Raceform

1995 FLAT ANNUAL

The BHB's Official Form Book

Complete record of all Turf and All-Weather Flat Racing in Great Britain from November 9th 1994 to November 6th 1995

Published by Raceform Ltd
Compton, Newbury, Berkshire, RG16 0NL
Tel: 01635 578080
Fax: 01635 578101

Registered as a newspaper at the Post Office

Printed by Woolnough Bookbinding Ltd,
Irthlingborough, Northants
Typeset by Raceform
Edited by Graham Wheldon

ISBN 0-900611-44-8

Cover Photo: A. Johnson

CONTENTS

The data contained in Raceform Flat Annual is available throughout the flat season in paper form or on computer disk.

The new-look paper formbook, known as Raceform, The Form Book, now available in A5 size, is updated weekly. Subscribers receive a binder with all the form to date and, thereafter, weekly sections and a new index are threaded into the binder to keep it up-to-date.

The disk service, Computer Raceform contains the same Data as Raceform, The Form Book. The system operates on any PC within a 'Windows' environment. The database is cleverly designed to allow you to access the information in a number of different ways, and is extremely quick and easy to use.

Full details of all Raceform services and publications are available from Raceform, Compton, Newbury, Berkshire, RG16 0NL. Tel: 01635 578080 Fax: 01635 578101.

How to read Raceform

3978 BEVERLEY H'CAP (0-80) (3-Y.O+) (Class D) £4,074.50 (£1,226.00: £593.00: £276.50)
1m 6f 19y Stalls: Low GOING minus 0.40 sec per fur (F) 3-40 (3-41)

3818[4] **Pretoria Dancer (65)**(79) *(JHMGosden)* 3-8-4b LDettori(2) (set stdy pce: qcknd over 4f out: hdd appr fnl f: sn led again: r.o) .... — 1
3723[7] Jadwal (USA) **(75)**(89) *(DMorley)* 3-9-0 RHills(4) (trckd ldrs: swtchd ins over 2f out: hung rt appr fnl f: sn led: hdd & no ex ins fnl f) .... nk 2
3799[3] High Patriarch (IRE) **(77)**(87)(Fav)*(JLDunlop)* 3-9-2v SWhitworth(8) (trckd ldrs: hdwy & ev ch 3f out: hung lft: btn appr fnl f) 3 3
3849[4] Star Rage (IRE) **(80)**(86) *(MJohnston)* 5-10-0 JWeaver(7) (trckd wnr: rdn over 3f out: btn whn n.m.r over 1f out) 4 4
3804[6] Moshaajir (USA) **(72)**(73) *(CSmith)* 5-9-3 (3) JStack(9) (hld up: effrt 4f out: no imp) 4 5
3935[2] Highfield Fizz **(54)**(55) *(CWFairhurst)* 3-7-0 (7) PDoe(1) (b.off hind: hld up: hdwy 4f out: outpcd fnl 2½f) .... ½ 6
1535[9] Rolling the Bones (USA) **(48)**(41) *(PSFelgate)* 6-7-10 ow3 AMackay(6) (hld up: outpcd fnl 4f) 4 7
LONG HANDICAP Highfield Fizz 7-5 Rolling the Bones (USA) 7-4

2/1 High Patriarch (IRE), **4/1** PRETORIA DANCER, **9/2** Star Rage (IRE), **11/2** Highfield Fizz, **7/1** Moshaajir (USA), **8/1** Jadwal (USA), **40/1** Rolling the Bones (USA), CSF £30.68 CT £72.43 TOTE £3.80: £2.50 £3.80 (£16.80) Trio £16.00 OWNER Sheikh Ahmed bin Saeed Al Maktoum (NEWMARKET) BRED Sheikh Mohammed bin Rashid al Maktoum 7 Rn

3m 7.6 (9.60) SF: 5/15/13/21/8/-/-
WEIGHT FOR AGE 3yo-9lb

RACE NUMBER TO WHICH INDEX WILL REFER

BLINKERS

HANDICAP FOR HORSES RATED 0-80

CLASS OF RACE ON SCALE A TO G

VALUE TO FIRST FOUR

RACE DISTANCE

RACE STARTED ONE MINUTE LATE

OFFICIAL HANDICAP RATING

COMMENT IN RUNNING

RACEFORM PRIVATE HANDICAP RATING

PLACING AND LENGTHS BEATEN

PREVIOUS RACE NUMBER

TOTE RETURNS

LONG HANDICAP WEIGHT FOR HORSE OUT OF HANDICAP

TIME OF RACE 9.6 SECS SLOWER THAN RACEFORM STANDARD

TRAINER, AGE, WEIGHT CARRIED AND JOCKEY

WINNER'S OWNER, LOCATION OF STABLE AND BREEDER

SPEED FIGURE RATINGS

How to read Raceform

Raceform, The Official Form Book records comprehensive race details of every domestic race, every French and Irish Group 1 and 2 race and every foreign event in which a British runner participated.

Meeting Back Reference Number is the Raceform number of the last meeting run at the track and is shown to the left of the course name. Abandoned meetings are signified by a †.

The Official Going, shown at the head of each meeting, is recorded as follows:
Turf: Hard; Firm; Good to firm; Good; Good to soft; Soft; Heavy.
All-Weather: Fast; Standard; Slow.

The Weather is shown below the date and is expressed as:
snowing; sleet; hail; stormy; thundery; raining; showers; drizzle; sea fret; foggy; misty; overcast; fair; sunny; hot.

The Wind is given as a strength and direction classified as follows:
Strengths: gale; v.str; str; fresh; mod; slt; almost nil; nil.
Directions: (half) against; (half) bhd; (half) across.

Visibility is good unless otherwise stated.

The Race Title gives the name of the race, the type of race, the weight range (if applicable) and the age range.

Competitive Racing Classifications are shown on a scale from Class A to Class G. All Pattern races are Class A.

Prize Money shows penalty values down to tenth place (where applicable).

The Position of the Starting Stalls is shown against each race, in the form `Stalls: Low', `Stalls: Centre', or 'Stalls: High' for races run on both the round course and the straight course. The actual position of the stalls can make a vital difference to a runner's chances and reference should be made to the *Effect of the Draw* summary (see page xv) when assessing a horse's performance.

The Going Allowance, expressed in seconds per furlong, is shown after the position of the stalls. A *minus* figure e.g (minus 0.62 sec per fur) indicates that the going was enabling the horses in that particular race to run 0.62 seconds per furlong faster than the Raceform Standard Time. Conversely, a *plus* figure e.g (0.05 sec per fur) indicates that the going was slowing the horses down, causing them to run 0.05 seconds per furlong slower than the Raceform Standard Time.

Raceform Going, which may differ from the Official Going, appears against each race to allow for changing conditions of the ground. It takes into account the race times compared with the Raceform Standard Times, the wind and other elements, and is recorded in the following stages:
Turf: H (Hard); F (Firm); GF (Good to firm); G (Good);
GS (Good to soft); S (Soft); HVY (Heavy).
All-Weather: FST (Fast); STD (Standard); SLW (Slow).

The Race Distance is given for all races. The suffix (rnd) is shown for races run on a round course, if there is a straight course of comparable distance. **(AWT)** after the distance signifies that such races were run on a Fibresand (Southwell or Wolverhampton) or Equitrack (Lingfield) surface.

Race Numbers for Foreign races carry the suffix 'a'.

In The Race Result, the figures to the left of each horse show the race number of its most recent listing in Raceform. A figure in *italics* indicates the previous performance was recorded on an All-Weather course. The superscript figures indicate its finishing position in that race and are coded as follows:

* - winner;

2..40 - finishing positions 2nd to 40th;

b - brought down; c - carried out; f - fell; p - pulled up; r - refused to race;

ro - ran out; s - slipped up; u - unseated rider; v - void race; w - withdrawn.

The Adjusted Official Rating is the figure in **bold type** directly after the horse's name in the race result. This figure indicates the Official BHB rating, at entry, after the following adjustments have been made:

(i) Overweight carried by the rider.

(ii) The number of pounds out of the handicap (if applicable).

(iii) Penalties incurred after the publication of the weights.

However, **no** adjustments have been made for:

(i) Weight-for-age.

(ii) Jockey's claims.

The Raceform Rating is the figure in *italics* directly after the horse's official rating. This figure takes into account Weight-for-age and Jockey's claims.

The Trainer is shown in parantheses for every runner.

The Horses Age is shown immediately before the weight carried.

Weights shown are actual weights carried. A figure in parantheses after the horse's weight denotes an apprentice jockey's claim, i.e $^{(7)}$. A figure next to the weight with an ^{ow} sign, is the amount of overweight put up by the jockey, i.e ^{ow4}.

Long Handicap Weights for runners allotted a lower-than-minimum weight at entry **(handicaps only)** are shown directly under the commentary of the last horse in each race.

Apprentice Allowances: The holders of apprentice jockeys' licences under the provisions of Rule 60 (iii) are permitted to claim the following allowances in Flat races:
7lbs until they have won 20 Flat races under the Rules of any recognised Turf Authority; thereafter 5lbs until they have won 50 such Flat races; thereafter 3lbs until they have won 95 such Flat races. These allowances can be claimed in the following Flat races, with the exception of races confined to apprentice jockeys:
a) All handicaps other than those Rated Stakes which are classified as Listed races.
b) All selling races.
c) All other races with *Money Added to Stakes* of not more than £8,000.

Headgear is shown after the actual weight carried and expressed as:

b (blinkers); **v** (visor); **e** (eyecover);

Eyeshield details are shown in the comments-on-running.

The Draw for places at the start is shown after each jockey's name.

The Official Distances are shown on the right-hand side immediately preceding the horse's position at the finish.

Starting Prices (SP) appear below the commentary of the last horse in the race. The race winner is shown in capitals.

Tote Returns, CSF's and CT's include a £1 stake. Dual Forecast dividends are shown in parentheses. The Tote Trio dividend is preceded by the word Trio.

The Owner, Trainer's Location and Breeder of the winner are shown immediately after the Tote returns.

Race Times in Great Britain, (except official times which are electronically recorded and shown to 100th of a second), are clocked by Raceform's own watch-holders at the Course. Figures in parentheses following the time show the number of seconds slower than the Raceform Standard Time for the course and distance.

Raceform Standard Times were originally compiled from times recorded on Good to firm going after adjustments had been made for weights carried above or below a norm of 9st. Times equal to the standard are shown as (equals standard). Times under the standard are preceded by a minus sign, for instance, 1.8 seconds under the standard would be shown as (-1.8). Record times are displayed either referring to the juvenile record (1.2 under 2y best; U2.3) or to the overall record (1.2 under best; -2.3).

Speed Figures(SF) appear for every horse that clocks a sufficiently fast time, and appear directly after the race time. The figures are adjusted to 9st, and calculations made for going, wind, and distance behind the winner. To apply Speed Figures to future races, add 1 point for each 1lb below 9st, and deduct 1 point for each 1lb above 9st. The highest resultant figure is best.

Withdrawn horses that fail to come under orders after entering the parade ring, are included in the index to past racing (with W after the race number); side reference, odds at the time of withdrawal and the reason for withdrawal (if known) are shown in italics below the bottom horse in the race.

Stewards' Enquiry, includes suspensions or fines handed out to trainers or jockeys. All objections are included.

Tote Jackpot, Placepot and Quadpot details appear at the end of the meeting to which they refer.

Selling Details (if applicable) are given below the speed figures. These show the result of the auction for sellers, and details of any claimed horse. Friendly claims are not detailed.

Index to Flat Racing - Please note that names of horses are indexed strictly as spelt and include suffixes, e.g. Elect (USA) would come **after** Electro.

KEY TO RACE READER INITIALS

AA..............Alan Amies
AK..............Anthony Kemp
AR..............Ashley Rumney
CR..............Colin Roberts
DG..............David Gowers
Dk...............David Dickinson
DS..............Desmond Stoneham
GB..............Gordon Brown
GW.............Graham Wheldon
Hn...............John Hanmer
IM................Ivor Markham
J..................Mike Jones
KH..............Keith Hewitt
KK..............Katie Knott
LM..............Lee McKenzie
NB..............Nicola Bowen
NR..............Neville Ring
P.................John Penney
RC..............Robert Carter
RL...............Richard Lowther
SC..............Steven Clarke
SM..............Stephen Mellish
T.................Mary Trueman
WG.............Walter Glynn

The utmost care is taken to ensure accuracy but the Proprietors accept no responsibility for error.

Table of Abbreviations

In The Parade Ring

b = bandaged fore
b.hind = bandaged hind
bkwd = backward in condition
gd sort = above average on looks
h.d.w = has done well: improved in looks
lt-f = light-framed
lw = looked very well
nice c = nice colt: very good sort
v nice c = outstanding on looks
nt grwn = not grown
scope = scope for development
str = strong
swtg = sweating
t = tubed
unf = unfurnished
wl grwn = well grown
w'like = workmanlike

The Running

a = always
a.p = always prominent
abt = about
appr = approaching
awrdd = awarded
b.b.v = broke blood vessel
b.d = brought down
bdly = badly
bef = before
bel = below
bhd = behind
bk = back
blkd = baulked
bmpd = bumped
bnd = bend
btn = beaten
bttr = better
c = came
ch = chance
chal = challenge(d)
chsd = chased
circ = circuit
cl = close
clr = clear
comf = comfortably
cpld = coupled
crse = course
ct = caught
dismntd = dismounted
disp = disputed
disq = disqualified
dist = distance (240y from finish)
div = division
drvn = driven
dwlt = dwelt
edgd = edged
effrt = effort
ent = entering
ev ch = every chance
ex = extra
f = furlong
fdd = faded
fin = finish(ed)
fnd = found
fnl = final
fr = from
gd = good
gng = going
grad = gradually
grnd = ground
hd = head
hdd = headed
hdwy = headway
hld = held
hmpd = hampered
hrd rdn = hard ridden
imp = impression
ins = inside
jnd = joined
jst = just
kpt = kept
l = length
ld = lead
ldr = leader
lft = left
m = mile
m.n.s = made no show
mde = made
mid div = mid division
n.d = no danger
n.g.t = not go through
n.m.r = not much room
nk = neck
no ex = no extra pace
no imp = no impression
nr = near
nrr = nearer
nrst fin = nearest at finish
nt = not
nvr = never
one pce = one paced
out = from finish
outpcd = outpaced
p.u = pulled up
pce = pace
pl = place
plcd = placed
plld = pulled
press = pressure
prog = progress
prom = prominent
qckly = quickly
qckn = quicken
r = race
r.o = ran on
racd = raced
rch = reach
rcvr = recover
rdn = ridden
rdr = rider
reard = reared
ref = refused
rn = ran
rnd = round
rn wl = ran well
rr = rear
rspnse = response
rt = right
s = start
slt = slight
sme = some
sn = soon
spd = speed
st = straight
stdd = steadied
stdy = steady
str = strong
styd = stayed
swtchd = switched
swvd = swerved
t.o = tailed off
tch = touch
thrght = throughout
thro = through
trckd = tracked
u.p = under pressure
w = with
w.r.s = whipped round start
wd = wide
whn = when
wknd = weakened
wl = well
wnr = winner
wnt = went
½-wy = half-way

THE OFFICIAL SCALE OF WEIGHT, AGE & DISTANCE (Flat)

The following scale of weight-for-age should be used only in conjunction with the Official ratings published in this book. Use of any other scale will introduce errors into calculations. The allowances are expressed as the number of pounds that is deemed the average horse in each group falls short of maturity at different dates and distances.

Distance Furlongs	Age	JAN 1/15	JAN 16/31	FEB 1/14	FEB 15/28	MARCH 1/15	MARCH 16/31	APRIL 1/15	APRIL 13/30	MAY 1/15	MAY 16/31	JUNE 1/15	JUNE 16/30	JULY 1/15	JULY 16/31	AUGUST 1/15	AUGUST 16/31	SEPT 1/15	SEPT 16/30	OCT 1/15	OCT 16/31	NOV 1/15	NOV 16/30	DEC 1/15	DEC 16/31
5	2	–	–	–	–	–	47	44	41	38	36	34	32	30	28	26	24	22	20	19	18	17	17	16	16
	3	15	15	15	15	14	13	12	11	10	9	8	7	6	5	4	3	2	2	1	1	–	–	–	–
6	2	–	–	–	–	–	–	–	–	44	41	38	36	33	31	28	26	24	22	21	20	19	18	17	17
	3	16	16	16	16	15	14	13	12	11	10	9	8	7	6	5	4	3	3	2	2	1	1	–	–
7	2	–	–	–	–	–	–	–	–	–	–	–	–	38	35	32	30	27	25	23	22	21	20	19	19
	3	18	18	18	18	17	16	15	14	12	11	10	9	8	7	6	5	4	4	3	3	2	2	1	1
8	2	–	–	–	–	–	–	–	–	–	–	–	–	–	–	37	34	31	28	26	24	23	22	21	20
	3	20	20	19	19	18	17	16	15	13	12	11	10	9	8	7	6	5	4	4	3	3	2	2	1
	4	1	1	–	–	–	–	–	–	–	–	–	–	–	–	–	–	–	–	–	–	–	–	–	–
9	3	22	22	21	20	20	19	18	17	15	14	12	11	10	9	8	7	6	5	5	4	4	3	2	2
	4	2	2	1	1	1	–	–	–	–	–	–	–	–	–	–	–	–	–	–	–	–	–	–	–
10	3	23	23	22	22	21	20	19	18	16	15	13	12	11	10	9	8	7	6	6	5	5	4	4	3
	4	3	3	2	2	1	1	–	–	–	–	–	–	–	–	–	–	–	–	–	–	–	–	–	–
11	3	–	–	–	–	23	22	21	20	18	17	15	14	12	11	10	9	8	7	7	6	6	5	4	4
	4	4	4	3	3	2	1	1	–	–	–	–	–	–	–	–	–	–	–	–	–	–	–	–	–
12	3	–	–	–	–	24	23	22	21	19	18	16	15	13	12	11	10	9	8	8	7	7	6	6	5
	4	5	4	4	3	3	2	2	1	–	–	–	–	–	–	–	–	–	–	–	–	–	–	–	–
13	3	–	–	–	–	25	24	23	22	20	19	17	16	14	13	12	11	10	9	8	8	7	6	6	5
	4	5	4	4	3	3	2	2	1	–	–	–	–	–	–	–	–	–	–	–	–	–	–	–	–
14	3	–	–	–	–	26	25	24	23	21	20	18	17	15	14	13	12	11	10	9	9	8	7	7	6
	4	6	5	5	4	4	3	3	2	1	–	–	–	–	–	–	–	–	–	–	–	–	–	–	–
15	3	–	–	–	–	28	27	26	25	23	21	19	18	16	15	14	13	12	11	10	9	9	8	7	6
	4	6	5	5	4	4	3	3	2	2	1	–	–	–	–	–	–	–	–	–	–	–	–	–	–
16	3	–	–	–	–	29	28	27	26	24	22	20	19	17	16	15	14	13	12	11	10	10	9	8	7
	4	7	7	6	6	5	5	4	4	3	2	1	–	–	–	–	–	–	–	–	–	–	–	–	–
18	3	–	–	–	–	31	30	29	28	26	24	22	21	19	18	17	16	15	14	13	12	11	10	9	8
	4	8	8	7	7	6	6	5	5	4	3	2	1	–	–	–	–	–	–	–	–	–	–	–	–
20	3	–	–	–	–	33	32	31	30	28	26	24	22	20	19	18	17	16	15	14	13	12	11	10	9
	4	9	9	8	8	7	7	6	6	5	4	3	2	1	–	–	–	–	–	–	–	–	–	–	–

RACEFORM RATINGS

Raceform Ratings for each horse are listed after the Starting Price and indicate the actual level of performance attained in that race. The figure in the back index represents the BEST public form that our handicappers still believe each horse is capable of reproducing.

To use the ratings constructively in determining those horses *best-in* in future events, the following procedure should be followed:

(i) In races where all runners are the same age and are set to carry the same weight, no calculations are necessary. The horse with the highest rating is the horse *best-in*.

(ii) In races where all runners are the same age but are set to carry different weights, add one point to the Raceform Rating for every pound less than 10 stone to be carried; deduct one point for every pound more than 10 stone.

For example,

Horse	Age & Weight	Adjustment from 10st	RR base rating	Adjusted rating
Sprouts	3-10-1	-1	78	77
Giant of Coldash	3-9-13	+1	80	81
Tangerine Army	3-9-7	+7	71	78
Mystic Clegg	3-8-11	+17	60	77

Therefore Giant of Coldash is top-rated (best-in)

(iii) In races concerning horses of different ages the procedure in example (ii) should again be followed, but reference must also be made to the Official Scale of Weight-For-Age.

For example,

12 furlongs July 20th

Horse	Age & Weight	Adjustment from 10st	RPH base rating	Adjusted rating	W-F-A deduction	Final rating
My Nipper	5-10-0	0	90	90	Nil	90
Beedotman	4-9-9	+5	83	88	Nil	88
Off-Road Ron	3-9-4	+10	85	95	-12	83
Kempo's Karpet	4-8-7	+21	73	94	Nil	94

Therefore Kempo's Karpet is top-rated (best-in)

(A 4-y-o is deemed 12lb less mature than a 5-y-o or older horse on 20th January over 2m. Therefore, the deduction of 12 points is necessary.)

The following symbols are used in conjunction with the ratings:

- **++** almost certain to prove better
- **+** likely to prove better
- **d** disappointing (has run well below best recently)
- **?** form hard to evaluate - rating may prove unreliable
- **t** tentative rating based on race-time

Weight adjusted ratings for every race are published daily in Raceform Private Handicap. For subscription terms please contact the Subscription Department on (01635) 578080.

EFFECT OF THE DRAW

(R.H.) denotes right-hand and (L.H.) left-hand courses.

RULES OF RACING No. 28(v): The Starter shall call over the names of the runners and for Flat races, assign the horses to the places drawn by lot, all horses taking their place at the Start in the order drawn for them. The rider who has drawn No. 1 must always be placed on the left and the other riders must take their places in consecutive numbers from the left. N.B. This being the left as looking from behind the stalls.
The stall position is displayed as either high, low or centre in Raceform. i.e. On a left-handed course, low would mean that stall No. 1 is situated directly next to the inside rail. If the stalls were given as high, stall No. 20 in a 20 runner race would be situated directly next to the outside rail.

ASCOT (R.H.) - On the straight course, the draw does not seem of great effect, although high numbers appear to have the edge on soft ground.
AYR (L.H.) - In big fields, low numbers have an advantage on the straight course when the ground is soft. However, in the past two years, the Ayr Gold Cup has been won by those drawn high, and in 1995 those drawn low never figured. In races over 7f and 8f, low numbers are favoured.
BATH (L.H.) - Low numbers are slightly favoured.
BEVERLEY (R.H.) - In races up to a mile, high numbers are favoured on firm ground.
BRIGHTON (L.H.) - Low numbers are slightly favoured in sprint races except in very wet conditions when jockeys tend to tack over to the stands' side.
CARLISLE (R.H.) - High numbers are marginally favoured, especially over sprint distances, although when the ground rides soft low numbers appear to have the edge.
CATTERICK (L.H.) - Low numbers are favoured, especially over 6f, although this can be negated by a slow start. In late season on soft ground, high numbers have the advantage on the straight course.
CHEPSTOW (L.H.) - No real advantage.
CHESTER (L.H.) - Low numbers have a distinct advantage, especially in sprint races, where a slow start from a high draw can be virtually impossible to overcome. However, after racing on soft ground, turf on the inside can become chewed up, and those with higher draws can be favoured.
DONCASTER (L.H.) - The draw is of little consequence on the straight course except when the ground is soft, when high numbers have an advantage. Low numbers are favoured on the round course.
EDINBURGH (R.H.) - High numbers are favoured over 7f & 8f. Over 5f when the stalls are on the stands' side, low numbers have a considerable advantage. When the stalls are on the far side, high numbers are favoured.
EPSOM (L.H.) - High numbers are marginally favoured on the 5f course. Low numbers are preferable on the round course, except when the ground is soft, when it is fashionable to tack over to the stands' rail.
FOLKESTONE (R.H.) - High numbers are favoured on the round course and, when the ground is soft, in sprints.
GOODWOOD (R.H.) - (L.H.) High numbers are slightly favoured on the round course, except in very wet conditions, when jockeys tend to tack over to the stands' side.
HAMILTON (R.H.) - On soft or heavy ground it is essential to be drawn middle to high in sprints, although ground can often be too heavy for the use of stalls. A high draw is also of advantage in races up to 1m 65y as there is a tight loop into the straight.

HAYDOCK (L.H.) - Low numbers are favoured over 7f & 8f. When the ground is soft, high numbers have an advantage over 5f and 6f.
KEMPTON (R.H.) - Over 5f & 6f, when the stalls are on the stands' side and the ground is soft, a low draw is a great advantage. When the stalls are placed on the far side, a high number is essential.
LEICESTER (R.H.) - Low numbers may have an advantage, especially when the ground is soft.
LINGFIELD (L.H.) - **Turf**: High numbers are generally favoured in races on the straight course.
AWT: Low numbers are favoured, an advantage which can be accentuated by a fast break.
LONGCHAMP (R.H.) - A low draw is important on the straight course (remembering that the French invariably number from the rail outwards).

NEWBURY (L.H.) - High numbers have a slight advantage on the straight course, an advantage accentuated by heavy ground.
NEWCASTLE (L.H.) - High numbers are favoured on the straight course, except on soft and heavy ground, when low numbers have a marked advantage.
NEWMARKET (R.H.) - **Rowley Mile Course**: When racing switches back from the July Course in the autumn, it is not uncommon to have races with 30 or more runners. When this is the case, runners drawn up against either rail can have a significant advantage.
July Course: No significant effect.
NOTTINGHAM (L.H.) - On the straight course, the position of stalls gives the best indication which side is favoured, i.e. when the stalls are positioned on the far side, low numbers are best. In big fields when the stalls are spread right across the course, those drawn low seem to have the overall edge. Low numbers are slightly favoured on the round course.
PONTEFRACT (L.H.) - Low numbers are favoured.
REDCAR (L.H.) - High numbers are favoured on the straight course when the ground is soft.
RIPON (R.H.) - Low numbers are favoured on the straight course, high numbers on the round course.
SALISBURY (R.H.) - Low numbers are favoured in sprints when the ground is soft, otherwise high numbers have some advantage, particularly over 6f.
SANDOWN (R.H.) - A high number is essential in 5f races when the ground is soft and the stalls are on the far side. However when the stalls are placed on the stands' side, low numbers have the advantage.
SOUTHWELL (L.H.) - **Turf**: Low numbers are favoured.
AWT: low numbers are favoured.
THIRSK (L.H.) - In sprint races, high numbers are usually favoured. However, this advantage can be negated by runners from low stalls tacking across to the far side.
WARWICK (L.H.) - Low numbers are favoured.
WINDSOR (R.H.) - It is generally considered that high numbers have the advantage in sprints but the advantage is not great.
WOLVERHAMPTON (L.H.) - **AWT**: High numbers had a marked advantage in the early stages on the new Fibresand course, but the effect seems to be diminishing, although on slow ground, the centre of the track can ride the fastest, and jockeys rarely seem to stick to the inside rail whatever the going.
YARMOUTH (L.H.) - High numbers have a slight advantage on the straight course.
YORK (L.H.) - Low numbers have an advantage on the straight course, especially when the ground is testing.

Raceform

WINTER
FLAT RACING 1994

Complete record of Foreign Turf Racing and All-Weather Flat Racing from November 9th to December 31st 1994

4140-LINGFIELD (L-H)
Wednesday November 9th (Standard)

4202
ROTHER APP'CE H'CAP (I) (0-70) (Class G) £2,442.00 (£687.00: £336.00)
7f (Equitrack) Stalls: Low GOING: minus 0.40 sec per fur (FS) 12-10 (12-12)

4034^{9} **Mr Nevermind (IRE) (67)***(68)*(Fav)*(GLMoore)* 4-9-6 (5) LSuthern(16) (hld up in tch: led appr fnl f: r.o wl)........— **1**

3426^{13} Greatest Hopes **(39)***(38) (CJBenstead)* 3-7-6 (3) CHawksley(9) (hdwy on outside over 4f out: ev ch appr fnl f: kpt on)........¾ **2**

4078^{13} Hawaii Storm (FR) **(52)***(46) (MissAJWhitfield)* 6-8-7 (3) RPainter(3) (s.i.s: wl bhd tl gd hdwy on outside fnl 2f: nrst fin)........2½ **3**

4078^{9} Our Shadee (USA) **(51)***(39) (KTIvory)* 4-8-4v(5)ow3 CScally(14) (a.p: led briefly over 1f out: sn hdd & one pce)........3 **4**

4101^{24} Ewar Gold (FR) **(42)***(25) (KOCunningham-Brown)* 4-7-9 (5)ow5 CTeague(7) (bhd: r.o one pce fnl 2f)........2½ **5**

3979^{14} Glenfield Greta **(48)***(30) (PSFelgate)* 6-8-6 PMcCabe(13) (s.s: bhd tl sme late hdwy: nvr nrr)........½ **6**

3806^{14} Lac de Gras (IRE) **(37)***(14) (RCurtis)* 3-7-7 NVarley(11) (a mid div)........2½ **7**

4059^{15} Maid Welcome **(56)***(33) (MrsNMacauley)* 7-8-9v(5) AmandaSanders(8) (chsd ldr 4f: one pce)........s.h **8**

3969^{3} Words of Wisdom (IRE) **(55)***(31) (CACyzer)* 4-8-13 SMulvey(1) (cl up tl wknd 1f out)........hd **9**

2813^{11} Asterix **(43)***(19) (JMBradley)* 6-7-10 (5) SLanigan(6) (nvr plcd to chal)........s.h **10**

3507^{12} Digpast (IRE) **(47)***(23) (RJO'Sullivan)* 4-8-2 (3) DGriffiths(10) (sn pushed along: rdn ent st: sn wknd)........s.h **11**

2009^{8} Personal Pride (IRE) **(52)***(24) (AGFoster)* 3-8-3 (5) SMcCarthy(4) (a bhd)........1¾ **12**

3963^{8} Obsidian Grey **(58)***(27) (MissLCSiddall)* 7-9-2 SDrowne(12) (prom tl wknd over 2f out)........1¼ **13**

3975^{11} Distant Dynasty **(51)***(14) (BAPearce)* 4-8-9 SSanders(15) (led tl over 1f out: wknd)........3 **14**

1699^{10} Papagos (IRE) **(57)***(14) (SDow)* 3-8-13 JDSmith(5) (eyeshield: m.n.s)........3 **15**

LONG HANDICAP Lac de Gras (IRE) 7-1

9/2 MR NEVERMIND (IRE) (6/1-4/1), **7/1** Words of Wisdom (IRE), Obsidian Grey, Digpast (IRE), **8/1** Glenfield Greta, **9/1** Maid Welcome, **12/1** Hawaii Storm (FR), Distant Dynasty, **14/1** Papagos (IRE), Asterix, **16/1** Ewar Gold (FR), Greatest Hopes, **20/1** Our Shadee (USA), **25/1** Lac de Gras (IRE), **33/1** Personal Pride (IRE), CSF £70.85 CT £760.91 TOTE £5.20: £2.00 £4.50 £3.80 (£53.10) OWNER Mr K. Higson (EPSOM) BRED Robert Corridan 15 Rn

1m 26.02 (3.02) SF: 39/10/19/11/-/1/-/-/-/-/-/-/-/-/-

WEIGHT FOR AGE 3yo-2lb

4203
E.B.F. WYE STKS (I) (Mdn 2-Y.O) (Class D) £3,243.90 (£982.20: £479.60: £228.30)
1m (Equitrack) Stalls: High GOING: minus 0.40 sec per fur (FS) 12-40 (12-40)

3997^{3} **Risky Romeo (75)***(85+)*(Fav)*(GCBravery)* 2-9-0 RCochrane(8) (s.s: last tl smooth hdwy over 4f out: led on bit over 1f out: sn clr: v.easily)........— **1**

3900^{6} Howqua River **(70)***(63) (PWChapple-Hyam)* 2-8-7 (7) RHavlin(7) (hld up: led over 2f out tl over 1f out: outpcd)........11 **2**

4095^{3} Komreyev Dancer **(66)***(58) (ABailey)* 2-8-9 (5) DWright(3) (led over 4f out: hdd briefly over 3f out: sn led again tl over 2f out: outpcd)........2½ **3**

3892^{7} Slytly Beveled **(49)***(52) (MPMuggeridge)* 2-9-0 TGMcLaughlin(6) (prom: led briefly over 3f out: wknd 2f out)........3 **4**

3987^{14} Pent-House Baby **(42)***(46) (JLSpearing)* 2-8-9 NAdams(9) (hld up: nt pce to chal)........nk **5**

4080^{11} Inn At the Top *(—) (MJohnston)* 2-9-0 TWilliams(4) (sn pushed along: lost pl ½-wy: sn wl bhd)........9 **6**

3281a^{25} Woolverstone Hall (IRE) *(—) (DJGMurraySmith)* 2-8-9 JWeaver(1) (led 7f out tl over 4f out: sn wknd)........5 **7**

3921^{21} Water Hazard (IRE) **(57)***(—) (SDow)* 2-9-0e StephenDavies(5) (led 1f: prom tl wknd 4f out)........6 **8**

3701^{13} Half Tone **(40)***(—) (RMFlower)* 2-9-0 MWigham(2) (a wl bhd)........6 **9**

9/4 RISKY ROMEO, **3/1** Howqua River, **7/2** Komreyev Dancer, Woolverstone Hall (IRE), **12/1** Inn At the Top, **20/1** Slytly Beveled, **33/1** Water Hazard (IRE), **50/1** Pent-House Baby, Half Tone, CSF £9.38 TOTE £3.10: £2.30 £1.10 £1.70 (£7.90) OWNER Miss Sonja Quince (NEWMARKET) BRED Mrs S. Quince 9 Rn

1m 38.99 (2.59) SF: 39/17/13/7/2/-/-/-/-

4204

ROTHER APP'CE H'CAP (II) (0-70) (Class G) £2,442.00 (£687.00: £336.00)
7f (Equitrack) Stalls: Low GOING: minus 0.40 sec per fur (FS) 1-10 (1-14)

4126* **Level Edge (49)***(55) (MJohnston)* 3-8-0 (7x) (5) OliverCasey(16) (a.p: rdn 1f out: r.o to ld wl ins fnl f) ...— 1
2924 6 Sharp Imp **(37)***(41) (RMFlower)* 4-7-4b(5)ow2 SLanigan(13) (led over 4f out: clr ent fnl f: hdd ins fnl f: no ex) ...1 2
4033 2 Milos **(69)***(71) (TJNaughton)* 3-9-8 (3) VHalliday(14) (hld up in tch: hdwy over 2f out: rdn & r.o one pce fnl f) ...¾ 3
3780 11 Dancing Lawyer **(69)***(70) (BJMeehan)* 3-9-6 (5) DaneO'Neill(3) (chsd ldrs: rdn over 1f out: one pce) ...nk 4
4101 8 Breckland (IRE) **(47)***(43) (KOCunningham-Brown)* 4-8-2 (3) DGriffiths(9) (hld up mid div: ev ch ent st: one pce) ...2½ 5
3594 22 Eatons **(46)***(38) (SDow)* 3-8-2e SSanders(15) (mid div: styd on one pce fnl 2f) 1¾ 6
3908 10 Super Benz **(65)***(56) (BBeasley)* 8-9-4 (5) CTeague(7) (chsd ldrs: one pce fnl 2f) ...hd 7
2923 12 Battling Bella (USA) **(44)***(31) (GLMoore)* 5-7-9 (7) CarolineHovington(10) (nvr plcd to chal) ...2 8
3891 7 Lucknam Style **(47)***(33) (MrsBarbaraWaring)* 6-8-5v SDrowne(5) (trckd ldrs: rdn 3f out: sn outpcd) ...nk 9
3777 2 King Parrot (IRE) **(54)***(39)*(Fav)*(LordHuntingdon)* 6-8-7 (5) JWilkinson(6) (led over 2f) ...nk 10
3439 11 Western Valley **(35)***(16) (CPWildman)* 4-7-2 (5) CAdamson(11) (a bhd) ...1¾ 11
4053 12 Mr Cube (IRE) **(45)***(22) (JMBradley)* 4-7-12 (5) AmandaSanders(2) (m.n.s) ...2 12
3507 10 Inspiration Point **(60)***(36) (MissBSanders)* 3-8-9 (7) AmandaBowen(4) (a bhd) ...nk 13
4105 7 No Speeches (IRE) **(64)***(36) (CACyzer)* 3-9-3 (3) JDSmith(1) (s.s: a in rr) ...1¾ 14
4083 16 Ezekiel **(49)***(20) (JWPayne)* 3-8-5 DWright(8) (s.s: sn pushed along & a in rr) ...½ 15

LONG HANDICAP Western Valley 7-2 Sharp Imp 7-0

3/1 King Parrot (IRE), **7/2** Milos, **8/1** LEVEL EDGE, **12/1** Mr Cube (IRE), Dancing Lawyer, Super Benz, **14/1** No Speeches (IRE), **16/1** Inspiration Point, Sharp Imp, Lucknam Style, Battling Bella (USA), **20/1** Breckland (IRE), **33/1** Eatons, Western Valley, Ezekiel, CSF £117.69 CT £480.87 TOTE £10.50: £2.20 £5.90 £1.80 (£80.40) OWNER Mr B. Coulthard (MIDDLEHAM) BRED Pinfold Stud and Farms Ltd 15 Rn 1m 26.85 (3.85) SF: 11/-/26/25/2/-/15/-/-/-/-/-/-/-/-
WEIGHT FOR AGE 3yo-2lb

4205

E.B.F. WYE STKS (II) (Mdn 2-Y.O) (Class D) £3,228.95 (£977.60: £477.30: £227.15) **1m (Equitrack)** Stalls: High GOING: minus 0.40 sec (FS) 1-40 (1-41)

3710 24 **Soldier's Leap (FR) (79)***(67) (CEBrittain)* 2-9-0b BDoyle(2) (led 1f: trckd ldrs: rdn to ld ins fnl f: r.o) ...— 1
4087 2 Crystal Gift *(65)*(Fav)*(PFICole)* 2-9-0 TQuinn(6) (chsd ldrs: led over 1f out: rdn, hdd & no ex ins fnl f) ...¾ 2
Frome Lad *(55) (WGMTurner)* 2-8-9 (5) JDSmith(9) (wl bhd tl gd hdwy over 4f out: styd on) ...5 3
4047 12 Just-Mana-Mou (IRE) *(51) (GLewis)* 2-9-0 SWhitworth(7) (bhd tl sme late hdwy) 1¾ 4
3358 8 Star Fighter **(62)***(49) (WAO'Gorman)* 2-8-11 (3) EmmaO'Gorman(8) (led after 1f tl over 1f out: wknd) ...¾ 5
4047 8 Most Welcome News **(58)***(46) (JRJenkins)* 2-9-0e CRutter(5) (prom: rdn 3f out: wknd 2f out) ...1¼ 6
3788 6 Fairy's Son *(42) (WRMuir)* 2-8-7 (7) SMcCarthy(3) (s.i.s: rdn 3f out: sn wknd) ...1¾ 7
3995 15 Kali Ro *(—) (ICampbell)* 2-8-9 DBiggs(4) (a bhd: t.o) ...11 8
4022 20 Magical Touch *(—) (RMFlower)* 2-8-9 StephenDavies(1) (rdn 3f out: sn outpcd: t.o) ...dist 9

1/3 Crystal Gift, **4/1** SOLDIER'S LEAP (FR), **16/1** Star Fighter, **33/1** Just-Mana-Mou (IRE), **50/1** Frome Lad, Most Welcome News, Fairy's Son, Kali Ro, Magical Touch, CSF £5.32 TOTE £6.10: £1.90 £1.10 £1.70 (£1.90) OWNER Mr A. J. Richards (NEWMARKET) BRED Ewar Stud Farm 9 Rn 1m 41.83 (5.43) SF: 11/10/-/-/-/-/-/-/-

4206

ARUN STKS (Mdn) (0-65) (Class F) £2,600.30 (£730.80: £356.90)
6f (Equitrack) Stalls: Low GOING: minus 0.40 sec per fur (FS) 2-10 (2-12)

3996 11 **Triple Joy (65)***(73+)*(Fav)*(SirMarkPrescott)* 3-8-9 GDuffield(11) (led after 1f: pushed clr over 1f out: easily) ...— 1
3700 13 Saxon King (IRE) **(44)***(64) (MDIUsher)* 4-9-0 RStreet(6) (hdwy to chse wnr over 3f out: ev ch ent st: sn outpcd) ...5 2
3707 5 Joint Effort (IRE) **(54)***(47) (AMoore)* 3-8-9 RCochrane(4) (chsd ldr 3f: one pce fnl 2f) ...5 3

3569[4] Secret Assignment (USA) **(42)***(45) (CACyzer)* 4-9-0v JReid(10) (plld hrd: mid div tl r.o fnl f) 2½ **4**
4102[6] Pakol (IRE) **(56)***(38) (MrsASwinbank)* 5-8-9 TIves(2) (in tch 3f: outpcd fnl 2f) ....½ **5**
3972[14] Thorniwama **(38)***(34) (JJBridger)* 3-8-9 TWilliams(12) (sn rdn along: nvr plcd to chal) 2 **6**
4101[22] Dance and Sing (IRE) **(36)***(38) (DLWilliams)* 4-8-9 (5) DGriffiths(9) (s.s: wl bhd tl r.o fnl 2f) ....s.h **7**
3978[17] Risk the Witch **(25)***(20) (DJSCosgrove)* 4-8-4 (5) LNewton(13) (chsd ldrs 2f: sn wl outpcd) 5 **8**
3598[13] Hall Bank Cottage **(29)***(17) (MrsALMKing)* 4-8-9 NCarlisle(14) (a mid div) ....¾ **9**
4064[18] Ewar Empress (IRE) **(45)***(14) (KOCunningham-Brown)* 3-8-9b JQuinn(7) (m.n.s)..1¼ **10**
3912[18] Crafty Cricketer **(36)***(13) (RVoorspuy)* 3-9-0b NAdams(8) (led 1f: wknd 3f out)....2½ **11**
3806[18] Hollington Song **(37)***(—) (MMadgwick)* 3-8-9 MFenton(3) (n.d) 3½ **12**
352[9] Ithkurni (USA) **(27)***(—) (PHayward)* 5-8-9 RPerham(5) (prom: drvn along & lost pl fnl 3f) ....nk **13**
4051[13] North to Glory **(38)***(—) (RVoorspuy)* 3-8-9 BDoyle(1) (a wl bhd) 2½ **14**

Evens TRIPLE JOY, **11/2** Secret Assignment (USA), **6/1** Pakol (IRE), **8/1** Joint Effort (IRE), **9/1** Saxon King (IRE), **25/1** Dance and Sing (IRE), **33/1** Hall Bank Cottage, Risk the Witch, North to Glory, **50/1** Thorniwama, Ewar Empress (IRE), Hollington Song, Ithkurni (USA), Crafty Cricketer, CSF £10.61 TOTE £1.60: £1.30 £2.00 £1.60 (£5.50) OWNER Hesmonds Stud (NEWMARKET) BRED Hesmonds Stud Ltd 14 Rn 1m 13.2 (2.60) SF: 24/15/-/-/-/-/-/-/-/-/-/-/-/-
WEIGHT FOR AGE 3yo-1lb

4207 MEDWAY CLAIMING STKS (2-Y.O) (Class F) £2,695.50 (£758.00: £370.50)
6f (Equitrack) Stalls: Low GOING: minus 0.40 sec per fur (FS) 2-40 (2-42)

4076[5] **Fairy Fay (IRE) (69)***(57)*(Jt-Fav)*(BJMcMath)* 2-8-8 RCochrane(14) (hld up in tch: rdn over 1f out: r.o to ld cl home) ....— **1**
3823[14] Robo Magic (USA) **(60)***(53) (GLewis)* 2-8-5b SWhitworth(5) (led: rdn over 1f out: hdd cl home) ....nk **2**
4104[5] Southern Dominion **(52)***(44) (WGMTurner)* 2-8-1b(5)ow1 JDSmith(10) (prom: ev ch 2f out: rdn & outpcd over 1f out) 4 **3**
4095[14] Rowlandsons Silver (FR) **(63)***(38) (DJGMurraySmith)* 2-8-3 StephenDavies(12) (wl bhd tl r.o wl fnl f) 1 **4**
3807[11] Tinker Amelia *(39) (WRMuir)* 2-8-6 JWeaver(8) (mid div: one pce fnl 2f) ....½ **5**
3566[8] Risky Rose **(37)***(34) (RHollinshead)* 2-7-11 (5) AGarth(4) (outpcd: styd on one pce fnl f) ....hd **6**
3815[4] Reponist **(50)***(36) (MJCamacho)* 2-8-6v LCharnock(9) (chsd ldrs: rdn over 2f out: wknd fnl f) ....½ **7**
3965[11] Jersey Belle *(31) (PJMakin)* 2-8-4 RPerham(7) (outpcd: sme late hdwy) ....¾ **8**
4055[11] Pagan Heights **(36)***(—) (JRJenkins)* 2-7-9b(7) MBaird(2) (a outpcd & bhd) 12 **9**
4106[8] Saxon Heir (IRE) **(53)***(—) (MDIUsher)* 2-7-10 (7) CAdamson(11) (m.n.s) 7 **10**
3020[14] Iron Man (IRE) **(67)***(—)*(Jt-Fav)*(LordHuntingdon)* 2-8-9 DHarrison(6) (outpcd) 1 **11**
Logie Pert Lad *(—) (JJBridger)* 2-8-11 TWilliams(3) (pushed along thrght: a outpcd) 9 **12**
1585[9] Foxhill Flyer *(—) (MDIUsher)* 2-7-10 JQuinn(13) (a wl bhd: t.o fnl 3f) 2½ **13**

3/1 FAIRY FAY (IRE), Iron Man (IRE), **5/1** Reponist, **6/1** Robo Magic (USA), **8/1** Rowlandsons Silver (FR), **12/1** Southern Dominion, **20/1** Jersey Belle, Saxon Heir (IRE), **25/1** Tinker Amelia, **33/1** Risky Rose, Foxhill Flyer, **50/1** Pagan Heights, Logie Pert Lad, CSF £20.66 TOTE £3.90: £2.70 £2.30 £3.00 (£20.90) OWNER Mr Brian Williams (NEWMARKET) BRED Thomas and Mary Shirley 13 Rn 1m 14.81 (4.21) SF: 2/-/-/-/-/-/-/-/-/-/-/-/-
STEWARDS' ENQUIRY Smith suspended 18-21/11/94 (excessive use of whip).

4208 STOUR H'CAP (0-65) (Class F) £2,600.30 (£730.80: £356.90)
2m (Equitrack) Stalls: Low GOING: minus 0.40 sec per fur (FS) 3-10 (3-11)

3937[21] **Art Form (USA) (63)***(75)*(Jt-Fav)*(CACyzer)* 7-10-0 TIves(3) (hld up & wl bhd: hdwy over 4f out: led over 3f out: sn clr: easily) ....— **1**
3964[6] Strat's Legacy **(57)***(63) (DWPArbuthnot)* 7-9-8 JWeaver(7) (hld up: hdwy 4f out: no ch w wnr) 6 **2**
4091[9] Arian Spirit (IRE) **(38)***(40) (WJMusson)* 3-7-7 NAdams(13) (hld up: led 4f out tl over 3f out: sn rdn & outpcd) 4 **3**
4141* Rose of Glenn **(53)***(54) (BPalling)* 3-8-8 (5x) StephenDavies(4) (hld up: r.o one pce fnl 2f) ....¾ **4**
4052[4] Glow Forum **(40)***(38) (GLMoore)* 3-7-9 NCarlisle(12) (hld up: hdwy over 4f out: rdn 3f out: wknd fnl 2f) 3½ **5**

41413 Scalp 'em (IRE) **(37)***(25) (PDEvans)* 6-7-11 (5)ow3 SSanders(2) (prom: rdn 4f out: wknd) 11 **6**
41418 Lajadhal (FR) **(31)***(17) (KBishop)* 5-7-5be(5)ow3 NVarley(8) (wl bhd tl sme late hdwy)....2½ **7**
413516 Duggan **(28)***(13) (MJohnston)* 7-7-0b(7) CAdamson(14) (led after 2f: sn clr: hdd 4f out: wknd) 1¼ **8**
40917 Tres Cher (IRE) **(56)***(32)*(Jt-Fav)*(BWHills)* 3-8-11b JReid(11) (hdwy to chse ldr 1f: wknd 4f out) 10 **9**
397611 Ragtime Song **(50)***(25) (AMoore)* 5-9-1 RCochrane(9) (m.n.s) ....¾ **10**
39524 Success Story **(61)***(28) (LordHuntingdon)* 3-9-2v DHarrison(5) (prom to ½-wy) 8 **11**
40528 La Reina Blanca (SPA) **(50)***(—) (TThomsonJones)* 3-8-5 ow3 SWhitworth(10) (chsd ldr to ½-wy: wknd qckly: t.o)....25 **12**
413512 Greystyle **(28)***(—) (MBrittain)* 4-7-7v GBardwell(6) (led 2f: wknd ½-wy: t.o)....dist **13**

LONG HANDICAP Lajadhal (FR) 6-11 Arian Spirit (IRE) 6-13 Duggan 7-4 Greystyle 7-4

9/2 ART FORM (USA), Tres Cher (IRE), **5/1** Scalp 'em (IRE), **11/2** Rose of Glenn, **7/1** Glow Forum, **10/1** Strat's Legacy, Success Story, **14/1** Ragtime Song, **25/1** Duggan, La Reina Blanca (SPA), **33/1** Lajadhal (FR), Arian Spirit (IRE), Greystyle, CSF £45.66 CT £1,189.29 TOTE £7.70: £2.30 £1.70 £28.60 (£23.80) OWNER Mr R. M. Cyzer (HORSHAM) BRED Morgan's Ford Farm and Elizabeth Thomas in USA 13 Rn

3m 28.22 (0.74 under best) (4.72) SF: 57/46/15/29/13/10/2/-/-/-/-/-/-
WEIGHT FOR AGE 3yo-10lb

4209 THAMES H'CAP (0-85) (Class D) £3,423.30 (£1,037.40: £507.20: £242.10)

1m 2f (Equitrack) Stalls: Low GOING: minus 0.40 sec per fur (FS) 3-40 (3-42)

34036 **Chatham Island (85)***(92+) (CEBrittain)* 6-10-0 BDoyle(12) (a.p: led 3f out: sn qcknd clr: comf)....— **1**
4140* Hillsdown Boy (IRE) **(56)***(59) (SDow)* 4-7-13 (6x) JQuinn(4) (a.p: n.m.r ent st: swtchd rt over 1f out: r.o fnl f) 2½ **2**
41033 Shabanaz **(62)***(64)*(Fav)*(WRMuir)* 9-8-5 JWeaver(14) (s.s: hdwy over 2f out: rdn ent st: styd on)....½ **3**
405214 Sarum **(53)***(54) (CPWildman)* 8-7-10 NAdams(10) (hld up: hdwy 3f out: one pce fnl 2f) ....nk **4**
25013 Sir Norman Holt (IRE) **(75)***(67) (RJO'Sullivan)* 5-9-4b JReid(9) (led 4f out to 3f out: rdn & wknd fnl 2f)....6 **5**
409114 Uncharted Waters **(67)***(58) (CACyzer)* 3-8-5 DeanMcKeown(13) (hld up & a in mid div) ....½ **6**
158714 Global Dancer **(73)***(61) (WAO'Gorman)* 3-8-8b(3) EmmaO'Gorman(5) (hld up in tch: ev ch 3f out: wknd fnl 2f)....2 **7**
40935 Sparkling Roberta **(55)***(40) (MDIUsher)* 3-7-0 (7) CAdamson(11) (nvr plcd to chal)...2 **8**
414010 Pink Brief (IRE) **(65)***(49) (BJMeehan)* 3-8-3 DHarrison(6) (hld up in rr: n.d) ....½ **9**
Strictly Personal (USA) **(72)***(55) (KRBurke)* 4-9-1 RCochrane(3) (hdwy over 4f out: sn wknd)....½ **10**
39204 Peaches Polly **(67)***(41) (GRimmer)* 4-8-10 RPrice(8) (led 5f)....6 **11**
40525 Kintwyn **(70)***(36) (DRLaing)* 4-8-13 SWhitworth(1) (led 5f out to 4f out: wknd qckly) 5 **12**
399311 Barahin (IRE) **(58)***(—) (JJBridger)* 5-8-1 TWilliams(2) (a in rr: t.o)....25 **13**

LONG HANDICAP Sparkling Roberta 6-3

3/1 Shabanaz, **9/2** CHATHAM ISLAND, **5/1** Hillsdown Boy (IRE), **7/1** Peaches Polly, **8/1** Sir Norman Holt (IRE), Kintwyn, **9/1** Barahin (IRE) (14/1-8/1), **12/1** Uncharted Waters, **16/1** Global Dancer, Pink Brief (IRE), **20/1** Sarum, Strictly Personal (USA), **33/1** Sparkling Roberta, CSF £29.26 CT £76.66 TOTE £4.10: £1.60 £1.90 £2.80 (£15.50) OWNER Mr B. H. Voak (NEWMARKET) BRED G. C. Hughes 13 Rn 2m 6.96 (3.96) SF: 47/17/21/13/24/11/14/-/-/-/-/-/-
WEIGHT FOR AGE 3yo-5lb

T/Plpt: £25.90 (333.91 Tckts). T/Qdpt: £4.00 (9.5 Tckts). TS

4140-LINGFIELD (L-H)
Friday November 11th (Standard)

4210 VALUATION CLAIMING STKS (I) (Class F) £2,078.60 (£584.60: £285.80)

7f (Equitrack) Stalls: Low GOING: minus 0.51 sec per fur (FS) 12-10 (12-12)

41433 **Soaking (62)***(62) (GLMoore)* 4-9-3 BRouse(10) (lw: a.p: led 3f out: clr over 1f out: r.o wl) ....— **1**
414310 Wave Hill **(70)***(52) (PRHedger)* 5-8-11v StephenDavies(12) (a.p: rdn over 2f out: r.o one pce)....2 **2**
39097 Knightrider **(48)***(51) (CJames)* 3-8-11b WNewnes(14) (a.p: rdn 2f out: one pce)....1½ **3**

3975[2] Masnun (USA) **(70)***(51) (RJO'Sullivan)* 9-8-13 RCochrane(2) (rdn thrght: a.p: 4th whn n.m.r & snatched up on ins over 1f out: r.o ins fnl f)................s.h **4**
3805[14] Monsieur Petong **(53)***(44) (DNicholls)* 3-8-9 AlexGreaves(6) (nvr nr to chal).........2½ **5**
4107[8] Island Knight (IRE) **(72)***(46)*(Fav)*(MJRyan)* 5-9-1 AClark(1) (lw: nvr nrr)..................1 **6**
4202[8] Maid Welcome **(56)***(35) (MrsNMacauley)* 7-7-13v(7) AmandaSanders(9) (led 4f: wknd over 1f out)..1 **7**
3909* Cape Pigeon (USA) **(58)***(35) (LGCottrell)* 9-8-7v NCarlisle(15) (lw: nvr nrr).............hd **8**
4064[13] Mrs Bizzybody **(35)***(23) (TJNaughton)* 3-8-0b JQuinn(13) (nvr nrr).........................3½ **9**
4078[10] Takenhall **(42)***(25) (MJFetherston-Godley)* 9-8-8 ow3 JWeaver(3) (bhd fnl 5f) 1¾ **10**
Poor Printer (IRE) *(27) (JAkehurst)* 3-9-0 DeanMcKeown(4) (s.s: a bhd) 3 **11**
3791[3] Galaxy Express **(44)***(11) (GHEden)* 6-8-5 NAdams(11) (b: lw: bhd fnl 2f)..............2½ **12**
Flash Appeal *(21) (RGuest)* 3-9-0 DHarrison(8) (w'like: bhd fnl 3f)........................hd **13**
3563[12] Annie's Own (IRE) *(14) (JBerry)* 3-8-10 SWilliams(16) (hdwy 6f out: wknd over 3f out)..1½ **14**
4064[17] Tremolante *(3) (CaptJWilson)* 3-8-4 MFenton(7) (prom over 2f) 2½ **15**

11/4 Island Knight (IRE), **4/1** Masnun (USA), **11/2** Wave Hill, **13/2** SOAKING, **10/1** Cape Pigeon (USA), **12/1** Maid Welcome, Galaxy Express, **14/1** Takenhall, **16/1** Monsieur Petong, Flash Appeal, Annie's Own (IRE), **20/1** Poor Printer (IRE), **25/1** Knightrider, **33/1** Mrs Bizzybody, Tremolante, CSF £44.62 TOTE £3.90: £1.10 £2.50 £4.00 (£28.80) OWNER Mr K. Higson (EPSOM) BRED David John Brown 15 Rn 1m 25.55 (4.95) SF: 28/18/16/17/8/11/1/1/-/-/-/-/-/-/-
WEIGHT FOR AGE 3yo-2lb

4211

BAKER LORENZ WINTER H'CAP (I) (0-70) (Class E) £2,211.00 (£621.00: £303.00) **5f** Stalls: High GOING: minus 0.51 sec per fur (FS) 12-40 (12-43)

3457[5] **Very Dicey (69)***(71)*(Jt-Fav)*(JBerry)* 6-9-7 (7) PRoberts(10) (mde virtually all: clr over 1f out: r.o wl)..— **1**
4078[19] Moujeeb (USA) **(59)***(53)*(Jt-Fav)*(PMitchell)* 4-9-4v AClark(1) (lw: outpcd: gd hdwy over 1f out: str run fnl f: fin wl) 2½ **2**
4133[5] My Cherrywell **(50)***(43) (LRLloyd-James)* 4-8-9 RCochrane(6) (b: b.hind: a.p: rdn over 2f out: unable qckn) ....nk **3**
4059[22] Green's Bid **(65)***(54) (DWChapman)* 4-9-10 JWeaver(3) (lw: a.p: rdn over 2f out: one pce)...1¼ **4**
4145[6] First Option **(64)***(50) (RBastiman)* 4-9-4 (5) HBastiman(5) (nvr nr to chal)..................1 **5**
4033[4] Four of Spades **(68)***(53) (BBeasley)* 3-9-10b(3) JTate(7) (lw: hdwy over 1f out: nvr nrr) ....hd **6**
4059[6] Born to Be **(60)***(40) (SDow)* 5-9-5 GDuffield(4) (bhd fnl 2f) 1¾ **7**
3978[19] Domino Queen (IRE) **(55)***(32) (JWPayne)* 3-9-0b GBardwell(2) (b.hind: spd over 2f)..¾ **8**
3969[12] Purbeck Centenary **(53)***(29) (PHowling)* 4-8-12 DeanMcKeown(8) (swtg: a.p: rdn over 2f out: wknd fnl f)...nk **9**
3969[11] Rankaidade **(54)***(19) (RHollinshead)* 3-8-8 (5) AGarth(9) (bhd fnl 2f) 3½ **10**

7/2 VERY DICEY, Moujeeb (USA), **11/2** Four of Spades, **13/2** My Cherrywell, **9/1** Born to Be, **10/1** First Option, **12/1** Green's Bid, **14/1** Domino Queen (IRE), Rankaidade, **16/1** Purbeck Centenary, CSF £15.60 CT £69.71 TOTE £3.90: £1.70 £1.50 £4.60 (£7.30) OWNER Mr J. Berry (COCKERHAM) BRED G. R. Smith (Thriplow) Ltd and Lord Edwin McAlpine 10 Rn
59.71 secs (1.51) SF: 42/25/16/27/22/25/14/-/-/-

4212

BAKER LORENZ WINTER H'CAP (II) (0-70) (Class E) £2,200.50 (£618.00: £301.50) **5f (Equitrack)** Stalls: High GOING: minus 0.51 sec per fur (FS) 1-10 (1-11)

3586[22] **Speedy Classic (USA) (49)***(64+) (MJHeaton-Ellis)* 5-9-0 StephenDavies(9) (lw: hdwy wl over 1f out: led ins fnl f: r.o wl)...— **1**
3969[4] Tee-Emm **(59)***(63)*(Fav)*(PHowling)* 4-9-10 JQuinn(10) (led over 2f: ev ch ins fnl f: unable qckn)..3½ **2**
4016[16] Super Rocky **(58)***(61) (RBastiman)* 5-9-4b(5) HBastiman(2) (rdn thrght: hdwy over 1f out: r.o ins fnl f) ....hd **3**
3446[14] Feather Face **(55)***(52) (CJames)* 4-9-6b WNewnes(4) (a.p: led over 2f out tl ins fnl f: sn wknd) 2 **4**
3969[7] Olifantsfontein **(50)***(46) (DNicholls)* 6-9-1 AlexGreaves(5) (hdwy over 1f out: nvr nrr)..nk **5**
4102[8] Manor Adventure **(55)***(46) (PTDalton)* 4-9-1b(5) PMcCabe(8) (s.i.s: outpcd: nvr nrr) 1½ **6**
3778[11] The Noble Oak (IRE) **(54)***(33) (MMcCormack)* 6-9-0b(5) RPainter(6) (spd over 3f)....4 **7**
3978[25] High Holme **(59)***(36) (DTThom)* 3-9-10 TIves(1) (bhd fnl 2f) ....½ **8**
4102[11] Miriam **(54)***(13) (MJFetherston-Godley)* 3-9-5 DHarrison(3) (spd over 2f) 6 **9**

3/1 Tee-Emm, **7/2** SPEEDY CLASSIC (USA), Super Rocky, **7/1** Miriam, **8/1** Feather Face, **10/1** Olifantsfontein, The Noble Oak (IRE), **12/1** Manor Adventure, **14/1** High Holme, CSF £14.97 CT £37.44 TOTE £6.00: £1.50 £1.20 £1.50 (£7.90) OWNER Stainless Design Services (WROUGHTON) BRED Lagrange Chance Partnership & Overbrook Farm 9 Rn

59.54 secs (1.34) SF: 32/30/28/19/13/14/-/-/-

4213 SURVEYORS (S) STKS (2-Y.O) (Class G) £1,752.30 (£492.80: £240.90)

7f (Equitrack) Stalls: Low GOING: minus 0.51 sec per fur (FS) 1-40 (1-41)

4203[4] **Slytly Beveled (49)***(52) (MPMuggeridge)* 2-8-6 (5) TGMcLaughlin(13) (lw: a.p: hrd rdn over 1f out: led nr fin)........— **1**
3965[5] Bon Secret (IRE) **(56)***(51) (TJNaughton)* 2-8-11 JWeaver(12) (lw: led: clr over 1f out: rdn fnl f: hdd nr fin)........nk **2**
4169[18] Water Bebe (IRE) **(55)***(39) (MJohnston)* 2-8-6 TWilliams(6) (a.p: rdn over 4f out: r.o ins fnl f)........3½ **3**
4106[11] Chadleigh Walk (IRE) **(44)***(37) (RHollinshead)* 2-8-11 TIves(9) (lw: a.p: hrd rdn over 2f out: one pce)........3½ **4**
4207[4] Rowlandsons Silver (FR) **(63)***(34)*(Fav)*(DJGMurraySmith)* 2-8-11 StephenDavies(16) (nvr nr to chal)........1¼ **5**
3892[11] Shanghai Lil **(40)***(26) (MJFetherston-Godley)* 2-8-6 DaleGibson(14) (hdwy over 4f out: wknd over 1f out)........1¼ **6**
4172[13] Final Spoof **(56)***(30) (MRChannon)* 2-8-6 (5) RPainter(7) (hld up: rdn over 2f out: wknd over 1f out)........½ **7**
3987[13] Havana Miss **(40)***(21) (BPalling)* 2-7-13 (7) WendyJones(5) (a mid div)........2 **8**
3788[11] Dancing-Alone *(25) (JWPayne)* 2-8-11 EGuest(15) (a mid div)........½ **9**
4066[16] Danny's Gift *(19) (DRLaing)* 2-8-6 GBardwell(10) (b: hrd rdn over 2f out: nvr nrr).hd **10**
4095[24] Lady Lucy Linnet **(40)***(14) (NAGraham)* 2-8-6 JWilliams(2) (nvr nrr)........2½ **11**
3350[11] Flatford Princess **(48)***(12) (GLMoore)* 2-8-6 BRouse(4) (a bhd)........¾ **12**
3970[9] Dismissive (IRE) *(10) (DrJDScargill)* 2-8-6 DHarrison(1) (bhd fnl 2f)........1 **13**
3239[13] Meesonette **(40)***(10) (DWChapman)* 2-8-6 DeanMcKeown(3) (a bhd)........s.h **14**
Knotty Scot *(7) (TMJones)* 2-8-6 RPerham(8) (b: neat: s.s: a bhd)........1½ **15**
4095[7] Qualitair Glory **(50)***(10) (JFBottomley)* 2-8-11v NKennedy(11) (prom 3f)........1 **16**

7/2 Rowlandsons Silver (FR), **9/2** Water Bebe (IRE), **6/1** Bon Secret (IRE), **8/1** Qualitair Glory, **9/1** Final Spoof, **10/1** SLYTLY BEVELED, Dancing-Alone, **12/1** Dismissive (IRE), Flatford Princess, **14/1** Havana Miss, **20/1** Lady Lucy Linnet, Shanghai Lil, **25/1** Danny's Gift, Knotty Scot, **33/1** Meesonette, Chadleigh Walk (IRE), CSF £71.84 TOTE £12.60: £3.20 £4.40 £3.00 (£39.90) OWNER Trojan Racing (NEWBURY) BRED Gordian Troeller Bloodstock Ltd 16 Rn

1m 26.58 (3.58) SF: 11/11/-/-/-/-/-/-/-/-/-/-/-/-/-/-

No bid

4214 VALUATION CLAIMING STKS (II) (Class F) £2,069.50 (£582.00: £284.50)

7f (Equitrack) Stalls: Low GOING: minus 0.51 sec per fur (FS) 2-10 (2-12)

3480[13] **Silent Expression (60)***(62) (BJMeehan)* 4-9-2 JWeaver(7) (a.p: led over 1f out: drvn out)........— **1**
3471[3] Mazeeka (IRE) **(70)***(58) (WAO'Gorman)* 3-8-9 (3) EmmaO'Gorman(14) (hdwy over 2f out: ev ch over 1f out: unable qckn)........¾ **2**
4202[3] Hawaii Storm (FR) **(52)***(49) (MissAJWhitfield)* 6-8-6 (5) RPainter(16) (hdwy 2f out: r.o)........3 **3**
3963[4] Make the Break **(66)***(38)*(Fav)*(GLMoore)* 3-8-9 BRouse(1) (hdwy over 2f out: one pce)........5 **4**
3979[17] After the Last **(70)***(38) (RHannon)* 4-8-6 (7) DaneO'Neill(10) (lost pl over 4f out: rallied fnl f: r.o)........¾ **5**
198[9] Arrasas Lady **(26)***(24) (RMFlower)* 4-8-0 StephenDavies(8) (rdn & lost pl over 3f out: edgd rt ins fnl f: r.o one pce)........hd **6**
4204[6] Eatons **(46)***(26) (SDow)* 3-7-11e(5)ow2 SSanders(12) (eyeshield: lw: a.p: hrd rdn over 1f out: sn wknd)........¾ **7**
2953[15] Bill Moon **(37)***(32) (PJFeilden)* 8-8-4 (7) JoHunnam(9) (lw: hdwy 4f out: wknd over 1f out)........nk **8**
1571[8] Komplicity **(57)***(26) (BobJones)* 3-8-5 DaleGibson(5) (lw: a.p: led over 3f out tl over 1f out: sn wknd)........1 **9**
4107[9] Alpine Johnny **(60)***(26) (RHollinshead)* 3-8-11b TIves(3) (led over 3f: wknd 2f out)...3 **10**
Rustic League (IRE) *(30) (TJNaughton)* 3-8-12 (7) VHalliday(2) (hdwy over 5f out: wknd over 3f out)........2 **11**
4126[19] Kentucky Flyer **(42)***(10) (JFBottomley)* 3-8-2 NKennedy(6) (bhd fnl 4f)........1½ **12**
3699[6] Fade Away (IRE) **(36)***(—) (KGWingrove)* 3-8-0b DBiggs(11) (lw: s.i.s: a bhd)........8 **13**
Swallow Ridge (IRE) *(—) (RJO'Sullivan)* 5-8-11 (5) JDSmith(15) (bit bkwd: a bhd) .8 **14**
Nigels Lady *(—) (NMBabbage)* 5-8-6 ow2 JWilliams(4) (a bhd)........7 **15**

4078[20] Letsbeonestaboutit **(52)***(—) (MrsNMacauley)* 8-8-11b DeanMcKeown(13) (hdwy over 3f out: wknd over 2f out: hmpd & uns rdr ins fnl f) .... **U**

5/2 Make the Break, **5/1** Mazeeka (IRE), **11/2** SILENT EXPRESSION, **6/1** After the Last, **7/1** Hawaii Storm (FR), **10/1** Alpine Johnny, **12/1** Komplicity, Eatons, **14/1** Letsbeonestaboutit, **20/1** Nigels Lady, **25/1** Swallow Ridge (IRE), Kentucky Flyer, Rustic League (IRE), **33/1** Bill Moon, Fade Away (IRE), **50/1** Arrasas Lady, CSF £36.08 TOTE £9.90: £3.00 £2.50 £1.80 (£23.70) OWNER Mr A. S. Reid (UPPER LAMBOURN) BRED J. B. H. Stevens 16 Rn
1m 25.34 (2.34) SF: 30/25/17/4/6/-/-/2/-/-/-/-/-/-/-/-

4215

BAKER LORENZ MEDIAN AUCTION STKS (Mdn 3-Y.O) (Class F) £1,969.40 (£553.40: £270.20)
1m 2f (Equitrack) Stalls: High GOING: minus 0.51 sec (FS) 2-45 (2-59)

4160[7] **Polly Peculiar** *(51+) (BSmart)* 3-8-9 DHarrison(9) (hdwy 8f out: led over 3f out: clr over 2f out: r.o wl)..— **1**
4023[9] Lady Reema **(48)***(46) (MissAJWhitfield)* 3-8-4 (5) RPainter(2) (hld up: rdn over 4f out: r.o one pce fnl 2f)..3 **2**
3977[11] Greggina **(49)***(46)*(Fav)*(PTWalwyn)* 3-8-9 RCochrane(8) (a.p: led over 4f out tl over 3f out: one pce) ....s.h **3**
3996[13] Premium Bond *(50) (ICampbell)* 3-9-0b DBiggs(10) (lw: a.p: rdn 4f out: one pce)...¾ **4**
Kingsfold Fountain *(47) (MJHaynes)* 3-9-0 BRouse(4) (b.hind: w'like: hdwy over 1f out: nvr nrr) 1¾ **5**
3463[10] Sweet Caroline **(40)***(41) (PMitchell)* 3-8-9 AClark(6) (hrd rdn 6f out: nvr nr to chal) ....nk **6**
Fleet Cadet *(41) (NAGraham)* 3-9-0 TIves(7) (w'like: nvr nrr) 3 **7**
3609[13] Little Miner (IRE) **(42)***(34) (BPalling)* 3-8-9 StephenDavies(5) (prom over 5f)...........1 **8**
4064[10] Dolly Dolittle *(30) (HJCollingridge)* 3-8-4 (5) CHawksley(11) (swtg: a bhd).............2½ **9**
4049[10] Tierra Colorada *(30) (RJRWilliams)* 3-8-9 NAdams(12) (lw: a bhd) ....hd **10**
3598[12] Slopes **(45)***(—) (TJNaughton)* 3-9-0 JWeaver(3) (a bhd)..25 **11**
4086[4] She's a Madam *(—) (LRLloyd-James)* 3-8-9 MDeering(1) (b: led over 5f: t.o) ....dist **12**

4/1 Greggina, **9/2** Fleet Cadet, **11/2** Premium Bond, **6/1** Lady Reema, Kingsfold Fountain, **8/1** POLLY PECULIAR, Little Miner (IRE), **20/1** Dolly Dolittle, She's a Madam, Slopes, **25/1** Tierra Colorada, **33/1** Sweet Caroline, CSF £53.82 TOTE £9.50: £3.20 £2.30 £1.10 (£36.50) OWNER The Big Eaters Partnership (LAMBOURN) BRED Aston Park Stud 12 Rn
2m 8.94 (5.94) SF: 6/2/2/5/4/-/-/-/-/-/-/-

4216

HANOVER SQUARE NURSERY (0-85) (Class D) £3,378.45 (£1,023.60: £500.30: £238.65)
1m (Equitrack) Stalls: High GOING: minus 0.51 sec per fur (FS) 3-20 (3-28)

4203* **Risky Romeo (75)***(87+)*(Fav)*(GCBravery)* 2-9-13 (6x) RCochrane(9) (stdy hdwy over 3f out: led over 1f out: pushed out) ....— **1**
4017* Failte Ro (56)*(64) (JEBanks)* 2-8-8 JQuinn(11) (hld up: led 3f out tl over 1f out: unable qckn) 2 **2**
3800[2] Dance So Suite **(59)***(55) (PFICole)* 2-8-11 TQuinn(4) (a.p: rdn 3f out: one pce).......6 **3**
4031[13] Tara Colleen (IRE) **(53)***(46) (CAHorgan)* 2-8-5 ow1 AClark(10) (hdwy over 3f out: one pce fnl 2f) 1½ **4**
3703[2] Kevasingo **(50)***(41) (SDow)* 2-7-11 (5)ow2 SSanders(2) (a.p: led over 3f out: sn hdd: one pce)..¾ **5**
3987[7] Mediate (IRE) **(50)***(33) (RHannon)* 2-8-2 GDuffield(7) (lw: a.p: ev ch 3f out: wknd wl over 1f out)..4 **6**
4129[5] Templemore (IRE) **(54)***(35) (NACallaghan)* 2-8-6 DHarrison(5) (rdn 6f out: nvr nr to chal)..¾ **7**
4142* No Pattern **(70)***(48) (GLMoore)* 2-9-8 (6x) BRouse(6) (a bhd)..............................1½ **8**
4122[3] Tabard Garden **(50)***(28) (DNicholls)* 2-8-2 GBardwell(3) (lw: hld up: rdn over 4f out: wknd over 3f out)..s.h **9**
4142[4] Poly Road **(50)***(25) (MRChannon)* 2-8-2 FNorton(8) (hdwy 4f out: wknd over 2f out)..1½ **10**
4031[9] Tonka **(59)***(31) (DJGMurraySmith)* 2-8-11 AMackay(12) (a bhd) 1¼ **11**
4106[2] Another Baileys **(49)***(21) (MJohnston)* 2-8-1 TWilliams(1) (led over 4f)..................s.h **12**

7/4 RISKY ROMEO, **5/1** Failte Ro, **11/2** Another Baileys, **6/1** Templemore (IRE), **7/1** Dance So Suite, **8/1** No Pattern, **12/1** Mediate (IRE), **16/1** Kevasingo, **20/1** Tonka, Poly Road, Tabard Garden, **33/1** Tara Colleen (IRE), CSF £12.70 CT £53.52 TOTE £2.10: £1.10 £2.80 £4.00 (£8.50) OWNER Miss Sonja Quince (NEWMARKET) BRED Mrs S. Quince 12 Rn
1m 38.2 (1.80) SF: 50/28/20/12/7/-/2/1/-/-/-/-

4217

BAKER LORENZ RELOCATION H'CAP (0-60) (Class F) £2,133.20 (£600.20: £293.60) **1m 4f (Equitrack)** Stalls: High GOING: minus 0.51 sec (FS) 3-50 (3-55)

4074[4] **Explosive Power (47)***(54) (GCBravery)* 3-8-13 TIves(2) (lw: gd hdwy over 3f out: hrd rdn fnl f: led nr fin)....— **1**
4091[4] Red Dancer **(49)***(56) (MBell)* 3-9-1b MFenton(16) (rdn over 4f out: hdwy over 3f out: hrd rdn & ev ch fnl f: r.o wl)....s.h **2**
3901[15] Stevie's Wonder (IRE) **(50)***(56)*(Fav)*(TGMills)* 4-9-9 JWeaver(4) (lw: led: hrd rdn over 1f out: hdd nr fin)....nk **3**
4091[6] Zuno Noelyn **(54)***(54) (GLewis)* 3-9-6 DHarrison(12) (a.p: rdn 2f out: wknd fnl f)......5 **4**
4091[5] Comtec's Legend **(40)***(38) (JFBottomley)* 4-8-13 NKennedy(15) (lw: hdwy over 3f out: one pce fnl 2f)....1½ **5**
4105[8] Kiyas **(46)***(42) (BJMcMath)* 3-8-12 AMackay(14) (lw: hdwy over 1f out: nvr nrr)....1¾ **6**
4139[6] Guesstimation (USA) **(51)***(43) (JPearce)* 5-9-10 GBardwell(8) (rdn over 4f out: nvr nr to chal)....3½ **7**
3902[11] Ann Hill (IRE) **(40)***(31) (RHollinshead)* 4-8-6 (7) DDenby(3) (nvr nrr)....nk **8**
3964[2] Telephus **(45)***(36) (BJMcMath)* 5-9-4 JWilliams(11) (nvr nrr)....s.h **9**
3660[7] Nadra (IRE) **(47)***(36) (PFICole)* 3-8-13 TQuinn(6) (a.p: hrd rdn 3f out: wknd 2f out)1½**10**
3708[7] Ajdar **(52)***(40) (PAKelleway)* 3-9-4 MWigham(5) (prom over 7f)....nk **11**
3771[10] Night Edition **(44)***(29) (SDow)* 4-9-3e GDuffield(13) (eyeshield: lw: prom over 9f)..2½ **12**
4052[12] Disputed Call (USA) **(47)***(23) (JWHills)* 5-9-6 RCochrane(1) (lw: a bhd)....7 **13**
3320[15] Little Miss Ribot **(35)***(9) (RJO'Sullivan)* 4-8-8 StephenDavies(17) (prom over 7f)..1½ **14**
3770[13] Kenyatta (USA) **(40)***(11) (AMoore)* 5-8-13 CandyMorris(7) (bhd fnl 5f)....2½ **15**
4053[16] Launchselect **(44)***(2) (DWChapman)* 3-8-10 JQuinn(18) (bhd fnl 5f)....11 **16**
158[7] Run to Au Bon (IRE) **(34)***(—) (AMoore)* 4-8-7 NAdams(9) (a bhd)....1¾ **17**
4140[7] Personimus **(42)***(—) (CaptJWilson)* 4-9-1 AClark(10) (t.o fnl 4f)....dist **18**

9/2 Stevie's Wonder (IRE), **6/1** Red Dancer, **13/2** Zuno Noelyn, Little Miss Ribot, Telephus, **10/1** Guesstimation (USA), **11/1** Comtec's Legend, **12/1** Nadra (IRE), **14/1** Night Edition, EXPLOSIVE POWER, **16/1** Ann Hill (IRE), Kiyas, Disputed Call (USA), Ajdar, **25/1** Kenyatta (USA), **33/1** Launchselect, Run to Au Bon (IRE), Personimus, CSF £103.18 CT £420.74 TOTE £106.70: £9.10 £1.50 £2.00 £3.10 (£83.90) OWNER Mr G. C. Bravery (NEWMARKET) BRED Mrs P. Hollingsworth 18 Rn 2m 32.33 (2.93) SF: 37/39/46/37/29/27/33/-/-/-/-/-/-/-/-/-/-/-
STEWARDS' ENQUIRY Fenton suspended 20-22/11/94 (excessive use of whip).

T/Plpt: £32.50 (226.08 Tckts). T/Qdpt: £5.40 (1.4 Tckts) AK

4102-WOLVERHAMPTON (L-H)
Saturday November 12th (Standard)

4218

ROWAN STKS (0-65) (Class F) £2,363.00 (£663.00: £323.00) **1m 4f (Fibresand)** Stalls: Low GOING: 0.05 sec per fur (Std) 7-00 (7-00)

4063[4] **Slmaat (64)***(67) (MrsMReveley)* 3-8-11 RCochrane(7) (hld up: hdwy 4f out: led over 2f out: all out)....— **1**
4093[2] Dakota Brave (IRE) **(64)***(70)*(Fav)*(JPearce)* 3-9-0 GBardwell(10) (b.nr fore: hld up & plld hrd: hdwy 4f out: 2nd st: rdn & ev ch fnl f: r.o wl)....hd **2**
4130[7] Noufari (FR) **(56)***(62) (RHollinshead)* 3-8-12 MWigham(3) (bhd tl hdwy over 1f out: r.o ins fnl f)....5 **3**
3570[3] Premier Dance **(57)***(64) (DHaydnJones)* 7-9-4 (5) SDrowne(2) (hld up & bhd: hdwy 2f out: r.o fnl f)....2 **4**
4062[6] Extra Time **(62)***(55) (LordHuntingdon)* 3-8-7v JWilliams(6) (prom: 5th st: no hdwy) hd **5**
4105[2] Buckley Boys **(42)***(53) (ABailey)* 3-8-2 (5) DWright(9) (hld up mid div: rdn over 4f out: 4th st: wknd over 1f out)....1¼ **6**
3427[13] Port Sunlight (IRE) **(61)***(57) (PDEvans)* 6-9-5 JWeaver(8) (led 6f: led over 4f out tl over 2f out: 3rd st: wknd wl over 1f out)....1 **7**
4177[7] Mr Devious **(62)***(59) (CNAllen)* 3-9-6 TIves(4) (chsd ldr 5f: wknd over 3f out)....5 **8**
4103* Donia (USA) **(54)***(32) (JLHarris)* 5-9-2 SWilliams(11) (lw: plld hrd: prom tl 6th & wkng st: t.o)....13 **9**
3979[18] Drummer's Dream (IRE) **(38)***(5) (TTBill)* 6-9-0 TWall(5) (plld hrd: hdwy on ins to ld 6f out: hdd over 4f out: sn wknd: t.o)....20 **10**

6/4 Dakota Brave (IRE), **2/1** SLMAAT, **8/1** Premier Dance, Extra Time, **9/1** Donia (USA), **12/1** Port Sunlight (IRE), **16/1** Mr Devious, Buckley Boys, **25/1** Noufari (FR), **40/1** Drummer's Dream (IRE), CSF £5.98 TOTE £3.30: £2.00 £1.30 £2.80 (£4.10) OWNER Mr G. A. Farndon (SALTBURN) BRED Ali K. Al Jafleh 10 Rn 2m 39.9 (8.90) SF: 41/44/35/43/28/27/37/-/-/-
STEWARDS' ENQUIRY Cochrane suspended 21-22/11/94 (excessive use of whip).

4219

BEECH STKS (Mdn 2-Y.O) (Class D) £2,853.00 (£864.00: £422.00: £201.00)
7f (Fibresand) Stalls: Low GOING: 0.05 sec per fur (Std) 7-30 (7-32)

4079[7] **Magna Carta** *(84+)*(Jt-Fav)*(MRStoute)* 2-9-0 JWeaver(2) (chsd ldrs: rdn to ld 3f out: sn clr: unchal)..........— **1**
4203[3] Komreyev Dancer **(66)***(58)*(Jt-Fav)*(ABailey)* 2-8-9 (5) DWright(11) (bhd tl hdwy over 1f out: r.o wl ins fnl f)..........12 **2**
4104[2] Chadleigh Lane (USA) **(62)***(57)* *(RHollinshead)* 2-9-0 TIves(7) (lw: dwlt: hdwy 4f out: 3rd st: chsd wnr over 1f out: no imp)..........nk **3**
4164[4] Bettergeton *(54)* *(GFierro)* 2-8-9 (5) JStack(6) (bhd tl hdwy over 1f out: n.d)..........1½ **4**
4123[2] Nigel's Lad (IRE) *(52)* *(PCHaslam)* 2-9-0 TWilliams(9) (prom: 4th st: no hdwy)..........1 **5**
4104[3] Pertemps Partner **(54)***(45)* *(BAMcMahon)* 2-8-4 (5) SSanders(12) (prom: led over 4f out to 3f out: 2nd st: wknd over 1f out)..........¾ **6**
3988[13] Knave of Diamonds *(39)* *(JWHills)* 2-9-0 RCochrane(10) (lw: nvr nr ldrs)..........5 **7**
4123[3] Silktail (IRE) *(28)* *(JBerry)* 2-8-9 SWilliams(1) (prom over 4f)..........3 **8**
4061[12] Crown My Chief *(27)* *(JEBanks)* 2-9-0 JQuinn(8) (prom: 5th & wkng st)..........3 **9**
4104[9] Franklinsboy *(26)* *(CaptJWilson)* 2-9-0 JWilliams(5) (led over 2f: 6th & wkng st)...nk **10**
1834[6] Kitty Waterjet **(50)***(8)* *(BEllison)* 2-8-9v AMackay(3) (a bhd)..........6 **11**
4104[11] Riva-Deva *(—)* *(SCoathup)* 2-8-7 (7) SharronJames(4) (a bhd: t.o)..........30 **12**

5/2 MAGNA CARTA, Komreyev Dancer, **7/2** Nigel's Lad (IRE), **7/1** Bettergeton, **11/1** Chadleigh Lane (USA), Silktail (IRE) (6/1-12/1), **16/1** Knave of Diamonds, **20/1** Pertemps Partner, **50/1** Crown My Chief, Franklinsboy, Kitty Waterjet, Riva-Deva, CSF £9.41 TOTE £3.00: £2.30 £1.80 £2.20 (£8.60) OWNER Mr R. Barnett (NEWMARKET) BRED W. and R. Barnett Ltd 12 Rn
1m 29.4 (5.40) SF: 39/12/11/8/6/-/-/-/-/-/-/-

4220

WILLOW H'CAP (0-80) (Class D) £2,814.00 (£852.00: £416.00: £198.00)
6f (Fibresand) Stalls: Low GOING: 0.05 sec per fur (Std) 8-00 (8-03)

4107[3] **Dawalib (USA) (73)***(72)* *(DHaydnJones)* 4-9-5v(5) SDrowne(8) (lw: hld up: wnt 2nd st: led ins fnl f: drvn out)..........— **1**
3671[5] Nordan Raider **(69)***(67)* *(MJCamacho)* 6-9-6 LCharnock(10) (s.i.s: sn chsng ldrs: 4th st: ev ch ins fnl f: r.o)..........nk **2**
4107[2] Rocketeer (IRE) **(78)***(76)* *(WRMuir)* 3-10-0b JWeaver(5) (led tl ins fnl f: r.o)..........s.h **3**
3986[16] The Old Chapel **(68)***(61)* *(BAMcMahon)* 5-9-0b(5) SSanders(12) (prom: 5th st: r.o one pce)..........2 **4**
4145* African Chimes **(72)***(61)*(Fav)*(WAO'Gorman)* 7-9-6 (3) EmmaO'Gorman(7) (lw: hld up: swtchd stands' side wl over 1f out: nvr nr to chal)..........1½ **5**
4133[7] Nordico Princess **(65)***(41)* *(GROldroyd)* 3-9-1 RCochrane(9) (lw: prom: 3rd st: wknd over 1f out)..........5 **6**
4170[18] Macfarlane **(75)***(50)* *(MJFetherston-Godley)* 6-9-12 FNorton(4) (lw: nvr trbld ldrs).hd **7**
4170[7] Domicksky **(70)***(41)* *(MRChannon)* 6-9-2 (5) RPainter(1) (chsd ldrs: 6th & wkng st)..........1¼ **8**
3240[15] Kid Ory **(69)***(36)* *(PCalver)* 3-9-5 DaleGibson(3) (rdn over 3f out: bhd fnl 2f)..........1½ **9**
4170[8] Leigh Crofter **(75)***(40)* *(PDCundell)* 5-9-7b(5) DGriffiths(6) (s.s: a wl bhd)..........½ **10**
4016[12] Mr M-E-N (IRE) **(70)***(31)* *(JBerry)* 3-8-13 (7) PRoberts(11) (prom: 7th & wkng st)...1¼ **11**
3885[20] Dark Eyed Lady (IRE) **(75)***(31)* *(DWPArbuthnot)* 4-9-12 JWilliams(2) (a bhd)..........2 **12**
4145[4] It Must Be Millie **(63)***(—)* *(GHEden)* 3-8-13 JQuinn(13) (b.off hind: bhd fnl 2f: t.o)...9 **13**

2/1 African Chimes, **9/4** Rocketeer (IRE), **11/1** Leigh Crofter, Nordan Raider, It Must Be Millie, **12/1** DAWALIB (USA), Domicksky, **14/1** The Old Chapel, **16/1** Macfarlane, **20/1** Mr M-E-N (IRE), **25/1** Kid Ory, Nordico Princess, **33/1** Dark Eyed Lady (IRE), CSF £134.15 CT £377.11 TOTE £23.70: £4.70 £3.00 £2.40 (£136.60) OWNER Jack Brown (Bookmaker) Ltd (PONTYPRIDD) BRED Hilary J. Boone Jnr in USA 13 Rn 1m 14.8 (3.60) SF: 62/58/64/50/51/30/39/-/-/-/-/-/-

4221

GILBERT CURRY ENGINEERS (COVENTRY) H'CAP (0-70) (Class E)
£2,866.00 (£868.00: £424.00: £202.00)
1m 6f 166y (Fibresand) Stalls: Low GOING: 0.05 sec per fur (Std) 8-30 (8-31)

3937[23] **Taroudant (65)***(73)* *(MrsMReveley)* 7-9-12 RCochrane(8) (hld up: stdy hdwy 6f out: 3rd st: hrd rdn to ld cl home)..........— **1**
4130* New Inn **(64)***(71)*(Fav)*(EWeymes)* 3-8-11 (5) JStack(4) (lw: hld up: 6th st: hdwy on ins over 1f out: led ins fnl f: hdd cl home)..........nk **2**
1007[2] Well and Truly **(50)***(57)* *(BAMcMahon)* 7-8-6 (5) SSanders(11) (a.p: 2nd st: ev ch 1f out: nt qckn)..........1 **3**
4124[6] El Nido **(56)***(63)* *(MJCamacho)* 6-9-3 LCharnock(10) (a.p: led 3f out tl ins fnl f)..........s.h **4**

4091[10] La Menorquina (USA) **(35)***(38) (DMarks)* 4-7-10e RStreet(1) (eyeshield: hld up & bhd: stdy hdwy 6f out: hrd rdn 4f out: 5th st: one pce) 3½ **5**
4019[4] Allmosa **(67)***(69) (TJNaughton)* 5-10-0 JWeaver(7) (b.nr hind: led after 2f: hdd 3f out: 4th st: wknd fnl f) ......½ **6**
3822[9] Sassiver (USA) **(43)***(39) (RHollinshead)* 4-7-13 (5) AGarth(9) (s.i.s: 7th st: no hdwy) 5 **7**
3786[11] Swordking (IRE) **(55)***(50) (JLHarris)* 5-9-2 AMackay(3) (lw: lost pl after 6f: hrd rdn 5f out: bhd fnl 2f) ......¾ **8**
2489[0] Broom Isle **(57)***(38) (DBurchell)* 6-8-13 (5)ow1 AProcter(12) (lw: prom tl wknd 3f out)13 **9**
3981[5] Tremendisto **(51)***(28) (CaptJWilson)* 4-8-12 JWilliams(2) (a bhd) 3½ **10**
3812[10] Beaumood **(34)***(2) (EJAlston)* 8-7-9 ow1 JQuinn(6) (led 2f: wknd 4f out) 8 **11**
4160[9] Truthful **(55)***(—) (TJNaughton)* 3-8-0b(7)ow3 VHalliday(5) (s.s: t.o fnl 5f) **12**

9/4 New Inn, **5/2** TAROUDANT, **9/2** Allmosa, **7/1** Well and Truly, **10/1** El Nido, **12/1** Swordking (IRE), Tremendisto, **20/1** La Menorquina (USA), Truthful, **25/1** Sassiver (USA), Broom Isle, **33/1** Beaumood, CSF £9.44 CT £36.08 TOTE £3.70: £1.60 £1.70 £2.30 (£5.80) OWNER Mr G.A. Farndon (SALTBURN) BRED Fieldspring Stud Ltd 12 Rn

3m 18.8 (11.40) SF: 53/44/38/43/20/49/22/-/-/-/-/-

WEIGHT FOR AGE 3yo-9lb

STEWARDS' ENQUIRY Cochrane suspended 23-25/11/94 (excessive use of whip).

4222

SILVER BIRCH (S) STKS (2-Y.O) (Class G) £2,085.00 (£585.00: £285.00)
5f (Fibresand) Stalls: Low GOING: 0.05 sec per fur (Std) 9-00 (9-04)

4029[7] **Rotherfield Park (IRE) (56)***(48) (CSmith)* 2-7-13 (7) MBaird(2) (lw: bhd: gd hdwy over 1f out: hrd rdn to ld wl ins fnl f: r.o) ......— **1**
4017[13] Pats Delight **(40)***(45) (SCoathup)* 2-8-6 TWilliams(4) (sn rdn along: led over 3f out tl wl ins fnl f) 1 **2**
3958[13] Curie Express (IRE) **(58)***(49) (JBerry)* 2-8-4 (7) PFessey(6) (a.p: 2nd st: ev ch ins fnl f: r.o) ......nk **3**
3954[18] Lady Pui **(73)***(46)*(Fav)*(JBerry)* 2-8-11 JWeaver(8) (a.p: 3rd st: rdn over 1f out: one pce) ......¾ **4**
4207[3] Southern Dominion **(52)***(44) (WGMTurner)* 2-8-6b(5) JDSmith(11) (led over 1f: 4th st: one pce) ......½ **5**
3790[8] Precious Times **(44)***(36) (MGMeagher)* 2-8-11 JQuinn(1) (nvr nr to chal) 2½ **6**
4142[5] Foxhill Blue **(45)***(27) (MDIUsher)* 2-8-6 RPerham(7) (no hdwy fnl 2f) 1¼ **7**
4128[5] Master M-E-N (IRE) **(65)***(36) (JBerry)* 2-9-2v SWilliams(13) (chsd ldrs: 6th st: wknd over 1f out) ......hd **8**
3974[12] Two Chalk **(55)***(29) (PDEvans)* 2-8-6v(5) JStack(12) (a bhd) ......½ **9**
4134[3] Lawnswood Lady **(50)***(26) (RHollinshead)* 2-8-1 (5) AGarth(9) (chsd ldrs: 7th st: wknd over 1f out) ......d.h **9**
4207[10] Saxon Heir (IRE) **(53)***(28) (MDIUsher)* 2-9-2b MWigham(10) (rdn over 2f out: sn bhd) 2 **11**
4104[10] Carnival of Light *(6) (JBalding)* 2-8-6 NAdams(3) (chsd ldrs: 5th st: wknd wl over 1f out) 4 **12**
4081[11] Ranger Sloane *(10) (GFierro)* 2-8-6 (5) DGriffiths(5) (s.i.s: a bhd) ......nk **13**

5/4 Lady Pui, **7/2** Southern Dominion, **7/1** Lawnswood Lady, **8/1** ROTHERFIELD PARK (IRE), **12/1** Two Chalk, Master M-E-N (IRE), **16/1** Curie Express (IRE), **20/1** Ranger Sloane, Saxon Heir (IRE), **25/1** Foxhill Blue, **50/1** Pats Delight, Carnival of Light, Precious Times, CSF £273.65 TOTE £10.20: £2.90 £6.40 £2.30 (£614.50) OWNER Miss Rosie Dean (WELLINGORE) BRED Ballymacarney Stud in Ireland 13 Rn

63.6 secs (5.60) SF: 1/-/3/-/-/-/-/-/-/-/-/-/-

Bt in 8,000 gns

4223

OAK H'CAP (0-85) (Class D) £2,801.00 (£848.00: £414.00: £197.00)
1m 100y (Fibresand) Stalls: Low GOING: 0.05 sec per fur (Std) 9-30 (9-31)

4063[13] **Wentbridge Lad (IRE) (74)***(81) (BAMcMahon)* 4-9-7b(5) SSanders(2) (a.p: 5th st: rdn to ld ins fnl f: r.o wl) ......— **1**
4018[13] Aitch N'Bee **(66)***(69) (LadyHerries)* 11-8-11 (7) ShonaCrombie(10) (mde most tl hdd ins fnl f) 2 **2**
4078[4] Polonez Prima **(67)***(70) (JEBanks)* 7-9-0 (5) LNewton(3) (a.p: 2nd st: ev ch ins fnl f: nt qckn) ......hd **3**
4083[2] Queens Stroller (IRE) **(66)***(67) (CCElsey)* 3-9-1 JQuinn(9) (hld up: hdwy & 4th st: r.o ins fnl f) ......¾ **4**
4139* Spring Flyer (IRE) **(66)***(64) (ABailey)* 4-8-13 (5) DWright(8) (a.p: 3rd st: ev ch over 1f out: one pce) 1½ **5**
4125[2] Gobsmacked (USA) **(78)***(72)*(Fav)*(WJHaggas)* 3-9-13 RCochrane(4) (6th st: no hdwy) 2 **6**

3787[6] So Rhythmical **(64)***(55) (GHEden)* 10-9-2 JWilliams(11) (hdwy over 3f out: 8th st: one pce) 1½ **7**
4140[4] Can Can Charlie **(64)***(58) (JPearce)* 4-9-2 GBardwell(5) (bhd: rdn 5f out: nvr nr to chal) ....d.h **7**
4139[2] Just Harry **(75)***(66) (MJRyan)* 3-9-10 DBiggs(12) (hdwy over 2f out: hrd rdn & 7th st: wknd over 1f out) ....hd **9**
4060[8] Tu Opes **(71)***(60) (JLHarris)* 3-9-6 DaleGibson(6) (hld up & bhd) 1 **10**
4064[4] Private Fixture (IRE) **(79)***(68) (DMarks)* 3-10-0e TIves(1) (eyeshield: w ldr over 4f: wknd 3f out) ....hd **11**
4024[11] Rose Elegance **(60)***(46) (OO'Neill)* 5-8-12b NAdams(7) (dwlt: hld up: bhd fnl 2f) ...1½ **12**

7/4 Gobsmacked (USA), **3/1** Polonez Prima, **9/2** Just Harry, **6/1** Spring Flyer (IRE), **9/1** Queens Stroller (IRE), **12/1** WENTBRIDGE LAD (IRE) (8/1-14/1), **16/1** Tu Opes, Can Can Charlie, **33/1** Aitch N'Bee, So Rhythmical, Private Fixture (IRE), **50/1** Rose Elegance, CSF £296.30 CT £1,370.60 TOTE £22.60: £4.40 £6.10 £1.90 (£232.30) OWNER Mr Peter Freeman (TAMWORTH) BRED Peter Doyle 12 Rn 1m 50.2 (6.20) SF: 54/43/44/39/39/44/30/30/-/-/-/-
WEIGHT FOR AGE 3yo-3lb
T/Plpt: £1,286.40 (10.76 Tckts). T/Qdpt: £69.00 (2.5 Tckts) KH

3693-SOUTHWELL (L-H)
Wednesday November 16th (Standard)

4224

RIVER IDLE CLAIMING STKS (I) (Class F) £2,398.00 (£673.00: £328.00)
1m (Fibresand) Stalls: Low GOING: minus 0.07 sec per fur (Std) 12-10 (12-13)

3634[21] **Millsolin (IRE) (68)***(60) (RAkehurst)* 6-8-5 TQuinn(16) (b: lw: trckd ldrs: smooth hdwy to ld over 1f out: shkn up: r.o) ....— **1**
4126[6] Nellie's Gamble **(60)***(50) (JLEyre)* 4-7-9 (5) DWright(2) (dwlt: hdwy 3f out: styd on u.p nr fin) 2½ **2**
4060[15] Spencer's Revenge **(72)***(61)*(Fav)*(LordHuntingdon)* 5-8-11 JWeaver(13) (s.i.s: hdwy on outside appr st: chal over 1f out: rdn & nt qckn) ....s.h **3**
3752[7] Broctune Gold **(65)***(49) (MrsMReveley)* 3-8-5 WWoods(12) (lw: a chsng ldrs: ev ch 2f out: r.o one pce) 4 **4**
3697[5] Charlies Dream (IRE) **(45)***(41) (KRBurke)* 3-8-0 JQuinn(14) (mde most to 2f out: one pce) 1½ **5**
4214[6] Arrasas Lady **(26)***(37) (RMFlower)* 4-7-12 ow2 StephenDavies(15) (cl up: led 2f out tl over 1f out: sn wknd) ....hd **6**
4126[12] Prime Mover **(45)***(37) (DWChapman)* 6-8-1b JFanning(1) (a chsng ldrs: rdn 3f out: no imp) 1½ **7**
4053[4] Puffy **(38)***(44) (MDods)* 7-8-9v DaleGibson(7) (b: s.i.s: sme hdwy ent st: n.d) ....½ **8**
2813[15] Ballad Dancer **(49)***(36) (JMackie)* 9-8-1 NCarlisle(3) (hld up & bhd: stdy hdwy 2f out: nvr nr to chal) ....s.h **9**
3562[4] Mary Macblain **(37)***(35) (JLHarris)* 5-7-11 (5) NVarley(5) (lw: sn pushed along: nvr trbld ldrs) 1 **10**
4033[10] Surprise Breeze **(49)***(32) (RMWhitaker)* 3-7-4 (7)ow3 SLanigan(6) (s.i.s: n.d) ....hd **11**
3902[13] Give In **(34)***(26) (MissGayKelleway)* 7-8-1 LCharnock(8) (w ldrs tl rdn & wknd over 2f out) 4 **12**
4012[19] Scottish Park **(51)***(31) (RWEmery)* 5-8-6 TWilliams(11) (chsd ldrs tl wknd fnl 3f) ...hd **13**
4012[18] Arctic Diamond **(59)***(36) (DNicholls)* 3-8-13 AlexGreaves(10) (sn bhd) 1¾ **14**
4124[14] King of the Horse (IRE) **(60)***(—) (WStorey)* 3-8-0v(5) DRMcCabe(9) (bhd fr ½-wy) **15**
4126[14] Genesis Four **(37)***(—) (AWPotts)* 4-8-3b BDoyle(4) (prom 5f: sn wknd) **16**

9/4 Spencer's Revenge, **6/1** MILLSOLIN (IRE), **7/1** Nellie's Gamble, **8/1** Broctune Gold, Scottish Park, **12/1** Mary Macblain, Arctic Diamond, Puffy, **14/1** Charlies Dream (IRE), Give In, **20/1** Surprise Breeze, Ballad Dancer, Prime Mover, **25/1** Arrasas Lady, King of the Horse (IRE), Genesis Four, CSF £51.12 TOTE £6.20: £2.30 £2.00 £2.00 (£15.30) OWNER Normandy Development (London) (EPSOM) BRED Lhasa Trading Ltd. in Ireland 16 Rn
1m 45.3 (6.00) SF: 25/15/26/12/5/2/3/9/-/-/-/-/-/-/-/-
WEIGHT FOR AGE 3yo-2lb

4225

SEVERN STKS (Mdn 2-Y.O) (Class D) £2,918.00 (£884.00: £432.00: £206.00)
7f (Fibresand) Stalls: High GOING: minus 0.07 sec per fur (Std) 12-40 (12-41)

4158[4] **Barrel of Hope** *(74)*(Jt-Fav)*(JLEyre)* 2-9-0 JFortune(1) (cl up: led 3f out: edgd rt: styd on gamely nr fin) ....— **1**
2225[4] Shooter *(73) (PFICole)* 2-9-0 TQuinn(13) (a.p: hdwy to disp ld 1f out: no ex nr fin) ½ **2**
4158[16] Shot the Sheriff *(66) (PFICole)* 2-9-0 AClark(16) (cl up: chal over 2f out: n.m.r & one pce) 3½ **3**

Winterbottom *(62+)*(Jt-Fav)*(RCharlton)* 2-9-0 JWeaver(2) (cmpt: bit bkwd: outpcd ½-wy: styd on nr fin)....2 **4**
2997³ Daily Challenger (USA) **(69)***(47) (RonaldThompson)* 2-9-0 TWilliams(15) (cl up tl rdn & btn appr fnl f)....7 **5**
4122⁵ Upex le Gold Too **(50)***(45) (MrsASwinbank)* 2-9-0 TIves(11) (led to 3f out: sn outpcd)....1 **6**
3995¹⁰ Bargash *(42) (PDEvans)* 2-9-0 DBiggs(9) (dwlt: bhd tl sme hdwy u.p fnl 2f)....1½ **7**
4164⁸ It Is Now *(38) (MHTompkins)* 2-8-9 (5) SMulvey(4) (s.i.s: styd on fnl 2f: n.d)....1¾ **8**
4095²⁷ Pendine *(32) (SCWilliams)* 2-8-4 (5) PMcCabe(5) (b.off fore: prom to st)....½ **9**
3897¹⁴ Mystoski *(31) (MHTompkins)* 2-8-9 WWoods(14) (outpcd fr ½-wy)....nk **10**
4174¹⁵ Music Please *(30) (SirMarkPrescott)* 2-9-0 GDuffield(12) (nvr bttr than mid div)....3 **11**
4122¹⁰ Here Comes Herbie *(—) (WStorey)* 2-8-9 (5) DRMcCabe(3) (sn outpcd & bhd)....8 **12**
4122¹³ Bracken *(—) (ASmith)* 2-8-4 (5) JStack(8) (s.s: a bhd)....2 **13**
Pink Petal *(—) (CJHill)* 2-8-9 NAdams(10) (neat: bkwd: sn outpcd & bhd)....15 **14**

9/4 BARREL OF HOPE (3/1-6/1), Winterbottom, **4/1** Shooter, **8/1** Daily Challenger (USA), **10/1** Shot the Sheriff, **12/1** Bargash, It Is Now, **14/1** Music Please, **16/1** Mystoski, **20/1** Pink Petal, **25/1** Upex le Gold Too, **33/1** Pendine, Here Comes Herbie, Bracken, CSF £14.17 TOTE £3.30: £1.40 £1.90 £6.50 (£6.60) OWNER Mr P. J. Watson (HAMBLETON) BRED Bolton Grange 14 Rn

1m 32.9 (6.10) SF: 24/23/15/10/-/-/-/-/-/-/-/-/-/-

4226 RIVER IDLE CLAIMING STKS (II) (Class F) £2,398.00 (£673.00: £328.00)

1m (Fibresand) Stalls: High GOING: minus 0.07 sec per fur (Std) 1-10 (1-10)

3979³ **Battle Colours (IRE) (64)***(66) (MrsJRRamsden)* 5-8-9 SWilliams(10) (trckd ldrs: led over 1f out: rdn & r.o)....— **1**
3985⁶ Majboor (IRE) **(59)***(70) (BAMcMahon)* 5-9-0 (5) SSanders(6) (hld up: hdwy 3f out: styd on u.p: nrst fin)....3 **2**
3667⁴ Langtonian **(28)***(47) (JLEyre)* 5-8-3 NCarlisle(14) (cl up: led wl over 2f out tl over 1f out: sn btn)....3½ **3**
3966¹⁰ Rad **(56)***(50) (SPCWoods)* 4-8-7 WWoods(13) (effrt ½-wy: styd on: nvr able to chal)....nk **4**
4102⁴ Certain Way (IRE) **(53)***(55) (NPLittmoden)* 4-8-7 (5) TGMcLaughlin(4) (chsd ldrs: rdn appr st: no imp)....hd **5**
4012¹⁰ No Submission (USA) **(66)***(48) (DWChapman)* 8-8-7 JQuinn(15) (prom: rdn 3f out: no imp after)....1 **6**
4101¹⁸ Allinson's Mate (IRE) **(77)***(53)*(Fav)*(TDBarron)* 6-8-13 JFortune(8) (a.p: shkn up over 1f out: r.o one pce)....½ **7**
4163⁹ Achares (IRE) **(73)***(37) (JLDunlop)* 3-8-9b JWeaver(16) (b.off fore: hdwy to ld after 2f: hdd wl over 2f out: wknd over 1f out)....7 **8**
4051¹⁰ Captain Marmalade **(54)***(29) (DTThom)* 5-8-2 (5) DRMcCabe(11) (sn wl bhd: hdwy ent st: n.d)....1¾ **9**
4053¹⁴ Midlin **(41)***(20) (JLHarris)* 4-7-8 (5)ow1 NVarley(1) (s.i.s: n.d)....½ **10**
3787² Gallery Artist (IRE) **(63)***(22) (RGuest)* 6-7-11 (5) DWright(9) (cl up tl wknd 3f out)....½ **11**
4064¹⁴ Screwball Anaconda **(45)***(20) (CJames)* 3-7-7 (7) CAdamson(3) (sn outpcd & bhd)..1 **12**
3979⁴ Across the Bay **(48)***(18) (RWEmery)* 7-8-3 GBardwell(12) (n.d)....1½ **13**
Amenable **(66)***(—) (BRichmond)* 9-8-0 (5) JStack(7) (b: bkwd: sn outpcd & bhd: t.o: fin lame).... **14**
3909²¹ Christian Warrior **(25)***(—) (REPeacock)* 5-8-1 NAdams(2) (b.off hind: led 2f: wknd qckly ½-wy: t.o).... **15**

4/1 Allinson's Mate (IRE), **9/2** Gallery Artist (IRE), Rad, **11/2** Achares (IRE), **6/1** No Submission (USA), BATTLE COLOURS (IRE), **12/1** Amenable, **14/1** Across the Bay, Majboor (IRE), Certain Way (IRE), **20/1** Langtonian, **25/1** Captain Marmalade, Screwball Anaconda, **33/1** Midlin, **50/1** Christian Warrior, CSF £92.96 TOTE £8.10: £2.90 £9.10 £4.70 (£135.40) OWNER Prestige Racing Club (THIRSK) BRED Stackallan Stud in Ireland 15 Rn

1m 44.5 (5.20) SF: 36/39/18/21/25/19/24/-/-/-/-/-/-/-/-

WEIGHT FOR AGE 3yo-2lb

4227 SHARPES INTERNATIONAL-SANCHO H'CAP (0-70) (Class E) £3,009.00 (£912.00: £446.00: £213.00)

7f (Fibresand) Stalls: High GOING: minus 0.07 sec per fur (Std) 1-40 (1-42)

4163⁵ **Mullitover (67)***(79) (MJHeaton-Ellis)* 4-9-13 StephenDavies(8) (trckd ldrs: led appr fnl f: r.o u.p)....— **1**
4101² Hawwam **(52)***(59) (EJAlston)* 8-8-12 JQuinn(10) (hdwy u.p over 2f out: styd on nr fin: nvr nrr)....2½ **2**

3966[5] Berge (IRE) **(64)***(67) (WAO'Gorman)* 3-9-8 TIves(1) (w ldrs: led 3f out tl over 1f out: rdn & no ex) 1¾ **3**
4163[2] Sandmoor Denim **(60)***(62)*(Fav)*(SRBowring)* 7-8-13 (7) GStrange(14) (b: trckd ldrs: effrt over 2f out: nt pce to chal) ....½ **4**
4139[13] Dream Carrier (IRE) **(68)***(66) (TDBarron)* 6-10-0 JFortune(6) (sn bhd: hdwy 2f out: nvr nr to chal) 2 **5**
3669[13] Bogart **(57)***(55) (CWFairhurst)* 3-8-10 (5) JStack(11) (led to 3f out: wknd over 1f out)s.h **6**
4093[20] Shuttlecock **(69)***(61) (NPLittmoden)* 3-9-6 (7) CTeague(9) (sn outpcd & bhd: sme late hdwy) 3 **7**
4083[9] Prim Lass **(57)***(46) (LordHuntingdon)* 3-9-1 AClark(5) (sn pushed along: nvr trbld ldrs) 1¼ **8**
4060[10] Phoenix Venture (IRE) **(69)***(58) (SPCWoods)* 3-9-13 WWoods(12) (a.p: one pce fnl 2f) ....s.h **9**
4163[18] Desert Lore **(67)***(54) (MrsJRRamsden)* 3-9-11 MWigham(15) (dwlt: hdwy 2f out: n.d) ....¾ **10**
4139[3] St Martha (IRE) **(55)***(41) (MHTompkins)* 4-8-10 (5) SMulvey(7) (s.i.s: bhd tl sme late hdwy) ....½ **11**
4059[12] Love Legend **(59)***(42) (DWPArbuthnot)* 9-9-5 JWeaver(13) (b: prom tl outpcd over 2f out) 1¼ **12**
3434[14] Off the Air (IRE) **(57)***(39) (ICampbell)* 3-9-1v DaleGibson(2) (chsd ldrs tl wknd over 2f out) ....½ **13**
4060[13] Marsh Arab **(54)***(19) (JRArnold)* 3-8-12 GDuffield(4) (lw: outpcd & bhd fr ½-wy)......8 **14**
4056[6] Rosina's Folly **(60)***(25) (RHollinshead)* 3-9-4 NCarlisle(16) (outpcd fr ½-wy).........s.h **15**

11/4 Sandmoor Denim, **11/2** Hawwam, **9/1** Phoenix Venture (IRE), **10/1** Dream Carrier (IRE), Desert Lore, St Martha (IRE), **12/1** MULLITOVER, Berge (IRE), **14/1** Love Legend, Prim Lass, **16/1** Bogart, **20/1** Shuttlecock, Off the Air (IRE), Marsh Arab, **33/1** Rosina's Folly, CSF £76.01 CT £763.64 TOTE £22.10: £4.90 £1.70 £3.50 (£42.90) OWNER Mrs D. B. Mulley (WROUGHTON) BRED Mrs D. B. Mulley 15 Rn 1m 31.4 (4.60) SF: 52/33/40/37/39/28/32/-/-/-/-/-/-/-/-
WEIGHT FOR AGE 3yo-2lb

4228

FIBRESAND NURSERY (0-85) (Class D) £2,905.00 (£880.00: £430.00: £205.00)
7f Stalls: High GOING: minus 0.07 sec per fur (Std) 2-10 (2-15)

4172* **Mister Fire Eyes (IRE) (66)***(83+)*(Jt-Fav)*(CEBrittain)* 2-8-9 (6x) BDoyle(14) (lw: in tch: hdwy ent st: led over 1f out: r.o) ....— **1**
3965[4] Tee Tee Too (IRE) **(73)***(77) (PCHaslam)* 2-9-2 JWeaver(13) (cl up: led over 2f out tl over 1f out: nt qckn) 6 **2**
4129[3] Saint Amigo **(59)***(59)*(Jt-Fav)*(JLEyre)* 2-8-2 GDuffield(15) (chsd ldrs: rdn 3f out: styd on one pce) 2 **3**
Jilly Jaffa Cake (IRE) **(63)***(57) (DWPArbuthnot)* 2-8-6 SWhitworth(4) (a.p: kpt on one pce fnl 2f) 3 **4**
3325[8] Qualitair Ridge **(54)***(37) (JFBottomley)* 2-7-11 NKennedy(2) (sn wl bhd: hdwy 2f out: nrst fin) 5 **5**
1461[4] Mac's Taxi **(59)***(39) (PCHaslam)* 2-8-2 DaleGibson(6) (a chsng ldrs: one pce fnl 3f) 1½ **6**
4156[9] Advance East **(66)***(45+) (MrsJRRamsden)* 2-8-9 MWigham(9) (s.i.s: hld up & bhd: stdy hdwy 2f out: nvr plcd to chal) ....½ **7**
3794[7] Westcourt Princess **(61)***(39) (MWEasterby)* 2-8-4b LCharnock(11) (chsd ldrs: effrt 3f out: one pce) ....hd **8**
3923[8] Prince Rudolf (IRE) **(59)***(31) (NPLittmoden)* 2-7-9b(7)ow1 CTeague(7) (led tl over 2f out: sn wknd) 3 **9**
3987[15] Needwood Newt **(62)***(32) (BAMcMahon)* 2-8-0 (5)ow7 SSanders(1) (prom tl grad wknd u.p fnl 3f) 1 **10**
4011[8] Emily-Mou (IRE) **(78)***(47) (EALDunlop)* 2-9-2 (5) JStack(8) (b: b.hind: s.i.s: n.d).......½ **11**
3585[16] Bold Palmella (IRE) **(63)***(30) (MrsJRRamsden)* 2-8-6 JFanning(5) (s.i.s: n.d) ....¾ **12**
3918[4] Boundary Express **(56)***(21) (MJohnston)* 2-7-13 TWilliams(10) (n.d) ....¾ **13**
4104* Crystal Loop **(63)***(21) (ABailey)* 2-8-1 (5) DWright(16) (spd 4f: sn wknd)....3½ **14**
4129[10] Shared Risk **(61)***(19) (SGNorton)* 2-8-4 JQuinn(3) (b: b.hind: pushed along ½-wy: sn lost tch) ....s.h **15**
4055[7] Bex Hill **(63)***(18) (DHaydnJones)* 2-8-1 (5)ow3 SDrowne(12) (sn outpcd & bhd).......1½ **16**

LONG HANDICAP Mister Fire Eyes (IRE) 8-3

4/1 MISTER FIRE EYES (IRE), Saint Amigo (5/2-9/2), **7/1** Emily-Mou (IRE), **9/1** Crystal Loop, **10/1** Bold Palmella (IRE), Shared Risk, Westcourt Princess, Tee Tee Too (IRE), **12/1** Boundary Express, Advance East, **14/1** Prince Rudolf (IRE), **16/1** Mac's Taxi, **20/1** Bex Hill, Qualitair Ridge, **25/1** Jilly Jaffa Cake (IRE), **33/1** Needwood Newt, CSF £47.60 CT £169.48 TOTE £4.50: £1.20 £1.90 £2.00 £14.40 (£18.80) OWNER Mr C. T. Olley (NEWMARKET) BRED Airlie Stud 16 Rn
1m 31.1 (4.30) SF: 39/32/14/11/-/-/-/-/-/-/-/-/-/-/-/-

4229 RIVER DEVON (S) STKS (Class G) £2,190.00 (£615.00: £300.00)
1m 6f (Fibresand) Stalls: Low GOING: minus 0.07 sec per fur (Std) 2-40 (2-42)

4221[7] **Sassiver (USA) (43)***(52+) (RHollinshead)* 4-9-3 TIves(7) (s.s: hdwy ½-wy: led 2f out: r.o)....— **1**
3982[6] Greenacres Star **(30)***(41) (BAMcMahon)* 4-8-12 JWeaver(15) (hdwy 7f out: styd on u.p fnl 2f: nrst fin)....5 **2**
3964[10] Dawn Rock **(60)***(50) (PAKelleway)* 3-9-1 MWigham(10) (b.off fore: hdwy 8f out: led 5f out to 2f out: one pce)....1¼ **3**
4136[7] Sunday News'n'echo (USA) **(57)***(44) (WStorey)* 3-8-5 (5) DRMcCabe(8) (cl up: effrt 4f out: one pce fnl 2f)....½ **4**
3343[10] Atlantic Way **(43)***(28)*(Fav)*(CJHill)* 6-9-3 JQuinn(2) (hdwy 6f out: sn prom & rdn: no imp fnl 2f)....15 **5**
3993[16] Cristal Springs **(41)***(17) (BJMcMath)* 3-8-5 AClark(5) (in tch: rdn 5f out: one pce)....5 **6**
3559[3] Cruising Chick **(46)***(11) (SGNorton)* 3-8-0 (5) NVarley(6) (w ldr: led 7f out to 5f out: sn outpcd)....5 **7**
4091[26] Fiaba **(42)***(8) (CNWilliams)* 6-8-12 RPerham(11) (hld up: prom & effrt ent st: sn rdn & one pce)....3 **8**
4221[11] Beaumood **(33)***(12) (EJAlston)* 8-9-3v JFortune(13) (chsd ldrs: outpcd 5f out: no imp after)....1 **9**
2548[6] Mr Geran (IRE) **(31)***(2) (BPalling)* 5-9-3b StephenDavies(14) (b: b.hind: effrt ½-wy: no imp)....9 **10**
4127[13] Glenvally **(49)***(—) (BWMurray)* 3-8-2b(5)ow2 DGriffiths(9) (trckd ldr tl rdn & wknd 4f out)....12 **11**
4127[14] Shawn Cuddy **(42)***(—) (JLHarris)* 3-8-10 SWilliams(3) (in tch to ½-wy: sn bhd: t.o) 9 **12**
3962[16] Top Villain **(31)***(—) (JDooler)* 8-9-3 SWebster(16) (sn drvn along & wl bhd: t.o) ..1½ **13**
4175[8] Flora Belle **(46)***(—) (LordHuntingdon)* 3-8-10v DaleGibson(1) (rdn & wl bhd fnl 6f: t.o)....2½ **14**
3694[11] Love of the North (IRE) **(43)***(—) (RTJuckes)* 3-8-5 (5) AGarth(4) (led to 7f out: sn wknd: t.o)....dist **15**
3699[9] Dupad **(28)***(—) (PHowling)* 4-8-12 (5) SDrowne(12) (sn outpcd & wl bhd: t.o) **16**

3/1 Atlantic Way, **5/1** Sunday News'n'echo (USA), **6/1** Dawn Rock, Greenacres Star, **8/1** Glenvally, **9/1** Flora Belle, **11/1** SASSIVER (USA), **12/1** Mr Geran (IRE), Fiaba, **14/1** Cruising Chick, **16/1** Shawn Cuddy, **20/1** Cristal Springs, Top Villain, Beaumood, Love of the North (IRE), **33/1** Dupad, CSF £84.38 TOTE £17.70: £4.70 £2.70 £3.30 (£35.40) OWNER Sinclair Developments Ltd (UPPER LONGDON) BRED Juddmonte Farms Inc in USA 16 Rn
No bid 3m 12.0 (12.30) SF: 28/18/20/15/6/-/-/-/-/-/-/-/-/-/-/-
WEIGHT FOR AGE 3yo-7lb

4230 BRITVIC STKS (Mdn 2-Y.O) (Class D) £2,892.00 (£876.00: £428.00: £204.00)
6f (Fibresand) Stalls: High GOING: minus 0.07 sec per fur (Std) 3-10 (3-15)

4219[3] **Chadleigh Lane (USA) (62)***(70) (RHollinshead)* 2-9-0 TIves(9) (a.p: n.m.r over 1f out: swtchd & qckn to ld ins fnl f)....— **1**
4164[12] Always Grace **(72)***(59)*(Fav)*(MissGayKelleway)* 2-8-9 JWeaver(14) (trckd ldrs: led over 1f out tl ins fnl f: no ex)....2½ **2**
Tael of Silver *(50) (KRBurke)* 2-8-9 StephenDavies(7) (neat: unf: in tch: styd on one pce fnl 3f)....3½ **3**
Tapping Feet *(49+) (SirMarkPrescott)* 2-8-9 GDuffield(10) (neat: bkwd: hdwy ½-wy: styd on: nrst fin)....nk **4**
4123[4] Shinerolla *(48) (MrsJRRamsden)* 2-9-0 JFanning(2) (dwlt: hdwy appr st: nt qckn appr fnl f)....2½ **5**
Wasblest *(38+) (MJohnston)* 2-8-9 TWilliams(16) (neat: scope: w ldrs tl wknd appr fnl f)....2 **6**
4058[11] Whittingham Girl *(35) (JBerry)* 2-8-9 LeTolboll(8) (led tl hdd & wknd over 1f out)....1 **7**
3784[5] Ism *(35) (MajorWRHern)* 2-9-0 AClark(5) (sme hdwy 2f out: nvr rchd ldrs)....2 **8**
Chase the Melody *(32) (MJHeaton-Ellis)* 2-9-0 RPerham(3) (leggy: outpcd & bhd tl sme late hdwy)....1 **9**
4123[9] Warwick Mist (IRE) *(22) (PCHaslam)* 2-8-9 MTebbutt(6) (chsd ldrs 4f: sn wknd) 2 **10**
4144[C] Magic Leader (IRE) **(45)***(19) (TTClement)* 2-8-7 (7) SLanigan(1) (b: n.d)....¾ **11**
3918[2] High Flown (USA) **(67)***(—) (MrsJRRamsden)* 2-9-0 SWilliams(12) (bhd fr ½-wy)....8 **12**
4164[14] Hoswinoname *(—) (DNicholls)* 2-9-0 AlexGreaves(4) (nvr trbld ldrs)....3 **13**
Hasty Bid (IRE) *(—) (CJHill)* 2-8-9 NAdams(13) (neat: nvr wnt pce)....3 **14**
948[13] Al Totseva *(—) (MPMuggeridge)* 2-8-9 JQuinn(11) (b: b.hind: a bhd)....nk **15**
3587[12] Bebe Pomme *(—) (MrsNMacauley)* 2-8-9 DaleGibson(15) (in tch 3f: sn lost pl)....11 **16**

11/4 Always Grace, **9/2** Wasblest, **5/1** Ism, **6/1** Shinerolla, High Flown (USA), **8/1** CHADLEIGH LANE (USA), **12/1** Tapping Feet, **14/1** Hasty Bid (IRE), **16/1** Chase the Melody, **20/1** Whittingham Girl, Hoswinoname, Tael of Silver, Magic Leader (IRE), **25/1** Warwick Mist (IRE), Bebe Pomme, **33/1** Al Totseva, CSF £34.81 TOTE £8.90: £2.80 £1.60 £13.60 (£18.90) OWNER Mr J. E. Bigg (UPPER LONGDON) BRED Windwoods Farm, Bruce Brown and Connie Brown 16 Rn
1m 18.3 (4.80) SF: 28/17/8/7/5/-/-/-/-/-/-/-/-/-/-/-

4231 TRENT NAVIGATION H'CAP (0-85) (Class D) £3,303.40 (£1,001.20: £489.60: £233.80) 5f (Fibresand) Stalls: Low GOING: minus 0.20 sec (Std) 3-40 (3-43)

4170[20] **Croft Pool (67)***(74) (JAGlover)* 3-9-3 TIves(13) (hdwy 2f out: led ins fnl f: r.o wl) ....— **1**
4078[5] Broadstairs Beauty (IRE) **(74)***(78) (SRBowring)* 4-9-3b(7) GStrange(9) (b: lw: s.i.s: hdwy to ld after 1f: hdd ins fnl f: kpt on) 1 **2**
4170* Press the Bell **(78)***(74) (JBerry)* 4-9-7 (7) PRoberts(3) (w ldrs: nt qckn ins fnl f) 2½ **3**
4170[4] Primula Bairn **(63)***(58) (MrsJRRamsden)* 4-8-13v SWilliams(8) (disp ld 1f: cl up tl rdn & btn over 1f out) ....nk **4**
3960[5] Bangles **(70)***(63)*(Fav)*(LordHuntingdon)* 4-9-6 JWeaver(1) (in tch far side tl rdn & btn over 1f out) ....½ **5**
3759[8] Delrob **(66)***(56) (DHaydnJones)* 3-8-11 (5) SDrowne(10) (disp ld 1f: chsd ldrs tl btn over 1f out) ....¾ **6**
3450[10] Rocky Two **(65)***(51) (PHowling)* 3-9-1b JQuinn(7) (b: lw: a chsng ldrs: nt qckn fnl f) 1¼ **7**
3978[12] Sir Tasker **(64)***(50) (JLHarris)* 6-8-9 (5) NVarley(14) (chsd ldrs stands' side: rdn & no imp fnl 2f) ....s.h **8**
3978[18] Spender **(75)***(60) (PWHarris)* 5-9-11 GDuffield(6) (cl up tl rdn & btn over 1f out)....hd **9**
3838* Saddlehome (USA) **(77)***(61) (TDBarron)* 5-9-13 JFortune(5) (outpcd fr ½-wy) ....hd **10**
3806[9] Pertemps Flyer **(63)***(46) (BAMcMahon)* 3-8-8 (5) SSanders(12) (in tch over 3f).......hd **11**
4145[3] Little Ibnr **(61)***(42) (PDEvans)* 3-8-6 (5) JStack(2) (trckd ldrs: nvr plcd to chal)..........½ **12**
3793[6] Grey Toppa **(61)***(39) (MrsJRRamsden)* 3-8-11 JFanning(16) (nvr trbld ldrs) ....¾ **13**
3960[11] Sison (IRE) **(72)***(47) (KGWingrove)* 4-9-8 DBiggs(4) (sn outpcd).......1 **14**
4059[11] Orthorhombus **(61)***(34) (DJSCosgrove)* 5-8-11b MWigham(15) (b: b.hind: s.s: a bhd) ....½ **15**
4170[16] Lovely Me (IRE) **(67)***(—) (RFJohnsonHoughton)* 3-9-3b SWhitworth(11) (lw: sn bhd) 15 **16**
3938[10] Bit of a Lark **(72)***(—) (DMorris)* 6-9-8 StephenDavies(17) (b: n.d).......½ **17**

4/1 Bangles, **11/2** Saddlehome (USA), **6/1** Broadstairs Beauty (IRE), **7/1** Primula Bairn, **8/1** Press the Bell, **9/1** Little Ibnr, **10/1** Orthorhombus, **12/1** Grey Toppa, Spender, **14/1** Delrob, **16/1** Lovely Me (IRE), Sir Tasker, **20/1** Rocky Two, Bit of a Lark, CROFT POOL, **33/1** Pertemps Flyer, Sison (IRE), CSF £145.48 CT £992.04 TOTE £19.80: £3.30 £3.10 £3.10 £1.70 (£111.00) OWNER Countrywide Classics Ltd (WORKSOP) BRED J. S. Bell 17 Rn
59.6 secs (1.60) SF: 56/60/56/40/45/39/35/-/-/-/-/-/-/-/-/-/-

T/Plpt: £409.70 (18.3 Tckts). T/Qdpt: Not won; £39.80 to Haydock 17/11/94 AA

4194a-SAINT-CLOUD (France) (L-H)
Friday November 11th (Good to soft)

4232a PRIX PERTH (Gp 3) £22,883.00 1m GOING: 1.10 sec per fur (S)

1490a* **Freedom Cry** *(120) (France)* 3-9-1 TJarnet ....— **1**
Scandinavian (FR) *(115) (France)* 3-8-11 GGuignard ....nk **2**
3867a[2] Misbegotten (IRE) *(108) (France)* 3-8-8 FHead 2 **3**
3928[2] Mistle Cat (USA) *(106) (SPCWoods)* 4-9-0b WWoods (btn further 2l) **6**

TOTE 5.40F: 1.80F 1.40F 2.50F (8.30F) OWNER Mr D. Wildenstein BRED Dayton Ltd 11 Rn
1m 49.8 (11.80) SF: 56/51/42/-

4195a-SAN SIRO (Milan, Italy) (R-H)
Friday November 11th (Heavy)

4233a PREMIO DORMELLO (Gp 3) (2-Y.O.F) £25,773.00 1m

Olimpia Dukakis (ITY) *(—) (Italy)* 2-8-11 GForte ....— **1**

4197a* Fanjica (IRE) *(—) (JLDunlop)* 2-8-11 JReid 3½ **2**
Coco Passion (FR) *(—) (France)* 2-8-11 FSanchez 2¾ **3**
3368a[3] Malafemmena (IRE) *(—) (JLDunlop)* 2-8-11 FJovine 1 **4**

TOTE 20L: 12L 19L 18L (112L) OWNER Scuderia Siba BRED Scuderia Siba in Italy 12 Rn
1m 52.5 SF: -/-/-/-

4198a-CAPANNELLE (Rome, Italy) (R-H)
Sunday November 13th (Heavy)

4234a PREMIO ROMA (Gp 1) (C & F) £86,983.00
1m 2f

3865a[17] **Big Tobin (ITY)** *(117) (Italy)* 5-8-13 MPasquale ....— **1**
2304a[2] Sugarland Express (IRE) *(117) (Italy)* 3-8-13 FJovine 3½ **2**
Scribano *(110) (Italy)* 4-8-13 EBotti 1¼ **3**
4152a* Wootton Rivers (USA) *(108) (PWChapple-Hyam)* 4-8-13 JReid 1 **4**
3920* Garden of Heaven (USA) *(103) (CEBrittain)* 5-8-13 MRoberts 3 **5**
4148a* Port Lucaya *(100) (DRLoder)* 4-8-13 JWeaver 1¾ **6**

TOTE 51L: 18L 23L 31L (327L) OWNER Lady Costanza 8 Rn 2m 7.5 SF: -/-/-/-/-/-

4194a-SAINT-CLOUD (France) (L-H)
Tuesday November 15th (Heavy)

4235a PRIX FILLE DE L'AIR (Gp 3) F £22,883.00
1m 2f 110y GOING: 1.40 sec per fur (Hvy)

3875a[3] **Hollywood Dream (GER)** *(115) (Germany)* 3-8-9 JReid ....— **1**
L'ile Tudy (IRE) *(—) (France)* 4-8-11 ABadel 5 **2**
4118a[3] Girl From Ipanema *(107) (PFICole)* 3-8-9 TQuinn ....nse **3**
3730[7] Maidment *(—) (LadyHerries)* 3-8-9 TIves (btn further 9*l) **11**

TOTE 11.80F: 7.70F 4.30F 9.20F (145.50F) OWNER Gestut Haus Ittlingen 15 Rn
2m 26.6 SF: 76/68/65/-

4236a PRIX MON TALISMAN £6,293.00
1m

Winning Smile (FR) *(101) (France)* 4-9-1 TGillet ....— **1**
Lost Prairie (USA) *(92) (France)* 4-8-8 TJarnet 1 **2**
Apyre (FR) *(97) (France)* 6-8-12 (3) SMaillot ....¾ **3**
3311[8] Metal Storm (FR) *(—) (KOCunningham-Brown)* 6-8-12 SGuillot (btn further 4½l) **7**

TOTE 4.00F: 2.30F 2.00F (9.50F) OWNER Mr Y. Asakawa BRED Kyowa Stud in France 7 Rn
1m 55.9 SF: -/-/-/-

4224-SOUTHWELL (L-H)
Tuesday November 22nd (Standard)

4237 BLUEBELL CLAIMING STKS (I) (Class F) £2,363.00 (£663.00: £323.00)
6f Stalls: Low GOING: minus 0.12 sec per fur (FS) 12-10 (12-12)

3986[20] **Walk the Beat (62)***(59) (RSimpson)* 4-8-3 (5) SDrowne(8) (b: chsd ldrs: chal over 1f out: styd on to ld wl ins fnl f) ....— **1**
3793* Frisky Miss (IRE) **(67)***(60) (JBerry)* 3-8-2 (7)ow1 PRoberts(16) (in tch: hdwy 2f out: styd on wl: nrst fin) ....nk **2**
4226[3] Langtonian **(28)***(57) (JLEyre)* 5-8-8v NCarlisle(6) (dwlt: bhd & nt clr run appr st: hdwy 2f out: hung lft: r.o wl nr fin) ....hd **3**
3972[7] Nakita **(60)***(53) (CNAllen)* 3-7-11 (7) MBaird(11) (s.i.s: c wd & hdwy 2f out: r.o wl nr fin) ....nk **4**
4145[10] Tyrian Purple (IRE) **(66)***(56) (TJNaughton)* 6-8-2b(7)ow1 VHalliday(2) (b: lw: led: clr ½-wy: hdd & no ex wl ins fnl f) ....hd **5**
3963[2] Sense of Priority **(61)***(51)*(Fav)*(MHEasterby)* 5-8-8 WWoods(4) (s.i.s: sn in tch: nt qckn fnl f) 1½ **6**
4231[13] Grey Toppa **(61)***(46) (MrsJRRamsden)* 3-8-6 MWigham(9) (in tch: styd on fnl 2f) 1½ **7**

3938[8] High Domain (IRE) **(76)***(52) (MMcCormack)* 3-8-12 (5) RPainter(14) (prom tl outpcd fnl 2f) 2 **8**
3586[5] Matthew David **(34)***(34) (SRBowring)* 4-8-4 SWilliams(5) (chsd ldrs: effrt 2f out: one pce) 1¼ **9**
4064[9] Dangerous Shadow **(51)***(32) (MrsMReveley)* 3-7-13 (5) DRMcCabe(7) (sn outpcd & bhd: sme hdwy 2f out: n.d) 1 **10**
4034[16] Gwernymynydd **(43)***(27) (SGNorton)* 3-7-9 (7)ow2 DDenby(3) (s.i.s: n.d) ....¾ **11**
4033[5] Vanessa Rose **(59)***(28) (ABailey)* 3-8-1b(5) DWright(13) (s.i.s: hdwy ½-wy: no imp) .1 **12**
843[6] Sea Devil **(76)***(30) (MJCamacho)* 8-8-7 (5) JStack(12) (chsd ldrs tl grad wknd fnl 2f: bttr for r) 1 **13**
3698* Grandee **(46)***(21) (BAMcMahon)* 3-8-2 (5) SSanders(1) (spd 4f) 2 **14**
2743[11] Shadow Jury **(60)***(20) (DWChapman)* 4-8-7 BDoyle(15) (outpcd & lost tch fr ½-wy) ....s.h **15**
4210[12] Galaxy Express **(44)***(2) (GHEden)* 6-8-2 JQuinn(10) (b: spd over 3f: sn wknd) 5 **16**

4/1 Sense of Priority, **5/1** Sea Devil, **11/2** Tyrian Purple (IRE), **15/2** Frisky Miss (IRE), **9/1** Vanessa Rose, **11/1** WALK THE BEAT, **12/1** Langtonian, Nakita, **14/1** Matthew David, High Domain (IRE), **16/1** Shadow Jury, Dangerous Shadow, **20/1** Galaxy Express, Grandee, Grey Toppa, **25/1** Gwernymynydd, CSF £95.22 TOTE £26.70: £4.90 £2.40 £2.40 (£102.40) OWNER The Country Life Partnership BRED R. B. Warren 16 Rn

1m 18.6 (5.10) SF: 15/16/14/10/13/9/3/8/-/-/-/-/-/-/-/-
WEIGHT FOR AGE 3yo-1lb

4238

ORCHID AUCTION STKS (Mdn 2-Y.O) (Class E) £2,716.20 (£763.20: £372.60)
5f (Fibresand) Stalls: High GOING: minus 0.12 sec per fur (FS) 12-40 (12-41)

3683[9] **Kung Frode** *(74) (BAMcMahon)* 2-8-2 (5) SSanders(5) (s.i.s: hdwy 2f out: hung lft: r.o to ld post) ....— **1**
4173[3] La Belle Dominique **(74)***(70) (SGKnight)* 2-7-12 (5)ow1 DRMcCabe(2) (mde most: qcknd over 1f out: no ex nr fin) ....s.h **2**
4164[10] Penny's Wishing *(63) (JPLeigh)* 2-8-2 DBiggs(7) (disp ld 3f: rdn & styd on one pce) 2 **3**
4230[4] Tapping Feet *(57) (SirMarkPrescott)* 2-8-2 GDuffield(12) (sn pushed along: styd on wl fr ½-wy: nrst fin) 2 **4**
4144[2] Das Island **(56)***(58) (JRJenkins)* 2-8-4e CRutter(6) (eyeshield: swtg: disp ld to ½-wy: grad wknd) ....nk **5**
4076[9] Risky Royal **(60)***(59) (TJNaughton)* 2-8-3 (7) VHalliday(9) (s.i.s: sn drvn along: nrst fin) 1½ **6**
4222[2] Pats Delight **(53)***(47) (SCoathup)* 2-7-8 (5) NVarley(8) (drvn along & sn chsng ldrs: nt qckn appr fnl f) ....hd **7**
4158[12] Keeper's Grey *(47) (RGuest)* 2-8-4 DHarrison(14) (sn drvn along & n.d) 1½ **8**
4079[8] Mr Slick **(70)***(52) (NACallaghan)* 2-8-10 TIves(11) (b.hind: hung lft & nvr wnt pce) hd **9**
3769[10] First Point (IRE) **(45)***(44) (CNAllen)* 2-8-4 GBardwell(4) (lw: sn outpcd) ....½ **10**
4230[2] Always Grace **(72)***(44)*(Fav)*(MissGayKelleway)* 2-8-5 TWilliams(10) (lw: in tch: sn drvn along: no imp fnl 2f) ....hd **11**
4134[4] Never Say so **(55)***(37) (CSmith)* 2-7-6 (7) MBaird(1) (w ldrs 3f: sn wknd) ....nk **12**
4066[13] Jessica's Secret (IRE) **(48)***(32) (ABailey)* 2-7-11 (5) DWright(3) (unruly gng to post: hung lft: sn outpcd & bhd) 2½ **13**
1703[4] Colston-C *(—) (CJHill)* 2-8-7 JQuinn(13) (s.i.s: sn wl bhd) 9 **14**

3/1 Always Grace, **7/2** La Belle Dominique, **4/1** Tapping Feet, **7/1** Mr Slick, **10/1** Das Island, **12/1** Pats Delight, **14/1** Penny's Wishing, Risky Royal, **16/1** Keeper's Grey, Jessica's Secret (IRE), Never Say so, **25/1** Colston-C, First Point (IRE), **33/1** KUNG FRODE, CSF £152.39 TOTE £52.90: £7.50 £1.60 £5.00 (£184.70) OWNER Mrs J. McMahon (TAMWORTH) BRED I. W. T. and Mrs Loftus 14 Rn 60.6 secs (2.60) SF: 37/33/26/19/20/21/10/-/-/-/-/-/-/-
No bid

4239

DAISY (S) STKS (Class G) £2,155.00 (£605.00: £295.00)
1m 3f (Fibresand) Stalls: Low GOING: minus 0.12 sec per fur (FS) 1-10 (1-11)

4209[3] **Shabanaz (62)***(67) (WRMuir)* 9-9-7 StephenDavies(14) (bhd: hdwy 6f out: led over 1f out: drvn clr) ....— **1**
4224[4] Broctune Gold **(65)***(49) (MrsMReveley)* 3-8-11 WWoods(3) (lw: trckd ldrs: rdn 4f out: one pce fnl 2f) 10 **2**
1507[3] Bold Pursuit (IRE) **(64)***(52)*(Fav)*(JGFitzGerald)* 5-9-7 TIves(4) (b: a chsng ldrs: one pce fnl 3f) 1¼ **3**
3902[5] Venture Fourth **(37)***(46) (EJAlston)* 5-8-11 (5) JStack(13) (cl up: led 8f out tl hdd & wknd over 1f out) ....½ **4**

4229[5] Atlantic Way **(43)**(42) (CJHill) 6-9-2 JQuinn(2) (hdwy appr st: styd on: nvr rchd ldrs)3 **5**
3961[6] Goodbye Millie **(47)**(40) (SGNorton) 4-9-2 TWilliams(6) (sn pushed along & bhd: hdwy 5f out: nvr rchd ldrs)....1¾ **6**
4229[3] Dawn Rock **(60)**(44) (PAKelleway) 3-9-2b MWigham(5) (b.off fore: outpcd & bhd tl styd on fnl 2f)....nk **7**
4217[8] Ann Hill (IRE) **(37)**(33) (RHollinshead) 4-8-4 (7) DDenby(10) (bhd: effrt 5f out: n.d)....½ **8**
4214[9] Komplicity **(54)**(40) (BobJones) 3-9-2 DaleGibson(7) (lw: led 3f: wknd 6f out)....2½ **9**
4226[10] Midlin **(41)**(29) (JLHarris) 4-8-11 AMackay(11) (prom tl wknd over 2f out)....1 **10**
4040[4] Greek Gold (IRE) **(56)**(32) (MrsJRRamsden) 5-9-2 DHarrison(1) (b.hind: lw: in tch: pushed along after 3f: no imp)....1¼ **11**
4215[8] Little Miner (IRE) **(40)**(22) (BPalling) 3-7-13 (7) WendyJones(12) (n.d)....4 **12**
4053[18] Taufeliane **(40)**(16) (JLHarris) 3-8-2b(5)ow1 SDrowne(9) (chsd ldrs: chal 7f out: wknd wl over 3f out)....5 **13**
3789[11] Swynford Flyer **(49)**(12) (JAHarris) 5-9-2 SWilliams(8) (chsd ldr tl wknd 5f out)....6 **14**

11/4 Bold Pursuit (IRE), **7/2** Greek Gold (IRE), **5/1** Broctune Gold, SHABANAZ, **11/2** Dawn Rock, **10/1** Atlantic Way, **11/1** Swynford Flyer, **20/1** Goodbye Millie, Komplicity, Ann Hill (IRE), **25/1** Venture Fourth, **33/1** Taufeliane, Little Miner (IRE), **40/1** Midlin, CSF £33.26 TOTE £11.90: £2.20 £2.20 £2.30 (£57.40) OWNER Fayzad Thoroughbred Ltd (LAMBOURN) BRED The Overbury Stud 14 Rn No bid
2m 30.2 (8.70) SF: 35/12/20/15/11/9/9/4/-/-/-/-/-/-
WEIGHT FOR AGE 3yo-5lb

4240 BUTTERCUP STKS (Mdn 2-Y.O) (Class D) £2,892.00 (£876.00: £428.00: £204.00) 1m (Fibresand) Stalls: Low GOING: minus 0.12 sec (FS) 1-40 (1-43)

4061[4] **What's the Verdict (IRE) (78)**(79)(Fav)(MJohnston) 2-9-0 TWilliams(12) (lw: cl up: led 3f out: styd on u.p fnl f)....— **1**
4219[2] Komreyev Dancer **(62)**(77) (ABailey) 2-8-9 (5) DWright(6) (lw: cl up: ev ch & rdn over 1f out: nt qckn nr fin)....1 **2**
4162[6] Ocean Hawk (USA) (67) (PFICole) 2-9-0 TQuinn(1) (a chsng ldrs: effrt over 2f out: r.o one pce)....5 **3**
Legally Delicious (58) (JEBanks) 2-8-9 JQuinn(10) (lt-f: bit bkwd: in tch: pushed along ½-wy: styd on: nvr nrr)....1¾ **4**
Framley Garth (50) (SirMarkPrescott) 2-8-9 GDuffield(4) (w'like: bit bkwd: led 5f: grad lost pl)....4 **5**
4205[3] Frome Lad (48) (WGMTurner) 2-8-9 (5) JDSmith(13) (hdwy on outside ½-wy: no imp)....3½ **6**
4106[5] Something Speedy (IRE) **(47)**(43) (PJBevan) 2-8-9 NCarlisle(9) (nvr trbld ldrs)....hd **7**
4156[6] Jalmaid (41) (BAMcMahon) 2-8-4 (5) SSanders(14) (effrt ½-wy: rdn & nt pce to chal)....1 **8**
Drama King (44) (SRBowring) 2-8-7 (7) CTeague(5) (lt-f: spd 4f: sn bhd)....1 **9**
3487[19] Fools Millyons (IRE) **(40)**(44) (WBentley) 2-9-0 DHarrison(2) (spd to ½-wy: sn bhd)....s.h **10**
4144[6] Instant Success (USA) **(55)**(31) (WAO'Gorman) 2-8-6 (3) EmmaO'Gorman(3) (s.i.s: nvr wnt pce)....4 **11**
4171[8] Lord Adriani (IRE) (29) (SirMarkPrescott) 2-9-0 CNutter(15) (s.i.s: n.d)....3½ **12**
Torrey Pines (IRE) (27) (DHaydnJones) 2-9-0 AMackay(8) (leggy: scope: s.s: wl bhd tl sme late hdwy)....¾ **13**
4213[4] Chadleigh Walk (IRE) **(44)**(26) (RHollinshead) 2-9-0 TIves(16) (effrt ½-wy: sn wknd)....½ **14**
3162[16] Simply Simon (KRBurke) 2-9-0 StephenDavies(7) (spd 5f: eased whn btn)....12 **15**
Daisy Madam (—) (MHEasterby) 2-8-9 AClark(11) (neat: bkwd: lost tch fnl 3f)....4 **16**

2/1 WHAT'S THE VERDICT (IRE), **4/1** Komreyev Dancer, **11/2** Ocean Hawk (USA), **9/1** Frome Lad, **10/1** Jalmaid, **12/1** Framley Garth, Instant Success (USA), **16/1** Legally Delicious, Lord Adriani (IRE), **20/1** Torrey Pines (IRE), **25/1** Drama King, Daisy Madam, **33/1** Fools Millyons (IRE), Chadleigh Walk (IRE), Something Speedy (IRE), **50/1** Simply Simon, CSF £11.60 TOTE £3.10: £1.90 £1.50 £2.90 (£7.50) OWNER Mr R. W. Huggins (MIDDLEHAM) BRED Islanmore Stud in Ireland 16 Rn
1m 45.5 (6.20) SF: 27/25/16/9/2/-/-/-/-/-/-/-/-/-/-/-

4241 TULIP H'CAP (0-80) (Class D) £2,918.00 (£884.00: £432.00: £206.00) 7f (Fibresand) Stalls: Low GOING: minus 0.12 sec per fur (FS) 2-10 (2-12)

4139[11] **Mustn't Grumble (IRE) (66)**(68) (WSCunningham) 4-9-2 AClark(3) (lw: trckd ldrs: nt clr run ent st: led 1f out: edgd rt: all out)....— **1**
4204[3] Milos **(69)**(70) (TJNaughton) 3-9-3 GDuffield(16) (trckd ldrs: led over 2f out to 1f out: kpt on wl nr fin)....hd **2**

4227[5] Dream Carrier (IRE) **(68)**_(67) (TDBarron)_ 6-8-11 (7) KimberleyHart(4) (lw: s.i.s: hdwy 2f out: r.o wl nr fin) ....¾ **3**
4227[6] Bogart **(57)**_(50) (CWFairhurst)_ 3-8-0 (5) JStack(6) (lw: cl up: effrt 3f out: kpt on one pce) 3 **4**
4223[9] Just Harry **(73)**_(65) (MJRyan)_ 3-9-7 DBiggs(13) (hdwy ½-wy: styd on fnl f: nvr able to chal) ....½ **5**
4226[6] No Submission (USA) **(66)**_(57) (DWChapman)_ 8-9-2 JQuinn(14) (lw: led tl over 2f out: r.o one pce) ....nk **6**
4224[2] Nellie's Gamble **(60)**_(48) (JLEyre)_ 4-8-5 (5) DWright(5) (s.i.s: hdwy ent st: nvr able to chal) 1½ **7**
4107[7] It's so Easy **(63)**_(44) (MJohnston)_ 3-8-11 TWilliams(7) (in tch: effrt & ch 2f out: sn rdn & grad wknd) 3½ **8**
4220[5] African Chimes **(72)**_(53)_(Fav)_(WAO'Gorman)_ 7-9-5 (3) EmmaO'Gorman(1) (lw: in tch: effrt ent st: no imp) ....s.h **9**
4202[13] Obsidian Grey **(56)**_(34) (MissLCSiddall)_ 7-8-6 DHarrison(2) (sme hdwy 2f out: n.d) 1½ **10**
4224[13] Scottish Park **(51)**_(26) (RWEmery)_ 5-7-10b(5) DarrenMoffatt(11) (s.i.s: n.d) 1¼ **11**
4223* Wentbridge Lad (IRE) **(78)**_(47) (BAMcMahon)_ 4-9-9b(5) SSanders(10) (cl up tl wknd fnl 2f) 3 **12**
4220[9] Kid Ory **(65)**_(21) (PCalver)_ 3-8-13 DaleGibson(8) (chsd ldrs tl wknd over 2f out) 6 **13**
543[20] Faez **(71)**_(23) (PSFelgate)_ 4-9-7 TIves(9) (a bhd) 1¾ **14**
3890[13] Matisse **(54)**_(—) (JDBethell)_ 3-8-2 StephenDavies(12) (s.i.s: a bhd) 3 **15**
486[9] I Fear Nothing **(80)**_(24) (SCWilliams)_ 3-9-9 (5) PMcCabe(15) (sn outpcd & bhd) ....¾ **16**

7/2 African Chimes, **13/2** Milos, **7/1** Nellie's Gamble, **8/1** Wentbridge Lad (IRE), Just Harry, **9/1** Dream Carrier (IRE), **12/1** MUSTN'T GRUMBLE (IRE), Bogart, **14/1** No Submission (USA), **16/1** Kid Ory, Scottish Park, **20/1** Obsidian Grey, It's so Easy, Matisse, I Fear Nothing, **25/1** Faez, CSF £89.88 CT £698.22 TOTE £15.30: £2.20 £2.10 £2.90 £3.80 (£62.40) OWNER Mr B. L. Cassidy (YARM) BRED Rathduff Stud 16 Rn 1m 31.7 (4.90) SF: 35/36/35/16/30/24/16/-/-/-/-/-/-/-/-/-
WEIGHT FOR AGE 3yo-2lb

4242 DAFFODIL NURSERY (0-75) (Class E) £2,866.00 (£868.00: £424.00: £202.00)
7f (Fibresand) Stalls: Low GOING: minus 0.12 sec per fur (FS) 2-40 (2-45)

4228* **Mister Fire Eyes (IRE) (64)**_(80+)_(Fav)_(CEBrittain)_ 2-9-12 (7x) BDoyle(6) (a.p: rdn to ld appr fnl f: r.o wl) ....— **1**
3923[11] Pleasure Beach **(59)**_(68) (WAO'Gorman)_ 2-9-4 (3) EmmaO'Gorman(8) (lw: trckd ldrs: effrt over 1f out: r.o one pce) 3½ **2**
4219[5] Nigel's Lad (IRE) **(53)**_(61) (PCHaslam)_ 2-9-1 TWilliams(14) (racd wd: outpcd ½-wy: hdwy 2f out: one pce ins fnl f) ....½ **3**
4169[9] Bellesonnette (IRE) **(57)**_(62) (DHaydnJones)_ 2-9-0 (5) SDrowne(5) (in tch: styd on fnl 2f: nt pce to chal) 1¼ **4**
4174[3] Mazilla **(54)**_(58) (WJHaggas)_ 2-9-2 WWoods(16) (racd wd in tch: outpcd ½-wy: kpt on fnl f) ....nk **5**
3965[8] Casper's Risk **(54)**_(56) (DNicholls)_ 2-9-2b AlexGreaves(4) (b.nr fore: disp ld tl led over 3f out: hdd appr fnl f: grad lost pl) 1 **6**
3829[7] Brownlows **(43)**_(42) (MPBielby)_ 2-8-0 (5) DarrenMoffatt(15) (sn outpcd & wl bhd tl hdwy fnl 2f) 1¼ **7**
4144[9] Miss Iron Heart (USA) **(48)**_(44) (DJSCosgrove)_ 2-8-10 MWigham(2) (b: disp ld tl hdd over 3f out: wknd 2f out) 1¼ **8**
4228[5] Qualitair Ridge **(47)**_(32) (JFBottomley)_ 2-8-9 NKennedy(9) (s.i.s: outpcd & bhd) 5 **9**
3212[6] Master Millfield (IRE) **(57)**_(41) (CJHill)_ 2-9-5 JQuinn(11) (sn bhd: sme late hdwy)..hd **10**
3951[3] Fahema **(49)**_(31) (RBoss)_ 2-8-11 StephenDavies(12) (chsd ldrs tl wknd over 2f out) ....¾ **11**
4095[12] Golden Fish **(45)**_(22) (JLEyre)_ 2-8-2 (5) DWright(3) (dwlt: hdwy appr st: sn wknd)..2½ **12**
4038[8] Our Tom **(49)**_(23) (JWharton)_ 2-8-11 AClark(1) (prom to ½-wy) 1¼ **13**
4203[2] Howqua River **(51)**_(22) (PWChapple-Hyam)_ 2-8-6 (7) RHavlin(7) (sn outpcd & bhd) 1½ **14**
4129* Flamboro **(46)**_(—) (JDBethell)_ 2-8-8 DHarrison(13) (sn outpcd & bhd) 5 **15**

2/1 MISTER FIRE EYES (IRE), **5/1** Flamboro, **6/1** Howqua River, **8/1** Pleasure Beach, **10/1** Fahema, Mazilla, **14/1** Nigel's Lad (IRE), Casper's Risk, Golden Fish, **16/1** Master Millfield (IRE), **20/1** Bellesonnette (IRE), Qualitair Ridge, **25/1** Our Tom, Miss Iron Heart (USA), **33/1** Brownlows, CSF £20.85 CT £188.97 TOTE £2.70: £1.50 £4.30 £7.40 (£20.90) OWNER Mr C. T. Olley (NEWMARKET) BRED Airlie Stud 15 Rn 1m 32.1 (5.30) SF: 39/27/20/22/18/16/4/-/-/-/-/-/-/-/-

4243

BLUEBELL CLAIMING STKS (II) (Class F) £2,363.00 (£663.00: £323.00)
6f (Fibresand) Stalls: Low GOING: minus 0.12 sec per fur (FS) 3-10 (3-16)

4227[3] **Berge (IRE) (64)***(66+)*(Fav)*(WAO'Gorman)* 3-8-11b TIves(5) (lw: trckd ldrs: led over 2f out: drvn clr: eased nr fin)......— 1
3978[20] Featherstone Lane **(57)***(58) (MissLCSiddall)* 3-8-13v DHarrison(1) (led after 2f tl over 2f out: one pce)......4 2
4214[10] Alpine Johnny **(58)***(48) (RHollinshead)* 3-8-2 (5) AGarth(4) (led 2f: cl up: nt qckn appr fnl f)......1½ 3
4212[5] Olifantsfontein **(50)***(49) (DNicholls)* 6-8-12 AlexGreaves(12) (in tch: styd on u.p fnl 2f: no imp)......¾ 4
4211[6] Four of Spades **(65)***(44) (WSCunningham)* 3-8-9b AClark(14) (hdwy ½-wy: styd on: nvr able to chal)......1 5
614[9] Dauntless Fort **(57)***(33) (BWMurray)* 3-7-13 NKennedy(2) (chsd ldrs: rdn ent st: r.o one pce)......nk 6
3978[9] Bradwell (IRE) **(52)***(36) (MHTompkins)* 3-8-0 (5)ow1 SMulvey(16) (racd wd: sn drvn along: hdwy ½-wy: no imp)......1 7
3748[3] Watheeqah (USA) **(60)***(39) (MBrittain)* 3-8-9b GBardwell(8) (s.i.s: hdwy 2f out: nvr rchd ldrs)......hd 8
3978[15] Grey Ancona (IRE) **(39)***(28) (EJAlston)* 5-8-8 JQuinn(6) (s.i.s: n.d)......3½ 9
Adwick Park **(76)***(38) (MJCamacho)* 6-8-13 (5) JStack(3) (hmpd after 1f: nvr nr to chal after)......s.h 10
4223[7] So Rhythmical **(61)***(24) (GHEden)* 10-8-6 AMackay(10) (b.off hind: in tch: effrt 3f out: no imp)......½ 11
4059[16] Ansellady **(61)***(20) (JBerry)* 3-7-11 (7) PFessey(13) (outpcd ½-wy: n.d after)......¾ 12
2965[15] Steel Sovereign **(40)***(11) (MrsMReveley)* 3-8-0 (5) DRMcCabe(11) (outpcd fr ½-wy).4 13
4218[10] Drummer's Dream (IRE) **(38)***(10) (TTBill)* 6-8-0 (5)ow1 SSanders(9) (in tch over 3f) s.h 14
3473* White Lady **(66)***(2) (RWEmery)* 3-7-9 (5) DarrenMoffatt(7) (prom 3f: sn lost pl)......1½ 15

7/4 BERGE (IRE), **7/1** Four of Spades, Ansellady, White Lady, **10/1** Olifantsfontein, Watheeqah (USA), **11/1** Bradwell (IRE), **14/1** Featherstone Lane, Alpine Johnny, Adwick Park, So Rhythmical, **16/1** Dauntless Fort, **20/1** Steel Sovereign, **33/1** Drummer's Dream (IRE), Grey Ancona (IRE), CSF £30.96 TOTE £3.00: £1.40 £4.80 £4.80 (£60.50) OWNER Mr S. Fustok (NEWMARKET) BRED S. Fustok 15 Rn 1m 17.4 (3.90) SF: 33/24/15/18/13/3/6/8/-/-/-/-/-/-/-
WEIGHT FOR AGE 3yo-1lb

4244

IRIS H'CAP (Amateurs) (0-60) (Class F) £2,601.00 (£731.00: £357.00)
1m 6f (Fibresand) Stalls: High GOING: minus 0.12 sec per fur (FS) 3-40 (3-44)

2048[4] **Absalom's Pillar (58)***(74) (JHetherton)* 4-11-11 (3) MissAElsey(12) (gd hdwy 7f out: led 3f out: r.o)......— 1
4221[8] Swordking (IRE) **(53)***(57) (JLHarris)* 5-11-6 (3) MrIMcLelland(3) (a.p: ev ch & rdn appr fnl f: kpt on one pce)......11 2
4135[8] Blowedifiknow **(45)***(45) (JWharton)* 4-10-8v(7) MrSWalker(16) (a chsng ldrs: led over 5f out to 3f out: one pce)......3½ 3
4221[10] Tremendisto **(48)***(47) (CaptJWilson)* 4-11-4 MrsGRees(11) (hdwy appr st: styd on: nvr nrr)......1 4
3964[5] Modest Hope (USA) **(52)***(50) (BRichmond)* 7-11-8 MissDianaJones(14) (mid div: hdwy 2f out: n.d)......½ 5
4217[9] Telephus **(45)***(37) (BJMcMath)* 5-11-1 MissPJones(2) (hdwy 7f out: sn prom: no imp fnl 3f)......6 6
3298[11] Augustan **(59)***(49) (JAHarris)* 3-11-8 MrDParker(4) (chsd ldrs tl rdn & btn 2f out) .1½ 7
3952[6] Golden Star (IRE) **(48)***(38) (MWEasterby)* 3-10-11 MrSSwiers(1) (prom tl grad wknd fnl 4f)......hd 8
Heliopsis **(42)***(31) (MDHammond)* 6-10-12 MrCBonner(13) (outpcd & bhd tl styd on fnl 3f)......½ 9
4014[8] Iron Baron (IRE) **(41)***(27) (MrsVAAconley)* 5-10-8 (3) MissADeniel(15) (hdwy 6f out: nvr rchd ldrs)......3 10
Legal Win (USA) **(38)***(12) (AGFoster)* 6-10-5 (3) MrGShenkin(5) (a outpcd & bhd)..11 11
4091[3] Deerlet **(59)***(24)*(Fav)*(JHMGosden)* 3-11-8v MrJDurkan(6) (lost tch fnl 4f)......8 12
4177[14] Birthplace (IRE) **(54)***(13) (NoTrainer)* 4-11-3 (7) MrJApiafi(10) (chsd ldrs tl wknd 5f out)......5 13
88[2] Smocking **(39)***(—) (JPearce)* 4-10-9 MrsLPearce(9) (chsd ldrs tl wknd over 4f out)......5 14
4125[13] Tempering **(52)***(1) (DWChapman)* 8-11-5 (3) MissRClark(17) (led & sn clr: hdd over 5f out: sn wknd)......3½ 15
3568* Sleeptite (FR) **(55)***(—) (WGMTurner)* 4-11-4 (7) MrsCPrice(8) (bhd fr ½-wy)......12 16

Mulled Ale (IRE) **(53)***(—) (SESherwood)* 4-11-9 MissSMitchell(7) .... **W**

3/1 Deerlet, **7/2** Smocking, **8/1** ABSALOM'S PILLAR, Blowedifiknow, **9/1** Modest Hope (USA), **10/1** Telephus, **12/1** Swordking (IRE), Golden Star (IRE), Sleeptite (FR), Tempering, Mulled Ale (IRE), **14/1** Birthplace (IRE), **16/1** Tremendisto, Augustan, **20/1** Iron Baron (IRE), Heliopsis, **50/1** Legal Win (USA), CSF £104.20 CT £664.38 TOTE £10.90: £1.80 £2.60 £2.30 £3.00 (£77.00) OWNER Mr N. Hetherton (MALTON) BRED Dunchurch Lodge Stud Co 16 Rn

3m 14.1 (14.40) SF: 49/33/22/24/27/14/19/-/-/-/-/-/-/-/-/-

WEIGHT FOR AGE 3yo-7lb

T/Plpt: £185.50 (48.1 Tckts). T/Qdpt: Not won; £51.20 to Cheltenham 23/11/94 AA

4200a-EVRY (France) (R-H)
Friday November 18th (Good to soft)

4245a PRIX SAINT-ROMAN (Gp 3) (2-Y.O) £22,883.00
1m 1f GOING: 1.40 sec per fur (Hvy)

Vaneyck (FR) *(—) (France)* 2-8-11 SGuillot ....— **1**
Bryntirion (USA) *(—) (France)* 2-8-11 TJarnet ....½ **2**
Beau Temps *(—) (France)* 2-8-11 FHead 1 **3**

TOTE8.70F: 3.10F 2.70F (SF: 42.50F) OWNER Mr M. Debeusscher in France BRED Haras de Bernesq in France 7 Rn 2m 9.13 (19.13) SF: -/-/-

4246a PRIX CONTESSINA (listed race) £13,730.00
6f

4165² **Branston Abby (IRE)** *(113) (MJohnston)* 5-8-13 JReid ....— **1**
Orage Noir (USA) *(107) (France)* 6-8-11 GGuignard 1½ **2**
4042⁵ Alzianah *(104) (JDBethell)* 3-8-8 TJarnet ....nk **3**
4165* Double Blue *(110) (MJohnston)* 5-9-2 JWeaver (btn further 1¼l).............................. **6**

TOTE 5.40F: 2.30F 1.50F 2.60F (20.90F) OWNER Mr J. D. Abell (MIDDLEHAM) BRED John David Abell 9 Rn 1m 19.59 (9.59) SF: 75/67/63/-

4234a-CAPANNELLE (Rome, Italy) (R-H)
Saturday November 19th (Good to soft)

4247a PREMIO ENCI (Mdn 2-Y.O.F) £6,909.00
1m

4182a⁹ **Pesce D'Aprile** *(—) (JLDunlop)* 2-8-11 FJovine ....— **1**
Artemisia (ITY) *(—) (Italy)* 2-8-11 VMezzatesta 5 **2**
Shamal (ITY) *(—) (Italy)* 2-8-11 ACorniani 2 **3**

TOTE26L: 13L 14L 27L (52L) OWNER Mr J. L. Dunlop (ARUNDEL) 13 Rn 1m 41.7 SF: -/-/-

CAPANNELLE (Rome, Italy) (R-H)
Sunday November 20th (Good to soft)

4248a PREMIO GUIDO BERARDELLI (Gp 2) (2-Y.O.C & F) £29,723.00
1m 2f

4119a³ **Court of Honour (IRE)** *(102) (PWChapple-Hyam)* 2-8-11 JReid ....— **1**
4096* Double Eclipse (IRE) *(99) (MJohnston)* 2-8-11 JWeaver 1¾ **2**
Red Paper (IRE) *(98) (Italy)* 2-8-11 BJovine ....s.h **3**

TOTE48L: 17L 13L 28L (43L) OWNER Mr R. E. Sangster (MARLBOROUGH) BRED Swettenham Stud in Ireland 11 Rn 2m 4.1 SF: -/-/-

4249a PREMIO UMBRIA (Gp 3) £25,429.00
6f

4008a³ **Thousla Rock (IRE)** *(113) (PWChapple-Hyam)* 5-9-6 JReid ....— **1**

Gentle Fan (USA) *(109) (Italy)* 5-9-6 DZarroli 1¼ 2
3864a[4] Late Parade (IRE) *(107) (Italy)* 3-9-6 ALuongo ....¾ 3

TOTE 33L: 15L 38L 150L (400L) OWNER Mr R. E. Sangster (MARLBOROUGH) BRED Swettenham Stud in Ireland 14 Rn 1m 10.5 SF: -/-/-

4250a PREMIO GARIM (2-Y.O.F) £5,922.00 **1m 1f**

4179a* **Alessandra Demarco (IRE)** *(82) (Italy)* 2-9-2 GBietolini ....— 1
Human Touch (ITY) *(81) (Italy)* 2-9-2 FJovine ....¾ 2
Gone On the Wind *(73) (Italy)* 2-8-9 JCaro ....½ 3
4179a[2] Kafkaienne (FR) *(72) (JLDunlop)* 2-8-9 JReid ....nk 4

TOTE 48L: 20L 22L 16L (358L) OWNER Scuderia Super King BRED E. J. Loder in Ireland 8 Rn 1m 55.4 SF: -/-/-/-

4183a-TESIO (Turin, Italy) (R-H)
Sunday November 20th (Good to soft)

4251a PREMIO AMEDEO PEYRON (listed race) £17,766.00 **1m**

4109a[2] **Ice and Glacial (IRE)** *(72) (Italy)* 2-8-11 EBotti ....— 1
So Sweet (IRE) *(68) (Italy)* 2-8-11 LSorrentino 2 2
Jimy's Grey *(53) (Italy)* 2-8-11 AMarcialis 8 3
4109a[3] Piccola Buddha (IRE) *(JLDunlop)* 2-8-11 MEsposito (btn further dist) 6

TOTE 22L: 19L 21L (192L) OWNER Scuderia Siba 6 Rn 1m 45.8 SF: -/-/-/-

4218-WOLVERHAMPTON (L-H)
Saturday November 26th (Standard)

4252 MANHATTAN H'CAP (0-85) (Class D) £2,814.00 (£852.00: £416.00: £198.00) **1m 4f (Fibresand)** GOING: minus 0.12 sec per fur (FS) Stalls: Low GOING: minus 0.05 sec per fur (Std) 7-00 (7-02)

4221[2] **New Inn** **(65)***(76)*(Fav)*(EWeymes)* 3-8-2 (5) JStack(6) (chsd ldr: led 5f out: clr fnl 2f: unchal)..— 1
4168[6] Star Rage (IRE) **(74)***(81) (MJohnston)* 4-9-1 (7) OliverCasey(5) (hld up: hdwy 4f out: 4th & rdn st: styd on)..3½ 2
3976[7] Meant to Be **(75)***(82) (LadyHerries)* 4-9-2 (7) ShonaCrombie(8) (hld up: hdwy on ins over 3f out: 6th st: r.o wl ins fnl f) ....hd 3
4218[4] Premier Dance **(57)***(61) (DHaydnJones)* 7-8-0 (5) SDrowne(3) (hld up: hdwy & 5th st: nvr able to chal)..2½ 4
4125[6] Mentalasanythin **(73)***(76) (ABailey)* 5-9-7 AMackay(12) (sn chsng ldrs: 3rd & hrd rdn ent st: wknd fnl f)..¾ 5
4107[5] Chief of Staff **(78)***(80) (JPearce)* 5-9-12 JMcLaughlin(10) (lw: s.s: hdwy 4f out: styd on ins fnl f: nvr nrr) ....½ 6
4028[12] Midyan Blue (IRE) **(67)***(67) (JMPEustace)* 4-8-12 (3) JTate(11) (chsd ldrs: 2nd st: rdn & wknd ins fnl f)..1¼ 7
4167[16] Hillzah (USA) **(80)***(71) (RBastiman)* 6-9-9 (5) HBastiman(9) (chsd ldrs 7f: sn hrd drvn & wknd: t.o)..7 8
4124[11] Mad Militant (IRE) **(75)***(53) (RHollinshead)* 5-9-9 TIves(1) (lw: chsd ldrs: hrd rdn & lost pl over 4f out: t.o)..11 9
4028[14] Holy Wanderer (USA) **(80)***(57) (DWPArbuthnot)* 5-10-0 SWhitworth(7) (a in rr: t.o) ¾ 10
4124[9] Philgun **(63)***(38) (CWCElsey)* 5-8-11v NKennedy(4) (led 7f: wknd qckly: t.o) 2 11
4159[4] Kerkura (USA) **(72)***(22) (MrsJCecil)* 4-9-6 AClark(2) (lost pl 7f out: t.o) 20 12

11/4 NEW INN, **9/2** Star Rage (IRE), **5/1** Mentalasanythin, **8/1** Kerkura (USA), **9/1** Hillzah (USA), **11/1** Chief of Staff, **12/1** Premier Dance, Midyan Blue (IRE), Mad Militant (IRE) (9/1-14/1), **14/1** Philgun, Meant to Be, **16/1** Holy Wanderer (USA), CSF £16.82 CT £147.66 TOTE £2.80: £1.80 £1.90 £4.60 (£8.50) OWNER Mrs Christine Sharratt (MIDDLEHAM) BRED Crockfords Stud 12 Rn 2m 38.4 (7.40) SF: 39/49/49/30/43/48/36/-/-/-/-/-
WEIGHT FOR AGE 3yo-6lb

4253 TEQUILA SUNRISE APP'CE H'CAP (0-60) (Class F) £2,398.00 (£673.00: £328.00) 5f Stalls: Low GOING: minus 0.05 sec per fur (Std) 7-30 (7-34)

3778[5] **Scored Again (50)***(61) (MJHeaton-Ellis)* 4-8-13 (5) AmandaSanders(2) (b: mde all: clr fnl 2f: unchal)......— 1
3969[5] Nineacres **(51)***(47) (DNicholls)* 3-9-0 (5) AEddery(3) (chsd ldrs: rdn ½-wy: kpt on appr fnl f: no ch w wnr)......5 2
3583[10] Kalar **(58)***(53) (DWChapman)* 5-9-12b CTeague(6) (a.p: rdn over 1f out: one pce).nk 3
3583[5] Lady Sheriff **(44)***(37) (MWEasterby)* 3-8-9b(3) OliverCasey(1) (chsd wnr 3f: rdn over 1f out: sn btn)......½ 4
4237[15] Shadow Jury **(60)***(52) (DWChapman)* 4-10-0 GStrange(12) (racd wd: outpcd tl r.o appr fnl f)......hd 5
3838[2] Hickory Blue **(59)***(50)*(Fav)*(JAGlover)* 4-9-8b(5) MrSRichardson(13) (racd wd: sme hdwy appr fnl f: nvr nrr)......nk 6
3222[13] Trioming **(50)***(38) (APJones)* 8-9-4 SLanigan(5) (bkwd: chsd ldrs: rdn & wknd wl over 1f out)......¾ 7
4170[5] Village Green (FR) **(48)***(34) (KOCunningham-Brown)* 4-9-2b MDwyer(8) (outpcd: a bhd)......1½ 8
3759[11] Paley Prince (USA) **(60)***(46) (MDIUsher)* 8-10-0 CAdamson(11) (b: outpcd)......s.h 9
3269[16] Zilzilah (USA) **(59)***(42) (NPLittmoden)* 3-9-8 (5) AimeeCook(7) (b.hind: s.s: wl bhd tl r.o ins fnl f)......¾ 10
3030[4] Bonny Melody **(51)***(32) (PDEvans)* 3-9-0 (5) DDenby(10) (outpcd: a bhd)......½ 11
4102* Arc Lamp **(52)***(—) (JAGlover)* 8-9-6 LSuthern(4) C
3133[6] Farndale **(58)***(—) (JBerry)* 7-9-12 PFessey(9) C

2/1 Hickory Blue, **5/1** Arc Lamp, **6/1** Nineacres, **8/1** Farndale, **9/1** SCORED AGAIN, **10/1** Bonny Melody, **12/1** Village Green (FR), Lady Sheriff, **14/1** Kalar, Trioming, **16/1** Zilzilah (USA), **20/1** Paley Prince (USA), **33/1** Shadow Jury, CSF £40.59 CT £309.37 TOTE £6.90: £1.40 £1.90 £5.80 (£54.50) OWNER Mrs Anna Sanders (WROUGHTON) BRED R. T. and Mrs Watson 11 Rn
62.9 secs (4.90) SF: 15/-/5/-/5/3/-/-/-/-/-/-

4254 BLUE MOON STKS (Mdn 2-Y.O) (Class D) £2,892.00 (£876.00: £428.00: £204.00) 7f (Fibresand) Stalls: Low GOING: minus 0.05 sec (Std) 8-00 (8-03)

4156[2] **Out on a Promise (IRE)** *(68+)*(Fav)*(GWragg)* 2-9-0 WWoods(10) (led over 4f out: clr appr fnl f: unchal)......— 1
4174[11] Bold Effort (FR) *(60) (KOCunningham-Brown)* 2-9-0 BDoyle(12) (chsd ldrs: 2nd st: ev ch 2f out: rdn & outpcd appr fnl f)......4 2
Posted Abroad (IRE) *(52+) (SirMarkPrescott)* 2-9-0 GDuffield(11) (unf: scope: a.p: 3rd st: one pce fnl 2f)......4 3
Mezzoramio *(48+) (SirMarkPrescott)* 2-9-0 RPerham(6) (w'like: bkwd: bhd & outpcd tl r.o wl fnl 2f)......2 4
3816[9] Bretton Princess **(50)***(42) (RHollinshead)* 2-8-9 TIves(4) (lw: chsd ldrs: 5th & outpcd 3f out: kpt on u.p appr fnl f)......nk 5
3807[8] Sharp Tern **(54)***(40) (BSmart)* 2-8-9 CRutter(3) (led over 2f: 4th & rdn st: sn btn)...¾ 6
4225[7] Bargash *(38) (PDEvans)* 2-8-9 (5) JStack(1) (s.s: bhd tl sme hdwy fnl 2f)......3½ 7
4225[4] Winterbottom *(21) (RCharlton)* 2-9-0 RCochrane(5) (bit bkwd: chsd ldrs: rdn ½-wy: sn outpcd: t.o)......8 8
3897[16] Maronetta *(8) (MJRyan)* 2-8-9 DBiggs(2) (in tch 4f: sn lost pl: t.o)......4 9
4164[17] Serious Fact *(12) (SirMarkPrescott)* 2-9-0 CNutter(9) (lw: dwlt: a bhd: t.o)......hd 10
Laureate *(6) (DHaydnJones)* 2-8-9 AMackay(7) (lt-f: unf: bkwd: s.s: a bhd & outpcd)......½ 11
4205[9] Magical Touch *(5) (RMFlower)* 2-8-4e(5) SDrowne(8) (eyeshield: lw: outpcd: t.o)....½ 12

4/5 OUT ON A PROMISE (IRE), **9/4** Winterbottom, **6/1** Posted Abroad (IRE), **20/1** Mezzoramio, **25/1** Bargash, **33/1** Maronetta, **40/1** Sharp Tern, Bretton Princess, Bold Effort (FR), Serious Fact, Laureate, Magical Touch, CSF £39.91 TOTE £1.90: £1.20 £7.30 £1.80 (£34.20) OWNER Mrs H. H. Morriss (NEWMARKET) BRED H. H. and Mrs Morriss 12 Rn
1m 30.9 (6.90) SF: 14/5/-/-/-/-/-/-/-/-/-/-

4255 PINA COLADA STKS (0-50) (Class F) £2,647.90 (£744.40: £363.70) 6f (Fibresand) Stalls: Low GOING: minus 0.05 sec per fur (Std) 8-30 (8-32)

3890[15] **Heathyards Lady (USA) (48)***(50) (RHollinshead)* 3-8-11 TIves(10) (hdwy ½-wy: led ins fnl f: hung lft: all out)......— 1
4204[2] Sharp Imp **(39)***(54) (RMFlower)* 4-8-12b(5) JDSmith(7) (mid div: hdwy ½-wy: led over 1f out tl ins fnl f: r.o)......nk 2

3720[10] Angelic Dancer **(43)***(41) (SRBowring)* 3-8-11b DaleGibson(2) (a.p: rdn 2f out: r.o one pce)........3 **3**
4224[5] Charlies Dream (IRE) **(45)***(35) (KRBurke)* 3-8-11 JQuinn(13) (in tch: hdwy u.p fnl 2f: nvr nrr)........2½ **4**
2243[7] Brisas **(49)***(37) (CWFairhurst)* 7-8-12v(5) JStack(9) (bit bkwd: a.p: rdn appr fnl f: grad wknd)........1 **5**
4237[14] Grandee **(46)***(34) (BAMcMahon)* 3-8-11 (5) SSanders(11) (outpcd tl r.o appr fnl f: nvr nrr)........¾ **6**
4202[5] Ewar Gold (FR) **(37)***(27) (KOCunningham-Brown)* 4-8-12 BDoyle(8) (chsd ldrs: eased whn btn over 1f out)........½ **7**
3576[5] Bee Dee Best (IRE) **(37)***(28) (JPSmith)* 3-8-13 SWebster(1) (nvr nrr)........hd **8**
3898[17] Ballyhays (IRE) **(38)***(26) (JAHarris)* 5-9-0 SWilliams(12) (outpcd)........½ **9**
3759[19] Daaniera (IRE) **(46)***(25) (PHowling)* 4-9-0b AMackay(5) (led: sn wl clr: wknd & hdd over 1f out)........nk **10**
4243[4] Olifantsfontein **(50)***(22)*(Fav)*(DNicholls)* 6-9-0 AlexGreaves(6) (nvr bttr than mid div)........1 **11**
4033[14] Bold Aristocrat (IRE) **(50)***(20) (RHollinshead)* 3-8-13 RCochrane(3) (spd 4f: sn rdn & wknd)........½ **12**
3507[8] Palacegate Gold (IRE) **(44)***(17) (RJHodges)* 5-8-12 (5) SDrowne(4) (outpcd)........2½ **13**

3/1 Olifantsfontein, **6/1** Sharp Imp, Angelic Dancer, Palacegate Gold (IRE), **9/1** Charlies Dream (IRE), **14/1** HEATHYARDS LADY (USA), Grandee, Bold Aristocrat (IRE), Bee Dee Best (IRE), **20/1** Brisas, Ewar Gold (FR), Daaniera (IRE), **25/1** Ballyhays (IRE), CSF £89.81 TOTE £21.90: £3.70 £1.90 £2.90 (£78.20) OWNER Mr L. A. Morgan (UPPER LONGDON) BRED S A'Long Farm and Dennis Swartz 13 Rn 1m 16.2 (5.00) SF: 22/28/13/7/10/8/2/2/-/-/-/-/-
WEIGHT FOR AGE 3yo-1lb

4256 BUCK'S FIZZ (S) STKS (2-Y.O) (Class G) £2,190.00 (£615.00: £300.00)
6f (Fibresand) Stalls: Low GOING: minus 0.05 sec per fur (Std) 9-00 (9-03)

4242[6] **Casper's Risk (61)***(56) (DNicholls)* 2-9-2b AlexGreaves(8) (a.p: led on bit 2f out: sn clr: hld on nr fin)........— **1**
One for Jeannie *(42+)*(Fav)*(ABailey)* 2-8-1 (5) DWright(7) (lengthy: lt-f: s.s: bhd & outpcd tl gd hdwy over 1f out: fin wl)........1¼ **2**
4213[3] Water Bebe (IRE) **(48)***(45) (GCBravery)* 2-8-11 TIves(4) (hdwy wl over 1f out: fin wl)........½ **3**
4207[7] Reponist **(50)***(40) (MJCamacho)* 2-8-7bow1 RCochrane(11) (hdwy ½-wy: rdn & r.o wl fnl f)........hd **4**
4238[9] Mr Slick **(70)***(35) (NACallaghan)* 2-8-11 GDuffield(9) (b.hind: lw: a.p: rdn over 1f out: sn outpcd)........3½ **5**
4222[11] Saxon Heir (IRE) **(53)***(30) (MDIUsher)* 2-9-2b MWigham(5) (gd spd over 4f)........4 **6**
3823[12] Sharp Shower (IRE) **(52)***(21) (BAMcMahon)* 2-8-6b(5) SSanders(2) (bhd & outpcd: hdwy u.p appr fnl f: nvr nrr)........1½ **7**
4222[6] Precious Times **(50)***(18) (MGMeagher)* 2-8-11 JQuinn(6) (b: spd 4f)........1 **8**
4222[4] Lady Pui **(56)***(15) (JBerry)* 2-8-11 SWilliams(3) (lw: led over 3f: rdn & wknd appr fnl f)........1 **9**
4106[10] Cranbrook Kate **(44)***(6) (JMackie)* 2-8-6 AMackay(13) (lw: outpcd)........1¼ **10**
4222[9] Lawnswood Lady **(45)***(—) (RHollinshead)* 2-8-1 (5) AGarth(1) (outpcd)........2½ **11**
4228[9] Prince Rudolf (IRE) **(54)***(8) (NPLittmoden)* 2-9-2b AClark(12) (a in rr: eased wl over 1f out)........½ **12**

9/4 One for Jeannie, **7/2** Lady Pui, **9/2** Mr Slick, **6/1** CASPER'S RISK, **7/1** Reponist, **10/1** Water Bebe (IRE), **16/1** Precious Times, Prince Rudolf (IRE), Lawnswood Lady, **25/1** Sharp Shower (IRE), Saxon Heir (IRE), **33/1** Cranbrook Kate, CSF £21.46 TOTE £8.10: £4.00 £1.20 £3.10 (£27.80) OWNER Mr John Gilbertson (THIRSK) BRED Roldvale Ltd 12 Rn No bid
1m 16.6 (5.40) SF: 21/10/13/9/4/-/-/-/-/-/-/-

4257 BLACK RUSSIAN H'CAP (0-70) (Class E) £2,905.00 (£880.00: £430.00: £205.00)
1m 100y (Fibresand) Stalls: Low GOING: minus 0.05 sec (Std) 9-30 (9-31)

4227[4] **Sandmoor Denim (59)***(72) (SRBowring)* 7-8-13 (7) GStrange(7) (b: hld up in tch: wnt 2nd st: led over 1f out: sn clr)........— **1**
4223[4] Queens Stroller (IRE) **(65)***(66) (CCElsey)* 3-9-10 JQuinn(10) (a.p: led over 3f out tl over 1f out: r.o one pce)........6 **2**
4217[7] Guesstimation (USA) **(50)***(49) (JPearce)* 5-8-11 GBardwell(2) (hld up: hdwy 3f out: 4th & rdn st: nt pce to chal)........1 **3**
4223[2] Aitch N'Bee **(66)***(65) (LadyHerries)* 11-9-6 (7) ShonaCrombie(5) (lw: hld up: hdwy wl over 1f out: rdn & r.o wl fnl f)........hd **4**

4204* Level Edge **(53)***(52)*(Fav)*(MJohnston)* 3-8-5 (7) OliverCasey(6) (led over 4f: 3rd st: one pce fnl f)....hd **5**
4226[2] Majboor (IRE) **(67)***(56) (BAMcMahon)* 5-9-9 (5) SSanders(1) (lw: chsd ldrs: 6th & rdn st: sn btn)....5 **6**
4223[10] Tu Opes **(68)***(50) (JLHarris)* 3-9-13 DaleGibson(9) (a bhd)....3½ **7**
4012[8] Lombard Ships **(51)***(30) (ABailey)* 7-8-12b AMackay(11) (chsd ldrs: rdn over 2f out: 5th st: sn wknd)....1¼ **8**
2171[6] Blushingbird (IRE) **(57)***(33) (LordHuntingdon)* 3-9-2 TIves(13) (a in rr)....1½ **9**
4218[7] Port Sunlight (IRE) **(59)***(33) (PDEvans)* 6-9-1 (5) JStack(12) (swtg: chsd ldrs 5f: sn wknd)....1¾ **10**
4227[7] Shuttlecock **(67)***(39) (NPLittmoden)* 3-9-12 AClark(8) (prom: rdn along ½-wy: sn lost tch)....¾ **11**
4103[2] Spring Loaded **(55)***(15) (JGMO'Shea)* 3-9-0 VSlattery(3) (chsd ldrs: sddle slipped & wknd 3f out: t.o)....6 **12**

7/2 Level Edge, **4/1** SANDMOOR DENIM, Queens Stroller (IRE), **7/1** Majboor (IRE), **10/1** Aitch N'Bee, Guesstimation (USA), Blushingbird (IRE), Spring Loaded, **14/1** Port Sunlight (IRE), Lombard Ships, **16/1** Shuttlecock, **33/1** Tu Opes, CSF £21.70 CT £147.10 TOTE £6.00: £1.70 £1.90 £2.70 (£19.70) OWNER Mr E. H. Lunness (EDWINSTOWE) BRED Rathasker Stud 12 Rn
1m 50.3 (0.1 under best) (6.30) SF: 40/33/19/34/19/25/17/-/-/-/-/-
WEIGHT FOR AGE 3yo-2lb

T/Plpt: £491.90 (26.05 Tckts). T/Qdpt: £53.40 (2.7 Tckts) IM

4202-LINGFIELD (L-H)
Saturday November 26th (Standard)

4258
BADAJOZ H'CAP (I) (0-85) (Class D) £3,273.80 (£991.40: £484.20: £230.60)
6f (Equitrack) GOING: minus 0.55 sec per fur (FS) 11-50 (11-51)

3424[7] **Rocky Waters (USA) (78)***(82) (GLMoore)* 5-9-11 BRouse(6) (chsd ldrs: r.o wl to ld ins fnl f)....— **1**
4231[9] Spender **(73)***(73)*(Fav)*(PWHarris)* 5-9-6 GDuffield(10) (trckd ldr: led appr fnl f tl rdn, hdd & no ex ins fnl f)....1¼ **2**
3748[5] Newington Butts (IRE) **(51)***(45) (RAkehurst)* 4-7-12e JQuinn(4) (led tl appr fnl f: one pce)....2½ **3**
4202[4] Our Shadee (USA) **(48)***(33) (KTIvory)* 4-7-9v GBardwell(3) (s.s: sn pushed along: hdwy ½-wy: r.o fnl f)....3½ **4**
4202[9] Words of Wisdom (IRE) **(56)***(40) (CACyzer)* 4-7-12 (5)ow1 DRMcCabe(5) (nvr nrr)..nk **5**
3446[4] Call to the Bar (IRE) **(74)***(55) (MMcCormack)* 5-9-7 AClark(8) (hdwy over 2f out: one pce fr over 1f out)....1 **6**
2923[9] Al Shaati (FR) **(54)***(31) (RJO'Sullivan)* 4-8-1 DBiggs(2) (nvr trbld ldrs)....1½ **7**
3910[5] Cradle Days **(77)***(54) (RCSpicer)* 5-9-10 TIves(9) (chsd ldrs 2f)....s.h **8**
1113[5] Victoria Hall **(60)***(22) (WGMTurner)* 4-8-2 (5)ow1 JDSmith(1) (sn lost tch)....6 **9**
3157[12] Thorny Bishop **(75)***(32) (JJBridger)* 3-9-7 TWilliams(7) (prom 3f)....1¾ **10**

100/30 Spender, **5/1** ROCKY WATERS (USA), **11/2** Call to the Bar (IRE), **6/1** Al Shaati (FR), **8/1** Newington Butts (IRE), **9/1** Words of Wisdom (IRE), Our Shadee (USA), **12/1** Cradle Days, Thorny Bishop, **14/1** Victoria Hall, CSF £21.79 CT £122.91 TOTE £5.00: £2.80 £1.90 £2.70 (£19.10) OWNER Mr K. Higson (EPSOM) BRED Dan C. Pitts 10 Rn
1m 11.11 (0.51) SF: 55/47/21/8/15/29/7/2/-/-
WEIGHT FOR AGE 3yo-1lb

4259
BUSACO RIDGE MEDIAN AUCTION STKS (Mdn 2-Y.O) (Class F)
£2,564.60 (£720.60: £351.80)
1m 2f (Equitrack) GOING: minus 0.55 sec per fur (FS) 12-20 (12-21)

4205[5] **Star Fighter (60)***(67) (WAO'Gorman)* 2-8-11 (3) EmmaO'Gorman(7) (hld up: hdwy to ld 6f out: rdn & r.o wl fr over 2f out)....— **1**
4174[7] Saterne Lady **(64)***(57)*(Fav)*(PFICole)* 2-8-9 TQuinn(8) (hdwy to chse ldr over 4f out: rdn & one pce fnl 2f)....3½ **2**
4203[5] Pent-House Baby **(42)***(43) (JLSpearing)* 2-8-9 TIves(6) (led after 2f to 6f out: outpcd)....9 **3**
3744[12] Joseno **(43)***(42) (BPalling)* 2-8-9 AClark(2) (nvr trbld ldrs)....¾ **4**
4205[6] Most Welcome News **(58)***(46) (JRJenkins)* 2-9-0e CRutter(4) (led 2f: bhd fnl 5f).....½ **5**
Desirous *(45) (BGubby)* 2-8-7 (7) AWhelan(1) (m.n.s)....½ **6**
4080[12] Elmer's Tune *(—) (RHannon)* 2-9-0 RPerham(5) (a bhd)....hd **7**
4171[6] Shy Paddy (IRE) *(—) (KOCunningham-Brown)* 2-9-0 BDoyle(3) (bhd fnl 5f).........¾ **8**

13/8 Saterne Lady, **5/2** Shy Paddy (IRE) (3/1-2/1), **6/1** STAR FIGHTER, **7/1** Elmer's Tune, **8/1** Pent-House Baby, **12/1** Joseno, Most Welcome News, **33/1** Desirous, CSF £16.63 TOTE £6.70: £1.60 £1.20 £2.10 (£6.70) OWNER Mr S. Fustok (NEWMARKET) BRED Deerfield Farm 8 Rn
2m 7.5 (4.50) SF: 19/9/-/-/-/-/-/-

4260 VITTORIA (S) STKS (Class G) £2,431.50 (£684.00: £334.50)
1m 2f (Equitrack) GOING: minus 0.55 sec per fur (FS) 12-50 (12-52)

4239* **Shabanaz (62)***(65)*(Fav)*(WRMuir)* 9-9-9 RCochrane(9) (s.s: hdwy over 2f out: led ins fnl f: comf)......— 1
4226⁹ Captain Marmalade **(49)***(57) (DTThom)* 5-8-13 (5) DRMcCabe(13) (hld up & bhd: effrt over 2f out: r.o wl fnl f)......1¾ 2
3604⁸ Ecu de France (IRE) **(73)***(61) (MMadgwick)* 4-9-9v AClark(3) (ev ch 3f out: nt qckn fnl f)......¾ 3
2664⁵ Vanroy **(58)***(60) (JRJenkins)* 10-9-9 SWhitworth(14) (eyeshield: chsd ldrs: rdn over 2f out: one pce)......nk 4
4224¹² Give In **(34)***(52) (MissGayKelleway)* 7-8-13 (5) SDrowne(7) (chsd ldrs: led 3f out tl hdd & no ex ins fnl f)......1¾ 5
4176³ Long Furlong **(37)***(54) (RAkehurst)* 6-9-9 TQuinn(2) (eyeshield: hld up & bhd: rdn 3f out: one pce fnl f)......1¾ 6
2551⁵ Rave-on-Hadley (IRE) **(48)***(46) (ABailey)* 4-9-4 WHawksley(6) (led after 2f to 3f out: sn wknd)......2 7
4126² Finjan **(54)***(44) (AGFoster)* 7-9-4 TIves(12) (in tch tl wknd over 1f out)......1 8
1092¹¹ Pop to Stans **(58)***(48) (JPearce)* 5-9-2 (7) ETurner(11) (a bhd)......½ 9
4210¹⁰ Takenhall **(42)***(38) (MJFetherston-Godley)* 9-9-4 CRutter(4) (a bhd)......3 10
4202⁶ Glenfield Greta **(45)***(34) (PSFelgate)* 6-9-4 AMackay(8) (m.n.s)......2½ 11
4214⁸ Bill Moon **(37)***(32) (PJFeilden)* 8-8-11 (7) JoHunnam(5) (prom tl wknd over 2f out).1½ 12
3359⁷ Mister O'Grady (IRE) **(48)***(31) (GLMoore)* 3-9-5v BRouse(10) (led 2f: wknd 4f out)..4 13
4214⁵ After the Last **(60)***(12) (RHannon)* 4-9-4 RPerham(1) (a bhd: t.o)......9 14

6/4 SHABANAZ, **5/1** After the Last, **15/2** Ecu de France (IRE), **8/1** Finjan, **10/1** Pop to Stans (8/1-12/1), Long Furlong (8/1-12/1), **12/1** Vanroy, **14/1** Captain Marmalade, **16/1** Rave-on-Hadley (IRE), **20/1** Mister O'Grady (IRE), Glenfield Greta, **25/1** Takenhall, **33/1** Give In, **50/1** Bill Moon, CSF £25.65 TOTE £2.80: £1.70 £2.80 £3.20 (£16.90) OWNER Fayzad Thoroughbred Ltd (LAMBOURN) BRED The Overbury Stud 14 Rn 2m 5.97 (2.97) SF: 39/32/36/35/29/32/25/-/-/-/-/-/-/-
WEIGHT FOR AGE 3yo-4lb
Bt in 6,000 gns

4261 CHAMPAGNE JACQUART CHALLENGE H'CAP (0-70) (Class E) £2,814.00 (£852.00: £416.00: £198.00)
1m 5f (Equitrack) GOING: minus 0.55 sec per fur (FS) 1-20 (1-21)

4074⁷ **Ela Man Howa (54)***(59) (RAkehurst)* 3-8-9 TQuinn(15) (hld up: hdwy 4f out: led over 2f out: r.o)......— 1
4159³ Miroswaki (USA) **(63)***(66) (PMMcEntee)* 4-9-10 JQuinn(5) (hld up mid div: effrt over 2f out: rdn ent fnl f: r.o)......1½ 2
499⁸ Dancing Diamond (IRE) **(47)***(50) (MissBSanders)* 4-8-3h(5) SSanders(9) (led over 3f out tl over 2f out: nt qckn fnl f)......nk 3
4208⁹ Tres Cher (IRE) **(53)***(56) (BWHills)* 3-8-8b RCochrane(11) (chsd ldrs: one pce fnl 2f)......hd 4
4217² Red Dancer **(52)***(51)*(Fav)*(MBell)* 3-8-7b GDuffield(3) (hld up: hdwy over 4f out: one pce)......3½ 5
4208⁴ Rose of Glenn **(51)***(47) (BPalling)* 3-8-6 CRutter(13) (in tch: rdn & one pce fr wl over 2f out)......2½ 6
3981⁷ Sir Thomas Beecham **(67)***(58) (SDow)* 4-9-7e(7) AWhelan(10) (outpcd 4f out: styd on one pce fnl 2f)......4 7
4131¹⁰ Sommersby (IRE) **(55)***(45) (ACStewart)* 3-8-10 SWhitworth(7) (chsd ldrs tl wknd over 2f out)......½ 8
4229⁶ Cristal Springs **(38)***(26) (BJMcMath)* 3-7-7 GBardwell(6) (nvr plcd to chal)......1¼ 9
3992¹¹ Bronze Maquette (IRE) **(42)***(28) (BJMcMath)* 4-7-12 (5) DRMcCabe(12) (a bhd)....1¾ 10
3777⁷ Lord Glenvara (IRE) **(44)***(28) (RJO'Sullivan)* 6-8-5 DBiggs(14) (chsd ldr tl wknd wl over 3f out)......1½ 11
4140⁵ Danielle Habibi (IRE) **(41)***(22) (CCElsey)* 3-7-10 DaleGibson(2) (a in rr)......2½ 12
3686¹² Shamwari (USA) **(58)***(33) (JWHills)* 3-8-13b AClark(1) (led tl over 3f out: wknd qckly)......5 13
4175⁶ Choir Master (CAN) **(55)***(26) (AMoore)* 7-9-2 CandyMorris(4) (nvr plcd to chal)....3½ 14
4209⁹ Pink Brief (IRE) **(55)***(9) (BJMeehan)* 3-8-10 BDoyle(8) (wl bhd fnl 4f: t.o)......15 15
LONG HANDICAP Cristal Springs 7-5

11/4 Red Dancer, **9/2** Rose of Glenn (7/1-4/1), **7/1** ELA MAN HOWA, **8/1** Tres Cher (IRE), **10/1** Miroswaki (USA), **12/1** Sir Thomas Beecham, Lord Glenvara (IRE), **14/1** Dancing Diamond (IRE), Pink Brief (IRE), Bronze Maquette (IRE), Sommersby (IRE), **16/1** Danielle Habibi (IRE), Shamwari (USA), Choir Master (CAN), **33/1** Cristal Springs, CSF £78.63 CT £910.24 TOTE £8.10: £2.20 £4.10 £4.40 (£46.00) OWNER Arlington Bloodstock (EPSOM) BRED Sheikh Ahmed bin Rashid al Maktoum 15 Rn 2m 43.82 (0.18 under best) (1.32) SF: 42/54/39/38/34/30/46/-/-/-/-
WEIGHT FOR AGE 3yo-6lb

4262

ANDREW KEENAN & CO. NURSERY (Class D) £3,393.40 (£1,028.20: £502.60: £239.80) **6f (Equitrack)** GOING: minus 0.55 sec per fur (FS) 1-55 (1-56)

4207[2] **Robo Magic (USA) (62)***(67)*(Jt-Fav)*(AMoore)* 2-8-0 (7) AWhelan(3) (w ldr: led over 2f out: rdn & r.o wl) — 1
4207* Fairy Fay (IRE) **(66)***(67)*(Jt-Fav)*(BJMcMath)* 2-8-11 RCochrane(2) (chsd ldrs: effrt 2f out: one pce fnl f) 1¼ 2
4228[14] Crystal Loop **(63)***(56) (ABailey)* 2-8-3 (5) DWright(1) (in tch tl outpcd 2f out: r.o ins fnl f) 3 3
4213[2] Bon Secret (IRE) **(58)***(51)*(Jt-Fav)*(TJNaughton)* 2-8-3 BDoyle(7) (led tl over 2f out: one pce) s.h 4
2677* First Crush **(76)***(63) (SirMarkPrescott)* 2-9-7 GDuffield(9) (in tch: one pce fnl 2f) 2½ 5
2414[8] Witney-de-Bergerac (IRE) **(67)***(53) (JSMoore)* 2-8-12 AClark(11) (m.n.s) hd 6
4164[9] Tiheros **(70)***(53) (RHannon)* 2-9-1 RPerham(10) (chsd ldrs tl wknd over 1f out) 1 7
4015[13] Red Spectacle (IRE) **(60)***(42) (PCHaslam)* 2-8-5 DaleGibson(6) (a bhd & outpcd) nk 8
4029[11] Solo Prize **(75)***(42) (PHowling)* 2-9-6b JQuinn(4) (s.s: a bhd) 6 9
4174[17] Bills Ploughgirl **(50)***(8) (JSMoore)* 2-7-4 (5)ow2 NVarley(5) (in tch 3f) 3½ 10
3974[14] Plucky Pet **(48)***(—) (CJBenstead)* 2-7-7 GBardwell(8) (a bhd: t.o) 5 11
LONG HANDICAP Bills Ploughgirl 7-4 Plucky Pet 7-4

9/2 ROBO MAGIC (USA), Fairy Fay (IRE), Bon Secret (IRE), **5/1** Crystal Loop, First Crush, **9/1** Solo Prize, **10/1** Tiheros, **16/1** Red Spectacle (IRE), **20/1** Witney-de-Bergerac (IRE), Plucky Pet, **25/1** Bills Ploughgirl, CSF £25.21 CT £99.50 TOTE £5.70: £2.10 £1.20 £2.40 (£7.20) OWNER Mr C. F. Sparrowhawk (BRIGHTON) BRED Curtis C. Green 11 Rn
1m 11.96 (1.36) SF: 26/28/17/12/22/13/14/-/-/-/-

4263

BADAJOZ H'CAP (II) (0-85) (Class D) £3,273.80 (£991.40: £484.20: £230.60) **6f (Equitrack)** GOING: minus 0.55 sec per fur (FS) 2-25 (2-26)

4214* **Silent Expression (65)***(73) (BJMeehan)* 4-8-12 RCochrane(10) (in tch: qcknd to ld wl over 1f out: easily) — 1
3975[10] Forgotten Dancer (IRE) **(61)***(54) (RIngram)* 3-8-7 WWoods(9) (mid div tl hdwy fnl f: no ch w wnr) 6 2
3986[6] La Petite Fusee **(62)***(50) (RJO'Sullivan)* 3-8-8 AClark(6) (chsd ldr: ev ch 2f out: sn outpcd) 2 3
4051[3] Formidable Liz **(59)***(44) (KRBurke)* 4-8-6 DaleGibson(4) (in tch: one pce fnl 2f) ¾ 4
4220[12] Dark Eyed Lady (IRE) **(70)***(51) (DWPArbuthnot)* 4-9-3 SWhitworth(5) (hld up & bhd: no hdwy fnl 2f) 1½ 5
3986[11] Rambold **(70)***(48) (TMJones)* 3-9-2 RPerham(8) (rdn ½-wy: sn btn) 1 6
4211[7] Born to Be **(55)***(33) (SDow)* 5-8-2 JQuinn(1) (led tl wl over 1f out: wknd qckly) s.h 7
4220[3] Rocketeer (IRE) **(82)***(50)*(Fav)*(WRMuir)* 3-9-7b(7) SMcCarthy(7) (a bhd) 4 8
3720[C] Circus Lodge **(55)***(17) (JARToller)* 3-8-1 TWilliams(2) (outpcd) 2½ 9

3/1 Rocketeer (IRE), **7/2** La Petite Fusee, **9/2** SILENT EXPRESSION, **11/2** Formidable Liz, **8/1** Born to Be, Circus Lodge, **12/1** Rambold, **16/1** Dark Eyed Lady (IRE), **20/1** Forgotten Dancer (IRE), CSF £74.39 CT £322.05 TOTE £5.10: £2.10 £3.90 £1.20 (£56.20) OWNER Mr A. S. Reid (UPPER LAMBOURN) BRED J. B. H. Stevens 9 Rn 1m 11.02 (0.42) SF: 44/23/19/15/21/17/5/-/-
WEIGHT FOR AGE 3yo-1lb

4264

LADBROKE ALL-WEATHER TROPHY (H'cap) (Qualifier) (I) (0-75) (Class D) £3,303.70 (£1,000.60: £448.80: £232.90) **1m (Equitrack)** GOING: minus 0.55 sec per fur (FS) 2-55 (2-57)

3966[3] **Present Situation (62)***(70)*(Jt-Fav)*(LordHuntingdon)* 3-8-7 (7) AWhelan(1) (a.p: led over 1f out: jst hld on) — 1
4202* Mr Nevermind (IRE) **(72)***(80)*(Jt-Fav)*(GLMoore)* 4-9-12 BRouse(7) (n.m.r 5f out: rdn 3f out: r.o wl fnl 2f) s.h 2
4105[3] Shansi (IRE) **(43)***(47) (MDIUsher)* 3-7-9v RStreet(9) (a.p: led over 3f out tl over 1f out: nt qckn fnl f) 2 3
3940b[9] Red Valerian **(71)***(75) (KMcAuliffe)* 3-9-6b(3) JTate(6) (hdwy 3f out: sn ev ch: no ex fnl f) s.h 4

4223³ Polonez Prima **(67)***(68) (JEBanks)* 7-9-7 JQuinn(3) (hld up: n.m.r ent st: styd on one pce) 1¼ **5**
4227* Mullitover **(74)***(71) (MJHeaton-Ellis)* 4-10-0 WWoods(4) (rdn over 3f out: one pce fnl 2f) 1¾ **6**
4204¹⁴ No Speeches (IRE) **(59)***(52) (CACyzer)* 3-8-11 TIves(5) (nvr plcd to chal) 1¾ **7**
3777⁶ Kissavos **(49)***(39) (CCElsey)* 8-8-3 CRutter(12) (a in rr) 1¼ **8**
4210⁶ Island Knight (IRE) **(70)***(60) (MJRyan)* 5-9-10 AClark(11) (hld up: rdn & no imp fnl 3f) ....hd **9**
3975⁴ World Traveller **(72)***(61) (WAO'Gorman)* 3-9-7 (3) EmmaO'Gorman(2) (nvr plcd to chal) ....½ **10**
4143⁴ Comanche Companion **(66)***(51) (TJNaughton)* 4-9-6 GDuffield(8) (led tl over 3f out) 1¾ **11**
4163¹⁴ True Precision **(64)***(42) (JDBethell)* 4-9-4 RCochrane(10) (a bhd) 3½ **12**

4/1 PRESENT SITUATION, Mr Nevermind (IRE), **5/1** Comanche Companion, **13/2** Polonez Prima, **7/1** Mullitover, Island Knight (IRE), **10/1** True Precision, **12/1** Kissavos, **14/1** Red Valerian, World Traveller, **20/1** Shansi (IRE), **33/1** No Speeches (IRE), CSF £21.62 CT £280.10 TOTE £4.10: £1.50 £2.50 £3.90 (£7.20) OWNER Mr Chris van Hoorn (WEST ILSLEY) BRED The Queen 12 Rn 1m 37.49 (1.09) SF: 42/53/20/46/42/47/29/-/-/-/-/-
WEIGHT FOR AGE 3yo-2lb

4265 LADBROKE ALL-WEATHER TROPHY (H'cap) (Qualifier) (II) (0-75) (Class D) £3,288.75 (£996.00: £486.50: £231.75)
1m (Equitrack) GOING: minus 0.55 sec per fur (FS) 3-25 (3-28)

4078* **Ertlon (72)***(88+) (CEBrittain)* 4-9-12 BDoyle(12) (hld up mid div: led 3f out: sn clr: comf) ....— **1**
4204⁴ Dancing Lawyer **(69)***(73) (BJMeehan)* 3-9-7 JQuinn(8) (chsd ldrs: styd on fnl 2f: no ch w wnr) 6 **2**
4099⁸ Northern Bird **(63)***(66) (BWHills)* 4-8-12 (5) JDSmith(3) (bhd: r.o fnl 2f: nvr plcd to chal) ....½ **3**
4101⁷ Spectacle Jim **(49)***(50) (JO'Donoghue)* 5-7-12b(5) DRMcCabe(5) (chsd ldrs: one pce fnl 2f) ....¾ **4**
4210⁴ Masnun (USA) **(66)***(67) (RJO'Sullivan)* 9-9-6 DBiggs(7) (rdn 3f out: kpt on fnl f) ....hd **5**
4210² Wave Hill **(63)***(63) (PRHedger)* 5-9-3v RPerham(4) (chsd ldr tl rdn & btn over 2f out) ....nk **6**
4209⁴ Sarum **(53)***(51) (CPWildman)* 8-8-7 RCochrane(6) (hld up mid div: rdn & no imp fnl 2f) ....¾ **7**
4209¹² Kintwyn **(66)***(63) (DRLaing)* 4-9-6 SWhitworth(1) (s.s: a bhd) ....nk **8**
4210* Soaking **(70)***(59)*(Fav)*(GLMoore)* 4-9-10 BRouse(11) (led ½-wy to 3f out: outpcd) ..4 **9**
4101¹¹ Zinbaq **(46)***(30) (CJBenstead)* 8-8-0 TWilliams(10) (nvr nr to chal) 2½ **10**
3729²⁶ Aljaz **(65)***(44) (DTThom)* 4-9-5 AMackay(9) (a in rr) 2½ **11**
4202¹⁵ Papagos (IRE) **(53)***(18) (SDow)* 3-7-12 (7) AWhelan(2) (led to 4f out: wknd: t.o) 7 **12**

11/4 Soaking, **4/1** ERTLON, **11/2** Dancing Lawyer, **6/1** Sarum, **13/2** Northern Bird, Wave Hill, **12/1** Masnun (USA), Papagos (IRE), **14/1** Kintwyn, **16/1** Zinbaq, **25/1** Spectacle Jim, **33/1** Aljaz, CSF £28.76 CT £139.24 TOTE £7.00: £1.90 £2.10 £2.20 (£34.80) OWNER Mr C. E. Brittain (NEWMARKET) BRED Hadi Al Tajir 12 Rn 1m 36.52 (0.12) SF: 63/46/42/28/43/39/29/-/-/-/-/-
WEIGHT FOR AGE 3yo-2lb

T/Plpt: £156.30 (44 Tckts). T/Qdpt: £60.20 (1 Tckt) TS

LINGFIELD (L-H)
Monday November 28th (Standard)

4266 SUNNINGDALE APP'CE H'CAP (I) (0-70) (Class G) £1,820.60 (£511.60: £249.80) **5f (Equitrack)** GOING: minus 0.60 sec per fur (FS) 12-10 (12-13)

4202¹⁴ **Distant Dynasty (49)***(58) (BAPearce)* 4-8-7 PRoberts(5) (s.i.s: hdwy over 3f out: led over 2f out: clr over 1f out: pushed out) ....— **1**
4253⁸ Village Green (FR) **(48)***(48) (KOCunningham-Brown)* 4-8-3b(3) CTeague(8) (outpcd: hdwy on ins over 1f out: r.o) 3 **2**
3806¹⁹ Swift Nick Nevison **(40)***(38) (KTIvory)* 3-7-7 (5) AmandaSanders(6) (led over 2f: unable qckn) ....½ **3**
3616¹⁰ Tommy Tempest **(42)***(40) (ABailey)* 5-7-11b(3) SLanigan(1) (s.i.s: hdwy over 3f out: rdn 2f out: one pce) ....s.h **4**
1170¹⁷ Pat Poindestres **(35)***(32) (RJO'Sullivan)* 4-7-7 MBaird(10) (hdwy over 1f out: r.o one pce) ....nk **5**

4231[7] Rocky Two **(63)***(59) (PHowling)* 3-9-7b AWhelan(7) (a.p: hrd rdn over 1f out: one pce)....hd **6**
4237[5] Tyrian Purple (IRE) **(66)***(57) (TJNaughton)* 6-9-10b VHalliday(9) (b: b.off hind: rdn & lost pl over 2f out: r.o one pce fnl f)....1½ **7**
1014[13] Not so Generous (IRE) **(65)***(55)*(Fav)*(WGMTurner)* 4-9-9 JDSmith(3) (no hdwy fnl 2f)....nk **8**
4206[11] Crafty Cricketer **(40)***(26) (RVoorspuy)* 3-7-7b(5)ow5 DDenby(2) (bhd fnl 2f)....1¼ **9**
3978[21] Hitchin a Ride **(35)***(—) (RAkehurst)* 7-7-7e IonaWands(4) .... **W**
LONG HANDICAP Pat Poindestres 7-0

3/1 Not so Generous (IRE), **7/2** DISTANT DYNASTY, **4/1** Tyrian Purple (IRE), Tommy Tempest, **6/1** Village Green (FR), **8/1** Hitchin a Ride, Rocky Two, **14/1** Swift Nick Nevison, **16/1** Pat Poindestres, **33/1** Crafty Cricketer, CSF £25.49 CT £251.02 TOTE £4.40: £1.50 £2.20 £4.20 (£12.30) OWNER Mr M. V. Kirby (LIMPSFIELD) BRED B. A. Pearce 9 Rn
59.6 secs (hand) (1.4) SF: 17/7/-/-/-/17/16/-/-/-

4267 WENTWORTH NURSERY (0-85) (Class D) £2,710.00 (£820.00: £400.00: £190.00) 5f (Equitrack) GOING: minus 0.60 sec per fur (FS) 12-40 (12-42)

4144* **Stoppes Brow (68)***(76)*(Fav)*(GLMoore)* 2-9-7v BRouse(2) (lw: hld up: n.m.r over 2f out: led ins fnl f: r.o wl)....— **1**
4238[5] Das Island **(56)***(61) (JRJenkins)* 2-8-9 CRutter(3) (a.p: led 1f out tl ins fnl f: unable qckn)....¾ **2**
4076[2] Nadwaty (IRE) **(58)***(57) (JDBethell)* 2-8-11 TWilliams(9) (led 4f: one pce)....2 **3**
4174[9] Lugana Vision **(46)***(36) (PMMcEntee)* 2-7-8 (5) NVarley(4) (no hdwy fnl 2f)....3 **4**
4230[11] Magic Leader (IRE) **(50)***(34) (TTClement)* 2-7-10 (7) SLanigan(6) (b: outpcd: nvr nrr)....2 **5**
4048[6] Royal Dancer **(45)***(29) (TTClement)* 2-7-7 (5)ow2 DWright(5) (a.p: hrd rdn over 1f out: sn wknd)....s.h **6**
3954[7] Fiery Footsteps **(65)***(46) (PHowling)* 2-9-4v AMackay(7) (outpcd)....1 **7**
4230[15] Al Totseva **(45)***(14) (MPMuggeridge)* 2-7-5 (7) CAdamson(1) (bhd fnl 3f)....4 **8**
4134* Super Sonata **(66)***(—) (MHTompkins)* 2-9-0v(5) SMulvey(8) (outpcd)....7 **9**

Evens STOPPES BROW, **4/1** Das Island, **5/1** Nadwaty (IRE), **6/1** Super Sonata, **12/1** Lugana Vision, **20/1** Fiery Footsteps, **33/1** Magic Leader (IRE), **50/1** Al Totseva, Royal Dancer, CSF £5.72 CT £12.73 TOTE £1.60: £1.10 £1.70 £2.30 (£4.10) OWNER Mr C. J. Pennick (EPSOM) BRED Dodford Stud 9 Rn
59.48 secs (1.28) SF: 32/19/14/-/-/-/1/-/-

4268 SUNNINGDALE APP'CE H'CAP (II) (0-70) (Class G) £1,812.20 (£509.20: £248.60) 5f (Equitrack) GOING: minus 0.60 sec per fur (FS) 1-10 (1-11)

4212[2] **Tee-Emm (59)***(63) (PHowling)* 4-8-12 (5) DBiggs(4) (led over 3f out tl ins fnl f: unable qckn: fin 2nd, 1l: awrdd r)....— **1**
3692[8] Warwick Warrior (IRE) **(70)***(63) (MrsLPiggott)* 3-9-7 (7) VictoriaAppleby(6) (b: b.hind: hld up: rdn over 1f out: one pce: fin 3rd, 3½l: plcd 2nd).... **2**
4220[13] It Must Be Millie **(63)***(53) (GHEden)* 3-9-7 AWhelan(10) (b.off hind: hld up: rdn over 1f out: one pce: fin 4th, 3/4 l: plcd 3rd).... **3**
4253[9] Paley Prince (USA) **(60)***(48) (MDIUsher)* 8-9-1 (3) CAdamson(2) (nvr nr to chal: fin 5th, ½l: plcd 4th).... **4**
4212[3] Super Rocky **(58)***(41) (RBastiman)* 5-9-2b HBastiman(1) (led over 1f: hrd rdn over 1f out: sn wknd)....1½ **6**
4220[6] Nordico Princess **(61)***(41) (GROldroyd)* 3-9-5 DGriffiths(9) (lw: s.s: nvr nr to chal)...1 **7**
4145[8] Granmas Delight **(60)***(32) (KTIvory)* 3-8-13 (5) CScally(5) (bhd fnl 2f)....2½ **8**
1741[9] Bandita **(47)***(14) (MissAJWhitfield)* 3-8-5 ow5 RPainter(3) (a bhd)....1¾ **9**
1586[6] As Such (IRE) **(64)***(25) (NACallaghan)* 3-9-3 (5) AEddery(8) (a bhd)....2 **10**
Crystal Heights (FR) **(40)***(47+)*(Fav)*(RJO'Sullivan)* 6-7-9 (3) SLanigan(7) (a.p: led ins fnl f: rdn out: fin 1st: disq: plcd last).... **0**

11/4 Crystal Heights (FR) (6/1-5/2), **100/30** TEE-EMM, **9/2** Super Rocky, **11/2** Nordico Princess, **13/2** Warwick Warrior (IRE), **8/1** It Must Be Millie, As Such (IRE), **10/1** Paley Prince (USA), **20/1** Bandita, Granmas Delight, CSF £14.20 CT £54.79 TOTE £4.40: £1.50 £1.30 £2.40 (£10.00) OWNER Mr Robert Carey (NEWMARKET) BRED Marquess Townshend 10 Rn
59.2 secs (1.00) SF: 16/30/29/20/9/8/-/-/-/-
STEWARDS' ENQUIRY: Wnr declared as Crystal Heights (8 ch g Wolver Heights-Crystal's Solo). Crystal Heights (FR) disq.

4269 WALTON HEATH STKS (I) (0-55) (Class F) £1,998.10 (£561.60: £274.30) 7f (Equitrack) GOING: minus 0.60 sec per fur (FS) 1-40 (1-41)

4078[11] **Bichette (47)***(49) (GLMoore)* 4-8-9 BRouse(13) (a.p: led 2f out: all out)....— **1**

4214[3] Hawaii Storm (FR) **(52)***(54)*(Fav)*(MissAJWhitfield)* 6-8-9 (5) RPainter(9) (hdwy over 3f out: hrd rdn fnl f: r.o wl)....s.h **2**
4265[4] Spectacle Jim **(49)***(51) (JO'Donoghue)* 5-8-9b(5) DRMcCabe(3) (s.s: hdwy over 5f out: rdn over 1f out: unable qckn ins fnl f)....1½ **3**
4255[4] Charlies Dream (IRE) **(45)***(48) (KRBurke)* 3-8-10 JQuinn(5) (a.p: rdn over 3f out: r.o one pce fnl 2f)....nk **4**
3508[14] Faynaz **(37)***(42) (AMoore)* 8-8-7 (7) AWhelan(2) (b: lw: hld up: hrd rdn over 1f out: one pce)....4 **5**
502[15] Titanium Honda (IRE) **(50)***(37) (CEBrittain)* 3-8-12 BDoyle(12) (a.p: led over 3f out to 2f out: wknd over 1f out)....2½ **6**
1272[5] Simon Ellis (IRE) **(28)***(36) (DRLaing)* 5-9-0 GBardwell(8) (b: lw: rdn thrght: nvr nr to chal)....nk **7**
4210[5] Monsieur Petong **(53)***(38) (DNicholls)* 3-9-1 AlexGreaves(4) (a.p: led 4f out tl over 3f out: wknd over 1f out)....½ **8**
3786[9] Remember This (IRE) **(41)***(33) (CACyzer)* 4-9-0 RCochrane(15) (nvr nrr)....¾ **9**
1413[5] Black Deed **(44)***(22) (DLWilliams)* 3-8-7 (5) DGriffiths(6) (lw: nvr nrr)....5 **10**
4206[8] Risk the Witch **(25)***(15) (DJSCosgrove)* 4-8-4 (5) LNewton(11) (a bhd)....1 **11**
3975[15] Katie's Kid **(30)***(20) (CJHemsley)* 4-9-0 RPerham(10) (bhd fnl 5f)....s.h **12**
3698[4] La Residence **(51)***(20) (MrsNMacauley)* 3-8-12 DaleGibson(16) (bhd fnl 2f)....s.h **13**
Amber Nectar **(40)***(—) (BAPearce)* 8-9-0 WNewnes(7) (b: bit bkwd: stumbled s: led 3f: wknd over 3f out)....10 **14**
2118[14] Top Tycoon (IRE) **(50)***(—) (JJBridger)* 3-8-12 AClark(14) (t: a bhd: virtually p.u over 1f out)....dist **15**

9/2 Hawaii Storm (FR), **5/1** Titanium Honda (IRE), **11/2** Spectacle Jim, **13/2** BICHETTE, **7/1** Charlies Dream (IRE), Monsieur Petong, **10/1** Amber Nectar, **14/1** Faynaz, Black Deed, La Residence, **20/1** Top Tycoon (IRE), Simon Ellis (IRE), **33/1** Remember This (IRE), Risk the Witch, Katie's Kid, CSF £37.34 TOTE £6.60: £2.20 £2.70 £2.50 (£18.10) OWNER Mr Peter Higson (EPSOM) BRED Exors of the late Mrs W. Wallace 15 Rn

1m 25.37 (2.37) SF: 16/21/18/13/8/-/2/2/-/-/-/-/-/-/-

WEIGHT FOR AGE 3yo-2lb

4270 WALTON HEATH STKS (II) (0-55) (Class F) £1,998.10 (£561.60: £274.30)
7f (Equitrack) GOING: minus 0.60 sec per fur (FS) 2-10 (2-11)

4210[7] **Maid Welcome (54)***(47) (MrsNMacauley)* 7-8-5v(7) AmandaSanders(12) (mde virtually all: pushed out)....— **1**
4202[11] Digpast (IRE) **(43)***(48) (RJO'Sullivan)* 4-9-0b DBiggs(14) (lw: hdwy over 3f out: hrd rdn over 1f out: r.o)....½ **2**
4258[4] Our Shadee (USA) **(48)***(49) (KTIvory)* 4-9-3v GBardwell(1) (lw: a.p: ev ch over 1f out: unable qckn)....¾ **3**
4206[3] Joint Effort (IRE) **(43)***(37) (AMoore)* 3-8-0 (7) AWhelan(3) (swtg: a.p: rdn over 2f out: one pce)....1¾ **4**
4265[7] Sarum **(53)***(44)*(Fav)*(CPWildman)* 8-9-3 RCochrane(6) (a.p: rdn over 3f out: one pce fnl f)....½ **5**
3697[9] On Y Va (USA) **(51)***(44) (RJRWilliams)* 7-8-11 (7) SarahThompson(11) (lost pl 4f out: rallied over 1f out: r.o)....½ **6**
2365[8] Canny Lad **(42)***(39) (DNicholls)* 4-9-0v AlexGreaves(16) (hdwy over 4f out: wknd over 1f out)....nk **7**
3910[9] Danseuse Davis (FR) **(55)***(33) (KMcAuliffe)* 3-8-4 (3) JTate(13) (b: nvr nr to chal)....½ **8**
4206[6] Thorniwama **(38)***(22) (JJBridger)* 3-8-7 AClark(7) (outpcd)....5 **9**
4255[7] Ewar Gold (FR) **(37)***(22) (KOCunningham-Brown)* 4-8-12 BDoyle(15) (lw: a mid div)....1¼ **10**
3972[10] Possibility **(47)***(23) (RIngram)* 3-8-8 (5) DRMcCabe(8) (a bhd)....¾ **11**
4241[15] Matisse **(54)***(16) (JDBethell)* 3-8-7 TWilliams(9) (prom over 4f)....hd **12**
4052[16] Dome Patrol **(53)***(22) (WRMuir)* 3-8-8 (7) SMcCarthy(4) (a bhd)....1 **13**
4206[4] Secret Assignment (USA) **(42)***(18) (CACyzer)* 4-9-0v TIves(2) (bhd fnl 5f)....hd **14**
3898[8] Miss Charlie **(40)***(5) (ABailey)* 4-8-9 WNewnes(5) (bhd fnl 2f)....4 **15**
4215[3] Greggina **(48)***(1) (PTWalwyn)* 3-8-7 DaleGibson(10) (prom over 3f)....1¾ **16**

9/2 Sarum, **5/1** Greggina (10/1-9/2), **6/1** Our Shadee (USA), **15/2** On Y Va (USA) (5/1-8/1), **8/1** Secret Assignment (USA), Digpast (IRE), **10/1** Joint Effort (IRE), **12/1** MAID WELCOME, **14/1** Possibility, **16/1** Dome Patrol, Matisse, **20/1** Ewar Gold (FR), Miss Charlie, **25/1** Danseuse Davis (FR), **33/1** Thorniwama, Canny Lad, CSF £106.67 TOTE £18.60: £3.10 £7.20 £2.80 (£196.70) OWNER Mrs Anna Sanders (MELTON MOWBRAY) BRED Doublet Ltd 16 Rn

1m 25.05 (2.05) SF: 22/23/25/13/21/21/17/-/-/-/-/-/-/-/-/-

WEIGHT FOR AGE 3yo-2lb

4271 GLENEAGLES STKS (Class D) £3,231.90 (£979.20: £478.60: £228.30)
1m (Equitrack) GOING: minus 0.60 sec per fur (FS) 2-40 (2-41)

4264[4] **Red Valerian (71)***(81) (KMcAuliffe)* 3-9-0b(3) JTate(6) (b.off hind: hld up: rdn over 1f out: led ins fnl f: r.o wl) — 1
2712[7] Buddy's Friend (IRE) **(63)***(71) (RJRWilliams)* 6-8-6 (7) SarahThompson(5) (a.p: led over 1f out tl ins fnl f: unable qckn) 2 2
4107* Everset (FR) **(88)***(80) (ABailey)* 6-9-6 (5) DWright(9) (stdy hdwy over 3f out: hrd rdn over 1f out: r.o one pce) 1¼ 3
4166[5] Cedez le Passage (FR) **(103)***(70)*(Fav)*(CEBrittain)* 3-9-3e BDoyle(10) (eyeshield: b.hind: lw: hdwy 4f out: rdn over 2f out: one pce) 1¾ 4
Masrah Dubai (USA) *(57) (MAJarvis)* 3-8-11 TIves(2) (w'like: bkwd: led 7f out tl over 1f out: sn wknd) 3½ 5
4023[7] Carpathian *(45) (LordHuntingdon)* 3-8-11 AClark(11) (hld up: rdn over 2f out: sn wknd) 6 6
3798[6] Feline (IRE) *(38) (RFJohnsonHoughton)* 3-8-6 JQuinn(4) (nvr nr to chal) ¾ 7
4105[5] Tudor Flight **(50)***(34) (AGNewcombe)* 3-8-1 (5) SDrowne(12) (nvr nrr) 1¾ 8
2852[12] Third Dam **(60)***(33) (BWHills)* 3-8-6 RStreet(1) (prom 3f) ½ 9
3925[25] Secundus (IRE) **(74)***(44) (BJMeehan)* 3-9-9 RCochrane(8) (led 1f: wknd 2f out) 3 10
4215[5] Kingsfold Fountain *(18) (MJHaynes)* 3-8-11 BRouse(7) (b: b.hind: lw: a bhd) 7 11
4210[11] Poor Printer (IRE) *(12) (JAkehurst)* 3-8-6 DaleGibson(3) (prom 3f) ½ 12

4/6 Cedez le Passage (FR), **5/1** Everset (FR), **10/1** RED VALERIAN, Feline (IRE), Secundus (IRE), **12/1** Masrah Dubai (USA), **14/1** Buddy's Friend (IRE) (10/1-16/1), **16/1** Third Dam, Kingsfold Fountain, **33/1** Carpathian, Tudor Flight, Poor Printer (IRE), CSF £141.63 TOTE £13.80: £2.10 £1.90 £2.10 (£44.90) OWNER Mr R. J. Cummings (LAMBOURN) BRED Mascalls Stud Farm 12 Rn 1m 36.81 (0.41) SF: 47/40/49/40/28/16/9/-/-/-/-/-
WEIGHT FOR AGE 3yo-2lb

4272 ROYAL ST GEORGE'S H'CAP (0-70) (Class E) £2,635.30 (£740.80: £361.90)
2m (Equitrack) GOING: minus 0.60 sec per fur (FS) 3-10 (3-11)

4208* **Art Form (USA) (70)***(84)*(Fav)*(CACyzer)* 7-10-0 TIves(2) (lw: hdwy over 4f out: chsd ldr over 2f out: led last strides) — 1
4261[2] Miroswaki (USA) **(63)***(77) (PMMcEntee)* 4-9-7 JQuinn(11) (hdwy over 5f out: led over 3f out: sn clr: hdd last strides) nk 2
4135[3] Milngavie (IRE) **(67)***(75) (MJohnston)* 4-9-11 TWilliams(8) (hrd rdn & no hdwy fnl 3f) 6 3
4221[5] La Menorquina (USA) **(37)***(42) (DMarks)* 4-7-2 (7)ow2 MBaird(7) (hdwy over 1f out: nvr nrr) 3 4
4221[6] Allmosa **(65)***(69) (TJNaughton)* 5-9-2 (7) VHalliday(10) (b: swtg: nvr nr to chal) ½ 5
4261[7] Sir Thomas Beecham **(67)***(67) (SDow)* 4-9-11e RCochrane(6) (eyeshield: b.hind: prom 13f) 4 6
4218[5] Extra Time **(56)***(53) (LordHuntingdon)* 3-7-12 (7) AWhelan(12) (prom over 11f) 3½ 7
4175[5] Bransby Road (IRE) **(40)***(37) (RAkehurst)* 4-7-12e GBardwell(9) (eyeshield: lw: bhd fnl 8f) s.h 8
4140[12] Tickerty's Gift **(53)***(49) (GLMoore)* 4-8-11v BRouse(4) (lw: prom 12f) 1½ 9
4217[6] Kiyas **(49)***(41) (BJMcMath)* 3-7-12 ow5 AMackay(5) (a bhd) 4 10
4208[7] Lajadhal (FR) **(38)***(27) (KBishop)* 5-7-5be(5)ow3 NVarley(3) (eyeshield: prom over 11f) 3 11
4052[6] Wicklow Boy (IRE) **(49)***(38) (TTClement)* 3-7-7v(5)ow5 DWright(1) (lw: led: sn clr: hdd over 3f out: sn wknd) nk 12
LONG HANDICAP La Menorquina (USA) 7-5 Lajadhal (FR) 6-4 Wicklow Boy (IRE) 7-5

2/1 ART FORM (USA), **7/2** Miroswaki (USA), **9/2** Allmosa, **7/1** Milngavie (IRE), **9/1** Bransby Road (IRE), **12/1** Tickerty's Gift, **16/1** La Menorquina (USA), Extra Time, **20/1** Sir Thomas Beecham, Kiyas, **50/1** Wicklow Boy (IRE), **100/1** Lajadhal (FR), CSF £9.95 CT £40.74 TOTE £3.30: £1.30 £1.30 £2.60 (£5.20) OWNER Mr R. M. Cyzer (HORSHAM) BRED Morgan's Ford Farm and Elizabeth Thomas in USA 12 Rn
3m 22.02 (-1.48) SF: 72/65/63/32/58/56/34/-/-/-/-/-
WEIGHT FOR AGE 3yo-9lb

4273 ST ANDREW'S H'CAP (0-65) (Class F) £2,483.00 (£698.00: £341.00)
1m 4f (Equitrack) GOING: minus 0.60 sec per fur (FS) 3-40 (3-41)

4244[6] **Telephus (45)***(49) (BJMcMath)* 5-8-12 RCochrane(8) (hdwy over 3f out: hrd rdn over 1f out: led nr fin) — 1

4131* Ballyranter **(52)***(56)*(Fav)*(HJCollingridge)* 5-9-5v JQuinn(3) (lw: hld up: stumbled bdly 2f out: led over 1f out: hrd rdn: hdd nr fin) ....hd **2**
4208[5] Glow Forum **(42)***(41) (GLMoore)* 3-7-12 (5)ow4 SSanders(5) (a.p: rdn over 3f out: one pce) 4 **3**
1412[2] Young Lucky **(37)***(34) (CPWildman)* 3-7-7 (5)ow5 DWright(4) (rdn & hdwy over 2f out: r.o) 1¾ **4**
4204[11] Western Valley **(30)***(27) (CPWildman)* 4-7-11 GBardwell(6) (nvr nr to chal) ....hd **5**
4215[2] Lady Reema **(48)***(45) (MissAJWhitfield)* 3-8-4 (5) RPainter(2) (a.p: led over 4f out tl over 1f out: sn wknd) ....hd **6**
4052[2] Beautete **(60)***(47) (SDow)* 3-9-7e BRouse(1) (eyeshield: b.hind: lw: prom 6f) 8 **7**
3426[10] Calisar **(49)***(34) (PHowling)* 4-9-2 AMackay(7) (prom 9f) 1½ **8**
4215[4] Premium Bond **(51)***(36) (ICampbell)* 3-8-12v DBiggs(9) (lw: led 1f: wknd 6f out) ....hd **9**
4209[6] Uncharted Waters **(63)***(47) (CACyzer)* 3-9-10 TIves(12) (hdwy over 5f out: wknd over 3f out) ....¾ **10**
4204[13] Inspiration Point **(57)***(16) (MissBSanders)* 3-9-4 WNewnes(10) (bhd fnl 6f) 20 **11**
4176[0] Wide Outside (IRE) **(34)***(—) (GLMoore)* 3-7-2 (7)ow2 MBaird(11) (led 11f out tl over 4f out: sn wknd) ....hd **12**

LONG HANDICAP Young Lucky 7-6 Wide Outside (IRE) 7-4

13/8 Ballyranter, **5/1** Beautete, **7/1** Glow Forum, **15/2** Uncharted Waters, **8/1** Lady Reema, TELEPHUS, **10/1** Premium Bond, **14/1** Inspiration Point, **16/1** Young Lucky, **25/1** Calisar, **50/1** Western Valley, Wide Outside (IRE), CSF £22.21 CT £95.96 TOTE £9.20: £2.20 £1.20 £3.90 (£17.00) OWNER Back Hill Bloodstock Ltd (NEWMARKET) BRED B. Alexander 12 Rn

2m 32.14 (2.74) SF: 31/37/17/12/10/21/22/-/-/-/-/-

WEIGHT FOR AGE 3yo-6lb

STEWARDS' ENQUIRY Quinn suspended 7-9/12/94 (excessive use of whip).

T/Plpt: £146.70 (47.55 Tckts). T/Qdpt: £25.10 (0.3 Tckts); £23.80 to Fontwell AK

4237-SOUTHWELL (L-H)
Wednesday November 30th (Standard)

4274 KING LEAR H'CAP (I) (0-60) (Class F) £2,398.00 (£673.00: £328.00)
1m (Fibresand) Stalls: Low GOING: minus 0.07 sec per fur (Std) 12-10 (12-10)

4257* **Sandmoor Denim (59)***(71+)*(Fav)*(SRBowring)* 7-9-12 (6x) (7) GStrange(13) (b: lw: sn trckng ldrs: led on bit over 2f out: rdn out) ....— **1**
4226[5] Certain Way (IRE) **(47)***(55) (NPLittmoden)* 4-9-2 (5) TGMcLaughlin(14) (trckd ldrs: chal over 2f out: hung lft: kpt on fnl f) 2 **2**
4102[9] Mislemani (IRE) **(42)***(48) (AGNewcombe)* 4-8-11 (5) NVarley(2) (chsd ldrs: kpt on same pce fnl 2f) ....¾ **3**
3789[10] Red Whirlwind **(47)***(50) (BJMcMath)* 4-9-7 RCochrane(1) (lw: hdwy over 2f out: styd on appr fnl f: nvr rchd ldrs) 1¼ **4**
4040[17] Mighty Kingdom (IRE) **(38)***(39) (RWEmery)* 3-8-10 BDoyle(10) (s.i.s: bhd tl styd on fnl 2f) ....¾ **5**
4257[8] Lombard Ships **(45)***(46) (ABailey)* 7-9-5b AMackay(5) (lw: s.i.s: bhd tl kpt on fnl 2f: n.d) ....s.h **6**
4131[8] Straw Thatch **(40)***(40) (MrsJRRamsden)* 5-9-0 JQuinn(3) (in tch: effrt over 2f out: nvr rchd ldrs) 1½ **7**
4260[9] Pop to Stans **(52)***(52) (JPearce)* 5-9-5 (7) ETurner(9) (b.nr fore: s.i.s: bhd & drvn along: sme hdwy 2f out: n.d) ....s.h **8**
4224[8] Puffy **(39)***(39) (MDods)* 7-8-13v DaleGibson(8) (b: s.i.s: bhd: effrt & hung lft 2f out: n.d) ....hd **9**
4243[8] Watheeqah (USA) **(54)***(47) (MBrittain)* 3-9-12b GBardwell(11) (led tl over 2f out: sn lost pl) 3½ **10**
275[8] Royal Acclaim **(44)***(31) (JMBradley)* 9-8-13v(5) DWright(16) (s.i.s: racd wd: a bhd) ...3 **11**
3707[10] Akabusi **(52)***(34) (LordHuntingdon)* 3-9-5 (5) AWhelan(7) (trckd ldrs: effrt over 2f out: sn wknd) 2½ **12**
363[2] Balmaha **(49)***(31) (WJHaggas)* 3-9-2 (5) BRussell(6) (lw: hld up & plld hrd: effrt over 2f out: nvr nr ldrs) ....hd **13**
4237[10] Dangerous Shadow **(45)***(24) (MrsMReveley)* 3-8-10 (7) GParkin(12) (chsd ldrs tl wknd 2f out) 1½ **14**
3655[17] Cheerful Groom (IRE) **(46)***(15) (JMackie)* 3-9-4 TWilliams(15) (trckd ldrs: effrt & edgd lft 2f out: sn wknd) 5 **15**
1393[7] Tanfirion Chief **(49)***(17) (RonaldThompson)* 3-9-7 GDuffield(4) (lost pl & drvn along after 2f out: sn wl bhd) ....½ **16**

9/4 SANDMOOR DENIM, **8/1** Straw Thatch, **9/1** Mislemani (IRE), Balmaha, Watheeqah (USA), **10/1** Certain Way (IRE), Red Whirlwind (8/1-12/1), **12/1** Puffy, Akabusi, **16/1** Dangerous Shadow, Lombard Ships, **20/1** Royal Acclaim, Pop to Stans, **25/1** Mighty Kingdom (IRE), **33/1** Cheerful Groom (IRE), Tanfirion Chief, CSF £26.96 CT £173.55 TOTE £2.80: £1.10 £1.90 £3.20 £2.60 (£12.90) OWNER Mr E. H. Lunness (EDWINSTOWE) BRED Rathasker Stud 16 Rn
1m 46.3 (7.00) SF: 41/26/20/23/11/20/14/-/-/-/-/-/-/-/-/-
WEIGHT FOR AGE 3yo-2lb

4275 JULIUS CAESAR NURSERY (0-75) (Class D) £3,378.45 (£1,023.60: £500.30: £238.65) **5f (Fibresand)** Stalls: High GOING: minus 0.13 sec (Std) 12-40 (12-43)

3572* **Hannah's Usher (70)***(70)*(Fav)*(PCHaslam)* 2-9-7 MTebbutt(13) (trckd ldrs gng wl: effrt 2f out: r.o to ld post)........— **1**
4161^{6} C-Yer-Simmie (IRE) **(58)***(57) (RHollinshead)* 2-8-4 (5) AGarth(10) (swvd lft s: led tl nr fin)........hd **2**
4203^{9} Half Tone **(45)***(26) (RMFlower)* 2-7-10b^{ow3} JQuinn(9) (hmpd & lost pl after 1f: effrt 2f out: styd on ins fnl f)........6 **3**
4222* Rotherfield Park (IRE) **(52)***(27) (CSmith)* 2-7-10 (7) MBaird(11) (chsd ldrs: outpcd ½-wy: kpt on u.p)........2 **4**
4134^{8} Fishy Affair **(49)***(22) (TDyer)* 2-7-9 (5) DWright(6) (in tch: effrt ½-wy: no imp)........½ **5**
4222^{3} Curie Express (IRE) **(54)***(15) (JBerry)* 2-8-5 LeTolboll(5) (chsd ldrs tl wknd 2f out)..4 **6**
3828^{18} Blaze Dewitt (USA) **(50)***(8) (SGNorton)* 2-7-10b(5) NVarley(7) (w ldrs tl wknd 2f out)........¾ **7**
3897^{17} Joyful Times **(54)***(10) (MrsNMacauley)* 2-8-2 (3)^{ow4} JTate(4) (s.i.s: wl outpcd & bhd: sme hdwy 2f out: n.d)........½ **8**
4128^{4} Red Hassett (IRE) **(55)***(7) (PABlockley)* 2-8-6b^{ow5} AClark(2) (s.i.s: sn chsng ldrs: wknd ½-wy)........1¼ **9**
4225^{5} Daily Challenger (USA) **(61)***(12) (RonaldThompson)* 2-8-12 TWilliams(1) (sn drvn along: outpcd ½-wy: wandered bdly & eased over 1f out)........nk **10**
4267^{5} Magic Leader (IRE) **(50)***(—) (TTClement)* 2-7-8 (7) SLanigan(12) (b: racd stands' side: sn bhd: hrd rdn 2f out)........1¾ **11**
1703^{5} Misstinger **(45)***(—) (WRMuir)* 2-7-10 GBardwell(8) (in tch early: outpcd & bhd fr ½-wy)........2½ **12**

LONG HANDICAP Half Tone 7-5

9/2 HANNAH'S USHER, **11/2** C-Yer-Simmie (IRE), Daily Challenger (USA), Rotherfield Park (IRE), **6/1** Curie Express (IRE), **12/1** Fishy Affair, Red Hassett (IRE), **14/1** Joyful Times, Misstinger, **16/1** Magic Leader (IRE), **20/1** Blaze Dewitt (USA), **33/1** Half Tone, CSF £27.92 CT £669.36 TOTE £3.70: £1.80 £1.60 £8.60 (£19.00) OWNER Mr Bill Fitzgerald (MIDDLEHAM) BRED P. Dowson 12 Rn
60.7 secs (2.70) SF: 47/36/5/5/-/-/-/-/-/-/-/-

4276 KING HENRY VI CLAIMING STKS (Class F) £2,398.00 (£673.00: £328.00) **1m 6f (Fibresand)** Stalls: High GOING: minus 0.07 sec per fur (Std) 1-10 (1-11)

3825^{10} **Pharly Dancer (65)***(71+)*(Fav)*(WWHaigh)* 5-9-4 (3) JTate(8) (trckd ldrs: led 8f out: rdn clr 3f out: eased nr fin)........— **1**
4208^{6} Scalp 'em (IRE) **(37)***(48) (PDEvans)* 6-8-5 (5) DRMcCabe(11) (sn prom: styd on fnl 3f: no ch w wnr)........11 **2**
2216^{5} Intention (USA) **(62)***(53) (ICampbell)* 4-9-4 RCochrane(10) (lw: hdwy ½-wy: styd on one pce fnl 3f)........2½ **3**
Dvorak (IRE) *(57+) (BJMcMath)* 3-9-3 AMackay(1) (hld up: hdwy ½-wy: effrt 3f out: r.o: nvr rchd ldrs)........1½ **4**
4217^{5} Comtec's Legend **(38)***(37) (JFBottomley)* 4-8-7 GDuffield(14) (sn prom: effrt & chsd wnr over 3f out: wknd over 1f out)........2½ **5**
4229^{2} Greenacres Star **(37)***(41) (BAMcMahon)* 4-8-6 (5) SSanders(16) (chsd ldrs tl wknd over 3f out)........nk **6**
4127^{3} Alcian Blue **(41)***(52) (RHollinshead)* 3-9-3 TIves(9) (sme hdwy ½-wy: lost pl 3f out)........1½ **7**
3574^{7} Fiery Sun **(22)***(42) (JLEyre)* 9-9-2 AClark(6) (in tch: outpcd 7f out: effrt over 3f out: sn wknd)........2 **8**
4239^{6} Goodbye Millie **(47)***(32) (SGNorton)* 4-8-9b TWilliams(12) (s.i.s: sn drvn along: wnt prom 9f out: wknd & eased 3f out)........3 **9**
4239^{3} Bold Pursuit (IRE) **(64)***(31) (JGFitzGerald)* 5-9-0 JQuinn(4) (b: lw: trckd ldrs: effrt over 4f out: wknd over 2f out)........5 **10**
4135^{14} Naawy **(34)***(20) (CSmith)* 4-8-9v(7) MBaird(3) (wl bhd fnl 4f)........12 **11**
Brigtina *(15) (JMBradley)* 6-8-9 (5) DGriffiths(13) (b: in tch tl lost pl 5f out)........2½ **12**
3091^{9} Northern Rainbow **(32)***(—) (RWEmery)* 6-8-10b DaleGibson(7) (w ldrs: led after 3f to 8f out: wknd over 4f out)........20 **13**
True Dancing *(—) (JDBethell)* 3-7-9 (5) DWright(5) (leggy: s.i.s: a bhd: t.o ½-wy)...6 **14**

1898[6] Volcanic Dancer (USA) **(32)***(—) (MrsNMacauley)* 8-9-10v SWilliams(2) (b: led 3f: sn drvn along & lost pl: t.o ½-wy)....20 **15**
Dear Madam *(—) (JMCarr)* 3-8-4 SMorris(15) (a bhd: t.o fr ½-wy)....30 **16**

9/4 PHARLY DANCER, **5/2** Bold Pursuit (IRE), **7/1** Intention (USA), **10/1** Dvorak (IRE), **12/1** Alcian Blue, Greenacres Star, Comtec's Legend, Goodbye Millie, **20/1** True Dancing, **25/1** Scalp 'em (IRE), Northern Rainbow, Naawy, **33/1** Brigtina, Dear Madam, Volcanic Dancer (USA), **50/1** Fiery Sun, CSF £59.97 TOTE £3.50: £1.90 £5.40 £2.10 (£34.70) OWNER Mr A. Marucci (MALTON) BRED Stud-On-The-Chart 16 Rn 3m 10.9 (11.20) SF: 38/16/21/18/6/10/14/-/-/-/-/-/-/-/-/-
WEIGHT FOR AGE 3yo-7lb

STEWARDS' ENQUIRY Trainer & rdr of Dvorak (IRE) fined £400 each under Rule 151 (ii) (failure to ensure best possible placing)

4277 MACBETH H'CAP (0-70) (Class E) £2,827.00 (£856.00: £418.00: £199.00)
1m 3f (Fibresand) Stalls: Low GOING: minus 0.07 sec per fur (Std) 1-40 (1-41)

4131[21] **Joseph's Wine (IRE) (55)***(65) (DNicholls)* 5-9-4b AlexGreaves(12) (hld up: stdy hdwy 5f out: rdn to ld 1f out: styd on)....— **1**
4244[15] Tempering **(52)***(59) (DWChapman)* 8-9-1 JQuinn(14) (led: clr 7f out: hdd 1f out: kpt on)....2½ **2**
4221[4] El Nido **(56)***(61)*(Fav)*(MJCamacho)* 6-9-5 RCochrane(3) (sn trckng ldrs: outpcd over 3f out: kpt on fnl 2f)....1¾ **3**
4209[7] Global Dancer **(68)***(71) (WAO'Gorman)* 3-9-9 (3) EmmaO'Gorman(2) (lw: trckd ldrs: effrt over 3f out: kpt on same pce)....1½ **4**
4221[9] Broom Isle **(54)***(55) (DBurchell)* 6-8-12 (5) DRMcCabe(8) (a chsng ldrs: one pce fnl 3f)....2 **5**
4244[5] Modest Hope (USA) **(52)***(45) (BRichmond)* 7-8-10 (5) NVarley(7) (s.i.s: bhd: rdn over 3f out: kpt on fnl 2f: nvr nr ldrs)....6 **6**
4063[7] Bentico **(60)***(51) (MrsNMacauley)* 5-9-9b SWhitworth(9) (hdwy ½-wy: rdn over 3f out: nvr nr ldrs)....1½ **7**
4252[4] Premier Dance **(57)***(40) (DHaydnJones)* 7-9-1 (5) DWright(11) (hdwy & in tch ½-wy: drvn along & outpcd 4f out: n.d after)....6 **8**
1431[10] Westfield Moves (IRE) **(56)***(35) (HJCollingridge)* 6-9-0 (5) CHawksley(6) (b: lw: s.i.s: wl bhd 5f out: sme late hdwy)....3 **9**
4124[3] In the Money (IRE) **(57)***(34) (RHollinshead)* 5-9-6 TIves(1) (chsd ldrs: rdn 5f out: lost pl over 3f out)....1¾ **10**
838[10] Alderney Prince (USA) **(65)***(40) (BAMcMahon)* 4-9-9 (5) SSanders(4) (in tch tl rdn & lost pl over 4f out)....1½ **11**
4227[9] Phoenix Venture (IRE) **(66)***(40) (SPCWoods)* 3-9-10 WWoods(13) (trckd ldrs tl rdn & wknd over 3f out)....¾ **12**
4239[2] Broctune Gold **(59)***(32) (MrsMReveley)* 3-8-10 (7) GParkin(5) (sn trckng ldrs: rdn & wknd 4f out)....¾ **13**
4218[9] Donia (USA) **(54)***(26) (JLHarris)* 5-9-3 SWilliams(10) (in tch tl rdn & lost pl over 4f out)....nk **14**

5/1 El Nido, **11/2** In the Money (IRE) (4/1-6/1), Broctune Gold, Modest Hope (USA), **7/1** Premier Dance, **8/1** JOSEPH'S WINE (IRE), **10/1** Westfield Moves (IRE), **12/1** Donia (USA), Bentico, **14/1** Global Dancer, **16/1** Tempering, Broom Isle, Phoenix Venture (IRE), **25/1** Alderney Prince (USA), CSF £129.29 CT £664.70 TOTE £15.20: £4.20 £4.8/ £1.70 (£107.10) OWNER Wetherby Racing Bureau Plc (THIRSK) BRED Michael Fennessy 14 Rn
2m 28.6 (7.10) SF: 47/41/43/47/36/26/32/-/-/-/-/-/-/-
WEIGHT FOR AGE 3yo-5lb

4278 TRAVIS PERKINS H'CAP (0-75) (Class D) £3,513.00 (£1,065.00: £521.00: £249.00) **6f (Fibresand)** Stalls: Low GOING: minus 0.07 sec (Std) 2-10 (2-15)

4206* **Triple Joy (58)***(75)*(Fav)*(SirMarkPrescott)* 3-9-5 GDuffield(11) (trckd ldrs: led 2f out: rdn along & r.o wl)....— **1**
4241* Mustn't Grumble (IRE) **(66)***(75) (WSCunningham)* 4-10-0 (7x) AClark(14) (lw: trckd ldrs: effrt 2f out: sn rdn & nt qckn)....3 **2**
4220[2] Nordan Raider **(66)***(67) (MJCamacho)* 6-9-7 (7) GParkin(4) (dwlt: hld up: hdwy ½-wy: styd on fnl 2f: nvr rchd ldrs)....3 **3**
4231[12] Little Ibnr **(54)***(55) (PDEvans)* 3-8-10v(5) DRMcCabe(9) (mde most to 2f out: kpt on same pce)....s.h **4**
4243[7] Bradwell (IRE) **(45)***(43) (MHTompkins)* 3-8-1 (5) SMulvey(6) (hdwy over 2f out: swtchd ins & styd on)....1 **5**
3562[2] Cledeschamps **(39)***(27) (MWEllerby)* 5-7-8 (7) ClaireBalding(13) (bhd tl kpt on fnl 2f)....4 **6**

4243[3] Alpine Johnny **(51)***(36) (RHollinshead)* 3-8-7 (5) AGarth(8) (prom early: sn outpcd & bhd: sme hdwy over 1f out: n.d) 1 7
3045[12] Nuclear Express **(43)***(23) (JMBradley)* 7-8-5 AMackay(10) (sn bhd: sme hdwy 2f out: n.d) 1¾ 8
4231[4] Primula Bairn **(56)***(32) (MrsJRRamsden)* 4-9-4v SWilliams(2) (w ldrs tl wknd over 2f out) 1½ 9
4231* Croft Pool **(65)***(40) (JAGlover)* 3-9-12 RCochrane(7) (s.i.s: bhd: effrt over 2f out: eased whn no ch) ....nk 10
4269[6] Titanium Honda (IRE) **(43)***(18) (CEBrittain)* 3-8-4 BDoyle(12) (sn outpcd) ....s.h 11
4243* Berge (IRE) **(64)***(36) (WAO'Gorman)* 3-9-11b (7x) TIves(3) (sn outpcd: sme hdwy over 2f out: nvr nr ldrs) ....¾ 12
4231[11] Pertemps Flyer **(54)***(22) (BAMcMahon)* 3-8-10 (5) SSanders(5) (w ldrs tl lost pl over 2f out) 1½ 13
4102[10] Farmer Jock **(45)***(12) (MrsNMacauley)* 12-8-4 (3) JTate(1) (b: in tch to ½-wy) ....nk 14
Wellsy Lad (USA) **(35)***(—) (DWChapman)* 7-7-11 JQuinn(16) (racd wd: in tch tl lost pl ½-wy: sn bhd & eased) 12 15

3/1 TRIPLE JOY, **9/2** Berge (IRE), **11/2** Croft Pool, **8/1** Mustn't Grumble (IRE), **9/1** Little Ibnr, Nordan Raider, **10/1** Primula Bairn, **16/1** Bradwell (IRE), **20/1** Titanium Honda (IRE), Alpine Johnny, Cledeschamps, **25/1** Pertemps Flyer, **33/1** Nuclear Express, Farmer Jock, Wellsy Lad (USA), CSF £27.89 CT £184.87 TOTE £4.20: £1.80 £4.00 £2.90 (£14.50) OWNE Hesmonds Stud (NEWMARKET) BRED Hesmonds Stud 15 Rn 1m 17.3 (3.80) SF: 46/46/38/26/15/-/7/-/-/-/-/-/-/-/-
WEIGHT FOR AGE 3yo-1lb

4279

ANTHONY & CLEOPATRA STKS (2-Y.O) (Class D) £3,288.75 (£996.00:£486.50: £231.75) **7f (Fibresand)** Stalls: Low GOING: minus 0.07 sec (Std) 2-40 (2-41)

4219[4] **Bettergeton (60)***(70) (GFierro)* 2-8-6 (5) SSanders(9) (w ldrs: led over 4f out: drvn along & styd on strly fnl f) ....— 1
4205* Soldier's Leap (FR) **(72)***(67) (CEBrittain)* 2-9-2b BDoyle(6) (chsd ldrs: ev ch & hrd rdn 2f out: one pce) 4 2
4164* Q Factor **(77)***(60) (DHaydnJones)* 2-8-9 AMackay(8) (b.off hind: dwlt: sn chsng ldrs: ev ch 2f out: kpt on one pce) ....½ 3
4242[2] Pleasure Beach **(66)***(58)*(Jt-Fav)*(WAO'Gorman)* 2-8-13 (3) EmmaO'Gorman(3) (hmpd & lost pl 4f out: hdwy u.p 2f out: styd on same pce) 3½ 4
3927[16] Norman Prince (IRE) **(67)***(53) (NPLittmoden)* 2-8-11 MFenton(5) (outpcd & lost pl ½-wy: kpt on fnl f) ....hd 5
4172[2] Cabcharge Blue **(79)***(40)*(Jt-Fav)*(TJNaughton)* 2-8-9 GDuffield(4) (plld hrd: led tl over 4f out: stdd, effrt & swtchd outside 2f out: sn rdn & wknd) 5 6
Charnwood Queen *(—) (RWArmstrong)* 2-8-6 WWoods(1) (w'like: leggy: s.i.s: sn prom: effrt over 2f out: sn rdn & wknd) 4 7
4225* Barrel of Hope **(75)***(36)*(Jt-Fav)*(JLEyre)* 2-9-2 TIves(7) (chsd ldrs: effrt 3f out: sn wknd) 1½ 8
4015[10] Bitch **(56)***(—) (DNicholls)* 2-8-6 AlexGreaves(2) (in tch: n.m.r: hmpd & lost pl 4f out: n.d after) 7 9

7/2 Cabcharge Blue, Barrel of Hope, Pleasure Beach, **5/1** Soldier's Leap (FR), Q Factor, **10/1** Charnwood Queen, **16/1** Bitch, **20/1** Norman Prince (IRE), BETTERGETON, CSF £113.37 TOTE £21.40: £3.30 £1.30 £2.40 (£83.20) OWNER Mr Derek Boulton (HEDNESFORD) BRED R. and Mrs Healy-Fenton 9 Rn 1m 32.3 (5.50) SF: 27/23/16/14/10/-/-/-/-
STEWARDS' ENQUIRY Doyle suspended 9-15/12/94 (excessive & improper use of whip).

4280

HAMLET STKS (Mdn 2-Y.O) (Class D) £3,408.35 (£1,032.80: £504.90: £240.95) **1m (Fibresand)** Stalls: Low GOING: minus 0.07 sec per fur (Std) 3-10 (3-13)

Just Lucky (IRE) *(72) (RWArmstrong)* 2-9-0 WWoods(6) (leggy: unf: chsd ldr: led over 1f out: sn clr: eased nr fin) ....— 1
4203[6] Inn At the Top *(60) (MJohnston)* 2-9-0 TWilliams(13) (chsd ldrs: led 3f out tl over 1f out: no ch w wnr) 6 2
3827[9] Northern Fan (IRE) *(58)*(Jt-Fav)*(ACStewart)* 2-9-0 SWhitworth(4) (trckd ldrs: effrt 2f out: kpt on same pce) 1 3
Hard Try *(52+) (MJCamacho)* 2-9-0 JQuinn(2) (rangy: unf: scope: bit bkwd: s.i.s: hdwy ½-wy: kpt on: nvr rchd ldrs) 3 4
4240[9] Drama King *(45) (SRBowring)* 2-8-7 (7) CTeague(14) (hung bdly lft thrght: mid div: kpt on fnl 2f: nvr rchd ldrs) 3½ 5
4240[5] Framley Garth *(44)*(Jt-Fav)*(SirMarkPrescott)* 2-8-9 GDuffield(8) (chsd ldrs tl outpcd over 2f out: eased) 3½ 6
4240[10] Fools Millyons (IRE) **(40)***(—) (WBentley)* 2-9-0 TIves(7) (bhd: kpt on fnl 2f: n.d) 2 7

3398 10 Scylla (—) (PCHaslam) 2-8-9 MTebbutt(10) (in tch: effrt 3f out: sn wknd: eased) ....nk **8**
4240 13 Torrey Pines (IRE) (—) (DHaydnJones) 2-9-0 AMackay(9) (chsd ldrs tl wknd 3f out) 1½ **9**
4242 7 Brownlows **(50)**(—) (MPBielby) 2-9-0 SWilliams(3) (led after 1f to 3f out: sn wknd) 1½ **10**
4213 9 Dancing-Alone (—) (JWPayne) 2-8-9 (5) LNewton(16) (a in rr) ....¾ **11**
4225 8 It Is Now (—) (MHTompkins) 2-8-9 (5) SMulvey(15) (s.i.s: bhd: sme hdwy ½-wy: sn wknd) 4 **12**
Docklands Courier (Jt-Fav)(BJMcMath) 2-9-0 RCochrane(5) (str: cmpt: s.i.s: a in rr) 2½ **13**
847 7 Fools Haven (IRE) **(44)**(—) (BSRothwell) 2-9-0 MFenton(11) (a bhd) ....¾ **14**
Amercius (—) (RHannon) 2-9-0 RPerham(12) (cmpt: bit bkwd: s.s: a wl bhd)....3½ **15**
4230 13 Hoswinoname (—) (DNicholls) 2-9-0 AlexGreaves(1) (led 1f: lost pl over 3f out: sn bhd) 8 **16**

4/1 Framley Garth (3/1-5/1), Northern Fan (IRE), Docklands Courier, **6/1** JUST LUCKY (IRE), **7/1** Inn At the Top, **8/1** Amercius, **9/1** Scylla (6/1-10/1), **12/1** Brownlows, **14/1** Drama King, Hard Try, **16/1** It Is Now, **25/1** Hoswinoname, **33/1** Dancing-Alone, Fools Haven (IRE), Torrey Pines (IRE), Fools Millyons (IRE), CSF £53.59 TOTE £7.50: £2.30 £2.70 £2.30 (£48.00) OWNER Mr Hugh Hart (NEWMARKET) BRED P.F.N.Fanning 16 Rn 1m 45.8 (6.50) SF: 28/17/15/9/3/-/-/-/-/-/-/-/-/-/-/-

4281

KING LEAR H'CAP (II) (0-60) (Class F) £2,398.00 (£673.00: £328.00)
1m (Fibresand) Stalls: Low GOING: minus 0.07 sec per fur (Std) 3-40 (3-43)

4237 3 **Langtonian (44)**(55+) (JLEyre) 5-8-12v TIves(2) (trckd ldrs gng wl: led on bit 2f out: sn pushed clr: hung lft: eased nr fin) ....— **1**
3667* Roar on Tour **(44)**(51) (MrsMReveley) 5-8-12 RCochrane(9) (lw: chsd ldrs: outpcd over 2f out: kpt on fnl f: no ch w wnr) 1¾ **2**
4099 20 Secret Aly (CAN) **(60)**(66)(Fav)(CEBrittain) 4-10-0 BDoyle(8) (mid div: sn pushed along: hdwy & swtchd outside 2f out: styd on ins fnl f)....nk **3**
4231 15 Orthorhombus **(58)**(52) (DJSCosgrove) 5-9-7b(5) LNewton(15) (trckd ldrs: led over 4f out to 2f out: grad wknd) 6 **4**
3891 5 Sharpening **(52)**(43) (LordHuntingdon) 3-8-13 (5) AWhelan(4) (in tch: effrt over 2f out: kpt on same pce u.p) 1¼ **5**
4059 9 Queen of Shannon (IRE) **(52)**(40) (BJMeehan) 6-9-6 MTebbutt(12) (mid div: hdwy over 2f out: kpt on: nvr nr ldrs)....1½ **6**
4224 9 Ballad Dancer **(47)**(31) (JMackie) 9-9-1 TWilliams(16) (sn bhd: sme hdwy 3f out: styd on: nvr nr ldrs) 2 **7**
4083 12 Valiant Man **(60)**(44) (JHetherton) 3-9-12 NKennedy(6) (hld up & bhd: nt clr run over 1f out: swtchd outside: nvr plcd to chal)....hd **8**
4257 3 Guesstimation (USA) **(50)**(33) (JPearce) 5-9-4 GBardwell(5) (rr div: effrt u.p over 2f out: n.d)....½ **9**
4270 7 Canny Lad **(42)**(20) (DNicholls) 4-8-10v AlexGreaves(3) (led tl over 4f out: wknd over 2f out) 2½ **10**
4126 5 Languedoc **(47)**(21) (MartynWane) 7-9-1 GDuffield(11) (hld up & plld hrd: effrt ½-wy: sn wknd)....2 **11**
4083 7 My Gallery (IRE) **(54)**(22) (ABailey) 3-9-1 (5) DWright(10) (prom: effrt over 2f out: sn wknd)....3 **12**
4083 5 Salska **(60)**(27) (PJBevan) 3-9-7 (5) CHawksley(13) (s.i.s: a wl bhd) ....½ **13**
4078 15 Lady Highfield **(52)**(18) (MJRyan) 3-9-4 AClark(7) (b.hind: mid div: drvn along ½-wy: sn wknd)....½ **14**
4126 13 Tolls Choice (IRE) **(55)**(—) (MWEasterby) 5-9-2 (7) CMunday(1) (s.i.s: bhd & drvn along: t.o)....20 **15**
4253 10 Zilzilah (USA) **(59)**(—) (NPLittmoden) 3-9-11 MFenton(14) (b.hind: ref to r: virtually t.n.p) .... **R**

7/2 Secret Aly (CAN), **5/1** Roar on Tour, **7/1** LANGTONIAN, **8/1** Guesstimation (USA), Sharpening, My Gallery (IRE), **14/1** Queen of Shannon (IRE), Languedoc, Salska, Canny Lad, **20/1** Orthorhombus, Ballad Dancer, Lady Highfield, **25/1** Valiant Man, Tolls Choice (IRE), Zilzilah (USA), CSF £43.56 CT £136.01 TOTE £9.00: £1.80 £1.40 £2.00 £5.70 (£18.90) OWNER Mr Roy Peebles (HAMBLETON) BRED Aldershawe Stud Farm 16 Rn
1m 45.1 (5.80) SF: 33/31/46/32/22/22/13/-/-/-/-/-/-/-/-/-
WEIGHT FOR AGE 3yo-2lb
STEWARDS' ENQUIRY Doyle suspended 16-21/12/94 (improper use of whip).

T/Plpt: £331.80 (21.97 Tckts). T/Qdpt: £30.70 (1.2 Tckts) WG

4258-LINGFIELD (L-H)
Thursday December 1st (Standard)

4282 THREE HOSTAGES STKS (I) (Mdn 2-Y.O) (Class D) £3,318.65 (£1,005.20: £491.10: £234.05) **6f (Equitrack)** GOING: minus 0.62 sec per fur (FS) 12-10 (12-11)

Rome to Nome (USA) *(75+) (JBerry)* 2-9-0 GDuffield(9) (bhd: hdwy on outside to ld over 2f out: rdn & r.o wl) — **1**
1107[7] Logie *(70) (MAJarvis)* 2-9-0 TIves(6) (chsd ldr: ev ch over 2f out: rdn & nt rch wnr) 2 **2**
3416[8] Friendly Lady (USA) **(60)***(64) (WAO'Gorman)* 2-8-6 (3) EmmaO'Gorman(4) (chsd ldrs: rdn & one pce fnl f) hd **3**
2585[6] The Cape Doctor (IRE) *(66) (BWHills)* 2-9-0 RCochrane(8) (chsd ldrs: rdn & no ex fnl f) 1 **4**
Anytime Baby *(57+) (KMcAuliffe)* 2-8-6 (3) JTate(2) (bhd: hdwy ½-wy: reminders over 1f out: nvr nr to chal) 1¼ **5**
4043[7] Gulf Shaadi **(82)***(57) (CEBrittain)* 2-9-0 BDoyle(5) (bhd: rdn ½-wy: n.d) 2 **6**
4205[2] Crystal Gift *(52)*(Fav)*(PFICole)* 2-9-0 TQuinn(3) (sn led: hdd over 2f out: wknd ins fnl f) 2 **7**
3768[13] Polly Garter **(65)***(39) (RHannon)* 2-8-9 RPerham(1) (led early: sn rdn & wknd: n.d after) 3 **8**
4158[2] Innocence *(34)*(Fav)*(GWragg)* 2-8-9 WWoods(7) (a bhd) 1¾ **9**
4157[17] Hylters Girl *(34) (MJRyan)* 2-8-9 DBiggs(11) (nvr wnt pce) s.h **10**
Iceblock *(32) (MMcCormack)* 2-8-9 AClark(12) (a bhd) ½ **11**
4142[6] Fair Ella (IRE) **(44)***(29) (JFfitch-Heyes)* 2-8-9 AMackay(10) (chsd ldrs tl wknd qckly over 2f out) ¾ **12**

6/4 Crystal Gift, Innocence, **8/1** Gulf Shaadi, The Cape Doctor (IRE), **12/1** ROME TO NOME (USA), **16/1** Polly Garter, **20/1** Friendly Lady (USA), **25/1** Anytime Baby, Iceblock, **33/1** Logie, **50/1** Hylters Girl, Fair Ella (IRE), CSF £297.89 TOTE £26.10: £4.90 £22.20 £6.50 (£541.70) OWNER Mr Daniel Murphy (COCKERHAM) BRED Mrs Clyde W. Hatfield in USA 12 Rn
1m 13.97 (4.97) SF: 1/-/-/-/-/-/-/-/-/-/-/-

4283 FLEURETS H'CAP (I) (0-60) (Class F) £2,612.20 (£734.20: £358.60) **6f (Equitrack)** GOING: minus 0.62 sec per fur (FS) 12-40 (12-40)

3806[2] **Double Splendour (IRE) (41)***(45) (PSFelgate)* 4-8-5 (5) PMcCabe(7) (bhd: hdwy ½-wy: rdn & fin fast: led last strides) — **1**
4266[5] Pat Poindestres **(28)***(31)*(Fav)*(RJO'Sullivan)* 4-7-4 (7) MBaird(2) (led: wl clr over 2f out: rdn & wknd ins fnl f: ct last strides) nk **2**
4243[2] Featherstone Lane **(57)***(55) (MissLCSiddall)* 3-9-7v(5) DRMcCabe(9) (chsd ldr: rdn 2f out: nt pce to chal) 1¾ **3**
4206[7] Dance and Sing (IRE) **(37)***(20) (DLWilliams)* 4-8-6 ow1 JWilliams(4) (mid div: rdn ½-wy: kpt on: nvr nr to chal) 6 **4**
3234[13] Europharm Lassie **(56)***(35) (GLMoore)* 3-9-11 BRouse(8) (chsd ldrs: pushed along 3f out: sn wknd) 1¼ **5**
4211[9] Purbeck Centenary **(48)***(22) (PHowling)* 4-9-3 JQuinn(10) (chsd ldrs tl wknd over 1f out) 1¾ **6**
4214[11] Rustic League (IRE) **(48)***(19) (TJNaughton)* 3-8-10 (7) VHalliday(3) (bhd: nvr nr to chal) ¾ **7**
4263[7] Born to Be **(55)***(21) (SDow)* 5-9-10 TQuinn(6) (nvr trbld ldrs) 1¾ **8**
3216[11] Banbury Flyer **(43)***(3) (MrsALMKing)* 6-8-12 AClark(1) (in tch early: sn outpcd & n.d after) 2½ **9**
3506[8] On the Wing Again **(44)***(3) (MarkCampion)* 3-8-13 RCochrane(5) (prom tl wknd qckly after 2f) hd **10**

5/2 Pat Poindestres, **4/1** Featherstone Lane, **6/1** DOUBLE SPLENDOUR (IRE), Born to Be, **8/1** Dance and Sing (IRE) (16/1-7/1), **10/1** Purbeck Centenary, **14/1** On the Wing Again, Europharm Lassie, Banbury Flyer, **20/1** Rustic League (IRE), CSF £21.14 CT £63.17 TOTE £5.80: £1.60 £1.60 £3.10 (£20.60) OWNER Yorkshire Racing Club Owners Group 1990 (MELTON MOWBRAY) BRED R. McQuillan 10 Rn 1m 12.5 (1.90) SF: 16/5/28/-/8/-/-/-/-/-

4284 THIRTY NINE STEPS H'CAP (Amateurs) (0-75) (Class F) £2,636.00 (£741.00: £362.00) **1m 4f (Equitrack)** GOING: minus 0.62 sec per fur (FS) 1-10 (1-11)

3757[4] **Carlton Express (IRE) (33)***(42+) (JLEyre)* 4-9-3 MissDianaJones(4) (bhd tl gd late hdwy: led 1f out: r.o wl) — **1**

4217[15] Kenyatta (USA) **(35)***(42) (AMoore)* 5-8-12 (7) MrsJoanMoore(14) (chsd ldrs: effrt over 2f out: r.o wl fnl f: nt rch wnr) 1¼ **2**
4273[7] Beautete **(60)***(65) (SDow)* 3-10-10 MrTCuff(12) (chsd ldrs: led 3f out: hdd 1f out: no ex) 2 **3**
4272[12] Wicklow Boy (IRE) **(42)***(47) (TTClement)* 3-9-2v(4) MrVLukaniuk(5) (bhd: rdn & hdwy 4f out: nrst fin) ....hd **4**
4208[2] Strat's Legacy **(57)***(60)*(Fav)*(DWPArbuthnot)* 7-10-13 MrsDArbuthnot(3) (in rr tl sme late hdwy: n.d) 1¾ **5**
2727[9] Marco Magnifico (USA) **(65)***(66) (BWHills)* 4-11-7 MrsMCowdrey(13) (led to 3f out: sn wknd) 1¾ **6**
4261[10] Bronze Maquette (IRE) **(42)***(37) (BJMcMath)* 4-9-12 MissPJones(7) (nvr gng pce)..5 **7**
4244[14] Smocking **(39)***(25) (JPearce)* 4-9-9 MrsLPearce(11) (a mid div) 7 **8**
3359[4] Malingerer **(36)***(18) (DAWilson)* 3-8-10 (4) MrsSBosley(8) (nvr nr to chal) 3 **9**
4261[12] Danielle Habibi (IRE) **(41)***(22) (CCElsey)* 3-9-5 MissAElsey(6) (mid div: wknd over 4f out) ....½ **10**
4239[8] Ann Hill (IRE) **(37)***(17) (RHollinshead)* 4-9-3 (4) MissJSouthall(9) (m.n.s) ....½ **11**
1139[9] Here He Comes **(51)***(29) (AMoore)* 8-10-7 MrTMcCarthy(1) (chsd ldrs tl rdn & wknd over 4f out) 1¼ **12**
1387[6] Mardood **(54)***(22) (DWChapman)* 9-10-6 (4) MissRClark(2) (a bhd) 8 **13**
4051[12] Regina Alicia **(36)***(—) (RIngram)* 3-8-10 (4) MissBCraven(10) (chsd ldr tl wknd over 4f out) 6 **14**

LONG HANDICAP Malingerer 8-11 Regina Alicia 8-13

9/4 Strat's Legacy, **9/2** CARLTON EXPRESS (IRE), **11/2** Smocking, **6/1** Beautete, **15/2** Marco Magnifico (USA), **12/1** Here He Comes, **16/1** Bronze Maquette (IRE), Mardood, **20/1** Ann Hill (IRE), Wicklow Boy (IRE), Danielle Habibi (IRE), **33/1** Kenyatta (USA), Malingerer, **66/1** Regina Alicia, CSF £127.99 CT £848.29 TOTE £5.00: £1.60 £12.00 £1.50 (£82.30) OWNER Mr A. Skelton (HAMBLETON) BRED A. Baxter 14 Rn 2m 33.76 SF: 23/24/39/22/40/46/19/-/-/-/-/-/-/-

WEIGHT FOR AGE 3yo-6lb

4285

RICHARD HANNAY NURSERY (0-85) (Class D) £3,288.75 (£996.00: £486.50: £231.75) **7f (Equitrack)** GOING: minus 0.62 sec per fur (FS) 1-40 (1-41)

4216[6] **Mediate (IRE) (51)***(58) (RHannon)* 2-7-13b TWilliams(2) (led early: chsd ldr: led over 1f out: rdn out) ....— **1**
4216[8] No Pattern **(73)***(69) (GLMoore)* 2-9-7v BRouse(1) (led after 2f: rdn & hdd over 1f out: r.o) 5 **2**
4106[12] Hever Golf Lady **(45)***(36) (TJNaughton)* 2-7-7 GBardwell(4) (mid div tl styd on fnl f: nvr able to chal) 2½ **3**
4047[4] Nordinex (IRE) **(70)***(59) (RWArmstrong)* 2-9-4 WWoods(3) (sn led: hdd after 2f: n.d after) ....¾ **4**
3416[7] Bally Wonder **(52)***(38) (DMorris)* 2-8-0 CRutter(9) (prom tl wknd over 2f out) 1¼ **5**
4216[7] Templemore (IRE) **(55)***(40) (NACallaghan)* 2-8-3 JQuinn(6) (bhd: nvr nr to chal)...hd **6**
4144[3] Sally Weld **(64)***(46) (CJBenstead)* 2-8-12 JWilliams(8) (chsd ldrs tl rdn & wknd over 2f out) 1¼ **7**
4174* Charlie Sillett **(73)***(54)*(Fav)*(BWHills)* 2-9-7 RCochrane(5) (hld up: sme hdwy ½-wy: sn wknd) ....hd **8**
4256* Casper's Risk **(68)***(44) (DNicholls)* 2-9-2b (7x) AlexGreaves(7) (n.d) 2½ **9**

LONG HANDICAP Hever Golf Lady 7-6

13/8 Charlie Sillett, **9/2** No Pattern, **6/1** Nordinex (IRE), Sally Weld, **9/1** MEDIATE (IRE), **11/1** Casper's Risk, **12/1** Templemore (IRE), **14/1** Hever Golf Lady, **16/1** Bally Wonder, CSF £48.30 CT £525.18 TOTE £9.20: £1.90 £1.90 £2.50 (£26.30) OWNER Mrs S. H. Spencer-Phillips (MARLBOROUGH) BRED Knocktoran Stud 9 Rn 1m 25.55 (2.55) SF: 3/12/-/2/-/-/-/-/-

4286

THREE HOSTAGES STKS (II) (Mdn 2-Y.O) (Class D) £3,318.65 (£1,005.20: £491.10: £234.05) **6f (Equitrack)** GOING: minus 0.62 sec (FS) 2-10 (2-11)

4225[3] **Shot the Sheriff** *(66)*(Fav)*(PFICole)* 2-9-0 TQuinn(4) (bhd: str run fnl f to ld post) ....— **1**
1882[4] Taylord *(66) (RHannon)* 2-9-0 RPerham(10) (chsd ldrs tl led ins fnl f: r.o: jst ct)...s.h **2**
3903[15] Kreef *(65) (RJO'Sullivan)* 2-9-0 DBiggs(3) (chsd ldr: led over 2f out: hdd ins fnl ff: r.o) ....nk **3**
4230[6] Wasblest *(52) (MJohnston)* 2-8-9 TWilliams(1) (led tl over 2f out: nt pce to chal after) 3 **4**
4100[17] Black Shadow *(44) (PJMcBride)* 2-8-4 (5) NVarley(2) (mid div: nvr nrr) 3 **5**
3905[10] Persian Conquest (IRE) *(48) (RIngram)* 2-9-0 JWilliams(7) (bhd tl mod late hdwy: n.d) ....hd **6**
3957[12] Jovale *(43) (SGNorton)* 2-8-7 (7) OliverCasey(5) (nvr nr to chal) 1¾ **7**
Mister Rm *(43) (RGuest)* 2-9-0 WWoods(11) (s.s: nvr rchd ldrs) ....s.h **8**

4161[9] Baby Bob **(50)**_(35) (JMPEustace)_ 2-8-9b MTebbutt(8) (prom tl outpcd over 2f out)..¾ **9**
4164[16] Call the Lifeboat _(30) (MHTompkins)_ 2-8-4 (5) SMulvey(6) (chsd ldrs: wknd 2f out)1¾ **10**
4207[12] Logie Pert Lad _(—) (JJBridger)_ 2-9-0 AClark(9) (nvr nr ldrs)................................12 **11**

11/8 SHOT THE SHERIFF, **7/2** Wasblest, **4/1** Taylord (6/1-7/2), **10/1** Mister Rm, **14/1** Persian Conquest (IRE), **20/1** Baby Bob, **33/1** Black Shadow, Jovale, Kreef, Call the Lifeboat, **50/1** Logie Pert Lad, CSF £7.18 TOTE £2.30: £1.60 £1.60 £3.20 (£4.20) OWNER Mr M. Arbib (WHATCOMBE) BRED Martyn Arbib 11 Rn 1m 13.81 (3.21) SF: 3/3/2/-/-/-/-/-/-/-/-

4287 DANCING FLOOR STKS (0-55) (Class F) £2,659.80 (£747.80: £365.40)
2m (Equitrack) GOING: minus 0.62 sec per fur (FS) 2-40 (2-43)

4140[6] **Stalled (IRE) (48)**_(60) (PTWalwyn)_ 4-9-4 RCochrane(1) (hld up & bhd: hdwy over 4f out: rdn to ld ent fnl f: rdn out)..— **1**
3937[22] Pride of Britain (CAN) **(55)**_(53)_(Fav)_(LGCottrell)_ 5-8-13 JQuinn(6) (chsd ldrs: rdn over 4f out: led over 2f out tl ent fnl f: no ex).................................2½ **2**
3505[2] Bo Knows Best (IRE) **(55)**_(55) (GLMoore)_ 5-9-4 BRouse(2) (mid div: hdwy over 3f out: nrst fin)..3 **3**
4221[3] Well and Truly **(50)**_(51) (BAMcMahon)_ 7-8-10 (5) SSanders(4) (prom: chsd ldr over 5f out: one pce)...1¼ **4**
4239[7] Dawn Rock **(55)**_(54) (PAKelleway)_ 3-8-12b MWigham(3) (mid div tl sme late hdwy: no imp)..2½ **5**
3609[12] Dinner At Eight **(47)**_(53) (RJO'Sullivan)_ 4-9-6 DBiggs(7) (chsd ldr: led 7f out tl over 2f out: sn wknd)...½ **6**
3062[7] Star Quest **(51)**_(50) (JRJenkins)_ 7-9-4e CRutter(8) (a mid div)..............................1½ **7**
1313[8] Mediator **(42)**_(53) (AMoore)_ 5-9-3 (5) AWhelan(9) (chsd ldrs tl rdn & wknd over 2f out)..1½ **8**
3812[11] Arc Bright (IRE) **(55)**_(52) (RHollinshead)_ 4-9-10 TIves(14) (chsd ldrs tl lost pl ½-wy: sn bhd)..3 **9**
3609[10] Tiger Claw (USA) **(40)**_(23) (ABarrow)_ 8-9-4 AMackay(12) (prom tl rdn & wknd over 5f out: eased)..25 **10**
4261[15] Pink Brief (IRE) **(55)**_(17) (BJMeehan)_ 3-8-7b BDoyle(10) (hld up: rdn over 4f out: sn wknd)..3½ **11**
4141[6] Princess Tateum (IRE) **(55)**_(8) (MrsMMcCourt)_ 4-8-13b GDuffield(5) (led to 7f out)..7 **12**
4244[11] Legal Win (USA) **(38)**_(—) (AGFoster)_ 6-9-4 JWilliams(13) (s.v.s: a wl t.o)...........dist **13**
Ballysparkle (IRE) **(55)**_(—) (JLEyre)_ 4-8-11 (7) GMacDonald(11) (reluctant to r: p.u after 3f)... **P**

15/8 Pride of Britain (CAN), **11/4** Bo Knows Best (IRE), **5/1** STALLED (IRE), **7/1** Well and Truly, **14/1** Princess Tateum (IRE), Arc Bright (IRE), **20/1** Star Quest, Mediator, Dawn Rock, Pink Brief (IRE), **25/1** Dinner At Eight, Ballysparkle (IRE), **33/1** Tiger Claw (USA), Legal Win (USA), CSF £15.80 TOTE £7.30: £2.50 £1.70 £2.20 (£8.60) OWNER Mrs P. T. Walwyn (LAMBOURN) BRED D. Aykroyd 14 Rn 3m 23.83 (0.33) SF: 52/45/47/43/38/45/42/-/-/-/-/-/-/-
WEIGHT FOR AGE 3yo-8lb

4288 FLEURETS H'CAP (II) (0-60) (Class F) £2,600.30 (£730.80: £356.90)
6f (Equitrack) GOING: minus 0.62 sec per fur (FS) 3-10 (3-13)

4212* **Speedy Classic (USA) (56)**_(68)_(Fav)_(MJHeaton-Ellis)_ 5-9-11 WWoods(5) (chsd ldrs: chal 2f out: led jst ins fnl f: jst hld on)...— **1**
4253[2] Nineacres **(51)**_(62) (DNicholls)_ 3-9-6 AlexGreaves(3) (chsd ldr tl led ½-wy: hdd jst ins fnl f: jst failed)..hd **2**
4270[4] Joint Effort (IRE) **(43)**_(46) (AMoore)_ 3-8-7 (5) AWhelan(4) (bhd tl styd on fnl f)..........3 **3**
4266* Distant Dynasty **(49)**_(49) (BAPearce)_ 4-8-11 (7) PRoberts(6) (chsd ldrs: chal over 2f out: rdn & no ex)..¾ **4**
829[10] Tassagh Bridge (IRE) **(29)**_(19) (RIngram)_ 4-7-7 (5)ow5 DWright(2) (nvr rchd ldrs)......4 **5**
4018[24] Waverley Star **(42)**_(30) (KOCunningham-Brown)_ 9-8-4 (7) CTeague(9) (a mid div) ..½ **6**
4204[8] Battling Bella (USA) **(42)**_(27) (GLMoore)_ 5-8-11v BRouse(1) (led to ½-wy: wknd fnl f)..¾ **7**
4033[12] Quiet Mission **(44)**_(26) (JLEyre)_ 3-8-13v MMcAndrew(8) (nvr wnt pce of ldrs)...........1 **8**
4241[10] Obsidian Grey **(56)**_(35) (MissLCSiddall)_ 7-9-6v(5) DRMcCabe(7) (bhd fr ½-wy)........1 **9**
LONG HANDICAP Tassagh Bridge (IRE) 7-6

6/4 SPEEDY CLASSIC (USA), **9/4** Distant Dynasty, **8/1** Nineacres, Quiet Mission (10/1-25/1), Battling Bella (USA), **9/1** Joint Effort (IRE), **16/1** Obsidian Grey, **20/1** Tassagh Bridge (IRE), **33/1** Waverley Star, CSF £15.01 CT £83.37 TOTE £2.30: £1.60 £1.40 £1.50 (£5.10) OWNER Stainless Design Services (WROUGHTON) BRED Lagrange Chance Partnership & Overbrook Farm 9 Rn 1m 12.79 (2.19) SF: 26/22/7/10/-/-/-/-/-

4289 LADBROKE ALL-WEATHER TROPHY (H'cap) (Qualifier) (0-70) (Class E) £3,009.00 (£912.00: £446.00: £213.00)
7f (Equitrack) GOING: minus 0.62 sec per fur (FS) 3-40 (3-43)

4265² **Dancing Lawyer (69)***(77) (BJMeehan)* 3-9-12 BDoyle(7) (mid div: str run to ld over 1f out: rdn out: easily)........— **1**
4226⁴ Rad **(55)***(56) (SPCWoods)* 4-8-13 WWoods(9) (mid div: r.o fnl 2f: nt pce of wnr)..3½ **2**
4255² Sharp Imp **(40)***(39) (RMFlower)* 4-7-5b(7)ow1 SLanigan(13) (bhd tl gd late hdwy: nt rch ldrs)........¾ **3**
4053¹³ Eastleigh **(50)***(48) (RHollinshead)* 5-8-8 ow1 TIves(11) (chsd ldrs: one pce fnl f)......nk **4**
4241² Milos **(69)***(66)*(Fav)*(TJNaughton)* 3-9-12 GDuffield(6) (led 2f out tl over 1f out: sn outpcd)........½ **5**
1707⁵ Flying Wind **(45)***(40) (GLMoore)* 5-7-12 (5)ow4 AWhelan(8) (sme late hdwy: n.d).......1 **6**
3777⁹ Ragazzo (IRE) **(44)***(24) (KOCunningham-Brown)* 4-7-9 (7) CTeague(16) (nvr nr to chal)........7 **7**
4265⁹ Soaking **(70)***(46) (GLMoore)* 4-10-0 BRouse(1) (led over 4f out to 2f out: sn wknd)........1¾ **8**
4270¹⁴ Secret Assignment (USA) **(42)***(17) (CACyzer)* 4-8-0v GBardwell(2) (m.n.s)............nk **9**
4257⁵ Level Edge **(53)***(25) (MJohnston)* 3-8-10 TWilliams(3) (led after 1f tl after 2f) 1¼ **10**
4059⁸ My Ruby Ring **(61)***(31) (DRLaing)* 7-9-5 AClark(12) (rdn ½-wy: outpcd)................¾ **11**
4202² Greatest Hopes **(42)***(12) (CJBenstead)* 3-7-13 JQuinn(4) (prom tl rdn & wknd ½-wy)........s.h **12**
4210³ Knightrider **(56)***(21) (CJames)* 3-8-13b WNewnes(14) (mid div: wknd over 2f out).2½ **13**
4253ᶜ Farndale **(58)***(22) (JBerry)* 7-8-9 (7) PRoberts(15) (a bhd)........½ **14**
4231¹⁷ Bit of a Lark **(68)***(31) (DMorris)* 6-9-9 (3) JTate(5) (led 1f: wknd qckly) ....nk **15**
94⁰ Lady Broker **(55)***(11) (ABailey)* 4-8-8 (5) DWright(10) (a bhd)........3½ **16**

4/1 Milos, **11/2** Greatest Hopes, **6/1** DANCING LAWYER, **13/2** Sharp Imp, **8/1** Soaking, **10/1** Farndale (16/1-9/1), Level Edge, **12/1** Lady Broker, **14/1** Flying Wind, Rad, **20/1** My Ruby Ring, Eastleigh, Knightrider, **25/1** Secret Assignment (USA), Bit of a Lark, Ragazzo (IRE), CSF £89.01 CT £529.52 TOTE £12.10: £2.10 £1.20 £2.20 £4.80 (£222.90) OWNER Vintage Services Ltd (UPPER LAMBOURN) BRED Vintage Services Ltd 16 Rn

1m 24.38 (1.38) SF: 41/22/7/15/30/7/-/1/-/-/-/-/-/-/-/-
WEIGHT FOR AGE 3yo-1lb

T/Plpt: £5,764.00 (1.27 Tckts). T/Qdpt: £27.30 (2.4 Tckts) AS

4234a-CAPANNELLE (Rome, Italy) (R-H)
Tuesday November 22nd (Good to soft)

4290a PREMIO TCHIN (2-Y.O.C &)G £5,922.00
1m 1f

Altola' (ITY) *(Italy)* 2-8-12 BJovine ....— **1**
Imco Gold (IRE) *(Italy)* 2-8-6 ACorniani 1¼ **2**
Roy (ITY) *(Italy)* 2-9-2 DZarroli ....¾ **3**
4121a* Sud (IRE) *(JLDunlop)* 2-8-13 FJovine (btn further 63/4l)........ **6**

TOTE 21L: 16L 30L (142L) OWNER Mr S. Parcu BRED U. Aletti in Italy 6 Rn 1m 54.0 SF: -/-/-/-

4235a-SAINT-CLOUD (France) (L-H)
Tuesday November 22nd (Heavy)

4291a PRIX PREDICATEUR £13,730.00
1m 2f 110y GOING: 1.50 sec per fur (Hvy)

Youngui (FR) *(115) (France)* 4-9-2 SGuillot ....— **1**
4200a² Le Conquet (FR) *(113) (France)* 6-9-2 SMaillot 1½ **2**
Sifacar (FR) *(109) (France)* 6-9-2 MCesandri 2½ **3**
3637⁸ Darrery *(104) (MRStoute)* 4-8-13 DBoeuf 1½ **4**

TOTE 7.50F: 2.00F 1.50F 1.90F (23.00F) OWNER Mr J. Jardel BRED J. Dolbeau in France 8 Rn
2m 29.7 (19.1) SF: 63/60/55/49

4245a-EVRY (France) (R-H)
Wednesday November 23rd (Heavy)

4292a PRIX ZEDDAAN (listed race) (2-Y.O) £13,730.00
6f GOING: 0.05 sec per fur (G)

Diffident (FR) *(101++) (France)* 2-8-11 TJarnet ....— **1**
Skip Lady (FR) *(88) (France)* 2-8-11 SGuillot 5 **2**
Struggler *(83) (France)* 2-8-11 FHead 2 **3**
4029* Wardara *(77) (MissGayKelleway)* 2-8-8 TWilliams (btn further 1¼l) **6**
4045[3] Leap for Joy *(77) (JHMGosden)* 2-8-8 JQuinn (btn 8½l by wnr) **7**
4173[2] Double Quick (IRE) *(57) (MJohnston)* 2-8-8 JReid (btn 16½l by wnr) **8**
TOTE 2.30F: 1.30F 4.10F 1.40F (73.70F) OWNER Sheikh Mohammed BRED Haras d'Etreham & R Ades in France 10 Rn
1m 11.98 (1.98) SF: 63/43/37/-/-/-

4293a PRIX ISOLA BESSA (listed race) (3-Y.O.F) £13,730.00
1m GOING: 1.15 sec per fur (S)

2300a[3] **Mrs Arkada (FR)** *(95+) (France)* 3-9-2 TJarnet ....— **1**
Estala *(93) (France)* 3-9-2 GGuignard ....¾ **2**
Alisa (GER) *(90) (Germany)* 3-9-2 OSchick 1½ **3**
4194a[3] Cherokee Rose (IRE) *(90) (France)* 3-9-2 SGuillot ....nse **4**
4133[6] Randonneur (IRE) *(89) (EWeymes)* 3-9-2 JReid ....½ **5**
4194a[4] Beaming *(—) (JRFanshawe)* 3-9-2 DBoeuf (btn further 3*l) **10**
TOTE 3.50F: 1.70F 5.40F 2.50F (39.50F) OWNER Mr J-L. Lagardere 12 Rn 1m 52.39 SF: 9/7/2

FUCHU (Tokyo, Japan) (L-H)
Sunday November 27th (Firm)

4294a JAPAN CUP (Gp 1) £1,023,498.00
1m 4f

Marvelous Crown (JPN) *(127) (Japan)* 4-9-0 KMinai (trckd ldrs: 3rd st: r.o to ld last strides) ....— **1**
4191a[3] Paradise Creek (USA) *(127) (USA)* 5-9-0 PDay (7th st: hdwy 2f out: led ins fnl f tl ct cl home) ....nse **2**
Royce and Royce (JPN) *(125) (Japan)* 4-9-0 NYokoyama (hdwy over 2f out: led over 1f out tl ins fnl f) 1¼ **3**
4191a[6] Hernando (FR) *(123) (France)* 4-9-0 CAsmussen (bhd: hdwy fnl 2f: nrst fin) 1¼ **4**
Sandpit (BRZ) *(122)(Fav)(USA)* 5-9-0 CNakatani (led 8f out tl over 1f out: one pce) ....nk **5**
4181a* Jeune *(121) (Australia)* 5-9-0 WHarris (hmpd after 2f: bhd tl styd on fnl 2f) ....nk **6**
Rough Habit (NZ) *(119) (NewZealand)* 8-9-0 JCassidy (hmpd after 2f: styd on fnl 2f: nvr nrr) 1½ **7**
401a[3] Grand Flotilla (USA) *(119) (USA)* 7-9-0 CBlack (in tch: one pce fnl 2f) ....nk **8**
Nice Nature (JPN) *(118) (Japan)* 6-9-0 MMatsunaga (5th st: rdn & one pce fnl 2f) ....d.h **8**
4191a[11] Fraise (USA) *(117) (USA)* 6-9-0 YTake (last st: sme late hdwy) ....nk **10**
Fujiyama Kenzan (JPN) *(116) (Japan)* 6-9-0 MEbina (led 4f: 4th st: wknd) ....nk **11**
4189a[2] Johann Quatz (FR) *(116) (USA)* 5-9-0 ASolis (prom whn hmpd after 2f: 2nd st: sn wknd) ....hd **12**
4191a[13] Raintrap *(115) (USA)* 4-9-0 PatEddery (a bhd) 1 **13**
3865a[3] Apple Tree (FR) *(112) (France)* 5-9-0 TJarnet (hdwy on ins 5f out: 6th st: wknd 2f out) 2½ **14**

7/2 Sandpit (BRZ), **4/1** Paradise Creek (USA), **49/10** Apple Tree (FR), **15/2** Hernando (FR), **86/10** Jeune, **96/10** MARVELOUS CROWN (JPN), **13/1** Raintrap, **18/1** Royce and Royce (JPN), **19/1** Fraise (USA), **22/1** Grand Flotilla (USA), **23/1** Nice Nature (JPN), **35/1** Rough Habit (NZ), **39/1** Johann Quatz (FR), **40/1** Fujiyama Kenzan (JPN), TOTE1060Y (inc 100Y stake): 290Y 190Y 310Y (3090Y) OWNER Mr S. Sasahara BRED K. Hayata in Japan 14 Rn
2m 23.6 SF: -/-/-/-/-/-/-/-/-/-/-/-/-/-

4291A-SAINT-CLOUD (France) (L-H)
Tuesday November 29th (Heavy)

4295a PRIX DES CHENES (Gp 3) (2-Y.O) £22,883.00
1m GOING: minus 1.55 sec per fur (Hvy)

4233a[3] **Coco Passion (FR)** *(96) (France)* 2-8-8 WMongil ....— **1**

4108a2 Privity (USA) *(96) (France)* 2-8-8 GDubroeucq ....nse **2**
Diamond Mix (IRE) *(97) (France)* 2-8-11 TGillet 1 **3**
4162* Royal Philosopher *(95) (KMcAuliffe)* 2-8-11 JTate (btn further 1l).... **5**
4154a5 Loch Bering (USA) *(92) (PAKelleway)* 2-8-11 JReid (btn 33/4l by wnr).... **7**

TOTE 24.90F: 4.00F 2.40F 3.50F (68.70F) OWNER Mr H. Chalhoub 11 Rn 1m 52.7 SF: 54/53/53

4282-LINGFIELD (L-H)
Wednesday December 7th (Standard)

4296 ART DECO STKS (I) (0-60) (Class F) £2,576.50 (£724.00: £353.50) **1m 2f (Equitrack)** GOING: minus 0.62 sec per fur (FS) 12-00 (12-02)

4209² **Hillsdown Boy (IRE) (57)***(61)*(Fav)*(SDow)* 4-8-11 (5) SSanders(5) (a.p: led over 3f out: sn hdd: led 2f out: hrd rdn over 1f out: r.o wl) ....— **1**
4281⁶ Queen of Shannon (IRE) **(52)***(51) (BJMeehan)* 6-8-9 MFenton(8) (hdwy over 4f out: led 3f out to 2f out: unable qckn)....1¾ **2**
4260² Captain Marmalade **(51)***(52) (DTThom)* 5-9-0 GDuffield(3) (lw: gd hdwy over 1f out: r.o wl ins fnl f)....2½ **3**
3913¹¹ Sushi Bar (IRE) **(60)***(51) (MrsMReveley)* 3-8-10 TIves(7) (lw: hld up: rdn over 4f out: r.o one pce fnl 2f)....nk **4**
3750⁴ Bo Knows Nigel (IRE) **(55)***(53) (ICampbell)* 3-9-0b RCochrane(4) (led over 5f out tl over 3f out: wknd over 2f out)....1½ **5**
605⁵ Doreen's Delight **(29)***(47) (HJCollingridge)* 8-8-9 (5) CHawksley(9) (b: bit bkwd: swtg: rdn over 3f out: nvr nr to chal)....1 **6**
3977¹⁰ Chancel (USA) **(60)***(41) (LordHuntingdon)* 3-8-5 DHarrison(10) (hld up: rdn over 5f out: wknd over 2f out)....nk **7**
4260⁴ Vanroy **(58)***(44) (JRJenkins)* 10-9-2e JWilliams(11) (eyeshield: a mid div)....2½ **8**
4223¹² Rose Elegance **(54)***(35) (OO'Neill)* 5-8-9 CRutter(12) (hld up: rdn over 4f out: sn wknd)....1¼ **9**
4270⁸ Danseuse Davis (FR) **(55)***(33) (KMcAuliffe)* 3-8-5 AClark(13) (prom over 7f)....1 **10**
4141⁵ Carlowitz (USA) **(57)***(32) (AMoore)* 6-9-2 BRouse(6) (eyeshield: a bhd)....5 **11**
4214¹⁴ Swallow Ridge (IRE) **(36)***(20) (RJO'Sullivan)* 5-8-9 DBiggs(2) (led over 4f)....3 **12**
4260¹⁴ After the Last **(60)***(18) (RHannon)* 4-8-8 (7)ow1 MDenaro(1) (prom over 4f)....5 **13**

3/1 HILLSDOWN BOY (IRE), **11/2** Sushi Bar (IRE), **6/1** Carlowitz (USA), **13/2** Chancel (USA), **7/1** Bo Knows Nigel (IRE), **10/1** Captain Marmalade, **12/1** Vanroy, **16/1** After the Last, Queen of Shannon (IRE), **33/1** Rose Elegance, Doreen's Delight, Swallow Ridge (IRE), **50/1** Danseuse Davis (FR), CSF £45.30 TOTE £3.80: £1.70 £12.40 £2.00 (£107.90) OWNER Mr J. E. Mills (EPSOM) BRED E. Daly 13 Rn 2m 4.95 (0.84 under best) (1.95) SF: 35/27/28/23/25/23/14/-/-/-/-
WEIGHT FOR AGE 3yo-4lb

4297 SEALAND QUALITY H'CAP (0-70) (Class E) £2,749.00 (£832.00: £406.00: £193.00) **5f (Equitrack)** GOING: minus 0.62 sec per fur (FS) 12-30 (12-34)

4268⁷ **Nordico Princess (61)***(65) (GROldroyd)* 3-9-5 RCochrane(5) (lw: mde all: drvn out)....— **1**
4145⁵ Little Saboteur **(67)***(69) (PJMakin)* 5-9-11 RPerham(10) (b.nr hind: lw: a.p: hrd rdn over 1f out: r.o ins fnl f)....½ **2**
4283³ Featherstone Lane **(60)***(61) (MissLCSiddall)* 3-8-13v(5) PMcCabe(9) (rdn & hdwy over 1f out: r.o wl ins fnl f)....nk **3**
4268* Tee-Emm **(59)***(55)*(Fav)*(PHowling)* 4-9-3 TIves(4) (chsd wnr: ev ch 2f out: hrd rdn over 1f out: unable qckn)....1¾ **4**
4231¹⁴ Sison (IRE) **(70)***(58) (KGWingrove)* 4-10-0 JMcLaughlin(1) (n.m.r on ins over 2f out: nvr nr to chal)....2½ **5**
4145⁷ Random **(64)***(51) (CJames)* 3-9-8 BRouse(7) (outpcd: nvr nrr)....nk **6**
4237⁸ High Domain (IRE) **(70)***(56) (MMcCormack)* 3-9-9 (5) TGMcLaughlin(3) (outpcd)....hd **7**
4266⁸ Not so Generous (IRE) **(65)***(50) (WGMTurner)* 4-9-4 (5) JDSmith(2) (outpcd)....hd **8**
4268³ It Must Be Millie **(63)***(48) (GHEden)* 3-9-2 (5) AWhelan(6) (b.off hind: hdwy over 2f out: hrd rdn over 1f out: wknd fnl f)....s.h **9**
4231⁵ Bangles **(70)***(52) (LordHuntingdon)* 4-10-0v DHarrison(8) (prom over 3f)....¾ **10**

15/8 Tee-Emm, **3/1** Bangles, **7/1** Featherstone Lane, **9/1** Little Saboteur, **10/1** Random, It Must Be Millie, **12/1** NORDICO PRINCESS, **14/1** High Domain (IRE), **16/1** Not so Generous (IRE), **33/1** Sison (IRE), CSF £107.19 CT £749.25 TOTE £25.20: £4.20 £3.10 £3.70 (£77.60) OWNER Mr M. S. Griffiths (YORK) 10 Rn 58.56 secs (0.36) SF: 44/48/41/37/38/32/37/-/-/-

4298 REGENCY NURSERY (0-75) (Class E) £2,879.00 (£872.00: £426.00: £203.00) **6f (Equitrack)** GOING: minus 0.62 sec per fur (FS) 1-00 (1-04)

3702[6] **Musical Fantasy (IRE) (50)***(55) (BJMeehan)* 2-7-7 (5) NVarley(3) (mde virtually all: drvn out) ....— 1
4267[2] Das Island **(56)***(61) (JRJenkins)* 2-8-4 CRutter(12) (lw: a.p: hrd rdn & swtchd rt over 1f out: r.o wl ins fnl f) ....s.h 2
4285* Mediate (IRE) **(58)***(59)*(Fav)*(RHannon)* 2-8-6b (7x) TWilliams(14) (rdn & hdwy over 3f out: hrd rdn 2f out: unable qckn fnl f) 1¼ 3
4285[2] No Pattern **(73)***(71) (GLMoore)* 2-9-7v BRouse(1) (lw: a.p: rdn over 3f out: one pce fnl f) ....¾ 4
4275[4] Rotherfield Park (IRE) **(52)***(49) (CSmith)* 2-7-7 (7) MBaird(7) (gd hdwy over 1f out: r.o wl ins fnl f) ....hd 5
4262[3] Crystal Loop **(63)***(57) (ABailey)* 2-8-6 (5) DWright(13) (a.p: nt clr run over 1f out: one pce) ....¾ 6
4164[7] Today Tonite **(60)***(49) (JPearce)* 2-8-8 GBardwell(11) (a mid div) 2 7
4203[8] Water Hazard (IRE) **(51)***(40) (SDow)* 2-7-6 (7)ow1 SLanigan(10) (b.hind: nvr plcd to chal) ....s.h 8
4275[5] Fishy Affair **(49)***(38) (TDyer)* 2-7-11 RStreet(9) (nvr plcd to chal) ....s.h 9
4219[10] Franklinsboy **(50)***(39) (CaptJWilson)* 2-7-12 AMackay(5) (nvr nrr) ....s.h 10
4228[12] Bold Palmella (IRE) **(60)***(45) (MrsJRRamsden)* 2-8-8 MWigham(4) (a bhd) 1½ 11
3973[5] Just Jesting **(62)***(45) (GLMoore)* 2-8-10 DHarrison(2) (lw: hld up: rdn over 3f out: wknd fnl f) ....½ 12
4262* Robo Magic (USA) **(69)***(50) (AMoore)* 2-8-12 (5) AWhelan(8) (bhd fnl 2f) ....½ 13
4267[8] Al Totseva **(47)***(15) (MPMuggeridge)* 2-7-2hb(7)ow2 CAdamson(6) (prom over 3f).....5 14

3/1 Mediate (IRE), **9/2** No Pattern, **5/1** Robo Magic (USA), **11/2** Das Island, **10/1** Crystal Loop, Rotherfield Park (IRE), **12/1** Bold Palmella (IRE), **14/1** Fishy Affair, **20/1** MUSICAL FANTASY (IRE), Just Jesting, **25/1** Today Tonite, **33/1** Franklinsboy, **40/1** Water Hazard (IRE), **50/1** Al Totseva, CSF £122.96 CT £398.26 TOTE £32.60: £5.50 £3.60 £1.20 (£135.30) OWNER Mr K. C. Gomm (UPPER LAMBOURN) BRED Prince Rose Stud 14 Rn

1m 12.7 (2.10) SF: 3/8/8/19/-/8/-/-/-/-/-/-/-/-

4299 SHERATON AUCTION STKS (Mdn 2-Y.O) (Class F) £2,588.40 (£727.40: £355.20) **7f (Equitrack)** GOING: minus 0.62 sec per fur (FS) 1-30 (1-32)

4216[4] **Tara Colleen (IRE) (54)***(61) (CAHorgan)* 2-8-2 TWilliams(5) (hdwy 4f out: hrd rdn over 1f out: led wl ins fnl f: r.o wl) ....— 1
4238[8] Keeper's Grey *(60) (RGuest)* 2-8-4 DHarrison(10) (a.p: led over 2f out: hrd rdn wl over 1f out: hdd wl ins fnl f: unable qckn) 1¼ 2
4238[4] Tapping Feet *(57)*(Fav)*(SirMarkPrescott)* 2-8-2 GDuffield(11) (led over 4f out: rdn 3f out: hdd over 2f out: n.m.r & swtchd lft 1f out: one pce) ....½ 3
4207[11] Iron Man (IRE) **(57)***(51) (LordHuntingdon)* 2-7-13v(5) AWhelan(6) (lw: nvr plcd to chal) 4 4
4285[3] Hever Golf Lady **(44)***(41) (TJNaughton)* 2-8-2 GBardwell(1) (hmpd & lost pl on ins over 5f out: r.o one pce fnl 2f) 4 5
3599[11] Ace Chapel (IRE) *(44) (CCElsey)* 2-8-7 MFenton(9) (b.hind: nvr nr to chal) 1 6
3415[6] Wings of Desire (IRE) **(53)***(36) (RChampion)* 2-8-7 MRimmer(8) (hld up: rdn 4f out: sn wknd) 4 7
4137[5] Harvest Reaper **(57)***(26) (JAHarris)* 2-8-4v SWilliams(3) (led over 2f: wknd over 2f out) 3½ 8
4066[8] Tigana **(47)***(—) (MrsLCJewell)* 2-7-13 CRutter(7) (bhd fnl 3f) 7 9
4282[11] Iceblock *(—) (MMcCormack)* 2-7-13 AMackay(4) (s.s: a wl bhd) 1 10
4282[2] Logie *(—) (MAJarvis)* 2-8-7 TIves(2) .... W

6/4 Tapping Feet, **2/1** Logie, **5/2** TARA COLLEEN (IRE), **5/1** Iron Man (IRE), **8/1** Hever Golf Lady, Ace Chapel (IRE), **10/1** Harvest Reaper, **12/1** Keeper's Grey, **16/1** Wings of Desire (IRE), **25/1** Iceblock, **33/1** Tigana, CSF £34.75 TOTE £4.40: £1.20 £3.60 £1.30 (£26.20) OWNER Friary Bloodstock Company Ltd (BILLINGBEAR) BRED John Malone 11 Rn

1m 26.47 (3.47) SF: -/-/-/-/-/-/-/-/-/-/-

4300 LLOYDS BANK PRIDE IN EXCELLENCE H'CAP (0-70) (Class E) £2,788.00 (£844.00: £412.00: £196.00) **1m 5f (Equitrack)** GOING: minus 0.62 sec per fur (FS) 2-00 (2-02)

4277[4] **Global Dancer (68)***(74) (WAO'Gorman)* 3-9-7 (3) EmmaO'Gorman(5) (a.p: led 3f out: clr over 1f out: r.o wl) ....— 1

4272[2] Miroswaki (USA) **(64)***(65)*(Fav)*(PMMcEntee)* 4-9-12 MFenton(8) (hdwy over 4f out: rdn over 2f out: chsd wnr fnl f: no imp)....4 **2**
4260* Shabanaz **(66)***(65) (WRMuir)* 9-10-0 RCochrane(3) (hdwy 9f out: rdn over 3f out: one pce)....1¼ **3**
4287[9] Arc Bright (IRE) **(55)***(52) (RHollinshead)* 4-9-3 AClark(2) (a.p: led over 3f out: sn hdd: hrd rdn over 1f out: wknd fnl f)....2 **4**
4261[3] Dancing Diamond (IRE) **(47)***(44) (MissBSanders)* 4-8-4h(5) SSanders(7) (hld up: rdn over 3f out: wknd over 2f out)....nk **5**
3812[9] Child Star (FR) **(36)***(26) (DMarks)* 5-7-7e(5) NVarley(1) (eyeshield: hdwy over 4f out: wknd over 3f out)....6 **6**
3131[4] Royal Circus **(37)***(23) (JGMO'Shea)* 5-7-6 (7) SLanigan(6) (led over 9f)....3½ **7**
4273[5] Western Valley **(31)***(15) (CPWildman)* 4-7-7v GBardwell(11) (bhd fnl 2f)....1¼ **8**
3901[19] Kiss Kincsem **(59)***(43) (PJMakin)* 3-9-1 RPerham(9) (lw: a bhd)....hd **9**
4257[12] Spring Loaded **(55)***(30) (JGMO'Shea)* 3-8-11 VSlattery(10) (a bhd)....8 **10**
4215[6] Sweet Caroline **(40)***(10) (PMitchell)* 3-7-3 (7) MBaird(4) (bhd fnl 8f)....4 **11**
939[12] Well Suited **(46)***(—) (BJMcMath)* 4-8-8 GDuffield(12) (b: b.hind: a bhd).... **12**

LONG HANDICAP Western Valley 7-6

9/4 Miroswaki (USA), **5/1** Shabanaz, **6/1** Dancing Diamond (IRE), **8/1** GLOBAL DANCER, Royal Circus, **12/1** Kiss Kincsem, Arc Bright (IRE), **14/1** Child Star (FR), Spring Loaded, **20/1** Western Valley, **25/1** Sweet Caroline, **33/1** Well Suited, CSF £25.89 CT £95.30 TOTE £9.30: £2.10 £1.40 £2.70 (£22.80) OWNER Mr N. S. Yong (NEWMARKET) BRED C. J. R. Trotter 12 Rn
2m 42.92 (0.90 under best) (0.42) SF: 56/53/54/41/33/16/13/-/-/-/-/-
WEIGHT FOR AGE 3yo-6lb

4301 ART DECO STKS (II) (0-60) (Class F) £2,576.50 (£724.00: £353.50)

1m 2f (Equitrack) GOING: minus 0.62 sec per fur (FS) 2-30 (2-30)

4143[9] **South Eastern Fred (57)***(62+) (HJCollingridge)* 3-8-12 MRimmer(9) (a.p: led over 3f out tl over 2f out: led over 1f out: rdn out)....— **1**
2957[10] Hatta Sunshine (USA) **(42)***(57) (AMoore)* 4-8-11 (5) AWhelan(4) (hdwy 4f out: led over 2f out tl over 1f out: unable qckn)....3½ **2**
4215* Polly Peculiar **(58)***(44)*(Fav)*(BSmart)* 3-8-7 DHarrison(8) (hdwy 5f out: rdn over 2f out: one pce)....5 **3**
4264[7] No Speeches (IRE) **(55)***(41) (CACyzer)* 3-8-10 MFenton(12) (no hdwy fnl 3f)....4 **4**
4273[6] Lady Reema **(48)***(34) (MissAJWhitfield)* 3-8-4 (5)ow4 RPainter(11) (hld up: rdn over 3f out: wknd over 2f out)....4 **5**
4227[8] Prim Lass **(53)***(30) (LordHuntingdon)* 3-8-6 ow1 AClark(6) (a.p: rdn over 4f out: wknd over 2f out)....½ **6**
2924[13] Pigalle Wonder **(40)***(32) (RJO'Sullivan)* 6-9-0b DBiggs(13) (nvr nrr)....1¼ **7**
3967* Rockstine (IRE) **(60)***(29) (PMitchell)* 3-8-9 GDuffield(1) (nvr nrr)....1½ **8**
4284[7] Bronze Maquette (IRE) **(38)***(24) (BJMcMath)* 4-8-9 RCochrane(3) (hdwy 4f out: wknd over 2f out)....¾ **9**
4040[12] Major Yaasi (USA) **(52)***(21) (JAGlover)* 4-9-0v SWilliams(5) (led 6f out tl over 3f out: sn wknd)....5 **10**
4271[9] Third Dam **(60)***(11) (BWHills)* 3-8-5 RStreet(2) (b: b.hind: led 4f: wknd 3f out)....3½ **11**
2516[10] Gallant Jack (IRE) **(49)***(16) (JGMO'Shea)* 5-9-0 AMackay(10) (a bhd)....hd **12**
4269[7] Simon Ellis (IRE) **(28)***(7) (DRLaing)* 5-9-0 GBardwell(7) (b: lw: prom 5f)....6 **13**

11/10 Polly Peculiar, **5/2** Rockstine (IRE), **7/1** SOUTH EASTERN FRED, **14/1** No Speeches (IRE), Lady Reema, Prim Lass, **16/1** Pigalle Wonder, Third Dam, **20/1** Major Yaasi (USA), Bronze Maquette (IRE), **25/1** Hatta Sunshine (USA), Gallant Jack (IRE), **33/1** Simon Ellis (IRE), CSF £161.12 TOTE £11.80: £2.80 £6.70 £1.10 (£101.60) OWNER South Eastern Electrical Plc (NEWMARKET) BRED L. Audus 13 Rn 2m 4.49 (1.30 under best) (1.49) SF: 34/33/17/14/7/3/9/2/-/-/-/-/-
WEIGHT FOR AGE 3yo-4lb

4302 LADBROKE ALL-WEATHER TROPHY (H'cap) (Qualifier) (I) (0-70) (Class E) £2,801.00 (£848.00: £414.00: £197.00)

1m (Equitrack) GOING: minus 0.62 sec per fur (FS) 3-00 (3-03)

4269[2] **Hawaii Storm (FR) (46)***(59) (MissAJWhitfield)* 6-8-7 (5) RPainter(1) (stdy hdwy over 3f out: str run fnl f: led nr fin)....— **1**
4265[5] Masnun (USA) **(59)***(71) (RJO'Sullivan)* 9-9-11 DBiggs(4) (hld up: led 2f out: rdn over 1f out: hdd nr fin)....nk **2**
4289* Dancing Lawyer **(69)***(74)*(Fav)*(BJMeehan)* 3-10-5 (6x) RCochrane(3) (a.p: led 4f out to 2f out: one pce)....3½ **3**
4289[4] Eastleigh **(42)***(40) (RHollinshead)* 5-8-8 DHarrison(10) (a.p: rdn 2f out: one pce) .3½ **4**
4273[8] Calisar **(43)***(29) (PHowling)* 4-8-9 AMackay(7) (lost pl 5f out: one pce fnl 2f)....6 **5**
4264[9] Island Knight (IRE) **(61)***(45) (MJRyan)* 5-9-13 AClark(12) (nvr plcd to chal)....1 **6**
4289[12] Greatest Hopes **(36)***(19) (CJBenstead)* 3-7-9 (5) CHawksley(11) (nvr nr to chal)....½ **7**
4177[17] Portolano (FR) **(46)***(28) (CNWilliams)* 3-8-10 MRimmer(6) (led 2f: rdn 4f out: wknd over 2f out)....½ **8**

4288[7] Battling Bella (USA) **(36)***(10) (GLMoore)* 5-8-2 AMorris(5) (prom over 5f) 4 **9**
3996[16] Nomogram **(32)***(—) (GLewis)* 3-7-5 (5) DWright(9) (s.s: a bhd) 3 **10**
3655[5] Mutinique **(43)***(9) (BAPearce)* 3-8-0 (7)ow5 PRoberts(8) (bhd fnl 4f)...........................¾ **11**
4212[6] Manor Adventure **(46)***(—) (PTDalton)* 4-8-7b(5) PMcCabe(2) (b: lw: led 6f out to 4f out: sn wknd)..9 **12**

13/8 Dancing Lawyer, **4/1** Eastleigh, **6/1** HAWAII STORM (FR), **7/1** Masnun (USA), **10/1** Island Knight (IRE), **14/1** Greatest Hopes, **20/1** Mutinique, Battling Bella (USA), Nomogram, **33/1** Calisar, Portolano (FR), Manor Adventure, CSF £45.58 CT £89.82 TOTE £4.90: £2.30 £3.00 £1.10 (£10.50) OWNER Mrs Renee Wheeler BRED Horse France 12 Rn

1m 36.83 (0.43) SF: 41/53/53/23/12/27/2/-/-/-/-/-

WEIGHT FOR AGE 3yo-2lb

4303 LADBROKE ALL-WEATHER TROPHY (H'cap) (Qualifier) (II) (0-70) (Class E) £2,788.00 (£844.00: £412.00: £196.00)

1m (Equitrack) GOING: minus 0.62 sec per fur (FS) 3-30 (3-33)

Sweet Supposin (IRE) (61)*(70+) (KMcAuliffe)* 3-9-5 RCochrane(10) (hdwy over 3f out: led 2f out: clr over 1f out: eased wl ins fnl f)..............................— **1**
4265[8] Kintwyn **(65)***(71) (DRLaing)* 4-9-11 GBardwell(11) (b.hind: outpcd: hdwy over 1f out: r.o ins fnl f)..1¼ **2**
3165[3] Invocation **(68)***(71) (AMoore)* 7-9-9 (5) AWhelan(7) (b.nr hind: hld up: rdn over 2f out: r.o one pce)..1½ **3**
4226* Battle Colours (IRE) **(64)***(64)*(Fav)*(MrsJRRamsden)* 5-9-10 SWilliams(3) (lost pl over 6f out: rallied over 1f out: one pce)..1¼ **4**
4270[5] Sarum **(52)***(50) (CPWildman)* 8-8-5 (7) SLanigan(6) (nvr nr to chal)..........................¾ **5**
4270[2] Digpast (IRE) **(43)***(41) (RJO'Sullivan)* 4-8-3b DBiggs(8) (b: lw: a.p: ev ch 2f out: wknd fnl f)..s.h **6**
4264[8] Kissavos **(46)***(42) (CCElsey)* 8-8-6 MFenton(4) (b.hind: a.p: rdn 3f out: wkng whn n.m.r 1f out)...¾ **7**
4271[2] Buddy's Friend (IRE) **(63)***(57) (RJRWilliams)* 6-9-2 (7) SarahThompson(2) (nvr nr to chal)..¾ **8**
4289[7] Ragazzo (IRE) **(44)***(34) (KOCunningham-Brown)* 4-8-4 DHarrison(5) (led 3f: led 4f out to 2f out: sn wknd)..1¾ **9**
4289[6] Flying Wind **(45)***(21) (GLMoore)* 5-8-0 (5)ow4 SSanders(9) (lw: bhd fnl 4f) 7 **10**
4264[3] Shansi (IRE) **(43)***(13) (MDIUsher)* 3-8-1v RStreet(1) (b: led 5f out to 4f out: wknd over 2f out) 3 **11**
4255[13] Palacegate Gold (IRE) **(41)***(7) (RJHodges)* 5-7-10 (5) DWright(12) (bhd fnl 5f)..........2 **12**

3/1 Battle Colours (IRE), **4/1** Digpast (IRE), **9/2** Buddy's Friend (IRE), **12/1** Kintwyn, Sarum, Invocation, Flying Wind, Shansi (IRE), **16/1** Palacegate Gold (IRE), Kissavos, **20/1** SWEET SUPPOSIN (IRE), **33/1** Ragazzo (IRE), CSF £213.81 CT £2,711.10 TOTE £58.60: £10.40 £4.20 £2.20 (£209.30) OWNER Mount Juliet Stud (LAMBOURN) BRED Ballylinch Stud Ltd 12 Rn

1m 37.91 (1.51) SF: 36/40/40/35/22/13/15/-/-/-/-/-

WEIGHT FOR AGE 3yo-2lb

T/Plpt: £119.20 (92.38 Tckts). T/Qdpt: £6.60 (10.7 Tckts) AK

4295a-SAINT-CLOUD (France) (L-H) Saturday December 3rd (Good to soft)

4304a PRIX GEORGES DE KERHALLET £6,293.00

1m

Astair (FR) *(92) (France)* 4-8-11 WMongil ....— **1**
Aladien (FR) *(92) (France)* 4-8-8 (3) SMaillot ....hd **2**
4236a[2] Lost Prairie (USA) *(92) (France)* 4-8-9 (3) CNora ....½ **3**
4236a[7] Metal Storm (FR) *(KOCunningham-Brown)* 6-8-11 GGuignard (btn further 9½l) **8**

TOTE3.80F: 1.50F 2.50F 1.20F (37.40F) OWNER Marquesa de Moratalla BRED Marquise Soledad de Moratalla in France 9 Rn 1m 56.6 SF: -/-/-/-

STERREBEEK (Brussels, Belgium) (L-H) Sunday December 4th (Standard)

4305a PRIX CAROLINE £1,122.00

1m (dirt)

4056[5] **Real Madrid** *(41) (GPEnright)* 3-8-2b VJanssen ....— **1**
Sovereign Rocket (USA) *(55) (Belgium)* 9-9-10b(4) PHenkens 5 **2**

Wonder Wood (GER) *(39) (Belgium)* 8-9-4b GAxler 3 **3**
TOTE 127BF: 27BF 26BF 18BF (475BF) OWNER Mr Chris Wall BRED Chris Wall 9 Rn 1m 40.1

4252-WOLVERHAMPTON (L-H)
Saturday December 10th (Standard)

4306 AS YOU LIKE IT H'CAP (0-70) (Class E) £2,801.00 (£848.00: £414.00: £197.00) **6f (Fibresand)** GOING: minus 0.13 sec per fur (FS) 7-00 (7-02)

4278[4] **Little Ibnr (60)***(67) (PDEvans)* 3-8-13 (5) SSanders(2) (w ldrs: led wl over 1f out: drvn out)....................— **1**
4278[2] Mustn't Grumble (IRE) **(75)***(78)*(Fav)*(WSCunningham)* 4-10-5 AClark(9) (a.p: 3rd st: r.o one pce fnl f)....................1¼ **2**
4099[6] Chinour (IRE) **(67)***(66) (EJAlston)* 6-9-11 JQuinn(12) (hdwy & 4th st: r.o ins fnl f)....................1½ **3**
4220[10] Leigh Crofter **(70)***(66) (PDCundell)* 5-9-9b(5) AProcter(4) (led after 1f: hdd & 2nd st: one pce fnl f)....................¾ **4**
4263[4] Formidable Liz **(57)***(45) (KRBurke)* 4-9-1 DaleGibson(3) (led 1f: 5th & wkng st)......3 **5**
4278[14] Farmer Jock **(50)***(34) (MrsNMacauley)* 12-8-8 MFenton(7) (hld up: c wd & hdwy over 1f out: nvr nr to chal)....................1½ **6**
4107[12] Jon's Choice **(69)***(50) (BPreece)* 6-9-13 TWall(10) (prom: 7th & wkng st)....................1 **7**
4241[8] It's so Easy **(61)***(36) (MJohnston)* 3-9-5 TWilliams(13) (chsd ldrs: hrd rdn over 2f out: 6th & wkng st)....................2½ **8**
4278[9] Primula Bairn **(62)***(32) (MrsJRRamsden)* 4-9-6v DHarrison(6) (n.d)....................1¾ **9**
4289[14] Farndale **(57)***(26) (JBerry)* 7-9-1 LeTolboll(11) (a bhd)....................hd **10**
4263[2] Forgotten Dancer (IRE) **(61)***(25) (RIngram)* 3-9-0 (5) SDrowne(5) (a bhd)....................1¾ **11**
4243[15] White Lady **(66)***(27) (RWEmery)* 3-9-10 RCochrane(1) (a bhd)....................1 **12**
3446[9] Anotherone to Note **(62)***(10) (MJHeaton-Ellis)* 3-9-6v RPerham(8) (a bhd)....................5 **13**

4/1 Mustn't Grumble (IRE), **11/2** LITTLE IBNR, **7/1** Chinour (IRE), Forgotten Dancer (IRE), **8/1** Leigh Crofter, **9/1** Primula Bairn (6/1-10/1), Jon's Choice, **12/1** It's so Easy, **14/1** Anotherone to Note, Farndale, **16/1** Formidable Liz, **20/1** White Lady, **25/1** Farmer Jock, CSF £27.57 CT £148.27 TOTE £5.40: £2.30 £1.80 £4.00 (£17.10) OWNER Swinnerton Transport Ltd (WELSHPOOL) BRED R. E. Waugh 13 Rn 1m 14.1 (2.90) SF: 51/62/51/52/32/21/36/-/-/-/-/-/-

4307 WINTER'S TALE CLAIMING STKS (2-Y.O) (Class F) £2,190.00 (£615.00: £300.00) **1m 100y (Fibresand)** GOING: minus 0.13 sec per fur (FS) 7-30 (7-34)

4240[7] **Something Speedy (IRE) (47)***(48) (PJBevan)* 2-8-5 NCarlisle(1) (bhd: hdwy over 1f out: str run to ld post)....................— **1**
4216[11] Tonka **(60)***(45) (DJGMurraySmith)* 2-8-2 AMackay(13) (plld hrd: a.p: 2nd st: hrd rdn to ld nr fin: hdd post)....................s.h **2**
4256[4] Reponist **(49)***(40)*(Fav)*(MJCamacho)* 2-7-13v DaleGibson(12) (plld hrd: led over 1f: led over 5f out: clr 2f out: wknd ins fnl f: hdd nr fin)....................¾ **3**
4280[10] Brownlows **(45)***(51) (MPBielby)* 2-8-7 (5) SDrowne(6) (bhd: hdwy & 6th st: nt qckn fnl f)....................1 **4**
3815[25] Dowdency **(45)***(36) (JAPickering)* 2-7-10 (5) DWright(8) (5th st: no hdwy)....................2 **5**
4279[9] Bitch **(56)***(36)*(Fav)*(DNicholls)* 2-8-0 (5)ow6 AWhelan(4) (hdwy 4f out: 4th st: wknd fnl f)....................2 **6**
4259[4] Joseno **(45)***(25) (BPalling)* 2-8-1 NAdams(5) (swtg: hdwy over 3f out: 3rd st: wknd over 1f out)....................3½ **7**
4298[11] Bold Palmella (IRE) **(60)***(23) (MrsJRRamsden)* 2-7-13 GBardwell(7) (nvr trbld ldrs)....................hd **8**
4240[14] Chadleigh Walk (IRE) **(44)***(18) (RHollinshead)* 2-8-8 RCochrane(11) (hdwy over 3f out: 7th & wkng st)....................7 **9**
4219[11] Kitty Waterjet **(45)***(13) (BEllison)* 2-7-11v(7)ow3 CTeague(3) (led 7f out tl over 5f out: wknd over 3f out)....................nk **10**
3438[8] Silent Sky **(54)***(12) (CJHill)* 2-8-3 TWilliams(2) (lw: prom: hrd rdn 4f out: wkng whn hmpd 3f out)....................s.h **11**
3566[7] Pennine Lady (IRE) **(37)***(—) (PABlockley)* 2-7-4b(7) SLanigan(9) (plld hrd: prom tl wknd over 3f out: t.o)....................10 **12**
4225[14] Pink Petal *(—) (CJHill)* 2-8-3 JQuinn(10) (a bhd: t.o)....................2½ **13**

9/2 Reponist, Bitch, **5/1** Bold Palmella (IRE), **11/2** Tonka, **6/1** Joseno, **14/1** SOMETHING SPEEDY (IRE), Chadleigh Walk (IRE), **16/1** Brownlows, Silent Sky, Pink Petal, **25/1** Dowdency, **33/1** Pennine Lady (IRE), Kitty Waterjet, CSF £84.41 TOTE £18.00: £3.90 £2.60 £1.80 (£43.50) OWNER Mrs Elisabeth Draper (UTTOXETER) BRED Tom Capehart 13 Rn
1m 52.1 (8.10) SF: 4/1/-/7/-/-/-/-/-/-/-/-/-

4308 MEASURE FOR MEASURE STKS (Mdn 2-Y.O) (Class D) £2,801.00 (£848.00: £414.00: £197.00) **1m 100y (Fibresand)** GOING: minus 0.13 sec (FS) 8-00 (8-04)

4162⁵ **Legitimate (78)***(83) (NACallaghan)* 2-9-0 TIves(12) (lw: hld up: hdwy 3f out: 2nd st: edgd rt & led ins fnl f: pushed out)......— **1**
4240² Komreyev Dancer **(63)***(77)*(Fav)*(ABailey)* 2-9-0 AMackay(10) (a.p: led wl over 2f out: rdn wl over 1f out: hdd ins fnl f: one pce)......3 **2**
4240⁶ Frome Lad *(53) (WGMTurner)* 2-9-0 RPerham(5) (bhd: hdwy & 5th st: one pce)..12 **3**
4254² Bold Effort (FR) *(50) (KOCunningham-Brown)* 2-9-0 DHarrison(3) (prom: 3rd & wkng st)......1½ **4**
1278⁴ Vade Retro Satanas (FR) **(53)***(36) (CTinkler)* 2-9-0 MFenton(9) (nvr nr ldrs)......7 **5**
4280¹³ Docklands Courier *(36) (BJMcMath)* 2-9-0 RCochrane(8) (chsd ldrs over 5f)......hd **6**
4279⁵ Norman Prince (IRE) **(62)***(35) (NPLittmoden)* 2-9-0 MRimmer(1) (plld hrd: prom: 6th & wkng st)......nk **7**
4256² One for Jeannie *(28+) (ABailey)* 2-8-4 (5) DWright(13) (hld up & bhd: carried wd st: nvr plcd to chal)......1 **8**
4254⁷ Bargash **(54)***(33) (PDEvans)* 2-9-0 JWilliams(2) (lw: prom 5f)......hd **9**
4254⁵ Bretton Princess **(55)***(23) (RHollinshead)* 2-8-9 MWigham(11) (a bhd)......2½ **10**
2885⁷ Ivy Lilian (IRE) **(49)***(21) (WMBrisbourne)* 2-8-4 (5) AGarth(4) (led over 5f: 4th & wkng st)......1 **11**
Parklife (IRE) *(—) (PCHaslam)* 2-9-0 TWilliams(6) (leggy: lt-f: s.s: a bhd: t.o)......14 **12**
664¹¹ Bordesley Belle *(—) (DNicholls)* 2-8-9 AlexGreaves(7) (prom over 4f: t.o)......7 **13**

7/4 Komreyev Dancer, **11/4** LEGITIMATE, **6/1** Bold Effort (FR), **13/2** One for Jeannie (3/1-7/1), **12/1** Docklands Courier, Parklife (IRE), **14/1** Bargash, Norman Prince (IRE), **20/1** Frome Lad, **25/1** Vade Retro Satanas (FR), **33/1** Bretton Princess, Ivy Lilian (IRE), Bordesley Belle, CSF £8.80 TOTE £4.20: £1.60 £1.30 £10.70 (£2.80) OWNER Mr F. M. Kalla (NEWMARKET) BRED P. D. and Mrs Player 13 Rn 1m 48.7 (4.70) SF: 43/37/16/12/-/-/-/-/-/-/-/-/-

4309 CORIOLANUS H'CAP (0-75) (Class D) £3,055.45 (£925.60: £452.30: £215.65) **1m 1f 79y (Fibresand)** GOING: minus 0.13 sec per fur (FS) 8-30 (8-30)

4277⁷ **Bentico (57)***(63) (MrsNMacauley)* 5-8-6 (5) SSanders(6) (hld up: hdwy & 5th st: rdn to ld ins fnl f: r.o wl)......— **1**
4274⁴ Red Whirlwind **(52)***(56) (BJMcMath)* 4-8-6 RCochrane(9) (a.p: led wl over 2f out tl ins fnl f)......1¼ **2**
4223⁵ Spring Flyer (IRE) **(64)***(65) (ABailey)* 4-8-13 (5) DWright(13) (led over 5f out: rdn & hdd wl over 2f out: 2nd st: one pce)......2 **3**
4274* Sandmoor Denim **(70)***(69)*(Fav)*(SRBowring)* 7-9-3 (7) GStrange(4) (hld up: hdwy over 3f out: 3rd st: btn whn swtchd lft ins fnl f)......1 **4**
4264⁵ Polonez Prima **(67)***(63) (JEBanks)* 7-9-2 (5) LNewton(10) (hdwy & 4th st: one pce)1¾ **5**
1649¹⁰ Hightown Cavalier **(58)***(50) (RJHodges)* 3-8-5 (5)ow1 SDrowne(3) (prom: 7th & wkng st)......2½ **6**
3925¹⁸ Sozzled **(67)***(53) (ABarrow)* 3-9-5 AMackay(2) (led over 6f: 6th & wkng st)......3½ **7**
4227¹⁰ Desert Lore **(64)***(43) (MrsJRRamsden)* 3-9-2 MWigham(7) (prom tl wknd over 3f out)......4 **8**
2330⁹ Palacegate Jo (IRE) **(66)***(41) (RHollinshead)* 3-9-4 TIves(11) (a bhd)......2½ **9**
4227¹³ Off the Air (IRE) **(54)***(20) (ICampbell)* 3-8-6v DHarrison(5) (a bhd)......1¼ **10**
Brief Respite (IRE) **(70)***(38) (EJAlston)* 3-9-8 JQuinn(12) (a bhd)......1¼ **11**
2328* Ivan the Terrible (IRE) **(55)***(25) (BEllison)* 6-8-9 RPerham(1) (hld up & plld hrd: a bhd)......3 **12**
2345* Mon Rouge (IRE) **(64)***(4) (BPJBaugh)* 3-9-2 TWall(8) (prom tl rdn & wknd 4f out: t.o)......15 **13**

7/4 Sandmoor Denim, **5/1** Spring Flyer (IRE), **6/1** Polonez Prima, **7/1** Red Whirlwind, **10/1** Ivan the Terrible (IRE), **12/1** Desert Lore, **14/1** Palacegate Jo (IRE), **16/1** BENTICO, Mon Rouge (IRE), **20/1** Off the Air (IRE), Brief Respite (IRE), **25/1** Sozzled, Hightown Cavalier, CSF £123.48 CT £598.57 TOTE £27.30: £5.30 £1.90 £1.50 (£110.70) OWNER Mr G. Wiltshire (MELTON MOWBRAY) BRED Britton House Stud 13 Rn 2m 1.3 (5.30) SF: 40/33/41/45/41/27/29/-/-/-/-/-/-
WEIGHT FOR AGE 3yo-2lb

4310 CYMBELINE (S) STKS (Class F) £2,190.00 (£615.00: £300.00) **7f (Fibresand)** GOING: minus 0.13 sec per fur (FS) 9-00 (9-04)

4243⁵ **Four of Spades (62)***(67) (WSCunningham)* 3-9-1b AClark(3) (a.p: led over 4f out: clr 1f out: drvn out)......— **1**

4278[7] Alpine Johnny **(54)***(64) (RHollinshead)* 3-8-10 (5) AGarth(12) (hdwy over 3f out: 4th st: r.o wl ins fnl f)....1¼ **2**
4237[4] Nakita **(60)***(50) (CNAllen)* 3-7-13 (7) MBaird(9) (s.i.s: hdwy & 5th st: one pce fnl f).2½ **3**
4237[6] Sense of Priority **(61)***(51) (MHEasterby)* 5-8-12 TIves(11) (a.p: jnd ldr over 2f out: 2nd st: one pce appr fnl f)....1¾ **4**
3854[18] So Intrepid (IRE) **(74)***(52) (JMBradley)* 4-9-2 AMackay(6) (lw: hld up & bhd: hdwy & 6th st: nvr nr to chal)....1½ **5**
4281[7] Ballad Dancer **(43)***(46) (JMackie)* 9-8-12 TWilliams(8) (nvr nr to chal)....¾ **6**
4226[11] Gallery Artist (IRE) **(63)***(49) (RGuest)* 6-8-9 (7) SEiffert(4) (7th st: no hdwy)....½ **7**
4237[2] Frisky Miss (IRE) **(67)***(43)*(Fav)*(JBerry)* 3-8-3 (7) PRoberts(10) (led 6f out tl over 4f out: 3rd st: wknd over 1f out)....½ **8**
4139[10] Ashdren **(59)***(42) (AHarrison)* 7-9-2 RCochrane(2) (sn outpcd)....3 **9**
4053[15] Noeprob (USA) **(48)***(32) (RJHodges)* 4-8-11 JWilliams(1) (swtg: a bhd)....2½ **10**
4278[8] Nuclear Express **(46)***(27) (JMBradley)* 7-8-7 (5) DWright(5) (led 1f: hrd rdn & wknd over 4f out)....3 **11**
4237* Walk the Beat **(66)***(—) (RSimpson)* 4-9-2 SDrowne(7) .... **W**

5/2 Frisky Miss (IRE), **3/1** Nakita, **5/1** Walk the Beat, Sense of Priority, **9/1** FOUR OF SPADES, **12/1** Alpine Johnny (8/1-14/1), **14/1** So Intrepid (IRE), **16/1** Gallery Artist (IRE), Noeprob (USA), **20/1** Ballad Dancer, Ashdren, **25/1** Nuclear Express, CSF £84.97 TOTE £10.00: £2.90 £2.90 £1.40 (£28.60) OWNER Mr B. L. Cassidy (YARM) BRED Hesmonds Stud Ltd 11 Rn No bid
1m 30.8 (6.80) SF: 10/8/-/-/-/-/-/-/-/-/-
WEIGHT FOR AGE 3yo-1lb

4311 COMEDY OF ERRORS H'CAP (0-60) (Class F) £2,398.00 (£673.00: £328.00)
1m 4f (Fibresand) GOING: minus 0.13 sec per fur (FS) 9-30 (9-30)

4218[3] **Noufari (FR) (56)***(65) (RHollinshead)* 3-9-4 TIves(12) (hdwy 4f out: 4th st: hrd rdn over 1f out: hung lft ins fnl f: r.o to ld cl home)....— **1**
4277[5] Broom Isle **(52)***(60) (DBurchell)* 6-9-1 (5) AProcter(11) (a.p: led 6f out: rdn 3f out: edgd rt ins fnl f: hdd cl home)....¾ **2**
4277* Joseph's Wine (IRE) **(61)***(65)*(Fav)*(DNicholls)* 5-10-1b AlexGreaves(6) (hld up & plld hrd: chsd ldr 6f out: 2nd st: ev ch 1f out: wknd fnl 100y)....3 **3**
4273* Telephus **(48)***(50) (BJMcMath)* 5-9-2 RCochrane(3) (hld up & bhd: hdwy 4f out: 3rd st: hrd rdn over 1f out: one pce)....1¼ **4**
4274[7] Straw Thatch **(44)***(42) (MrsJRRamsden)* 5-8-12 MWigham(4) (lw: bhd: hdwy & 6th st: nvr trbld ldrs)....3 **5**
4287[4] Well and Truly **(50)***(46) (BAMcMahon)* 7-9-4 AClark(9) (5th st: no hdwy)....1½ **6**
3786[7] Carrolls Marc (IRE) **(50)***(27) (PCHaslam)* 6-9-4 TWilliams(2) (prom: rdn over 5f out: wknd over 3f out)....15 **7**
4281[13] Salska **(56)***(32) (PJBevan)* 3-9-4 TWall(10) (hrd rdn over 4f out: bhd fnl 3f)....nk **8**
3909[16] Rocky Bay **(44)***(19) (BJLlewellyn)* 5-8-7 (5) SDrowne(8) (bhd fnl 3f)....1 **9**
Wassl's Nanny (IRE) **(52)***(14) (BEllison)* 5-9-6v RPerham(7) (led 6f: wknd over 4f out: t.o)....11 **10**
4239[4] Venture Fourth **(45)***(—) (EJAlston)* 5-8-13 JQuinn(1) (a bhd: t.o)....11 **11**
4301[12] Gallant Jack (IRE) **(49)***(—) (JGMO'Shea)* 5-9-3 AMackay(5) (prom: rdn over 5f out: wknd over 4f out: t.o)....20 **12**

5/2 Joseph's Wine (IRE), **4/1** Telephus, **6/1** Well and Truly, **7/1** NOUFARI (FR), **10/1** Broom Isle, Straw Thatch, Carrolls Marc (IRE), **16/1** Venture Fourth, **20/1** Rocky Bay, Salska, Gallant Jack (IRE), **33/1** Wassl's Nanny (IRE), CSF £71.33 CT £206.60 TOTE £6.60: £1.60 £3.80 £2.30 (£37.60) OWNER Ed Weetman (Haulage & Storage) Ltd (UPPER LONGDON) BRED His Highness The Aga Khans Studs S.C. in France 12 Rn 2m 39.6 (8.60) SF: 35/36/41/28/20/24/5/-/-/-/-/-
WEIGHT FOR AGE 3yo-6lb

T/Plpt: £583.80 (21.03 Tckts). T/Qdpt: £149.20 (1.1 Tckts) KH

4296-LINGFIELD (L-H)
Wednesday December 14th (Standard)

4312 ROBERT MARCKS 75th BIRTHDAY H'CAP (Amateurs) (0-75) (Class G) £2,400.00 (£675.00: £330.00)
1m 2f (Equitrack) GOING: minus 0.57 sec per fur (FS) 12-10 (12-12)

3137[9] **Our Eddie (66)***(77+) (BGubby)* 5-11-3v(3) MrsMBusby(3) (a.p: led over 1f out: r.o wl)....— **1**
4140[2] Conspicuous (IRE) **(64)***(71) (LGCottrell)* 4-11-1 (3) MrLJefford(5) (a.p: led over 4f out tl over 1f out: unable qckn)....2½ **2**

4012[11] Credit Squeeze **(68)***(74) (RFJohnsonHoughton)* 4-11-5 (3) MissEJohnsonHoughton(11) (lw: hld up: shkn up fnl f: r.o wl)........................½ **3**
4223[7] Can Can Charlie **(63)***(63) (JPearce)* 4-11-3 MrsLPearce(4) (hdwy over 1f out: r.o)..4 **4**
4296[3] Captain Marmalade **(51)***(49) (DTThom)* 5-10-5 MissDianaJones(2) (gd hdwy over 1f out: r.o wl: too much to do)..1 **5**
3785[2] Mulciber **(74)***(72) (GHarwood)* 6-12-0 MissAHarwood(7) (b: rdn over 4f out: no hdwy fnl 3f)..hd **6**
4296[9] Rose Elegance **(54)***(51) (OO'Neill)* 5-10-1 (7) MrAMitchell(9) (s.s: nvr nrr)................½ **7**
4301[2] Hatta Sunshine (USA) **(45)***(39)*(Fav)*(AMoore)* 4-9-10 (3)ow3 MrTMcCarthy(12) (hdwy 5f out: rdn over 2f out: wknd 1f out)..2 **8**
4260[13] Mister O'Grady (IRE) **(46)***(39) (GLMoore)* 3-9-3v(7) MrsJoanMoore(13) (led over 5f: wknd over 2f out) ....¾ **9**
Inzar **(58)***(51) (PMitchell)* 3-10-1 (7) MissFBurke(14) (rdn over 6f out: bhd fnl 2f).....hd **10**
4284[9] Malingerer **(43)***(17) (DAWilson)* 3-9-7 MissElaineBronson(6) (b.off hind: a bhd) 12 **11**
4260[12] Bill Moon **(39)***(9) (PJFeilden)* 8-9-4 (3) MissJFeilden(1) (lw: prom 5f)......................2½ **12**

LONG HANDICAP Malingerer 8-8 Bill Moon 9-5

100/30 Hatta Sunshine (USA), **7/2** Captain Marmalade, **5/1** Mulciber, Conspicuous (IRE), **10/1** Can Can Charlie, OUR EDDIE, **12/1** Credit Squeeze, **14/1** Inzar, **20/1** Mister O'Grady (IRE), **25/1** Bill Moon, **33/1** Rose Elegance, Malingerer, CSF £58.00 CT £563.35 TOTE £8.10: £2.40 £2.30 £4.50 (£50.60) OWNER Brian Gubby Ltd (BAGSHOT) BRED Brian Gubby Ltd 12 Rn

2m 6.11 (3.11) SF: 59/53/56/45/33/54/35/-/-/-/-/-

WEIGHT FOR AGE 3yo-4lb

4313 MADAGANS COMPANY SERVICES H'CAP (I) (0-60) (Class F) £2,624.10 (£737.60: £360.30) 7f (Equitrack) GOING: minus 0.57 sec (FST) 12-40 (12-44)

4241[4] **Bogart (54)***(63) (CWFairhurst)* 3-9-7 RCochrane(16) (a.p: led & edgd lft over 1f out: drvn out)..— **1**
4289[3] Sharp Imp **(43)***(51)*(Fav)*(RMFlower)* 4-8-11b JQuinn(6) (hdwy over 2f out: hung lft over 1f out: ev ch ins fnl f: r.o)..nk **2**
4303[6] Digpast (IRE) **(48)***(51) (RJO'Sullivan)* 4-9-2b DBiggs(15) (b: a.p: led 3f out tl hdd & hmpd on ins over 1f out: unable qckn) 2½ **3**
4270[3] Our Shadee (USA) **(49)***(49) (KTIvory)* 4-9-3v GBardwell(4) (a.p: rdn over 3f out: one pce)...1½ **4**
4269* Bichette **(47)***(36)*(Fav)*(GLMoore)* 4-9-1 BRouse(12) (b.off fore: led 1f: lost pl over 4f out: rallied over 3f out: one pce)..5 **5**
4269[5] Faynaz **(37)***(23) (AMoore)* 8-8-5 TWilliams(1) (b: lw: lost pl 5f out: r.o one pce fnl 2f)..1¼ **6**
4101[21] Ebony Blaze **(58)***(42) (CPWildman)* 3-9-11 DHarrison(2) (nvr nr to chal) 1 **7**
4266[9] Crafty Cricketer **(35)***(17) (RVoorspuy)* 3-7-9b(7) DDenby(13) (led 6f out to 5f out: wknd over 2f out) ....¾ **8**
1901[14] Prince Rodney **(46)***(22) (CJDrewe)* 5-9-0b RPerham(7) (b: lw: led 5f out to 3f out: sn wknd)...3 **9**
2690[9] Storm Bidder **(48)***(23) (BGubby)* 3-8-10 (5) AWhelan(3) (prom over 3f)....................nk **10**
3219[8] Quinzii Martin **(43)***(17) (DHaydnJones)* 6-8-11v JWilliams(11) (bhd fnl 2f) ....½ **11**
4302[11] Mutinique **(44)***(14) (BAPearce)* 3-8-4 (7) PRoberts(5) (prom 4f) 2 **12**
4302[5] Calisar **(46)***(15) (PHowling)* 4-9-0b AMackay(10) (hdwy 3f out: wknd over 2f out)...hd **13**
4053[19] Oakley Manor **(42)***(—) (PDEvans)* 3-8-4 (5) SSanders(9) (lw: a bhd)........................8 **14**
4253[7] Trioming **(49)***(—) (APJones)* 8-9-3 NAdams(14) (bhd fnl 5f)..................................¾ **15**
3707[12] No What I Mean (IRE) **(35)***(—) (JSMoore)* 3-7-11b(5) DWright(8) (a bhd)...............nk **16**

7/2 Sharp Imp, Bichette, **5/1** BOGART, **7/1** Digpast (IRE), Our Shadee (USA), **12/1** Faynaz, **14/1** Quinzii Martin, **16/1** Calisar, **20/1** Ebony Blaze, Mutinique, **25/1** Storm Bidder, Trioming, **33/1** No What I Mean (IRE), Oakley Manor, Prince Rodney, **50/1** Crafty Cricketer, CSF £23.47 CT £120.93 TOTE £6.50: £1.90 £1.10 £2.10 £2.10 (£13.30) OWNER A P Development Products (N. E) Ltd (MIDDLEHAM) BRED Robert T. Cartwright 16 Rn

1m 25.1 (2.10) SF: 32/23/22/19/6/-/11/-/-/-/-/-/-/-/-/-

WEIGHT FOR AGE 3yo-1lb

4314 ARCHFORM ORTHODONTIC LABORATORIES CLAIMING STKS (2-Y.O) (Class E) £2,788.00 (£844.00: £412.00: £196.00) 7f (Equitrack) GOING: minus 0.57 sec per fur (FS) 1-10 (1-16)

4299[4] **Iron Man (IRE) (57)***(58) (LordHuntingdon)* 2-7-11v(5) AWhelan(11) (a.p: rdn over 2f out: led wl ins fnl f: r.o wl)..— **1**
4279[4] Pleasure Beach **(67)***(65)*(Fav)*(WAO'Gorman)* 2-8-7 (3) EmmaO'Gorman(9) (hld up: rdn over 1f out: led ins fnl f: sn hdd: r.o)..nk **2**

4282[12] Fair Ella (IRE) **(44)***(49) (JFfitch-Heyes)* 2-7-12b NAdams(10) (rdn over 3f out: lost pl over 2f out: rallied over 1f out: r.o wl ins fnl f)....2 **3**
4262[4] Bon Secret (IRE) **(58)***(55) (TJNaughton)* 2-8-5 DHarrison(3) (lw: led 6f out tl ins fnl f: 3rd & btn whn squeezed out nr fin)....½ **4**
4054[12] Irie Mon (IRE) *(51) (JWHills)* 2-8-8 ow3 RCochrane(5) (hdwy over 1f out: nvr nrr)..3½ **5**
4286[6] Persian Conquest (IRE) **(55)***(48) (RIngram)* 2-8-7 JWilliams(4) (hdwy over 1f out: nvr nrr)....¾ **6**
4267[7] Fiery Footsteps **(60)***(39) (PHowling)* 2-7-13 JQuinn(12) (a.p: ev ch wl over 1f out: wknd fnl f)....½ **7**
4286[9] Baby Bob **(48)***(33) (JMPEustace)* 2-7-6b(5)ow1 NVarley(2) (prom over 4f)....1¾ **8**
4222[9] Two Chalk **(50)***(41) (PDEvans)* 2-8-1 (5)ow2 SSanders(13) (led 1f: wknd 2f out)......hd **9**
3768[11] Kirov Protege (IRE) **(52)***(28) (RWArmstrong)* 2-8-4 MFenton(7) (bhd fnl 5f)....5 **10**
Dingo Warrior *(25) (JFfitch-Heyes)* 2-8-3 AMackay(8) (w'like: bit bkwd: s.s: a bhd) 1 **11**
4262[6] Witney-de-Bergerac (IRE) **(64)***(23) (JSMoore)* 2-8-9 AClark(1) (bhd fnl 4f)....4 **12**
4254[6] Sharp Tern **(54)***(10) (BSmart)* 2-7-13 GBardwell(14) (hld up: rdn over 4f out: wknd 3f out)....1½ **13**
4256[3] Water Bebe (IRE) **(53)***(10) (GCBravery)* 2-8-4 TWilliams(6) (bhd fnl 5f)....2½ **14**

9/4 Pleasure Beach, **5/1** Bon Secret (IRE), **11/2** IRON MAN (IRE), Fiery Footsteps, **13/2** Witney-de-Bergerac (IRE), **8/1** Water Bebe (IRE), **14/1** Persian Conquest (IRE), **25/1** Fair Ella (IRE), Two Chalk, Kirov Protege (IRE), Baby Bob, Irie Mon (IRE), Sharp Tern, Dingo Warrior, CSF £18.11 TOTE £8.70: £2.60 £1.80 £12.00 (£14.60) OWNER Mrs Amanda Simmons (WEST ILSLEY) BRED Conquering Hero Syndicate in Ireland 14 Rn 1m 25.88 (2.88) SF: 6/13/-/3/-/-/-/-/-/-/-/-/-/-
Iron Man (IRE) clmd F Freeman £3,000

4315 HUDSON DENTAL EQUIPMENT STKS (Mdn 2-Y.O) (Class D) £3,288.75 (£996.00: £486.50: £231.75) 6f (Equitrack) GOING: minus 0.57 (FST) 1-40 (1-41)

3605[10] **Go Hever Golf (68)***(74+) (TJNaughton)* 2-9-0 GCarter(7) (b.nr hind: lw: mde all: clr 2f out: unchal)....— **1**
4077[7] Komodo (USA) **(68)***(54) (DRCElsworth)* 2-9-0 DHarrison(6) (lw: chsd wnr over 1f: rdn 4f out: chsd wnr over 1f out: no imp)....8 **2**
4308[8] One for Jeannie *(46) (ABailey)* 2-8-4 (5) DWright(3) (hld up: rdn 3f out: one pce).....1 **3**
3460[12] Alka International **(55)***(46) (JWhite)* 2-9-0 JWilliams(4) (outpcd: nvr nrr)....1¾ **4**
Fallal (IRE) *(28) (KMcAuliffe)* 2-8-9 AClark(5) (unf: bit bkwd: chsd wnr over 4f out tl over 1f out: sn wknd)....5 **5**
4282[3] Friendly Lady (USA) **(67)***(—)*(Fav)*(WAO'Gorman)* 2-8-6 (3) EmmaO'Gorman(1) (stumbled s: a bhd)....9 **6**
4254[11] Laureate *(—) (DHaydnJones)* 2-8-9 AMackay(2) (bit bkwd: a bhd)....5 **7**

9/4 Friendly Lady (USA), **3/1** GO HEVER GOLF, Komodo (USA), One for Jeannie, **9/1** Fallal (IRE), **14/1** Alka International, **50/1** Laureate, CSF £13.03 TOTE £3.20: £1.90 £2.00 (£5.30) OWNER Hever Racing Club (EPSOM) BRED Ronald Popely 7 Rn
1m 11.67 (1.07) SF: 35/14/7/9/-/-/-

4316 MADAGANS H'CAP (0-85) (Class D) £3,228.95 (£977.60: £477.30: £227.15) 5f (Equitrack) GOING: minus 0.57 sec per fur (FS) 2-10 (2-13)

4278[10] **Croft Pool (72)***(75) (JAGlover)* 3-9-8 TIves(7) (lw: hld up: rdn over 3f out: led ins fnl f: r.o wl)....— **1**
4263* Silent Expression **(75)***(78)*(Fav)*(BJMeehan)* 4-9-11 RCochrane(8) (lw: hld up: rdn over 2f out: ev ch ins fnl f: r.o wl)....s.h **2**
4231[3] Press the Bell **(78)***(75)*(Fav)*(JBerry)* 4-9-7 (7) PRoberts(5) (w ldr: led over 2f out tl ins fnl f: unable qckn)....2 **3**
4266[3] Swift Nick Nevison **(43)***(31) (KTIvory)* 3-7-7 GBardwell(6) (led over 2f: wknd ins fnl f)....3 **4**
4268[8] Granmas Delight **(57)***(42) (KTIvory)* 3-8-2 (5) NVarley(4) (outpcd: nvr nr to chal) .....¾ **5**
4258[8] Cradle Days **(75)***(59) (RCSpicer)* 5-9-11 MFenton(1) (a bhd)....nk **6**
4266[6] Rocky Two **(62)***(41) (PHowling)* 3-8-12b AMackay(3) (squeezed out over 4f out: a bhd)....1¾ **7**
3506[12] Baton Bleu **(48)***(26) (PHowling)* 3-7-12 JQuinn(2) (lw: hld up: rdn over 2f out: wknd over 1f out)....nk **8**
LONG HANDICAP Swift Nick Nevison 7-3

2/1 Silent Expression, Press the Bell, **5/1** CROFT POOL, **10/1** Swift Nick Nevison, **12/1** Rocky Two, **14/1** Cradle Days, **20/1** Granmas Delight, **50/1** Baton Bleu, CSF £14.52 CT £23.20 TOTE £5.70: £1.60 £1.80 £1.20 (£7.80) OWNER Countrywide Classics Ltd (WORKSOP) BRED J. S. Bell 8 Rn 59.4 secs (1.20) SF: 37/40/36/-/5/20/5/-

4317

MADAGANS COMPANY SERVICES H'CAP (II) (0-60) (Class F) £2,624.10 (£737.60: £360.30) **7f (Equitrack)** GOING: minus 0.57 sec per fur (FS) 2-40 (2-44)

4270* **Maid Welcome (54)***(56) (MrsNMacauley)* 7-9-1v(7) AmandaSanders(16) (racd wd: mde virtually all: r.o wl)........— **1**
4289² Rad **(56)***(56)*(Fav)*(SPCWoods)* 4-9-5 (5) NVarley(10) (b.hind: hdwy over 2f out: hrd rdn over 1f out: r.o)........1 **2**
4265¹⁰ Zinbaq **(44)***(39) (CJBenstead)* 8-8-12 TWilliams(15) (a.p: ev ch wl over 1f out: unable qckn)........2½ **3**
4296¹² Swallow Ridge (IRE) **(36)***(29) (RJO'Sullivan)* 5-8-4 DBiggs(1) (rdn over 2f out: hdwy over 1f out: r.o wl ins fnl f)........¾ **4**
4283⁵ Europharm Lassie **(51)***(42) (GLMoore)* 3-9-4 BRouse(5) (hdwy over 3f out: hrd rdn over 1f out: one pce)........1 **5**
4303⁷ Kissavos **(46)***(36) (CCElsey)* 8-9-0 MFenton(6) (b.hind: lw: hld up: hrd rdn over 1f out: wknd ins fnl f)........½ **6**
4018²³ Pirates Gold (IRE) **(60)***(49) (JWhite)* 4-9-9 (5) SDrowne(14) (lw: hdwy over 4f out: hrd rdn over 2f out: wknd fnl f)........nk **7**
4269⁴ Charlies Dream (IRE) **(45)***(33) (KRBurke)* 3-8-12 JQuinn(2) (nvr nr to chal)........½ **8**
4288³ Joint Effort (IRE) **(41)***(18) (AMoore)* 3-8-3 (5) AWhelan(13) (prom over 5f)........5 **9**
4283⁷ Rustic League (IRE) **(43)***(18) (TJNaughton)* 3-8-3 (7) VHalliday(9) (b.hind: prom 4f).1 **10**
4268¹⁰ As Such (IRE) **(59)***(28) (NACallaghan)* 3-9-12 TIves(4) (bhd fnl 2f)........3 **11**
4274¹² Akabusi **(54)***(21) (LordHuntingdon)* 3-9-7 DHarrison(11) (prom 4f)........¾ **12**
3707¹¹ Lady Valient **(43)***(6) (MJHaynes)* 3-8-10 AClark(3) (s.i.s: a bhd)........1¾ **13**
4102¹² Hi Penny **(45)***(6) (KTIvory)* 3-8-12 JWilliams(8) (a bhd)........1 **14**
4258⁹ Victoria Hall **(55)***(8) (WGMTurner)* 4-9-4 (5) JDSmith(7) (swtg: bhd fnl 4f)........4 **15**
4289¹⁶ Lady Broker **(55)***(6) (ABailey)* 4-9-4 (5) DWright(12) (hdwy over 4f out: wknd over 3f out)........¾ **16**

3/1 Rad, **11/2** Charlies Dream (IRE), **6/1** Joint Effort (IRE), **9/1** MAID WELCOME, **10/1** Kissavos, Lady Broker, **12/1** Rustic League (IRE), **14/1** Akabusi, **16/1** Europharm Lassie, **20/1** Zinbaq, As Such (IRE), Victoria Hall, Pirates Gold (IRE), **25/1** Swallow Ridge (IRE), **33/1** Hi Penny, Lady Valient, CSF £36.15 CT £506.78 TOTE £7.40: £2.00 £1.80 £4.70 £30.20 (£12.10) OWNER Mrs Anna Sanders (MELTON MOWBRAY) BRED Doublet Ltd 16 Rn

1m 25.49 (2.49) SF: 29/28/12/4/14/9/21/6/-/-/-/-/-/-/-/-

WEIGHT FOR AGE 3yo-1lb

4318

MADAGANS LEGAL SERVICES APP'CE H'CAP (0-65) (Class F) £2,540.80 (£713.80: £348.40)
1m 5f (Equitrack) GOING: minus 0.57 sec per fur (FS) 3-10 (3-11)

4276² **Scalp 'em (IRE) (42)***(49) (PDEvans)* 6-8-3 (3) GMilligan(7) (hld up: led over 3f out: hrd rdn over 1f out: r.o wl)........— **1**
4124⁴ Admirals Secret (USA) **(64)***(70)*(Fav)*(CFWall)* 5-9-9 (5) CWebb(5) (b.hind: lw: stdy hdwy over 2f out: hrd rdn over 1f out: r.o)........1 **2**
4296² Queen of Shannon (IRE) **(49)***(53) (BJMeehan)* 6-8-13 DaneO'Neill(11) (b.hind: hdwy over 4f out: rdn over 1f out: unable qckn)........2 **3**
4273³ Glow Forum **(39)***(43) (GLMoore)* 3-7-4 (7)ow1 CarolineHovington(2) (lw: hld up: hrd rdn over 1f out: r.o)........hd **4**
4300⁷ Royal Circus **(37)***(39) (JGMO'Shea)* 5-7-10 (5) DDenby(9) (led over 9f: wknd fnl f)........1½ **5**
4300⁵ Dancing Diamond (IRE) **(47)***(46) (MissBSanders)* 4-8-4h(7) AmandaBowen(10) (lw: chsd ldr 7f out to 3f out: wknd over 1f out)........2½ **6**
4208³ Arian Spirit (IRE) **(35)***(33) (WJMusson)* 3-7-7 MDwyer(8) (nvr nr to chal)........½ **7**
4273⁴ Young Lucky **(35)***(31) (CPWildman)* 3-7-7 SLanigan(12) (chsd ldr 6f: wknd over 2f out)........2 **8**
3707⁸ Priscilla Rose **(43)***(39) (CNAllen)* 3-7-10 (5) AEddery(4) (a bhd)........nk **9**
3120¹² Cone Lane **(36)***(31) (BGubby)* 8-8-0 ow1 GMitchell(3) (bit bkwd: prom 8f)........1 **10**
1313⁴ Nearly Honest **(39)***(32) (RJHodges)* 6-8-0 (3) AmandaSanders(6) (lw: a bhd)........1½ **11**
3440⁷ Dawn Flight **(50)***(43) (JRJenkins)* 5-9-0 CAdamson(1) (bhd fnl 11f)........nk **12**

LONG HANDICAP Arian Spirit (IRE) 7-6 Young Lucky 7-3

15/8 Admirals Secret (USA), **7/1** Queen of Shannon (IRE), **8/1** Dancing Diamond (IRE), **10/1** SCALP 'EM (IRE), Glow Forum, Dawn Flight, Young Lucky, **12/1** Arian Spirit (IRE), **14/1** Royal Circus, Cone Lane, Nearly Honest, **20/1** Priscilla Rose, CSF £29.32 CT £138.43 TOTE £9.30: £2.80 £1.80 £2.70 (£20.60) OWNER Mrs L. A. Windsor (WELSHPOOL) BRED Ivan Allen 12 Rn

2m 45.65 (3.15) SF: 26/46/30/15/17/23/6/-/-/-/-/-

WEIGHT FOR AGE 3yo-6lb

T/Plpt: £49.80 (230.47 Tckts). T/Qdpt: £6.10 (4.35 Tckts) AK

4274-SOUTHWELL (L-H)
Thursday December 15th (Standard)
No Tote returns 1st race - electrical failure

4319
BERKSHIRE H'CAP (I) (0-65) (Class F) £2,398.00 (£673.00: £328.00)
1m (Fibresand) Stalls: Low GOING: minus 0.06 sec per fur (Std) 11-50 (11-51)

3259 12 **Cicerone (46)***(52) (JLHarris)* 4-9-1 RCochrane(7) (chsd ldrs: led 3f out: sn clr: drvn out) ....— **1**
4281 9 Guesstimation (USA) **(50)***(51) (JPearce)* 5-9-5 GBardwell(14) (hdwy & 5th st: rdn over 1f out: r.o one pce) 2½ **2**
4224 6 Arrasas Lady **(40)***(36) (RMFlower)* 4-8-4 (5) SDrowne(2) (w ldrs: 3rd st: one pce fnl 2f) 2½ **3**
4227 2 Hawwam **(55)***(48)*(Fav)*(EJAlston)* 8-9-10 JQuinn(11) (lw: hld up: hdwy over 2f out: styd on same pce fnl f) 1½ **4**
4281 8 Valiant Man **(57)***(49) (JHetherton)* 3-9-10 TIves(3) (lw: hld up: hdwy 3f out: rdn over 2f out: nt rch ldrs) ....s.h **5**
4270 13 Dome Patrol **(49)***(25) (WRMuir)* 3-9-2 MFenton(4) (sme hdwy fnl 2f: n.d) 8 **6**
4274 2 Certain Way (IRE) **(54)***(19) (NPLittmoden)* 4-9-4 (5) TGMcLaughlin(1) (chsd ldrs: btn whn hmpd wl over 1f out) 6 **7**
4260 7 Rave-on-Hadley (IRE) **(46)***(9) (ABailey)* 4-8-10 (5) DWright(15) (swtg: lw: nvr nrr) ...¾ **8**
195 9 Jolly Swagman **(45)***(6) (LordHuntingdon)* 3-8-12 DHarrison(5) (lw: s.i.s: effrt over 3f out: wknd over 1f out) ....½ **9**
4296 10 Danseuse Davis (FR) **(47)***(4) (KMcAuliffe)* 3-9-0 AClark(12) (hdwy over 3f out: wknd fnl 2f) 2 **10**
4288 9 Obsidian Grey **(50)***(4) (MissLCSiddall)* 7-9-0 (5) PMcCabe(9) (swtchd ½-wy: n.d) 2 **11**
4269 8 Monsieur Petong **(50)***(—) (DNicholls)* 3-9-3 AlexGreaves(8) (lw: hld up & a bhd) 2½ **12**
4212 8 High Holme **(55)***(—) (DTThom)* 3-9-8v SWebster(10) (led after 2f to 3f out: eased whn btn appr fnl f) 4 **13**
4241 11 Scottish Park **(45)***(—) (RWEmery)* 5-9-0 TWilliams(13) (drvn along: chsd ldrs: 4th st: sn wknd: t.o) ....dist **14**
4214 12 Kentucky Flyer **(42)***(—) (JFBottomley)* 3-8-9 GCarter(6) (led 2f: lost pl over 3f out: t.o) 1¾ **15**

3/1 Hawwam, **7/2** Certain Way (IRE), **7/1** Guesstimation (USA), **8/1** Arrasas Lady, **9/1** Jolly Swagman, **14/1** Rave-on-Hadley (IRE), CICERONE, Scottish Park, Dome Patrol, **16/1** Valiant Man, Monsieur Petong, **20/1** Obsidian Grey, **25/1** Danseuse Davis (FR), High Holme, **33/1** Kentucky Flyer, CSF £109.44 CT £788.76 OWNER Dr C. W. Ashpole (MELTON MOWBRAY) BRED Aldershawe Stud Farm 15 Rn 1m 45.4 (6.10) SF: 34/33/19/30/29/6/1/-/-/-/-/-/-/-/-
WEIGHT FOR AGE 3yo-2lb

4320
BERKSHIRE H'CAP (II) (0-65) (Class F) £2,398.00 (£673.00: £328.00)
1m (Fibresand) Stalls: Low GOING: minus 0.06 sec per fur (Std) 12-20 (12-20)

4309* **Bentico (62)***(65) (MrsNMacauley)* 5-9-8 (5x) (5) SSanders(9) (a.p: 5th st: rdn to ld over 1f out: hld on wl) ....— **1**
4241 6 No Submission (USA) **(62)***(64) (DWChapman)* 8-9-13 JQuinn(14) (lw: w ldr: 2nd st: ev ch fnl f: r.o) ....nk **2**
2553 8 Sharp Gazelle **(40)***(37) (BSmart)* 4-8-5 DHarrison(3) (swtg: mde most tl hdd over 1f out: one pce) 2½ **3**
351 6 Camden's Ransom (USA) **(60)***(55) (GBBalding)* 7-9-6 (5) SDrowne(11) (lw: hdwy over 3f out: rdn & kpt on fnl f) 1 **4**
4281* Langtonian **(51)***(44)*(Fav)*(JLEyre)* 5-9-2v NCarlisle(15) (lw: chsd ldrs gng wl: 4th st: chal 2f out: sn rdn: grad wknd) ....¾ **5**
1005 8 Gallop to Glory **(40)***(27) (ALForbes)* 4-8-5 ow2 SWilliams(10) (swtg: chsd ldrs: sn drvn along: no hdwy fnl 2f) 3 **6**
4214 2 Mazeeka (IRE) **(62)***(45) (WAO'Gorman)* 3-9-8 (3) EmmaO'Gorman(13) (lw: hld up: effrt over 2f out: nt rch ldrs) 1½ **7**
4163 8 Ochos Rios (IRE) **(61)***(44) (BSRothwell)* 3-9-10 MFenton(5) (sn bhd: sme late hdwy: nvr nrr) ....hd **8**
4274 3 Mislemani (IRE) **(48)***(30) (AGNewcombe)* 4-8-8 (5) NVarley(7) (chsd ldrs: 3rd & rdn st: wknd wl over 1f out) 1 **9**
4265 11 Aljaz **(60)***(39) (DTThom)* 4-9-11 AMackay(4) (b: hdwy ½-wy: 6th st: wknd 2f out).1½ **10**
4274 5 Mighty Kingdom (IRE) **(43)***(13) (RWEmery)* 3-8-6 ow1 AClark(8) (lw: nvr nr ldrs) 4 **11**
4300 12 Well Suited **(46)***(11) (BJMcMath)* 4-8-11 RCochrane(6) (b: b.hind: s.i.s: a bhd) 3 **12**
4255* Heathyards Lady (USA) **(52)***(10) (RHollinshead)* 3-9-1 TIves(12) (chsd ldrs: rdn & wknd over 2f out) 3 **13**

4243[9] Grey Ancona (IRE) **(39)***(—) (EJAlston)* 5-8-4 GBardwell(2) (a in rr) 1½ **14**
3331[10] Hay Dance **(52)***(—) (JPLeigh)* 3-9-1 GCarter(16) (a bhd: t.o) 5 **15**
4257[7] Tu Opes **(65)***(—) (JLHarris)* 3-10-0 DaleGibson(1) (lw: reard s: a wl bhd: t.o).......10 **16**

13/8 Langtonian, **6/1** Aljaz, **7/1** Camden's Ransom (USA), **9/1** Mazeeka (IRE), BENTICO, **10/1** Mislemani (IRE), **12/1** Ochos Rios (IRE), No Submission (USA), **14/1** Heathyards Lady (USA), Mighty Kingdom (IRE), Tu Opes, Grey Ancona (IRE), **25/1** Well Suited, Sharp Gazelle, **33/1** Hay Dance, Gallop to Glory, CSF £122.21 CT £2,450.17 TOTE £15.20: £2.80 £2.80 £3.70 £2.50 (£39.50) OWNER Mr G. Wiltshire (MELTON MOWBRAY) BRED Britton House Stud 16 Rn
1m 45.8 (6.50) SF: 41/41/15/32/22/7/22/-/-/-/-/-/-/-/-/-
WEIGHT FOR AGE 3yo-2lb

4321 BUCKINGHAM (S) STKS (2-Y.O) (Class G) £2,190.00 (£615.00: £300.00)
1m (Fibresand) Stalls: Low GOING: minus 0.06 sec per fur (Std) 12-50 (12-52)

4216[10] **Poly Road (51)***(54) (MRChannon)* 2-8-6 DHarrison(9) (chsd ldrs: 4th st: rdn to ld ins fnl f: r.o wl) ....— **1**
4308[7] Norman Prince (IRE) **(62)***(54) (NPLittmoden)* 2-8-11 MRimmer(8) (bhd: hdwy over 3f out: led over 1f out tl ins fnl f: no ex)....................2½ **2**
3345[10] Runforaction (IRE) **(56)***(48) (BSRothwell)* 2-8-11 MFenton(11) (a.p: 2nd st: led over 2f out tl over 1f out: one pce) 3 **3**
4230[12] High Flown (USA) **(60)***(43)*(Fav)*(MrsJRRamsden)* 2-8-11 SWilliams(15) (lw: a.p: 5th st: sn rdn: r.o one pce)....................2½ **4**
4043[13] Samana Cay **(48)***(43) (DNicholls)* 2-8-11 RCochrane(13) (s.i.s: hdwy fnl 2f: nrst fin)....................hd **5**
4207[6] Risky Rose **(48)***(38) (RHollinshead)* 2-8-1 (5) AGarth(12) (mid div tl styd on fnl f: nvr nrr)....................s.h **6**
4280[7] Fools Millyons (IRE) **(46)***(40) (WBentley)* 2-8-11 JFanning(16) (lw: chsd ldrs: 3rd st: wknd over 1f out)....................1¼ **7**
4307[6] Bitch **(56)***(38) (DNicholls)* 2-8-11 AlexGreaves(2) (lw: hdwy 4f out: rdn & wknd over 1f out) ....¾ **8**
4299[5] Hever Golf Lady **(42)***(33) (TJNaughton)* 2-8-6 GBardwell(4) (sn outpcd & rdn along: n.d)....................hd **9**
4106[4] Magical Belle (IRE) **(47)***(37) (CASmith)* 2-8-11v TIves(5) (nvr nr ldrs)....................½ **10**
4219[8] Silktail (IRE) **(50)***(29)*(Fav)*(JBerry)* 2-8-6 GCarter(6) (sn pushed along: chsd ldrs tl lost pl over 3f out) 1¼ **11**
4307[7] Joseno **(45)***(21) (BPalling)* 2-8-6 AClark(7) (hmpd after 100y: gd hdwy & 6th st: sn wknd)....................4 **12**
4207[8] Jersey Belle **(48)***(11) (PJMakin)* 2-8-6 RPerham(1) (led ½-wy tl over 2f out: sn rdn & wknd) 5 **13**
3951[7] Pash **(45)***(—) (CWCElsey)* 2-8-6v NKennedy(14) (a bhd: t.o)....................10 **14**
3744[10] Singleton Barn (IRE) **(45)***(—) (CNAllen)* 2-8-4 (7) MBaird(3) (hmpd after 1f: a bhd: t.o)....................nk **15**
4213[14] Meesonette **(40)***(—) (DWChapman)* 2-8-6 NCarlisle(10) (led 4f: sn lost pl: t.o).....10 **16**

4/1 High Flown (USA), Silktail (IRE), **8/1** Bitch, Magical Belle (IRE), Jersey Belle, **9/1** Norman Prince (IRE), **10/1** Runforaction (IRE), Samana Cay, Hever Golf Lady, **14/1** Joseno, Pash, POLY ROAD, **20/1** Risky Rose, **33/1** Fools Millyons (IRE), Singleton Barn (IRE), Meesonette, CSF £141.73 TOTE £22.20: £5.00 £5.70 £5.10 (£225.00) OWNER Sheet & Roll Convertors Ltd (UPPER LAMBOURN) BRED W. Beasley 16 Rn 1m 47.2 (7.90) SF: 8/9/3/-/-/-/-/-/-/-/-/-/-/-/-/-
Bt in 5,600 gns. Silktail (IRE) clmd R Emery £6,000

4322 PLUTO STKS (0-60) (Class F) £2,398.00 (£673.00: £328.00)
6f (Fibresand) Stalls: Low GOING: minus 0.06 sec per fur (Std) 1-20 (1-25)

4306* **Little Ibnr (60)***(67)*(Fav)*(PDEvans)* 3-8-9 (5) SSanders(16) (lw: a.p: led 2f out: drvn clr fnl f) ....— **1**
4204[7] Super Benz **(60)***(61) (FJO'Mahony)* 8-9-0 GCarter(15) (b: mid div: outpcd ½-wy: hdwy over 2f out: r.o wl ins fnl f)....................2½ **2**
4253* Scored Again **(59)***(56) (MJHeaton-Ellis)* 4-8-7 (7) AmandaSanders(14) (b: led tl hdd & hung lft 2f out: one pce)....................2 **3**
4306[5] Formidable Liz **(57)***(48) (KRBurke)* 4-8-9 DaleGibson(1) (w ldrs: rdn 2f out: r.o one pce)....................1 **4**
4102[3] Panther (IRE) **(50)***(52) (JHetherton)* 4-9-0 NKennedy(7) (bhd tl r.o wl appr fnl f: nvr nrr)....................nk **5**
4243[6] Dauntless Fort **(52)***(42) (BWMurray)* 3-8-9 TIves(4) (swvd rt s: chsd ldrs: one pce appr fnl f) 2 **6**
4255[6] Grandee **(44)***(45) (BAMcMahon)* 3-9-0 RCochrane(5) (hmpd s: r.o fnl 2f: nrst fin) ..½ **7**

4253[5] Shadow Jury **(60)**_(40) (DWChapman)_ 4-8-11 JQuinn(11) (chsd ldrs tl rdn & outpcd over 2f out)........½ **8**
3698[3] Miss Tipsy **(37)**_(30) (WWHaigh)_ 3-8-6 AClark(6) (lw: in tch: rdn 2f out: sn btn).........2 **9**
4281[4] Orthorhombus **(56)**_(32) (DJSCosgrove)_ 5-8-6b(5) LNewton(2) (chsd ldrs: sn drvn along: wknd over 2f out)........1 **10**
4297[3] Featherstone Lane **(60)**_(27) (MissLCSiddall)_ 3-8-11v DHarrison(8) (a in rr)...........1¾ **11**
4283[4] Dance and Sing (IRE) **(34)**_(22) (DLWilliams)_ 4-8-11 NAdams(3) (s.i.s: outpcd)........2 **12**
Meeson Times **(53)**_(14) (RBastiman)_ 6-8-6 NCarlisle(9) (chsd ldrs over 3f).............1 **13**
2935[8] Joellise **(31)**_(10) (JBalding)_ 4-7-13 (7) ClaireBalding(10) (a bhd)........1¼ **14**
4214[4] Make the Break **(60)**_(5) (SCoathup)_ 3-9-0 TWilliams(13) (chsd ldrs tl wknd qckly over 2f out)........5 **15**
3494[10] Oscar the Second (IRE) **(30)**_(—) (CWFairhurst)_ 4-8-11 MFenton(12) (a bhd & outpcd)........1 **16**

4/1 LITTLE IBNR, **5/1** Featherstone Lane, **11/2** Scored Again, **6/1** Dauntless Fort, **10/1** Make the Break, Super Benz, **12/1** Formidable Liz, Orthorhombus, Shadow Jury, **14/1** Panther (IRE), Meeson Times, **25/1** Dance and Sing (IRE), Grandee, **33/1** Joellise, Miss Tipsy, Oscar the Second (IRE), CSF £45.62 TOTE £3.90: £2.00 £3.70 £3.30 (£37.40) OWNER Swinnerton Transport Ltd (WELSHPOOL) BRED R. E. Waugh 16 Rn

1m 18.1 (4.60) SF: 32/25/20/13/17/7/10/-/-/-/-/-/-/-/-/-

4323

MONTGOMERY H'CAP (0-65) (Class F) £2,398.00 (£673.00: £328.00)
1m 6f (Fibresand) Stalls: High GOING: minus 0.06 sec per fur (Std) 1-50 (1-54)

4277[3] **El Nido (56)**_(66) (MJCamacho)_ 6-9-5 RCochrane(2) (trckd ldrs: led 2f out: drvn out)........— **1**
4244[4] Tremendisto **(47)**_(55) (CaptJWilson)_ 4-8-5 (5) NVarley(9) (chsd ldrs: drvn along 8f out: styd on u.p fnl 2f)........1½ **2**
4244* Absalom's Pillar **(65)**_(71)_(Fav)_(JHetherton)_ 4-10-0 NCarlisle(11) (lw: hld up & bhd: hdwy 5f out: edgd lft: nvr rchd ldrs)........1¾ **3**
3343[3] Mrs Jawleyford (USA) **(54)**_(58) (CSmith)_ 6-8-10 (7) MBaird(13) (b: hdwy ½-wy: led 3f out to 2f out: one pce)........2 **4**
4276[6] Greenacres Star **(37)**_(38) (BAMcMahon)_ 4-8-0 TWilliams(6) (lw: prom early: sn outpcd: hdwy to chse ldrs 4f out: sn rdn & no imp)........2½ **5**
4261[6] Rose of Glenn **(51)**_(50) (BPalling)_ 3-8-2 (5)ow2 SSanders(3) (prom: outpcd over 2f out: n.d after)........½ **6**
4276[8] Fiery Sun **(35)**_(34) (JLEyre)_ 9-7-12 JQuinn(12) (a in tch: reminders 4f out: outpcd over 2f out)........¾ **7**
4229* Sassiver (USA) **(47)**_(43) (RHollinshead)_ 4-8-10 TIves(14) (lw: s.i.s: bhd: hdwy & in tch 3f out: wknd 2f out)........2½ **8**
4244[3] Blowedifiknow **(44)**_(26) (JWharton)_ 4-8-7v AClark(16) (led after 3f to 7f out: lost pl over 2f out)........13 **9**
4277[6] Modest Hope (USA) **(50)**_(28) (BRichmond)_ 7-8-13 NAdams(10) (lw: hld up & bhd: hdwy over 3f out: wknd 2f out)........4 **10**
4244[2] Swordking (IRE) **(54)**_(26) (JLHarris)_ 5-9-3 SWilliams(5) (led 3f: led 7f out to 3f out: wknd & eased over 1f out)........5 **11**
4272[10] Kiyas **(44)**_(5) (BJMcMath)_ 3-8-0 AMackay(7) (hdwy & in tch 5f out: wknd 2f out).....9 **12**
3981[14] Lord Nitrogen (USA) **(44)**_(—) (RWEmery)_ 4-8-7 DHarrison(15) (sn drvn along: hdwy to chse ldrs 10f out: wknd 4f out)........8 **13**
4274[16] Tanfirion Chief **(49)**_(—) (RonaldThompson)_ 3-8-5 ow1 MFenton(4) (t.o 3f out)........11 **14**
Mill de Lease **(30)**_(—) (JDooler)_ 9-7-7 GBardwell(8) (b: chsd ldrs tl drvn along & lost pl 9f out: sn wl bhd: t.o)........13 **15**
3169[14] Marinos **(40)**_(—) (HJCollingridge)_ 3-7-5 (5) CHawksley(1) (t.o 7f out)........dist **16**

LONG HANDICAP Mill de Lease 6-11

11/4 Absalom's Pillar, **5/1** EL NIDO, **7/1** Sassiver (USA), **9/1** Blowedifiknow, **10/1** Swordking (IRE), Mrs Jawleyford (USA), **11/1** Modest Hope (USA), Rose of Glenn, **14/1** Kiyas, Tremendisto, **16/1** Greenacres Star, **33/1** Fiery Sun, Lord Nitrogen (USA), Tanfirion Chief, Marinos, **50/1** Mill de Lease, CSF £72.28 CT £219.21 TOTE £6.20: £2.10 £7.00 £1.70 £3.60 (£61.00) OWNER M K Slinger & A Stuart (MALTON) BRED M. J. Camacho 16 Rn

3m 11.7 (12.00) SF: 32/23/38/26/8/14/4/1/-/-/-/-/-/-/-/-

WEIGHT FOR AGE 3yo-7lb

4324

ESSEX STKS (Mdn 2-Y.O) (Class D) £3,408.35 (£1,032.80: £504.90: £240.95)
5f (Fibresand) Stalls: High GOING: minus 0.06 sec per fur (Std) 2-20 (2-27)

4286[4] **Wasblest** _(56) (MJohnston)_ 2-8-9 TWilliams(10) (mde virtually all: styd on wl fnl f)........— **1**
2812[6] Avant Huit **(58)**_(51) (MrsNMacauley)_ 2-8-9 MFenton(6) (lw: a chsng ldrs: nt qckn fnl f)........1½ **2**

4254[3] Posted Abroad (IRE) *(56+)* *(SirMarkPrescott)* 2-9-0 CNutter(11) (s.i.s: sn outpcd: hdwy over 1f out: styd on wl nr fin)....s.h **3**
4137[4] Pursuance (IRE) **(60)***(51)* *(JBalding)* 2-8-7 (7) JEdmunds(8) (a in tch: effrt ½-wy: styd on same pce appr fnl f)....1½ **4**
4238[2] La Belle Dominique **(64)***(46)*(Fav)*(SGKnight)* 2-8-4 (5) SDrowne(2) (w ldrs: ev ch over 1f out: wknd ins fnl f)....s.h **5**
Merrie le Bow *(44)* *(PatMitchell)* 2-8-9 JMcLaughlin(16) (scope: bit bkwd: dwlt: bhd tl kpt on fnl f)....½ **6**
4267[3] Nadwaty (IRE) **(58)***(36)* *(JDBethell)* 2-8-9 RCochrane(4) (trckd ldrs tl grad wknd over 1f out)....2½ **7**
3951[9] Komlucky **(52)***(35)* *(FJO'Mahony)* 2-8-9 GCarter(15) (hmpd s: bhd tl kpt on appr fnl f)....hd **8**
4267[6] Royal Dancer **(40)***(31)* *(TTClement)* 2-8-4 (5) NVarley(3) (prom 3f: sn wknd)....1¼ **9**
4238[7] Pats Delight **(50)***(31)* *(SCoathup)* 2-8-4 (7)ow2 SharronJames(14) (swvd rt s: in tch tl outpcd 2f out)....½ **10**
Pc's Cruiser (IRE) *(31)* *(MCChapman)* 2-9-0 SWebster(12) (w'like: bit bkwd: s.i.s: outpcd tl sme hdwy over 1f out)....¾ **11**
4256[11] Lawnswood Lady **(40)***(26)* *(RHollinshead)* 2-8-10 ow1 TIves(13) (nvr wnt pce)....nk **12**
4286[7] Jovale **(52)***(24)* *(SGNorton)* 2-9-0 SWilliams(9) (nvr wnt pce)....2 **13**
4254[8] Winterbottom *(19)* *(ICampbell)* 2-9-0 AMackay(1) (dwlt: nvr nr ldrs)....1¾ **14**
4222[12] Carnival of Light *(—)* *(JBalding)* 2-8-9 NAdams(7) (trckd ldrs tl lost pl ½-wy: sn bhd & eased)....9 **15**
4123[11] Branston Kristy **(52)***(—)* *(CSmith)* 2-8-2v(7) MBaird(5) (b.hind: in tch: rdn & wnt lft ½-wy: sn bhd)....4 **16**

2/1 La Belle Dominique, **9/4** Posted Abroad (IRE), **6/1** WASBLEST, **8/1** Nadwaty (IRE), **10/1** Avant Huit, **12/1** Branston Kristy, **14/1** Pursuance (IRE), Winterbottom, **16/1** Pats Delight, **20/1** Lawnswood Lady, **25/1** Merrie le Bow, **33/1** Komlucky, Jovale, Royal Dancer, Carnival of Light, Pc's Cruiser (IRE), CSF £70.03 TOTE £7.80: £2.50 £2.30 £1.60 (£92.90) OWNER Mrs S.E.Dingwall (MIDDLEHAM) BRED M. B. Small 16 Rn
61.8 secs (3.80) SF: 24/20/24/19/14/12/4/-/-/-/-/-/-/-/-/-

4325 CHURCHILL H'CAP (0-70) (Class E) £2,905.00 (£880.00: £430.00: £205.00)
5f (Fibresand) Stalls: High GOING: minus 0.06 sec per fur (Std) 2-50 (2-57)

4253[3] **Kalar** **(58)***(67)* *(DWChapman)* 5-8-9b(7) CTeague(4) (racd far side: mde all: rdn & edgd rt over 1f out: kpt on wl)....— **1**
4288[2] Nineacres **(54)***(61)*(Fav)*(DNicholls)* 3-8-12b AlexGreaves(2) (lw: racd far side: a chsng wnr: nt qckn ins fnl f)....½ **2**
2630[9] Samson-Agonistes **(70)***(74)* *(PDEvans)* 8-9-9 (5) SSanders(5) (b.off fore: racd far side: chsd ldr: sn drvn along: kpt on fnl f)....1 **3**
3791[8] Black Boy (IRE) **(41)***(40)* *(RFMarvin)* 5-7-6b(7) ClaireBalding(1) (racd far side: hdwy ½-wy: styd on wl fnl f)....1½ **4**
3806[13] Cheeky Chappy **(39)***(37)* *(DWChapman)* 3-7-11b JQuinn(3) (racd far side: prom over 3f: grad wknd)....nk **5**
Dundeelin **(50)***(45)* *(JLEyre)* 3-8-8v NCarlisle(17) (racd stands' side: bhd tl kpt on wl fnl f)....¾ **6**
4255[10] Daaniera (IRE) **(46)***(41)* *(PHowling)* 4-8-4b AMackay(14) (dwlt: racd centre: bhd tl kpt on fnl f)....s.h **7**
4255[5] Brisas **(47)***(41)* *(CWFairhurst)* 7-8-5v JFanning(8) (racd centre: in tch: outpcd ½-wy: n.d after)....hd **8**
4253[4] Lady Sheriff **(43)***(36)* *(MWEasterby)* 3-8-1b DaleGibson(12) (sltly hmpd s: nvr wnt pce)....hd **9**
3978[16] Tauber **(51)***(42)* *(PatMitchell)* 10-8-9 RCochrane(13) (racd stands' side: outpcd fr ½-wy)....½ **10**
4266[4] Tommy Tempest **(41)***(31)* *(ABailey)* 5-7-8 (5) DWright(7) (racd centre: chsd ldrs 3f: sn wknd)....nk **11**
4231[8] Sir Tasker **(62)***(46)* *(JLHarris)* 6-9-6 TIves(16) (racd stands' side: nvr wnt pce)....2 **12**
4253[C] Arc Lamp **(52)***(33)* *(JAGlover)* 8-8-10 SWilliams(10) (bmpd s: racd centre: nvr wnt pce)....1 **13**
4268[6] Super Rocky **(59)***(37)* *(RBastiman)* 5-8-12 (5)ow1 HBastiman(6) (racd far side: chsd ldrs tl wknd over 1f out)....1 **14**
3838[17] Muzz (IRE) **(70)***(47)* *(MJohnston)* 3-9-7 (7) OliverCasey(15) (lw: racd stands' side: a outpcd)....hd **15**
4266[7] Tyrian Purple (IRE) **(64)***(38)* *(TJNaughton)* 6-9-1b(7) VHalliday(11) (lw: sltly hmpd s: a bhd)....1 **16**
4255[12] Bold Aristocrat (IRE) **(44)***(—)* *(RHollinshead)* 3-7-11 (5) AGarth(9) (racd centre: bhd: hung bdly lft over 1f out: eased)....6 **17**

4/1 Nineacres, **7/1** KALAR, Arc Lamp, **8/1** Sir Tasker, Tommy Tempest, **9/1** Tyrian Purple (IRE), **10/1** Brisas, Dundeelin, **11/1** Lady Sheriff, Super Rocky, **12/1** Samson-Agonistes, **16/1** Muzz (IRE), **25/1** Black Boy (IRE), Cheeky Chappy, Daaniera (IRE), **33/1** Tauber, Bold Aristocrat (IRE), CSF £37.86 CT £326.79 TOTE £11.40: £2.10 £1.80 £4.90 £3.40 (£20.00) OWNER Mr E. Stockdale (YORK) BRED C. C. and Mrs Pryor 17 Rn

61.1 secs (3.10) SF: 42/37/49/16/13/21/18/-/-/-/-/-/-/-/-/-/-

4326

HAMPSHIRE H'CAP (0-80) (Class D) £3,393.40 (£1,028.20: £502.60: £239.80)
1m 3f Stalls: Low GOING: minus 0.06 sec per fur (Std) 3-20 (3-25)

4311[3] **Joseph's Wine (IRE) (61)**_(71+)_(Fav)_(DNicholls)_ 5-8-9b AlexGreaves(6) (hld up gng wl: smooth hdwy over 4f out: led over 1f out: shkn up & sn clr)........— **1**
4252[8] Hillzah (USA) **(78)**_(83) (RBastiman)_ 6-9-7 (5) HBastiman(10) (hld up: hdwy & in tch over 3f out: kpt on fnl 2f: no ch w wnr)........4 **2**
4252[6] Chief of Staff **(77)**_(75) (JPearce)_ 5-9-11 JMcLaughlin(13) (hld up & bhd: styd on fnl 3f: nvr nr to chal)........5 **3**
4252[9] Mad Militant (IRE) **(73)**_(71) (RHollinshead)_ 5-9-7 TIves(3) (hld up: hdwy ½-wy: styd on fnl 2f: nvr rchd ldrs)........hd **4**
4091[15] Broughton's Pride (IRE) **(49)**_(36) (JAGlover)_ 3-7-7 GBardwell(8) (lw: sn trckng ldrs: effrt & chal over 2f out: sn wknd)........8 **5**
4300* Global Dancer **(71)**_(56) (WAO'Gorman)_ 3-8-12 (5x) (3) EmmaO'Gorman(1) (lw: trckd ldrs: effrt over 3f out: rdn & wknd over 2f out)........2 **6**
4300[3] Shabanaz **(66)**_(50) (WRMuir)_ 9-9-0 RCochrane(2) (hdwy to trck ldrs ½-wy: led over 2f out tl hdd & wknd over 1f out)........nk **7**
4252* New Inn **(72)**_(53)_(Fav)_(EWeymes)_ 3-8-11 (5) JMarshall(11) (chsd ldrs: effrt & n.m.r over 2f out: grad wknd)........2½ **8**
4277[2] Tempering **(54)**_(34) (DWChapman)_ 8-8-2 JQuinn(7) (w ldrs: led 6f out tl over 2f out: grad wknd)........1 **9**
4277[9] Westfield Moves (IRE) **(53)**_(32) (HJCollingridge)_ 6-7-10 (5) CHawksley(5) (b: lw: sn outpcd & drvn along: n.d)........nk **10**
4287[11] Pink Brief (IRE) **(52)**_(24) (BJMeehan)_ 3-7-5 (5)ow3 NVarley(12) (b.hind: sn drvn along: led over 8f out to 6f out: lost pl over 4f out: sn bhd)........5 **11**
3850[16] Vishnu (USA) **(80)**_(48) (JLEyre)_ 4-10-0 AClark(9) (a bhd: drvn along ½-wy)........3 **12**
1930[3] View From Above **(79)**_(45) (NJHWalker)_ 8-9-8 (5) SDrowne(14) (in tch tl lost pl over 4f out: sn bhd)........1½ **13**
4241[16] I Fear Nothing **(72)**_(37) (SCWilliams)_ 3-9-2 GCarter(4) (led tl over 8f out: sn drvn along: lost pl 5f out: sn bhd)........nk **14**

LONG HANDICAP Pink Brief (IRE) 7-4

3/1 JOSEPH'S WINE (IRE), New Inn, **5/1** Global Dancer, **6/1** Tempering, **10/1** Westfield Moves (IRE), Chief of Staff, **12/1** Shabanaz, **14/1** Vishnu (USA), View From Above, **16/1** Hillzah (USA), Broughton's Pride (IRE), Mad Militant (IRE), **33/1** Pink Brief (IRE), I Fear Nothing, CSF £54.98 CT £431.11 TOTE £3.70: £1.90 £5.50 £2.80 (£51.60) OWNER Wetherby Racing Bureau Plc (THIRSK) BRED Michael Fennessy 14 Rn 2m 26.8 (5.30) SF: 52/62/54/50/13/30/29/-/-/-/-/-/-/-

WEIGHT FOR AGE 3yo-4lb

T/Plpt: £852.10 (11.34 Tckts). T/Qdpt: £21.00 (4 Tckts) IM/WG

SHA TIN (Kowloon, Hong Kong) (L-H)
Saturday December 10th (Good)

4327a

HONG KONG INTERNATIONAL VASE (Stks) £228,346.00
1m 4f

4005a[3] **Red Bishop (USA)** _(120) (France)_ 6-8-11 CAsmussen ....— **1**
4010a[5] Urgent Request (IRE) _(116) (RAkehurst)_ 4-8-11 TQuinn 2¾ **2**
Wonderful Way (IRE) _(112) (HongKong)_ 4-8-11 BMarcus 2¾ **3**
4002a[2] Alriffa _(114) (RHannon)_ 3-8-10 PatEddery (btn further 1¼l)........ **6**
4183a* Double Trigger (IRE) _(MJohnston)_ 3-8-10 LDettori (btn approx 7l by wnr)........ **7**

TOTE HK134.50: HK37.00 HK20.00 HK29.50 (HK275.50) OWNER Mr Ahmad Saeed BRED Pillar Stud Inc 14 Rn 2m 25.1 SF: -/-/-/-/-/-

4328a

HONG KONG INTERNATIONAL BOWL (Stks) (Gp 3) £228,346.00
7f

3924[2] **Soviet Line (IRE)** _(123) (MRStoute)_ 4-8-11 WRSwinburn ....— **1**
Nijinsky's Gold (USA) _(119) (America)_ 5-8-11b JSantos 1¾ **2**

3051a⁰ Heart Lake *(118) (Ireland)* 3-8-10 LDettori ....hd 3
4006a⁰ Young Ern *(116+) (SDow)* 4-8-11 TQuinn 1 4

TOTE HK56.00: HK21.50 HK23.50 HK18.00 (HK221.00) OWNER Maktoum Al Maktoum (NEWMARKET) BRED Cheveley Park Stud Ltd 14 Rn 1m 22.0 SF: -/-/-/-

4329a HONG KONG INTERNATIONAL CUP (Stks) (Gp 2) £279,090.00 **1m 1f**

State Taj (AUS) *(123) (Australia)* 5-8-11 DOlivier ....— 1
River Majesty (USA) *(122) (USA)* 5-8-11 JSantos ....¾ 2
4191a9 Volochine (IRE) *(121) (France)* 3-8-10 TJarnet 1 3
3394 4 Emperor Jones (USA) *(120) (JHMGosden)* 4-9-0 LDettori (btn further 2l) 5
2992 7 Alflora (IRE) *(CEBrittain)* 5-9-0 MRoberts (btn approx 6 3/4l by wnr) 9

TOTE HK213.70: HK66.10 HK28.20 HK30.10 (HK910.80) OWNER H. T & Mrs L Croll et al BRED Mr P. Mantzaris in Australia 14 Rn 1m 48.4 SF: -/-/-/-

4312-LINGFIELD (L-H)
Saturday December 17th (Standard)

4330 ACE AMBULANCE CLAIMING STKS (2-Y.O) (Class F) £2,552.70 (£717.20: £350.10) 5f (Equitrack) GOING: minus 0.53 sec per fur (FS) 11-40 (11-41)

4256 9 **Lady Pui (46)***(48) (JBerry)* 2-7-8b(5) DarrenMoffatt(2) (chsd ldrs: hrd rdn over 1f out: led nr fin) ....— 1
4314 4 Bon Secret (IRE) **(58)***(55) (TJNaughton)* 2-8-3 (5) SSanders(1) (chsd ldr: hrd rdn & led ins fnl f: hdd nr fin) ....½ 2
4298* Musical Fantasy (IRE) **(54)***(47)*(Fav)*(BJMeehan)* 2-7-12 (5) NVarley(4) (led tl ins fnl f: one pce) ....¾ 3
4144 5 Baileys Sunset (IRE) **(65)***(50)*(Fav)*(MJohnston)* 2-8-12 TWilliams(3) (sn rdn along: hdwy 3f out: rdn & one pce fnl 2f) 2 4
4230 7 Whittingham Girl **(50)***(35) (JBerry)* 2-8-1 LeTolboll(10) (rdn & outpcd early: r.o fnl f: nvr nrr) 1¼ 5
3573 4 Abbey House **(49)***(27) (RGuest)* 2-7-6b(5)ow2 DWright(7) (sn outpcd: nvr nrr) 1¼ 6
4256 5 Mr Slick **(48)***(31) (NACallaghan)* 2-8-4b DHarrison(8) (sn rdn along: a bhd) 1 7
4298 12 Just Jesting **(58)***(31) (GLMoore)* 2-8-1 (5)ow2 AWhelan(5) (mid div: rdn over 2f out: wknd over 1f out) ....½ 8
4275 12 Misstinger **(45)***(20) (WRMuir)* 2-7-11 GBardwell(9) (a bhd) ....½ 9
4262 10 Bills Ploughgirl **(45)***(10) (JSMoore)* 2-7-13 NAdams(6) (mid div: rdn over 2f out: wknd over 1f out) 4 10

7/2 Baileys Sunset (IRE), Musical Fantasy (IRE), **6/1** Bon Secret (IRE), **7/1** Just Jesting, **9/1** LADY PUI (6/1-10/1), Mr Slick (6/1-10/1), **10/1** Abbey House (7/1-12/1), **20/1** Whittingham Girl, **33/1** Misstinger,Bills Ploughgirl, CSF £53.95 TOTE £11.40: £2.20 £1.30 £1.60 (£30.50) OWNERMr John Hulme (COCKERHAM) BRED Bearstone Stud 10 Rn 60.65 secs (2.45) SF: -/6/-/1/-/-/-/-/-/-

4331 ALEX GORRIE STKS (I) (Mdn 2-Y.O) (Class D) £3,258.85 (£986.80: £481.90: £229.45) 7f (Equitrack) GOING: minus 0.53 sec per fur (FS) 12-10 (12-12)

3927 21 **Dark Shot (IRE) (85)***(73+)*(Fav)*(JBerry)* 2-9-0 GCarter(6) (lw: mde all: clr 2f out: comf) ....— 1
4238 11 Always Grace **(57)***(57) (MissGayKelleway)* 2-8-9 TWilliams(2) (chsd ldr: rdn over 2f out: one pce) 5 2
3398 11 Sabicas *(54) (SCWilliams)* 2-8-9 (5) PMcCabe(3) (bhd & outpcd: hdwy over 1f out: r.o) 4 3
See You Again *(46) (RHannon)* 2-9-0 BRouse(5) (w'like: bit bkwd: chsd ldrs: rdn & lost pl over 4f out: r.o one pce fnl f) 4 4
3794 13 Cuban Reef **(53)***(41) (DJSCosgrove)* 2-8-5 (5)ow1 LNewton(9) (chsd ldrs: rdn 3f out: wknd over 1f out) ....½ 5
4285 5 Bally Wonder **(48)***(38) (DMorris)* 2-8-4 (5) DWright(10) (mid div: rdn 4f out: no hdwy fnl 2f) 1 6
4104 4 Storm Flash *(—) (LordHuntingdon)* 2-8-9 DHarrison(11) (chsd ldrs tl rdn & wknd over 2f out) 12 7
4299 10 Iceblock *(—) (MMcCormack)* 2-8-9 AClark(1) (a bhd) 5 8
Fosters Top *(—) (JFfitch-Heyes)* 2-9-0 NAdams(8) (cmpt: bit bkwd: dwlt: a bhd) .nk 9
4173 10 Maple Leaf Candy **(45)***(—) (JAkehurst)* 2-8-9b JQuinn(7) (bhd fnl 4f) 4 10

11/8 DARK SHOT (IRE), **3/1** Storm Flash, **11/2** Always Grace, **6/1** See You Again, **10/1** Bally Wonder, **20/1** Cuban Reef, **33/1** Sabicas, Iceblock, Fosters Top, Maple Leaf Candy, CSF £9.51 TOTE £2.30: £1.50 £1.30 £10.60 (£6.30) OWNER Laurel (Leisure) Ltd (COCKERHAM) BRED Mrs Amanda Skiffington and W. Macauley 10 Rn 1m 27.56 (4.56) SF: 2/-/-/-/-/-/-/-/-/-

4332 MODENA MERCHANTS H'CAP (Amateurs) (0-60) (Class F) £2,600.30 (£730.80: £356.90) **2m (Equitrack)** GOING: minus 0.53 sec per fur (FS) 12-40 (12-44)

4287* **Stalled (IRE) (58)***(69) (PTWalwyn)* 4-11-0 (7) MarchionesBlandford(13) (hld up: hdwy 6f out: led ins fnl f: r.o) — **1**
4287[7] Star Quest **(46)***(56) (JRJenkins)* 7-10-2 (7) MrCAppleby(7) (a.p: chsd ldr fr 6f out: hrd rdn 2f out: ev ch fnl f: r.o) ½ **2**
4287[2] Pride of Britain (CAN) **(52)***(61)*(Fav)*(LGCottrell)* 5-10-10 (5) MrLJefford(5) (lw: led 8f out: hrd rdn & hdd ins fnl f: unable qckn) ¾ **3**
4284[5] Strat's Legacy **(55)***(61) (DWPArbuthnot)* 7-11-1 (3) MrsDArbuthnot(3) (b: b.hind: hld up: hdwy 5f out: rdn over 2f out: one pce) 3½ **4**
4300[4] Arc Bright (IRE) **(53)***(58) (RHollinshead)* 4-11-2b MrTCuff(9) (led 10f out to 8f out: one pce fnl 3f) 1½ **5**
4284[2] Kenyatta (USA) **(38)***(41) (AMoore)* 5-9-8 (7) MrsJoanMoore(12) (nvr nrr) 2½ **6**
4208[10] Ragtime Song **(47)***(45) (AMoore)* 5-10-7 (3) MissJWinter(14) (chsd ldrs: rdn over 2f out: wknd fnl f) 5 **7**
4284[13] Mardood **(51)***(42) (DWChapman)* 9-10-9 (5) MissRClark(10) (nvr nrr) 7 **8**
4318[12] Dawn Flight **(50)***(39) (JRJenkins)* 5-10-6 (7) MrsKHills(4) (chsd ldrs: rdn 4f out: wknd 3f out) 2½ **9**
3976[5] Woodmans Star **(39)***(20) (JJSheehan)* 4-9-11 (5) MrPClose(11) (b: b.hind: prom 3f) 8 **10**
4175[4] Carfax **(36)***(8) (RPCHoad)* 9-9-6b(7) MissLMcIntosh(6) (s.s: a bhd) 10 **11**
4287[6] Dinner At Eight **(50)***(19) (RJO'Sullivan)* 4-10-13 MissAHarwood(1) (prom to ½-wy) 3½ **12**
4318[11] Nearly Honest **(39)***(—) (RJHodges)* 6-9-9 (7) MrsBTory(2) (led 6f) 20 **13**

100/30 Pride of Britain (CAN), **4/1** STALLED (IRE), **5/1** Arc Bright (IRE), **8/1** Strat's Legacy, **12/1** Carfax, Kenyatta (USA), Dinner At Eight, **16/1** Nearly Honest, Dawn Flight, **20/1** Ragtime Song, Star Quest, Woodmans Star, **40/1** Mardood, CSF £72.30 CT £272.99 TOTE £5.00: £2.00 £6.30 £1.80 (£53.60) OWNER Mrs P. T. Walwyn (LAMBOURN) BRED D. Aykroyd 13 Rn
3m 32.04 (8.54) SF: 48/37/42/41/38/22/26/-/-/-/-/-/-

4333 EVANS HALSHAW H'CAP (0-90) (Class C) £4,901.75 (£1,484.00: £724.50: £344.75) **6f (Equitrack)** GOING: minus 0.53 sec per fur (FS) 1-10 (1-15)

4263[8] **Rocketeer (IRE) (80)***(90) (WRMuir)* 3-9-6b DHarrison(5) (sn rdn along: chsd ldrs: hdwy to ld over 1f out: r.o) — **1**
4133[10] Inherent Magic (IRE) **(82)***(87) (MMcCormack)* 5-9-3 (5) TGMcLaughlin(6) (chsd ldrs gng wl: hdwy & ev ch 1f out: unable qckn) 2 **2**
4288* Speedy Classic (USA) **(60)***(56) (MJHeaton-Ellis)* 5-8-0 StephenDavies(10) (chsd ldrs: rdn 3f out: hrd rdn over 1f out: one pce) 3½ **3**
4303[3] Invocation **(68)***(62) (AMoore)* 7-8-3 (5) AWhelan(4) (outpcd early: hdwy over 1f out: nvr nrr) ½ **4**
4271[3] Everset (FR) **(88)***(74) (ABailey)* 6-9-9 (5) DWright(9) (nvr nrr) 3 **5**
4258[2] Spender **(74)***(55)*(Fav)*(PWHarris)* 5-9-0 TIves(1) (led tl over 1f out: wknd fnl f) 2 **6**
4211[4] Green's Bid **(63)***(41) (DWChapman)* 4-8-3 JQuinn(7) (nvr nrr) ¾ **7**
4258* Rocky Waters (USA) **(83)***(60) (GLMoore)* 5-9-9 BRouse(13) (chsd ldrs: rdn & ev ch 1f out: eased whn btn fnl f) hd **8**
4220* Dawalib (USA) **(77)***(53) (DHaydnJones)* 4-8-12v(5) SDrowne(12) (prom tl rdn & wknd wl over 1f out) hd **9**
4211* Very Dicey **(75)***(49) (JBerry)* 6-8-8 (7) PRoberts(3) (chsd ldr tl wknd over 1f out) ½ **10**
4099[9] Mr Martini (IRE) **(88)***(52) (CEBrittain)* 4-10-0 MRimmer(2) (a bhd) 4 **11**
4268[0] Crystal Heights (FR) **(56)***(—) (RJO'Sullivan)* 6-7-3 (7)ow1 SLanigan(11) (s.v.s: reluctant to r: a t.o: fin lame) 30 **12**

9/2 Spender, **11/2** Very Dicey, **6/1** Rocky Waters (USA), Speedy Classic (USA), **8/1** ROCKETEER (IRE), **9/1** Inherent Magic (IRE), **10/1** Invocation, Dawalib (USA), **12/1** Everset (FR), **14/1** Mr Martini (IRE), **16/1** Green's Bid, **20/1** Crystal Heights (FR), CSF £74.80 CT £429.88 TOTE £7.70: £2.30 £3.20 £2.90 (£70.90) OWNER Mrs J. M. Muir (LAMBOURN) BRED Mrs T. Bracken in Ireland 12 Rn 1m 12.72 (2.12) SF: 30/26/-/3/13/-/-/-/-/-/-/-

4334 ALEX GORRIE STKS (II) (Mdn 2-Y.0) (Class D) £3,243.90 (£982.20: £479.60: £228.30) **7f (Equitrack)** GOING: minus 0.53 sec per fur (FS) 1-40 (1-41)

4282[6] **Gulf Shaadi (75)***(71) (CEBrittain)* 2-9-0 MRimmer(3) (a.p: led ins fnl f: r.o) — **1**
2247[7] Chewit *(66) (AMoore)* 2-9-0 CandyMorris(9) (led 6f out tl over 4f out: led over 1f out tl ins fnl f: unable qckn) 2½ **2**

4282[4] The Cape Doctor (IRE) *(59)*(Fav)*(BWHills)* 2-9-0 RCochrane(2) (led 1f: led over 4f out tl over 1f out: one pce)....3½ **3**
4282[5] Anytime Baby *(49) (KMcAuliffe)* 2-8-9 AClark(4) (hld up: hdwy 3f out: rdn & one pce fnl 2f)....2½ **4**
3584[4] Oakbury (IRE) **(84)***(37) (RHannon)* 2-8-7 (7) DaneO'Neill(5) (prom tl rdn & lost pl 5f out: mod hdwy fnl f)....8 **5**
2888[10] Portelet *(21) (RJRWilliams)* 2-8-9 DBiggs(6) (mid div tl rdn & wknd 3f out)....5 **6**
4279[7] Charnwood Queen *(19) (RWArmstrong)* 2-8-9 TIves(1) (mid div: rdn & wknd 3f out)1 **7**
4164[15] Adjacent Too *(16) (DRLaing)* 2-8-9 GBardwell(8) (a bhd)....1½ **8**
4314[3] Fair Ella (IRE) **(44)***(16) (JFfitch-Heyes)* 2-8-9b NAdams(7) (bhd fnl 4f)....s.h **9**

2/1 The Cape Doctor (IRE), **3/1** Oakbury (IRE), **9/2** Anytime Baby, **7/1** GULF SHAADI, Charnwood Queen, **8/1** Portelet, **16/1** Fair Ella (IRE), **33/1** Chewit, **50/1** Adjacent Too, CSF £153.56 TOTE £7.90: £2.20 £5.50 £1.70 (£73.70) OWNER Mr C. E. Brittain (NEWMARKET) BRED Sheikh Mohammed bin Rashid al Maktoum 9 Rn 1m 28.49 (5.49) SF: -/-/-/-/-/-/-/-/-

4335 BIFFA WASTE SERVICES RECYCLING STKS (0-60) (Class F) £2,564.60 (£720.60: £351.80) **1m 4f (Equitrack)** GOING: minus 0.53 sec (FST) 2-10 (2-10)

4273[2] **Ballyranter (55)***(64)*(Fav)*(HJCollingridge)* 5-9-6v JQuinn(8) (hld up: led 4f out: clr 2f out: rdn out)....— **1**
4277[10] In the Money (IRE) **(54)***(60) (RHollinshead)* 5-9-4 TIves(9) (a.p: chsd wnr 4f out: rdn over 2f out: r.o fnl f)....1¼ **2**
4261* Ela Man Howa **(58)***(51) (RAkehurst)* 3-9-1e GCarter(4) (eyeshield: hld up: hdwy 3f out: sn rdn: one pce fnl 3f)....9 **3**
4287[8] Mediator **(46)***(38) (AMoore)* 5-9-1 (5) AWhelan(6) (chsd ldr 8f: wknd 3f out)....11 **4**
2779[8] Galejade **(38)***(26) (DHaydnJones)* 4-8-11 AMackay(2) (chsd ldrs: rdn 7f out: wknd 3f out)....2½ **5**
4301[8] Rockstine (IRE) **(59)***(28) (PMitchell)* 3-8-10 GBardwell(5) (hld up: rdn 6f out: hdwy 4f out: wknd 3f out)....1½ **6**
4091[18] One Wild Oat **(56)***(1) (CFWall)* 3-8-8 StephenDavies(7) (prom over 7f)....20 **7**
4217[13] Disputed Call (USA) **(42)***(—) (JWHills)* 5-9-2 RCochrane(1) (led 8f)....6 **8**
3466[6] Bigwheel Bill (IRE) **(52)***(—) (JRJenkins)* 5-9-2v CRutter(3) (dwlt: a bhd)....s.h **9**

13/8 BALLYRANTER, **7/4** Ela Man Howa, **15/2** One Wild Oat, **8/1** Rockstine (IRE), **12/1** In the Money (IRE), **25/1** Galejade, Mediator, Disputed Call (USA), Bigwheel Bill (IRE), CSF £19.49 TOTE £2.80: £1.80 £1.10 £1.50 (£12.30) OWNER Mr P. J. Byrnes (NEWMARKET) BRED Llety Stud 9 Rn 2m 33.85 (4.45) SF: 32/29/16/7/-/-/-/-/-
WEIGHT FOR AGE 3yo-5lb

4336 LADBROKE ALL-WEATHER TROPHY (H'cap) (Qualifier) (I) (0-75) (Class D) £3,303.70 (£1,000.60: £488.80: £232.90) **7f (Equitrack)** GOING: minus 0.53 sec per fur (FS) 2-40 (2-41)

4278* **Triple Joy (73)***(81+)*(Fav)*(SirMarkPrescott)* 3-9-11 WWoods(1) (mde all: clr 2f out: eased ins fnl f: comf)....— **1**
4271* Red Valerian **(73)***(78) (KMcAuliffe)* 3-9-11 RCochrane(9) (s.i.s: hdwy 2f out: r.o fnl f)....1¼ **2**
4264[10] World Traveller **(69)***(69) (WAO'Gorman)* 3-9-4b(3) EmmaO'Gorman(10) (a.p: ev ch 3f out: hrd rdn 2f out: one pce)....2½ **3**
3726[11] Waldo **(66)***(65) (LordHuntingdon)* 3-9-4v DHarrison(5) (sn rdn along mid div: r.o one pce fnl f)....nk **4**
4263[6] Rambold **(66)***(61) (TMJones)* 3-9-4 RPerham(3) (chsd ldrs: rdn over 2f out: one pce)....2 **5**
4313* Bogart **(60)***(51) (CWFairhurst)* 3-8-12 (6x) TIves(12) (hld up: rdn 1f out: nvr nrr)....2 **6**
Perilous Plight **(65)***(51) (WRMuir)* 3-9-3 TWilliams(4) (dwlt: a bhd)....2½ **7**
4264[6] Mullitover **(74)***(60) (MJHeaton-Ellis)* 4-9-13 StephenDavies(11) (mid div: rdn 4f out: sltly hmpd 3f out: no hdwy fnl 2f)....s.h **8**
4302* Hawaii Storm (FR) **(59)***(42) (MissAJWhitfield)* 6-8-7 (5)ow2 RPainter(2) (a bhd)....1¼ **9**
4263[3] La Petite Fusee **(60)***(32) (RJO'Sullivan)* 3-8-12 JQuinn(7) (mid div: rdn 3f out: wknd)....5 **10**
3478[4] Myjinka **(42)***(—) (JO'Donoghue)* 4-7-2b(7)ow2 MBaird(8) (prom over 4f)....20 **11**
LONG HANDICAP Myjinka 6-1

7/4 TRIPLE JOY, **5/1** Red Valerian, Waldo, **6/1** Hawaii Storm (FR), **8/1** Bogart, **10/1** La Petite Fusee, **12/1** Mullitover (8/1-14/1), **14/1** Perilous Plight, **16/1** World Traveller, **25/1** Rambold, **33/1** Myjinka, CSF £12.12 CT £108.69 TOTE £2.60: £1.80 £1.90 £3.50 (£9.10) OWNER HesmondsStud (NEWMARKET) BRED Hesmonds Stud Ltd 11 Rn 1m 26.66 (3.66) SF: 22/19/11/7/3/-/-/1/-/-/-
WEIGHT FOR AGE 3yo-1lb

4337 LADBROKE ALL-WEATHER TROPHY (H'cap) (Qualifier) (II) (0-75) (Class D) £3,288.75 (£996.00: £486.50: £231.75)
7f (Equitrack) GOING: minus 0.53 sec per fur (FS) 3-10 (3-11)

4281[3] **Secret Aly (CAN) (62)***(71)*(Fav)*(CEBrittain)* 4-9-1 MRimmer(8) (s.i.s: hdwy 3f out: led over 1f out: hrd rdn fnl f: r.o)........— **1**
4241[5] Just Harry **(72)***(76) (MJRyan)* 3-9-10 DBiggs(7) (hld up: hdwy 2f out: rdn & ev ch ins fnl f: unable qckn)........2½ **2**
4302[4] Eastleigh **(48)***(46) (RHollinshead)* 5-7-10 (5) AGarth(10) (a.p: led 2f out tl over 1f out: one pce)........3 **3**
2399[4] Friendly Brave (USA) **(73)***(70) (TGMills)* 4-9-5b(7) DToole(5) (led 6f out to 2f out: ev ch over 1f out: one pce)........nk **4**
4313[4] Our Shadee (USA) **(44)***(34) (KTIvory)* 4-7-11v GBardwell(4) (a mid div)........3½ **5**
4320[7] Mazeeka (IRE) **(62)***(51) (WAO'Gorman)* 3-8-11 (3) EmmaO'Gorman(3) (mid div: rdn & lost pl 3f out: r.o one pce fnl f)........hd **6**
4289[11] My Ruby Ring **(58)***(47) (DRLaing)* 7-8-11 TWilliams(1) (led 1f: chsd ldrs to 2f out: wknd 1f out)........s.h **7**
4241[14] Faez **(69)***(57) (PSFelgate)* 4-9-8 TIves(2) (prom 5f)........hd **8**
4268[2] Warwick Warrior (IRE) **(70)***(55) (MrsLPiggott)* 3-9-1 (7) VictoriaAppleby(9) (a bhd) 1½ **9**
4289[5] Milos **(70)***(50) (TJNaughton)* 3-9-8 GCarter(6) (a bhd)........2½ **10**
4209[5] Sir Norman Holt (IRE) **(72)***(51) (RJO'Sullivan)* 5-9-11b AClark(11) (mid div: rdn 3f out: sn wknd)........nk **11**

5/2 SECRET ALY (CAN), **5/1** Sir Norman Holt (IRE), **6/1** Mazeeka (IRE), **13/2** Milos, Our Shadee (USA), **10/1** Eastleigh, **12/1** Warwick Warrior (IRE), Just Harry, **20/1** Friendly Brave (USA), **25/1** My Ruby Ring, **33/1** Faez, CSF £30.89 CT £242.48 TOTE £2.80: £2.00 £3.20 £2.90 (£19.70) OWNER Mr B. H. Voak (NEWMARKET) BRED Northern Equine Thoroughbred Productions 11 Rn
1m 26.53 (3.53) SF: 14/17/-/11/-/-/-/-/-/-/-
WEIGHT FOR AGE 3yo-1lb

T/Plpt: £44.90 (146.47 Tckts). T/Qdpt: £16.90 (1.3 Tckts) SM

LINGFIELD (L-H)
Tuesday December 20th (Standard)

4338 SEVASTOPOL APP'CE H'CAP (0-70) (Class G) £2,326.50 (£654.00: £319.50)
1m 5f (Equitrack) GOING: minus 0.42 sec per fur (FS) 12-00 (12-01)

4176[2] **Wottashambles (37)***(45) (GLewis)* 3-7-9 AGarth(8) (hld up: chsd wnr over 2f out: led ins fnl f: r.o wl)........— **1**
4318[7] Arian Spirit (IRE) **(35)***(43) (WJMusson)* 3-7-2 (5) MDwyer(10) (hdwy 12f out: led over 4f out tl ins fnl f: r.o)........hd **2**
4318[4] Glow Forum **(40)***(39) (GLMoore)* 3-7-12 ow2 SSanders(9) (a.p: rdn over 4f out: unable qckn)........8 **3**
Prosequendo (USA) **(65)***(61) (MDixon)* 7-9-11 (3) AWhelan(11) (b: b.hind: nvr nr to chal)........2½ **4**
4261[9] Cristal Springs **(36)***(31) (BJMcMath)* 3-7-5 (3)ow1 CHawksley(5) (led over 8f: wknd over 3f out)........½ **5**
3937[11] Arctic Guest (IRE) **(64)***(57) (CSmith)* 4-9-10 (3) MBaird(3) (nvr nrr)........1½ **6**
4318[2] Admirals Secret (USA) **(64)***(56)*(Fav)*(CFWall)* 5-9-8 (5) CWebb(2) (b.hind: lw: chsd ldr 8f: wknd over 3f out)........½ **7**
Grecian Lady (IRE) **(39)***(31) (KRBurke)* 5-8-2 SDrowne(7) (rdn & hdwy over 4f out: wknd over 3f out)........s.h **8**
4284[11] Ann Hill (IRE) **(35)***(25) (RHollinshead)* 4-7-7 (5) DDenby(6) (swtg: a bhd)........2 **9**
4272[11] Lajadhal (FR) **(30)***(—) (KBishop)* 5-7-7 NVarley(1) (eyeshield: bhd fnl 12f)........20 **10**
4269[11] Risk the Witch **(32)***(—) (DJSCosgrove)* 4-7-4 (5)ow2 SLanigan(4) (a bhd)........20 **11**

LONG HANDICAP Arian Spirit (IRE) 7-6 Cristal Springs 7-4 Lajadhal (FR) 6-9 Risk the Witch 7-2
11/10 Admirals Secret (USA), **9/2** WOTTASHAMBLES, **11/2** Arctic Guest (IRE), **6/1** Glow Forum, **10/1** Prosequendo (USA) (8/1-12/1), **14/1** Grecian Lady (IRE), **16/1** Arian Spirit (IRE), **33/1** Ann Hill (IRE), **66/1** Cristal Springs, Lajadhal (FR), Risk the Witch, CSF £67.56 CT £401.01 TOTE £5.80: £2.40 £2.70 £1.70 (£55.30) OWNER Dream On Racing Partnership (EPSOM) BRED Arthur Sims 11 Rn
2m 48.11 (5.61) SF: 13/11/7/32/-/28/28/-/-/-/-
WEIGHT FOR AGE 3yo-5lb

4339 KNIGHT, FRANK & RUTLEY H'CAP (I) (0-70) (Class E) £2,775.00 (£840.00: £410.00: £195.00) **1m 2f (Equitrack)** GOING: minus 0.42 sec (FS) 12-30 (12-30)

4326* **Joseph's Wine (IRE) (61)***(73)*(Fav)*(DNicholls)* 5-9-11b (6x) AlexGreaves(10) (lw: stdy hdwy 3f out: led ins fnl f: r.o wl)........— **1**

4303* Sweet Supposin (IRE) **(64)***(70) (KMcAuliffe)* 3-9-11 RCochrane(8) (lw: a.p: rdn over 3f out: led over 2f out tl ins fnl f: unable qckn) 4 **2**
4271[6] Carpathian **(44)***(46) (LordHuntingdon)* 3-8-5 DHarrison(6) (hdwy over 3f out: hrd rdn 2f out: one pce)....2½ **3**
4261[11] Lord Glenvara (IRE) **(36)***(33) (RJO'Sullivan)* 6-8-0 DBiggs(14) (lw: hld up: rdn over 4f out: one pce fnl 2f)....3 **4**
4317[7] Pirates Gold (IRE) **(54)***(48) (JWhite)* 4-8-13 (5) SDrowne(4) (lw: hdwy over 1f out: nvr nrr) 1¾ **5**
2367[10] Pearly River **(61)***(54) (DrJDScargill)* 3-9-8 MRimmer(3) (a.p: rdn over 3f out: wknd over 2f out) ....½ **6**
4320[9] Mislemani (IRE) **(42)***(34) (AGNewcombe)* 4-8-1 (5) NVarley(9) (prom 8f) ....¾ **7**
4303[2] Kintwyn **(61)***(52) (DRLaing)* 4-9-11 GBardwell(7) (b.hind: lw: nvr nr to chal) ....¾ **8**
4217[12] Night Edition **(36)***(21) (SDow)* 4-8-0e ow1 StephenDavies(2) (eyeshield: a mid div)....4 **9**
4202[7] Lac de Gras (IRE) **(38)***(18) (RCurtis)* 3-7-8 (5)ow6 DWright(13) (bhd fnl 3f) 3 **10**
2988[20] Whatone Bell **(29)***(8) (PHayward)* 4-7-7 RStreet(1) (a bhd) ....½ **11**
4318[9] Priscilla Rose **(37)***(16) (CNAllen)* 3-7-12 JQuinn(5) (led over 5f: wknd over 3f out)s.h **12**
4271[10] Secundus (IRE) **(62)***(39) (BJMeehan)* 3-9-9 RPerham(12) (chsd ldr: led over 4f out tl over 2f out: wknd over 1f out: dead)....1 **13**
Jake the Pake (IRE) **(54)***(—) (GCBravery)* 4-9-4 GCarter(11) (bhd fnl 5f) 25 **14**
LONG HANDICAP Lac de Gras (IRE) 7-6 Whatone Bell 6-13

9/4 JOSEPH'S WINE (IRE), **7/2** Sweet Supposin (IRE), **6/1** Lord Glenvara (IRE), Kintwyn, **8/1** Carpathian, **14/1** Pearly River, **16/1** Pirates Gold (IRE), **20/1** Mislemani (IRE), Night Edition, Secundus (IRE), **25/1** Jake the Pake (IRE), **50/1** Priscilla Rose, Lac de Gras (IRE), Whatone Bell, CSF £10.92 CT £51.57 TOTE £2.90: £1.20 £2.00 £4.00 (£4.30) OWNER Wetherby Racing Bureau Plc (THIRSK) BRED Michael Fennessy 14 Rn 2m 6.72 (3.72) SF: 45/39/17/8/23/25/10
WEIGHT FOR AGE 3yo-3lb

4340 LIGHT BRIGADE MEDIAN AUCTION STKS (Mdn 2-Y.O) (Class F) £2,647.90 (£744.40: £363.70)

7f (Equitrack) GOING: minus 0.42 sec per fur (FS) 1-00 (1-02)

4242[10] **Master Millfield (IRE) (60)***(63) (CJHill)* 2-8-9 (5) SSanders(9) (chsd ldr: led over 3f out: rdn out)....— **1**
4308[4] Bold Effort (FR) **(60)***(60) (KOCunningham-Brown)* 2-9-0 AClark(3) (a.p: rdn over 3f out: r.o ins fnl f)....1½ **2**
Montanelli (FR) *(58) (KMcAuliffe)* 2-9-0 RCochrane(10) (neat: bit bkwd: a.p: rdn over 3f out: ev ch over 1f out: one pce)....1 **3**
4106[3] Little Scarlett **(54)***(34) (PJMakin)* 2-8-9 RPerham(1) (lost pl over 5f out: nt clr run over 3f out & wl over 1f out: nvr plcd to chal)....9 **4**
4157[2] Meghdoot *(32)*(Fav)*(HJCollingridge)* 2-8-9 JQuinn(8) (hdwy over 4f out: wknd over 2f out) 1 **5**
Zesti *(29) (TTClement)* 2-8-7 (7) PBowe(5) (neat: prom over 3f) 4 **6**
4315[6] Friendly Lady (USA) **(65)***(24) (WAO'Gorman)* 2-8-6 (3) EmmaO'Gorman(4) (a mid div) ....s.h **7**
4298[10] Franklinsboy **(46)***(18) (CaptJWilson)* 2-8-9 (5) NVarley(2) (nvr nrr) 5 **8**
Lanesra Breeze *(16) (TJNaughton)* 2-8-7 (7) VHalliday(13) (leggy: s.s: a bhd) 1 **9**
Governor's Lass *(6) (SDow)* 2-8-9e StephenDavies(12) (eyeshield: str: bkwd: hdwy over 3f out: wknd over 2f out)....2½ **10**
Vibro (IRE) *(—) (GCBravery)* 2-9-0 GCarter(7) (bit bkwd: led over 3f)....7 **11**
4299[9] Tigana **(42)***(—) (MrsLCJewell)* 2-8-2b(7) HoneyPearce(11) (s.s: a wl bhd) 5 **12**
Prime Silver (IRE) *(—) (DJSCosgrove)* 2-8-9 (5) LNewton(6) (leggy: lt-f: bhd fnl 4f)....3 **13**

5/4 Meghdoot, **11/2** Friendly Lady (USA), **13/2** Montanelli (FR) (10/1-6/1), **15/2** MASTER MILLFIELD (IRE), **10/1** Zesti, **12/1** Bold Effort (FR), **14/1** Little Scarlett, Vibro (IRE), **16/1** Governor's Lass, **25/1** Lanesra Breeze, Franklinsboy, Prime Silver (IRE), **33/1** Tigana, CSF £94.42 TOTE £18.40: £2.20 £2.40 £3.00 (£171.60) OWNER Mr John Hill (BARNSTAPLE) BRED A. M. F. Persse 13 Rn 1m 25.81 (2.81) SF: 30/27/25/-/-/-/-/-/-/-/-/-/-

4341 KNIGHT, FRANK & RUTLEY H'CAP (II) (0-70) (Class E) £2,775.00 (£840.00: £410.00: £195.00)

1m 2f GOING: minus 0.42 sec per fur (FS) 1-30 (1-30)

4301* **South Eastern Fred (56)***(72)*(Fav)*(HJCollingridge)* 3-9-3 MRimmer(8) (a.p: led wl over 1f out: rdn out)....— **1**
3251[2] Awesome Power **(63)***(75) (JWHills)* 8-9-13 AClark(1) (hdwy over 4f out: rdn over 1f out: r.o)....2½ **2**

43125 Captain Marmalade **(45)***(54) (DTThom)* 5-8-9 MFenton(4) (lw: nt clr run on ins over 2f out: hdwy over 1f out: r.o one pce)....1¾ **3**
4312* Our Eddie **(66)***(70) (BGubby)* 5-9-11v (6x) (5) AWhelan(13) (lw: a.p: led 3f out tl wl over 1f out: eased whn btn wl ins fnl f)....3 **4**
36978 My Minnie **(46)***(44) (BJMeehan)* 4-8-10 DHarrison(6) (rdn over 3f out: hdwy over 1f out: nvr nrr)....4 **5**
33567 Bag of Tricks (IRE) **(64)***(60) (SDow)* 4-10-0e StephenDavies(3) (eyeshield: hld up: rdn over 2f out: eased whn btn fnl f)....1½ **6**
43028 Portolano (FR) **(42)***(30) (CNWilliams)* 3-8-3 JQuinn(14) (led 7f)....5 **7**
43017 Pigalle Wonder **(36)***(23) (RJO'Sullivan)* 6-8-0bow2 DBiggs(5) (prom over 7f)....nk **8**
420415 Ezekiel **(38)***(23) (JWPayne)* 3-7-13 GBardwell(9) (rdn & hdwy over 3f out: wknd wl over 1f out)....1 **9**
43092 Red Whirlwind **(49)***(33) (BJMcMath)* 4-8-13 RCochrane(12) (bhd fnl 2f)....¾ **10**
30126 Charlistiona **(33)***(17) (MJohnston)* 3-7-8 NAdams(11) (stdy hdwy 8f out: wknd 3f out)....s.h **11**
42746 Lombard Ships **(42)***(24) (ABailey)* 7-8-6b AMackay(10) (lw: s.s: a bhd)....1½ **12**
42603 Ecu de France (IRE) **(59)***(38) (MMadgwick)* 4-9-9v WWoods(7) (lw: bhd fnl 4f)....1¾ **13**
42718 Tudor Flight **(41)***(15) (AGNewcombe)* 3-8-2 CRutter(2) (b: prom over 5f)....3½ **14**

100/30 SOUTH EASTERN FRED, **9/2** Red Whirlwind, **5/1** Our Eddie, **13/2** Captain Marmalade, **9/1** Awesome Power, **12/1** Ecu de France (IRE), **14/1** My Minnie, Lombard Ships, Portolano (FR), **16/1** Tudor Flight, **20/1** Pigalle Wonder, **25/1** Bag of Tricks (IRE), **33/1** Charlistiona, **50/1** Ezekiel, CSF £33.17 CT £177.93 TOTE £4.10: £2.40 £3.20 £1.90 (£16.50) OWNER South Eastern Electrical Plc (NEWMARKET) BRED L. Audus 14 Rn 2m 7.22 (4.22) SF: 33/39/21/36/11/25
WEIGHT FOR AGE 3yo-3lb

4342 COMMERCIAL CEILING FACTORS NURSERY (Class C) £4,765.25 (£1,442.00: £703.50: £334.25) 6f (Equitrack) GOING: minus 0.42 sec per fur (FS) 2-00 (2-00)

4315* **Go Hever Golf (68)***(95+)*(Fav)*(TJNaughton)* 2-9-8 (7x) GCarter(7) (b.nr fore: lw: mde all: qcknd wl over 1f out: easily)....— **1**
4267* Stoppes Brow **(67)***(76) (GLMoore)* 2-9-7v BRouse(1) (chsd wnr: rdn over 3f out: no imp)....7 **2**
42985 Rotherfield Park (IRE) **(45)***(49) (CSmith)* 2-7-6 (7) MBaird(4) (hdwy over 1f out: r.o one pce)....2 **3**
43142 Pleasure Beach **(60)***(60) (WAO'Gorman)* 2-8-11b(3) EmmaO'Gorman(2) (hld up: rdn over 3f out: one pce)....1¼ **4**
37889 Keys Seminar **(43)***(28) (NACallaghan)* 2-7-11b JQuinn(3) (a bhd)....6 **5**
42625 First Crush **(66)***(50) (SirMarkPrescott)* 2-9-6 CNutter(6) (lw: hdwy over 4f out: wknd over 2f out)....hd **6**
42982 Das Island **(52)***(26) (JRJenkins)* 2-8-6 CRutter(5) (hld up: rdn over 3f out: wknd over 2f out)....4 **7**

Evens GO HEVER GOLF, **9/2** Stoppes Brow, **13/2** Pleasure Beach, **7/1** Rotherfield Park (IRE), Das Island, **10/1** First Crush, **20/1** Keys Seminar, CSF £6.37 TOTE £1.80: £1.50 £2.80 (£3.10) OWNER Hever Racing Club (EPSOM) BRED Ronald Popely 7 Rn 1m 12.7 (2.10) SF: 41/21/-/7

4343 THIN RED LINE STKS (I) (Mdn) (Class D) £3,273.80 (£991.40: £484.20: £230.60) 7f (Equitrack) GOING: minus 0.42 sec per fur (FS) 2-30 (2-32)

9159 **Kaafih Homm (IRE)** *(66) (NACallaghan)* 3-8-13 DHarrison(7) (lw: a.p: hrd rdn over 1f out: led nr fin)....— **1**
42583 Newington Butts (IRE) **(49)***(60) (RAkehurst)* 4-8-4 (5) SSanders(3) (led: hrd rdn over 1f out: hdd nr fin)....nk **2**
43179 Joint Effort (IRE) **(41)***(59) (AMoore)* 3-8-3 (5) AWhelan(9) (hdwy over 2f out: r.o ins fnl f)....nk **3**
38064 Dynamis (IRE) **(64)***(48) (KOCunningham-Brown)* 3-8-8 RCochrane(2) (hdwy over 4f out: rdn 2f out: one pce)....5 **4**
42715 Masrah Dubai (USA) *(45)*(Fav)*(MAJarvis)* 3-8-13 WWoods(5) (a.p: ev ch over 2f out: 3rd & btn whn squeezed out 2f out)....4 **5**
Ela Palikari Mou (IRE) *(43) (RAkehurst)* 3-8-13 GCarter(10) (w'like: s.s: hdwy over 1f out: nvr nrr)....1 **6**
38969 Quick Million *(41) (BJMeehan)* 3-8-5 (7)ow4 DaneO'Neill(4) (nvr nr to chal)....hd **7**
421013 Flash Appeal *(32) (RGuest)* 3-8-8 MRimmer(8) (prom over 4f)....2½ **8**
432212 Dance and Sing (IRE) **(34)***(34) (DLWilliams)* 4-8-9b(5) DGriffiths(1) (bhd fnl 2f)....1¼ **9**
380612 David Blue (IRE) **(51)***(27) (JWhite)* 3-8-8 (5) SDrowne(12) (bhd fnl 3f)....3½ **10**
Esperer *(25) (JO'Donoghue)* 4-8-9 (5) TGMcLaughlin(11) (s.s: a wl bhd)....¾ **11**
323612 Mutiara *(7) (MissGayKelleway)* 3-8-8 StephenDavies(6) (b.hind: bhd fnl 5f)....6 **12**

2/1 Masrah Dubai (USA), **100/30** KAAFIH HOMM (IRE), Dynamis (IRE), **6/1** Newington Butts (IRE), **10/1** Ela Palikari Mou (IRE), **16/1** Joint Effort (IRE), **20/1** Flash Appeal, **25/1** David Blue (IRE), **33/1** Mutiara, Quick Million, **50/1** Esperer, Dance and Sing (IRE), CSF £23.86 TOTE £6.00: £2.10 £2.10 £2.60 (£27.80) OWNER Gallagher Materials Ltd (NEWMARKET) BRED Sheikh Ahmed bin Rashid al Maktoum 12 Rn 1m 26.75 (3.75) SF: 18/15/13/2/-/-/-/-/-/-/-/-
WEIGHT FOR AGE 3yo-1lb

4344 THIN RED LINE STKS (II) (Mdn) (Class D) £3,258.85 (£986.80: £481.90: £229.45) **7f (Equitrack)** GOING: minus 0.42 sec per fur (FS) 3-00 (3-03)

2690[14] **Krayyan Dawn (22)***(50) (RAkehurst)* 4-9-0 GCarter(8) (lw: hdwy over 2f out: hrd rdn over 1f out: led ins fnl f: r.o wl)........— **1**
4317[5] Europharm Lassie **(51)***(41) (GLMoore)* 3-8-8v BRouse(6) (chsd ldr 5f out: led over 1f out tl ins fnl f: unable qckn)........1¾ **2**
4270[9] Thorniwama **(36)***(38) (JJBridger)* 3-8-8 AClark(4) (rdn over 3f out: hdwy over 1f out: r.o wl ins fnl f)........1½ **3**
2545[4] Eqtesaad (USA) *(42) (SCWilliams)* 3-8-13 AMackay(5) (s.s: hdwy 5f out: rdn over 3f out: r.o one pce)........½ **4**
4313[7] Ebony Blaze **(58)***(40)*(Fav)*(CPWildman)* 3-8-13 DHarrison(1) (rdn over 4f out: hdwy over 1f out: r.o)........¾ **5**
3912[13] Gingerillo **(35)***(39) (TGMills)* 3-8-6b(7) DToole(7) (lw: led 6f out: clr 5f out: hdd over 1f out: wknd fnl f)........hd **6**
4336[11] Myjinka **(20)***(29) (JO'Donoghue)* 4-8-2b(7) MBaird(2) (nvr nr to chal)........2½ **7**
4288[5] Tassagh Bridge (IRE) **(23)***(5) (RIngram)* 4-8-4 (5) SDrowne(11) (a bhd)........11 **8**
Celestial Faith *(—) (MJohnston)* 3-8-8 TWilliams(9) (neat: bit bkwd: bhd fnl 6f)..3½ **9**
1742[7] Excelled (IRE) **(30)***(—) (CJDrewe)* 5-8-9b RPerham(3) (b: a bhd)........¾ **10**
1284[4] Chardonnay Girl *(—) (JMCarr)* 3-8-8 JQuinn(10) (bhd fnl 3f)........s.h **11**
4206[9] Hall Bank Cottage **(29)***(—) (MrsALMKing)* 4-8-9 NCarlisle(12) (led 1f: wknd over 4f out)........4 **12**

3/1 Ebony Blaze, **7/2** Eqtesaad (USA), Celestial Faith, Europharm Lassie, **7/1** KRAYYAN DAWN, **14/1** Myjinka, **16/1** Gingerillo, Tassagh Bridge (IRE), Chardonnay Girl, **25/1** Thorniwama, **33/1** Excelled (IRE), Hall Bank Cottage, CSF £34.62 TOTE £8.50: £2.10 £1.10 £11.00 (£17.30) OWNER Mr R. E. Greatorex (EPSOM) BRED R. Voorspuy 12 Rn
1m 26.52 (3.52) SF: 22/14/11/14/13/13/3/-/-/-/-/-
WEIGHT FOR AGE 3yo-1lb

4345 INKERMAN H'CAP (0-60) (Class F) £2,564.60 (£720.60: £351.80) **5f (Equitrack)** GOING: minus 0.42 sec per fur (FS) 3-30 (3-32)

4325[2] **Nineacres (54)***(62)*(Fav)*(DNicholls)* 3-9-1b(7) AEddery(7) (hld up: hrd rdn over 1f out: led ins fnl f: r.o wl)........— **1**
4322[11] Featherstone Lane **(60)***(63) (MissLCSiddall)* 3-10-0v DHarrison(1) (s.i.s: outpcd: gd hdwy over 1f out: str run fnl f: fin wl)........1½ **2**
4316[5] Granmas Delight **(55)***(53) (KTIvory)* 3-9-9 RCochrane(4) (hdwy over 1f out: r.o ins fnl f)........1½ **3**
4325[7] Daaniera (IRE) **(46)***(42) (PHowling)* 4-9-0b JQuinn(10) (b.hind: lw: led over 2f: led over 1f out tl ins fnl f: nt r.o)........½ **4**
4288[4] Distant Dynasty **(52)***(45) (BAPearce)* 4-8-13 (7) PRoberts(2) (hld up: rdn over 2f out: one pce)........1 **5**
4297[4] Tee-Emm **(59)***(41) (PHowling)* 4-9-6 (7) DBiggs(8) (prom over 3f)........3½ **6**
4325[11] Tommy Tempest **(41)***(19) (ABailey)* 5-8-4b(5) DWright(3) (w ldr: led over 2f out tl over 1f out: wknd fnl f)........1¼ **7**
4265[12] Papagos (IRE) **(46)***(21) (SDow)* 3-9-0 StephenDavies(6) (b.hind: a bhd)........¾ **8**
4325[17] Bold Aristocrat (IRE) **(44)***(14) (RHollinshead)* 3-8-12b WWoods(9) (outpcd)........1½ **9**
1810[7] Patacake (IRE) **(39)***(—) (AMoore)* 3-8-7 CandyMorris(5) (b.hind: a bhd)........25 **10**

2/1 NINEACRES, **7/2** Distant Dynasty, **4/1** Tee-Emm, **8/1** Tommy Tempest, Featherstone Lane, **9/1** Granmas Delight, Daaniera (IRE), **20/1** Papagos (IRE), Bold Aristocrat (IRE), **33/1** Patacake (IRE), CSF £19.68 CT £119.05 TOTE £2.60: £1.90 £2.20 £2.20 (£12.10) OWNER Mr John Gilbertson (THIRSK) BRED David Nicholls 10 Rn 60.03 secs (1.83) SF: 39/40/30/21/23/17/-/-/-/-

T/Plpt: £290.40 (43.07 Tckts). T/Qdpt: Not won; £246.00 to Ludlow 21/12/94. AK

NAKAYAMA (L-H) (Japan)
Sunday December 18th (Firm)

4346a SPRINTERS STKS (Gp 1) £563,227.00 **6f**

Sakura Bakushin O (JPN) *(—) (Japan)* 5-9-0 FKojima........— **1**
Biko Pegasus (USA) *(—) (Japan)* 3-8-9 HMatoba........4 **2**

Kyoei Keyman (JPN) *(—) (Japan)* 5-9-0b MMatsunaga ....nk **3**
3924* Zieten (USA) *(—) (JHMGosden)* 4-9-0 YTake (btn further 3 3/4l) **9**
TOTE(inc 100 Yen stake) 160Y: 120Y 310Y 1220Y (950Y) OWNER Sakura Commerce Co Ltd
BRED Shadai Farm in Japan 14 Rn 1m 7.1

4306-WOLVERHAMPTON (L-H)
Monday December 26th (Standard)

4347 BURNLEY ALL-WEATHER STKS (Mdn 2-Y.O) (Class D) £3,243.90 (£982.20: £479.60: £228.30) **1m 100y (Fibresand)** GOING: 0.29 sec per fur (SL) 1-25 (1-26)

4308[2] **Komreyev Dancer (68)***(74)*(Fav)*(ABailey)* 2-8-9 (5) DWright(3) (hld up on ins: swtchd rt & hdwy over 2f out: 3rd st: led wl ins fnl f) ....— **1**
4132[6] Forgotten Empress *(65) (JLEyre)* 2-8-9 AClark(6) (b.hind: racd wd: hld up: hdwy to ld over 3f out: rdn & hdd wl ins fnl f) 2 **2**
4280[4] Hard Try *(66) (MJCamacho)* 2-9-0 RCochrane(7) (racd wd: hld up: hdwy 3f out: 2nd & ev ch ent st: rdn & one pce appr fnl f) 2 **3**
4205[7] Fairy's Son **(56)***(54) (WRMuir)* 2-9-0 DHarrison(4) (chsd ldrs: rdn & 4th st: wknd appr fnl f) 6 **4**
4240[8] Jalmaid **(45)***(37) (BAMcMahon)* 2-8-9 GCarter(5) (prom tl wknd qckly over 2f out: 5th & btn st) 6 **5**
4307[5] Dowdency **(45)***(36) (JAPickering)* 2-8-9 NCarlisle(1) (led 5f: wknd over 2f out: 6th & btn ent st: t.o) ....½ **6**
4307[9] Chadleigh Walk (IRE) **(40)***(37) (RHollinshead)* 2-8-9 (5) AGarth(2) (w ldrs 5f: wknd & 7th st: t.o) 2 **7**

Evens KOMREYEV DANCER, **7/2** Forgotten Empress, **9/2** Hard Try, **6/1** Jalmaid, **20/1** Dowdency, **25/1** Fairy's Son, **33/1** Chadleigh Walk (IRE), CSF £5.02 TOTE £2.00: £1.20 £2.40 (£3.50) OWNER Mr Denis Gallagher (TARPORLEY) BRED G. and Mrs Whittaker 7 Rn
1m 53.7 (9.70) SF: 29/21/22/11/-/-/-

4348 LEEDS CLAIMING STKS (Class F) £2,398.00 (£673.00: £328.00) **7f (Fibresand)** GOING: 0.29 sec per fur (SL) 1-55 (1-57)

4333[5] **Everset (FR) (87)***(80+)*(Fav)*(ABailey)* 6-9-1 (5) DWright(4) (hld up: hdwy to ld 2f out: clr fnl f: eased: unchal) ....— **1**
4310[2] Alpine Johnny **(57)***(64) (RHollinshead)* 3-8-4 (5) AGarth(7) (a.p: led 3f out to 2f out: 3rd st: one pce appr fnl f) 3 **2**
4310[4] Sense of Priority **(61)***(59) (MHEasterby)* 5-8-7 TWilliams(11) (a.p: rdn & 2nd st: r.o one pce) ....¾ **3**
4322[2] Super Benz **(60)***(61) (FJO'Mahony)* 8-8-13 GCarter(8) (b: a.p: rdn & 5th st: nt pce to chal) 1¾ **4**
4317[8] Charlies Dream (IRE) **(45)***(51) (KRBurke)* 3-8-4 NAdams(9) (hdwy 3f out: nvr plcd to chal) ....¾ **5**
4243[10] Adwick Park **(73)***(62) (MJCamacho)* 6-9-2 MFenton(12) (prom: 6th & rdn st: sn btn) ....s.h **6**
4322[7] Grandee **(44)***(50) (BAMcMahon)* 3-8-11 RCochrane(5) (a bhd & outpcd) 4 **7**
4255[8] Bee Dee Best (IRE) **(37)***(48) (JPSmith)* 3-8-13 SWebster(10) (bhd: effrt 3f out: no imp) 2 **8**
4253[11] Bonny Melody **(49)***(35) (PDEvans)* 3-7-13 (5) SSanders(3) (slt ld 4f: 4th & wkng st: sn btn) 2 **9**
1408[14] Dissident Dancer **(32)***(10) (JHPeacock)* 5-8-6v AMackay(2) (bkwd: a bhd & outpcd: t.o) 12 **10**
4309[13] Mon Rouge (IRE) **(59)***(21) (BPJBaugh)* 3-8-12v(5) SDrowne(6) (b: chsd ldrs: rdn along ½-wy: sn lost tch: t.o) ....½ **11**

4/5 EVERSET (FR), **5/1** Alpine Johnny, **7/1** Sense of Priority, Super Benz, **12/1** Bonny Melody, **14/1** Mon Rouge (IRE), Grandee, Adwick Park, **16/1** Charlies Dream (IRE), **33/1** Dissident Dancer, Bee Dee Best (IRE), CSF £6.84 TOTE £1.90: £1.50 £1.40 £2.00 (£4.00) OWNER Mr G. Mytton (TARPORLEY) BRED Societe Aland 11 Rn 1m 31.6 (7.60) SF: 38/21/18/21/12/23/8/-/-/-
WEIGHT FOR AGE 3yo-1lb

4349 J. GIDDINGS ALLOYS H'CAP (0-65) (Class F) £2,624.10 (£757.60: £360.30) **6f (Fibresand)** GOING: 0.29 sec per fur (SL) 2-25 (2-27)

3612[11] **Arndilly (63)***(74) (BJMeehan)* 3-9-12 RCochrane(6) (b: hld up: hdwy 2f out: str run to ld ins fnl f: sn clr) ....— **1**

2641[8] Pretonic **(46)***(49) (BPalling)* 6-8-9 StephenDavies(8) (bit bkwd: a.p: led over 1f out tl hdd & no ex ins fnl f) 3 **2**
4320[13] Heathyards Lady (USA) **(50)***(52) (RHollinshead)* 3-8-13 GCarter(2) (chsd ldrs on ins: rdn & r.o wl fnl f) ....hd **3**
4322* Little Ibnr **(66)***(63)*(Fav)*(PDEvans)* 3-9-10 (5) SSanders(3) (led after 2f tl over 1f out: rdn & wknd fnl f) 1¾ **4**
4343[9] Dance and Sing (IRE) **(34)***(30) (DLWilliams)* 4-7-11 NAdams(10) (bhd & outpcd tl r.o strly ins fnl f) ....nk **5**
4306[10] Farndale **(55)***(45) (JBerry)* 7-8-11 (7) PRoberts(11) (hdwy fnl 2f: nvr rchd ldrs)....2½ **6**
4034[18] Swinging Tich **(46)***(18) (BAMcMahon)* 5-8-9 DHarrison(1) (dwlt: a bhd & outpcd)....7 **7**
4274[15] Cheerful Groom (IRE) **(47)***(11) (JMackie)* 3-8-10 MFenton(13) (prom tl rdn & outpcd wl over 1f out)....3 **8**
4337[7] My Ruby Ring **(55)***(6) (DRLaing)* 7-9-4 TWilliams(5) (b.hind: in tch: rdn ½-wy: wknd over 2f out)....5 **9**
4325[6] Dundeelin **(50)***(—) (JLEyre)* 3-8-13v AClark(7) (b.hind: slt ld 2f: wknd qckly appr fnl f)....¾ **10**
4322[3] Scored Again **(59)***(5) (MJHeaton-Ellis)* 4-9-1 (7) AmandaSanders(12) (b: lw: disp ld to ½-wy: wknd over 2f out) ....½ **11**
4317[16] Lady Broker **(52)***(—) (ABailey)* 4-8-10 (5) DWright(9) (chsd ldrs early: rdn & wknd over 2f out)....3½ **12**

7/4 Little Ibnr, **6/1** Scored Again, Dundeelin, **7/1** Pretonic, **8/1** ARNDILLY, **10/1** My Ruby Ring, Heathyards Lady (USA), **12/1** Lady Broker, **14/1** Farndale, **16/1** Cheerful Groom (IRE), **20/1** Swinging Tich, **33/1** Dance and Sing (IRE), CSF £65.12 CT £537.69 TOTE £12.30: £3.40 £2.00 £2.90 (£57.90) OWNER Mr A. S. Reid (UPPER LAMBOURN) BRED Hilborough Stud Farm Ltd
12 Rn 1m 18.1 (6.90) SF: 38/14/18/30/-/12/-/-/-/-/-/-

4350 LPK UPHOLSTERY NURSERY (Class E) £2,788.00 (£844.00: £412.00: £196.00)
6f (Fibresand) GOING: 0.29 sec per fur (SL) 2-55 (2-55)

4340* **Master Millfield (IRE) (69)***(71)*(Fav)*(CJHill)* 2-8-0 (6x) (5)ow3 SSanders(2) (lw: a.p: led over 3f out: rdn & edgd lft fnl f: r.o wl) ....— **1**
4298[6] Crystal Loop **(63)***(61) (ABailey)* 2-7-13 ow1 AMackay(7) (hdwy over 2f out: rdn over 1f out: kpt on)....1½ **2**
4331* Dark Shot (IRE) **(85)***(79) (JBerry)* 2-9-7 GCarter(1) (lw: a.p: ev ch over 1f out: rdn & unable qckn fnl f)....1½ **3**
4172[7] Poly Laureon (IRE) **(67)***(60) (RHollinshead)* 2-8-3 NCarlisle(5) (sn bhd & outpcd: hdwy ½-wy: rdn & kpt on wl fnl f)....nk **4**
Fools of Pride (IRE) **(65)***(40) (RHollinshead)* 2-7-10 (5) AGarth(3) (outpcd: a bhd)....7 **5**
3769[9] Poly Lane **(59)***(24) (WRMuir)* 2-7-9 GBardwell(4) (slt ld over 2f: wknd qckly over 2f out)....4 **6**
4256[12] Prince Rudolf (IRE) **(62)***(—) (NPLittmoden)* 2-7-7b(5)ow5 DWright(6) (spd to ½-wy: sn wknd: t.o)....9 **7**

LONG HANDICAP Prince Rudolf (IRE) 7-0

7/4 MASTER MILLFIELD (IRE), **5/2** Dark Shot (IRE), **3/1** Crystal Loop, **5/1** Poly Laureon (IRE), **12/1** Poly Lane, **14/1** Fools of Pride (IRE), **25/1** Prince Rudolf (IRE), CSF £8.07 TOTE £4.00: £2.00 £2.50 (£12.70) OWNER Mr John Hill (BARNSTAPLE) BRED A. M. F. Persse 7 Rn
1m 17.6 (6.40) SF: 25/16/32/15/-/-/-

4351 SOLIHULL H'CAP (0-65) (Class F) £2,398.00 (£673.00: £328.00)
2m 46y (Fibresand) GOING: 0.29 sec per fur (SL) 3-25 (3-28)

4323[4] **Mrs Jawleyford (USA) (52)***(61) (CSmith)* 6-9-1 (7) MBaird(4) (b: hld up & bhd: hdwy 5f out: 3rd st: styd on to ld wl ins fnl f) ....— **1**
4323[2] Tremendisto **(48)***(55) (CaptJWilson)* 4-8-13 (5) NVarley(6) (a.p: led over 4f out tl wl ins fnl f) 1¾ **2**
4323[8] Sassiver (USA) **(45)***(49) (RHollinshead)* 4-8-10 (5) AGarth(2) (hld up: hdwy 6f out: 2nd st: one pce appr fnl f) 3½ **3**
4332[3] Pride of Britain (CAN) **(53)***(57) (LGCottrell)* 5-9-9 NCarlisle(3) (unruly bef s: led after 2f tl over 4f out: 4th & rdn st: one pce)....hd **4**
4311[6] Well and Truly **(48)***(51)*(Fav)*(BAMcMahon)* 7-9-4 RCochrane(9) (chsd ldrs: 5th st: rdn over 1f out: one pce)....¾ **5**
4338[5] Cristal Springs **(32)***(34) (BJMcMath)* 3-7-9 GBardwell(11) (chsd ldrs: 6th & rdn st: no imp)....1¼ **6**
4318* Scalp 'em (IRE) **(46)***(48) (PDEvans)* 6-8-11 (5) SSanders(8) (hld up: hdwy 6f out: rdn over 2f out: sn btn)....hd **7**
4323[7] Fiery Sun **(31)***(30) (JLEyre)* 9-8-1 TWilliams(7) (b.hind: led 2f: wknd over 2f out) .3½ **8**

4332[10] Woodmans Star **(37)***(17) (JJSheehan)* 4-8-2 (5) AWhelan(10) (hld up mid div: wknd 4f out: t.o) 20 **9**
4332[2] Star Quest **(48)***(14) (JRJenkins)* 7-9-4 BDoyle(1) (prom 12f: sn wknd: t.o) 15 **10**
2131[6] Persian Bud (IRE) **(29)***(—) (JRBosley)* 6-7-13 NAdams(5) (bit bkwd: a in rr: t.o fnl 3f) 10 **11**
3952[8] Epica **(65)***(21) (ABailey)* 3-10-0b AClark(12) (b: prom: rdn ½-wy: wknd 4f out: t.o) 1¼ **12**
7/2 Well and Truly, **4/1** Pride of Britain (CAN), **5/1** Scalp 'em (IRE), **11/2** Star Quest (7/2-6/1), MRS JAWLEYFORD (USA), **8/1** Tremendisto, Epica (6/1-10/1), **16/1** Fiery Sun, Sassiver (USA), Persian Bud (IRE), **20/1** Woodmans Star, **25/1** Cristal Springs, CSF £52.18 CT £640.39 TOTE £7.80: £2.00 £3.00 £4.90 (£126.50) OWNER Mr Clifford Smith (WELLINGORE) BRED Bruce Hundley and John J. Greely III 12 Rn 3m 45.6 (18.6) SF: 39/35/29/36/31/9/28/-/-/-/-/-
WEIGHT FOR AGE 3yo-7lb

4352 LIVERPOOL (S) STKS (2-Y.O) (Class G) £2,190.00 (£615.00: £300.00)
5f (Fibresand) GOING: 0.29 sec per fur (SL) 3-55 (4-00)

4330[5] **Whittingham Girl (49)***(66) (JBerry)* 2-8-6 GCarter(7) (a.p: led ins fnl f: r.o wl) ....— **1**
3666[7] David James' Girl **(59)***(66) (ABailey)* 2-8-6 (5) DWright(2) (chsd ldrs: rdn & kpt on ins fnl f: no ch w wnr) 1½ **2**
4324[12] Lawnswood Lady **(40)***(59) (RHollinshead)* 2-8-6b NCarlisle(10) (hdwy over 2f out: rdn & r.o fnl f) ....½ **3**
4324[10] Pats Delight **(48)***(56) (SCoathup)* 2-8-6 TWilliams(11) (sn rdn along: led over 2f out: sn clr: wknd & hdd ins fnl f) ....¾ **4**
4230[14] Hasty Bid (IRE) *(32) (CJHill)* 2-8-6 NAdams(3) (dwlt: nvr rchd ldrs) 8 **5**
4307[13] Pink Petal *(30) (CJHill)* 2-8-1 (5) SSanders(4) (nvr nrr) ....½ **6**
4330[3] Musical Fantasy (IRE) **(54)***(31) (BJMeehan)* 2-8-6 (5) NVarley(5) (b: a in rr: effrt & nt clr run over 2f out: n.d) 1¼ **7**
4330* Lady Pui **(52)***(29)*(Fav)*(JBerry)* 2-8-8b(3) DarrenMoffatt(8) (disp ld 3f: wknd qckly appr fnl f) ....½ **8**
4219[6] Pertemps Partner **(54)***(21) (BAMcMahon)* 2-8-6 DHarrison(1) (outpcd) 1 **9**
4308[11] Ivy Lilian (IRE) **(45)***(17) (WMBrisbourne)* 2-8-1 (5) AGarth(9) (led to ½-wy: sn rdn & wknd) 1¼ **10**
4324[16] Branston Kristy **(48)***(—) (CSmith)* 2-7-13v(7) MBaird(6) (b.hind: outpcd: t.o) 10 **11**
7/4 Lady Pui, **7/2** Musical Fantasy (IRE), David James' Girl, **5/1** WHITTINGHAM GIRL, **13/2** Pertemps Partner, **10/1** Branston Kristy, **14/1** Ivy Lilian (IRE), Lawnswood Lady, Pats Delight, Pink Petal, **20/1** Hasty Bid (IRE), CSF £27.93 TOTE £9.50: £2.00 £2.50 £7.20 (£24.60) OWNER T & M A Bibby (COCKERHAM) BRED Cheveley Park Stud Ltd 11 Rn No bid
64.9 secs (6.90) SF: -/-/-/-/-/-/-/-/-/-/-

4353 BIRMINGHAM H'CAP (0-85) (Class D) £3,288.75 (£996.00: £486.50: £231.75)
1m 1f 79y (Fibresand) GOING: 0.29 sec per fur (SL) 4-25 (4-31)

4131[17] **Mam'zelle Angot (61)***(67) (JLEyre)* 4-8-9 AClark(6) (chsd ldrs: 4th st: rdn & r.o to ld cl home) ....— **1**
4336[4] Waldo **(66)***(72)*(Fav)*(LordHuntingdon)* 3-8-12v DHarrison(12) (hdwy 6f out: 3rd st: ev ch fnl f: r.o) ....hd **2**
4312[2] Conspicuous (IRE) **(65)***(71) (LGCottrell)* 4-8-13 NCarlisle(1) (led: rdn ent fnl f: ct nr fin) ....s.h **3**
3726[14] Sieve of Time (USA) **(82)***(86) (CEBrittain)* 3-10-0 BDoyle(8) (a.p: 2nd st: rdn & n.m.r 1f out: unable qckn) 1¼ **4**
1750[13] Salbus **(80)***(83) (FJYardley)* 4-10-0 JWilliams(2) (bkwd: prom tl outpcd & 6th st: rdn & kpt on nr fin) ....½ **5**
4326[2] Hillzah (USA) **(80)***(82) (RBastiman)* 6-9-9 (5) HBastiman(5) (s.i.s: hdwy over 2f out: nrst fin) ....½ **6**
4339[8] Kintwyn **(67)***(66) (DRLaing)* 4-9-1 SWhitworth(10) (chsd ldrs over 7f: 5th & wkng st) 2 **7**
Haroldon (IRE) **(62)***(60) (BPalling)* 5-8-5 (5) SSanders(9) (b: nvr nr ldrs) ....nk **8**
4257[11] Shuttlecock **(64)***(43) (NPLittmoden)* 3-8-5 (5) TGMcLaughlin(7) (chsd ldrs 6f: sn rdn & wknd: t.o) 11 **9**
3406[17] Veloce (IRE) **(64)***(7) (ABailey)* 6-8-12 AMackay(3) (b: bkwd: a bhd: t.o) 20 **10**
5/2 Waldo, **3/1** Hillzah (USA), **4/1** Sieve of Time (USA), **9/2** Conspicuous (IRE), **8/1** Veloce (IRE), MAM'ZELLE ANGOT, Kintwyn, **12/1** Haroldon (IRE), **14/1** Shuttlecock, Salbus, CSF £33.48 CT £104.89 TOTE £11.40: £1.90 £1.70 £1.40 (£27.40) OWNER Mr R. Fenwick-Gibson (HAMBLETON) 10 Rn 2m 4.9 (8.90) SF: 40/43/44/57/56/55/39/-/-/-
WEIGHT FOR AGE 3yo-2lb

T/Plpt: £579.20 (11.94 Tckts). T/Qdpt: Not won; £53.80 to Wolverhampton 27/12/95. IM

4347-WOLVERHAMPTON (L-H)
Tuesday December 27th (Standard)

Vis: misty

4354 HIMLEY H'CAP (0-65) (Class F) £2,398.00 (£673.00: £328.00)
1m 4f (Fibresand) GOING: 0.07 sec per fur (Std) 1-25 (1-26)

4311* **Noufari (FR) (61)***(71)*(Fav)*(RHollinshead)* 3-9-9 MWigham(3) (bhd: rdn 4f out: gd hdwy 2f out: r.o to ld wl ins fnl f)........— 1
4277[8] Premier Dance **(54)***(61) (DHaydnJones)* 7-9-7 JWilliams(11) (lw: chsd ldrs: 5th st: ev ch ins fnl f: unable qckn)........2½ 2
1353[14] Mr Bean **(45)***(50) (KRBurke)* 4-8-7 (5) SDrowne(1) (bit bkwd: a.p: 3rd st: ev ch ent fnl f: one pce)........1¾ 3
4323[10] Modest Hope (USA) **(48)***(52) (BRichmond)* 7-9-1 NAdams(10) (hld up: hdwy & 4th st: led wl over 1f out tl ins fnl f)........1 4
3795[7] Manolete **(45)***(48) (CWCElsey)* 3-8-7b NKennedy(7) (bit bkwd: hld up & bhd: hdwy fnl 2f: nvr nrr)........½ 5
4312[4] Can Can Charlie **(61)***(62) (JPearce)* 4-10-0b GBardwell(12) (led over 7f out tl hdd & wknd over 1f out)........1¼ 6
4277[14] Donia (USA) **(52)***(42) (JLHarris)* 5-9-5 SWilliams(8) (prom: 2nd st: hrd rdn & wknd over 1f out)........9 7
4323* El Nido **(59)***(48)*(Fav)*(MJCamacho)* 6-9-12 MRimmer(5) (lw: led over 4f: rdn & 6th st: sn btn)........1 8
4320[11] Mighty Kingdom (IRE) **(41)***(24) (RWEmery)* 3-8-3 BDoyle(9) (s.i.s: a bhd)........5 9
4326[5] Broughton's Pride (IRE) **(45)***(23) (JAGlover)* 3-8-7 GCarter(6) (lw: chsd ldrs 8f: sn lost tch)........4 10
4284* Carlton Express (IRE) **(39)***(11)*(Fav)*(JLEyre)* 4-8-6 AClark(2) (b.hind: hld up & bhd: hdwy over 3f out: wknd fnl 2f: fin lame)........5 11
2464[11] Derricks Refusal **(40)***(—) (CaptJWilson)* 3-7-11 (5) NVarley(4) (rdn & lost pl 5f out: t.o)........dist 12

4/1 NOUFARI (FR), El Nido, Carlton Express (IRE), **11/2** Premier Dance, **8/1** Broughton's Pride (IRE), **10/1** Can Can Charlie, **14/1** Donia (USA), Modest Hope (USA), **16/1** Mr Bean, **25/1** Derricks Refusal, **33/1** Mighty Kingdom (IRE), Manolete, CSF £25.79 CT £294.17 TOTE £4.60: £1.90 £1.70 £3.00 (£14.80) OWNER Ed Weetman (Haulage & Storage) Ltd (UPPER LONGDON) BRED His Highness The Aga Khans Studs S.C. in France 12 Rn

2m 40.2 (9.20) SF: 52/47/37/39/30/49/29/-/-/-/-/-

WEIGHT FOR AGE 3yo-5lb

4355 DUNSTON CLAIMING STKS (Class F) £2,398.00 (£673.00: £328.00)
6f (Fibresand) GOING: 0.07 sec per fur (Std) 1-55 (1-57)

4310[8] **Frisky Miss (IRE) (67)***(68) (JBerry)* 3-8-4 ow1 GCarter(11) (chsd ldrs: rdn to ld ins fnl f: hld on wl)........— 1
4310[C] Walk the Beat **(66)***(70) (RSimpson)* 4-8-2 (5) SDrowne(9) (b: a.p: slt ld ins fnl f: sn hdd: r.o)........hd 2
4348* Everset (FR) **(87)***(82)*(Fav)*(ABailey)* 6-9-2 (5) DWright(1) (in tch: hrd rdn over 1f out: r.o wl ins fnl f)........½ 3
4325[3] Samson-Agonistes **(70)***(70) (PDEvans)* 8-8-8 (5) SSanders(2) (b.off fore: a.p: led 2f out tl ins fnl f)........1¼ 4
4231[6] Delrob **(66)***(57) (DHaydnJones)* 3-7-13 (5) NVarley(12) (chsd ldrs: rdn & one pce appr fnl f)........1½ 5
4237[13] Sea Devil **(76)***(55) (MJCamacho)* 8-8-7 MRimmer(8) (led 4f: rdn & wknd ins fnl f) 1¾ 6
2222[3] Needwood Swift **(33)***(43) (BAMcMahon)* 3-8-0 TWilliams(13) (chsd ldrs: no hdwy fnl 2f)........2 7
Bold Cyrano (IRE) *(47) (BPalling)* 3-8-7 AClark(6) (bkwd: dwlt: sn rcvrd: chsd ldrs over 4f)........1 8
4322[6] Dauntless Fort **(50)***(33) (BWMurray)* 3-7-11 JQuinn(4) (b.off hind: in tch: effrt 2f out: no imp)........1¼ 9
2827[10] Educated Pet **(66)***(40) (BPreece)* 5-8-7 JWilliams(5) (bit bkwd: outpcd & a bhd)......1 10
4255[11] Olifantsfontein **(50)***(34) (DNicholls)* 6-7-11 (7)ow3 AEddery(3) (a bhd & outpcd)........¾ 11
4313[15] Trioming **(46)***(13) (APJones)* 8-8-3v NAdams(10) (dwlt: a bhd & outpcd: t.o)........8 12

10/11 Everset (FR), **6/1** Sea Devil, **7/1** FRISKY MISS (IRE) (5/1-8/1), **10/1** Walk the Beat, **12/1** Samson-Agonistes, Educated Pet, **14/1** Delrob, Olifantsfontein, **20/1** Bold Cyrano (IRE), **25/1** Dauntless Fort, **33/1** Needwood Swift, Trioming, CSF £74.42 TOTE £5.70: £1.70 £3.40 £1.30 (£41.70) OWNER Mrs Margaret Sinanan (COCKERHAM) BRED Mrs Margaret Sinanan 12 Rn

1m 14.7 (3.50) SF: 46/49/60/50/38/38/26/-/-/-/-/-

4356
CANNOCK NURSERY (0-85) (Class E) £2,788.00 (£844.00: £412.00: £196.00)
7f (Fibresand) GOING: 0.07 sec per fur (Std) 2-25 (2-26)

4350* **Master Millfield (IRE) (67)***(69) (CJHill)* 2-8-5 (7x) (5) SSanders(10) (a.p: 2nd st: brought wd: r.o wl to ld nr fin)......— **1**
4340² Bold Effort (FR) **(62)***(61) (KOCunningham-Brown)* 2-8-5 ow2 AClark(2) (led: hrd rdn fnl f: ct cl home)......1¼ **2**
4334* Gulf Shaadi **(78)***(74) (CEBrittain)* 2-9-7 BDoyle(5) (lw: chsd ldrs: 4th st: rdn & kpt on ins fnl f)......1½ **3**
4347* Komreyev Dancer **(75)***(71) (ABailey)* 2-8-13 (7x) (5) DWright(1) (hld up: effrt & 5th st: nt pce to chal)......s.h **4**
4216² Failte Ro **(64)***(57)*(Fav)*(JEBanks)* 2-8-7 JQuinn(11) (chsd ldrs: 6th st: rdn & one pce appr fnl f)......1½ **5**
4340⁸ Franklinsboy **(54)***(39) (CaptJWilson)* 2-7-6 (5)ow4 NVarley(7) (chsd ldr tl 3rd & wkng st)......4 **6**
4307³ Reponist **(52)***(30) (MJCamacho)* 2-7-6v(3)ow2 DarrenMoffatt(8) (a in rr)......3½ **7**
4286⁵ Black Shadow **(50)***(11) (PJMcBride)* 2-7-0 (7) RMullen(3) (a bhd & outpcd: t.o)......8 **8**
4055⁴ Never Time (IRE) **(63)***(23) (MrsVAAconley)* 2-8-1 (5)ow7 SDrowne(9) (lw: prom over 4f: sn wknd: t.o)......hd **9**
4285⁹ Casper's Risk **(61)***(10) (DNicholls)* 2-7-11b(7) AEddery(12) (dwlt: a bhd & outpcd: t.o)......5 **10**

LONG HANDICAP Franklinsboy 7-3 Reponist 7-4

3/1 Failte Ro, **9/2** MASTER MILLFIELD (IRE), **5/1** Komreyev Dancer, **11/2** Gulf Shaadi, **8/1** Bold Effort (FR), Reponist, Casper's Risk, **20/1** Black Shadow, **25/1** Never Time (IRE), **33/1** Franklinsboy, CSF £37.63 CT £185.67 TOTE £4.80: £2.20 £1.80 £2.00 (£14.20) OWNER Mr John Hill (BARNSTAPLE) BRED A. M. F. Persse 10 Rn 1m 29.4 (5.40) SF: 36/30/41/39/25/7/-/-/-/-

4357
DUDLEY H'CAP (0-65) (Class F) £2,398.00 (£673.00: £328.00)
7f (Fibresand) GOING: 0.07 sec per fur (Std) 2-55 (2-57)

2966⁸ **Tilly Owl (33)***(35+) (JAHarris)* 3-7-13 JO'Reilly(12) (b.off hind: a.p: 2nd st: led over 1f out: sn clr: rdn out)......— **1**
3481⁷ Kinnegad Kid **(40)***(37)*(Fav)*(RIngram)* 5-8-7 GCarter(2) (hld up: hdwy over 2f out: r.o strly fnl f: nt rch wnr)......2½ **2**
4313¹¹ Quinzii Martin **(40)***(37) (DHaydnJones)* 6-8-7 JWilliams(4) (hld up: hdwy & 6th st: rdn & r.o wl fnl f)......s.h **3**
4288⁶ Waverley Star **(38)***(24) (KOCunningham-Brown)* 9-8-5 AClark(8) (chsd ldrs: 5th st: wknd over 1f out)......5 **4**
4313⁹ Prince Rodney **(42)***(24) (CJDrewe)* 5-8-9b RPerham(7) (b: chsd ldrs: 3rd & rdn st: wknd over 1f out)......1¾ **5**
4034¹⁷ Beckyhannah **(32)***(14) (RBastiman)* 4-7-8 (5) DWright(9) (led over 4f out tl over 1f out: wknd fnl f)......s.h **6**
4278¹¹ Titanium Honda (IRE) **(45)***(14) (CEBrittain)* 3-8-11 BDoyle(1) (led 1f: wknd over 2f out)......6 **7**
4348⁵ Charlies Dream (IRE) **(45)***(10) (KRBurke)* 3-8-11 NAdams(6) (led after 1f tl over 4f out: rdn & 4th st: sn btn)......2 **8**
3234^C Belmont Princess (IRE) **(41)***(—) (APJones)* 4-8-3 (5) SDrowne(10) (s.s: a bhd & outpcd: t.o)......6 **9**
4306⁶ Farmer Jock **(48)***(—) (MrsNMacauley)* 12-9-1 MFenton(11) (b: a bhd: t.o)......4 **10**
2228⁶ Farastrada **(62)***(—) (BPreece)* 3-10-0 TWall(3) (bkwd: outpcd & bhd: t.o)......5 **11**
2311⁶ Princess Shera (IRE) **(45)***(—) (EJAlston)* 3-8-11 JQuinn(5) (bkwd: a bhd: t.o)......4 **12**

7/2 Kinnegad Kid, **4/1** TILLY OWL, **11/2** Quinzii Martin, **15/2** Charlies Dream (IRE), **8/1** Farmer Jock, **10/1** Beckyhannah, Farastrada, Princess Shera (IRE), Belmont Princess (IRE), **12/1** Titanium Honda (IRE), Waverley Star, **16/1** Prince Rodney, CSF £20.42 CT £78.13 TOTE £6.40: £1.90 £2.40 £2.30 (£11.90) OWNER Burntwood Sports Ltd (SOUTHWELL) BRED C. J. and Mrs J. E. Small 12 Rn 1m 29.2 (5.20) SF: 28/31/31/17/19/9/7/2/-/-/-/-

WEIGHT FOR AGE 3yo-1lb

4358
GAILEY STKS (Mdn) (Class D) £3,288.75 (£996.00: £486.50: £231.75)
1m 100y (Fibresand) GOING: 0.07 sec per fur (Std) 3-25 (3-26)

4255⁹ **Ballyhays (IRE) (37)***(52+) (JAHarris)* 5-9-0 SWilliams(10) (chsd ldrs: led over 3f out: sn clr: rdn out)......— **1**
4056⁴ Supercool *(40)*(Fav)*(BAMcMahon)* 3-8-8 (5) SSanders(8) (chsd ldrs: rdn & effrt 2f out: kpt on fnl f: nt rch wnr)......6 **2**
4270¹⁵ Miss Charlie **(36)***(35) (ABailey)* 4-8-9 GBardwell(13) (hld up: hdwy over 2f out: nrst fin)......hd **3**

4078[14] Ziggy's Dancer (USA) **(69)***(39) (EJAlston)* 3-8-8 (5) DWright(9) (led 5f: rdn & one pce appr fnl f)........nk 4
4320[6] Gallop to Glory **(38)***(36) (ALForbes)* 4-8-9 (5) BRussell(6) (bhd: rdn 4f out: styd on ins fnl f)........1½ 5
3191[14] Rock to Sleep (USA) **(60)***(23) (LordHuntingdon)* 3-8-8 DHarrison(5) (hld up: effrt 2f out: wknd appr fnl f)........4 6
4288[8] Quiet Mission **(41)***(25) (JLEyre)* 3-8-13 AClark(3) (chsd ldrs: rdn over 2f out: sn btn)........1¼ 7
4064[16] Dragonflight *(23) (DHaydnJones)* 3-8-8 (5) SDrowne(12) (bit bkwd: nvr trbld ldrs)....1 8
Amlak (USA) *(23) (TKersey)* 5-9-0 BDoyle(4) (bkwd: a in rr)........s.h 9
4140[9] Sky Diver **(41)***(22) (BJLlewellyn)* 3-8-13 JQuinn(2) (prom 5f)........½ 10
Great Bond *(10) (BAMcMahon)* 3-8-13 GCarter(7) (w'like: bkwd: a bhd: t.o)........6 11
4344[9] Celestial Faith *(3) (MJohnston)* 3-8-8 TWilliams(1) (dwlt: sn chsng ldrs: wknd 3f out: t.o)........1 12
D K Reunion *(—) (RHollinshead)* 4-8-7 (7) AEddery(11) (s.i.s: a bhd: t.o)........4 13

9/4 Supercool, **3/1** Ziggy's Dancer (USA), **4/1** Rock to Sleep (USA), **9/1** Celestial Faith, **14/1** Gallop to Glory, Great Bond, **16/1** Miss Charlie, **20/1** BALLYHAYS (IRE), Quiet Mission, Amlak (USA), **25/1** Sky Diver, D K Reunion, **33/1** Dragonflight, CSF £65.73 TOTE £50.80: £7.10 £1.50 £3.20 (£39.40) OWNER Mrs T. L. Martin (SOUTHWELL) BRED James M. Egan 13 Rn
1m 51.4 (7.40) SF: 33/22/18/21/19/6/9/7/-/-/-/-/-
WEIGHT FOR AGE 3yo-1lb

4359 MORVILLE (S) STKS (2-Y.O) (Class G) £2,190.00 (£615.00: £300.00)
6f (Fibresand) GOING: 0.07 sec per fur (Std) 3-55 (3-58)

4324[8] **Komlucky (49)***(59) (FJO'Mahony)* 2-8-6b JQuinn(9) (a.p: shkn up to ld over 1f out: hld on gamely)........— 1
4352[3] Lawnswood Lady **(40)***(59) (RHollinshead)* 2-8-6b DHarrison(12) (hdwy on outside over 2f out: str chal fnl f: jst failed)........s.h 2
4228[10] Needwood Newt **(55)***(55) (BAMcMahon)* 2-8-6 GBardwell(11) (bhd: hdwy 2f out: fin wl)........1½ 3
3666[25] Superbit **(50)***(58) (BAMcMahon)* 2-8-6 (5) SSanders(3) (bit bkwd: led tl hdd over 1f out: no ex fnl f)........½ 4
4352[2] David James' Girl **(59)***(57)*(Fav)*(ABailey)* 2-8-6 (5) DWright(4) (chsd ldrs: rdn over 1f out: one pce)........hd 5
4275[6] Curie Express (IRE) **(53)***(52) (JBerry)* 2-8-11 GCarter(6) (prom tl rdn & wknd over 1f out)........2 6
4299[7] Wings of Desire (IRE) **(46)***(43) (RChampion)* 2-8-11b MRimmer(2) (lw: hdwy over 2f out: rdn over 1f out: nvr able to chal)........3½ 7
4314[9] Two Chalk **(47)***(34) (PDEvans)* 2-8-11 AClark(5) (prom tl rdn & outpcd over 2f out: sn bhd)........3½ 8
3345[14] Princess in Blue (IRE) **(46)***(25) (CJHill)* 2-8-6 TWilliams(1) (outpcd: a bhd)........1¼ 9
4307[11] Silent Sky **(46)***(19) (CJHill)* 2-8-6 NAdams(8) (a bhd & outpcd)........2½ 10
Garadice Girl (IRE) *(—) (KRBurke)* 2-8-6 ATucker(10) (dwlt: a bhd & outpcd: t.o)15 11

5/4 David James' Girl, **5/1** Curie Express (IRE), Two Chalk, **6/1** Lawnswood Lady, **12/1** KOMLUCKY, **14/1** Superbit, Silent Sky, Needwood Newt, Princess in Blue (IRE), Garadice Girl (IRE), **20/1** Wings of Desire (IRE), CSF £87.13 TOTE £16.30: £2.30 £2.60 £3.70 (£40.30) OWNER Hambleton Racing Partnership (HAMBLETON) BRED T. Barratt 11 Rn No bid
1m 17.0 (5.80) SF: 17/17/13/16/16/10/1/-/-/-/-

4360 BRIDGETOWN H'CAP (0-80) (Class D) £3,199.05 (£968.40: £472.70: £224.85)
1m 100y (Fibresand) GOING: 0.07 sec per fur (Std) 4-25 (4-26)

4337* **Secret Aly (CAN) (69)***(74)*(Fav)*(CEBrittain)* 4-9-6 MRimmer(4) (lw: a.p: led over 2f out: sn clr: drvn out)........— 1
4281[2] Roar on Tour **(47)***(46)*(Fav)*(MrsMReveley)* 5-7-7 (5)ow1 DWright(6) (lw: a.p: 3rd st: chsd wnr appr fnl f: no imp)........3 2
4303[9] Ragazzo (IRE) **(44)***(40) (KOCunningham-Brown)* 4-7-6 (3)ow2 DarrenMoffatt(1) (led tl hdd & 2nd st: rdn & one pce appr fnl f)........1¼ 3
4333[9] Dawalib (USA) **(77)***(57) (DHaydnJones)* 4-9-9 (5) SDrowne(5) (lw: prom: 4th & rdn st: sn outpcd)........8 4
4309[9] Palacegate Jo (IRE) **(63)***(21) (RHollinshead)* 3-8-13 GCarter(2) (a bhd & outpcd: poor 6th st: t.o)........11 5
4309[11] Brief Respite (IRE) **(65)***(18) (EJAlston)* 3-9-1 JQuinn(3) (a in rr: rdn 3f out: 5th & btn st: t.o)........2½ 6
LONG HANDICAP Ragazzo (IRE) 7-6

6/4 SECRET ALY (CAN), Roar on Tour, **6/1** Dawalib (USA), **7/1** Palacegate Jo (IRE), **20/1** Ragazzo (IRE), Brief Respite (IRE), CSF £4.21 TOTE £2.70: £1.30 £1.50 (£2.00) OWNER Mr B. H. Voak (NEWMARKET) BRED Northern Equine Thoroughbred Productions 6 Rn

1m 49.7 (5.70) SF: 55/29/24/40/6/3
WEIGHT FOR AGE 3yo-1lb

T/Plpt: £442.00 (25.08 Tckts). T/Qdpt: £94.90 (2 Tckts) IM

4319-SOUTHWELL (L-H)
Tuesday December 27th (Slow)

Abandoned after 2nd race - course deemed unsafe after persistent rain

4361 STRIDER CLAIMING STKS (I) (Class F) £2,398.00 (£673.00: £328.00)
5f (Fibresand) GOING: minus 0.17 sec per fur (FS) 11-50 (11-53)

4237⁹ **Matthew David (34)***(59) (SRBowring)* 4-7-12 (7) CTeague(10) (chsd ldrs: sn hrd rdn: kpt on fnl f: led post) ....— **1**
4306⁹ Primula Bairn **(60)***(58) (MrsJRRamsden)* 4-8-4v AMackay(9) (swtchd lft s: sn chsng ldrs: led wl ins fnl f: jst ct).......s.h **2**
4333⁷ Green's Bid **(61)***(65) (DWChapman)* 4-9-0 DaleGibson(4) (led far side tl hdd & no ex wl ins fnl f).......¾ **3**
4333¹⁰ Very Dicey **(75)***(61)*(Fav)*(JBerry)* 6-8-6 (7) PRoberts(11) (lw: racd stands' side: chsd ldrs: kpt on wl fnl f).......¾ **4**
4345³ Granmas Delight **(53)***(36) (KTIvory)* 3-8-0 DBiggs(1) (s.v.s: bhd tl kpt on appr fnl f).......4 **5**
3583¹² Miss Siham (IRE) **(39)***(40) (JBalding)* 5-7-13 (7) ClaireBalding(5) (in tch: drvn along ½-wy: grad wknd).......½ **6**
4227¹⁵ Rosina's Folly **(54)***(39) (JLHarris)* 3-8-6 NCarlisle(8) (outpcd fr ½-wy).......nk **7**
1014¹⁶ My Foxy Lady **(38)***(19) (JAHarris)* 4-7-5 (7) SLanigan(2) (chsd ldr far side 3f: sn wknd).......4 **8**
Bassetlaw Belle **(20)***(—) (NPLittmoden)* 5-7-7 (7) CAdamson(7) (sn outpcd & bhd) .7 **9**
Northgate Raver *(—) (RonaldThompson)* 3-8-7 (5) LNewton(6) (uns rdr gng to s: sn drvn along: in tch: outpcd ½-wy: t.o) 25 **10**

Evens Very Dicey, **9/2** Primula Bairn, **5/1** Granmas Delight, **8/1** Green's Bid, **12/1** MATTHEW DAVID, **20/1** Miss Siham (IRE), Rosina's Folly, My Foxy Lady, **33/1** Northgate Raver, **50/1** Bassetlaw Belle, CSF £63.25 TOTE £6.70: £1.30 £2.50 £2.20 (£17.40) OWNER Mrs Katherine Fogg (EDWINSTOWE) BRED MDM Racing (Thoroughbreds) Ltd 10 Rn

60.8 secs (2.80) SF: 28/27/34/31/6/9/8/-/-/-

4362 ROHAN NURSERY (0-75) (Class E) £2,671.00 (£808.00: £394.00: £187.00)
5f (Fibresand) GOING: minus 0.17 sec per fur (FS) 12-20 (12-20)

4342* **Go Hever Golf (75)***(96+)*(Fav)*(TJNaughton)* 2-9-7 (7x) (7) VHalliday(1) (w ldr: led ½-wy: rdn over 1f out: r.o strly nr fin) ....— **1**
4275³ Half Tone **(42)***(58?) (RMFlower)* 2-7-2b(7)ow2 MDwyer(4) (outpcd after 2f out: hdwy & ev ch over 1f out: nt qckn ins fnl f) 1½ **2**
3605⁸ Bold Frontier **(58)***(66) (KTIvory)* 2-8-11b RCochrane(2) (b: trckd ldrs: effrt & rdn over 1f out: kpt on same pce).......2½ **3**
4275² C-Yer-Simmie (IRE) **(56)***(53) (RHollinshead)* 2-8-4 (5) AGarth(3) (led to ½-wy: wknd over 1f out).......3½ **4**
4298⁹ Fishy Affair **(44)***(17) (TDyer)* 2-7-4 (7)ow4 SLanigan(5) (s.i.s: sn outpcd stands' side) 8 **5**
LONG HANDICAP Fishy Affair 7-5 Half Tone 7-0

4/5 GO HEVER GOLF, **3/1** C-Yer-Simmie (IRE), **9/2** Bold Frontier, **14/1** Half Tone, Fishy Affair, CSF £9.97 TOTE £1.60: £1.20 £1.70 (£7.90) OWNER Hever Racing Club (EPSOM) BRED Ronald Popely 5 Rn 60.0 secs (2.00) SF: 62/27/33/20/-

4363 STRIDER CLAIMING STKS (II) (Class F)
5f (Fibresand) - 12-50 **Abandoned** - course deemed unsafe

4364 DAVY MINING H'CAP (0-70) (Class E)
1m 6f (Fibresand) - 1-20 **Abandoned** - course deemed unsafe

4365 SARUMAN (S) STKS (I) (Class G)
1m 3f (Fibresand) - 1-55 - **Abandoned** - course deemed unsafe

4366 CARPET CONTRACTORS NOTTINGHAM STKS (Mdn 2-Y.O) (Class D)
6f (Fibresand) (2-30) - **Abandoned** - course deemed unsafe

4367 SARUMAN (S) STKS (II) (Class G)
1m 3f (Fibresand) (3-00) - **Abandoned** - course deemed unsafe

4368 ELROND H'CAP (0-70) (Class E)
7f (Fibresand) (3-30) - **Abandoned** - course deemed unsafe
T/Plpt: £5.70 (989.38 Tckts) WG

4338-LINGFIELD (L-H)
Saturday December 31st (Standard)

4369 'ANY PORT' MEDIAN AUCTION STKS (Mdn 2-Y.O) (Class F) £2,481.30 (£696.80: £339.90) **5f (Equitrack)** GOING: minus 0.55 sec (FS) 11-55 (11-56)

4330⁶ **Abbey House (45)***(55) (RGuest)* 2-8-4b(5) AWhelan(4) (s.i.s: hdwy over 1f out: str run fnl f: led nr fin) ....— **1**
4324² Avant Huit **(56)***(51)*(Fav)*(MrsNMacauley)* 2-8-9b JWeaver(1) (lw: a.p: led over 2f out: hrd rdn over 1f out: hdd nr fin) 1¼ **2**
4324⁶ Merrie le Bow *(47) (PatMitchell)* 2-8-9 JMcLaughlin(6) (lost pl over 2f out: rallied fnl f: r.o) 1¼ **3**
4330⁸ Just Jesting **(55)***(52) (GLMoore)* 2-9-0b RPerham(3) (lw: a.p: rdn over 2f out: r.o one pce fnl f) ....s.h **4**
4314⁷ Fiery Footsteps **(56)***(46) (PHowling)* 2-8-9 JQuinn(2) (led over 2f: hrd rdn over 1f out: one pce) ....nk **5**
4340¹⁰ Governor's Lass *(42) (SDow)* 2-8-9e StephenDavies(5) (eyeshield: lost pl over 2f out: one pce) 1¼ **6**

8/11 Avant Huit, **5/1** Merrie le Bow, Fiery Footsteps **9/1** ABBEY HOUSE **14/1** Just Jesting, **25/1** Governor's Lass CSF £15.61 TOTE £7.60: £2.30 £1.30 (£4.70) OWNER Mr A. P. Davies (NEWMARKET) BRED M. G. T. Stokes 6 Rn 60.56 secs (2.36) SF: 8/5/2/6/1/-

4370 'ALL'S FAIR' H'CAP (0-85) (Class D) £3,420.00 (£1,035.00: £505.00: £240.00) **5f (Equitrack)** GOING: minus 0.55 sec per fur (FS) 12-25 (12-26)

4345⁴ **Daaniera (IRE) (55)***(61) (PHowling)* 4-7-7b(5)ow5 DWright(2) (b.hind: lw: led 4f out: hrd rdn fnl f: r.o wl) ....— **1**
4297* Nordico Princess **(64)***(65)*(Fav)*(GROldroyd)* 3-8-7 ow1 RCochrane(5) (led 1f: hrd rdn over 1f out: unable qckn) 1¾ **2**
4316³ Press the Bell **(77)***(75) (JBerry)* 4-9-6 GCarter(7) (a.p: hrd rdn over 1f out: r.o ins fnl f) ....¾ **3**
4345² Featherstone Lane **(60)***(46) (MissLCSiddall)* 3-8-3v DHarrison(1) (a.p: rdn over 3f out: wknd ins fnl f) 4 **4**
4316⁷ Rocky Two **(60)***(45) (PHowling)* 3-8-3b JQuinn(9) (prom over 3f) ....nk **5**
4241⁹ African Chimes **(71)***(56) (WAO'Gorman)* 7-8-11b(3) EmmaO'Gorman(8) (nvr nr to chal) ....s.h **6**
3457* Moscow Road **(76)***(53) (MissBSanders)* 3-9-0 (5) SSanders(3) (lw: outpcd) 2½ **7**
3449⁴ Farfelu **(85)***(61) (WRMuir)* 7-10-0b JWeaver(6) (outpcd) ....nk **8**
240² Riskie Things **(65)***(14) (JSMoore)* 3-8-8 NAdams(4) (lw: bhd fnl 4f) 9 **9**
LONG HANDICAP Daaniera (IRE) 7-1

3/1 Nordico Princess, **5/1** Feathersone Lane, **6/1** Press the Bell, Moscow Road, **13/2** African Chimes, Farfelu, **14/1** Rocky Two, **20/1** DAANIERA (IRE), **25/1** Riskie Things CSF £71.96 CT £371.77 TOTE £17.10: £3.40 £1.90 £1.50 (£53.20) OWNER The Hammond Partnership (GUILDFORD) BRED Andrew Bannon 9 Rn 58.5 secs (0.30) SF: 31/36/46/17/16/26/22/-/-

4371 'COLD AS CHARITY' CLAIMING STKS (I) (Class E) £2,762.00 (£836.00: £408.00: £194.00) **1m (Equitrack)** GOING: minus 0.55 sec (FS) 12-55 (12-56)

4304a⁸ **Metal Storm (FR) (95)***(82) (KOCunningham-Brown)* 6-9-5 RCochrane(2) (chsd ldr 5f out: led 1f out: pushed out) ....— **1**
4224³ Spencer's Revenge **(70)***(70)*(Fav)*(LordHuntingdon)* 5-8-9 JWeaver(8) (lw: led 7f: unable qckn) ....¾ **2**
2724⁹ Medland (IRE) **(56)***(48) (WGMTurner)* 4-7-8 (7) SLanigan(6) (lw: stdd s: stdy hdwy over 3f out: nvr plcd to chal) 7 **3**
4319¹⁴ Scottish Park **(40)***(38) (RWEmery)* 5-7-12 GBardwell(3) (lost pl 5f out: r.o one pce fnl 2f) 3½ **4**
4343³ Joint Effort (IRE) **(42)***(36) (AMoore)* 3-7-8 (5) AWhelan(7) (no hdwy fnl 4f) 1¾ **5**
4265⁶ Wave Hill **(62)***(39) (PRHedger)* 5-8-5v StephenDavies(5) (lw: a.p: rdn over 3f out: eased whn btn fnl f) 1 **6**

Val D'Authie (FR) *(21) (RJO'Sullivan)* 6-8-7 MRimmer(10) (nvr nr to chal)............10 7
Victoria Princess **(30)***(4) (MMadgwick)* 7-7-12 NAdams(11) (bit bkwd: a bhd)..........4 8
1732[21] Youcanstoplooking (IRE) **(50)***(11) (SDow)* 3-8-1 (5) SSanders(1) (eyeshield: a bhd) ¾ 9
4320[12] Well Suited **(40)***(13) (BJMcMath)* 4-8-11 TWilliams(9) (b: b.hind: prom over 2f)......¾ 10
Forbidden Gem *(—) (SWoodman)* 3-9-0 DHarrison(4) (unf: prom over 3f)...........15 11

2/1 Spencer's Revenge, **11/4** Wave Hill, **4/1** METAL STORM (FR), **6/1** Joint Effort (IRE), **14/1** Medland (IRE), **16/1** Val D'Authie (FR), **25/1** Scottish Park, **66/1** Ors CSF £11.62 TOTE £5.50: £2.30 £1.10 £3.90 (£8.80) OWNER Mr A. J. Richards (STOCKBRIDGE) BRED Mme Yolande Seydoux de Clausonne 11 Rn 1m 37.73 (1.33) SF: 44/33/13/3/2/5/-/-/-/-/-

4372 `GIFT HORSE' NURSERY (Class C) £4,810.75 (£1,456.00: £710.50: £337.75)
1m (Equitrack) GOING: minus 0.55 sec per fur (FS) 1-25 (1-26)

3688* **Battleship Bruce (56)***(72+)*(Fav)*(NACallaghan)* 2-8-1 DHarrison(2) (a.p: led over 1f out: pushed out)...........— 1
4356* Master Millfield (IRE) **(68)***(77) (CJHill)* 2-8-8 (5x) (5) SSanders(10) (lw: a.p: led over 3f out tl over 1f out: unable qckn)...........3½ 2
4259* Star Fighter **(64)***(67) (WAO'Gorman)* 2-8-6 (3) EmmaO'Gorman(9) (hdwy over 3f out: one pce fnl 2f)...........3 3
4279[2] Soldier's Leap (FR) **(72)***(67) (CEBrittain)* 2-9-3b BDoyle(5) (a.p: rdn over 2f out: sn wknd)...........4 4
4314[12] Witney-de-Bergerac (IRE) **(61)***(36) (JSMoore)* 2-8-1 (5)ow1 SDrowne(7) (nt clr run on ins over 3f out: nvr nr to chal)...........10 5
4228[4] Jilly Jaffa Cake (IRE) **(60)***(30) (DWPArbuthnot)* 2-8-5 SWhitworth(11) (prom 3f) ..2½ 6
4314* Iron Man (IRE) **(59)***(28) (JWhite)* 2-7-13b(5) AWhelan(8) (bhd fnl 4f)...........½ 7
3927[10] Star Witness (IRE) **(76)***(42) (JSMoore)* 2-9-7 NAdams(6) (bhd fnl 5f)...........1½ 8
4356[2] Bold Effort (FR) **(60)***(24) (KOCunningham-Brown)* 2-8-5 AClark(1) (led over 4f)......1 9
4334[2] Chewit **(74)***(32) (AMoore)* 2-9-5 CandyMorris(12) (b.hind: lw: s.s: hdwy over 4f out: wknd over 3f out)...........3 10

7/4 BATTLESHIP BRUCE, **100/30** Master Millfield (IRE), **6/1** Bold Effort (FR), **13/2** Soldier's Leap (FR), **8/1** Iron Man (IRE), **12/1** Star Fighter, **25/1** Ors CSF £7.88 CT £44.18 TOTE £3.20: £1.60 £1.10 £2.90 (£5.20) OWNER Mr T. A. Foreman (NEWMARKET) BRED Highfield Stud Ltd 10 Rn 1m 37.23 (0.83) SF: 32/37/27/27/-/-/-/-/-/-

4373 `APPLE A DAY' H'CAP (0-65) (Class F) £2,933.60 (£824.60: £402.80)
1m 5f (Equitrack) GOING: minus 0.55 sec per fur (FS) 1-55 (1-56)

4284[3] **Beautete (60)***(67) (SDow)* 3-9-6 DHarrison(4) (a.p: chsd ldr 4f out: hrd rdn over 1f out: led nr fin)...........— 1
4284[6] Marco Magnifico (USA) **(63)***(69) (BWHills)* 4-9-9 (5) JDSmith(12) (b: b.hind: led: rdn over 1f out: hdd nr fin)...........½ 2
4338* Wottashambles **(42)***(45)*(Fav)*(GLewis)* 3-7-11 (5) AGarth(2) (lost pl 6f out: rallied over 2f out: r.o one pce)...........2½ 3
4318[6] Dancing Diamond (IRE) **(45)***(47) (MissBSanders)* 4-8-5hb(5) SSanders(13) (a.p: rdn over 4f out: one pce)...........½ 4
4335[2] In the Money (IRE) **(55)***(57) (RHollinshead)* 5-9-6 TIves(3) (a.p: rdn over 4f out: one pce)...........s.h 5
4311[4] Telephus **(48)***(35) (BJMcMath)* 5-8-13b RCochrane(7) (no hdwy fnl 3f)...........13 6
1825[11] Upper Mount Clair **(62)***(47) (CEBrittain)* 4-9-13 BDoyle(9) (nvr nr to chal)...........1¼ 7
4338[3] Glow Forum **(42)***(26) (GLMoore)* 3-7-11 (5)ow4 AWhelan(6) (hdwy 3f out: sn wknd) .½ 8
4341[13] Ecu de France (IRE) **(59)***(36) (MMadgwick)* 4-9-5 (5) DRMcCabe(11) (lw: a bhd) 6 9
307[8] Colin's Pride **(46)***(—) (MrsSDWilliams)* 3-8-1 (5)ow1 SDrowne(10) (prom 4f)...........25 10
4338[4] Prosequendo (USA) **(63)***(6) (MDixon)* 7-10-0 AClark(8) (b: lw: a bhd)...........4 11
3993[19] Karon Beach **(50)***(—) (JPearce)* 3-8-10 GBardwell(1) (bhd fnl 11f)...........15 12

9/4 Wottashambles, **9/2** In the Money (IRE), **5/1** Telephus, Proseqendo (USA), **10/1** Glow Forum, **12/1** BEAUTETE, Marco Magnifico (USA), **16/1** Karon Beach, Dancing Diamond (IRE), **20/1** Upper Mount Clair, Ecu de France (IRE), **33/1** Colin's Pride CSF £141.84 CT £409.85 TOTE £11.40: £4.00 £4.30 £2.00 (£89.20) OWNER Mr D. G. Churston (EPSOM) BRED Hollow Hole Stud 12 Rn 2m 45.16 (2.66) SF: 44/51/24/31/40/18/30/-/-/-/-/-
WEIGHT FOR AGE 3yo-5lb

4374 `COLD AS CHARITY' CLAIMING STKS (II) (Class E) £2,762.00 (£836.00: £408.00: £194.00) **1m (Equitrack)** GOING: minus 0.55 sec per fur (FS) 2-25 (2-25)

4302[2] **Masnun (USA) (69)***(68) (RJO'Sullivan)* 9-8-7 DBiggs(9) (hld up: hrd rdn over 1f out: led last strides)...........— 1
4264[2] Mr Nevermind (IRE) **(76)***(80)*(Fav)*(GLMoore)* 4-8-12 (7) LSuthern(2) (lw: hld up: led over 1f out: hrd rdn: hdd last strides)...........hd 2

4343[7] Quick Million *(62) (BJMeehan)* 3-8-1 (7)ow7 DaneO'Neill(6) (led 3f: led 2f out tl over 1f out: unable qckn)....4 **3**
4260[5] Give In **(42)***(50) (MissGayKelleway)* 7-7-10 (5) DWright(5) (lost pl over 4f out: r.o one pce fnl 2f)....2 **4**
1884[4] Respectable Jones **(48)***(54) (RHollinshead)* 8-8-0 (7) RGordon(7) (lw: hdwy over 3f out: wknd wl over 1f out)....1 **5**
4260[8] Finjan **(51)***(41) (AGFoster)* 7-8-1 StephenDavies(4) (b.hind: led 5f out to 2f out: wknd 1f out)....3½ **6**
3899[6] Miss Mah-Jong **(65)***(43) (JWhite)* 3-8-1b(5)ow1 SDrowne(3) (bhd fnl 4f)....1¾ **7**
4344[3] Thorniwama **(36)***(41) (JJBridger)* 3-8-5 ow2 AClark(8) (prom over 3f)....nk **8**
4306[12] White Lady **(61)***(1) (RWEmery)* 3-7-9 JQuinn(10) (lw: bhd fnl 4f)....15 **9**
3783[9] Super Assignation (IRE) *(7) (DRCElsworth)* 3-8-13 JWilliams(1) (lw: a bhd)....6 **10**

13/8 Mr Nevermind (IRE), **2/1** MASNUN (USA), **8/1** Super Assignation (IRE), **10/1** Miss Mah-Jong, **14/1** Respectable Jones, Thorniwama, Finjan, **20/1** Give In, **25/1** White Lady, **33/1** Quick Million, CSF £5.77 TOTE £3.50: £1.80 £1.20 £6.20 (£3.00) OWNER Mr I.W. Page (BOGNOR REGIS) BRED Glencrest Farm 10 Rn 1m 38.35 (1.95) SF: 27/38/20/10/13/1/3/2/-/-

4375 LADBROKE ALL-WEATHER TROPHY (H'cap) (Qualifier) (I) (0-70) (Class E) £2,697.00 (£816.00: £398.00: £189.00)

7f (Equitrack) GOING: minus 0.55 sec per fur (FS) 2-55 (2-57)

4336[3] **World Traveller (69)***(74)(WAO'Gorman)* 3-9-11b(3) EmmaO'Gorman(5) (lw: hld up: hrd rdn over 2f out: led nr fin)....— **1**
4317[11] As Such (IRE) **(55)***(59) (NACallaghan)* 3-9-0b MRimmer(2) (led over 3f: led over 2f out: hrd rdn fnl f: hdd nr fin)....½ **2**
4270[11] Possibility **(43)***(44) (RIngram)* 3-7-11b(5) DWright(3) (rdn over 3f out: hdwy over 1f out: r.o ins fnl f)....1¼ **3**
4349* Arndilly **(69)***(69) (BJMeehan)*(Fav) 3-10-0 (6x) RCochrane(9) (b: hdwy over 3f out: hrd rdn over 1f out: unable qckn ins fnl f)....nk **4**
4289[8] Soaking **(68)***(65) (GLMoore)* 4-9-7 (7) LSuthern(8) (nvr nr to chal)....1¼ **5**
4269[3] Spectacle Jim **(48)***(42) (JO'Donoghue)* 5-8-3 (5) DRMcCabe(7) (rdn over 3f out: hdwy fnl f: nvr nrr)....1¼ **6**
4319[11] Obsidian Grey **(46)***(40) (MissLCSiddall)* 7-8-6 DHarrison(6) (prom over 4f)....s.h **7**
4357[7] Titanium Honda (IRE) **(45)***(35) (CEBrittain)* 3-8-4b BDoyle(1) (chsd ldr: led over 3f out tl over 2f out: wknd over 1f out)....1¾ **8**
4345[8] Papagos (IRE) **(42)***(21) (SDow)* 3-8-1 StephenDavies(4) (bhd fnl 2f)....5 **9**

7/4 Arndilly, **9/2** Spectacle Jim, Soaking (6/1-4/1), **5/1** WORLD TRAVELLER, **10/1** Possibility, **14/1** As Such (IRE), **16/1** Obsidian Grey, **20/1** Titanium Honda (IRE), **25/1** Papagos (IRE) CSF £62.77 CT £615.48 TOTE £5.50: £1.60 £3.00 £3.80 (£30.80) OWNER Mr N. S. Yong (NEWMARKET) BRED N. E. and Mrs Poole 9 Rn 1m 25.5 (2.50) SF: 36/22/9/32/30/9/8/4/-
WEIGHT FOR AGE 3yo-1lb

4376 LADBROKE ALL-WEATHER TROPHY (H'cap) (Qualifier) (II) (0-70) (Class E) £2,697.00 (£816.00: £398.00: £189.00)

7f (Equitrack) GOING: minus 0.55 sec per fur (FS) 3-25 (3-25)

4313[3] **Digpast (IRE) (47)***(54) (RJO'Sullivan)* 4-8-7b DBiggs(8) (b: lw: gd hdwy over 2f out: led over 1f out: edgd lft: all out)....— **1**
4313[2] Sharp Imp **(46)***(52)*(Fav)*(RMFlower)* 4-8-1b(5) JDSmith(6) (hdwy over 1f out: str run fnl f: fin wl)....hd **2**
4317* Maid Welcome **(58)***(63) (MrsNMacauley)* 7-8-11v(7) AmandaSanders(3) (led 2f: nt clr run over 1f out: r.o wl ins fnl f)....½ **3**
4337[10] Milos **(69)***(66) (TJNaughton)* 3-10-0 GCarter(2) (lw: nvr nr to chal)....4 **4**
4344[7] Myjinka **(35)***(31) (JO'Donoghue)* 4-7-2b(7)ow2 MBaird(4) (lw: led 5f out tl over 1f out: sn wknd)....½ **5**
4051[9] Apollo Red **(54)***(49) (AMoore)* 5-9-0 CandyMorris(1) (b.hind: a.p: rdn over 1f out: wknd fnl f)....nk **6**
4317[3] Zinbaq **(43)***(25) (CJBenstead)* 8-8-3 TWilliams(7) (outpcd)....6 **7**
4343[4] Dynamis (IRE) **(57)***(26) (KOCunningham-Brown)* 3-9-2 MWigham(5) (bhd fnl 2f)....6 **8**
LONG HANDICAP Myjinka 6-8

3/1 Sharp Imp, **7/2** DIGPAST (IRE), **9/2** Maid Welcome, **11/2** Zinbaq, **7/1** Milos, Dynamis (IRE), **14/1** Apollo Red, **50/1** Myjinka CSF £13.61 CT £42.16 TOTE £5.50: £1.80 £1.50 £1.90 (£8.40) OWNER Mr Les Randall (BOGNOR REGIS) BRED Somerville Stud 8 Rn
1m 25.08 (2.08) SF: 21/20/30/30/-/16/-/-

T/Plpt: £13.80 (583.13 Tckts). T/Qdpt: £5.60 (8.6 Tckts). AK

4347-WOLVERHAMPTON (L-H)
Saturday December 31st

4377 `FAREWELL 1994' H'CAP (0-80) (Class D) £2,682.60 (£753.60: £367.80)
6f (Fibresand) GOING: minus 0.05 sec per fur (Std) 6-00 (6-01)

4310* **Four of Spades (62)***(67) (WSCunningham)* 3-8-13b AClark(3) (lw: led over 4f out: hrd rdn ent fnl f: r.o wl)........— 1
4349⁴ Little Ibnr **(66)***(67)*(Fav)*(PDEvans)* 3-8-12 (5) TGMcLaughlin(5) (a.p: rdn over 1f out: unable qckn fnl f)........1½ 2
4360⁴ Dawalib (USA) **(77)***(72) (DHaydnJones)* 4-9-9v(5) SDrowne(6) (lw: chsd ldrs: hrd drvn 2f out: nt pce to chal)........2½ 3
4349⁸ Cheerful Groom (IRE) **(47)***(36) (JMackie)* 3-7-12 NCarlisle(2) (lw: dwlt: sn rdn along: nvr trbld ldrs)........2½ 4
4310⁵ So Intrepid (IRE) **(69)***(43) (JMBradley)* 4-9-6 AMackay(4) (outpcd: a bhd: t.o)........6 5
4059¹⁹ Hiltons Travel (IRE) **(55)***(11) (EJAlston)* 3-8-6 JQuinn(1) (led over 1f: lost pl ½-wy: t.o)........7 6

6/4 Little Ibnr, **3/1** FOUR OF SPADES, **7/2** Dawalib (USA), **8/1** Hiltons Travel (IRE), **10/1** So Intrepid (IRE), **20/1** Cheerful Groom (IRE) CSF £7.62 TOTE £4.10: £1.80 £1.90 (£2.80) OWNER Mr B. L. Cassidy (YARM) BRED Hesmonds Stud Ltd 6 Rn 1m 14.9 (3.70) SF: 41/42/45/11/15/-

4378 NEW YEAR CLAIMING STKS (Class F) £2,085.00 (£585.00: £285.00)
1m 100y (Fibresand) GOING: minus 0.05 sec per fur (Std) 6-30 (6-32)

4034¹¹ **Northern Celadon (IRE) (68)***(76+)(MJHeaton-Ellis)* 3-9-2 StephenDavies(2) (mde all: clr appr fnl f: unchal)........— 1
4320³ Sharp Gazelle **(40)***(57) (BSmart)* 4-8-1 (5) SSanders(3) (lw: chsd wnr: 2nd & rdn st: sn outpcd)........4 2
1624⁵ Zahran (IRE) **(79)***(42) (JMBradley)* 3-8-4 JQuinn(7) (b: hld up: hdwy & 6th st: styd on one pce fnl f: nvr nrr)........7 3
4341¹² Lombard Ships **(45)***(37) (ABailey)* 7-8-0bow2 AMackay(12) (hld up & bhd: styd on fr appr fnl f: nrst fin)........s.h 4
4358⁸ Dragonflight *(47) (DHaydnJones)* 3-8-7 (5) SDrowne(4) (chsd ldrs: 5th & rdn st: sn btn)........1½ 5
4303⁴ Battle Colours (IRE) **(63)***(45)*(Fav) *(MrsJRRamsden)* 5-8-13 SWilliams(6) (lw: chsd ldrs 5f: sn rdn & wknd)........¾ 6
4274¹¹ Royal Acclaim **(47)***(30) (JMBradley)* 9-7-8v(7) AmandaSanders(8) (bhd: hdwy on outside fnl 2f: nvr nrr)........1½ 7
4257¹⁰ Port Sunlight (IRE) **(55)***(33) (PDEvans)* 6-8-5 AClark(13) (swtg: hdwy 4f out: nt rch ldrs)........nk 8
4322¹⁵ Make the Break **(56)***(40) (SCoathup)* 3-8-5 (7) SharronJames(5) (hdwy ½-wy: 3rd st: wknd over 1f out)........nk 9
3570¹² Nigelschinapalace **(28)***(33) (MissSJWilton)* 5-8-7 JWilliams(9) (b: outpcd: a bhd)..nk 10
4349⁶ Farndale **(55)***(27) (JBerry)* 7-8-2 (3) DarrenMoffatt(1) (prom: 4th & rdn st: sn wknd)1¾ 11
3116⁷ City Rhythm *(—) (JMBradley)* 4-8-0 (5) DWright(11) (bit bkwd: outpcd: a bhd: t.o) 20 12
4348² Alpine Johnny **(57)***(—) (RHollinshead)* 3-8-8 AGarth(10) .... W

11/4 Battle Colours (IRE), **6/1** NORTHERN CELADON (IRE), **7/1** Sharp Gazelle, **15/2** Zahran (IRE), **10/1** Farndale, **11/1** Lombard Ships, **12/1** Port Sunlight (IRE), **14/1** Royal Acclaim, Make the Break, **33/1** Ors CSF £34.10 TOTE £5.10: £1.30 £1.50 £2.80 (£40.40) OWNER The Over The Bridge Partnership (WROUGHTON) BRED A.O'Callaghan 12Rn 1m 50.9 (6.90) SF: 31/14/-/-/4/4
WEIGHT FOR AGE 3yo-1lb

4379 HOGMANAY H'CAP (0-80) (Class D) £2,695.20 (£757.20: £369.60)
1m 1f 79y (Fibresand) GOING: minus 0.05 sec per fur (Std) 7-00 (7-01)

4320* **Bentico (66)***(73)*(Fav)*(MrsNMacauley)* 5-9-9 (5) SSanders(7) (hdwy 4f out: led over 2f out: rdn out)........— 1
4319⁷ Certain Way (IRE) **(53)***(57) (NPLittmoden)* 4-8-10 (5) TGMcLaughlin(4) (lw: chsd ldrs: slt ld 3f out: sn hdd: 2nd st: r.o one pce)........2 2
4319⁴ Hawwam **(54)***(58) (EJAlston)* 8-9-2 JQuinn(1) (a.p: 3rd & rdn st: kpt on ins fnl f) ...hd 3
4360⁵ Palacegate Jo (IRE) **(63)***(55) (RHollinshead)* 3-9-9 GCarter(5) (chsd ldrs: rdn 3f out: 5th & btn st)........7 4
4311⁸ Salska **(52)***(41) (PJBevan)* 3-8-12 NCarlisle(3) (a in rr: 6th st: rdn & no imp)........2 5
3205¹³ Sharp Thrill **(43)***(30) (BSmart)* 3-8-3v StephenDavies(2) (lw: chsd ldr 5f: 4th st: eased whn btn appr fnl f)........1½ 6

4341⁹ Ezekiel **(40)***(—) (JWPayne)* 3-8-0 GBardwell(6) (lw: led: sn clr: wknd & hdd 3f out: 7th st: t.o)........20 **7**

Evens BENTICO, **5/2** Hawwam, **13/2** Certain Way (IRE), **12/1** Palacegate Jo (IRE), **16/1** Salska, **25/1** Ors CSF £7.63 TOTE £2.10: £1.20 £2.30 (£6.40) OWNER Mr G. Wiltshire (MELTON MOWBRAY) BRED Britton House Stud 7 Rn 2m 4.1 (8.10) SF: 38/23/24/19/6/-/-
WEIGHT FOR AGE 3yo-2lb

4380 RESOLUTIONS STKS (Mdn 2-Y.O) (Class D) £2,658.00 (£804.00: £392.00: £186.00) **1m 1f 79y (Fibresand)** GOING: minus 0.05 sec per fur (Std) 7-30 (7-31)

4259⁸ **Shy Paddy (IRE)** *(64)(KOCunningham-Brown)* 2-9-0 AClark(3) (s.i.s: a.p: 2nd & rdn st: led ent fnl f: edgd lft: all out)........— **1**
4342⁵ Keys Seminar **(45)***(63) (NACallaghan)* 2-9-0 GCarter(4) (led 1f: 3rd st: shkn up to ld over 1f out: sn hdd: r.o)........½ **2**
3956³ Sandra Dee (IRE) *(50)* (Fav) *(BAPearce)* 2-8-9 StephenDavies(1) (bit bkwd: led after 1f tl over 1f out: wknd fnl f)........5 **3**
4280⁶ Framley Garth *(36) (SirMarkPrescott)* 2-8-9 CNutter(2) (hld up: effrt 4f out: sn outpcd: 4th & btn st)........8 **4**
1996⁸ Rockfield Lady (IRE) *(30) (ICampbell)* 2-8-9 AMackay(5) (bkwd: racd wd: chsd ldrs: rdn & outpcd over 3f out: 5th st)........3½ **5**

7/4 Sandra Dee (IRE), **9/4** Framley Garth, **11/4** SHY PADDY (IRE), **7/1** Keys Seminar, **16/1** Rockfield Lady (IRE) CSF £17.92 TOTE £3.60: £1.70 £2.70 (£16.10) OWNER Danebury Racing Stables Ltd (STOCKBRIDGE) BRED Somerville Stud 5 Rn 2m 6.2 (10.20) SF: 9/8/-/-/-

4381 WULFRUNA (S) STKS (2-Y.O) (Class G) £2,085.00 (£585.00: £285.00) **7f (Fibresand)** GOING: minus 0.05 sec per fur (Std) 8-00 (8-03)

4359⁵ **David James' Girl (59)***(66)*(Fav)*(ABailey)* 2-8-11 GCarter(2) (mde all: clr over 1f out: unchal)........— **1**
4347⁶ Dowdency **(45)***(53) (JAPickering)* 2-8-6 NCarlisle(3) (a.p: 2nd st: one pce appr fnl f)........4 **2**
4321² Norman Prince (IRE) **(58)***(51) (NPLittmoden)* 2-8-11 MRimmer(1) (lw: hld up: hdwy ½-wy: rdn 3f out: 4th st: nt pce to chal)........3½ **3**
4359⁸ Two Chalk **(47)***(44) (PDEvans)* 2-8-11 AClark(7) (b: b.hind: prom: 3rd st: sn hrd rdn: r.o one pce)........3½ **4**
4321⁶ Risky Rose **(48)***(38) (RHollinshead)* 2-8-1 (5) AGarth(8) (in tch: effrt & 6th st: n.d) ..nk **5**
4321⁴ High Flown (USA) **(53)***(42) (MrsJRRamsden)* 2-8-11v SWilliams(5) (chsd ldrs: 5th & rdn st: sn btn)........½ **6**
4275⁸ Joyful Times **(50)***(—) (MrsNMacauley)* 2-8-1b(5) SSanders(6) (chsd ldrs 4f: sn lost tch: t.o)........14 **7**
4315⁷ Laureate *(—) (DHaydnJones)* 2-8-6 AMackay(4) (a bhd: t.o)........20 **8**

7/4 DAVID JAMES' GIRL, **5/2** Norman Prince (IRE), **4/1** High Flown (IRE), **9/1** Risky Rose, **16/1** Dowdency, Two Chalk, Joyful Times, **25/1** Laureate CSF £25.63 TOTE £3.60: £1.70 £2.50 £1.30 (£7.00) OWNER David James Racing Services (TARPORLEY) BRED Miss P. E. Decker 8 Rn
No bid 1m 31.0 (7.00) SF: -/-/-/-/-/-/-/-

4382 OLD YEAR HANDICAP £2,528.20 (£710.20: £346.60) **1m 2f (Fibresand)** GOING: minus 0.05 sec per fur (Std) 8-30 (8-30)

4351⁷ **Scalp 'em (IRE) (43)***(53) (PDEvans)* 6-9-0 AClark(3) (led over 8f: 3rd st: led over 1f out: rdn out)........— **1**
4311² Broom Isle **(52)***(61)*(Jt-Fav)*(DBurchell)* 6-9-4 (5) DWright(5) (a.p: led over 3f out: hdd & 2nd st: rdn to ld appr fnl f: sn hdd: r.o)........¾ **2**
4354² Premier Dance **(51)***(60) (DHaydnJones)* 7-9-8 JWilliams(4) (lw: prom tl outpcd & 4th st: swtchd rt over 1f out: fin wl)........hd **3**
4354⁵ Manolete **(40)***(50) (CWCElsey)* 3-8-8b NKennedy(6) (hld up: hdwy 3f out: led 2f out tl appr fnl f: no ex fnl f)........nk **4**
4354* Noufari (FR) **(61)***(68)*(Jt-Fav)*(RHollinshead)* 3-10-1(5x) MWigham(2) (lw: bhd: rdn 4f out: 5th st: no imp)........2½ **5**
2838⁸ General Chase **(52)***(32) (ICampbell)* 4-9-9 StephenDavies(1) (dwlt: a in rr: 6th & btn st: t.o)........20 **6**

2/1 Broom Isle, Noufari (FR), **4/1** Premier Dance, **7/1** SCALP 'EM (IRE), **12/1** Manolete, **16/1** General Chase CSF £20.35 TOTE £7.00: £2.20 £1.80 (£11.60) OWNER Mrs L. A. Windsor (WELSHPOOL) BRED Ivan Allen 6 Rn 2m 41.8 (10.80) SF: -/-/-/-/-/-
WEIGHT FOR AGE 3yo-3lb

T/Plpt: £164.30 (52.63 Tckts). T/Qdpt: £71.20 (1.8 Tckts). IM

ALL-WEATHER INDEX 1994

COVERING RACES FROM NOVEMBER 9th TO DECEMBER 31st 1994. FOR ALL PEDIGREES NOT LISTED PLEASE REFER TO RACEFORM 1994.

A

Abbey House 3 b f 4330^{6} (4369) >**71a 50f**<
Absalom's Pillar 5 ch g (4244) 4323^{3} >**70a 55f**<
Ace Chapel (IRE) 3 br g 4299^{6} >**39a 53f**<
Achares (IRE) 4 ch c 4226^{8} >**37a 76f**<
Across the Bay 8 ch h 4226^{13} >**39a 33f**<
Adjacent Too 3 gr f 4334^{8} >**16a 22f**<
Admirals Secret (USA) 6 ch h 4318^{2} 4338^{7} >**63da 78df**<
Advance East 3 b c 4228^{7} >**45+a 76f**<
Adwick Park 7 b h 4243^{10} 4348^{6} >**54a f**<
African Chimes 8 b h 4220^{5} 4241^{9} 4370^{6} >**67a 75f**<
After the Last 5 b or br h 4214^{5} 4260^{14} 4296^{13} >**38da 66df**<
Aitch N'Bee 12 ch h 4223^{2} 4257^{4} >**74a 73f**<
Ajdar 4 b g 4217^{11} >**44a 47f**<
Akabusi 4 gr c 4274^{12} 4317^{12} >**21da 39f**<
Aladien (FR) 5 b h Kadrou (FR)-Army Life (FR) (Brigadier Gerard) 4304a^{2} >**92f**<
Alcian Blue 4 b c 4276^{7} >**52a 58f**<
Alderney Prince (USA) 5 ch h 4277^{11} >**55f**<
Alessandra Demarco (IRE) 3 b f (4250a) >**69f**<
Alflora (IRE) 6 b h 4327a^{9} >**122f**<
Alisa (GER) 4 b f Daun (GER)-Altura (GER) (Luciano) 4293a^{3} >**90f**<
Aljaz 5 b g 4265^{11} 4320^{10} >**57a 68f**<
Alka International 3 b g 4315^{4} >**51a 52f**<
Allinson's Mate (IRE) 7 b h 4226^{7} >**66a 84f**<
Allmosa 6 b m 4221^{6} 4272^{5} >**69a 65f**<
Alpine Johnny 4 b c 4214^{10} 4243^{3} 4278^{7} 4310^{2} 4348^{2} 4378^{C} >**60a 53df**<
Alriffa 4 b c 4327a^{6} >**116f**<
Al Shaati (FR) 5 b m 4258^{7} >**52da 54f**<
Altola' (ITY) 3 b c Waajib-Associance (USA) (Alleged (USA)) (4290a)
Al Totseva 3 b f 4230^{15} 4267^{8} 4298^{14} >**15a 19f**<
Always Grace 3 b f 4230^{2} 4238^{11} 4331^{2} >**50a 80f**<
Alzianah 4 b f 4246a^{3} >**108f**<
Amber Nectar 9 ch h Sallust-Curtana 4269^{14} >**18f**<
Amenable 10 b h 4226^{14}
Amercius 3 ch c Old Vic-Elarrih (USA) (Sharpen Up) 4280^{15} >**9a 63f**<
Amlak (USA) 6 b h 4358^{9} >**14a 19f**<
Angelic Dancer 4 b f 4255^{3} >**41a 50f**<
Ann Hill (IRE) 5 ch m 4217^{8} 4239^{8} 4284^{11} 4338^{9} >**39a 42f**<
Annie's Own (IRE) 4 b f 4210^{14} >**14a 51f**<
Another Baileys 3 ch f 4216^{12} >**48a 55f**<
Anotherone to Note 4 ch c 4306^{13} >**37a 47f**<
Ansellady 4 ch f 4243^{12} >**60da 68f**<
Anytime Baby 3 b f Bairn (USA)-Cindys Gold (Sonnen Gold) 4282^{5} 4334^{4} >**49a 61f**<
Apollo Red 6 ch h 4376^{6} >**57a 58f**<
Apple Tree (FR) 6 ch h 4294a^{14} >**127f**<
Apyre (FR) 7 ch h Vacarme (USA)-Pierre de Feu (FR) (Jean-Pierre) 4236a^{3} >**97f**<
Arc Bright (IRE) 5 b h 4287^{9} 4300^{4} 4332^{5} >**73a 57f**<
Arc Lamp 9 b h 4253^{C} 4325^{13} >**56a 50f**<
Arctic Diamond 4 b c 4224^{14} >**36a 61f**<
Arctic Guest (IRE) 5 ch m 4338^{6} >**57a 68f**<
Arian Spirit (IRE) 4 b f 4208^{3} 4318^{7} 4338^{2} >**44a 48f**<
Arndilly 4 b f (4349) 4375^{4} >**65a 79f**<
Arrasas Lady 5 ch m 4214^{6} 4224^{6} 4319^{3} >**36a 13f**<
Artemisia (ITY) 3 b f Tender King-Antifona (Nabirpour (USA)) 4247a^{2}
Art Form (USA) 8 b g (4208) (4272) >**85+a 81f**<
Ashdren 8 b h 4310^{9} >**40a 60f**<
As Such (IRE) 4 b c 4268^{10} 4317^{11} 4375^{2} >**59a 57f**<
Astair (FR) 5 b h (4304a)
Asterix 7 ch h 4202^{10} >**19a 61f**<
Atlantic Way 7 gr m 4229^{5} 4239^{5} >**39a f**<
Augustan 4 b c 4244^{7} >**64da 68f**<
Avant Huit 3 ch f 4324^{2} 4369^{2} >**51a 61f**<
Awesome Power 9 b g 4341^{2} >**75a 56f**<

B

Baby Bob 3 b f 4286^{9} 4314^{8} >**33da 35f**<
Bag of Tricks (IRE) 5 br h 4341^{6} >**71a 59f**<
Baileys Sunset (IRE) 3 b c 4330^{4} >**73a 61df**<
Ballad Dancer 10 ch h 4224^{9} 4281^{7} 4310^{6} >**44a 45df**<
Ballyhays (IRE) 6 ch g 4255^{9} (4358) >**52a 34f**<
Ballyranter 6 ch h 4273^{2} (4335) >**74a 68f**<
Ballysparkle (IRE) 5 b g Flash of Steel-Ballysnip (Ballymore) 4287^{0}
Bally Wonder 3 b f 4285^{5} 4331^{6} >**39a 44f**<
Balmaha 4 b f 4274^{13} >**58a 64f**<
Banbury Flyer 7 b g 4283^{9} >**27a 42f**<
Bandita 4 ch f 4268^{9} >**51a 46f**<
Bangles 5 ch m 4231^{5} 4297^{10} >**63a 75f**<
Barahin (IRE) 6 b h 4209^{13} >**60a 39f**<
Bargash 3 ch c 4225^{7} 4254^{7} 4308^{9} >**38a 74f**<
Barrel of Hope 3 b c (4225) 4279^{8} >**69a 79f**<
Bassetlaw Belle 6 b m 4361^{9} >**23a f**<
Baton Bleu 4 b c 4316^{8} >**38a 4f**<
Battle Colours (IRE) 6 b h (4226) 4303^{4} 4378^{6} >**69a 67df**<
Battleship Bruce 3 b c (4372) >**73a 74f**<
Battling Bella (USA) 6 b m 4204^{8} 4288^{7} 4302^{9} >**31a 39f**<
Beaming 4 b or br f 4293a^{10} >**90f**<
Beaumood 9 b h 4221^{11} 4229^{9} >**12a 52f**<
Beau Temps 3 br c Mtoto-Shimmer (FR) (Green Dancer (USA)) 4245a^{3} >**107f**<
Beautete 4 b c 4273^{7} 4284^{3} (4373) >**73a 66f**<
Bebe Pomme 3 b f 4230^{16} >**17a 47f**<
Beckyhannah 5 b m 4357^{6} >**36a 43df**<
Bee Dee Best (IRE) 4 b c 4255^{8} 4348^{8} >**40a 48f**<
Bellesonnette (IRE) 3 br f 4242^{4} >**73a 59f**<
Belmont Princess (IRE) 5 b m 4357^{9} >**3a 42f**<
Bentico 6 b h 4277^{7} (4309) (4320) (4379) >**78a 76f**<
Berge (IRE) 4 b c 4227^{3} (4243) 4278^{12} >**84a 68+f**<
Bettergeton 3 ch c 4219^{4} (4279) >**70+a 100f**<
Bex Hill 3 ch f 4228^{16} >**39a 39f**<
Bichette 5 b m (4269) 4313^{5} >**44a 49f**<
Big Tobin (ITY) 6 ch h (4234a) >**119f**<
Bigwheel Bill (IRE) 6 br h 4335^{9} >**55da 45f**<
Biko Pegasus (USA) 4 b c Danzig (USA)-Condessa (Condorcet (FR)) 4346a^{2}

Bill Moon 9 ch h 4214^{8} 4260^{12} 4312^{12} **>32da 32f<**

Bills Ploughgirl 3 gr f 4262^{10} 4330^{10} **>10a 45f<**

Birthplace (IRE) 5 b or br h 4244^{13} **>57da 62df<**

Bitch 3 ch f 4279^{9} 4307^{6} 4321^{8} **>38a 49f<**

Bit of a Lark 7 b h 4231^{17} 4289^{15} **>31a 57f<**

Black Boy (IRE) 6 br g 4325^{4} **>30a 57f<**

Black Deed 4 b g 4269^{10} **>30a 47f<**

Black Shadow 3 b f 4286^{5} 4356^{8} **>49a 36f<**

Blaze Dewitt (USA) 3 b f 4275^{7} **>8a 18f<**

Blowedifiknow 5 b h 4244^{3} 4323^{9} **>44a 50f<**

Blushingbird (IRE) 4 b f 4257^{9} **>33a 54f<**

Bogart 4 gr g 4227^{6} 4241^{4} (4313) 4336^{6} **>54a 62f<**

Bo Knows Best (IRE) 6 ch g 4287^{3} **>51a 64f<**

Bo Knows Nigel (IRE) 4 b c 4296^{5} **>48a 57f<**

Bold Aristocrat (IRE) 4 b c 4255^{12} 4325^{17} 4345^{9} **>61a 47f<**

Bold Cyrano (IRE) 4 b c 4355^{8} **>47da 63f<**

Bold Effort (FR) 3 b g 4254^{2} 4308^{4} 4340^{2} 4356^{2} 4372^{9} **>80a 102f<**

Bold Frontier 3 gr c 4362^{3} **>76a 57f<**

Bold Palmella (IRE) 3 b f 4228^{12} 4298^{11} 4307^{8} **>45a 63f<**

Bold Pursuit (IRE) 6 b h 4239^{3} 4276^{10} **>74da 64f<**

Bonny Melody 4 b f 4253^{11} 4348^{9} **>42a 43f<**

Bon Secret (IRE) 3 b c 4213^{2} 4262^{4} 4314^{4} 4330^{2} **>77a 32f<**

Bordesley Belle 3 b f 4308^{13} **>14f<**

Born to Be 6 b m 4211^{7} 4263^{7} 4283^{8} **>40da 57f<**

Boundary Express 3 b g 4228^{13} **>51a 67f<**

Bracken 3 b f 4225^{13}

Bradwell (IRE) 4 b f 4243^{7} 4278^{5} **>51a 55f<**

Bransby Road (IRE) 5 ch h 4272^{8} **>28a 55?f<**

Branston Abby (IRE) 6 ch m (4246a) **>118f<**

Branston Kristy 3 b f 4324^{16} 4352^{11} **>39a 53f<**

Breckland (IRE) 5 b h 4204^{5} **>56a 40f<**

Bretton Princess 3 ch f 4254^{5} 4308^{10} **>52a 36f<**

Brief Respite (IRE) 4 b or br g Simply Great (FR)-No Time To Dance (Shareef Dancer (USA)) 4309^{11} 4360^{6} **>43da f<**

Brigtina 7 b g Tina's Pet-Bristle-Moss (Brigadier Gerard) 4276^{12} **>15a f<**

Brisas 8 ch h 4255^{5} 4325^{8} **>51a 44f<**

Broadstairs Beauty (IRE) 5 ch h 4231^{2} **>78a 81f<**

Broctune Gold 4 b c 4224^{4} 4239^{2} 4277^{13} **>49a 52f<**

Bronze Maquette (IRE) 5 b m 4261^{10} 4284^{7} 4301^{9} **>37a 54f<**

Broom Isle 7 b m 4221^{9} 4277^{5} 4311^{2} 4382^{2} **>73a 60df<**

Broughton's Pride (IRE) 4 b f 4326^{5} 4354^{10} **>36a 62f<**

Brownlows 3 b c 4242^{7} 4280^{10} 4307^{4} **>51a 43f<**

Bryntirion (USA) 3 b c Bering-Aletta Maria (USA) (Diesis) 4245a^{2}

Buckley Boys 4 gr f 4218^{6} **>53a 57f<**

Buddy's Friend (IRE) 7 ch h 4271^{2} 4303^{8} **>67a 68f<**

C

Cabcharge Blue 3 b f 4279^{6} **>40a 76f<**

Calisar 5 br h 4273^{8} 4302^{5} 4313^{13} **>45a 48f<**

Call the Lifeboat 3 b f 4286^{10} **>25a f<**

Call to the Bar (IRE) 6 b h 4258^{6} **>52a 77f<**

Camden's Ransom (USA) 8 b h 4320^{4} **>62a 53f<**

Can Can Charlie 5 gr h 4223^{7} 4312^{4} 4354^{6} **>67a 53f<**

Canny Lad 5 b h 4270^{7} 4281^{10} **>39a 55f<**

Cape Pigeon (USA) 10 ch h 4210^{8} **>74f<**

Captain Marmalade 6 ch g 4226^{9} 4260^{2} 4296^{3} 4312^{5} 4341^{3} **>58a 56f<**

Carfax 10 ch h 4332^{11} **>37a 46f<**

Carlowitz (USA) 7 b h 4296^{11} **>61da 31df<**

Carlton Express (IRE) 5 b h (4284) 4354^{11} **>42a 47f<**

Carnival of Light 3 b f 4222^{12} 4324^{15} **>6a f<**

Carpathian 4 b c 4271^{6} 4339^{3} **>73a 70f<**

Carrolls Marc (IRE) 7 b h 4311^{7} **>55a 57f<**

Casper's Risk 3 ch c 4242^{6} (4256) 4285^{9} 4356^{10} **>60a 55f<**

Cedez le Passage (FR) 4 b c 4271^{4} **>95a 106f<**

Celestial Faith 4 b f Celestial Storm (USA)-All Gold Rose (Rheingold) 4344^{9} 4358^{12} **>35a f<**

Certain Way (IRE) 5 ch h 4226^{5} 4274^{2} 4319^{7} 4379^{2} **>51a 56?f<**

Chadleigh Lane (USA) 3 ch c 4219^{3} (4230) **>52a 56f<**

Chadleigh Walk (IRE) 3 b or br c 4213^{4} 4240^{14} 4307^{9} 4347^{7} **>53da 41f<**

Chancel (USA) 4 b f 4296^{7} **>56a 53f<**

Chardonnay Girl 4 b f 4344^{11} **>12a 37f<**

Charlies Dream (IRE) 4 b f 4224^{5} 4255^{4} 4269^{4} 4317^{8} 4348^{5} 4357^{8} **>43da f<**

Charlie Sillett 3 ch c 4285^{8} **>54a 90f<**

Charlistiona 4 ch f 4341^{11} **>17a 34df<**

Charnwood Queen 3 ch f Cadeaux Genereux-Florentynna Bay (Aragon) 4279^{7} 4334^{7} **>34a 63f<**

Chase the Melody 3 b c Sizzling Melody-Odilese (Mummy's Pet) 4230^{9} **>32a 31f<**

Chatham Island 7 ch g (4209) **>99a 78f<**

Cheeky Chappy 4 b c 4325^{5} **>42a 49f<**

Cheerful Groom (IRE) 4 ch g 4274^{15} 4349^{8} 4377^{4} **>44a 39f<**

Cherokee Rose (IRE) 4 b f 4293a^{4} **>123f<**

Chewit 3 gr c 4334^{2} 4372^{10} **>80a 85f<**

Chief of Staff 6 ch h 4252^{6} 4326^{3} **>76a 78f<**

Child Star (FR) 6 gr m 4300^{6} **>50a 38f<**

Chinour (IRE) 7 b g 4306^{3} **>59a 75f<**

Choir Master (CAN) 8 b g 4261^{14} **>26a 35f<**

Christian Warrior 6 gr h 4226^{15} **>9a 39f<**

Cicerone 5 br h (4319) **>48a 53f<**

Circus Lodge 4 b f 4263^{9} **>8a 55f<**

City Rhythm 5 b g 4378^{12} **>42f<**

Cledeschamps 6 b m 4278^{6} **>42da 41f<**

Coco Passion (FR) 3 ch f Groom Dancer (USA)-Gaiete de Coeur (Lomond (USA)) 4233a^{3} (4295a) **>100f<**

Colin's Pride 4 b f 4373^{10} **>30a 52f<**

Colston-C 3 gr c 4238^{14} **>43da 71f<**

Comanche Companion 5 b m 4264^{11} **>66a 88f<**

Comtec's Legend 5 ch m 4217^{5} 4276^{5} **>40a 39f<**

Cone Lane 9 ch h 4318^{10} **>28a 39f<**

Conspicuous (IRE) 5 b h 4312^{2} 4353^{3} **>60+a 90f<**

Court of Honour (IRE) 3 b c (4248a) **>122f<**

Cradle Days 6 b h 4258^{8} 4316^{6} **>59a 64f<**

Crafty Cricketer 4 ch c 4206^{11} 4266^{9} 4313^{8} **>21a 42f<**

Cranbrook Kate 3 b f 4256^{10} **>26a 22f<**

Credit Squeeze 5 ch h 4312^{3} **>74a 85f<**

Cristal Springs 4 b f 4229^{6} 4261^{9} 4338^{5} 4351^{6} **>34a 45f<**

Croft Pool 4 b c (4231) 4278^{10} (4316) **>84a 105f<**

Crown My Chief 3 b c 4219^{9} **>27a 44f<**
Cruising Chick 4 b f 4229^{7} **>30a 36f<**
Crystal Gift 3 b c 4205^{2} 4282^{7} **>57a 64f<**
Crystal Heights (FR) 7 ch h Crystal Glitters (USA)-Fahrenheit (Mount Hagen (FR)) 4268^{0} 4333^{12} **>67a 77f<**
Crystal Loop 3 b f 4228^{14} 4262^{3} 4298^{6} 4350^{2} **>76a 72f<**
Cuban Reef 3 b f 4331^{5} **>32a 57f<**
Curie Express (IRE) 3 ch f 4222^{3} 4275^{6} 4359^{6} **>46a 66f<**
C-Yer-Simmie (IRE) 3 b f 4275^{2} 4362^{4} **>63a 64f<**

D

Daaniera (IRE) 5 gr h 4255^{10} 4325^{7} 4345^{4} (4370) **>49a 23f<**
Daily Challenger (USA) 3 b c 4225^{5} 4275^{10} **>37a 74f<**
Daisy Madam 3 b f Shavian-Pride of Paris (Troy) 4240^{16}
Dakota Brave (IRE) 4 b c 4218^{2} **>70a 66f<**
Dance and Sing (IRE) 5 b g 4206^{7} 4283^{4} 4322^{12} 4343^{9} 4349^{5} **>30a 25f<**
Dance So Suite 3 b c 4216^{3} **>55a 86f<**
Dancing-Alone 3 ch c 4213^{9} 4280^{11} **>25a f<**
Dancing Diamond (IRE) 5 b m 4261^{3} 4300^{5} 4318^{6} 4373^{4} **>59a 47f<**
Dancing Lawyer 4 b c 4204^{4} 4265^{2} (4289) 4302^{3} **>77a 80f<**
Dangerous Shadow 4 gr f 4237^{10} 4274^{14} **>32a 43f<**
Danielle Habibi (IRE) 4 b f 4261^{12} 4284^{10} **>29a 45f<**
Danny's Gift 3 ch f 4213^{10} **>30a 23f<**
Danseuse Davis (FR) 4 b f 4270^{8} 4296^{10} 4319^{10} **>33a 52f<**
Dark Eyed Lady (IRE) 5 b m 4220^{12} 4263^{5} **>55a 48f<**
Dark Shot (IRE) 3 b c (4331) 4350^{3} **>67a 67f<**
Darrery 5 b m 4291a^{4} **>104f<**
Das Island 3 b c 4238^{5} 4267^{2} 4298^{2} 4342^{7} **>63a 55f<**
Dauntless Fort 4 gr f 4243^{6} 4322^{6} 4355^{9} **>42da 47f<**
David Blue (IRE) 4 b c 4343^{10} **>17a 54df<**
David James' Girl 3 b f 4352^{2} 4359^{5} (4381) **>73a 70f<**
Dawalib (USA) 5 ch h (4220) 4333^{9} 4360^{4} 4377^{3} **>73a 75f<**
Dawn Flight 6 b g 4318^{12} 4332^{9} **>36a 52f<**
Dawn Rock 4 b c 4229^{3} 4239^{7} 4287^{5} **>50a 29f<**
Dear Madam 4 gr f 4276^{16}
Deerlet 4 br f 4244^{12} **>24a 67f<**
Delrob 4 b f 4231^{6} 4355^{5} **>62a 54f<**
Derricks Refusal 4 b c 4354^{12} **>21a 33f<**
Desert Lore 4 b c 4227^{10} 4309^{8} **>54a 69f<**
Desirous 3 gr g Grey Desire-Clairwood (Final Straw) 4259^{6} **>45a f<**
Diamond Mix (IRE) 3 gr c Linamix (FR)-Diamond Seal (Persian Bold) 4295a^{3} **>119f<**
Diffident (FR) 3 b c Nureyev (USA)-Shy Princess (USA) (Irish River (FR)) (4292a) **>117f<**
Digpast (IRE) 5 ch h 4202^{11} 4270^{2} 4303^{6} 4313^{3} (4376) **>72a 47df<**
Dingo Warrior 3 ch c Roman Warrior-Patsy Pennall (Celtic Cone) 4314^{11} **>28a 38f<**
Dinner At Eight 5 b g 4287^{6} 4332^{12} **>49a 42f<**
Dismissive (IRE) 3 ch f 4213^{13} **>10a 22f<**
Disputed Call (USA) 6 b h 4217^{13} 4335^{8} **>43da 52f<**
Dissident Dancer 6 b g 4348^{10} **>3a 16f<**
Distant Dynasty 5 br h 4202^{14} (4266) 4288^{4} 4345^{5} **>67a 53f<**
D K Reunion 5 b g Welsh Captain-Thetford Chase (Relkino) 4358^{13}
Docklands Courier 3 b c Dominion-High Quail (USA) (Blushing Groom (FR)) 4280^{13} 4308^{6} **>56a 54f<**
Dolly Dolittle 4 ch f 4215^{9} **>30a 24f<**
Dome Patrol 4 gr c 4270^{13} 4319^{6} **>52a 43f<**
Domicksky 7 b h 4220^{8} **>67a 61f<**
Domino Queen (IRE) 4 b f 4211^{8} **>32a 56f<**
Donia (USA) 6 ch m 4218^{9} 4277^{14} 4354^{7} **>48a f<**
Doreen's Delight 9 ch h 4296^{6} **>42a 33?f<**
Double Blue 6 ch h 4246a^{6} **>112df<**
Double Eclipse (IRE) 3 b c 4248a^{2} **>122f<**
Double Quick (IRE) 3 b f 4292a^{8} **>106f<**
Double Splendour (IRE) 5 b g (4283) **>45a 76f<**
Double Trigger (IRE) 4 ch c 4327a^{7} **>127f<**
Dowdency 3 b f 4307^{5} 4347^{6} 4381^{2} **>49a 60f<**
Dragonflight 4 b c 4358^{8} 4378^{5} **>65a 17f<**
Drama King 3 b c Tragic Role (USA)-Consistent Queen (Queen's Hussar) 4240^{9} 4280^{5} **>45a 19f<**
Dream Carrier (IRE) 7 b h 4227^{5} 4241^{3} **>62a 52f<**
Drummer's Dream (IRE) 7 b m 4218^{10} 4243^{14} **>19a 15f<**
Duggan 8 b h 4208^{8} **>13a 42f<**
Dundeelin 4 ch f 4325^{6} 4349^{10} **>34a 41f<**
Dupad 5 br g 4229^{16}
Dvorak (IRE) 4 b c Darshaan-Grace Note (FR) (Top Ville) 4276^{4} **>62a 75f<**
Dynamis (IRE) 4 b f 4343^{4} 4376^{8} **>38a 74f<**

E

Eastleigh 6 b h 4289^{4} 4302^{4} 4337^{3} **>68a 31f<**
Eatons 4 br f 4204^{6} 4214^{7} **>38a 40f<**
Ebony Blaze 4 b c 4313^{7} 4344^{5} **>40a 52f<**
Ecu de France (IRE) 5 ch h 4260^{3} 4341^{13} 4373^{9} **>61da 58f<**
Educated Pet 6 gr h 4355^{10} **>56a 53f<**
Ela Man Howa 4 b c (4261) 4335^{3} **>59da 65f<**
Ela Palikari Mou (IRE) 4 b g Lomond (USA)-Ionian Raja (USA) (Raja Baba (USA)) 4343^{6} **>33a 30f<**
Elmer's Tune 3 b c 4259^{7} **>42f<**
El Nido 7 ch h 4221^{4} 4277^{3} (4323) 4354^{8} **>75a 53f<**
Emily-Mou (IRE) 3 b f 4228^{11} **>47a 83f<**
Emperor Jones (USA) 5 b h 4329a^{5} **>120f<**
Epica 4 b c 4351^{12} **>54da 49f<**
Eqtesaad (USA) 4 b or br c 4344^{4} **>80a 78f<**
Ertlon 5 b h (4265) **>95a 88f<**
Esperer 5 b g Full of Hope-Priory Maid (Malinowski (USA)) 4343^{11} **>29a f<**
Estala 4 ch f Be My Guest (USA)-Roupala (USA) (Vaguely Noble) 4293a^{2} **>93f<**
Europharm Lassie 4 b f 4283^{5} 4317^{5} 4344^{2} **>33a 28f<**
Everset (FR) 7 b h 4271^{3} 4333^{5} (4348) 4355^{3} **>95a 63f<**
Ewar Empress (IRE) 4 b f 4206^{10} **>6a 17f<**
Ewar Gold (FR) 5 ch m 4202^{5} 4255^{7} 4270^{10} **>27a 51f<**
Excelled (IRE) 6 gr m 4344^{10} **>28a 55f<**
Explosive Power 4 br c (4217) **>54a 41f<**
Extra Time 4 b f 4218^{5} 4272^{7} **>55a 81f<**

Ezekiel 4 ch c 4204^{15} 4341^{9} 4379^{7} **>23da 36f<**

F

Fade Away (IRE) 4 ch f 4214^{13} **>36da 29f<**

Faez 5 b h 4241^{14} 4337^{8} **>53a 78?f<**

Fahema 3 b f 4242^{11} **>49a 61f<**

Failte Ro 3 bl f 4216^{2} 4356^{5} **>64a 52f<**

Fair Ella (IRE) 3 ch f 4282^{12} 4314^{3} 4334^{9} **>49a 43f<**

Fairy Fay (IRE) 3 b f (4207) 4262^{2} **>63a 65f<**

Fairy's Son 3 b c 4205^{7} 4347^{4} **>42a 32f<**

Fallal (IRE) 3 b f Fayruz-Lady Bidder 4315^{5} **>28a 55f<**

Fanjica (IRE) 3 b f 4233a^{2} **>114f<**

Farastrada 4 b f 4357^{11} **>54a 40f<**

Farfelu 8 b h 4370^{8} **>68a 66f<**

Farmer Jock 13 ch h 4278^{14} 4306^{6} 4357^{10} **>43a 48f<**

Farndale 8 gr h 4253^{C} 4289^{14} 4306^{10} 4349^{6} 4378^{11} **>50a 42f<**

Faynaz 9 ch h 4269^{5} 4313^{6} **>32a 38f<**

Feather Face 5 b h 4212^{4} **>47a 58f<**

Featherstone Lane 4 b c 4243^{2} 4283^{3} 4297^{3} 4322^{11} 4345^{2} 4370^{4} **>67a 60df<**

Feline (IRE) 4 ch f 4271^{7} **>41a 45f<**

Fiaba 7 b m 4229^{8} **>49a 49df<**

Fiery Footsteps 3 ro f 4267^{7} 4314^{7} 4369^{5} **>46a 59f<**

Fiery Sun 10 b g 4276^{8} 4323^{7} 4351^{8} **>31a 72—f<**

Final Spoof 3 b c 4213^{7} **>37da 56f<**

Finjan 8 b h 4260^{8} 4374^{6} **>44a 50f<**

First Crush 3 b f 4262^{5} 4342^{6} **>59da 73f<**

First Option 5 ch g 4211^{5} **>62a 57f<**

First Point (IRE) 3 b c 4238^{10} **>28a 27f<**

Fishy Affair 3 ch c 4275^{5} 4298^{9} 4362^{5} **>38a 56f<**

Flamboro 3 ch c 4242^{15} **>68f<**

Flash Appeal 4 b f Tate Gallery (USA)-Camomilla (Targowice (USA)) 4210^{13} 4343^{8} **>22a f<**

Flatford Princess 3 b f 4213^{12} **>12a 47f<**

Fleet Cadet 4 ch c Bairn (USA)-Pirogue 4215^{7} **>50a 54f<**

Flora Belle 4 b f 4229^{14} **>15a 57df<**

Flying Wind 6 b m 4289^{6} 4303^{10} **>40a 39f<**

Fools Haven (IRE) 3 b c 4280^{14} **>10a 46f<**

Fools Millyons (IRE) 3 ch c 4240^{10} 4280^{7} 4321^{7} **>51a 39f<**

Fools of Pride (IRE) 3 ch f Al Hareb (USA)-I'll Take Paris (USA) (Vaguely Noble) 4350^{5} **>55a 49f<**

Forbidden Gem 4 b g Formidable-Emerald Ring (Auction Ring (USA)) 4371^{11} **>31a 16f<**

Forgotten Dancer (IRE) 4 ch c 4263^{2} 4306^{11} **>36a 64f<**

Forgotten Empress 3 b f 4347^{2} **>68a 68df<**

Formidable Liz 5 ch m 4263^{4} 4306^{5} 4322^{4} **>48a 66f<**

Fosters Top 3 ch g Pharly (FR)-More Sparkle (Morston (FR)) 4331^{9} **>1a 44f<**

Four of Spades 4 ch c 4211^{6} 4243^{5} (4310) (4377) **>73a 60f<**

Foxhill Blue 3 b f 4222^{7} **>27a 40f<**

Foxhill Flyer 3 b f 4207^{13} **>22f<**

Fraise (USA) 7 b h 4294a^{10}

Framley Garth 3 ch f Belmez (USA)-Heavenly Abode (FR) (Habitat) 4240^{5} 4280^{6} 4380^{4} **>46da f<**

Franklinsboy 3 b c 4219^{10} 4298^{10} 4340^{8} 4356^{6} **>45a 3f<**

Freedom Cry 4 b c (4232a) **>131f<**

Friendly Brave (USA) 5 b h 4337^{4} **>67a 63f<**

Friendly Lady (USA) 3 b f 4282^{3} 4315^{6} 4340^{7} **>56da 64f<**

Frisky Miss (IRE) 4 b f 4237^{2} 4310^{8} (4355) **>66a 70f<**

Frome Lad 3 ch g Buzzards Bay-Groundsel (Reform) 4205^{3} 4240^{6} 4308^{3} **>61a 54f<**

Fujiyama Kenzan (JPN) 7 b h Lucky Cast (JPN)-Waka Suzuran (JPN) (Contrite (USA)) 4294a^{11}

G

Galaxy Express 7 ch g 4210^{12} 4237^{16} **>47a 18f<**

Galejade 5 b m 4335^{5} **>40a 56df<**

Gallant Jack (IRE) 6 b g 4301^{12} 4311^{12} **>34a 31f<**

Gallery Artist (IRE) 7 ch h 4226^{11} 4310^{7} **>57a 58f<**

Gallop to Glory 5 b h 4320^{6} 4358^{5} **>27a 12f<**

Garadice Girl (IRE) 3 b f Gallic League-Columbian Sand (IRE) (Salmon Leap (USA)) 4359^{11}

Garden of Heaven (USA) 6 ch h 4234a^{5} **>109f<**

General Chase 5 ch m 4382^{6} **>53a 13f<**

Genesis Four 5 b h 4224^{16} **>48a 44f<**

Gentle Fan (USA) 6 b h Lear Fan (USA)-Gay Bentley (USA) (Riverman (USA)) 4249a^{2} **>109f<**

Gingerillo 4 ch c 4344^{6} **>37a 39f<**

Girl From Ipanema 4 b f 4235a^{3} **>108df<**

Give In 8 gr h 4224^{12} 4260^{5} 4374^{4} **>44a 47f<**

Glenfield Greta 7 ch m 4202^{6} 4260^{11} **>34a 52f<**

Glenvally 4 gr f 4229^{11} **>55da 59df<**

Global Dancer 4 b c 4209^{7} 4277^{4} (4300) 4326^{6} **>77a 85f<**

Glow Forum 4 b f 4208^{5} 4273^{3} 4318^{4} 4338^{3} 4373^{8} **>36a 46f<**

Gobsmacked (USA) 4 b c 4223^{6} **>75a 83f<**

Go Hever Golf 3 ch c (4315) (4342) (4362) **>100+a 97+f<**

Golden Fish 3 b g 4242^{12} **>22a 52f<**

Golden Star (IRE) 4 ch c 4244^{8} **>55a 49f<**

Gone On the Wind 3 b f Law Society (USA)-Salette (Sallust) 4250a^{3}

Goodbye Millie 5 b or br m 4239^{6} 4276^{9} **>37a 52f<**

Governor's Lass 3 b f Governor General-Belle Tower (Tower Walk) 4340^{10} 4369^{6} **>42a 43f<**

Grandee 4 b c 4237^{14} 4255^{6} 4322^{7} 4348^{7} **>42a f<**

Grand Flotilla (USA) 8 ro h 4294a^{8} **>119f<**

Granmas Delight 4 b f 4268^{8} 4316^{5} 4345^{3} 4361^{5} **>53a 31f<**

Great Bond 4 b g Cree Song-May Bond (Good Bond) 4358^{11} **>41a f<**

Greatest Hopes 4 ch c 4202^{2} 4289^{12} 4302^{7} **>32a 38f<**

Grecian Lady (IRE) 6 b m Be My Guest (USA)-Grecian Sky (African Sky) 4338^{8} **>26a f<**

Greek Gold (IRE) 6 b h 4239^{11} **>64da 56f<**

Greenacres Star 5 ch m 4229^{2} 4276^{6} 4323^{5} **>51a 58f<**

Green's Bid 5 gr h 4211^{4} 4333^{7} 4361^{3} **>62a 64df<**

Greggina 4 b f 4215^{3} 4270^{16} **>46a 51f<**

Grey Ancona (IRE) 6 gr h 4243^{9} 4320^{14} **>28a f<**

Greystyle 5 b h 4208^{13} **>30f<**

Grey Toppa 4 gr f 4231^{13} 4237^{7} **>46da 65df<**

Guesstimation (USA) 6 b h 4217^{7} 4257^{3} 4281^{9} 4319^{2} **>51a 74f<**

Gulf Shaadi 3 b c 4282^{6} (4334) 4356^{3} **>87a 62f<**

Gwernymynydd 4 b f 4237^{11} **>27a 25f<**

H

Half Tone 3 gr c 4203^{9} 4275^{3} 4362^{2} **>60a 44f<**
Hall Bank Cottage 5 br m 4206^{9} 4344^{12} **>9a 31f<**
Hannah's Usher 3 b g (4275) **>83a 64f<**
Hard Try 3 ro c Sharrood (USA)-Trynova (Tyrnavos) 4280^{4} 4347^{3} **>63a 62f<**
Haroldon (IRE) 6 ch h 4353^{8} **>49da 82f<**
Harvest Reaper 3 gr c 4299^{8} **>43a 57f<**
Hasty Bid (IRE) 3 b f Cyrano de Bergerac-Hedwige 4230^{14} 4352^{5} **>28a f<**
Hatta Sunshine (USA) 5 b h 4301^{2} 4312^{8} **>53a 50f<**
Havana Miss 3 b f 4213^{8} **>38a 49f<**
Hawaii Storm (FR) 7 b h 4202^{3} 4214^{3} 4269^{2} (4302) 4336^{9} **>61da 33f<**
Hawwam 9 b h 4227^{2} 4319^{4} 4379^{3} **>77a 59f<**
Hay Dance 4 b c 4320^{15} **>27a 56f<**
Heart Lake 4 ch c 4328a^{3} **>123f<**
Heathyards Lady (USA) 4 b f (4255) 4320^{13} 4349^{3} **>77a 64f<**
Heliopsis 7 b g 4244^{9} **>31a f<**
Here Comes Herbie 3 ch g 4225^{12} **>45f<**
Here He Comes 9 b g 4284^{12} **>49a 85f<**
Hernando (FR) 5 b h 4294a^{4} **>128f<**
Hever Golf Lady 3 b f 4285^{3} 4299^{5} 4321^{9} **>52+a 67f<**
Hickory Blue 5 ch h 4253^{6} **>50a 71f<**
High Domain (IRE) 4 b c 4237^{8} 4297^{7} **>56a 64f<**
High Flown (USA) 3 b g 4230^{12} 4321^{4} 4381^{6} **>64da 63f<**
High Holme 4 ch c 4212^{8} 4319^{13} **>31a 30f<**
Hightown Cavalier 4 b g 4309^{6} **>50a 43f<**
Hillsdown Boy (IRE) 5 ch h 4209^{2} (4296) **>44a f<**
Hillzah (USA) 7 ch h 4252^{8} 4326^{2} 4353^{6} **>86a 84f<**
Hiltons Travel (IRE) 4 b g 4377^{6} **>26a 40f<**
Hi Penny 4 b f 4317^{14} **>43a 50f<**
Hitchin a Ride 8 b g 4266^{C} **>51?a f<**
Hollington Song 4 gr f 4206^{12} **>42da 36df<**
Hollywood Dream (GER) 4 ch f (4235a) **>117f<**
Holy Wanderer (USA) 6 b h 4252^{10} **>81da 96f<**
Hoswinoname 3 ch g 4230^{13} 4280^{16} **>16f<**
Howqua River 3 b c 4203^{2} 4242^{14} **>63da 47f<**
Human Touch (ITY) 3 b f Love the Groom (USA)-Heba (Artaius (USA)) 4250a^{2} **>82f<**
Hylters Girl 3 b f 4282^{10} **>26a 37f<**

I

Ice and Glacial (IRE) 3 b c (4251a) **>103f<**
Iceblock 3 gr f Green Ruby (USA)-True Liberty (Indian King (USA)) 4282^{11} 4299^{10} 4331^{8} **>24da f<**
I Fear Nothing 4 gr f 4241^{16} 4326^{14} **>37da 76df<**
Imco Gold (IRE) 3 b c Groom Dancer (USA)-Philyra (FR) (Fabulous Dancer (USA)) 4290a^{2}
Inherent Magic (IRE) 6 ch m 4333^{2} **>87a 98f<**
Inn At the Top 3 b c 4203^{6} 4280^{2} **>69a 68f<**
Innocence 3 b f 4282^{9} **>26a 74df<**
Inspiration Point 4 ch f 4204^{13} 4273^{11} **>36da 56f<**
Instant Success (USA) 3 ch f 4240^{11} **>47a 62f<**
Intention (USA) 5 b h 4276^{3} **>61a 71f<**
In the Money (IRE) 6 b h 4277^{10} 4335^{2} 4373^{5} **>64a 71f<**
Invocation 8 ch h 4303^{3} 4333^{4} **>71a 61f<**
Inzar 4 b c 4312^{10} **>51a f<**
Irie Mon (IRE) 3 b c 4314^{5} **>62a 62f<**
Iron Baron (IRE) 6 b h 4244^{10} **>27a 50f<**
Iron Man (IRE) 3 b c 4207^{11} 4299^{4} (4314) 4372^{7} **>65a 62f<**
Island Knight (IRE) 6 b h 4210^{6} 4264^{9} 4302^{6} **>60a 75f<**
Ism 3 b c 4230^{8} **>71a 65f<**
Ithkurni (USA) 6 b m 4206^{13} **>8a f<**
It Is Now 3 ch c 4225^{8} 4280^{12} **>33a 33f<**
It Must Be Millie 4 b f 4220^{13} 4268^{3} 4297^{9} **>59a 64f<**
It's so Easy 4 b f 4241^{8} 4306^{8} **>32a 57f<**
Ivan the Terrible (IRE) 7 ch h 4309^{12} **>59a 67f<**
Ivy Lilian (IRE) 3 b f 4308^{11} 4352^{10} **>52a 46f<**

J

Jake the Pake (IRE) 5 b g 4339^{14} **>39a 42f<**
Jalmaid 3 ch f 4240^{8} 4347^{5} **>61a 60f<**
Jersey Belle 3 b f 4207^{8} 4321^{13} **>56a 53f<**
Jessica's Secret (IRE) 3 ch f 4238^{13} **>32a 50f<**
Jeune 6 ch h 4294a^{6} **>121f<**
Jilly Jaffa Cake (IRE) 3 ch f Waajib-Lady Fandet (Gay Fandango (USA)) 4228^{4} 4372^{6} **>57a f<**
Jimy's Grey 3 gr c Sharrood (USA)-Fair Test (Fair Season) 4251a^{3} **>53f<**
Joellise 5 b m 4322^{14} **>37da 12f<**
Johann Quatz (FR) 6 b h 4294a^{12} **>128f<**
Joint Effort (IRE) 4 b f 4206^{3} 4270^{4} 4288^{3} 4317^{9} 4343^{3} 4371^{5} **>45a 65f<**
Jolly Swagman 4 b g 4319^{9} **>34a f<**
Jon's Choice 7 b g 4306^{7} **>53a 60f<**
Joseno 3 b f 4259^{4} 4307^{7} 4321^{12} **>25a 53f<**
Joseph's Wine (IRE) 6 b h (4277) 4311^{3} (4326) (4339) **>86da 76f<**
Jovale 3 ch c 4286^{7} 4324^{13} **>38da 36f<**
Joyful Times 3 br f 4275^{8} 4381^{7} **>47a 24f<**
Just Harry 4 ch c 4223^{9} 4241^{5} 4337^{2} **>84da 72f<**
Just Jesting 3 ch g 4298^{12} 4330^{8} 4369^{4} **>39a 65f<**
Just Lucky (IRE) 3 b c Fools Holme (USA)-Miss Victoria (Auction Ring (USA)) (4280) **>72da 37f<**
Just-Mana-Mou (IRE) 3 b c 4205^{4} **>51a 60f<**

K

Kaafih Homm (IRE) 4 b g (4343) **>69a 73f<**
Kafkaienne (FR) 3 b f 4250a^{4} **>72f<**
Kalar 6 b h 4253^{3} (4325) **>71a 54f<**
Kali Ro 3 b f 4205^{8}
Karon Beach 4 ch f 4373^{12} **>32a 12f<**
Katie's Kid 5 br g 4269^{12} **>15a 44f<**
Keeper's Grey 3 gr c 4238^{8} 4299^{2} **>56a 54f<**
Kentucky Flyer 4 ch f 4214^{12} 4319^{15} **>10a 23f<**
Kenyatta (USA) 6 b h 4217^{15} 4284^{2} 4332^{6} **>42a 34f<**
Kerkura (USA) 5 ch m 4252^{12} **>18a 77f<**
Kevasingo 3 b c 4216^{5} **>55a 66f<**
Keys Seminar 3 b c 4342^{5} 4380^{2} **>53a 55f<**
Kid Ory 4 ch g 4220^{9} 4241^{13} **>28a 76f<**
King of the Horse (IRE) 4 ch g 4224^{15} **>55a 39df<**
King Parrot (IRE) 7 br g 4204^{10} **>63da 55f<**
Kingsfold Fountain 4 b g Thowra (FR)-Bella Lisa 4215^{5} 4271^{11} **>47a f<**
Kinnegad Kid 6 b m 4357^{2} **>78a 49f<**
Kintwyn 5 b h 4209^{12} 4265^{8} 4303^{2} 4339^{8} 4353^{7} **>77a 65f<**
Kirov Protege (IRE) 3 b c 4314^{10} **>63a 63f<**
Kissavos 9 ch h 4264^{8} 4303^{7} 4317^{6} **>40a 42f<**
Kiss Kincsem 4 b f 4300^{9} **>43da 73df<**
Kitty Waterjet 3 ch f 4219^{11} 4307^{10} **>13a 22f<**
Kiyas 4 ch c 4217^{6} 4272^{10} 4323^{12} **>46a 47f<**

Knave of Diamonds **3** b c 4219^{7} **>39a 59df<**
Knightrider **4** b c 4210^{3} 4289^{13} **>51da 51f<**
Knotty Scot **3** b f Scottish Reel-Ballyreef (Ballymore) 4213^{15} **>7a 11f<**
Komlucky **3** b f 4324^{8} (4359) **>51a 40f<**
Komodo (USA) **3** ch c 4315^{2} **>54a 75f<**
Komplicity **4** b c 4214^{9} 4239^{9} **>37a 34df<**
Komreyev Dancer **3** b g 4203^{3} 4219^{2} 4240^{2} 4308^{2} (4347) 4356^{4} **>82a 76f<**
Krayyan Dawn **5** ch h (4344) **>50a 58f<**
Kreef **3** b c 4286^{3} **>61a 41f<**
Kung Frode **3** ch c (4238) **>74a 65f<**
Kyoei Keyman (JPN) **6** b h Petoski-Sweet Emma (Welsh Saint) 4346a^{3}

L

La Belle Dominique **3** b f 4238^{2} 4324^{5} **>49a 65f<**
Lac de Gras (IRE) **4** gr g 4202^{7} 4339^{10} **>18a 25f<**
Lady Broker **5** b m 4289^{16} 4317^{16} 4349^{12} **>55da f<**
Lady Highfield **4** br f 4281^{14} **>54a 63f<**
Lady Lucy Linnet **3** b f 4213^{11} **>14a 27f<**
Lady Pui **3** b f 4222^{4} 4256^{9} (4330) 4352^{8} **>39a 62f<**
Lady Reema **4** b f 4215^{2} 4273^{6} 4301^{5} **>66a 46f<**
Lady Sheriff **4** b f 4253^{4} 4325^{9} **>37++a 88f<**
Lady Valient **4** b f 4317^{13} **>6a 50df<**
Lajadhal (FR) **6** gr h 4208^{7} 4272^{11} 4338^{10} **>18a 35f<**
La Menorquina (USA) **5** b m 4221^{5} 4272^{4} **>56a 45f<**
Lanesra Breeze **3** b g Petoski-Constant Companion (Pas de Seul) 4340^{9} **>16a 48f<**
Langtonian **6** br h 4226^{3} 4237^{3} (4281) 4320^{5} **>55a 29f<**
Languedoc **8** b h 4281^{11} **>21a 52f<**
La Petite Fusee **4** br f 4263^{3} 4336^{10} **>78+a 75f<**
La Reina Blanca (SPA) **4** b f 4208^{12} **>29a 60df<**
La Residence **4** b c 4269^{13} **>53a 60f<**
Late Parade (IRE) **4** b c 4249a^{3} **>113f<**
Launchselect **4** b g 4217^{16} **>31a 27f<**
Laureate **3** br f Statoblest-Indian Wells 4254^{11} 4315^{7} 4381^{8}
Lawnswood Lady **3** b f 4222^{9} 4256^{11} 4324^{12} 4352^{3} 4359^{2} **>46a 50f<**
Leap for Joy **3** ch f 4292a^{7} **>108f<**
Le Conquet (FR) **7** b h 4291a^{2} **>113f<**
Legally Delicious **3** b f Law Society (USA)-Bold Apple (Bold Lad (IRE)) 4240^{4} **>72a 9f<**
Legal Win (USA) **7** ch h 4244^{11} 4287^{13} **>12a f<**
Legitimate **3** b c (4308) **>83a 79f<**
Leigh Crofter **6** ch h 4220^{10} 4306^{4} **>78a 75f<**
Letsbeonestaboutit **9** b h 4214^{0} **>58a 48f<**
Level Edge **4** b f (4204) 4257^{5} 4289^{10} **>52da 40f<**
L'ile Tudy (IRE) **5** b m Wassl-Melinte (Caerleon (USA)) 4235a^{2} **>113f<**
Little Ibnr **4** b g 4231^{12} 4278^{4} (4306) (4322) 4349^{4} 4377^{2} **>87a 68f<**
Little Miner (IRE) **4** b or br f 4215^{8} 4239^{12} **>34a f<**
Little Miss Ribot **5** b m 4217^{14} **>38a 48f<**
Little Saboteur **6** ch m 4297^{2} **>74a 64f<**
Little Scarlett **3** b f 4340^{4} **>59+a 29f<**
Loch Bering (USA) **3** ch c 4295a^{7} **>92f<**
Logie **3** ch c 4282^{2} 4299^{C} **>63a 37f<**
Logie Pert Lad **3** b g Green Ruby (USA)-Rhazya (Rousillon (USA)) 4207^{12} 4286^{11} **>20f<**
Lombard Ships **8** ch m 4257^{8} 4274^{6} 4341^{12} 4378^{4} **>30da 45f<**
Long Furlong **7** b g 4260^{6} **>54a 54f<**
Lord Adriani (IRE) **3** b c 4240^{12} **>25a 53f<**
Lord Glenvara (IRE) **7** ch g 4261^{11} 4339^{4} **>33a 48f<**
Lord Nitrogen (USA) **5** b or br h 4323^{13} **>51da 46f<**
Lost Prairie (USA) **5** b m Lyphard (USA)-Lady Lianga (USA) (Secretariat (USA)) 4236a^{2} 4304a^{3} **>92f<**
Love Legend **10** ch h 4227^{12} **>61a 61f<**
Lovely Me (IRE) **4** b f 4231^{16} **>27a 62f<**
Love of the North (IRE) **4** b g 4229^{15} **>49da 39f<**
Lucknam Style **7** b g 4204^{9} **>52a 54f<**
Lugana Vision **3** b f 4267^{4} **>42a 57f<**

M

Macfarlane **7** br h 4220^{7} **>50a 73f<**
Mac's Taxi **3** b g 4228^{6} **>63a 74f<**
Mad Militant (IRE) **6** b h 4252^{9} 4326^{4} **>79a 70f<**
Magical Belle (IRE) **3** ch f 4321^{10} **>39a 38f<**
Magical Touch **3** gr f 4205^{9} 4254^{12} **>5a f<**
Magic Leader (IRE) **3** b or br c 4230^{11} 4267^{5} 4275^{11} **>25a 47f<**
Magna Carta **3** b c (4219) **>84+a 81f<**
Maidment **4** b f 4235a^{11} **>92f<**
Maid Welcome **8** br m 4202^{8} 4210^{7} (4270) (4317) 4376^{3} **>66a 59f<**
Majboor (IRE) **6** b h 4226^{2} 4257^{6} **>70a 68f<**
Major Yaasi (USA) **5** b h 4301^{10} **>21a 54f<**
Make the Break **4** b c 4214^{4} 4322^{15} 4378^{9} **>41da 48f<**
Malafemmena (IRE) **3** b f 4233a^{4} **>88f<**
Malingerer **4** gr f 4284^{9} 4312^{11} **>34da 37f<**
Mam'zelle Angot **5** b m (4353) **>66a 69f<**
Manolete **4** b c 4354^{5} 4382^{4} **>61a 36f<**
Manor Adventure **5** ch m 4212^{6} 4302^{12} **>41a 32f<**
Maple Leaf Candy **3** b f 4331^{10}
Marco Magnifico (USA) **5** b or br h 4284^{6} 4373^{2} **>70a 59df<**
Mardood **10** b h 4284^{13} 4332^{8} **>38a 71df<**
Marinos **4** b f 4323^{16} **>46f<**
Maronetta **3** ch f 4254^{9} **>30a 56f<**
Marsh Arab **4** b g 4227^{14} **>19a 47f<**
Marvelous Crown (JPN) **5** ch g Miswaki (USA)-Maurita (NZ) (Harbor Prince (USA)) (4294a) **>127f<**
Mary Macblain **6** b m 4224^{10} **>35a 43f<**
Masnun (USA) **10** gr h 4210^{4} 4265^{5} 4302^{2} (4374) **>74a 68f<**
Masrah Dubai (USA) **4** b g Theatrical-Roycon (High Top) 4271^{5} 4343^{5} **>61a f<**
Master M-E-N (IRE) **3** ch c 4222^{8} **>36a 62f<**
Master Millfield (IRE) **3** b c 4242^{10} (4340) (4350) (4356) 4372^{2} **>79a 71f<**
Matisse **4** b f 4241^{15} 4270^{12} **>16a 49f<**
Matthew David **5** ch h 4237^{9} (4361) **>49a 34f<**
Mazeeka (IRE) **4** ch f 4214^{2} 4320^{7} 4337^{6} **>58da 66f<**
Mazilla **3** b f 4242^{5} **>66a 54df<**
Meant to Be **5** b m 4252^{3} **>78a 90f<**
Mediate (IRE) **3** b c 4216^{6} (4285) 4298^{3} **>69a 72f<**
Mediator **6** b h 4287^{8} 4335^{4} **>39a 49f<**
Medland (IRE) **5** ch h 4371^{3} **>58a 36f<**
Meesonette **3** ch f 4213^{14} 4321^{16} **>10a f<**
Meeson Times **7** b m 4322^{13} **>46da 27f<**
Meghdoot **3** b f 4340^{5} **>32a 79f<**
Mentalasanythin **6** b g 4252^{5} **>80a 75f<**

Merrie le Bow **3** b f Merdon Melody-Arch Sculptress (Arch Sculptor) 4324^{6} 4369^{3} **>51a 49f<**
Metal Storm (FR) **7** b h 4236a^{7} 4304a^{8} (4371) **>86a 89f<**
Mezzoramio **3** ch g Cadeaux Genereux-Hopeful Search (USA) (Vaguely Noble) 4254^{4} **>60a f<**
Midlin **5** ch m 4226^{10} 4239^{10} **>46da 32f<**
Midyan Blue (IRE) **5** ch h 4252^{7} **>63a 89f<**
Mighty Kingdom (IRE) **4** b f 4274^{5} 4320^{11} 4354^{9} **>29a 53f<**
Mill de Lease **10** b g Milford-Melting Snows (High Top) 4323^{15}
Millsolin (IRE) **7** b h (4224) **>60da 60f<**
Milngavie (IRE) **5** ch h 4272^{3} **>66da 43f<**
Milos **4** b c 4204^{3} 4241^{2} 4289^{5} 4337^{10} 4376^{4} **>62a 71f<**
Miriam **4** br f 4212^{9} **>27a 54df<**
Miroswaki (USA) **5** br h 4261^{2} 4272^{2} 4300^{2} **>68a 75f<**
Misbegotten (IRE) **4** b f 4232a^{3} **>112f<**
Mislemani (IRE) **5** b h 4274^{3} 4320^{9} 4339^{7} **>54a 65f<**
Miss Charlie **5** ch m 4270^{15} 4358^{3} **>43da 69f<**
Miss Iron Heart (USA) **3** b f 4242^{8} **>17a 50f<**
Miss Mah-Jong **4** b f 4374^{7} **>37a 58f<**
Miss Siham (IRE) **6** ch m 4361^{6} **>28a 50+f<**
Misstinger **3** b f 4275^{12} 4330^{9} **>29a 37f<**
Miss Tipsy **4** b f 4322^{9} **>34a 38f<**
Mister Fire Eyes (IRE) **3** b c (4228) (4242) **>83a 81f<**
Mister O'Grady (IRE) **4** b c 4260^{13} 4312^{9} **>39a 57f<**
Mister Rm **3** b c Dominion-La Cabrilla (Carwhite) 4286^{8} **>38a 82f<**
Mistle Cat (USA) **5** gr h 4232a^{6} **>117f<**
Modest Hope (USA) **8** b h 4244^{5} 4277^{6} 4323^{10} 4354^{4} **>55a 56f<**
Mon Rouge (IRE) **4** b c 4309^{13} 4348^{11} **>13a 72f<**
Monsieur Petong **4** b c 4210^{5} 4269^{8} 4319^{12} **>47a 37f<**
Montanelli (FR) **3** b c Dowsing (USA)-Honeymooning (USA) (Blushing Groom (FR)) 4340^{3} **>86a 63f<**
Moscow Road **4** b c 4370^{7} **>74a 69df<**
Most Welcome News **3** b c 4205^{6} 4259^{5} **>47a 55f<**
Moujeeb (USA) **5** b h 4211^{2} **>62a 71f<**
Mr Bean **5** b g 4354^{3} **>67a 75f<**
Mr Cube (IRE) **5** ch h 4204^{12} **>41a 70f<**
Mr Devious **4** b c 4218^{8} **>59a 63f<**
Mr Geran (IRE) **6** b g 4229^{10} **>18a 40f<**
Mr Martini (IRE) **5** b h 4333^{11} **>78a 118f<**
Mr M-E-N (IRE) **4** ch c 4220^{11} **>31a 67f<**
Mr Nevermind (IRE) **5** b h (4202) 4264^{2} 4374^{2} **>81a 70f<**
Mrs Arkada (FR) **4** b f (4293a) **>107f<**
Mrs Bizzybody **4** b f 4210^{9} **>23a 18f<**
Mrs Jawleyford (USA) **7** b m 4323^{4} (4351) **>55da 51f<**
Mr Slick **3** ch c 4238^{9} 4256^{5} 4330^{7} **>52a 53f<**
Mulciber **7** b h 4312^{6} **>72a 69f<**
Mulled Ale (IRE) **5** b m 4244^{C} **>55f<**
Mullitover **5** ch h (4227) 4264^{6} 4336^{8} **>65a 93f<**
Musical Fantasy (IRE) **3** b f (4298) 4330^{3} 4352^{7} **>45a 46f<**
Music Please **3** ch g 4225^{11} **>25a 39f<**
Mustn't Grumble (IRE) **5** b g (4241) 4278^{2} 4306^{2} **>54a 63f<**
Mutiara **4** b f 4343^{12} **>21a 49df<**
Mutinique **4** br f 4302^{11} 4313^{12} **>27a 50f<**
Muzz (IRE) **4** br c 4325^{15} **>47a 64df<**
My Cherrywell **5** br m 4211^{3} **>54a 49f<**
My Foxy Lady **5** b m 4361^{8} **>7a 35f<**
My Gallery (IRE) **4** ch f 4281^{12} **>62a 58f<**
Myjinka **5** gr m 4336^{11} 4344^{7} 4376^{5} **>42a 29f<**
My Minnie **5** b m 4341^{5} **>75+a 52f<**
My Ruby Ring **8** b m 4289^{11} 4337^{7} 4349^{9} **>67df<**
Mystoski **3** b f 4225^{10} **>26a 47f<**

N

Naawy **5** b h 4276^{11} **>32a 43f<**
Nadra (IRE) **4** b f 4217^{10} **>36a 56f<**
Nadwaty (IRE) **3** b f 4267^{3} 4324^{7} **>40a 49f<**
Nakita **4** ch f 4237^{4} 4310^{3} **>53a 58f<**
Nearly Honest **7** ch m 4318^{11} 4332^{13} **>25a 47f<**
Needwood Newt **3** ch f 4228^{10} 4359^{3} **>45a 48f<**
Needwood Swift **4** ch f 4355^{7} **>43a 30f<**
Nellie's Gamble **5** b m 4224^{2} 4241^{7} **>50a 42f<**
Never Say so **3** ch f 4238^{12} **>37a 46f<**
Never Time (IRE) **3** b c 4356^{9} **>29a 62f<**
Newington Butts (IRE) **5** br m 4258^{3} 4343^{2} **>48a 45f<**
New Inn **4** b c 4221^{2} (4252) 4326^{8} **>72da 57f<**
Nice Nature (JPN) **7** b h 4294a^{8}
Nigelschinapalace **6** b g 4378^{10} **>44a 10f<**
Nigel's Lad (IRE) **3** b g 4219^{5} 4242^{3} **>81a 93f<**
Nigels Lady **6** ch m Ra Nova-Curzon House (Green God) 4214^{15}
Night Edition **5** b h 4217^{12} 4339^{9} **>44a 54f<**
Nijinsky's Gold (USA) **6** ro h Lot O'Gold (USA)-Super Jamie (USA) (Nijinsky (CAN)) 4328a^{2} **>119f<**
Nineacres **4** b g 4253^{2} 4288^{2} 4325^{2} (4345) **>62a 53f<**
Noeprob (USA) **5** b m 4310^{10} **>30a 51f<**
Nomogram **4** b g 4302^{10} **>8a 44f<**
No Pattern **3** ch c 4216^{8} 4285^{2} 4298^{4} **>88a 84f<**
Nordan Raider **7** ch m 4220^{2} 4278^{3} **>78a 64f<**
Nordico Princess **4** b f 4220^{6} 4268^{7} (4297) 4370^{2} **>74a 58f<**
Nordinex (IRE) **3** b c 4285^{4} **>73a 86f<**
Norman Prince (IRE) **3** b c 4279^{5} 4308^{7} 4321^{2} 4381^{3} **>54a 62f<**
Northern Bird **5** ch m 4265^{3} **>66a 66+f<**
Northern Celadon (IRE) **4** b c (4378) **>76a 75f<**
Northern Fan (IRE) **3** b c 4280^{3} **>58a 79f<**
Northern Rainbow **7** b h 4276^{13} **>47da 47f<**
Northgate Raver **4** ch f 4361^{10}
North to Glory **4** b f 4206^{14} **>14a 3f<**
No Speeches (IRE) **4** b c 4204^{14} 4264^{7} 4301^{4} **>63a 63df<**
No Submission (USA) **9** b h 4226^{6} 4241^{6} 4320^{2} **>76a 74f<**
Not so Generous (IRE) **5** b m 4266^{8} 4297^{8} **>55a 59f<**
Noufari (FR) **4** b g 4218^{3} (4311) (4354) 4382^{5} **>85a 85f<**
No What I Mean (IRE) **4** b f 4313^{16} **>21f<**
Nuclear Express **8** b h 4278^{8} 4310^{11} **>25a 61df<**

O

Oakbury (IRE) **3** ch c 4334^{5} **>37a 75f<**
Oakley Manor **4** ch f 4313^{14} **>21f<**
Obsidian Grey **8** gr h 4202^{13} 4241^{10} 4288^{9} 4319^{11} 4375^{7} **>40a 56f<**
Ocean Hawk (USA) **3** b c 4240^{3} **>63a 49f<**

Ochos Rios (IRE) 4 br g 4320^{8} **>59a 65f<**
Off the Air (IRE) 4 b f 4227^{13} 4309^{10} **>48a 36f<**
Olifantsfontein 7 b h 4212^{5} 4243^{4} 4255^{11} 4355^{11} **>49a 57f<**
Olimpia Dukakis (ITY) 3 b f Isopach (USA)-Jaana (Cure The Blues (USA)) (4233a) **>100f<**
One for Jeannie 3 b f Clantime-Miss Henry (Blue Cashmere) 4256^{2} 4308^{8} 4315^{3} **>72a 64f<**
One Wild Oat 4 b f 4335^{7} **>1a 59f<**
On the Wing Again 4 b f 4283^{10} **>36da 37f<**
On Y Va (USA) 8 ch m 4270^{6} **>56da 71f<**
Orage Noir (USA) 7 b h 4246a^{2}
Orthorhombus 6 b h 4231^{15} 4281^{4} 4322^{10} **>64a 67f<**
Oscar the Second (IRE) 5 b g 4322^{16} **>27da 44f<**
Our Eddie 6 ch g (4312) 4341^{4} **>68a 57f<**
Our Shadee (USA) 5 b h 4202^{4} 4258^{4} 4270^{3} 4313^{4} 4337^{5} **>58a 52f<**
Our Tom 3 br c 4242^{13} **>68a 61f<**
Out on a Promise (IRE) 3 b c (4254) **>68a 96f<**

P

Pagan Heights 3 b f 4207^{9} **>28?f<**
Pakol (IRE) 6 b m 4206^{5} **>45a 44f<**
Palacegate Gold (IRE) 6 b h 4255^{13} 4303^{12} **>19a 47f<**
Palacegate Jo (IRE) 4 b f 4309^{9} 4360^{5} 4379^{4} **>59da 67f<**
Paley Prince (USA) 9 b h 4253^{9} 4268^{4} **>48a 65f<**
Panther (IRE) 5 ch h 4322^{5} **>56a 54f<**
Papagos (IRE) 4 b c 4202^{15} 4265^{12} 4345^{8} 4375^{9} **>22a 42f<**
Paradise Creek (USA) 6 b h 4294a^{2}
Parklife (IRE) 3 ch g Double Schwartz-Silk Trade (Auction Ring (USA)) 4308^{12} **>26a 44f<**
Pash 3 b f 4321^{14} **>52f<**
Patacake (IRE) 4 ch f 4345^{10} **>33f<**
Pat Poindestres 5 b m 4266^{5} 4283^{2} **>36a 36df<**
Pats Delight 3 ch f 4222^{2} 4238^{7} 4324^{10} 4352^{4} **>47a 16f<**
Pc's Cruiser (IRE) 3 b g Homo Sapien-Ivy Holme (Silly Season) 4324^{11} **>65a 58df<**
Peaches Polly 5 b m 4209^{11} **>41a 93?f<**
Pearly River 4 b f 4339^{6} **>60da 78f<**
Pendine 3 b f 4225^{9} **>27a 40f<**
Pennine Lady (IRE) 3 b f 4307^{12} **>15a 35f<**
Penny's Wishing 3 b f 4238^{3} **>63a 69df<**
Pent-House Baby 3 ch f 4203^{5} 4259^{3} **>46a 27f<**
Perilous Plight 4 ch g Siberian Express (USA)-Loveskate (USA) (Overskate (CAN)) 4336^{7} **>81a 75f<**
Persian Bud (IRE) 7 b or br h 4351^{11} **>27a 48f<**
Persian Conquest (IRE) 3 b c 4286^{6} 4314^{6} **>84a 66f<**
Personal Pride (IRE) 4 br c 4202^{12} **>24a 48df<**
Personimus 5 b h 4217^{18} **>35a 35f<**
Pertemps Flyer 4 b c 4231^{11} 4278^{13} **>46a 56df<**
Pertemps Partner 3 b f 4219^{6} 4352^{9} **>47a 47f<**
Pesce D'Aprile 3 b f (4247a) **>88f<**
Pharly Dancer 6 b h (4276) **>84a 68f<**
Philgun 6 b h 4252^{11} **>64a 75f<**
Phoenix Venture (IRE) 4 ch f 4227^{9} 4277^{12} **>58a 65f<**
Piccola Buddha (IRE) 3 b c 4251a^{6} **>72f<**
Pigalle Wonder 7 br h 4301^{7} 4341^{8} **>39a 35f<**
Pink Brief (IRE) 4 b f 4209^{9} 4261^{15} 4287^{11} 4326^{11} **>49da 69f<**
Pink Petal 3 gr f Northern Game-Gratclo (Belfort (FR)) 4225^{14} 4307^{13} 4352^{6} **>27a 28f<**
Pirates Gold (IRE) 5 ch h 4317^{7} 4339^{5} **>56da 56f<**
Pleasure Beach 3 br g 4242^{2} 4279^{4} 4314^{2} 4342^{4} **>65a 45f<**
Plucky Pet 3 br f 4262^{11} **>28a 46f<**
Polly Garter 3 gr f 4282^{8} **>46a 57f<**
Polly Peculiar 4 b f (4215) 4301^{3} **>51a 73f<**
Polonez Prima 8 ch h 4223^{3} 4264^{5} 4309^{5} **>68a 70f<**
Poly Lane 3 b c 4350^{6} **>64a 62df<**
Poly Laureon (IRE) 3 b f 4350^{4} **>64a 56f<**
Poly Road 3 b f 4216^{10} (4321) **>64da 66f<**
Poor Printer (IRE) 4 ch f Digamist (USA)-No Reproach (Northfields (USA)) 4210^{11} 4271^{12} **>27a 28f<**
Pop to Stans 6 b h 4260^{9} 4274^{8} **>59a 48f<**
Portelet 3 b f 4334^{6} **>53a 85f<**
Port Lucaya 5 ch h 4234a^{6} **>117f<**
Portolano (FR) 4 b c 4302^{8} 4341^{7} **>38a 59f<**
Port Sunlight (IRE) 7 ch h 4218^{7} 4257^{10} 4378^{8} **>53a 75f<**
Possibility 4 b f 4270^{11} 4375^{3} **>44a 57f<**
Posted Abroad (IRE) 3 b g Cyrano de Bergerac-Postie (Sharpo) 4254^{3} 4324^{3} **>71a f<**
Precious Times 3 b c 4222^{6} 4256^{8} **>39a 33f<**
Premier Dance 8 ch h 4218^{4} 4252^{4} 4277^{8} 4354^{2} 4382^{3} **>70a 52f<**
Premium Bond 4 br g 4215^{4} 4273^{9} **>50a 47f<**
Present Situation 4 ch c (4264) **>77a 59f<**
Press the Bell 5 br g 4231^{3} 4316^{3} 4370^{3} **>73a 80f<**
Pretonic 7 b m 4349^{2} **>49a 23f<**
Pride of Britain (CAN) 6 ch m 4287^{2} 4332^{3} 4351^{4} **>57a 70f<**
Prime Mover 7 b h 4224^{7} **>37a 50f<**
Prime Silver (IRE) 3 gr g Standaan (FR)-Avital (Pitskelly) 4340^{13}
Prim Lass 4 b f 4227^{8} 4301^{6} **>46a 55f<**
Primula Bairn 5 b m 4231^{4} 4278^{9} 4306^{9} 4361^{2} **>51a 50f<**
Prince Rodney 6 gr h 4313^{9} 4357^{5} **>34a 32f<**
Prince Rudolf (IRE) 3 b g 4228^{9} 4256^{12} 4350^{7} **>54a 59f<**
Princess in Blue (IRE) 3 b f 4359^{9} **>19a 36f<**
Princess Shera (IRE) 4 b f 4357^{12} **>29da 35df<**
Princess Tateum (IRE) 5 b m 4287^{12} **>30a 73f<**
Priscilla Rose 4 b f 4318^{9} 4339^{12} **>32a 55f<**
Private Fixture (IRE) 4 ch c 4223^{11} **>68a 69f<**
Privity (USA) 14 ch h 4295a^{2} **>112f<**
Prosequendo (USA) 8 b h 4338^{4} 4373^{11} **>56da 44f<**
Puffy 8 ch g 4224^{8} 4274^{9} **>52a 50f<**
Purbeck Centenary 5 b h 4211^{9} 4283^{6} **>50a 44f<**
Pursuance (IRE) 3 b c 4324^{4} **>68a 51f<**

Q

Q Factor 3 br f 4279^{3} **>60a 76f<**
Qualitair Glory 3 b g 4213^{16} **>10a 50f<**
Qualitair Ridge 3 ch f 4228^{5} 4242^{9} **>41a 55f<**
Queen of Shannon (IRE) 7 b m 4281^{6} 4296^{2} 4318^{3} **>46da 43f<**
Queens Stroller (IRE) 4 b f 4223^{4} 4257^{2} **>72a 62f<**
Quick Million 4 b f 4343^{7} 4374^{3} **>56da 41f<**
Quiet Mission 4 ch c 4288^{8} 4358^{7} **>22a 45f<**
Quinzii Martin 7 b h 4313^{11} 4357^{3} **>64a 51f<**

R

Rad 5 b h 4226^{4} 4289^{2} 4317^{2} **>59a 58f<**

Ragazzo (IRE) 5 b g 4289^{7} 4303^{9} 4360^{3} **>53da 44f<**
Ragtime Song 6 b h 4208^{10} 4332^{7} **>29f<**
Raintrap 5 ch h 4294a^{13} **>124f<**
Rambold 4 b f 4263^{6} 4336^{5} **>61a 70df<**
Random 4 ch f 4297^{6} **>64a 69f<**
Randonneur (IRE) 4 ch f 4293a^{5} **>91f<**
Ranger Sloane 3 ch c 4222^{13} **>51a 24f<**
Rankaidade 4 b f 4211^{10} **>25a 38f<**
Rave-on-Hadley (IRE) 5 b g 4260^{7} 4319^{8} **>46a 26f<**
Real Madrid 4 b g (4305a) **>56df<**
Red Bishop (USA) 7 b or br h (4327a) **>123f<**
Red Dancer 4 ch f 4217^{2} 4261^{5} **>56a 55f<**
Red Hassett (IRE) 3 b c 4275^{9} **>12a 55f<**
Red Paper (IRE) 3 b c Emmson-Gold Slipper (Glint of Gold) 4248a^{3} **>109f<**
Red Spectacle (IRE) 3 b c 4262^{8} **>59a 65f<**
Red Valerian 4 b c 4264^{4} (4271) 4336^{2} **>90a 93f<**
Red Whirlwind 5 b h 4274^{4} 4309^{2} 4341^{10} **>68a 56f<**
Regina Alicia 4 b f 4284^{14} **>16a 34f<**
Remember This (IRE) 5 b g 4269^{9} **>48a 47df<**
Reponist 3 b f 4207^{7} 4256^{4} 4307^{3} 4356^{7} **>36a 53f<**
Respectable Jones 9 ch h 4374^{5} **>50a 50f<**
Riskie Things 4 ch f 4370^{9} **>55da 47f<**
Risk the Witch 5 b m 4206^{8} 4269^{11} 4338^{11} **>12a 16f<**
Risky Romeo 3 b g (4203) (4216) **>87+a 68f<**
Risky Rose 3 b f 4207^{6} 4321^{6} 4381^{5} **>40a 60f<**
Risky Royal 3 ch g 4238^{6} **>59a 40f<**
Riva-Deva 3 b c 4219^{12}
River Majesty (USA) 6 b m 4329a^{2} **>122f<**
Roar on Tour 6 b h 4281^{2} 4360^{2} **>74a 50f<**
Robo Magic (USA) 3 b c 4207^{2} (4262) 4298^{13} **>73a 60f<**
Rocketeer (IRE) 4 ch c 4220^{3} 4263^{8} (4333) **>90a 78f<**
Rockfield Lady (IRE) 3 b f 4380^{5} **>20a f<**
Rockstine (IRE) 4 b f 4301^{8} 4335^{6} **>52a 47f<**
Rock to Sleep (USA) 4 ch f 4358^{6} **>14a 66df<**
Rocky Bay 6 ch m 4311^{9} **>27a 13f<**
Rocky Two 4 b c 4231^{7} 4266^{6} 4316^{7} 4370^{5} **>59a 56df<**
Rocky Waters (USA) 6 b or br h (4258) 4333^{8} **>74da 64f<**
Rome to Nome (USA) 3 b c Far Out East (USA)-Lithia's Dantan (USA) (Prince Dantan (USA)) (4282) **>67+a f<**
Rose Elegance 6 ch m 4223^{12} 4296^{9} 4312^{7} **>51a 62df<**
Rose of Glenn 4 b f 4208^{4} 4261^{6} 4323^{6} **>55a 57f<**
Rosina's Folly 4 b f 4227^{15} 4361^{7} **>58a 49f<**
Rotherfield Park (IRE) 3 b f (4222) 4275^{4} 4298^{5} 4342^{3} **>43a 34f<**
Rough Habit (NZ) 9 b g Roughcast (USA)-Certain Habit (NZ) (Ashabit) 4294a^{7} **>119f<**
Rowlandsons Silver (FR) 3 b c 4207^{4} 4213^{5} **>37a 61f<**
Royal Acclaim 10 ch h 4274^{11} 4378^{7} **>50a 41f<**
Royal Circus 6 b h 4300^{7} 4318^{5} **>43a 46f<**
Royal Dancer 3 ch f 4267^{6} 4324^{9} **>31a 39f<**
Royal Philosopher 3 b c 4295a^{5} **>104df<**
Royce and Royce (JPN) 5 b h Toby Bin-That's My Pal (USA) (Key To The Mint (USA)) 4294a^{3} **>125f<**
Roy (ITY) 3 b c Victory Piper (USA)-Rocca d'Aspide (ITY) (Droll Role (USA)) 4290a^{3}
Runforaction (IRE) 3 b f 4321^{3} **>44a 48f<**
Run to Au Bon (IRE) 5 b h 4217^{17}
Rustic League (IRE) 4 b g Gallic League-Walnut Lass (Tap On Wood) 4214^{11} 4283^{7} 4317^{10} **>36a 35f<**

S

Sabicas 3 b c 4331^{3} **>45da 45f<**
Saddlehome (USA) 6 b h 4231^{10} **>85a 82f<**
Saint Amigo 3 gr c 4228^{3} **>59a 57f<**
Sakura Bakushin O (JPN) 6 b h Sakura Yutaka O (JPN)-Sakura Hagoromo (JPN) (Northern Taste (CAN)) (4346a)
Salbus 5 b h 4353^{5} **>70a 42f<**
Sally Weld 3 ch f 4285^{7} **>64a 62f<**
Salska 4 b f 4281^{13} 4311^{8} 4379^{5} **>41a 56f<**
Samana Cay 3 ch f 4321^{5} **>63a 46f<**
Samson-Agonistes 9 b h 4325^{3} 4355^{4} **>64a 46df<**
Sandmoor Denim 8 b g 4227^{4} (4257) (4274) 4309^{4} **>71a 72f<**
Sandpit (BRZ) 6 ch h Baynoun-Sand Dancer (FR) (Green Dancer (USA)) 4294a^{5} **>122f<**
Sandra Dee (IRE) 3 ch f 4380^{3} **>31a 35df<**
Sarum 9 b h 4209^{4} 4265^{7} 4270^{5} 4303^{5} **>51a f<**
Sassiver (USA) 5 b h 4221^{7} (4229) 4323^{8} 4351^{3} **>54a 42f<**
Saterne Lady 3 b f 4259^{2} **>57a 50f<**
Saxon Heir (IRE) 3 b g 4207^{10} 4222^{11} 4256^{6} **>30da 47f<**
Saxon King (IRE) 5 ch g 4206^{2} **>56a 46f<**
Scalp 'em (IRE) 7 b g 4208^{6} 4276^{2} (4318) 4351^{7} (4382) **>62a 52f<**
Scandinavian (FR) 4 b c Always Fair (USA)-Sarietta (GER) (Windwurf (GER)) 4232a^{2} **>115f<**
Scored Again 5 b h (4253) 4322^{3} 4349^{11} **>62a 52f<**
Scottish Park 6 ch m 4224^{13} 4241^{11} 4319^{14} 4371^{4} **>49a 50f<**
Screwball Anaconda 4 ch c 4226^{12} **>20a 54df<**
Scribano 5 b h Pharly (FR)-Biograph (USA) (Riverman (USA)) 4234a^{3} **>111f<**
Scylla 3 b f 4280^{8} **>28a 42f<**
Sea Devil 9 gr h 4237^{13} 4355^{6} **>78a 63f<**
Secret Aly (CAN) 5 b h 4281^{3} (4337) (4360) **>86a 89f<**
Secret Assignment (USA) 5 ch g 4206^{4} 4270^{14} 4289^{9} **>38a 33f<**
Secundus (IRE) 4 gr g 4271^{10} 4339^{13} **>44a 84df<**
See You Again 3 b c Then Again-Down the Valley (Kampala) 4331^{4} **>49a 63f<**
Sense of Priority 6 ch g 4237^{6} 4310^{4} 4348^{3} **>67a 63f<**
Serious Fact 3 b c 4254^{10} **>25a 39f<**
Shabanaz 10 b h 4209^{3} (4239) (4260) 4300^{3} 4326^{7} **>67a 72f<**
Shadow Jury 5 ch h 4237^{15} 4253^{5} 4322^{8} **>75a 72f<**
Shamal (ITY) 3 b f Nacacyte (USA)-Blizzard (Viani) 4247a^{3}
Shamwari (USA) 4 ch f 4261^{13} **>58da 71df<**
Shanghai Lil 3 b f 4213^{6} **>48a 35f<**
Shansi (IRE) 4 b g 4264^{3} 4303^{11} **>50a 30f<**
Shared Risk 3 ch c 4228^{15} **>66da 40f<**
Sharpening 4 ch f 4281^{5} **>43da 53f<**
Sharp Gazelle 5 ch m 4320^{3} 4378^{2} **>50a 54f<**
Sharp Imp 5 b h 4204^{2} 4255^{2} 4289^{3} 4313^{2} 4376^{2} **>52a 56f<**
Sharp Shower (IRE) 3 b c 4256^{7} **>41a 48df<**

Sharp Tern 3 gr f 4254^{6} 4314^{13} **>40a 48f<**
Sharp Thrill 4 ch c 4379^{6} **>51a 47f<**
Shawn Cuddy 4 ch c 4229^{12} **>37a 38f<**
She's a Madam 4 b f 4215^{12} **>36a 10tf<**
Shinerolla 3 b g 4230^{5} **>48a 91f<**
Shooter 3 b c 4225^{2} **>68a 63f<**
Shot the Sheriff 3 b c 4225^{3} (4286) **>61a 41f<**
Shuttlecock 4 ch c 4227^{7} 4257^{11} 4353^{9} **>75da 54f<**
Shy Paddy (IRE) 3 b g 4259^{8} (4380) **>54a 64f<**
Sieve of Time (USA) 4 br c 4353^{4} **>86a 90df<**
Sifacar (FR) 7 b g Cariellor (FR)-Sifana (Double-U-Jay) 4291a^{3} **>109f<**
Silent Expression 5 gr m (4214) (4263) 4316^{2} **>86a 92f<**
Silent Sky 3 b f 4307^{11} 4359^{10} **>38a 30f<**
Silktail (IRE) 3 b f 4219^{8} 4321^{11} **>29a 79f<**
Simon Ellis (IRE) 6 ch h 4269^{7} 4301^{13} **>31a 33f<**
Simply Simon 3 b c 4240^{15} **>27a 42f<**
Singleton Barn (IRE) 3 b c 4321^{15} **>35f<**
Sir Norman Holt (IRE) 6 b h 4209^{5} 4337^{11} **>67a 62f<**
Sir Tasker 7 b h 4231^{8} 4325^{12} **>65a 62df<**
Sir Thomas Beecham 5 b g 4261^{7} 4272^{6} **>68a 67f<**
Sison (IRE) 5 b h 4231^{14} 4297^{5} **>58a 61f<**
Skip Lady (FR) 3 gr f Gairloch-Alta River (FR) (Kautokeino (FR)) 4292a^{2} **>88f<**
Sky Diver 4 b c 4358^{10} **>21a 46f<**
Sleeptite (FR) 5 gr g 4244^{16} **>77a 10f<**
Slmaat 4 ch f (4218) **>71a 69f<**
Slopes 4 b c 4215^{11} **>8a 21f<**
Slytly Beveled 3 ch c 4203^{4} (4213) **>66a 63f<**
Smocking 5 ch m 4244^{14} 4284^{8} **>47da 43f<**
Soaking 5 b h (4210) 4265^{9} 4289^{8} 4375^{5} **>74a 60f<**
So Intrepid (IRE) 5 ch h 4310^{5} 4377^{5} **>44a 79f<**
Soldier's Leap (FR) 3 b c (4205) 4279^{2} 4372^{4} **>85a 80f<**
Solo Prize 3 b c 4262^{9} **>38a 73f<**
Something Speedy (IRE) 3 b f 4240^{7} (4307) **>50a 37f<**
Sommersby (IRE) 4 b c 4261^{8} **>75a 54f<**
So Rhythmical 11 b g 4223^{7} 4243^{11} **>55a 72df<**
So Sweet (IRE) 3 ch c Doulab (USA)-Rip Roaring (Royal And Regal (USA)) 4251a^{2} **>68f<**
South Eastern Fred 4 b c (4301) (4341) **>86a 59df<**
Southern Dominion 3 ch c 4207^{3} 4222^{5} **>53a 68f<**
Sovereign Rocket (USA) 10 b h Sovereign Dancer (USA)-Jeffs Miss Rocket (USA) (Jeff D) 4305a^{2} **>55f<**
Soviet Line (IRE) 5 b h (4328a) **>129f<**
Sozzled 4 gr c 4309^{7} **>53a 65df<**
Sparkling Roberta 4 b f 4209^{8} **>40a 45f<**
Spectacle Jim 6 b h 4265^{4} 4269^{3} 4375^{6} **>46a 53f<**
Speedy Classic (USA) 6 br g (4212) (4288) 4333^{3} **>64a 64df<**
Spencer's Revenge 6 ch g 4224^{3} 4371^{2} **>80a 79f<**
Spender 6 b or br g 4231^{9} 4258^{2} 4333^{6} **>82a 74f<**
Spring Flyer (IRE) 5 b m 4223^{5} 4309^{3} **>65a 62f<**
Spring Loaded 4 b c 4257^{12} 4300^{10} **>30a 62f<**
Stalled (IRE) 5 b h (4287) (4332) **>65a 63f<**
Star Fighter 3 gr c 4205^{5} (4259) 4372^{3} **>54a 58f<**
Star Quest 8 b h 4287^{7} 4332^{2} 4351^{10} **>52a 58f<**
Star Rage (IRE) 5 b h 4252^{2} **>77a 91f<**
Star Witness (IRE) 3 b c 4372^{8} **>42a 76f<**
State Taj (AUS) 6 b g True Statement (USA)-Feltaj (AUS) (Taj Rossi (AUS)) (4329a) **>123f<**
Steel Sovereign 4 gr c 4243^{13} **>11a 36df<**
Stevie's Wonder (IRE) 5 ch h 4217^{3} **>76a 69f<**
St Martha (IRE) 5 b m 4227^{11} **>41a 64f<**
Stoppes Brow 3 b c (4267) 4342^{2} **>87a 77f<**
Storm Bidder 4 b g 4313^{10} **>41da 40f<**
Storm Flash 3 b f 4331^{7} **>43a 64+f<**
Strat's Legacy 8 b g 4208^{2} 4284^{5} 4332^{4} **>60a 51f<**
Straw Thatch 6 b h 4274^{7} 4311^{5} **>42a 52f<**
Strictly Personal (USA) 5 b or br h 4209^{10} **>71a 46f<**
Struggler 3 b c Night Shift (USA)-Dreamawhile (Known Fact (USA)) 4292a^{3} **>121f<**
Success Story 4 gr f 4208^{11} **>62da 53f<**
Sud (IRE) 3 br c 4290a^{6}
Sugarland Express (IRE) 4 br c 4234a^{2} **>117f<**
Sunday News'n'echo (USA) 4 b f 4229^{4} **>44a 66f<**
Super Assignation (IRE) 4 ch f 4374^{10} **>43a 64f<**
Super Benz 9 ch h 4204^{7} 4322^{2} 4348^{4} **>66a 73f<**
Superbit 3 b c 4359^{4} **>51da 51f<**
Supercool 4 ch g 4358^{2} **>42a 68f<**
Super Rocky 6 b h 4212^{3} 4268^{6} 4325^{14} **>56da 80f<**
Super Sonata 3 b f 4267^{9} **>39a 60f<**
Surprise Breeze 4 gr f 4224^{11} **>32a 33f<**
Sushi Bar (IRE) 4 gr c 4296^{4} **>64a 63f<**
Swallow Ridge (IRE) 6 ch m 4214^{14} 4296^{12} 4317^{4} **>34a f<**
Sweet Caroline 4 br f 4215^{6} 4300^{11} **>37a 35f<**
Sweet Supposin (IRE) 4 b c Posen (USA)-Go Honey Go (General Assembly (USA)) (4303) 4339^{2} **>87a 67f<**
Swift Nick Nevison 4 b c 4266^{3} 4316^{4} **>38a 35f<**
Swinging Tich 6 b m 4349^{7} **>48da 47f<**
Swordking (IRE) 6 ch g 4221^{8} 4244^{2} 4323^{11} **>57a 54f<**
Swynford Flyer 6 b m 4239^{14} **>45a 45f<**

T

Tabard Garden 3 ch f 4216^{9} **>28a 42f<**
Tael of Silver 3 b f Today and Tomorrow-Schula (Kala Shikari) 4230^{3} **>56a 68f<**
Takenhall 10 b h 4210^{10} 4260^{10} **>38a 48f<**
Tanfirion Chief 4 b or br c 4274^{16} 4323^{14} **>12a 44f<**
Tapping Feet 3 b f Dominion-Vitry (Vitiges (FR)) 4230^{4} 4238^{4} 4299^{3} **>42a 14f<**
Tara Colleen (IRE) 3 b f 4216^{4} (4299) **>56da 54f<**
Taroudant 8 b g (4221) **>74a 82df<**
Tassagh Bridge (IRE) 5 b m 4288^{5} 4344^{8} **>19a 22df<**
Tauber 11 b h 4325^{10} **>42a 32f<**
Taufeliane 4 b f 4239^{13} **>13a 32df<**
Taylord 3 ch c 4286^{2} **>61a 73f<**
Tee-Emm 5 b h 4212^{2} (4268) 4297^{4} 4345^{6} **>58a 45f<**
Tee Tee Too (IRE) 3 ch g 4228^{2} **>77da 67df<**
Telephus 6 b g 4217^{9} 4244^{6} (4273) 4311^{4} 4373^{6} **>50a 49f<**
Tempering 9 b h 4244^{15} 4277^{2} 4326^{9} **>64a 26f<**
Templemore (IRE) 3 gr f 4216^{7} 4285^{6} **>40a 47f<**
The Cape Doctor (IRE) 3 b c 4282^{4} 4334^{3} **>64da 64f<**
The Noble Oak (IRE) 7 ch h 4212^{7} **>45a 42f<**
The Old Chapel 6 b h 4220^{4} **>76a 66f<**
Third Dam 4 b f 4271^{9} 4301^{11} **>33a 53f<**
Thorniwama 4 b f 4206^{6} 4270^{9} 4344^{3} 4374^{8} **>38a 20f<**
Thorny Bishop 4 b g 4258^{10} **>38a 39f<**
Thousla Rock (IRE) 6 ch h (4249a) **>113f<**

Tickerty's Gift **5** b h 4272^{9} **>40a 59f<**

Tierra Colorada **4** b f 4215^{10} **>30a 3f<**

Tigana **3** b f 4299^{9} 4340^{12} **>52f<**

Tiger Claw (USA) **9** b h 4287^{10} **>19a 31f<**

Tiheros **3** ch c 4262^{7} **>49a 61df<**

Tilly Owl **4** b f (4357) **>50a 38f<**

Tinker Amelia **3** b f 4207^{5} **>49a f<**

Titanium Honda (IRE) **4** gr c 4269^{6} 4278^{11} 4357^{7} 4375^{8} **>50a 42f<**

Today Tonite **3** b f 4298^{7} **>49a 57f<**

Tolls Choice (IRE) **6** ch g 4281^{15} **>61f<**

Tommy Tempest **6** ch g 4266^{4} 4325^{11} 4345^{7} **>54a 42f<**

Tonka **3** b c 4216^{11} 4307^{2} **>45a 71f<**

Top Tycoon (IRE) **4** b or br c 4269^{15} **>53f<**

Top Villain **9** b h 4229^{13} **>30a 25f<**

Torrey Pines (IRE) **3** b g Red Sunset-Yukon Baby (USA) (Northern Dancer) 4240^{13} 4280^{9} **>59a 61f<**

Tremendisto **5** b h 4221^{10} 4244^{4} 4323^{2} 4351^{2} **>57a 64f<**

Tremolante **4** b f 4210^{15} **>33a 4f<**

Tres Cher (IRE) **4** b f 4208^{9} 4261^{4} **>56a 57f<**

Trioming **9** b g 4253^{7} 4313^{15} 4355^{12} **>38da 44f<**

Triple Joy **4** b f (4206) (4278) (4336) **>99a 110f<**

True Dancing **4** b f Mashhor Dancer (USA)-True Queen (USA) (Silver Hawk (USA)) 4276^{14}

True Precision **5** b m 4264^{12} **>53a 67f<**

Truthful **4** b f 4221^{12}

Tudor Flight **4** b f 4271^{8} 4341^{14} **>41a 62f<**

Tu Opes **4** ch g 4223^{10} 4257^{7} 4320^{16} **>76a 81f<**

Two Chalk **3** b c 4222^{9} 4314^{9} 4359^{8} 4381^{4} **>44a 29f<**

Tyrian Purple (IRE) **7** b h 4237^{5} 4266^{7} 4325^{16} **>65a 62f<**

U

Uncharted Waters **4** b f 4209^{6} 4273^{10} **>58a 64f<**

Upex le Gold Too **3** ch g 4225^{6} **>40a 50f<**

Upper Mount Clair **5** b m 4373^{7} **>55a 73f<**

Urgent Request (IRE) **5** gr h 4327a^{2} **>125f<**

V

Vade Retro Satanas (FR) **3** b c 4308^{5} **>36da 53df<**

Val D'Authie (FR) **7** b h Truculent (USA)-Viva Bella (FR) (Cap Martin (FR)) 4371^{7} **>21a f<**

Valiant Man **4** br c 4281^{8} 4319^{5} **>49a 52f<**

Vanessa Rose **4** ro f 4237^{12} **>28a 58f<**

Vaneyck (FR) **3** ch c Romildo-Miss Brandish (USA) (Elocutionist (USA)) (4245a)

Vanroy **11** b h 4260^{4} 4296^{8} **>60a 61df<**

Veloce (IRE) **7** b h 4353^{10} **>51a 77f<**

Venture Fourth **6** b h 4239^{4} 4311^{11} **>32da 54f<**

Very Dicey **7** b g (4211) 4333^{10} 4361^{4} **>67a 78df<**

Vibro (IRE) **3** b c Sharp Victor (USA)-Binnissima (USA) (Tilt Up (USA)) 4340^{11} **>31a f<**

Victoria Hall **5** b m 4258^{9} 4317^{15} **>34a 59f<**

Victoria Princess **8** b m King of Spain-Renira (Relkino) 4371^{8} **>4a 28f<**

View From Above **9** b m 4326^{13} **>73a 84f<**

Village Green (FR) **5** gr h 4253^{8} 4266^{2} **>56a 65f<**

Vishnu (USA) **5** b h 4326^{12} **>62a 64f<**

Volcanic Dancer (USA) **9** b h 4276^{15} **>2a 32f<**

Volochine (IRE) **4** ch c 4329a^{3} **>122f<**

W

Waldo **4** ch g 4336^{4} 4353^{2} **>68a 76f<**

Walk the Beat **5** b h (4237) 4310^{C} 4355^{2} **>65a 67f<**

Wardara **3** ch f 4292a^{6} **>77f<**

Warwick Mist (IRE) **3** ch f 4230^{10} **>35a 38f<**

Warwick Warrior (IRE) **4** b g 4268^{2} 4337^{9} **>72a 66f<**

Wasblest **3** b f Statoblest-Safety First (Wassl) 4230^{6} 4286^{4} (4324) **>57a 62f<**

Wassl's Nanny (IRE) **6** b m Wassl-Granny's Bank (Music Boy) 4311^{10} **>14a 48f<**

Water Bebe (IRE) **3** b f 4213^{3} 4256^{3} 4314^{14} **>66+a 51df<**

Water Hazard (IRE) **3** b c 4203^{8} 4298^{8} **>62a 59f<**

Watheeqah (USA) **4** b f 4243^{8} 4274^{10} **>42a 64f<**

Wave Hill **6** b h 4210^{2} 4265^{6} 4371^{6} **>63a 75f<**

Waverley Star **10** br h 4288^{6} 4357^{4} **>41da 50f<**

Well and Truly **8** b m 4221^{3} 4287^{4} 4311^{6} 4351^{5} **>60a 41f<**

Well Suited **5** b h 4300^{12} 4320^{12} 4371^{10} **>24a 14f<**

Wellsy Lad (USA) **8** ch h 4278^{15} **>46a 52f<**

Wentbridge Lad (IRE) **5** b h (4223) 4241^{12} **>82a 74f<**

Westcourt Princess **3** b f 4228^{8} **>41a 65+f<**

Western Valley **5** ch m 4204^{11} 4273^{5} 4300^{8} **>27a 41f<**

Westfield Moves (IRE) **7** b h 4277^{9} 4326^{10} **>35a 57f<**

Whatone Bell **5** b h 4339^{11} **>32df<**

What's the Verdict (IRE) **3** b g (4240) **>75a 81f<**

White Lady **4** ch f 4243^{15} 4306^{12} 4374^{9} **>20a 68f<**

Whittingham Girl **3** b f 4230^{7} 4330^{5} (4352) **>66a 29f<**

Wicklow Boy (IRE) **4** b c 4272^{12} 4284^{4} **>43da 44f<**

Wide Outside (IRE) **4** b f 4273^{12} **>24f<**

Wings of Desire (IRE) **3** b c 4299^{7} 4359^{7} **>39a 59df<**

Winning Smile (FR) **5** br h Never so Bold-Funny Reef (FR) (Mill Reef (USA)) (4236a) **>101f<**

Winterbottom **3** gr c Reference Point-Snowing (USA) (Icecapade (USA)) 4225^{4} 4254^{8} 4324^{14} **>19a f<**

Witney-de-Bergerac (IRE) **3** b c 4262^{6} 4314^{12} 4372^{5} **>61a 69f<**

Wonderful Way (IRE) **5** b g Dance of Life (USA)-Tender and True (USA) (Prove Out (USA)) 4327a^{3} **>112f<**

Wonder Wood (GER) **9** b h Mlolshan-Wandering Ways (Will Somers) 4305a^{3} **>39f<**

Woodmans Star **5** ch h 4332^{10} 4351^{9} **>37da 49f<**

Woolverstone Hall (IRE) **3** b f 4203^{7} **>47a 66f<**

Wootton Rivers (USA) **5** ch h 4234a^{4} **>113f<**

Words of Wisdom (IRE) **5** b g 4202^{9} 4258^{5} **>66a 48f<**

World Traveller **4** ch c 4264^{10} 4336^{3} (4375) **>74a 64f<**

Wottashambles **4** b or br c (4338) 4373^{3} **>47a 53f<**

Y

Youcanstoplooking (IRE) **4** ch c 4371^{9} **>16a 30f<**

Young Ern **5** b h 4328a^{4} **>125f<**

Young Lucky **4** b g 4273^{4} 4318^{8} **>34a 32f<**

Youngui (FR) **5** ch h Lightning (FR)-Crystala (FR) (Crystal Palace (FR)) (4291a) **>115f<**

Z

Zahran (IRE) **4** b c 4378^{3} **>56a 66f<**

Zesti **3** br g Charmer-Lutine Royal (Formidable) 4340^{6} **>33a 56f<**

Zieten (USA) **5** b h 4346a^{9} **>123f<**

Ziggy's Dancer (USA) **4** b c 4358^{4} **>75a 92f<**

Zilzilah (USA) **4** ch f 4253^{10} 4281^{0} **>42a 65f<**

Zinbaq **9** ch h 4265^{10} 4317^{3} 4376^{7} **>32a 36f<**

Zuno Noelyn **4** b f 4217^{4} **>59a 63f<**

Raceform

TURF AND ALL-WEATHER FLAT RACING 1995

Complete record of Turf and All-Weather Flat Racing from January 1st to November 7th 1995

SOUTHWELL (L-H)
Monday January 2nd (Standard)

1 FARTHING H'CAP (0-80) (Class D) £3,741.40 (£1,133.20: £553.60: £263.80)
1m (Fibresand) GOING minus 0.04 sec per fur (STD) 1-00 (1-02)

Just Harry (74)*(79) (MJRyan)* 4-9-9 AClark(3) (lw: gd hdwy & 4th st: led over 1f out: rdn out)....— **1**
Orthorhombus **(54)***(55) (DJSCosgrove)* 6-8-4b AShoults(9) (disp ld tl led 5f out: hdd over 1f out: kpt on)....2 **2**
Sandmoor Denim **(70)***(70) (SRBowring)* 8-8-13 (7) GStrange(4) (b: chsd ldrs: 3rd st: rdn 2f out: kpt on same pce)....nk **3**
Mullitover **(72)***(65) (MJHeaton-Ellis)* 5-9-8 StephenDavies(6) (chsd ldrs: 5th st: no ex appr fnl f)....3½ **4**
Queens Consul (IRE) **(70)***(57)*(Fav)*(BSRothwell)* 5-9-6 MFenton(5) (prom tl lost pl ½-wy: 7th st: r.o again appr fnl f)....3 **5**
Karinska **(66)***(49) (MCChapman)* 5-8-11 (5) DRMcCabe(10) (wl bhd: poor 6th st: r.o fnl 2f)....1¾ **6**
Cicerone **(52)***(27) (JLHarris)* 5-8-2 AMackay(8) (lw: led 3f: 2nd st: wknd 2f out)....4 **7**
Warhurst (IRE) **(75)***(42) (DNicholls)* 4-9-10 AlexGreaves(1) (dwlt: a bhd)....4 **8**
Haroldon (IRE) **(62)***(—) (BPalling)* 6-8-7 (5) SSanders(7) (chsd ldrs: rdn ½-wy: sn bhd)....25 **9**
Wild Adventure **(43)***(—) (DWChapman)* 6-7-7 JQuinn(2) (Withdrawn).... **W**
LONG HANDICAP Wild Adventure 7-1

7/2 Queens Consul (IRE), **4/1** JUST HARRY, Sandmoor Denim, **9/2** Cicerone, **9/1** Mullitover, **12/1** Karinska, Haroldon (IRE), **14/1** Warhurst (IRE), **16/1** Orthorhombus, **33/1** Wild Adventure, CSF £55.83 CT £248.09 TOTE £3.60: £1.60 £4.50 £1.90 (£32.90) OWNER Miss Laura Shally (NEWMARKET) BRED Mrs S. T. Shally 9 Rn 1m 45.4 (6.10) SF: 49/27/42/37/29/24/3/-/-/-

2 HALF-CROWN CLAIMING STKS (Class F) £2,537.00 (£712.00: £347.00)
7f (Fibresand) GOING minus 0.04 sec per fur (STD) 1-30 (1-33)

Super Benz (60)*(66) (FJO'Mahony)* 9-8-10 GCarter(7) (hld up in tch: 7th st: led 2f out: sn qcknd clr: pushed out)....— **1**
Dream Carrier (IRE) **(68)***(58)*(Fav)*(TDBarron)* 7-8-13 LDettori(11) (chsd ldrs: 5th & rdn st: outpcd appr fnl f)....5 **2**
Bradwell (IRE) **(50)***(46) (MHTompkins)* 4-8-0 (5)ow3 SMulvey(13) (hdwy over 3f out: kpt on wl fnl f)....1¾ **3**
Bold Mick **(64)***(49) (DJGMurraySmith)* 4-8-9 StephenDavies(8) (wl bhd tl gd hdwy fnl 2f)....½ **4**
Jamaica Bridge **(48)***(51) (SGNorton)* 5-8-8 (5) JStack(12) (bit bkwd: hld up: hdwy & 3rd st: sn ev ch: wknd fnl f)....1 **5**
Monsieur Petong **(47)***(39) (DNicholls)* 4-7-11 (7)ow3 AEddery(10) (bhd: hdwy over 2f out: nvr rchd ldrs)....1½ **6**
Perilous Plight **(63)***(45) (WRMuir)* 4-8-11 JWeaver(14) (prom 4f: sn rdn & no imp).½ **7**
Ballad Dancer **(43)***(34) (JMackie)* 10-8-1 NCarlisle(2) (prom 4f)....hd **8**
Asmarina *(29) (SRBowring)* 5-7-11 (7) CTeague(3) (s.i.s: wl bhd tl sme late hdwy)..4 **9**
Profit Release (IRE) *(28) (MJohnston)* 4-8-4 TWilliams(6) (prom: 4th st: sn ev ch: wknd appr fnl f)....nk **10**
Sense of Priority **(61)***(25) (MHEasterby)* 6-8-4 WWoods(1) (lw: led 5f: eased whn btn)....1½ **11**
It's so Easy **(59)***(20) (MJohnston)* 4-8-4 JFanning(4) (prom: 6th st: sn btn: eased)2½ **12**
Bold Cyrano (IRE) *(28) (BPalling)* 4-9-3 AClark(9) (n.m.r & dropped rr after 1f: n.d after)....2½ **13**
Britannia Mills **(49)***(10) (MCChapman)* 4-8-0 GBardwell(5) (bit bkwd: prom: 2nd st: sn wknd & eased)....hd **14**

5/4 Dream Carrier (IRE), **7/1** Sense of Priority, Profit Release (IRE), Jamaica Bridge, **10/1** SUPER BENZ, Perilous Plight, **12/1** It's so Easy (7/1-14/1), Bold Mick, **20/1** Asmarina, Bradwell (IRE), Ballad Dancer, **25/1** Monsieur Petong, **33/1** Bold Cyrano (IRE), **40/1** Britannia Mills, CSF £24.73 TOTE £9.20: £2.20 £1.50 £6.20 (£9.90) OWNER Whitestonecliffe Racing Partnership (HAMBLETON) BRED Scarteen Stud 14 Rn 1m 31.5 (4.70) SF: 44/35/26/29/30/18/24/-/-/-/-/-/-/-

3 ALEXANDRA MOTORS H'CAP (0-70) (Class E) £3,066.80 (£928.40: £453.20: £215.60) **2m (Fibresand)** GOING minus 0.04 sec per fur (STD) 2-00 (2-00)

Argyle Cavalier (IRE) (64)*(75+)*(Fav)*(MJohnston)* 5-9-4 (7) OliverCasey(1) (hld up: smooth hdwy 8f out: 2nd st: sn led on bit: qcknd clr appr fnl f)....— **1**

Mizyan (IRE) **(65)***(68) (JEBanks)* 7-9-12 SKeightley(2) (lw: hld up: hdwy & 3rd st: rdn 2f out: kpt on: no ch w wnr)..8 **2**
Shaffic (FR) **(52)***(47) (MrsMReveley)* 8-8-13 LDettori(5) (chsd ldrs: rdn 7f out: 4th st: kpt on fnl 2f)..8 **3**
Fiery Sun **(34)***(27) (JLEyre)* 10-7-9vow2 JQuinn(8) (led: shkn up 4f out: hdd over 2f out: sn btn)..2½ **4**
Arctic Guest (IRE) **(62)***(36) (CSmith)* 5-9-2 (7) MBaird(4) (bhd: sn pushed along: hdwy & 6th st: nvr nr ldrs)..20 **5**
Top Prize **(37)***(5) (MBrittain)* 7-7-12 GBardwell(7) (chsd ldrs: pushed along 8f out: poor 5th & btn st)..6 **6**
Electrolyte **(66)***(25) (BPalling)* 5-9-13 StephenDavies(6) (b: bkwd: chsd ldr 8f: bhd fnl 5f)..10 **7**
Betty Kenwood **(44)***(—) (MrsJRRamsden)* 5-8-5 SWilliams(3) (chsd ldrs tl rdn & wknd 8f out)..dist **8**

LONG HANDICAP Fiery Sun 7-6

15/8 ARGYLE CAVALIER (IRE), **9/4** Mizyan (IRE), **9/2** Shaffic (FR), **8/1** Arctic Guest (IRE), **9/1** Top Prize, **12/1** Fiery Sun, Betty Kenwood, **25/1** Electrolyte, CSF £6.95 CT £15.70 TOTE £2.80: £1.40 £1.30 £1.90 (£4.30) OWNER E H Jones (Paints) Ltd (MIDDLEHAM) BRED Oldtown Bloodstock Holdings Ltd in Ireland 8 Rn 3m 45.1 (19.10) SF: 21/15/-/-/-/-/-/-

4

EAST MIDLAND ELECTRICITY-LINCOLN MEDIAN AUCTION STKS (Mdn 4, 5 & 6-Y.O) (Class E) £3,023.90 (£915.20: £446.60: £212.30)
1m 3f (Fibresand) GOING minus 0.04 sec per fur (STD) 2-30 (2-30)

Shakiyr (FR) *(54)*(Fav)*(RHollinshead)* 4-8-12 LDettori(8) (bhd: hung rt after 2f: hdwy to ld over 4f out: hdd 2f out: sn led again: rdn out)................— **1**
Uckerby Lad **(35)***(53) (NPLittmoden)* 4-8-7 (5) TGMcLaughlin(2) (hld up: hdwy & 4th st: ev ch whn rdn & wnt lft 1f out: r.o)..1 **2**
Feline (IRE) *(41) (RFJohnsonHoughton)* 4-8-7 JQuinn(7) (hdwy after 4f: 2nd st: led 2f out: sn hdd: no ex whn nt clr run 1f out)..5 **3**
Murphys Way *(39) (JLEyre)* 6-8-6 (5) JStack(3) (b: bit bkwd: chsd ldrs tl lost pl over 4f out: r.o wl fnl 2f)..1½ **4**
Dallai (IRE) **(55)***(34) (MrsNMacauley)* 4-8-7 (5) SSanders(6) (lw: prom: shkn up & 3rd st: sn btn)..7 **5**
Dolly Dolittle *(25) (HJCollingridge)* 4-8-2 (5) CHawksley(4) (in tch: 6th st: no hdwy) .3 **6**
I Fear Nothing **(65)***(15) (SCWilliams)* 4-8-7 GCarter(9) (led over 6f: sn wknd)..7 **7**
Comfortable **(35)***(19) (SGollings)* 5-9-2e StephenDavies(5) (eyeshield: lw: a bhd)....1 **8**
Fleet Cadet *(—) (NAGraham)* 4-8-12 JWeaver(1) (dwlt: plld hrd & sn chsng ldr: rdn, wkng & 5th st)..15 **9**

Evens SHAKIYR (FR), **5/1** Fleet Cadet (3/1-11/2), **13/2** Murphys Way, **7/1** Feline (IRE), **12/1** I Fear Nothing, **14/1** Dallai (IRE), **20/1** Comfortable, **25/1** Dolly Dolittle, **33/1** Uckerby Lad, CSF £28.98 TOTE £2.00: £1.50 £3.20 £2.00 (£39.00) OWNER L & R Roadlines (UPPER LONGDON) BRED S. A. Aga Khan in France 9 Rn 2m 32.0 (10.50) SF: 26/25/14/15/7/-/-/-/-
WEIGHT FOR AGE 4yo-4lb

5

FLORIN (S) STKS (3-Y.O) (Class G) £2,259.00 (£634.00: £309.00)
1m (Fibresand) GOING minus 0.04 sec per fur (STD) 3-00 (3-02)

Durgams First (IRE) (64)*(75)*(Fav)*(MrsMReveley)* 3-8-10 (7) GParkin(2) (a.p: 3rd st: led wl over 1f out: rdn clr fnl f)..— **1**
Lawbuster (IRE) **(51)***(62) (WRMuir)* 3-8-12 DHarrison(1) (lw: prom: 4th st: pulled out over 1f out: kpt on u.p)..4 **2**
Pc's Cruiser (IRE) *(58) (MCChapman)* 3-8-12 JWeaver(6) (led over 5f: no ex) 2 **3**
Runforaction (IRE) **(56)***(44) (BSRothwell)* 3-8-7 (5) JStack(7) (chsd ldrs tl lost pl & 7th st: n.d after)..7 **4**
Bretton Princess **(50)***(39) (RHollinshead)* 3-8-7 LDettori(13) (hld up: pushed along & 6th st: nvr nr ldrs)..hd **5**
Madam Sunpak *(33) (MrsVAAconley)* 3-8-2 (5) SDrowne(3) (neat: in tch: poor 5th st: sn btn)..3 **6**
Miss Suzy *(23) (JPLeigh)* 3-8-7 StephenDavies(12) (neat: lt-f: sn pushed along & outpcd: effrt 4f out: btn 2f out)..5 **7**
Vade Retro Satanas (FR) **(49)***(23) (CTinkler)* 3-8-12 MFenton(5) (sn prom: 2nd st: wknd 2f out: eased fnl f)..2½ **8**
Nanny Doon *(17) (MJohnston)* 3-8-7 TWilliams(10) (neat: w'like: nvr nr ldrs).........½ **9**
Mayday Kitty *(12) (WGMTurner)* 3-8-7 NAdams(11) (lw: chsd ldrs 3f: sn rdn & btn)..2½ **10**

Visual Illusion (IRE) *(2) (BSRothwell)* 3-8-7 JQuinn(9) (cmpt: a bhd)........................5 **11**
Joint Prospect **(43)***(3) (CCElsey)* 3-8-12 CRutter(8) (bit bkwd: sn pushed along: chsd ldrs over 3f)........................2 **12**
Dent's Delight (IRE) *(—) (DWChapman)* 3-8-7 MRimmer(4) (leggy: dwlt: a bhd: t.o)........................dist **13**

9/4 DURGAMS FIRST (IRE), **9/2** Vade Retro Satanas (FR), Runforaction (IRE), **11/2** Lawbuster (IRE) (4/1-6/1), **10/1** Nanny Doon, **14/1** Joint Prospect, Bretton Princess, **16/1** Pc's Cruiser (IRE), **20/1** Dent's Delight (IRE), **25/1** Miss Suzy, Mayday Kitty, Visual Illusion (IRE), Madam Sunpak, CSF £15.58 TOTE £3.00: £1.70 £2.00 £5.30 (£16.00) OWNER Mrs S. Todd (SALTBURN) BRED William McGladdery in Ireland 13 Rn Bt in 4,800 gns 1m 47.9 (8.60) SF: 19/7/3/-/-/-/-/-/-/-/-/-/-

6 CAMILLA H'CAP (0-80) (Class D) £3,640.00 (£1,102.00: £538.00: £256.00)
6f (Fibresand) GOING minus 0.04 sec per fur (STD) 3-30 (3-30)

Croft Pool (75)*(84) (JAGlover)* 4-10-0 LDettori(3) (lw: chsd ldrs: 5th st: rdn to ld ins fnl f)........................— **1**
Matthew David **(42)***(49) (SRBowring)* 5-7-9 ow1 JQuinn(10) (w ldr: 2nd st: led 2f out tl hdd & no ex ins fnl f)........................½ **2**
Langtonian **(51)***(52) (JLEyre)* 6-8-4v NCarlisle(7) (hdwy & 4th st: ev ch over 1f out: edgd lft & nt qckn)........................2½ **3**
Faez **(65)***(53) (PSFelgate)* 5-9-4 TIves(5) (lw: bhd tl styd on fnl 2f)........................5 **4**
Warwick Warrior (IRE) **(69)***(55) (MrsLPiggott)* 4-9-1e(7) VictoriaAppleby(11) (eyeshield: b: b.hind: prom: 3rd st: btn appr fnl f)........................½ **5**
Green's Bid **(61)***(42) (DWChapman)* 5-9-0 DaleGibson(4) (led 4f: sn wknd)........................2 **6**
Watheeqah (USA) **(58)***(37) (MBrittain)* 4-8-11b GBardwell(9) (sn rdn along: nvr on terms)........................½ **7**
Chardonnay Girl **(42)***(12) (JMCarr)* 4-7-9 NAdams(8) (chsd ldrs tl 6th & btn st)....3½ **8**
Nineacres **(58)***(19)*(Fav)*(DNicholls)* 4-8-4b(7) AEddery(2) (sn pushed along: nvr nr to chal)........................3½ **9**
Nez Carrera **(50)***(—) (RMWhitaker)* 4-7-12 (5) DWright(6) (lw: outpcd & sn wl bhd)12 **10**
LONG HANDICAP Matthew David 7-1

9/4 Nineacres, **9/2** Matthew David, CROFT POOL, **5/1** Langtonian, **8/1** Green's Bid, **14/1** Warwick Warrior (IRE), Faez, **16/1** Watheeqah (USA), **33/1** Chardonnay Girl, Nez Carrera, CSF £24.06 CT £95.09 TOTE £5.40: £1.90 £1.70 £1.80 (£9.00) OWNER Countrywide Classics Ltd (WORKSOP) BRED J. S. Bell 10 Rn 1m 17.1 (3.60) SF: 66/34/35/35/38/25/20/-/-/-

T/Plpt: £17.30 (1,184.97 Tckts). T/Qdpt: £7.40 (7.2 Tckts). Dk

LINGFIELD (L-H)
Tuesday January 3rd (Standard)

7 TENNYSON CLAIMING STKS (3-Y.O) (Class E) £2,981.00 (£902.00: £440.00: £209.00) **5f (Equitrack)** GOING minus 0.54 sec per fur (FST) 12-45 (12-47)

Baileys Sunset (IRE) (62)*(73) (MJohnston)* 3-8-9 TWilliams(3) (mde all: clr over 1f out: rdn out)........................— **1**
Abbey House **(45)***(57)*(Fav)*(RGuest)* 3-7-7b(3) DWright(7) (rn wd bnd & lost pl wl over 1f out: rallied & chsd wnr fnl f: r.o wl)........................1 **2**
Prince Rudolf (IRE) **(50)***(53) (NPLittmoden)* 3-8-3b MFenton(8) (outpcd: hdwy fnl f: r.o)........................3½ **3**
Curie Express (IRE) **(53)***(45) (JBerry)* 3-8-4b GCarter(4) (lw: chsd wnr 4f: sn wknd) 3 **4**
Lady Pui **(52)***(39) (JBerry)* 3-7-12b GBardwell(2) (a.p: rdn 3f out: wknd over 1f out)s.h **5**
Black Shadow **(50)***(46) (PJMcBride)* 3-8-8 (5) NVarley(1) (a bhd)........................2½ **6**
More Bills (IRE) **(50)***(34) (AMoore)* 3-8-3bow2 CandyMorris(6) (a bhd)........................½ **7**
Vibro (IRE) **(55)***(31) (GCBravery)* 3-8-11 TIves(5) (prom 3f)........................3½ **8**

2/1 Abbey House, **5/2** Lady Pui, **100/30** BAILEYS SUNSET (IRE), **15/2** Curie Express (IRE), **10/1** Vibro (IRE), **16/1** Prince Rudolf (IRE), **25/1** More Bills (IRE), **33/1** Black Shadow, CSF £10.34 TOTE £3.70: £1.10 £1.30 £4.20 (£4.90) OWNER G R Bailey Ltd (Baileys Horse Feeds) (MIDDLEHAM) BRED Vincent and Joseph Fitzpatrick in Ireland 8 Rn 60.4 secs (2.20) SF: 11/-/-/-/-/-/-/-

8 DAILY STAR AWT 1M 2F CHALLENGE SERIES H'CAP (Qualifier) (I) (0-80) (Class D) £3,741.05 (£1,132.40: £552.70: £262.85)
1m 2f (Equitrack) GOING minus 0.54 sec per fur (FST) 1-15 (1-15)

South Eastern Fred (67)*(83+)*(Fav)*(HJCollingridge)* 4-8-12 MRimmer(1) (hld up: shkn up to ld over 1f out: comf)........................— **1**

Rawya (USA) **(71)***(82) (BWHills)* 4-9-2 JWeaver(7) (a.p: led over 2f out tl over 1f out: unable qckn) 3½ **2**
Our Eddie **(71)***(68) (BGubby)* 6-9-5v TIves(3) (lw: rdn over 4f out: nvr nr to chal) 9 **3**
Surprise Guest (IRE) **(74)***(71) (MJohnston)* 4-9-5 TWilliams(5) (lw: rdn over 5f out: lost pl over 3f out: one pce)....s.h **4**
Canary Falcon **(65)***(60) (RJO'Sullivan)* 4-8-10 StephenDavies(6) (lw: a.p: led over 3f out tl over 2f out: wknd over 1f out)....1½ **5**
Tondres (USA) **(71)***(64) (RIngram)* 4-9-2 WWoods(4) (hdwy 4f out: wknd 3f out) .1½ **6**
View From Above **(76)***(60) (NJHWalker)* 9-9-10 NAdams(8) (hdwy over 4f out: wknd over 2f out) 6 **7**
Wahem (IRE) **(45)***(18) (CEBrittain)* 5-7-7 GBardwell(2) (lw: led over 6f: wknd over 2f out) 7 **8**

LONG HANDICAP Wahem (IRE) 7-6

6/4 SOUTH EASTERN FRED, **11/4** Rawya (USA), **4/1** Canary Falcon, **7/1** Our Eddie, **15/2** Surprise Guest (IRE), **14/1** Tondres (USA), **16/1** View From Above, **33/1** Wahem (IRE), CSF £6.70 CT £21.81 TOTE £3.30: £1.10 £1.10 £3.20 (£5.30) OWNER South Eastern Electrical Plc (NEWMARKET) BRED L. Audus 8 Rn 2m 6.26 (3.26) SF: 27/26/15/14/4/7/5/-

WEIGHT FOR AGE 4yo-3lb

9

SHELLEY H'CAP (0-60) (Class F) £2,688.20 (£755.20: £368.60)
2m (Equitrack) GOING minus 0.54 sec per fur (FST) 1-45 (1-46)

Arian Spirit (IRE) (36)*(44) (WJMusson)* 4-8-1 (5) DRMcCabe(5) (hdwy over 1f out: rdn fnl f: led nr fin) ....— **1**
Arc Bright (IRE) **(51)***(59)*(Fav)*(RHollinshead)* 5-10-0 LDettori(7) (a.p: hrd rdn over 3f out: led wl ins fnl f: hdd nr fin) ....nk **2**
Rose of Glenn **(49)***(55) (BPalling)* 4-9-5 StephenDavies(1) (hdwy over 3f out: hrd rdn over 1f out: one pce)....2½ **3**
Disputed Call (USA) **(37)***(43) (JWHills)* 6-9-0 RCochrane(6) (lw: a.p: led over 2f out: hrd rdn over 1f out: hdd wl ins fnl f: one pce)....nk **4**
Star Quest **(48)***(52) (JRJenkins)* 8-9-11 TIves(10) (lw: hdwy over 6f out: lost pl over 2f out: r.o one pce fnl f)....2½ **5**
Wicklow Boy (IRE) **(42)***(42) (TTClement)* 4-8-12v JWeaver(2) (hdwy 9f out: led 5f out tl hdd & n.m.r on ins over 2f out: wknd over 1f out)....4 **6**
Royal Circus **(35)***(32) (JGMO'Shea)* 6-8-7 (5)ow2 DGriffiths(8) (w ldr: led 7f out to 5f out: wknd over 2f out) 3 **7**
Malingerer **(30)***(19) (DAWilson)* 4-8-0 NGwilliams(11) (hld up: rdn 5f out: sn wknd).9 **8**
Ragtime Song **(44)***(31) (AMoore)* 6-9-7 CandyMorris(9) (b.off hind: hdwy over 6f out: wknd 5f out) 2 **9**
Kiss Kincsem **(54)***(37) (PJMakin)* 4-9-10 DHarrison(4) (a bhd)....4 **10**
Mediator **(46)***(18) (AMoore)* 6-9-4 (5) AWhelan(3) (led 9f) 12 **11**

5/2 Arc Bright (IRE), **4/1** ARIAN SPIRIT (IRE), **11/2** Royal Circus, **7/1** Star Quest, **8/1** Mediator, **9/1** Rose of Glenn, **11/1** Wicklow Boy (IRE), **20/1** Kiss Kincsem, **25/1** Ragtime Song, Disputed Call (USA), **33/1** Malingerer, CSF £14.06 CT £78.84 TOTE £5.10: £1.20 £2.00 £4.40 (£16.90) OWNER Broughton Thermal Insulation (NEWMARKET) BRED M. Ervine in Ireland 11 Rn

3m 28.79 (5.29) SF: 23/44/33/28/36/20/17/-/-/-/-

WEIGHT FOR AGE 4yo-7lb

10

WORDSWORTH STKS (3-Y.O) (0-60) (Class F) £2,801.60 (£586.20: £586.20)
1m (Equitrack) GOING minus 0.54 sec per fur (FST) 2-15 (2-18)

Battleship Bruce (56)*(68+)*(Fav)*(NACallaghan)* 3-9-0 LDettori(7) (b.off hind: lw: led over 5f out: comf) ....— **1**
Water Bebe (IRE) **(53)***(59) (GCBravery)* 3-8-10 ow1 TIves(2) (rdn over 4f out: hdwy 2f out: r.o ins fnl f)....d.h **2**
Mazilla **(60)***(58) (WJHaggas)* 3-8-4 (5) BRussell(8) (lw: chsd wnr over 5f out: hrd rdn over 1f out: unable qckn)....d.h **2**
Poly Road **(56)***(57) (MRChannon)* 3-8-9 DHarrison(3) (hld up: rdn over 3f out: one pce fnl 2f) ....nk **4**
Tara Colleen (IRE) **(58)***(31) (CAHorgan)* 3-8-9 AClark(1) (nvr nr to chal)....13 **5**
Red Spectacle (IRE) **(57)***(34) (PCHaslam)* 3-9-0 JWeaver(9) (prom over 4f)....1 **6**
Go Likecrazy **(53)***(23) (KTIvory)* 3-8-2 (7) CScally(5) (bhd fnl 5f)....3 **7**
Jemthorn Bishop **(52)***(16) (JJBridger)* 3-9-0 TWilliams(4) (led over 1f)....6 **8**

1/3 BATTLESHIP BRUCE, **6/1** Tara Colleen (IRE), **10/1** Mazilla, Poly Road, **25/1** Water Bebe (IRE), Red Spectacle (IRE), Go Likecrazy, **66/1** Jemthorn Bishop, CSF £2.67 w M, £5.58 w WB TOTE £1.40: £1.10 £2.60 M £3.60 WB (£2.20 w M, £5.10 w WB) OWNER Mr T. A. Foreman (NEWMARKET) BRED Highfield Stud Ltd 8 Rn 1m 40.49 (4.09) SF: 13/4/4/3/-/-/-/-

11 DAILY STAR AWT 1M 2F CHALLENGE SERIES H'CAP (Qualifier) (II) (0-80) (Class D) £3,741.05 (£1,132.40: £552.70: £262.85)
1m 2f (Equitrack) GOING minus 0.54 sec per fur (FST) 2-45 (2-46)

Birequest (65)*(71) (RBoss)* 4-8-13 LDettori(1) (lw: mde virtually all: drvn out)......— **1**
Awesome Power **(70)***(75)*(Fav)*(JWHills)* 9-9-7 DHarrison(6) (hld up: rdn over 4f out: ev ch wl ins fnl f: r.o)......nk **2**
Global Dancer **(73)***(77) (WAO'Gorman)* 4-9-4 (3) EmmaO'Gorman(7) (w wnr: rdn over 3f out: ev ch over 1f out: unable qckn)......¾ **3**
Herr Trigger **(76)***(76) (DrJDScargill)* 4-9-10b RCochrane(4) (lw: rdn over 4f out: hdwy over 1f out: nvr nrr)......2½ **4**
Mulciber **(72)***(71) (GHarwood)* 7-9-9 AClark(3) (b: b.hind: rdn over 4f out: hdwy 3f out: one pce)......nk **5**
Bag of Tricks (IRE) **(68)***(62) (SDow)* 5-9-0e(5) SSanders(5) (eyeshield: bhd fnl 4f) 3½ **6**
Shepherd Market (IRE) **(75)***(57) (DAWilson)* 4-9-9 GCarter(2) (a bhd)......8 **7**
Knightrider **(54)***(33) (CJames)* 4-8-2b GBardwell(8) (dwlt: hdwy over 7f out: rdn over 4f out: wknd over 3f out)......1¾ **8**

7/4 Awesome Power, **7/2** BIREQUEST, **4/1** Mulciber, **6/1** Global Dancer, **9/1** Herr Trigger, **20/1** Bag of Tricks (IRE), Shepherd Market (IRE), Knightrider, CSF £9.85 CT £29.80 TOTE £5.80: £1.60 £1.20 £1.60 (£7.60) OWNER Mr J. Ellis (NEWMARKET) BRED Langham Hall Bloodstock
8 Rn 2m 7.7 (4.70) SF: 17/24/23/22/21/11/3/-
WEIGHT FOR AGE 4yo-3lb

12 COLERIDGE H'CAP (0-75) (Class D) £3,673.80 (£1,112.40: £543.20: £258.60)
1m (Equitrack) GOING minus 0.54 sec per fur (FST) 3-15 (3-16)

Kinnegad Kid (43)*(54) (RIngram)* 6-7-7 (3)ow3 DWright(9) (led 4f out: clr over 1f out: r.o wl)......— **1**
Hatta Sunshine (USA) **(49)***(50) (AMoore)* 5-7-11 (5)ow1 AWhelan(1) (dwlt: hdwy over 2f out: rdn & r.o one pce)......5 **2**
Sweet Supposin (IRE) **(72)***(70) (KMcAuliffe)* 4-9-10 RCochrane(2) (lw: hld up: rdn over 3f out: one pce)......1½ **3**
Hawaii Storm (FR) **(57)***(52) (MissAJWhitfield)* 7-8-5 (5) RPainter(11) (hdwy 2f out: rn wd bnd wl over 1f out: r.o one pce)......1¼ **4**
Eastleigh **(47)***(40) (RHollinshead)* 6-7-9 (5) AGarth(3) (lost pl 5f out: one pce fnl 2f).¾ **5**
Buddy's Friend (IRE) **(62)***(53) (RJRWilliams)* 7-8-8 (7) SarahThompson(5) (hld up: rdn over 2f out: one pce)......¾ **6**
Krayyan Dawn **(48)***(36)*(Fav)*(RAkehurst)* 5-8-1 JQuinn(4) (lw: lost pl 5f out: rallied over 1f out: wknd fnl f)......1¼ **7**
Rad **(56)***(40) (SPCWoods)* 5-8-9 WWoods(8) (nvr nr to chal)......2 **8**
Level Edge **(52)***(31) (MJohnston)* 4-8-4 TWilliams(7) (prom over 4f)......2½ **9**
Breckland (IRE) **(45)***(22) (KOCunningham-Brown)* 5-7-12 GBardwell(10) (hdwy over 4f out: wknd wl over 1f out)......¾ **10**
Friendly Brave (USA) **(72)***(37) (TGMills)* 5-9-11b JWeaver(6) (led 4f: wknd over 1f out)......6 **11**
Pearly River **(64)***(3) (DrJDScargill)* 4-9-2 LDettori(12) (lw: prom over 4f)......13 **12**

7/2 Krayyan Dawn, **5/1** Sweet Supposin (IRE), Rad, **13/2** KINNEGAD KID, **8/1** Hawaii Storm (FR), **11/1** Eastleigh, **12/1** Level Edge, **14/1** Buddy's Friend (IRE), Friendly Brave (USA), **16/1** Pearly River, **20/1** Hatta Sunshine (USA), **33/1** Breckland (IRE), CSF £112.40 CT £644.62 TOTE £7.60: £2.60 £4.70 £2.60 (£101.30) OWNER Mr J. B. Wilcox (EPSOM) BRED Airlie Stud and Miss K. Rausing 12 Rn 1m 38.1 (1.70) SF: 20/16/33/19/8/20/5/9/-/-/-/-
WEIGHT FOR AGE 4yo-1lb

13 SHAKESPEARE H'CAP (Amateurs) (0-70) (Class E) £3,052.50 (£924.00: £451.00: £214.50)
1m 5f (Equitrack) GOING minus 0.54 sec per fur (FST) 3-45 (3-46)

Beautete (65)*(73)*(Fav)*(SDow)* 4-11-4 5x MrTCuff(2) (b: lw: a.p: led over 3f: clr over 1f out: r.o wl)......— **1**
Sir Thomas Beecham **(63)***(68) (SDow)* 5-11-7e MrTMcCarthy(8) (eyeshield: b: b.hind: a.p: led over 5f out tl over 3f out: unable qckn fnl 2f)......2½ **2**
Kadiri (IRE) **(55)***(59) (JRBosley)* 4-10-4 (4) MrsSBosley(9) (hdwy over 3f out: r.o one pce)......½ **3**
Kenyatta (USA) **(38)***(37) (AMoore)* 6-9-3 (7) MrsJoanMoore(4) (led over 7f: dropped rr 4f out: r.o one pce fnl 2f)......4 **4**

Captain Marmalade **(51)***(50)*(Fav)*(DTThom)* 6-10-9 MissDianaJones(7) (lw: nvr nr to chal: b.b.v) ....s.h **5**
Persian Bud (IRE) **(29)***(26) (JRBosley)* 7-8-8 (7) MrsLBarrett(3) (no hdwy fnl 3f)....1½ **6**
Strat's Legacy **(54)***(49) (DWPArbuthnot)* 8-10-12 MrsDArbuthnot(1) (b: b.hind: a bhd)....2 **7**
Cone Lane **(33)***(28) (BGubby)* 9-9-1 (4) MrsMBusby(5) (w ldr over 7f)....s.h **8**
Sweet Caroline **(34)***(27) (PMitchell)* 4-9-1 MissAHarwood(6) (lw: rdn over 9f out: bhd fnl 2f)....2 **9**

5/2 BEAUTETE, Captain Marmalade, **7/2** Strat's Legacy, **9/1** Kenyatta (USA), **10/1** Cone Lane, **12/1** Sir Thomas Beecham, **16/1** Persian Bud (IRE), **25/1** Kadiri (IRE), **33/1** Sweet Caroline, CSF £29.52 CT £560.49 TOTE £4.20: £2.60 £4.00 £3.80 (£23.00) OWNER Mr D. G. Churston (EPSOM) BRED Hollow Hole Stud 9 Rn 2m 52.17 (9.67) SF: 28/28/15/-/12/-/10/-/-
WEIGHT FOR AGE 4yo-5lb

T/Jkpt: £3,292.10 (0.1 Tckts); £4,173.16 to Wolverhampton 4/1/95. T/Plpt: 8.50 (2,561.4Tckts). T/Qdpt: £4.70 (12.25 Tckts). AK

WOLVERHAMPTON (L-H)
Wednesday January 4th (Standard)

14 CEDAR CLAIMING STKS (I) (Class E) £2,995.30 (£906.40: £442.20: £210.10)
5f (Fibresand) GOING minus 0.36 sec per fur (FST) 1-30 (1-30)

Very Dicey (75)*(67) (JBerry)* 7-8-0 (7) PFessey(2) (mde all: rdn & r.o wl fnl f)....— **1**
Farastrada **(62)***(54) (BPreece)* 4-7-12b JQuinn(4) (hdwy ½-wy: kpt on u.p fnl f)....1¼ **2**
Little Saboteur **(68)***(64) (PJMakin)* 6-8-8 JWeaver(3) (b.nr hind: a.p: ev ch ent fnl f: unable qckn)....s.h **3**
Leigh Crofter **(70)***(69) (PDCundell)* 6-9-0b(5) DGriffiths(6) (dwlt: r.o appr fnl f)....2 **4**
Primula Bairn **(60)***(46) (MrsJRRamsden)* 5-8-0v JFanning(5) (s.s: hdwy ½-wy: rdn & one pce appr fnl f)....1¼ **5**
Samson-Agonistes **(70)***(58)*(Fav)*(PDEvans)* 9-8-13 AClark(7) (nvr gng pce)....hd **6**
Tommy Tempest **(40)***(38) (ABailey)* 6-7-12b(3) DWright(1) (chsd wnr over 3f & wknd qckly)....2½ **7**
My Foxy Lady **(38)***(7) (JAHarris)* 5-7-4 (7)ow1 SLanigan(8) (outpcd: a bhd: t.o)....9 **8**

11/4 Samson-Agonistes, **3/1** Primula Bairn, **7/2** Little Saboteur, VERY DICEY, **9/1** Leigh Crofter, **25/1** Tommy Tempest, **33/1** Farastrada, **40/1** My Foxy Lady, CSF £74.24 TOTE £2.70: £2.30 £3.90 £1.40 (£31.50) OWNER Mr J. Berry (COCKERHAM) BRED G. R. Smith (Thriplow) Ltd and Lord Edwin McAlpine 8 Rn 61.5 secs (3.50) SF: 3/-/1/4/-/-/-/-

15 BEECH H'CAP (0-80) (Class D) £3,606.20 (£1,091.60: £532.80: £253.40)
1m 6f 166y (Fibresand) GOING minus 0.36 sec per fur (FST) 2-00 (2-00)

Noufari (FR) (65)*(75+) (RHollinshead)* 4-8-11 4x TIves(2) (hld up in rr: hdwy 4f out: 3rd st: led appr fnl f: sn clr)....— **1**
Iota **(64)***(68) (JLHarris)* 6-9-2 LDettori(8) (bit bkwd: hld up: hdwy 5f out: led over 2f out tl appr fnl f: one pce)....5 **2**
Pride of May (IRE) **(68)***(69) (RHannon)* 4-9-0 RPerham(3) (led 1f: lost pl ½-wy: rallied & 4th st: styd on)....2½ **3**
Meant to Be **(76)***(75) (LadyHerries)* 5-9-7 (7) ShonaCrombie(9) (led after 1f tl over 2f out: styd on same pce)....1¾ **4**
Milngavie (IRE) **(65)***(55)*(Fav)*(MJohnston)* 5-9-3 TWilliams(5) (lw: prom tl rdn & outpcd 3f out: 5th & btn st)....8 **5**
Absalom's Pillar **(65)***(51) (JHetherton)* 5-9-3 NCarlisle(1) (hld up: rdn & 6th st: nvr nr to chal)....4 **6**
Lobilio (USA) **(64)***(34) (DBurchell)* 6-9-2v JWeaver(6) (b.nr fore: hld up: effrt & rdn 5f out: no imp: t.o)....15 **7**
Vishnu (USA) **(75)***(43) (JLEyre)* 5-9-13 AClark(7) (hld up: effrt over 3f out: no imp: t.o)....2 **8**
Jean de Florette (USA) **(47)***(—) (RWEmery)* 4-7-7b GBardwell(4) (bkwd: chsd ldrs 10f: sn wknd: t.o)....15 **9**

LONG HANDICAP Jean de Florette (USA) 7-0

3/1 Milngavie (IRE), **4/1** NOUFARI (FR), **9/2** Absalom's Pillar, **5/1** Meant to Be, Pride of May (IRE), **6/1** Iota, **12/1** Lobilio (USA), Vishnu (USA), **33/1** Jean de Florette (USA), CSF £29.06 CT £117.26 TOTE £4.90: £2.30 £2.00 £1.40 (£17.60) OWNER Ed Weetman (Haulage & Storage) Ltd (UPPER LONGDON) BRED His Highness The Aga Khans Studs S.C. in France 9 Rn
3m 11.3 SF: 46/46/42/54/35/31/15/-/-
WEIGHT FOR AGE 4yo-6lb

16

CEDAR CLAIMING STKS (II) (Class E) £2,995.30 (£906.40: £442.20: £210.10)
5f (Fibresand) GOING minus 0.36 sec per fur (FST) 2-30 (2-30)

Sir Tasker (60)*(68) (JLHarris)* 7-8-7 LDettori(5) (mde all: clr 2f out: pushed out)..— 1
Walk the Beat **(66)***(61)*(Fav)*(RSimpson)* 5-8-1 (5)ow1 SDrowne(2) (a.p: chsd wnr fnl 2f: no imp fnl f)....2 2
Delrob **(66)***(50) (DHaydnJones)* 4-8-4 AMackay(7) (chsd ldrs: rdn & kpt on fnl f: nt pce to chal)....3 3
Tyrian Purple (IRE) **(62)***(44) (TJNaughton)* 7-8-1b(5) VHalliday(8) (b: b.off hind: chsd wnr 3f: sn hrd rdn: one pce)....2½ 4
Ragazzo (IRE) **(41)***(41) (KOCunningham-Brown)* 5-8-9b LCharnock(1) (drvn along ½-wy: nvr nr ldrs)....2 5
Florac (IRE) **(32)***(26) (JBalding)* 5-7-7 (7) ClaireBalding(6) (bit bkwd: outpcd: a bhd).2 6
Woodlands Electric **(18)***(3) (PAPritchard)* 5-8-1 NAdams(4) (outpcd & bhd: t.o)....8 7
Lunar Prince *(8) (TTClement)* 5-8-4 (3) DWright(3) (hmpd sn after s: a bhd & outpcd: t.o)....nk 8

Evens Walk the Beat, **4/1** SIR TASKER, Delrob, Tyrian Purple (IRE), **14/1** Ragazzo (IRE), **33/1** Florac (IRE), **50/1** Lunar Prince, **66/1** Woodlands Electric, CSF £8.74 TOTE £4.10: £1.70 £1.10 £1.10 (£6.10) OWNER Mr J. F. Coupland (MELTON MOWBRAY) BRED W. H. Joyce 8 Rn
60.5 secs (2.50) SF: 19/11/-/-/-/-/-/-

17

ROWAN STKS (Mdn 3-Y.O) (Class D) £3,538.60 (£1,070.80: £522.40: £248.20) **1m 100y (Fibresand)** GOING minus 0.36 sec per fur (FST) 3-00 (3-00)

Contrafire (IRE) (57)*(49+) (WJarvis)* 3-9-0 LDettori(6) (bit bkwd: led tl hdd over 3f out: 2nd st: led appr fnl f: comf)....— 1
Biya (IRE) *(43+)*(Fav)*(MJohnston)* 3-9-0 TWilliams(1) (gd sort: bkwd: dwlt: plld hrd: led over 3f out tl appr fnl f: rdn & no ex fnl f)....3 2
Zesti *(31) (TTClement)* 3-9-0 RCochrane(2) (chsd ldrs: rdn 2f out: 3rd & wkng st)..6 3
Amercius *(9) (RHannon)* 3-9-0 RPerham(3) (bit bkwd: s.i.s: chsd ldrs tl lost tch ½-wy: 4th & btn st)....11 4
Solor Dancer *(—) (CBBBooth)* 3-9-0 GCarter(5) (bit bkwd: lost pl after 3f: 5th & rdn st: t.o)....5 5
Lanesra Breeze *(—) (TJNaughton)* 3-8-9 (5) VHalliday(4) (b: lw: a bhd: lost tch ½-wy: 6th & t.o st)....11 6

4/5 Biya (IRE), **7/4** CONTRAFIRE (IRE), **8/1** Zesti, **14/1** Amercius, **20/1** Solor Dancer, **33/1** Lanesra Breeze, CSF £3.60 TOTE £2.80: £1.10 £1.50 (£1.80) OWNER Miss V. R. Jarvis (NEWMARKET) BRED Thoroughbred Trust in Ireland 6 Rn 1m 48.6 SF: 26/20/10/-/-/-

18

ASH H'CAP (0-75) (Class D) £4,182.00 (£1,266.00: £618.00: £294.00)
1m 1f 79y (Fibresand) GOING minus 0.36 sec per fur (FST) 3-30 (3-30)

Aitch N'Bee (61)*(71) (LadyHerries)* 12-9-6 (7) ShonaCrombie(9) (a.p: led ent st: rdn & hld on gamely nr fin)....— 1
Pillow Talk (IRE) **(54)***(64) (KRBurke)* 4-9-4 RCochrane(5) (hld up: hdwy 5f out: 3rd st: hrd rdn & str chal fnl f: jst failed)....hd 2
Rockstine (IRE) **(52)***(60) (PMitchell)* 4-9-2 LDettori(6) (in tch: hdwy & 5th st: rdn & r.o wl fnl f)....1 3
Bentico **(66)***(73)*(Fav)*(MrsNMacauley)* 6-9-13 (5) 5x SSanders(2) (lw: hld up: hdwy over 3f out: 6th st: kpt on u.p ins fnl f: nt pce to chal)....½ 4
Ballyhays (IRE) **(38)***(41) (JAHarris)* 6-8-4 ow1 5x SWilliams(11) (chsd ldrs: led 3f out : hdd & 2nd st: wknd ent fnl f)....2½ 5
Tu Opes **(60)***(62) (JLHarris)* 4-9-10 DaleGibson(7) (hld up: hdwy fnl 2f: nvr nrr)....½ 6
Tapis Rouge (IRE) **(62)***(56) (THCaldwell)* 6-10-0 JWeaver(12) (prom tl rdn & wknd over 3f out)....5 7
Bold Acre **(49)***(36) (DBurchell)* 5-8-10 (5) DRMcCabe(4) (b.off fore: chsd ldrs 6f)....4 8
Ziggy's Dancer (USA) **(64)***(50) (EJAlston)* 4-9-11 (3) DWright(10) (led over 9f: 4th & wkng st)....½ 9
Salska **(47)***(12) (PJBevan)* 4-8-11v NCarlisle(3) (a bhd: t.o)....12 10
Turtle Power **(35)***(—) (APJames)* 5-8-1 GBardwell(8) (b: a bhd: t.o)....20 11
Personal Pride (IRE) **(40)***(—) (AGFoster)* 4-8-4 StephenDavies(1) (a in rr: t.o)....25 12

7/4 Bentico, **9/4** Ballyhays (IRE), **6/1** Rockstine (IRE), **10/1** AITCH N'BEE, **12/1** Pillow Talk (IRE), **14/1** Tapis Rouge (IRE), Salska, **20/1** Tu Opes, Bold Acre, Ziggy's Dancer (USA), **33/1** Turtle Power, Personal Pride (IRE), CSF £120.18 CT £725.29 TOTE £16.00: £4.30 £2.20 £3.70 (£27.20) OWNER Lady Herries (LITTLEHAMPTON) BRED Liam Ward 12 Rn
1m 59.3 (3.30) SF: 53/45/41/55/25/43/38/-/-/-/-/-
WEIGHT FOR AGE 4yo-2lb

19

ACORN CLAIMING STKS (Class F) £2,537.00 (£712.00: £347.00)
1m 4f (Fibresand) GOING minus 0.36 sec per fur (FST) 4-00 (4-03)

Mad Militant (IRE) (71)*(72)*(Fav)*(RHollinshead)* 6-9-3 LDettori(2) (hld up: hdwy over 3f out: 4th st: led ins fnl f: rdn out) ....—- 1
Salbus **(80)***(70) (FJYardley)* 5-9-3 JWilliams(4) (a.p: led over 2f out tl ins fnl f: no ex) 1¼ 2
Strictly Personal (USA) **(65)***(71) (KRBurke)* 5-9-7 RCochrane(7) (lw: hld up: hdwy 3f out: 5th st: rdn & edgd lft fnl f: nt qckn) 2½ 3
Taahhub (IRE) *(53) (NATwiston-Davies)* 5-8-7 JWeaver(3) (led 1f: chal & 3rd st: one pce appr fnl f) 3 4
Abu Dancer (IRE) *(49) (KOCunningham-Brown)* 5-8-11 LCharnock(8) (bit bkwd: led after 1f tl over 2f out: 2nd & rdn st: sn wknd) 6 5
Soneeto *(33) (DRLaing)* 9-8-11 GBardwell(5) (bkwd: hld up: outpcd 4f out: poor 6th st: t.o) 13 6
Chapel Haven (IRE) **(30)***(22) (JParkes)* 5-8-4b JQuinn(1) (chsd ldrs over 8f: sn lost tch: t.o) 3 7
Almost a Princess *(22) (WGMTurner)* 7-7-11 (7) SLanigan(6) (dwlt: a bhd: t.o) ......hd 8
Smart Debutante (IRE) *(—) (MissSJWilton)* 6-8-6 AMackay(9) (bit bkwd: a bhd: t.o fr ½-wy) 30 9

2/5 MAD MILITANT (IRE), **6/1** Salbus, Strictly Personal (USA), **12/1** Taahhub (IRE), **16/1** Almost a Princess, **33/1** Smart Debutante (IRE), **50/1** Abu Dancer (IRE), **66/1** Chapel Haven (IRE), Soneeto, CSF £3.99 TOTE £1.50: £1.10 £1.10 £2.20 (£3.70) OWNER Mr J. E. Bigg (UPPER LONGDON) BRED Cloghran Stud Farm Co in Ireland 9 Rn 2m 39.7 (8.70) SF: 17/15/16/-/-/-/-/-/-

20

OAK H'CAP (0-90) (Class C) £5,602.00 (£1,696.00: £828.00: £394.00)
7f (Fibresand) GOING minus 0.36 sec per fur (FST) 4-30 (4-32)

Rocketeer (IRE) (87)*(90) (WRMuir)* 4-10-0b JWeaver(3) (lw: bhd: rapid hdwy appr fnl f: str run to ld cl home) ....—- 1
Everset (FR) **(93)***(95) (ABailey)* 7-10-3 (3) 6x DWright(9) (hld up: gd hdwy over 1f out: fin wl) ....½ 2
Milos **(69)***(70) (TJNaughton)* 4-8-5 (5) VHalliday(1) (b.off fore: chsd ldrs: 3rd st: led wl ins fnl f: ct cl home) ....hd 3
Aljaz **(56)***(54) (DTThom)* 5-7-11 AMackay(4) (b: led after 1f tl over 4f out: led over 2f out tl wl ins fnl f) 1½ 4
2[2] Dream Carrier (IRE) **(68)***(64) (TDBarron)* 7-8-9 TIves(5) (hld up: gd hdwy appr fnl f: nrst fin) ....¾ 5
Mr Martini (IRE) **(85)***(78) (CEBrittain)* 5-9-12 BDoyle(7) (chsd ldrs: 4th st: wknd over 1f out) 1½ 6
Beware of Agents **(71)***(61) (MJohnston)* 6-8-12 TWilliams(2) (bit bkwd: led 1f: led over 4f out: hdd & 2nd st: wknd wl over 1f out) 1½ 7
Chinour (IRE) **(67)***(56) (EJAlston)* 7-8-8 JQuinn(10) (chsd ldrs: 6th, rdn & btn st) ..nk 8
On Y Va (USA) **(52)***(40) (RJRWilliams)* 8-7-7 GBardwell(6) (nvr plcd to chal) ....hd 9
Mustn't Grumble (IRE) **(77)***(54) (WSCunningham)* 5-9-4 AClark(8) (chsd ldrs: 5th st: rdn & wknd qckly appr fnl f) 5 10
Bassmaat (USA) **(77)***(35)*(Fav)*(MrsLPiggott)* 4-9-4e LDettori(11) (b: b.hind: bhd: hrd rdn 4f out: no imp: t.o) 9 11

LONG HANDICAP On Y Va (USA) 7-5

3/1 Bassmaat (USA) (2/1-7/2), **9/2** Chinour (IRE), **5/1** ROCKETEER (IRE), **11/2** Everset (FR), Mustn't Grumble (IRE), **8/1** Aljaz, **10/1** On Y Va (USA), **12/1** Beware of Agents, Milos, Dream Carrier (IRE), **20/1** Mr Martini (IRE), CSF £35.83 CT £308.13 TOTE £8.40: £2.10 £2.60 £1.90 (£24.60) OWNER Mrs J. M. Muir (LAMBOURN) BRED Mrs T. Bracken in Ireland 11 Rn 1m 27.3 (3.30) SF: 43/48/25/10/19/31/15/-/-/-/-

T/Jkpt: Not won; £10,917.52 to Lingfield 5/1/95. T/Plpt: £24.60 (911.05 Tckts). T/Qdpt: £8.70 (3.6 Tckts). IM

0007-LINGFIELD (L-H)
Thursday January 5th (Standard)

21

BAD PENNY STKS (I) (Mdn) (Class D) £3,572.40 (£1,081.20: £527.60: £250.80) **1m 2f (Equitrack)** GOING minus 0.37 sec per fur (FST) 12-30 (12-31)

Eqtesaad (USA) (60)*(57) (SCWilliams)* 4-8-11 TIves(9) (plld hrd: a.p: led over 3f out: rdn over 1f out: r.o wl) ....—- 1

Kedwick (IRE) *(56) (PRHedger)* 6-9-0b JWilliams(6) (b: b.hind: dwlt: hdwy over 6f out: chsd wnr over 2f out: rdn over 1f out: r.o) .... ¾ **2**
13[9] Sweet Caroline **(34)***(37) (PMitchell)* 4-8-6b JMcLaughlin(4) (lost pl 8f out: r.o one pce fnl 2f) 9 **3**
Celestial Faith *(34) (MJohnston)* 4-8-6 TWilliams(5) (hld up: rdn over 4f out: one pce) 2 **4**
Joyce E Jackson *(29) (RIngram)* 5-8-9 WWoods(1) (lw: lost pl 7f out: one pce fnl 3f) 3 **5**
Ela Palikari Mou (IRE) *(30)*(Fav)*(RAkehurst)* 4-8-11 GCarter(2) (led over 6f: wknd over 2f out) 2½ **6**
Liffeyside Leader (IRE) *(23) (HJCollingridge)* 4-8-1 (5) CHawksley(7) (a bhd) 1½ **7**
Indian Fire *(23) (KOCunningham-Brown)* 5-9-0 LCharnock(8) (lw: w ldr over 6f: wknd over 2f out) 3 **8**
Esperer *(12) (JO'Donoghue)* 5-8-9 (5) TGMcLaughlin(3) (hdwy 6f out: wknd over 4f out) 7 **9**

6/4 Ela Palikari Mou (IRE), **7/4** EQTESAAD (USA), **9/2** Kedwick (IRE), **10/1** Liffeyside Leader (IRE), **14/1** Celestial Faith, **25/1** Joyce E Jackson, Sweet Caroline, **33/1** Indian Fire, Esperer, CSF £10.55 TOTE £2.60: £1.10 £1.40 £2.10 (£9.50) OWNER Miss L.J.Ward (NEWMARKET) BRED Shadwell Estate Co Ltd & Shadwell Farm in USA 9 Rn 2m 9.87 (6.87) SF: 11/13/-/-/-/-/-/-/-
WEIGHT FOR AGE 4yo-3lb

22

ROLLING STONE H'CAP (0-60) (Class F) £2,700.80 (£758.80: £370.40)
1m 4f (Equitrack) GOING minus 0.37 sec per fur (FST) 1-00 (1-00)

Long Furlong (45)*(52) (RAkehurst)* 7-9-7e GCarter(5) (eyeshield: lw: stdy hdwy over 3f out: led over 1f out: rdn out) .... — **1**
Wottashambles **(42)***(47)*(Fav)*(GLewis)* 4-8-8 (5) AGarth(7) (hld up: led over 3f out tl over 1f out: unable qckn) 1¼ **2**
9[8] Malingerer **(30)***(34) (DAWilson)* 4-8-1 NGwilliams(1) (hld up: rdn over 4f out: ev ch over 2f out: one pce) 1 **3**
Mr Bean **(45)***(39) (KRBurke)* 5-9-2 (5) SDrowne(2) (led over 8f: wknd over 2f out) 8 **4**
Lady Bunting **(26)***(16) (MissBSanders)* 8-8-2v GBardwell(3) (b: chsd ldr over 8f: wknd over 2f out) 3 **5**
Head Turner **(48)***(30) (CPWildman)* 7-9-10 NAdams(10) (rdn over 4f out: nvr nr to chal) 6 **6**
Mighty Kingdom (IRE) **(41)***(22) (RWEmery)* 4-8-12 JWilliams(4) (lw: bhd fnl 8f) .... ½ **7**
Annabella Baggins (IRE) **(48)***(26) (RBoss)* 4-9-5 LDettori(8) (hdwy over 6f out: wknd over 3f out) 2½ **8**
Nomogram **(33)***(8) (GLewis)* 4-8-4 StephenDavies(6) (bhd fnl 5f) 2½ **9**
One Wild Oat **(50)***(—) (CFWall)* 4-9-7b WWoods(9) (dwlt: a bhd) 20 **10**

13/8 Wottashambles, **4/1** Mr Bean, **9/2** LONG FURLONG, **6/1** Annabella Baggins (IRE), **7/1** Head Turner, **12/1** One Wild Oat, **25/1** Malingerer, **33/1** Mighty Kingdom (IRE), Nomogram, Lady Bunting, CSF £12.33 CT £148.78 TOTE £5.70: £2.80 £1.10 £6.80 (£4.50) OWNER Mr R. Akehurst (EPSOM) BRED J. Dunlop 10 Rn 2m 35.73 (6.33) SF: 34/25/13/21/-/13/1/-/-/-
WEIGHT FOR AGE 4yo-5lb

23

TOO MANY COOKS H'CAP (0-70) (Class E) £3,009.60 (£910.80: £444.40: £211.20) **6f (Equitrack)** GOING minus 0.37 sec per fur (FST) 1-30 (1-30)

Pageboy (62)*(69+)*(Fav)*(PCHaslam)* 6-9-6 JWeaver(6) (mde all: clr over 1f out: pushed out) .... — **1**
Distant Dynasty **(51)***(49)*(Fav)*(BAPearce)* 5-8-9 LDettori(3) (hld up: rdn over 2f out: unable qckn) 3½ **2**
Cheerful Groom (IRE) **(47)***(40) (JMackie)* 4-8-5 GCarter(2) (lw: hrd rdn & hdwy over 2f out: r.o one pce fnl f) 2 **3**
Waverley Star **(38)***(28) (KOCunningham-Brown)* 10-7-10 LCharnock(8) (b: a.p: rdn over 3f out: one pce) .... ¾ **4**
Rambold **(64)***(52) (TMJones)* 4-9-8 RPerham(1) (hld up: rdn over 2f out: one pce) ½ **5**
Thorny Bishop **(70)***(38) (JJBridger)* 4-10-0 GBardwell(4) (rdn thrght: bhd fnl 3f) 8 **6**
Hinari Video **(57)***(21) (MJohnston)* 10-9-1 TWilliams(5) (bit bkwd: stumbled s: prom over 2f) 1½ **7**
Crafty Cricketer **(39)***(—) (RVoorspuy)* 4-7-11 ow4 NAdams(7) (a bhd) 4 **8**
LONG HANDICAP Crafty Cricketer 7-3

7/4 PAGEBOY, Distant Dynasty, **7/1** Hinari Video, **8/1** Rambold, **14/1** Cheerful Groom (IRE), Thorny Bishop, **16/1** Waverley Star, **66/1** Crafty Cricketer, CSF £5.15 CT £26.65 TOTE £3.30: £1.90 £1.70 £1.40 (£3.40) OWNER Lord Scarsdale (MIDDLEHAM) BRED K. T. Ivory and Partners 8 Rn 1m 13.58 (2.98) SF: 31/12/4/-/15/-/-/-

24

BIRD IN THE HAND H'CAP (3-Y.O) (0-80) (Class D) £3,555.50 (£1,076.00: £525.00: £249.50) **7f (Equitrack)** GOING minus 0.37 sec per fur (FST)2-00 (2-00)

Sarasi (63)*(77) (PFICole)* 3-9-7 CRutter(3) (b.nr fore: lw: hld up: rdn over 2f out: led ins fnl f: r.o wl)........— **1**
Mac's Taxi **(56)***(63) (PCHaslam)* 3-9-0 JWeaver(4) (lw: led 2f: led wl over 1f out tl ins fnl f: unable qckn)........3½ **2**
Master Millfield (IRE) **(69)***(73)*(Fav)*(CJHill)* 3-9-8 (5) 6x SSanders(2) (lw: led 5f out: rdn over 2f out: hdd wl over 1f out: one pce)........1½ **3**
Mediate (IRE) **(59)***(57) (RHannon)* 3-9-3b LDettori(6) (hld up: rdn over 3f out: wknd over 1f out)........3 **4**
Rowlandsons Silver (FR) **(60)***(32) (DJGMurraySmith)* 3-9-4 StephenDavies(5) (lw: a bhd)........12 **5**
The Aspecto Girl (IRE) **(50)***(18) (MJohnston)* 3-8-8 TWilliams(1) (lw: a bhd)........2 **6**

1/2 Master Millfield (IRE), **5/1** Mediate (IRE), **11/2** SARASI (6/1-4/1), **11/1** Mac's Taxi, **16/1** Rowlandsons Silver (FR), **25/1** The Aspecto Girl (IRE), CSF £49.69 TOTE £5.50: £2.90 £3.30 (£13.70) OWNER The Blue Chip Group (WHATCOMBE) BRED C. J. R. Trotter 6 Rn
1m 27.73 (4.73) SF: 18/5/13/-/-/-

25

STITCH IN TIME CLAIMING STKS (3-Y.O) (Class E) £3,138.30 (£950.40: £464.20: £221.10) **1m (Equitrack)** GOING minus 0.37 sec (FST) 2-30 (2-31)

Good so Fa (IRE) (58)*(62) (MHTompkins)* 3-8-3 (5) SMulvey(8) (hmpd s: stdy hdwy 4f out: rdn over 1f out: led ins fnl f: r.o wl)........— **1**
Irie Mon (IRE) **(54)***(59) (JWHills)* 3-8-8 RCochrane(10) (lw: hdwy 6f out: led over 3f out: clr over 1f out: hdd ins fnl f: unable qckn)........1½ **2**
The Cape Doctor (IRE) **(70)***(64) (BWHills)* 3-8-13 (5) JDSmith(6) (b.hind: lw: hdwy over 3f out: hrd rdn over 1f out: one pce)........2½ **3**
Tachycardia **(56)***(39) (RJO'Sullivan)* 3-8-3 DBiggs(2) (a.p: rdn over 3f out: wknd 1f out)........5 **4**
Fahema **(52)***(41)*(Fav)*(RBoss)* 3-8-7 LDettori(9) (lw: hld up: rdn over 3f out: wknd over 1f out)........¾ **5**
Presto Boy **(60)***(38) (MBell)* 3-8-7b MFenton(3) (led over 4f: wknd over 2f out)......1¼ **6**
Baby Bob **(44)***(11) (JMPEustace)* 3-7-6b(5)ow2 NVarley(4) (bhd fnl 3f)........9 **7**
Colston-C **(45)***(15) (CJHill)* 3-8-1 (5) SSanders(5) (bhd fnl 3f)........2½ **8**
Fairy's Son **(56)***(12) (WRMuir)* 3-8-8 JWeaver(1) (bhd fnl 4f)........2½ **9**
Double Booking (IRE) *(—) (CJHill)* 3-8-2 JQuinn(7) (a bhd)........5 **10**

9/4 Fahema, **3/1** The Cape Doctor (IRE), **9/2** Presto Boy, **5/1** Tachycardia, **7/1** Irie Mon (IRE), **15/2** GOOD SO FA (IRE), **16/1** Colston-C, Fairy's Son, **33/1** Baby Bob, Double Booking (IRE), CSF £60.46 TOTE £21.00: £5.10 £1.10 £2.10 (£27.90) OWNER Mark Tompkins Racing (NEWMARKET) BRED Frank Dunne in Ireland 10 Rn 1m 41.82 (5.42) SF: 8/5/9/-/-/-/-/-/-/-

26

BAD PENNY STKS (II) (Mdn) (Class D) £3,555.50 (£1,076.00: £525.00: £249.50) **1m 2f (Equitrack)** GOING minus 0.37 sec per fur (FST) 3-00 (3-01)

El Atrevido (FR) *(51+) (NJHWalker)* 5-9-0 RCochrane(8) (lw: a.p: led over 4f out: clr over 1f out: eased ins fnl f)........— **1**
Regal Pursuit (IRE) **(57)***(46) (CAHorgan)* 4-8-6h AClark(7) (rdn over 4f out: gd hdwy over 2f out: hung lft over 1f out: r.o wl ins fnl f)........hd **2**
Tropical Jungle (USA) **(61)***(45)*(Fav)*(PJMakin)* 5-9-0 LDettori(4) (led over 5f: rdn over 2f out: unable qckn)........4 **3**
Thorniwama **(36)***(38) (JJBridger)* 4-8-6 GBardwell(6) (lw: plld hrd: rdn over 4f out: one pce)........1½ **4**
Chili Lady **(39)***(37) (JSMoore)* 5-8-4 (5) SDrowne(3) (a.p: rdn 3f out: wknd over 1f out)........½ **5**
King's Gold *(31) (TMJones)* 5-9-0 RPerham(1) (lw: s.i.s: a bhd)........7 **6**
Oaks Star (USA) *(20) (PFICole)* 4-8-11 CRutter(2) (a bhd)........7 **7**
Chapter Two *(16) (SDow)* 4-8-11 JWeaver(5) (lw: chsd ldr over 5f)........2½ **8**

7/4 Tropical Jungle (USA), **2/1** EL ATREVIDO (FR), **11/4** Regal Pursuit (IRE), **11/2** Oaks Star (USA), **12/1** Chili Lady, Thorniwama, **25/1** Chapter Two, **33/1** King's Gold, CSF £9.25 TOTE £2.90: £1.10 £1.40 £1.30 (£8.10) OWNER Herald Sporting Club Ltd (WANTAGE) BRED France Foal Investments in France 8 Rn 2m 9.07 (6.07) SF: 20/13/14/5/7/-/-/-
WEIGHT FOR AGE 4yo-3lb

27 MANY HANDS STKS (0-60) (Class F) £2,688.20 (£755.20: £368.60)
1m 2f (Equitrack) GOING minus 0.37 sec per fur (FST) 3-30 (3-31)

Ballyranter (60)*(74+)*(Fav)*(HJCollingridge)* 6-9-0v JQuinn(3) (hld up: led 3f out: clr over 2f out: comf) ....— **1**
Camden's Ransom (USA) **(60)***(62) (GBBalding)* 8-8-9 (5) SDrowne(5) (hld up: rdn over 4f out: unable qckn) 8 **2**
My Minnie **(50)***(56) (BJMeehan)* 5-8-9 BDoyle(4) (chsd ldr: led over 5f out to 3f out: one pce) ....nk **3**
Hillsdown Boy (IRE) **(60)***(44) (SDow)* 5-8-9 (5) SSanders(2) (b: b.hind: lw: hld up: rdn over 4f out: wknd over 2f out) 11 **4**
Lac de Gras (IRE) **(31)***(4) (RCurtis)* 4-8-11 GBardwell(1) (led over 4f: wknd 3f out)25 **5**

8/15 BALLYRANTER, **5/2** Hillsdown Boy (IRE), **9/2** Camden's Ransom (USA), **14/1** My Minnie, **66/1** Lac de Gras (IRE), CSF £3.90 TOTE £1.70: £1.50 £3.90 (£3.10) OWNER Mr P. J. Byrnes (NEWMARKET) BRED Llety Stud 5 Rn 2m 8.25 (5.25) SF: 27/15/10/-/-
WEIGHT FOR AGE 4yo-3lb

T/Jkpt: £14,940.90 (1.09 Tckts). T/Plpt: £138.90 (133.36 Tckts). T/Qdpt: Not won; £30.40 to Uttoxeter 6/1/95. AK

0001-SOUTHWELL (L-H)
Friday January 6th (Standard)

28 STAFFORDSHIRE H'CAP (I) (Mdn) (0-60) (Class F) £2,537.00 (£712.00: £347.00) **7f (Fibresand)** Stalls: Low GOING minus 0.22 sec (FST) 12-00 (12-01)

Harry Browne (IRE) (50)*(56) (MrsJRRamsden)* 3-8-7 SWilliams(7) (hld up & bhd: hdwy 2f out: r.o wl to ld nr fin: cleverly) ....— **1**
Genesis Four **(37)***(42) (SRBowring)* 5-8-12b SWebster(6) (a cl up: led over 1f out: styd on u.p: jst ct) ....hd **2**
Indian Serenade **(49)***(52)*(Fav)*(PWHarris)* 4-9-10 LDettori(5) (cl up: led 2f out: sn hdd & one pce) ....¾ **3**
Kiyas **(40)***(35) (BJMcMath)* 4-9-1 AMackay(2) (led to 2f out: grad wknd) 4 **4**
Venture Fourth **(42)***(32) (EJAlston)* 6-8-10 (7) SKnott(10) (hdwy ½-wy: rdn & no imp fnl 2f) 2½ **5**
Clear Look **(47)***(34) (MissHCKnight)* 5-9-8 DHarrison(3) (nvr bttr than mid div).....1½ **6**
Quiet Mission **(41)***(22) (JLEyre)* 4-9-2b AClark(9) (chsd ldr tl wknd over 2f out) 3 **7**
Miss Tipsy **(37)***(10) (WWHaigh)* 4-8-12b DaleGibson(12) (hdwy to chse ldrs after 2f: rdn appr st: sn wknd) 4 **8**
Tassagh Bridge (IRE) **(23)***(—) (RIngram)* 5-7-12b GBardwell(1) (sn drvn along & bhd: n.d) 2½ **9**
David Blue (IRE) **(46)***(12) (JWhite)* 4-9-7 JWilliams(8) (lw: outpcd fr ½-wy) 1 **10**
Charlistiona **(35)***(—) (MJohnston)* 4-8-10 TWilliams(11) (prom over 4f) 3½ **11**
Charlotte Penny **(42)***(—) (NPLittmoden)* 4-8-12 (5) TGMcLaughlin(4) (drvn along ½-wy: n.d) 1¼ **12**

6/4 Indian Serenade, **5/1** HARRY BROWNE (IRE), **7/1** Miss Tipsy, **8/1** Venture Fourth, **10/1** Clear Look, **11/1** Charlistiona, **12/1** David Blue (IRE), Genesis Four, **16/1** Tassagh Bridge (IRE), Quiet Mission, Kiyas, **33/1** Charlotte Penny, CSF £63.94 CT £125.56 TOTE £5.50: £2.10 £4.30 £1.10 (£58.40) OWNER Mrs J. R. Ramsden (THIRSK) BRED Patrick Whelan in Ireland 12 Rn
1m 31.6 (4.80) SF: 20/24/34/16/13/14/2/-/-/-/-/-
WEIGHT FOR AGE 3yo-18lb

29 YORKSHIRE (S) STKS (I) (Class G) £2,259.00 (£634.00: £309.00)
1m 3f (Fibresand) GOING minus 0.22 sec per fur (FST) 12-30 (12-30)

Greek Gold (IRE) (55)*(57) (MrsJRRamsden)* 6-9-2 JWeaver(4) (lw: mde all: rdn out fnl 2f) ....— **1**
Off the Air (IRE) **(49)***(48) (ICampbell)* 4-8-7v DHarrison(5) (a chsng wnr: drvn along over 4f out: kpt on one pce) 3 **2**
Top Shiel **(74)***(46)*(Fav)*(KRBurke)* 7-9-2 GCarter(6) (trckd ldrs: outpcd 5f out: no imp after) 5 **3**
Trail of Tears **(25)***(41) (WWHaigh)* 5-9-2 DaleGibson(3) (a chsng ldrs: rdn appr st: one pce) 4 **4**
Well Suited **(40)***(24) (BJMcMath)* 5-9-2 RCochrane(2) (prom tl outpcd over 4f out: n.d after) 12 **5**

Comtec's Legend **(37)***(17) (JFBottomley)* 5-8-11 LDettori(7) (sn pushed along: sme hdwy appr st: eased whn btn fnl 2½f)........1¾ 6
Speedy Snapper **(48)***(21) (PDCundell)* 4-8-12b JWilliams(9) (lw: sn outpcd & bhd)........¾ 7
Pop to Stans **(56)***(18) (JPearce)* 6-9-2 GBardwell(8) (in tch: pushed along after 4f: sn btn)........2½ 8
Kush **(23)***(10) (JLHarris)* 4-8-7 AMackay(1) (a bhd)........2½ 9

4/6 Top Shiel, **4/1** GREEK GOLD (IRE), **6/1** Comtec's Legend, **11/1** Pop to Stans, **12/1** Off the Air (IRE), **16/1** Speedy Snapper, **25/1** Kush, Well Suited, **33/1** Trail of Tears, CSF £48.19 TOTE £4.70: £2.00 £2.80 £1.10 (£14.60) OWNER Mrs J. R. Ramsden (THIRSK) BRED Ballymacoll Stud Farm Ltd in Ireland 9 Rn 2m 29.1 (7.60) SF: 30/18/19/14/-/-/-/-/-
WEIGHT FOR AGE 4yo-4lb
Sold D Nicholls 5,000 gns

30

LINCOLNSHIRE H'CAP (Amateurs) (0-70) (Class E) £3,052.50 (£924.00: £451.00: £214.50)**1m (Fibre)** Stalls: Low GOING minus 0.22 sec (FST) 1-00 (1-01)

Roar on Tour (46)*(51)*(Fav)*(MrsMReveley)* 6-9-7b(4) MrMHNaughton(5) (lw: a cl up: led over 2f out: pushed out)........— 1
No Submission (USA) **(65)***(68) (DWChapman)* 9-10-12 (4) MissRClark(8) (led after 1f tl over 2f out: sn outpcd: styd on wl nr fin)........¾ 2
Larn Fort **(47)***(46) (CWFairhurst)* 5-9-8v(4) MrsSBosley(2) (trckd ldrs: effrt 3f out: r.o one pce)........1¾ 3
Kissavos **(43)***(40) (CCElsey)* 9-9-8 MissJWinter(1) (b: bhd: gd hdwy appr st: sn chsng ldrs: nt qckn fnl f)........¾ 4
Educated Pet **(66)***(56) (BPreece)* 6-10-10 (7) MissLBoswell(3) (c wd & hdwy appr st: styd on one pce fnl f)........3½ 5
*1*5 Queens Consul (IRE) **(70)***(59) (BSRothwell)* 5-11-0 (7) MissAlexMcCabe(12) (cl up tl wknd fr over 2f out)........½ 6
Perdition (IRE) **(49)***(34) (KRBurke)* 5-9-7 (7) MrsEBurke(6) (dwlt: hdwy appr st: sn btn)........2 7
Charlies Dream (IRE) **(45)***(22) (KRBurke)* 4-9-9v MrTCuff(9) (prom to st: sn rdn & btn)........4 8
Rosy Lydgate **(50)***(7) (SEKettlewell)* 4-9-10 (4) MrsDKettlewell(4) (in tch: effrt ent st: sn btn)........10 9
Winagins (IRE) **(36)***(—) (TRWatson)* 4-8-7 (7) MrsCWatson(7) (led 1f: chsd ldrs tl rdn & wknd appr st)........1¾ 10
Azubah **(45)***(—) (GMMoore)* 8-9-10 MrCBonner(10) (lost tch fr ½-wy)........5 11
Chantry Bellini **(37)***(—) (MrsSMAustin)* 6-8-9b(7) MrsDWilkinson(11) (b: b.hind: chsd ldrs tl wknd 3f out)........6 12

9/4 ROAR ON TOUR, **3/1** No Submission (USA) (2/1-7/2), **11/2** Queens Consul (IRE), **9/1** Azubah, **11/1** Kissavos, **12/1** Larn Fort, Charlies Dream (IRE), **14/1** Perdition (IRE), **16/1** Rosy Lydgate, **20/1** Educated Pet, **33/1** Chantry Bellini, **40/1** Winagins (IRE), CSF £9.81 CT £64.94 TOTE £3.40: £1.70 £1.70 £4.50 (£3.60) OWNER Mrs S. D. Murray (SALTBURN) BRED Pitts Farm Stud 12 Rn 1m 46.7 (7.40) SF: 18/34/16/11/25/28/5/-/-/-/-/-
WEIGHT FOR AGE 4yo-1lb

31

LEICESTERSHIRE CLAIMING STKS (Class F) £2,814.20 (£791.20: £386.60) **1m (Fibresand)** GOING minus 0.22 sec per fur (FST) 1-30 (1-31)

Shuttlecock (64)*(59) (NPLittmoden)* 4-8-7 MFenton(4) (sn cl up: rdn over 2f out: styd on to ld wl ins fnl f)........— 1
Battle Colours (IRE) **(63)***(61)*(Fav)*(MrsJRRamsden)* 6-8-10 LDettori(7) (in tch: rdn ent st: swtchd over 1f out: hrd rdn & styd on wl nr fin)........hd 2
*2*10 Profit Release (IRE) **(83)***(55) (MJohnston)* 4-8-6 TWilliams(2) (led: rdn over 1f out: hdd & no ex wl ins fnl f)........1¼ 3
Brackenthwaite **(77)***(63) (LRLloyd-James)* 5-9-2 JWeaver(3) (s.i.s: hdwy & c wd st: styd on nr fin)........nk 4
*2*6 Monsieur Petong **(47)***(46) (DNicholls)* 4-7-10 (7)ow2 AEddery(5) (in tch: hdwy 2f out: sn rdn & no imp)........2½ 5
Valiant Man **(56)***(49) (JHetherton)* 4-8-9 TIves(8) (trckd ldrs: effrt over 2f out: grad wknd)........1½ 6
Red March Hare **(31)***(33) (DMoffatt)* 4-7-12 JQuinn(6) (trckd ldrs: rdn 2f out: sn btn)........2½ 7
Roodmas (IRE) **(30)***(—) (JParkes)* 4-7-11 ow1 NAdams(1) (sn outpcd & bhd)........20 8

10/11 Battle Colours (IRE), **4/1** Profit Release (IRE), **13/2** Valiant Man, **7/1** Brackenthwaite, **10/1** Monsieur Petong, **14/1** SHUTTLECOCK, **20/1** Red March Hare, **33/1** Roodmas (IRE), CSF £27.86 TOTE £25.80: £3.50 £1.10 £1.80 (£13.00) OWNER Mr James Colling (NEWARK) BRED A. B. Phipps 8 Rn
1m 45.4 (6.10) SF: 14/17/11/20/3/6/-/-
WEIGHT FOR AGE 4yo-1lb
STEWARDS' ENQUIRY Dettori suspended 15-17/1/95 (excessive use of whip).

32

STAFFORDSHIRE H'CAP (II) (Mdn) (0-60) (Class F) £2,537.00 (£712.00: £347.00) **7f (Fibresand)** GOING minus 0.22 sec per fur (FST) 2-00 (2-05)

La Residence (47)*(53) (MrsNMacauley)* 4-8-13 (5) SSanders(4) (mde most: hld on wl fnl f)......— **1**
Rosina's Folly **(54)***(58) (JLHarris)* 4-9-11 RCochrane(2) (hdwy over 1f out: styd on wl nr fin)......¾ **2**
Slip a Coin **(55)***(58) (RHollinshead)* 4-9-7 (5) AGarth(1) (a w ldrs: nt qckn ins fnl f)..hd **3**
Bassetlaw Belle **(25)***(23) (NPLittmoden)* 6-7-3 (7)ow3 CAdamson(8) (bhd: hdwy on ins 2f out: n.m.r: styd on wl)......2½ **4**
Arrasas Lady **(40)***(35)*(Fav)*(RMFlower)* 5-8-11 StephenDavies(11) (prom: rdn 3f out: one pce)......1¼ **5**
Tenor **(57)***(50) (DNicholls)* 4-10-0 AlexGreaves(7) (sn w ldrs: shkn up 2f out: wknd ins fnl f)......¾ **6**
5[12] Joint Prospect **(43)***(35) (CCElsey)* 3-7-10b JQuinn(3) (hdwy 2f out: sn rdn: no imp)nk **7**
Qualitair Ridge **(50)***(41) (JFBottomley)* 3-8-3v GCarter(6) (bhd: hdwy over 1f out: nvr able to chal)......hd **8**
Amlak (USA) **(44)***(13) (TKersey)* 6-9-1 BDoyle(10) (nvr wnt pce)......10 **9**
Belmont Princess (IRE) **(41)***(—) (APJones)* 5-8-7 (5) SDrowne(5) (chsd ldr tl wknd 3f out)......10 **10**
6[10] Nez Carrera **(50)***(—) (RMWhitaker)* 4-9-7b AClark(9) (sn outpcd & wl bhd)......dist **11**
LONG HANDICAP Bassetlaw Belle 7-5

5/2 Arrasas Lady, **5/1** Slip a Coin, **6/1** LA RESIDENCE, **7/1** Qualitair Ridge, **15/2** Belmont Princess (IRE), **12/1** Tenor, **14/1** Rosina's Folly, **16/1** Amlak (USA), Joint Prospect, **20/1** Nez Carrera, **33/1** Bassetlaw Belle, CSF £75.35 CT £408.65 TOTE £8.10: £2.00 £4.30 £1.70 (£32.30) OWNER Mr Brian Pollins (MELTON MOWBRAY) BRED D. A. and Mrs Hicks 11 Rn
1m 33.4 (6.60) SF: 11/16/16/-/-/9/-/-/-/-/-
WEIGHT FOR AGE 3yo-18lb

33

NOTTINGHAMSHIRE H'CAP (3-Y.O) (0-75) (Class D) £3,589.30 (£1,086.40: £530.20: £252.10) **6f (Fibresand)** GOING minus 0.22 sec (FST) 2-30 (2-33)

Portend (47)*(59) (SRBowring)* 3-7-2 (7)ow2 ClaireBalding(4) (cl up: led over 2f out: edgd lft: styd on wl)......— **1**
Tee Tee Too (IRE) **(73)***(77)*(Fav)*(PCHaslam)* 3-9-7 JWeaver(6) (led tl over 2f out: one pce)......3 **2**
Keeper's Grey **(57)***(56) (RGuest)* 3-8-5 DHarrison(5) (a.p: effrt 3f out: styd on one pce)......1¾ **3**
Samana Cay **(51)***(42) (DNicholls)* 3-7-13 CRutter(1) (a chsng ldrs: nt qckn fnl 2f) ...3 **4**
Rotherfield Park (IRE) **(50)***(28) (CSmith)* 3-7-5 (7) MBaird(2) (bhd: effrt ½-wy: rdn & no imp)......5 **5**
Never Time (IRE) **(56)***(19) (MrsVAAconley)* 3-8-4 JQuinn(3) (lw: outpcd & bhd ½-wy: n.d)......6 **6**
Seenthelight **(56)***(—) (DMoffatt)* 3-8-4 DaleGibson(7) (in tch tl outpcd fnl 3f)......8 **7**
LONG HANDICAP Portend 7-4

Evens Tee Tee Too (IRE), **7/2** Keeper's Grey, **11/2** Rotherfield Park (IRE), **7/1** Seenthelight, **10/1** PORTEND, **14/1** Samana Cay, **16/1** Never Time (IRE), CSF £21.27 TOTE £9.80: £2.10 £1.10 (£9.30) OWNER Mr D. H. Bowring (EDWINSTOWE) BRED Hollow Hole Stud 7 Rn
1m 16.4 (2.90) SF: 23/40/22/9/-/-/-

34

YORKSHIRE (S) STKS (II) (Class G) £2,259.00 (£634.00: £309.00) **1m 3f (Fibresand)** GOING minus 0.22 sec per fur (FST) 3-00 (3-00)

Rousitto (54)*(58)*(Fav)*(RHollinshead)* 7-9-2 LDettori(5) (lw: a.p: led 2f out: pushed clr: eased nr fin)......— **1**
Greek Night Out (IRE) **(44)***(46) (JAHarris)* 4-8-7 SWilliams(6) (led to 2f out: one pce)......5 **2**
Puffy **(43)***(46) (MDods)* 8-9-2v WWoods(4) (b: trckd ldrs: chal over 2f out: rdn & nt r.o)......3½ **3**
2[14] Britannia Mills **(49)***(37) (MCChapman)* 4-8-2 (5) DRMcCabe(8) (bhd: hdwy appr st: one pce fnl 2f)......3 **4**

Little Miner (IRE) **(36)***(20) (BPalling)* 4-8-2 (5) SSanders(9) (chsd ldrs: rdn 4f out: sn outpcd)....12 **5**
Amy's Star **(21)***(10) (PWigham)* 9-8-11 MDeering(7) (cl up tl rdn & wknd 5f out)......7 **6**
Awestruck **(40)***(15) (BPreece)* 5-9-2b TWall(1) (sn outpcd & bhd)....hd **7**
Betabetcorbett **(49)***(11) (BPJBaugh)* 4-8-5 (7) PRoberts(3) (prom tl wknd appr st) 3 **8**
Arrogant Boy *(4) (DWChapman)* 6-9-2 SWebster(2) (s.s: a bhd)....5 **9**

5/6 ROUSITTO, **7/2** Greek Night Out (IRE), **7/1** Puffy, Awestruck, **8/1** Betabetcorbett, **14/1** Britannia Mills, **20/1** Little Miner (IRE), **25/1** Arrogant Boy, **50/1** Amy's Star, CSF £5.08 TOTE £2.40: £1.50 £1.30 £1.30 (£4.20) OWNER Mr J. Pattison (UPPER LONGDON) BRED White Lodge Stud Ltd 9 Rn No bid 2m 29.6 (8.10) SF: 27/12/16/3/-/-/-/-/-
WEIGHT FOR AGE 4yo-4lb

35 DERBYSHIRE H'CAP (0-70) (Class E) £3,109.70 (£941.60: £459.80: £218.90)
1m 4f (Fibresand) GOING minus 0.22 sec per fur (FST) 3-30 (3-31)

Pharly Dancer (67)*(76)*(Fav)*(WWHaigh)* 6-9-11 DaleGibson(2) (mde all: rdn & styd on wl fnl 2f)....— **1**
Royal Citizen (IRE) **(60)***(67) (JFBottomley)* 6-9-4 LDettori(7) (trckd ldrs: chal over 2f out: rdn & nt qckn)....2 **2**
Modest Hope (USA) **(48)***(52) (BRichmond)* 8-8-6 NAdams(8) (lw: in tch: hdwy 4f out: styd on: nt pce to chal)....2½ **3**
Nothing Doing (IRE) **(40)***(43) (WJMusson)* 6-7-9 (3)ow3 DWright(6) (lw: cl up: effrt 3f out: wknd appr fnl f)....½ **4**
Non Vintage (IRE) **(63)***(63) (MCChapman)* 4-8-11 (5) DRMcCabe(5) (bhd: effrt appr st: sme late hdwy)....2½ **5**
Blowedifiknow **(42)***(33) (JWharton)* 5-8-0 JQuinn(1) (lw: chsd ldrs tl outpcd over 4f out: n.d after)....7 **6**
Broughton's Pride (IRE) **(45)***(31) (JAGlover)* 4-7-12v GBardwell(3) (lw: in tch: effrt 5f out: wknd 3f out)....4 **7**
Aldington Chapple **(37)***(—) (BPreece)* 7-7-2 (7) MBaird(4) (a bhd)....20 **8**

2/1 PHARLY DANCER, **3/1** Royal Citizen (IRE), **4/1** Modest Hope (USA), **8/1** Broughton's Pride (IRE), Non Vintage (IRE), **9/1** Blowedifiknow, **20/1** Nothing Doing (IRE), Aldington Chapple, CSF £8.57 CT £18.97 TOTE £2.70: £1.20 £2.00 £1.90 (£5.50) OWNER Mr A. Marucci (MALTON) BRED Stud-On-The-Chart 8 Rn 2m 41.7 (7.50) SF: 43/34/20/12/26/3/-/-
WEIGHT FOR AGE 4yo-5lb
T/Plpt: £12.30 (642.36 Tckts). T/Qdpt: £11.30 (1.6 Tckts). AA

0021-LINGFIELD (L-H)
Saturday January 7th (Standard)

36 SNOWDROP APP'CE CLAIMING STKS (Class F) £2,637.80 (£740.80: £361.40)
1m 4f (Equitrack) GOING minus 0.44 sec per fur (FST) 12-45 (12-46)

Stevie's Wonder (IRE) (53)*(70) (TGMills)* 5-8-6 (3) DToole(2) (lw: mde all: clr over 1f out: easily)....— **1**
8[4] Surprise Guest (IRE) **(74)***(75)*(Fav)*(MJohnston)* 4-9-5 OliverCasey(3) (chsd ldr over 8f: hrd rdn over 3f out: one pce)....8 **2**
Quick Million **(55)***(50) (BJMeehan)* 4-7-13 DaneO'Neill(1) (hld up: hdwy over 4f out: chsd ldr over 3f out: wknd over 1f out)....4 **3**
Whatone Bell **(21)** *(PHayward)* 5-8-3b(3) AmandaSanders(5) (chsd ldrs tl rdn & wknd over 3f: t.o)....dist **4**
Honest Dave *(BAPearce)* 5-8-10 (5) GinaFaulkner(6) (w'like: s.s: sn rdn along: wl bhd fnl 6f: t.o)....s.h **5**

Evens Surprise Guest (IRE), **6/4** STEVIE'S WONDER (IRE), **4/1** Quick Million, **50/1** Whatone Bell, Honest Dave, CSF £3.39 TOTE £2.30: £1.10 £1.10 (£1.40) OWNER Mr T. G. Mills (EPSOM) BRED Ovidstown Investments Ltd in Ireland 5 Rn 2m 35.07 (5.67) SF: 21/21/-/-/-
WEIGHT FOR AGE 4yo-5lb
Stevie's Wonder (IRE) clmd K Ramsden £4,000

37 DAFFODIL H'CAP (0-80) (Class D) £3,538.60 (£1,070.80: £522.40: £248.20)
1m 4f (Equitrack) GOING minus 0.44 sec per fur (FST) 1-15 (1-15)

Benfleet (69)*(75) (RWArmstrong)* 4-9-6 LDettori(5) (hld up: hdwy 4f out: rdn 2f out: led ins fnl f: r.o wl)....— **1**

In the Money (IRE) **(54)***(59) (RHollinshead)* 6-8-10 TIves(3) (led 2f: chsd ldr: rdn 2f out: led 1f out: sn hdd: r.o) ....nk **2**
Pharamineux **(56)***(56) (RAkehurst)* 9-8-12e GCarter(1) (eyeshield: chsd ldrs: rdn over 3f out: r.o one pce fnl 2f) 4 **3**
11³ Global Dancer **(73)***(71)*(Fav)*(WAO'Gorman)* 4-9-7 (3) EmmaO'Gorman(6) (chsd ldr 2f: led 10f out: hrd rdn 2f out: hdd 1f out: sn wknd) 1¾ **4**
Admirals Secret (USA) **(66)***(45) (CFWall)* 6-9-8 WWoods(2) (hld up: rdn over 4f out: sn wknd) 15 **5**
In Behind (IRE) **(52)***(26) (GLMoore)* 4-8-3 AMorris(4) (rdn 7f out: a bhd) 4 **6**

13/8 Global Dancer, **9/2** In the Money (IRE), BENFLEET, **11/2** Pharamineux (4/1-6/1), **6/1** Admirals Secret (USA), **14/1** In Behind (IRE), CSF £22.00 TOTE £5.90: £2.00 £1.80 (£9.30) OWNER Mr C. G. Donovan (NEWMARKET) BRED Aston Park Stud 6 Rn
2m 33.55 (4.15) SF: 41/32/28/38/18/-
WEIGHT FOR AGE 4yo-5lb

38 COWSLIP MEDIAN AUCTION STKS (Mdn 3-Y.O) (Class E) £3,109.70 (£941.60: £459.80: £218.90)
1m 2f (Equitrack) GOING minus 0.44 sec per fur (FST) 1-45 (1-46)

Bardon Hill Boy (IRE) *(67+) (BHanbury)* 3-9-0 MRimmer(9) (hld up in tch: hdwy to ld 2f out: pushed out) ....— **1**
Shaft of Light *(62) (LordHuntingdon)* 3-9-0 DHarrison(4) (leggy: dwlt: bhd: rdn along: hdwy over 3f out: chsd wnr over 1f out: unable qckn) 3 **2**
5² Lawbuster (IRE) **(51)***(60) (WRMuir)* 3-9-0b JWeaver(1) (rdn in rr 4f out: hdwy 3f out: n.m.r over 2f out: swtchd rt: styd on wl fnl f) 1½ **3**
Mr Lowry **(54)***(57) (RBoss)* 3-9-0 LDettori(6) (a.p: led over 2f out: sn hdd: wknd ins fnl f) 1¾ **4**
Pennine Wind (IRE) **(73)***(54)*(Fav)*(MJohnston)* 3-9-0 TWilliams(2) (chsd ldrs: rdn 3f out: one pce) 1¾ **5**
See You Again *(49) (RHannon)* 3-8-7 (7) DaneO'Neill(7) (a.p: led over 3f out tl over 2f out: sn rdn: wknd fnl f) 3 **6**
Sabicas **(56)***(35) (SCWilliams)* 3-9-0 GCarter(8) (a bhd) 9 **7**
Cuban Reef **(48)***(10) (DJSCosgrove)* 3-8-9 AShoults(3) (mid div: rdn & wknd 5f out)13 **8**
Pent-House Baby **(45)***(5) (JLSpearing)* 3-8-9 NAdams(5) (led over 8f: sn wknd) 3 **9**

2/1 Pennine Wind (IRE), **5/2** BARDON HILL BOY (IRE), **7/1** Lawbuster (IRE), Mr Lowry, Sabicas, **8/1** Shaft of Light, **10/1** See You Again, **20/1** Pent-House Baby, **25/1** Cuban Reef, CSF £23.46 TOTE £3.50: £1.10 £2.80 £1.20 (£11.00) OWNER The Finsbury Partnership (NEWMARKET) BRED John McNamee in Ireland 9 Rn 2m 9.07 (6.07) SF: 15/11/9/7/6/1/-/-/-

39 BLUEBELL H'CAP (0-60) (Class F) £2,738.60 (£769.60: £375.80)
6f (Equitrack) GOING minus 0.44 sec per fur (FST) 2-15 (2-16)

Myjinka (28)*(36) (JO'Donoghue)* 5-7-5b(7) MBaird(1) (led 4f out tl over 1f out: edgd rt & led ins fnl f: r.o) ....— **1**
Pat Poindestres **(32)***(36)*(Fav)*(RJO'Sullivan)* 5-8-2 DBiggs(8) (led 2f: led over 1f out tl ins fnl f: unable qckn) 1¼ **2**
Spectacle Jim **(48)***(46)*(Fav)*(JO'Donoghue)* 6-8-13b(5) DRMcCabe(2) (mid div: rdn 2f out: r.o one pce fnl f) 2½ **3**
Faynaz **(35)***(29) (AMoore)* 9-8-0 (5) AWhelan(10) (mid div: rdn over 2f out: r.o one pce fnl f) 1¼ **4**
Anotherone to Note **(57)***(47) (MJHeaton-Ellis)* 4-9-13v LDettori(11) (chsd ldrs: rdn 2f out: wknd fnl f) 1¼ **5**
6⁹ Nineacres **(58)***(44) (DNicholls)* 4-9-7b(7) AEddery(6) (mid div: hld up: rdn 2f out: one pce) 1¼ **6**
Prince Rodney **(38)***(23) (CJDrewe)* 6-8-8v DHarrison(5) (rdn 3f out: nvr nrr) ....nk **7**
Splash of Salt (IRE) **(54)***(33) (TJNaughton)* 5-9-5 (5) VHalliday(12) (a bhd) 2½ **8**
Europharm Lassie **(48)***(23) (GLMoore)* 4-9-4v AClark(7) (chsd ldrs: rdn 2f out: wknd over 1f out) 1¼ **9**
23⁸ Crafty Cricketer **(31)***(—) (RVoorspuy)* 4-8-1 NAdams(9) (a bhd) 3½ **10**
Glitter Bay **(32)***(—) (CDBroad)* 4-8-2 ow1 MFenton(4) (bhd fnl 4f) 20 **11**

3/1 Pat Poindestres, Spectacle Jim, **4/1** Nineacres, **5/1** Europharm Lassie, **12/1** MYJINKA, **14/1** Anotherone to Note, Splash of Salt (IRE), **16/1** Faynaz, **20/1** Prince Rodney, **33/1** Crafty Cricketer, Glitter Bay, CSF £47.33 CT £128.01 TOTE £12.30: £2.40 £1.80 £1.70 (£23.60) OWNER Miss P. I. Westbrook (REIGATE) BRED Miss Prue Westbrook and Bob Pettis 11 Rn
1m 13.73 (3.13) SF: 4/5/13/-/16/14/-/3/-/-/-

40

VIOLET H'CAP (3-Y.O) (0-80) (Class D) £3,572.40 (£1,081.20: £527.60: £250.80) **5f (Equitrack)** GOING minus 0.44 sec per fur (FST) 2-45 (2-46)

Stoppes Brow (74)*(77)*(Fav)*(GLMoore)* 3-8-12v(7) LSuthern(1) (sn pushed along: hdwy over 1f out: led ins fnl f: r.o) ....— **1**
Hannah's Usher **(76)***(71) (PCHaslam)* 3-9-7 JWeaver(3) (hdwy over 2f out: ev ch ins fnl f: unable qckn) 2½ **2**
Wasblest **(59)***(42) (MJohnston)* 3-8-4 TWilliams(5) (w ldr: rdn over 1f out: ev ch ins fnl f: sn wknd) 4 **3**
Dolly Face **(65)***(44) (WRMuir)* 3-8-10 LDettori(2) (led tl hdd & wknd ins fnl f) 1¼ **4**
Russian Heroine **(74)***(47) (MJohnston)* 3-8-12 (7) OliverCasey(4) (chsd ldrs: rdn 3f out: sn wknd) 2 **5**

2/1 STOPPES BROW, **9/4** Hannah's Usher, **11/4** Wasblest, **8/1** Dolly Face, **10/1** Russian Heroine, CSF £6.55 TOTE £3.00: £1.80 £1.30 (£2.90) OWNER Mr C. J. Pennick (EPSOM) BRED Dodford Stud 5 Rn 59.43 secs (1.23) SF: 44/39/10/12/14

41

LADBROKE ALL-WEATHER TROPHY (H'cap) (Qualifier) (0-70) (Class E) £3,009.60 (£910.80: £444.40: £211.20) **7f (Equitrack)** GOING minus 0.44 sec per fur (FST) 3-20 (3-20)

16⁵ **Ragazzo (IRE) (41)***(50) (KOCunningham-Brown)* 5-7-13b LCharnock(5) (chsd ldr: led 3f out tl over 1f out: hrd rdn fnl f: led again nr fin) ....— **1**
Digpast (IRE) **(49)***(58) (RJO'Sullivan)* 5-8-7b DBiggs(9) (chsd ldrs gng wl: led over 1f out: hrd rdn fnl f: hdd nr fin) ....s.h **2**
Invocation **(68)***(71) (AMoore)* 8-9-12 NAdams(3) (sltly hmpd s: hld up: hdwy 4f out: rdn over 1f out: one pce) 3 **3**
Gingerillo **(35)***(37) (TGMills)* 4-7-7b GBardwell(7) (sn rdn along: chsd ldrs: r.o one pce fnl f) ....½ **4**
World Traveller **(72)***(72) (WAO'Gorman)* 4-9-13b(3) EmmaO'Gorman(2) (a.p: hrd rdn 2f out: one pce) ....¾ **5**
12⁵ Eastleigh **(47)***(46) (RHollinshead)* 6-8-0 (5) AGarth(6) (chsd ldrs: rdn & wknd 2f out)nk **6**
Kindergarten Boy (IRE) **(60)***(52)*(Fav)*(RBoss)* 4-9-4 LDettori(8) (sn rdn along: sme hdwy 2f out: wknd over 1f out) 3½ **7**
Greatest Hopes **(39)***(30) (CJBenstead)* 4-7-6 (5) CHawksley(4) (edgd lft s: a bhd)..hd **8**
Newington Butts (IRE) **(49)***(12) (RAkehurst)* 5-8-2 (5) SSanders(1) (led 4f) 13 **9**

3/1 Kindergarten Boy (IRE), **100/30** Digpast (IRE), **6/1** Invocation (5/1-8/1), World Traveller, **13/2** Newington Butts (IRE), **10/1** Gingerillo, Eastleigh, **14/1** RAGAZZO (IRE), **25/1** Greatest Hopes, CSF £57.59 CT £289.28 TOTE £16.70: £4.00 £1.30 £2.20 (£107.80) OWNER Mr S. Pedersen (STOCKBRIDGE) BRED Cleaboy Stud 9 Rn 1m 26.17 (3.17) SF: 10/18/28/-/29/6/10/-/-

T/Plpt: £43.30 (141.09 Tckts). T/Qdpt: £14.80 (0.8 Tckts); £4.00 to Lingfield 10/1/95. SM

0014-WOLVERHAMPTON (L-H)
Saturday January 7th (Standard)

42

OPAL H'CAP (Mdn 3-Y.O) (0-65) (Class F) £2,259.00 (£634.00: £309.00) **5f (Fibresand)** 7-00 (7-00)

Half Tone (48)*(60) (RMFlower)* 3-8-12b LDettori(3) (led 2f: dwlt: hdwy & nt clr run over 2f out: nvr rchd ldrs) ....— **1**
One for Jeannie **(54)***(66)*(Fav)*(ABailey)* 3-9-1 (3) DWright(6) (hld up: rdn over 2f out: r.o wl appr fnl f: jst failed) ....s.h **2**
Pursuance (IRE) **(57)***(63) (JBalding)* 3-9-7 LCharnock(5) (trckd ldrs: kpt on wl appr fnl f) 2 **3**
Ultra Beet **(55)***(57) (PCHaslam)* 3-9-5 JWeaver(2) (lw: w ldrs tl no ex appr fnl f) 1¾ **4**
Superbit **(50)***(51) (BAMcMahon)* 3-8-9 (5) SSanders(7) (w wnr tl slt ld after 2f: hdd 2f out: ev ch over 1f out: sn btn) ....hd **5**
Pats Delight **(48)***(19) (SCoathup)* 3-8-12b TWilliams(4) (lw: sn bhd) 10 **6**

11/10 One for Jeannie, **9/4** HALF TONE, **5/1** Ultra Beet, **12/1** Pats Delight, **14/1** Superbit, **16/1** Pursuance (IRE), CSF £5.12 TOTE £3.60: £1.60 £1.50 (£3.00) OWNER Mrs G. M. Temmerman (JEVINGTON) BRED T. M. Jennings 6 Rn 63.2 secs (5.20) SF: 1/7/3/-/-/-

43 TOPAZ CLAIMING STKS (3-Y.O) (Class F) £2,085.00 (£585.00: £285.00)
6f (Fibresand) 7-30 (7-31)

Crystal Loop (63)*(65)*(Fav)*(ABailey)* 3-8-7 (3) DWright(2) (lw: mde all: rdn out).....— 1
Poly Laureon (IRE) **(65)***(63)*(Fav)*(RHollinshead)* 3-8-10 LDettori(9) (rdn & hdwy over 2f out: r.o wl fnl f)........½ 2
Whittingham Girl **(54)***(57) (JBerry)* 3-8-6 GCarter(1) (prom: ev ch over 1f out: no ex)........½ 3
Komlucky **(49)***(51) (FJO'Mahony)* 3-8-4b JQuinn(7) (b.hind: lw: chsd ldrs: effrt & ev ch wl over 1f out: nt qckn fnl f)........1¼ 4
Dowdency **(47)***(47) (JAPickering)* 3-8-4 NCarlisle(4) (chsd wnr tl rdn & wknd wl over 1f out)........1½ 5
Tael of Silver *(56) (KRBurke)* 3-9-0 StephenDavies(6) (bhd: effrt 2f out: no imp) ..nk 6
Boldly So *(50) (WJMusson)* 3-8-8 MWigham(3) (leggy: unf: hdwy & nt clr run over 2f out: nvr rchd ldrs)........s.h 7
Poly Lane **(53)***(49) (WRMuir)* 3-8-9 JWeaver(8) (lw: chsd ldrs over 3f: sn rdn & btn)........½ 8
Shartel *(34) (MJohnston)* 3-8-9 TWilliams(5) (lw: sn pushed along: bhd fnl 3f)........6 9

11/4 CRYSTAL LOOP (2/1-3/1), Poly Laureon (IRE), **7/2** Whittingham Girl, **8/1** Komlucky, **9/1** Tael of Silver, **16/1** Dowdency, Poly Lane, **20/1** Shartel, **33/1** Boldly So, CSF £10.26 TOTE £3.60: £1.40 £1.80 £2.00 (£5.00) OWNER Mr Roy Matthews (TARPORLEY) BRED B. Long 9 Rn 1m 16.6 (5.40) SF: 12/11/6/2/-/6/1/-/-

OFFICIAL EXPLANATION **Boldly So, became upset, outpaced and resented the kick-back. She suffered slight interference going into the final bend and was hanging.**

44 DIAMOND H'CAP (0-80) (Class D) £3,673.80 (£1,112.40: £543.20: £258.60)
7f (Fibresand) 8-00 (8-00)

*1** **Just Harry (80)***(84)*(Fav)*(MJRyan)* 4-9-12 (7) 6x MBaird(1) (lw: hld up: hdwy & 5th st: sn rdn: r.o wl to ld wl ins fnl f)........— 1
Little Ibnr **(66)***(69) (PDEvans)* 4-9-5 LDettori(10) (led: rdn over 1f out: hdd & no ex wl ins fnl f)........hd 2
Hawwam **(55)***(57) (EJAlston)* 9-8-8 ow1 JWeaver(9) (chsd ldrs: rdn & 4th st: kpt on fnl f)........½ 3
Heathyards Lady (USA) **(50)***(50) (RHollinshead)* 4-8-3 GCarter(11) (prom: 3rd st: no ex appr fnl f)........¾ 4
Dawalib (USA) **(75)***(73) (DHaydnJones)* 5-10-0 AMackay(8) (w ldr: 2nd st: ev ch over 1f out: no ex fnl f)........1 5
20[8] Chinour (IRE) **(67)***(57) (EJAlston)* 7-8-13 (7) SKnott(7) (dwlt: r.o fnl 2f: nvr trbld ldrs)........4 6
Quinzii Martin **(43)***(26) (DHaydnJones)* 7-7-7v(3)ow3 DWright(5) (hld up: effrt over 1f out: nvr nr ldrs)........3½ 7
Pretonic **(46)***(25) (BPalling)* 7-7-13 JQuinn(4) (lw: chsd ldrs: pushed along ½-wy: 6th & btn st)........2 8
Sharp N' Smooth **(42)***(16) (WTKemp)* 8-7-9 ow1 LCharnock(3) (sn rdn along: bhd fnl 4f)........2½ 9
Veloce (IRE) **(61)***(34) (ABailey)* 7-9-0 TIves(6) (prom tl 7th & btn st)........hd 10
2[4] Bold Mick **(64)***(36) (DJGMurraySmith)* 4-9-3 StephenDavies(2) (sn rdn along: bhd fr ½-wy)........½ 11

3/1 JUST HARRY, **5/1** Little Ibnr, **6/1** Pretonic, Quinzii Martin, **13/2** Chinour (IRE), **8/1** Hawwam, **10/1** Heathyards Lady (USA) (8/1-12/1), Dawalib (USA), Bold Mick, **20/1** Veloce (IRE), **25/1** Sharp N'Smooth, CSF £19.47 CT £106.97 TOTE £5.50: £2.00 £2.00 £2.30 (£6.00) OWNER Miss Laura Shally (NEWMARKET) BRED Mrs S.T.Shally 11 Rn 1m 29.1 (5.10) SF: 48/35/23/17/38/21

45 RUBY H'CAP (0-60) (Class F) £2,433.00 (£683.00: £333.00)
2m 46y (Fibresand) 8-30 (8-31)

Well and Truly (47)*(60) (BAMcMahon)* 8-9-0 (5) SSanders(7) (a.p: led 6f out: rdn & hld on wl fnl f)........— 1
Nahri (USA) **(51)***(64) (JMackie)* 4-9-2 GCarter(8) (lw: in tch: hdwy 6f out: 2nd st: rdn & ev ch over 1f out: kpt on fnl f)........s.h 2
Carrolls Marc (IRE) **(48)***(55) (PCHaslam)* 7-9-6 JWeaver(2) (hld up & bhd: hdwy 7f out: 3rd st: no imp fnl f: eased nr fin)........6 3
Sassiver (USA) **(45)***(46)*(Fav)*(RHollinshead)* 5-9-3 LDettori(10) (lw: bhd: rdn 6f out: 6th st: kpt on: nvr able to chal)........6 4

Mrs Jawleyford (USA) **(56)***(55) (CSmith)* 7-9-7 (7) MBaird(6) (b: lw: plld hrd: trckd ldrs tl 5th & wkng st)....2 5
Castle Secret **(52)***(50) (DBurchell)* 9-9-10 TIves(3) (b.off fore: bhd: pushed along ½-wy: r.o fnl 2f: nvr nrr)....¾ 6
Tilty (USA) **(56)***(43) (ALForbes)* 5-9-9v(5) AProcter(9) (s.i.s: hdwy over 5f out: rdn 7f out: sn btn)....12 7
Flim Flam Aly (USA) **(32)***(17) (LJBarratt)* 6-8-4b GBardwell(11) (n.d: collapsed & died after r)....2 8
Shamwari (USA) **(53)***(37) (JWHills)* 4-9-4 MFenton(4) (prom tl 7th & wkng st)....½ 9
Royal Print (IRE) **(45)***(21) (WRMuir)* 6-9-3 DHarrison(12) (in tch 11f: sn rdn & btn)....8 10
Regal Rambler (CAN) **(45)***(20) (LJBarratt)* 4-8-10 JQuinn(5) (prom tl wknd over 3f out)....¾ 11
Joe Jagger (IRE) **(54)***(6) (MissMKMilligan)* 4-9-5 TWilliams(13) (led 10f: wknd qckly)....25 12
Crab 'n Lobster (IRE) **(31)***(—) (BPreece)* 5-7-10 (7)ow5 AEddery(1) (rdn ½-wy: a bhd)....hd 13

11/4 Sassiver (USA), **9/2** Nahri (USA), **5/1** Mrs Jawleyford (USA), **13/2** WELL AND TRULY, **8/1** Carrolls Marc (IRE), **10/1** Shamwari (USA), **14/1** Tilty (USA), Castle Secret, Royal Print (IRE), **16/1** Regal Rambler (CAN), **25/1** Flim Flam Aly (USA), **33/1** Joe Jagger (IRE), Crab 'n Lobster (IRE), CSF £36.46 CT £225.17 TOTE £6.30: £1.80 £2.80 £3.00 (£37.40) OWNER Mr Peter Freeman (TAMWORTH) BRED Littleton Stud 13 Rn 3m 41.1 SF: 28/25/24/16/24/19/12/-/-/-/-/-/-
WEIGHT FOR AGE 4yo-7lb

46

GARNET (S) STKS (Class G) £2,085.00 (£585.00: £285.00)
1m 4f (Fibresand) 9-00 (9-01)

Gold Surprise (IRE) (56)*(54+)*(Fav)*(SEKettlewell)* 6-9-3 LDettori(9) (sn trckng ldrs: 2nd st: led on bit wl over 1f out: hrd hld)....— 1
Sharp Thrill **(38)***(51) (BSmart)* 4-8-12v DHarrison(7) (prom: led 6f out tl wl over 1f out: no ch w wnr)....2½ 2
Daphnis (USA) *(47) (WTKemp)* 6-9-3 JWeaver(5) (hdwy 7f out: kpt on u.p fnl 2f)....3½ 3
Aerial View **(46)***(36) (WGMTurner)* 4-8-12 RPerham(2) (lw: plld hrd: prom: 3rd st: one pce)....9 4
Blue Pennant *(25) (TTBill)* 4-8-7 SWebster(11) (dwlt: bhd: sn pushed along: r.o u.p fnl 2f)....5 5
Haydon Hill **(34)***(16) (PDEvans)* 4-8-7 JQuinn(12) (s.i.s: hdwy & poor 6th st: nvr trbld ldrs)....7 6
Lombard Ships **(45)***(8) (ABailey)* 8-8-12 AMackay(10) (lw: hdwy over 7f out: shkn up 4f out: wknd & 5th st)....6 7
Falcons Dawn *(10) (MGMeagher)* 8-9-0v(3) DWright(8) (led after 2f to 6f out: sn wknd)....2½ 8
Springtime Affair **(40)***(—) (MrsNMacauley)* 4-8-2 (5) SSanders(1) (sn pushed along: in tch 7f)....4 9
Prince Palacio *(—) (DBurchell)* 5-9-3 StephenDavies(4) (n.m.r & rdn 7f out: sn bhd)....6 10
*34*8 Betabetcorbett **(49)***(—) (BPJBaugh)* 4-8-5 (7) PRoberts(3) (sn pushed along: wl bhd fr ½-wy)....25 11
D K Reunion *(—) (RHollinshead)* 5-9-3 TIves(6) (bit bkwd: led 2f: wknd qckly 7f out)....6 12

4/5 GOLD SURPRISE (IRE), **3/1** Lombard Ships (9/2-5/2), **8/1** Springtime Affair, **9/1** Prince Palacio, **16/1** Daphnis (USA), **20/1** Betabetcorbett, Haydon Hill, Sharp Thrill, Aerial View, **25/1** Falcons Dawn, **33/1** Blue Pennant, D K Reunion, CSF £21.37 TOTE £1.90: £1.30 £4.20 £4.90 (£22.40) OWNER Mr J. S. Calvert (MIDDLEHAM) BRED Lodge Park Stud in Ireland 12 Rn
2m 44.7 (13.70) SF: 5/-/-/-/-/-/-/-/-/-/-/-
WEIGHT FOR AGE 4yo-5lb
Bt in 4,800 gns

47

EMERALD H'CAP £2,814.00 (£852.00: £416.00: £198.00)
1m 100y (Fibresand) 9-30 (9-31)

Grand Selection (IRE) (50)*(55) (MBell)* 3-8-1 MFenton(3) (chsd ldr tl led 4f out: rdn & hld on wl fnl f)....— 1
Komreyev Dancer **(74)***(77)*(Fav)*(ABailey)* 3-9-11 TIves(5) (trckd ldrs: wnt 2nd st: rdn & unable qckn fnl f)....1 2

Nigel's Lad (IRE) **(60)***(61) (PCHaslam)* 3-8-11 JWeaver(2) (chsd ldrs: 4th st: kpt on u.p fnl 2f) 1 3
10² Water Bebe (IRE) **(54)***(54) (GCBravery)* 3-8-0 (5)ow1 DRMcCabe(4) (hdwy & 5th st: kpt on fnl 2f) ....½ 4
Rose Chime (IRE) **(48)***(26) (MJohnston)* 3-7-13 TWilliams(8) (prom: 3rd & rdn st: sn btn) 11 5
Fools of Pride (IRE) **(60)***(14) (RHollinshead)* 3-8-11 LDettori(6) (lw: pushed along over 3f out: nvr trbld ldrs) 12 6
Tapping Feet **(54)***(3) (SirMarkPrescott)* 3-8-5 CNutter(1) (led over 4f: 6th & wkng st) 2½ 7
Blackpool Festival (IRE) **(55)***(—) (JBerry)* 3-8-6 GCarter(7) (lw: s.i.s: a bhd: eased fnl 2f) 25 8

9/4 Komreyev Dancer, **3/1** Nigel's Lad (IRE), **4/1** GRAND SELECTION (IRE), **5/1** Tapping Feet (4/1-8/1), **9/1** Water Bebe (IRE), **10/1** Rose Chime (IRE), Fools of Pride (IRE), **12/1** Blackpool Festival (IRE), CSF £14.46 CT £29.84 TOTE £4.20: £2.00 £1.10 £1.40 (£7.60) OWNER Mr M. B. Hawtin (NEWMARKET) BRED Mount Coote Stud in Ireland 8 Rn 1m 50.5 SF: 17/37/22/16/-/-/-/-

T/Plpt: £19.90 (617.67 Tckts). T/Qdpt: £56.90 (1.7 Tckts). Dk

0028-SOUTHWELL (L-H)
Monday January 9th (Standard)

48

KERRY (S) STKS (I) (3-Y.O) (Class G) £2,259.00 (£634.00: £309.00)
7f (Fibresand) GOING minus 0.07 sec per fur (STD) 12-15 (12-15)

High Flown (USA) (49)*(64) (MrsJRRamsden)* 3-9-0 JWeaver(9) (hdwy 5f out: led wl over 1f out: hrd rdn & sn clr: eased nr fin) ....— 1
33⁴ Samana Cay **(51)***(44) (DNicholls)* 3-9-2 AlexGreaves(2) (lw: bhd: hdwy over 2f out: styd on u.p: nrst fin) 10 2
Joyful Times **(43)***(37) (MrsNMacauley)* 3-8-4 (5) SSanders(4) (a.p: effrt over 2f out: one pce appr fnl f) ....s.h 3
Wings of Desire (IRE) **(43)***(39) (RChampion)* 3-9-0b LDettori(6) (cl up: led 3f out tl wl over 1f out: sn outpcd) 1½ 4
Daily Challenger (USA) **(60)***(33) (RonaldThompson)* 3-9-0 MFenton(3) (cl up tl outpcd after 2f: n.d after) 3 5
Reponist **(46)***(26) (MJCamacho)* 3-8-9v LCharnock(8) (led tl hdd 3f out: sn rdn & btn) 1 6
Sweet Mate *(28) (SRBowring)* 3-8-7 (7) CTeague(7) (prom tl wknd 2f out) 1¼ 7
David James' Girl **(60)***(30)*(Fav)*(ABailey)* 3-9-2 GCarter(5) (prom: pushed along ½-wy: hung lft: eased whn btn fnl f) ....s.h 8
Western Ploy *(—) (JLHarris)* 3-8-9 DaleGibson(10) (s.i.s: n.d) 13 9
Doulily *(—) (GHolmes)* 3-8-9 JQuinn(1) (bit bkwd: s.i.s: a bhd) 2 10

11/10 David James' Girl, **100/30** Samana Cay, **13/2** HIGH FLOWN (USA), Reponist, **15/2** Daily Challenger (USA), **14/1** Sweet Mate, **16/1** Wings of Desire (IRE), **20/1** Joyful Times, Western Ploy, Doulily, CSF £31.17 TOTE £5.40: £2.10 £1.70 £4.70 (£10.90) OWNER Mr M. R. Charlton (THIRSK) BRED Newgate Stud Farm Inc in USA 10 Rn 1m 34.0 (7.20) SF: 22/2/-/-/-/-/-/-/-/-
Sold R Thompson 4,200 gns

OFFICIAL EXPLANATION **David James' Girl is normally very fast out of the stalls, but on this occassion did not take hold of the bridle and was not travelling freely. The jockey added that when he let her down in the home straight, she began to hang badly to the left.**

49

TIPPERARY APP'CE H'CAP (I) (0-60) (Class F) £2,537.00 (£712.00: £347.00)
1m (Fibresand) GOING minus 0.07 sec per fur (STD) 12-45 (12-45)

King Parrot (IRE) (51)*(63) (LordHuntingdon)* 7-9-2 (5) JWilkinson(2) (w ldr: led 2f out: hld on wl) ....— 1
Glenvally **(43)***(55) (BWMurray)* 4-8-7b(5) CScudder(1) (led tl hdd 2f out: rallied to disp ld ins fnl f: no ex cl home) ....s.h 2
Early Star **(49)***(51) (KBishop)* 6-9-0b(5) LSuthern(9) (lost pl & bhd after 3f: r.o u.p fnl 2f) 5 3
Give In **(42)***(43) (MissGayKelleway)* 8-8-9 (3) AmandaSanders(6) (cl up: chal over 2f out: no ex fnl f) ....½ 4
1² Orthorhombus **(54)***(54)*(Fav)*(DJSCosgrove)* 6-9-10b MDwyer(4) (s.i.s: hdwy appr st: nt qckn fnl f) ....nk 5
32⁴ Bassetlaw Belle **(23)***(13) (NPLittmoden)* 6-7-7 CAdamson(8) (trckd ldrs: effrt over 2f out: sn rdn & btn) 5 6

Gallop to Glory **(38)***(20) (ALForbes)* 5-8-1 (7) RGordon(3) (b.hind: dwlt: a outpcd & bhd)....4 **7**
Bescaby Girl **(42)***(—) (JSWainwright)* 4-8-11b SKnott(5) (outpcd & lost tch ½-wy) 15 **8**
Lady Broker **(49)***(—) (ABailey)* 5-8-12 (7) AngelaGallimore(7) (prom tl outpcd ½-wy: sn no ch)....dist **9**

LONG HANDICAP Bassetlaw Belle 7-4

5/2 Orthorhombus, **7/2** KING PARROT (IRE), **5/1** Lady Broker, Give In, **10/1** Bassetlaw Belle, **12/1** Gallop to Glory, **16/1** Glenvally, Bescaby Girl, **20/1** Early Star, CSF £49.09 CT £888.00 TOTE £5.20: £1.70 £4.70 £6.40 (£61.60) OWNER Lord Huntingdon (WEST ILSLEY) BRED W. Hastings-Bass in Ireland 9 Rn 1m 47.5 (8.20) SF: 29/21/18/11/21/-/-/-/-

WEIGHT FOR AGE 4yo-1lb

50 TIPPERARY APP'CE H'CAP (II) (0-60) (Class F) £2,537.00 (£712.00: £347.00)
1m (Fibresand) GOING minus 0.07 sec per fur (STD) 1-15 (1-15)

28² **Genesis Four (37)***(47) (SRBowring)* 5-8-7b CAdamson(6) (chsd ldrs: led over 2f out: kpt on wl)....— **1**
Certain Way (IRE) **(53)***(57) (NPLittmoden)* 5-9-9 OliverCasey(1) (cl up: led over 3f out tl over 2f out: wknd ins fnl f)....3 **2**
Oozlem (IRE) **(34)***(34)*(Fav)*(RMFlower)* 6-8-4b SLanigan(9) (s.s: hdwy & prom ½-wy: nt qckn appr fnl f)....2 **3**
31⁵ Monsieur Petong **(47)***(42) (DNicholls)* 4-8-11 (5) AEddery(5) (trckd ldrs: effrt over 2f out: rdn & one pce)....2½ **4**
Derricks Refusal **(36)***(21) (CaptJWilson)* 4-7-12 (7)ow3 RGordon(2) (led tl hdd over 3f out: grad wknd)....5 **5**
4⁸ Comfortable **(35)***(13) (SGollings)* 5-8-0e(5) GinaFaulkner(7) (eyeshield: gd spd 5f: sn lost pl)....3½ **6**
Anorak (USA) **(58)***(26) (GMMoore)* 5-9-7 (7) JGracey(4) (sn bhd & drvn along: n.d)..5 **7**
T O O Mamma's (IRE) **(42)***(10) (JBerry)* 4-8-8 (3) PFessey(3) (rr div: hrd rdn 2f out: no imp)....hd **8**
Sav-Ed **(33)***(—) (APJarvis)* 6-8-3 MDwyer(8) (prom 4f: sn wknd & eased)....20 **9**

100/30 Oozlem (IRE), **7/2** GENESIS FOUR, **4/1** Certain Way (IRE), **5/1** Anorak (USA), **7/1** T O O Mamma's (IRE), Monsieur Petong, **16/1** Sav-Ed, **25/1** Comfortable, **33/1** Derricks Refusal, CSF £17.44 CT £46.23 TOTE £5.00: £1.10 £1.10 £1.80 (£6.70) OWNER Mrs M. Fanous (EDWINSTOWE) BRED Mrs C. P. Evans 9 Rn 1m 47.5 (8.20) SF: 16/25/4/10/-/-/-/-/-

WEIGHT FOR AGE 4yo-1lb

51 LIMERICK CLAIMING STKS (3-Y.O) (Class F) £2,537.00 (£712.00: £347.00)
1m (Fibresand) GOING minus 0.07 sec per fur (STD) 1-45 (1-45)

10⁴ **Poly Road (56)***(64) (MRChannon)* 3-8-4 CRutter(6) (a.p: slt ld 2f out: rdn & r.o wl)....— **1**
Inn At the Top **(62)***(68) (MJohnston)* 3-8-11 TWilliams(7) (lw: led after 3f to 2f out: rdn & r.o)....1¼ **2**
*25** Good so Fa (IRE) **(58)***(50)*(Fav)*(MHTompkins)* 3-8-4 (5) SMulvey(11) (in tch: effrt 3f out: no imp)....8 **3**
5⁴ Runforaction (IRE) **(56)***(39) (BSRothwell)* 3-8-1 ow1 MFenton(8) (in tch: rdn over 3f out: styd on: no imp)....1¼ **4**
Slapy Dam *(37) (MrsJRRamsden)* 3-8-9 JWeaver(2) (lw: trckd ldrs: rdn over 2f out: one pce)....5 **5**
Risky Rose **(43)***(25) (RHollinshead)* 3-7-11 (5) AGarth(5) (lw: in tch: effrt 3f out: no imp)....2½ **6**
5¹¹ Visual Illusion (IRE) *(9) (BSRothwell)* 3-7-10 JQuinn(10) (sn outpcd & bhd: n.d)....5 **7**
5⁷ Miss Suzy *(15) (JPLeigh)* 3-8-4 LCharnock(3) (w ldrs tl rdn & wknd 3f out)....1 **8**
Sweet Cheap Pet **(53)***(11) (JBerry)* 3-8-4 GCarter(1) (led 3f: cl up tl wknd over 2f out)....2 **9**
Sergio (IRE) *(—) (MCChapman)* 3-8-8 (5) DRMcCabe(4) (s.s: a bhd)....15 **10**
Pash **(42)***(—) (CWCElsey)* 3-7-12v DaleGibson(9) (outpcd & bhd fr ½-wy)....3 **11**

13/8 Good so Fa (IRE), **7/2** POLY ROAD, **5/1** Inn At the Top, **6/1** Slapy Dam, **8/1** Sweet Cheap Pet, **10/1** Runforaction (IRE), **16/1** Risky Rose, **20/1** Pash, **25/1** Sergio (IRE), **33/1** Visual Illusion (IRE), Miss Suzy, CSF £22.68 TOTE £4.50: £1.50 £1.60 £1.10 (£10.90) OWNER Sheet & Roll Convertors Ltd (LAMBOURN) BRED W. Beasley 11 Rn 1m 47.0 (7.70) SF: 18/23/6/-/-/-/-/-/-/-/-

52 KILDARE H'CAP (0-80) (Class D) £3,538.60 (£1,070.80: £522.40: £248.20)
1m 3f (Fibresand) GOING minus 0.07 sec per fur (STD) 2-15 (2-15)

Joseph's Wine (IRE) (75)*(86)*(Fav)*(DNicholls)* 6-9-9b AlexGreaves(7) (lw: trckd ldrs gng wl: led 2f out: shkn up & r.o wl)....— **1**

My Handy Man **(56)***(64) (RAllan)* 4-8-0 JQuinn(6) (in tch: qcknd to disp ld 2f out: sn hdd: r.o)........2½ 2
35[5] Non Vintage (IRE) **(63)***(60) (MCChapman)* 4-8-2b(5) DRMcCabe(3) (w ldr tl outpcd fnl 2f)........8 3
Tiger Shoot **(70)***(64) (DTThom)* 8-9-4 LDettori(2) (set str pce tl hdd 2f out: sn btn)........2½ 4
12[3] Sweet Supposin (IRE) **(72)***(64) (KMcAuliffe)* 4-9-2 RCochrane(1) (lw: cl up tl grad wknd fnl 2f)........1¾ 5
Charlie Bigtime **(53)***(43) (BJMcMath)* 5-8-1 AMackay(5) (dwlt: bhd tl hdwy 6f out: nvr nr to chal)........1¼ 6
Hillzah (USA) **(80)***(42) (RBastiman)* 7-9-9 (5) HBastiman(4) (in tch: rdn along 6f out: wknd appr st)........20 7

10/11 JOSEPH'S WINE (IRE), **5/1** Hillzah (USA), **11/2** Tiger Shoot, **7/1** Sweet Supposin (IRE), **12/1** Non Vintage (IRE), Charlie Bigtime, **20/1** My Handy Man, CSF £17.07 TOTE £2.10: £1.60 £4.70 (£33.40) OWNER Wetherby Racing Bureau Plc (THIRSK) BRED Michael Fennessy 7 Rn
2m 27.8 (6.30) SF: 68/43/38/45/42/26/23
WEIGHT FOR AGE 4yo-4lb

53

WATERFORD STKS (Mdn) (Class D) £3,690.70 (£1,117.60: £545.80: £259.90)
1m 4f (Fibresand) GOING minus 0.07 sec per fur (STD) 2-45 (2-46)

Thaleros (67)*(76) (GMMoore)* 5-9-3 LDettori(5) (sn prom: led 6f out: hld on wl fnl f)........— 1
Crown Prosecutor *(75)*(Fav)*(WRMuir)* 5-9-3 JWeaver(3) (b: b.hind: trckd ldrs gng wl: chal over 1f out: wandered u.p: nt qckn)........¾ 2
Handmaiden *(64) (JLEyre)* 5-8-12 TIves(12) (lw: bhd: hdwy after 5f: sn prom: effrt over 2f out: r.o one pce)........5 3
Tristan's Comet **(38)***(66) (JLHarris)* 8-8-12 (5) NVarley(7) (outpcd & bhd: hdwy 5f out: styd on one pce appr fnl f)........2½ 4
All on *(49) (JHetherton)* 4-8-7 NCarlisle(11) (bhd: effrt over 4f out: styd on: no imp)........10 5
3[8] Betty Kenwood **(44)***(37) (MrsJRRamsden)* 5-8-12 SWilliams(13) (hdwy 7f out: sn rdn: one pce fnl 4f)........10 6
19[6] Soneeto *(40) (DRLaing)* 9-9-3 GBardwell(14) (prom tl rdn & no imp fnl 2½f)........1½ 7
4[2] Uckerby Lad **(35)***(39) (NPLittmoden)* 4-8-7 (5) TGMcLaughlin(8) (outpcd 6f out: n.d after)........¾ 8
Zaaheyah (USA) **(38)***(29) (MDHammond)* 5-8-12v GCarter(6) (in tch: drvn along 5f out: sn btn)........4 9
2[9] Asmarina *(16) (SRBowring)* 5-8-5 (7) CTeague(10) (bhd: effrt 5f out: n.d)........11 10
Cut Adrift **(73)***(15) (MRChannon)* 4-8-7 CRutter(9) (in tch: effrt 4f out: wknd over 2f out)........½ 11
King of Show (IRE) **(70)***(11) (RAllan)* 4-8-12 RCochrane(4) (led 3f: cl up tl wknd 3f out)........7 12
Hay Dance **(45)***(—) (JPLeigh)* 4-8-7 (5) JStack(2) (led 9f out to 6f out: wknd qckly)20 13
Homebeforemidnight *(—) (RHollinshead)* 4-8-0 (7) RGordon(1) (rdn & wknd after 4f: wl t.o)........dist 14

2/1 Crown Prosecutor (7/4-3/1), **100/30** THALEROS, **11/2** Handmaiden, **7/1** Cut Adrift, **8/1** King of Show (IRE), **14/1** All on, **16/1** Asmarina, Uckerby Lad, **20/1** Betty Kenwood, Tristan's Comet, Zaaheyah (USA), **33/1** Homebeforemidnight, Hay Dance, **50/1** Soneeto,CSF £11.21 TOTE £3.80: £2.10 £1.20 £2.50 (£7.90) OWNER Mr M. Gleason (MIDDLEHAM) BRED A.Christodoulou 14 Rn
2m 43.8 (9.60) SF: 45/44/33/34/13/5/7/2/-/-/-/-/-/-
WEIGHT FOR AGE 4yo-5lb

54

KERRY (S) STKS (II) (3-Y.O) (Class G) £2,259.00 (£634.00: £309.00)
7f (Fibresand) GOING minus 0.07 sec per fur (STD) 3-15 (3-19)

47[4] **Water Bebe (IRE) (53)***(66+)*(Fav)*(GCBravery)* 3-9-2 TIves(9) (unruly gng to s: sn prom: led over 2f out: qcknd: comf)........— 1
5[5] Bretton Princess **(50)***(52) (RHollinshead)* 3-8-9 LDettori(2) (a.p: effrt over 2f out: kpt on: nt pce of wnr)........3½ 2
5[3] Pc's Cruiser (IRE) *(53) (MCChapman)* 3-8-9 (5) DRMcCabe(1) (hld up: effrt appr st: hrd rdn appr fnl f: no ex)........2 3
Needwood Newt **(50)***(45) (BAMcMahon)* 3-8-9 GBardwell(6) (cl up: led 4f out tl over 2f out: sn btn)........1¼ 4
Tyreless (IRE) **(42)***(41) (APJarvis)* 3-8-4 (5) NVarley(3) (in tch: sn drvn along: styd on fnl 2f: no imp)........1¾ 5

Lotties Bid *(28) (PSFelgate)* 3-8-9 AMackay(7) (s.s: hdwy on outside appr st: sn btn)....6 **6**
Travel Out *(20) (MrsMReveley)* 3-8-9 JQuinn(4) (prom tl rdn & wknd 2f out)....4 **7**
Wendy's Way **(53)***(14) (JBerry)* 3-9-2 GCarter(5) (led 3f: wknd over 2f out)....6 **8**
Benten **(50)***(—) (DNicholls)* 3-8-9 AlexGreaves(8) (chsd ldrs tl wknd & eased fnl 2½f)....20 **9**

85/40 WATER BEBE (IRE) (6/4-9/4), **7/2** Pc's Cruiser (IRE), **9/2** Travel Out, **6/1** Wendy's Way, **9/1** Benten, **10/1** Bretton Princess, **12/1** Needwood Newt, **16/1** Lotties Bid, **33/1** Tyreless (IRE), CSF £22.91 TOTE £2.70: £1.30 £3.50 £1.40 (£12.50) OWNER Mr G. C. Bravery (NEWMARKET) BRED Maple Bloodstock 9 Rn No bid 1m 33.8 (7.00) SF: 26/12/13/6/4/-/-/-/-

OFFICIAL EXPLANATION **Benten returned with a cut on her near-fore.**

55

WICKLOW H'CAP (0-70) (Class E) £3,009.60 (£910.80: £444.40: £211.20)
7f (Fibresand) GOING minus 0.07 sec per fur (STD) 3-45 (3-46)

44[7] **Quinzii Martin (40)***(52+) (DHaydnJones)* 7-7-12 TWilliams(11) (a.p: led 2f out: rdn & r.o)....— **1**
Sharp Imp **(47)***(48)*(Fav)*(RMFlower)* 5-8-5b LDettori(3) (hld up: hdwy over 2f out: hung lft fnl f: nt r.o)....5 **2**
20[4] Aljaz **(56)***(56) (DTThom)* 5-9-0 AMackay(10) (b: cl up: led over 2f out: sn hdd & grad wknd)....½ **3**
*2** Super Benz **(65)***(64) (FJO'Mahony)* 9-9-9 6x GCarter(1) (b: hld up & bhd: effrt & nt clr run over 2f out: swtchd & styd on)....½ **4**
Aquado **(38)***(26) (ALForbes)* 6-7-10 NAdams(4) (lw: led tl hdd over 2f out: sn btn)..5 **5**
1[3] Sandmoor Denim **(70)***(57) (SRBowring)* 8-9-7 (7) GStrange(9) (b: lw: in tch: hdwy appr st: rdn & btn over 1f out)....½ **6**
Black Boy (IRE) **(40)***(23) (RFMarvin)* 6-7-12b JQuinn(6) (lw: a outpcd & bhd)....2 **7**
Efficacy **(39)***(18) (APJarvis)* 4-7-6 (5)ow3 NVarley(7) (bhd: hdwy on outside appr st: sn btn)....2 **8**
Cledeschamps **(44)***(12) (MWEllerby)* 6-7-9 (7) ClaireBalding(2) (in tch tl outpcd fnl 2f)....5 **9**
Grey Toppa **(56)***(13) (MrsJRRamsden)* 4-9-0 JWeaver(5) (cl up tl wknd over 2f out)5 **10**
6[4] Faez **(65)***(21) (PSFelgate)* 5-9-9 TIves(8) (b.hind: lost tch fnl 2½f)....½ **11**

9/4 Sharp Imp, **3/1** Aljaz, **5/1** Sandmoor Denim, **11/2** Super Benz, **8/1** Grey Toppa, Faez, **10/1** QUINZII MARTIN, **14/1** Aquado, **20/1** Black Boy (IRE), **25/1** Cledeschamps, **33/1** Efficacy, CSF £36.02 CT £85.27 TOTE £10.30: £2.90 £1.40 £1.90 (£22.40) OWNER Monolithic Refractories Ltd (PONTYPRIDD) BRED Lord Fairhaven 11 Rn 1m 32.3 (5.50) SF: 26/21/29/36/-/28/-/-/-/-/-

T/Plpt £95.70 (91.84 Tckts). T/Qdpt: £3.10 (11.1 Tckts). AA

0036-LINGFIELD (L-H)
Tuesday January 10th (Standard)

56

WARSPITE H'CAP (I) (0-65) (Class F) £2,713.40 (£762.40: £372.20)
1m (Equitrack) GOING minus 0.45 sec per fur (FST) 1-00 (1-01)

*12** **Kinnegad Kid (46)***(54+)*(Fav)*(RIngram)* 6-8-9 (3) 6x DWright(9) (a.p: led over 3f out: rdn over 1f out: r.o wl)....— **1**
41[6] Eastleigh **(47)***(47) (RHollinshead)* 6-8-13 LDettori(8) (lw: a.p: chsd wnr over 3f out: ev ch over 2f out: unable qckn)....4 **2**
26[5] Chili Lady **(40)***(37) (JSMoore)* 5-8-1 (5)ow1 SDrowne(4) (lw: a.p: rdn over 4f out: r.o one pce fnl f)....1½ **3**
Zinbaq **(41)***(32) (CJBenstead)* 9-8-7 TWilliams(5) (a.p: rdn 4f out: one pce fnl 2f)....3 **4**
The Little Ferret **(62)***(51) (GLMoore)* 5-10-0 AMorris(3) (hld up: rdn over 2f out: one pce)....¾ **5**
Swallow Ridge (IRE) **(35)***(23) (RJO'Sullivan)* 6-8-1 DBiggs(2) (rdn over 4f out: hdwy over 2f out: one pce)....½ **6**
*39** Myjinka **(34)***(17) (JO'Donoghue)* 5-7-7b(7) 6x IonaWands(7) (a bhd)....2½ **7**
Pair of Jacks (IRE) **(45)***(20) (DAWilson)* 5-8-11 GCarter(6) (a bhd)....4 **8**
Great Hall **(58)***(29) (PDCundell)* 6-9-10 JWilliams(10) (bit bkwd: a bhd)....1¾ **9**
32[5] Arrasas Lady **(40)***(—) (RMFlower)* 5-8-6b StephenDavies(1) (led over 4f)....7 **10**

1/2 KINNEGAD KID, **8/1** Swallow Ridge (IRE), **12/1** Eastleigh, Myjinka, **16/1** Chili Lady, Zinbaq, **20/1** The Little Ferret, Great Hall, **25/1** Pair of Jacks (IRE), Arrasas Lady, CSF £8.31 CT £48.36 TOTE £1.50: £1.10 £2.00 £3.50 (£4.70) OWNER Mr J. B. Wilcox (EPSOM) BRED Airlie Stud and Miss K. Rausing 10 Rn 1m 39.63 (3.23) SF: 26/20/11/6/23/-/-/-/-/-

57 VICTORY MEDIAN AUCTION STKS (Mdn 3-Y.O) (Class F) £2,675.60 (£751.60: £366.80) **5f (Equitrack)** GOING minus 0.45 sec per fur (FST) 1-30 (1-31)

Bon Secret (IRE) (60)*(57) (TJNaughton)* 3-8-9 (5) SSanders(5) (lw: mde all: rdn over 2f out: all out) ....— **1**
Merrie le Bow *(51) (PMitchell)* 3-8-9 JMcLaughlin(6) (a.p: rdn over 1f out: r.o wl ins fnl f) ....nk **2**
Avant Huit **(55)***(50) (MrsNMacauley)* 3-8-9v JWeaver(4) (lw: chsd wnr: hrd rdn over 1f out: unable qckn ins fnl f) ....hd **3**
Fiveaday *(53)*(Fav)*(BHanbury)* 3-9-0 MRimmer(3) (lw: rdn over 3f out: hdwy over 2f out: r.o wl ins fnl f) ....½ **4**
10⁸ Jemthorn Bishop **(52)***(35) (JJBridger)* 3-9-0b TWilliams(2) (a bhd) 6 **5**
Kings of Canvey Is *(—) (JWhite)* 3-8-9 JWilliams(1) (a bhd) 15 **6**

7/4 Fiveaday, **2/1** BON SECRET (IRE), **11/4** Avant Huit, **8/1** Merrie le Bow, **25/1** Kings of Canvey Is, **33/1** Jemthorn Bishop, CSF £16.00 TOTE £3.10: £1.30 £4.60 (£17.60) OWNER Mr F.R. Jackman (EPSOM) BRED Sean Mc Donnell in Ireland 6 Rn 60.22 secs (2.02) SF: 26/21/20/23/3
STEWARDS' ENQUIRY Weaver suspended 19-20/1/95 (excessive use of whip).

58 HOOD (S) H'CAP (0-60) (Class G) £2,449.40 (£688.40: £336.20) **1m 5f (Equitrack)** GOING minus 0.45 sec per fur (FST) 2-00 (2-01)

Carlowitz (USA) (53)*(61) (AMoore)* 7-9-13 CandyMorris(8) (b: hld up: led over 3f out: clr over 2f out: unchal) ....— **1**
Dancing Diamond (IRE) **(44)***(30)*(Fav)*(MissBSanders)* 5-8-13hv(5) SSanders(10) (a.p: led over 5f out tl over 3f out: unable qckn) 10 **2**
22³ Malingerer **(30)***(22)*(Fav)*(DAWilson)* 4-7-13 NGwilliams(7) (b.hind: hld up: rdn over 4f out: one pce) 3½ **3**
Super Assignation (IRE) **(58)***(42) (DRCElsworth)* 4-9-13 JWilliams(9) (lw: rdn over 8f out: hdwy wl over 1f out: nvr nrr) 7 **4**
Tokanda **(21)***(—) (FJYardley)* 11-7-2 (7)ow1 MBaird(11) (nvr nr to chal) 9 **5**
Feeling Foolish (IRE) **(28)***(2) (BForsey)* 6-7-9v(7) SLanigan(1) (b.off hind: nvr nrr)..hd **6**
Cristal Springs **(31)***(4) (BJMcMath)* 4-8-0 GBardwell(3) (b.off hind: a mid div) ....½ **7**
28¹¹ Charlistiona **(35)***(8) (MJohnston)* 4-8-4 TWilliams(5) (led over 7f) ....hd **8**
Highland Flame **(34)***(—) (KTIvory)* 6-8-8 JQuinn(6) (bhd fnl 2f) 10 **9**
Rita's Joy **(40)***(—) (WGMTurner)* 4-8-9 RPerham(2) (a bhd) 5 **10**
Princerullah **(42)***(—) (CDBroad)* 4-8-11b MFenton(4) (prom 8f: t.o) ....dist **11**

5/2 Dancing Diamond (IRE), Malingerer, **8/1** Super Assignation (IRE), Rita's Joy, **9/1** CARLOWITZ (USA), **12/1** Cristal Springs, **14/1** Feeling Foolish (IRE), Charlistiona, **25/1** Highland Flame, Princerullah, **33/1** Tokanda, CSF £30.70 CT £68.89 TOTE £5.20: £3.90 £1.00 £2.10 (£11.70) OWNER Mr K. Higson (BRIGHTON) BRED John C. and Mrs Mabee 11 Rn No bid
2m 49.65 (7.15) SF: 32/3/-/8/-/-/-/-/-/-/-
WEIGHT FOR AGE 4yo-5lb

59 DAILY STAR AWT 1M 2F CHALLENGE SERIES H'CAP (Qualifier) (3-Y.O) (0-75) (Class D) £3,881.45 (£1,175.60: £574.30: £273.65) **1m 2f (Equitrack)** GOING minus 0.45 sec per fur (FST) 2-30 (2-31)

47³ **Nigel's Lad (IRE) (60)***(66)*(Fav)*(PCHaslam)* 3-8-7 JWeaver(7) (hld up: chsd ldr over 4f out: led over 1f out: rdn out) ....— **1**
Persian Conquest (IRE) **(53)***(53) (RIngram)* 3-7-11 (3) DWright(2) (rdn over 4f out: hdwy 2f out: r.o wl ins fnl f) 4 **2**
What's the Verdict (IRE) **(74)***(71)*(Fav)*(MJohnston)* 3-9-7 TWilliams(4) (lw: led over 4f: rdn over 4f out: r.o one pce) 2 **3**
Star Fighter **(64)***(60)*(Fav)*(WAO'Gorman)* 3-8-8 (3) EmmaO'Gorman(10) (lw: hdwy over 8f out: led over 5f out tl over 1f out: one pce) ....½ **4**
Mo's Main Man (IRE) **(55)***(46) (SDow)* 3-7-11 (5)ow4 AWhelan(1) (nvr nr to chal) ...3½ **5**
Elite Number (USA) **(55)***(45) (PFICole)* 3-8-2 CRutter(3) (rdn over 4f out: no hdwy fnl 3f) ....¾ **6**
25⁴ Tachycardia **(56)***(37) (RJO'Sullivan)* 3-8-3 DBiggs(9) (nvr nrr) 6 **7**
Soldier's Leap (FR) **(70)***(50) (CEBrittain)* 3-9-3 BDoyle(11) (lw: hdwy 7f out: wknd 3f out) ....nk **8**
Mrs Tigger **(55)***(33) (RWArmstrong)* 3-8-2 JQuinn(8) (bhd fnl 4f) 1¼ **9**
Shy Paddy (IRE) **(64)***(39) (KOCunningham-Brown)* 3-8-11 LDettori(5) (lw: prom over 5f) 1¾ **10**
Kindred Greeting **(55)***(29) (DMorris)* 3-8-2 StephenDavies(6) (bit bkwd: a bhd) ....½ **11**

9/2 NIGEL'S LAD (IRE), What's the Verdict (IRE), Star Fighter, **11/2** Shy Paddy (IRE), **6/1** Elite Number (USA), **7/1** Mo's Main Man (IRE), **8/1** Persian Conquest (IRE), **10/1** Soldier's Leap (FR), **12/1** Tachycardia, **20/1** Mrs Tigger, **33/1** Kindred Greeting, CSF £41.54 CT £164.44 TOTE £3.30: £1.80 £3.00 £2.30 (£20.80) OWNER Mr N. C. Dunnington (MIDDLEHAM) BRED Nikita Investments 11 Rn 2m 9.36 (6.36) SF: 6/-/10/-/-/-/-/-/-/-/-

OFFICIAL EXPLANATION **Shy Paddy showed no interest when headed. The trainer stated that on his next outing he would be fitted with either blinkers or a visor.**

60

RENOWN CLAIMING STKS (3-Y.O) (Class E) £3,009.60 (£910.80: £444.40: £211.20) **7f (Equitrack)** GOING minus 0.45 sec per fur (FST) 3-00 (3-00)

Gulf Shaadi (78)*(74)*(Fav)*(CEBrittain)* 3-8-13 BDoyle(4) (lw: a.p: rdn over 2f out: led over 1f out: r.o wl) — **1**
Sandra Dee (IRE) **(58)***(55) (BAPearce)* 3-7-11 (5) AWhelan(3) (lw: a.p: led 3f out tl over 1f out: unable qckn) 4 **2**
Robo Magic (USA) **(69)***(56) (AMoore)* 3-8-7b LDettori(2) (b.hind: led 4f: one pce fnl 2f) 1¾ **3**
Star Information **(45)***(30) (JSMoore)* 3-7-10 NAdams(1) (lw: a bhd) 7 **4**
Bills Ploughgirl **(38)***(—) (JSMoore)* 3-7-9b(3) DWright(5) (prom over 3f) 15 **5**

4/5 GULF SHAADI, **9/4** Robo Magic (USA), **9/2** Sandra Dee (IRE), **25/1** Star Information, **50/1** Bills Ploughgirl, CSF £4.57 TOTE £1.70: £1.10 £2.10 (£2.20) OWNER Mr C. E. Brittain (NEWMARKET) BRED Sheikh Mohammed bin Rashid al Maktoum 5 Rn 1m 27.25 (4.25) SF: 10/-/-/-/-

61

REPULSE H'CAP (0-80) (Class D) £3,606.20 (£1,091.60: £532.80: £253.40) **6f (Equitrack)** GOING minus 0.45 sec per fur (FST) 3-30 (3-30)

Silent Expression (78)*(86) (BJMeehan)* 5-10-0 RCochrane(1) (hld up: led over 1f out: rdn out) — **1**
23* Pageboy **(69)***(69)*(Fav)*(PCHaslam)* 6-9-5 7x JWeaver(3) (sddle slipped s: hld up: rdn 2f out: r.o one pce) 3 **2**
Spender **(74)***(68) (PWHarris)* 6-9-10 LDettori(5) (chsd ldr over 4f out: led over 2f out tl over 1f out: one pce) 2½ **3**
Forgotten Dancer (IRE) **(60)***(34) (RIngram)* 4-8-10 WWoods(2) (lw: a bhd) 8 **4**
23[6] Thorny Bishop **(70)***(26) (JJBridger)* 4-9-6 TWilliams(4) (led over 3f) 7 **5**

5/6 Pageboy, **11/4** Spender, **4/1** SILENT EXPRESSION, **14/1** Forgotten Dancer (IRE), **33/1** Thorny Bishop, CSF £7.56 TOTE £5.50: £1.70 £1.50 (£2.40) OWNER Mr A. S. Reid (UPPER LAMBOURN) BRED J. B. H. Stevens 5 Rn 1m 12.76 (2.16) SF: 43/27/25/-/-

62

WARSPITE H'CAP (II) (0-65) (Class F) £2,700.80 (£758.80: £370.40) **1m (Equitrack)** GOING minus 0.45 sec per fur (FST) 4-00 (4-01)

Dome Patrol (45)*(50) (WRMuir)* 4-8-10 JWeaver(8) (a.p: led & edgd lft over 2f out: clr over 1f out: rdn out) — **1**
A Million Watts **(60)***(63)*(Fav)*(LadyHerries)* 4-9-11 TIves(1) (hld up: rdn over 3f out: r.o wl ins fnl f) ¾ **2**
Hi Penny **(41)***(41) (KTIvory)* 4-8-6b DBiggs(3) (a.p: rdn over 3f out: bmpd over 2f out: unable qckn) 1¼ **3**
12[4] Hawaii Storm (FR) **(57)***(52) (MissAJWhitfield)* 7-9-4 (5) RPainter(2) (lw: hdwy over 1f out: nvr nrr) 2½ **4**
Pigalle Wonder **(38)***(27) (RJO'Sullivan)* 7-8-4b WWoods(9) (w ldr over 4f: wkng whn n.m.r over 2f out) 3 **5**
Main Brace **(46)***(34) (KRBurke)* 4-8-11 RCochrane(7) (lw: nvr nr to chal) nk **6**
Possibility **(43)***(29) (RIngram)* 4-8-5b(3) DWright(6) (stdd s: hdwy over 3f out: wknd over 2f out) 1 **7**
12[10] Breckland (IRE) **(45)***(9) (KOCunningham-Brown)* 5-8-11 BDoyle(4) (led over 5f) 11 **8**
Panchellita (USA) **(58)***(19) (GLMoore)* 6-9-3 (7) LSuthern(5) (a bhd) 1¼ **9**

9/4 A Million Watts, **3/1** Hawaii Storm (FR), Possibility, **10/1** Panchellita (USA), DOME PATROL, **16/1** Pigalle Wonder, Main Brace, **20/1** Breckland (IRE), **33/1** Hi Penny, CSF £31.74 CT £668.13 TOTE £14.20: £1.10 £2.30 £6.80 (£28.90) OWNER Mr Duncan Wiltshire (LAMBOURN) BRED Mrs M. Chaworth Musters 9 Rn 1m 40.07 (3.67) SF: 20/33/14/25/2/7/3/-/-
WEIGHT FOR AGE 4yo-1lb

T/Plpt: £17.00 (625.99 Tckts). T/Qdpt: £28.00 (4.5 Tckts). AK

0042-**WOLVERHAMPTON (L-H)**
Wednesday January 11th (Standard)

63 BASIL (S) STKS (I) (Class F) £2,537.00 (£712.00: £347.00)
1m 100y (Fibresand) GOING: minus 0.18 sec per fur (Std) 1-30 (1-30)

*21** **Eqtesaad (USA) (60)***(66)*(Fav)*(SCWilliams)* 4-9-4 TIves(11) (a gng wl: led wl over 2f out: easily) .....— **1**
2[7] Perilous Plight **(63)***(55) (WRMuir)* 4-8-13 JWeaver(2) (hld up & bhd: gd hdwy 4f out: wnt 2nd st: no imp) 3 **2**
Alpine Johnny **(57)***(49) (RHollinshead)* 4-8-8 (5) AGarth(4) (hdwy over 3f out: 6th st: r.o one pce fnl f) 3 **3**
Zahran (IRE) **(60)***(46) (JMBradley)* 4-8-13 LCharnock(6) (b: led 4f: led over 3f out tl wl over 2f out: 3rd st: wknd 1f out) 1¼ **4**
2[8] Ballad Dancer **(43)***(44) (JMackie)* 10-9-0 GCarter(5) (bhd: hdwy & 7th st: styd on fnl f: nvr nrr) .....¾ **5**
Cyprus Point **(64)***(31) (GHEden)* 4-8-8 JQuinn(8) (prom: 5th st: wknd over 1f out) ..4 **6**
Fashionable Dancer **(28)***(33) (CEBrittain)* 5-9-0b BDoyle(9) (w ldr: led over 4f out tl over 3f out: wknd over 1f out) 1½ **7**
Buckley Boys **(42)***(22) (ABailey)* 4-8-5b(3) DWright(3) (mid div: bhd fnl 3f) 3 **8**
Aragona *(12) (PDCundell)* 6-8-9 JWilliams(7) (prom 5f) 5 **9**
Dissident Dancer **(32)***(3) (JHPeacock)* 6-9-0 TWall(1) (a bhd) 7 **10**
Princess Shera (IRE) **(41)***(—) (EJAlston)* 4-8-3b(5) JStack(10) (hld up & plld hrd: sn mid div: bhd fnl 4f: t.o) 10 **11**

11/8 EQTESAAD (USA), **5/2** Alpine Johnny, **11/2** Perilous Plight, **10/1** Zahran (IRE), Buckley Boys, **14/1** Cyprus Point, **16/1** Princess Shera (IRE), **25/1** Fashionable Dancer, Ballad Dancer, **33/1** Aragona, **50/1** Dissident Dancer, CSF £10.44 TOTE £2.60: £1.10 £3.10 £1.70 (£16.70) OWNER Miss L. J. Ward (NEWMARKET) BRED Shadwell Estate Co Ltd & Shadwell Farm Inc in USA 11 Rn Bt in 9,200 gns 1m 50.5 SF: 35/25/20/18/18/5/8/-/-/-/-
WEIGHT FOR AGE 4yo-1lb

64 JAMUNA STKS (Mdn 3-Y.O) (Class D) £3,741.40 (£1,133.20: £553.60: £263.80) **7f (Fibresand)** GOING: minus 0.18 sec per fur (Std) 2-00 (2-02)

Montanelli (FR) *(64)*(Fav)*(KMcAuliffe)* 3-9-0 RCochrane(10) (w ldrs: 2nd st: led 1f out: rdn out) .....— **1**
Bold Effort (FR) **(65)***(63) (KOCunningham-Brown)* 3-9-0 JWeaver(4) (led: rdn 2f out: hdd 1f out: r.o wl) .....½ **2**
Jalmaid **(45)***(47) (BAMcMahon)* 3-8-4 (5) SSanders(5) (w ldrs: ev ch 2f out: 3rd st: one pce) 5 **3**
Almuhtaram **(78)***(44)*(Fav)*(WWHaigh)* 3-9-0 DaleGibson(9) (bit bkwd: chsd ldrs: rdn over 3f out: 5th st: one pce) 4 **4**
Logie *(33) (MAJarvis)* 3-9-0 WWoods(6) (prom: 4th & wkng st) 5 **5**
Lawnswood Lady **(48)***(25) (RHollinshead)* 3-8-9 LDettori(2) (prom over 3f) 1½ **6**
Concer Un *(27) (SCWilliams)* 3-9-0 GCarter(3) (unf: s.i.s: plld hrd: mid div whn rn wd bnd over 2f out: sn bhd) 1½ **7**
Inchkeith *(19)*(Fav)*(GWragg)* 3-8-2 (7) DGibbs(7) (neat: lw: a bhd) 1¼ **8**
Sand Star *(16) (DHaydnJones)* 3-8-9 AMackay(1) (neat: s.s: gd hdwy 4f out: 6th & wkng st) 1¼ **9**
Crocodile Rock *(—) (MJHeaton-Ellis)* 3-9-0 StephenDavies(8) (unf: lw: s.s: a bhd: t.o) 10 **10**

7/2 MONTANELLI (FR), Inchkeith, Almuhtaram, **4/1** Bold Effort (FR), **9/2** Logie, **8/1** Lawnswood Lady, **10/1** Crocodile Rock, **12/1** Jalmaid, **25/1** Concer Un, **33/1** Sand Star, CSF £20.52 TOTE £3.20: £2.00 £1.90 £1.70 (£7.70) OWNER Delamere Cottage Racing Syndicate (LAMBOURN) BRED Crest Stud Ltd in France 10 Rn 1m 29.6 (5.60) SF: 28/27/11/7/-/-/-/-/-/-

65 BAILEY CLAIMING STKS £2,537.00 (£712.00: £347.00)
6f (Fibresand) GOING: minus 0.18 sec per fur (Std) 2-30 (2-30)

Lift Boy (USA) (57)*(66) (AMoore)* 6-9-3 CandyMorris(3) (b: a.p: 2nd st: led wl over 1f out: r.o wl) .....— **1**
Sea Devil **(69)***(66) (MJCamacho)* 9-9-4 LCharnock(5) (sn pushed along: chsd ldrs: 3rd st: hrd rdn over 1f out: ev ch fnl f: r.o wl) .....hd **2**
Frisky Miss (IRE) **(67)***(66) (JBerry)* 4-9-5 GCarter(7) (lw: led over 4f: ev ch ins fnl f: r.o) .....hd **3**

16^{2} Walk the Beat **(69)***(65)*(Fav)*(RSimpson)* 5-9-1 (5) SDrowne(2) (a.p: 4th st: ev ch over 1f out: nt qckn ins fnl f)....½ **4**
Arc Lamp **(52)***(56) (JAGlover)* 9-8-9 (7) MrSRichardson(9) (hld up: gd hdwy fnl f: fin wl)....2 **5**
6^{6} Green's Bid **(61)***(57) (DWChapman)* 5-9-5 AlexGreaves(8) (prom: 6th st: no hdwy)½ **6**
Rossini Blue **(76)***(56) (RHannon)* 4-9-8 LDettori(4) (prom: 5th st: wknd over 1f out)....1½ **7**
Sison (IRE) **(68)***(48) (KGWingrove)* 5-9-4 JMcLaughlin(13) (hld up: 7th st: no hdwy)....1½ **8**
So Intrepid (IRE) **(62)***(44) (JMBradley)* 5-9-4 RCochrane(11) (b: bhd fnl 2f)....1½ **9**
Arawa **(49)***(34) (DMarks)* 5-9-0 (7) MBaird(6) (hld up: hmpd after 1f: sn bhd)....5 **10**
Caherass Court (IRE) **(62)***(24) (BPreece)* 4-8-13 JWeaver(1) (hld up: hdwy 4f out: wknd 3f out)....½ **11**
Bessie's Will *(—) (DHaydnJones)* 4-8-13 AMackay(12) (a bhd: t.o)....12 **12**
16^{7} Woodlands Electric **(18)***(—) (PAPritchard)* 5-9-0v NAdams(10) (spd over 2f: t.o)....5 **13**

2/1 Walk the Beat (3/1-7/4), **7/2** Frisky Miss (IRE), **4/1** Rossini Blue, **5/1** Sea Devil, **8/1** Caherass Court (IRE), **10/1** Green's Bid, **12/1** So Intrepid (IRE), **14/1** Arc Lamp, **16/1** Sison (IRE), Arawa, **20/1** LIFT BOY (USA), **33/1** Bessie's Will, Woodlands Electric, CSF £131.89 TOTE £138.40: £12.60 £2.00 £1.90 (£116.10) OWNER Mr A. Moore (BRIGHTON) BRED Paul & Arnold Bryant in USA 13 Rn
1m 15.3 (4.10) SF: 39/40/40/40/31/32/31/-/-/-/-/-/-
Rossini Blue clmd A Bailey £6,000. Frisky Miss (IRE) clmd K Cunningham-Brown £7,000.

66

JAFFA H'CAP (0-90) (Class C) £5,706.00 (£1,728.00: £844.00: £402.00)
1m 1f 79y (Fibresand) GOING: minus 0.18 sec per fur (Std) 3-00 (3-01)

*8** **South Eastern Fred (72)***(86)*(Fav)*(HJCollingridge)* 4-8-8 5x MRimmer(1) (a gng wl: qcknd to ld 2f out: sn clr: drvn out)....— **1**
Chatham Island **(90)***(97) (CEBrittain)* 7-10-0 BDoyle(3) (led 1f: 3rd st: r.o one pce).4 **2**
Northern Celadon (IRE) **(72)***(76) (MJHeaton-Ellis)* 4-8-8 StephenDavies(7) (lw: led after 1f to 2f out: 2nd st: one pce)....1¾ **3**
18^{4} Bentico **(70)***(72) (MrsNMacauley)* 6-8-3 (5) SSanders(11) (lw: hld up: hdwy over 4f out: rdn over 3f out: 5th st: one pce)....1½ **4**
31^{4} Brackenthwaite **(77)***(77) (LRLloyd-James)* 5-9-1b JWeaver(12) (hld up & bhd: c stands' side st: hdwy fnl f: nvr nrr)....1½ **5**
Second Chance (IRE) **(82)***(80) (PMitchell)* 5-9-6 LDettori(8) (a.p: 4th st: wknd over 1f out)....1½ **6**
Mentalasanythin **(72)***(64) (ABailey)* 6-8-10 AMackay(4) (prom tl wknd over 2f out)....3½ **7**
Metal Storm (FR) **(88)***(78) (KOCunningham-Brown)* 7-9-12 RCochrane(5) (chsd ldrs: 6th st: wknd over 1f out)....1 **8**
Dubai Falcon (USA) **(65)***(48) (RDickin)* 4-8-1 CRutter(13) (lw: plld hrd: hdwy 6f out: wknd 3f out)....4 **9**
Nick the Biscuit **(72)***(54) (MDIUsher)* 4-8-1 (7) CAdamson(9) (b: a bhd)....½ **10**
Palacegate Jo (IRE) **(59)***(39) (RHollinshead)* 4-7-9 ow1 JQuinn(10) (bhd fnl 4f)....1 **11**
One Off the Rail (USA) **(81)***(58) (AMoore)* 5-9-5 CandyMorris(6) (lw: bhd fnl 4f)...1¾ **12**
Rainbow Walk (IRE) **(88)***(65) (JGMO'Shea)* 5-9-7 (5) JStack(2) (a bhd)....hd **13**

5/2 SOUTH EASTERN FRED, **4/1** Chatham Island, **6/1** Northern Celadon (IRE), Bentico, **7/1** Second Chance (IRE), **10/1** Brackenthwaite, Mentalasanythin, Metal Storm (FR), **12/1** Rainbow Walk (IRE), **14/1** Palacegate Jo (IRE), **20/1** Dubai Falcon (USA), **25/1** One Off the Rail (USA), Nick the Biscuit, CSF £15.27 CT £57.25 TOTE £3.60: £2.00 £2.90 £1.10 (£14.40) OWNER South Eastern Electrical Plc (NEWMARKET) BRED L. Audus 13 Rn
2m 0.2 (4.20) SF: 52/64/43/41/45/48/32/-/-/-/-/-/-
WEIGHT FOR AGE 4yo-2lb

67

JERICHO H'CAP (0-75) (Class E) £4,279.50 (£1,296.00: £633.00: £301.50)
1m 6f 166y (Fibresand) GOING: minus 0.18 sec per fur (Std) 3-30 (3-30)

*3** **Argyle Cavalier (IRE) (68)***(74)*(Fav)*(MJohnston)* 5-9-0 (7) 4x OliverCasey(3) (a.p: rdn to ld over 2f out: r.o wl)....— **1**
15^{2} Iota **(64)***(69) (JLHarris)* 6-9-3 LDettori(5) (a.p: led 5f out tl over 2f out: 2nd st: rallied fnl f: r.o wl)....1 **2**
Child Star (FR) **(42)***(43) (DMarks)* 6-7-2 (7)ow2 MBaird(11) (a.p: 4th st: one pce)....4 **3**
Secret Serenade **(71)***(71) (CWFairhurst)* 4-9-4 RCochrane(7) (lw: led to 5f out: 3rd st: one pce)....¾ **4**
Manolete **(47)***(44) (CWCElsey)* 4-7-8bow1 NKennedy(4) (hld up & bhd: hdwy over 3f out: 5th st: wknd fnl f)....2½ **5**

18[7] Tapis Rouge (IRE) **(67)***(62) (THCaldwell)* 6-9-6 JWeaver(6) (hld up: 6th st: no hdwy) 2 **6**
Upper Mount Clair **(59)***(53) (CEBrittain)* 5-8-12 BDoyle(9) (prom tl wknd 3f out) .....½ **7**
Brief Respite (IRE) **(60)***(43) (EJAlston)* 4-8-2 (5)ow2 JStack(1) (hld up: sddle slipped: a bhd: t.o) 10 **8**
Scorched Air **(49)***(16) (JGMO'Shea)* 5-7-11 (5) NVarley(2) (hld up: hdwy 6f out: wknd qckly 4f out: t.o) 15 **9**

LONG HANDICAP Manolete 7-6 Child Star (FR) 7-1

8/13 ARGYLE CAVALIER (IRE), **3/1** Iota, **10/1** Scorched Air, **12/1** Manolete, **14/1** Secret Serenade, **20/1** Tapis Rouge (IRE), **25/1** Child Star (FR), **33/1** Upper Mount Clair, Brief Respite (IRE), CSF £3.36 CT £21.36 TOTE £1.70: £1.10 £1.70 £2.60 (£2.10) OWNER E H Jones (Paints) Ltd (MIDDLEHAM) BRED Oldtown Bloodstock Holdings Ltd in Ireland 9 Rn

3m 20.8 SF: 30/25/1/21/-/19/11/-/-

WEIGHT FOR AGE 4yo-6lb

68 BASIL (S) STKS (II) (Class F) £2,537.00 (£712.00: £347.00)

1m 100y (Fibresand) GOING: minus 0.18 sec per fur (Std) 4-00 (4-00)

29[2] **Off the Air (IRE) (49)***(47) (ICampbell)* 4-8-8v RCochrane(9) (a.p: 2nd st: led over 1f out: r.o wl) ....— **1**
Miss Charlie **(36)***(43) (ABailey)* 5-8-9 GCarter(11) (plld hrd: a.p: led over 4f out tl over 1f out: nt qckn) 2 **2**
20[7] Beware of Agents **(71)***(38)*(Fav)*(MJohnston)* 6-9-0 LDettori(6) (hld up: rdn & hdwy over 3f out: wnt 3rd st: one pce) 5 **3**
Nigelschinapalace **(28)***(36) (MissSJWilton)* 6-9-0 JWilliams(5) (hld up: hdwy & 5th st: nvr nr to chal) ....¾ **4**
Royal Acclaim **(45)***(31) (JMBradley)* 10-8-7v(7) AmandaSanders(4) (wl bhd tl hdwy & 6th st: nvr nrr) 2½ **5**
29[8] Pop to Stans **(56)***(27) (JPearce)* 6-9-0 GBardwell(3) (lw: nvr trbld ldrs) 1¾ **6**
21[8] Indian Fire *(15) (KOCunningham-Brown)* 5-9-0 LCharnock(10) (led 4f: 4th st: eased whn btn over 1f out) 6 **7**
18[5] Ballyhays (IRE) **(51)***(12) (JAHarris)* 6-9-5 SWilliams(2) (prom: rdn & wknd over 3f out) 4 **8**
Dance and Sing (IRE) **(33)***(4) (DLWilliams)* 5-9-0 NAdams(1) (bhd fnl 3f) 1½ **9**
City Rhythm **(32)***(—) (JMBradley)* 5-8-11v(3) DWright(8) (prom 5f) 7 **10**
Coniston Lake (IRE) **(45)***(—) (GLMoore)* 6-8-7 (7) CarolineHovington(7) (a bhd: t.o) 6 **11**

Evens Beware of Agents, **3/1** OFF THE AIR (IRE), **5/1** Ballyhays (IRE), **8/1** Miss Charlie, **12/1** Pop to Stans, **20/1** Indian Fire, Coniston Lake (IRE), **25/1** Royal Acclaim, **33/1** Nigelschinapalace, Dance and Sing (IRE), City Rhythm, CSF £28.75 TOTE £5.60: £2.10 £1.40 £1.40 (£36.90) OWNER Mr John O'Malley (NEWMARKET) BRED Edward Doyle 11 Rn No bid

1m 50.8 SF: 23/21/16/15/10/9/-/-/-/-/-

WEIGHT FOR AGE 4yo-1lb

69 MALIBU H'CAP (0-75) (Class D) £3,707.60 (£1,122.80: £548.40: £261.20)

5f (Fibresand) GOING: minus 0.18 sec per fur (Std) 4-30 (4-32)

14[4] **Leigh Crofter (70)***(78) (PDCundell)* 6-10-0b JWeaver(1) (hld up: hdwy & 4th st: led ins fnl f: r.o wl) ....— **1**
Kalar **(61)***(64) (DWChapman)* 6-8-12b(7) CTeague(7) (led tl ins fnl f) 1¾ **2**
39[6] Nineacres **(58)***(59) (DNicholls)* 4-9-2b CRutter(3) (hdwy on ins & 5th st: r.o one pce fnl f) ....½ **3**
Bella Parkes **(67)***(66) (DNicholls)* 4-9-11 AlexGreaves(8) (a.p: 6th & c wd st: edgd rt over 1f out: r.o fnl f) ....½ **4**
16[3] Delrob **(63)***(59) (DHaydnJones)* 4-9-7 AMackay(6) (lw: bhd tl hdwy on ins 1f out: nt rch ldrs) 1 **5**
Scored Again **(57)***(50) (MJHeaton-Ellis)* 5-8-8 (7) AmandaSanders(11) (b: lw: mid div: carried wd st: r.o fnl f: nvr nrr) ....¾ **6**
55[7] Black Boy (IRE) **(40)***(30) (RFMarvin)* 6-7-5b(7) ClaireBalding(12) (nvr nr to chal) 1 **7**
Brisas **(46)***(35) (CWFairhurst)* 8-8-4v JFanning(5) (no hdwy fnl 2f) ....nk **8**
23[7] Hinari Video **(57)***(38) (MJohnston)* 10-8-8 (7) OliverCasey(4) (prom 3f) 2½ **9**
16* Sir Tasker **(67)***(47)*(Fav)*(JLHarris)* 7-9-11 7x LDettori(2) (lw: prom: sn rdn along: 3rd st: edgd rt & wknd over 1f out) ....nk **10**
14[7] Tommy Tempest **(40)***(18) (ABailey)* 6-7-9b(3) DWright(13) (w ldr: 2nd st: wknd over 1f out) ....½ **11**
Jon's Choice **(67)***(21) (BPreece)* 7-9-11 TWall(10) (n.m.r 4f out: a bhd: t.o) 8 **12**

4/1 Sir Tasker, **9/2** LEIGH CROFTER, **13/2** Kalar, **15/2** Nineacres, **12/1** Delrob, Scored Again, Tommy Tempest, **14/1** Hinari Video, **16/1** Brisas, Bella Parkes, Jon's Choice, **25/1** Black Boy (IRE), CSF £30.08 CT £192.26 TOTE £4.30: £2.20 £1.60 £2.80 (£15.90) OWNER Mr Peter Dimmock (NEWBURY) BRED Richard Castle 12 Rn 62.0 secs (4.00) SF: 38/27/23/29/22/14
T/Plpt: £23.90 (528.34 Tckts). T/Qdpt: £12.00 (3.1 Tckts). KH

0056-LINGFIELD (L-H)
Thursday January 12th (Standard)

70
GUY MANNERING CLAIMING STKS (Class E) £3,081.10 (£932.80: £455.40: £216.70) **5f (Equitrack)** GOING: minus 0.30 sec per fur (FS) 1-00 (1-00)

14[3] **Little Saboteur (68)***(67) (PJMakin)* 6-8-5bow1 AClark(8) (b.nr hind: hld up: chsd ldr over 2f out: hrd drvn over 1f out: led last stride)......— **1**
Press the Bell **(77)***(73)*(Fav)*(JBerry)* 5-8-11 GCarter(1) (led: hrd rdn fnl f: hdd last stride)......s.h **2**
14[6] Samson-Agonistes **(70)***(64) (PDEvans)* 9-8-7 RCochrane(5) (chsd ldr over 2f: one pce)......1½ **3**
23[2] Distant Dynasty **(51)***(67) (BAPearce)* 5-9-1 LDettori(6) (b.hind: hld up: rdn over 2f out: one pce)......1¾ **4**
Farfelu **(82)***(68) (WRMuir)* 8-9-3b JWeaver(7) (nvr nr to chal)......nk **5**
Another Episode (IRE) **(74)***(55) (JBerry)* 6-8-12 (7) PRoberts(3) (hdwy over 3f out: wknd over 1f out)......5 **6**
Baton Bleu **(43)***(37) (PHowling)* 4-8-3 JQuinn(4) (bhd fnl 3f)......½ **7**
Not so Generous (IRE) **(63)***(29) (WGMTurner)* 5-7-7 (7) MBaird(2) (a bhd)......1½ **8**

5/2 Press the Bell, **9/2** Farfelu, **5/1** LITTLE SABOTEUR, **11/2** Samson-Agonistes, **13/2** Distant Dynasty, **8/1** Another Episode (IRE), **14/1** Not so Generous (IRE), **33/1** Baton Bleu, CSF £16.67 TOTE £4.50: £2.00 £1.40 £1.10 (£4.00) OWNER Mrs C. R. Walford (MARLBOROUGH) BRED Courtown Stud Co 8 Rn 60.14 secs (1.94) SF: 31/37/29/33/34/19/2/-
STEWARDS' ENQUIRY Clark suspended 21-22/1/95 (excessive use of whip).

71
REDGAUNTLET (S) STKS (Class G) £2,259.00 (£634.00: £309.00) **7f (Equitrack)** GOING: minus 0.30 sec per fur (FS) 1-30 (1-34)

Spencer's Revenge (70)*(63+)*(Fav)*(LordHuntingdon)* 6-8-12 JWeaver(12) (lw: a.p: led over 2f out: clr wl over 1f out: easily)......— **1**
Respectable Jones **(48)***(50) (RHollinshead)* 9-8-12 LDettori(3) (lw: stdy hdwy over 3f out: chsd wnr wl over 1f out: no imp)......6 **2**
Joint Effort (IRE) **(42)***(37) (AMoore)* 4-8-2 (5) AWhelan(11) (b.hind: hdwy over 1f out: nvr nrr)......4 **3**
16[4] Tyrian Purple (IRE) **(62)***(39) (TJNaughton)* 7-8-7b(5) VHalliday(13) (b.off hind: led over 4f)......1¼ **4**
62[5] Pigalle Wonder **(38)***(39) (RJO'Sullivan)* 7-8-12 DBiggs(1) (lost pl over 4f out: r.o one pce fnl 2f)......s.h **5**
2[12] It's so Easy **(59)***(32) (MJohnston)* 4-8-7 TWilliams(5) (no hdwy fnl 2f)......¾ **6**
Waders Dream (IRE) **(39)***(37) (PMitchell)* 6-8-12v RCochrane(6) (nvr nr to chal)...s.h **7**
44[10] Veloce (IRE) **(61)***(35) (ABailey)* 7-8-9b(3) DWright(9) (b: lw: prom 5f)......1 **8**
Farndale **(52)***(34) (JBerry)* 8-8-5 (7) CLowther(10) (prom 5f)......hd **9**
Youcanstoplooking (IRE) **(47)***(6) (SDow)* 4-8-7e(5) SSanders(8) (eyeshield: b: a bhd)......13 **10**
Morjinski *(—) (DJSffrenchDavis)* 5-8-7 NAdams(4) (lw: a bhd)......4 **11**
Victoria Princess **(30)***(—) (MMadgwick)* 8-8-7 MFenton(2) (bhd fnl 4f)......30 **12**

8/13 SPENCER'S REVENGE, **8/1** Respectable Jones (5/1-9/1), Pigalle Wonder, **9/1** Tyrian Purple (IRE), **10/1** Veloce (IRE) (5/1-12/1), **12/1** It's so Easy, **14/1** Joint Effort (IRE), **20/1** Waders Dream (IRE), Farndale, **50/1** Morjinski, **100/1** Youcanstoplooking (IRE), Victoria Princess, CSF £7.68 TOTE £1.20: £1.10 £1.10 £3.20 (£3.10) OWNER Lord Crawshaw (WEST ILSLEY) BRED Lord Crawshaw 12 Rn 1m 25.29 (2.29) SF: 44/30/17/19/19/13/17/-/-/-/-/-
Bt in 5,200 gns

72
QUENTIN DURWARD STKS (Mdn 3-Y.O) (Class D) £3,758.30 (£1,138.40: £556.20: £265.10) **1m (Equitrack)** GOING: minus 0.30 sec per fur (FS) 2-00 (2-05)

17[2] **Biya (IRE)** *(62)*(Fav)*(MJohnston)* 3-9-0 TWilliams(12) (lw: a.p: rdn 5f out: led over 3f out: r.o wl)......— **1**

Pleasant Memories *(53) (LordHuntingdon)* 3-8-9 LDettori(9) (leggy: bit bkwd: rdn over 4f out: hdwy over 3f out: r.o ins fnl f)....2 **2**
Portelet *(53) (RJRWilliams)* 3-8-9 DBiggs(11) (hdwy over 4f out: ev ch over 1f out: one pce)....hd **3**
Frome Lad **(58)***(55) (WGMTurner)* 3-9-0 RPerham(8) (a.p: led 4f out tl over 3f out: one pce)....1¼ **4**
La Fille de Cirque *(38) (RJRWilliams)* 3-8-9 RCochrane(7) (b: hmpd over 6f out: hdwy over 3f out: one pce)....6 **5**
*51*² Inn At the Top **(62)***(38) (MJohnston)* 3-9-0 GCarter(4) (nvr nr to chal)....2½ **6**
Beau Matelot *(38) (JDBethell)* 3-9-0 JWeaver(5) (nvr nrr)....s.h **7**
*17*³ Zesti *(33) (TTClement)* 3-9-0 MRimmer(1) (led 1f: wknd 3f out)....2½ **8**
Dingo Warrior *(28) (JFfitch-Heyes)* 3-9-0 AMackay(2) (bit bkwd: a bhd)....2½ **9**
Anytime Baby *(19) (KMcAuliffe)* 3-8-9 MFenton(10) (b.hind: bhd fnl 2f)....1¾ **10**
Don't Mean a Thing (IRE) **(56)***(24) (RHannon)* 3-8-7 (7) DaneO'Neill(3) (bhd fnl 5f)....s.h **11**
Charnwood Queen *(9) (RWArmstrong)* 3-8-9 WWoods(6) (led 7f out tl 4f out: sn wknd)....5 **12**

9/4 BIYA (IRE), **9/2** Pleasant Memories, Inn At the Top, **7/1** Beau Matelot, **10/1** Anytime Baby (8/1-12/1), Frome Lad, **12/1** Don't Mean a Thing (IRE), **14/1** La Fille de Cirque, Charnwood Queen, Portelet, **16/1** Zesti, **50/1** Dingo Warrior, CSF £14.06 TOTE £3.10: £1.60 £1.80 £5.20 (£8.20) OWNER Julian Clopet and Associates (MIDDLEHAM) BRED Kirtlington Stud Ltd 12 Rn
1m 41.32 (4.92) SF: 24/15/15/18/2/1/1/-/-/-/-/-

73

DAILY STAR AWT 1M 2F CHALLENGE SERIES H'CAP (Qualifier) (I) (0-65) (Class F) £2,910.50 (£818.00: £399.50)
1m 2f (Equitrack) GOING: minus 0.30 sec per fur (FS) 2-30 (2-30)

Scottish Park (40)*(46) (RWEmery)* 6-9-0 JWilliams(5) (hdwy over 2f out: rdn over 1f out: led nr fin)....— **1**
Night Edition **(39)***(44) (SDow)* 5-8-13e StephenDavies(1) (b: b.hind: led: hrd rdn fnl f: hdd nr fin)....nk **2**
Lexus (IRE) **(40)***(44) (RJRWilliams)* 7-8-7 (7) SarahThompson(2) (bit bkwd: rdn & lost pl 3f out: swtchd rt & n.m.r 1f out: str run fnl f: fin wl)....¾ **3**
General Chase **(50)***(53) (ICampbell)* 5-9-5 (5) SSanders(8) (lw: hld up: rdn over 3f out: r.o one pce fnl f)....½ **4**
Calisar **(42)***(45) (PHowling)* 5-9-2 JQuinn(6) (lost pl over 4f out: rallied fnl f: r.o)....nk **5**
*49*⁴ Give In **(42)***(44)*(Fav)*(MissGayKelleway)* 8-9-2b RCochrane(10) (hld up: rdn over 2f out: one pce)....d.h **5**
Lady Sabina **(40)***(39) (WJMusson)* 5-9-0 MWigham(7) (hld up: rdn over 3f out: one pce)....1¾ **7**
Mogwai (IRE) **(45)***(41) (MartynMeade)* 6-9-5 AClark(3) (a bhd)....1¾ **8**
*8*⁸ Wahem (IRE) **(44)***(35) (CEBrittain)* 5-9-4b MRimmer(9) (prom over 8f)....3½ **9**
Silver Brief **(36)***(5) (DJSffrenchDavis)* 4-8-7b LDettori(4) (prom over 7f)....15 **10**

11/4 Give In, **4/1** Night Edition, **9/2** Lexus (IRE), **5/1** Lady Sabina, SCOTTISH PARK, **12/1** Calisar, Silver Brief, **16/1** Wahem (IRE), **20/1** General Chase, **25/1** Mogwai (IRE), CSF £26.09 CT £92.15 TOTE £5.60: £2.30 £2.60 £1.40 (£29.90) OWNER Cleartherm Ltd (RUGBY) BRED J. B. H. Stevens 10 Rn
2m 10.21 (7.21) SF: 17/16/15/24/16/16/13/-/-/-
WEIGHT FOR AGE 4yo-3lb

74

WAVERLEY H'CAP (3-Y.O) (0-80) (Class D) £3,538.60 (£1,070.80: £522.40: £248.20) **6f (Equitrack)** GOING: minus 0.30 sec per fur (FS) 3-00 (3-01)

*40** **Stoppes Brow (81)***(83)*(Fav)*(GLMoore)* 3-9-5v(7) 7x LSuthern(4) (lw: hld up: squeezed thro & jinked 1f out: led wl ins fnl f: rdn out)....— **1**
*40*² Hannah's Usher **(76)***(78) (PCHaslam)* 3-9-7 JWeaver(5) (hld up: rdn over 2f out: led over 1f out tl wl ins fnl f: r.o wl)....s.h **2**
Pleasure Beach **(65)***(62) (WAO'Gorman)* 3-8-7v(3) EmmaO'Gorman(2) (chsd ldr: led 2f out tl over 1f out: unable qckn)....2 **3**
Polly Garter **(59)***(46) (RHannon)* 3-8-4 TWilliams(1) (led 4f: 4th & btn whn hmpd on ins 1f out)....4 **4**
*43** Crystal Loop **(70)***(52) (ABailey)* 3-8-12 (3) 7x DWright(3) (hld up: rdn 2f out: sn wknd)2 **5**

10/11 STOPPES BROW, **9/4** Hannah's Usher, **5/1** Pleasure Beach, **10/1** Crystal Loop, **12/1** Polly Garter, CSF £3.53 TOTE £1.80: £1.10 £1.40 (£1.60) OWNER Mr C. J. Pennick (EPSOM) BRED Dodford Stud 5 Rn
1m 14.25 (3.65) SF: 33/29/13/-/2
STEWARDS' ENQUIRY Suthern suspended 21-22/1/95 (careless riding).

75

IVANHOE H'CAP (0-60) (Class F) £2,726.00 (£766.00: £374.00)
1m 5f (Equitrack) GOING: minus 0.30 sec per fur (FS) 3-30 (3-30)

9[7] **Royal Circus (33)***(43) (JGMO'Shea)* 6-8-4 BDoyle(9) (mde all: rdn out)........— 1
Scalp 'em (IRE) **(49)***(56) (PDEvans)* 7-9-6 AClark(3) (chsd wnr 9f out: rdn over 4f out: unable qckn)........2½ 2
22[6] Head Turner **(48)***(53) (CPWildman)* 7-9-5 NAdams(5) (lw: hld up: rdn over 3f out: one pce)........1¾ 3
Intention (USA) **(57)***(61) (ICampbell)* 5-10-0 RCochrane(8) (lw: hld up: rdn over 4f out: one pce)........½ 4
22[7] Mighty Kingdom (IRE) **(37)***(29) (RWEmery)* 4-7-12 (5) SSanders(6) (lw: no hdwy fnl 4f)........10 5
22[2] Wottashambles **(42)***(32)*(Fav)*(GLewis)* 4-8-3b(5) AGarth(2) (prom over 9f)........1¾ 6
Holiday Island **(51)***(18) (RAkehurst)* 6-9-8 GCarter(1) (lw: a bhd)........20 7
Heathyards Crusade (IRE) **(37)***(2) (RHollinshead)* 4-8-3 JQuinn(7) (prom 5f)........1¾ 8
Marketing Man **(39)***(1) (PMitchell)* 5-8-10 JMcLaughlin(4) (prom 5f)........2½ 9

7/4 Wottashambles, **7/2** Scalp 'em (IRE), **6/1** Holiday Island, **13/2** Head Turner, **8/1** Heathyards Crusade (IRE), Intention (USA), **11/1** ROYAL CIRCUS, **33/1** Mighty Kingdom (IRE), Marketing Man, CSF £48.65 CT £252.29 TOTE £12.10: £3.10 £1.10 £1.50 (£28.00) OWNER Mr P. W. Hiatt (REDDITCH) BRED Snailwell Stud Co Ltd 9 Rn 2m 50.85 (8.35) SF: 15/27/25/32/-/2/-/-/-
WEIGHT FOR AGE 4yo-5lb

76

DAILY STAR AWT 1M 2F CHALLENGE SERIES H'CAP (Qualifier) (II) (0-65) (Class F) £2,897.20 (£814.20: £397.60)
1m 2f (Equitrack) GOING: minus 0.30 sec per fur (FS) 4-00 (4-03)

Zuno Noelyn (52)*(59) (RAkehurst)* 4-9-2 GCarter(4) (lw: hld up: rdn over 3f out: led 1f out: r.o wl)........— 1
Kaafih Homm (IRE) **(55)***(59)*(Fav)*(NACallaghan)* 4-9-5 RCochrane(1) (lw: a.p: rdn over 4f out: led over 3f out tl over 1f out: unable qckn ins fnl f)........2 2
18[3] Rockstine (IRE) **(57)***(59) (PMitchell)* 4-9-7 LDettori(6) (led over 6f: ev ch ins fnl f: one pce)........1¼ 3
Carpathian **(48)***(48) (LordHuntingdon)* 4-8-12 JWeaver(3) (hld up: rdn over 3f out: r.o one pce)........1½ 4
27[2] Camden's Ransom (USA) **(60)***(55) (GBBalding)* 8-9-8 (5) SDrowne(8) (hld up: hrd rdn over 3f out: wknd over 2f out)........3½ 5
Golden Hadeer **(47)***(34) (MJRyan)* 4-8-11 DBiggs(9) (hld up: rdn over 4f out: wknd over 3f out)........5 6
Queen of Shannon (IRE) **(49)***(24) (BJMeehan)* 7-9-2 MTebbutt(7) (b: b.hind: bhd fnl 4f)........8 7
Papagos (IRE) **(38)***(—) (SDow)* 4-8-2 StephenDavies(2) (b: prom over 6f)........11 8
Kelly's Kite **(32)***(—) (HJCollingridge)* 7-7-8 (5) CHawksley(5) (b: bkwd: bhd fnl 5f: t.o)........30 9

11/10 Kaafih Homm (IRE), **4/1** Carpathian, **6/1** Rockstine (IRE), ZUNO NOELYN, **10/1** Camden's Ransom (USA), Queen of Shannon (IRE), **14/1** Golden Hadeer, **33/1** Papagos (IRE), Kelly's Kite, CSF £13.72 CT £41.02 TOTE £6.10: £1.80 £1.10 £2.20 (£4.50) OWNER Planflow (Leasing) Ltd (EPSOM) BRED R. B. Warren 9 Rn 2m 7.74 (4.74) SF: 38/37/38/28/36/14/6/-/-
WEIGHT FOR AGE 4yo-3lb
T/Ppt: £28.40 (440.02 Tckts). T/Qdpt: £8.50 (0.5 Tckts); £5.80 to Ascot 13/1/95. AK

0048-SOUTHWELL (L-H)
Friday January 13th (Standard)

77

BUTTERCUP H'CAP (Amateurs) (I) (0-65) (Class F) £2,537.00 (£712.00: £347.00) **1m 3f (Fibresand)** GOING minus 0.08 sec per fur (STD) 12-50 (12-51)

Sudden Spin (40)*(50+)*(Fav)*(SGNorton)* 5-10-1 (4) MrMNaughton(1) (trckd ldrs: wnt 2nd st: led over 2f out: sn pushed clr)........— 1
Gold Blade **(56)***(59) (JPearce)* 6-11-7 MrsLPearce(8) (racd wd: chsd ldrs: 5th st: rdn & kpt on appr fnl f)........5 2
35[3] Modest Hope (USA) **(47)***(48)*(Fav)*(BRichmond)* 8-10-12 MissDianaJones(5) (hld up: hdwy & 4th st: rdn wl over 1f out: kpt on)........1¼ 3
Donia (USA) **(49)***(40) (JLHarris)* 6-10-10 (4) MrIMcLelland(6) (plld hrd: chsd ldr tl 3rd st: rdn & one pce fnl 2f)........7 4

Don't Drop Bombs (USA) **(34)***(23) (PJFeilden)* 6-9-13 MissJFeilden(4) (led: rdn & hdd over 2f out: sn wknd)........1¾ **5**
Medland (IRE) **(56)***(38) (WGMTurner)* 5-11-3 (4) MrsCPrice(3) (lw: in tch: pushed along 5f out: 7th & btn st)........5 **6**
35[8] Aldington Chapple **(37)***(8) (BPreece)* 7-9-12 (4) MissLBoswell(7) (bhd fnl 4f)........8 **7**
Mabthul (USA) **(36)***(7) (RTJuckes)* 7-9-11 (4) MissSHiggins(2) (lw: a bhd)........hd **8**
Goldenberry **(44)***(8) (JParkes)* 4-10-1 (4) MrRJohnson(9) (prom tl 6th & wkng st)........5 **9**

9/4 SUDDEN SPIN, Modest Hope (USA), **9/2** Gold Blade, **8/1** Donia (USA), Medland (IRE), **10/1** Don't Drop Bombs (USA), **20/1** Goldenberry, **25/1** Aldington Chapple, **33/1** Mabthul (USA), CSF £13.03 CT £23.52 TOTE £4.90: £1.60 £1.50 £1.10 (£11.60) OWNER Mr Billy Parker (BARNSLEY) BRED The Arrow Farm and Stud 9 Rn 2m 31.5 (10.00) SF: 40/48/38/30/16/28/1/-/-
WEIGHT FOR AGE 4yo-4lb

78

RYEGRASS H'CAP (0-65) (Class F) £2,827.00 (£856.00: 418.00: £199.00)
6f (Fibresand) GOING minus 0.08 sec per fur (STD) 1-20 (1-27)

*33** **Portend (49)***(63+) (SRBowring)* 3-7-6 (7) 7x ClaireBalding(9) (lw: a.p: led & qcknd clr over 2f out: unchal)........— **1**
23[3] Cheerful Groom (IRE) **(42)***(41) (JMackie)* 4-8-8 GCarter(5) (hld up & bhd: gd hdwy fnl 2f: fin wl: no ch w wnr)........6 **2**
Meeson Times **(53)***(46) (RBastiman)* 7-9-0 (5) HBastiman(8) (bit bkwd: hdwy 2f out: nrst fin)........2½ **3**
Shadow Jury **(58)***(47) (DWChapman)* 5-9-3b(7) OliverCasey(14) (sn chsng ldrs: no ex fnl 2f)........1¼ **4**
61[2] Pageboy **(69)***(55)*(Fav)*(PCHaslam)* 6-10-7 7x JWeaver(15) (chsd ldrs: rdn over 1f out: no imp whn n.m.r ins fnl f)........¾ **5**
Swinging Tich **(43)***(26) (BAMcMahon)* 6-8-4 (5) SSanders(1) (dwlt: rdn & r.o fnl 2f: nvr nrr)........1 **6**
Fairey Firefly **(58)***(41) (MJCamacho)* 4-9-10 LCharnock(13) (bit bkwd: chsd ldrs 4f: sn rdn & btn)........s.h **7**
Henry the Hawk **(50)***(29) (MDods)* 4-8-11v(5) JStack(12) (hung rt early: bhd tl sme late hdwy)........1¼ **8**
Hiltons Travel (IRE) **(50)***(26) (EJAlston)* 4-9-2b SWebster(2) (led over 3f: rdn & wknd)........1 **9**
Rapier Point (IRE) **(60)***(33) (PCHaslam)* 4-9-12 MTebbutt(7) (nvr plcd to chal: fin lame)........1 **10**
Last Straw **(37)***(32) (BPreece)* 7-7-10 (7) AEddery(11) (bkwd: prom tl wknd 2f out)2½ **11**
Winterbottom **(48)***(—) (ICampbell)* 3-7-12 AMackay(4) (s.i.s: a in rr)........10 **12**
Three of Hearts **(50)***(—) (MrsNMacauley)* 4-9-2 LDettori(3) (b: sn pushed along & outpcd)........3 **13**
Wellsy Lad (USA) **(39)***(—) (DWChapman)* 8-8-5 JQuinn(10) (dwlt: nvr rchd ldrs) .hd **14**
Twice in Bundoran (IRE) **(53)***(—) (PSFelgate)* 4-9-5 TIves(6) (in tch over 3f)........nk **15**

2/1 Pageboy, **5/2** PORTEND, **10/1** Three of Hearts, Cheerful Groom (IRE) (8/1-12/1), **12/1** Fairey Firefly, Hiltons Travel (IRE), **14/1** Swinging Tich, **16/1** Rapier Point (IRE), Winterbottom, **20/1** Shadow Jury, **25/1** Henry the Hawk, Last Straw, Meeson Times, Twice in Bundoran (IRE), **33/1** Wellsy Lad (USA), CSF £29.90 CT £515.57 TOTE £3.50: £1.90 £2.10 £6.60 (£17.70) OWNER Mr D. H. Bowring (EDWINSTOWE) BRED Hollow Hole Stud 15 Rn
1m 17.8 (4.30) SF: 20/13/16/18/25/-/13/-/-/-/-/-/-/-/-
WEIGHT FOR AGE 3yo-16lb

79

DAISY CLAIMING STKS (Class F) £2,537.00 (£712.00: £347.00)
2m (Fibresand) GOING minus 0.08 sec per fur (STD) 1-55 (1-57)

El Nido (59)*(67)*(Fav)*(MJCamacho)* 7-9-3 LCharnock(11) (hld up: stumbled 9f out: 3rd st: rdn to ld 2f out: edgd lft & sn qcknd clr)........— **1**
Brodessa **(59)***(66)*(Fav)*(MrsMReveley)* 9-9-7 RCochrane(7) (trckd ldrs: led 3f out to 2f out: kpt on)........5 **2**
45[4] Sassiver (USA) **(45)***(54) (RHollinshead)* 5-9-1 LDettori(4) (hld up: hdwy 5f out: 4th st: kpt on u.p)........6 **3**
53[9] Zaaheyah (USA) **(38)***(43) (MDHammond)* 5-8-6v GCarter(5) (led 13f: 2nd st: sn btn)........2½ **4**
Dawn Rock **(51)***(44) (PAKelleway)* 4-8-1v(7) AdelleGibbons(1) (hld up & bhd: rdn 7f out: styd on fnl 4f: nvr nrr)........8 **5**
Greenacres Star **(34)***(28) (BAMcMahon)* 5-8-8 JWeaver(8) (bhd: rdn 6f out: kpt on wl fnl 2f: nrst fin)........10 **6**
29[9] Kush **(23)***(15) (JLHarris)* 4-7-8 (5) NVarley(3) (prom tl btn & 7th st)........12 **7**

Mac's Boy **(45)***(15) (BPalling)* 6-9-1 AClark(2) (plld hrd: in tch: rdn 5f out: btn & 6th st)....10 **8**
9[10] Kiss Kincsem **(54)***(—) (PJMakin)* 4-7-10b ow1 DaleGibson(10) (plld hrd: chsd ldrs tl poor 5th & wkng st)....3 **9**
19[7] Chapel Haven (IRE) **(30)***(—) (JParkes)* 5-8-4b NAdams(6) (chsd ldr 9f)....5 **10**
30[10] Winagins (IRE) **(30)***(—) (TRWatson)* 4-7-10 ow1 JQuinn(9) (prom 9f: sn rdn & wknd qckly)....dist **11**

9/4 EL NIDO, Brodessa, **11/2** Sassiver (USA) (8/1-5/1), **6/1** Kiss Kincsem (5/1-8/1), **12/1** Dawn Rock, Greenacres Star, **20/1** Winagins (IRE), Zaaheyah (USA), **33/1** Kush, Chapel Haven (IRE), Mac's Boy, CSF £7.92 TOTE £3.70: £1.70 £1.00 £1.90 (£4.70) OWNER M K Slinger & A Stuart (MALTON) BRED M. J. Camacho 11 Rn 3m 48.1 (22.10) SF: -/-/-/-/-/-/-/-/-/-/-
WEIGHT FOR AGE 4yo-7lb

80

COWSLIP STKS (0-55) (Class F) £2,537.00 (£712.00: £347.00)
1m (Fibresand) GOING minus 0.08 sec per fur (STD) 2-25 (2-26)

44[3] **Hawwam (54)***(62) (EJAlston)* 9-8-12 JWeaver(8) (hdwy & 5th st: led wl over 1f out: rdn out)....— **1**
49[5] Orthorhombus **(54)***(55) (DJSCosgrove)* 6-8-12b AShoults(5) (bhd & sn rdn along: gd hdwy & 2nd st: sn rdn & hung rt 2f out: no ex fnl f)....3½ **2**
34[3] Puffy **(43)***(47) (MDods)* 8-8-12v WWoods(4) (b: s.i.s: bhd tl r.o fnl 3f: nrst fin)....4 **3**
1[7] Cicerone **(52)***(47) (JLHarris)* 5-8-12 RCochrane(3) (b.hind: chsd ldrs: 6th st: kpt on fnl 2f)....hd **4**
Exclusion **(49)***(43) (JHetherton)* 6-8-12 TIves(2) (bit bkwd: hdwy over 2f out: nrst fin)....1¾ **5**
Sharpening **(50)***(35) (LordHuntingdon)* 4-8-1v(5) AWhelan(10) (prom: led 3f out tl wl over 1f out: sn wknd)....1¼ **6**
Tilly Owl **(39)***(23)*(Fav)*(JAHarris)* 4-8-6 JO'Reilly(9) (b.hind: lw: prom tl 8th st: sn rdn: eased whn btn fnl f)....6 **7**
12[9] Level Edge **(52)***(20) (MJohnston)* 4-8-6 TWilliams(6) (prom tl 7th & btn st)....1½ **8**
Supercool **(50)***(23) (BAMcMahon)* 4-8-6 (5) SSanders(7) (prom: led 4f out to 3f out: 3rd st: sn btn)....¾ **9**
32[3] Slip a Coin **(55)***(4) (RHollinshead)* 4-8-6 LDettori(1) (lw: led 4f: 4th st: sn wknd)....7 **10**

7/2 Tilly Owl, **4/1** Sharpening, Slip a Coin (3/1-9/2), **9/2** HAWWAM, **7/1** Supercool, **8/1** Orthorhombus, **10/1** Level Edge, Cicerone (8/1-12/1), **20/1** Puffy, **33/1** Exclusion, CSF £40.74 TOTE £7.00: £2.10 £2.50 £4.00 (£13.50) OWNER North West Racing Club Owners Club (PRESTON) BRED G. Franco 10 Rn 1m 45.8 (6.50) SF: 25/19/12/11/9/2/-/-/-/-
WEIGHT FOR AGE 4yo-1lb

81

FOXGLOVE H'CAP (0-80) (Class D) £3,555.50 (£1,076.00: £525.00: £249.50)
1m 4f (Fibresand) GOING minus 0.08 sec per fur (STD) 2-55 (2-55)

35* **Pharly Dancer (72)***(84) (WWHaigh)* 6-9-11 5x DaleGibson(1) (mde all: rdn & hld on wl fnl 2f)....— **1**
67* Argyle Cavalier (IRE) **(69)***(76)*(Fav)*(MJohnston)* 5-9-1 (7) 5x OliverCasey(5) (chsd wnr: 2nd st: sn rdn & ev ch: no ex fnl f)....4 **2**
34* Rousitto **(59)***(65) (RHollinshead)* 7-8-12 5x LDettori(2) (lw: hld up: hdwy & 3rd st: sn rdn & no imp)....1 **3**
3[2] Mizyan (IRE) **(65)***(67) (JEBanks)* 7-9-4 JWeaver(4) (chsd ldrs: outpcd & 4th st: n.d after)....3 **4**
52* Joseph's Wine (IRE) **(80)***(70) (DNicholls)* 6-10-5b 5x AlexGreaves(3) (lw: 5th st: a bhd)....10 **5**

2/1 Argyle Cavalier (IRE), **5/2** Joseph's Wine (IRE), **3/1** PHARLY DANCER, **6/1** Mizyan (IRE), **8/1** Rousitto, CSF £9.02 TOTE £4.30: £1.80 £1.90 (£4.20) OWNER Mr A. Marucci (MALTON) BRED Stud-On-The-Chart 5 Rn 2m 42.4 (8.20) SF: 50/42/31/33/34

82

BLUEBELL (S) STKS (Class G) £2,259.00 (£634.00: £309.00)
7f (Fibresand) GOING minus 0.08 sec per fur (STD) 3-25 (3-27)

63[3] **Alpine Johnny (57)***(60) (RHollinshead)* 4-8-7 (5) AGarth(14) (plld hrd: a.p: led 3f out: all out)....— **1**
2[5] Jamaica Bridge **(48)***(60)*(Fav)*(SGNorton)* 5-8-7 (5) JStack(12) (lw: plld hrd: prom: 4th st: ev ch over 1f out: nt qckn nr fin)....s.h **2**
2[3] Bradwell (IRE) **(50)***(51) (MHTompkins)* 4-8-2 (5) SMulvey(8) (lw: led 4f: 2nd st: kpt on u.p)....2 **3**

1[8] Warhurst (IRE) **(75)***(45) (DNicholls)* 4-8-12 AlexGreaves(7) (lw: bhd: shkn up & hdwy over 2f out: edgd lft & r.o appr fnl f)....5 **4**
Obsidian Grey **(43)***(39) (MissLCSiddall)* 8-8-12 RCochrane(9) (racd wd: chsd ldrs: 8th st: kpt on)....3 **5**
Grandee **(44)***(38) (BAMcMahon)* 4-8-12 JWeaver(15) (chsd ldrs: effrt & 3rd st: btn 2f out)....nk **6**
Spanish Stripper (USA) *(37) (MCChapman)* 4-8-7 (5) DRMcCabe(2) (lw: stdd s: wl bhd tl r.o fnl 2f)....nk **7**
Killing Time **(59)***(37) (MrsNMacauley)* 4-8-12v MFenton(4) (lw: chsd ldrs: 7th st: sn rdn & no imp)....s.h **8**
At the Savoy (IRE) **(38)***(29) (TDBarron)* 4-8-5 (7) KimberleyHart(1) (hld up: rdn over 1f out: nvr plcd to chal)....4 **9**
Make the Break **(54)***(28) (SCoathup)* 4-8-5 (7) SharronJames(13) (hld up: effrt 4f out: no imp)....½ **10**
Mister Blake **(56)***(26) (ICampbell)* 5-8-12b AMackay(3) (a bhd)....1 **11**
Lon Isa **(49)***(20) (BPalling)* 4-8-7 AClark(5) (sn pushed along: a bhd)....½ **12**
34[9] Arrogant Boy *(24) (DWChapman)* 6-8-12 SWebster(6) (prom tl 5th & wkng st)....½ **13**
The Real Whizzbang (IRE) **(38)***(21) (PSFelgate)* 4-8-12 TIves(11) (sn rdn along: bhd fnl 3f)....1¼ **14**
Premier Star **(40)***(—) (MDods)* 5-8-12b DaleGibson(10) (sn prom: 6th st: wknd qckly)....20 **15**

5/2 Jamaica Bridge, **4/1** ALPINE JOHNNY (3/1-9/2), **5/1** Bradwell (IRE), **7/1** Warhurst (IRE), Grandee, **11/1** Killing Time, **12/1** Spanish Stripper (USA), Mister Blake, **14/1** At the Savoy (IRE), **16/1** Obsidian Grey, **20/1** Make the Break, Lon Isa, **25/1** The Real Whizzbang (IRE), Premier Star, **33/1** Arrogant Boy, CSF £16.59 TOTE £3.30: £1.90 £1.60 £2.00 (£10.60) OWNER Mr J. E. Bigg (UPPER LONGDON) BRED Tally Ho Stud (England) & L. Boyd-Rochfort S'Ment 15 Rn
1m 32.3 (5.50) SF: 27/27/18/12/5/5/4/4/-/-/-/-/-/-/-
No bid

83

BUTTERCUP H'CAP (Amateurs) (II) (0-65) (Class F) £2,537.00 (£712.00: £347.00) **1m 3f (Fibresand)** GOING minus 0.08 sec per fur (STD) 3-55 (3-55)

Tempering (54)*(64)*(Fav)*(DWChapman)* 9-11-3 (4) MissRClark(3) (led after 2f: hld on wl fnl 2f)....— **1**
Killick **(46)***(54) (ABailey)* 7-10-9 (4) MissBridgetGatehouse(6) (lw: a.p: 2nd st: ev ch 2f out: no ex fnl f)....2 **2**
Ozzie Jones **(44)***(51) (MCChapman)* 4-10-3 (4) MrTonyHughes(5) (lw: led 2f: 4th & rdn st: kpt on u.p fnl f)....1 **3**
58[3] Malingerer **(30)***(34)*(Fav)*(DAWilson)* 4-9-7 MissDianaJones(1) (hld up: hdwy & 5th st: styd on u.p: nt pce to chal)....2½ **4**
Midlin **(37)***(40) (JLHarris)* 5-10-0 (4) MrIMcLelland(7) (trckd ldrs: 3rd st: sn rdn: wknd fnl f)....nk **5**
13[6] Persian Bud (IRE) **(26)***(27) (JRBosley)* 7-9-3 (4) MrsSBosley(4) (chsd ldrs: 6th st: rdn & no imp fnl 2f)....1½ **6**
Mrs Jogglebury **(41)***(—) (CSmith)* 4-10-0 (4)ow6 MissSSempers(8) (a bhd: t.o)....dist **7**
Sharp Sensation **(52)***(—) (DNicholls)* 5-11-1 (4) MrSBrisby(9) (rdn ½-wy: sn wl bhd: t.o)....10 **8**
30[11] Azubah **(45)***(—) (JAHarris)* 8-10-12 MrTCuff(2) (prom 5f: t.o)....25 **9**

3/1 TEMPERING, Malingerer, **4/1** Persian Bud (IRE), **6/1** Ozzie Jones, **8/1** Killick, Azubah, **9/1** Sharp Sensation, **20/1** Mrs Jogglebury, Midlin, CSF £27.12 CT £126.37 TOTE £2.80: £1.30 £2.50 £2.10 (£17.70) OWNER Mr Richard Berenson (YORK) BRED Lord Howard de Walden 9 Rn
2m 32.9 (11.40) SF: 45/35/28/13/22/10/-/-/-
WEIGHT FOR AGE 4yo-4lb
T/Plpt: £13.30 (609.62 Tckts). T/Qdpt: £19.40 (3.85 Tckts). Dk

0070-LINGFIELD (L-H)
Saturday January 14th (Standard)

84

TYRONE STKS (Mdn) (Class D) £3,623.10 (£1,096.80: £535.40: £254.70) **1m 5f (Equitrack)** GOING minus 0.47 sec per fur (FST) 12-55 (12-55)

Hattaafeh (IRE) *(53) (MAJarvis)* 4-8-9 WWoods(3) (hld up: hdwy 4f out: led over 1f out: hrd rdn: jst hld on)....— **1**
Dvorak (IRE) *(58)*(Fav)*(BJMcMath)* 4-9-0 AMackay(1) (hld up: hdwy 4f out: hrd rdn over 1f out: str run fnl f: jst failed)....s.h **2**

26[2] Regal Pursuit (IRE) **(57)***(52) (CAHorgan)* 4-8-9h AClark(4) (chsd ldrs: led 3f out tl over 1f out: hrd rdn: one pce)....................¾ 3
8[6] Tondres (USA) **(64)***(52) (RIngram)* 4-9-0 LDettori(2) (chsd ldrs 9f out: led 4f out to 3f out: wknd over 1f out)....................4 4
21[3] Sweet Caroline **(40)***(35) (PMitchell)* 4-8-9b JMcLaughlin(5) (chsd ldr 4f: rdn 5f out: sn wknd)....................10 5
26[4] Thorniwama **(40)***(29) (JJBridger)* 4-8-9 GBardwell(6) (prom 9f)....................5 6
19[5] Abu Dancer (IRE) **(50)***(24) (KOCunningham-Brown)* 5-9-5 LCharnock(7) (led 9f)....9 7
26[8] Chapter Two **(35)***(18) (SDow)* 4-9-0 JWeaver(8) (a bhd)....................5 8

6/4 Dvorak (IRE), **3/1** Tondres (USA), Regal Pursuit (IRE), **6/1** HATTAAFEH (IRE), **20/1** Thorniwama, Abu Dancer (IRE), **33/1** Sweet Caroline, Chapter Two, CSF £15.45 TOTE £8.80: £1.50 £1.30 £2.10 (£9.20) OWNER Mr Michael Jarvis (NEWMARKET) BRED Sheikh Ahmed bin Rashid al Maktoum in Ireland 8 Rn 2m 49.69 (7.19) SF: 13/18/13/13/-/-/-/-
WEIGHT FOR AGE 4yo-5lb

85

LONDONDERRY H'CAP (3-Y.O) (0-60) (Class F) £2,763.80 (£776.80: £379.40)
7f (Equitrack) GOING minus 0.47 sec per fur (FST) 1-30 (1-30)

Water Hazard (IRE) (47)*(55) (SDow)* 3-8-9 StephenDavies(6) (b.hind: chsd ldrs: rdn over 1f out: swtchd lft & r.o fnl f: led nr fin)....................— 1
24[2] Mac's Taxi **(56)***(63)*(Fav)*(PCHaslam)* 3-9-4 JWeaver(9) (chsd ldrs: led 2f out: rdn fnl f: ct fin)....................hd 2
24[4] Mediate (IRE) **(59)***(58) (RHannon)* 3-9-7b LDettori(3) (led 5f: rdn over 1f out: wknd ins fnl f)....................4 3
Always Grace **(57)***(45) (MissGayKelleway)* 3-9-5 TIves(1) (chsd ldr over 4f: rdn & wknd over 1f out)....................5 4
47[5] Rose Chime (IRE) **(43)***(29) (MJohnston)* 3-8-5 TWilliams(4) (chsd ldrs: rdn over 3f out: one pce fnl 2f)....................¾ 5
Just Jesting **(55)***(39) (GLMoore)* 3-9-3 RPerham(7) (hdwy fr rr 3f out: sn rdn: wknd over 1f out)....................1 6
Plucky Pet **(45)***(28) (CJBenstead)* 3-8-7 MRimmer(5) (nvr nrr)....................½ 7
Bitter N Twisted **(46)***(27) (SEKettlewell)* 3-8-3 (5) DRMcCabe(10) (sn outpcd & wl bhd: nvr nrr)....................¾ 8
60[4] Star Information **(45)***(4) (JSMoore)* 3-8-7 NAdams(8) (sme hdwy fr rr over 3f: wknd over 2f out)....................10 9
Rockfield Lady (IRE) **(44)***(—) (ICampbell)* 3-8-6v RCochrane(2) (bhd fnl 4f)............8 10

5/4 Mac's Taxi, **4/1** Mediate (IRE), **5/1** Rose Chime (IRE), **7/1** Always Grace, **14/1** WATER HAZARD (IRE), Just Jesting, Rockfield Lady (IRE), **33/1** Bitter N Twisted, Star Information, Plucky Pet, CSF £31.83 CT £80.38 TOTE £17.80: £3.00 £1.20 £1.40 (£38.10) OWNER Mr Ken Butler (EPSOM) BRED Mrs A. C. Belcher and P. B. Hayden in Ireland 10 Rn
1m 27.05 (4.05) SF: 7/16/10/-/-/-/-/-/-/-

86

ANTRIM STKS (3-Y.O) (0-60) (Class F) £2,637.80 (£740.80: £361.40)
5f (Equitrack) GOING minus 0.47 sec per fur (FST) 2-05 (2-06)

42[4] **Ultra Beet (54)***(77) (PCHaslam)* 3-8-11 JWeaver(6) (chsd ldr: led over 1f out: sn clr: comf)....................— 1
40[3] Wasblest **(58)***(57) (MJohnston)* 3-8-6 TWilliams(2) (led tl hdd over 1f out: wknd fnl f)....................5 2
57* Bon Secret (IRE) **(60)***(64) (TJNaughton)* 3-8-9 (5) SSanders(4) (rdn along thrght: styd on fnl f)....................nk 3
7[2] Abbey House **(54)***(41)*(Fav)*(RGuest)* 3-8-6b LDettori(3) (chsd ldrs: rdn over 2f out: wknd over 1f out)....................5 4
Magic Leader (IRE) **(44)***(25) (TTClement)* 3-8-11 AMackay(7) (sn outpcd: a bhd)...7 5
57[5] Jemthorn Bishop **(47)***(14) (JJBridger)* 3-8-11b GBardwell(1) (sn outpcd: a bhd)....3½ 6

11/8 Abbey House, **7/4** Wasblest, **7/2** Bon Secret (IRE), **7/1** ULTRA BEET, **33/1** Magic Leader (IRE), Jemthorn Bishop, CSF £19.88 TOTE £10.70: £2.10 £2.00 (£9.80) OWNER Pet Express Ltd T/A Nutrimix (MIDDLEHAM) BRED Rockhouse Farms Ltd 6 Rn
58.83 secs (0.63) SF: 44/23/30/6/-/-

87

FERMANAGH H'CAP (Amateurs) (0-70) (Class E) £3,066.80 (£928.40: £453.20: £215.60) **2m (Equitrack)** GOING minus 0.47 sec per fur (FST) 2-40 (2-40)

13[3] **Kadiri (IRE) (55)***(64+) (JRBosley)* 4-9-9 (5) MrsSBosley(3) (hld up: hdwy 3f out: led over 1f out: pushed out)....................— 1

15[3] Pride of May (IRE) **(68)***(72) (RHannon)* 4-10-6b(7) MissCHyde(5) (chsd ldr 10f out: led 2f out tl over 1f out: one pce) 5 **2**
Elburg (IRE) **(62)***(65) (RPCHoad)* 5-10-7 (7) MissLMcIntosh(4) (chsd ldr 6f: rdn 4f out: r.o one pce fnl f) 1¼ **3**
Marco Magnifico (USA) **(69)***(70) (BWHills)* 5-11-7 MrsMCowdrey(7) (led tl hdd 2f out: rdn over 1f out: wknd fnl f) 2½ **4**
46* Gold Surprise (IRE) **(59)***(53) (SEKettlewell)* 6-10-6 (5) MrsDKettlewell(1) (hld up: rdn 4f out: wknd over 2f out) 7 **5**
13* Beautete **(70)***(64)*(Fav)*(SDow)* 4-11-1 MrTCuff(2) (B; b.hind: chsd ldrs tl rdn & wknd 2f out) ....nk **6**
King William **(42)***(25) (JLSpearing)* 10-9-3 (5) MissTSpearing(6) (dwlt: a bhd) 12 **7**

2/1 Beautete, **4/1** Marco Magnifico (USA) (5/2-9/2), **5/1** KADIRI (IRE), **11/2** Gold Surprise (IRE), **6/1** Pride of May (IRE), **9/1** Elburg (IRE), **20/1** King William, CSF £31.21 TOTE £7.20: £2.20 £3.20 (£17.70) OWNER Mr J. R. Bosley (WANTAGE) BRED His Highness The Aga Khans Studs S.C. 7 Rn 3m 28.66 (5.16) SF: 49/57/57/61/45/49/18
WEIGHT FOR AGE 4yo-7lb

88

ARMAGH H'CAP (0-70) (Class E) £3,023.90 (£915.20: £446.60: £212.30)
1m 4f (Equitrack) GOING minus 0.47 sec per fur (FST) 3-10 (3-10)

37* **Benfleet (75)***(82+)*(Fav)*(RWArmstrong)* 4-10-0 LDettori(4) (hld up: hdwy 3f out: led over 1f out: easily) ....— **1**
11[6] Bag of Tricks (IRE) **(63)***(66) (SDow)* 5-9-7 JWeaver(3) (b: b.hind: chsd ldr 9f out: led over 3f out tl over 1f out: one pce) 3 **2**
15[5] Milngavie (IRE) **(65)***(66) (MJohnston)* 5-9-2 (7) OliverCasey(6) (led over 8f: hrd rdn 2f out: one pce) 2 **3**
9[9] Ragtime Song **(40)***(31) (AMoore)* 6-7-12 NAdams(2) (chsd ldr 3f: rdn 4f out: wknd 3f out) 8 **4**
Doreen's Delight **(40)***(25) (HJCollingridge)* 9-7-7 (5) CHawksley(1) (b: swtg: sn outpcd: a bhd) 5 **5**
Inzar **(54)***(39) (PMitchell)* 4-8-7b JQuinn(5) (chsd ldrs: rdn 4f out: wknd 3f out) ....s.h **6**

8/11 BENFLEET, **4/1** Doreen's Delight, **11/2** Milngavie (IRE), **9/1** Bag of Tricks (IRE), **12/1** Ragtime Song, **25/1** Inzar, CSF £7.59 TOTE £1.60: £1.10 £3.10 (£3.90) OWNER Mr C. G. Donovan (NEWMARKET) BRED Aston Park Stud 6 Rn 2m 33.96 (4.56) SF: 44/34/33/-/-/2
WEIGHT FOR AGE 4yo-5lb

89

LADBROKE ALL-WEATHER TROPHY (H'cap) (Final) (Class B)
£9,649.50 (£2,886.00: £1,383.00: £631.50)
7f (Equitrack) GOING minus 0.47 sec per fur (FST) 3-40 (3-41)

Red Valerian (75)*(84) (KMcAuliffe)* 4-9-5b RCochrane(4) (edgd lft s: sn chsng ldrs: led ins fnl f: all out) ....— **1**
Ertlon **(84)***(92)*(Fav)*(CEBrittain)* 5-10-0 BDoyle(7) (lw: last over 4f out: c wd & hdwy over 2f out: str run fnl f: jst failed) ....hd **2**
Triple Joy **(81)***(86) (SirMarkPrescott)* 4-9-11 WWoods(3) (sltly hmpd s: sn rcvrd: led 5f out tl ins fnl f: one pce) 1¼ **3**
Maid Welcome **(58)***(63) (MrsNMacauley)* 8-7-9v(7) AmandaSanders(14) (a.p: ev ch ins fnl f: one pce) ....s.h **4**
Mr Nevermind (IRE) **(76)***(78) (GLMoore)* 5-8-13 (7) LSuthern(13) (lw: dwlt: hld up & bhd: styd on wl fnl f: too much to do) 1½ **5**
41[2] Digpast (IRE) **(53)***(50) (RJO'Sullivan)* 5-7-11b JQuinn(11) (b: mid div: rdn 2f out: one pce) 2½ **6**
44* Just Harry **(82)***(79) (MJRyan)* 4-9-5 (7) MBaird(15) (rdn 4f out: nvr nrr) ....s.h **7**
55[3] Aljaz **(55)***(49) (DTThom)* 5-7-13 AMackay(5) (b: led 2f: chsd ldr: ev ch 2f out: 5th & btn whn eased ins fnl f) 1½ **8**
Secret Aly (CAN) **(74)***(68) (CEBrittain)* 5-9-4 MRimmer(12) (lw: dwlt: sn rdn along: nvr nrr) ....s.h **9**
41[3] Invocation **(67)***(59) (AMoore)* 8-8-11 NAdams(8) (chsd ldrs: rdn 2f out: wknd over 1f out) ....¾ **10**
1[4] Mullitover **(70)***(61) (MJHeaton-Ellis)* 5-9-0 StephenDavies(10) (bhd fnl 2f) ....nk **11**
12[11] Friendly Brave (USA) **(69)***(59) (TGMills)* 5-8-13 TIves(16) (mid div: rdn 3f out: wknd over 1f out) ....nk **12**
Masnun (USA) **(69)***(58) (RJO'Sullivan)* 10-8-13 DBiggs(9) (bhd & outpcd: mod hdwy into mid div whn n.m.r ins fnl f) ....½ **13**
41[5] World Traveller **(71)***(60) (WAO'Gorman)* 4-8-12v(3) EmmaO'Gorman(2) (sltly hmpd s: hmpd after 2f: a bhd) ....s.h **14**

Waldo **(67)***(54) (LordHuntingdon)* 4-8-11v LDettori(6) (bhd fr ½-wy)..........¾ **15**
Dancing Lawyer **(75)***(54) (BJMeehan)* 4-9-5 JWeaver(1) (lw: chsd ldrs tl rdn & wknd 2f out)..........4 **16**

9/2 Ertlon, **6/1** Triple Joy, **7/1** RED VALERIAN (5/1-8/1), Just Harry, **10/1** Dancing Lawyer, Digpast (IRE), Secret Aly (CAN), **12/1** Mr Nevermind (IRE), Waldo, Aljaz, **16/1** Maid Welcome, Masnun (USA), **20/1** Invocation, **25/1** World Traveller, Mullitover, **33/1** Friendly Brave (USA), CSF £39.42 CT £194.17 TOTE £8.60: £2.20 £2.50 £3.00 £2.30 (£23.60) OWNER Mr R. J. Cummings (LAMBOURN) BRED Mascalls Stud Farm 16 Rn
1m 24.64 (1.64) SF: 44/52/47/26/39/12/38/-/-/-/-/-/-/-/-/-

T/Plpt: £101.10 (72.2 Tckts). T/Qdpt: £29.10 (0.5 Tckts); £19.68 to Fontwell 16/1/95. SM

0077-SOUTHWELL (L-H)
Monday January 16th (Standard)

90

SHETLAND (S) STKS (I) (3-Y.O) (Class G) £2,259.00 (£634.00: £309.00)
1m (Fibresand) GOING: 0.08 sec per fur (STD) 1-00 (1-01)

Legally Delicious *(49+) (JEBanks)* 3-8-9 JQuinn(9) (trckd ldrs: led 2f out: pushed clr 1f out: eased nr fin)..........— **1**
Kirov Protege (IRE) **(46)***(46) (RWArmstrong)* 3-9-0 MRimmer(2) (led tl over 2f out: swtchd & kpt on one pce appr fnl f)..........4 **2**
43⁸ Poly Lane **(51)***(53) (WRMuir)* 3-9-7 JWeaver(7) (chsd ldrs: outpcd ½-wy: kpt on u.p fnl 2f)..........hd **3**
51⁶ Risky Rose **(43)***(37) (RHollinshead)* 3-8-4 (5) AGarth(6) (hdwy ½-wy: styd on fnl 2f: nt rch ldrs)..........2 **4**
25⁶ Presto Boy **(56)***(39)*(Fav)*(MBell)* 3-9-0b MFenton(12) (chsd ldrs: led over 2f out: sn hdd: edgd lft & wknd over 1f out)..........1¼ **5**
Recovery Lad (IRE) *(29) (KRBurke)* 3-9-0 RCochrane(3) (in tch: outpcd over 2f out: n.d after)..........5 **6**
Havana Miss **(40)***(30) (BPalling)* 3-9-2 GDuffield(1) (chsd ldrs tl wknd 2f out)..........nk **7**
5⁸ Vade Retro Satanas (FR) **(45)***(20) (CTinkler)* 3-9-0 TIves(4) (chsd ldrs: drvn along ½-wy: wknd over 2f out)..........4 **8**
51⁴ Runforaction (IRE) **(50)***(11) (BSRothwell)* 3-8-11 (5) JStack(10) (sn drvn along: chsd ldrs: outpcd ½-wy: n.d after)..........2 **9**
51⁸ Miss Suzy *(8) (JPLeigh)* 3-8-9 LCharnock(11) (sn outpcd & pushed along)..........3½ **10**
51¹⁰ Sergio (IRE) *(—) (MCChapman)* 3-8-9 (5) DRMcCabe(13) (s.i.s: a outpcd & sn wl bhd)..........14 **11**
Royal Addiction (IRE) *(—) (PABlockley)* 3-9-0 AClark(8) (bkwd: racd wd: sn outpcd & bhd)..........5 **12**
Aisling's Image *(—) (SGNorton)* 3-8-9 GCarter(5) (leggy: dwlt: a bhd)..........hd **13**

9/4 Presto Boy, **11/4** LEGALLY DELICIOUS, **7/1** Poly Lane, **15/2** Runforaction (IRE), **9/1** Aisling's Image, **10/1** Recovery Lad (IRE), Vade Retro Satanas (FR), **12/1** Risky Rose, Kirov Protege (IRE) (10/1-16/1), Havana Miss, **25/1** Sergio (IRE), **33/1** Royal Addiction (IRE), Miss Suzy, CSF £39.92 TOTE £3.20: £1.80 £2.30 £2.70 (£46.70) OWNER Mr P. A. Philipps (NEWMARKET) BRED E. Landi 13 Rn
1m 47.8 (8.50) SF: 16/13/19/5/7/-/-/-/-/-/-/-/-
No bid

91

MULL H'CAP (0-70) (Class E) £3,166.90 (£959.20: £468.60: £223.30)
1m 3f (Fibresand) GOING: 0.08 sec per fur (STD) 1-30 (1-30)

Barti-Ddu **(57)***(58) (SCWilliams)* 4-8-10 (5) JStack(9) (chsd ldrs: drvn along & styd on to ld 1f out: r.o)..........— **1**
35² Royal Citizen (IRE) **(63)***(62)*(Fav)*(JFBottomley)* 6-9-11 GCarter(1) (mid div: hdwy over 3f out: styd on u.p fnl f: no imp)..........1¼ **2**
*83** Tempering **(59)***(56) (DWChapman)* 9-9-7 5x JQuinn(8) (swtg: led: clr over 4f out: hdd 1f out: no ex)..........1¼ **3**
66¹¹ Palacegate Jo (IRE) **(58)***(55) (RHollinshead)* 4-9-2 WWoods(11) (bhd: hdwy on outside 5f out: edgd lft & styd on fnl 2f: nt rch ldrs)..........hd **4**
Atherton Green (IRE) **(58)***(50) (JAGlover)* 5-9-6 TIves(7) (sn bhd: styd on fnl 2f: nt rch ldrs)..........4 **5**
Let's Get Lost **(66)***(57) (MrsJRRamsden)* 6-10-0 JWeaver(12) (lw: stdd s: hld up & bhd: hdwy 5f out: effrt & swtchd ins 2f out: nvr nr ldrs)..........½ **6**
*29** Greek Gold (IRE) **(59)***(50) (GPKelly)* 6-9-7 AlexGreaves(4) (lw: trckd ldrs: effrt over 2f out: wknd & eased over 1f out)..........2½ **7**

52³ Non Vintage (IRE) **(63)***(51) (MCChapman)* 4-9-2 (5) DRMcCabe(6) (sn bhd: styd on fnl 3f: nvr nr ldrs)........d.h **7**
Imperial Bid (FR) **(55)***(40) (DenysSmith)* 7-8-10 (7) CTeague(2) (sn bhd & drvn along: n.m.r over 3f out: hdwy & hung lft over 2f out: nvr nr ldrs)........2½ **9**
30⁷ Perdition (IRE) **(45)***(10) (KRBurke)* 5-8-7 RCochrane(5) (nvr nr ldrs)........7 **10**
Westfield Moves (IRE) **(49)***(16) (HJCollingridge)* 7-8-11 MRimmer(14) (lw: sn bhd & drvn along: n.d)........6 **11**
28⁶ Clear Look **(44)***(10) (MissHCKnight)* 5-8-6 AClark(13) (rr div: sme hdwy u.p over 3f out: sn wknd)........½ **12**
76⁷ Queen of Shannon (IRE) **(49)***(24) (BJMeehan)* 7-8-4v(7) DaneO'Neill(3) (w ldr tl wknd over 4f out: sn bhd: t.o)........20 **13**
Mister Beat **(62)***(—) (JGFitzGerald)* 4-8-13 (7) FLynch(10) (chsd ldrs: rdn 5f out: sn wknd: broke leg over 1f out: dead)........ **0**

7/2 Royal Citizen (IRE), **6/1** Tempering, **7/1** Let's Get Lost, **8/1** Greek Gold (IRE), **10/1** Atherton Green (IRE), **11/1** Non Vintage (IRE), Westfield Moves (IRE), Perdition (IRE), **12/1** BARTI-DDU, Imperial Bid (FR), Palacegate Jo (IRE), **14/1** Queen of Shannon (IRE), **16/1** Mister Beat, **33/1** Clear Look, CSF £54.91 CT £270.66 TOTE £17.20: £3.40 £1.50 £2.40 (£37.70) OWNER Miss L. J. Ward (NEWMARKET) BRED Lloyd Bros 14 Rn 2m 31.8 (10.30) SF: 33/41/36/32/30/36/27/27/-/-
WEIGHT FOR AGE 4yo-4lb

92

ISLE OF SKYE CLAIMING STKS (Class F) £2,537.00 (£712.00: £347.00)
7f (Fibresand) GOING: 0.08 sec per fur (STD) 2-00 (2-01)

20⁵ **Dream Carrier (IRE) (67)***(75) (TDBarron)* 7-8-0 (7) KimberleyHart(8) (hld up & bhd: hdwy over 3f out: rdn to ld over 1f out: styd on)........— **1**
20² Everset (FR) **(93)***(79)*(Fav)*(ABailey)* 7-9-2 (3) DWright(7) (lw: chsd ldrs: led over 3f out tl over 1f out: nt qckn)........4 **2**
55⁴ Super Benz **(66)***(53) (FJO'Mahony)* 9-8-1 (5) JStack(4) (s.s: hld up & bhd: hdwy over 3f out: sn prom: rdn & r.o same pce fnl 2f)........6 **3**
Millsolin (IRE) **(69)***(42) (RAkehurst)* 7-8-3 GCarter(3) (b: sn outpcd & pushed along: sme hdwy over 2f out: n.d)........4 **4**
32² Rosina's Folly **(54)***(38) (JLHarris)* 4-8-6 RCochrane(1) (outpcd tl kpt on fnl 2f)........3½ **5**
82¹³ Arrogant Boy *(28) (DWChapman)* 6-7-9 (7)ow1 CTeague(5) (nvr nr ldrs)........3 **6**
Great Bond *(41) (BAMcMahon)* 4-8-10 (5) SSanders(6) (bit bkwd: chsd ldrs 2f: sn outpcd & bhd: sme hdwy 2f out: n.d)........s.h **7**
Curie Crusader (IRE) **(47)***(36) (MDods)* 4-8-11 WWoods(10) (chsd ldrs: led over 4f out tl over 3f out: wknd 2f out)........hd **8**
53¹³ Hay Dance **(45)***(21) (JPLeigh)* 4-8-7 JFanning(2) (led 1f: chsd ldr tl lost pl over 3f out: sn bhd)........5 **9**
65¹² Bessie's Will **(46)***(13) (DHaydnJones)* 4-8-0 AMackay(9) (bit bkwd: led after 1f tl over 4f out: drvn along & wknd over 3f out: sn bhd)........nk **10**

10/11 Everset (FR), **3/1** Millsolin (IRE), **5/1** Super Benz, **7/1** DREAM CARRIER (IRE), **12/1** Rosina's Folly, **33/1** Hay Dance, Curie Crusader (IRE), **66/1** Great Bond, Arrogant Boy, Bessie's Will, CSF £14.03 TOTE £9.90: £1.40 £1.10 £1.20 (£8.80) OWNER Mr Stephen Woodall (THIRSK) BRED Mellon Stud 10 Rn 1m 32.2 (5.40) SF: 36/38/13/1/-/-/-/-/-/-

93

LUNDY H'CAP (0-80) (Class D) £3,724.50 (£1,128.00: £551.00: £262.50)
6f (Fibresand) GOING: 0.08 sec per fur (STD) 2-30 (2-32)

Nordan Raider (71)*(78) (MJCamacho)* 7-9-5 LCharnock(10) (lw: a.p: led 2f out: r.o wl fnl f)........— **1**
6* Croft Pool **(80)***(82) (JAGlover)* 4-10-0 TIves(12) (a.p: ev ch 1f out: nt qckn)........1¾ **2**
44⁵ Dawalib (USA) **(73)***(71) (DHaydnJones)* 5-9-7 AMackay(8) (sn bhd: hdwy & prom 2f out: kpt on one pce)........1½ **3**
Elton Ledger (IRE) **(73)***(70) (MrsNMacauley)* 6-9-2v(5) SSanders(5) (b: effrt & swtchd outside over 2f out: styd on fnl f)........nk **4**
6² Matthew David **(46)***(33)*(Fav)*(SRBowring)* 5-7-8 GBardwell(4) (b: bhd whn hmpd over 3f out: kpt on wl fnl 2f: nt rch ldrs)........4 **5**
32⁶ Tenor **(55)***(41) (DNicholls)* 4-8-3 CRutter(11) (dwlt: hdwy to chse ldrs over 2f out: sn outpcd)........hd **6**
Arndilly **(69)***(51) (BJMeehan)* 4-9-3 RCochrane(2) (bhd whn hmpd over 3f out: sme hdwy 2f out: n.d)........1¼ **7**
Cradle Days **(70)***(46) (RCSpicer)* 6-9-4 JWeaver(7) (in tch: effrt & hmpd over 2f out: n.d after)........2½ **8**
Four of Spades **(66)***(37) (WSCunningham)* 4-9-0b AClark(13) (lw: w ldrs: led over 2f out: sn hdd & wknd)........2 **9**
55⁵ Aquado **(48)***(16) (ALForbes)* 6-7-5 (5)ow3 NVarley(1) (sn drvn along: nvr nr ldrs)........¾ **10**

65[6] Green's Bid **(59)***(24) (DWChapman)* 5-8-7 AlexGreaves(9) (chsd ldrs: ev ch over 2f out: sn wknd)....¾ **11**
41[9] Newington Butts (IRE) **(49)***(—) (RAkehurst)* 5-7-11 JQuinn(6) (w ldrs tl wknd over 2f out: sn bhd)....8 **12**
Boursin (IRE) **(72)***(2) (PCalver)* 6-9-6 DaleGibson(3) (mde most tl over 2f out: sn wknd)....6 **13**

LONG HANDICAP Aquado 7-0

4/1 Matthew David, **9/2** Croft Pool, **6/1** NORDAN RAIDER, **13/2** Arndilly, **8/1** Four of Spades, **9/1** Dawalib (USA), **10/1** Elton Ledger (IRE), **12/1** Cradle Days, Boursin (IRE), **14/1** Green's Bid, Newington Butts (IRE), **16/1** Tenor, **25/1** Aquado, CSF £34.80 CT £234.62 TOTE £9.20: £2.80 £2.20 £3.40 (£35.20) OWNER Miss J. A. Camacho (MALTON) BRED B. Nordan 13 Rn
1m 18.7 (5.20) SF: 39/45/35/34/-/6/16/-/-/-/-/-/-

94

FAIR ISLE H'CAP (0-70) (Class E) £3,238.40 (£981.20: £479.60: £228.80)
1m (Fibresand) GOING: 0.08 sec per fur (STD) 3-00 (3-01)

30* **Roar on Tour (49)***(59)*(Fav)*(MrsMReveley)* 6-8-4b(7) SCopp(7) (lw: trckd ldrs: led on bit over 2f out: pushed out)....— **1**
62[4] Hawaii Storm (FR) **(56)***(61) (MissAJWhitfield)* 7-8-13 (5) RPainter(14) (chsd ldrs: ev ch & edgd lft u.p 2f out: nt qckn)....2½ **2**
12[6] Buddy's Friend (IRE) **(60)***(61) (RJRWilliams)* 7-9-1 (7) SarahThompson(11) (lw: bhd: gd hdwy on outside over 3f out: kpt on same pce fnl 2f)....2 **3**
Polonez Prima **(65)***(64) (JEBanks)* 8-9-13 JWeaver(10) (lw: s.i.s: bhd tl hdwy on outside over 2f out: styd on nr fin)....¾ **4**
30[6] Queens Consul (IRE) **(65)***(59) (BSRothwell)* 5-9-8 (5) JStack(13) (in tch: effrt 2f out: no imp)....2½ **5**
18[6] Tu Opes **(64)***(57) (JLHarris)* 4-9-11 DaleGibson(6) (s.i.s: hld up & bhd: stdy hdwy 2f out: fin strly)....½ **6**
30[2] No Submission (USA) **(66)***(57) (DWChapman)* 9-10-0 TIves(1) (chsd ldrs: reminders & lost pl over 4f out: kpt on appr fnl f)....¾ **7**
50* Genesis Four **(40)***(28) (SRBowring)* 5-7-9b(7)ow1 CTeague(9) (prom: outpcd over 2f out: n.d after)....1½ **8**
80[7] Tilly Owl **(39)***(22) (JAHarris)* 4-8-0 JO'Reilly(3) (b.hind: led tl over 2f out: sn wknd)2½ **9**
55* Quinzii Martin **(46)***(26) (DHaydnJones)* 7-8-8 6x TWilliams(8) (chsd ldrs: ev ch & rdn over 2f out: sn wknd)....1¼ **10**
18[2] Pillow Talk (IRE) **(61)***(39) (KRBurke)* 4-9-8 RCochrane(15) (prom: effrt over 2f out: sn rdn & wknd)....¾ **11**
Christian Flight (IRE) **(47)***(19) (SGollings)* 6-8-9 JQuinn(12) (in tch: effrt over 2f out: sn wknd)....3 **12**
Titania's Dance (IRE) **(58)***(23) (MBell)* 4-9-5 MFenton(2) (bit bkwd: w ldrs tl wknd over 2f out)....3½ **13**
The Country Dancer **(40)***(—) (KTIvory)* 5-8-2 GDuffield(4) (sn bhd: t.o)....20 **14**

9/2 ROAR ON TOUR, **5/1** Genesis Four, Titania's Dance (IRE), **7/1** Polonez Prima, **8/1** Pillow Talk (IRE), Quinzii Martin, **9/1** Tilly Owl, **10/1** No Submission (USA), Hawaii Storm (FR), **12/1** Buddy's Friend (IRE), Queens Consul (IRE), **16/1** Tu Opes, **33/1** Christian Flight (IRE), The Country Dancer, CSF £52.91 CT £492.62 TOTE £6.90: £2.90 £4.50 £3.90 (£23.20) OWNER Mrs S.Murray (SALTBURN) BRED Pitts Farm Stud 14 Rn 1m 47.2 (7.90) SF: 23/25/25/29/23/20/22/-
WEIGHT FOR AGE 4yo-1lb

95

SHETLAND (S) STKS (II) (3-Y.O) (Class G) £2,259.00 (£634.00: £309.00)
1m (Fibresand) GOING: 0.08 sec per fur (STD) 3-30 (3-32)

10[2] **Mazilla (57)***(57)*(Fav)*(WJHaggas)* 3-8-9 WWoods(4) (mde all: drvn along 2f out: jst hld on)....— **1**
Jilly Jaffa Cake (IRE) **(55)***(57) (DWPArbuthnot)* 3-8-9 SWhitworth(3) (b: a chsng wnr: kpt on wl u.p ins fnl f)....hd **2**
48[7] Sweet Mate *(62) (SRBowring)* 3-8-7 (7) CTeague(5) (hld up & bhd: effrt on outside 3f out: edgd rt & styd on wl fnl f)....hd **3**
48[2] Samana Cay **(50)***(63) (DNicholls)* 3-9-2 AlexGreaves(9) (lw: chsd ldrs: ev ch over 1f out: kpt on same pce)....½ **4**
51[5] Slapy Dam *(60) (MrsJRRamsden)* 3-9-0 JWeaver(1) (hld up & bhd: hdwy over 2f out: kpt on fnl f: nvr rchd ldrs)....nk **5**
48[3] Joyful Times **(43)***(47) (MrsNMacauley)* 3-8-4 (5) SSanders(12) (hdwy over 3f out: hrd rdn & hung bdly lft 2f out: sn wknd)....4 **6**
Fools Millyons (IRE) **(46)***(51) (WBentley)* 3-9-0 JFanning(11) (in tch: drvn along over 3f out: one pce)....nk **7**
48[5] Daily Challenger (USA) **(60)***(37) (RonaldThompson)* 3-9-0 TWilliams(8) (trckd ldrs tl wknd over 2f out)....7 **8**

Princess Kamina **(35)***(29) (MJCamacho)* 3-8-9 LCharnock(6) (sn outpcd & drvn along: in tch tl lost pl over 3f out)....1½ **9**
10[7] Go Likecrazy **(49)***(24) (KTIvory)* 3-8-9b(7) CScally(2) (sn wl bhd) 6 **10**
Jovale **(48)***(14) (SGNorton)* 3-8-9 (5) JStack(7) (chsd ldrs: rdn over 3f out: wknd over 2f out) 4 **11**
Red Hassett (IRE) **(48)***(12) (PABlockley)* 3-9-0 AClark(10) (s.i.s: bhd tl hdwy over 3f out: sn wknd) 1 **12**

Evens MAZILLA, **11/2** Slapy Dam, **6/1** Jilly Jaffa Cake (IRE), **7/1** Samana Cay, **12/1** Joyful Times, **14/1** Daily Challenger (USA), **16/1** Sweet Mate, Jovale, **20/1** Princess Kamina, Red Hassett (IRE), **25/1** Go Likecrazy, **33/1** Fools Millyons (IRE), CSF £9.07 TOTE £2.00: £1.10 £2.90 £7.60 (£6.10) OWNER . Flying Fillies (NEWMARKET) BRED Mrs H. MacFarlane 12 Rn
1m 48.5 (9.20) SF: 9/9/13/15/12/-/4/-/-/-/-/-
Bt in 6,800 gns

96

BARRA APP'CE H'CAP (Mdn) (0-60) (Class F) £2,537.00 (£712.00: £347.00)
1m 4f (Fibresand) GOING: 0.08 sec per fur (STD) 4-00 (4-01)

Borocay (33)*(42) (MJCamacho)* 7-8-6 GParkin(13) (bhd: hdwy 4f out: styd on wl u.p appr fnl f: led nr fin)....— **1**
45[9] Shamwari (USA) **(50)***(58) (JWHills)* 4-9-5b RPainter(4) (chsd ldrs: led over 5f out tl nr fin)....½ **2**
9[6] Wicklow Boy (IRE) **(40)***(43) (TTClement)* 4-8-6v(3) SLanigan(5) (a.p: one pce fnl 3f)....4 **3**
Tuscania **(22)***(25) (JWharton)* 5-7-9 MBaird(12) (lw: hld up: hdwy over 3f out: styd on fnl f: nt rch ldrs)....hd **4**
Mr Moriarty (IRE) **(34)***(35)*(Fav)*(SRBowring)* 4-8-3 CTeague(11) (chsd ldrs: rdn & hung lft 2f out: one pce)....1¾ **5**
21[4] Celestial Faith **(38)***(35) (MJohnston)* 4-8-4 (3) OliverCasey(2) (a.p: effrt over 3f out: grad wknd)....3½ **6**
Jihaad (USA) **(50)***(46) (JNorton)* 5-9-2v(7) AmyGosden(15) (s.i.s: bhd: kpt on fnl 3f: n.d)....1 **7**
Petite Bijou **(42)***(29) (RBrotherton)* 4-8-11 DGriffiths(16) (bhd: sme hdwy over 2f out: n.d)....7 **8**
Premier Blues (FR) **(35)***(20) (RJRWilliams)* 5-8-5 (3) SarahThompson(1) (b.hind: nvr nr ldrs)....1½ **9**
Shamaka **(48)***(31) (JAGlover)* 4-8-12 (5) MrSRichardson(10) (chsd ldrs tl wknd over 2f out)....1¼ **10**
50[6] Comfortable **(35)***(16) (SGollings)* 5-8-8e SCopp(3) (eyeshield: dwlt: sn mid div: rdn 4f out: sn wknd)....1¼ **11**
46[6] Haydon Hill **(34)***(14) (PDEvans)* 4-8-0 (3) DaneO'Neill(14) (hdwy 5f out: sn rdn: wknd 3f out)....¾ **12**
Grecian Lady (IRE) **(36)***(11) (KRBurke)* 6-8-6b(3) CAdamson(9) (a in rr)....4 **13**
Flying Imp **(37)***(—) (RHollinshead)* 4-8-1 (5) AEddery(17) (a bhd: t.o)....25 **14**
Red Whirlwind **(55)***(—) (BJMcMath)* 5-10-0 VHalliday(8) (lw: bhd fnl 3f: t.o)....4 **15**
Nord Lys (IRE) **(35)***(—) (FHLee)* 4-8-4b ClaireBalding(6) (led tl over 5f out: sn lost pl: t.o 3f out)....½ **16**
Strolling Minstrel (IRE) **(47)***(—) (BSRothwell)* 4-8-11b(5) GinaFaulkner(7) (lw: chsd ldrs tl wknd 6f out: wl t.o 3f out)....dist **17**

7/2 Mr Moriarty (IRE), **6/1** Celestial Faith, **7/1** Red Whirlwind, **15/2** Shamaka, **8/1** Wicklow Boy (IRE), **9/1** Shamwari (USA), BOROCAY, **10/1** Petite Bijou, **12/1** Jihaad (USA), **14/1** Tuscania, Grecian Lady (IRE), **20/1** Nord Lys (IRE), Flying Imp, Strolling Minstrel (IRE), Haydon Hill, **25/1** Comfortable, Premier Blues (FR), CSF £95.70 CT £647.35 TOTE £14.90: £2.50 £4.10 £1.70 £4.30 (£114.00) OWNER Mrs S. Camacho (MALTON) BRED Mrs S. Camacho 17 Rn
2m 48.1 (13.90) SF: 9/20/6/-/-/-/12/-/-/-/-/-/-/-/-/-/-
WEIGHT FOR AGE 4yo-4lb
T/Plpt: £46.90 (198.53 Tckts). T/Qdpt: £17.60 (2.2 Tckts). WG

0084-LINGFIELD (L-H)
Tuesday January 17th (Standard)

97

YARMOUTH CLAIMING STKS (Class E) £2,981.00 (£902.00:£440.00: £209.00)
1m 5f (Equitrack) GOING minus 0.30 sec per fur (FST) 1-30 (1-30)

Elementary (73)*(71+) (NJHWalker)* 12-9-5 RCochrane(4) (a.p: led over 3f out: sn clr: easily)....— **1**
Cliburnel News (IRE) **(49)***(54) (WRMuir)* 5-8-10 JWeaver(7) (b: b.hind: rdn & hdwy over 3f out: unable qckn)....7 **2**

37[2] In the Money (IRE) **(59)***(64) (RHollinshead)* 6-9-7 TIves(5) (w ldr over 9f: one pce) ¾ **3**
36[2] Surprise Guest (IRE) **(67)***(60) (MJohnston)* 4-9-1 TWilliams(3) (lw: led over 9f: one pce) 1½ **4**
58* Carlowitz (USA) **(53)***(42)*(Fav)*(AMoore)* 7-8-9 CandyMorris(1) (b: a wl bhd) 7 **5**
37[3] Pharamineux **(57)***(9) (RAkehurst)* 9-8-11e GCarter(6) (eyeshield: lw: bhd fnl 5f) 30 **6**

3/1 Carlowitz (USA), **7/2** ELEMENTARY, Pharamineux, **6/1** Surprise Guest (IRE), In the Money (IRE), **7/1** Cliburnel News (IRE),CSF £23.39 TOTE £4.40: £3.00 £8.70 (£42.80) OWNER Mr Paul Green (WANTAGE) BRED Ballymaglassan Stud 6 Rn 2m 47.92 (5.42) SF: 46/30/39/32/18/-
WEIGHT FOR AGE 4yo-4lb

98

VENTNOR (S) STKS (3-Y.O) (Class G) £2,483.00 (£698.00: £341.00)
7f (Equitrack) GOING minus 0.30 sec per fur (FST) 2-00 (2-04)

25[5] **Fahema (50)***(49+) (RBoss)* 3-8-6 GDuffield(3) (mde all: clr over 1f out: r.o wl) .....— **1**
Iron Man (IRE) **(59)***(51) (JWhite)* 3-8-11b(5) SDrowne(6) (a.p: chsd wnr over 3f out: hrd rdn over 1f out: unable qckn) 4 **2**
25[9] Fairy's Son **(46)***(42) (WRMuir)* 3-8-11b StephenDavies(8) (b: plld hrd: hdwy over 3f out: one pce fnl 2f) 2 **3**
7[7] More Bills (IRE) **(46)***(40) (AMoore)* 3-8-11 CandyMorris(7) (b.hind: a.p: one pce fnl 2f) 1 **4**
24[5] Rowlandsons Silver (FR) **(54)***(37) (DJGMurraySmith)* 3-8-11 CRutter(9) (rdn over 4f out: hdwy over 1f out: r.o one pce) 1¼ **5**
Griffin's Girl *(21) (RPCHoad)* 3-8-6 GCarter(4) (lw: nvr nr to chal) 5 **6**
5[9] Nanny Doon *(17) (MJohnston)* 3-8-6 TWilliams(10) (bhd fnl 5f) 1¾ **7**
85[10] Rockfield Lady (IRE) **(44)***(14) (ICampbell)* 3-8-6v RCochrane(1) (b.nr hind: prom over 3f) 1½ **8**
Slybird *(9) (MJRyan)* 3-8-6 AClark(2) (neat: bit bkwd: bhd fnl 4f) 2½ **9**
54* Water Bebe (IRE) **(53)***(—)*(Fav)*(GCBravery)* 3-8-1 (5) DRMcCabe(5) (a.p: rdn over 4f out: 5th whn p.u over 2f out: broke leg: dead) **0**

1/2 Water Bebe (IRE), **5/1** Iron Man (IRE), **13/2** FAHEMA, **9/1** Rowlandsons Silver (FR), **20/1** Fairy's Son, Slybird, Rockfield Lady (IRE), **25/1** More Bills (IRE), Nanny Doon, **33/1** Griffin's Girl, CSF £40.62 TOTE £5.60: £1.30 £2.00 £2.20 (£11.10) OWNER Mr A. Foustok (NEWMARKET) BRED Ahmed M. Foustok 10 Rn 1m 29.43 (6.43) SF: -/-/-/-/-/-/-/-/-/-
No bid

99

SHANKLIN H'CAP (3-Y.O) (0-75) (Class D) £3,555.50 (£1,076.00: £525.00: £249.50) **1m (Equitrack)** GOING minus 0.30 sec per fur (FST) 2-30 (2-30)

No Pattern (74)*(78) (GLMoore)* 3-9-0 (7) LSuthern(3) (lw: stdd s: hdwy 5f out: chsd ldr ins fnl f: str run to ld last stride) ....— **1**
10* Battleship Bruce **(69)***(73++) (NACallaghan)* 3-8-11 (5) SSanders(1) (b.hind: lw: led: clr over 4f out: eased fnl f: rdn nr fin: hdd last stride) .... s.h **2**
85* Water Hazard (IRE) **(53)***(53) (SDow)* 3-8-0 6x StephenDavies(5) (b.hind: chsd ldr over 4f out tl ins fnl f: r.o) 1¾ **3**
24* Sarasi **(70)***(42)*(Fav)*(PFICole)* 3-9-3 CRutter(4) (b.nr fore: lw: rdn: dropped rr & stumbled over 4f out: no hdwy fnl 3f) 14 **4**
Star Witness (IRE) **(70)***(42) (JSMoore)* 3-9-3 AShoults(2) (chsd ldr over 3f) .... hd **5**

5/4 Sarasi, **11/8** Battleship Bruce, **6/1** Water Hazard (IRE), **16/1** NO PATTERN, **25/1** Star Witness (IRE), CSF £36.47 TOTE £21.90: £3.20 £1.10 (£18.40) OWNER Mr K. Higson (EPSOM) BRED Mrs N. F. M. Sampson 5 Rn 1m 41.16 (4.76) SF: 32/27/10/-/-
STEWARDS' ENQUIRY Sanders fined £375 under Rule 151 (ii) (failure to ensure best poss placing).

100

NEWPORT H'CAP (0-70) (Class E) £3,081.10 (£932.80: £455.40: £216.70)
1m 2f (Equitrack) GOING minus 0.30 sec per fur (FST) 3-00 (3-02)

76[2] **Kaafih Homm (IRE) (55)***(62)*(Fav)*(NACallaghan)* 4-9-6 RCochrane(11) (lw: hdwy over 4f out: led over 1f out: drvn out) ....— **1**
27[3] My Minnie **(50)***(55) (BJMeehan)* 5-9-4 JWeaver(12) (hld up: led over 3f out tl over 1f out: unable qckn) 1¼ **2**
Braveboy **(60)***(64) (CEBrittain)* 7-10-0 BDoyle(10) (hdwy over 4f out: rdn over 3f out: r.o ins fnl f) .... ½ **3**
73[2] Night Edition **(39)***(38) (SDow)* 5-8-7 GCarter(5) (b.hind: a.p: rdn 3f out: one pce) .3½ **4**
63* Eqtesaad (USA) **(65)***(64)*(Fav)*(SCWilliams)* 4-10-2 5x TIves(9) (s.s: hdwy 7f out: rdn over 3f out: one pce) .... hd **5**
56[3] Chili Lady **(39)***(30) (JSMoore)* 5-8-2 (5) SDrowne(7) (lw: led 4f out tl over 3f out: sn wknd) 5 **6**
Little Miss Ribot **(33)***(19) (RJO'Sullivan)* 5-8-1 StephenDavies(2) (prom 6f) 3½ **7**
Coalisland **(37)***(14) (RIngram)* 5-8-5 WWoods(4) (led 5f) 6 **8**

41[8] Greatest Hopes **(36)***(13) (CJBenstead)* 4-8-1 TWilliams(8) (a bhd)........................hd **9**
Ezekiel **(34)***(—) (JWPayne)* 4-7-13 GBardwell(6) (led 5f out to 4f out: sn wknd)...30 **10**
Tina's Charm (IRE) **(38)***(—) (JSMoore)* 6-8-6 AClark(3) (a bhd)..........................1¾ **11**

2/1 KAAFIH HOMM (IRE), Eqtesaad (USA), **6/1** Night Edition, **10/1** Braveboy, Little Miss Ribot, **11/1** Chili Lady, My Minnie, **16/1** Greatest Hopes, **20/1** Tina's Charm (IRE), **25/1** Coalisland, **33/1** Ezekiel, CSF £26.12 CT £183.50 TOTE £3.70: £1.90 £3.50 £4.80 (£17.70) OWNER Gallagher Materials Ltd (NEWMARKET) BRED Sheikh Ahmed bin Rashid al Maktoum 11 Rn
2m 8.88 (5.88) SF: 33/29/38/13/34/6/-/-/-/-/-
WEIGHT FOR AGE 4yo-3lb

101

COWES STKS (Mdn) (Class D) £3,555.50 (£1,076.00: £525.00: £249.50)
6f (Equitrack) GOING minus 0.30 sec per fur (FST) 3-30 (3-34)

Hoist (IRE) (66)*(61+)*(Fav)*(SirMarkPrescott)* 4-9-2 GDuffield(7) (lw: hld up: led over 3f out: clr wl over 1f out: easily)..— **1**
Jersey Belle **(48)***(48) (PJMakin)* 3-8-0 StephenDavies(6) (led over 4f out tl over 3f out: unable qckn)..5 **2**
71[3] Joint Effort (IRE) **(42)***(45) (AMoore)* 4-8-11 (5) SSanders(1) (b.hind: led 5f out tl over 4f out: 3rd & btn whn hmpd on ins over 2f out).............................¾ **3**
Friendly Lady (USA) **(58)***(32) (WAO'Gorman)* 3-7-11 (3) DWright(3) (led 1f: wknd over 3f out)..5 **4**
21[6] Ela Palikari Mou (IRE) *(32) (RAkehurst)* 4-9-7 GCarter(2) (lw: a bhd)..................1¾ **5**
Forbidden Gem *(31) (SWoodman)* 4-9-7 TIves(5) (bhd fnl 4f)...............................nk **6**

1/2 HOIST (IRE), **5/1** Ela Palikari Mou (IRE), **6/1** Joint Effort (IRE), **7/1** Friendly Lady (USA), **25/1** Jersey Belle, **33/1** Forbidden Gem, CSF £12.17 TOTE £1.60: £1.10 £6.10 (£16.60) OWNER Exors of the late Lord Derby (NEWMARKET) BRED Barronstown Bloodstock and Swettenham Stud 6 Rn
1m 14.8 (4.20) SF: 17/-/2/-/-/-
WEIGHT FOR AGE 3yo-16lb

102

RYDE APP'CE H'CAP (0-70) (Class F) £2,663.00 (£748.00: £365.00)
5f (Equitrack) GOING minus 0.30 sec per fur (FST) 4-00 (4-05)

69[3] **Nineacres (57)***(62)*(Fav)*(DNicholls)* 4-9-0b(5) AEddery(7) (chsd ldr: led 1f out: drvn out)...— **1**
70[4] Distant Dynasty **(51)***(54)*(Fav)*(BAPearce)* 5-8-13 SSanders(2) (hdwy over 2f out: ev ch ins fnl f: r.o)..½ **2**
Cheeky Chappy **(38)***(39) (DWChapman)* 4-7-11b(3) CTeague(9) (racd wd: hld up: shkn up over 1f out: r.o ins fnl f)...½ **3**
Banbury Flyer **(37)***(27) (MrsALMKing)* 7-7-13 NVarley(5) (rdn thrght: a.p: unable qckn fnl 2f)..3½ **4**
Daaniera (IRE) **(60)***(49) (PHowling)* 5-9-3 (5) DBiggs(1) (b.hind: led 4f)..................hd **5**
6[5] Warwick Warrior (IRE) **(66)***(50) (MrsLPiggott)* 4-9-9e(5) GMilligan(6) (eyeshield: b: b.hind: lw: outpcd: hdwy fnl f: nvr nrr)................................1½ **6**
69[9] Hinari Video **(55)***(38) (MJohnston)* 10-8-12 (5) OliverCasey(3) (7th & no ch whn hmpd over 2f out)..nk **7**
39[2] Pat Poindestres **(36)***(18)*(Fav)*(RJO'Sullivan)* 5-7-9 (3) CHawksley(8) (prom 3f).......nk **8**
As Such (IRE) **(56)***(33) (NACallaghan)* 4-9-4b DRMcCabe(4) (b.nr hind: a bhd)....1¾ **9**

7/2 NINEACRES, Distant Dynasty, Pat Poindestres, **11/2** As Such (IRE), Daaniera (IRE), **8/1** Warwick Warrior (IRE), **12/1** Hinari Video, **20/1** Cheeky Chappy, Banbury Flyer, CSF £16.73 CT £197.52 TOTE £6.30: £1.20 £1.10 £7.10 (£12.00) OWNER Mr John Gilbertson (THIRSK) BRED David Nicholls 9 Rn
60.49 secs (2.29) SF: 38/32/18/6/26/27/16/-/-
T/Plpt: £354.90 (65.98 Tckts). T/Qdpt: £27.40 (2.1 Tckts). AK

0063-WOLVERHAMPTON (L-H)
Wednesday January 18th (Standard)

103

COPTHORNE HOTELS STKS £3,656.90 (£1,107.20: £540.60: £257.30)
1m 100y (Fibresand) GOING: nil sec per fur (STD) 2-00 (2-01)

Sharp Conquest (67)*(69) (WRMuir)* 4-8-13 JWeaver(11) (lw: a.p: led 3f out: r.o: comf)..— **1**
80[10] Slip a Coin **(55)***(54) (RHollinshead)* 4-8-8 LDettori(6) (led to 3f out: one pce)...........5 **2**
Ship of the Line **(62)***(55)*(Fav)*(JRFanshawe)* 5-8-9 (5) NVarley(7) (pushed along thrght: hung bdly rt over 1f out: styd on sme pce)..................................2 **3**

Severn Gale *(48) (KWhite)* 5-8-9 JWilliams(2) (sn outpcd & wl bhd: hdwy appr st: nrst fin) ...... ¾ **4**
Lady Valensina (IRE) **(59)***(48) (BJLlewellyn)* 4-8-8 RCochrane(9) (chsd ldrs tl wknd fnl 2f) ...... hd **5**
4⁹ Fleet Cadet *(50) (NAGraham)* 4-8-13 GDuffield(8) (chsd ldrs tl wknd over 1f out) 1¼ **6**
68² Miss Charlie **(36)***(39) (ABailey)* 5-8-9 GBardwell(5) (chsd ldrs: outpcd 3f out: sn btn) 3 **7**
68⁴ Nigelschinapalace **(28)***(36) (MissSJWilton)* 6-9-0 AMackay(1) (b: hld up: hdwy 3f out: n.d) 4 **8**
Seraphic **(61)***(29) (BRCambidge)* 4-8-8 NAdams(3) (outpcd ½-wy: n.d) 1 **9**
Tanah Merah (IRE) **(61)***(27) (EJAlston)* 4-8-10 (3) DWright(10) (bhd: effrt 4f out: n.d) 3½ **10**
Honest Achiever (IRE) *(—) (APJames)* 4-8-3 (5) SSanders(4) (cl up over 4f: wknd qckly) 15 **11**

9/4 Ship of the Line, **3/1** SHARP CONQUEST, **13/2** Lady Valensina (IRE), **9/1** Slip a Coin (6/1-10/1), **11/1** Seraphic, Tanah Merah (IRE), **12/1** Miss Charlie, **16/1** Severn Gale, **20/1** Fleet Cadet, **33/1** Nigelschinapalace, Honest Achiever (IRE), CSF £28.28 TOTE £3.30: £1.20 £2.00 £1.80 (£16.60) OWNER Mrs H. Levy (LAMBOURN) BRED Hill Rivers Ltd 11 Rn
1m 49.4 SF: 46/32/34/28/26/29/20/-/-/-/-
WEIGHT FOR AGE 4yo-1lb

104 COPTHORNE MERRY HILL DUDLEY CLAIMING STKS (Class E) £3,009.60 (£910.80: £444.40: £211.20)
1m 4f (Fibresand) GOING:nil sec per fur (STD) 2-30 (2-33)

19² **Salbus (77)***(66)*(Fav)*(FJYardley)* 5-9-2 JWilliams(2) (trckd ldrs: led over 4f out tl over 2f out: led over 1f out: drvn out) ...... — **1**
66¹⁰ Nick the Biscuit **(72)***(65) (MDIUsher)* 4-8-12v MWigham(6) (lw: led tl over 4f out: outpcd 2f out: hdwy 1f out: hung lft: styd on nr fin) ...... nk **2**
34⁷ Awestruck **(37)***(54) (BPreece)* 5-8-1 (5) SSanders(8) (cl up: rdn to ld over 2f out: hdd over 1f out: kpt on one pce) ...... nk **3**
Chapel Hill (IRE) *(42) (BJLlewellyn)* 7-8-5 RCochrane(7) (cl up tl outpcd 6f out: sn no ch) 9 **4**
Culrain **(43)***(49) (MGMeagher)* 4-8-3 (5) VHalliday(1) (outpcd 4f out: n.d after) ...... hd **5**
Ginka **(51)***(21) (PJBevan)* 4-8-5 NCarlisle(4) (outpcd & wl bhd fnl 6f) 20 **6**

4/9 SALBUS, **7/2** Nick the Biscuit, **8/1** Ginka, **14/1** Awestruck, **33/1** Chapel Hill (IRE), Culrain, CSF £2.62 TOTE £1.40: £1.10 £1.80 (£2.90) OWNER Mr Graham Parker (DROITWICH) BRED Juddmonte Farms 6 Rn
2m 40.3 (9.30) SF: 39/35/29/17/20/-
WEIGHT FOR AGE 4yo-4lb

105 COPTHORNE BIRMINGHAM H'CAP (3-Y.O) (0-75) (Class D) £4,201.50 (£1,272.00: £621.00: £295.50)
7f (Fibresand) GOING: nil sec per fur (STD) 3-00 (3-00)

Our Tom (52)*(62) (JWharton)* 3-7-13 JQuinn(2) (lw: cl up: led 2f out: styd on wl) .— **1**
42² One for Jeannie **(57)***(59) (ABailey)* 3-8-4 GCarter(3) (trckd ldrs: effrt 3f out: styd on: no imp) 4 **2**
43² Poly Laureon (IRE) **(63)***(64) (RHollinshead)* 3-8-10 LDettori(5) (led to 2f out: one pce) ...... hd **3**
Opera Fan (IRE) **(64)***(59)*(Fav)*(SirMarkPrescott)* 3-8-11 GDuffield(1) (cl up: shkn up 3f out: one pce) 3 **4**
33² Tee Tee Too (IRE) **(74)***(66) (PCHaslam)* 3-9-7 JWeaver(8) (hld up: hdwy 3f out: nvr able to chal) 1¼ **5**
54⁸ Wendy's Way **(53)***(41) (JBerry)* 3-8-0 LCharnock(7) (in tch: drvn along 3f out: sn btn) 1¾ **6**
60³ Robo Magic (USA) **(69)***(54) (AMoore)* 3-9-2 RCochrane(4) (lw: chsd ldrs: effrt over 3f out: wknd 2f out) 1½ **7**
Happy Brave **(52)***(36) (PDCundell)* 3-7-13 AMackay(9) (dwlt: hld up: outpcd 4f out: n.d) ...... hd **8**
Gigfy **(63)***(30) (BJLlewellyn)* 3-8-5 (5) SDrowne(6) (lw: in tch: drvn along 4f out: sn btn) 8 **9**

2/1 Opera Fan (IRE), **7/2** One for Jeannie, **4/1** Poly Laureon (IRE), **9/2** Tee Tee Too (IRE), **12/1** Robo Magic (USA), Happy Brave, **16/1** Wendy's Way, **33/1** OUR TOM, Gigfy, CSF £139.31 CT £526.98 TOTE £23.20: £2.80 £1.50 £2.40 (£52.40) OWNER Mr J. M. Berry (MELTON MOWBRAY) BRED Bylon Farmers Ltd 9 Rn 1m 29.3 (5.30) SF: 22/18/23/17/24/3/14/-/-

106

COPTHORNE MANCHESTER H'CAP (0-90) (Class C) £5,524.00 (£1,672.00: £816.00: £388.00) **1m 4f (Fibresand)** GOING: nil sec per fur (STD) 3-30 (3-30)

*52*7 **Hillzah (USA) (80)***(86) (RBastiman)* 7-9-3 (5) HBastiman(8) (stdd s: wnt prom after 3f out: led wl over 1f out: drvn out)......— **1**
Cedez le Passage (FR) **(90)***(95)*(Fav)*(CEBrittain)* 4-10-0 BDoyle(6) (hld up: effrt 2f out: hung lft: styd on nr fin)......½ **2**
Philgun **(60)***(63) (CWCElsey)* 6-8-2v NKennedy(3) (cl up: led 6f out tl wl over 1f out: one pce)......1¼ **3**
Johns Act (USA) **(69)***(71) (DHaydnJones)* 5-8-11 AMackay(7) (lw: hld up: effrt over 2f out: kpt on: nt pce to chal)......¾ **4**
*8*7 View From Above **(72)***(73) (NJHWalker)* 9-9-0 RCochrane(4) (trckd ldrs: effrt over 2f out: styd on one pce)......½ **5**
*83*2 Killick **(52)***(52) (ABailey)* 7-7-1 (7)ow1 MBaird(1) (b: lw: trckd ldrs: chal 4f out: sn rdn: wknd fnl 2f)......½ **6**
*67*6 Tapis Rouge (IRE) **(62)***(57) (THCaldwell)* 6-8-4 GCarter(5) (bhd: pushed along 6f out: n.d)......4 **7**
*66*12 One Off the Rail (USA) **(81)***(74) (AMoore)* 5-9-9 CandyMorris(2) (led to 6f out: lost tch 3f out)......1½ **8**

LONG HANDICAP Killick 7-2

2/1 Cedez le Passage (FR), **11/4** Killick, **4/1** Johns Act (USA), **7/1** HILLZAH (USA), **9/1** Philgun (6/1-10/1), **14/1** View From Above, **16/1** Tapis Rouge (IRE), **25/1** One Off the Rail (USA), CSF £21.13 CT £118.73 TOTE £9.00: £2.50 £1.10 £2.50 (£14.30) OWNER Mrs P.Churm (WETHERBY) BRED Helen M.Polinger, Benjamin Polinger et al 8 Rn 2m 41.2 (10.20) SF: 39/44/19/26/28/9/14/-

WEIGHT FOR AGE 4yo-4lb

107

COPTHORNE WINDSOR (S) STKS (Class F) £2,801.60 (£787.60: £384.80) **5f (Fibresand)** GOING: nil sec per fur (STD) 4-00 (4-01)

*14*5 **Primula Bairn (58)***(64) (MrsJRRamsden)* 5-9-2v JWeaver(11) (lw: w ldrs: led 2f out: kpt on u.p)......— **1**
*70*3 Samson-Agonistes **(70)***(64)*(Fav)*(PDEvans)* 9-9-7 RCochrane(3) (lw: sn chsng ldrs & pushed along: ev ch 2f out: r.o one pce)......1¾ **2**
*65** Lift Boy (USA) **(57)***(66) (AMoore)* 6-9-12 5x CandyMorris(6) (b: b.hind: mid div: drvn along ½-wy: styd on: nvr able to chal)......1 **3**
*71*9 Farndale **(52)***(50) (JBerry)* 8-9-0 (7) CLowther(1) (lw: outpcd tl styd on fnl 2f: nvr nrr)......3½ **4**
Ivy Lilian (IRE) **(40)***(37) (WMBrisbourne)* 3-7-10 (5) AGarth(4) (led 3f: grad wknd) .2½ **5**
*14*2 Farastrada **(60)***(34) (BPreece)* 4-8-11 (5) SSanders(10) (chsd ldrs: rdn ½-wy: btn 2f out)......¾ **6**
Precious Times **(46)***(34) (MGMeagher)* 3-8-1 (5) VHalliday(12) (prom: rdn ½-wy: wknd fnl 2f)......1½ **7**
*92*10 Bessie's Will **(46)***(26) (DHaydnJones)* 4-9-2 AMackay(2) (sn pushed along: a rr div)......¾ **8**
Super Rocky **(57)***(28) (RBastiman)* 6-9-2 (5) HBastiman(5) (nvr wnt pce)......¾ **9**
Muzz (IRE) **(67)***(25) (MJohnston)* 4-9-7 TWilliams(9) (chsd ldr to ½-wy: sn rdn & wknd)......1 **10**
Distinctive Lady **(30)***(16) (REPeacock)* 5-9-2 GDuffield(7) (s.i.s: n.d)......1¼ **11**
Oriental Song **(23)***(—) (KSBridgwater)* 6-9-2 TWall(8) (lost tch after 2f)......9 **12**

11/10 Samson-Agonistes, **11/4** PRIMULA BAIRN, **6/1** Farastrada, **13/2** Lift Boy (USA), **9/1** Muzz (IRE), **14/1** Super Rocky, **16/1** Ivy Lilian (IRE), Farndale, **33/1** Bessie's Will, Precious Times, Distinctive Lady, Oriental Song, CSF £7.12 TOTE £4.00: £1.70 £1.60 £3.10 (£5.20) OWNER Mr M. A. Bagnall (THIRSK) BRED Kavli Ltd 12 Rn 62.0 secs (4.00) SF: 32/33/35/19/-/4/-/-/-/-/-/-

WEIGHT FOR AGE 3yo-15lb

No bid

108

DUDLEY H'CAP (0-75) (Class D) £3,640.00 (£1,102.00: £538.00: £256.00) **2m 46y (Fibresand)** GOING: nil sec per fur (STD) 4-30 (4-30)

*67*4 **Secret Serenade (71)***(79) (CWFairhurst)* 4-9-6 LDettori(2) (lw: a.p: led over 2f out: kpt on u.p)......— **1**
*67*3 Child Star (FR) **(38)***(45) (DMarks)* 6-7-1 (7)ow1 MBaird(6) (effrt 4f out: hdwy on ins to chal ins fnl f: kpt on one pce)......¾ **2**
*45** Well and Truly **(53)***(60) (BAMcMahon)* 8-8-4 (5) SSanders(7) (cl up: led over 6f out tl over 2f out: kpt on)......hd **3**
Reggae Beat **(45)***(52) (ICampbell)* 10-8-1 JQuinn(8) (trckd ldrs: hdwy 4f out: rdn 2f out: styd on nr fin)......hd **4**

Taroudant **(67)***(71)*(Fav)*(MrsMReveley)* 8-9-9 RCochrane(4) (lw: hld up: effrt 4f out: rdn 3f out: btn fnl 2f)....3 **5**
Ibsen **(68)***(64) (RAkehurst)* 7-9-10 GCarter(1) (b: hld up: effrt 4f out: sn rdn & no imp)....9 **6**
66[7] Mentalasanythin **(72)***(65) (ABailey)* 6-10-0 AMackay(5) (cl up tl wknd 4f out)....3 **7**
79[3] Sassiver (USA) **(45)***(37) (RHollinshead)* 5-7-10 (5) AGarth(10) (bhd: drvn along 4f out: n.d)....½ **8**
3[5] Arctic Guest (IRE) **(60)***(52) (CSmith)* 5-8-13 (3) KRutter(3) (a bhd)....nk **9**
Flass Vale **(45)***(—) (CWFairhurst)* 7-7-12 (3) DWright(9) (led tl over 6f out: wknd qckly 4f out)....dist **10**

LONG HANDICAP Child Star (FR) 7-4

11/8 Taroudant, **4/1** Well and Truly, **11/2** SECRET SERENADE, Ibsen, **7/1** Child Star (FR), **10/1** Sassiver (USA), **16/1** Arctic Guest (IRE), Mentalasanythin, **20/1** Reggae Beat, **50/1** Flass Vale, CSF £45.32 CT £163.40 TOTE £8.70: £2.30 £1.20 £1.70 (£22.20) OWNER Glasgow House Racing Syndicate (MIDDLEHAM) BRED C. R. Mason 10 Rn

3m 39.3 SF: 45/20/34/26/44/37/38/-/-/-
WEIGHT FOR AGE 4yo-7lb
T/Plpt: £20.60 (489.8 Tckts). T/Qdpt: £17.20 (2.2 Tckts). AA

0097-LINGFIELD (L-H)
Thursday January 19th (Standard)

Abandoned after 1st race due to high winds

109

CAVEAT EMPTOR H'CAP (I) (0-65) (Class F) £2,713.40 (£762.40: £372.20)
2m (Equitrack) GOING minus 0.30 sec per fur (FST) 1-10 (1-10)

9[2] **Arc Bright (IRE) (57)***(67)*(Fav)*(RHollinshead)* 5-9-7 LDettori(2) (mde all: rdn over 3f out: r.o wl)....— **1**
Jawani (IRE) **(53)***(55) (DrJDScargill)* 7-9-3v RCochrane(6) (a.p: rdn over 6f out: chsd wnr 4f out: ev ch wl over 1f out: unable qckn)....9 **2**
75[4] Intention (USA) **(57)***(51) (ICampbell)* 5-9-7 TIves(9) (a.p: rdn 9f out: wknd over 3f out)....8 **3**
Ikhtiraa (USA) **(60)***(53) (RJO'Sullivan)* 5-9-10 MRimmer(8) (b: a.p: rdn over 3f out: sn wknd)....1 **4**
67[7] Upper Mount Clair **(59)***(50) (CEBrittain)* 5-9-9b BDoyle(5) (chsd wnr 11f)....2½ **5**
75[6] Wottashambles **(46)***(24) (GLewis)* 4-8-3 StephenDavies(4) (a bhd)....14 **6**
37[6] In Behind (IRE) **(50)***(26) (GLMoore)* 4-8-7 RPerham(1) (a bhd)....2½ **7**
Prosequendo (USA) **(58)***(32) (MDixon)* 8-9-3 (5) SSanders(3) (hdwy 12f out: wknd over 3f out)....2½ **8**
21[5] Joyce E Jackson **(38)***(—) (RIngram)* 5-7-13 (3) DWright(7) (bhd fnl 9f: t.o fnl 5f)....dist **9**

5/2 ARC BRIGHT (IRE), **9/2** Jawani (IRE), Intention (USA), **11/2** Wottashambles, **6/1** Ikhtiraa (USA), **7/1** Prosequendo (USA) (5/1-8/1), **10/1** In Behind (IRE) (8/1-12/1), **33/1** Upper Mount Clair, Joyce E Jackson, CSF £14.27 CT £44.00 TOTE £2.80: £2.40 £1.20 £2.00 (£3.60) OWNER Mr J. E. Bigg (UPPER LONGDON) BRED Tsarina Stud 9 Rn

3m 30.2 (6.70) SF: 41/29/25/27/24/-/-/-/-
WEIGHT FOR AGE 4yo-7lb
T/Plpt: £1.10 (14,015.79 Tckts). AK

0090-SOUTHWELL (L-H)
Friday January 20th (Standard)

116

CRAB H'CAP (3-Y.0) (0-70) (Class E) £3,023.90 (£915.20: £446.60: £212.30)
1m (Fibresand) GOING minus 0.23 sec per fur (FST) 1-40 (1-40)

*28** **Harry Browne (IRE) (53)***(68) (MrsJRRamsden)* 3-9-7 SWilliams(7) (hld up: hdwy to ld 2f out: styd on)....— **1**
*47** Grand Selection (IRE) **(53)***(66)*(Fav)*(MBell)* 3-9-7 MFenton(1) (hdwy 3f out: edgd lft u.p over 1f out: styd on strly nr fin)....1 **2**
95[4] Samana Cay **(50)***(58) (DNicholls)* 3-8-11 (7) AEddery(5) (lw: s.i.s: hdwy ½-wy: led over 3f out: hung lft & hdd 2f out: sn btn)....2½ **3**
*48** High Flown (USA) **(55)***(43) (RonaldThompson)* 3-9-9 6x LDettori(2) (lw: led early: sn outpcd and bhd: hdwy 3f out: hung lft & one pce fnl 2f)....10 **4**
Tonka **(51)***(29) (DJGMurraySmith)* 3-9-5 AMackay(6) (prom: outpcd 3f out: sn btn) 5 **5**
Miss Toffee Nose (IRE) **(40)***(—) (DJSCosgrove)* 3-8-3 (5) LNewton(3) (sn led: hdd over 3f out: wknd over 2f out)....6 **6**

*98*³ Fairy's Son **(46)***(—) (WRMuir)* 3-9-0b StephenDavies(4) (cl up tl wknd qckly over 3f out)....15 **7**

13/8 Grand Selection (IRE), **85/40** HARRY BROWNE (IRE), **5/1** High Flown (USA), **6/1** Samana Cay, **9/1** Tonka, **16/1** Fairy's Son, **20/1** Miss Toffee Nose (IRE), CSF £6.30 TOTE £4.00: £1.50 £1.60 (£3.90) OWNER Mrs J. R. Ramsden (THIRSK) BRED Patrick Whelan in Ireland 7 Rn
1m 48.5 (9.20) SF: -/-/-/-/-/-/-

117

HALIBUT CLAIMING STKS (Class F) £2,537.00 (£712.00: £347.00)
1m (Fibresand) GOING minus 0.23 sec per fur (FST) 2-10 (2-10)

*31** **Shuttlecock (59)***(75) (MrsNMacauley)* 4-9-2 MFenton(12) (a cl up: slt ld appr fnl f: styd on)....— **1**
*94*⁷ No Submission (USA) **(66)***(69)*(Fav)*(DWChapman)* 9-9-0 LDettori(10) (lw: led tl appr fnl f: kpt on)....1½ **2**
*92*³ Super Benz **(66)***(59) (FJO'Mahony)* 9-9-0 GCarter(9) (b: trckd ldrs: effrt & ev ch 2f out: sn rdn & no ex)....5 **3**
*31*² Battle Colours (IRE) **(61)***(60) (MrsJRRamsden)* 6-8-12 (5) SSanders(5) (a chsng ldrs: nt qckn fnl 2f)....1 **4**
Sharp Gazelle **(47)***(39) (BSmart)* 5-8-12 RCochrane(8) (in tch: effrt 3f out: styd on one pce)....8 **5**
Ivan the Terrible (IRE) **(53)***(26) (BEllison)* 7-8-5 AMackay(4) (b: sme hdwy on outside over 3f out: rdn & no imp)....3 **6**
*53*¹⁰ Asmarina *(22) (SRBowring)* 5-7-10 (7) CTeague(3) (sn outpcd: racd wd: styd on fnl 3f: nrst fin)....1 **7**
*82*⁴ Warhurst (IRE) **(70)***(31) (DNicholls)* 4-8-13 AlexGreaves(1) (sn bhd: sme hdwy fnl 2f)....¾ **8**
Major Mouse **(56)***(27) (WWHaigh)* 7-8-11 DaleGibson(7) (prom tl wknd 2f out) ....½ **9**
Allinson's Mate (IRE) **(73)***(36) (TDBarron)* 7-8-13 (7) JennyBenson(2) (sn bhd: sme late hdwy)....hd **10**
*36*³ Quick Million **(45)***(2) (BJMeehan)* 4-8-0 (7)ow5 DaneO'Neill(13) (spd 5f: sn wknd) ...11 **11**
*78*⁹ Hiltons Travel (IRE) **(50)***(—) (EJAlston)* 4-8-13b SWebster(11) (hld up: hdwy 5f out: wknd 3f out)....6 **12**
Monkey Boy (IRE) **(40)***(—) (MartynWane)* 4-8-1 JFanning(6) (outpcd & bhd after 3f)....15 **13**

2/1 No Submission (USA), **4/1** Battle Colours (IRE), **7/1** Super Benz, Warhurst (IRE), **10/1** SHUTTLECOCK, Ivan the Terrible (IRE), **12/1** Allinson's Mate (IRE), Sharp Gazelle, **14/1** Quick Million, **20/1** Major Mouse, **33/1** Asmarina, Hiltons Travel (IRE), Monkey Boy (IRE), CSF £31.39 TOTE £11.80: £5.30 £1.40 £2.80 (£24.50) OWNER Mr James Colling (MELTON MOWBRAY) BRED A. B. Phipps 13 Rn 1m 44.3 (5.00) SF: 32/28/18/19/-/-/-/-/-/-/-/-/-
WEIGHT FOR AGE 4yo-1lb

118

SHARK H'CAP (3-Y.O) (0-70) (Class E) £3,066.80 (£928.40: £453.20: £215.60)
6f (Fibresand) GOING minus 0.23 sec per fur (FST) 2-40 (2-40)

*78** **Portend (63)***(70)*(Fav)*(SRBowring)* 3-8-7 (7) 7x CTeague(3) (lw: hmpd s: hdwy ent st: led jst ins fnl f: r.o)....— **1**
Bold Frontier **(62)***(67) (KTIvory)* 3-8-13 RCochrane(7) (b: wnt rt s: hld up: nt clr run over 2f out: swtchd & r.o nr fin)....½ **2**
*40*⁵ Russian Heroine **(70)***(73) (MJohnston)* 3-9-7 TWilliams(4) (chsd ldrs: slt ld appr fnl f: sn hdd & no ex)....½ **3**
*40*⁴ Dolly Face **(63)***(61) (WRMuir)* 3-9-0 StephenDavies(5) (led tl appr fnl f: grad wknd ins fnl f)....2 **4**
*54*⁴ Needwood Newt **(52)***(41) (BAMcMahon)* 3-7-12 (5)ow2 SSanders(2) (effrt ½-wy: no imp)....3½ **5**
*43*⁴ Komlucky **(51)***(30) (FJO'Mahony)* 3-8-2 JQuinn(1) (b: b.hind: sn chsng ldrs: nt clr run over 2f out: wknd over 1f out)....4 **6**
Chaldon Herring **(66)***(41) (TDBarron)* 3-8-10 (7) KimberleyHart(8) (hmpd s: racd wd: hdwy appr st: sn wknd)....1¼ **7**
*43*⁵ Dowdency **(47)***(20) (JAPickering)* 3-7-12 NCarlisle(6) (spd over 3f: sn wknd) ....½ **8**
Branston Kristy **(44)***(15) (CSmith)* 3-7-4 (5) NVarley(9) (b: b.hind: spd 3f: sn outpcd)....½ **9**

4/5 PORTEND, **11/2** Bold Frontier, **10/1** Komlucky, **11/1** Dolly Face, Russian Heroine, **12/1** Dowdency, **14/1** Chaldon Herring, **16/1** Needwood Newt, **40/1** Branston Kristy, CSF £6.02 CT £27.41 TOTE £1.80: £1.30 £1.80 £2.80 (£4.40) OWNER Mr D. H. Bowring (EDWINSTOWE) BRED Hollow Hole Stud 9 Rn 1m 17.5 (4.00) SF: 26/24/30/18/-/-/-/-/-

119

OYSTER STKS (Mdn) (Class D) £3,606.20 (£1,091.60: £532.80: £253.40)
7f (Fibresand) GOING minus 0.23 sec per fur (FST) 3-10 (3-10)

Legal Fiction (64)*(69) (MJohnston)* 4-9-0 TWilliams(4) (lw: trckd ldrs: led over 2f out: shkn up & r.o) — **1**
82⁹ At the Savoy (IRE) **(38)***(47) (TDBarron)* 4-8-7 (7) KimberleyHart(8) (hdwy to chse ldrs after 3f: styd on fnl 2f: no imp) 10 **2**
18⁹ Ziggy's Dancer (USA) **(55)***(39)*(Fav)*(EJAlston)* 4-8-11 (3) DWright(5) (led tl over 2f out: sn outpcd) 4 **3**
82⁷ Spanish Stripper (USA) *(35) (MCChapman)* 4-8-9 (5) DRMcCabe(7) (sn outpcd & bhd: hdwy over 2f out: hung lft: n.d) 1¾ **4**
Bandita **(42)***(29) (MissAJWhitfield)* 4-8-6 (5)ow2 RPainter(6) (prom tl grad wknd fnl 3f) 1½ **5**
92⁵ Rosina's Folly **(54)***(16) (JLHarris)* 4-8-9 RCochrane(1) (s.i.s: nvr trbld ldrs) 5 **6**
Inovar **(29)***(—) (CBBBooth)* 5-9-0 LDettori(3) (bit bkwd: effrt 3f out: sn btn) 15 **7**
Pratique (USA) **(63)***(—) (PCalver)* 4-8-9 DaleGibson(2) (b: b.hind: spd 4f: sn wknd) 2½ **8**

5/2 Ziggy's Dancer (USA), **3/1** LEGAL FICTION, **7/2** Rosina's Folly, **5/1** Pratique (USA), **12/1** Spanish Stripper (USA), At the Savoy (IRE), Inovar, **20/1** Bandita, CSF £34.51 TOTE £3.80: £2.00 £2.00 £1.60 (£24.00) OWNER Mr J. S. Morrison (MIDDLEHAM) BRED Fares Stables Ltd
8 Rn 1m 29.3 (2.50) SF: 51/28/19/17/11/-/-/-

120

LOBSTER (S) STKS (Class G) £2,259.00 (£634.00: £309.00)
1m 3f (Fibresand) GOING minus 0.23 sec per fur (FST) 3-40 (3-40)

82⁸ **Killing Time (59)***(59) (MrsNMacauley)* 4-8-12v MFenton(1) (mde all: drvn out) — **1**
81³ Rousitto **(58)***(63)*(Fav)*(RHollinshead)* 7-9-7 LDettori(4) (lw: bhd: hdwy 6f out: outpcd over 2f out: styd on ins fnl f: nrst fin) 1 **2**
91⁷ Greek Gold (IRE) **(59)***(61) (GPKelly)* 6-9-7 AlexGreaves(6) (lw: a cl up: chal & effrt 2f out: nt qckn fnl f) 1¾ **3**
*68** Off the Air (IRE) **(49)***(53) (ICampbell)* 4-8-12v RCochrane(9) (lw: a.p: one pce fnl 2f) 2½ **4**
83⁵ Midlin **(37)***(46) (JLHarris)* 5-8-11 TIves(2) (prom: pushed along 5f out: one pce) 2 **5**
63⁵ Ballad Dancer **(43)***(39) (JMackie)* 10-9-2 GCarter(5) (effrt 6f out: nvr bttr than mid div) 9 **6**
34² Greek Night Out (IRE) **(44)***(32) (JAHarris)* 4-8-7 SWilliams(7) (b.nr hind: lw: chsd ldrs tl wknd fnl 3f) 1¾ **7**
34⁴ Britannia Mills **(40)***(21) (MCChapman)* 4-8-2 (5) DRMcCabe(11) (bhd tl sme late hdwy) 8 **8**
46² Sharp Thrill **(45)***(16) (BSmart)* 4-8-7v(5) SSanders(13) (chsd ldrs: drvn along 4f out: wknd ent st) 7 **9**
29⁴ Trail of Tears **(35)***(11) (WWHaigh)* 5-9-2 DaleGibson(12) (in tch: effrt 3f out: sn btn) 3½ **10**
28⁵ Venture Fourth **(40)***(—) (EJAlston)* 6-8-11 (5) JStack(3) (bhd: rdn 6f out: n.d) 30 **11**
29³ Top Shiel **(71)***(—) (KRBurke)* 7-9-2 MRimmer(8) (prom tl wknd 4f out: fin lame) 15 **12**
Dancing Reef *(—) (EJAlston)* 6-8-8 (3) DWright(10) (dwlt: a bhd) 12 **13**

2/1 Rousitto, **3/1** Top Shiel, **9/2** Off the Air (IRE), **8/1** Greek Gold (IRE), **9/1** Greek Night Out (IRE), **10/1** KILLING TIME, **16/1** Sharp Thrill, **20/1** Britannia Mills, Dancing Reef, Venture Fourth, **25/1** Midlin, **33/1** Trail of Tears, Ballad Dancer, CSF £32.46 TOTE £11.20 £2.90 £2.10 £2.30 (£31.30) OWNER Mr James Colling (MELTON MOWBRAY) BRED L. H. J. Ward 13 Rn
2m 27.7 (6.20) SF: 35/42/41/29/26/18/8/-/-/-/-/-/-
WEIGHT FOR AGE 4yo-4lb
Bt in 3,200 gns

121

OCTOPUS H'CAP (0-70) (Class E) £3,009.60 (£910.80: £444.40: £211.20)
1m 4f (Fibresand) GOING minus 0.23 sec per fur (FST) 4-10 (4-11)

*36** **Stevie's Wonder (IRE) (62)***(75) (MJRyan)* 5-9-13 GCarter(2) (a.p: slt ld over 2f out: kpt on wl) — **1**
96⁵ Mr Moriarty (IRE) **(34)***(46) (SRBowring)* 4-7-2 (7) ClaireBalding(5) (led tl over 2f out: rallied fnl f: nt qckn nr fin) nk **2**
*77** Sudden Spin **(45)***(48)*(Fav)*(SGNorton)* 5-8-5 (5) 5x JStack(6) (hld up: hdwy gng wl 5f out: shkn up over 2f out: sn btn) 7 **3**
83³ Ozzie Jones **(44)***(45) (MCChapman)* 4-8-0 (5) DRMcCabe(3) (stdd after s: sn wl bhd: styd on fnl 4f: nvr nrr) 2 **4**

*91*2 Royal Citizen (IRE) **(63)***(63) (JFBottomley)* 6-10-0 RCochrane(1) (effrt 4f out: sn rdn & no imp)....½ **5**
*4** Shakiyr (FR) **(60)***(57) (RHollinshead)* 4-9-7 LDettori(4) (in tch: outpcd 5f out: n.d after)....2½ **6**
*96*7 Jihaad (USA) **(50)***(45) (JNorton)* 5-9-1v JQuinn(7) (chsd ldrs tl rdn & wknd 4f out)...2 **7**
Lightning Quest (IRE) **(40)***(10) (JSWainwright)* 4-8-1 LCharnock(8) (cl up: pushed along 7f out: wknd 5f out)....20 **8**

5/4 Sudden Spin, **7/2** Shakiyr (FR), **11/2** Royal Citizen (IRE), **6/1** STEVIE'S WONDER (IRE), **10/1** Ozzie Jones, **11/1** Mr Moriarty (IRE), **14/1** Lightning Quest (IRE), **20/1** Jihaad (USA), CSF £63.30 CT £123.41 TOTE £6.10: £1.70 £1.70 £1.40 (£31.30) OWNER Newmarket Consortium(NEWMARKET) BRED Ovidstown Investments Ltd in Ireland 8 Rn2m 40.7 (6.50) SF: 51/21/26/19/40/30/22
WEIGHT FOR AGE 4yo-4lb

T/Plpt: £17.20 (1,003.98 Tckts). T/Qdpt: Not won; £29.20 to Haydock 21/1/95. AA

0109-LINGFIELD (L-H)
Saturday January 21st (Standard)

122 STUBBS H'CAP (Amateurs) (0-65) (Class F) £2,776.40 (£780.40: £381.20)
1m 4f (Equitrack) GOING minus 0.49 sec per fur (FST) 1-25 (1-32)

*77*5 **Don't Drop Bombs (USA) (29)***(43)*(Fav)*(PJFeilden)* 6-9-2v MissJFeilden(5) (chsd ldr: led over 5f out: clr over 2f out: comf)....— **1**
*75** Royal Circus **(37)***(39)*(Fav)*(JGMO'Shea)* 6-9-5 (5) MrsSBosley(6) (led over 6f: rdn over 4f out: one pce fnl 3f)....10 **2**
Can Can Charlie **(59)***(53) (JPearce)* 5-11-4 MrsLPearce(9) (bhd: mod hdwy over 2f out: nvr nrr)....6 **3**
The Frog Lady (IRE) **(47)***(40) (DWPArbuthnot)* 4-10-2 MrsDArbuthnot(10) (mid div: mod hdwy over 2f out: nvr nrr)....½ **4**
*83*4 Malingerer **(33)***(14) (DAWilson)* 4-9-2 ow2 MissAHarwood(7) (outpcd: a mid div)....10 **5**
*13*8 Cone Lane **(30)***(11) (BGubby)* 9-8-12 (5) MrsMBusby(2) (outpcd: nvr nrr)....hd **6**
Storm Bidder **(44)***(25) (BGubby)* 4-9-13h MrsMCowdrey(8) (a bhd)....s.h **7**
*106*6 Killick **(49)***(28) (ABailey)* 7-10-3 (5) MissBridgetGatehouse(4) (chsd ldrs tl rdn & wknd over 3f out)....2 **8**
*71*11 Morjinski **(27)***(—) (DJSffrenchDavis)* 5-9-0 MissSMitchell(11) (a wl bhd)....6 **9**
Written Agreement **(41)***(7) (REPeacock)* 7-9-9 (5)ow14 MrsCPeacock(3) (bhd fnl 7f)..4 **10**
*97*5 Carlowitz (USA) **(62)***(—) (AMoore)* 7-11-2 (5) MrsJoanMoore(1) (ref to r: t.n.p).... **0**

LONG HANDICAP Written Agreement 8-5 Malingerer 8-13

7/2 DON'T DROP BOMBS (USA), Royal Circus, **4/1** Killick, **11/2** The Frog Lady (IRE), **9/1** Can Can Charlie, Carlowitz (USA), **12/1** Malingerer, **14/1** Cone Lane, **33/1** Storm Bidder, **40/1** Morjinski, **50/1** Written Agreement, CSF £15.79 CT £94.43 TOTE £4.90: £1.10 £1.80 £2.30 (£7.30) OWNER Miss J. Feilden (NEWMARKET) BRED Hurstland Farm Incorporated 11 Rn
2m 36.7 (7.30) SF: 14/9/21/6/-/-/-/-/-/-/-
WEIGHT FOR AGE 4yo-4lb

123 HARRINGTON BIRD CLAIMING STKS (Class E) £3,109.70 (£941.60: £459.80: £218.90) **6f (Equitrack)** GOING minus 0.49 sec per fur (FST) 1-55 (2-17)

*92*2 **Everset (FR) (93)***(81)*(Fav)*(ABailey)* 7-9-3 LDettori(4) (chsd ldrs: rdn 3f out: hrd rdn over 1f out: led ins fnl f: r.o)....— **1**
*61*3 Spender **(73)***(73) (PWHarris)* 6-9-1 RCochrane(6) (chsd ldr: led over 2f out tl ins fnl f: unable qckn)....2½ **2**
Rocky Waters (USA) **(83)***(74) (GLMoore)* 6-9-7 AMorris(1) (reard s: sn chsng ldrs: rdn over 1f out: one pce)....1¾ **3**
*70*5 Farfelu **(79)***(45) (WRMuir)* 8-9-3b JWeaver(3) (led over 3f: wknd over 1f out)....10 **4**
*76*8 Papagos (IRE) **(32)***(22) (SDow)* 4-8-3 StephenDavies(5) (sn outpcd: a bhd)....3½ **5**
*71*10 Youcanstoplooking (IRE) **(35)***(16) (SDow)* 4-8-0 (5)ow2 SSanders(7) (bhd fnl 3f)....3 **6**

4/5 EVERSET (FR), **7/2** Rocky Waters (USA), **5/1** Spender, Farfelu, **66/1** Papagos (IRE), Youcanstoplooking (IRE), CSF £5.26 TOTE £1.80: £1.40 £1.20 (£2.40) OWNER Mr Gordon Mytton (TARPORLEY) BRED Societe Aland 6 Rn 1m 12.1 (1.50) SF: 39/31/34/3/-/-

124 SNAFFLES MEDIAN AUCTION STKS (Mdn 3-Y.O) (Class E) £2,966.70 (£897.60: £437.80: £207.90)
6f (Equitrack) GOING minus 0.49 sec per fur (FST) 2-25 (2-46)

*64*2 **Bold Effort (FR)** *(70)*(Fav)*(KOCunningham-Brown)* 3-9-0 JWeaver(6) (chsd ldr: led over 3f out tl over 1f out: led ins fnl f: r.o)....— **1**

Chewit **(74)**_(66) (AMoore)_ 3-9-0 CandyMorris(2) (hld up: hdwy 3f out: led over 1f out tl ins fnl f: unable qckn) 1¼ **2**
_57²_ Merrie le Bow **(53)**_(41) (PMitchell)_ 3-8-9 JMcLaughlin(8) (outpcd & bhd: nvr nrr) 8 **3**
Fiery Footsteps **(50)**_(32) (PHowling)_ 3-8-6 (3) DWright(4) (led over 2f: wknd 2f out) 3½ **4**
_85⁶_ Just Jesting _(35) (GLMoore)_ 3-9-0 RPerham(7) (chsd ldrs: rdn over 3f out: wknd 2f out) ....½ **5**
_57⁴_ Fiveaday **(57)**_(31)_(Fav)_(BHanbury)_ 3-9-0 MRimmer(3) (s.i.s: sn outpcd: a bhd) 1½ **6**
_64⁵_ Logie **(65)**_(25) (MAJarvis)_ 3-9-0b WWoods(5) (chsd ldrs tl stumbled over 4f out: bhd fnl 3f) 2½ **7**

9/4 BOLD EFFORT (FR), Fiveaday, **100/30** Merrie le Bow, **13/2** Chewit, **8/1** Logie, **14/1** Fiery Footsteps, **16/1** Just Jesting, CSF £16.90 TOTE £3.10: £2.30 £2.60 (£10.60) OWNER Mr A. J. Richards (STOCKBRIDGE) BRED Ewar Stud Farm 7 Rn 1m 12.1 (1.50) SF: 36/33/8/-/1/-/-

125 CECIL ALDIN H'CAP (0-80) (Class D) £3,724.50 (£1,128.00: £551.00: £262.50)
1m (Equitrack) GOING minus 0.49 sec per fur (FST) 2-55 (3-17)

_56*_ **Kinnegad Kid (51)**_(59)_(Fav)_(RIngram)_ 6-7-12 (3) DWright(8) (a.p: led over 1f out: hrd rdn & edgd rt ins fnl f: r.o) ....— **1**
_89*_ Red Valerian **(79)**_(87) (KMcAuliffe)_ 4-10-0b RCochrane(9) (hld up: hdwy 4f out: rdn over 2f out: ev ch ins fnl f: hrd rdn & r.o) ....hd **2**
_89⁵_ Mr Nevermind (IRE) **(76)**_(80) (GLMoore)_ 5-9-12 SWhitworth(4) (chsd ldrs: rdn 1f out: one pce) 1¾ **3**
_12²_ Hatta Sunshine (USA) **(49)**_(52) (AMoore)_ 5-7-13 TWilliams(1) (led 1f: chsd ldr: led 2f out tl over 1f out: one pce) ....½ **4**
_12⁷_ Krayyan Dawn **(46)**_(49) (RAkehurst)_ 5-7-10 JQuinn(2) (chsd ldrs: rdn over 3f out: r.o one pce fnl f) ....s.h **5**
Roman Reel (USA) **(64)**_(59) (GLMoore)_ 4-8-13 AMorris(7) (led 7f out: hrd rdn 2f out: wknd over 1f out: eased whn btn ins fnl f) 4 **6**
_11⁷_ Shepherd Market (IRE) **(68)**_(59) (DAWilson)_ 4-9-3 NGwilliams(10) (bhd: hrd rdn over 2f out: nvr nrr) 1¾ **7**
_30⁴_ Kissavos **(45)**_(31) (CCElsey)_ 9-7-2v(7)ow2 MBaird(6) (a bhd) 2½ **8**
_56⁸_ Pair of Jacks (IRE) **(43)**_(25) (DAWilson)_ 5-7-7 GBardwell(3) (a bhd) 1¾ **9**
_18*_ Aitch N'Bee **(69)**_(45) (LadyHerries)_ 12-8-12 (7) ShonaCrombie(5) (bhd fnl 5f) 3 **10**

LONG HANDICAP Kissavos 7-6 Pair of Jacks (IRE) 7-4

5/4 KINNEGAD KID, **4/1** Red Valerian, **11/2** Mr Nevermind (IRE), **9/1** Krayyan Dawn, **10/1** Hatta Sunshine (USA), Aitch N'Bee, Kissavos, **20/1** Roman Reel (USA), **33/1** Pair of Jacks (IRE), Shepherd Market (IRE), CSF £7.46 CT £20.49 TOTE £2.50: £1.10 £1.80 £2.30 (£3.40) OWNER Mr J. B. Wilcox (EPSOM) BRED Airlie Stud and Miss K. Rausing 10 Rn
1m 38.5 (2.10) SF: 24/49/46/19/16/25/26/-/-/-
WEIGHT FOR AGE 4yo-1lb

126 HERRING H'CAP (3-Y.O) (0-70) (Class E) £3,638.80 (£893.20)
7f (Equitrack) GOING minus 0.49 sec per fur (FST) 3-25 (3-45)

_85²_ **Mac's Taxi (60)**_(55+)_(Fav)_(PCHaslam)_ 3-9-7 JWeaver(2) (mde all: clr over 1f out: pushed out) ....— **1**
_74⁴_ Polly Garter **(56)**_(46) (RHannon)_ 3-9-3 LDettori(1) (chsd wnr: rdn over 3f out: hrd rdn over 1f out: one pce) 2½ **2**

1/2 MAC'S TAXI, **13/8** Polly Garter, TOTE £1.20 OWNER Mr J. McMurdo (MIDDLEHAM) BRED Mrs C. J. Proctor 2 Rn 1m 26.9 (3.90) SF: 18/10

127 MUNNINGS STKS (0-65) (Class F) £2,663.00 (£748.00: £365.00)
1m 2f (Equitrack) GOING minus 0.49 sec per fur (FST) 3-55 (4-18)

_100*_ **Kaafih Homm (IRE) (56)**_(68)_(Fav)_(NACallaghan)_ 4-9-2 RCochrane(6) (hld up gng wl: hdwy 3f out: led ins fnl f: r.o) ....— **1**
_94⁶_ Tu Opes **(64)**_(65) (JLHarris)_ 4-9-0 DaleGibson(5) (plld hrd: a.p: led over 1f out: hrd rdn ins fnl f: unable qckn) ....¾ **2**
_88²_ Bag of Tricks (IRE) **(63)**_(61) (SDow)_ 5-9-3 JWeaver(7) (hld up: hdwy 2f out: rdn over 1f out: r.o one pce) 2½ **3**
_31³_ Profit Release (IRE) **(65)**_(54) (MJohnston)_ 4-8-9 TWilliams(3) (chsd ldr: led 4f out tl over 1f out: wknd ins fnl f) 1½ **4**
_8⁵_ Canary Falcon **(61)**_(56) (RJO'Sullivan)_ 4-9-0 WWoods(2) (chsd ldrs: rdn over 2f out: one pce) 2 **5**

12[12] Pearly River **(60)***(46) (DrJDScargill)* 4-8-9 MRimmer(4) (rdn over 3f out: a bhd)...3½ **6**
26[3] Tropical Jungle (USA) **(61)***(37) (PJMakin)* 5-9-3 RPerham(1) (led 6f)........................9 **7**

4/5 KAAFIH HOMM (IRE), **4/1** Tu Opes, **5/1** Bag of Tricks (IRE), **7/1** Tropical Jungle (USA), **9/1** Canary Falcon, Profit Release (IRE), **20/1** Pearly River, CSF £5.50 TOTE £2.30: £1.60 £2.80 (£6.10) OWNER Gallagher Materials Ltd (NEWMARKET) BRED Sheikh Ahmed bin Rashid al Maktoum 7 Rn 2m 8.2 (5.20) SF: 20/17/16/6/8/-/-

WEIGHT FOR AGE 4yo-3lb

T/Plpt: £4.30 (1,856.45 Tckts). T/Qdpt: £4.20 (2.8 Tckts). SM

0103-WOLVERHAMPTON (L-H)
Saturday January 21st (Standard)

128

MARS MEDIAN AUCTION STKS (Mdn 3-Y.O) (Class E) £2,710.00 (£820.00: £400.00: £190.00)
1m 1f 79y (Fibresand) GOING minus 0.40 sec per fur (FST) 7-00 (7-00)

Mr Mactavish (77)*(64) (MrsJCecil)* 3-9-0 TIves(7) (chsd ldr: rdn over 4f out: 3rd st: led 1f out: r.o wl)..— **1**
38[2] Shaft of Light *(63)*(Fav)*(LordHuntingdon)* 3-9-0 LDettori(4) (hld up: hdwy 4f out: 2nd st: led over 1f out: sn hdd: edgd rt ins fnl f: r.o)...........................nk **2**
38[3] Lawbuster (IRE) **(56)***(55) (WRMuir)* 3-9-0b JWeaver(3) (lw: led: rdn over 3f out: hdd over 1f out: wknd fnl f)...5 **3**
95[7] Fools Millyons (IRE) **(46)***(50) (WBentley)* 3-9-0v JFanning(6) (hdwy 6f out: wknd over 2f out: 4th & btn st)..3 **4**
Parklife (IRE) *(26) (PCHaslam)* 3-8-9 (5) JStack(1) (poor 6th st: a bhd: t.o) 14 **5**
25[3] The Cape Doctor (IRE) **(63)***(18) (AGFoster)* 3-8-9 (5) JDSmith(2) (lw: prom tl wknd 3f out: poor 5th st: t.o) 5 **6**
Haya Ya Kefaah *(15) (SirMarkPrescott)* 3-9-0 MFenton(5) (w'like: bit bkwd: s.i.s: plld hrd: a bhd: t.o fnl 3f) 2 **7**

11/8 Shaft of Light, **3/1** MR MACTAVISH, **11/2** Lawbuster (IRE), **6/1** Haya Ya Kefaah, **12/1** The Cape Doctor (IRE), **33/1** Parklife (IRE), **50/1** Fools Millyons (IRE), CSF £6.93 TOTE £3.60: £1.90 £1.50 (£5.50) OWNER Mrs D. MacRae (NEWMARKET) BRED D. MacRae 7 Rn

2m 0.5 (4.50) SF: 28/28/20/15/-/-/-

129

JUPITER H'CAP (0-65) (Class F) £2,433.00 (£683.00: £333.00)
6f (Fibresand) GOING minus 0.40 sec per fur (FST) 7-30 (7-30)

Beckyhannah (34)*(36) (RBastiman)* 5-7-8b(3)ow4 DWright(8) (mde all: clr 4f out: hrd rdn & edgd rt over 1f out: r.o wl) ....— **1**
107[4] Farndale **(50)***(50) (JBerry)* 8-8-6 (7) CLowther(4) (hld up: hdwy over 3f out: wnt 2nd st: ev ch fnl f: no ex nr fin) ....½ **2**
44[4] Heathyards Lady (USA) **(50)***(50) (RHollinshead)* 4-8-13 TIves(7) (prom: 4th & rdn st: r.o wl ins fnl f)..s.h **3**
28[3] Indian Serenade **(49)***(45)*(Fav)*(PWHarris)* 4-8-12 LDettori(13) (chsd ldrs: 6th st: r.o one pce fnl f) 1½ **4**
Farmer Jock **(46)***(36) (MrsNMacauley)* 13-8-9 MFenton(6) (b: prom: 3rd st: wknd over 1f out) 2½ **5**
78[10] Rapier Point (IRE) **(60)***(47) (PCHaslam)* 4-9-9 JWeaver(9) (prom: 5th st: no hdwy)¾ **6**
69[5] Delrob **(62)***(44) (DHaydnJones)* 4-9-11 AMackay(1) (hld up & bhd: hdwy fnl f: nvr nrr) 2 **7**
65[5] Arc Lamp **(53)***(34) (JAGlover)* 9-8-9 (7) MrSRichardson(5) (lw: prom: 6th & wkng st)..hd **8**
68[9] Dance and Sing (IRE) **(35)***(16) (DLWilliams)* 5-7-12 ow2 TWilliams(11) (lw: n.d).....s.h **9**
93[10] Aquado **(35)***(3) (ALForbes)* 6-7-12v JQuinn(2) (lw: prom 5f).....................................5 **10**
2[13] Bold Cyrano (IRE) **(58)***(22) (BPalling)* 4-9-7 StephenDavies(3) (prom 3f)..............1¼ **11**
Hershebar **(56)***(11) (GFierro)* 5-9-0 (5) SSanders(12) (bit bkwd: a bhd) 3½ **12**
65[11] Caherass Court (IRE) **(60)***(—) (BPreece)* 4-9-4 (5) JStack(10) (bhd fnl 3f: t.o)..6 **13**

2/1 Indian Serenade, **6/1** Heathyards Lady (USA), **7/1** Arc Lamp, Rapier Point (IRE), **8/1** BECKY-HANNAH, **10/1** Delrob, **12/1** Farndale, **16/1** Aquado, **20/1** Farmer Jock, Hershebar, Caherass Court (IRE), **33/1** Bold Cyrano (IRE), Dance and Sing (IRE), CSF £94.20 CT £567.19 TOTE £8.90: £2.20 £2.90 £2.10 (£50.40) OWNER Mr Terry Pitts (WETHERBY) BRED A. D. Redhead 13 Rn

1m 15.2 (4.00) SF: -/9/9/4/-/5/1/-/-/-/-/-/-

130

PLUTO H'CAP (0-70) (Class E) £2,788.00 (£844.00: £412.00: £196.00)
7f (Fibresand) GOING minus 0.40 sec per fur (FST) 8-00 (8-01)

44[2] **Little Ibnr (67)***(79)*(Fav)*(PDEvans)* 4-10-0 LDettori(9) (lw: mde all: pushed out)........— 1
94[10] Quinzii Martin **(50)***(58) (DHaydnJones)* 7-8-11v TWilliams(6) (hld up: hdwy over 3f out: 2nd st: hrd rdn over 1f out: no imp)........2 2
82* Alpine Johnny **(56)***(53) (RHollinshead)* 4-8-12 (5) AGarth(2) (w ldrs: 3rd st: wknd over 1f out)........5 3
44[6] Chinour (IRE) **(65)***(59) (EJAlston)* 7-9-12 JWeaver(7) (hld up: rdn 3f out: 4th st: wknd wl over 1f out)........1½ 4
49[7] Gallop to Glory **(35)***(25) (ALForbes)* 5-7-10be JQuinn(3) (eyeshield: b: b.hind: s.s: hdwy & 5th st: nvr nr ldrs)........2 5
30[5] Educated Pet **(59)***(34) (BPreece)* 6-9-6 TWall(8) (6th st: a bhd)........7 6
Welsh Heritage (IRE) **(47)***(7) (RJPrice)* 5-8-8 StephenDavies(4) (lw: prom over 3f: t.o)........7 7
Come on Lucy **(52)***(—) (SCoathup)* 6-8-6 (7)ow4 SharronJames(1) (lw: sn bhd: t.o)..9 8

7/4 LITTLE IBNR, **9/4** Chinour (IRE), **6/1** Alpine Johnny, **9/1** Quinzii Martin, **12/1** Educated Pet, **16/1** Gallop to Glory, **33/1** Come on Lucy, **50/1** Welsh Heritage (IRE), CSF £15.46 CT £63.30 TOTE £2.10: £1.30 £2.10 £1.30 (£13.30) OWNER Swinnerton Transport Ltd (WELSHPOOL) BRED R. E. Waugh 8 Rn 1m 28.4 (4.40) SF: 27/7/2/7/-/-/-/-

131

BIRMINGHAM CITY BLUE NOSE H'CAP (0-70) (Class E) £2,710.00 (£820.00: £400.00: £190.00)
1m 6f 166y (Fibresand) GOING minus 0.40 sec per fur (FST) 8-30 (8-30)

Premier Dance (55)*(64+) (DHaydnJones)* 8-9-5 AMackay(2) (a gng wl: led on bit wl over 1f out: easily)........— 1
75[2] Scalp 'em (IRE) **(49)***(57) (PDEvans)* 7-8-13 TIves(7) (prom: rdn to ld 4f out: sn hdd: 3rd st: r.o one pce fnl f: no ch w wnr)........½ 2
67[2] Iota **(64)***(71)*(Fav)*(JLHarris)* 6-10-0 LDettori(5) (lw: hld up & bhd: hdwy 5f out: led over 3f out: hdd & 2nd st: styd on ins fnl f)........¾ 3
45[3] Carrolls Marc (IRE) **(48)***(46) (PCHaslam)* 7-8-12 JWeaver(4) (lw: hld up in rr: hdwy over 3f out: 4th st: wknd over 1f out)........8 4
88[3] Milngavie (IRE) **(63)***(58) (MJohnston)* 5-9-6 (7) OliverCasey(6) (jnd ldr 8f out: wknd 3f out: poor 5th st)........2½ 5
Suivez **(54)***(45) (MrsNMacauley)* 5-8-13 (5) SSanders(3) (led to 4f out: sn wknd: poor 6th st)........4 6
3[7] Electrolyte **(64)***(—) (BPalling)* 5-10-0 StephenDavies(1) (b: w ldr over 6f: wknd over 5f out: t.o fnl 3f)........dist 7

7/4 Iota, **3/1** Carrolls Marc (IRE), **5/1** Scalp 'em (IRE) (3/1-6/1), **6/1** PREMIER DANCE (5/1-8/1), Milngavie (IRE) (5/1-8/1), **16/1** Suivez, **66/1** Electrolyte, CSF £32.49 TOTE £8.10: £3.20 £2.10 (£25.00) OWNER J S Fox and Sons (PONTYPRIDD) 7 Rn 3m 18.7 SF: 13/8/21/-/9/-/-

132

MERCURY CLAIMING STKS (3-Y.O) (Class F) £2,433.00 (£683.00: £333.00)
5f (Fibresand) GOING minus 0.40 sec per fur (FST) 9-00 (9-00)

86* **Ultra Beet (66)***(77)*(Fav)*(PCHaslam)* 3-8-12 JWeaver(2) (a.p: 2nd st: led 1f out: r.o wl)........— 1
C-Yer-Simmie (IRE) **(63)***(62) (RHollinshead)* 3-7-10 (5) AGarth(7) (led 4f out to 1f out: nt qckn)........1¼ 2
42[5] Superbit **(49)***(51) (BAMcMahon)* 3-8-3 (5) SSanders(4) (prom: 3rd st: hrd rdn over 1f out: one pce)........6 3
42[6] Pats Delight **(46)***(42) (SCoathup)* 3-8-1 NAdams(3) (dwlt: rdn & hdwy 3f out: one pce)........½ 4
107[7] Precious Times **(46)***(39) (MGMeagher)* 3-7-13 (3) DWright(5) (a bhd)........1¼ 5
7* Baileys Sunset (IRE) **(68)***(37) (MJohnston)* 3-8-8 TWilliams(6) (chsd ldrs: hrd rdn over 3f out: 6th & wkng st)........2½ 6
7[5] Lady Pui **(52)***(21) (JBerry)* 3-7-11b LCharnock(1) (b: led 1f: 4th & wkng st)........1½ 7

Evens ULTRA BEET, **100/30** Baileys Sunset (IRE), **9/2** C-Yer-Simmie (IRE), **7/1** Lady Pui, **16/1** Superbit, **25/1** Pats Delight, **66/1** Precious Times, CSF £5.93 TOTE £2.10: £1.70 £2.10 (£4.60) OWNER Pet Express Ltd T/A Nutrimix (MIDDLEHAM) BRED Rockhouse Farms Ltd 7 Rn 61.3 secs (3.30) SF: 7/-/-/-/-/-/-

133 VENUS APP'CE H'CAP (3-Y.O) (0-60) (Class F) £2,433.00 (£683.00: £333.00)
1m 1f 79y (Fibresand) GOING minus 0.40 sec per fur (FST) 9-30 (9-31)

10[6] **Red Spectacle (IRE) (54)***(59) (PCHaslam)* 3-9-0 (5) NicolaHowarth(9) (hld up: hdwy 5f out: led wl over 1f out: rdn & edgd rt fnl f: r.o wl)......— **1**
Boundary Express **(50)***(51) (MJohnston)* 3-8-12 (3) OliverCasey(10) (led tl hdd & 2nd st: nt qckn fnl f)......2½ **2**
Hever Golf Lady **(42)***(29) (TJNaughton)* 3-8-7 VHalliday(4) (chsd ldrs: outpcd over 2f out: 5th st: styd on fnl f)......8 **3**
47[6] Fools of Pride (IRE) **(55)***(42) (RHollinshead)* 3-9-1 (5) AEddery(5) (prom: 3rd & wkng st)......s.h **4**
Something Speedy (IRE) **(54)***(37)*(Fav)*(PJBevan)* 3-9-5 CHawksley(1) (chsd ldrs: hrd rdn: 4th & wkng st)......2½ **5**
38[7] Sabicas **(54)***(36) (SCWilliams)* 3-9-0b(5) GinaFaulkner(6) (dwlt: sme hdwy 3f out: nvr nr ldrs)......½ **6**
Scylla **(49)***(19) (PCHaslam)* 3-8-9 (5) CarolDavison(11) (prom: wknd over 2f out: poor 6th st)......7 **7**
Commanche Storm (IRE) **(45)***(10) (KGWingrove)* 3-8-7 (3) SLanigan(8) (dwlt: wl bhd fnl 4f)......3 **8**
Our Bairn **(56)***(16) (WBentley)* 3-9-0 (7) JGracey(7) (prom tl wknd over 3f out: t.o)..10 **9**
Centaur Express **(41)***(—) (ALForbes)* 3-8-6 GParkin(2) (plld hrd: bhd fnl 3f: t.o)...nk **10**
Lady Lucy Linnet **(40)***(—) (NAGraham)* 3-8-5 MBaird(3) (plld hrd: a bhd: t.o) 1 **11**

11/4 Something Speedy (IRE), **5/1** Hever Golf Lady, **6/1** Sabicas (3/1-13/1), **7/1** RED SPECTACLE (IRE), **8/1** Our Bairn, Boundary Express, **10/1** Fools of Pride (IRE), **12/1** Scylla, **20/1** Lady Lucy Linnet, **25/1** Centaur Express, Commanche Storm (IRE), CSF £57.86 CT £277.49 TOTE £7.90: £1.80 £3.10 £2.00 (£74.20) OWNER Mr David Morgan (MIDDLEHAM) BRED J. Beckett 11 Rn
2m 2.3 (6.30) SF: 18/11/-/2/-/-/-/-/-/-/-
T/Plpt: £168.10 (72.16 Tckts). T/Qdpt: £52.20 (3 Tckts). KH

0116-SOUTHWELL (L-H)
Monday January 23rd (Standard)

134 SILVER ICE (S) STKS (I) (Class G) £2,259.00 (£634.00: £309.00)
6f (Fibresand) GOING minus 0.09 sec per fur (STD) 12-45 (12-45)

43[3] **Whittingham Girl (56)***(60) (JBerry)* 3-8-5 SWilliams(5) (mde all: styd on wl fnl f)......— **1**
69[4] Bella Parkes **(67)***(51)*(Fav)*(DNicholls)* 4-9-2 AlexGreaves(9) (hld up: hdwy ½-wy: effrt 2f out: styd on nr fin)......1¼ **2**
78[6] Swinging Tich **(41)***(47) (BAMcMahon)* 6-8-11 (5) SSanders(1) (bhd: hdwy 3f out: styd on one pce fnl f)......1½ **3**
39[8] Splash of Salt (IRE) **(51)***(42) (TJNaughton)* 5-8-11b(5) VHalliday(8) (a chsng ldrs: one pce fnl 2f)......1¾ **4**
82[14] The Real Whizzbang (IRE) **(36)***(43) (PSFelgate)* 4-9-2 (5) PMcCabe(3) (s.i.s: hdwy over 2f out: nvr rchd ldrs)......1¼ **5**
44[8] Pretonic **(46)***(34) (BPalling)* 7-9-2 StephenDavies(7) (chsd ldrs tl outpcd fnl 2f)....1¼ **6**
Letsbeonestaboutit **(52)***(29) (MrsNMacauley)* 9-9-7b DeanMcKeown(4) (prom tl outpcd ½-wy: n.d after)......4 **7**
54[7] Travel Out *(22) (MrsMReveley)* 3-8-0 JQuinn(6) (hld up: effrt over 2f out: sn rdn & btn)......½ **8**
48[4] Wings of Desire (IRE) **(43)***(23) (RChampion)* 3-8-6bow1 MRimmer(2) (chsd ldrs 4f: sn wknd)......1¾ **9**

Evens Bella Parkes, **9/2** WHITTINGHAM GIRL, **7/1** Pretonic, **8/1** Splash of Salt (IRE), **9/1** Letsbeonestaboutit, **11/1** Swinging Tich, **16/1** Travel Out, **20/1** The Real Whizzbang (IRE), **33/1** Wings of Desire (IRE), CSF £9.66 TOTE £3.30: £1.10 £1.10 £2.00 (£4.20) OWNER T & M A Bibby (COCKERHAM) BRED Cheveley Park Stud Ltd 9 Rn
1m 18.3 (4.80) SF: 18/26/22/22/14/8/-/-/-
WEIGHT FOR AGE 3yo-16lb
Bt in 4,800 gns

135 SCARLET FLAME H'CAP (I) (3-Y.O) (0-60) (Class F) £2,537.00 (£712.00: £347.00) **1m (Fibresand)** GOING minus 0.09 sec per fur (STD) 1-15 (1-15)

54[3] **Pc's Cruiser (IRE) (48)***(56) (MCChapman)* 3-8-6 (5) DRMcCabe(3) (s.i.s: hdwy ½-wy: slt ld appr fnl f: drvn out)......— **1**

59² Persian Conquest (IRE) **(55)***(62)*(Fav)*(RIngram)* 3-9-4 WWoods(1) (lw: led tl hdd appr fnl f: kpt on) ..... ½ **2**
90³ Poly Lane **(51)***(55) (WRMuir)* 3-9-0 JWeaver(9) (in tch: hdwy ½-wy: styd on one pce fnl f) 1½ **3**
Warwick Mist (IRE) **(35)***(35) (PCHaslam)* 3-7-12 TWilliams(5) (prom: effrt & ev ch 2f out: no ex) 1¾ **4**
90² Kirov Protege (IRE) **(46)***(43) (RWArmstrong)* 3-8-9 MRimmer(2) (lw: cl up: hrd rdn over 2f out: wknd over 1f out) 1½ **5**
95³ Sweet Mate **(42)***(29) (SRBowring)* 3-7-12 (7) CTeague(4) (prom: hung bdly rt most of wy: rn v.wd st: sn btn) 5 **6**
86⁵ Magic Leader (IRE) **(40)***(13) (TTClement)* 3-7-10 (7) SLanigan(6) (b: prom tl rn wd & wknd fr ½-wy) 7 **7**
85⁸ Bitter N Twisted **(39)***(6) (SEKettlewell)* 3-8-2 JFanning(8) (a outpcd & bhd) 3 **8**
116⁴ High Flown (USA) **(58)***(23) (RonaldThompson)* 3-9-7 DeanMcKeown(7) (prom to ½-wy: sn bhd) ..... ¾ **9**

100/30 Persian Conquest (IRE), **7/2** Poly Lane (5/2-4/1), **4/1** Sweet Mate, **9/2** Kirov Protege (IRE), **9/1** High Flown (USA) (6/1-10/1), **11/1** Warwick Mist (IRE), **12/1** PC'S CRUISER (IRE), **33/1** Magic Leader (IRE), Bitter N Twisted, CSF £48.24 CT £154.31 TOTE £10.10: £2.10 £1.50 £1.50 (£19.70) OWNER P. C Racing Partners (MARKET RASEN) BRED Mrs Maureen Graham
9 Rn 1m 46.8 (7.50) SF: 14/20/13/-/4/-/-/-/-

136

JADE JEWEL MEDIAN AUCTION STKS (Mdn 4, 5 & 6-Y.O) (Class F) £2,537.00 (£712.00: £347.00)
1m 4f (Fibresand) GOING minus 0.09 sec per fur (STD) 1-45 (1-46)

53⁵ **All on** *(63+) (JHetherton)* 4-8-7 NKennedy(10) (in tch: hdwy 4f out: led 2f out: styd on wl) ..... — **1**
4⁴ Murphys Way **(42)***(57) (JLEyre)* 6-8-11v TIves(3) (b: led tl hdd 2f out: one pce) 5 **2**
96⁴ Tuscania **(22)***(51) (JWharton)* 5-8-11 JQuinn(1) (chsd ldrs tl outpcd over 4f out: kpt on fnl 2f) 5 **3**
96² Shamwari (USA) **(50)***(51)*(Fav)*(JWHills)* 4-8-8b(5)ow6 RPainter(2) (lw: cl up: effrt & hung lft ent st: sn btn) 5 **4**
53⁸ Uckerby Lad **(50)***(44) (NPLittmoden)* 4-8-12 JWeaver(6) (lw: bhd: effrt 6f out: styd on: n.d) 5 **5**
Jolly Swagman **(45)***(34) (LordHuntingdon)* 4-8-12 LDettori(9) (chsd ldrs tl rdn & btn over 2f out) 8 **6**
96⁸ Petite Bijou **(42)***(29) (RBrotherton)* 4-8-7 AMackay(8) (nvr wnt pce) ..... s.h **7**
Minster Glory *(30) (MWEasterby)* 4-8-12 LCharnock(11) (in tch tl wknd 3f out) 3 **8**
84⁵ Sweet Caroline **(40)***(15) (PMitchell)* 4-8-7b JMcLaughlin(7) (wl bhd fnl 7f) 8 **9**
83⁷ Mrs Jogglebury **(35)***(—) (CSmith)* 4-8-2 (5) JStack(4) (a bhd) 25 **10**
96¹⁶ Nord Lys (IRE) **(35)***(—) (FHLee)* 4-8-12 AClark(5) (prom tl outpcd over 5f out: sn bhd) 30 **11**

Evens Shamwari (USA), **6/1** ALL ON, **7/1** Murphys Way, **8/1** Jolly Swagman, **10/1** Uckerby Lad, **12/1** Tuscania, **16/1** Petite Bijou, Minster Glory, **25/1** Sweet Caroline, **33/1** Mrs Jogglebury, Nord Lys (IRE), CSF £46.66 TOTE £8.00: £2.70 £1.60 £4.50 (£24.70) OWNER Mr N. Hetherton (MALTON) BRED N. Hetherton 11 Rn 2m 43.9 (9.70) SF: 23/20/14/10/3/-/-/-/-/-/-
WEIGHT FOR AGE 4yo-4lb

137

BLUE VELVET H'CAP (0-80) (Class D) £3,606.20 (£1,091.60: £532.80: £253.40) **1m 3f (Fibresand)** GOING minus 0.09 sec per fur (STD) 2-15 (2-15)

Slmaat (64)*(69+)*(Fav)*(MrsMReveley)* 4-9-2 RCochrane(3) (lw: hld up: hdwy 4f out: led 2f out: r.o) ..... — **1**
91⁴ Palacegate Jo (IRE) **(54)***(54) (RHollinshead)* 4-8-6 LDettori(5) (led 2f: cl up: kpt on u.p fnl f) 3½ **2**
91⁹ Imperial Bid (FR) **(55)***(54) (DenysSmith)* 7-8-11 MFenton(1) (led after 2f to 2f out: one pce) ..... nk **3**
91⁶ Let's Get Lost **(66)***(58) (MrsJRRamsden)* 6-9-8 MWigham(4) (lw: in tch: pushed along 5f out: one pce fnl 3f) 5 **4**
66⁵ Brackenthwaite **(72)***(62) (LRLloyd-James)* 5-10-0b JWeaver(2) (b.hind: hld up: hdwy 4f out: rdn & btn 2f out) 1½ **5**
Santana Lady (IRE) **(72)***(34) (MJHeaton-Ellis)* 6-10-0 StephenDavies(8) (cl up tl wknd 2f out) 20 **6**
50⁷ Anorak (USA) **(55)***(16) (GMMoore)* 5-8-11 TWilliams(7) (in tch tl drvn along & wknd 4f out) ..... ½ **7**
67⁸ Brief Respite (IRE) **(55)***(12) (EJAlston)* 4-8-7v JQuinn(6) (chsd ldrs tl wknd 2f out) ... 3 **8**

7/4 SLMAAT, **7/2** Brackenthwaite, **11/2** Let's Get Lost, Palacegate Jo (IRE), **15/2** Santana Lady (IRE) (5/1-8/1), **10/1** Imperial Bid (FR), **12/1** Anorak (USA), **33/1** Brief Respite (IRE), CSF £11.95 CT £70.72 TOTE £2.80: £1.20 £1.80 £3.00 (£5.00) OWNER Mr G. A. Farndon (SALTBURN) BRED Ali K. Al Jafleh 8 Rn 2m 28.1 (6.60) SF: 47/33/37/40/44/16/-/-

WEIGHT FOR AGE 4yo-4lb

138

CHAMPAGNE GOLD H'CAP (0-70) (Class E) £3,138.30 (£950.40: £464.20: £221.10) **1m (Fibresand)** GOING minus 0.09 sec per fur (STD) 2-45 (2-45)

*80** **Hawwam (57)***(74) (EJAlston)* 9-9-5 JWeaver(9) (lw: hld up: hdwy ent st: led wl over 1f out: r.o wl).......— **1**

Mam'zelle Angot **(63)***(66) (JLEyre)* 5-9-11 AClark(4) (stdd s: hdwy on outside appr st: r.o fnl f: nvr able to chal).......7 **2**

94[2] Hawaii Storm (FR) **(56)***(55) (MissAJWhitfield)* 7-8-13 (5) RPainter(2) (chsd ldrs: led over 2f out tl wl over 1f out: one pce).......2 **3**

*94** Roar on Tour **(55)***(53)*(Fav)*(MrsMReveley)* 6-8-10b(7) 6x SCopp(11) (lw: s.i.s: hdwy on outside appr st: rdn & nvr able to chal).......nk **4**

119[2] At the Savoy (IRE) **(38)***(26) (TDBarron)* 4-7-13 AMackay(1) (lw: led tl hdd over 2f out: grad wknd).......5 **5**

61[4] Forgotten Dancer (IRE) **(56)***(34) (RIngram)* 4-9-3 WWoods(6) (chsd ldrs tl grad wknd over 2f out).......5 **6**

49[3] Early Star **(47)***(22) (KBishop)* 6-8-9b RPerham(12) (in tch: effrt over 3f out: no imp).......1¼ **7**

55[8] Efficacy **(34)***(8) (APJarvis)* 4-7-4 (5)ow1 NVarley(3) (chsd ldrs tl wknd over 2f out)...nk **8**

94[8] Genesis Four **(44)***(15) (SRBowring)* 5-7-13b(7) CTeague(7) (lw: cl up tl wknd over 2f out).......1½ **9**

Scoffera **(38)***(4) (NTinkler)* 5-8-0 KimTinkler(8) (chsd ldrs: rdn appr st: sn wknd)..2½ **10**

Sure to Win (IRE) **(44)***(8) (JMCarr)* 6-8-6 SMorris(13) (b: prom tl rdn & lost pl ½-wy).......¾ **11**

Media Messenger **(50)***(12) (DenysSmith)* 6-8-12 MFenton(5) (in tch tl wknd ent st).......1 **12**

96[10] Shamaka **(48)***(—) (JAGlover)* 4-8-9 SWilliams(10) (prom tl wknd 5f out).......6 **13**

13/8 Roar on Tour, **5/1** HAWWAM, **8/1** Mam'zelle Angot, Hawaii Storm (FR), At the Savoy (IRE), **12/1** Genesis Four, **14/1** Early Star, **16/1** Forgotten Dancer (IRE), Shamaka, Media Messenger, **20/1** Scoffera, **33/1** Efficacy, **50/1** Sure to Win (IRE), CSF £44.64 CT £299.16 TOTE £6.90: £2.20 £2.60 £1.80 (£31.70) OWNER North West Racing Club Owners Club (PRESTON) BRED G. Franco 13 Rn 1m 45.6 (6.30) SF: 33/25/15/13/-/-/-/-/-/-/-/-/-

WEIGHT FOR AGE 4yo-1lb

139

BEAMISH H'CAP (0-70) (Class E) £3,066.80 (£928.40: £453.20: £215.60) **6f (Fibresand)** GOING minus 0.09 sec per fur (STD) 3-15 (3-15)

102[6] **Warwick Warrior (IRE) (66)***(72) (MrsLPiggott)* 4-10-0 JWeaver(3) (b: b.hind: bhd: hdwy over 2f out: str run to ld wl ins fnl f).......— **1**

78[7] Fairey Firefly **(56)***(57) (MJCamacho)* 4-9-4 LCharnock(11) (lw: cl up: slt ld appr fnl f: sn hdd: nt qckn nr fin).......1¾ **2**

78[2] Cheerful Groom (IRE) **(44)***(42)*(Fav)*(JMackie)* 4-8-6 LDettori(9) (lw: a.p: effrt over 2f out: styd on one pce).......¾ **3**

93[5] Matthew David **(46)***(43) (SRBowring)* 5-8-8 SWilliams(5) (b: led tl hdd appr fnl f: kpt on same pce).......nk **4**

102[3] Cheeky Chappy **(38)***(26) (DWChapman)* 4-8-0b JQuinn(10) (cl up tl wknd wl over 1f out).......3½ **5**

Mr B Reasonable (IRE) **(48)***(31) (SWCampion)* 4-8-10b RCochrane(6) (bhd: sme hdwy fnl 3f: no imp).......2 **6**

Chiliola **(65)***(44) (MHEasterby)* 4-9-13 TIves(7) (a.p: effrt over 2f out: r.o one pce)1½ **7**

50[9] Sav-Ed **(33)***(—) (APJarvis)* 6-7-4 (5)ow2 NVarley(4) (spd over 3f: sn rdn & btn).......5 **8**

Kid Ory **(60)***(21) (PCalver)* 4-9-8 DaleGibson(8) (prom 3f).......1¾ **9**

14[8] My Foxy Lady **(38)***(—) (JAHarris)* 5-8-0 AMackay(1) (prom to ½-wy).......15 **10**

Akabusi **(50)***(—) (MCChapman)* 4-8-7 (5) DRMcCabe(2) (a outpcd & bhd).......2½ **11**

LONG HANDICAP Sav-Ed 7-4

9/4 Cheerful Groom (IRE) (2/1-3/1), **3/1** Matthew David, **11/2** Cheeky Chappy, **6/1** Fairey Firefly, **7/1** WARWICK WARRIOR (IRE), **12/1** Chiliola, **16/1** Kid Ory, **25/1** Akabusi, **33/1** Sav-Ed, My Foxy Lady, Mr B Reasonable (IRE), CSF £47.13 CT £113.28 TOTE £7.30: £2.00 £2.00 £1.40 (£12.60) OWNER Wetherby Racing Bureau Plc BRED Mrs Aine O'Farrell 11 Rn

1m 18.2 (4.70) SF: 41/29/16/17/1/5/16/-/-/-/-

140 SILVER ICE (S) STKS (II) (Class G) £2,259.00 (£634.00: £309.00)
6f (Fibresand) GOING minus 0.09 sec per fur (STD) 3-45 (3-45)

822 **Jamaica Bridge (55)***(65) (SGNorton)* 5-9-2 (5) JStack(5) (hld up: hdwy ½-wy: led over 1f out: r.o)........— **1**
652 Sea Devil **(67)***(59)*(Fav)*(MJCamacho)* 9-9-7 LCharnock(6) (chsd ldrs: effrt over 2f out: styd on one pce)........2½ **2**
211 Sense of Priority **(57)***(53) (MHEasterby)* 6-9-7 WWoods(2) (a.p: effrt 2f out: nt qckn fnl f)........2½ **3**
714 Tyrian Purple (IRE) **(58)***(40) (TJNaughton)* 7-9-2b(5) VHalliday(4) (b.off hind: mde most tl hdd over 1f out: sn btn)........5 **4**
5510 Grey Toppa **(54)***(17) (MrsJRRamsden)* 4-9-2 JWeaver(7) (effrt ½-wy: nvr trbld ldrs)........7 **5**
697 Black Boy (IRE) **(39)***(14) (RFMarvin)* 6-9-2v(5) DGriffiths(1) (w ldrs tl wknd over 1f out)........3 **6**
717 Waders Dream (IRE) **(39)***(12) (PMitchell)* 6-9-7v JMcLaughlin(8) (nvr wnt pce).......½ **7**
Bold Aristocrat (IRE) **(38)***(11) (RHollinshead)* 4-9-7 LDettori(3) (chsd ldrs tl hung lft & hit rail ent st: eased fnl 2f)........hd **8**

10/11 Sea Devil, **7/2** JAMAICA BRIDGE, **7/1** Tyrian Purple (IRE), **8/1** Sense of Priority, Grey Toppa, **20/1** Bold Aristocrat (IRE), **25/1** Black Boy (IRE), Waders Dream (IRE), CSF £7.27 TOTE £5.20: £1.10 £1.30 £2.10 (£2.50) OWNER Mr Billy Parker (BARNSLEY) BRED Sir Stephen Hastings 8 Rn 1m 18.5 (5.00) SF: 30/24/17/4/-/-/-/-
No bid

OFFICIAL EXPLANATION Bold Aristocrat had hung into the rail on the home turn, causing the saddle to slip.

141 SCARLET FLAME H'CAP (II) (3-Y.O) (0-60) (Class F) £2,537.00 (£712.00: £347.00) **1m (Fibresand)** GOING minus 0.09 sec per fur (STD) 4-15 (4-15)

1162 **Grand Selection (IRE) (53)***(78+)*(Fav)*(MBell)* 3-9-6 MFenton(5) (mde all: qcknd 2f out: sn clr)........— **1**
Warrior Lady (IRE) **(45)***(56) (PJMcBride)* 3-8-12 JQuinn(8) (chsd ldrs: kpt on fnl 2f: no ch w wnr)........7 **2**
*51** Poly Road **(53)***(48) (MRChannon)* 3-9-6 RHughes(9) (chsd wnr tl rdn & btn 2f out)........8 **3**
477 Tapping Feet **(53)***(42) (SirMarkPrescott)* 3-9-6 WWoods(2) (prom: outpcd ½-wy: no imp after)........3 **4**
545 Tyreless (IRE) **(40)***(27) (APJarvis)* 3-8-2 (5) NVarley(3) (chsd ldrs: rdn 3f out: no imp)1 **5**
646 Lawnswood Lady **(48)***(30) (RHollinshead)* 3-9-1b LDettori(1) (chsd ldrs tl wknd over 2f out)........2½ **6**
Friar's Oak **(45)***(25) (MHTompkins)* 3-8-5 (7) JGotobed(7) (outpcd fr ½-wy)........1 **7**
Lass of Kinloch **(40)***(—) (MBrittain)* 3-8-7 GBardwell(6) (s.i.s: sme hdwy ½-wy: sn wknd)........15 **8**
*133** Red Spectacle (IRE) **(54)***(4) (PCHaslam)* 3-9-7 JWeaver(4) (lw: s.i.s: rdn 3f out: a bhd)........s.h **9**

11/10 GRAND SELECTION (IRE), **3/1** Poly Road, **11/2** Red Spectacle (IRE), **10/1** Lawnswood Lady, Tapping Feet, **12/1** Warrior Lady (IRE), **33/1** Tyreless (IRE), Friar's Oak, Lass of Kinloch, CSF £15.20 CT £30.65 TOTE £2.10: £1.30 £3.10 £1.50 (£14.60) OWNER Mr M. B. Hawtin (NEWMARKET) BRED Mount Coote Stud in Ireland 9 Rn 1m 46.7 (7.40) SF: 24/3/-/-/-/-/-/-/-

OFFICIAL EXPLANATION Red Spectacle: jockey reported that the race must have come too soon after the gelding's win at Wolverhampton.

T/Jkpt: Not won; £4,271.51 to Lingfield 24/1/95. T/Plpt: £103.70 (199.5 Tckts). T/Qdpt: £65.00 (1.6 Tckts). AA

0122-LINGFIELD (L-H)
Tuesday January 24th (Standard)

142 HUNGERFORD APP'CE H'CAP (I) (0-60) (Class F) £2,700.80 (£758.80: £370.40) **7f (Equitrack)** GOING minus 0.57 sec per fur (FST) 1-15 (1-17)

894 **Maid Welcome (59)***(66)*(Fav)*(MrsNMacauley)* 8-9-8v(5) AmandaSanders(3) (led 1f: led wl ins fnl f: rdn out)........— **1**
Our Shadee (USA) **(44)***(50) (KTIvory)* 5-8-7v(5) CScally(10) (hld up: rdn over 1f out: ev ch wl ins fnl f: r.o)........hd **2**

55² Sharp Imp **(47)***(50) (RMFlower)* 5-8-12b(3) JDSmith(7) (led over 4f out tl wl ins fnl f: unable qckn)....1¼ **3**
56⁷ Myjinka **(35)***(36) (JO'Donoghue)* 5-7-12b(5) IonaWands(11) (a.p: rdn over 1f out: one pce)....1 **4**
39¹⁰ Crafty Cricketer **(28)***(21) (RVoorspuy)* 4-7-5 (5)ow2 CAdamson(9) (nvr nr to chal)......4 **5**
101³ Joint Effort (IRE) **(42)***(34) (AMoore)* 4-8-10 SSanders(5) (b.hind: hld up: rdn over 3f out: wknd wl over 1f out)....nk **6**
39⁹ Europharm Lassie **(43)***(33) (GLMoore)* 4-8-4 (7) CarolineHovington(2) (a bhd) ....¾ **7**
Bonny Melody **(45)***(11) (PDEvans)* 4-8-13 JStack(6) (led 6f out tl over 4f out: wknd over 2f out) 11 **8**
36⁴ Whatone Bell **(25)***(—) (PHayward)* 5-7-7 DWright(8) (b.hind: a bhd)....4 **9**
76⁹ Kelly's Kite **(26)***(—) (HJCollingridge)* 7-7-5 (3) CHawksley(4) (b: swtg: dwlt: a bhd) 2 **10**

LONG HANDICAP Whatone Bell 7-3

5/2 MAID WELCOME, **4/1** Sharp Imp, **11/2** Joint Effort (IRE), **6/1** Our Shadee (USA), **8/1** Bonny Melody, **12/1** Europharm Lassie, **16/1** Myjinka, **25/1** Kelly's Kite, **50/1** Whatone Bell, Crafty Cricketer, CSF £15.73 CT £48.39 TOTE £2.30: £1.10 £2.10 £1.70 (£7.00) OWNER Mrs Anna Sanders (MELTON MOWBRAY) BRED Doublet Ltd 10 Rn 1m 25.91 (2.91) SF: 29/15/16/2/-/-/-/-/-/-

143

WESTMINSTER CLAIMING STKS (Class E) £2,966.70 (£897.60: £437.80: £207.90) **1m 4f (Equitrack)** GOING minus 0.57 sec per fur (FST) 1-45 (1-45)

Prince Danzig (IRE) (76)*(65+) (DJGMurraySmith)* 4-8-13 LDettori(4) (chsd ldr: led 5f out: rdn over 2f out: r.o wl) ....— **1**
82¹² Lon Isa **(42)***(55) (BPalling)* 4-8-5 ow1 AClark(7) (hdwy over 4f out: chsd wnr over 1f out: unable qckn) 2 **2**
22* Long Furlong **(50)***(54) (RAkehurst)* 7-8-4 (5) SSanders(6) (eyeshield: lw: hld up: ev ch over 2f out: one pce) ....¾ **3**
97* Elementary **(73)***(56)*(Fav)*(NJHWalker)* 12-9-5 RCochrane(5) (lw: hld up: rdn & ev ch over 3f out: wknd over 2f out) 6 **4**
9¹¹ Mediator **(42)***(39) (AMoore)* 6-8-11b DHarrison(3) (b.hind: led 7f) 7 **5**
Forever Blushing **(32)** *(PButler)* 4-7-10 GBardwell(2) (bhd fnl 5f)....25 **6**
Bernie's Sister (IRE) **(33)***(—) (CNAllen)* 4-7-10 JQuinn(1) (prom 7f) 1¼ **7**

1/2 Elementary, **3/1** Long Furlong, **5/1** PRINCE DANZIG (IRE), **16/1** Mediator, **50/1** Lon Isa, Forever Blushing, Bernie's Sister (IRE), CSF £111.95 TOTE £8.60: £2.10 £7.60 (£123.40) OWNER Mr A. H. Ulrick (LAMBOURN) BRED J. N. McCaffrey in Ireland 7 Rn
2m 33.96 (4.56) SF: 22/12/15/17/1/-/-
WEIGHT FOR AGE 4yo-4lb
Long Furlong clmd J Bosley £4,000
OFFICIAL EXPLANATION **Elementary: jockey reported that the horse seemed flat.**

144

VAUXHALL (S) STKS (3-Y.O) (Class G) £2,483.00 (£698.00: £341.00) **1m (Equitrack)** GOING minus 0.57 sec per fur (FST) 2-15 (2-18)

98² **Iron Man (IRE) (59)***(63) (JWhite)* 3-8-11b(5) SDrowne(5) (hld up: rdn over 4f out: led ins fnl f: drvn out)....— **1**
51³ Good so Fa (IRE) **(58)***(62) (MHTompkins)* 3-8-11 (5) SMulvey(4) (hdwy over 3f out: hrd rdn over 2f out: r.o wl ins fnl f) ....½ **2**
Witney-de-Bergerac (IRE) **(57)***(61) (JSMoore)* 3-9-2 RHughes(11) (b.hind: hdwy over 1f out: r.o wl ins fnl f: too much to do)....½ **3**
98* Fahema **(50)***(44)*(Fav)*(RBoss)* 3-8-6 LDettori(3) (rdn & lost pl over 4f out: one pce fnl 2f) 3½ **4**
59⁷ Tachycardia **(52)***(44) (RJO'Sullivan)* 3-8-6 JWeaver(2) (lw: led: clr over 2f out: hdd ins fnl f: sn wknd)....hd **5**
Little Scarlett **(52)***(36) (PJMakin)* 3-8-6 RPerham(9) (a.p: rdn over 3f out: eased whn btn ins fnl f)....4 **6**
85⁷ Plucky Pet **(38)***(14) (CJBenstead)* 3-8-6 MRimmer(6) (prom over 4f) 11 **7**
38⁸ Cuban Reef **(43)***(11) (DJSCosgrove)* 3-8-1 (5) LNewton(8) (prom over 4f) 1½ **8**
Red Owa Lady (IRE) *(8) (CJHill)* 3-8-1 (5) SSanders(7) (bhd fnl 5f) 1½ **9**
Fosters Top *(1) (JFfitch-Heyes)* 3-8-11 NAdams(10) (lw: a bhd)....6 **10**
Two Way Stretch *(—) (GLMoore)* 3-8-6 AClark(12) (a bhd) ....½ **11**

13/8 Fahema, **4/1** Good so Fa (IRE), **5/1** Little Scarlett, Tachycardia, **10/1** IRON MAN (IRE), **16/1** Witney-de-Bergerac (IRE), **20/1** Two Way Stretch, **25/1** Cuban Reef, **33/1** Fosters Top, **50/1** Red Owa Lady (IRE), **66/1** Plucky Pet, CSF £47.71 TOTE £5.70: £3.90 £1.10 £3.40 (£17.10) OWNER Mr J. R. White (WENDOVER) BRED Conquering Hero Syndicate in Ireland 11 Rn
1m 40.99 (4.59) SF: 8/7/6/-/-/-/-/-/-/-/-
Sold M Johnston 5,000 gns; Good So Fa (IRE) clmd M Dunne £6,000

145

DAILY STAR AWT 1M 2F CHALLENGE SERIES H'CAP (Qualifier) (0-75) (Class D) £3,916.55 (£1,186.40: £579.70: £276.35)
1m 2f (Equitrack) GOING minus 0.57 sec per fur (FST) 2-45 (2-47)

*11** **Birequest (68)***(79+) (RBoss)* 4-9-5 LDettori(4) (lw: mde all: clr over 1f out: r.o wl) — **1**
8² Rawya (USA) **(75)***(82) (BWHills)* 4-9-12 JWeaver(9) (b: rdn & nt clr run 3f out: hdwy over 2f out: r.o one pce) 2½ **2**
89⁹ Secret Aly (CAN) **(74)***(80) (CEBrittain)* 5-10-0 MRimmer(10) (lw: rdn & hdwy over 1f out: r.o ins fnl f) ¾ **3**
*27** Ballyranter **(66)***(68)*(Fav)*(HJCollingridge)* 6-9-6v JQuinn(5) (a.p: chsd wnr over 4f out: fly-jumped 2f out: hrd rdn over 1f out: wknd fnl f) 2½ **4**
Zacaroon **(67)***(65) (LordHuntingdon)* 4-9-4 DHarrison(8) (hld up: rdn over 3f out: one pce) 2½ **5**
37⁴ Global Dancer **(73)***(66) (WAO'Gorman)* 4-9-7 (3) EmmaO'Gorman(11) (stdy hdwy over 6f out: wknd over 2f out) 3 **6**
89¹² Friendly Brave (USA) **(66)***(57) (TGMills)* 5-9-6 TWilliams(1) (bhd fnl 2f) 1¼ **7**
8³ Our Eddie **(68)***(57) (BGubby)* 6-9-3v(5) JStack(6) (lw: prom over 6f) 1 **8**
Ultimate Warrior **(74)***(63) (CACyzer)* 5-10-0 RCochrane(7) (bhd fnl 2f) s.h **9**

9/4 Ballyranter, **3/1** Rawya (USA), **4/1** BIREQUEST, **11/2** Secret Aly (CAN), **7/1** Our Eddie, **12/1** Global Dancer, **14/1** Zacaroon, **20/1** Ultimate Warrior, **25/1** Friendly Brave (USA), CSF £17.12 CT £63.49 TOTE £5.50: £1.50 £2.20 £1.40 (£10.60) OWNER Mr J. Ellis (NEWMARKET) BRED Langham Hall Bloodstock 9 Rn 2m 6.1 (3.10) SF: 32/35/36/25/19/20/15/-/-
WEIGHT FOR AGE 4yo-3lb

146

LINGFIELD PARK AWT SPRINT SERIES H'CAP (Qualifier) (3-Y.O) (0-60) (Class F) £2,963.70 (£833.20: £407.10)
6f (Equitrack) GOING minus 0.57 sec per fur (FST) 3-15 (3-19)

105² **One for Jeannie (57)***(69)*(Fav)*(ABailey)* 3-9-4 JWeaver(5) (a.p: led 1f out: rdn out) — **1**
7³ Prince Rudolf (IRE) **(50)***(54) (MrsNMacauley)* 3-8-11v MFenton(10) (a.p: carried wd bnd wl over 1f out: r.o ins fnl f) 3 **2**
86³ Bon Secret (IRE) **(59)***(59) (TJNaughton)* 3-9-1 (5) SSanders(1) (lw: led 5f: unable qckn) 1¼ **3**
Nomadic Dancer (IRE) **(60)***(51) (MSSaunders)* 3-9-7 ADicks(3) (hrd rdn & hdwy on ins over 1f out: r.o one pce) 3½ **4**
43⁹ Shartel **(40)***(27) (MJohnston)* 3-8-1b TWilliams(7) (w ldr: rdn over 3f out: rn wd bnd wl over 1f out: sn wknd) 1½ **5**
Two Chalk **(44)***(30) (PDEvans)* 3-8-0v(5) JStack(11) (lw: nvr nr to chal) nk **6**
First Point (IRE) **(50)***(28) (CNAllen)* 3-8-11 EGuest(6) (hld up: rdn over 2f out: sn wknd) 3 **7**
Royal Uprising (IRE) **(52)***(12) (GLMoore)* 3-8-13 SWhitworth(8) (a bhd) 7 **8**
Princess in Blue (IRE) **(40)***(—) (CJHill)* 3-8-1b JQuinn(9) (a bhd) 5 **9**
33⁵ Rotherfield Park (IRE) **(48)***(—) (CSmith)* 3-8-9 WWoods(2) (mid div whn sddle slipped over 3f out: nt rcvr: virtually p.u over 1f out: t.o) dist **10**

5/4 ONE FOR JEANNIE, **4/1** Bon Secret (IRE) (3/1-9/2), **9/2** Rotherfield Park (IRE), **7/1** Prince Rudolf (IRE), **20/1** Princess in Blue (IRE), Two Chalk, Shartel, **25/1** Nomadic Dancer (IRE), **33/1** Royal Uprising (IRE), First Point (IRE), CSF £10.48 CT £25.51 TOTE £2.30: £1.10 £2.00 £1.70 (£6.90) OWNER Mrs Julia Jones (TARPORLEY) BRED A. Saccomando 10 Rn
1m 13.95 (3.35) SF: 9/-/-/-/-/-/-/-/-/-
OFFICIAL EXPLANATION **Rotherfield Park(IRE): saddle slipped half a mile from home.**

147

TOWER H'CAP (0-80) (Class D) £3,589.30 (£1,086.40: £530.20: £252.10)
2m (Equitrack) GOING minus 0.57 sec per fur (FST) 3-45 (3-46)

Art Form (USA) (74)*(81+) (CACyzer)* 8-10-0 TIves(3) (hdwy 5f out: led over 3f out: clr over 1f out: r.o wl) — **1**
81² Argyle Cavalier (IRE) **(72)***(76)*(Fav)*(MJohnston)* 5-9-5 (7) OliverCasey(6) (a.p: ev ch 3f out: unable qckn) 3½ **2**
*109** Arc Bright (IRE) **(59)***(61) (RHollinshead)* 5-8-13 4x LDettori(2) (led over 12f: hrd rdn over 2f out: eased whn btn wl ins fnl f) 1¾ **3**
87³ Elburg (IRE) **(62)***(61) (RPCHoad)* 5-9-2 RCochrane(5) (hld up: rdn over 4f out: one pce) 3 **4**
108⁹ Arctic Guest (IRE) **(60)***(57) (CSmith)* 5-9-0 WWoods(1) (lw: rdn & no hdwy fnl 4f) 2½ **5**

88[4] Ragtime Song **(41)** *(AMoore)* 6-7-2 (7)ow2 MBaird(7) (b.hind: chsd ldr 8f out to 6f out: sn wknd: t.o)....dist **6**
94[14] The Country Dancer **(41)***(—)* *(KTIvory)* 5-7-9 ow1 JQuinn(4) (chsd ldr 8f: t.o)....12 **7**

LONG HANDICAP Ragtime Song 7-4

15/8 Argyle Cavalier (IRE), **5/2** Arc Bright (IRE), **3/1** ART FORM (USA), **5/1** Elburg (IRE), **25/1** Arctic Guest (IRE), Ragtime Song, **50/1** The Country Dancer, CSF £8.78 TOTE £2.90: £2.00 £1.90 (£3.60) OWNER Mr R. M. Cyzer (HORSHAM) BRED Morgan's Ford Farm and Elizabeth Thomas in USA 7 Rn
3m 24.22 (0.72) SF: 63/58/45/45/41/-/-

148

HUNGERFORD APP'CE H'CAP (II) (0-60) (Class F) £2,700.80 (£758.80: £370.40) **7f (Equitrack)** GOING minus 0.57 sec per fur (FST) 4-15 (4-17)

Words of Wisdom (IRE) (53)*(57)* *(CACyzer)* 5-9-7 DRMcCabe(2) (a.p: hrd rdn 1f out: led ins fnl f: r.o wl)....— **1**
56[5] The Little Ferret **(60)***(60)* *(GLMoore)* 5-9-9 (5) LSuthern(8) (lw: led tl ins fnl f: unable qckn)....1¾ **2**
56[6] Swallow Ridge (IRE) **(31)***(28)* *(RJO'Sullivan)* 6-7-13 SMulvey(5) (b: rdn & lost pl over 4f out: rallied fnl f: r.o wl)....1¼ **3**
Bogart **(58)***(54)*(Fav)*(CWFairhurst)* 4-9-12 JStack(3) (w ldr: ev ch ins fnl f: one pce)....nk **4**
71[8] Veloce (IRE) **(54)***(46)* *(ABailey)* 7-9-1b(7) AngelaGallimore(6) (b: hdwy 3f out: one pce fnl 2f)....1¾ **5**
78[3] Meeson Times **(51)***(39)* *(RBastiman)* 7-9-2 (3) HBastiman(4) (nvr nr to chal)....1¾ **6**
Rustic League (IRE) **(39)***(26)* *(TJNaughton)* 4-8-4 (3) VHalliday(7) (b.hind: hld up: stumbled over 2f out: hrd rdn over 1f out: sn wknd)....nk **7**
41[4] Gingerillo **(34)***(20)* *(TGMills)* 4-7-11b(5) DToole(9) (lw: a.p: ev ch over 2f out: wknd over 1f out)....½ **8**
Scots Law **(42)***(4)* *(JELong)* 8-8-10b PMcCabe(10) (b: bhd fnl 3f)....11 **9**
Darakah **(60)***(17)* *(CJHill)* 8-10-0 SSanders(1) (bit bkwd: a bhd)....2½ **10**

3/1 Bogart (4/1-2/1), **4/1** The Little Ferret, **9/2** Meeson Times, **13/2** Gingerillo, **8/1** Swallow Ridge (IRE), **9/1** WORDS OF WISDOM (IRE), **10/1** Darakah, **12/1** Veloce (IRE), **14/1** Rustic League (IRE), **25/1** Scots Law, CSF £44.63 CT £282.73 TOTE £16.70: £3.80 £1.10 £2.90 (£18.30) OWNER Mr M. J. Morrison (HORSHAM) BRED Stackallan Stud in Ireland 10 Rn
1m 26.34 (3.34) SF: 18/23/-/19/12/7/-/-/-/-

T/Jpt: £9,207.30 (0.3 Tckts); £9,077.64 to Sedgefield 25/1/95. T/Plpt: £161.80 (160.14 Tckts). T/Qdpt: £5.80 (14 Tckts). AK

0128-WOLVERHAMPTON (L-H)
Wednesday January 25th (Standard)

149

HADDOCK STKS (Mdn) (Class D) £3,589.30 (£1,086.40: £530.20: £252.10) **6f (Fibresand)** GOING minus 0.29 sec per fur (FST) 2-00 (2-01)

Posted Abroad (IRE) *(60+)*(Fav)*(SirMarkPrescott)* 3-8-8 WWoods(8) (chsd ldr: led over 1f out: sn clr: easily)....— **1**
64[3] Jalmaid **(50)***(48)* *(BAMcMahon)* 3-7-13 (5)ow1 SSanders(3) (led: rdn & veered lft over 1f out: sn hdd: one pce)....3 **2**
Nuthatch (IRE) *(27)* *(MDIUsher)* 3-7-10 (7) CAdamson(5) (bit bkwd: lt-f: chsd ldrs: kpt on one pce fnl 2f)....8 **3**
64[9] Sand Star *(22)* *(DHaydnJones)* 3-8-3 AMackay(6) (chsd ldrs: rdn & outpcd over 2f out)....1¾ **4**
103[5] Lady Valensina (IRE) **(59)***(18)* *(BJLlewellyn)* 4-9-5b JWeaver(2) (outpcd: bhd tl styd on appr fnl f)....1¼ **5**
Winning Wonder *(—)* *(CEBrittain)* 3-8-3 BDoyle(7) (bit bkwd: sn chsng ldrs: rdn ½-wy: sn wknd: t.o)....12 **6**
Captain Sinbad *(—)* *(KSBridgwater)* 3-8-8 NAdams(4) (w'like: leggy: bkwd: s.i.s: a bhd & outpcd)....3 **7**
103[11] Honest Achiever (IRE) *(—)* *(APJames)* 4-9-5 DHarrison(1) (spd to ½-wy: sn outpcd: t.o)....7 **8**

4/11 POSTED ABROAD (IRE), **15/2** Jalmaid, **10/1** Lady Valensina (IRE), **12/1** Winning Wonder, **16/1** Sand Star, **25/1** Nuthatch (IRE), **33/1** Honest Achiever (IRE), **50/1** Captain Sinbad, CSF £4.11 TOTE £1.50: £1.10 £2.00 £3.80 (£3.90) OWNER Mr Neil Greig (NEWMARKET) BRED John Kent in Ireland 8 Rn
1m 14.3 (3.10) SF: 25/14/-/-/1/-/-/-
WEIGHT FOR AGE 3yo-16lb

150

MACKEREL CLAIMING STKS (Class F) £2,580.00 (£780.00: £380.00: £180.00)
7f (Fibresand) GOING minus 0.29 sec per fur (FST) 2-30 (2-32)

93[7] **Arndilly (69)***(65) (BJMeehan)* 4-8-11b RCochrane(6) (b: drvn along thrght: hdwy & 3rd st: rdn to ld ins fnl f: r.o)........— 1
65[4] Walk the Beat **(68)***(57) (RSimpson)* 5-8-1 (5) SDrowne(5) (a.p: led 2f out tl hdd & unable qckn ins fnl f)........1¼ 2
92* Dream Carrier (IRE) **(67)***(63)*(Fav)*(TDBarron)* 7-8-5 (7) KimberleyHart(9) (dwlt: wl bhd & outpcd: gd hdwy appr fnl f: fin wl)........s.h 3
130[3] Alpine Johnny **(56)***(54) (RHollinshead)* 4-8-1 (5) AGarth(10) (sn chsng ldrs: 4th st: rdn & one pce fnl f)........1¼ 4
41* Ragazzo (IRE) **(46)***(53) (KOCunningham-Brown)* 5-8-10b LCharnock(7) (w ldr: led over 3f out: sn hdd: 2nd st: rdn & wknd appr fnl f)........2½ 5
Titanium Honda (IRE) **(41)***(40) (CEBrittain)* 4-8-0b BDoyle(8) (chsd ldrs tl 6th & btn st)........1¼ 6
44[11] Bold Mick **(60)***(39) (DJGMurraySmith)* 4-7-13 (5) DRMcCabe(3) (outpcd: a bhd)....2½ 7
107[8] Bessie's Will **(42)***(23) (DHaydnJones)* 4-7-13 AMackay(2) (outpcd: a bhd: t.o)........5 8
82[6] Grandee **(43)***(26) (BAMcMahon)* 4-8-6 JWeaver(1) (led tl over 2f out: 5th & wkng st: t.o)........1¾ 9

13/8 Dream Carrier (IRE), **7/2** ARNDILLY, Walk the Beat, **8/1** Alpine Johnny, **10/1** Bold Mick, **12/1** Ragazzo (IRE), **20/1** Grandee, **25/1** Titanium Honda (IRE), **50/1** Bessie's Will, CSF £16.02 TOTE £5.30: £1.80 £1.50 £1.40 (£10.70) OWNER Mr A. S. Reid (UPPER LAMBOURN) BRED Hilborough Stud Farm Ltd 9 Rn 1m 28.8 (4.80) SF: 16/9/14/7/5/-/-/-/-

Dream Carrier (IRE) clmd T G K Construction £8,000

151

TROUT H'CAP £5,368.00 (£1,624.00: £792.00: £376.00)
1m 100y (Fibresand) GOING minus 0.29 sec per fur (FST) 3-00 (3-00)

47[2] **Komreyev Dancer (75)***(80) (ABailey)* 3-8-13 TIves(1) (a.p: 2nd st: rdn to ld wl ins fnl f)........— 1
59* Nigel's Lad (IRE) **(67)***(71) (PCHaslam)* 3-8-5 JWeaver(4) (hdwy 6f out: led 3f out: sn clr: rdn & ct nr fin)........½ 2
17* Contrafire (IRE) **(66)***(56) (WJarvis)* 3-8-4 WWoods(3) (b.hind: lw: chsd ldrs: 4th st: one pce fnl f)........7 3
99[2] Battleship Bruce **(69)***(49)*(Fav)*(NACallaghan)* 3-8-7 LDettori(2) (b.hind: led early: disp ld 4f out to 3f out: 3rd & rdn st: sn btn)........5 4
Dark Shot (IRE) **(83)***(13) (JBerry)* 3-9-0 (7) PRoberts(5) (plld hrd: led 7f out to 3f out: sn wknd: 5th & t.o st)........25 5

5/4 Battleship Bruce, **2/1** KOMREYEV DANCER, **11/2** Nigel's Lad (IRE), **8/1** Contrafire (IRE), **14/1** Dark Shot (IRE), CSF £11.50 TOTE £3.30: £1.10 £4.40 (£6.50) OWNER Mr Denis Gallagher (TARPORLEY) BRED G. and Mrs Whittaker 5 Rn 1m 49.6 SF: 21/13/-/-/-

OFFICIAL EXPLANATION Battleship Bruce: appeared too soon after his hard race at Lingfield on January 17th.

152

SALMON H'CAP 0-80) (Class D £4,045.50 (£1,224.00: £597.00: £283.50)
1m 1f 79y (Fibresand) GOING: minus 0.29 sec per fur (FS) 3-00 (3-31)

127* **Kaafih Homm (IRE) (61)***(69)*(Fav)*(NACallaghan)* 4-8-7 5x RCochrane(7) (b.hind: lw: hld up: hdwy 4f out: 3rd st: led 1f out: r.o wl)........— 1
Folly Finnesse **(73)***(78) (BRMillman)* 4-9-5 JWilliams(1) (led: clr after 2f: hdd appr fnl f: wnt lft ins fnl f: r.o: fin 3rd, ½l: plcd 2nd)........ 2
66[4] Bentico **(68)***(74) (MrsNMacauley)* 6-8-11 (5) SSanders(4) (lw: hld up: led appr fnl f: sn hdd: wnt lft fnl f: no ex: fin 2nd, 1½l: plcd 3rd)........ 3
120[4] Off the Air (IRE) **(49)***(52) (ICampbell)* 4-7-9v JQuinn(3) (chsd ldrs: 4th st: rdn over 1f out: one pce)........1½ 4
100[3] Braveboy **(60)***(61) (CEBrittain)* 7-8-8 BDoyle(6) (chsd ldrs: 5th st: nt pce to chal).1¼ 5
66[13] Rainbow Walk (IRE) **(80)***(75) (JGMO'Shea)* 5-9-9 (5) JStack(5) (a bhd: 6th & t.o st: sme late hdwy)........3½ 6
Jonjas Chudleigh **(80)***(—) (WGMTurner)* 8-10-0 MWigham(2) (lw: prom to ½-wy: sn rdn & wknd: t.o)........dist 7

6/4 KAAFIH HOMM (IRE), **11/4** Bentico, **7/2** Braveboy, **7/1** Folly Finnesse, **10/1** Off the Air (IRE), **14/1** Rainbow Walk (IRE), **33/1** Jonjas Chudleigh, CSF £12.36 TOTE £2.40: £1.40 £2.00 (£5.20) OWNER Gallagher Materials Ltd (NEWMARKET) BRED Sheikh Ahmed bin Rashid al Maktoum 7 Rn 2m 2.9 (6.90) SF: 11/17/18/-/5/17/-

WEIGHT FOR AGE 4yo-2lb

STEWARDS' ENQUIRY Sanders suspended 3-4/2/95 (careless riding).

153 BREAM £2,537.00 (£712.00: £347.00)
1m 6f 166y (Fibresand) GOING minus 0.29 sec per fur (FST) 4-00 (4-00)

Epica (62)*(54) (ABailey)* 4-8-11b TIves(10) (b: sn led & clr: rdn 4f out: styd on strly)— **1**
*79*4 Zaaheyah (USA) **(36)***(46) (MDHammond)* 5-8-11 RCochrane(7) (lw: led 1f: 2nd st: rdn & nt qckn fnl f)..........2½ **2**
*97*2 Cliburnel News (IRE) **(49)***(46) (WRMuir)* 5-8-11 StephenDavies(6) (b.hind: hld up & bhd: hdwy 5f out: 5th & rdn st: styd on fnl f)..........hd **3**
*108*8 Sassiver (USA) **(45)***(53) (RHollinshead)* 5-9-7 LDettori(5) (lw: hld up & bhd: hdwy 5f out: 3rd st: rdn & one pce appr fnl f)..........2½ **4**
*131*4 Carrolls Marc (IRE) **(48)***(45)*(Fav)*(PCHaslam)* 7-9-2 JWeaver(8) (hld up & bhd: smooth hdwy 4f out: 4th st: sn rdn: no imp)..........2½ **5**
*83*8 Sharp Sensation **(47)***(35) (DNicholls)* 5-9-2 AlexGreaves(1) (lw: chsd ldrs: 6th & rdn st: sn btn)..........9 **6**
*46*5 Blue Pennant *(27) (TTBill)* 4-8-6 SWebster(11) (a in rr)..........2½ **7**
*104*4 Chapel Hill (IRE) *(11) (BJLlewellyn)* 7-8-11 DHarrison(12) (b: chsd ldrs: rdn ½-wy: sn wknd: t.o)..........15 **8**
*46*4 Aerial View **(45)***(6) (WGMTurner)* 4-8-11 RPerham(2) (chsd wnr after 3f: wknd 4f out: t.o)..........9 **9**
*63*10 Dissident Dancer **(28)***(—) (JHPeacock)* 6-9-2 TWall(3) (a in rr: t.o)..........15 **10**
*46*11 Betabetcorbett **(40)***(—) (BPJBaugh)* 4-8-4 (7) PRoberts(9) (b.hind: prom 8f: sn rdn & wknd: t.o)..........20 **11**
*19*8 Almost a Princess **(41)***(—) (WGMTurner)* 7-8-6b(5) DRMcCabe(4) (lost tch ½-wy: t.o)..........2½ **12**

2/1 Carrolls Marc (IRE), **9/4** Cliburnel News (IRE), **11/2** EPICA (5/2-7/1), **8/1** Sassiver (USA), **12/1** Chapel Hill (IRE), **14/1** Zaaheyah (USA), **16/1** Sharp Sensation, Aerial View, **20/1** Betabetcorbett, Almost a Princess, **33/1** Blue Pennant, Dissident Dancer, CSF £78.01 TOTE £6.40: £2.10 £2.70 £1.10 (£33.00) OWNER Mr J. B. Wilcox (TARPORLEY) BRED N. G. Halsey 12 Rn No bid
3m 20.5 SF: 5/3/3/9/2/-/-/-/-/-/-/-
WEIGHT FOR AGE 4yo-5lb

154 HALIBUT H'CAP (0-75) (Class D) £3,707.60 (£1,122.80:£548.40: £261.20) **5f (Fibresand)** GOING minus 0.29 sec per fur (FST) 4-30 (4-30)

*69*6 **Scored Again (56)***(61) (MJHeaton-Ellis)* 5-8-2 (7) AmandaSanders(1) (chsd ldrs: led ins fnl f: hld on gamely)..........— **1**
*69*2 Kalar **(62)***(66) (DWChapman)* 6-9-1b LDettori(3) (led tl ins fnl f: rallied cl home).....hd **2**
*69** Leigh Crofter **(75)***(78)*(Fav)*(PDCundell)* 6-10-0b TIves(10) (hdwy 2f out: rdn & r.o wl nr fin)..........nk **3**
*129*7 Delrob **(62)***(62) (DHaydnJones)* 4-9-1 AMackay(2) (hld up: hdwy on ins over 2f out: ev ch ins fnl f: unable qckn nr fin)..........¾ **4**
*102** Nineacres **(58)***(55) (DNicholls)* 4-8-11b AlexGreaves(4) (in tch: effrt & rdn over 2f out: kpt on fnl f)..........¾ **5**
*14** Very Dicey **(74)***(65) (JBerry)* 7-9-6 (7) PRoberts(5) (chsd wnr: rdn & no ex ins fnl f)..2 **6**
*107*2 Samson-Agonistes **(69)***(60) (PDEvans)* 9-9-3 (5) JStack(7) (chsd ldng pair over 3f: sn rdn & outpcd)..........s.h **7**
*69*11 Tommy Tempest **(40)***(30) (ABailey)* 6-7-7b GBardwell(6) (s.i.s: effrt wl over 1f out: no imp)..........nk **8**
*78*5 Pageboy **(70)***(52) (PCHaslam)* 6-9-9 JWeaver(9) (outpcd: rdn wl over 1f out: no imp)..........2½ **9**
*107*6 Farastrada **(60)***(18) (BPreece)* 4-8-6b(7) AEddery(8) (mid div: rdn along ½-wy: sn outpcd: t.o)..........8 **10**

7/2 Leigh Crofter, **4/1** Pageboy, Kalar, **6/1** Nineacres, **7/1** Very Dicey, **8/1** SCORED AGAIN, **10/1** Samson-Agonistes, **12/1** Delrob, **14/1** Farastrada, **16/1** Tommy Tempest, CSF £41.28 CT £126.50 TOTE £7.60: £2.50 £2.20 £1.10 (£29.30) OWNER Mrs Anna Sanders (WROUGHTON) BRED R. T. and Mrs Watson 10 Rn 62.2 secs (4.20) SF: -/5/15/1/-/3/-/-/-/-
T/Plpt: £55.00 (504.71 Tckts). T/Qdpt: £13.70 (2.45 Tckts). IM

0142-LINGFIELD (L-H)
Thursday January 26th (Standard)

155 DAILY STAR AWT 1M 2F CHALLENGE SERIES H'CAP (Qualifier) (I) 0-60) (Class F) £2,897.20 (£814.20: £397.60)
1m 2f (Equitrack) GOING minus 0.53 sec per fur (FST) 1-10 (1-13)

*100*7 **Little Miss Ribot (33)***(38) (RJO'Sullivan)* 5-8-1 StephenDavies(4) (hdwy over 3f out: led ins fnl f: rdn out)..........— **1**

120³ Greek Gold (IRE) **(59)***(63) (GPKelly)* 6-9-13 LDettori(10) (led 9f out: hrd rdn over 1f out: hdd ins fnl f: unable qckn)....¾ **2**
21² Kedwick (IRE) **(58)***(60)*(Fav)*(PRHedger)* 6-9-12v JWilliams(3) (b.hind: hld up: rdn over 2f out: r.o one pce)....1¼ **3**
13⁵ Captain Marmalade **(51)***(52) (DTThom)* 6-9-0 (5) DRMcCabe(9) (nt clr run on ins over 2f out: hdwy over 1f out: r.o wl ins fnl f)....½ **4**
73³ Lexus (IRE) **(43)***(41) (RJRWilliams)* 7-8-4b(7)ow3 SarahThompson(8) (hdwy over 8f out: hrd rdn over 1f out: one pce)....1¾ **5**
80⁵ Exclusion **(46)***(42) (JHetherton)* 6-9-0 TIves(6) (b: b.hind: lw: rdn 7f out: nvr nr to chal)....1¼ **6**
73⁵ Calisar **(40)***(22) (PHowling)* 5-8-8 JQuinn(5) (prom 6f)....9 **7**
62³ Hi Penny **(43)***(23) (KTIvory)* 4-8-8b DHarrison(1) (prom over 5f)....1¼ **8**
63⁶ Cyprus Point **(48)***(25) (GHEden)* 4-8-13 JWeaver(7) (led 1f: chsd ldr over 4f out tl wl over 1f out: eased whn btn fnl f)....1¾ **9**
Playing Tricks **(38)***(—) (PDEvans)* 4-8-3v BDoyle(2) (a wl bhd)....12 **10**

9/4 Kedwick (IRE), **7/2** Lexus (IRE), **6/1** Captain Marmalade, **13/2** Hi Penny, **7/1** Exclusion, **9/1** Calisar, **10/1** LITTLE MISS RIBOT, **12/1** Greek Gold (IRE), **20/1** Cyprus Point, **25/1** Playing Tricks, CSF £115.70 CT £337.41 TOTE £8.00: £5.00 £2.00 £1.30 (£59.00) OWNER Christopher Lane (BOGNOR REGIS) BRED H. Powis 10 Rn 2m 7.58 (4.58) SF: 8/30/28/21/12/13/-/-/-/-
WEIGHT FOR AGE 4yo-3lb

156 DISRAELI STKS (Mdn 3-Y.O) (Class D) £3,690.70 (£1,117.60: £545.80: £259.90) 7f (Equitrack) GOING minus 0.53 sec per fur (FST) 1-40 (1-43)

Mr Frosty *(62) (WJarvis)* 3-9-0 JWeaver(11) (chsd ldr over 3f out: hrd rdn & led over 1f out: r.o wl)....— **1**
72³ Portelet **(55)***(50)*(Fav)*(RJRWilliams)* 3-8-9 LDettori(10) (led over 4f out tl over 1f out: unable qckn)....3½ **2**
Bally Wonder **(46)***(39) (DMorris)* 3-8-9 DHarrison(5) (hld up: rdn over 4f out: wknd over 1f out)....5 **3**
Docklands Courier *(41) (BJMcMath)* 3-9-0 RCochrane(3) (led over 2f: hrd rdn over 3f out: wknd over 1f out)....1½ **4**
Athinar *(33) (CPWildman)* 3-8-9 StephenDavies(6) (lt-f: nvr nr to chal)....1¼ **5**
Sailors Moon **(49)***(32) (HJCollingridge)* 3-8-9 MRimmer(7) (b: bit bkwd: hld up: rdn over 4f out: wknd over 2f out)....nk **6**
Maronetta *(30) (MJRyan)* 3-8-9 AClark(2) (rdn over 4f out: nvr nrr)....¾ **7**
Alka International **(55)***(33) (JWhite)* 3-9-0 JWilliams(1) (b: b.hind: prom 3f)....¾ **8**
Zeliba *(20) (CEBrittain)* 3-8-9 BDoyle(4) (a bhd)....4 **9**
Okay Baby (IRE) *(18) (MHTompkins)* 3-8-4 (5) SMulvey(9) (a bhd)....¾ **10**
Our Dorothy *(1) (CNWilliams)* 3-8-9 JQuinn(8) (neat: s.s: a bhd)....8 **11**

2/1 Portelet, **11/4** MR FROSTY, **9/2** Alka International (8/1-12/1), **9/1** Okay Baby (IRE), **14/1** Docklands Courier, Our Dorothy, **16/1** Bally Wonder, Zeliba, **20/1** Sailors Moon, **25/1** Maronetta, **33/1** Athinar, CSF £8.90 TOTE £4.20: £1.20 £1.60 £4.60 (£7.10) OWNER Mr D. G. Wright (NEWMARKET) BRED D. G. and Miss C. M. Wright 11 Rn 1m 25.92 (2.92) SF: 20/8/-/-/-/-/-/-/-/-/-

157 GLADSTONE CLAIMING STKS (Class E) £3,066.80 (£928.40: £453.20: £215.60) 1m (Equitrack) GOING minus 0.53 sec per fur (FST) 2-10 (2-12)

89¹³ **Masnun (USA) (66)***(62)*(Fav)*(RJO'Sullivan)* 10-8-8 AClark(8) (hld up: rdn over 4f out: led 1f out: r.o wl)....— **1**
52⁵ Sweet Supposin (IRE) **(70)***(73) (KMcAuliffe)* 4-9-7b RCochrane(3) (lw: led over 6f out to 1f out: unable qckn)....1½ **2**
Gallery Artist (IRE) **(60)***(55) (RGuest)* 7-7-13 (5) SSanders(9) (a.p: rdn over 4f out: r.o ins fnl f)....hd **3**
63² Perilous Plight **(58)***(57) (WRMuir)* 4-8-9 JWeaver(1) (lw: s.s: rdn over 3f out: hdwy over 2f out: r.o wl ins fnl f)....1¾ **4**
12⁸ Rad **(55)***(51) (SPCWoods)* 5-8-10 WWoods(6) (led over 1f out: rdn over 3f out: wknd over 1f out)....3 **5**
39⁴ Faynaz **(33)***(32) (AMoore)* 9-8-3 ow1 DHarrison(4) (b: lw: rdn 5f out: nvr nr to chal)...6 **6**
Lunar Mission (IRE) **(78)***(46) (JMPEustace)* 4-9-3 LDettori(10) (lw: no hdwy fnl 3f)....½ **7**
50⁴ Monsieur Petong **(43)***(20) (DNicholls)* 4-8-1 DaleGibson(12) (prom over 5f)....5 **8**
Miss Mah-Jong **(59)***(25) (JWhite)* 4-8-3 (5) SDrowne(5) (lw: a bhd)....¾ **9**
11⁸ Knightrider **(50)***(21) (CJames)* 4-8-7b JWilliams(11) (stumbled s: bhd fnl 2f)....1¼ **10**
Night Fantasy (IRE) **(40)***(—) (NJHWalker)* 7-7-13v NAdams(7) (bhd fnl 4f)....7 **11**
Helmsley Palace *(2) (MPMuggeridge)* 6-8-3 MFenton(2) (a bhd)....s.h **12**

2/1 MASNUN (USA), **100/30** Lunar Mission (IRE), **4/1** Sweet Supposin (IRE), **8/1** Rad, **10/1** Perilous Plight, **12/1** Gallery Artist (IRE), Monsieur Petong, **16/1** Miss Mah-Jong, Knightrider, **25/1** Faynaz, Night Fantasy (IRE), **33/1** Helmsley Palace, CSF £11.69 TOTE £3.80: £1.10 £3.40 £8.20 (£7.40) OWNER Mr I. W. Page (BOGNOR REGIS) BRED Glencrest Farm 12 Rn

1m 37.65 (1.25) SF: 36/46/29/32/27/9/21/-/-/-/-/-

WEIGHT FOR AGE 4yo-1lb

158

DAILY STAR AWT 1M 2F CHALLENGE SERIES H'CAP (Qualifier) (II)(0-60) (Class F) £2,897.20 (£814.20: £397.60)
1m 2f (Equitrack) GOING minus 0.53 sec per fur (FST) 2-40 (2-41)

Shansi (IRE) (43)*(50) (MDIUsher)* 4-8-8v RStreet(4) (b: chsd ldr: led over 3f out: drvn out)........— 1
122³ Can Can Charlie **(59)***(65) (JPearce)* 5-9-13 JWeaver(8) (hld up: chsd wnr over 2f out: hrd rdn over 1f out: r.o ins fnl f)........½ 2
76* Zuno Noelyn **(56)***(59)*(Fav)*(RAkehurst)* 4-9-2 (5) SSanders(7) (rdn over 4f out: hdwy over 2f out: rn wd bnd wl over 1f out: r.o wl)........1¾ 3
100⁴ Night Edition **(40)***(42) (SDow)* 5-8-8e LDettori(3) (eyeshield: led over 6f: hrd rdn over 1f out: eased whn btn nr fin)........nk 4
100⁸ Coalisland **(37)***(38) (RIngram)* 5-8-5b WWoods(5) (hdwy over 3f out: rdn over 2f out: r.o ins fnl f)........¾ 5
96⁶ Celestial Faith **(38)***(34) (MJohnston)* 4-8-3 TWilliams(2) (a.p: rdn over 3f out: wknd over 1f out)........3 6
73⁷ Lady Sabina **(37)***(33) (WJMusson)* 5-8-0 (5) PMcCabe(9) (lw: hdwy over 3f out: wknd over 2f out)........s.h 7
Barahin (IRE) **(53)***(38) (MDixon)* 6-9-7 AClark(1) (a bhd)........7 8
Stipple **(38)***(14) (SWoodman)* 4-8-3 MFenton(10) (prom over 7f)........6 9
Nearly Honest **(37)***(7) (RJHodges)* 7-8-0 (5)ow2 SDrowne(6) (a bhd)........4 10

10/11 Zuno Noelyn, **4/1** Night Edition, **6/1** Can Can Charlie, **10/1** SHANSI (IRE), Lady Sabina, **14/1** Barahin (IRE), Celestial Faith, **25/1** Nearly Honest, **33/1** Stipple, Coalisland, CSF £68.38 CT £99.70 TOTE £12.70: £2.90 £1.60 £1.30 (£26.30) OWNER Mr Trevor Barker (SWINDON) BRED Sheikh Mohammed bin Rashid al Maktoum in Ireland 10 Rn

2m 7.18 (4.18) SF: 17/34/27/14/11/5/6/1/-/-

WEIGHT FOR AGE 4yo-3lb

159

LINGFIELD PARK AWT SPRINT SERIES H'CAP (Qualifier) (3-Y.O) (0-70) (Class E) £3,149.00 (£953.00: £465.00: £221.00)
5f (Equitrack) GOING minus 0.53 sec per fur (FST) 3-10 (3-10)

118⁴ **Dolly Face (63)***(66)*(Fav)*(WRMuir)* 3-9-5 JWeaver(4) (hld up: rdn over 2f out: led ins fnl f: r.o wl)........— 1
86² Wasblest **(55)***(56)*(Fav)*(MJohnston)* 3-8-11 TWilliams(3) (chsd ldr: led 2f out tl ins fnl f: r.o)........½ 2
124* Bold Effort (FR) **(72)***(72)*(Fav)*(KOCunningham-Brown)* 3-10-0 7x LDettori(2) (outpcd: hdwy over 2f out: hrd rdn over 1f out: r.o wl ins fnl f)........nk 3
146³ Bon Secret (IRE) **(59)***(54) (TJNaughton)* 3-8-10 (5) SSanders(5) (lw: led 3f: unable qckn)........1¾ 4

5/2 DOLLY FACE, Wasblest, Bold Effort (FR), **3/1** Bon Secret (IRE), CSF £8.26 TOTE £2.70 (£4.90) OWNER Mr Stanley Meadows (LAMBOURN) BRED Lode Moors Farm 4 Rn

59.68 secs (1.48) SF: 33/24/39/24

160

LLOYD GEORGE H'CAP (0-80) (Class D) £3,656.90 (£1,107.20: £540.60: £257.30) **7f (Equitrack)** GOING minus 0.53 sec per fur (FST) 3-40 (3-40)

Moon Strike (FR) (77)*(85) (WJarvis)* 5-10-0 JWeaver(3) (gd hdwy over 1f out: str run fnl f: led nr fin)........— 1
142* Maid Welcome **(59)***(66) (MrsNMacauley)* 8-8-3v(7) AmandaSanders(2) (led: rdn over 1f out: hdd nr fin)........½ 2
89⁶ Digpast (IRE) **(51)***(56) (RJO'Sullivan)* 5-8-2b StephenDavies(6) (b: lw: s.s: nt clr run wl over 1f out: gd hdwy over 1f out: r.o wl ins fnl f)........¾ 3
Present Situation **(66)***(69) (LordHuntingdon)* 4-9-3 DHarrison(4) (a.p: hrd rdn & ev ch over 1f out: one pce)........¾ 4
Greatest **(54)***(53)*(Fav)*(RAkehurst)* 4-8-0 (5) SSanders(10) (a.p: rdn over 3f out: ev ch over 1f out: one pce)........1¾ 5
89¹⁰ Invocation **(64)***(57) (AMoore)* 8-9-1 MRimmer(9) (b.hind: rdn over 4f out: no hdwy fnl 3f)........3 6
Pirates Gold (IRE) **(57)***(43) (JWhite)* 5-8-3 (5) SDrowne(11) (lw: nvr nr to chal)......3½ 7
62⁹ Panchellita (USA) **(54)***(36) (GLMoore)* 6-8-5 ow1 AClark(5) (prom over 4f)........2 8

41[7] Kindergarten Boy (IRE) **(58)***(38) (RBoss)* 4-8-9 LDettori(7) (rdn thrght: mid div: hrd rdn over 1f out: eased whn btn fnl f)....¾ **9**
Sullamell **(48)***(—) (RJHodges)* 4-7-10 (3) DWright(1) (bit bkwd: s.s: a bhd)....25 **10**
65[3] Frisky Miss (IRE) **(67)***(—) (KOCunningham-Brown)* 4-9-4 BDoyle(8) (lw: prom over 4f)....3½ **11**

4/1 Greatest, **9/2** Kindergarten Boy (IRE), Maid Welcome, **5/1** Digpast (IRE), Present Situation, **8/1** MOON STRIKE (FR), **12/1** Frisky Miss (IRE), Invocation, **14/1** Pirates Gold (IRE), **16/1** Panchellita (USA), **50/1** Sullamell, CSF £45.19 CT £189.59 TOTE £17.90: £4.20 £2.70 £1.80 (£58.40) OWNER Mr A. Foustok (NEWMARKET) BRED Haras de Manneville in France 11 Rn
1m 24.71 (1.71) SF: 47/29/20/32/19/21/7/-/-/-/-

161

THATCHER STKS (0-50) (Class F) £2,839.40 (£798.40: £390.20)
1m 4f (Equitrack) GOING minus 0.53 sec per fur (FST) 4-10 (4-10)

75[3] **Head Turner (46)***(56) (CPWildman)* 7-8-9 NAdams(2) (lw: hld up: led over 1f out: rdn out)....— **1**
131[2] Scalp 'em (IRE) **(49)***(60) (PDEvans)* 7-9-0 LDettori(3) (a.p: rdn 4f out: led 3f out tl over 1f out: r.o)....½ **2**
100[2] My Minnie **(50)***(51)*(Fav)*(BJMeehan)* 5-8-9 JWeaver(1) (hld up: rdn over 3f out: ev ch over 1f out: unable qckn)....3½ **3**
9[3] Rose of Glenn **(50)***(46) (BPalling)* 4-8-5 StephenDavies(4) (a.p: rdn over 3f out: lost pl over 2f out: one pce)....4 **4**
Glowing Path **(49)***(49) (RJHodges)* 5-8-9b(5) SDrowne(11) (rdn 5f out: nvr nr to chal)....2 **5**
Port Sunlight (IRE) **(50)***(48) (PDEvans)* 7-9-0 AClark(8) (nvr nrr)....½ **6**
9[4] Disputed Call (USA) **(37)***(42) (JWHills)* 6-9-0 RCochrane(7) (lw: a.p: ev ch 3f out: wknd 2f out)....5 **7**
Portolano (FR) **(44)***(38) (CNWilliams)* 4-8-10 MRimmer(6) (led 9f)....3½ **8**
Kentavrus Way (IRE) **(50)***(33) (AMoore)* 4-8-10 CandyMorris(12) (b.hind: bhd fnl 9f)....4 **9**
53[7] Soneeto **(30)***(8) (DRLaing)* 9-9-0 GBardwell(9) (bhd fnl 9f)....20 **10**
Little Luke (IRE) **(42)***(—) (PButler)* 4-8-10 JWilliams(5) (a bhd: t.o fnl 6f)....12 **11**

7/4 My Minnie, **4/1** HEAD TURNER, Scalp 'em (IRE), **9/2** Rose of Glenn, **14/1** Disputed Call (USA), **16/1** Glowing Path, Kentavrus Way (IRE), Portolano (FR), **20/1** Port Sunlight (IRE), Little Luke (IRE), **33/1** Soneeto, CSF £21.55 TOTE £4.70: £1.20 £1.90 £1.10 (£8.80) OWNER I. Jerrard (SALISBURY) BRED M. B. O'Gorman 11 Rn 2m 33.46 (4.06) SF: 25/29/20/11/17/17/11/-/-/-/-
WEIGHT FOR AGE 4yo-4lb
T/Plpt: £75.90 (194.94 Tckts). T/Qdpt: £10.90 (3.6 Tckts). AK

CAGNES-SUR-MER (Nice, France) (L-H) Wednesday January 18th (Good to soft)

162a

PRIX DE JUAN-LES-PINS £6,587.00 **1m**

Confronter *(—) (SDow)* 6-8-5 ESaint-Martin....— **1**
Hundred Hours (IRE) *(—) (France)* 6-8-8 SDupouy....nk **2**
Celestial Way (USA) *(—) (France)* 4-8-5 FSanchez....1½ **3**

TOTE12.00F: 3.80F 15.80F 1.90F (779.90F) OWNER Hatfield Ltd (EPSOM) BRED Hamilton Bloodstock (UK) Ltd 18 Rn
1m 44.4 SF: -/-/-

163a

PRIX DU CANNET 3-Y.O.C & G £5,988.00 **1m**

Le Pilat (USA) *(—) (France)* 3-8-8 (5) J-BEyquem....— **1**
Rey (FR) *(—) (France)* 3-9-2 GElorriaga-Santos....nk **2**
Sharpest Image (IRE) *(—) (France)* 3-8-4 (3) CHanotel....4 **3**
Courbaril *(—) (SDow)* 3-8-7 FSanchez (btn further 3*l)....6

TOTE6.00F: 2.70F 4.10F 7.80F (29.20F) OWNER Mme S. Desmarais BRED Dakotah Thoroughbred Farm in USA 17 Rn
1m 53.9 SF: -/-/-/-

0162A-CAGNES-SUR-MER (Nice, France) (L-H) Friday January 20th (Soft)

164a

PRIX D'AJACCIO (3-Y.O) £5,988.00 **1m 2f**

Musilumieres (FR) *(—) (France)* 3-9-0 ABarzalona....— **1**

Tha Tidja (FR) *(—) (France)* 3-8-6 FBlondel ....½ 2
L'Arpege (USA) *(—) (France)* 3-8-9 WMongil 1 3
59[5] Mo's Main Man (IRE) *(—) (SDow)* 3-8-9 FSanchez 1½ 4

TOTE7.10F: 1.70F 2.10F 1.20F (29.10F) OWNER Mr J. Damas BRED Haras de Bernesq in France 10 Rn 2m 16.3 SF: -/-/-/-

0149-WOLVERHAMPTON (L-H)
Friday January 27th (Standard)
Transferred from Southwell

165
ANNESLEY STKS (I) (0-55) (Class F) £2,537.00 (£712.00: £347.00)
6f (Fibresand) GOING: 0.37 sec per fur (SLW) 12-50 (12-51)

Panther (IRE) (50)*(56) (JHetherton)* 5-8-11 NKennedy(10) (b: b.hind: sn pushed along: hdwy 3f out: led over 1f out: rdn out)....— 1
134[3] Swinging Tich **(41)***(48) (BAMcMahon)* 6-8-1 (5) SSanders(7) (lw: bhd: c wd & hdwy over 2f out: ev ch 1f out: edgd lft & nt qckn)....1 2
78[4] Shadow Jury **(55)***(49) (DWChapman)* 5-8-6b(5) DRMcCabe(9) (chsd ldrs: ev ch wl over 1f out: kpt on)....1½ 3
69[8] Brisas **(44)***(40) (CWFairhurst)* 8-8-11 JFanning(2) (prom: no hdwy fnl 2f)....3½ 4
138[8] Efficacy **(33)***(32) (APJarvis)* 4-8-1 (5) NVarley(6) (lw: prom: led 2f out: sn hdd & btn)¾ 5
129[8] Arc Lamp **(53)***(33) (JAGlover)* 9-8-11 RCochrane(1) (chsd ldrs: pushed along over 2f out: no imp)....1¼ 6
139[4] Matthew David **(46)***(32)*(Fav)*(SRBowring)* 5-8-11b SWilliams(5) (led 4f: wknd fnl f)....hd 7
78[11] Last Straw **(34)***(9) (BPreece)* 7-8-4v(7) ClaireBalding(11) (prom over 3f: sn bhd)....9 8
134[4] Splash of Salt (IRE) **(51)***(—) (TJNaughton)* 5-8-1b(5) VHalliday(4) (b: lw: sn pushed along: a bhd)....2½ 9
129[5] Farmer Jock **(46)***(—) (MrsNMacauley)* 13-8-11 AClark(3) (b: hld up: c wd st: nvr nr ldrs)....6 10

7/4 Matthew David, **3/1** Arc Lamp (2/1-7/2), **5/1** Shadow Jury, **6/1** Swinging Tich, **7/1** PANTHER (IRE), **10/1** Splash of Salt (IRE), **14/1** Farmer Jock, Brisas, **16/1** Last Straw, **33/1** Efficacy, CSF £51.67 TOTE £7.50: £3.10 £2.80 £2.10 (£15.40) OWNER Mrs Elizabeth Milner (MALTON) BRED My Treasure Ltd 10 Rn 1m 19.2 (8.00) SF: 16/9/10/-/-/-/-/-/-/-

166
BALDERTON H'CAP (Amateurs) (I) (0-60) (Class F) £2,537.00 (£712.00: £347.00) **1m 4f (Fibresand)** GOING: 0.37 sec per fur (SLW) 1-20 (1-22)

77[2] **Gold Blade (57)***(69)*(Fav)*(JPearce)* 6-11-11 MrsLPearce(11) (lw: wnt prom after 3f: led 2f out: pushed out)....— 1
96* Borocay **(33)***(45) (MJCamacho)* 7-10-1 MrMHNaughton(12) (hld up: hdwy over 5f out: 3rd st: sn rdn & ev ch: kpt on nr fin)....hd 2
121[2] Mr Moriarty (IRE) **(34)***(36) (SRBowring)* 4-9-12 MrsMMorris(8) (lw: prom: led over 7f out tl hdd & 3rd st: nt qckn)....8 3
35[6] Blowedifiknow **(40)***(23) (JWharton)* 5-10-8 MrSWalker(10) (lw: chsd ldrs: sn rdn along: 5th & btn st)....15 4
120[5] Midlin **(36)***(17) (JLHarris)* 5-10-4 MrIMcLelland(5) (hdwy 5f out: wknd & 6th st)....2 5
77[3] Modest Hope (USA) **(47)***(28) (BRichmond)* 8-11-1 MissDianaJones(2) (lw: hld up: hdwy 5f out: poor 4th & btn st)....hd 6
Rejects Reply **(38)***(11) (WJMusson)* 5-10-6 MrTMcCarthy(9) (nvr nr to chal)....6 7
Kentucky Flyer **(35)***(—) (JFBottomley)* 4-9-13v MissPRobson(6) (prom tl wknd 3f out)....15 8
Mamalama **(30)***(—) (BJLlewellyn)* 7-9-7 (5) MissEJJones(3) (in tch 5f)....3 9
15[9] Jean de Florette (USA) **(40)***(—) (RWEmery)* 4-10-4 MrMRimell(1) (led over 4f: wknd qckly)....1¼ 10
96[3] Wicklow Boy (IRE) **(40)***(—) (TTClement)* 4-10-4v MrVLukaniuk(4) (prom over 4f: sn bhd)....15 11

100/30 GOLD BLADE, **7/2** Borocay, **4/1** Mr Moriarty (IRE), Modest Hope (USA), **12/1** Blowedifiknow, Wicklow Boy (IRE), **20/1** Mamalama, **25/1** Rejects Reply, Midlin, **33/1** Jean de Florette (USA), Kentucky Flyer, CSF £14.72 CT £42.86 TOTE £4.40: £2.20 £2.10 £1.10 (£8.40) OWNER Rochford Racing Ltd (NEWMARKET) BRED Ballymacoll Stud Co 11 Rn
2m 49.5 (18.50) SF: 43/21/9/-/-/3/-/-/-/-/-
WEIGHT FOR AGE 4yo-4lb

167 ANNESLEY STKS (II) (0-55) (Class F) £2,537.00 (£712.00: £347.00)
6f (Fibresand) GOING: 0.37 sec per fur (SLW) 1-50 (1-52)

134[7] **Letsbeonestaboutit (52)***(51) (MrsNMacauley)* 9-8-11 DeanMcKeown(10) (prom tl lost pl over 2f out: rallied u.p over 1f out: led nr fin) — 1
129[2] Farndale **(50)***(48) (JBerry)* 8-8-4 (7) CLowther(7) (hdwy over 2f out: led ins fnl f tl ct nr fin) ¾ 2
89[8] Aljaz **(55)***(43)*(Fav)*(DTThom)* 5-8-11 AMackay(11) (b: a.p: ev ch over 1f out: one pce) 2 3
Chadwell Hall **(38)***(42) (SRBowring)* 4-8-4b(7) CTeague(8) (led after 1f tl ins fnl f: wknd nr fin) nk 4
82[10] Make the Break **(47)***(41) (SCoathup)* 4-8-4b(7) SharronJames(5) (bhd tl rdn & hdwy over 2f out: nt rch ldrs) hd 5
Miss Siham (IRE) **(39)***(26) (JBalding)* 6-8-6 NAdams(6) (bkwd: chsd ldrs 4f) 4 6
93[6] Tenor **(55)***(29) (DNicholls)* 4-8-11 AlexGreaves(9) (prom tl wknd over 1f out) ½ 7
78[15] Twice in Bundoran (IRE) **(48)***(6) (PSFelgate)* 4-8-1 (5) PMcCabe(2) (b.hind: plld hrd: in tch 3f) 7 8
139[3] Cheerful Groom (IRE) **(44)***(7) (JMackie)* 4-8-11 MFenton(4) (s.i.s: a bhd) 1½ 9
Dauntless Fort **(46)***(—) (BWMurray)* 4-8-1v(5) JStack(1) (lw: led 1f: bhd fr ½-wy) 2½ 10
139[8] Sav-Ed **(28)***(—) (APJarvis)* 6-8-11b TIves(3) (lw: dwlt: a bhd) 4 11

7/4 Aljaz, **2/1** Farndale, **9/2** Cheerful Groom (IRE), **6/1** Tenor, **8/1** Chadwell Hall, **12/1** LETSBEONESTABOUTIT, **16/1** Miss Siham (IRE), **20/1** Make the Break, Twice in Bundoran (IRE), Dauntless Fort, **50/1** Sav-Ed, CSF £41.50 TOTE £10.50: £2.60 £1.90 £1.10 (£16.30) OWNER Mr Stephen Roots (MELTON MOWBRAY) BRED Mrs R. D. Peacock 11 Rn
1m 19.6 (8.40) SF: 11/9/4/3/3/-/-/-/-/-/-

168 DANETHORPE MEDIAN AUCTION STKS (Mdn 3-Y.O) (Class F) £2,537.00 (£712.00: £347.00) **1m 100y (Fibresand)** GOING: 0.37 sec (SLW) 2-20 (2-21)

64[4] **Almuhtaram (74)***(59) (WWHaigh)* 3-9-0 DaleGibson(3) (chsd ldrs: rdn & 2nd st: led over 1f out: rdn & ducked lft ins fnl f: hld on wl) — 1
Wisdom *(58) (PFICole)* 3-9-0 TIves(6) (bit bkwd: sn pushed along: bhd tl hdwy & 3rd st: r.o ins fnl f) nk 2
Hard Try *(54)*(Fav)*(MJCamacho)* 3-9-0 LCharnock(1) (led tl over 1f out: sn bdly hmpd: no ch after) 2 3
141[5] Tyreless (IRE) **(40)***(42) (APJarvis)* 3-8-4 (5) NVarley(5) (plld hrd: prom: 4th & rdn st: sn wknd) 3½ 4
90[11] Sergio (IRE) *(35) (MCChapman)* 3-8-9 (5) DRMcCabe(2) (in tch 4f: wknd & 5th st) 6 5
51[7] Visual Illusion (IRE) *(—) (BSRothwell)* 3-8-9 JQuinn(4) (lw: sn pushed along & bhd: last st) 30 6

5/4 Hard Try, **6/4** ALMUHTARAM, **7/2** Wisdom, **33/1** Tyreless (IRE), Sergio (IRE), Visual Illusion (IRE), CSF £7.10 TOTE £1.70: £1.10 £1.10 (£4.50) OWNER Mr A. M. Al-Midani (MALTON) BRED A. M. Midani 6 Rn 1m 56.2 SF: 13/13/9/-/-/-

169 CARLTON-ON-TRENT H'CAP (0-70) (Class E) £3,152.60 (£954.80: £466.40: £222.20) **1m 100y (Fibresand)** GOING: 0.09 sec per fur (STD) 2-50 (2-51)

94[3] **Buddy's Friend (IRE) (60)***(63) (RJRWilliams)* 7-9-3 (7) SarahThompson(8) (lw: hdwy ½-wy: led ent st: sn qcknd clr: pushed out) — 1
119[4] Spanish Stripper (USA) **(48)***(48) (MCChapman)* 4-8-6 (5) DRMcCabe(4) (lw: led 3f: led 3f out tl hdd & 2nd st: kpt on) 1½ 2
56[2] Eastleigh **(47)***(45) (RHollinshead)* 6-8-11 TIves(6) (chsd ldrs: 6th st: r.o wl fnl f) ¾ 3
68[5] Royal Acclaim **(44)***(41) (JMBradley)* 10-8-1v(7) AmandaSanders(9) (hdwy 4f out: 4th st: rdn & kpt on appr fnl f) nk 4
80[2] Orthorhombus **(53)***(50) (DJSCosgrove)* 6-8-12b(5) LNewton(7) (trckd ldrs: 3rd & rdn st: fnd nil) hd 5
63[4] Zahran (IRE) **(55)***(40) (JMBradley)* 4-9-4 JQuinn(5) (lw: chsd ldrs: 5th st: wknd fnl f) 6 6
73[9] Wahem (IRE) **(38)***(6) (CEBrittain)* 5-8-2b BDoyle(3) (lw: led after 3f tl 3f out: wknd) 9 7
*117** Shuttlecock **(65)***(26)*(Fav)*(MrsNMacauley)* 4-10-0 6x MFenton(2) (prom: rdn ½-wy: sn lost pl: eased whn btn) 3½ 8
138[3] Hawaii Storm (FR) **(56)***(5) (MissAJWhitfield)* 7-9-1 (5) RPainter(1) (a bhd) 6 9

9/4 Shuttlecock, **7/2** BUDDY'S FRIEND (IRE), **4/1** Eastleigh, **5/1** Hawaii Storm (FR), Orthorhombus, **12/1** Spanish Stripper (USA), **14/1** Wahem (IRE), **16/1** Zahran (IRE), Royal Acclaim, CSF £44.52 CT £169.47 TOTE £8.40: £1.80 £6.90 £1.10 (£88.90) OWNER Mr Colin Booth (NEWMARKET) BRED John and Mrs McNamara 9 Rn 1m 53.3 SF: 27/13/11/8/16/6/-/-/-
WEIGHT FOR AGE 4yo-1lb

170

EAST MIDLANDS ELECTRICITY H'CAP (3-Y.O) (0-80) (Class D)
£3,487.90 (£1,055.20: £514.60: £244.30)
7f (Fibresand) GOING: 0.09 sec per fur (STD) 3-20 (3-20)

*60** **Gulf Shaadi (78)***(85) (CEBrittain)* 3-9-7 BDoyle(5) (s.i.s: bhd tl hdwy & 4th st: led over 1f out: rdn out) — **1**
*105** Our Tom **(58)***(62+)*(Fav)*(JWharton)* 3-8-1 6x JQuinn(4) (lw: chsd ldrs: 2nd st: sn rdn & edgd lft: plld out 1f out: r.o wl nr fin) 1½ **2**
*118** Portend **(67)***(70) (SRBowring)* 3-8-3 (7) 6x CTeague(3) (lw: chsd ldr tl led 3f out: rdn wl over 1f out: sn hdd & no ex) nk **3**
118² Bold Frontier **(63)***(64) (KTIvory)* 3-8-6 ow1 RCochrane(1) (chsd ldrs: 3rd st: sn rdn & btn) 1 **4**
*126** Mac's Taxi **(66)***(41) (PCHaslam)* 3-8-4 (5) 6x JStack(2) (lw: led 4f: sn wknd:last st) 12 **5**

9/4 Our Tom, **5/2** Bold Frontier, **7/2** Portend, **5/1** GULF SHAADI, **7/1** Mac's Taxi (5/1-8/1), CSF £15.40 TOTE £5.30: £2.20 £1.40 (£5.70) OWNER Mr C. E. Brittain (NEWMARKET) BRED Sheikh Mohammed bin Rashid al Maktoum 5 Rn 1m 30.9 (6.90) SF: 31/10/17/12/-

171

FACKLEY (S) STKS (3-Y.O) (Class G) £2,259.00 (£634.00: £309.00)
7f (Fibresand) GOING: 0.09 sec per fur (STD) 3-50 (3-51)

*95** **Mazilla (57)***(66)*(Fav)*(WJHaggas)* 3-8-13 WWoods(9) (in tch: hdwy & 2nd st: led over 1f out: shkn up & sn clr) — **1**
90⁵ Presto Boy **(56)***(59) (MBell)* 3-8-12v MFenton(10) (led over 5f: no ch w wnr) 3 **2**
54² Bretton Princess **(45)***(49) (RHollinshead)* 3-8-7 RCochrane(7) (chsd ldrs: 4th st: kpt on one pce appr fnl f) 2½ **3**
43⁷ Boldly So *(48) (WJMusson)* 3-8-7 MWigham(6) (lw: bhd: sn pushed along: rdn 2f out: kpt on wl fnl f) ½ **4**
54⁶ Lotties Bid *(45) (PSFelgate)* 3-8-2 (5) PMcCabe(3) (hdwy & 5th st) 1¼ **5**
105⁹ Gigfy **(63)***(51) (BJLlewellyn)* 3-8-13 (5) DRMcCabe(11) (prom: 3rd st: sn rdn & btn) 2½ **6**
47⁸ Blackpool Festival (IRE) **(55)***(43) (JBerry)* 3-9-4b TIves(8) (s.i.s: nvr trbld ldrs) 4 **7**
95⁶ Joyful Times **(43)***(31) (MrsNMacauley)* 3-8-2v(5) SSanders(2) (chsd ldr tl wknd qckly & 6th st) hd **8**
128⁷ Haya Ya Kefaah *(28) (SirMarkPrescott)* 3-8-12 CNutter(4) (lw: sn bhd & pushed along: nvr nr ldrs) 4 **9**
105⁶ Wendy's Way **(43)***(14) (JBerry)* 3-8-13 SWilliams(1) (prom 2f: sn lost pl) 7 **10**
48¹⁰ Doulily *(—) (GHolmes)* 3-8-7 JQuinn(5) (sn bhd: t.o) 30 **11**

2/1 MAZILLA, **5/2** Boldly So, **6/1** Presto Boy, **10/1** Bretton Princess, Blackpool Festival (IRE), **14/1** Wendy's Way, Joyful Times, **16/1** Haya Ya Kefaah, **20/1** Gigfy, **25/1** Lotties Bid, **50/1** Doulily, CSF £14.68 TOTE £3.60: £2.10 £3.60 £3.10 (£8.00) OWNER . Flying Fillies (NEWMARKET) BRED Mrs H. MacFarlane 11 Rn 1m 31.9 (7.90) SF: 13/5/-/-/-/-/-/-/-/-/-
Bt in 6,800 gns

172

BALDERTON H'CAP (Amateurs) (II) (0-60) (Class F) £2,537.00 (£712.00: £347.00) **1m 4f (Fibresand)** GOING: 0.09 sec per fur (STD) 4-20 (4-21)

29⁶ **Comtec's Legend (33)***(40) (JFBottomley)* 5-11-5 MrsLPearce(1) (hld up: hdwy 6f out: led 3f out: sn clr: pushed out) — **1**
121⁴ Ozzie Jones **(46)***(49) (MCChapman)* 4-12-0 MrTonyHughes(7) (lw: in tch: sn rdn along: 4th st: chsd wnr fnl f: no imp) 3 **2**
Who's the Best (IRE) **(36)***(35) (APJarvis)* 5-11-8 MrMRimell(4) (lw: prom: pushed along 6f out: 5th st: kpt on) 3½ **3**
77⁹ Goldenberry **(37)***(34) (JParkes)* 4-11-5 MrRJohnson(9) (s.i.s: hdwy 6f out: 2nd st: wknd fnl f) 1¾ **4**
*122** Don't Drop Bombs (USA) **(34)***(28)*(Fav)*(PJFeilden)* 6-11-6v 5x MissJFeilden(2) (prom: led 7f out to 3f out: rdn & 3rd st: sn wknd) 2½ **5**
76⁶ Golden Hadeer **(42)***(34) (MJRyan)* 4-11-5 (5) MrWDixon(11) (chsd ldrs: 6th & btn st) 1½ **6**
122¹⁰ Written Agreement **(18)***(—) (REPeacock)* 7-9-13 (5) MrsCPeacock(5) (lw: a bhd) 25 **7**
67⁵ Manolete **(44)***(—) (CWCElsey)* 4-11-12b MissAElsey(6) (t.o fnl 5f) dist **8**
68¹⁰ City Rhythm **(28)***(—) (JMBradley)* 5-11-0v MrTMcCarthy(10) (prom: led over 8f out to 7f out: sn wknd: t.o) 3 **9**
Mendip Mist **(27)***(—) (BRMillman)* 7-10-8 (5) MrAHoldsworth(8) (led over 3f: sn wknd: t.o) dist **10**

4/5 Don't Drop Bombs (USA), **3/1** Manolete, **7/1** Golden Hadeer, **10/1** COMTEC'S LEGEND, **12/1** Ozzie Jones, Who's the Best (IRE), **20/1** Goldenberry, Mendip Mist, City Rhythm, **33/1** Written Agreement, CSF £120.42 CT £1,354.58 TOTE £9.40: £1.20 £2.70 £5.50 (£22.10) OWNER Qualitair Holdings Ltd (MALTON) BRED Qualitair Stud Ltd 10 Rn

2m 48.8 (17.80) SF: 21/26/16/12/10/12/-/-/-/-
WEIGHT FOR AGE 4yo-4lb

T/Jkpt: £12,020.40 (0.1 Tckts); £15,237.24 to Ayr 28/1/95. T/Plpt: £73.60 (317.86 Tckts). T/Qdpt: Not won; £25.00 to Ayr 28/1/95. Dk

0155-LINGFIELD (L-H)
Saturday January 28th (Standard)

173
LINDSAY CORREA BIRTHDAY CLAIMING STKS (3-Y.O) (Class F) £2,688.20 (£755.20: £368.60) **5f (Equitrack)** GOING minus 0.55 sec (FST) 1-40 (1-41)

*132** **Ultra Beet (72)***(74)*(Fav)*(PCHaslam)* 3-8-9 (5) JStack(5) (racd wd: a.p: rdn over 1f out: led ins fnl f: r.o wl)........— **1**
132⁶ Baileys Sunset (IRE) **(68)***(64) (MJohnston)* 3-8-8 TWilliams(7) (racd wd: rdn & hdwy over 1f out: unable qckn wl ins fnl f)........1¼ **2**
Musical Fantasy (IRE) **(54)***(45) (BJMeehan)* 3-7-4 (5) NVarley(1) (b: led 3f out tl ins fnl f: one pce)........2 **3**
Superlao (BEL) *(49) (AndreHermans,Belgium)* 3-8-5 RCochrane(4) (lt-f: bit bkwd: a.p: hrd rdn over 1f out: one pce)........2 **4**
124⁴ Fiery Footsteps **(50)***(38) (PHowling)* 3-7-10v(3) DWright(3) (b.hind: led 2f: rdn over 2f out: wknd over 1f out)........1½ **5**
Derry Queen **(42)***(31) (PDCundell)* 3-7-11 JQuinn(2) (s.i.s: a bhd)........1½ **6**
Foxhill Blue **(45)***(26) (MDIUsher)* 3-7-3v(7)ow1 CAdamson(6) (a bhd)........1¼ **7**

4/6 ULTRA BEET, **4/1** Musical Fantasy (IRE), **11/2** Superlao (BEL), **6/1** Baileys Sunset (IRE), **25/1** Foxhill Blue, **33/1** Fiery Footsteps, **66/1** Derry Queen, CSF £5.54 TOTE £1.50: £1.20 £1.90 (£2.70) OWNER Pet Express Ltd T/A Nutrimix (MIDDLEHAM) BRED Rockhouse Farms Ltd 7 Rn

59.4 secs (1.20) SF: 31/22/4/7/-/-/-

174
CHIEFTAIN MEDIAN AUCTION STKS (Mdn 3-Y.O) (Class E) £3,009.60 (£910.80: £444.40: £211.20)
1m (Equitrack) GOING minus 0.55 sec per fur (FST) 2-10 (2-11)

Whackford Squeers *(72) (CACyzer)* 3-9-0 AClark(1) (leggy: hdwy 4f out: led over 2f out: rdn out)........— **1**
25² Irie Mon (IRE) **(54)***(62) (JWHills)* 3-9-0 RCochrane(4) (led over 5f: unable qckn fnl 2f)........5 **2**
105⁴ Opera Fan (IRE) **(62)***(56)*(Fav)*(SirMarkPrescott)* 3-9-0 WWoods(2) (a.p: rdn over 4f out: one pce)........3 **3**
Semi Serious *(55) (WJarvis)* 3-9-0 TIves(5) (scope: bkwd: plld hrd: rdn over 4f out: lost pl over 3f out: r.o one pce fnl f)........nk **4**
Death by Chocolate *(50) (DrJDScargill)* 3-9-0 MRimmer(6) (small: a.p: rdn over 3f out: wknd over 2f out)........2½ **5**
Emerald Dream (IRE) *(43) (CCElsey)* 3-8-9 DHarrison(3) (hld up: rdn over 4f out: wknd over 3f out)........¾ **6**

11/8 Opera Fan (IRE), **2/1** Irie Mon (IRE), **4/1** Semi Serious, **8/1** WHACKFORD SQUEERS (10/1-16/1), **16/1** Death by Chocolate, **33/1** Emerald Dream (IRE), CSF £23.69 TOTE £16.40: £3.50 £1.40 (£21.10) OWNER Trilby Racing (HORSHAM) BRED Philip T. Dyke 6 Rn

1m 40.55 (4.15) SF: 12/2/-/-/-/-

175
CHURCHILL CLAIMING STKS (Class E) £3,066.80 (£928.40: £453.20: £215.60)
1m 2f (Equitrack) GOING minus 0.55 sec per fur (FST) 2-45 (2-47)

77⁶ **Medland (IRE) (50)***(56) (WGMTurner)* 5-8-3 DHarrison(5) (lw: a.p: chsd ldr 4f out: led over 1f out: r.o wl)........— **1**
155² Greek Gold (IRE) **(57)***(64) (GPKelly)* 6-8-12 AlexGreaves(7) (led over 8f: unable qckn)........¾ **2**
11² Awesome Power **(71)***(69)*(Fav)*(JWHills)* 9-9-4 AClark(2) (hld up: rdn over 3f out: r.o one pce fnl 2f)........nk **3**
73⁸ Mogwai (IRE) **(41)***(40) (MartynMeade)* 6-8-6 WWoods(1) (no hdwy fnl 3f)........11 **4**
84⁶ Thorniwama **(39)***(32) (JJBridger)* 4-7-12 GBardwell(3) (rdn thrght: nvr nr to chal)....2 **5**

157[11] Night Fantasy (IRE) **(40)***(20) (NJHWalker)* 7-7-12 NAdams(6) (led over 1f: wknd 4f out) 6 **6**
21[7] Liffeyside Leader (IRE) *(—) (HJCollingridge)* 4-7-13 (5) CHawksley(8) (lw: dwlt: bhd fnl 5f) .... s.h **7**
Clancy's Express **(35)***(—) (GBBalding)* 4-8-1 (5)ow3 SDrowne(4) (bhd fnl 4f) 20 **8**

8/13 Awesome Power, **3/1** Greek Gold (IRE), **15/2** MEDLAND (IRE), **11/1** Mogwai (IRE), **12/1** Clancy's Express, **20/1** Thorniwama, **25/1** Liffeyside Leader (IRE), **33/1** Night Fantasy (IRE), CSF £31.24 TOTE £7.10: £2.00 £1.40 £1.40 (£13.00) OWNER Mrs A. G. Sims (SHERBORNE) BRED S. W. D. McIlveen 8 Rn 2m 6.98 (3.98) SF: 12/20/25/-/-/-/-/-
WEIGHT FOR AGE 4yo-3lb

176

CHALLENGER H'CAP (3-Y.O) (0-80) (Class D) £3,555.50 (£1,076.00: £525.00: £249.50) **1m (Equitrack)** GOING minus 0.55 sec per fur (FST) 3-15 (3-16)

Nordinex (IRE) (68)*(73) (RWArmstrong)* 3-8-11 WWoods(5) (lw: chsd ldr: led 5f out: rdn out) .... — **1**
99* No Pattern **(78)***(81)*(Fav)*(GLMoore)* 3-9-0 (7) LSuthern(4) (lw: hdwy over 4f out: chsd wnr over 2f out: ev ch ins fnl f: unable qckn) .... ¾ **2**
59[8] Soldier's Leap (FR) **(67)***(63) (CEBrittain)* 3-8-10 RCochrane(1) (hld up: hrd rdn over 4f out: swtchd rt over 1f out: r.o one pce) 3½ **3**
99[3] Water Hazard (IRE) **(53)***(46) (SDow)* 3-7-10 JQuinn(7) (hld up: rdn over 2f out: one pce) 1½ **4**
144[3] Witney-de-Bergerac (IRE) **(57)***(45) (JSMoore)* 3-7-9 (5) NVarley(6) (b.hind: hdwy over 4f out: wknd over 1f out) 2½ **5**
133[2] Boundary Express **(54)***(32) (MJohnston)* 3-7-11 TWilliams(3) (led 3f: wknd over 3f out: in rr whn hmpd on ins over 2f out) 5 **6**
105[8] Happy Brave **(50)***(26) (PDCundell)* 3-7-7 GBardwell(2) (plld hrd: prom over 3f) 1 **7**
LONG HANDICAP Happy Brave 7-5

7/2 No Pattern, **4/1** Water Hazard (IRE), Soldier's Leap (FR), **6/1** Witney-de-Bergerac (IRE), **13/2** NORDINEX (IRE), **8/1** Boundary Express, **9/1** Happy Brave, CSF £26.66 TOTE £8.40: £3.80 £1.40 (£15.70) OWNER Mr R. J. Arculli (NEWMARKET) BRED Howard Kaskel in Ireland 7 Rn
1m 39.86 (3.46) SF: 16/23/7/-/-/-/-

177

LINGFIELD PARK AWT SPRINT SERIES H'CAP (Qualifier) (0-70) (Class E £3,095.40 (£937.20: £457.60: £217.80)
6f (Equitrack) GOING minus 0.55 sec per fur (FST) 3-45 (3-50)

Nordico Princess (65)*(69) (GROldroyd)* 4-9-9 RCochrane(9) (mde all: all out) .... — **1**
Speedy Classic (USA) **(60)***(63)*(Fav)*(MJHeaton-Ellis)* 6-9-4 WWoods(12) (hld up: rdn over 2f out: chsd wnr fnl f: r.o wl) .... hd **2**
Red Admiral **(67)***(66) (PCHaslam)* 5-9-4 (7) NicolaHowarth(8) (b.hind: lw: chsd wnr 5f: r.o one pce) 1¼ **3**
93[9] Four of Spades **(66)***(64) (WSCunningham)* 4-9-10b AClark(4) (lw: hld up: rdn over 2f out: r.o ins fnl f) .... hd **4**
Apollo Red **(52)***(50) (AMoore)* 6-8-10 CandyMorris(7) (b.hind: nt clr run 4f out: hdwy over 1f out: r.o) .... s.h **5**
African Chimes **(70)***(67)*(Fav)*(WAO'Gorman)* 8-9-11 (3) EmmaO'Gorman(6) (hdwy over 1f out: r.o wl ins fnl f) .... hd **6**
71[2] Respectable Jones **(49)***(44) (RHollinshead)* 9-8-0 (7) RGordon(2) (lw: nt clr run 4f out: hdwy over 1f out: r.o one pce) .... ½ **7**
My Lifetime Lady (IRE) **(45)***(15) (KTIvory)* 4-8-3 DHarrison(11) (b.hind: lw: bhd fnl 2f) 10 **8**
102[5] Daaniera (IRE) **(60)***(27) (PHowling)* 5-9-1b(3) DWright(3) (b.hind: lw: spd 4f) 1 **9**
Glowing Account (IRE) **(63)***(22) (JWMullins)* 4-9-7 StephenDavies(10) (bhd fnl 4f) .. 3 **10**
Cranfield Cracker **(46)***(2) (DWPArbuthnot)* 4-8-4 BDoyle(1) (b: a bhd) .... ¾ **11**

4/1 African Chimes, Speedy Classic (USA), **5/1** NORDICO PRINCESS, **6/1** Respectable Jones, **13/2** Four of Spades, **9/1** Daaniera (IRE) (6/1-10/1), **12/1** Red Admiral, **14/1** Apollo Red, **25/1** My Lifetime Lady (IRE), Glowing Account (IRE), Cranfield Cracker, CSF £24.18 CT £201.38 TOTE £6.30: £2.20 £1.70 £3.00 (£19.90) OWNER Mr M. S. Griffiths (YORK) 11 Rn
1m 13.1 (2.50) SF: 26/21/25/23/11/26/6/-/-/-/-

178

CENTURION H'CAP (0-70) (Class E) £3,023.90 (£915.20: £446.60: £212.30)
1m 4f (Equitrack) GOING minus 0.55 sec per fur (FST) 4-20 (4-20)

76[4] **Carpathian (46)***(57)*(Fav)*(LordHuntingdon)* 4-8-9 DHarrison(1) (a.p: led over 3f out: clr over 1f out: r.o wl) .... — **1**

97³ In the Money (IRE) **(59)***(62) (RHollinshead)* 6-9-12 TIves(5) (hld up: rdn over 4f out: chsd wnr over 2f out: no imp)....6 2
58² Dancing Diamond (IRE) **(44)***(44) (MissBSanders)* 5-8-6hv(5) SSanders(8) (chsd ldr 8f: one pce fnl 2f)....2½ 3
122² Royal Circus **(37)***(32) (JGMO'Shea)* 6-8-4 BDoyle(4) (led over 8f: wknd wl over 1f out)....4 4
Sheltered Cove (IRE) **(54)***(43) (KOCunningham-Brown)* 4-9-3 AClark(7) (lw: hld up: rdn over 4f out: wknd over 3f out)....5 5
35⁴ Nothing Doing (IRE) **(38)***(26) (WJMusson)* 6-8-0 (5) PMcCabe(3) (stdy hdwy over 6f out: wknd over 4f out)....¾ 6
4⁶ Dolly Dolittle **(35)***(—) (HJCollingridge)* 4-7-12 JQuinn(2) (a bhd: t.o)....dist 7
131⁵ Milngavie (IRE) **(61)***(—) (MJohnston)* 5-10-0 RCochrane(6) (a bhd: t.o whn p.u ins fnl f: dismntd).... 0

6/4 CARPATHIAN, **7/2** Royal Circus, **4/1** In the Money (IRE), **8/1** Nothing Doing (IRE), **9/1** Sheltered Cove (IRE), Milngavie (IRE), **10/1** Dancing Diamond (IRE), **33/1** Dolly Dolittle, CSF £8.65 CT £43.93 TOTE £2.40: £1.40 £1.10 £2.20 (£4.30) OWNER The Queen (WEST ILSLEY) BRED Sheikh Mohammed bin Rashid al Maktoum 8 Rn 2m 32.11 (2.71) SF: 32/40/23/12/17/6/-/-

WEIGHT FOR AGE 4yo-4lb

OFFICIAL EXPLANATION **Mingavie(IRE): jockey reported that the horse felt wrong. The gelding has suffered from intermittent lameness.**

T/Plpt: £26.00 (482.26 Tckts). T/Qdpt: £97.00 (4.05 Tckts). AK

0134-SOUTHWELL (L-H)
Monday January 30th (Standard)

179 LONDONDERRY H'CAP (I) (0-65) (Class F) £2,537.00 (£712.00: £347.00)
1m (Fibresand) GOING minus 0.25 sec per fur (FST) 1-00 (1-00)

30³ **Larn Fort (47)***(53) (CWFairhurst)* 5-9-2v RCochrane(6) (a.p: rdn 3f out: styd on to ld wl ins fnl f)....— 1
127⁴ Profit Release (IRE) **(56)***(60)*(Fav)*(MJohnston)* 4-9-10 TWilliams(9) (trckd ldrs: led over 2f out tl wl ins fnl f: no ex u.p cl home)....1 2
Fletcher's Bounty (IRE) **(49)***(47) (WSCunningham)* 6-9-4 AClark(3) (trckd ldrs: chal over 2f out: sn rdn & one pce)....3 3
62* Dome Patrol **(51)***(47)*(Fav)*(WRMuir)* 4-9-5 JWeaver(8) (in tch: effrt ent st: rdn & one pce appr fnl f)....1 4
138¹⁰ Scoffera **(38)***(32) (NTinkler)* 5-8-7 KimTinkler(4) (led 1f: chsd ldrs: rdn over 2f out: kpt on same pce)....1 5
45¹¹ Regal Rambler (CAN) **(40)***(22) (LJBarratt)* 4-8-8b LCharnock(7) (led after 1f tl over 2f out: sn btn: eased fnl f)....6 6
92⁶ Arrogant Boy **(45)***(11) (DWChapman)* 6-8-7 (7) CTeague(5) (s.i.s: nvr nr to chal)....8 7
La Belle Shyanne **(41)***(—) (CJHill)* 4-8-4 (5) SSanders(2) (a rr div)....10 8
139¹¹ Akabusi **(50)***(—) (MCChapman)* 4-8-13 (5) DRMcCabe(1) (stdd s: bhd: rdn appr st: no imp)....nk 9

5/2 Dome Patrol, Profit Release (IRE), **11/4** LARN FORT, **7/1** Fletcher's Bounty (IRE), **8/1** La Belle Shyanne, **10/1** Scoffera, **20/1** Akabusi, **25/1** Regal Rambler (CAN), **33/1** Arrogant Boy, CSF £10.81 CT £42.54 TOTE £3.60: £1.10 £1.30 £1.90 (£7.90) OWNER A P Development Products (N.E) Ltd (MIDDLEHAM) BRED Robert Cartwright 9 Rn 1m 44.9 (5.60) SF: 25/30/19/18/5/-/-/-/-

WEIGHT FOR AGE 4yo-1lb

STEWARDS' ENQUIRY Williams suspended 8-9/2/95 (excessive use of whip).

180 TYRONE (S) H'CAP (I) (3-Y.O) (0-60) (Class G) £2,259.00 (£634.00: £309.00)
1m (Fibresand) GOING minus 0.25 sec per fur (FST) 1-30 (1-30)

135⁵ **Kirov Protege (IRE) (46)***(49) (RWArmstrong)* 3-8-11 MRimmer(1) (mde all: styd on wl fnl 2f)....— 1
135⁴ Warwick Mist (IRE) **(35)***(35)*(Fav)*(PCHaslam)* 3-8-0 JQuinn(7) (in tch: rdn appr st: styd on wl fnl f: nrst fin)....1½ 2
90⁹ Runforaction (IRE) **(45)***(43) (BSRothwell)* 3-8-10 MFenton(2) (chsd ldrs tl outpcd ½-wy: swtchd over 1f out: styd on nr fin)....¾ 3
85⁵ Rose Chime (IRE) **(39)***(37) (MJohnston)* 3-8-4 TWilliams(5) (lw: a chsng ldrs: hrd rdn ent st: one pce)....s.h 4
133⁴ Fools of Pride (IRE) **(51)***(39) (RHollinshead)* 3-9-2 LDettori(9) (effrt ½-wy: styd on: nvr trbld ldrs)....5 5

128[4] Fools Millyons (IRE) **(44)***(28)* *(WBentley)* 3-8-9v JFanning(3) (s.i.s: hdwy appr st: no imp)....2 **6**
128[3] Lawbuster (IRE) **(56)***(37)* *(WRMuir)* 3-9-7b JWeaver(6) (chsd ldrs: rdn appr st: wknd 2f out)....1½ **7**
72[10] Anytime Baby **(54)***(—)* *(KMcAuliffe)* 3-9-5 AClark(8) (b.hind: stdd after s: hdwy 1f out: sn btn)....25 **8**
25[7] Baby Bob **(40)***(—)* *(JMPEustace)* 3-8-5b NKennedy(4) (outpcd & bhd fr ½-wy)....1¼ **9**
Spanish Girl (USA) **(56)***(—)* *(PAKelleway)* 3-9-0 (7) AdelleGibbons(10) (unruly leaving paddock: ref to r: t.n.p).... **0**

100/30 Warwick Mist (IRE), **4/1** Lawbuster (IRE), **9/2** KIROV PROTEGE (IRE), **6/1** Rose Chime (IRE), **7/1** Fools Millyons (IRE), **8/1** Fools of Pride (IRE), **9/1** Runforaction (IRE), **10/1** Anytime Baby, **12/1** Spanish Girl (USA), **20/1** Baby Bob, CSF £21.13 CT £126.30 TOTE £5.50: £1.70 £1.80 £5.90 (£8.10) OWNER Mr M. J. Polglase (NEWMARKET) BRED Irish National Stud Co Ltd 10 Rn No bid 1m 46.7 (7.40) SF: 4/-/-/-/-/-/-/-/-/-

181 LONDONDERRY H'CAP (II) (0-65) (Class F) £2,537.00 (£712.00: £347.00)
1m (Fibresand) GOING minus 0.25 sec per fur (FST) 2-00 (2-00)

Broughtons Turmoil (49)*(68)* *(WJMusson)* 6-8-9 (5) DRMcCabe(5) (cl up: led wl over 2f out & qcknd: styd on wl)....— **1**
138* Hawwam **(63)***(77)*(Fav)*(EJAlston)* 9-10-0 6x JWeaver(2) (hld up & bhd: hdwy appr st: hrd rdn 2f out: styd on: nvr able to chal)....2½ **2**
165[7] Matthew David **(46)***(46)* *(SRBowring)* 5-8-11 JQuinn(4) (led tl hdd wl over 2f out: sn btn)....7 **3**
169[3] Eastleigh **(47)***(44)* *(RHollinshead)* 6-8-12 LDettori(3) (lw: a.p: rdn ½-wy: one pce)1¼ **4**
169[5] Orthorhombus **(53)***(49)* *(DJSCosgrove)* 6-9-4b TIves(1) (cl up after 3f tl rdn & wknd over 2f out)....nk **5**
Twin Creeks **(60)***(49)* *(MDHammond)* 4-9-10 RCochrane(8) (lw: hld up & bhd: hdwy 4f out: wknd over 2f out)....3½ **6**
125[8] Kissavos **(40)***(17)* *(CCElsey)* 9-8-5 BDoyle(6) (b.hind: prom to ½-wy: sn outpcd)....6 **7**
49[2] Glenvally **(45)***(12)* *(BWMurray)* 4-8-4b(5) JStack(7) (outpcd ½-wy: rn wd st: n.d)....5 **8**

Evens Hawwam, **6/1** Eastleigh, **7/1** Glenvally, Kissavos, **8/1** Orthorhombus, **12/1** Twin Creeks, Matthew David, **20/1** BROUGHTONS TURMOIL, CSF £41.01 CT £257.35 TOTE £18.70: £4.10 £1.40 £1.40 (£61.40) OWNER Broughton Thermal Insulation (NEWMARKET) BRED Tally Ho Stud Co (U.K.) Ltd and Ninevah Ltd 8 Rn 1m 43.3 (4.00) SF: 38/47/18/17/21/20/-/-
WEIGHT FOR AGE 4yo-1lb

182 DOWN CLAIMING STKS (Class F) £2,537.00 (£712.00: £347.00)
6f (Fibresand) GOING minus 0.25 sec per fur (FST) 2-30 (2-31)

Pine Ridge Lad (IRE) (64)*(64)* *(JLEyre)* 5-8-6 SWilliams(12) (mde all: drvn out)..— **1**
140[2] Sea Devil **(67)***(52)*(Fav)*(MJCamacho)* 9-8-2 LCharnock(4) (lw: a chsng ldrs: effrt over 2f out: kpt on same pce)....3 **2**
140[8] Bold Aristocrat (IRE) **(38)***(50)* *(RHollinshead)* 4-7-13 (5) AGarth(11) (cl up: effrt over 2f out: one pce)....1¼ **3**
165[5] Efficacy **(33)***(42)* *(APJarvis)* 4-7-5 (5)ow1 NVarley(7) (chsd ldrs: effrt 2f out: hung rt & nt r.o)....s.h **4**
134[2] Bella Parkes **(67)***(49)* *(DNicholls)* 4-8-5 AlexGreaves(8) (lw: a chsng ldrs: rdn over 2f out: one pce)....½ **5**
150[2] Walk the Beat **(68)***(40)* *(RSimpson)* 5-8-1 (5)ow2 SDrowne(1) (b: s.i.s: hdwy ent st: rdn & nvr able to chal)....4 **6**
82[3] Bradwell (IRE) **(49)***(29)* *(MHTompkins)* 4-7-13v(5)ow5 SMulvey(6) (lw: outpcd ½-wy: n.d)....3½ **7**
139[7] Chiliola **(65)***(21)* *(MHEasterby)* 4-7-13b JQuinn(2) (s.i.s: sme hdwy ½-wy: sn rdn & btn)....1 **8**
150[8] Bessie's Will **(37)***(17)* *(DHaydnJones)* 4-7-13 ow2 AMackay(3) (in tch: rdn ½-wy: sn btn)....1½ **9**
Angelic Dancer **(45)***(9)* *(SRBowring)* 4-7-6b(7) ClaireBalding(9) (spd 4f)....3 **10**
148[10] Darakah **(60)***(9)* *(CJHill)* 8-8-0 (5) SSanders(5) (a outpcd & bhd)....2½ **11**
139[6] Mr B Reasonable (IRE) **(48)***(—)* *(SWCampion)* 4-7-9b(7) CTeague(10) (racd wd: outpcd & lost tch fr ½-wy)....4 **12**

7/4 Sea Devil, **4/1** Walk the Beat, Bella Parkes, **6/1** Chiliola, **9/1** Bradwell (IRE), **14/1** Angelic Dancer, Darakah, PINE RIDGE LAD (IRE), **20/1** Bold Aristocrat (IRE), Efficacy, **25/1** Mr B Reasonable (IRE), **50/1** Bessie's Will, CSF £41.75 TOTE £19.60: £4.80 £1.90 £6.90 (£31.40) OWNER Whitestonecliffe Racing Partnership (HAMBLETON) BRED Whitechurch Stud in Ireland 12 Rn 1m 15.9 (2.40) SF: 38/26/25/18/26/15/4/-/-/-/-/-

183

FERMANAGH MEDIAN AUCTION STKS (Mdn 4, 5 & 6-Y.O) (Class E)
£2,981.00 (£902.00: £440.00: £209.00)
2m (Fibresand) GOING minus 0.25 sec per fur (FST) 3-00 (3-00)

*4*5 **Dallai (IRE) (40)***(56) (MrsNMacauley)* 4-8-4 (7) AmandaSanders(6) (lw: chsd ldr: disp ld over 4f out: kpt on wl cl home)........— 1
*79*6 Greenacres Star **(34)***(51) (BAMcMahon)* 5-8-13 JWeaver(8) (trckd ldrs: disp ld over 4f out: hrd drvn fnl f: nt qckn nr fin)........nk 2
Romalito **(55)***(47) (MBlanshard)* 5-9-4 StephenDavies(1) (in tch: drvn along appr st: nt pce to chal)........10 3
*109*3 Intention (USA) **(55)***(43)*(Fav)*(ICampbell)* 5-9-4 RCochrane(5) (lw: hld up: hdwy ½-wy: rdn appr st: no imp)........4 4
Most Beautiful **(42)***(24) (KSBridgwater)* 4-8-6b NAdams(2) (led tl hdd over 4f out: sn outpcd)........15 5
Stephanentse **(32)***(23) (EJAlston)* 5-8-13 SWebster(7) (outpcd ½-wy: n.d after).....¾ 6
Hold Your Hat on *(14) (CWThornton)* 6-9-4 GDuffield(3) (prom: hrd drvn 7f out: sn btn)........15 7
*96*14 Flying Imp **(30)***(—) (RHollinshead)* 4-8-11 LDettori(4) (hrd drvn & bhd 7f out: n.d after)........dist 8

10/11 Intention (USA), **7/2** Romalito, **13/2** Most Beautiful (10/1-5/1), **8/1** Greenacres Star, **12/1** Hold Your Hat on, Flying Imp, **20/1** Stephanentse, DALLAI (IRE), CSF £155.70 TOTE £19.40: £3.80 £1.10 £2.10 (£25.70) OWNER Mr Donald Cooper (MELTON MOWBRAY) BRED R. Hodgins 8 Rn
3m 43.6 (17.60) SF: -/-/-/-/-/-/-/-
WEIGHT FOR AGE 4yo-7lb
STEWARDS' ENQUIRY Weaver suspended 8-9/2/95 (excessive use of whip).

184

ARMAGH H'CAP (0-80) (Class D) £3,589.30 (£1,086.40: £530.20: £252.10)
6f (Fibresand) GOING minus 0.25 sec per fur (FST) 3-30 (3-31)

*130** **Little Ibnr (73)***(80) (PDEvans)* 4-9-7 LDettori(3) (lw: cl up: led 2f out: r.o)........— 1
*139** Warwick Warrior (IRE) **(70)***(71)*(Fav)*(MrsLPiggott)* 4-9-4 7x JWeaver(4) (b: b.hind: sn outpcd & bhd: hdwy over 1f out: r.o nr fin)........2½ 2
*165*3 Shadow Jury **(55)***(53) (DWChapman)* 5-7-12b(5) DRMcCabe(6) (chsd ldrs: effrt 2f out: edgd lft & nt qckn)........1 3
*93*3 Dawalib (USA) **(72)***(67) (DHaydnJones)* 5-9-6v AMackay(5) (lw: sn chsng ldrs: effrt over 2f out: nt qckn)........¾ 4
*93*2 Croft Pool **(82)***(76) (JAGlover)* 4-10-2 TIves(2) (lw: in tch: drvn along ½-wy: r.o one pce)........nk 5
*117*3 Super Benz **(63)***(56) (FJO'Mahony)* 9-8-11 GCarter(7) (b: in tch: rdn ½-wy: no imp)........nk 6
*167*7 Tenor **(53)***(28) (DNicholls)* 4-8-1 CRutter(1) (lw: led 4f: sn btn)........7 7

9/4 Warwick Warrior (IRE), **11/4** LITTLE IBNR, **4/1** Croft Pool, **11/2** Dawalib (USA), **9/1** Super Benz, **10/1** Shadow Jury, **20/1** Tenor, CSF £9.25 TOTE £3.70: £2.10 £2.10 (£4.70) OWNER Swinnerton Transport Ltd (WELSHPOOL) BRED R. E. Waugh 7 Rn
1m 15.6 (2.10) SF: 56/47/30/44/53/34/6

185

TYRONE (S) H'CAP (II) (3-Y.O) (0-60) (Class G) £2,259.00 (£634.00: £309.00)
1m (Fibresand) GOING minus 0.25 sec per fur (FST) 4-00 (4-00)

*135*3 **Poly Lane (51)***(64)*(Fav)*(WRMuir)* 3-9-6b JWeaver(8) (lw: cl up: slt ld 2f out: styd on strly)........— 1
Vindaloo **(46)***(49) (MJohnston)* 3-9-1 TWilliams(1) (bit bkwd: a chsng ldrs: sn pushed along: ev ch over 2f out: one pce)........5 2
*116*3 Samana Cay **(50)***(51) (DNicholls)* 3-9-5v AlexGreaves(2) (s.i.s: hdwy appr st: edgd lft & styd on fnl 2f)........¾ 3
*95*2 Jilly Jaffa Cake (IRE) **(52)***(46) (DWPArbuthnot)* 3-9-7 SWhitworth(7) (s.i.s: effrt & in tch ½-wy: one pce fnl 2f)........3½ 4
*90*10 Miss Suzy **(29)***(20) (JPLeigh)* 3-7-9 (3) DWright(3) (sn outpcd & bhd: styd on fnl 3f: nrst fin)........1¼ 5
*48*6 Reponist **(39)***(30) (MJCamacho)* 3-8-8b LCharnock(6) (led tl hdd 2f out: wknd fnl f)........s.h 6
Pink Petal **(40)***(27) (CJHill)* 3-8-4 (5) SSanders(5) (b.off fore: chsd ldrs tl rdn & btn over 2f out)........2 7
*133*11 Lady Lucy Linnet **(33)***(—) (NAGraham)* 3-8-2 JQuinn(4) (outpcd & bhd fr ½-wy)..15 8
*168*4 Tyreless (IRE) **(40)***(—) (APJarvis)* 3-8-4 (5) NVarley(9) (prom to ½-wy)........7 9

11/4 POLY LANE, **3/1** Pink Petal (5/1-5/2), **7/2** Samana Cay, **4/1** Jilly Jaffa Cake (IRE), **10/1** Reponist, **12/1** Vindaloo, **20/1** Tyreless (IRE), **25/1** Miss Suzy, Lady Lucy Linnet, CSF £33.39 CT £109.10 TOTE £3.60: £1.90 £3.70 £1.20 (£21.60) OWNER Mrs H. Levy (LAMBOURN) BRED G. Harris 9 Rn 1m 46.1 (6.80) SF: 17/3/6/-/-/-/-/-/-
No bid

186 ANTRIM H'CAP (0-70) (Class E) £3,124.00 (£946.00: £462.00: £220.00) **1m 3f (Fibresand)** GOING minus 0.25 sec per fur (FST) 4-30 (4-30)

137[2] **Palacegate Jo (IRE) (57)***(63) (RHollinshead)* 4-8-13 LDettori(8) (a.p: led over 3f out & qcknd: styd on wl: eased nr fin) ....— 1
172[3] Who's the Best (IRE) **(36)***(39) (APJarvis)* 5-7-5 (5) NVarley(3) (lw: outpcd & bhd tl styd on strly fnl 3f: nrst fin) 2½ 2
137* Slmaat **(69)***(71)*(Fav)*(MrsMReveley)* 4-9-11 5x RCochrane(6) (lw: hld up: hdwy 5f out: nt qckn fnl 2f) 1 3
137[4] Let's Get Lost **(64)***(56) (JAHarris)* 6-9-10b DaleGibson(7) (a.p: drvn along 4f out: r.o one pce) 7 4
91* Barti-Ddu **(61)***(51) (SCWilliams)* 4-8-12 (5) JStack(5) (lw: led 3f: chsd ldrs & pushed along: outpcd fnl 2½f) 2 5
91[3] Tempering **(59)***(47) (DWChapman)* 9-9-5 DeanMcKeown(9) (cl up: led after 3f tl over 3f out: sn btn) 2 6
Polly Peculiar **(53)***(40) (BSmart)* 4-8-9 DHarrison(4) (lw: chsd ldrs: ev ch 3f out: wknd fnl 2f) ....nk 7
Joyrider **(56)***(42) (MissMKMilligan)* 4-8-12 MFenton(2) (prom tl wknd appr st) ....¾ 8
Bures (IRE) **(65)***(51) (MHTompkins)* 4-9-2v(5) SMulvey(13) (outpcd 6f out: sn bhd)s.h 9
76[5] Camden's Ransom (USA) **(55)***(41) (HGRowsell)* 8-9-1 BDoyle(12) (lw: effrt 5f out: sn rdn & btn) ....s.h 10
Risky Tu **(59)***(42) (PAKelleway)* 4-8-8 (7) AdelleGibbons(14) (racd wd: in tch tl wknd over 4f out) 2½ 11
Sagasan **(61)***(3) (WRMuir)* 4-9-3 JWeaver(10) (b: b.hind: a bhd: t.o) 30 12
Mhemeanles **(62)***(3) (MHEasterby)* 5-9-8b JQuinn(1) (b: outpcd & bhd fnl 7f: t.o)....¾ 13

15/8 Slmaat, **4/1** Barti-Ddu, **6/1** PALACEGATE JO (IRE), **9/1** Polly Peculiar, **12/1** Tempering, Let's Get Lost, Sagasan, **14/1** Camden's Ransom (USA), **16/1** Risky Tu, **20/1** Bures (IRE), **25/1** Joyrider, Who's the Best (IRE), Mhemeanles, CSF £132.27 CT £354.64 TOTE £7.00: £1.80 £8.10 £1.40 (£56.20) OWNER Palacegate Corporation Ltd (UPPER LONGDON) BRED Brendan and Sheila Powell 13 Rn 2m 26.8 (5.30) SF: 41/22/47/37/28/27/17/-/-/-/-/-/-
WEIGHT FOR AGE 4yo-4lb
T/Jkpt: Not won; £48,417.43 to Lingfield 31/1/95. T/Plpt: £159.00 (167.95 Tckts). T/Qdpt: £104.70 (1.8 Tckts). AA

0173-LINGFIELD (L-H)
Tuesday January 31st (Standard)

187 DOG CART CLAIMING STKS (Class E) £3,109.70: £459.80: £218.90 **1m (Equitrack)** GOING minus 0.42 sec per fur (FST) 1-40 (1-42)

157[4] **Perilous Plight (54)***(70) (WRMuir)* 4-8-6 JWeaver(8) (lw: hdwy over 4f out: ev ch fnl 2f: carried rt fnl f: r.o: fin 2nd, hd: awrdd r) ....— 1
157* Masnun (USA) **(66)***(72)*(Fav)*(RJO'Sullivan)* 10-8-9 AClark(12) (hld up: led over 3f out: hung rt fnl f: drvn out: fin 1st: disq: plcd 2nd) 2
150* Arndilly **(68)***(61) (BJMeehan)* 4-8-13b RCochrane(3) (b: b.hind: hld up: rdn over 2f out: r.o one pce) 8 3
150[6] Titanium Honda (IRE) **(41)***(40) (CEBrittain)* 4-8-2 BDoyle(4) (a.p: rdn over 3f out: one pce) 5 4
68[3] Beware of Agents **(64)***(44) (MJohnston)* 6-8-11 DeanMcKeown(9) (s.s: rdn & hdwy over 3f out: one pce) 2 5
Claret Bumble *(37) (AndreHermans,Belgium)* 4-8-0 (5)ow2 JStack(1) (s.s: racd wd: hdwy over 3f out: one pce) ....¾ 6
Victoria Hall **(51)***(19) (WGMTurner)* 5-8-2 ow2 GDuffield(11) (led over 4f out tl over 3f out: wknd over 2f out) 7 7
21[9] Esperer *(29) (JO'Donoghue)* 5-8-8 (5) DRMcCabe(10) (s.s: nvr nrr) ....nk 8
Secret Assignment (USA) **(40)***(25) (CACyzer)* 5-8-13v GBardwell(5) (bhd fnl 4f)...1¾ 9
Belfort Ruler **(52)***(15) (BGubby)* 8-8-5h JQuinn(6) (bit bkwd: bhd fnl 4f) 1 10
22[8] Annabella Baggins (IRE) **(40)***(—) (RBoss)* 4-8-7b LDettori(2) (led over 3f: wknd over 3f out) 12 11

68⁷ Indian Fire **(39)***(—) (KOCunningham-Brown)* 5-8-13 GCarter(7) (lw: prom 4f) 8 **12**
2/1 Masnun (USA), **3/1** PERILOUS PLIGHT, **9/2** Arndilly, **8/1** Beware of Agents, Claret Bumble, **14/1** Annabella Baggins (IRE), **20/1** Secret Assignment (USA), **25/1** Victoria Hall, Titanium Honda (IRE), Belfort Ruler, **50/1** Esperer, Indian Fire, CSF £9.50 TOTE £5.30: £1.90 £1.50 £1.10 (£6.20) OWNER Mr J. Jannaway (LAMBOURN) BRED Crest Stud Ltd 12 Rn

1m 38.34 (1.94) SF: 39/-/27/7/11/4/-/-/-/-/-/-

WEIGHT FOR AGE 4yo-1lb

OFFICIAL EXPLANATION **Claret Bumble: missed the break and then appeared to resent the kick-back so the jockey took her to the outside of the track.**

188

LINGFIELD PARK AWT SPRINT SERIES H'CAP (Qualifier) (0-80) (Class D) £3,776.15 (£1,143.20: £558.10: £265.55)
5f (Equitrack) GOING minus 0.42 sec per fur (FST) 2-10 (2-11)

123² **Spender (73)***(79) (PWHarris)* 6-9-6 (5) JStack(5) (hld up: rdn over 1f out: led ins fnl f: r.o wl) ....— **1**
102² Distant Dynasty **(55)***(58) (BAPearce)* 5-8-7 StephenDavies(6) (b.hind: rdn 2f out: hdwy over 1f out: r.o wl ins fnl f) ....¾ **2**
Moscow Road **(74)***(74) (MissBSanders)* 4-9-7 (5) SSanders(3) (b.hind: led: hrd rdn 1f out: hdd ins fnl f: unable qckn) 1 **3**
Tee-Emm **(59)***(58) (PHowling)* 5-8-11 JQuinn(4) (w ldr: hrd rdn over 1f out: ev ch ins fnl f: one pce) ....nk **4**
69¹⁰ Sir Tasker **(67)***(62) (JLHarris)* 7-9-5 RCochrane(1) (hld up: rdn over 2f out: r.o one pce) 1¼ **5**
70⁶ Another Episode (IRE) **(72)***(56) (JBerry)* 6-9-10 GCarter(2) (s.s: a bhd) 3½ **6**
154² Kalar **(63)***(32)*(Fav)*(DWChapman)* 6-9-1b LDettori(7) (s.s: a bhd) 5 **7**
7/4 Kalar, **7/2** SPENDER, **5/1** Distant Dynasty, **8/1** Another Episode (IRE), Sir Tasker, **10/1** Tee-Emm, **14/1** Moscow Road, CSF £19.38 TOTE £3.60: £2.60 £2.00 (£12.60) OWNER The Entrepreneurs (BERKHAMSTED) BRED The Mount Coote Partnership 7 Rn

58.83 secs (0.63) SF: 62/43/57/42/46/40/14

OFFICIAL EXPLANATION **Kalar: missed the break and was unable to get into the contest.**

189

DAILY STAR AWT 1M 2F CHALLENGE SERIES H'CAP (Qualifier) (3-Y.O) (0-70) (Class E) £3,268.60 (£989.80: £483.40: £230.20)
1m 2f (Equitrack) GOING minus 0.42 sec per fur (FST) 2-40 (2-40)

151² **Nigel's Lad (IRE) (67)***(81)*(Fav)*(PCHaslam)* 3-9-7 JWeaver(1) (hdwy over 4f out: led wl over 1f out: rdn out) ....— **1**
72⁶ Inn At the Top **(57)***(69) (MJohnston)* 3-8-11 TWilliams(9) (led 5f out tl wl over 1f out: unable qckn fnl f) 1½ **2**
*116** Harry Browne (IRE) **(59)***(62) (MrsJRRamsden)* 3-8-13 SWilliams(10) (rdn & hdwy over 3f out: one pce) 6 **3**
59⁴ Star Fighter **(63)***(55) (WAO'Gorman)* 3-9-0 (3) EmmaO'Gorman(7) (dwlt: hdwy over 8f out: ev ch over 2f out: sn wknd) 7 **4**
98⁵ Rowlandsons Silver (FR) **(48)***(37) (DJGMurraySmith)* 3-8-2 CRutter(4) (lw: hrd rdn & no hdwy fnl 4f) 2 **5**
Keys Seminar **(60)***(34) (NACallaghan)* 3-9-0 GCarter(3) (nvr nr to chal) 10 **6**
78¹² Winterbottom **(48)***(19) (ICampbell)* 3-8-2 AMackay(8) (lw: s.i.s: a bhd) 2 **7**
85⁹ Star Information **(43)***(2) (JSMoore)* 3-7-8 (3)ow4 DWright(2) (led 5f) 8 **8**
32⁷ Joint Prospect **(41)***(—) (CCElsey)* 3-7-9bow1 JQuinn(5) (bhd fnl 5f) 12 **9**

LONG HANDICAP Star Information 7-6

7/4 NIGEL'S LAD (IRE), **5/2** Harry Browne (IRE), **6/1** Inn At the Top, **7/1** Star Fighter, **12/1** Keys Seminar, **20/1** Rowlandsons Silver (FR), Winterbottom, **25/1** Joint Prospect, **33/1** Star Information, CSF £12.04 CT £23.38 TOTE £2.30: £1.30 £1.10 £1.30 (£7.40) OWNER Mr N. C. Dunnington (MIDDLEHAM) BRED Nikita Investments 9 Rn2m 8.35 (5.35) SF: 28/17/10/3/-/-/-/-/-

190

SULKY STKS (Mdn) (Class D) £3,690.70 (£1,117.60: £545.80: £259.90)
1m 2f (Equitrack) GOING minus 0.42 sec per fur (FST) 3-10 (3-10)

135² **Persian Conquest (IRE) (55)***(68) (RIngram)* 3-8-3bow1 WWoods(1) (mde all: qcknd over 2f out: clr over 1f out: r.o wl) ....— **1**
Masrah Dubai (USA) *(58) (MAJarvis)* 4-9-8 TIves(4) (dwlt: hdwy to chse wnr over 3f out: no imp) 6 **2**
Field of Stars **(68)***(54)*(Fav)*(NACallaghan)* 5-9-11 RCochrane(3) (hld up: hrd rdn over 3f out: one pce) 2½ **3**
Come on Dancer (IRE) **(49)***(52) (JWhite)* 7-9-6 (5) SDrowne(2) (lw: chsd wnr over 6f) 1½ **4**
Mountain Boy *(18t) (MJohnston)* 4-9-8 AProud(5) (lw: bhd fnl 5f) 12 **5**

6/4 Field of Stars, **13/8** PERSIAN CONQUEST (IRE), **11/2** Masrah Dubai (USA), **12/1** Mountain Boy, **14/1** Come on Dancer (IRE), CSF £9.28 TOTE £2.50: £1.20 £2.30 (£5.00) OWNER Mrs A. V. Cappuccini (EPSOM) BRED Louis A. Walshe 5 Rn 2m 7.21 (4.21) SF: 20/29/28/26/5
WEIGHT FOR AGE 3yo-23lb, 4yo-3lb

191

HANSOM STKS (0-70) (Class E) £2,981.00 (£902.00: £440.00: £209.00)
7f (Equitrack) GOING minus 0.42 sec per fur (FST) 3-40 (3-41)

*71** **Spencer's Revenge (70)***(72+) (LordHuntingdon)* 6-9-10 LDettori(5) (lw: hld up: led on bit over 1f out: easily)......— **1**
89¹¹ Mullitover **(67)***(63) (MJHeaton-Ellis)* 5-9-7 StephenDavies(6) (rdn & hdwy over 2f out: r.o one pce)......3 **2**
20³ Milos **(69)***(62) (TJNaughton)* 4-9-7 JWeaver(8) (lw: a.p: led 3f out tl over 1f out: eased whn btn wl ins fnl f)......nk **3**
160⁷ Pirates Gold (IRE) **(57)***(56) (JWhite)* 5-9-2 (5) SDrowne(2) (lw: rdn over 3f out: hdwy fnl f: nvr nrr)......3 **4**
Desert Invader (IRE) **(70)***(54) (DWChapman)* 4-9-2 (5) DRMcCabe(3) (bit bkwd: dwlt: nvr nr to chal)......¾ **5**
*101** Hoist (IRE) **(66)***(48)*(Fav)*(SirMarkPrescott)* 4-9-5 GDuffield(4) (lw: led 5f out to 3f out: wknd over 1f out)......2 **6**
160¹¹ Frisky Miss (IRE) **(67)***(43) (KOCunningham-Brown)* 4-9-2 GCarter(7) (led 2f: wknd over 2f out)......¾ **7**
Admirals Flame (IRE) **(65)***(47) (CFWall)* 4-9-7 WWoods(1) (b: bit bkwd: a bhd).....hd **8**

15/8 Hoist (IRE), **100/30** Milos, **4/1** SPENCER'S REVENGE, **6/1** Admirals Flame (IRE) (8/1-9/2), **10/1** Mullitover, **14/1** Desert Invader (IRE), **20/1** Frisky Miss (IRE), **33/1** Pirates Gold (IRE), CSF £37.77 TOTE £4.30: £1.10 £3.40 £1.90 (£53.50) OWNER Mr P. A. Leonard (WEST ILSLEY) BRED Lord Crawshaw 8 Rn 1m 26.05 (3.05) SF: 36/27/26/19/18/12/8/-

192

PHAETON H'CAP (0-65) (Class F) £2,763.80 (£776.80: £379.40)
6f (Equitrack) GOING minus 0.42 sec per fur (FST) 4-10 (4-11)

Crystal Heights (FR) (55)*(60) (RJO'Sullivan)* 7-8-13 (5) SMulvey(1) (b: dwlt: n.m.r 2f out: hdwy over 1f out: str run fnl f: hung lft & led nr fin)......— **1**
Purbeck Centenary **(44)***(46) (PHowling)* 5-8-7 JQuinn(4) (led over 2f: led over 2f out: hrd rdn fnl f: hdd nr fin)......¾ **2**
142⁴ Myjinka **(35)***(34) (JO'Donoghue)* 5-7-5b(7) MBaird(10) (hdwy over 1f out: r.o ins fnl f)......1 **3**
139⁵ Cheeky Chappy **(40)***(37) (DWChapman)* 4-7-10b(7) CTeague(8) (led over 3f out tl over 2f out: hrd rdn over 1f out: one pce)......½ **4**
Sweet Whisper **(48)***(44) (KMcAuliffe)* 4-8-6v(5) JStack(9) (a.p: hrd rdn over 1f out: one pce)......nk **5**
102⁷ Hinari Video **(50)***(40) (MJohnston)* 10-8-13 TWilliams(5) (prom 4f)......2½ **6**
129⁶ Rapier Point (IRE) **(55)***(45)*(Fav)*(PCHaslam)* 4-9-4 JWeaver(2) (lw: hld up: hrd rdn over 1f out: wknd fnl f)......s.h **7**
138⁶ Forgotten Dancer (IRE) **(56)***(36) (RIngram)* 4-9-5b RCochrane(6) (lw: a bhd)......4 **8**
39⁵ Anotherone to Note **(54)***(26) (MJHeaton-Ellis)* 4-9-3v WWoods(3) (hld up: rdn 2f out: sn wknd)......3 **9**
Riskie Things **(65)***(12) (JSMoore)* 4-9-7 (7) HannahFox(7) (lw: a bhd)......10 **10**

5/2 Rapier Point (IRE), **4/1** Myjinka, **6/1** Cheeky Chappy, **15/2** Sweet Whisper (5/1-8/1), **8/1** Anotherone to Note, **9/1** Hinari Video (6/1-10/1), Forgotten Dancer (IRE), **12/1** CRYSTAL HEIGHTS (FR), **14/1** Purbeck Centenary, **20/1** Riskie Things, CSF £149.79 CT £726.08 TOTE £15.70: £5.70 £4.30 £1.60 (£78.00) OWNER Mr Jack Joseph (BOGNOR REGIS) BRED Ahmad Fustok 10 Rn 1m 12.94 (2.34) SF: 34/22/11/15/21/16/21/-/-/-

T/Jkpt: £13,753.00 (4.65 Tckts). T/Plpt: £21.70 (1,083.89 Tckts). T/Qdpt: £36.20 (2.2 Tckts). AK

0165-WOLVERHAMPTON (L-H)
Wednesday February 1st (Standard)

193

THYME H'CAP (0-80) (Class D) £3,572.40 (£1,081.20: £527.60: £250.80)
1m 4f (Fibresand) GOING: 0.03 sec per fur (STD) 2-10 (2-11)

121⁶ **Shakiyr (FR) (56)***(63) (RHollinshead)* 4-8-5 ow1 LDettori(8) (hld up: hdwy 5f out: jnd ldr 3f out: 2nd st: edgd rt & led ins fnl f: all out)......— **1**

121* Stevie's Wonder (IRE) **(67)***(73)*(Fav)*(MJRyan)* 5-9-6 GCarter(5) (led: rdn over 3f out: edgd rt & hdd ins fnl f: r.o) ....nk **2**
106⁴ Johns Act (USA) **(68)***(69) (DHaydnJones)* 5-9-7 AMackay(4) (prom: rdn over 4f out: 3rd st: one pce) 4 **3**
How's it Goin (IRE) **(73)***(58) (WRMuir)* 4-9-8 JWeaver(2) (bit bkwd: hld up in rr: 7th st: sme late hdwy) 13 **4**
104* Salbus **(75)***(58) (FJYardley)* 5-10-0 JWilliams(7) (hld up: hdwy over 4f out: 5th & wkng st) 1½ **5**
Wannaplantatree **(67)***(48) (GHYardley)* 4-9-2 SWhitworth(1) (bit bkwd: hld up: 6th & wkng st) 1½ **6**
106⁵ View From Above **(71)***(52) (NJHWalker)* 9-9-10 RCochrane(6) (prom: 4th & wkng st) ....s.h **7**
106³ Philgun **(60)***(37) (CWCElsey)* 6-8-13v NKennedy(3) (hld up: rdn over 4f out: sn bhd) 3 **8**

5/2 Stevie's Wonder (IRE), **3/1** Philgun, **5/1** Johns Act (USA), **7/1** View From Above, **9/1** Salbus, **10/1** SHAKIYR (FR), **14/1** Wannaplantatree, How's it Goin (IRE), CSF £33.39 CT £128.81 TOTE £9.40: £3.60 £1.40 £1.10 (£12.70) OWNER L & R Roadlines (UPPER LONGDON) BRED S. A. Aga Khan in France 8 Rn 2m 40.5 (9.50) SF: 30/44/39/24/28/15/22/-
WEIGHT FOR AGE 4yo-4lb

194 SAGE CLAIMING STKS (Class E) £3,023.90 (£915.20: £446.60: £212.30)
5f (Fibresand) GOING: 0.03 sec per fur (STD) 2-40 (2-40)

107* **Primula Bairn (60)***(56) (MrsJRRamsden)* 5-9-1v JWeaver(3) (led early: led wl over 1f out: r.o wl) ....— **1**
154⁶ Very Dicey **(74)***(51)*(Fav)*(JBerry)* 7-9-1 (7) PRoberts(1) (sn led: hdd & 2nd st: edgd rt & wknd fnl f) 4 **2**
154⁸ Tommy Tempest **(40)***(35) (ABailey)* 6-9-0 WHawksley(4) (sn outpcd: 3rd st: r.o fnl f: n.d) 2½ **3**
107¹² Oriental Song **(23)***(—) (KSBridgwater)* 6-9-1b NAdams(2) (outpcd: poor 4th st) 15 **4**

Evens Very Dicey, **11/10** PRIMULA BAIRN, **11/1** Tommy Tempest, **200/1** Oriental Song, CSF £2.41 TOTE £2.10 (£1.10) OWNER Mr M. A. Bagnall (THIRSK) BRED Kavli Ltd 4 Rn
63.0 secs (5.00) SF: 17/11/-/-

195 ROSEMARY H'CAP (0-90) (Class C) £5,602.00 (£1,696.00: £828.00: £394.00)
1m 1f 79y (Fibresand) GOING: 0.03 sec per fur (STD) 3-10 (3-12)

119* **Legal Fiction (64)***(76+) (MJohnston)* 4-8-7 TWilliams(3) (a.p: rdn to ld wl over 2f out: clr over 1f out: drvn out) ....— **1**
127² Tu Opes **(65)***(71) (JLHarris)* 4-8-8 DaleGibson(7) (bhd: rdn & hdwy over 4f out: 5th st: r.o fnl f: nt trble wnr) 3½ **2**
Sieve of Time (USA) **(82)***(86) (CEBrittain)* 4-9-11 LDettori(5) (lw: hld up: hdwy 4f out: 2nd & hrd rdn st: one pce) 1½ **3**
152³ Bentico **(67)***(68) (MrsNMacauley)* 6-8-7 (5) SSanders(6) (hld up: hdwy 5f out: 4th st: one pce) 2½ **4**
Conspicuous (IRE) **(65)***(56) (LGCottrell)* 5-8-10 NCarlisle(1) (led over 6f out to 5f out: 3rd & rdn st: wknd over 1f out) 6 **5**
89⁷ Just Harry **(82)***(68) (MJRyan)* 4-9-4 (7) MBaird(9) (hld up: hdwy 4f out: 7th & wkng st) 2½ **6**
66³ Northern Celadon (IRE) **(71)***(56) (MJHeaton-Ellis)* 4-9-0 StephenDavies(2) (lw: led over 1f: led 5f out tl wl over 2f out: 6th & wkng st) ....¾ **7**
Noblely (USA) **(71)***(36) (NJHWalker)* 8-9-2v RCochrane(10) (b: b.hind: led 8f out tl over 6f out: wknd qckly 4f out: sn t.o) 12 **8**
125⁶ Roman Reel (USA) **(62)***(22) (GLMoore)* 4-8-5 AClark(11) (a bhd: t.o fnl 3f) 2½ **9**
103* Sharp Conquest **(69)***(26)*(Fav)*(WRMuir)* 4-8-12 JWeaver(8) (mid div: eased whn btn wl over 1f out) 1¾ **10**
The Power of One **(64)***(21) (RWEmery)* 6-8-9 JWilliams(4) (a bhd: t.o fnl 5f) ....¾ **11**

9/2 Sharp Conquest, **5/1** Sieve of Time (USA), **6/1** LEGAL FICTION, **7/1** Northern Celadon (IRE), **15/2** Bentico, Just Harry, **8/1** Tu Opes, **12/1** Roman Reel (USA), Conspicuous (IRE), **14/1** Noblely (USA), **50/1** The Power of One, CSF £49.44 CT £236.26 TOTE £7.20: £1.80 £1.30 £3.90 (£26.10) OWNER Mr J. S. Morrison (MIDDLEHAM) BRED Fares Stables Ltd 11 Rn
2m 1.0 (5.00) SF: 51/47/60/44/32/41/30/-/-/-/-
WEIGHT FOR AGE 4yo-2lb

OFFICIAL EXPLANATION **Sharp Conquest: did not show any life, ran flat and did not respond when under pressure.**

196 PARSLEY H'CAP (3-Y.O) (0-90) (Class C) £5,498.00 (£1,664.00: £812.00: £386.00) 6f (Fibresand) GOING: 0.03 sec per fur (STD) 3-40 (3-41)

Go Hever Golf (89)*(100)*(Fav)*(TJNaughton)* 3-9-7 GCarter(6) (b.nr hind: chsd ldr: rdn to ld 2f out: r.o wl).......— 1
74⁵ Crystal Loop **(64)***(65) (ABailey)* 3-7-10 GBardwell(1) (lw: led: rdn 3f out: hdd 2f out: 2nd st: one pce fnl f).......4 2
*74** Stoppes Brow **(85)***(80) (GLMoore)* 3-8-10v(7) LSuthern(8) (hld up: hdwy & 3rd st: r.o one pce fnl f).......2½ 3
24³ Master Millfield (IRE) **(73)***(65) (CJHill)* 3-8-0 (5) SSanders(7) (prom: rdn & outpcd over 3f out: 6th st: rallied over 1f out: one pce).......¾ 4
105⁵ Tee Tee Too (IRE) **(74)***(61) (PCHaslam)* 3-8-6 JWeaver(2) (prom: 4th st: wknd over 1f out).......2 5
105³ Poly Laureon (IRE) **(63)***(46) (RHollinshead)* 3-7-9 NCarlisle(4) (no hdwy fnl 2f)....1½ 6
*146** One for Jeannie **(64)***(44) (ABailey)* 3-7-10v 7x LCharnock(3) (s.i.s: sn rdn: hdwy on ins & 5th st: wknd over 1f out).......¾ 7
Noosa (IRE) **(82)***(39) (MJohnston)* 3-9-0 TWilliams(5) (t.o fnl 4f).......9 8

9/4 GO HEVER GOLF, **9/2** One for Jeannie, **6/1** Stoppes Brow, Master Millfield (IRE), Tee Tee Too (IRE), **8/1** Noosa (IRE), **12/1** Poly Laureon (IRE), Crystal Loop (8/1-14/1), CSF £26.27 CT £132.85 TOTE £2.80: £1.30 £4.30 £1.60 (£18.60) OWNER Hever Racing Club (EPSOM) BRED Ronald Popely 8 Rn 1m 14.7 (3.50) SF: 58/24/38/25/19/6/5/-

197 MARJORAM (S) STKS (3-Y.O) (Class G) £2,433.00 (£683.00: £333.00) 6f (Fibresand) GOING: 0.03 sec per fur (STD) 4-10 (4-11)

*134** **Whittingham Girl (56)***(66)*(Fav)*(JBerry)* 3-8-12 GCarter(4) (a.p: led 4f out: clr over 1f out: eased nr fin).......— 1
48⁸ David James' Girl **(60)***(64) (ABailey)* 3-8-12 SWhitworth(1) (hdwy on ins & 4th st: r.o wl fnl f).......½ 2
Nadwaty (IRE) **(57)***(56) (JDBethell)* 3-8-7 JWeaver(9) (bit bkwd: led 2f: 2nd st: r.o one pce).......1 3
132⁴ Pats Delight **(45)***(47) (SCoathup)* 3-8-7 NAdams(3) (prom: 3rd st: wknd over 1f out).......3½ 4
141⁶ Lawnswood Lady **(48)***(46) (RHollinshead)* 3-8-7 LDettori(8) (lw: w ldrs: outpcd over 2f out: 7th st: styd on fnl f).......nk 5
107⁵ Ivy Lilian (IRE) **(40)***(43) (WMBrisbourne)* 3-8-2b(5) AGarth(5) (n.m.r s: gd hdwy 4f out: 5th st: wknd over 1f out).......1 6
118⁶ Komlucky **(49)***(38) (FJO'Mahony)* 3-8-12b JQuinn(6) (hld up & plld hrd: 6th & wkng st).......4 7
149⁷ Captain Sinbad *(28) (KSBridgwater)* 3-8-12 JWilliams(2) (a bhd).......4 8
146⁶ Two Chalk **(44)***(25) (PDEvans)* 3-8-12v AClark(7) (b: a bhd).......¾ 9

11/10 WHITTINGHAM GIRL, **3/1** David James' Girl, **9/2** Nadwaty (IRE), **8/1** Komlucky, **10/1** Lawnswood Lady, **16/1** Ivy Lilian (IRE), **25/1** Pats Delight, Two Chalk, **33/1** Captain Sinbad, CSF £5.48 TOTE £2.70: £1.40 £1.30 £1.50 (£4.70) OWNER T & M A Bibby (COCKERHAM) BRED Cheveley Park Stud Ltd 9 Rn Bt in 6,800 gns 1m 16.0 (4.80) SF: 32/31/24/14/13/11/5/-/-

198 CHIVE H'CAP (I) (Mdn) (0-70) (Class E) £2,966.70 (£897.60: £437.80: £207.90) 7f (Fibresand) GOING: 0.03 sec per fur (STD) 4-40 (4-41)

119³ **Ziggy's Dancer (USA) (50)***(66+) (EJAlston)* 4-9-6 JWeaver(1) (mde all: clr 2f out: unchal).......— 1
129⁴ Indian Serenade **(49)***(41)*(Fav)*(PWHarris)* 4-9-5 RCochrane(7) (hld up: hrd rdn & hdwy over 3f out: 3rd st: r.o fnl f: no ch w wnr).......11 2
142⁷ Europharm Lassie **(43)***(31) (GLMoore)* 4-8-13v AClark(5) (lw: hld up: chsd wnr over 3f out: 2nd st: no imp).......1¾ 3
Mrs Bizzybody **(35)***(19) (TJNaughton)* 4-8-5b JQuinn(6) (bkwd: dropped rr 4f out: sme hdwy & 4th st: n.d).......2 4
Rainbows Rhapsody **(43)***(10) (MJCamacho)* 4-8-13 LCharnock(4) (chsd ldrs: rdn 4f out: sn wknd: poor 6th st).......8 5
103⁶ Fleet Cadet **(54)***(16) (NAGraham)* 4-9-10 GDuffield(2) (chsd ldrs: rdn 4f out: wknd 3f out).......2½ 6
107¹¹ Distinctive Lady **(30)***(—) (REPeacock)* 5-7-11b(3) DWright(3) (chsd wnr over 3f: 5th & wkng st).......4 7

11/10 Indian Serenade, **3/1** ZIGGY'S DANCER (USA), **11/2** Rainbows Rhapsody, **7/1** Fleet Cadet, **9/1** Europharm Lassie, **20/1** Mrs Bizzybody, **50/1** Distinctive Lady, CSF £6.71 CT £22.63 TOTE £3.00: £2.00 £1.10 (£2.20) OWNER Mr John Patrick Barry (PRESTON) BRED Warren W. Rosenthal 7 Rn 1m 29.6 (5.60) SF: 40/15/7/-/-/-/-

199 CHIVE H'CAP (II) (Mdn) (0-70) (Class E) £2,966.70 (£897.60: £437.80: £207.90) **7f (Fibresand)** GOING: 0.03 sec per fur (STD) 5-10 (5-11)

*127*5 **Canary Falcon (59)***(63) (RJO'Sullivan)* 4-9-9 WWoods(4) (a.p: led 2f out: clr 1f out: r.o wl).......— **1**
*138*5 At the Savoy (IRE) **(44)***(42) (TDBarron)* 4-8-1 (7) KimberleyHart(1) (lw: hmpd on ins & lost pl over 3f out: plld out & 4th st: hdwy 1f out: r.o wl).......3 **2**
*148*7 Rustic League (IRE) **(39)***(35) (TJNaughton)* 4-7-12 (5) SSanders(3) (plld hrd: led 4f out to 2f out: 2nd st: one pce).......¾ **3**
*103*2 Slip a Coin **(53)***(44)*(Fav)*(RHollinshead)* 4-9-3 LDettori(2) (led 3f: 3rd st: wknd over 1f out).......2½ **4**
*130*7 Welsh Heritage (IRE) **(41)***(21) (RJPrice)* 5-8-5 StephenDavies(5) (hld up: 6th & wkng st).......5 **5**
Dragonflight **(45)***(8) (DHaydnJones)* 4-8-4 (5) SDrowne(6) (lw: bhd fnl 3f).......8 **6**
Dahiyah (USA) **(64)***(24) (GLMoore)* 4-10-0 AClark(7) (hld up: hdwy on ins over 4f out: 5th & wkng st).......1¼ **7**
16[8] Lunar Prince **(40)***(—) (TTClement)* 5-8-4 AMackay(8) (lame at s)....... **W**

7/4 Slip a Coin, **2/1** CANARY FALCON, **3/1** At the Savoy (IRE), **12/1** Dahiyah (USA), **14/1** Dragonflight, **16/1** Rustic League (IRE), **50/1** Welsh Heritage (IRE), Lunar Prince, CSF £8.36 CT £65.74 TOTE £3.60: £2.00 £1.10 (£4.70) OWNER Mrs N. Aqil (BOGNOR REGIS) BRED Gainsborough Stud Management Ltd 7 Rn 1m 30.1 (6.10) SF: 37/17/11/18/-/-/-/-

T/Jkpt: £3,419.90 (1.38 Tckts). T/Plpt: £24.00 (1,198.16 Tckts). T/Qdpt: £5.70 (12.1 Tckts). KH

0187-LINGFIELD (L-H)
Thursday February 2nd (Standard)

200 ALBERTA (S) H'CAP (I) (0-60) (Class G) £2,427.00 (£682.00: £333.00) **1m 5f (Equitrack)** GOING minus 0.51 sec per fur (FST) 1-30 (1-30)

*178*3 **Dancing Diamond (IRE) (44)***(57) (MissBSanders)* 5-9-0hv(5) SSanders(6) (mde all: clr over 8f out: unchal).......— **1**
*3*4 Fiery Sun **(28)***(29) (JLEyre)* 10-8-3v JQuinn(4) (a.p: chsd wnr fnl f: no imp).......10 **2**
*153*3 Cliburnel News (IRE) **(49)***(47)*(Fav)*(WRMuir)* 5-9-10 JWeaver(2) (hdwy over 4f out: hrd rdn over 3f out: one pce).......3 **3**
*175*4 Mogwai (IRE) **(41)***(35) (MartynMeade)* 6-9-2 VSlattery(1) (a.p: rdn 5f out: wknd over 3f out).......3½ **4**
*122*6 Cone Lane **(27)***(19) (BGubby)* 9-8-2h GBardwell(3) (b.hind: rdn 7f out: nvr nr to chal).......1¼ **5**
*172*7 Written Agreement **(20)***(12) (REPeacock)* 7-7-2 (7)ow2 MBaird(5) (lw: nvr nrr).......nk **6**
*83*6 Persian Bud (IRE) **(24)***(15) (JRBosley)* 7-7-13v CRutter(10) (a mid div).......½ **7**
*122*5 Malingerer **(30)***(18) (DAWilson)* 4-8-0 NGwilliams(8) (b.hind: a bhd).......1¾ **8**
*161*5 Glowing Path **(49)***(9) (RJHodges)* 5-9-10b LDettori(9) (prom over 7f).......25 **9**
*84*8 Chapter Two **(33)***(—) (SDow)* 4-8-3 StephenDavies(7) (lw: bhd fnl 8f: t.o).......dist **10**

7/4 Cliburnel News (IRE), **5/1** DANCING DIAMOND (IRE), Glowing Path, **8/1** Fiery Sun, **10/1** Malingerer, **14/1** Mogwai (IRE), Persian Bud (IRE), **16/1** Cone Lane, **33/1** Chapter Two, **50/1** Written Agreement, CSF £39.41 CT £86.29 TOTE £4.20: £1.10 £1.90 £1.10 (£18.70) OWNER Mrs J. M. Laycock (EPSOM) BRED Kiltinan Farms Inc 10 Rn No bid
2m 46.5 (4.00) SF: 38/12/28/16/3/-/-/-/-/-
WEIGHT FOR AGE 4yo-5lb

201 ALBERTA (S) H'CAP (II) (0-60) (Class G) £2,415.80 (£678.80: £331.40) **1m 5f (Equitrack)** GOING minus 0.51 sec per fur (FST) 2-00 (2-01)

Side Bar (28)*(40) (MJRyan)* 5-8-1b DBiggs(3) (mde all: clr over 4f out: unchal).......— **1**
So Discreet (USA) **(48)***(50) (JWhite)* 7-9-2 (5) SDrowne(5) (bit bkwd: hld up: rdn 7f out: chsd wnr over 3f out: no imp).......9 **2**
*143*2 Lon Isa **(43)***(36)*(Fav)*(BPalling)* 4-8-11 AClark(1) (hdwy over 4f out: 5th whn nt clr run over 3f out tl over 2f out: one pce).......7 **3**
*109*5 Upper Mount Clair **(54)***(48) (CEBrittain)* 5-9-13b BDoyle(6) (chsd wnr 8f: lost pl over 4f out: one pce).......nk **4**
Ann Hill (IRE) **(31)***(23) (RHollinshead)* 5-7-11 (7) AEddery(7) (nvr nr to chal).......1½ **5**
*58*4 Super Assignation (IRE) **(55)***(43) (DRCElsworth)* 4-9-9 DHarrison(10) (lw: a.p: chsd wnr 5f out tl over 3f out: wknd over 2f out).......2½ **6**

136[9] Sweet Caroline **(41)**_(29) (PMitchell)_ 4-8-9e JMcLaughlin(4) (nvr nrr) ....s.h **7**
158[6] Celestial Faith **(37)**_(24) (MJohnston)_ 4-8-5 TWilliams(9) (hld up: hrd rdn over 4f out: wknd over 2f out) ....¾ **8**
Zonk **(42)**_(22) (RGFrost)_ 5-8-10 (5) PMcCabe(2) (b.hind: bhd fnl 4f) 7 **9**
58[5] Tokanda **(22)**_(—) (FJYardley)_ 11-7-2 (7)ow2 MBaird(8) (b: bhd fnl 9f) 25 **10**

LONG HANDICAP Tokanda 7-2

7/4 Lon Isa, **6/1** SIDE BAR, **7/1** So Discreet (USA), **8/1** Upper Mount Clair, Ann Hill (IRE), Super Assignation (IRE) (9/2-9/1), Celestial Faith, Zonk, **16/1** Sweet Caroline, **33/1** Tokanda, CSF £47.21 CT £97.19 TOTE £9.80: £2.90 £4.00 £1.10 (£32.60) OWNER Mr M. J. Baxter (NEWMARKET) BRED Mrs M. A. Ryan 10 Rn 2m 46.53 (4.03) SF: 21/30/12/27/4/18/6/1/-/-

WEIGHT FOR AGE 4yo-5lb

No bid

202

BRITISH COLUMBIA CLAIMING STKS (Class F) £2,713.40 (£762.40: £372.20) **6f (Equitrack)** GOING minus 0.51 sec per fur (FST) 2-30 (2-31)

140[4] **Tyrian Purple (IRE) (58)**_(57) (TJNaughton)_ 7-8-5b DHarrison(1) (b.off hind: mde all: all out) ....— **1**
107[3] Lift Boy (USA) **(62)**_(58) (AMoore)_ 6-8-6 CandyMorris(6) (b.hind: a.p: hrd rdn over 2f out: r.o wl ins fnl f) ....s.h **2**
123[4] Farfelu **(76)**_(67) (WRMuir)_ 8-9-5b JWeaver(5) (chsd wnr: hrd rdn over 1f out: ev ch ins fnl f: unable qckn) 1½ **3**
177[7] Respectable Jones **(49)**_(42)_(Fav)_(RHollinshead)_ 9-8-7 LDettori(8) (lw: no hdwy fnl 3f) 5 **4**
167[2] Farndale **(52)**_(39) (JBerry)_ 8-8-3 (7) CLowther(2) (hld up: rdn over 2f out: sn wknd)2½ **5**
Mheanmetoo **(61)**_(23) (DLWilliams)_ 4-8-2 (5) DGriffiths(3) (lw: bhd fnl 3f) 5 **6**
101[6] Forbidden Gem _(12) (SWoodman)_ 4-8-9 MFenton(4) (a bhd) 5 **7**

9/4 Respectable Jones, **5/2** Lift Boy (USA), **4/1** Farfelu, **13/2** TYRIAN PURPLE (IRE), **7/1** Farndale, **10/1** Mheanmetoo, **33/1** Forbidden Gem, CSF £22.51 TOTE £7.00: £3.40 £1.60 (£11.40) OWNER Mr T. O'Flaherty (EPSOM) BRED Niels Schibbye 7 Rn

1m 12.73 (2.13) SF: 18/18/27/2/-/-/-

203

DAILY STAR AWT 1M 2F CHALLENGE SERIES H'CAP (Qualifier) (0-65) (Class F) £2,788.00 (£844.00: £412.00: £196.00) **1m 2f (Equitrack)** GOING minus 0.51 sec per fur (FST) 3-00 (3-00)

155* **Little Miss Ribot (33)**_(37) (RJO'Sullivan)_ 5-7-12 5x StephenDavies(4) (hdwy 2f out: swtchd rt over 1f out: hrd rdn & led wl ins fnl f: r.o wl) ....— **1**
155[4] Captain Marmalade **(51)**_(54) (DTThom)_ 6-8-13 (3) DRMcCabe(9) (lw: lost pl over 6f out: rallied 2f out: r.o wl ins fnl f) ....nk **2**
152[5] Braveboy **(61)**_(63) (CEBrittain)_ 7-9-12b BDoyle(6) (hdwy 6f out: rdn over 4f out: r.o one pce fnl f) ....½ **3**
100[9] Greatest Hopes **(32)**_(32) (CJBenstead)_ 4-7-9 JQuinn(5) (a.p: led over 4f out: clr over 1f out: hdd wl ins fnl f: one pce) 1¼ **4**
62[2] A Million Watts **(64)**_(63)_(Fav)_(LadyHerries)_ 4-9-13 TIves(2) (a.p: rdn over 4f out: one pce fnl f) ....¾ **5**
125[9] Pair of Jacks (IRE) **(36)**_(24) (DAWilson)_ 5-8-1 NGwilliams(3) (lw: led over 5f: wknd over 2f out) 7 **6**
158[5] Coalisland **(31)**_(19) (RIngram)_ 5-7-7b(3)ow1 DWright(7) (a bhd) ....hd **7**
27[4] Hillsdown Boy (IRE) **(58)**_(44) (SDow)_ 5-9-4 (5) SSanders(8) (a.p: rdn over 4f out: wknd over 1f out) 1¼ **8**
Sozzled **(63)**_(38) (ABarrow)_ 4-9-7v(5) SDrowne(1) (bhd fnl 4f) 7 **9**

11/4 A Million Watts, **100/30** LITTLE MISS RIBOT, **11/2** Coalisland, **6/1** Braveboy, **13/2** Hillsdown Boy (IRE), **8/1** Captain Marmalade, **20/1** Sozzled, Greatest Hopes, **25/1** Pair of Jacks (IRE), CSF £27.64 CT £139.71 TOTE £3.50: £1.10 £2.40 £2.30 (£11.10) OWNER Mr Christopher Lane (BOGNOR REGIS) BRED H. Powis 9 Rn 2m 7.4 (4.40) SF: 8/24/32/2/31/-/-/1/-

WEIGHT FOR AGE 4yo-2lb

204

QUEBEC STKS (Mdn 3-Y.O) (Class D) £3,572.40 (£1,081.20: £527.60: £250.80) **1m (Equitrack)** GOING minus 0.51 sec per fur (FST) 3-30 (3-31)

Peutetre _(58+)_(Fav)_(CEBrittain)_ 3-9-0 BDoyle(1) (str: hld up: rdn over 3f out: led 2f out: r.o wl) ....— **1**
64[8] Inchkeith _(51) (GWragg)_ 3-8-2 (7) DGibbs(5) (led over 4f: hrd rdn over 1f out: ev ch ins fnl f: unable qckn) ....¾ **2**
156[5] Athinar _(35) (CPWildman)_ 3-8-9 StephenDavies(2) (hld up: rdn over 4f out: wknd wl over 1f out) 8 **3**

72[5] La Fille de Cirque *(28) (RJRWilliams)* 3-8-9 RCochrane(7) (b: w ldr: led over 3f out to 2f out: 3rd & btn whn hmpd wl over 1f out)............................3½ 4
Welsh Wizzard *(—) (CNWilliams)* 3-9-0 MRimmer(4) (w'like: bit bkwd: s.s: a wl bhd)..20 5

13/8 PEUTETRE, **5/2** Athinar, **7/2** La Fille de Cirque, **6/1** Welsh Wizzard, **8/1** Inchkeith, CSF £12.59 TOTE £2.70: £1.10 £2.70 (£5.70) OWNER The Dayspring Company Ltd (NEWMARKET) BRED Dayspring Co Ltd 5 Rn 1m 40.44 (4.04) SF: 16/10/-/-/-

205

ONTARIO H'CAP (0-70) (Class E) £3,095.40 (£937.20: £457.60: £217.80)
1m (Equitrack) GOING minus 0.51 sec per fur (FST) 4-00 (4-03)

*187** **Perilous Plight (60)***(75)*(Fav)*(WRMuir)* 4-9-10 6x JWeaver(4) (lw: hdwy over 4f out: led over 1f out: comf)..— 1
148[3] Swallow Ridge (IRE) **(30)***(34) (RJO'Sullivan)* 6-7-9 NAdams(7) (b: lw: rdn & hdwy over 4f out: ev ch over 1f out: unable qckn)..6 2
*158** Shansi (IRE) **(49)***(45) (MDIUsher)* 4-8-13v 6x RStreet(1) (b: led over 6f: 3rd & btn whn n.m.r on ins 1f out)..3½ 3
Mr Browning (USA) **(54)***(46) (MarkCampion)* 4-9-4 RCochrane(3) (hld up: hrd rdn 3f out: 5th whn hmpd & lost pl on ins over 2f out: r.o one pce).............1¾ 4
56[4] Zinbaq **(38)***(27) (CJBenstead)* 9-8-3 TWilliams(8) (a.p: rdn over 3f out: wknd wl over 1f out)...1¾ 5
71[5] Pigalle Wonder **(33)***(19) (RJO'Sullivan)* 7-7-12b ow1 StephenDavies(5) (nvr plcd to chal)...1½ 6
62[7] Possibility **(41)***(24) (RIngram)* 4-8-5b WWoods(2) (chsd ldrs 7f out tl over 2f out: sn wknd)...1 7
181[4] Eastleigh **(46)***(26)*(Fav)*(RHollinshead)* 6-8-11 LDettori(6) (prom over 5f).............1¾ 8
125[7] Shepherd Market (IRE) **(63)***(28) (DAWilson)* 4-9-13 GCarter(11) (a bhd)................7 9
94[13] Titania's Dance (IRE) **(56)***(7) (MBell)* 4-9-6 MFenton(9) (bhd fnl 4f).........................7 10
28[7] Quiet Mission **(36)***(—) (JLEyre)* 4-8-0 JQuinn(10) (lw: bhd fnl 5f)...........................8 11
27[5] Lac de Gras (IRE) **(31)***(—) (RCurtis)* 4-7-9 GBardwell(12).. W

3/1 PERILOUS PLIGHT, Eastleigh, **6/1** Swallow Ridge (IRE), **7/1** Shansi (IRE), **9/1** Shepherd Market (IRE), **10/1** Titania's Dance (IRE), **12/1** Pigalle Wonder, **14/1** Possibility, Zinbaq, **16/1** Mr Browning (USA), **33/1** Quiet Mission, **50/1** Lac de Gras (IRE), CSF £21.52 CT £110.99 TOTE £2.80: £2.10 £1.80 £4.60 (£16.70) OWNER Mr J. Jannaway (LAMBOURN) BRED Crest Stud Ltd 11 Rn 1m 38.34 (1.94) SF: 46/7/17/20/5/-/1/5/-/-/-

WEIGHT FOR AGE 4yo-1lb

206

MANITOBA H'CAP (0-80) (Class D) £3,589.30 (£1,086.40: £530.20: £252.10)
1m 4f (Equitrack) GOING minus 0.51 sec per fur (FST) 4-30 (4-30)

*147** **Art Form (USA) (79)***(85)*(Fav)*(CACyzer)* 8-10-3 5x TIves(4) (lw: rdn 9f out: gd hdwy fnl f: led wl ins fnl f: r.o wl)..— 1
106[8] One Off the Rail (USA) **(74)***(78) (AMoore)* 5-9-12 CandyMorris(3) (b.hind: a.p: led over 3f out tl wl ins fnl f: unable qckn)..1¼ 2
127[3] Bag of Tricks (IRE) **(62)***(64) (SDow)* 5-9-0 DHarrison(2) (led over 8f out tl over 3f out: wknd ins fnl f)..2 3
145[8] Our Eddie **(68)***(66) (BGubby)* 6-9-6v LDettori(7) (hld up: rdn over 4f out: r.o one pce fnl f)..3 4
Mr Copyforce **(62)***(56) (MissBSanders)* 5-8-7 (7) AmandaBowen(1) (led over 3f: wknd over 4f out)...3½ 5
15[8] Vishnu (USA) **(70)***(62) (JLEyre)* 5-9-8v AClark(5) (bhd fnl 5f)...................................1¾ 6
Rapporteur (USA) **(76)***(37) (CCElsey)* 9-10-0 CRutter(6) (b: stumbled s: bhd fnl 7f)...25 7

4/5 ART FORM (USA), **5/1** Our Eddie, **11/2** Bag of Tricks (IRE), **15/2** One Off the Rail (USA), **10/1** Rapporteur (USA), **20/1** Mr Copyforce, Vishnu (USA), CSF £7.58 TOTE £1.60: £1.10 £7.80 (£6.10) OWNER Mr R. M. Cyzer (HORSHAM) BRED Morgan's Ford Farm and Elizabeth Thomas in USA 7 Rn 2m 32.97 (3.57) SF: 50/44/30/32/22/29/2

£13.90 (1,145.68 Tckts). T/Qdpt: £22.90 (1.25 Tckts). AK

0164A-CAGNES-SUR-MER (Nice, France) (L-H)
Friday January 27th (Soft)

207a

PRIX RENOIR (3-Y.O) £5,988.00 **1m 2f**

163a[3] **Sharpest Image (IRE)** *(—) (France)* 3-8-12 SMaillot...— 1
Tzar Rodney (FR) *(—) (France)* 3-9-1 ODoleuze...½ 2
164a[3] L'Arpege (USA) *(—) (France)* 3-8-9 WMongil...nk 3

163a6 Courbaril *(—) (SDow)* 3-8-9 FSanchez (btn further 2l) 5

TOTE4.20F: 1.10F 1.20F 1.10F (8.70F) OWNER Mr R. C. Strauss 12 Rn 2m 11.9 SF: -/-/-/-

208a PRIX DES PEUPLIERS (H'cap) £8,982.00 **1m**

Charme Slave (FR) *(—) (France)* 7-8-10 ABarzalona .... — 1
162a* Confronter *(—) (SDow)* 6-9-5 ESaint-Martin 1 2
Relaunchrette (CAN) *(—) (France)* 5-8-8 WMongil .... ½ 3

TOTE18.70F OWNER Mr J. Nahoum BRED R. Ades in France 15 Rn 1m 43.9 SF: -/-/-

0207A-CAGNES-SUR-MER (Nice, France) (L-H) Sunday January 29th (Good)

209a PRIX DE BASTIA (3-Y.O) £4,790.00 **1m 2f**

164a4 **Mo's Main Man (IRE)** *(—) (SDow)* 3-9-2 FSanchez .... — 1
Papaly (FR) *(—) (France)* 3-9-2 MCesandri .... nse 2
Kabanova (FR) *(—) (France)* 3-8-13 MBoutin 1½ 3

TOTE4.50F: 2.80F 23.30F 2.70F (332.50F) OWNER Hatfield Ltd (EPSOM) BRED Gaberson Ltd 19 Rn 2m 10.6 SF: -/-/-

0179-SOUTHWELL (L-H) Friday February 3rd (Standard)

210 LADBROKE ALL WEATHER BOWL SERIES H'CAP (Qualifier) (3-Y.O) (0-70) (Class E) £3,517.50 (£1,065.00: £520.00: £247.50) **6f (Fibresand)** GOING minus 0.21 sec per fur (FST) 2-10 (2-10)

1703 **Portend (68)***(76+)*(Fav)*(SRBowring)* 3-8-12 (7) CTeague(5) (chsd ldrs: led over 2f out: sn clr: edgd lft: easily) .... — 1
1323 Superbit **(49)***(39) (BAMcMahon)* 3-8-0 DaleGibson(4) (chsd ldrs: led 3f out: sn hdd: no ch w wnr) 7 2
Nite-Owl Dancer **(60)***(46) (JAHarris)* 3-8-11 JO'Reilly(7) (s.i.s: hdwy & prom ½-wy: styd on same pce fnl 2f) 1¼ 3
423 Pursuance (IRE) **(56)***(36) (JBalding)* 3-8-7 LDettori(6) (sn outpcd: styd on u.p fnl 2f: nvr nr ldrs) 2½ 4
1187 Chaldon Herring **(62)***(42) (TDBarron)* 3-8-6 (7) KimberleyHart(1) (s.i.s: hdwy ½-wy: kpt on fnl 2f) .... s.h 5
7212 Charnwood Queen **(45)***(15) (RWArmstrong)* 3-7-10 GBardwell(2) (sn chsng ldrs: rdn over 2f out: grad wknd) 4 6
1183 Russian Heroine **(70)***(35) (MJohnston)* 3-9-7 TWilliams(9) (prom early: sn in rr) 2 7
1702 Our Tom **(59)***(11) (JWharton)* 3-8-10 JQuinn(10) (lw: sn bhd: effrt on outside over 2f out: n.d) 5 8
Another Nightmare (IRE) **(62)***(1) (RMMcKellar)* 3-8-6 (7) RHavlin(8) (led to 3f out: sn lost pl) 5 9

5/2 PORTEND, **3/1** Our Tom, **4/1** Russian Heroine, **7/1** Pursuance (IRE), **10/1** Charnwood Queen, **12/1** Chaldon Herring, Nite-Owl Dancer, **16/1** Superbit, Another Nightmare (IRE), CSF £37.84 CT £382.59 TOTE £3.60: £1.20 £5.70 £2.40 (£55.60) OWNER Mr D. H. Bowring (EDWINSTOWE) BRED Hollow Hole Stud 9 Rn 1m 17.0 (3.50) SF: 39/3/10/-/5/-/-/-/-

211 LANGFORD CLAIMING STKS (Class F) £2,537.00 (£712.00: £347.00) **7f (Fibresand)** GOING minus 0.21 sec per fur (FST) 2-40 (2-42)

1172 **No Submission (USA) (66)***(69)*(Fav)*(DWChapman)* 9-9-6 LDettori(7) (mde virtually all: rdn over 3f out: styd on wl ins fnl f) .... — 1
1174 Battle Colours (IRE) **(61)***(69) (MrsJRRamsden)* 6-9-8 JWeaver(2) (a chsng wnr: disp ld over 3f out: nt qckn ins fnl f) .... ¾ 2
1846 Super Benz **(63)***(61) (FJO'Mahony)* 9-9-7 GCarter(4) (b: trckd ldrs: effrt over 2f out: hung lft: kpt on same pce) 3½ 3
11710 Allinson's Mate (IRE) **(70)***(55) (TDBarron)* 7-9-5 (7) JennyBenson(5) (hdwy ½-wy: kpt on fnl 2f: nvr nr to chal) 5 4

148[5] Veloce (IRE) **(54)**_(40) (ABailey)_ 7-8-9 (7) AngelaGallimore(1) (lw: sn chsng ldrs: effrt over 2f out: grad wknd) 2½ **5**
146[7] First Point (IRE) **(50)**_(—) (CNAllen)_ 3-7-5 (7) MBaird(3) (in tch to ½-wy: sn wl bhd: t.o) 25 **6**
Corky's Girl _(—) (RMMcKellar)_ 3-7-10 ow3 DaleGibson(6) (a bhd: t.o) 6 **7**
150[4] Alpine Johnny **(55)**_(—) (RHollinshead)_ 4-9-6 AGarth(8) (Withdrawn: v.unruly & ref to ent stalls: not under orders: rule 4 applies) .... **W**

5/6 NO SUBMISSION (USA), **5/1** Battle Colours (IRE), Super Benz, **9/1** Alpine Johnny, **10/1** Veloce (IRE), **12/1** Allinson's Mate (IRE), **33/1** First Point (IRE), **50/1** Corky's Girl, CSF £4.84 TOTE £1.50: £1.10 £2.40 (£3.10) OWNER Mr T. S. Redman (YORK) BRED Mr. Francis X. Weber 7 Rn 1m 30.7 (3.90) SF: 42/43/34/27/13/-/-/-
WEIGHT FOR AGE 3yo-18lb

212 FIBRESAND APP'CE H'CAP (0-70) (Class E) £3,009.60 (£910.80: £444.40: £211.20) **1m (Fibresand)** GOING minus 0.21 sec per fur (FST) 3-10 (3-10)

157[5] **Rad (55)**_(59) (SPCWoods)_ 5-8-10 (5) CWebb(1) (hld up: hdwy ½-wy: led 1f out: hung lft: styd on wl) .... — **1**
169* Buddy's Friend (IRE) **(65)**_(67) (RJRWilliams)_ 7-9-11 6x SarahThompson(3) (lw: chsd ldrs: led over 3f out to 2f out: kpt on same pce fnl f) 1 **2**
135* Pc's Cruiser (IRE) **(54)**_(54)_(Fav)_(MCChapman)_ 3-7-9 6x AmandaSanders(5) (w ldrs: led 4f out: sn hdd: kpt on same pce appr fnl f) .... ¾ **3**
125[10] Aitch N'Bee **(68)**_(60) (LadyHerries)_ 12-9-7 (7) PDoe(6) (led to 4f out: sn rdn: wknd over 1f out) 4 **4**
Benjarong **(52)**_(39) (RMMcKellar)_ 3-7-7 CAdamson(4) (chsd ldrs: rdn 2f out: grad wknd) 2½ **5**
139[10] My Foxy Lady **(38)**_(—) (JAHarris)_ 5-7-12 SLanigan(2) (sn outpcd: sme hdwy ½-wy: sn wknd) 15 **6**
LONG HANDICAP Benjarong 7-4

15/8 Pc's Cruiser (IRE), **2/1** Buddy's Friend (IRE), **4/1** Aitch N'Bee, **9/2** RAD, **16/1** Benjarong, **33/1** My Foxy Lady, CSF £13.59 TOTE £5.30: £1.80 £1.50 (£4.10) OWNER Mr S. P. C. Woods (NEWMARKET) BRED Mrs D. Whittingham 6 Rn 1m 46.6 (7.30) SF: 11/18/-/12/-/-
WEIGHT FOR AGE 3yo-19lb

213 OLD CLIPSTONE MEDIAN AUCTION STKS (Mdn 3-Y.O) (Class E) £3,081.10 (£932.80: £455.40: £216.70) **1m 3f (Fibresand)** GOING minus 0.21 sec per fur (FST) 3-40 (3-42)

128[2] **Shaft of Light** _(66+)_(Fav)_(LordHuntingdon)_ 3-9-0v LDettori(2) (mde all: pushed along over 2f out: clr over 1f out: eased nr fin) .... — **1**
72[7] Beau Matelot **(57)**_(61) (JDBethell)_ 3-9-0 JWeaver(4) (sn chsng wnr: drvn along 4f out: kpt on: no ch w wnr) 3½ **2**
168[2] Wisdom _(58) (PFICole)_ 3-9-0 CRutter(10) (sn drvn along: hdwy & prom 7f out: kpt on one pce fnl 3f) 2½ **3**
Darling Clover _(51) (DMorley)_ 3-8-9 MFenton(1) (lengthy: unf: chsd ldrs: hrd drvn over 3f out: sn outpcd: kpt on fnl f) 1¼ **4**
176[6] Boundary Express **(54)**_(45) (MJohnston)_ 3-9-0 TWilliams(5) (chsd ldrs: rdn 5f out: wknd over 2f out) 8 **5**
59[11] Kindred Greeting **(48)**_(40) (DMorris)_ 3-9-0 TIves(9) (in tch: sn drvn along: outpcd over 3f out: n.d after) 3½ **6**
Vaslav Nijinsky _(39) (GRimmer)_ 3-9-0 MRimmer(6) (w'like: scope: bit bkwd: unruly s: chsd ldrs: drvn 3f out: sn wknd: eased fnl f) .... ¾ **7**
168[5] Sergio (IRE) _(19) (MCChapman)_ 3-8-11 (3) DRMcCabe(3) (sn bhd) 15 **8**
17[5] Solor Dancer _(17) (CBBBooth)_ 3-9-0 JFanning(8) (sn bhd) 1¼ **9**
90[13] Aisling's Image _(—) (SGNorton)_ 3-8-9 DeanMcKeown(7) (hld up: bhd fnl 7f: t.o) .... dist **10**

10/11 SHAFT OF LIGHT, **3/1** Wisdom, **6/1** Vaslav Nijinsky, **12/1** Beau Matelot, **14/1** Darling Clover, **16/1** Boundary Express, Kindred Greeting, **25/1** Solor Dancer, **50/1** Sergio (IRE), Aisling's Image, CSF £13.56 TOTE £1.70: £1.10 £4.00 £1.80 (£8.30) OWNER The Queen (WEST ILSLEY) BRED The Queen 10 Rn 2m 29.7 (8.20) SF: 25/21/17/11/5/-/-/-/-/-

214 NEW BALDERTON (S) STKS (Class G) £2,259.00 (£634.00: £309.00) **1m 3f (Fibresand)** GOING minus 0.21 sec per fur (FST) 4-10 (4-10)

120* **Killing Time (59)**_(61) (MrsNMacauley)_ 4-9-2v MFenton(4) (mde all: clr 3f out: unchal) .... — **1**

4[3] Feline (IRE) **(43)***(41) (RFJohnsonHoughton)* 4-8-6 JQuinn(3) (a.p: chsd wnr fnl 2f: no imp)....7 **2**
Durham **(76)***(42)*(Fav)*(NTinkler)* 4-8-11 LDettori(1) (chsd ldrs: rdn & lost pl over 3f out: hung lft & kpt on fnl 2f)....3 **3**
Days of Thunder **(42)***(41) (JWhite)* 7-8-9 (5) SDrowne(6) (hdwy to chse ldrs ½-wy: one pce fnl 2f)....1 **4**
50[8] T O O Mamma's (IRE) **(37)***(35) (JBerry)* 4-7-13 (7) PFessey(7) (hld up & bhd: hdwy 3f out: nvr nr to chal)....1 **5**
92[9] Hay Dance **(39)***(27) (JPLeigh)* 4-8-11b DeanMcKeown(2) (hld up: hdwy & prom 7f out: rdn & wknd over 2f out)....10 **6**
119[6] Rosina's Folly **(52)***(17) (JLHarris)* 4-8-6 AMackay(10) (hdwy to chse ldrs 7f out: rdn & wknd over 2f out)....3½ **7**
Derisbay (IRE) *(19) (JJBridger)* 7-9-0b JFanning(5) (b: chsd ldrs tl lost pl 5f out: sn bhd)....2½ **8**
Miss Freebie (IRE) **(36)***(12) (BAMcMahon)* 4-8-6 JO'Reilly(8) (drvn along & prom 6f out: lost pl 4f out)....1¼ **9**
Brigadore Gold **(24)***(11) (ABailey)* 5-8-9 GBardwell(9) (lw: a bhd)....¾ **10**

2/1 Durham, **9/4** KILLING TIME, **7/1** Feline (IRE), Rosina's Folly, T O O Mamma's (IRE), **10/1** Miss Freebie (IRE), Days of Thunder, Brigadore Gold, **16/1** Derisbay (IRE), **20/1** Hay Dance, CSF £21.25 TOTE £3.20: £1.10 £1.70 £1.70 (£7.60) OWNER Mr James Colling (MELTON MOWBRAY) BRED L. H. J. Ward 10 Rn 2m 29.7 (8.20) SF: 27/8/9/10/2/-/-/-/-/-
WEIGHT FOR AGE 4yo-3lb
No bid

215 MANSFIELD H'CAP (0-70) (Class E) £3,109.70 (£941.60: £459.80: £218.90) **1m 4f (Fibresand)** GOING minus 0.21 sec per fur (FST) 4-40 (4-40)

186* **Palacegate Jo (IRE) (62)***(69+)*(Fav)*(RHollinshead)* 4-9-2 5x LDettori(6) (lw: sn trckng ldr: led over 4f out: pushed clr 3f out: unchal)....— **1**
186[2] Who's the Best (IRE) **(36)***(41) (APJarvis)* 5-7-3 (5) NVarley(4) (sn bhd & drvn: hdwy 3f out: swtchd outside & styd on appr fnl f: no ch w wnr)....2 **2**
53* Thaleros **(67)***(71) (GMMoore)* 5-9-11 JWeaver(8) (led after 1f tl over 4f out: kpt on: no ch w wnr: eased nr fin)....¾ **3**
52[6] Charlie Bigtime **(50)***(48) (BJMcMath)* 5-8-8 AMackay(3) (sn drvn along: hdwy to chse ldrs 4f out: one pce)....5 **4**
172[2] Ozzie Jones **(47)***(33) (MCChapman)* 4-7-12 (3)ow3 DRMcCabe(7) (sn bhd: sme hdwy 4f out: n.d)....10 **5**
91[5] Atherton Green (IRE) **(56)***(37) (JAGlover)* 5-9-0 TIves(1) (trckd ldrs: drvn along 5f out: sn wknd)....4 **6**
With Gusto **(41)***(13) (JJBridger)* 8-7-13 ow1 JFanning(5) (b: prom tl lost pl over 4f out: sn bhd)....7 **7**
136[5] Uckerby Lad **(56)***(13) (NPLittmoden)* 4-8-5 (5)ow6 TGMcLaughlin(2) (prom tl lost pl over 4f out: sn bhd)....12 **8**

7/4 PALACEGATE JO (IRE), **7/2** Thaleros, **11/2** Who's the Best (IRE), **7/1** Ozzie Jones, Atherton Green (IRE), **15/2** Charlie Bigtime, **20/1** With Gusto, Uckerby Lad, CSF £11.88 CT £27.38 TOTE £2.80: £1.10 £1.60 £2.40 (£8.40) OWNER Palacegate Corporation Ltd (UPPER LONGDON) BRED Brendan and Sheila Powell 8 Rn 2m 41.1 (6.90) SF: 40/17/45/23/4/11/-/-
WEIGHT FOR AGE 4yo-4lb
T/Jkpt: £823.70 (13.07 Tckts). T/Plpt: £6.20 (3,277.07 Tckts). T/Qdpt: £2.90 (9.7 Tckts). WG

0200-LINGFIELD (L-H)
Saturday February 4th (Standard)

216 BLACKWOOD CLAIMING STKS (Class E) £2,981.00 (£902.00: £440.00: £209.00) **5f (Equitrack)** GOING minus 0.44 sec per fur (FST) 1-50 (1-50)

159[4] **Bon Secret (IRE) (58)***(66) (TJNaughton)* 3-8-6 DHarrison(6) (b: hld up: hdwy over 2f out: edgd lft over 1f out: r.o fnl f: led last strides)....— **1**
173[4] Superlao (BEL) *(59) (AndreHermans,Belgium)* 3-7-13 JQuinn(2) (b.hind: chsd ldr: led over 2f out: rdn & edgd lft ins fnl f: hdd last strides)....s.h **2**
65[8] Sison (IRE) **(65)***(57) (KGWingrove)* 5-9-3 JMcLaughlin(1) (b.hind: hld up: hdwy over 2f out: n.m.r fnl f: ev ch whn hmpd nr fin: nt rcvr)....1½ **3**
70* Little Saboteur **(70)***(55)*(Fav)*(PJMakin)* 6-9-2b AClark(3) (b.nr hind: hld up: hdwy & n.m.r 2f out: swtchd rt over 1f out: r.o one pce)....nk **4**
Amazing News **(56)***(40) (MarkCampion)* 4-8-12 JWeaver(4) (led over 2f: 4th & wkng whn hmpd over 1f out)....3½ **5**

70[2] Press the Bell **(76)***(33) (JBerry)* 5-9-9 GCarter(5) (b.off hind: chsd ldrs: rdn 3f out: wknd 2f out) 6 **6**

5/4 Little Saboteur, **6/4** Press the Bell, **8/1** Superlao (BEL), **10/1** BON SECRET (IRE), **16/1** Sison (IRE), **25/1** Amazing News, CSF £70.24 TOTE £13.90: £6.10 £2.60 (£88.20) OWNER Mr F.R. Jackman (EPSOM) BRED Sean Mc Donnell in Ireland 6 Rn 60.17 secs (1.97) SF: 20/14/26/24/8/-
WEIGHT FOR AGE 3yo-15lb

217 PELLEW APP'CE H'CAP (0-60) (Class G) £2,550.20 (£717.20: £350.60)

1m (Equitrack) GOING minus 0.44 sec per fur (FST) 2-20 (2-22)

*148** **Words of Wisdom (IRE) (57)***(66) (CACyzer)* 5-9-11 MBaird(4) (a.p: led over 1f out: r.o) ....— **1**
192[3] Myjinka **(33)***(39) (JO'Donoghue)* 5-7-10b(5) IonaWands(5) (chsd ldr: ev ch over 1f out: unable qckn) 1½ **2**
76[3] Rockstine (IRE) **(57)***(59) (PMitchell)* 4-9-7 (3) LSuthern(10) (dwlt: outpcd & bhd: hdwy & edgd lft over 1f out: r.o fnl f) 1½ **3**
155[5] Lexus (IRE) **(40)***(42) (RJRWilliams)* 7-8-5b(3) SarahThompson(12) (hld up: hdwy 3f out: hrd rdn over 1f out: r.o one pce) ....½ **4**
*49** King Parrot (IRE) **(54)***(53)*(Fav)*(LordHuntingdon)* 7-9-5 (3) AmandaSanders(6) (chsd ldrs: rdn over 1f out: one pce) 1¼ **5**
177[8] My Lifetime Lady (IRE) **(41)***(37) (KTIvory)* 4-8-3 (5) CScally(7) (mid div: rdn 4f out: hrd rdn over 1f out: one pce) 1 **6**
Blue Ensign **(41)***(34) (HGRowsell)* 10-8-9b DGibbs(3) (dwlt: bhd & rdn over 2f out: nvr nrr) 2 **7**
Doodies Pool (IRE) **(52)***(40) (GLMoore)* 5-8-13 (7) CarolineHovington(9) (a bhd)...2½ **8**
187[6] Claret Bumble **(55)***(40) (AndreHermans,Belgium)* 4-9-8 RPainter(8) (mid div: rdn over 4f out: wknd 2f out) ....¾ **9**
157[12] Helmsley Palace **(30)***(12) (MPMuggeridge)* 6-7-9b(3) SLanigan(1) (chsd ldrs tl rdn & wknd 2f out) 1¾ **10**
Christian Spirit **(35)***(3) (BAPearce)* 5-8-3b PRoberts(2) (led over 6f) 7 **11**
143[7] Bernie's Sister (IRE) **(31)***(—) (CNAllen)* 4-7-5v(7)ow1 KarenMarkham(11) (bhd fnl 4f) 5 **12**

11/4 King Parrot (IRE), **3/1** WORDS OF WISDOM (IRE), **7/2** Rockstine (IRE), **5/1** Lexus (IRE), **8/1** Myjinka, **9/1** Blue Ensign, **16/1** Claret Bumble, **20/1** Doodies Pool (IRE), My Lifetime Lady (IRE), **33/1** Christian Spirit, **50/1** Helmsley Palace, Bernie's Sister (IRE), CSF £28.96 CT £85.81 TOTE £4.10: £1.80 £2.10 £1.80 (£21.70) OWNER Mr M. J. Morrison (HORSHAM) BRED Stackallan Stud in Ireland 12 Rn 1m 39.98 (3.58) SF: 36/11/29/14/25/10/7/-/-/-/-/-
WEIGHT FOR AGE 4yo-1lb

218 GAMBIER STKS (Mdn) (Class D) £3,555.50 (£1,076.00: £525.00: £249.50)

1m (Equitrack) GOING minus 0.44 sec per fur (FST) 2-50 (2-52)

145[9] **Ultimate Warrior (67)***(60+) (CACyzer)* 5-9-0 TIves(3) (hld up: hdwy over 2f out: led over 1f out: sn clr: comf) ....— **1**
Song of Years (IRE) *(41)*(Fav)*(JWHills)* 4-8-9 LDettori(2) (led: hrd rdn & hdd over 1f out: one pce) 7 **2**
175[5] Thorniwama **(35)***(38) (JJBridger)* 4-8-9b GBardwell(7) (sn rdn along: a.p: hrd rdn & ev ch over 2f out: one pce) 1½ **3**
Thames Side **(55)***(43) (MMadgwick)* 4-8-11 (3) DRMcCabe(4) (hld up: hdwy 2f out: r.o one pce fnl f) ....hd **4**
158[9] Stipple **(31)***(26) (SWoodman)* 4-8-9 MFenton(5) (chsd ldrs: rdn 3f out: wknd over 1f out) 6 **5**
Inspiration Point **(51)***(20) (MissBSanders)* 4-8-4 (5) NVarley(6) (rdn 3f out: a bhd) 3 **6**
Added Dimension (IRE) **(41)***(1) (CTNash)* 4-9-0 RPerham(1) (prom 4f) 12 **7**

2/5 Song of Years (IRE), **11/4** ULTIMATE WARRIOR, **10/1** Inspiration Point, **20/1** Added Dimension (IRE), **25/1** Thorniwama, Thames Side, **50/1** Stipple, CSF £4.39 TOTE £3.20: £1.20 £1.10 (£1.80) OWNER Mr R. M. Cyzer (HORSHAM) BRED D. O'Dell and J. S. Delahooke 7 Rn 1m 39.31 (2.91) SF: 32/14/12/16/-/-/-
WEIGHT FOR AGE 4yo-1lb

219 JERVIS H'CAP (0-80) (Class D) £3,623.10 (£1,096.80: £535.40: £254.70)

7f (Equitrack) GOING minus 0.44 sec per fur (FST) 3-20 (3-21)

160[3] **Digpast (IRE) (52)***(59)*(Fav)*(RJO'Sullivan)* 5-8-6b DBiggs(4) (dwlt: bhd: rdn 3f out: hdwy 2f out: swtchd rt over 1f out: led wl ins fnl f: r.o) ....— **1**

150[5] Ragazzo (IRE) **(46)***(50) (KOCunningham-Brown)* 5-8-0b LCharnock(5) (chsd ldr: rdn 3f out: led over 1f out: hdd wl ins fnl f: r.o)....1½ **2**
179[2] Profit Release (IRE) **(56)***(58) (MJohnston)* 4-8-10 TWilliams(1) (a.p: rdn 4f out: hrd rdn fnl f: r.o)....¾ **3**
Prima Silk **(74)***(70)*(Fav)*(MJRyan)* 4-10-0 AClark(2) (sn rdn along: hdwy over 2f out: hrd rdn over 1f out: r.o one pce)....3 **4**
160[2] Maid Welcome **(61)***(51)*(Fav)*(MrsNMacauley)* 8-8-8v(7) AmandaSanders(3) (led tl over 1f out: wknd ins fnl f)....3 **5**
160[8] Panchellita (USA) **(50)***(32) (GLMoore)* 6-8-4 JQuinn(7) (chsd ldrs tl rdn & wknd over 2f out)....4 **6**
71[6] It's so Easy **(53)***(18) (APJames)* 4-8-7 WWoods(6) (a bhd)....8 **7**

11/4 DIGPAST (IRE), Maid Welcome, Prima Silk, **4/1** Profit Release (IRE) (3/1-9/2), **9/1** Ragazzo (IRE), **10/1** Panchellita (USA), **33/1** It's so Easy, CSF £25.57 TOTE £3.30: £2.00 £3.20 (£8.10) OWNER Mr Les Randall (BOGNOR REGIS) BRED Somerville Stud 7 Rn
1m 24.73 (1.73) SF: 33/25/32/42/23/4/-

220 COCHRANE STKS (0-50) (Class F) £2,826.80 (£794.80: £388.40) **6f (Equitrack)** GOING minus 0.44 sec per fur (FST) 3-55 (3-56)

142[2] **Our Shadee (USA) (45)***(56) (KTIvory)* 5-9-0v(7) CScally(9) (mid div: hdwy 2f out: r.o fnl f: led nr fin)....— **1**
192[5] Sweet Whisper **(48)***(50) (KMcAuliffe)* 4-9-2v JWeaver(4) (led: clr over 1f out: hrd rdn fnl f: hdd nr fin)....nk **2**
Carte Blanche **(43)***(47) (CACyzer)* 4-8-13 (3) DRMcCabe(11) (chsd ldrs: rdn 2f out: hrd rdn over 1f out: r.o)....1 **3**
146[2] Prince Rudolf (IRE) **(51)***(46)*(Fav)*(MrsNMacauley)* 3-8-5v MFenton(6) (chsd ldrs: hrd rdn over 1f out: one pce)....2½ **4**
Sherblu **(40)***(46) (JFfitch-Heyes)* 4-9-7b MWigham(2) (dwlt: bhd: hdwy over 1f out: swtchd rt & r.o wl fnl f: nrst fin)....s.h **5**
Lady Roxanne **(45)***(38) (LordHuntingdon)* 6-9-2v DHarrison(7) (hld up: hdwy 2f out: chsd ldr over 1f out: wknd ins fnl f)....¾ **6**
167[5] Make the Break **(47)***(40) (SCoathup)* 4-9-0b(7) SharronJames(10) (bhd: rdn 4f out: nvr nrr)....¾ **7**
Finjan **(46)***(35) (AGFoster)* 8-9-7 MRimmer(12) (nvr nrr)....2 **8**
148[8] Gingerillo **(32)***(29) (TGMills)* 4-9-7b WWoods(1) (chsd ldr over 4f: rdn 2f out: wknd fnl f)....2½ **9**
102[8] Pat Poindestres **(36)***(21) (RJO'Sullivan)* 5-9-2 DBiggs(14) (mid div: rdn over 2f out: wknd over 1f out)....1 **10**
140[7] Waders Dream (IRE) **(39)***(25) (PMitchell)* 6-9-7e JMcLaughlin(13) (a bhd)....hd **11**
182[12] Mr B Reasonable (IRE) **(43)***(17) (SWCampion)* 4-9-7b TIves(8) (a bhd)....3 **12**
102[4] Banbury Flyer **(35)***(11) (MrsALMKing)* 7-9-2 (5) NVarley(3) (chsd ldrs tl rdn & wknd over 2f out)....2½ **13**
148[9] Scots Law **(36)***(6) (JELong)* 8-9-2b(5) PMcCabe(5) (a bhd)....1¾ **14**

4/1 Prince Rudolf (IRE), **9/2** Lady Roxanne (4/1-6/1), **5/1** Sweet Whisper, OUR SHADEE (USA), **6/1** Carte Blanche, **10/1** Finjan, Make the Break, Pat Poindestres, **12/1** Gingerillo, **20/1** Sherblu, Banbury Flyer, **25/1** Waders Dream (IRE), Mr B Reasonable (IRE), Scots Law, CSF £33.35 TOTE £5.20: £2.30 £2.60 £3.00 (£15.40) OWNER Mr K. T. Ivory (RADLETT) BRED Overbury Stud 14 Rn 1m 13.03 (2.43) SF: 34/29/27/10/24/17/20/-/-/-/-/-/-/-
WEIGHT FOR AGE 3yo-16lb

221 COLLINGWOOD H'CAP (0-70) (Class E) £3,023.90 (£915.20: £446.60: £212.30) **1m 5f (Equitrack)** GOING minus 0.44 sec per fur (FST) 4-25 (4-26)

161* **Head Turner (47)***(57+)*(Fav)*(CPWildman)* 7-8-7 NAdams(1) (hld up: hdwy & n.m.r over 2f out: swtchd rt & led over 1f out: r.o wl)....— **1**
84* Hattaafeh (IRE) **(60)***(66) (MAJarvis)* 4-9-1 WWoods(5) (chsd ldrs: rdn 6f out: hrd rdn 2f out: r.o)....2½ **2**
Princely Gait **(70)***(73) (CACyzer)* 4-9-11 TIves(3) (dwlt: hld up: hdwy 3f out: led 2f out tl over 1f out: one pce)....2½ **3**
178[4] Royal Circus **(37)***(39) (JGMO'Shea)* 6-7-11 JQuinn(4) (led 3f: led over 5f out to 2f out: ev ch over 1f out: one pce)....1¼ **4**
52[4] Tiger Shoot **(66)***(65) (DTThom)* 8-9-7 (5) LNewton(2) (a.p: chsd ldr over 5f out: hrd rdn 3f out: ev ch over 1f out: wknd fnl f)....3 **5**
83[9] Azubah **(37)***(1) (JAHarris)* 8-7-6 (5) NVarley(6) (chsd ldr: led 10f out tl over 5f out: wknd qckly: t.o)....30 **6**

2/1 HEAD TURNER, **5/2** Hattaafeh (IRE), **3/1** Princely Gait, **6/1** Tiger Shoot (4/1-7/1), **13/2** Royal Circus, **25/1** Azubah, CSF £7.57 TOTE £2.60: £1.40 £1.20 (£3.90) OWNER Mr I. Jerrard (SALISBURY) BRED M. B. O'Gorman 6 Rn
2m 46.72 (4.22) SF: 31/36/42/15/38/-
WEIGHT FOR AGE 4yo-5lb
T/Plpt: £176.00 (72.74 tckts). T/Qdpt: £32.70 (2.05 Tckts). SM

0193-WOLVERHAMPTON (L-H)
Saturday February 4th (Standard)

222
OSPREY H'CAP (0-65) (Class F) £2,502.00 (£702.00: £342.00)
1m 1f 79y (Fibresand) GOING: 0.01 sec per fur (STD) 7-00 (7-00)

77⁴ **Donia (USA) (46)***(48) (JLHarris)* 6-8-9b GDuffield(8) (hld up: hdwy on outside 4f out: led over 2f out: sn clr: rdn out)....— 1
First Century (IRE) **(54)***(51) (MCPipe)* 6-9-3b JWeaver(5) (led 6f: 2nd & ev ch st: rdn & unable qckn fnl f)....3 2
138² Mam'zelle Angot **(65)***(60)*(Fav)*(JLEyre)* 5-9-11 (3) OPears(1) (b.hind: hld up: smooth hdwy 4f out: 4th st: sn ev ch: r.o one pce)....1½ 3
131⁶ Suivez **(51)***(45) (MrsNMacauley)* 5-9-0 DeanMcKeown(9) (a.p: 5th & outpcd ent st: styd on u.p ins fnl f)....nk 4
Tremolante **(35)***(26) (CaptJWilson)* 4-7-7 (3)ow3 DWright(10) (bit bkwd: chsd ldrs: led 3f out: sn hdd: 3rd st: wknd appr fnl f)....1½ 5
103³ Ship of the Line **(60)***(37) (JRFanshawe)* 5-9-9e DHarrison(3) (eyeshield: lw: bhd: rdn along ½-wy: nvr nr to chal)....9 6
175² Greek Gold (IRE) **(60)***(35) (GPKelly)* 6-9-9 AlexGreaves(2) (b.hind: chsd ldrs: rdn 3f out: 6th & btn st)....1¼ 7
Doon Ridge **(53)***(12) (JJO'Neill)* 4-8-9 (5) JStack(11) (in tch over 5f: sn wknd: t.o)....9 8
103⁷ Miss Charlie **(43)***(—) (ABailey)* 5-8-6 JFanning(4) (a bhd: t.o)....3 9
*73** Scottish Park **(42)***(—) (RWEmery)* 6-8-5 GBardwell(7) (lost pl 4f out: t.o)....dist 10
LONG HANDICAP Tremolante 7-5

5/2 Mam'zelle Angot, **4/1** Suivez, **11/2** First Century (IRE) (7/2-13/2), **6/1** Scottish Park, **7/1** Greek Gold (IRE), **8/1** Ship of the Line, **12/1** DONIA (USA), **14/1** Miss Charlie, **16/1** Doon Ridge, **66/1** Tremolante, CSF £73.88 CT £202.83 TOTE £10.60: £3.40 £1.80 £1.50 (£101.20) OWNER Mr J. S. Gowling (MELTON MOWBRAY) BRED Petelain Stables 10 Rn
2m 3.6 (7.60) SF: 30/32/40/27/7/18/16/-/-/-
WEIGHT FOR AGE 4yo-2lb
OFFICIAL EXPLANATION Scottish Park: was found to be in a distressed condition after the race.

223
THRUSH CLAIMING STKS (Class F) £2,085.00 (£585.00: £285.00)
1m 6f 166y (Fibresand) GOING: 0.01 sec per fur (STD) 7-30 (7-30)

121⁵ **Royal Citizen (IRE) (64)***(67) (JFBottomley)* 6-9-4 TIves(6) (lw: hld up & bhd: hdwy 4f out: 2nd st: rdn to ld ins fnl f: r.o)....— 1
Lone Risk **(51)***(68) (MCPipe)* 4-9-1 DHarrison(3) (hld up: a.p: led 3f out: hrd rdn & hdd ins fnl f: kpt on nr fin)....½ 2
Acrow Line **(52)***(45) (DBurchell)* 10-8-12 StephenDavies(1) (led 11f: 3rd & rdn st: sn outpcd)....14 3
79² Brodessa **(59)***(44) (MrsMReveley)* 9-9-1 (7) GParkin(5) (hld up: hdwy 8f out: led over 3f out: sn hdd: 4th & btn ent st)....10 4
155¹⁰ Playing Tricks **(32)***(—) (PDEvans)* 4-7-10 JQuinn(2) (b: chsd ldr 8f: sn wknd: 5th & t.o ent st)....25 5
Noon Air *(—) (RHollinshead)* 4-8-12 MWigham(4) (leggy: lt-f: bit bkwd: s.s: lost tch ½-wy: 6th & t.o st)....dist 6
53² Crown Prosecutor *(—)*(Fav)*(WRMuir)* 5-9-8 JWeaver(7) (b: hld up in tch: p.u lame after 5f: destroyed).... 0

13/8 Crown Prosecutor, **3/1** Lone Risk, **4/1** Brodessa, **11/2** ROYAL CITIZEN (IRE), **10/1** Acrow Line, **20/1** Noon Air, **50/1** Playing Tricks, CSF £21.06 TOTE £6.50: £3.40 £2.00 (£12.40) OWNER Mr John Bottomley (MALTON) BRED Whitechurch Stud 7 Rn 3m 21.5 SF: 29/26/9/8/-/-/-
WEIGHT FOR AGE 4yo-6lb

224
STEWART MATTHEWS 21st H'CAP (0-70) (Class E) £2,788.00 (£844.00: £412.00: £196.00)
6f (Fibresand) GOING: 0.01 sec per fur (STD) 8-00 (8-00)

167⁴ **Chadwell Hall (41)***(49) (SRBowring)* 4-7-9b(7) CTeague(2) (chsd ldr: shkn up to ld 1f out: r.o wl)....— 1

177[4] Four of Spades **(66)***(71)*(Fav)*(WSCunningham)* 4-9-13b AClark(10) (lw: led: rdn & hdd 1f out: no ex nr fin) 1 **2**
129[3] Heathyards Lady (USA) **(51)***(46)*(Fav)*(RHollinshead)* 4-8-12 MWigham(8) (sme hdwy fnl 2f: nvr nrr) 4 **3**
191[7] Frisky Miss (IRE) **(67)***(61) (KOCunningham-Brown)* 4-10-0 JWeaver(6) (prom: rdn 2f out: r.o one pce) ....hd **4**
Fighter Squadron **(53)***(45) (REPeacock)* 6-9-0b GDuffield(7) (b.hind: bkwd: dwlt: bhd & outpcd tl r.o appr fnl f) ....½ **5**
167* Letsbeonestaboutit **(54)***(37) (MrsNMacauley)* 9-9-1 DeanMcKeown(4) (outpcd: a bhd) 3½ **6**
154[7] Samson-Agonistes **(67)***(49) (PDEvans)* 9-10-0v TIves(9) (b.off fore: chsd ldrs: rdn along ½-wy: wknd over 1f out) ....hd **7**
65[10] Arawa **(49)***(26) (DMarks)* 5-8-3 (7) MBaird(5) (swtg: outpcd) 2 **8**
Soba Guest (IRE) **(56)***(31) (RTJuckes)* 6-9-0 (3) EmmaO'Gorman(3) (b: b.nr hind: bkwd: in tch: drvn along ½-wy: sn lost pl) ....½ **9**
129* Beckyhannah **(38)***(12) (RBastiman)* 5-7-10b(3) DWright(1) (s.s: effrt ½-wy: wknd fnl 2f) ....hd **10**

3/1 Four of Spades, Heathyards Lady (USA), **9/2** CHADWELL HALL, **6/1** Beckyhannah, **10/1** Frisky Miss (IRE), Letsbeonestaboutit, **12/1** Samson-Agonistes, **20/1** Arawa, Fighter Squadron, **25/1** Soba Guest (IRE), CSF £18.14 CT £43.46 TOTE £7.70: £2.50 £1.60 £1.70 (£14.90) OWNER Mr D. H. Bowring (EDWINSTOWE) BRED J. C. and Mrs C. L. Owen 10 Rn
1m 15.9 (4.70) SF: 23/43/19/33/19/11/22/-/-/-

225

ROBIN MEDIAN AUCTION STKS (Mdn 3, 4, 5 & 6-Y.O) (Class D)
£3,023.90 (£915.20: £446.60: £212.30)
1m 100y (Fibresand) GOING: 0.01 sec per fur (STD) 8-30 (8-31)

Forgotten Empress (65)*(52)*(Fav)*(JLEyre)* 3-8-0 JFanning(2) (b.hind: hdwy over 6f out: 2nd st: led appr fnl f: sn clr) ....— **1**
149[4] Sand Star *(44) (DHaydnJones)* 3-8-0 AMackay(6) (led tl appr fnl f: one pce) 4 **2**
Dynamis (IRE) **(51)***(38) (KOCunningham-Brown)* 4-9-5 AClark(5) (hld up & bhd: hdwy 4f out: 3rd st: rdn & one pce appr fnl f) 3 **3**
80[9] Supercool **(43)***(42) (BAMcMahon)* 4-9-10 JWeaver(10) (prom: rdn & 4th st: sn btn) ....½ **4**
Bentham's About *(12) (DrJDScargill)* 3-8-5 DHarrison(7) (bit bkwd: prom 5f: outpcd & 5th st) 15 **5**
28[12] Charlotte Penny **(35)***(5) (NPLittmoden)* 4-9-0b(5) TGMcLaughlin(8) (lw: chsd ldrs over 4f: 6th & rdn ent st: sn btn) 1 **6**
171[9] Haya Ya Kefaah *(—) (SirMarkPrescott)* 3-8-5 GDuffield(3) (lw: bhd: effrt & drvn along 5f out: no imp: t.o) 15 **7**
156[11] Our Dorothy *(—) (CNWilliams)* 3-8-0 JQuinn(1) (b.nr hind: lost pl ½-wy: t.o) ....½ **8**
64[10] Crocodile Rock *(—) (MJHeaton-Ellis)* 3-8-5 StephenDavies(4) (bit bkwd: a rr div: t.o) ....nk **9**

1/2 FORGOTTEN EMPRESS, **5/1** Supercool, **9/1** Dynamis (IRE), **12/1** Sand Star, **16/1** Crocodile Rock, **20/1** Bentham's About, Haya Ya Kefaah, **40/1** Our Dorothy, Charlotte Penny, CSF £8.22 TOTE £1.60: £1.30 £1.90 £1.40 (£8.60) OWNER Mr R. Fenwick-Gibson (HAMBLETON) BRED Lord Bolton 9 Rn
1m 52.7 SF: 4/-/9/13/-/-/-/-/-
WEIGHT FOR AGE 3yo-19lb, 4yo-1lb

226

FINCH (S) STKS (Class G) £2,085.00 (£585.00: £285.00)
1m 100y (Fibresand) GOING: 0.01 sec per fur (STD) 9-00 (9-01)

152[4] **Off the Air (IRE) (49)***(59)*(Fav)*(ICampbell)* 4-9-8v DHarrison(3) (chsd ldrs: drvn along fr ½-wy: 3rd st: led wl ins fnl f: r.o) ....— **1**
117[6] Ivan the Terrible (IRE) **(50)***(58) (BEllison)* 7-9-9 TIves(6) (b: hld up: hdwy ½-wy: 2nd st: led over 1f out tl wl ins fnl f) ....¾ **2**
117[5] Sharp Gazelle **(47)***(50) (BSmart)* 5-8-11 (7) MDenaro(7) (lw: led over 5f out tl over 1f out: rdn & no ex nr fin) 1½ **3**
62[6] Main Brace **(41)***(39) (KRBurke)* 4-9-9 JQuinn(4) (sn wl bhd & outpcd: effrt & 4th st: no imp) 8 **4**
Saxon Heir (IRE) **(51)***(25) (MDIUsher)* 3-7-11 (7) CAdamson(5) (led 3f: wknd over 3f out: 5th & btn st) 7 **5**
142[8] Bonny Melody **(42)***(10) (PDEvans)* 4-9-4v AClark(2) (b.hind: a in rr: lost tch & 6th st: t.o) 5 **6**
Pinatubo **(43)***(—) (MCPipe)* 4-9-9 JWeaver(1) (bit bkwd: chsd ldrs over 4f: sn lost tch: t.o) ....dist **7**

7/4 OFF THE AIR (IRE), **11/4** Sharp Gazelle, **7/2** Pinatubo, **8/1** Ivan the Terrible (IRE), **14/1** Bonny Melody, **16/1** Saxon Heir (IRE), **20/1** Main Brace, CSF £14.57 TOTE £2.90: £1.50 £2.90 (£6.30) OWNER Mr John O'Malley (NEWMARKET) BRED Edward Doyle 7 Rn No bid
1m 53.9 SF: 14/13/7/-/-/-/-
WEIGHT FOR AGE 3yo-19lb, 4yo-1lb

227

A. JAEBAN BUDGET RENTACAR H'CAP (0-60) (Class F) £2,791.80 (£784.80: £383.40) **1m 4f (Fibresand)** GOING: 0.01 sec per fur (STD) 9-30 (9-30)

*104*3 **Awestruck (40)***(51) (BPreece)* 5-8-8 GDuffield(6) (hld up in tch: hdwy 4f out: 3rd st: rdn to ld ins fnl f: r.o strly)........— **1**
*161*2 Scalp 'em (IRE) **(51)***(61)*(Fav)*(PDEvans)* 7-9-5v AClark(12) (a.p: led over 2f out: hrd rdn & hdd ins fnl f: r.o)........¾ **2**
*131** Premier Dance **(60)***(68) (DHaydnJones)* 8-9-9 (5) SDrowne(4) (lw: chsd ldrs: 5th st: effrt appr fnl f: unable qckn nr fin)........2 **3**
*138*9 Genesis Four **(40)***(44) (SRBowring)* 5-8-1b(7) CTeague(8) (plld hrd: led after 2f tl over 2f out: 2nd & rdn st: r.o one pce)........3 **4**
*153*6 Sharp Sensation **(43)***(47) (DNicholls)* 5-8-11 AlexGreaves(10) (hld up: hdwy 5f out: 6th st: rdn & one pce appr fnl f)........hd **5**
Opera Buff (IRE) **(56)***(60) (MCPipe)* 4-9-6 DHarrison(9) (bit bkwd: dwlt: hdwy 7f out: 4th st: wknd appr fnl f)........hd **6**
Winn's Pride (IRE) **(55)***(56) (RHollinshead)* 4-9-5 TIves(2) (nvr nr to chal)........2½ **7**
Spring Loaded **(46)***(30) (JGMO'Shea)* 4-8-5 (5) JStack(11) (a in rr: t.o)........14 **8**
King's Shilling (USA) **(54)***(30) (HOliver)* 8-9-8 VSlattery(7) (bit bkwd: prom over 7f: sn wknd: t.o)........6 **9**
Dormston Boyo **(32)***(8) (KWhite)* 5-8-0 JQuinn(3) (bit bkwd: chsd ldrs to ½-wy: sn rdn & wknd: t.o)........s.h **10**
*108*2 Child Star (FR) **(39)***(5) (DMarks)* 6-8-0 (7) MBaird(1) (a bhd: t.o)........8 **11**
*75*5 Mighty Kingdom (IRE) **(33)***(—) (RWEmery)* 4-7-11 GBardwell(5) (led 2f: wknd over 5f out: t.o)........13 **12**

5/2 Scalp 'em (IRE), **11/4** Premier Dance, **5/1** Opera Buff (IRE), **7/1** Child Star (FR) (5/1-8/1), **10/1** AWESTRUCK, **12/1** King's Shilling (USA), **16/1** Spring Loaded, Winn's Pride (IRE), Genesis Four, **20/1** Sharp Sensation, **25/1** Dormston Boyo, **33/1** Mighty Kingdom (IRE), CSF £36.28 CT £85.93 TOTE £9.90: £2.20 £1.10 £1.70 (£12.10) OWNER Mr D. Portman (TELFORD) BRED Cheveley Park Stud Ltd 12 Rn 2m 42.7 (11.70) SF: 17/27/32/10/13/21/17/-/-/-/-/-
WEIGHT FOR AGE 4yo-4lb
T/Plpt: £62.40 (221.37 Tckts). T/Qdpt: £3.40 (64.3 Tckts). IM

0210-SOUTHWELL (L-H)
Monday February 6th (Standard)

228

ABBEY BUSINESS DEVELOPMENT H'CAP (I) (0-60) (Class F) £2,738.60 (£769.60: £375.80) **7f (Fibresand)** GOING minus 0.09 sec (STD) 1-30 (1-31)

*129*10 **Aquado (30)***(41) (ALForbes)* 6-8-0 JQuinn(10) (hld up: stdy hdwy ent st: chal 1f out: styd on to ld nr fin)........— **1**
*199*2 At the Savoy (IRE) **(37)***(47)*(Fav)*(TDBarron)* 4-8-7 DeanMcKeown(6) (lw: cl up: led over 2f out: hdd & no ex nr fin)........hd **2**
*148*4 Bogart **(58)***(51) (CWFairhurst)* 4-10-0 RCochrane(7) (lw: trckd ldrs: effrt 2f out: r.o one pce)........8 **3**
*167*9 Cheerful Groom (IRE) **(44)***(30) (JMackie)* 4-9-0 MFenton(4) (lw: hld up: effrt 3f out: styd on: nvr rchd ldrs)........3½ **4**
*130*6 Educated Pet **(56)***(39) (BPreece)* 6-9-12v JWeaver(9) (sn chsng ldrs: rdn over 2f out: grad wknd)........1½ **5**
*148*6 Meeson Times **(50)***(31) (RBastiman)* 7-9-1e(5) HBastiman(8) (eyeshield: cl up tl wknd over 2f out)........¾ **6**
*169*2 Spanish Stripper (USA) **(49)***(19) (MCChapman)* 4-9-2 (3) DRMcCabe(3) (rdn to ld after 1f tl over 2f out: sn btn)........5 **7**
*28*8 Miss Tipsy **(34)***(—) (WWHaigh)* 4-8-4b DaleGibson(5) (nvr wnt pce)........10 **8**
Grey Kingdom **(46)***(—) (MBrittain)* 4-9-2 GBardwell(1) (led 1f: drvn along & wknd 4f out)........3½ **9**

7/4 At the Savoy (IRE), **7/2** Bogart, **13/2** Cheerful Groom (IRE), Spanish Stripper (USA), **10/1** Meeson Times, **12/1** Educated Pet, **16/1** Grey Kingdom, **20/1** Miss Tipsy, AQUADO, CSF £53.19 CT £142.19 TOTE £34.70: £5.00 £1.10 £1.50 (£24.20) OWNER Mr K. Nicholls (UTTOXETER) BRED Lord Howard de Walden 9 Rn 1m 31.7 (4.90) SF: 22/29/30/9/16/9/-/-/-

229 AMAZON H'CAP (0-70) (Class E) £3,081.10 (£932.80: £455.40: £216.70)
1m 3f (Fibresand) GOING minus 0.09 sec per fur (STD) 2-00 (2-00)

Ashover (60)*(66) (TDBarron)* 5-8-13 (7) KimberleyHart(4) (a.p: led over 2f out: r.o)......— 1
Mr Towser **(70)***(74) (WWHaigh)* 4-9-13 DaleGibson(3) (a cl up: led over 2f out: sn hdd: kpt on)......1½ 2
*137*3 Imperial Bid (FR) **(55)***(52) (DenysSmith)* 7-9-1 JWeaver(2) (lw: trckd ldrs: chal 3f out: n.m.r over 2f out: r.o one pce)......5 3
In a Moment (USA) **(62)***(57) (TDBarron)* 4-9-5 DeanMcKeown(6) (outpcd appr st: styd on fnl f: n.d)......1½ 4
*215** Palacegate Jo (IRE) **(60)***(48)*(Fav)*(RHollinshead)* 4-9-3 5x LDettori(7) (lw: led tl over 2f out: sn btn)......5 5
Missus Murhill (IRE) **(60)***(30) (NTinkler)* 4-9-3 KimTinkler(1) (bhd: hdwy 4f out: sn wknd)......13 6
Jonbel **(35)***(—) (TTClement)* 7-7-9 ow2 JQuinn(5) (cl up tl outpcd 5f out: sn bhd)...25 7
LONG HANDICAP Jonbel 7-4

1/2 Palacegate Jo (IRE), **100/30** Imperial Bid (FR), **17/2** Mr Towser, **14/1** ASHOVER, **16/1** In a Moment (USA), **20/1** Missus Murhill (IRE), **66/1** Jonbel, CSF £108.90 TOTE £20.90: £4.20 £3.60 (£54.40) OWNER Mr Thomas Cox (THIRSK) BRED Bridge End Bloodstock 7 Rn
2m 29.6 (8.10) SF: 40/45/27/28/20/2/-
WEIGHT FOR AGE 4yo-3lb

230 ORINOCO H'CAP (0-80) (Class D) £3,589.30 (£1,086.40: £530.20: £252.10)
1m (Fibresand) GOING minus 0.09 sec per fur (STD) 2-30 (2-30)

*138*4 **Roar on Tour (55)***(61)*(Fav)*(MrsMReveley)* 6-8-10 RCochrane(5) (lw: trckd ldr: led over 3f out: r.o)......— 1
*80*4 Cicerone **(48)***(48) (JLHarris)* 5-8-3 GDuffield(4) (b: prom: hdwy to chse wnr over 2f out: rdn & nt qckn)......3 2
*117*9 Major Mouse **(55)***(50) (WWHaigh)* 7-8-10 DaleGibson(2) (lw: chsd ldrs: effrt 3f out: rdn & r.o one pce)......2½ 3
*150*3 Dream Carrier (IRE) **(73)***(68) (JGMO'Shea)* 7-9-9 (5) JStack(1) (hdwy ½-wy: outpcd ent st: n.d after)......hd 4
*55*11 Faez **(60)***(33) (PSFelgate)* 5-9-1 TIves(3) (led tl over 3f out: sn btn)......11 5

6/4 ROAR ON TOUR, **11/4** Cicerone, **7/2** Dream Carrier (IRE), **17/2** Major Mouse, **10/1** Faez, CSF £5.55 TOTE £2.20: £1.60 £1.70 (£2.10) OWNER Mrs S. D. Murray (SALTBURN) BRED Pitts Farm Stud 5 Rn
1m 45.7 (6.40) SF: 24/12/14/29/-

231 ABBEY BUSINESS DEVELOPMENT H'CAP (II) (0-60) (Class F) £2,738.60 (£769.60: £375.80) **7f (Fibresand)** GOING minus 0.09 sec (STD) 3-00 (3-02)

*130*2 **Quinzii Martin (52)***(64) (DHaydnJones)* 7-9-8 TWilliams(8) (a.p: led appr fnl f: drvn out)......— 1
*94*9 Tilly Owl **(36)***(47) (JAHarris)* 4-8-6 JO'Reilly(9) (cl up: led over 2f out tl over 1f out: rallied nr fin)......nk 2
*181*3 Matthew David **(46)***(44) (SRBowring)* 5-9-2 JQuinn(7) (cl up: led 3f out: sn hdd & one pce)......6 3
*50*2 Certain Way (IRE) **(54)***(51) (NPLittmoden)* 5-9-5 (5) TGMcLaughlin(2) (in tch: rdn 3f out: styd on one pce)......nk 4
*78*14 Wellsy Lad (USA) **(35)***(31) (DWChapman)* 8-7-12b(7)ow1 CTeague(6) (racd wd: chsd ldrs tl outpcd fnl 2f)......½ 5
Achilles Heel **(45)***(33)*(Fav)*(CNAllen)* 4-9-1 EGuest(1) (bhd: effrt over 2f out: rdn & no imp)......4 6
*134*5 The Real Whizzbang (IRE) **(38)***(19) (PSFelgate)* 4-8-3 (5) PMcCabe(3) (outpcd & bhd ½-wy: n.d)......3½ 7
Tyrone Flyer **(57)***(30) (PMMcEntee)* 6-9-13 StephenDavies(4) (b: bit bkwd: led tl hdd & wknd 3f out)......4 8
*179*3 Fletcher's Bounty (IRE) **(49)***(15) (WSCunningham)* 6-9-5 AClark(5) (hdwy & prom after 2f: wknd over 2f out)......3½ 9

9/4 Achilles Heel, **9/2** QUINZII MARTIN, **5/1** Tilly Owl (4/1-6/1), **8/1** Certain Way (IRE), Matthew David, Fletcher's Bounty (IRE), **17/2** The Real Whizzbang (IRE) (12/1-8/1), **9/1** Tyrone Flyer (7/1-12/1), **33/1** Wellsy Lad (USA), CSF £26.75 CT £162.70 TOTE £4.70: £1.60 £1.60 £1.80 (£18.00) OWNER Monolithic Refractories Ltd (PONTYPRIDD) BRED Lord Fairhaven 9 Rn
1m 31.6 (4.80) SF: 44/29/24/31/12/13/-/-/-

232

MISSOURI MEDIAN AUCTION STKS (Mdn 3-Y.O) (Class E)
£3,052.50 (£924.00: £451.00: £214.50)
6f (Fibresand) GOING minus 0.09 sec per fur (STD) 3-30 (3-31)

Montague Dawson (IRE) *(59) (MrsNMacauley)* 3-8-9 (5) SDrowne(4) (a.p: led over 1f out: styd on) ....— 1
85[4] Always Grace **(54)***(50) (MissGayKelleway)* 3-8-9 JWeaver(2) (a.p: ev ch over 1f out: styd on one pce) 1¼ 2
124[3] Merrie le Bow **(53)***(48) (PMitchell)* 3-8-9 JMcLaughlin(7) (bhd: hdwy 2f out: styd on wl nr fin) ....½ 3
149[2] Jalmaid **(50)***(45)*(Fav)*(BAMcMahon)* 3-8-4 (5) SSanders(8) (a chsng ldrs: nt qckn appr fnl f) ....¾ 4
210[4] Pursuance (IRE) **(56)***(47) (JBalding)* 3-8-7v(7) JEdmunds(3) (led: clr ½-wy: hdd over 1f out: wknd) 1 5
Ladybower (IRE) *(12) (LordHuntingdon)* 3-8-9 DHarrison(6) (small: neat: bit bkwd: sn outpcd & bhd) 12 6
Paronomasia *(12) (MBell)* 3-9-0 MFenton(1) (w'like: lw: sn outpcd & bhd) 1¾ 7
197[8] Captain Sinbad *(—) (KSBridgwater)* 3-9-0 NAdams(5) (chsd ldrs to ½-wy: sn wknd) 6 8

11/4 Jalmaid, **7/2** Always Grace, Paronomasia, **6/1** Merrie le Bow, Ladybower (IRE), **7/1** Pursuance (IRE), **20/1** MONTAGUE DAWSON (IRE), **33/1** Captain Sinbad, CSF £85.35 TOTE £37.90: £5.60 £1.70 £2.10 (£60.10) OWNER Mrs N. Macauley (MELTON MOWBRAY) BRED Christopher Flynn in Ireland 8 Rn 1m 19.0 (5.50) SF: 18/11/10/8/10/-/-/-

233

RIO GRANDE (S) STKS (Class G) £2,259.00 (£634.00: £309.00)
6f (Fibresand) GOING minus 0.09 sec per fur (STD) 4-00 (4-03)

182[5] **Bella Parkes (67)***(63) (DNicholls)* 4-9-5b AlexGreaves(6) (lw: hld up & bhd: hdwy over 2f out: qcknd to ld ins fnl f) ....— 1
182[2] Sea Devil **(67)***(62) (MJCamacho)* 9-9-10 LCharnock(16) (sn chsng ldrs: disp ld over 2f out: hdd & no ex ins fnl f) 2½ 2
182[3] Bold Aristocrat (IRE) **(38)***(61) (RHollinshead)* 4-9-5 (5) AGarth(9) (bhd & hmpd ent st: hdwy over 1f out: r.o wl nr fin) ....hd 3
140[3] Sense of Priority **(53)***(61) (MHEasterby)* 6-9-10 WWoods(15) (hdwy over 2f out: ch appr fnl f: styd on one pce) ....s.h 4
140* Jamaica Bridge **(60)***(60)*(Fav)*(SGNorton)* 5-9-9 (5) JStack(8) (lw: cl up: disp ld over 2f out tl wknd appr fnl f) 1¾ 5
165[4] Brisas **(42)***(50) (CWFairhurst)* 8-9-10 JFanning(4) (led tl hdd & wknd ins fnl f) 2½ 6
165[2] Swinging Tich **(45)***(41) (BAMcMahon)* 6-9-0 (5) SSanders(11) (nvr rchd ldrs) 1¼ 7
93[11] Green's Bid **(59)***(41) (DWChapman)* 5-9-7 (3) OPears(3) (hld up: hdwy on ins ent st: no imp) 1¾ 8
140[5] Grey Toppa **(50)***(32) (MrsJRRamsden)* 4-9-5 JWeaver(7) (hmpd after 1f: n.d after) 1¼ 9
Life's a Breeze **(49)***(35) (PSFelgate)* 6-9-5 (5) PMcCabe(10) (lw: nvr trbld ldrs) ....½ 10
187[7] Victoria Hall **(51)***(25) (WGMTurner)* 5-9-5v GDuffield(12) (n.d) 2 11
Dundeelin **(48)***(19) (JLEyre)* 4-9-5v TIves(1) (w ldrs over 3f: sn wknd) 2½ 12
165[6] Arc Lamp **(51)***(23) (JAGlover)* 9-9-10 SWilliams(5) (chsd ldrs to st: sn wknd) ....nk 13
Mockingbird **(35)***(12) (BPreece)* 4-9-5 TWall(2) (lw: prom to st) 2½ 14
182[9] Bessie's Will **(37)***(—) (DHaydnJones)* 4-9-5v AMackay(14) (hmpd after s: n.d) 15 15
Northgate Raver *(—) (RonaldThompson)* 4-9-5 MFenton(13) (rn v.wd & t.o fr ½-wy) 25 16

7/4 Jamaica Bridge, **11/2** Sea Devil, **6/1** BELLA PARKES, **12/1** Grey Toppa, Sense of Priority, Swinging Tich, **14/1** Victoria Hall, **16/1** Green's Bid, Bold Aristocrat (IRE), Brisas, **20/1** Life's a Breeze, Arc Lamp, **25/1** Dundeelin, Mockingbird, **33/1** Bessie's Will, Northgate Raver, CSF £40.37 TOTE £5.20: £2.30 £1.70 £7.30 (£12.50) OWNER Mr J. Barton (THIRSK) 16 Rn
1m 18.3 (4.80) SF: 31/30/29/29/30/19/12/-/-/-/-/-/-/-/-/-
Bt in 4,400 gns

234

NILE H'CAP (Amateurs) (0-60) (Class F) £2,537.00 (£712.00: £347.00)
2m (Fibresand) GOING minus 0.09 sec per fur (STD) 4-30 (4-32)

Flashman (30)*(39) (BJLlewellyn)* 5-10-1 MrJLLlewellyn(6) (hdwy ½-wy: sn trckng ldrs: qcknd to ld wl ins fnl f) ....— 1
45[6] Castle Secret **(50)***(58) (DBurchell)* 9-11-0 (7) MissEJJones(7) (cl up: chal 7f out: styd on fnl f) 1¼ 2

166[2] Borocay **(38)***(44)*(Fav)*(MJCamacho)* 7-10-9 MrsLPearce(9) (hld up: smooth hdwy ½-wy: ev ch over 1f out: nt qckn)....2 **3**
Desert President **(34)***(38) (RPCHoad)* 4-9-6 (7) MissLMcIntosh(8) (cl up: led 7f out tl hdd & no ex wl ins fnl f)....2 **4**
Alternation (FR) **(43)***(42) (JWebber)* 6-10-7 (7) MrPScott(11) (cl up: led 9f out to 7f out: one pce fnl 3f)....5 **5**
172[4] Goldenberry **(36)***(29) (JParkes)* 4-9-12 (3)ow1 MrIMcLelland(3) (hld up & bhd: hdwy ½-wy: one pce fnl 3f)....6 **6**
200[6] Written Agreement **(30)***(2) (REPeacock)* 7-9-8v(7)ow15 MrsCPeacock(2) (led 7f: sn outpcd & lost pl: styd on nr fin)....15 **7**
Kausar (USA) **(35)***(7) (JLEyre)* 8-10-6 MissDianaJones(5) (b: n.d)....nk **8**
Gunmaker **(35)***(5) (BJLlewellyn)* 6-10-3 (3) MrsBethWilliams(12) (racd wd: prom to ½-wy)....2½ **9**
87[7] King William **(39)***(6) (JLSpearing)* 10-10-7 (3) MissTSpearing(13) (hld up & bhd: hdwy ½-wy: rdn & no imp fnl 3f)....3 **10**
108[10] Flass Vale **(40)***(26) (CWFairhurst)* 7-10-8v(3) MrsSBosley(14) (lw: prom tl outpcd 6f out: n.d after)....7 **11**
Baybeejay **(31)***(—) (RBrotherton)* 8-9-9 (7) MissVHill(4) (cl up to ½-wy: sn bhd)....10 **12**
Comaneci (IRE) **(34)***(—) (KSBridgwater)* 7-10-5 MrDParker(15) (prom tl wknd appr st)....1¼ **13**
Kismetim **(46)***(2) (FJordan)* 5-11-0 (3) MrLSquire(10) (hdwy ½-wy: rdn & wknd over 2f out)....1 **14**
Asaaf (USA) **(37)***(—) (NPLittmoden)* 12-10-1 (7) MrMSalaman(1) (b: sn bhd: t.o).dist **15**

LONG HANDICAP Written Agreement 8-12

5/4 Borocay, **8/1** Castle Secret, **10/1** Kismetim, **12/1** FLASHMAN, Kausar (USA), King William, **14/1** Goldenberry, Gunmaker, Desert President, **16/1** Alternation (FR), **20/1** Written Agreement, Comaneci (IRE), **25/1** Baybeejay, Flass Vale, **33/1** Asaaf (USA), CSF £104.45 CT £191.77 TOTE £14.80: £4.60 £3.20 £1.10 (£36.40) OWNER Mr Colin Simpson (BARGOED) BRED P. Asquith 15 Rn 3m 52.2 (26.20) SF: -/1/-/-/-/-/-/-/-/-/-/-/-/-/-

WEIGHT FOR AGE 4yo-6lb

T/Plpt: £470.40 (23.3 Tckts). T/Qdpt: £10.50 (6.75 Tckts). AA

0216-LINGFIELD (L-H)
Tuesday February 7th (Standard)

235
PLUM CLAIMING STKS (Class E) £3,095.40 (£937.20: £457.60: £217.80)
1m 2f (Equitrack) GOING minus 0.43 sec per fur (FST) 1-50 (1-51)

187[2] **Masnun (USA) (66)***(62)*(Fav)*(RJO'Sullivan)* 10-8-4 AClark(10) (stdy hdwy over 4f out: hrd rdn over 1f out: led wl ins fnl f: r.o wl)....— **1**
143* Prince Danzig (IRE) **(76)***(73) (DJGMurraySmith)* 4-9-0 JWeaver(1) (led over 7f: led over 1f out tl wl ins fnl f: r.o)....½ **2**
175* Medland (IRE) **(53)***(55) (WGMTurner)* 5-8-1 ow1 DHarrison(2) (lw: a.p: led over 2f out tl over 1f out: unable qckn ins fnl f)....1¾ **3**
158[8] Barahin (IRE) **(44)***(42) (MDixon)* 6-8-0 AMackay(8) (rdn thrght: hdwy 6f out: wknd over 2f out)....8 **4**
203[8] Hillsdown Boy (IRE) **(58)***(42) (SDow)* 5-8-3 (5) SSanders(3) (lw: a.p: rdn over 4f out: wknd over 2f out)....5 **5**
120[7] Greek Night Out (IRE) **(40)***(30) (JAHarris)* 4-7-4 (5) NVarley(11) (b.nr hind: nvr nr to chal)....¾ **6**
119[5] Bandita **(40)***(32) (MissAJWhitfield)* 4-7-9 (3)ow3 DWright(4) (lw: prom 5f)....¾ **7**
Call Me Blue **(53)***(38) (TJNaughton)* 5-8-5 (5) VHalliday(5) (lw: s.s: a bhd)....2½ **8**
182[11] Darakah **(60)***(9) (CJHill)* 8-8-1 JQuinn(6) (lw: a bhd)....13 **9**
Prairie Grove **(52)***(14) (JSKing)* 5-8-6b GBardwell(7) (bhd fnl 5f)....s.h **10**
73[5] Give In **(37)***(—) (MissGayKelleway)* 8-8-2bow2 GDuffield(9) (prom over 5f)....9 **11**

2/1 MASNUN (USA), **5/2** Prince Danzig (IRE), **4/1** Medland (IRE), **8/1** Hillsdown Boy (IRE), **16/1** Give In, **20/1** Call Me Blue, Greek Night Out (IRE), **25/1** Barahin (IRE), Darakah, **33/1** Bandita, Prairie Grove, CSF £7.42 TOTE £2.70: £1.10 £1.30 £1.70 (£3.50) OWNER Mr I. W. Page (BOGNOR REGIS) BRED Glencrest Farm 11 Rn 2m 6.38 (3.38) SF: 27/36/22/9/9/-/-/5/-/-/-

WEIGHT FOR AGE 4yo-2lb

Medland (IRE) clmd S Olley £3,000

236
DAMSON (S) STKS (3-Y.O) (Class G) £2,393.40 (£672.40: £328.20)
6f (Equitrack) GOING minus 0.43 sec per fur (FST) 2-20 (2-20)

105[7] **Robo Magic (USA) (64)***(73) (AMoore)* 3-9-5 RCochrane(4) (b.hind: w ldr: led over 3f out: clr over 1f out: r.o wl)....— **1**

173² Baileys Sunset (IRE) **(68)**_(60)_(Fav)_(MJohnston)_ 3-9-5 TWilliams(2) (hld up: rdn over 3f out: chsd wnr over 1f out: no imp) 5 **2**
197³ Nadwaty (IRE) **(57)**_(39) (JDBethell)_ 3-8-7 JWeaver(6) (led over 2f: rdn over 2f out: wknd over 1f out) 3½ **3**
90⁷ Havana Miss **(40)**_(38) (BPalling)_ 3-9-0 GDuffield(5) (b: hld up: rdn over 4f out: wknd over 2f out) 3 **4**
173⁶ Derry Queen **(42)**_(27) (PDCundell)_ 3-8-7 JQuinn(1) (a bhd) 1½ **5**
98⁶ Griffin's Girl **(37)**_(17) (RPCHoad)_ 3-8-7 AMackay(3) (lw: a bhd) 4 **6**

6/4 Baileys Sunset (IRE), **2/1** Nadwaty (IRE), **9/4** ROBO MAGIC (USA), **14/1** Havana Miss, **33/1** Derry Queen, Griffin's Girl, CSF £6.10 TOTE £2.90: £1.10 £1.90 (£4.30) OWNER Mr C. F. Sparrowhawk (BRIGHTON) BRED Curtis C. Green 6 Rn 1m 12.89 (2.29) SF: 35/21/2/-/-/-
Bt in 4,000 gns

237

LINGFIELD PARK AWT SPRINT SERIES H'CAP (Qualifier) (0-75) (Class D) £3,723.50 (£1,127.00: £550.00: £261.50)
6f (Equitrack) GOING minus 0.43 sec per fur (FST) 2-50 (2-51)

188⁵ **Sir Tasker (67)**_(69) (JLHarris)_ 7-9-3 (5) SSanders(9) (a.p: hrd rdn & led 1f out: r.o wl) ....— **1**
23⁴ Waverley Star **(40)**_(41) (KOCunningham-Brown)_ 10-7-9 ow2 LCharnock(4) (rdn over 4f out: hdwy over 2f out: hrd rdn over 1f out: r.o wl ins fnl f) ....nk **2**
177⁵ Apollo Red **(52)**_(49) (AMoore)_ 6-8-7 CandyMorris(5) (b.hind: hld up: rdn over 2f out: r.o one pce) 1¼ **3**
192* Crystal Heights (FR) **(62)**_(55)_(Fav)_(RJO'Sullivan)_ 7-8-12 (5) 7x SMulvey(2) (b: s.s: hdwy over 1f out: r.o wl ins fnl f) 1½ **4**
177* Nordico Princess **(69)**_(62) (GROldroyd)_ 4-9-10 RCochrane(3) (led 5f) ....s.h **5**
154⁹ Pageboy **(69)**_(58) (PCHaslam)_ 6-9-10 JWeaver(6) (w ldr over 3f: eased whn btn fnl f) 1½ **6**
220⁹ Gingerillo **(38)**_(17) (TGMills)_ 4-7-7hb GBardwell(7) (b.nr hind: lw: hld up: rdn over 4f out: wknd over 3f out) 4 **7**
146⁴ Nomadic Dancer (IRE) **(56)**_(30) (MSSaunders)_ 3-7-4 (5) NVarley(1) (bhd fnl 5f) 1¾ **8**
188² Distant Dynasty **(55)**_(24) (BAPearce)_ 5-8-10 StephenDavies(8) (b.nr hind: spd 3f) 2 **9**

LONG HANDICAP Gingerillo 7-1 Waverley Star 7-3

11/4 Crystal Heights (FR), **7/2** Pageboy, **5/1** Nordico Princess (7/2-11/2), **11/2** Distant Dynasty, **7/1** Apollo Red, **9/1** Nomadic Dancer (IRE), **20/1** Waverley Star, SIR TASKER, **25/1** Gingerillo, CSF £281.40 CT £2,756.82 TOTE £18.70: £4.40 £11.40 £2.30 (£55.10) OWNER Mr J.F. Coupland (MELTON MOWBRAY) BRED W. H. Joyce 9 Rn 1m 12.4 (1.80) SF: 44/19/28/32/39/34/-/-/-
WEIGHT FOR AGE 3yo-16lb

238

CHERRY H'CAP (0-70) (Class E) £2,952.40 (£893.20: £435.60: £206.80)
1m 4f (Equitrack) GOING minus 0.43 sec per fur (FST) 3-20 (3-22)

Majal (IRE) (52)_(60) (JSWainwright)_ 6-9-3 DeanMcKeown(7) (hdwy over 5f out: rdn over 2f out: qcknd & led ins fnl f: r.o wl) ....— **1**
221* Head Turner **(52)**_(58)_(Fav)_(CPWildman)_ 7-9-3 5x NAdams(2) (lw: hdwy over 5f out: led over 1f out tl ins fnl f: unable qckn) 1¾ **2**
127⁶ Pearly River **(55)**_(60) (DrJDScargill)_ 4-9-2 MRimmer(5) (a.p: ev ch ins fnl f: one pce) ....nk **3**
178² In the Money (IRE) **(59)**_(60) (RHollinshead)_ 6-9-10 TIves(4) (led over 10f) 3 **4**
La Menorquina (USA) **(33)**_(29) (DMarks)_ 5-7-7 (5) MBaird(3) (rdn 7f out: nvr nr to chal) 4 **5**
1⁹ Haroldon (IRE) **(57)**_(28) (BPalling)_ 6-9-8 StephenDavies(1) (b: lw: w ldr over 8f) ...20 **6**
179⁸ La Belle Shyanne **(41)**_(—) (CJHill)_ 4-8-2 JQuinn(6) (a bhd: t.o) 25 **7**

10/11 Head Turner, **4/1** In the Money (IRE), **13/2** MAJAL (IRE), **7/1** La Menorquina (USA), **14/1** La Belle Shyanne, **25/1** Pearly River, Haroldon (IRE), CSF £12.33 TOTE £11.20: £2.60 £1.10 (£4.60) OWNER Mrs P. Wake (MALTON) BRED Lodge Park Stud 7 Rn
2m 33.86 (4.46) SF: 37/36/35/38/9/7/-
WEIGHT FOR AGE 4yo-4lb

239

NECTARINE STKS (Mdn) (Class D) £3,555.50 (£1,076.00: £525.00: £249.50)
7f (Equitrack) GOING minus 0.43 sec per fur (FST) 3-50 (3-52)

Wild Rice _(63++)_(Fav)_(GWragg)_ 3-8-6 WWoods(1) (b: w'like: bkwd: mde all: clr over 1f out: comf) ....— **1**

149[3] Nuthatch (IRE) *(51) (MDIUsher)* 3-7-8 (7) CAdamson(2) (chsd wnr: rdn 2f out: no imp)....3½ **2**
62[8] Breckland (IRE) **(37)***(43) (KOCunningham-Brown)* 5-9-10b LCharnock(3) (hdwy over 4f out: wknd wl over 1f out)....6 **3**
Considerable Charm *(23) (LordHuntingdon)* 3-8-1 DHarrison(8) (neat: hdwy over 3f out: wknd 2f out)....7 **4**
72[9] Dingo Warrior *(26) (JFfitch-Heyes)* 3-8-6 SWhitworth(4) (lw: hld up: rdn over 4f out: wknd over 2f out)....¾ **5**
Ever Friends *(23) (BJMcMath)* 3-8-6 AMackay(6) (unf: lw: hld up: rdn over 4f out: wknd over 2f out: bhd whn hmpd over 1f out)....1¼ **6**
Balrath Cross (IRE) *(—) (RPCHoad)* 4-9-10b NAdams(7) (bhd whn reluctant to r 5f out: t.o fnl 4f)....dist **7**

10/11 WILD RICE, **3/1** Ever Friends, **7/2** Considerable Charm, **8/1** Nuthatch (IRE) (7/1-14/1), **25/1** Breckland (IRE), **66/1** Dingo Warrior, Balrath Cross (IRE), CSF £8.76 TOTE £3.10: £1.10 £2.20 (£7.20) OWNER Sir Philip Oppenheimer (NEWMARKET) BRED Hascombe and Valiant Studs 7 Rn
1m 26.83 (3.83) SF: 10/-/6/-/-/-/-
WEIGHT FOR AGE 3yo-18lb

240

PEACH H'CAP (Amateurs) (0-70) (Class E) £3,038.20 (£919.60: £448.80: £213.40) **1m (Equitrack)** GOING minus 0.43 sec per fur (FST) 4-20 (4-22)

108[7] **Mentalasanythin (65)***(80) (ABailey)* 6-11-9 (5) MissBridgetGatehouse(9) (a.p: led over 3f out: sn clr: unchal)....— **1**
Bold Habit **(54)***(53) (JPearce)* 10-11-3 MrsLPearce(7) (b: bit bkwd: stdd s: hdwy over 2f out: chsd wnr over 1f out: no imp)....8 **2**
217[3] Rockstine (IRE) **(57)***(52)*(Fav)*(PMitchell)* 4-11-5 MrRTeal(10) (dwlt: hdwy over 3f out: one pce fnl 2f)....1½ **3**
177[10] Glowing Account (IRE) **(58)***(43) (JWMullins)* 4-11-6 MrTMcCarthy(1) (led over 4f)..5 **4**
171[6] Gigfy **(53)***(31) (BJLlewellyn)* 3-9-8b(3) MrsBethWilliams(4) (chsd ldr over 4f)....4 **5**
Remember This (IRE) **(41)***(19) (CACyzer)* 5-9-13 (5) MissAWilcox(3) (dropped rr 5f out: nvr nr to chal)....hd **6**
149[5] Lady Valensina (IRE) **(53)***(25) (BJLlewellyn)* 4-11-1 MrJLLlewellyn(8) (lw: sme hdwy over 4f out: wknd over 3f out)....2½ **7**
177[11] Cranfield Cracker **(40)***(—) (DWPArbuthnot)* 4-10-2 MrsDArbuthnot(5) (b: bhd fnl 3f)....6 **8**
142[10] Kelly's Kite **(30)***(—) (HJCollingridge)* 7-9-4 (3) MrPClose(2) (b: dwlt: bhd fnl 4f)....2½ **9**
203[6] Pair of Jacks (IRE) **(36)***(—) (DAWilson)* 5-9-13 MissElaineBronson(6) (veterinary advice).... **W**
LONG HANDICAP Kelly's Kite 8-11

6/4 Rockstine (IRE), **7/2** MENTALASANYTHIN, Bold Habit, **10/1** Lady Valensina (IRE), **12/1** Gigfy, Glowing Account (IRE), **14/1** Pair of Jacks (IRE), **20/1** Remember This (IRE), **33/1** Cranfield Cracker, Kelly's Kite, CSF £15.81 CT £22.82 TOTE £7.60: £3.60 £1.10 £1.10 (£6.00) OWNER Mrs M. O'Donnell (TARPORLEY) BRED R. B. Warren 9 Rn
1m 40.31 (3.91) SF: 62/36/35/26/-/4/8/-/-/-
WEIGHT FOR AGE 3yo-19lb, 4yo-1lb
T/Plpt: £102.60 (116.3 Tckts). T/Qdpt: Not won; £16.60 to Ascot 8/2/95. AK

0222-WOLVERHAMPTON (L-H)
Wednesday February 8th (Standard)

241

WELLAND CLAIMING STKS (3-Y.O) (Class F) £2,537.00 (£712.00: £347.00) **1m 1f 79y (Fibresand)** GOING: 0.06 sec per fur (STD) 2-10 (2-11)

176[3] **Soldier's Leap (FR) (66)***(85) (CEBrittain)* 3-9-5v RCochrane(1) (lw: mde all: rdn clr over 2f out: unchal)....— **1**
5* Durgams First (IRE) **(66)***(71)*(Fav)*(MrsMReveley)* 3-8-8 (7) GParkin(8) (lw: hdwy 5f out: 3rd st: sn rdn & chsng wnr: no imp)....6 **2**
90[6] Recovery Lad (IRE) *(59) (KRBurke)* 3-8-2 (3) DRMcCabe(9) (plld hrd: prom tl 4th & outpcd st: kpt on again fnl f)....1½ **3**
185* Poly Lane **(51)***(55)*(Fav)*(WRMuir)* 3-8-3b DHarrison(2) (chsd wnr: 2nd st: wknd fnl f)....1¼ **4**
180[5] Fools of Pride (IRE) **(51)***(51) (RHollinshead)* 3-7-9 (5) AGarth(6) (bhd tl hdwy 4f out: 6th st: kpt on fnl f)....¾ **5**
141[3] Poly Road **(50)***(17) (MRChannon)* 3-8-2 CRutter(4) (in tch: effrt & 5th st: sn btn)...20 **6**
32[8] Qualitair Ridge **(47)***(7) (JFBottomley)* 3-8-2v JQuinn(5) (rdn over 4f out: a bhd)....6 **7**

144[9] Red Owa Lady (IRE) **(37)***(—) (CJHill)* 3-7-10 GBardwell(7) (sn rdn along: a bhd)...7 **8**
116[5] Tonka **(45)***(—) (DJGMurraySmith)* 3-8-3v AMackay(3) (prom over 4f: sn wknd)......1 **9**
5/2 Poly Lane, Durgams First (IRE), **4/1** SOLDIER'S LEAP (FR), **11/2** Poly Road, **10/1** Tonka, Qualitair Ridge, **14/1** Fools of Pride (IRE), **20/1** Recovery Lad (IRE), **33/1** Red Owa Lady (IRE), CSF £14.91 TOTE £6.90: £1.60 £1.50 £6.80 (£11.80) OWNER Mr A. J. Richards (NEWMARKET) BRED Ewar Stud Farm 9 Rn 2m 4.7 (8.70) SF: 34/20/9/6/1/-/-/-/-

242

TYNE H'CAP (0-90) (Class C) £5,602.00 (£1,696.00: £828.00: £394.00)
1m 100y (Fibresand) GOING: 0.06 sec per fur (STD) 2-40 (2-40)

195* **Legal Fiction (71)***(88)*(Fav)*(MJohnston)* 4-8-9 6x DeanMcKeown(8) (lw: chsd ldr tl led 3f out: rdn clr wl over 1f out)..........— **1**
89[2] Ertlon **(89)***(93) (CEBrittain)* 5-10-0 BDoyle(3) (hld up: hdwy 5f out: wnt 2nd st: no ch w wnr)..........7 **2**
152[2] Folly Finnesse **(76)***(71) (BRMillman)* 4-9-0 TIves(7) (b.hind: prom: 3rd st: one pce) 4 **3**
151* Komreyev Dancer **(81)***(74) (ABailey)* 3-8-1 GBardwell(1) (hld up: hdwy & 4th st: no imp)..........1¼ **4**
181[2] Hawwam **(70)***(51) (EJAlston)* 9-8-9 LDettori(4) (lost pl after 3f: last st: n.d)..........6 **5**
66[9] Dubai Falcon (USA) **(61)***(34) (RDickin)* 4-7-13 CRutter(6) (lw: led over 5f: wknd qckly & 6th st)..........3½ **6**
20* Rocketeer (IRE) **(89)***(62) (WRMuir)* 4-9-13b DHarrison(5) (b: lw: prom: rdn ½-wy: 5th & btn st)..........s.h **7**
9/4 LEGAL FICTION, **3/1** Ertlon, **9/2** Komreyev Dancer, **5/1** Hawwam, **11/2** Rocketeer (IRE), **10/1** Folly Finnesse, **20/1** Dubai Falcon (USA), CSF £9.60 CT £51.14 TOTE £2.60: £1.90 £1.30 (£5.20) OWNER Mr J. S. Morrison (MIDDLEHAM) BRED Fares Stables Ltd 7 Rn
1m 49.0 SF: 50/55/35/21/17/2/27
WEIGHT FOR AGE 3yo-19lb, 4yo-1lb

243

DIXONS THE ESTATE AGENTS CHALLENGE 95 H'CAP (3-Y.O) (0-75) (Class D) £3,589.30 (£1,086.40: £530.20: £252.10)
7f (Fibresand) GOING: 0.06 sec per fur (STD) 3-15 (3-16)

196[2] **Crystal Loop (64)***(74) (ABailey)* 3-8-12 GBardwell(5) (lw: mde all: rdn out)..........— **1**
144* Iron Man (IRE) **(59)***(65) (MJohnston)* 3-8-0v(7) OliverCasey(8) (dwlt: hdwy 4f out: 2nd st: kpt on u.p fnl f)..........2 **2**
196[4] Master Millfield (IRE) **(73)***(75) (CJHill)* 3-9-7 RCochrane(7) (chsd ldrs: 3rd st: sn rdn & no ex)..........1¾ **3**
171* Mazilla **(57)***(42)*(Fav)*(WJHaggas)* 3-8-5 WWoods(2) (chsd wnr: sn pushed along: 4th & btn st)..........8 **4**
Chadleigh Lane (USA) **(65)***(49) (RHollinshead)* 3-8-13 TIves(4) (in tch: 5th st: no imp)..........nk **5**
Al Corniche (IRE) **(52)***(25) (MRChannon)* 3-7-9 (5) PPMurphy(3) (lw: sn rdn & bhd: nvr rchd ldrs)..........5 **6**
141[4] Tapping Feet **(47)***(18) (SirMarkPrescott)* 3-7-9 ow1 JQuinn(6) (lw: chsd ldrs over 3f).1 **7**
Ho Mei Surprise **(50)***(—) (BPreece)* 3-7-12 LCharnock(1) (rdn & 6th st: sn wl bhd)25 **8**
9/4 Mazilla, **5/2** CRYSTAL LOOP, **11/2** Master Millfield (IRE), **7/1** Iron Man (IRE), Chadleigh Lane (USA), Tapping Feet, **16/1** Al Corniche (IRE), **33/1** Ho Mei Surprise, CSF £19.75 CT £82.65 TOTE £5.30: £1.10 £2.50 £2.30 (£18.10) OWNER Mr Roy Matthews (TARPORLEY) BRED B. Long 8 Rn 1m 29.4 (5.40) SF: 38/28/39/7/13/-/-/-

244

LADBROKE ALL WEATHER BOWL SERIES H'CAP (Qualifier) (0-70) (Class E) £3,452.50 (£1,045.00: £510.00: £242.50)
5f (Fibresand) GOING: 0.06 sec per fur (STD) 3-45 (3-45)

154* **Scored Again (58)***(62)*(Fav)*(MJHeaton-Ellis)* 5-8-12 (7) AmandaSanders(5) (b: w ldr tl led over 2f out: hld on wl fnl f)..........— **1**
Rocky Two **(58)***(59) (PHowling)* 4-9-5b WWoods(9) (chsd ldrs: ev ch over 1f out: rdn & no ex fnl f)..........¾ **2**
154[4] Delrob **(61)***(61) (DHaydnJones)* 4-9-8 AMackay(4) (lw: hmpd s: sn bhd: hdwy over 2f out: kpt on fnl f)..........nk **3**
70[7] Baton Bleu **(43)***(38) (PHowling)* 4-8-4 JQuinn(8) (plld hrd: chsd ldrs: ev ch wl over 1f out: rdn & btn fnl f)..........1¾ **4**
69[12] Jon's Choice **(65)***(33) (BPreece)* 7-9-12 TWall(2) (sn rdn along: chsd ldrs: ev ch wl over 1f out: sn wknd)..........9 **5**
Gondo **(67)***(31) (EJAlston)* 8-9-7 (7) SKnott(3) (hmpd s: a bhd)..........1¼ **6**
Grand Time **(45)***(6) (CJHill)* 6-8-6 GBardwell(7) (sn pushed along: a bhd)..........¾ **7**
177[3] Red Admiral **(67)***(27) (PCHaslam)* 5-9-7 (7) NicolaHowarth(1) (b.hind: led over 2f: ev ch wl over 1f out: sn wknd)..........hd **8**

5/2 SCORED AGAIN, **11/4** Red Admiral, **3/1** Delrob, **9/1** Grand Time, **10/1** Gondo, **12/1** Rocky Two, Jon's Choice, **33/1** Baton Bleu, CSF £28.67 CT £85.77 TOTE £2.80: £1.40 £1.50 £1.30 (£19.90) OWNER Mrs Anna Sanders (WROUGHTON) BRED R. T. and Mrs Watson 8 Rn
63.5 secs (5.50) SF: 15/13/15/-/-/-/-/-

245 NENE MEDIAN AUCTION STKS (Mdn 4, 5 & 6-Y.O) (Class E)
£2,995.30 (£906.40: £442.20: £210.10)
1m 4f (Fibresand) GOING: 0.06 sec per fur (STD) 4-15 (4-15)

Harlequin Walk (IRE) (52)*(71) (AHide)* 4-8-7b JQuinn(10) (plld hrd: led after 4f: rdn clr 2f out: eased nr fin)........— **1**
Nirvana Prince *(72) (BPreece)* 6-9-2 TWall(8) (sn pushed along: hdwy 5f out: 3rd st: kpt on: nrst fin)........3½ **2**
227⁶ Opera Buff (IRE) **(56)***(60)*(Fav)*(MCPipe)* 4-8-12 GCarter(7) (lw: chsd ldrs: rdn 4f out: 2nd st: wknd appr fnl f)........10 **3**
Turfmans Vision **(45)***(58) (RHollinshead)* 5-9-2 TIves(2) (lw: bhd: hdwy & 4th st: nvr rchd ldrs)........1½ **4**
Moonlight Calypso *(47) (EJAlston)* 4-8-7 MFenton(4) (prom 6f: 6th & btn st)........5 **5**
120⁹ Sharp Thrill **(43)***(42) (BSmart)* 4-8-12v DHarrison(3) (led 4f: 5th & wkng st)........8 **6**
46³ Daphnis (USA) *(39) (WTKemp)* 6-9-2b RCochrane(1) (lw: chsd ldrs 7f)........2½ **7**
103⁴ Severn Gale *(33) (KWhite)* 5-8-11 AClark(6) (lw: effrt 5f out: 7th & btn st)........nk **8**
Mollinsburn (IRE) **(40)***(—) (JAHarris)* 4-8-5 (7) CTeague(5) (b: lw: a bhd: t.o fnl 4f)........dist **9**
53¹⁴ Homebeforemidnight *(—) (RHollinshead)* 4-8-0 (7) RGordon(9) (t.o fnl 7f)........dist **10**

7/4 Opera Buff (IRE), **3/1** Nirvana Prince, **5/1** HARLEQUIN WALK (IRE) (4/1-6/1), Severn Gale, **12/1** Moonlight Calypso, **16/1** Daphnis (USA), Sharp Thrill, **20/1** Turfmans Vision, **33/1** Mollinsburn (IRE), Homebeforemidnight, CSF £20.61 TOTE £8.60: £2.70 £1.60 £1.60 (£15.70) OWNER Charlcombe Racing (NEWMARKET) BRED Ronnie Boland in Ireland 10 Rn
2m 41.7 (10.70) SF: 26/31/15/16/2/-/-/-/-/-
WEIGHT FOR AGE 4yo-4lb

246 THAMES H'CAP (0-80) (Class D) £4,182.00 (£1,266.00: £618.00: £294.00)
1m 4f (Fibresand) GOING: 0.06 sec per fur (STD) 4-45 (4-45)

*15** **Noufari (FR) (72)***(84)*(Fav)*(RHollinshead)* 4-9-7 TIves(7) (hld up: hdwy 5f out: rdn & wnt 3rd st: sn led: edgd lft & styd on wl)........— **1**
193² Stevie's Wonder (IRE) **(67)***(76)*(Fav)*(MJRyan)* 5-9-6 GCarter(6) (prom: qcknd to ld 6f out: hdd wl over 1f out: kpt on)........2½ **2**
215³ Thaleros **(67)***(72) (GMMoore)* 5-9-6 AClark(5) (trckd ldrs: 2nd st: one pce)........3½ **3**
145⁴ Ballyranter **(65)***(66) (HJCollingridge)* 6-9-4v JQuinn(10) (trckd ldrs tl rdn, outpcd & 5th st)........3½ **4**
*172** Comtec's Legend **(40)***(40) (JFBottomley)* 5-7-7 GBardwell(1) (hdwy over 5f out: 6th & btn st)........¾ **5**
193⁸ Philgun **(60)***(55) (CWCElsey)* 6-8-13v NKennedy(9) (led 4f: 4th st: sn btn)........4 **6**
178⁰ Milngavie (IRE) **(61)***(54) (MJohnston)* 5-9-0 DeanMcKeown(8) (in tch 8f)........2 **7**
New Inn **(72)***(63) (EWeymes)* 4-9-2 (5) JStack(2) (prom tl rdn & outpcd 5f out)........1¾ **8**
152⁶ Rainbow Walk (IRE) **(75)***(66)*(Fav)*(JGMO'Shea)* 5-10-0 RCochrane(4) (nvr nr to chal)........s.h **9**

LONG HANDICAP Comtec's Legend 7-5

4/1 NOUFARI (FR), Stevie's Wonder (IRE), Rainbow Walk (IRE), **9/2** Ballyranter, **5/1** Comtec's Legend, **13/2** Thaleros, **7/1** New Inn, **12/1** Philgun, **16/1** Milngavie (IRE), CSF £22.39 CT £100.78 TOTE £2.60: £1.50 £1.10 £2.70 (£5.30) OWNER Ed Weetman (Haulage & Storage) Ltd (UPPER LONGDON) BRED His Highness The Aga Khans Studs S.C. in France 9 Rn
2m 43.2 (12.20) SF: 30/26/22/16/-/5/3/9/-
WEIGHT FOR AGE 4yo-4lb

T/Plpt: £16.30 (832.64 Tckts). T/Qdpt: £6.60 (9 Tckts). Dk

0235-LINGFIELD (L-H)
Thursday February 9th (Standard)

247 LINGFIELD PARK AWT SPRINT SERIES H'CAP (Qualifier) (0-60)
(Class F) £2,870.60 (£806.60: £393.80)
5f (Equitrack) GOING minus 0.41 sec per fur (FST) 1-50 (1-51)

184⁷ **Tenor (51)***(61) (DNicholls)* 4-9-6 AlexGreaves(1) (lw: hdwy over 2f out: hrd rdn over 1f out: led ins fnl f: r.o wl)........— **1**

2379 Distant Dynasty **(55)**_(57) (BAPearce)_ 5-9-5 (5) SSanders(10) (b.hind: a.p: led 1f out tl ins fnl f: unable qckn) 2½ **2**
1884 Tee-Emm **(59)**_(53) (PHowling)_ 5-10-0 JQuinn(8) (w ldr: ev ch 2f out: hrd rdn over 1f out: one pce) 2½ **3**
1943 Tommy Tempest **(37)**_(30)_(Fav)_(ABailey)_ 6-8-1v(5) MBaird(6) (led 4f: sn wknd) ....nk **4**
1824 Efficacy **(33)**_(26) (APJarvis)_ 4-7-11 (5) NVarley(2) (rdn & hdwy over 2f out: one pce) ....s.h **5**
216* Bon Secret (IRE) **(65)**_(58) (TJNaughton)_ 3-9-5 7x DHarrison(7) (lw: outpcd: nvr nr to chal) ....s.h **6**
Halliard **(55)**_(47) (TMJones)_ 4-9-10 RPerham(4) (b: squeezed out 4f out: nvr nrr)..nk **7**
Swift Nick Nevison **(39)**_(22) (KTIvory)_ 4-8-1 (7) AmandaSanders(9) (spd over 3f) 3 **8**
1676 Miss Siham (IRE) **(39)**_(10) (JBalding)_ 6-8-1 (7) ClaireBalding(5) (outpcd) 4 **9**
2165 Amazing News **(56)**_(22) (MarkCampion)_ 4-9-11 RCochrane(3) (bhd fnl 2f) 1¾ **10**

4/1 Tommy Tempest, **9/2** Efficacy, **5/1** Tee-Emm, Bon Secret (IRE), **11/2** Distant Dynasty, **10/1** Swift Nick Nevison, **11/1** Miss Siham (IRE), Halliard, **12/1** Amazing News, **14/1** TENOR, CSF £87.87 CT £411.43 TOTE £13.30: £3.80 £2.40 £1.70 (£52.70) OWNER Mr G. Thompson (THIRSK) BRED Lord Victor Matthews 10 Rn 60.02 secs (1.82) SF: 38/34/29/8/4/20/23/-/-/-
WEIGHT FOR AGE 3yo-15lb

248 WISTERIA CLAIMING STKS (Class F) £2,700.80 (£758.80:£370.40)
7f (Equitrack) GOING minus 0.41 sec per fur (FST) 2-20 (2-20)

1572 **Sweet Supposin (IRE) (70)**_(74) (KMcAuliffe)_ 4-9-3b RCochrane(4) (lw: rdn thrght: hdwy & n.m.r over 2f out: hrd rdn 1f out: led ins fnl f: r.o wl) ....— **1**
1233 Rocky Waters (USA) **(81)**_(62)_(Fav)_(GLMoore)_ 6-9-2 AMorris(7) (hdwy to ld 4f out: clr 2f out: hdd ins fnl f: unable qckn) 5 **2**
2115 Veloce (IRE) **(51)**_(46) (ABailey)_ 7-7-10v(7) AngelaGallimore(8) (b: s.s: gd hdwy over 1f out: r.o wl ins fnl f) 1¼ **3**
32* La Residence **(49)**_(44) (MrsNMacauley)_ 4-8-1 (5) SSanders(3) (a.p: rdn over 4f out: one pce) 2½ **4**
1794 Dome Patrol **(51)**_(37) (WRMuir)_ 4-8-3 DHarrison(9) (a.p: rdn over 3f out: one pce)1¾ **5**
2249 Soba Guest (IRE) **(56)**_(37) (RTJuckes)_ 6-8-1 (5)ow1 SDrowne(11) (lw: a.p: rdn over 3f out: wknd over 1f out) 1½ **6**
1879 Secret Assignment (USA) **(40)**_(38) (CACyzer)_ 5-8-2 (5) SMulvey(10) (prom over 5f) ....s.h **7**
2037 Coalisland **(35)**_(25) (RIngram)_ 5-8-9b WWoods(2) (a bhd) 7 **8**
21711 Christian Spirit **(35)**_(4) (BAPearce)_ 5-8-3b StephenDavies(1) (b: led 3f) 7 **9**
Arras Royale **(22)**_(—) (JELong)_ 5-7-13 (5) PMcCabe(5) (b: bhd fnl 4f) 8 **10**

11/8 Rocky Waters (USA), **15/8** SWEET SUPPOSIN (IRE), **7/1** Dome Patrol, **8/1** Veloce (IRE) (6/1-10/1), **10/1** La Residence, **25/1** Soba Guest (IRE), **33/1** Secret Assignment (USA), **40/1** Coalisland, **66/1** Christian Spirit, Arras Royale, CSF £4.86 TOTE £2.60: £4.10 £1.00 £3.30 (£2.60) OWNER Mount Juliet Stud (LAMBOURN) BRED Ballylinch Stud Ltd 10 Rn
1m 25.5 (2.50) SF: 37/25/11/8/3/2/3/-/-/-

249 DAILY STAR AWT 1M 2F CHALLENGE SERIES H'CAP (Qualifier) (0-80) (Class D) £3,811.25 (£1,154.00: £563.50: £268.25)
1m 2f (Equitrack) GOING minus 0.41 sec per fur (FST) 2-50 (2-50)

1453 **Secret Aly (CAN) (74)**_(85) (CEBrittain)_ 5-9-12 MRimmer(7) (lw: chsd ldr: rdn over 2f out: led last strides) ....— **1**
145* Birequest **(73)**_(84)_(Fav)_(RBoss)_ 4-9-9 LDettori(3) (lw: led: hrd rdn fnl f: hdd last strides) ....hd **2**
8915 Waldo **(66)**_(65) (LordHuntingdon)_ 4-9-2v DHarrison(9) (a.p: rdn over 3f out: one pce)8 **3**
2032 Captain Marmalade **(50)**_(47) (DTThom)_ 6-7-13 (3) DRMcCabe(6) (lw: nvr nr to chal) 1½ **4**
2054 Mr Browning (USA) **(55)**_(47) (MarkCampion)_ 4-8-5 ow1 RCochrane(2) (bhd fnl 4f) .3½ **5**
1918 Admirals Flame (IRE) **(65)**_(56) (CFWall)_ 4-9-1 GDuffield(4) (b: a bhd) ....½ **6**
Blurred Image (IRE) **(78)**_(61) (MissGayKelleway)_ 4-9-7 (7) DGibbs(5) (b.hind: bhd fnl 4f) 5 **7**

Evens Birequest, **7/2** SECRET ALY (CAN), **5/1** Captain Marmalade, **7/1** Waldo, **9/1** Admirals Flame (IRE), **16/1** Mr Browning (USA), **20/1** Blurred Image (IRE), CSF £7.77 CT £21.63 TOTE £4.80: £2.30 £1.50 (£3.40) OWNER Mr B. H. Voak (NEWMARKET) BRED Northern Equine Thoroughbred Productions 7 Rn 2m 4.74 (1.74) SF: 62/59/41/25/22/31/35
WEIGHT FOR AGE 4yo-2lb
STEWARDS' ENQUIRY Dettori suspended 18-20/2/95 (excessive use of whip).

250

FORSYTHIA STKS (3-Y.O) (Class D) £3,572.40 (£1,081.20: £527.60: £250.80)
1m (Equitrack) GOING minus 0.41 sec per fur (FST) 3-20 (3-21)

*64** **Montanelli (FR) (72)***(86) (KMcAuliffe)* 3-9-2 RCochrane(5) (hld up: led over 3f out: rdn out)........— **1**
176² No Pattern **(82)***(88) (GLMoore)* 3-8-12 (7) LSuthern(4) (lw: hdwy over 4f out: rdn over 1f out: hung lft ins fnl f: r.o)........nk **2**
*170** Gulf Shaadi **(82)***(85)*(Fav)*(CEBrittain)* 3-9-7 BDoyle(2) (a.p: ev ch 2f out: nt r.o)...2½ **3**
Renown *(68) (LordHuntingdon)* 3-8-11 DHarrison(1) (led over 1f: 4th whn hmpd & dropped rr 5f out: one pce fnl 3f)........3½ **4**
*174** Whackford Squeers *(64) (CACyzer)* 3-9-0 TIves(3) (led over 6f out tl over 3f out: wknd over 2f out)........3½ **5**
Just Lucky (IRE) *(52) (RWArmstrong)* 3-9-2 WWoods(6) (b: lw: bhd fnl 4f)........7 **6**

11/4 Gulf Shaadi, **4/1** MONTANELLI (FR), Whackford Squeers, Just Lucky (IRE), **9/2** No Pattern, **12/1** Renown, CSF £19.99 TOTE £5.90: £1.20 £3.90 (£40.20) OWNER Delamere Cottage Racing Syndicate (LAMBOURN) BRED Crest Stud Ltd in France 6 Rn
1m 39.85 (3.45) SF: 31/34/31/14/11/-

251

JAPONICA H'CAP (3-Y.O) (0-70) (Class E) £3,023.90 (£915.20: £446.60: £212.30) **7f (Equitrack)** GOING minus 0.41 sec per fur (FST) 3-50 (3-50)

176⁴ **Water Hazard (IRE) (52)***(57) (SDow)* 3-8-2 (5) SSanders(5) (hld up: rdn 3f out: hit rail over 2f out: squeezed thro & led ins fnl f: r.o wl)........— **1**
*156** Mr Frosty **(66)***(66)*(Fav)*(WJarvis)* 3-9-7 LDettori(6) (stumbled s: stdy hdwy over 3f out: led over 1f out tl ins fnl f: unable qckn)........2½ **2**
220⁴ Prince Rudolf (IRE) **(51)***(46) (MrsNMacauley)* 3-8-6v MFenton(4) (led over 4f out tl over 1f out: wknd fnl f)........2½ **3**
38⁴ Mr Lowry **(54)***(38) (RBoss)* 3-8-9b GDuffield(2) (a.p: rdn over 3f out: 4th & btn whn hmpd over 2f out)........5 **4**
146⁸ Royal Uprising (IRE) **(46)***(30) (GLMoore)* 3-8-1 CRutter(1) (led over 2f: wknd over 2f out)........s.h **5**
156⁹ Zeliba **(42)***(24) (CEBrittain)* 3-7-11 JQuinn(3) (bhd fnl 4f)........¾ **6**

11/10 Mr Frosty, **4/1** WATER HAZARD (IRE), Mr Lowry, **9/2** Prince Rudolf (IRE), **16/1** Zeliba, **25/1** Royal Uprising (IRE), CSF £8.82 TOTE £5.20: £2.30 £1.10 (£2.40) OWNER Mr Ken Butler (EPSOM) BRED Mrs A.C.Belcher and P.B.Hayden in Ireland 6 Rn 1m 27.1 (4.10) SF: 10/17/-/-

252

BUDDLEIA STKS (Mdn) (Class D) £3,606.20 (£1,091.60: £532.80: £253.40)
1m 4f (Equitrack) GOING minus 0.41 sec per fur (FST) 4-20 (4-21)

Power *(63+) (CEBrittain)* 4-8-12 BDoyle(2) (lw: hld up: nt clr run over 1f out: squeezed thro to ld ins fnl f: r.o wl)........— **1**
84² Dvorak (IRE) *(62)*(Fav)*(BJMcMath)* 4-8-12 AMackay(6) (hdwy 7f out: rdn over 4f out: ev ch over 1f out: unable qckn fnl f)........1 **2**
Ginger Jim **(49)***(62) (PRHedger)* 4-8-12v GDuffield(7) (lw: led 1f: rdn over 4f out: ev ch ins fnl f: one pce)........hd **3**
Tervel (USA) *(62) (JPearce)* 4-8-12 JMcLaughlin(11) (led 11f out tl ins fnl f: one pce)........s.h **4**
190² Masrah Dubai (USA) **(65)***(61) (MAJarvis)* 4-8-12 TIves(5) (stdy hdwy over 3f out: rdn over 1f out: one pce)........¾ **5**
84³ Regal Pursuit (IRE) **(57)***(54) (CAHorgan)* 4-8-7h WWoods(3) (hld up: rdn over 3f out: eased whn btn ins fnl f)........1½ **6**
Jadidh *(29) (CPWildman)* 7-8-11 StephenDavies(1) (b: bhd fnl 6f)........20 **7**
Mutiara **(34)***(21) (MissGayKelleway)* 4-8-7 RCochrane(4) (b.hind: lw: bhd fnl 4f).....6 **8**
Snow Dream *(10) (MJRyan)* 5-8-11 AClark(9) (bit bkwd: bhd fnl 5f)........9 **9**
218⁷ Added Dimension (IRE) **(41)***(12) (CTNash)* 4-8-12 RPerham(8) (s.s: plld hrd: hdwy over 9f out: wknd over 4f out)........2½ **10**
The Leaf Sweeper *(—) (MJBolton)* 4-8-7 CRutter(10) (bhd fnl 5f)........6 **11**

2/1 Dvorak (IRE), **3/1** Masrah Dubai (USA), **4/1** POWER, **11/2** Regal Pursuit (IRE), **12/1** Tervel (USA), **14/1** Snow Dream, **16/1** Jadidh, **20/1** Ginger Jim, **33/1** Mutiara, **50/1** Added Dimension (IRE), The Leaf Sweeper, CSF £12.61 TOTE £5.70: £2.50 £1.10 £1.60 (£9.70) OWNER The Dayspring Company Ltd (NEWMARKET) BRED Bloomsbury Stud 11 Rn
2m 34.08 (4.68) SF: 33/32/32/32/30/24/3/-/-/-/-
WEIGHT FOR AGE 4yo-4lb

T/Plpt: £33.00 (337.05 Tckts). T/Qdpt: £249.50 (0.8 Tckts); £67.44 to Newbury 10/2/95. AK

0209A-CAGNES-SUR-MER (Nice, France) (L-H)
Wednesday February 1st (Good)

253a PRIX DE LA MADELEINE £6,587.00 **1m**

Roi Ho (FR) (—) *(France)* 4-9-4 PDumortier .... — **1**
208a[2] Confronter (—) *(SDow)* 6-9-0 ESaint-Martin 1 **2**
Le Vivarois (USA) (—) *(France)* 4-9-0 SMaillot .... nse **3**

TOTE3.30F: 1.70F 1.50F 1.80F (8.00F) OWNER Mme M. de Chambure BRED H. Rouillere & Therese Louveau in France 11 Rn
1m 43.3 SF: -/-/-

0228-SOUTHWELL (L-H)
Friday February 10th (Standard)

254 SEA GOAT CLAIMING STKS (Class F) £2,537.00 (£712.00: £347.00)
1m 4f (Fibresand) GOING minus 0.44 sec per fur (FST) 2,10 (2-18)

*214** **Killing Time (59)***(59)*(Fav)*(MrsNMacauley)* 4-8-12v MFenton(4) (mde all: styd on wl u.p fnl 2f) .... — **1**
161[6] Port Sunlight (IRE) **(45)***(53) (PDEvans)* 7-8-12 AClark(1) (jnd ldrs ½-wy: ev ch 2f out: nt qckn ins fnl f) 1¼ **2**
172[8] Manolete **(44)***(50) (CWCElsey)* 4-8-6b NKennedy(6) (a chsng ldrs: ev ch 2f out: kpt on one pce) .... ¾ **3**
200[3] Cliburnel News (IRE) **(49)***(39) (WRMuir)* 5-8-7 JWeaver(7) (b.hind: jnd ldr 7f out: drvn along & outpcd 3f out: hdwy & prom 2f out: no imp) 6 **4**
Not for Sale **(39)***(6) (JWharton)* 4-7-9 JQuinn(2) (hld up: hmpd after 1f: effrt over 4f out: sn rdn & wknd) 20 **5**
Binlaboon (IRE) *(17) (KGWingrove)* 4-8-12b JMcLaughlin(3) (b: b.hind: plld hrd: hld up: effrt over 4f out: sn drvn along: lost pl 3f out) 5 **6**
Aspirant (—) *(JRBostock)* 7-8-4 AMackay(5) (sn bhd: drvn along 7f out: t.o 4f out) .... dist **7**

Evens KILLING TIME, **9/4** Cliburnel News (IRE), **6/1** Port Sunlight (IRE), **12/1** Manolete, **16/1** Not for Sale, **20/1** Binlaboon (IRE), **66/1** Aspirant, CSF £7.35 TOTE £1.80: £1.40 £3.20 (£5.30) OWNER Mr James Colling (MELTON MOWBRAY) BRED L. H. J. Ward 7 Rn
2m 40.0 (5.80) SF: 26/24/18/12/-/-/-
WEIGHT FOR AGE 4yo-4lb

255 GREAT BEAR H'CAP (0-70) (Class E) £3,181.20 (£963.60:£470.80: £224.40)
1m (Fibresand) GOING minus 0.44 sec per fur (FST) 2-40 (2-47)

*230** **Roar on Tour (61)***(74) (MrsMReveley)* 6-10-0 6x RCochrane(8) (lw: chsd ldrs: hung lft & led over 1f out: drvn out) .... — **1**
189[3] Harry Browne (IRE) **(59)***(68)*(Fav)*(MrsJRRamsden)* 3-8-7 JWeaver(5) (lw: hld up: hdwy on outside over 2f out: rdn & hung lft over 1f out: no imp) 2 **2**
219[3] Profit Release (IRE) **(57)***(63) (MJohnston)* 4-9-9 TWilliams(1) (chsd ldrs: rdn & outpcd over 2f out: kpt on wl fnl f) .... ¾ **3**
Salinger **(33)***(36) (JParkes)* 7-8-0 JFanning(7) (chsd ldr: led over 2f out tl over 1f out: one pce) 1¾ **4**
*181** Broughtons Turmoil **(55)***(53) (WJMusson)* 6-9-5 (3) 6x DRMcCabe(9) (b: swtg: trckd ldrs: effrt over 2f out: sn rdn & btn over 1f out) 2½ **5**
179[5] Scoffera **(33)***(31) (NTinkler)* 5-8-0 KimTinkler(11) (outpcd & drvn along 4f out: kpt on fnl 2f: nvr nr to chal) .... hd **6**
*212** Rad **(55)***(47) (SPCWoods)* 5-9-8 WWoods(3) (in tch: effrt 2f out: nvr nr to chal) 3 **7**
231[8] Tyrone Flyer **(57)***(47) (PMMcEntee)* 6-9-3 (7) SarahThompson(4) (led tl over 2f out: wknd over 1f out) .... ¾ **8**
137[8] Brief Respite (IRE) **(46)***(23) (EJAlston)* 4-8-12 JQuinn(12) (s.s: a bhd & sn drvn along) 6 **9**
33[6] Never Time (IRE) **(50)***(24) (MrsVAAconley)* 3-7-7b(5) NVarley(10) (s.s: a outpcd & bhd) 1¾ **10**
120[11] Venture Fourth **(30)***(—) (EJAlston)* 6-7-8b(3) DWright(6) (prom tl lost pl 3f out) 5 **11**
231[7] The Real Whizzbang (IRE) **(39)***(—) (PSFelgate)* 4-8-5b PMcCabe(2) .... **W**

11/4 Harry Browne (IRE), **3/1** Broughtons Turmoil, **5/1** ROAR ON TOUR, **6/1** Profit Release (IRE), **13/2** Rad, **16/1** Scoffera, Salinger, The Real Whizzbang (IRE), **20/1** Tyrone Flyer, Venture Fourth, **33/1** Never Time (IRE), Brief Respite (IRE), CSF £18.90 CT £78.05 TOTE £4.90: £1.50 £1.10 £2.80 (£6.80) OWNER Mrs S. D. Murray (SALTBURN) BRED Pitts Farm Stud 11 Rn
1m 42.5 (3.20) SF: 44/21/35/11/27/6/21/-/-/-/-/-
WEIGHT FOR AGE 3yo-19lb, 4yo-1lb

256 EAST MIDLANDS ELECTRICITY STKS (Mdn) (Class D) £3,741.40 (£1,133.20: £553.60: £263.80) 7f (Fibresand) GOING minus 0.44 sec (FST) 3-10 (3-16)

181[6] **Twin Creeks (60)***(59) (MDHammond)* 4-9-10 RCochrane(13) (trckd ldrs: led over 2f out: styd on wl fnl f: drvn out) — 1
210[3] Nite-Owl Dancer **(60)***(46) (JAHarris)* 3-8-1 JO'Reilly(14) (led tl over 2f out: kpt on fnl f: no ch w wnr) 4 2
228[7] Spanish Stripper (USA) **(49)***(48) (MCChapman)* 4-9-7 (3) DRMcCabe(4) (swtg: hdwy ½-wy: styd on fnl 2f: nvr nr to chal) 1¼ 3
Anjou *(42+)*(Fav)*(GWragg)* 3-8-6 LDettori(7) (leggy: scope: dwlt: hdwy ½-wy: kpt on fnl 2f: nvr nr ldrs) 3 4
Tovarich **(60)***(42) (DNicholls)* 4-9-10 SWhitworth(11) (hld up & bhd: kpt on fnl 2f: nvr nr ldrs) s.h 5
Silver Rondo (USA) *(34) (LordHuntingdon)* 3-8-1 DHarrison(8) (leggy: unf: chsd ldrs tl lost pl over 2f out) 1½ 6
Callonescy (IRE) *(35) (CEBrittain)* 3-8-6 BDoyle(5) (w'like: str: bit bkwd: sn outpcd & drvn along: styd on fnl 2f: nt rch ldrs) 1¾ 7
Lovely Me (IRE) **(64)***(27) (RFJohnsonHoughton)* 4-9-5 GDuffield(2) (chsd ldrs tl wknd over 2f out) 1¼ 8
53[12] King of Show (IRE) **(64)***(27) (RAllan)* 4-9-10b JWeaver(1) (chsd ldrs tl drvn along & outpcd 3f out: sn wknd) 2½ 9
136[8] Minster Glory *(12) (MWEasterby)* 4-9-10 LCharnock(10) (s.i.s: a in rr) 7 10
Rory John *(9) (SWCampion)* 7-9-10 TIves(12) (s.s: a bhd) 1¼ 11
Noble Canonire *(5) (NPLittmoden)* 3-8-3 ow2 MFenton(9) (unf: s.i.s: a bhd) hd 12
103[10] Tanah Merah (IRE) **(56)***(—) (EJAlston)* 4-9-10 JQuinn(3) (sn bhd) 5 13

Evens Anjou, **9/2** Callonescy (IRE), **9/1** Nite-Owl Dancer, King of Show (IRE), **10/1** Silver Rondo (USA), **14/1** Tovarich, Lovely Me (IRE), **16/1** TWIN CREEKS, Spanish Stripper (USA), **25/1** Tanah Merah (IRE), **33/1** Noble Canonire, **40/1** Minster Glory, **50/1** Rory John, CSF £151.49 TOTE £27.50: £8.30 £3.60 £4.70 (£62.90) OWNER The Armchair Jockeys (MIDDLEHAM) BRED Crest Stud Ltd 13 Rn
1m 28.6 (1.80) SF: 52/21/40/17/34/9/11/-/-/-/-/-/-
WEIGHT FOR AGE 3yo-18lb

OFFICIAL EXPLANATION **Tovarich: was outpaced in the early stages. The jockey reported that the gelding would not have finished any closer for more vigorous riding early on. The horse may be better suited by a longer trip.**

257 LADBROKE ALL WEATHER BOWL SERIES (H'cap) (Qualifier) (3-Y.O) (0-70) (Class E) £3,355.00 (£1,015.00: £495.00: £235.00) 6f (Fibresand) GOING minus 0.44 sec per fur (FST) 3-40 (3-45)

212[3] **Pc's Cruiser (IRE) (52)***(65) (MCChapman)* 3-8-0 (3) DRMcCabe(2) (sn outpcd & drvn along: hdwy over 2f out: led 1f out: drvn out) — 1
*149** Posted Abroad (IRE) **(63)***(71)*(Fav)*(SirMarkPrescott)* 3-9-0 GDuffield(1) (lw: chsd ldrs: drvn along 3f out: led over 1f out: sn hdd & nt qckn) 2 2
*210** Portend **(75)***(74) (SRBowring)* 3-9-5 (7) 7x CTeague(4) (trckd ldr: led over 2f out: hdd over 1f out: sn wknd) 3½ 3
170[4] Bold Frontier **(64)***(59) (KTIvory)* 3-8-8 (7) CScally(6) (b: unruly in stalls: s.s: effrt on outside over 2f out: nvr nr ldrs) 1¼ 4
134[8] Travel Out **(43)***(25) (MrsMReveley)* 3-7-1 (7)ow1 ClaireBalding(3) (b.off hind: led tl over 2f out: sn wknd) 5 5

LONG HANDICAP Travel Out 7-0

5/4 Posted Abroad (IRE), **11/8** Portend, **7/1** Bold Frontier, **11/1** PC'S CRUISER (IRE), **16/1** Travel Out, CSF £24.67 TOTE £8.90: £2.40 £1.40 (£5.70) OWNER P. C Racing Partners (MARKET RASEN) BRED Mrs Maureen Graham 5 Rn
1m 15.1 (1.60) SF: 31/36/38/25/-

258 PEACOCK (S) STKS (3-Y.O) (Class G) £2,259.00 (£634.00: £309.00) 6f (Fibresand) GOING minus 0.44 sec per fur (FST) 4-10 (4-17)

171[8] **Joyful Times (40)***(46) (MrsNMacauley)* 3-7-13 (7) AmandaSanders(1) (swtchd rt s: bhd: gd hdwy over 1f out: fin wl: led post) — 1
118[8] Dowdency **(45)***(46) (JAPickering)* 3-8-6 NCarlisle(10) (bhd: gd hdwy over 1f out: styd on wl nr fin) s.h 2

210[2] Superbit **(49)***(51) (BAMcMahon)* 3-8-8 (3) SSanders(7) (lw: chsd ldr: led 1f out tl nr fin)....s.h **3**
171[5] Lotties Bid *(43) (PSFelgate)* 3-8-1 (5) PMcCabe(9) (chsd ldrs: rdn & kpt on same pce fnl 2f)....¾ **4**
118[9] Branston Kristy **(38)***(38) (CSmith)* 3-8-6 WWoods(5) (b.hind: led to 1f out: wknd).1¾ **5**
54[9] Benten **(46)***(37) (DNicholls)* 3-8-6 GDuffield(13) (chsd ldrs: ev ch tl wknd fnl f)......hd **6**
171[2] Presto Boy **(50)***(36)*(Fav)*(MBell)* 3-8-11v MFenton(12) (bhd & reminders 4f out: kpt on fnl 2f: nvr nr ldrs)....2½ **7**
118[5] Needwood Newt **(43)***(27) (BAMcMahon)* 3-8-6 DaleGibson(8) (hdwy u.p ½-wy: kpt on fnl 2f: nvr nr to chal)....1¼ **8**
Tinker Amelia *(19) (WRMuir)* 3-8-6 JWeaver(11) (s.s: a in rr)....3 **9**
51[9] Sweet Cheap Pet **(53)***(18) (JBerry)* 3-8-11 GCarter(6) (b.nr hind: chsd ldr tl wknd over 2f out)....2½ **10**
197[5] Lawnswood Lady **(43)***(—) (RHollinshead)* 3-8-6b LDettori(2) (unruly gng to s: hmpd s: iron broke: nt rcvr)....6 **11**
189[8] Star Information **(38)***(—) (JSMoore)* 3-8-1b(5) SDrowne(4) (swvd lft s: bhd fr ½-wy)....hd **12**
Tappen Lady (IRE) **(45)***(—) (JSWainwright)* 3-8-6v LCharnock(3) (hmpd s: hmpd bnd after 2f: sn in tch: wknd over 2f out)....2½ **13**

3/1 Presto Boy, **5/1** Superbit, **6/1** Lawnswood Lady, Lotties Bid, **9/1** Sweet Cheap Pet, **10/1** Needwood Newt, **11/1** Tinker Amelia, **12/1** Dowdency, **16/1** Benten, **20/1** Star Information, JOYFUL TIMES, Tappen Lady (IRE), **33/1** Branston Kristy, CSF £225.23 TOTE £23.30: £3.50 £4.30 £2.40 (£121.10) OWNER Joyful Times Racing (MELTON MOWBRAY) BRED Mrs K. E. Naylor
13 Rn No bid 1m 16.6 (3.10) SF: 14/14/19/12/10/9/7/-/-/-/-/-/-

OFFICIAL EXPLANATION Lawnswood Lady: an iron broke as the filly left the stalls. causing the jockey to ride without the aid of stirrups.

259

MILKY WAY H'CAP (0-65) (Class F) £2,537.00 (£712.00: £347.00)
2m (Fibresand) GOING minus 0.44 sec per fur (FST) 4-40 (4-46)

215[2] **Who's the Best (IRE) (34)***(48) (APJarvis)* 5-7-6 (5) NVarley(6) (hld up: hdwy ½-wy: sn prom: led 1f out: styd on strly)....— **1**
186[11] Risky Tu **(59)***(71) (PAKelleway)* 4-8-9 (7) AdelleGibbons(14) (a.p: styd on fnl 2f: nt qckn ins fnl f)....2 **2**
15[6] Absalom's Pillar **(65)***(73) (JHetherton)* 5-10-0 NCarlisle(10) (hdwy ½-wy: sn prom: rdn 3f out: kpt on same pce appr fnl f)....4 **3**
136[2] Murphys Way **(44)***(51) (JLEyre)* 6-8-7 TIves(7) (b: w ldrs: led 10f out: hdd over 1f out: one pce)....1½ **4**
166[4] Blowedifiknow **(38)***(44) (JWharton)* 5-8-1b JQuinn(8) (a.p: led over 1f out: sn hdd & wknd)....1½ **5**
215[4] Charlie Bigtime **(50)***(47) (BJMcMath)* 5-8-13 AMackay(16) (chsd ldrs: rdn 4f out: wknd over 1f out: eased)....10 **6**
45[5] Mrs Jawleyford (USA) **(56)***(52) (CSmith)* 7-9-5 WWoods(3) (b: hdwy ½-wy: sn prom: drvn along 4f out: wknd 2f out)....½ **7**
186[9] Bures (IRE) **(65)***(52) (MHTompkins)* 4-9-3v(5) SMulvey(13) (plld hrd: trckd ldrs: disp ld 7f out: wknd 2f out)....10 **8**
Moonshine Dancer **(48)***(35) (MrsMReveley)* 5-8-4 (7) SCopp(15) (bhd: sme hdwy 6f out: nvr rchd ldrs)....hd **9**
183* Dallai (IRE) **(44)***(29) (MrsNMacauley)* 4-7-8 (7) 4x AmandaSanders(11) (hld up: bhd ½-wy: sme hdwy 6f out: n.d)....1¾ **10**
Jolis Absent **(50)***(32)*(Fav)*(MJRyan)* 5-8-13 AClark(4) (b: in tch: reminders 10f out: sn lost pl)....3½ **11**
108[3] Well and Truly **(53)***(24) (BAMcMahon)* 8-9-2 JWeaver(1) (sn bhd & drvn along: sme hdwy ½-wy: n.d)....12 **12**
Have a Nightcap **(35)***(—) (NPLittmoden)* 6-7-9 (3) DWright(9) (led 6f: chsd ldrs tl wknd qckly 4f out: sn wl bhd: t.o)....dist **13**
Eightandahalf (IRE) **(63)***(—) (MrsVAAconley)* 6-9-7 (5) JStack(12) (bhd fnl 5f: t.o).25 **14**
Durshan (USA) **(54)***(—) (JRJenkins)* 6-9-3 LDettori(2) (prom tl wknd qckly 6f out: sn wl bhd: t.o)....20 **15**

4/1 Jolis Absent, **5/1** WHO'S THE BEST (IRE), **6/1** Well and Truly, **7/1** Murphys Way, **10/1** Dallai (IRE), **11/1** Absalom's Pillar, **12/1** Moonshine Dancer, Durshan (USA), **14/1** Mrs Jawleyford (USA), **16/1** Charlie Bigtime, **20/1** Risky Tu, Blowedifiknow, Eightandahalf (IRE), **25/1** Bures (IRE), **33/1** Have a Nightcap, CSF £94.57 CT £985.05 TOTE £4.30: £2.90 £5.90 £3.30 (£343.00) OWNER Mrs Ann Jarvis (ASTON UPTHORPE) BRED F. Feeney 15 Rn
3m 40.1 (14.10) SF: -/-/6/-/-/-/-/-/-/-/-/-/-/-/-
WEIGHT FOR AGE 4yo-6lb

T/Plpt: £292.50 (71.32 Tckts). T/Qdpt: £88.30 (0.4 Tckts); £71.64 to Newbury 11/02/95. WG

0247-LINGFIELD (L-H)
Saturday February 11th (Standard)

260 RED ROSE (S) H'CAP (0-60) (Class G) £2,460.60 (£691.60: £337.80)
1m 5f (Equitrack) GOING minus 0.36 sec per fur (FST) 2-05 (2-07)

Sleeptite (FR) (53)*(63) (WGMTurner)* 5-9-4 (5) JDSmith(2) (hld up: hdwy 4f out: led over 1f out: drvn out) ....— 1
*200** Dancing Diamond (IRE) **(50)***(59)*(Fav)*(MissBSanders)* 5-9-3hv(3) SSanders(3) (chsd ldrs: rdn & lost pl 5f out: hrd rdn 3f out: r.o fnl f) 1 2
201[5] Ann Hill (IRE) **(33)***(39) (RHollinshead)* 5-7-10 (7)ow6 AEddery(1) (hld up: hdwy 3f out: ev ch over 1f out: one pce) 2½ 3
58[7] Cristal Springs **(30)***(27) (BJMcMath)* 4-7-9 ow2 JQuinn(6) (b: b.hind: mid div: rdn over 2f out: r.o one pce fnl f) 7 4
Aviator's Dream **(50)***(47) (JPearce)* 5-9-6 JMcLaughlin(9) (led tl over 1f out: wknd fnl f) ....½ 5
201[2] So Discreet (USA) **(48)***(44) (JWhite)* 7-8-13 (5) SDrowne(5) (bhd: hrd rdn & hdwy 2f out: one pce) ....½ 6
Quadrant **(58)***(49) (AMoore)* 6-10-0 CandyMorris(11) (b: chsd ldrs 6f out: rdn 2f out: wknd over 1f out) 4 7
183[4] Intention (USA) **(50)***(41) (ICampbell)* 5-9-6v RCochrane(7) (hdwy 6f out: rdn over 2f out: wknd over 1f out: eased whn btn fnl f) ....nk 8
*201** Side Bar **(34)***(17) (MJRyan)* 5-8-4b DBiggs(13) (dwlt: hdwy 4f out: wknd 3f out) 7 9
Call Me Albi (IRE) **(52)***(20) (GLMoore)* 4-9-3 AClark(12) (bhd fnl 5f) 12 10
Pierre Blanco (USA) **(41)***(6) (MBradstock)* 6-8-11b NCarlisle(4) (chsd ldrs 3f out: wknd 5f out) 3½ 11
136[6] Jolly Swagman **(41)***(2) (LordHuntingdon)* 4-8-6 DHarrison(10) (dwlt: a bhd) 2½ 12
178[6] Nothing Doing (IRE) **(35)***(—) (WJMusson)* 6-8-0b(5) PMcCabe(8) (chsd ldr 12f out to 6f out: sn wknd) 5 13

7/2 Dancing Diamond (IRE), **4/1** Intention (USA), Side Bar, **13/2** Call Me Albi (IRE) (4/1-7/1), **8/1** So Discreet (USA), **10/1** Aviator's Dream, **12/1** Ann Hill (IRE), SLEEPTITE (FR), **16/1** Cristal Springs, Jolly Swagman, **20/1** Nothing Doing (IRE), **25/1** Pierre Blanco (USA), Quadrant, CSF £56.46 CT £496.55 TOTE £33.50: £5.40 £1.80 £3.60 (£55.30) OWNER Mr David Chown (SHERBORNE) BRED Ronald Reeves in France 13 Rn 2m 48.19 (5.69) SF: 43/39/21/6/28/26/30/-/-/-
WEIGHT FOR AGE 4yo-5lb
No bid

261 ROMEO CLAIMING STKS (3-Y.O) (Class F) £2,713.40 (£762.40: £372.20) 7f (Equitrack) GOING minus 0.36 sec per fur (FST) 2-35 (2-37)

151[5] **Dark Shot (IRE) (80)***(71)*(Fav)*(JBerry)* 3-9-0 GCarter(4) (mde all: hrd rdn fnl f: all out) ....— 1
124[7] Logie **(58)***(63) (MAJarvis)* 3-8-6 WWoods(6) (chsd ldr: rdn 3f out: r.o fnl f: jst failed) ....s.h 2
174[5] Death by Chocolate *(54) (DrJDScargill)* 3-7-11 (3) DWright(1) (chsd ldrs: hrd rdn over 1f out: r.o) 1¼ 3
Fair Ella (IRE) **(44)***(34) (JFfitch-Heyes)* 3-7-9 JQuinn(2) (chsd ldrs: rdn 3f out: sn wknd) 7 4
141[2] Warrior Lady (IRE) **(45)***(42) (PJMcBride)* 3-8-2 (7) JustineReader(5) (a bhd) 3 5
174[2] Irie Mon (IRE) **(59)***(—) (JWHills)* 3-8-8 RCochrane(3) (Withdrawn: broke out of stalls: not under orders: rule 4 applies) .... W

10/11 DARK SHOT (IRE), **3/1** Irie Mon (IRE), **7/1** Logie, **8/1** Warrior Lady (IRE), **10/1** Death by Chocolate, **14/1** Fair Ella (IRE), CSF £4.46 TOTE £1.30: £1.10 £2.30 (£1.90) OWNER Laurel (Leisure) Ltd (COCKERHAM) BRED Mrs Amanda Skiffington and W. Macauley 5 Rn
1m 27.77 (4.77) SF: 12/5/-/-/-/-

262 JACK & JILL COLE H'CAP (0-85) (Class D) £3,589.30 (£1,086.40: £530.20: £252.10) 1m (Equitrack) GOING minus 0.36 sec per fur (FST) 3-05 (3-06)

*125** **Kinnegad Kid (56)***(63) (RIngram)* 6-7-10 (3) 5x DWright(7) (chsd ldrs: hrd rdn wl over 1f out: led ins fnl f: all out) ....— 1
125[2] Red Valerian **(84)***(90) (KMcAuliffe)* 4-9-12b RCochrane(6) (hld up: rdn 4f out: hdwy over 2f out: hrd rdn over 1f out: r.o: jst failed) ....s.h 2
66[8] Metal Storm (FR) **(83)***(86) (KOCunningham-Brown)* 7-9-12 AClark(1) (hld up: hdwy over 2f out: led over 1f out tl ins fnl f: unable qckn) 1¾ 3
*242** Legal Fiction **(76)***(76)*(Fav)*(MJohnston)* 4-9-4 5x TWilliams(4) (chsd ldr: led over 4f out tl over 1f out: one pce) ....¾ 4

160* Moon Strike (FR) **(80)***(76) (WJarvis)* 5-9-9 JWeaver(5) (b.hind: chsd ldrs: rdn over 2f out: one pce fnl 2f)........2½ **5**
195⁵ Conspicuous (IRE) **(63)***(58) (LGCottrell)* 5-8-6 NCarlisle(3) (led over 3f: hrd rdn over 2f out: one pce fnl 2f)........nk **6**
My Best Valentine **(85)***(50) (JWhite)* 5-9-9 (5) SDrowne(2) (hld up: rdn over 4f out: sn wknd)........15 **7**

13/8 Legal Fiction, **5/2** Moon Strike (FR), **7/2** KINNEGAD KID, **5/1** Red Valerian, **12/1** Conspicuous (IRE), **14/1** My Best Valentine, **16/1** Metal Storm (FR), CSF £21.62 TOTE £6.30: £3.00 £2.20 (£6.30) OWNER Mr J. B. Wilcox (EPSOM) BRED Airlie Stud and Miss K. Rausing 7 Rn
1m 39.59 (3.19) SF: 22/47/45/36/36/20/11
WEIGHT FOR AGE 4yo-1lb

263

DAILY STAR AWT 1M 2F CHALLENGE SERIES H'CAP (Qualifier) (3-Y.O) (0-65) (Class F) £3,152.60 (£954.80: £466.40: £222.20)
1m 2f (Equitrack) GOING minus 0.36 sec per fur (FST) 3-35 (3-41)

141* **Grand Selection (IRE) (65)***(74)*(Fav)*(MBell)* 3-9-7 MFenton(9) (a.p: led over 1f out: hrd rdn: r.o)........— **1**
156⁴ Docklands Courier **(49)***(56) (BJMcMath)* 3-8-5 RCochrane(10) (mid div: hdwy 4f out: hrd rdn over 1f out: r.o)........1½ **2**
190* Persian Conquest (IRE) **(70)***(75) (RIngram)* 3-9-12b WWoods(6) (led 3f: led 4f out tl over 1f out: one pce)........1½ **3**
176⁵ Witney-de-Bergerac (IRE) **(57)***(51) (JSMoore)* 3-8-13 RHughes(3) (bhd early: nvr nrr)........7 **4**
185² Vindaloo **(46)***(39) (MJohnston)* 3-8-2 TWilliams(2) (chsd ldrs: rdn over 3f out: one pce fnl 2f)........nk **5**
5¹⁰ Mayday Kitty **(41)***(29) (WGMTurner)* 3-7-4v(7)ow3 SLanigan(12) (hdwy over 3f out: r.o one pce fnl 2f)........3 **6**
144² Good so Fa (IRE) **(58)***(34) (CNAllen)* 3-9-0 EGuest(8) (s.v.s: nvr nrr)........8 **7**
Framley Garth **(46)***(20) (SirMarkPrescott)* 3-8-2 ow1 GDuffield(7) (chsd ldr: led 9f out to 4f out: sn wknd)........1 **8**
189⁵ Rowlandsons Silver (FR) **(43)***(—) (DJGMurraySmith)* 3-7-13bow1 CRutter(13) (chsd ldrs: hrd rdn 4f out: sn wknd)........15 **9**
144⁷ Plucky Pet **(37)***(—) (CJBenstead)* 3-7-2 (5) MBaird(1) (a bhd)........2 **10**
Green Green Ruby **(42)***(—) (GLMoore)* 3-7-12 JQuinn(4) (bhd fnl 3f)........12 **11**
156⁷ Maronetta **(42)***(—) (MJRyan)* 3-7-12 ow3 DBiggs(5) (a bhd)........3 **12**
141⁷ Friar's Oak **(39)***(—) (MHTompkins)* 3-7-6 (3)ow1 DWright(11) (Withdrawn: bolted bef s: not under orders)........ **W**

7/4 GRAND SELECTION (IRE), **4/1** Persian Conquest (IRE), **7/1** Vindaloo, **15/2** Good so Fa (IRE), **10/1** Witney-de-Bergerac (IRE), **11/1** Docklands Courier, **12/1** Framley Garth, **16/1** Rowlandsons Silver (FR), **20/1** Green Green Ruby, **25/1** Maronetta, **33/1** Friar's Oak, **50/1** Plucky Pet, Mayday Kitty, CSF £21.34 CT £66.14 TOTE £2.40: £1.70 £2.90 £1.40 (£14.50) OWNER Mr M. B. Hawtin (NEWMARKET) BRED Mount Coote Stud in Ireland 12 Rn
2m 8.27 (5.27) SF: 34/17/34/11/1/-/-/-/-/-/-/-

264

JULIET MEDIAN AUCTION STKS (Mdn 3-Y.O) (Class E) £2,995.30 (£906.40: £442.20: £210.10)
1m 2f (Equitrack) GOING minus 0.36 sec per fur (FST) 4-05 (4-08)

Tribal Peace (IRE) (62)*(66) (BGubby)* 3-8-9 (5) JStack(5) (chsd ldr: led over 3f out: clr over 1f out: pushed out)........— **1**
38⁵ Pennine Wind (IRE) **(53)***(60) (MJohnston)* 3-9-0 RCochrane(6) (a.p: rdn 4f out: ev ch 2f out: edgd lft 1f out: one pce)........4 **2**
213³ Wisdom **(60)***(58) (PFICole)* 3-9-0b CRutter(1) (led over 6f: hrd rdn over 1f out: one pce)........1½ **3**
Chastleton **(45)***(48) (MRChannon)* 3-8-9 CandyMorris(2) (chsd ldrs: hrd rdn 2f out: one pce)........3 **4**
Rocky Forum *(47) (GLMoore)* 3-8-9 RPerham(3) (w'like: hld up: rdn 3f out: r.o one pce fnl f)........nk **5**
Yet Again *(47)*(Fav)*(BHanbury)* 3-9-0 MRimmer(8) (w'like: mid div: rdn over 5f out: no hdwy fnl 3f)........3½ **6**
174⁴ Semi Serious *(WJarvis)* 3-9-0 TIves(4) (bhd fnl 4f: t.o fnl 2f)........dist **7**
98⁹ Slybird *(MJRyan)* 3-8-9 AClark(7) (bhd fnl 4f: t.o fnl 3f)........dist **8**

6/4 Yet Again, **3/1** Pennine Wind (IRE), **5/1** TRIBAL PEACE (IRE), **11/2** Wisdom, **6/1** Semi Serious, **12/1** Chastleton, **25/1** Rocky Forum, **50/1** Slybird, CSF £20.98 TOTE £4.80: £1.30 £1.70 £1.10 (£14.10) OWNER Brian Gubby Ltd (BAGSHOT) BRED Mrs P. H. Burns in Ireland 8 Rn
2m 9.18 (6.18) SF: 20/14/12/3/3/2/-/-

265 DEMPSTER'S DIARY H'CAP (0-70) (Class E) £3,081.10 (£932.80: £455.40: £216.70) **7f (Equitrack)** GOING minus 0.36 sec per fur (FST) 4-35 (4-38)

205[7] **Possibility (37)***(41) (RIngram)* 4-8-3b TWilliams(1) (hld up: hdwy 2f out: str run fnl f: led nr fin)......— **1**
*219** Digpast (IRE) **(57)***(59)*(Fav)*(RJO'Sullivan)* 5-9-9b DBiggs(3) (chsd ldrs: hrd rdn & swtchd rt over 1f out: r.o)......¾ **2**
202[4] Respectable Jones **(48)***(48) (RHollinshead)* 9-8-7 (7) RGordon(4) (chsd ldrs: sddle slipped 4f out: led 1f out tl ins fnl f: r.o)......1 **3**
219[6] Panchellita (USA) **(45)***(44) (GLMoore)* 6-8-11v SWhitworth(6) (led to 1f out: r.o)......½ **4**
240[W] Pair of Jacks (IRE) **(30)***(25) (DAWilson)* 5-7-10 JQuinn(12) (a.p: hrd rdn over 1f out: one pce)......1¾ **5**
167[3] Aljaz **(54)***(41) (DTThom)* 5-9-6 AMackay(8) (chsd ldr: ev ch 1f out: eased whn btn fnl f)......4 **6**
219[2] Ragazzo (IRE) **(48)***(34) (KOCunningham-Brown)* 5-9-0b LCharnock(7) (chsd ldrs: sn rdn along: one pce fnl 2f)......nk **7**
Kingchip Boy **(60)***(45) (MJRyan)* 6-9-12v AClark(9) (rdn over 2f out: nvr nr to chal)nk **8**
80[6] Sharpening **(47)***(21) (LordHuntingdon)* 4-8-13v DHarrison(5) (mid div: rdn over 4f out: wknd 2f out)......5 **9**
224[6] Letsbeonestaboutit **(54)***(20) (MrsNMacauley)* 9-9-6 DeanMcKeown(11) (a bhd)......4 **10**
220[14] Scots Law **(33)***(—) (JELong)* 8-7-13 NAdams(2) (a bhd)......1¾ **11**
142[9] Whatone Bell **(30)***(—) (PHayward)* 5-7-7 (3)ow3 DWright(10) (a bhd)......20 **12**
LONG HANDICAP Whatone Bell 6-13

2/1 Digpast (IRE), **11/2** Ragazzo (IRE), Sharpening, **6/1** Respectable Jones, **7/1** Aljaz, **9/1** Kingchip Boy, **10/1** Letsbeonestaboutit, **11/1** Pair of Jacks (IRE), **14/1** Panchellita (USA), **16/1** POSSIBILITY, **33/1** Scots Law, **50/1** Whatone Bell, CSF £51.61 CT £218.37 TOTE £27.90: £2.70 £1.70 £2.10 (£37.30) OWNER Mrs A. V. Cappuccini (EPSOM) BRED Britton House Stud 12 Rn
1m 27.02 (4.02) SF: 11/28/17/14/-/11/5/-/-/-/-/-
T/Plpt: £16.60 (757.94 Tckts). T/Qdpt: £8.40 (7.5 Tckts). SM

0254-SOUTHWELL (L-H)
Monday February 13th (Standard)

266 NEVADA STKS (0-60) (Class F) £2,537.00 (£712.00: £347.00) **1m 4f (Fibresand)** GOING minus 0.41 sec per fur (FST) 2-10 (2-15)

*229** **Ashover (60)***(74) (TDBarron)* 5-8-10 (7) KimberleyHart(5) (lw: bhd: gd hdwy ½-wy: led over 2f out: styd on)......— **1**
229[5] Palacegate Jo (IRE) **(70)***(65)*(Fav)*(RHollinshead)* 4-8-10 LDettori(1) (chsd ldrs: rdn to chal ent st: no ex appr fnl f)......5 **2**
246[6] Philgun **(59)***(64) (CWCElsey)* 6-9-1v NKennedy(4) (chsd ldrs: led 5f out tl over 2f out: one pce)......1¼ **3**
Jemima Puddleduck **(60)***(55) (DWPArbuthnot)* 4-8-6 SWhitworth(6) (chsd ldrs: rdn 4f out: one pce fnl 3f)......3 **4**
158[2] Can Can Charlie **(58)***(56) (JPearce)* 5-9-1 RCochrane(9) (in tch: effrt 5f out: no imp)......3 **5**
229[6] Missus Murhill (IRE) **(60)***(26) (NTinkler)* 4-8-6 KimTinkler(3) (led to 5f out: sn wknd)......20 **6**
Art Deco Lady **(54)***(24) (NMBabbage)* 4-8-6 GDuffield(8) (s.i.s: a outpcd & bhd)......2 **7**
52[2] My Handy Man **(57)***(17) (RAllan)* 4-8-11 JWeaver(2) (prom tl rdn & wknd 5f out)...10 **8**

2/1 Palacegate Jo (IRE), **100/30** ASHOVER, **4/1** My Handy Man, **7/1** Can Can Charlie, **9/1** Philgun, **11/1** Jemima Puddleduck, **16/1** Art Deco Lady, **25/1** Missus Murhill (IRE), CSF £10.19 TOTECSF £10.19 TOTE £5.00: £1.70 £1.70 £3.10 (£5.70) (£5.70) OWNER Mr Thomas Cox (THIRSK) BRED Bridge End Bloodstock 8 Rn 2m 38.8 (4.60) SF: 40/27/31/19/23/-/-/-
WEIGHT FOR AGE 4yo-4lb

267 SYRIAN DESERT CLAIMING STKS (Class F) £2,537.00 (£712.00: £347.00) **7f (Fibresand)** GOING minus 0.41 sec per fur (FST) 2-40 (2-50)

*182** **Pine Ridge Lad (IRE) (67)***(72) (JLEyre)* 5-8-9 SDWilliams(12) (trckd ldrs: hdwy to ld 1f out: styd on wl)......— **1**
*211** No Submission (USA) **(66)***(67)*(Fav)*(DWChapman)* 9-8-7b LDettori(10) (sn led & clr: hdd 1f out: kpt on)......1½ **2**
Zanzara (IRE) *(56) (MrsVAAconley)* 4-8-2 TWilliams(13) (a.p: outpcd 3f out: styd on fnl f)......3 **3**
211[2] Battle Colours (IRE) **(65)***(61)*(Fav)*(MrsJRRamsden)* 6-8-9 JWeaver(7) (sn drvn along: styd on fnl 2f: nvr rchd ldrs)......¾ **4**

230[4] Dream Carrier (IRE) **(73)***(57) (JGMO'Shea)* 7-8-12 (5) JStack(6) (bhd tl styd on fnl 2f: no imp) .6 **5**
120[8] Britannia Mills **(33)***(32) (MCChapman)* 4-7-12 NKennedy(8) (in tch: rdn ½-wy: no imp).........2½ **6**
157[8] Monsieur Petong **(40)***(26) (JParkes)* 4-8-3 JFanning(9) (chsd ldrs tl grad wknd fnl 2f)..............5 **7**
Petal's Jarred **(32)***(15) (WStorey)* 5-7-10 JQuinn(1) (s.i.s: n.d)..1¾ **8**
233[14] Mockingbird **(35)***(20) (BPreece)* 4-7-13 (3)ow2 SSanders(3) (prom to st)..................................nk **9**
214[7] Rosina's Folly **(50)***(18) (JLHarris)* 4-8-2bow2 GDuffield(2) (s.i.s: n.d)..1 **10**
Kristis Girl *(14) (DHaydnJones)* 8-8-2 AMackay(4) (s.i.s: a bhd)..2 **11**
Cramona (IRE) **(27)***(—) (WStorey)* 5-7-7 (7) ClaireBalding(5) (s.i.s: a bhd)..............................6 **12**
211[W] Alpine Johnny **(55)***(—) (RHollinshead)* 4-8-7 AGarth(11) (Withdrawn not under Starter's orders).. **W**

100/30 Battle Colours (IRE), No Submission (USA), **7/2** PINE RIDGE LAD (IRE), **6/1** Dream Carrier (IRE), **10/1** Alpine Johnny, **12/1** Petal's Jarred, **16/1** Rosina's Folly, **20/1** Monsieur Petong, **25/1** Kristis Girl, **33/1** Mockingbird, Zanzara (IRE), Cramona (IRE), Britannia Mills, CSF £13.62 TOTE £3.70: £2.00 £1.00 £8.60 (£6.30) OWNER Whitestonecliffe Racing Partnership (HAMBLETON) BRED Whitechurch Stud in Ireland 12 Rn 1m 29.0 (2.20) SF: 36/31/19/24/19/-/-/-/-/-/-/-

268

SAHARA H'CAP (0-70) (Class E) £2,952.40 (£893.20: £435.60: £206.80)
6f (Fibresand) GOING minus 0.41 sec per fur (FST) 3-10 (3-16)

184[3] **Shadow Jury (53)***(58) (DWChapman)* 5-9-5b LDettori(3) (trckd ldrs: rdn to ld wl ins fnl f)......— **1**
224* Chadwell Hall **(48)***(51) (SRBowring)* 4-8-7b(7) CTeague(7) (b.off hind: cl up: led over 3f out: rdn ins fnl f: hdd & no ex nr fin)...½ **2**
94[12] Christian Flight (IRE) **(40)***(39) (SGollings)* 6-8-6 DHarrison(4) (a chsng ldrs: rdn & nt qckn appr fnl f)..1¼ **3**
228[2] At the Savoy (IRE) **(44)***(38)*(Fav)*(TDBarron)* 4-8-10 DeanMcKeown(2) (lw: dwlt: hmpd after 1f: hdwy ½-wy: hrd rdn 1f out: nt qckn)..1¾ **4**
192[4] Cheeky Chappy **(40)***(30) (DWChapman)* 4-8-6b AlexGreaves(1) (hld up: effrt over 2f out: no imp)...1½ **5**
233[10] Life's a Breeze **(49)***(24) (PSFelgate)* 6-9-1 JQuinn(6) (lw: nvr plcd to chal)..............................6 **6**
228[5] Educated Pet **(56)***(—) (BPreece)* 6-9-8b JWeaver(8) (led over 2f: eased whn btn fnl 2f)........25 **7**

9/4 At the Savoy (IRE), **11/4** Chadwell Hall (2/1-3/1), **100/30** SHADOW JURY, **8/1** Life's a Breeze, Cheeky Chappy, **9/1** Educated Pet, **25/1** Christian Flight (IRE), CSF £12.61 CT £174.74 TOTE £6.10: £3.90 £2.00 (£6.70) OWNER Mrs Jeanne Chapman (YORK) BRED J. S. Bell 7 Rn
1m 16.6 (3.10) SF: 28/23/13/14/6/-/-

269

GREAT SANDY H'CAP (0-70) (Class E) £3,166.90 (£959.20: £468.60: £223.30)
1m (Fibresand) GOING minus 0.41 sec per fur (FST) 3-40 (3-48)

195[4] **Bentico (67)***(77) (MrsNMacauley)* 6-9-11 JWeaver(3) (lw: trckd ldrs: led over 2f out: r.o u.p)— **1**
228* Aquado **(37)***(44) (ALForbes)* 6-7-9 ow1 6x JQuinn(4) (b.off hind: lw: trckd ldrs gng wl: effrt over 2f out: rdn & one pce fnl f)..1½ **2**
255* Roar on Tour **(61)***(68)*(Fav)*(MrsMReveley)* 6-9-5 6x RCochrane(9) (lw: trckd ldrs: c wd st: rdn & edgd lft appr fnl f: kpt on)..s.h **3**
212[2] Buddy's Friend (IRE) **(65)***(60) (RJRWilliams)* 7-9-2 (7) SarahThompson(10) (hld up: hdwy 3f out: sn prom & rdn: nt qckn fnl f)..6 **4**
1[6] Karinska **(63)***(56) (MCChapman)* 5-9-4 (3) DRMcCabe(8) (unruly bef s: bhd: hdwy ½-wy: styd on fnl f)...¾ **5**
222[5] Tremolante **(38)***(18) (CaptJWilson)* 4-7-4 (5)ow2 NVarley(11) (nvr bttr than mid div)..................6 **6**
46[8] Falcons Dawn **(40)***(14) (MGMeagher)* 8-7-9v(3)ow5 DWright(2) (led 3f: cl up tl wknd over 2f out)...3½ **7**
199[6] Dragonflight **(42)***(15) (DHaydnJones)* 4-7-13 ow2 AMackay(12) (lw: stumbled after s: nt rcvr)..hd **8**
Marowins **(65)***(39) (EJAlston)* 6-9-9 RHughes(13) (hld up & bhd: gd hdwy 3f out: wknd fnl f) s.h **9**
139[9] Kid Ory **(55)***(28) (PCalver)* 4-8-12 DaleGibson(7) (chsd ldrs: hrd drvn over 3f out: sn btn).....s.h **10**
167[8] Twice in Bundoran (IRE) **(47)***(10) (PSFelgate)* 4-7-13 (5)ow4 PMcCabe(5) (b: b.hind: in tch 5f)..5 **11**
68[8] Ballyhays (IRE) **(44)***(4) (JAHarris)* 6-8-2 ow1 GDuffield(1) (cl up: slt ld 5f out: hdd wl over 2f out: sn btn)..2 **12**
220[12] Mr B Reasonable (IRE) **(40)***(—) (SWCampion)* 4-7-11 ow1 NAdams(6) (sn bhd)....................10 **13**
LONG HANDICAP Falcons Dawn 7-1 Tremolante 7-1

6/4 Roar on Tour, **5/1** BENTICO, Buddy's Friend (IRE), **7/1** Aquado, **12/1** Karinska, Marowins, Ballyhays (IRE), **14/1** Tremolante, **16/1** Kid Ory, **20/1** Twice in Bundoran (IRE), **33/1** Falcons Dawn, Dragonflight, Mr B Reasonable (IRE), CSF £41.74 CT £72.81 TOTE £5.70: £1.90 £1.70 £1.30 (£14.50) Trio £9.80 OWNER Mr G. Wiltshire (MELTON MOWBRAY) BRED Britton House Stud 13 Rn 1m 42.4 (3.10) SF: 45/14/37/28/25/-/-/-/-/-/-/-/-
WEIGHT FOR AGE 4yo-1lb

270 NUBIAN (S) STKS (3-Y.O) (Class G) £2,259.00 (£634.00: £309.00)
1m (Fibresand) GOING minus 0.41 sec per fur (FST) 4-10 (4-16)

Bakers Daughter (48)*(55) (JRArnold)* 3-8-6 JQuinn(5) (trckd ldrs: led 2f out: rdn & r.o) ....— 1
*144*6 Little Scarlett **(49)***(50) (PJMakin)* 3-8-6 LDettori(3) (cl up: led after 3f to 2f out: wandered u.p)2½ 2
Summer Villa **(42)***(46) (PCHaslam)* 3-8-6 JWeaver(2) (led 3f: chsd ldrs: one pce fnl 2f)............2 3
*241*4 Poly Lane **(56)***(39) (WRMuir)* 3-9-2b DHarrison(7) (cl up tl wknd fnl 2f)....................................9 4
*90*4 Risky Rose **(38)***(22) (RHollinshead)* 3-8-1 (5) AGarth(1) (effrt ½-wy: nvr trbld ldrs) 3½ 5
*204*5 Welsh Wizzard *(22) (CNWilliams)* 3-8-11 MWigham(10) (sn drvn along: nvr trbld ldrs).........2½ 6
*189*7 Winterbottom **(41)***(14) (ICampbell)* 3-8-11v AMackay(6) (shkn up after s: in tch to st) 4 7
*90*12 Royal Addiction (IRE) *(—) (PABlockley)* 3-8-11 NCarlisle(8) (nvr wnt pce) 7 8
*5*6 Madam Sunpak *(—) (MrsVAAconley)* 3-8-3 (3) DWright(9) (prom to ½-wy: sn outpcd & bhd)..2 9
*171*4 Boldly So *(—)*(Fav)*(WJMusson)* 3-8-1 (5) PMcCabe(4) (lw: sn outpcd & wl bhd: p.u appr st)..... P

2/1 Boldly So, **3/1** Poly Lane, **4/1** Little Scarlett, **9/1** Risky Rose, **10/1** Winterbottom, **12/1** Summer Villa, BAKERS DAUGHTER, **14/1** Welsh Wizzard, **20/1** Madam Sunpak, **25/1** Royal Addiction (IRE), CSF £60.37 TOTE £18.10: £2.60 £2.00 £1.70 (£57.00) OWNER Mr J. R. Arnold (UPPER LAMBOURN) BRED C. C. Bromley and Son and A. O. Nerses 10 Rn 1m 44.4 (5.10) SF: 8/4/-/-/-/-/-/-/-/-
Bt in 4,000 gns

271 KALAHARI H'CAP (0-70) (Class E) £3,066.80 (£928.40: £453.20: £215.60)
1m 3f (Fibresand) GOING minus 0.41 sec per fur (FST) 4-40 (4-47)

*186*10 **Camden's Ransom (USA) (50)***(60) (HGRowsell)* 8-8-11 BDoyle(7) (trckd ldrs gng wl: led 3f out: shkn up & kpt on) ....— 1
*195*2 Tu Opes **(66)***(74) (JLHarris)* 4-9-10 JWeaver(8) (mde most to 3f out: kpt on) 1¾ 2
*222*4 Suivez **(49)***(55) (MrsNMacauley)* 5-8-10 LDettori(10) (sn chsng ldrs: effrt over 3f out: styd on one pce)...1¼ 3
*229*2 Mr Towser **(70)***(71) (WWHaigh)* 4-10-0 DaleGibson(12) (lw: a.p: hdwy 4f out: one pce fnl 2f)3½ 4
*166*6 Modest Hope (USA) **(45)***(38) (BRichmond)* 8-8-6 JMcLaughlin(2) (bhd: hdwy 5f out: one pce fnl 2f)...6 5
*227*4 Genesis Four **(39)***(31) (SRBowring)* 5-7-7b(7) ClaireBalding(9) (disp ld 7f out tl rdn & wknd 3f out) ....¾ 6
*229*4 In a Moment (USA) **(62)***(53) (TDBarron)* 4-9-6 DeanMcKeown(6) (chsd ldrs: rdn 6f out: outpcd fnl 4f)...1 7
Personimus **(36)***(16) (CaptJWilson)* 5-7-11 NCarlisle(4) (nvr trbld ldrs).................................8 8
*227** Awestruck **(45)***(23) (BPreece)* 5-8-6 GDuffield(5) (prom to ½-wy) 1¼ 9
Ijab (CAN) **(32)***(5) (JParkes)* 5-7-2 (5) MBaird(11) (a bhd)...3½ 10
Ho-Joe (IRE) **(41)***(9) (JMCarr)* 5-8-2 ow2 SMorris(3) (a bhd) 4 11
Sunday News'n'echo (USA) **(51)***(18)*(Fav)*(WStorey)* 4-8-6 (3) DRMcCabe(1) (a outpcd & bhd)¾ 12
Guards Brigade **(60)***(22) (JHetherton)* 4-9-4 NKennedy(13) (drvn along ½-wy: sn bhd)............4 13
LONG HANDICAP Ijab (CAN) 7-2

7/2 Sunday News'n'echo (USA), **4/1** Tu Opes, **5/1** Suivez, **11/2** Mr Towser, **9/1** In a Moment (USA), Awestruck, **12/1** Modest Hope (USA), **14/1** Ho-Joe (IRE), Genesis Four, **16/1** CAMDEN'S RANSOM (USA), **20/1** Guards Brigade, **33/1** Personimus, Ijab (CAN), CSF £80.29 CT £349.50 TOTE £33.00: £3.90 £3.30 £1.60 (£50.50) Trio £25.10 OWNER Mr E. Cobelli (WINCHESTER) BRED Dr and Mrs Chris Elia and Phil Needham 13 Rn 2m 24.6 (3.10) SF: 42/53/38/50/22/15/32/-/-/-/-/-/-
WEIGHT FOR AGE 4yo-3lb

T/Jkpt: Not won; £5,044.37 to Lingfield 14/2/95. T/Plpt: £41.50 (527.06 Tckts). T/Qdpt: £36.10 (3.7 Tckts). WG

0260-LINGFIELD (L-H)
Tuesday February 14th (Standard)

272 REID MINTY H'CAP (0-85) (Class D) £3,490.10 (£1,062.80: £523.40: £253.70)
6f (Equitrack) GOING minus 0.44 sec per fur (FST) 1-50 (1-51)

*89*3 **Triple Joy (84)***(99)*(Fav)*(SirMarkPrescott)* 4-9-13 GDuffield(4) (a.p: led 3f out: clr 1f out: r.o wl)...— 1
*237*4 Crystal Heights (FR) **(63)***(60) (RJO'Sullivan)* 7-8-6 ow2 JWeaver(3) (b: lw: led over 4f out to 3f out: hrd rdn over 1f out: unable qckn)...7 2
*177*2 Speedy Classic (USA) **(63)***(56) (MJHeaton-Ellis)* 6-8-6 LDettori(1) (led over 1f: rdn over 3f out: one pce) 1¼ 3
*188** Spender **(77)***(64) (PWHarris)* 6-9-1 (5) JStack(5) (hld up: rdn over 2f out: one pce) 2½ 4
*61*5 Thorny Bishop **(60)***(34) (JJBridger)* 4-8-3 GBardwell(2) (a bhd) 5 5
*188*3 Moscow Road **(73)***(37) (MissBSanders)* 4-8-13 (3) SSanders(6) (b.hind: lw: hld up: rdn over 3f out: wknd over 2f out)...4 6

2/1 TRIPLE JOY, **3/1** Crystal Heights (FR), **7/2** Speedy Classic (USA), **9/2** Spender, **10/1** Moscow Road, **25/1** Thorny Bishop, TOTE £2.40: £1.30 £2.20 (£6.00) OWNER Hesmonds Stud (NEWMARKET) BRED Hesmonds Stud Ltd 6 Rn 1m 11.43 (0.83) SF: 62/23/20/27/-/-

273 REID MINTY LIBEL & SLANDER CLAIMING STKS (3-Y.O) (Class E) £3,081.10 (£932.80: £455.40: £216.70) **1m 2f (Equitrack)** GOING minus 0.44 sec per fur (FST) 2-20 (2-21)

*189*4 **Star Fighter (58)***(71+)*(Fav)*(WAO'Gorman)* 3-8-8 (3) EmmaO'Gorman(1) (lw: hdwy over 6f out: led over 3f out: sn clr) — 1
*243*6 Al Corniche (IRE) **(52)***(48) (MRChannon)* 3-7-11 (5) PPMurphy(10) (hdwy over 4f out: unable qckn fnl 3f) 9 2
*263*4 Witney-de-Bergerac (IRE) **(57)***(57) (JSMoore)* 3-8-13 RHughes(2) (b.hind: hld up: chsd wnr over 2f out tl ins fnl f: one pce) 1½ 3
*180*7 Lawbuster (IRE) **(51)***(36) (WRMuir)* 3-8-1 DHarrison(5) (s.s: rdn & hdwy over 3f out: one pce) 6 4
*189*6 Keys Seminar **(50)***(24) (NACallaghan)* 3-8-9 LDettori(8) (b.hind: led over 1f: led 5f out tl over 3f out: wknd over 2f out) 13 5
Bellara *(28) (NMBabbage)* 3-9-0 VSlattery(9) (s.s: nvr nr to chal) ¾ 6
*239*5 Dingo Warrior *(14) (JFfitch-Heyes)* 3-8-1 JQuinn(7) (bhd fnl 3f) ½ 7
*144*4 Fahema **(50)***(—) (RBoss)* 3-8-2b GDuffield(6) (plld hrd: prom over 6f) 11 8
*59*6 Elite Number (USA) **(51)***(—) (PFICole)* 3-8-0b CRutter(4) (b.hind: led over 8f out to 5f out: wknd over 3f out) 1¼ 9
*211*6 First Point (IRE) **(40)***(—) (CNAllen)* 3-7-10v(5) MBaird(3) (plld hrd: hdwy over 8f out: wknd 5f out: t.o fnl 3f) dist 10

3/1 STAR FIGHTER, **7/2** Elite Number (USA), **9/2** Witney-de-Bergerac (IRE), **6/1** Fahema, **13/2** Lawbuster (IRE), **8/1** Keys Seminar, **12/1** Al Corniche (IRE), **25/1** First Point (IRE), **33/1** Bellara, Dingo Warrior, TOTE £2.80: £2.00 £2.30 £1.70 (£27.40) OWNER Mr S. Fustok (NEWMARKET) BRED Deerfield Farm 10 Rn 2m 6.68 (3.68) SF: 30/9/17/-/-/-/-/-/-/-

274 REID MINTY MOVE TO MAYFAIR MEDIAN AUCTION STKS (Mdn 3-Y.O) (Class F) £2,612.60 (£733.60: £357.80) **6f (Equitrack)** GOING minus 0.44 sec per fur (FST) 2-50 (2-51)

Das Island (58)*(63)*(Fav)*(JRJenkins)* 3-9-0 LDettori(1) (mde all: rdn over 1f out: r.o wl) — 1
*258*9 Tinker Amelia *(49) (WRMuir)* 3-8-9 JWeaver(2) (chsd wnr: ev ch wl over 1f out: unable qckn) 3½ 2
*232*3 Merrie le Bow **(53)***(40) (PMitchell)* 3-8-9 JMcLaughlin(6) (hdwy over 3f out: one pce) 3½ 3
*232*7 Paronomasia *(32) (MBell)* 3-8-7 (7) GinaFaulkner(5) (in rr whn nt clr run over 3f out: one pce) .5 4
*237*8 Nomadic Dancer (IRE) **(56)***(—) (MSSaunders)* 3-8-9 ADicks(4) (hld up: rdn over 3f out: wknd over 2f out) 12 5
*264*8 Slybird *(—) (MJRyan)* 3-8-9 AClark(3) (lw: bhd fnl 3f) ½ 6

11/8 DAS ISLAND (Evens-6/4), **5/2** Merrie le Bow, **4/1** Nomadic Dancer (IRE), **7/1** Tinker Amelia, **10/1** Paronomasia, **33/1** Slybird, TOTE £1.80: £1.60 £2.00 (£7.90) OWNER Mrs Eliza Long (ROYSTON) BRED D. H. Jones 6 Rn 1m 13.5 (2.90) SF: 21/8/-/-/-/-

275 REID MINTY 15th ANNIVERSARY STKS (0-65) (Class F) £2,663.00 (£748.00: £365.00) **1m (Equitrack)** GOING minus 0.44 sec per fur (FST) 3-20 (3-21)

Kintwyn (65)*(76) (CCElsey)* 5-9-0 DHarrison(3) (b.hind: lw: mde all: rdn out) — 1
*205** Perilous Plight **(64)***(78)*(Fav)*(WRMuir)* 4-9-6 JWeaver(6) (lw: stdd s: hdwy over 3f out: chsd wnr fnl 2f: unable qckn) 2 2
*145*5 Zacaroon **(63)***(64) (LordHuntingdon)* 4-8-9 LDettori(1) (lw: hld up: rdn over 3f out: nt clr run over 2f out: one pce) 1¼ 3
*240** Mentalasanythin **(65)***(64)*(Fav)*(ABailey)* 6-9-3 AMackay(8) (hld up: rdn over 4f out: one pce) ..4 4
*94*11 Pillow Talk (IRE) **(59)***(55) (KRBurke)* 4-8-9 RCochrane(2) (chsd wnr 6f) ½ 5
*191*5 Desert Invader (IRE) **(65)***(56) (DWChapman)* 4-8-11b(3) DRMcCabe(4) (lw: hld up: rdn over 2f out: wknd over 1f out) 1¾ 6
*148*2 The Little Ferret **(60)***(34) (GLMoore)* 5-9-0 SWhitworth(5) (lw: bhd fnl 4f) 11 7
*191*4 Pirates Gold (IRE) **(53)***(26) (JWhite)* 5-8-9 (5) SDrowne(7) (lw: bhd fnl 5f) 4 8

9/4 Mentalasanythin, Perilous Plight, **9/2** Zacaroon, **8/1** The Little Ferret, **11/1** KINTWYN, **12/1** Desert Invader (IRE), **16/1** Pillow Talk (IRE), **25/1** Pirates Gold (IRE), TOTE £23.50: £3.90 £1.00 £1.30 (£19.20) OWNER Mrs F. E. Bacon (LAMBOURN) BRED A. Baxter 8 Rn
1m 37.84 (1.44) SF: 47/49/37/36/28/31/9/-
WEIGHT FOR AGE 4yo-1lb

276

REID MINTY LITIGATORS STKS (Class D) £3,673.80 (£1,112.40: £543.20: £258.60) **1m 2f (Equitrack)** GOING minus 0.44 sec per fur (FST) 3-50 (3-51)

239* **Wild Rice** *(82+)*(Fav)*(GWragg)* 3-8-4 WWoods(2) (b: hld up: led over 2f out: clr over 1f out: r.o wl) — 1
11[4] Herr Trigger **(75)***(77) (DrJDScargill)* 4-9-7b MRimmer(4) (lw: stmbld s: rdn 4f out: hdwy over 3f out: chsd wnr over 1f out: r.o one pce) 1¼ 2
26* El Atrevido (FR) *(72) (NJHWalker)* 5-9-10 RCochrane(3) (lw: chsd ldr: led over 4f out tl over 2f out: one pce) 4 3
Speedybird (IRE) *(51) (BJMeehan)* 3-7-9 JQuinn(1) (neat: hld up: rdn 3f out: wknd 2f out) 9 4
250[6] Just Lucky (IRE) *(20) (RWArmstrong)* 3-8-4 LDettori(6) (b: led over 5f) 25 5
Tip the Dove *(—) (RJPrice)* 6-9-1 StephenDavies(5) (bhd fnl 8f) 10 6

6/4 WILD RICE, **15/8** El Atrevido (FR), **100/30** Herr Trigger, **10/1** Just Lucky (IRE), **40/1** Speedybird (IRE), Tip the Dove, TOTE £2.40: £1.50 £1.90 (£5.60) OWNER Sir Philip Oppenheimer (NEWMARKET) BRED Hascombe and Valiant Studs 6 Rn 2m 6.62 (3.62) SF: 24/39/35/-/-/-
WEIGHT FOR AGE 3yo-22lb, 4yo-2lb

277

REID MINTY FURTHER & BETTER PARTICULARS H'CAP (0-65) (Class F) £2,751.20 (£773.20: £377.60)
2m (Equitrack) GOING minus 0.44 sec per fur (FST) 4-20 (4-22)

178[5] **Sheltered Cove (IRE) (50)***(61)*(Fav)*(KOCunningham-Brown)* 4-8-10 JWeaver(2) (lw: led 1f: lost pl over 13f out: rallied over 4f out: led ins fnl f: r.o wl) — 1
147[3] Arc Bright (IRE) **(62)***(70)*(Fav)*(RHollinshead)* 5-10-0 LDettori(5) (a.p: led over 6f out tl ins fnl f: unable qckn) 3½ 2
161[4] Rose of Glenn **(50)***(53) (BPalling)* 4-8-10 GDuffield(8) (rdn & hdwy over 4f out: chsd wnr over 3f out tl over 2f out: one pce) 5 3
147[4] Elburg (IRE) **(60)***(63) (RPCHoad)* 5-9-12 JQuinn(12) (rdn over 6f out: hdwy over 3f out: r.o one pce) s.h 4
South Sands **(40)***(40) (AMForte)* 9-8-1b(5)ow2 SDrowne(6) (b: hdwy over 3f out: one pce) 3½ 5
206[5] Mr Copyforce **(60)***(52) (MissBSanders)* 5-9-9v(3) SSanders(11) (a.p: led over 8f out tl over 6f out: wknd over 3f out) 9 6
109[7] In Behind (IRE) **(48)***(38) (GLMoore)* 4-8-8 RPerham(1) (nvr nr to chal) 2 7
109[6] Wottashambles **(44)***(33) (GLewis)* 4-8-4 StephenDavies(3) (prom 11f) ½ 8
161[7] Disputed Call (USA) **(40)***(18) (JWHills)* 6-8-6bow3 RCochrane(10) (lw: hdwy 8f out: wknd 3f out) 12 9
238[3] Pearly River **(55)***(24) (DrJDScargill)* 4-9-1 MRimmer(4) (bhd fnl 4f) 10 10
Doc's Coat **(38)***(1) (CPWildman)* 10-8-4 DHarrison(7) (bkwd: dwlt: a bhd) 6 11
235[10] Prairie Grove **(52)***(2) (JSKing)* 5-9-4 GBardwell(9) (led 15f out tl over 8f out: sn wknd) 14 12

4/1 SHELTERED COVE (IRE), Arc Bright (IRE), **9/2** Elburg (IRE), **6/1** Rose of Glenn, Disputed Call (USA), **8/1** Pearly River, **14/1** Wottashambles, Mr Copyforce, **20/1** In Behind (IRE), **33/1** South Sands, Doc's Coat, **50/1** Prairie Grove, TOTE £3.00: £1.20 £2.20 £2.80 (£6.90) OWNER Mr A. J. Richards (STOCKBRIDGE) BRED Ewar Stud Farm International 12 Rn
3m 25.36 (1.86) SF: 33/47/26/40/19/29/10/-/-/-/-/-
WEIGHT FOR AGE 4yo-6lb

278

REID MINTY SOLICITORS SPRINT H'CAP (3-Y.O) (0-80) (Class D) £3,723.50 (£1,127.00: £550.00: £261.50)
6f (Equitrack) GOING minus 0.44 sec per fur (FST) 4-50 (4-50)

159[3] **Bold Effort (FR) (72)***(80)*(Fav)*(KOCunningham-Brown)* 3-9-7 JWeaver(3) (led 4f out: rdn over 2f out: r.o wl) — 1
247[6] Bon Secret (IRE) **(65)***(67) (TJNaughton)* 3-8-11 (3) SSanders(2) (lw: rdn 3f out: hdwy over 1f out: r.o wl ins fnl f) 2½ 2
159* Dolly Face **(65)***(63) (WRMuir)* 3-9-0 LDettori(6) (hld up: chsd wnr 2f out tl ins fnl f: unable qckn) 1¼ 3
146[10] Rotherfield Park (IRE) **(48)***(43) (CSmith)* 3-7-6 (5) NVarley(4) (hld up: rdn 3f out: one pce) ¾ 4
173[3] Musical Fantasy (IRE) **(53)***(23) (BJMeehan)* 3-8-2 BDoyle(1) (led 2f: wknd over 2f out) 10 5
197* Whittingham Girl **(60)***(25) (JBerry)* 3-8-9 GCarter(5) (prom over 3f) 1¾ 6

6/4 BOLD EFFORT (FR), **100/30** Whittingham Girl, **9/2** Musical Fantasy (IRE), **11/2** Dolly Face, **10/1** Rotherfield Park (IRE), Bon Secret (IRE), TOTE £2.90: £1.50 £4.50 (£18.30) OWNER Mr A. J. Richards (STOCKBRIDGE) BRED Ewar Stud Farm 6 Rn 1m 12.86 (2.26) SF: 36/24/21/4/-/-
T/Jkpt: £12,200.50 (0.38 Tckts); £10,654.00 to Wolverhampton 15/2/95. T/Plpt: £16.00 (1,687.20 Tckts). T/Qdpt: £5.70 (19.4 Tckts). AK

0241-WOLVERHAMPTON (L-H)
Wednesday February 15th (Standard)

279
HEARTS AND ROSES APP'CE H'CAP (0-70) (Class E) £2,981.00 (£902.00: £440.00: £209.00) **1m 4f (Fibresand)** GOING: 0.05 sec per fur (STD) 2-20 (2-22)

271[9] **Awestruck (45)***(57) (BPreece)* 5-8-2 (5) AEddery(9) (hld up: hdwy to ld over 2f out: sn clr: hld on)......— **1**
275[4] Mentalasanythin **(70)***(80) (ABailey)* 6-9-11 (7) 5x AngelaGallimore(7) (hld up: hdwy 4f out: 3rd st: chsd wnr appr fnl f: r.o)......1½ **2**
227[11] Child Star (FR) **(39)***(39) (DMarks)* 6-7-12e(3) MBaird(4) (eyeshield: bhd: hdwy 3f out: r.o u.p fnl f: nt rch ldrs)......8 **3**
Bodantree **(36)***(34) (HOliver)* 4-7-3 (5) PFessey(8) (bkwd: chsd ldrs: led over 3f out: hdd & 2nd st: sn wknd)......nk **4**
254[2] Port Sunlight (IRE) **(45)***(40)*(Fav)*(PDEvans)* 7-8-2 (5) DaneO'Neill(2) (bhd: effrt & 6th st: no imp)......3 **5**
*136** All on **(51)***(41) (JHetherton)* 4-8-9 JStack(5) (chsd ldr: led over 5f out tl over 3f out: 4th, rdn & wkng st)......3 **6**
214[5] T O O Mamma's (IRE) **(35)***(15) (JBerry)* 4-7-2 (5) BHalligan(3) (prom tl rdn &wknd over 2f out: t.o)......8 **7**
227[8] Spring Loaded **(42)***(—) (JGMO'Shea)* 4-7-9b(5) SLanigan(6) (bit bkwd: led & sn clr: hdd & wknd over 5f out: t.o)......dist **8**
Riva's Book (USA) **(55)***(—) (SCoathup)* 4-8-8b(5) SharronJames(1) (outpcd: a bhd: t.o)......8 **9**

100/30 Port Sunlight (IRE), **7/2** All on, **5/1** Spring Loaded, **11/2** Mentalasanythin (4/1-6/1), **6/1** AWESTRUCK, **10/1** Child Star (FR), **12/1** Riva's Book (USA), **14/1** T O O Mamma's (IRE), **25/1** Bodantree, TOTE £6.70: £2.70 £5.00 £2.10 (£11.60) OWNER Mr D. Portman (TELFORD) BRED Cheveley Park Stud Ltd 9 Rn 2m 39.6 (8.60) SF: 39/61/22/15/23/21/-/-/-
WEIGHT FOR AGE 4yo-4lb

280
CUPID CLAIMING STKS (Class F) £2,580.00 (£780.00: £380.00: £180.00) **1m 6f 166y (Fibresand)** GOING: 0.05 sec per fur (STD) 2-50 (2-50)

*223** **Royal Citizen (IRE) (64)***(59) (JFBottomley)* 6-9-2 TIves(7) (hdwy 5f out: led ent st: rdn out).— **1**
193[4] How's it Goin (IRE) **(70)***(62) (WRMuir)* 4-9-2 JWeaver(8) (lw: hld up: hdwy & 4th st: rdn & r.o wl ins fnl f)......½ **2**
183[2] Greenacres Star **(42)***(44) (BAMcMahon)* 5-8-2 (3) SSanders(4) (lw: a.p: led over 3f out: sn hdd: 3rd & rdn st: one pce)......2½ **3**
153[2] Zaaheyah (USA) **(41)***(43) (MDHammond)* 5-8-5 ow2 RCochrane(3) (lw: led tl over 3f out: sn led again: hdd & 2nd st: rdn & wknd appr fnl f)......1¼ **4**
104[6] Ginka **(46)***(31) (PJBevan)* 4-8-5b NCarlisle(5) (bit bkwd: chsd ldr 10f: sn lost tch: t.o)......15 **5**
223[2] Lone Risk **(64)***(39)*(Fav)*(MCPipe)* 4-9-0 DHarrison(6) (dwlt: plld hrd: hld up & bhd: 6th st: nvr plcd to chal: t.o)......½ **6**
227[2] Scalp 'em (IRE) **(54)***(40) (PDEvans)* 7-9-6 LDettori(1) (hld up in tch: effrt over 3f out: 5th st: eased whn btn: t.o)......½ **7**
214[9] Miss Freebie (IRE) **(30)***(19) (BAMcMahon)* 4-7-13 JO'Reilly(2) (hdwy 8f out: wknd over 3f out: t.o)......4 **8**

7/4 Lone Risk, **7/2** ROYAL CITIZEN (IRE), **4/1** How's it Goin (IRE), **5/1** Scalp 'em (IRE), **8/1** Zaaheyah (USA), **14/1** Greenacres Star, **33/1** Ginka, Miss Freebie (IRE), TOTE £4.40: £1.60 £1.80 £4.10 (£19.90) OWNER Mr John Bottomley (MALTON) BRED Whitechurch Stud 8 Rn
3m 20.4 SF: 35/35/22/21/6/14/19/-
WEIGHT FOR AGE 4yo-6lb

281
SWEETHEART H'CAP (0-90) (Class C) £5,602.00 (£1,696.00: £828.00: £394.00) **7f (Fibresand)** GOING: 0.05 sec per fur (STD) 3-20 (3-21)

*184** **Little Ibnr (80)***(87) (PDEvans)* 4-9-5 LDettori(7) (a.p: led 2f out: rdn & hld on wl)......— **1**
242[2] Ertlon **(89)***(95) (CEBrittain)* 5-10-0 BDoyle(3) (b: lw: chsd ldrs: 5th st: rdn & r.o wl ins fnl f).....½ **2**
184[4] Dawalib (USA) **(71)***(72) (DHaydnJones)* 5-8-10 DHarrison(1) (hld up: hdwy 3f out: 4th st: rdn & unable qckn fnl f)......2½ **3**
219[5] Maid Welcome **(61)***(61) (MrsNMacauley)* 8-7-7v(7) AmandaSanders(4) (led to 2f out: 2nd st: one pce appr fnl f)......nk **4**
262[4] Legal Fiction **(76)***(75)*(Fav)*(MJohnston)* 4-9-1 6x TWilliams(6) (prom: ev ch & 3rd st: rdn & no ex appr fnl f)......½ **5**
211[4] Allinson's Mate (IRE) **(68)***(63) (TDBarron)* 7-8-7 DeanMcKeown(2) (lw: hld up: hdwy over 2f out: nt pce to chal)......1¾ **6**

187[3] Arndilly **(68)**(60) (BJMeehan) 4-8-7b RCochrane(5) (b: b.hind: chsd ldrs: rdn & wknd over 2f out) 1½ **7**
Highborn (IRE) **(86)**(75) (PSFelgate) 6-9-6 (5) PMcCabe(11) (bkwd: hld up: effrt ½-wy: wknd 2f out) 1½ **8**
Bold Street (IRE) **(70)**(56) (ABailey) 5-8-9b SWhitworth(9) (bkwd: hld up & bhd: effrt 3f out: 6th & rdn st: sn wknd) 1¼ **9**
Master Beveled **(78)**(60) (PDEvans) 5-8-12 (5) JStack(8) (bit bkwd: chsd ldrs over 4f: sn outpcd) 1¾ **10**
242[3] Folly Finnesse **(75)**(44) (BRMillman) 4-9-0 TIves(10) (b.hind: prom 4f: sn lost tch: t.o) 6 **11**

4/1 Legal Fiction, **11/2** LITTLE IBNR, Highborn (IRE), Bold Street (IRE), **7/1** Ertlon, **9/1** Master Beveled, **11/1** Dawalib (USA), **12/1** Allinson's Mate (IRE), **14/1** Arndilly, **16/1** Maid Welcome, Folly Finnesse, TOTE £5.80: £2.70 £2.90 £2.70 (£13.60) OWNER Swinnerton Transport Ltd (WELSHPOOL) BRED R. E. Waugh 11 Rn 1m 28.7 (4.70) SF: 51/59/36/26/39/30/26/-/-/-/-

282 SWEET NOTHINGS STKS (Mdn 3-Y.0) (Class D) £3,538.60 (£1,070.80: £522.40: £248.20) 1m 1f 79y (Fibresand) GOING: 0.05 sec per fur (STD) 3-50 (3-50)

204[2] **Inchkeith** (63+) (GWragg) 3-8-2 (7) DGibbs(1) (mde all: rdn over 1f out: kpt on wl fnl f) ....— **1**
256[7] Callonescy (IRE) (61) (CEBrittain) 3-9-0 BDoyle(5) (b.hind: bit bkwd: hld up: hdwy ½-wy: 2nd & ev ch ent st: one pce fnl f) 4 **2**
72[2] Pleasant Memories (51)(Fav)(LordHuntingdon) 3-8-9 LDettori(4) (hld up: hdwy 4f out: 3rd & rdn st: r.o one pce) 3 **3**
Handson (20?) (BRMillman) 3-9-0 TIves(3) (w'like: bit bkwd: reard s: sn chsng wnr: wknd over 3f out: 4th & btn st) 20 **4**
Hot Breeze (—) (LJBarratt) 3-9-0 GBardwell(2) (leggy: lt-f: dwlt: sn rcvrd: wknd 4f out: 5th & t.o st) 30 **5**

4/9 Pleasant Memories, **5/2** INCHKEITH, **7/1** Callonescy (IRE), **33/1** Handson, **100/1** Hot Breeze, TOTE £4.10: £1.00 £4.20 (£8.50) OWNER Sir Philip Oppenheimer (NEWMARKET) BRED Hascombe and Valiant Studs 5 Rn 2m 3.0 (7.00) SF: 38/36/26/-/-

283 BE MY VALENTINE (S) STKS (3-Y.O) (Class G) £2,433.00 (£683.00: £333.00) 7f (Fibresand) GOING: 0.05 sec per fur (STD) 4-20 (4-20)

258[2] **Dowdency (45)**(49) (JAPickering) 3-8-6 NCarlisle(9) (hld up: hdwy over 2f out: rdn to ld cl home) ....— **1**
Beecham **(57)**(53) (AHide) 3-8-11b JQuinn(4) (bit bkwd: a.p: led 2f out tl ct fnl strides) ....nk **2**
258[10] Sweet Cheap Pet **(53)**(50) (JBerry) 3-8-11v DeanMcKeown(8) (a.p: led 3f out to 2f out: rdn & unable qckn fnl f) 1¼ **3**
171[3] Bretton Princess **(45)**(32+) (RHollinshead) 3-8-6 LDettori(5) (hld up: r.o fnl 2f: nt pce to chal)..6 **4**
240[5] Gigfy **(53)**(38) (BJLlewellyn) 3-8-13b(3) DRMcCabe(1) (s.s: nvr nr to chal) 2 **5**
101[2] Jersey Belle **(46)**(24) (PJMakin) 3-8-6 JWeaver(6) (led after 2f to 3f out: rdn & wknd fnl 2f) 2 **6**
251[4] Mr Lowry **(54)**(22) (RBoss) 3-8-11b GDuffield(10) (sn drvn along: chsd ldrs over 4f) 3½ **7**
Bernard Star (IRE) (—) (BJLlewellyn) 3-8-6 SWhitworth(7) (bkwd: s.v.s: a bhd: t.o) 8 **8**
226[5] Saxon Heir (IRE) **(41)**(7) (MDIUsher) 3-9-2b MWigham(3) (led 2f: rdn along ½-wy: sn btn) 1¼ **9**
197[2] David James' Girl **(58)**(—)(Fav)(ABailey) 3-8-11 GBardwell(2) (hld up: gd hdwy 3f out: ev ch whn fell 2f out) **0**

5/4 David James' Girl, **3/1** Mr Lowry, **6/1** Jersey Belle, **8/1** Bretton Princess, **10/1** Beecham, **12/1** Sweet Cheap Pet, DOWDENCY, Gigfy, **14/1** Saxon Heir (IRE), **33/1** Bernard Star (IRE), TOTE £11.10: £2.50 £1.70 £4.00 (£47.40) OWNER Mr P.W.Till (HINCKLEY) BRED R.G.R. Chapman 10 Rn 1m 31.4 (7.40) SF: 9/13/11/-/-/-/-/-/-/-
No bid

284 LADBROKE ALL WEATHER BOWL SERIES (H'cap) (Qualifier) (3-Y.O) (0-80) (Class D) £4,026.00 (£1,218.00: £594.00: £282.00) 5f (Fibresand) GOING: 0.05 sec per fur (STD) 4-50 (4-51)

74[2] **Hannah's Usher (79)**(83)(Fav)(PCHaslam) 3-9-7 JWeaver(3) (hld up: effrt 2f out: shkn up to ld post) ....— **1**
132[2] C-Yer-Simmie (IRE) **(60)**(63) (RHollinshead) 3-7-11 (5) AGarth(4) (led: rdn appr fnl f: ct post).hd **2**
278[3] Dolly Face **(65)**(63) (WRMuir) 3-8-7 DeanMcKeown(1) (hld up: hdwy over 1f out: fin wl) 1½ **3**
243* Crystal Loop **(73)**(53) (ABailey) 3-9-1 7x GBardwell(5) (disp ld: rdn 2f out: wknd appr fnl f) 6 **4**
Oneineverycolour **(51)**(4) (PDEvans) 3-7-2 (5) MBaird(6) (s.i.s: a outpcd) 9 **5**
Double Glow **(72)**(20) (NBycroft) 3-9-0 GDuffield(2) (bit bkwd: prom 3f: sn rdn & outpcd) 1½ **6**
LONG HANDICAP Oneineverycolour 7-6

6/4 HANNAH'S USHER, **5/2** Crystal Loop, **7/2** C-Yer-Simmie (IRE), **8/1** Dolly Face, **14/1** Double Glow, **33/1** Oneineverycolour, TOTE £2.70: £1.80 £1.20 (£2.80) OWNER Mr Bill Fitzgerald (MIDDLEHAM) BRED P. Dowson 6 Rn 61.9 secs (3.90) SF: 42/25/24/12/-/-

T/Jkpt: £20,089.40 (0.87 Tckts); £3,678.07 to Lingfield 16/2/95. T/Plpt: £299.30 (106.61 Tckts). T/Qdpt: Not won; £81.80 to Lingfield 16/2/95.

0272-LINGFIELD (L-H)
Thursday February 16th (Standard)

285 NEEDLES H'CAP (Amateurs) (0-70) (Class E) £3,052.50 (£924.00: £451.00: £214.50) **1m 5f (Equitrack)** GOING minus 0.49 sec per fur (FST) 1-50 (1-53)

221[4] **Royal Circus (35)***(41) (JGMO'Shea)* 6-8-10 (4) MrsSBosley(7) (chsd ldr: led 4f out: rdn 2f out: r.o) — 1
172[5] Don't Drop Bombs (USA) **(36)***(36)*(Fav)*(DTThom)* 6-9-1v MissJFeilden(4) (led 9f: rdn over 2f out: one pce) 5 2
22[5] Lady Bunting **(35)***(29) (MissBSanders)* 8-8-7 (7) MissHMitchell(9) (mid div: rdn 4f out: r.o one pce fnl 2f) 5 3
200[2] Fiery Sun **(37)***(31) (JLEyre)* 10-9-2vow2 MissDianaJones(10) (chsd ldrs: outpcd fnl f) nk 4
240[6] Remember This (IRE) **(45)***(35) (CACyzer)* 5-9-3 (7)ow4 MissAWilcox(2) (a mid div) 3½ 5
193[7] View From Above **(70)***(59) (NJHWalker)* 9-11-3 (4) MrsDMcHale(6) (mid div: rdn over 4f out: one pce fnl 3f) ¾ 6
234[5] Alternation (FR) **(50)***(27) (JWebber)* 6-9-8 (7)ow7 MrPScott(1) (a bhd) 10 7
166[11] Wicklow Boy (IRE) **(40)***(17) (TTClement)* 4-8-12v(4) MrVLukaniuk(3) (s.s: a bhd) hd 8
Brilliant **(58)***(28) (JPearce)* 7-10-9 MrsLPearce(8) (bhd fnl 5f) 6 9
187[8] Esperer **(44)***(5) (JO'Donoghue)* 5-9-2 (7)ow1 MrsTEustance(5) (a bhd) 8 10

LONG HANDICAP Lady Bunting 8-0 Fiery Sun 8-7

9/4 Don't Drop Bombs (USA), **7/2** Brilliant, **9/2** ROYAL CIRCUS, **15/2** View From Above, **9/1** Fiery Sun, **14/1** Wicklow Boy (IRE), **20/1** Remember This (IRE), **25/1** Alternation (FR), Lady Bunting, **33/1** Esperer, TOTE £7.60: £2.20 £1.10 £6.70 (£5.30) OWNER Mr P. W. Hiatt (REDDITCH) BRED Snailwell Stud Co Ltd 10 Rn 2m 48.84 (6.34) SF: 21/17/10/12/15/36/7/-/-/-

WEIGHT FOR AGE 4yo-3lb

286 DURLSTON HEAD MEDIAN AUCTION STKS (Mdn 3-Y.O.F) (Class F) £2,625.20 (£737.20: £359.60) **7f (Equitrack)** GOING minus 0.49 sec per fur (FST) 2-25 (2-27)

225[2] **Sand Star (53)***(44) (DHaydnJones)* 3-8-11 AMackay(5) (lw: chsd ldrs: n.m.r 2f out: swtchd rt over 1f out: hrd rdn fnl f: led nr fin) — 1
239[4] Considerable Charm *(43) (LordHuntingdon)* 3-8-11 DHarrison(3) (a.p: led over 1f out: hrd rdn fnl f: hdd nr fin) nk 2
Solianna **(69)***(39)*(Fav)*(MRChannon)* 3-8-11 RHughes(1) (led over 5f out tl over 1f out: hrd rdn fnl f: one pce) 2 3
57[6] Kings of Canvey Is **(35)***(15) (JWhite)* 3-8-6 (5) SDrowne(4) (led over 1f: wknd over 2f out) 11 4
Brooke Wood *(7) (MissBSanders)* 3-8-4 (7) AmandaBowen(2) (rdn 3f out: a bhd) 4 5

8/11 Solianna, **11/4** SAND STAR, **7/2** Considerable Charm, **33/1** Kings of Canvey Is, Brooke Wood, TOTE £3.70: £1.40 £2.70 (£4.00) OWNER Mrs T. M. Parry (PONTYPRIDD) BRED Mrs M. L. Parry and P. M. Steele-Mortimer 5 Rn 1m 28.66 (5.66) SF: -/-/-/-/-

287 LINGFIELD PARK AWT SPRINT SERIES H'CAP (Qualifier) (0-60) (Class F) £2,963.70 (£833.20: £407.10) **6f (Equitrack)** GOING minus 0.49 sec per fur (FST) 2-55 (2-57)

217[2] **Myjinka (35)***(42) (JO'Donoghue)* 5-8-3b(5) PMcCabe(9) (a.p: led over 1f out: r.o wl) — 1
220* Our Shadee (USA) **(52)***(54) (KTIvory)* 5-9-4v(7) CScally(10) (s.i.s: bhd: hdwy 2f out: str run fnl f: r.o) 1¾ 2
192[2] Purbeck Centenary **(47)***(45) (PHowling)* 5-9-6 JQuinn(6) (b.hind: led over 4f out: hdd over 1f out: one pce) 1½ 3
7[6] Black Shadow **(47)***(41) (PJMcBride)* 3-7-13 (5) LNewton(2) (mid div: hrd rdn over 1f out: r.o one pce fnl f) 1½ 4
220[11] Waders Dream (IRE) **(35)***(24) (PMitchell)* 6-8-8v RCochrane(4) (mid div: hdwy over 2f out: rdn over 1f out: one pce) 1¾ 5
165[9] Splash of Salt (IRE) **(45)***(34) (TJNaughton)* 5-9-4 JWeaver(11) (b: mid div: rdn 2f out: r.o one pce fnl f) s.h 6
192[6] Hinari Video **(47)***(35) (MJohnston)* 10-9-6 TWilliams(5) (led over 1f: rdn over 2f out: one pce) hd 7
144[5] Tachycardia **(50)***(30) (RJO'Sullivan)* 3-8-7 WWoods(8) (chsd ldrs tl rdn & wknd over 2f out) 3 8

*237*2 Waverley Star **(34)***(13)*(Fav)*(KOCunningham-Brown)* 10-8-7 LCharnock(1) (lw: sn outpcd: bhd fnl 5f) ....nk **9**
*220*10 Pat Poindestres **(34)***(8) (BAPearce)* 5-8-7 StephenDavies(3) (b.hind: dwlt: a bhd) 2 **10**
*202*6 Mheanmetoo **(55)***(19) (DLWilliams)* 4-9-11 (3) DWright(7) (a bhd) 4 **11**

5/2 Waverley Star, **3/1** Tachycardia, **11/2** Purbeck Centenary, **7/1** Our Shadee (USA) (5/1-8/1), Black Shadow, **9/1** MYJINKA, **16/1** Pat Poindestres, Splash of Salt (IRE), **20/1** Hinari Video, **25/1** Waders Dream (IRE), Mheanmetoo, TOTE £10.80: £2.20 £1.80 £2.00 (£17.00) OWNER Miss P. I. Westbrook (REIGATE) BRED Miss Prue Westbrook and Bob Pettis 11 Rn

1m 12.58 (1.98) SF: 24/37/29/10/11/20/21/-/-/-/-

WEIGHT FOR AGE 3yo-16lb

288 HURST POINT (S) H'CAP (0-60) (Class G) £2,449.40 (£688.40: £336.20) **2m (Equitrack)** GOING minus 0.72 sec per fur (FST) 3-30 (3-31)

*260*2 **Dancing Diamond (IRE) (50)***(59) (MissBSanders)* 5-9-7hv(3) SSanders(5) (a.p: led 6f out to 2f out: led over 1f out: hrd rdn & r.o) ....— **1**
*260*13 Nothing Doing (IRE) **(35)***(43) (WJMusson)* 6-8-9 RCochrane(12) (hld up: hdwy 8f out: led 2f out tl over 1f out: unable qckn) 1½ **2**
*201*4 Upper Mount Clair **(50)***(55) (CEBrittain)* 5-9-10 BDoyle(4) (hld up: hdwy 6f out: chsd ldr 4f out: hrd rdn over 2f out: r.o one pce fnl f) 3 **3**
*277*5 South Sands **(38)***(38) (AMForte)* 9-8-12e AMackay(11) (eyeshield: b: chsd ldrs: rdn 3f out: one pce fnl 2f) 5 **4**
*9** Arian Spirit (IRE) **(41)***(36)*(Fav)*(JLEyre)* 4-8-6 (3) DRMcCabe(6) (mid div & rdn along: hdwy 8f out: lost pl 5f out: hrd rdn 3f out: one pce fnl 2f) 5 **5**
*260*6 So Discreet (USA) **(48)***(42) (JWhite)* 7-9-3 (5) SDrowne(8) (chsd ldrs: hrd rdn 4f out: wknd over 1f out) 1½ **6**
*153*7 Blue Pennant **(34)***(20) (TTBill)* 4-8-2 NCarlisle(3) (a bhd) 9 **7**
Mexican Dancer **(27)***(12) (PHowling)* 6-8-1 JQuinn(2) (b.hind: a bhd) ....½ **8**
Dragonmist (IRE) **(29)***(13) (MMadgwick)* 5-8-3 TWilliams(1) (chsd ldr: led 9f out to 6f out: wknd 4f out) 1½ **9**
*260*9 Side Bar **(34)***(4) (MJRyan)* 5-8-8b DBiggs(10) (bhd fnl 8f) 15 **10**
*58*9 Highland Flame **(28)***(—) (KTIvory)* 6-8-2v GBardwell(7) (b: chsd ldrs tl rdn & wknd qckly 5f out: t.o) ....dist **11**
*248*10 Arras Royale **(22)***(—) (JELong)* 5-7-10 NAdams(9) (b: led 7f: sn wknd: t.o) 7 **12**

13/8 Arian Spirit (IRE), **11/4** DANCING DIAMOND (IRE), **7/1** Side Bar, **9/1** Upper Mount Clair, **10/1** So Discreet (USA), **20/1** Nothing Doing (IRE), South Sands, Dragonmist (IRE), **33/1** Mexican Dancer, Blue Pennant, **40/1** Highland Flame, Arras Royale, TOTE £4.60: £1.00 £8.20 £4.30 (£37.20) OWNER Mrs J. M. Laycock (EPSOM) BRED Kiltinan Farms Inc 12 Rn

3m 26.23 (2.73) SF: 38/23/34/19/12/22/-/-/-/-/-/-

WEIGHT FOR AGE 4yo-6lb

No bid

289 EDDYSTONE H'CAP (3-Y.O) (0-70) (Class E) £3,242.80 (£910.80: £444.40) **1m (Equitrack)** GOING minus 0.49 sec per fur (FST) 4-00 (4-01)

*241** **Soldier's Leap (FR) (66)***(82)*(Fav)*(CEBrittain)* 3-9-13v RCochrane(3) (led 2f: led 4f out: clr 2f out: pushed out) ....— **1**
Never so Rite (IRE) **(44)***(46) (DWPArbuthnot)* 3-8-5 JQuinn(2) (chsd ldrs: rdn over 3f out: no imp) 7 **2**
*60*2 Sandra Dee (IRE) **(52)***(50) (BAPearce)* 3-8-13 JWeaver(1) (plld hrd: led 6f out to 4f out: rdn over 1f out: wknd fnl f) 2 **3**

8/13 SOLDIER'S LEAP (FR), **5/2** Sandra Dee (IRE), **4/1** Never so Rite (IRE), TOTE £1.40 (£2.90) OWNER Mr A. J. Richards (NEWMARKET) BRED Ewar Stud Farm 3 Rn 1m 40.61 (4.21) SF: 28/-/-

290 DUNGENESS POINT STKS (Mdn) (Class D) £3,589.30 (£1,086.40: £530.20: £252.10) **1m 4f (Equitrack)** GOING minus 0.49 sec per fur (FST) 4-30 (4-33)

Old Rouvel (USA) *(67) (DJGMurraySmith)* 4-8-13 JWeaver(7) (small: lw: a.p: led over 4f out: clr over 1f out: r.o) ....— **1**
*252*6 Regal Pursuit (IRE) **(57)***(58)*(Fav)*(CAHorgan)* 4-8-8h WWoods(4) (in rr: rdn 4f out: hdwy 2f out: r.o fnl f) 3½ **2**
*190*4 Come on Dancer (IRE) **(53)***(58) (JWhite)* 7-8-11 (5) SDrowne(5) (a.p: rdn 4f out: one pce fnl 2f) 4 **3**
*235*7 Bandita **(40)***(51) (MissAJWhitfield)* 4-8-5 (3) SSanders(3) (led 2f: rdn over 3f out: one pce fnl 2f) 1¾ **4**

155[3] Kedwick (IRE) **(57)***(53) (PRHedger)* 6-9-2b StephenDavies(6) (b.hind: hld up: hdwy 5f out: chsd wnr over 3f out tl rdn & wknd over 1f out)........2½ 5
Admiral Hood (USA) *(48) (LordHuntingdon)* 4-8-13 DHarrison(2) (unf: bkwd: nvr nrr)........4 6
218[3] Thorniwama **(35)***(31) (JJBridger)* 4-8-8b GBardwell(9) (mid div: rdn 3f out: wknd over 2f out).10 7
190[5] Mountain Boy *(34) (MJohnston)* 4-8-13 AProud(8) (led 10f out tl over 4f out: sn wknd)........2 8
Il Fratello *(30) (NACallaghan)* 4-8-13 RHughes(1) (w'like: bhd fnl 4f)........3 9
A New Flame *(30) (RGuest)* 4-8-13 RCochrane(10) (w'like: bit bkwd: s.s: a bhd)........hd 10

9/4 Regal Pursuit (IRE), **5/2** OLD ROUVEL (USA), **11/4** Kedwick (IRE), **12/1** Admiral Hood (USA), **14/1** Il Fratello, Come on Dancer (IRE), **20/1** A New Flame, **33/1** Mountain Boy, Bandita, Thorniwama, TOTE £3.80: £1.80 £1.90 £3.70 (£8.20) OWNER Ms Diane Wilder (LAMBOURN) BRED The Bloodstock Agency in USA 10 Rn 2m 33.16 (3.76) SF: 33/25/27/19/23/15/-/-/-/-
WEIGHT FOR AGE 4yo-3lb

T/Jkpt: £6,098.70 (1.38 Tckts). T/Plpt: £42.10 (411.78 Tckts). T/Qdpt: £131.20 (0.5 Tckts); £88.70 to Southwell 17/2/95.

0253A-CAGNES-SUR-MER (Nice, France) (L-H)
Tuesday February 7th (Soft)

291a PRIX DU TRAYAS (3-Y.O) £5,988.00
1m 2f

207a[5] **Courbaril** *(—) (SDow)* 3-8-7 FSanchez ....— 1
207a* Sharpest Image (IRE) *(—) (France)* 3-9-2 SMaillot 2 2
Minervitta *(—) (France)* 3-8-8 ESaint-Martin 1 3

TOTE 8.70F: 3.00F 1.90F 2.50F (31.60F) OWNER G.Steinberg (EPSOM) BRED George & Mrs Steinberg 19 Rn 2m 10.7 SF: -/-/-

0266-SOUTHWELL (L-H)
Friday February 17th (Standard)

292 GIRTON H'CAP (3-Y.O) (0-60) (Class F) £2,537.00 (£712.00: £347.00)
1m 3f (Fibresand) GOING minus 0.36 sec per fur (FST) 1-50 (1-52)

Fen Terrier (55)*(58) (WJHaggas)* 3-9-7 WWoods(5) (lw: sn chsng ldrs: led over 2f out: hld on wl)........— 1
133[3] Hever Golf Lady **(39)***(41)*(Fav)*(TJNaughton)* 3-8-5 JWeaver(4) (lw: cl up early: lost pl appr st: ev ch ins fnl f: no ex nr fin)........½ 2
241[5] Fools of Pride (IRE) **(48)***(42) (RHollinshead)* 3-9-0 LDettori(8) (chsd ldrs: effrt appr st: one pce appr fnl f)........6 3
116[7] Fairy's Son **(46)***(38) (WRMuir)* 3-8-12 DHarrison(11) (hld up & bhd: stdy hdwy 5f out: ev ch 2f out: rdn & nt qckn)........2 4
185[5] Miss Suzy **(30)***(20) (JPLeigh)* 3-7-7 (3)ow3 DWright(3) (lw: bhd: hdwy on outside 7f out: chsng ldrs 3f out: rdn & grad wknd fnl 2f)........1½ 5
180[3] Runforaction (IRE) **(45)***(32) (BSRothwell)* 3-8-11 MFenton(2) (led 2f: chsd ldrs tl outpcd appr st)........2½ 6
263[W] Friar's Oak **(39)***(24) (MHTompkins)* 3-8-0 (5)ow1 SMulvey(1) (drvn along & bhd 5f out: n.d)....1½ 7
213[6] Kindred Greeting **(46)***(28) (DMorris)* 3-8-12 TIves(7) (bhd & rdn 5f out: no imp)........2½ 8
95[9] Princess Kamina **(35)***(9) (MJCamacho)* 3-8-1v LCharnock(12) (bit bkwd: prom: led 6f out tl over 2f out: sn wknd)........6 9
185[4] Jilly Jaffa Cake (IRE) **(48)***(21) (DWPArbuthnot)* 3-9-0 SWhitworth(13) (a chsng ldrs: effrt 4f out: one pce fnl 2f)........¾ 10
133[10] Centaur Express **(35)***(—) (ALForbes)* 3-8-1 JQuinn(10) (cl up early: outpcd 6f out: sn wknd) .7 11
225[7] Haya Ya Kefaah **(35)***(—) (SirMarkPrescott)* 3-8-1 ow1 GDuffield(6) (led after 2f to 6f out: sn wknd)........7 12
133[5] Something Speedy (IRE) **(50)***(—) (PJBevan)* 3-9-2 NCarlisle(9) C
LONG HANDICAP Miss Suzy 7-4

3/1 Hever Golf Lady, **4/1** FEN TERRIER, **6/1** Jilly Jaffa Cake (IRE), **7/1** Runforaction (IRE), **10/1** Fools of Pride (IRE), Haya Ya Kefaah, **12/1** Something Speedy (IRE), **16/1** Kindred Greeting, Princess Kamina, Friar's Oak, Miss Suzy, **20/1** Fairy's Son, **25/1** Centaur Express, TOTE £5.80: £1.10 £1.60 £2.90 (£7.10) OWNER Jolly Farmers Racing (NEWMARKET) BRED Racing Thoroughbreds P L C 13 Rn 2m 30.6 (9.10) SF: 15/-/-/-/-/-/-/-/-/-/-/-/-

293

HARDWICK CLAIMING STKS (Class F) £2,537.00 (£712.00: £347.00)
1m (Fibresand) GOING minus 0.36 sec per fur (FST) 2-25 (2-25)

267[2] **No Submission (USA) (66)***(72)*(Fav)*(DWChapman)* 9-8-5 LDettori(4) (mde all: shkn up 2f out: r.o)........— 1
267[4] Battle Colours (IRE) **(65)***(68) (MrsJRRamsden)* 6-8-8b JWeaver(5) (trckd wnr: chal & effrt 2f out: no ex fnl f)........3½ 2
169[8] Shuttlecock **(65)***(69) (MrsNMacauley)* 4-8-9 MFenton(2) (cl up: rdn over 2f out: one pce)......hd 3
Private Fixture (IRE) **(74)***(49) (DMarks)* 4-9-1 TIves(7) (in tch: outpcd ½-wy: no imp after).....13 4
92[4] Millsolin (IRE) **(67)***(25) (RAkehurst)* 7-8-3 GCarter(6) (b: lost tch ½-wy: n.d after)........6 5
Try Again Jane *(12) (DEddy)* 5-8-2vow2 GDuffield(1) (a outpcd & bhd)........6 6

9/4 NO SUBMISSION (USA), **11/4** Millsolin (IRE) (2/1-3/1), **3/1** Shuttlecock, **9/2** Battle Colours (IRE), **14/1** Private Fixture (IRE), **25/1** Try Again Jane, TOTE £3.40: £1.70 £1.90 (£3.60) OWNER Mr T. S. Redman (YORK) BRED Mr. Francis X. Weber 6 Rn 1m 43.2 (3.90) SF: 22/19/19/-/-/-

294

KIRKBY-IN-ASHFIELD H'CAP (3-Y.O) (0-70) (Class E) £3,052.50 (£924.00: £451.00: £214.50) **7f (Fibresand)** GOING minus 0.36 sec per fur (FST) 2-55 (2-56)

257[2] **Posted Abroad (IRE) (63)***(70)*(Fav)*(SirMarkPrescott)* 3-9-5 GDuffield(7) (plld hrd: hdwy appr st: led appr fnl f: r.o u.p)........— 1
Three Arch Bridge **(53)***(59) (MJohnston)* 3-8-9 TWilliams(3) (s.i.s: hdwy to ld after 1f: hdd over 1f out: rallied nr fin)........hd 2
Speedy Snaps Pride **(45)***(45) (PDCundell)* 3-8-1 AMackay(6) (bhd tl hdwy 2f out: styd on wl nr fin)........3 3
210[5] Chaldon Herring **(58)***(57) (TDBarron)* 3-9-0 DeanMcKeown(2) (lw: plld hrd: cl up: effrt 2f out: one pce)........nk 4
243[5] Chadleigh Lane (USA) **(65)***(61) (RHollinshead)* 3-9-7 TIves(4) (lw: prom tl outpcd appr st: no imp after)........1¼ 5
156[3] Bally Wonder **(46)***(35) (DMorris)* 3-8-2 CRutter(5) (chsd ldrs tl outpcd fnl 2½f)........3½ 6
*257** Pc's Cruiser (IRE) **(59)***(47) (MCChapman)* 3-8-8 (7) 6x CMunday(1) (led 1f: chsd ldrs tl wknd fnl 2f)........½ 7

Evens POSTED ABROAD (IRE), **4/1** Chaldon Herring, Pc's Cruiser (IRE), **9/1** Chadleigh Lane (USA), **12/1** Bally Wonder, **16/1** Three Arch Bridge, **33/1** Speedy Snaps Pride, TOTE £1.90: £1.10 £5.10 (£18.50) OWNER Mr Neil Greig (NEWMARKET) BRED John Kent in Ireland 7 Rn
1m 31.9 (5.10) SF: 17/8/-/5/9/-/-

295

LAXTON H'CAP (0-70) (Class E) £3,109.70 (£941.60: £459.80: £218.90)
2m (Fibresand) GOING minus 0.36 sec per fur (FST) 3-30 (3-30)

238[5] **La Menorquina (USA) (33)***(44) (DMarks)* 5-7-3 (5) MBaird(8) (bhd: hdwy 6f out: chal ins fnl f: r.o to ld nr fin)........— 1
45[2] Nahri (USA) **(57)***(68) (JMackie)* 4-8-12 GCarter(6) (in tch: drvn along 5f out: led over 1f out: rdn ins fnl f: r.o: jst ct)........hd 2
259[2] Risky Tu **(54)***(61) (PAKelleway)* 4-8-2 (7) AdelleGibbons(1) (lw: a chsng ldrs: one pce fnl 3f)....4 3
108[5] Taroudant **(67)***(74) (MrsMReveley)* 8-10-0 RCochrane(10) (lw: hld up: hdwy on bit to ld over 3f out: sn qcknd clr: hdd over 1f out: sn btn)........hd 4
*259** Who's the Best (IRE) **(40)***(33)*(Fav)*(APJarvis)* 5-7-10 (5) 4x NVarley(11) (prom: drvn along 7f out: led 5f out tl over 3f out: eased whn btn)........15 5
259[12] Well and Truly **(53)***(40) (BAMcMahon)* 8-9-0 JWeaver(5) (led 3f: cl up tl wknd over 2f out: eased whn btn)........6 6
259[9] Moonshine Dancer **(48)***(33) (MrsMReveley)* 5-8-2 (7) SCopp(3) (lw: bhd: hdwy 5f out: nvr nr to chal)........2½ 7
206[6] Vishnu (USA) **(65)***(37) (JLEyre)* 5-9-12 AClark(9) (nvr trbld ldrs)........14 8
259[7] Mrs Jawleyford (USA) **(56)***(20) (CSmith)* 7-9-3 WWoods(4) (b: trckd ldrs: led 6f out to 5f out: sn wknd)........8 9
215[5] Ozzie Jones **(43)***(5) (MCChapman)* 4-7-12b NKennedy(12) (hdwy to ld after 3f: hdd 6f out: sn lost pl)........1¾ 10
245[4] Turfmans Vision **(45)***(3) (RHollinshead)* 5-8-6 LDettori(2) (in tch tl wknd 5f out)........4 11
131[7] Electrolyte **(58)***(14) (BPalling)* 5-9-5 DHarrison(13) (b: chsd ldrs 7f: sn wl bhd)........2 12
Surcoat **(42)***(—) (RJBaker)* 8-8-3 JQuinn(7) (wl bhd fr ½-wy)........1 13

3/1 Who's the Best (IRE), **4/1** Taroudant, **11/2** Risky Tu, Nahri (USA), **10/1** Well and Truly, **12/1** Vishnu (USA), Mrs Jawleyford (USA), **14/1** Ozzie Jones, LA MENORQUINA (USA), Turfmans Vision, **16/1** Moonshine Dancer, **33/1** Surcoat, **50/1** Electrolyte, TOTE £17.30: £3.00 £2.10 £2.00 (£29.10) OWNER Mr Joe Arden (UPPER LAMBOURN) BRED R. L. Elam 13 Rn
3m 42.0 (16.00) SF: -/-/-/5/-/-/-/-/-/-/-/-/-
WEIGHT FOR AGE 4yo-6lb
STEWARDS' ENQUIRY Carter suspended 26-27/2/95 (excessive use of whip).

296 MAPLEBECK (S) STKS (Class G) £2,259.00 (£634.00: £309.00)
1m 4f (Fibresand) GOING minus 0.36 sec per fur (FST) 4-00 (4-02)

Red Indian (50)*(68) (WWHaigh)* 9-9-0 DeanMcKeown(4) (hld up: qcknd to ld wl over 1f out: hung lft & hld on wl)........— 1
*19** Mad Militant (IRE) **(71)***(72)*(Fav)*(RHollinshead)* 6-9-5 LDettori(1) (lw: trckd ldrs on bit: n.m.r & swtchd 2f out: qcknd to chal ins fnl f: no ex)........nk 2
260[5] Aviator's Dream **(50)***(51) (JPearce)* 5-9-0 GBardwell(6) (trckd ldrs: effrt 3f out: rdn & btn wl over 1f out)........13 3
*254** Killing Time **(60)***(56) (MrsNMacauley)* 4-9-2v MFenton(5) (led tl wl over 1f out: sn outpcd)....s.h 4
222[7] Greek Gold (IRE) **(58)***(31) (GPKelly)* 6-9-5 AlexGreaves(2) (b: b.hind: cl up tl wknd 3f out)...20 5
256[11] Rory John *(20) (SWCampion)* 7-9-0 RCochrane(3) (a bhd)........5 6

Evens Mad Militant (IRE), **3/1** Killing Time, **5/1** RED INDIAN, **15/2** Greek Gold (IRE) (6/1-9/1), **12/1** Aviator's Dream, **50/1** Rory John, TOTE £7.30: £2.20 £1.30 (£5.40) OWNER Mr Dave Marshall (MALTON) BRED A. O'Brien 6 Rn 2m 40.2 (6.00) SF: 32/37/16/17/-/-
WEIGHT FOR AGE 4yo-3lb
No bid

297 LADBROKE ALL WEATHER BOWL SERIES H'CAP (Qualifier) (0-75) (Class D) £3,640.00 (£1,102.00: £538.00: £256.00)
6f (Fibresand) GOING minus 0.36 sec per fur (FST) 4-30 (4-31)

White Sorrel (62)*(68) (JLEyre)* 4-8-10 (5) JStack(7) (trckd ldrs: led & hung lft 2f out: r.o)........— 1
*233** Bella Parkes **(72)***(75) (DNicholls)* 4-9-11b 7x AlexGreaves(9) (lw: bhd: effrt & hung lft over 2f out: hdwy over 1f out: nrst fin)........1 2
265[6] Aljaz **(54)***(57) (DTThom)* 5-8-7 AMackay(3) (b: in tch: hdwy 3f out: sn chsng ldrs: kpt on one pce fnl f)........s.h 3
268[2] Chadwell Hall **(49)***(42)*(Fav)*(SRBowring)* 4-7-9b(7)ow1 CTeague(4) (b.off hind: w ldrs: effrt over 2f out: one pce)........4 4
154[3] Leigh Crofter **(75)***(64)*(Fav)*(PDCundell)* 6-10-0b JWeaver(6) (chsd ldrs tl wknd fnl 2f)........1½ 5
184[2] Warwick Warrior (IRE) **(71)***(59) (MrsLPiggott)* 4-9-3 (7) VictoriaAppleby(2) (b: b.hind: led to 2f out: grad wknd)........hd 6
228[4] Cheerful Groom (IRE) **(44)***(22) (JMackie)* 4-7-11 JQuinn(1) (s.i.s: effrt ½-wy: no imp)........4 7
Hello Hobson's (IRE) **(56)***(—) (RBastiman)* 5-8-9 DeanMcKeown(8) (s.i.s: a bhd)........15 8
224[4] Frisky Miss (IRE) **(65)***(1) (KOCunningham-Brown)* 4-9-4 LDettori(5) (spd over 3f: eased whn btn fnl 2f)........1½ 9

7/2 Chadwell Hall, Leigh Crofter, **11/2** Warwick Warrior (IRE), **6/1** WHITE SORREL, **7/1** Aljaz, **8/1** Bella Parkes, **9/1** Frisky Miss (IRE), **14/1** Cheerful Groom (IRE), **50/1** Hello Hobson's (IRE), TOTE £10.00: £3.90 £3.10 £2.00 (£48.10) OWNER Mr R. Fenwick-Gibson (HAMBLETON) BRED Stud-On-The-Chart 9 Rn 1m 16.2 (2.70) SF: 34/40/24/9/28/24/-/-/-

T/Jkpt: Not won; £5,642.26 to Newcastle 18/2/95. T/Plpt: £120.10 (139.4 Tckts). T/Qdpt: £153.80 (1.05 Tckts).

0285-LINGFIELD (L-H)
Saturday February 18th (Standard)

298 DOROTHY L. SAYERS APP'CE H'CAP (0-70) (Class E) £3,081.10 (£932.80: £455.40: £216.70) **7f (Equitrack)** GOING minus 0.55 sec per fur (FST) 2-20 (2-21)

160[4] **Present Situation (65)***(74) (LordHuntingdon)* 4-9-11 (3) AWhelan(9) (a.p: rdn over 1f out: led ins fnl f: r.o wl)........— 1
275[7] The Little Ferret **(60)***(64) (GLMoore)* 5-9-4 (5) LSuthern(3) (chsd ldrs: rdn over 1f out: r.o).....2½ 2
93[12] Newington Butts (IRE) **(47)***(48) (RAkehurst)* 5-8-5b(5) RMoogan(2) (led: rdn over 1f out: hdd ins fnl f: wknd nr fin)........1½ 3
*217** Words of Wisdom (IRE) **(62)***(59)*(Fav)*(CACyzer)* 5-9-11 SMulvey(1) (hld up: hdwy over 2f out: rdn over 1f out: r.o one pce fnl f)........2 4
Mary's Case (IRE) **(57)***(53) (MJohnston)* 5-9-1 (5) OliverCasey(5) (mid div: rdn over 3f out: one pce fnl 2f)........½ 5
181[5] Orthorhombus **(52)***(46) (DJSCosgrove)* 6-9-1b LNewton(7) (mid div: rdn 3f out: one pce fnl 2f) 1 6
Courting Newmarket **(51)***(41) (MrsAKnight)* 7-8-9 (5) SarahThompson(4) (chsd ldrs over 4f: wknd over 1f out)........2 7
192[8] Forgotten Dancer (IRE) **(50)***(35) (RIngram)* 4-8-13 SDrowne(8) (a bhd)........2½ 8
Giggleswick Girl **(62)***(14) (MRChannon)* 4-9-8 (3) PPMurphy(6) (dwlt: a bhd)........15 9

9/4 Words of Wisdom (IRE), **5/2** PRESENT SITUATION, **5/1** The Little Ferret, **12/1** Orthorhombus, Courting Newmarket, **14/1** Mary's Case (IRE), Newington Butts (IRE), **16/1** Forgotten Dancer (IRE), Giggleswick Girl, TOTE £3.20: £1.90 £2.10 £6.60 (£9.60) OWNER Mr Chris van Hoorn (WEST ILSLEY) BRED The Queen 9 Rn 1m 24.94 (1.94) SF: 42/32/17/26/21/14/9/-/-

299 HELEN McINNES STKS (Mdn) (Class D) £3,538.60 (£1,070.80: £522.40: £248.20) **5f (Equitrack)** GOING minus 0.55 sec per fur (FST) 2-50 (2-50)

247[7] **Halliard (53)***(60) (TMJones)* 4-9-10 RPerham(4) (chsd ldr: led 1f out: r.o) — 1
57[3] Avant Huit **(53)***(50) (MrsNMacauley)* 3-7-11 (7) AmandaSanders(6) (sn outpcd & bhd: hdwy over 1f out: str run fnl f: fin wl) 1½ 2
258[5] Branston Kristy **(38)***(39) (CSmith)* 3-8-4 WWoods(3) (b.hind: chsd ldrs: rdn & sltly outpcd 3f out: hdwy 1f out: r.o one pce) 3½ 3
La Suquet **(66)***(34)*(Fav)*(MRChannon)* 3-8-4 CRutter(2) (chsd ldrs: rdn & sltly outpcd 3f out: hdwy over 1f out: one pce) 1½ 4
124[5] Just Jesting **(53)***(35) (GLMoore)* 3-8-9v SWhitworth(5) (led to 1f out: wknd fnl f) 1¼ 5
Fairlight Magic *(3) (PCHaslam)* 3-7-11 (7) NicolaHowarth(1) (b: w'like: s.i.s: outpcd: a bhd) 9 6

11/10 La Suquet, **7/4** Avant Huit, **9/2** HALLIARD, **14/1** Just Jesting, **20/1** Branston Kristy, Fairlight Magic, TOTE £9.50: £2.80 £1.70 (£7.20) OWNER The Rest Hill Partnership (GUILDFORD) BRED Mrs J. Brookes 6 Rn 59.76 secs (1.56) SF: 34/12/-/-/-/-
WEIGHT FOR AGE 3yo-15lb

300 GEORGETTE HEYER CLAIMING STKS (3-Y.O) (Class F) £2,663.00 (£748.00: £365.00) **7f (Equitrack)** GOING minus 0.55 sec per fur (FST) 3-20 (3-20)

261[W] **Irie Mon (IRE) (59)***(62) (JWHills)* 3-7-13 (7) MHenry(4) (chsd ldr: led 1f out: r.o) — 1
First Crush **(68)***(54) (SirMarkPrescott)* 3-8-2 GDuffield(2) (led: rdn over 1f out: hdd 1f out: unable qckn) 1¾ 2
251[3] Prince Rudolf (IRE) **(50)***(50) (MrsNMacauley)* 3-8-4v MFenton(3) (hld up: rdn & hdwy over 2f out: hrd rdn over 1f out: one pce) 3 3
Call Tophorse *(38) (PCHaslam)* 3-8-7 JWeaver(5) (unf: chsd ldrs: rdn 3f out: wknd over 2f out) 7 4
236* Robo Magic (USA) **(69)***(33)*(Fav)*(AMoore)* 3-8-7 RCochrane(1) (b.hind: chsd ldrs: rdn 3f out: wknd over 2 out) 2½ 5

5/4 Robo Magic (USA), **7/4** First Crush, **7/1** IRIE MON (IRE), **8/1** Prince Rudolf (IRE), Call Tophorse, TOTE £8.20: £2.60 £1.10 (£6.00) OWNER Mr J. Hawkes (LAMBOURN) BRED Stan Policky 5 Rn 1m 25.2 (2.20) SF: 19/13/8/-/-

301 EVELYN ANTHONY H'CAP (3-Y.O) (0-90) (Class C) £5,550.00 (£1,680.00: £820.00: £390.00) **1m 2f (Equitrack)** GOING minus 0.55 sec (FST) 3-50 (3-51)

151[3] **Contrafire (IRE) (66)***(76) (WJarvis)* 3-8-2 (3) SSanders(6) (chsd ldr: led over 1f out: hrd rdn fnl f: r.o) — 1
264* Tribal Peace (IRE) **(66)***(75)*(Fav)*(BGubby)* 3-8-0 (5)ow4 JStack(8) (a.p: rdn over 1f out: edgd lft & r.o fnl f) nk 2
250[3] Gulf Shaadi **(82)***(87) (CEBrittain)* 3-9-7 BDoyle(2) (hld up: hdwy 4f out: rdn over 2f out: r.o one pce fnl f) 2½ 3
189* Nigel's Lad (IRE) **(72)***(76)*(Fav)*(PCHaslam)* 3-8-11 JWeaver(4) (led tl over 1f out: one pce) ¾ 4
263[3] Persian Conquest (IRE) **(70)***(69) (RIngram)* 3-8-9b WWoods(1) (chsd ldrs: rdn over 1f out: eased whn btn fnl f) 3 5
242[4] Komreyev Dancer **(80)***(74)*(Fav)*(ABailey)* 3-9-5 TIves(7) (hld up: rdn over 3f out: no hdwy) 3½ 6
273* Star Fighter **(63)***(49)*(Fav)*(WAO'Gorman)* 3-8-2 DHarrison(5) (hld up: hdwy over 4f out: sn rdn: wknd 3f out) 5 7
128* Mr Mactavish **(70)***(41)*(Fav)*(MrsJCecil)* 3-8-9 AClark(3) (a bhd) 10 8

9/2 Komreyev Dancer, Tribal Peace (IRE), Mr Mactavish, Nigel's Lad (IRE), Star Fighter, **7/1** Persian Conquest (IRE), **10/1** Gulf Shaadi, **12/1** CONTRAFIRE (IRE), TOTE £25.80: £3.80 £1.40 £1.80 (£84.60) OWNER Miss V. R. Jarvis (NEWMARKET) BRED Thoroughbred Trust in Ireland 8 Rn 2m 7.5 (4.50) SF: 10/10/21/11/5/8/-/-

302 AGATHA CHRISTIE (S) STKS (Class G) £2,505.40 (£704.40: £344.20) **1m (Equitrack)** GOING minus 0.55 sec per fur (FST) 4-20 (4-20)

255[3] **Profit Release (IRE) (57)***(54+)*(Fav)*(MJohnston)* 4-8-9 RCochrane(3) (a.p: led wl over 2f out: clr over 1f out: r.o) — 1
205[8] Eastleigh **(45)***(52) (RHollinshead)* 6-9-0 TIves(2) (led over 5f: rdn 2f out: one pce) 3½ 2

Fiaba **(35)***(47) (MrsNMacauley)* 7-8-2 (7) AmandaSanders(10) (hld up: rdn 3f out: hdwy over 1f out: r.o fnl f)....s.h **3**
217[8] Doodies Pool (IRE) **(49)***(44) (GLMoore)* 5-9-0 SWhitworth(1) (chsd ldrs: rdn over 2f out: one pce)....4 **4**
26[6] King's Gold *(41) (TMJones)* 5-9-0b RPerham(6) (dwlt: rdn over 4f out: hdwy 3f out: hrd rdn 2f out: one pce)....1½ **5**
157[3] Gallery Artist (IRE) **(59)***(39) (RGuest)* 7-8-9 (5) CHawksley(8) (chsd ldrs: rdn 3f out: one pce fnl 2f)....¾ **6**
217[6] My Lifetime Lady (IRE) **(37)***(30) (KTIvory)* 4-8-2b(7) CScally(4) (dwlt: nvr nrr)....2 **7**
249[6] Admirals Flame (IRE) **(60)***(15) (CFWall)* 4-9-0 GDuffield(5) (chsd ldr tl rdn & wknd 3f out)....10 **8**
224[8] Arawa **(47)***(—) (DMarks)* 5-8-4 (5) MBaird(12) (chsd ldrs tl rdn & wknd 3f out)....10 **9**
Predictable **(44)***(—) (MrsAKnight)* 9-8-9 (5) SDrowne(9) (bhd fnl 5f)....1½ **10**
265[11] Scots Law **(27)***(—) (JELong)* 8-9-0b NAdams(7) (bhd fnl 5f)....½ **11**
226[3] Sharp Gazelle **(43)***(—) (BSmart)* 5-8-9 DHarrison(11) (prom: rdn 5f out: wknd 3f out)....s.h **12**

15/8 PROFIT RELEASE (IRE), **5/2** Admirals Flame (IRE), **4/1** Gallery Artist (IRE), **6/1** Sharp Gazelle, **10/1** Doodies Pool (IRE) (8/1-12/1), Eastleigh, **20/1** My Lifetime Lady (IRE), **25/1** Fiaba, **33/1** Arawa, Predictable, Scots Law, King's Gold, TOTE £3.30: £1.60 £2.20 £1.80 (£14.90) OWNER G R Bailey Ltd (Baileys Horse Feeds) (MIDDLEHAM) BRED Moyglare Stud Farm Ltd 12 Rn No bid
1m 39.59 (3.19) SF: 16/15/10/6/4/3/-/-/-/-/-/-

303

MARGERY ALLINGHAM H'CAP (0-75) (Class D) £3,555.50 (£1,076.00: £525.00: £249.50) **1m 4f (Equitrack)** GOING minus 0.55 sec per fur (FST) 4-50 (4-50)

221[3] **Princely Gait (69)***(75) (CACyzer)* 4-9-7 TIves(1) (hld up: hdwy 4f out: rdn over 1f out: led wl ins fnl f: r.o)....— **1**
109[4] Ikhtiraa (USA) **(60)***(64)*(Fav)*(RJO'Sullivan)* 5-9-1 JWeaver(7) (b: a.p: rdn over 1f out: ev ch wl ins fnl f: unable qckn)....1¼ **2**
238[4] In the Money (IRE) **(57)***(59) (RHollinshead)* 6-8-12 RCochrane(4) (a.p: led over 3f out tl wl ins fnl f: one pce)....2 **3**
259[8] Bures (IRE) **(60)***(57) (MHTompkins)* 4-8-7v(5) SMulvey(5) (mid div: rdn over 2f out: one pce)...4 **4**
238[2] Head Turner **(53)***(46) (CPWildman)* 7-8-8 NAdams(9) (hld up: hdwy over 3f out: rdn over 2f out: one pce)....3 **5**
206[3] Bag of Tricks (IRE) **(62)***(50) (SDow)* 5-9-3 TQuinn(3) (led over 8f: rdn over 2f out: wknd over 1f out)....4 **6**
206[7] Rapporteur (USA) **(73)***(42) (CCElsey)* 9-10-0 CRutter(2) (b: a bhd)....15 **7**
Magic Times **(70)***(31) (MJohnston)* 4-9-8 TWilliams(6) (chsd ldr: rdn 5f out: wknd over 3f out).6 **8**
246[3] Thaleros **(66)***(25) (GMMoore)* 5-9-7 AClark(8) (mid div: rdn 4f out: sn wknd)....2 **9**

5/2 Ikhtiraa (USA), **7/2** Head Turner, **11/2** PRINCELY GAIT, **6/1** In the Money (IRE), Thaleros, **7/1** Bag of Tricks (IRE), **20/1** Rapporteur (USA), **25/1** Magic Times, Bures (IRE), TOTE £5.60: £3.10 £1.60 £1.70 (£15.20) OWNER Mr R. M. Cyzer (HORSHAM) BRED Somerhall Bloodstock Ltd 9 Rn
2m 30.38 (0.98) SF: 54/47/42/37/30/33/24/-/-
WEIGHT FOR AGE 4yo-3lb
T/Plpt: £142.70 (65.59 Tckts). T/Qdpt: £28.40 (2.1 Tckts).

0279-WOLVERHAMPTON (L-H)
Saturday February 18th (Standard)

304

DALMATION H'CAP (Amateurs) (0-65) (Class F) £2,537.00 (£712.00: £347.00) **1m 4f (Fibresand)** GOING: nil sec per fur (STD) 7-00 (7-00)

Pontynyswen (34)*(49) (DBurchell)* 7-9-2b(7) MissEJJones(6) (chsd ldrs: led over 6f: rdn out)— **1**
22[4] Mr Bean **(41)***(52) (KRBurke)* 5-9-9 (7) MrsEBurke(5) (a.p: chsd wnr 6f out: 2nd st: no imp appr fnl f)....3½ **2**
246[5] Comtec's Legend **(37)***(29) (JFBottomley)* 5-9-12 MrsLPearce(11) (hld up: hdwy & 4th st: nvr able to chal)....15 **3**
Rocky Bay **(40)***(27) (BJLlewellyn)* 6-10-1 MrJLLlewellyn(12) (bhd: hdwy over 2f out: 6th st: nvr trbld ldrs)....4 **4**
186[4] Let's Get Lost **(60)***(43) (JAHarris)* 6-11-0 (7) MrJApiafi(10) (chsd ldrs: hrd rdn over 2f out: 3rd & wkng st)....3 **5**
179[6] Regal Rambler (CAN) **(36)***(15) (LJBarratt)* 4-9-8b MissDianaJones(7) (prom: rdn over 3f out: 5th & wkng st)....3½ **6**
234[9] Gunmaker **(33)***(11) (BJLlewellyn)* 6-9-4 (4)ow1 MrsBethWilliams(3) (hld up: a in rr)....1 **7**
222[2] First Century (IRE) **(55)***(31)*(Fav)*(MCPipe)* 6-11-2b MrJDurkan(8) (led over 5f: sn hrd rdn & grad wknd: poor 7th st)....2 **8**
143[3] Long Furlong **(50)***(24) (JRBosley)* 7-10-7 (4) MrsSBosley(4) (a in rr)....1½ **9**

*260*3 Ann Hill (IRE) **(31)***(—) (RHollinshead)* 5-9-2 (4) MissJSouthall(2) (a bhd: t.o)..........20 **10**
*103*9 Seraphic **(52)***(—) (BRCambidge)* 4-10-10 MrJCambidge(9) (mid div: rdn over 6f out: grad wknd: t.o)..........10 **11**
*234*14 Kismetim **(43)***(—) (FJordan)* 5-10-0 (4) MrLSquire(1) (a in rr: t.o)..........dist **12**

11/4 First Century (IRE), **3/1** Comtec's Legend, **6/1** Long Furlong, **8/1** Mr Bean, **10/1** Let's Get Lost, **12/1** Ann Hill (IRE), Kismetim, **16/1** PONTYNYSWEN, **20/1** Rocky Bay, Regal Rambler (CAN), **25/1** Seraphic, **33/1** Gunmaker, TOTE £76.90: £17.30 £2.10 £2.10 (£78.50) OWNER Mr J. L. Thomas (EBBW VALE) BRED J. L. Thomas 12 Rn 2m 41.4 (10.40) SF: 39/41/18/16/30/2/-/-/-/-/-/-
WEIGHT FOR AGE 4yo-3lb

305 COLLIE CLAIMING STKS (Class F) £2,433.00 (£683.00: £333.00)
5f (Fibresand) GOING: nil sec per fur (STD) 7-30 (7-31)

Sigama (USA) (60)*(57) (DNicholls)* 9-9-3 AlexGreaves(8) (mde all: rdn out)..........— **1**
*197*6 Ivy Lilian (IRE) **(40)***(52) (WMBrisbourne)* 3-7-9 (5) AGarth(10) (chsd wnr: 2nd & rdn st: no ex nr fin)..........¾ **2**
*194*2 Very Dicey **(73)***(54)*(Fav)*(JBerry)* 7-8-12 (7) PFessey(6) (chsd ldrs: 3rd & rdn st: unable qckn ins fnl f)..........½ **3**
*196*6 Poly Laureon (IRE) **(62)***(55) (RHollinshead)* 3-8-6 GCarter(5) (hld up: hdwy ½-wy: r.o u.p ins fnl f)..........nk **4**
*258*6 Benten **(42)***(39) (DNicholls)* 3-7-4 (5)ow2 NVarley(9) (mid div: 6th st: no hdwy appr fnl f)..........1¾ **5**
*202*3 Farfelu **(73)***(53) (WRMuir)* 8-9-11b JWeaver(7) (lw: prom: 4th st: rdn over 1f out: no imp)..........hd **6**
*78*8 Henry the Hawk **(46)***(39) (MDods)* 4-8-10v(5) JStack(4) (hld up: styd on u.p appr fnl f: nvr nrr)..........1¼ **7**
*216*3 Sison (IRE) **(61)***(39) (KGWingrove)* 5-9-3 JMcLaughlin(3) (b.hind: nvr trbld ldrs)..........½ **8**
*132*5 Precious Times **(44)***(24) (MGMeagher)* 3-7-12 JQuinn(1) (sn outpcd & bhd)..........3½ **9**
*258*3 Superbit **(49)***(14) (BAMcMahon)* 3-8-3b(3) SSanders(2) (chsd ldrs to ½-wy)..........6 **10**

11/8 Very Dicey, **5/1** Farfelu, **6/1** Superbit, **9/1** Poly Laureon (IRE), Sison (IRE), SIGAMA (USA), **10/1** Benten, **20/1** Ivy Lilian (IRE), **25/1** Precious Times, **33/1** Henry the Hawk, TOTE £9.00: £2.40 £4.60 £1.30 (£99.10) OWNER Mr Ian Glenton (THIRSK) BRED Welcome Farm 10 Rn
63.3 secs (5.30) SF: 12/-/11/-/-/11/-/-/-/-
WEIGHT FOR AGE 3yo-15lb

306 LURCHER STKS (0-60) (Class F) £2,433.00 (£683.00: £333.00)
6f (Fibresand) GOING: nil sec per fur (STD) 8-00 (8-01)

*92*8 **Curie Crusader (IRE) (47)***(59) (MDods)* 4-9-9 WWoods(4) (hld up: hdwy & 5th st: r.o to ld nr fin)..........— **1**
The Institute Boy **(53)***(58) (MissJFCraze)* 5-9-9 SWebster(3) (bit bkwd: led 5f out: rdn & edgd rt 1f out: hdd nr fin)..........hd **2**
*194** Primula Bairn **(60)***(55)*(Fav)*(MrsJRRamsden)* 5-9-8v JWeaver(9) (hld up in tch: 6th st: rdn & ev ch ins fnl f: nt qckn nr fin)..........½ **3**
*278*6 Whittingham Girl **(60)***(51) (JBerry)* 3-8-6 GCarter(8) (b: chsd ldrs: 2nd st: no ex appr fnl f)....1½ **4**
*232*4 Jalmaid **(50)***(49) (BAMcMahon)* 3-8-2 (3)ow3 SSanders(5) (led 1f: 3rd st: ev ch 1f out: no ex)..hd **5**
*202*5 Farndale **(51)***(42) (JBerry)* 8-9-2 (7) CLowther(2) (s.i.s: a in rr)..........3½ **6**
*224*3 Heathyards Lady (USA) **(51)***(34) (RHollinshead)* 4-9-4 TIves(1) (chsd ldrs tl 7th & btn st)......¾ **7**
*233*11 Victoria Hall **(40)***(34) (WGMTurner)* 5-9-4v GDuffield(10) (chsd ldrs: 4th & rdn st: wknd fnl f).s.h **8**
*129*13 Caherass Court (IRE) **(57)***(19) (BPreece)* 4-8-11 (7) AEddery(7) (sn outpcd & bhd)..........6 **9**
197*4* Pats Delight **(44)***(—) (SCoathup)* 3-8-2 TWilliams(6) (Withdrawn not under Starter's orders).... **W**

6/4 Primula Bairn, **7/2** Whittingham Girl, **9/2** Heathyards Lady (USA), **9/1** Jalmaid, **11/1** Farndale, **14/1** Victoria Hall, **16/1** Caherass Court (IRE), **20/1** The Institute Boy, **25/1** CURIE CRUSADER (IRE), **33/1** Pats Delight, TOTE £27.20: £3.80 £2.70 £1.50 (£126.40) OWNER Three Plus One Racing (DARLINGTON) BRED E. O'Leary 9 Rn 1m 16.9 (5.70) SF: 28/28/25/7/5/13/6/6/-/-
WEIGHT FOR AGE 3yo-16lb

307 AIREDALE H'CAP (0-70) (Class E) £2,788.00 (£844.00: £412.00: £196.00)
7f (Fibresand) GOING: nil sec per fur (STD) 8-30 (8-31)

*231*2 **Tilly Owl (41)***(50) (JAHarris)* 4-8-0 JO'Reilly(8) (hld up: 5th st: str burst to ld cl home)..........— **1**
*198** Ziggy's Dancer (USA) **(64)***(68)*(Fav)*(EJAlston)* 4-9-9 JWeaver(7) (chsd ldr: led over 4f out: rdn clr over 1f out: hdd wl ins fnl f)..........2½ **2**
*231** Quinzii Martin **(58)***(59) (DHaydnJones)* 7-9-3 TWilliams(3) (hld up in tch: 3rd & rdn st: styd on same pce)..........1¼ **3**
Cronk's Courage **(43)***(41) (MGMeagher)* 9-8-2v JQuinn(5) (bit bkwd: chsd ldrs: 2nd & rdn st: styd on same pce)..........1½ **4**

224[5] Fighter Squadron **(53)***(45) (REPeacock)* 6-8-12b GDuffield(9) (b.hind: hld up: hdwy ½-wy: 4th & rdn st: no imp) 3 **5**
160[5] Greatest **(53)***(19) (RAkehurst)* 4-8-12 GCarter(4) (mid div: effrt over 6f out: 6th & wkng st) 12 **6**
Timely Example (USA) **(69)***(34) (BRCambidge)* 4-10-0 TIves(6) (sn outpcd & bhd) ....hd **7**
244[5] Jon's Choice **(62)***(26) (BPreece)* 7-9-7 TWall(2) (lw: hmpd sn after s: prom: rdn 4f out: grad lost pl) ....hd **8**
225[3] Dynamis (IRE) **(48)***(10) (KOCunningham-Brown)* 4-8-7 RCochrane(1) (led over 2f: wknd 3f out) ....¾ **9**

5/2 Ziggy's Dancer (USA), **3/1** TILLY OWL, **4/1** Quinzii Martin, **5/1** Greatest, **8/1** Dynamis (IRE), Jon's Choice, **12/1** Fighter Squadron, **20/1** Cronk's Courage, **33/1** Timely Example (USA), TOTE £5.40: £1.60 £1.70 £1.80 (£7.10) OWNER Burntwood Sports Ltd (SOUTHWELL) BRED C. J. and Mrs J. E. Small 9 Rn 1m 30.9 (6.90) SF: 5/21/13/-/-/-/-/-/-

STEWARDS' ENQUIRY Cochrane suspended 27/2-4/3/95 (irresponsible riding).

308 DOBERMAN (S) STKS (Class G) £2,085.00 (£585.00: £285.00)
1m 1f 79y (Fibresand) GOING: nil sec per fur (STD) 9-00 (9-01)

199[4] **Slip a Coin (51)***(55) (RHollinshead)* 4-8-8 TIves(12) (mde virtually all: edgd lft over 1f out: rdn out) ....— **1**
279[7] T O O Mamma's (IRE) **(35)***(55) (JBerry)* 4-8-2 (7)ow1 PRoberts(7) (a.p: 2nd st: kpt on u.p ins fnl f) ....¾ **2**
117[8] Warhurst (IRE) **(60)***(55) (DNicholls)* 4-8-13 AlexGreaves(1) (bhd: hdwy over 2f out: 7th st: styd on u.p ins fnl f: nrst fin) 2½ **3**
193[5] Salbus **(72)***(57) (FJYardley)* 5-9-5v GDuffield(6) (chsd ldrs: chal over 3f out: 3rd & rdn st: no ex) 1¾ **4**
*226** Off the Air (IRE) **(50)***(48)*(Fav)*(ICampbell)* 4-8-13v RCochrane(8) (prom: drvn along & lost pl 7f out: hdwy over 3f out: 5th st: eased whn btn fnl f) 2½ **5**
248[6] Soba Guest (IRE) **(50)***(41) (RTJuckes)* 6-8-9 (5) SDrowne(4) (lw: prom: 4th & rdn st: sn wknd).4 **6**
269[12] Ballyhays (IRE) **(43)***(43) (JAHarris)* 6-9-5 SDWilliams(9) (hld up: hdwy 4f out: 6th & rdn st: sn wknd) 1¾ **7**
80[3] Puffy **(45)***(30) (MDods)* 8-9-0v WWoods(2) (b: a in rr) 5 **8**
254[6] Binlaboon (IRE) *(24) (KGWingrove)* 4-8-13b JMcLaughlin(10) (b.nr hind: prom over 6f) 3½ **9**
Eglwys Newydd *(—) (KSBridgwater)* 4-8-8 NCarlisle(3) (s.i.s: sn outpcd & bhd) 25 **10**
220[7] Make the Break **(47)***(—) (SCoathup)* 4-8-13b TWilliams(5) (prom 5f) 3½ **11**

2/1 Off the Air (IRE), **5/2** Salbus, **5/1** Warhurst (IRE), SLIP A COIN, **10/1** Puffy, **12/1** Make the Break, **14/1** Ballyhays (IRE), Soba Guest (IRE), **20/1** T O O Mamma's (IRE), **33/1** Binlaboon (IRE), Eglwys Newydd, TOTE £4.80: £2.00 £3.60 £3.50 (£33.00) OWNER Mr T. G. Holdcroft (UPPER LONGDON) BRED Bearstone Stud 11 Rn 2m 2.7 (6.70) SF: 35/35/35/39/29/24/26/-/-/-/-

WEIGHT FOR AGE 4yo-1lb
Sold E O'Malley 5,400gns

309 LABRADOR H'CAP (3-Y.O) (0-70) (Class E) £2,684.00 (£812.00: £396.00: £188.00) **1m (Fibresand)** GOING: nil sec per fur (STD) 9-30 (9-30)

*263** **Grand Selection (IRE) (70)***(81+)*(Fav)*(MBell)* 3-9-7 MFenton(4) (lw: chsd ldr: led 4f out: rdn out) ....— **1**
210[8] Our Tom **(59)***(67) (JWharton)* 3-8-10 JQuinn(1) (lw: hld up in tch: chsd wnr over 2f out: 2nd st: r.o) 1¼ **2**
59[10] Shy Paddy (IRE) **(61)***(47) (KOCunningham-Brown)* 3-8-12 JWeaver(3) (led over 4f: 3rd & wkng st) 11 **3**
263[5] Vindaloo **(42)***(14) (MJohnston)* 3-7-7 NCarlisle(2) (trckd ldrs: rdn over 4f out: sn lost tch: poor 4th st) 7 **4**

1/2 GRAND SELECTION (IRE), **9/2** Our Tom, Shy Paddy (IRE), **10/1** Vindaloo, TOTE £1.60 (£2.90) OWNER Mr M. B. Hawtin (NEWMARKET) BRED Mount Coote Stud in Ireland 4 Rn
1m 51.1 SF: 37/25/7/-
T/Plpt: £107.10 (109.52 Tckts). T/Qdpt: £79.10 (3.45 Tckts).

0292-SOUTHWELL (L-H)
Monday February 20th (Standard)

310 ADRIATIC H'CAP (Mdn 3-Y.O) (0-60) (Class F) £2,537.00 (£712.00: £347.00)
1m (Fibresand) GOING minus 0.16 sec per fur (FST) 2-20 (2-26)

270[3] **Summer Villa (42)***(56)*(Fav)*(PCHaslam)* 3-9-3 JWeaver(7) (trckd ldrs: led over 2f out: rdn & styd on wl to draw clr fnl f) ....— **1**

264[4] Chastleton **(45)***(42) (MRChannon)* 3-9-6 CandyMorris(4) (trckd ldrs: effrt 2f out: one pce appr fnl f) 9 2
176[7] Happy Brave **(43)***(37) (PDCundell)* 3-9-4 AMackay(2) (hmpd on ins after 1½f: effrt over 2f out: sn rdn: kpt on one pce) 1½ 3
Gulf Bay **(45)***(37) (MBell)* 3-9-6 MFenton(1) (dwlt: sn pushed along: hdwy ½-wy: ev ch & rdn 2f out: wknd ins fnl f) 1 4
116[6] Miss Toffee Nose (IRE) **(38)***(9) (DJSCosgrove)* 3-8-8 (5) LNewton(3) (outpcd & bhd after 3f) 8 5
292[4] Fairy's Son **(46)***(16) (WRMuir)* 3-9-7 DHarrison(5) (hld up: hdwy over 3f out: rdn, hung lft & wknd 2f out) 3 6
258[13] Tappen Lady (IRE) **(38)***(—) (JSWainwright)* 3-8-13v TIves(6) (led tl over 2f out: sn lost pl) 12 7

7/4 SUMMER VILLA, **3/1** Chastleton, **6/1** Fairy's Son, **8/1** Gulf Bay, **10/1** Happy Brave, Tappen Lady (IRE), **12/1** Miss Toffee Nose (IRE), TOTE £2.00: £1.20 £2.20 (£3.20) OWNER Mr K. E. Williamson (MIDDLEHAM) BRED Mrs R. D. Peacock 7 Rn 1m 46.4 (7.10) SF: 18/4/-/-/-/-/-

311 BALTIC CLAIMING STKS (Class F) £2,537.00 (£712.00: £347.00)
1m 4f (Fibresand) GOING minus 0.16 sec per fur (FST) 2-50 (2-55)

296[2] **Mad Militant (IRE) (71)***(64+)*(Fav)*(RHollinshead)* 6-8-13 TIves(3) (lw: trckd ldrs: led on bit 2f out: canter) ....— 1
186[12] Sagasan **(58)***(68) (WRMuir)* 4-9-4 JWeaver(4) (lw: hld up & plld hrd: wnt 2nd after 2f: led 3f out to 2f out: no ch w wnr) 3½ 2
254[3] Manolete **(44)***(49) (CWCElsey)* 4-8-4b NKennedy(7) (chsd ldrs: effrt over 2f out: one pce) 4 3
Garboni (USA) *(48) (DMoffatt)* 6-8-11 GDuffield(8) (led to 3f out: wknd over 1f out) 9 4
234[6] Goldenberry **(33)***(34) (JParkes)* 4-7-11 (5) MBaird(2) (hld up & plld hrd: stdd after 3f: wnt prom ½-wy: effrt 4f out: wknd over 2f out) 2½ 5
Winter Gem *(—) (RTJuckes)* 6-8-8 (5) SDrowne(6) (hld up: rdn & outpcd 5f out: sn bhd: t.o) ....dist 6
Munnasib (FR) *(—) (PMMcEntee)* 5-8-5 (3) DWright(1) (b: hld up: effrt & lost pl 6f out: sn bhd: t.o) ....nk 7
Placid-Warrior *(—) (JCMcConnochie)* 5-9-7 JQuinn(5) (prom: pushed along 7f out: sn lost pl & bhd: t.o 3f out) 20 8

1/2 MAD MILITANT (IRE), **6/1** Sagasan, **7/1** Garboni (USA), **15/2** Manolete, **10/1** Placid-Warrior, **25/1** Munnasib (FR), Goldenberry, **33/1** Winter Gem, TOTE £1.80: £1.10 £1.70 £1.70 (£4.90) OWNER Mr J. E. Bigg (UPPER LONGDON) BRED Cloghran Stud Farm Co in Ireland 8 Rn
2m 44.3 (10.10) SF: 21/21/4/5/-/-/-/-
WEIGHT FOR AGE 4yo-3lb

312 BERING H'CAP (0-65) (Class F) £2,789.00 (£784.00: £383.00)
1m 3f (Fibresand) GOING minus 0.16 sec per fur (FST) 3-20 (3-25)

271[3] **Suivez (42)***(59) (MrsNMacauley)* 5-9-3 JWeaver(2) (lw: chsd ldr: led 5f out: styd on strly fnl 2f: drvn out) ....— 1
Fearless Wonder **(60)***(62) (MrsMReveley)* 4-9-11b(7) SCopp(6) (lost pl after 3f: sn wl bhd: hdwy on outside 2f out: styd on strly nr fin) 6 2
227[7] Winn's Pride (IRE) **(45)***(53) (RHollinshead)* 4-9-3 TIves(12) (lw: sn bhd & pushed along: hdwy 5f out: kpt on one pce fnl 2f) ....½ 3
271* Camden's Ransom (USA) **(48)***(56) (HGRowsell)* 8-9-9 5x DaleGibson(9) (trckd ldrs: effrt & ev ch over 2f out: kpt on same pce) ....hd 4
169[4] Royal Acclaim **(44)***(44) (JMBradley)* 10-8-12v(7) AmandaSanders(11) (sn bhd & pushed along: hdwy over 2f out: styd on nr fin) ....¾ 5
Eurotwist **(34)***(40)*(Fav)*(JLEyre)* 6-8-9 AClark(3) (sn bhd: hdwy 5f out: effrt 2f out: sn rdn: no imp) 1 6
203[3] Braveboy **(53)***(57) (CEBrittain)* 7-10-0v BDoyle(4) (b.hind: hdwy 5f out: rdn over 2f out: nvr rchd ldrs) 1½ 7
271[5] Modest Hope (USA) **(38)***(41) (BRichmond)* 8-8-13 JMcLaughlin(8) (dwlt: chsd ldrs: one pce fnl 3f) 1 8
227[5] Sharp Sensation **(34)***(33) (DNicholls)* 5-8-9 AlexGreaves(5) (hdwy 5f out: effrt over 2f out: nvr nr to chal) 3 9
238[6] Haroldon (IRE) **(53)***(25) (BPalling)* 6-9-7 (7) OliverCasey(13) (b: hdwy 5f out: effrt over 3f out: wknd over 2f out) 15 10
255[8] Tyrone Flyer **(54)***(24) (PMMcEntee)* 6-9-8 (7) SarahThompson(1) (b: led to 5f out: lost pl over 2f out) 1½ 11
267[9] Mockingbird **(28)***(5) (BPreece)* 4-8-0 ow2 GDuffield(14) (a bhd) 2 12
256[13] Tanah Merah (IRE) **(43)***(17) (EJAlston)* 4-9-1 JQuinn(10) (nvr nr ldrs) 1 13
Classic Exhibit **(31)***(—) (ALForbes)* 6-8-3 (3) SSanders(7) (sn bhd) 4 14

9/4 Eurotwist, **11/4** SUIVEZ, **5/1** Camden's Ransom (USA), **7/1** Braveboy, **9/1** Winn's Pride (IRE), **12/1** Fearless Wonder, **14/1** Royal Acclaim, Modest Hope (USA), Sharp Sensation, **25/1** Haroldon (IRE), Tyrone Flyer, **33/1** Tanah Merah (IRE), **40/1** Mockingbird, Classic Exhibit, TOTE £5.00: £1.80 £3.10 £3.00 (£40.00) OWNER Mr G. Wiltshire (MELTON MOWBRAY) BRED Theakston Stud 14 Rn
2m 28.5 (7.00) SF: 40/39/31/36/25/21/36/-/-/-/-/-/-/-
WEIGHT FOR AGE 4yo-3lb

313

CASPIAN H'CAP (0-70) (Class E) £3,124.00 (£946.00: £462.00: £220.00)
1m (Fibresand) GOING minus 0.16 sec per fur (FST) 3-50 (3-55)

242[5] **Hawwam (67)**(*75*) (*EJAlston*) 9-9-11 (5) AProcter(3) (lw: s.i.s: sn prom: led jst ins fnl f: hld on wl) ....— 1
230[3] Major Mouse **(49)**(*59*) (*WWHaigh*) 7-8-12 DaleGibson(10) (hld up: hdwy & prom 4f out: hrd rdn & ev ch ins fnl f: no ex) ....nk 2
269[2] Aquado **(35)**(*42*)(Fav)(*ALForbes*) 6-7-12 JQuinn(7) (lw: a.p: led over 1f out: hdd & nt qckn ins fnl f) 1¼ 3
195[7] Northern Celadon (IRE) **(64)**(*63*) (*MJHeaton-Ellis*) 4-9-13 StephenDavies(12) (swtg: a chsng ldrs: kpt on same pce fnl 2f) 4 4
256[3] Spanish Stripper (USA) **(53)**(*43*) (*MCChapman*) 4-8-9 (7) CMunday(14) (sn bhd & pushed along: kpt on: nt rch ldrs) 1 5
256[5] Tovarich **(57)**(*53*) (*DNicholls*) 4-9-6 SWhitworth(5) (trckd ldrs: led over 2f out tl over 1f out: grad wknd) ....nk 6
255[7] Rad **(60)**(*44*) (*SPCWoods*) 5-9-2 (7) CWebb(6) (hld up & bhd: hdwy on outside over 2f out: nt rch ldrs) 2½ 7
249[3] Waldo **(61)**(*52*) (*LordHuntingdon*) 4-9-10v DHarrison(13) (b.hind: sn drvn along: hdwy & prom 5f out: hung lft & wknd 2f out) ....hd 8
169[6] Zahran (IRE) **(52)**(*36*) (*JMBradley*) 4-8-10 (5) SDrowne(1) (chsd ldrs: drvn along ½-wy: outpcd fnl 2f) ....¾ 9
Sacred Mirror (IRE) **(53)**(*34*) (*CEBrittain*) 4-9-2 BDoyle(11) (bit bkwd: sn rdn along: nvr bttr than mid div) 4 10
Rafter-J **(53)**(*31*) (*MissJacquelineDoyle*) 4-9-2 GBardwell(8) (s.i.s: hdwy on outside 4f out: sn prom: hung lft & wknd 2f out) 1¼ 11
195[10] Sharp Conquest **(65)**(*41*) (*WRMuir*) 4-10-0 JWeaver(2) (led tl over 2f out: wknd over 1f out) ...1 12
Environmentalist (IRE) **(57)**(*—*) (*SCWilliams*) 4-9-6 AMackay(4) (a bhd) 20 13
Penny Ramble (IRE) **(49)**(*—*) (*SGNorton*) 4-8-7 (5) JStack(9) (b.nr hind: prom tl lost pl over 3f out: sn bhd) 15 14

5/2 Aquado, **11/2** Waldo, **7/1** HAWWAM, **10/1** Sacred Mirror (IRE), Major Mouse, Sharp Conquest, **11/1** Spanish Stripper (USA), **12/1** Northern Celadon (IRE), Environmentalist (IRE), Rad, **14/1** Rafter-J, **16/1** Tovarich, **20/1** Zahran (IRE), **25/1** Penny Ramble (IRE), TOTE £7.70: £3.90 £1.90 £1.40 (£95.00) OWNER North West Racing Club Owners Club (PRESTON) BRED G. Franco 14 Rn
1m 44.5 (5.20) SF: 46/32/17/35/17/26/18/-/-/-/-/-/-/-

314

PERSIAN GULF (S) STKS (Class G) £2,259.00 (£634.00: £309.00)
6f (Fibresand) GOING minus 0.16 sec per fur (FST) 4-20 (4-26)

233[2] **Sea Devil (63)**(*64*)(Fav)(*MJCamacho*) 9-9-7 LCharnock(7) (trckd ldrs: hmpd ½-wy: led over 2f out: rdn out) ....— 1
233[5] Jamaica Bridge **(60)**(*64*) (*SGNorton*) 5-9-12 (7) TMarsden(5) (hld up: nt clr run & swtchd 2f out: kpt on u.p fnl f: no imp) 2 2
265[10] Letsbeonestaboutit **(52)**(*58*) (*MrsNMacauley*) 9-9-12v DeanMcKeown(2) (chsd ldrs: hmpd ½-wy: styd on same pce fnl 2f) 2½ 3
65[9] So Intrepid (IRE) **(58)**(*44*) (*JMBradley*) 5-9-7 JWeaver(6) (b: hld up: effrt over 2f out: swtchd outside over 1f out: nvr rchd ldrs) 3½ 4
258[8] Needwood Newt **(41)**(*34*) (*BAMcMahon*) 3-8-0 DaleGibson(4) (chsd ldrs tl wknd over 1f out)1¾ 5
236[4] Havana Miss **(40)**(*32*) (*BPalling*) 3-8-0 ow2 GDuffield(3) (led: swvd rt ½-wy: sn hdd: wknd over 1f out) 1¼ 6
233[7] Swinging Tich **(45)**(*20*) (*BAMcMahon*) 6-9-2 (3) SSanders(1) (chsd ldrs tl wknd over 2f out)......4 7
267[7] Monsieur Petong **(40)**(*22*) (*JParkes*) 4-9-7 (5) JStack(8) (s.s: hdwy on outside over 2f out: sn rdn & wknd) ....¾ 8
268[7] Educated Pet **(53)**(*21*) (*BPreece*) 6-9-7 TWall(9) (in tch: sn drvn along: bhd fnl 2f) ....nk 9

Evens SEA DEVIL, **3/1** Jamaica Bridge, **8/1** So Intrepid (IRE), Swinging Tich, **10/1** Letsbeonestaboutit, Educated Pet, **16/1** Needwood Newt, **20/1** Monsieur Petong, Havana Miss, TOTE £2.20: £1.30 £1.40 £1.60 (£2.70) OWNER Mr A. N. Goacher (MALTON) BRED A. L. Goacher and E. G. Noble 9 Rn
1m 17.5 (4.00) SF: 38/37/31/17/-/-/-/-/-
WEIGHT FOR AGE 3yo-16lb
Bt in 4,400 gns

315 HUDSON BAY MEDIAN AUCTION STKS (Mdn 3, 4 & 5-Y.O) (Class F) £2,789.00 (£784.00: £383.00)
6f (Fibresand) GOING minus 0.16 sec per fur (FST) 4-50 (4-59)

Denbrae (IRE) (66)*(63) (DJGMurraySmith)* 3-8-8 JWeaver(4) (chsd ldrs: led over 1f out: hld on nr fin).......— 1
South Forest (IRE) **(68)***(62) (SRBowring)* 4-9-10 (7) CTeague(9) (b: effrt on outside 2f out: swtchd ins & styd on wl fnl f).......nk 2
Reverand Thickness **(69)***(60) (SCWilliams)* 4-9-10b TIves(11) (trckd ldrs: effrt 2f out: sn ev ch: hung lft & nt qckn ins fnl f).......½ 3
Statius *(57) (TDBarron)* 3-8-8 DeanMcKeown(10) (rangy: scope: bit bkwd: hdwy ½-wy: n.m.r 2f out: styd on: hmpd fnl f: kpt on wl).......¾ 4
256² Nite-Owl Dancer **(56)***(49)*(Fav)*(JAHarris)* 3-8-3 JO'Reilly(2) (led over 4f out tl over 1f out: wknd nr fin).......1 5
Robaty's Law (IRE) *(36) (MJHeaton-Ellis)* 3-8-8 StephenDavies(7) (led over 1f: chsd ldrs tl wknd over 1f out).......7 6
232⁶ Ladybower (IRE) *(21) (LordHuntingdon)* 3-8-3 DHarrison(3) (chsd ldrs: wandered & wknd over 1f out).......4 7
274⁴ Paronomasia *(22) (MBell)* 3-8-8 (7) RMullen(6) (nvr nr ldrs).......1¼ 8
256¹⁰ Minster Glory *(18) (MWEasterby)* 4-9-10 LCharnock(8) (s.i.s: a outpcd & bhd).......1½ 9
Airbourne Ron (IRE) **(59)***(15) (SGNorton)* 3-8-8v GBardwell(12) (sn drvn along: lost pl after 1f: sn bhd).......1 10
Prime Property (IRE) **(59)***(7) (GPKelly)* 3-8-3 JQuinn(1) (s.i.s: a bhd).......1 11
306⁹ Caherass Court (IRE) **(57)***(—) (BPreece)* 4-9-5 GDuffield(13) (mid div: effrt 3f out: sn wknd).......3 12
Angelic Belle *(—) (NPLittmoden)* 3-8-3 NCarlisle(5) (unruly s: s.s: a wl bhd).......3 13

11/4 Nite-Owl Dancer, **7/2** Reverand Thickness, **9/2** South Forest (IRE), **11/2** DENBRAE (IRE), **11/1** Ladybower (IRE) (8/1-12/1), **14/1** Paronomasia, **16/1** Angelic Belle, Statius, Caherass Court (IRE), Airbourne Ron (IRE), **20/1** Prime Property (IRE), Robaty's Law (IRE), **33/1** Minster Glory, TOTE £6.50: £2.00 £2.00 £2.30 (£25.10) OWNER Mr Michael Mellersh (LAMBOURN) BRED Mellon Stud 13 Rn 1m 18.4 (4.90) SF: 14/29/27/11/4/-/-/-/-/-/-/-/-
WEIGHT FOR AGE 3yo-16lb

T/Plpt: £10.40 (1,679.4 Tckts). T/Qdpt: £20.70 (2 Tckts).

0298-LINGFIELD (L-H)
Tuesday February 21st (Standard)

316 DORDOGNE MEDIAN AUCTION MAIDEN STKS (3-Y.O) (Class F) £2,751.20 (£773.20: £377.60)
1m (Equitrack) Stalls: High GOING minus 0.55 sec per fur (FST) 2-20 (2-23)

Cannizaro (IRE) *(64) (RJRWilliams)* 3-8-9 LDettori(7) (leggy: a.p: led over 1f out: r.o wl).......— 1
213⁷ Vaslav Nijinsky *(63) (GRimmer)* 3-9-0 MRimmer(2) (lw: led over 1f: led over 3f out tl over 1f out: unable qckn).......3 2
Top Fella (USA) **(64)***(60)*(Fav)*(WAO'Gorman)* 3-8-11 (3) EmmaO'Gorman(11) (hdwy 5f out: hrd rdn over 1f out: r.o wl ins fnl f).......1½ 3
264⁵ Rocky Forum *(41) (GLMoore)* 3-8-9 RPerham(5) (rdn over 3f out: nvr nr to chal).......7 4
261³ Death by Chocolate *(40) (DrJDScargill)* 3-8-11 (3) DWright(8) (outpcd: hdwy over 3f out: one pce).......3 5
156⁸ Alka International **(55)***(39) (JWhite)* 3-8-9 (5) SDrowne(6) (b.hind: a.p: rdn 4f out: wknd over 2f out).......nk 6
He's Special *(27) (CACyzer)* 3-9-0 TIves(9) (lt-f: nvr nrr).......6 7
Danny's Gift *(14) (MissAJWhitfield)* 3-8-6 (3) SSanders(1) (prom over 3f).......4 8
Guymichelle (IRE) *(14) (RIngram)* 3-8-9 TWilliams(4) (bhd fnl 6f).......nk 9
Rookery Girl *(7) (DMorris)* 3-8-9 CRutter(12) (lt-f: hdwy over 4f out: wknd over 2f out).......3½ 10
225⁹ Crocodile Rock *(6) (MJHeaton-Ellis)* 3-9-0v StephenDavies(10) (led over 6f out tl over 3f out: sn wknd).......3 11
286⁵ Brooke Wood *(MissBSanders)* 3-8-2 (7) AmandaBowen(3) (a bhd).......15 12

11/4 Top Fella (USA), **7/2** Death by Chocolate (5/2-4/1), **9/2** CANNIZARO (IRE), **11/2** He's Special, **13/2** Vaslav Nijinsky (op 12/1), **10/1** Rocky Forum (op 6/1), **14/1** Alka International (7/1-16/1), **20/1** Rookery Girl, **33/1** Crocodile Rock, Guymichelle (IRE), Brooke Wood, **50/1** Danny's Gift, CSF £33.64 TOTE £5.90: £1.20 £2.10 £1.20 (£20.80) OWNER Wimbledon Racing Club (NEWMARKET) BRED Mrs Ian Fox 12 Rn 1m 39.54 (3.14) SF: 17/16/13/-/-/-/-/-/-/-/-/-

317

SEINE CLAIMING STKS (4-Y.O+) (Class E) £2,966.70 (£897.60: £437.80: £207.90)
1m 2f (Equitrack) Stalls: Low GOING minus 0.55 sec per fur (FST) 2-50 (2-50)

235* **Masnun (USA) (66)***(72)*(Fav)*(RJO'Sullivan)* 10-8-11 AClark(1) (lw: hld up: chsd ldr over 3f out: led ins fnl f: rdn out) .....— 1
175³ Awesome Power **(70)***(75)*(Fav)*(JWHills)* 9-9-1 LDettori(3) (led 1f: led over 4f out: rdn over 3f out: hdd ins fnf f: r.o) .....½ 2
Tapatch (IRE) **(52)***(73) (JSWainwright)* 7-9-7 DeanMcKeown(5) (s.s: hld up: rdn over 2f out: unable qckn) 5 3
Arafel **(50)***(40) (CJames)* 4-8-6 ow1 JWeaver(4) (lw: led 9f out tl over 4f out: sn wknd) 12 4
187¹⁰ Belfort Ruler **(47)***(6) (BGubby)* 8-8-0 (5) JStack(2) (bhd fnl 4f) 20 5

11/10 MASNUN (USA) (op 8/13), Awesome Power, **10/1** Tapatch (IRE), **50/1** Arafel, Belfort Ruler, CSF £2.49 TOTE £1.80: £1.00 £10.00 (£1.20) OWNER Mr I. W. Page (BOGNOR REGIS) BRED Glencrest Farm 5 Rn 2m 6.29 (3.29) SF: 25/28/26/-/-
WEIGHT FOR AGE 4yo-2lb

318

DAILY STAR AWT 1M 2F CHALLENGE SERIES (QUALIFIER) H'CAP (0-80) (4-Y.O+) (Class D) £3,863.90 (£1,170.20: £571.60: £272.30)
1m 2f (Equitrack) Stalls: Low GOING minus 0.55 sec per fur (FST) 3-20 (3-22)

195⁹ **Roman Reel (USA) (57)***(63) (GLMoore)* 4-8-3 JQuinn(2) (hld up: nt clr run on ins over 2f out: hrd rdn over 1f out: led nr fin) .....— 1
249* Secret Aly (CAN) **(80)***(86) (CEBrittain)* 5-10-0 MRimmer(6) (lw: rdn 5f out: lost pl over 3f out: rallied over 1f out: led ins fnf f: hdd nr fin) .....hd 2
235² Prince Danzig (IRE) **(76)***(79) (DJGMurraySmith)* 4-9-8 JWeaver(5) (lost pl over 7f out: rallied over 1f out: r.o wl ins fnl f) 2 3
249² Birequest **(77)***(78)*(Fav)*(RBoss)* 4-9-9 LDettori(3) (lw: led: rdn over 2f out: hdd ins fnl f: sn wknd) 1 4
Father Dan (IRE) **(49)***(48) (MissGayKelleway)* 6-7-8 (3) DWright(9) (lw: rdn & hdwy over 3f out: one pce fnl 2f) 1 5
145⁶ Global Dancer **(71)***(70) (WAO'Gorman)* 4-9-0 (3) EmmaO'Gorman(7) (hdwy over 7f out: rdn over 3f out: lost pl over 2f out: r.o ins fnl f) .....s.h 6
Able Choice (IRE) **(74)***(65) (RWArmstrong)* 5-9-8 RCochrane(8) (hdwy over 7f out: rdn & ev ch over 2f out: wknd wl over 1f out) 5 7
84⁴ Tondres (USA) **(60)***(42) (RIngram)* 4-8-6 TWilliams(1) (lw: a bhd) 6 8
Misty Silks **(74)***(37) (MJRyan)* 5-9-8 AClark(4) (bhd fnl 3f) 12 9

9/4 Birequest, **5/2** Secret Aly (CAN), **7/1** Prince Danzig (IRE) (5/1-8/1), **10/1** ROMAN REEL (USA) (16/1-8/1), Tondres (USA) (8/1-12/1), **12/1** Misty Silks (op 8/1), **14/1** Global Dancer, **16/1** Father Dan (IRE), **25/1** Able Choice (IRE), CSF £32.77 CT £170.81 TOTE £11.70: £2.40 £1.20 £2.50 (£29.50) Trio £67.90 OWNER Mr K. Higson (EPSOM) BRED Dorothy Price, Jackie W. Ramos & Ken Hickson 9 Rn 2m 5.44 (2.44) SF: 24/49/40/39/11/31/28/3/-
WEIGHT FOR AGE 4yo-2lb

319

LINGFIELD PARK AWT SPRINT SERIES (QUALIFIER) H'CAP (0-70) (3-Y.O) (Class E) £3,119.10 (£943.80: £460.40: £218.70)
6f (Equitrack) Stalls: Low GOING minus 0.55 sec per fur (FST) 3-50 (3-50)

232* **Montague Dawson (IRE) (62)***(67)*(Fav)*(MrsNMacauley)* 3-9-1 (5) SDrowne(1) (lw: hld up: hrd rdn over 2f out: led ins fnl f: r.o wl) .....— 1
278² Bon Secret (IRE) **(63)***(66) (TJNaughton)* 3-9-4 (3) SSanders(6) (lw: a.p: hrd rdn over 1f out: ev ch ins fnl f: unable qckn) .....¾ 2
287⁴ Black Shadow **(47)***(49) (PJMcBride)* 3-8-5 JQuinn(3) (a.p: led over 2f out tl ins fnl f: one pce) ½ 3
274* Das Island **(65)***(63)*(Fav)*(JRJenkins)* 3-9-9 7x LDettori(4) (lw: hdwy over 2f out: hrd rdn over 1f out: one pce) 1½ 4
300³ Prince Rudolf (IRE) **(50)***(45) (MrsNMacauley)* 3-8-3v(5) JStack(8) (hdwy over 3f out: hrd rdn over 1f out: one pce) 1 5
204⁴ La Fille de Cirque **(45)***(32) (RJRWilliams)* 3-8-3 DHarrison(5) (b: nvr nr to chal) 3 6
287⁸ Tachycardia **(50)***(35) (RJO'Sullivan)* 3-8-8 StephenDavies(7) (lw: led over 3f) .....¾ 7
Woolverstone Hall (IRE) **(60)***(24)*(Fav)*(DJGMurraySmith)* 3-9-4 JWeaver(2) (spd over 2f) 8 8

9/2 MONTAGUE DAWSON (IRE), Woolverstone Hall (IRE) (6/1-4/1), Das Island, **5/1** Bon Secret (IRE), Black Shadow, **8/1** La Fille de Cirque, Prince Rudolf (IRE), **10/1** Tachycardia, CSF £26.03 CT £106.82 TOTE £5.90: £3.20 £1.50 £1.50 (£15.90) OWNER Mr G. Wiltshire (MELTON MOWBRAY) BRED Christopher Flynn in Ireland 8 Rn 1m 13.52 (2.92) SF: 18/17/-/14/-/-/-/-
OFFICIAL EXPLANATION Woolverstone Hall (IRE): lost his action and was subsequently eased.

320 RHONE H'CAP (0-70) (4-Y.O+) (Class E) £3,138.30 (£950.40: £464.20: £221.10)
1m (Equitrack) Stalls: High GOING minus 0.55 sec per fur (FST) 4-20 (4-21)

275² **Perilous Plight (64)***(75)*(Fav)*(WRMuir)* 4-9-11 JWeaver(7) (lw: hdwy 3f out: led ins fnl f: rdn out) — 1
*262** Kinnegad Kid **(61)***(71) (RIngram)* 6-9-5 (3) DWright(2) (a.p: rdn over 2f out: led over 1f out tl ins fnl f: r.o) ½ 2
265⁴ Panchellita (USA) **(45)***(48) (GLMoore)* 6-8-6b SWhitworth(6) (lw: led over 6f: unable qckn) ...3½ 3
Dutosky **(49)***(49) (RJRWilliams)* 5-8-10 LDettori(3) (lw: hld up: rdn 3f out: one pce) 1½ 4
205⁵ Zinbaq **(37)***(29) (CJBenstead)* 9-7-12 ow2 TWilliams(8) (a.p: rdn over 3f out: wknd over 2f out) 3 5
Lady Williams (IRE) **(60)***(49) (LordHuntingdon)* 4-9-7 DHarrison(10) (lw: nvr nr to chal) 2½ 6
*287** Myjinka **(41)***(30) (JO'Donoghue)* 5-7-9b(7) 6x IonaWands(4) (chsd ldr over 6f) s.h 7
*218** Ultimate Warrior **(67)***(46) (CACyzer)* 5-10-0 TIves(12) (hdwy over 4f out: wknd over 3f out) 5 8
205⁶ Pigalle Wonder **(33)***(1) (RJO'Sullivan)* 7-7-8bow1 NAdams(9) (s.s: a bhd) 5 9
249⁵ Mr Browning (USA) **(51)***(18) (MarkCampion)* 4-8-12 NCarlisle(11) (a bhd) 1 10
265⁵ Pair of Jacks (IRE) **(32)** *(DAWilson)* 5-7-7 GBardwell(5) (lw: bhd fnl 3f) nk 11
265⁸ Kingchip Boy **(58)***(24) (MJRyan)* 6-9-5v AClark(1) (hld up: rdn over 3f out: wknd over 2f out) .nk 12
LONG HANDICAP Pair of Jacks (IRE) 7-3 Pigalle Wonder 7-6

9/4 PERILOUS PLIGHT, **4/1** Kinnegad Kid, **8/1** Dutosky, Ultimate Warrior, **10/1** Panchellita (USA), Kingchip Boy, **12/1** Lady Williams (IRE), **14/1** Myjinka (op 9/1), Pair of Jacks (IRE), **20/1** Mr Browning (USA), **25/1** Zinbaq, **33/1** Pigalle Wonder, CSF £11.71 TC £71.27 TOTE £3.10: £1.10 £1.90 £2.60 (£5.80) Trio £43.00 OWNER Mr J. Jannaway (LAMBOURN) BRED Crest Stud Ltd 12 Rn 1m 37.95 (1.55) SF: 47/43/20/21/1/21/2/18/-/-/-/-

321 GIRONDE H'CAP (0-60) (4-Y.O+) (Class F) £2,864.60 (£805.60: £393.80)
1m 4f (Equitrack) Stalls: Low GOING minus 0.55 sec per fur (FST) 4-50 (4-51)

Jaraab (41)*(49) (GLewis)* 4-8-6 SWhitworth(11) (lw: a.p: rdn over 3f out: led over 1f out: r.o wl) — 1
*260** Sleeptite (FR) **(58)***(62) (WGMTurner)* 5-9-7 (5) JDSmith(2) (hdwy over 3f out: r.o wl ins fnl f)....3 2
303² Ikhtiraa (USA) **(60)***(63)*(Fav)*(RJO'Sullivan)* 5-10-0 JWeaver(12) (b: led over 10f out tl over 1f out: unable qckn) ½ 3
259⁶ Charlie Bigtime **(47)***(46) (BJMcMath)* 5-9-1 AMackay(10) (lw: hld up: rdn 7f out: one pce fnl 2f) 3½ 4
158³ Zuno Noelyn **(56)***(52) (RAkehurst)* 4-9-7 TQuinn(4) (lw: hld up: rdn over 3fout: wknd over 1f out) 1¾ 5
285⁵ Remember This (IRE) **(35)***(27) (CACyzer)* 5-8-3 MFenton(6) (hld up: rdn over 4f out: wknd over 1f out) 3½ 6
*285** Royal Circus **(40)***(27) (JGMO'Shea)* 6-8-8 5x BDoyle(8) (led over 1f: wknd 3f out) 3½ 7
Telephus **(47)***(31) (BJMcMath)* 6-9-1 RCochrane(3) (nvr nrr) 2 8
*238** Majal (IRE) **(57)***(41) (JSWainwright)* 6-9-11 DeanMcKeown(7) (lw: bhd fnl 3f) hd 9
Glow Forum **(37)***(19) (GLMoore)* 4-8-2 JQuinn(5) (bhd fnl 4f) 2 10
Lady Reema **(45)***(26) (MissAJWhitfield)* 4-8-7 (3) SSanders(1) (bhd fnl 5f) ½ 11
200⁸ Malingerer **(28)***(6) (DAWilson)* 4-7-7 GBardwell(9) (b.hind: bhd fnl 3f) 2 12
LONG HANDICAP Malingerer 7-5

5/2 Ikhtiraa (USA), **3/1** Zuno Noelyn, **5/1** Majal (IRE), **9/1** JARAAB (14/1-8/1), Sleeptite (FR) (6/1-10/1), **10/1** Royal Circus, **12/1** Telephus (op 8/1), **16/1** Charlie Bigtime, Glow Forum, **20/1** Malingerer, Lady Reema, **25/1** Remember This (IRE), CSF £87.17 CT £246.82 TOTE £9.70: £1.90 £1.50 £1.90 (£93.10) Trio £90.10 OWNER Mr S. I. Ross (EPSOM) BRED Shadwell Estate Company Limited 12 Rn 2m 31.3 (1.90) SF: 34/50/51/34/37/15/15/19/29/4/11/-
WEIGHT FOR AGE 4yo-3lb

T/Jkpt: Not won; £28,670.69 to Wolverhampton 22/2/95. T/Plpt: £34.00 (619.2 Tckts). T/Qdpt: £13.90 (11 Tckts). AK

0304-WOLVERHAMPTON (L-H)
Wednesday February 22nd (Standard)
Paddock not used Race 5 - adverse weather conditions.

322 PHILMAC VALVE MEDIAN AUCTION MAIDEN STKS (3 & & 5-Y.O)
(Class E) £3,009.60 (£910.80: £444.40: £211.20)
7f (Fibresand) Stalls: Low GOING minus 0.03 sec per fur (STD) 2-00 (2-01)

Hand Craft (IRE) *(81)*(Fav)*(WJHaggas)* 3-8-6 LDettori(3) (w'like: bit bkwd: s.i.s: hld up: hdwy over 4f out: 3rd st: led over 1f out: pushed out) — 1

Dont Forget Curtis (IRE) *(78) (JRFanshawe)* 3-8-6 DHarrison(6) (chsd ldrs: 2nd st: sn ev ch: no ex fnl f)....1½ **2**
298[5] Mary's Case (IRE) **(57)***(64) (MJohnston)* 5-9-10 TWilliams(5) (led 1f: led 4f out: rdn & hdd over 1f out: no ex)....6 **3**
Sharp Holly (IRE) **(52)***(45) (JABennett)* 3-7-13 (3)ow1 SSanders(4) (prom: jnd ldrs 5f out: 4th st: sn rdn & wknd)....6 **4**
239[2] Nuthatch (IRE) *(34) (MDIUsher)* 3-7-8 (7) CAdamson(1) (trckd ldrs: rdn over 3f out: grad wknd: poor 5th st)....5 **5**
245[8] Severn Gale *(11) (KWhite)* 5-9-5b JWeaver(2) (led 6f out: hdd over 4f out: grad wknd: poor 6th st)....10 **6**

5/4 HAND CRAFT (IRE) (4/5-6/4), **9/4** Dont Forget Curtis (IRE), **6/1** Mary's Case (IRE) (op 4/1), **8/1** Nuthatch (IRE), **12/1** Sharp Holly (IRE) (20/1-33/1), **14/1** Severn Gale, CSF £4.49 TOTE £1.90: £1.80 £1.60 (£3.50) OWNER Mrs M. M. Haggas (NEWMARKET) BRED D. and N. Wallace 6 Rn
1m 30.4 (6.40) SF: 14/11/15/-/-/-
WEIGHT FOR AGE 3yo-18lb

323 PHILMAC FITTING CLAIMING STKS (4-Y.O+) (Class F) £2,749.00 (£832.00: £406.00: £193.00)

7f (Fibresand) Stalls: Low GOING minus 0.03 sec per fur (STD) 2-30 (2-30)

191* **Spencer's Revenge (77)***(73)*(Fav)*(LordHuntingdon)* 6-8-11 LDettori(2) (hld up: hdwy over 3f out: led 2f out: pushed clr: eased cl home)....— **1**
281[7] Arndilly **(68)***(63) (BJMeehan)* 4-8-8b RCochrane(1) (led 1f: led 3f out: hdd & 2nd st: sn outpcd)3 **2**
244[3] Delrob **(61)***(55) (DHaydnJones)* 4-8-4 AMackay(4) (trckd ldrs: 3rd & rdn st: styd on same pce)2 **3**
267[5] Dream Carrier (IRE) **(70)***(60) (JGMO'Shea)* 7-8-5 (7) AmandaSanders(6) (hld up: 5th st: nvr able to chal)....1¼ **4**
248[3] Veloce (IRE) **(49)***(51) (ABailey)* 7-7-13v(7) AngelaGallimore(3) (b: hld up: hdwy 4f out: 4th & rdn st: no imp)....1¼ **5**
Backstabber **(38)***(19) (MissSJWilton)* 5-8-3 (5) JStack(5) (led 6f out: hdd 3f out: sn rdn & wknd: poor 6th st)....15 **6**

4/9 SPENCER'S REVENGE, **4/1** Arndilly, **5/1** Dream Carrier (IRE) (7/2-6/1), **10/1** Delrob, **16/1** Veloce (IRE), **50/1** Backstabber, CSF £3.32 TOTE £1.30: £1.10 £2.60 (£2.30) OWNER Mr P. A. Leonard (WEST ILSLEY) BRED Lord Crawshaw 6 Rn 1m 30.0 (6.00) SF: 23/13/5/10/1/-

324 PHILMAC CONNECTOR H'CAP (0-80) (3-Y.O) (Class D) £4,045.50 (£1,224.00: £597.00: £283.50)

1m 1f 79y (Fibresand) Stalls: Low GOING minus 0.03 sec per fur (STD) 3-00 (3-00)

Mister Fire Eyes (IRE) (79)*(82) (CEBrittain)* 3-9-6 BDoyle(1) (bit bkwd: trckd ldrs: led 2f out: r.o wl)....— **1**
301[6] Komreyev Dancer **(80)***(82)*(Fav)*(ABailey)* 3-9-7 JWeaver(4) (led: hdd 2f out: 2nd st: styd on u.p nr fin)....¾ **2**
309* Grand Selection (IRE) **(75)***(74) (MBell)* 3-8-9 (7) 5x GFaulkner(3) (lw: chsd ldr: 3rd st: rdn over 1f out: no imp)....1½ **3**
What a Nightmare (IRE) **(70)***(65) (JAGlover)* 3-8-11 DeanMcKeown(2) (bit bkwd: hld up in tch: plld hrd: effrt & 4th st: kpt on u.p)....2½ **4**
99[4] Sarasi **(70)***(44) (PFICole)* 3-8-11 TQuinn(5) (plld hrd: hld up: outpcd over 2f out: poor 5th st) 12 **5**

2/1 Komreyev Dancer, **5/2** Grand Selection (IRE), Sarasi, **11/4** MISTER FIRE EYES (IRE) (6/4-3/1), **14/1** What a Nightmare (IRE), CSF £9.25 TOTE £3.80: £2.20 £1.30 (£4.50) OWNER Mr C. T. Olley (NEWMARKET) BRED Airlie Stud 5 Rn 2m 6.0 (10.00) SF: 17/17/9/-/-

325 PHILMAC STOPCOCK H'CAP (0-90) (4-Y.O+) (Class C) £5,602.00 (£1,696.00: £828.00: £394.00)

1m 4f (Fibresand) Stalls: Low GOING minus 0.03 sec per fur (STD) 3-30 (3-31)

246* **Noufari (FR) (80)***(85) (RHollinshead)* 4-9-1 TIves(4) (lw: hld up: rdn along 8f out: hdwy over 5f out: 3rd st: led & edgd lft 1f out: styd on wl)....— **1**
66[2] Chatham Island **(90)***(93)*(Fav)*(CEBrittain)* 7-10-0 BDoyle(1) (lw: chsd ldrs: led over 5f out: hdd 1f out: unable qckn)....1¼ **2**
193[3] Johns Act (USA) **(68)***(70) (DHaydnJones)* 5-8-6v JWeaver(9) (chsd ldrs: led 8f out to 6f out: 2nd st: ev ch whn n.m.r 1f out: no ex)....¾ **3**
106* Hillzah (USA) **(83)***(79) (RBastiman)* 7-9-2 (5) HBastiman(3) (s.i.s: hld up: hdwy 6f out: 4th & rdn st: sn btn)....5 **4**
Chimborazo **(74)***(67) (BJMcMath)* 4-8-9 RCochrane(6) (prom: rdn along over 3f out: 6th & btn st)....1¾ **5**

*279*2 Mentalasanythin **(73)***(53) (ABailey)* 6-8-11 AMackay(5) (led: hdd 9f out: rdn over 3f out: grad wknd) 10 **6**
*88** Benfleet **(80)***(56) (RWArmstrong)* 4-9-1 LDettori(8) (hld up: hdwy over 3f out: 5th & wkng st) ..3 **7**
*186*3 Slmaat **(69)***(34) (MrsMReveley)* 4-8-4 JQuinn(2) (prom: rdn 4f out: grad wknd) 8 **8**
*246*8 New Inn **(72)***(35) (EWeymes)* 4-8-2 (5) JStack(7) (chsd ldr tl led 9f out: sn hdd: led 6f out to 5f out: rdn & grad wknd) 1¾ **9**

100/30 Chatham Island, **4/1** NOUFARI (FR), Slmaat, **5/1** Benfleet, **8/1** Johns Act (USA), **9/1** Mentalasanythin (5/1-10/1), Hillzah (USA) (6/1-10/1), **12/1** New Inn (10/1-16/1), **16/1** Chimborazo, CSF £18.09 CT £96.26 TOTE £5.80: £2.00 £1.30 £2.10 (£15.90) Trio £44.60 OWNER Ed Weetman (Haulage & Storage) Ltd (UPPER LONGDON) BRED His Highness The Aga Khans Studs S.C. in France 9 Rn 2m 39.4 SF: 42/53/30/39/24/13/13/-/-

WEIGHT FOR AGE 4yo-3lb

326

PHILMAC PLUGCOCK (S) STKS (3-Y.O) (Class G) £2,611.50 (£734.00: £358.50)
1m 100y (Fibresand) Stalls: Low GOING minus 0.03 sec per fur (STD) 4-00 (4-01)

*310** **Summer Villa (42)***(57)*(Fav)*(PCHaslam)* 3-8-12 JWeaver(5) (hld up in tch: 3rd st: rdn over 1f out: styd on to ld last strides) ....— **1**
*180** Kirov Protege (IRE) **(49)***(62) (RWArmstrong)* 3-9-3 MRimmer(9) (led: hdd & 2nd st: rallied to ld over 1f out: edgd rt & ct nr fin) ....s.h **2**
Chadleigh Walk (IRE) **(40)***(53) (RHollinshead)* 3-8-12 TIves(10) (chsd ldr: led 2f out tl hdd & hmpd over 1f out: unable qckn) 2 **3**
*283** Dowdency **(44)***(41) (JAPickering)* 3-8-12 NCarlisle(3) (hld up: hdwy & 5th st: styd on u.p) 6 **4**
*283*5 Gigfy **(47)***(41) (BJLlewellyn)* 3-9-3b DHarrison(4) (chsd ldrs: 4th & rdn st: sn btn) 2½ **5**
*283*3 Sweet Cheap Pet **(47)***(22) (JBerry)* 3-8-12v GCarter(6) (prom: 6th & rdn st: sn btn) 7 **6**
*273*8 Fahema **(50)***(8) (RBoss)* 3-8-12 GDuffield(2) (chsd ldrs 6f) 7 **7**
*273*4 Lawbuster (IRE) **(51)***(4) (WRMuir)* 3-8-12b LDettori(8) (hld up: effrt over 3f out: sn btn) 2 **8**
*283*8 Bernard Star (IRE) *(BJLlewellyn)* 3-8-4 (3) DRMcCabe(1) (s.i.s: sn outpcd & bhd) 3 **9**

4/5 SUMMER VILLA (tchd Evens), **5/1** Kirov Protege (IRE) (op 3/1), **7/1** Fahema, **8/1** Lawbuster (IRE), Gigfy, Sweet Cheap Pet, **9/1** Dowdency, **20/1** Chadleigh Walk (IRE), **33/1** Bernard Star (IRE), CSF £6.90 TOTE £2.00: £1.60 £2.40 £5.60 (£5.70) OWNER Mr K. E. Williamson (MIDDLEHAM) BRED Mrs R. D. Peacock 9 Rn 1m 51.1 (7.10) SF: 27/32/23/12/12/-/-/-/-

No bid

327

PHILMAC RAPIDFIX H'CAP (0-80) (3-Y.O+) (Class D) £3,538.60 (£1,070.80: £522.40: £248.20)
5f (Fibresand) Stalls: Low GOING minus 0.03 sec per fur (STD) 4-30 (4-31)

Lord Sky (68)*(72) (ABailey)* 4-9-7 LDettori(2) (trckd ldrs: 2nd st: rdn to ld wl ins fnl f: r.o) ....— **1**
*297*5 Leigh Crofter **(75)***(77)*(Fav)*(PDCundell)* 6-10-0b JWeaver(4) (hld up: 4th st: r.o ins fnl f) ....½ **2**
*188*7 Kalar **(63)***(65) (DWChapman)* 6-8-9b(7) CTeague(5) (led: clr 2f out: hdd & unable qckn wl ins fnl f) ....hd **3**
*244** Scored Again **(62)***(48) (MJHeaton-Ellis)* 5-8-8 (7) AmandaSanders(3) (prom: 3rd & rdn st: r.o one pce) 5 **4**
*216*6 Press the Bell **(75)** *(JBerry)* 5-10-0 GCarter(1) (chsd ldrs tl 5th & wkng st) 20 **5**

7/4 Leigh Crofter (6/1-9/4), **11/4** Scored Again, **3/1** Kalar, LORD SKY (op 2/1), **12/1** Press the Bell (op 8/1), CSF £9.05 TOTE £5.10: £1.10 £2.10 (£3.80) OWNER Mr Ray Bailey (TARPORLEY) BRED R. Barber 5 Rn 61.2 secs (3.20) SF: 47/52/40/23/-

T/Jkpt: £1,407.20 (34.22 Tckts). T/Plpt: £11.10 (1,769.43 Tckts). T/Qdpt £9.30 (6.9 Tckts). CR

0316-LINGFIELD (L-H)
Thursday February 23rd (Standard)

328

LINGFIELD PARK AWT SPRINT SERIES (QUALIFIER) H'CAP (0-70) (4-Y.O+) (Class E) £3,104.15 (£939.20: £458.10: £217.55)
5f (Equitrack) Stalls: High GOING minus 0.56 sec per fur (FST) 2-15 (2-15)

*247** **Tenor (58)***(65)*(Fav)*(DNicholls)* 4-9-10 AlexGreaves(1) (hld up: led over 1f out: hrd rdn: r.o wl)— **1**
*306*2 The Institute Boy **(53)***(55) (MissJFCraze)* 5-9-5 SWebster(4) (rdn & hdwy over 1f out: r.o one pce) 1½ **2**
*247*3 Tee-Emm **(57)***(58) (PHowling)* 5-9-9 JQuinn(5) (led over 3f: one pce) ....½ **3**
*305*8 Sison (IRE) **(61)***(58) (KGWingrove)* 5-9-13 JMcLaughlin(6) (b.hind: lw: hld up: rdn over 1f out: one pce) 1¼ **4**

Random **(62)***(58) (CJames)* 4-10-0 JWeaver(3) (lw: rdn & hdwy over 1f out: one pce ins fnl f) ....nk 5
*307*⁹ Dynamis (IRE) **(48)***(24) (KOCunningham-Brown)* 4-9-0 TQuinn(2) (chsd ldr over 3f) 6 6

11/8 TENOR, **3/1** The Institute Boy, **9/2** Tee-Emm, **9/1** Sison (IRE), **12/1** Random (8/1-14/1), **16/1** Dynamis (IRE), CSF £5.44 TOTE £2.30: £1.20 £2.20 (£3.20) OWNER Mr Geoffrey Thompson (THIRSK) BRED Lord Victor Matthews 6 Rn 58.94 secs (0.74) SF: 47/37/40/40/40/6

329 BARNABY RUDGE CLAIMING STKS (4-Y.O+) (Class F) £2,738.60 (£769.60: £375.80) 1m 4f (Equitrack) Stalls: Low GOING minus 0.56 sec (FST) 2-45 (2-45)

*245** **Harlequin Walk (IRE) (53)***(53)*(Fav)*(AHide)* 4-8-6b JQuinn(1) (mde virtually all: all out) ....— 1
*201*³ Lon Isa **(47)***(50) (BPalling)* 4-8-5 ow1 AClark(5) (rdn & hdwy over 3f out: r.o wl ins fnl f) ....½ 2
*254*⁴ Cliburnel News (IRE) **(45)***(49) (WRMuir)* 5-8-7v JWeaver(9) (b.hind: stdy hdwy over 2f out: r.o wl ins fnl f) ....¾ 3
*290*⁴ Bandita **(40)***(45) (MissAJWhitfield)* 4-7-12 (3)ow1 SSanders(2) (lw: chsd wnr tl ins fnl f: one pce) ....s.h 4
*235*⁸ Call Me Blue **(50)***(44) (TJNaughton)* 5-8-12 GCarter(8) (hdwy over 4f out: rdn over 3f out: eased whn btn ins fnl f) 8 5
*260*⁷ Quadrant **(56)***(34) (AMoore)* 6-8-10 CandyMorris(10) (b: hdwy over 4f out: wknd over 3f out)..6 6
*157*¹⁰ Knightrider **(48)***(29) (CJames)* 4-8-7 TQuinn(4) (b: prom over 9f) 3½ 7
*296*⁴ Killing Time **(60)***(28) (MrsNMacauley)* 4-8-7v MFenton(3) (b: prom over 7f) ....½ 8
*288*⁹ Dragonmist (IRE) **(29)** *(MMadgwick)* 5-8-3v TWilliams(7) (stdy hdwy over 6f out: hrd rdn over 4f out: sn wknd: t.o) 30 9
*200*⁵ Cone Lane **(24)** *(BGubby)* 9-8-0 (5)ow1 JStack(6) (b.hind: lw: prom over 5f: t.o fnl 4f) 10 10
*109*⁹ Joyce E Jackson **(33)** *(RIngram)* 5-8-4b(3) DWright(11) (lw: a bhd: t.o fnl 4f) 9 11

13/8 HARLEQUIN WALK (IRE), **100/30** Killing Time, **8/1** Lon Isa, **9/1** Cliburnel News (IRE) (6/1-10/1), **12/1** Bandita, Call Me Blue, **14/1** Knightrider, **20/1** Quadrant, **33/1** Dragonmist (IRE), **50/1** Cone Lane, Joyce E Jackson, CSF £14.08 TOTE £2.50: £1.10 £1.60 £1.90 (£11.00) OWNER Charlcombe Racing (NEWMARKET) BRED Ronnie Boland in Ireland 11 Rn
2m 31.88 (2.48) SF: 30/27/29/22/24/14/6/5/-/-/-
WEIGHT FOR AGE 4yo-3lb
Harlequin Walk (IRE) clmd K Catchpole £7,000.

330 DAILY STAR AWT 1M 2F CHALLENGE SERIES (QUALIFIER) H'CAP (0-70) (4-Y.O+) (Class E) £3,253.65 (£985.20: £481.10: £229.05) 1m 2f (Equitrack) Stalls: Low GOING minus 0.56 sec per fur (FST) 3-15 (3-17)

Young Freeman (USA) (70)*(88)*(Fav)*(DRLoder)* 6-10-0 JWeaver(3) (lw: mde all: clr over 2f out: unchal) ....— 1
*231*⁶ Achilles Heel **(45)***(49) (CNAllen)* 4-8-1 JQuinn(5) (hdwy over 4f out: chsd wnr fnl 3f: no imp)...9 2
*249*⁴ Captain Marmalade **(50)***(49) (DTThom)* 6-8-5 (3) DRMcCabe(11) (lw: bhd whn hmpd over 2f out: gd hdwy over 1f out: fin wl) 3 3
*203** Little Miss Ribot **(36)***(35) (RJO'Sullivan)* 5-7-8 NAdams(8) (dwlt: rdn over 4f out: hdwy over 3f out: one pce) ....hd 4
*205*³ Shansi (IRE) **(45)***(44) (MDIUsher)* 4-8-1v RStreet(2) (b: b.hind: a.p: rdn over 3f out: one pce)s.h 5
*161*³ My Minnie **(50)***(49) (BJMeehan)* 5-8-8 BDoyle(6) (hld up: rdn over 4f out: r.o one pce fnl f)...s.h 6
Uncharted Waters **(59)***(26) (CACyzer)* 4-9-1 TIves(9) (a bhd) 20 7
*235*⁵ Hillsdown Boy (IRE) **(54)***(17) (SDow)* 5-8-12 TQuinn(4) (prom over 6f) 2½ 8
*125*⁵ Krayyan Dawn **(45)***(7) (RAkehurst)* 5-8-3 GCarter(10) (lw: a bhd) ....s.h 9
*217*⁴ Lexus (IRE) **(39)***(1) (RJRWilliams)* 7-7-11b GBardwell(1) (bhd fnl 3f) ....nk 10
*203*⁴ Greatest Hopes **(40)** *(CJBenstead)* 4-7-5 (5)ow3 CHawksley(7) (prom over 6f) 1¾ 11
LONG HANDICAP Greatest Hopes 7-0

5/2 YOUNG FREEMAN (USA) (7/4-11/4), **4/1** Little Miss Ribot, **6/1** Lexus (IRE), Krayyan Dawn, **8/1** Achilles Heel (op 9/2), **10/1** Captain Marmalade, Shansi (IRE), My Minnie, **20/1** Hillsdown Boy (IRE), **25/1** Uncharted Waters, **33/1** Greatest Hopes, CSF £23.25 CT £166.13 TOTE £3.20: £1.10 £4.70 £3.10 (£18.70) TRIO £187.80 OWNER Lucayan Stud (NEWMARKET) BRED Allen E. Paulson 11 Rn
2m 3.19 (0.19) SF: 65/24/26/12/19/26/1/-/-/-/-
WEIGHT FOR AGE 4yo-2lb

331 BLEAK HOUSE (S) STKS (3-Y.O+) (Class G) £2,471.80 (£694.80: £339.40) 6f (Equitrack) Stalls: Low GOING minus 0.56 sec per fur (FST) 3-45 (3-47)

*202** **Tyrian Purple (IRE) (61)***(65) (TJNaughton)* 7-9-12b DHarrison(4) (mde all: clr over 4f out: edgd rt over 1f out: r.o wl) ....— 1
*236*² Baileys Sunset (IRE) **(67)***(60)*(Fav)*(MJohnston)* 3-8-10 RCochrane(8) (a.p: chsd wnr fnl 3f: hrd rdn fnl f: unable qckn) 1¾ 2

192[9] Anotherone to Note **(52)***(49) (MJHeaton-Ellis)* 4-9-7 JWeaver(5) (stdd s: gd hdwy over 1f out: str run fnl f: fin wl)....2½ **3**
202[2] Lift Boy (USA) **(62)***(52) (AMoore)* 6-9-12 CandyMorris(2) (b.hind: a.p: one pce fnl 2f)....½ **4**
287[5] Waders Dream (IRE) **(35)***(39) (PatMitchell)* 6-9-7v JMcLaughlin(10) (outpcd: no hdwy fnl 3f)....3 **5**
287[9] Waverley Star **(42)***(33) (KOCunningham-Brown)* 10-9-7 TQuinn(7) (outpcd: nvr nr to chal)....2½ **6**
248[7] Secret Assignment (USA) **(40)***(32) (CACyzer)* 5-9-2 (5) SMulvey(6) (outpcd)....nk **7**
25[8] Colston-C **(44)***(27) (CJHill)* 3-8-5 JQuinn(9) (a bhd)....1¾ **8**
185[7] Pink Petal **(35)***(12) (CJHill)* 3-8-0 GBardwell(1) (b: outpcd)....4 **9**
287[10] Pat Poindestres **(34)***(6) (BAPearce)* 5-8-11 (5) AWhelan(3) (b: b.hind: spd over 3f)....2 **10**
198[7] Distinctive Lady **(23)** *(REPeacock)* 5-9-2v GDuffield(11) (a bhd)....13 **11**

9/4 Baileys Sunset (IRE), **5/2** Lift Boy (USA) (op 6/4), **7/2** TYRIAN PURPLE (IRE), **11/1** Waverley Star, **12/1** Anotherone to Note, **16/1** Pink Petal, **20/1** Waders Dream (IRE), Secret Assignment (USA), Colston-C, Pat Poindestres, **33/1** Distinctive Lady, CSF £11.99 TOTE £5.10: £1.40 £1.60 £2.30 (£5.00) OWNER Mr T. O'Flaherty (EPSOM) BRED Niels Schibbye 11 Rn

1m 12.29 (1.69) SF: 39/18/23/26/13/7/6/-/-/-/-
WEIGHT FOR AGE 3yo-16lb
No bid

332 HARD TIMES MAIDEN STKS (3-Y.O+) (Class D) £3,640.00 (£1,102.00: £538.00: £256.00) 7f (Equitrack) Stalls: Low GOING minus 0.56 sec (FST) 4-15 (4-16)

250[4] **Renown (68)***(57)*(Fav)*(LordHuntingdon)* 3-8-5 DHarrison(4) (a.p: hrd rdn over 1f out: led nr fin)....— **1**
239[3] Breckland (IRE) **(37)***(56) (KOCunningham-Brown)* 5-9-9 JWeaver(6) (led: hrd rdn fnl f: hdd nr fin)....½ **2**
286[3] Solianna **(69)***(50) (MRChannon)* 3-8-0 CRutter(1) (a.p: hrd rdn over 1f out: r.o one pce)....½ **3**
64[7] Concer Un *(55) (SCWilliams)* 3-8-2 (3) DWright(8) (lw: plld hrd: rdn & hdwy over 1f out: r.o wl ins fnl f)....s.h **4**
289[3] Sandra Dee (IRE) **(58)***(49) (BAPearce)* 3-8-0 StephenDavies(9) (lw: hdwy over 4f out: rdn over 2f out: r.o ins fnl f)....½ **5**
Full Cover (IRE) **(78)***(44) (DRCElsworth)* 3-8-5b BDoyle(2) (nvr nr to chal)....4 **6**
Margaret Modes *(33) (CACyzer)* 3-8-2 ow2 GDuffield(5) (neat: a bhd)....3 **7**
276[4] Speedybird (IRE) *(31) (BJMeehan)* 3-8-0 JQuinn(3) (prom over 5f)....¾ **8**
Tarjumaan (USA) *(32) (RJO'Sullivan)* 4-9-9 AClark(11) (s.s: a bhd)....1½ **9**
308[9] Binlaboon (IRE) *(23) (KGWingrove)* 4-9-9b JMcLaughlin(7) (b.hind: bhd fnl 3f)....4 **10**
Foreshore (IRE) **(53)***(2) (RIngram)* 5-9-4 TWilliams(10) (bhd fnl 3f)....7 **11**

6/5 RENOWN, **5/1** Solianna, Full Cover (IRE) (7/2-11/2), **7/1** Speedybird (IRE), **10/1** Sandra Dee (IRE) (op 6/1), **12/1** Margaret Modes (8/1-14/1), **20/1** Tarjumaan (USA), Foreshore (IRE), **25/1** Concer Un, **33/1** Breckland (IRE), **50/1** Binlaboon (IRE), CSF £38.36 TOTE £2.10: £1.30 £3.30 £1.80 (£27.20) OWNER The Queen (WEST ILSLEY) BRED The Queen 11 Rn

1m 25.91 (2.91) SF: 9/26/2/7/1/-/-/-/2/-/-
WEIGHT FOR AGE 3yo-18lb

333 NICHOLAS NICKLEBY H'CAP (0-80) (3-Y.O) (Class D) £3,538.60 (£1,070.80: £522.40: £248.20) 7f (Equitrack) Stalls: Low GOING minus 0.56 sec per fur (FST) 4-45 (4-45)

243[3] **Master Millfield (IRE) (72)***(79) (CJHill)* 3-9-7 JWeaver(2) (led 2f: led 2f out: rdn out)....— **1**
294[2] Three Arch Bridge **(53)***(57) (MJohnston)* 3-8-2 TWilliams(3) (led 5f out to 2f out: unable qckn fnl f)....1¼ **2**
Greenwich Again **(66)***(69) (TGMills)* 3-9-1 TQuinn(6) (hdwy over 3f out: rdn over 2f out: r.o ins fnl f)....½ **3**
*319** Montague Dawson (IRE) **(68)***(64)*(Fav)*(MrsNMacauley)* 3-8-12 (5) 6x SDrowne(4) (b.hind: lw: hld up: rdn over 2f out: wknd fnl f)....3 **4**
*251** Water Hazard (IRE) **(57)***(53) (SDow)* 3-8-3 (3) SSanders(5) (nvr nr to chal)....s.h **5**
Scissor Ridge **(65)** *(JJBridger)* 3-9-0 GDuffield(1) (lw: bhd fnl 4f)....30 **6**

5/2 Montague Dawson (IRE), **3/1** Three Arch Bridge, **7/2** Water Hazard (IRE), **4/1** MASTER MILLFIELD (IRE), **11/2** Greenwich Again, **25/1** Scissor Ridge, CSF £15.63 TOTE £6.70: £1.50 £1.70 (£9.00) OWNER Mr John Hill (BARNSTAPLE) BRED A. M. F. Persse 6 Rn

1m 24.95 (1.95) SF: 35/13/25/20/9/-

T/Plpt: £26.30 (460.25 Tckts). T/Qdpt: ££27.90 (2.1 Tckts). AK

0310-**SOUTHWELL (L-H)**
Friday February 24th (Standard)
WIND: slight across

334
FARNSFIELD MAIDEN APPRENTICE H'CAP (0-60) (I) (4-Y.O+)
(Class F) £2,537.00 (£712.00: £347.00)
1m (Fibresand) Stalls: Low GOING minus 0.14 sec per fur (FST) 1-40 (1-40)

268[4] **At the Savoy (IRE) (44)***(48)*(Fav)*(TDBarron)* 4-9-2 (3) KimberleyHart(2) (lw: led after 1f: rdn over 2f out: jst hld on)....— 1
155[8] Hi Penny **(40)***(43) (KTIvory)* 4-8-12b(3) CScally(7) (chsd ldrs: rdn & ev ch wl ins fnl f: no ex nr fin)....nk 2
269[6] Tremolante **(30)***(33) (CaptJWilson)* 4-8-5 MHenry(4) (sn outpcd & bhd: gd hdwy appr fnl f: fin fast)....s.h 3
Intrepid Fort **(25)***(28) (BWMurray)* 6-8-0v MartinDwyer(9) (bhd: hdwy appr st: styd on one pce appr fnl f)....nk 4
166[3] Mr Moriarty (IRE) **(38)***(38) (SRBowring)* 4-8-13b AmandaSanders(3) (swtg: s.i.s: hdwy 2f out: styd on nr fin)....1¼ 5
226[4] Main Brace **(40)***(35) (KRBurke)* 4-8-12 (3) RWaterfield(1) (lw: chsd ldrs: outpcd ent st: no imp after)....2½ 6
313[5] Spanish Stripper (USA) **(49)***(42) (MCChapman)* 4-9-5 (5) GFaulkner(8) (led 1f: cl up: rdn over 2f out: wknd appr fnl f)....1 7
198[3] Europharm Lassie **(41)***(26) (GLMoore)* 4-9-2v LSuthern(5) (w ldrs tl wknd over 1f out)....4 8
225[6] Charlotte Penny **(30)***(3) (NPLittmoden)* 4-8-5b CAdamson(6) (b.nr fore: s.i.s: a bhd)....6 9

2/1 AT THE SAVOY (IRE), **11/4** Mr Moriarty (IRE), **6/1** Spanish Stripper (USA) (4/1-7/1), **13/2** Main Brace (10/1-6/1), **9/1** Europharm Lassie (6/1-10/1), **10/1** Tremolante, **12/1** Intrepid Fort, Hi Penny, **33/1** Charlotte Penny, CSF £25.66 CT £190.11 TOTE £3.10: £1.60 £2.80 £2.20 (£22.90) Trio £75.50 OWNER Mr Stephen Woodall (THIRSK) BRED Frank Towey 9 Rn
1m 46.9 (7.60) SF: 18/13/3/-/8/5/12/-/-

335
FARNSFIELD MAIDEN APPRENTICE H'CAP (0-60) (II) (4-Y.O+)
(Class F) £2,537.00 (£712.00: £347.00)
1m (Fibresand) Stalls: Low GOING minus 0.14 sec per fur (FST) 2-10 (2-10)

181[8] **Glenvally (43)***(47)*(Fav)*(BWMurray)* 4-9-4b(5) CScudder(6) (bhd: gd hdwy appr st: led wl over 2f out: r.o)....— 1
Coven Moon **(31)***(32) (DMorris)* 5-8-6 (5) CWebb(4) (outpcd & lost tch appr st: hdwy over 1f out: styd on wl)....1½ 2
215[8] Uckerby Lad **(44)***(44) (NPLittmoden)* 4-9-10b CAdamson(3) (s.i.s: sn chsng ldrs: ev ch over 1f out: nt qckn)....¾ 3
Rambollina **(41)***(38) (MWEasterby)* 4-9-7 RuthCoulter(7) (w ldrs: one pce fnl 2f)....1½ 4
179[7] Arrogant Boy **(38)***(29) (DWChapman)* 6-9-1 (3) AEddery(5) (pushed along ½-wy: hdwy over 2f out: no imp)....3 5
Blaster Bates (USA) **(39)***(25) (RBrotherton)* 4-9-2b(3) RWaterfield(1) (chsd ldrs: outpcd appr st: no imp after)....2½ 6
Saxon Magic **(29)** *(JABennett)* 5-8-9 MHenry(2) (led over 6f out tl wl over 2f out: sn wknd)....8 7
271[8] Personimus **(36)** *(CaptJWilson)* 5-9-2 AmandaSanders(8) (led over 1f: cl up tl wknd qckly over 2f out)....dist 8

5/2 GLENVALLY, **11/2** Saxon Magic, Personimus, **6/1** Coven Moon (op 14/1), Uckerby Lad, **7/1** Rambollina (op 7/2), **8/1** Arrogant Boy, **10/1** Blaster Bates (USA), CSF £17.51 CT £75.91 TOTE £2.20: £1.90 £2.00 £1.20 (£10.40) OWNER Mrs M. Lingwood (MALTON) BRED Norton Grove Stud Ltd 8 Rn
1m 47.0 (7.70) SF: 22/7/19/13/4/-/-/-

336
BEESTHORPE CLAIMING STKS (3-Y.O+) (Class F) £2,537.00 (£712.00: £347.00)
7f (Fibresand) Stalls: Low GOING minus 0.14 sec per fur (FST) 2-40 (2-40)

*293** **No Submission (USA) (66)***(74)*(Fav)*(DWChapman)* 9-9-6 DeanMcKeown(4) (lw: led after 1f: qcknd over 2f out: styd on wl)....— 1
293[2] Battle Colours (IRE) **(65)***(67) (MrsJRRamsden)* 6-9-5b JWeaver(2) (disp ld after 2f: brt wd st: hrd rdn & ltl rspnse)....2½ 2
248[2] Rocky Waters (USA) **(80)***(64) (GLMoore)* 6-9-9 AMorris(1) (lw: trckd ldrs: effrt over 1f out: rdn & no rspnse)....3 3
267[11] Kristis Girl *(11) (DHaydnJones)* 8-9-1 AMackay(5) (outpcd & bhd fr ½-wy)....20 4
Tiddy Oggie *(22) (NAGraham)* 4-9-13 TQuinn(3) (led 1f: cl up tl btn over 1f out & eased)....nk 5

13/8 NO SUBMISSION (USA), **85/40** Rocky Waters (USA), **5/2** Battle Colours (IRE), **11/2** Tiddy Oggie, **33/1** Kristis Girl, CSF £6.19 TOTE £2.30: £1.70 £1.60 (£2.20) OWNER Mr T. S. Redman (YORK) BRED Mr. Francis X. Weber 5 Rn 1m 31.4 (4.60) SF: 41/34/31/-/-

337 PARK HOSPITAL H'CAP (0-80) (3-Y.O+) (Class D) £3,707.60 (£1,122.80: £548.40: £261.20) **7f (Fibresand)** Stalls: Low GOING minus 0.14 sec (FST) 3-10 (3-11)

Flowing Ocean (70)_(84) (MissGayKelleway)_ 5-9-8 RCochrane(1) (lw: trckd ldrs: led over 2f out: shkn up & sn clr) .... — 1
_298⁶_ Orthorhombus **(52)**_(55) (DJSCosgrove)_ 6-8-1b(3) DRMcCabe(6) (bhd: hdwy on outside 2f out: styd on: no imp) 5 2
Belleminette (IRE) **(70)**_(70) (DHaydnJones)_ 4-9-8 AMackay(3) (bhd: hdwy & prom ½-wy: nt qckn appr fnl f) 1¼ 3
_315²_ South Forest (IRE) **(68)**_(67) (SRBowring)_ 4-8-13 (7) CTeague(8) (b: cl up tl rdn & grad wknd fnl 2½f) .... ½ 4
_281⁶_ Allinson's Mate (IRE) **(68)**_(59) (TDBarron)_ 7-9-6 KDarley(7) (prom: outpcd appr st: no imp after) 3½ 5
_256*_ Twin Creeks **(58)**_(49)_(Fav)_(MDHammond)_ 4-8-10 GDuffield(2) (lw: led tl over 2f out: wknd)..s.h 6
Taufan Blu (IRE) **(74)**_(49) (FJO'Mahony)_ 6-9-12 GCarter(4) (sn drvn along & bhd) 7 7
Macs Maharanee **(76)**_(44) (PSFelgate)_ 8-9-9 (5) JStack(5) (bit bkwd: chsd ldrs tl rdn & wknd wl over 2f out) 3 8

5/2 Twin Creeks, **3/1** FLOWING OCEAN, **100/30** South Forest (IRE), **7/2** Allinson's Mate (IRE), **14/1** Orthorhombus, **16/1** Belleminette (IRE), **20/1** Taufan Blu (IRE), **25/1** Macs Maharanee, CSF £38.47 CT £533.74 TOTE £5.00: £1.90 £2.60 £4.80 (£27.60) OWNER Mr A. Al-Radi (WHITCOMBE) BRED London Thoroughbred Services Ltd 8 Rn 1m 30.9 (4.10) SF: 49/20/35/32/24/14/14/9

338 CROPS H'CAP (0-70) (4-Y.O+) (Class E) £3,009.60 (£910.80: £444.40: £211.20) **6f (Fibresand)** Stalls: Low GOING minus 0.14 sec per fur (FST) 3-40 (3-40)

_220⁶_ **Lady Roxanne (43)**_(46) (LordHuntingdon)_ 6-8-3v DHarrison(3) (a.p: hdwy to ld ins fnl f: kpt on wl) .... — 1
_297²_ Bella Parkes **(64)**_(67)_(Fav)_(DNicholls)_ 4-9-10b AlexGreaves(6) (lw: trckd ldrs gng wl: chal & rdn wl over 1f out: kpt on nr fin) .... s.h 2
_268³_ Christian Flight (IRE) **(40)**_(39) (SGollings)_ 6-7-11 (3) DWright(7) (cl up: slt ld ½-wy: hdd & no ex ins fnl f) 1½ 3
_231⁵_ Wellsy Lad (USA) **(34)**_(30) (DWChapman)_ 8-7-8bow1 NCarlisle(2) (s.i.s: hdwy 2f out: styd on: nt pce to chal) .... ¾ 4
_231³_ Matthew David **(45)**_(41) (SRBowring)_ 5-8-5 JQuinn(1) (trckd ldrs: nt clr run & swtchd over 1f out: nt rcvr) .... ½ 5
_228⁶_ Meeson Times **(48)**_(40) (RBastiman)_ 7-8-8 SDWilliams(4) (led to ½-wy: grad wknd fnl 2f) 1½ 6
_233⁹_ Grey Toppa **(46)**_(37) (MrsJRRamsden)_ 4-8-6 DeanMcKeown(5) (w ldrs tl wknd appr fnl f).....nk 7

5/6 Bella Parkes, **5/1** Matthew David, **8/1** LADY ROXANNE, **9/1** Christian Flight (IRE), **10/1** Meeson Times (7/1-11/1), **12/1** Grey Toppa, **14/1** Wellsy Lad (USA), CSF £14.97 TOTE £6.60: £3.00 £1.40 (£6.20) OWNER Lord Huntingdon (WEST ILSLEY) BRED W. Hastings-Bass 7 Rn 1m 17.6 (4.10) SF: 20/41/13/4/15/14/11

339 WELLOW (S) STKS (3-Y.O) (Class G) £2,259.00 (£634.00: £309.00) **1m 3f (Fibresand)** Stalls: Low GOING minus 0.14 sec per fur (FST) 4-10 (4-11)

_264³_ **Wisdom (58)**_(65)_(Fav)_(PFICole)_ 3-8-11b TQuinn(10) (b.hind: lw: mde all: styd on wl fnl 2f)...— 1
_241⁶_ Poly Road **(47)**_(58) (MRChannon)_ 3-8-11 RHughes(3) (lw: hdwy 6f out: chsd wnr fnl 2½f: hung lft & nt qckn) 5 2
_241³_ Recovery Lad (IRE) _(53) (KRBurke)_ 3-8-8 (3) DRMcCabe(11) (hld up: effrt 4f out: edgd lft & no imp) 3½ 3
_144¹¹_ Two Way Stretch **(35)**_(45) (GLMoore)_ 3-8-6 SWhitworth(4) (chsd ldrs: one pce fnl 3f) 2 4
_292³_ Fools of Pride (IRE) **(48)**_(41) (RHollinshead)_ 3-8-6 WRyan(8) (sme hdwy 3f out: nvr rchd ldrs) 2½ 5
_292²_ Hever Golf Lady **(39)**_(39) (TJNaughton)_ 3-8-6 JWeaver(5) (prom: effrt appr st: sn btn) 1½ 6
_292⁶_ Runforaction (IRE) **(45)**_(38) (BSRothwell)_ 3-8-11 MFenton(12) (drvn along ½-wy: nvr trbld ldrs) 4 7
_292⁵_ Miss Suzy **(24)**_(31) (JPLeigh)_ 3-8-6 DeanMcKeown(2) (nvr nr ldrs) 1½ 8
_292^C_ Something Speedy (IRE) **(50)**_(29) (PJBevan)_ 3-8-11 NCarlisle(1) (chsd ldrs tl wknd appr st)...5 9
Drama King _(24) (SRBowring)_ 3-8-4b(7) CTeague(9) (a outpcd & bhd) 3 10
_95⁸_ Daily Challenger (USA) **(42)**_(21) (RonaldThompson)_ 3-8-11 AMackay(6) (plld hrd: chsd wnr tl wknd 2f out) 2 11
_225⁵_ Bentham's About _(DrJDScargill)_ 3-8-11 DHarrison(7) (a t.o) 25 12

2/1 WISDOM, **11/4** Hever Golf Lady, **7/1** Recovery Lad (IRE), **8/1** Something Speedy (IRE), **9/1** Fools of Pride (IRE) (6/1-10/1), **10/1** Poly Road, **12/1** Drama King, **16/1** Runforaction (IRE), **25/1** Miss Suzy, Two Way Stretch, Daily Challenger (USA), Bentham's About, CSF £23.07 TOTE £2.80: £1.20 £2.10 £3.20 (£7.00) Trio £31.00 OWNER Prince Fahd Salman (WHATCOMBE) BRED Newgate Stud Co 12 Rn 2m 29.6 (8.10) SF: 28/21/16/8/4/2/1/-/-/-/-/-
Sold K Morgan 8,200 gns.

340 THORGATON H'CAP (0-70) (4-Y.O+) (Class E) £3,052.50 (£924.00: £451.00: £214.50) **1m 4f (Fibresand)** GOING minus 0.14 sec per fur (FST) 4-40 (4-41)

304² **Mr Bean (42)***(54)*(Fav)*(KRBurke)* 5-8-3 ow1 MFenton(6) (w ldrs: led 4f out: qcknd clr over 2f out: unchal) — 1
312⁸ Modest Hope (USA) **(45)***(42) (BRichmond)* 8-7-13 (7) ClaireBalding(8) (in tch: hdwy 4f out: styd on: no ch w wnr) 12 2
312³ Winn's Pride (IRE) **(52)***(46) (RHollinshead)* 4-8-10 WRyan(2) (lw: trckd ldrs: effrt over 3f out: one pce) 2 3
234⁸ Kausar (USA) **(34)***(17) (JLEyre)* 8-7-9 ow1 JQuinn(5) (b: led tl hdd 4f out: outpcd fnl 3f) 8 4
252⁹ Snow Dream **(48)***(25) (MJRyan)* 5-8-9 AClark(4) (prom tl wknd 4f out) 5 5
280² How's it Goin (IRE) **(70)***(46)*(Fav)*(WRMuir)* 4-10-0b JWeaver(1) (plld hrd: chsd ldrs tl wknd 3f out) ½ 6
32⁹ Amlak (USA) **(41)** *(TKersey)* 6-8-2vow2 BDoyle(7) (b: a bhd) 25 7

5/2 MR BEAN (op 6/4), How's it Goin (IRE), **3/1** Winn's Pride (IRE), **5/1** Modest Hope (USA), **10/1** Kausar (USA), **12/1** Snow Dream, **33/1** Amlak (USA), CSF £14.93 CT £35.48 TOTE £2.30: £2.10 £2.10 (£7.30) OWNER Mr K. Powell (WANTAGE) BRED M. L. Page 7 Rn
2m 41.8 (7.60) SF: 28/16/17/-/-/17/-
WEIGHT FOR AGE 4yo-3lb
T/Plpt: £236.50 (49.95 Tckts). T/Qdpt: £37.30 (1.4 Tckts). AA

0328-LINGFIELD (L-H)
Saturday February 25th (Standard)

341 MERLIN (S) H'CAP (0-60) (I) (4-Y.O+) (Class F) £2,751.20 (£773.20: £377.60) **1m (Equitrack)** Stalls: High GOING minus 0.44 sec per fur (FST) 1-50 (1-52)

255⁵ **Broughtons Turmoil (55)***(60) (WJMusson)* 6-9-7 (5) PMcCabe(4) (b: prom: chsd ldr over 2f out: led ins fnl f: r.o) — 1
205² Swallow Ridge (IRE) **(31)***(34)*(Fav)*(RJO'Sullivan)* 6-8-2 NAdams(11) (b: chsd ldrs: rdn 3f out: hrd rdn over 1f out: r.o fnl f) 1¼ 2
217⁵ King Parrot (IRE) **(52)***(54) (LordHuntingdon)* 7-9-4 (5) AWhelan(6) (chsd ldrs: hrd rdn over 2f out: r.o fnl f) s.h 3
187⁴ Titanium Honda (IRE) **(41)***(43) (CEBrittain)* 4-8-12 BDoyle(12) (chsd ldr: led over 4f out tl ins fnl f: one pce) s.h 4
312⁵ Royal Acclaim **(44)***(40) (JMBradley)* 10-8-8v(7) AmandaSanders(1) (nvr nrr) 3 5
323⁵ Veloce (IRE) **(49)***(41) (ABailey)* 7-8-13v(7) AngelaGallimore(3) (b: hld up: hdwy over 2f out: sn rdn: hung lft over 1f out: nt r.o) 2 6
302⁷ My Lifetime Lady (IRE) **(37)***(27) (KTIvory)* 4-8-8 NCarlisle(5) (b.hind: nvr nrr) 1 7
320¹¹ Pair of Jacks (IRE) **(28)***(18) (DAWilson)* 5-7-13 NGwilliams(9) (led over 3f: wknd over 1f out) hd 8
302⁴ Doodies Pool (IRE) **(46)***(34) (GLMoore)* 5-9-3 SWhitworth(10) (b.hind: hld up: rdn 4f out: no hdwy fnl 3f) 1 9
142⁵ Crafty Cricketer **(24)***(6) (RMFlower)* 4-7-9 JQuinn(7) (mid div: hdwy 3f out: btn over 1f out) 3 10
248⁴ La Residence **(49)***(7) (MrsNMacauley)* 4-9-3 (3) SSanders(8) (bhd fnl 4f) 12 11
265¹² Whatone Bell **(22)** *(PHayward)* 5-7-7b GBardwell(2) (b.hind: dwlt: a bhd) 14 12

LONG HANDICAP Whatone Bell 7-4

7/2 Swallow Ridge (IRE), **5/1** King Parrot (IRE) (op 11/4), **11/2** BROUGHTONS TURMOIL, Veloce (IRE), **7/1** Doodies Pool (IRE), **10/1** La Residence, **12/1** Crafty Cricketer, **14/1** Royal Acclaim, **20/1** Pair of Jacks (IRE), My Lifetime Lady (IRE), Titanium Honda (IRE), **33/1** Whatone Bell, CSF £24.31 CT £95.83 TOTE £10.80: £3.20 £1.80 £2.60 (£28.00) Trio £29.50 OWNER Broughton Thermal Insulation (NEWMARKET) BRED Tally Ho Stud Co (U.K.) Ltd and Ninevah Ltd 12 Rn No bid
1m 39.45 (3.05) SF: 42/16/36/25/22/23/9/-/16/-/-/-

342 LINGFIELD PARK AWT SPRINT SERIES (QUALIFIER) H'CAP (0-80) (3-Y.O) (Class D) £3,688.40 (£1,116.20: £544.60: £258.80) **5f (Equitrack)** GOING minus 0.44 sec per fur (FST) 2-20 (2-21)

*173** **Ultra Beet (76)***(85)*(Fav)*(PCHaslam)* 3-9-7 JWeaver(1) (mde all: clr over 1f out: r.o) — 1
284³ Dolly Face **(65)***(66) (WRMuir)* 3-8-10 TQuinn(6) (sn pushed along: chsd ldrs: hdwy over 2f out: chsd wnr over 1f out: one pce) 2½ 2

284[2] C-Yer-Simmie (IRE) **(62)***(60) (RHollinshead)* 3-8-2 (5) AGarth(2) (chsd wnr over 3f: ev ch 2f out: rn wd over 1f out: one pce)....1 3
319[4] Das Island **(60)***(52) (JRJenkins)* 3-8-5 CRutter(3) (chsd ldrs: rdn & outpcd over 2f out: r.o one pce fnl f)....1¾ 4
Saltz (IRE) **(73)***(52) (PTDalton)* 3-9-1 (3) SSanders(7) (chsd ldrs: rdn & outpcd over 2f out: no hdwy fnl 2f)....4 5
299[5] Just Jesting **(52)***(29) (GLMoore)* 3-7-11v JQuinn(4) (chsd ldrs: rdn & outpcd over 2f out: no hdwy fnl 2f)....¾ 6
283[9] Saxon Heir (IRE) **(48)***(15) (MDIUsher)* 3-7-7b GBardwell(5) (b: sn outpcd: a bhd)....3 7

LONG HANDICAP Saxon Heir (IRE) 7-0

7/4 ULTRA BEET, **100/30** Dolly Face (5/2-4/1), **4/1** C-Yer-Simmie (IRE), **5/1** Das Island, **12/1** Saltz (IRE) (op 6/1), **25/1** Just Jesting, **50/1** Saxon Heir (IRE), CSF £7.31 TOTE £2.00: £1.20 £2.20 (£4.60) OWNER Pet Express Ltd T/A Nutrimix (MIDDLEHAM) BRED Rockhouse Farms Ltd 7 Rn
59.32 secs (1.12) SF: 48/29/23/15/15/-/-

343 MERLIN (S) H'CAP (0-60) (II) (4-Y.O+) (Class F) £2,751.20 (£773.20: £377.60)
1m (Equitrack) GOING minus 0.44 sec per fur (FST) 2-50 (2-51)

302[2] **Eastleigh (46)***(53) (RHollinshead)* 6-9-6 TIves(8) (led 1f: styd prom: chsd ldr 4f out: rdn over 1f out: led wl ins fnl f: r.o)....— 1
313[9] Zahran (IRE) **(50)***(57) (JMBradley)* 4-9-5 (5) SDrowne(11) (mid div: hdwy 3f out: hrd rdn over 1f out: ev ch wl ins fnl f: r.o)....hd 2
302[3] Fiaba **(41)***(47) (MrsNMacauley)* 7-8-8 (7) AmandaSanders(9) (outpcd & bhd: hdwy over 1f out: str run fnl f: fin wl)....nk 3
248[5] Dome Patrol **(47)***(50)*(Fav)*(WRMuir)* 4-9-7b JWeaver(3) (led 7f out: clr over 1f out: rdn, hung lft & hdd wl ins fnl f: nt r.o)....1½ 4
117[11] Quick Million **(42)***(42) (BJMeehan)* 4-8-9 (7) DaneO'Neill(10) (nvr nrr)....1¾ 5
56[10] Arrasas Lady **(35)***(34) (RMFlower)* 5-8-4 (5) JDSmith(4) (a.p: rdn over 3f out: hrd rdn over 1f out: one pce)....½ 6
217[7] Blue Ensign **(39)***(33) (HGRowsell)* 10-8-6b(7) DGibbs(1) (nvr nrr)....2½ 7
198[4] Mrs Bizzybody **(32)***(22) (TJNaughton)* 4-8-6 JQuinn(2) (b: prom: rdn over 3f out: wknd 2f out) 2 8
308[7] Ballyhays (IRE) **(40)***(22) (JAHarris)* 6-9-0b SDWilliams(6) (chsd ldrs: rdn over 3f out: wknd over 2f out)....4 9
147[7] The Country Dancer **(30)***(9) (KTIvory)* 5-8-4 NCarlisle(7) (a bhd)....1½ 10
252[11] The Leaf Sweeper **(25)** *(MJBolton)* 4-7-13 CRutter(5) (sn outpcd: a bhd)....20 11

3/1 Dome Patrol, **4/1** Blue Ensign, **9/2** Fiaba, EASTLEIGH, **7/1** Quick Million (6/1-9/1), **14/1** Zahran (IRE), Mrs Bizzybody (op 9/1), **16/1** Ballyhays (IRE), **20/1** Arrasas Lady, **50/1** The Country Dancer, The Leaf Sweeper, CSF £59.57 CT £274.23 TOTE £2.30: £1.50 £2.80 £1.20 (£33.80) Trio £66.90 OWNER Mr J. E. Bigg (UPPER LONGDON) BRED Hever Castle Stud 11 Rn No bid
1m 40.55 (4.15) SF: 26/30/20/23/15/7/6/-/-/-/-

344 HARRIER LIMITED STKS (0-65) (3-Y.O+) (Class F) £2,713.40 (£762.40: £372.20)
7f (Equitrack) GOING minus 0.44 sec per fur (FST) 3-25 (3-26)

320* **Perilous Plight (70)***(81) (WRMuir)* 4-10-1 2x JWeaver(4) (hld up gng wl: led over 1f out: r.o wl)....— 1
298* Present Situation **(69)***(73)*(Fav)*(LordHuntingdon)* 4-9-4 (5) AWhelan(7) (sn pushed along in rr: hdwy over 2f out: hrd rdn over 1f out: r.o fnl f)....¾ 2
281[4] Maid Welcome **(61)***(60) (MrsNMacauley)* 8-8-11v(7) AmandaSanders(6) (a.p: ev ch over 1f out: one pce)....3½ 3
199* Canary Falcon **(65)***(64) (RJO'Sullivan)* 4-9-11 WWoods(2) (chsd ldr: led 3f out: hdd over 1f out: one pce fnl f)....1½ 4
298[4] Words of Wisdom (IRE) **(62)***(55) (CACyzer)* 5-9-6 (3) DRMcCabe(5) (chsd ldrs: rdn & outpcd 4f out: no hdwy fnl 2f)....3 5
237[3] Apollo Red **(51)***(39) (AMoore)* 6-9-9v CandyMorris(1) (led 4f: wknd 1f out)....7 6
298[9] Giggleswick Girl **(60)** *(MRChannon)* 4-9-4 RHughes(3) (dwlt: a bhd)....20 7

6/4 Present Situation, **5/2** PERILOUS PLIGHT, **13/2** Canary Falcon, **9/1** Words of Wisdom (IRE) (4/1-10/1), **10/1** Maid Welcome (op 5/1), **20/1** Giggleswick Girl, **25/1** Apollo Red, CSF £6.13 TOTE £3.40: £1.90 £1.30 (£2.60) OWNER Mr J. Jannaway (LAMBOURN) BRED Crest Stud Ltd 7 Rn
1m 25.17 (2.17) SF: 49/41/28/32/23/7/-

345 SPARROWHAWK H'CAP (0-90) (3-Y.O+) (Class C) £5,446.00 (£1,648.00: £804.00: £382.00) **6f (Equitrack)** GOING minus 0.44 sec per fur (FST) 3-55 (3-56)

196[3] **Stoppes Brow (84)***(87) (GLMoore)* 3-8-6v SWhitworth(4) (dwlt: hdwy 3f out: chsd ldr over 1f out: led ins fnl f: r.o)....— 1

327* Lord Sky **(74)***(76)*(Fav)*(ABailey)* 4-8-9 (3) 6x SSanders(1) (led: rdn over 1f out: hdd ins fnl f: r.o) ....nk 2
184[5] Croft Pool **(80)***(78) (JAGlover)* 4-9-4 Tlves(7) (chsd ldrs: rdn & outpcd 2f out: r.o ins fnl f) 1¾ 3
160[6] Invocation **(65)***(59) (AMoore)* 8-7-12 (5)ow2 AWhelan(3) (a.p: chsd ldr briefly 2f out: rdn over 1f out: one pce) ....½ 4
237* Sir Tasker **(69)***(64) (JLHarris)* 7-8-7 RCochrane(6) (hld up: hdwy over 2f out: rdn over 1f out: one pce fnl f) ....nk 5
242[7] Rocketeer (IRE) **(88)***(77) (WRMuir)* 4-9-12b JWeaver(5) (b: sn outpcd: hdwy over 1f out: nvr nrr) 2½ 6
278* Bold Effort (FR) **(77)***(60) (KOCunningham-Brown)* 3-7-13 JQuinn(2) (chsd ldr 4f: btn over 1f out) 2 7
281* Little Ibnr **(85)***(50) (PDEvans)* 4-9-4 (5) JStack(8) (racd wd: chsd ldrs: wknd 2f out) 7 8

4/1 Lord Sky, **9/2** Rocketeer (IRE), Bold Effort (FR) (3/1-5/1), **5/1** STOPPES BROW, **11/2** Little Ibnr (op 7/2), **9/1** Croft Pool (5/1-10/1), **10/1** Sir Tasker, **20/1** Invocation, CSF £22.98 CT £154.74 TOTE £6.90: £2.30 £1.30 £2.40 (£25.20) OWNER Mr C. J. Pennick (EPSOM) BRED Dodford Stud 8 Rn
1m 11.86 (1.26) SF: 36/41/43/24/29/42/9/15
WEIGHT FOR AGE 3yo-16lb

346

OSPREY H'CAP (0-70) (4-Y.O+) (Class E) £3,152.60 (£954.80: £466.40: £222.20)
2m (Equitrack) GOING minus 0.67 sec per fur (FST) 4-30 (4-31)

303* **Princely Gait (74)***(80) (CACyzer)* 4-10-0 Tlves(4) (a.p: rdn over 1f out: led wl ins fnl f: r.o) ..— 1
277* Sheltered Cove (IRE) **(56)***(62)*(Fav)*(KOCunningham-Brown)* 4-8-10 JWeaver(6) (chsd ldr: rdn over 1f out: led ins fnl f: sn hdd: r.o) ....nk 2
277[2] Arc Bright (IRE) **(65)***(69) (RHollinshead)* 5-9-11 WRyan(8) (led: rdn over 1f out: hdd ins fnl f: unable qckn) 1½ 3
Wild Strawberry **(65)***(69) (MissBSanders)* 6-9-8 (3) SSanders(9) (plld hrd: a.p: rdn over 1f out: r.o fnl f) ....s.h 4
288[2] Nothing Doing (IRE) **(37)***(41) (WJMusson)* 6-7-11 JQuinn(12) (hld up: hdwy over 4f out: rdn 2f out: r.o one pce fnl f) ....½ 5
303[5] Head Turner **(53)***(55) (CPWildman)* 7-8-13 NAdams(10) (hld up: hdwy 4f out: rdn over 1f out: r.o one pce fnl f: eased nr fin) 1½ 6
Maradonna (USA) **(62)***(64) (JWhite)* 6-9-8 MFenton(2) (a.p: rdn over 2f out: one pce) ....hd 7
277[7] In Behind (IRE) **(44)***(45) (GLMoore)* 4-7-12 CRutter(1) (mid div: rdn 5f out: r.o one pce fnl f) ..¾ 8
108[6] Ibsen **(68)***(69) (RAkehurst)* 7-10-0 TQuinn(13) (hld up: rdn 4f out: nvr nrr) ....¾ 9
288[3] Upper Mount Clair **(50)***(42) (CEBrittain)* 5-8-10 BDoyle(5) (chsd ldrs: rdn & wknd 3f out) 9 10
147[6] Ragtime Song **(36)***(16) (AMoore)* 6-7-5 (5) MBaird(11) (a bhd: t.o) 12 11
285[10] Esperer **(36)***(1) (JO'Donoghue)* 5-7-10 NCarlisle(7) (dwlt: a bhd: t.o) 15 12

2/1 Sheltered Cove (IRE), **9/4** PRINCELY GAIT, **6/1** Arc Bright (IRE), **8/1** Ibsen (op 5/1), **10/1** Wild Strawberry, Head Turner, **12/1** Nothing Doing (IRE) (op 6/1), **14/1** Upper Mount Clair, **16/1** Maradonna (USA), **25/1** Ragtime Song, **33/1** In Behind (IRE), **50/1** Esperer, CSF £8.09 CT £25.27 TOTE £3.30: £1.90 £1.40 £1.60 (£5.00) Trio £4.50 OWNER Mr R. M. Cyzer (HORSHAM) BRED Somerhall Bloodstock Ltd 12 Rn 3m 25.48 (1.98) SF: 49/31/44/44/16/30/39/14/44/17/-/-
WEIGHT FOR AGE 4yo-6lb

347

LYNN SPAULDING MEMORIAL MAIDEN STKS (4-Y.O+) (Class D)
£3,623.10 (£1,096.80: £535.40: £254.70)
1m (Equitrack) GOING minus 0.44 sec per fur (FST) 5-00 (5-02)

220[3] **Carte Blanche (43)***(54) (CACyzer)* 4-8-9 Tlves(2) (a.p: rdn 3f out: hrd rdn over 1f out: led 1f out: r.o wl) ....— 1
290[5] Kedwick (IRE) **(54)***(58) (PRHedger)* 6-9-0v StephenDavies(1) (b.hind: hld up gng wl: hdwy 2f out: led over 1f out: sn hdd: r.o) ....nk 2
218[2] Song of Years (IRE) **(60)***(41)*(Fav)*(JWHills)* 4-8-9 TQuinn(3) (a.p: rdn 3f out: hrd rdn & hung lft over 1f out: one pce) 6 3
220[5] Sherblu **(42)***(46) (JFfitch-Heyes)* 4-9-0b RCochrane(4) (hld up: hdwy over 2f out: hrd rdn over 1f out: r.o one pce fnl f) ....hd 4
313[10] Sacred Mirror (IRE) **(56)***(36) (CEBrittain)* 4-8-9 BDoyle(6) (chsd ldrs: rdn 5f out: hrd rdn over 2f out: one pce) 2½ 5
53[11] Cut Adrift **(62)***(36) (MRChannon)* 4-8-9 RHughes(5) (led 1f: chsd ldr over 4f out: ev ch over 1f out: wknd fnl f) ....nk 6
302[5] King's Gold **(40)***(40) (TMJones)* 5-9-0b RPerham(9) (b: plld hrd: led 7f out: hdd over 1f out: wknd fnl f) ....½ 7
290[7] Thorniwama **(35)***(23) (JJBridger)* 4-8-9b GBardwell(10) (chsd ldrs: sn rdn: wknd 4f out) 6 8
Kingsfold Fountain *(18) (MJHaynes)* 4-8-11 (3) SSanders(7) (a bhd) 5 9

Anzio (IRE) **(75)***(2) (BAPearce)* 4-9-0 JWeaver(8) (b: chsd ldr over 3f: wknd over 2f out: eased over 1f out: virtually p.u) 8 **10**

6/4 Song of Years (IRE) (tchd 9/4), **5/1** Sacred Mirror (IRE) (op 3/1), **11/2** CARTE BLANCHE (4/1-6/1), **6/1** Anzio (IRE), **15/2** Kedwick (IRE), **9/1** Sherblu, **12/1** Cut Adrift (op 7/1), **20/1** Thorniwama, Kingsfold Fountain, **33/1** King's Gold, CSF £46.14 TOTE £8.60: £2.40 £1.80 £1.30 (£12.80) OWNER Mr R. M. Cyzer (HORSHAM) BRED Cotswold Stud 10 Rn
1m 38.67 (2.27) SF: 34/38/21/26/16/16/20/3/-/-

T/Plpt: £17.00 (682.63 Tckts). T/Qdpt: £4.30 (8 Tckts). SM

0334-SOUTHWELL (L-H)
Monday February 27th (Standard)

348 APENNINES (S) H'CAP (0-60) (I) (3-Y.O+) (Class G) £2,259.00 (£634.00: £309.00)
6f (Fibresand) GOING: minus 0.04 sec per fur (STD) 1-50 (1-57)

233[6] **Brisas (42)***(51) (CWFairhurst)* 8-9-0 JFanning(7) (led 1f: cl up led over 2f out: jst hld on) ....— **1**
314[8] Monsieur Petong **(38)***(47) (JParkes)* 4-8-5 (5) PMcCabe(9) (bhd: hdwy 2f out: hung lft: styd on wl nr fin) ....s.h **2**
233[4] Sense of Priority **(56)***(62) (MHEasterby)* 6-10-0 KDarley(2) (w ldrs: disp ld over 2f out: sn rdn & r.o one pce) 1¼ **3**
258* Joyful Times **(45)***(44)*(Fav)*(MrsNMacauley)* 3-7-8 (7) AmandaSanders(1) (lw: s.i.s: styd on fnl 2f: n.d) 2½ **4**
Pretty Chic **(30)***(29) (DWChapman)* 6-7-9b(7) CTeague(10) (bt bkwd: outpcd & bhd tl sme late hdwy) ....s.h **5**
224[10] Beckyhannah **(38)***(35) (RBastiman)* 5-8-10b DeanMcKeown(3) (rdn to ld after 1f: hdd over 2f out: sn btn) ....¾ **6**
283[2] Beecham **(50)***(43)*(Fav)*(AHide)* 3-8-6b JQuinn(4) (lw: sn drvn alng & bhd: n.d) 1¼ **7**
331[6] Waverley Star **(42)***(14) (KOCunningham-Brown)* 10-9-0 LCharnock(5) (chsd ldrs: sn drvn along: wknd over 2f out) 8 **8**
305[9] Precious Times **(45)***(8) (MGMeagher)* 3-7-12 (3)ow1 SSanders(6) (in tch tl outpcd fr ½-wy) 3 **9**
165[8] Last Straw **(30)** *(BPreece)* 7-8-2b GDuffield(8) (chsd ldrs over 3f: sn rdn & wknd) 5 **10**

7/2 Joyful Times, Beecham, **5/1** Sense of Priority, **11/2** BRISAS, **7/1** Beckyhannah, **9/1** Last Straw, **10/1** Waverley Star, **16/1** Monsieur Petong, Precious Times, **33/1** Pretty Chic, CSF £79.03 CT £430.67 TOTE £8.10: £2.10 £3.00 £2.50 (£28.70) Trio £38.60 OWNER Mr C. W. Fairhurst (MIDDLEHAM) BRED Mrs J. E. Young 10 Rn No bid 1m 18.5 (5.00) SF: 28/24/39/5/6/12/4/-/-/-
WEIGHT FOR AGE 3yo-16lb

349 ALPS H'CAP (0-70) (3-Y.O+) (Class E) £3,124.00 (£946.00: £462.00: £220.00)
1m (Fibresand) GOING: minus 0.04 sec per fur (STD) 2-20 (2-26)

275[6] **Desert Invader (IRE) (60)***(68) (DWChapman)* 4-9-5 DeanMcKeown(11) (lw: trkd ldrs gng wl: led over 1f out & hung lft: kpt on) ....— **1**
313[2] Major Mouse **(52)***(59) (WWHaigh)* 7-8-11 DaleGibson(6) (hld up & bhd: hdwy 3f out: ev ch & edgd lft ins fnl f: nt qckn) ....¾ **2**
275[3] Zacaroon **(59)***(64)*(Fav)*(LordHuntingdon)* 4-9-4v DHarrison(3) (chsd ldrs: ev ch over 1f out: nt qckn) ....¾ **3**
269[9] Marowins **(61)***(65) (EJAlston)* 6-9-6 JQuinn(9) (bhd: hdwy 2f out: hung lft & no imp) ....¾ **4**
293[3] Shuttlecock **(65)***(67) (MrsNMacauley)* 4-9-10 MFenton(8) (disp ld 1f: led over 2f out: hdd wl over 1f out: grad wknd) ....¾ **5**
267[3] Zanzara (IRE) **(57)***(51) (MrsVAAconley)* 4-9-2 TWilliams(10) (chsd ldrs: hrd rdn over 3f: one pce) 4 **6**
55[6] Sandmoor Denim **(69)***(60) (SRBowring)* 8-9-7 (7) CTeague(1) (b: hld up: hdwy whn n.m.r 2f out: nvr able to chal) 1½ **7**
269[3] Roar on Tour **(65)***(52) (MrsMReveley)* 6-9-10 KDarley(7) (in tch: pushed along ½-wy: sn btn) .2 **8**
137[5] Brackenthwaite **(66)***(51) (LRLloyd-James)* 5-9-6 (5) JStack(4) (b.hind: effrt ½-wy: n.d) 1¼ **9**
265[7] Ragazzo (IRE) **(48)***(17) (KOCunningham-Brown)* 5-8-7b LCharnock(5) (disp ld tl wknd over 2f out) 8 **10**
Slytly Beveled **(59)***(18) (NPLittmoden)* 3-7-13 NCarlisle(2) (b: disp ld to ½-wy: sn rdn & wknd)5 **11**

5/2 Zacaroon, **9/2** Major Mouse, Roar on Tour, **8/1** Shuttlecock, **10/1** DESERT INVADER (IRE), **12/1** Brackenthwaite, Sandmoor Denim, Ragazzo (IRE), **14/1** Zanzara (IRE), Marowins, **16/1** Slytly Beveled, CSF £54.63 CT £139.02 TOTE £19.80: £3.80 £2.00 £1.70 (£34.10) Trio £62.40 OWNER Mr Michael Hill (YORK) BRED Gainsborough Stud Management Ltd 11 Rn
1m 45.7 (6.40) SF: 39/30/35/36/38/22/31/23/22/-/-
WEIGHT FOR AGE 3yo-19lb

350 ROCKY CLAIMING STKS (3-Y.O) (Class F) £2,537.00 (£712.00: £347.00)
1m (Fibresand) GOING: minus 0.04 sec per fur (STD) 2-50 (2-56)

241² **Durgams First (IRE) (66)***(68)*(Fav)*(MrsMReveley)* 3-8-13 KDarley(3) (lw: a gng wl: led on bit over 2f out: shkn up & styd on fnl f)— **1**
270⁴ Poly Lane **(52)***(50) (WRMuir)* 3-7-12b(3) SSanders(4) (led tl hdd over 2f out: styd on one pce) .3 **2**
Lucky Peg **(50)***(46) (FJO'Mahony)* 3-7-12 JQuinn(6) (trckd ldrs: effrt 3f out: nt qckn) nk **3**
273⁵ Keys Seminar **(45)***(41) (NACallaghan)* 3-8-2b(5) JStack(9) (b: b.hind: w ldrs tl rdn & btn over 1f out) 7 **4**
292¹¹ Centaur Express **(30)***(27) (ALForbes)* 3-8-1 StephenDavies(2) (unruly s: in tch: hdwy u.p ½-wy: n.d) 4 **5**
261⁵ Warrior Lady (IRE) **(45)***(24) (PJMcBride)* 3-8-3 (7) JustineReader(8) (s.i.s: n.d) 6 **6**
Kitty Waterjet **(36)***(11) (BEllison)* 3-7-10 (7)ow5 CTeague(1) (hld up & bhd: outpcd ½-wy: n.d) ..½ **7**
El Taurus *(KGWingrove)* 3-8-1 DBiggs(10) (leggy: unf: spd 5f: sn lost pl) 10 **8**
Beyaateh *(MCChapman)* 3-7-11 (7) CMunday(7) (bkwd: s.s: a bhd) 5 **9**
Evan Can Wait (IRE) *(JLEyre)* 3-7-13 (7)ow4 GMacDonald(5) (leggy: lt-f: s.i.s: a bhd) 15 **10**

8/11 DURGAMS FIRST (IRE), **7/2** Poly Lane, **11/2** Keys Seminar, **14/1** Warrior Lady (IRE), **16/1** Evan Can Wait (IRE), **20/1** Lucky Peg, **33/1** Centaur Express, **40/1** Beyaateh, Kitty Waterjet, **50/1** El Taurus, CSF £4.07 TOTE £1.80: £1.00 £1.30 £3.40 (£3.00) OWNER The Mary Reveley Racing Club (SALTBURN) BRED William McGladdery in Ireland 10 Rn 1m 47.6 (8.30) SF: 13/-/-/-/-/-/-/-/-/-

351 PYRENEES H'CAP (0-80) (3-Y.O+) (Class D) £3,640.00 (£1,102.00: £538.00: £256.00) **1m 3f (Fibresand)** GOING: minus 0.04 sec per fur (STD) 3-20 (3-25)

312* **Suivez (54)***(64) (MrsNMacauley)* 5-8-9 5x SDWilliams(3) (led tl hdd over 2f out: rallied u.p to ld wl ins fnl f) — **1**
266* Ashover **(69)***(79)*(Fav)*(TDBarron)* 5-9-3 (7) KimberleyHart(8) (hld up: gd hdwy 4f out: slt ld over 2f out: no ex twrds fin) hd **2**
186⁵ Barti-Ddu **(60)***(68) (SCWilliams)* 4-8-12 KDarley(7) (cl up: chl appr 5f: onepce fnl 2f) 1¼ **3**
266² Palacegate Jo (IRE) **(65)***(67) (RHollinshead)* 4-9-3 TIves(5) (in tch: outpcd 3f out: styd on appr fnl f) 4 **4**
296* Red Indian **(58)***(60) (WWHaigh)* 9-8-13 DeanMcKeown(9) (lw: hld up: hdwy 5f out: effrt 2f out: nt qcknd) ½ **5**
137⁷ Anorak (USA) **(50)***(46) (GMMoore)* 5-8-5 TWilliams(6) (chsd ldrs: rdn 4f out: outpcd fnl 2½f) ..4 **6**
155⁶ Exclusion **(42)***(37) (JHetherton)* 6-7-11 NKennedy(4) (prom tl outpcd 6f out: n.d after) nk **7**

11/4 Ashover, **3/1** SUIVEZ, **5/1** Red Indian, **6/1** Palacegate Jo (IRE), **7/1** Barti-Ddu, **14/1** Exclusion, **16/1** Anorak (USA), CSF £11.18 CT £46.70 TOTE £3.40: £1.20 £1.50 £2.10 (£3.70) OWNER Mr G. Wiltshire (MELTON MOWBRAY) BRED Theakston Stud 7 Rn
2m 27.9 (6.40) SF: 45/60/46/45/41/27/18
WEIGHT FOR AGE 4yo-3lb

352 SIERRA MADRE MEDIAN AUCTION MAIDEN STKS (4, 5, & 6-Y.O) (Class E) £3,023.90 (£915.20: £446.60: £212.30)
1m 4f (Fibresand) GOING: minus 0.04 sec per fur (STD) 3-50 (3-56)

53³ **Handmaiden** *(61)*(Fav)*(JLEyre)* 5-8-10 TIves(10) (a.p: hdwy 6f out: led 3f out: rdn & styd on)— **1**
136⁴ Shamwari (USA) **(53)***(58) (JWHills)* 4-8-0 (7) MHenry(3) (cl up: led 6f out to 3f out: one pce) 2 **2**
Always Greener (IRE) *(58) (MrsNMacauley)* 4-8-2 (5) SDrowne(6) (a chsng ldrs: outpcd ent st: kpt on wl nr fin) nk **3**
311³ Manolete **(44)***(61) (CWCElsey)* 4-8-12b NKennedy(2) (bhd: stdy hdwy 6f out: effrt 2f out: one pce) 1½ **4**
290² Regal Pursuit (IRE) **(57)***(51) (CAHorgan)* 4-8-7h AClark(1) (bhd: hdwy ½-wy: no imp fnl 3f) 4 **5**
290¹⁰ A New Flame *(42) (RGuest)* 4-8-12v GBardwell(8) (s.i.s: sn rcvrd & prom: rdn appr st: sn btn)10 **6**
Lord Wellington (IRE) **(32)***(32) (JRJenkins)* 4-8-12 CRutter(9) (effrt ½-wy: btn 3f out) 8 **7**
290⁸ Mountain Boy *(26) (MJohnston)* 4-8-12 TWilliams(7) (lw: led tl hdd 6f out: sn wknd) 4 **8**
Danson *(25) (THCaldwell)* 4-8-12 GDuffield(5) (dwlt: hdwy ½-wy: wknd over 2f out) ¾ **9**
269⁸ Dragonflight **(38)** *(DHaydnJones)* 4-8-12 AMackay(4) (plld hrd: n.d) 20 **10**
Madam Chairman *(NPLittmoden)* 6-8-10 NCarlisle(11) (cl up tl wknd over 4f out) 3 **11**

13/8 HANDMAIDEN, **3/1** Regal Pursuit (IRE), **4/1** Shamwari (USA), **8/1** Always Greener (IRE), Manolete, **12/1** Lord Wellington (IRE), **16/1** Mountain Boy, **20/1** Dragonflight, **25/1** A New Flame, Madam Chairman, **33/1** Danson, CSF £9.86 TOTE £2.30: £1.10 £2.20 £2.90 (£7.70) OWNER Mr R. Fenwick-Gibson (HAMBLETON) BRED Sheikh Mohammed bin Rashid al Maktoum 11 Rn
2m 44.2 (10.00) SF: 29/23/23/26/16/7/-/-/-/-/-
WEIGHT FOR AGE 4yo-3lb

353

APENNINES (S) H'CAP (0-60) (II) (3-Y.O+) (Class G) £2,259.00 (£634.00: £309.00)
6f (Fibresand) GOING: minus 0.04 sec per fur (STD) 4-20 (4-26)

165[10] **Farmer Jock (40)***(43) (MrsNMacauley)* 13-8-12 AClark(6) (b: in tch: hdwy over 2f out: hrd rdn fnl f: r.o to ld post) ....— **1**
297[4] Chadwell Hall **(49)***(52)*(Fav)*(SRBowring)* 4-9-0b(7) CTeague(5) (b.hind: trckd ldrs: hmpd after 2f: led over 1f out: rdn & r.o) ....s.h **2**
*165** Panther (IRE) **(53)***(56)*(Fav)*(JHetherton)* 5-9-11 NKennedy(1) (s.i.s: hdwy 2f out: styd on wl nr fin) ....hd **3**
199[3] Rustic League (IRE) **(37)***(36) (TJNaughton)* 4-8-9 DHarrison(8) (disp ld tl led ½-wy: hdd over 1f out: no ex) 1½ **4**
267[6] Britannia Mills **(33)***(27) (MCChapman)* 4-7-12 (7) CMunday(9) (drvn alng thrght: sn bhd: sme late hdwy) 1¾ **5**
287[7] Hinari Video **(45)***(36) (MJohnston)* 10-8-10 (7) OliverCasey(7) (spd 2f: sn rdn & btn) 1 **6**
314[6] Havana Miss **(42)***(5) (BPalling)* 3-7-12bow2 StephenDavies(3) (disp ld to ½-wy: sn wknd) 10 **7**
305[7] Henry the Hawk **(46)***(9) (MDods)* 4-8-13 (5) JStack(2) (lw: stdd s: outpcd & bhd fr ½-wy) ....½ **8**
Domybly **(50)** *(MHEasterby)* 3-8-6 GDuffield(4) (spd to ½-wy: sn wknd) 9 **9**

3/1 Chadwell Hall, Panther (IRE), **5/1** Domybly, **11/2** Rustic League (IRE), **7/1** Hinari Video, **9/1** Henry the Hawk, **12/1** Havana Miss, FARMER JOCK, **16/1** Britannia Mills, CSF £48.74 CT £130.02 TOTE £16.80: £3.10 £1.40 £2.00 (£31.40) Trio £32.80 OWNER Mr S. Thompson (MELTON MOWBRAY) 9 Rn 1m 19.3 (5.80) SF: 18/27/31/11/2/11/-/-/-

WEIGHT FOR AGE 3yo-16lb

No bid

354

CAUCASUS H'CAP (0-60) (3-Y.O+) (Class F) £2,537.00 (£712.00: £347.00)
7f (Fibresand) GOING: minus 0.04 sec per fur (STD) 4-50 (4-57)

313[3] **Aquado (41)***(49)*(Fav)*(ALForbes)* 6-8-11 JQuinn(11) (trckd ldrs: led 2f out: rdn out) ....— **1**
271[6] Genesis Four **(37)***(44) (SRBowring)* 5-8-0b(7) CTeague(9) (b: c v.wd st: r.o wl fnl 2f: too much to do) ....½ **2**
314[3] Letsbeonestaboutit **(52)***(51) (MrsNMacauley)* 9-9-8v DeanMcKeown(13) (chsd ldrs: ev ch over 1f out: nt qckn) 3½ **3**
338[3] Christian Flight (IRE) **(40)***(30) (SGollings)* 6-8-10 DHarrison(2) (cl up: chal over 2f out: nt qckn fnl f) 4 **4**
*334** At the Savoy (IRE) **(47)***(36) (TDBarron)* 4-8-10 (7) KimberleyHart(10) (in tch: hdwy 2½f out: no imp) ....nk **5**
230[2] Cicerone **(48)***(33) (JLHarris)* 5-9-4 GDuffield(8) (a chsng ldrs: led over 2f out: sn hdd & one pce) 2 **6**
20[9] On Y Va (USA) **(50)***(32) (RJRWilliams)* 8-8-13 (7) SarahThompson(7) (hdwy u.p 2f out: nvr able to chal) 1 **7**
294[4] Chaldon Herring **(56)***(37) (TDBarron)* 3-8-8 KDarley(6) (lw: sn outpcd & bhd: styd on fnl 2f: n.d) ....½ **8**
167[10] Dauntless Fort **(42)***(12) (BWMurray)* 4-8-5 (7) CScudder(4) (prom 4f) 5 **9**
335[6] Blaster Bates (USA) **(39)***(5) (RBrotherton)* 4-8-9b AMackay(14) (sn outpcd & wl bhd: styd on fnl f) 1½ **10**
307[3] Quinzii Martin **(58)***(24) (DHaydnJones)* 7-10-0 TWilliams(1) (chsd ldrs tl outpcd fnl 2f) ....nk **11**
307[4] Cronk's Courage **(43)***(4) (MGMeagher)* 9-8-8v(5) JStack(12) (led tl hdd & wknd over 2f out) 2 **12**
312[11] Tyrone Flyer **(54)***(15) (PMMcEntee)* 6-9-7 (3) DWright(15) (b: lw: sn chsng ldrs: rdn over 3f out: sn btn) ....hd **13**
Penny's Wishing **(59)***(19) (JPLeigh)* 3-8-11 ACulhane(3) (s.i.s: a outpcd & bhd) ....½ **14**
Foist **(52)***(10) (MWEasterby)* 3-8-4 LCharnock(5) (a bhd) ....¾ **15**

4/1 AQUADO, **9/2** Cicerone, **7/1** Chaldon Herring, **15/2** Quinzii Martin, **10/1** At the Savoy (IRE), Cronk's Courage, **12/1** Genesis Four, Letsbeonestaboutit, Christian Flight (IRE), **14/1** On Y Va (USA), Tyrone Flyer, Penny's Wishing, **20/1** Dauntless Fort, Blaster Bates (USA), **40/1** Foist, CSF £52.71 CT £514.56 TOTE £5.90: £1.70 £2.90 £3.90 (£44.20) Trio £408.30 OWNER Mr K. Nicholls (UTTOXETER) BRED Lord Howard de Walden 15 Rn

1m 32.5 (5.70) SF: 25/20/27/6/12/9/8/-/-/-/-/-/-/-/-

WEIGHT FOR AGE 3yo-18lb

T/Jkpt: Not won; £5,840.80 to Nottingham 28/2/95. T/Plpt: £30.60 (649.18 Tckts). T/Qdpt: £9.00 (19.1 Tckts). AA

0341-**LINGFIELD (L-H)**
Tuesday February 28th (Standard)

355
COOK LIMITED STKS (I) (4-Y.O+) (Class F) £2,688.20 (£755.20: £368.60)
1m 2f (Equitrack) Stalls: Low GOING minus 0.44 sec per fur (FST) 2-00 (2-01)

318[5] **Father Dan (IRE) (49)***(62)*(Fav)*(MissGayKelleway)* 6-9-0 SWhitworth(5) (lw: hld up: hrd rdn over 1f out: led ins fnl f: r.o wl) ....— 1
330[3] Captain Marmalade **(50)***(59) (DTThom)* 6-8-11 (3) DRMcCabe(7) (gd hdwy over 3f out: led over 1f out tl ins fnl f: edgd lft: unable qckn) 2 2
330[2] Achilles Heel **(45)***(56)*(Fav)*(CNAllen)* 4-8-12 TIves(9) (lw: hld up: led over 3f out tl over 1f out: one pce) 1½ 3
296[3] Aviator's Dream **(50)***(45) (JPearce)* 5-9-0 GBardwell(8) (hdwy 4f out: rdn over 3f out: one pce)7 4
320[4] Dutosky **(49)***(36) (RJRWilliams)* 5-8-9 DBiggs(4) (led over 5f out tl over 3f out: wknd 2f out) 2½ 5
341[7] My Lifetime Lady (IRE) **(37)***(25) (KTIvory)* 4-8-7 NCarlisle(2) (b.hind: lw: led 1f: wknd 6f out) ..7 6
231[9] Fletcher's Bounty (IRE) **(47)***(22) (WSCunningham)* 6-9-0 AClark(1) (hdwy 4f out: wknd over 2f out) 5 7
341[9] Doodies Pool (IRE) **(46)***(22) (GLMoore)* 5-8-9v(5) AWhelan(6) (b.hind: prom over 7f) ....s.h 8
222[9] Miss Charlie **(40)***(4) (ABailey)* 5-8-9 GCarter(3) (b.hind: led 9f out tl over 5f out: sn wknd) 8 9

3/1 FATHER DAN (IRE), Achilles Heel, **100/30** Dutosky (2/1-7/2), **11/2** Captain Marmalade, **8/1** Fletcher's Bounty (IRE) (6/1-10/1), **20/1** Doodies Pool (IRE), **25/1** Aviator's Dream, **33/1** My Lifetime Lady (IRE), Miss Charlie, CSF £18.18 TOTE £3.10: £1.30 £1.60 1.90 (£6.10) OWNER Wessex Fm (Whitcombe) Racing Club Ltd (WHITCOMBE) BRED John Michael 9 Rn

2m 5.52 (2.52) SF: 42/39/34/25/16/3/2/2/-
WEIGHT FOR AGE 4yo-2lb

356
MARCO POLO APPRENTICE H'CAP (0-75) (4-Y.O+) (Class F) £2,700.80 (£758.80: £370.40)
1m 5f (Equitrack) Stalls: Low GOING minus 0.44 sec per fur (FST) 2-30 (2-30)

Warm Spell (73)*(78)*(Fav)*(GLMoore)* 5-10-0 LSuthern(2) (lw: chsd ldr: rdn over 3f out: led ins fnl f: r.o wl) ....— 1
321[7] Royal Circus **(39)***(43) (JGMO'Shea)* 6-7-8 CAdamson(4) (led: rdn over 2f out: hdd ins fnl f: unable qckn) ....¾ 2
Dancing Sensation (USA) **(50)***(37) (RAkehurst)* 8-8-0e(5) RMoogan(1) (stdd s: hld up: a wl bhd) 14 3
329[3] Cliburnel News (IRE) **(51)***(32) (WRMuir)* 5-7-13v(7)ow6 RPooles(3) (b: b.hind: s.s: a wl bhd) ...hd 4

13/8 WARM SPELL, **2/1** Dancing Sensation (USA), **7/2** Royal Circus, **11/2** Cliburnel News (IRE) (op 3/1), CSF: £6.70 TOTE £2.60 (£3.30) OWNER Mr K. Higson (EPSOM) BRED R. H. Cowell and Mrs R. B. Collie 4 Rn

2m 46.55 (4.05) SF: 52/17/11/6

357
VASCO DA GAMA MAIDEN STKS (3-Y.O+) (Class D) £3,741.40 (£1,133.20: £553.60: £263.80) **1m 2f (Equitrack)** GOING minus 0.44 sec (FST) 3-00 (3-03)

Mega Tid *(71) (BAPearce)* 3-7-13 (3) SSanders(3) (neat: s.s: hdwy over 4f out: led 3f out: drvn out) ....— 1
321[11] Lady Reema **(45)***(66) (MissAJWhitfield)* 4-8-12 (5) RPainter(5) (hld up: swtchd rt over 1f out: r.o wl ins fnl f) ....nk 2
256[4] Anjou *(70)*(Fav)*(GWragg)* 3-8-2 WWoods(6) (led 7f: ev ch ins fnl f: unable qckn) ....½ 3
290[6] Admiral Hood (USA) *(70) (LordHuntingdon)* 4-9-8 DHarrison(2) (w ldr 7f: ev ch ins fnl f: one pce) ....hd 4
Brave Spy **(63)***(65) (CACyzer)* 4-9-8 MFenton(10) (rdn & hdwy over 4f out: n.m.r over 2f out: one pce) 3 5
252[3] Ginger Jim **(64)***(33) (PRHedger)* 4-9-8v GDuffield(9) (lw: prom 7f) 20 6
Torrey Pines (IRE) *(30) (DHaydnJones)* 3-8-2 AMackay(4) (bhd fnl 4f) 2 7
332[9] Tarjumaan (USA) *(27) (RJO'Sullivan)* 4-9-8 AClark(7) (b: a bhd) 1½ 8
Bellateena *(13) (HJCollingridge)* 3-7-11 JQuinn(1) (w'like: bkwd: a bhd) 6 9
290[9] Il Fratello *(16) (NACallaghan)* 4-9-8 TIves(8) (lw: prom over 4f) 1¼ 10

4/6 Anjou (Evens-6/4), **7/2** Brave Spy, **7/1** Ginger Jim (op 4/1), **14/1** MEGA TID (op 33/1), **16/1** Admiral Hood (USA), **25/1** Lady Reema, Tarjumaan (USA), **50/1** Torrey Pines (IRE), Bellateena, Il Fratello, CSF: £249.60 TOTE £28.00: £3.80 £5.00 £1.00 (£131.10) Trio £297.20 OWNER Mr P. C. J. Saunders (LIMPSFIELD) BRED Sheikh Mohammed bin Rashid al Maktoum 10 Rn

2m 6.97 (3.97) SF: 20/35/19/39/34/2/-/-/-/-
WEIGHT FOR AGE 3yo-22lb, 4yo-2lb

358 COLOMBUS CLAIMING STKS (4-Y.O+) (Class F) £2,688.20 (£755.20: £368.60)
7f (Equitrack) Stalls: Low GOING minus 0.44 sec per fur (FST) 3-30 (3-30)

*248** **Sweet Supposin (IRE) (72)***(74) (KMcAuliffe)* 4-9-2b TIves(3) (lw: hdwy to chse ldr over 2f out: hrd rdn over 1f out: led wl ins fnl f: r.o wl) — 1
*323** Spencer's Revenge **(77)***(74)*(Fav)*(LordHuntingdon)* 6-8-11 (5) AWhelan(1) (lw: lost pl over 4f out: rallied over 2f out: r.o wl ins fnl f) hd 2
*307*6 Greatest **(50)***(65) (RAkehurst)* 4-8-8 GCarter(5) (led: rdn 2f out: hdd wl ins fnl f: unable qckn) ½ 3
*308*6 Soba Guest (IRE) **(50)***(33) (RTJuckes)* 6-8-1v(5) SDrowne(4) (lw: hld up: rdn over 2f out: sn wknd) 13 4
*129*11 Bold Cyrano (IRE) **(52)***(24) (BPalling)* 4-8-4 GDuffield(7) (prom over 4f) 3 5
Halbert **(54)***(16) (MRChannon)* 6-7-13 (5) PPMurphy(6) (prom over 3f) 3½ 6
*332*11 Foreshore (IRE) **(53)** *(RIngram)* 5-7-10 (3) DWright(2) (a bhd) 10 7

4/6 Spencer's Revenge, **13/8** SWEET SUPPOSIN (IRE), **14/1** Greatest (op 8/1), **25/1** Foreshore (IRE), Halbert, **33/1** Bold Cyrano (IRE), Soba Guest (IRE), CSF: £3.09 TOTE £2.90: £1.70 £1.10 (£1.10) OWNER Mount Juliet Stud (LAMBOURN) BRED Ballylinch Stud Ltd 7 Rn
1m 24.43 (1.43) SF: 46/46/37/5/-/-/-

359 LINGFIELD PARK SPRINT SERIES (QUALIFIER) H'CAP (0-70) (3-Y.O+) (Class E) £3,119.10 (£943.80: £460.40: £218.70)
6f (Equitrack) Stalls: Low GOING minus 0.44 sec per fur (FST) 4-00 (4-00)

*287*2 **Our Shadee (USA) (53)***(57) (KTIvory)* 5-8-11v(7) CScally(1) (hmpd on ins 5f out: hdwy over 1f out: str run fnl f: led nr fin) — 1
*287*3 Purbeck Centenary **(47)***(50) (PHowling)* 5-8-12 JQuinn(5) (b.hind: led: rdn over 1f out: hdd nr fin) ½ 2
*272*2 Crystal Heights (FR) **(63)***(64) (RJO'Sullivan)* 7-10-0 WWoods(4) (b: a.p: rdn over 1f out: unable qckn) ½ 3
*287*6 Splash of Salt (IRE) **(42)***(41) (TJNaughton)* 5-8-7 DHarrison(6) (a.p: hrd rdn 2f out: r.o one pce fnl f) ¾ 4
*220*2 Sweet Whisper **(47)***(41)*(Fav)*(KMcAuliffe)* 4-8-12v TIves(2) (hld up: one pce fnl 2f) 2 5
*319*3 Black Shadow **(45)***(32) (PJMcBride)* 3-7-3 (5) NVarley(3) (prom over 3f) 2½ 6

100/30 Sweet Whisper, **7/2** OUR SHADEE (USA), Crystal Heights (FR), **4/1** Black Shadow (3/1-9/2), **6/1** Purbeck Centenary (op 4/1), **10/1** Splash of Salt (IRE) (op 16/1), CSF £21.14 TOTE £4.50: £2.50 £3.20 (£6.40) OWNER Mr K. T. Ivory (RADLETT) BRED Overbury Stud 6 Rn
1m 12.45 (1.85) SF: 39/32/46/23/23/-
WEIGHT FOR AGE 3yo-16lb

360 LIVINGSTONE H'CAP (0-80) (3-Y.O) (Class D) £3,589.30 (£1,086.40: £530.20: £252.10) **1m (Equitrack)** Stalls: High GOING minus 0.44 sec (FST) 4-30 (4-30)

*333*3 **Greenwich Again (66)***(77)*(Fav)*(TGMills)* 3-8-7 GCarter(2) (a.p: led over 2f out: clr over 1f out: hrd rdn: r.o wl) — 1
*250** Montanelli (FR) **(80)***(86)*(Fav)*(KMcAuliffe)* 3-9-7v TIves(7) (rdn over 4f out: hdwy over 2f out: chsd wnr over 1f out: r.o) 2½ 2
*176** Nordinex (IRE) **(74)***(73) (RWArmstrong)* 3-9-1 WWoods(5) (b: lw: hld up: rdn over 3f out: unable qckn fnl f) 3½ 3
*324*5 Sarasi **(70)***(68) (PFICole)* 3-8-11 CRutter(4) (b: lw: hld up: rdn over 3f out: hmpd on ins wl over 1f out: r.o one pce fnl f) nk 4
*301*5 Persian Conquest (IRE) **(70)***(63) (RIngram)* 3-8-8b(3) DWright(3) (led 7f out tl over 2f out: wknd over 1f out) 2½ 5
*286** Sand Star **(55)***(20) (DHaydnJones)* 3-7-10 ow2 AMackay(1) (dwlt: bhd fnl 3f) 13 6
Don't Forget Ruby (IRE) **(54)***(18) (DWPArbuthnot)* 3-7-4 (5)ow2 NVarley(6) (led 1f: wknd 3f out) ½ 7
LONG HANDICAP Don't Forget Ruby (IRE) 7-2

9/4 GREENWICH AGAIN (op 7/2), Montanelli (FR) (op 6/4), **4/1** Nordinex (IRE), **9/1** Sarasi, Persian Conquest (IRE), Sand Star, **33/1** Don't Forget Ruby (IRE), CSF £7.50 TOTE £3.10: £1.80 £1.20 (£4.00) OWNER John Humphreys (Turf Accountants) Ltd (EPSOM) BRED T. G. Mills Ltd 7 Rn
1m 38.7 (2.30) SF: 32/41/28/23/18/-/-

361 COOK LIMITED STKS (0-50) (II) (4-Y.O+) (Class F) £2,675.60 (£751.60: £366.80)
1m 2f (Equitrack) Stalls: Low GOING minus 0.44 sec per fur (FST) 5-00 (5-00)

*329*5 **Call Me Blue (50)***(61) (TJNaughton)* 5-9-0 SWhitworth(5) (hld up: hrd rdn over 1f out: led ins fnl f: all out) — 1

Chancel (USA) **(50)***(56) (LordHuntingdon)* 4-8-2v(5) AWhelan(7) (a.p: led 3f out tl ins fnl f: r.o)s.h **2**
*73*4 General Chase **(49)***(35) (ICampbell)* 5-8-6 (3) SSanders(2) (lw: rdn 5f out: hdwy fnl f: nvr nrr).13 **3**
*186*7 Polly Peculiar **(50)***(34)*(Fav)*(BSmart)* 4-8-7 DHarrison(1) (b.off hind: hld up: hdwy 4f out: wknd 2f out)....½ **4**
Wollboll **(36)***(39) (PJMakin)* 5-9-0b WRyan(4) (b: hdwy 7f out: wknd over 2f out)....s.h **5**
Smart Teacher (USA) **(50)***(33) (KRBurke)* 5-9-0 RHughes(6) (led over 6f)....4 **6**
*343*10 The Country Dancer **(30)** *(KTIvory)* 5-8-2 (7) CScally(8) (chsd ldr 3f)....25 **7**

11/4 Polly Peculiar, **3/1** Chancel (USA) (op 6/4), **4/1** Smart Teacher (USA) (op 8/1), **9/2** General Chase (op 11/4), **12/1** CALL ME BLUE (op 8/1), **14/1** Wollboll, **40/1** The Country Dancer, CSF £42.01 TOTE £9.60: £3.40 £1.20 (£13.50) OWNER Mr D. Borrows (EPSOM) BRED J. A. Redmond 7 Rn
2m 6.82 (3.82) SF: 32/25/6/3/10/4/-
WEIGHT FOR AGE 4yo-2lb

T/Plpt: £24.50 (403.83 Tckts). T/Qdpt: £7.00 (11.5 Tckts). AK

0322-WOLVERHAMPTON (L-H)
Wednesday March 1st (Standard)

362 CAPRICORN MAIDEN STKS (3-Y.O) (Class D) £3,640.00 (£1,102.00: £538.00: £256.00) **1m 100y (Fibresand)** GOING minus 0.02 sec per fur (STD) 2-10 (2-13)

Heathyards Rock *(61) (RHollinshead)* 3-9-0 TIves(1) (trckd ldrs: 4th st: plld out 2f out: qcknd to ld 1f out: comf)....— **1**
Hand Woven *(56)*(Fav)*(WJHaggas)* 3-9-0 WWoods(6) (led: shkn up over 3f out: hdd 2f out: led over 1f out: sn hdd & unable qckn)....2½ **2**
*332*4 Concer Un *(55) (SCWilliams)* 3-8-11 (3) DWright(5) (dwlt: hdwy 4f out: 3rd st: no ex appr fnl f)....¾ **3**
Acquittal (IRE) *(55) (JRFanshawe)* 3-9-0 DHarrison(3) (a.p: 2nd st: led 2f out: sn hdd: no ex appr fnl f)....hd **4**
Malzoom *(26) (SEKettlewell)* 3-8-9 (5) JStack(7) (prom tl 5th & wkng st)....15 **5**
*282*4 Handson *(19) (BRMillman)* 3-9-0 MFenton(4) (b: chsd ldrs: rdn 4f out: 6th & btn st)....4 **6**
*315*13 Angelic Belle *(NPLittmoden)* 3-8-9 NCarlisle(2) (plld hrd: in tch 4f: sn rdn & wl bhd)....dist **7**

4/5 Hand Woven, **100/30** Concer Un, **7/2** HEATHYARDS ROCK, **14/1** Acquittal (IRE), **33/1** Handson, **50/1** Malzoom, **66/1** Angelic Belle, CSF £6.49 TOTE £4.40 £1.20 £1.30 [£3.10] OWNER Mr L. A. Morgan (UPPER LONGDON) BRED N. E. and Mrs Poole 7 Rn
1m 51.0 (7.00) SF: 30/25/24/24/-/-/-

363 ARIES CLAIMING STKS (3-Y.O) (Class F) £2,580.00 (£780.00: £380.00: £180.00) **5f (Fibresand)** GOING minus 0.02 sec per fur (STD) 2-40 (2-41)

*342** **Ultra Beet (76)***(81)*(Fav)*(PCHaslam)* 3-9-0 (5) JStack(6) (lw: w ldr tl led after 1f: shkn up & qcknd clr 2f out: unchal)....— **1**
*305*4 Poly Laureon (IRE) **(62)***(60) (RHollinshead)* 3-8-6 WRyan(4) (chsd ldrs: kpt on wl fnl 2f: no ch w wnr)....2½ **2**
*261** Dark Shot (IRE) **(80)***(60) (JBerry)* 3-9-5 JCarroll(9) (hdwy over 2f out: r.o fnl f)....4 **3**
*305*5 Benten **(46)***(37) (DNicholls)* 3-7-7 (5) NVarley(2) (lw: led 1f: ev ch 2f out: sn outpcd: wknd fnl f)¾ **4**
Jessica's Secret (IRE) **(48)***(30) (ABailey)* 3-7-13 (3) SSanders(3) (lw: in tch: no hdwy fnl 2f) ..3½ **5**
*197*7 Komlucky **(47)***(19) (FJO'Mahony)* 3-8-4b JQuinn(8) (in tch 3f)....4 **6**
My Lady Brady *(12) (GROldroyd)* 3-8-7 MMcAndrew(1) (spd 3f)....3 **7**
*284*5 Oneineverycolour **(43)** *(PDEvans)* 3-8-0 CRutter(10) (dwlt: rdn ½-wy: nvr trbld ldrs)....2½ **8**
Positive Result (IRE) *(RJPrice)* 3-9-0 StephenDavies(5) (w'like: unf: s.i.s: a bhd)....3½ **9**
*299*3 Branston Kristy **(38)** *(CSmith)* 3-8-4 WWoods(7) (b: a bhd)....7 **10**

10/11 ULTRA BEET, **3/1** Dark Shot (IRE), **6/1** Poly Laureon (IRE), **12/1** My Lady Brady, **20/1** Benten, **25/1** Komlucky, **33/1** Branston Kristy, **40/1** Jessica's Secret (IRE), **50/1** Oneineverycolour, Positive Result (IRE), CSF £6.88 TOTE £1.30 £1.10 £2.10 £1.10 [£3.70] OWNER Pet Express Ltd T/A Nutrimix (MIDDLEHAM) BRED Rockhouse Farms Ltd 10 Rn
61.7 secs (3.70) SF: 33/12/12/-/-/-/-/-/-/-

364 POST A LITTLE HAPPINESS H'CAP (0-100) (4-Y.O+) (Class C) £7,021.50 (£2,112.00: £1,021.00: £475.50) **1m 1f 79y (Fibresand)** GOING minus 0.02 sec per fur (STD) 3-10 (3-10)

*275** **Kintwyn (68)***(77) (CCElsey)* 5-8-10 DHarrison(9) (b.hind: lw: hld up: hdwy 5f out: 5th st: rdn to ld appr fnl f: hld on wl)....— **1**

308* Slip a Coin **(58)***(65) (ICampbell)* 4-7-13 ow1 StephenDavies(3) (led tl hdd over 2f out: 2nd st: kpt on wl fnl f) ....½ 2
281⁵ Legal Fiction **(76)***(82)*(Fav)*(MJohnston)* 4-9-3 TWilliams(7) (lw: trckd ldr: rdn to ld over 2f out: hdd & one pce appr fnl f) 1 3
Celestial Choir **(72)***(78) (JLEyre)* 5-9-0 JFanning(4) (hld up: hdwy & 5th st: kpt on fnl f) ....½ 4
349⁴ Marowins **(61)***(66) (EJAlston)* 6-8-3 JQuinn(2) (hld up: rdn & hdwy 3f out: no ex appr fnl f) ....¾ 5
269* Bentico **(73)***(76) (MrsNMacauley)* 6-9-1 TIves(8) (chsd ldrs: 6th & rdn st: no imp) 1¾ 6
337³ Belleminette (IRE) **(70)***(67) (DHaydnJones)* 4-8-11 AMackay(11) (plld hrd: sn chsng ldrs: 3rd st: rdn 2f out: eased whn btn fnl f) 3½ 7
281¹⁰ Master Beveled **(75)***(65) (PDEvans)* 5-8-12 (5) JStack(5) (hld up: effrt over 3f out: no imp fnl f) .4 8
Sweet Trentino (IRE) **(68)***(53) (CASmith)* 4-8-6 (3) DRMcCabe(10) (lw: prom tl rdn & btn 3f out) 3 9
Promise Fulfilled (USA) **(87)***(71) (SGNorton)* 4-10-0 GCarter(6) (prom: rdn 4f out: sn wknd)...¾ 10
308⁵ Off the Air (IRE) **(52)***(31) (ICampbell)* 4-7-7v GBardwell(1) (lw: pushed along after 4f: a bhd) ...3 11

LONG HANDICAP Off the Air (IRE) 7-5

4/1 Legal Fiction, **9/2** Bentico, **11/2** KINTWYN, **6/1** Marowins, **7/1** Master Beveled, **8/1** Celestial Choir, **11/1** Slip a Coin, **12/1** Belleminette (IRE), **20/1** Sweet Trentino (IRE), Promise Fulfilled (USA), Off the Air (IRE), CSF £59.37 TC £238.68 TOTE £6.20 £3.50 £2.70 £1.80 [29.20] Trio £36.60 OWNER Mrs F. E. Bacon (LAMBOURN) BRED A. Baxter 11 Rn

2m 0.5 (4.50) SF: 54/41/58/55/42/51/41/41/27/45/5

WEIGHT FOR AGE 4yo-1lb

365 PLEASE USE YOUR POSTCODE H'CAP (0-90) (3-Y.O+) (Class C)

£5,524.00 (£1,672.00: £816.00: £388.00)
7f (Fibresand) GOING minus 0.02 sec per fur (STD) 3-40 (3-42)

Mahool (USA) (86)*(91) (JLEyre)* 6-9-9 (3) DWright(7) (led 1f: led over 2f out tl over 1f out: r.o wl to ld ins fnl f) ....— 1
Castel Rosselo **(84)***(88)*(Fav)*(SCWilliams)* 5-9-10 AMackay(1) (lw: trckd ldrs: 4th st: led over 1f out: hdd & no ex ins fnl f) ....½ 2
281³ Dawalib (USA) **(71)***(72) (DHaydnJones)* 5-8-11 DHarrison(4) (in tch: effrt & 5th st: ev ch appr fnl f: no ex) 1¼ 3
333* Master Millfield (IRE) **(78)***(71) (CJHill)* 3-8-1 6x JQuinn(10) (lw: chsd ldrs: rdn & 6th st: kpt on one pce) 3½ 4
281⁸ Highborn (IRE) **(85)***(70) (PSFelgate)* 6-9-6 (5) PMcCabe(9) (s.s: wl bhd tl r.o wl fnl 2f) 3½ 5
Cee-Jay-Ay **(61)***(46) (JBerry)* 8-8-1 LCharnock(11) (bkwd: bhd: rdn 5f out: kpt on fnl 2f)....hd 6
345⁸ Little Ibnr **(85)***(69) (PDEvans)* 4-9-6 (5) JStack(12) (led after 1f tl over 2f out: 2nd st: eased whn btn appr fnl f) ....nk 7
219⁴ Prima Silk **(74)***(54) (MJRyan)* 4-9-0 AClark(3) (prom: 3rd & rdn st: sn wknd) 2 8
345⁶ Rocketeer (IRE) **(88)***(65) (WRMuir)* 4-10-0b KDarley(2) (b: in tch: rdn 4f out: btn over 2f out) ...1 9
302* Profit Release (IRE) **(57)***(31) (MJohnston)* 4-7-11 TWilliams(8) (chsd ldrs: rdn 3f out: sn btn)1½ 10
Persian Affair (IRE) **(77)***(48) (DHaydnJones)* 4-9-3 MFenton(6) (lw: dwlt: nvr nr to chal)....1¼ 11
65⁷ Rossini Blue **(72)***(32) (ABailey)* 4-8-12 WHawksley(5) (dwlt: sn outpcd & wl bhd) 5 12

9/4 Castel Rosselo, **7/1** Master Millfield (IRE), **8/1** Dawalib (USA), MAHOOL (USA), Little Ibnr, **10/1** Highborn (IRE), Rocketeer (IRE), Profit Release (IRE), **12/1** Prima Silk, **16/1** Cee-Jay-Ay, **25/1** Persian Affair (IRE), Rossini Blue, CSF £26.09 CT £140.84 TOTE £6.50 £1.90 £1.60 £3.00 [£12.20] Trio £105.00 OWNER Mr M. Gleason (HAMBLETON) BRED Wooden Horse Investments in USA 12 Rn 1m 28.3 (4.30) SF: 58/55/39/21/37/13/36/21/32/-/15/-

WEIGHT FOR AGE 3yo-17lb

366 AQUARIUS (S) STKS (3-Y.O+) (Class G) £2,433.00 (£683.00: £333.00)

7f (Fibresand) GOING minus 0.02 sec per fur (STD) 4-10 (4-12)

314* **Sea Devil (63)***(70) (MJCamacho)* 9-9-12 LCharnock(3) (trckd ldrs: effrt on ins 3f out: 2nd st: led over 1f out: sn rdn clr) ....— 1
314² Jamaica Bridge **(60)***(64) (SGNorton)* 5-9-5 (7) TMarsden(8) (in tch: hdwy 4f out: led over 2f out tl over 1f out: no ex) 2½ 2
Second Colours (USA) **(73)***(55)*(Fav)*(MrsMReveley)* 5-9-7 KDarley(4) (lw: hdwy & 4th st: kpt on u.p appr fnl f) 1¾ 3
354³ Letsbeonestaboutit **(52)***(57) (MrsNMacauley)* 9-9-12v DeanMcKeown(7) (hmpd s: bhd tl r.o fnl 2f) 1¼ 4
323³ Delrob **(61)***(44) (DHaydnJones)* 4-9-2 AMackay(5) (chsd ldrs: 3rd st: one pce) 1½ 5
182⁶ Walk the Beat **(65)***(53) (RSimpson)* 5-9-7v(5) SDrowne(2) (chsd ldrs: n.m.r over 3f out: 5th st: no hdwy) ....½ 6
350² Poly Lane **(52)***(52) (WRMuir)* 3-8-6b(3) SSanders(10) (prom tl lost pl over 3f out: n.d after).....nk 7
28⁴ Kiyas **(37)***(46) (BJMcMath)* 4-9-4 (3) DWright(9) (lw: led over 4f out: hdd over 2f out: n.m.r & 6th st: no ch after) ....¾ 8

326[5] Gigfy **(47)***(27) (BJLlewellyn)* 3-8-0 (5)ow1 JStack(6) (hmpd after 2f: sn bhd)....8 9
Melling *(22) (RJHodges)* 4-9-7 JQuinn(11) (lw: dwlt: a bhd)....2½ 10
194[4] Oriental Song **(23)** *(KSBridgwater)* 6-9-2 NAdams(1) (led over 2f out: wkng whn hmpd over 3f out: sn wl bhd)....25 11

7/4 Second Colours (USA), **7/2** Jamaica Bridge, **5/1** SEA DEVIL, **6/1** Delrob, **8/1** Letsbeonestaboutit, **11/1** Walk the Beat, **12/1** Poly Lane, **20/1** Gigfy, **25/1** Kiyas, **50/1** Melling, Oriental Song, CSF £23.66 TOTE £5.20 £1.40 £1.60 £1.80 [£7.60] OWNER Mr A. N. Goacher (MALTON) BRED A.L.Goacher and E.G.Noble 11 Rn 1m 30.1 (6.10) SF: 33/27/18/20/7/16/-/9/-/-/-
WEIGHT FOR AGE 3yo-17lb
No bid

367

KEN BROWN FELLOWSHIP H'CAP (4-Y.O+) (Class E) £3,124.00 (£946.00: £462.00: £220.00) **1m 4f (Fibresand)** GOING minus 0.02 sec (STD) 4-40 (4-41)

303[3] **In the Money (IRE) (57)***(64)*(Fav)*(RHollinshead)* 6-9-2 TIves(7) (chsd ldrs: 2nd st: sn ev ch: rdn to ld wl ins fnl f)....— 1
Clifton Game **(47)***(49) (PGMurphy)* 5-7-13 (7)ow5 RWaterfield(3) (led after 2f: rdn 2f out: hdd & no ex wl ins fnl f)....nk 2
227[3] Premier Dance **(60)***(63) (DHaydnJones)* 8-9-5 AMackay(9) (lw: hld up: hdwy 5f out: 4th st: sn rdn & r.o)....2½ 3
277[8] Wottashambles **(41)***(34) (GLewis)* 4-7-11 JQuinn(1) (a.p: 3rd st: sn rdn & btn)....8 4
329[4] Bandita **(46)***(36) (MissAJWhitfield)* 4-7-13 (3) SSanders(4) (led 2f: 6th & btn st)....2 5
279[5] Port Sunlight (IRE) **(46)***(35) (PDEvans)* 7-8-5v AClark(11) (hld up: effrt 3f out: nvr rchd ldrs) .s.h 6
279[4] Bodantree **(37)***(25) (HOliver)* 4-7-0 (7) BHalligan(8) (lw: plld hrd: prom: rdn 4f out: sn btn)....1 7
131[3] Iota **(65)***(52) (JLHarris)* 6-9-10 KDarley(12) (lw: in tch: rdn & lost pl over 4f out: n.d after)....½ 8
312[14] Classic Exhibit **(35)***(22) (ALForbes)* 6-7-8 GBardwell(5) (lw: a bhd)....hd 9
311[2] Sagasan **(58)***(32) (WRMuir)* 4-9-0 DHarrison(10) (w ldrs tl 5th & wkng st: eased whn btn appr fnl f)....10 10
Golden Torque **(65)***(34) (RBastiman)* 8-9-5 (5) HBastiman(6) (a bhd)....3½ 11
LONG HANDICAP Bodantree 7-3

3/1 IN THE MONEY (IRE), **7/2** Premier Dance, **9/2** Sagasan, **11/2** Iota, **7/1** Bodantree, **8/1** Golden Torque, **12/1** Wottashambles, Bandita, Port Sunlight (IRE), **20/1** Clifton Game, **25/1** Classic Exhibit, CSF £60.66 CT £216.75 TOTE £4.60 £1.30 £7.90 £1.50 [£311.10] Trio: Not won; £298.21 to Lingfield 2/3/95. OWNER Mr J. E. Bigg (UPPER LONGDON) BRED Cheveley Park Stud Ltd 11 Rn
2m 39.8 SF: 41/26/40/8/10/13/-/30/-/6/12
WEIGHT FOR AGE 4yo-3lb
T/Plpt: £12.40 (1,049.37 Tckts). T/Qdpt: £32.40 (1 Tckt). Dk

0355-LINGFIELD (L-H)
Thursday March 2nd (Standard)

368

STAINLESS CATERING SINKS CLAIMING APPRENTICE STKS (3-Y.O) (Class E) £2,966.70 (£897.60: £437.80: £207.90)
1m 4f (Equitrack) Stalls: Low GOING minus 0.46 sec per fur (FST) 2-10 (2-11)

339[2] **Poly Road (47)***(54)*(Fav)*(MRChannon)* 3-8-2 PPMurphy(7) (a gng wl: stdy hdwy 3f out: led on bit over 2f out: sn clr: easily)....— 1
263[6] Mayday Kitty **(36)***(37) (WGMTurner)* 3-7-10v MBaird(6) (lw: rdn over 6f out: hdwy over 5f out: r.o one pce ins fnl f)....8 2
339[6] Hever Golf Lady **(44)***(35) (TJNaughton)* 3-7-11 ow1 CTeague(3) (lw: hdwy over 4f out: rdn over 2f out: one pce)....1½ 3
316[8] Danny's Gift *(30) (MissAJWhitfield)* 3-7-5 (3) CAdamson(4) (lw: led 3f: rdn 2f out: one pce) ..2½ 4
326[8] Lawbuster (IRE) **(50)***(31) (WRMuir)* 3-7-10 (3) MHenry(1) (w ldr: led 9f out tl over 2f out: wknd ins fnl f)....3 5
135[8] Bitter N Twisted **(32)***(26) (SEKettlewell)* 3-7-7b(3) AmandaSanders(2) (bhd fnl 3f)....1¼ 6
273[7] Dingo Warrior **(30)***(24) (JFfitch-Heyes)* 3-7-13 CHawksley(5) (bhd fnl 3f)....4 7

13/8 POLY ROAD, **3/1** Lawbuster (IRE), **7/2** Hever Golf Lady, **6/1** Bitter N Twisted, **12/1** Mayday Kitty, **33/1** Danny's Gift, Dingo Warrior, CSF £18.28 TOTE £1.90: £1.90 £2.50 (£9.10) OWNER Sheet & Roll Convertors Ltd (UPPER LAMBOURN) BRED W. Beasley 7 Rn
2m 35.45 (6.05) SF: 11/-/-/-/-/-/-

369

STAINLESS DESIGN SERVICES H'CAP (0-80) (3-Y.O+) (Class D) £3,538.60 (£1,070.80: £522.40: £248.20)
5f (Equitrack) Stalls: High GOING minus 0.46 sec per fur (FST) 2-40 (2-42)

327[3] **Kalar (63)***(71) (DWChapman)* 6-8-7b(7) CTeague(4) (mde virtually all: rdn out)....— 1
• 237[5] Nordico Princess **(68)***(68) (GROldroyd)* 4-9-5 MMcAndrew(6) (a.p: rdn 3f out: r.o ins fnl f) ...2½ 2

272⁴ Spender **(77)***(74)* *(PWHarris)* 6-9-9 (5) JStack(1) (outpcd: hdwy on ins 2f out: unable qckn ins fnl f) 1 **3**
272³ Speedy Classic (USA) **(62)***(57)*(Fav)*(MJHeaton-Ellis)* 6-8-13 WWoods(2) (outpcd: rdn & bhd wl over 1f out: hdwy fnl f: r.o wl) ....½ **4**
272⁶ Moscow Road **(72)***(62)* *(MissBSanders)* 4-9-6 (3) SSanders(7) (b.hind: lw: no hdwy fnl 3f) 1½ **5**
305* Sigama (USA) **(62)***(51)* *(DNicholls)* 9-8-13 AlexGreaves(5) (lw: prom: rdn over 1f out: wknd fnl f) ....½ **6**
177⁹ Daaniera (IRE) **(58)***(41)* *(PHowling)* 5-8-6b(3) DWright(8) (b.hind: lw: spd over 3f) 1¾ **7**
Prince Belfort **(58)***(9)* *(JLEyre)* 7-8-2b(7) GMacDonald(3) (a wl bhd) 10 **8**

3/1 Speedy Classic (USA), **4/1** KALAR, **5/1** Spender, Sigama (USA), **7/1** Nordico Princess, Prince Belfort, **12/1** Moscow Road, **20/1** Daaniera (IRE), CSF £29.02 CT £128.47 TOTE £3.00: £1.50 £2.20 £2.10 (£18.90) OWNER Mr E. Stockdale (YORK) BRED C. C. and Mrs Pryor 8 Rn
58.49 secs (0.29) SF: 54/51/57/40/45/34/24/-

370 STAINLESS REFURBISHMENT H'CAP (0-60) (I) (4-Y.O+) (Class F)
£2,776.40 (£780.40: £381.20)
2m (Equitrack) Stalls: Low GOING minus 0.69 sec per fur (FST) 3-10 (3-12)

346⁶ **Head Turner (53)***(60)* *(CPWildman)* 7-9-7 StephenDavies(8) (b.off fore: stdy hdwy over 6f out: rdn over 2f out: led over 1f out: r.o wl) ....— **1**
96¹⁵ Red Whirlwind **(53)***(57)* *(RJO'Sullivan)* 5-9-7 WWoods(2) (b: a.p: led over 4f out tl over 1f out: unable qckn) 3½ **2**
260¹⁰ Call Me Albi (IRE) **(49)***(50)* *(GLMoore)* 4-8-12 AClark(10) (lw: hdwy 6f out: one pce fnl 2f) 2½ **3**
303⁴ Bures (IRE) **(56)***(56)* *(MHTompkins)* 4-9-0v(5) SMulvey(4) (led 2f: led 9f out: hdd over 4f out: rdn over 3f out: one pce) ....¾ **4**
321¹⁰ Glow Forum **(37)***(32)* *(GLMoore)* 4-8-0 JQuinn(12) (rdn & hdwy over 3f out: one pce) 5 **5**
Master Reach **(36)***(31)* *(BJMeehan)* 6-8-4 MFenton(5) (b: a.p: rdn 6f out: wknd over 3f out) s.h **6**
246⁷ Milngavie (IRE) **(57)***(44)* *(MJohnston)* 5-9-11 TWilliams(9) (a mid div) 8 **7**
285³ Lady Bunting **(26)***(12)* *(MissBSanders)* 8-7-8v GBardwell(1) (b.off fore: prom over 12f) 1½ **8**
346² Sheltered Cove (IRE) **(56)***(41)*(Fav)*(KOCunningham-Brown)* 4-9-5 BDoyle(7) (b.hind: rdn over 8f out: nvr nr to chl) ....nk **9**
Marjons Boy **(28)** *(CAHorgan)* 8-7-5 (5)ow3 NVarley(6) (a bhd: t.o) 30 **10**
Real Popcorn (IRE) **(51)***(5)* *(KMcAuliffe)* 4-8-11hv(3) JTate(14) (lw: led 14f out to 9f out: sn wknd: t.o: sddle slipped) 1 **11**
302¹⁰ Predictable **(44)** *(MrsAKnight)* 9-8-12 AlexGreaves(11) (a bhd: t.o) ....½ **12**
18¹¹ Turtle Power **(35)** *(APJames)* 5-8-0b(3)ow7 SSanders(13) (bhd fnl 9f: t.o) 20 **13**

11/10 Sheltered Cove (IRE), **11/2** HEAD TURNER, **8/1** Bures (IRE), **10/1** Milngavie (IRE), **12/1** Call Me Albi (IRE), Lady Bunting, **14/1** Red Whirlwind, Real Popcorn (IRE), **33/1** Master Reach, Marjons Boy, Glow Forum, **50/1** Predictable, Turtle Power, CSF £74.03 CT £814.99 TOTE £7.40: £1.80 £7.10 £3.40 (£81.10) Trio £371.80 OWNER Mr I. Jerrard (SALISBURY) BRED M. B. O'Gorman 13 Rn
3m 25.43 (1.93) SF: 42/39/27/33/9/13/26/-/18/-/-/-/-
WEIGHT FOR AGE 4yo-5lb

OFFICIAL EXPLANATION **Real Popcorn: the jockey reported that the saddle had slipped.**

371 STAINLESS SPECIALIST'S H'CAP (0-70) (3-Y.O+) (Class E)
£3,124.00 (£946.00: £462.00: £220.00)
7f (Equitrack) Stalls: Low GOING minus 0.46 sec per fur (FST) 3-40 (3-40)

265² **Digpast (IRE) (59)***(71)*(Fav)*(RJO'Sullivan)* 5-9-3b DBiggs(9) (b: lw: s.s: rdn thrght: gd hdwy over 3f out: led 1f out: r.o wl) ....— **1**
198² Indian Serenade **(49)***(53)* *(PWHarris)* 4-8-2 (5) JStack(1) (lw: led 6f: unable qckn) 3½ **2**
322³ Mary's Case (IRE) **(56)***(59)* *(MJohnston)* 5-9-0 TWilliams(4) (rdn & hdwy over 4f out: ev ch over 1f out: one pce) ....½ **3**
298³ Newington Butts (IRE) **(47)***(38)* *(RAkehurst)* 5-8-2b(3) SSanders(3) (a.p: ev ch over 1f out: wknd fnl f) 5 **4**
320³ Panchellita (USA) **(45)***(20)* *(GLMoore)* 6-8-3v JQuinn(7) (lw: a.p: rdn over 3f out: wknd 2f out) .7 **5**
323² Arndilly **(66)***(38)* *(BJMeehan)* 4-9-10b WWoods(2) (nvr nr to chal) 1½ **6**
267* Pine Ridge Lad (IRE) **(70)***(38)* *(JLEyre)* 5-10-0 SDWilliams(8) (lw: bhd fnl 4f) 1¾ **7**
298⁷ Courting Newmarket **(51)***(12)* *(MrsAKnight)* 7-8-9 AlexGreaves(5) (bhd fnl 3f) 3 **8**
287¹¹ Mheanmetoo **(48)** *(DLWilliams)* 4-8-3 (3) DWright(6) (lw: prom over 2f) 25 **9**

11/4 DIGPAST (IRE), **7/2** Panchellita (USA), **9/2** Pine Ridge Lad (IRE), **7/1** Newington Butts (IRE), **8/1** Arndilly, Indian Serenade, **10/1** Courting Newmarket, **12/1** Mary's Case (IRE), **33/1** Mheanmetoo, CSF £24.09 CT £212.21 TOTE £5.10: £1.50 £2.90 £4.80 (£20.50) Trio £57.80 OWNER Mr Les Randall (BOGNOR REGIS) BRED Somerville Stud 9 Rn
1m 24.31 (1.31) SF: 47/29/35/14/-/14/14/-/-

372

STAINLESS HOSPITAL EQUIPMENT MAIDEN STKS (3-Y.O) (Class D) £3,690.70 (£1,117.60: £545.80: £259.90)
1m 2f (Equitrack) Stalls: Low GOING minus 0.46 sec per fur (FST) 4-10 (4-11)

Vin St Koola (92)*(55)*(Fav)*(HJCollingridge)* 3-9-0 MRimmer(8) (lw: a.p: led over 2f out: rdn out) — **1**
Komodo (USA) **(63)***(54) (DRCElsworth)* 3-8-9 (5) SDrowne(3) (lw: a.p: hrd rdn over 2f out: chsd wnr over 1f out: r.o fnl f) ½ **2**
256⁶ Silver Rondo (USA) *(44) (LordHuntingdon)* 3-8-9 DHarrison(10) (hdwy 8f out: led over 3f out tl over 2f out: one pce) 3½ **3**
Simposa (IRE) *(46) (JEBanks)* 3-9-0 JQuinn(9) (w'like: hld up: rdn over 1f out: one pce) 1¾ **4**
174⁶ Emerald Dream (IRE) *(40) (CCElsey)* 3-8-9 TIves(7) (led over 8f out tl over 3f out: wknd over 1f out) ½ **5**
316⁴ Rocky Forum *(40) (GLMoore)* 3-8-9 RPerham(2) (nvr nr to chal) s.h **6**
239⁶ Ever Friends *(40) (BJMcMath)* 3-9-0 AMackay(5) (lw: a bhd) 3 **7**
282² Callonescy (IRE) *(31) (CEBrittain)* 3-9-0 BDoyle(1) (a bhd) 6 **8**
316⁷ He's Special *(30) (CACyzer)* 3-9-0 MFenton(6) (led over 1f: wknd over 3f out) hd **9**
Roadsweeper (FR) *(29) (KOCunningham-Brown)* 3-9-0 AClark(4) (leggy: s.i.s: hdwy over 7f out: wknd over 3f out) ¾ **10**

15/8 VIN ST KOOLA, **9/2** Callonescy (IRE), **5/1** Simposa (IRE), **11/2** Rocky Forum, **6/1** Komodo (USA), **7/1** Silver Rondo (USA), **20/1** Ever Friends, **25/1** Roadsweeper (FR), **33/1** He's Special, Emerald Dream (IRE), CSF £14.26 TOTE £2.80: £1.20 £2.10 £1.90 (£12.10) OWNER Mr D. C. G. Cooper (NEWMARKET) BRED David Cooper 10 Rn 2m 8.76 (5.76) SF: 16/15/5/7/1/1/1/-/-/-

373

STAINLESS SANITARY WARE H'CAP (0-65) (3-Y.O+) (Class F) £2,801.60 (£787.60: £384.80)
1m (Equitrack) Stalls: High GOING minus 0.46 sec per fur (FST) 4-40 (4-42)

125⁴ **Hatta Sunshine (USA) (48)***(53)*(Fav)*(AMoore)* 5-8-9 (3) SSanders(2) (b.hind: a.p: led over 1f out: drvn out) — **1**
341⁸ Pair of Jacks (IRE) **(31)***(32) (DAWilson)* 5-7-9 ow2 JQuinn(1) (lw: ld over 6f: hrd rdn: r.o) 1 **2**
*265** Possibility **(40)***(42)*(Fav)*(RIngram)* 4-8-4b WWoods(9) (hdwy over 1f out: r.o wl ins fnl f) nk **3**
320⁶ Lady Williams (IRE) **(60)***(61) (LordHuntingdon)* 4-9-10 DHarrison(10) (hld up: ev ch over 2f out: one pce) ¾ **4**
347⁴ Sherblu **(42)***(42) (JFfitch-Heyes)* 4-8-6 BDoyle(3) (a.p: rdn over 2f out: one pce) nk **5**
269⁴ Buddy's Friend (IRE) **(63)***(62) (RJRWilliams)* 7-9-6 (7) SarahThompson(7) (lw: hdwy over 1f out: r.o) ¾ **6**
320⁵ Zinbaq **(35)***(30) (CJBenstead)* 9-7-13 TWilliams(8) (lw: a.p: rdn over 2f out: wknd wl over 1f out) 2 **7**
Calder King **(64)***(58) (JLEyre)* 4-9-11 (3) OPears(4) (nvr nr to chl) ½ **8**
298² The Little Ferret **(60)***(44)*(Fav)*(GLMoore)* 5-9-3 (7) LSuthern(6) (lw: prom 5f) 5 **9**
Power Share **(52)***(12) (MrsAKnight)* 4-9-2 AlexGreaves(5) (bhd fnl 4f) 12 **10**

LONG HANDICAP Pair of Jacks (IRE) 7-6

4/1 HATTA SUNSHINE (USA), Possibility, The Little Ferret, **5/1** Lady Williams (IRE), **8/1** Buddy's Friend (IRE), **12/1** Zinbaq, Sherblu, Calder King, **25/1** Pair of Jacks (IRE), **33/1** Power Share, CSF £78.74 CT £386.51 TOTE £3.90: £2.10 £3.60 £1.90 (£54.60) Trio £120.50 OWNER Mr R. Kieman (BRIGHTON) BRED Daniel M. Galbreath 10 Rn 1m 39.77 (3.37) SF: 24/3/13/32/13/33/1/29/15/-

374

STAINLESS REFURBISHMENT H'CAP (0-60) (II) (4-Y.O+) (Class F) £2,776.40 (£780.40: £381.20)
2m (Equitrack) Stalls: Low GOING minus 0.46 sec per fur (FST) 5-10 (5-12)

*321** **Jaraab (45)***(57)*(Fav)*(GLewis)* 4-8-8 4x SWhitworth(13) (hld up: led over 2f out: clr over 1f out) — **1**
321² Sleeptite (FR) **(58)***(68) (WGMTurner)* 5-9-7 (5) JDSmith(3) (hdwy on ins over 3f out: chsd wnr over 1f out: r.o) 1¾ **2**
295³ Risky Tu **(59)***(62) (PAKelleway)* 4-9-1 (7) AdelleGibbons(7) (hdwy over 3f out: eased whn btn over 1f out) 7 **3**
352⁵ Regal Pursuit (IRE) **(57)***(51) (CAHorgan)* 4-9-6h WWoods(10) (hdwy over 3f out: eased whn btn over 1f out) 9 **4**
Sure Pride (USA) **(45)***(38) (AMoore)* 7-8-13 CandyMorris(9) (b: nvr nr to chl) 1¾ **5**
Debacle (USA) **(56)***(48) (BJMcMath)* 6-9-10 TIves(5) (nvr nrr) 1 **6**
346⁸ In Behind (IRE) **(44)***(35) (GLMoore)* 4-8-7 CRutter(14) (b.hnd: hdwy over 3f out: wknd over 2f out) hd **7**
321⁶ Remember This (IRE) **(35)***(25) (CACyzer)* 5-8-3 MFenton(2) (b.hnd: hld up: rdn over 7f out: wknd over 2f out) 1½ **8**

2958 Vishnu (USA) **(60)***(47) (JLEyre)* 5-9-11b(3) OPears(6) (hdwy over 13 f out: wknd over 2f out) 2½ 9
2212 Hattaafeh (IRE) **(60)***(47) (MAJarvis)* 4-9-4 (5) JStack(8) (hdwy over 3f out: wknd over 2f out)..nk 10
288* Dancing Diamond (IRE) **(54)***(26) (MissBSanders)* 5-9-5hv(3) SSanders(4) (bhd fnl 3f) 15 11
Bayphia **(37)***(4) (RJO'Sullivan)* 7-8-5 StephenDavies(11) (b: led over 11f)..............................5 12
Pip's Dream **(44)** *(MJRyan)* 4-8-7 AClark(12) (prom over 11f)..13 13
Super Heights **(48)** *(DLWilliams)* 7-8-11 (5) DGriffiths(1) (bhd fnl 8f)..7 14

5/2 JARAAB, **9/2** Dancing Diamond (IRE), **5/1** Sleeptite (FR), Hattaafeh (IRE), **7/1** Regal Pursuit (IRE), **9/1** Risky Tu, **12/1** In Behind (IRE), **14/1** Bayphia, **16/1** Pip's Dream, Vishnu (USA), **25/1** Super Heights, Sure Pride (USA), Debacle (USA), **33/1** Remember This (IRE), CSF £17.92 CT £103.44 TOTE £2.20: £1.90 £2.50 £2.20 (£11.10) Trio £21.00 OWNER Mr S. I. Ross (EPSOM) BRED Shadwell Estate Company Limited 14 Rn

3m 25.62 (2.12) SF: 29/45/34/23/15/25/7/2/24/19/3/-/-/-
WEIGHT FOR AGE 4yo-5lb

T/Jkpt: £5,107.90 (1.39 Tckts). T/Plpt: £195.50 (87.32 Tckts). T/Qdpt: £252.80 (0.9 Tckts); £34.17 to Newbury 3/3/95. AK

0348-SOUTHWELL (L-H)
Friday March 3rd (Standard)

375 NORMANTON CLAIMING STKS (4-Y.O+) (Class F) £2,537.00 (£712.00: £347.00)
1m 6f (Fibresand) Stalls: High GOING minus 0.04 sec per fur (STD) 2-10 (2-12)

79* **El Nido (59)***(66)*(Fav)*(MJCamacho)* 7-9-3 LCharnock(2) (lw: trckd ldrs: r.o wl to ld ins fnl f: drvn out).................................— 1
280* Royal Citizen (IRE) **(64)***(67) (JFBottomley)* 6-9-7 TIves(11) (hdwy & prom 6f out: led 2f out: edgd rt: hdd & nt qckn ins fnl f).........................2½ 2
3406 How's it Goin (IRE) **(67)***(59) (WRMuir)* 4-9-1 DHarrison(1) (hld up & bhd: hdwy 7f out: styd on fnl 2f: nvr rchd ldrs)...........................5 3
Bud's Bet (IRE) **(32)***(50) (WWHaigh)* 7-8-11 DaleGibson(13) (lw: bhd & pushed along: hdwy on outside over 2f out: hung lft: kpt on: nvr nr to chal) 1 4
Swordking (IRE) **(52)***(56) (JLHarris)* 6-9-3 GDuffield(12) (drvn along & hdwy on outside 8f out: one pce fnl 2f).......................................nk 5
Criminal Record (USA) **(49)***(44) (WClay)* 5-8-13b MWigham(10) (chsd ldrs tl lost pl 2f out) 7 6
Eulogy (FR) *(38) (KRBurke)* 8-9-1v RHughes(9) (trckd ldrs: led over 2f out: sn hdd: wknd over 1f out)..7 7
2773 Rose of Glenn **(47)***(28) (BPalling)* 4-8-4 StephenDavies(3) (hdwy & prom 6f out: wknd over 3f out)..3 8
29511 Turfmans Vision **(41)***(26) (RHollinshead)* 5-8-11b WRyan(8) (lw: prom: effrt 4f out: wknd over 2f out)......................................4 9
2604 Cristal Springs **(26)***(14) (BJMcMath)* 4-7-8 (3)ow1 DWright(4) (b: b.hind: led tl over 5f out: sn lost pl).....................................1¾ 10
3115 Goldenberry **(33)***(5) (JParkes)* 4-7-12 ow2 TWilliams(15) (hdwy ½-way: lost pl over 2f out: eased) 8 11
2804 Zaaheyah (USA) **(41)***(1) (MDHammond)* 5-8-4 GCarter(7) (w ldr: led over 5f out tl over 2f out: sn lost pl & eased).................................7 12
Beaumood **(29)** *(EJAlston)* 9-8-7b JQuinn(6) (in tch: effrt 4f out: sn lost pl)..............................3 13
25913 Have a Nightcap **(30)***(2) (NPLittmoden)* 6-9-2 (5) TGMcLaughlin(14) (s.i.s: a bhd & sn drvn along)...11 14
3118 Placid-Warrior *(JCMcConnochie)* 5-8-8 (3) DRMcCabe(5) (t.o fnl 5f).................................dist 15

11/8 EL NIDO, **7/2** Royal Citizen (IRE), **7/1** How's it Goin (IRE), **10/1** Rose of Glenn, **14/1** Eulogy (FR), Zaaheyah (USA), Swordking (IRE), **20/1** Criminal Record (USA), Have a Nightcap, **25/1** Bud's Bet (IRE), Cristal Springs, Turfmans Vision, Goldenberry, **33/1** Beaumood, Placid-Warrior, CSF £7.58 TOTE £2.80: £1.30 £2.00 £1.90 (£5.20) Trio £6.30 OWNER M K Slinger & A Stuart (MALTON) BRED M. J. Camacho 15 Rn 3m 10.5 (10.80) SF: 38/39/27/22/28/16/10/-/-/-/-/-/-/-/-
WEIGHT FOR AGE 4yo-4lb

376 SKEGBY MAIDEN STKS (3-Y.O) (Class D) £3,572.40 (£1,081.20: £527.60: £250.80) **1m 4f (Fibresand)** Stalls: High GOING minus 0.04 sec (STD) 2-40 (2-41)

Warluskee *(72)*(Fav)*(MJohnston)* 3-8-9 WRyan(7) (trckd ldrs: drvn along over 3f out: sn hmpd & led: r.o strly fnl 2f).................................— 1
Toy Princess (USA) *(64) (CEBrittain)* 3-8-9 BDoyle(6) (led: rn wd & hdd 3f out: kpt on: no ch w wnr)..6 2
2132 Beau Matelot **(62)***(57) (JDBethell)* 3-9-0 TIves(2) (chsd ldrs: hrd drvn over 4f out: one pce) 9 3

213[4] Darling Clover *(48) (DMorley)* 3-8-9 MFenton(4) (chsd ldrs: drvn along 5f out: wknd over 3f out) 3 **4**
339[5] Fools of Pride (IRE) **(47)***(41) (RHollinshead)* 3-8-9 AClark(8) (prom: drvn along 5f out: lost pl over 3f out) 5 **5**
Fabillion *(46) (CASmith)* 3-9-0 MWigham(3) (rangy: s.i.s: sn in tch: drvn along & lost pl over 3f out) ....nk **6**
256[12] Noble Canonire *(NPLittmoden)* 3-8-4 (5) TGMcLaughlin(5) (hld up & plld hrd: rn wd bnd over 3f out: t.o whn rn v.wd st: sddle & bit slipped) ....dist **7**

13/8 WARLUSKEE, **11/4** Beau Matelot, **3/1** Toy Princess (USA), **5/1** Darling Clover, **14/1** Fools of Pride (IRE), Fabillion, **33/1** Noble Canonire, CSF £7.40 TOTE £2.20: £1.10 £3.80 (£3.30) OWNER Sheikh Mohammed (MIDDLEHAM) BRED Sheikh Mohammed bin Rashid al Maktoum 7 Rn
2m 43.7 (9.50) SF: 30/22/15/6/-/4/-

OFFICIAL EXPLANATION **Noble Canonire: jockey reported that his saddle had slipped forward and that his mount's bit had slipped through her mouth.**

377 BRITISH GYPSUM CLUB 2000 H'CAP (0-80) (4-Y.O+) (Class D)

£3,606.20 (£1,091.60: £532.80: £253.40)
1m 4f (Fibresand) Stalls: High GOING minus 0.04 sec per fur (STD) 3-10 (3-11)

81* **Pharly Dancer (79)***(83)*(Fav)*(WWHaigh)* 6-10-0 DaleGibson(2) (mde all: hrd rdn 3f out: styd on wl appr fnl f) ....— **1**
252* Power **(76)***(78) (CEBrittain)* 4-9-8 BDoyle(1) (unruly in stalls: effrt over 3f out: sn hrd rdn: styd on same pce fnl f) 1¾ **2**
311* Mad Militant (IRE) **(75)***(71) (RHollinshead)* 6-9-10 5x TIves(4) (hld up: smooth hdwy & ev ch 3f out: shkn up over 1f out: kpt on same pce) 4 **3**
Mint a Million (IRE) **(49)***(37) (MBlanshard)* 4-7-9 ow2 JQuinn(3) (prom: drvn along 4f out: sn wl outpcd) 5 **4**

LONG HANDICAP Mint a Million (IRE) 7-3

10/11 PHARLY DANCER, **9/4** Power, **3/1** Mad Militant (IRE), **25/1** Mint a Million (IRE), CSF £3.30 TOTE £1.90 (£1.90) OWNER Mr A. Marucci (MALTON) BRED Stud-On-The-Chart 4 Rn
2m 44.1 (9.90) SF: 45/37/33/-
WEIGHT FOR AGE 4yo-3lb

378 EAST MIDLANDS ELECTRICITY H'CAP (0-70) (3-Y.O+) (Class E)

£3,209.80 (£972.40: £475.20: £226.60)
1m (Fibresand) Stalls: Low GOING minus 0.04 sec per fur (STD) 3-40 (3-40)

203[5] **A Million Watts (61)***(70) (LadyHerries)* 4-9-5 TIves(8) (lw: chsd ldrs: r.o to ld jst ins fnl f: drvn out) ....— **1**
Self Expression **(57)***(59) (MrsJRRamsden)* 7-9-1 SDWilliams(13) (a.p: shkn up to ld 2f out: hdd & nt qckn ins fnl f) 3½ **2**
308[8] Puffy **(40)***(39) (MDods)* 8-7-12v DaleGibson(12) (b: s.i.s: bhd: hdwy 2f out: styd on u.p ins fnl f) 1¾ **3**
313* Hawwam **(73)***(71) (EJAlston)* 9-9-12 (5) 6x AProcter(9) (lw: reard s: bhd tl styd on fnl 2f: nvr nr to chal) ....nk **4**
341[4] Titanium Honda (IRE) **(41)***(36) (CEBrittain)* 4-7-13 CRutter(11) (chsd ldrs tl wknd over 1f out)1½ **5**
349[5] Shuttlecock **(65)***(59) (MrsNMacauley)* 4-9-4 (5) JStack(1) (w ldr: led over 4f out tl over 2f out: wknd over 1f out) ....½ **6**
349* Desert Invader (IRE) **(66)***(59)*(Fav)*(DWChapman)* 4-9-10 6x DeanMcKeown(6) (mid div: rdn ent st: no hdwy appr fnl f) ....nk **7**
335[4] Rambollina **(41)***(26) (MWEasterby)* 4-7-13b LCharnock(10) (prom: lost pl & hmpd 2f out: styd on u.p ins fnl f) 4 **8**
354* Aquado **(47)***(28) (ALForbes)* 6-8-5 6x JQuinn(4) (b.off hind: bhd: sme hdwy 2f out: n.d) 2 **9**
Sea Spouse **(49)***(24) (MBlanshard)* 4-8-0 (7) SMcCarthy(7) (rr div: sme hdwy over 2f out: sn wknd) 3 **10**
The Happy Loon (IRE) **(62)***(33) (DenysSmith)* 4-9-6 MFenton(5) (mid div: effrt 3f out: nvr nr to chal) 2 **11**
334[7] Spanish Stripper (USA) **(47)***(17) (MCChapman)* 4-7-12 (7) CMunday(3) (swtg: a bhd) ....s.h **12**
Phase One (IRE) **(38)** *(JLEyre)* 5-7-7 (3)ow2 DWright(2) (led tl over 4f out: lost pl over 2f out) 11 **13**

7/2 Desert Invader (IRE), **11/2** Aquado, **6/1** Phase One (IRE), A MILLION WATTS, Hawwam, **8/1** Self Expression, **9/1** Shuttlecock, **12/1** Titanium Honda (IRE), **16/1** Spanish Stripper (USA), **20/1** Rambollina, The Happy Loon (IRE), Puffy, **50/1** Sea Spouse, CSF £53.67 CT £852.02 TOTE £8.60: £2.20 £3.30 £4.30 (£54.30) Trio £474.20 OWNER Mr John Constable (LITTLEHAMPTON) BRED Peter Nash 13 Rn 1m 44.7 (5.40) SF: 46/35/15/47/12/35/35/2/4/-/9/-/-

379
RUFFORD (S) STKS (4-Y.O+) (Class G) £2,433.00 (£683.00: £333.00)
1m (Fibresand) Stalls: Low GOING minus 0.04 sec per fur (STD) 4-10 (4-10)

336* **No Submission (USA) (69)**(63)(Fav)(DWChapman) 9-9-3 DeanMcKeown(5) (lw: chsd ldr: led over 4f out: styd on wl fnl f) — 1
68[6] Pop to Stans **(50)**(56) (JPearce) 6-8-5 (7) ElizabethTurner(1) (s.i.s: bhd: hdwy on outside 2f out: styng on fin) 2½ 2
226[2] Ivan the Terrible (IRE) **(50)**(55) (BEllison) 7-8-12 TIves(2) (b: reard s: sn chsg ldrs: one pce fnl f) nk 3
343[3] Fiaba **(41)**(49) (MrsNMacauley) 7-8-0 (7) AmandaSanders(7) (lw: bhd tl styd on fnl 2f: nvr nr to chal) ¾ 4
Roseate Lodge **(60)**(48) (KRBurke) 9-8-12 AClark(3) (chsd ldrs tl wknd over 1f out) 3 5
335[2] Coven Moon **(31)**(36) (DMorris) 5-8-1 (7)ow1 CWebb(8) (hdwy ½-wy: wknd 2f out) 3½ 6
335[3] Uckerby Lad **(44)**(39) (NPLittmoden) 4-8-7 (5) TGMcLaughlin(9) (prom: drvn along 3f out: sn wl outpcd) ¾ 7
313[7] Rad **(55)**(38) (SPCWoods) 5-8-12 WWoods(4) (lw: trckd ldrs: ev ch tl rdn & wknd over 1f out) ½ 8
353[5] Britannia Mills **(33)**(13) (MCChapman) 4-8-0 (7) CMunday(6) (led to 4f out: lost pl over 2f out) 10 9
Wassl's Nanny (IRE) **(46)**(3) (BEllison) 6-8-7 WRyan(10) (prom to ½-wy: sn bhd) 5 10

4/6 NO SUBMISSION (USA), **13/2** Rad, Ivan the Terrible (IRE), **9/1** Fiaba, **10/1** Roseate Lodge, Coven Moon, **20/1** Uckerby Lad, Pop to Stans, Wassl's Nanny (IRE), **25/1** Britannia Mills, CSF £17.87 TOTE £2.30: £1.50 £4.20 £1.60 (£17.90) Trio £27.30 OWNER Mr T. S. Redman (YORK) BRED Mr. Francis X. Weber 10 Rn 1m 45.2 (5.90) SF: 39/29/28/22/21/9/12/11/-/-
Bt in 5,200 gns

380
LADBROKE ALL WEATHER BOWL SERIES FINAL H'CAP (0-100) (3-Y.O+) (Class C) £5,368.00 (£1,624.00: £792.00: £376.00)
6f (Fibresand) Stalls: Low GOING minus 0.04 sec per fur (STD) 4-40 (4-40)

338[2] **Bella Parkes (73)**(81)(Fav)(DNicholls) 4-9-12b AlexGreaves(8) (trckd ldrs: shkn up 2f out: r.o to ld ins fnl f: drvn out) — 1
327[2] Leigh Crofter **(75)**(78) (PDCundell) 6-9-9v(5) DGriffiths(4) (trckd ldrs: led over 2f out tl ins fnl f: no ex) 2 2
257[3] Portend **(80)**(79) (SRBowring) 3-8-11 (7) CTeague(7) (lw: hld up gng wl: hdwy on outside 2f out: rdn & hung lft over 1f out: kpt on same pce) 1½ 3
294[7] Pc's Cruiser (IRE) **(58)**(47) (MCChapman) 3-7-10 GBardwell(5) (sn outpcd & drvn along: kpt on fnl 2f: swtchd lft: nvr nr to chal) 3½ 4
297[9] Frisky Miss (IRE) **(64)**(29) (KOCunningham-Brown) 4-9-3 AClark(3) (mde most tl over 2f out: sn wknd) 9 5
284[6] Double Glow **(66)**(18) (NBycroft) 3-8-4 GDuffield(2) (w ldrs on ins tl bdly hmpd over 3f out: nt rcvr) 5 6
244[6] Gondo **(60)**(7) (EJAlston) 8-8-13v JQuinn(6) (trckd ldrs tl rdn & wknd 2f out) 2 7

15/8 BELLA PARKES, **3/1** Leigh Crofter, **7/2** Portend, **4/1** Pc's Cruiser (IRE), **10/1** Gondo, **16/1** Frisky Miss (IRE), **20/1** Double Glow, CSF £8.31 CT £16.93 TOTE £2.60: £1.80 £2.20 (£6.60) OWNER Mr John Barton (THIRSK) 7 Rn 1m 17.0 (20.20 under best) (-22.30) SF: 59/56/42/10/7/-/-
WEIGHT FOR AGE 3yo-15lb

T/Plpt: £65.50 (533.36 Tckts). T/Qdpt: £12.10 (7.45 Tckts). WG

0368-LINGFIELD (L-H)
Saturday March 4th (Standard)

381
ZOE HURWORTH 'WILL YOU MARRY ME?' MAIDEN STKS (3-Y.O) (Class F) £2,650.40 (£744.40: £363.20)
7f (Equitrack) Stalls: High GOING minus 0.42 sec per fur (FST) 2-10 (2-12)

Lyford Law (IRE) (74)(Fav)(JHMGosden) 3-9-0 JCarroll(7) (b.hind: bit bkwd: hld up: hdwy 3f out: rdn over 1f out: led nr fin) — 1
124[2] Chewit **(70)**(74) (AMoore) 3-9-0 CandyMorris(5) (plld hrd: a.p: led over 4f out: rdn ins fnl f: hdd nr fin) hd 2
Dance King **(67)**(62) (JEBanks) 3-9-0 JQuinn(2) (hld up: hdwy 3f out: rdn over 1f out: one pce) 5 3
286[2] Considerable Charm (44) (LordHuntingdon) 3-8-9 DHarrison(4) (lw: chsd ldrs tl rdn & wknd 3f out) 6 4
43[6] Tael of Silver (44) (KRBurke) 3-8-9 MFenton(1) (a bhd) s.h 5

332³ Solianna **(58)**(43) (MRChannon) 3-8-9 CRutter(3) (lw: led over 2f: rdn & ev ch 2f out: wknd over 1f out) ....s.h 6
Governor's Lass (37) (SDow) 3-8-9e StephenDavies(6) (bhd fnl 3f) 3 7

11/10 LYFORD LAW (IRE), **3/1** Dance King, **13/2** Chewit, **8/1** Considerable Charm, Solianna, **25/1** Tael of Silver, **50/1** Governor's Lass, CSF £8.36 TOTE £1.70: £1.10 £2.60 (£4.10) OWNER Sheikh Mohammed (NEWMARKET) BRED T. A. Ryan 7 Rn 1m 25.83 (2.83) SF: 30/30/18/-/-/-/-

382

TAURUS CLAIMING STKS (3-Y.O) (Class F) £2,700.80 (£758.80: £370.40)
1m (Equitrack) Stalls: Low GOING minus 0.42 sec per fur (FST) 2-40 (2-40)

301³ **Gulf Shaadi (83)**(85)(Fav)(CEBrittain) 3-9-1 BDoyle(5) (plld hrd: hld up: hdwy over 3f out: led 2f out: rdn over 1f out: sn clr: comf) ....— 1
243⁴ Mazilla **(53)**(61) (WJHaggas) 3-7-7 (5) NVarley(3) (led: hdd 2f out: rdn over 1f out: one pce)..3½ 2
310² Chastleton **(41)**(45) (MRChannon) 3-8-2 CandyMorris(4) (chsd ldr 5f: rdn over 2f out: sn wknd) 10 3
333⁶ Scissor Ridge **(60)**(42) (JJBridger) 3-8-4 (3) SSanders(7) (a.p: rdn over 2f out: sn wknd) 4 4
251⁵ Royal Uprising (IRE) **(40)**(23) (GLMoore) 3-7-10 JQuinn(6) (bhd fnl 4f) 4 5
Ketchican (30) (SGKnight) 3-8-7 DHarrison(1) (dwlt: sn rcvrd: rdn & wknd 4f out) 2 6

4/9 GULF SHAADI, **100/30** Mazilla, **16/1** Chastleton, **25/1** Scissor Ridge, **33/1** Royal Uprising (IRE), Ketchican, CSF £2.16 TOTE £1.40: £1.10 £1.60 (£1.90) OWNER Mr C. E. Brittain (NEWMARKET) BRED Sheikh Mohammed bin Rashid al Maktoum 6 Rn 1m 39.12 (2.72) SF: 37/13/-/-/-/-
Gulf Shaadi clmd S Dow £12,000

383

CAPRICORN H'CAP (0-95) (4-Y.O+) (Class C) £5,550.00 (£1,680.00: £820.00: £390.00) **1m (Equitrack)** Stalls: Low GOING minus 0.42 sec per fur (FST) 3-10 (3-11)

Dune River (90)(95)(Fav)(DRLoder) 6-9-8 (3) DRMcCabe(2) (lw: mde all: rdn over 1f out: r.o wl) ....— 1
66⁶ Second Chance (IRE) **(76)**(78) (PMitchell) 5-8-8 (3) SSanders(6) (chsd ldr: rdn 2f out: unable qckn) 1½ 2
281² Ertlon **(93)**(95) (CEBrittain) 5-10-0 BDoyle(1) (lw: chsd ldrs gng wl: rdn over 1f out: one pce) hd 3
125³ Mr Nevermind (IRE) **(75)**(72) (GLMoore) 5-8-10 SWhitworth(4) (chsd ldrs: rdn over 1f out: one pce) 2½ 4
344* Perilous Plight **(77)**(72) (WRMuir) 4-8-12 DHarrison(7) (hld up: rdn & hdwy 2f out: one pce fnl 2f) 1 5
262² Red Valerian **(87)**(79) (KMcAuliffe) 4-9-5b(3) JTate(3) (hld up: rdn & outpcd 4f out: r.o one pce fnl 2f) 1¼ 6
61* Silent Expression **(85)**(76) (BJMeehan) 5-9-6 JCarroll(5) (chsd ldrs: rdn over 3f out: one pce fnl 2f) ....½ 7

11/4 DUNE RIVER, **3/1** Ertlon, **7/2** Perilous Plight, **6/1** Red Valerian, **7/1** Mr Nevermind (IRE), **12/1** Silent Expression, **16/1** Second Chance (IRE), CSF £35.58 TOTE £3.80: £1.80 £4.90 (£14.10) OWNER Mrs P. T. Fenwick (NEWMARKET) BRED Hesmonds Stud Ltd 7 Rn
1m 37.6 (1.20) SF: 61/44/61/38/38/45/42

384

DAILY STAR AWT 1M 2F CHALLENGE SERIES (QUALIFIER) H'CAP (0-70) (3-Y.O) (Class E) £3,163.95 (£957.60: £467.30: £222.15)
1m 2f (Equitrack) Stalls: High GOING minus 0.42 sec per fur (FST) 3-45 (3-46)

213* **Shaft of Light (65)**(75)(Fav)(LordHuntingdon) 3-9-7v DHarrison(9) (mde all: clr 2f out: r.o) ...— 1
270* Bakers Daughter **(52)**(59) (JRArnold) 3-8-8 JQuinn(6) (a.p: hrd rdn over 1f out: r.o fnl f) 1¾ 2
289² Never so Rite (IRE) **(50)**(54) (DWPArbuthnot) 3-8-6 BDoyle(7) (a.p: chsd ldr over 3f out: rdn over 1f out: one pce) 1¾ 3
263² Docklands Courier **(51)**(51) (BJMcMath) 3-8-7 TIves(3) (b.hind: mid div: rdn over 4f out: one pce fnl 2f) 3 4
273² Al Corniche (IRE) **(42)**(41) (KOCunningham-Brown) 3-7-12 StephenDavies(8) (nvr nrr) ....hd 5
263⁷ Good so Fa (IRE) **(55)**(54) (CNAllen) 3-8-6 (5) MBaird(4) (dwlt: hld up: nvr nr to chal) ....s.h 6
273³ Witney-de-Bergerac (IRE) **(52)**(48) (JSMoore) 3-8-3 (5) SDrowne(2) (b.hind: hld up: rdn over 4f out: nvr nrr) 1½ 7
326* Summer Villa **(48)**(35) (PCHaslam) 3-7-13 (5)ow1 JStack(1) (chsd ldrs over 6f: wknd 2f out) 5 8
Brownlows **(50)**(22) (MPBielby) 3-8-3 (3) SSanders(5) (bhd fnl 3f) 10 9

5/2 SHAFT OF LIGHT, **7/2** Summer Villa, Docklands Courier, **8/1** Witney-de-Bergerac (IRE), **9/1** Bakers Daughter, **11/1** Good so Fa (IRE), **12/1** Al Corniche (IRE), **14/1** Never so Rite (IRE), **25/1** Brownlows, CSF £24.03 CT £245.09 TOTE £2.80: £1.40 £2.30 £2.60 (£13.10) Trio £64.30 OWNER The Queen (WEST ILSLEY) BRED The Queen 9 Rn 2m 7.57 (4.57) SF: 34/18/13/10/-/13/7/-/-

385 RAPPORTEUR STKS (4-Y.O+) (Class D) £3,589.30 (£1,086.40: £530.20: £252.10)
1m 2f (Equitrack) Stalls: High GOING minus 0.42 sec per fur (FST) 4-15 (4-15)

Ionio (USA) (114)_(96)_(Fav)_(CEBrittain)_ 4-9-5 BDoyle(4) (b.hind: lw: chsd ldr: led over 2f out: clr 1f out: idled fnl f: rdn & r.o cl home)......— 1
_330*_ Young Freeman (USA) **(80)**_(88) (DRLoder)_ 6-8-11 (3) DRMcCabe(1) (lw: led over 9f out: rdn over 1f out: r.o)......1¼ 2
Latahaab (USA) _(57) (RAkehurst)_ 0-9-1 GCarter(3) (stdd s: a bhd)......20 3
Irish Emerald _(32) (GCBravery)_ 8-8-12 SWhitworth(2) (b: bit bkwd: chsd ldrs: bhd fnl 5f)......14 4

10/11 IONIO (USA), **Evens** Young Freeman (USA), **16/1** Latahaab (USA), **100/1** Irish Emerald, CSF £2.09 TOTE £1.80 (£1.10) OWNER The Dayspring Company Ltd (NEWMARKET) BRED Flaxman Holdings Ltd 4 Rn 2m 3.43 (0.43) SF: 66/59/28/3
WEIGHT FOR AGE 4yo-1lb

386 LINGFIELD PARK AWT SPRINT SERIES (QUALIFIER) H'CAP (0-80) (4-Y.O+) (Class D) £3,705.95 (£1,121.60: £547.30: £260.15)
6f (Equitrack) Stalls: High GOING minus 0.42 sec per fur (FST) 4-45 (4-46)

_345⁴_ **Invocation (63)**_(66) (AMoore)_ 8-9-0 TWilliams(5) (b.hind: chsd ldr: rdn over 1f out: led ins fnl f: r.o)......— 1
_331*_ Tyrian Purple (IRE) **(66)**_(65)_(Fav)_(TJNaughton)_ 7-9-3b DHarrison(3) (led: clr over 1f out: hdd ins fnl f: unable to qckn)......1½ 2
_281⁹_ Bold Street (IRE) **(68)**_(66) (ABailey)_ 5-9-5b SWhitworth(1) (dwlt: sn rcvrd: hdwy over 2f out: rdn over 1f out: r.o)......½ 3
Assignment **(61)**_(48) (JFfitch-Heyes)_ 9-8-12 BDoyle(2) (b.hind: outpcd & bhd: hdwy over 1f out: nvr nrr)......4 4
Martinosky **(55)**_(40) (GCBravery)_ 9-8-6 GCarter(6) (bit bkwd: chsd ldrs: rdn & outpcd over 3f out: r.o one pce fnl f)......¾ 5
_359⁵_ Sweet Whisper **(47)**_(32) (KMcAuliffe)_ 4-7-12v JQuinn(7) (chsd ldrs: rdn over 1f out: one pce) hd 6
_365¹¹_ Persian Affair (IRE) **(77)**_(52) (DHaydnJones)_ 4-10-0 AMackay(4) (a bhd)......3½ 7
_337⁸_ Macs Maharanee **(76)**_(38) (PSFelgate)_ 8-9-8 (5) JStack(8) (a bhd)......5 8

9/4 Tyrian Purple (IRE), **11/4** INVOCATION, **100/30** Bold Street (IRE), **5/1** Sweet Whisper, **14/1** Macs Maharanee, **20/1** Persian Affair (IRE), **25/1** Assignment, Martinosky, CSF £9.10 CT £17.74 TOTE £3.80: £1.20 £1.40 £1.60 (£4.40) OWNER Mr R. Kiernan (BRIGHTON) BRED Juddmonte Farms 8 Rn 1m 12.57 (1.97) SF: 19/18/19/1/-/-/5/-

T/Jkpt: £254.10 (36.3 Tckts). T/Plpt: £23.10 (1,111 Tckts). T/Qdpt: £36.20 (3.2 Tckts). SM

0362-WOLVERHAMPTON (L-H)
Saturday March 4th (Standard)

387 BUTCHER AMATEUR H'CAP (0-70) (4-Y.O+) (Class E) £2,814.00 (£852.00: £416.00: £198.00)
1m 1f 79y (Fibresand) Stalls: Low GOING: 0.10 sec per fur (STD) 7-00 (7-01)

Queens Stroller (IRE) (66)_(72) (CCElsey)_ 4-11-0 (5) MissAElsey(9) (hld up in rr: hdwy & 5th st: styd on to ld cl home)......— 1
_212⁴_ Aitch N'Bee **(67)**_(73) (LadyHerries)_ 12-11-7 MrsMCowdrey(11) (hld up: hdwy 3f out: 2nd st: led ent fnl f: ct nr fin)......nk 2
_341⁵_ Royal Acclaim **(43)**_(48) (JMBradley)_ 10-9-6v(5) MrsDMcHale(8) (hld up & bhd: hdwy 3f out: ev ch ins fnl f: unable qckn)......hd 3
_343²_ Zahran (IRE) **(51)**_(51) (JMBradley)_ 4-9-13 (5) MrRJohnson(10) (b: chsd ldrs: led over 3f out tl over 1f out: rdn & hung lft: no ex fnl f)......3 4
_229⁷_ Jonbel **(35)**_(27) (TTClement)_ 7-8-12 (5)ow3 MrVLukaniuk(12) (b: bkwd: disp ld early: 4th & rdn st: sn btn)......3 5
_275⁵_ Pillow Talk (IRE) **(56)**_(48) (KRBurke)_ 4-10-2 (7) MrsEBurke(3) (hld up: hdwy over 4f out: 6th st: one pce fnl 2f)......2 6
_364²_ Slip a Coin **(57)**_(37)_(Fav)_(ICampbell)_ 4-10-10 MrJLLlewellyn(4) (led tl over 3f out: sn btn)......7 7
Rave-on-Hadley (IRE) **(42)**_(20) (SWCampion)_ 5-9-3 (7) MrsSJCampion(6) (plld hrd: prom tl rdn & wknd over 3f out)......1 8
Swynford Flyer **(69)**_(21) (JAHarris)_ 6-11-2 (7)ow21 MrJApiafi(7) (a in rr)......3 9
_314⁹_ Educated Pet **(46)**_(17) (BPreece)_ 6-9-7 (7) MissLBoswell(1) (hld up in tch: wknd 3f out)......1 10
Balmaha **(53)**_(17) (WJHaggas)_ 4-10-6 MrsLPearce(2) (bkwd: prom 6f: sn lost tch: t.o)......4 11
Northern Chief **(49)**_(6) (RWEmery)_ 5-9-12 (5) MrIMcLelland(5) (chsd ldrs 5f: sn wknd: t.o)......4 12

LONG HANDICAP Jonbel 8-9

7/4 Slip a Coin, **6/1** Aitch N'Bee, **13/2** Balmaha, **8/1** Pillow Talk (IRE), **10/1** Zahran (IRE), **12/1** Royal Acclaim, Swynford Flyer, **14/1** QUEENS STROLLER (IRE), **25/1** Northern Chief, **33/1** Educated Pet, Rave-on-Hadley (IRE), **50/1** Jonbel, CSF £87.02 CT £948.63 TOTE £12.20: £2.50 £2.20 £3.50 (£63.40) Trio £140.50 OWNER Mr Richard Berenson (LAMBOURN) BRED Ardenode Stud Ltd 12 Rn 2m 5.9 (9.90) SF: 53/55/30/32/9/29/18/2/3/-/-/-

WEIGHT FOR AGE 4yo-1lb

388

BLACKSMITH CLAIMING STKS (3-Y.O) (Class F) £2,433.00 (£683.00: £333.00)
1m 1f 79y (Fibresand) Stalls: Low GOING: 0.10 sec per fur (STD) 7-30 (7-30)

*368** **Poly Road (50)***(64) (MRChannon)* 3-7-9hbc(5) PPMurphy(4) (hld up gng wl: hdwy to ld over 2f out: edgd lft fnl f: r.o wl) — 1
326² Kirov Protege (IRE) **(51)***(63) (RWArmstrong)* 3-8-4b WWoods(1) (lw: led tl hdd over 2f out: 2nd st: rdn & one pce fnl f) 3 2
324⁴ What a Nightmare (IRE) **(70)***(59)*(Fav)*(JAGlover)* 3-8-5 DeanMcKeown(3) (hld up: wnt 2nd over 3f out: 3rd & rdn st: one pce) 3 3
326³ Chadleigh Walk (IRE) **(42)***(35) (RHollinshead)* 3-8-7 TIves(2) (chsd ldr: pushed along ½-wy: wknd & 4th st: t.o) 15 4

Evens What a Nightmare (IRE), **5/2** POLY ROAD, **3/1** Kirov Protege (IRE), **10/1** Chadleigh Walk (IRE), CSF £9.27 TOTE £3.50 (£4.30) OWNER Sheet & Roll Convertors Ltd (UPPER LAMBOURN) BRED W. Beasley 4 Rn 2m 4.6 (8.60) SF: 20/19/15/-

389

WHEELWRIGHT H'CAP (0-70) (4-Y.O+) (Class E) £2,788.00 (£844.00: £412.00: £196.00)
1m 4f (Fibresand) Stalls: Low GOING: 0.10 sec per fur (STD) 8-00 (8-01)

321⁴ **Charlie Bigtime (44)***(54) (BJMcMath)* 5-8-2 AMackay(6) (a.p: led over 3f out: drvn along & styd on wl: readily) — 1
367³ Premier Dance **(60)***(67) (DHaydnJones)* 8-8-13 (5) SDrowne(11) (hdwy ½-wy: 3rd st: chsd wnr appr fnl f: no imp) 2 2
*340** Mr Bean **(50)***(54)*(Fav)*(KRBurke)* 5-8-8 MFenton(5) (a.p: led ½-wy tl over 3f out: 2nd & rdn st: one pce) 2½ 3
Homemaker **(48)***(39) (PGMurphy)* 5-7-13 (7)ow8 RWaterfield(9) (b: chsd ldrs: 4th & rdn st: kpt on same pce) 4 4
340³ Winn's Pride (IRE) **(52)***(51) (RHollinshead)* 4-8-7 TIves(2) (chsd ldrs: effrt & 5th st: one pce fnl 2f) s.h 5
*279** Awestruck **(50)***(41) (BPreece)* 5-8-8 GDuffield(4) (pushed along mid div ½-wy: nvr nr ldrs) 6 6
347⁵ Sacred Mirror (IRE) **(51)***(38) (CEBrittain)* 4-8-6 BDoyle(1) (b.hind: lw: chsd ldrs: drvn along & 6th st: sn btn) 2½ 7
Hill Farm Dancer **(53)***(36) (WMBrisbourne)* 4-8-3 (5) AGarth(8) (bit bkwd: s.i.s: a bhd) 3 8
367⁹ Classic Exhibit **(35)***(6) (ALForbes)* 6-7-7 GBardwell(7) (a in rr: t.o fnl 4f) 9 9
308⁴ Salbus **(70)***(32) (FJYardley)* 5-10-0 JQuinn(10) (bhd: rdn over 3f out: no rspnse: t.o) 7 10
Petitjean (IRE) **(45)***(7) (DBurchell)* 4-8-0 StephenDavies(3) (bit bkwd: mde most 6f: wknd 4f out: t.o) hd 11

LONG HANDICAP Classic Exhibit 7-2

7/4 Mr Bean, **4/1** Premier Dance, **9/2** CHARLIE BIGTIME, **11/2** Awestruck, **12/1** Sacred Mirror (IRE), Winn's Pride (IRE), Hill Farm Dancer, **14/1** Homemaker, **16/1** Petitjean (IRE), **20/1** Salbus, **40/1** Classic Exhibit, CSF £24.35 CT £41.84 TOTE £5.10: £1.50 £1.80 £1.80 (£10.50) Trio £12.00 OWNER Mr Ron Dawson (NEWMARKET) BRED Sir Stanley Grinstead 11 Rn 2m 41.9 SF: 23/36/23/8/17/10/4/2/-/1/-

WEIGHT FOR AGE 4yo-3lb

390

GROCER MAIDEN H'CAP (0-65) (3-Y.O+) (Class F) £2,433.00 (£683.00: £333.00)
7f (Fibresand) Stalls: High GOING: 0.10 sec per fur (STD) 8-30 (8-31)

214¹⁰ **Brigadore Gold (24)***(29) (ABailey)* 5-8-5b LCharnock(9) (led 5f out: pushed clr appr fnl f: unchal) — 1
335⁵ Arrogant Boy **(34)***(30) (DWChapman)* 6-9-1 DeanMcKeown(10) (hdwy 4f out: 2nd st: rdn & outpcd fnl 2f) 4 2
315⁵ Nite-Owl Dancer **(58)***(51)*(Fav)*(JAHarris)* 3-9-8 GDuffield(11) (a.p: 4th & drvn along ent st: kpt on) 1¼ 3
Noble Neptune **(60)***(47) (WJMusson)* 3-9-5 (5) PMcCabe(3) (hld up: effrt over 2f out: 5th & rdn st: nt rch ldrs) 2½ 4
33³ Keeper's Grey **(56)***(23)*(Fav)*(RGuest)* 3-9-6b DHarrison(7) (chsd ldrs: 3rd st: rdn & wknd wl over 1f out) 9 5

*341*10 Crafty Cricketer **(19)** *(RMFlower)* 4-7-7 (7) CAdamson(2) (effrt & poor 6th st: sn rdn: no imp)...8 6
*199*W Lunar Prince **(40)** *(TTClement)* 5-9-7 AMackay(5) (s.s: nvr nrr)....1 7
*328*6 Dynamis (IRE) **(42)** *(KOCunningham-Brown)* 4-9-9 AClark(8) (s.i.s: a in rr)....2 8
*332*5 Sandra Dee (IRE) **(57)** *(BAPearce)* 3-9-4 (3) SSanders(1) (chsd ldrs: wkng whn hmpd 3f out)1¾ 9
Miss Katie Louise **(30)** *(APJames)* 4-8-11 JQuinn(4) (led 2f: wknd over 3f out: t.o)....20 10

5/2 Keeper's Grey, Nite-Owl Dancer, **5/1** Noble Neptune, Sandra Dee (IRE), **10/1** BRIGADORE GOLD, Dynamis (IRE), **12/1** Crafty Cricketer, **14/1** Arrogant Boy, **16/1** Miss Katie Louise, **25/1** Lunar Prince, CSF £132.97 CT £425.79 TOTE £49.70: £6.30 £2.90 £1.50 (£83.70) Trio £229.00; £203.22 to 6/3/95 OWNER Mr Alan Hart (TARPORLEY) BRED Mrs R. D. Peacock 10 Rn
1m 33.3 (9.30) SF: -/1/5/1/-/-/-/-/-/-
WEIGHT FOR AGE 3yo-17lb

391

COBBLER (S) STKS (4-Y.O+) (Class G) £2,085.00 (£585.00: £285.00)
5f (Fibresand) Stalls: High GOING: 0.10 sec per fur (STD) 9-00 (9-04)

*305*6 **Farfelu (72)***(57) (WRMuir)* 8-8-11b DHarrison(4) (lw: sn chsng ldr: rdn appr fnl f: r.o to ld wl ins fnl f)....— 1
*305*3 Very Dicey **(70)***(63)*(Fav)*(JBerry)* 7-8-11 (7) PRoberts(2) (led tl hdd wl ins fnl f: kpt on nr fin)...nk 2
*224*7 Samson-Agonistes **(65)***(45) (PDEvans)* 9-8-11 AClark(1) (b: disp ld early: rdn along ½-wy: r.o one pce)....3½ 3
331 10 Pat Poindestres **(30)** *(BAPearce)* 5-8-3 (3) SSanders(3) (lame at s) .... W

evens Very Dicey, **2/1** FARFELU, **3/1** Samson-Agonistes, **20/1** Pat Poindestres, CSF £4.05 TOTE £2.70: (£1.70) OWNER Mr John O'Mulloy (LAMBOURN) BRED Sean Collins 3 Rn
64.1 secs (6.10) SF: 2/8/-/-
No bid

392

BAKER H'CAP (0-70) (3-Y.O) (Class E) £2,775.00 (£840.00: £410.00: £195.00)
6f (Fibresand) Stalls: High GOING: 0.10 sec per fur (STD) 9-30 (9-33)

*284*4 **Crystal Loop (69)***(76)*(Fav)*(ABailey)* 3-9-2 (5) VHalliday(8) (led after 2f: clr ent st: v.easily)...— 1
*322*4 Sharp Holly (IRE) **(50)***(49) (JABennett)* 3-7-13 (3) DWright(9) (lw: dwlt: hdwy over 2f out: chsd wnr appr fnl f: no imp)....3 2
*258*11 Lawnswood Lady **(43)***(38) (RHollinshead)* 3-7-9 NCarlisle(4) (s.i.s: bhd tl hdwy fnl 2f: nrst fin)1½ 3
Rockcracker (IRE) **(65)***(55) (RCharlton)* 3-9-3 DHarrison(5) (bkwd: mid div: effrt & drvn along over 2f out: nvr able chal) 2 4
*274*2 Tinker Amelia **(48)***(27) (WRMuir)* 3-8-0 JQuinn(1) (chsd ldrs: nt clr run ent st: nt rcvr)....4 5
*305*2 Ivy Lilian (IRE) **(48)***(8) (WMBrisbourne)* 3-7-9 (5)ow3 AGarth(7) (led 2f: prom tl wknd ent st) 6 6
*306*4 Whittingham Girl **(60)***(22) (JBerry)* 3-8-12 JCarroll(3) (prom over 4f: sn outpcd) ....nk 7
*236*3 Nadwaty (IRE) **(52)***(13) (JDBethell)* 3-8-4 TWilliams(6) (disp ld 2f: wknd wl over 1f out)....½ 8
*243*8 Ho Mei Surprise **(48)** *(BPreece)* 3-8-0 LCharnock(2) (rdn along ½-wy: a in rr)....6 9
Jet Classic **(50)** *(RWEmery)* 3-8-2 GBardwell(10) (bkwd: spd to ½-wy: sn lost tch)....s.h 10

7/4 CRYSTAL LOOP, **3/1** Rockcracker (IRE), **9/2** Whittingham Girl, **5/1** Ivy Lilian (IRE), **12/1** Tinker Amelia, Nadwaty (IRE), **16/1** Sharp Holly (IRE), Lawnswood Lady, **25/1** Ho Mei Surprise, Jet Classic, CSF £30.60 CT £340.66 TOTE £3.00: £1.70 £2.70 £2.20 (£18.00) OWNER Mr Roy Matthews (TARPORLEY) BRED B. Long 10 Rn 1m 17.1 (5.90) SF: 31/4/-/10/-/-/-/-/-/-

T/Plpt £479.10. T/Qdpt £36.00 IM

0387-WOLVERHAMPTON (L-H)
Wednesday March 8th (Standard)

393

SANDSTORM H'CAP (0-70) (I) (4-Y.O+) (Class E) £3,023.90 (£915.20: £446.60: £212.30) **6f (Fibresand)** Stalls: Low GOING minus 0.05 sec (STD) 2-10 (2-10)

*307*2 **Ziggy's Dancer (USA) (66)***(75)*(Fav)*(EJAlston)* 4-9-12 DHolland(9) (chsd ldr: led over 3f out: qcknd clr appr fnl f: unchal)....— 1
The Old Chapel **(68)***(68) (BAMcMahon)* 6-10-0b JWeaver(5) (bkwd: led over 2f out: outpcd appr fnl f) 3½ 2
*233*8 Green's Bid **(55)***(48) (DWChapman)* 5-9-1 ACulhane(3) (hdwy fr over 1f out: nvr nrr) 2½ 3
*348*2 Monsieur Petong **(36)***(26) (JParkes)* 4-7-7 (3) DarrenMoffatt(8) (chsd ldrs: rdn over 2f out: kpt on one pce) 1¼ 4
Souperficial **(46)***(26) (JAGlover)* 4-8-6v MFenton(6) (chsd ldrs: no hdwy fnl 2f) 3½ 5
*328*2 The Institute Boy **(53)***(32) (MissJFCraze)* 5-8-13 SWebster(7) (chsd ldrs tl rdn & wknd over 1f out) ....½ 6
*386*5 Martinosky **(55)***(34) (GCBravery)* 9-9-1 GCarter(2) (bit bkwd: outpcd) ....hd 7

366[4] Letsbeonestaboutit **(56)***(31) (MrsNMacauley)* 9-9-2v DeanMcKeown(1) (sn rdn along: a bhd) 1½ **8**
338* Lady Roxanne **(47)***(11)*(Fav)*(LordHuntingdon)* 6-8-7v LDettori(4) (in tch: rdn & wknd wl over 1f out) 4 **9**

3/1 ZIGGY'S DANCER (USA) (op 2/1), Lady Roxanne, **4/1** The Institute Boy, **7/1** Monsieur Petong, **9/1** Souperficial, **10/1** The Old Chapel, Letsbeonestaboutit, **14/1** Martinosky, **25/1** Green's Bid, CSF £30.89 TOTE £3.90: £1.70 £2.70 £9.40 [£15.20] OWNER Mr John Patrick Barry (PRESTON) BRED Warren W. Rosenthal 9 Rn 1m 15.0 (3.80) SF: 52/45/25/3/3/9/11/8/-

394

TEMPEST MAIDEN STKS (3-Y.O+) (Class D) £3,775.20 (£1,143.60: £558.80: £266.40) **1m 100y (Fibresand)** Stalls: Low GOING minus 0.05 sec(STD) 2-40 (2-42)

Allemande (IRE) *(77)*(Fav)*(JHMGosden)* 3-8-6 LDettori(2) (unf: scope: mde all: shkn up & r.o wl fnl f) ....— **1**
Tatika *(74) (GWragg)* 5-9-10 WWoods(10) (bit bkwd: hld up & prom: 2nd st: ev ch appr fnl f: no ex) 1½ **2**
Howqua River **(54)***(59) (PWChapple-Hyam)* 3-8-3 (7)ow4 RHavlin(7) (bit bkwd: chsd ldrs: rdn over 3f out: 3rd st: r.o one pce) 8 **3**
Daleria *(47) (JLEyre)* 4-9-0 (5) JStack(6) (bit bkwd: a.p: rdn 3f out: 4th st: r.o one pce) 4 **4**
Adilov *(49) (JRFanshawe)* 3-8-1 (5) NVarley(9) (bkwd: hdwy ½-wy: 6th st: rdn & no imp fr bel dist) 1½ **5**
310[3] Happy Brave **(38)***(44) (PDCundell)* 3-8-6 RPrice(1) (prom tl 5th & wkng st) 2½ **6**
Asking *(37) (JABennett)* 3-8-6 DHolland(12) (leggy: lt-f: chsd ldrs on outside: rdn ½-wy: wknd 3f out) 3½ **7**
Miss Jemmima *(31) (LordHuntingdon)* 3-8-1 DaleGibson(13) (w'like: bkwd: chsd ldrs over 4f: sn lost tch) ....½ **8**
Pretty Scarce *(27) (SESherwood)* 4-9-0 (5) MFenton(11) (b.hind: mid div tl wknd over 2f out) 2½ **9**
Fraise du Roi (IRE) *(21) (LordHuntingdon)* 3-8-1 NCarlisle(4) (w'like: bkwd: a bhd & outpcd) 3 **10**
294[3] Speedy Snaps Pride **(45)***(11) (PDCundell)* 3-8-6 AMackay(5) (lost pl ½-wy: t.o) 8 **11**
352[9] Danson *(THCaldwell)* 4-9-10 GDuffield(8) (prom tl wknd over 3f out: t.o) 15 **12**
223[6] Noon Air *(RHollinshead)* 4-9-5 MWigham(3) (s.i.s: a bhd: t.o) 5 **13**

4/7 ALLEMANDE (IRE), **7/1** Tatika (op 7/2), **9/1** Adilov, **14/1** Howqua River, Daleria, Speedy Snaps Pride, **16/1** Pretty Scarce, **20/1** Fraise du Roi (IRE), Miss Jemmima, **25/1** Happy Brave, **33/1** Danson, **50/1** Asking, **66/1** Noon Air, CSF £6.52 TOTE: £1.70 £1.10 £1.50 £2.40 [£3.00] OWNER Sheikh Mohammed (NEWMARKET) 13 Rn 1m 49.3 (5.30) SF: 36/51/18/24/8/3/-/-/4/-/-/-/-
WEIGHT FOR AGE 3yo-18lb

395

CYCLONE H'CAP (0-80) (3-Y.O+) (Class D) £4,045.50 (£1,224.00: £597.00: £283.50) **1m 100y (Fibresand)** Stalls: Low GOING: 0.05 sec (STD) 3-10 (3-11)

309[2] **Our Tom (59)***(68) (JWharton)* 3-8-2 NCarlisle(3) (lw: hld up: effrt & 3rd st: led jst ins fnl f: veered rt: sn clr: readily) ....— **1**
332* Renown **(65)***(69)*(Fav)*(LordHuntingdon)* 3-8-8 LDettori(6) (w ldr tl led over 4f out: rdn & hdd ins fnl f: no ex) 2½ **2**
Grey Again **(54)***(55) (SRBowring)* 3-7-11 ow1 TWilliams(4) (swtg: chsd ldrs: 2nd & ev ch st: one pce fnl f) 1¼ **3**
384[2] Bakers Daughter **(53)***(44) (JRArnold)* 3-7-7 (3)ow1 DWright(5) (led over 4f: 4th & wkng st) 5 **4**
90* Legally Delicious **(54)***(24) (JEBanks)* 3-7-6 (5) MBaird(1) (hld up: hdwy 5f out: 5th & btn st: t.o)12 **5**
Owdbetts (IRE) **(78)***(33) (GLMoore)* 3-9-0 (7) LSuthern(2) (chsd ldrs 5f: sn lost tch: 6th st: t.o) .8 **6**

5/4 Renown, **4/1** OUR TOM, Bakers Daughter, Legally Delicious, **14/1** Owdbetts (IRE), **25/1** Grey Again, CSF £9.35 TOTE: £6.10 £2.50 £1.10 [£3.10] OWNER Mr J. M. Berry (MELTON MOWBRAY) BRED Bylon Farmers Ltd 6 Rn 1m 50.7 (6.70) SF: 19/20/6/-/-/-

396

HURRICANE H'CAP (0-90) (4-Y.O+) (Class C) £5,576.00 (£1,688.00: £824.00: £392.00)
1m 4f (Fibresand) Stalls: Low GOING minus 0.05 sec per fur (STD) 3-40 (3-41)

325[3] **Johns Act (USA) (68)***(74) (DHaydnJones)* 5-8-13v KDarley(12) (a.p: led over 3f out: rdn & r.o wl towards fin) ....— **1**
377[3] Mad Militant (IRE) **(70)***(75) (RHollinshead)* 6-9-1 WRyan(9) (hld up & bhd: hdwy 5f out: wnt 2nd st: ev ch fnl f: jst hld) ....½ **2**
325[6] Mentalasanythin **(72)***(73) (ABailey)* 6-9-3 AMackay(8) (chsd ldrs: rdn 5f out: 5th st: styd on fnl f) 3½ **3**

325* Noufari (FR) **(85)***(82)*(Fav)*(RHollinshead)* 4-9-13 MWigham(3) (bmpd s: bhd: rdn ½-wy: hdwy 5f out: 6th st: styd on appr fnl f)....2½ 4
325⁴ Hillzah (USA) **(83)***(78) (RBastiman)* 7-9-9 (5) HBastiman(4) (prom: 3rd st: wknd over 1f out)..1½ 5
318³ Prince Danzig (IRE) **(77)***(67) (DJGMurraySmith)* 4-9-5 JWeaver(7) (led 7f: 7th & wkng st) 4 6
389⁶ Awestruck **(51)***(35) (BPreece)* 5-7-10 ow1 LCharnock(10) (a in rr) 4 7
364³ Legal Fiction **(76)***(61) (MJohnston)* 4-9-4 DHolland(11) (prom: led 5f out tl over 3f out: 4th st: eased whn btn bel dist)....hd 8
303⁹ Thaleros **(64)***(22) (GMMoore)* 5-8-9 TWilliams(6) (prom 9f: wknd qckly: t.o)....20 9
304* Pontynyswen **(51)** *(DBurchell)* 7-7-7b(3)ow3 DWright(2) (a bhd: rdn 8f out: t.o)....5 10
206² One Off the Rail (USA) **(77)***(24) (AMoore)* 5-9-8 CandyMorris(5) (b.hind: prom 7f: sn wknd: t.o)....3½ 11
325⁵ Chimborazo **(72)***(12) (BJMcMath)* 4-9-0 LDettori(1) (hld up: rdn ½-wy: sn bhd: t.o)....5 12

LONG HANDICAP Pontynyswen 7-2

7/2 Noufari (FR), **5/1** JOHNS ACT (USA), **11/2** Legal Fiction, **6/1** Pontynyswen, **13/2** Chimborazo, **8/1** Prince Danzig (IRE), **10/1** Mad Militant (IRE), **12/1** Hillzah (USA), **14/1** Mentalasanythin, **16/1** Awestruck, One Off the Rail (USA), Thaleros, CSF £55.43 TC £628.16 TOTE £8.30: £2.00 £2.90 £5.60 [£19.00] Trio £166.90 OWNER Jack Brown (Bookmaker) Ltd (PONTYPRIDD) BRED Galloping Acres Farm 12 Rn 2m 38.4 SF: 45/46/44/50/49/35/6/29/-/-/-/-

WEIGHT FOR AGE 4yo-3lb

397

BLIZZARD (S) STKS (I) (4-Y.O+) (Class G) £2,433.00 (£683.00: £333.00)
1m 1f 79y (Fibresand) Stalls: Low GOING minus 0.05 sec per fur (STD) 4-10 (4-12)

302⁶ **Gallery Artist (IRE) (55)***(53)*(Fav)*(RGuest)* 7-8-12 LDettori(2) (a.p: led over 2f out: rdn ins fnl f: r.o wl)....— 1
387⁹ Swynford Flyer **(48)***(45) (JAHarris)* 6-8-7 DHolland(5) (hld up: hdwy 5f out: 3rd st: ev ch 1f out: nt qckn)....1½ 2
343* Eastleigh **(48)***(53) (RHollinshead)* 6-9-4 WRyan(8) (hld up: 5th st: styd on fnl f) 1¾ 3
Hill Farm Katie **(45)***(42) (WMBrisbourne)* 4-8-1 (5) AGarth(9) (a.p: jnd ldrs tl over 3f out: sn rdn: 2nd st: ev ch 1f out: one pce)....½ 4
Fabulous Princess (IRE) **(42)***(33) (CLPopham)* 4-8-6 BDoyle(1) (nvr nr to chal)....5 5
142⁶ Joint Effort (IRE) **(43)***(26) (AMoore)* 4-8-6 TWilliams(3) (b.hind: lw: hdwy & 6th st: no imp)......4 6
334² Hi Penny **(43)***(24) (KTIvory)* 4-8-1b(7)ow2 CScally(7) (prom: led over 4f out tl over 2f out: 4th st: wknd over 1f out)....1¼ 7
Deputy Tim **(30)***(9) (RBastiman)* 12-8-12 LCharnock(6) (bit bkwd: led over 4f: wknd over 2f out: t.o)....12 8
Boxboy **(25)***(8) (GHYardley)* 5-8-12 RPrice(4) (bit bkwd: a bhd: t.o)....hd 9
Cobbs Cross **(42)** *(THCaldwell)* 5-8-12 GDuffield(10) (plld hrd: prom tl wknd 4f out: t.o) 8 10

2/1 GALLERY ARTIST (IRE), **3/1** Eastleigh, **4/1** Swynford Flyer, Hi Penny, **7/1** Joint Effort (IRE), **16/1** Deputy Tim, **20/1** Fabulous Princess (IRE), **25/1** Cobbs Cross, **33/1** Hill Farm Katie, **50/1** Boxboy, CSF £11.47 TOTE: £3.80 £1.80 £1.70 £1.50 [£9.50] OWNER Mr Rae Guest (NEWMARKET) BRED Viscount de Vesci 10 Rn 2m 2.7 (6.70) SF: 35/27/35/23/14/7/5/-/-/-

WEIGHT FOR AGE 4yo-1lb

No bid

398

TORNADO H'CAP (0-80) (3-Y.O+) (Class D) £3,707.60 (£1,122.80: £548.40: £261.20) **5f (Fibresand)** Stalls: Low GOING minus 0.05 sec (STD) 4-40 (4-42)

Saddlehome (USA) (75)*(85) (TDBarron)* 6-9-12 KDarley(2) (a gng wl: shkn up to ld ins fnl f: r.o wl)....— 1
353² Chadwell Hall **(49)***(55) (SRBowring)* 4-8-0b TWilliams(11) (b.hind: w ldrs: ev ch 1f out: nt qckn)....1¼ 2
306³ Primula Bairn **(60)***(60) (MrsJRRamsden)* 5-8-11v JWeaver(3) (lw: led tl ins fnl f)....2 3
King Rambo **(63)***(62) (RHollinshead)* 4-9-0 WRyan(10) (bkwd: a.p: nt qckn appr fnl f)............nk 4
327⁴ Scored Again **(62)***(59) (MJHeaton-Ellis)* 5-8-6 (7) AmandaSanders(6) (b: a.p: ev ch wl over 1f out: r.o one pce)....½ 5
380² Leigh Crofter **(76)***(65) (PDCundell)* 6-9-8v(5) DGriffiths(9) (nvr nr to chal)....2½ 6
345² Lord Sky **(77)***(64)*(Fav)*(ABailey)* 4-10-0v LDettori(5) (chsd ldrs: rdn 2f out: no hdwy)....¾ 7
My Cherrywell **(50)***(36) (LRLloyd-James)* 5-8-1b NKennedy(7) (b.hind: bkwd: dwlt: nvr nrr)....nk 8
369* Kalar **(71)***(56) (DWChapman)* 6-9-1b(7) 7x CTeague(4) (hld up & plld hrd: nvr plcd to chal)......nk 9
Swan At Whalley **(80)***(58) (JBerry)* 3-9-3 JCarroll(13) (prom tl wknd qckly over 1f out)....2 10
380⁷ Gondo **(60)** *(EJAlston)* 8-8-11 DHolland(8) (a bhd: t.o)....13 11
La Belle Dominique **(64)** *(SGKnight)* 3-7-12 (3) DarrenMoffatt(1) (a bhd)....4 12
342⁵ Saltz (IRE) **(70)** *(PTDalton)* 3-8-4 (3) SSanders(12) (b.hind: racd wd: prom tl wknd over 2f out)....1½ 13

2/1 Lord Sky, **3/1** Primula Bairn (op 5/1), **5/1** Leigh Crofter, **9/1** Chadwell Hall, **10/1** SADDLEHOME (USA), Kalar, **12/1** Scored Again, **16/1** Swan At Whalley, **20/1** King Rambo, **25/1** My Cherrywell, Gondo, La Belle Dominique, Saltz (IRE), CSF £97.18 TC £310.92 TOTE £12.80: £3.80 £3.30 £2.50 [£286.80] Trio £78.40 OWNER Mr Kevin Shaw (THIRSK) BRED Saddle Home Farm in USA
13 Rn 61.6 secs (3.60) SF: 44/14/19/21/18/24/23/-/15/3/-/-/-
WEIGHT FOR AGE 3yo-14lb

399

BLIZZARD (S) STKS (II) (4-Y.O+) (Class G) £2,433.00 (£683.00: £333.00)
1m 1f 79y (Fibresand) Stalls: Low GOING minus 0.05 sec per fur (STD) 5-10 (5-10)

*379** **No Submission (USA) (70)***(75)*(Fav)*(DWChapman)* 9-9-4 DeanMcKeown(8) (chsd ldr: led over 3f out: clr over 1f out: drvn out)..........— **1**
*336*4 Kristis Girl **(42)***(42) (DHaydnJones)* 8-8-7 AMackay(4) (hld up & bhd: rdn & hdwy over 4f out: 3rd st: r.o wl fnl f: no ch w wnr)..........13 **2**
*343*9 Ballyhays (IRE) **(38)***(52) (JAHarris)* 6-9-4 DaleGibson(9) (a.p: hrd rdn & 2nd st: one pce)......nk **3**
*308*2 T O O Mamma's (IRE) **(57)***(29) (JBerry)* 4-8-6 JCarroll(3) (prom: hrd rdn 4f out: 5th & btn st)..........7 **4**
*351*6 Anorak (USA) **(50)***(33) (GMMoore)* 5-8-12v JWeaver(1) (bhd: rdn 5f out: hdwy 4f out: 6th & wkng st)..........½ **5**
*323*6 Backstabber **(38)***(31) (MissSJWilton)* 5-8-7 (5) JStack(7) (bit bkwd: led tl over 3f out: 4th & wkng st)..........1½ **6**
Delmour **(25)** *(WMBrisbourne)* 4-8-6 (5) AGarth(6) (swtg: s.s: a wl bhd: t.o)..........dist **7**
Bustle'em (IRE) **(45)** *(DMcCain)* 4-8-6 KDarley(5) (bit bkwd: s.s: a wl bhd: t.o)..........25 **8**

Evens NO SUBMISSION (USA), **15/8** T O O Mamma's (IRE), **11/4** Anorak (USA) (op 5/1), **14/1** Bustle'em (IRE), **25/1** Kristis Girl, **33/1** Delmour, Ballyhays (IRE), **40/1** Backstabber, CSF £25.57 TOTE £2.00: £1.10 £2.00 £4.60 [£17.40] OWNER Mr T. S. Redman (YORK) BRED Mr. Francis X. Weber 8 Rn 2m 2.0 (6.00) SF: 52/19/29/5/10/8/-/-
WEIGHT FOR AGE 4yo-1lb
No bid

400

SANDSTORM H'CAP (0-70) (II) (4-Y.O+) (Class E) £3,023.90 (£915.20: £446.60: £212.30)
6f (Fibresand) Stalls: Low GOING minus 0.05 sec per fur (STD) 5-40 (5-40)

*297** **White Sorrel (66)***(82)*(Fav)*(JLEyre)* 4-9-7 (5) JStack(8) (mde all: clr over 1f out: easily)..........— **1**
*338*4 Wellsy Lad (USA) **(33)***(28) (DWChapman)* 8-7-7b NCarlisle(3) (w ldrs: 2nd st: btn whn edgd rt fnl f)..........8 **2**
*306*7 Heathyards Lady (USA) **(50)***(40) (RHollinshead)* 4-8-10 WRyan(9) (chsd ldrs: 6th st: r.o one pce fnl f)..........1¾ **3**
Plum First **(52)***(39) (LRLloyd-James)* 5-8-12 NKennedy(2) (b: b.hind: bit bkwd: hdwy over 1f out: r.o one pce fnl f)..........1 **4**
*307*8 Jon's Choice **(59)***(46) (BPreece)* 7-9-5 TWall(4) (prom: rdn 3f out: 3rd st: wknd over 1f out)..........s.h **5**
*338*5 Matthew David **(44)***(28) (SRBowring)* 5-8-4 TWilliams(6) (b: b.hind: s.s: rdn st: no hdwy).....1¼ **6**
*344*6 Apollo Red **(51)***(33) (AMoore)* 6-8-11 CandyMorris(5) (w wnr 3f: 4th & wkng st)..........¾ **7**
*353** Farmer Jock **(47)** *(MrsNMacauley)* 13-8-7 7x AClark(1) (bhd whn hung bdly rt 2f out: t.o)......12 **8**
*337*2 Orthorhombus **(52)** *(DJSCosgrove)* 6-8-9b(3) DRMcCabe(7) (b: lw: s.s: a t.o)..........11 **9**

4/5 WHITE SORREL, **6/1** Matthew David, **7/1** Wellsy Lad (USA), Orthorhombus, **9/1** Farmer Jock, Heathyards Lady (USA), **10/1** Apollo Red, **25/1** Jon's Choice, Plum First, CSF £8.56 TC £34.23 TOTE £1.70: £1.50 £1.90 £1.10 [£17.90] Trio £39.20 OWNER Mr R. Fenwick-Gibson (HAMBLETON) BRED Stud-On-The-Chart 9 Rn 1m 13.8 (2.60) SF: 69/15/27/26/33/15/20/-/-

T/Plpt: £93.30 (228.94 Tckts). T/Qdpt: £64.00 (0.4 Tckts); £51.96 to Wincanton 9/3/95. KH

0381-LINGFIELD (L-H)
Thursday March 16th (Standard)

401

MOSQUITO CLAIMING STKS (I) (3-Y.O+) (Class E) £3,066.80 (£928.40: £453.20: £215.60)
7f (Equitrack) Stalls: High GOING minus 0.57 sec per fur (FST) 1-40 (1-41)

*358*3 **Greatest (60)***(73) (RAkehurst)* 4-9-3 GCarter(1) (led over 5f: hrd rdn: led last strides)..........— **1**
*383*4 Mr Nevermind (IRE) **(75)***(78) (GLMoore)* 5-9-8 BRouse(5) (hdwy: rdn over 3f out: hdwy over 1f out: hrd rdn fnl f: r.o wl)..........s.h **2**
*358*2 Spencer's Revenge **(75)***(77)*(Fav)*(LordHuntingdon)* 6-9-7 LDettori(6) (hdwy over 3f out: led over 1f out: hrd rdn: hdd last strides)..........hd **3**

*349*11 Slytly Beveled **(55)***(66) (NPLittmoden)* 3-8-3 (5)ow4 TGMcLaughlin(2) (lw: hdwy over 1f out: r.o)....4 4
*383*5 Perilous Plight **(76)***(70) (WRMuir)* 4-9-12 JWeaver(3) (lw: hdwy wl over 1f out: hrd rdn: one pce)....1¼ 5
*390*9 Sandra Dee (IRE) **(54)***(56) (BAPearce)* 3-7-9 (3)ow1 SSanders(9) (lw: a.p: rdn over 3f out: wknd over 1f out)....¾ 6
*400*7 Apollo Red **(51)***(57) (AMoore)* 6-9-4v CandyMorris(4) (b.hind: w ldr over 4f)....1¼ 7
Aragrove **(52)***(52) (JWPayne)* 5-9-8 GBardwell(7) (prom over 3f)....4 8
*332*2 Breckland (IRE) **(47)***(35) (KOCunningham-Brown)* 5-9-2b TIves(8) (b.hind: a bhd)....5 9

13/8 Spencer's Revenge, **3/1** Mr Nevermind (IRE), Perilous Plight, **8/1** GREATEST, **14/1** Breckland (IRE), Sandra Dee (IRE), **20/1** Apollo Red, **25/1** Slytly Beveled, **33/1** Aragrove, CSF £32.47 TOTE £9.30: £1.50 £1.50 £1.10 [£23.10] OWNER Invoshire Ltd (EPSOM) BRED Bloomsbury Stud 9 Rn
1m 25.12 (2.12) SF: 28/33/32/5/25/-/12/7/-
WEIGHT FOR AGE 3yo-16lb

402

WELLINGTON AMATEUR H'CAP (0-60) (I) (3-Y.O+) (Class F)
£2,726.00 (£766.00: £374.00)
1m (Equitrack) Stalls: Low GOING minus 0.57 sec per fur (FST) 2-10 (2-12)

*393*3 **Green's Bid (55)***(62) (DWChapman)* 5-11-0 (5) MissRClark(9) (lw: a.p: led wl over 1f out: all out)....— 1
*373*5 Sherblu **(42)***(49) (JFfitch-Heyes)* 4-10-3 (3) MrTMcCarthy(1) (dwlt: hdwy over 3f out: ev ch over fnl 2f: r.o wl)....s.h 2
*285*2 Don't Drop Bombs (USA) **(35)***(30) (DTThom)* 6-9-13v MissJFeilden(8) (lw: led over 6f: unable to qckn)....6 3
*387*4 Zahran (IRE) **(57)***(49) (JMBradley)* 4-11-7 MrTCuff(4) (b: lw: lost pl over 5f out: r.o one pce fnl f)....1½ 4
*343*4 Dome Patrol **(47)***(31) (WRMuir)* 4-10-4 (7) MissSDalton(2) (lw: hmpd & dropped rr over 6f out: rallied over 1f out: one pce)....4 5
*248*9 Christian Spirit **(48)***(25) (BAPearce)* 5-10-5 (7)ow20 MrRBlyth(10) (b: a.p: rdn over 3f out: wknd over 2f out)....hd 6
*122*7 Storm Bidder **(41)***(25) (BGubby)* 4-10-0v(5) MrsMBusby(7) (led over 1f: hmpd 5f out: wknd over 2f out)....s.h 7
*265*3 Respectable Jones **(49)***(30)*(Fav)*(RHollinshead)* 9-10-8 (5) MissJSouthall(6) (lw: hld up: r.o wl over 1f out: sn wknd)....1¼ 8
*267*10 Rosina's Folly **(47)***(21) (JLHarris)* 4-10-6 (5) MrIMcLelland(5) (dwlt: a bhd)....3½ 9
*161*9 Kentavrus Way (IRE) **(45)***(11) (AMoore)* 4-10-2 (7) MrsJMoore(3) (b.hind: a bhd)....4 10
*234*15 Asaaf (USA) **(25)** *(NPLittmoden)* 12-8-10b(7)ow1 MrMSalaman(11) (a bhd)....15 11
LONG HANDICAP Asaaf (USA) 9-8

5/2 Respectable Jones, **100/30** Don't Drop Bombs (USA), **9/2** Dome Patrol, **6/1** Zahran (IRE), **7/1** Sherblu, **10/1** GREEN'S BID, **12/1** Rosina's Folly, **20/1** Kentavrus Way (IRE), **33/1** Storm Bidder, **66/1** Christian Spirit, Asaaf (USA), CSF £74.70 CT £261.49 TOTE £11.70: £1.70 £2.30 £1.60 [£32.20] OWNER Mr J. M. Chapman (YORK) BRED Stud-On-The-Chart 11 Rn
1m 40.33 (3.93) SF: 42/29/10/29/11/5/5/10/1/-/-

403

MK ELECTRIC H'CAP (0-80) (4-Y.O+) (Class D) £3,690.70
(£1,117.60: £545.80: £259.90)
1m 4f (Equitrack) Stalls: High GOING minus 0.57 sec per fur (FST) 2-40 (2-44)

*396*6 **Prince Danzig (IRE) (77)***(84) (DJGMurraySmith)* 4-9-12 JWeaver(10) (lw: hdwy over 2f out: str run fnl f: led wl ins fnl f: r.o wl)....— 1
*318*7 Able Choice (IRE) **(70)***(75) (RWArmstrong)* 5-9-7 LDettori(1) (led over 8f: led over 2f out tl wl ins fnl f: unable to qckn)....1¾ 2
*396*11 One Off the Rail (USA) **(77)***(80) (AMoore)* 5-9-7 (7) LSuthern(6) (b.hind: lw: a.p: led over 3f out to over 2f out: hrd rdn over 1f out: one pce)....1¼ 3
*367** In the Money (IRE) **(60)***(60) (RHollinshead)* 6-8-11 WRyan(3) (chsd ldr over 8f: one pce)....2 4
*318*6 Global Dancer **(69)***(61) (WAO'Gorman)* 4-9-1 (3) EmmaO'Gorman(5) (hld up: rdn over 3f out: wknd over 2f out)....6 5
*87*6 Beautete **(70)***(58) (SDow)* 4-9-5 DHarrison(7) (lw: hdwy over 4f out: wknd over 2f out)....3½ 6
*367*5 Bandita **(46)***(33) (MissAJWhitfield)* 4-7-9 ow1 JQuinn(11) (lw: nvr nr to chal)....nk 7
*321*8 Telephus **(45)***(29) (BJMcMath)* 6-7-3 (7) MartinDwyer(13) (nvr nrr)....2½ 8
*377*2 Power **(76)***(58)*(Fav)*(CEBrittain)* 4-9-11 MRimmer(14) (b.hind: prom over 7f)....1¾ 9
*356*3 Dancing Sensation (USA) **(50)***(31) (RAkehurst)* 8-7-12e(3) SSanders(2) (prom over 8f)....nk 10
*321*3 Ikhtiraa (USA) **(62)***(42) (RJO'Sullivan)* 5-8-13 WWoods(8) (b: lw: bhd fnl 5f)....1¼ 11
*329*2 Lon Isa **(50)***(27) (BPalling)* 4-7-6 (7) CAdamson(12) (prom over 7f)....2 12
*361*3 General Chase **(42)***(15) (ICampbell)* 5-7-7 GBardwell(9) (lw: a bhd)....3 13

347[9] Kingsfold Fountain **(44)** *(MJHaynes)* 4-7-7 NAdams(4) (b.hind: a bhd) 20 **14**
LONG HANDICAP Kingsfold Fountain 7-5

3/1 Power, **4/1** Ikhtiraa (USA), **9/2** Able Choice (IRE), **7/1** Dancing Sensation (USA), **8/1** Global Dancer, In the Money (IRE), **10/1** PRINCE DANZIG (IRE), **12/1** Beautete, Lon Isa, **14/1** General Chase, **20/1** One Off the Rail (USA), Telephus, **25/1** Bandita, Kingsfold Fountain, CSF £61.13 TC £860.90 TOTE £18.20: £4.00 £3.60 £7.10 [£75.00] OWNER Mr A. H. Ulrick (LAMBOURN) BRED J. N. McCaffrey in Ireland 14 Rn 2m 30.89 (1.49) SF: 54/47/52/32/31/28/3/1/28/3/14/-/-/-
WEIGHT FOR AGE 4yo-2lb

OFFICIAL EXPLANATION Ikhtiraa (USA): The jockey reported that Ikhtiraa had been outpaced and, unable to race in a prominent position, disliked the kickback and did not respond when asked to quicken.

404 LANCASTER CLAIMING STKS (3-Y.O+) (Class F) £2,839.40 (£798.40: £390.20)
6f (Equitrack) Stalls: High GOING: minus 0.57 sec per fur (FST) 3-10 (3-13)

345[5] **Sir Tasker (69)***(80) (JLHarris)* 7-9-3 (3) SSanders(14) (mde all: clr 3f out: unchal)....— **1**
336[3] Rocky Waters (USA) **(78)***(67)*(Fav)*(GLMoore)* 6-9-9 BRouse(3) (hdwy over 2f out: chsd wnr over 2f out: r.o)....6 **2**
269[11] Twice in Bundoran (IRE) **(42)***(44) (PSFelgate)* 4-8-4 (5) PMcCabe(1) (hdwy over 1f out: r.o)....3½ **3**
386[4] Assignment **(58)***(47) (JFfitch-Heyes)* 9-8-12 DBiggs(2) (b: lost pl 3f out: rallied over 1f out: one pce)....s.h **4**
363[3] Dark Shot (IRE) **(76)***(53) (JBerry)* 3-8-10 JCarroll(11) (a.p: rdn over 4f out: wknd over 1f out)..2 **5**
348[8] Waverley Star **(40)***(37) (KOCunningham-Brown)* 10-8-12b GCarter(4) (a.p: rdn over 3f out: wknd over 1f out)....1½ **6**
Pearl Dawn (IRE) *(33) (NoelChance)* 5-9-3 TIves(10) (outpcd)....3½ **7**
Father Tim (IRE) *(37) (JMBradley)* 5-9-7 (5) SDrowne(9) (s.s: a bhd)....1¾ **8**
391[3] Samson-Agonistes **(63)***(27) (PDEvans)* 9-9-2 LDettori(6) (b: prom over 2f)....hd **9**
Flutter With Life **(30)***(8) (MrsAEJermy)* 4-8-10 JWilliams(7) (a bhd)....5 **10**
358[5] Bold Cyrano (IRE) **(46)** *(BPalling)* 4-8-12 JWeaver(5) (lw: a bhd)....10 **11**

9/4 Rocky Waters (USA), **4/1** Pearl Dawn (IRE), Dark Shot (IRE), **6/1** SIR TASKER, Samson-Agonistes, **7/1** Assignment, **20/1** Waverley Star, **33/1** Twice in Bundoran (IRE), Flutter With Life, **50/1** Father Tim (IRE), Bold Cyrano (IRE), CSF £20.20 TOTE £8.90: £2.10 £1.70 £33.80 [£18.70] OWNER Mr J. F. Coupland (MELTON MOWBRAY) BRED W. H. Joyce 11 Rn
1m 11.33 (0.73) SF: 45/32/9/12/4/2/-/2/-/-/-
WEIGHT FOR AGE 3yo-14lb

405 MOSQUITO CLAIMING STKS (II) (3-Y.O+) (Class E) £3,052.50 (£924.00: £451.00: £214.50)
7f (Equitrack) Stalls: High GOING minus 0.57 sec per fur (FST) 3-45 (3-45)

382* **Gulf Shaadi (83)***(81)*(Fav)*(GLewis)* 3-8-10 SWhitworth(1) (lw: hdwy over 2f out: hrd rdn over 1f out: led last strides)....— **1**
Soaking **(66)***(74) (GLMoore)* 5-9-5 BRouse(7) (led 6f out: hrd rdn fnl f: hdd last strides) ....hd **2**
358* Sweet Supposin (IRE) **(75)***(78) (KMcAuliffe)* 4-9-6b(3) JTate(9) (lw: hdwy over 4f out: hrd rdn over 1f out: r.o wl)....hd **3**
359[3] Crystal Heights (FR) **(63)***(53) (RJO'Sullivan)* 7-9-5 WWoods(8) (b: hdwy over 4f out: wknd over 1f out)....9 **4**
397[6] Joint Effort (IRE) **(43)***(29) (AMoore)* 4-8-6 (3) SSanders(5) (b.hind: hld up: rdn over 4f out: wknd over 3f out)....6 **5**
353[7] Havana Miss **(38)***(29) (BPalling)* 3-7-8 ow1 NCarlisle(2) (lw: led 1f: wknd 4f out)....½ **6**
Marjorie's Orchid **(47)***(20) (MJHeaton-Ellis)* 4-9-3 StephenDavies(4) (prom 4f)....7 **7**
Noor El Houdah (IRE) **(63)***(15) (JBerry)* 3-8-3 JCarroll(6) (bhd fnl 4f)....3 **8**

4/5 GULF SHAADI, **3/1** Sweet Supposin (IRE), **9/2** Crystal Heights (FR), **5/1** Noor El Houdah (IRE), **12/1** Soaking, **20/1** Marjorie's Orchid, Joint Effort (IRE), **33/1** Havana Miss, CSF £13.56 TOTE £1.90: £1.10 £3.50 £1.60 [£18.40] OWNER Laurel (Leisure) Ltd (EPSOM) BRED Sheikh Mohammed bin Rashid al Maktoum 8 Rn 1m 24.72 (1.72) SF: 27/36/40/15/-/-/-/-
WEIGHT FOR AGE 3yo-16lb

406 BEAUFORT H'CAP (0-80) (4-Y.O+) (Class D) £3,673.80 (£1,112.40: £543.20: £258.60)
1m 2f (Equitrack) Stalls: High GOING: minus 0.57 sec per fur (FST) 4-15 (4-20)

312[4] **Camden's Ransom (USA) (55)** *(HGRowsell)* 8-8-5 BDoyle(2) (a.p: rdn 2f out: led ins fnl f: r.o wl)....— **1**

3215 Zuno Noelyn **(54)** *(RAkehurst)* 4-8-3 GCarter(6) (rdn over 3f out: hdwy 2f out: r.o wl ins fnl f) ....nk 2
364* Kintwyn **(75)***(17) (CCElsey)* 5-9-11 DHarrison(3) (b.hind: chsd ldr: led over 7f out tl ins fnl f: unable qckn) 1½ 3
3552 Captain Marmalade **(50)** *(DTThom)* 6-8-0 JQuinn(7) (lw: hdwy on ins over 1f out: r.o) ....hd 4
3733 Possibility **(45)** *(RIngram)* 4-7-8bow1 NCarlisle(9) (hdwy over 1f out: r.o wl ins fnl f) 1 5
3572 Lady Reema **(50)** *(MissAJWhitfield)* 4-7-6 (7) CAdamson(4) (a.p: rdn over 3f out: one pce) ...1½ 6
3648 Master Beveled **(70)***(6) (PDEvans)* 5-9-1 (5) JStack(12) (lw: a.p: rdn over 3f out: wknd over 1f out) 1½ 7
3127 Braveboy **(59)** *(CEBrittain)* 7-8-9 MRimmer(10) (b.hind: hld up: rdn 4f out: wknd over 2f out) 1¼ 8
3734 Lady Williams (IRE) **(59)** (Fav)*(LordHuntingdon)* 4-8-8 LDettori(1) (led over 2f: ev ch over 1f out: wknd fnl f) 1¼ 9
318* Roman Reel (USA) **(62)** *(GLMoore)* 4-8-11 BRouse(13) (lw: hdwy over 3f out: wknd over 2f out) 2½ 10
3646 Bentico **(74)** *(MrsNMacauley)* 6-9-10 JWeaver(11) (a bhd) 1 11
3172 Awesome Power **(70)** *(JWHills)* 9-8-13 (7) MHenry(8) (prom over 7f) 1 12
3854 Irish Emerald **(60)** *(GCBravery)* 8-8-10 SWhitworth(14) (b: bit bkwd: a bhd) 2 13
Ebony Blaze **(49)** *(CPWildman)* 4-7-12 ow2 StephenDavies(5) (bhd fnl 8f) 7 14

LONG HANDICAP Possibility 7-3

5/1 Lady Williams (IRE), **6/1** Kintwyn, Zuno Noelyn, **8/1** Bentico, **9/1** CAMDEN'S RANSOM (USA), Captain Marmalade, Roman Reel (USA), **10/1** Possibility, **11/1** Awesome Power, Master Beveled, **12/1** Braveboy, **14/1** Lady Reema, **20/1** Ebony Blaze, **25/1** Irish Emerald, CSF £63.99 TC £334.33 TOTE £23.50: £4.00 £5.20 £3.50 [£66.80] OWNER Mr E. Cobelli (WINCHESTER) BRED Dr and Mrs Chris Elia and Phil Needham 14 Rn 2m 5.37 (2.37) SF: -/-/17/-/-/-/6/-/-/-/-/-/-/-
WEIGHT FOR AGE 4yo-1lb

407 STIRLING H'CAP (0-70) (3-Y.O+) (Class E) £3,052.50 (£924.00: £451.00: £214.50)
5f (Equitrack) Stalls: Low GOING minus 0.57 sec per fur (FST) 4-45 (4-47)

3422 **Dolly Face (66)***(72) (WRMuir)* 3-8-11 JWeaver(8) (chsd ldr: hrd rdn fnl f: led last stride) ....— 1
3692 Nordico Princess **(68)***(74)*(Fav)*(GROldroyd)* 4-9-12 LDettori(3) (led: hrd rdn fnl f: hdd last stride) ....s.h 2
2472 Distant Dynasty **(56)***(51) (BAPearce)* 5-8-11 (3) SSanders(7) (hdwy over 3f out: hrd rdn over 1f out: one pce) 3½ 3
36512 Rossini Blue **(67)***(62) (ABailey)* 4-9-6 (5) VHalliday(5) (hld up: rdn over 2f out: one pce) ....s.h 4
268* Shadow Jury **(57)***(49) (DWChapman)* 5-9-1b DeanMcKeown(6) (nvr nr to chal) ....¾ 5
1776 African Chimes **(69)***(60) (WAO'Gorman)* 8-9-10b(3) EmmaO'Gorman(2) (hdwy on ins over 1f out: one pce) ....½ 6
3936 The Institute Boy **(53)***(32) (MissJFCraze)* 5-8-11 JMcLaughlin(4) (s.s: a bhd) 3½ 7
2444 Baton Bleu **(43)** *(PHowling)* 4-8-1 JQuinn(10) (b: a bhd) 9 8
Lincstone Boy (IRE) **(51)** *(MissJFCraze)* 7-8-9b SWebster(9) (5th whn hmpd & uns rdr over 2f out) .... U

9/4 Nordico Princess, **7/2** DOLLY FACE, African Chimes, **8/1** The Institute Boy, Shadow Jury, Distant Dynasty, **20/1** Rossini Blue, Lincstone Boy (IRE), **25/1** Baton Bleu, CSF £11.19 CT £54.76 TOTE £3.20: 1.40 £1.90 £3.50 [£3.90] OWNER Mr Stanley Meadows (LAMBOURN) BRED Lode Moors Farm 9 Rn 58.49 secs (0.29) SF: 42/57/34/45/32/43/15/-/-
WEIGHT FOR AGE 3yo-13lb

408 WELLINGTON AMATEUR H'CAP (0-60) (II) (3-Y.O+) (Class F)
£2,726.00 (£766.00: £374.00)
1m (Equitrack) Stalls: Low GOING minus 0.57 sec per fur (FST) 5-15 (5-16)

3712 **Indian Serenade (49)***(54) (PWHarris)* 4-10-9 (3) MissAElsey(8) (lw: hdwy over 2f out: led ins fnl f: r.o wl) ....— 1
3732 Pair of Jacks (IRE) **(32)***(35) (DAWilson)* 5-9-9 MrTCuff(5) (lw: chsd ldr over 5f out: led over 2f out tl ins fnl f: unable qckn) 1 2
2402 Bold Habit **(54)***(55)*(Fav)*(JPearce)* 10-11-3 MrsLPearce(4) (b: lw: hdwy over 3f out: hrd rdn over 1f out: r.o) 1¼ 3
1997 Dahiyah (USA) **(58)***(47) (GLMoore)* 4-11-2v(5) MrKGoble(2) (led over 5f: wknd over 1f out) 6 4
3873 Royal Acclaim **(47)***(29) (JMBradley)* 10-10-5v(5) MrsDMcHale(10) (s.s: hdwy fnl 2f: nvr nrr) 3½ 5
3902 Arrogant Boy **(35)***(16) (DWChapman)* 6-9-7 (5) MissRClark(7) (nvr nr to chal) ....nk 6
Air Command (BAR) **(40)***(2) (CTNash)* 5-9-12 (5)ow6 MrPPhillips(6) (nvr nrr) 7 7
390* Brigadore Gold **(34)** *(ABailey)* 5-9-6b(5) MissBridgetGatehouse(1) (chsd ldr 7f out to over 5f out: sn wknd) 9 8

Chloes Diamond (IRE) **(39)** *(APJames)* 7-9-11 (5) MissSHiggins(3) (bhd fnl 3f) .... ¾ **9**
*302*11 Scots Law **(37)** *(JELong)* 8-9-7b(7)ow10 MrTWaters(9) (a bhd) 1½ **10**
*361*6 Smart Teacher (USA) **(50)** *(KRBurke)* 5-10-6 (7) MrsEBurke(11) (bhd fnl 4f)............................. 5 **11**

9/4 Bold Habit, **3/1** Pair of Jacks (IRE), **5/1** INDIAN SERENADE, Royal Acclaim, **15/2** Brigadore Gold, **8/1** Smart Teacher (USA), **12/1** Arrogant Boy, **16/1** Dahiyah (USA), **25/1** Air Command (BAR), Chloes Diamond (IRE), **33/1** Scots Law, CSF £22.39 CT £42.75 TOTE £5.30: £2.10 £1.40 £1.50 [£14.30] OWNER The Management (BERKHAMSTED) BRED B. Minty 11 Rn
1m 40.12 (3.72) SF: 38/19/39/31/13/-/-/-/-/-/-

T/Plpt: £224.30 (45.9 Tckts). T/Qdpt: £12.90 (5.2 Tckts). AK

0393-WOLVERHAMPTON (L-H)
Saturday March 18th (Standard)

409 CORNWALL-LEIGH MEDIAN AUCTION MAIDEN STKS (3 & & 5-Y.O) (Class E) £2,710.00 (£820.00: £400.00: £190.00)
1m 1f 79y (Fibresand) GOING: 0.07 sec per fur (STD) 7-00 (7-01)

Enchanteur *(60) (TJEtherington)* 4-9-5 KDarley(2) (hld up: hdwy & 4th st: r.o wl to ld nr fin) .... — **1**
*352*10 Dragonflight **(32)***(65) (DHaydnJones)* 4-9-10 AMackay(7) (lw: plld hrd: prom tl led 4f out: rdn over 1f out: hdd & no ex nr fin) .... nk **2**
Sian Wyn *(53) (KRBurke)* 5-9-5 ATucker(9) (bhd: hdwy & 5th st: kpt on fnl f) 4 **3**
Ju Ju's Girl (IRE) *(53) (BSmart)* 5-9-5 DHarrison(3) (b.hind: prom: 3rd st: sn rdn: no ex appr fnl f) .... s.h **4**
*394*3 Howqua River **(56)***(46)*(Fav)*(PWChapple-Hyam)* 3-8-3 (7)ow5 RHavlin(1) (trckd ldrs: pushed along 5f out: 2nd st: sn wknd) 7 **5**
*362*5 Malzoom *(32) (SEKettlewell)* 3-8-0 (5) JStack(8) (lw: nvr trbld ldrs) 8 **6**
*310*6 Fairy's Son **(41)***(29) (WRMuir)* 3-8-2 (3) SSanders(6) (lw: led over 3f: wknd & 6th st) 2 **7**
*316*9 Guymichelle (IRE) *(RIngram)* 3-8-0 NAdams(5) (a bhd) 15 **8**

1/2 Howqua River, **8/1** ENCHANTEUR (op 5/1), Fairy's Son (op 4/1), **9/1** Ju Ju's Girl (IRE) (op 5/1), **33/1** Guymichelle (IRE), Malzoom, Dragonflight, **50/1** Sian Wyn, CSF £149.44 TOTE £6.60: £1.40 £5.60 £6.50 (£54.80) OWNER Mr N.S.Yong (MALTON) 8 Rn 2m 5.6 (9.60) SF: 27/32/20/20/-/-/-/-
WEIGHT FOR AGE 3yo-19lb

410 HUMPHREYS CLAIMING APPRENTICE STKS (3-Y.O+) (Class G) £2,242.50 (£630.00: £307.50)
6f (Fibresand) GOING: 0.07 sec per fur (STD) 7-30 (7-35)

*86*4 **Abbey House (53)***(71) (RGuest)* 3-7-7b CHawksley(10) (led after 1f: clr ½-wy: kpt on wl appr fnl f) .... — **1**
*366** Sea Devil **(66)***(78)*(Fav)*(MJCamacho)* 9-9-5 GParkin(1) (hld up: hdwy over 2f out: sn rdn: kpt on: nt rch wnr) 2 **2**
Legatee **(66)***(62) (BJMeehan)* 4-8-10 PPMurphy(3) (prom: rdn & one pce fr ½-wy) 2½ **3**
*404*7 Pearl Dawn (IRE) *(53) (NoelChance)* 5-9-3 VHalliday(7) (hdwy over 2f out: nrst fin) 6 **4**
*344*7 Giggleswick Girl **(56)***(46) (MRChannon)* 4-8-6 (5) JDennis(4) (lw: bhd tl r.o fnl 2f) .... nk **5**
*392*5 Tinker Amelia **(48)***(43) (WRMuir)* 3-7-5 (3) CAdamson(2) (led 1f: wknd over 2f out) .... hd **6**
*392*3 Lawnswood Lady **(42)***(44) (RHollinshead)* 3-7-12 (5) AEddery(11) (nvr nr ldrs) 3 **7**
Mister Raider *(53) (SMellor)* 3-8-7 (5) ADaly(6) (chsd ldrs 3f: sn rdn & bhd) .... hd **8**
*366*8 Kiyas **(37)***(31) (BJMcMath)* 4-8-5 (7) JustineReader(8) (lw: chsd ldrs 3f: wknd over 1f out) 3 **9**
Cerbera **(35)***(16) (JPSmith)* 6-9-2 CTeague(12) (sn bhd) 7 **10**
Logie Pert Lad *(JJBridger)* 3-8-2 ow2 DGriffiths(13) (in tch over 3f: eased whn btn) 12 **11**

6/4 Sea Devil, **5/1** ABBEY HOUSE, Legatee, **11/2** Pearl Dawn (IRE) (4/1-6/1), **10/1** Tinker Amelia, **16/1** Giggleswick Girl, Lawnswood Lady, **25/1** Mister Raider, Kiyas, **33/1** Logie Pert Lad, **50/1** Cerbera, CSF £12.69 TOTE £5.70: £1.90 £1.30 £2.00 (£3.80) OWNER Mr A. P. Davies (NEWMARKET) BRED M. G. T. Stokes 11 Rn 1m 15.8 (4.60) SF: 20/41/25/16/9/-/-/2/-/-/-
WEIGHT FOR AGE 3yo-14lb

411 SOLARI BIRTHDAY H'CAP (0-70) (3-Y.O) (Class E) £2,775.00 (£840.00: £410.00: £195.00)
7f (Fibresand) GOING: 0.07 sec per fur (STD) 8-00 (8-02)

*283*0 **David James' Girl (58)***(73) (ABailey)* 3-9-0 KDarley(5) (w ldr tl led after 3f: clr 2f out: comf) .... — **1**

2945 Chadleigh Lane (USA) **(62)**_(68) (RHollinshead)_ 3-9-4 TIves(1) (trckd ldrs: hmpd & dropped rr over 3f out: rallied over 2f out: r.o wl fnl f) 4 **2**
3822 Mazilla **(53)**_(58) (WJHaggas)_ 3-8-4 (5) NVarley(4) (trckd ldrs: n.m.r over 3f out: chsd wnr 2f out: sn rdn & no imp) ....nk **3**
3824 Scissor Ridge **(55)**_(56) (JJBridger)_ 3-8-11 GDuffield(9) (chsd ldrs: 3rd st: kpt on u.p) 2 **4**
2125 Benjarong **(47)**_(48) (RMMcKellar)_ 3-8-3 DaleGibson(8) (dwlt: rdn & hdwy 2f out: nvr rchd ldrs) ....s.h **5**
3815 Tael of Silver **(57)**_(53) (KRBurke)_ 3-8-13 MFenton(6) (lw: prom: 4th st: sn btn) 2 **6**
395* Our Tom **(65)**_(59) (JWharton)_ 3-9-7 JQuinn(3) (prom: hmpd after 1f: 5th st: no imp) ....¾ **7**
Exclusive Assembly **(53)**_(29) (APJames)_ 3-8-9 FNorton(2) (led 3f) 8 **8**
3332 Three Arch Bridge **(55)**_(29)_(Fav)_(MJohnston)_ 3-8-11 DHolland(10) (chsd ldrs: 6th st: eased whn btn appr fnl f) ....¾ **9**
3924 Rockcracker (IRE) **(63)**_(36) (RCharlton)_ 3-9-5 DHarrison(7) (lw: sn outpcd: rdn ½-wy: nvr able to chal: eased whn btn fnl f) ....½ **10**
1246 Fiveaday **(56)**_(28) (BHanbury)_ 3-8-12 MRimmer(11) (dwlt: effrt over 3f out: wknd 2f out) ....½ **11**

2/1 Three Arch Bridge, **4/1** Rockcracker (IRE), **5/1** Our Tom, **7/1** Mazilla, **8/1** Tael of Silver (7/2-10/1), **10/1** DAVID JAMES' GIRL, Fiveaday (7/1-12/1), **12/1** Chadleigh Lane (USA), **16/1** Exclusive Assembly, **20/1** Benjarong, **25/1** Scissor Ridge, CSF £121.24 CT £835.43 TOTE £9.80: £2.00 £2.10 £2.00 (£66.90) OWNER One In Ten Racing Club (TARPORLEY) BRED Miss P. E. Decker 11 Rn
1m 31.9 (7.90) SF: 12/7/-/-/-/-/-/-/-/-/-

412 BALLARD-ABERDEEN ANGUS H'CAP (0-70) (4-Y.O+) (Class E)
£2,866.00 (£868.00: £424.00: £202.00)
1m 6f 166y (Fibresand) GOING: 0.07 sec per fur (STD) 8-30 (8-31)

Broom Isle (56)_(73) (DBurchell)_ 7-9-3 FNorton(10) (trckd ldrs: 2nd st: sn led: rdn out) ....— **1**
3467 Maradonna (USA) **(60)**_(76) (JWhite)_ 6-9-7 MFenton(5) (in tch: rdn & poor 4th st: styd on wl appr fnl f) 1 **2**
3742 Sleeptite (FR) **(61)**_(77) (WGMTurner)_ 5-9-3 (5) JDSmith(1) (hld up: hdwy 6f out: led over 2f out: sn hdd: eased cl home) ....hd **3**
389* Charlie Bigtime **(50)**_(60) (BJMcMath)_ 5-8-11 AMackay(6) (hdwy after 4f: led over 3f out tl over 2f out: rdn & 3rd st: one pce) 5 **4**
2954 Taroudant **(67)**_(64)_(Fav)_(MrsMReveley)_ 8-10-0 KDarley(4) (lw: in tch: rdn 5f out: no imp & 5th st) 12 **5**
3746 Debacle (USA) **(54)**_(39) (BJMcMath)_ 6-8-8 (7) JustineReader(8) (lw: wnt poor 6th st: nvr nr to chal) 11 **6**
3463 Arc Bright (IRE) **(65)**_(50) (RHollinshead)_ 5-9-12 TIves(3) (lw: led 1f: wknd 7f out) ....½ **7**
153* Epica **(57)**_(34) (ABailey)_ 4-9-1b JWeaver(9) (led after 1f to 5f out: sn wknd) 7 **8**
Jalore **(47)**_(3) (SCoathup)_ 6-8-8 NAdams(12) (s.i.s: t.o tl kpt on fnl 3f) 20 **9**
3307 Uncharted Waters **(57)**_(11) (CACyzer)_ 4-9-1 GDuffield(7) (rdn 7f out: sn bhd) 1½ **10**
3892 Premier Dance **(62)**_(15)_(Fav)_(DHaydnJones)_ 8-9-4 (5) SDrowne(2) (sn pushed along: wl bhd fnl 6f) 1 **11**
3755 Swordking (IRE) **(52)** _(JLHarris)_ 6-8-13 DHolland(11) (lw: chsd ldrs tl led 5f out: hdd over 3f out: wknd qckly & eased) 20 **12**

4/1 Premier Dance, Taroudant, **9/2** Charlie Bigtime, **11/2** Sleeptite (FR), **6/1** Epica, **8/1** Swordking (IRE), **9/1** Arc Bright (IRE), **12/1** BROOM ISLE (8/1-14/1), **16/1** Maradonna (USA), **33/1** Debacle (USA), Uncharted Waters, Jalore, CSF £176.77 CT £1076.06 TOTE £12.50: £3.20 £4.50 £2.00 (£131.30) OWNER Mr Vivian Guy (EBBW VALE) BRED Lord Bolton 12 Rn
3m 21.0 (13.60) SF: 35/38/39/22/26/1/12/-/-/-/-/-
WEIGHT FOR AGE 4yo-3lb

413 HORROCKS (S) STKS (3-Y.O+) (Class G) £2,326.50 (£654.00: £319.50)
1m 100y (Fibresand) GOING: 0.07 sec per fur (STD) 9-00 (9-02)

3663 **Second Colours (USA) (70)**_(69) (MrsMReveley)_ 5-9-8 KDarley(9) (trckd ldrs: led on bit over 2f out: easily) ....— **1**
399* No Submission (USA) **(70)**_(69)_(Fav)_(DWChapman)_ 9-9-13 DeanMcKeown(5) (prom: led 3f out: sn hdd: 2nd st: kpt on fnl f) 2½ **2**
3973 Eastleigh **(50)**_(68) (RHollinshead)_ 6-9-13 TIves(7) (prom: led 5f out to 3f out: 3rd st: sn chsng wnr: btn fnl f) ....¾ **3**
3994 T O O Mamma's (IRE) **(57)**_(55) (JBerry)_ 4-8-10v(7) PRoberts(13) (lw: chsd ldrs: 4th st: btn appr fnl f) 1¾ **4**
3992 Kristis Girl **(38)**_(47) (DHaydnJones)_ 8-9-3 AMackay(10) (hdwy 5f out: 5th st: rdn & no imp fnl 2f) 4 **5**
3234 Dream Carrier (IRE) **(68)**_(57) (JGMO'Shea)_ 7-9-6 (7) KimberleyHart(4) (hdwy over 3f out: rdn & no imp fnl 2f) ....s.h **6**

379² Pop to Stans **(51)***(39) (JPearce)* 6-9-1 (7) ElizabethTurner(1) (bhd tl sme hdwy fnl 2f) 7 **7**
387¹² Northern Chief **(49)***(37) (RWEmery)* 5-9-8 JWilliams(8) (lw: nvr trbld ldrs) ....¾ **8**
379³ Ivan the Terrible (IRE) **(50)***(26) (BEllison)* 7-9-8 SWhitworth(2) (b: chsd ldrs: rdn ½-wy: wkng & 6th st) 6 **9**
Across the Bay **(43)***(23) (RWEmery)* 8-9-8b JQuinn(11) (a bhd) 1¾ **10**
Golden Memories (IRE) **(60)** *(MJHeaton-Ellis)* 4-9-8 DHolland(6) (led over 4f: sn wknd) 12 **11**
379⁴ Fiaba **(44)** *(MrsNMacauley)* 7-9-3 JWeaver(3) (prom 3f: eased whn btn fnl 3f) ....s.h **12**
397⁸ Deputy Tim **(30)** *(RBastiman)* 12-9-3 (5) HBastiman(12) (sn rdn along: a bhd) ....½ **13**

6/4 No Submission (USA), **2/1** SECOND COLOURS (USA), **9/1** Dream Carrier (IRE) (6/1-10/1), **10/1** Pop to Stans, Fiaba, Eastleigh (6/1-11/1), **12/1** Ivan the Terrible (IRE) (op 8/1), **14/1** T O O Mamma's (IRE) (8/1-16/1), **20/1** Golden Memories (IRE), Across the Bay, **25/1** Northern Chief, Deputy Tim, **33/1** Kristis Girl, CSF £6.50 TOTE £3.90: £1.70 £1.30 £2.80 (£4.30) OWNER Mr P. D. Savill (SALTBURN) BRED Dinnaken Farm in USA 13 Rn

1m 52.0 (8.00) SF: 35/35/34/21/13/23/5/3/-/-/-/-/-
Bt in 6,400 gns

414 BEEFCAKE H'CAP (0-70) (4-Y.O+) (Class E) £2,827.00 (£856.00: £418.00: £199.00) 1m 1f 79y (Fibresand) GOING: 0.07 sec per fur (STD) 9-30 (9-30)

320² **Kinnegad Kid (66)***(74)*(Fav)*(RIngram)* 6-9-9 (3) DWright(7) (trckd ldrs: led on bit over 2f out: rdn appr fnl f: hld on wl) .... — **1**
271² Tu Opes **(68)***(76) (JLHarris)* 4-10-0 DaleGibson(8) (dwlt: sn chsng ldrs: wnt 2nd st: sn rdn: kpt on fnl f) ....nk **2**
330⁶ My Minnie **(50)***(57) (BJMeehan)* 5-8-10 JWeaver(2) (lw: led 2f: 4th st: kpt on u.p) ....½ **3**
334³ Tremolante **(40)***(23) (CaptJWilson)* 4-7-7 (7)ow7 MHenry(11) (lw: rdn & hdwy over 4f out: r.o fnl 2f: nvr nr ldrs) 10 **4**
Northern Trial (USA) **(49)***(37) (KRBurke)* 7-8-6v(3)ow1 JTate(4) (in tch: 6th st: no imp) ....hd **5**
374¹⁴ Super Heights **(47)***(31) (DLWilliams)* 7-8-2 (5)ow1 DGriffiths(5) (hld up: effrt 3f out: nvr rchd ldrs) 2½ **6**
364⁵ Marowins **(62)***(46) (EJAlston)* 6-9-8 JQuinn(6) (dwlt: rdn & hdwy 5f out: no imp fnl 3f) ....½ **7**
313⁴ Northern Celadon (IRE) **(66)***(44) (MJHeaton-Ellis)* 4-9-7 (5) SDrowne(12) (lw: w ldrs tl led over 5f out: hdd over 2f out: 3rd st: sn btn) 3½ **8**
367¹¹ Golden Torque **(62)***(37) (RBastiman)* 8-9-3 (5) HBastiman(10) (a bhd) 1¾ **9**
389⁴ Homemaker **(43)** *(PGMurphy)* 5-7-10 (7)ow3 RWaterfield(1) (b.nr fore: a bhd) 10 **10**
387⁵ Jonbel **(33)** *(TTClement)* 7-7-2 (5) MBaird(9) (b: lw: led after 2f tl over 5f out: 5th st: sn wknd & eased) 2½ **11**
387⁷ Slip a Coin **(62)***(9) (ICampbell)* 4-9-8 DHarrison(3) (w ldrs tl wknd qckly over 3f out) 4 **12**

LONG HANDICAP Jonbel 7-1

11/4 KINNEGAD KID, **3/1** Marowins, **9/2** Tu Opes, **7/1** My Minnie, Slip a Coin, **9/1** Northern Celadon (IRE) (op 6/1), **10/1** Homemaker (8/1-12/1), **16/1** Tremolante, **20/1** Northern Trial (USA), **25/1** Super Heights, Golden Torque, **33/1** Jonbel, CSF £17.11 CT £79.65 TOTE £3.90: £1.90 £1.90 £1.70 (£9.20) Trio£14.70 OWNER Mr J. B. Wilcox (EPSOM) BRED Airlie Stud and Miss K. Rausing 12 Rn

2m 2.9 (6.90) SF: 56/58/39/5/19/13/28/26/19/-/-/-

T/Plpt: £374.10. T/Qdpt: £16.00 Dk

0375-SOUTHWELL (L-H)
Monday March 20th (Standard)

415 TROON APPRENTICE H'CAP (0-60) (I) (4-Y.O+) (Class F) £2,550.00 (£725.00: £360.00) 1m (Fibresand) Stalls: Low GOING minus 0.08 sec per fur (STD) 2-00 (2-01)

Whitelock Quest (25)*(41) (NEBerry)* 7-7-7 AdelleGibbons(4) (chsd ldrs: led over 1f out: sn clr) .... — **1**
371³ Mary's Case (IRE) **(56)***(62) (MJohnston)* 5-9-10b BHalligan(3) (trckd ldrs: chal 2f out: sn rdn & hung lft: no imp fnl f) 5 **2**
413⁷ Pop to Stans **(51)***(56) (JPearce)* 6-9-5 ElizabethTurner(1) (sn wl bhd: hdwy on outside 2f out: nrst fin) ....¾ **3**
397* Gallery Artist (IRE) **(55)***(57) (RGuest)* 7-9-9 DToole(10) (trckd ldrs: effrt & outpcd over 2f: edgd lft & hung on fnl f) 1½ **4**
406⁴ Captain Marmalade **(50)***(51) (DTThom)* 6-9-4 GMilligan(13) (sn bhd: hdwy on outside over 2f out: nvr nr ldrs) ....nk **5**
341³ King Parrot (IRE) **(52)***(50) (LordHuntingdon)* 7-9-6v JWilkinson(8) (led tl over 1f out: sn wknd) 1½ **6**
354² Genesis Four **(42)***(34)*(Fav)*(SRBowring)* 5-8-10b PFessey(9) (prom: hrd rdn 2f out: sn wknd) 3 **7**

379[6] Coven Moon **(32)***(22) (DMorris)* 5-8-0 GFaulkner(5) (outpcd & bhd: sme hdwy on outside over 2f out: eased whn no ch fnl f)....¾ 8
379[7] Uckerby Lad **(44)***(28) (NPLittmoden)* 4-8-12b SMcCarthy(7) (stdd s: hdwy & prom ½-wy: wknd 2f out)....3 9
Murphy's Gold (IRE) **(49)***(27) (RAFahey)* 4-9-3 JGotobed(6) (hld up & plld hrd: effrt over 2f out: n.d)....3 10
334[4] Intrepid Fort **(41)***(12) (BWMurray)* 6-8-9vow7 CScudder(11) (s.s: a in rr)....nk 11
397[4] Hill Farm Katie **(45)***(17) (WMBrisbourne)* 4-8-13 AEddery(14) (chsd ldrs tl wknd over 2f out)...3 12
355[7] Fletcher's Bounty (IRE) **(43)***(14) (WSCunningham)* 6-8-11 ADaly(2) (chsd ldrs tl wknd over 2f out)....nk 13
Soda Popinski (USA) **(36)** *(JLHarris)* 7-8-4 RWaterfield(12) (lw: bhd: effrt on outside over 2f out: n.d)....6 14

7/2 Genesis Four, **5/1** King Parrot (IRE), **11/2** Captain Marmalade, **9/1** Coven Moon, Pop to Stans, **10/1** Mary's Case (IRE), Gallery Artist (IRE), Murphy's Gold (IRE), **14/1** Intrepid Fort, Uckerby Lad, Hill Farm Katie, Fletcher's Bounty (IRE), **33/1** WHITELOCK QUEST, Soda Popinski (USA), CSF £322.73 CT £2,935.00 TOTE £32.60: £6.20 £4.50 £2.50 (£156.20) OWNER Mr B. Beale (UPPER LAMBOURN) BRED Patrick Eddery Ltd 14 Rn 1m 46.8 (7.50) SF: -/21/15/16/10/9/-/-/-/-/-/-/-/-

416

TROON APPRENTICE H'CAP (0-60) (II) (4-Y.O+) (Class F)
£2,550.00 (£725.00: £360.00)
1m (Fibresand) Stalls: Low GOING minus 0.08 sec per fur (STD) 2-30 (2-30)

378[9] **Aquado (48)***(58)*(Fav)*(ALForbes)* 6-9-4 DDenby(5) (bhd: chsd ldrs: led over 1f out: hld on wl towards fin)....— 1
Daytona Beach (IRE) **(54)***(63) (MJAhern)* 5-9-10 JDennis(14) (w ldr: led over 4f out tl over 1f out: nt qckn nr fin)....½ 2
198[5] Rainbows Rhapsody **(40)***(48) (MJCamacho)* 4-8-10 AEddery(8) (b: b.hind: sn pushed along: hdwy ½-wy: ev ch fnl f: nt qckn cl home)....nk 3
402[5] Dome Patrol **(47)***(52) (WRMuir)* 4-8-12 (5) RPooles(12) (chsd ldrs: ev ch tl wknd ins fnl f)......1¾ 4
397[7] Hi Penny **(43)***(41) (KTIvory)* 4-8-13b RWaterfield(4) (chsd ldrs: one pce fnl 2f)....3½ 5
117[7] Asmarina **(38)***(32) (SRBowring)* 5-8-8b PFessey(11) (sn bhd: hdwy on outside over 2f out: nrst fin)....2 6
343[6] Arrasas Lady **(33)***(27) (JELong)* 5-7-12 (5) TField(2) (chsd ldrs: outpcd over 3f out: kpt on fnl 2f)....hd 7
242[6] Dubai Falcon (USA) **(53)***(40) (RDickin)* 4-9-4 (5) MichelleThomas(6) (sn outpcd & pushed along: kpt on fnl 2f: n.d)....3½ 8
379[8] Rad **(50)***(36) (SPCWoods)* 5-9-6 CWebb(1) (lw: mid-div: effrt over 2f out: nvr nr ldrs)....nk 9
288[8] Mexican Dancer **(25)***(7) (PHowling)* 6-7-4 (5)ow1 TThomas(9) (sn hmpd: bhd: sme hdwy over 1f out: n.d)....1½ 10
399[3] Ballyhays (IRE) **(46)***(26) (JAHarris)* 6-9-2 JEdmunds(10) (bhd & hrd rdn over 2f out: n.d).....1¾ 11
302[12] Sharp Gazelle **(40)***(16) (BSmart)* 5-8-10 ADaly(3) (led tl over 4f out: wknd 3f out)....2 12
340[7] Amlak (USA) **(33)** *(TKersey)* 6-8-3 JGotobed(13) (bhd)....5 13
335* Glenvally **(47)** *(BWMurray)* 4-9-3b CScudder(7) (s.s: sn t.o: p.u ½-wy: lame).... P

LONG HANDICAP Mexican Dancer 7-5

7/2 AQUADO, **4/1** Rad, **11/2** Rainbows Rhapsody, Glenvally, **7/1** Dome Patrol, **11/1** Hi Penny, **12/1** Sharp Gazelle, **14/1** Dubai Falcon (USA), Ballyhays (IRE), **16/1** Asmarina, **20/1** Arrasas Lady, **25/1** Mexican Dancer, Daytona Beach (IRE), **50/1** Amlak (USA), CSF £84.90 CT £460.49 TOTE £5.80: £2.20 £4.90 £2.40 (£126.90) Trio £328.90 OWNER Mr K. Nicholls (UTTOXETER) BRED Lord Howard de Walden 14 Rn 1m 46.6 (7.30) SF: 23/28/13/17/6/-/-/5/1/-/-/-/-/-

OFFICIAL EXPLANATION **Glenvally: The trainer reported that the filly had pulled up lame on her off-fore and this was confirmed to the Stewards by the Vet.**

417

CARNOUSTIE CLAIMING STKS (3-Y.O+) (Class F) £2,537.00 (£712.00: £347.00)
7f (Fibresand) Stalls: Low GOING minus 0.08 sec per fur (STD) 3-00 (3-02)

Berge (IRE) (67)*(79)*(Fav)*(WAO'Gorman)* 4-9-4 (3) EmmaO'Gorman(4) (lw: s.i.s: hld up & bhd: gd hdwy on outside over 2f out: edgd lft: led over 1f out: eased nr fin)....— 1
388[3] What a Nightmare (IRE) **(68)***(72) (JAGlover)* 3-8-4v GCarter(10) (led tl over 1f out: no ch w wnr)....2½ 2
365[8] Prima Silk **(70)***(70)*(Fav)*(MJRyan)* 4-9-7 DBiggs(2) (hdwy ½-wy: kpt on fnl 2f: nvr nr to chal)....1½ 3
378[7] Desert Invader (IRE) **(66)***(59)*(Fav)*(DWChapman)* 4-9-8b DeanMcKeown(9) (sn trckng ldr: effrt 2f out: sn wknd)....5 4
134[6] Pretonic **(44)***(46) (BPalling)* 7-8-13 JWeaver(3) (sn drvn along: chsd ldrs tl outpcd 4f out: sn lost pl & wandered: n.d after)....2 5
413[6] Dream Carrier (IRE) **(68)***(52) (JGMO'Shea)* 7-9-6v TIves(1) (sn bhd: sme hdwy over 2f out: kpt on: nvr nr ldrs)....½ 6

96[11] Comfortable (30)*(14)* *(SGollings)* 5-8-12b(5) JStack(11) (sn reminders: drvn along: sn wl outpcd) 15 7
233[3] Bold Aristocrat (IRE) **(50)***(12)* *(RHollinshead)* 4-9-0 (5) AGarth(6) (sn chsng ldrs: drvn along over 2f out: sn wknd) 2 8
Waterlord (IRE) *(DNicholls)* 5-9-5 AlexGreaves(7) (a in rr) 7 9
Malsisio *(SGNorton)* 3-7-13 FNorton(8) (bhd fr ½-wy) 2 10

3/1 BERGE (IRE), Prima Silk, Desert Invader (IRE), **11/2** What a Nightmare (IRE), **6/1** Dream Carrier (IRE), **12/1** Bold Aristocrat (IRE), **14/1** Pretonic, **20/1** Waterlord (IRE), **25/1** Malsisio, **33/1** Comfortable, CSF £21.10 TOTE £5.30: £1.50 £1.70 £1.50 (£19.30) OWNER Mr S. Fustok (NEWMARKET) BRED S. Fustok 10 Rn 1m 31.8 (5.00) SF: 41/18/32/21/8/14/-/-/-/-
WEIGHT FOR AGE 3yo-16lb

418

MUIRFIELD MAIDEN STKS (3-Y.O) (Class D) £3,707.60 (£1,122.80: £548.40: £261.20) **1m (Fibresand)** Stalls: Low GOING minus 0.08 sec (STD) 3-30 (3-31)

Sheer Danzig (IRE) *(73)* *(RWArmstrong)* 3-9-0 RPrice(7) (trckd ldrs: styd on wl fnl 2f: led wl ins fnl f) ....— 1
Abu Simbel (USA) *(72)*(Fav)*(JHMGosden)* 3-9-0 JCarroll(9) (b.all round: sn chsng ldrs: hrd drvn & led over 2f out: hdd & nt qckn ins fnl f) ....¾ 2
Yoush (IRE) **(83)***(62)* *(MAJarvis)* 3-9-0 PRobinson(1) (prom tl outpcd & drvn along ½-wy: gd hdwy 2f out: kpt on same pce appr fnl f) 5 3
Alute (IRE) *(53)* *(CEBrittain)* 3-8-9 BDoyle(2) (chsd ldrs: kpt on same pce fnl f) 2 4
Doddington Flyer **(52)***(50)* *(RHollinshead)* 3-9-0 TIves(10) (hdwy to chse ldrs ½-wy: grad wknd fnl 2f) 4 5
316[2] Vaslav Nijinsky *(46)* *(GRimmer)* 3-9-0 MRimmer(11) (chsd ldr: led over 4f out to over 2f out: wknd over 1f out) 1¾ 6
372[4] Simposa (IRE) *(42)* *(JEBanks)* 3-9-0 JQuinn(8) (outpcd & drvn along ½-wy: n.d) 2 7
357[9] Bellateena *(23)* *(HJCollingridge)* 3-8-9 DaleGibson(4) (bit bkwd: s.i.s: a bhd) 7 8
372[7] Ever Friends *(27)* *(BJMcMath)* 3-9-0 AMackay(3) (swtg: sn outpcd & bhd) ....½ 9
350[9] Beyaateh *(14)* *(MCChapman)* 3-8-2 (7) CMunday(5) (dwlt s: a bhd) 4 10
Rubislaw **(50)***(19)* *(CWFairhurst)* 3-9-0 DeanMcKeown(6) (bit bkwd: hmpd s: a bhd) ....hd 11
Hunza Story *(11)* *(NPLittmoden)* 3-8-9 DHolland(12) (bkwd: led tl over 4f out: wknd qckly over 3f out: sn bhd) 1¼ 12

6/4 Abu Simbel (USA), **7/4** SHEER DANZIG (IRE), **11/2** Yoush (IRE), **7/1** Vaslav Nijinsky, **12/1** Simposa (IRE), **14/1** Doddington Flyer, **16/1** Alute (IRE), **25/1** Ever Friends, **33/1** Rubislaw, **50/1** Beyaateh, Bellateena, Hunza Story, CSF £5.46 TOTE £3.70: £1.30 £1.20 £1.50 (£3.80) OWNER Mr R. J. Arculli (NEWMARKET) BRED Mrs Max Morris 12 Rn
1m 45.2 (5.90) SF: 33/32/22/13/10/6/2/-/-/-/-/-

419

ST ANDREWS H'CAP (0-65) (3-Y.O+) (Class F) £2,537.00 (£712.00: £347.00) **6f (Fibresand)** Stalls: Low GOING minus 0.08 sec per fur (STD) 4-05 (4-06)

393[5] **Souperficial (43)***(51)*(Fav)*(JAGlover)* 4-8-11v JWeaver(12) (s.i.s: hdwy on outside 2f out: r.o wl u.p to ld ins fnl f) ....— 1
378[5] Titanium Honda (IRE) **(40)***(43)* *(CEBrittain)* 4-8-8 BDoyle(9) (in tch: styd on fnl f: no ch w wnr) 2 2
354[5] At the Savoy (IRE) **(47)***(48)* *(TDBarron)* 4-8-8 (7) KimberleyHart(16) (a chsng ldrs: ev ch ins fnl f: nt qckn) ....¾ 3
354[4] Christian Flight (IRE) **(39)***(39)* *(SGollings)* 6-8-7 DHarrison(2) (a chsng ldrs: ev ch over 1f out: kpt on one pce) ....hd 4
353[3] Panther (IRE) **(55)***(51)* *(JHetherton)* 5-9-9 NKennedy(4) (sn bhd: swtchd outside over 2f out: styd on wl: nt rch ldrs) 1½ 5
348* Brisas **(47)***(39)* *(CWFairhurst)* 8-9-1 JFanning(10) (led tl wknd & hdd ins fnl f) 1½ 6
Shared Risk **(57)***(44)* *(SGNorton)* 3-8-11 JFortune(14) (nvr rchd ldrs) 2 7
400[8] Farmer Jock **(43)***(27)* *(MrsNMacauley)* 13-8-11 AClark(5) (b: sn bhd: hdwy on wd outside over 2f out: nvr nr ldrs) 1¼ 8
407[5] Shadow Jury **(57)***(39)* *(DWChapman)* 5-9-11b DeanMcKeown(6) (in tch tl lost pl 3f out) ....½ 9
Scent of Power **(44)***(20)* *(MartynWane)* 5-8-12 JCarroll(15) (nvr nr ldrs) 2½ 10
400[6] Matthew David **(43)***(16)* *(SRBowring)* 5-8-11 JQuinn(3) (s.i.s: bhd: sme hdwy 2f out: n.d) 1 11
393[4] Monsieur Petong **(42)***(14)* *(JParkes)* 4-8-5 (5) PMcCabe(13) (in tch: drvn along over 2f out: sn wknd) ....½ 12
353[4] Rustic League (IRE) **(37)***(5)* *(TJNaughton)* 4-8-5 DHolland(11) (w ldr tl wknd 2f out) 1½ 13
Polli Pui **(57)***(22)* *(PDEvans)* 3-8-6 (5) JStack(8) (chsd ldrs tl wknd over 2f out) 1 14
297[3] Aljaz **(58)***(21)* *(DTThom)* 5-9-12 AMackay(1) (b: a in rr) ....¾ 15
Royal Comedian **(41)** *(BWMurray)* 6-8-2 (7)ow1 CScudder(7) (a bhd) 5 16

4/1 SOUPERFICIAL, **13/2** Panther (IRE), **8/1** Aljaz, Titanium Honda (IRE), **10/1** Shadow Jury, **12/1** At the Savoy (IRE), Brisas, Matthew David, Christian Flight (IRE), **14/1** Shared Risk, Monsieur Petong, **16/1** Farmer Jock, Rustic League (IRE), Scent of Power, Royal Comedian, **20/1** Polli Pui, CSF £37.71 CT £346.92 TOTE £4.80: £1.60 £3.00 £2.20 £2.80 (£16.50) Trio £207.40 OWNER Mr M. G. Ridley (WORKSOP) BRED C. L. Loyd 16 Rn

1m 17.7 (4.20) SF: 32/24/29/20/32/20/11/8/20/1/-/-/-/-/2/-

WEIGHT FOR AGE 3yo-14lb

420 SANDWICH (S) STKS (3-Y.O) (Class G) £2,259.00 (£634.00: £309.00)
5f (Fibresand) Stalls: High GOING minus 0.39 sec per fur (FST) 4-35 (4-36)

*392*8 **Nadwaty (IRE) (50)***(57) (JDBethell)* 3-8-7b JWeaver(1) (mde all: shkn up over 1f out: sn drvn clr) — 1
*210*7 Russian Heroine **(70)***(47)*(Fav)*(MJohnston)* 3-8-13 DHolland(9) (lw: a chsng ldrs: effrt 2f out: kpt on: no imp) 5 2
*392*6 Ivy Lilian (IRE) **(45)***(36) (WMBrisbourne)* 3-8-2 (5) AGarth(4) (a chsng ldrs: kpt on same pce fnl 2f) 1½ 3
*319*5 Prince Rudolf (IRE) **(48)***(45) (MrsNMacauley)* 3-9-4v MFenton(10) (chsd ldrs: rdn & hung lft ½-wy: no imp) ¾ 4
*410*7 Lawnswood Lady **(42)***(32) (RHollinshead)* 3-8-8 ow1 TIves(7) (in tch: rdn ½-wy: kpt on fnl f) ½ 5
Tish **(40)***(27) (ASmith)* 3-8-7 DeanMcKeown(3) (s.i.s: hdwy ½-wy: kpt on fnl f) 1¾ 6
*405*6 Havana Miss **(38)***(28) (BPalling)* 3-8-13 TSprake(2) (chsd ldrs tl wknd over 1f out) 1½ 7
Bebe Pomme **(45)***(17) (MrsNMacauley)* 3-8-4 (3) SSanders(6) (s.i.s: outpcd & bhd tl kpt on fnl f) 1½ 8
*339*11 Daily Challenger (USA) **(42)***(22) (RonaldThompson)* 3-8-12 CRutter(8) (s.s: bhd tl sme late hdwy) hd 9
*363*4 Benten **(46)***(11) (DNicholls)* 3-8-7 GDuffield(5) (chsd ldrs tl lost pl ½-wy: eased) 1¾ 10
*270*9 Madam Sunpak *(3) (MrsVAAconley)* 3-8-7 TWilliams(11) (nvr wnt pce) 2½ 11
*362*7 Angelic Belle *(NPLittmoden)* 3-8-7b RPrice(12) (swvd rt s: hung bdly lft thrght: a bhd) 2½ 12
Tarsid *(SCoathup)* 3-8-5 (7) SJames(13) (unf: s.i.s: sn hmpd & bhd) 3½ 13

8/11 Russian Heroine, **13/2** NADWATY (IRE), **7/1** Prince Rudolf (IRE), **8/1** Ivy Lilian (IRE), **10/1** Lawnswood Lady, **12/1** Benten, **14/1** Bebe Pomme, Havana Miss, **20/1** Tish, Daily Challenger (USA), Madam Sunpak, **33/1** Angelic Belle, **50/1** Tarsid, CSF £13.24 TOTE £7.00: £1.80 £1.20 £1.80 (£6.10) OWNER Sheikh Amin Dahlawi (MIDDLEHAM) BRED Al Dahlawi Stud Co Ltd 13 Rn

59.3 secs (1.30) SF: 36/26/15/24/11/6/7/-/1/-/-/-/-

Sold H V Ward 4,200 gns

421 TURNBERRY H'CAP (0-60) (I) (4-Y.O+) (Class F) £2,537.00 (£712.00: £347.00)
1m 3f (Fibresand) Stalls: Low GOING minus 0.08 sec per fur (STD) 5-05 (5-06)

*340*2 **Modest Hope (USA) (45)***(55) (BRichmond)* 8-8-13 JWeaver(10) (lw: hld up: stdy hdwy 5f out: shkn up to ld over 1f out: drvn clr) — 1
*186*6 Tempering **(57)***(63)*(Fav)*(DWChapman)* 9-9-11 JQuinn(1) (led: clr 3f out: hdd & no ex over 1f out) 2½ 2
*375*9 Turfmans Vision **(40)***(25) (RHollinshead)* 5-8-8b ow1 TIves(3) (hdwy & drvn along 5f out: one pce fnl 3f) 14 3
*397*2 Swynford Flyer **(48)***(30) (JAHarris)* 6-9-2 DaleGibson(2) (in tch tl lost pl ....4f out: kpt on appr fnl f) 2½ 4
*334*5 Mr Moriarty (IRE) **(38)***(18) (SRBowring)* 4-7-12b(7) CTeague(7) (w ldrs tl wknd over 2f out) 1½ 5
*389*8 Hill Farm Dancer **(53)***(29) (WMBrisbourne)* 4-9-1 (5) AGarth(6) (chsd ldrs: outpcd over 3f out: wknd 2f out) 3 6
Salutation (IRE) **(40)***(7) (TKersey)* 4-8-7v GDuffield(8) (b: sn bhd) 6 7
*367*6 Port Sunlight (IRE) **(43)***(9) (PDEvans)* 7-8-11 AClark(9) (sn bhd) 1 8
Silver Samurai **(57)***(18) (MrsVAAconley)* 6-9-11 DeanMcKeown(4) (in tch tl wknd over 3f out: eased) 5 9
Mr Abbot **(36)** *(GROldroyd)* 5-8-4 DHolland(5) (w ldrs: sn drvn along: wknd over 4f out) 4 10
Dontbetalking (IRE) **(33)** *(ALForbes)* 5-8-1v JFanning(11) (prom early: sn bhd: t.o 4f out) dist 11

7/2 Tempering, **4/1** MODEST HOPE (USA), Mr Moriarty (IRE), **5/1** Port Sunlight (IRE), **11/2** Swynford Flyer, **10/1** Hill Farm Dancer, Mr Abbot, **12/1** Silver Samurai, **25/1** Turfmans Vision, **33/1** Salutation (IRE), Dontbetalking (IRE), CSF £19.28 TC £295.62 TOTE £3.40: £1.70 £1.60 £6.00 (£10.50) Trio £163.60 OWNER Mr J. McManamon BRED Ralph Wilson 11 Rn

2m 29.7 (8.20) SF: 34/42/4/9/-/7/-/-/-/-/-

WEIGHT FOR AGE 4yo-1lb

422

TURNBERRY H'CAP (0-60) (II) (4-Y.O+) (Class F) £2,537.00 (£712.00: £347.00)
1m 3f (Fibresand) Stalls: Low GOING minus 0.08 sec per fur (STD) 5-35 (5-35)

*389*3 **Mr Bean (50)***(61)*(Fav)*(KRBurke)* 5-9-4 MFenton(1) (mde virtually all: styd on wl fnl 2f: drvn out) — 1
*271*10 Ijab (CAN) **(27)***(37) (JParkes)* 5-7-6b(3) DarrenMoffatt(8) (w ldrs: rdn 3f out: kpt on wl fnl f) ¾ 2
*374*10 Hattaafeh (IRE) **(60)***(68) (MAJarvis)* 4-9-13 PRobinson(5) (a chsng ldrs: effrt over 2f out: kpt on one pce) 1½ 3
I'm a Dreamer (IRE) **(59)***(62) (WWHaigh)* 5-9-13 DeanMcKeown(9) (lw: hld up: hdwy 6f out: effrt 4f out: one pce fnl 2f: nvr able chal) 3½ 4
*304*3 Comtec's Legend **(36)***(34) (JFBottomley)* 5-8-4 GCarter(4) (sn in tch: effrt 4f out: one pce) 3½ 5
*361** Call Me Blue **(57)***(36) (TJNaughton)* 5-9-11 SWhitworth(3) (hdwy ½-wy: sn drvn along: wknd 2f out) 13 6
Gold Desire **(37)***(8) (MBrittain)* 5-8-5 JLowe(2) (hld up & plld hrd: bhd fnl 5f) 5 7
*378*8 Rambollina **(41)***(7) (MWEasterby)* 4-8-8 LCharnock(11) (w ldr: drvn along 6f out: lost pl over 3f out) 3½ 8
Marble **(49)** *(MartynWane)* 4-9-2 AMackay(6) (reard s: chsd ldrs: drvn along 6f out: wknd over 3f out) 15 9
Bite the Bullet **(36)** *(DJSffrenchDavis)* 4-8-3 NAdams(7) (b: a in rr) 1 10
Alizarin **(28)** *(JLHarris)* 6-7-5 (5)ow1 NVarley(10) (bit bkwd: a bhd: drvn along 5f out: sn t.o) 20 11

9/4 MR BEAN, **9/2** Call Me Blue, I'm a Dreamer (IRE), **5/1** Hattaafeh (IRE), **11/2** Comtec's Legend, **12/1** Ijab (CAN), **14/1** Gold Desire, Rambollina, Marble, **25/1** Bite the Bullet, **33/1** Alizarin, CSF £31.13 CT £125.02 TOTE £3.10: £1.40 £6.80 £1.80 (£39.70) Trio £52.50 OWNER Mr K. Powell (WANTAGE) BRED M. L. Page 11 Rn 2m 28.9 (7.40) SF: -/-/6/1/-/-/-/-/-/-/-
WEIGHT FOR AGE 4yo-1lb

T/Jkpt: Not won; £537,620.79 to Stratford 21/3/95. T/Plpt: £321.70 (109.28 Tckts). T/Qdpt: £44.00 (1.7 Tckts) WG

DONCASTER (L-H)
Thursday March 23rd (Good)
WIND: almost nil

423

RACEFORM APPRENTICE H'CAP (0-80) (4-Y.O+) (Class E) £3,201.60 (£976.80: £482.40: £235.20)
1m 4f Stalls: Low GOING minus 0.09 sec per fur (G) 2-05 (2-08)

*355*3 **Achilles Heel (47)***(62) (CNAllen)* 4-7-2 (5) MBaird(6) (hdwy on ins 4f out: led wl ins fnl f: kpt on) — 1
Shadow Leader **(70)***(85) (MissAJWhitfield)* 4-8-11 (5) RPainter(3) (hdwy ent st: ev ch 2f out: hung lft u.p: nt qckn cl home) nk 2
*374*3 Risky Tu **(49)***(63) (PAKelleway)* 4-7-4 (5) AdelleGibbons(2) (lw: a.p: led 1½f out tl wl ins fnl f: no ex: uns rdr after fin) nk 3
*351*2 Ashover **(50)***(58)*(Fav)*(TDBarron)* 5-7-9 (3) NVarley(7) (chsd ldrs: led wl over 1f out: sn hdd & one pce) 5 4
*396*3 Mentalasanythin **(56)***(60) (ABailey)* 6-7-11 (7)ow3 AngelaGallimore(5) (in tch: hdwy & swtchd over 2f out: styd on nr fin) nk 5
Top Cees **(73)***(80) (MrsJRRamsden)* 5-9-0 (7) TFinn(22) (lw: hdwy over 4f out: styd on: nrst fin) nk 6
*403*4 In the Money (IRE) **(64)***(67) (RHollinshead)* 6-8-9 (3) AGarth(21) (cl up: led ent st tl wl over 1f out: grad wknd) 2½ 7
Stalled (IRE) **(56)***(57) (PTWalwyn)* 5-7-13 (5) MHenry(9) (in tch: effrt ent st: no imp fnl 2f) 1½ 8
*396** Johns Act (USA) **(69)***(67) (DHaydnJones)* 5-9-0v(3) SDrowne(12) (chsd ldrs: rdn 4f out: grad wknd fnl 2f) 2½ 9
*245*3 Opera Buff (IRE) **(58)***(54) (MCPipe)* 4-8-1 (3)ow2 SMulvey(4) (sme hdwy 4f out: n.d) s.h 10
Bit on the Side (IRE) **(76)***(71) (WJMusson)* 6-9-7 (3) PMcCabe(23) (bit bkwd: nvr trbld ldrs) 2½ 11
General Mouktar **(80)***(74) (MCPipe)* 5-10-0 OPears(13) (hdwy appr st: sn rdn & no imp) nk 12
Cutthroat Kid (IRE) **(63)***(53) (MrsMReveley)* 5-8-6 (5) DDenby(1) (lw: s.s: n.d) 3 13
*377** Pharly Dancer **(60)***(49)*(Fav)*(WWHaigh)* 6-8-8 JTate(17) (swtg: chsd ldrs tl wknd fnl 3f) 1¼ 14
Uncle Oswald **(80)***(69) (RHannon)* 4-9-7 (5) MarkDenaro(8) (lw: hmpd after 4f: n.d) s.h 15
*313*13 Environmentalist (IRE) **(59)***(47) (SCWilliams)* 4-8-5 DWright(20) (chsd ldrs: effrt 4f out: sn wknd) nk 16
Classic Model (IRE) **(62)***(50) (BWHills)* 4-8-3 (5) JDSmith(15) (n.d) ½ 17
Wadada **(48)***(31) (SWCampion)* 4-7-3b(5)ow1 PFessey(24) (racd wd: led tl ent st: sn wknd) 3 18

Hit the Canvas (USA) **(69)***(52) (MrsMReveley)* 4-8-10 (5) GParkin(10) (cl up: hrd rdn 4f out: no imp) ....nk **19**
Sunderland Echo **(78)***(53) (MrsMReveley)* 6-9-7 (5) SCopp(18) (chsd ldr tl wknd over 3f out)....6 **20**
The Premier Expres **(47)***(20) (FJO'Mahony)* 5-7-6 (3)ow2 DarrenMoffatt(11) (bit bkwd: led tl hdd ent st) ....hd **21**
403[10] Dancing Sensation (USA) **(57)***(29) (RAkehurst)* 8-8-5 SSanders(16) (mid div: effrt ent st: sn wknd) 2½ **22**
High Five (IRE) **(60)** *(DAWilson)* 5-8-8 DRMcCabe(19) (hdwy appr st: sn wknd) 25 **23**

LONG HANDICAP Wadada 7-3 The Premier Expres 7-4 Achilles Heel 7-6

15/2 Ashover, Pharly Dancer, **8/1** Hit the Canvas (USA), **9/1** Top Cees, **10/1** Bit on the Side (IRE), **12/1** In the Money (IRE), Stalled (IRE), Johns Act (USA), **14/1** Dancing Sensation (USA), General Mouktar, **16/1** Opera Buff (IRE), Cutthroat Kid (IRE), Mentalasanythin, Sunderland Echo, Classic Model (IRE), **20/1** Shadow Leader, Risky Tu, ACHILLES HEEL, Uncle Oswald, **25/1** High Five (IRE), **33/1** The Premier Expres, Environmentalist (IRE), **50/1** Wadada, CSF £375.83 CT £7,150.93 TOTE £37.00: £5.10 £8.10 £7.10 £2.00 (£319.90) Trio Not won; £1,309.90 to Doncaster 25/3/95. OWNER Four J's Syndicate (NEWMARKET) BRED Winning Post Racing Ltd 23 Rn

2m 35.28 (4.68) SF: 40/63/41/38/40/60/47/37/47/32/51/54/33/29/47/25/28/9/30/33/-/9/-

WEIGHT FOR AGE 4yo-2lb

424

BROCKLESBY STKS (2-Y.O) (Class C) £5,348.80 (£1,979.20: £949.60: £388.00: £154.00: £60.40)
5f Stalls: High GOING: 0.15 sec per fur (G) 2-35 (2-38)

World Premier *(77t)*(Fav)*(CEBrittain)* 2-8-11 MRimmer(7) (neat: a cl up: chal 2f out: r.o u.p to ld cl home) ....— **1**
Johayro *(77) (WGMTurner)* 2-8-11 GDuffield(11) (cmpt: mde most tl hdd cl home) ....hd **2**
Don't Forget Mikie (IRE) *(69) (MJHeaton-Ellis)* 2-8-11 StephenDavies(8) (cmpt: in tch: hdwy over 1f out: r.o nr fin) 2½ **3**
Pleasure Time *(68) (CSmith)* 2-8-11 WWoods(9) (neat: bit bkwd: in tch: styd on wl fnl f)....nk **4**
Gwespyr *(66) (JBerry)* 2-8-11 JCarroll(5) (cmpt: lw: chsd ldrs: effrt & hung lft 2f out: no ex) ....½ **5**
Dungeon Master (IRE) *(63) (MRChannon)* 2-8-11 RHughes(1) (leggy: scope: w ldrs tl rdn & btn appr fnl f) 1 **6**
Ramsey Hope *(60) (CWFairhurst)* 2-8-11 NKennedy(2) (cmpt: a in tch: kpt on same pce fnl 2f) 1 **7**
Thai Morning *(57) (PWHarris)* 2-8-11 PatEddery(6) (small: str: bit bkwd: s.i.s: hdwy after 2f: nvr plcd to chal) ....¾ **8**
Clint *(41) (JFfitch-Heyes)* 2-8-11 TQuinn(4) (leggy: unf: dwlt: n.d) 5 **9**
Whittle Rock *(35) (EJAlston)* 2-8-6 JFortune(10) (str: cmpt: bkwd: dwlt: hdwy after 1½f: wandered u.p: wknd over 1f out) ....½ **10**
Yellow Dragon (IRE) *(38) (MissGayKelleway)* 2-8-11 SWhitworth(12) (neat: a outpcd & bhd) ....½ **11**
Go-Go-Power-Ranger *(13) (BEllison)* 2-8-11 TIves(3) (leggy: s.i.s: a outpcd & bhd)....8 **12**

9/4 WORLD PREMIER, **3/1** Gwespyr, **7/2** Thai Morning, **5/1** Dungeon Master (IRE), **10/1** Yellow Dragon (IRE), Johayro, **14/1** Whittle Rock, **16/1** Ramsey Hope, **20/1** Clint, Pleasure Time, **25/1** Don't Forget Mikie (IRE), Go-Go-Power-Ranger, CSF £28.91 TOTE £4.20: £1.60 £3.10 £4.60 (£46.60) Trio £211.50 OWNER Mrs C. E. Brittain (NEWMARKET) BRED Mrs C. E. Brittain 12 Rn

63.49 secs (5.09) SF: 22/22/14/13/11/8/5/2/-/-/-/-

425

STONES BITTER DONCASTER MILE STKS (Listed) (4-Y.O+) (Class A) £12,690.00 (£3,780.00: £1,305.00: £1,305.00)
1m (round) Stalls: High GOING minus 0.09 sec per fur (G) 3-05 (3-07)

Airport (USA) (100)*(110) (JHMGosden)* 4-8-12 JCarroll(4) (lw: b: b.hind: hld up & bhd: hdwy to ld over 1f out: r.o wl) ....— **1**
Fraam **(109)***(112) (EALDunlop)* 6-9-1 WRSwinburn(8) (lw: b: hld up: nt clr run over 2f out tl appr fnl f: r.o wl) ....¾ **2**
Missed Flight **(117)***(115)*(Fav)*(CFWall)* 5-9-5 GDuffield(3) (plld hrd: nt clr run 3f out tl ins fnl f: r.o wl) ....s.h **3**
Alanees **(110)***(108) (CEBrittain)* 4-8-12 MRimmer(6) (a.p: qcknd to chal over 1f out: no ex ins fnl f) ....d.h **3**
Our Rita **(94)***(103) (DrJDScargill)* 6-8-7 DHolland(7) (hld up & bhd: hdwy over 2f out: nt qckn fnl f) ....nk **5**
Penny Drops **(110)***(107) (LordHuntingdon)* 6-9-0 DHarrison(2) (cl up: outpcd over 2f out: btn whn hmpd ins fnl f) 1¼ **6**
Jafeica (IRE) **(100)***(103) (RHannon)* 4-8-12 PatEddery(5) (mde most tl hdd & wknd over 1f out) 1 **7**

Risk Master **(92)***(99) (CAHorgan)* 6-8-12 WWoods(1) (in tch: effrt over 2f out: no imp) 1¾ 8
Bin Ajwaad (IRE) **(109)***(100) (BHanbury)* 5-9-3 WRyan(9) (lw: plld hrd: sn w ldr: disp ld 3f out: wknd over 1f out) 2 9

6/4 Missed Flight, **4/1** Fraam, **7/1** Bin Ajwaad (IRE), **9/1** Penny Drops, Alanees, **11/1** Our Rita, **12/1** AIRPORT (USA), **14/1** Jafeica (IRE), **50/1** Risk Master, CSF £55.73 TOTE £13.10: £2.60 £1.90 £0.50 MF £1.70 A (£16.80) Trio £7.40 A, F & MF, £14.60 A, F & AL OWNER Sheikh Mohammed (NEWMARKET) BRED E. A. Seltzer Irrevocable Trust in USA 9 Rn
1m 42.68 (6.38) SF: 24/26/29/22/17/21/17/14/15

426 RACEFORM UPDATE H'CAP (0-90) (3-Y.O) (Class C) £6,108.00 (£1,824.00: £872.00: £396.00)

5f Stalls: High GOING: 0.15 sec per fur (G) 3-40 (3-41)

380[3] **Portend (71)***(78) (SRBowring)* 3-7-10 (7)ow1 CTeague(11) (bhd: hdwy ½-wy: squeezed thro to ld 1f out: r.o) ....— 1
Double Quick (IRE) **(84)***(84) (MJohnston)* 3-9-2 DHolland(1) (chsd ldrs: chal over 1f out: nt qckn) 2½ 2
Shinerolla **(61)***(61) (MrsJRRamsden)* 3-7-7 JLowe(10) (bhd: nt clr run 2f out: r.o wl fnl f) ....hd 3
398[10] Swan At Whalley **(75)***(69) (JBerry)* 3-8-7 JCarroll(12) (lw: led tl hdd & wknd fnl f: fin 5th: ½l: plcd 4th) 4
That Man Again **(84)***(70) (GLewis)* 3-9-2b SWhitworth(13) (chsd ldrs: nt qckn appr fnl f: fin 6th: 2½l: plcd 5th) 5
Superpride **(72)***(53) (TDBarron)* 3-8-4 JFortune(3) (chsd ldrs over 3f) 1½ 7
Leap for Joy **(89)***(67) (JHMGosden)* 3-9-7 JQuinn(14) (chsd ldrs: rdn 2f out: grad wknd) 1 8
A Million to One (IRE) **(78)***(48) (MBell)* 3-8-10 MFenton(6) (effrt ½-wy: edgd lft & sn btn) 2½ 9
*363** Ultra Beet **(75)***(39)*(Fav)*(PCHaslam)* 3-8-7 JWeaver(8) (cl up tl wknd & hmpd appr fnl f) 2 10
*392** Crystal Loop **(70)***(31) (ABailey)* 3-8-2 KDarley(4) (spd 3f: btn whn hmpd wl over 1f out) ....¾ 11
342[3] C-Yer-Simmie (IRE) **(61)***(18) (RHollinshead)* 3-7-7 NCarlisle(7) (spd over 3f) 1½ 12
380[6] Double Glow **(66)***(22) (NBycroft)* 3-7-12 JFanning(5) (bit bkwd: effrt ½-wy: n.d) ....nk 13
173[5] Fiery Footsteps **(65)***(15) (PHowling)* 3-7-4v(7)ow4 SLanigan(2) (bit bkwd: w ldrs tl wknd over 1f out) ....½ 14
257[4] Bold Frontier **(61)***(57) (KTIvory)* 3-7-7b GBardwell(9) (b: bhd: nt clr run 2f out: swtchd lft: r.o fnl f: fin 4th: 1¼l: disq: pl last) 0

LONG HANDICAP Shinerolla 7-4 C-Yer-Simmie (IRE) 7-4 Fiery Footsteps 7-4 Bold Frontier 7-4
100/30 Ultra Beet, **6/1** Double Quick (IRE), **8/1** A Million to One (IRE), That Man Again, Shinerolla, **9/1** Leap for Joy, **10/1** Crystal Loop, PORTEND, **16/1** C-Yer-Simmie (IRE), **20/1** Superpride, Swan At Whalley, **25/1** Bold Frontier, **33/1** Double Glow, Fiery Footsteps, CSF £65.14 CT £464.15 TOTE £10.20: £2.30 £2.00 £3.10 (£26.10) Trio £882.60 OWNER Mr D. H. Bowring (EDWINSTOWE) BRED Hollow Hole Stud 14 Rn
62.13 secs (3.73) SF: 37/43/20/-/-/-/-/-/-/-/-/-/-/-
STEWARDS' ENQUIRY Bold Frontier disq. (interf. to Shinerolla). Bardwell susp. 1 & 3-5/4/95

427 'BACK A WINNER BY TRAIN' H'CAP (0-85) (3-Y.O) (Class D) £4,698.00 (£1,404.00: £672.00: £306.00)

1m 2f 60y Stalls: Low GOING minus 0.09 sec per fur (G) 4-10 (4-14)

Inquisitor (USA) (83)*(101+)*(Fav)*(JHMGosden)* 3-9-7 PatEddery(17) (lw: b: b.hind: mde all: qcknd over 2f out: r.o wl) ....— 1
*301** Contrafire (IRE) **(57)***(68) (WJarvis)* 3-7-4 (5)ow2 NVarley(4) (lw: a chsng ldrs: pushed along appr st: r.o wl fnl f) 3 2
Danegold (IRE) **(71)***(68) (MRChannon)* 3-8-9 ow1 RHughes(12) (hdwy over 4f out: sn chsng ldrs: one pce fnl 2f) 10 3
324[2] Komreyev Dancer **(70)***(67) (ABailey)* 3-8-3 (5) VHalliday(2) (a in tch: drvn along 4f out: one pce) ....¾ 4
Euro Forum **(58)***(54) (GLMoore)* 3-7-10 JQuinn(15) (bit bkwd: hdwy ent st: swtchd 3f out: styd on one pce) ....½ 5
488a[9] Courbaril **(60)***(54) (SDow)* 3-7-12 GCarter(14) (styd on fnl 4f: nrst fin) 1¼ 6
418[5] Doddington Flyer **(63)***(55) (RHollinshead)* 3-7-10 (5)ow1 AGarth(1) (hld up: hdwy 3f out: nvr rchd ldrs) ....nk 7
Clifton Fox **(77)***(67) (JAGlover)* 3-9-1 MBirch(11) (chsd ldrs: effrt 4f out: grad wknd fnl 3f) 2½ 8
*350** Durgams First (IRE) **(64)***(53) (MrsMReveley)* 3-7-9 (7) DDenby(6) (lw: bhd: effrt 4f out: n.d) ....½ 9
Busy Banana **(70)***(59) (RHannon)* 3-8-8 KDarley(5) (h.d.w: trckd ldrs: effrt over 3f out: wknd fnl 2f) ....hd 10
Dr Edgar **(73)***(59) (GWragg)* 3-8-11 FNorton(8) (hdwy appr st: nvr trbld ldrs) 1½ 11
Elpidos **(71)***(57) (CEBrittain)* 3-8-9 BDoyle(18) (prom: effrt over 4f out: sn btn) ....nk 12
354[8] Chaldon Herring **(65)***(51) (TDBarron)* 3-8-3 WCarson(3) (bhd: hdwy on ins 3f out: n.m.r: n.d) ....hd 13

Toshiba Talk (IRE) **(55)***(39) (BEllison)* 3-7-7 JLowe(10) (chsd ldrs tl wknd fnl 3f)....................1 **14**
Fame Again **(80)***(61) (MrsJRRamsden)* 3-9-4 JWeaver(9) (hld up & bhd: hmpd 3f out: n.d)....................1¾ **15**
Rambo Waltzer **(65)***(32) (SGNorton)* 3-8-3 JFanning(16) (chsd ldrs: ev ch 4f out: wknd over 2f out)....................9 **16**
Crested Knight (IRE) **(70)***(37) (CAHorgan)* 3-8-8 JReid(7) (stdd s: a bhd)....................nk **17**
Lucidity **(70)***(37) (CWThornton)* 3-8-8 DeanMcKeown(13) (bit bkwd: bhd fnl 3f)....................hd **18**

LONG HANDICAP Contrafire (IRE) 7-5 Toshiba Talk (IRE) 7-5

100/30 INQUISITOR (USA), **5/1** Contrafire (IRE), **11/2** Fame Again, **9/1** Clifton Fox, **10/1** Courbaril, **12/1** Komreyev Dancer, Chaldon Herring, Durgams First (IRE), **14/1** Busy Banana, Elpidos, **16/1** Dr Edgar, **20/1** Lucidity, Danegold (IRE), **25/1** Crested Knight (IRE), Euro Forum, **33/1** Toshiba Talk (IRE), Rambo Waltzer, Doddington Flyer, CSF £22.25 CT £289.23 TOTE £3.60: £1.90 £2.20 £8.10 £1.90 (£14.00) Trio £477.90 OWNER Mr K. Abdullah (NEWMARKET) BRED Juddmonte Farms 18 Rn 2m 11.39 (4.39) SF: 63/30/30/29/16/16/17/29/15/21/21/19/13/1/23/-/-/-

428

HALL GATE MAIDEN STKS (3-Y.O) (Class D) £4,171.70 (£1,247.60: £597.80: £272.90) **1m 2f 60y** Stalls: Low GOING minus 0.09 sec per fur (G) 4-40 (4-42)

Sea Victor *(93) (JHMGosden)* 3-9-0 PatEddery(8) (lw: a cl up: rdn over 3f out: led wl over 1f out: edgd lft: r.o)....................— **1**
Menshood (IRE) *(89) (BHanbury)* 3-9-0 WRyan(5) (w'like: scope: led tl hdd wl over 1f out: kpt on)....................2½ **2**
Astrolabe *(80)*(Fav)*(BWHills)* 3-9-0 MHills(4) (lw: a.p: outpcd over 3f out: styd on fnl f)....................6 **3**
Paper Cloud *(74) (CEBrittain)* 3-8-9 BDoyle(1) (bit bkwd: hdwy 4f out: styd on: no imp)....................nk **4**
Daffaq *(75) (PTWalwyn)* 3-9-0 WCarson(2) (trckd ldrs: chal over 2f out: btn whn hmpd wl over 1f out)....................½ **5**
China Mail (IRE) *(52) (JMPEustace)* 3-9-0 BThomson(12) (bhd: hdwy 4f out: nvr rchd ldrs)....................15 **6**
Antarctica (USA) *(42) (PAKelleway)* 3-8-9 JWeaver(3) (leggy: unf: dwlt: bhd tl sme late hdwy)....................3½ **7**
17[4] Amercius *(39) (RHannon)* 3-9-0 RHughes(10) (a rr div)....................5 **8**
Homecrest *(35) (BEllison)* 3-9-0 TIves(6) (lengthy: bkwd: chsd ldrs tl wknd fnl 3½f)....................2½ **9**
Trauma (IRE) *(29) (WJarvis)* 3-8-9 JReid(7) (lengthy: unf: effrt & prom appr st: wknd over 3f out)....................¾ **10**
Roscommon Lad (IRE) *(RHollinshead)* 3-9-0 WRSwinburn(11) (sn outpcd & wl bhd)....................30 **11**
90[8] Vade Retro Satanas (FR) **(49)** *(BSRothwell)* 3-9-0 MBirch(9) (chsd ldrs to st)....................1½ **12**

3/1 Astrolabe, **100/30** Daffaq, **4/1** SEA VICTOR, **6/1** Paper Cloud, **7/1** Trauma (IRE), **10/1** Menshood (IRE), **12/1** Antarctica (USA), **20/1** Amercius, **33/1** China Mail (IRE), **50/1** Homecrest, Roscommon Lad (IRE), Vade Retro Satanas (FR), CSF £42.05 TOTE £5.20: £2.00 £4.10 £2.00 (£50.10) Trio £169.40 OWNER Mr K. Abdullah (NEWMARKET) BRED Juddmonte Farms 12 Rn 2m 13.36 (6.36) SF: 37/33/24/18/23/-/-/-/-/-/-/-

T/Jkpt: Not won; £10,225.93 to Doncaster 24/3/95. T/Plpt: £747.30 (51.3 Tckts). T/Qdpt: £24.90 (9.2 Tckts). AA

0423-DONCASTER (L-H)
Friday March 24th (Good)

WIND: fresh,half against

429

RIVA BINGO (S) MAIDEN STKS (2-Y.O) (Class F) £2,519.00 (£694.00: £329.00) **5f** Stalls: High GOING: 0.19 sec per fur (G) 1-30 (1-33)

Penny Parkes *(59t) (JBerry)* 2-8-9 JCarroll(3) (b.hind: leggy: scope: lw: chsd ldrs: effrt 2f out: r.o u.p to ld nr fin)....................— **1**
Swiss Valley Lady *(58) (WGMTurner)* 2-8-9 TSprake(2) (leggy: unf: led: shkn up over 1f out: jst ct)....................nk **2**
Don't Tell Vicki *(47) (JSMoore)* 2-8-9 JWeaver(8) (unf: stdd s: sn wl bhd: hdwy & switched outside over 1f out: r.o)....................3½ **3**
Poly Static (IRE) *(43) (MRChannon)* 2-8-9 RHughes(6) (neat: scope: chsd ldr: rdn 2f out: sn wknd)....................1¼ **4**
Double Or Bust *(32) (RJBaker)* 2-8-9 SRaymont(1) (small: lt-f: s.s: sn drvn along: hdwy ½-wy: wknd over 1f out)....................3½ **5**
Power Dee *(25) (MWEasterby)* 2-8-9 LCharnock(9) (unf: prom: sn drvn along: lost pl ½-wy)..2 **6**
Iron And Steel *(28)*(Fav)*(GLewis)* 2-9-0 SWhitworth(5) (small: lt-f: prom: drvn along ½-wy: sn wknd)....................¾ **7**
Seven Kisses (IRE) *(BAMcMahon)* 2-8-9 LDettori(4) (neat: scope: bit bkwd: wandered & sn wl bhd: t.o)....................25 **8**

2/1 Iron And Steel, **11/4** Poly Static (IRE), **4/1** PENNY PARKES (op 9/4), **5/1** Swiss Valley Lady, **8/1** Seven Kisses (IRE) (op 5/1), **10/1** Don't Tell Vicki, **12/1** Power Dee, **20/1** Double Or Bust, CSF £25.35 TOTE £3.70: £1.60 £1.60 £2.60 (£14.80) Trio £91.10 OWNER Mr Joseph Heler (COCKERHAM) BRED Joseph Heler 8 Rn
64.84 secs (6.44) SF: 2/1/-/-/-/-/-/-
Bt in 7,400 gns

430 127 SPITFIRE SQUADRON LADIES' H'CAP (0-80) (4-Y.O+) (Class E)
£3,200.00 (£950.00: £450.00: £200.00)
1m 2f 60y Stalls: Low GOING minus 0.15 sec per fur (GF) 2-05 (2-07)

Children's Choice (IRE) (55)*(66) (PJMcBride)* 4-9-11 (5)ow2 MrsDKettlewell(1) (b.off hind: in tch: nt clr run & swtchd 2f out: r.o wl u.p to ld wl ins fnl f) — 1
*81*5 Joseph's Wine (IRE) **(65)***(76)*(Fav)*(DNicholls)* 6-10-13b MissAHarwood(8) (lw: trckd ldrs gng wl: led over 2f out tl wl ins fnl f) 1¼ 2
Teen Jay **(72)***(82) (SESherwood)* 5-11-6 MissSMitchell(15) (bhd tl hdwy over 3f out: styd on wl u.p fnl f: nt rch ldrs) ¾ 3
*179** Larn Fort **(47)***(54) (CWFairhurst)* 5-9-9v MrsSBosley(7) (chsd ldr: led over 5f out tl over 2f out: one pce fnl 2f) 2 4
*303*7 Rapporteur (USA) **(60)***(65) (CCElsey)* 9-10-8 MissAElsey(21) (b: prom tl lost pl 6f out: styd on again fnl 2f) 1¼ 5
Prenonamoss **(67)***(71) (DWPArbuthnot)* 7-11-1v MrsDArbuthnot(3) (b.hind: a chsng ldrs: kpt on one pce fnl 2f) ½ 6
Eskimo Nel (IRE) **(43)***(44) (JLSpearing)* 4-8-13 (5) MissTSpearing(4) (mid div: styd on fnl 2f: nt rch ldrs) 1¾ 7
Stoproveritate **(42)***(43) (MrsMReveley)* 6-8-13 (5) MissSBainbridge(23) (bhd: gd hdwy on ins 3f out: nt rch ldrs) ½ 8
*408*5 Royal Acclaim **(43)***(39) (JMBradley)* 10-9-0v(5)ow3 MrsDMcHale(9) (prom: effrt 3f out: grad wknd) ¾ 9
*100*11 Tina's Charm (IRE) **(38)***(35) (JSMoore)* 6-8-9 (5) MrsSMoore(26) (mid div: hdwy 5f out: nvr rchd ldrs) 1½ 10
Sweet Mignonette **(73)***(70) (MrsMReveley)* 7-11-2 (5) MissCSpearing(18) (s.s: bhd tl sme hdwy fnl 2f) nk 11
*166** Gold Blade **(45)***(41) (JPearce)* 6-9-7 MrsLPearce(13) (mid div: hdwy 5f out: rdn over 2f out: wknd over 1f out) ½ 12
Hazard a Guess (IRE) **(70)***(66) (MrsJRRamsden)* 5-11-4 MissDianaJones(2) (bhd: sme hdwy over 2f out: n.d) hd 13
Bookcase **(58)***(51) (DRCElsworth)* 8-10-6 MissJAllison(17) (mid div: effrt over 3f out: wknd over 2f out) ¾ 14
4235 Mentalasanythin **(53)***(45) (ABailey)* 6-9-10 (5) MissBridgetGatehouse(25) (chsd ldrs: ev ch tl wknd over 2f out) ½ 15
*266*6 Missus Murhill (IRE) **(47)***(37) (NTinkler)* 4-9-8 MissPJones(5) (in tch tl outpcd fnl 3f) 1¼ 16
Credit Squeeze **(61)***(50) (RFJohnsonHoughton)* 5-10-9 MissEJohnsonHoughton(24) (trckd ldrs: led over 3f out tl over 2f out: sn wknd) ½ 17
Allesca **(61)***(50) (MDIUsher)* 5-10-4 (5) MrsAUsher(20) (b: a bhd) hd 18
North Ardar **(56)***(41) (MrsMReveley)* 5-9-13 (5) MissMCarson(6) (sn bhd) 2½ 19
*387*8 Rave-on-Hadley (IRE) **(42)***(26) (SWCampion)* 5-8-13 (5) MrsSJCampion(22) (led tl over 5f out: one pce fnl 3f) 1 20
Alpine Skier (IRE) **(47)***(30) (MrsMReveley)* 4-9-8 MissJWinter(16) (lw: nvr nr ldrs) nk 21
Gallardini (IRE) **(72)***(55) (BSRothwell)* 6-11-1 (5) MissAlexMcCabe(10) (a rr div) nk 22
Avishayes (USA) **(53)***(35) (MrsMReveley)* 8-10-1 MrsAFarrell(12) (sn bhd & pushed along) nk 23
Zahid (USA) **(56)***(37) (BobJones)* 4-9-12 (5) MissDJJones(14) (prom tl lost pl 4f out) ¾ 24
*379*9 Britannia Mills **(40)***(21) (MCChapman)* 4-8-10 (5) MissEFolkes(19) (a bhd) s.h 25
*387*2 Aitch N'Bee **(65)***(46) (LadyHerries)* 12-10-13 MrsMCowdrey(27) (s.i.s: a bhd) nk 26
Reed My Lips (IRE) **(46)***(13) (BPJBaugh)* 4-9-2 (5)ow4 MissLBoswell(11) (b.nr hind: chsd ldrs tl wknd over 3f out) 6 27

LONG HANDICAP Tina's Charm (IRE) 8-9

11/2 Joseph's Wine (IRE), **8/1** Hazard a Guess (IRE), Gold Blade, **12/1** Aitch N'Bee, **14/1** Stoproveritate, Larn Fort, Mentalasanythin, Credit Squeeze, Sweet Mignonette, **20/1** Eskimo Nel (IRE), Teen Jay, Gallardini (IRE), North Ardar, Alpine Skier (IRE), Bookcase, Allesca, Avishayes (USA), **25/1** CHILDREN'S CHOICE (IRE), Zahid (USA), **33/1** Royal Acclaim, Prenonamoss, Rapporteur (USA), **50/1** Missus Murhill (IRE), Rave-on-Hadley (IRE), Britannia Mills, Tina's Charm (IRE), Reed My Lips (IRE), CSF £154.83 CT £2,618.78 TOTE £97.60: £14.40 £1.60 £8.50 £4.80 (£386.90) Trio £976.80 OWNER Mr P. C. Totman (NEWMARKET) BRED M. J. Cassidy 27 Rn
2m 13.82 (6.82) SF: 48/59/65/37/48/54/26/26/22/18/53/24/49/36/30/21/35/35/26/10/14/39/20/21/5/30/-
WEIGHT FOR AGE 4yo-1lb

431

MARC WHEATLEY MAIDEN STKS (I) (3-Y.O) (Class D) £3,360.50 (£998.00: £473.00: £210.50) **7f** Stalls: High GOING: 0.19 sec per fur (G) 2-35 (2-37)

Torrential (USA) *(96+)*(Fav)*(JHMGosden)* 3-9-0 LDettori(3) (gd sort: scope: s.s: stdy hdwy ½-wy: n.m.r: swtchd ins: r.o strly to ld ins fnl f: readily)............— 1
Silver Sting *(93) (IABalding)* 3-9-0 WRyan(1) (swvd lft s: sn trckng ldrs: led wl over 1f out tl ins fnl f: no ch w wnr)............1½ 2
Sanoosea (USA) *(86) (MRStoute)* 3-9-0 WRSwinburn(8) (w'like: lengthy: scope: hld up: stdy hdwy 2f out: kpt on wl fnf f: improve)............3 3
Christmas Kiss **(85)***(76) (RHannon)* 3-8-9 PatEddery(12) (w ldrs: ev ch 2f out: wknd appr fnl f)2 4
Henry Koehler *(81) (CEBrittain)* 3-9-0 MRimmer(7) (w'like: w ldrs: led 3f out tl wl over 1f out: grad wknd)............nk 5
Fawj (USA) *(71) (RWArmstrong)* 3-9-0 RPrice(11) (s.s: bhd: sme hdwy ½-wy: nvr nr ldrs)......4 6
Stand Tall *(63) (CWThornton)* 3-9-0 DeanMcKeown(6) (w'like: str: bit bkwd: s.i.s: hdwy to chse ldrs ½-wy: n.m.r & wknd 2f out)............3½ 7
Alltime Dancer (IRE) *(63) (MrsJRRamsden)* 3-9-0 SDWilliams(2) (w'like: str: bkwd: s.s: outpcd & bhd: sme hdwy 2f out: nvr nr ldrs)............s.h 8
Spirituelle **(72)***(57) (MMcCormack)* 3-8-9 BThomson(9) (led to 3f out: sn wknd)............½ 9
Shared (IRE) *(51) (WJHaggas)* 3-9-0 MTebbutt(10) (b.nr hind: w'like: outpcd fr ½-wy)............5 10
Bulsara **(60)***(43) (CWFairhurst)* 3-9-0 JFanning(5) (w ldrs tl lost pl over 2f out)............3½ 11
*255*10 Never Time (IRE) **(55)***(20) (MrsVAAconley)* 3-9-0b GDuffield(4) (sn w ldrs: wknd qckly 3f out: sn bhd)............10 12

7/4 TORRENTIAL (USA) (Evens-4/5), **11/2** Christmas Kiss, **6/1** Silver Sting, Henry Koehler (op 7/2), **13/2** Sanoosea (USA) (5/1-8/1), **15/2** Fawj (USA), **16/1** Shared (IRE), **25/1** Alltime Dancer (IRE), Spirituelle, **50/1** Stand Tall, Bulsara, Never Time (IRE), CSF £13.02 TOTE £2.30: £1.50 £2.60 £1.60 (£17.30) Trio £36.90 OWNER Sheikh Mohammed (NEWMARKET) BRED Peter M. Brant 12 Rn
1m 29.72 (6.32) SF: 39/36/29/19/24/14/6/6/-/-/-/-

432

CYSTIC FIBROSIS RESEARCH CUP H'CAP (0-90) (4-Y.O+) (Class C) £6,400.00 (£1,900.00: £900.00: £400.00)
2m 2f Stalls: Low GOING minus 0.15 sec per fur (GF) 3-05 (3-08)

*346*10 **Upper Mount Clair (57)***(71) (CEBrittain)* 5-8-7 BDoyle(12) (in tch: hdwy to ld over 2f out: styd on wl fnl f)............— 1
*396*4 Noufari (FR) **(70)***(83) (RHollinshead)* 4-9-0 TIves(13) (bhd: gd hdwy 4f out: chsd wnr 2f out: hung lft: nt qckn fnl f)............1½ 2
Roberty Lea **(65)***(72) (MrsMReveley)* 7-9-1 KDarley(11) (hld up: styd on fnl 2f: nt rch ldrs)......6 3
*277*4 Elburg (IRE) **(60)***(66) (RPCHoad)* 5-8-10 JQuinn(9) (chsd ldrs: pushed along 6f out: sn wl outpcd: hrd rdn & styd on fnl 2f)............1 4
Ambuscade (USA) **(55)***(61) (EJAlston)* 9-8-5 JFortune(15) (bhd tl hdwy 7f out: styd on fnl 3f: nt rch ldrs)............1 5
Googly **(75)***(79) (JWhite)* 6-9-6b(5) SDrowne(14) (b: bhd: drvn along ½-wy: kpt on fnl 3f: nvr nr ldrs)............1¼ 6
*375*3 How's it Goin (IRE) **(62)***(66) (WRMuir)* 4-8-6 DHarrison(6) (in tch: hdwy to chse ldrs over 3f out: rdn & wandered over 2f out: sn wknd)............¾ 7
Ballymac Girl **(54)***(57) (JMBradley)* 7-8-4 JoannaMorgan(1) (b: bhd: hdwy 3f out: kpt on: nvr nr ldrs)............½ 8
*271*13 Guards Brigade **(56)***(59) (JHetherton)* 4-8-0 NKennedy(2) (led: clr 4f out: hdd over 2f out: sn wknd)............nk 9
*147*2 Argyle Cavalier (IRE) **(65)***(68)*(Fav)*(MJohnston)* 5-9-1 DHolland(7) (chsd ldrs: drvn along 5f out: lost pl 3f out)............hd 10
Brandon Prince (IRE) **(73)***(76) (IABalding)* 7-9-4b(5) DGriffiths(5) (hld up & bhd: sme hdwy over 2f out: n.d)............½ 11
*234** Flashman **(46)***(45) (BJLlewellyn)* 5-7-10 ow3 TWilliams(8) (sn chsng ldr: rdn & wknd 3f out).....¾ 12
Mondragon **(76)***(69) (MrsMReveley)* 5-9-12 RCochrane(4) (bhd: effrt over 3f out: sn wknd & eased)............10 13
*87*2 Pride of May (IRE) **(68)***(39) (RHannon)* 4-8-12b TQuinn(10) (plld hrd: trckd ldrs tl lost pl 5f out: sn bhd: t.o)............25 14

LONG HANDICAP Flashman 6-12

7/2 Argyle Cavalier (IRE), **9/2** Roberty Lea, **13/2** Noufari (FR), **7/1** Mondragon, **15/2** Googly, **10/1** Pride of May (IRE), **12/1** Ballymac Girl, Brandon Prince (IRE), **14/1** Ambuscade (USA), Elburg (IRE), **16/1** How's it Goin (IRE), **33/1** Flashman, UPPER MOUNT CLAIR, **50/1** Guards Brigade, CSF £227.01 CT £1,072.50 TOTE £41.60: £8.60 £1.90 £2.10 (£153.40) Trio £719.20 OWNER Mr C. E. Brittain (NEWMARKET) BRED J. Ward Hill 14 Rn
4m 3.0 (10.30) SF: 36/42/37/31/26/44/25/22/18/33/41/10/34/-
WEIGHT FOR AGE 4yo-6lb

433

WILLIAM HILL SPRING MILE H'CAP (4-Y.O+) (Class B) £15,920.00 (£4,760.00: £2,280.00: £1,040.00)
1m (straight) Stalls: High GOING: 0.19 sec per fur (G) 3-40 (3-41)

Sharp Prospect (74)*(85) (RAkehurst)* 5-9-2 TQuinn(22) (hdwy ½-wy: r.o wl to ld ins fnl f: drvn clr) ....— 1
Set Table (USA) **(71)***(76) (JHMGosden)* 6-8-13 LDettori(10) (trckd ldrs centre: effrt 2f out: edgd rt: kpt on fnl f: no ch w wnr) 3 2
Gadge **(72)***(74) (DMorris)* 4-9-0 WRSwinburn(15) (hdwy over 2f out: styd on wl fnl f: nt rch ldrs) 1¼ 3
Garnock Valley **(74)***(75) (JBerry)* 5-9-2 GCarter(18) (a.p: qcknd to ld over 2f out: hdd & no ex ins fnl f) ....½ 4
Samah **(69)***(67) (DNicholls)* 5-8-11 NConnorton(17) (hdwy over 2f out: styd on wl fnl f: nt rch ldrs) 1¼ 5
Sheppard's Cross **(79)***(77) (PTWalwyn)* 4-9-7 PRobinson(19) (hld up: hdwy over 1f out: r.o wl nr fin) ....s.h 6
Sandmoor Chambray **(71)***(69) (MHEasterby)* 4-8-13 MBirch(13) (chsd ldrs tl outpcd fnl 2f) ...hd 7
365⁶ Cee-Jay-Ay **(73)***(67) (JBerry)* 8-9-1 JCarroll(23) (lw: s.i.s: hdwy ½-wy: wknd over 1f out)......1¾ 8
Roi de la Mer (IRE) **(70)***(64) (JAkehurst)* 4-8-12 SWhitworth(9) (s.i.s: swtchd lft & racd far side: nvr wnt pce) ....hd 9
*337** Flowing Ocean **(71)***(65)*(Fav)*(MissGayKelleway)* 5-8-13 RCochrane(14) (in tch: effrt over 2f out: hung rt: grad wknd) ....s.h 10
302⁸ Admirals Flame (IRE) **(65)***(57) (CFWall)* 4-8-7 GDuffield(4) (b: racd far side: led wl over 1f out: no ch w stands' side) 1¾ 11
383⁶ Red Valerian **(74)***(66) (KMcAuliffe)* 4-8-13b(3) JTate(8) (b.off hind: racd centre: chsd ldrs tl wknd 2f out) ....hd 12
383³ Ertlon **(77)***(68) (CEBrittain)* 5-9-5 BDoyle(6) (prom centre over 5f) ....¾ 13
130⁴ Chinour (IRE) **(66)***(47) (EJAlston)* 7-8-8 JQuinn(24) (bhd fnl 2f) 5 14
Pride of Pendle **(68)***(46) (DNicholls)* 6-8-10 AlexGreaves(2) (chsd ldrs far side 5f: eased)....1¼ 15
Harpoon Louie (USA) **(79)***(52) (MHEasterby)* 5-9-7 KDarley(16) (lw: chsd ldrs: drvn along ½-wy: wknd over 2f out) 2½ 16
313¹² Sharp Conquest **(65)***(37) (WRMuir)* 4-8-7b JWeaver(1) (lw: led far side tl wknd wl over 1f out)¾ 17
386⁷ Persian Affair (IRE) **(73)***(39) (DHaydnJones)* 4-9-1 AMackay(3) (racd far side: prom: drvn along ½-wy: sn wknd) 3 18
Kaitak (IRE) **(72)***(37) (JMCarr)* 4-9-0 SMorris(11) (b.off hind: racd centre: chsd ldrs tl wknd 2f out) ....½ 19
Braille (IRE) **(75)***(39) (MGMeagher)* 4-9-3 JFortune(20) (w ldrs tl wknd 3f out) ....½ 20
94⁵ Queens Consul (IRE) **(77)***(38) (BSRothwell)* 5-9-5 MFenton(21) (led tl hdd & wknd over 2f out) 1½ 21
347¹⁰ Anzio (IRE) **(75)***(6) (BAPearce)* 4-9-3 StephenDavies(12) (b: racd centre: prom tl lost pl ½-wy: sn bhd & eased) 15 22
Another Fiddle (IRE) **(70)** *(RAkehurst)* 5-8-9 (3) SSanders(5) (b.off hind: racd centre: bhd & eased fr ½-wy) 1½ 23

5/1 Flowing Ocean (op 3/1), **11/2** Ertlon, **8/1** SHARP PROSPECT (op 16/1), **9/1** Set Table (USA), **12/1** Red Valerian, Harpoon Louie (USA), **14/1** Another Fiddle (IRE), **16/1** Chinour (IRE), **20/1** Samah, Cee-Jay-Ay, Gadge, **25/1** Sharp Conquest, Garnock Valley, Kaitak (IRE), Admirals Flame (IRE), **33/1** Sandmoor Chambray, Sheppard's Cross, Pride of Pendle, Roi de la Mer (IRE), Persian Affair (IRE), Queens Consul (IRE), **50/1** Braille (IRE), **66/1** Anzio (IRE), CSF £73.45 CT £1,298.30 TOTE £8.30: £2.20 £1.90 £4.50 £6.60 (£37.50) Trio £397.30 OWNER Future Prospectors - Four Seasons Racing (EPSOM) BRED Crest Stud Ltd 23 Rn
1m 42.21 (5.71) SF: 57/48/47/48/40/50/42/40/37/38/30/39/41/20/19/25/10/12/10/12/11/-/-

434

HOLROYD CONSTRUCTION GROUP H'CAP (0-90) (3-Y.O+) (Class C) £5,120.00 (£1,120.00: £1,120.00: £320.00)
6f Stalls: High GOING: 0.19 sec per fur (G) 4-10 (4-12)

Castlerea Lad (76)*(79) (RHollinshead)* 6-9-4 WRyan(11) (lw: sn wl bhd: gd hdwy centre 2f out: r.o wl to ld ins fnl f) ....— 1
Domulla **(82)***(83) (RAkehurst)* 5-9-10 TQuinn(9) (trckd ldrs: qcknd to ld over 1f out: hdd & no ex ins fnl f) ....¾ 2
Sailormaite **(72)***(73) (SRBowring)* 4-9-0 SWebster(21) (led stands side: kpt on wl appr fnl f) d.h 2
Jigsaw Boy **(63)***(63) (PGMurphy)* 6-8-5 DHarrison(22) (in tch stands' side: styd on wl fnl f)....nk 4
400⁴ Plum First **(58)***(58) (LRLloyd-James)* 5-8-0 NKennedy(14) (b.hind: a chsng ldrs stands' side: kpt on same pce appr fnl f) ....hd 5
314⁴ So Intrepid (IRE) **(74)***(72) (JMBradley)* 5-8-11 (5) SDrowne(13) (a in tch: kpt on same pce fr ½-wy) ....¾ 6

Sagebrush Roller **(86)***(82) (JWWatts)* 7-10-0 GDuffield(19) (racd stands' side: s.s: hdwy 2f out: styd on ins fnl f)........¾ 7
365[5] Highborn (IRE) **(85)***(79) (PSFelgate)* 6-9-13 KDarley(8) (hdwy over 2f out: styd on fnl 2f)........¾ 8
Mister Jolson **(85)***(77) (RJHodges)* 6-9-13 RCochrane(16) (racd stands' side: hdwy & prom ½-wy: rdn & nt qckn appr fnl f)........¾ 9
341[6] Veloce (IRE) **(70)***(61) (ABailey)* 7-8-7 (5) VHalliday(7) (b: bhd: kpt on fnl 2f: n.d)........½ 10
Champagne Grandy **(75)***(64) (MRChannon)* 5-9-3 RHughes(12) (in tch: effrt over 2f out: eased whn btn ins fnl f)........¾ 11
380* Bella Parkes **(70)***(57) (DNicholls)* 4-8-12b AlexGreaves(6) (chsd ldrs tl wknd over 1f out)........½ 12
Kildee Lad **(74)***(59) (APJones)* 5-9-2 JWilliams(17) (racd stands' side: outpcd: hmpd & kpt on ins fnl f)........1 13
Ansellman **(79)***(58) (JBerry)* 5-9-7 JCarroll(20) (racd stands' side: outpcd fr ½-wy)........2 14
Elle Shaped (IRE) **(75)***(51) (DNicholls)* 5-9-3 NConnorton(15) (gd spd stands' side 4f)........1¼ 15
Barato **(65)***(38) (MrsJRRamsden)* 4-8-7 JWeaver(5) (b.nr hind: in tch: hdwy to ld over 2f out: hdd over 1f out: eased whn btn)........1¼ 16
Two Moves in Front (IRE) **(78)***(37) (JBerry)* 5-9-6 GCarter(2) (sn outpcd & pushed along)........5 17
393* Ziggy's Dancer (USA) **(68)***(25) (EJAlston)* 4-8-10 DHolland(3) (w ldrs far side tl wknd 2f out) .¾ 18
Eagle Day (USA) **(78)***(33) (DRCElsworth)* 4-9-6v PatEddery(10) (racd centre: gd spd over 3f: sn lost pl)........¾ 19
Oggi **(70)***(25) (PJMakin)* 4-8-12 JFortune(18) (racd stands' side: s.i.s: hdwy ½-wy: rdn & wknd 2f out)........hd 20
400* White Sorrel **(72)***(25)*(Fav)*(JLEyre)* 4-8-9 (5) JStack(4) (trckd ldrs: led over 3f out tl over 2f out: wknd qckly)........¾ 21
Captain Carat **(69)***(14) (MrsJRRamsden)* 4-8-11 DeanMcKeown(1) (w ldrs far side tl wknd 2f out)........3 22

4/1 White Sorrel, **10/1** Sailormaite, Highborn (IRE), **11/1** Bella Parkes, **12/1** Ziggy's Dancer (USA), Captain Carat, Domulla, **14/1** Eagle Day (USA), CASTLEREA LAD, Barato, Sagebrush Roller, **16/1** Ansellman, Mister Jolson, **25/1** Two Moves in Front (IRE), Oggi, Jigsaw Boy, Champagne Grandy, Kildee Lad, **33/1** Plum First, Elle Shaped (IRE), Veloce (IRE), So Intrepid (IRE), CSF £83.39 CL & D, £71.69 CL & S, CT £807.02 CL, D & S, £797.37 CL, S & D TOTE £13.40: £2.60 £6.00 D, £2.30 S, £4.00 (£53.90 CL & D, £40.20 CL & S) Trio £442.50 OWNER Mrs Tess Graham (UPPER LONGDON) BRED J. D. Hurd 22 Rn
1m 15.89 (4.89) SF: 49/53/43/33/28/42/52/49/47/31/34/27/29/28/21/8/7/-/3/-/-/-

435 MARC WHEATLEY MAIDEN STKS (II) (3-Y.O) (Class D) £3,360.50 (£998.00: £473.00: £210.50)

7f Stalls: High GOING: 0.19 sec per fur (G) 4-40 (4-45)

Blomberg (IRE) (90)*(84+) (JRFanshawe)* 3-9-0 DHarrison(9) (lw: mde all: qcknd clr 2f out: r.o strly)........— 1
Maeterlinck (IRE) *(73) (BWHills)* 3-9-0 MHills(1) (bit bkwd: s.i.s: hld up: rdn over 2f out: styd on wl fnl f: no ch w wnr)........5 2
Hakiki (IRE) **(98)***(67)*(Fav)*(PTWalwyn)* 3-9-0 WCarson(11) (bit bkwd: trckd ldrs: plld v.hrd: effrt over 2f out: wknd over 1f out)........2½ 3
Prolific Lady (IRE) *(56) (GROldroyd)* 3-8-9 RCochrane(5) (w'like: lengthy: sn in rr: hdwy over 2f out: styd on fnl f: nvr nr to chal)........2½ 4
Yubralee (USA) *(54) (MRStoute)* 3-9-0 WRSwinburn(6) (lw: sn chsng ldrs: effrt over 2f out: sn rdn & wknd)........3 5
Leading Spirit (IRE) *(53) (CFWall)* 3-9-0 WWoods(8) (in tch: rdn ½-wy: sn wl outpcd)........¾ 6
Nordic Breeze (IRE) *(51) (ABailey)* 3-8-9 (5) VHalliday(3) (bit bkwd: in tch: outpcd ½-wy: n.d after)........½ 7
Magical Bid (IRE) **(57)***(50) (JMBradley)* 3-8-9 (5) SDrowne(10) (chsd ldrs tl wknd over 2f out)........¾ 8
Mr Personality *(50) (MrsMReveley)* 3-9-0 KDarley(2) (w'like: unf: s.i.s: hld up & plld hrd: bhd: sme hdwy 2f out: nvr nr ldrs)........s.h 9
Corrievarkie *(44) (MissGayKelleway)* 3-8-9 SWhitworth(4) (unf: s.i.s: bhd fnl 2f)........hd 10
Outstayed Welcome *(49) (MJHaynes)* 3-9-0 JReid(12) (b.hind: in tch tl outpcd fnl 3f)........s.h 11
Indian Rhapsody *(44) (MRChannon)* 3-8-9 RHughes(7) (hld up & a bhd)........s.h 12

15/8 Hakiki (IRE) (op 3/1), **7/2** BLOMBERG (IRE), **4/1** Yubralee (USA) (op 5/2), **11/2** Maeterlinck (IRE), **14/1** Corrievarkie, **20/1** Leading Spirit (IRE), Indian Rhapsody, **25/1** Nordic Breeze (IRE), Mr Personality, **33/1** Magical Bid (IRE), Prolific Lady (IRE), Outstayed Welcome, CSF £22.87 TOTE £3.80: £1.50 £1.70 £1.40 (£17.10) Trio £9.60 OWNER Comet Group Plc (NEWMARKET) BRED Mrs Chris Harrington 12 Rn 1m 29.75 (6.35) SF: 39/28/22/11/9/8/6/5/5/-/4/-

T/Jkpt: Not won; £19,489.18 to Doncaster 25/3/95. T/Plpt: £1,171.10 (28.73 Tckts). T/Qdpt: £157.50 (0.65 Tckts); £74.53 to Doncaster 25/3/95. WG

0429-**DONCASTER (L-H)**
Saturday March 25th (Good to firm)
WEATHER: overcast WIND: slt half against

436 GREY FRIARS MAIDEN AUCTION STKS (2-Y.O) (Class D) £3,651.50 (£1,091.00: £522.00: £237.50)
5f Stalls: High GOING: 0.12 sec per fur (G) 2-00 (2-02)

Kustom Kit (IRE) *(77t) (BAMcMahon)* 2-8-8 FNorton(9) (small: outpcd tl hdwy 2f out: led ins fnl f: r.o)....— **1**
Ortolan *(75) (RHannon)* 2-8-2 (7)ow1 DaneO'Neill(13) (leggy: unf: hdwy ½-wy: n.m.r over 1f out: r.o ins fnl f: hung lft)....½ **2**
Arvzees (IRE) *(67) (MRChannon)* 2-8-4 TQuinn(12) (small: a w ldrs: nt qckn ins fnl f)....1¼ **3**
Bedside Mail *(68) (JMPEustace)* 2-8-5 BThomson(10) (cmpt: led to ½-wy: kpt on wl)....hd **4**
Afisiak *(62) (MJohnston)* 2-7-13 TWilliams(2) (leggy: unf: w ldrs: led wl over 1f out tl ins fnl f: hrd drvn: no ex)....hd **5**
Worldwide Elsie (USA) *(63) (PAKelleway)* 2-8-2 AMackay(8) (unf: s.i.s: sn in tch: nt clr run fnl 2f)....½ **6**
Mono Lady (IRE) *(63) (DHaydnJones)* 2-8-2 DHarrison(7) (leggy: chsd ldrs: outpcd 2f out: styd on fnl f)....s.h **7**
Oriel Lad *(59) (KRBurke)* 2-8-6 MRimmer(6) (cmpt: w ldrs: led ½-wy tl hdd & wknd wl over 1f out)....2½ **8**
Lady of The Mist (IRE) *(52) (JSMoore)* 2-7-13 GBardwell(3) (neat: unf: s.s: hmpd after s: wl bhd tl styd on fnl f)....s.h **9**
Stealth Attack (IRE) *(59)*(Fav)*(JBerry)* 2-8-6 JCarroll(5) (leggy: scope: w ldrs: hrd drvn 2f out: wknd appr fnl f)....hd **10**
Vanishing Point *(47) (GLewis)* 2-8-7 PatEddery(1) (cmpt: bit bkwd: spd to ½-wy: sn bhd)....4 **11**
Magical Midnight *(36) (NTinkler)* 2-7-13 KimTinkler(4) (neat: bit bkwd: dwlt & wnt lft s: a bhd)....1 **12**
Go Like West *(13) (JHetherton)* 2-8-5 NKennedy(11) (cmpt: bkwd: sn outpcd & bhd)....9 **13**

5/2 Stealth Attack (IRE), **7/2** Afisiak, **6/1** Vanishing Point, **13/2** Arvzees (IRE), **8/1** Oriel Lad, **10/1** Worldwide Elsie (USA), **11/1** Ortolan, **14/1** Lady of The Mist (IRE), Mono Lady (IRE), **16/1** Bedside Mail, **20/1** KUSTOM KIT (IRE), **25/1** Magical Midnight, Go Like West, CSF £224.67 TOTE £54.40: £10.00 £3.70 £2.50 (£210.00) Trio £465.10 OWNER Charterhouse Holdings Plc (TAMWORTH) BRED Gay O'Callaghan 13 Rn 63.08 secs (4.68) SF: 24/22/14/15/9/10/10/6/-/6/-/-/-

437 NORTHERN H'CAP (0-85) (3-Y.O) (Class D) £4,737.00 (£1,416.00: £678.00: £309.00) **7f** Stalls: High GOING: 0.12 sec per fur (G) 2-30 (2-31)

*324** **Mister Fire Eyes (IRE) (64)***(71)*(Fav)*(CEBrittain)* 3-8-0 BDoyle(13) (lw: hdwy 3f out: led wl over 1f out: carried rt: r.o wl)....— **1**
Tiler (IRE) **(83)***(83) (MJohnston)* 3-9-5 DHolland(11) (w ldrs: led over 2f out: wandered u.p: hdd over 1f out: kpt on)....3 **2**
251² Mr Frosty **(67)***(60) (WJarvis)* 3-8-3 WCarson(7) (b.hind: in tch: rdn ½-wy: kpt on wl)....3 **3**
Risky Romeo **(73)***(66) (GCBravery)* 3-8-9 MHills(5) (s.i.s: hdwy over 2f out: nrst fin)....hd **4**
Roy Boy **(74)***(67) (MrsMReveley)* 3-8-10 PaulEddery(15) (lw: chsd ldrs: rdn whn hmpd over 1f out: sn wknd)....hd **5**
255² Harry Browne (IRE) **(57)***(50) (MrsJRRamsden)* 3-7-7 JLowe(12) (s.i.s: hdwy ½-wy: kpt on: nvr able to chal)....hd **6**
At Liberty (IRE) **(78)***(67) (RHannon)* 3-9-0 TQuinn(4) (chsd lrds: hrd rdn over 3f out: no hdwy)....1½ **7**
380⁴ Pc's Cruiser (IRE) **(57)***(45) (MCChapman)* 3-7-4 (3) DWright(16) (outpcd & bhd: styd on fnl 2f)....½ **8**
Katya (IRE) **(85)***(70) (MRChannon)* 3-9-7 RHughes(6) (trckd ldrs: effort over 2f out: r.o one pce)....1¼ **9**
Kildrummy Castle **(60)***(38) (MrsJRRamsden)* 3-7-10 JFanning(9) (bkwd: s.i.s: a bhd)....3 **10**
Flyaway Blues **(67)***(42) (MrsMReveley)* 3-8-3 ow2 KDarley(14) (bhd: sme hdwy 2f out: n.d)....¾ **11**
Casper's Risk **(59)***(28) (DNicholls)* 3-7-4b(5)ow2 NVarley(3) (w ldrs over 4f: sn wknd)....2½ **12**
196⁵ Tee Tee Too (IRE) **(73)***(33) (PCHaslam)* 3-8-4 (5) JStack(2) (led tl hdd over 2f out: grad wknd)....5 **13**
360² Montanelli (FR) **(83)***(37) (KMcAuliffe)* 3-9-5 PatEddery(1) (in tch: drvn along ½-wy: one pce)2½ **14**
315¹⁰ Airbourne Ron (IRE) **(57)** *(SGNorton)* 3-7-7 GBardwell(10) (sn outpcd & bhd)....7 **15**

LONG HANDICAP Casper's Risk 7-5 Harry Browne (IRE) 7-6 Pc's Cruiser (IRE) 7-6 Airbourne Ron (IRE) 7-5

100/30 MISTER FIRE EYES (IRE), **11/2** Tiler (IRE), **13/2** Risky Romeo, **8/1** Harry Browne (IRE), **10/1** Mr Frosty, Montanelli (FR), **12/1** At Liberty (IRE), Katya (IRE), **14/1** Roy Boy, **16/1** Kildrummy Castle, Flyaway Blues, **20/1** Pc's Cruiser (IRE), **25/1** Tee Tee Too (IRE), **33/1** Casper's Risk, **50/1** Airbourne Ron (IRE), CSF £21.94 CT £160.11 TOTE £3.90: £2.20 £2.30 £2.70 (£6.60) Trio £36.80 OWNER Mr C. T. Olley (NEWMARKET) BRED Airlie Stud 15 Rn

1m 28.29 (4.89) SF: 37/49/26/32/33/16/33/11/36/4/8/-/-/3/-

438 GLOBAL SHOPFITTERS STKS (3-Y.O) (Class C) £6,420.20

(£2,391.80: £1,160.90: £489.50: £209.75: £97.85)
1m (straight) Stalls: High GOING: 0.12 sec per fur (G) 3-00 (3-00)

Juyush (USA) **(115)***(98+)*(Fav)*(BWHills)* 3-8-13 WCarson(7) (lw: mde all: hung lft 2f out: r.o wl) — 1
*362** Heathyards Rock **(82)***(96) (RHollinshead)* 3-8-13 TIves(5) (hdwy over 2f out: r.o: nrst fin) 1¼ 2
Moments of Fortune (USA) *(95) (BHanbury)* 3-8-13 WRyan(10) (hdwy 3f out: styd on wl: nt pce to chal) nk 3
Dee-Lady **(100)***(89) (WGMTurner)* 3-8-8 TSprake(8) (chsd wnr: effrt over 2f out: r.o one pce) nk 4
Welton Arsenal **(98)***(90) (MRChannon)* 3-9-1 RHughes(6) (trckd ldrs: effort over 2f out: btn appr fnl f) 3 5
Twilight Sleep (USA) **(107)***(83) (LordHuntingdon)* 3-8-13 WRSwinburn(9) (chsd ldrs tl rdn & outpcd wl over 2f out) 2½ 6
Baltic Raider **(104)***(87) (GWragg)* 3-9-3 MHills(4) (lw: chsd ldr tl outpcd fnl 2½f) nk 7
Anniversarypresent **(94)***(85) (GLewis)* 3-9-1 PatEddery(3) (hld up: effort 3f out: no imp) s.h 8
Luso *(79) (CEBrittain)* 3-8-11 MRimmer(2) (prom: effort 3f out: sn btn) 1 9
*357** Mega Tid *(51) (BAPearce)* 3-8-13 SSanders(1) (b: wnt lft s: effrt u.p ½-wy: sn btn) 15 10

11/10 JUYUSH (USA), **5/1** Anniversarypresent, **8/1** Baltic Raider, Twilight Sleep (USA), **10/1** Moments of Fortune (USA), **11/1** Welton Arsenal, **12/1** Dee-Lady, Luso, **20/1** Heathyards Rock, **33/1** Mega Tid, CSF £24.12 TOTE £2.00: £1.30 £6.80 £2.80 (£50.60) Trio £92.10 OWNER Mr Hamdan Al Maktoum (LAMBOURN) BRED Corbin J. Robertson 10 Rn

1m 40.74 (4.24) SF: 64/62/61/55/56/49/53/51/45/17

439 WILLIAM HILL LINCOLN H'CAP (4-Y.O+) (Class B) £46,332.50

(£13,910.00: £6,705.00: £3,102.50)
1m (straight) Stalls: High GOING: 0.12 sec per fur (G) 3-40 (3-44)

Roving Minstrel **(82)***(92) (BAMcMahon)* 4-8-3 KDarley(11) (lw: chsd ldrs: led over 2f out: r.o wl u.p) — 1
Moving Arrow **(87)***(97) (MissSEHall)* 4-8-8 NConnorton(12) (hdwy over 3f out: chal ins fnl f: nt qckn nr fin) s.h 2
20⁶ Mr Martini (IRE) **(87)***(96) (CEBrittain)* 5-8-8 MRimmer(4) (lw: racd far side: chsd ldrs: led over 2f out: r.o) ½ 3
Leif the Lucky (USA) **(84)***(89) (MissSEHall)* 6-8-5 NCarlisle(10) (a chsng ldrs: kpt on wl fnl 2f) 1¾ 4
Royal Hill **(79)***(83) (LordHuntingdon)* 4-8-0 DHarrison(13) (a chsng ldrs: kpt on same pce fnl 3f) ½ 5
Bagshot **(83)***(87) (RHannon)* 4-8-4 BThomson(8) (lw: racd far side: in tch: hdwy & ev ch over 1f out: no ex) hd 6
Indian Fly **(94)***(90) (RHannon)* 4-9-1 PatEddery(21) (lw: bhd: hdwy 2f out: rdn & btn appr fnl f) 4 7
Cameron Highland (IRE) **(82)***(77) (PFICole)* 4-8-3b TQuinn(20) (effort ½-wy: sn chsng ldrs: rdn & nt qckn fnl f) ½ 8
Mellottie **(95)***(89) (MrsMReveley)* 10-9-2 JLowe(2) (racd far side: bhd & rdn ½-wy: nrst fin) ¾ 9
406⁷ Master Beveled **(88)***(81) (PDEvans)* 5-8-4 (5) JStack(17) (b: w ldrs: led ½-wy: hung lft: hdd over 2f out: sn btn) ½ 10
365² Castel Rosselo **(84)***(76) (SCWilliams)* 5-8-5 AMackay(3) (lw: led far side tl hdd & wknd over 2f out) ½ 11
Robsera (IRE) **(82)***(69) (GLewis)* 4-8-3 PaulEddery(15) (lw: effort ½-wy: nvr trbld ldrs) 2½ 12
364⁴ Celestial Choir **(82)***(68) (JLEyre)* 5-8-3 JFanning(23) (effort ½-wy: sn rdn & n.d) ½ 13
246⁹ Rainbow Walk (IRE) **(85)***(70) (JGMO'Shea)* 5-8-6v BDoyle(22) (w ldrs to ½-wy: sn outpcd) nk 14
364¹⁰ Promise Fulfilled (USA) **(87)***(71) (SGNorton)* 4-8-8 WRyan(16) (hdwy ½-wy: sn rdn & btn) ¾ 15
General Chaos (IRE) **(86)***(67) (JJO'Neill)* 5-8-7 JFortune(1) (b.hind: racd far side: prom 5f) 1½ 16
Chickawicka (IRE) **(88)***(61) (MCPipe)* 4-8-9 MHills(14) (led to ½-wy: wknd over 2f out) 4 17
Country Lover **(87)***(60)*(Fav)*(LordHuntingdon)* 4-8-8 LDettori(19) (lw: effort over 3f out: n.d) s.h 18

365* Mahool (USA) **(84)***(55) (JLEyre)* 6-8-2 (3) 5x DWright(7) (racd far side: chsd ldrs tl wknd over 2f out) .... ¾ **19**
383² Second Chance (IRE) **(82)***(43) (PMitchell)* 5-8-0 (3) SSanders(6) (racd far side: cl up tl wknd qckly over 2f out) 1 **20**
Knave's Ash (USA) **(89)***(52) (MRStoute)* 4-8-10 DHolland(5) (swtg: racd far side: rdn ½-wy: a bhd) .... hd **21**
Neither Nor **(87)***(45) (DAWilson)* 6-8-8 GCarter(9) (swtg: racd far side: outpcd & bhd fr ½-wy) 1¼ **22**
Realities (USA) **(103)***(66) (GHarwood)* 5-9-10 WRSwinburn(24) (chsd ldrs over 4f) 4 **23**
262³ Metal Storm (FR) **(90)** *(KOCunningham-Brown)* 7-8-11 JReid(18) (withdrawn: lame at s) .... **W**

15/2 Country Lover, **8/1** Celestial Choir, **10/1** Mellottie, **12/1** Knave's Ash (USA), Castel Rosselo, Mahool (USA), **14/1** Master Beveled, Royal Hill, Moving Arrow, Bagshot, **16/1** Indian Fly, Cameron Highland (IRE), Chickawicka (IRE), **20/1** Realities (USA), Robsera (IRE), **28/1** Second Chance (IRE), **33/1** ROVING MINSTREL, Neither Nor, Mr Martini (IRE), Leif the Lucky (USA), General Chaos (IRE), **50/1** Metal Storm (FR), Promise Fulfilled (USA), **66/1** Rainbow Walk (IRE), CSF £399.50 CT £12,933.56 TOTE £51.70: £8.80 £5.90 £7.30 £8.20 (£637.70) Trio £7,696.90 (0.39 Tckts); £6,612.89 to Folkestone 27/3/95. OWNER Mrs J. McMahon (TAMWORTH) BRED Mrs J. McMahon 23 Rn

1m 40.11 (3.61) SF: 61/66/65/58/52/56/59/46/58/50/45/38/37/39/40/36/30/29/24/20/27/22/30/-

440

MIDLAND COPYING DONCASTER SHIELD STKS (4-Y.O+) (Class B)
£8,299.24 (£3,069.16: £1,471.08: £599.40: £236.20: £90.92)
1m 4f Stalls: Low GOING minus 0.10 sec per fur (G) 4-15 (4-15)

Fire Worshipper (IRE) *(105) (JHMGosden)* 4-8-10 LDettori(9) (b: b.hind: hld up & bhd: smooth hdwy over 2f out: led 1½f out: sn hdd: led wl ins fnl f: r.o) .... — **1**
Cotteir Chief (IRE) **(107)***(117) (MCPipe)* 4-9-8 PatEddery(8) (hld up & bhd: hdwy to ld over 1f out: hung lft & hdd wl ins fnl f: r.o) .... s.h **2**
Khamaseen **(113)***(101)*(Fav)*(JLDunlop)* 4-9-0 WCarson(1) (led: rdn over 3f out: hdd 1½f out: one pce) 6 **3**
Dreams End *(97) (BJLlewellyn)* 7-8-12 JWilliams(4) (in tch: effrt 3f out: styd on: nvr able to chal) .... nk **4**
Charity Crusader **(95)***(98) (PWChapple-Hyam)* 4-8-12 JReid(2) (chsd ldrs: outpcd 4f out: sn lost pl: kpt on fnl f) .... hd **5**
Linpac West **(103)***(100) (CWCElsey)* 9-9-5 JCarroll(6) (lw: chsd ldrs: chal 4f out: wknd over 1f out) 2½ **6**
Sue's Artiste **(84)***(83) (BWHills)* 4-8-5 MHills(11) (hld up: stdy hdwy over 3f out: sn chsng ldrs: wknd over 1f out) 3½ **7**
106² Cedez le Passage (FR) **(103)***(85) (CEBrittain)* 4-8-10 MRimmer(7) (in tch: effrt 4f out: wknd over 1f out) 2½ **8**
385³ Latahaab (USA) *(73) (RAkehurst)* 4-8-10 TQuinn(10) (chsd ldrs tl wknd 4f out) 9 **9**
Slasher Jack (IRE) **(83)***(77) (SGNorton)* 4-9-0 JFortune(3) (bit bkwd: bhd & rdn ent st: n.d after) .... hd **10**
Windrush Lady *(71) (MMcCormack)* 5-8-11 BThomson(5) (chsd ldr tl wknd 4f out) 1 **11**

5/4 Khamaseen, **5/1** Cotteir Chief (IRE), **11/2** FIRE WORSHIPPER (IRE), **8/1** Cedez le Passage (FR), **9/1** Sue's Artiste, **10/1** Linpac West, **14/1** Latahaab (USA), Charity Crusader, **25/1** Dreams End, **33/1** Slasher Jack (IRE), Windrush Lady, CSF £34.02 TOTE £6.50: £2.00 £1.80 £1.30 (£14.90) Trio £10.90 OWNER Sheikh Mohammed (NEWMARKET) BRED Sheikh Mohammed bin Rashid al Maktoum in Ireland 11 Rn 2m 32.66 (2.06) SF: 73/85/69/67/66/70/51/53/41/45/41

WEIGHT FOR AGE 4yo-2lb

441

MITSUBISHI DIAMOND VISION CAMMIDGE TROPHY STKS (Listed)
(3-Y.O+) (Class A) £12,720.00 (£3,810.00: £1,830.00: £840.00)
6f Stalls: High GOING: 0.12 sec per fur (G) 4-45 (4-46)

Montendre (108)*(108) (MMcCormack)* 8-9-2 JReid(3) (hdwy over 2f out: qcknd to ld ins fnl f: r.o) .... — **1**
Sharp Prod (USA) **(107)***(112) (LordHuntingdon)* 5-9-7 WRSwinburn(2) (chsd ldrs & hung rt: ev ch 2f out: kpt on wl nr fin) .... nk **2**
Double Blue **(104)***(109)*(Fav)*(MJohnston)* 6-9-5 DHolland(10) (bhd: hdwy over 1f out: r.o wl: too much to do) .... nk **3**
Hard to Figure **(108)***(107) (RJHodges)* 9-9-5 PatEddery(11) (pushed along & hdwy after 2f: rdn to ld ins fnl f: sn hdd: no ex) .... ¾ **4**
Daring Destiny **(94)***(99) (KRBurke)* 4-8-11b TQuinn(8) (trckd ldrs: led wl over 1f out: sn rdn: hdd & wknd ins fnl f) .... hd **5**

Venture Capitalist **(90)***(100) (DNicholls)* 6-9-2 AlexGreaves(6) (dwlt: hdwy over 1f out: nvr nr to chal) 1¾ 6
Amron **(94)***(96) (JBerry)* 8-9-5 NCarlisle(1) (bhd: effrt 2f out: no imp) 2½ 7
Cool Jazz **(105)***(90) (CEBrittain)* 4-9-2v LDettori(9) (in tch: effrt over 2f out: sn btn) 1 8
Regal Chimes **(97)***(74) (BAMcMahon)* 6-9-2 TIves(5) (gd spd 4f) 6 9
Palacegate Jack (IRE) **(98)***(70) (JBerry)* 4-9-2v JCarroll(4) (led over 4f: sn wknd) 1¾ 10
Call Me I'm Blue (IRE) **(102)***(64) (NTinkler)* 5-9-2 MBirch(7) (chsd ldrs over 4f) 2 11

11/4 Double Blue, **5/1** Cool Jazz, **6/1** Hard to Figure, **13/2** MONTENDRE, Amron, **9/1** Sharp Prod (USA), Daring Destiny, **14/1** Palacegate Jack (IRE), **20/1** Call Me I'm Blue (IRE), Regal Chimes, **33/1** Venture Capitalist, CSF £60.06 TOTE £8.20: £3.00 £2.60 £1.60 (£42.90) Trio £63.00 OWNER Mr David Mort (WANTAGE) BRED A. B. Phipps 11 Rn
1m 14.44 (3.44) SF: 62/66/63/61/53/54/50/44/28/24/18

442

SOUTH YORKSHIRE MAIDEN STKS (3-Y.O) (Class D) £4,273.10 (£1,278.80: £613.40: £280.70)
6f Stalls: High GOING: 0.12 sec per fur (G) 5-15 (5-18)

Fata (IRE) (77)*(79) (PTWalwyn)* 3-9-0 WCarson(7) (mde all: drvn out) ....— 1
Forzair **(75)***(76) (MMcCormack)* 3-9-0 JReid(11) (chsd ldrs: kpt on u.p fnl f) 1¼ 2
Mistress Thames *(70) (JRFanshawe)* 3-8-9 DHarrison(16) (str: cmpt: bit bkwd: bhd tl hdwy 2f out: r.o wl nr fin) ....nk 3
Rokeby Bowl *(73) (IABalding)* 3-9-0 WRyan(13) (plld hrd: effrt over 2f out: styd on one pce fnl f) ....¾ 4
Taylord *(73) (RHannon)* 3-9-0 TQuinn(14) (a cl up: nt qckn appr fnl f) ....hd 5
Perfect World *(67) (BAMcMahon)* 3-9-0 KDarley(1) (prom tl rdn & btn appr fnl f) 2 6
Daysman (USA) *(67) (BWHills)* 3-9-0 MHills(17) (w'like: hdwy ½-wy: kpt on wl nr fin) ....s.h 7
Assumpsit (IRE) **(66)***(64) (SDow)* 3-8-7 (7) ADaly(10) (mid div: styd on steadily fnl 2f) 1¼ 8
Lough Erne *(50) (CFWall)* 3-8-9 NCarlisle(6) (bit bkwd: in tch: no imp fnl 2f) ....¾ 9
*315*4 Statius *(55) (TDBarron)* 3-9-0 JFortune(4) (chsd ldrs over 3f) ....s.h 10
Peggy Spencer *(50) (CWThornton)* 3-8-9 DeanMcKeown(12) (bit bkwd: stdy hdwy 2f out: nvr plcd to chal) ....s.h 11
Cool Tactician *(54) (RHollinshead)* 3-9-0 TIves(15) (bhd: sme hdwy 2f out: n.d) ....½ 12
Summer Retreat (USA) *(43)*(Fav)*(JHMGosden)* 3-8-9 PatEddery(5) (small: bit bkwd: b.hind: effrt ½-wy: sn in tch: rdn & btn appr fnl f: eased) 2 13
Ching *(37) (JHMGosden)* 3-8-9 LDettori(18) (racd stands' side: a bhd) 2½ 14
Frontiersman *(38) (JWWatts)* 3-9-0 BThomson(21) (leggy: scope: nvr trbld ldrs) 1½ 15
Hot Snap *(34) (CFWall)* 3-8-9 (5) LNewton(9) (lengthy: bkwd: outpcd fr ½-wy) 1¼ 16
Maybank (IRE) *(34) (BAMcMahon)* 3-9-0 MWigham(20) (rangy: dwlt: n.d) ....hd 17
Bollin Sophie *(26) (MHEasterby)* 3-8-9 MBirch(19) (str: lengthy: bkwd: a bhd) 1¼ 18
Red O'Reilly *(27) (MrsNMacauley)* 3-9-0 SDWilliams(2) (lengthy: unf: b: nvr wnt pce) 1¼ 19
Dromalane (IRE) *(JMCarr)* 3-9-0 SMorris(8) (chsd ldrs 3f: wknd qckly) 15 20

11/4 Summer Retreat (USA), **7/2** Rokeby Bowl, **5/1** Ching, **8/1** FATA (IRE), **9/1** Forzair, Daysman (USA), **12/1** Taylord, **14/1** Statius, **16/1** Mistress Thames, Cool Tactician, Frontiersman, **20/1** Bollin Sophie, **25/1** Lough Erne, Hot Snap, Assumpsit (IRE), **33/1** Perfect World, Peggy Spencer, Maybank (IRE), Red O'Reilly, Dromalane (IRE), CSF £88.28 TOTE £12.70: £2.90 £2.40 £11.60 (£44.10) Trio £289.20 OWNER Mr Hamdan Al Maktoum (LAMBOURN) BRED Shadwell Estate Company Limited 20 Rn 1m 15.89 (4.89) SF: 40/37/31/34/34/28/28/25/11/16/11/15/4/-/-/-/-/-/-/-

T/Jkpt: Not won; £36.013.58 to Folkestone 27/3/95. T/Plpt: £1,115.90 (46.99 Tckts). T/Qdpt: £124.50 (3.8 Tckts). AA

0401-LINGFIELD (L-H)
Saturday March 25th (Standard)

443

WAVELL MEDIAN AUCTION MAIDEN STKS (3-Y.O) (Class F) £2,796.20 (£773.20: £368.60)
1m (Equitrack) GOING minus 0.47 sec per fur (FST) 2-25 (2-26)

Indrapura (IRE) (66)*(74) (PFICole)* 3-9-0b CRutter(8) (mde all: clr over 2f out: unchal) ....— 1
Secret Spring (FR) *(71) (RCharlton)* 3-9-0 RCochrane(5) (leggy: s.s: gd hdwy over 3f out: r.o wl ins fnl f) 1½ 2
Fairelaine *(65) (APJarvis)* 3-8-2 (7) BHunter(7) (hdwy 6f out: rdn over 3f out: r.o ins fnl f) ....½ 3
Himalayan Blue **(64)***(65) (MRChannon)* 3-8-9 (5) PPMurphy(4) (bit bkwd: chsd wnr 7f: one pce) 2½ 4
Claireswan (IRE) *(63) (SCWilliams)* 3-9-0 MFenton(2) (scope: lost pl 6f out: rallied over 1f out: r.o) 1¼ 5

316^{3} Top Fella (USA) **(63)***(60) (WAO'Gorman)* 3-8-11b$^{(3)}$ EmmaO'Gorman(9) (outpcd: nvr nr to chal) 1¼ **6**
381^{3} Dance King **(67)***(59) (JEBanks)* 3-9-0b JQuinn(1) (b.hind: a.p: rdn over 3f out: wknd over 1f out) .... ¾ **7**
Norfolk Glory *(49)*(Fav)*(DJGMurraySmith)* 3-9-0 JWeaver(3) (lw: hld up: rdn over 3f out: r.o wl ins fnl f) 5 **8**
17^{6} Lanesra Breeze *(TJNaughton)* 3-9-0 StephenDavies(6) (bit bkwd: a wl bhd: t.o) .... dist **9**

5/2 Norfolk Glory, **4/1** Top Fella (USA), **5/1** INDRAPURA (IRE), **15/2** Secret Spring (FR), Himalayan Blue, **8/1** Fairelaine, Dance King, **33/1** Claireswan (IRE), **50/1** Lanesra Breeze, CSF £38.02 TOTE £5.80: £1.50 £2.00 £3.80 (£8.00) OWNER H.R.H. Sultan Ahmad Shah (WHATCOMBE) BRED John Burns 9 Rn
1m 39.76 (3.36) SF: 25/22/16/16/14/11/10/-/-
STEWARDS' ENQUIRY Rutter suspended 3-4/4/95 (careless riding).

444

PATRICK HASLAM RACING CLUB (S) H'CAP (0-60) (3-Y.O) (Class G)
£2,623.80 (£726.80: £347.40)
1m 2f (Equitrack) GOING minus 0.47 sec per fur (FST) 2-55 (2-57)

368^{3} **Hever Golf Lady (40)***(46) (TJNaughton)* 3-8-6 StephenDavies(5) (lw: hdwy over 3f out: led ins fnl f: rdn out) .... — **1**
368^{2} Mayday Kitty **(37)***(38) (WGMTurner)* 3-8-3v GDuffield(3) (a.p: led over 3f out: hrd rdn over 1f out: hdd ins fnl f: unable qckn) 3 **2**
316^{6} Alka International **(53)***(51) (JWhite)* 3-9-0 $^{(5)}$ SDrowne(2) (b: b.hind: a.p: led over 4f out tl over 3f out: hrd rdn over 1f out: one pce) 1¾ **3**
309^{4} Vindaloo **(39)***(36) (MJohnston)* 3-8-5 AMcGlone(9) (lw: a.p: rdn over 4f out: one pce) 1 **4**
261^{4} Fair Ella (IRE) **(42)***(37) (JFfitch-Heyes)* 3-8-8v DBiggs(1) (a.p: rdn 5f out: one pce) 1¼ **5**
Royal Rabbit **(51)***(43) (GLMoore)* 3-9-3 BRouse(4) (bit bkwd: bhd whn hmpd on ins over 7f out: hdwy over 2f out: one pce) 1½ **6**
388* Poly Road **(55)***(43)*(Fav)*(MRChannon)* 3-9-2 $^{(5)}$ PPMurphy(12) (rdn 7f out: nvr nrr) 2½ **7**
339^{4} Two Way Stretch **(36)***(23) (GLMoore)* 3-8-2 JQuinn(8) (dwlt: hdwy over 3f out: wknd over 2f out) .... ¾ **8**
Pendine **(50)***(23) (SCWilliams)* 3-9-2 MFenton(7) (bhd fnl 3f) 9 **9**
372^{5} Emerald Dream (IRE) **(50)***(21) (CCElsey)* 3-9-2 WWoods(11) (lw: hdwy over 3f out: wknd over 2f out) 1 **10**
350^{6} Warrior Lady (IRE) **(40)** *(PJMcBride)* 3-8-1 $^{(5)}$ PMcCabe(14) (hdwy over 7f out: wknd over 3f out) 8 **11**
98^{4} More Bills (IRE) **(44)** *(AMoore)* 3-8-10v CandyMorris(13) (b.hind: bhd fnl 6f) 4 **12**
360^{7} Don't Forget Ruby (IRE) **(47)** *(DWPArbuthnot)* 3-8-13v JWeaver(6) (led over 5f: wknd over 3f out) 2½ **13**
316^{5} Death by Chocolate **(50)** *(DrJDScargill)* 3-8-9v$^{(7)}$ CDomergue(10) (s.s: a t.o) 30 **14**

2/1 Poly Road, **13/2** Death by Chocolate, **7/1** Warrior Lady (IRE), **8/1** Mayday Kitty, **9/1** Vindaloo, **10/1** Two Way Stretch, **12/1** Emerald Dream (IRE), Don't Forget Ruby (IRE), HEVER GOLF LADY, **14/1** Royal Rabbit, **25/1** Pendine, More Bills (IRE), Fair Ella (IRE), **33/1** Alka International, CSF £104.81 CT £2,847.84 TOTE £6.20: £2.20 £2.50 £16.30 (£43.90) Trio Not won; £255.91 to Folkestone 27/3/95. OWNER Mrs E. Jackman (EPSOM) BRED M. M. Allen 14 Rn
2m 8.82 (5.82) SF: 7/-/12/-/-/4/4/-/-/-/-/-/-/-
No bid

445

DAILY STAR AWT 1M 2F CHALLENGE SERIES FINAL H'CAP (3-Y.O+)
(Class B) £10,503.75 (£3,180.00: £1,552.50: £738.75)
1m 2f (Equitrack) GOING minus 0.47 sec per fur (FST) 3-30 (3-31)

385^{2} **Young Freeman (USA) (84)***(99)*(Fav)*(DRLoder)* 6-10-0 JWeaver(2) (lw: mde all: clr over 2f out: comf) .... — **1**
276^{2} Herr Trigger **(72)***(76) (DrJDScargill)* 4-9-1b MFenton(5) (hld up: chsd wnr over 3f out: no imp) 7 **2**
403* Prince Danzig (IRE) **(83)***(79) (DJGMurraySmith)* 4-9-12 WWoods(1) (lw: a.p: rdn over 3f out: one pce) 5 **3**
152* Kaafih Homm (IRE) **(69)***(64) (NACallaghan)* 4-8-12 RCochrane(13) (b.hind: lw: hdwy over 4f out: rdn over 3f out: one pce) .... ½ **4**
246^{4} Ballyranter **(64)***(59) (HJCollingridge)* 6-8-8v JQuinn(8) (rdn over 4f out: hdwy over 3f out: r.o one pce fnl 2f) .... hd **5**
206^{4} Our Eddie **(66)***(53) (BGubby)* 6-8-10v WNewnes(3) (a.p: rdn over 3f out: eased whn btn fnl f) 5 **6**
415^{5} Captain Marmalade **(50)***(36) (DTThom)* 6-7-3 $^{(5)}$ MBaird(14) (lw: nvr nr to chal) .... ½ **7**
406* Camden's Ransom (USA) **(59)***(35) (HGRowsell)* 8-8-3 AMcGlone(6) (chsd wnr over 5f: wknd over 3f out) 6 **8**

406² Zuno Noelyn **(57)***(29) (RAkehurst)* 4-8-0 DBiggs(12) (lw: a bhd) 3 9
330⁵ Shansi (IRE) **(50)***(21) (MDIUsher)* 4-7-7v RStreet(11) (b: b.hind: prom over 7f) ....½ 10
355* Father Dan (IRE) **(56)***(24) (MissGayKelleway)* 6-8-0 StephenDavies(7) (lw: bhd fnl 3f) 1¾ 11
406¹² Awesome Power **(69)***(29) (JWHills)* 9-8-13 AClark(10) (a bhd) 5 12
318⁴ Birequest **(77)***(16) (RBoss)* 4-9-6 GDuffield(4) (lw: prom over 6f) 13 13
LONG HANDICAP Shansi (IRE) 7-2

11/10 YOUNG FREEMAN (USA), **11/2** Kaafih Homm (IRE), **8/1** Zuno Noelyn, Ballyranter, **12/1** Birequest, Herr Trigger, Father Dan (IRE), **14/1** Camden's Ransom (USA), **16/1** Captain Marmalade, **20/1** Prince Danzig (IRE), **25/1** Our Eddie, **33/1** Awesome Power, Shansi (IRE), CSF £17.44 CT £192.22 TOTE £2.10: £1.10 £3.60 £7.20 (£12.80) Trio £147.10 OWNER Lucayan Stud (NEWMARKET) BRED Allen E. Paulson 13 Rn 2m 3.66 (0.66) SF: 68/44/47/32/28/22/5/4/-/-/-/-/-
WEIGHT FOR AGE 4yo-1lb

446

LINGFIELD PARK AWT SPRINT SERIES FINAL H'CAP (3-Y.O+) (Class B) £10,260.00 (£3,105.00: £1,515.00: £720.00)
6f (Equitrack) GOING minus 0.47 sec per fur (FST) 4-00 (4-02)

404* **Sir Tasker (75)***(81) (JLHarris)* 7-9-13 RCochrane(5) (a.p: rdn over 2f out: led ins fnl f: r.o wl) ....— 1
359* Our Shadee (USA) **(56)***(58) (KTIvory)* 5-8-1v(7) CScally(1) (lost pl over 4f out: rallied fnl f: r.o wl) 1½ 2
333⁴ Montague Dawson (IRE) **(68)***(66) (MrsNMacauley)* 3-8-1 (5)ow3 SDrowne(7) (hdwy over 3f out: rdn over 2f out: r.o ins fnl f) ....nk 3
369⁴ Speedy Classic (USA) **(61)***(61) (MJHeaton-Ellis)* 6-8-13 WWoods(10) (hld up: rdn over 2f out: r.o ins fnl f) ....½ 4
386* Invocation **(68)***(68) (AMoore)* 8-9-6 GDuffield(4) (chsd ldr: led over 2f out tl ins fnl f: r.o wl) ..s.h 5
369³ Spender **(76)***(66) (PWHarris)* 6-9-9 (5) PMcCabe(8) (outpcd: nvr nrr) 3½ 6
407* Dolly Face **(71)***(61) (WRMuir)* 3-8-9 JWeaver(11) (outpcd) ....nk 7
407⁶ African Chimes **(67)***(50)*(Fav)*(WAO'Gorman)* 8-9-2 (3) EmmaO'Gorman(6) (outpcd) 2½ 8
404⁴ Assignment **(56)***(30) (JFfitch-Heyes)* 9-8-8 DBiggs(3) (outpcd) 3½ 9
359² Purbeck Centenary **(48)***(15) (PHowling)* 5-8-0 JQuinn(9) (b.hind: bhd fnl 3f) 2½ 10
386² Tyrian Purple (IRE) **(67)***(33) (TJNaughton)* 7-9-5b MFenton(2) (led over 3f) ....½ 11

9/2 African Chimes, **6/1** SIR TASKER, Our Shadee (USA), **13/2** Speedy Classic (USA), **7/1** Dolly Face, **8/1** Invocation, Tyrian Purple (IRE), Montague Dawson (IRE), **10/1** Spender, **12/1** Purbeck Centenary, **16/1** Assignment, CSF £42.15 CT £274.04 TOTE £8.50: £2.30 £2.30 £4.10 (£33.90) OWNER Mr J. F. Coupland (MELTON MOWBRAY) BRED W. H. Joyce 11 Rn
1m 11.84 (1.24) SF: 53/30/24/33/40/38/19/22/2/-/5
WEIGHT FOR AGE 3yo-14lb

447

STARFORM LIMITED STKS (0-60) (3-Y.O+) (Class F) £3,023.00 (£838.00: £401.00) **7f (Equitrack)** GOING minus 0.47 sec per fur (FST) 4-30 (4-31)

344³ **Maid Welcome (60)***(61)*(Fav)*(MrsNMacauley)* 8-8-9v(7) AmandaSanders(7) (mde all: rdn over 1f out: r.o wl) ....— 1
342⁴ Das Island **(60)***(61) (JRJenkins)* 3-8-8 JWeaver(5) (lw: chsd wnr: rdn over 3f out: unable qckn fnl 2f) 3½ 2
401⁷ Apollo Red **(50)***(56) (AMoore)* 6-9-7v CandyMorris(3) (b.hind: a.p: rdn over 1f out: one pce) 1 3
275⁸ Pirates Gold (IRE) **(53)***(55) (JWhite)* 5-9-2 (5) SDrowne(6) (lw: lost pl 3f out: r.o one pce fnl f) ....½ 4
402² Sherblu **(45)***(53) (JFfitch-Heyes)* 4-9-7v DBiggs(2) (lw: hdwy 4f out: rdn over 3f out: one pce) .¾ 5
Mazeeka (IRE) **(60)***(42) (WAO'Gorman)* 4-8-13 (3) EmmaO'Gorman(4) (nvr nr to chal) 2½ 6
401⁸ Aragrove **(52)***(38) (JWPayne)* 5-9-7 MTebbutt(1) (a bhd) 4 7
401⁴ Slytly Beveled **(59)***(32) (NPLittmoden)* 3-8-2 (5)ow2 TGMcLaughlin(8) (lw: bhd fnl 6f) 2½ 8
347⁷ King's Gold **(40)***(21) (TMJones)* 5-9-7b RPerham(9) (b: lw: prom over 2f) 5 9

2/1 MAID WELCOME, **7/2** Das Island, **4/1** Slytly Beveled, **5/1** Mazeeka (IRE), **7/1** Sherblu, **16/1** Pirates Gold (IRE), **25/1** Aragrove, Apollo Red, **50/1** King's Gold, CSF £9.49 TOTE £2.30: £1.10 £1.20 £3.20 (£4.10) OWNER Mrs Anna Sanders (MELTON MOWBRAY) BRED Doublet Ltd 9 Rn
1m 24.98 (1.98) SF: 37/21/32/31/29/18/14/-/-
WEIGHT FOR AGE 3yo-16lb

448

ELITE RACING CLUB H'CAP (0-70) (3-Y.O) (Class E) £3,388.00 (£1,012.00: £484.00: £220.00)
1m (Equitrack) GOING minus 0.47 sec per fur (FST) 5-05 (5-06)

Kevasingo (51)*(55) (SDow)* 3-8-3 GDuffield(8) (lw: rdn over 6f out: hdwy 4f out: led 1f out: r.o wl) ....— 1

3504 Keys Seminar **(46)***(48) (NACallaghan)* 3-7-12bow1 StephenDavies(4) (b.hind: lw: a.p: rdn over 3f out: r.o ins fnl f) ....½ 2
3762 Toy Princess (USA) **(69)***(71)*(Fav)*(CEBrittain)* 3-9-7 JWeaver(5) (wl bhd over 5f: gd hdwy over 1f out: str run fnl f: fin wl) ....nk 3
4119 Three Arch Bridge **(55)***(55) (MJohnston)* 3-8-7 WWoods(7) (rdn over 6f out: hdwy over 1f out: r.o) 1¼ 4
3843 Never so Rite (IRE) **(50)***(46) (DWPArbuthnot)* 3-8-2b JQuinn(9) (a.p: led over 3f out to 1f out: sn wknd) 2 5
3487 Beecham **(50)***(42) (AHide)* 3-7-11 (5) MBaird(3) (lw: hld up: rdn over 4f out: n.m.r on ins over 1f out: one pce fnl f) 2 6
Kreef **(65)***(51) (RJO'Sullivan)* 3-9-3 DBiggs(1) (bit bkwd: led over 4f: wknd over 1f out) 3 7
246 The Aspecto Girl (IRE) **(45)***(25) (MJohnston)* 3-7-11 NAdams(2) (lw: s.s: a bhd) 3 8
3882 Kirov Protege (IRE) **(52)***(10) (HJCollingridge)* 3-8-4 DaleGibson(6) (lw: prom tl hmpd & wknd 5f out) 11 9

3/1 Toy Princess (USA), **4/1** Kreef, **9/2** Kirov Protege (IRE), **11/2** Never so Rite (IRE), Three Arch Bridge, **10/1** KEVASINGO, **12/1** Beecham, **14/1** Keys Seminar, **20/1** The Aspecto Girl (IRE), CSF £121.56 CT £477.84 TOTE £16.80: £3.60 £4.60 £1.50 (£84.70) Trio £178.50 OWNER Mr G. Steinberg (EPSOM) BRED Miss Caroline Dickson 9 Rn 1m 39.76 (3.36) SF: 15/8/31/15/6/2/11/-/-

T/Plpt: £330.10 (39.59 Tckts). T/Qdpt: £8.70 (11.8 Tckts). AK

FOLKESTONE (R-H)
Monday March 27th (Good, Soft patches)

WEATHER: snow showers WIND: str half against

449 ALDINGTON RATING RELATED MAIDEN STKS (3-Y.O) (Class F)
£2,519.00 (£694.00: £329.00)
6f 189y Stalls: Low GOING: 0.79 sec per fur (S) 1-50 (1-56)

Double Rush (IRE) (60)*(64) (TGMills)* 3-9-0 JReid(5) (b.hind: rdn over 2f out: 2nd st: led over 1f out: edgd rt ins fnl f: r.o wl) ....— 1
Sharp 'n Smart **(65)***(63)*(Fav)*(BSmart)* 3-9-0 DHarrison(1) (lw: chsd ldr: led over 3f out tl over 1f out: carried rt & bmpd ins fnl f: r.o) ....nk 2
Sobeloved **(51)***(62) (MRChannon)* 3-9-0 RHughes(6) (4th st: hrd rdn over 1f out: hmpd ins fnl f: r.o) ....¾ 3
Western Horizon (USA) **(65)***(56) (CEBrittain)* 3-8-9 BDoyle(4) (5th st: hrd rdn over 1f out: r.o wl ins fnl f) ....nk 4
Moonee Valley **(65)***(14) (RHannon)* 3-9-0 LDettori(3) (led over 3f: 3rd st: eased whn btn fnl f) 20 5
3826 Ketchican **(40)** *(SGKnight)* 3-9-0 JQuinn(2) (dwlt: a bhd) 10 6
Tolent (IRE) **(50)** *(HVanderdussen,Belgium)* 3-8-9 LionelDelacruz(7) (bkwd: bhd fnl 5f) 10 7

7/4 Sharp 'n Smart, **100/30** DOUBLE RUSH (IRE) (6/1-3/1), **4/1** Moonee Valley (op 2/1), **5/1** Western Horizon (USA) (op 5/2), **16/1** Tolent (IRE), **20/1** Sobeloved, **50/1** Ketchican, CSF £8.74 TOTE £3.10: £1.80 £1.30 (£3.20) OWNER Mr Tony Murray (EPSOM) BRED Dermot Finnegan 7 Rn 1m 33.7 (12.10) SF: 18/17/16/10/-/-/-

450 LEVY BOARD H'CAP (0-70) (3-Y.O+) (Class E) £3,445.20
(£1,029.60: £492.80: £224.40)
6f 189y Stalls: Low GOING: 0.79 sec per fur (S) 2-20 (2-25)

4009 **Orthorhombus (60)***(67) (DJSCosgrove)* 6-9-4b MRimmer(9) (hdwy on ins over 2f out: led wl ins fnl f: r.o wl) ....— 1
1956 Just Harry **(60)***(66) (MJRyan)* 4-8-13 (5) MBaird(6) (lw: hdwy 2f out: ev ch ins fnl f: r.o) ....nk 2
2059 Shepherd Market (IRE) **(55)***(61) (DAWilson)* 4-8-13 GCarter(5) (hwdy over 1f out: r.o wl ins fnl f) ....s.h 3
3937 Martinosky **(55)***(58) (GCBravery)* 9-8-13 MHills(15) (hdwy over 3f out: 4th st: led ins fnl f: sn hdd: unable qckn) 1½ 4
569 Great Hall **(58)***(61) (PDCundell)* 6-9-2 WNewnes(3) (bit bkwd: hdwy over 1f out: r.o wl ins fnl f) ....hd 5
4103 Legatee **(63)***(64) (BJMeehan)* 4-9-7 BDoyle(1) (6th st: hrd rdn over 1f out: one pce) ....½ 6
Media Express **(59)***(54) (TGMills)* 3-8-1 JQuinn(8) (hdwy over 1f out: nvr nrr) 1¾ 7
1507 Bold Mick **(60)***(57) (DJGMurraySmith)* 4-9-4 JWeaver(2) (lw: nvr nr to chal) ....nk 8
Silktail (IRE) **(60)***(54) (JohnBerry)* 3-8-2 SRaymont(12) (dwlt: nvr nrr) ....nk 9
4012 Mr Nevermind (IRE) **(65)***(56)*(Fav)*(GLMoore)* 5-9-2 (7) LSuthern(13) (2nd st: wknd over 1f out) 2 10

Noeprob (USA) **(49)***(39) (RJHodges)* 5-8-2 (5)ow1 SDrowne(11) (7th st: wknd over 2f out)......s.h **11**
371[4] Newington Butts (IRE) **(50)***(41) (KMcAuliffe)* 5-8-5 (3) SSanders(14) (led 6f out tl ins fnl f: sn wknd)........s.h **12**
Dia Georgy **(57)***(40) (RGuest)* 4-9-1 LDettori(4) (5th st: sn wknd over 1f out)........3½ **13**
Duckey Fuzz **(70)***(32) (RMFlower)* 7-9-7 (7) MarkDenaro(16) (bkwd: bhd fnl 3f)........9 **14**
*401** Greatest **(60)** (Fav)*(RAkehurst)* 4-9-4 TQuinn(7) (led 1f: 3rd st: wknd over 1f out)........11 **15**
349[10] Ragazzo (IRE) **(44)** *(KOCunningham-Brown)* 5-8-2b GDuffield(10) (prom over 3f)........¾ **16**

9/2 Mr Nevermind (IRE), Greatest (op 3/1), **6/1** Just Harry, **7/1** Dia Georgy, **11/1** Legatee, **14/1** Duckey Fuzz, **16/1** Shepherd Market (IRE), Martinosky, Newington Butts (IRE), **20/1** Media Express, Noeprob (USA), ORTHORHOMBUS, Bold Mick, Ragazzo (IRE), **25/1** Great Hall, **33/1** Silktail (IRE), CSF £127.99 CT £1,819.34 TOTE £25.30: £3.90 £2.10 £3.80 £7.10 (£43.50) Trio £993.80 OWNER Mr Alexander MacGillivray (NEWMARKET) BRED Cliveden Stud 16 Rn
1m 31.8 (10.20) SF: 44/43/38/35/38/41/17/34/17/33/16/18/17/9/-/-
WEIGHT FOR AGE 3yo-16lb
OFFICIAL EXPLANATION Greatest: no explanation offered

451

SHORNECLIFFE MEDIAN AUCTION MAIDEN STKS (3-Y.O) (Class F) £2,519.00 (£694.00: £329.00)
6f Stalls: Low GOING: 0.11 sec per fur (G) 2-50 (2-57)

Tiheros (65)*(69) (RHannon)* 3-9-0 TQuinn(3) (a.p: led 2f out: rdn out)........— **1**
299[4] La Suquet **(64)***(64) (MRChannon)* 3-8-9 RHughes(1) (a.p: ev ch fnl 2f: r.o wl)........s.h **2**
Woodrising *(57) (LadyHerries)* 3-8-9 GDuffield(2) (outpcd: hdwy fnl f: r.o wl)........2½ **3**
Crimson Shower *(55)*(Fav)*(JRFanshawe)* 3-8-9 DHarrison(6) (bkwd: a.p: ev ch 2f out: wknd fnl f)........1 **4**
Kellaire Girl (IRE) *(47) (GLewis)* 3-8-9 PaulEddery(4) (lw: led 4f)........3 **5**
Care And Comfort *(44) (GWragg)* 3-8-9 FNorton(5) (neat: s.s: a bhd)........1 **6**

15/8 Crimson Shower (5/4-2/1), **11/4** La Suquet (3/1-9/2), **7/2** TIHEROS (5/2-4/1), **10/1** Care And Comfort (op 3/1), **12/1** Woodrising (op 8/1), **14/1** Kellaire Girl (IRE), CSF £12.06 TOTE £4.90: £1.80 £1.90 (£4.30) OWNER Mr T. Anthony (MARLBOROUGH) BRED Roldvale Ltd 6 Rn
1m 16.8 (5.10) SF: 37/32/25/23/15/12

452

ROCHESTER H'CAP (0-70) (3-Y.O+) (Class E) £3,187.80 (£950.40: £453.20: £204.60) **5f** Stalls: Low GOING: 0.11 sec per fur (G) 3-20 (3-26)

407[2] **Nordico Princess (60)***(71)*(Fav)*(GROldroyd)* 4-9-12 RCochrane(4) (b.hind: mde all: rdn out)........— **1**
Harry's Coming **(46)***(49) (RJHodges)* 11-8-7 (5) SDrowne(8) (bit bkwd: hld up: hrd rdn over 1f out: unable qckn)........2½ **2**
419[13] Rustic League (IRE) **(37)***(35) (TJNaughton)* 4-8-0 (3) SSanders(7) (a.p: hrd rdn over 1f out: onepce)........1½ **3**
410[8] Mister Raider **(48)***(46) (SMellor)* 3-7-8 (7) ADaly(6) (lw: hld up: rdn over 1f out: r.o one pce) ...hd **4**
Texas Cowgirl (IRE) **(45)***(41) (HVanderdussen,Belgium)* 5-8-11 LionelDelacruz(2) (lw: s.s: swtchd rt over 1f out: hdwy fnl f: nvr nrr)........½ **5**
244[2] Rocky Two **(62)***(58) (PHowling)* 4-10-0v WWoods(5) (a.p: rdn over 2f out: one pce)........hd **6**
*299** Halliard **(55)***(50) (TMJones)* 4-9-7 RPerham(1) (rdn thrght: nt clr run 2f out, over 1f out & ins fnl f: nvr nr to chal)........nk **7**
Lloc **(66)***(55) (JohnBerry)* 3-9-5 CDwyer(3) (a.p: hrd rdn over 1f out: eased whn btn ins fnl f)1¾ **8**

6/4 NORDICO PRINCESS, **4/1** Lloc, **6/1** Halliard, **13/2** Rocky Two (op 4/1), **9/1** Texas Cowgirl (IRE) (op 5/1), **16/1** Harry's Coming, Rustic League (IRE), **25/1** Mister Raider, CSF £21.75 CT £249.92 TOTE £2.20: £1.20 £2.00 £3.20 (£11.20) OWNER Mr M. S. Griffiths (YORK) 8 Rn
62.6 secs (4.00) SF: 51/29/15/13/21/38/30/22
WEIGHT FOR AGE 3yo-13lb

453

KINGSNORTH H'CAP (0-70) (3-Y.O) (Class E) £3,216.40 (£959.20: £457.60: £206.80) **1m 4f** Stalls: Low GOING: 0.79 sec per fur (S) 3-50 (3-56)

Iron N Gold (41)*(48) (SDow)* 3-7-10 ow1 FNorton(9) (gd hdwy over 1f out: led 1f out: r.o wl)........— **1**
372[6] Rocky Forum **(50)***(54) (GLMoore)* 3-8-5 RPerham(8) (led: wandered over 1f out: hdd 1f out: unable to qckn)........2½ **2**
384[5] Al Corniche (IRE) **(45)***(45) (KOCunningham-Brown)* 3-7-11 (3) SSanders(7) (5th st: hrd rdn over 1f out: one pce)........3 **3**
Mim-Lou-and **(40)***(39) (BRMillman)* 3-7-11 ow2 AMackay(6) (bit bkwd: 4th st: rdn over 1f out: one pce)........2 **4**

Tommyknocker (IRE) **(42)***(36) (JRJenkins)* 3-7-11 ow2 JQuinn(10) (lw: nvr nr to chal) 2 **5**
*444*7 Poly Road **(50)***(43) (MRChannon)* 3-8-0 (5) PPMurphy(11) (6th st: wknd over 1f out) 1¼ **6**
*282** Inchkeith **(66)***(57)*(Fav)*(GWragg)* 3-9-0 (7) DGibbs(3) (2nd st: wknd over 1f out)........................1 **7**
*72*11 Don't Mean a Thing (IRE) **(56)***(38) (RHannon)* 3-8-11 RHughes(1) (bit bkwd: a bhd) 7 **8**
Maysann **(65)***(47) (JLDunlop)* 3-9-6 TQuinn(4) (bit bkwd: chsd ldr over 9f: 3rd st: wknd 2f out) ....s.h **9**
Stoneham Girl **(40)***(5) (PButler)* 3-7-4 (5) MBaird(5) (a bhd)..13 **10**
*156*10 Okay Baby (IRE) **(55)***(18) (MHTompkins)* 3-8-10 PRobinson(2) (bhd fnl 3f)...........................1½ **11**

3/1 Inchkeith (op 2/1), **11/2** Maysann (3/1-6/1), **6/1** Poly Road (op 4/1), Rocky Forum, **7/1** Al Corniche (IRE), **8/1** Tommyknocker (IRE), **12/1** Don't Mean a Thing (IRE), **25/1** IRON N GOLD, Okay Baby (IRE), **33/1** Mim-Lou-and, Stoneham Girl, CSF £148.05 CT 1,055.48 TOTE £31.90: £4.80 £1.20 £2.80 (£114.20) Trio £199.60 OWNER A Family Affair Partnership (EPSOM) BRED M. F. Kentish 11 Rn 2m 52.3 (21.10) SF: -/6/-/-/-/-/9/-/-/-/-

454

ALKHAM H'CAP (0-70) (4-Y.O+) (Class E) £3,388.00 (£1,012.00: £484.00: £220.00) **1m 1f 149y** Stalls: Low GOING: 0.79 sec per fur (S) 4-20 (4-26)

*387** **Queens Stroller (IRE) (56)***(63) (CCElsey)* 4-8-13 DHarrison(3) (3rd st: hrd rdn over 1f out: led nr fin) ....— **1**
*266*4 Jemima Puddleduck **(57)***(64) (DWPArbuthnot)* 4-9-0 JWeaver(5) (b.hind: led: edgd lft over 1f out: hdd nr fin) ....hd **2**
*330*9 Krayyan Dawn **(45)***(50) (RAkehurst)* 5-8-3 GCarter(13) (lw: hld up: rdn over 1f out: r.o ins fnl f)...........1½ **3**
Cheveley Dancer (USA) **(46)***(49) (DAWilson)* 7-8-4 NGwilliams(10) (b: hld up: rdn over 1f out: r.o ins fnl f) 1¾ **4**
*389*7 Sacred Mirror (IRE) **(56)***(57) (CEBrittain)* 4-8-13 MRimmer(4) (hdwy over 1f out: nvr nrr).......hd **5**
Grand Salt (IRE) **(53)***(53) (MJHaynes)* 4-8-10 JReid(7) (5th st: hrd rdn over 1f out: one pce).¾ **6**
Morstock **(49)***(50) (RJHodges)* 5-8-2 (5) SDrowne(6) (no hdwy fnl 2f).......................................s.h **7**
Shoofk **(61)***(59)*(Fav)*(SDow)* 4-9-4 TQuinn(14) (lw: nvr nr to chal) 1 **8**
Lucky Tucky **(63)***(61) (JRJenkins)* 4-9-6 PaulEddery(2) (2nd st: ev ch over 1f out: sn wknd)..nk **9**
Pink Brief (IRE) **(60)***(55) (MJRyan)* 4-9-3 RCochrane(9) (hdwy over 2f out: wknd over 1f out)...........1½ **10**
Desiderata **(58)***(51) (BWHills)* 4-9-1 MHills(12) (b.hind: a bhd)..1½ **11**
*403*2 Able Choice (IRE) **(58)***(40) (RWArmstrong)* 5-9-2 LDettori(1) (4th st: wknd over 1f out) 7 **12**
Amber Valley (USA) **(66)***(43) (DLWilliams)* 4-9-4 (5) DGriffiths(11) (b.hind: 6th st: wknd over 2f out)...........2½ **13**
Al Moulouki **(70)***(32) (JWPayne)* 5-10-0 BThomson(15) (bhd fnl 5f) 10 **14**

3/1 Shoofk, **11/2** Able Choice (IRE), **7/1** Desiderata, Jemima Puddleduck, QUEENS STROLLER (IRE) (op 9/2), **8/1** Morstock, **14/1** Krayyan Dawn, **16/1** Lucky Tucky, Sacred Mirror (IRE), **20/1** Pink Brief (IRE), **25/1** Amber Valley (USA), **33/1** Cheveley Dancer (USA), Grand Salt (IRE), Al Moulouki, CSF £52.67 CT £608.95 TOTE £7.30: £2.60 £1.60 £2.20 (£22.60) Trio £88.40 OWNER Mr Richard Berenson (LAMBOURN) BRED Ardenode Stud Ltd 14 Rn
2m 12.8 (15.10) SF: 35/36/22/21/29/25/22/31/33/27/23/12/15/4
WEIGHT FOR AGE 4yo-1lb

455

HEADCORN MAIDEN AUCTION STKS (2-Y.O F) (Class F) £2,771.00 (£766.00: £365.00) **5f** Stalls: Low GOING: 0.11 sec per fur (G) 4-50 (4-56)

Maggi For Margaret *(72?t)*(Fav)*(MRChannon)* 2-8-1 CRutter(2) (neat: mde all: clr 2f out: unchal) ....— **1**
Dancing Lottie (IRE) *(52)*(Fav)*(PAKelleway)* 2-8-0 FNorton(7) (leggy: bit bkwd: a.p: rdn over 2f out: unable qckn) 6 **2**
Lincon Twenty One *(45) (MJHaynes)* 2-8-1 JQuinn(3) (neat: hdwy 4f out: rdn over 2f out: one pce) 2½ **3**
Deaken Dancer *(37) (KTIvory)* 2-7-12 GBardwell(4) (neat: a.p: rdn over 2f out: one pce).....1½ **4**
Shanoora (IRE) *(32) (BPalling)* 2-8-3 TSprake(6) (neat: bit bkwd: a.p: rdn over 2f out: wknd) .3 **5**
Bites *(16) (GLewis)* 2-7-13 ow1 GCarter(1) (neat: a bhd)..3½ **6**
Red Sky Delight (IRE) *(PButler)* 2-7-7 (5) MBaird(5) (neat: bit bkwd: a bhd) 8 **7**

2/1 MAGGI FOR MARGARET (op 4/5), Dancing Lottie (IRE) (11/4-5/1), **5/1** Lincon Twenty One (op 2/1), **11/2** Shanoora (IRE) (12/1-5/1), **6/1** Bites (op 7/2), **20/1** Deaken Dancer, Red Sky Delight (IRE), CSF £6.81 TOTE £2.60: £1.80 £2.40 (£5.40) OWNER Mr Michael Foy (UPPER LAMBOURN) BRED Brook Stud Ltd 7 Rn 63.1 secs (4.50) SF: 20/-/-/-/-/-/-

T/Jkpt: Not won; £58,629.77 to Catterick 29/3/95. T/Plpt: £415.00 (55.02 Tckts). T/Qdpt: £57.80 (1 Tckt). AK

NEWCASTLE (L-H) Tuesday March 28th

0456 Abandoned-Waterlogged

CATTERICK (L-H) Wednesday March 29th

0462 Abandoned-Frost

0443-LINGFIELD (L-H)
Wednesday March 29th (Standard)

WEATHER: sunny

468 SAN SEBASTIAN MAIDEN STKS (3-Y.O) (Class D) £3,799.90 (£1,133.20: £540.60: £244.30)
7f (Equitrack) Stalls: Low GOING minus 0.42 sec per fur (FST) 2-10 (2-16)

Bencher Q C (USA) *(75)*(Fav)*(JHMGosden)* 3-9-0 LDettori(6) (leggy: scope: lw: s.s: hdwy over 3f out: rdn 2f out: str run fnl f: led last strides)....— 1
Shen Yang (USA) **(75)***(75) (GLMoore)* 3-9-0 BRouse(3) (lw: led over 2f out: clr over 1f out: hdd last strides)....s.h 2
418[4] Alute (IRE) *(64) (CEBrittain)* 3-8-9 BDoyle(8) (a.p: rdn over 2f out: r.o ins fnl f)....2½ 3
448[7] Kreef **(65)***(61) (RJO'Sullivan)* 3-9-0 DBiggs(1) (hld up: rdn over 2f out: one pce)....3½ 4
394[8] Miss Jemmima *(51) (LordHuntingdon)* 3-8-9 DHarrison(5) (nvr nr to chal)....2½ 5
Rubylee **(70)***(49) (KMcAuliffe)* 3-8-9 RCochrane(4) (led over 1f: wknd wl over 1f out)....½ 6
332[6] Full Cover (IRE) **(70)***(36) (DRCElsworth)* 3-9-0v WNewnes(9) (prom over 3f)....8 7
372[9] He's Special *(32) (CACyzer)* 3-9-0 GDuffield(2) (a bhd)....2 8
243[7] Tapping Feet **(41)***(8) (DMHyde)* 3-8-2 (7) RHavlin(7) (prom 2f)....8 9

10/11 BENCHER Q C (USA) (4/5-6/5), **5/2** Shen Yang (USA) (op 6/4), **10/1** Kreef, **12/1** Alute (IRE) (op 8/1), Full Cover (IRE) (op 8/1), **14/1** Miss Jemmima (20/1-12/1), Rubylee, **33/1** He's Special, Tapping Feet, CSF £3.99 TOTE £2.00: £1.00 £1.60 £3.10 (£2.70) OWNER Sheikh Mohammed (NEWMARKET) BRED Tri-Star Stable 9 Rn 1m 25.63 (2.63) SF: 32/32/21/18/8/6/-/-/-

469 VIGO CLAIMING STKS (4-Y.O+) (Class F) £2,720.60 (£751.60: £357.80)
2m (Equitrack) Stalls: Low GOING minus 0.65 sec per fur (FST) 2-40 (2-47)

412[2] **Maradonna (USA) (62)***(73) (JWhite)* 6-9-8 MFenton(7) (hdwy over 6f out: w ldr 5f out: led over 1f out: bmpd ins fnl f: hdd last stride: fin 2nd, s.h: awrdd r)....— 1
412[7] Arc Bright (IRE) **(65)***(73)*(Fav)*(RHollinshead)* 5-9-8 LDettori(1) (led 1f: led 5f out: hrd rdn & hdd over 1f out: edgd rt ins fnl f: led last stride: fin 1st: disq: plcd 2nd)....½ 2
403[12] Lon Isa **(47)** *(BPalling)* 4-8-6 AClark(3) (lw: hdwy over 6f out: wknd 5f out: t.o)....dist 3
370[3] Call Me Albi (IRE) **(49)** *(GLMoore)* 4-8-7v BRouse(2) (lw: led over 9f out to 5f out: sn wknd: t.o)....2 4
153[9] Aerial View **(39)** *(WGMTurner)* 4-8-5 GDuffield(6) (hld up: rdn 5f out: sn wknd: t.o)....9 5
352[6] A New Flame *(RGuest)* 4-8-2v(5) CHawksley(5) (led 15f out: sn clr: hdd over 9f out: sn wknd: t.o)....dist 6
329[6] Quadrant **(49)** *(AMoore)* 6-8-12 CandyMorris(4) (b: 5th & no ch whn p.u over 4f out: broke down).... P

11/8 Arc Bright (IRE), **15/8** MARADONNA (USA), **5/1** Call Me Albi (IRE), **8/1** Lon Isa, **20/1** Quadrant, **33/1** Aerial View, A New Flame, CSF £4.76 TOTE £2.60: £2.10 £1.70 (£2.60) OWNER Mr Alan Spargo (WENDOVER) BRED Gerald W. Leigh 7 Rn 3m 26.15 (2.65) SF: 42/-/-/-/-/-/-
WEIGHT FOR AGE 4yo-5lb
STEWARDS' ENQUIRY Arc Bright (IRE) disq. (interference to Maradonna (USA) ins fnl f).

470 BILBAO LIMITED STKS (0-65) (4-Y.O+) (Class F) £2,720.60 (£751.60: £357.80)
1m 2f (Equitrack) Stalls: Low GOING minus 0.42 sec per fur (FST) 3-10 (3-17)

276[3] **El Atrevido (FR) (65)***(72) (NJHWalker)* 5-9-3 RCochrane(2) (b: chsd ldr: led over 2f out: drvn out)....— 1
349[3] Zacaroon **(61)***(65)*(Fav)*(LordHuntingdon)* 4-8-9 LDettori(5) (hld up: rdn over 3f out: chsd wnr over 1f out: r.o)....nk 2
357[5] Brave Spy **(46)***(63) (CACyzer)* 4-9-0 GDuffield(7) (lw: rdn & hdwy over 3f out: r.o one pce fnl f)....4 3
406[10] Roman Reel (USA) **(62)***(64) (GLMoore)* 4-9-2 BRouse(4) (lw: n.m.r on ins 5f out: rdn over 3f out: hdwy over 1f out: r.o one pce)....½ 4
General Shirley (IRE) **(55)***(60) (PRHedger)* 4-9-0 StephenDavies(1) (led over 7f)....1¼ 5

222[10] Scottish Park **(41)***(49) (RWEmery)* 6-8-12 JWilliams(6) (lw: a bhd) 5 **6**
Shuttlingslow **(47)***(43) (NAGaselee)* 4-8-9 TQuinn(3) (prom 7f) 3 **7**

7/4 Zacaroon (6/4-5/2), **9/4** EL ATREVIDO (FR), **4/1** Brave Spy (11/2-7/2), **11/2** Roman Reel (USA), **14/1** Shuttlingslow, **20/1** General Shirley (IRE), **33/1** Scottish Park, CSF £6.59 TOTE £2.20: £2.10 £1.30 (£1.70) OWNER Mrs Alison Brooks (WANTAGE) BRED France Foal Investments in France 7 Rn 2m 6.13 (3.13) SF: 42/34/32/33/29/19/12
WEIGHT FOR AGE 4yo-1lb

471

SANTIAGO H'CAP (0-70) (4-Y.O+) (Class E) £3,044.80 (£906.40: £431.20: £193.60) **1m 4f (Equitrack)** Stalls: Low GOING minus 0.42 sec per fur (FST) 3-40 (3-45)

303[6] **Bag of Tricks (IRE) (60)***(71) (SDow)* 5-10-0 DHarrison(6) (hld up: led over 4f out: clr 2f out: rdn out) ....— **1**
421* Modest Hope (USA) **(50)***(54)*(Fav)*(BRichmond)* 8-9-4 5x LDettori(7) (lw: hdwy over 4f out: rdn over 3f out: chsd wnr over 1f out: no imp) 5 **2**
357[6] Ginger Jim **(55)***(56) (PRHedger)* 4-9-7v GDuffield(3) (lw: led over 7f: rdn 3f out: wknd fnl f)...2½ **3**
320[9] Pigalle Wonder **(30)***(30) (RJO'Sullivan)* 7-7-12 NAdams(1) (nvr nr to chal) ....½ **4**
304[9] Long Furlong **(48)***(47) (JRBosley)* 7-9-2 CRutter(5) (prom over 9f) 1¼ **5**
414[5] Northern Trial (USA) **(46)***(42) (KRBurke)* 7-8-11v(3) JTate(4) (bhd fnl 5f) 1¾ **6**
413[10] Across the Bay **(40)***(20) (RWEmery)* 8-8-8b JWilliams(2) (chsd ldr over 6f) 12 **7**

11/8 Modest Hope (USA), **4/1** BAG OF TRICKS (IRE) (3/1-9/2), **6/1** Northern Trial (USA) (op 4/1), **7/1** Long Furlong, **11/1** Pigalle Wonder (16/1-10/1), **12/1** Ginger Jim (op 8/1), **14/1** Across the Bay (op 8/1), CSF £9.36 TOTE £4.40: £2.10 £1.60 (£4.40) OWNER Eurostrait Ltd (EPSOM) BRED Hesmonds Stud Ltd 7 Rn 2m 38.09 (8.69) SF: 21/4/4/-/-/-/-
WEIGHT FOR AGE 4yo-2lb

472

LIMA H'CAP (0-70) (4-Y.O+) (Class E) £3,187.80 (£950.40: £453.20: £204.60) **1m (Equitrack)** Stalls: Low GOING minus 0.42 sec per fur (FST) 4-10 (4-16)

413[3] **Eastleigh (50)***(58) (RHollinshead)* 6-8-11 LDettori(4) (chsd ldr over 6f out: led 3f out: rdn out) ....— **1**
347[2] Kedwick (IRE) **(54)***(60) (PRHedger)* 6-9-1b StephenDavies(7) (b: b.hind: s.s: hdwy wl over 1f out: r.o wl ins fnl f) 1¼ **2**
371* Digpast (IRE) **(67)***(72)*(Fav)*(RJO'Sullivan)* 5-10-0b DBiggs(8) (b: lw: dwlt: hld up: rdn over 2f out: ev ch ins fnl f: unable qckn) ....s.h **3**
408[2] Pair of Jacks (IRE) **(33)***(32) (DAWilson)* 5-7-8 JQuinn(5) (lw: led 5f: ev ch over 1f out: wknd fnl f) 3 **4**
413[12] Fiaba **(44)***(37) (MrsNMacauley)* 7-7-12 (7) AmandaSanders(3) (bhd fnl 5f) 3 **5**
402* Green's Bid **(59)***(42) (DWChapman)* 5-9-6 ACulhane(2) (lw: a.p: nt clr run on ins over 6f out: rdn over 4f out: wknd over 2f out) 5 **6**
Melody Dancer **(53)***(12) (RWEmery)* 4-9-0 JWilliams(1) (a bhd) 12 **7**
408* Indian Serenade **(52)** *(PWHarris)* 4-8-8 (5) JStack(6) (lw: uns rdr s) .... **U**

9/4 Digpast (IRE), **4/1** EASTLEIGH (3/1-5/1), **5/1** Kedwick (IRE), Indian Serenade, **15/2** Pair of Jacks (IRE) (op 5/1), **10/1** Green's Bid (op 6/1), **14/1** Fiaba, **25/1** Melody Dancer, CSF £22.53 CT £49.51 TOTE £6.00: £2.20 £1.40 £1.10 (£28.50) OWNER Mr J. E. Bigg (UPPER LONGDON) BRED Hever Castle Stud 8 Rn 1m 38.41 (2.01) SF: 40/42/54/14/19/24/-/-

473

SANTANDER H'CAP (0-65) (3-Y.O) (Class F) £2,821.40 (£780.40: £372.20) **6f (Equitrack)** Stalls: Low GOING minus 0.42 sec per fur (FST) 4-40 (4-46)

319[2] **Bon Secret (IRE) (64)***(77)*(Fav)*(TJNaughton)* 3-9-4 (3) SSanders(3) (lw: hdwy over 1f out: str run to ld ins fnl f: r.o wl) ....— **1**
426[0] Bold Frontier **(62)***(67) (KTIvory)* 3-9-5b GDuffield(4) (b: led over 3f out: clr 2f out: hdd ins fnl f: unable qckn) 3 **2**
411[8] Exclusive Assembly **(53)***(47) (APJames)* 3-8-10 FNorton(1) (lost pl over 3f out: r.o one pce fnl 2f) 4 **3**
319[8] Woolverstone Hall (IRE) **(54)***(47) (DJGMurraySmith)* 3-8-11 TQuinn(8) (hld up: rdn over 2f out: one pce) ....½ **4**
410* Abbey House **(58)***(46) (RGuest)* 3-8-10b(5) CHawksley(7) (a.p: rdn over 2f out: wknd 1f out) 2 **5**
False Pretences (IRE) **(40)***(21) (BAPearce)* 3-7-6 (5) MBaird(5) (lw: dwlt: outpcd: nvr nrr) 2½ **6**
319[7] Tachycardia **(45)***(24) (RJO'Sullivan)* 3-8-2 StephenDavies(6) (led over 3f: wknd over 2f out) ....¾ **7**
Deardaw **(43)** *(MDIUsher)* 3-7-7 (7) CAdamson(9) (b: a bhd) 10 **8**

Gilpa Trinkets **(40)** *(DWChapman)* 3-7-11 JQuinn(2) (dwlt: a bhd) ....hd 9

2/1 BON SECRET (IRE), **11/4** Bold Frontier, **7/2** Abbey House, **8/1** Woolverstone Hall (IRE), **10/1** Exclusive Assembly, **11/1** Tachycardia, **16/1** Deardaw, **33/1** False Pretences (IRE), Gilpa Trinkets, CSF £8.18 CT £40.02 TOTE £4.00: £1.40 £1.10 £3.70 (£3.60) Trio £21.80 OWNER Mr F. R. Jackman (EPSOM) BRED Sean Mc Donnell in Ireland 9 Rn 1m 13.49 (2.89) SF: 29/19/-/-/-/-/-/-/-

T/Plpt: £3.10 (5,955.30 Tckts). T/Qdpt: £2.40 (22.2 Tckts). AK

EDINBURGH (R-H)
Thursday March 30th (Good to soft)
WEATHER: overcast WIND: mod across

474 TUCK SHOP MAIDEN AUCTION STKS (2-Y.O) (Class F) £2,634.50 (£742.00: £363.50) 5f Stalls: High GOING: 0.39 sec per fur (GS) 2-10 (2-11)

Whicksey Perry *(71+t) (JBerry)* 2-8-4 JCarroll(5) (w'like: reard s: hdwy ½-wy: led wl over 1f out: comf) ....— 1
Unconditional Love (IRE) *(63)*(Fav)*(MJohnston)* 2-8-2 TWilliams(7) (cmpt: scope: chsd ldrs: led 2f out: sn hdd & kpt on) 1¾ 2
436[3] Arvzees (IRE) *(57)*(Fav)*(MRChannon)* 2-8-4 CRutter(3) (led 3f: sn rdn & btn) 2½ 3
In A Tizzy *(46) (PCHaslam)* 2-7-13 LCharnock(6) (leggy: scope: a chsng ldrs: rdn & no imp fr ½-wy) 2 4
Dance To Victory *(18) (TDBarron)* 2-7-11 JFanning(2) (lt-f: s.i.s: a outpcd) 8 5
Braes'O'Shieldhill *(20) (ABailey)* 2-8-2 GBardwell(1) (small: neat: lw: s.s: nt rcvr) 1 6
436[13] Go Like West *(JHetherton)* 2-8-7 NKennedy(4) (prom early: sn wl bhd) 11 7

5/2 Unconditional Love (IRE), Arvzees (IRE), **11/4** WHICKSEY PERRY, **7/2** Braes'O'Shieldhill, **12/1** In A Tizzy (op 6/1), **33/1** Dance To Victory, **100/1** Go Like West, CSF £10.00 TOTE £4.00: £1.80 £2.20 (£5.30) OWNER Mr J. Berry (COCKERHAM) BRED D. H. Jones 7 Rn
63.9 secs (6.20) SF: 16/8/2/-/-/-/-

475 BOOKER CASH & CARRY H'CAP (0-70) (3-Y.O+) (Class E) £3,501.25 (£1,060.00: £517.50: £246.25) 5f Stalls: High GOING: 0.39 sec per fur (GS) 2-40 (2-42)

398[8] **My Cherrywell (50)***(57) (LRLloyd-James)* 5-9-7v TWilliams(5) (b.hind: a chsng ldrs: led ins fnl f: all out) ....— 1
Sonderise **(47)***(54)*(Fav)*(NTinkler)* 6-9-4 JLowe(7) (s.i.s: hdwy ½-wy: squeezed thro' to chal ins fnl f: hrd rdn: no ex nr fin) ....hd 2
398[9] Kalar **(43)***(44) (DWChapman)* 6-9-0b DeanMcKeown(6) (cl up: wandered u.p: led 1½f out tl ins fnl f: no ex) 1¾ 3
369[6] Sigama (USA) **(51)***(51) (DNicholls)* 9-9-8 AlexGreaves(1) (lw: racd stands' side: led tl hdd ½f out: kpt on one pce) ....½ 4
353[8] Henry the Hawk **(50)***(45) (MDods)* 4-9-2v(5) JStack(8) (lw: hdwy u.p ½-wy: no imp) 1½ 5
Sunday Mail Too (IRE) **(54)***(49) (MissLAPerratt)* 3-8-12 JWeaver(3) (chsd ldr stands' side over 3f) ....s.h 6
Uppance **(30)***(21) (DANolan)* 7-7-10 (5) NVarley(2) (t: s.i.s: racd stands' side: hdwy ½-wy: n.d) 1 7
Rich Glow **(44)***(34) (NBycroft)* 4-9-1b JFortune(11) (cl up 3f: btn whn hmpd ent fnl f) ....nk 8
338[6] Meeson Times **(46)***(27) (RBastiman)* 7-9-3 ACulhane(4) (racd centre: wl outpcd fr ½-wy) 3 9
Daily Starshine (IRE) **(63)***(33) (JBerry)* 3-9-7 JCarroll(9) (spd to ½-wy: sn bhd) 3½ 10
Serious Hurry **(53)** *(RMMcKellar)* 7-9-3 (7) NKinnon(10) (bkwd: spd 2f: sn wknd & wl bhd) 15 11

3/1 Sonderise (op 7/1), **4/1** Kalar (op 5/2), **5/1** Daily Starshine (IRE), **15/2** Sigama (USA) (5/1-8/1), **9/1** Sunday Mail Too (IRE), **10/1** MY CHERRYWELL, Rich Glow, Meeson Times, **20/1** Henry the Hawk, **50/1** Uppance, **100/1** Serious Hurry, CSF £37.77 CT £130.11 TOTE £17.40: £1.90 £1.50 £1.50 (£19.90) Trio £30.00 OWNER Mrs Cheryl Owen (MALTON) BRED J. C. and Mrs C. L. Owen 11 Rn
64.2 secs (6.50) SF: 27/24/14/21/15/6/-/4/-/-/-
WEIGHT FOR AGE 3yo-13lb

476 GOLD MARK CLAIMING H'CAP (0-60) (4-Y.O+) (Class F) £2,655.50 (£748.00: £366.50) 1m 4f 31y Stalls: High GOING: 0.39 sec per fur (GS) 3-10 (3-10)

234[3] **Borocay (38)***(49)*(Fav)*(MJCamacho)* 7-8-10 LCharnock(6) (chsd ldrs: led wl over 3f out: wandered u.p: styd on) ....— 1
Doubling Dice **(32)***(39) (RAllan)* 4-8-2 JFanning(8) (hld up: hdwy 3f out: styd on fnl f) 3 2

Funny Rose **(22)***(28) (PMonteith)* 5-7-8 JMarshall(1) (hld up: gd hdwy over 2f out: rdn & no ex appr fnl f) ...¾ 3
Rebeccas Secret (IRE) **(58)***(62) (RFFisher)* 4-10-0 NConnorton(2) (in tch: effrt 3f out: r.o one pce) ...1½ 4
422[7] Gold Desire **(37)***(41) (MBrittain)* 5-8-9 JLowe(4) (trckd ldrs: effrt over 3f out: sn rdn & btn) ...s.h 5
44[9] Sharp N' Smooth **(51)***(55) (WTKemp)* 8-9-9b JWeaver(7) (hld up & bhd: c wd & effrt over 2f out: no imp) ...nk 6
422[2] Ijab (CAN) **(27)***(31) (JParkes)* 5-7-10b(3) DarrenMoffatt(5) (lw: cl up: effrt & ev ch 3f out: wknd over 2f out) ...s.h 7
Doctor Roy **(34)***(37) (NBycroft)* 7-8-6 JFortune(3) (chsd ldrs tl wknd fnl 3f) ...½ 8
Judge and Jury **(38)***(21) (LLungo)* 6-8-10b DaleGibson(9) (led tl hdd wl over 3f out: sn rdn & btn) ...15 9

3/1 BOROCAY, **100/30** Ijab (CAN), **6/1** Judge and Jury, Gold Desire, **7/1** Rebeccas Secret (IRE), **9/1** Doubling Dice (14/1-8/1), **10/1** Funny Rose, **20/1** Doctor Roy, Sharp N' Smooth, CSF £27.61 CT £212.70 TOTE £4.10: £1.30 £1.90 £2.30 (£26.70) Trio £235.61 OWNER Mrs S. Camacho (MALTON) BRED Mrs S. Camacho 9 Rn 2m 49.5 (17.00) SF: 16/4/-/27/8/22/-/4/-

WEIGHT FOR AGE 4yo-2lb

477

CHEFS LARDER MEDIAN AUCTION MAIDEN STKS (3-Y.O) (Class F)
£2,634.50 (£742.00: £363.50)
1m 3f 32y Stalls: High GOING: 0.39 sec per fur (GS) 3-40 (3-42)

Sarasota Storm *(73)*(Fav)*(MBell)* 3-9-0 MFenton(7) (lw: a.p: led over 3f out: rdn & styd on strly) ...— 1
Stone Cross (IRE) *(66) (RFFisher)* 3-9-0 JFanning(4) (leggy: in tch: hdwy on bit to chal over 2f out: rdn over 1f out: sn wknd) ...5 2
168[3] Hard Try *(62) (MJCamacho)* 3-9-0 LCharnock(2) (led 2f: cl up tl outpcd fnl 2½f) ...2½ 3
Ricana **(48)***(47) (WTKemp)* 3-8-9 JWeaver(5) (unruly s: s.s: sme hdwy fnl 3f: n.d) ...7 4
368[6] Bitter N Twisted **(40)***(30) (SEKettlewell)* 3-8-9b TWilliams(1) (led after 2f tl over 3f out: sn outpcd) ...12 5
Robellina *(24) (MDods)* 3-9-0 DaleGibson(3) (lost tch appr st: n.d) ...8 6
Carondra *(4) (RMMcKellar)* 3-8-9b JCarroll(6) (in tch to st) ...10 7

4/11 SARASOTA STORM, **7/2** Hard Try, **7/1** Stone Cross (IRE), **25/1** Ricana, **33/1** Bitter N Twisted, **66/1** Robellina, **100/1** Carondra, CSF £3.98 TOTE £1.30: £1.10 £4.30 (£6.80) OWNER Mr B. J. Warren (NEWMARKET) BRED B. J. Warren 7 Rn 2m 33.3 (13.60) SF: 33/26/22/7/-/-/-

478

MALT HOUSE VINTNERS (S) H'CAP (0-60) (3-Y.O+) (Class G)
£2,480.50 (£698.00: £341.50)
1m 16y Stalls: High GOING: 0.39 sec per fur (GS) 4-10 (4-11)

51[11] **Pash (42)***(53) (CWCElsey)* 3-7-7v NKennedy(7) (in tch: led over 1f out: styd on u.p) ...— 1
400[2] Wellsy Lad (USA) **(44)***(52) (DWChapman)* 8-8-12b DeanMcKeown(5) (chsd ldrs: ev ch over 1f out: nt qckn) ...1½ 2
415[2] Mary's Case (IRE) **(56)***(63)*(Fav)*(MJohnston)* 5-9-10b JWeaver(10) (hdwy over 2f out: hung lft: ev ch 1f out: hrd rdn & no ex) ...½ 3
233[12] Dundeelin **(42)***(41) (JLEyre)* 4-8-10 JFortune(3) (styd on u.p fnl 3f: n.d) ...4 4
379[10] Wassl's Nanny (IRE) **(52)***(48) (BEllison)* 6-9-6 JCarroll(2) (lw: rr div: rdn over 3f out: n.d) ...1¾ 5
378[3] Puffy **(38)***(33) (MDods)* 8-8-6v DaleGibson(4) (b: s.i.s: stumbled after s: rdn 3f out: n.d) ...½ 6
Portite Sophie **(37)***(30) (MBrittain)* 4-8-5 JLowe(6) (cl up tl wknd over 2fout) ...1 7
411[5] Benjarong **(50)***(41) (RMMcKellar)* 3-8-1 TWilliams(8) (chsd ldrs: led over 2f out tl hdd & wknd over 1f out) ...1 8
Languedoc **(47)***(24) (MartynWane)* 8-9-1 LCharnock(1) (dwlt: hdwy to chse ldrs ent st: sn wknd) ...7 9
408[8] Brigadore Gold **(30)***(2) (ABailey)* 5-7-12b GBardwell(9) (led tl hdd & wknd over 2f out) ...2½ 10

LONG HANDICAP Pash 7-5

2/1 Mary's Case (IRE), **5/1** Puffy, **6/1** Wellsy Lad (USA), Brigadore Gold, **8/1** Languedoc, **9/1** Benjarong, **12/1** Portite Sophie, **14/1** Dundeelin, **33/1** PASH, **50/1** Wassl's Nanny (IRE), CSF £200.64 CT £534.85 TOTE £53.80: £9.60 £2.30 £1.10 (£84.50) Trio £107.40 OWNER Mr C. D. Barber-Lomax (MALTON) BRED Mrs M. Morley 10 Rn

1m 47.9 (9.30) SF: 17/33/44/22/29/14/11/5/5/-

WEIGHT FOR AGE 3yo-17lb

No bid

479

FAMILY CHOICE MAIDEN H'CAP (0-70) (3-Y.O+) (Class E)
£3,035.00 (£920.00: £450.00: £215.00)
7f 15y Stalls: High GOING: 0.39 sec per fur (GS) 4-40 (4-44)

3153 **Reverand Thickness (69)***(77) (SCWilliams)* 4-10-0 JFortune(6) (lw: led: hung bdly lft 2f out: hdd ins fnl f: rallied to ld nr fin) .....— 1
Equerry **(60)***(67)*(Fav)*(MJohnston)* 4-9-5 JWeaver(9) (bhd: gd hdwy 3f out: led ins fnl f: no ex nr fin) .....nk 2
Bedazzle **(36)***(34) (MBrittain)* 4-7-9 JLowe(5) (effrt on outside appr st: hdwy 2f out: nt pce to chal) 4 3
41910 Scent of Power **(37)***(32) (MartynWane)* 5-7-10 DaleGibson(7) (in tch: effrt over 3f out: one pce) 1½ 4
Sul Fosso **(50)***(39) (JBerry)* 3-7-0 (7) PFessey(3) (in tch: rdn 3f out: one pce) 2½ 5
4163 Rainbows Rhapsody **(44)***(22) (MJCamacho)* 4-8-3 LCharnock(4) (b: b.hind: chsd ldrs: tl rdn & grad wknd fnl 3f) 5 6
Kenesha (IRE) **(62)***(36) (DANolan)* 5-9-2 (5) NVarley(2) (chsd ldrs 4f: sn lost pl) 1¾ 7
Pegs **(52)***(15) (CWThornton)* 4-8-11 DeanMcKeown(8) (cl up tl lost pl appr st: sn rcvrd: wknd 2f out) 5 8
Strathtore Dream (IRE) **(59)***(18) (MissLAPerratt)* 4-9-4 JFanning(1) (bit bkwd: a bhd) 1½ 9

5/2 Equerry (2/1-3/1), **7/2** REVERAND THICKNESS, **4/1** Pegs, **11/2** Rainbows Rhapsody, **12/1** Scent of Power, Strathtore Dream (IRE), **14/1** Bedazzle, **20/1** Kenesha (IRE), **25/1** Sul Fosso, CSF £12.16 CT £97.30 TOTE £3.00: £1.70 £1.40 £4.10 (£3.70) Trio £15.70 OWNER The Waresley Partnership (NEWMARKET) BRED S. J. Mear 9 Rn 1m 33.6 (7.60) SF: 55/45/12/10/1/-/14/-/-
WEIGHT FOR AGE 3yo-16lb

T/Plpt: £54.90 (187.76 Tckts). T/Qdpt: £6.30 (4.5 Tckts). AA

LEICESTER (R-H)
Thursday March 30th (Soft)
WIND: slt half bhd

480

KNIGHTON MEDIAN AUCTION MAIDEN STKS (2-Y.O) (Class F)
£2,821.40 (£780.40: £372.20)
5f 2y Stalls: High GOING: 0.44 sec per fur (GS) 2-20 (2-21)

Cabcharge Striker *(87?t) (MRChannon)* 2-9-0 RHughes(8) (w'like: bit bkwd: chsd ldrs: rdn over 1f out: r.o to ld wl ins fnl f) .....— 1
Dankeston (USA) *(86)*(Fav)*(MBell)* 2-9-0 MHills(7) (w'like: leggy: chsd ldrs: drvn along ½-wy: rdn & r.o wl ins fnl f) .....nk 2
Passion For Life *(82) (GLewis)* 2-9-0 PaulEddery(6) (leggy: scope: bit bkwd: led: clr over 1f out: wknd & ct wl ins fnl f) 1¼ 3
Capilano Princess *(61) (DHaydnJones)* 2-8-9 KDarley(5) (leggy: unf: swtchd lft s: spd 3f) 5 4
Monsieur Culsyth *(53) (JBerry)* 2-9-0 GCarter(3) (leggy: lt-f: unf: dwlt: sn rcvrd to chse ldrs: rdn & wknd wl over 1f out) 4 5
Kenny Davis (IRE) *(42) (MrsHParrott)* 2-9-0 TSprake(2) (lt-f: bkwd: spd to ½-wy: sn lost tch) 3½ 6
Ebony Boy *(29) (JWharton)* 2-9-0 JWilliams(1) (leggy: bit bkwd: sn outpcd & bhd) 4 7
Digwana (IRE) *(25) (TMJones)* 2-9-0 RPerham(4) (lt-f: unf: s.s: a bhd & outpcd) 1¼ 8

4/7 Dankeston (USA), **6/1** CABCHARGE STRIKER (op 7/2), **13/2** Passion For Life (op 7/2), Monsieur Culsyth (op 4/1), **7/1** Ebony Boy (5/1-8/1), **12/1** Capilano Princess (tchd 20/1), **16/1** Kenny Davis (IRE), **20/1** Digwana (IRE), CSF £11.33 TOTE £10.50: £1.30 £1.20 £2.30 (£7.80) OWNER Computer Cab Racing Club (UPPER LAMBOURN) BRED J. K. Keegan 8 Rn
64.3 secs (5.80) SF: 37/36/32/11/3/-/-/-

481

HARBOROUGH H'CAP (0-80) (4-Y.O+ F & M) (Class D) £3,732.30
(£1,112.40: £530.20: £239.10)
1m 8y Stalls: High GOING: 0.44 sec per fur (GS) 2-50 (2-50)

3189 **Misty Silks (74)***(83) (MJRyan)* 5-9-11 AClark(9) (hld up: swtchd rt & hdwy over 2f out: led appr fnl f: sn clr) .....— 1
Celtic Ceilidh **(51)***(52) (JWharton)* 4-8-2 PRobinson(3) (in tch tl outpcd ½-wy: rallied 2f out: r.o wl ins fnl f) 4 2
Forgetful **(49)***(38) (DBurchell)* 6-8-0 ow7 RPrice(1) (chsd ldrs: rdn & outpcd over 3f out: kpt on fnl f) 2½ 3

20[11] Bassmaat (USA) **(77)***(71) (MrsLPiggott)* 4-9-7 (7) GMilligan(6) (b: b.hind: bit bkwd: a.p: led over 3f out tl over 1f out: sn wknd) 1 **4**
410[5] Giggleswick Girl **(56)***(40) (MRChannon)* 4-8-7 PatEddery(4) (lw: a.p: jnd ldr over 2f out: sn rdn: wknd appr fnl f)....5 **5**
Ikis Girl **(56)***(35) (SGollings)* 4-8-7 TQuinn(10) (bkwd: prom 5f)....2½ **6**
Fabriana **(51)***(2) (TJNaughton)* 5-8-2 DHarrison(2) (bit bkwd: led over 4f: sn wknd: t.o) 14 **7**
414* Kinnegad Kid **(52)** (Fav)*(RIngram)* 6-8-0 (3) DWright(8) (lw: chsd ldrs tl rdn & wknd 3f out: t.o) 4 **8**
364[7] Belleminette (IRE) **(57)** *(DHaydnJones)* 4-8-8 AMackay(7) (hld up in tch: rdn over 3f out: eased whn btn wl over 1f out: t.o) 25 **9**
365[10] Profit Release (IRE) **(56)** *(MJohnston)* 4-8-7 DHolland(5) (spd early: lost pl ½-wy: sn bhd: t.o) 15 **10**
LONG HANDICAP Forgetful 7-5

9/4 Kinnegad Kid (op 6/4), **4/1** MISTY SILKS, **6/1** Profit Release (IRE), **9/1** Bassmaat (USA), **10/1** Celtic Ceilidh, Ikis Girl, Fabriana, Giggleswick Girl, **12/1** Belleminette (IRE), **25/1** Forgetful, CSF £41.14 CT £819.32 TOTE £4.70: £1.30 £2.10 £6.00 (£21.30) Trio £290.10 OWNER Mr P. E. Axon (NEWMARKET) BRED R. M. Scott 10 Rn 1m 46.3 (11.30) SF: 28/-/-/16/-/-/-/-/-/-
OFFICIAL EXPLANATION **Kinnegad Kid: the jockey reported the mare was unable to handle the patches of holding ground on lower-lying parts of the course.**
Profit Release (IRE): the jockey reported his mount ran a lifeless race.

482 BURTON OVERY (S) STKS (3-Y.O) (Class G) £2,735.80 (£758.80: £363.40)
5f 218y Stalls: High GOING: 0.44 sec per fur (GS) 3-20 (3-22)

405[8] **Noor El Houdah (IRE) (63)***(65) (JBerry)* 3-9-0 GCarter(8) (lw: chsd ldrs: shkn up 2f out: hdwy to ld wl ins fnl f: r.o)....— **1**
326[4] Dowdency **(44)***(61) (JAPickering)* 3-9-0 NCarlisle(10) (hdwy 2f out: rdn & r.o wl fnl f)....1½ **2**
420[2] Russian Heroine **(70)***(61)*(Fav)*(MJohnston)* 3-9-0 DHolland(15) (led tl hdd & no ex ins fnl f) ....s.h **3**
331[2] Baileys Sunset (IRE) **(63)***(66) (MJohnston)* 3-9-5 WRSwinburn(7) (w ldrs: rdn over 1f out: one pce) ....s.h **4**
394[11] Speedy Snaps Pride **(45)***(61) (PDCundell)* 3-9-0 WNewnes(9) (hld up & bhd: hdwy 2f out: nrst fin)....hd **5**
Rupert's Princess (IRE) **(58)***(57) (MJHeaton-Ellis)* 3-9-0 StephenDavies(5) (lw: sn pushed along: in tch: kpt on fnl f) 1½ **6**
437[12] Casper's Risk **(55)***(53) (DNicholls)* 3-9-5b PaulEddery(18) (hld up: hdwy ½-wy: rdn 2f out: sn btn)....3 **7**
420[4] Prince Rudolf (IRE) **(55)***(49) (MrsNMacauley)* 3-9-5b JReid(17) (chsd ldrs over 4f: eased whn btn)....1½ **8**
Aston Manor (IRE) *(44) (RHannon)* 3-9-0 PatEddery(4) (bkwd: rdn along ½-wy: nvr plcd to chal)....s.h **9**
283[6] Jersey Belle *(35) (PJMakin)* 3-8-9 LDettori(3) (lw: bhd tl sme late hdwy)....1¾ **10**
Simply Simon **(40)***(36) (KRBurke)* 3-9-0v RCochrane(2) (bhd: rdn 2f out: no imp) 1¼ **11**
381[7] Governor's Lass *(25) (SDow)* 3-8-9 TQuinn(13) (bit bkwd: spd 4f) 2½ **12**
411[4] Scissor Ridge **(53)***(24) (JJBridger)* 3-9-5 GDuffield(12) (w ldrs over 3f)....4 **13**
283[4] Bretton Princess **(45)***(11) (RHollinshead)* 3-8-9 WRyan(16) (hmpd after 1f: eased whn btn wl over 1f out) 1¼ **14**
258[4] Lotties Bid *(PSFelgate)* 3-8-9 KDarley(6) (a in rr: t.o)....8 **15**
435[12] Indian Rhapsody *(MRChannon)* 3-8-9 RHughes(1) (hrd rdn 3f out: sn bhd: t.o)....2 **16**
420[6] Tish **(40)** *(ASmith)* 3-8-9 MBirch(11) (hmpd after 1f: sn bhd: t.o) 2½ **17**

7/2 Russian Heroine, **6/1** NOOR EL HOUDAH (IRE) (op 4/1), Casper's Risk, Aston Manor (IRE), Indian Rhapsody, **7/1** Baileys Sunset (IRE), **8/1** Rupert's Princess (IRE), **10/1** Lotties Bid, **12/1** Jersey Belle, **14/1** Dowdency, Prince Rudolf (IRE), **20/1** Bretton Princess, **25/1** Scissor Ridge, Speedy Snaps Pride, Tish, **33/1** Simply Simon, Governor's Lass, CSF £98.57 TOTE £7.60: £2.70 £6.30 £1.60 (£104.50) Trio £196.70 OWNER Mr Basheer Kielany (COCKERHAM) BRED Mrs Margaret Sinanan 17 Rn 1m 18.6 (8.60) SF: 15/11/11/16/11/7/3/-/-/-/-/-/-/-/-/-/-
Bt in 4,400 gns

483 GADSBY H'CAP (0-90) (3-Y.O) (Class C) £5,796.00 (£1,728.00: £824.00: £372.00)
5f 2y Stalls: High GOING: 0.44 sec per fur (GS) 3-50 (3-50)

426* **Portend (77)***(86) (SRBowring)* 3-8-5 (7) 7x CTeague(7) (lw: a.p: led over 1f out: r.o wl)....— **1**
Total Stranger **(71)***(77) (MrsLPiggott)* 3-8-6 KDarley(5) (b: b.hind: lw: a.p: led wl over 1f out: sn hdd: unable qckn fnl f) 1 **2**

Musica **(79)***(83) (MRChannon)* 3-9-0 RHughes(4) (led 3f out tl wl over 1f out: sn rdn: no ex) ½ **3**
426³ Shinerolla **(58)***(61)*(Fav)*(MrsJRRamsden)* 3-7-7 JQuinn(1) (s.i.s: swtchd far side: effrt 2f out: sn rdn: nt pce to chal) ½ **4**
426¹² C-Yer-Simmie (IRE) **(58)***(59) (RHollinshead)* 3-7-7 NCarlisle(2) (hdwy over 1f out: nrst fin) ½ **5**
Jo Maximus **(70)***(65) (SDow)* 3-8-5 TQuinn(6) (dwlt: nvr trbld ldrs) 1¾ **6**
426² Double Quick (IRE) **(84)***(73) (MJohnston)* 3-9-5 DHolland(3) (spd centre 3f) 2 **7**
Endless Wave **(86)***(40) (MBell)* 3-9-7 PRobinson(8) (b.hind: bkwd: led 2f: lost tch fnl 2f: t.o) 11 **8**

13/8 Shinerolla, **7/2** Double Quick (IRE), PORTEND, **6/1** Musica (op 4/1), **10/1** Total Stranger, **12/1** Endless Wave, **16/1** Jo Maximus, **20/1** C-Yer-Simmie (IRE), CSF £35.84 CT £191.38 TOTE £4.90 £1.60 £2.20 £2.20 (£54.40) OWNER Mr D. H. Bowring (EDWINSTOWE) BRED Hollow Hole Stud 8 Rn 64.5 secs (6.00) SF: 32/23/29/7/5/11/19/-

484

LANGHAM MAIDEN STKS (3-Y.O) (Class D) £3,698.50 (£1,102.00: £525.00: £236.50)
1m 3f 183y Stalls: High GOING: 0.94 sec per fur (S) 4-20 (4-21)

Lord Jim (IRE) (70)*(78) (MissGayKelleway)* 3-9-0 RCochrane(2) (bkwd: mde all: clr fnl 3f: unchal) — **1**
Arctic Charmer (USA) *(66) (JLDunlop)* 3-9-0 WCarson(3) (h.d.w: hld up: 4th st: sn rdn: chsd wnr over 1f out: no imp) 9 **2**
Noonday Gun (IRE) **(78)***(60)*(Fav)*(RHannon)* 3-9-0 BRouse(5) (plld hrd: chsd ldrs: 3rd st: rdn 3f out: no imp) 4 **3**
Blue Smoke (IRE) *(55) (BAMcMahon)* 3-9-0 MWigham(6) (wl grwn: bkwd: s.s: bhd: 6th st: nvr nr ldrs) 4 **4**
Elation *(21) (PFICole)* 3-9-0 TQuinn(4) (hld up: 5th st: effrt & wnt lft 3f out: sn bhd: t.o) 25 **5**
Tenpenny *(GRimmer)* 3-8-9 MRimmer(1) (bit bkwd: chsd wnr: 2nd st: wknd over 2f out: eased: t.o) 15 **6**

13/8 Noonday Gun (IRE), **5/2** Elation, **4/1** LORD JIM (IRE) (3/1-9/2), **6/1** Arctic Charmer (USA), **14/1** Blue Smoke (IRE), **16/1** Tenpenny, CSF £24.47 TOTE £6.50: £2.10 £2.60 (£12.70) OWNER Mrs S. Y. Thomas (WHITCOMBE) BRED Woodcote Stud Ltd 6 Rn 2m 49.2 (20.40) SF: 36/24/18/13/-/-

485

SIMON DE MONTFORT MAIDEN STKS (3-Y.O+) (Class D) £4,205.50 (£1,258.00: £603.00: £275.50)
1m 1f 218y Stalls: High GOING: 0.94 sec per fur (S) 4-50 (4-52)

Parthian Springs *(91+)*(Fav)*(JHMGosden)* 4-9-13 PatEddery(7) (a.p: 2nd st: led over 3f out: clr ent fnl f: comf) — **1**
Motakabber (IRE) *(85) (JHMGosden)* 3-8-8 LDettori(15) (scope: b.hind: hld up & bhd: hdwy 3f out: styd on wl fnl f) 4 **2**
Orchestra Stall *(80) (JLDunlop)* 3-8-8 KDarley(10) (chsd ldrs: 5th st: ev ch 3f out: one pce appr fnl f) 3 **3**
He Knows The Rules *(73) (MRChannon)* 3-8-9 ow1 RHughes(12) (leggy: a.p: 4th st: hrd rdn 2f out: no imp) 4 **4**
Crespo (IRE) *(73) (JRFanshawe)* 3-8-8 DHarrison(13) (hld up: hdwy 3f out: nvr nr to chal) s.h **5**
Rushaway *(67) (RHannon)* 4-9-13 RPerham(16) (hld up: hdwy 4f out: one pce fnl 2f) 4 **6**
Legendra *(39) (PGMurphy)* 5-9-2 (7) RWaterfield(3) (chsd ldrs on outside: no imp fnl 3f) 15 **7**
Catempo (IRE) *(42) (SDow)* 5-10-0 StephenDavies(5) (chsd ldrs: 3rd st: hmpd over 3f out: eased whn btn) 1½ **8**
Salaman (FR) *(37) (JLDunlop)* 3-8-8 WCarson(11) (bit bkwd: nvr trbld ldrs) 2 **9**
Ray of Hope *(28) (GWragg)* 3-8-3 FNorton(1) (plld hrd: hld up & bhd: effrt 4f out: no rspnse) 2½ **10**
276⁶ Tip the Dove *(29) (RJPrice)* 6-9-9 TSprake(2) (lw: chsd ldrs to ½-wy) ½ **11**
Chocolate Charlie *(30) (RCharlton)* 4-9-13 PaulEddery(14) (leggy: unf: chsd ldrs: 6th & rdn st: sn lost tch) 1¾ **12**
Ismeno *(23) (SDow)* 4-9-13 TQuinn(6) (bit bkwd: nvr nr ldrs: t.o) 4 **13**
Jimbo *(18) (JRJenkins)* 4-9-13 JWilliams(9) (unf: dwlt: a bhd: t.o) 3½ **14**
Boundless (IRE) *(6) (BJMeehan)* 3-8-3 BDoyle(8) (a bhd: rdn over 4f out: t.o) 4 **15**
Super Sharp (NZ) *(8) (HOliver)* 7-10-0 TWall(4) (led: clr ½-wy: hdd over 3f out: wknd qckly: t.o) 2½ **16**

6/4 PARTHIAN SPRINGS, **4/1** Motakabber (IRE) (op 5/2), **9/2** Salaman (FR) (op 3/1), Crespo (IRE) (op 3/1), **10/1** Chocolate Charlie, He Knows The Rules, **16/1** Orchestra Stall, Ismeno, Ray of Hope, **20/1** Rushaway, **33/1** Tip the Dove, Jimbo, **40/1** Legendra, **50/1** Catempo (IRE), Boundless (IRE), Super Sharp (NZ), CSF £10.21 TOTE £2.60: £1.80 £1.70 £13.60 (£3.00) Trio £198.00 OWNER Hesmonds Stud (NEWMARKET) BRED Hesmonds Stud Ltd 16 Rn

2m 17.3 (14.60) SF: 68/43/38/31/31/44/16/19/-/-/6/7/-/-/-/-

WEIGHT FOR AGE 3yo-20lb, 4yo-1lb

486 KIBWORTH H'CAP (0-85) (3-Y.O+) (Class D) £4,002.70 (£1,195.60: £571.80: £259.90)

7f 9y Stalls: High GOING: 0.44 sec per fur (GS) 5-20 (5-23)

*349*7 **Sandmoor Denim (64)***(72) (SRBowring)* 8-8-2 (7) CTeague(8) (b: hld up & bhd: hdwy over 2f out: rdn to ld ins fnl f:) — 1

4505 Great Hall **(58)***(65) (PDCundell)* 6-8-3 DHarrison(2) (hld up & bhd: gd hdwy fr wl over 1f out: fin wl) ½ 2

Sharp Rebuff **(66)***(72) (PJMakin)* 4-8-11 LDettori(4) (lw: led: qcknd ½-wy: hdd & no ex ins fnl f) ½ 3

First Gold **(63)***(65) (JWharton)* 6-8-8 JWilliams(1) (hld up: hdwy over 2f out: one pce appr fnl f) 1¾ 4

Knobbleeneeze **(75)***(77) (MRChannon)* 5-9-6v RHughes(3) (chsd ldrs: effrt over 1f out: n.m.r: one pce fnl f) s.h 5

4333 Gadge **(72)***(70)*(Fav)*(DMorris)* 4-9-3 KDarley(6) (chsd ldrs: rdn 3f out: wknd appr fnl f) 1¾ 6

Saifan **(66)***(52) (DMorris)* 6-8-8 (3) CHodgson(7) (bit bkwd: chsd ldrs: no imp fnl 2f) 5 7

Tawafij (USA) **(82)***(65) (TDyer)* 6-9-13 WCarson(9) (hld up: nvr nr to chal) 1½ 8

Panikin **(72)***(46) (JWharton)* 7-9-3 JQuinn(5) (plld hrd: prom over 4f) 4 9

Serious Option (IRE) **(83)***(50) (PFICole)* 4-10-0 TQuinn(10) (bit bkwd: chsd ldr 5f: wknd wl over 1f out) 3 10

Halmanerror **(63)***(14) (MrsJRRamsden)* 5-8-8 JReid(11) (s.s: sn chsng ldrs: wknd over 2f out: eased: t.o) 7 11

East Barns (IRE) **(50)** *(SGollings)* 7-7-2b(7)ow2 MartinDwyer(12) (Withdrawn not under Starter's orders: lame) W

LONG HANDICAP East Barns (IRE) 7-4

, **5/2** Gadge, **4/1** Sharp Rebuff, **9/2** Halmanerror, **7/1** SANDMOOR DENIM, **8/1** Great Hall, **10/1** Tawafij (USA), Knobbleeneeze, **14/1** First Gold, **16/1** Serious Option (IRE), Panikin, **25/1** Saifan, CSF £62.10 TC £239.87 TOTE £7.30: £2.10 £3.10 £2.40 (£35.90) Trio £72.60 OWNER Mr E. H. Lunness (EDWINSTOWE) BRED Rathasker Stud 11 Rn 1m 33.2 (10.70) SF: 4/-/4/-/9/2/-/-/-/-/-

T/Jkpt: £53,460.70 (1.28 Tckts). T/Plpt: £246.80 (112.52 Tckts). T/Qdpt; £50.00 (0.2 Tckts); £54.08 to Huntingdon 31/3/95 IM

0291A-CAGNES-SUR-MER (Nice, France) (L-H) Sunday February 19th (Soft)

487a PRIX DE PASSAU £7,186.00

1m

Fort Commander (FR) *(RCollet,France)* 4-8-12 WMongil — 1

Banco Prime (IRE) *(France)* 5-9-2 PCourty ½ 2

Le Silicon (FR) *(France)* 5-9-0 SMaillot ½ 3

253a2 Confronter *(SDow)* 6-9-6 ESaint-Martin 1 4

TOTE 8.50f: 2.90f 6.20f 2.60f (71.90f) 4 Rn 1m 42.8 SF: -/-/-/-

488a PRIX POLICEMAN £11,976.00

1m 2f

Narazyyani (FR) *(PKhozian,France)* 3-9-0 GElorriaga-Santos — 1

207a2 Tzar Rodney (FR) *(France)* 3-9-3 ODoleuze 2 2

291a3 Minervitta *(France)* 3-8-10 WMongil 1 3

291a* Courbaril *(SDow)* 3-9-0 ESaint-Martin 9

209a* Mo's Main Man (IRE) *(SDow)* 3-8-10 FSanchez (btn more than 6l by wnr) 12

TOTE 3.40f: 2.50f 3.20f 4.10f (10.50f) 5 Rn 2m 9.4 SF: -/-/-/-/-

SAINT-CLOUD (France) (L-H)
Sunday March 19th (Heavy)

489a
PRIX EXBURY (Gp 3) (4-Y.O+) £26,374.00
1m 2f

Tuesday's Special (USA) *(AFabre,France)* 5-8-9 TJarnet ....— 1
En Cascade (FR) *(France)* 4-8-9 CAsmussen 1 2
Matarun (IRE) *(France)* 7-9-2 DBoeuf ....hd 3

3.60f: 1.70f 3.40f 2.30f (29.60f) OWNER Not Known (FRANCE) 2m 24.7 (21.20) SF: -/-/-

HAMILTON (R-H)
Friday March 31st (Heavy)
WEATHER: overcast WIND: mod across

490
DUNWAN MEDIAN AUCTION MAIDEN STKS (2-Y.O) (Class F)
£2,720.60 (£751.60: £357.80)
5f 4y Stalls: High GOING: 0.56 sec per fur (GS) 2-00 (2-02)

Precious Girl *(66t) (DMoffatt)* 2-8-6 (3) DarrenMoffatt(3) (leggy: scope: lw: sn outpcd & bhd: hdwy ½-wy: swtchd twice: led ins fnl f: r.o) ....— 1
Miss Offset *(63) (MJohnston)* 2-8-9 TWilliams(7) (w'like: scope: bit bkwd: mde most tl ins fnl f: kpt on wl).................................1 2
Red Simba *(46)(Fav)(JBerry)* 2-9-0 JCarroll(2) (disp ld: rdn ½-wy: btn appr fnl f).................................7 3
Just Rory *(14) (EJAlston)* 2-9-0 KFallon(5) (leggy: s.s: hdwy to jn ldrs ½-wy: wknd appr fnl f) 10 4
Annagh *(WTKemp)* 2-8-9 KDarley(1) (small: neat: unf: s.s: a outpcd & bhd).................................7 5
Vales Ales *(RMMcKellar)* 2-8-7 (7) NKinnon(4) (lt-f: bkwd: s.i.s: jnd ldrs after 1½f: wandered u.p ½-wy: wknd 1f out) 5 6
Saturiba (USA) *(MJohnston)* 2-9-0 DHolland(6) (leggy: unf: w ldrs to ½-wy: sn rdn & btn)..2½ 7

Evens Red Simba, **7/2** Saturiba (USA) (op 2/1), **9/2** Just Rory, **11/2** PRECIOUS GIRL, **20/1** Miss Offset, **33/1** Annagh, **200/1** Vales Ales, CSF £75.81 TOTE £9.60: £2.50 £3.90 (£26.70) OWNER Mr P. G. Airey (CARTMEL) BRED P. G. Airey and R. R. Whitton 7 Rn
65.6 secs (7.30) SF: 18/15/-/-/-/-/-

491
NEW TOTE SPRINT H'CAP (0-75) (3-Y.O+) (Class D) £5,020.00
(£1,510.00: £730.00: £340.00)
6f 5y Stalls: High GOING: 0.56 sec per fur (GS) 2-30 (2-31)

*419*15 **Aljaz (60)***(68) (DTThom)* 5-9-4 AMackay(11) (a cl up: led appr fnl f: styd on) ....— 1
4753 Kalar **(48)***(40) (DWChapman)* 6-7-13b(7)ow5 CTeague(9) (led tl hdd appr fnl f: no ex).................................4 2
Birchwood Sun **(56)***(43) (MDods)* 5-9-0b JFortune(4) (s.i.s: styd on fnl 2f: nrst fin).................................4 3
*354*12 Cronk's Courage **(56)***(24)(Fav)(MGMeagher)* 9-9-0v MFenton(8) (cl up to ½-wy: grad wknd) ...7 4
*348*6 Beckyhannah **(44)***(8) (RBastiman)* 5-8-2b LCharnock(6) (chsd ldrs tl rdn & wknd 2f out) 1½ 5
Cavers Yangous **(67)***(21)(Fav)(MJohnston)* 4-9-11 DHolland(10) (in tch: swtchd lft ½-wy: sn no ch).................................4 6
Densben **(58)***(6) (DenysSmith)* 11-9-2 KDarley(7) (s.i.s: nvr wnt pce).................................2 7
Miss Whittingham (IRE) **(56)***(4) (JBerry)* 5-9-0 JCarroll(2) (nvr wnt pce) ....hd 8
*371*7 Pine Ridge Lad (IRE) **(53)** *(JLEyre)* 5-8-11 SDWilliams(1) (a bhd) 1¼ 9
*117*12 Hiltons Travel (IRE) **(54)** *(EJAlston)* 4-8-12 KFallon(3) (outpcd after 2f).................................3 10
Diet **(47)** *(MissLAPerratt)* 9-8-5b JFanning(5) (w ldrs to ½-wy: sn wknd).................................3 11

5/1 Cavers Yangous, Cronk's Courage, **11/2** Beckyhannah, **6/1** Pine Ridge Lad (IRE) (op 4/1), **9/1** Diet, **10/1** Densben, **11/1** ALJAZ, Birchwood Sun, **12/1** Miss Whittingham (IRE), **16/1** Hiltons Travel (IRE), **20/1** Kalar, CSF £172.76 CT £2,218.74 TOTE £8.10: £3.10 £2.90 £5.00 (£73.60) Trio £372.00 OWNER Mr Ron Dawson (NEWMARKET) BRED Side Hill Stud 11 Rn
1m 17.0 (7.00) SF: 50/22/25/6/-/3/-/-/-/-/-

492
SPRINGFIELD RATING RELATED MAIDEN LIMITED STKS (0-60)
(3-Y.O) (Class F) £2,771.00 (£766.00: £365.00)
1m 65y Stalls: High GOING: 0.68 sec per fur (GS) 3-00 (3-00)

*362*3 **Concer Un (60)***(62) (SCWilliams)* 3-9-0 KDarley(3) (trckd ldrs: led over 4f out: hld on wl fnl 2f) ....— 1

362[4] Acquittal (IRE) **(60)***(61) (JRFanshawe)* 3-9-0 DHarrison(4) (hld up: hdwy 3f out: chsd wnr fnl 2f: styd on u.p) ....nk 2
427[14] Toshiba Talk (IRE) **(53)***(40) (BEllison)* 3-9-0 JCarroll(6) (hdwy & ch 3f out: one pce fnl 2f) 11 3
Hamilton Silk **(55)***(37) (MGMeagher)* 3-9-0 JFortune(2) (lw: cl up tl outpcd & lost pl 4f out: swtchd & hmpd 2f out: n.d) 1½ 4
Cool Steel (IRE) **(60)***(35)*(Fav)*(MissSEHall)* 3-9-0v NConnorton(5) (lw: hld up: nt clr run 3f out: swtchd & no imp after) 1¼ 5
Achill Princess **(42)***(20) (WTKemp)* 3-8-9 JMarshall(1) (led tl hdd over 4f out: wknd 2f out) 5 6

6/4 Cool Steel (IRE), **9/4** Acquittal (IRE), **3/1** CONCER UN, **14/1** Toshiba Talk (IRE) (op 8/1), **25/1** Achill Princess, **33/1** Hamilton Silk, CSF £9.37 TOTE £4.50: £2.20 £2.00 (£6.40) OWNER Miss L. J. Ward (NEWMARKET) BRED Lloyd Bros 6 Rn 1m 57.6 (14.30) SF: 16/15/-/-/-/-

493 CALDER H'CAP (0-70) (3-Y.O+) (Class E) £3,850.00 (£1,150.00: £550.00: £250.00)

1m 65y Stalls: High GOING: 0.68 sec per fur (GS) 3-30 (3-30)

Scaraben (47)*(62) (SEKettlewell)* 7-8-7 JFortune(8) (hld up: stdy hdwy on ins 3f out: led ins fnl f: drvn out) ....— 1
Sarmatian (USA) **(60)***(74) (MDHammond)* 4-9-6 JCarroll(3) (prom: led over 2f out tl ins fnl f: r.o) ....nk 2
378[4] Hawwam **(52)***(51)*(Fav)*(EJAlston)* 9-8-12 KFallon(11) (bhd: hdwy 3f out: styd on: nvr rchd ldrs) 8 3
378[11] The Happy Loon (IRE) **(62)***(51) (DenysSmith)* 4-9-8 MBirch(7) (lw: led tl hdd over 2f out: one pce) 5 4
413[2] No Submission (USA) **(51)***(40) (DWChapman)* 9-8-11 DeanMcKeown(4) (lw: a chsng ldrs: one pce fnl 3f) ....s.h 5
413[13] Deputy Tim **(38)***(12) (RBastiman)* 12-7-12 LCharnock(5) (w ldrs tl wknd 2f out) 8 6
222[3] Mam'zelle Angot **(63)***(14) (JLEyre)* 5-9-4 (5) JStack(2) (hld up: c wd st: sn rdn & btn) 12 7
349[8] Roar on Tour **(54)***(1) (MrsMReveley)* 6-9-0b KDarley(6) (swtg: trckd ldrs tl wknd over 2f out) 1¾ 8
Fools Haven (IRE) **(53)** *(BSRothwell)* 3-7-7 (3)ow3 DarrenMoffatt(9) (c wd st: sn no ch) 30 9
Princess Maxine (IRE) **(68)** *(JJO'Neill)* 6-9-7 (7) GParkin(1) (chsd ldrs tl wknd over 3f out) 1¾ 10

LONG HANDICAP Fools Haven (IRE) 6-11

9/4 Hawwam, **4/1** Mam'zelle Angot, **5/1** SCARABEN (op 8/1), **7/1** Roar on Tour (op 4/1), **12/1** Sarmatian (USA), No Submission (USA), **16/1** Deputy Tim, The Happy Loon (IRE), **20/1** Princess Maxine (IRE), **50/1** Fools Haven (IRE), CSF £54.10 CT £152.98 TOTE £9.50: £2.40 £2.00 £2.00 (£27.80) Trio £48.40 OWNER Mr J. Tennant (MIDDLEHAM) BRED Burton Agnes Stud Co Ltd 10 Rn 1m 55.8 (12.50) SF: 26/38/15/15/4/-/-/-/-/-
WEIGHT FOR AGE 3yo-17lb

494 GLEN LIMITED STKS (0-60) (4-Y.O+) (Class F) £2,846.60 (£787.60: £375.80)

1m 4f 17y Stalls: High GOING: 0.68 sec per fur (GS) 4-00 (4-00)

351[3] **Barti-Ddu (58)***(70) (SCWilliams)* 4-9-0 KDarley(8) (b.nr fore: trckd ldrs: led wl over 3f out: hld on gamely cl home) ....— 1
312[13] Tanah Merah (IRE) **(59)***(68) (EJAlston)* 4-8-12 KFallon(1) (s.i.s: bhd: hdwy 3f out: qcknd to chal wl ins fnl f: no ex cl home) ....hd 2
423[21] The Premier Expres **(42)***(65) (FJO'Mahony)* 5-9-0 JFortune(7) (a.p: hdwy to disp ld over 2f out: wknd over 1f out) 2½ 3
Virkon Venture (IRE) **(55)***(63) (MHTompkins)* 7-9-0 PRobinson(3) (b: in tch: effrt 3f out: rdn & one pce) 1½ 4
Persuasive **(53)***(48)*(Fav)*(MrsMReveley)* 8-8-2 (7) SCopp(2) (a.p: c wd st: rdn 3f out: btn 2f out) 7 5
Friendly Knight **(28)***(40) (JSHaldane)* 5-9-0 DeanMcKeown(9) (bhd: sme hdwy 3f out: n.d) ...10 6
Balnibarbi **(50)***(27) (TDyer)* 6-9-0 MFenton(4) (cl up tl wknd 3f out) 10 7
422[9] Marble **(49)***(19) (MartynWane)* 4-8-7 AMackay(5) (chsd ldrs: pushed along appr st: wknd 4f out) 2 8
303[8] Magic Times **(60)** *(MJohnston)* 4-8-12 DHolland(6) (led tl hdd over 3f out:wknd qckly: b.b.v) 30 9

9/4 Persuasive, **5/2** Virkon Venture (IRE), **3/1** BARTI-DDU, **14/1** Magic Times (op 8/1), Balnibarbi, **20/1** The Premier Expres, Tanah Merah (IRE), Marble, **100/1** Friendly Knight, CSF £48.42 TOTE £3.60: £1.70 £2.30 £2.90 (£27.70) Trio £162.20 OWNER Miss L. J. Ward (NEWMARKET) BRED Lloyd Bros 9 Rn 2m 49.7 (17.70) SF: 36/34/33/31/16/8/-/-/-

WEIGHT FOR AGE 4yo-2lb

OFFICIAL EXPLANATION **Magic Times: broke a blood-vessel.**

495

EARN H'CAP (0-70) (4-Y.O+) (Class E) £3,785.00 (£1,130.00: £540.00: £245.00)
1m 5f 9y Stalls: High GOING: 0.68 sec per fur (GS) 4-30 (4-30)

*375*12 **Zaaheyah (USA) (39)***(46) (MDHammond)* 5-8-0 ow1 PRobinson(4) (mde all: kpt on strly fnl f) — **1**
423 13 Cutthroat Kid (IRE) **(63)***(68) (MrsMReveley)* 5-9-10b KDarley(7) (wnt prom 7f out: disp ld over 2f out: hrd rdn & btn ins fnl f) 2½ **2**
*252*2 Dvorak (IRE) **(65)***(59)*(Fav)*(BJMcMath)* 4-9-10 AMackay(6) (lw: a in tch: pushed along appr st: one pce fnl 2f) 9 **3**
*375** El Nido **(54)***(45) (MJCamacho)* 7-9-1 LCharnock(8) (cl up: effrt 4f out: edgd lft & outpcd fnl 2f) 2½ **4**
*414*9 Golden Torque **(58)***(49) (RBastiman)* 8-9-0 (5) HBastiman(2) (hld up & bhd: nvr nr to chal) hd **5**
*79*5 Dawn Rock **(47)***(29) (RMMcKellar)* 4-8-6 TWilliams(1) (chsd ldrs to st: sn outpcd) 7 **6**
Explore Mondial (IRE) **(50)***(21) (TDyer)* 4-8-6 (3) DarrenMoffatt(3) (lw: bhd fnl 6f) 9 **7**
*370*7 Milngavie (IRE) **(46)***(5) (MJohnston)* 5-8-7 DHolland(5) (prom to st: sn btn) 10 **8**

9/4 Dvorak (IRE), **3/1** El Nido, **4/1** Cutthroat Kid (IRE), **7/1** ZAAHEYAH (USA), **8/1** Milngavie (IRE), **10/1** Golden Torque, **20/1** Explore Mondial (IRE), **50/1** Dawn Rock, CSF £32.62 CT £74.86 TOTE £9.10: £1.60 £2.20 £1.30 (£7.80) OWNER The Zed Team (MIDDLEHAM) BRED Gainsborough Farm Inc 8 Rn 3m 8.0 (22.30) SF: 6/28/17/5/9/-/-/-

WEIGHT FOR AGE 4yo-2lb

T/Plpt: £1,022.90 (12.95 Tckts). T/Qdpt: £48.80 (2 Tckts) AA

0468-LINGFIELD (L-H)
Friday March 31st (Standard)

496

COLD AS CHARITY CLAIMING STKS (4-Y.O+) (Class F) £2,745.80 (£758.80: £361.40)
1m 4f (Equitrack) Stalls: Low GOING minus 0.49 sec per fur (FST) 2-10 (2-10)

*403*3 **One Off the Rail (USA) (78)***(72) (AMoore)* 5-9-3 (7) LSuthern(5) (b.hind: lw: a.p: w ldr over 5f out: hrd rdn over 2f out: led ins fnl f: r.o wl) — **1**
*143*4 Elementary **(73)***(63)*(Fav)*(NJHWalker)* 12-9-2 RCochrane(2) (lw: a.p: led over 5f out: rdn over 2f out: hdd ins fnl f: unable qckn) ¾ **2**
*471*5 Long Furlong **(48)***(41) (JRBosley)* 7-8-7 (3) SSanders(3) (lw: rdn over 4f out: no hdwy fnl 3f) 12 **3**
*374*12 Bayphia **(35)***(36) (RJO'Sullivan)* 7-8-6 WWoods(4) (rdn over 4f out: no hdwy fnl 3f) 1 **4**
*374*8 Remember This (IRE) **(30)***(48) (CACyzer)* 5-9-6 TIves(1) (led over 6f) 1¼ **5**

10/11 Elementary, **5/4** ONE OFF THE RAIL (USA), **9/1** Long Furlong, **25/1** Bayphia, **33/1** Remember This (IRE), CSF £2.75 TOTE £2.10: £1.10 £1.10 (£1.10) OWNER Mr K. Higson (BRIGHTON) BRED Parrish Hill Farm 5 Rn 2m 33.98 (4.58) SF: 38/29/7/2/14

497

APPLE A DAY (S) STKS (4-Y.O+) (Class G) £2,467.00 (£682.00: £325.00)
1m 2f (Equitrack) Stalls: Low GOING minus 0.49 sec per fur (FST) 2-40 (2-42)

*235*4 **Barahin (IRE) (44)***(60) (JJBridger)* 6-8-12 AClark(5) (hld up: led wl over 1f out: rdn out) — **1**
*127*7 Tropical Jungle (USA) **(55)***(56) (PJMakin)* 5-8-12b LDettori(7) (b: a.p: led over 3f out tl wl over 1f out: unable qckn) 2½ **2**
*218*4 Thames Side **(48)***(45) (MMadgwick)* 4-8-11 TQuinn(2) (a.p: rdn over 3f out: one pce) 7 **3**
*415*3 Pop to Stans **(51)***(37)*(Fav)*(JPearce)* 6-8-5b(7) ElizabethTurner(6) (hdwy over 4f out: wknd over 2f out) 5 **4**
*214*4 Days of Thunder **(41)***(36) (JWhite)* 7-8-7 (5) SDrowne(3) (lw: nvr nr to chal) nk **5**
*331*7 Secret Assignment (USA) **(40)***(14) (CACyzer)* 5-8-12 GDuffield(8) (hld up: rdn over 4f out: wknd over 3f out) 14 **6**

19[4] Taahhub (IRE) **(51)***(13) (RJO'Sullivan)* 5-8-12 JWeaver(4) (lw: led over 2f: led 5f out tl over 3f out: sn wknd) .....½ 7
404[8] Father Tim (IRE) *(JMBradley)* 5-8-9 (3) DWright(1) (lw: s.i.s: hdwy to ld over 7f out: hdd 5f out: sn wknd) 25 8

100/30 Pop to Stans, **7/2** Tropical Jungle (USA), **4/1** Taahhub (IRE), **9/2** BARAHIN (IRE) (4/1-6/1), **15/2** Thames Side (8/1-5/1), **14/1** Days of Thunder (op 6/1), Father Tim (IRE), **20/1** Secret Assignment (USA), CSF £19.07 TOTE £7.30: £1.80 £1.30 £1.60 (£13.60) OWNER Mr J. J. Bridger (LIPHOOK) BRED Stowell Hill Ltd and A. J. Tree 8 Rn 2m 6.35 (3.35) SF: 30/26/14/7/6/-/-/-
WEIGHT FOR AGE 4yo-1lb
No bid

OFFICIAL EXPLANATION Taahhub (IRE): the jockey reported his instructions were to ride the race as he found it. His mount had changed his legs several times when in front and he had felt it might have sustained an injury. The Vet added that the horse had a swelling under the saddle which might have caused discomfort.

498

ALL'S FAIR H'CAP (0-90) (3-Y.O+) (Class C) £5,588.00 (£1,664.00: £792.00: £356.00)
5f (Equitrack) Stalls: High GOING minus 0.49 sec per fur (FST) 3-10 (3-16)

446[6] **Spender (76)***(82) (PWHarris)* 6-10-0 RCochrane(8) (hld up: rdn over 2f out: led nr fin) .....— 1
216[4] Little Saboteur **(69)***(74) (PJMakin)* 6-9-7b LDettori(1) (b.nr hind: lw: a.p: led over 1f out: hrd rdn fnl f: hdd nr fin) .....nk 2
328* Tenor **(63)***(68)*(Fav)*(DNicholls)* 4-9-1 AlexGreaves(4) (lw: hld up: hrd rdn over 1f out: r.o) .....hd 3
328[5] Random **(60)***(54) (CJames)* 4-8-12 JWeaver(5) (nvr nr to chal) 3½ 4
Sally Slade **(76)***(69) (CACyzer)* 3-9-1 JReid(6) (nvr nrr) .....s.h 5
426[5] That Man Again **(84)***(73) (GLewis)* 3-9-9b SWhitworth(3) (lw: a.p: rdn over 2f out: wknd over 1f out) 1¼ 6
369[7] Daaniera (IRE) **(56)***(41) (PHowling)* 5-8-5b(3) DWright(7) (b.hind: lw: led over 3f) 1¼ 7
345* Stoppes Brow **(88)** *(GLMoore)* 3-9-13v BRouse(2) (Withdrawn not under Starter's orders: veterinary advice) ..... W

2/1 Tenor, **9/4** That Man Again, **4/1** Stoppes Brow, **9/2** Little Saboteur, **11/2** SPENDER, **8/1** Sally Slade, **10/1** Random, **25/1** Daaniera (IRE), CSF £29.60 CT £61.06 TOTE £6.70: £3.30 £2.20 (£12.40) OWNER The Entrepreneurs (BERKHAMSTED) BRED The Mount Coote Partnership 7 Rn
58.77 secs (0.57) SF: 60/52/46/32/34/38/19/-
WEIGHT FOR AGE 3yo-13lb

499

BALD COOT H'CAP (0-80) (3-Y.O+) (Class D) £3,867.50 (£1,154.00: £551.00: £249.50)
6f (Equitrack) Stalls: Low GOING minus 0.49 sec per fur (FST) 3-40 (3-42)

381[2] **Chewit (73)***(80) (AMoore)* 3-8-11 CandyMorris(2) (b.hind: hld up: led over 1f out: rdn out) ...— 1
405[4] Crystal Heights (FR) **(63)***(62) (RJO'Sullivan)* 7-9-1 LDettori(7) (b: nt clr run over 2f out: hdwy over 1f out: unable qckn ins fnl f) 3 2
405[3] Sweet Supposin (IRE) **(75)***(74) (KMcAuliffe)* 4-9-13b RCochrane(1) (b.nr hind: lw: lost pl 5f out: rallied over 1f out: str run fnl f: fin wl) .....hd 3
Maiandros (GR) **(80)***(72) (RCharlton)* 3-9-4 JWeaver(4) (stdd s: rdn & hdwy over 1f out: r.o) 2½ 4
404[2] Rocky Waters (USA) **(76)***(65) (GLMoore)* 6-10-0 BRouse(10) (rdn over 3f out: nvr nr to chal) 1¼ 5
359[4] Splash of Salt (IRE) **(41)***(30) (TJNaughton)* 5-7-7b GBardwell(5) (prom over 4f) .....hd 6
Dark Eyed Lady (IRE) **(68)***(55) (DWPArbuthnot)* 5-9-6 TQuinn(6) (b: bit bkwd: a.p: led 3f out tl over 1f out: sn wknd) .....¾ 7
446[2] Our Shadee (USA) **(56)***(42)*(Fav)*(KTIvory)* 5-8-1v(7) CScally(8) (lw: hld up: rdn wl over 1f out: sn wknd) .....nk 8
Pab's Choice **(62)***(37) (MMcCormack)* 4-9-0 JReid(9) (prom over 3f) 4 9
Cork Street Girl (IRE) **(65)***(39) (BJMeehan)* 3-8-3 BDoyle(3) (bit bkwd: led 3f) .....nk 10
LONG HANDICAP Splash of Salt (IRE) 7-6

3/1 Our Shadee (USA), **7/2** Pab's Choice, **11/2** Maiandros (GR) (op 7/2), **6/1** Crystal Heights (FR), **7/1** Sweet Supposin (IRE) (op 9/2), **8/1** Dark Eyed Lady (IRE) (op 5/1), Rocky Waters (USA), **12/1** CHEWIT, Splash of Salt (IRE), **33/1** Cork Street Girl (IRE), CSF £82.60 CT £510.77 TOTE £16.60: £3.60 £2.70 £4.10 (£79.60) Trio £42.20 OWNER Ballard (1834) Ltd (BRIGHTON) BRED B. Minty 10 Rn
1m 11.97 (1.37) SF: 35/31/43/27/34/-/24/11/6/-
WEIGHT FOR AGE 3yo-14lb

500 ANY PORT MAIDEN STKS (3-Y.O+) (Class D) £3,867.50 (£1,154.00: £551.00: £249.50) **1m 2f (Equitrack)** Stalls: Low GOING minus 0.49 sec (FST) 4-10 (4-11)

Proposing (IRE) *(80+)*(Fav)*(JHMGosden)* 3-8-4 LDettori(1) (w'like: lw: hld up: chsd ldr over 3f out: led over 1f out: comf) ....— **1**
Worldnews Extra (USA) *(77) (PFICole)* 3-8-4 TQuinn(2) (b.hind: leggy: lw: led: rdn over 2f out: hdd over 1f out: unable qckn) 2 **2**
427³ Danegold (IRE) **(58)***(67) (MRChannon)* 3-8-4 CRutter(5) (hld up: rdn over 2f out: sn wknd) 6 **3**
Marchant Ming (IRE) *(56) (MAJarvis)* 3-8-4 WWoods(7) (a bhd) 7 **4**
Bambara *(51) (CEBrittain)* 3-7-13 JQuinn(4) (chsd ldr over 6f) ....nk **5**
*357*⁸ Tarjumaan (USA) *(55) (RJO'Sullivan)* 4-9-9 AClark(6) (swtg: bhd fnl 4f) ....s.h **6**

Evens PROPOSING (IRE), **2/1** Danegold (IRE), **6/1** Bambara, **8/1** Worldnews Extra (USA) (op 3/1), **16/1** Marchant Ming (IRE), **50/1** Tarjumaan (USA), CSF £9.16 TOTE £1.90: £1.10: £2.30 (£4.40) OWNER Sheikh Mohammed (NEWMARKET) BRED Sheikh Mohammed bin Rashid al Maktoum 6 Rn 2m 7.36 (4.36) SF: 15/12/2/-/-/9
WEIGHT FOR AGE 3yo-20lb, 4yo-1lb

501 GIFT HORSE H'CAP (0-65) (3-Y.O+) (Class F) £3,023.00 (£838.00: £401.00) **1m (Equitrack)** Stalls: High GOING minus 0.49 sec per fur (FST) 4-40 (4-40)

*402*⁴ **Zahran (IRE) (53)***(61) (JMBradley)* 4-9-0 (5) SDrowne(2) (b: lw: a.p: rdn over 3f out: led ins fnl f: r.o wl) ....— **1**
*341*¹¹ La Residence **(47)***(52) (MrsNMacauley)* 4-8-10 (3) SSanders(10) (led over 6f out tl over 4f out: ev ch over 1f out: unable qckn) 1¾ **2**
*472*⁴ Pair of Jacks (IRE) **(33)***(37) (DAWilson)* 5-7-13 JQuinn(3) (lw: led over 1f: led over 4f out tl ins fnl f: one pce) ....s.h **3**
*417*⁵ Pretonic **(44)***(38) (BPalling)* 7-8-10 TSprake(7) (rdn over 4f out: hdwy wl over 1f out: r.o one pce) 5 **4**
*373*⁷ Zinbaq **(33)***(24) (CJBenstead)* 9-7-13 CRutter(6) (nvr nr to chal) 1¾ **5**
*344*⁵ Words of Wisdom (IRE) **(61)***(45) (CACyzer)* 5-9-10 (3) DRMcCabe(9) (prom over 2f) 3½ **6**
*341** Broughtons Turmoil **(58)***(40) (WJMusson)* 6-9-5 (5) PMcCabe(11) (dwlt: hld up: rdn over 2f out: sn wknd) 1 **7**
*404*⁶ Waverley Star **(40)***(17) (KOCunningham-Brown)* 10-8-6 BDoyle(5) (bhd fnl 5f) 2½ **8**
*445*¹⁰ Shansi (IRE) **(45)***(19) (MDIUsher)* 4-8-11v RStreet(1) (b: b.hind: bhd fnl 6f) 1½ **9**
*341*² Swallow Ridge (IRE) **(32)***(4)*(Fav)*(RJO'Sullivan)* 6-7-12bow1 StephenDavies(12) (prom over 5f) ....nk **10**
*331*³ Anotherone to Note **(52)***(25) (MJHeaton-Ellis)* 4-9-4 JWeaver(4) (a bhd) ....hd **11**

5/2 Swallow Ridge (IRE), **3/1** Broughtons Turmoil (2/1-100/30), **7/1** Words of Wisdom (IRE), Pair of Jacks (IRE), **8/1** Anotherone to Note, **10/1** Zinbaq, **12/1** Shansi (IRE), ZAHRAN (IRE), **14/1** Pretonic, **25/1** La Residence, Waverley Star, CSF £234.10 CT £2,048.38 TOTE £15.30: £2.00 £13.10 £2.00 (£311.10) Trio £265.60 OWNER Mr D. Smith(Saul) (CHEPSTOW) BRED S. Niarchos 11 Rn 1m 38.25 (1.85) SF: 43/34/19/20/6/27/22/-/1/-/7

T/Plpt: £184.80 (62.5 Tckts). T/Qdpt: £45.50 (1 Tckt) AK

WARWICK (L-H)
Saturday April 1st (Good to soft)

502 CHILDISH PRANK MAIDEN STKS (3-Y.O+) (Class D) £2,775.95 (£2,775.95: £613.40: £280.70) **5f** Stalls: Low GOING: 0.04 sec per fur (G) 1-50 (1-56)

General Sir Peter (IRE) *(70) (PFICole)* 3-8-9 TQuinn(10) (leggy: scope: a.p: led over 1f out: r.o wl) ....— **1**
Port Augusta (IRE) *(70) (BWHills)* 3-8-4 (5) JDSmith(4) (lw: dwlt: rdn & gd hdwy 2f out: str run fnl f: fin wl) ....— **1**
Honey Trader **(58)***(68) (JBerry)* 3-8-9 JCarroll(6) (lw: led over 3f: r.o wl) ....½ **3**
*419*¹⁴ Polli Pui **(57)***(62) (PDEvans)* 3-8-4 DHolland(3) (a.p: r.o fnl f) ....½ **4**
Lorelei Lee (IRE) *(57) (JohnBerry)* 3-7-13 (7)ow2 GFaulkner(2) (a chsng ldrs: one pce fnl 2f) .1½ **5**
*337*⁴ South Forest (IRE) **(68)***(56) (SRBowring)* 4-9-0 (7) CTeague(7) (b: hdwy over 1f out: r.o ins fnl f) 2 **6**
*305*¹⁰ Superbit **(50)***(48) (BAMcMahon)* 3-8-6 (3) SSanders(12) (prom 3f) 2½ **7**
434¹⁹ Eagle Day (USA) **(74)***(43)*(Fav)*(DRCElsworth)* 4-9-7v PatEddery(16) (prom over 3f) 1½ **8**
Coastal Bluff *(42) (TDBarron)* 3-8-9 JFortune(5) (plld hrd: prom: wkng whn n.m.r over 1f out) ....nk **9**

Secret Miss (35) (APJarvis) 3-7-11 (7) BHunter(13) (dwlt: a bhd) ½ 10
Scharnhorst **(58)**(36) (SDow) 3-8-2 (7) ADaly(9) (dwlt: a in rr) 1¼ 11
Express Routing (35) (RAkehurst) 3-8-9 AClark(14) (bit bkwd: s.s: a in rr) ½ 12
442[17] Maybank (IRE) (33) (BAMcMahon) 3-8-9 MWigham(17) (s.s: a bhd) ½ 13
247[8] Swift Nick Nevison **(40)**(31) (KTIvory) 4-9-0 (7) CScally(11) (bit bkwd: w ldr tl wknd qckly wl over 1f out) ¾ 14
442[5] Taylord **(72)**(24) (RHannon) 3-8-9 LDettori(1) (chsd ldrs over 2f) 2 15
Name That Tune (17) (CJHill) 3-8-4 JQuinn(8) (cmpt: bkwd: dwlt: a bhd) ¾ 16
Vintage Taittinger (IRE) (22) (MBell) 3-8-2 (7) RMullen(15) (a bhd) s.h 17

5/2 Eagle Day (USA), **3/1** Taylord (op 5/1), **7/1** South Forest (IRE), **9/1** GENERAL SIR PETER (IRE) (4/1-10/1), **12/1** Coastal Bluff, Honey Trader, **16/1** PORT AUGUSTA (IRE), Polli Pui, Scharnhorst, **20/1** Superbit, Vintage Taittinger (IRE), **25/1** Express Routing, **33/1** Lorelei Lee (IRE), Maybank (IRE), Secret Miss, Name That Tune, Swift Nick Nevison, CSF £69.02 GSP & PA, £74.73 PA & GSP TOTE £4.40 GSP £19.90 PA: £2.70 GSP £8.80 PA £3.30 (£102.40) OWNER Mr Yahya Nasib (WHATCOMBE)/Mr R. E. Sangster (LAMBOURN) BRED Hamilton Bloodstock (UK) Ltd 17 Rn 62.3 secs (4.30) SF: 24/24/22/16/11/22/2/9/-/-/-/-/-/-/-/-/-

WEIGHT FOR AGE 3yo-12lb

503

YOU'VE BEEN HAD! CLAIMING STKS (4-Y.O+) (Class F) £3,158.00 (£944.00: £452.00: £206.00) **1m** Stalls: Low GOING: 0.16 sec per fur (G) 2-20 (2-26)

414[8] **Northern Celadon (IRE) (68)**(74) (MJHeaton-Ellis) 4-8-13 StephenDavies(16) (racd wd: mde virtually all: drvn out) — 1
Duello **(56)**(70) (MBlanshard) 4-8-11 WRyan(17) (racd wd: chsd wnr: 2nd st: ev ch 1f out: unable qckn) 1 2
Montone (IRE) **(58)**(52) (KRBurke) 5-8-13 TQuinn(9) (lw: hdwy over 3f out: 5th st: r.o one pce fnl 2f) 10 3
220[8] Finjan **(54)**(43) (AGFoster) 8-8-5 JFortune(6) (chsd ldrs: 6th st: one pce fnl 2f) ½ 4
336[2] Battle Colours (IRE) **(64)**(23) (MrsJRRamsden) 6-8-7 KFallon(8) (chsd ldrs over 4f) 11 5
Lady Lacey **(53)**(17) (GBBalding) 8-8-4 JWilliams(5) (bhd tl sme late hdwy: nrst fin) 1½ 6
235[9] Darakah (17) (CJHill) 8-8-6 JQuinn(4) (s.s: nvr nr ldrs) 1 7
103[8] Nigelschinapalace **(35)**(10) (MissSJWilton) 6-8-5 AMackay(13) (b: n.d) 3 8
Blockade (USA) **(70)**(13)(Fav)(MBell) 6-8-13 MFenton(14) (t: prom tl 7th & wkng st) 2½ 9
Millridge (IRE) **(39)** (RLee) 4-7-12 FNorton(1) (b: chsd ldrs over 4f) 3 10
The Merry Monk (8) (CNAllen) 4-9-3 TIves(7) (a bhd) 1¾ 11
408[9] Chloes Diamond (IRE) **(39)** (APJames) 7-7-7 (7)ow2 MHenry(11) (n.d) hd 12
Not the Nadger **(46)** (PDEvans) 4-8-13 JWeaver(2) (b: b.hind: prom: 4th st: wknd qckly 2f out: t.o) 12 13
404[3] Twice in Bundoran (IRE) **(49)** (PSFelgate) 4-8-1 ow1 RPrice(3) (prom: 3rd st: wknd 2f out: eased whn btn: t.o) 1 14
Kimberley Boy **(65)** (GROldroyd) 5-8-13 DHolland(15) (b: bhd fnl 3f: t.o) 8 15
225[4] Supercool (BAMcMahon) 4-9-0 (3) SSanders(12) (a bhd: t.o) 2 16
Westcoast (MTate) 4-8-13 PatEddery(10) (a bhd: t.o) 6 17

4/1 Blockade (USA), **9/2** Battle Colours (IRE), **7/1** Lady Lacey, **8/1** NORTHERN CELADON (IRE), **10/1** Duello, Finjan, Kimberley Boy, **12/1** Not the Nadger, Montone (IRE), **14/1** Supercool, Twice in Bundoran (IRE), **20/1** Darakah, **25/1** Westcoast, The Merry Monk, **33/1** Chloes Diamond (IRE), Millridge (IRE), Nigelschinapalace, CSF £87.62 TOTE £11.50: £2.30 £9.00 £4.90 (£75.00) Trio £238.80 OWNER The Over The Bridge Partnership (WROUGHTON) BRED A. F. O'Callaghan 17 Rn 1m 43.0 (6.00) SF: 49/45/27/18/-/-/-/-/-/-/-/-/-/-/-/-/-

504

APRIL FOOLS H'CAP (0-95) (3-Y.O) (Class C) £9,285.25 (£2,812.00: £1,373.50: £654.25) **1m** Stalls: Low GOING: 0.16 sec per fur (G) 2-50 (2-54)

El Supremo (USA) (90)(99) (DRLoder) 3-9-2 JWeaver(16) (a.p: led wl over 2f out: wandered over 1f out: drvn out) — 1
437* Mister Fire Eyes (IRE) **(76)**(84)(Fav)(CEBrittain) 3-8-2 BDoyle(19) (lw: a.p: hrd rdn & 4th st: ev ch fnl f: unable qckn) ¾ 2
King Balant (IRE) **(75)**(72) (MRStoute) 3-8-1 ow1 PaulEddery(20) (racd wd: w ldr: 2nd st: one pce fnl 2f) 5 3
427[4] Komreyev Dancer **(69)**(66) (ABailey) 3-7-9 NAdams(18) (hdwy 2f out: r.o ins fnl f) ½ 4
322[2] Dont Forget Curtis (IRE) **(80)**(76) (JRFanshawe) 3-8-6 DHarrison(13) (hdwy 4f out: 5th st: one pce appr fnl f) hd 5
372[2] Komodo (USA) **(70)**(58) (DRCElsworth) 3-7-7 (3) DWright(17) (racd wd: led over 5f: 3rd st: wknd 2f out) 4 6
Beauchamp Jazz **(93)**(80) (JLDunlop) 3-9-5 JReid(7) (hdwy 4f out: 6th st: no imp fnl 2f) ½ 7

Cabcharge Blue **(78)***(49) (TJNaughton)* 3-8-4 StephenDavies(12) (lw: bhd tl sme late hdwy) ..8 **8**
Emirates Express **(79)***(43) (JWHills)* 3-8-5 LDettori(11) (lw: hdwy & 7th st: sn rdn: eased whn btn over 1f out)....3½ **9**
Cyrus the Great (IRE) **(78)***(41) (MBell)* 3-8-4 MFenton(14) (chsd ldrs tl wknd over 2f out).......½ **10**
Out on a Promise (IRE) **(80)***(43) (GWragg)* 3-8-6 MHills(4) (hmpd over 3f out: n.d)................nk **11**
Fantasy Racing (IRE) **(81)***(40) (MRChannon)* 3-8-7 CRutter(6) (hmpd over 3f out: a bhd) 2 **12**
Kemo Sabo **(81)***(37) (MrsJRRamsden)* 3-8-7 KFallon(8) (a bhd)....1½ **13**
Thaljanah (IRE) **(80)***(35) (ACStewart)* 3-8-6 KDarley(10) (chsd ldrs 4f)....½ **14**
Duffertoes **(83)***(36) (MJRyan)* 3-8-9 GCarter(1) (prom: 8th st: wknd 2f out) ....¾ **15**
437[4] Risky Romeo **(73)***(6) (GCBravery)* 3-7-13 FNorton(3) (s.s: a bhd: t.o)....10 **16**
428[5] Daffaq **(76)***(4) (PTWalwyn)* 3-8-2 WCarson(2) (prom 4f: t.o) 2½ **17**
Last Roundup **(95)***(13) (CWThornton)* 3-9-7 DeanMcKeown(9) (lw: prom: wkng whn hmpd & lost pl over 3f out)....5 **18**
488a[12] Mo's Main Man (IRE) **(70)** *(SDow)* 3-7-3 (7)ow3 SLanigan(5) (s.s: hmpd over 3f out: t.o) 13 **19**

LONG HANDICAP Mo's Main Man (IRE) 7-2

5/2 Mister Fire Eyes (IRE), **7/1** Daffaq, **8/1** EL SUPREMO (USA), Risky Romeo, **12/1** Beauchamp Jazz, Duffertoes, Emirates Express, **14/1** King Balant (IRE), Kemo Sabo (op 8/1), Cabcharge Blue, **16/1** Out on a Promise (IRE), Thaljanah (IRE), **20/1** Cyrus the Great (IRE), Dont Forget Curtis (IRE), Komodo (USA), Komreyev Dancer, Fantasy Racing (IRE), **25/1** Last Roundup, Mo's Main Man (IRE), CSF £31.33 CT £285.46 TOTE £11.10 £2.30 £1.10 £3.50 £4.50 (£24.80) Trio £74.80 OWNER Mr Wafic Said (NEWMARKET) BRED Miss K. Rausing 19 Rn
1m 42.9 (5.90) SF: 53/38/26/20/30/12/34/3/-/-/-/-/-/-/-/-/-/-/-

505 JOKE'S ON YOU H'CAP (0-85) (4-Y.O+) (Class D) £4,171.70 (£1,247.60: £597.80: £272.90)
1m 2f 169y Stalls: Low GOING: 0.16 sec per fur (G) 3-20 (3-21)

Gone for a Burton (IRE) (80)*(92) (PJMakin)* 5-10-0 PatEddery(6) (hdwy 5f out: 3rd st: led ins fnl f: drvn out)....— **1**
433[12] Red Valerian **(72)***(82) (KMcAuliffe)* 4-9-5b RCochrane(5) (b.off hind: hdwy 4f out: 6th st: ev ch whn hmpd wl over 1f out: hrd rdn: r.o ins fnl f)....¾ **2**
454[10] Pink Brief (IRE) **(60)***(69) (MJRyan)* 4-8-2 (5) MBaird(4) (hld up & bhd: hdwy over 3f out: 5th st: led 2f out tl ins fnl f: nt qckn)....½ **3**
430[13] Hazard a Guess (IRE) **(68)***(72) (MrsJRRamsden)* 5-9-2 KFallon(13) (s.s: hdwy 4f out: 7th st: hmpd wl over 1f out: hung lft ins fnl f: r.o one pce)....4 **4**
Wentbridge Lad (IRE) **(49)***(41) (BAMcMahon)* 5-7-11b FNorton(10) (hld up: hdwy 4f out: 4th st: hung rt over 2f out: sn wknd)....8 **5**
Un Parfum de Femme (IRE) **(72)***(62) (JPearce)* 4-9-5 JMcLaughlin(14) (chsd ldrs 6f: n.d after) 1 **6**
433[8] Cee-Jay-Ay **(72)***(59) (JBerry)* 8-9-6 JCarroll(12) (s.s: hdwy & 8th st: nt rch ldrs)....2½ **7**
Myfontaine **(53)***(38) (KTIvory)* 8-8-1 GDuffield(2) (hdwy over 3f out: nt trble ldrs) 1¾ **8**
Precious Wonder **(47)***(29) (PButler)* 6-7-9 ow2 JLowe(11) (lw: prom: 2nd st: ev ch whn hmpd 2f out: wknd qckly)....nk **9**
281[11] Folly Finnesse **(73)***(19) (BRMillman)* 4-9-6 JWeaver(15) (plld hrd: led 2f: led over 3f out: hdd & bmpd 2f out: virtually p.u fnl f: t.o) 25 **10**
Fox Sparrow **(73)***(19) (NTinkler)* 5-9-7 KDarley(9) (rdn 4f out: sn bhd: t.o)....¾ **11**
Ketabi (USA) **(70)***(11)*(Fav)*(RAkehurst)* 4-9-3 TQuinn(7) (racd ins: prom 6f: sn wknd: t.o) 2½ **12**
413[8] Northern Chief **(49)** *(RWEmery)* 5-7-11 JQuinn(3) (racd ins: bhd fnl 4f: t.o) 2½ **13**
445[13] Birequest **(65)** *(RBoss)* 4-8-12b LDettori(8) (led over 8f out tl over 3f out: wknd qckly: t.o)....30 **14**
Kardelle **(53)** *(MrsALMKing)* 5-7-10 (5)ow4 AGarth(1) (s.s: t.o fnl 6f)....13 **15**

LONG HANDICAP Precious Wonder 7-4

2/1 Ketabi (USA), **6/1** Hazard a Guess (IRE) (op 4/1), **13/2** Myfontaine, **7/1** GONE FOR A BURTON (IRE) (op 4/1), **9/1** Birequest, **10/1** Un Parfum de Femme (IRE), **12/1** Folly Finnesse (7/1-14/1), Cee-Jay-Ay, **14/1** Fox Sparrow, **20/1** Wentbridge Lad (IRE), Pink Brief (IRE), Red Valerian, **33/1** Precious Wonder, Northern Chief, **66/1** Kardelle, CSF £134.43 CT £2478.93 TOTE £9.20 £2.80 £3.20 £10.10 (£53.10) Trio £361.00 OWNER Mr H. P. Carrington (MARLBOROUGH) 15 Rn
2m 25.8 (12.30) SF: 33/23/10/13/-/3/-/-/-/-/-/-/-/-/-
WEIGHT FOR AGE 4yo-1lb

506 PRIVATE JOKE H'CAP (0-95) (4-Y.O+) (Class C) £6,193.00 (£1,864.00: £902.00: £421.00) **1m 6f 194y** Stalls: Low GOING: 0.16 sec per fur (G) 3-55 (3-55)

Lalindi (IRE) (64)*(83) (DRCElsworth)* 4-8-9 PatEddery(13) (racd wd: a.p: 6th st: rdn to ld 1f out: r.o) ....— **1**

Smuggling **(64)***(83) (RAkehurst)* 4-8-9 TQuinn(6) (a.p: led over 3f out to 1f out: r.o)..............hd **2**
Purple Splash **(80)***(90) (PJMakin)* 5-10-0b MHills(5) (b: bit bkwd: hdwy to ld 6f out: hdd 3f out: outpcd fnl 2f)..............8 **3**
Phil's Time **(72)***(79) (TGMills)* 4-9-3b JReid(9) (lw: hld up: 7th st: hdwy fnl 2f: n.d)..............3 **4**
*108** Secret Serenade **(72)***(75) (CWFairhurst)* 4-9-3 RCochrane(11) (hdwy & 8th st: nvr nr to chal)..............3½ **5**
259[3] Absalom's Pillar **(54)***(55) (JHetherton)* 5-8-2 NKennedy(14) (led after 2f: hdd 6f out: 4th st: wkng whn edgd rt over 1f out)..............2½ **6**
432[11] Brandon Prince (IRE) **(71)***(70) (IABalding)* 7-9-5 LDettori(7) (hld up & bhd: rdn 6f out: hdwy 2f out: eased whn btn ins fnl f)..............1½ **7**
432[2] Noufari (FR) **(74)***(71)*(Fav)*(RHollinshead)* 4-9-5 TIves(15) (hld up & bhd: nvr rchd ldrs)..............1¾ **8**
13[2] Sir Thomas Beecham **(59)***(52) (SDow)* 5-8-0 (7) ADaly(10) (chsd ldrs: 5th st: wknd 2f out).....3½ **9**
Lookingforarainbow (IRE) **(77)***(65) (BobJones)* 7-9-11 MWigham(2) (hld up & bhd: stdy hdwy over 4f out: wknd 3f out)..............5 **10**
Bandar Perak **(63)***(46) (MJHaynes)* 4-8-8 JWeaver(12) (led 2f: wknd 4f out)..............5 **11**
Polo Kit (IRE) **(82)***(57) (JRFanshawe)* 4-9-13 DHarrison(4) (lw: a.p: jnd ldr 4f out: sn hdd: 2nd st: wknd 2f out)..............7 **12**
Chimanimani **(81)***(54) (NTinkler)* 4-9-12 GDuffield(3) (plld hrd: prom 11f)..............2 **13**
193[6] Wannaplantatree **(67)***(25) (GHYardley)* 4-8-12 AClark(8) (a bhd: t.o)..............14 **14**

9/2 Noufari (FR), **11/2** Smuggling (5/2-6/1), **6/1** Brandon Prince (IRE), **13/2** Polo Kit (IRE), **9/1** Chimanimani, LALINDI (IRE), **10/1** Secret Serenade, **14/1** Phil's Time, Lookingforarainbow (IRE), Absalom's Pillar, Sir Thomas Beecham, **16/1** Purple Splash, **25/1** Bandar Perak, **33/1** Wannaplantatree, CSF £57.35 CT £735.06 TOTE £10.40 £2.70 £1.90 £8.20 (£26.90) Trio part won OWNER White Horse Racing Ltd (WHITCOMBE) BRED Hascombe and Valiant Studs 14 Rn
3m 26.9 (17.90) SF: 13/13/23/9/5/-/3/1/-/-/-/-/-/-
WEIGHT FOR AGE 4yo-3lb

507 PERCHCOURT STAINLESS STEEL H'CAP (0-70) (3-Y.O+) (Class E)

£3,786.75 (£1,134.00: £544.50: £249.75)
5f Stalls: Low GOING: 0.04 sec per fur (G) 4-25 (4-29)

Canovas Heart (53)*(60)*(Fav)*(BobJones)* 6-8-11 GDuffield(8) (w ldrs: led over 2f out: all out)..............— **1**
Grey Charmer (IRE) **(50)***(55) (CJames)* 6-8-8 WNewnes(20) (chsd ldrs: effrt over 1f out: ev ch ins fnl f: r.o)..............¾ **2**
407[3] Distant Dynasty **(51)***(43) (BAPearce)* 5-8-9 PatEddery(16) (a.p: ev ch 2f out: one pce)..............4 **3**
420[3] Ivy Lilian (IRE) **(51)***(37) (WMBrisbourne)* 3-7-4 (7)ow4 SLanigan(18) (led over 2f: r.o one pce fnl 2f)..............½ **4**
419[11] Matthew David **(35)***(23) (SRBowring)* 5-7-7b NKennedy(19) (chsd ldrs: rdn over 2f out: styd on fnl f)..............¾ **5**
244[7] Grand Time **(37)***(22) (CJHill)* 6-7-9bow2 JQuinn(4) (hld up in rr: gd hdwy fnl f: nvr plcd to chal)..............nk **6**
Bright Paragon (IRE) **(50)***(34) (HJCollingridge)* 6-8-8 MRimmer(11) (chsd ldrs: no hdwy fnl 2f)..............¾ **7**
The Kings Ransom **(56)***(35) (MrsJRRamsden)* 3-8-2 ow1 DHarrison(14) (s.i.s: sn chsng ldrs: no hdwy fnl 2f)..............1¼ **8**
Abigails Boy (HOL) **(43)***(21) (DrJDScargill)* 6-7-12 (3) DWright(2) (nvr nrr)..............¾ **9**
Domicksky **(70)***(48) (MRChannon)* 7-10-0 RHughes(13) (nvr nr to chal)..............s.h **10**
Most Uppitty **(65)***(38) (JBerry)* 3-8-11 JCarroll(17) (chsd ldrs 3f)..............1½ **11**
Petraco (IRE) **(61)***(29) (NASmith)* 7-8-12 (7) GMitchell(12) (bit bkwd: bhd fnl 2f)..............1½ **12**
Followmegirls **(61)***(27)*(Fav)*(MrsALMKing)* 6-9-5 LDettori(5) (chsd ldrs 3f)..............¾ **13**
268[6] Life's a Breeze **(43)***(9) (PSFelgate)* 6-8-1 AMackay(15) (bhd fnl 2f)..............hd **14**
Patsy Grimes **(69)***(31) (LJHolt)* 5-9-13 JReid(9) (a bhd)..............1¼ **15**
The Fed **(60)***(6) (RMWhitaker)* 5-9-4 ACulhane(1) (hdwy over 2f out: wknd wl over 1f out)......5 **16**
Hong Kong Dollar **(60)***(1) (BJMeehan)* 3-8-6 BDoyle(7) (lw: a bhd)..............1½ **17**
451* Tiheros **(72)** *(RHannon)* 3-9-4 7x TQuinn(6) (bhd fnl 2f)..............6 **18**
407[8] Baton Bleu **(37)** *(PHowling)* 4-7-9 ow2 JLowe(10) (bhd fnl 2f)..............1¼ **19**
LONG HANDICAP Matthew David 7-5 Ivy Lilian (IRE) 7-5 Baton Bleu 7-6

5/1 CANOVAS HEART (4/1-13/2), Followmegirls, **6/1** Distant Dynasty, **13/2** Tiheros, **12/1** Domicksky (op 8/1), **14/1** Most Uppitty, Bright Paragon (IRE), The Fed, Patsy Grimes (10/1-16/1), **16/1** Grey Charmer (IRE), The Kings Ransom, **20/1** Hong Kong Dollar, Matthew David, **25/1** Life's a Breeze, Grand Time, Ivy Lilian (IRE), Petraco (IRE), Abigails Boy (HOL), **33/1** Baton Bleu, CSF £83.13 CT £472.28 TOTE £5.90 £1.50 £4.90 £1.90 £6.50 (£241.30) OWNER Mr Bob Jones (NEWMARKET) BRED M. J. Hall 19 Rn 61.3 secs (3.30) SF: 42/37/25/7/5/4/16/5/3/30/8/11/9/-/13/-/-/-/-
WEIGHT FOR AGE 3yo-12lb

508 LAST LAUGH MAIDEN STKS (2-Y.O F) (Class D) £3,529.30 (£1,053.40: £503.20: £228.10) **5f** Stalls: Low GOING: 0.04 sec per fur (G) 4-55 (4-56)

Miss Bigwig *(63) (JBerry)* 2-8-11 JCarroll(6) (leggy: bit bkwd: sn prom: led wl over 1f out: sn hdd: lft in ld ins fnl f: edgd lft nr fin: r.o) — 1
Kandavu *(58) (MMcCormack)* 2-8-11 AClark(3) (leggy: unf: dwlt: hdwy 2f out: r.o wl ins fnl f: carried lft nr fin) 1½ 2
Solo Symphony (IRE) *(53)*(Fav)*(PWChapple-Hyam)* 2-8-11 JReid(5) (w'like: scope: a.p: led over 1f out tl jinked lft & hit rails ins fnl f: nt rcvr) 1¾ 3
Lussuria (IRE) *(51) (BJMeehan)* 2-8-11 BDoyle(11) (unf: bkwd: hdwy over 2f out: r.o ins fnl f: n.m.r cl home) ½ 4
Miss Waterline *(49) (PDEvans)* 2-8-11 LDettori(1) (w'like: neat: s.s: swtchd outside: gd hdwy over 1f out: r.o) ¾ 5
Just Lady *(48) (WGMTurner)* 2-8-11 GDuffield(10) (lengthy: led over 3f: wknd fnl f) s.h 6
Apartments Abroad *(48) (KMcAuliffe)* 2-8-11 RCochrane(4) (lt-f: unf: dwlt: hdwy fnl f: r.o) s.h 7
429³ Don't Tell Vicki *(40) (JSMoore)* 2-8-11 JWeaver(2) (chsd ldrs over 3f) 2½ 8
Rhumba Dancer *(36) (RHannon)* 2-8-11 PatEddery(8) (unf: s.i.s: swtchd outside: hdwy over 2f out: wknd over 1f out) 1¼ 9
429⁴ Poly Static (IRE) *(17) (MRChannon)* 2-8-11 RHughes(9) (unf: w ldrs over 3f) 6 10
Magic Bird (IRE) *(4) (JLSpearing)* 2-8-11 KDarley(13) (lt-f: unf: prom 3f) 4 11
Alistover *(3) (RDickin)* 2-8-11 TQuinn(12) (unf: scope: bit bkwd: s.i.s: outpcd) nk 12
Zuno Princess (IRE) *(GLewis)* 2-8-11 PaulEddery(7) (unf: bit bkwd: s.s: a in rr: t.o) 14 13

15/8 Solo Symphony (IRE), **4/1** MISS BIGWIG (op 5/2), Miss Waterline, **5/1** Rhumba Dancer, **9/1** Poly Static (IRE), **10/1** Don't Tell Vicki, **16/1** Zuno Princess (IRE), Magic Bird (IRE), **20/1** Kandavu, Just Lady, Alistover, **25/1** Lussuria (IRE), Apartments Abroad, CSF £84.61 TOTE £4.10 £2.10 £4.90 £1.50 (£41.30) Trio £76.10 OWNER Bigwigs Entertainments (COCKERHAM) BRED Ravenstonedale Fold and Bloodstock 13 Rn 63.6 secs (5.60) SF: 5/-/-/-/-/-/-/-/-/-/-/-/-

T/Plpt: £7,242.30 (4.04 Tckts). T/Qdpt: £60.30 (3 Tckts). T/Jkpt: Not won; £20,813.84 to 3/4/95 KH

0409-WOLVERHAMPTON (L-H)
Saturday April 1st (Standard)

509 TRESCOTT MEDIAN AUCTION MAIDEN STKS (3-Y.O) (Class E) £2,795.20 (£772.20: £367.60) **1m 4f (Fibresand)** Stalls: High GOING minus 0.02 sec per fur (STD) 7-00 (7-02)

Last Corner (58)*(67) (RHollinshead)* 3-9-0 KDarley(5) (hld up: hdwy 5f out: sn rdn: 2nd st: styd on to ld ins fnl f) — 1
376⁴ Darling Clover *(61) (DMorley)* 3-8-9 MFenton(6) (a.p: led over 5f out: hrd rdn & hdd ins fnl f) ½ 2
Peter Monamy *(40)*(Fav)*(PFICole)* 3-9-0 TQuinn(2) (bit bkwd: unruly s: bhd: hdwy & 3rd st: nvr nr to chal) 20 3
372¹⁰ Roadsweeper (FR) *(36) (KOCunningham-Brown)* 3-9-0 TIves(4) (dwlt: bhd tl hdwy 4f out: 6th st: nvr nrr) 2½ 4
Emnala (IRE) **(58)***(27) (MRChannon)* 3-8-9 RHughes(8) (lw: chsd ldrs: led over 6f out tl over 5f out: 4th & btn st) 3 5
Rainy Day Woman *(13) (DrJDScargill)* 3-8-9 DHarrison(1) (bkwd: led 2f: wknd over 4f out: t.o) 11 6
418⁷ Simposa (IRE) *(15) (JEBanks)* 3-9-0 JQuinn(3) (chsd ldrs: reminders 5f out: sn wknd: 5th st: t.o) 2 7
Lady Kuynder *(DrJDScargill)* 3-8-9 DHolland(7) (lengthy: bkwd: s.s: led after 2f: sn drvn clr: hdd over 6f out: wknd qckly: t.o) dist 8

11/4 Peter Monamy, **4/1** Emnala (IRE), **11/2** Simposa (IRE), **6/1** Darling Clover, **7/1** LAST CORNER, **8/1** Lady Kuynder (op 5/1), **20/1** Rainy Day Woman, **33/1** Roadsweeper (FR), CSF £41.03 TOTE £10.00 £2.30 £1.90 £2.00 (£7.50) OWNER Mr P. D. Savill (UPPER LONGDON) BRED Aston Park Stud 8 Rn 2m 43.0 (12.00) SF: 19/13/-/-/-/-/-/-
STEWARDS' ENQUIRY Holland suspended 10-13/4/95 & 15-17/4/95 (failure to acquaint himself with course).

510 PERTON CLAIMING STKS (3-Y.O+) (Class F) £2,243.00 (£618.00: £293.00) **5f (Fibresand)** Stalls: Low GOING minus 0.02 sec per fur (STD) 7-30 (7-32)

398³ **Primula Bairn (58)***(63)*(Fav)*(MrsJRRamsden)* 5-8-11v KFallon(3) (lw: hld up: hdwy & rdn 2f out: r.o strly to ld wl ins fnl f) — 1

475[4] Sigama (USA) **(62)***(62) (DNicholls)* 9-9-0 AlexGreaves(4) (lw: chsd ldr: led over 2f out tl wl ins fnl f)......1¼ 2
446[11] Tyrian Purple (IRE) **(67)***(60) (TJNaughton)* 7-9-2b DHarrison(2) (b: led over 2f: hrd rdn ent fnl f: kpt on nr fin)......1¼ 3
She's a Madam *(36) (LRLloyd-James)* 4-8-11 NKennedy(5) (bit bkwd: outpcd: a bhd & rdn: no imp)......6 4
391[2] Very Dicey **(70)** (Fav)*(JBerry)* 7-8-9 (7) PRoberts(1) (chsd ldrs tl broke down & p.u 2f out: dead)...... P

7/4 PRIMULA BAIRN, Very Dicey, **4/1** Tyrian Purple (IRE) (op 5/2), **9/2** Sigama (USA), **33/1** She's a Madam, CSF £9.26 TOTE £2.60: £1.20 £2.00 (£5.80) OWNER Mr M. A. Bagnall (THIRSK) BRED Kavli Ltd 5 Rn
63.3 secs (5.30) SF: 5/4/2/-/-
Primula Bairn clmd Mrs C Wadsworth £5,000.

511

PORTOBELLO H'CAP (0-70) (3-Y.O+) (Class E) £2,768.00 (£824.00: £392.00: £176.00) **6f (Fibresand)** Stalls: Low GOING minus 0.02 sec (STD) 8-00 (8-00)

Another Jade (57)*(65) (APJarvis)* 5-10-0 KDarley(2) (bit bkwd: s.i.s: drvn to ld after 2f: drew clr ins fnl f)......— 1
400[3] Heathyards Lady (USA) **(48)***(49)*(Fav)*(RHollinshead)* 4-9-5 TIves(6) (lw: hdwy ½-wy: rdn to chal 1f out: hung lft: one pce)......2½ 2
419[3] At the Savoy (IRE) **(51)***(46) (TDBarron)* 4-9-1 (7) KimberleyHart(3) (a.p: rdn wl over 1f out: r.o one pce)......2½ 3
419[4] Christian Flight (IRE) **(42)***(32) (SGollings)* 6-8-13 DHarrison(5) (b.hind: lw: hld up: hdwy 3f out: rdn wl over 1f out: nvr able to chal)......1¾ 4
Brookhead Lady **(57)***(43) (PDEvans)* 4-10-0 DHolland(7) (b: b.hind: bit bkwd: led 2f: wknd 2f out: eased fnl f)......1½ 5
404[11] Bold Cyrano (IRE) **(40)***(22) (BPalling)* 4-8-11 GDuffield(1) (lw: outpcd & bhd)......1½ 6
400[5] Jon's Choice **(56)***(31) (BPreece)* 7-9-13 TWall(4) (prom: shkn up ½-wy: wknd over 2f out)......2½ 7

2/1 Heathyards Lady (USA) (op 3/1), **7/2** ANOTHER JADE, **4/1** Jon's Choice, **5/1** At the Savoy (IRE), **6/1** Christian Flight (IRE), **12/1** Brookhead Lady, **16/1** Bold Cyrano (IRE), CSF £11.13 TOTE £4.50: £2.30 £1.80 (£5.00) OWNER Mrs Ann Jarvis (ASTON UPTHORPE) BRED J. R. C. and Mrs Wren 7 Rn
1m 15.7 (4.50) SF: 47/31/28/14/25/4/13

512

BILSTON H'CAP (0-70) (3-Y.O+) (Class E) £3,348.00 (£999.00: £477.00: £216.00) **1m 100y (Fibresand)** Stalls: High GOING minus 0.02 sec per fur (STD) 8-30 (8-31)

100[5] **Eqtesaad (USA) (66)***(80) (SCWilliams)* 4-9-12 KDarley(5) (a.p: led 3f out: clr fnl f: unchal)......— 1
*378** A Million Watts **(68)***(73)*(Fav)*(LadyHerries)* 4-10-0 TIves(3) (chsd ldrs: outpcd over 3f out: 4th st: r.o wl fnl f)......5 2
399[6] Backstabber **(35)***(39) (MissSJWilton)* 5-7-9 JQuinn(8) (led over 5f: 2nd & rdn st: wknd fnl f)......s.h 3
414[6] Super Heights **(45)***(45) (DLWilliams)* 7-8-0b(5)ow1 DGriffiths(7) (lw: bhd: hdwy ½-wy: 3rd & rdn st: sn btn)......2 4
*307** Tilly Owl **(47)***(43) (JAHarris)* 4-8-7 JO'Reilly(1) (b.hind: outpcd: a bhd: 5th st)......2½ 5
Portland Way **(54)***(24) (APJarvis)* 3-7-5 (7)ow5 BHunter(4) (chsd ldr to ½-wy: 6th & wkng st: t.o)......11 6
130[5] Gallop to Glory **(33)** *(ALForbes)* 5-7-7be NAdams(6) (b.hind: bit bkwd: dwlt: a bhd & outpcd: t.o)......30 7
354[11] Quinzii Martin **(58)** *(DHaydnJones)* 7-9-4 TWilliams(2) (stumbled & uns rdr sn after s)...... U
LONG HANDICAP Portland Way 6-12 Gallop to Glory 7-5

2/1 A Million Watts, **9/4** EQTESAAD (USA), **3/1** Tilly Owl, **7/1** Quinzii Martin, **10/1** Super Heights, **16/1** Gallop to Glory, **25/1** Portland Way, Backstabber, CSF £7.61 CT £79.42 TOTE £3.20: £1.40 £1.50 £2.50 (£4.20) OWNER Mr J. W. Lovitt (NEWMARKET) BRED Shadwell Estate Co Ltd & Shadwell Farm Inc in USA 8 Rn
1m 50.8 (6.80) SF: 43/36/2/8/6/-/-/-
WEIGHT FOR AGE 3yo-16lb

513

SEISDON (S) STKS (3-Y.O+) (Class G) £2,243.00 (£618.00: £293.00) **1m 1f 79y (Fibresand)** Stalls: High GOING minus 0.02 sec per fur (STD) 9-00 (9-05)

382[3] **Chastleton (41)***(57) (MRChannon)* 3-8-6 CandyMorris(4) (lw: chsd ldrs: outpcd over 4f out: rdn & 5th st: qcknd to ld wl over 1f out: sn clr)......— 1
418[12] Hunza Story **(38)***(49) (NPLittmoden)* 3-8-6 DHolland(7) (chsd ldrs: 4th st: kpt on fnl f: no ch w wnr)......5 2

*448*2 Keys Seminar **(45)***(53) (NACallaghan)* 3-8-11b StephenDavies(2) (b.hind: chsd ldrs: rdn & 2nd st: outpcd appr fnl f) ....nk 3
*447*8 Slytly Beveled **(59)***(57) (NPLittmoden)* 3-8-11b(5) TGMcLaughlin(5) (lw: led tl hdd wl over 1f out: sn rdn & wknd) ....¾ 4
*376*5 Fools of Pride (IRE) **(44)***(36) (RHollinshead)* 3-8-6 KDarley(6) (prom: rdn & 3rd st: wknd over 1f out) 6 5
Norman Prince (IRE) **(56)** *(MrsNMacauley)* 3-8-11 MFenton(1) (lw: a bhd & outpcd: 7th st: t.o) 25 6
431 10 Shared (IRE) (Fav)*(WJHaggas)* 3-8-11b MTebbutt(3) (b.nr hind: lw: bhd: rdn along ½-wy: 6th st: t.o) ....nk 7

5/2 Shared (IRE), **11/4** Keys Seminar, **9/2** Slytly Beveled, Norman Prince (IRE), **7/1** CHASTLETON, **8/1** Fools of Pride (IRE), **40/1** Hunza Story, CSF £135.73 TOTE £5.50: £2.70 £8.20 (£135.30) OWNER Mr M.Channon (UPPER LAMBOURN) BRED M.P.Allen 7 Rn 2m 8.1 (12.10) SF: -/-/-/-/-/-/-
No bid

514 BUSHBURY H'CAP (0-65) (4-Y.O+) (Class F) £2,243.00 (£618.00: £293.00)
2m 46y (Fibresand) Stalls: High GOING minus 0.02 sec per fur (STD) 9-30 (9-31)

*279*3 **Child Star (FR) (38)***(50) (DMarks)* 6-7-12e(5) MBaird(11) (hdwy ½-wy: rdn to ld appr fnl f: hld on: all out) ....— 1
*370*2 Red Whirlwind **(55)***(67) (RJO'Sullivan)* 5-9-6 WWoods(1) (chsd ldrs: hdwy to ld 5f out: sn clr: hdd ent fnl f: rallied gamely cl home) ....hd 2
*346*5 Nothing Doing (IRE) **(36)***(42) (WJMusson)* 6-8-1 JQuinn(10) (dwlt: hdwy after 7f: 3rd st: one pce fnl 2f) 6 3
*396*7 Awestruck **(49)***(49) (BPreece)* 5-9-0 GDuffield(13) (hld up & bhd: hdwy over 3f out: 6th st: styd on fnl f) 6 4
*375*2 Royal Citizen (IRE) **(63)***(62) (JFBottomley)* 6-10-0 TIves(3) (hld up: hdwy 6f out: 4th & rdn st: sn btn) 1½ 5
*295*5 Who's the Best (IRE) **(37)***(34)*(Fav)*(APJarvis)* 5-7-9 (7) BHunter(7) (sn chsng ldrs: wnt 2nd 5f out: lost pl & 5th st: sn btn) 1¼ 6
432 7 How's it Goin (IRE) **(60)***(55) (WRMuir)* 4-9-7 DHarrison(12) (a in rr) 2 7
*153*4 Sassiver (USA) **(48)***(19) (PAKelleway)* 5-8-6 (7) AdelleGibbons(9) (lw: in tch on ins: wknd over 4f out: t.o) 25 8
*412*12 Swordking (IRE) **(52)***(21) (JLHarris)* 6-9-3 PaulEddery(2) (chsd ldrs: drvn along ½-wy: wknd over 4f out: t.o) 1¾ 9
Dugort Strand (IRE) **(52)***(20) (JLHarris)* 4-8-10 (3) SSanders(4) (bit bkwd: prom tl wknd 7f out: t.o) 1¼ 10
Rasayel (USA) **(52)***(19) (PDEvans)* 5-9-3 DHolland(8) (bit bkwd: led over 11f: sn rdn & wknd: t.o) 1 11
*375*4 Bud's Bet (IRE) **(42)***(7) (WWHaigh)* 7-8-7 DaleGibson(5) (bit bkwd: mid div tl wknd 2f out: t.o) 1½ 12

3/1 Who's the Best (IRE), **9/2** Royal Citizen (IRE), **5/1** CHILD STAR (FR), **7/1** Red Whirlwind, **8/1** Swordking (IRE), **9/1** Awestruck, How's it Goin (IRE), Nothing Doing (IRE), **11/1** Bud's Bet (IRE) (8/1-12/1), **20/1** Sassiver (USA), Dugort Strand (IRE), **25/1** Rasayel (USA), CSF £41.99 CT £296.54 TOTE £8.40: £2.90 £2.80 £2.50 (£19.90) Trio £173.40 OWNER Mr P. J. Pearson (UPPER LAMBOURN) BRED Darley Stud Management 12 Rn 3m 40.2 SF: 23/40/15/22/35/7/24/-/-/-/-/-
WEIGHT FOR AGE 4yo-4lb

T/Plpt: £258.30 (48.71 Tckts). T/Qdpt: £63.60 (3.3 Tckts). IM

0415-SOUTHWELL (L-H)
Monday April 3rd (Standard)
WIND: fresh half bhd

515 KING ARTHUR MEDIAN AUCTION MAIDEN STKS (3-Y.O) (Class F) £2,519.00 (£694.00: £329.00)
7f (Fibresand) Stalls: Low GOING: 0.05 sec per fur (STD) 2-20 (2-22)

Cloette *(73)*(Fav)*(WAO'Gorman)* 3-8-6 (3) EmmaO'Gorman(5) (trckd ldrs: led over 4f out to 2f out: r.o to ld ins fnl f: jst hld on) ....— 1
Bellesonnette (IRE) **(62)***(73) (DHaydnJones)* 3-8-9 AMackay(8) (sn drvn along: sn chsd ldrs: led 2f out: hrd rdn: jst failed) ....s.h 2
*350*3 Lucky Peg **(48)***(39) (FJO'Mahony)* 3-8-9 JQuinn(7) (outpcd & drvn along ½-wy: kpt on fnl 2f) 15 3
482 14 Bretton Princess **(42)***(39) (RHollinshead)* 3-8-9 WRyan(4) (in tch: drvn along ½-wy: no imp) ....s.h 4

443[4] Himalayan Blue **(63)***(39) (MRChannon)* 3-9-0 RHughes(1) (led tl over 4f out: hrd rdn & outpcd fnl 2f)....2 5
428[10] Trauma (IRE) *(32) (WJarvis)* 3-8-9 LDettori(6) (trckd ldrs: effrt over 2f out: sn rdn: grad wknd)¾ 6
Nyali Beach (IRE) *(16) (BJMeehan)* 3-8-9 BDoyle(9) (outpcd & drvn along ½-wy: n.d)....7 7
443[8] Norfolk Glory *(20) (DJGMurraySmith)* 3-9-0b JWeaver(2) (s.s: hld up: effrt wy: sn hrd rdn & no response)....¾ 8
394[7] Asking *(16) (JABennett)* 3-9-0 DHolland(3) (bit bkwd: chsd ldrs tl lost pl ½-wy)....1½ 9
All Honour *(DWChapman)* 3-9-0 DeanMcKeown(10) (leggy: scope: s.i.s: racd wd & a bhd: t.o)....dist 10

5/2 CLOETTE, **9/2** Trauma (IRE), **5/1** Himalayan Blue (op 3/1), **11/2** Bellesonnette (IRE), **7/1** Norfolk Glory, **9/1** Nyali Beach (IRE), **16/1** Lucky Peg, **20/1** Bretton Princess, **25/1** All Honour, **50/1** Asking, CSF £15.83 TOTE £3.90: £1.90 £3.10 £1.10 (£9.70) Trio £40.60 OWNER Mr S. Fustok (NEWMARKET) BRED Deerfield Farm 10 Rn 1m 32.2 (5.40) SF: 36/36/2/2/2/-/-/-/-/-

516 HOLY GRAIL (S) APPRENTICE STKS (4-Y.O+) (Class G) £2,243.00 (£618.00: £293.00) **1m 4f (Fibresand)** Stalls: High GOING: 0.05 sec (STD) 2-50 (2-50)

378[10] **Sea Spouse (45)***(67) (MBlanshard)* 4-8-5 (6) SMcCarthy(1) (trckd ldr: led over 4f out: styd on wl u.p to ld ins fnl f)....— 1
396[2] Mad Militant (IRE) **(75)***(71)*(Fav)*(RHollinshead)* 6-8-13 (6) AEddery(3) (lw: hld up: stdy hdwy & prom ½-wy: slt ld over 1f out: hdd & no ex ins fnl f)....1¼ 2
375[7] Eulogy (FR) *(59) (KRBurke)* 8-8-13 SLanigan(5) (led tl over 4f out: sn hrd rdn: kpt on one pce fnl 2f)....5 3
351[5] Red Indian **(55)***(59) (WWHaigh)* 9-9-5 MartinDwyer(4) (chsd ldrs: pushed along 5f out: wknd over 1f out)....4 4
234[4] Desert President **(34)***(35) (RPCHoad)* 4-8-11 GMitchell(6) (sn pushed along: bhd fnl 8f)....14 5
375[6] Criminal Record (USA) **(45)***(25) (WClay)* 5-8-10b(3) PFessey(2) (sn bhd & pushed along: lost tch 8f out)....7 6

8/15 Mad Militant (IRE), **7/2** Red Indian, **10/1** Eulogy (FR), **14/1** Desert President, **16/1** Criminal Record (USA), **33/1** SEA SPOUSE, CSF £50.57 TOTE £64.20: £15.60 £1.10 (£39.40) OWNER Seven Seas Racing (UPPER LAMBOURN) BRED Cheveley Park Stud Ltd 6 Rn
2m 45.8 (11.60) SF: 25/31/19/19/-/-
WEIGHT FOR AGE 4yo-2lb
Bt in 4,800gns. Mad Militant (IRE) clmd K Nicholls £6,000.

OFFICIAL EXPLANATION **Sea Spouse: the trainer's representative reported that the gelding had blown up on his last run and needed further. Today's trip, and the drop to a seller had been beneficial and a routine test was ordered.**

517 PERCEVAL H'CAP (0-70) (3-Y.O+) (Class E) £3,102.00 (£924.00: £440.00: £198.00) **1m 3f (Fibresand)** Stalls: High GOING: 0.05 sec (STD) 3-20 (3-20)

414[3] **My Minnie (50)***(59) (BJMeehan)* 5-9-2 BDoyle(1) (lw: led 3f: drvn along ½-wy: led 2f out: styd on wl)....— 1
422* Mr Bean **(55)***(62) (KRBurke)* 5-9-7 MFenton(6) (lw: trckd ldrs: led over 3f out to 2f out: nt qckn fnl f)....1½ 2
351[4] Palacegate Jo (IRE) **(63)***(66) (RHollinshead)* 4-10-0 TIves(4) (hld up & bhd: stdy hdwy 4f out: r.o over 1f out: kpt on same pce)....2½ 3
421[2] Tempering **(58)***(54) (DWChapman)* 9-9-10 JQuinn(2) (led after 3f tl over 3f out: wknd over 1f out)....5 4
351* Suivez **(57)***(44)*(Fav)*(MrsNMacauley)* 5-9-9 JWeaver(5) (lw: chsd ldrs: drvn along ½-wy: sn wl outpcd)....6 5
414[4] Tremolante **(35)** *(CaptJWilson)* 4-7-7 (7)ow2 MHenry(3) (a bhd: sn drvn along: t.o fr 4f out)....15 6

6/4 Suivez, **4/1** Mr Bean, **11/2** MY MINNIE, **6/1** Palacegate Jo (IRE), Tempering (op 4/1), **14/1** Tremolante, CSF £24.57 TOTE £4.70: £3.90 £1.60 (£14.50) WNER Mrs W.Protheroe-Beynon (UPPER LAMBOURN) BRED Mrs Wilma Protheroe-Beynon 6 Rn 2m 30.7 (9.20) SF: 39/42/45/34/24/-
WEIGHT FOR AGE 4yo-1lb

OFFICIAL EXPLANATION **Suivez: the jockey reported that the gelding, who was hanging and never travelling well, had not responded to encouragement. He may also have trapped a nerve behind the saddle.**

518 LANCELOT LIMITED STKS (0-55) (3-Y.O+) (Class F) £3,073.40 (£852.40: £408.20) **7f (Fibresand)** Stalls: Low GOING: 0.05 sec per fur (STD) 3-50 (3-51)

473[3] **Exclusive Assembly (53)***(63) (APJames)* 3-8-7 FNorton(11) (plld hrd: trckd ldrs: led over 2f out: drvn out)....— 1

450* Orthorhombus **(52)***(64)* *(DJSCosgrove)* 6-9-11b MRimmer(12) (s.i.s: hdwy on outside over 2f out: ev ch ins fnl f: nt qckn nr fin) ... ¾ 2
*448*4 Three Arch Bridge **(54)***(48)*(Fav)*(MJohnston)* 3-8-2 DHolland(8) (mde most tl over 4f out: led 3f out: sn hdd: one pce) ... 3½ 3
*416** Aquado **(51)***(55)* *(ALForbes)* 6-10-0 JQuinn(7) (b.hind: hld up: stdy hdwy over 2f out: effrt over 1f out: nvr nr to chal) ... 2 4
*501*4 Pretonic **(44)***(30)* *(BPalling)* 7-9-3 TSprake(5) (w ldrs tl wknd 2f out) ... 6 5
*393*8 Letsbeonestaboutit **(55)***(35)* *(MrsNMacauley)* 9-9-11v DeanMcKeown(9) (w ldrs: rdn & hung lft over 2f out: wandered & sn wknd) ... 1¼ 6
*448*6 Beecham **(48)***(32)* *(AHide)* 3-8-7b AMackay(1) (s.i.s: bhd tl kpt on fnl 2f) ... nk 7
Kilnamartyra Girl **(47)***(23)* *(JParkes)* 5-8-12b(5) PMcCabe(2) (sn pushed along: outpcd ½-wy: kpt on fnl 2f: n.d) ... 1½ 8
*336*5 Tiddy Oggie **(55)***(19)* *(NAGraham)* 4-9-8 JWeaver(4) (in tch: drvn along ½-wy: sn outpcd) ... 4 9
Lord Vivienne (IRE) **(43)***(17)* *(JIACharlton)* 6-9-5 (3) DarrenMoffatt(10) (outpcd & pushed along ½-wy) ... ¾ 10
481 5 Giggleswick Girl **(51)** *(MRChannon)* 4-9-3 RHughes(6) (wl bhd: sme hdwy over 2f out: sn wknd) ... 8 11
Sapphire Son (IRE) **(48)** *(CNWilliams)* 3-8-7 PRobinson(3) (w ldrs: led over 4f out: hdd 3f out: wknd) ... 13 12

7/2 Three Arch Bridge, **5/1** Orthorhombus, Tiddy Oggie, **11/2** Aquado, **9/1** Giggleswick Girl, Letsbeonestaboutit (op 6/1), **11/1** Sapphire Son (IRE) (7/1-12/1), **12/1** EXCLUSIVE ASSEMBLY, Kilnamartyra Girl, **20/1** Pretonic, **25/1** Beecham, **33/1** Lord Vivienne (IRE), CSF £69.46 TOTE £12.20: £1.20 £2.90 £2.30 (£84.80) Trio £55.30 OWNER Mrs Brenda Rooney (TENBURY WELLS) BRED Brian Winn 12 Rn 1m 32.6 (5.80) SF: 30/46/15/37/12/17/-/5/1/-/-/-
WEIGHT FOR AGE 3yo-15lb

519

GALAHAD CLAIMING MAIDEN STKS (3-Y.O+) (Class F) £2,519.00 (£694.00: £329.00) **6f (Fibresand)** Stalls: Low GOING: 0.05 sec per fur (STD) 4-20 (4-23)

502 6 **South Forest (IRE) (68)***(64)*(Fav)*(SRBowring)* 4-8-10 (7) CTeague(4) (b: hld up: hdwy ½-wy: rdn & hung lft 1f out: styd on to ld ins fnl f: sn clr) ... — 1
Cretan Gift **(54)***(57)* *(NPLittmoden)* 4-9-4 (5) TGMcLaughlin(7) (sn bhd: hdwy on outside over 2f out: styd on fnl f) ... 5 2
*255*W The Real Whizzbang (IRE) **(36)***(45)* *(PSFelgate)* 4-8-8b(5) PMcCabe(9) (led: clr ½-wy: wknd whn hdd ins fnl f) ... ½ 3
Hi Rock **(52)***(41)* *(MJCamacho)* 3-7-13 LCharnock(5) (sn chsng ldrs: wnt 2nd ½-wy: wknd over 1f out) ... 1¼ 4
*420*5 Lawnswood Lady **(45)***(32)* *(RHollinshead)* 3-7-10 (5) AGarth(2) (chsd ldrs: drvn along ½-wy: wknd 2f out) ... 4 5
Chilly Time **(32)***(5)* *(PGMurphy)* 4-8-1b(7) RWaterfield(6) (bit bkwd: in tch: drvn along ½-wy: sn wknd) ... 8 6
442 19 Red O'Reilly *(19)* *(MrsNMacauley)* 3-8-12v JWeaver(8) (b: w ldrs ½-wy: sn lost pl) ... 1¼ 7
452 3 Rustic League (IRE) **(36)***(5)* *(TJNaughton)* 4-8-10 (3) SSanders(1) (hld up: effrt ½-wy: sn drvn along: nvr nr ldrs) ... ½ 8
*1*W Wild Adventure **(37)** *(DWChapman)* 6-8-11 DeanMcKeown(3) (s.i.s: a outpcd & bhd) ... 8 9

5/6 SOUTH FOREST (IRE) (10/11-Evens), **6/1** Hi Rock, **7/1** Red O'Reilly, **10/1** Rustic League (IRE) (6/1-12/1), Lawnswood Lady, Chilly Time (12/1-20/1), **11/1** Cretan Gift (8/1-12/1), **14/1** The Real Whizzbang (IRE) (20/1-12/1), **33/1** Wild Adventure, CSF £11.93 TOTE £1.50: £1.10 £2.70 £3.60 (£9.00) Trio £152.80 OWNER South Forest Racing (EDWINSTOWE) BRED Miss B. Galway-Greer 9 Rn 1m 18.2 (4.70) SF: 42/35/23/6/-/-/-/-/-
WEIGHT FOR AGE 3yo-13lb

520

EXCALIBUR H'CAP (0-65) (3-Y.O+) (Class F) £2,519.00 (£694.00: £329.00) **1m (Fibresand)** Stalls: Low GOING: 0.05 sec per fur (STD) 4-50 (4-52)

*416*2 **Daytona Beach (IRE) (56)***(62)* *(PBurgoyne)* 5-9-1 (7) GParkin(16) (prom: rdn & outpcd ½-wy: styd on wl to ld ins fnl f: all out) ... — 1
*415*7 Genesis Four **(42)***(48)* *(SRBowring)* 5-8-1b(7) CTeague(13) (chsd ldrs: rdn ½-wy: hung lft: ev ch fnl f: nt qckn nr fin) ... hd 2
*443*6 Top Fella (USA) **(59)***(61)* *(WAO'Gorman)* 3-8-6b(3) EmmaO'Gorman(3) (s.s: bhd: gd hdwy on outside 2f out: rdn & kpt on wl ins fnl f) ... 2 3
*416*6 Asmarina **(35)***(37)* *(SRBowring)* 5-7-8 (7) PFessey(2) (s.i.s: wl bhd: gd hdwy on outside 2f out: styd on wl ins fnl f) ... s.h 4
*419*2 Titanium Honda (IRE) **(45)***(43)* *(CEBrittain)* 4-8-11 BDoyle(5) (w ldr: led 2f out tl ins fnl f) ... 2 5

354[6] Cicerone **(48)***(45) (JLHarris)* 5-9-0 RCochrane(12) (b: a.p: effrt & n.m.r 2f out: nt clr run: swtchd rt over 1f out: kpt on same pce) ....½ **6**
Dante's Rubicon (IRE) **(47)***(41) (JDBethell)* 4-8-13 JWeaver(4) (bit bkwd: mde most to 2f out: wknd fnl f) 1½ **7**
415* Whitelock Quest **(33)***(25) (NEBerry)* 7-7-6 (7) AdelleGibbons(11) (n.m.r & lost pl after 2f: sme hdwy 2f out: n.d) ....¾ **8**
255[4] Salinger **(32)***(18) (JParkes)* 7-7-12 JFanning(14) (chsd ldrs: sn drvn along: lost pl over 2f out) 3 **9**
313[6] Tovarich **(59)***(42)*(Fav)*(DNicholls)* 4-9-11 SWhitworth(6) (unruly in stalls: hdwy on ins to chse ldrs ½-wy: rdn & wknd over 1f out: eased) 1¾ **10**
349[6] Zanzara (IRE) **(53)***(34) (MrsVAAconley)* 4-9-5 TWilliams(8) (in tch: rdn & outpcd ½-wy: n.d after) ....¾ **11**
409[2] Dragonflight **(39)***(12) (DHaydnJones)* 4-8-5 AMackay(10) (in tch to ½-wy: sn lost pl) 4 **12**
408[6] Arrogant Boy **(34)** *(DWChapman)* 6-8-0b NCarlisle(15) (chsd ldrs tl rdn & lost pl over 2f out) 5 **13**
296[5] Greek Gold (IRE) **(57)***(18) (GPKelly)* 6-9-9 AlexGreaves(7) (lw: in tch tl lost pl over 3f out) 1 **14**
Hickleton Lady (IRE) **(62)***(17) (CaptJWilson)* 4-9-7 (7) MHenry(1) (s.i.s: a bhd) 3 **15**
358[6] Halbert **(48)** *(MRChannon)* 6-9-0 RHughes(9) (chsd ldrs tl rdn & wknd 2f out: eased) 2½ **16**

9/4 Tovarich, **7/1** Titanium Honda (IRE), Whitelock Quest, Cicerone, **8/1** Salinger, DAYTONA BEACH (IRE), **12/1** Genesis Four, Top Fella (USA), **14/1** Asmarina, Dragonflight, **16/1** Zanzara (IRE), Dante's Rubicon (IRE), **25/1** Arrogant Boy, Greek Gold (IRE), Hickleton Lady (IRE), Halbert, CSF £105.22 CT £1,073.91 TOTE £11.00: £2.50 £2.30 £4.20 £2.80 (£53.70) Trio £173.10 OWNER Mrs J. E. Radburn (WANTAGE) BRED Miss H. Dean 16 Rn

1m 47.1 (7.80) SF: 32/18/15/7/13/15/11/-/-/12/4/-/-/-/-/-
WEIGHT FOR AGE 3yo-16lb

T/Plpt: £129.70 (85.28 Tckts). T/Qdpt £35.80 (2 Tckts). WG

NOTTINGHAM (L-H)
Tuesday April 4th (Good, Good to firm patches)
WEATHER: sunny WIND: slt across

521 LANGWITH (S) H'CAP (0-60) (3-Y.O) (Class G) £2,243.00 (£618.00: £293.00)
1m 1f 213y Stalls: High GOING minus 0.30 sec per fur (GF) 2-30 (2-31)

270[P] **Boldly So (38)***(46+) (WJMusson)* 3-8-3 JQuinn(2) (lw: hld up in tch: hdwy to ld over 2f out: sn clr: hld on) ....— **1**
95[5] Slapy Dam **(48)***(54)*(Fav)*(MrsJRRamsden)* 3-8-13 KFallon(17) (hld up: effrt & outpcd over 3f out: rallied u.p bel dist: kpt on twrds fin) 1¼ **2**
444[13] Don't Forget Ruby (IRE) **(44)***(44) (DWPArbuthnot)* 3-8-9 TQuinn(13) (lw: led after 3f tl over 2f out: kpt on same pace) 4 **3**
236[6] Griffin's Girl **(32)***(31) (RPCHoad)* 3-7-11 JLowe(7) (hld up: hdwy over 2f out: styd on wl fnl f) ....½ **4**
270[5] Risky Rose **(40)***(37) (RHollinshead)* 3-8-5 DHarrison(12) (dwlt: hdwy 3f out: styd on fnl f: nvr nrr) 1 **5**
331[9] Pink Petal **(32)***(28) (CJHill)* 3-7-11 TWilliams(18) (b: s.s: hdwy on ins fnl 2f: nrst fin) ....½ **6**
350[5] Centaur Express **(32)***(25) (ALForbes)* 3-7-6 (5)ow2 CHawksley(19) (reard s: effrt on outside ent st: nt trbld ldrs) ....¾ **7**
292[8] Kindred Greeting **(46)***(38) (DMorris)* 3-8-11b GDuffield(16) (hld up & bhd: hdwy over 2f out: nt rch ldrs) 2 **8**
Absolute Folly **(56)***(38) (JBerry)* 3-9-7 GCarter(11) (bit bkwd: chsd ldrs: 6th st: rdn 3f out: sn btn) 6 **9**
444[9] Pendine **(40)***(20) (SCWilliams)* 3-8-5 MFenton(4) (prom: 2nd st: wknd over 2f out) 1½ **10**
Elsies Bar **(53)***(28) (RMWhitaker)* 3-9-4 ACulhane(5) (bkwd: chsd ldrs 6f: sn lost tch) 3 **11**
339[10] Drama King **(45)***(19) (SRBowring)* 3-8-10b SDWilliams(1) (swtg: nvr trbld ldrs) ....¾ **12**
Lilac Rain **(45)***(18) (JRArnold)* 3-8-10 JWeaver(8) (nt grwn: led 3f: 3rd st: wknd over 3f out) ....½ **13**
453[11] Okay Baby (IRE) **(55)***(27) (MHTompkins)* 3-9-6 PRobinson(9) (prom: 5th st: wknd over 2f out) ....¾ **14**
368[4] Danny's Gift **(32)***(4) (MissAJWhitfield)* 3-7-4 (7) CAdamson(15) (swtg: hdwy 8f out: wknd over 3f out) ....s.h **15**
156[6] Sailors Moon **(49)***(18) (HJCollingridge)* 3-9-0 MRimmer(10) (in tch 6f: sn rdn & wknd) 2 **16**
Fly the Eagle **(48)***(10) (DJSffrenchDavis)* 3-8-13 JWilliams(3) (t: a in rr: t.o) 4 **17**
453[8] Don't Mean a Thing (IRE) **(56)***(10) (RHannon)* 3-9-7 LDettori(14) (a bhd: t.o) 5 **18**
263[11] Green Green Ruby **(41)** *(GLMoore)* 3-8-6 AClark(6) (a in rr: t.o) 3 **19**

4/1 Slapy Dam (op 5/2), **11/2** Absolute Folly, **7/1** BOLDLY SO (op 3/1), **10/1** Don't Mean a Thing (IRE), Pendine, **12/1** Kindred Greeting, **14/1** Elsies Bar, Risky Rose, Lilac Rain, Drama King, **16/1** Green Green Ruby, Sailors Moon, **20/1** Don't Forget Ruby (IRE), Pink Petal, Okay Baby (IRE), **33/1** Danny's Gift, Fly the Eagle, Griffin's Girl, Centaur Express, CSF £35.55 CT £510.13 TOTE £6.40: £2.90 £1.10 £4.40 £28.80 (£55.60) Trio £105.80 OWNER Miss Therese Sevremont (NEWMARKET) BRED Fares Stables Ltd 19 Rn 2m 9.5 (7.00) SF: 8/16/6/-/-/-/-/-/-/-/-/-/-/-/-/-/-/-/-
Bt in 3,600 gns.

522

FLYING HORSE MAIDEN STKS (3-Y.O F) (Class D) £4,110.00 (£1,230.00: £590.00: £270.00) **5f 13y** Stalls: High GOING minus 0.30 sec (GF) 3-00 (3-02)

Karina Heights (USA) *(73) (JWWatts)* 3-8-11 JReid(2) (w'like: led 3f: swtchd rt & rallied to ld cl home)....— **1**
451[2] La Suquet **(64)***(71) (MRChannon)* 3-8-11 RHughes(12) (w ldrs: led 2f out: rdn & hung lft fnl f: hdd nr fin)....¾ **2**
Nottash (IRE) *(63)*(Fav)*(JRFanshawe)* 3-8-11 DHarrison(9) (lw: hdwy 2f out: rdn & edgd lft bel dist: kpt on fnl f)....2½ **3**
Blue Sioux **(72)***(56) (JWharton)* 3-8-11 JWilliams(14) (bit bkwd: wnt w ldrs: rdn & one pce appr fnl f)....2 **4**
Fairy Wind (IRE) *(55) (NACallaghan)* 3-8-11 LDettori(17) (b: b.hind: lt-f: chsd ldrs: effrt 2f out: nt plcd to chal)....½ **5**
442[11] Peggy Spencer *(52) (CWThornton)* 3-8-11 DeanMcKeown(13) (hdwy ½-wy: one pce appr fnl f)....1 **6**
Never Such Bliss *(48) (JDBethell)* 3-8-11 TIves(15) (bkwd: sme hdwy fnl 2f: nvr nrr)....1¼ **7**
502[10] Secret Miss *(40) (APJarvis)* 3-8-4 (7) BHunter(1) (s.i.s: hdwy u.p 2f out: nvr nrr)....2½ **8**
Ganador **(60)***(34) (JBerry)* 3-8-11 GCarter(6) (prom over 3f)....1¾ **9**
Squires Mount *(30) (MBell)* 3-8-11 MFenton(7) (leggy: bkwd: nvr nr ldrs)....1½ **10**
420[8] Bebe Pomme *(29) (MrsNMacauley)* 3-8-8b(3) JTate(16) (bit bkwd: outpcd)....nk **11**
Nisya *(28) (MissGayKelleway)* 3-8-11 SWhitworth(4) (bkwd: spd to ½-wy)....s.h **12**
Samsung Lovelylady (IRE) *(27) (EWeymes)* 3-8-11 GHind(3) (w'like: bkwd: dwlt: hdwy ½-wy: wknd wl over 1f out)....½ **13**
502[16] Name That Tune *(26) (CJHill)* 3-8-11 JQuinn(5) (a outpcd)....nk **14**
Princess Gay (IRE) *(15) (MBell)* 3-8-4 (7) GFaulkner(8) (b.hind: lt-f: unf: outpcd)....3½ **15**
398[12] La Belle Dominique **(70)***(13) (SGKnight)* 3-8-11 WNewnes(10) (a outpcd)....½ **16**
299[2] Avant Huit **(55)***(12) (MrsNMacauley)* 3-8-11 JWeaver(11) (a outpcd)....nk **17**

11/4 Nottash (IRE), **6/1** Blue Sioux, La Suquet, Ganador, **13/2** Fairy Wind (IRE) (op 5/2), **8/1** Avant Huit, **10/1** KARINA HEIGHTS (USA), Squires Mount, **11/1** Peggy Spencer (8/1-12/1), **12/1** Nisya, **16/1** La Belle Dominique, **20/1** Never Such Bliss, **25/1** Name That Tune, **33/1** Samsung Lovelylady (IRE), Princess Gay (IRE), Bebe Pomme, Secret Miss, CSF £78.10 TOTE £19.60: £3.60 £3.60 £1.50 (£52.40) Trio £131.00 OWNER Mr R. E. Sangster (RICHMOND) BRED Brereton C. Jones 17 Rn 61.9 secs (3.20) SF: 17/15/7/-/-/-/-/-/-/-/-/-/-/-/-/-/-

523

EUROPEAN BREEDERS FUND CINDERHILL MAIDEN STKS (2-Y.O) (Class D) £3,655.00 (£1,090.00: £520.00: £235.00)
5f 13y Stalls: High GOING minus 0.30 sec per fur (GF) 3-30 (3-32)

424[6] **Dungeon Master (IRE)** *(75) (MRChannon)* 2-9-0 RHughes(2) (hdwy 2f out: shkn up to ld ins fnl f: r.o wl)....— **1**
Dance of The Moon *(65)*(Fav)*(MBell)* 2-8-9 MFenton(4) (cmpt: bkwd: w ldr: led 1f out: hdd & no ex ins fnl f)....1½ **2**
424[8] Thai Morning *(66) (PWHarris)* 2-9-0 PatEddery(6) (led to 1f out: rdn & unable qckn fnl f)....1½ **3**
Kala Sunrise *(65) (CSmith)* 2-9-0 WWoods(9) (unf: scope: bit bkwd: s.i.s: hdwy 2f out: rdn & kpt on ins fnl f)....hd **4**
Uncle George *(54) (MHTompkins)* 2-9-0 PRobinson(8) (neat: bkwd: chsd ldrs over 3f: sn outpcd)....3½ **5**
Amaretto Bay (IRE) *(54) (BJMeehan)* 2-9-0 BDoyle(3) (small: chsd ldrs fr ½-wy: rdn wl over 1f out: sn btn)....s.h **6**
Richard House Lad *(46) (CASmith)* 2-9-0 MWigham(7) (lt-f: bkwd: s.i.s: outpcd)....2½ **7**
Albert The Bear *(44) (JBerry)* 2-9-0 GCarter(1) (leggy: lt-f: bit bkwd: a bhd & outpcd)....¾ **8**
Everyone Can Dream *(33) (MJohnston)* 2-9-0 DHolland(5) (cmpt: bkwd: sn drvn along: nvr gng pce of ldrs)....3½ **9**

2/1 Dance of The Moon, **7/2** Thai Morning, **5/1** DUNGEON MASTER (IRE) (5/2-11/2), Everyone Can Dream, **6/1** Albert The Bear (op 3/1), **10/1** Uncle George, **16/1** Amaretto Bay (IRE), **25/1** Kala Sunrise, **33/1** Richard House Lad, CSF £15.91 TOTE £6.10: £2.50 £1.40 £1.10 (£12.20) Trio £11.10 OWNER The Classicstone Partnership (UPPER LAMBOURN) BRED T. J. Monaghan 9 Rn
62.6 secs (3.90) SF: 8/-/-/-/-/-/-/-/-

524 BAGTHORPE H'CAP (0-70) (3-Y.O) (Class E) £3,473.80 (£1,038.40: £497.20: £226.60) **6f 15y** Stalls: High GOING minus 0.30 sec per fur (GF) 4-00 (4-01)

*315** **Denbrae (IRE) (66)***(70) (DJGMurraySmith)* 3-9-5 JWeaver(9) (in tch: hdwy 2f out: str run to ld nr fin) — **1**
156[2] Portelet **(55)***(58) (RJRWilliams)* 3-8-8 GDuffield(8) (hld up: hdwy over 1f out: rdn to ld wl ins fnl f: caught nr fin) nk **2**
450[7] Media Express **(59)***(61) (TGMills)* 3-8-12 JReid(2) (mde most far side: rdn bel dist: hdd wl ins fnl f) nk **3**
Tafahhus **(60)***(57) (RWArmstrong)* 3-8-13 WCarson(3) (bit bkwd: chsd ldr far side: ev ch ins fnl f: wknd cl home) 2 **4**
411[10] Rockcracker (IRE) **(65)***(61) (RCharlton)* 3-9-4b DHarrison(7) (led centre: rdn over 1f out: one pce) nk **5**
Garlande D'Or **(54)***(47) (JLSpearing)* 3-8-7 GHind(4) (still unf: prom far side: rdn & one pce appr fnl f) 1¼ **6**
South Sound (IRE) **(65)***(56) (RHannon)* 3-8-11 (7) DaneO'Neill(1) (bkwd: swrvd lft s: chsd ldrs far side over 4f) ¾ **7**
365[4] Master Millfield (IRE) **(68)***(59) (CJHill)* 3-9-7 JQuinn(14) (lw: chsd ldrs: no hdwy ins fnl 2f) s.h **8**
Miss Felixstowe (USA) **(58)***(41) (MrsMReveley)* 3-8-11 GCarter(18) (bit bkwd: hdwy u.p stand's side bel dist: nvr nrr) 3 **9**
Nafta **(65)***(47) (SEKettlewell)* 3-9-4 JFortune(11) (bkwd: swtchd lft s: r.o appr fnl f: nvr nrr) nk **10**
442[8] Assumpsit (IRE) **(65)***(46) (SDow)* 3-9-4 TQuinn(10) (nvr trbld ldrs) ½ **11**
482[7] Casper's Risk **(55)***(35) (DNicholls)* 3-8-8b AlexGreaves(17) (mid div: rdn over 2f out: nt pce to chal) ½ **12**
Tharwa (IRE) **(59)***(39)*(Fav)*(NACallaghan)* 3-8-12 PatEddery(16) (b.hind: spd 4f: sn rdn & wknd) s.h **13**
409[6] Malzoom **(40)***(18) (SEKettlewell)* 3-7-7 NCarlisle(13) (prom over 3f: sn lost pl) ¾ **14**
Perfect Bertie (IRE) **(58)***(35) (MrsJRRamsden)* 3-8-11 KFallon(19) (bkwd: a in rr) hd **15**
Voila Premiere (IRE) **(64)***(33) (MHTompkins)* 3-9-3 PRobinson(15) (bkwd: sn rdn along: a outpcd) 3 **16**
426[13] Double Glow **(62)***(27) (NBycroft)* 3-9-1 DeanMcKeown(12) (swtg: hmpd after 2f: a in rr) 1½ **17**
363[2] Poly Laureon (IRE) **(57)***(15) (RHollinshead)* 3-8-10 LDettori(6) (outpcd) 3 **18**
Raticosa **(41)** *(DonEnricoIncisa)* 3-7-8vow1 KimTinkler(5) (swtg: outpcd) 4 **19**

LONG HANDICAP Malzoom 7-2

6/1 Tharwa (IRE), **13/2** Master Millfield (IRE) (tchd 4/1), **7/1** DENBRAE (IRE), **15/2** Perfect Bertie (IRE), **10/1** Assumpsit (IRE), Rockcracker (IRE), Poly Laureon (IRE), **12/1** Tafahhus, Media Express, Portelet, **14/1** Miss Felixstowe (USA), Malzoom, **16/1** South Sound (IRE), Voila Premiere (IRE), **20/1** Casper's Risk, Nafta, **25/1** Double Glow, **33/1** Garlande D'Or, **66/1** Raticosa, CSF £92.89 CT £951.36 TOTE £10.90: £2.40 £3.20 £2.10 £2.90 (£91.50) Trio £557.80 OWNER Mr Michael Mellersh (LAMBOURN) BRED Mellon Stud 19 Rn

1m 15.9 (4.90) SF: 11/-/2/-/2/-/-/-/-/-/-/-/-/-/-/-/-/-/-

525 FOREST H'CAP (0-70) (3-Y.O) (Class E) £3,273.60 (£976.80: £466.40: £211.20) **1m 6f 15y** Stalls: High GOING minus 0.30 sec per fur (GF) 4-30 (4-31)

427[7] **Doddington Flyer (60)***(65)*(Fav)*(RHollinshead)* 3-9-2 TIves(5) (hld up: 3rd st: chsd ldr 4f out: hrd rdn 2f out: led 1f out: all out) — **1**
453[3] Al Corniche (IRE) **(45)***(49) (KOCunningham-Brown)* 3-8-1 JQuinn(7) (led tl hdd over 2f out: rdn & styd on ins fnl f) ¾ **2**
428[8] Amercius **(49)***(51) (RHannon)* 3-8-5b RPerham(3) (chsd ldr: rdn ½-wy: 2nd st: one pce fr bel dist) 1¾ **3**
453[4] Mim-Lou-and **(40)***(42) (BRMillman)* 3-7-10 JLowe(8) (dwlt: hld up & bhd: 6th st: hdwy to ld over 2f out: hdd appr fnl f: sn btn) s.h **4**
453[5] Tommyknocker (IRE) **(40)***(42) (JRJenkins)* 3-7-10 FNorton(1) (hld up: 5th st: rdn 2f out: kpt on) hd **5**
Clean Edge (USA) **(65)***(61) (MHTompkins)* 3-9-7 PRobinson(6) (bit bkwd: chsd ldrs: 4th st: wknd over 2f out) 5 **6**
213[9] Solor Dancer **(37)***(16) (CBBBooth)* 3-7-7 NKennedy(4) (lost tch ½-wy: 7th st: t.o) 15 **7**

LONG HANDICAP Solor Dancer 7-5

11/4 DODDINGTON FLYER (2/1-3/1), **9/2** Al Corniche (IRE), **11/2** Clean Edge (USA) (op 3/1), **6/1** Mim-Lou-and, Tommyknocker (IRE), **7/1** Amercius, **25/1** Solor Dancer, CSF £13.16 CT £52.59 TOTE £3.30: £2.40 £1.80 (£7.20) OWNER Mr J. F. Bower (UPPER LONGDON) BRED Worksop Manor Stud Farm 7 Rn

3m 10.3 (11.80) SF: 13/-/-/-/9/-

526 LANGWORTH APPRENTICE H'CAP (0-70) (3-Y.O+) (Class G)
£2,270.00 (£645.00: £320.00)
1m 54y Stalls: High GOING minus 0.30 sec per fur (GF) 5-00 (5-05)

Muferr (IRE) (70)*(84)*(Fav)*(LMCumani)* 3-9-0 JoHunnam(5) (lw: hld up: hdwy to ld over 2f out: pushed out)........— 1
445⁷ Captain Marmalade **(38)***(49) (DTThom)* 6-7-12 GMilligan(3) (hld up & bhd: hdwy fnl 2f: fin wl)........1¾ 2
Last Laugh (IRE) **(65)***(68) (RHannon)* 3-8-4 (5) EGreehy(1) (hld up: hdwy on ins fnl 3f: nt rch ldrs)........4 3
Chairmans Choice **(46)***(45) (APJarvis)* 5-8-6 BHunter(14) (swtg: w ldrs: 3rd st: one pce appr fnl f)........2 4
430²³ Avishayes (USA) **(51)***(48) (MrsMReveley)* 8-8-11 DDenby(6) (bit bkwd: hld up: hdwy over 2f out: nrst fin)........1 5
402⁸ Respectable Jones **(43)***(32) (RHollinshead)* 9-8-3 AEddery(9) (prom: 2nd st: wknd wl over 1f out)........4 6
Maurangi **(57)***(46) (BWMurray)* 4-9-3 CScudder(16) (bkwd: prom: 5th st: rdn & wknd over 2f out)........s.h 7
Total Rach (IRE) **(69)***(58) (MrsLPiggott)* 3-8-8 (5) VictoriaAppleby(12) (b: b.hind: a.p: 4th st: rdn & wknd ent fnl f)........s.h 8
235⁶ Greek Night Out (IRE) **(48)***(37) (JAHarris)* 4-8-8b ADaly(15) (b.hind: led tl hdd over 2f out: grad wknd)........hd 9
430²⁶ Aitch N'Bee **(60)***(49) (LadyHerries)* 12-9-1 (5) PDoe(7) (hld up: effrt 3f out: nvr nr to chal)........hd 10
Brandonhurst **(65)***(51)*(Fav)*(LadyHerries)* 5-9-6 (5) LisaHackett(11) (bkwd: hld up in tch: wknd fnl 2f)........1½ 11
Delgarth Lady **(38)***(23) (JLSpearing)* 4-7-12 AdelleGibbons(8) (mid div tl wknd over 2f out)........½ 12
378² Self Expression **(57)***(41) (MrsJRRamsden)* 7-8-12 (5) TFinn(4) (a in rr)........½ 13
Pewter Lass **(60)***(42) (MBlanshard)* 3-8-4 SMcCarthy(18) (nvr nr ldrs)........¾ 14
238⁷ La Belle Shyanne **(41)***(20) (CJHill)* 4-8-1 JWilkinson(20) (a in rr)........2 15
Talented Ting (IRE) **(68)***(44) (PCHaslam)* 6-10-0 CarolDavison(2) (chsd ldrs: 6th st: wknd 3f out)........1¼ 16
Just Fizzy **(50)***(22) (JWharton)* 3-7-3 (5) TThomas(17) (prom tl wknd over 3f out)........2 17
Lawnswood Junior **(62)***(23) (JLSpearing)* 8-9-8 CWebb(10) (bit bkwd: a in rr: t.o)........6 18
Cafe Solo **(47)** *(NBycroft)* 4-8-7 PFessey(19) (bit bkwd: lost pl ½-wy: t.o)........9 19
179⁹ Akabusi **(40)** *(JNorton)* 4-7-9 (5) AmyGosden(13) (bolted bef s: dwlt: a bhd: t.o)........dist 20

9/2 MUFERR (IRE) (op 5/2), Brandonhurst (op 10/1), **5/1** Self Expression, **10/1** Chairmans Choice (op 25/1), Captain Marmalade, Maurangi, **11/1** Total Rach (IRE) (8/1-12/1), **12/1** Avishayes (USA) (op 8/1), **14/1** Greek Night Out (IRE), Aitch N'Bee, Last Laugh (IRE) (12/1-20/1), **20/1** Respectable Jones, Pewter Lass, Talented Ting (IRE), Cafe Solo, **25/1** La Belle Shyanne, Lawnswood Junior, **33/1** Just Fizzy, Delgarth Lady, Akabusi, CSF £55.02 CT £579.39 TOTE £6.90: £2.70 £1.30 £6.30 £7.50 (£30.30) Trio £90.30 OWNER Sheikh Ahmed Al Maktoum (NEWMARKET) BRED Mrs T. V. Ryan 20 Rn 1m 44.9 (5.30) SF: 22/3/6/-/2/-/-/-/-/3/5/-/-/-/-/-/-/-/-/-
WEIGHT FOR AGE 3yo-16lb

T/Jkpt: Not won; £44,527.46 to Ripon 5/4/95. T/Plpt: £111.60 (192.78 Tckts). T/Qdpt: Not won; £31.20 to Ripon 5/4/95. IM

0509-WOLVERHAMPTON (L-H)
Tuesday April 4th (Standard)
WIND: nil

527 THAILAND MEDIAN AUCTION MAIDEN STKS (3-Y.O) (Class F)
£2,519.00 (£694.00: £329.00)
6f (Fibresand) Stalls: Low GOING: nil sec per fur (STD) 2-20 (2-21)

Heathyards Magic (IRE) *(64) (RHollinshead)* 3-9-0 WRyan(4) (sn pushed along: last st: rdn & edgd lft 1f out: led ins fnl f: r.o wl)........— 1
449² Sharp 'n Smart **(65)***(57)*(Fav)*(BSmart)* 3-8-11 (3) SSanders(2) (led tl ins fnl f)........2½ 2
392² Sharp Holly (IRE) **(52)***(52) (JABennett)* 3-8-6 (3) DWright(3) (chsd ldr: rdn 2f out: 2nd st: ev ch 1f out: r.o one pce)........s.h 3

6/5 Sharp 'n Smart, **7/4** HEATHYARDS MAGIC (IRE), **7/2** Sharp Holly (IRE), CSF £3.69 TOTE £2.00 (£1.20) OWNER Mr L. A. Morgan (UPPER LONGDON) BRED Patrick Walshe 3 Rn
1m 15.9 (4.70) SF: 33/26/21

528

CHINA H'CAP (0-70) (3-Y.O F) (Class E) £3,044.80 (£906.40: £431.20: £193.60)
7f (Fibresand) Stalls: Low GOING: nil sec per fur (STD) 2-50 (2-51)

Dominion's Dream (66)(72) (BSmart) 3-9-0 (7) ADaly(6) (a.p: led 3f out: all out) ....— 1
395[3] Grey Again **(53)**(58) (SRBowring) 3-8-1b(7) CTeague(2) (hld up: hdwy over 2f out: 2nd & racd wd st: edgd rt & ev ch fnl f: r.o) ....½ 2
Remontant (IRE) **(45)**(43) (RHollinshead) 3-7-9 (5) AGarth(1) (lw: outpcd & bhd: hdwy & 4th st: nt rch ldrs) 3 3
411* David James' Girl **(65)**(58)(Fav)(ABailey) 3-9-6 KDarley(4) (prom: rdn 4f out: 3rd st: wknd wl over 1f out) 2 4
Instant Success (USA) **(50)**(9) (WAO'Gorman) 3-8-2 (3) SSanders(3) (bkwd: prom: rdn over 3f out: 5th & wknd st: t.o) 15 5
We're Joken **(50)** (JBerry) 3-8-5 JCarroll(5) (b.hind: bkwd: led 4f : sn wknd: 6th & btn st: t.o)11 6

5/4 David James' Girl, **3/1** Grey Again, **9/2** We're Joken (op 3/1), **12/1** DOMINION'S DREAM (op 6/1), Instant Success (USA) (op 6/1), **16/1** Remontant (IRE), CSF £42.66 TOTE £34.10: £3.60 £1.40 (£174.90) OWNER Mrs Bernice Cuthbert (LAMBOURN) BRED Aston Park Stud 6 Rn
1m 31.6 (7.60) SF: 16/2/-/2/-/-

529

SINGAPORE LIMITED STKS (0-60) (3-Y.O+) (Class F) £2,796.20 (£773.20: £368.60) **1m 100y (Fibresand)** Stalls: Low GOING: nil sec (STD) 3-20 (3-21)

414[7] **Marowins (60)**(69+) (EJAlston) 6-9-7 KDarley(1) (bhd tl hdwy over 4f out: slt ld on bit 2f out: v.easily) ....— 1
479[2] Equerry **(60)**(68)(Fav)(MJohnston) 4-9-7 MHills(5) (a.p: led over 4f out to 2f out: r.o & no ch w wnr) ....¾ 2
413[5] Kristis Girl **(40)**(55) (DHaydnJones) 8-9-2 AMackay(7) (a.p: hrd rdn over 3f out: 3rd st: r.o one pce) 4 3
Sooty Tern **(60)**(51) (JMBradley) 8-9-2 (5) SDrowne(3) (lw: prom: outpcd 3f out: 4th st: wknd over 1f out) 5 4
301[7] Star Fighter **(60)**(54) (WAO'Gorman) 3-8-6 (3) EmmaO'Gorman(2) (lw: prom over 4f: 6th & bhd st) ....½ 5
Jackatack (IRE) **(57)**(44) (MRChannon) 3-8-5 PaulEddery(4) (lw: rdn 5f out: bhd fnl 3f: 5th & no ch st) 3 6
Fitzroy Lad **(31)**(29) (RJBaker) 5-9-7 SRaymont(6) (lw: led 4f: wknd 3f out: 7th & bhd st) 8 7

Evens Equerry, **4/1** MAROWINS, Star Fighter, **7/1** Jackatack (IRE), **10/1** Sooty Tern (op 6/1), **16/1** Kristis Girl, **40/1** Fitzroy Lad, CSF £8.64 TOTE £5.10: £2.80 £1.10 (£3.80) OWNER Whitehills Racing Syndicate (PRESTON) BRED W. M. Lidsey 7 Rn 1m 52.6 (8.60) SF: 24/23/10/6/-/-/-
WEIGHT FOR AGE 3yo-16lb

530

INDIA H'CAP (0-70) (3-Y.O+) (Class E) £3,159.20 (£941.60: £448.80: £202.40)
1m 4f (Fibresand) Stalls: Low GOING: nil sec per fur (STD) 3-50 (3-52)

193* **Shakiyr (FR) (61)**(72) (RHollinshead) 4-9-11 WRyan(7) (prom: hrd rdn: 4th & rcd wd st: styd on ins fnl f: led post) ....— 1
412* Broom Isle **(60)**(71)(Fav)(DBurchell) 7-9-9 (3) DRMcCabe(8) (led tl hdd 2f out: hrd rdn to ld ins fnl f: hdd post) ....s.h 2
421[6] Hill Farm Dancer **(48)**(59) (WMBrisbourne) 4-8-7 (5) AGarth(6) (hld up & bhd: hdwy 3f out: led 2f out tl ins fnl f: r.o) ....hd 3
514[4] Awestruck **(49)**(55) (BPreece) 5-9-1v PaulEddery(5) (chsd ldr: 2nd st: wknd over 1f out) 4 4
444* Hever Golf Lady **(49)**(44) (TJNaughton) 3-7-7 NAdams(10) (bhd: sme hdwy over 1f out: n.d)..8 5
412[11] Premier Dance **(62)**(56) (DHaydnJones) 8-9-9 (5) SDrowne(1) (prom tl wknd over 3f out: poor 6th st) 1 6
421[4] Swynford Flyer **(43)**(26) (JAHarris) 6-8-4 (5) JStack(2) (hld up & plld hrd: hdwy on ins over 4f out: 5th & wkng st) 8 7
409* Enchanteur **(40)**(8) (TJEtherington) 4-8-4 KDarley(4) (hld up & plld hrd: rdn over 4f out: sn bhd: t.o) 11 8
Western Fleet (USA) **(52)**(12) (JHPeacock) 4-8-13 (3) SSanders(9) (drppd rr & rdn 5f out: t.o)..6 9
LONG HANDICAP Hever Golf Lady 7-4

5/2 Broom Isle, **3/1** SHAKIYR (FR), **11/2** Hever Golf Lady, **7/1** Enchanteur (op 4/1), **9/1** Swynford Flyer, **10/1** Premier Dance (op 6/1), **14/1** Awestruck, **20/1** Hill Farm Dancer, **33/1** Western Fleet (USA), CSF £10.31 CT £110.48 TOTE £5.80: £2.50 £1.10 £3.50 (£3.80) Trio £96.20 OWNER L & R Roadlines (UPPER LONGDON) BRED S. A. Aga Khan in France 9 Rn
2m 43.1 (12.10) SF: 30/31/17/15/-/16/-/-/-
WEIGHT FOR AGE 3yo-22lb, 4yo-2lb
STEWARDS' ENQUIRY McCabe suspended 13-15/4/95 (excessive use of whip).

531 MALAYSIA (S) STKS (2-Y.O) (Class G) £2,277.00 (£627.00: £297.00)
5f (Fibresand) Stalls: Low GOING: nil sec per fur (STD) 4-20 (4-22)

429² **Swiss Valley Lady** *(55)*(Fav)*(WGMTurner)* 2-8-6 TSprake(1) (mde all: clr over 1f out: easily) ....— 1
508⁸ Don't Tell Vicki *(29) (JSMoore)* 2-8-6 KDarley(3) (chsd wnr tl rdn over 2f out: 3rd st: r.o one pce fnl f) 8 2
Gi La High *(29) (JBerry)* 2-8-6 JCarroll(2) (lengthy: unf: dwlt: sn rcvrd: chsd wnr over 2f out: 2nd st: one pce) ....s.h 3
Exactly (IRE) *(7) (MJohnston)* 2-8-6 MHills(4) (unf: bit bkwd: sn rdn & outpcd: poor 4th st) 7 4

6/5 SWISS VALLEY LADY, **9/4** Exactly (IRE), **11/4** Gi La High, **7/2** Don't Tell Vicki, CSF £6.11 TOTE £2.30 (£2.10) OWNER Swiss Valley Racing Associates (SHERBORNE) BRED R. Navarra and Mrs J. Pike 4 Rn
63.7 secs (5.70) SF: -/-/-/-
Bt in 7,200 gns.

532 HONG KONG H'CAP (0-65) (3-Y.O+) (Class F) £2,519.00 (£694.00: £329.00)
6f (Fibresand) Stalls: Low GOING: nil sec per fur (STD) 4-50 (4-51)

*419** **Souperficial (52)***(61) (JAGlover)* 4-9-3v KDarley(4) (hdwy 3f out: led 2f out: drvn out) ....— 1
Sakharov **(52)***(60) (MJohnston)* 6-9-3 MHills(11) (lw: hdwy 3f out: 2nd st: ev ch fnl f: r.o) ....nk 2
398⁴ King Rambo **(63)***(62)*(Fav)*(RHollinshead)* 4-10-0 WRyan(6) (a.p: 1st st: wknd 1f out) 3½ 3
Saxon King (IRE) **(47)***(39) (MDIUsher)* 5-8-12 RStreet(8) (b.hind: hld up & bhd: hdwy over 1f out: nvr nrr) 2½ 4
*473** Bon Secret (IRE) **(71)***(62)*(Fav)*(TJNaughton)* 3-9-6 (3) 7x SSanders(5) (lw: nvr nr to chal) ....½ 5
182¹⁰ Angelic Dancer **(45)***(35) (SRBowring)* 4-8-3b(7) CTeague(12) (hld up & sn bhd: hdwy over 1f out: nt rch ldrs) ....½ 6
511⁷ Jon's Choice **(56)***(42) (BPreece)* 7-9-7b TWall(9) (rdn & hdwy on outside 3f out: 5th st: wknd over 1f out) 1¼ 7
407⁷ The Institute Boy **(51)***(35) (MissJFCraze)* 5-9-2 SWebster(7) (prom: 4th st: wknd over 1f out) ....¾ 8
415¹² Hill Farm Katie **(42)***(22) (WMBrisbourne)* 4-8-2b(5) AGarth(10) (s.i.s: outpcd) 1½ 9
Red Five **(58)***(29) (JBerry)* 4-9-9 JCarroll(3) (s.i.s: a bhd) 3½ 10
Our Mica **(32)** *(LJBarratt)* 5-7-11bow1 TWilliams(2) (bit bkwd: led 4f: 6th & wkng st) 4 11
519⁶ Chilly Time **(34)** *(PGMurphy)* 4-7-6b(7)ow2 SLanigan(1) (chsd ldr 2f: wknd over 2f out: t.o) 15 12

3/1 Bon Secret (IRE), King Rambo, **4/1** SOUPERFICIAL, **13/2** Sakharov (4/1-7/1), **7/1** Red Five, **10/1** Jon's Choice, **12/1** The Institute Boy, **16/1** Angelic Dancer, Saxon King (IRE), **20/1** Chilly Time, **25/1** Hill Farm Katie, **33/1** Our Mica, CSF £32.38 CT £86.87 TOTE £3.90: £1.50 £3.80 £1.70 (£15.10) Trio £30.70 OWNER Mr M. G. Ridley (WORKSOP) BRED C. L. Loyd 12 Rn
1m 15.7 (4.50) SF: 38/37/39/16/26/12/19/12/-/6/-/-
WEIGHT FOR AGE 3yo-13lb

T/Plpt: £95.10 (82.23 Tckts). T/Qdpt: £16.40 (2.7 Tckts). KH

RIPON (R-H)
Wednesday April 5th (Good to soft, Soft patches)
WEATHER: cloudy WIND: fresh half bhd

533 EUROPEAN BREEDERS FUND SPA WELTER MAIDEN STKS (2-Y.O) (Class D) £4,240.50 (£1,284.00: £627.00: £298.50)
5f Stalls: High GOING: 0.14 sec per fur (G) 2-25 (2-28)

Playmaker *(83+t)*(Fav)*(JBerry)* 2-9-0 JCarroll(10) (leggy: unf: scope: mde all: rdn & r.o wl fnl f) ....— 1
424⁷ Ramsey Hope *(78) (CWFairhurst)* 2-9-0 NKennedy(5) (lw: chsd ldrs: r.o wl u.p fnl f) 1½ 2
424¹⁰ Whittle Rock *(73) (EJAlston)* 2-8-9 KFallon(6) (sn chsng ldrs: kpt on wl u.p appr fnl f) ....s.h 3
Mallia *(78) (TDBarron)* 2-9-0 JFortune(3) (dipped-back: hdwy ½-wy: rn green: kpt on wl fnl f) ....hd 4

4244 Pleasure Time *(70) (CSmith)* 2-9-0 WWoods(16) (a chsng ldrs: nt qckn appr fnl f) 2½ 5
Martara (IRE) *(68) (MRChannon)* 2-9-0 RHughes(13) (cmpt: a.p: hdwy over 1f out: styd on same pce) ....½ 6
Goretski (IRE) *(59) (NTinkler)* 2-9-0 KDarley(14) (w'like: chsd ldrs tl wknd 2f out) 3 7
Margi Boo *(46) (GMMoore)* 2-8-9 JFanning(11) (unf: styd on fnl 2f: nvr nr ldrs) 2½ 8
4243 Don't Forget Mikie (IRE) *(46) (MJHeaton-Ellis)* 2-9-0 StephenDavies(2) (lw: chsd ldrs: hung rt ½-wy: sn wknd) 1½ 9
Oriole *(38) (NTinkler)* 2-9-0 KimTinkler(12) (unf: s.i.s: hung bdly rt thrght: n.d) 2½ 10
Abduction *(33) (EWeymes)* 2-9-0 GHind(4) (w'like: bit bkwd: s.s: a wl outpcd & bhd) 1½ 11
Lucky Bea *(30) (MWEasterby)* 2-9-0 LCharnock(8) (cmpt: bkwd: s.s: a bhd) 1 12
Sharp Monty *(27) (RHollinshead)* 2-9-0 LDettori(9) (leggy: scope: s.i.s: a rr div) 1 13
Euro Express *(19) (MHEasterby)* 2-9-0 MBirch(1) (cmpt: s.i.s: a wl bhd) 2½ 14
Capo Bay (IRE) *(11) (PCHaslam)* 2-9-0 JWeaver(15) (lt-f: sn outpcd) 2½ 15
Hobbs Choice *(MissJFCraze)* 2-8-9 SWebster(7) (neat: bit bkwd: sn wl bhd) 10 16

15/8 PLAYMAKER, **4/1** Martara (IRE) (op 9/4), Don't Forget Mikie (IRE) (op 5/2), **6/1** Sharp Monty, **10/1** Ramsey Hope (op 6/1), Pleasure Time (op 6/1), Capo Bay (IRE), **16/1** Euro Express, Mallia, **20/1** Margi Boo, Whittle Rock, Oriole, Abduction, **25/1** Goretski (IRE), Hobbs Choice, **33/1** Lucky Bea, CSF £27.40 TOTE £3.10: £1.50 £2.90 £3.20 (£38.10) Trio £216.70 OWNER Mr Robert Hughes (COCKERHAM) BRED Mrs V. E. Hughes 16 Rn

62.0 secs (4.00) SF: 42/37/32/37/29/27/18/5/5/-/-/-/-/-/-/-

534

MARKINGTON (S) H'CAP (0-60) (4-Y.O+) (Class F) £2,905.00 (£880.00: £430.00: £205.00)
1m 4f 60y Stalls: High GOING: 0.14 sec per fur (G) 2-55 (2-57)

Merry Mermaid (37)*(47)*(Fav)*(JFBottomley)* 5-8-5 KFallon(5) (hld up: hdwy over 3f out: led over 1f out: r.o wl) ....— 1
1667 Rejects Reply **(35)***(39) (WJMusson)* 5-7-12 (5)ow1 PMcCabe(4) (a.p: outpcd 3f out: styd on wl appr fnl f) 3½ 2
476* Borocay **(43)***(48) (MJCamacho)* 7-8-11 5x LCharnock(14) (chsd ldrs: led over 3f out tl over 1f out: nt pce of wnr) ....½ 3
2885 Arian Spirit (IRE) **(34)***(36) (JLEyre)* 4-8-0 JFanning(11) (chsd ldr: led over 4f out tl over 3f out: one pce) 2 4
2007 Persian Bud (IRE) **(42)***(42) (JRBosley)* 7-8-10 CRutter(10) (a.p: effrt over 3f out: grad wknd) 1¾ 5
4768 Doctor Roy **(34)***(34) (NBycroft)* 7-8-2 FNorton(9) (hdwy over 3f out: kpt on u.p: nt rch ldrs) ....nk 6
4213 Turfmans Vision **(39)***(32) (RHollinshead)* 5-8-7b WRyan(7) (a.p: effrt over 3f out: grad wknd) 5 7
Mac Rambler **(32)***(20) (NBycroft)* 8-8-0 SMaloney(12) (b: effrt over 4f out:kpt on: nvr rchd ldrs) 3½ 8
45011 Noeprob (USA) **(48)***(29) (RJHodges)* 5-8-11 (5) SDrowne(6) (bhd: effrt 4f out: no imp) 6 9
Aljadeer (USA) **(60)***(38) (MWEasterby)* 6-9-7 (7) RuthCoulter(3) (rr div: kpt on fnl 3f: n.d) 2 10
Nuveen (IRE) **(48)***(23) (MrsJJordan)* 4-9-0 ACulhane(17) (dwlt: a bhd) 2½ 11
25511 Venture Fourth **(28)** *(EJAlston)* 6-7-7 (3)ow3 DWright(16) (s.s: a rr div) 2½ 12
4956 Dawn Rock **(47)***(15) (RMMcKellar)* 4-8-13 TWilliams(15) (led tl over 4f out: wknd over 3f out) 2½ 13
Don't Cry **(26)** *(DonEnricoIncisa)* 7-7-8 ow1 KimTinkler(13) (a bhd) 1¼ 14
Demurrer **(45)** *(MrsAMNaughton)* 5-8-13 JWeaver(1) (prom: effrt 4f out: sn wknd) 12 15
Skolern **(25)** *(AHarrison)* 11-7-7v NCarlisle(2) (a bhd) 6 16
12010 Trail of Tears **(27)** *(WWHaigh)* 5-7-9bow2 DaleGibson(8) (plld hrd: trckd ldrs tl lost pl 4f out: sn wl bhd) ....¾ 17

LONG HANDICAP Venture Fourth 7-4

7/2 MERRY MERMAID, **9/2** Borocay, **8/1** Skolern, Arian Spirit (IRE), Dawn Rock (op 12/1), Noeprob (USA), **10/1** Rejects Reply, Persian Bud (IRE), **12/1** Turfmans Vision (op 8/1), Aljadeer (USA), **14/1** Doctor Roy, Mac Rambler, **16/1** Venture Fourth, Demurrer, **20/1** Don't Cry, **25/1** Nuveen (IRE), **33/1** Trail of Tears, CSF £45.65 CT £167.36 TOTE £4.70: £1.40 £4.30 £1.60 £2.00 (£72.50) Trio £183.00 OWNER Mrs O. K. Steele (MALTON) BRED Mrs L. Steele 17 Rn

2m 45.5 (11.50) SF: 27/19/28/14/22/14/12/-/9/18/1/-/-/-/-/-/-

WEIGHT FOR AGE 4yo-2lb

Bt in 5,600 gns

535

FOUNTAINS H'CAP (0-90) (3-Y.O+) (Class C) £5,888.00 (£1,784.00: £872.00: £188.00: £188.00) **6f** Stalls: High GOING: 0.14 sec per fur (G) 3-30 (3-31)

Palacegate Touch (86)*(96) (JBerry)* 5-9-10v JCarroll(20) (lw: racd far side: w ldr: rdn to ld over 1f out: edgd lft: sn clr) ....— 1

398* Saddlehome (USA) **(75)***(76) (TDBarron)* 6-8-13 JFortune(8) (racd stands' side: hld up: effrt & swtchd 2f out: r.o strly fnl f) 3½ **2**
393[2] The Old Chapel **(58)***(55) (BAMcMahon)* 6-7-10b[ow1] FNorton(17) (racd far side: led tl over 1f out: kpt on same pce) 1 **3**
434[2] Sailormaite **(75)***(70)*(Fav)*(SRBowring)* 4-8-13 SWebster(3) (lw: racd stands' side: chsd ldrs: drvn along & outpcd ½-wy: kpt on fnl f) 1¼ **4**
437[13] Tee Tee Too (IRE) **(70)***(65) (PCHaslam)* 3-7-9 DaleGibson(5) (led stands' side tl over 1f out: kpt on same pce) ....d.h **4**
491[9] Pine Ridge Lad (IRE) **(58)***(48) (JLEyre)* 5-7-10 [ow3] JFanning(16) (racd far side: sn drvn along: a.p: kpt on fnl 2f) ....½ **6**
434[12] Bella Parkes **(69)***(59) (DNicholls)* 4-8-7 [ow1] AlexGreaves(18) (racd far side: chsd ldrs tl wknd over 1f out) 1 **7**
Tshusick **(80)***(67) (JRFanshawe)* 4-9-4 DHarrison(2) (b.hind: lw: racd stands' side: in tch: r.o fnl f) 1¼ **8**
Colway Rake **(64)***(45) (JWWatts)* 4-8-2b[ow1] GDuffield(10) (racd centre: hdwy ½-wy: nvr nr ldrs) 2 **9**
434[5] Plum First **(59)***(40) (LRLloyd-James)* 5-7-11 NKennedy(6) (b.hind: racd stands' side: spd to ½-wy: sn wknd) ....nk **10**
Samsolom **(71)***(51) (PHowling)* 7-8-9 KDarley(21) (a mid div) ....½ **11**
Truthful Image **(77)***(56) (RJHodges)* 6-9-1b LDettori(19) (b: racd far side: chsd ldrs over 3f: eased) ....nk **12**
Maid O'Cannie **(70)***(46) (MWEasterby)* 4-8-8b LCharnock(22) (racd far side: hld up & bhd: sme hdwy 2f out) 1¼ **13**
Rankaidade **(58)***(30) (DonEnricoIncisa)* 4-7-10 KimTinkler(23) (lw: racd far side: prom over 3f: sn outpcd) 1¼ **14**
417[4] Desert Invader (IRE) **(72)***(44) (DWChapman)* 4-8-10b DeanMcKeown(15) (racd far side: nvr nr ldrs) ....nk **15**
434[15] Elle Shaped (IRE) **(71)***(43) (DNicholls)* 5-8-9 NConnorton(4) (swtg: racd stands' side: chsd ldrs to ½-wy) ....s.h **16**
Whittle Woods Girl **(77)***(47) (EJAlston)* 4-9-1 JQuinn(9) (racd stands' side: w ldrs tl rdn & wknd over 2f out) ....¾ **17**
Just Bob **(81)***(46) (SEKettlewell)* 6-9-0 (5) JStack(1) (racd stands' side: sn outpcd: n.m.r ½-wy: n.d) 1¾ **18**
Mu-Arrik **(58)***(19) (GROldroyd)* 7-7-10v JLowe(7) (racd stands' side: sn bhd) 1½ **19**
434* Castlerea Lad **(80)***(40) (RHollinshead)* 6-9-4 WRyan(14) (lw: racd towards centre: sn bhd) ....nk **20**
433[20] Braille (IRE) **(70)***(26) (MGMeagher)* 4-8-8 JWeaver(12) (racd centre: spd to ½-wy: sn lost pl) 1½ **21**
Pete Afrique (IRE) **(90)***(33) (MWEasterby)* 4-10-0 MBirch(13) (b: racd far side: in tch to ½-wy: sn wknd) 5 **22**
434[22] Captain Carat **(66)***(6) (MrsJRRamsden)* 4-8-4 [ow1] KFallon(11) (racd far side: prom to ½-wy: sn bhd) ....½ **23**
LONG HANDICAP Pine Ridge Lad (IRE) 7-5

9/2 Sailormaite, **13/2** Saddlehome (USA), **9/1** PALACEGATE TOUCH, **10/1** Tshusick, Castlerea Lad, **12/1** The Old Chapel, Truthful Image, Whittle Woods Girl, Captain Carat, **14/1** Plum First, **20/1** Pete Afrique (IRE), Bella Parkes, Colway Rake, Pine Ridge Lad (IRE), Maid O'Cannie, Just Bob, **25/1** Mu-Arrik, **33/1** Elle Shaped (IRE), Tee Tee Too (IRE), Samsolom, Braille (IRE), Desert Invader (IRE), **50/1** Rankaidade, CSF £69.20 CT £684.02 TOTE £7.70: £2.70 £2.80 £3.30 £1.00 S £9.70 TTT (£40.20) Trio £224.00 OWNER Palacegate Corporation Ltd (COCKERHAM) BRED The Woodhaven Stud 23 Rn
1m 13.9 (3.70) SF: 67/47/26/41/23/19/30/38/16/11/22/27/17/1/15/14/18/17/-/11/-/4/-
WEIGHT FOR AGE 3yo-13lb

536 GALPHAY CONDITIONS STKS (3-Y.O) (Class C) £4,832.00 (£1,808.00: £884.00: £380.00: £170.00: £86.00)
1m 1f Stalls: High GOING: 0.14 sec per fur (G) 4-00 (4-00)

431* **Torrential (USA)** *(96+)*(Fav)*(JHMGosden)* 3-9-2 LDettori(7) (lw: trckd ldrs: chal over 2f out: shkn up to ld wl over 1f out: pushed clr fnl f) ....— **1**
438[2] Heathyards Rock **(93)***(90) (RHollinshead)* 3-9-2 TIves(3) (outpcd & drvn along over 4f out: hdwy 3f out: styd on fnl f: no ch w wnr) 3½ **2**
Dance Band (USA) *(85) (BHanbury)* 3-9-2 WRSwinburn(6) (bit bkwd: led tl wl over 1f out: kpt on same pce) 2½ **3**
Grey Shot *(84) (IABalding)* 3-9-2 RCochrane(4) (lw: hld up: effrt 4f out: hung rt: kpt on: nvr trbld ldrs) ....½ **4**
Lancer (USA) *(84) (MBell)* 3-9-2 MFenton(1) (hld up: hdwy on outside 4f out: effrt & edgd rt u.p over 2f out: grad wknd) ....nk **5**

Manful **(88)***(78) (JHetherton)* 3-9-2 NKennedy(2) (bhd & drvn along 5f out: n.d) 3½ 6
Captain's Day **(96)***(67) (TGMills)* 3-9-4 JWeaver(5) (lw: w ldrs: reminders over 4f out: wknd over 2f out: eased) 7 7

4/7 TORRENTIAL (USA), **6/1** Heathyards Rock, **7/1** Dance Band (USA), Grey Shot, **8/1** Lancer (USA), **14/1** Captain's Day, **33/1** Manful, CSF £5.38 TOTE £1.40: £1.10 £2.60 (£3.50) OWNER Sheikh Mohammed (NEWMARKET) BRED Peter M. Brant 7 Rn

1m 56.5 (6.30) SF: 55/49/44/43/43/37/26

537 STUDLEY ROYAL H'CAP (0-70) (3-Y.O) (Class E) £3,017.40 (£913.20: £445.60: £211.80) 1m 4f 60y Stalls: Low GOING: 0.14 sec per fur (G) 4-30 (4-31)

Executive Design (70)*(77+) (MrsMReveley)* 3-9-7 KDarley(5) (h.d.w: unruly s: trckd ldrs: smooth hdwy to ld on bit over 3f out: shkn up 1f out: easily) ....— 1
427² Contrafire (IRE) **(64)***(69)*(Fav)*(WJarvis)* 3-9-1 MTebbutt(4) (lw: trckd ldr: eff & ev ch over 3f out: kpt on u.p fnl f) 1¾ 2
376³ Beau Matelot **(60)***(58) (JDBethell)* 3-8-11 JWeaver(3) (led tl over 3f out: wl outpcd fnl 2f) 5 3
453⁹ Maysann **(65)***(57) (JLDunlop)* 3-9-2 WCarson(1) (effrt over 4f out: kpt on fnl 2f: nvr nr to chal) 5 4
427¹² Elpidos **(69)***(60) (CEBrittain)* 3-9-6b MRimmer(7) (hld up: effrt & hung rt 4f out: nvr nr to chal) ....nk 5
Coneygree **(44)***(29) (JWharton)* 3-7-9 ow2 JQuinn(6) (bit bkwd: effrt over 4f out: sn wl outpcd) 3 6
Sedvicta **(57)***(12) (MrsMReveley)* 3-8-8 JFortune(2) (s.s: a wl bhd) 25 7

LONG HANDICAP Coneygree 7-6

Evens Contrafire (IRE), **4/1** Elpidos (op 7/1), **6/1** EXECUTIVE DESIGN (9/2-7/1), **9/1** Beau Matelot (op 6/1), Maysann (op 6/1), **16/1** Sedvicta, **25/1** Coneygree, CSF £12.08 TOTE £7.40: £2.30 £1.40 (£4.60) OWNER Mr W. H. Strawson (SALTBURN) BRED L. T. and M. Foster 7 Rn

2m 46.7 (12.70) SF: 34/26/15/14/17/-/-

538 SAWLEY H'CAP (0-70) (3-Y.O) (Class E) £3,203.30 (£970.40: £474.20: £226.10) 1m 2f Stalls: Low GOING: 0.14 sec per fur (G) 5-00 (5-05)

Silently (70)*(76+) (IABalding)* 3-9-7 LDettori(14) (trckd ldrs: nt clr run 3f out: swtchd outside: qcknd to ld over 1f out: went rt: drvn out) ....— 1
411⁷ Our Tom **(58)***(61) (JWharton)* 3-8-9 JQuinn(10) (trckd ldrs: nt clr run over 2f out: styng on u.p fnl f: nt rch wnr) 2 2
448³ Toy Princess (USA) **(69)***(71) (CEBrittain)* 3-9-6 MRimmer(5) (mde most tl over 2f out: one pce appr fnl f) ....¾ 3
427¹³ Chaldon Herring **(63)***(63) (TDBarron)* 3-9-0 JFortune(6) (hld up: gd hdwy on ins over 3f out: nt qckn over 1f out) 1¼ 4
453⁶ Poly Road **(50)***(49) (MRChannon)* 3-7-10 (5) PPMurphy(11) (mid div: effrt on outside 3f out: styd on appr fnl f) ....hd 5
Tessajoe **(54)***(53) (MJCamacho)* 3-8-5 LCharnock(15) (stdd s: hld up & bhd: hdwy & nt clr run over 2f out: kpt on wl fnl f) ....hd 6
On a Pedestal (IRE) **(53)***(46) (MrsJRRamsden)* 3-8-4 ow1 KFallon(8) (hld up: effrt & nt clr run over 2f out: kpt on fnl f: nvr rch ldrs) 3½ 7
Hong Kong Designer **(55)***(48) (SGNorton)* 3-8-3 (3) JTate(3) (bhd tl kpt on fnl 2f: n.d) ....nk 8
Grate British (IRE) **(65)***(54) (EWeymes)* 3-9-2 GHind(1) (hdwy & prom 7f out: slight ld over 2f out: hdd & wknd over 1f out) 2½ 9
437³ Mr Frosty **(67)***(55)*(Fav)*(WJarvis)* 3-9-4 JWeaver(12) (lw: chsd ldrs: wkng whn slightly hmpd over 2f out) ....¾ 10
Green Land (BEL) **(62)***(49) (SCWilliams)* 3-8-10 (3) DWright(2) (lw: b: rr div: effrt over 4f out: sn lost pl) ....¾ 11
301⁴ Nigel's Lad (IRE) **(70)***(54) (PCHaslam)* 3-9-7 MTebbutt(4) (hld up: nt clr run fr 3f out: nt rcvr) 1½ 12
437¹¹ Flyaway Blues **(65)***(49) (MrsMReveley)* 3-9-2 KDarley(13) (a in rr: drvn along 3f out: n.d) ....½ 13
Euro Sceptic (IRE) **(45)***(23) (MHEasterby)* 3-7-10bow1 JFanning(9) (sn chsng ldrs: lost pl over 3f out) 3 14
Labibeh (USA) **(70)** *(JLDunlop)* 3-9-7 WCarson(7) (Withdrawn not under Starter's orders: unruly & ref to ent stalls) .... W

, **11/2** Mr Frosty, **13/2** On a Pedestal (IRE), **7/1** SILENTLY, Toy Princess (USA), **11/1** Nigel's Lad (IRE), **12/1** Flyaway Blues, Our Tom, Grate British (IRE), Chaldon Herring, **20/1** Green Land (BEL), Euro Sceptic (IRE), **25/1** Poly Road, Hong Kong Designer, **33/1** Tessajoe, CSF £64.30 CT £355.28 TOTE £6.80: £3.20 £2.10 £2.10 (£52.00) Trio £52.50 OWNER Mr Paul Mellon (KINGSCLERE) BRED Paul Mellon 14 Rn 2m 13.6 (10.10) SF: 35/20/30/22/8/12/5/7/13/14/8/13/8/-/-

539 GRANTLEY MAIDEN STKS (3-Y.O+) (Class D) £4,056.95 (£1,229.60: £601.30: £287.15) **1m** Stalls: High GOING: 0.14 sec per fur (G) 5-30 (5-35)

Lucky Di (USA) *(98)*(Fav)*(LMCumani)* 3-8-12 JWeaver(15) (w'like: unf: lw: led 1f: led over 3f out: styd on strly fnl f: pushed out) — 1
Amanah (USA) *(92)* *(JHMGosden)* 3-8-7 WCarson(18) (b.hind: chsd ldrs: styd on wl u.p) ½ 2
Bernard Seven (IRE) *(81)* *(SPCWoods)* 3-8-12 WWoods(1) (unruly s: gd hdwy over 3f out: kpt on fnl 2f) 8 3
Samsonesque *(62)* *(JRFanshawe)* 4-9-9 DHarrison(17) (chsd ldrs: drvn along over 3f out: kpt on fnl 2f) 7 4
Tregaron (USA) *(67)* *(PCalver)* 4-10-0 MBirch(4) (hld up: stdy hdwy over 3f out: kpt on wl fnl f: nvr plcd to chal) s.h 5
Safey Ana (USA) **(72)***(64)* *(BHanbury)* 4-10-0 WRyan(11) (b: a in tch: kpt on one pce fnl 3f) 1¼ 6
Zaralaska *(64)* *(LMCumani)* 4-9-11 (3) CHodgson(13) (sn bhd: stdy hdwy 3f out: nvr plcd to chal) hd 7
Kaf *(54)* *(JLDunlop)* 3-8-12 GDuffield(6) (mid div: hdwy u.p on ins over 3f out: sn wknd) 5 8
Final Fling *(49)* *(JWWatts)* 3-8-7 NConnorton(3) (bhd: swtchd ins over 2f out: kpt on: nvr nr ldrs) s.h 9
Never So Fit *(52)* *(RBastiman)* 4-9-9b(5) HBastiman(16) (w'like: plld hrd: led after 1f: sn clr: hdd over 3f out: sn wknd) 1¼ 10
442[18] Bollin Sophie *(39)* *(MHEasterby)* 3-8-7 SMaloney(8) (a in rr) 4 11
Cross Talk (IRE) *(37)* *(RHollinshead)* 3-8-12 TIves(12) (w'like: a in rr) 3½ 12
Operatic Dancer *(33)* *(RMMcKellar)* 4-10-0 TWilliams(14) (chsd ldrs tl rdn & wknd 3f out) 2 13
Anastina *(27)* *(JHMGosden)* 3-8-7 LDettori(2) (w'like: swrvd lft s: a rr div) hd 14
Brother Barnabas *(31)* *(CWThornton)* 4-10-0 DeanMcKeown(7) (s.i.s: a bhd) ½ 15
Hutchies Lady *(8)* *(RMMcKellar)* 3-8-4 (7)ow4 NKinnon(5) (lt-f: bhd & rn wd ent str) 9 16
435[9] Mr Personality *(1)* *(MrsMReveley)* 3-8-12 KDarley(10) (bhd & plld hrd: hung bdly lft 3f out: nt r.o) 6 17
Crucis (IRE) *(BAMcMahon)* 4-10-0 MWigham(9) (s.i.s: a wl bhd: t.o) dist 18

13/8 LUCKY DI (USA) (9/4-6/4), **9/4** Amanah (USA) (11/8-5/2), **6/1** Anastina (op 4/1), **13/2** Bernard Seven (IRE), **16/1** Zaralaska, Kaf, **20/1** Safey Ana (USA), Samsonesque, Final Fling, Tregaron (USA), **33/1** Mr Personality, **50/1** Brother Barnabas, Crucis (IRE), Bollin Sophie, Cross Talk (IRE), **100/1** Never So Fit, Hutchies Lady, Operatic Dancer, CSF £6.40 TOTE £2.80: £1.40 £1.60 £2.00 (£3.00) Trio £6.50 OWNER Mrs Virginia Knott Bender (NEWMARKET) BRED Mrs Virginia K. Bender
18 Rn 1m 42.5 (4.80) SF: 59/53/42/39/44/41/41/15/10/29/-/-/10/-/8/-/-/-
WEIGHT FOR AGE 3yo-16lb

T/Jkpt: £42,274.10 (1.09 Tckts). T/Plpt: £26.20 (831.59 Tckts). T/Qdpt: £12.60 (8.8 Tckts). WG

BRIGHTON (L-H)
Thursday April 6th (Good, Good to firm patches)
WEATHER: overcast WIND: almost nil.

540 EUROPEAN BREEDERS FUND SOUTHWICK MEDIAN AUCTION MAIDEN STKS (2-Y.O) (Class F) £2,820.00 (£840.00: £400.00: £180.00) **5f 59y** Stalls: Low GOING minus 0.61 sec per fur (F) 2-15 (2-16)

General Rose *(55t)* *(RHannon)* 2-9-0 RPerham(2) (neat: 3rd st: nt clr run & swtchd rt over 1f out: led wl ins fnl f: rdn out) — 1
474[3] Arvzees (IRE) *(54)* *(MRChannon)* 2-9-0 RHughes(1) (4th st: chsd ldr over 2f out: shkn up to ld ins fnl f: sn hdd: r.o) nk 2
490[2] Miss Offset *(39)*(Fav)*(MJohnston)* 2-8-9 TWilliams(3) (2nd st: rdn 3f out: swtchd rt over 2f out: unable qckn) 3½ 3
Bath Knight *(42)* *(DJSffrenchDavis)* 2-9-0 NAdams(4) (b.hind: wl grwn: bkwd: led tl ins fnl f: one pce) ½ 4
455[4] Deaken Dancer *(37)* *(KTIvory)* 2-8-2 (7) CScally(5) (5th st: hrd rdn over 2f out: one pce) hd 5

5/4 Miss Offset, **11/4** GENERAL ROSE, Arvzees (IRE) (op 13/8), **16/1** Deaken Dancer, **33/1** Bath Knight, CSF £9.48 TOTE £3.90: £2.00 £1.10 (£6.60) OWNER Mr D. B. Gallop (MARLBOROUGH) BRED P. Balding 5 Rn 63.3 secs (3.30) SF: -/-/-/-/-

541 ELM GROVE CLAIMING STKS (4-Y.O+) (Class F) £2,519.00(£694.00: £329.00)
5f 213y Stalls: Low GOING minus 0.61 sec per fur (F) 2-45 (2-46)

Shikari's Son (87)*(73)*(Fav)*(JWhite)* 8-9-7 RHughes(14) (hdwy over 2f out: led ins fnl f: pushed out) — 1
*447*3 Apollo Red **(49)***(58) (AMoore)* 6-8-7 CandyMorris(9) (swtg: 2nd st: led wl over 1f out tl ins fnl f: r.o) nk 2
*501*8 Waverley Star **(40)***(50) (KOCunningham-Brown)* 10-8-3 WWoods(10) (lost pl over 4f out: rallied over 1f out: r.o) 1¾ 3
Billy Cruncheon **(60)***(53) (MCPipe)* 4-8-7 AMcGlone(15) (5th st: ev ch over 1f out: unable qckn) nk 4
*408*4 Dahiyah (USA) *(52) (GLMoore)* 4-8-0v(7) CTeague(2) (lw: 4th st: hrd rdn over 1f out: one pce) nk 5
*501*3 Pair of Jacks (IRE) **(34)***(46) (DAWilson)* 5-8-1 JQuinn(4) (lw: 6th st: one pce fnl 2f) hd 6
*419*8 Farmer Jock *(48) (MrsNMacauley)* 13-8-7 AClark(8) (b: hmpd over 3f out: nt clr run over 1f out: nvr nr to chal) 1¼ 7
*510*3 Tyrian Purple (IRE) **(60)***(45) (TJNaughton)* 7-8-7b JWeaver(6) (b: b.hind: lw: led over 4f: wknd fnl f) 1¼ 8
Starsport (IRE) **(56)***(38) (DJSffrenchDavis)* 4-7-12b(7) RWaterfield(3) (bit bkwd: no hdwy fnl 2f) 1¾ 9
*499*6 Splash of Salt (IRE) **(57)***(34) (TJNaughton)* 5-7-13b(3) SSanders(12) (3rd st: wknd wl over 1f out) ½ 10
*71*12 Victoria Princess *(28) (MMadgwick)* 8-8-0 TWilliams(13) (a bhd) 1½ 11
*390*6 Crafty Cricketer **(34)***(28) (RMFlower)* 4-7-8b(7) SLanigan(7) (swtg: s.s: hdwy 3f out: wknd 2f out) nk 12
Grecian Garden **(29)***(14) (RCSpicer)* 4-7-7 (3) DWright(1) (a bhd) 3½ 13
Amber Nectar **(40)***(12) (BAPearce)* 9-8-5 StephenDavies(11) (b: bit bkwd: a bhd) 4 14
*404*10 Flutter With Life **(30)** *(MrsAEJermy)* 4-7-12 NAdams(5) (a bhd) 15 15

7/4 SHIKARI'S SON, **7/2** Tyrian Purple (IRE), **15/2** Dahiyah (USA), **12/1** Pair of Jacks (IRE), Billy Cruncheon, **14/1** Apollo Red, **20/1** Splash of Salt (IRE), Farmer Jock, Starsport (IRE), **33/1** Amber Nectar, Crafty Cricketer, **40/1** Waverley Star, **50/1** Grecian Garden, Victoria Princess, Flutter With Life, CSF £24.99 TOTE £2.20: £1.90 £2.20 £11.30 (£16.40) Trio £178.80 OWNER Mr Alan Spargo (WENDOVER) BRED W. H. Joyce 15 Rn 69.4 secs (1.00) SF: 38/23/15/18/17/11/13/10/3/-/-/-/-/-/-

542 BRIGHTON SPRING H'CAP (0-80) (3-Y.O+) (Class D) £3,732.30 (£1,112.40: £530.20: £239.10) **5f 213y** Stalls: Low GOING minus 0.61 sec (F) 3-20 (3-21)

Golden Lady (IRE) (75)*(83) (RHannon)* 3-8-11 WCarson(8) (led 1f: 2nd st: swtchd rt 2f out: led 1f out: edgd lft: rdn out) — 1
*499** Chewit **(80)***(85) (AMoore)* 3-9-2 7x CandyMorris(4) (6th st: swtchd lft over 1f out: ev ch ins fnl f: unable qckn) 1¼ 2
Paddy's Rice **(49)***(53) (LJHolt)* 4-7-5 (7) IonaWands(5) (swtg: hdwy 2f out: r.o wl ins fnl f) ¾ 3
*511** Another Jade **(64)***(64)*(Fav)*(APJarvis)* 5-8-13 7x JWeaver(7) (hdwy over 1f out: r.o) 1¼ 4
*447*7 Aragrove **(52)***(50) (JWPayne)* 5-7-12b(3) DWright(2) (led 5f out to 1f out: 3rd & btn whn hmpd ins fnl f) ¾ 5
434 11 Champagne Grandy **(75)***(65) (MRChannon)* 5-9-10 RHughes(6) (lw: nvr nr to chal) 3 6
La Petite Fusee **(62)***(49) (RJO'Sullivan)* 4-8-11 AClark(9) (b: b.hind: 3rd st: wknd over 1f out) 1¼ 7
*446*4 Speedy Classic (USA) **(62)***(45) (MJHeaton-Ellis)* 6-8-11 WWoods(3) (5th st: wknd over 1f out) 1½ 8
*447** Maid Welcome **(56)***(28) (MrsNMacauley)* 8-7-12v(7) AmandaSanders(1) (4th st: wknd over 2f out) 4 9

7/2 Another Jade, **4/1** Chewit, **5/1** Speedy Classic (USA), GOLDEN LADY (IRE), **9/1** Aragrove, Champagne Grandy, Maid Welcome (op 5/1), **16/1** La Petite Fusee, **25/1** Paddy's Rice, CSF £23.51 CT £408.82 TOTE £4.00: £1.60 £2.00 £6.60 (£10.90) Trio £205.30 OWNER Prince Fahd Salman (MARLBOROUGH) BRED Newgate Stud Co 9 Rn 1m 8.9 (0.50) SF: 35/37/17/28/14/29/13/9/-
WEIGHT FOR AGE 3yo-13lb

OFFICIAL EXPLANATION **Another Jade: the jockey reported that he had broken well, steadied the horse as ordered, but could not hold his position in the early stages of the race.**

543 HOLLINGBURY CONDITIONS STKS (3-Y.O) (Class D) £4,002.70 (£1,195.60: £571.80: £259.90)
6f 209y Stalls: Low GOING minus 0.61 sec per fur (F) 3-55 (3-57)

Sergeyev (IRE) (90)*(85)*(Fav)*(RHannon)* 3-9-2 RHughes(6) (lw: stdd s: a gng wl: hdwy over 4f out: 4th st: shkn up to ld 1f out: easily) — 1

Emerging Market *(80) (JLDunlop)* 3-9-4 WCarson(8) (lw: led over 1f: 2nd st: led over 2f out to 1f out: unable qckn) 3 **2**
Willie Conquer *(74) (RAkehurst)* 3-8-12 AClark(5) (bit bkwd: hdwy 4f out: 6th st: ev ch over 1f out: one pce) ....s.h **3**
442[2] Forzair **(74)***(71) (MMcCormack)* 3-8-12 JWeaver(7) (3rd st: ev ch over 1f out: one pce) 1¼ **4**
Easy Dollar *(55) (BGubby)* 3-8-12b JQuinn(4) (bkwd: led over 5f out to over 2f out: ev ch over 1f out: sn wknd) 7 **5**
Ballestro (IRE) **(40)***(41) (JFfitch-Heyes)* 3-8-12 DBiggs(2) (bhd fnl 3f) 6 **6**
R Dragon *(27) (MMadgwick)* 3-8-7 TWilliams(9) (lw: a bhd) 4 **7**
Dissentor (IRE) *(28) (LMCumani)* 3-8-5 (7) GMitchell(1) (bit bkwd: bhd fnl 4f) 1¾ **8**
473[6] False Pretences (IRE) **(35)***(28) (BAPearce)* 3-8-12 StephenDavies(3) (5th st: wknd over 2f out) ....s.h **9**

7/4 SERGEYEV (IRE), **9/4** Forzair, **5/1** Emerging Market (op 5/2), **10/1** Willie Conquer, **12/1** Dissentor (IRE), **20/1** Easy Dollar, **66/1** Ballestro (IRE), R Dragon, False Pretences (IRE), CSF £9.73 TOTE £2.90: £1.10 £1.60 £1.50 (£3.80) Trio £22.60 OWNER Mr B. T. Stewart-Brown (MARLBOROUGH) BRED Hugo Merry and Michael Stanley 9 Rn 1m 21.1 (1.10) SF: 34/29/23/20/4/-/-/-/-

544 VARDEAN MEDIAN AUCTION MAIDEN STKS (3-Y.O) (Class E)

£3,216.40 (£959.20: £457.60: £206.80)
1m 1f 209y Stalls: Low GOING minus 0.61 sec per fur (F) 4-30 (4-31)

Raased *(77) (JLDunlop)* 3-9-0 WCarson(7) (lw: mde virtually all: clr over 1f out: easily) ....— **1**
264[6] Yet Again *(56) (BHanbury)* 3-9-0 JQuinn(3) (bit bkwd: mod 4th st: rdn over 3f out: r.o one pce fnl 2f) 13 **2**
Jumairah Sun (IRE) *(49)*(Fav)*(LMCumani)* 3-8-9 JWeaver(9) (w wnr: rdn over 3f out: wknd over 1f out) 1½ **3**
Shanuke (IRE) **(54)***(42) (JSMoore)* 3-8-9 AClark(8) (mod 6th st: nvr nr to chal) 4 **4**
Share the Secret **(50)***(47) (BHanbury)* 3-9-0 WWoods(6) (mod 5th st: rdn over 3f out: one pce) ....nk **5**
286[4] Kings of Canvey Is *(34) (JWhite)* 3-8-4 (5) SDrowne(1) (mod 3rd st: wknd over 2f out) 5 **6**
Elmer's Tune *(32) (RHannon)* 3-9-0 RHughes(2) (bkwd: bhd fnl 5f) 4 **7**
Paddy's Storm *(16) (RMFlower)* 3-8-9 (5) JDSmith(4) (w'like: bit bkwd: s.s: a bhd) 10 **8**

1/2 Jumairah Sun (IRE), **9/4** RAASED, **25/1** Yet Again, **33/1** Share the Secret, **40/1** Shanuke (IRE), Kings of Canvey Is, Elmer's Tune, **66/1** Paddy's Storm, CSF £42.06 TOTE £3.30: £1.10 £2.20 £1.00 (£20.60) Trio £2.90 OWNER Mr Hamdan Al Maktoum (ARUNDEL) BRED Shadwell Estate Company Limited 8 Rn 2m 1.5 (3.50) SF: 19/-/-/-/-/-/-/-

545 SHEEPCOTE VALLEY H'CAP (0-60) (3-Y.O+) (Class F) £3,199.40 (£888.40:

£426.20) **1m 3f 196y** Stalls: High GOING minus 0.61 sec per fur (F) 5-00 (5-02)

430[17] **Credit Squeeze (59)***(74) (RFJohnsonHoughton)* 5-9-13 JQuinn(17) (lw: stdy hdwy over 4f out: led over 1f out: r.o wl) ....— **1**
320[10] Mr Browning (USA) **(51)***(58)*(Fav)*(RAkehurst)* 4-9-3 AClark(14) (4th st: led over 2f out tl over 1f out: unable qckn) 5 **2**
422[3] Hattaafeh (IRE) **(57)***(60) (MAJarvis)* 4-9-9 WWoods(16) (lw: 3rd st: ev ch over 1f out: wknd fnl f) 3 **3**
*370** Head Turner **(48)***(52) (CPWildman)* 7-9-2 StephenDavies(6) (hdwy over 1f out: r.o ins fnl f) ..nk **4**
403[6] Beautete **(60)***(61) (SDow)* 4-9-12 GHind(18) (lw: hdwy 6f out: 6th st: one pce fnl 2f) 1¾ **5**
406[6] Lady Reema **(45)***(43) (MissAJWhitfield)* 4-8-6 (5) RPainter(2) (nvr nr to chal) 1¾ **6**
Mirador **(49)***(47) (RCurtis)* 4-8-12 (3) DWright(5) (2nd st: hrd rdn over 3f out: wknd over 1f out) ....s.h **7**
414[10] Homemaker **(40)***(24) (PGMurphy)* 5-8-1 (7) RWaterfield(4) (a mid div) 11 **8**
Granby Bell **(53)***(34) (PHayward)* 4-8-12 (7) MarkDenaro(15) (a mid div) 1½ **9**
Ivanhoe **(40)***(15) (JRArnold)* 4-8-6 BRouse(8) (a mid div) 5 **10**
438[10] Mega Tid **(60)***(31) (BAPearce)* 3-8-3 (3) SSanders(3) (5th st: rdn over 3f out: eased whn btn over 1f out) 2½ **11**
Rosscoyne **(39)***(9) (JFfitch-Heyes)* 5-8-7 DBiggs(13) (a bhd) 1¾ **12**
454[6] Grand Salt (IRE) **(53)***(15) (MJHaynes)* 4-9-5 WCarson(7) (lw: bhd fnl 5f) 5 **13**
329[9] Dragonmist (IRE) **(34)** *(MMadgwick)* 5-8-2v NAdams(12) (lw: bhd fnl 6f) ....s.h **14**
Hillswick **(53)***(10) (JSKing)* 4-9-5 RHughes(9) (prom over 6f) 3½ **15**
346[11] Ragtime Song **(36)** *(AMoore)* 6-8-4 TWilliams(11) (lw: prom over 7f) 6 **16**
454[12] Able Choice (IRE) **(58)***(6) (RWArmstrong)* 5-9-12 JWeaver(10) (led over 9f) 1½ **17**

7/4 Mr Browning (USA) (op 3/1), **4/1** Mega Tid (10/1-16/1), **5/1** Head Turner, **7/1** Granby Bell, **8/1** Beautete, **12/1** Hattaafeh (IRE), Able Choice (IRE) (8/1-14/1), CREDIT SQUEEZE (op 8/1), **14/1** Mirador, **16/1** Grand Salt (IRE), **20/1** Lady Reema, Homemaker, **33/1** Ivanhoe, Dragonmist (IRE), Hillswick, Ragtime Song, Rosscoyne, CSF £38.54 CT £275.10 TOTE £24.90: £4.20 £1.20 £1.30 £3.20 (£32.10) Trio £70.40 OWNER Mr R. C. Naylor (DIDCOT) BRED Home Stud Ltd 17 Rn

2m 29.9 (0.90) SF: 56/39/41/34/42/24/28/6/15/-/-/-/-/-/-/-/-

WEIGHT FOR AGE 3yo-22lb, 4yo-2lb

OFFICIAL EXPLANATION **Mega Tid: the jockey reported that the horse had run well through the race, but he lost his action at the two-furlong marker and so thought it best not to exert any pressure, when he noticeably eased him down. The trainer confirmed that the horse has a bad action.**

546

CHURCHILL SQUARE H'CAP (0-70) (3-Y.O+) (Class E) £3,588.20 (£1,073.60: £514.80: £235.40)
7f 214y Stalls: Low GOING minus 0.61 sec per fur (F) 5-30 (5-32)

487a[4] **Confronter (63)***(78) (SDow)* 6-9-12 RHughes(3) (5th st: led 2f out: hrd rdn: r.o wl)........— **1**
450[2] Just Harry **(60)***(74) (MJRyan)* 4-9-9 AClark(13) (lw: 7th st: ev ch ins fnl f: unable qckn)........¾ **2**
Runic Symbol **(42)***(49) (MBlanshard)* 4-8-5 StephenDavies(1) (hdwy wl over 1f out: one pce)........3½ **3**
406[3] Kintwyn **(42)***(45)*(Fav)*(CCElsey)* 5-8-5 ow2 JWeaver(5) (hdwy over 1f out: r.o)........¾ **4**
Old Swinford (IRE) **(66)***(70) (BJMeehan)* 3-8-13 SWhitworth(15) (3rd st: ev ch 2f out: wknd over 1f out)........hd **5**
344[4] Canary Falcon **(65)***(68) (RJO'Sullivan)* 4-10-0 WWoods(4) (b: lw: 6th st: one pce fnl 3f)........¾ **6**
Pistol (IRE) **(61)***(61) (CAHorgan)* 5-9-10 PWaldron(8) (b.hind: nvr nr to chal)........1½ **7**
355[6] My Lifetime Lady (IRE) **(44)***(41) (KTIvory)* 4-8-0 (7)ow2 CScally(7) (bhd: nvr nrr)........¾ **8**
50[3] Oozlem (IRE) **(42)***(39) (RMFlower)* 6-8-0b(5) JDSmith(14) (bit bkwd: dwlt: hdwy over 4f out: 4th st: wknd 2f out)........¾ **9**
450[13] Dia Georgy **(57)***(48) (RGuest)* 4-9-6 GHind(9) (a.p: led over 4f out to 2f out: sn wknd)........3 **10**
Jobber's Fiddle **(60)***(42) (DJSffrenchDavis)* 3-8-7 NAdams(10) (bhd fnl 3f)........4 **11**
446[9] Assignment **(54)***(37) (JFfitch-Heyes)* 9-9-3 DBiggs(11) (bhd fnl 3f)........hd **12**
202[7] Forbidden Gem **(35)***(11) (SWoodman)* 4-7-12 TWilliams(2) (s.s: a bhd)........3½ **13**
418[9] Ever Friends **(49)***(21) (BJMcMath)* 3-7-7 (3) DWright(6) (lw: a bhd)........1¾ **14**
Dalcross **(50)** *(HJCollingridge)* 4-8-13 JQuinn(12) (led over 3f: 2nd st: wknd over 2f out)........12 **15**

5/2 Kintwyn, **100/30** Old Swinford (IRE), **5/1** Just Harry, **6/1** CONFRONTER, **10/1** Oozlem (IRE), **14/1** Dia Georgy, Pistol (IRE), Canary Falcon (op 6/1), **16/1** Ever Friends, **20/1** Runic Symbol, Jobber's Fiddle, **25/1** Forbidden Gem, **33/1** Assignment, My Lifetime Lady (IRE), Dalcross, CSF £38.66 CT £543.55 TOTE £6.60: £2.00 £1.90 £4.30 (£22.00) Trio £69.90 OWNER Hatfield Ltd (EPSOM) BRED Hamilton Bloodstock (UK) Ltd 15 Rn

1m 34.2 (2.00) SF: 36/32/7/3/13/26/19/-/-/6/-/-/-/-/-

WEIGHT FOR AGE 3yo-16lb

T/Plpt: £61.90 (141.59 Tckts). T/Qdpt: £6.20 (12.4 Tckts) AK

0480-LEICESTER (R-H)
Thursday April 6th (Good.)
WEATHER: sunny WIND: slt bhd

547

KEYTHORPE MAIDEN STKS (3-Y.O F) (Class D) £4,036.50 (£1,206.00: £577.00: £262.50)
7f 9y Stalls: Low GOING: 0.07 sec per fur (G) 2-25 (2-27)

Cask *(86) (JHMGosden)* 3-8-11 LDettori(12) (w'like: scope: chsd ldrs: led 3f out: sn hdd: r.o to ld again nr fin)........— **1**
A la Carte (IRE) *(85)*(Fav)*(JLDunlop)* 3-8-11 PatEddery(10) (trckd ldrs: led over 2f out: rdn & no ex nr fin)........nk **2**
Cap And Gown (IRE) *(85) (PFICole)* 3-8-11 TQuinn(7) (lengthy: unf: prom: rdn over 1f out: kpt on wl ins fnl f)........nk **3**
Russian Maid *(83) (JRFanshawe)* 3-8-11 DHarrison(5) (leggy: unf: bkwd: b.hind: bhd: hdwy 2f out: kpt on fnl f)........¾ **4**
Self Reliance *(76) (MBell)* 3-8-11 MFenton(3) (lt-f: unf: bhd tl r.o fnl 2f)........3 **5**
Anita's Contessa (IRE) *(73) (BPalling)* 3-8-11 TSprake(8) (lt-f: plld hrd: led 4f: no ex fnl f)........1½ **6**

431[4] Christmas Kiss **(85)***(73) (RHannon)* 3-8-11 WRSwinburn(6) (plld hard: trckd ldrs: rdn over 2f out: eased whn btn) ....hd 7
316[10] Rookery Girl *(67) (DMorris)* 3-8-8 (3) CHodgson(11) (nvr trbld ldrs) 2½ 8
435[10] Corrievarkie *(63) (MissGayKelleway)* 3-8-11 RCochrane(1) (plld hard: prom tl rdn over 2f out: sn wknd) 1½ 9
443[3] Fairelaine *(57) (APJarvis)* 3-8-11 BThomson(4) (bhd fnl 3f) 3 10
Carnbrea Belle (IRE) *(56) (MBell)* 3-8-4 (7) RMullen(2) (bit bkwd: w ldr 4f) ....nk 11
Hard Love **(73)***(53) (SPCWoods)* 3-8-4 (7) CWebb(9) (plld hard: bhd fnl 3f) 1½ 12

4/5 A la Carte (IRE) (op 6/4), **7/2** Christmas Kiss (2/1-4/1), **7/1** CASK (op 5/2), **14/1** Cap And Gown (IRE) (5/1-20/1), **16/1** Russian Maid, **20/1** Self Reliance, Hard Love, **25/1** Corrievarkie, Fairelaine, **33/1** Rookery Girl, Anita's Contessa (IRE), **50/1** Carnbrea Belle (IRE), CSF £13.22 TOTE £3.00: £1.90 £1.90 £2.70 (£2.60) Trio £14.40 OWNER Lord Hartington (NEWMARKET) 12 Rn
1m 28.3 (5.80) SF: 32/31/31/29/22/19/19/13/9/3/2/-

548 BILLESDON (S) STKS (3-Y.O+) (Class G) £2,892.60 (£803.60: £385.80) **7f 9y** Stalls: Low GOING: 0.07 sec per fur (G) 2-55 (2-56)

379[5] **Roseate Lodge (56)***(68) (KRBurke)* 9-9-7 TIves(2) (hld up: n.m.r over 2f out: strng run appr fnl f: led wl ins fnl f) ....— 1
187[5] Beware of Agents **(70)***(65) (MDHammond)* 6-9-7 DeanMcKeown(15) (hdwy over 3f out: led 2f out: sn clr: nt qckn & caught wl ins fnl f) 1½ 2
Nakita **(60)***(58) (CNAllen)* 4-8-11 (5) MBaird(1) (bhd: gd hdwy over 1f out: r.o fnl f) ....¾ 3
410[2] Sea Devil **(63)***(63) (MJCamacho)* 9-9-12 LCharnock(14) (held up: hdwy over 2f out: no ex appr fnl f) 2 4
Code of Silence **(43)***(58) (BPalling)* 3-8-6v TSprake(4) (led: sn clr: hdd 2f out: sn btn) ....s.h 5
482[2] Dowdency **(44)***(54)*(Fav)*(JAPickering)* 3-8-6 NCarlisle(5) (in tch: rdn 2f out: no imp) 2 6
Nabjelsedr *(51) (AGNewcombe)* 5-9-2 (5) DGriffiths(12) (chsd ldrs: no hdwy fnl 2f) 1¼ 7
402[9] Rosina's Folly **(55)***(45) (JLHarris)* 4-9-2 PaulEddery(7) (trckd ldrs: ev ch over 2f out: eased whn btn ins fnl f) ....nk 8
Export Mondial *(41) (PBurgoyne)* 5-9-7 TQuinn(8) (rdn 3f out: nvr trbld ldrs) 4 9
Infantry Glen *(37) (PDCundell)* 5-9-7 WNewnes(16) (prom 4f) 2 10
450[8] Bold Mick **(60)***(35) (DJGMurraySmith)* 4-9-7 LDettori(13) (sn pushed along: in tch 5f) ....¾ 11
417[8] Bold Aristocrat (IRE) **(47)***(35) (RHollinshead)* 4-9-2 (5) AGarth(11) (n.d) ....hd 12
423[18] Wadada **(40)***(30) (SWCampion)* 4-9-7b WRSwinburn(6) (prom 4f) 2 13
Glen Miller **(43)***(27) (JWPayne)* 5-9-7 MTebbutt(17) (rdn over 2f out: nvr nr ldrs) 1¼ 14
308[11] Make the Break **(64)***(20) (SCoathup)* 4-9-7 KDarley(10) (chsd ldr: rdn ½-wy: sn wknd) 3 15
302[9] Arawa **(38)***(11) (DMarks)* 5-9-2 MRimmer(3) (prom tl wknd 2f out) 1¾ 16
Corina's Glow *(MissJFCraze)* 3-8-5 ow4 SWebster(9) (sn t.o) 15 17

7/2 Dowdency, **5/1** Sea Devil, **11/2** Bold Mick, **6/1** Nakita, **8/1** Glen Miller, Beware of Agents, **10/1** Make the Break, ROSEATE LODGE, **12/1** Bold Aristocrat (IRE), **14/1** Nabjelsedr, **16/1** Arawa, **20/1** Rosina's Folly, Export Mondial, Code of Silence, **25/1** Infantry Glen, Wadada, **33/1** Corina's Glow, CSF £99.27 TOTE £14.90: £4.10 £4.00 £2.30 (£53.20) Trio £62.30 OWNER Astaire & Partners (Holdings) Ltd (WANTAGE) BRED Barrettstown Stud Farms Ltd 17 Rn
1m 28.5 (6.00) SF: 39/36/29/34/14/10/22/16/12/8/6/6/1/-/-/-/-
WEIGHT FOR AGE 3yo-15lb
No bid.

549 KINGFISHER H'CAP (0-70) (4-Y.O+) (Class E) £3,817.00 (£1,144.00: £550.00: £253.00) **1m 3f 183y** Stalls: Low GOING: 0.07 sec per fur (G) 3-30 (3-33)

356[4] **Cliburnel News (IRE) (53)***(63) (ALForbes)* 5-8-11 PRobinson(6) (b.hind: prom: 5th st: led over 1f out: hrd rdn & hld on wl) ....— 1
325[8] Slmaat **(70)***(79) (MrsMReveley)* 4-9-12 KDarley(15) (in tch: hdwy 3f out: r.o wl appr fnl f: nt rch wnr) ....nk 2
454[2] Jemima Puddleduck **(57)***(64) (DWPArbuthnot)* 4-8-13 TQuinn(12) (led after 3f to over 1f out: kpt on) 1¼ 3
430[5] Rapporteur (USA) **(58)***(64) (CCElsey)* 9-9-2 DHarrison(13) (chsd ldrs 7f: rdn: edged lft & styd on fnl 3f) 1¾ 4
423[16] Environmentalist (IRE) **(55)***(59) (SCWilliams)* 4-8-11 AMackay(14) (dwlt: bhd tl stdy hdwy fnl 3f) ....hd 5
Exemption **(69)***(68) (HCandy)* 4-9-11 WNewnes(16) (trckd ldrs tl lost pl 5f out: n.d after) 4 6
312[10] Haroldon (IRE) **(60)***(60) (BPalling)* 6-9-4v TSprake(3) (plld hrd: chsd ldrs: 7th st: no imp fnl 3f) ....hd 7
Aljawab (USA) **(62)***(54)*(Fav)*(JLDunlop)* 4-9-4 PatEddery(18) (prom: 4th str: rdn 3f out: eased whn btn fnl f) 5 8
Southampton **(38)***(27) (GBBalding)* 5-7-5 (5)ow2 NVarley(19) (r.o fnl 3f: nvr rchd ldrs) 1½ 9

Bayrak (USA) **(70)***(60) (MJRyan)* 5-10-0 RCochrane(7) (chsd ldrs: 8th st: no hdwy) ....¾ **10**
Allahrakha **(53)***(40) (DRTucker)* 4-8-9 JWilliams(5) (in tch: pushed along ½-wy: no imp) 1½ **11**
Double Echo (IRE) **(60)***(47) (JDBethell)* 7-9-4 WRSwinburn(10) (nvr nr to chal) ....s.h **12**
423[7] In the Money (IRE) **(62)***(47) (RHollinshead)* 6-9-6 LDettori(17) (chsd ldrs: 6th st: rdn 3f out: btn whn stumbled & hit rails over 1f out) 2 **13**
367[2] Clifton Game **(42)***(27) (PGMurphy)* 5-8-0 GCarter(2) (led 3f: 3rd st: wknd over 2f out) ....hd **14**
Art Tatum **(62)***(44) (RHannon)* 4-9-4 MHills(4) (hdwy & 9th st:wknd over 2f out)....................1¼ **15**
Requested **(65)***(32) (PBurgoyne)* 8-9-6 (3) JTate(9) (dwlt: a bhd) 12 **16**
Broughtons Formula **(54)***(17) (WJMusson)* 5-8-7 (5) PMcCabe(8) (a bhd)..................................3 **17**
Jarrow **(50)** *(MrsAMNaughton)* 4-8-6 ow1 ACulhane(1) (bit bkwd: prom: 2nd st: rdn & btn 3f out)...8 **18**
422[11] Alizarin **(38)** *(JLHarris)* 6-7-5 (5)ow3 CHawksley(11) (prom 4f: t.o fnl 5f) 2 **19**

LONG HANDICAP Alizarin 6-6

9/2 Aljawab (USA), **6/1** Exemption, **15/2** In the Money (IRE) (5/1-8/1), **8/1** Slmaat (5/1-9/1), Jemima Puddleduck, **9/1** Double Echo (IRE), Clifton Game, **12/1** Bayrak (USA), Environmentalist (IRE) (op 8/1), Rapporteur (USA), Broughtons Formula, **14/1** Art Tatum, **20/1** Southampton, Requested, CLIBURNEL NEWS (IRE), Jarrow, **33/1** Haroldon (IRE), Allahrakha, **50/1** Alizarin, CSF £185.31 CT £1,314.49 TOTE £65.00: £7.60 £3.60 £2.00 £5.20 (£366.50) Trio £273.40 OWNER Target Racing (UTTOXETER) BRED St Simon Foundation 19 Rn

2m 37.2 (8.40) SF: 45/60/45/46/40/49/42/35/9/42/21/29/29/9/25/14/-/-/-

WEIGHT FOR AGE 4yo-2lb

550 GREYHOUND H'CAP (0-80) (4-Y.O+) (Class D) £4,137.90 (£1,237.20: £592.60: £270.30)

1m 1f 218y Stalls: Low GOING: 0.07 sec per fur (G) 4-05 (4-06)

325[7] **Benfleet (74)***(85) (RWArmstrong)* 4-9-10 LDettori(11) (7th st: hdwy over 1f out: rdn & r.o gamely to ld nr fin) ....— **1**
Superluminal **(69)***(80) (GRimmer)* 4-9-5 MRimmer(14) (a.p: 3rd st: led over 2f out: edgd lft over 1f out: caught cl home) ....s.h **2**
Show Faith (IRE) **(78)***(87) (RHannon)* 5-10-0 PatEddery(6) (hdwy over 2f out: r.o fnl f).........1½ **3**
Sadler's Walk **(70)***(76) (GWragg)* 4-9-6 MHills(9) (bit bkwd: sn prom: 4th st: rdn 3f out: styng on whn n.m.r over 1f out: r.o)...1¾ **4**
Sharp Falcon (IRE) **(69)***(74) (JWharton)* 4-9-5 RCochrane(3) (bit bkwd: s.i.s: stdy hdwy 4f out: nvr plcd to chal)...¾ **5**
Lord of a Dance **(50)***(49) (WJHaggas)* 4-8-0 RHills(16) (led: hung rt 5f out: hdd over 2f out: wknd fnl f) 3½ **6**
454* Queens Stroller (IRE) **(61)***(54)*(Fav)*(CCElsey)* 4-8-11 5x DHarrison(2) (chsd ldrs: 6th st: edgd rt over 2f out no imp)...3½ **7**
Bescaby Boy **(61)***(54) (JWharton)* 9-8-11 KFallon(15) (hld up: effrt 4f out: eased whn btn over 1f out)...s.h **8**
470[6] Scottish Park **(45)***(37) (RWEmery)* 6-7-9 GBardwell(7) (prom 3f: rallied u.p 3f out: n.d) ....½ **9**
433[9] Roi de la Mer (IRE) **(70)***(61) (JAkehurst)* 4-9-6 GCarter(13) (chsd ldrs: 5th st: sn rdn: wknd over 2f out)...1 **10**
Total Joy (IRE) **(62)***(52) (PFICole)* 4-8-12 TQuinn(4) (bit bkwd: bhd fnl 3f)..............................nk **11**
Platini (IRE) **(59)***(48) (GBBalding)* 4-8-9 JWilliams(10) (nvr trbld ldrs) ....¾ **12**
Rock The Barney (IRE) **(48)***(35) (PBurgoyne)* 6-7-12 NCarlisle(12) (nvr plcd to chal)............1¼ **13**
Eden's Close **(68)***(55) (MHTompkins)* 6-9-4 PRobinson(5) (chsd ldr: 2nd st: ev ch 3f out: sn wknd)..nk **14**
Sharaar (USA) **(70)***(57) (JLSpearing)* 5-9-6b KDarley(17) (dwlt : a bhd) ....hd **15**
145[7] Friendly Brave (USA) **(68)***(54) (TGMills)* 5-9-4 PaulEddery(1) (rdn over 3f out: a bhd) ....½ **16**
Colonel Colt **(66)***(36) (RDickin)* 4-9-2 WRSwinburn(8) (a bhd) 10 **17**

9/2 Queens Stroller (IRE), **5/1** Superluminal (op 10/1), **6/1** Lord of a Dance, BENFLEET, **7/1** Sadler's Walk, **10/1** Sharp Falcon (IRE), **12/1** Show Faith (IRE) (7/1-14/1), Bescaby Boy, Roi de la Mer (IRE), **14/1** Scottish Park, **16/1** Total Joy (IRE), **20/1** Platini (IRE), Rock The Barney (IRE), Eden's Close, Sharaar (USA), Friendly Brave (USA), Colonel Colt, CSF £37.82 CT £327.43 TOTE £5.00: £1.50 £1.90 £3.20 £3.20 (£20.20) Trio £51.40 OWNER Mr C. G. Donovan (NEWMARKET) BRED Aston Park Stud 17 Rn 2m 10.1 (7.40) SF: 53/48/55/44/42/17/22/22/5/29/20/16/3/23/25/22/4

551 LODDINGTON CONDITIONS STKS (3-Y.O) (Class C) £5,302.40 (£1,961.60: £940.80: £384.00: £152.00: £59.20)

5f 218y Stalls: Low GOING: 0.07 sec per fur (G) 4-40 (4-41)

Baaderah (IRE) (100)*(88) (LMCumani)* 3-8-9 LDettori(4) (mde virtually all: rdn & hld on wl ins fnl f) ....— **1**
Paris Babe *(83) (DMorris)* 3-8-5 GDuffield(5) (trckd ldrs: qcknd to chal 1f out: r.o).................nk **2**
The Jotter **(105)***(77)*(Fav)*(WJarvis)* 3-9-1 WRSwinburn(6) (w wnr: rdn 2f out: wknd fnl f) 6 **3**

527[3] Sharp Holly (IRE) **(48)***(64) (JABennett)* 3-8-5 TSprake(1) (plld hrd: chsd ldrs tl wknd appr fnl f)....1¼ 4
Coffee 'n Cream **(84)***(68) (RHannon)* 3-8-10 PatEddery(3) (bit bkwd: trckd ldrs: ev ch 2f out: btn & eased ins fnl f)....nk 5
Fakhira (IRE) *(35) (JPearce)* 3-8-9 GBardwell(2) (rdn over 2f out: a bhd)....12 6

11/8 The Jotter, **7/4** BAADERAH (IRE), **3/1** Coffee 'n Cream, **10/1** Fakhira (IRE), **16/1** Paris Babe, **50/1** Sharp Holly (IRE), CSF £23.55 TOTE £2.60: £1.20 £2.70 (£22.90) OWNER Sheikh Ahmed Al Maktoum (NEWMARKET) BRED Sheikh Ahmed bin Rashid al Maktoum 6 Rn
1m 13.9 (3.90) SF: 44/39/33/20/24/-

552

BESCABY MAIDEN STKS (I) (3-Y.O) (Class D) £3,935.10 (£1,174.80: £561.40: £254.70) **1m 8y** Stalls: Low GOING: 0.07 sec per fur (G) 5-10 (5-11)

Daunt *(90++) (JHMGosden)* 3-9-0 LDettori(5) (a gng wl: qcknd to ld wl over 1f out: sn clr: easily)....— 1
Viyapari (IRE) *(85)*(Fav)*(LMCumani)* 3-9-0 KDarley(2) (plld hrd: prom: rdn 3f out: chsd wnr over 1f out: eased whn btn ins fnl f)....2½ 2
Al Safeer (IRE) *(80) (JWHills)* 3-9-0 RHills(12) (chsd ldrs tl wknd over 1f out)....2½ 3
River Keen (IRE) *(76) (RWArmstrong)* 3-9-0 RPrice(11) (hld up: hdwy over 3f out: sn rdn: wknd 2f out)....2 4
Empower (IRE) *(75) (RHannon)* 3-9-0 MHills(7) (in tch 3f: styd on fnl 2f)....¾ 5
332[8] Speedybird (IRE) *(69) (BJMeehan)* 3-8-9 BDoyle(1) (prom: led 4f out tl wl over 1f out: sn wknd)....hd 6
468[7] Full Cover (IRE) **(75)***(64) (DRCElsworth)* 3-9-0v WNewnes(6) (swrvd lft s: led 4f: btn over 2f out)....5 7
Barbason *(47) (JRFanshawe)* 3-9-0 DHarrison(9) (unf: scope: bkwd: hld up: plld hard: bhd fnl 3f)....9 8
Superflex *(40) (DMorris)* 3-8-6 (3) CHodgson(4) (w'like: lt-f: s.i.s: a bhd)....¾ 9
Tirlie (IRE) *(44) (JWPayne)* 3-9-0 BThomson(8) (a bhd)....¾ 10
Ahaalee (USA) *(40) (EALDunlop)* 3-9-0 WRSwinburn(3) (leggy: scope: bit bkwd: hld up: a bhd)....2 11
Miss Biarritz *(MBell)* 3-8-9 MFenton(10) (s.s: sn t.o: p.u 3f out).... P

Evens Viyapari (IRE), **7/2** DAUNT, **13/2** River Keen (IRE), **8/1** Al Safeer (IRE) (op 14/1), Ahaalee (USA), **10/1** Barbason, **33/1** Speedybird (IRE), Full Cover (IRE), Miss Biarritz, Empower (IRE), **50/1** Tirlie (IRE), Superflex, CSF £7.87 TOTE £3.70: £1.10 £1.60 £2.20 (£2.40) Trio £18.30 OWNER Lord Hartington (NEWMARKET) BRED Side Hill Stud 12 Rn
1m 41.4 (6.40) SF: 37/32/27/23/22/16/11/-/-/-/-/-

553

BESCABY MAIDEN STKS (II) (3-Y.O) (Class D) £3,901.30 (£1,164.40: £556.20: £252.10) **1m 8y** Stalls: Low GOING: 0.07 sec per fur (G) 5-40 (5-41)

Orsay *(75) (WRMuir)* 3-9-0 MHills(9) (mde virtually all: qcknd over 2f out: hld on wl fnl f)....— 1
Banadam (USA) *(74) (BHanbury)* 3-9-0 WRyan(8) (b.hind: cmpt: chsd ldrs: rdn & ev ch 1f out: r.o)....nk 2
Dances With Hooves *(74) (DJSffrenchDavis)* 3-9-0 JWilliams(6) (chsd ldrs: rdn over 2f out: kpt on fnl f)....hd 3
Heboob Alshemaal (IRE) *(68) (JHMGosden)* 3-8-9 LDettori(4) (w'like: s.i.s: hdwy 4f out: rdn over 2f out: r.o wl fnl f)....½ 4
Blisland *(72)*(Fav)*(RCharlton)* 3-9-0 PatEddery(5) (trckd ldrs: rdn over 2f out: wknd ins fnl f) .½ 5
Sayitagain *(67) (TGMills)* 3-9-0 PaulEddery(10) (unf: prom 6f)....2½ 6
Invest Wisely *(61) (JMPEustace)* 3-9-0 RCochrane(11) (scope: chsd ldrs over 5f: eased whn btn ins fnl f)....3 7
Equity's Darling (IRE) *(50) (MBell)* 3-8-9 MFenton(3) (bit bkwd: in tch: pushed along ½-wy: sn wknd)....3 8
My Boy Josh *(43) (RGuest)* 3-9-0 GDuffield(1) (weak: scope: bkwd: plld hard: jnd wnr after 1f: wknd over 3f out)....6 9
Le Bal **(45)** *(MrsNMacauley)* 3-8-9 JFortune(2) (bit bkwd: a bhd: t.o fnl 4f)....20 10

11/8 Blisland, **2/1** Heboob Alshemaal (IRE) (op 4/5), **100/30** Banadam (USA), **8/1** Dances With Hooves (op 5/1), **14/1** ORSAY (14/1-33/1), **20/1** Sayitagain, **33/1** Invest Wisely, Equity's Darling (IRE), My Boy Josh, **50/1** Le Bal, CSF £63.24 TOTE £40.90: £3.60 £2.70 £3.80 (£34.50) Trio £78.30; £46.34 to Aintree race 5 7/4/95 OWNER Mr D. J. Deer (LAMBOURN) BRED D. J. and Mrs Deer 10 Rn 1m 42.4 (7.40) SF: 27/26/26/20/24/19/13/2/-/-

T/Plpt: £119.90 (88.07 Tckts). T/Qdpt: £22.70 (0.6 Tckts); £12.32 to Aintree 7/4/95 DK

BEVERLEY (R-H)
Friday April 7th (Good to firm)
WEATHER: cloudy WIND: fresh half against

554 SCARBOROUGH (S) STKS (2-Y.O) (Class F) £2,861.00 (£796.00: £383.00)
5f Stalls: Centre GOING minus 0.20 sec per fur (GF) 2-20 (2-25)

The Frisky Farmer *(62+t) (WGMTurner)* 2-8-11 TSprake(7) (w'like: leggy: mde virtually all: rdn clr over 1f out: eased towards fin) .....— 1
429* Penny Parkes *(52)*(Fav)*(JBerry)* 2-8-9 GCarter(2) (b.hind: w ldrs: rdn over 1f out: nt able qckn) 2½ 2
Ghostly Apparition *(41) (JohnUpson)* 2-8-11 KFallon(3) (leggy: unf: sn wl outpcd: hdwy over 1f out: styd on) 4 3
Mysterious Times *(30) (MWEasterby)* 2-8-6 LCharnock(8) (small: cmpt: bkwd: sltly hmpd s: sn wl outpcd: kpt on appr fnl f) 2 4
Brogans Brush *(33) (CWFairhurst)* 2-8-11 JFanning(1) (s.s: swtchd rt & wl outpcd: kpt on fnl f) .....½ 5
474[5] Dance To Victory *(25) (TDBarron)* 2-8-6 JFortune(6) (swrvd rt s: chsd ldrs tl wknd 2 out) 1 6
Static Love *(19) (SCWilliams)* 2-8-6 KDarley(4) (leggy: chsd ldrs: effrt ½-wy: sn wknd) 2 7
429[6] Power Dee *(15) (MWEasterby)* 2-8-6 MBirch(5) (w ldrs tl rdn & wknd 2f out) 1 8

5/4 Penny Parkes, **6/4** Static Love, **6/1** THE FRISKY FARMER, **12/1** Ghostly Apparition, **14/1** Brogans Brush, **16/1** Mysterious Times, Power Dee, **20/1** Dance To Victory, CSF £15.22 TOTE £9.90: £1.10 £1.10 £3.30 (£4.70) OWNER Mr G. J. Bush (SHERBORNE) BRED Miss Claire Farrow, Dame Elizabeth and Alexander C 8 Rn 66.4 secs (4.90) SF: 2/-/-/-/-/-/-/-
Bt in for 9,200gns.

555 HUTTON CRANSWICK MAIDEN STKS (3-Y.O+) (Class D) £4,048.50 (£1,218.00: £589.00: £274.50)
5f Stalls: Centre GOING minus 0.20 sec per fur (GF) 2-50 (2-50)

Bolshoi (IRE) *(72) (JBerry)* 3-8-12 GCarter(2) (lw: trckd ldrs: hdwy to ld 1f out: r.o wl) .....— 1
Showery *(61) (JWWatts)* 3-8-7 BThomson(4) (hdwy ½-wy: effrt & swtchd rt 1f out: r.o) 1¾ 2
Sing With the Band **(47)***(58) (BAMcMahon)* 4-9-5 JFortune(5) (led: rdn & edgd rt over 1f out: sn hdd & no ex) 1 3
Michellisa **(54)***(50) (JDBethell)* 4-9-5 KDarley(10) (chsd ldrs: effrt & n.m.r over 1f out: kpt on same pce) 2½ 4
431[8] Alltime Dancer (IRE) *(30) (MrsJRRamsden)* 3-8-12 KFallon(6) (sn outpcd & bhd: sme hdwy 2f out: n.d) 8 5
482[17] Tish **(40)***(23) (ASmith)* 3-8-7b DHarrison(1) (swvd lft s: a in rr) .....½ 6
442[15] Frontiersman *(25) (JWWatts)* 3-8-12 NConnorton(7) (sn outpcd & drvn along) 1 7
Bajan Frontier (IRE) *(19) (FHLee)* 3-8-7 TIves(3) (b.hind: trckd ldrs: rdn 2f out: sn wknd) .....nk 8
Yaa Wale *(21)*(Fav)*(JHMGosden)* 3-8-12 LDettori(9) (b.hind: chsd ldrs: sn drvn along: edgd lft & lost pl 2f out: eased fnl f) 1 9
Skiptamaloo **(38)***(10) (DonEnricoIncisa)* 4-9-5 KimTinkler(8) (a outpcd) 1¾ 10

Evens Yaa Wale, **9/2** Michellisa, **6/1** Showery, **7/1** BOLSHOI (IRE), Frontiersman (9/2-8/1), **9/1** Bajan Frontier (IRE), **10/1** Sing With the Band, **12/1** Alltime Dancer (IRE) (op 7/1), **20/1** Skiptamaloo, **25/1** Tish, CSF £54.13 TOTE £9.30: £2.20 £1.70 £4.30 (£39.70) Trio £133.00 OWNER Mrs David Brown (COCKERHAM) BRED David John Brown 10 Rn
63.9 secs (2.40) SF: 41/30/39/31/-/-/-/-/-/-
WEIGHT FOR AGE 3yo-12lb

OFFICIAL EXPLANATION Yaa Wale: the jockey stated that the horse did not move well, hung left and so had therefore eased him when there was no more to come. The horse had also lost his near-fore plate.

556 BRIDLINGTON BAY H'CAP (0-70) (4-Y.O+) (Class E) £3,621.25 (£1,090.00: £527.50: £246.25)
2m 35y Stalls: Centre GOING minus 0.40 sec per fur (F) 3-20 (3-21)

Moonlight Quest (63)*(76) (BHanbury)* 7-9-10 TIves(18) (hld up: stdy hdwy 3f out: swtchd rt & led over 1f out: sn clr: easily) .....— 1
Rolling the Bones (USA) **(35)***(43) (PSFelgate)* 6-7-10 GBardwell(11) (bhd: hdwy over 2f out: hung rt: styd on wl fnl f: no ch w wnr) 5 2
White Willow **(67)***(75) (MrsMReveley)* 6-10-0v KDarley(3) (lw: hld up: hdwy 6f out: rdn & n.m.r over 2f out: edgd rt & kpt on appr fnl f) .....½ 3

432[8] Ballymac Girl **(53)***(57) (JMBradley)* 7-8-9 (5) SDrowne(17) (b: hld up: hdwy 6f out: nt clr run over 1f out: styd on wl) 3½ **4**
432[9] Guards Brigade **(50)***(53) (JHetherton)* 4-8-7 NKennedy(15) (led tl hdd & wknd over 1f out) 1 **5**
259[4] Murphys Way **(44)***(46) (JLEyre)* 6-8-2 (3) JTate(20) (bhd: hdwy to chse ldrs ½-wy: one pce fnl 3f) 1 **6**
469[2] Arc Bright (IRE) **(40)***(42) (RHollinshead)* 5-7-10 (5) AGarth(24) (chsd ldrs tl outpcd fnl 2f) ....nk **7**
*87** Kadiri (IRE) **(61)***(62) (JRBosley)* 4-9-4 PaulEddery(6) (bhd tl kpt on u.p fnl 3f) ....¾ **8**
295[2] Nahri (USA) **(52)***(52) (JMackie)* 4-8-9 GCarter(2) (lw: hld up: styd on fnl 3f: nvr nr to chal) 1¼ **9**
396[9] Thaleros **(67)***(66) (GMMoore)* 5-10-0 LDettori(22) (hld up in tch: stdy hdwy 6f out: effrt 3f out: sn wknd) 1¼ **10**
325[9] New Inn **(60)***(56) (EWeymes)* 4-9-3v DHarrison(1) (chsd ldrs tl wknd 2f out) 2½ **11**
432[5] Ambuscade (USA) **(53)***(47) (EJAlston)* 9-9-0 KFallon(14) (bhd: swtchd outside & kpt on fnl 3f: n.d) 1¾ **12**
271[7] In a Moment (USA) **(50)***(44) (TDBarron)* 4-8-7 JFortune(12) (nvr rchd ldrs) ....nk **13**
223[3] Acrow Line **(43)***(34) (DBurchell)* 10-8-4 RPrice(7) (in tch tl lost pl 5f out) 3½ **14**
53[4] Tristan's Comet **(45)***(34) (JLHarris)* 8-8-6 WWoods(8) (lw: sn bhd & drvn along) 1¼ **15**
Sir Dickie Cox (IRE) **(51)***(37) (FHLee)* 4-8-8 JWilliams(23) (trckd ldrs: effrt 6f out: sn wknd) 3 **16**
412[9] Jalore **(50)***(23) (SCoathup)* 6-8-11 TSprake(13) (chsd ldrs tl lost pl over 3f out) 14 **17**
121[8] Lightning Quest (IRE) **(40)***(11) (JSWainwright)* 4-7-11 JFanning(9) (b.hind: bhd: hdwy on outside 6f out: sn wknd) 2 **18**
259[14] Eightandahalf (IRE) **(63)***(31) (MrsVAAconley)* 6-9-10 TWilliams(16) (sn bhd) 3 **19**
Burntwood Melody **(43)***(8) (JAHarris)* 4-8-0 JO'Reilly(21) (chsd ldrs tl lost pl 6f out) 2½ **20**
Briggs Lad (IRE) **(52)***(15) (PTDalton)* 6-8-13 LCharnock(10) (chsd ldrs: drvn along ½-wy: lost pl over 4f out) 2½ **21**
Fryup Satellite **(44)***(4) (LRLloyd-James)* 4-8-1 DaleGibson(4) (bit bkwd: hdwy ½-wy: drvn along & lost pl 5f out) 2½ **22**
412[3] Sleeptite (FR) **(54)***(10)*(Fav)*(WGMTurner)* 5-8-10 (5) JStack(19) (hdwy & prom ½-wy: effrt 4f out: sn lost pl) 4 **23**

11/2 Sleeptite (FR), **6/1** White Willow (op 4/1), Nahri (USA) (op 4/1), **7/1** Ballymac Girl, **8/1** Rolling the Bones (USA), Arc Bright (IRE), MOONLIGHT QUEST, **10/1** Kadiri (IRE), **12/1** Ambuscade (USA), New Inn, **14/1** Guards Brigade, Acrow Line, **16/1** Thaleros, Murphys Way, **20/1** Tristan's Comet, Eightandahalf (IRE), Jalore, In a Moment (USA), Burntwood Melody, Lightning Quest (IRE), **25/1** Sir Dickie Cox (IRE), Briggs Lad (IRE), **33/1** Fryup Satellite, CSF £89.16 CT £417.81 TOTE: £27.20: £4.60 £3.20 £1.90 £2.90 (£121.90) Trio £224.20 OWNER Mr B. Hanbury (NEWMARKET) BRED Raintree Stud 23 Rn
3m 37.4 (6.90) SF: 45/12/44/26/18/15/11/27/17/35/21/16/9/3/3/2/-/-/-/-/-/-/-
WEIGHT FOR AGE 4yo-4lb

557 LECONFIELD CONDITIONS STKS (3-Y.O F) (Class C) £5,075.50 (£1,765.50: £855.25: £358.75) **1m 1f 207y** Stalls: High GOING minus 0.40 sec (F) 3-50 (3-50)

Bunting *(91)*(Fav)*(JHMGosden)* 3-9-0 LDettori(1) (chsd ldr: drvn along 3f out: styd on to ld over 1f out) ....— **1**
438[4] Dee-Lady **(98)***(89) (WGMTurner)* 3-9-0 TSprake(2) (hld up: stdy hdwy 3f out: ev ch over 1f out: sn rdn & nt qckn) 1 **2**
College Night (IRE) *(38) (JohnBerry)* 3-8-10 CDwyer(4) (bit bkwd: led tl over 1f out: kpt on) ..½ **3**
273[6] Bellara *(21) (NMBabbage)* 3-8-10 PaulEddery(3) (chsd ldrs: drvn along over 3f out: sn wl outpcd) 11 **4**

2/5 BUNTING, **2/1** Dee-Lady, **25/1** College Night (IRE), Bellara, CSF £1.64 TOTE £1.40 (£1.10) OWNER Mohammed Al Nabouda (NEWMARKET) BRED Sheikh Mohammed bin Rashid al Maktoum 4 Rn
2m 9.1 (6.60) SF: 14/12/8/-

558 HORNSEA MERE H'CAP (0-85) (4-Y.O+) (Class D) £3,996.50 (£1,202.00: £581.00: £270.50) **1m 1f 207y** Stalls: High GOING minus 0.40 sec per fur (F) 4-25 (4-25)

Wayne County (IRE) (79)*(87) (GFierro)* 5-9-10 LDettori(12) (lw: trckd ldrs: effrt over 2f out: r.o u.p to ld ins fnl f) ....— **1**
Southern Power (IRE) **(75)***(82) (MrsMReveley)* 4-9-6 GCarter(10) (b.hind: trckd ldrs: led over 1f out: nt qckn towards fin) ....½ **2**
Retender (USA) **(67)***(70) (MrsJRRamsden)* 6-8-12 KFallon(14) (lw: hld up: hdwy over 2f out: styd on fnl f: nt rch ldrs) 2½ **3**
Rory **(82)***(84)*(Fav)*(MrsJCecil)* 4-9-13 PaulEddery(15) (lw: trckd ldrs: effrt 3f out: kpt on same pce appr fnl f) 1 **4**

Kalou **(53)***(53) (CWCElsey)* 4-7-12v LCharnock(3) (chsd ldrs: kpt on same pce fnl 2f)............¾ 5
433[21] Queens Consul (IRE) **(75)***(71) (BSRothwell)* 5-9-1 (5) JStack(9) (led tl over 1f out: grad wknd)..........2½ 6
439[13] Celestial Choir **(80)***(74) (JLEyre)* 5-9-11 JFortune(8) (in tch: hdwy over 2f out: kpt on: nvr rchd ldrs)..........1¼ 7
Faal Mario (USA) **(82)***(70) (MrsJRRamsden)* 4-9-13 DHarrison(7) (unruly in stalls: nvr bttr than mid div)..........4 8
Walsham Whisper (IRE) **(79)***(63) (JWharton)* 4-9-10 JWilliams(4) (bhd: sme hdwy 2f out: n.d)..........2½ 9
440[10] Slasher Jack (IRE) **(83)***(66) (SGNorton)* 4-9-11 (3) JTate(13) (bit bkwd: mid div: drvn along over 5f out: outpcd fnl 3f)..........nk 10
Sarawat **(80)***(59) (DNicholls)* 7-9-11 AlexGreaves(11) (bit bkwd: trckd ldrs tl edgd lft & wknd over 2f out)..........2½ 11
Sushi Bar (IRE) **(60)***(39) (MrsMReveley)* 4-8-5 KDarley(2) (bhd: effrt over 2f out: n.d)..........½ 12
421[9] Silver Samurai **(70)***(46) (MrsVAAconley)* 6-9-1 DeanMcKeown(5) (s.s: hld up & a bhd)..........1½ 13
Muzrak (CAN) **(72)***(46) (MDHammond)* 4-9-3 TIves(6) (sn outpcd & drvn along)..........1½ 14
304[5] Let's Get Lost **(66)***(40) (JAHarris)* 6-8-11 DaleGibson(1) (a bhd)..........hd 15

3/1 Rory, **5/1** Celestial Choir, **7/1** Retender (USA), **8/1** WAYNE COUNTY (IRE), **10/1** Southern Power (IRE) (op 6/1), Sushi Bar (IRE), Slasher Jack (IRE), **12/1** Walsham Whisper (IRE), Faal Mario (USA), **14/1** Queens Consul (IRE), Kalou, Let's Get Lost, **20/1** Sarawat, Silver Samurai, Muzrak (CAN), CSF £90.34 CT £551.99 TOTE £10.20:£2.10 £5.40 £2.80 (£34.20) Trio £239.20 OWNER Old School House Racing Ltd (HEDNESFORD) BRED Swettenham Stud 15 Rn
2m 4.0 (1.50) SF: 63/58/46/60/29/47/50/46/39/42/35/15/22/22/16

559 WITHERNSEA H'CAP (0-80) (4-Y.O+) (Class D) £4,178.50 (£1,258.00: £609.00: £284.50) 7f 100y Stalls: High GOING minus 0.40 sec per fur (F) 5-00 (5-02)

433[7] **Sandmoor Chambray (71)***(79) (MHEasterby)* 4-9-5b MBirch(9) (mde virtually all: styd on u.p fnl f)..........— 1
Sea-Ayr (IRE) **(48)***(53) (MrsSMAustin)* 5-7-10 JMarshall(2) (b.hind: gd hdwy on outside 2f out: r.o strly ins fnl f: nt rch wnr)..........1½ 2
394[2] Tatika **(70)***(73)*(Fav)*(GWragg)* 5-9-4 WWoods(18) (plld hrd: trckd ldrs: kpt on same pce over 1f out)..........1 3
Tolls Choice (IRE) **(55)***(57) (MWEasterby)* 6-7-10 (7) RuthCoulter(14) (a in tch: kpt on same pce fnl 2f)..........nk 4
434[10] Veloce (IRE) **(68)***(70) (ABailey)* 7-8-11 (5) VHalliday(17) (hdwy over 2f out: kpt on: nvr nr to chal)..........hd 5
Ochos Rios (IRE) **(64)***(64) (BSRothwell)* 4-8-12 LCharnock(7) (hld up: hdwy & n.m.r over 2f out: nvr rchd ldrs)..........1 6
*413** Second Colours (USA) **(60)***(60) (MrsMReveley)* 5-8-8 KDarley(11) (lw: effrt on outside 3f out: kpt on u.p: nvr rch ldrs)..........s.h 7
269[5] Karinska **(52)***(48) (MCChapman)* 5-7-7 (7)ow2 CMunday(4) (chsd wnr tl wknd over 1f out)..........½ 8
Yoxall Lodge **(63)***(60) (HJCollingridge)* 5-8-11 DaleGibson(5) (bhd tl styd on fnl 2f)..........¾ 9
Up in Flames (IRE) **(65)***(61) (MDHammond)* 4-8-13 TIves(3) (bhd tl kpt on fnl 2f)..........½ 10
518[8] Kilnamartyra Girl **(47)***(42) (JParkes)* 5-7-9b GBardwell(1) (bhd: kpt on u.p appr fnl f: n.d)..........nk 11
481[6] Ikis Girl **(56)***(49) (SGollings)* 4-8-4 DHarrison(12) (rr div: effrt u.p 3f out: n.d)..........1 12
Ashdren **(59)***(52) (AHarrison)* 8-8-2 (5) JStack(8) (hld up & bhd: stdy hdwy 2f out: nvr plcd to chal)..........s.h 13
Ballard Ring (IRE) **(75)***(63) (JSWainwright)* 4-9-9 DeanMcKeown(16) (hld up & a bhd)..........2½ 14
228[3] Bogart **(57)***(42) (CWFairhurst)* 4-8-5 KFallon(6) (trckd ldrs tl lost pl 2f out)..........1 15
Pendolino (IRE) **(65)***(50) (MBrittain)* 4-8-13 JLowe(13) (plld hrd: trckd ldrs tl lost pl 3f out)..........hd 16
417[9] Waterlord (IRE) **(56)***(41) (DNicholls)* 5-8-4 NConnorton(15) (in tch: hmpd 6f out: effrt over 3f out: sn wknd)..........nk 17
439[19] Mahool (USA) **(80)** *(JLEyre)* 6-10-0 LDettori(10) (s.s: hdwy to chse ldrs ½-wy: wknd & eased 3f out: virtually p.u ins fnl f: b.b.v)..........dist 18

4/1 Tatika (op 7/1), **9/2** SANDMOOR CHAMBRAY (op 3/1), Mahool (USA), **7/1** Second Colours (USA), **10/1** Up in Flames (IRE), **12/1** Sea-Ayr (IRE), Veloce (IRE), **16/1** Ochos Rios (IRE), Karinska, Ashdren, Waterlord (IRE), Yoxall Lodge, Bogart, **20/1** Ikis Girl, Tolls Choice (IRE), **25/1** Kilnamartyra Girl, Pendolino (IRE), Ballard Ring (IRE), CSF £64.05 CT £229.15 TOTE £9.10: £1.70 £2.50 £1.90 £16.00 (£60.30) Trio £137.40 OWNER Sandmoor Textiles Co Ltd (MALTON) BRED P. and Mrs Venner 18 Rn 1m 32.9 (0.90) SF: 61/35/55/39/52/46/42/30/42/43/24/31/34/45/24/32/23/-
OFFICIAL EXPLANATION Mahool (USA): broke a blood-vessel.

T/Plpt: £433.90 (22.85 Tckts). T/Qdpt: £28.70 (2 Tckts). WG

0496-LINGFIELD (L-H)
Friday April 7th (AWT Standard, Turf Good becoming Good to firm)
WEATHER: sunny WIND: almost nil

560
APRIL LIMITED STKS (0-65) (3-Y.O) (Class F) £2,745.80 (£758.80: £361.40)
1m (Equitrack) Stalls: High GOING minus 0.52 sec per fur (FST) 2-15 (2-16)

529[6] **Jackatack (IRE) (57)***(63) (MRChannon)* 3-8-11 RHughes(2) (chsd ldr: led over 3f out: rdn out) — 1
532[5] Bon Secret (IRE) **(64)***(71)*(Fav)*(TJNaughton)* 3-9-3 (3) SSanders(4) (b: lw: hld up: chsd wnr fnl 2f: r.o ins fnf f) ½ 2
Spitfire Bridge (IRE) **(58)***(48) (MMcCormack)* 3-8-11 JReid(1) (bit bkwd: dwlt: racd wd: hdwy over 1f out: r.o) 7 3
449[4] Western Horizon (USA) **(65)***(33) (CEBrittain)* 3-8-6 BDoyle(5) (rdn over 4f out: bhd fnl 3f) 5 4
449[5] Moonee Valley **(65)***(32) (RHannon)* 3-8-11b WRyan(3) (lw: led over 4f: wknd wl over 1f out) 3 5
482[13] Scissor Ridge **(53)***(24) (JJBridger)* 3-8-11 GDuffield(6) (bhd fnl 3f) 4 6

2/1 Bon Secret (IRE), **5/2** Western Horizon (USA) (op 13/8), **4/1** Moonee Valley, **6/1** JACKATACK (IRE), **8/1** Spitfire Bridge (IRE), **33/1** Scissor Ridge, CSF £17.14 TOTE £9.90: £3.30 £1.40 (£8.40) OWNER Mr Peter Taplin (UPPER LAMBOURN) BRED Mrs C. A. Moore 6 Rn
1m 40.2 (3.80) SF: 15/23/-/-/-/-

561
EUROPEAN BREEDERS FUND TANDRIDGE MAIDEN STKS (2-Y.O) (Class D) £3,525.00 (£1,050.00: £500.00: £225.00)
5f Stalls: High GOING minus 0.13 sec per fur (G) 2-45 (2-47)

424[5] **Gwespyr** *(78t)*(Fav)*(JBerry)* 2-9-0 JCarroll(6) (lw: a.p: led wl over 1f out: rdn out) — 1
Cyrillic *(67) (PAKelleway)* 2-8-9 MWigham(2) (unf: a.p: led over 2f out tl over 1f out: unable qckn) 2 2
455[6] Bites *(47) (GLewis)* 2-8-9 GHind(5) (hld up: rdn over 3f out: unable qckn) 6 3
Never Think Twice *(48) (KTIvory)* 2-8-7 (7) CScally(3) (lt-f: hld up: rdn over 2f out: one pce) 1½ 4
Baluteer (IRE) *(45) (MRChannon)* 2-9-0 RHughes(8) (w'like: bit bkwd: hld up: hrd rdn over 2f out: wknd fnl f) ¾ 5
Solva Mist *(32) (LJHolt)* 2-8-9 AScobie(4) (neat: bkwd: a bhd) 2½ 6
Heights of Love *(32) (MSSaunders)* 2-8-9 PatEddery(1) (neat: led over 2f) hd 7
Caveat Emptor (IRE) *(31) (SDow)* 2-9-0 TQuinn(7) (cmpt: bkwd: bhd fnl 3f) 2 8

Evens GWESPYR, **7/2** Cyrillic (4/1-2/1), **9/2** Baluteer (IRE) (3/1-5/1), **9/1** Heights of Love (5/1-10/1), **14/1** Caveat Emptor (IRE) (op 6/1), **40/1** Solva Mist, Never Think Twice, Bites, CSF £4.83 TOTE £1.60: £1.10 £1.90 £4.10 (£10.50) OWNER Lord Mostyn (COCKERHAM) BRED R. and Mrs Heathcote 8 Rn 60.74 secs (3.74) SF: 23/12/-/-/-/-/-/-

562
BAKERS LANE CONDITIONS STKS (2-Y.O) (Class C) £4,610.62 (£1,657.50: £791.25: £318.75: £121.88)
5f Stalls: High GOING minus 0.13 sec per fur (G) 3-15 (3-16)

474* **Whicksey Perry** *(85t) (JBerry)* 2-8-11 JCarroll(5) (chsd ldr: rdn 3f out: led wl over 1f out: r.o wl) — 1
Repertory *(83)*(Fav)*(MRChannon)* 2-8-11 RHughes(1) (leggy: led over 3f: r.o) ¾ 2
436[6] Worldwide Elsie (USA) *(52) (PAKelleway)* 2-8-6 AMackay(3) (lw: s.s: outpcd) 8 3
Friendly Forester (USA) *(57) (RCharlton)* 2-8-11 JWeaver(2) (w'like: bit bkwd: outpcd) hd 4
Daily Risk *(57) (SDow)* 2-8-11 TQuinn(4) (w'like: outpcd) s.h 5

7/4 Repertory, **2/1** WHICKSEY PERRY (11/10-9/4), **4/1** Worldwide Elsie (USA) (3/1-5/1), Friendly Forester (USA) (3/1-5/1), **33/1** Daily Risk, CSF £5.77 TOTE £2.20: £1.60 £1.10 (£3.40) OWNER Mr J. Henderson (COCKERHAM) BRED D. H. Jones 5 Rn 60.06 secs (3.06) SF: 31/29/-/3/3

563
DEC-FAX H'CAP (0-90) (3-Y.O+) (Class C) £6,212.00 (£1,856.00: £888.00: £404.00) **7f** Stalls: High GOING minus 0.13 sec per fur (G) 3-45 (3-46)

433[6] **Sheppard's Cross (79)***(86)*(Fav)*(PTWalwyn)* 4-9-3 PatEddery(3) (a.p: led over 2f out: rdn out) — 1

450³ Shepherd Market (IRE) **(56)***(59) (DAWilson)* 4-7-8 ow1 JQuinn(7) (nt clr run over 2f out: hdwy & nt clr run over 1f out: r.o) 1½ 2
434⁷ Sagebrush Roller **(86)***(86) (JWWatts)* 7-9-10 GDuffield(6) (swtchd lft 2f out: hdwy over 1f out: r.o one pce) 1¾ 3
486⁵ Knobbleeneeze **(75)***(74) (MRChannon)* 5-8-13v RHughes(10) (lw: hld up: nt clr run 2f out: hrd rdn over 1f out: one pce) ....hd 4
417³ Prima Silk **(74)***(72) (MJRyan)* 4-8-12 DBiggs(2) (hld up: hrd rdn over 1f out: one pce) ....½ 5
*405** Gulf Shaadi **(84)***(82) (GLewis)* 3-8-7 SWhitworth(11) (s.s: rdn over 2f out: hdwy over 1f out: nvr nrr) ....hd 6
433² Set Table (USA) **(73)***(71) (JHMGosden)* 6-8-11 GHind(1) (led over 4f: hrd rdn over 1f out: one pce) ....d.h 6
Adolescence (IRE) **(81)***(76) (KMcAuliffe)* 5-9-5 RCochrane(12) (nvr nr to chal) 1¼ 8
433⁴ Garnock Valley **(74)***(68) (JBerry)* 5-8-12 JCarroll(8) (hdwy over 2f out: hrd rdn over 1f out: wknd ins fnl f) ....½ 9
Absolute Magic **(83)***(56) (WJHaggas)* 5-9-7 MHills(9) (lw: prom over 4f) 9 10
Nagnagnag (IRE) **(90)***(63) (SDow)* 3-8-6 (7) ADaly(4) (bhd fnl 2f) ....nk 11
Deeply Vale (IRE) **(76)***(42) (GLMoore)* 4-9-0 BRouse(13) (prom over 4f) 3 12
491* Aljaz **(66)***(29) (DTThom)* 5-8-4 6x AMackay(5) (b: prom over 5f) 1¼ 13

9/2 SHEPPARD'S CROSS (6/1-4/1), **11/2** Garnock Valley, Set Table (USA), **6/1** Shepherd Market (IRE), **15/2** Gulf Shaadi (5/1-8/1), **8/1** Sagebrush Roller, **10/1** Knobbleeneeze, **12/1** Adolescence (IRE), Absolute Magic (op 8/1), **14/1** Deeply Vale (IRE), Aljaz, **20/1** Nagnagnag (IRE), Prima Silk, CSF £32.80 CT £199.42 TOTE £6.60: £2.40 £2.80 £2.00 (£16.60) Trio £44.90. OWNER Major & Mrs R B Kennard and Partners (LAMBOURN) BRED Mrs R. B. Kennard 13 Rn
1m 24.57 (3.97) SF: 41/14/41/29/27/22/26/31/23/11/3/-/-
WEIGHT FOR AGE 3yo-15lb

564 KENTUCKY DERBY TRIAL CONDITIONS STKS (3-Y.O) (Class B)
£8,103.80 (£3,024.20: £1,472.10: £625.50: £272.75: £131.65)
1m 2f (Equitrack) Stalls: Low GOING minus 0.52 sec per fur (FST) 4-15 (4-18)

Maralinga (IRE) (89)*(98) (MBell)* 3-8-10 JReid(3) (lw: w ldr: rdn over 2f out: led ins fnl f: r.o wl) ....— 1
*500** Proposing (IRE) *(98)*(Fav)*(JHMGosden)* 3-8-12 JCarroll(8) (lw: s.s: rdn thrght: hdwy over 3f out: r.o wl ins fnl f) 1¼ 2
Off'n'away (IRE) *(98) (DKWeld,Ireland)* 3-8-12 PatEddery(2) (w'like: scope: lw: led: rdn over 2f out: hdd ins fnl f: unable qckn) ....hd 3
*289** Soldier's Leap (FR) **(79)***(79) (CEBrittain)* 3-8-12v RCochrane(5) (b.hind: hld up: rdn over 4f out: wknd over 2f out) 12 4
*38** Bardon Hill Boy (IRE) *(73) (BHanbury)* 3-8-10 MRimmer(6) (hdwy over 3f out: sn wknd) 2½ 5
Mentor (GR) **(97)***(71) (RCharlton)* 3-8-12 JWeaver(4) (bit bkwd: bhd fnl 8f) 2 6
Nero Kris *(PAKelleway)* 3-8-10 MHills(1) (swtg: w'like: lw: bhd fnl 4f: t.o) ....dist 7

2/1 Proposing (IRE), **9/4** Off'n'away (IRE) (op 6/4), **5/1** MARALINGA (IRE), **7/1** Bardon Hill Boy (IRE) (9/2-8/1), **10/1** Nero Kris (7/1-20/1), **12/1** Soldier's Leap (FR) (7/1-14/1), **14/1** Mentor (GR) (op 9/2), CSF £15.14 TOTE £14.20: £3.90 £1.70 (£13.40) OWNER Mr D K R & Mrs J B C Oliver (NEWMARKET) BRED W. H. Elliott 7 Rn 2m 5.15 (2.15) SF: 35/35/35/16/10/8/-

565 AINTREE H'CAP (0-80) (3-Y.O+) (Class D) £4,104.10 (£1,226.80: £587.40: £267.70) **5f** Stalls: High GOING minus 0.13 sec per fur (G) 4-45 (4-46)

452* **Nordico Princess (67)***(73) (GROldroyd)* 4-9-1 7x RCochrane(8) (mde all: rdn out) ....— 1
Allthruthenight (IRE) **(80)***(85) (LJHolt)* 6-10-0 JReid(1) (swtg: rdn & hdwy over 1f out: r.o wl ins fnl f) ....nk 2
507¹⁰ Domicksky **(70)***(70) (MRChannon)* 7-9-4 RHughes(6) (rdn & hdwy 1f out: r.o wl ins fnl f) 1½ 3
Name the Tune **(74)***(73) (PHowling)* 4-9-8 PRobinson(11) (b.hind: a.p: hrd rdn 2f out: unable qckn) ....½ 4
507⁷ Bright Paragon (IRE) **(50)***(48) (HJCollingridge)* 6-7-12 NCarlisle(4) (hld up: rdn over 2f out: edgd rt over 1f out: one pce) ....hd 5
Fangio **(80)***(77) (WGMTurner)* 6-9-9 (5) PMcCabe(12) (a.p: hrd rdn over 1f out: one pce) ....nk 6
Myasha (USA) **(78)***(71) (AlexVanderhaeghen,Belgium)* 6-9-12 MServranckx(10) (a.p: hrd rdn over 1f out: eased whn btn wl ins fnl f) 1¼ 7
Ann's Pearl (IRE) **(80)***(69) (JWHills)* 4-10-0 MHills(7) (hld up: rdn over 1f out: wknd fnl f) 1½ 8
434²⁰ Oggi **(65)***(52) (PJMakin)* 4-8-13 GDuffield(9) (a bhd) ....½ 9
93⁸ Cradle Days **(75)***(59) (RCSpicer)* 6-9-9 JWeaver(3) (bhd fnl 2f) 1 10
498² Little Saboteur **(63)***(44)*(Fav)*(PJMakin)* 6-8-11b PatEddery(2) (b.hind: lw: a bhd) ....¾ 11

7/2 Little Saboteur, **9/2** NORDICO PRINCESS, **11/2** Fangio, **8/1** Myasha (USA), **9/1** Name the Tune, **10/1** Domicksky, Allthruthenight (IRE), Cradle Days, **14/1** Ann's Pearl (IRE), **16/1** Bright Paragon (IRE), **20/1** Oggi, CSF £45.49 CT £394.23 TOTE £4.10: £1.90 £3.10 £3.00 (£39.80) Trio £172.70 OWNER Mr M. S. Griffiths (YORK) 11 Rn

59.26 secs (2.26) SF: 48/60/45/48/23/52/46/44/27/34/19

566

BLACKBERRY LANE H'CAP (0-80) (3-Y.O) (Class D) £3,901.30 (£1,164.40: £556.20: £252.10)
1m 2f (Equitrack) Stalls: Low GOING minus 0.52 sec per fur (FST) 5-15 (5-16)

427[10] **Busy Banana (68)***(84) (RHannon)* 3-9-0 WRyan(1) (lw: mde all: drvn out)...— 1
360[5] Persian Conquest (IRE) **(68)***(83) (RIngram)* 3-9-0b AMcGlone(2) (lw: chsd wnr: rdn over 3f out: ev ch over 2f out: r.o ins fnl f)...½ 2
Dont Shoot Fairies **(65)***(56) (CEBrittain)* 3-8-11 BDoyle(6) (no hdwy fnl 3f)...15 3
453[7] Inchkeith **(66)***(56) (GWragg)* 3-8-5 (7) DGibbs(7) (lw: hdwy over 6f out: rdn over 4f out: one pce fnl 3f)...¾ 4
500[3] Danegold (IRE) **(58)***(44) (MRChannon)* 3-8-4v CRutter(4) (nvr nr to chal)...2½ 5
*372** Vin St Koola **(75)***(57)*(Fav)*(HJCollingridge)* 3-9-7 MRimmer(3) (lw: rdn thrght: bhd fnl 4f)...2½ 6
418[3] Yoush (IRE) **(69)***(40) (MAJarvis)* 3-9-1 PRobinson(8) (b.hind: lw: bhd fnl 4f)...7 7
Amboyna Burl (IRE) **(54)** *(DAWilson)* 3-8-0 JQuinn(5) (dwlt: a bhd)...20 8

2/1 Vin St Koola, **100/30** Yoush (IRE), **4/1** Danegold (IRE), **7/1** BUSY BANANA, **9/1** Persian Conquest (IRE), **10/1** Inchkeith (7/1-11/1), **16/1** Dont Shoot Fairies, **50/1** Amboyna Burl (IRE), CSF £59.20 CT £876.10 TOTE £4.80: £2.90 £2.60 £3.30 (£27.50) OWNER Mr P. D. Savill (MARLBOROUGH) BRED Lingfield Lodge Farm 8 Rn 2m 6.04 (3.04) SF: 32/31/4/4/-/5/-/-

T/Plpt: £72.40 (119.87 Tckts). T/Qdpt: £92.30 (0.80 Tckts). AK

AINTREE (L-H)
Saturday April 8th (Good to firm)

WEATHER: fine WIND: almost nil

567

MARTELL BOB CHAMPION CANCER TRUST CELEBRITY H'CAP (0-70) (4-Y.O+) (Class E) £3,383.00 (£1,034.00: £512.00: £251.00)
6f GOING: minus 0.06 sec per fur (G) 12-30 (12-30)

433[14] **Chinour (IRE) (65)***(75) (EJAlston)* 7-11-11 MBarnes(7) (trckd ldrs: led over 1f out: r.o)...— 1
446[5] Invocation **(68)***(74) (AMoore)* 8-12-0 RChampion(1) (b.hind: chsd ldrs: rdn ½-wy: kpt on fnl f)1½ 2
433[17] Sharp Conquest **(64)***(68) (WRMuir)* 4-11-10v ow1 TStack(4) (lw: led tl over 1f out: one pce)...nk 3
486[2] Great Hall **(60)***(59) (PDCundell)* 6-11-6b TCarberry(5) (bhd tl styd on u.p fnl 1½f: nrst fin)...2½ 4
434[4] Jigsaw Boy **(65)***(62)*(Fav)*(PGMurphy)* 6-11-11 HDavies(6) (in tch: effrt ½-wy: nt qckn fnl f)...½ 5
493[10] Princess Maxine (IRE) **(66)***(62) (JJO'Neill)* 6-11-12 PBuckley(2) (lw: in tch: effrt & nt clr run over 1f out: sn btn)...½ 6
Clarion Call (IRE) **(65)***(56) (GThorner)* 4-11-11b GThorner(3) (chsd ldrs 4f)...2 7
365[7] Little Ibnr **(65)***(40) (PDEvans)* 4-11-11 MScudamore(10) (chsd ldrs over 3f: grad wknd)...6 8
338[7] Grey Toppa **(61)***(34) (NPLittmoden)* 4-11-7 SCKnight(8) (nvr wnt pce)...½ 9
Pampered Guest (IRE) **(69)***(15) (KCBailey)* 4-12-1 ow11 BRDavies(9) (s.i.s: a outpcd & bhd)...6 10

100/30 Jigsaw Boy, **4/1** Great Hall, **11/2** Little Ibnr, Invocation, **10/1** Sharp Conquest, **12/1** Grey Toppa, **14/1** CHINOUR (IRE), **16/1** Princess Maxine (IRE), **20/1** Clarion Call (IRE), Pampered Guest (IRE), CSF £78.68 CT £726.68 TOTE £15.10: £3.10 £2.50 £3.50 (£47.60) OWNER Mr Frank McKevitt (PRESTON) BRED His Highness The Aga Khans Studs S.C. 10 Rn

1m 16.1 SF: -/-/-/-/-/-/-/-/-/-

T/Jkpt: Not won; £59,931.08 to Folkestone 10/4/95 T/Plpt: £1,662.30 (45.65 Tckts). T/Qdpt: £429.50 (0.1 Tckts); £522.41 to Folkestone 10/4/95 AA

0554-BEVERLEY (R-H)
Saturday April 8th (Good to firm)

Wind: almost nil. Weather: fine

568

MELLING ROAD H'CAP (0-60) (4-Y.O+) (Class F) £3,309.00 (£924.00: £447.00)
1m 1f 207y Stalls: High GOING minus 0.61 sec per fur (F) 1-00 (1-02)

430[4] **Larn Fort (47)***(56) (CWFairhurst)* 5-9-1v RCochrane(7) (trckd ldrs: n.m.r on ins 2f out: swtchd & r.o wl to ld ins fnl f)...— 1

315[9] Minster Glory **(39)***(47) (MWEasterby)* 4-8-7 LCharnock(14) (b.hind: trckd ldrs: outpcd 3f out: nt clr run & swtchd over 1f out: chal ins fnl f) ..... ¾ **2**
Augustan **(57)***(64) (SGollings)* 4-9-11 RHughes(10) (bit bkwd: trckd ldrs: led over 2f out tl ins fnl f: nt qckn nr fin) ..... ½ **3**
505[5] Wentbridge Lad (IRE) **(49)***(55) (BAMcMahon)* 5-9-3b LDettori(1) (trckd ldrs: chal over 1f out: hung rt: nt qckn ins fnl f) ..... ½ **4**
430[19] North Ardar **(52)***(56) (MrsMReveley)* 5-8-13 (7) GParkin(5) (hld up & bhd: hdwy & n.m.r 2f out: kpt on same pce appr fnl f: nt rch ldrs) 1¼ **5**
Thatched (IRE) **(43)***(46) (REBarr)* 5-8-11 SWebster(15) (in tch: hdwy on outside 2f out: hung rt: nvr nr to chal) ..... ½ **6**
430[8] Stoproveritate **(40)***(42)*(Fav)*(MrsMReveley)* 6-8-8 KDarley(12) (hld up & bhd: hdwy on ins 2f out: styd on: nt rch ldrs) ..... ¾ **7**
35[7] Broughton's Pride (IRE) **(49)***(51) (JAGlover)* 4-9-3 DeanMcKeown(8) (in tch: racd wd & lost pl over 3f out: styd on appr fnl f) ..... nk **8**
Bold Elect **(49)***(51) (PWigham)* 7-9-3 MWigham(19) (bit bkwd: hld up: hdwy & prom 4f out: grad wknd fnl 2f) ..... hd **9**
271[11] Ho-Joe (IRE) **(45)***(44) (JMCarr)* 5-8-13 SMorris(13) (b: b.hind: s.s: a bhd) 1½ **10**
471[2] Modest Hope (USA) **(50)***(49) (BRichmond)* 8-9-4 JWeaver(9) (lw: hld up: sme hdwy 3f out: sn wknd) ..... s.h **11**
Lord Hastie (USA) **(63)***(61) (CWThornton)* 7-10-0 (3) OPears(4) (a bhd) ..... ½ **12**
520[10] Tovarich **(60)***(57) (DNicholls)* 4-10-0 AlexGreaves(11) (hdwy over 3f out: sn chsng ldrs: wknd 2f out) ..... ¾ **13**
Glenugie **(55)***(50) (GMMoore)* 4-9-6 (3) JTate(16) (a in rr) 1¼ **14**
520[14] Greek Gold (IRE) **(53)***(43) (GPKelly)* 6-9-0 (7) BPeel(17) (lw: led tl over 2f out: wknd qckly over 1f out) 3 **15**
Kalko **(40)***(13) (AHarrison)* 6-8-3v(5) JStack(6) (trckd ldrs tl wknd over 2f out: sn bhd) 11 **16**
Friar Street (IRE) **(50)** *(EJAlston)* 5-9-4 KFallon(2) (Withdrawn not under Starter's orders: kicked at s) ..... **W**

, **11/4** Stoproveritate, **7/2** LARN FORT, **5/1** Wentbridge Lad (IRE), **8/1** Tovarich (op 4/1), Modest Hope (USA), **10/1** Glenugie, **12/1** Minster Glory, **16/1** Bold Elect, Thatched (IRE), **20/1** Augustan, Broughton's Pride (IRE), North Ardar, **25/1** Ho-Joe (IRE), Kalko, **33/1** Greek Gold (IRE), Lord Hastie (USA), CSF £49.57 CT £731.19 TOTE £5.50: £1.60 £2.60 £5.30 £1.80 (£61.00) Trio : Not won ; £336.81 to 2.45 Folkestone 10/04/95. OWNER A P Development Products (NE) Ltd (MIDDLEHAM) BRED Robert T. Cartwright 16 Rn 2m 6.5 (4.00) SF: 19/10/27/18/19/9/5/14/14/7/12/24/20/13/6/-/-

569

VALENTINES (S) STKS (4-Y.O+) (Class G) £2,425.00 (£675.00: £325.00)
1m 3f 216y Stalls: High GOING minus 0.61 sec per fur (F) 1-30 (1-30)

503[15] **Kimberley Boy (65)***(55) (GROldroyd)* 5-8-13 RCochrane(3) (hld up: hdwy over 2f out: r.o to ld ins fnl f: drvn out) ..... — **1**
497[2] Tropical Jungle (USA) **(50)***(53)*(Fav)*(PJMakin)* 5-8-13b LDettori(2) (trckd ldrs: qcknd to ld over 1f out: hdd & no ex ins fnl f) 1¼ **2**
Irish Senor (IRE) **(66)***(54) (JLSpearing)* 4-9-2 DeanMcKeown(6) (chsd ldrs: ev ch fnl 2f: sn rdn kpt on one pce) 2½ **3**
304[10] Ann Hill (IRE) **(36)***(42) (RHollinshead)* 5-8-8 WRyan(4) (hld up & bhd: gd hdwy on outside & ev ch over 2f out: wknd over 1f out) 2 **4**
Antartictern (USA) **(53)***(49) (NTinkler)* 5-9-4b KDarley(5) (trckd ldrs: hmpd & lost pl over 3f out: styd on fnl 2f) 2½ **5**
Persian Linnet **(45)***(43) (MrsMReveley)* 4-8-4 (7) SCopp(8) (t: lw: chsd ldr tl wknd 2f out) ..... nk **6**
Sottises (IRE) *(35) (PTDalton)* 4-8-6 LCharnock(9) (led tl over 2f out: sn lost pl) 2 **7**
Ttyfran *(40) (BPJBaugh)* 5-8-13 ACulhane(1) (b: hld up & bhd: effrt over 3f out: sn rdn & wknd) ..... ½ **8**
King Optimist **(23)***(7) (ASmith)* 6-8-13 MBirch(7) (b: chsd ldrs: drvn along & n.m.r 4f out: sn lost pl & bhd: eased) 25 **9**

6/4 Tropical Jungle (USA), **11/4** Irish Senor (IRE), **5/1** Antartictern (USA), **11/2** Persian Linnet, **10/1** Ann Hill (IRE), **12/1** KIMBERLEY BOY, **25/1** Ttyfran, **33/1** Sottises (IRE), King Optimist, CSF £31.35 TOTE £13.90: £2.30 £1.20 £1.50 (£16.30) Trio £14.60 OWNER Consultco Ltd (YORK) BRED Kessly Bloodstock Ltd 9 Rn 2m 39.0 (7.50) SF: 3/1/1/-/-/-/-/-/-
WEIGHT FOR AGE 4yo-2lb
No bid.

570

CHAIR MAIDEN AUCTION STKS (2-Y.O F) (Class F) £2,952.00 (£822.00: £396.00)
5f Stalls: Centre GOING minus 0.41 sec per fur (F) 2-00 (2-02)

474[2] **Unconditional Love (IRE)** *(75+t)*(Fav)*(MJohnston)* 2-8-6 DHolland(1) (chsd ldr: rdn to ld over 1f out: edgd rt: sn clr) ..... — **1**

Badger Bay (IRE) *(57) (JohnBerry)* 2-8-4 JQuinn(7) (v.unf: chsd ldrs: rdn & edgd lft 1f out: wnt rt ins fnl f) 5 **2**
Mystique Smile *(50) (JBerry)* 2-8-7 JCarroll(2) (leggy: unf: led: hdd & hmpd over 1f out: grad wknd: n.m.r nr fin) 3 **3**
Takapuna (IRE) *(47) (RHannon)* 2-8-5 RPerham(8) (unf: scope: sn outpcd & wl bhd: styd on fnl 2f) ....½ **4**
Fortuitious (IRE) *(40) (JRJenkins)* 2-8-6 LDettori(6) (unf: unruly s: hmpd sn after s: drvn along: a outpcd) 2½ **5**
Lady Eclat *(29) (JAGlover)* 2-8-3 GCarter(3) (cmpt: bkwd: s.s: a bhd) 2½ **6**
508[12] Alistover *(22) (RDickin)* 2-8-3 JLowe(4) (a outpcd) 2 **7**
Skelton Countess (IRE) *(RHollinshead)* 2-8-3 KDarley(5) (cmpt: bit bkwd: sn trckng ldrs: wknd qckly 2f out) 9 **8**

6/4 UNCONDITIONAL LOVE (IRE) (op 9/4), **9/4** Mystique Smile (op 6/4), **5/1** Takapuna (IRE) (op 3/1), **9/1** Fortuitious (IRE) (op 6/1), **12/1** Badger Bay (IRE), **14/1** Lady Eclat, Skelton Countess (IRE) (op 8/1), **20/1** Alistover, CSF £19.43 TOTE £2.40: £1.30 £3.50 £1.30 (£21.70). OWNER Mrs H. Conroy (MIDDLEHAM) BRED Rathbarry Stud 8 Rn 63.6 secs (2.10) SF: 24/6/-/-/-/-/-/-

571

EAST RIDING STKS (Listed) (3-Y.O+) (Class A) £12,838.50 (£3,888.00: £1,899.00: £904.50) **5f** Stalls: Centre GOING minus 0.41 sec per fur (F) 2-30 (2-32)

El Yasaf (IRE) (92)*(111) (GFierro)* 7-9-3 MWigham(11) (lw: prom: effrt & sltly hmpd over 1f out: r.o to ld ins fnl f: just ct: fin 2nd, s.h: awrdd r) ....— **1**
Blue Siren **(113)***(110)*(Fav)*(IABalding)* 4-9-2 LDettori(7) (chds ldrs: drvn along 2f out: led 1f out tl ins fnl f: r.o to ld post: fin 1st: disq: plcd 2nd) **2**
Branston Abby (IRE) **(105)***(109) (MJohnston)* 6-9-2 JReid(2) (s.i.s: outpcd & bhd: gd hdwy 2f out: swtchd ins & r.o strly ins fnl f) ....nk **3**
441[6] Venture Capitalist **(98)***(104) (DNicholls)* 6-9-3 AlexGreaves(13) (sn bhd: styd on wl fnl 2f) 1¾ **4**
Lucky Parkes **(100)***(95) (JBerry)* 5-8-12 JCarroll(6) (w ldr: edgd lft over 1f out: wknd jst ins fnl f) 1½ **5**
Alzianah **(92)***(93) (JDBethell)* 4-8-12 BThomson(12) (bit bkwd: in tch: effrt 2f out: grad wknd) ½ **6**
Snipe Hall *(92) (TRWatson)* 4-8-12 DeanMcKeown(8) (b.hind: hdwy ½-wy: n.m.r: styd on nr fin) ....nk **7**
Averti (IRE) *(97) (WRMuir)* 4-9-3 JWeaver(5) (bit bkwd: unruly in stalls: reard s: bhd tl kpt on appr fnl f: n.d) ....s.h **8**
Eveningperformance **(97)***(95) (HCandy)* 4-9-2 WNewnes(9) (led tl hdd & wknd 1f out) ....nk **9**
441[9] Regal Chimes **(95)***(95) (BAMcMahon)* 6-9-3 TIves(4) (sn pushed along: hdwy & prom ½-wy: wknd over 1f out) ....nk **10**
441[11] Call Me I'm Blue (IRE) **(100)***(95) (NTinkler)* 5-9-3 MBirch(10) (hld up: effrt 3 out: nvr rchd ldrs) ....hd **11**
Welsh Mist **(100)***(93) (RBoss)* 4-9-2 WRyan(3) (hld up: effrt ½-wy: n.d) ....hd **12**

5/4 Blue Siren, **5/1** Eveningperformance, Lucky Parkes, **10/1** Averti (IRE), Branston Abby (IRE), **12/1** Welsh Mist, **14/1** Venture Capitalist, **20/1** Regal Chimes, EL YASAF (IRE), Call Me I'm Blue (IRE), Alzianah, **25/1** Snipe Hall, CSF £47.95 TOTE £35.20: £4.50 £1.50 £3.30 (£26.80) Trio £212.80 OWNER Old School House Racing Ltd (HEDNESFORD) BRED Deepwood Farm Stud 12 Rn 62.3 secs (0.80) SF: 53/54/51/47/37/35/35/39/37/37/37/36

572

GRAND NATIONAL DAY H'CAP (0-85) (3-Y.O) (Class D) £3,762.50 (£1,130.00: £545.00: £252.50)
1m 100y Stalls: High GOING minus 0.61 sec per fur (F) 3-00 (3-02)

427[8] **Clifton Fox (76)***(80) (JAGlover)* 3-9-3 MBirch(7) (trckd ldrs: nt clr run over 1f out: r.o wl u.p to ld ins fnl f) ....— **1**
*381** Lyford Law (IRE) **(80)***(81) (JHMGosden)* 3-9-7 LDettori(1) (b: b.hind: hld up: stdy hdwy over 2f out: chal over 1f out: rdn & nt qckn ins fnl f) 1½ **2**
Blasted **(60)***(60) (RHannon)* 3-8-1 GCarter(4) (led tl ins fnl f: r.o same pce) ....½ **3**
437[10] Kildrummy Castle **(58)***(52) (MrsJRRamsden)* 3-7-13 JFanning(5) (chsd ldrs: kpt on same pce fnl 2f) 3½ **4**
Raise the Stakes **(80)***(72) (IABalding)* 3-9-7 RCochrane(8) (lw: mstkes: effrt over 3f out: kpt on: nvr nr to chal) ....¾ **5**
437[5] Roy Boy **(74)***(61)*(Fav)*(MrsMReveley)* 3-9-1 KDarley(3) (lw: hld up: hdwy & prom 3f out: sn rdn: wknd 1f out) 3 **6**
427[15] Fame Again **(78)***(55) (MrsJRRamsden)* 3-9-5 KFallon(2) (hld up: effrt on outside 3f out: sn prom: wknd 2f out) 5 **7**
Shining Edge **(66)***(36) (MHEasterby)* 3-8-7 SMaloney(6) (plld hrd: trckd ldrs: rdn & outpcd 3f out: sn lost pl) 4 **8**

2/1 Roy Boy, **3/1** Lyford Law (IRE) (op 7/4), **5/1** CLIFTON FOX, **7/1** Fame Again, **8/1** Raise the Stakes, **9/1** Kildrummy Castle, **12/1** Blasted (op 8/1), **16/1** Shining Edge, CSF £20.51 CT £159.70 TOTE £6.00: £1.80 £1.70 £2.80 (£4.40). OWNER P and S Partnership (WORKSOP) BRED Crest Stud Ltd 8 Rn
1m 45.8 (1.80) SF: 35/36/15/7/27/16/10/-

573 CANAL TURN H'CAP (0-70) (3-Y.O) (Class E) £3,276.75 (£984.00: £474.50: £219.75) 7f 100y Stalls: High GOING minus 0.61 sec per fur (F) 3-30 (3-30)

The Stager (IRE) **(65)***(73) (JRJenkins)* 3-9-2 LDettori(1) (lw: trckd ldrs: r.o u.p to ld ins fnl f) .... — 1
Blaze of Song **(59)***(65)*(Fav)*(RHannon)* 3-8-10 RPerham(6) (led tl over 5f out: led over 1f out: nt qckn nr fin) 1 2
Chiming In **(67)***(60) (MrsJRRamsden)* 3-9-4 KFallon(8) (effrt & drvn along over 3f out: sn prom: nt qckn appr fnl f) 6 3
Euro Rebel **(62)***(52) (MHEasterby)* 3-8-13 MBirch(10) (chsd ldrs: kpt on same pce fnl 2f) 1¼ 4
427[16] Rambo Waltzer **(60)***(50) (SGNorton)* 3-8-11 MTebbutt(7) (chsd ldrs: sn drvn along: outpcd fnl 2f) .... nk 5
431[9] Spirituelle **(70)***(53) (MMcCormack)* 3-9-7b JReid(3) (trckd ldrs: led over 5f out tl over 1f out: hung rt & sn wknd) 3 6
Prudent Pet **(62)***(40) (CWFairhurst)* 3-8-13 JFanning(9) (lw: sn bhd: sme hdwy 2f out: n.d) .. 2½ 7
Ballard Lady (IRE) **(44)***(15) (JSWainwright)* 3-7-9 ow2 JQuinn(4) (effrt ½-wy: sn in tch: wknd over 2f out) 2½ 8
315[11] Prime Property (IRE) **(59)***(28) (MWEasterby)* 3-8-10 KDarley(5) (sn bhd) 1½ 9
354[15] Foist **(50)** *(MWEasterby)* 3-8-1 LCharnock(2) (bit bkwd: a wl bhd) 15 10

LONG HANDICAP Ballard Lady (IRE) 7-5

9/4 Blaze of Song, **4/1** Rambo Waltzer, **5/1** THE STAGER (IRE) (op 3/1), Euro Rebel, **13/2** Prudent Pet, **7/1** Chiming In (op 3/1), **12/1** Foist, **14/1** Spirituelle, **16/1** Prime Property (IRE), **25/1** Ballard Lady (IRE), CSF £18.29 CT £79.40 TOTE £5.40: £2.30 £1.50 £2.20 (£8.20) Trio £22.30. OWNER Mr T. Long (ROYSTON) BRED Barronstown Bloodstock and Swettenham Stud 10 Rn
1m 32.0 (equals standard) SF: 51/43/38/30/28/31/18/-/6/-

T/Plpt: £11.20 (1,099.36 Tckts). T/Qdpt: £7.20 (13.55 Tckts). WG

0474-EDINBURGH (R-H)
Monday April 10th (Good, Good to soft patches)
WEATHER: sunny WIND: moderate against

574 CARBERRY MAIDEN AUCTION STKS (2-Y.O) (Class F) £2,634.50 (£742.00: £363.50) 5f Stalls: High GOING minus 0.34 sec per fur (GF) 2-00 (2-01)

Tropical Beach *(51t) (JBerry)* 2-8-5 JCarroll(4) (leggy: scope: s.i.s: hdwy ½-wy: led ins fnl f: r.o) .... — 1
436[5] Afisiak *(42)*(Fav)*(MJohnston)* 2-8-0 TWilliams(5) (lw: disp ld after 1f tl hdd ins fnl f: kpt on u.p) 1¼ 2
540[2] Arvzees (IRE) *(45) (MRChannon)* 2-8-0 (5) PPMurphy(3) (led tl disp ld after 1f: no ex u.p ins fnl f) .... ½ 3
533[11] Abduction *(39) (EWeymes)* 2-8-5 KDarley(1) (chsd ldrs: rdn ½-wy: outpcd fnl 2f) 2 4
Royal Rigger *(28) (CSmith)* 2-7-10 JFanning(6) (leggy: lt-f: chsd ldrs: n.m.r 2f out: wknd appr fnl f) .... ½ 5
Tiny Astro *(21) (MHEasterby)* 2-8-1 SMaloney(2) (cmpt: s.i.s: hdwy u.p ½-wy: sn wknd) 4 6

5/4 Afisiak (op 2/1), **5/2** Arvzees (IRE), **11/4** TROPICAL BEACH (13/8-3/1), **14/1** Abduction (12/1-20/1), **33/1** Tiny Astro, **66/1** Royal Rigger, CSF £6.27 TOTE £2.60: £2.40 £1.70 (£3.40) OWNER Contact One & Torrisholme Travel (COCKERHAM) BRED P. Balding 6 Rn
62.5 secs (4.80) SF: -/-/-/-/-/-

575 COLONEL AND MAUDE MONTEITH'S 80TH BIRTHDAY CELEBRATION H'CAP (0-70) (3-Y.O) (Class E) £2,944.00 (£892.00: £436.00: £208.00) 1m 3f 32y Stalls: High GOING minus 0.34 sec per fur (GF) 2-30 (2-30)

521[2] **Slapy Dam (48)***(59)*(Fav)*(MrsJRRamsden)* 3-8-6 KFallon(3) (bhd: pushed along ent st: led appr fnl f: r.o wl) .... — 1
538[4] Chaldon Herring **(63)***(71) (TDBarron)* 3-9-7 JFortune(5) (hld up: smooth hdwy to ld over 2f out: hdd appr fnl f: kpt on wl) 2 2
427[9] Durgams First (IRE) **(60)***(66) (MrsMReveley)* 3-9-4 KDarley(4) (lw: hdwy 6f out: ev ch over 2f out: rdn & nt qckn) 1¾ 3
213[5] Boundary Express **(55)***(56) (MJohnston)* 3-8-13 TWilliams(6) (led tl hdd over 2f out: sn outpcd) 3 4

Jackmanii **(54)***(50) (WTKemp)* 3-8-12 DeanMcKeown(1) (racd wd: chsd ldrs to st) 4 **5**
Raindeer Quest **(52)***(19) (CSmith)* 3-8-5 (5) JStack(2) (cl up tl wknd qckly over 3f out) 20 **6**

6/5 SLAPY DAM, **3/1** Chaldon Herring, Durgams First (IRE), **16/1** Boundary Express, **20/1** Raindeer Quest, **50/1** Jackmanii, CSF £4.76 TOTE £2.20: £1.20 £1.70 (£4.40) OWNER Mr M. R. Charlton (THIRSK) BRED Hesmonds Stud Ltd 6 Rn 2m 26.0 (6.30) SF: 20/32/27/17/11/-

576

INVERESK RATING RELATED MAIDEN LIMITED STKS (0-60) (3-Y.O) (Class F) £2,645.00 (£745.00: £365.00)
1m 16y Stalls: High GOING minus 0.34 sec per fur (GF) 3-00 (3-00)

Eden Dancer (59)*(62) (MrsMReveley)* 3-9-0 KDarley(6) (lw: mde all: qcknd clr over 3f out: pushed out)..— **1**
451³ Woodrising **(55)***(50)*(Fav)*(LadyHerries)* 3-8-9 JCarroll(5) (lw: chsd ldrs: rdn ent st: styd on: nt pce to chal) 3½ **2**
477⁴ Ricana **(48)***(45) (WTKemp)* 3-8-9 DeanMcKeown(2) (cl up tl outpcd over 3f out: no imp after) 2½ **3**
482¹⁶ Indian Rhapsody **(40)***(37) (MRChannon)* 3-8-9 RHughes(4) (effrt over 3f out: rdn & no imp)...4 **4**
515³ Lucky Peg **(45)***(35) (FJO'Mahony)* 3-8-9 JFortune(1) (prom tl outpcd fnl 3f) 1¼ **5**
Miss Tri Colour **(45)***(17) (FHLee)* 3-8-9 MBirch(3) (hld up & bhd: n.d)..9 **6**

8/11 Woodrising, **2/1** EDEN DANCER, **16/1** Ricana, Indian Rhapsody, **20/1** Lucky Peg, **50/1** Miss Tri Colour, CSF £3.58 TOTE £3.20: £1.60 £1.10 (£1.70) OWNER Mr Ashley Graham (SALTBURN) BRED B. D. Cantle 6 Rn 1m 42.9 (4.30) SF: 28/16/11/3/1/-

577

NORTH BERWICK MEDIAN AUCTION MAIDEN STKS (3-Y.O) (Class F) £2,624.00 (£739.00: £362.00)
7f 15y Stalls: High GOING minus 0.34 sec per fur (GF) 3-30 (3-31)

Shaffishayes *(51)*(Fav)*(MrsMReveley)* 3-9-0 KDarley(1) (w'like: plld hrd: cl up tl ran wd appr st: hdwy 3f out: carried lft: rdn to ld wl ins fnl f) ....— **1**
519⁴ Hi Rock **(54)***(43) (MJCamacho)* 3-8-9 LCharnock(2) (hdwy to ld appr st: hung lft fnl 2f: hdd & no ex wl ins fnl f)...1¼ **2**
Royal Dome (IRE) *(45) (MartynWane)* 3-9-0 JFortune(4) (bit bkwd: hdwy to chal ent st: hung lft fnl 2f: nt qckn fnl f)..1¼ **3**
Bollin Frank **(65)***(36) (MHEasterby)* 3-9-0 MBirch(3) (led tl ran wd & hdd appr st: hdwy 3f out: wknd fnl 2f)..4 **4**

11/8 SHAFFISHAYES, **7/4** Bollin Frank, **3/1** Hi Rock, **16/1** Royal Dome (IRE), CSF £5.33 TOTE £1.80 (£2.50) OWNER Mr P. Davidson-Brown (SALTBURN) BRED W. G. Barker 4 Rn 1m 31.5 (5.50) SF: 9/1/3/-

578

ABERLADY (S) H'CAP (0-60) (3-Y.O+) (Class G) £2,512.00 (£707.00: £346.00)
7f 15y Stalls: High GOING minus 0.34 sec per fur (GF) 4-00 (4-01)

444⁴ **Vindaloo (42)***(50) (JLHarris)* 3-7-12 DaleGibson(13) (lw: in tch: hdwy on ins to ld ins fnl f: r.o) ....— **1**
476⁶ Sharp N' Smooth **(50)***(56) (WTKemp)* 8-9-7b KDarley(12) (lw: bhd: gd hdwy 2f out: ev ch ins fnl f: r.o)...1 **2**
Guesstimation (USA) **(57)***(63) (JPearce)* 6-10-0 GBardwell(15) (hdwy over 2f out: ev ch & rdn ins fnl f: kpt on)..hd **3**
511³ At the Savoy (IRE) **(46)***(50) (TDBarron)* 4-9-3 JFortune(2) (lw: a chsng ldrs: ev ch ins fnl f: nt qckn)...½ **4**
476³ Funny Rose **(23)***(23) (PMonteith)* 5-7-8 JMarshall(3) (hdwy 3f out: nt clr run wl over 1f out: styd on nr fin)...2 **5**
Samaka Hara (IRE) **(42)***(40) (WSCunningham)* 3-7-12 JFanning(6) (hdwy on outside 3f out: edgd rt & nt qckn appr fnl f) ....¾ **6**
Never so True **(40)***(37) (MartynWane)* 4-8-11 KFallon(10) (chsd ldrs: ev ch 2f out: hung lft: r.o one pce)..½ **7**
478⁴ Dundeelin **(37)***(30) (JLEyre)* 4-8-8 RLappin(16) (cl up: led over 2f out tl ins fnl f: wknd)..2 **8**
267⁸ Petal's Jarred **(35)***(18) (WStorey)* 5-7-13 (7)ow3 CTeague(8) (bhd tl sme late hdwy)......................3 **9**
82⁵ Obsidian Grey **(48)***(25) (MissLCSiddall)* 8-9-2 (3) DRMcCabe(7) (effrt over 3f out: n.d) 4 **10**
136¹¹ Nord Lys (IRE) **(35)***(8) (FHLee)* 4-8-6b MBirch(5) (lw: n.d) 1½ **11**
528⁶ We're Joken **(50)***(20) (JBerry)* 3-8-6 JCarroll(4) (b.hind: unruly in stalls: in tch 4f) 1¼ **12**
420¹⁰ Benten **(44)***(5) (DWChapman)* 3-8-0b SMaloney(11) (led tl hdd & wknd over 2f out)....................4 **13**
Shropshire Blue **(37)** *(DANolan)* 5-8-8 TWilliams(14) (n.d) 1¼ **14**

366[2] Jamaica Bridge **(49)***(3)*(Fav)*(SGNorton)* 5-9-1 (5) JStack(9) (b.off.hind: chsd ldrs tl wknd 2f out) 2 15
My Godson **(47)** *(FJO'Mahony)* 5-9-4b SDWilliams(1) (cl up tl wknd 3f out) 6 16

4/1 Jamaica Bridge, **11/2** Samaka Hara (IRE), **7/1** At the Savoy (IRE), Sharp N' Smooth, **8/1** Guesstimation (USA), **9/1** We're Joken, **10/1** Dundeelin, **14/1** Obsidian Grey (12/1-20/1), Petal's Jarred, **16/1** VINDALOO, **20/1** My Godson, Funny Rose, **25/1** Never so True, Benten, **33/1** Nord Lys (IRE), **66/1** Shropshire Blue, CSF £120.94 CT £900.53 TOTE £18.40: £2.70 £1.70 £3.80 £2.30 (£77.60) Trio £373.70 OWNER Mr J. D. Abell (MELTON MOWBRAY) BRED Green Park Investments Ltd 16 Rn 1m 29.4 (3.40) SF: 17/38/45/32/5/7/19/12/-/7/-/-/-/-/-/-
WEIGHT FOR AGE 3yo-15lb
No bid

579 TENNENTS SPRING H'CAP (0-70) (3-Y.O+) (Class E) £3,126.00 (£948.00: £464.00: £222.00) 7f 15y Stalls: High GOING minus 0.34 sec (GF) 4-30 (4-31)

Don Pepe (64)*(71) (RBoss)* 4-9-11 JCarroll(5) (mde all: clr 3f out: rdn & r.o fnl f) ....— 1
486[3] Sharp Rebuff **(67)***(73)*(Fav)*(PJMakin)* 4-10-0 JFortune(11) (a.p: swtchd & effrt 3f out: rdn ins fnl f: styd on u.p) ....½ 2
529[2] Equerry **(62)***(68) (MJohnston)* 4-9-9 KDarley(4) (bhd: hdwy 2f out: r.o wl nr fin) ....s.h 3
518[2] Orthorhombus **(64)***(65) (DJSCosgrove)* 6-9-11b MWigham(6) (bhd: effrt ½-wy: hdwy appr fnl f: fin wl) 2 4
Blue Grit **(55)***(52) (MDods)* 9-9-2 DaleGibson(3) (a chsng ldrs: effrt 3f out: r.o one pce) 2 5
Spanish Verdict **(66)***(57) (DenysSmith)* 8-9-6 (7) CTeague(10) (in tch: outpcd over 3f out: no imp after) 2½ 6
Peacefull Reply (USA) **(53)***(42) (FHLee)* 5-9-0 MBirch(8) (chsd wnr: one pce fnl 3f) ....¾ 7
369[8] Prince Belfort **(64)***(50) (JLEyre)* 7-9-8b(3) OPears(9) (nvr trbld ldrs) 1½ 8
Just Flamenco **(52)***(30) (MJRyan)* 4-8-13 DBiggs(7) (nvr wnt pce) 3½ 9
224[2] Four of Spades **(49)***(21) (WSCunningham)* 4-8-10b KFallon(1) (chsd ldrs 4f: sn lost pl) 2½ 10

3/1 Sharp Rebuff, **9/2** Equerry, **5/1** DON PEPE, **11/2** Four of Spades, **6/1** Orthorhombus, **9/1** Just Flamenco, **12/1** Spanish Verdict, **16/1** Blue Grit, Prince Belfort, **20/1** Peacefull Reply (USA), CSF £20.42 CT £68.17 TOTE £6.00: £2.70 £1.40 £1.80 (£10.20) Trio £25.90 OWNER Mrs Elaine Aird (NEWMARKET) BRED Patrick Eddery Ltd 10 Rn 1m 28.6 (2.60) SF: 51/53/48/45/32/37/22/30/10/1

T/Plpt: £25.60 (434.8 Tckts). T/Qdpt: £21.30 (10.55 Tckts) AA

0449-FOLKESTONE (R-H)
Monday April 10th (Good to firm)
WEATHER: overcast WIND: almost nil

580 LEVY BOARD APPRENTICE H'CAP (0-60) (3-Y.O) (Class G) £2,312.00 (£657.00: £326.00) 6f Stalls: Low GOING minus 0.61 sec per fur (F) 1-45 (1-47)

Bonita (53)*(54) (MrsLPiggott)* 3-8-13 (8) VictoriaAppleby(2) (b: b.hind: dwlt: led over 4f out: r.o wl) ....— 1
452[4] Mister Raider **(47)***(47) (SMellor)* 3-9-1 ADaly(7) (swtg: hdwy over 1f out: ev ch ins fnl f: r.o) ....nk 2
Cedar Dancer **(44)***(44) (RJHodges)* 3-8-12 JoHunnam(1) (a.p: hrd rdn over 1f out: ev ch ins fnl f: r.o) ....s.h 3
42* Half Tone **(44)***(39)*(Fav)*(RMFlower)* 3-8-12b RWaterfield(6) (bit bkwd: lost pl over 2f out: rallied over 1f out: unable qckn ins fnl f) 2 4
Ilustre (IRE) **(53)***(48) (LJHolt)* 3-9-4 (3) IonaWands(3) (lw: nvr nr to chal) ....hd 5
Deceit the Second **(50)***(37) (GLewis)* 3-9-1 (3) ALakeman(4) (lw: led over 1f: wknd over 2f out) 3 6
359[6] Black Shadow **(47)***(23) (PJMcBride)* 3-9-1 GFaulkner(5) (dwlt: bhd fnl 2f) 4 7

11/4 Half Tone (2/1-3/1), **100/30** Mister Raider, **4/1** Black Shadow, **7/1** Ilustre (IRE), **8/1** BONITA (5/1-10/1), **10/1** Cedar Dancer (op 6/1), Deceit the Second (op 4/1), CSF £31.69 TOTE £7.40: £3.30 £2.20 (£10.80) OWNER Mr Tony Hirschfeld BRED Mrs S. E. Piggott 7 Rn
1m 14.0 (2.30) SF: 23/16/13/8/17/6/-

581 CHATHAM CLAIMING STKS (3-Y.O) (Class F) £2,519.00 (£694.00: £329.00) 5f Stalls: Low GOING minus 0.61 sec per fur (F) 2-15 (2-16)

482[4] **Baileys Sunset (IRE) (62)***(67)*(Fav)*(MJohnston)* 3-8-3 PRobinson(9) (chsd ldr: led over 1f out: hrd rdn: r.o wl) ....— 1

196[8] Noosa (IRE) **(79)***(67) (MJohnston)* 3-8-8 JReid(1) (hdwy over 1f out: hrd rdn: unable qckn) 1½ 2
483[8] Endless Wave **(80)***(73) (MBell)* 3-9-0 DHarrison(3) (hmpd s: hld up: rdn over 1f out: one pce) ....s.h 3
363[7] My Lady Brady **(57)***(55) (GROldroyd)* 3-8-7 RCochrane(2) (swvd rt s: led over 3f) 3½ 4
Kencol **(69)***(58) (AGFoster)* 3-8-9 (5)ow3 RPainter(7) (b.hind: hld up: hung bdly rt 2f out: ev ch over 1f out: eased whn btn ins fnl f) ....nk 5
482[12] Governor's Lass **(40)***(43) (SDow)* 3-7-12 StephenDavies(6) (hld up: rdn 3f out: wknd wl over 1f out) ....½ 6
410[11] Logie Pert Lad **(30)***(25) (JJBridger)* 3-8-2 (3) SSanders(8) (prom over 2f) 8 7
Il Furetto *(25) (JSKing)* 3-8-13 LDettori(4) (unf: hmpd s: outpcd) 2½ 8

9/4 BAILEYS SUNSET (IRE), **5/2** Noosa (IRE), **100/30** Endless Wave (9/4-7/2), **6/1** My Lady Brady, **9/1** Il Furetto (5/1-10/1), **12/1** Kencol, **25/1** Governor's Lass, Logie Pert Lad, CSF £8.60 TOTE £3.30: £1.20 £1.50 £1.60 (£3.00) Trio £2.10 OWNER G R Bailey Ltd (Baileys Horse Feeds) (MIDDLEHAM) BRED Vincent and Joseph Fitzpatrick in Ireland 8 Rn

60.0 secs (1.40) SF: 13/13/19/1/4/-/-/-

582

GRAVESEND H'CAP (0-70) (4-Y.O+) (Class E) £3,531.00 (£1,056.00: £506.00: £231.00) **1m 7f 92y** Stalls: Low GOING minus 0.27 sec per fur (GF) 2-45 (2-47)

Soojama (IRE) (35)*(44) (RMFlower)* 5-8-0 (5) JDSmith(15) (6th st: led over 1f out: hrd rdn: r.o wl) ....— 1
556[4] Ballymac Girl **(53)***(60) (JMBradley)* 7-9-4 (5) SDrowne(11) (b: 3rd st: led 2f out tl over 1f out: unable qckn) 1½ 2
By Arrangement (IRE) **(40)***(47) (SWoodman)* 6-8-10 RCochrane(5) (5th st: hrd rdn over 1f out: one pce) ....nk 3
340[5] Snow Dream **(41)***(48) (MJRyan)* 5-8-11 WCarson(3) (2nd st: ev ch over 1f out: one pce) ....nk 4
259[15] Durshan (USA) **(54)***(59) (JRJenkins)* 6-9-10 LDettori(2) (lw: rdn over 3f out: hdwy over 1f out: r.o wl ins fnl f) 1¾ 5
514[2] Red Whirlwind **(51)***(56) (RJO'Sullivan)* 5-9-7 WWoods(16) (4th st: hrd rdn over 1f out: one pce) ....s.h 6
*514** Child Star (FR) **(34)***(38) (DMarks)* 6-7-13 (5) MBaird(14) (hdwy over 1f out: nvr nrr) 1¼ 7
Dakota Girl **(52)***(54) (GBBalding)* 4-9-5v JWeaver(6) (lw: no hdwy fnl 2f) 1¾ 8
377[4] Mint a Million (IRE) **(41)***(42) (MBlanshard)* 4-8-8 JQuinn(1) (nvr nr to chal) 1¼ 9
*374** Jaraab **(46)***(44)*(Fav)*(GLewis)* 4-8-8 (5) AWhelan(4) (rdn & hdwy 6f out: wknd over 2f out) 2½ 10
Access Sun **(44)***(42) (JSKing)* 8-9-0 TQuinn(9) (led over 13f out to 6f out: wknd over 3f out) ....nk 11
Kingsfold Pet **(48)***(45) (MJHaynes)* 6-9-4 BRouse(8) (led 2f: led 6f out to 2f out: sn wknd) ....nk 12
Lunar Risk **(50)***(47) (MissBSanders)* 5-9-6 WNewnes(7) (plld hrd: hmpd over 12f out: bhd fnl 10f) ....s.h 13
Fruitful Affair (IRE) **(44)***(33) (TThomsonJones)* 6-9-0 StephenDavies(12) (a bhd) 8 14
Sports View **(40)***(27) (RJHodges)* 6-8-10 FNorton(13) (a bhd) 1½ 15
430[24] Zahid (USA) **(53)***(40) (BobJones)* 4-9-6 GDuffield(10) (hmpd over 12f out: bhd fnl 6f) ....½ 16

11/8 Jaraab, **13/2** Red Whirlwind, **15/2** Ballymac Girl (5/1-8/1), **8/1** Dakota Girl (5/1-9/1), **9/1** Child Star (FR) (6/1-10/1), **12/1** By Arrangement (IRE), Snow Dream, Kingsfold Pet (8/1-14/1), **14/1** Fruitful Affair (IRE) (10/1-16/1), **16/1** Lunar Risk, **20/1** Access Sun, Durshan (USA), Zahid (USA), **25/1** Mint a Million (IRE), Sports View, SOOJAMA (IRE), CSF £219.24 CT £2,206.67 TOTE £76.20: £8.10 £1.60 £2.90 £3.40 (£313.80) Trio £1,110.30 OWNER Mr N. G. Castleton (JEVINGTON) BRED E. and Mrs Hanley 16 Rn 3m 27.7 (10.80) SF: 15/31/18/19/30/27/9/22/10/12/13/16/18/4/-/8

WEIGHT FOR AGE 4yo-3lb

583

GILLINGHAM LIMITED STKS (0-55) (4-Y.O+) (Class F) £2,871.80 (£794.80: £379.40) **5f** Stalls: Low GOING minus 0.61 sec per fur (F) 3-15 (3-16)

Bashful Brave (55)*(60) (JWPayne)* 4-8-11 MRimmer(2) (lw: a.p: led over 1f out: rdn out) ....— 1
507[3] Distant Dynasty **(51)***(52) (BAPearce)* 5-8-11 StephenDavies(4) (hdwy over 2f out: hrd rdn over 1f out: unable qckn) 2½ 2
452[2] Harry's Coming **(49)***(50) (RJHodges)* 11-8-6 (5) SDrowne(1) (hld up: rdn over 2f out: r.o ins fnl f) ....½ 3
507* Canovas Heart **(62)***(52)*(Fav)*(BobJones)* 6-9-0 GDuffield(9) (led over 3f: one pce) ....nk 4
452[7] Halliard **(55)***(48) (TMJones)* 4-9-0 LDettori(8) (a.p: hrd rdn over 1f out: wknd fnl f) 1¼ 5
Judgement Call **(51)***(41) (PHowling)* 8-8-11 NCarlisle(3) (b: bkwd: no hdwy fnl 2f) 1¼ 6
248[8] Coalisland **(35)***(32) (RIngram)* 5-8-11v WWoods(7) (a bhd) 3 7
Mazzarello (IRE) **(29)***(32) (RCurtis)* 5-8-11 JWeaver(5) (bit bkwd: a bhd) ....s.h 8
Superlativemaximus (IRE) **(53)***(9) (JABennett)* 7-8-11 TSprake(6) (spd over 2f) 7 9

Evens Canovas Heart, **7/2** Halliard, **11/2** Distant Dynasty (3/1-6/1), **7/1** Harry's Coming, **12/1** BASHFUL BRAVE (8/1-14/1), Judgement Call (7/1-14/1), **20/1** Superlativemaximus (IRE), **33/1** Coalisland, Mazzarello (IRE), CSF £75.27 TOTE £19.40: £2.90 £2.40 £1.70 (£37.30) Trio £178.40 OWNER Mrs G. M. Hay (NEWMARKET) BRED Mrs G. M. Hay 9 Rn

58.95 secs (0.35) SF: 39/31/29/31/27/20/11/11/-

584

DARTFORD MAIDEN STKS (3-Y.O+) (Class D) £4,171.70 (£1,247.60: £597.80: £272.90) **1m 4f** Stalls: Low GOING minus 0.27 sec per fur (GF) 3-45 (3-47)

Mokhtar (IRE) *(71)*(Fav)*(JLDunlop)* 4-9-12 WCarson(3) (bit bkwd: hld up: led over 5f out: pushed out)......— 1
Artic Courier **(76)***(68) (DJSCosgrove)* 4-9-12b MRimmer(12) (3rd st: rdn over 1f out: r.o one pce)......2½ 2
Crowned Glory (USA) **(80)***(68) (PFICole)* 3-8-6 TQuinn(9) (lw: 5th st: rdn over 2f out: one pce)......hd 3
Fearless Venture *(64) (SPCWoods)* 3-8-6 WWoods(1) (rdn over 3f out: 2nd st: wknd fnl f)......2½ 4
Tadellal (IRE) *(54) (MDixon)* 4-9-4 (3) SSanders(7) (bit bkwd: 4th st: wknd over 1f out)......4 5
Chahaya Timor (IRE) *(58) (PFICole)* 3-7-13 (7) DavidO'Neill(8) (nvr nr to chal)......¾ 6
509^{5} Emnala (IRE) **(58)***(53) (MRChannon)* 3-8-1 CRutter(6) (s.s: nvr nrr)......nk 7
Sharazi (USA) *(55) (DJSCosgrove)* 4-9-12 JQuinn(14) (bit bkwd: nvr nrr)......2 8
485^{13} Ismeno *(54) (SDow)* 4-9-12 WRyan(5) (nvr plcd to chal)......¾ 9
Trapeze *(51) (CLPopham)* 4-9-12 JReid(11) (bhd fnl 3f)......2 10
485^{8} Catempo (IRE) *(46) (SDow)* 5-10-0 StephenDavies(13) (led over 6f: wknd over 3f out: 6th st)......4 11
428^{7} Antarctica (USA) *(41) (PAKelleway)* 3-8-2 ow1 PaulEddery(10) (prom 7f)......s.h 12
485^{12} Chocolate Charlie *(45) (RCharlton)* 4-9-12 TSprake(2) (s.s: a bhd)......nk 13
366^{10} Melling *(25) (RJHodges)* 4-9-7 (5) SDrowne(4) (bhd fnl 6f)......15 14

Evens MOKHTAR (IRE), **13/2** Artic Courier (4/1-7/1), **15/2** Fearless Venture (10/1-6/1), **8/1** Crowned Glory (USA) (op 4/1), Tadellal (IRE), **10/1** Trapeze, **14/1** Chahaya Timor (IRE) (10/1-16/1), **16/1** Ismeno, **20/1** Sharazi (USA), Emnala (IRE), Antarctica (USA), Chocolate Charlie, **50/1** Catempo (IRE), Melling, CSF £10.27 TOTE £3.10: £1.90 £4.40 £4.40 (£5.60) Trio £4.50 OWNER Mr Hamdan Al Maktoum (ARUNDEL) BRED Kilcarn Stud 14 Rn

2m 39.8 (8.60) SF: 32/29/9/5/15/-/-/16/15/12/9/-/6/-
WEIGHT FOR AGE 3yo-22lb, 4yo-2lb

OFFICIAL EXPLANATION **Ismeno: the trainer reported that the gelding was immature, has had all the associated problems and was not suited by the course.**

585

'PRIVY COUNCILLOR' MAIDEN STKS (3-Y.O) (Class D) £4,137.90 (£1,237.20: £592.60: £270.30)
6f 189y Stalls: Low GOING minus 0.27 sec per fur (GF) 4-15 (4-16)

435^{3} **Hakiki (IRE) (94)***(76)*(Fav)*(PTWalwyn)* 3-9-0 WCarson(5) (lw: led over 5f: led ins fnl f: pushed out)......— 1
Midnight Spell *(70) (MrsJCecil)* 3-8-9 PaulEddery(4) (2nd st: led over 1f out tl ins fnl f: r.o)...nk 2
443^{2} Secret Spring (FR) *(72) (RCharlton)* 3-9-0 JWeaver(9) (5th st: hrd rdn over 1f out: r.o ins fnl f)......1¼ 3
435^{4} Prolific Lady (IRE) *(66) (GROldroyd)* 3-8-9 RCochrane(3) (3rd st: rdn over 1f out: unable qckn)......¾ 4
Northern Fan (IRE) *(70) (ACStewart)* 3-9-0 SWhitworth(10) (bit bkwd: hdwy over 1f out: nvr nrr)......½ 5
Berkeley Bounder (USA) *(69) (PFICole)* 3-9-0 TQuinn(11) (lw: rdn 3f out: 6th st: one pce fnl 2f)......s.h 6
442^{4} Rokeby Bowl *(64) (IABalding)* 3-9-0 LDettori(8) (lw: rdn 3f out: 4th st: wknd over 1f out)......2½ 7
Zine Lane *(58) (MajorWRHern)* 3-9-0 TSprake(2) (lw: nvr nr to chal)......2½ 8
Zuno Flyer (USA) *(56) (GLewis)* 3-9-0 WRyan(12) (neat: bit bkwd: a mid div)......¾ 9
Jovie King (IRE) *(56) (PMitchell)* 3-9-0 TIves(13) (bhd fnl 5f)......hd 10
Sharpical *(49) (JRFanshawe)* 3-9-0 DHarrison(7) (unf: bhd fnl 2f)......3 11
451^{6} Care And Comfort *(38) (GWragg)* 3-8-9 FNorton(1) (lw: a bhd)......2½ 12
Tennyson Bay *(27) (RMFlower)* 3-8-9 (5) JDSmith(6) (a bhd)......7 13

15/8 HAKIKI (IRE), **9/4** Midnight Spell, **100/30** Rokeby Bowl, **15/2** Secret Spring (FR) (5/1-8/1), **12/1** Berkeley Bounder (USA), **14/1** Prolific Lady (IRE), **16/1** Zuno Flyer (USA), **20/1** Zine Lane, **25/1** Northern Fan (IRE), Sharpical, Care And Comfort, **33/1** Jovie King (IRE), **50/1** Tennyson Bay, CSF £7.71 TOTE £3.40: £1.50 £1.90 £2.60 (£5.90) Trio £15.00 OWNER Mr Hamdan Al Maktoum (LAMBOURN) BRED Philip De Vere Hunt 13 Rn

1m 24.3 (2.70) SF: 43/37/39/33/37/36/31/25/23/23/16/5/-

586 BOLLINGER CHAMPAGNE CHALLENGE SERIES AMATEUR H'CAP (0-70) (4-Y.O+) (Class E) £3,273.60 (£976.80: £466.40: £211.20)
1m 1f 149y Stalls: Low GOING minus 0.27 sec per fur (GF) 4-45 (4-46)

454[3] **Krayyan Dawn (46)***(53)*(Fav)*(RAkehurst)* 5-10-7 MrTMcCarthy(7) (lw: 3rd st: shkn up to ld ins fnl f: r.o wl) — 1
503[3] Montone (IRE) **(58)***(63) (KRBurke)* 5-11-1 (4) MrMMannish(12) (led tl ins fnl f: unable qckn) 1¼ 2
470[4] Roman Reel (USA) **(64)***(69) (GLMoore)* 4-11-7 (4) MrKGoble(11) (lw: 2nd st: ev ch over 1f out: one pce) hd 3
Shaarid (USA) **(67)***(72) (IABalding)* 7-11-10 (4) MrABalding(15) (bit bkwd: lost pl over 3f out: rallied over 1f out: r.o) hd 4
526[2] Captain Marmalade **(42)***(41)*(Fav)*(DTThom)* 6-9-13 (4)ow4 MrPPritchard-Gordon(5) (lw: hrd rdn & hdwy over 1f out: nvr nrr) 1¼ 5
454[8] Shoofk **(59)***(61) (SDow)* 4-11-6 MrTCuff(9) (lw: 4th st: one pce fnl 2f) ½ 6
430[9] Royal Acclaim **(40)***(41) (JMBradley)* 10-10-1v MrRJohnson(13) (nvr nr to chal) ¾ 7
454[4] Cheveley Dancer (USA) **(44)***(43) (DAWilson)* 7-10-1 (4) MrCAppleby(4) (b: lw: 6th st: one pce fnl 2f) 1 8
Starlight Flyer **(37)***(27) (JELong)* 8-9-8b(4)ow5 MrTWaters(14) (b: bit bkwd: a mid div) 2½ 9
414[11] Jonbel **(32)***(23) (TTClement)* 7-9-3 (4) MrVLukaniuk(10) (b: w ldr 7f: 5th st: wknd 2f out) 2 10
Brown Carpet **(36)***(22) (CAHorgan)* 8-9-7b(4)ow4 MrHEssaied(1) (b.hind: a bhd) 1 11
505[9] Precious Wonder **(42)***(29) (PButler)* 6-9-13 (4) MrKSantana(8) (a bhd) 1¾ 12
416[7] Arrasas Lady **(32)***(13) (JELong)* 5-9-3 (4) MrJO'Brien(3) (prom 7f) 3½ 13
408[7] Air Command (BAR) **(49)***(20) (CTNash)* 5-10-6 (4) MrPPhillips(2) (prom 7f) 6 14
402[6] Christian Spirit **(45)** *(BAPearce)* 5-10-2 (4)ow13 MrRBlyth(6) (b: s.i.s: a bhd) 13 15
LONG HANDICAP Jonbel 9-0 Starlight Flyer 9-0 Arrasas Lady 9-5 Brown Carpet 9-2 Christian Spirit 9-3

11/4 KRAYYAN DAWN, Captain Marmalade, **3/1** Shoofk, **10/1** Montone (IRE) (6/1-12/1), Roman Reel (USA) (5/1-12/1), **12/1** Cheveley Dancer (USA) (op 5/1), **14/1** Shaarid (USA) (7/1-16/1), **16/1** Royal Acclaim, **25/1** Precious Wonder, Air Command (BAR), **50/1** Jonbel, Starlight Flyer, Arrasas Lady, Brown Carpet, Christian Spirit, CSF £31.27 CT £230.84 TOTE £3.70: £2.20 £3.40 £2.70 (£29.50) Trio £121.10 OWNER Mr R. E. Greatorex (EPSOM) BRED R. Voorspuy 15 Rn
2m 6.3 (8.60) SF: 25/35/41/44/13/33/13/15/-/-/-/1/-/-/-

T/Jkpt: Not won; £97,161.76 to Bangor 11/4/95. T/Plpt: £61.20 (331.96 Tckts). T/Qdpt: £38.40 (18.5 Tckts) AK

0515-SOUTHWELL (L-H)
Tuesday April 11th (Standard)
WEATHER: sunny WIND: slt half bhd

587 PEACOCK H'CAP (0-65) (3-Y.O) (Class F) £2,519.00 (£694.00: £329.00)
7f (Fibresand) Stalls: Low GOING minus 0.03 sec per fur (STD) 2-00 (2-01)

518[3] **Three Arch Bridge (54)***(65+)*(Fav)*(MJohnston)* 3-9-1b JReid(8) (n.m.r after 2f: sn chsng ldrs: led over 2f out: drvn clr over 1f out) — 1
419[7] Shared Risk **(55)***(50) (SGNorton)* 3-8-13 (3) JTate(10) (hdwy ½-wy: kpt on fnl 2f: no ch w wnr) 7 2
482[5] Speedy Snaps Pride **(42)***(35) (PDCundell)* 3-8-3 AMackay(11) (hdwy u.p ½-wy: one pce fnl 2f) 1 3
348[4] Joyful Times **(45)***(32) (MrsNMacauley)* 3-7-13 (7) AmandaSanders(5) (lw: hld up & bhd: hdwy on outside 2f out: hung lft: kpt on) 2½ 4
Mixed Mood **(50)***(37) (BPalling)* 3-8-11 TSprake(9) (bit bkwd: chsd ldrs tl grad wknd fnl 2f) s.h 5
513[4] Slytly Beveled **(50)***(33) (NPLittmoden)* 3-8-6b(5) TGMcLaughlin(6) (in tch tl lost pl over 2f out) 1¾ 6
515[4] Bretton Princess **(42)***(11) (RHollinshead)* 3-8-3 DHarrison(7) (mid div: rdn over 2f out: sn wknd) 6 7
418[6] Vaslav Nijinsky **(60)***(27)*(Fav)*(GRimmer)* 3-9-7b MRimmer(12) (lw: trckd ldrs: effrt over 2f out: sn wknd) 1 8
502[11] Scharnhorst **(57)***(20) (SDow)* 3-9-4 TQuinn(1) (hmpd & lost pl after 2f: hrd rdn 2f out: n.d) 1¾ 9
Westcourt Princess **(57)***(19) (MWEasterby)* 3-9-4b LCharnock(13) (led tl over 2f out: sn wknd) nk 10
Gentle Irony **(60)***(22) (PJMakin)* 3-9-7 RCochrane(2) (nt grwn: prom early: bhd fnl 4f) s.h 11
Civil **(53)** *(RHannon)* 3-9-0 RPerham(4) (bit bkwd: plld hrd: trckd ldrs tl lost pl ½-wy: sn bhd) 9 12
135[6] Sweet Mate **(42)** *(SRBowring)* 3-7-10c(7) CTeague(3) (Withdrawn not under Starter's orders: incorrect headgear declared) W

4/1 THREE ARCH BRIDGE, Vaslav Nijinsky, **6/1** Scharnhorst (op 10/1), **7/1** Shared Risk, Joyful Times, **8/1** Speedy Snaps Pride (op 5/1), **10/1** Civil (op 6/1), Sweet Mate, **12/1** Westcourt Princess, Slytly Beveled (op 8/1), Gentle Irony (op 8/1), **16/1** Mixed Mood, **25/1** Bretton Princess, CSF £33.38 CT £207.24 TOTE £4.50: £2.10 £3.20 £2.20 (£22.20) Trio £28.40 OWNER Mr R. N. Pennell (MIDDLEHAM) BRED R. Taylor 12 Rn 1m 32.5 (5.70) SF: 32/17/2/-/4/-/-/-/-/-/-/-

588

SWAN CLAIMING APPRENTICE STKS (4-Y.O+) (Class F) £2,550.00 (£725.00: £360.00) **1m 6f (Fibresand)** Stalls: High GOING minus 0.03 sec (STD) 2-30 (2-30)

503[8] **Nigelschinapalace (28)***(44) (MissSJWilton)* 6-8-7 GFaulkner(6) (b: chsd ldr: led 5f out: rdn clr 3f out: unchal) ....— **1**
495[4] El Nido **(60)***(43)*(Fav)*(MJCamacho)* 7-9-5 GMilligan(2) (trckd ldrs: effrt over 4f out: chsd wnr 2f out: hung lft: no imp) 11 **2**
416[10] Mexican Dancer **(17)***(25) (PHowling)* 6-7-11 (5) TThomas(10) (sn bhd & drvn along: hdwy over 3f out: styd on same pce) 1½ **3**
Kalakate *(25) (JJBridger)* 10-8-5 ADaly(3) (drvn along & sme hdwy 7f out: kpt on fnl 2f) 2½ **4**
Homile *(23) (GFierro)* 7-8-5 JoHunnam(1) (led to 5f out: wknd over 2f out) 2 **5**
534[7] Turfmans Vision **(35)***(21) (RHollinshead)* 5-8-11b AEddery(7) (sltly hmpd s: hdwy to chse ldrs 8f out: wknd over 3f out) 7 **6**
514[10] Dugort Strand (IRE) **(44)***(7) (JLHarris)* 4-8-8b RWaterfield(8) (swvd lft s: plld hrd early: in tch tl drvn along & wknd 5f out) 12 **7**
Cloghran Lad *(MrsMMcCourt)* 8-8-5b(5) RStudholme(4) (hld up & a bhd) 5 **8**
288[7] Blue Pennant **(28)** *(TTBill)* 4-7-11 BHalligan(9) (lost tch 9f out) ....nk **9**
29[7] Speedy Snapper **(40)** *(PDCundell)* 4-8-3 (5)ow2 NLovelock(5) (sltly hmpd s: sn bhd & drvn along) 11 **10**

2/5 El Nido, **7/1** Dugort Strand (IRE), **11/1** Kalakate, **12/1** Turfmans Vision (op 7/1), **14/1** Homile, **16/1** Cloghran Lad, **20/1** Speedy Snapper, **25/1** NIGELSCHINAPALACE, Mexican Dancer, **33/1** Blue Pennant, CSF £37.40 TOTE £45.90: £7.40 £1.00 £6.70 (£18.00) Trio £56.10 OWNER Rock House Training & Consultancy Ltd (STOKE-ON-TRENT) BRED Mrs Barbara Molins 10 Rn
3m 14.1 (14.40) SF: 11/10/-/-/-/-/-/-/-/-
WEIGHT FOR AGE 4yo-3lb

589

STARLING H'CAP (0-65) (4-Y.O+) (Class F) £2,519.00 (£694.00: £329.00) **1m 6f (Fibresand)** Stalls: High GOING minus 0.03 sec per fur (STD) 3-00 (3-00)

81[4] **Mizyan (IRE) (63)***(75) (JEBanks)* 7-10-0 LDettori(6) (lw: trckd ldrs: led over 3f out: clr 2f out: drvn out) ....— **1**
*295** La Menorquina (USA) **(38)***(49) (DMarks)* 5-7-12 (5) MBaird(9) (hld up & bhd: hdwy 7f out: chsd wnr fnl 2f: styd on ins fnl f) 1 **2**
Bold Pursuit (IRE) **(57)***(45) (JGFitzGerald)* 6-9-8 KFallon(10) (chsd ldrs: drvn along 7f out: wknd 2f out) 20 **3**
514[9] Swordking (IRE) **(47)***(32) (JLHarris)* 6-8-12v PaulEddery(5) (lw: chsd ldrs: drvn along & lost pl 7f out: hrd rdn & kpt on fnl 3f: n.d) 2½ **4**
Hasta la Vista **(57)***(36) (MWEasterby)* 5-9-8b LCharnock(3) (led 1f: led 8f out tl over 3f out: wknd over 2f out) 5 **5**
517[3] Palacegate Jo (IRE) **(63)***(31)*(Fav)*(RHollinshead)* 4-9-11 TIves(4) (in tch: effrt 4f out: sn wknd) 10 **6**
470[7] Shuttlingslow **(44)***(2) (NAGaselee)* 4-8-6 TQuinn(1) (sn drvn along: sme hdwy 5f out: wknd 3f out) 9 **7**
Vaigly Sunthyme **(41)** *(JMCarr)* 5-8-6 SMorris(7) (sn drvn along: lost tch 5f out) 9 **8**
Ballad Ruler **(32)** *(PAPritchard)* 9-7-11 ow4 TWilliams(2) (s.i.s: bhd: t.o 5f out: virtually p.u ins fnl f) ....dist **9**
Masai Man (USA) **(51)** *(SRBowring)* 4-8-13b SDWilliams(8) (plld hrd: led after 1f to 8f out: sn drvn along & lost pl: t.o 4f out: virtually p.u ins fnl f) 25 **10**

3/1 Palacegate Jo (IRE), **4/1** MIZYAN (IRE), **5/1** Hasta la Vista, Bold Pursuit (IRE), **6/1** Masai Man (USA), La Menorquina (USA), **14/1** Swordking (IRE), **16/1** Shuttlingslow, **25/1** Vaigly Sunthyme, **50/1** Ballad Ruler, CSF £28.12 CT £115.30 TOTE £3.80: £1.70 £2.30 £1.70 (£12.10) Trio £13.30 OWNER Mr J. A. Bianchi (NEWMARKET) BRED S. Niarchos in Ireland 10 Rn
3m 10.8 (11.10) SF: 48/22/18/5/9/1/-/-/-/-
WEIGHT FOR AGE 4yo-3lb

590

PUFFIN H'CAP (0-65) (4-Y.O+) (Class F) £2,846.60 (£787.60: £375.80) **6f (Fibresand)** Stalls: Low GOING minus 0.03 sec per fur (STD) 3-30 (3-33)

519[2] **Cretan Gift (54)***(62) (NPLittmoden)* 4-9-3 (5) TGMcLaughlin(12) (a.p: effrt 2f out: wandered: styd on to ld wl ins fnl f) ....— **1**

Beveled Edge **(51)***(58) (BPalling)* 6-9-5 TSprake(9) (a chsng ldrs: kpt on same pce ins fnl f) ....nk **2**

*532** Souperficial **(59)***(60) (JAGlover)* 4-9-13v 7x JWeaver(7) (hld up & bhd: effrt on outside over 2f out: edgd lft & kpt on same pce fnl f: nvr nr to chal) 2½ **3**

519³ The Real Whizzbang (IRE) **(36)***(33) (PSFelgate)* 4-7-13b(5) PMcCabe(8) (lw: led: clr over 1f out: hdd & wknd nr fin) 1½ **4**

541⁷ Farmer Jock **(43)***(38) (MrsNMacauley)* 13-8-11 LDettori(10) (b.hind: swtchd rt & styd on appr fnl f: nt rch ldrs) ....¾ **5**

532² Sakharov **(52)***(40)*(Fav)*(MJohnston)* 6-9-6 JReid(1) (lw: in tch: effrt over 2f out: nvr rchd ldrs)2½ **6**

419⁶ Brisas **(46)***(34) (CWFairhurst)* 8-9-0 JFanning(5) (chsd ldrs tl wknd over 1f out) ....s.h **7**

511⁴ Christian Flight (IRE) **(42)***(23) (SGollings)* 6-8-10 DHarrison(6) (chsd ldrs tl lost pl 2f out) 2½ **8**

450⁴ Martinosky **(52)***(24) (GCBravery)* 9-9-6 MHills(4) (s.i.s: sn bhd & drvn along) 3½ **9**

154⁵ Nineacres **(60)***(32) (DNicholls)* 4-9-7 (7) BPeel(3) (chsd ldrs tl lost pl over 2f out) ....s.h **10**

478² Wellsy Lad (USA) **(34)** *(DWChapman)* 8-8-2b NCarlisle(11) (nvr wnt pce) 6 **11**

Lukes Brother (IRE) **(37)** *(RFMarvin)* 4-8-5 FNorton(2) (outpcd after 2f) 1½ **12**

6/4 Sakharov, **9/2** Souperficial, **7/1** Martinosky, **10/1** Wellsy Lad (USA), **12/1** CRETAN GIFT, The Real Whizzbang (IRE), Nineacres, **14/1** Farmer Jock, Christian Flight (IRE), **20/1** Beveled Edge, Brisas, **50/1** Lukes Brother (IRE), CSF £203.49 CT £1,139.01 TOTE £21.90: £4.10 £11.50 £1.80 (£143.50) Trio £29.20 OWNER R A M Racecourses Ltd (NEWARK) BRED Hesmonds Stud Ltd 12 Rn
1m 18.1 (4.60) SF: 41/37/39/12/17/19/13/2/3/11/-/-

591 JAY (S) STKS (3-Y.O) (Class G) £2,243.00 (£618.00: £293.00)

6f (Fibresand) Stalls: Low GOING minus 0.03 sec per fur (STD) 4-00 (4-03)

404⁵ **Dark Shot (IRE) (72)***(67)*(Fav)*(JBerry)* 3-9-2 JCarroll(4) (lw: mde virtually all: styd on u.p fnl f: edgd rt: all out) ....— **1**

482⁹ Aston Manor (IRE) **(50)***(61) (RHannon)* 3-8-11 RPerham(8) (sn prom: hdwy & ev ch fnl f: nt qckn nr fin) ....nk **2**

524¹² Casper's Risk **(59)***(60) (DNicholls)* 3-9-2b AlexGreaves(1) (trckd ldrs: hrd rdn 2f out: styd on one pce appr fnl f) 2½ **3**

482³ Russian Heroine **(65)***(54) (MJohnston)* 3-8-11 JReid(2) (a chsng ldrs: ev ch 2f out: nt qckn appr fnl f) ....nk **4**

Shazanni (IRE) *(47) (JGFitzGerald)* 3-8-6 KFallon(12) (unf: scope: bit bkwd: sn bhd: styd on fnl 2f: nt rch ldrs) ....¾ **5**

482¹⁰ Jersey Belle **(44)***(45) (PJMakin)* 3-8-6 LDettori(9) (mid div: effrt 2f out: hung lft u.p: kpt on: nt rch ldrs) ....½ **6**

Komiamaite *(44) (SRBowring)* 3-8-4b(7) CTeague(11) (bit bkwd: s.s: bhd: rn wd ent st: hdwy over 1f out: kpt on) 2½ **7**

417² What a Nightmare (IRE) **(68)***(45) (JAGlover)* 3-9-2v SDWilliams(7) (w ldrs: rdn 2f out: wknd over 1f out) 1½ **8**

519⁵ Lawnswood Lady **(45)***(33) (RHollinshead)* 3-8-6 DHarrison(6) (chsd ldrs tl rdn & wknd 2f out) ....¾ **9**

418¹⁰ Beyaateh *(1) (MCChapman)* 3-7-13 (7) CMunday(5) (s.i.s: a bhd) 12 **10**

431¹¹ Bulsara **(58)***(1) (CWFairhurst)* 3-8-11 JFanning(14) (sn outpcd) 1¾ **11**

Little Tyson (IRE) *(JJBridger)* 3-8-11 GBardwell(3) (leggy: unf: s.s: a bhd) 4 **12**

264⁷ Semi Serious *(DWChapman)* 3-8-11 ACulhane(10) (a bhd: hung bdly rt & rn wd ent st) 13 **13**

515¹⁰ All Honour *(DWChapman)* 3-8-11 DeanMcKeown(13) (sn outpcd: rn wd ent st) 1¼ **14**

13/8 DARK SHOT (IRE) (9/4-6/4), **4/1** Russian Heroine (op 5/2), **5/1** What a Nightmare (IRE) (7/2-11/2), **7/1** Aston Manor (IRE), **11/1** Lawnswood Lady (op 7/1), **12/1** Casper's Risk (op 8/1), Jersey Belle, **14/1** Komiamaite, Shazanni (IRE), **20/1** Semi Serious, **25/1** Bulsara, Little Tyson (IRE), Beyaateh, All Honour, CSF £16.06 TOTE £2.20: £1.50 £3.50 £3.50 (£19.70) Trio £150.00 OWNER Laurel (Leisure) Ltd (COCKERHAM) BRED Mrs Amanda Skiffington and W. Macauley 14 Rn
1m 18.7 (5.20) SF: 28/22/21/15/8/6/5/6/-/-/-/-/-/-
No bid

592 HERON MAIDEN H'CAP (0-70) (3-Y.O+) (Class E) £3,330.80 (£994.40: £475.20: £215.60)

1m 3f (Fibresand) Stalls: Low GOING minus 0.03 sec per fur (STD) 4-30 (4-34)

476⁷ **Ijab (CAN) (30)***(41) (JParkes)* 5-7-7b GBardwell(9) (sn bhd & drvn along: hdwy on outside 5f out: styd on fnl 2f to ld nr fin) ....— **1**

477³ Hard Try **(54)***(63) (MJCamacho)* 3-7-10 LCharnock(7) (chsd ldrs: chal 3f out: slt ld ins fnl f: hdd nr fin) 1¼ **2**

Monarch **(68)***(77)*(Fav)*(PFICole)* 3-8-10 TQuinn(2) (b: b.hind: led tl ins fnl f: no ex) ....½ **3**

166⁵ Midlin **(34)***(35) (JLHarris)* 5-7-6 (5) NVarley(13) (sn bhd: hdwy 6f out: one pce fnl 3f) 5 **4**

421[5] Mr Moriarty (IRE) **(35)***(28) (SRBowring)* 4-7-11 NKennedy(10) (bhd & drvn along 6f out: n.d) 6 **5**
352[3] Always Greener (IRE) **(54)***(44) (MrsNMacauley)* 4-9-2 JWeaver(1) (chsd ldrs: drvn along 7f out: wknd over 3f out) 2 **6**
520[3] Top Fella (USA) **(59)***(41) (WAO'Gorman)* 3-8-1b GCarter(11) (lw: sn bhd: hdwy on outside 5f out: sn rdn: wknd over 2f out) 5 **7**
378[12] Spanish Stripper (USA) **(44)***(21) (MCChapman)* 4-7-13 (7) CMunday(6) (unruly in stalls: nvr nr ldrs) 3½ **8**
Glitter of Gold **(61)***(35) (SCWilliams)* 4-9-6 (3) DWright(4) (chsd ldrs: hrd rdn & lost pl over 3f out) 2½ **9**
Divertimiento **(60)***(16) (JGFitzGerald)* 4-9-8 KFallon(3) (lw: unruly in stalls: chsd ldr: rdn over 3f out: wknd over 2f out: eased) 12 **10**
Chita Rivera **(51)** *(PJMakin)* 4-8-13v LDettori(12) (lost tch ½-wy) 10 **11**
Monte Cavo **(60)** *(MBrittain)* 4-9-8 JLowe(5) (in tch tl wknd qckly over 4f out: eased: t.o) 5 **12**
The Chairman (IRE) **(66)** *(FJordan)* 4-9-9 (5) TGMcLaughlin(8) (sn bhd: t.o 5f out) ....dist **13**

LONG HANDICAP Ijab (CAN) 7-6

5/2 Monarch, **4/1** Always Greener (IRE) (3/1-5/1), **11/2** Top Fella (USA), **7/1** Chita Rivera, **9/1** Hard Try, Glitter of Gold, **10/1** Mr Moriarty (IRE), **11/1** IJAB (CAN) (6/1-12/1), **12/1** Divertimiento, **14/1** The Chairman (IRE), **20/1** Spanish Stripper (USA), Midlin, Monte Cavo, CSF £112.79 CT £305.03 TOTE £18.30: £3.50 £1.60 £2.00 (£30.70) Trio £58.90 OWNER Mrs Lynn Parkes (MALTON) BRED R. M. Anderson 13 Rn 2m 29.8 (8.30) SF: 18/19/33/12/4/20/-/-/11/-/-/-/-

WEIGHT FOR AGE 3yo-21lb, 4yo-1lb

T/Plpt: £99.60 (116.53 Tckts). T/Qdpt: Not won; £53.00 to Worcester 12/4/95. WG

0490-HAMILTON (R-H)
Wednesday April 12th (Soft, Good to soft patches)
WEATHER: sunny WIND: almost nil

593
AUCHINGRAMOT CLAIMING STKS (3-Y.O+) (Class F) £2,759.00 (£774.00: £377.00) **1m 1f 36y** Stalls: High GOING: 0.14 sec per fur (G) 2-10 (2-11)

413[9] **Ivan the Terrible (IRE) (39)***(57) (BEllison)* 7-9-2 SWhitworth(9) (b: mde all: clr over 3f out: styd on wl) ....— **1**
Stash the Cash (IRE) **(90)***(65)*(Fav)*(TDyer)* 4-9-13 KDarley(13) (swtg: in tch: rdn ½-wy: hdwy over 2f out: styd on one pce fnl f) 2 **2**
Running Green *(57) (TDyer)* 4-9-6 KFallon(3) (mid div: hdwy ½-wy: sn chsng ldrs: nt qckn fnl f) ....s.h **3**
539[10] Never So Fit *(53) (RBastiman)* 4-9-5 (5) HBastiman(6) (lw: hld up & bhd: hdwy ½-wy: nvr rchd ldrs) 5 **4**
Gospel Song **(50)***(44) (WTKemp)* 3-8-4 GCarter(8) (in tch: effrt 4f out: rdn & no imp) 4 **5**
493[6] Deputy Tim **(34)***(35) (RBastiman)* 12-9-3 DeanMcKeown(7) (cl up tl wknd fnl 3f) 2 **6**
Wali (USA) **(67)***(33) (VThompson)* 5-9-1 (5) JStack(11) (chsd ldrs: effrt ½-wy: wknd over 2f out) 3 **7**
539[16] Hutchies Lady *(29) (RMMcKellar)* 3-8-1 DaleGibson(1) (nvr trbld ldrs) 1½ **8**
539[13] Operatic Dancer *(24) (RMMcKellar)* 4-9-10 TWilliams(5) (a bhd) 6 **9**
Keith's Pride (IRE) *(18) (TDyer)* 3-8-2 JFanning(12) (sn chsng ldrs: wknd over 3f out) 1¼ **10**
Funny Worry *(24) (PMonteith)* 6-9-13 JMarshall(10) (s.s: sme hdwy ½-wy: sn wknd) ....nk **11**
Miss Greenyards *(JSHaldane)* 4-8-13 NConnorton(4) (chsd ldrs over 4f: sn wknd) 14 **12**
Best of Times *(DMoffatt)* 4-8-9 (3) DarrenMoffatt(2) (ref to r after leaving stalls) .... **R**

5/4 Stash the Cash (IRE) (10/11-11/8), **5/1** Wali (USA), **6/1** Gospel Song, **8/1** IVAN THE TERRIBLE (IRE), **12/1** Deputy Tim, **16/1** Keith's Pride (IRE), Never So Fit, Best of Times, **33/1** Funny Worry, Running Green, **100/1** Operatic Dancer, Hutchies Lady, Miss Greenyards, CSF £17.38 TOTE £10.10: £1.90 £1.60 £3.40 (£5.90) Trio £120.10 OWNER Mrs Jean Stapleton (CONSETT) BRED Stud-On-The-Chart 13 Rn 2m 2.7 (8.40) SF: 38/46/38/34/7/16/14/-/5/-/5/-/-

WEIGHT FOR AGE 3yo-18lb

OFFICIAL EXPLANATION **Never So Fit: was settled by his rider early in the race, as instructed, but ran green and became unbalanced on the home turn, only to run on well in the later stages.**

594
CHARLIE ANDERSON HALF CENTURY SPRINT H'CAP (0-60) (3-Y.O+) (Class F) £3,550.00 (£1,075.00: £525.00: £250.00) **6f 5y** Stalls: High GOING: 0.14 sec per fur (G) 2-40 (2-43)

419[5] **Panther (IRE) (53)***(59) (JHetherton)* 5-9-7 NKennedy(15) (lw: mde all: r.o wl fnl f) ....— **1**

55[9] Cledeschamps **(37)***(36) (MWEllerby)* 6-8-5 SMorris(13) (a.p: kpt on fnl f: nt pce of wnr)........2½ **2**
507[9] Abigails Boy (HOL) **(40)***(38) (DrJDScargill)* 6-8-8 JFanning(8) (in tch: styd on fnl 2f: nvr able to chal) ....½ **3**
Blow Dry (IRE) **(60)***(47) (MartynWane)* 5-10-0 KDarley(6) (a.p: kpt on one pce fnl 2f) 4 **4**
Millemay **(32)***(19) (PMonteith)* 5-8-0 JMarshall(12) (in tch: effrt over 1f out: styd on) ....nk **5**
532[10] Red Five **(58)***(41) (JBerry)* 4-9-5 (7) PRoberts(16) (in tch: rdn ½-wy: no imp) 1½ **6**
491[3] Birchwood Sun **(56)***(29)*(Fav)*(MDods)* 5-9-10b JFortune(11) (s.i.s: nvr nrr) 3½ **7**
479[9] Strathtore Dream (IRE) **(55)***(24) (MissLAPerratt)* 4-9-9 NConnorton(17) (sn outpcd: sme hdwy 2f out: n.d) 1½ **8**
491[5] Beckyhannah **(40)***(1) (RBastiman)* 5-8-8b DeanMcKeown(14) (chsd ldrs over 4f) 3 **9**
524[14] Malzoom **(40)** *(SEKettlewell)* 3-7-9 ow2 LCharnock(9) (lw: drvn along ½-wy: n.d) 1¼ **10**
475[6] Sunday Mail Too (IRE) **(54)***(9) (MissLAPerratt)* 3-8-9 GCarter(7) (lw: cl up 4f) 1 **11**
226[6] Bonny Melody **(59)***(4) (PDEvans)* 4-9-13 SWhitworth(5) (sn bhd) 4 **12**
478[8] Benjarong **(46)** *(RMMcKellar)* 3-8-1 TWilliams(4) (nvr wnt pce) 3 **13**
479[7] Kenesha (IRE) **(57)** *(DANolan)* 5-9-6 (5) NVarley(2) (chsd ldrs stands' side: no ch fr ½-wy) 1¼ **14**
33[7] Seenthelight **(54)** *(DMoffatt)* 3-8-6 (3) DarrenMoffatt(10) (swtchd stands' side after s: a bhd) 2½ **15**
491[4] Cronk's Courage **(52)** *(MGMeagher)* 9-9-6v KFallon(1) (led stands' side: no ch fr ½-wy) 2 **16**
Seconds Away **(45)** *(AHarrison)* 4-8-8 (5) JStack(3) (racd stands' side: a bhd) 6 **17**

LONG HANDICAP Malzoom 7-4

5/1 Birchwood Sun, **6/1** PANTHER (IRE), Abigails Boy (HOL), Red Five, **10/1** Seenthelight, **11/1** Beckyhannah, Sunday Mail Too (IRE), **14/1** Malzoom, **16/1** Benjarong, Blow Dry (IRE), Cronk's Courage, **20/1** Cledeschamps, **25/1** Bonny Melody, Strathtore Dream (IRE), **33/1** Seconds Away, Kenesha (IRE), **50/1** Millemay, CSF £111.88 CT £700.73 TOTE £6.20: £2.00 £11.90 £1.50 £2.90 (£84.30) Trio £126.50 OWNER Mr Paul Dancer (MALTON) BRED My Treasure Ltd 17 Rn
1m 15.3 (5.30) SF: 42/19/21/30/2/24/12/7/-/-/-/-/-/-/-/-/-
WEIGHT FOR AGE 3yo-13lb

595 WHITEMOSS MEDIAN AUCTION MAIDEN STKS (2-Y.O F) (Class F) £2,661.00 (£746.00: £363.00)

5f 4y Stalls: High GOING: 0.14 sec per fur (G) 3-10 (3-12)

Chilibang Bang *(66t)*(Fav)*(JBerry)* 2-8-10 GCarter(3) (w'like: a cl up: rdn to ld wl ins fnl f: jst hld on) ....— **1**
Gagajulu *(66) (PDEvans)* 2-8-10 JFortune(6) (unf: lw: dwlt: sn outpcd & wl bhd: hdwy 2f out: swtchd outside: r.o wl) ....hd **2**
Itsinthepost *(65) (MJohnston)* 2-8-10 TWilliams(5) (w'like: scope: bit bkwd: led: qcknd 2f out: hdd & no ex wl ins fnl f) ....nk **3**
533[8] Margi Boo *(39) (GMMoore)* 2-8-10 JFanning(1) (chsd ldrs 3f: sn btn) 8 **4**
Ned's Contessa (IRE) *(38) (MDods)* 2-8-10 DaleGibson(4) (neat: spd 3f: sn btn) ....nk **5**
Supergal *(10) (MWEasterby)* 2-8-10 LCharnock(2) (neat: bit bkwd: spd to ½-wy: sn wknd) 9 **6**

2/1 CHILIBANG BANG, **5/2** Margi Boo, **3/1** Gagajulu (op 7/4), **7/2** Itsinthepost, **14/1** Supergal (op 8/1), **25/1** Ned's Contessa (IRE), CSF £8.63 TOTE £2.30: £1.30 £2.10 (£6.00) OWNER Mr Ian Crawford (COCKERHAM) BRED G. W. Hampson 6 Rn 63.5 secs (5.20) SF: -/-/-/-/-/-

596 WHIRLIES (S) STKS (3-Y.O) (Class G) £2,381.00 (£666.00: £323.00)

1m 65y Stalls: High GOING: 0.14 sec per fur (G) 3-40 (3-41)

492[4] **Hamilton Silk (49)***(56) (MGMeagher)* 3-8-11 JFortune(5) (a.p: led over 2f out: sn clr) ....— **1**
576[3] Ricana **(48)***(39) (WTKemp)* 3-8-6 DeanMcKeown(1) (led tl hdd over 3f out: kpt on one pce) 6 **2**
479[5] Sul Fosso **(47)***(38) (JBerry)* 3-8-11 GCarter(2) (swtg: cl up: rdn 3f out: one pce fnl 2f) 3½ **3**
Mr Slick **(60)***(37) (WStorey)* 3-8-11 SWhitworth(6) (a.p: one pce fnl 3f) ....nk **4**
513[*] Chastleton **(45)***(28)*(Fav)*(MRChannon)* 3-8-4 (7) JDennis(7) (lw: s.i.s: bhd: gd hdwy on outside to ld over 3f out: hdd over 2f out: sn btn) 5 **5**
509[8] Lady Kuynder *(9) (DrJDScargill)* 3-8-6 KDarley(4) (prom tl rdn & wknd over 2f out) 7 **6**
420[13] Tarsid *(SCoathup)* 3-8-5 (7)ow1 SJames(3) (dwlt: c.wd st: t.o) ....dist **7**

6/4 Chastleton, **9/2** Mr Slick, Ricana, **6/1** HAMILTON SILK, **8/1** Lady Kuynder, **9/1** Sul Fosso (op 5/1), **66/1** Tarsid, CSF £29.99 TOTE £6.00: £2.00 £2.80 (£16.70) OWNER Haydock Exhibitions Ltd (ORMSKIRK) BRED Haydock Exhibitions Ltd 7 Rn 1m 53.7 (10.40) SF: 8/-/-/-/-/-/-
Bt in 5,200 gns.

597 BARNCLUITH H'CAP (0-75) (3-Y.O+) (Class D) £3,589.30 (£1,086.40: £530.20: £252.10) **1m 3f 16y** Stalls: High GOING: 0.14 sec per fur (G) 4-10 (4-10)

Cool Luke (IRE) (63)*(74)*(Fav)*(GMMoore)* 6-9-6 MTebbutt(6) (lw: trckd ldrs: swtchd ins 3f out: led wl over 1f out: kpt on)........— **1**
*396*5 Hillzah (USA) **(66)***(73) (RBastiman)* 7-9-4 (5) HBastiman(7) (chsd ldrs: led over 2f out tl wl over 1f out: kpt on)........2½ **2**
4942 Tanah Merah (IRE) **(59)***(53) (EJAlston)* 4-9-1 KFallon(1) (lw: hld up: effrt & swtchd ins over 3f out: sn rdn: nvr rchd ldrs)........9 **3**
Monkey Wench (IRE) **(54)***(43) (JBerry)* 4-8-10v GCarter(3) (hld up: hdwy 4f out: outpcd fnl 2½f)........3½ **4**
53413 Dawn Rock **(40)***(24) (RMMcKellar)* 4-7-10b TWilliams(5) (s.i.s: n.d)........3½ **5**
Rapid Mover **(39)***(20) (DANolan)* 8-7-5b(5)ow3 NVarley(2) (led tl hdd & wknd over 2f out)........nk **6**
Izza **(72)***(40) (WStorey)* 4-10-0 SWhitworth(4) (cl up tl wknd 3f out)........11 **7**

LONG HANDICAP Rapid Mover 7-0

4/5 COOL LUKE (IRE), **4/1** Hillzah (USA), Tanah Merah (IRE), **12/1** Monkey Wench (IRE), **25/1** Dawn Rock, Rapid Mover, Izza, CSF £4.49 TOTE £1.60: £1.50 £1.90 (£3.00) OWNER Mr B. Batey (MIDDLEHAM) BRED Lodge Park Stud 7 Rn 2m 28.4 (9.40) SF: 48/47/26/16/-/-/13

WEIGHT FOR AGE 4yo-1lb

598 CARFIN APPRENTICE H'CAP (0-70) (3-Y.O+) (Class E) £2,884.25 (£884.00: £439.50: £217.25) **1m 4f 17y** Stalls: High GOING: 0.14 sec per fur (G) 4-40 (4-40)

4943 **The Premier Expres (40)***(59)*(Fav)*(FJO'Mahony)* 5-8-6 GMacDonald(2) (a cl up: led wl over 3f out: all out)........— **1**
495* Zaaheyah (USA) **(45)***(55) (MDHammond)* 5-8-3 (8) MMathers(4) (lw: led 4f: led 6f out tl wl over 3f out: one pce)........7 **2**
4958 Milngavie (IRE) **(43)***(44) (MJohnston)* 5-8-9 SMcCarthy(1) (styd on fnl 4f: no imp)........7 **3**
Devilry **(62)***(60) (GMMoore)* 5-9-6 (8) IGrantham(5) (rdn over 4f out: styd on: no imp)........1¾ **4**
Zamhareer (USA) **(53)***(43) (WStorey)* 4-9-3 GFaulkner(7) (b: lw: bhd: c wd & rdn ent st: n.d)........6 **5**
Juice Plus **(34)***(15) (JParkes)* 4-7-12 AEddery(3) (lw: in tch to st: sn wl outpcd)........7 **6**
55617 Jalore **(50)***(22) (SCoathup)* 6-8-13 (3) SJames(8) (led after 4f to 6f out: wknd 4f out)........7 **7**
*186*8 Joyrider **(46)***(12) (MissMKMilligan)* 4-8-10 CarolDavison(6) (b: prom to st: sn wknd)........4 **8**

9/4 THE PREMIER EXPRES, **5/2** Zamhareer (USA), **4/1** Zaaheyah (USA), **8/1** Devilry (op 5/1), **14/1** Milngavie (IRE), **16/1** Juice Plus, Joyrider, **66/1** Jalore, CSF £10.55 CT £81.76 TOTE £4.20: £2.10 £1.20 £2.20 (£8.30) OWNER Mr Ron Davison (HAMBLETON) BRED J. Weinfeld 8 Rn

2m 44.6 (12.60) SF: 20/16/5/21/2/-/-/-

WEIGHT FOR AGE 4yo-2lb

T/Plpt : £49.50 (216.5 Tckts). T/Qdpt : £22.30 (4.2 Tckts). AA

0527-WOLVERHAMPTON (L-H)
Thursday April 13th (Standard)

WEATHER: Fine & sunny WIND: nil

599 RASPBERRY TART LIMITED LIMITED STKS (0-65) (3-Y.O) (Class F) £2,519.00 (£694.00: £329.00) **7f (Fibresand)** Stalls: High GOING: 0.03 sec per fur (STD) 2-00 (2-00)

*411*2 **Chadleigh Lane (USA) (63)***(70)*(Fav)*(RHollinshead)* 3-9-2 TIves(2) (lw: s.i.s: hdwy 4f out: 2nd st: qcknd to ld over 1f out: eased cl home)........— **1**
Sue Me (IRE) **(65)***(66) (WRMuir)* 3-9-0 JWeaver(3) (still unf: hld up: led over 4f out tl over 1f out: kpt on u.p)........1 **2**
5229 Ganador **(60)***(47) (JBerry)* 3-8-9 GCarter(1) (led over 2f: rdn & outpcd over 2f out: 3rd st)........6 **3**

5/4 CHADLEIGH LANE (USA), **13/8** Sue Me (IRE) (11/10-7/4), **100/30** Ganador (9/4-7/2), CSF £3.19 TOTE £2.20: (£1.10). OWNER Mr J. E. Bigg (UPPER LONGDON) BRED Windwoods Farm, Bruce Brown and Connie Brown 3 Rn 1m 31.9 (7.90) SF: 11/7/-

600 TRUFFLE CLAIMING APPRENTICE STKS (4-Y.O+) (Class F) £2,519.00 (£694.00: £329.00) **1m 4f (Fibresand)** Stalls: Low GOING: 0.03 sec per fur (STD) 2-30 (2-30)

*516*2 **Mad Militant (IRE) (75)***(73)*(Fav)*(ALForbes)* 6-8-8 (5) DDenby(7) (lw: hld up: hdwy 7f out: led ent st: drifted lft fnl f: hld on)........— **1**

*530*3 Hill Farm Dancer **(48)***(66) (WMBrisbourne)* 4-8-4 MartinDwyer(4) (stdd s: sn chsng ldrs: 3rd st: rdn & styd on wl ins fnl f)....nk **2**
556 23 Sleeptite (FR) **(63)***(66) (WGMTurner)* 5-8-8 (5) ADaly(1) (a.p: led wl over 3f out tl hdd & 2nd st: kpt on one pce)....5 **3**
*530*4 Awestruck **(46)***(56) (BPreece)* 5-8-8 (3) AEddery(3) (sn wl bhd & pushed along: effrt & 6th st: nvr nrr)....6 **4**
*512*4 Super Heights **(43)***(52) (DLWilliams)* 7-8-9 SLanigan(6) (hld up: rdn along 3f out: 4th st: sn btn)....1½ **5**
*514*11 Rasayel (USA) **(44)***(34) (PDEvans)* 5-8-0 MHenry(5) (chsd ldr 9f: 4th & rdn st: sn t.o)....7 **6**
*304*4 Rocky Bay **(37)***(17) (BJLlewellyn)* 6-7-12 CAdamson(2) (led tl hdd wl over 3f out: wknd & 7th st: t.o)....11 **7**

6/4 MAD MILITANT (IRE) (Evens-13/8), **3/1** Sleeptite (FR) (op 2/1), **4/1** Hill Farm Dancer, **9/1** Awestruck, **12/1** Super Heights, **14/1** Rocky Bay (12/1-20/1), **33/1** Rasayel (USA), CSF £7.48 TOTE £2.20: £1.10 £2.20 (£4.10). OWNER Mr K. Nicholls (UTTOXETER) BRED Cloghran Stud Farm Co in Ireland 7 Rn 2m 42.9 (11.90) SF: 16/7/9/-/-/-/-
WEIGHT FOR AGE 4yo-2lb

601

BOWMER AND KIRKLAND H'CAP (0-70) (3-Y.O+) (Class E) £3,245.00 (£968.00: £462.00: £209.00)
1m 100y (Fibresand) Stalls: Low GOING: 0.03 sec per fur (STD) 3-00 (3-01)

*529** **Marowins (65)***(73)*(Fav)*(EJAlston)* 6-9-9 5x KFallon(6) (dwlt: hld up: hdwy over 3f out: 4th st: rdn to ld ins fnl f: all out)....— **1**
559 7 Second Colours (USA) **(70)***(77) (MrsMReveley)* 5-10-0 KDarley(11) (lw: chsd ldrs: 2nd st: led over 1f out tl ins fnl f: kpt on)....nk **2**
503 2 Duello **(64)***(71) (MBlanshard)* 4-9-8 WRyan(12) (hld up: hdwy ½-wy: 3rd st: hmpd over 1f out: swtchd rt fnl f: fin wl)....nk **3**
Love Legend **(56)***(60) (DWPArbuthnot)* 10-9-0 TQuinn(8) (b: bkwd: hld up: hdwy 4f out: 5th & rdn st: unable qckn fnl f)....1½ **4**
486* Sandmoor Denim **(65)***(68) (SRBowring)* 8-9-2 (7) CTeague(3) (b: bhd: effrt u.p 3f out: nvr nr to chal)....½ **5**
503* Northern Celadon (IRE) **(64)***(67) (MJHeaton-Ellis)* 4-9-8 GCarter(7) (led tl hdd over 1f out: rdn & r.o one pce)....s.h **6**
Flashfeet **(54)***(44) (KBishop)* 5-8-12 JWilliams(4) (bit bkwd: chsd ldrs over 5f: sn outpcd)....7 **7**
*181*7 Kissavos **(38)***(24) (CCElsey)* 9-7-3 (7)ow3 CAdamson(5) (b.hind: bit bkwd: a bhd)....nk **8**
433 19 Kaitak (IRE) **(70)***(46) (JMCarr)* 4-10-0 SMorris(2) (chsd ldrs over 5f: sn rdn & wknd: t.o)....7 **9**
*471*7 Across the Bay **(37)***(11) (RWEmery)* 8-7-9bow2 JQuinn(13) (a in rr: t.o)....s.h **10**
526 16 Talented Ting (IRE) **(66)***(34) (PCHaslam)* 6-9-10 JWeaver(10) (bit bkwd: prom tl 6th & btn st: t.o)....4 **11**
*501** Zahran (IRE) **(59)***(26) (JMBradley)* 4-8-12 (5) SDrowne(1) (chsd ldr to ½-wy: rdn & wknd over 2f out: t.o)....¾ **12**
*518*6 Letsbeonestaboutit **(55)***(20) (MrsNMacauley)* 9-8-13 DeanMcKeown(9) (a bhd: t.o)....1 **13**

7/2 MAROWINS, **4/1** Sandmoor Denim, **13/2** Northern Celadon (IRE), **7/1** Second Colours (USA), **8/1** Talented Ting (IRE), Duello (6/1-10/1), **10/1** Zahran (IRE), **12/1** Kaitak (IRE), **16/1** Love Legend, **20/1** Letsbeonestaboutit, **25/1** Across the Bay, Kissavos, **33/1** Flashfeet, CSF £28.37 CT £175.73 TOTE £6.90: £2.40 £1.30 £2.30 (£15.20) Trio £67.30. OWNER Whitehills Racing Syndicate (PRESTON) BRED W. M. Lidsey 13 Rn 1m 50.9 (6.90) SF: 43/47/41/30/38/37/14/-/16/-/4/-/-

602

BREAD PUDDING H'CAP (0-70) (3-Y.O+) (Class E) £3,044.80 (£906.40: £431.20: £193.60)
5f (Fibresand) Stalls: Low GOING: 0.03 sec per fur (STD) 3-30 (3-30)

*398*2 **Chadwell Hall (51)***(65+)*(Fav)*(SRBowring)* 4-8-9b(7) CTeague(8) (b.off hind: led over 3f out: sn clr: unchal)....— **1**
*398*5 Scored Again **(60)***(61) (MJHeaton-Ellis)* 5-9-4 (7) AmandaSanders(4) (b: a.p: chsd wnr fnl 2f: no imp)....4 **2**
*306*6 Farndale **(50)***(46) (RonaldThompson)* 8-9-1 JWeaver(7) (outpcd: rdn & effrt over 1f out: kpt on)....1¾ **3**
507 4 Ivy Lilian (IRE) **(45)***(40) (WMBrisbourne)* 3-7-5 (7) SLanigan(6) (hdwy u.p 2f out: kpt on ins fnl f: nvr nrr)....s.h **4**
452 6 Rocky Two **(59)***(50) (PHowling)* 4-9-10b WWoods(5) (chsd ldrs: rdn over 2f out: outpcd appr fnl f)....1½ **5**
*532*3 King Rambo **(63)***(44)*(Fav)*(RHollinshead)* 4-10-0 WRyan(1) (outpcd: a bhd)....3 **6**
*532*11 Our Mica **(31)***(10) (LJBarratt)* 5-7-10b JQuinn(2) (outpcd: a bhd)....¾ **7**
Lady Quinta (IRE) **(55)** *(JBerry)* 3-8-8 GCarter(3) (broke wl: led over 1f: outpcd fnl 2f: t.o)....12 **8**

11/4 CHADWELL HALL (2/1-3/1), King Rambo, **6/1** Scored Again (op 4/1), Rocky Two, **8/1** Ivy Lilian (IRE), **9/1** Farndale, **10/1** Lady Quinta (IRE), **25/1** Our Mica, CSF £18.27 CT £117.62 TOTE £3.70: £1.50 £2.30 £2.20 (£14.00). OWNER Mr D. H. Bowring (EDWINSTOWE) BRED J. C. and Mrs C. L. Owen 8 Rn
62.8 secs (4.80) SF: 21/17/2/-/6/-/-/-
WEIGHT FOR AGE 3yo-12lb

603 SPOTTED DICK MAIDEN STKS (3-Y.O+) (Class D) £3,799.90 (£1,133.20: £540.60: £244.30) 6f (Fibresand) GOING: 0.03 sec per fur (STD) 4-00 (4-03)

442[12] **Cool Tactician** *(68) (RHollinshead)* 3-8-11 TIves(9) (a.p: rdn to ld wl ins fnl f: r.o)........— 1
555[3] Sing With the Band **(47)***(62) (BAMcMahon)* 4-9-5 JWeaver(13) (led tl hdd wl ins fnl f)........½ 2
442[10] Statius *(56)*(Fav)*(TDBarron)* 3-8-11 JFortune(6) (swtg: chsd ldrs: stmbld over 3f out: effrt u.p fnl 2f: nt pce to chal)........4 3
Mamma's Due *(46) (JBerry)* 3-8-6 GCarter(12) (cmpt: s.i.s: hdwy ½-wy: nvr nrr)........1¾ 4
Pacific Spirit **(45)***(40) (MTate)* 5-9-5 JWilliams(4) (bit bkwd: outpcd tl sme hdwy appr fnl f)...2½ 5
502[4] Polli Pui **(55)***(33) (PDEvans)* 3-8-6 KDarley(7) (outpcd)........2½ 6
390[5] Keeper's Grey **(53)***(35) (RGuest)* 3-8-11b WWoods(8) (prom 4f: sn rdn & outpcd)........1 7
520[16] Halbert **(48)***(34) (MRChannon)* 6-9-3 (7) DSweeney(2) (rdn along & outpcd ½-wy: nvr nrr)........½ 8
420[9] Daily Challenger (USA) **(42)***(31) (RonaldThompson)* 3-8-11 DeanMcKeown(10) (outpcd).....1¼ 9
357[10] Il Fratello *(21) (NACallaghan)* 4-9-10 PaulEddery(11) (outpcd)........3½ 10
590[8] Christian Flight (IRE) **(42)***(13) (SGollings)* 6-9-0v(5) JStack(5) (prom: hrd rdn 2f out: sn lost tch)........1¼ 11
524[11] Assumpsit (IRE) **(65)***(17) (SDow)* 3-8-11 TQuinn(3) (outpcd)........nk 12
Rinus Manor (IRE) **(46)***(7) (DMcCain)* 4-9-10 KFallon(1) (sn pushed along: a outpcd)........4 13

9/4 Statius, **4/1** Polli Pui, **5/1** COOL TACTICIAN (4/1-6/1), **6/1** Sing With the Band (4/1-13/2), **13/2** Assumpsit (IRE) (4/1-7/1), **10/1** Keeper's Grey (8/1-12/1), **12/1** Mamma's Due (op 8/1), **16/1** Christian Flight (IRE), **25/1** Daily Challenger (USA), Rinus Manor (IRE), **33/1** Halbert, **50/1** Pacific Spirit, Il Fratello, CSF £36.10 TOTE £9.30: £2.50 £2.00 £1.70 (£23.20) Trio £55.00. OWNER Mr J. D. Graham (UPPER LONGDON) BRED M. C. Collins and N. Bycroft 13 Rn
1m 15.6 (4.40) SF: 37/44/25/15/22/2/4/16/-/3/-/-/-
WEIGHT FOR AGE 3yo-13lb

OFFICIAL EXPLANATION **Il Fratello: jockey reported that the gelding hung throughout and was almost unrideable, and that the trip was inadequate.**

604 CREME CARAMEL (S) STKS (2-Y.O) (Class G) £2,243.00 (£618.00: £293.00) 5f (Fibresand) Stalls: Low GOING: 0.03 sec per fur (STD) 4-30 (4-31)

531[3] **Gi La High** *(50t)*(Fav)*(JBerry)* 2-8-6 GCarter(6) (s.i.s: sn rcvrd to chse ldrs: led over 2f out: rdn out)........— 1
Nameless *(48) (DJSCosgrove)* 2-8-6 JQuinn(5) (b.hind: lt-f: unf: a.p: rdn to chal fnl f: unable qckn nr fin)........¾ 2
Tymeera *(22) (BPalling)* 2-8-6 TSprake(7) (neat: bit bkwd: bhd & rdn along: kpt on appr fnl f: nvr nrr)........8 3
Mustaffa (IRE) *(16) (MRChannon)* 2-8-11 RHughes(2) (leggy: unf: bit bkwd: s.i.s: sn pushed along & bhd: nvr nrr)........3½ 4
531[2] Don't Tell Vicki *(7) (JSMoore)* 2-8-6 KDarley(3) (lw: outpcd: a bhd)........1¼ 5
554[7] Static Love *(7) (SCWilliams)* 2-8-6 JFortune(4) (spd over 3f)........s.h 6
533[15] Capo Bay (IRE) *(PCHaslam)* 2-8-11 JWeaver(1) (led to ½-wy: wknd qckly: t.o)........14 7

5/2 GI LA HIGH, **9/2** Static Love (op 3/1), Mustaffa (IRE) (9/4-5/1), **5/1** Don't Tell Vicki, **6/1** Capo Bay (IRE), **7/1** Tymeera, **8/1** Nameless, CSF £21.15 TOTE £2.80: £3.20 £2.30 (£8.90). OWNER Mr Basheer Kielany (COCKERHAM) BRED J. H. Heath 7 Rn 64.2 secs (6.20) SF: -/-/-/-/-/-/-
Bt in 3,600 gns

605 SOUFFLE H'CAP (0-60) (3-Y.O+) (Class F) £2,519.00 (£694.00: £329.00) 1m 1f 79y (Fibresand) Stalls: Low GOING: 0.03 sec per fur (STD) 5-00 (5-00)

*517** **My Minnie (55)***(75+)*(Fav)*(BJMeehan)* 5-9-13 5x BDoyle(8) (mde all: clr 2f out: unchal)........— 1
512[3] Backstabber **(35)***(41) (MissSJWilton)* 5-8-7 JQuinn(7) (a.p: 2nd st: kpt on u.p fnl f: no ch w wnr)........8 2
Mazirah **(56)***(58)*(Fav)*(PJMakin)* 4-10-0 JWeaver(11) (hld up: effrt 3f out: r.o wl fnl f: nvr nrr)........2½ 3
530[8] Enchanteur **(40)***(40) (TJEtherington)* 4-8-12 KDarley(5) (lw: s.s: hdwy 4f out: 5th st: kpt on one pce)........1½ 4

501[2] La Residence **(49)***(46) (MrsNMacauley)* 4-9-4 (3) SSanders(10) (prom: 3rd & rdn st: no imp) 1¼ 5
141[9] Red Spectacle (IRE) **(59)***(53) (PCHaslam)* 3-8-13 JFortune(12) (hdwy fnl 2f: nvr nrr) 2 6
501[9] Shansi (IRE) **(43)***(36) (MDIUsher)* 4-9-1v RStreet(13) (chsd ldrs: 4th & rdn st: sn btn) ....½ 7
529[3] Kristis Girl **(40)***(31) (DHaydnJones)* 8-8-12 AMackay(4) (chsd ldrs over 6f: sn lost pl) 1¼ 8
550[9] Scottish Park **(41)***(32) (RWEmery)* 6-8-13 JWilliams(6) (b.hind: nvr nr to chal) ....s.h 9
530[7] Swynford Flyer **(43)***(33) (JAHarris)* 6-8-10 (5) JStack(9) (in tch: rdn & 6th st: wknd wl over 1f out) ....½ 10
497[4] Pop to Stans **(50)***(31)*(Fav)*(JPearce)* 6-9-8 PaulEddery(2) (a bhd & outpcd: t.o) 5 11
520[2] Genesis Four **(42)***(23) (SRBowring)* 5-8-7b(7) CTeague(3) (chsd ldrs over 5f: sn lost tch) ....nk 12
503[17] Westcoast **(48)***(3) (MTate)* 4-9-6 TIves(1) (swtg: a in rr: t.o fnl 3f) 15 13

9/2 MY MINNIE, Mazirah (op 3/1), Pop to Stans, **6/1** Genesis Four (op 4/1), **8/1** Swynford Flyer (6/1-10/1), **10/1** Red Spectacle (IRE), La Residence, **14/1** Backstabber, Kristis Girl, Shansi (IRE), **16/1** Scottish Park, **20/1** Enchanteur, **33/1** Westcoast, CSF £64.89 CT £285.19 TOTE £8.50: £2.90 £1.90 £3.00 (£102.50) Trio £201.80. OWNER Mrs W. Protheroe-Beynon (UPPER LAMBOURN) BRED Mrs Wilma Protheroe-Beynon 13 Rn 2m 3.9 (7.90) SF: 45/11/28/10/16/5/6/1/2/3/1/-/-

WEIGHT FOR AGE 3yo-18lb

T/Plpt: £28.80 (10.51 Tckts). T/Qdpt: £31.00 (1.55 Tckts). IM

SHA TIN (Kowloon, Hong Kong) (L-H)
Saturday April 1st (Good to soft)

606a QUEEN ELIZABETH II CUP (3-Y.O+)
1m 3f

Red Bishop (USA) *(123) (HIbrahim,Dubai)* 7-9-0 MJKinane ....— 1
Volochine (IRE) *(121) (France)* 4-9-0 MrRCollet 2¼ 2
Survey King (NZ) *(116) (HongKong)* 5-9-0 GChilds 3½ 3
385* Ionio (USA) *(114) (CEBrittain)* 4-9-0 BMarcus (btn approx 8l) 6

OWNER Godolphin BRED Pillar Stud Inc 2m 17.2 SF: -/-/-/-

LONGCHAMP (Paris, France) (R-H)
Sunday April 2nd (Soft)

607a PRIX D'HARCOURT (Gp 2) (4-Y.O+)
1m 2f

Freedom Cry *(122)*(Fav)*(AFabre,France)* 4-8-11 OPeslier (a.p: 2nd st: rdn to ld over 1f out: r.o wl u.p fnl f) ....— 1
Pelder (IRE) *(122) (PAKelleway)* 5-8-11 LDettori (5th st: effrt to ld over 1f out: sn hdd: r.o wl) ....nk 2
489a* Tuesday's Special (USA) *(119) (France)* 5-8-11 TJarnet (hld up: 8th st: sn rdn & outpcd: r.o strly nr fin) 1½ 3
Green Tune (USA) *(125) (France)* 4-9-4 ODoleuze (a.p: 3rd st: rdn 2f out: outpcd fnl f) ....½ 4
Millkom *(125) (France)* 4-9-4 J-RDubosc (6th st: swtchd over 1f out: wknd ins fnl f) ....½ 5
Nononito (FR) *(115) (France)* 4-8-11 GMosse (9th st: rdn over 2f out: sme late hdwy) 1½ 6
Alderbrook *(119) (MrsJCecil)* 6-9-1 PaulEddery (4th st: sn rdn: one pce) ....s.h 7
Suave Tern (USA) *(109) (France)* 4-8-11 JReid (10th st: n.d) 4 8
Marildo (FR) *(114) (DSmaga,France)* 8-9-4b GGuignard (led tl over 1f out: sn wknd) 1 9
Truly a Dream (IRE) *(105) (France)* 4-8-11 WMongil (7th st: n.d) 1 10

OWNER Mr D. Wildenstein (FRANCE) BRED Dayton Ltd DS

EVRY (France) (R-H)
Friday April 7th (Good)

608a PRIX COR DE CHASSE (Listed)
5f 110y

Struggler *(118) (CLaffon-Parias,France)* 3-8-7 FSanchez ....— 1
Neverneyev (USA) *(115) (France)* 5-9-8 ODoleuze 2 2

Poplar Bluff (IRE) *(104) (France)* 3-8-7 OPeslier 3 3
Imperial Bailiwick (IRE) *(98) (MDIUsher)* 4-9-1 WRSwinburn ....½ 4

OWNER Mr Hamad Ali

CURRAGH (Newbridge, Ireland) (R-H)
Saturday April 8th

609a SEAN COUGHLAN GLADNESS (Gp 3)
7f

425⁹ **Bin Ajwaad (IRE)** *(119) (BHanbury)* 5-9-11 PatEddery ....— 1
Ridgewood Ben *(117) (JOxx,Ireland)* 4-9-11 JPMurtagh 1 2
Nordic Oak (IRE) *(101) (Ireland)* 7-9-8 KJManning 5½ 3
Soreze (IRE) *(98) (Ireland)* 3-8-5 ow1 PVGilson ....hd 4
Jahid (USA) *(98) (Ireland)* 3-8-10 MJKinane 2½ 5
Port Lucaya *(DRLoder)* 5-10-1b JWeaver 6
Quintiliani (IRE) *(Ireland)* 4-9-11 JFEgan 7

OWNER Mr A. Merza (NEWMARKET) BRED Tullamaine Castle Stud and Partners in Ireland 7 Rn
1m 28.9 (5.70) SF: -/-/-/-/-/-/-

HAYDOCK (L-H)
Saturday April 15th (Good)
WEATHER: fine WIND: mod half against

610 BNFL EASTER CONDITIONS STKS (4-Y.O+) (Class B) £7,885.50
(£2,944.50: £1,434.75: £611.25: £268.13: £130.87)
2m 45y Stalls: Low GOING minus 0.17 sec per fur (GF) 2-00 (2-02)

Further Flight (107)*(98) (BWHills)* 9-9-12 MHills(7) (bit bkwd: dwlt: hld up & bhd: 6th st: hdwy over 1f out: styd on to ld wl ins fnl f) ....— 1
*290** Old Rouvel (USA) *(88) (DJGMurraySmith)* 4-8-12 KDarley(1) (lw: hld up: 3rd st: ev ch whn n.m.r 1f out: rdn & fin wl) ....nk 2
Silence in Court (IRE) **(93)***(97) (BAMcMahon)* 4-9-8 JFortune(8) (lw: s.i.s: hld up & bhd: 7th st: shkn up over 2f out: ev ch ent fnl f: unable qckn) ....nk 3
440⁵ Charity Crusader **(95)***(87)*(Fav)*(PWChapple-Hyam)* 4-8-13 BThomson(3) (lw: hld up: 5th st: hdwy to ld 2f out: hdd & no ex wl ins fnl f) 1¾ 4
Dato Star (IRE) *(82)*(Fav)*(JMJefferson)* 4-8-10 WRSwinburn(2) (chsd ldr: 2nd st: rdn & ev ch 1f out: one pce) 1½ 5
440⁹ Latahaab (USA) *(84) (RAkehurst)* 4-8-12 TIves(4) (b: lw: led to 2f out: rdn & ev ch tl wknd ins fnl f) ....hd 6
485¹¹ Tip the Dove *(62) (RJPrice)* 6-8-9 TSprake(5) (chsd ldrs 12f: sn lost tch: t.o) 15 7

3/1 Charity Crusader, Dato Star (IRE), **100/30** FURTHER FLIGHT, **7/2** Silence in Court (IRE), **14/1** Old Rouvel (USA), **20/1** Latahaab (USA), **50/1** Tip the Dove, CSF £36.96 TOTE £4.10: £2.20 £5.00 (£25.30) OWNER Mr S. WingfieldDigby (LAMBOURN) BRED S. Wingfield Digby 7 Rn
3m 31.69 (4.49) SF: 75/61/70/60/55/57/39
WEIGHT FOR AGE 4yo-4lb

611 BNFL FAMILY DAY H'CAP (0-95) (4-Y.O+) (Class C) £5,654.00
(£1,712.00: £836.00: £398.00)
6f Stalls: High GOING minus 0.17 sec per fur (GF) 2-30 (2-33)

434² **Domulla (85)***(91)*(Fav)*(RAkehurst)* 5-9-6 WRSwinburn(8) (b: hld up: swtchd rt 1f out: str run to ld ins fnl f: readily) ....— 1
434¹⁶ Barato **(65)***(68) (MrsJRRamsden)* 4-8-0 JFanning(12) (hld up: hdwy & n.m.r 2f out: swtchd lft & ev ch fnl f: r.o) 1 2
434⁸ Highborn (IRE) **(83)***(85) (PSFelgate)* 6-9-4 KDarley(9) (chsd ldrs: rdn & outpcd over 1f out: kpt on ins fnl f) ....½ 3
535³ The Old Chapel **(61)***(60) (BAMcMahon)* 6-7-10bow3 FNorton(10) (mde most tl hdd & no ex ins fnl f) ....hd 4
567* Chinour (IRE) **(65)***(64) (EJAlston)* 7-8-0 NCarlisle(7) (hld up: hdwy appr fnl f: nrst fin) 1 5
535²⁰ Castlerea Lad **(80)***(79) (RHollinshead)* 6-9-1 WRyan(11) (hld up: hdwy over 1f out: nvr nrr) ..hd 6
Madly Sharp **(86)***(84) (JWWatts)* 4-9-7 BThomson(13) (bit bkwd: hld up in tch: hdwy & ev ch appr fnl f: one pce) ....nk 7
535¹⁷ Whittle Woods Girl **(77)***(62) (EJAlston)* 4-8-12 JQuinn(5) (nvr trbld ldrs) 5 8

434[6] So Intrepid (IRE) **(74)***(52) (JMBradley)* 5-8-4 (5) SDrowne(2) (prom tl wknd over 1f out) 2½ 9
Bayin (USA) **(68)***(45) (MDIUsher)* 6-8-3 RStreet(3) (b: lw: a in rr) ....½ 10
Benzoe (IRE) **(73)***(39) (MrsJRRamsden)* 5-8-8 KFallon(6) (unruly s: prom tl wknd fnl 2f) 4 11
Selhurstpark Flyer (IRE) **(91)***(54) (JBerry)* 4-9-12 JCarroll(4) (lw: spd over 3f) 1¼ 12
Caspian Gold **(65)***(28) (CNAllen)* 4-7-9 (5) MBaird(1) (bit bkwd: outpcd) ....s.h 13
LONG HANDICAP The Old Chapel 7-6

5/1 DOMULLA, **6/1** Selhurstpark Flyer (IRE), **7/1** Highborn (IRE), **8/1** Madly Sharp, Castlerea Lad, **9/1** Barato, **10/1** The Old Chapel, Whittle Woods Girl, Chinour (IRE), **12/1** Benzoe (IRE), So Intrepid (IRE), **14/1** Bayin (USA), **33/1** Caspian Gold, CSF £48.44 CT £296.98 TOTE £4.00: £2.60 £5.80 £2.10 (£62.70) Trio £92.70 OWNER Mr A. W. Boon (EPSOM) BRED Alan Boon 13 Rn
1m 13.69 (1.99) SF: 62/39/56/31/35/50/55/33/23/16/10/25/-

612

BNFL FIELD MARSHAL STKS (Listed) (3-Y.O) (Class A) £12,136.50 (£3,672.00: £1,791.00: £850.50)
5f Stalls: High GOING minus 0.17 sec per fur (GF) 3-00 (3-00)

Mind Games (115)*(111)*(Fav)*(JBerry)* 3-9-4 JCarroll(4) (lw: mde all: qcknd clr over 1f out: impressive) ....— 1
Wavian **(104)***(96) (RCharlton)* 3-8-11 KDarley(1) (nt grwn: hld up: hdwy to chse wnr fnl 2f: no imp) 2½ 2
Millstream (USA) **(109)***(97) (MJohnston)* 3-8-13 WRSwinburn(3) (lw: swtg: a.p: shkn up over 1f out: r.o one pce) ....nk 3
Hinton Rock (IRE) **(96)***(94) (MBell)* 3-8-11 MFenton(2) (bit bkwd: dwlt: rdn & effrt 2f out: nt pce to chal) ....nk 4
551[5] Coffee 'n Cream **(84)***(86) (RHannon)* 3-8-11 BThomson(5) (effrt ½-wy: rdn wl over 1f out: sn outpcd) 2½ 5

Evens MIND GAMES, **3/1** Millstream (USA), **4/1** Wavian, **9/1** Hinton Rock (IRE), **16/1** Coffee 'n Cream, CSF £5.13 TOTE £1.80: £1.10 £1.90 (£3.00) OWNER Mr Robert Hughes (COCKERHAM) BRED Mrs V. E. Hughes 5 Rn 60.47 secs (1.47) SF: 63/48/49/46/38

613

BNFL FAMILY DAY MAIDEN STKS (I) (3-Y.O) (Class D) £3,837.50 (£1,160.00: £565.00: £267.50)
7f 30y Stalls: Low GOING minus 0.17 sec per fur (GF) 3-30 (3-33)

431[3] **Sanoosea (USA)** *(86)*(Fav)*(MRStoute)* 3-9-0 WRSwinburn(6) (mde virtually all: hrd rdn fnl 2f: all out) ....— 1
Amrak Ajeeb (IRE) *(85) (BHanbury)* 3-9-0 WRyan(7) (bit bkwd: chsd wnr: 2nd st: disp ld 3f out: hrd rdn & unable qckn cl home) ....½ 2
Carol's Dream (USA) *(76) (JWHills)* 3-8-7 (7) MHenry(9) (bit bkwd: hld up: hdwy 2f out: styd on ins fnl f: nvr nrr) 4 3
Splintercat (USA) *(70) (JHMGosden)* 3-8-9 GHind(5) (lengthy: unf: bit bkwd: s.s: sn rcvrd to chse ldrs: 3rd st: rdn & hung lft over 1f out: one pce) ....nk 4
524[10] Nafta **(63)***(64) (SEKettlewell)* 3-9-0 JFortune(3) (prom: 5th st: rdn & one pce fnl 2f) 5 5
Good Match (IRE) *(63) (NTinkler)* 3-9-0 KDarley(1) (bkwd: nvr nr to chal) ....½ 6
Cupronickel (IRE) *(56) (JWWatts)* 3-8-9 BThomson(2) (w'like: leggy: bit bkwd: prom: 4th st: wknd 2f out) 1 7
435[7] Nordic Breeze (IRE) *(59) (ABailey)* 3-8-9 (5) VHalliday(10) (a bhd: rdn 3f out: no rspnse) ....¾ 8
435[8] Magical Bid (IRE) **(57)***(51) (JMBradley)* 3-8-9 (5) SDrowne(8) (chsd ldrs: 6th st: wknd over 2f out) 3½ 9
Northern Charmer *(51) (MGMeagher)* 3-9-0 MFenton(4) (bit bkwd: chsd ldrs 4f: sn lost tch) ....hd 10

1/2 SANOOSEA (USA), **5/1** Splintercat (USA), **12/1** Cupronickel (IRE) (op 7/1), **14/1** Nafta, **16/1** Amrak Ajeeb (IRE), **20/1** Carol's Dream (USA), Good Match (IRE), **33/1** Nordic Breeze (IRE), Magical Bid (IRE), **50/1** Northern Charmer, CSF £10.38 TOTE £1.60: £1.10 £2.90 £2.20 (£5.50) Trio £32.30 OWNER Maktoum Al Maktoum (NEWMARKET) BRED Gainsborough Farm Inc 10 Rn
1m 32.0 (4.70) SF: 31/30/21/15/9/8/1/4/-/-

614

BNFL CHILDRENS' CHARITY H'CAP (0-95) (3-Y.O) (Class C) £5,602.00 (£1,696.00: £828.00: £394.00)
1m 2f 120y Stalls: Low GOING minus 0.17 sec per fur (GF) 4-00 (4-02)

Murajja (USA) (86)*(96)*(Fav)*(PTWalwyn)* 3-9-0 MHills(8) (h.d.w: prom: 2nd st: led over 3f out: clr appr fnl f: unchal) ....— 1
538[12] Nigel's Lad (IRE) **(68)***(74) (PCHaslam)* 3-7-10 TWilliams(9) (hld up & bhd: hdwy 2f out: rdn & one pce fnl f) 2½ 2

572* Clifton Fox **(81)***(86) (JAGlover)* 3-8-9 MBirch(7) (hld up: hdwy over 2f out: kpt on ins fnl f) ... ¾ 3
301[2] Tribal Peace (IRE) **(66)***(70) (BGubby)* 3-7-8 ow1 JQuinn(10) (hld up: hdwy & 4th st: styd on one pce fnl 2f) ... s.h 4
New Century (USA) **(90)***(94) (HRACecil)* 3-9-4 WRyan(6) (b.hind: bit bkwd: hld up: hung lft & styd on appr fnl f) ... 1 5
Mistinguett (IRE) **(76)***(77) (RHannon)* 3-8-4 ow1 BThomson(1) (chsd ldrs: 3rd st: outpcd 2f out: kpt on ins fnl f) ... 1¼ 6
Tidal Reach (USA) **(67)***(67) (ABailey)* 3-7-9 LCharnock(5) (chsd ldrs: 5th st: rdn over 2f out: sn wknd) ... 1 7
504[13] Kemo Sabo **(79)***(73) (MrsJRRamsden)* 3-8-7 KFallon(11) (lw: hld up: effrt & rdn over 2f out: no imp) ... 4 8
536[6] Manful **(88)***(79) (JHetherton)* 3-9-2 NKennedy(4) (a bhd) ... 2 9
Percy Braithwaite (IRE) **(93)***(84) (MJohnston)* 3-9-7 JCarroll(3) (chsd ldrs 6f: sn rdn & wknd) ... nk 10
504[10] Cyrus the Great (IRE) **(77)***(54) (MBell)* 3-8-5 MFenton(2) (led tl over 3f out: sn rdn & wknd: t.o) ... 9 11

LONG HANDICAP Tribal Peace (IRE) 7-3

100/30 MURAJJA (USA), **4/1** Mistinguett (IRE), **9/2** New Century (USA), **13/2** Clifton Fox, **9/1** Tribal Peace (IRE), **12/1** Tidal Reach (USA), Percy Braithwaite (IRE), Kemo Sabo, **14/1** Manful, Nigel's Lad (IRE), Cyrus the Great (IRE), CSF £47.47 CT £275.35 TOTE £3.30: £1.70 £4.10 £2.60 (£77.60) Trio £47.80 OWNER Mr Hamdan Al Maktoum (LAMBOURN) BRED Shadwell Farm Inc & Shadwell Estate Co Ltd in USA 11 Rn 2m 14.12 (2.62) SF: 65/43/55/39/63/46/36/42/48/53/23

STEWARDS' ENQUIRY Charnock suspended 24-27/4/95 (irresponsible riding).

615 BNFL RISLEY MAIDEN AUCTION STKS (2-Y.O) (Class E) £3,338.75 (£1,010.00: £492.50: £233.75)

5f Stalls: High GOING minus 0.17 sec per fur (GF) 4-30 (4-37)

480[3] **Passion For Life** *(86+t)*(Fav)*(GLewis)* 2-8-7 MHills(3) (mde all: clr fnl 2f: unchal) ... — 1
533[4] Mallia *(71) (TDBarron)* 2-8-5 JFortune(14) (hdwy stands' side ½-wy: rdn & drifted lft fnl f: r.o) ... 4 2
533[13] Sharp Monty *(65) (RHollinshead)* 2-8-5 WRyan(17) (a.p stands' side: rdn & one pce appr fnl f) ... 2 3
533[2] Ramsey Hope *(60) (CWFairhurst)* 2-8-7 NKennedy(2) (chsd wnr far side: rdn & wknd appr fnl f) ... 2 4
Rapid Liner *(56) (AHarrison)* 2-8-2 (5) JStack(4) (leggy: unf: spd far side over 3f) ... 1½ 5
436[4] Bedside Mail *(46) (JMPEustace)* 2-8-5 BThomson(6) (chsd ldrs far side over 3f) ... 2½ 6
Eights High (USA) *(47) (RHannon)* 2-8-7 KDarley(1) (neat: cmpt: b.hind: racd far side: nvr trbld ldrs) ... hd 7
Royal Rapport *(45) (BAMcMahon)* 2-8-7 TIves(16) (w'like: bkwd: chsd ldr stands' side 3f) ... ¾ 8
523[7] Richard House Lad *(44) (CASmith)* 2-8-7 MWigham(7) (dwlt: nvr nr to chal) ... nk 9
Anshan's Deity *(38) (CWFairhurst)* 2-8-5 WWoods(12) (lt-f: led stands' side 3f: sn rdn & wknd) ... 1¼ 10
533[10] Oriole *(38) (NTinkler)* 2-8-5 KimTinkler(18) (a in rr) ... s.h 11
Traceability *(35) (JBerry)* 2-8-7 JCarroll(15) (leggy: unf: s.s: a in rr) ... 1½ 12
480[6] Kenny Davis (IRE) *(31) (MrsHParrott)* 2-8-5 TSprake(13) (m.n.s) ... ½ 13
Topaglow (IRE) *(30) (PTDalton)* 2-8-5 LCharnock(11) (lt-f: outpcd) ... nk 14
455[2] Dancing Lottie (IRE) *(22) (PAKelleway)* 2-7-12 FNorton(8) (prom: rdn 2f out: sn wknd) ... nk 15
Merlin's Honour *(15) (PCHaslam)* 2-8-2 TWilliams(9) (lt-f: unf: s.i.s: a in rr) ... 3½ 16
Russian Rascal (IRE) *(13) (MHEasterby)* 2-8-5 MBirch(5) (unf: bkwd: outpcd) ... 1½ 17
490[4] Just Rory *(EJAlston)* 2-8-3 JQuinn(10) (Withdrawn not under Starter's orders: unruly at s) ... W

2/1 PASSION FOR LIFE, **100/30** Traceability (op 2/1), **5/1** Mallia, **8/1** Ramsey Hope, **12/1** Dancing Lottie (IRE), Bedside Mail, Eights High (USA), **14/1** Sharp Monty, **16/1** Royal Rapport, Merlin's Honour, Russian Rascal (IRE), **20/1** Rapid Liner, Just Rory, **25/1** Kenny Davis (IRE), Richard House Lad, Topaglow (IRE), **33/1** Oriole, Anshan's Deity, CSF £15.63 TOTE £3.40: £1.60 £2.50 £5.70 (£12.80) Trio £131.00 OWNER Mr David Waters (EPSOM) BRED G. R. Smith (Thriplow) Ltd 17 Rn 61.69 secs (2.69) SF: 32/17/11/6/2/-/-/-/-/-/-/-/-/-/-/-/-

616 BNFL FAMILY DAY MAIDEN STKS (II) (3-Y.O) (Class D) £3,837.50 (£1,160.00: £565.00: £267.50)

7f 30y Stalls: Low GOING minus 0.17 sec per fur (GF) 5-00 (5-03)

Zeb (IRE) (100)*(81)*(Fav)*(BAMcMahon)* 3-9-0 TIves(5) (chsd ldrs: 5th st: led over 1f out: rdn out) ... — 1

Khamseh *(70) (JWWatts)* 3-8-9 BThomson(10) (bit bkwd: hld up: hdwy 2f out: r.o fnl f: no ch w wnr) 2½ 2
Dosses Dan (IRE) *(74) (BWHills)* 3-9-0 MHills(6) (bit bkwd: chsd ldr: 2nd st: led over 2f out tl over 1f out: one pce) ....½ 3
Houghton Venture (USA) *(74) (SPCWoods)* 3-9-0 WWoods(4) (w'like: bit bkwd: a.p: 3rd st: rdn 2f out: one pce) ....s.h 4
Jam N Shadeed (USA) *(66) (PFICole)* 3-9-0 CRutter(9) (hld up: 6th st: effrt on outside 2f out: nt pce to chal) 3½ 5
4317 Stand Tall *(60) (CWThornton)* 3-9-0 DeanMcKeown(1) (hld up: swtchd ins 3f out: nvr plcd to chal) 3 6
Smolensk (IRE) *(54) (JBerry)* 3-9-0 JCarroll(8) (led tl hdd over 2f out: wknd over 1f out) 2½ 7
Carlito Brigante *(50) (MrsJRRamsden)* 3-9-0 KFallon(3) (w'like: s.s: a in rr) 2 8
Show Flair (IRE) *(29) (JSWainwright)* 3-9-0 JFanning(2) (bkwd: a bhd: t.o) 9 9
Social Register *(28) (HThomsonJones)* 3-9-0 NCarlisle(7) (bit bkwd: chsd ldrs: 4th st: wknd 3f out: t.o) ....½ 10

13/8 ZEB (IRE) (Evens-7/4), **7/2** Khamseh, **5/1** Dosses Dan (IRE), **6/1** Jam N Shadeed (USA), **10/1** Houghton Venture (USA), **11/1** Social Register, **14/1** Smolensk (IRE), **20/1** Stand Tall, Carlito Brigante, **50/1** Show Flair (IRE), CSF £8.37 TOTE £2.20: £1.20 £1.80 £1.40 (£2.70) Trio £18.00 OWNER Barouche Stud Ltd (TAMWORTH) BRED Mrs M. Cross 10 Rn
1m 30.78 (3.48) SF: 45/34/38/38/30/24/18/14/-/-

T/Plpt: £33.30 (689.14 Tckts). T/Qdpt: £6.50 (31.85 Tckts). IM

KEMPTON (R-H)
Saturday April 15th (St course Good, Rest Good to firm)
WEATHER: overcast WIND: almost nil

617
E.B.F. REDFERN MAIDEN STKS (2-Y.O) (Class D) £3,649.00 (£1,102.00: £536.00: £253.00)
5f Stalls: High GOING minus 0.41 sec per fur (F) 1-45 (1-48)

5236 **Amaretto Bay (IRE)** *(67t) (BJMeehan)* 2-9-0 BDoyle(14) (a.p: led ins fnl f: rdn out) ....— 1
4242 Johayro *(67)*(Fav)*(WGMTurner)* 2-9-0 GDuffield(7) (led: rdn 2f out: hdd ins fnl f: r.o) ....hd 2
5085 Miss Waterline *(61) (PDEvans)* 2-8-9 LDettori(2) (hld up: rdn over 2f out: r.o wl ins fnl f) ....nk 3
Tapintime (USA) *(65) (PFICole)* 2-9-0 TQuinn(20) (leggy: a.p: rdn over 2f out: ev ch ins fnl f: unable qckn) ....nk 4
Sonic Mail *(63) (KMcAuliffe)* 2-9-0 RCochrane(4) (unf: stmbld over 3f out: hdwy & nt clr run 1f out: nt clr run ins fnl f: r.o) ....½ 5
Sky Dome (IRE) *(58) (MHTompkins)* 2-9-0 PRobinson(9) (scope: lw: a.p: rdn over 2f out: eased whn btn wl ins fnl f) 1½ 6
Tropical Dance (USA) *(53) (MrsJCecil)* 2-8-9 JReid(3) (unf: hdwy over 1f out: nvr nrr) ....hd 7
Jolis Present *(56) (MJRyan)* 2-9-0 WCarson(12) (neat: bit bkwd: gd hdwy over 1f out: r.o wl ins fnl f) ....½ 8
Sporting Fantasy *(53) (MRChannon)* 2-9-0 RHughes(6) (neat: bit bkwd: a.p: hrd rdn over 1f out: wknd fnl f) 1 9
The Imps (IRE) *(52) (BWHills)* 2-8-9 (5) JDSmith(13) (neat: hld up: rdn over 2f out: wknd over 1f out) ....½ 10
Pride of Kashmir *(48) (PWHarris)* 2-9-0 RHills(19) (neat: bit bkwd: hld up: rdn over 3f out: wknd fnl f) 1 11
Hever Golf Express *(43) (TJNaughton)* 2-9-0 GCarter(16) (neat: bit bkwd: dwlt: nvr nrr) 1¾ 12
Navigate (USA) *(40) (RHannon)* 2-9-0 PatEddery(5) (neat: lw: s.s: a mid div) 1 13
Arctic Romancer (IRE) *(39) (GLewis)* 2-8-9 (5) AWhelan(10) (neat: dwlt: nvr nrr) ....nk 14
Back By Dawn *(35) (DRCElsworth)* 2-9-0 JWilliams(17) (b.hind: leggy: a bhd) 1¼ 15
All She Surveys *(30) (JAkehurst)* 2-8-9 SWhitworth(11) (neat: bit bkwd: bhd fnl 2f) ....s.h 16
Babylon Blues *(34) (RHannon)* 2-8-7 (7) DaneO'Neill(15) (neat: bit bkwd: a bhd) ....hd 17
4553 Lincon Twenty One *(26) (MJHaynes)* 2-8-9 AMcGlone(1) (bhd fnl 2f) 1 18
Mandy's Risk *(30) (TMJones)* 2-9-0 RPerham(8) (neat: bit bkwd: bhd fnl 2f) ....nk 19
Sharp Night *(29) (MSSaunders)* 2-9-0 ADicks(18) (leggy: lt-f: bhd fnl 2f) ....nk 20

7/2 Johayro, **5/1** Tapintime (USA) (9/4-11/2), **11/2** Navigate (USA) (4/1-6/1), **15/2** Sonic Mail (5/1-8/1), **10/1** Pride of Kashmir, Sporting Fantasy (op 5/1), Tropical Dance (USA), Miss Waterline, **14/1** The Imps (IRE), **16/1** AMARETTO BAY (IRE), Jolis Present, **20/1** Sky Dome (IRE), **25/1** Hever Golf Express, Lincon Twenty One, All She Surveys, **33/1** Arctic Romancer (IRE), Babylon Blues, Back By Dawn, Mandy's Risk, Sharp Night, CSF £77.36 TOTE £20.50: £4.50 £2.50 £3.90 (£38.60) Trio £369.70 OWNER The Harlequin Partnership (UPPER LAMBOURN) BRED Gay O'Callaghan 20 Rn
61.36 secs (3.56) SF: 4/4/-/2/-/-/-/-/-/-/-/-/-/-/-/-/-/-/-/-

618

MIDDLESEX H'CAP (0-90) (3-Y.O) (Class C) £5,862.00 (£1,776.00: £868.00: £414.00) **1m 1f (round)** Stalls: High GOING minus 0.41 sec per fur (F) 2-15 (2-20)

Rockforce (75)*(83) (MRChannon)* 3-8-11 RHughes(16) (hdwy on ins over 3f out: 6th st: led 1f out: rdn out)........—- **1**
437[7] At Liberty (IRE) **(78)***(85) (RHannon)* 3-9-0 JReid(11) (rdn over 3f out: 4th st: ev ch 1f out: unable qckn)........½ **2**
State Law **(84)***(91) (GHarwood)* 3-9-6 AClark(4) (hdwy over 1f out: r.o wl ins fnl f)........nk **3**
250[2] No Pattern **(72)***(78) (GLMoore)* 3-8-8v BRouse(14) (lw: rdn over 2f out: hdwy over 1f out: r.o wl ins fnl f)........hd **4**
Kimbridge Knight (IRE) **(71)***(76) (PTWalwyn)* 3-8-7 ow1 RCochrane(5) (hld up: rdn over 2f out: r.o ins fnl f)........nk **5**
504[5] Dont Forget Curtis (IRE) **(80)***(84) (JRFanshawe)* 3-9-2 DHarrison(10) (hld up: rdn over 3f out: one pce)........1¼ **6**
504[15] Duffertoes **(83)***(86) (MJRyan)* 3-9-5 GCarter(3) (led over 7f out to 1f out: wknd ins fnl f)........½ **7**
*360** Greenwich Again **(68)***(70) (TGMills)* 3-8-4 RHills(13) (3rd st: rdn over 2f out: 4th & btn whn hmpd ins fnl f)........nk **8**
428[4] Paper Cloud **(73)***(73) (CEBrittain)* 3-8-9 BDoyle(15) (5th st: hrd rdn over 2f out: one pce)........1 **9**
John Lee Hooker **(72)***(71) (DWPArbuthnot)* 3-8-8 SWhitworth(17) (nvr nrr)........1 **10**
Night Dance **(84)***(74) (GLewis)* 3-9-6 PatEddery(1) (lw: nvr nrr)........5 **11**
Snowy Petrel (IRE) **(85)***(69) (JLDunlop)* 3-9-7 WCarson(7) (swtg: a bhd)........3 **12**
Hi-Aud **(65)***(39) (JAkehurst)* 3-7-12 (3) SSanders(8) (a bhd)........6 **13**
Orchidarma **(69)***(32) (RJRWilliams)* 3-8-5 GDuffield(2) (a bhd: hmpd over 1f out)........6 **14**
Bellas Gate Boy **(75)***(35) (MissHCKnight)* 3-8-11 JWeaver(12) (led over 1f: 2nd st: wknd over 2f out)........1¾ **15**
Bob's Ploy **(72)** *(RAkehurst)* 3-8-8 TQuinn(6) (bit bkwd: mid div whn stumbled 8f out: bhd fnl 7f)........25 **16**
526* Muferr (IRE) **(77)** (Fav)*(LMCumani)* 3-8-13 LDettori(9) (hld up: rdn over 2f out: 8th whn fell over 1f out)........ **F**

9/4 Muferr (IRE), **6/1** Bob's Ploy, **7/1** Night Dance, **9/1** Kimbridge Knight (IRE), Greenwich Again, **12/1** Dont Forget Curtis (IRE), No Pattern, Duffertoes, At Liberty (IRE), **16/1** Bellas Gate Boy, State Law, **20/1** Paper Cloud, ROCKFORCE, Snowy Petrel (IRE), John Lee Hooker, **33/1** Hi-Aud, Orchidarma, CSF £248.75 CT £3,592.09 TOTE £71.40: £6.80 £3.10 £2.70 £2.40 (£192.40) Trio £570.00 OWNER Mr G. Z. Mizel (UPPER LAMBOURN) BRED Guest Leasing and Bloodstock Co 17 Rn
1m 51.69 (1.69) SF: 47/49/55/42/40/48/50/34/37/35/38/33/3/-/-/-/-

619

DURANTE STKS (3-Y.O) (Class C) £4,971.20 (£1,860.80: £910.40: £392.00: £176.00: £89.60) **1m 2f** Stalls: High GOING minus 0.41 sec per fur (F) 2-45 (2-48)

Presenting *(103)*(Fav)*(JHMGosden)* 3-9-7 LDettori(1) (bit bkwd: 3rd st: rdn over 2f out: led ins fnl f: r.o wl)........— **1**
Commoner (USA) *(93) (RHannon)* 3-8-13 PatEddery(3) (led 7f: 2nd st: led 2f out tl ins fnl f: unable qckn)........1 **2**
Warning Order **(100)***(88) (JLDunlop)* 3-8-10 WCarson(7) (rdn over 2f out: nt clr run & swtchd lft wl over 1f out: hdwy over 1f out: r.o wl ins fnl f)........1¾ **3**
Dreamer (USA) **(103)***(95) (PFICole)* 3-9-4 TQuinn(10) (lw: rdn & hdwy on ins over 2f out: one pce fnl f)........nk **4**
438[7] Baltic Raider **(104)***(94) (GWragg)* 3-9-4 PRobinson(6) (5th st: rdn over 2f out: one pce)........½ **5**
Korambi *(82) (CEBrittain)* 3-8-10 MRimmer(5) (lw: 4th st: rdn over 2f out: wknd over 1f out)...3 **6**
Al Widyan (IRE) **(107)***(88) (HRACecil)* 3-9-4 AMcGlone(2) (b.hind: lw: a.p: led 3f out to 2f out: sn wknd)........¾ **7**
Taipan (IRE) *(83) (JLDunlop)* 3-8-13 JReid(8) (a bhd)........hd **8**
438[6] Twilight Sleep (USA) **(100)***(82) (LordHuntingdon)* 3-8-13 JWeaver(4) (lw: wknd over 2f out)....1 **9**
Tira Heights (USA) **(107)***(76) (RWArmstrong)* 3-8-13 RPrice(9) (bit bkwd: a bhd)........3½ **10**

5/4 PRESENTING, **4/1** Al Widyan (IRE) (5/2-9/2), **13/2** Commoner (USA), **10/1** Baltic Raider, **12/1** Warning Order, Twilight Sleep (USA), Taipan (IRE), Tira Heights (USA), **14/1** Dreamer (USA), **33/1** Korambi, CSF £10.85 TOTE £2.00: £1.30 £2.10 £2.50 (£8.70) Trio £39.70 OWNER Mr George Strawbridge (NEWMARKET) BRED George Strawbridge 10 Rn
2m 3.15 (0.65) SF: 66/56/51/58/57/45/51/46/45/39

620

BONUSPRINT MASAKA STKS (Listed) (3-Y.O F) (Class A) £13,118.75 (£3,950.00: £1,912.50: £893.75) **1m (round)** Stalls: High GOING minus 0.41 sec(F) 3-15 (3-18)

Subya (104)*(104) (JLDunlop)* 3-8-11 JReid(3) (hdwy over 3f out: 4th st: led 2f out: clr over 1f out: rdn out)........— **1**

Poppy Carew (IRE) **(107)***(100) (PWHarris)* 3-8-8 RCochrane(6) (hdwy over 1f out: r.o wl ins fnl f) ... ¾ **2**
547* Cask *(98) (JHMGosden)* 3-8-8 LDettori(1) (hdwy over 2f out: hrd rdn over 1f out: r.o wl ins fnl f) ... 1 **3**
Fleet Hill (IRE) **(102)***(98) (MRChannon)* 3-8-11 RHughes(8) (hld up: nt clr run over 2f out: rallied over 1f out: nt clr run ins fnl f: r.o) ... 1¼ **4**
Shefoog *(89) (RWArmstrong)* 3-8-8 RPrice(5) (lw: hdwy over 2f out: hrd rdn over 1f out: unable qckn) ... 3 **5**
Mandarina (USA) *(88) (LMCumani)* 3-8-8 JWeaver(11) (lw: 6th st: nt clr run & lost pl on ins over 2f out: nt rcvr) ... nk **6**
Bring on the Choir *(88) (RBoss)* 3-8-8 TQuinn(9) (lw: 5th st: rdn over 2f out: wknd over 1f out) ... hd **7**
Hiwaya **(106)***(86) (HThomsonJones)* 3-8-11 RHills(4) (nt grwn: lw: 3rd st: ev ch 2f out: wknd fnl f) ... 2½ **8**
Menas Gold **(100)***(82) (SDow)* 3-8-8 StephenDavies(13) (nvr nr to chal) ... ½ **9**
Spout *(79)*(Fav)*(RCharlton)* 3-8-8 PatEddery(10) (chsd ldr: led over 3f out to 2f out: sn wknd) ... 1¾ **10**
Karayib (USA) **(86)***(76) (JLDunlop)* 3-8-8 WCarson(7) (led over 4f: 2nd st: ev ch 2f out: eased whn btn over 1f out) ... 1½ **11**
Regal Fanfare (IRE) **(103)***(73) (JWHills)* 3-8-8 AClark(12) (a bhd) ... 1¼ **12**
Musetta (IRE) **(106)***(53) (CEBrittain)* 3-8-8 MRimmer(2) (prom 5f) ... 10 **13**

100/30 Spout, **5/1** SUBYA, **11/2** Hiwaya, **8/1** Mandarina (USA), **9/1** Cask, Poppy Carew (IRE), **12/1** Bring on the Choir, Shefoog, Musetta (IRE), **14/1** Fleet Hill (IRE), **16/1** Menas Gold, **20/1** Karayib (USA), Regal Fanfare (IRE), CSF £49.77 TOTE £8.00: £2.50 £3.10 £3.10 (£70.10) Trio £301.20
OWNER Prince A. A. Faisal (ARUNDEL) BRED Nawara Stud Co Ltd 13 Rn
1m 37.59 (0.39) SF: 56/52/50/50/41/40/40/38/34/31/28/25/5

621 QUEEN ELIZABETH H'CAP (0-90) (3-Y.O) (Class C) £5,732.00 (£1,736.00: £848.00: £404.00)
6f Stalls: High GOING minus 0.41 sec per fur (F) 3-45 (3-49)

437⁹ **Katya (IRE) (85)***(89) (MRChannon)* 3-9-2 RHughes(2) (lw: plld hrd: hdwy 3f out: led ins fnl f: r.o wl) ... — **1**
524* Denbrae (IRE) **(72)***(75) (DJGMurraySmith)* 3-8-3 ow1 RHills(14) (a.p: led over 1f out tl ins fnl f: r.o wl) ... s.h **2**
543⁵ Easy Dollar **(78)***(81) (BGubby)* 3-8-9v RCochrane(15) (rdn over 3f out: hdwy over 1f out: r.o ins fnl f) ... ½ **3**
Star Tulip **(90)***(91) (JLDunlop)* 3-9-7 GDuffield(12) (hdwy over 2f out: ev ch over 1f out: unable qckn ins fnl f) ... ½ **4**
Astral Invader (IRE) **(72)***(70) (MSSaunders)* 3-8-3 RPrice(8) (a.p: led over 2f out: sn hdd: one pce) ... 1¼ **5**
442* Fata (IRE) **(77)***(75) (PTWalwyn)* 3-8-8 WCarson(5) (swtg: a.p: led 2f out to over 1f out: one pce ins fnl f) ... hd **6**
Quintus Decimus **(78)***(75) (LordHuntingdon)* 3-8-9 LDettori(4) (hld up: rdn over 2f out: nt clr run over 1f out: r.o one pce) ... hd **7**
*196** Go Hever Golf **(85)***(77)*(Fav)*(TJNaughton)* 3-9-2 GCarter(7) (b.hind: a mid div) ... 2 **8**
345⁷ Bold Effort (FR) **(77)***(69) (KOCunningham-Brown)* 3-8-8 BDoyle(10) (dwlt: nvr nrr) ... s.h **9**
Gallows Corner (IRE) **(85)***(76) (RHannon)* 3-9-2 PatEddery(1) (nvr nrr) ... nk **10**
Squire Corrie **(70)***(60) (LJHolt)* 3-8-1 ow1 AMcGlone(9) (hdwy 1f out: wknd ins fnl f) ... s.h **11**
499⁴ Maiandros (GR) **(85)***(74) (RCharlton)* 3-9-2 JWeaver(3) (lw: prom over 3f) ... ¾ **12**
498⁵ Sally Slade **(76)***(63) (CACyzer)* 3-8-7 JReid(13) (hdwy over 1f out: sn wknd) ... ¾ **13**
Classic Pet (IRE) **(64)***(41) (CAHorgan)* 3-7-4 (5)ow2 NVarley(11) (led over 3f) ... 3 **14**
498ᵂ Stoppes Brow **(75)***(54) (GLMoore)* 3-8-6v BRouse(6) (spd over 4f) ... hd **15**

LONG HANDICAP Classic Pet (IRE) 7-0

100/30 Go Hever Golf (9/4-7/2), **5/1** Fata (IRE), **7/1** Denbrae (IRE), Stoppes Brow, **8/1** Sally Slade, **12/1** Quintus Decimus, Maiandros (GR), **14/1** Gallows Corner (IRE), KATYA (IRE), Star Tulip, **20/1** Bold Effort (FR), Easy Dollar, Astral Invader (IRE), **25/1** Squire Corrie, **33/1** Classic Pet (IRE), CSF £107.66 CT £1,821.54 TOTE £14.90: £2.30 £3.50 £7.70 (£81.50) Trio £1,154.50; £195.13 to 3.10 Kempton 17/4/95 OWNER Mr John Mitchell (UPPER LAMBOURN) BRED Lodge Park Stud in Ireland
15 Rn 1m 13.09 (1.79) SF: 41/27/33/43/22/27/27/29/21/28/12/26/15/-/6

622 BONUSPRINT EASTER STKS (Listed) (3-Y.O C & G) (Class A) £12,875.00 (£3,875.00: £1,875.00: £875.00)
1m (round) Stalls: High GOING minus 0.41 sec per fur (F) 4-15 (4-16)

Two O'Clock Jump (IRE) (90)*(103) (RHannon)* 3-8-8 PatEddery(3) (rdn & hdwy 2f out: led ins fnl f: r.o wl) ... — **1**

435* Blomberg (IRE) **(94)***(100) (JRFanshawe)* 3-8-8 DHarrison(4) (4th st: rdn over 2f out: led over 1f out tl ins fnl f: unable qckn)....1½ 2
Stiletto Blade *(96)*(Fav)*(IABalding)* 3-8-8 LDettori(1) (6th st: nt clr run 2f out: hrd rdn over 1f out: one pce)....2 3
Dahik **(100)***(93) (MajorWRHern)* 3-8-8 WCarson(9) (swtg: 2nd st: led over 2f out tl over 1f out: wknd fnl f)....1½ 4
Missel **(110)***(92) (PWChapple-Hyam)* 3-8-8 JReid(10) (led over 5f)....½ 5
431[5] Henry Koehler *(90) (CEBrittain)* 3-8-8 MRimmer(2) (lw: 5th st: rdn over 2f out: wknd fnl f)....1 6
Sotoboy (IRE) **(106)***(88) (PWHarris)* 3-8-8 RCochrane(5) (hdwy over 1f out: wknd fnl f)....1¼ 7
Magna Carta *(81) (MRStoute)* 3-8-8 JWeaver(7) (hdwy over 2f out: wknd fnl f)....3½ 8
Bahith (USA) *(75) (HThomsonJones)* 3-8-8 RHills(6) (2nd st: wkng whn n.m.r 2f out)....3 9
Albinor (IRE) *(74) (JLDunlop)* 3-8-8 GDuffield(8) (bhd fnl 3f)....s.h 10

4/1 Stiletto Blade (op 5/2), **9/2** Sotoboy (IRE), Blomberg (IRE), Missel, **7/1** Magna Carta, **15/2** Dahik, **10/1** Bahith (USA), **16/1** TWO O'CLOCK JUMP (IRE), **20/1** Albinor (IRE), **25/1** Henry Koehler, CSF £83.28 TOTE £20.10: £4.00 £1.50 £2.60 (£41.00) Trio £115.20 OWNER Mr Bob Lalemant (MARLBOROUGH) BRED D Hollyday 10 Rn 1m 37.69 (0.49) SF: 52/49/45/42/41/39/37/30/24/23

623

CHATSWORTH H'CAP (0-95) (4-Y.O+) (Class C) £5,810.00 (£1,760.00: £860.00: £410.00) **1m 4f** Stalls: High GOING minus 0.41 sec per fur (F) 4-45 (4-53)

Wishing (USA) (85)*(97)*(Fav)*(RAkehurst)* 4-9-2 GCarter(9) (lw: rdn over 3f out: 2nd st: led over 1f out: r.o wl)....— 1
423[2] Shadow Leader **(73)***(85) (MissAJWhitfield)* 4-8-4 DHarrison(10) (4th st: rdn over 2f out: ev ch fnl f: r.o)....nk 2
Glide Path (USA) **(95)***(106) (JWHills)* 6-10-0 RHills(5) (lw: hdwy over 2f out: nt clr run over 1f out: unable qckn)....¾ 3
325[2] Chatham Island **(67)***(74) (CEBrittain)* 7-8-0 ow2 BDoyle(4) (lw: led over 10f out tl over 1f out: one pce)....1½ 4
558* Wayne County (IRE) **(84)***(92) (GFierro)* 5-9-3 LDettori(16) (5th st: ev ch over 1f out: 5th whn nt clr run ins fnl f: one pce)....nk 5
Backgammon **(85)***(91) (JABOld)* 4-9-2 JReid(17) (lw: 6th st: rdn over 1f out: one pce)....1½ 6
Endless Light (USA) **(88)***(94) (PFICole)* 4-9-5 TQuinn(15) (hdwy on ins over 2f out: wknd fnl f)....nk 7
Pembridge Place **(77)***(81) (JLDunlop)* 4-8-8 WCarson(1) (b: swtg: nvr plcd to chal)....1½ 8
423[12] General Mouktar **(77)***(78) (MCPipe)* 5-8-10 AMcGlone(14) (a mid div)....2 9
430[18] Allesca **(61)***(60) (MDIUsher)* 5-7-1 (7)ow1 CAdamson(12) (b: uns rdr & bolted bef s: nvr nrr)....1¼ 10
Flight Lieutenant (USA) **(84)***(82) (RHannon)* 6-9-3 RHughes(11) (lw: nvr nrr)....1 11
Beauman **(74)***(72) (PDEvans)* 5-8-4 (3) SSanders(6) (3rd st: wknd over 2f out)....½ 12
423[11] Bit on the Side (IRE) **(75)***(71) (WJMusson)* 6-8-3 (5) PMcCabe(2) (s.s: a bhd)....1 13
430[14] Bookcase **(63)***(54) (DRCElsworth)* 8-7-7 (3)ow3 DWright(3) (bhd fnl 3f)....1½ 14
Statajack (IRE) **(85)***(76) (DRCElsworth)* 7-9-4b PatEddery(8) (swtg: a bhd)....2½ 15
Without a Flag (USA) **(62)***(51) (JWhite)* 5-7-4 (5)ow2 NVarley(7) (lw: bhd fnl 2f)....s.h 16
Dallachio (IRE) **(72)***(61) (PJHobbs)* 4-8-3 GDuffield(13) (led over 1f: wknd over 3f out)....1¼ 17

LONG HANDICAP Allesca 7-5 Without a Flag (USA) 7-5 Bookcase 7-2
3/1 WISHING (USA), **5/1** Wayne County (IRE), **11/2** Backgammon (4/1-6/1), **8/1** Chatham Island, Statajack (IRE), **10/1** Shadow Leader, **14/1** Pembridge Place, **16/1** Bit on the Side (IRE), General Mouktar, Endless Light (USA), **20/1** Flight Lieutenant (USA), Beauman, Glide Path (USA), Bookcase, **25/1** Allesca, **33/1** Without a Flag (USA), Dallachio (IRE), CSF £36.02 CT £512.32 TOTE £4.30: £2.00 £2.40 £7.50 £1.60 (£24.20) Trio £386.00 OWNER Mr A. D. Spence (EPSOM) BRED C. L. Kidder & N. L. Kidder 17 Rn
2m 32.09 (1.89) SF: 55/43/66/34/52/49/52/39/38/20/42/32/31/14/36/11/19
WEIGHT FOR AGE 4yo-2lb

T/Jkpt: Not won; £26,677.89 to Kempton 17/4/95. T/Plpt: £873.20 (35.95 Tckts). T/Qdpt: £180.70 (1 Tckt). AK

0599-WOLVERHAMPTON (L-H)
Saturday April 15th (Standard)

WEATHER: fine WIND: mod against

624

CODSALL MAIDEN H'CAP (0-70) (3-Y.O+) (Class E) £2,845.80 (£788.80: £377.40) **1m 1f 79y (Fibresand)** Stalls: Low GOING: 0.02 sec (STD) 7-00 (7-01)

520[4] **Asmarina (36)***(43) (SRBowring)* 5-8-1 (7) CTeague(13) (hld up & bhd: hdwy & 5th st: led ins fnl f: r.o wl)....— 1

601[7] Flashfeet **(54)***(56) (KBishop)* 5-9-12 JWilliams(1) (hld up: hdwy over 4f out: ev ch whn edgd rt over 1f out: r.o one pce)....3 2
500[4] Marchant Ming (IRE) **(53)***(54) (MAJarvis)* 3-8-7 WWoods(5) (lw: chsd ldrs: rdn over 3f out: 3rd st: hung lft over 1f out: r.o ins fnl f)....½ 3
Olivia Val **(24)***(21) (AGNewcombe)* 5-7-5 (5)ow3 CHawksley(9) (hld up & bhd: hdwy over 4f out: led wl over 3f out tl ins fnl f)....½ 4
526[12] Delgarth Lady **(35)***(34) (JLSpearing)* 4-8-7 DeanMcKeown(12) (prom: hmpd over 3f out: 4th st: ev ch over 1f out: one pce)....½ 5
546[5] Old Swinford (IRE) **(66)***(40)*(Fav)*(BJMeehan)* 3-9-6 SWhitworth(7) (lw: bhd fnl 3f)....15 6
547[10] Fairelaine **(60)***(34) (APJarvis)* 3-9-0 KDarley(6) (prom tl wknd 3f out)....hd 7
Studio Thirty **(54)***(27) (RHollinshead)* 3-8-8 TIves(4) (sn wl bhd)....½ 8
543[6] Ballestro (IRE) **(41)***(11) (JFfitch-Heyes)* 3-7-9 ow1 JQuinn(10) (prom: 6th & wkng st)....¾ 9
Montagne **(33)***(4) (MWEckley)* 6-8-5 TWilliams(8) (w ldr: led 6f out tl wl over 3f out: wknd qckly)....nk 10
Our Bessie **(44)***(11) (DMarks)* 4-8-11 (5) MBaird(3) (sn wl bhd)....2½ 11
503[10] Millridge (IRE) **(39)** *(RLee)* 4-8-11 JFortune(11) (b: led 3f: bhd fnl 3f: t.o)....dist 12

3/1 Old Swinford (IRE), **7/2** Fairelaine, **4/1** ASMARINA, **7/1** Marchant Ming (IRE), Our Bessie, **12/1** Olivia Val (op 33/1), **20/1** Ballestro (IRE), **25/1** Delgarth Lady, Flashfeet, Montagne, Studio Thirty, **33/1** Millridge (IRE), CSF £85.62 CT £629.94 TOTE £5.10: £2.00 £5.00 £1.90 (£46.90) Trio £26.40 OWNER Mr S. R. Bowring (EDWINSTOWE) BRED S. R. Bowring 12 Rn
2m 4.5 (8.50) SF: 22/35/15/-/13/1/-/-/-/-/-/-
WEIGHT FOR AGE 3yo-18lb

625 OAKEN CLAIMING STKS (4-Y.O+) (Class F) £2,243.00 (£618.00: £293.00)
6f (Fibresand) Stalls: Low GOING: 0.02 sec per fur (STD) 7-30 (7-31)

247[5] **Efficacy (33)***(47) (APJarvis)* 4-7-7 (7)ow1 BHunter(8) (plld hrd: a.p: led 3f out: pushed out)....— 1
548[4] Sea Devil **(66)***(53)*(Fav)*(MJCamacho)* 9-8-8 LCharnock(6) (chsd ldrs: 2nd st: rdn & ev ch over 1f out: r.o)....1 2
Best Kept Secret **(74)***(59) (JBerry)* 4-9-0 JCarroll(4) (bhd: rdn & outpcd 4f out: hdwy fnl f: r.o)....s.h 3
511[5] Brookhead Lady **(52)***(44) (PDEvans)* 4-8-1 JQuinn(2) (b: led early: 3rd st: r.o one pce fnl f)....¾ 4
602[3] Farndale **(50)***(25) (RonaldThompson)* 8-8-8 JWeaver(1) (sn led: hdd 4f out: 4th & wkng st)....10 5
Top Show (IRE) *(KWHogg)* 4-9-0 KDarley(7) (prom: led 4f out to 3f out: sn wknd & eased: 6th & t.o st)....dist 6

5/4 Sea Devil (op Evens), **9/4** Best Kept Secret, **5/1** Farndale, **14/1** Brookhead Lady, **16/1** EFFICACY, **20/1** Top Show (IRE), CSF £34.26 TOTE £26.70: £5.50 £1.40 (£24.30) OWNER Mrs Ann Jarvis (ASTON UPTHORPE) BRED Hever Castle Stud Farm Ltd 6 Rn 1m 16.3 (5.10) SF: 15/21/27/12/-/-

626 BOWMER AND KIRKLAND (LONDON) H'CAP (0-70) (3-Y.O) (Class E)
£2,794.00 (£832.00: £396.00: £178.00)
1m 4f (Fibresand) Stalls: Low GOING: 0.02 sec per fur (STD) 8-00 (8-01)

502[17] **Vintage Taittinger (IRE) (40)***(48) (MBell)* 3-7-9 JFanning(8) (a.p: led over 2f out: rdn over 1f out: r.o wl)....— 1
*509** Last Corner **(65)***(68) (RHollinshead)* 3-9-6 KDarley(1) (hld up: rdn 4f out: 3rd st: r.o one pce fnl f)....3½ 2
301[8] Mr Mactavish **(65)***(62)*(Fav)*(MrsJCecil)* 3-9-6 TIves(5) (lw: prom: rdn 3f out: 4th st: one pce)....5 3
537[5] Elpidos **(66)***(62) (CEBrittain)* 3-9-7 MRimmer(9) (b.hind: lw: led over 9f: 2nd st: wknd fnl f)....¾ 4
560[3] Spitfire Bridge (IRE) **(58)***(38) (MMcCormack)* 3-8-13 GDuffield(3) (chsd ldr: hrd rdn 4f out: 5th & wkng st)....12 5
537[3] Beau Matelot **(60)***(34) (JDBethell)* 3-9-1 JWeaver(4) (plld hrd: rdn 4f out: poor 6th st)....4 6
513[2] Hunza Story **(42)***(4) (NPLittmoden)* 3-7-11 NCarlisle(6) (bhd fnl 4f: t.o)....9 7
444[5] Fair Ella (IRE) **(40)***(2) (JFfitch-Heyes)* 3-7-9b JQuinn(7) (reard st: a bhd: t.o)....hd 8
544[4] Shanuke (IRE) **(55)***(7) (JSMoore)* 3-8-10 ow1 RHughes(2) (lw: rdn over 4f out: sn bhd: t.o)....7 9

5/2 Mr Mactavish, **3/1** Last Corner, **9/2** Beau Matelot, **10/1** Shanuke (IRE), **14/1** Spitfire Bridge (IRE) (op 8/1), Elpidos (op 8/1), Hunza Story, **16/1** VINTAGE TAITTINGER (IRE), **25/1** Fair Ella (IRE), CSF £57.03 CT £140.59 TOTE £14.80: £2.30 £1.40 £1.70 (£79.80) Trio £119.00 OWNER Mr P. T. Fenwick (NEWMARKET) BRED Carrigbeg Stud Co Ltd 9 Rn
2m 42.5 (11.50) SF: 7/27/21/21/-/-/-/-/-
OFFICIAL EXPLANATION **Shanuke (IRE): was eased when she gurgled badly.**

627 HEATH TOWN H'CAP (0-70) (3-Y.O+) (Class E) £3,028.00 (£904.00: £432.00: £196.00) **7f (Fibresand)** Stalls: Low GOING: 0.02 sec per fur (STD) 8-30 (8-31)

479* **Reverand Thickness (67)***(71)*(Fav)*(SCWilliams)* 4-10-0 JCarroll(3) (lw: a.p: rdn 4f out: led over 2f out: clr over 1f out: r.o) — 1
472U Indian Serenade **(52)***(54) (PWHarris)* 4-8-8 (5) JStack(6) (a.p: 3rd st: r.o fnl f) ¾ 2
3375 Allinson's Mate (IRE) **(64)***(66) (TDBarron)* 7-9-11 JFortune(12) (hdwy & 6th st: r.o ins fnl f) nk 3
5112 Heathyards Lady (USA) **(50)***(48) (RHollinshead)* 4-8-11 TIves(2) (hdwy & 5th st: r.o one pce fnl f) 1½ 4
Court Nap (IRE) **(65)***(55) (SMellor)* 3-8-11 MWigham(9) (lw: dwlt: hdwy over 1f out: nvr nrr) 3½ 5
548[16] Arawa **(44)***(34) (DMarks)* 5-8-2e(3) SSanders(11) (nvr nr to chal) nk 6
4475 Sherblu **(45)***(28) (JFfitch-Heyes)* 4-8-6b DBiggs(7) (led 3f: 4th & wkng st) 3 7
5424 Another Jade **(64)***(47) (APJarvis)* 5-9-11 KDarley(5) (lw: w ldr: led 4f out tl over 2f out: 2nd st: wknd ins fnl f) s.h 8
5483 Nakita **(60)***(40) (CNAllen)* 4-9-2 (5) MBaird(4) (b.hind: hld up: hdwy over 3f out: wknd over 2f out) 1¼ 9
512U Quinzii Martin **(58)***(35) (DHaydnJones)* 7-9-5v TWilliams(1) (7th st: n.d) 1¼ 10
Shaynes Domain **(48)***(11) (RMFlower)* 4-8-4 (5) JDSmith(10) (a bhd) 6 11
*528** Dominion's Dream **(71)***(33) (BSmart)* 3-8-10 (7) ADaly(8) (chsd ldrs: hrd rdn over 3f out: sn bhd) ½ 12

7/2 REVERAND THICKNESS, **4/1** Another Jade (3/1-9/2), **6/1** Allinson's Mate (IRE), **8/1** Heathyards Lady (USA) (6/1-9/1), **9/1** Indian Serenade, **11/1** Nakita (8/1-12/1), Dominion's Dream (8/1-12/1), **14/1** Quinzii Martin, **16/1** Sherblu, Shaynes Domain, **25/1** Arawa, Court Nap (IRE), CSF £32.66 CT £165.92 TOTE £4.90: £2.00 £2.90 £2.40 (£25.60) Trio £127.90; £90.08 to 3.10 Kempton 17/4/95 OWNER The Waresley Partnership (NEWMARKET) BRED S. J. Mear 12 Rn

1m 31.9 (7.90) SF: 21/4/16/-/-/-/-/-/-/-/-/-

WEIGHT FOR AGE 3yo-15lb

628 TETTENHALL (S) STKS (3-Y.O) (Class G) £2,243.00 (£618.00: £293.00) **1m 100y (Fibresand)** Stalls: Low GOING: 0.02 sec per fur (STD) 9-00 (9-01)

2702 **Little Scarlett (48)***(59+) (PJMakin)* 3-8-7 RPerham(4) (lw: hld up: rdn & hdwy 3f out: led ins fnl f: r.o wl) — 1
Little Wilma *(54) (APJarvis)* 3-8-7 KDarley(5) (lt-f: unf: hld up: hdwy 5f out: led on bit over 2f out: hdd ins fnl f) 2½ 2
3577 Torrey Pines (IRE) **(44)***(59) (DHaydnJones)* 3-8-12 AMackay(11) (rdn 5f out: hdwy & 4th st: r.o ins fnl f) s.h 3
5096 Rainy Day Woman *(54) (DrJDScargill)* 3-8-7 JFanning(12) (prom: led over 4f out: hdd over 2f out: 2nd st: one pce) nk 4
4435 Claireswan (IRE) *(53) (SCWilliams)* 3-8-9 (3) DWright(10) (lw: prom: 5th & lost pl st: styd on ins fnl f) 3 5
5877 Bretton Princess **(42)***(44) (RHollinshead)* 3-8-7 JFortune(6) (prom: hmpd & lost pl over 3f out: 6th st: no hdwy) 2 6
5217 Centaur Express **(30)***(40) (ALForbes)* 3-8-7 (5) CHawksley(7) (s.i.s: sme hdwy & 7th st: n.d) 5 7
*560** Jackatack (IRE) **(64)***(29)*(Fav)*(MRChannon)* 3-9-4 RHughes(9) (lw: prom: rdn over 4f out: wknd 3f out) 9 8
5486 Dowdency **(45)***(23) (JAPickering)* 3-8-13 NCarlisle(3) (a bhd) ½ 9
4489 Kirov Protege (IRE) **(51)***(20) (HJCollingridge)* 3-9-4v MRimmer(8) (lw: led 4f: wknd qckly: t.o) 4 10
Lady Davenport (IRE) **(75)***(6) (RonaldThompson)* 3-8-13 JWeaver(1) (dwlt: a bhd: t.o fnl 3f) 5 11

2/1 Jackatack (IRE), **4/1** Claireswan (IRE) (9/2-3/1), **6/1** Lady Davenport (IRE), **7/1** LITTLE SCARLETT, **8/1** Kirov Protege (IRE), **10/1** Dowdency, **20/1** Little Wilma, Bretton Princess, **25/1** Centaur Express, **33/1** Rainy Day Woman, Torrey Pines (IRE), CSF £115.84 TOTE £5.70: £1.40 £3.70 £7.00 (£63.30) OWNER Mrs P. J. Makin (MARLBOROUGH) BRED Mrs J. McColl 11 Rn

1m 53.3 (9.30) SF: 6/1/6/1/-/-/-/-/-/-/-

No bid

OFFICIAL EXPLANATION **Jackatack (IRE): was unable to race prominently, which he needs to do, and resented the kick-back.**

629 BLAKENHALL H'CAP (0-65) (3-Y.O) (Class F) £2,243.00 (£618.00: £293.00) **5f (Fibresand)** Stalls: Low GOING: 0.02 sec per fur (STD) 9-30 (9-37)

4732 **Bold Frontier (62)***(76) (KTIvory)* 3-9-6b GDuffield(1) (s.i.s: gd hdwy over 2f out: 3rd st: led over 1f out: drvn out) — 1

580[4] Half Tone **(52)***(53) (RMFlower)* 3-8-5b(5) JDSmith(10) (hdwy over 1f out: wandered ins fnl f: r.o: nt trble wnr) 4 2
475[10] Daily Starshine (IRE) **(60)***(58) (JBerry)* 3-9-4b JCarroll(5) (a.p: led 2f out tl over 1f out: one pce) 1 3
499[10] Cork Street Girl (IRE) **(62)***(52) (BJMeehan)* 3-9-6 BDoyle(2) (chsd ldrs: 5th st: one pce) 2½ 4
524[18] Poly Laureon (IRE) **(62)***(52) (RHollinshead)* 3-9-6 KDarley(3) (nvr nr to chal) ....s.h 5
482[6] Rupert's Princess (IRE) **(53)***(37) (MJHeaton-Ellis)* 3-8-11 StephenDavies(7) (lw: led over 1f: 4th st: wknd over 1f out) 1¾ 6
602[4] Ivy Lilian (IRE) **(45)***(29) (WMBrisbourne)* 3-7-12 (5) AGarth(9) (chsd ldrs: 6th st: n.d) ....s.h 7
159[2] Wasblest **(55)***(35)*(Fav)*(MJohnston)* 3-8-13 JWeaver(4) (w ldrs: led over 3f out to 2f out: 2nd st: wknd qckly) 1¼ 8
502[7] Superbit **(49)***(10) (BAMcMahon)* 3-8-4 (3) SSanders(6) (w ldrs tl wknd qckly 2f out) 6 9
Top Pearl **(63)***(24) (NAGraham)* 3-9-2 (5) JStack(8) (bhd fnl 3f) ....hd 10

9/4 Wasblest (4/1-2/1), **6/1** BOLD FRONTIER, Top Pearl, **13/2** Half Tone, **8/1** Daily Starshine (IRE) (op 5/1), **9/1** Cork Street Girl (IRE), **10/1** Rupert's Princess (IRE) (op 6/1), **12/1** Poly Laureon (IRE), **14/1** Ivy Lilian (IRE), **20/1** Superbit, CSF £42.67 CT £290.06 TOTE £7.50: £2.10 £3.40 £2.80 (£16.30) Trio £59.00 OWNER Mr K. T. Ivory (RADLETT) BRED J. Weinfeld 10 Rn
63.2 secs (5.20) SF: 18/-/-/-/-/-/-/-/-/-

OFFICIAL EXPLANATION **Wasblest: her jockey eased her when she started gulping for air.**

T/Plpt: £330.90 (36.96 Tckts). T/Qdpt: £98.90 (1.2 Tckts). KH

0617-KEMPTON (R-H)
Monday April 17th (Good to firm)
WEATHER: drizzle WIND: mod across

630 STARK MAIDEN STKS (I) (3-Y.O+) (Class D) £3,772.50 (£1,140.00: £555.00: £262.50) **7f (Jubilee)** Stalls: High GOING minus 0.32 sec per fur (GF) 2-10 (2-13)

431[6] **Fawj (USA)** *(82)*(Fav)*(RWArmstrong)* 3-8-10 WCarson(8) (3rd st: led 2f out: drvn out) ....— 1
Summertown (USA) *(76)*(Fav)*(JHMGosden)* 3-8-5 GHind(7) (lw: s.s: hdwy 6f out: 4th st: rdn over 2f out: r.o wl ins fnl f) ....nk 2
Godmersham Park *(81) (MJHeaton-Ellis)* 3-8-10 DHarrison(5) (6th st: rdn over 2f out: r.o wl ins fnl f) ....s.h 3
Francfurter *(75) (RCharlton)* 3-8-5 TSprake(12) (bit bkwd: w ldr: led over 3f out to 2f out: unable qckn fnl f) ....½ 4
Rasmi (CAN) *(73) (ACStewart)* 4-9-10 RHills(9) (bkwd: led over 3f: 2nd st: ev ch 2f out: wknd fnl f) 3 5
553[8] Equity's Darling (IRE) *(67) (MBell)* 3-8-5 MFenton(11) (5th st: shkn up over 2f out: one pce) .½ 6
435[5] Yubralee (USA) *(69) (MRStoute)* 3-8-10 WRSwinburn(4) (lw: nvr nr to chal) 1½ 7
Edan Heights *(64) (SDow)* 3-8-10 GDuffield(2) (str: bhd fnl 3f) 2 8
Ironic (IRE) *(64) (RHannon)* 3-8-10 BThomson(1) (w'like: bit bkwd: a bhd) ....s.h 9
Bid for a Rainbow **(47)***(50) (MrsMELong)* 4-9-3 (7) TField(10) (bit bkwd: a bhd) 6 10
Partenaire *(46) (KMcAuliffe)* 3-8-10 RCochrane(6) (b: neat: prom over 3f) 1¾ 11
101[5] Ela Palikari Mou (IRE) *(30) (RAkehurst)* 4-9-7 (3) SSanders(3) (prom over 3f) 7 12

11/4 FAWJ (USA) (4/1-5/2), Summertown (USA) (5/4-3/1), **11/2** Yubralee (USA), **8/1** Ironic (IRE) (6/1-10/1), Rasmi (CAN), Francfurter (op 5/1), **20/1** Partenaire, **33/1** Equity's Darling (IRE), Edan Heights, **50/1** Ela Palikari Mou (IRE), **100/1** Bid for a Rainbow, Godmersham Park, CSF £9.93: TOTE £4.50: £1.60 £1.50 £5.50 (£5.60) Trio £217.70 OWNER Mr Hamdan Al Maktoum (NEWMARKET) BRED Joan C. Johnson 12 Rn 1m 26.54 (2.34) SF: 40/34/39/33/45/25/27/22/22/22/4/2
WEIGHT FOR AGE 3yo-14lb

631 MAGNOLIA STKS (Listed) (4-Y.O+) (Class A) £12,712.50 (£3,825.00: £1,850.00: £862.50) **1m 2f (Jubilee)** Stalls: High GOING minus 0.32 sec (GF) 2-40 (2-42)

Captain Horatius (IRE) (110)*(123) (JLDunlop)* 6-9-5 WRSwinburn(7) (hdwy on ins over 3f out: 5th st: led 2f out: r.o wl) ....— 1
Golden Ball (IRE) **(105)***(113) (MRStoute)* 4-8-11 WCarson(2) (lw: hdwy over 2f out: rdn over 1f out: unable qckn) 1¼ 2
Young Buster (IRE) **(113)***(113)*(Fav)*(GWragg)* 7-9-0 MHills(4) (lw: hdwy over 4f out: 2nd st: led over 2f out: sn hdd: one pce) 1¾ 3
Alriffa **(116)***(110) (RHannon)* 4-9-0b PatEddery(6) (lw: nt clr run & lost pl over 3f out: rallied 2f out: one pce) 2 4
440[8] Cedez le Passage (FR) **(100)***(97) (CEBrittain)* 4-8-11 BDoyle(9) (lw: nvr nr to chal) 6 5
Florid (USA) **(107)***(96) (HRACecil)* 4-8-11 WRyan(8) (lw: w ldr: led 7f out tl over 2f out: sn wknd) 1 6

Girl From Ipanema **(104)***(90) (PFICole)* 4-8-9 TQuinn(10) (lw: 3rd st: wknd over 2f out) 2½ 7
Old Hickory (IRE) **(100)***(94) (LMCumani)* 4-9-0 RCochrane(3) (6th st: wknd 3f out) ....½ 8
Mediterraneo **(95)***(59) (RAkehurst)* 4-8-11 AClark(1) (lw: bhd fnl 4f) 20 9
Persian Brave (IRE) **(108)***(58) (MBell)* 5-9-2 MFenton(5) (lw: led 3f: 4th st: wknd 3f out) 3½ 10

100/30 Young Buster (IRE), **7/2** Florid (USA), Alriffa, **13/2** CAPTAIN HORATIUS (IRE), **8/1** Golden Ball (IRE), **9/1** Persian Brave (IRE) (op 6/1), **12/1** Girl From Ipanema, **14/1** Old Hickory (IRE), **33/1** Cedez le Passage (FR), **50/1** Mediterraneo, CSF £53.74 TOTE £10.10: £2.40 £2.60 £1.60 (£54.50) Trio £76.10 OWNER Mr D. R. Hunnisett (ARUNDEL) BRED B. W. Hills and Mrs V. Shaw 10 Rn
2m 2.46 (-0.04) SF: 78/68/68/65/52/51/45/49/14/13
OFFICIAL EXPLANATION **Persian Brave (IRE): the trainer reported that the horse was unable to stride out on the firm ground.**

632 QUEEN'S PRIZE H'CAP (0-90) (4-Y.O+) (Class C) £11,088.75 (£3,360.00: £1,642.50: £783.75)
2m Stalls: High GOING minus 0.32 sec per fur (GF) 3-10 (3-11)

Always Aloof (USA) (86)*(99) (MRStoute)* 4-9-12 WRSwinburn(11) (hdwy over 3f out: 6th st: led over 1f out: rdn out) ....— 1
556* Moonlight Quest **(70)***(81)*(Fav)*(BHanbury)* 7-9-0 TIves(19) (rdn 7f out: hdwy over 2f out: r.o one pce) 2 2
Blaze Away (USA) **(77)***(88) (IABalding)* 4-9-3 MFenton(2) (lw: 3rd st: hrd rdn over 2f out: ev ch over 1f out: one pce) ....nk 3
Doyce **(68)***(76) (RJRWilliams)* 6-8-12 GDuffield(10) (hld up: led over 3f out tl over 1f out: 5th & btn whn hmpd ins fnl f: fin 5th, 3l: plcd 4th) 4
506* Lalindi (IRE) **(70)***(77) (DRCElsworth)* 4-8-10 JWilliams(12) (lw: no hdwy fnl 3f: fin 6th, nk: plcd 5th) 5
*346*4 Wild Strawberry **(65)***(71) (MissBSanders)* 6-8-6 (3) SSanders(5) (hmpd & lost pl on ins over 4f out: rallied over 2f out: one pce) 1¾ 7
Stoney Valley **(74)***(79) (JRJenkins)* 5-9-4 PatEddery(8) (hdwy over 2f out: 8th whn nt clr run 1f out) ....¾ 8
Harlestone Brook **(84)***(86) (JLDunlop)* 5-10-0 WCarson(14) (hdwy over 4f out: 4th st: wknd over 1f out) 3 9
Chief's Song **(69)***(64) (SDow)* 5-8-13 DHarrison(7) (a mid div) 7 10
Well Arranged (IRE) **(80)***(72) (RAkehurst)* 4-9-6 TQuinn(18) (lw: a.p: led over 4f out tl over 3f out: 2nd st: wknd over 2f out) 2½ 11
Paradise Navy **(75)***(65) (CREgerton)* 6-9-5b BThomson(3) (chsd ldr over 10f: led 6f out tl over 4f out: 5th st: wknd 3f out) 2½ 12
*396*12 Chimborazo **(74)***(63) (BJMcMath)* 4-9-0 RCochrane(15) (swtg: a mid div) 1¼ 13
*370*9 Sheltered Cove (IRE) **(56)***(42) (KOCunningham-Brown)* 4-7-7 (3) DarrenMoffatt(1) (b: lw: prom over 10f) 3 14
5064 Phil's Time **(69)***(55) (TGMills)* 4-8-9b RHills(13) (bhd fnl 9f) ....hd 15
43210 Argyle Cavalier (IRE) **(62)***(44) (MJohnston)* 5-8-6 MHills(20) (bhd fnl 6f) 3½ 16
Top Spin **(62)***(44) (JRJenkins)* 6-8-6 GHind(4) (a bhd) ....nk 17
Chakalak **(64)***(45) (SDow)* 7-8-8 AMartinez(17) (bhd fnl 14f) ....¾ 18
Triple Tie (USA) **(73)***(53) (MBlanshard)* 4-8-13 WRyan(6) (swtg: s.s: a bhd) ....¾ 19
432* Upper Mount Clair **(63)***(42) (CEBrittain)* 5-8-7 BDoyle(16) (led over 9f: wkng whn hmpd on ins over 4f out) 1¼ 20
4238 Stalled (IRE) **(54)** *(PTWalwyn)* 5-7-12 AMackay(9) (lw: nt clr run on ins 4f out: hdwy over 1f out: swtchd rt ins fnl f: one pce: fin 4th, 1¼l: disq: plcd last) 0

6/1 Moonlight Quest, **8/1** Well Arranged (IRE), **10/1** Chief's Song, Blaze Away (USA), Stoney Valley, **11/1** Stalled (IRE), Lalindi (IRE), **14/1** Phil's Time, Doyce, ALWAYS ALOOF (USA), Argyle Cavalier (IRE), **16/1** Wild Strawberry, Upper Mount Clair, Harlestone Brook, **20/1** Triple Tie (USA), **25/1** Paradise Navy, **33/1** Chimborazo, Sheltered Cove (IRE), Top Spin, Chakalak, CSF £92.22 CT £815.91 TOTE £16.40: £3.50 £1.70 £2.60 £3.20 (£55.00) Trio £176.30 OWNER Mr S. Hanson (NEWMARKET) BRED Northern and Pacific Investments 20 Rn
3m 27.85 (3.45) SF: 68/54/57/49/46/44/52/59/37/41/38/32/11/24/17/17/18/22/15/-
WEIGHT FOR AGE 4yo-4lb
STEWARDS' ENQUIRY Mackay suspended 26-29/4/95 (irresponsible riding).

633 QUAIL STKS (3-Y.O) (Class B) £7,996.20 (£2,995.80: £1,467.90: £634.50: £287.25: £148.35)
6f Stalls: High GOING minus 0.32 sec per fur (GF) 3-40 (3-52)

543* **Sergeyev (IRE) (90)***(98+) (RHannon)* 3-8-12 TQuinn(5) (lw: hld up: nt clr run over 2f out & over 1f out: qcknd to ld wl ins fnl f: r.o wl) ....— 1

438[5] Welton Arsenal **(98)***(97) (MRChannon)* 3-9-0 MHills(8) (lw: stdy hdwy on ins over 2f out: led 1f out tl wl ins fnl f: unable qckn) 1 2
Fire Dome (IRE) **(99)***(98) (TGMills)* 3-9-4 WRSwinburn(9) (hld up: hrd rdn over 1f out: unable qckn ins fnl f) 1¼ 3
Overbrook **(92)***(82)*(Fav)*(IABalding)* 3-8-7 RCochrane(2) (hld up: hrd rdn over 1f out: one pce) 1¾ 4
Lennox Lewis **(91)***(93) (APJarvis)* 3-9-4 BThomson(6) (led over 1f: led over 2f out to 1f out: one pce) ....nk 5
Kayrawan (USA) *(85) (HThomsonJones)* 3-8-12 RHills(4) (lw: rdn over 2f out: hdwy over 1f out: one pce) ....½ 6
Al Rawda (FR) **(98)***(78) (HRACecil)* 3-8-7 WRyan(3) (led over 4f out tl over 2f out: wknd fnl f) 1 7
Al Nufooth (IRE) **(101)***(85) (MajorWRHern)* 3-9-2 WCarson(7) (swtchd lft 1f out: nvr nr to chal) ....½ 8
Rockville Pike (IRE) *(39) (SDow)* 3-8-10 DHarrison(1) (bhd fnl 2f) 15 9

7/2 Overbrook, **4/1** SERGEYEV (IRE), **5/1** Kayrawan (USA), **11/2** Al Nufooth (IRE), **6/1** Welton Arsenal, **7/1** Fire Dome (IRE), Al Rawda (FR), **14/1** Lennox Lewis, **33/1** Rockville Pike (IRE), CSF £27.67 TOTE £5.40: £2.00 £2.00 £2.30 (£16.50) Trio £64.50 OWNER Mr B. T. Stewart-Brown (MARLBOROUGH) BRED Hugo Merry and Michael Stanley 9 Rn
1m 13.05 (1.75) SF: 45/44/45/29/40/32/25/32/-

634

WESTMINSTER-MOTOR TAXI INSURANCE ROSEBERY H'CAP (0-90) (4-Y.O+) (Class C) £13,588.00 (£5,092.00: £2,496.00: £1,080.00: £490.00: £254.00)
1m 2f (Jubilee) Stalls: High GOING minus 0.32 sec per fur (GF) 4-15 (4-21)

Special Dawn (IRE) (78)*(90)*(Fav)*(JLDunlop)* 5-9-6 PatEddery(3) (lw: 6th st: led over 1f out: drvn out) ....— 1
Blushing Flame (USA) **(84)***(96)*(Fav)*(MRStoute)* 4-9-12 WRSwinburn(16) (rdn & gd hdwy on ins over 2f out: r.o wl ins fnl f) ....nk 2
550* Benfleet **(78)***(87) (RWArmstrong)* 4-9-6 AMackay(23) (lw: rdn over 2f out: hdwy over 1f out: r.o wl ins fnl f) 1¾ 3
318[2] Secret Aly (CAN) **(70)***(79) (CEBrittain)* 5-8-12 BDoyle(14) (lw: lost pl over 3f out: rallied over 1f out: r.o) ....hd 4
423[15] Uncle Oswald **(77)***(85) (RHannon)* 4-9-5 BThomson(2) (2nd st: led 2f out tl wl over 1f out: one pce fnl f) ....nk 5
440[7] Sue's Artiste **(84)***(92) (BWHills)* 4-9-12 MHills(12) (hdwy over 2f out: led wl over 1f out: sn hdd: one pce) ....hd 6
505[2] Red Valerian **(74)***(81) (KMcAuliffe)* 4-9-2b RCochrane(13) (swtchd lft over 2f out: hdwy over 1f out: r.o) ....¾ 7
No Speeches (IRE) **(61)***(67) (CACyzer)* 4-7-12 (5)ow1 PMcCabe(19) (rdn over 2f out: hdwy over 1f out: nvr nrr) ....s.h 8
550[3] Show Faith (IRE) **(78)***(83) (RHannon)* 5-8-13 (7) DaneO'Neill(18) (3rd st: wknd wl over 1f out) 1 9
439[18] Country Lover **(86)***(91) (LordHuntingdon)* 4-10-0 DHarrison(24) (lw: nvr nrr) ....hd 10
Laxford Bridge **(82)***(85) (PWHarris)* 4-9-10 GDuffield(8) (lw: lost pl over 4f out: r.o one pce fnl 2f) 1 11
*512** Eqtesaad (USA) **(76)***(78) (SCWilliams)* 4-9-4 GHind(17) (hdwy over 1f out: eased whn btn ins fnl f) 1 12
558[4] Rory **(82)***(82) (MrsJCecil)* 4-9-5 (5) SMulvey(22) (hdwy over 3f out: wknd over 2f out) 1 13
512[2] A Million Watts **(60)***(59)*(Fav)*(LadyHerries)* 4-8-2 WCarson(9) (nvr nrr) ....¾ 14
Proton **(75)***(73)*(Fav)*(RAkehurst)* 5-9-3 TQuinn(6) (lw: led 8f) ....¾ 15
550[10] Roi de la Mer (IRE) **(68)***(65) (JAkehurst)* 4-8-7 (3) SSanders(15) (a bhd) ....¾ 16
505[10] Folly Finnesse **(72)***(67) (BRMillman)* 4-9-0 JWilliams(4) (a bhd) 1¼ 17
Zermatt (IRE) **(68)***(40) (MDIUsher)* 5-8-10 TSprake(21) (4th st: wknd over 2f out) 14 18
Locorotondo (IRE) **(78)***(45) (MBell)* 4-9-6 MFenton(20) (b.hind: bhd fnl 2f) 3½ 19
440[11] Windrush Lady **(83)***(46) (MMcCormack)* 5-9-11 TIves(1) (prom 7f) 2½ 20
*470** El Atrevido (FR) **(68)***(16) (NJHWalker)* 5-8-10 RHills(5) (prom 8f) 9 21
430[6] Prenonamoss **(65)** *(DWPArbuthnot)* 7-8-2v(5) AWhelan(7) (b.hind: stmbld & uns rdr over 8f out) .... U

8/1 SPECIAL DAWN (IRE), Blushing Flame (USA), A Million Watts, Proton, **10/1** Secret Aly (CAN), **12/1** Sue's Artiste, Red Valerian, Benfleet, **14/1** Rory, Country Lover, Show Faith (IRE), **16/1** Locorotondo (IRE), El Atrevido (FR), **20/1** Eqtesaad (USA), Uncle Oswald, Prenonamoss, **33/1** Folly Finnesse, Zermatt (IRE), Laxford Bridge, Windrush Lady, Roi de la Mer (IRE), **50/1** No Speeches (IRE), CSF £70.61 CT £729.77 TOTE £6.60: £2.20 £2.70 £3.10 £3.00 (£27.40) Trio £87.80 OWNER Windflower Overseas Holdings Inc (ARUNDEL) BRED Windflower Overseas 22 Rn
2m 5.29 (2.79) SF: 55/61/52/44/50/57/46/32/48/56/50/43/47/24/38/30/32/5/10/11/-/-

635

FIFIELD MAIDEN STKS (3-Y.O) (Class D) £4,065.00 (£1,230.00: £600.00: £285.00) **1m 2f (Jubilee)** Stalls: High GOING minus 0.32 sec (GF) 4-45 (4-57)

Minds Music (USA) *(89) (HRACecil)* 3-9-0 WRyan(20) (w'like: nt clr run on ins over 2f out: hdwy over 1f out: str run fnl f: led last stride) — **1**
Istidaad (USA) **(106)***(89)*(Fav)*(ACStewart)* 3-9-0 WCarson(8) (2nd st: led 2f out: hdd last stride) s.h **2**
Riyadian *(87) (PFICole)* 3-9-0 TQuinn(16) (w'like: scope: lw: plld hrd: led 4f out to 2f out: ev ch 1f out: one pce) 1¼ **3**
Mackook (USA) *(83) (MRStoute)* 3-9-0 WRSwinburn(21) (rdn over 3f out: hdwy over 2f out: r.o ins fnl f) 2½ **4**
Main Offender *(80) (HRACecil)* 3-9-0 RHills(12) (rdn over 3f out: hdwy over 2f out: one pce) 1¾ **5**
High Patriarch (IRE) *(75) (JLDunlop)* 3-9-0 GHind(19) (bkwd: rdn over 4f out: hdwy over 1f out: one pce) 3½ **6**
Snow Princess (IRE) *(69) (LordHuntingdon)* 3-8-9 DHarrison(15) (6th st: wknd over 2f out) s.h **7**
Tadjoni *(74) (IABalding)* 3-9-0 RCochrane(7) (w'like: s.s: rdn over 4f out: nvr nrr) s.h **8**
Stormaway (ITY) *(71) (TGMills)* 3-9-0 TIves(9) (w'like: scope: lw: a mid div) 2 **9**
Stone Ridge (IRE) *(66) (RHannon)* 3-9-0 PatEddery(6) (hdwy over 5f out: 4th st: hrd rdn over 2f out: 6th & btn whn hmpd over 1f out) 3½ **10**
Turquoise Sea (USA) *(60) (JLDunlop)* 3-8-9 GDuffield(3) (nvr nrr) ½ **11**
428[6] China Mail (IRE) *(61) (JMPEustace)* 3-8-11 (3) SSanders(10) (3rd st: wknd over 2f out) 2½ **12**
Maplestead (IRE) *(60) (CEBrittain)* 3-9-0 BDoyle(5) (bit bkwd: hdwy over 5f out: wknd over 2f out) nk **13**
Western Playboy *(60) (RHannon)* 3-9-0 BThomson(14) (w'like: prom over 6f) s.h **14**
Greycoat Boy *(55) (BJMeehan)* 3-9-0 MFenton(18) (bhd fnl 4f) 3½ **15**
Lamp of Phoebus (USA) *(50) (JHMGosden)* 3-8-4 (5) PMcCabe(2) (b: b.hind: w'like: bkwd: a bhd) s.h **16**
Red Dragon *(51) (GWragg)* 3-9-0 MHills(17) (w'like: a bhd) 2½ **17**
Bowcliffe Court (IRE) *(48) (BWHills)* 3-8-7 (7) GBrace(11) (bit bkwd: led 6f) 1½ **18**
Coggle *(40) (NAGraham)* 3-8-9 TSprake(1) (bhd fnl 6f) 1¾ **19**
Blazing Miracle *(29) (BRMillman)* 3-8-9 JWilliams(13) (unf: bhd fnl 6f) 7 **20**
Burnt Sienna (IRE) *(21) (JSMoore)* 3-8-9 AClark(4) (a bhd) 5 **21**

15/8 Istidaad (USA), **5/1** Mackook (USA), Riyadian (op 3/1), **7/1** Stone Ridge (IRE), **14/1** MINDS MUSIC (USA), Lamp of Phoebus (USA) (op 8/1), Main Offender, **16/1** Tadjoni, **20/1** Western Playboy, Red Dragon, **25/1** Snow Princess (IRE), **33/1** Turquoise Sea (USA), **50/1** China Mail (IRE), Stormaway (ITY), Greycoat Boy, Maplestead (IRE), High Patriarch (IRE), Bowcliffe Court (IRE), Coggle, Blazing Miracle, Burnt Sienna (IRE), CSF £40.97 TOTE £10.90: £3.80 £1.50 £2.20 (£14.40) Trio £42.50. OWNER Mr S. S. Niarchos (NEWMARKET) BRED Flaxman Holdings Ltd 21 Rn 2m 4.38 (1.88) SF: 57/57/55/51/48/43/37/42/39/34/28/29/28/28/23/18/19/16/8/-/-

636

TEAL H'CAP (0-85) (4-Y.O+) (Class D) £4,849.75 (£1,468.00: £716.50: £340.75) **6f** Stalls: High GOING minus 0.32 sec per fur (GF) 5-15 (5-26)

Gone Savage (62)*(64) (WJMusson)* 7-8-0 (5) PMcCabe(13) (a.p: hrd rdn over 2f out: led ins fnl f: r.o wl) — **1**
542[7] La Petite Fusee **(62)***(64) (RJO'Sullivan)* 4-8-5 AClark(12) (b.hind: led over 3f: led over 1f out tl ins fnl f: r.o) hd **2**
Fionn de Cool (IRE) **(70)***(70)*(Fav)*(RAkehurst)* 4-8-13 TQuinn(15) (lw: hrd rdn & hdwy 2f out: r.o wl ins fnl f) ½ **3**
Yet More Roses **(69)***(68) (LadyHerries)* 4-8-12 TIves(3) (b.hind: a.p: led over 2f out tl over 1f out: unable qckn) ½ **4**
Bryan Robson (USA) **(68)***(65) (GBBalding)* 4-8-11 JWilliams(17) (bit bkwd: hdwy over 2f out: r.o ins fnl f) ¾ **5**
434[13] Kildee Lad **(74)***(58) (APJones)* 5-9-3 WRyan(16) (lw: hdwy 3f out: one pce fnl f) 5 **6**
499[3] Sweet Supposin (IRE) **(65)***(49) (KMcAuliffe)* 4-8-8b RCochrane(11) (lw: rdn over 3f out: nvr nr to chal) s.h **7**
Chili Heights **(65)***(42) (GBBalding)* 5-8-8 TSprake(2) (nvr nrr) 2½ **8**
How's Yer Father **(85)***(62) (RJHodges)* 9-10-0 PatEddery(1) (no hdwy fnl 3f) s.h **9**
542[6] Champagne Grandy **(72)***(46) (MRChannon)* 5-9-1 MHills(9) (nvr nrr) 1¼ **10**
499[7] Dark Eyed Lady (IRE) **(70)***(33) (DWPArbuthnot)* 5-8-13 BDoyle(14) (b: prom over 3f) 4 **11**
297[6] Warwick Warrior (IRE) **(68)***(28) (MrsLPiggott)* 4-8-4 (7) GMilligan(7) (b: b.hind: bhd fnl 2f) 1 **12**
567[2] Invocation **(68)***(27) (AMoore)* 8-8-11 GDuffield(10) (b.hind: bhd fnl 2f) ½ **13**

Madurai **(67)***(25) (JLDunlop)* 4-8-10 WCarson(4) (bit bkwd: prom over 3f) ....nk **14**
Zifta (USA) **(76)***(30) (SCWilliams)* 4-9-5 AMackay(5) (a bhd) 1½ **15**
535[12] Truthful Image **(74)***(25) (RJHodges)* 6-9-3 WRSwinburn(6) (a bhd) 1¼ **16**
Peter Rowley **(75)***(26) (RHannon)* 4-9-4 RHills(8) (bhd fnl 4f) ....s.h **17**

13/2 Fionn de Cool (IRE), **8/1** Kildee Lad, Truthful Image (op 14/1), How's Yer Father, Madurai, **9/1** Sweet Supposin (IRE), Warwick Warrior (IRE), Yet More Roses, **10/1** Invocation, **11/1** Dark Eyed Lady (IRE), **16/1** Zifta (USA), Champagne Grandy, Bryan Robson (USA), **20/1** Peter Rowley, La Petite Fusee, **25/1** GONE SAVAGE, **33/1** Chili Heights, CSF £432.17 CT £3,289.94 TOTE £57.70: £12.50 £4.50 £2.50 £3.60 (£255.40) Trio £355.40 OWNER The On The Floor Partnership (NEWMARKET) BRED Mrs C. F. Van Straubenzee and R. Mead 17 Rn
1m 12.78 (1.48) SF: 42/42/48/46/43/36/27/20/40/24/11/6/5/3/8/3/4

637

STARK MAIDEN STKS (II) (3-Y.O+) (Class D) £3,772.50 (£1,140.00: £555.00: £262.50) **7f (Jubilee)** Stalls: High GOING minus 0.32 sec per fur (GF) 5-45 (5-54)

Atlaal (USA) *(84) (HThomsonJones)* 3-8-10 RHills(6) (6th st: nt clr run 2f out: swtchd lft over 1f out: str run fnl f: led last strides) ....— **1**
553[2] Banadam (USA) *(83) (BHanbury)* 3-8-10 WRyan(11) (lw: 2nd st: led 3f out: edgd lft fnl f: hdd last strides) ....nk **2**
431[2] Silver Sting *(78)*(Fav)*(IABalding)* 3-8-10 PatEddery(9) (lw: 4th st: rdn over 2f out: one pce) 2½ **3**
543[4] Forzair **(74)***(77) (MMcCormack)* 3-8-10 AClark(4) (rdn over 3f out: 3rd st: ev ch over 2f out: one pce) ....½ **4**
Floridante (USA) *(72) (PFICole)* 3-8-10 TQuinn(5) (hdwy over 1f out: r.o) 2 **5**
Roderick Hudson *(71) (JARToller)* 3-8-10 MHills(7) (bit bkwd: nvr nr to chal) ....½ **6**
Victory Team (IRE) *(71) (JRFanshawe)* 3-8-10 DHarrison(1) (w'like: 5th st: rdn over 2f out: wknd over 1f out) ....hd **7**
Lucky Coin *(58) (CEBrittain)* 3-8-5 BDoyle(8) (a bhd) 3½ **8**
Rumpelstiltskin *(56) (MartynMeade)* 3-8-3 (7) CTinel(12) (w'like: bit bkwd: bhd fnl 3f) 3 **9**
Poor Printer (IRE) *(28) (JAkehurst)* 4-9-5 RCochrane(3) (lw: bhd fnl 4f) 10 **10**
485[14] Jimbo *(33) (JRJenkins)* 4-9-10 JWilliams(2) (bhd fnl 4f) ....hd **11**
Hasaid Lady (IRE) *(27) (RHannon)* 3-8-6 ow1 BThomson(10) (led 4f) ....hd **12**

15/8 Silver Sting, **3/1** Victory Team (IRE), **4/1** Banadam (USA), **9/1** ATLAAL (USA) (op 6/1), Floridante (USA) (op 5/1), **14/1** Forzair, **16/1** Hasaid Lady (IRE), **33/1** Lucky Coin, Roderick Hudson, Rumpelstiltskin, **66/1** Poor Printer (IRE), Jimbo, CSF £43.68 TOTE £13.60: £2.90 £2.00 £1.40 (£32.30) Trio £11.20 OWNER Mr Hamdan Al Maktoum (NEWMARKET) BRED Shadwell Farm Inc 12 Rn
1m 26.68 (2.48) SF: 39/38/33/32/27/26/26/13/11/-/2/-
WEIGHT FOR AGE 3yo-14lb

T/Jkpt: Not won; £39,548.29 to Newmarket 18/4/95. T/Plpt: £45.40 (850.86 Tckts). T/Qdpt: £9.40 (12.6 Tckts) AK

0456-NEWCASTLE (L-H)
Monday April 17th (Good to firm)

WEATHER: overcast WIND: mod against

638

E.B.F. CAP HEATON MAIDEN STKS (2-Y.O F) (Class D) £3,258.85 (£986.80: £481.90: £229.45)
5f Stalls: Centre GOING minus 0.33 sec per fur (GF) 2-25 (2-27)

My Melody Parkes *(65t)*(Fav)*(JBerry)* 2-8-11 JCarroll(2) (w'like: lengthy: cl up: rdn to ld over 1f out: edgd lft: r.o) ....— **1**
Top Cat (FR) *(54) (EWeymes)* 2-8-11 DeanMcKeown(3) (cmpt: scope: bit bkwd: dwlt: sn rcvrd & trckd ldrs: nt qckn fnl f) 3½ **2**
Kunucu (IRE) *(54) (TDBarron)* 2-8-11 KDarley(5) (w'like: led tl hdd over 1f out: no ex) ....s.h **3**
Clary Sage *(6) (CWFairhurst)* 2-8-11 JFanning(4) (str: bit bkwd: prom to ½-wy: sn rdn & btn) 15 **4**
Baileys Bride (IRE) *(MJohnston)* 2-8-11 TWilliams(7) (unf: n.d) 2½ **5**
490[5] Annagh *(WTKemp)* 2-8-11 DaleGibson(6) (prom tl outpcd ½-wy: sn bhd) 2 **6**
Siger Water *(RFFisher)* 2-8-11 NConnorton(1) (leggy: unf: s.s: a outpcd & wl bhd) 12 **7**

4/6 MY MELODY PARKES, **5/2** Kunucu (IRE), **7/1** Baileys Bride (IRE), **12/1** Clary Sage, Top Cat (FR), **20/1** Siger Water, **100/1** Annagh, CSF £10.00 TOTE £1.40: £1.10 £2.80 (£5.00) OWNER Mr Joseph Heler (COCKERHAM) BRED Joseph Heler 7 Rn 62.07 secs (3.67) SF: 7/-/-/-/-/-/-

639

BLAGDON H'CAP (0-80) (3-Y.O+) (Class D) £3,656.90 (£1,107.20: £540.60: £257.30) **5f** Stalls: Centre GOING minus 0.33 sec per fur (GF) 2-55 (2-57)

Perryston View (67)*(78+)*(Fav)*(PCalver)* 3-8-6v MBirch(9) (cl up: led ½-wy: hung lft: r.o wl) .— **1**
*498*3 Tenor **(60)***(63) (DNicholls)* 4-8-10 AlexGreaves(8) (in tch: hdwy 2f out: styd on wl) 2½ **2**
535 9 Colway Rake **(61)***(64) (JWWatts)* 4-8-11b NConnorton(6) (lw: prom: effrt ½-wy: r.o one pce) s.h **3**
475 2 Sonderise **(52)***(48) (NTinkler)* 6-8-2 JLowe(5) (lw: hld up: hdwy over 1f out: r.o).......................2 **4**
*590*10 Nineacres **(56)***(48) (DNicholls)* 4-8-6 SMaloney(7) (chsd ldrs: nt qckn fnl 2f) 1¼ **5**
My Abbey **(57)***(45) (EJAlston)* 6-8-4 (3) JTate(3) (unruly s: dwlt: nvr trbld ldrs).........................1¼ **6**
*398*7 Lord Sky **(70)***(57)*(Fav)*(ABailey)* 4-9-6 KDarley(4) (lw: chsd ldrs: effrt ½-wy: grad wknd).........½ **7**
Stephensons Rocket **(78)***(61) (JBerry)* 4-10-0 JCarroll(10) (lw: led to ½-wy: sn wknd) 1¼ **8**
Bells of Longwick **(66)***(47) (WWHaigh)* 6-9-2 DaleGibson(1) (hung lft: sn outpcd & bhd).........½ **9**
475* My Cherrywell **(55)***(27) (LRLloyd-James)* 5-8-5v TWilliams(2) (b.hind: s.i.s: hmpd s: a bhd) 3 **10**

9/2 PERRYSTON VIEW, Lord Sky, **5/1** Tenor, **6/1** Stephensons Rocket, **7/1** Sonderise, **15/2** My Cherrywell, **10/1** Colway Rake, **12/1** Bells of Longwick, **14/1** My Abbey, Nineacres, CSF £26.47 CT £198.15 TOTE £5.40: £1.90 £1.90 £3.70 (£12.30) Trio £107.90 OWNER Mrs Janis MacPherson (RIPON) BRED Mrs V. E. Hughes 10 Rn 60.81 secs (2.41) SF: 22/18/19/3/3/-/12/16/2/-
WEIGHT FOR AGE 3yo-11lb

640

BYWELL H'CAP (0-85) (3-Y.O) (Class D) £3,606.20 (£1,091.60: £532.80: £253.40) **7f** Stalls: Centre GOING minus 0.33 sec per fur (GF) 3-25 (3-26)

Shahid (78)*(87+)*(Fav)*(JLDunlop)* 3-9-7 KDarley(2) (a gng wl: led on bit appr fnl f: qcknd: easily)..— **1**
483 4 Shinerolla **(60)***(61) (MrsJRRamsden)* 3-8-3 DeanMcKeown(7) (lw: hld up & bhd: hdwy over 2f out: r.o fnl f: no ch w wnr)...3½ **2**
Hawa Al Nasamaat (USA) **(75)***(70) (EALDunlop)* 3-9-1 (3) JTate(3) (b: lw: chsd ldrs: rdn over 2f out: r.o one pce) 2½ **3**
Persian Fayre **(65)***(60) (JBerry)* 3-8-8 JCarroll(5) (led tl hdd appr fnl f: sn btn) ....s.h **4**
524 15 Perfect Bertie (IRE) **(56)***(48) (MrsJRRamsden)* 3-7-13 JFanning(4) (bhd: effrt & hung lft 2f out: no imp) 1¼ **5**
Hotspur Street **(75)***(61) (MJohnston)* 3-9-4 TWilliams(1) (prom tl rdn & btn 2f out) 3 **6**
573 4 Euro Rebel **(62)***(42) (MHEasterby)* 3-8-5 MBirch(6) (cl up tl rdn & wknd over 2f out) 2½ **7**
492 5 Cool Steel (IRE) **(58)***(34) (MissSEHall)* 3-8-1v DaleGibson(8) (lw: sn pushed along: wl outpcd fnl 2f) 1¾ **8**

Evens SHAHID, **7/2** Shinerolla, **7/1** Hawa Al Nasamaat (USA), **8/1** Euro Rebel, Hotspur Street (op 5/1), **10/1** Persian Fayre, **12/1** Perfect Bertie (IRE), **16/1** Cool Steel (IRE), CSF £5.88 CT £17.60 TOTE £1.90: £1.10 £1.80 £1.80 (£2.50) Trio Not won OWNER Mr Hamdan Al Maktoum (ARUNDEL) BRED Somerhall Bloodstock Ltd and Lord Chelsea 8 Rn 1m 27.27 (2.97) SF: 43/17/26/16/4/17/-/-

641

BELSAY MEDIAN AUCTION MAIDEN STKS (3-Y.O) (Class E) £2,952.40 (£893.20: £435.60: £206.80) **1m 4f 93y** Stalls: Low GOING minus 0.33 sec per fur (GF) 3-55 (3-57)

Embryonic (IRE) *(77)*(Fav)*(RFFisher)* 3-9-0 NConnorton(5) (hld up: stdy hdwy appr st: led over 2f out: rn green: r.o fnl f)...— **1**
Toraja *(76) (JLDunlop)* 3-9-0 KDarley(7) (w'like: str: a.p: led 3f out: sn hdd: r.o u.p) ....½ **2**
Dawn Mission *(64) (MHEasterby)* 3-9-0 MBirch(1) (w'like: lengthy: hld up: hdwy 3f out: ev ch 2f out: sn wknd)...10 **3**
575 5 Jackmanii **(54)***(62) (WTKemp)* 3-9-0 DeanMcKeown(2) (lw: led 2f: cl up tl lost pl appr st: sme hdwy 2f out: no imp)..1¼ **4**
Battery Boy **(58)***(59) (CWCElsey)* 3-9-0 JCarroll(3) (prom: effrt ent st: rdn & outpcd final 2½f) 2 **5**
524 19 Raticosa **(32)***(16) (DonEnricoIncisa)* 3-8-9v KimTinkler(4) (swtg: a bhd) 30 **6**
525 7 Solor Dancer **(27)***(20) (CBBBooth)* 3-9-0v ACulhane(6) (led after 2f: sn clr: hdd & wknd qckly 3f out) ....½ **7**

11/10 EMBRYONIC (IRE), **7/2** Toraja (op 2/1), **9/2** Battery Boy, **6/1** Dawn Mission (op 3/1), **33/1** Jackmanii, **50/1** Raticosa, Solor Dancer, CSF £4.93 TOTE £2.10: £1.10 £1.80 (£2.00) OWNER Mrs D. Miller (ULVERSTON) BRED Tsarina Stud 7 Rn 2m 42.38 (3.88) SF: 48/47/35/33/30/-/-

642

ANGERTON APPRENTICE H'CAP (0-70) (3-Y.O+) (Class F) £2,620.00 (£745.00: £370.00) **1m** Stalls: Low GOING minus 0.33 sec per fur (GF) 4-25 (4-27)

568 6 **Thatched (IRE) (42)***(50) (REBarr)* 5-7-11 (3) PFessey(7) (a.p: led appr fnl f: r.o) ....— **1**

493[3] Hawwam **(52)***(58)*(Fav)*(EJAlston)* 9-8-10 SLanigan(12) (mid div: hdwy over 2f out: styd on wl nr fin) 1¼ 2
579[6] Spanish Verdict **(66)***(70)* *(DenysSmith)* 8-9-10 GMitchell(1) (cl up: effrt 3f out: kpt on nr fin) ....¾ 3
454[11] Desiderata **(55)***(59)* *(BWHills)* 4-8-13 MHenry(8) (b.hind: led tl hdd appr fnl f: no ex) ....hd 4
559[10] Up in Flames (IRE) **(63)***(67)* *(MDHammond)* 4-8-11 (10) MMathers(13) (lw: mid div: effrt 3f out: styd on: nt pce to chal) ....hd 5
505[7] Cee-Jay-Ay **(70)***(73)* *(JBerry)* 8-9-4 (10) CLowther(4) (dwlt: hdwy appr st: styd on) ....nk 6
559[11] Kilnamartyra Girl **(47)***(49)* *(JParkes)* 5-8-0 (5)ow1 GFaulkner(3) (chsd ldrs: one pce fnl 3f) ....s.h 7
526[13] Self Expression **(55)***(57)*(Fav)*(MrsJRRamsden)* 7-8-5 (8) SBuckley(14) (hld up & bhd: nt clr run 2½f out: swtchd & r.o: nrst fin) ....nk 8
578[2] Sharp N' Smooth **(50)***(52)* *(WTKemp)* 8-8-3b(5) BHalligan(11) (hld up: effrt 3f out: rdn & no imp) ....nk 9
526[5] Avishayes (USA) **(51)***(50)* *(MrsMReveley)* 8-8-3 (6) DDenby(6) (s.i.s: hld up & bhd: sme hdwy whn n.m.r over 2f out: n.d) 1½ 10
578[7] Never so True **(45)***(35)* *(MartynWane)* 4-7-12 (5)ow5 CarolDavison(9) (in tch tl wknd fnl 2½f) 2 11
Tanseeq **(69)***(64)* *(HThomsonJones)* 4-9-5 (8) CatherineCooper(5) (effrt ent st: sn wknd) ....s.h 12
256[9] King of Show (IRE) **(69)***(52)* *(RAllan)* 4-9-13 SarahThompson(15) (in tch tl c wd st & lost pl) 6 13
Suedoro **(35)***(14)* *(GPKelly)* 5-7-0 (7) PDoe(10) (swtg: chsd ldrs to st: sn lost pl) 2 14
King of the Horse (IRE) **(42)***(17)* *(WStorey)* 4-8-0v RuthCoulter(2) (chsd ldrs to st: wknd qckly) 2 15

LONG HANDICAP Suedoro 7-5

6/1 Self Expression, Hawwam, **13/2** Avishayes (USA), THATCHED (IRE), **7/1** Sharp N' Smooth, **8/1** Spanish Verdict, Tanseeq, **10/1** Desiderata, Cee-Jay-Ay, **11/1** Up in Flames (IRE), **20/1** Kilnamartyra Girl, **25/1** Never so True, King of Show (IRE), Suedoro, King of the Horse (IRE), CSF £46.24 CT £295.61 TOTE £11.00: £3.30 £2.00 £3.70 (£14.80) Trio £95.60 OWNER Mr J. C. Garbutt (MIDDLESBROUGH) BRED D. P. O'Brien 15 Rn

1m 44.2 (5.20) SF: 8/16/28/17/25/31/7/15/10/8/-/22/10/-/-

643

NEWBROUGH MAIDEN STKS (3-Y.O) (Class D) £3,775.20 (£1,143.60: £558.80: £266.40)
1m Stalls: Low GOING minus 0.33 sec per fur (GF) 4-55 (4-59)

Medaille Militaire *(60++)*(Fav)*(JLDunlop)* 3-9-0 KDarley(4) (dwlt: sn rcvrd: led on bit 2f out: v.easily) ....— 1
Mithraic (IRE) *(56)* *(JWWatts)* 3-9-0 MBirch(2) (wl grwn: a.p: effrt 3f out: styd on wl: no ch w wnr) 2 2
539[9] Final Fling *(46)* *(JWWatts)* 3-8-9 NConnorton(3) (hld up: shkn up over 2f out: styd on: nvr nr to chal) 2½ 3
552[11] Ahaalee (USA) *(49)* *(EALDunlop)* 3-8-11 (3) JTate(1) (cl up: led appr st: hdd 2f out: sn btn) 1 4
River Wye (IRE) *(46)* *(JMCarr)* 3-9-0 SMorris(5) (plld hrd: led tl hdd appr st: outpcd fnl 2½f) 1¾ 5
Island Cascade *(27)* *(DonEnricoIncisa)* 3-8-9 KimTinkler(6) (w'like: s.s: a bhd) 7 6
Undawaterscubadiva *(MPBielby)* 3-9-0 ACulhane(7) (leggy: unf: prom to st: wknd qckly) ...25 7

4/6 MEDAILLE MILITAIRE (op 1/3), **9/2** Final Fling, **5/1** Mithraic (IRE) (op 8/1), **8/1** Ahaalee (USA), **33/1** River Wye (IRE), Undawaterscubadiva, **50/1** Island Cascade, CSF £4.50 TOTE £1.40: £1.10 £2.60 (£2.60) OWNER Mr James Hartnett (ARUNDEL) BRED Fares Stables Ltd 7 Rn

1m 44.82 (5.82) SF: 15/11/1/4/1/-/-

T/Plpt: £7.60 (669.35 Tckts). T/Qdpt: £3.50 (15.8 Tckts). AA

0521-NOTTINGHAM (L-H)
Monday April 17th (Good to firm, Good patches)

WEATHER: rain WIND: fresh half against

644

EASTER EGG CLAIMING STKS (2-Y.O) (Class F) £2,139.00 (£589.00: £279.00)
5f 13y Stalls: Low GOING: 0.01 sec per fur (G) 2-20 (2-20)

Orange And Blue *(60t)* *(MAJarvis)* 2-8-1c PRobinson(2) (eyecover: lt-f: chsd ldrs: qcknd to ld jst ins fnl f: sn clr) ....— 1
574[3] Arvzees (IRE) *(62)*(Fav)*(MRChannon)* 2-8-8 RHughes(6) (w ldr: led 2f out tl jst ins fnl f: no ex) 1¾ 2

570[4] Takapuna (IRE) *(51) (RHannon)* 2-8-1 SRaymont(4) (bhd: hdwy 2f out: rdn & kpt on fnl f)....1¼ 3
490[3] Red Simba *(55) (JBerry)* 2-8-12 GCarter(1) (led 3f: rdn over 1f out: one pce)....2 4
Donington Park *(43) (JAHarris)* 2-7-10 (5) NVarley(3) (leggy: lt-f: chsd ldrs: rdn over 1f out: one pce)....½ 5
Rowhome *(24) (MRChannon)* 2-8-8 CandyMorris(7) (small: lt-f: swvd rt s: spd to ½-wy: t.o)....8 6
540[5] Deaken Dancer *(KTIvory)* 2-7-12 ow1 DBiggs(5) (Withdrawn not under Starter's orders: lame at s).... W

, **7/4** Arvzees (IRE), **2/1** Red Simba, **3/1** Takapuna (IRE), **8/1** ORANGE AND BLUE (op 5/1), **12/1** Donington Park, **14/1** Rowhome, CSF £21.88 TOTE £10.10: £3.60 £1.90 (£9.10) OWNER Mr M. A. Jarvis (NEWMARKET) BRED Mrs Mary Taylor 6 Rn 64.7 secs (6.00) SF: 10/12/1/5/-/-/-

645 ROBIN HOOD MEDIAN AUCTION MAIDEN STKS (3-Y.O) (Class E)

£2,888.00 (£798.00: £380.00)
5f 13y Stalls: Low GOING: 0.01 sec per fur (G) 2-50 (2-50)

502[9] **Coastal Bluff** *(85+) (TDBarron)* 3-9-0 JFortune(6) (b.hind: a.p: shkn up to ld ins fnl f: r.o strly)....— 1
522[2] La Suquet **(70)***(69)*(Fav)*(MRChannon)* 3-8-9 RHughes(2) (led tl hdd & nt qckn ins fnl f)....3½ 2
483[6] Jo Maximus **(70)***(68) (SDow)* 3-9-0 StephenDavies(3) (chsd ldrs: effrt 2f out: sn rdn: r.o nr fin)....2 3
580[2] Mister Raider **(47)***(67) (SMellor)* 3-8-7 (7) ADaly(1) (chsd ldrs: rdn along ½-wy: kpt on ins fnl f)....s.h 4
442[6] Perfect World **(68)***(64) (BAMcMahon)* 3-9-0 KFallon(7) (s.i.s: bhd & outpcd tl r.o ins fnl f)....1¼ 5
Sizzling *(56) (RHannon)* 3-9-0 PRobinson(5) (bkwd: prom: rdn 2f out: sn wknd)....2½ 6
451[5] Kellaire Girl (IRE) *(38) (GLewis)* 3-8-9 SWhitworth(8) (nvr nr to chal)....4 7
502[3] Honey Trader **(66)***(35) (JBerry)* 3-9-0 GCarter(10) (wnt rt s: hdwy ½wy: rdn 2f out: sn btn)....2½ 8
Miss Laughter *(30) (JWHills)* 3-8-9 NAdams(9) (a bhd)....d.h 8
L'Eglise Belle **(50)***(14) (MrsALMKing)* 3-8-4 (5) AGarth(4) (still unf: dwlt: a bhd & outpcd: t.o)....5 10

11/8 La Suquet, **5/1** Jo Maximus, Honey Trader (op 3/1), **6/1** Perfect World, **8/1** COASTAL BLUFF, **10/1** Sizzling, **11/1** Mister Raider, **14/1** Kellaire Girl (IRE), **16/1** Miss Laughter, **33/1** L'Eglise Belle, CSF £21.22 TOTE £15.40: £2.40 £1.50 £1.50 (£12.50) Trio £19.30 OWNER Mrs D. E. Sharp (THIRSK) BRED R. M. West 10 Rn 62.6 secs (3.90) SF: 57/41/40/39/36/28/10/7/2/-

646 'FAMILY DAY OUT' H'CAP (0-70) (3-Y.O+) (Class E) £3,340.20

(£927.20: £444.60)
6f 15y Stalls: Low GOING: 0.01 sec per fur (G) 3-20 (3-24)

Double Splendour (IRE) (41)*(52) (PSFelgate)* 5-8-0 (3) DWright(13) (chsd ldrs: qcknd to ld ins fnl f: sn clr)....— 1
518[11] Giggleswick Girl **(52)***(59) (MRChannon)* 4-9-0 RHughes(5) (hld up: n.m.r & swtchd rt 2f out: rdn & r.o wl fnl f)....1½ 2
Asterix **(43)***(45) (JMBradley)* 7-8-5v LCharnock(6) (bhd: hdwy over 1f out: fin wl)....2 3
486[4] First Gold **(63)***(65)*(Fav)*(JWharton)* 6-9-11 JQuinn(11) (hld up: hdwy wl over 1f out: rdn & one pce fnl f)....s.h 4
Cool Edge (IRE) **(66)***(65) (MHTompkins)* 4-10-0 PRobinson(18) (bit bkwd: prom tl wknd appr fnl f)....1 5
532[6] Angelic Dancer **(47)***(46) (SRBowring)* 4-8-4b(5) CTeague(7) (hld up: n.m.r 2f out: rdn & kpt on fnl f)....hd 6
535[19] Mu-Arrik **(58)***(57) (GROldroyd)* 7-9-1v(5) DGriffiths(9) (lw: hld up: hdwy over 1f out: nt pce to chal)....s.h 7
535[23] Captain Carat **(65)***(50) (MrsJRRamsden)* 4-9-13 KFallon(2) (chsd ldrs: rdn 2f out: grad wknd)....5 8
*446** Sir Tasker **(61)***(45)*(Fav)*(JLHarris)* 7-9-4 (5) NVarley(3) (disp ld over 4f: sn wknd)....½ 9
503[14] Twice in Bundoran (IRE) **(49)***(33) (PSFelgate)* 4-8-11 JFortune(16) (prom tl wknd over 1f out)....s.h 10
Gate of Heaven **(31)***(14) (JohnBerry)* 5-7-7 NKennedy(10) (bit bkwd: spd 4f)....½ 11
532[4] Saxon King (IRE) **(44)***(26) (MDIUsher)* 5-8-6 RStreet(4) (b: b.hind: hld up: hdwy to ld over 1f out: hdd, hmpd & eased ins fnl f)....nk 12
Killy's Filly **(48)***(25) (JMBradley)* 5-8-5 (5) SDrowne(14) (bit bkwd: bhd: rdn 2f out: no imp)....1¾ 13

*387*10 Educated Pet **(55)***(32) (BPreece)* 6-8-12 (5) JStack(12) (a in rr)....hd **14**
507 11 Most Uppitty **(62)***(39) (JBerry)* 3-8-12 GCarter(1) (chsd ldrs 4f: sn lost tch)....hd **15**
*532*12 Chilly Time **(31)** *(MrsLAMurphy)* 4-7-7v NAdams(8) (a bhd: t.o)....6 **16**
*518*9 Tiddy Oggie **(50)** *(NAGraham)* 4-8-12 MTebbutt(17) (slt ld over 4f: wknd qckly: t.o)....6 **17**
Fairy Fay (IRE) **(58)** *(BJMcMath)* 3-8-8 MWigham(15) (a bhd: t.o fnl 2f)....15 **18**

LONG HANDICAP Chilly Time 7-6 Gate of Heaven 6-10

9/2 First Gold, Sir Tasker, **6/1** Captain Carat, **8/1** Fairy Fay (IRE), DOUBLE SPLENDOUR (IRE) (op 5/1), **9/1** Saxon King (IRE) (op 6/1), **10/1** Most Uppitty, Angelic Dancer, **14/1** Giggleswick Girl, Tiddy Oggie, Cool Edge (IRE), **20/1** Asterix, Mu-Arrik, Twice in Bundoran (IRE), **25/1** Chilly Time, Educated Pet, Killy's Filly, **33/1** Gate of Heaven, CSF £123.24 CT £2,051.75 TOTE £9.20: £1.70 £4.20 £21.20 £1.50 (£556.10) Trio: Not won OWNER Yorkshire Racing Club Owners Group 1990 (MELTON MOWBRAY) BRED R. McQuillan 18 Rn

1m 17.7 (6.70) SF: 19/26/12/32/32/13/24/17/12/-/-/-/-/-/-/-/-/-
WEIGHT FOR AGE 3yo-12lb

647

EASTER BONNET H'CAP (0-80) (3-Y.O) (Class D) £4,070.30 (£1,216.40: £582.20: £265.10)
1m 1f 213y Stalls: Low GOING: 0.01 sec per fur (G) 3-50 (3-53)

*515*5 **Himalayan Blue (64)***(70) (MRChannon)* 3-8-5 CandyMorris(6) (chsd ldrs: 5th st: rdn to ld appr fnl f: hld on)....— **1**
Elfin Laughter **(73)***(78) (RHannon)* 3-9-0 RHughes(9) (lt-f: hld up & bhd: hdwy u.p 2f out: str run fnl f: fin wl)....½ **2**
Kristal's Paradise (IRE) **(73)***(78) (JLDunlop)* 3-9-0 GCarter(12) (hld up & bhd: hdwy 3f out: rdn & r.o ins fnl f)....nk **3**
Imlak (IRE) **(65)***(69) (DMorley)* 3-8-6 MTebbutt(3) (wl grwn: led after 2f: clr 2f out: wknd & hdd ent fnl f: one pce)....½ **4**
Red Bustaan **(77)***(78) (ACStewart)* 3-9-4 SWhitworth(13) (bkwd: s.i.s: sn chsng ldrs: drvn along ent st: hdwy over 2f out: one pce appr fnl f)....2 **5**
Advance East **(66)***(67) (MrsJRRamsden)* 3-8-7 KFallon(4) (hld up: hdwy over 2f out: one pce appr fnl f)....hd **6**
575 2 Chaldon Herring **(63)***(56) (TDBarron)* 3-8-4 JFortune(8) (plld hrd: hld up: effrt 3f out: nt rch ldrs)....5 **7**
427 11 Dr Edgar **(71)***(61) (GWragg)* 3-8-5 (7) DGibbs(1) (bit bkwd: led 2f: 6th st: wknd 2f out)....1¾ **8**
538* Silently **(76)***(65)*(Fav)*(IABalding)* 3-8-12 (5) DGriffiths(7) (lw: lost pl after 3f: wl bhd tl styd on appr fnl f)....nk **9**
Shining High **(80)***(69) (JLDunlop)* 3-9-7 StephenDavies(10) (hld up: effrt & rdn over 2f out: no imp)....nk **10**
Tucan (USA) **(76)***(55) (HRACecil)* 3-8-10 (7) DLockhart(5) (bit bkwd: plld hrd: hld up mid div: wknd over 2f out: t.o)....6 **11**
538 2 Our Tom **(60)***(31) (JWharton)* 3-8-1 JQuinn(11) (chsd ldrs: 4th st: wknd 2f out: t.o)....5 **12**
Million Dancer **(72)***(40) (MCPipe)* 3-8-8 (5) JStack(14) (chsd ldr: 2nd st: ev ch 3f out: sn rdn & wknd: t.o)....1¾ **13**
Eden's Star (IRE) **(67)***(35) (MHTompkins)* 3-8-8 PRobinson(2) (still unf: prom: 3rd st: wknd over 3f out: t.o)....½ **14**

3/1 Silently, **11/2** Advance East, **6/1** Our Tom, **13/2** Chaldon Herring, **9/1** Red Bustaan, **10/1** Imlak (IRE), Shining High, Elfin Laughter, **12/1** Tucan (USA), **14/1** Kristal's Paradise (IRE), Million Dancer, Eden's Star (IRE), **16/1** Dr Edgar, **25/1** HIMALAYAN BLUE, CSF £263.32 CT £3,338.33 TOTE £25.20: £4.50 £3.90 £4.20 (£221.20) Trio £116.10 OWNER Miss C. Fagerstrom (UPPER LAMBOURN) 14 Rn 2m 9.7 (7.20) SF: 32/40/40/31/40/29/18/23/27/31/17/-/2/-

STEWARDS' ENQUIRY Hughes suspended 26-27/4/95 (excessive use of whip).
OFFICIAL EXPLANATION Silently: no explanation offered.

648

EASTER MONDAY H'CAP (0-70) (3-Y.O) (Class E) £3,553.00 (£988.00: £475.00)
1m 54y Stalls: Low GOING: 0.01 sec per fur (G) 4-20 (4-26)

*566** **Busy Banana (69)***(81) (RHannon)* 3-9-6 JFortune(16) (mde all: clr 3f out: eased fnl f)....— **1**
437 6 Harry Browne (IRE) **(56)***(58) (MrsJRRamsden)* 3-8-7 KFallon(14) (hld up & bhd: styd on fnl 2f: nvr nrr)....5 **2**
*448** Kevasingo **(54)***(54) (SDow)* 3-8-5 StephenDavies(12) (lw: hld up in tch: hdwy 3f out: kpt on u.p fnl f)....1¼ **3**
450 9 Silktail (IRE) **(59)***(59) (JohnBerry)* 3-8-10 SRaymont(13) (stdd s: hld up & bhd: hdwy fnl 2f: fin wl)....s.h **4**
Soviet Bride (IRE) **(54)***(54) (EALDunlop)* 3-8-0 (5) JStack(18) (lw: a.p: 3rd st: sn chsng wnr: rdn over 1f out: wknd fnl f)....hd **5**
Delightful Dancer (IRE) **(62)***(57) (BWHills)* 3-8-8 (5) JDSmith(8) (bhd: hdwy over 2f out: nt rch ldrs)....2½ **6**

449* Double Rush (IRE) **(60)***(51)*(Fav)*(TGMills)* 3-8-11 GCarter(11) (chsd ldrs: 6th st: rdn over 2f out: no imp) 1¾ **7**
Bury the Hatchet **(59)***(47) (MHTompkins)* 3-8-10 PRobinson(7) (bit bkwd: r.o fnl 2f: nvr nrr) 1½ **8**
Embezzler **(58)***(33) (GLewis)* 3-8-9 SWhitworth(1) (chsd ldrs: 4th st: rdn & wknd 3f out) 7 **9**
435 11 Outstayed Welcome **(57)***(30) (MJHaynes)* 3-8-8 DBiggs(17) (b.hind: nvr plcd to chal) 1 **10**
Red River Rose (IRE) **(50)***(15) (NPLittmoden)* 3-8-1 NKennedy(15) (s.s: a in rr) 4 **11**
Shot the Sheriff **(66)***(30) (PFICole)* 3-9-0 (3) DWright(10) (nt grwn: nvr nr ldrs) ....½ **12**
504 16 Risky Romeo **(70)***(33) (GCBravery)* 3-9-4 (3) CHodgson(3) (s.i.s: a in rr) ....½ **13**
Dance of Joy **(65)***(25) (JLDunlop)* 3-9-2 MTebbutt(20) (s.s: a bhd) 1¾ **14**
Kristal Breeze **(60)***(12) (WRMuir)* 3-8-4 (7) RPooles(19) (lw: chsd ldrs: 5th st: wknd over 3f out: t.o) 4 **15**
Anna Bannanna **(70)***(22) (MCPipe)* 3-9-7 JQuinn(6) (a in rr: t.o) ....nk **16**
261 2 Logie **(58)***(8) (MAJarvis)* 3-8-9 MWigham(4) (a bhd: t.o) ....¾ **17**
Can't Say (IRE) **(45)** *(JMBradley)* 3-7-5 (5) NVarley(2) (chsd ldrs 5f: sn wknd: t.o) 3 **18**
Prince Pellinore **(58)***(1) (MBell)* 3-8-9 CDwyer(9) (bolted bef s: sn chsng ldrs: 2nd st: wknd over 3f out: t.o) ....½ **19**

3/1 Double Rush (IRE), **4/1** BUSY BANANA, **6/1** Harry Browne (IRE), **11/1** Risky Romeo, **12/1** Kevasingo, Dance of Joy, Delightful Dancer (IRE), Anna Bannanna, Embezzler, Shot the Sheriff, **14/1** Soviet Bride (IRE), **16/1** Silktail (IRE), Bury the Hatchet, Logie, **20/1** Red River Rose (IRE), **25/1** Kristal Breeze, Outstayed Welcome, Prince Pellinore, **33/1** Can't Say (IRE), CSF £33.64 CT £279.05 TOTE £5.00: £2.10 £1.90 £2.80 £4.50 (£15.70) Trio £81.30 OWNER Mr P. D. Savill (MARLBOROUGH) BRED Lingfield Lodge Farm 19 Rn

1m 46.4 (6.80) SF: 37/14/10/15/10/13/7/3/-/-/-/-/-/-/-/-/-/-/-

649

EASTER BUNNY H'CAP (0-70) (4-Y.O+) (Class E) £3,579.60 (£995.60: £478.80)
1m 6f 15y Stalls: Low GOING: 0.01 sec per fur (G) 4-50 (4-53)

589 4 **Swordking (IRE) (41)***(54) (JLHarris)* 6-8-10v PRobinson(6) (hld up: hdwy on ins & hmpd home turn: hdwy 3f out: hrd rdn to ld cl home) ....— **1**
Seize the Day (IRE) **(55)***(68) (CDBroad)* 7-9-10 MWigham(4) (hld up & bhd: hdwy over 2f out: rdn to ld wl ins fnl f: ct cl home) ....nk **2**
556 7 Arc Bright (IRE) **(37)***(47) (RHollinshead)* 5-8-6 JQuinn(3) (led: rdn over 3f out: wknd & hdd wl ins fnl f) 2½ **3**
549 5 Environmentalist (IRE) **(55)***(64)*(Fav)*(BJMcMath)* 4-9-5 (3) DWright(7) (hld up: hdwy 2f out: styd on ins fnl f: nvr nrr) ....½ **4**
600 4 Awestruck **(46)***(46) (BPreece)* 5-8-8b(7) AEddery(1) (bhd: hdwy over 3f out: nt rch ldrs) 8 **5**
Memorable **(43)***(43) (JHetherton)* 4-8-10 NKennedy(8) (hld up: hdwy 3f out: nvr nr to chal) ....nk **6**
370 5 Glow Forum **(34)***(28) (GLMoore)* 4-8-1 DBiggs(10) (prom: 3rd st: rdn 3f out: grad wknd) 5 **7**
556 13 In a Moment (USA) **(47)***(41) (TDBarron)* 4-9-0 JFortune(2) (chsd ldrs: 4th st: wnt 2nd 3f out: wknd appr fnl f) ....hd **8**
Lajadhal (FR) **(27)***(16) (KBishop)* 6-7-5 (5)ow3 CHawksley(16) (nvr nrr) 1¾ **9**
582 2 Ballymac Girl **(51)***(43) (JMBradley)* 7-9-1 (5) SDrowne(15) (b: 6th st: rdn & wknd over 2f out) ....nk **10**
520 9 Salinger **(32)***(23) (JParkes)* 7-8-1 StephenDavies(14) (chsd ldrs 10f: sn wknd) ....½ **11**
582 10 Jaraab **(46)***(37) (GLewis)* 4-8-13 SWhitworth(5) (chsd ldrs: 5th st: rdn & wknd over 2f out) ....½ **12**
588 7 Dugort Strand (IRE) **(44)***(23) (JLHarris)* 4-8-6b(5) NVarley(12) (a in rr: t.o) 10 **13**
Naawy **(34)***(5) (CSmith)* 5-8-3 NAdams(11) (bhd fnl 4f: t.o) 7 **14**
592 5 Mr Moriarty (IRE) **(36)***(3) (SRBowring)* 4-7-12b(5)ow1 CTeague(17) (prom: 4th st: wknd 3f out: t.o) 2½ **15**
569 8 Ttyfran **(43)** *(BPJBaugh)* 5-8-12 RLappin(9) (b: a bhd: t.o) 13 **16**
423 10 Opera Buff (IRE) **(55)** *(MCPipe)* 4-9-8 RHughes(13) (lw: prom: 2nd st: wknd 3f out: t.o) 30 **17**

LONG HANDICAP Lajadhal (FR) 7-6

5/2 Environmentalist (IRE) (op 4/1), **4/1** Ballymac Girl, **9/2** Jaraab, **7/1** Memorable, **8/1** Salinger, Arc Bright (IRE), **10/1** Opera Buff (IRE), **12/1** SWORDKING (IRE), Mr Moriarty (IRE), Seize the Day (IRE), **14/1** In a Moment (USA), Awestruck, **20/1** Dugort Strand (IRE), Glow Forum, **25/1** Naawy, **33/1** Ttyfran, Lajadhal (FR), CSF £174.73 CT £1,171.00 TOTE £17.00: £2.70 £4.10 £1.70 £2.30 (£215.70) Trio: Not won OWNER Lavender Hill Leisure Ltd (MELTON MOWBRAY) BRED Barronstown Bloodstock and Swettenham Stud 17 Rn

3m 9.2 (10.70) SF: 36/50/29/44/28/23/8/21/-/25/5/17/3/-/-/-/-

WEIGHT FOR AGE 4yo-2lb

T/Plpt: £1,525.80 (4.5 Tckts). T/Qdpt: Not won; £35.30 to Newmarket 18/4/95. IM

0502-**WARWICK (L-H)**
Monday April 17th (Good, Good to firm patches)
WEATHER: rain WIND: mod bhd

650 LIONS CLUB INTERNATIONAL MEDIAN AUCTION MAIDEN STKS (2-Y.O F) (Class E) £3,377.25 (£1,008.00: £481.50: £218.25)
5f Stalls: Low GOING minus 0.40 sec per fur (F) 2-05 (2-09)

Anotheranniversary *(76+t)*(Fav)*(GLewis)* 2-8-11 PaulEddery(10) (b.hind: w'like: scope: bit bkwd: s.s: wnt rt: sn chsng ldrs: rdn over 1f out: led ins fnl f: r.o wl)........................— 1
Kossolian *(74) (BPalling)* 2-8-11 JWeaver(1) (unf: bit bkwd: dwlt: swtchd rt over 2f out: hdwy over 1f out: r.o wl ins fnl f)........................¾ 2
Gracious Gretclo *(67) (CJHill)* 2-8-11 MRimmer(3) (leggy: chsd ldrs: led over 2f out: hdd & no ex ins fnl f)........................2 3
Mrs McBadger *(62) (BSmart)* 2-8-11 RPerham(2) (lt-f: s.s: hdwy over 2f out: r.o ins fnl f).....1½ 4
Satellite Star (IRE) *(54) (MRChannon)* 2-8-11 CRutter(6) (unf: chsd ldrs: wknd over 1f out).2½ 5
Victoria Venture *(52) (SPCWoods)* 2-8-11 WWoods(4) (small: dwlt: hdwy over 1f out: nvr nrr)........................¾ 6
508[9] Rhumba Dancer *(50) (RHannon)* 2-8-11 JReid(11) (led over 2f: wknd over 1f out)........................¾ 7
Sam Coles (USA) *(43) (BJMeehan)* 2-8-11 WNewnes(8) (small: bit bkwd: sn outpcd)........................2 8
Swifty Nifty (IRE) *(30) (JBerry)* 2-8-11 SDWilliams(5) (small: unf: bhd fnl 2f)........................4 9
Melos *(14) (RonaldThompson)* 2-8-11 FNorton(7) (leggy: unf: s.s: outpcd)........................5 10
Ping-Pong Ball *(TRWatson)* 2-8-11 NCarlisle(9) (neat: bkwd: bhd fnl 3f: t.o)........................6 11

11/8 ANOTHERANNIVERSARY (9/4-5/4), **5/1** Gracious Gretclo, Swifty Nifty (IRE) (op 3/1), **6/1** Rhumba Dancer (op 7/2), **9/1** Satellite Star (IRE) (op 6/1), **16/1** Victoria Venture, Kossolian, **20/1** Sam Coles (USA), Mrs McBadger, **25/1** Ping-Pong Ball, **50/1** Melos, CSF £24.33 TOTE £2.60: £1.30 £3.60 £2.20 (£23.10) Trio £33.50 OWNER Mr David Barker (EPSOM) BRED Capt A. L. Smith-Maxwell 11 Rn 59.1 secs (1.10) SF: 32/30/23/18/10/8/6/-/-/-/-

651 B.B.C. C.W.R. H'CAP (0-70) (3-Y.O) (Class E) £3,465.00 (£1,035.00: £495.00: £225.00) **1m 2f 169y** Stalls: Low GOING minus 0.40 sec per fur (F) 2-35 (2-39)

538[5] **Poly Road (48)***(55) (MRChannon)* 3-7-13 CRutter(9) (dwlt: hld up & bhd: hdwy 5f out: 5th st: led over 1f out: sn clr: r.o wl)........................— 1
Matamoros **(65)***(70)*(Fav)*(JLDunlop)* 3-9-2 JReid(7) (hld up: nt clr run 3f out: hdwy 2f out: r.o wl ins fnl f)........................1½ 2
526[17] Just Fizzy **(47)***(46) (JWharton)* 3-7-7 (5) MBaird(12) (hdwy 5f out: 3rd st: one pce fnl f)........................4 3
427[17] Crested Knight (IRE) **(65)***(60) (CAHorgan)* 3-9-2 PaulEddery(1) (hld up & bhd: gd hdwy 2f out: one pce fnl f)........................2½ 4
Much Too High **(60)***(53) (TJNaughton)* 3-8-11 RPerham(3) (hld up & bhd: hdwy 3f out: nt rch ldrs)........................1¾ 5
566[3] Dont Shoot Fairies **(65)***(55) (CEBrittain)* 3-9-2 MRimmer(6) (lw: w ldr: slt ld over 4f out: hdd over 1f out: wknd)........................1½ 6
521[6] Pink Petal **(42)***(28) (CJHill)* 3-7-7 GBardwell(5) (hld up & plld hrd: nvr nr to chal)........................3 7
504[19] Mo's Main Man (IRE) **(60)***(46) (SDow)* 3-8-11 FNorton(14) (s.s: hld up & bhd: hdwy 2f out: nvr nrr)........................s.h 8
409[5] Howqua River **(60)***(44) (PWChapple-Hyam)* 3-8-4 (7) RHavlin(15) (hld up: hdwy 5f out: 4th st: wknd over 1f out)........................1¼ 9
Specialize **(51)***(33) (KRBurke)* 3-7-13 (3)ow2 DRMcCabe(2) (led tl hdd over 4f out: 2nd st: wknd 2f out)........................hd 10
310[4] Gulf Bay **(42)***(23) (MBell)* 3-7-0 (7) RMullen(10) (hld up: 7th st: wknd 2f out)........................1¾ 11
Most Welcome News **(51)***(21) (JRJenkins)* 3-8-2 ow1 RPrice(16) (hld up: hdwy 4f out: 6th st: wknd 2f out)........................7 12
Oakbury (IRE) **(70)***(40) (RHannon)* 3-9-7 JWeaver(13) (b.hind: hld up: lost pl over 3f out: bhd whn hung lft over 2f out)........................¾ 13
Little Secret (IRE) **(51)***(8) (TMJones)* 3-8-2 ow1 AMcGlone(11) (bit bkwd: hld up: bhd whn bdly hmpd 3f out: nt rcvr)........................8 14
Romantic Folly **(47)***(5) (BJMeehan)* 3-7-12 NCarlisle(4) (prom tl wknd over 3f out)........................s.h 15
Arctic Poppy (USA) **(65)** *(IABalding)* 3-9-2 WNewnes(8) (b.hind: prom over 5f: t.o)........................25 16

LONG HANDICAP Gulf Bay 7-5 Pink Petal 6-11

4/1 Matamoros, **9/2** Oakbury (IRE), **6/1** POLY ROAD, **8/1** Dont Shoot Fairies, Arctic Poppy (USA), **10/1** Pink Petal, **12/1** Crested Knight (IRE), Howqua River, **14/1** Mo's Main Man (IRE), **16/1** Specialize, **20/1** Just Fizzy, Gulf Bay, **25/1** Most Welcome News, Romantic Folly, **33/1** Little Secret (IRE), Much Too High, CSF £31.01 CT £435.50 TOTE £5.70: £1.70 £1.70 £3.40 £2.40 (£16.90) Trio £104.80 OWNER Sheet & Roll Convertors Ltd (UPPER LAMBOURN) BRED W. Beasley 16 Rn 2m 18.1 (4.60) SF: 18/33/9/23/16/18/-/9/7/-/-/-/3/-/-/-

652

450TH ANNIVERSARY STKS (4-Y.O+) (Class C) £5,163.20 (£1,908.80: £914.40: £372.00: £146.00: £55.60)
7f Stalls: Low GOING minus 0.40 sec per fur (F) 3-05 (3-08)

Star Talent (USA) (99)(*114*) (*DRCElsworth*) 4-9-1 PaulEddery(2) (lw: hld up: wnt 3rd st: slt ld over 1f out: shkn up: r.o wl) — 1
441[8] Cool Jazz **(105)**(*108*) (*CEBrittain*) 4-8-12 MRimmer(5) (sn pushed along: chsd ldr 4f out: led over 2f out: hdd over 1f out: nt qckn) 1½ 2
Storiths (IRE) **(109)**(*103*)(Fav)(*JWWatts*) 5-9-3b JReid(7) (b.hind: sn bhd: 5th st: hdwy over 1f out: r.o) 4 3
Masnad (USA) (*87*) (*RWArmstrong*) 4-9-0 RPrice(1) (4th st: nt clr run 2f out: wknd over 1f out) 6 4
535* Palacegate Touch **(92)**(*87*) (*JBerry*) 5-9-9v SDWilliams(4) (led 5f out tl over 2f out: 2nd st: wknd over 1f out: eased whn btn ins fnl f) 4 5
Damier Blanc (FR) (*62*) (*MCPipe*) 6-8-10 AMcGlone(3) (sn outpcd) 5 6
Weather Break **(80)**(*48*) (*HCandy*) 4-9-0 WNewnes(6) (slt ld 2f: wkng whn hung rt & 6th st) 8 7

5/2 Storiths (IRE), **11/4** Masnad (USA), **7/2** Cool Jazz, **4/1** Palacegate Touch, **7/1** Weather Break (14/1-6/1), **14/1** STAR TALENT (USA), **50/1** Damier Blanc (FR), CSF £59.66 TOTE £11.20: £3.00 £1.90 (£24.60) OWNER Mr J. C. Smith (WHITCOMBE) BRED Mrs Afaf A. Al Essa 7 Rn
1m 24.7 (0.50) SF: 60/54/49/33/33/8/-

653

HIGH TENSILE BOLTS H'CAP (0-80) (4-Y.O+) (Class D) £4,137.90 (£1,237.20: £592.60: £270.30)
1m 2f 169y Stalls: Low GOING minus 0.40 sec per fur (F) 3-35 (3-38)

Son of Sharp Shot (IRE) (75)(*85*) (*JLDunlop*) 5-9-10 PaulEddery(4) (lw: hld up: gd hdwy & 4th st: led over 1f out: drvn out) — 1
600[2] Hill Farm Dancer **(48)**(*55*) (*WMBrisbourne*) 4-7-4 (7) MartinDwyer(8) (stdy hdwy 5f out: led over 2f out: hdd over 1f out: nt qckn) 2 2
558[2] Southern Power (IRE) **(79)**(*82*)(Fav)(*MrsMReveley*) 4-10-0 JWeaver(3) (lw: b.hind: stdy hdwy 5f out: 5th st: rdn & edgd lft over 1f out: one pce) 2½ 3
586[6] Shoofk **(59)**(*56*) (*SDow*) 4-8-8 FNorton(5) (bolted bef s: s.i.s: hld up & bhd: hdwy on ins & n.m.r over 1f out: one pce) 4 4
445[12] Awesome Power **(59)**(*55*) (*JWHills*) 9-8-8 JReid(2) (hld up: stdy hdwy 4f out: one pce fnl 2f) ¾ 5
505[6] Un Parfum de Femme (IRE) **(71)**(*67*) (*JPearce*) 4-9-6 GBardwell(12) (hld up & bhd: hdwy 2f out: rdn over 1f out: one pce) nk 6
550[11] Total Joy (IRE) **(60)**(*55*) (*PFICole*) 4-8-9 CRutter(9) (led tl hdd 3f out: 3rd st: wknd 2f out) nk 7
Tony's Mist **(70)**(*63*) (*JMBradley*) 5-9-5 RPrice(1) (bit bkwd: bhd fnl 3f) 1½ 8
Midnight Jazz (IRE) **(79)**(*66*) (*WAO'Gorman*) 5-10-0 EmmaO'Gorman(10) (bit bkwd: plld hrd: sn chsng ldr: led 3f out: sn hdd: 2nd st: hung lft & wknd wl over 1f out) 4 9
Conic Hill (IRE) **(73)**(*55*) (*RJBaker*) 4-9-8b WNewnes(7) (chsd ldr: 7th & wkng st) 3½ 10
403[9] Power **(76)**(*56*) (*CEBrittain*) 4-9-11 MRimmer(6) (hdwy over 4f out: 6th & rdn st: wknd 2f out) 1¼ 11
546[7] Pistol (IRE) **(61)**(*37*) (*CAHorgan*) 5-8-10 WWoods(11) (b.hind: a bhd) 2½ 12

3/1 Southern Power (IRE), **5/1** SON OF SHARP SHOT (IRE), **6/1** Un Parfum de Femme (IRE), **7/1** Hill Farm Dancer, Total Joy (IRE) (6/1-10/1), **9/1** Pistol (IRE), **11/1** Shoofk, **14/1** Power, Midnight Jazz (IRE), **16/1** Conic Hill (IRE), Awesome Power, **33/1** Tony's Mist, CSF £39.49 CT £115.72 TOTE £4.50: £1.70 £2.00 £1.80 (£12.80) Trio £6.90 OWNER Windflower Overseas Holdings Inc (ARUNDEL) BRED Windflower Overseas 12 Rn
2m 18.1 (4.60) SF: 41/11/38/12/11/23/11/19/22/11/12/-

654

JETCASH DASH CLAIMING STKS (3-Y.O) (Class E) £3,318.75 (£990.00: £472.50: £213.75) **1m 4f 115y** Stalls: Low GOING minus 0.40 sec per fur (F) 4-05 (4-08)

509[3] **Peter Monamy** (*70*) (*PFICole*) 3-8-13 JReid(6) (unruly s: a.p: led 4f out: hrd rdn over 1f out: r.o wl) — 1
339[3] Recovery Lad (IRE) (*61*) (*KRBurke*) 3-8-2 (3) DRMcCabe(1) (hld up: hdwy over 4f out: 3rd st: hung lft & ev ch fnl 2f: nt r.o) 1 2
575[3] Durgams First (IRE) **(60)**(*68*) (*MrsMReveley*) 3-8-13 JWeaver(3) (lw: hld up & bhd: stdy hdwy 5f out: 2nd st: rdn & ev ch whn edgd rt over 1f out: nt qckn) ½ 3
529[5] Star Fighter **(60)**(*49*) (*WAO'Gorman*) 3-8-7 EmmaO'Gorman(8) (a.p: led 6f out to 4f out: 4th st: wknd 2f out) 10 4

*530*5 Hever Golf Lady **(43)***(37) (TJNaughton)* 3-8-0 GBardwell(7) (b.hind: hld up & bhd: nvr nr ldrs) 4 5
*509*4 Roadsweeper (FR) *(48) (KOCunningham-Brown)* 3-8-13 MRimmer(5) (dwlt: hdwy & 5th st: wknd 2f out) 2 6
Darius The Great (IRE) *(31) (DMarks)* 3-7-12 (5) MBaird(12) (lt-f: bkwd: s.s: a bhd) 5 7
Calling Jamaica **(58)***(30) (MCPipe)* 3-8-2 PaulEddery(10) (led 2f: lost pl & 6th st: eased whn btn over 1f out) ....s.h 8
Backview *(40) (BJLlewellyn)* 3-8-13 RPrice(2) (neat: prom over 6f) 1 9
526 14 Pewter Lass **(60)***(19) (MBlanshard)* 3-7-11 (7)ow6 SMcCarthy(4) (hdwy 4f out: 7th & wkng st) 5 10
5847 Emnala (IRE) **(58)***(17) (MRChannon)* 3-8-2 CRutter(9) (hld up: hdwy 5f out: wknd 4f out) 4 11
Smiling Thru *(22)*(Fav)*(HRACecil)* 3-8-13 AMcGlone(11) (led after 2f: hdd 6f out: wknd over 4f out) 5 12

3/1 Smiling Thru, **100/30** Durgams First (IRE), **4/1** Calling Jamaica, **8/1** PETER MONAMY (6/1-9/1), **9/1** Emnala (IRE), **11/1** Hever Golf Lady, **12/1** Pewter Lass, Recovery Lad (IRE), Star Fighter, **25/1** Roadsweeper (FR), **33/1** Darius The Great (IRE), Backview, CSF £96.62 TOTE £9.60: £2.80 £3.60 £1.50 (£81.70) Trio £44.20 OWNER Richard Green (Fine Paintings) Ltd (WHATCOMBE) BRED R. Green 12 Rn
2m 45.2 (7.70) SF: 18/9/16/-/-/-/-/-/-/-/-/-
Peter Monamy clmd M Pipe £10,000

655 BRYANT HOMES LIMITED STKS (0-70) (3-Y.O) (Class E) £3,172.50 (£945.00: £450.00: £202.50)
1m 4f 115y Stalls: Low GOING minus 0.40 sec per fur (F) 4-35 (4-37)

538 3 **Toy Princess (USA) (70)***(70) (CEBrittain)* 3-8-6 MRimmer(7) (lw: chsd ldr: 2nd st: rdn 2f out: r.o to ld last strides) ....— 1
537* Executive Design **(78)***(77)*(Fav)*(MrsMReveley)* 3-8-13 JWeaver(3) (lw: hld up: stdy hdwy 5f out: carried wd & 6th st: ev ch whn wandered over 1f out & ins fnl f: r.o wl cl home) ....hd 2
*241*9 Tonka **(62)***(75) (DJGMurraySmith)* 3-8-7 (5)ow1 RPainter(6) (plld hrd: a.p: 3rd st: led 2f out: hrd rdn & hdd last strides) ....s.h 3
Vizard (IRE) **(70)***(70) (MJHeaton-Ellis)* 3-8-11b PaulEddery(5) (plld hrd: chsd ldrs: 4th st: ev ch over 1f out: wknd ins fnl f) 3½ 4
525 3 Amercius **(48)***(63) (RHannon)* 3-8-11b RPerham(2) (a.p: rdn to ld over 4f out: hdd 2f out: eased whn btn ins fnl f) 6 5
525* Doddington Flyer **(62)***(57) (RHollinshead)* 3-8-13 JReid(4) (hmpd s: hdwy 4f out: hung rt & 5th st: wkng whn hung lft over 1f out) 6 6
*566*2 Persian Conquest (IRE) **(68)** *(RIngram)* 3-8-13b WWoods(1) (lw: led 8f: 7th & wkng st: eased whn btn fnl 2f: t.o) ....dist 7

4/7 Executive Design (Evens-8/15), **11/2** TOY PRINCESS (USA), **7/1** Doddington Flyer, **8/1** Persian Conquest (IRE), **12/1** Vizard (IRE), **20/1** Amercius, Tonka, CSF £9.32 TOTE £5.20: £2.50 £1.10 (£3.20) OWNER Mr C. E. Brittain (NEWMARKET) BRED Northmore Stud 7 Rn
2m 45.4 (7.90) SF: 11/18/16/11/4/-/-

656 HENRY VIII H'CAP (0-70) (3-Y.O+) (Class E) £3,494.25 (£1,044.00: £499.50: £227.25) **5f** Stalls: Low GOING minus 0.40 sec per fur (F) 5-05 (5-11)

583 5 **Halliard (55)***(62) (TMJones)* 4-8-13 RPerham(1) (a.p: led over 2f out: clr over 1f out: drvn out) ....— 1
507 6 Grand Time **(35)***(34) (CJHill)* 6-7-2b(5) MBaird(9) (s.i.s: hdwy & hung lft over 1f out: plld out, edgd lft & r.o wl ins fnl f) 2½ 2
*498** Spender **(70)***(66)*(Fav)*(PWHarris)* 6-10-0 PaulEddery(7) (a.p: hrd rdn over 2f out: r.o one pce) 1 3
507 2 Grey Charmer (IRE) **(58)***(50) (CJames)* 6-9-2 WNewnes(8) (hdwy over 1f out: r.o ins fnl f) 1¼ 4
507 12 Petraco (IRE) **(58)***(47) (NASmith)* 7-9-2 MRimmer(10) (no hdwy fnl 2f) ....¾ 5
Windrush Boy **(60)***(49) (JRBosley)* 5-9-4 JReid(11) (led over 2f: wknd ins fnl f) ....s.h 6
John O'Dreams **(55)***(41) (MrsALMKing)* 10-8-8 (5) AGarth(12) (b: rdr lost irons s: sn rcvrd: wknd ins fnl f) 1 7
*328*3 Tee-Emm **(45)***(28) (PHowling)* 5-8-3 WWoods(5) (prom over 3f: eased whn btn ins fnl f) 1 8
Kensington Freight **(50)***(28) (JAkehurst)* 3-7-11 GBardwell(3) (dwlt: a bhd) 1½ 9
*233*16 Northgate Raver **(40)** *(RonaldThompson)* 4-7-5 (7)ow5 CAdamson(2) (bhd fnl 2f) 5 10
Kangra Valley **(51)***(7) (TRWatson)* 4-8-9 NCarlisle(6) (b: a bhd) 2 11
LONG HANDICAP Northgate Raver 6-11

100/30 Spender, **4/1** Grey Charmer (IRE), **5/1** Tee-Emm, **11/2** Grand Time (op 7/2), **8/1** Windrush Boy, **10/1** HALLIARD, **14/1** John O'Dreams, **16/1** Petraco (IRE), **20/1** Kensington Freight, Kangra Valley, **50/1** Northgate Raver, CSF £59.73 CT £204.62 TOTE £12.80: £3.30 £2.00 £1.60 (£38.30) Trio £237.20 OWNER The Rest Hill Partnership (GUILDFORD) BRED Mrs J. Brookes 11 Rn
58.5 secs (0.50) SF: 44/16/48/32/29/31/23/10/-/-/-
WEIGHT FOR AGE 3yo-11lb
T/Plpt: £345.40 (17.83 Tckts). T/Qdpt: £19.30 (3 Tckts). KH

NEWMARKET (R-H)
Tuesday April 18th (Good to firm)
WEATHER: overcast WIND: mod half bhd

657
CONSTANT SECURITY MAIDEN STKS (3-Y.O) (Class D) £5,117.00 (£1,526.00: £728.00: £329.00)
1m 4f (Rowley) Stalls: High GOING minus 0.37 sec per fur (F) 2-00 (2-02)

Sebastian *(95+)*(Fav)*(HRACecil)* 3-9-0 WRyan(2) (gd sort: s.i.s: sn rcvrd: led wl over 2f out: rdn & r.o wl fnl f) — 1
Royal Scimitar (USA) **(104)***(95) (PFICole)* 3-9-0 TQuinn(6) (trckd ldrs: led 3f out: sn hdd: rallied ins fnl f: r.o wl) s.h 2
General Assembly (IRE) *(91) (HRACecil)* 3-9-0 AMcGlone(7) (wl grwn: bkwd: s.i.s: hdwy 5f out: styd on: nt pce to chal) 3 3
Anchor Clever *(84) (PAKelleway)* 3-9-0 JWeaver(10) (leggy: scope: led tl hdd 3f out: one pce) 5 4
Foresworn (USA) *(76) (MrsJCecil)* 3-9-0 PaulEddery(12) (w'like: scope: in tch: shkn up over 4f out: styd on one pce) 6 5
Torch Vert (IRE) *(73) (BWHills)* 3-9-0 RHills(5) (trckd ldr tl wknd fnl 3f) 2½ 6
Solatium (IRE) *(64) (JHMGosden)* 3-9-0 LDettori(3) (lw: in tch: outpcd 4f out: n.d after) 7 7
539[12] Cross Talk (IRE) *(59) (RHollinshead)* 3-9-0 TIves(9) (bhd tl sme late hdwy) 3½ 8
484[4] Blue Smoke (IRE) *(57) (BAMcMahon)* 3-9-0 KFallon(11) (nvr trbld ldrs) 1¾ 9
Vaugrenier (IRE) *(57) (RHannon)* 3-9-0 PatEddery(4) (h.d.w: cl up tl wknd wl over 2f out) s.h 10
428[3] Astrolabe *(53) (BWHills)* 3-9-0 MHills(1) (lw: trckd ldrs tl wknd 3f out) 2½ 11
Shawahin *(JLDunlop)* 3-9-0 WCarson(8) (a outpcd & bhd) dist 12

6/5 SEBASTIAN (Evens-11/8), **4/1** Royal Scimitar (USA) (op 9/4), **8/1** Vaugrenier (IRE), **10/1** Astrolabe (7/1-12/1), **12/1** Solatium (IRE) (8/1-14/1), **14/1** Foresworn (USA), Shawahin, **20/1** Anchor Clever, General Assembly (IRE), **25/1** Torch Vert (IRE), **33/1** Blue Smoke (IRE), **50/1** Cross Talk (IRE), CSF £6.82 TOTE £2.20: £1.20 £1.50 £7.00 (£3.70) Trio £28.60 OWNER Lord Howard de Walden (NEWMARKET) BRED Lord Howard de Walden 12 Rn
2m 31.85 (2.55) SF: 52/52/48/41/33/30/21/16/14/14/10/-
OFFICIAL EXPLANATION **Shawahin: no explanation offered.**

658
RACING & FOOTBALL OUTLOOK MAIDEN STKS (3-Y.O) (Class D) £5,208.00 (£1,554.00: £742.00: £336.00)
6f (Rowley) Stalls: High GOING minus 0.37 sec per fur (F) 2-35 (2-36)

Magnificent Devil (USA) *(87) (JWWatts)* 3-9-0 BThomson(9) (lw: trckd ldrs: smooth hdwy to ld 1f out: qcknd clr: comf) — 1
Twice as Sharp **(85)***(80) (PWHarris)* 3-9-0 PatEddery(3) (h.d.w: led tl hdd 1f out: kpt on same pce) 2½ 2
Alarming *(73)*(Fav)*(JHMGosden)* 3-8-9 LDettori(4) (w ldrs: chal 2f out: no ex fnl f) ¾ 3
Double Matt (IRE) *(72) (RHannon)* 3-9-0 JReid(10) (in tch: styd on wl fnl 2f: nvr rchd ldrs) 2½ 4
Bedouin Invader *(69) (MRStoute)* 3-9-0 WRSwinburn(12) (h.d.w: in tch: sme hdwy 2f out: nvr nr to chal) 1 5
Mutabassim (IRE) *(66) (ACStewart)* 3-9-0 WCarson(1) (cl up tl wknd appr fnl f) 1¼ 6
442[16] Hot Snap *(65) (CFWall)* 3-9-0 GDuffield(11) (bkwd: bhd tl sme late hdwy) nk 7
522[5] Fairy Wind (IRE) *(58) (NACallaghan)* 3-8-9 RCochrane(2) (b: s.i.s: stdy hdwy 2f out: nvr plcd to chal) ¾ 8
Distant Princess *(58) (BWHills)* 3-8-9 MHills(5) (s.i.s: n.d) s.h 9
Mister Rm *(63) (RGuest)* 3-9-0 KFallon(6) (s.i.s: shkn up over 2f out: sme late hdwy) hd 10
Sooty (IRE) *(47) (HThomsonJones)* 3-8-9 RHills(7) (prom over 4f: eased whn btn) 4 11
Mousehole *(41) (RGuest)* 3-9-0 WWoods(8) (bhd fr ½-wy) 4 12

11/4 Alarming, **100/30** Twice as Sharp, **7/1** Double Matt (IRE), **15/2** MAGNIFICENT DEVIL (USA), **10/1** Fairy Wind (IRE) (6/1-12/1), Mutabassim (IRE), **12/1** Bedouin Invader (op 8/1), **25/1** Distant Princess, Sooty (IRE), **40/1** Hot Snap, Mister Rm, Mousehole, CSF £29.52 TOTE £9.50: £2.40 £1.40 £1.70 (£18.20) Trio £31.80 OWNER Mr Joe Allbritton (RICHMOND) BRED Lazy Lane Stables Inc. 12 Rn 1m 13.11 (1.81) SF: 42/35/28/27/24/21/20/13/13/18/2/-

659

ABERNANT STKS (Listed) (3-Y.O+) (Class A) £12,034.80
(£4,453.20: £2,136.60: £873.00: £346.50: £135.90)
6f (Rowley) Stalls: Centre GOING minus 0.37 sec per fur (F) 3-05 (3-05)

Lake Coniston (IRE) (117)*(120)*(Fav)*(GLewis)* 4-9-8 PatEddery(11) (lw: trckd ldrs: led 2f out: sn clr) — 1
272* Triple Joy **(84)***(100) (SirMarkPrescott)* 4-8-11 GDuffield(10) (a.p: effrt ½-wy: styd on wl: no ch w wnr) 3½ 2
441* Montendre **(103)***(108) (MMcCormack)* 8-9-6 MJKinane(4) (prom: hdwy u.p over 2f out: no imp) nk 3
Tajannub (USA) **(109)***(105) (RWArmstrong)* 3-8-5 WCarson(6) (a chsng ldrs: kpt on u.p fnl 2f) s.h 4
441⁴ Hard to Figure **(104)***(101) (RJHodges)* 9-9-6 RCochrane(5) (bhd tl styd on fnl 2f) 2½ 5
571¹² Welsh Mist **(97)***(87) (RBoss)* 4-9-1 WRyan(7) (chsd ldrs: rdn ½-wy: one pce) 3½ 6
441³ Double Blue **(104)***(85) (MJohnston)* 6-9-6 DHolland(1) (lw: chsd ldrs: rdn over 2f out: sn btn) 2½ 7
571³ Branston Abby (IRE) **(105)***(73) (MJohnston)* 6-9-1 JReid(2) (nvr nr to chal) 2½ 8
Windmachine (SWE) *(71) (BjoernOlsen,Norway)* 4-9-1 YvonneDurant(8) (b: wl grwn: led 4f: wknd qckly) ¾ 9
441⁷ Amron **(94)***(72) (JBerry)* 8-9-6 NCarlisle(9) (dwlt: nvr wnt pce) 1¾ 10
Cim Bom Bom (IRE) **(99)***(64) (MBell)* 3-8-4 MFenton(3) (nvr plcd to chal) 1¼ 11

7/4 LAKE CONISTON (IRE), **13/2** Double Blue, **8/1** Triple Joy (11/2-9/1), **9/1** Branston Abby (IRE) (6/1-10/1), **10/1** Montendre (7/1-12/1), **12/1** Hard to Figure (op 8/1), **14/1** Tajannub (USA) (12/1-20/1), **20/1** Windmachine (SWE), **25/1** Cim Bom Bom (IRE), **33/1** Amron, Welsh Mist, CSF £13.80 TOTE £2.50: £1.30 £2.60 £2.90 (£15.80) Trio £47.20 OWNER Highclere Thoroughbred Racing Ltd (EPSOM) BRED J. P. McManus 11 Rn
1m 10.25 (0.41 under best) (-1.05) SF: 90/70/78/63/71/57/55/43/41/42/22
WEIGHT FOR AGE 3yo-12lb

660

SHADWELL STUD NELL GWYN STKS (Gp 3) (3-Y.O F) (Class A)
£22,589.00 (£8,351.00: £4,000.50: £1,627.50: £638.75: £243.25)
7f (Rowley) Stalls: Centre GOING minus 0.37 sec per fur (F) 3-40 (3-40)

Myself (111)*(106+) (PWChapple-Hyam)* 3-8-9 JReid(9) (lw: b.hind: hld up: stdy hdwy 2f out: led appr fnl f: qcknd: comf) — 1
Epagris *(100)*(Fav)*(HRACecil)* 3-8-9 WRyan(1) (lw: hld up & bhd: gd hdwy to chal 2f out: kpt on wl fnl f) 2½ 2
Red Carnival (USA) *(102) (MRStoute)* 3-8-12 WRSwinburn(5) (h.d.w: trckd ldrs: led & qcknd 2f out: hdd appr fnl f: no ex) ½ 3
Germane **(105)***(98) (MBell)* 3-8-12 MFenton(3) (trckd ldrs: effrt over 2f out: r.o one pce) 2 4
With the Fairies **(85)***(89) (RHannon)* 3-8-9 MJKinane(6) (h.d.w: led 1½f: cl up tl outpcd fnl 2f) 2½ 5
Dashing Water **(98)***(85) (IABalding)* 3-8-9 LDettori(2) (unf: chsd ldr tl outpcd fnl 2f) 1½ 6
Trimming (IRE) *(83) (JHMGosden)* 3-8-9 PatEddery(8) (b.hind: hld up: stdy hdwy ½-wy: shkn up 2f out: sn btn) 1 7
551² Paris Babe *(81) (DMorris)* 3-8-9 GDuffield(7) (led after 1½f to 2f out: n.m.r & sn lost pl) ¾ 8

9/4 Epagris, **5/2** Red Carnival (USA) (7/4-11/4), **5/1** MYSELF, **7/1** Trimming (IRE), **10/1** Germane, **12/1** With the Fairies, **25/1** Dashing Water, **33/1** Paris Babe, CSF £15.44 TOTE £5.80: £1.50 £1.60 £1.50 (£10.90) Trio £7.30 OWNER Bloomsbury Stud (MARLBOROUGH) BRED Bloomsbury Stud 8 Rn
1m 24.34 (0.64) SF: 55/49/51/47/38/34/32/30

OFFICIAL EXPLANATION **Paris Babe: the jockey reported that she had appeared to lose her action at the furlong pole. The vet and trainer confirmed that she had knocked her off-hind.**

661

NGK SPARK PLUGS SWAFFHAM H'CAP (0-90) (4-Y.O+) (Class C)
£8,155.00 (£2,440.00: £1,170.00: £535.00)
1m 6f (Rowley) Stalls: High GOING minus 0.37 sec per fur (F) 4-15 (4-15)

Tudor Island (73)*(86) (CEBrittain)* 6-8-11 MRimmer(9) (chsd ldrs: led over 3f out: all out) — 1
Thunderheart **(75)***(87) (LMCumani)* 4-8-11 LDettori(5) (bit bkwd: in tch: hdwy 5f out: kpt on fnl 2f) 1 2
Well Beloved **(79)***(91) (HRACecil)* 4-9-1 WRyan(13) (lw: bhd tl styd on strly fnl 3f: gng on fin) s.h 3
506¹² Polo Kit (IRE) **(79)***(89) (JRFanshawe)* 4-9-1 DHarrison(11) (lw: hdwy 5f out: chsng ldrs 2f out: kpt on) 1¼ 4

423[6] Top Cees **(71)***(81)*(Fav)*(MrsJRRamsden)* 5-8-9 KFallon(12) (hld up & bhd: stdy hdwy 4f out: nt clr run 2f out: nvr plcd to chal)........hd **5**
Island Blade (IRE) **(59)***(68) (RAkehurst)* 6-7-11 JQuinn(7) (a.p: rdn & ev ch over 2f out: hmpd over 1f out: sn btn)........¾ **6**
Sword Master **(70)***(73) (BobJones)* 6-8-8 RCochrane(6) (b: styd on fnl 4f: nvr trbld ldrs)........6 **7**
Microlite (USA) **(73)***(69) (MDHammond)* 4-8-9b TQuinn(16) (chsd ldrs: n.m.r 3f out: sn wknd)........6 **8**
545[4] Head Turner **(55)***(47) (CPWildman)* 7-7-7 NAdams(1) (nvr rchd ldrs)........3½ **9**
Not in Doubt (USA) **(90)***(81) (HCandy)* 6-10-0 WNewnes(4) (lw: hdwy 6f out: sn prom: wknd over 2f out)........¾ **10**
Trans Siberia **(80)***(71) (SPCWoods)* 4-9-2 WWoods(3) (h.d.w: hld up: hdwy 5f out: ev ch over 3f out: wknd over 2f out)........s.h **11**
Simafar (IRE) **(80)***(70) (NAGraham)* 4-9-2 PatEddery(8) (nvr trbld ldrs)........¾ **12**
Rumi **(77)***(60) (CREgerton)* 4-8-13 BThomson(10) (trckd ldrs: effrt 4f out: wknd over 2f out)........6 **13**
556[5] Guards Brigade **(57)***(17) (JHetherton)* 4-7-7 NKennedy(14) (led tl hdd 5f out: sn wknd)........20 **14**
506[13] Chimanimani **(78)***(37) (NTinkler)* 4-9-0 GDuffield(2) (a bhd)........¾ **15**
440[4] Dreams End **(86)***(45) (BJLlewellyn)* 7-9-10 JWeaver(15) (b: chsd ldrs: led 5f out tl over 3f out: sn wknd)........nk **16**
LONG HANDICAP Guards Brigade 6-11 Head Turner 6-13

5/1 Top Cees, **7/1** TUDOR ISLAND, Trans Siberia, **9/1** Well Beloved, Dreams End, Island Blade (IRE), **10/1** Thunderheart, **12/1** Polo Kit (IRE), **14/1** Simafar (IRE), **16/1** Chimanimani, **20/1** Microlite (USA), Rumi, **25/1** Head Turner, Not in Doubt (USA), **33/1** Sword Master, **50/1** Guards Brigade, CSF £68.91 CT £585.05 TOTE £7.90: £2.30 £2.40 £2.30 £3.00 (£55.50) Trio £127.50 OWNER Mr D. Sieff (NEWMARKET) BRED David Sieff 16 Rn
2m 59.52 (3.52) SF: 46/45/49/47/41/28/33/27/7/41/29/28/18/-/-/5
WEIGHT FOR AGE 4yo-2lb

OFFICIAL EXPLANATION **Dreams End: the trainer reported that the gelding lost his action coming down the hill and has also had leg trouble in the past.**
Top Cees: the jockey reported that he'd been ordered to hold the horse up but was unable to find room to make a challenge in the latter stages. A routine test was ordered.

662

CHRIS BLACKWELL MEMORIAL H'CAP (0-95) (3-Y.O) (Class C)
£5,952.00 (£1,776.00: £848.00: £384.00)
7f (Rowley) Stalls: High GOING minus 0.37 sec per fur (F) 4-45 (4-46)

Iblis (IRE) (80)*(94) (GWragg)* 3-8-6 MHills(2) (hld up: stdy hdwy to ld wl over 1f out: shkn up & qcknd)........— **1**
Noble Kingdom **(84)***(84) (RAkehurst)* 3-8-10 TQuinn(1) (lw: plld hrd: cl up: led 4f out tl wl over 1f out: no ch w wnr)........6 **2**
Otterbourne (IRE) **(86)***(81)*(Fav)*(JHMGosden)* 3-8-12 LDettori(8) (cl up far side: chal 2f out: r.o one pce)........2½ **3**
Jawlaat (USA) **(80)***(70) (JLDunlop)* 3-8-6 WCarson(7) (cl up far side: rdn & nt qckn fnl 2f)........2 **4**
Axeman (IRE) **(95)***(83) (RHannon)* 3-9-7 PatEddery(4) (lw: led 3f: grad wknd fnl 2f)........¾ **5**
Singing Rock (IRE) **(70)***(58) (RHannon)* 3-7-10 TWilliams(3) (in tch: effrt over 2f out: r.o one pce)........hd **6**
Sue's Return **(88)***(76) (APJarvis)* 3-9-0 BThomson(11) (cl up far side tl rdn & btn wl over 1f out)........s.h **7**
Iltimas (USA) **(88)***(75) (PTWalwyn)* 3-9-0 RHills(5) (chsd ldrs tl wknd fnl 2f)........½ **8**
572[7] Fame Again **(75)***(55) (MrsJRRamsden)* 3-8-1 DHarrison(6) (in tch far side: rdn over 2f out: no imp)........3 **9**
437[2] Tiler (IRE) **(88)***(59)*(Fav)*(MJohnston)* 3-9-0 DHolland(9) (hld up far side: effrt over 2f out: rdn & no imp)........4 **10**
Miss Mercy (IRE) **(69)***(34) (CNAllen)* 3-7-9 ow2 JQuinn(10) (outpcd far side fnl 2f)........1½ **11**

7/2 Tiler (IRE), Otterbourne (IRE), **6/1** IBLIS (IRE), **13/2** Jawlaat (USA), **7/1** Fame Again, **9/1** Axeman (IRE), **10/1** Noble Kingdom, Iltimas (USA) (7/1-12/1), **25/1** Sue's Return, **33/1** Singing Rock (IRE), Miss Mercy (IRE), CSF £60.08 CT £220.68 TOTE £5.70: £2.20 £4.20 £1.60 (£79.00) Trio £130.10 OWNER Mrs Nicola Bscher (NEWMARKET) 11 Rn
1m 23.53 (-0.17) SF: 62/52/49/38/51/26/44/43/23/27/2

663

MUSEUM MAIDEN STKS (3-Y.O) (Class D) £5,390.00 (£1,610.00: £770.00: £350.00) **1m 2f (Rowley)** Stalls: High GOING minus 0.37 sec (F) 5-20 (5-21)

Burning (USA) *(91) (GHarwood)* 3-9-0 MHills(10) (hld up & bhd: smooth hdwy to ld over 1f out: r.o)........— **1**

438⁹ Luso *(91) (CEBrittain)* 3-9-0 BDoyle(1) (in tch: hdwy & ev ch 2f out: r.o u.p fnl f) ....nk **2**
Prussian Blue (USA) *(90) (HRACecil)* 3-9-0 WRyan(6) (a cl up: chal 2f out: r.o u.p fnl f) ....nk **3**
Sanmartino (IRE) *(86) (BWHills)* 3-9-0 PatEddery(8) (wl grwn: bit bkwd: trckd ldrs: hdwy u.p & ev ch over 1f out: sn btn) 2½ **4**
Mezaan (IRE) *(81) (MRStoute)* 3-9-0 WRSwinburn(9) (lw: led: qcknd 3f out: hdd & wknd over 1f out) 3 **5**
Okavango (USA) *(79) (JHMGosden)* 3-9-0 LDettori(5) (lw: trckd ldr: styd on fnl f) 1¼ **6**
Nine Barrow Down (IRE) *(78) (HRACecil)* 3-9-0 AMcGlone(12) (cl up: disp ld over 3f out tl wknd over 2f out) 1 **7**
Birthday Boy (IRE) *(75) (RHannon)* 3-9-0 TQuinn(13) (h.d.w: in tch: pushed along 4f out: no imp) 1¾ **8**
San Pietra (IRE) *(69)*(Fav)*(PWChapple-Hyam)* 3-8-9 JReid(3) (leggy: scope: hld up: shkn up 3f out: rn green: n.d) ....nk **9**
Coburg *(72) (HRACecil)* 3-9-0 MJKinane(2) (gd sort: a bhd) 1¾ **10**
504⁶ Komodo (USA) **(68)***(62) (DRCElsworth)* 3-9-0 DHarrison(11) (nvr trbld ldrs) 6 **11**
Chalk Circle (IRE) *(61) (JHMGosden)* 3-9-0 JCarroll(4) (cmpt: scope: a outpcd & bhd) ....¾ **12**
Snow Valley *(61) (LMCumani)* 3-8-11 (3) CHodgson(7) (a bhd) ....s.h **13**

5/2 San Pietra (IRE), **9/2** Sanmartino (IRE) (2/1-5/1), Mezaan (IRE) (2/1-7/1), **6/1** Prussian Blue (USA), Okavango (USA) (3/1-8/1), **10/1** Coburg (5/1-12/1), **14/1** Nine Barrow Down (IRE) (6/1-16/1), **16/1** BURNING (USA), **25/1** Luso, **33/1** Chalk Circle (IRE), **50/1** Birthday Boy (IRE), Komodo (USA), Snow Valley, CSF £313.07 TOTE £32.30: £3.60 £5.60 £2.20 (£169.50) Trio £626.00; £617.25 to 4.15 Newmarket 19/04/95 OWNER Mr Khalifa Dasmal (PULBOROUGH) BRED Mill Ridge Farm Ltd
13 Rn 2m 4.16 (1.56) SF: 55/55/54/50/45/43/42/39/33/36/26/25/25

T/Jpkt: £43,830.90 (0.19 Tckts); £50,004.30 to Newmarket 19/4/95. T/Plpt: £23.30 (1,589.56 Tckts). T/Qdpt: £31.10 (9.25 Tckts). AA

0657-NEWMARKET (R-H)
Wednesday April 19th (Good to firm)
WEATHER: sunny WIND: almost nil races 1-4, rest fresh half bhd

664

GEOFFREY BARLING MAIDEN STKS (3-Y.O F) (Class D) £5,253.50 (£1,568.00: £749.00: £339.50)
7f (Rowley) Stalls: High GOING minus 0.34 sec per fur (GF) 2-00 (2-05)

Warning Shadows (IRE) *(91) (CEBrittain)* 3-8-11 BDoyle(8) (w'like: hmpd st: swtchd lft ½-way: hdwy to ld wl ins fnl f) ....— **1**
Tinashaan (IRE) *(88) (JRFanshawe)* 3-8-11 DHarrison(11) (w'like: scope: bkwd: a.p: slt ld over 1f out: rdn & ct wl ins fnl f) 1½ **2**
Dream Ticket (USA) *(88) (MRStoute)* 3-8-11 WRSwinburn(3) (hld up: effrt over 2f out: kpt on wl ins fnl f) ....s.h **3**
Avignon (IRE) *(87)*(Fav)*(PWChapple-Hyam)* 3-8-11 JReid(4) (led 3f: styd on u.p wl ins fnl f) ....s.h **4**
Vena (IRE) **(100)***(87)*(Fav)*(JLDunlop)* 3-8-11 PatEddery(1) (led after 3f tl appr fnl f: rallied u.p cl home) ....nk **5**
Persian Butterfly *(86) (JEBanks)* 3-8-11 JQuinn(7) (leggy: scope: hdwy over 2f out: hung rt bel dist: styd on nr fin) ....hd **6**
Merry Festival (USA) *(86) (JHMGosden)* 3-8-11 LDettori(6) (w'like: leggy: prom: ev ch over 1f out: checked & eased nr fin) ....nk **7**
Miss Haversham *(82) (CACyzer)* 3-8-11 KFallon(10) (w'like: str: w ldrs tl out pcd over 2f out: effrt & carried rt ins fnl f: nt rcvr) 1½ **8**
Jurassic Sue *(74) (BWHills)* 3-8-11 MHills(9) (a in rr) 3½ **9**
Anna-Jane *(68) (RHannon)* 3-8-11 TQuinn(2) (prom 5f: sn rdn & outpcd) 3 **10**
418⁸ Bellateena *(62) (HJCollingridge)* 3-8-11 MRimmer(5) (a in rr) 2½ **11**
Kewaashi (USA) *(56) (LMCumani)* 3-8-11 MJKinane(12) (unf: hld up: effrt whn hmpd wl over 1f out: eased whn btn) 2½ **12**

5/1 Avignon (IRE) (op 5/2), Vena (IRE) (op 5/2), **6/1** Miss Haversham (8/1-14/1), Merry Festival (USA) (3/1-13/2), **13/2** Kewaashi (USA), **7/1** WARNING SHADOWS (IRE), Dream Ticket (USA) (5/1-8/1), **16/1** Tinashaan (IRE), Jurassic Sue, Anna-Jane, **33/1** Persian Butterfly, **100/1** Bellateena, CSF £100.51 TOTE £15.30: £3.10 £7.00 £2.30 (£150.40) Trio £297.50 OWNER Sheikh Marwan Al Maktoum (NEWMARKET) BRED Sheikh Marwan al Maktoum 12 Rn
1m 26.55 (2.85) SF: 34/31/31/30/30/29/29/25/17/11/5/-
STEWARDS' ENQUIRY J.Quinn suspended 28-29/4/95 & 1-2/5/95 (irresponsible riding).

665

BOADICEA RATED STKS H'CAP (0-105) (4-Y.O+) (Class B)
£9,174.36 (£3,399.24: £1,634.62: £672.10: £271.05: £110.63)
7f (Rowley) Stalls: High GOING minus 0.34 sec per fur (GF) 2-35 (2-40)

Governor George (USA) (100)*(110)*(Fav)*(JLDunlop)* 4-9-4 PatEddery(4) (lw: hld up stands' side: hdwy 2f out: str run to ld cl home)........— 1
Classic Sky (IRE) **(97)***(107) (BHanbury)* 4-9-1 RHills(17) (chsd ldrs far side: led bel dist tl ct nr fin)........hd 2
Belfry Green (IRE) **(94)***(104) (CAHorgan)* 5-8-12 WWoods(11) (s.s: gd hdwy 2f out: chal ins fnl f: r.o)........hd 3
439[11] Castel Rosselo **(86)***(86) (BJMcMath)* 5-8-4 AMackay(20) (in tch far side: kpt on appr fnl f: nt pce to chal)........4 4
Gymcrak Premiere **(90)***(89) (GHolmes)* 7-8-8 KFallon(19) (b.hind: hld up: hdwy appr fnl f: fin wl)........½ 5
Moccasin Run (USA) **(103)***(101) (IABalding)* 4-9-7 LDettori(10) (lw: chsd ldrs far side: rdn & one pce appr fnl f)........½ 6
Crazy Paving (IRE) **(90)***(88) (CACyzer)* 4-8-8 JReid(12) (chsd ldrs: rdn 2f out: kpt on)........hd 7
Band on the Run **(88)***(85) (BAMcMahon)* 8-8-6 TQuinn(2) (bit bkwd: racd stands' side: outpcd fnl 2f)........½ 8
439[3] Mr Martini (IRE) **(91)***(86) (CEBrittain)* 5-8-9 MRimmer(9) (lw: prom: rdn ½-way: no imp)........¾ 9
Desert Green (FR) **(86)***(80) (RHannon)* 6-8-4 RPerham(6) (a.p: led stands' side ½-way: outpcd fnl 2f)........nk 10
Caleman **(86)***(80) (RBoss)* 6-8-4 JCarroll(15) (led far side 4f: wknd bel dist)........s.h 11
262[7] My Best Valentine **(86)***(80) (JWhite)* 5-8-1 (3) DWright(21) (nvr trbld ldrs)........hd 12
New Capricorn (USA) **(95)***(86) (MAJarvis)* 5-8-13 PRobinson(8) (chsd ldrs over 5f)........1¼ 13
Calling Collect (USA) **(97)***(88) (LMCumani)* 6-8-12 (3) CHodgson(14) (lw: prom far side: slt ld 3f out tl over 1f out: wknd appr fnl f)........hd 14
Be Warned **(86)***(77) (NACallaghan)* 4-8-4 DHarrison(16) (nvr bttr than mid div)........s.h 15
Saseedo (USA) **(86)***(74) (WAO'Gorman)* 5-8-4 PaulEddery(13) (dwlt: a bhd)........1¼ 16
439[23] Realities (USA) **(102)***(82) (GHarwood)* 5-9-6 MJKinane(1) (lw: led stands' side to ½-way: sn rdn & wknd)........3½ 17
Top Guide (USA) **(90)***(70) (EALDunlop)* 4-8-8 WRSwinburn(18) (b: prom far side 5f)........hd 18
Waikiki Beach (USA) **(97)***(65) (GLMoore)* 4-9-1 BRouse(3) (b.nr hind: racd stands' side: bhd fr ½-wy: t.o)........5 19
Queenbird **(95)***(61) (MJRyan)* 4-8-13 WCarson(7) (bhd fnl 3f: t.o)........1 20
Hello Mister **(101)***(44) (JO'Donoghue)* 4-9-0 (5) PMcCabe(5) (bkwd: swtchd rt st: hld up & bhd: t.o)........10 21

LONG HANDICAP My Best Valentine 8-3 Castel Rosselo 8-2 Be Warned 8-0 Desert Green (FR) 8-3

13/2 GOVERNOR GEORGE (USA), **10/1** Desert Green (FR), Realities (USA), Mr Martini (IRE), **12/1** Crazy Paving (IRE), Top Guide (USA), Saseedo (USA), Castel Rosselo (8/1-14/1), **14/1** Belfry Green (IRE), New Capricorn (USA), **16/1** Caleman, Moccasin Run (USA), **20/1** Band on the Run, Classic Sky (IRE), Gymcrak Premiere, **25/1** Calling Collect (USA), Queenbird, Be Warned, Waikiki Beach (USA), **33/1** My Best Valentine, Hello Mister, CSF £121.17 CT £1,623.92 TOTE £6.50: £2.00 £4.10 £2.90 £1.80 (£76.50) Trio £627.30 OWNER Mr O. Zawawi (ARUNDEL) BRED Warren L. King and Mark Rash in USA 21 Rn

1m 25.2 (1.50) SF: 56/53/50/32/35/47/34/31/32/26/26/26/32/34/23/20/28/16/11/7/-

666

EARL OF SEFTON STKS (Gp 3) (4-Y.O+) (Class A) £21,574.00
(£7,966.00: £3,808.00: £1,540.00: £595.00: £217.00)
1m 1f (Rowley) Stalls: Centre GOING minus 0.34 sec per fur (GF) 3-05 (3-09)

Desert Shot (111)*(114) (MRStoute)* 5-8-10 WRSwinburn(4) (lw: hld up: hdwy 2f out: rdn to ld wl ins f: hld on)........— 1
Overbury (IRE) **(112)***(119)*(Fav)*(DRLoder)* 4-9-1 MJKinane(2) (h.d.w: chsd ldr: led over 2f out: hrd rdn & hdd wl ins fnl f: rallied cl home)........hd 2
425* Airport (USA) **(102)***(105) (JHMGosden)* 4-8-10 LDettori(3) (b.hind: chsd ldng pair: effrt 3f out: styd on one pce fnl f)........5 3
Nicolotte *(102) (GWragg)* 4-8-10 MHills(1) (hld up: hdwy 3f out: rdn & btn appr fnl f)........1½ 4
Fitzrovian (IRE) **(95)***(100) (DRLoder)* 4-8-10 MTebbutt(7) (lw: led over 6f: outpcd appr fnl f)........1¼ 5
425[7] Jafeica (IRE) **(100)***(88) (RHannon)* 4-8-10 PatEddery(5) (sn bhd & pushed along: nvr wnt pce of ldrs)........7 6
Garden of Heaven (USA) **(105)***(86) (CEBrittain)* 6-8-10 MRimmer(6) (chsd ldrs: rdn 3f out: sn btn)........¾ 7

6/4 Overbury (IRE), **5/2** DESERT SHOT, **6/1** Airport (USA) (op 4/1), **7/1** Nicolotte (5/1-8/1), **11/1** Garden of Heaven (USA), **25/1** Jafeica (IRE), **50/1** Fitzrovian (IRE), CSF £6.12 TOTE £3.00: £1.80 £1.30 (£3.50) OWNER Maktoum Al Maktoum (NEWMARKET) BRED The Lavington Stud 7 Rn
1m 48.73 (-0.97) SF: 76/81/67/64/62/50/48

667

EUROPEAN FREE H'CAP (Listed) (3-Y.O) (Class A) £16,425.00
(£6,075.00: £2,912.50: £1,187.50: £468.75: £181.25)
7f (Rowley) Stalls: Centre GOING minus 0.34 sec per fur (GF) 3-40 (3-42)

Diffident (FR) (110)*(116++)*(Fav)*(AFabre,France)* 3-9-5 MJKinane(5) (neat: gd sort: lw: hld up & bhd: hdwy bel dist: shkn up & qcknd to ld wl ins fnl f)......— 1
Harayir (USA) **(112)***(115+) (MajorWRHern)* 3-9-7 WCarson(9) (hld up: hdwy to ld over 1f out: qcknd clr: hdd ins fnl f)......1¼ 2
Citadeed (USA) **(108)***(104) (PWChapple-Hyam)* 3-9-3 PatEddery(1) (lw: a.p: ev ch over 1f out: unable qckn)......3 3
Alami (USA) **(108)***(104) (HThomsonJones)* 3-9-3 RHills(4) (hld up: hdwy & nt clr run 2f out: kpt on fnl f)......nk 4
Inzar (USA) **(108)***(101) (PFICole)* 3-9-3 TQuinn(3) (lw: hld up: swtchd & hdwy 3f out: rdn & one pce appr fnl f)......1¼ 5
Sonic Boy **(108)***(99) (RFJohnsonHoughton)* 3-9-3 MHills(6) (chsd ldr: effrt 3f out: one pce fnl 2f)......¾ 6
Bin Nashwan (USA) **(112)***(102) (CEBrittain)* 3-9-7 WRSwinburn(10) (led tl hdd over 1f out: wknd fnl f)......½ 7
Helmsman (USA) **(110)***(98) (PWChapple-Hyam)* 3-9-5 JReid(12) (prom tl rdn & outpcd appr fnl f)......¾ 8
Be Mindful **(108)***(96) (JRFanshawe)* 3-9-3 DHarrison(2) (hld up & bhd: nvr lcd to chal)......s.h 9
Silca Blanka (IRE) **(109)***(96) (MRChannon)* 3-9-4 RHughes(8) (chsd ldrs tl outpcd fnl 2f)......nk 10
Smart Guest **(104)***(89) (MBell)* 3-8-13 MFenton(7) (a bhd)......1¼ 11
551³ The Jotter **(105)***(86) (WJarvis)* 3-9-0 LDettori(11) (chsd ldrs: rdn along ½-wy: sn btn)......1½ 12

11/10 DIFFIDENT (FR), **9/1** Inzar (USA), Alami (USA), Bin Nashwan (USA), **10/1** Harayir (USA), Helmsman (USA), **16/1** Citadeed (USA), **20/1** The Jotter, **33/1** Smart Guest, **40/1** Sonic Boy, Silca Blanka (IRE), Be Mindful, CSF £12.07 CT £100.27 TOTE £1.80: £1.30 £1.90 £4.90 (£5.50) Trio £51.10 OWNER Sheikh Mohammed (FRANCE) BRED Haras d'Etreham & R Ades in France 12 Rn
1m 22.93 (-0.77) SF: 85/84/73/73/70/68/71/67/65/65/58/55

668

BABRAHAM RACING H'CAP (0-90) (4-Y.O+) (Class C) £6,212.00
(£1,856.00: £888.00: £404.00)
1m 4f (Rowley) Stalls: High GOING minus 0.34 sec per fur (GF) 4-15 (4-22)

485* **Parthian Springs (86)***(103)*(Fav)*(JHMGosden)* 4-10-0 LDettori(10) (lw: hld up in tch: shkn up to ld ins fnl f: pushed clr)......— 1
430* Children's Choice (IRE) **(60)***(74) (PJMcBride)* 4-7-13 (3) DWright(12) (b.off hind: a.p: led over 3f out tl hdd & no ex ins fnl f)......2 2
550⁵ Sharp Falcon (IRE) **(69)***(82) (JWharton)* 4-8-11 JReid(2) (hld up: hdwy over 3f out: one pce fnl f)......1 3
432¹⁴ Pride of May (IRE) **(65)***(73) (RHannon)* 4-8-7b RPerham(13) (rdn & hdwy over 3f out: styd on wl fnl f)......4 4
Riparius (USA) **(78)***(85) (HCandy)* 4-9-6 WNewnes(1) (a.p: ev ch 2f out: wknd fnl f)......nk 5
584² Artic Courier **(76)***(80) (DJSCosgrove)* 4-9-4b MRimmer(6) (prom: rdn over 2f out: kpt on u.p)......2½ 6
423* Achilles Heel **(52)***(56) (CNAllen)* 4-7-8 JQuinn(8) (hld up: hdwy 5f out: ev ch 2f out: wknd appr fnl f)......nk 7
558⁹ Walsham Whisper (IRE) **(77)***(76) (JWharton)* 4-9-5 JWilliams(17) (hld up: hdwy over 2f out: nvr nrr)......3½ 8
Northern Union (CAN) **(80)***(78) (MAJarvis)* 4-9-8 PRobinson(15) (hld up mid div: effrt 2f out: no imp)......¾ 9
545⁵ Beautete **(60)***(54) (SDow)* 4-8-2 ow2 DHarrison(4) (nvr trbld ldrs)......1¼ 10
Lear Dancer (USA) **(66)***(61) (PMitchell)* 4-8-8 MJKinane(7) (prom over 9f)......¾ 11
506¹⁰ Lookingforarainbow (IRE) **(75)***(68) (BobJones)* 7-9-4 MWigham(14) (bhd tl sme late hdwy: n.d)......1½ 12
558³ Retender (USA) **(67)***(60) (MrsJRRamsden)* 6-8-10 KFallon(20) (hld up: hdwy on ins over 3f out: hmpd 2f out: nt rcvr)......½ 13
Rising Spray **(68)***(59) (CAHorgan)* 4-8-10 GHind(16) (s.s: a in rr)......1 14
505¹² Ketabi (USA) **(68)***(58) (RAkehurst)* 4-8-10 TQuinn(19) (hld up: hdwy ½-way: wknd wl over 1f out)......1 15
Silver Hunter (USA) **(78)***(67) (GCBravery)* 4-9-6 MHills(3) (bkwd: n.d)......¾ 16

445[4] Kaafih Homm (IRE) **(68)***(57) (NACallaghan)* 4-8-10 PatEddery(11) (b.hind: mid div tl wknd 3f out).....hd **17**
Faugeron **(73)***(54) (RAkehurst)* 6-9-2 AClark(18) (lw: led: sn clr: hdd over 3f out & wknd qckly: t.o).....6 **18**
Jermyn Street (USA) **(80)***(58) (MrsJCecil)* 4-9-8 PaulEddery(9) (a in rr).....2 **19**
Dusty Point (IRE) **(68)***(33) (JPearce)* 5-8-11 RHills(5) (bhd fnl 4f: t.o).....10 **20**

3/1 PARTHIAN SPRINGS (5/2-4/1), **6/1** Retender (USA), **9/1** Ketabi (USA), **10/1** Northern Union (CAN) (12/1-8/1), Achilles Heel, **12/1** Sharp Falcon (IRE), **14/1** Kaafih Homm (IRE), **16/1** Children's Choice (IRE), **20/1** Lookingforarainbow (IRE), **25/1** Riparius (USA), Beautete, Lear Dancer (USA), Walsham Whisper (IRE), Artic Courier, Dusty Point (IRE), Faugeron, **33/1** Silver Hunter (USA), Jermyn Street (USA), Pride of May (IRE), **50/1** Rising Spray, CSF £48.51 CT £489.09 TOTE £3.90: £1.90 £5.80 £2.30 £13.20 (£107.00) Trio £396.90 OWNER Hesmonds Stud (NEWMARKET) BRED Hesmonds Stud Ltd 20 Rn

2m 31.33 (2.03) SF: 71/42/50/41/53/48/24/44/46/22/29/37/29/27/26/35/25/23/26/2

WEIGHT FOR AGE 4yo-1lb

669 NGK SPARK PLUGS BARTLOW MAIDEN STKS (2-Y.O F) (Class D) £5,117.00 (£1,526.00: £728.00: £329.00)

5f (Rowley) Stalls: High GOING minus 0.34 sec per fur (GF) 4-45 (4-53)

Incarvillea (USA) *(93?t) (DRLoder)* 2-8-11 MJKinane(10) (cmpt: chsd ldrs: rdn bel dist: r.o to ld cl home).....— **1**
Hear The Music (IRE) *(92) (BWHills)* 2-8-11 MHills(3) (leggy: scope: hld up: hdwy on bit to ld over 1f out: hdd cl home).....nk **2**
523[2] Dance of The Moon *(82)*(Fav)*(MBell)* 2-8-11 MFenton(4) (a.p: disp ld ½-way tl over 1f out: rdn & one pce fnl f).....3 **3**
Capture The Moment *(76) (RJRWilliams)* 2-8-11 TQuinn(9) (lt-f: unf: s.i.s: hdwy ½-way: nt qckn appr fnl f).....2 **4**
533[3] Whittle Rock *(72) (EJAlston)* 2-8-11 KFallon(11) (chsd ldrs: rdn & outpcd over 1f out).....1¼ **5**
Lillibella *(71) (IABalding)* 2-8-11 LDettori(6) (neat: prom: disp ld ½-way tl over 1f out: sn outpcd).....nk **6**
Green Bentley (IRE) *(69) (RHannon)* 2-8-11 RPerham(7) (lt-f: unf: b.hind: s.s: a bhd & outpcd).....¾ **7**
Limerick Princess (IRE) *(68) (JBerry)* 2-8-11 JCarroll(1) (neat: unruly s: s.s: jnd ldrs ½-way: wknd wl over 1f out).....hd **8**
561[2] Cyrillic *(64) (PAKelleway)* 2-8-11 MWigham(8) (led far side: wknd over 1f out).....1¼ **9**
Mystic Dawn *(60) (RBoss)* 2-8-11 PatEddery(5) (lt-f: unf: led to ½-way: wknd wl over 1f out).....1¼ **10**
Sound Check *(BJMeehan)* 2-8-11 BDoyle(2) (w'like: s.s: lost action & virtually p.u: t.o).....dist **11**

5/2 Dance of The Moon, **3/1** INCARVILLEA (USA), **11/2** Limerick Princess (IRE) (4/1-6/1), **8/1** Mystic Dawn (10/1-6/1), **10/1** Lillibella (5/1-12/1), Green Bentley (IRE) (8/1-14/1), **12/1** Hear The Music (IRE) (8/1-20/1), **14/1** Whittle Rock, **16/1** Cyrillic, **33/1** Capture The Moment, Sound Check, CSF £37.13 TOTE £3.40: £1.70 £3.00 £1.70 (£26.60) Trio £38.40 OWNER Sheikh Mohammed (NEWMARKET) BRED Darley Stud Management Inc 11 Rn

59.66 secs (0.96) SF: 50/49/39/33/29/28/26/25/21/17/-

670 WOOD DITTON MAIDEN STKS (3-Y.O) (Class D) £5,952.00 (£1,776.00: £848.00: £384.00)

1m (Rowley) Stalls: High GOING minus 0.34 sec per fur (GF) 5-20 (5-23)

Solar Flight *(92t) (BWHills)* 3-9-0 PatEddery(1) (w'like: scope: hmpd s: led after 1f: rdn appr fnl f: styd on strly).....— **1**
Tertium (IRE) *(87t) (PWChapple-Hyam)* 3-9-0 JReid(3) (w'like: scope: chsd ldrs: rdn over 1f out: styd on).....2½ **2**
Kazaki *(86t)*(Fav)*(JHMGosden)* 3-9-0 LDettori(6) (gd sort: b.hind: dwlt: hdwy 3f out: ev ch & rdn 2f out: wandered appr fnl f: nt qckn).....¾ **3**
Prophets Honour *(85t) (CACyzer)* 3-9-0 KFallon(11) (w'like: chsd ldrs: rdn & kpt on appr fnl f).....s.h **4**
Horesti *(83t) (CEBrittain)* 3-9-0 BDoyle(10) (w'like: str: hld up & bhd: shkn up 2f out: r.o wl fnl f).....1¼ **5**
Krystallos *(81t) (RHannon)* 3-9-0 MJKinane(2) (wl grwn: bkwd: swtchd lft st: led 1f: prom tl wknd over 1f out).....¾ **6**
Kutta *(77t) (RWArmstrong)* 3-9-0 WCarson(4) (w'like: bit bkwd: hld up: shkn up 2f out: no imp).....2 **7**
Catercap (IRE) *(73t) (JHMGosden)* 3-9-0 GHind(5) (wl grwn: hld up: hdwy over 3f out: wknd qckly bel dist).....2 **8**

Raayaat (USA) *(67t) (ACStewart)* 3-9-0 RHills(7) (w'like: prom over 5f) 3 9
Md Thompson *(32t) (SCWilliams)* 3-8-6 (3) DWright(9) (leggy: bkwd: a bhd: lost tch 3f out: t.o) 15 10
Farmer's Tern (IRE) *(WJarvis)* 3-8-9 MTebbutt(8) (Withdrawn not under Starter's orders: ref to enter stalls) .... W

, **8/11** Kazaki, **13/2** SOLAR FLIGHT (4/1-7/1), **7/1** Kutta (5/1-8/1), **9/1** Tertium (IRE) (4/1-10/1), **14/1** Horesti (10/1-16/1), Krystallos (8/1-16/1), **16/1** Raayaat (USA), **25/1** Catercap (IRE), **50/1** Prophets Honour, Md Thompson, CSF £58.64 TOTE £5.10: £1.50 £3.00 £1.10 (£30.60) Trio £7.40 OWNER Mr K. Abdullah (LAMBOURN) BRED Juddmonte Farms 10 Rn
1m 38.11 (1.11) SF: 59/54/53/52/50/48/44/40/34/-/-

T/Jkpt £29,087.30 (1.7 Tckts). T/Plpt £210.30 (168.47 Tckts). T/Qdpt £4.50 (43.2 Tckts). IM

PONTEFRACT (L-H)
Wednesday April 19th (Firm becoming Good to firm)

2nd race - snowstorm
WEATHER: fine, snow showers WIND: almost nil

671 STRAWBERRY HILL MEDIAN AUCTION MAIDEN STKS (2-Y.O) (Class E) £3,269.00 (£992.00: £486.00: £233.00)
5f Stalls: Low GOING minus 0.45 sec per fur (F) 2-45 (2-50)

523[4] **Kala Sunrise** *(77t) (CSmith)* 2-9-0 JFortune(4) (a chsng ldrs: styd on wl to ld ins fnl f) ....— 1
Butterwick Belle (IRE) *(66) (RAFahey)* 2-8-9 ACulhane(6) (leggy: unf: chsd ldrs: styd on wl ins fnl f) 1¾ 2
Manolo (FR) *(70) (JBerry)* 2-9-0 JWeaver(3) (cmpt: led tl hdd & no ex ins fnl f: eased nr fin) ....½ 3
Princely Sound *(62)*(Fav)*(MBell)* 2-8-7 (7) GFaulkner(13) (w'like: leggy: fractious in stalls: chsd ldrs: nt qckn appr fnl f) 2½ 4
Cinnamon Stick (IRE) *(49) (WJarvis)* 2-9-0 AMcGlone(1) (leggy: unf: sn outpcd & pushed along) 4 5
615[7] Eights High (USA) *(48) (RHannon)* 2-9-0 KDarley(7) (b.hind: sn rdn along: nvr nr ldrs) ....nk 6
U-No-Harry (IRE) *(43) (RHollinshead)* 2-9-0 TIves(5) (cmpt: prom tl wknd over 1f out) 1½ 7
533[12] Lucky Bea *(42) (MWEasterby)* 2-9-0 LCharnock(10) (bit bkwd: unruly in stalls: reard s: bhd tl sme hdwy fnl f) ....nk 8
Blessingindisguise *(34) (MWEasterby)* 2-9-0 MBirch(2) (w'like: str: bkwd: sn outpcd & pushed along) 2½ 9
Rustic Song (IRE) *(17) (JWharton)* 2-8-9 JFanning(9) (cmpt: chsd ldrs 3f: sn wknd) 4 10
Comrade Chinnery (IRE) *(21) (JMPEustace)* 2-9-0 RCochrane(8) (cmpt: outpcd & a bhd) ....hd 11
Bear To Dance *(8) (JohnBerry)* 2-8-9 CDwyer(11) (unf: bit bkwd: outpcd fr ½-wy) 2½ 12
Dispol Sapphire *(MrsVAAconley)* 2-8-9 GDuffield(12) (small: unf: outpcd & hung bdly rt 2f out: sn wl bhd: t.o) 20 13

7/2 Princely Sound, **4/1** Manolo (FR), **5/1** Cinnamon Stick (IRE), Eights High (USA) (op 3/1), **11/2** KALA SUNRISE, **10/1** Butterwick Belle (IRE) (op 9/2), **14/1** Comrade Chinnery (IRE) (op 8/1), **16/1** U-No-Harry (IRE), Blessingindisguise, **20/1** Rustic Song (IRE), Bear To Dance, **50/1** Lucky Bea, Dispol Sapphire, CSF £59.51 TOTE £7.10: £1.60 £2.70 £1.60 (£47.40) Trio £149.70; £126.52 to Newmarket 20/04/95 OWNER Mr A. E. Needham (WELLINGORE) BRED Green Park Investments Ltd 13 Rn
63.6 secs (2.10) SF: 28/17/21/13/-/-/-/-/-/-/-/-/-

672 OSSETT (S) H'CAP (0-60) (3-Y.O+) (Class G) £2,959.00 (£824.00: £397.00)
1m 4y Stalls: Low GOING minus 0.45 sec per fur (F) 3-20 (3-21)

155[7] **Calisar (38)***(48) (PHowling)* 5-8-9 KDarley(10) (hdwy on outside ½-wy: styd on to ld ins fnl f) ....— 1
481[10] Profit Release (IRE) **(56)***(61) (MJohnston)* 4-9-13 DHolland(14) (trckd ldrs: led over 2f out: hung rt & hdd ins fnl f) 2½ 2
605[11] Pop to Stans **(46)***(48) (JPearce)* 6-8-10 (7) ElizabethTurner(19) (lw: s.i.s: bhd: hdwy on outside 2f out: styd on wl ins fnl f) 1¾ 3
575[4] Boundary Express **(55)***(56) (MJohnston)* 3-8-11 TWilliams(11) (chsd ldrs: sn drvn along: n.m.r over 2f out: styd on same pce appr fnl f) ....nk 4
578[3] Guesstimation (USA) **(57)***(53) (JPearce)* 6-10-0 GBardwell(20) (in tch: effrt over 2f out: styd on same pce fnl f) 2½ 5

Corona Gold **(44)***(38) (JGFitzGerald)* 5-9-1 LCharnock(2) (led 1f: chsd ldrs: n.m.r over 2f out: one pce) 1 **6**
505 13 Northern Chief **(45)***(33) (RWEmery)* 5-9-2 StephenDavies(3) (led after 1f tl over 4f out: chsd ldrs tl wknd over 1f out) 3 **7**
Resolute Bay **(45)***(31) (RMWhitaker)* 9-9-2 ACulhane(6) (bhd: styd on u.p fnl 3f) 1 **8**
578 8 Dundeelin **(37)***(22) (JLEyre)* 4-8-8 RLappin(12) (bhd: sme hdwy ½-wy: nvr nr ldrs) ....½ **9**
430 27 Reed My Lips (IRE) **(39)***(24) (BPJBaugh)* 4-8-10 RPrice(16) (b.hind: hdwy on outside ½-wy: wknd 2f out) ....s.h **10**
526 9 Greek Night Out (IRE) **(46)***(27) (JAHarris)* 4-9-0b(3) DRMcCabe(17) (b.hind: bhd: effrt over 3f out: n.d) 1¾ **11**
419 12 Monsieur Petong **(42)***(17) (JParkes)* 4-8-13 JWeaver(15) (s.i.s: bhd tl sme hdwy 2f out) 3 **12**
559 4 Tolls Choice (IRE) **(55)***(29)*(Fav)*(MWEasterby)* 6-9-5 (7) RuthCoulter(5) (w ldrs: led over 4f out tl over 2f out: wknd over 1f out) ....½ **13**
548 8 Rosina's Folly **(53)***(27) (JLHarris)* 4-9-10 RCochrane(1) (mid div: effrt & n.m.r over 3f out: sn wknd) ....s.h **14**
Tancred Mischief **(37)***(9) (WLBarker)* 4-8-8 DeanMcKeown(13) (bhd: rdn ½-wy: n.d) 1¼ **15**
559 17 Waterlord (IRE) **(53)***(21) (DNicholls)* 5-9-10 NConnorton(9) (lw: in tch tl lost pl ½-wy) 2 **16**
605 12 Genesis Four **(40)***(6) (SRBowring)* 5-8-6b(5) CTeague(4) (chsd ldrs tl wknd over 2f out) 1 **17**
Icanspell **(46)***(2) (WStorey)* 4-9-3v SWhitworth(18) (hdwy to chse ldrs ½-wy: sn lost pl) 5 **18**
568 15 Greek Gold (IRE) **(49)** *(GPKelly)* 6-9-6 AlexGreaves(7) (lw: prom tl wknd 3f out) 3 **19**
Lady Highfield **(45)** *(MJRyan)* 4-8-11 (5) MBaird(22) (prom tl wknd over 2f out) 6 **20**
478 5 Wassl's Nanny (IRE) **(47)** *(BEllison)* 6-9-4 TIves(8) (a rr div) 1¾ **21**
416 5 Hi Penny **(40)** *(KTIvory)* 4-8-11b GDuffield(21) (sn bhd & drvn along: p.u 3f out: b.b.v) .... **P**

5/1 Tolls Choice (IRE), **8/1** Guesstimation (USA), **9/1** Greek Gold (IRE) (20/1-8/1), **11/1** Hi Penny, Waterlord (IRE) (8/1-16/1), **12/1** Boundary Express, Genesis Four, Resolute Bay, **14/1** Greek Night Out (IRE), **16/1** Wassl's Nanny (IRE), Pop to Stans, Monsieur Petong, Profit Release (IRE), Lady Highfield, CALISAR, Corona Gold, Rosina's Folly, **20/1** Dundeelin, Icanspell, Northern Chief, **25/1** Reed My Lips (IRE), **33/1** Tancred Mischief, CSF £261.48 CT £3,810.77 TOTE £30.40: £5.00 £3.50 £4.20 £2.80 (£149.10) Trio Not won; £538.03 to Newmarket 20/04/95 OWNER Six Furlongs Racing (NEWMARKET) BRED W. M. Comerford 22 Rn

1m 46.3 (4.30) SF: 17/30/17/10/22/7/2/-/-/-/-/-/-/-/-/-/-/-/-/-/-/-

WEIGHT FOR AGE 3yo-15lb

No bid

673 LADY BALK MAIDEN STKS (3-Y.O+) (Class D) £4,021.25 (£1,220.00: £597.50: £286.25)

1m 2f 6y Stalls: Low GOING minus 0.45 sec per fur (F) 3-50 (3-58)

552 3 **Al Safeer (IRE) (75)***(85) (JWHills)* 3-8-9 DHolland(1) (chsd ldrs: led over 2f out: hrd rdn & styd on wl fnl f) ....— **1**
Godwin (USA) *(78)*(Fav)*(HRACecil)* 4-9-8 WRyan(12) (sn chsng ldr: led over 4f out tl over 2f out: ev ch 1f out: unable qckn) 1¼ **2**
Sugar Mill *(67) (MrsMReveley)* 5-9-13 KDarley(18) (lw: hdwy ½-wy: kpt on wl fnl 2f: improve) 10 **3**
Analogue (IRE) *(66) (MRStoute)* 3-8-9 JWeaver(5) (stdd s: bhd: stdy hdwy over 2f out: nvr trbld ldrs) ....¾ **4**
Turnpole (IRE) *(60) (MrsMReveley)* 4-9-13 JFanning(13) (str: bkwd: s.i.s: hdwy ½-wy: styd on fnl 2f: nvr nr to chal) 3½ **5**
Tabdeel *(59) (ACStewart)* 3-8-9 SWhitworth(10) (rangy: bit bkwd: mid div: kpt on fnl 2f: nvr nr ldrs) 1 **6**
Saleel (IRE) *(54) (ACStewart)* 3-8-4 (5) MHumphries(3) (str: bkwd: s.i.s: hld up: sme hdwy 3f out: rn green: nvr nr ldrs) 3 **7**
Little Redwing *(48) (MrsJCecil)* 3-8-4 GDuffield(14) (str: bit bkwd: in tch: effrt 3f out: grad wknd) ....nk **8**
Shamekh *(51) (JEBanks)* 3-8-9 RCochrane(8) (s.s: hld up & bhd: stdy hdwy over 2f out: nvr plcd to chal) 1¼ **9**
553 9 My Boy Josh *(40) (RGuest)* 3-8-4 (5) CHawksley(9) (prom 6f: sn rdn & wknd) 7 **10**
539 11 Bollin Sophie *(35) (MHEasterby)* 3-8-4 MBirch(17) (nvr nr ldrs) ....s.h **11**
Lawful Love (IRE) *(39) (TWDonnelly)* 5-9-13 SDWilliams(2) (in tch tl rdn & wknd 4f out) ....½ **12**
Laal (USA) *(37) (EALDunlop)* 3-8-6 (3) JTate(4) (hld up: effrt 4f out: grad wknd) 1¼ **13**
Surgiva *(16) (JRArnold)* 3-8-4 CRutter(7) (chsd ldrs tl wknd over 3f out) 10 **14**
Be My Choice *(15) (MrsJCecil)* 3-8-4 StephenDavies(16) (rangy: scope: bkwd: racd wd: a bhd) ....¾ **15**

Oleron (9) (JNorton) 3-8-4 RPrice(15) (unf: led & sn clr: hdd over 4f out: sn wknd)..................4 16
Amy's Dream (RDEWoodhouse) 4-9-8 NConnorton(6) (Withdrawn not under Starter's orders: v.unruly: ref to enter stalls) .... W

5/6 Godwin (USA), **9/2** Analogue (IRE), **13/2** AL SAFEER (IRE) (4/1-7/1), **12/1** Little Redwing, **14/1** Shamekh, **16/1** Sugar Mill, Tabdeel, Laal (USA), **20/1** Be My Choice, **25/1** Saleel (IRE), **33/1** Turnpole (IRE), **50/1** Surgiva, Lawful Love (IRE), **66/1** My Boy Josh, Oleron, **100/1** Bollin Sophie, CSF £12.86 TOTE £8.50: £1.80 £1.20 £3.10 (£5.10) Trio £33.00 OWNER Mr Ziad Galadari (LAMBOURN) BRED Mrs K. Twomey 16 Rn 2m 13.6 (5.30) SF: 18/29/18/-/11/-/-/-/-/-/-/-/-/-/-/-
WEIGHT FOR AGE 3yo-18lb

674

ST GILES H'CAP (0-80) (3-Y.O F) (Class D) £6,160.00 (£1,840.00: £880.00: £400.00) **6f** Stalls: Low GOING minus 0.45 sec per fur (F) 4-25 (4-27)

573[3] **Chiming In (67)***(73) (MrsJRRamsden)* 3-8-8 JFortune(4) (hld up: hdwy over 1f out: effrt, nt clr rn & swtchd over 1f out: r.o wl to ld ins fnl f: readily) ....— 1
Arasong **(70)***(72) (EWeymes)* 3-8-11 KDarley(6) (chsd ldrs: led 2f out tl ins fnl f: nt qckn).....1½ 2
Brockton Flame **(65)***(64) (JMPEustace)* 3-8-6 ow1 RCochrane(8) (chsd ldrs: outpcd over 2f out: styd on wl fnl f)..¾ 3
Stolen Kiss (IRE) **(65)***(65) (MWEasterby)* 3-8-6 LCharnock(2) (a.p: sltly hmpd over 1f out: kpt on same pce)..s.h 4
542* Golden Lady (IRE) **(80)***(79)*(Fav)*(RHannon)* 3-9-7 JWeaver(1) (led to 2f out: kpt on same pce fnl f) ....nk 5
504[12] Fantasy Racing (IRE) **(80)***(76) (MRChannon)* 3-9-7 CRutter(10) (chsd ldrs: wl outpcd over 2f out: kpt on wl fnl f)..1¼ 6
482* Noor El Houdah (IRE) **(60)***(55) (JBerry)* 3-8-1 GCarter(9) (lw: chsd ldrs tl wknd appr fnl f) .....nk 7
504[8] Cabcharge Blue **(77)***(67) (TJNaughton)* 3-9-4 DHolland(12) (hld up: trckd ldrs: outpcd over 2f out: kpt on fnl f) 1¾ 8
Delight of Dawn **(75)***(65) (KTIvory)* 3-9-2 GDuffield(7) (bhd & drvn along: hdwy on outside over 2f out: wknd over 1f out)...hd 9
Dominelle **(52)***(29) (MHEasterby)* 3-7-7 NCarlisle(11) (unf: chsd ldrs tl wknd 2f out) 5 10
Miss Zanzibar **(58)***(32) (RAFahey)* 3-7-13 SMaloney(5) (bhd & outpcd ½-wy: n.d) 1 11
426[11] Crystal Loop **(68)** *(ABailey)* 3-8-4 (5) VHalliday(3) (chsd ldrs: drvn along & lost pl over 2f out: virtually p.u fnl f: b.b.v) ....dist 12
LONG HANDICAP Dominelle 7-6

5/2 Golden Lady (IRE), **13/2** Noor El Houdah (IRE), **7/1** CHIMING IN, Cabcharge Blue (5/1-8/1), **8/1** Brockton Flame, **10/1** Crystal Loop, **11/1** Delight of Dawn, **12/1** Dominelle, **14/1** Fantasy Racing (IRE), Stolen Kiss (IRE), **16/1** Arasong, **20/1** Miss Zanzibar, CSF £104.43 CT £845.73 TOTE £9.60: £1.90 £4.40 £2.50 (£64.20) Trio £199.30; £140.41 to Newmarket 20/04/95 OWNER Mr Bernard Hathaway (THIRSK) BRED B. Hathaway 12 Rn 1m 17.7 (3.40) SF: 12/11/3/4/18/15/-/6/4/-/-/-
OFFICIAL EXPLANATION Crystal Loop: jockey reported that the filly had bled from the nose.

675

WEFT GATE STKS (3-Y.O+) (Class D) £3,582.50 (£1,085.00: £530.00: £252.50) **1m 4y** Stalls: Low GOING minus 0.45 sec per fur (F) 5-00 (5-05)

504[7] **Beauchamp Jazz (93)***(87+)*(Fav)*(JLDunlop)* 3-8-11 GDuffield(6) (lw: mde all: qcknd clr over 1f out: v.easily)..— 1
Prize Pupil (IRE) *(65) (CFWall)* 3-8-0 (5) LNewton(5) (hld up: effrt & chsd wnr over 2f out: rdn & hung lft over 1f out)...8 2
577* Shaffishayes *(68) (MrsMReveley)* 3-8-9 KDarley(4) (hld up: hdwy to chse ldrs over 3f out: kpt on same pce fnl 2f) ....nk 3
539[18] Crucis (IRE) *(45) (BAMcMahon)* 4-9-6 TIves(3) (trckd ldrs: outpcd over 3f out: n.d after) 10 4
Taro Card (IRE) *(RDEWoodhouse)* 4-9-6 NConnorton(2) (bit bkwd: chsd ldrs tl lost pl ½-wy: sn wl bhd) 30 5
Lelise (IRE) *(APJarvis)* 3-7-8 (7)ow1 BHunter(1) (uns rdr gng to s: sn w wnr: rdn & wknd qckly 3f out: sn bhd) 4 6

8/11 BEAUCHAMP JAZZ, **2/1** Prize Pupil (IRE), **11/2** Shaffishayes (6/1-9/1), **100/1** Crucis (IRE), Lelise (IRE), **250/1** Taro Card (IRE), CSF £2.37 TOTE £1.70: £1.10 £1.60 (£1.60) OWNER Mr E. Penser (ARUNDEL) BRED E. Penser 6 Rn 1m 44.6 (2.60) SF: 35/13/16/8/-/-
WEIGHT FOR AGE 3yo-15lb

676

GARFORTH H'CAP (0-70) (3-Y.O+) (Class E) £3,903.75 (£1,170.00: £562.50: £258.75) **1m 2f 6y** Stalls: Low GOING minus 0.45 sec per fur (F) 5-30 (5-38)

Obelos (USA) (62)*(71) (MrsJCecil)* 4-9-8 TIves(6) (a.p: styd on wl to ld over 1f out: drvn out)— 1
558[5] Kalou **(52)***(59) (CWCElsey)* 4-8-12v LCharnock(12) (led after 1f tl over 1f out: kpt on wl).......1½ 2

597[2] Hillzah (USA) **(66)***(71) (RBastiman)* 7-9-7 (5) HBastiman(9) (hld up: hdwy ½-wy: effrt over 2f out: kpt on same pce fnl f) 1 **3**
Sommersby (IRE) **(51)***(54) (ACStewart)* 4-8-11 SWhitworth(18) (hld up & bhd: hdwy & swtchd outside 2f out: kpt on wl fnl f) 1 **4**
481[2] Celtic Ceilidh **(51)***(46) (JWharton)* 4-8-11 RCochrane(2) (in tch: effrt 3f out: kpt on fnl f: nvr nr to chal) 5 **5**
Douce Maison (IRE) **(56)***(50) (APJarvis)* 4-9-2 KDarley(1) (led: hmpd & hdd after 1f: chsd ldrs: n.m.r & wknd over 1f out) 1 **6**
550[14] Eden's Close **(64)***(56) (MHTompkins)* 6-9-5 (5) SMulvey(5) (hld up: hdwy 2f out: nvr nr ldrs) 1 **7**
550[8] Bescaby Boy **(59)***(51) (JWharton)* 9-9-5 MBirch(8) (hld up & bhd: stdy hdwy over 1f out: nvr plcd to chal) ....nk **8**
505[8] Myfontaine **(51)***(41) (KTIvory)* 8-8-11 GDuffield(10) (lw: hld up: hdwy to chse ldrs 4f out: effrt over 2f out: wknd over 1f out) 1¼ **9**
Hunters' Heaven (USA) **(59)***(47) (JMackie)* 4-9-5 GCarter(11) (mid div: effrt 4f out: wknd over 2f out) 1 **10**
373[8] Calder King **(64)***(52) (JLEyre)* 4-9-10 JFortune(3) (bhd: effrt on ins 3f out: n.d) ....nk **11**
558[14] Muzrak (CAN) **(66)***(51) (MDHammond)* 4-9-5 (7) MMathers(4) (hld up: a rr div) 1½ **12**
Sallyoreally (IRE) **(61)***(46) (WStorey)* 4-9-4 (3) DRMcCabe(7) (s.i.s: bhd: hdwy 2f out: n.d) ....½ **13**
520[11] Zanzara (IRE) **(53)***(37) (MrsVAAconley)* 4-8-13 TWilliams(13) (prom: drvn along 5f out: wknd 2f out) ....s.h **14**
Drummer Hicks **(54)***(37)*(Fav)*(EWeymes)* 6-9-0 DeanMcKeown(15) (chsd ldrs: effrt over 3f out: wknd 2f out) 1 **15**
King Curan (USA) **(61)***(37) (ABailey)* 4-9-2 (5) VHalliday(16) (hld up & a bhd) 4 **16**
568[3] Augustan **(58)***(25) (SGollings)* 4-9-4 DHolland(14) (chsd ldrs tl lost pl over 2f out) 6 **17**
Lochore **(54)***(19) (MrsVAAconley)* 5-9-0 DaleGibson(17) (hdwy on outside 4f out: wknd over 2f out) 1 **18**
550[17] Colonel Colt **(61)** *(RDickin)* 4-9-7 JLowe(19) (racd wd: chsd ldrs: drvn along 5f out: sn lost pl: t.o 3f out) ....dist **19**

7/2 Drummer Hicks, **6/1** Augustan, **10/1** Douce Maison (IRE) (op 6/1), **11/1** Myfontaine, Hillzah (USA), **12/1** Calder King, Celtic Ceilidh, Kalou, **14/1** Sommersby (IRE), Bescaby Boy (op 8/1), OBELOS (USA), **16/1** Eden's Close, Hunters' Heaven (USA), **25/1** Lochore, **33/1** Zanzara (IRE), King Curan (USA), Colonel Colt, **50/1** Sallyoreally (IRE), **66/1** Muzrak (CAN), CSF £164.54 CT £1,765.65 TOTE £20.60: £3.90 £4.00 £2.50 £6.50 (£172.70) Trio £521.90 OWNER Lord Howard de Walden (NEWMARKET) 19 Rn 2m 12.8 (4.50) SF: 36/24/36/19/11/15/21/16/6/12/17/16/11/2/2/2/-

T/Plpt £204.00 (58.78 Tckts). T/Qdpt £30.70 (3 Tckts). WG

0664-NEWMARKET (R-H)
Thursday April 20th (Good to firm)
WEATHER: sunny WIND: mod half bhd

677
GRANBY MAIDEN STKS (3-Y.O C & G) (Class D) £5,390.00 (£1,610.00: £770.00: £350.00) **7f (Rowley)** Stalls: High GOING minus 0.44 sec per fur (F) 2-00 (2-00)

Charnwood Forest (IRE) *(99+)*(Fav)*(HRACecil)* 3-8-11 MJKinane(1) (h.d.w: trckd ldrs: led wl over 1f out: r.o wl) ....— **1**
Prince Arthur (IRE) *(95) (PWChapple-Hyam)* 3-8-11 JReid(4) (b.hind: trckd ldrs: led wl over 2f out tl wl over 1f out: no ex ins fnl f) 1¾ **2**
Bin Rosie *(81) (DRLoder)* 3-8-11 JWeaver(5) (leggy: scope: a.p: kpt on fnl 2f: nt pce to chal) 6 **3**
Samwar *(77) (BWHills)* 3-8-11 PatEddery(3) (bit bkwd: hld up & bhd: hdwy over 3f out: chsng ldrs 2f out: nt qckn) 1¾ **4**
Royal Solo (IRE) *(76) (PWChapple-Hyam)* 3-8-11 BThomson(2) (gd sort: cl up: rdn over 2f out: grad wknd) ....½ **5**
Rug *(70) (GWragg)* 3-8-11 MHills(6) (w'like: scope: bit bkwd: hld up: effrt over 2f out: r.o nr fin) 2½ **6**
552[2] Viyapari (IRE) *(67) (LMCumani)* 3-8-11 LDettori(9) (bkwd: prom: rdn 2f out: sn outpcd) 1½ **7**
Time Leader *(66) (MRStoute)* 3-8-11 WRSwinburn(8) (lw: bhd: shkn up 2f out: styd on nr fin) ....nk **8**
City Run (USA) *(61) (DJSCosgrove)* 3-8-11 MRimmer(10) (led tl wl over 2f out: sn wknd) ...2½ **9**
Bergholt *(49) (GLMoore)* 3-8-11 SWhitworth(7) (b.off hind: leggy: unf: s.i.s: n.d) 5 **10**

4/6 CHARNWOOD FOREST (IRE), **7/2** Prince Arthur (IRE) (5/2-4/1), **10/1** Rug (12/1-7/1), Viyapari (IRE) (7/1-11/1), **20/1** Samwar, **25/1** Royal Solo (IRE), Time Leader, **33/1** Bin Rosie, **100/1** City Run (USA), Bergholt, CSF £3.52 TOTE £1.60: £1.10 £1.40 £4.10 (£1.80) Trio £20.30 OWNER Sheikh Mohammed (NEWMARKET) BRED Sheikh Mohammed bin Rashid al Maktoum 10 Rn
1m 23.79 (0.09) SF: 58/54/40/36/35/29/26/25/20/8

678
NGK SPARK PLUGS H'CAP (0-95) (3-Y.O) (Class C) £7,375.00
(£2,200.00: £1,050.00: £475.00)
1m 2f (Rowley) Stalls: High GOING minus 0.44 sec per fur (F) 2-35 (2-38)

Indonesian (IRE) (79)*(86) (MBell)* 3-8-5 MFenton(10) (a.p: hdwy over 2f out: styd on to ld ins fnl f)......— 1
In Camera (IRE) **(80)***(85)*(Fav)*(MRStoute)* 3-8-6 MJKinane(11) (lw: lost pl after 2f: outpcd over 3f out: hdwy over 1f out: fin wl)......1½ 2
*418** Sheer Danzig (IRE) **(77)***(81) (RWArmstrong)* 3-8-3 RPrice(9) (led: qcknd over 3f out: hdd & no ex ins fnl f)......nk 3
536[3] Dance Band (USA) **(95)***(95) (BHanbury)* 3-9-7 WRSwinburn(3) (a chsng ldrs: effrt 3f out: r.o one pce)......2½ 4
Leontios (IRE) **(76)***(68) (MHTompkins)* 3-8-2 PRobinson(4) (a.p: effrt 3f out: one pce)......5 5
564[4] Soldier's Leap (FR) **(75)***(43) (CEBrittain)* 3-8-1b BDoyle(1) (lw: chsd ldrs tl wknd over 2f out).15 6
Yacht **(79)***(41) (BWHills)* 3-8-5b MHills(6) (bhd: effrt 3f out: n.d)......4 7
Zingibar **(76)***(36) (BWHills)* 3-8-2 ow1 JCarroll(8) (hld up: hmpd over 2f out: n.d)......nk 8
151[4] Battleship Bruce **(75)***(32) (NACallaghan)* 3-8-1 StephenDavies(7) (b.hind: prom: effrt 3f out: wknd 2f out)......2½ 9
484[3] Noonday Gun (IRE) **(71)** *(RHannon)* 3-7-11 WCarson(2) (hld up: hdwy on outside over 3f out: fell 3f out: dead)...... F

11/4 In Camera (IRE), **9/2** Dance Band (USA), **5/1** Sheer Danzig (IRE), **11/1** Noonday Gun (IRE), **12/1** Yacht, **14/1** Battleship Bruce (op 8/1), INDONESIAN (IRE) (10/1-16/1), Leontios (IRE) (6/1-16/1), **16/1** Zingibar, Soldier's Leap (FR), CSF £46.15 CT £184.16 TOTE £14.70: £3.10 £1.60 £1.60 (£23.30) Trio £44.50 OWNER Mr J. L. C. Pearce (NEWMARKET) BRED J. L. C. Pearce 10 Rn
2m 3.35 (0.75) SF: 48/47/43/57/30/5/3/-/-/-

679
FEILDEN STKS (Listed) (3-Y.O) (Class A) £11,199.60
(£4,136.40: £1,978.20: £801.00: £310.50: £114.30)
1m 1f (Rowley) Stalls: Centre GOING minus 0.44 sec per fur (F) 3-05 (3-07)

Munwar *(114+) (PTWalwyn)* 3-8-11 WCarson(1) (mde most: qcknd 3f out: rdn & r.o wl fnl f)......— 1
Flemensfirth (USA) *(110) (JHMGosden)* 3-8-11 LDettori(2) (b.hind: trckd ldrs: hdwy over 3f out: ev ch over 1f out: nt qckn ins fnl f)......2½ 2
Eltish (USA) **(120)***(115)*(Fav)*(HRACecil)* 3-9-5 PatEddery(7) (h.d.w: w wnr: rdn 2f out: nt qckn)......1¼ 3
Indian Light **(91)***(101) (JLDunlop)* 3-8-11 TQuinn(4) (chsd ldrs tl outpcd 3f out: kpt on fnl f)..3½ 4
Wijara (IRE) *(98) (RHannon)* 3-8-11 RPerham(6) (lw: cl up: pushed along over 3f out: btn 2f out)......2 5
536[2] Heathyards Rock **(98)***(93) (RHollinshead)* 3-8-11 TIves(5) (drvn along ½-wy: n.d after)......2½ 6
Seckar Vale (USA) **(88)***(79) (JHanson)* 3-8-11 MHills(3) (plld hrd: bhd fnl 4f)......8 7

11/8 Eltish (USA), **3/1** Flemensfirth (USA), **9/2** MUNWAR, **8/1** Indian Light (6/1-9/1), **10/1** Wijara (IRE), **50/1** Heathyards Rock, Seckar Vale (USA), CSF £16.59 TOTE £4.80: £1.80 £2.20 (£17.50) OWNER Mr Hamdan Al Maktoum (LAMBOURN) BRED W. and R. Barnett Ltd 7 Rn
1m 48.53 (-1.17) SF: 70/66/71/57/54/49/35

680
CRAVEN STKS (Gp 3) (3-Y.O C & G) (Class A) £22,141.00
(£7,966.00: £3,808.00: £1,540.00: £595.00)
1m (Rowley) Stalls: Centre GOING minus 0.44 sec per fur (F) 3-40 (3-41)

Painter's Row (IRE) *(111) (PWChapple-Hyam)* 3-8-12 JReid(2) (lw: cl up: led over 2f out: rdn & r.o gamely fnl f)......— 1
Montjoy (USA) **(113)***(107) (PFICole)* 3-8-9 TQuinn(6) (h.d.w: hld up: hdwy over 2f out: swtchd over 1f out: hrd rdn: r.o wl)......nk 2
Nwaamis (USA) *(107)*(Fav)*(JLDunlop)* 3-8-9 WCarson(1) (lw: trckd ldrs: chal over 1f out: hrd rdn fnl f: r.o)......hd 3
Chilly Billy **(116)***(102) (MrsJRRamsden)* 3-9-0 KFallon(3) (lw: plld hrd: effrt over 2f out: btn appr fnl f)......5 4
Denebola Way (GR) *(86) (RCharlton)* 3-9-0 PatEddery(5) (led tl over 2f out: wknd over 1f out)......8 5

11/8 Nwaamis (USA), **7/2** Chilly Billy, Montjoy (USA), **5/1** PAINTER'S ROW (IRE) (3/1-6/1), **20/1** Denebola Way (GR), CSF £19.58 TOTE £4.40: £2.00 £2.00 (£8.90) OWNER Lord Weinstock & The Hon Simon Weinstock (MARLBOROUGH) BRED Ballymacoll Stud Farm Ltd in Ireland 5 Rn
1m 37.08 (0.08) SF: 59/55/55/50/34

681
WISBECH H'CAP (0-90) (3-Y.O) (Class C) £5,900.00 (£1,760.00: £840.00: £380.00) **6f (Rowley)** Stalls: High GOING minus 0.44 sec per fur (F) 4-10 (4-11)

Cheyenne Spirit (85)*(92) (BHanbury)* 3-9-7 WRyan(2) (b.off hind: led after 1½f: qcknd clr over 1f out: rdn & r.o wl) — 1
Kabil **(84)***(84)*(Fav)*(HThomsonJones)* 3-9-6 WCarson(5) (bit bkwd: in tch: pushed along & hdwy 2f out: r.o: nt pce to chal) 2½ 2
522[6] Peggy Spencer **(60)***(55) (CWThornton)* 3-7-10 AMackay(7) (lw: chsd ldrs: rdn ½-wy: r.o one pce) 2 3
Cats Bottom **(74)***(66) (DJSCosgrove)* 3-8-10 MRimmer(8) (prom: effrt over 2f out: rdn & nvr able to chal) 1¼ 4
426[9] A Million to One (IRE) **(78)***(66) (MBell)* 3-9-0 MFenton(9) (led over 1f: cl up tl outpcd fnl 2f) 1½ 5
483[3] Musica **(81)***(59)*(Fav)*(MRChannon)* 3-9-3 RHughes(6) (chsd ldrs tl wknd fnl 2f) 3½ 6
Here Comes Risky **(84)***(58) (MJohnston)* 3-9-6 JReid(4) (nvr plcd to chal) 1½ 7
524[7] South Sound (IRE) **(65)***(37) (RHannon)* 3-8-1 BDoyle(3) (lw: nvr wnt pce) ¾ 8
446[3] Montague Dawson (IRE) **(70)***(40) (MrsNMacauley)* 3-8-6 JWeaver(1) (b.hind: prom early: wl outpcd fr ½-wy) ¾ 9

3/1 Musica, Kabil, **11/2** Peggy Spencer (7/2-6/1), **8/1** A Million to One (IRE), **10/1** Here Comes Risky (8/1-14/1), CHEYENNE SPIRIT, South Sound (IRE), **14/1** Cats Bottom, Montague Dawson (IRE), CSF £38.06 CT £168.19 TOTE £15.00: £3.20 £1.30 £2.30 (£18.10) Trio £49.00 OWNER Mr C. Mauritzon (NEWMARKET) BRED J. McGarry 9 Rn 1m 11.7 (0.40) SF: 62/54/25/36/36/29/28/7/10

682
E.B.F. STUNTNEY MAIDEN STKS (2-Y.O C & G) (Class D) £5,071.50 (£1,512.00: £721.00: £325.50)
5f (Rowley) Stalls: High GOING minus 0.44 sec per fur (F) 4-45 (4-47)

Lucayan Prince (USA) *(91+t)*(Fav)*(DRLoder)* 2-8-11 JWeaver(2) (cmpt: leggy: lw: trckd ldrs: hdwy to ld over 1f out: rn green: rdn & r.o) — 1
L'Ami Louis (USA) *(85) (JHMGosden)* 2-8-11 LDettori(5) (w'like: scope: a chsng ldrs: kpt on wl fnl f) 2 2
Centurion *(83) (RHannon)* 2-8-11 PatEddery(3) (leggy: scope: led tl over 1f out: no ex) ½ 3
Deadline Time (IRE) *(75) (MHTompkins)* 2-8-11 WRyan(6) (neat: bhd: hdwy 2f out: r.o) 2½ 4
Red Nose (IRE) *(64) (MHTompkins)* 2-8-11 PRobinson(4) (cmpt: cl up over 3f: grad wknd) 3½ 5
Oberons Boy (IRE) *(51) (BJMeehan)* 2-8-11 BDoyle(7) (neat: bkwd: outpcd & bhd after 2f) 4 6
Incapol *(47) (MJRyan)* 2-8-11 DBiggs(1) (w'like: bkwd: spd to ½-wy: sn outpcd) 1¼ 7

5/6 LUCAYAN PRINCE (USA), **4/1** L'Ami Louis (USA) (op 5/2), **6/1** Centurion (5/2-13/2), **12/1** Incapol (op 8/1), **14/1** Oberons Boy (IRE) (8/1-16/1), **25/1** Red Nose (IRE), **33/1** Deadline Time (IRE), CSF £4.30 TOTE £1.80: £1.20 £2.00 (£2.40) OWNER Lucayan Stud (NEWMARKET) BRED Airdrie Partnership 7 Rn 59.6 secs (0.90) SF: 43/37/35/27/16/3/-

683
THETFORD STKS (2-Y.O) (Class C) £5,156.00 (£1,856.00: £888.00: £360.00: £140.00)
5f (Rowley) Stalls: High GOING minus 0.44 sec per fur (F) 5-20 (5-20)

523* **Dungeon Master (IRE)** *(84t) (MRChannon)* 2-9-4 RHughes(3) (trckd ldrs: effrt over 1f out: r.o wl u.p to ld cl home) — 1
Night Parade (USA) *(76) (PWChapple-Hyam)* 2-8-12 JReid(1) (gd sort: cl up: hdwy to ld over 1f out: rn green: hdd & no ex nr fin) ½ 2
436* Kustom Kit (IRE) *(73) (BAMcMahon)* 2-9-4 FNorton(2) (outpcd & bhd tl styd on wl fnl f) 3 3
561* Gwespyr *(71) (JBerry)* 2-9-4 JCarroll(4) (lw: cl up tl rdn & wknd over 1f out) ½ 4
617[13] Navigate (USA) *(61)*(Fav)*(RHannon)* 2-8-12 PatEddery(5) (lw: led tl hdd & wknd over 1f out) 1¼ 5

9/4 Navigate (USA) (op 4/1), **5/2** Night Parade (USA) (op 11/8), **11/4** DUNGEON MASTER (IRE) (3/1-9/2), **11/2** Gwespyr (3/1-6/1), **12/1** Kustom Kit (IRE) (6/1-14/1), CSF 9.18 TOTE £4.30: £1.70 £1.50 (£5.10) OWNER The Classicstone Partnership (UPPER LAMBOURN) BRED T. J. Monaghan 5 Rn 60.74 secs (2.04) SF: 31/23/20/18/8

T/Jkpt £7,504.00 (0.7 Tckts); £3,107.72 to Newbury 21/4/95. T/Plpt £42.40 (714.5 Tckts). T/Qdpt £28.90 (4.8 Tckts). AA

0533-**RIPON (R-H)**
Thursday April 20th (Good to firm)
WEATHER: overcast WIND: almost nil

684
E.B.F. SHAROW MAIDEN STKS (2-Y.O) (Class D) £4,045.50 (£1,224.00: £597.00: £283.50)
5f Stalls: Low GOING minus 0.51 sec per fur (F) 2-30 (2-31)

Montrestar *(67t) (PDEvans)* 2-9-0 JFortune(2) (cmpt: trckd ldrs: led over 1f out: edgd rt: hld on wl) — 1
Scathebury *(67)(Fav)(SPCWoods)* 2-9-0 WWoods(6) (cmpt: trckd ldrs: led wl over 1f out: sn hdd: r.o wl u.p nr fin) hd 2
Don't Tell Anyone *(57) (JBerry)* 2-9-0 GCarter(5) (neat: led tl over 1f out: kpt on same pce) 3 3
Tadeo *(56) (MRChannon)* 2-9-0 KDarley(1) (w'like: cmpt: s.s: sn pushed along: hdwy whn hmpd on ins over 1f out: swtchd & hung rt: styd on nr fin) nk 4
Mooncusser *(48) (JGFitzGerald)* 2-9-0 DeanMcKeown(8) (unf: hmpd after 1½f: sme hdwy ½-wy: nvr nr ldrs) 2½ 5
Borana Lodge (USA) *(43) (MrsJRRamsden)* 2-9-0 DHarrison(4) (leggy: unf: scope: bit bkwd: sn trckng ldrs: outpcd fnl 2f) 1½ 6
531⁴ Exactly (IRE) *(27) (MJohnston)* 2-8-9 DHolland(3) (s.i.s: sn drvn along & a outpcd) 3½ 7
Briganoone *(19) (SRBowring)* 2-8-9 (5) CTeague(7) (str: cmpt: bit bkwd: prom: rn green & hung rt: outpcd fr ½-wy) 4 8

2/1 Scathebury (op 7/2), **4/1** Tadeo, Don't Tell Anyone (2/1-9/2), **7/1** MONTRESTAR (5/1-8/1), **8/1** Mooncusser, Borana Lodge (USA), **10/1** Briganoone, **16/1** Exactly (IRE), CSF £21.89 TOTE £16.20: £3.00 £1.10 £1.50 (£14.00) OWNER Mr John Pugh (WELSHPOOL) BRED D. Newton 8 Rn
60.6 secs (2.60) SF: 12/12/2/1/-/-/-/-

685
COPT HEWICK CLAIMING STKS (3-Y.O+) (Class F) £2,879.00 (£872.00: £426.00: £203.00) **5f** Stalls: Low GOING minus 0.51 sec per fur (F) 3-00 (3-05)

565⁶ **Fangio (78)***(76+) (WGMTurner)* 6-9-1 (5) PMcCabe(4) (w ldr: led 2f out: r.o strly) — 1
407⁴ Rossini Blue **(75)***(72) (ABailey)* 4-9-4 KDarley(5) (mid div: styd on wl ins fnl f: nt rch wnr) ¾ 2
Gorinsky (IRE) **(97)***(73)*(Fav)*(JBerry)* 7-9-6 GCarter(2) (w ldrs: rdn over 1f out: unable qckn) s.h 3
510² Sigama (USA) **(50)***(61) (DNicholls)* 9-9-0 AlexGreaves(7) (lw: led 3f: kpt on same pce fnl f) 2 4
Thick as Thieves **(72)***(70) (RonaldThompson)* 3-9-0 NConnorton(12) (in tch: effrt 2f out: kpt on fnl f) ½ 5
Lugana Vision **(43)***(54) (GFierro)* 3-7-12 (3)ow2 SSanders(13) (bhd tl kpt on wl fnl 2f) ½ 6
Sunshine Belle **(45)***(38) (GMMoore)* 3-7-13 JFanning(1) (w ldrs: hung bdly rt & lost pl wl over 1f out) 5 7
210⁹ Another Nightmare (IRE) **(60)***(39) (RMMcKellar)* 3-8-1 TWilliams(10) (s.s: bhd: hdwy 2f out: nvr nr to chal) nk 8
497⁸ Father Tim (IRE) *(32) (JMBradley)* 5-8-8 (5) SDrowne(11) (sn outpcd) 2½ 9
Red Hot Risk **(58)***(36) (MDods)* 3-8-9 DaleGibson(8) (sn outpcd & pushed along) 1 10
Supreme Desire **(35)***(3) (GROldroyd)* 7-8-10 MMcAndrew(9) (s.s: veered rt ½-wy: a bhd) 7 11
Novocento *(JDooler)* 5-8-6 (7) AngelaGallimore(3) (nvr wnt pce) 2½ 12
535²² Pete Afrique (IRE) **(84)** *(MWEasterby)* 4-9-8 LCharnock(14) (b: sn outpcd: wl bhd fnl 2f) 7 13
Bettykimvic **(72)** *(EJAlston)* 4-8-13 JFortune(6) (Withdrawn not under Starter's orders: uns rdr & bolted gng to s) **W**

4/5 Gorinsky (IRE), **11/4** FANGIO, **11/1** Thick as Thieves, **12/1** Pete Afrique (IRE) (op 6/1), **14/1** Sigama (USA), Rossini Blue, **20/1** Bettykimvic, **25/1** Red Hot Risk, Lugana Vision, **33/1** Another Nightmare (IRE), Father Tim (IRE), Supreme Desire, Novocento, Sunshine Belle, CSF £40.30 TOTE £4.70: £1.60 £2.30 £1.10 (£27.90) Trio £8.80 OWNER Mr Malcolm Heygate-Browne (SHERBORNE) BRED Melbury Park Stud 13 Rn 58.7 secs (0.70) SF: 48/44/45/33/31/15/-/-/4/-/-/-/-
WEIGHT FOR AGE 3yo-11lb

686
COCKED HAT 'COCK O'THE NORTH' H'CAP (0-90) (3-Y.O) (Class C) £5,576.00 (£1,688.00: £824.00: £392.00)
1m Stalls: High GOING minus 0.51 sec per fur (F) 3-30 (3-32)

Bettergeton (73)*(75) (PJBevan)* 3-8-5 (3) SSanders(3) (trckd ldrs: led 1f out: hld on wl) — 1
Barrel of Hope **(75)***(76) (JLEyre)* 3-8-10 JFortune(6) (led: qcknd over 3f out: hdd 1f out: r.o wl ins fnl f) ½ 2

Hujjab (USA) **(78)***(77)*(Fav)*(JLDunlop)* 3-8-13 KDarley(5) (lw: hld up & plld hrd: outpcd over 3f out: styd on wl fnl f)....1¼ 3
Kings Assembly **(69)***(67) (PWHarris)* 3-8-4 DHolland(7) (trckd ldrs: outpcd over 3f out: kpt on wl ins fnl f)....hd 4
Rock Foundation **(73)***(61) (PCHaslam)* 3-8-8 TWilliams(2) (stdd s: hld up & plld hrd: effrt over 3f out: nvr nr ldrs)....5 5
437[14] Montanelli (FR) **(76)***(63) (KMcAuliffe)* 3-8-11 GDuffield(1) (plld hrd: trckd ldrs: outpcd & n.m.r 2f out: swtchd: n.d after)....¾ 6
In Good Faith **(86)***(67) (JJQuinn)* 3-9-7 MBirch(4) (hld up: effrt over 3f out: wknd over 1f out)..3 7

11/8 Hujjab (USA), **3/1** Kings Assembly, **7/1** Montanelli (FR), **8/1** Rock Foundation, In Good Faith, **9/1** BETTERGETON (op 6/1), **14/1** Barrel of Hope, CSF £98.77 TOTE £11.10: £3.30 £4.70 (£42.40) OWNER Mr Derek Boulton (UTTOXETER) BRED R. and Mrs Healy-Fenton 7 Rn
1m 41.2 (3.50) SF: 16/17/18/8/2/4/8

687

FARM FED CHICKEN H'CAP (0-80) (3-Y.O) (Class D) £3,723.50 (£1,127.00: £550.00: £261.50) **1m 4f 60y** Stalls: High GOING minus 0.51 sec (F) 4-00 (4-00)

538[6] **Tessajoe (54)***(63) (MJCamacho)* 3-7-13 LCharnock(1) (hld up: smooth hdwy over 4f out: swtchd ins & led on bit over 3f out: shkn up & edgd lft 1f out: drvn out)....— 1
Westminster (IRE) **(60)***(67) (MHTompkins)* 3-8-0 (5) SMulvey(6) (hld up: hdwy on bit to chal 3f out: edgd left & nt qckn ins fnl f)....1¼ 2
485[9] Salaman (FR) **(73)***(74) (JLDunlop)* 3-9-4 GCarter(2) (lw: hld up: rn wd & lost pl ent st: kpt on u.p fnl f)....5 3
538[13] Flyaway Blues **(60)***(61) (MrsMReveley)* 3-8-5 KDarley(4) (hld up: outpcd & bhd 5f out: kpt on fnl 2f: nvr nr to chal)....hd 4
59[3] What's the Verdict (IRE) **(76)***(57) (MJohnston)* 3-9-7 TWilliams(5) (plld hrd: led tl over 4f out: lost pl 3f out: eased)....15 5
537[2] Contrafire (IRE) **(68)***(17)*(Fav)*(WJarvis)* 3-8-13 MTebbutt(3) (plld hrd: w ldr: led over 4f out tl over 3f out: sn wl bhd & eased)....25 6

6/4 Contrafire (IRE), **7/2** TESSAJOE, **4/1** Salaman (FR), **5/1** What's the Verdict (IRE), **8/1** Flyaway Blues, **10/1** Westminster (IRE), CSF £31.60 TOTE £4.90: £2.20 £3.80 (£31.70) OWNER Riley Partnership (MALTON) BRED A. and Mrs Rhodes 6 Rn 2m 36.1 (2.10) SF: 30/34/41/28/24/-

688

NEWBY APPRENTICE H'CAP (0-70) (4-Y.O+) (Class E) £2,985.00 (£915.00: £455.00: £225.00) **5f** Stalls: Low GOING minus 0.51 sec per fur (F) 4-30 (4-30)

579[8] **Prince Belfort (64)***(68) (JLEyre)* 7-9-1b(8) GMacDonald(9) (s.i.s: hdwy ½-wy: effrt over 1f out: r.o to ld ins fnl f)....— 1
247[9] Miss Siham (IRE) **(39)***(41) (DNicholls)* 6-7-12 SLanigan(8) (led: edgd rt over 1f out: hdd & nt qckn ins fnl f)....¾ 2
Leading Princess (IRE) **(44)***(42) (MissLAPerratt)* 4-7-12b(5)ow1 GFaulkner(5) (bit bkwd: in tch stands' side: styd on fnl f)....¾ 3
491[2] Kalar **(43)***(42) (DWChapman)* 6-7-13b(3) DDenby(6) (w ldrs: nt qckn ins fnl f)....s.h 4
*602** Chadwell Hall **(48)***(47)*(Fav)*(SRBowring)* 4-8-7b 7x PFessey(13) (b.off hind: lw: w ldrs: carried rt & nt qckn ins fnl f)....hd 5
565[3] Domicksky **(69)***(66) (MRChannon)* 7-9-4 (10) DSweeney(1) (lw: racd stands' side: sn chsng ldrs: effrt 2f out: r.o ins fnl f)....½ 6
475[8] Rich Glow **(44)***(41) (NBycroft)* 4-8-3 GMitchell(4) (chsd ldrs stands' side 3f: kpt on nr fin)....hd 7
639[5] Nineacres **(56)***(43) (DNicholls)* 4-8-5 (10) BPeel(12) (sn wl outpcd & bhd: hdwy 1f out: n.d)....3 8
398[11] Gondo **(66)***(53) (EJAlston)* 8-9-11 MartinDwyer(7) (outpcd tl kpt on fnl 2f)....s.h 9
Barbezieux **(44)***(31) (MDods)* 8-8-0 (3) SMcCarthy(2) (b.nr hind: sn pushed along & outpcd stands' side)....s.h 10
446[10] Purbeck Centenary **(50)***(35) (PHowling)* 5-8-1 (8) DebbieBiggs(10) (chsd ldrs tl wknd over 1f out)....½ 11
475[5] Henry the Hawk **(45)***(26) (MDods)* 4-8-1v(3) AEddery(3) (b: racd stands' side: rdn & outpcd fr ½-wy)....1¼ 12
Covent Garden Girl **(50)***(15) (MWEasterby)* 5-8-6 (3) RuthCoulter(11) (b.off hind: in tch far side tl wknd 2f out)....5 13

100/30 Chadwell Hall (9/4-7/2), **4/1** Domicksky, **9/2** Kalar, **10/1** Nineacres, Purbeck Centenary, Henry the Hawk, **12/1** PRINCE BELFORT, **14/1** Covent Garden Girl, Gondo, Miss Siham (IRE), **16/1** Barbezieux, Leading Princess (IRE), **20/1** Rich Glow, CSF £162.20 CT £2,467.94 TOTE £21.40: £4.20 £3.90 £4.40 (£179.70) Trio Not won; £814.31 to Newbury 21/4/95 OWNER Mrs Carole Sykes (HAMBLETON) BRED Concorde Bloodstock Agency Ltd 13 Rn
60.9 secs (2.90) SF: 15/-/-/-/-/13/-/-/-/-/-/-/-

689 LITTLETHORPE RATING RELATED MAIDEN LIMITED STKS (0-70) (3-Y.O) (Class E) £3,046.00 (£922.00: £450.00: £214.00)
1m Stalls: High GOING minus 0.51 sec per fur (F) 5-00 (5-01)

*566*5 **Danegold (IRE)** **(70)***(70)*(Fav)*(MRChannon)* 3-9-0v KDarley(7) (lw: trckd ldrs: led over 2f out: styd on wl u.p fnl f) — 1
*443*7 Dance King **(67)***(68) (JEBanks)* 3-9-0 JQuinn(8) (led tl over 2f out: kpt on wl: nt qckn ins fnl f) 1 2
Spanish Steps (IRE) **(62)***(66) (MWEasterby)* 3-9-0 LCharnock(3) (trckd ldrs: ev ch 2f out: nt qckn fnl f) 1¼ 3
Court Joker (IRE) **(69)***(62) (MHTompkins)* 3-8-9 (5) SMulvey(2) (hld up: slipped ent st: hdwy over 3f out: ev ch 2f out: grad wknd) 1¾ 4
Harvey White (IRE) **(68)***(59) (JPearce)* 3-9-0 GBardwell(4) (lw: trckd ldrs: effrt over 3f out: sn outpcd: nvr able to chal) 1¾ 5
553 10 Le Bal **(43)***(40) (MrsNMacauley)* 3-8-9b JFortune(9) (trckd ldrs: drvn along over 3f out: wknd over 2f out) 7 6
Percy Parrot **(50)***(35) (RMWhitaker)* 3-9-0 ACulhane(6) (hld up & bhd: effrt 4f out: n.d) 5 7
521 16 Sailors Moon **(42)***(25) (HJCollingridge)* 3-8-9 MTebbutt(1) (s.i.s: a outpcd & bhd) 2½ 8

2/1 DANEGOLD (IRE), **7/2** Dance King, **4/1** Court Joker (IRE), Harvey White (IRE) (3/1-9/2), **7/1** Spanish Steps (IRE), **20/1** Le Bal, Percy Parrot, Sailors Moon, CSF £9.79 TOTE £2.60: £1.80 £1.10 £2.70 (£4.30) Trio £27.20 OWNER The Dream Team (UPPER LAMBOURN) BRED Barronstown Stud and Ron Con Ltd 8 Rn 1m 41.3 (3.60) SF: 21/19/17/13/10/-/-/-

T/Plpt £8,456.50 (1.28 Tckts). T/Qdpt: Not won; £48.60 to Newbury 21/4/95. WG

NEWBURY (L-H)
Friday April 21st (Good to firm)
WEATHER: sunny WIND: slt half bhd

690 BECKHAMPTON MAIDEN STKS (2-Y.O) (Class D) £3,850.00 (£1,150.00: £550.00: £250.00) **5f 34y** Stalls: Centre GOING minus 0.42 sec (F) 2-10 (2-11)

Polish Legion *(86+t) (JHMGosden)* 2-9-0 LDettori(5) (str: a.p: rdn over 2f out: led ins fnl f: r.o wl) — 1
Caricature (IRE) *(86) (GLewis)* 2-9-0 PaulEddery(2) (neat: bit bkwd: a.p: rdn over 2f out: led over 1f out: edgd rt & hdd ins fnl f: r.o) hd 2
April The Eighth *(82) (BWHills)* 2-9-0 MHills(7) (leggy: rdn over 3f out: hdwy over 1f out: r.o) 1¼ 3
5624 Friendly Forester (USA) *(79) (RCharlton)* 2-9-0 WRyan(6) (led over 3f: 3rd whn hmpd ins fnl f: one pce) 1 4
5336 Martara (IRE) *(74) (MRChannon)* 2-9-0 RHughes(9) (a.p: hrd rdn & ev ch over 1f out: one pce ins fnl f) 1½ 5
Man of Wit (IRE) *(63) (APJarvis)* 2-9-0 BThomson(3) (unf: a.p: ev ch over 1f out: wknd fnl f) 3½ 6
Extra Hour (IRE) *(59) (WRMuir)* 2-9-0 MJKinane(4) (neat: bit bkwd: no hdwy fnl 2f) 1½ 7
Woodborough (USA) *(57)*(Fav)*(PWChapple-Hyam)* 2-9-0 JReid(12) (scope: lw: rdn over 3f out: nvr nr to chal: fin lame) ½ 8
Two Socks *(52) (MMcCormack)* 2-9-0 WRSwinburn(8) (neat: bhd fnl 3f) 1¾ 9
Hoh Returns (IRE) *(50) (MBell)* 2-9-0 MFenton(14) (b.hind: scope: lw: prom over 2f) ½ 10
Current Leader *(46) (RHannon)* 2-9-0 KDarley(1) (neat: bit bkwd: bhd fnl 3f) 1¼ 11
Blue Delight (IRE) *(34) (GLewis)* 2-9-0 SWhitworth(10) (str: bit bkwd: s.s: a bhd) 4 12
Bozeman (IRE) *(29) (RHannon)* 2-9-0 PatEddery(11) (neat: bit bkwd: bhd fnl 2f) 1½ 13

8/11 Woodborough (USA), **6/1** Martara (IRE), **7/1** POLISH LEGION (op 3/1), **12/1** April The Eighth (7/1-16/1), Hoh Returns (IRE) (9/2-14/1), **16/1** Bozeman (IRE), **20/1** Friendly Forester (USA), **25/1** Caricature (IRE), Extra Hour (IRE), Current Leader, **33/1** Two Socks, Man of Wit (IRE), **50/1** Blue Delight (IRE), CSF £151.13 TOTE £6.20: £1.80 £12.90 £2.40 (£247.10) Trio £444.70 OWNER Sheikh Mohammed (NEWMARKET) BRED Sheikh Mohammed bin Rashid al Maktoum 13 Rn
61.71 secs (1.41) SF: 39/39/35/32/27/16/12/10/5/3/-/-/-

691 PETER SMITH MEMORIAL MAIDEN STKS (3-Y.O) (Class D) £4,402.50 (£1,320.00: £635.00: £292.50)
1m 3f 5y Stalls: Low GOING minus 0.42 sec per fur (F) 2-40 (2-47)

Tamure (IRE) *(100+)*(Fav)*(JHMGosden)* 3-9-0 LDettori(7) (b.hind: w'like: scope: hdwy over 2f out: led over 1f out: comf)........— **1**
Royal Circle *(92) (RCharlton)* 3-8-9 KDarley(3) (leggy: unf: 6th st: ev ch over 1f out: unable qckn)........2 **2**
Montejurra *(96) (HRACecil)* 3-9-0 MJKinane(6) (w'like: scope: 4th st: rdn over 3f out: led over 2f out tl over 1f out: one pce)........¾ **3**
Candle Smile (USA) *(94) (MRStoute)* 3-9-0 WRSwinburn(1) (bit bkwd: 3rd st: ev ch over 1f out: eased whn btn ins fnl f)........1¾ **4**
Cypress Avenue (IRE) *(86) (RHannon)* 3-9-0 RPerham(15) (w'like: scope: bit bkwd: plld hrd: led over 8f out tl over 2f out: sn wknd)........5 **5**
Taklif (IRE) *(85) (BWHills)* 3-9-0 WCarson(14) (stdy hdwy over 3f out: shkn up over 2f out: sn wknd)........1 **6**
Vitus *(85) (HRACecil)* 3-9-0 WRyan(5) (w'like: scope: hdwy over 2f out: wknd over 1f out)........s.h **7**
Heath Robinson (IRE) *(83) (JHMGosden)* 3-9-0 GHind(2) (b: b.hind: w'like: bkwd: led over 2f: 2nd st: wknd over 2f out)........1 **8**
Typhoon Eight (IRE) *(80) (BWHills)* 3-9-0 MHills(9) (bit bkwd: nvr nrr)........2 **9**
Streaky Hawk (USA) *(75) (PFICole)* 3-9-0 TQuinn(13) (nvr nrr)........3½ **10**
United Force (IRE) *(73) (PWChapple-Hyam)* 3-9-0 JReid(11) (lw: nvr nr to chal)........1¼ **11**
Corradini *(71) (HRACecil)* 3-9-0 PatEddery(4) (w'like: scope: hdwy over 5f out: 5th st: wknd over 3f out)........2 **12**
485[4] He Knows The Rules *(68) (MRChannon)* 3-9-0 RHughes(12) (a bhd)........2 **13**
Zalament *(53) (APJarvis)* 3-8-9 BThomson(10) (prom over 5f)........7 **14**
Peatsville (IRE) *(36) (MRChannon)* 3-9-0 CRutter(8) (leggy: scope: bit bkwd: bhd fnl 5f)........15 **15**

9/4 TAMURE (IRE) (op 5/4), **9/2** Vitus, **7/1** Taklif (IRE) (5/1-8/1), **8/1** United Force (IRE) (tchd 12/1), **12/1** Royal Circle, Corradini (8/1-14/1), Typhoon Eight (IRE) (7/1-14/1), **14/1** Candle Smile (USA) (10/1-16/1), Montejurra (op 5/1), **20/1** Streaky Hawk (USA), He Knows The Rules, **25/1** Heath Robinson (IRE), **33/1** Peatsville (IRE), **50/1** Zalament, Cypress Avenue (IRE), CSF £29.71 TOTE £3.10: £1.70 £3.20 £4.30 (£37.90) Trio £225.10 OWNER Sheikh Mohammed (NEWMARKET) BRED Sheikh Mohammed bin Rashid al Maktoum 15 Rn
2m 20.29 (4.29) SF: 33/25/29/27/19/18/18/16/13/8/6/4/1/-/-

692 GAINSBOROUGH STUD FRED DARLING STKS (Gp 3) (3-Y.O F) (Class A) £22,740.00 (£8,532.00: £4,116.00: £1,812.00)
7f 64y (round) Stalls: Low GOING minus 0.42 sec per fur (F) 3-10 (3-15)

Aqaarid (USA) *(113)*(Fav)*(JLDunlop)* 3-9-0 WCarson(5) (2nd st: led 2f out: rdn out)........— **1**
Hoh Magic **(117)***(108) (MBell)* 3-9-0 MHills(4) (lw: stdy hdwy over 2f out: rdn over 1f out: r.o ins fnl f)........2½ **2**
Autumn Affair **(87)***(107) (CEBrittain)* 3-9-0 BDoyle(1) (rdn & hdwy over 1f out: r.o ins fnl f)........hd **3**
All Time Great *(104) (LMCumani)* 3-9-0 LDettori(3) (5th st: rdn over 1f out: one pce)........1½ **4**
Gay Gallanta (USA) **(116)***(103)*(Fav)*(MRStoute)* 3-9-0 WRSwinburn(6) (lw: 4th st: hrd rdn over 1f out: one pce)........nk **5**
Fiendish (USA) **(90)***(100) (PFICole)* 3-9-0 TQuinn(2) (led over 1f: 3rd st: wknd over 1f out)........1½ **6**
Signs **(93)***(100) (RHannon)* 3-9-0 PatEddery(8) (plld hrd: led 6f out to 2f out: wknd fnl f)........hd **7**
Loyalize (USA) **(109)***(92) (DRLoder)* 3-9-0 MJKinane(7) (lw: 6th st: wknd over 2f out)........3½ **8**

9/4 AQAARID (USA), Gay Gallanta (USA), **3/1** Hoh Magic, **13/2** Loyalize (USA), **14/1** All Time Great, **20/1** Signs, **33/1** Fiendish (USA), **50/1** Autumn Affair, CSF £9.16 TOTE £3.00: £1.30 £1.10 £4.50 (£6.70) OWNER Mr Hamdan Al Maktoum (ARUNDEL) BRED Shadwell Farm Inc in USA 8 Rn
1m 28.37 (-0.13) SF: 65/60/59/56/55/52/52/44

693 NEWBURY RACECOURSE SHOPPING ARCADE H'CAP (0-100) (4-Y.O+) (Class B) £8,460.80 (£3,147.20: £1,523.60: £638.00: £269.00: £121.40)
5f 34y Stalls: Centre GOING minus 0.42 sec per fur (F) 3-40 (3-42)

Royale Figurine (IRE) (88)*(96) (MJFetherston-Godley)* 4-9-0 WRSwinburn(7) (lw: hld up: rdn over 1f out: led nr fin)........— **1**

Brave Edge **(86)***(94) (RHannon)* 4-8-12 RHughes(6) (hld up: led over 1f out: hrd rdn & hdd nr fin) ....hd 2
434[9] Mister Jolson **(85)***(87)*(Fav)*(RJHodges)* 6-8-11 RCochrane(9) (hdwy over 1f out: r.o ins fnl f)....1¾ 3
Humbert's Landing (IRE) **(90)***(88) (PFICole)* 4-9-2 TQuinn(1) (bit bkwd: hdwy over 1f out: nvr nrr) 1¼ 4
Crystal Magic **(94)***(92) (RHannon)* 4-9-6 JReid(10) (lw: led over 1f: ev ch over 1f out: one pce) ....hd 5
Sir Joey (USA) **(85)***(83) (PGMurphy)* 6-8-6 (5) SDrowne(11) (lw: nt clr run over 1f out: hdwy fnl f: nvr nrr) ....s.h 6
565[2] Allthruthenight (IRE) **(83)***(76) (LJHolt)* 6-8-9 AMcGlone(3) (nvr nr to chal) 1½ 7
502[8] Eagle Day (USA) **(78)***(70) (DRCElsworth)* 4-7-13b(5) NVarley(4) (no hdwy fnl 2f) ....nk 8
Spaniards Close **(93)***(79) (PJMakin)* 7-9-5 PatEddery(5) (nvr nrr) 2 9
571[10] Regal Chimes **(95)***(80) (BAMcMahon)* 6-9-7 KDarley(14) (w ldr: ev ch wl over 1f out: wknd fnl f) ....½ 10
Darren Boy (IRE) **(90)***(74) (PFICole)* 4-8-11 (5) PMcCabe(2) (swtg: s.s: a bhd) ....nk 11
Lord High Admiral (CAN) **(92)***(75) (MJHeaton-Ellis)* 7-9-4 RPerham(12) (lw: led over 3f out tl wl over 1f out: one pce) ....hd 12
Ashtina **(89)***(65) (RJHodges)* 10-9-1 LDettori(8) (prom over 2f) 2½ 13
565[8] Ann's Pearl (IRE) **(78)***(47) (JWHills)* 4-8-4 MHills(13) (bhd fnl 2f) 2 14

LONG HANDICAP Eagle Day (USA) 7-10

11/2 Mister Jolson, **6/1** Humbert's Landing (IRE), **7/1** Allthruthenight (IRE), **10/1** Crystal Magic, Sir Joey (USA), **11/1** Lord High Admiral (CAN), **12/1** Spaniards Close, ROYALE FIGURINE (IRE), Regal Chimes, Ashtina, **14/1** Darren Boy (IRE), Ann's Pearl (IRE), Brave Edge, **20/1** Eagle Day (USA), CSF £153.41 CT £941.73 TOTE £11.70: £3.50 £5.10 £2.60 (£166.70) Trio £312.40 OWNER Mr Craig Pearman (EAST ILSLEY) BRED Craig Pearman 14 Rn

60.3 secs (equals standard) SF: 63/61/54/55/59/50/43/37/46/47/41/42/32/14

694

STROUD GREEN H'CAP (0-100) (3-Y.O) (Class C) £5,949.00 (£1,782.00: £856.00: £393.00) **1m (straight)** Stalls: Low GOING minus 0.42 sec per fur (F) 4-10 (4-12)

Crumpton Hill (IRE) (75)*(81+) (NAGraham)* 3-8-1 PaulEddery(6) (lw: hdwy 2f out: led 1f out: comf) ....— 1
Ihtiram (IRE) **(95)***(97) (JLDunlop)* 3-9-7 WCarson(10) (hdwy over 1f out: r.o ins fnl f) 2 2
Bedivere (USA) **(82)***(83) (PWChapple-Hyam)* 3-8-8 JReid(4) (bit bkwd: a.p: led over 1f out: sn hdd & unable qckn) ....nk 3
Lipizzaner (IRE) **(88)***(87) (BWHills)* 3-9-0 MJKinane(1) (rdn & hdwy 2f out: ev ch over 1f out: one pce) 1 4
543[3] Willie Conquer **(78)***(75)*(Fav)*(RAkehurst)* 3-8-4 GCarter(9) (hld up: nt clr run wl over 1f out: r.o one pce) 1 5
Myrtle Quest **(86)***(82) (RCharlton)* 3-8-12 KDarley(12) (a.p: led over 2f out tl over 1f out: wknd fnl f) ....¾ 6
Noble Sprinter (IRE) **(78)***(71) (RHannon)* 3-8-4 RPerham(13) (a.p: hrd rdn over 1f out: sn wknd) 1¼ 7
Midwich Cuckoo **(84)***(77) (PTWalwyn)* 3-8-10 PatEddery(3) (nvr nrr) ....nk 8
Shifting Moon **(80)***(70) (IABalding)* 3-8-6 RCochrane(8) (nvr nrr) 1¼ 9
564[6] Mentor (GR) **(92)***(82) (RCharlton)* 3-9-4 DHarrison(11) (led over 5f) ....s.h 10
Santa Fan (IRE) **(80)***(67) (PFICole)* 3-8-6 TQuinn(5) (bit bkwd: bhd fnl 3f) 1¾ 11
Bobanlyn (IRE) **(78)***(65) (DMorris)* 3-8-4 StephenDavies(7) (lw: bhd fnl 3f) ....hd 12
Chattaroy (IRE) **(92)***(74) (JHMGosden)* 3-9-4 LDettori(2) (bit bkwd: prom over 5f) 2½ 13
Sylvandra **(94)***(64) (PGMurphy)* 3-9-6 JWilliams(14) (bit bkwd: a bhd) 6 14

7/2 Willie Conquer, **13/2** Lipizzaner (IRE), **8/1** Bedivere (USA), Ihtiram (IRE) (6/1-9/1), Chattaroy (IRE) (5/1-9/1), **9/1** Midwich Cuckoo, **12/1** Myrtle Quest, CRUMPTON HILL (IRE), Shifting Moon, Bobanlyn (IRE), **20/1** Santa Fan (IRE), **33/1** Noble Sprinter (IRE), Mentor (GR), Sylvandra, CSF £97.20 CT £741.02 TOTE £16.10: £3.00 £2.70 £2.00 (£66.90) Trio £127.00 OWNER Mr T. H. Chadney (NEWMARKET) BRED Michael Doyle 14 Rn

1m 37.9 (0.90) SF: 42/58/44/48/36/43/32/38/31/43/28/26/35/25

695

BRIDGET MAIDEN STKS (3-Y.O F) (Class D) £4,240.00 (£1,270.00: £610.00: £280.00) **7f (straight)** Stalls: Centre GOING minus 0.42 sec per fur (F) 4-40 (4-44)

Tarhhib *(94+)*(Fav)*(JHMGosden)* 3-8-11 WCarson(7) (str: scope: hld up: led over 1f out: rdn out) ....— 1
Farani *(94) (RCharlton)* 3-8-11 KDarley(12) (w'like: bit bkwd: rdn over 2f out: hdwy over 1f out: r.o wl ins fnl f) ....hd 2
Courageous Dancer (IRE) *(89) (BHanbury)* 3-8-11 WRyan(16) (w'like: scope: bit bkwd: hdwy 2f out: ev ch over 1f out: unable qckn) 2 3

All The Time *(80) (PFICole)* 3-8-11 TQuinn(8) (leggy: unf: led over 5f: wknd fnl f) 4 **4**
Mighty Squaw *(79) (MissGayKelleway)* 3-8-11 RCochrane(9) (w'like: bit bkwd: a.p: ev ch over 2f out: wknd over 1f out) ....nk **5**
Academy Life *(78) (PFICole)* 3-8-11 PatEddery(17) (leggy: unf: lw: hdwy over 4f out: wknd wl over 1f out) ....½ **6**
Lovely Lyca *(78) (JWHills)* 3-8-11 BThomson(6) (w'like: bkwd: nt clr run over 2f out: nvr nr to chal) ....hd **7**
Proud Destiny *(78) (MRStoute)* 3-8-11 WRSwinburn(11) (w'lke: bit bkwd: no hdwy fnl 2f) ....hd **8**
Brave Princess *(74) (MAJarvis)* 3-8-11 PRobinson(13) (w'like: scope: bit bkwd: hld up: rdn over 2f out: wknd over 1f out) 1½ **9**
Prickwillow (USA) *(69) (JHMGosden)* 3-8-11 LDettori(15) (w'like: scope: a mid div) 2½ **10**
Lobana (IRE) *(68) (JWHills)* 3-8-11 MHills(2) (w'like: nvr nrr) ....hd **11**
Indescent Blue *(63) (DWPArbuthnot)* 3-8-11 RHughes(3) (w'like: scope: bit bkwd: a mid div) 2½ **12**
Sadler's Pearl *(63) (BJMeehan)* 3-8-11 BDoyle(1) (w'like: bkwd: hld up: rdn over 4f out: sn wknd) ....s.h **13**
Easter Coul (IRE) *(57) (MJFetherston-Godley)* 3-8-11 JReid(18) (unf: a bhd) 2½ **14**
Lidhama (USA) *(57) (GLewis)* 3-8-11 SWhitworth(5) (wl grwn: bkwd: s.s: a bhd) ....hd **15**
Roka *(57) (RHannon)* 3-8-11 MJKinane(14) (cmpt: hdwy over 4f out: wknd over 2f out) ....s.h **15**
Amany (IRE) *(53) (GLewis)* 3-8-11 PaulEddery(19) (str: scope: bit bkwd: s.s: a bhd) 1½ **17**
Pacific Overture *(47) (CRBarwell)* 3-8-11 JWilliams(4) (neat: a bhd) 2½ **18**
Lorsanginner (IRE) *(31) (SDow)* 3-8-11 StephenDavies(10) (w'like: bit bkwd: prom over 3f) ...7 **19**

13/8 TARHHIB, **7/1** Prickwillow (USA) (4/1-15/2), **8/1** Farani, **10/1** Brave Princess, **12/1** Proud Destiny (op 7/1), **14/1** Academy Life (6/1-16/1), Roka (10/1-16/1), All The Time (8/1-16/1), **16/1** Courageous Dancer (IRE), **25/1** Amany (IRE), **33/1** Mighty Squaw, Lobana (IRE), Sadler's Pearl, Indescent Blue, Lidhama (USA), Lovely Lyca, **50/1** Easter Coul (IRE), Lorsanginner (IRE), **66/1** Pacific Overture, CSF £15.60 TOTE £2.70: £1.50 £2.80 £4.70 (£12.00) Trio £161.10 OWNER Mr Hamdan Al Maktoum (NEWMARKET) BRED Shadwell Estate Company Limited 19 Rn
1m 24.4 (-0.10) SF: 62/62/57/48/47/46/46/46/42/37/36/31/31/25/25/25/21/15/-

696 THATCHAM H'CAP (0-95) (4-Y.O+) (Class C) £6,131.00 (£1,838.00: £884.00: £407.00)
2m Stalls: Low GOING minus 0.42 sec per fur (F) 5-10 (5-12)

Bold Gait **(95)***(108) (JRFanshawe)* 4-9-10 DHarrison(7) (lw: 6th st: led over 2f out: r.o wl)...— **1**
Shadirwan (IRE) **(70)***(80)*(Fav)*(RAkehurst)* 4-7-13 GCarter(9) (b.off fore: 4th st: led over 4f out tl over 2f out: unable qckn) 3½ **2**
Bardolph (USA) **(76)***(84) (PFICole)* 8-8-9 TQuinn(2) (bit bkwd: 3rd st: rdn over 2f out: one pce) 1¼ **3**
Father Sky **(77)***(84) (OSherwood)* 4-8-6 BThomson(1) (2nd st: ev ch over 2f out: one pce) ..1½ **4**
Tarthooth (IRE) **(67)***(70) (CJBenstead)* 4-7-10 ow1 WCarson(6) (5th st: wknd over 3f out) 3 **5**
432[4] Elburg (IRE) **(62)***(62) (RPCHoad)* 5-7-9 ow2 JQuinn(8) (led over 11f) 1½ **6**
183[3] Romalito **(60)***(62) (MBlanshard)* 5-7-2 (5) MBaird(5) (bkwd: a bhd) ....nk **7**
506[7] Brandon Prince (IRE) **(70)***(71) (IABalding)* 7-8-3 KDarley(10) (a bhd) 1 **8**
Sight'n Sound **(65)***(63) (DRCElsworth)* 4-7-3 (5)ow1 NVarley(3) (a bhd) 2 **9**
549[16] Requested **(60)***(56) (PBurgoyne)* 8-7-7 GBardwell(4) (a bhd) 2½ **10**
LONG HANDICAP Elburg (IRE) 7-5 Romalito 7-2 Sight'n Sound 7-3 Requested 7-5

7/2 Shadirwan (IRE), **4/1** BOLD GAIT, **5/1** Father Sky, **11/2** Tarthooth (IRE), **9/1** Elburg (IRE), **12/1** Bardolph (USA), Sight'n Sound, **14/1** Brandon Prince (IRE), **33/1** Romalito, Requested, CSF £16.54 CT £134.66 TOTE £3.90: £1.40 £1.80 £3.30 (£9.00) Trio £28.90 OWNER Mrs I. Phillips (NEWMARKET) BRED Ian H. Wills 10 Rn 3m 28.9 (2.40) SF: 64/36/44/40/26/22/22/31/19/16
WEIGHT FOR AGE 4yo-4lb

T/Jkpt: Not won; £9,085.65 to Newbury 22/4/95. T/Plpt: £1,320.20 (22.42 Tckts). T/Qdpt: £113.90 (2.2 Tckts). AK

THIRSK (L-H)
Friday April 21st (Good to firm, Firm patches)
WEATHER: showers WIND: mod half against

697 BRITON RATING RELATED MAIDEN LIMITED STKS (0-75) (3-Y.O) (Class D) £3,968.90 (£1,185.20: £566.60: £257.30)
6f Stalls: High GOING minus 0.07 sec per fur (G) 2-15 (2-17)

Pelleman **(72)***(84) (RBoss)* 3-9-0 JWeaver(1) (mde all: edgd lft over 1f out: r.o u.p) ....— **1**

572[6] Roy Boy **(71)***(81) (MrsMReveley)* 3-9-0 JFortune(3) (lw: a chsng ldrs: effrt 2f out: nt qckn ins fnl f) 1¼ 2
Rolling (IRE) **(70)***(72) (BWHills)* 3-8-4 (5) JDSmith(2) (unf: sn outpcd & bhd: hdwy over 2f out: styd on ins fnl f) 1½ 3
354[14] Penny's Wishing **(56)***(69) (JPLeigh)* 3-8-9 GDuffield(8) (chsd wnr: kpt on one pce fnl 2f) 1 4
Rasas (IRE) **(73)***(73) (HThomsonJones)* 3-9-0 NCarlisle(10) (lw: trckd ldrs: plld hrd: nt clr run over 2f out: effrt & hmpd over 1f out: styd on) ....nk 5
South Rock **(74)***(66) (JAGlover)* 3-8-9 DeanMcKeown(7) (bit bkwd: hld up & bhd: stdy hdwy 2f out: nvr plcd to chal) ....¾ 6
Brecongill Lad **(70)***(63) (MissSEHall)* 3-9-0 NConnorton(5) (bit bkwd: dwlt: hld up & plld hrd: effrt & nt clr run over 2f out: kpt on fnl f) 3 7
522[4] Blue Sioux **(70)***(57) (JWharton)* 3-8-9 KFallon(12) (hld up: effrt & nt clr run over 1f out: swtchd: n.d) ....½ 8
Just Dissident (IRE) **(68)***(60) (RMWhitaker)* 3-9-0 ACulhane(9) (prom: rdn & hung lft over 2f out: sn wknd) ....¾ 9
468[2] Shen Yang (USA) **(75)***(55) (GLMoore)* 3-9-0 BRouse(6) (chsd ldrs: rdn over 2f out: sn wknd) 2 10
Shady Deed (USA) **(73)***(49)*(Fav)*(JWHills)* 3-8-9 DHolland(11) (chsd ldrs: hung lft ½-wy: wknd 2f out) ....hd 11
Hey Up Dolly (IRE) **(68)***(49) (JBerry)* 3-8-9 JCarroll(4) (bit bkwd: chsd ldrs: rdn ½-wy: sn wknd) ....nk 12

5/2 Shady Deed (USA) (7/2-9/4), **6/1** Shen Yang (USA), **7/1** Roy Boy, Rasas (IRE), **8/1** Rolling (IRE) (op 5/1), South Rock, **9/1** PELLEMAN (op 6/1), Blue Sioux, **12/1** Hey Up Dolly (IRE) (op 8/1), **16/1** Just Dissident (IRE), **25/1** Brecongill Lad, **33/1** Penny's Wishing, CSF £70.64 TOTE £16.00: £3.30 £2.70 £3.00 (£66.40) Trio £374.40; £189.87 to Thirsk 22/4/95 OWNER Mr M. Berger (NEWMARKET) 12 Rn 1m 12.4 (2.70) SF: 54/51/42/39/43/36/33/27/30/25/19/19
OFFICIAL EXPLANATION Shady Deed (USA): the jockey stated that his orders were to lay up but, that after three furlongs, the filly was in trouble. The trainer's representative added that the filly might be slightly ungenuine.

698

SOWERBY MAIDEN STKS (3-Y.O) (Class D) £3,833.70 (£1,143.60: £545.80: £246.90) **1m 4f** Stalls: High GOING minus 0.07 sec per fur (G) 2-50 (2-51)

500[5] **Bambara** *(63) (CEBrittain)* 3-8-9 MRimmer(8) (plld hrd: chsd ldrs: outpcd over 3f out: styd on wl to ld ins fnl f: eased nr fin) ....— 1
True Bird (IRE) *(63) (JDBethell)* 3-8-9 JCarroll(2) (cmpt: unf: bhd: drvn along & rn green 7f out: gd hdwy 2f out: styd on wl nr fin) ....nk 2
Mansur (IRE) *(66)*(Fav)*(DRLoder)* 3-9-0v JWeaver(3) (lw: led: clr 3f out: wknd & hdd ins fnl f) 1 3
Tonnerre *(62) (CWFairhurst)* 3-9-0 JFanning(7) (plld hrd: trckd ldrs: effrt 3f out: kpt on one pce) 3 4
477[2] Stone Cross (IRE) *(62) (RFFisher)* 3-9-0 KFallon(5) (hld up & plld hrd: hdwy on outside over 2f out: swtchd ins: shkn up: nvr plcd to chal) ....½ 5
591[10] Beyaateh *(53) (MCChapman)* 3-8-2 (7) CMunday(4) (bhd: edgd lft & kpt on fnl 2f: n.d) 3 6
Kraton Garden (USA) *(56) (WJarvis)* 3-9-0 MTebbutt(1) (bit bkwd: prom: drvn along & outpcd 6f out: n.d after) 1½ 7
Indiscretion (IRE) *(32) (MrsJCecil)* 3-8-9 AClark(6) (tall: leggy: s.s: hdwy to chse ldrs 8f out: wknd over 2f out: sn bhd & eased) 14 8

4/9 Mansur (IRE), **6/1** Indiscretion (IRE), **9/1** Kraton Garden (USA), **10/1** Stone Cross (IRE), **16/1** BAMBARA, True Bird (IRE), **33/1** Tonnerre, **66/1** Beyaateh, CSF £193.62 TOTE £22.90: £2.60 £3.00 £1.10 (£76.10) OWNER Mr Saeed Manana (NEWMARKET) BRED Saeed Manana 8 Rn
2m 39.8 (9.80) SF: 24/24/27/23/23/14/17/-

699

KNAYTON CLAIMING STKS (2-Y.O) (Class F) £3,182.40 (£881.40: £421.20) **5f** Stalls: High GOING minus 0.07 sec per fur (G) 3-20 (3-23)

508[6] **Just Lady** *(67t)*(Fav)*(WGMTurner)* 2-8-5 GDuffield(7) (mde all: hung lft & sn clr: unchal) ....— 1
Double Point (IRE) *(64) (MBell)* 2-8-5 (7) GFaulkner(8) (cmpt: unf: unruly in stalls: s.s: swtchd lft: hdwy to chse wnr 2f out: no imp) 3 2
Patrington Park *(60) (MWEasterby)* 2-8-12 MBirch(3) (leggy: unf: stdd s: hld up & bhd: stdy hdwy 2f out: kpt on ins fnl f) 1¼ 3
574* Tropical Beach *(58) (JBerry)* 2-9-0 JCarroll(2) (outpcd & bhd tl styd on u.p appr fnl f) 1¼ 4
Thorntoun Jewel (IRE) *(44) (MJohnston)* 2-8-1 TWilliams(6) (neat: unf: chsd ldrs 2f: sn lost pl: kpt on fnl f) ....nk 5

Harsh Times *(36) (MHEasterby)* 2-8-1 SMaloney(9) (b.hind: cmpt: unf: s.s: outpcd & bhd tl kpt on u.p appr fnl f) 2½ 6
554[4] Mysterious Times *(33) (MWEasterby)* 2-7-13 LCharnock(5) (sn wl outpcd & bhd: kpt on appr fnl f) ....½ 7
574[5] Royal Rigger *(35) (CSmith)* 2-8-1 JFanning(10) (chsd wnr tl wknd 2f out) ....s.h 8
595[5] Ned's Contessa (IRE) *(31) (MDods)* 2-7-13 DaleGibson(4) (chsd ldrs: rdn ½-wy: sn lost pl) ....½ 9
615[16] Merlin's Honour *(31) (PCHaslam)* 2-8-5 JWeaver(1) (swvd lft s: hld up in tch: n.m.r 2f out: eased) 2 10

7/4 JUST LADY (op 3/1), **11/4** Tropical Beach (2/1-7/2), **7/2** Double Point (IRE), **10/1** Harsh Times, Merlin's Honour, **14/1** Ned's Contessa (IRE) (16/1-25/1), **16/1** Thorntoun Jewel (IRE), **20/1** Royal Rigger, Patrington Park, Mysterious Times, CSF £9.24 TOTE £3.50: £1.30 £1.90 £3.80 (£6.40) £183.70 OWNER Somerset and Dorset Racing (SHERBORNE) BRED Mrs M. S. Teversham 10 Rn
61.1 secs (3.90) SF: 17/14/10/8/-/-/-/-/-/-

700

HAMBLETON STKS (3-Y.O+) (Class C) £5,163.20 (£1,908.80: £914.40: £372.00: £146.00: £55.60)
5f Stalls: High GOING minus 0.07 sec per fur (G) 3-50 (3-50)

571* **El Yasaf (IRE) (106)***(112) (GFierro)* 7-9-12 MWigham(1) (chsd ldrs: hdwy over 1f out: led wl ins fnl f: pushed out) ....— 1
Mistertopogigo (IRE) **(116)***(112)*(Fav)*(WSCunningham)* 5-9-12 AClark(5) (b.off hind: stdd s: hdwy to chse ldrs ½-wy: led 1f out tl wl ins fnl f: r.o nr fin) ....hd 2
Ya Malak **(100)***(102) (JWPayne)* 4-9-12 DHolland(2) (trckd ldr: led over 1f out: sn hdd & nt qckn) 3 3
571[7] Snipe Hall **(97)***(94) (TRWatson)* 4-9-4 DeanMcKeown(6) (b.hind: hmpd s: bhd & drvn along: hdwy 2f out: kpt on) ....s.h 4
Palacegate Episode (IRE) **(109)***(91) (JBerry)* 5-9-7 JCarroll(3) (led tl over 1f out: sn wknd) 2 5
571[11] Call Me I'm Blue (IRE) **(97)***(93) (NTinkler)* 5-9-10 MTebbutt(4) (hld up: effrt ½-wy: sn outpcd & hung lft: kpt on nr fin) ....hd 6

10/11 Mistertopogigo (IRE), **9/2** EL YASAF (IRE), **5/1** Palacegate Episode (IRE), **6/1** Ya Malak (op 4/1), **14/1** Snipe Hall, **16/1** Call Me I'm Blue (IRE), CSF £8.92 TOTE £6.50: £2.90 £1.10 (£3.00) OWNER Old School House Racing Ltd (HEDNESFORD) BRED Deepwood Farm Stud 6 Rn
59.3 secs (2.10) SF: 67/67/57/49/46/48

701

OAKSTRIPE CLAIMING H'CAP (0-70) (3-Y.O+) (Class F) £3,701.10 (£1,029.60: £495.30)
6f Stalls: High GOING minus 0.07 sec per fur (G) 4-20 (4-22)

*417** **Berge (IRE) (53)***(68+)*(Fav)*(WAO'Gorman)* 4-8-11b EmmaO'Gorman(14) (lw: in tch: hdwy to ld over 1f out: sn clr) ....— 1
591[4] Russian Heroine **(57)***(61) (MJohnston)* 3-8-3 DHolland(5) (chsd ldrs: led over 2f out: hdd over 1f out: nt qckn) 4 2
491[8] Miss Whittingham (IRE) **(56)***(56) (JBerry)* 5-9-0 JCarroll(11) (a chsng ldrs: kpt on wl u.p fnl 2f) 1½ 3
688[4] Kalar **(43)***(43) (DWChapman)* 6-7-12b(3) DarrenMoffatt(3) (led far side: kpt on wl fnl f) ....nk 4
535[10] Plum First **(58)***(55) (LRLloyd-James)* 5-9-2b NKennedy(19) (b.hind: lw: chsd ldrs: hung lft ½-wy: kpt on one pce fnl 2f) 1 5
419[9] Shadow Jury **(56)***(53) (DWChapman)* 5-9-0b DeanMcKeown(4) (racd far side: chsd ldr: styd on appr fnl f) ....s.h 6
491[7] Densben **(54)***(49) (DenysSmith)* 11-8-12 KFallon(8) (styd on fnl 2f: nvr nr to chal) ....¾ 7
192[7] Rapier Point (IRE) **(70)***(63) (PCHaslam)* 4-10-0 JWeaver(2) (b: racd far side: sn outpcd: kpt on appr fnl f) ....¾ 8
646[6] Angelic Dancer **(47)***(38) (SRBowring)* 4-8-0b(5) CTeague(1) (racd far side: edgd rt fr ½-wy: n.d) ....½ 9
646[2] Giggleswick Girl **(52)***(41) (MRChannon)* 4-8-10 CandyMorris(16) (hld up: effrt on ins & nt clr run over 2f out: n.d) ....¾ 10
603[6] Polli Pui **(60)***(44) (PDEvans)* 3-8-6 SMaloney(18) (chsd ldrs over 3f: sn wknd) 2 11
Boost **(50)***(29) (CWThornton)* 3-7-10 JLowe(10) (outpcd: sme hdwy 2f out: eased) 2 12
532[8] The Institute Boy **(47)***(23) (MissJFCraze)* 5-8-5vow1 SWebster(7) (lw: trckd ldrs: effrt over 2f out: sn wknd) ....½ 13
Fyne Song **(47)***(21) (WJMusson)* 3-7-7 NCarlisle(17) (a outpcd & sn drvn along) 1½ 14
567[3] Sharp Conquest **(63)***(34) (WRMuir)* 4-9-7v JFortune(15) (chsd ldrs: drvn along ½-wy: sn wknd) 1¼ 15

Shotley Again **(38)***(6) (NBycroft)* 5-7-10 ow3 JFanning(12) (bit bkwd: rr div: effrt & n.m.r over 2f out: sn wknd) ....d.h **15**
646[10] Twice in Bundoran (IRE) **(49)***(16) (PSFelgate)* 4-8-7 RPrice(9) (b.hind: led over 3f: wknd)....1¼ **17**
555[10] Skiptamaloo **(38)** *(DonEnricoIncisa)* 4-7-10 KimTinkler(13) (bit bkwd: unruly in stalls: s.s: a bhd) 3 **18**
107[10] Muzz (IRE) **(59)** *(RMMcKellar)* 4-9-3 TWilliams(6) (swtchd rt s: t.o) 15 **19**

LONG HANDICAP Shotley Again 7-4 Fyne Song 7-5

6/1 BERGE (IRE), **13/2** Sharp Conquest, **7/1** Plum First, Giggleswick Girl, **8/1** Russian Heroine (op 12/1), **10/1** Fyne Song, **12/1** Miss Whittingham (IRE), Angelic Dancer, **14/1** Rapier Point (IRE), Kalar, **16/1** Densben, Shadow Jury, The Institute Boy, Polli Pui, **20/1** Twice in Bundoran (IRE), **25/1** Shotley Again, Boost, Muzz (IRE), **33/1** Skiptamaloo, CSF £56.83 CT £545.41 TOTE £5.90: £1.90 £1.80 £4.10 £3.00 (£31.80) Trio £523.20 OWNER Mr S. Fustok (NEWMARKET) BRED S. Fustok 19 Rn 1m 12.6 (2.90) SF: 48/29/36/23/35/33/29/43/18/21/12/-/3/-/14/-/-/-/-

WEIGHT FOR AGE 3yo-12lb

702

BIRDFORTH H'CAP (0-70) (3-Y.O+) (Class E) £3,753.90 (£1,123.20: £538.60: £246.30) **7f** Stalls: Low GOING minus 0.07 sec per fur (G) 4-50 (4-53)

446[8] **African Chimes (70)***(75) (WAO'Gorman)* 8-10-0 EmmaO'Gorman(4) (lw: a.p: led 2f out: rdn out) ....— **1**
590[3] Souperficial **(52)***(54)*(Fav)*(JAGlover)* 4-8-10v JWeaver(1) (lw: hld up: hrd rdn & hdwy on outside over 2f out: styd on wl fnl f: nt rch wnr) 1¼ **2**
Sycamore Lodge (IRE) **(66)***(65) (PCalver)* 4-9-10 MBirch(7) (hld up: stdy hdwy on outside 2f out: nt clr run & swtchd ins: fin strly) 1½ **3**
Sobering Thoughts **(66)***(58) (JLEyre)* 9-9-7 (3) OPears(12) (in tch: styd on u.p fnl 2f: nvr nr to chal) 3 **4**
535[7] Bella Parkes **(66)***(58) (DNicholls)* 4-9-10b AlexGreaves(10) (trckd ldrs: ev ch over 2f out: kpt on same pce) ....s.h **5**
579[7] Peacefull Reply (USA) **(53)***(45) (FHLee)* 5-8-11 NConnorton(2) (in tch: hmpd bnd 4f out: hung lft & kpt on u.p fnl f) ....hd **6**
Johnnie the Joker **(60)***(49) (JPLeigh)* 4-9-4 DeanMcKeown(8) (bkwd: chsd ldrs: drvn along ½-wy: outpcd fnl 2f) 1¼ **7**
535[15] Desert Invader (IRE) **(70)***(56) (DWChapman)* 4-9-11 (3) JTate(16) (s.i.s: bhd tl hdwy on outside 2f out: kpt on) 1¼ **8**
Light Movement (IRE) **(58)***(44) (WSCunningham)* 5-9-2 ACulhane(9) (b.nr fore: bkwd: nvr nr ldrs) ....s.h **9**
Different Times (IRE) **(53)***(39) (MissLCSiddall)* 5-8-8 (3) DRMcCabe(3) (s.i.s: bhd tl sme late hdwy) ....hd **10**
646[4] First Gold **(63)***(47) (JWharton)* 6-9-7 KFallon(6) (s.i.s: bhd: hdwy on ins 2f out: n.m.r: eased nr fin) ....½ **11**
405[2] Soaking **(65)***(46) (GLMoore)* 5-9-9 BRouse(5) (lw: chsd ldrs: n.m.r on ins over 2f out: sn wknd) 1½ **12**
354[13] Tyrone Flyer **(57)***(31) (GFierro)* 6-9-1 MWigham(14) (chsd ldrs: led 3f out to 2f out: sn wknd) 3 **13**
Comeonup **(54)***(24) (JMBradley)* 4-8-12 LCharnock(13) (b: chsd ldrs: wkng whn hmpd over 2f out) 1¾ **14**
Awesome Venture **(57)***(26) (MCChapman)* 5-8-8 (7) CMunday(11) (led to 3f out: sn wknd) ....½ **15**
579[4] Orthorhombus **(65)** *(DJSCosgrove)* 6-9-9b MRimmer(15) (b.off hind: lw: s.s: a bhd & sn drvn along) 15 **16**

11/2 Souperficial, **6/1** Soaking, **7/1** First Gold, **10/1** Sobering Thoughts, Comeonup, Orthorhombus, **12/1** AFRICAN CHIMES, Bella Parkes, Light Movement (IRE), **14/1** Different Times (IRE), Desert Invader (IRE), Sycamore Lodge (IRE), **16/1** Tyrone Flyer, Peacefull Reply (USA), **20/1** Johnnie the Joker, **33/1** Awesome Venture, CSF £75.93 CT £882.00 TOTE £31.90: £5.70 £1.40 £4.00 £2.20 (£37.10) Trio £246.30 OWNER Mr D. G. Wheatley (NEWMARKET) BRED Noel Cogan 16 Rn 1m 26.7 (4.00) SF: 57/36/47/40/40/27/31/38/26/21/29/28/13/6/8/-

T/Plpt: £299.80 (34.61 Tckts). T/Qdpt: £23.40 (3.3 Tckts) WG

0607a-LONGCHAMP (Paris, France) (R-H)
Tuesday April 11th (Good to firm)

703a

PRIX LORD SEYMOUR (Listed) (4-Y.O+)
1m 4f

Tot Ou Tard (IRE) *(110) (JForesi,France)* 5-8-11 ESaint-Martin ....— **1**
Danseur Landais *(109) (France)* 5-8-11 GMosse 1 **2**

Petralona (IRE) *(102) (France)* 4-8-8 TJarnet 4 3
440* Fire Worshipper (IRE) *(104) (JHMGosden)* 4-8-11 CAsmussen (btn approx further 3/4l).......... 5
OWNER Ecurie Kura BRED M.Kura 2m 33.1 SF: -/-/-/-
DS

0489a-SAINT-CLOUD (France) (L-H)
Friday April 14th (Good)

704a PRIX EDMOND BLANC (Gp 3) (4-Y.O+)
1m

Kaldouneeves (FR) *(111) (JEHammond,France)* 4-8-11 CAsmussen ....— 1
Agathe (USA) *(111) (AFabre,France)* 4-8-13 OPeslier 1 2
Les Boyer *(106) (GBotti,Italy)* 4-8-11 EBotti 1½ 3
Salt Lake *(PWChapple-Hyam)* 4-8-11 JReid (btn further 5½l by wnr).................... 6
OWNER Ecurie Chalhoub 1m 41.8 SF: -/-/-/-
DS

0608a-EVRY (France) (R-H)
Saturday April 15th (Good)

705a PRIX IMPRUDENCE (Listed) (3-Y.O F)
6f 110y

Macoumba (USA) *(107+) (MmeCHead,France)* 3-9-2 FHead ....— 1
Smolensk (USA) *(107) (AFabre,France)* 3-9-2 SGuillot ....hd 2
Take Liberties *(105) (AFabre,France)* 3-9-2 PaulEddery ....¾ 3
Tereshkova (USA) *(103) (AFabre,France)* 3-9-2 TJarnet ....½ 4
OWNER Haras d'Etreham (FRANCE) BRED Janus Bloodstock Inc. in USA 1m 20.5 SF: -/-/-/-

706a PRIX DJEBEL (Listed) (3-Y.O C)
6f 110y

Pennekamp (USA) *(100++) (AFabre,France)* 3-9-2 TJarnet ....— 1
Bene Erit (USA) *(96) (CLaffon-Parias,France)* 3-9-2 ODoleuze 1½ 2
Viva Nureyev (USA) *(94) (AFabre,France)* 3-9-2 SGuillot 1 3
OWNER Sheikh Mohammed (FRANCE) BRED Mrs M. O. Bryant in USA 1m 17.4 SF: -/-/-
DS

LEOPARDSTOWN (Dublin, Ireland) (L-H)
Saturday April 15th (Good)

707a LEOPARDSTOWN 1,000 GUINEAS TRIAL (Listed) (3-Y.O F)
7f

Khaytada (IRE) *(110) (JOxx,Ireland)* 3-8-10 JPMurtagh ....— 1
Mediation (IRE) *(102) (JOxx,Ireland)* 3-8-10 PVGilson 3½ 2
Sharp Point (IRE) *(96) (DKWeld,Ireland)* 3-8-10 MJKinane 2½ 3
Eva Luna (IRE) *(101) (JSBolger,Ireland)* 3-9-3 KJManning 2 4
OWNER Aga Khan 1m 33.2 (8.20) SF: -/-/-/-

708a LEOPARDSTOWN 2,000 GUINEAS TRIAL (Listed) (3-Y.O C)
1m

Adjareli (IRE) *(104+) (JOxx,Ireland)* 3-8-10 JPMurtagh ....— 1
Oscar Schindler (IRE) *(97) (KPrendergast,Ireland)* 3-8-10 WJSupple 3½ 2
Free To Speak (IRE) *(96) (DKWeld,Ireland)* 3-8-10 MJKinane ....nk 3
OWNER Aga Khan 1m 44.6 (7.60) SF: -/-/-

709a BALLYSAX (Listed) (3-Y.O)
1m 2f

Humbel (USA) *(98?) (DKWeld,Ireland)* 3-9-3 MJKinane ....— 1
Zabadi (IRE) *(93) (JOxx,Ireland)* 3-9-0 JPMurtagh 1 2
Rawy (USA) *(93) (JSBolger,Ireland)* 3-9-0 KJManning ....s.h 3
OWNER Dr Michael Smurfit BRED A. E. Paulson 2m 13.8 (9.80) SF: -/-/-
NR

CAPANNELLE (Rome, Italy) (R-H)
Sunday April 16th (Heavy)

710a
PREMIO NATALE DI ROMA (Gp 3) (4-Y.O+)
1m

Lear White (USA) *(FBrogi,Italy)* 4-8-9 JCaro ......— **1**
425[2] Fraam *(EALDunlop)* 6-8-9 WRSwinburn ......¾ **2**
Golden Bechett (IRE) *(GFratini,Italy)* 5-8-9 VMezzatesta 3 **3**
OWNER Scuderia Gen Horse 1m 42.2 SF: -/-/-

0690-NEWBURY (L-H)
Saturday April 22nd (Good)
WEATHER: overcast WIND: slt bhd

711
ARLINGTON INTERNATIONAL RACECOURSE STKS (3-Y.O) (Class B)
£8,600.00 (£3,200.00: £1,550.00: £650.00: £275.00: £125.00)
1m 3f 5y Stalls: Low GOING minus 0.30 sec per fur (GF) 2-00 (2-01)

Posidonas *(99) (PFICole)* 3-8-13 TQuinn(7) (h.d.w: 3rd st: rdn & n.m.r over 3f out: hrd rdn & hdwy over 1f out: led ins fnl f: r.o wl) ......— **1**
539* Lucky Di (USA) *(97)*(Fav)*(LMCumani)* 3-8-13 JWeaver(6) (hdwy 6th & c wd st: led wl over 1f out: hrd rdn & hdd ins fnl f) 1¼ **2**
Nash Terrace (IRE) *(94) (RCharlton)* 3-8-13 JReid(8) (hld up & bhd: 5th st: hdwy over 2f out: one pce fnl f) 2½ **3**
Stelvio *(91) (HRACecil)* 3-8-13 WRyan(4) (lw: 2nd st: rdn 3f out: ev ch 2f out: one pce) 1¾ **4**
Stiffelio (IRE) **(105)***(91) (RHannon)* 3-9-1 LDettori(3) (led tl hdd wl over 1f out: wknd fnl f) 1¼ **5**
536[4] Grey Shot *(89) (IABalding)* 3-8-13 RCochrane(1) (hld up & bhd: last st: nvr trbld ldrs) ......½ **6**
Evezio Rufo *(85) (JLDunlop)* 3-8-11 KDarley(5) (hld up: 7th st: hrd rdn over 2f out: sn bhd)...¾ **7**
Great Crusader **(104)***(77) (CACyzer)* 3-8-13 TIves(2) (lw: 4th st: nt clr run & swtchd rt 4f out: sn wknd) 7 **8**

13/8 Lucky Di (USA), **5/2** Stelvio, **6/1** Nash Terrace (IRE), **8/1** Stiffelio (IRE) (11/2-9/1), **16/1** POSIDONAS, **20/1** Great Crusader, **25/1** Grey Shot, Evezio Rufo, CSF £38.96 TOTE £18.40: £2.40 £1.10 £1.80 (£29.30) OWNER Mr Athos Christodoulou (WHATCOMBE) BRED A. Christodoulou 8 Rn
2m 21.54 (5.54) SF: 33/31/28/25/25/23/19/11

712
LANES END JOHN PORTER STKS (Gp 3) (4-Y.O+) (Class A)
£22,020.00 (£8,256.00: £3,978.00: £1,746.00)
1m 4f 5y Stalls: Low GOING minus 0.30 sec per fur (GF) 2-30 (2-31)

Strategic Choice (USA) (115)*(119) (PFICole)* 4-8-11 TQuinn(9) (b.off hind: a gng wl: 3rd st: rdn to ld ins fnl f: r.o) ......— **1**
Broadway Flyer (USA) **(114)***(122)*(Fav)*(JWHills)* 4-9-0 MHills(10) (lw: led: clr 5f out: rdn over 2f out: hdd wl ins fnl f: r.o) ......nk **2**
Shambo **(108)***(118) (CEBrittain)* 8-9-1 BDoyle(7) (lw: hld up & bhd: 9th st: hdwy over 2f out: styd on fnl f) 3 **3**
Right Win (IRE) **(120)***(117) (RHannon)* 5-9-3 PatEddery(2) (lw: plld hrd: 4th st: one pce fnl 2f) 1¾ **4**
Linney Head (USA) **(108)***(115) (JHMGosden)* 4-9-0 LDettori(1) (lw: chsd ldr: 2nd st: rdn & ev ch over 2f out: wknd over 1f out) ......hd **5**
440[2] Cotteir Chief (IRE) **(107)***(111) (MCPipe)* 4-8-11 RCochrane(8) (8th st: rdn 3f out: hdwy over 1f out: r.o one pce fnl f) ......¾ **6**
Zilzal Zamaan (USA) **(109)***(107) (MRStoute)* 4-8-11 WRSwinburn(5) (hld up: sltly hmpd on ins & 7th st: rdn & n.m.r over 2f out & over 1f out: one pce) 3 **7**
River North (IRE) **(120)***(112) (LadyHerries)* 5-9-5 KDarley(3) (b: hld up: 6th st: rdn & hdwy over 3f out: edgd rt over 2f out: sn wknd) 1½ **8**
Escarpment (USA) *(105) (PWChapple-Hyam)* 4-8-11 JReid(6) (hld up: 5th st: wknd over 3f out) ......½ **9**
623[5] Wayne County (IRE) **(84)***(91) (GFierro)* 5-8-12 JWeaver(4) (last st: a in rr) 10 **10**

100/30 Broadway Flyer (USA), **7/2** Zilzal Zamaan (USA), **9/2** Linney Head (USA), **11/2** River North (IRE), **15/2** Right Win (IRE), **12/1** Cotteir Chief (IRE), STRATEGIC CHOICE (USA) (8/1-14/1), **20/1** Escarpment (USA), **25/1** Shambo, **66/1** Wayne County (IRE), CSF £48.16 TOTE £16.30: £2.50 £1.60 £6.10 (£18.60) OWNER Mr M. Arbib (WHATCOMBE) BRED M. Arbib 10 Rn
2m 32.36 (3.06) SF: 51/54/51/50/47/43/39/45/37/24
WEIGHT FOR AGE 4yo-1lb

713 TRIPLEPRINT GREENHAM STKS (Gp 3) (3-Y.O C & G) (Class A)
£21,840.00 (£8,187.00: £3,943.50: £1,729.50)
7f (straight) Stalls: Centre GOING minus 0.30 sec per fur (GF) 3-00 (3-02)

Celtic Swing (130)*(121+)*(Fav)*(LadyHerries)* 3-9-0 KDarley(7) (lw: h.d.w: chsd ldr: led over 2f out: qcknd clr over 1f out: rdn out) .....— 1
Bahri (USA) **(98)***(118) (JLDunlop)* 3-9-0 WCarson(5) (lw: hld up & plld hrd: hdwy 2f out: chsd wnr over 1f out: r.o wl ins fnl f) 1¼ 2
Moon King (IRE) **(110)***(98) (RHannon)* 3-9-0 WRSwinburn(9) (a.p: rdn & one pce fnl 2f) 9 3
Peace Envoy *(96) (HRACecil)* 3-9-0 PatEddery(2) (hld up: hdwy over 2f out: one pce) .....½ 4
Rambrino **(106)***(93) (PWChapple-Hyam)* 3-9-0 JReid(1) (lw: prom: rdn & wknd 2f out) 1½ 5
622[6] Henry Koehler *(87) (CEBrittain)* 3-9-0 MRimmer(6) (hld up: rdn over 2f out: sn wknd) 2½ 6
Knight Commander (USA) **(95)***(79) (RHannon)* 3-9-0 LDettori(4) (prom: rdn over 2f out: wknd wl over 1f out) 3½ 7
Bishop of Cashel **(112)***(68) (JRFanshawe)* 3-9-0 DHarrison(8) (hld up & plld hrd: rdn over 2f out: sn bhd) 5 8
Art of War **(109)***(52) (RCharlton)* 3-9-0 JWeaver(3) (plld hrd: led over 4f: eased whn btn & hmpd over 1f out) 7 9

4/9 CELTIC SWING, **9/1** Peace Envoy, **12/1** Bishop of Cashel (8/1-14/1), Art of War (op 8/1), **14/1** Bahri (USA), **16/1** Rambrino, Moon King (IRE), **33/1** Knight Commander (USA), **100/1** Henry Koehler, CSF £7.97 TOTE £1.40: £1.10 £2.00 £4.00 (£5.10) Trio £36.00 OWNER Mr P. D. Savill (LITTLEHAMPTON) BRED Lavinia Duchess of Norfolk 9 Rn
1m 24.31 (-0.19) SF: 76/73/53/51/48/42/34/23/7

714 LADBROKES SPRING CUP H'CAP (0-105) (4-Y.O+) (Class B) £18,237.50
(£5,525.00: £2,700.00: £1,287.50)
1m 7y (round) Stalls: Low GOING minus 0.30 sec per fur (GF) 3-30 (3-34)

Star Manager (USA) (78)*(88) (PFICole)* 5-8-5 TQuinn(4) (bhd: plld out 4f out: hrd rdn over 2f out: gd hdwy over 1f out: str run to ld wl ins fnl f) .....— 1
Jawaal **(80)***(87) (LadyHerries)* 5-8-7 JReid(15) (lw: s.i.s: gd hdwy over 2f out: ev ch ins fnl f: nt qckn) 1½ 2
486[6] Gadge **(72)***(78) (DMorris)* 4-7-13 RPrice(5) (4th st: led ins fnl f: sn hdd & nt qckn) .....½ 3
563[4] Knobbleeneeze **(75)***(81) (MRChannon)* 5-8-2v BDoyle(19) (lw: led 2f: 5th st: ev ch fnl 2f: nt qckn last 100 yards) .....s.h 4
Czarna (IRE) **(87)***(93) (CEBrittain)* 4-9-0 MRimmer(16) (3rd st: led 2f out tl ins fnl f: nt qckn) s.h 5
439[9] Mellottie **(95)***(99) (MrsMReveley)* 10-9-8 KDarley(20) (7th st: ev ch over 1f out: r.o ins fnl f) ...¾ 6
439[10] Master Beveled **(87)***(91) (PDEvans)* 5-9-0 MHills(3) (hld up & bhd: swtchd rt 4f out: sn rdn: gd hdwy over 1f out: fin wl) .....hd 7
433* Sharp Prospect **(82)***(86)*(Fav)*(RAkehurst)* 5-8-9 WRSwinburn(14) (lw: 5th st: ev ch fnl f: nt qckn) .....s.h 8
439[5] Royal Hill **(79)***(83) (LordHuntingdon)* 4-8-6 DHarrison(2) (hld up & bhd: hdwy on ins over 2f out: one pce fnl f) .....s.h 9
439[17] Chickawicka (IRE) **(85)***(88) (MCPipe)* 4-8-12 GCarter(7) (led 6f out to 2f out: wknd fnl f) .....nk 10
439[7] Indian Fly **(94)***(95) (RHannon)* 4-9-7 PatEddery(10) (hld up mid div: rdn 2f out: no hdwy) 1¼ 11
563* Sheppard's Cross **(85)***(83) (PTWalwyn)* 4-8-12 BThomson(13) (hdwy 3f out: ev ch over 1f out: wknd fnl f) 1½ 12
Embankment (IRE) **(88)***(83) (RHannon)* 5-9-1 RHughes(9) (hld up & bhd: nvr plcd to chal) ..1¼ 13
439* Roving Minstrel **(88)***(79) (BAMcMahon)* 4-9-1 JWeaver(8) (plld hrd: 2nd st: rdn & ev ch over 2f out: wknd over 1f out) 2 14
Dance Turn **(101)***(87) (RWArmstrong)* 4-10-0 WWoods(11) (lw: a bhd) 2½ 15
Pay Homage **(88)***(74) (IABalding)* 7-9-1 LDettori(1) (s.i.s: a bhd) .....s.h 16
Geisway (CAN) **(95)***(74) (NJHWalker)* 5-9-8 RCochrane(17) (a bhd) 3½ 17
401[5] Perilous Plight **(75)***(38) (WRMuir)* 4-7-13 (3) SSanders(18) (8th st: wknd over 2f out) 8 18
Brave Patriarch (IRE) **(83)***(40) (JLDunlop)* 4-8-10 WCarson(12) (lw: prom: 6th st: wknd 3f out)3 19
Highland Magic (IRE) **(74)***(12) (MJFetherston-Godley)* 7-8-1 FNorton(6) (bkwd: a bhd) 10 20

11/2 Sharp Prospect, **13/2** Indian Fly, **7/1** Royal Hill, **9/1** Jawaal, **10/1** Sheppard's Cross (8/1-12/1), Brave Patriarch (IRE), **11/1** Roving Minstrel, **12/1** Pay Homage, **14/1** Gadge, **16/1** Czarna (IRE), **20/1** STAR MANAGER (USA), **25/1** Dance Turn, Master Beveled, Mellottie, Knobbleeneeze, **33/1** Chickawicka (IRE), Highland Magic (IRE), Perilous Plight, Embankment (IRE), **40/1** Geisway (CAN), CSF £180.43 CT £2,392.31 TOTE £23.10: £4.40 £2.50 £3.20 £4.00 (£150.80) Trio £1,152.30 OWNER Mr M. Arbib (WHATCOMBE) BRED Hickory Tree Farm 20 Rn
1m 37.11 (1.11) SF: 53/52/43/46/58/64/56/51/48/53/60/48/48/44/52/39/39/3/5/-
OFFICIAL EXPLANATION Highland Magic (IRE): the trainer reported that the gelding had received a blow to it's near-fore.

715 GET AWAY DAY MAIDEN STKS (3-Y.O) (Class D) £4,695.00 (£1,410.00: £680.00: £315.00) 1m (straight) Stalls: Centre GOING minus 0.30 sec (GF) 4-00 (4-09)

Lyrikos (USA) *(94+) (HRACecil)* 3-9-0 WRyan(17) (w'like: b.nr fore: hld up: gd hdwy over 2f out: led over 1f out: r.o wl)........— 1
418² Abu Simbel (USA) *(84) (JHMGosden)* 3-9-0 LDettori(1) (b.hind: a.p: ev ch over 1f out: one pce)........5 2
Pinzon (USA) *(83)*(Fav)*(PWChapple-Hyam)* 3-9-0 JReid(5) (w'like: lw: a.p: rdn & ev ch over 1f out: one pce)........nk 3
Office Hours *(78) (CACyzer)* 3-9-0 TIves(13) (led over 6f: one pce)........2½ 4
Cap Juluca (IRE) *(78) (RCharlton)* 3-9-0 SRaymont(6) (wl grwn: a.p: ev ch 2f out: wknd 1f out)........nk 5
Desert Harvest *(74) (RCharlton)* 3-9-0 JWeaver(7) (h.d.w: hdwy 3f out: one pce fnl 2f)........1¾ 6
Northern Law *(70) (BWHills)* 3-9-0 MHills(21) (w'like: prom: rdn 3f out: r.o one pce fnl f)........2 7
Dawsha (IRE) *(62) (SDow)* 3-8-2 (7) ADaly(10) (hdwy fnl 2f: nvr nrr)........1½ 8
Western Fame (USA) *(67) (JLDunlop)* 3-9-0 WCarson(18) (lw: nvr plcd to chal)........nk 9
Arcatura *(65) (CJames)* 3-9-0 WNewnes(2) (no hdwy fnl 2f)........1 10
553³ Dances With Hooves *(65) (DJSffrenchDavis)* 3-9-0 RCochrane(25) (prom tl wknd over 1f out)........s.h 11
High Commotion (IRE) *(59) (DRCElsworth)* 3-8-9 JWilliams(14) (lengthy: hld up: sn bhd: nvr plcd to chal)........nk 12
468⁵ Miss Jemmima *(59) (LordHuntingdon)* 3-8-9 DHarrison(20) (prom: ev ch over 2f out: sn wknd)........hd 13
En Vacances (IRE) *(54) (AGFoster)* 3-8-9 MRimmer(22) (unf: prom: rdn 3f out: sn wknd)....2½ 14
Proud Image *(56) (APJarvis)* 3-9-0 RHughes(12) (neat: w ldrs over 5f)........1½ 15
Pharly Reef *(55) (IABalding)* 3-9-0 KDarley(19) (unf: bhd fnl 2f)........nk 16
Queens Theatre *(45) (BWHills)* 3-8-9 MFenton(4) (scope: a bhd)........2½ 17
Admiral's Guest (IRE) *(49) (GHarwood)* 3-9-0 AClark(3) (a bhd)........¾ 18
Rock Oyster *(48) (BJMeehan)* 3-9-0 BDoyle(15) (a bhd)........nk 19
Merit (IRE) *(48) (PFICole)* 3-9-0 TQuinn(24) (rdn 3f out: a in rr)........s.h 20
Thomas Crown (IRE) *(48) (NJHWalker)* 3-9-0 GCarter(8) (a bhd)........s.h 21
Selmeston (IRE) *(46) (ACStewart)* 3-8-9 (5) MHumphries(11) (cmpt: a bhd)........1 22
Sunoma Valley *(44) (JMPEustace)* 3-9-0 BThomson(9) (leggy: prom: rdn 3f out: sn wknd).....1 23
Yosif (IRE) *(36) (RHannon)* 3-9-0 PatEddery(16) (w'like: scope: bkwd: bhd fnl 3f)........4 24
Night Flare (FR) *(RHannon)* 3-9-0 WWoods(23) (Withdrawn not under Starter's orders: burst through stalls)........ W

, **6/5** Pinzon (USA) (5/4-Evens), **7/1** Merit (IRE) (6/1-12/1), Abu Simbel (USA) (8/1-5/1), **10/1** Desert Harvest (op 5/1), Western Fame (USA) (op 6/1), **14/1** LYRIKOS (USA) (10/1-16/1), Yosif (IRE) (10/1-16/1), **16/1** Dances With Hooves, **20/1** Dawsha (IRE), **33/1** Office Hours, Cap Juluca (IRE), Northern Law, Admiral's Guest (IRE), Pharly Reef, **50/1** En Vacances (IRE), Arcatura, Proud Image, Rock Oyster, Miss Jemmima, Thomas Crown (IRE), Selmeston (IRE), Sunoma Valley, Queens Theatre, High Commotion (IRE), CSF £110.24 TOTE £18.20: £5.10 £2.30 £1.10 (£44.80) Trio £34.00 OWNER Mr L. Marinopoulos (NEWMARKET) BRED Hickory Tree Farm 24 Rn
1m 38.14 (1.14) SF: 61/51/50/45/45/41/37/29/34/32/32/26/26/21/23/22/12/16/15/15/15/13/11/3/-
OFFICIAL EXPLANATION **High Commotion (IRE): had lost her action when the far-side and stands-side groups had joined, then encountered traffic problems later on.**

716 NETHERAVON MAIDEN AUCTION STKS (2-Y.O F) (Class D) £3,622.50 (£1,080.00: £515.00: £232.50) 5f 34y Stalls: Centre GOING minus 0.30 sec per fur (GF) 4-30 (4-37)

508² **Kandavu** *(73t) (MMcCormack)* 2-7-13 StephenDavies(1) (mde all: rdn out)........— 1
508⁴ Lussuria (IRE) *(69) (BJMeehan)* 2-8-1 BDoyle(3) (w wnr: ev ch 2f out: nt qckn)........2 2
Windswept (IRE) *(65) (DJSffrenchDavis)* 2-8-2 NAdams(4) (unf: a.p: r.o one pce fnl f)........1½ 3
436⁷ Mono Lady (IRE) *(64) (DHaydnJones)* 2-8-3 ow1 DHarrison(8) (chsd ldrs: one pce fnl f)........nk 4
Evidence In Chief *(63) (PFICole)* 2-8-4 ow3 TQuinn(9) (scope: hdwy fnl f: r.o)........s.h 5
Cd Super Targeting (IRE) *(50)*(Fav)*(MRChannon)* 2-8-3 WCarson(2) (unf: prom: rdn 2f out: wknd over 1f out)........5 6
Compensate (IRE) *(25) (MJHaynes)* 2-7-11 (3) SSanders(5) (lt-f: unf: sn rdn & outpcd)........7 7
Little Lucky *(21) (GLewis)* 2-7-10 (5)ow1 AWhelan(7) (neat: dwlt: outpcd)........1¼ 8

6/4 Cd Super Targeting (IRE), **3/1** KANDAVU, **6/1** Evidence In Chief (op 4/1), **13/2** Lussuria (IRE), **12/1** Little Lucky, **14/1** Mono Lady (IRE), **33/1** Compensate (IRE), Windswept (IRE), CSF £20.41 TOTE £4.10: £1.60 £1.90 £3.50 (£8.40) Trio £31.40 OWNER Mrs H. Corr (WANTAGE) BRED R. Burton 8 Rn 62.25 secs (1.95) SF: 27/23/19/18/17/4/-/-

717
LEVY BOARD SEVENTH RACE H'CAP (0-85) (3-Y.O) (Class D)
£3,777.00 (£1,131.00: £543.00: £249.00)
1m 4f 5y Stalls: Low GOING minus 0.30 sec per fur (GF) 5-00 (5-03)

592^{3} **Monarch (68)***(76) (PFICole)* 3-8-6 TQuinn(3) (lw: a gng wl: 4th st: led over 1f out: r.o wl)............— **1**
427^{6} Courbaril **(60)***(65) (SDow)* 3-7-12 GCarter(1) (hld up & bhd: 7th st: hdwy over 3f out: ev ch over 1f out: nt qckn)............2½ **2**
Deano's Beeno **(79)***(83) (MJohnston)* 3-9-3 JReid(7) (lw: led tl hdd over 1f out: nt qckn)........¾ **3**
484* Lord Jim (IRE) **(82)***(84) (MissGayKelleway)* 3-9-6 RCochrane(2) (3rd st: rdn over 3f out: ev ch over 1f out: one pce)............1¼ **4**
Better Offer (IRE) **(78)***(71) (GHarwood)* 3-9-2 AClark(4) (hld up: 6th st: hdwy over 3f out: ev ch 2f out: wknd over 1f out)............7 **5**
614^{6} Mistinguett (IRE) **(75)***(66)*(Fav)*(RHannon)* 3-8-13 PatEddery(5) (last st: a bhd)............1½ **6**
427^{5} Euro Forum **(59)***(21) (GLMoore)* 3-7-11v^{ow2} WCarson(8) (chsd ldr: 2nd st: wknd over 3f out: t.o)............20 **7**
477* Sarasota Storm **(83)***(21) (MBell)* 3-9-7 MFenton(6) (hld up: rdn & 5th st: bhd 3f: t.o)............20 **8**

15/8 Mistinguett (IRE), **4/1** Deano's Beeno, **6/1** Lord Jim (IRE) (op 4/1), **13/2** Sarasota Storm (7/2-7/1), **8/1** Better Offer (IRE), MONARCH, **11/1** Euro Forum (8/1-12/1), **12/1** Courbaril (7/1-14/1), CSF £85.19 CT £402.77 TOTE £11.10: £1.90 £3.70 £1.50 (£39.50) OWNER Prince Fahd Salman (WHATCOMBE) BRED Newgate Stud Co 8 Rn 2m 34.23 (4.93) SF: 34/23/41/42/29/24/-/-
OFFICIAL EXPLANATION Mistinguett (IRE): never picked up.

T/Jkpt: Not won; £21,537.47 to Nottingham 24/4/95. T/Plpt: £164.30 (235.71 Tckts). T/Qdpt: £160.20 (1.5 Tckts). KH

0697-THIRSK (L-H)
Saturday April 22nd (Good)
WEATHER: showers WIND: mod half against

718
CLIFTON STKS (2-Y.O) (Class C) £4,789.12 (£1,723.50: £824.25: £333.75: £129.38) **5f** Stalls: High GOING: 0.12 sec per fur (G) 2-15 (2-15)

Safio *(67t) (CSmith)* 2-8-7 JFortune(2) (neat: s.s: sn chsng ldrs: nt clr run on ins 2f out: swtchd: led 1f out: rn green & drvn out)............— **1**
554* The Frisky Farmer *(71) (WGMTurner)* 2-8-11 TSprake(3) (lw: hung lft u.p: nt qckn wl ins fnl f)............hd **2**
455* Maggi For Margaret *(58)*(Fav)*(MRChannon)* 2-8-6 CRutter(4) (w ldr: rdn 2f out: nt qckn appr fnl f)............2½ **3**
508* Miss Bigwig *(52) (JBerry)* 2-8-10 JCarroll(5) (sn chsng ldrs: wkng whn sltly hmpd over 1f out)............3 **4**
615^{3} Sharp Monty *(44) (RHollinshead)* 2-8-11 PaulEddery(1) (s.i.s: sn chsng ldrs: rdn ½-wy: wandered & wknd 2f out)............3 **5**

11/8 Maggi For Margaret, **11/4** Miss Bigwig (op 7/4), **4/1** Sharp Monty, **9/2** The Frisky Farmer (op 3/1), **14/1** SAFIO (8/1-16/1), CSF £63.53 TOTE £22.80: £3.50 £2.90 (£30.40) OWNER Mrs M. A. Clayton (WELLINGORE) BRED Mrs M. A. Clayton 5 Rn 62.7 secs (5.50) SF: 8/12/-/-/-

719
MICHAEL FOSTER MEMORIAL STKS (3-Y.O+) (Class C) £5,910.90
(£2,183.10: £1,044.05: £422.75: £163.88: £60.32)
6f Stalls: High GOING: 0.12 sec per fur (G) 2-50 (2-50)

571^{4} **Venture Capitalist (100)***(105) (DNicholls)* 6-9-6 AlexGreaves(6) (hld up: effrt & nt clr run over 2f out: squeezed thro & r.o wl to ld nr fin)............— **1**
Lago Di Varano **(98)***(106) (JBerry)* 3-8-12b JCarroll(3) (reard s: hdwy & swtchd outside over 2f out: led over 1f out tl nr fin)............1¼ **2**
Don't Worry Me (IRE) **(102)***(90) (FHLee)* 3-8-3 PRobinson(4) (trckd ldrs: plld hard: effrt & ev ch over 1f out: wknd jst ins fnl f)............2½ **3**
Monaassib (IRE) **(98)***(86) (EALDunlop)* 4-9-6 PaulEddery(1) (trckd ldrs: ev ch over 1f out: kpt on same pce)............3½ **4**
522* Karina Heights (USA) *(75) (JWWatts)* 3-7-13 JLowe(5) (lw: w ldr: led over 2f out tl hdd & wknd over 1f out)............½ **5**
Lord Olivier (IRE) **(95)***(64)*(Fav)*(WJarvis)* 5-9-2 MTebbutt(7) (led over 3f: hung lft & sn lost pl)............6 **6**
Bunty Boo **(106)***(55)*(Fav)*(RHannon)* 6-8-13 RPerham(2) (bit bkwd: trckd ldr tl wknd 2f out)............2½ **7**

100/30 Bunty Boo, Lord Olivier (IRE), **4/1** Monaassib (IRE), **11/2** VENTURE CAPITALIST, **13/2** Don't Worry Me (IRE), **17/2** Karina Heights (USA), **10/1** Lago Di Varano, CSF £48.84 TOTE £5.20: £2.60 £4.20 (£33.20) OWNER Mr W. G. Swiers (THIRSK) BRED Brook Bloodstock Plc 7 Rn
1m 14.2 (4.50) SF: 50/39/23/31/8/9/-
WEIGHT FOR AGE 3yo-12lb

720 THIRSK CLASSIC TRIAL STKS (3-Y.O) (Class B) £11,236.50 (£4,153.50: £1,989.25: £808.75: £316.88: £120.12)
1m Stalls: Low GOING: 0.12 sec per fur (G) 3-20 (3-22)

438[3] **Moments of Fortune (USA) (92)***(101)*(Fav)*(BHanbury)* 3-8-12 PaulEddery(5) (mde virtually all: styd on u.p fnl 2f: hld on wl) — 1
667[9] Be Mindful **(108)***(104) (JRFanshawe)* 3-9-2 KFallon(2) (hld up: effrt over 2f out: styd on wl fnl f) nk 2
Sayeh (IRE) *(98) (HThomsonJones)* 3-8-10 NCarlisle(6) (lw: trckd ldrs: effrt & outpcd: sltly hmpd over 2f out: styd on wl ins fnl f) nk 3
619[5] Baltic Raider **(104)***(98) (GWragg)* 3-9-2 PRobinson(3) (lw: trckd ldrs: effrt & swtchd rt over 2f out: sn ev ch: nt qckn appr fnl f) 3 4
Impulsive Air (IRE) **(98)***(89) (EWeymes)* 3-8-12 JFortune(4) (pushed along & outpcd over 3f out: styd on fnl f: n.d) 2½ 5
557[2] Dee-Lady **(92)***(83) (WGMTurner)* 3-8-7 GDuffield(1) (trckd ldrs: disp ld over 2f out: sn rdn: wknd over 1f out) nk 6

2/1 MOMENTS OF FORTUNE (USA), **7/2** Be Mindful, **9/2** Baltic Raider, **11/2** Sayeh (IRE), **13/2** Dee-Lady, **10/1** Impulsive Air (IRE), CSF £8.78 TOTE £2.80: £1.50 £2.00 (£5.80) OWNER Mr Abdullah Ali (NEWMARKET) BRED Mrs Hardie Scott 6 Rn 1m 41.3 (5.70) SF: 47/50/44/44/35/29

721 STRAIGHTLACE LIMITED STKS (0-70) (3-Y.O+) (Class E) £3,215.70 (£957.60: £455.80: £204.90) **1m 4f** Stalls: High GOING: 0.12 sec per fur (G) 3-50 (3-53)

549[10] **Bayrak (USA) (65)***(83+) (MJRyan)* 5-9-10 PaulEddery(3) (led 2f: led over 2f out: drvn clr over 1f out: eased nr fin) — 1
505[11] Fox Sparrow **(69)***(76) (NTinkler)* 5-9-10 MBirch(1) (hld up: effrt over 2f out: rdn over 1f out: no ch w wnr) 5 2
Surrey Dancer **(70)***(73)*(Fav)*(MrsMReveley)* 7-9-3 (7) GParkin(2) (lw: hld up: stdy hdwy over 3f out: effrt & swtchd outside wl over 1f out: kpt on same pce) 2½ 3
557[4] Bellara **(47)***(63) (NMBabbage)* 3-7-12 JQuinn(6) (unruly s: led after 2f tl over 3f out: sn lost pl) 4 4
Sariyaa **(70)***(62) (MBrittain)* 4-9-4 GDuffield(5) (plld hard: sn trckng ldr: led over 3f out tl over 2f out: sn wknd) nk 5
Greenfinch (CAN) **(35)***(27) (MrsAMNaughton)* 4-9-4v(5) JStack(4) (drvn along 5f out: sn wl bhd) 30 6

6/4 Surrey Dancer, **5/2** BAYRAK (USA), **4/1** Sariyaa, **9/2** Fox Sparrow, **33/1** Bellara, **66/1** Greenfinch (CAN), CSF £12.75 TOTE £3.10: £1.70 £2.90 (£17.00) OWNER Mr A. S. Reid (NEWMARKET) BRED Swettenham Stud 6 Rn 2m 39.4 (9.40) SF: 55/48/45/14/33/-
WEIGHT FOR AGE 3yo-21lb, 4yo-1lb

722 BYLAND MAIDEN LIMITED STKS (0-65) (3-Y.O+) (Class F) £3,428.10 (£951.60: £456.30)
7f Stalls: Low GOING: 0.12 sec per fur (G) 4-20 (4-22)

Nordic Doll (IRE) (65)*(71)*(Fav)*(BWHills)* 3-8-2 (5) JDSmith(7) (prom: led & hung lft over 1f out: rdn clr) — 1
Takeshi (IRE) **(65)***(62) (EALDunlop)* 3-8-7 PaulEddery(1) (led tl over 1f out: kpt on same pce) 4 2
603[3] Statius **(64)***(61)*(Fav)*(TDBarron)* 3-8-12 JFortune(10) (hdwy 3f out: kpt on appr fnl f: nvr nr to chal) 2½ 3
592[8] Spanish Stripper (USA) **(44)***(57) (MCChapman)* 4-9-5 (7) CMunday(6) (a in tch: hrd rdn 2f out: hung lft: kpt on one pce) 2 4
Spara Tir **(59)***(55) (BobJones)* 3-8-12 MWigham(3) (w ldr: ev ch tl wknd over 1f out) ¾ 5
Fresh Look (IRE) **(62)***(45) (RFJohnsonHoughton)* 3-8-7 JQuinn(8) (b.hind: sme hdwy 3f out: nvr nr ldrs) 2 6
613[5] Nafta **(63)***(47) (SEKettlewell)* 3-8-9 (3) DRMcCabe(2) (chsd ldrs tl wknd 2f out) 1¼ 7
572[3] Blasted **(61)***(39)*(Fav)*(RHannon)* 3-8-12 RPerham(11) (prom: effrt 3f out: wknd 2f out) 3½ 8
Lady Ploy **(44)***(30) (MissLCSiddall)* 3-8-7 DeanMcKeown(9) (stdd s: hld up & bhd: n.d) 2 9

Upex le Gold Too **(50)***(34) (MrsASwinbank)* 3-8-12 JMarshall(12) (in tch: effrt over 2f out: grad wknd) ....½ **10**
Qualitair Pride **(63)***(26) (JFBottomley)* 3-8-7 KFallon(4) (hdwy ½-wy: effrt over 2f out: sn wknd) 1¼ **11**
Blackspot (IRE) **(35)***(19) (FHLee)* 3-8-7b RLappin(5) (unruly: in tch tl lost pl 3f out) 3 **12**
Bairn Glen **(34)** *(GROldroyd)* 4-9-7 MMcAndrew(13) (s.i.s: a wl bhd) 11 **13**
205[11] Quiet Mission **(43)** *(JLEyre)* 4-9-9b(3) JTate(14) (unruly in stalls: s.i.s: a wl bhd) 4 **14**

4/1 NORDIC DOLL (IRE), Blasted, Statius, **11/2** Fresh Look (IRE), **6/1** Takeshi (IRE), **10/1** Nafta, Spara Tir, **11/1** Qualitair Pride, **25/1** Lady Ploy, **33/1** Upex le Gold Too, Blackspot (IRE), **50/1** Spanish Stripper (USA), Bairn Glen, Quiet Mission, CSF £28.96 TOTE £6.40: £2.30 £2.00 £1.80 (£30.50) Trio £35.70 OWNER Mr Peter Williams (LAMBOURN) BRED Tony Butler 14 Rn
1m 27.9 (5.20) SF: 39/30/29/39/23/13/15/7/-/2/-/-/-/-
WEIGHT FOR AGE 3yo-14lb

723 THOMAS LORD H'CAP (0-90) (3-Y.O+) (Class C) £6,434.50 (£1,921.00: £918.00: £416.50)
5f Stalls: High GOING: 0.12 sec per fur (G) 4-50 (4-53)

639[2] **Tenor (60)***(69)*(Fav)*(DNicholls)* 4-8-5 AlexGreaves(7) (lw: hld up: hdwy whn nt clr run ½-wy: r.o wl u.p fnl f: led cl home) ....— **1**
Broadstairs Beauty (IRE) **(63)***(72) (SRBowring)* 5-8-8b SDWilliams(16) (b: b.hind: led tl cl home) ....hd **2**
Ned's Bonanza **(69)***(67) (MDods)* 6-9-0 SWhitworth(6) (hld up: stdy hdwy ½-wy: r.o wl nr fin) 3½ **3**
French Grit (IRE) **(80)***(77) (MDods)* 3-9-0 DaleGibson(8) (a chsng ldrs: hung rt & kpt on wl appr fnl f) ....s.h **4**
Croft Imperial **(68)***(64) (MJohnston)* 8-8-13 DHolland(5) (bit bkwd: chsd ldrs tl wknd over 1f out) ....½ **5**
535[2] Saddlehome (USA) **(76)***(72) (TDBarron)* 6-9-7 JFortune(1) (lw: hld up: hdwy on outside over 1f out: nvr nr to chal) ....s.h **6**
Magic Pearl **(73)***(68) (EJAlston)* 5-9-4 KFallon(4) (bit bkwd: chsd ldrs tl outpcd fnl f) ....s.h **7**
602[6] King Rambo **(63)***(56) (RHollinshead)* 4-8-3 (5) AGarth(3) (chsd ldrs over 3f: grad wknd) ....¾ **8**
Beau Venture (USA) **(74)***(63) (FHLee)* 7-9-5 PRobinson(14) (hld up: effrt ½-wy: n.m.r over 1f out: n.d) 1¼ **9**
565[10] Cradle Days **(72)***(59) (RCSpicer)* 6-9-3 JO'Reilly(11) (prom: hung bdly rt 2f out: sn lost pl) ....½ **10**
Craigie Boy **(61)***(37) (NBycroft)* 5-8-6 JQuinn(12) (s.i.s: outpcd & bhd: sme hdwy ½-wy: nvr nr ldrs) 3½ **11**
639[8] Stephensons Rocket **(78)***(49) (JBerry)* 4-9-9 JCarroll(13) (b.off hind: chsd ldrs tl wknd 2f out) 1½ **12**
*510*** Primula Bairn **(63)***(31) (JMackie)* 5-8-8v PaulEddery(15) (unruly in stalls: s.i.s: a bhd) 1 **13**
685* Fangio **(85)***(50) (WGMTurner)* 6-9-11 (5) 7x PMcCabe(10) (unruly in stalls: chsd ldrs tl rdn & lost pl ½-wy) 1 **14**
535[18] Just Bob **(80)** *(SEKettlewell)* 6-9-6 (5) JStack(9) (v.upset in stalls: s.s: a wl t.o) ....dist **15**

4/1 TENOR (op 8/1), **5/1** Saddlehome (USA), **11/2** Broadstairs Beauty (IRE) (7/2-6/1), **8/1** Fangio, Primula Bairn, **10/1** Beau Venture (USA), **11/1** Stephensons Rocket, **12/1** Craigie Boy, French Grit (IRE), **14/1** Croft Imperial, King Rambo, Just Bob, **16/1** Magic Pearl, **20/1** Cradle Days, Ned's Bonanza, CSF £29.14 CT £389.33 TOTE £8.80: £2.00 £3.60 £8.80 (£39.40) Trio £876.10; £1,110.62 to Nottingham 24/4/95 OWNER Mr Geoffrey Thompson (THIRSK) BRED Lord Victor Matthews 15 Rn 61.2 secs (4.00) SF: 31/34/29/28/26/34/30/18/25/21/-/11/-/12/-
WEIGHT FOR AGE 3yo-11lb

724 LEVY BOARD H'CAP (0-80) (3-Y.O+ F & M) (Class D) £4,070.30 (£1,216.40: £582.20: £265.10)
1m Stalls: Low GOING: 0.12 sec per fur (G) 5-20 (5-21)

559[8] **Karinska (50)***(59) (MCChapman)* 5-7-7 (7) CMunday(6) (s.s: hdwy on ins over 3f out: led just ins fnl f: jst hld on) ....— **1**
558[6] Queens Consul (IRE) **(73)***(82) (BSRothwell)* 5-9-4 (5) JStack(7) (led after 2f to 2f out: kpt on wl u.p: nt qckn nr fin) ....hd **2**
Donna Viola **(72)***(80) (CFWall)* 3-8-7 NCarlisle(11) (mid div: outpcd: hdwy over 1f out: r.o wl nr fin) ....nk **3**
558[7] Celestial Choir **(78)***(83) (JLEyre)* 5-10-0 JFortune(2) (hdwy on ins over 2f out: nt clr run & swtchd over 1f out: no imp) 1½ **4**
567[6] Princess Maxine (IRE) **(66)***(71) (JJO'Neill)* 6-9-2 JCarroll(9) (a chsng ldrs: kpt on same pce fnl 2f) ....s.h **5**

Willshe Gan **(48)***(53) (DenysSmith)* 5-7-12 JQuinn(4) (lw: led 2f: led 2f out tl jst ins fnl f: sn wknd) ....hd 6
*528*2 Grey Again **(58)***(61) (SRBowring)* 3-7-0b(7) PFessey(8) (w ldrs tl outpcd over 1f out) 1 7
526 3 Last Laugh (IRE) **(65)***(64) (RHannon)* 3-8-0 PRobinson(5) (bhd & drvn along ½-wy: n.d) 1¾ 8
433 15 Pride of Pendle **(68)***(64)*(Fav)*(DNicholls)* 6-9-4 AlexGreaves(1) (lw: hld up: smooth hdwy over 2f out: sn rdn: nvr nr to chal) 1½ 9
481* Misty Silks **(78)***(68) (MJRyan)* 5-10-0 PaulEddery(10) (sn bhd: sme hdwy over 2f out: n.d) 3 10
559 14 Ballard Ring (IRE) **(70)***(42) (JSWainwright)* 4-9-6 DeanMcKeown(3) (hld up & a bhd) 9 11
LONG HANDICAP Grey Again 7-1

9/4 Pride of Pendle (op 6/1), **9/2** Misty Silks (op 3/1), Last Laugh (IRE) (op 3/1), **7/1** Donna Viola, Celestial Choir, **10/1** Willshe Gan, Queens Consul (IRE), **12/1** Princess Maxine (IRE), **14/1** Grey Again, **16/1** KARINSKA, Ballard Ring (IRE), CSF £166.53 CT £1,139.05 TOTE £29.20: £6.00 £3.40 £2.10 (£76.80) Trio £304.40; £12.86 to Nottingham 24/4/95 OWNER Mr Geoff Whiting (MARKET RASEN) BRED Sheikh Mohammed bin Rashid al Maktoum 11 Rn
1m 41.6 (6.00) SF: 33/56/39/57/45/27/20/23/38/42/16
WEIGHT FOR AGE 3yo-15lb

T/Plpt: £1,152.40 (7.84 Tckts). T/Qdpt: £51.40 (2.4 Tckts). WG

0540-BRIGHTON (L-H)
Monday April 24th (Good to firm)
WEATHER: misty WIND: str half bhd

725
SIDNEY THOMPSON MEMORIAL MAIDEN AUCTION STKS (2-Y.O) (Class F) £1,829.50 (£1,829.50: £383.00)
5f 59y Stalls: Low GOING minus 0.59 sec per fur (F) 2-00 (2-01)

650 5 **Satellite Star (IRE)** *(55)*(Fav)*(MRChannon)* 2-8-2 CRutter(4) (6th st: hdwy 1f out:str run fnl f: jnd wnr post) ....— 1
650 8 **Sam Coles (USA)** *(53t) (BJMeehan)* 2-8-0 BDoyle(3) (w ldr: led over 1f out: all out) ....— 1
Crimson And Clover *(55) (MBell)* 2-8-2 MFenton(5) (unf: outpcd: 6th st: hdwy 1f out: str run fnl f: fin wl) ....hd 3
617 16 All She Surveys *(46) (JAkehurst)* 2-8-1 GCarter(2) (led over 3f: one pce) 2½ 4
Sharp Shuffle (IRE) *(42) (RHannon)* 2-8-6 PatEddery(7) (lw: w'like: outpcd: hdwy fnl f: nvr nrr) 3 5
561 8 Caveat Emptor (IRE) *(43) (SDow)* 2-8-9 TQuinn(1) (4th st: rdn over 2f out: wknd over 1f out) ....¾ 6
617 19 Mandy's Risk *(28) (TMJones)* 2-8-5 RPerham(6) (lw: 3rd st: hrd rdn over 2f out: wknd over 1f out) 3½ 7

7/4 SATELLITE STAR (IRE), **9/4** Sharp Shuffle (IRE) (6/4-5/2), **6/1** Crimson And Clover (5/2-13/2), All She Surveys (op 3/1), **10/1** SAM COLES (USA) (8/1-12/1), **20/1** Caveat Emptor (IRE), **25/1** Mandy's Risk, CSF Satellite Star, Sam Coles £8.56; Sam Coles, Satellite Star £13.30 TOTE S.S. £1.50; S.C. £2.40: S.S. £2.10, S.C £1.10 (£8.70) OWNER Express Newspapers Plc (UPPER LAMBOURN)/Mr Gary Catchpole (UPPER LAMBOURN) BRED Rathasker Stud 7 Rn
62.7 secs (2.70) SF: -/-/-/-/-/-/-

726
LEVY BOARD H'CAP (0-70) (3-Y.O+) (Class E) £3,302.20 (£985.60: £470.80: £213.40) **5f 59y** Stalls: Low GOING minus 0.59 sec per fur (F) 2-30 (2-32)

542 5 **Aragrove (52)***(59) (JWPayne)* 5-9-4b MTebbutt(1) (hld up: nt clr run over 2f out: led over 1f out: drvn out) ....— 1
*627*8 Another Jade **(62)***(63) (APJarvis)* 5-10-0 BThomson(5) (lw: hld up: led 2f out to over 1f out: unable qckn) 2 2
656* Halliard **(62)***(58) (TMJones)* 4-10-0 7x RPerham(4) (dwlt: nt clr run over 2f out: hdwy over 1f out: r.o ins fnl f) 1½ 3
701 10 Giggleswick Girl **(52)***(45) (MRChannon)* 4-9-4 RHughes(10) (lw: hdwy over 1f out: r.o) 1¼ 4
583 2 Distant Dynasty **(51)***(38) (BAPearce)* 5-9-3 RCochrane(11) (hld up: rdn over 2f out: unable qckn) 1¾ 5
656 2 Grand Time **(35)***(21)*(Fav)*(CJHill)* 6-8-1b GDuffield(8) (4th st: wknd 2f out) ....nk 6
*603*8 Halbert **(47)***(28) (MRChannon)* 6-8-6 (7) DSweeney(13) (lw: 6th st: wknd 2f out) 1¾ 7
*331*4 Lift Boy (USA) **(45)***(26) (AMoore)* 6-8-11 CandyMorris(7) (3rd st: wknd over 1f out) ....d.h 7
565 5 Bright Paragon (IRE) **(47)***(26) (HJCollingridge)* 6-8-13 MRimmer(12) (5th st: wknd 2f out) ....¾ 9

519[8] Rustic League (IRE) **(37)***(10) (TJNaughton)* 4-8-0 (3) SSanders(2) (b.hind: led over 3f out to 2f out: wknd over 1f out) 1¾ 10
391W Pat Poindestres **(35)***(3) (BAPearce)* 5-7-10 (5)ow5 AWhelan(6) (a bhd) ....nk 11
Little Hooligan **(47)***(10) (JAkehurst)* 4-8-13 GBardwell(9) (a bhd) 3 12
The Noble Oak (IRE) **(58)***(14) (MJBolton)* 7-9-10 PatEddery(3) (led over 1f: 2nd st: wknd 2f out) 2½ 13

5/1 Grand Time (3/1-11/2), **6/1** ARAGROVE (4/1-7/1), Halliard (4/1-13/2), **13/2** Another Jade, Distant Dynasty, **8/1** Bright Paragon (IRE) (6/1-9/1), **9/1** Giggleswick Girl, **10/1** The Noble Oak (IRE) (7/1-12/1), **12/1** Lift Boy (USA), **14/1** Little Hooligan (10/1-16/1), **16/1** Rustic League (IRE), **25/1** Pat Poindestres, **33/1** Halbert, CSF £44.60 CT £230.99 TOTE TOTE £7.00: £3.20 £2.00 £3.50 (£31.00) Trio £59.70 OWNER Mr Dennis Purkiss (NEWMARKET) BRED Mrs J. R. Hine and Miss J. Bunting 13 Rn
60.8 secs (0.80) SF: 37/41/36/23/16/-/6/4/4/-/-/-/-

727 ORLEANS LIMITED STKS (0-65) (3-Y.O) (Class F) £2,922.20 (£809.20: £386.60)
5f 213y Stalls: Low GOING minus 0.59 sec per fur (F) 3-00 (3-01)

524[4] **Tafahhus (60)***(61+)*(Fav)*(RWArmstrong)* 3-8-11 WCarson(7) (lw: mde virtually all: pushed out) ....— 1
629[4] Cork Street Girl (IRE) **(65)***(52) (BJMeehan)* 3-8-6 BDoyle(2) (w wnr: rdn over 2f out: unable qckn) 1½ 2
603[12] Assumpsit (IRE) **(65)***(55) (SDow)* 3-8-11v GDuffield(4) (outpcd: 5th st: hrd rdn & hdwy over 1f out: r.o) ....¾ 3
126[2] Polly Garter **(60)***(50) (RHannon)* 3-8-6 TQuinn(5) (outpcd: hdwy over 1f out: r.o wl ins fnl f) ....hd 4
Midnight Break **(65)***(39) (PTWalwyn)* 3-8-6 PatEddery(1) (lw: 3rd st: rdn over 2f out: eased whn btn ins fnl f) 4 5
468[4] Kreef **(60)***(28) (RJO'Sullivan)* 3-8-11 DBiggs(3) (lw: 4th st: rdn over 2f out: wknd over 1f out) 6 6
381[6] Solianna **(65)***(22) (MRChannon)* 3-8-1 (5) PPMurphy(6) (lw: bhd fnl 4f) ....½ 7

11/8 TAFAHHUS (Evens-6/4), **15/8** Midnight Break, **7/1** Polly Garter (5/1-8/1), **10/1** Kreef (8/1-16/1), Solianna (op 6/1), **16/1** Cork Street Girl (IRE), Assumpsit (IRE), CSF £20.69 TOTE £2.20: £1.30 £2.30 (£15.70) OWNER Mr Hamdan Al Maktoum (NEWMARKET) BRED Shadwell Estate Company Limited 7 Rn
69.3 secs (0.90) SF: 31/22/25/20/9/-/-

728 A R DENNIS BOOKMAKERS APRIL H'CAP (0-90) (3-Y.O+) (Class C)
£6,264.00 (£1,872.00: £896.00: £408.00)
6f 209y Stalls: Low GOING minus 0.59 sec per fur (F) 3-30 (3-31)

433[13] **Ertlon (75)***(92) (CEBrittain)* 5-9-2 BDoyle(7) (lw: mde virtually all: clr over 2f out: unchal) ....— 1
563[2] Shepherd Market (IRE) **(59)***(60)*(Fav)*(DAWilson)* 4-8-0 GCarter(9) (6th st: n.m.r 2f out & over 1f out: unable qckn) 7 2
546[6] Canary Falcon **(64)***(65) (RJO'Sullivan)* 4-8-5 WWoods(8) (lw: 4th st: rdn over 2f out: one pce) ....hd 3
Walnut Burl (IRE) **(59)***(57) (LJHolt)* 5-8-0 ow2 AMcGlone(1) (rdn & hdwy 2f out: one pce) ....nk 4
Dom Pennion **(68)***(59) (RGuest)* 4-8-9 GHind(6) (lw: hdwy over 1f out: nvr nrr) 4 5
499[2] Crystal Heights (FR) **(65)***(54) (RJO'Sullivan)* 7-8-6 MRimmer(5) (b: 5th st: chsd wnr over 2f out to 1f out: sn wknd) ....¾ 6
Top Pet (IRE) **(65)***(52) (RAkehurst)* 5-8-6 TQuinn(11) (nvr nr to chal) 1 7
433[18] Persian Affair (IRE) **(71)***(49) (DHaydnJones)* 4-8-12 AMackay(2) (lw: a bhd) 4 8
439[12] Robsera (IRE) **(81)***(55) (GLewis)* 4-9-8 PaulEddery(3) (lw: 3rd st: wknd over 2f out) 1½ 9
499[5] Rocky Waters (USA) **(80)***(51) (GLMoore)* 6-9-7 BRouse(4) (b.hind: 2nd st: wknd over 2f out) 1½ 10
541* Shikari's Son **(87)***(56) (JWhite)* 8-10-0 RHughes(10) (a bhd) ....¾ 11

4/1 Shepherd Market (IRE), **5/1** ERTLON, Robsera (IRE), **6/1** Shikari's Son, **13/2** Top Pet (IRE) (7/2-7/1), **7/1** Crystal Heights (FR), **10/1** Walnut Burl (IRE), **20/1** Rocky Waters (USA), Canary Falcon, **33/1** Dom Pennion, Persian Affair (IRE), CSF £23.69 CT £329.81 TOTE £6.30: £1.60 £2.00 £5.80 (£16.50) Trio £68.60 OWNER Mr C. E. Brittain (NEWMARKET) BRED Hadi Al Tajir 11 Rn
1m 19.8 (-0.20) SF: 52/20/25/17/19/14/12/9/15/11/16

729 ROYAL PAVILION CLAIMING STKS (4-Y.O+) (Class F) £2,947.40 (£816.40: £390.20) **1m 3f 196y** Stalls: High GOING minus 0.59 sec per fur (F) 4-00 (4-03)

97[6] **Pharamineux (71)***(57+) (RAkehurst)* 9-8-4 TQuinn(7) (lw: hdwy over 2f out: led 1f out: pushed out) ....— 1

496[2] Elementary **(76)***(65)*(Fav)*(NJHWalker)* 12-9-0 PatEddery(5) (lw: 4th st: led over 2f out to 1f out: unable qckn) 1¾ 2
569* Kimberley Boy **(58)***(55)* *(GROldroyd)* 5-8-10 RCochrane(6) (hdwy over 4f out: 6th st: rdn over 2f out: one pce) 4 3
375[10] Cristal Springs **(40)***(32)* *(BJMcMath)* 4-7-10 GBardwell(2) (led over 4f: led over 4f out tl over 2f out: sn wknd) 7 4
496[5] Remember This (IRE) **(30)***(40)* *(CACyzer)* 5-9-0 GDuffield(8) (hdwy 3f out: wknd over 2f out) 7 5
545[16] Ragtime Song **(27)***(27)* *(AMoore)* 6-8-4 CandyMorris(1) (lw: 2nd st: wknd over 2f out) 2½ 6
75[7] Holiday Island **(51)***(20)* *(RAkehurst)* 6-8-8 GCarter(10) (bhd fnl 5f) 8 7
586[9] Starlight Flyer **(25)***(14)* *(JELong)* 8-7-9b(7) TField(4) (b: led over 7f out tl over 4f out: 3rd st: wknd 3f out) .... hd 8
497[3] Thames Side **(50)***(19)* *(MMadgwick)* 4-8-7 MFenton(3) (5th st: wknd over 2f out) .... nk 9
Moled Again *(19)* *(JRBosley)* 4-8-7 AClark(9) (a bhd) .... s.h 10

11/8 Elementary (4/5-6/4), **11/4** PHARAMINEUX (2/1-3/1), **5/1** Kimberley Boy, **13/2** Holiday Island, **20/1** Thames Side, **33/1** Remember This (IRE), Cristal Springs, **50/1** Starlight Flyer, Ragtime Song, Moled Again, CSF £6.47 TOTE £3.00: £1.60 £1.50 £1.20 (£2.40) Trio £3.10 OWNER Mr K. R. Snellings (EPSOM) BRED J.L.C.Pearce 10 Rn 2m 31.8 (2.80) SF: 24/32/22/-/7/-/-/-/-/-
WEIGHT FOR AGE 4yo-1lb

730 CONFLANS MAIDEN STKS (3-Y.O+) (Class D) £3,935.10 (£1,174.80: £561.40: £254.70)
7f 214y Stalls: Low GOING minus 0.59 sec per fur (F) 4-30 (4-33)

635[10] **Stone Ridge (IRE)** *(86)*(Fav)*(RHannon)* 3-8-11 PatEddery(1) (5th st: led over 1f out: rdn out) .... — 1
539[3] Bernard Seven (IRE) **(83)***(81)*(Fav)*(SPCWoods)* 3-8-11 WWoods(6) (lw: 4th st: led 3f out tl over 1f out: unable qckn) 2½ 2
585[6] Berkeley Bounder (USA) *(78)* *(PFICole)* 3-8-11 TQuinn(8) (lw: 6th st: rdn over 2f out: r.o ins fnl f) 1½ 3
Crystal Gift **(90)***(68)* *(PFICole)* 3-8-11 CRutter(10) (hdwy over 2f out: rdn over 1f out: one pce) 5 4
Domitia (USA) *(55)* *(MBell)* 3-8-6 MFenton(5) (b: 3rd st: wknd 2f out) 4 5
585[9] Zuno Flyer (USA) *(59)* *(GLewis)* 3-8-11 PaulEddery(3) (led 5f) .... ½ 6
Silks and Studs *(59)* *(JWhite)* 3-8-11 RPrice(9) (lw: bhd fnl 4f) .... s.h 7
564[7] Nero Kris *(51)* *(PAKelleway)* 3-8-11 MWigham(4) (lw: 2nd st: wknd over 2f out) 4 8
Alpine Storm (IRE) *(39)* *(MDIUsher)* 3-8-6 RPerham(2) (bit bkwd: bhd fnl 4f) 3½ 9
Return To Brighton *(33)* *(PCClarke)* 3-8-6 AMackay(7) (leggy: s.s: a wl bhd) 3 10

2/1 STONE RIDGE (IRE), Bernard Seven (IRE), **5/1** Berkeley Bounder (USA) (2/1-11/2), **9/1** Crystal Gift (6/1-10/1), **10/1** Zuno Flyer (USA), **12/1** Domitia (USA) (7/1-14/1), **20/1** Nero Kris, **50/1** Silks and Studs, Alpine Storm (IRE), **66/1** Return To Brighton, CSF £6.36 TOTE £2.90: £1.60 £1.40 £1.30 (£3.30) Trio £3.10 OWNER Mrs Chris Harrington (MARLBOROUGH) BRED Mrs Chris Harrington 10 Rn 1m 34.2 (2.00) SF: 24/19/16/6/-/-/-/-/-/-

731 TOWN PURSE H'CAP (0-70) (4-Y.O+) (Class E) £3,502.40 (£1,047.20: £501.60: £228.80)
7f 214y Stalls: Low GOING minus 0.59 sec per fur (F) 5-00 (5-04)

Mr Rough (58)*(70)* *(DMorris)* 4-9-3 RCochrane(11) (6th st: led over 1f out: edgd lft: drvn out) .... — 1
653[12] Pistol (IRE) **(61)***(70)* *(CAHorgan)* 5-9-6 PaulEddery(14) (b.hind: hdwy over 2f out: hrd rdn over 1f out: unable qckn) 1¾ 2
546* Confronter **(69)***(75+)*(Fav)*(SDow)* 6-10-0 RHughes(8) (lw: 7th st: nt clr run over 2f out: hmpd over 1f out: swtchd rt: r.o wl ins fnl f) 1½ 3
497[7] Taahhub (IRE) **(51)***(50)* *(RJO'Sullivan)* 5-8-10 WWoods(9) (lw: led 5f out tl over 1f out: sn wknd) 3½ 4
447[4] Pirates Gold (IRE) **(53)***(50)* *(JWhite)* 5-8-12 AMackay(10) (lw: 5th st: rdn over 2f out: one pce) .... ¾ 5
546[10] Dia Georgy **(54)***(44)* *(RGuest)* 4-8-13 GHind(15) (hdwy over 1f out: nvr nrr) 3½ 6
501[6] Words of Wisdom (IRE) **(50)***(39)* *(CACyzer)* 5-8-9 GDuffield(6) (4th st: rdn over 2f out: hmpd over 1f out: nt rcvr) .... nk 7
433[23] Another Fiddle (IRE) **(69)***(55)* *(RAkehurst)* 5-10-0 TQuinn(2) (b.hind: nvr nr to chal) 1½ 8
550[16] Friendly Brave (USA) **(65)***(29)* *(TGMills)* 5-9-10 GCarter(5) (led 3f: 2nd st: wkng whn n.m.r on ins wl over 1f out) 11 9

Araboybill **(61)***(17) (MartynMeade)* 4-9-6 AClark(3) (nvr nrr) 4 **10**
Dragon Bold (IRE) **(50)** *(LJHolt)* 4-8-9 AMcGlone(4) (lw: a mid div)....................3 **11**
500[6] Tarjumaan (USA) **(47)** *(RJO'Sullivan)* 4-8-6 MRimmer(7) (s.s: a bhd) 2½ **12**
Audrey Grace **(51)** *(BJMeehan)* 4-8-10 BDoyle(12) (bhd fnl 4f)....................2½ **13**
Whatever's Right (IRE) **(62)***(1) (MDIUsher)* 6-9-7 PatEddery(1) (3rd st: wknd 3f out)....................¾ **14**
Mutinique **(53)** *(BAPearce)* 4-8-9 (3) SSanders(13) (bit bkwd: bhd fnl 3f)....................8 **15**

4/1 Confronter (op 5/2), **5/1** Whatever's Right (IRE), **11/2** MR ROUGH (4/1-6/1), **8/1** Words of Wisdom (IRE) (5/1-9/1), **10/1** Another Fiddle (IRE) (op 6/1), **12/1** Dia Georgy, Araboybill (tchd 20/1), **14/1** Pirates Gold (IRE) (10/1-16/1), Taahhub (IRE) (10/1-16/1), Audrey Grace (op 8/1), **16/1** Friendly Brave (USA), **25/1** Pistol (IRE), Tarjumaan (USA), Dragon Bold (IRE), **33/1** Mutinique, CSF £121.78 CT £566.98 TOTE £7.20: £3.00 £7.50 £2.10 (£84.50) Trio £37.50 OWNER Mr Robin Akehurst (NEWMARKET) BRED Ahmed M. Foustok 15 Rn

1m 33.5 (1.30) SF: 37/37/42/17/17/11/6/22/-/-/-/-/-/-/-

T/Plpt: £31.80 (369.19 Tckts). T/Qdpt: £3.10 (26.45 Tckts). AK

0644-NOTTINGHAM (L-H)

Monday April 24th (Good, Good to soft patches)

WEATHER: dull WIND: Slt across

732

OVAL (S) STKS (3-Y.O) (Class G) £2,243.00 (£618.00: £293.00)
6f 15y Stalls: High GOING minus 0.14 sec per fur (G) 2-15 (2-18)

411[6] **Tael of Silver** *(64) (KRBurke)* 3-8-6 DHolland(16) (a.p: shkn up to ld 2f out: clr fnl f)....................— **1**
591[*] Dark Shot (IRE) **(80)***(61)(Fav)(JBerry)* 3-9-2v JCarroll(6) (led 4f: sn rdn: kpt on one pce)..........5 **2**
Saatchmo *(55) (JLSpearing)* 3-8-11 DeanMcKeown(10) (hld up: hdwy wl over 1f out: kpt on fnl f: nvr nrr)....................½ **3**
629[6] Rupert's Princess (IRE) **(53)***(47) (MJHeaton-Ellis)* 3-8-11 StephenDavies(3) (prom: rdn & outpcd bel dist: sn btn)....................3 **4**
628[9] Dowdency **(57)***(45) (JAPickering)* 3-8-11 NCarlisle(15) (chsd ldrs stands side: rdn over 2f out: nt pce to chal)....................½ **5**
603[9] Daily Challenger (USA) **(65)***(42) (RonaldThompson)* 3-8-11 NConnorton(11) (mid div: r.o u.p appr fnl f: nvr nrr)....................1¼ **6**
581[5] Kencol **(65)***(41) (AGFoster)* 3-8-11 JWeaver(13) (sme late hdwy: nvr nrr)....................½ **7**
591[9] Lawnswood Lady **(50)***(34) (RHollinshead)* 3-8-6 DHarrison(4) (prom tl rdn & wknd over 2f out)....................¾ **8**
581[6] Governor's Lass **(40)***(18) (SDow)* 3-8-6 WRyan(14) (in tch 4f: sn lost pl)....................6 **9**
519[7] Red O'Reilly *(20) (MrsNMacauley)* 3-8-11 DaleGibson(12) (outpcd)....................1¼ **10**
350[8] El Taurus *(19) (KGWingrove)* 3-8-11 JMcLaughlin(8) (a in rr)....................nk **11**
Fortunes Leap **(60)***(15) (MrsLAMurphy)* 3-8-6 (5) SDrowne(2) (hdwy ½-wy: rdn 2f out: sn btn)....................1½ **12**
La Dama (USA) **(55)** *(GROldroyd)* 3-8-6 MMcAndrew(5) (s.i.s: a bhd: t.o)....................8 **13**
Fuzzy *(SEKettlewell)* 3-8-11 NRodgers(9) (lt-fr: outpcd: a bhd: t.o)....................hd **14**
Daniel's Lass *(CNAllen)* 3-8-6 JQuinn(17) (b: lt-fr: s.s: a bhd: t.o)....................4 **15**
Chosen Man *(MWEllerby)* 3-8-11 SMorris(7) (s.s: a bhd: t.o)....................nk **16**
555[6] Tish **(40)** *(ASmith)* 3-8-6b MBirch(1) (s.s: a bhd & outpcd: t.o)....................11 **17**

9/4 Dark Shot (IRE), **6/1** Kencol, **7/1** TAEL OF SILVER (op 9/2), **8/1** Dowdency, Rupert's Princess (IRE), **12/1** Fortunes Leap, Daniel's Lass, La Dama (USA), **14/1** Lawnswood Lady, **20/1** Fuzzy, Saatchmo, Red O'Reilly, Daily Challenger (USA), **25/1** Governor's Lass, **33/1** Chosen Man, **50/1** El Taurus, Tish, CSF £24.27 TOTE £10.40: £2.60 £1.50 £5.00 (£18.50) Trio £220.80; £279.90 to Pontefract 25/04/95 OWNER Mr A. H. Boodoo (WANTAGE) BRED Mrs V. O'Brien 17 Rn

1m 15.1 (4.10) SF: 22/19/13/5/3/-/-/-/-/-/-/-/-/-/-/-/-

No bid.

733

EDGBASTON H'CAP (0-70) (3-Y.O) (Class E) £3,731.20 (£1,117.60: £536.80: £246.40)
6f 15y Stalls: High GOING minus 0.14 sec per fur (G) 2-45 (2-48)

524[3] **Media Express (62)***(71) (TGMills)* 3-8-13 JReid(16) (mde virtually all: clr whn edgd lft fnl f)....................— **1**
Magical Manoeuvers **(55)***(57) (BAMcMahon)* 3-8-6 JFortune(19) (swtg: a.p: ev ch bel dist: one pce fnl f)....................2½ **2**
507[8] The Kings Ransom **(55)***(54) (MrsJRRamsden)* 3-8-6 KFallon(18) (hdwy ½-wy: rdn wl over 1f out: kpt on)....................1¼ **3**

548[5] Code of Silence **(48)***(34) (BPalling)* 3-7-13v TSprake(10) (chsd ldrs: r.o one pce fnl 2f)....5 **4**
Runs in the Family **(66)***(52) (PGMurphy)* 3-9-3 DHarrison(11) (bit bkwd: hdwy fnl 2f: nvr nrr)....s.h **5**
The Mestral **(45)***(23) (MJRyan)* 3-7-5 (5) MBaird(12) (mid div: hdwy wl over 1f out: nvr nrr)....3 **6**
Rosa Bonheur **(60)***(33) (MAJarvis)* 3-8-11 LDettori(2) (chsd ldrs: drvn along bel dist: sn outpcd)....1¾ **7**
580[3] Cedar Dancer **(48)***(19) (RJHodges)* 3-7-6 (7)ow2 AmandaSanders(9) (chsd ldrs: rdn & one pce fnl 2f)....hd **8**
La Bossette (IRE) **(58)***(27) (JRArnold)* 3-8-9 JWeaver(17) (nvr trbld ldrs)....1½ **9**
555* Bolshoi (IRE) **(70)***(35)*(Fav)*(JBerry)* 3-9-7 JCarroll(1) (lw: prom: rdn along 2f out: sn wknd)....1½ **10**
468[3] Alute (IRE) **(53)***(17) (CEBrittain)* 3-8-4 MBirch(13) (a bhd & outpcd)....nk **11**
Blushing Grenadier (IRE) **(60)***(21) (MJFetherston-Godley)* 3-8-11 FNorton(6) (a in rr)....1¼ **12**
524[16] Voila Premiere (IRE) **(58)***(18) (MHTompkins)* 3-8-9 PRobinson(20) (in tch over 3f: sn wknd)....nk **13**
681[8] South Sound (IRE) **(65)***(23) (RHannon)* 3-9-2 KDarley(7) (prom to ½-wy: sn rdn & lost tch)....¾ **14**
Bowden Rose **(60)***(12) (MBlanshard)* 3-8-11 StephenDavies(5) (s.s: a bhd)....2½ **15**
128[6] The Cape Doctor (IRE) **(60)***(9) (AGFoster)* 3-8-11 DHolland(3) (bit bkwd: outpcd: a bhd)....1 **16**

5/1 Bolshoi (IRE), **11/2** MEDIA EXPRESS, **7/1** The Kings Ransom (12/1-6/1), **8/1** Code of Silence, **9/1** Alute (IRE), Runs in the Family, **12/1** Cedar Dancer, **14/1** Rosa Bonheur, **16/1** Bowden Rose, South Sound (IRE), Magical Manoeuvers, Voila Premiere (IRE), **20/1** Blushing Grenadier (IRE), The Mestral, **25/1** La Bossette (IRE), The Cape Doctor (IRE), CSF £86.42 CT £580.26 TOTE £4.90: £1.60 £4.00 £1.70 £3.20 (£42.10) Trio £221.30 OWNER Mr Mahmood Al-Shuaibi (EPSOM) BRED Fulling Mill Farm and Stud 16 Rn 1m 13.3 (2.30) SF: 53/39/36/16/34/5/15/1/9/17/-/3/-/5/-/-

734

LORDS CLAIMING STKS (3-Y.O+) (Class F) £2,947.40 (£816.40: £390.20)
5f 13y Stalls: High GOING: 0.18 sec per fur (G) 3-15 (3-15)

583[3] **Harry's Coming (49)***(59) (RJHodges)* 11-8-5 (5) SDrowne(9) (hld up: hdwy ½-wy: ld wl over 1f out: clr whn drifted lft appr fnl f: unchal)....— **1**
625[3] Best Kept Secret **(74)***(68) (JBerry)* 4-9-10 JCarroll(5) (hld up & bhd: hdwy over 1f out: fin wl)....1¾ **2**
328[4] Sison (IRE) **(68)***(56) (KGWingrove)* 5-9-0 JMcLaughlin(4) (b.hind: dwlt: hdwy 2f out: rdn & one pce fnl f)....½ **3**
581* Baileys Sunset (IRE) **(66)***(56)*(Fav)*(MJohnston)* 3-8-5 DHolland(6) (chsd ldrs: effrt & rdn bel dist: nt pce to chal)....½ **4**
498[4] Random **(60)***(42) (CJames)* 4-8-13 JWeaver(2) (w ldr: led over 2f out tl wl over 1f out: wknd fnl f)....3½ **5**
363[8] Oneineverycolour **(50)***(30) (PDEvans)* 3-7-2 (7)ow1 MartinDwyer(7) (dwlt: rdn over 2f out: n.d)....1¼ **6**
567[9] Grey Toppa **(61)***(32) (NPLittmoden)* 4-8-6 (5) TGMcLaughlin(3) (outpcd: a bhd)....1½ **7**
Lucy's Gold **(36)***(24) (MJRyan)* 4-8-0 (5) MBaird(8) (bit bkwd: gd spd 3f: sn wknd)....¾ **8**
348[10] Last Straw **(38)***(23) (BPreece)* 7-8-5 (5) JStack(1) (b: slt ld over 2f: sn hrd rdn & wknd)....1¾ **9**

7/4 Baileys Sunset (IRE) (5/4-2/1), **4/1** Best Kept Secret, **5/1** Random, **6/1** HARRY'S COMING, **8/1** Sison (IRE) (6/1-9/1), **12/1** Oneineverycolour, **20/1** Grey Toppa, Lucy's Gold, **33/1** Last Straw, CSF £28.84 TOTE £7.00: £1.80 £1.20 £3.30 (£15.30) Trio £30.30 OWNER Mr R. J. Hodges (SOMERTON) BRED T. E. Herring 9 Rn 62.2 secs (3.50) SF: 24/33/21/10/7/-/-/-/-
WEIGHT FOR AGE 3yo-11lb

735

'MICHELOZZO' STKS (4-Y.O+) (Class C) £4,909.00 (£1,831.00: £890.50: £377.50: £163.75: £78.25)
1m 6f 15y Stalls: Low GOING: 0.18 sec per fur (G) 3-45 (3-45)

440[3] **Khamaseen (107)***(103)*(Fav)*(JLDunlop)* 4-8-11 LDettori(6) (led tl rn wd & hdd bnd 11f out: 2nd st: led 2f out: r.o wl)....— **1**
440[6] Linpac West **(100)***(105) (CWCElsey)* 9-9-2 JCarroll(3) (lw: chsd ldrs: 3rd st: styd on wl ins fnl f)....1¼ **2**
Poltarf (USA) **(101)***(111) (HRACecil)* 4-9-6 WRyan(2) (bkwd: led over 11f out to 2f out: rallied bel dist: no ex fnl f)....hd **3**
Castle Courageous **(106)***(110) (LadyHerries)* 8-9-10 JReid(4) (bkwd: hld up & bhd: 5th st: hdwy over 3f out: wknd appr fnl f)....2½ **4**

The Flying Phantom **(90)***(99) (MHTompkins)* 4-9-2 PRobinson(5) (bit bkwd: hld up: 4th st: effrt over 3f out: outpcd fnl 2f) 4 5
Blue Judge (IRE) *(85) (RThompson)* 5-8-10 JWeaver(1) (bkwd: hld up & bhd: 6th st: lost tch fnl 3f) 5 6

11/8 KHAMASEEN, **7/2** Castle Courageous, **4/1** Poltarf (USA) (3/1-9/2), **13/2** The Flying Phantom, **8/1** Linpac West, **16/1** Blue Judge (IRE), CSF £11.64 TOTE £1.40: £1.70 £3.40 (£9.20) OWNER Prince A. A. Faisal (ARUNDEL) BRED Nawara Stud Co Ltd 6 Rn
3m 8.4 (9.90) SF: 54/58/62/63/50/38
WEIGHT FOR AGE 4yo-2lb

736 HEADINGLEY LIMITED STKS (0-70) (3-Y.O) (Class E) £3,302.20 (£985.60: £470.80: £213.40)
1m 1f 213y Stalls: Low GOING: 0.18 sec per fur (G) 4-15 (4-16)

614[2] **Nigel's Lad (IRE) (70)***(78) (PCHaslam)* 3-8-10 (5) JStack(1) (a.p: 4th st: veered rt & led jst ins fnl f: rdn & wnt lft fin: r.o) ....— 1
648* Busy Banana **(69)***(77)*(Fav)*(RHannon)* 3-9-1 KDarley(6) (lw: led: rdn over 1f out: hdd ins fnl f: unable qckn) ....½ 2
539[8] Kaf **(65)***(62) (JLDunlop)* 3-8-11 LDettori(5) (bit bkwd: chsd ldr: 2nd st: ev ch 2f out: wknd bel dist) 7 3
Mutazz (USA) **(65)***(60) (MajorWRHern)* 3-8-11 MBirch(3) (chsd ldrs: 5th st: one pce fnl 3f) 1¼ 4
427[18] Lucidity **(67)***(57) (CWThornton)* 3-8-8 DeanMcKeown(4) (hld up & bhd: 7th st: rdn 3f out: nvr nr ldrs) ....s.h 5
482[11] Simply Simon **(40)** *(KRBurke)* 3-8-4 (7) SO'Shea(7) (s.i.s: hld up: wnt 3rd st: outpcd fnl 3f: t.o) ....dist 6
Cranbrook Kate **(44)** *(JMackie)* 3-8-6 JQuinn(2) (bit bkwd: a bhd: 6th st: t.o) 6 7

6/4 Busy Banana (op Evens), **15/8** Kaf, **9/2** NIGEL'S LAD (IRE), **7/1** Mutazz (USA), Lucidity, **66/1** Simply Simon, Cranbrook Kate, CSF £12.02 TOTE £5.70: £1.30 £1.70 (£4.00) OWNER Mr N. C. Dunnington (MIDDLEHAM) BRED Nikita Investments 7 Rn 2m 11.6 (9.10) SF: 40/39/24/22/19/-/-

737 TRENT BRIDGE H'CAP (0-80) (4-Y.O+) (Class D) £4,036.50 (£1,206.00: £577.00: £262.50)
1m 6f 15y Stalls: Low GOING: 0.18 sec per fur (G) 4-45 (4-46)

556[11] **New Inn (55)***(67) (EWeymes)* 4-8-3 KDarley(1) (a.p: 4th st: led 3f out: rdn & styd on wl) ....— 1
*589** Mizyan (IRE) **(60)***(71) (JEBanks)* 7-8-10 LDettori(9) (hld up: hdwy ½-wy: 3rd st: ev ch 3f out: rdn & outpcd over 1f out: kpt on twrds fin) 1¼ 2
Cuango (IRE) **(76)***(85) (RHollinshead)* 4-9-10 WRyan(13) (swtg: bit bkwd: hld up & bhd: hdwy 3f out: styd on ins fnl f: nrst fin) 1¼ 3
649[6] Memorable **(45)***(54) (JHetherton)* 4-7-7 NCarlisle(8) (a.p: 5th st: kpt on u.p appr fnl f) ....hd 4
Wings Cove **(76)***(82) (LadyHerries)* 5-9-12 JReid(5) (chsd ldrs: 6th st: rdn over 2f out: one pce) 3 5
549[4] Rapporteur (USA) **(58)***(52) (CCElsey)* 9-8-8 DHarrison(2) (b: mid div: rdn & outpcd ½-wy: n.d after) 10 6
La Spezia **(60)***(53) (MBlanshard)* 5-8-10 StephenDavies(10) (hld up: effrt 3f out: no imp) 1¼ 7
Moshaajir (USA) **(70)***(61) (CSmith)* 5-9-1 (5) JStack(7) (bkwd: chsd ldr: 2nd st: led over 3f out: sn hdd & wknd) 1¼ 8
Smuggler's Point (USA) **(65)***(56) (JJBridger)* 5-9-1 JWeaver(6) (bkwd: led tl hdd over 3f out: sn wknd) ....s.h 9
Special Risk (IRE) **(50)***(40)*(Fav)*(RAkehurst)* 5-8-0 JQuinn(11) (bkwd: hld up in tch: pushed along over 3f out: sn btn) 1½ 10
Vasiliev **(55)***(43) (SGollings)* 7-8-5v DeanMcKeown(12) (bit bkwd: a bhd) 1½ 11
649* Swordking (IRE) **(45)***(10) (JLHarris)* 6-7-9v 4x DaleGibson(3) (a bhd: t.o) 20 12
LONG HANDICAP Memorable 7-5

100/30 Special Risk (IRE), **7/2** Mizyan (IRE) (op 9/4), **13/2** Swordking (IRE), **10/1** Cuango (IRE), Wings Cove, **11/1** Rapporteur (USA) (8/1-12/1), **12/1** Moshaajir (USA) (op 20/1), Memorable, Smuggler's Point (USA), **14/1** NEW INN, **16/1** La Spezia, **20/1** Vasiliev, CSF £61.49 CT £486.00 TOTE £23.00: £3.90 £1.30 £3.80 (£43.90) Trio £246.10 OWNER Mrs Christine Sharratt (MIDDLEHAM) BRED Crockfords Stud 12 Rn 3m 9.2 (10.70) SF: 42/48/60/29/59/29/30/38/33/17/20/-
WEIGHT FOR AGE 4yo-2lb

738 NOTTINGHAM LADIES' H'CAP (0-75) (3-Y.O+) (Class F) £2,519.00 (£694.00: £329.00)
1m 1f 213y Stalls: Low GOING: 0.18 sec per fur (G) 5-15 (5-16)

586[5] **Captain Marmalade (41)**_(52)_(Fav)_(DTThom)_ 6-9-1 ow1 MissDianaJones(10) (hld up: hdwy 4f out: shkn up to ld wl over 1f out: comf) ....— 1
568[8] Broughton's Pride (IRE) **(48)**_(58)_ _(JAGlover)_ 4-9-8 MissPJones(23) (hld up: hdwy over 2f out: fin wl) 1 2
545* Credit Squeeze **(69)**_(77)_ _(RFJohnsonHoughton)_ 5-11-1 MissEJohnsonHoughton(22) (hld up: 6th st: led bel dist: sn hdd: kpt on one pce) 1½ 3
549[7] Haroldon (IRE) **(56)**_(61)_ _(BPalling)_ 6-9-12 (4) MissEJJones(7) (b: in tch: hdwy & ev ch 2f out: rdn & no ex ins fnl f) 1¾ 4
Bajan (IRE) **(52)**_(57)_ _(LadyHerries)_ 4-9-12 MrsMCowdrey(2) (chsd ldrs: ev ch wl over 1f out: one pce) ....hd 5
550[7] Queens Stroller (IRE) **(59)**_(64)_ _(CCElsey)_ 4-10-5 MissAElsey(19) (chsd ldrs: 5th st: ev ch wl over 1f out: unable qckn fnl f) ....hd 6
Telopea **(75)**_(78)_ _(HCandy)_ 4-11-0 (7) MrsCDunwoody(12) (led tl hdd & wknd bel dist)....1 7
568* Larn Fort **(51)**_(49)_ _(CWFairhurst)_ 5-9-11v MrsSBosley(3) (chsd ldr: 2nd st: n.m.r bel dist: sn btn)....3½ 8
493[5] No Submission (USA) **(49)**_(44)_ _(DWChapman)_ 9-9-5 (4) MissRClark(15) (mid div: effrt 2f out: no imp) 1¾ 9
_605_[9] Scottish Park **(43)**_(28)_ _(RWEmery)_ 6-9-3 MissJWinter(5) (b.hind: nvr trbld ldrs)....6 10
Breezed Well **(54)**_(27)_ _(BRCambidge)_ 9-9-10 (4)ow11 MrsHNoonan(9) (prom: 3rd st: wknd over 2f out) 1 11
559[12] Ikis Girl **(53)**_(36)_ _(SGollings)_ 4-9-6 (7) MrsJMGollings(16) (prom: 4th st: wknd over 2f out)....½ 12
430[22] Gallardini (IRE) **(65)**_(47)_ _(BSRothwell)_ 6-10-4 (7) MissAlexMcCabe(8) (nvr btr than mid div) ....½ 13
Ayunli **(58)**_(36)_ _(SCWilliams)_ 4-9-11 (7) MissKWright(18) (bit bkwd: chsd ldrs: effrt & rdn 2f out: grad wknd) 2½ 14
_138_[11] Sure to Win (IRE) **(40)**_(18)_ _(JMCarr)_ 6-8-7 (7) MrsLBarrett(21) (b: a in rr) ....hd 15
586[7] Royal Acclaim **(46)**_(15)_ _(JMBradley)_ 10-9-2v(4)ow6 MrsDMcHale(11) (nvr trbld ldrs)....1½ 16
586[8] Cheveley Dancer (USA) **(42)**_(11)_ _(DAWilson)_ 7-9-2 MissJAllison(17) (swtg: b: mid div tl wknd 3f out)....4 17
Allmosa **(57)**_(25)_ _(TJNaughton)_ 6-9-13 (4) MrsJNaughton(13) (b: a in rr) ....¾ 18
Bill and Win **(40)**_(7)_ _(KWhite)_ 4-8-7 (7) MissAAnderson(20) (bit bkwd: a in rr) ....½ 19
550[15] Sharaar (USA) **(66)**_(33)_ _(JLSpearing)_ 5-10-8b(4) MissTSpearing(1) (s.s: a bhd: t.o) ....nk 20
Ripsnorter (IRE) **(57)**_(20)_ _(JABennett)_ 6-9-13 (4) MissAPurdy(4) (bit bkwd: s.s: a bhd: t.o)....2 21
Bresil (USA) **(66)** _(KRBurke)_ 6-10-5 (7)ow26 MrsHSweeting(14) (s.s: a bhd: t.o)....11 22
Mr Devious **(58)** _(PJHobbs)_ 4-10-0 (4) MrsSHobbs(6) (chsd ldrs tl stmbld & uns rdr 6f out) .... U
LONG HANDICAP Bill and Win 8-8 Sure to Win (IRE) 8-9 Royal Acclaim 8-12

4/1 CAPTAIN MARMALADE, **11/2** Bajan (IRE), **7/1** Larn Fort, **10/1** Queens Stroller (IRE), **11/1** Credit Squeeze (7/1-12/1), **12/1** Ayunli, Mr Devious, **14/1** Broughton's Pride (IRE), No Submission (USA), Cheveley Dancer (USA), Telopea, **16/1** Allmosa, **20/1** Haroldon (IRE), **25/1** Ripsnorter (IRE), Gallardini (IRE), Royal Acclaim, Ikis Girl, **33/1** Breezed Well, Sure to Win (IRE), Bill and Win, Scottish Park, Sharaar (USA), **50/1** Bresil (USA), CSF £64.10 CT £575.16 TOTE £6.30: £1.40 £2.20 £1.20 £5.10 (£90.10) Trio £203.80 OWNER Mrs Carol Whitwood (NEWMARKET) BRED Mrs C. Whitwood and N. E. C Sherwood 23 Rn
2m 12.5 (10.00) SF: 33/39/58/42/38/45/59/30/25/9/8/17/28/17/-/-/-/6/-/14/1/-/-

T/Jkpt: Not won; £30,628.33 to Pontefract 26/4/95: T/Plpt £84.00 (184.26 Tckts). T/Qdpt: £20.20 (2.45 Tckts) . IM

0580-FOLKESTONE (R-H)
Tuesday April 25th (Good to firm)
WEATHER: sunny WIND: slt half against

739 WALMER MAIDEN APPRENTICE STKS (3-Y.O+) (Class G) £2,364.50 (£672.00: £333.50)
6f 189y Stalls: High GOING minus 0.10 sec per fur (G) 2-30 (2-36)

Ma Petite Anglaise (75)_(73)_(Fav)_(WJarvis)_ 3-8-5 MHenry(9) (hdwy over 2f out: 6th st: led ins fnl f: r.o wl)....— 1
502[5] Lorelei Lee (IRE) _(69)_ _(JohnBerry)_ 3-8-4 (5)ow4 GFaulkner(3) (3rd st: led 1f out to ins fnl f: unable qckn) 1¾ 2

Mo's Star **(59)***(68) (SDow)* 3-7-11 (8) ADaly(5) (hdwy on ins over 1f out: ev ch ins fnl f: one pce) ....½ **3**
Emphatic Candidate (IRE) **(77)***(72) (RAkehurst)* 3-8-3 (8)ow1 RMoogan(2) (lw: hdwy 2f out: hrd rdn over 1f out: one pce) ....½ **4**
630[5] Rasmi (CAN) *(67)*(Fav)*(ACStewart)* 4-9-5 (5) JoHunnam(14) (lw: led 6f) 2 **5**
I'm Outa Here (IRE) *(65) (RHannon)* 3-8-1 (10)ow1 EGreehy(13) (bit bkwd: 4th st: wknd over 2f out) ....¾ **6**
527[2] Sharp 'n Smart **(60)***(59) (BSmart)* 3-8-10 MartinDwyer(4) (2nd st: wknd over 1f out) 2½ **7**
511[6] Bold Cyrano (IRE) *(58) (BPalling)* 4-9-10 DaneO'Neill(10) (5th st: wknd over 1f out) ....½ **8**
401[6] Sandra Dee (IRE) **(65)***(50) (BAPearce)* 3-7-12 (7) TField(11) (lw: a bhd) 1½ **9**
543[8] Dissentor (IRE) *(51) (LMCumani)* 3-8-7 (3) GMitchell(12) (lw: bhd fnl 3f) 1¾ **10**
Colt D'Or *(47) (JWhite)* 3-8-10 SLanigan(8) (lw: a bhd) 1½ **11**
541[9] Starsport (IRE) **(55)***(39) (DJSffrenchDavis)* 4-9-7v(3) RWaterfield(6) (lw: bhd fnl 5f) 3½ **12**
628[2] Little Wilma *(APJarvis)* 3-7-11 (8) BHunter(7) (Withdrawn not under Starter's orders: bolted bef s) .... **W**

5/2 MA PETITE ANGLAISE, Rasmi (CAN) (2/1-3/1), **5/1** Sharp 'n Smart, **9/1** Emphatic Candidate (IRE), **12/1** Little Wilma, Lorelei Lee (IRE), **14/1** Dissentor (IRE) (7/1-16/1), I'm Outa Here (IRE), **20/1** Bold Cyrano (IRE), Sandra Dee (IRE), Starsport (IRE), **25/1** Colt D'Or, **33/1** Mo's Star, CSF £30.72 TOTE £5.00: £2.00 £2.60 £4.50 (£19.40) Trio £228.60; £32.21 to Kempton 26/04/95
OWNER Mr K. P. Seow (NEWMARKET) BRED R. P. Williams 12 Rn
1m 26.2 (4.60) SF: 26/22/21/25/34/18/12/25/3/4/-/6/-
WEIGHT FOR AGE 3yo-14lb

740 SANDLING (S) STKS (2-Y.O) (Class G) £2,489.40 (£688.40: £328.20)
5f Stalls: Low GOING minus 0.40 sec per fur (F) 3-00 (3-01)

644[2] **Arvzees (IRE)** *(62t)*(Fav)*(MRChannon)* 2-8-11 RHughes(6) (a.p: led over 1f out: pushed out) ....— **1**
604[4] Mustaffa (IRE) *(57) (MRChannon)* 2-8-6 (5) PPMurphy(1) (lw: s.s: hdwy 2f out: ev ch 1f out: unable qckn) 1½ **2**
561[6] Solva Mist *(30) (LJHolt)* 2-8-7 ow1 AScobie(5) (bit bkwd: nvr nr to chal) 7 **3**
Sakti (AUS) *(28) (WJarvis)* 2-8-7 ow1 JReid(3) (neat: bit bkwd: led over 3f) ....½ **4**
617[17] Babylon Blues *(32) (RHannon)* 2-8-11 PatEddery(2) (bit bkwd: w ldr: ev ch wl over 1f out: sn wknd) ....½ **5**
Touch of Fantasy *(20) (JohnBerry)* 2-8-7 ow1 CDwyer(4) (neat: bit bkwd: a bhd) 2 **6**

5/4 ARVZEES (IRE) (Evens-11/8), **2/1** Babylon Blues, **4/1** Sakti (AUS) (op 2/1), **8/1** Mustaffa (IRE) (6/1-10/1), **20/1** Touch of Fantasy, **25/1** Solva Mist, CSF £11.09 TOTE £1.70: £1.20 £4.20 (£7.30)
OWNER . Albion Investments (UPPER LAMBOURN) BRED Topazio Est Vaduz 6 Rn
61.7 secs (3.10) SF: 10/5/-/-/-/-
Bt in 7,100gns.

741 LEVY BOARD H'CAP (0-70) (4-Y.O+) (Class E) £3,531.00 (£1,056.00: £506.00: £231.00)
1m 7f 92y Stalls: Low GOING minus 0.10 sec per fur (G) 3-30 (3-31)

556[2] **Rolling the Bones (USA) (36)***(50) (PSFelgate)* 6-8-1 AMackay(10) (3rd st: led 2f out: r.o wl) ....— **1**
582* Soojama (IRE) **(40)***(49) (RMFlower)* 5-8-0 (5)ow2 JDSmith(8) (s.s: hdwy 3f out: 6th st: chsd wnr over 1f out: edgd rt: unable qckn) 2½ **2**
661[9] Head Turner **(47)***(57) (CPWildman)* 7-8-12 StephenDavies(12) (hdwy 5f out: 5th st: hrd rdn over 1f out: 3rd & btn whn hmpd on ins, ins fnl f) 1¾ **3**
582[3] By Arrangement (IRE) **(40)***(42)*(Fav)*(SWoodman)* 6-8-5 RCochrane(11) (7th st: hmpd on ins over 1f out: nt rcvr) 7 **4**
514[6] Who's the Best (IRE) **(34)***(33) (APJarvis)* 5-7-6 (7) BHunter(5) (2nd st: wknd over 1f out) 3 **5**
Captain Starlight (IRE) **(43)***(42) (RAkehurst)* 4-8-6 GCarter(14) (4th st: wknd 2f out) ....s.h **6**
*329** Harlequin Walk (IRE) **(38)***(35) (RJO'Sullivan)* 4-8-1 DBiggs(6) (led 8f out to 2f out: sn wknd) 2½ **7**
Simply (IRE) **(35)***(26) (TPMcGovern)* 6-8-0 NCarlisle(15) (led over 7f) 5 **8**
Limosa **(57)***(41) (RFJohnsonHoughton)* 4-9-6 JReid(3) (lost pl 10f out: rallied 5f out: wknd over 2f out) 7 **9**
All in the Mind **(50)***(26) (AlexVanderhaeghen,Belgium)* 4-8-13 MServranckx(13) (a bhd) 8 **10**
506[9] Sir Thomas Beecham **(58)***(31) (SDow)* 5-9-9 RHughes(9) (bhd fnl 2f) 2½ **11**

649[2] Seize the Day (IRE) **(55)***(23) (CDBroad)* 7-9-6v MWigham(1) (lw: bhd fnl 3f)....5 **12**
Mendip Son **(45)** *(JFfitch-Heyes)* 5-8-10 JWilliams(4) (b: a bhd: t.o)....dist **13**
497[6] Secret Assignment (USA) **(42)** *(RCurtis)* 5-8-7 GBardwell(7) (lw: prom over 8f: t.o).... **14**

7/2 By Arrangement (IRE), **6/1** Captain Starlight (IRE) (3/1-13/2), **7/1** Soojama (IRE), Seize the Day (IRE), Head Turner, **8/1** ROLLING THE BONES (USA), **10/1** Harlequin Walk (IRE) (7/1-12/1), Limosa, **12/1** Simply (IRE), **14/1** Sir Thomas Beecham, **16/1** Who's the Best (IRE), **25/1** All in the Mind, **33/1** Mendip Son, Secret Assignment (USA), CSF £63.84 CT £387.51 TOTE £6.70: £2.10 £2.60 £2.80 (£35.90) Trio £97.40 OWNER Mr M. F. Hyman (MELTON MOWBRAY) BRED Holtsinger Incorporated 14 Rn 3m 26.3 (9.40) SF: 31/30/38/23/14/21/14/7/20/5/12/4/-/-
WEIGHT FOR AGE 4yo-2lb

742

BARHAM MEDIAN AUCTION MAIDEN STKS (3-Y.O) (Class E) £3,216.40 (£959.20: £457.60: £206.80)
6f Stalls: Low GOING minus 0.40 sec per fur (F) 4-00 (4-01)

585[4] **Prolific Lady (IRE)** *(67) (GROldroyd)* 3-8-9 RCochrane(2) (lw: mde virtually all: drvn out)....— **1**
645[3] Jo Maximus **(70)***(69) (SDow)* 3-9-0 StephenDavies(10) (a.p: hrd rdn & ev ch over 1f out: unable qckn)....1¼ **2**
658[4] Double Matt (IRE) *(69)*(Fav)*(RHannon)* 3-9-0 JReid(8) (hdwy over 4f out: hrd rdn & ev ch over 1f out: one pce)....s.h **3**
Aoife Alainn (IRE) *(54) (JWHills)* 3-8-9 MHills(3) (hld up: swtchd rt over 2f out: hrd rdn over 1f out: one pce)....3½ **4**
Glorious Aragon *(48) (RFJohnsonHoughton)* 3-8-9 AClark(11) (w'like: bit bkwd: hdwy over 4f out: hrd rdn & ev ch over 1f out: wknd fnl f)....2½ **5**
Anegre (IRE) **(62)***(45) (LJHolt)* 3-9-0 AMcGlone(1) (nvr plcd to chal)....3 **6**
547[6] Anita's Contessa (IRE) *(39) (BPalling)* 3-8-9 TSprake(5) (outpcd)....s.h **7**
She Said No *(33) (LordHuntingdon)* 3-8-9 DHarrison(6) (w'like: lw: a bhd)....2½ **8**
Solano (IRE) *(28) (AlexVanderhaeghen,Belgium)* 3-9-0 MServranckx(4) (swtg: spd over 3f)....3½ **9**
581[7] Logie Pert Lad **(30)***(12) (JJBridger)* 3-8-11 (3) SSanders(7) (outpcd)....6 **10**

Evens Double Matt (IRE), **100/30** PROLIFIC LADY (IRE) (5/2-4/1), **7/1** Jo Maximus (op 7/2), **10/1** Anita's Contessa (IRE) (5/1-12/1), She Said No (op 6/1), **12/1** Aoife Alainn (IRE) (op 5/1), **20/1** Anegre (IRE), **33/1** Glorious Aragon, **50/1** Solano (IRE), Logie Pert Lad, CSF £26.28 TOTE £4.10: £1.30 £1.70 £1.20 (£11.80) Trio £8.30 OWNER Mr M. S. Griffiths (YORK) BRED Gainsborough Stud Management Ltd 10 Rn 1m 13.4 (1.70) SF: 37/39/39/24/18/15/9/3/-/-

743

FOLKESTONE TOWN STKS (3-Y.O+) (Class D) £3,833.70 (£1,143.60: £545.80: £246.90)
6f Stalls: Low GOING minus 0.40 sec per fur (F) 4-30 (4-31)

543[2] **Emerging Market (84)***(84) (JLDunlop)* 3-8-12 WCarson(4) (lw: hld up: led 2f out: r.o wl)....— **1**
Prima Cominna **(94)***(74)*(Fav)*(MBell)* 3-8-7 MFenton(2) (w ldr: ev ch 2f out: unable qckn)....1¾ **2**
433[22] Anzio (IRE) **(68)***(60) (BAPearce)* 4-9-4 RCochrane(3) (b: lw: led 4f)....5 **3**
612[5] Coffee 'n Cream **(88)***(63) (RHannon)* 3-8-10 PatEddery(1) (hld up: rdn over 2f out: wknd over 1f out)....½ **4**

13/8 Prima Cominna, **7/4** Coffee 'n Cream (5/4-15/8), **2/1** EMERGING MARKET, **33/1** Anzio (IRE), CSF £5.39 TOTE £2.70: (£2.60) OWNER Mr Philip Wroughton (ARUNDEL) BRED R. T. and Mrs Watson 4 Rn 1m 13.1 (1.40) SF: 44/34/32/23
WEIGHT FOR AGE 3yo-12lb

744

DOVER H'CAP (0-70) (3-Y.O+) (Class E) £3,359.40 (£1,003.20: £479.60: £217.80)
1m 4f Stalls: Low GOING minus 0.10 sec per fur (G) 5-00 (5-02)

623[14] **Bookcase (55)***(66) (DRCElsworth)* 8-9-4 JWilliams(6) (lw: hdwy over 1f out: squeezed thro to ld ins fnl f: r.o wl)....— **1**
*471** Bag of Tricks (IRE) **(55)***(65) (SDow)* 5-9-4 DHarrison(4) (hdwy over 2f out: 6th st: ev ch ins fnl f: unable qckn)....½ **2**
545[2] Mr Browning (USA) **(54)***(64)*(Fav)*(RAkehurst)* 4-9-2 AClark(11) (2nd st: led over 1f out to ins fnl f: one pce)....nk **3**
Shabanaz **(65)***(72) (WRMuir)* 10-10-0 RHughes(1) (5th st: hrd rdn over 1f out: one pce)....2½ **4**
549[3] Jemima Puddleduck **(58)***(64) (DWPArbuthnot)* 4-9-6 RPrice(2) (b.hind: lw: a.p: led over 4f out to over 1f out: wknd fnl f)....¾ **5**

549[15] Art Tatum **(55)***(59) (RHannon)* 4-9-3 JReid(3) (3rd st: wknd over 1f out)....1¼ **6**
355[5] Dutosky **(56)***(59) (RJO'Sullivan)* 5-9-5 DBiggs(9) (b.hind: lw: nvr nr to chal)....½ **7**
649[7] Glow Forum **(39)***(34) (GLMoore)* 4-7-10 (5)ow5 AWhelan(8) (bhd fnl 2f)....2½ **8**
729[3] Kimberley Boy **(58)***(53) (GROldroyd)* 5-9-7 RCochrane(5) (hdwy over 3f out: 4th st: wknd over 1f out)....3½ **9**
471[4] Pigalle Wonder **(31)***(26) (RJO'Sullivan)* 7-7-3 (5) MBaird(10) (led over 7f)....nk **10**
Kala Star **(52)***(7) (JFfitch-Heyes)* 4-9-0 BDoyle(7) (bhd fnl 5f)....30 **11**

11/4 Mr Browning (USA), **7/2** Bag of Tricks (IRE), Jemima Puddleduck, **15/2** Kimberley Boy, **8/1** Art Tatum (6/1-9/1), **14/1** Dutosky (10/1-16/1), **16/1** Shabanaz, **20/1** BOOKCASE, **33/1** Glow Forum, Pigalle Wonder, Kala Star, CSF £84.20 CT £233.26 TOTE £9.50: £1.50 £2.40 £1.50 (£31.50) Trio £76.70 OWNER Adept (80) Ltd (WHITCOMBE) BRED The Sussex Stud 11 Rn
2m 39.8 (8.60) SF: 38/37/35/44/35/30/31/5/25/-/-
WEIGHT FOR AGE 4yo-1lb

745

TIM FREEMAN H'CAP (0-65) (3-Y.O) (Class F) £2,519.00 (£694.00: £329.00)
1m 1f 149y Stalls: High GOING minus 0.10 sec per fur (G) 5-30 (5-32)

Fujiyama Crest (IRE) (55)*(63) (MRStoute)* 3-8-8 (3) JTate(9) (b.hind: a.p: led 3f out: edgd rt over 1f out: jinked lft ins fnl f: rdn out)....— **1**
547[11] Carnbrea Belle (IRE) **(57)***(62) (MBell)* 3-8-13 MFenton(15) (bit bkwd: 4th st: hrd rdn over 1f out: unable qckn)....2 **2**
492[2] Acquittal (IRE) **(59)***(63)*(Fav)*(JRFanshawe)* 3-9-1 DHarrison(10) (5th st: hrd rdn over 1f out: one pce)....¾ **3**
Flight Master **(63)***(62) (PJMakin)* 3-9-5 RPerham(5) (lw: 2nd st: hrd rdn over 1f out: one pce)....3 **4**
560[4] Western Horizon (USA) **(55)***(52) (CEBrittain)* 3-8-11 BDoyle(13) (lw: nvr nr to chal)....1 **5**
Pioneer Princess **(55)***(52) (MJRyan)* 3-8-11 DBiggs(3) (6th st: one pce fnl 2f)....hd **6**
Wet Patch (IRE) **(60)***(52) (RHannon)* 3-9-2 PatEddery(2) (bit bkwd: a mid div)....3 **7**
628[8] Jackatack (IRE) **(57)***(48) (MRChannon)* 3-8-13 RHughes(11) (led over 6f: 3rd st: wknd over 1f out)....nk **8**
648[15] Kristal Breeze **(60)***(48) (WRMuir)* 3-9-2 RCochrane(4) (lw: a mid div)....2 **9**
444[3] Alka International **(53)***(36) (JWhite)* 3-8-4 (5) SDrowne(1) (a mid div)....3 **10**
618[13] Hi-Aud **(62)***(45) (JAkehurst)* 3-9-1 (3) SSanders(14) (bhd fnl 3f)....s.h **11**
My Mum Said **(65)***(46) (LadyHerries)* 3-9-0 (7) JO'Dwyer(12) (lw: a bhd)....1¼ **12**
First Bite (IRE) **(61)***(42) (JLDunlop)* 3-9-3 WCarson(6) (a bhd)....s.h **13**
485[10] Ray of Hope **(53)***(33) (GWragg)* 3-8-9 FNorton(7) (prom over 6f)....½ **14**

4/1 Acquittal (IRE), **5/1** First Bite (IRE), **6/1** FUJIYAMA CREST (IRE) (op 7/2), Flight Master, **13/2** Wet Patch (IRE), **8/1** Jackatack (IRE), Hi-Aud, **10/1** My Mum Said, **14/1** Western Horizon (USA), **16/1** Alka International, Carnbrea Belle (IRE), Ray of Hope, **33/1** Kristal Breeze, Pioneer Princess, CSF £99.95 CT £408.27 TOTE £6.10: £3.50 £16.20 £1.90 (£180.90) Trio £340.30; £71.80 to Kempton 26/04/95 OWNER Mr Seisuke Hata (NEWMARKET) BRED B. Kennedy 14 Rn
2m 5.4 (7.70) SF: 23/22/23/22/12/12/12/8/8/-/5/6/2/-

T/Plpt: £130.30 (99.11 Tckts). T/Qdpt: £12.90 (3 Tckts). AK

0671-PONTEFRACT (L-H)
Tuesday April 25th (Good)

WEATHER: sunny WIND: str across

746

PONTEFRACT SERIES APPRENTICE LIMITED STKS (0-70) (3-Y.O+) (Class E) £2,929.75 (£898.00: £446.50: £220.75)
5f Stalls: Low GOING minus 0.46 sec per fur (F) 2-45 (2-47)

701[5] **Plum First (58)***(62) (LRLloyd-James)* 5-9-5 KimberleyHart(6) (lw: a.p: styd on to ld wl ins fnl f)....— **1**
390[3] Nite-Owl Dancer **(63)***(55) (JAHarris)* 3-8-3 PFessey(4) (a chsng ldrs: hdwy to disp ld wl ins fnl f: kpt on)....½ **2**
688* Prince Belfort **(62)***(59) (JLEyre)* 7-9-3b(5) 3x GMacDonald(1) (cl up: led ½-wy tl hdd & no ex wl ins fnl f)....1¼ **3**
535[13] Maid O'Cannie **(70)***(46)*(Fav)*(MWEasterby)* 4-9-0b RuthCoulter(10) (in tch: hdwy 2f out: nt pce to chal)....1¾ **4**
580* Bonita **(55)***(49) (MrsLPiggott)* 3-8-1 (5) VictoriaAppleby(9) (lw: b: b.hind: effrt ½-wy: edgd lft & nvr rch ldrs)....hd **5**
685[4] Sigama (USA) **(50)***(52) (DNicholls)* 9-9-1 (7) BPeel(7) (lw: led to ½-wy: wknd over 1f out)....½ **6**
702[8] Desert Invader (IRE) **(70)***(49) (DWChapman)* 4-9-5b(3) DDenby(3) (lw: s.i.s: sme hdwy whn hmpd over 1f out: no imp)....1 **7**

132[7] Lady Pui **(70)***(43) (JBerry)* 3-7-13 (7) JoanneWebster(8) (in tch tl rdn & btn over 1f out)...........nk 8
672[12] Monsieur Petong **(42)***(37) (JParkes)* 4-9-5 CAdamson(2) (cl up over 3f: sn lost pl)................2½ 9
656[11] Kangra Valley **(51)***(28) (TRWatson)* 4-8-9 (5) SBuckley(11) (b: dwlt: a bhd) 1¼ 10
Rennyholme **(20)***(10) (MWEllerby)* 4-9-0 (5) JEdmunds(5) (spd 2f: wl bhd fr ½-wy) 7 11

11/4 Maid O'Cannie, **3/1** Prince Belfort, **6/1** Bonita, **7/1** Sigama (USA), Nite-Owl Dancer, **8/1** PLUM FIRST, **16/1** Desert Invader (IRE), Lady Pui, **25/1** Kangra Valley, **50/1** Monsieur Petong, **150/1** Rennyholme, CSF £58.56 TOTE £8.20: £2.20 £1.90 £1.80 (£63.70) Trio £34.80 OWNER Mr J. B. Slatcher (MALTON) BRED Limestone Stud 11 Rn 63.5 secs (2.00) SF: 34/16/31/18/10/24/21/4/9/-/-
WEIGHT FOR AGE 3yo-11lb
STEWARDS' ENQUIRY Edmunds suspended 4-5/5/95 (excessive use of whip).

747

AMEC DEVELOPMENTS MEDIAN AUCTION MAIDEN STKS (3-Y.O) (Class E) £3,061.00 (£928.00: £454.00: £217.00)
1m 2f 6y Stalls: Low GOING minus 0.46 sec per fur (F) 3-15 (3-18)

500[2] **Worldnews Extra (USA)** *(80) (PFICole)* 3-9-0 TQuinn(1) (lw: mde all: styd on strly fnl 2f).......................................— 1
553[4] Heboob Alshemaal (IRE) *(72)*(Fav)*(JHMGosden)* 3-8-9 LDettori(5) (trckd ldrs: chal 2f out: rdn & fnd nil fnl f)...........................1¾ 2
553[7] Invest Wisely *(75) (JMPEustace)* 3-9-0 RHills(4) (in tch: styd on wl fnl 2f: nrst fin) 1¼ 3
Junior Ben (IRE) **(80)***(74) (JBerry)* 3-9-0 JCarroll(10) (bit bkwd: prom: hdwy u.p 3f out: nt qckn fnl f) ....½ 4
Oneofthеoldones **(82)***(62) (SGNorton)* 3-9-0 JFortune(2) (bit bkwd: hdwy ½-wy: effrt 3f out: sn outpcd)...........................8 5
The Banshee (FR) *(52) (JMPEustace)* 3-9-0 MTebbutt(11) (outpcd & bhd tl sme late hdwy)...........................6 6
Catiche *(47) (MrsJCecil)* 3-8-9 PaulEddery(3) (rangy: unf: a chsng ldrs: effrt over 3f out: wknd wl over 1f out) ....nk 7
Last Spin *(46) (JRJenkins)* 3-8-9 WRyan(8) (in tch: effrt over 3f out: sn btn)...........................hd 8
Mill Thyme *(35) (MrsMReveley)* 3-8-9 KDarley(6) (lengthy: bit bkwd: dwlt: outpcd & wl bhd tl sme late hdwy)...........................7 9
Call Me Flash **(54)***(29) (MrsPSly)* 3-9-0 DeanMcKeown(7) (cl up tl wknd qckly 4f out)...........................7 10

15/8 Heboob Alshemaal (IRE), **7/2** WORLDNEWS EXTRA (USA), **6/1** Oneofthеoldones, **13/2** Last Spin, **8/1** Catiche (6/1-10/1), **10/1** The Banshee (FR) (12/1-8/1), **16/1** Junior Ben (IRE), **20/1** Invest Wisely, **33/1** Mill Thyme, **66/1** Call Me Flash, CSF £10.25 TOTE £4.60: £1.50 £1.40 £4.80 (£3.20) Trio £19.00 OWNER Prince Fahd Salman (WHATCOMBE) 10 Rn
2m 12.2 (3.90) SF: 33/25/28/27/15/5/-/-/-/-

748

WAKEFIELD EUROPORT (S) STKS (3-Y.O+) (Class G) £2,665.00 (£740.00: £355.00) **6f** Stalls: Low GOING minus 0.46 sec per fur (F) 3-45 (3-46)

625[4] **Brookhead Lady (57)***(62) (PDEvans)* 4-9-2 KDarley(8) (b: a chsng ldrs: led ½-wy: hld on wl)...........................— 1
Six for Luck **(75)***(64)*(Fav)*(JBerry)* 3-8-9 JCarroll(7) (b.hind: in tch: hdwy to chal over 1f out: rdn & nt qckn)...........................1¼ 2
269[10] Kid Ory **(68)***(62) (PCalver)* 4-9-7 MBirch(6) (hdwy 2f out: styd on wl twrds fin)...........................¾ 3
548* Roseate Lodge **(64)***(66) (KRBurke)* 9-9-12 TIves(14) (in tch: hdwy 2f out: nt qckn ins fnl f) ....nk 4
640[5] Perfect Bertie (IRE) **(56)***(54)*(Fav)*(MrsJRRamsden)* 3-8-9 KFallon(10) (lw: sn pushed along & bhd: hdwy 2f out: nt qckn ins fnl f) 2½ 5
578[10] Obsidian Grey **(44)***(48) (MissLCSiddall)* 8-9-7 TQuinn(11) (a chsng ldrs: rdn ½-wy: one pce)...........................2½ 6
594[12] Bonny Melody **(56)***(39) (PDEvans)* 4-9-2 JFortune(15) (led to ½-wy: wknd over 1f out) 1½ 7
548[15] Make the Break **(60)***(40) (SCoathup)* 4-9-7 WRyan(12) (effrt on outside 2f out: nvr rch ldrs)...........................1½ 8
501[11] Anotherone to Note **(58)***(34) (MJHeaton-Ellis)* 4-9-7 JWeaver(2) (bhd tl sme late hdwy)...........................2 9
526[6] Respectable Jones **(40)***(29) (RHollinshead)* 9-9-7 LDettori(9) (in tch tl outpcd fnl 2f)................2 10
Drum Sergeant **(38)***(13) (JParkes)* 8-9-7 MDeering(5) (a bhd) 6 11
416[13] Amlak (USA) **(34)***(8) (TKersey)* 6-9-7 GDuffield(4) (s.i.s: a bhd)...........................2 12
431[12] Never Time (IRE) **(51)***(6) (MrsVAAconley)* 3-8-9b TWilliams(1) (a rr div) ....¾ 13
Daring Gift **(36)** *(JRBosley)* 4-9-2v PaulEddery(13) (bit bkwd: chsd ldrs 4f: sn wknd) ....¾ 14
685[W] Bettykimvic **(72)** *(EJAlston)* 4-9-2 DeanMcKeown(3) (cl up 3f: wknd qckly) ....nk 15

7/2 Six for Luck, Perfect Bertie (IRE), **5/1** Roseate Lodge, **6/1** BROOKHEAD LADY, **9/1** Kid Ory, **12/1** Anotherone to Note, Respectable Jones, **14/1** Bettykimvic, **16/1** Bonny Melody, **20/1** Make the Break, **25/1** Obsidian Grey, Never Time (IRE), **33/1** Drum Sergeant, Daring Gift, **100/1** Amlak (USA), CSF £27.82 TOTE £7.20: £2.10 £1.70 £2.70 (£13.40) Trio £111.90 OWNER Mr J. E. Abbey (WELSHPOOL) BRED Theakston Stud 15 Rn

1m 15.9 (1.60) SF: 42/32/42/46/22/28/19/20/14/9/-/-/-/-/-

WEIGHT FOR AGE 3yo-12lb

No bid.

749 WAKEFIELD EUROPORT H'CAP (0-90) (3-Y.O+) (Class C) £6,472.00 (£1,936.00: £928.00: £424.00)

1m 4y Stalls: Low GOING minus 0.46 sec per fur (F) 4-15 (4-16)

	Western General (78)*(87) (MissSEHall)* 4-9-13 NConnorton(4) (a in tch: hdwy 2f out: styd on to ld cl home)	—	1
724²	Queens Consul (IRE) **(73)***(81) (BSRothwell)* 5-9-3 (5) JStack(2) (led: rdn 2f out: r.o: no ex cl home)	nk	2
	Mo-Addab (IRE) **(74)***(80) (ACStewart)* 5-9-9 RHills(3) (bit bkwd: chsd ldrs: effrt 2f out: styd on)	1¼	3
433¹¹	Admirals Flame (IRE) **(63)***(66) (CFWall)* 4-8-12 GDuffield(18) (b: bhd tl stdy hdwy fnl 3f: r.o)	1½	4
539⁶	Safey Ana (USA) **(70)***(73) (BHanbury)* 4-9-5 WRyan(1) (b: a chsng ldrs: nt qckn fnl 2f)	hd	5
	Unprejudice **(68)***(66) (GRimmer)* 4-9-3 MRimmer(13) (b: hdwy over 2f out: nvr rch ldrs)	2½	6
559⁹	Yoxall Lodge **(63)***(54) (HJCollingridge)* 5-8-12 JQuinn(15) (bhd tl styd on fnl 2f)	3½	7
601⁵	Sandmoor Denim **(67)***(53) (SRBowring)* 8-8-11 (5) CTeague(5) (lw: b: effrt 3f out: n.m.r & no imp)	2½	8
	Move Smartly (IRE) **(56)***(42) (FHLee)* 5-8-5 KDarley(16) (prom: effrt 3f out: wknd wl over 1f out)	hd	9
	Somerton Boy (IRE) **(69)***(45) (PCalver)* 5-9-4 MBirch(12) (lw: chsd ldrs tl grad wknd fnl 2½f)	5	10
559¹⁶	Pendolino (IRE) **(62)***(35) (MBrittain)* 4-8-11 JLowe(17) (bit bkwd: nvr trbld ldrs)	1½	11
433⁵	Samah **(69)***(39)*(Fav)*(DNicholls)* 5-9-4 LDettori(10) (lw: chsd ldr tl wknd 2f out)	1¼	12
559²	Sea-Ayr (IRE) **(50)***(17) (MrsSMAustin)* 5-7-13 JMarshall(8) (b: effrt ½-wy: n.d)	1¾	13
486¹¹	Halmanerror **(63)***(28) (MrsJRRamsden)* 5-8-12 KFallon(14) (bhd & pushed along: hdwy 2f out: eased appr fnl f)	1	14
676¹¹	Calder King **(64)***(26) (JLEyre)* 4-8-13 JFortune(11) (prom: btn whn hung lft over 1f out)	1¼	15
349²	Major Mouse **(57)***(11) (WWHaigh)* 7-8-6 DaleGibson(6) (a rr div)	4	16
454¹⁴	Al Moulouki **(66)***(4) (JWPayne)* 5-9-1b BThomson(7) (a bhd)	8	17

5/2 Samah, **8/1** Sea-Ayr (IRE), Queens Consul (IRE), Mo-Addab (IRE), Sandmoor Denim, **9/1** Safey Ana (USA), **14/1** Major Mouse, WESTERN GENERAL, Halmanerror, Yoxall Lodge, **16/1** Somerton Boy (IRE), Move Smartly (IRE), Admirals Flame (IRE), **20/1** Calder King, **25/1** Al Moulouki, **33/1** Unprejudice, **50/1** Pendolino (IRE), CSF £125.56 CT £905.12 TOTE £20.90: £3.30 £1.40 £2.10 £6.40 (£162.90) Trio £150.70 OWNER Mrs James McAllister (MIDDLEHAM) BRED Fluorocarbon Bloodstock 17 Rn

1m 42.6 (0.60) SF: 69/63/62/48/55/48/36/35/24/27/17/21/-/10/8/-/-

750 WAKEFIELD EUROPORT AGENTS STKS (4-Y.O+) (Class C) £5,118.40 (£1,790.40: £875.20: £376.00)

1m 2f 6y Stalls: Low GOING minus 0.46 sec per fur (F) 4-45 (4-50)

631⁶	**Florid (USA) (107)***(111) (HRACecil)* 4-9-4 WRyan(2) (lw: mde all: pushed along & styd on strly fnl 3f)	—	1
	Waiting **(100)***(99)*(Fav)*(PFICole)* 4-8-12 TQuinn(4) (chsd wnr: rdn over 2f out: one pce)	4	2
	Moneghetti *(49) (RHollinshead)* 4-8-10 LDettori(3) (outpcd & no ch fnl 5f)	30	3
	Young Steven *(41) (WTKemp)* 4-8-10 KDarley(1) (bit bkwd: outpcd & bhd after 3f)	5	4

10/11 Waiting (Evens-11/10), **Evens** FLORID (USA), **40/1** Moneghetti, **150/1** Young Steven, CSF £2.06 TOTE £1.80: (£1.10) OWNER Lord Howard de Walden (NEWMARKET) BRED Lord Howard de Walden 4 Rn

2m 10.0 (1.70) SF: 53/41/-/-

751 EUROPEAN LINK H'CAP (0-80) (4-Y.O+) (Class D) £3,980.00 (£1,190.00: £570.00: £260.00)
2m 1f 22y Stalls: Centre GOING minus 0.46 sec per fur (F) 5-15 (5-18)

432[3] **Roberty Lea (64)***(75)*(Fav)*(MrsMReveley)* 7-9-5 KDarley(2) (lw: chsd ldrs tl outpcd 5f out: hdwy 3f out: led wl over 1f out: r.o) — 1
506[8] Noufari (FR) **(72)***(82) (RHollinshead)* 4-9-9 TIves(1) (hld up & bhd: hdwy 7f out: ev ch 2f out: r.o) ¾ 2
556[8] Kadiri (IRE) **(57)***(67) (JRBosley)* 4-8-8 PaulEddery(3) (bhd: hdwy 6f out: chsng ldrs 2f out: swtchd over 1f out: r.o wl) hd 3
Northern Kingdom (USA) **(49)***(54) (SGNorton)* 6-8-4 JQuinn(6) (led tl wl over 1f out: one pce) 6 4
556[12] Ambuscade (USA) **(51)***(54) (EJAlston)* 9-8-6 KFallon(5) (bhd tl styd on fnl 4f: nt pce to chal) 1¼ 5
534[10] Aljadeer (USA) **(50)***(50) (MWEasterby)* 6-8-5b MBirch(12) (hld up: hdwy 8f out: nt clr run over 2f out: sn btn) 4 6
556[6] Murphys Way **(41)***(37) (JLEyre)* 6-7-10 JFanning(10) (chsd ldrs tl wknd fnl 3f) 3½ 7
632[20] Upper Mount Clair **(63)***(58) (CEBrittain)* 5-9-4 MRimmer(4) (bhd: hdwy ½-wy: wknd over 2f out) 1¾ 8
374[9] Vishnu (USA) **(62)***(53) (JLEyre)* 5-9-3 JFortune(8) (chsd ldrs tl wknd fnl 3½f) 4 9
Mystic Memory **(69)***(60) (MrsMReveley)* 6-9-3 (7) SCopp(7) (nvr trbld ldrs) ½ 10
Efaad (IRE) **(59)***(47) (JNorton)* 4-8-10 ACulhane(13) (chsd ldrs tl wknd 4f out) 3 11
556[19] Eightandahalf (IRE) **(56)** *(MrsVAAconley)* 6-8-11 TWilliams(11) (in tch tl wknd qckly 3f out: t.o) dist 12
Mandalay Prince **(38)** *(TKersey)* 11-7-7 NKennedy(9) (b: outpcd & bhd fr ½-wy: t.o) 20 13

LONG HANDICAP Mandalay Prince 6-5

11/4 ROBERTY LEA, **9/2** Aljadeer (USA), **7/1** Ambuscade (USA), **8/1** Noufari (FR), Mystic Memory, **10/1** Kadiri (IRE), **11/1** Vishnu (USA), **12/1** Murphys Way, Upper Mount Clair, **20/1** Eightandahalf (IRE), **25/1** Northern Kingdom (USA), Efaad (IRE), **100/1** Mandalay Prince, CSF £24.80 CT £184.11 TOTE £4.30: £1.80 £3.30 £2.40 (£12.20) Trio £46.10 OWNER Wentdale Const Ltd (SALTBURN) BRED Stud-On-The-Chart 13 Rn3m 50.0 (10.00) SF: 23/26/11/2/2/-/-/6/1/8/-/-/-

WEIGHT FOR AGE 4yo-4lb

752 INTERMODAL MAIDEN STKS (3-Y.O F) (Class D) £3,631.25 (£1,100.00: £537.50: £256.25) **6f** Stalls: Low GOING minus 0.46 sec per fur (F) 5-45 (5-48)

Rosebud (70)*(78) (RHannon)* 3-8-11 KDarley(8) (a cl up: r.o u.p to ld wl ins fnl f) — 1
Intiaash (IRE) *(77) (PTWalwyn)* 3-8-11 JWeaver(10) (led: hung lft fnl 2f: no ex twrds fin) ½ 2
Allyana (IRE) *(66)*(Fav)*(IABalding)* 3-8-11 LDettori(1) (a chsng ldrs: rdn ½-wy: one pce) 4 3
442[9] Lough Erne *(65) (CFWall)* 3-8-11 GDuffield(5) (plld hrd: trckd ldrs: effrt 2f out: r.o one pce) ½ 4
It's Academic *(55) (MrsJRRamsden)* 3-8-11 KFallon(2) (outpcd ½-wy: styd on fnl f) 3½ 5
Sweet Pavlova (USA) *(47) (PFICole)* 3-8-11 TQuinn(3) (b.hind: chsd ldrs tl wknd wl over 1f out) 3 6
Just Whistle *(38) (CWThornton)* 3-8-11 DeanMcKeown(6) (str: bkwd: outpcd ½-wy: n.d after) 3½ 7
Miles Away (IRE) *(27) (JRFanshawe)* 3-8-6 (5) NVarley(9) (nvr wnt pce) 4 8
Barriyah *(27) (HThomsonJones)* 3-8-11 RHills(7) (rangy: unf: stdd s: plld hrd & hung rt most of wy: a bhd) s.h 9
Merlin's Fancy *(6) (WJarvis)* 3-8-11 BThomson(4) (a rr div) 8 10

6/4 Allyana (IRE), **9/2** Intiaash (IRE) (op 3/1), **5/1** Sweet Pavlova (USA), **6/1** Barriyah (op 4/1), **9/1** ROSEBUD, **12/1** Lough Erne, **16/1** Merlin's Fancy, **20/1** It's Academic, Miles Away (IRE), **50/1** Just Whistle, CSF £48.41 TOTE £12.50: £2.90 £1.80 £1.60 (£60.30) Trio £12.70 OWNER Lord Carnarvon (MARLBOROUGH) BRED R. Powell-Tuck and Partners 10 Rn

1m 15.1 (0.80) SF: 48/47/36/35/25/17/8/-/-/-

T/Jkpt: Not won; £49,935.12 to Kempton 26/4/95. T/Plpt: £42.70 (543.98 Tckts). T/Qdpt: £48.20 (1.8 Tckts). AA

0462-CATTERICK (L-H)
Wednesday April 26th (Good)

WEATHER: overcast WIND: fresh half against

753 BELLE ISLE APPRENTICE LIMITED STKS (0-55) (3-Y.O+) (Class F) £2,776.00 (£786.00: £388.00)
5f 212y Stalls: High GOING: 0.10 sec per fur (G) 2-10 (2-16)

578[12] **We're Joken (46)***(46) (JBerry)* 3-7-10 (7) CLowther(13) (b.hind: mde all: clr over 1f out: styd on strly) — 1

5964 Mr Slick **(52)***(46) (WStorey)* 3-8-8 DRMcCabe(1) (wl bhd tl styd on wl fnl 2f: nt rch wnr) 2 **2**
4514 Crimson Shower **(53)***(39)*(Fav)*(JRFanshawe)* 3-8-3 NVarley(9) (lw: rr div: swtchd & hdwy over 1f out: styd on: nt rch ldrs) ....¾ **3**
6856 Lugana Vision **(43)***(37) (GFierro)* 3-7-12v(5) JoHunnam(2) (mid div: effrt & swtchd ins 2f out: kpt on appr fnl f) ....½ **4**
64214 Suedoro **(33)***(36) (GPKelly)* 5-8-8 (7) NKinnon(7) (bit bkwd: in tch: kpt on same pce fnl 2f) ....½ **5**
57816 My Godson **(45)***(39) (FJO'Mahony)* 5-9-1b(5) GMacDonald(8) (sn drvn along: chsd wnr to wknd over 1f out) ....¾ **6**
486W East Barns (IRE) **(45)***(39) (SGollings)* 7-9-1b(5) MartinDwyer(3) (sn bhd & pushed along: hdwy & hung lft 2f out: nvr nr ldrs) ....s.h **7**
6295 Poly Laureon (IRE) **(55)***(30) (RHollinshead)* 3-7-12 (5) AEddery(12) (prom tl wknd 2f out) 1¼ **8**
6394 Sonderise **(52)***(31) (NTinkler)* 6-9-6 JStack(4) (hld up & bhd: carried wd ent st: sme hdwy over 2f out: nvr nr ldrs) 1½ **9**
5907 Brisas **(42)***(33) (CWFairhurst)* 8-9-8 AGarth(6) (prom: effrt 2f out: edgd lft & sn wknd) ....nk **10**
Hi Kiki **(52)***(20) (MrsMMcCourt)* 4-8-8 (7) RStudholme(11) (chsd ldrs tl wknd 2f out) 2 **11**
68812 Henry the Hawk **(45)***(19) (MDods)* 4-9-3v(3) VHalliday(5) (b.nr fore: mid div: rdn & bhd over 2f out) 2½ **12**
Silver Will **(30)** *(WLBarker)* 5-9-6 DarrenMoffatt(10) (unruly s: mid div: rn wd ent st: sn wl bhd) 8 **13**

5/2 Crimson Shower, **4/1** Sonderise, **7/1** Lugana Vision, **8/1** Poly Laureon (IRE), **10/1** WE'RE JOKEN, **11/1** My Godson, Hi Kiki, **12/1** East Barns (IRE), Brisas, **20/1** Mr Slick, Henry the Hawk, **33/1** Silver Will, **50/1** Suedoro, CSF £174.28 TOTE £14.60: £4.30 £4.30 £1.30 (£715.00; £312.20 to Beverley 27/04/95) Trio £174.90 OWNER Mr J. K. M. Oliver (COCKERHAM) BRED James Thom and Sons 13 Rn 1m 16.1 (5.60) SF: 18/18/11/9/20/23/23/2/15/17/4/3/-
WEIGHT FOR AGE 3yo-12lb

754 SEDBURY H'CAP (0-80) (3-Y.O) (Class D) £3,935.10 (£1,174.80: £561.40: £254.70) 5f Stalls: Low GOING: 0.10 sec per fur (G) 2-45 (2-46)

639* **Perryston View (74)***(82+)*(Fav)*(PCalver)* 3-9-3v 7x MBirch(9) (lw: chsd ldrs: led over 1f out: pushed out) ....— **1**
4835 C-Yer-Simmie (IRE) **(58)***(63) (RHollinshead)* 3-7-10 (5) AGarth(2) (chsd ldrs: styd on fnl f: no ch w wnr) 1 **2**
*420** Nadwaty (IRE) **(57)***(48) (MCChapman)* 3-7-7b(7)ow3 CMunday(3) (led tl over 1f out: kpt on same pce) 3½ **3**
Absolutely Fabulus **(52)***(41) (JLSpearing)* 3-7-6 (3)ow2 DarrenMoffatt(1) (unruly in stalls: sn outpcd & bhd: styd on u.p fnl 2f) ....¾ **4**
42610 Ultra Beet **(70)***(61) (PCHaslam)* 3-8-13 JWeaver(4) (swvd rt s: stdy hdwy over 1f out: nvr plcd to chal) ....hd **5**
Able Sheriff **(52)***(41) (MWEasterby)* 3-7-9bow1 JFanning(7) (chsd ldrs: rdn & hung lft 2f out: wknd over 1f out) ....nk **6**
4528 Lloc **(63)***(40) (JohnBerry)* 3-8-1b(5)ow3 JStack(5) (b: hmpd s: bhd tl sme hdwy fnl 2f: sn wl outpcd) 3 **7**
High Ranking **(78)***(56) (MHEasterby)* 3-9-7 SMaloney(11) (lw: in tch: effrt ½-wy: grad wknd) ....¾ **8**
Statomist **(62)***(30) (GFierro)* 3-8-5 MWigham(8) (bit bkwd: hld up & bhd: sme hdwy 2f out: n.d) 3 **9**
4264 Swan At Whalley **(71)***(33) (JBerry)* 3-9-0 JCarroll(6) (chsd ldrs: drvn along ½-wy: wknd 2f out) 2 **10**
Pemley **(59)***(11) (RMWhitaker)* 3-8-2 DaleGibson(10) (sn wl outpcd) 3 **11**
LONG HANDICAP Absolutely Fabulus 7-6

11/8 PERRYSTON VIEW, **9/2** Swan At Whalley, **6/1** Ultra Beet, **10/1** Nadwaty (IRE), **11/1** Able Sheriff, **12/1** C-Yer-Simmie (IRE), **14/1** Lloc, High Ranking, **20/1** Statomist, Absolutely Fabulus, Pemley, CSF £19.32 CT £113.32 TOTE £2.30: £1.10 £3.00 £3.10 (£14.70) Trio £70.20 OWNER Mrs Janis MacPherson (RIPON) BRED Mrs V. E. Hughes 11 Rn
63.3 secs (5.80) SF: 11/-/-/-/-/-/-/-/-/-/-

755 JOCKEY CAP (S) STKS (2-Y.O) (Class G) £2,467.00 (£682.00: £325.00) 5f Stalls: Low GOING: 0.10 sec per fur (G) 3-20 (3-22)

4805 **Monsieur Culsyth** *(48+t)*(Fav)*(JBerry)* 2-8-11 JCarroll(5) (b.nr fore: lw: mde all: pushed clr over 1f out: comf) ....— **1**

699[5] Thorntoun Jewel (IRE) *(38) (MJohnston)* 2-8-6 DHolland(4) (sn drvn along & outpcd: styd on appr fnl f: no ch w wnr) 1½ **2**
684[7] Exactly (IRE) *(29) (MJohnston)* 2-8-6 TWilliams(2) (sn drvn along & outpcd: hdwy ½-wy: kpt on fnl f) 3 **3**
554[8] Power Dee *(26) (MWEasterby)* 2-8-6 MBirch(6) (swvd rt s: chsd ldrs tl wknd fnl f) ....¾ **4**
490[6] Vales Ales *(RMMcKellar)* 2-8-4 (7) NKinnon(1) (s.i.s: a wl outpcd & bhd) 20 **5**
671[13] Dispol Sapphire *(MrsVAAconley)* 2-8-6 JWeaver(3) (bit bkwd: w wnr: hung badly lft ½-wy: nt rcvr & eased) 1¼ **6**

4/9 MONSIEUR CULSYTH, **4/1** Thorntoun Jewel (IRE) (op 5/2), **9/1** Exactly (IRE) (6/1-10/1), **14/1** Power Dee (op 8/1), **20/1** Dispol Sapphire, **50/1** Vales Ales, CSF £2.74 TOTE £1.30: £1.10 £1.60 (£1.50) OWNER Forsyth Cully Racing (COCKERHAM) BRED J. Forsyth 6 Rn
64.8 secs (7.30) SF: -/-/-/-/-/-
No bid.
OFFICIAL EXPLANATION **Dispol Sapphire: no explanation offered.**

756

RICHMOND STKS (3-Y.O) (Class C) £5,024.00 (£1,856.00: £888.00: £360.00: £140.00: £52.00)
1m 3f 214y Stalls: Low GOING: 0.10 sec per fur (G) 3-50 (3-50)

Wot-If-We (IRE) (92)*(94) (TGMills)* 3-9-2 JCarroll(3) (lw: trckd ldrs: rdn & outpcd 2f out: squeezed thro, carried lft & styd on wl to ld wl ins fnl f) ....— **1**
619[4] Dreamer (USA) **(103)***(100) (PFICole)* 3-9-8 JFortune(4) (lw: b: b.hind: hld up: smooth hdwy over 3f out: led 2f out: rdn & hung lft jst ins fnl f: hdd nr fin) ....nk **2**
544* Raased **(92)***(85)*(Fav)*(JLDunlop)* 3-9-0 WCarson(5) (lw: led after 1f: rdn over 2f out: sn hdd: wkng whn sltly hmpd ins fnl f: eased) 5 **3**
428* Sea Victor *(80) (JHMGosden)* 3-9-2 LDettori(2) (lw: b.hind: trckd ldrs: effrt & rdn 4f out: wknd 2f out) 5 **4**
614[9] Manful **(85)***(78) (JHetherton)* 3-9-4 NKennedy(6) (unruly in stalls: bhd: reminders 5f out: n.d) 3 **5**
557[3] College Night (IRE) *(55) (JohnBerry)* 3-8-7 CDwyer(1) (led 1f: chsd ldrs tl lost pl over 3f out) .9 **6**

6/4 Raased, **2/1** Sea Victor, **7/2** Dreamer (USA), **14/1** WOT-IF-WE (IRE), **20/1** College Night (IRE), **25/1** Manful, CSF £55.54 TOTE £26.30: £6.80 £1.90 (£27.70) OWNER Mr Bob Merrick (EPSOM) BRED Hermes Services Ltd in Ireland 6 Rn 2m 42.5 (11.50) SF: 33/39/24/19/17/-

757

'WIN WITH THE TOTE' H'CAP (0-85) (4-Y.O+) (Class D) £3,867.50 (£1,154.00: £551.00: £249.50)
1m 3f 214y Stalls: Low GOING: 0.10 sec per fur (G) 4-20 (4-21)

423[14] **Pharly Dancer (56)***(68) (WWHaigh)* 6-8-1 DaleGibson(10) (lw: led tl over 2f out: edgd rt & styd on wl to ld jst ins fnl f: all out) ....— **1**
George Dillingham **(83)***(95) (DenysSmith)* 5-10-0 JCarroll(12) (trckd ldrs: outpcd over 3f out: styd on wl & ev ch ins fnl f: edgd lft: bmpd nr fin) ....s.h **2**
Soba Up **(50)***(54) (TJEtherington)* 5-7-9 ow1 JFanning(5) (trckd ldr: led over 3f out to jst ins fnl f: wknd) 5 **3**
653[3] Southern Power (IRE) **(79)***(82) (MrsMReveley)* 4-9-9 JWeaver(6) (b.nr hind: hld up & bhd: styd on fnl 3f: nvr nr ldrs) 1½ **4**
597* Cool Luke (IRE) **(68)***(70)*(Fav)*(GMMoore)* 6-8-13 MTebbutt(9) (hld up: outpcd 7f out: hdwy over 2f out: nt rch ldrs) ....¾ **5**
558[10] Slasher Jack (IRE) **(81)***(81) (SGNorton)* 4-9-11 JFortune(4) (in tch tl outcd 7f out: sn drvn along: kpt on fnl 2f: nvr nr to chal) 1½ **6**
534* Merry Mermaid **(48)***(44) (JFBottomley)* 5-7-7 NKennedy(3) (in tch tl outpcd 4f out: n.d after) ...3 **7**
676[13] Sallyoreally (IRE) **(61)***(55) (WStorey)* 4-8-2 (3) DRMcCabe(8) (hld up & bhd: sme hdwy over 2f out: n.d) 1¾ **8**
Kinoko **(50)***(23) (KWHogg)* 7-7-6 (3)ow2 DarrenMoffatt(2) (hld up & a bhd: eased whn no ch) ..14 **9**
549[13] In the Money (IRE) **(60)***(33) (RHollinshead)* 6-8-0 (5) AGarth(7) (trckd ldrs: outpcd over 3f out: sn lost pl) 1½ **10**
549[12] Double Echo (IRE) **(57)***(29)*(Fav)*(JDBethell)* 7-8-2 WCarson(13) (hld up & bhd: drvn along 5f out: sme hdwy over 2f out: eased) 1 **11**
Chowpor **(60)***(5) (MDHammond)* 4-8-4 JMarshall(11) (bhd & drvn along 5f out: eased) 20 **12**
LONG HANDICAP Merry Mermaid 7-5

9/2 Double Echo (IRE), Cool Luke (IRE), **5/1** Southern Power (IRE), **7/1** Merry Mermaid, **9/1** George Dillingham, **10/1** Kinoko, **11/1** In the Money (IRE), **12/1** PHARLY DANCER, Slasher Jack (IRE), **16/1** Soba Up, **20/1** Chowpor, **33/1** Sallyoreally (IRE), CSF £106.35 CT £1,579.35 TOTE £16.00: £4.50 £2.90 £4.10 (£71.30) Trio £351.50; £445.65 to Beverley 27/04/95 OWNER Mr A. Marucci (MALTON) BRED Stud-On-The-Chart 12 Rn 2m 42.9 (11.90) SF: 16/43/2/29/18/28/-/2/-/-/-/-
WEIGHT FOR AGE 4yo-1lb

758 HURGILL LODGE MAIDEN STKS (3-Y.O) (Class D) £4,104.10 (£1,226.80: £587.40: £267.70)
7f Stalls: Low GOING: 0.10 sec per fur (G) 4-50 (4-53)

Classicy *(74)*(Fav)*(MRStoute)* 3-9-0 JWeaver(8) (lw: plld hrd: led over 1f: qcknd to ld over 1f out: sn clr: readily)........— **1**
Dr Caligari (IRE) *(68)* *(JBerry)* 3-9-0 JCarroll(2) (a.p: kpt on fnl 2f: no ch w wnr)........2½ **2**
Harry's Treat *(56)* *(JLEyre)* 3-8-9 JFortune(5) (rangy: unf: bit bkwd: chsd ldrs: led over 2f out tl over 1f out: kpt on same pce)........3 **3**
Skedaddle *(52)* *(JGFitzGerald)* 3-8-9 DHolland(4) (lengthy: unf: bit bkwd: sn prom: one pce fnl 2f)........2 **4**
732[3] Saatchmo *(55)* *(JLSpearing)* 3-8-9 (5) JStack(9) (s.i.s: bhd: stdy hdwy on outside 2f out: nvr plcd to chal)........1 **5**
613[7] Cupronickel (IRE) *(49)* *(JWWatts)* 3-8-9 MBirch(6) (sn bhd: hdwy on ins whn hmpd over 1f out: styd on twrds fin)........nk **6**
593[8] Hutchies Lady *(43)* *(RMMcKellar)* 3-8-3 (7)ow1 NKinnon(13) (b.off hind: sn wl bhd: styd on fnl 2f)........2½ **7**
Ligurian (USA) *(38)* *(JWWatts)* 3-8-9 BThomson(1) (prom: effrt over 2f out: grad wknd)........2½ **8**
555[5] Alltime Dancer (IRE) *(42)* *(MrsJRRamsden)* 3-9-0 SMaloney(7) (outpcd & rr div: sme hdwy 2f out: n.d)........nk **9**
Farfields Prince *(38)* *(DNicholls)* 3-9-0 NConnorton(3) (led over 5f out tl over 2f out: grad wknd)........1¾ **10**
Highfield Fizz *(33)* *(CWFairhurst)* 3-8-9 JFanning(15) (unf: in tch: outpcd & drvn along ½-wy: sn bhd)........hd **11**
522[13] Samsung Lovelylady (IRE) *(25)* *(EWeymes)* 3-8-9 GHind(10) (bit bkwd: plld hrd: w ldrs tl wknd over 1f out)........3½ **12**
643[7] Undawaterscubadiva *(27)* *(MPBielby)* 3-9-0 ACulhane(14) (in tch tl lost pl ½-wy)........1¼ **13**
Thrushwood *(NChamberlain)* 3-8-9 SWebster(11) (leggy: unf: s.i.s: sn wl bhd)........11 **14**
Charlie-Don't Surf *(RThompson)* 3-9-0 MWigham(12) (compt: s.s: hld up & plld hrd: a wl bhd)........15 **15**

8/13 CLASSICY (Evens-11/10), **4/1** Ligurian (USA) (op 2/1), **10/1** Alltime Dancer (IRE) (op 6/1), **16/1** Cupronickel (IRE), Skedaddle, Dr Caligari (IRE), Saatchmo, **25/1** Farfields Prince, **33/1** Highfield Fizz, **50/1** Harry's Treat, Undawaterscubadiva, Samsung Lovelylady (IRE), Charlie-Don't Surf, **100/1** Hutchies Lady, Thrushwood, CSF £13.69 TOTE £1.50: £1.30 £2.10 £5.40 (£8.90) Trio £58.20 OWNER Maktoum Al Maktoum (NEWMARKET) BRED S. P. and Major B. P. Hornung 15 Rn
1m 30.3 (7.10) SF: 23/17/5/1/4/-/-/-/-/-/-/-/-/-/-

759 SPRING H'CAP (0-70) (3-Y.O) (Class E) £3,702.60 (£1,108.80: £532.40: £244.20)
7f Stalls: Low GOING: 0.10 sec per fur (G) 5-20 (5-23)

170[5] **Mac's Taxi (56)***(74)* *(PCHaslam)* 3-8-10 (5) JStack(8) (mde all: rdn clr over 2f out: unchal)........— **1**
555[2] Showery **(60)***(60)*(Fav)*(JWWatts)* 3-9-5 BThomson(7) (chsd ldrs: kpt on same pce appr fnl f: no ch w wnr)........8 **2**
437[8] Pc's Cruiser (IRE) **(54)***(51)* *(MCChapman)* 3-8-6 (7) CMunday(5) (mid div: styd on wl fnl 2f: nrst fin)........1¼ **3**
Our Robert **(60)***(56)* *(JGFitzGerald)* 3-9-5 JWeaver(12) (a.p: styd on same pce u.p fnl 2f)........nk **4**
578* Vindaloo **(46)***(40)* *(JLHarris)* 3-8-5 DaleGibson(10) (lw: bhd tl styd on wl fnl 2f)........1 **5**
538[14] Euro Sceptic (IRE) **(42)***(36)* *(MHEasterby)* 3-8-1b SMaloney(6) (prom: rdn over 2f out: wknd over 1f out)........s.h **6**
594[10] Malzoom **(37)***(24)* *(SEKettlewell)* 3-7-5 (5)ow3 NVarley(16) (in tch: rdn over 2f out: no imp)........1½ **7**
Simand **(53)***(41)* *(EWeymes)* 3-8-12 GHind(18) (mid div: kpt on fnl 2f: n.d)........1 **8**
Tobago Boy **(40)***(26)* *(MGMeagher)* 3-7-6 (7) MartinDwyer(3) (s.i.s: bhd tl styd on fnl 2f)........1 **9**
Champagne N Dreams **(54)***(40)* *(DNicholls)* 3-8-13 AlexGreaves(19) (nvr bttr than mid div)........s.h **10**
685[10] Red Hot Risk **(58)***(44)* *(MDods)* 3-9-3v SWebster(17) (bit bkwd: s.s: bhd tl styd on u.p appr fnl f)........s.h **11**
576* Eden Dancer **(62)***(45)* *(MrsMReveley)* 3-9-7 JFortune(9) (lw: chsd ldrs: rdn over 2f out: wknd over 1f out)........1 **12**
478* Pash **(45)***(23)* *(CWCElsey)* 3-8-4v NKennedy(4) (sn wl bhd: sme late hdwy)........2½ **13**
573[9] Prime Property (IRE) **(54)***(29)* *(MWEasterby)* 3-8-13 MBirch(11) (s.i.s: hld up & bhd: stdy hdwy 2f out: nvr plcd to chal)........1¼ **14**

Tinklers Folly **(46)***(21) (DenysSmith)* 3-8-5 NConnorton(15) (sn wl bhd: sme hdwy 2f out: n.d) ....s.h **15**
Bad News **(55)***(24) (GFierro)* 3-9-0 MWigham(14) (s.i.s: a bhd) 2½ **16**
Leap Year Baby (IRE) **(43)***(8) (MDHammond)* 3-8-2 JMarshall(2) (s.i.s: a in rr) 1½ **17**
573[10] Foist **(43)***(6) (MWEasterby)* 3-8-2 JFanning(1) (prom: lost pl over 2f out) 1 **18**
Longcroft **(42)** *(KWHogg)* 3-8-1 TWilliams(13) (sddle slipped leaving stalls: sn virtually p.u) ....dist **19**

LONG HANDICAP Malzoom 7-6

11/4 Showery, **7/2** Eden Dancer, **10/1** Pash, Vindaloo, **12/1** MAC'S TAXI, Pc's Cruiser (IRE), Bad News (op 8/1), Simand, **14/1** Our Robert, **20/1** Euro Sceptic (IRE), Longcroft, Prime Property (IRE), Champagne N Dreams, Leap Year Baby (IRE), Tinklers Folly, **25/1** Foist, **33/1** Red Hot Risk, Tobago Boy, Malzoom, CSF £48.33 CT £405.70 TOTE £18.70: £2.00 £1.80 £3.70 £2.20 (£19.20) Trio £138.90 OWNER Mr J. McMurdo (MIDDLEHAM) BRED Mrs C. J. Proctor 19 Rn
1m 28.8 (5.60) SF: 41/27/18/23/7/3/-/8/-/7/11/12/-/-/-/-/-/-/-

T/Plpt £233.60 (50.88 Tckts). T/Qdpt £47.00 (1.4 Tckts). WG

0630-**KEMPTON (R-H)**
Wednesday April 26th (Good, Good to firm patches Rnd Course)

WEATHER: overcast WIND: almost nil

760 EUROPEAN BREEDERS FUND POLYANTHUS MAIDEN STKS (2-Y.O) (Class D) £3,454.00 (£1,042.00: £506.00: £238.00)
5f Stalls: Low GOING minus 0.16 sec per fur (GF) 5-30 (5-32)

High Hope Henry (USA) *(73+t) (PFICole)* 2-9-0 TQuinn(3) (cmpt: hdwy 2f out: led ins fnl f: r.o) ....— **1**
617[5] Sonic Mail *(65) (KMcAuliffe)* 2-9-0 RCochrane(9) (led: edgd lft 1f out: hdd ins fnl f) 2½ **2**
682[3] Centurion *(59)*(Fav)*(RHannon)* 2-9-0 PatEddery(6) (w ldrs: btn whn sltly hmpd ins fnl f) 1¾ **3**
617[15] Back By Dawn *(55) (DRCElsworth)* 2-9-0 JWilliams(7) (b.hind: gd late hdwy: nvr nrr) 1¼ **4**
Eastern Prophets *(51) (GLewis)* 2-9-0 PaulEddery(4) (cmpt: w ldrs: wkng whn hmpd ins fnl f) 1¼ **5**
562[5] Daily Risk *(50) (SDow)* 2-9-0 MHills(8) (no hdwy fnl 2f) ....nk **6**
Isla Glen *(45) (MMcCormack)* 2-8-9 JReid(1) (neat: nrst fin) ....nk **7**
617[9] Sporting Fantasy *(44) (MRChannon)* 2-9-0 CRutter(2) (rdn along bhd most of wy) 1¾ **8**
Dancing Jack *(42) (JJBridger)* 2-9-0 GDuffield(5) (w'like: a bhd) ....½ **9**

9/4 Centurion (5/4-5/2), **11/4** HIGH HOPE HENRY (USA), Sonic Mail, **10/1** Eastern Prophets (9/2-12/1), **12/1** Sporting Fantasy (op 8/1), **16/1** Isla Glen, **25/1** Back By Dawn, **33/1** Daily Risk, **66/1** Dancing Jack, CSF £10.15 TOTE £4.90: £1.50 £1.40 £1.30 (£5.80) Trio £3.70 OWNER Lucayan Stud (WHATCOMBE) BRED Frank and J. Cosentino 9 Rn 62.11 secs (4.31) SF: 12/4/-/-/-/-/-/-/-

761 HAWTHORN MAIDEN STKS (3-Y.O+) (Class D) £3,909.00 (£1,182.00: £576.00: £273.00)
7f (Jubilee) Stalls: High GOING minus 0.31 sec per fur (GF) 6-00 (6-06)

Sulb (USA) *(86)*(Fav)*(ACStewart)* 3-8-10 JReid(10) (str: scope: lw: hld up: hdwy to ld over 1f out: comf) ....— **1**
Storm Bid (USA) *(80) (EALDunlop)* 3-8-7 (3) JTate(13) (w'like: 4th st: ev ch 1f out: nt qckn) 2½ **2**
Takhlid (USA) *(76) (HThomsonJones)* 4-9-10 RHills(7) (gd sort: lw: plld hrd: wnt 4th st: led over 2f out tl over 1f out) 1¾ **3**
Mokuti *(76) (GWragg)* 3-8-10 MHills(1) (w'like: scope: gd hdwy fnl 2f: nrst fin) ....nk **4**
Shift Again (IRE) *(69) (WJarvis)* 3-8-5 AMcGlone(14) (hdwy over 1f out: nt qckn ins fnl f) ....¾ **5**
Quinwood (USA) *(62) (JHMGosden)* 3-8-5 PatEddery(5) (lw: 3rd st: ev ch 2f out: sn wknd) 3 **6**
547[8] Rookery Girl *(61) (DMorris)* 3-8-5 RPrice(2) (no hdwy fnl 2f) ....nk **7**
Backhander (IRE) *(63) (JARToller)* 3-8-10 PaulEddery(6) (str: scope: nvr plcd to chal) 1½ **8**

Baddi Quest *(62) (BHanbury)* 3-8-10 MRimmer(11) (w'like: nvr nr to chal) ....nk **9**
Sporting Risk *(62) (PWHarris)* 3-8-10 RCochrane(17) (5th st: wknd 2f out) ....s.h **10**
658[7] Hot Snap *(58) (CFWall)* 3-8-10 GDuffield(12) (nvr trbld ldrs) 1¾ **11**
Jigadee Creek *(57) (GHarwood)* 3-8-10 AClark(9) (led over 4f: wkng whn hmpd over 1f out) ....½ **12**
Dixit Dominus *(54) (GBBalding)* 4-9-10 JWilliams(8) (outpcd) 1½ **13**
Napoleon's Law *(48) (RHannon)* 3-8-10 TQuinn(16) (w'like: 2nd st: wkng whn hmpd over 1f out) 2½ **14**
Autumn Cover *(40) (RMFlower)* 3-8-5 (5) JDSmith(4) (w'like: scope: bkwd: b: s.s: a bhd) 3½ **15**
552[9] Superflex *(29) (DMorris)* 3-8-5 (3)ow3 CHodgson(3) (chsd ldrs: 7th & wkng st) 2½ **16**
630[3] Godmersham Park *(MJHeaton-Ellis)* 3-8-10 DHarrison(15) (Withdrawn not under Starter's orders: ref ent stalls) .... **W**

, **3/1** SULB (USA) (6/4-100/30), **5/1** Quinwood (USA) (op 3/1), **8/1** Mokuti (5/1-9/1), **10/1** Takhlid (USA) (8/1-12/1), **12/1** Storm Bid (USA) (8/1-14/1), Baddi Quest (7/1-14/1), **16/1** Jigadee Creek, Sporting Risk, **20/1** Napoleon's Law, **25/1** Backhander (IRE), **33/1** Hot Snap, Dixit Dominus, **50/1** Shift Again (IRE), Superflex, Rookery Girl, **100/1** Autumn Cover, CSF £28.20 TOTE £3.20: £1.90 £5.20 £3.10 (£25.90) Trio £72.80 OWNER Mr Hamdan Al Maktoum (NEWMARKET) BRED Allan Mactier 16 Rn 1m 27.64 (3.44) SF: 29/23/33/19/12/5/4/6/5/5/1/-/11/-/-/-/-
WEIGHT FOR AGE 3yo-14lb

762 FLORENCE NAGLE (GIRL APPRENTICES) APPRENTICE H'CAP (0-70) (3-Y.O+) (Class F) £2,944.00 (£892.00: £436.00: £208.00)
1m 1f (round) Stalls: High GOING minus 0.31 sec per fur (GF) 6-30 (6-37)

*520** **Daytona Beach (IRE) (56)***(70) (PBurgoyne)* 5-9-0 DebbieBiggs(16) (mde all: qcknd clr over 2f out: edgd lft: unchal) ....— **1**
586[2] Montone (IRE) **(58)***(61) (KRBurke)* 5-9-2 VictoriaAppleby(15) (3rd st: chsd wnr fnl 2f: no imp) 6 **2**
Progression **(65)***(62) (PCHaslam)* 4-9-9 NicolaHowarth(14) (gd hdwy fnl 2f: nvr nrr) 3½ **3**
545[6] Lady Reema **(42)***(36) (MissAJWhitfield)* 4-8-0 RuthCoulter(2) (gd late hdwy: nrst fin) 1½ **4**
529[4] Sooty Tern **(66)***(60) (JMBradley)* 8-9-10 AmandaSanders(18) (6th st: r.o one pce fnl 2f) ....s.h **5**
*373** Hatta Sunshine (USA) **(40)***(32) (AMoore)* 5-7-7 (5) CarolineHovington(12) (5th st: no hdwy fnl 2f) 1¼ **6**
Positivo **(68)***(59) (LordHuntingdon)* 4-9-12 AimeeCook(13) (styd on fnl 2f: nt rch ldrs) ....½ **7**
373[6] Buddy's Friend (IRE) **(60)***(48) (RJRWilliams)* 7-9-4 SarahThompson(6) (7th st: wknd over 1f out) 1¾ **8**
My Gallery (IRE) **(54)***(40) (ABailey)* 4-8-7 (5) AngelaGallimore(20) (8th st: wknd 2f out) 1¼ **9**
Anlace **(56)***(39) (SMellor)* 6-9-0 JoHunnam(5) (nvr nr to chal) 1½ **10**
403[5] Global Dancer **(68)***(51) (WAO'Gorman)* 4-9-12b EmmaO'Gorman(8) (9th st: wknd over 2f out) ....s.h **11**
526[11] Brandonhurst **(65)***(45) (LadyHerries)* 5-9-4 (5) LisaHackett(3) (nvr trbld ldrs) 1¾ **12**
627[11] Shaynes Domain **(42)***(18) (RMFlower)* 4-7-9 (5)ow3 SallyWall(19) (plld hrd: 2nd st: wknd over 2f out) ....½ **13**
Nanton Point (USA) **(60)***(38) (LadyHerries)* 3-8-1 ShonaCrombie(10) (a bhd) ....½ **14**
503[6] Lady Lacey **(53)***(30)*(Fav)*(GBBalding)* 8-8-11v IonaWands(11) (a bhd) ....½ **15**
738* Captain Marmalade **(45)***(20) (DTThom)* 6-8-3 5x AdelleGibbons(4) (a bhd) 1¼ **16**
642[12] Tanseeq **(69)***(43) (HThomsonJones)* 4-9-13 CatherineCooper(9) (4th st: wknd over 2f out) ....¾ **17**
Santella Boy (USA) **(65)***(38) (GHarwood)* 3-8-6 MissGHarwood(17) (s.s: plld hrd: wknd 4f out) ....¾ **18**
Tuigamala **(44)***(8) (RIngram)* 4-7-11 (5)ow4 AmandaBowen(7) (outpcd) 2½ **19**
Indefence (IRE) **(70)***(35) (MRChannon)* 4-10-0 ElizabethTurner(1) (outpcd) 2 **20**

13/2 Lady Lacey, **7/1** Santella Boy (USA) (5/1-8/1), **8/1** Global Dancer, Sooty Tern, **9/1** DAYTONA BEACH (IRE), Montone (IRE), **10/1** Buddy's Friend (IRE), Captain Marmalade (7/1-11/1), Brandonhurst, **11/1** Progression (20/1-10/1), **12/1** Tanseeq, **14/1** Positivo, Hatta Sunshine (USA), **16/1** Anlace, **20/1** My Gallery (IRE), Nanton Point (USA), **25/1** Lady Reema, Shaynes Domain, Indefence (IRE), **33/1** Tuigamala, CSF £97.54 CT £874.04 TOTE £15.30: £2.60 £2.70 £3.20 £2.60 (£73.70) Trio £286.40 OWNER Mrs J. E. Radburn (WANTAGE) BRED Miss H. Dean 20 Rn
1m 52.33 (2.33) SF: 52/43/44/18/42/14/41/30/22/21/33/27/-/3/12/2/25/3/-/17
WEIGHT FOR AGE 3yo-17lb

763 CHESTNUT H'CAP (0-85) (4-Y.O+) (Class D) £3,728.75 (£1,130.00: £552.50: £263.75) **1m 4f** Stalls: High GOING minus 0.31 sec per fur (GF) 7-00 (7-06)

Roisin Clover (62)*(75) (SDow)* 4-8-10 TQuinn(5) (hld up & bhd: gd hdwy over 1f out: led ins fnl f: r.o) — 1
423[22] Dancing Sensation (USA) **(55)***(65) (RAkehurst)* 8-8-1 (3) SSanders(15) (5th st: ev ch fnl f: nt qckn) 2½ 2
582[5] Durshan (USA) **(52)***(62) (JRJenkins)* 6-8-1 DBiggs(6) (cl up: ev ch fnl 2f: nt qckn) s.h 3
721* Bayrak (USA) **(70)***(79)*(Fav)*(MJRyan)* 5-9-5 5x PaulEddery(11) (hdwy & 6th st: ev ch 2f out: r.o ins fnl f) ½ 4
623[2] Shadow Leader **(76)***(85) (MissAJWhitfield)* 4-9-5 (5) RPainter(4) (gd hdwy over 1f out: r.o ins fnl f) s.h 5
668[7] Achilles Heel **(52)***(61) (CNAllen)* 4-8-0 JQuinn(2) (led tl ins fnl f) s.h 6
549[6] Exemption **(67)***(71)*(Fav)*(HCandy)* 4-9-1 WNewnes(13) (4th st: one pce fnl 3f) 3½ 7
Trade Wind **(73)***(75) (DRCElsworth)* 4-9-7b JWilliams(12) (nvr nrr) 1½ 8
668[2] Children's Choice (IRE) **(60)***(62)*(Fav)*(PJMcBride)* 4-8-5 (3) DWright(3) (nrst fin) hd 9
623[10] Allesca **(58)***(60) (MDIUsher)* 5-8-0 (7) CAdamson(7) (nvr nr to chal) nk 10
Pilib (IRE) **(50)***(52) (JPearce)* 4-7-12 GBardwell(14) (nvr trbld ldrs) hd 11
Wildfire (SWI) **(59)***(56) (RAkehurst)* 4-8-7 AMcGlone(10) (hdwy & 2nd st: wknd over 2f out) 3½ 12
549[17] Broughtons Formula **(52)***(47) (WJMusson)* 5-7-10 (5)ow1 AWhelan(8) (a bhd) ¾ 13
545[9] Granby Bell **(50)***(35) (PHayward)* 4-7-12 RStreet(1) (bhd most of wy: t.o) 8 14
Saahi (USA) **(50)***(34) (CWeedon)* 6-7-13 NAdams(9) (t.o) 1¼ 15

5/1 Bayrak (USA), Children's Choice (IRE), Exemption (8/1-9/2), **15/2** Shadow Leader, **9/1** Achilles Heel, Wildfire (SWI) (6/1-10/1), **12/1** Pilib (IRE), **14/1** Allesca, Dancing Sensation (USA), **16/1** Trade Wind, Granby Bell, **20/1** Durshan (USA), Broughtons Formula, ROISIN CLOVER, **33/1** Saahi (USA), CSF £259.32 CT £5,070.09 TOTE £25.00: £5.00 £4.20 £7.40 (£162.60) Trio £263.00 OWNER Brighthelm Racing (EPSOM) BRED D. A. and Mrs Hicks 15 Rn
2m 34.83 (4.63) SF: 39/30/27/44/49/25/35/39/26/25/16/20/12/-/-
WEIGHT FOR AGE 4yo-1lb

764 LABURNUM MAIDEN STKS (3-Y.O+) (Class D) £4,045.50 (£1,224.00: £597.00: £283.50) **1m 2f (Jubilee)** Stalls: High GOING minus 0.31 sec per fur (GF)7-30 (7-38)

635[3] **Riyadian** *(90)*(Fav)*(PFICole)* 3-8-8 TQuinn(21) (a gng wl: 5th st: led over 1f out: comf) — 1
Quandary (USA) *(79) (HRACecil)* 4-9-7 PatEddery(20) (2nd st: led wl over 21f out: sn hdd: nt qckn) 3½ 2
670[7] Kutta *(81) (RWArmstrong)* 3-8-8 RHills(15) (rapid hdwy fnl 2f: fin fast) 2 3
Zidac *(81) (PJMakin)* 3-8-8 RPerham(6) (led tl wl over 1f out: r.o one pce) s.h 4
Tibetan *(70) (LadyHerries)* 3-8-8 TIves(1) (str: scope: gd hdwy fnl 2f: nrst fin) 7 5
Moscow Mist (IRE) *(70) (LadyHerries)* 4-9-12 KDarley(22) (w'like: scope: 4th st: wknd over 1f out) s.h 6
Polydamas *(69) (MRStoute)* 3-8-8 JReid(14) (mid div: styd on fnl 2f) ¾ 7
Braydon Forest *(68) (CJDrewe)* 3-8-8 DHarrison(3) (nvr nrr) ½ 8
Sea Freedom *(68) (GBBalding)* 4-9-12 JWilliams(18) (7th st: one pce fnl 2f) s.h 9
Jagellon (USA) *(66) (WRMuir)* 4-9-12 MHills(7) (6th st: wknd 2f out) 1 10
Pedaltothemetal (IRE) **(46)***(61) (PMitchell)* 3-7-12 (5) AWhelan(2) (nvr nr to chal) hd 11
Istabraq (IRE) *(65) (JHMGosden)* 3-8-8 WCarson(5) (nvr plcd to chal) ¾ 12
Pending *(64) (IABalding)* 3-8-8 RCochrane(13) (nvr bttr than mid div) nk 13
Pampas Breeze (IRE) *(58) (WJarvis)* 3-8-3 AMcGlone(10) (scope: 8th st: wknd over 2f out) ¾ 14
Dahlenburg (IRE) *(62) (JHMGosden)* 3-8-8 LDettori(8) (str: scope: no hdwy fnl 3f) ½ 15
553[6] Sayitagain *(60) (TGMills)* 3-8-8 WNewnes(4) (3rd st: wknd over 2f out) 1¼ 16
Grandes Oreilles (IRE) **(72)***(55) (NJHWalker)* 3-8-3 CRutter(9) (outpcd) d.h 16
Elpida (USA) *(60) (JPearce)* 3-8-8 JMcLaughlin(23) (a bhd) nk 18
I Recall (IRE) *(57) (PHayward)* 4-9-12 SRaymont(19) (outpcd) 1½ 19
Caerle Lad (IRE) *(57) (GHarwood)* 4-9-12 AClark(12) (outpcd) nk 20
Great Expectations (FR) *(53) (KOCunningham-Brown)* 4-9-12 MRimmer(11)(bkwd: prom 5f) 3½ 21
Wizzy Lizzy (IRE) *(40) (DRCElsworth)* 4-9-7 PaulEddery(16) (t.o fnl 4f) 5 22
544[8] Paddy's Storm *(29) (RMFlower)* 3-8-3 (5) JDSmith(17) (t.o fnl 4f) 10 23

11/8 RIYADIAN, **7/1** Polydamas (op 4/1), Jagellon (USA), **8/1** Quandary (USA), **10/1** Istabraq (IRE), Dahlenburg (IRE) (op 6/1), **14/1** Pending, **16/1** Kutta, Sea Freedom, **20/1** Moscow Mist (IRE), **33/1** Tibetan, Pampas Breeze (IRE), Zidac, **50/1** Braydon Forest, Pedaltothemetal (IRE), Sayitagain, Grandes Oreilles (IRE), Elpida (USA), I Recall (IRE), Caerle Lad (IRE), Great Expectations (FR), Wizzy Lizzy (IRE), Paddy's Storm, CSF £14.65 TOTE £2.30: £1.20 £3.90 £4.70 (£10.20) Trio £148.50 OWNER Prince Fahd Salman (WHATCOMBE) BRED Newgate Stud Co. 23 Rn
2m 5.74 (3.24) SF: 41/48/32/32/21/39/20/19/37/35/12/16/15/9/13/11/6/11/26/26/22/9/-

WEIGHT FOR AGE 3yo-18lb
STEWARDS' ENQUIRY Perham suspended 5-7/5/95 (failure to ensure best possible place).
OFFICIAL EXPLANATION Tibetan: the jockey reported that the gelding who was slow out of the stalls, ran green and ran on through beaten horses.

765

SYRINGA H'CAP (0-80) (3-Y.O+) (Class D) £3,777.50 (£1,145.00: £560.00: £267.50) **6f** Stalls: Low GOING minus 0.16 sec per fur (GF) 8-00 (8-10)

Teetotaller (IRE) (66)_(72) (GBBalding)_ 4-9-5 JWilliams(8) (hdwy over 1f out: led wl ins fnl f: r.o) — 1
Ahjay **(42)**_(45) (DAWilson)_ 5-7-9 ow2 JQuinn(5) (hdwy over 1f out: r.o wl ins fnl f) ½ 2
Napoleon Star (IRE) **(71)**_(75) (MSSaunders)_ 4-9-10 RPrice(15) (chsd ldr: led wl over 1f out tl wl ins fnl f) hd 3
Moujeeb (USA) **(60)**_(64) (PatMitchell)_ 5-8-13v LDettori(7) (hdwy 2f out: nt qckn ins fnl f) nk 4
Dashing Dancer (IRE) **(55)**_(58) (RAkehurst)_ 4-8-8 TQuinn(13) (hdwy 2f out: ev ch 1f out: nt qckn) hd 5
Efra **(73)**_(74) (RHannon)_ 6-9-12 SRaymont(9) (hdwy 2f out: ev ch 1f out: wknd ins fnl f) 1 6
542[3] Paddy's Rice **(49)**_(49) (LJHolt)_ 4-7-9 (7) IonaWands(14) (hdwy 2f out: wknd ins fnl f) hd 7
611[10] Bayin (USA) **(66)**_(66) (MDIUsher)_ 6-9-5 RStreet(1) (late hdwy: nrst fin) hd 8
Make Time **(73)**_(72) (JPearce)_ 3-9-0 GBardwell(3) (prom 4f) ½ 9
507[15] Patsy Grimes **(65)**_(61) (LJHolt)_ 5-9-4 AMcGlone(6) (nvr nr to chal) 1¼ 10
Face the Future **(67)**_(62)_(Fav)_(LJHolt)_ 6-9-6 JReid(4) (nvr trbld ldrs) nk 11
535[11] Samsolom **(70)**_(61) (PHowling)_ 7-9-9 KDarley(10) (prom 4f) 1½ 12
636[12] Warwick Warrior (IRE) **(68)**_(58) (MrsLPiggott)_ 4-9-7b RCochrane(11) (hdwy & hrd rdn 2f out: sn wknd) nk 13
688[6] Domicksky **(69)**_(52)_(Fav)_(MRChannon)_ 7-9-8 PatEddery(16) (gd spd 4f) 2½ 14
_244_[8] Red Admiral **(60)**_(41) (PCHaslam)_ 5-8-6 (7) NicolaHowarth(17) (led tl hdd & wknd qckly over 1f out) ¾ 15
Landlord **(80)**_(55) (JARToller)_ 3-9-7 WNewnes(2) (prom 4f) 2½ 16
Vanessa Rose **(59)**_(26) (ABailey)_ 4-8-7 (5) VHalliday(12) (outpcd) 3 17

6/1 Face the Future, Domicksky, **13/2** Bayin (USA), **8/1** Moujeeb (USA), Make Time, **9/1** Landlord, **11/1** Samsolom (8/1-12/1), **12/1** Efra, Paddy's Rice, Warwick Warrior (IRE), Dashing Dancer (IRE) (8/1-14/1), **16/1** Vanessa Rose, Patsy Grimes, TEETOTALLER (IRE), **20/1** Red Admiral, **33/1** Ahjay, Napoleon Star (IRE), CSF £424.33 CT £14,260.75 TOTE £19.70: £3.10 £11.10 £12.80 £2.50 (£1,721.30) Trio £929.00; £1,177.60 to 28/04/95 OWNER Highflyers (ANDOVER) BRED David John Brown 17 Rn 1m 14.33 (3.03) SF: 47/20/50/39/33/49/24/41/35/36/37/36/33/27/16/18/1
WEIGHT FOR AGE 3yo-12lb

T/Jkpt: Not won; £63,583.83 to Beverley 27/4/95. T/Plpt: £3,189.90 (6.27 Tckts). T/Qdpt: £62.90 (0.1 Tckts); £76.50 to Beverley 27/4/95. Hn

0587-SOUTHWELL (L-H)
Wednesday April 26th

WEATHER: fine & dull WIND: strong across

766

NEPTUNE MAIDEN H'CAP (0-65) (3-Y.O+) (Class F) £2,519.00 (£694.00: £329.00) **7f (Fibresand)** Stalls: Low GOING minus 0.09 sec (STD) 2-25 (2-29)

_520_[5] **Titanium Honda (IRE) (44)**_(50)_(Fav)_(CEBrittain)_ 4-9-8 BDoyle(15) (hld up: hdwy to ld ent st: clr 1f out: hrd rdn: jst hld on) — 1
Nautical Jewel **(54)**_(60) (MDIUsher)_ 3-9-4 RPrice(9) (leggy: bhd: hdwy bel dist: str run fnl f: jst failed) hd 2
Faustino **(55)**_(58) (PFICole)_ 3-9-5 MFenton(5) (bit bkwd: hld up & bhd: pushed along over 2f out: gd hdwy appr fnl f: r.o) 1¼ 3
_513_[3] Keys Seminar **(42)**_(42) (JohnBerry)_ 3-8-6 StephenDavies(7) (hld up: effrt & rdn over 1f out: nt pce to chal) 1¼ 4
_520_[7] Dante's Rubicon (IRE) **(47)**_(45) (JDBethell)_ 4-9-11 WRyan(4) (led tl hdd & 2nd st: rdn over 1f out: one pce) ¾ 5
479[3] Bedazzle **(35)**_(31) (MBrittain)_ 4-8-13 JLowe(14) (prom: 3rd st: rdn & one pce fnl 2f) 1 6
479[6] Rainbows Rhapsody **(41)**_(23) (MJCamacho)_ 4-9-5 JQuinn(8) (b: prom tl rdn & 6th st: sn btn) 6 7
_322_[5] Nuthatch (IRE) **(43)**_(25) (MDIUsher)_ 3-8-0 (7) CAdamson(11) (prom: 5th st: wknd wl over 1f out) nk 8

Lancashire Life (IRE) **(50)***(27) (EJAlston)* 4-10-0 KFallon(1) (bkwd: prom to ½-wy: sn lost tch) 2 **9**
519[9] Wild Adventure **(35)***(12) (DWChapman)* 6-8-13 DeanMcKeown(13) (chsd ldrs 4f: 4th & rdn st: sn wknd) ....hd **10**
479[4] Scent of Power **(42)***(3) (MartynWane)* 5-9-6 KDarley(10) (hdwy ½-wy: rdn over 2f out: grad wknd) 7 **11**
603[10] Il Fratello **(40)** *(NACallaghan)* 4-9-4 GCarter(6) (a in rr) ....½ **12**
Gamzatti **(30)** *(CBBBooth)* 4-8-8 SWhitworth(12) (a in rr) 1¾ **13**
534[11] Nuveen (IRE) **(42)** *(MrsJJordan)* 4-9-6b ACulhane(3) (chsd ldrs: 5th st: sn rdn & wknd: t.o) 10 **14**
Colosse **(51)** *(MAJarvis)* 3-9-1 PRobinson(2) (lw: prom 4f: sn wknd: t.o) 6 **15**

100/30 TITANIUM HONDA (IRE), **7/1** Dante's Rubicon (IRE), **8/1** Faustino (5/1-10/1), Keys Seminar (op 5/1), **10/1** Nuthatch (IRE), **12/1** Bedazzle, Rainbows Rhapsody, Lancashire Life (IRE), Colosse, **14/1** Scent of Power, **16/1** Nautical Jewel, **20/1** Il Fratello, **33/1** Wild Adventure, Gamzatti, Nuveen (IRE), CSF £51.59 CT £361.48 TOTE £3.30: £1.60 £13.00 £4.20 (£369.90) Trio £106.90 OWNER Eddy Grimstead Honda Ltd (NEWMARKET) BRED Wellington House Stud 15 Rn

1m 33.3 (6.50) SF: 25/21/19/3/20/6/-/-/2/-/-/-/-/-/-
WEIGHT FOR AGE 3yo-14lb

767

APHRODITE CLAIMING STKS (3-Y.O+) (Class F) £2,519.00 (£694.00: £329.00)
1m (Fibresand) Stalls: Low GOING minus 0.09 sec per fur (STD) 3-00 (3-01)

395[5] **Legally Delicious (54)***(72) (JEBanks)* 3-7-9 JQuinn(11) (dwlt: hdwy & 5th st: led bel dist: sn clr: unchal) ....— **1**
601[6] Northern Celadon (IRE) **(63)***(73) (MJHeaton-Ellis)* 4-9-9 StephenDavies(10) (a.p: 4th st: led over 2f out to bel dist: one pce) 6 **2**
738[9] No Submission (USA) **(70)***(66) (DWChapman)* 9-9-5 DeanMcKeown(9) (lw: sn disp ld: 2nd st: ev ch 2f out: rdn & one pce fnl f) 1¾ **3**
591[8] What a Nightmare (IRE) **(65)***(63) (JAGlover)* 3-8-2 GCarter(7) (bhd: hdwy 2f out: nrst fin) ....½ **4**
648[17] Logie **(58)***(61) (MAJarvis)* 3-8-2 PRobinson(6) (prom: 3rd st: ev ch 2f out: rdn & kpt on same pce) 1 **5**
578[6] Samaka Hara (IRE) **(42)***(43) (WSCunningham)* 3-8-2 NCarlisle(3) (nvr trbld ldrs) 9 **6**
378[6] Shuttlecock **(65)***(39) (MrsNMacauley)* 4-9-3 MFenton(8) (lw: chsd ldrs: 6th st: wknd wl over 1f out) 1¾ **7**
601[2] Second Colours (USA) **(72)***(41)*(Fav)*(MrsMReveley)* 5-9-13 KDarley(2) (lw: sn drvn along & bhd: nvr nr to chal) 4 **8**
503[5] Battle Colours (IRE) **(65)***(27) (MrsJRRamsden)* 6-9-1b KFallon(4) (led: hrd drvn & hdd over 2f out: sn wknd & eased) 1¼ **9**
548[10] Infantry Glen **(42)***(23) (PDCundell)* 5-8-13b WNewnes(1) (bit bkwd: bhd most of wy) 1 **10**
547[9] Corrievarkie *(MissGayKelleway)* 3-8-0 (3) SSanders(5) (prom to ½-wy: wknd qckly: t.o) 30 **11**

7/2 Second Colours (USA), **4/1** No Submission (USA), **6/1** Battle Colours (IRE), Shuttlecock, **7/1** LEGALLY DELICIOUS, **15/2** Logie, **8/1** What a Nightmare (IRE), **10/1** Northern Celadon (IRE), **14/1** Corrievarkie, **33/1** Samaka Hara (IRE), **50/1** Infantry Glen, CSF £71.81 TOTE £10.60: £2.20 £2.60 £2.20 (£62.50) Trio £159.20 OWNER Mr J. A. Bianchi (NEWMARKET) BRED E. Landi 11 Rn

1m 44.9 (5.60) SF: 18/34/27/9/7/-/-/2/-/-/-
WEIGHT FOR AGE 3yo-15lb
Clmd T. Dawson £4,000

OFFICIAL EXPLANATION **Corrievarkie: the trainer reported that the filly had lost her action on the bend and was not persevered with.**
Second Colours: the jockey reported that the gelding seemed unsuited by the deep surface and resented the kickback and a routine test was ordered.

768

HERA MEDIAN AUCTION MAIDEN STKS (3-Y.O) (Class F) £2,519.00 (£694.00: £329.00)
6f (Fibresand) Stalls: Low GOING minus 0.09 sec per fur (STD) 3-35 (3-36)

587[5] **Mixed Mood (48)***(55) (BPalling)* 3-8-9 TSprake(2) (hld up: hdwy to ld wl over 1f out: rdn clr fnl f) ....— **1**
603[4] Mamma's Due *(44) (JBerry)* 3-8-9 GCarter(6) (lw: a.p: slt ld over 2f out: sn hdd: r.o one pce) 4 **2**
547[5] Self Reliance *(41)*(Fav)*(MBell)* 3-8-9 MFenton(5) (a.p: ev ch 2f out: rdn & unable qckn) 1¼ **3**
587[10] Westcourt Princess **(53)***(22) (MWEasterby)* 3-8-9b JQuinn(1) (bit bkwd: prom over 3f: sn outpcd) 7 **4**
577[3] Royal Dome (IRE) *(18) (MartynWane)* 3-9-0 KDarley(4) (sn led: rdn & hdd over 2f out: wknd) 3½ **5**

522[12] Nisya *(MissGayKelleway)* 3-8-9 SWhitworth(3) (half reard s: a bhd: t.o) 20 6

5/4 Self Reliance (8/11-11/8), **11/4** Mamma's Due, **7/1** Royal Dome (IRE), **10/1** MIXED MOOD, Westcourt Princess (8/1-12/1), Nisya, CSF £34.38 TOTE £11.30: £5.00 £1.40 (£14.90) OWNER Millstream Associates (COWBRIDGE) BRED Edward Gregory 6 Rn 1m 18.9 (5.40) SF: 14/3/-/-/-/-

769

ACHILLES H'CAP (0-65) (3-Y.O+) (Class F) £2,519.00 (£694.00: £329.00)
6f (Fibresand) Stalls: Low GOING minus 0.09 sec per fur (STD) 4-10 (4-15)

578[4] **At the Savoy (IRE) (50)***(70) (TDBarron)* 4-8-6b(7) KimberleyHart(4) (a.p: led ½-wy: clr fr bel dist: unchal) .... — 1
*625** Efficacy **(40)***(33) (APJarvis)* 4-7-10 (7) BHunter(5) (lw: a.p: rdn & one pce fnl 2f) 10 2
590[5] Farmer Jock **(41)***(33) (MrsNMacauley)* 13-7-13 (5) CTeague(13) (b: lw: bhd: hdwy 2f out: fin wl) ....½ 3
590[2] Beveled Edge **(55)***(40) (BPalling)* 6-9-4 TSprake(7) (chsd ldrs: kpt on u.p ins fnl f: nrst fin) 2½ 4
210[6] Charnwood Queen **(45)***(26) (RWArmstrong)* 3-7-3 (7)ow3 SLanigan(8) (chsd ldrs: kpt on ins fnl f) ....½ 5
646[11] Gate of Heaven **(36)***(9) (JohnBerry)* 5-7-13 ow6 GCarter(10) (chsd ldrs: rdn over 2f out: one pce) 1¾ 6
590[4] The Real Whizzbang (IRE) **(41)***(15) (PSFelgate)* 4-7-13b(5)ow1 PMcCabe(15) (lw: s.s: nvr nrr) 1½ 7
702[2] Souperficial **(58)***(32)*(Fav)*(JAGlover)* 4-9-7v KDarley(3) (effrt on ins over 2f out: sn rdn: nvr able to chal) ....½ 8
*590** Cretan Gift **(59)***(32) (NPLittmoden)* 4-9-3 (5) TGMcLaughlin(2) (chsd ldrs over 4f: sn outpcd) ....nk 9
611[8] Whittle Woods Girl **(65)***(37) (EJAlston)* 4-10-0 JQuinn(11) (a in rr: hrd drvn over 2f out: no imp) ....½ 10
578[13] Benten **(46)** *(DWChapman)* 3-7-6b(5) MBaird(6) (a bhd & outpcd: t.o) 7 11
583[8] Mazzarello (IRE) **(30)** *(RCurtis)* 5-7-7 JLowe(12) (bit bkwd: a bhd & outpcd: t.o) 4 12
590[11] Wellsy Lad (USA) **(32)** *(DWChapman)* 8-7-9b NCarlisle(1) (lw: led to ½-wy: wknd 2f out: t.o) 3 13
Lady Khadija **(30)** *(GPKelly)* 9-7-7 ClaireBalding(14) (bkwd: s.s: a bhd: t.o) 8 14

LONG HANDICAP Charnwood Queen 7-3 Mazzarello (IRE) 7-6 Gate of Heaven 6-11 Lady Khadija 6-7

7/2 Souperficial, **11/2** Beveled Edge, **13/2** Cretan Gift, **7/1** Whittle Woods Girl, **9/1** Efficacy (op 6/1), **10/1** The Real Whizzbang (IRE), **12/1** AT THE SAVOY (IRE) (op 8/1), Farmer Jock, **16/1** Wellsy Lad (USA), **20/1** Charnwood Queen, Mazzarello (IRE), **25/1** Benten, **33/1** Gate of Heaven, **100/1** Lady Khadija, CSF £105.14 CT £1,208.47 TOTE £12.10: £2.90 £3.10 £3.70 (£47.00) Trio £214.60 OWNER Mr Stephen Woodall (THIRSK) BRED Frank Towey 14 Rn
1m 16.3 (2.80) SF: 53/16/16/23/-/-/-/15/15/20/-/-/-/-
WEIGHT FOR AGE 3yo-12lb

770

APOLLO (S) STKS (2-Y.O) (Class G) £2,243.00 (£618.00: £293.00)
5f (Fibresand) Stalls: High GOING minus 0.09 sec per fur (STD) 4-40 (4-42)

455[5] **Shanoora (IRE)** *(56t) (BPalling)* 2-8-7v TSprake(2) (chsd ldrs: shkn up 2f out: qcknd to ld wl ins fnl f) .... — 1
*604** Gi La High *(58) (JBerry)* 2-8-12 GCarter(4) (a.p: led ½-wy: hdd nr fin) 1 2
604[2] Nameless *(30)*(Fav)*(DJSCosgrove)* 2-8-7 JQuinn(6) (b.hind: slt ld to ½-wy: rdn & outpcd appr fnl f) 7 3
554[5] Brogans Brush *(34) (CWFairhurst)* 2-8-12 SWhitworth(3) (outpcd: a bhd) ....½ 4
699[7] Mysterious Times *(6) (MWEasterby)* 2-8-7 KFallon(1) (s.i.s: a bhd & outpcd) 7 5
Snitch *(CSmith)* 2-8-12 WWoods(5) (neat: bkwd: gd spd 3f: sn wknd) 3½ 6

2/1 Nameless, **5/2** Gi La High (op 6/4), **7/2** Brogans Brush, **5/1** SHANOORA (IRE), **12/1** Snitch, **14/1** Mysterious Times, CSF £17.22 TOTE £11.10: £2.60 £1.30 (£9.20) OWNER Windsor Associates (COWBRIDGE) BRED Graigueshoneen Stud 6 Rn 62.7 secs (4.70) SF: 5/7/-/-/-/-
No bid.

771

GREEK GOD H'CAP (0-70) (3-Y.O+) (Class E) £3,388.00 (£1,012.00: £484.00: £220.00)
1m 4f (Fibresand) Stalls: High GOING minus 0.09 sec per fur (STD) 5-10 (5-12)

271[4] **Mr Towser (70)***(84) (WWHaigh)* 4-9-8 (5) CTeague(13) (chsd ldrs: 2nd st: led over 2f out: hrd rdn: all out) .... — 1

*592** Ijab (CAN) **(35)***(49) (JParkes)* 5-7-7b NCarlisle(16) (lw: chsd ldrs: 3rd st: jnd wnr over 2f out: rdn & no ex nr fin) ....nk 2
545[3] Hattaafeh (IRE) **(59)***(63) (MAJarvis)* 4-9-2 WWoods(4) (a.p: 5th st: one pce fnl 2f) 7 3
589[6] Palacegate Jo (IRE) **(60)***(61) (RHollinshead)* 4-9-3 WRyan(15) (hld up: hdwy over 3f out: kpt on u.p ins fnl f) 2½ 4
423[3] Risky Tu **(57)***(49) (PAKelleway)* 4-9-0 SWhitworth(9) (chsd ldrs: wnt 2nd st: wknd wl over 1f out) 7 5
556[22] Fryup Satellite **(36)***(23) (LRLloyd-James)* 4-7-2 (5) MBaird(6) (b.hind: hdwy fnl 3f: nvr nrr) 3½ 6
*605** My Minnie **(65)***(49) (BJMeehan)* 5-9-9 BDoyle(5) (chsd ldrs over 8f: sn lost tch) 2 7
568[11] Modest Hope (USA) **(50)***(32) (BRichmond)* 8-8-8 ClaireBalding(11) (lw: wl bhd tl sme late hdwy) 1½ 8
*516** Sea Spouse **(58)***(32) (MBlanshard)* 4-9-1 StephenDavies(14) (chsd ldr: led ½-wy tl over 2f out: wknd qckly) 6 9
589[5] Hasta la Vista **(50)***(7)*(Fav)*(MWEasterby)* 5-8-8b MFenton(2) (prom 7f: wknd qckly: t.o) 13 10
59[9] Mrs Tigger **(59)***(12) (RWArmstrong)* 3-7-3 (7)ow3 SLanigan(7) (a rr div: t.o) ....½ 11
Bardia **(37)** *(DonEnricoIncisa)* 5-7-9 ow2 KimTinkler(10) (bkwd: a bhd: t.o) 2½ 12
Gymcrak Diamond (IRE) **(40)** *(GHolmes)* 5-7-12 GCarter(3) (bit bkwd: b.nr hind: hdwy ½-wy: 6th st: wknd over 2f out: t.o) ....s.h 13
517[4] Tempering **(56)***(6) (DWChapman)* 9-9-0b DeanMcKeown(12) (lw: led to ½-wy: wknd qckly: t.o) 2 14
558[13] Silver Samurai **(54)** *(MrsVAAconley)* 6-8-12 KFallon(1) (hld up: hdwy 6f out: wknd over 3f out: t.o) 5 15
549[18] Jarrow **(42)** *(MrsAMNaughton)* 4-7-13e JLowe(8) (Withdrawn not under Starter's orders) .... W

LONG HANDICAP Bardia 7-4 Fryup Satellite 7-5 Mrs Tigger 7-3

, **5/1** Hasta la Vista, **13/2** My Minnie, **7/1** Risky Tu, **15/2** Ijab (CAN), **8/1** Hattaafeh (IRE), Palacegate Jo (IRE), Gymcrak Diamond (IRE) (op 14/1), MR TOWSER, **10/1** Tempering (op 6/1), **12/1** Sea Spouse, Modest Hope (USA) (op 8/1), **20/1** Silver Samurai, **33/1** Bardia, Fryup Satellite, Mrs Tigger, CSF £68.82 CT £466.77 TOTE £12.70: £2.70 £3.40 £2.90 (£56.60) Trio £112.40 OWNER Mrs I. Gibson (MALTON) BRED Miss H. K. Monteith 15 Rn 2m 45.7 (11.50) SF: 30/-/9/7/-/-/-/-/-/-/-/-/-/-/-

WEIGHT FOR AGE 3yo-21lb, 4yo-1lb

T/Plpt: £515.60 (17.07 Tckts). T/Qdpt: Not won; £89.00 to Beverley 27/4/95. IM

0568-BEVERLEY (R-H)
Thursday April 27th (Good to firm)

WEATHER: overcast WIND: mod half bhd

772 CAPTAIN STORIE MAIDEN STKS (3-Y.O+) (Class D) £3,788.50 (£1,138.00: £549.00: £254.50)

5f Stalls: Centre GOING minus 0.45 sec per fur (F) 2-10 (2-15)

658[8] **Fairy Wind (IRE)** *(73+)*(Fav)*(NACallaghan)* 3-8-8 LDettori(10) (b.hind: trckd ldrs: nt clr run & swtchd outside 2f out: led 1f out: pushed out) ....— 1
Cemaes Bay **(59)***(74) (JBerry)* 3-8-13 JCarroll(13) (a chsng ldrs: kpt on same pce fnl f) 1¼ 2
697[2] Roy Boy **(71)***(70) (MrsMReveley)* 3-8-13 KDarley(3) (lw: sn outpcd & pushed along: hdwy ½-wy: styd on fnl f) 1¼ 3
522[7] Never Such Bliss *(63) (JDBethell)* 3-8-8 TIves(8) (small: in tch: effrt ½-wy: kpt on same pce fnl f) ....½ 4
645[2] La Suquet **(70)***(63) (MRChannon)* 3-8-8 DHarrison(7) (w ldrs: led 2f out to 1f out: grad wknd) ....hd 5
Premium Gift *(63) (CBBBooth)* 3-8-8 MBirch(1) (sn prom: rdn & outpcd fnl f) ....hd 6
Master Charter *(63) (MrsJRRamsden)* 3-8-13 KFallon(2) (lengthy: unf: s.i.s: bhd: stdy hdwy over 1f out: snatched up ins fnl f: nvr plcd to chal) 1½ 7
603[2] Sing With the Band **(55)***(56) (BAMcMahon)* 4-9-5 JWeaver(11) (led 3f: n.m.r & wknd 1f out) ....¾ 8
Surprise Mission *(60) (RMWhitaker)* 3-8-13 ACulhane(5) (leggy: uns rdr gng to s: sn trckng ldrs: edgd rt & wknd fnl f) ....nk 9
555[7] Frontiersman *(50) (JWWatts)* 3-8-13 BThomson(4) (sn pushed along: outpcd fr ½-wy) 3 10
613[6] Good Match (IRE) *(42) (NTinkler)* 3-8-13 KimTinkler(6) (sn wl outpcd) 2½ 11
140[6] Black Boy (IRE) **(33)***(23) (RFMarvin)* 6-9-10b SDWilliams(14) (b: prom tl wknd ½-wy) 6 12
Power Mouse *(4) (HJCollingridge)* 3-8-13 MRimmer(9) (unf: b.hind: s.s: a bhd) 6 13
Come on Winn *(MissSJWilton)* 3-8-8 JQuinn(12) (v unruly s: swvd rt & uns rdr s) .... U

11/4 FAIRY WIND (IRE), **3/1** Roy Boy, **13/2** Sing With the Band, **7/1** La Suquet, **10/1** Cemaes Bay, **14/1** Never Such Bliss, Frontiersman, **16/1** Surprise Mission, Master Charter, **20/1** Premium Gift, Good Match (IRE), Power Mouse, Come on Winn, **50/1** Black Boy (IRE), CSF £31.57 TOTE £4.30: £1.20 £2.40 £1.40 (£15.10) Trio £26.20 OWNER Mr N. A. Callaghan (NEWMARKET) BRED Ron Con Ltd 14 Rn 62.4 secs (0.90) SF: 42/43/39/32/32/32/32/36/29/19/11/3/-/-

WEIGHT FOR AGE 3yo-11lb

773 BRIAN BOYES CLAIMING STKS (3-Y.O) (Class F) £2,798.00 (£778.00: £374.00)
1m 1f 207y Stalls: High GOING minus 0.45 sec per fur (F) 2-40 (2-47)

655[3] **Tonka (62)***(65+)*(Fav)*(DJGMurraySmith)* 3-8-5 JWeaver(11) (hld up & bhd: smooth hdwy 4f out: led over 1f out: drvn out) — 1
651[3] Just Fizzy **(47)***(56) (JWharton)* 3-7-11 (5) MBaird(7) (trckd ldrs: led over 2f out tl over 1f out: kpt on same pce) 4 2
654[3] Durgams First (IRE) **(60)***(68)*(Fav)*(MrsMReveley)* 3-9-1 KDarley(4) (hld up: hdwy 6f out: effrt over 2f out: styd on fnl f) hd 3
587[11] Gentle Irony **(60)***(50) (PJMakin)* 3-7-12 StephenDavies(1) (hdwy & prom over 3f out: kpt on one pce fnl 2f) 1 4
521[8] Kindred Greeting **(41)***(49) (DMorris)* 3-8-7b GDuffield(10) (chsd ldrs: rdn over 3f out: wknd over 1f out) 6 5
Cuillin Caper *(45) (TRWatson)* 3-8-4 DeanMcKeown(9) (rangy: bit bkwd: led early: chsd ldrs tl lost pl 4f out: kpt on fnl 2f) ½ 6
628[6] Bretton Princess **(40)***(35) (RHollinshead)* 3-8-2 ow2 DHarrison(13) (hdwy to trck ldrs 6f out: wknd 2f out) 4 7
Kings Vision **(65)***(38) (BSRothwell)* 3-8-7 MFenton(12) (t: uns rdr gng to s: sn led: hdd over 2f out: wknd over 1f out) 2½ 8
698[6] Beyaateh *(25) (MCChapman)* 3-7-11 (7) CMunday(2) (sn bhd & drvn along: sme hdwy fnl 2f) 6 9
515[9] Asking *(11) (JABennett)* 3-8-1 (3) DWright(5) (racd wd: bhd fr ½-wy) 9 10
Granny's Legacy **(35)***(5) (JDBethell)* 3-8-2 WCarson(6) (bhd fr ½-wy) 2½ 11
Lady Lancer (IRE) *(4) (CNAllen)* 3-8-6 TIves(3) (leggy: s.s: a bhd) 3 12
417[10] Malsisio *(SGNorton)* 3-8-0 JQuinn(8) (chsd ldrs tl wknd 3f out) ¾ 13

5/2 TONKA, Durgams First (IRE), **6/1** Just Fizzy, **8/1** Kings Vision (op 5/1), **9/1** Gentle Irony, **12/1** Kindred Greeting, Granny's Legacy, **16/1** Lady Lancer (IRE), **20/1** Bretton Princess, Malsisio, Beyaateh, **33/1** Asking, Cuillin Caper, CSF £19.35 TOTE £2.70: £1.80 £2.50 £1.40 (£10.60) Trio £4.00 OWNER Lady D M Watts (LAMBOURN) BRED Mrs J. Murray-Smith and N. Bowyer 13 Rn

2m 6.3 (3.80) SF: 22/13/25/7/6/2/-/-/-/-/-/-/-

774 BRIAN OUGHTRED H'CAP (0-85) (3-Y.O) (Class D) £3,944.50 (£1,186.00: £573.00: £266.50)
1m 1f 207y Stalls: High GOING minus 0.45 sec per fur (F) 3-10 (3-13)

651[6] **Dont Shoot Fairies (65)***(72) (CEBrittain)* 3-8-8 BDoyle(6) (trckd ldrs: effrt over 2f out: led over 1f out: drvn out) — 1
504[4] Komreyev Dancer **(69)***(75) (ABailey)* 3-8-7 (5) VHalliday(7) (chsd ldrs: drvn along & outpcd over 4f out: styd on wl ins fnl f: nt qckn nr fin) ½ 2
736* Nigel's Lad (IRE) **(75)***(79) (PCHaslam)* 3-8-13 (5) 5x JStack(4) (trckd ldrs: effrt & wnt lft over 2f out: ev ch 1f out: nt qckn) 1½ 3
647[4] Imlak (IRE) **(65)***(68)*(Fav)*(DMorley)* 3-8-8 WCarson(1) (sn w ldr: led over 2f out tl over 1f out: kpt on same pce: b.b.v) nk 4
648[2] Harry Browne (IRE) **(56)** *(MrsJRRamsden)* 3-7-10 (3) SSanders(3) (hld up: effrt, hmpd & bmpd over 2f out: kpt on: nvr rch ldrs: fin 6th 2½l, plcd 5th) 5
Penbola (IRE) **(60)** *(MHEasterby)* 3-8-3 SMaloney(10) (bit bkwd: hld up & plld hrd: bhd fnl 3f) 10 7
538[9] Grate British (IRE) **(64)** *(EWeymes)* 3-8-7 KDarley(9) (hld up: effrt over 3f out: sn wl outpcd & bhd) ½ 8
614[8] Kemo Sabo **(75)** *(MrsJRRamsden)* 3-9-4 KFallon(2) (mde most tl over 2f out:sn wknd) 2½ 9
596* Hamilton Silk **(58)** *(MGMeagher)* 3-8-1 JQuinn(8) (chsd ldrs tl wknd over 2f out) nk 10
504[14] Thaljanah (IRE) **(78)** *(ACStewart)* 3-9-2 (5) MHumphries(5) (in tch: c wd & bmpd twice over 2f out: kpt on wl: fin 5th 2l, disq & plcd last). 0

15/8 Imlak (IRE), **7/2** Nigel's Lad (IRE), **5/1** Harry Browne (IRE), **8/1** Grate British (IRE), Komreyev Dancer, **9/1** Kemo Sabo, **12/1** Thaljanah (IRE), **14/1** Hamilton Silk, **16/1** DONT SHOOT FAIRIES, **20/1** Penbola (IRE), CSF £135.43 CT £513.63 TOTE £17.50: £4.00 £2.30 £1.60 (£66.60) Trio £57.50 OWNER Mrs Celia Miller (NEWMARKET) BRED Mrs Celia Miller 10 Rn

2m 5.8 (3.30) SF: 30/33/37/26/-/-/-/-/-/-

STEWARDS' ENQUIRY Humphries suspended 6-9/5/95 (irresponsible riding).
OFFICIAL EXPLANATION Imlak: bled from the nose.

775

CHARLES GREIG H'CAP (0-95) (3-Y.O) (Class B) £7,767.40
(£2,896.60: £1,408.30: £596.50: £258.25: £122.95)
7f 100y Stalls: High GOING minus 0.45 sec per fur (F) 3-40 (3-41)

640* **Shahid (81)**(87+)(Fav)*(JLDunlop)* 3-8-12 3x WCarson(2) (lw: hld up: nt clr run over 2f out: swtchd ins: qcknd to ld ins fnl f: readily)......— 1
585[7] Rokeby Bowl **(76)***(79) (IABalding)* 3-8-0 (7) MartinDwyer(7) (chsd ldrs: drvn along & outpcd over 3f out: styd on u.p fnl f: no ch w wnr)......1¼ 2
Pengamon **(90)***(92) (HJCollingridge)* 3-9-7 MRimmer(4) (a chsng ldrs: ev ch 1f out: kpt on wl)......¾ 3
573* The Stager (IRE) **(76)***(78) (JRJenkins)* 3-8-7 LDettori(8) (lw: trckd ldrs: effrt & n.m.r 2f out: edgd rt: kpt on same pce fnl f)......hd 4
504[2] Mister Fire Eyes (IRE) **(84)***(85) (CEBrittain)* 3-9-1 BDoyle(6) (lw: led tl jst ins fnl f: r.o same pce)......nk 5
Neverending (USA) **(85)***(86) (HRACecil)* 3-9-2 WRyan(1) (b.off hind: swrvd lft s: effrt on outside over 2f out: kpt on fnl f)......s.h 6
Flight Soundly (IRE) **(78)***(64) (MRStoute)* 3-8-6 (3) JTate(3) (bit bkwd: hld up & plld hrd: effrt over 2f out: sn lost pl & eased)......7 7
Made in Heaven **(85)***(71) (JWHills)* 3-9-2 KDarley(5) (w ldrs: edgd lft & wknd over 1f out: eased)......s.h 8
LONG HANDICAP The Stager (IRE) 8-2 Rokeby Bowl 8-3

4/5 SHAHID, **6/1** Mister Fire Eyes (IRE), **7/1** The Stager (IRE), **9/1** Neverending (USA), Flight Soundly (IRE), **14/1** Made in Heaven, **20/1** Rokeby Bowl, Pengamon, CSF £16.45 CT £186.32 TOTE £1.60: £1.10 £3.50 £4.40 (£21.20) OWNER Mr Hamdan Al Maktoum (ARUNDEL) BRED Somerhall Bloodstock Ltd and Lord Chelsea 8 Rn 1m 33.2 (1.20) SF: 42/34/47/33/40/41/19/26

776

GEORGE CULLINGTON H'CAP (0-70) (4-Y.O+ F & M) (Class E)
£3,234.50 (£971.00: £468.00: £216.50)
1m 1f 207y Stalls: High GOING minus 0.45 sec per fur (F) 4-10 (4-10)

Wonderful Day (63)*(70)*(Fav)*(SCWilliams)* 4-9-8 KDarley(8) (lw: trckd ldrs: led over 2f out: r.o wl u.p fnl f)......— 1
122[8] Killick **(46)***(52) (ABailey)* 7-8-0 (5) VHalliday(10) (chsd ldrs: drvn along 4f out: hrd rdn & ev ch 1f out: unable qckn)......½ 2
539[4] Samsonesque **(65)***(70) (JRFanshawe)* 4-9-10 DHarrison(9) (chsd ldr: led 3f out: sn hdd: kpt on same pce fnl f)......1 3
642[7] Kilnamartyra Girl **(46)***(45) (JParkes)* 5-8-5 MDeering(5) (hld up: effrt on outside 3f out: edgd lft: kpt on same pce)......3½ 4
430[16] Missus Murhill (IRE) **(42)***(41) (NTinkler)* 4-8-1 WCarson(7) (bhd tl styd on fnl 3f)......s.h 5
*624** Asmarina **(44)***(38) (SRBowring)* 5-7-12 (5)ow2 CTeague(1) (s.i.s: bhd: effrt on outside 3f out: nvr nr to chal)......2 6
676[5] Celtic Ceilidh **(51)***(45) (JWharton)* 4-8-10 JWilliams(4) (lw: chsd ldrs: rdn 3f out: sn wknd)......1 7
738[12] Ikis Girl **(53)***(41) (SGollings)* 4-8-7 (5) JStack(3) (racd wd: a bhd)......4 8
753[5] Suedoro **(41)***(12) (GPKelly)* 5-7-7 (7)ow7 CMunday(11) (trckd ldrs: rdn & edgd lft 3f out: sn wknd)......6 9
569[7] Sottises (IRE) **(36)** *(PTDalton)* 4-7-4b(5)ow2 CHawksley(6) (led & sn clr: hdd 3f out: wandered & sn wl bhd: t.o)......20 10
LONG HANDICAP Suedoro 7-6 Sottises (IRE) 7-5

5/2 WONDERFUL DAY, **4/1** Samsonesque (op 7/4), **5/1** Asmarina, **6/1** Killick, Celtic Ceilidh, **12/1** Ikis Girl, Kilnamartyra Girl, **16/1** Missus Murhill (IRE), **25/1** Suedoro, **33/1** Sottises (IRE), CSF £17.67 CT £54.71 TOTE £3.40: £1.80 £2.40 £1.80 (£16.50) Trio £37.80 OWNER Mr Maurice Kirby (NEWMARKET) BRED M. Kirby 10 Rn 2m 6.3 (3.80) SF: 39/21/39/14/10/7/14/10/-/-

777

ALD. WILLIAM HODGSON MAIDEN STKS (3-Y.O+) (Class D)
£3,788.50 (£1,138.00: £549.00: £254.50)
1m 100y Stalls: High GOING minus 0.45 sec per fur (F) 4-40 (4-42)

Romanzof *(75) (HRACecil)* 3-8-11 WRyan(3) (lw: trckd ldr: led over 2f out: edgd lft: styd on strly)......— 1
Tillandsia (IRE) *(69)*(Fav)*(DRLoder)* 3-8-6 JWeaver(2) (rangy: lengthy: hld up: hdwy to trck ldrs over 3f out: effrt 2f out: rn green: kpt on wl twrds fin)......½ 2
585[11] Sharpical *(59) (JRFanshawe)* 3-8-11 DHarrison(5) (hld up: effrt 3f out: wandered over 1f out: no ch w 1st 2)......8 3
643[4] Ahaalee (USA) *(52) (EALDunlop)* 3-8-8 (3) JTate(7) (ld tl over 2f out: sn wl outpcd)......3½ 4
Alerting *(48) (IABalding)* 3-8-11 LDettori(1) (hld up: effrt over 3f out: kpt on: nvr nr to chal)......2½ 5

Mr Christie **(67)***(42) (MissLCSiddall)* 3-8-11 DeanMcKeown(10) (bit bkwd: sn chsng ldrs: drvn along over 3f out: sn wknd)....3 **6**
Beauchief *(36) (RFMarvin)* 3-8-11 AProud(8) (unf: a bhd)....3 **7**
643[2] Mithraic (IRE) *(32) (JWWatts)* 3-8-11 BThomson(9) (prom tl outpcd over 2f out)....2½ **8**
616[8] Carlito Brigante *(31) (MrsJRRamsden)* 3-8-11 KFallon(6) (bhd: drvn along ½-wy: n.d)....s.h **9**
Bali Tender *(MWEasterby)* 4-9-12 MBirch(4) (Withdrawn not under Starter's orders: unruly in stalls).... **W**

, **10/11** Tillandsia (IRE) (Evens-11/10), **2/1** ROMANZOF, **10/1** Mithraic (IRE) (6/1-11/1), Alerting (7/1-11/1), **20/1** Mr Christie, Ahaalee (USA), Sharpical, Carlito Brigante, **33/1** Beauchief, CSF £4.43 TOTE £2.70: £1.10 £1.10 £8.10 (£1.10) Trio £18.70 OWNER Sheikh Mohammed (NEWMARKET) BRED Sheikh Mohammed bin Rashid al Maktoum 9 Rn 1m 45.8 (1.80) SF: 42/36/26/19/15/9/3/-/-/-
WEIGHT FOR AGE 3yo-15lb
T/Jkpt: £14,774.60 (5.1 Tckts). T/Plpt: £6.90 (3,378.7 Tckts). T/Qdpt: £13.40 (15.05 Tckts). WG

0650-WARWICK (L-H)
Thursday April 27th (Good to firm)
WEATHER: Fine & dry WIND: Slight against

778
BOLLINGER CHAMPAGNE CHALLENGE SERIES GENTLEMENS' H'CAP (0-70) (3-Y.O+) (Class F) £3,023.00 (£838.00: £401.00)
1m 4f 115y Stalls: Low GOING minus 0.50 sec per fur (F) 5-30 (5-31)

653[7] **Total Joy (IRE) (60)***(72) (PFICole)* 4-11-5 MrJDurkan(6) (a.p: wnt 2nd st: rdn to ld 1f out: r.o wl)....— **1**
Daily Sport Girl **(37)***(47) (BJLlewellyn)* 6-9-11 MrJLLlewellyn(8) (b: a.p: led 6f out tl hdd & no ex fnl f)....1¾ **2**
Preston Guild (IRE) **(52)***(57) (ALForbes)* 5-10-8 (4) MrNBradley(13) (b: bit bkwd: hld up & bhd: hdwy over 2f out: nrst fin)....4 **3**
*600** Mad Militant (IRE) **(68)***(70) (ALForbes)* 6-11-10 (4) MrBLeavy(5) (hld up in tch: outpcd ent st: rdn & styd on fnl f)....2 **4**
586[14] Air Command (BAR) **(44)***(43) (CTNash)* 5-10-0 (4) MrPPhillips(4) (lw: hld up: hdwy over 3f out: nvr nr to chal)....2½ **5**
Parish Walk (IRE) **(47)***(42) (KWHogg)* 4-10-2 (4)ow4 MrKDrewry(7) (bit bkwd: led over 6f: 5th & wkng st)....hd **6**
545[15] Hillswick **(46)***(38) (JSKing)* 4-10-1 (4)ow3 MrLBaker(9) (prom: 3rd & rdn st: wknd wl over 1f out)....3 **7**
317[4] Arafel **(49)***(35) (CJames)* 4-10-4 (4)ow7 MrEJames(1) (bit bkwd: nvr trbld ldrs)....1¼ **8**
421[8] Port Sunlight (IRE) **(56)***(46) (PDEvans)* 7-10-12 (4) MrWMcLaughlin(10) (hld up mid div: effrt 3f out: no imp)....3 **9**
598[7] Jalore **(43)***(27) (SCoathup)* 6-9-13 (4)ow3 MrIMcLelland(12) (prom tl wknd over 3f out)....2 **10**
558[15] Let's Get Lost **(62)***(47) (JAHarris)* 6-11-4 (4) MrJApiafi(11) (effrt 7f out: wknd over 3f out)....1¼ **11**
653[4] Shoofk **(57)***(36)*(Fav)*(SDow)* 4-11-2 MrTCuff(3) (plld hrd: wnt prom 8f out: 4th & rdn st: wknd: t.o)....5 **12**
Spice and Sugar **(45)** *(BRCambidge)* 5-10-5 MrJCambidge(2) (Withdrawn not under Starter's orders: kicked at s).... **W**
LONG HANDICAP Hillswick 10-3

, **3/1** Shoofk, **7/2** Daily Sport Girl (9/4-4/1), **9/2** TOTAL JOY (IRE), **6/1** Mad Militant (IRE), **8/1** Preston Guild (IRE), **14/1** Port Sunlight (IRE), **16/1** Let's Get Lost, **20/1** Arafel, **33/1** Hillswick, Air Command (BAR), **40/1** Parish Walk (IRE), **50/1** Jalore, CSF £19.26 CT £111.73 TOTE £5.50: £1.30 £2.10 £3.40 (£15.80) Trio £56.00 OWNER Hon Piers Portman (WHATCOMBE) BRED Mrs Kiki Ward Platt 12 Rn 2m 44.4 (6.90) SF: 46/22/32/45/18/16/12/9/21/2/22/10/-
WEIGHT FOR AGE 4yo-1lb

779
KENILWORTH CASTLE MAIDEN STKS (3-Y.O+ F & M) (Class D) £4,408.30 (£1,320.40: £634.20: £291.10)
1m Stalls: Low GOING minus 0.50 sec per fur (F) 6-00 (6-04)

Stinging Reply *(75) (IABalding)* 3-8-8 TQuinn(12) (b: mde virtually all: drvn clr appr fnl f: easily)....— **1**
Incha *(70) (HThomsonJones)* 3-8-8 RHills(3) (lt-f: unf: hld up: hdwy & 6th st: r.o fnl f: no ch w wnr)....2½ **2**
Cyphell (IRE) *(67) (MRStoute)* 3-8-8 DHolland(2) (leggy: lt-f: b.hind: dwlt: hdwy over 2f out: swtchd rt & kpt on wl fnl f)....1¾ **3**
Sheama (USA) *(66) (WJarvis)* 3-8-8 WWoods(7) (a.p: 4th st: kpt on u.p appr fnl f)....nk **4**

Built for Comfort (IRE) *(65) (RHannon)* 3-8-8 RPerham(13) (b.hind: hld up: hdwy & 7th st: rdn & one pce fnl f) ....½ **5**
Dream Wedding *(63) (EALDunlop)* 3-8-8 PaulEddery(4) (w'like: scope: w ldrs: 2nd st: wknd appr fnl f) ....¾ **6**
Web of Intrigue **(70)***(60) (HRACecil)* 3-8-8 AMcGlone(14) (swtg: s.i.s: hdwy ½-wy: 3rd st: wknd wl over 1f out) 1¾ **7**
585[12] Care And Comfort *(59) (GWragg)* 3-8-8 FNorton(11) (lw: r.o appr fnl f: nvr nrr) ....½ **8**
Marzipan (IRE) *(55)*(Fav)*(JWHills)* 3-8-8 MHills(9) (still unf: chsd ldrs: sn drvn along: 5th st: wknd wl over 1f out) 1¾ **9**
695[13] Sadler's Pearl *(47) (BJMeehan)* 3-8-8 WNewnes(8) (bit bkwd: chsd ldrs 3f: sn outpcd) 4 **10**
Love The Blues *(42) (DNicholson)* 3-8-8 GCarter(1) (w'like: str: bkwd: a in rr) 2½ **11**
Pinkerton Polka *(39) (CEBrittain)* 3-8-8 DaleGibson(5) (str: cmpt: bkwd: a bhd) 1¾ **12**
282[3] Pleasant Memories *(38) (LordHuntingdon)* 3-8-3 (5) AWhelan(10) (chsd ldrs over 5f: sn lost tch) ....nk **13**
Midnight Mass *(12) (AGFoster)* 3-8-8 NAdams(6) (lt-f: outpcd: t.o) 13 **14**

7/2 Marzipan (IRE), **9/2** Web of Intrigue, **11/2** Incha, **6/1** Cyphell (IRE) (op 4/1), **8/1** Dream Wedding, **9/1** STINGING REPLY, **10/1** Pinkerton Polka (op 4/1), **12/1** Love The Blues, Pleasant Memories (8/1-14/1), **14/1** Sheama (USA) (op 7/1), **25/1** Built for Comfort (IRE), **33/1** Care And Comfort, Sadler's Pearl, Midnight Mass, CSF £59.70 TOTE £9.90: £2.10 £3.00 £2.50 (£25.60) Trio £53.40 OWNER The Queen (KINGSCLERE) BRED The Queen 14 Rn
1m 37.9 (0.90) SF: 42/37/34/33/32/30/27/26/22/14/9/6/5/-

780 LORD LEYCESTER HOSPITAL H'CAP (0-75) (3-Y.O+) (Class D)

£4,780.10 (£1,434.80: £691.40: £319.70)
7f Stalls: Low GOING minus 0.50 sec per fur (F) 6-30 (6-36)

365[3] **Dawalib (USA) (51)***(68) (DHaydnJones)* 5-8-7 TQuinn(15) (lw: hld up: 3rd st: led bel dist: drvn clr fnl f: readily) ....— **1**
518[4] Aquado **(45)***(57) (ALForbes)* 6-8-1 JQuinn(6) (hld up: hdwy & 5th st: ev ch over 1f out: unable qckn) 2 **2**
*627** Reverand Thickness **(72)***(82) (SCWilliams)* 4-10-0 JFortune(18) (a.p: 4th st: r.o ins fnl f) 1¼ **3**
Pusey Street Boy **(56)***(58) (JRBosley)* 8-8-12 RPerham(7) (t: bit bkwd: chsd ldrs: 6th & rdn ent st: kpt on ins fnl f) 3½ **4**
579* Don Pepe **(67)***(62) (RBoss)* 4-9-9 JCarroll(20) (lw: chsd ldr: 2nd st: ev ch over 1f out: one pce) 3 **5**
198[6] Fleet Cadet **(47)***(39) (NAGraham)* 4-8-3 PaulEddery(3) (hdwy 2f out: styd on fnl f: nvr nrr) 1¼ **6**
701* Berge (IRE) **(59)***(50)*(Fav)*(WAO'Gorman)* 4-9-1b 6x EmmaO'Gorman(10) (s.s: hdwy fnl 2f: nvr nrr: fin lame) ....½ **7**
Comanche Companion **(68)***(58) (TJNaughton)* 5-9-10 GCarter(1) (mid div tl styd on appr fnl f) ....nk **8**
Leguard Express (IRE) **(52)***(38) (OO'Neill)* 7-8-8bow1 WNewnes(16) (bkwd: led tl hdd & wknd bel dist) 1¼ **9**
590[9] Martinosky **(55)***(42) (GCBravery)* 9-8-11 MHills(8) (a in rr) ....hd **10**
507[17] Hong Kong Dollar **(60)***(41) (BJMeehan)* 3-8-2 ow3 BDoyle(5) (prom to ½-wy: sn lost tch) 1¼ **11**
548[7] Nabjelsedr **(60)***(47) (AGNewcombe)* 5-8-11 (5) DGriffiths(4) (b.hind: dwlt: nvr nr ldrs) ....d.h **11**
532[9] Hill Farm Katie **(41)***(24) (WMBrisbourne)* 4-7-4 (7)ow1 MartinDwyer(2) (s.s: a bhd) ....hd **13**
Broughton Singer (IRE) **(58)***(41) (WJMusson)* 4-9-0 AMcGlone(13) (s.i.s: hld up mid div: carried wd ent st: n.d) ....nk **14**
526[18] Lawnswood Junior **(62)***(43) (JLSpearing)* 8-9-4 GHind(11) (dwlt: a in rr) 1 **15**
Goody Four Shoes **(44)***(18) (AGNewcombe)* 7-8-0 RPrice(9) (a in rr) 3 **16**
601[12] Zahran (IRE) **(72)***(43) (JMBradley)* 4-9-9 (5) SDrowne(19) (chsd ldrs: 7th & outpcd ent st: sn bhd) 1¼ **17**
548[14] Glen Miller **(43)***(11) (JWPayne)* 5-7-13 GBardwell(14) (a bhd) 1½ **18**
Daring Ryde **(44)***(2) (JPSmith)* 4-7-9 (5)ow1 AGarth(17) (bit bkwd: chsd ldrs tl 8th & wkng st) 4 **19**
Persian Heritage **(45)** *(AJChamberlain)* 4-7-10 (5) NVarley(12) (b: bkwd: a bhd: t.o) ....dist **20**

7/2 Berge (IRE), **7/1** DAWALIB (USA), Aquado, Don Pepe, **9/1** Reverand Thickness, **12/1** Glen Miller, **14/1** Pusey Street Boy, **16/1** Leguard Express (IRE), Comanche Companion, Broughton Singer (IRE), **20/1** Goody Four Shoes, Nabjelsedr, Martinosky, **25/1** Zahran (IRE), Hill Farm Katie, Hong Kong Dollar, **33/1** Fleet Cadet, Lawnswood Junior, **50/1** Daring Ryde, Persian Heritage, CSF £55.57 CT £425.28 TOTE £7.80: £1.80 £2.20 £2.50 £1.60 (£25.10) Trio £82.50 OWNER Jack Brown (Bookmaker) Ltd (PONTYPRIDD) BRED Hilary J. Boone Jnr 20 Rn
1m 25.1 (0.90) SF: 40/29/54/30/34/11/22/30/10/14/-/19/-/13/15/-/15/-/-/-
WEIGHT FOR AGE 3yo-14lb

OFFICIAL EXPLANATION Berge (IRE): the jockey reported that the colt had finished sore due to the going and a routine test was ordered.

781

MOTOR HERITAGE TRUST STKS (2-Y.O) (Class D) £4,023.40 (£1,112.40: £530.20) **5f** Stalls: Low GOING minus 0.50 sec per fur (F) 7-00 (7-01)

615* **Passion For Life** *(74+t)*(Fav)*(GLewis)* 2-9-3 PaulEddery(1) (lw: mde all: clr whn hung rt fnl f)........— **1**
*531** Swiss Valley Lady *(57) (WGMTurner)* 2-8-10 TSprake(3) (chsd wnr: rdn & effrt bel dist: no imp)........3 **2**
540[4] Bath Knight *(49) (DJSffrenchDavis)* 2-8-6 (5) RPainter(2) (dwlt: a bhd & outpcd)........3 **3**

1/6 PASSION FOR LIFE, **6/1** Swiss Valley Lady (op 4/1), **12/1** Bath Knight, CSF £1.60 TOTE £1.20: (£1.10) OWNER Mr David Waters (EPSOM) BRED G. R. Smith (Thriplow) Ltd 3 Rn
59.9 secs (1.90) SF: 26/9/1

782

HATTON COUNTRY WORLD MAIDEN AUCTION STKS (2-Y.O) (Class F) £3,073.40 (£852.40: £408.20)
5f Stalls: Low GOING minus 0.50 sec per fur (F) 7-30 (7-31)

Hotlips Houlihan *(54t) (RJRWilliams)* 2-7-12 DBiggs(3) (lt-f: unf: chsd ldrs: led ½-wy: rdn & r.o wl fnl f)........— **1**
570[2] Badger Bay (IRE) *(53) (JohnBerry)* 2-8-2 JQuinn(7) (w ldrs: rdn & kpt on ins fnl f)........1½ **2**
Clan Chief *(56)*(Fav)*(JRArnold)* 2-8-7 RHills(4) (cmpt: bit bkwd: s.i.s: hdwy ½-wy: ev ch fnl f: r.o)........¾ **3**
650[4] Mrs McBadger *(46) (BSmart)* 2-7-10 (3)ow1 SSanders(13) (led over 2f: rdn over 1f out: one pce)........nk **4**
Lady Dignity (IRE) *(44) (PJMakin)* 2-7-12 StephenDavies(6) (small: bit bkwd: bhd: hdwy over 1f out: fin wl)........½ **5**
Pride of Whalley (IRE) *(45)*(Fav)*(JBerry)* 2-8-2 JCarroll(12) (lt-f: unf: bit bkwd: dwlt: sn chsng ldrs: one pce fnl 2f)........1 **6**
Masbro Bird *(39) (BRMillman)* 2-7-10 (5)ow3 AWhelan(2) (lt-f: unf: outpcd tl sme late hdwy)........¾ **7**
Credite Risque *(33) (MMcCormack)* 2-8-2 DHarrison(11) (leggy: lt-f: unf: s.i.s: rdn over 2f out: no imp)........3 **8**
570[5] Fortuitious (IRE) *(33) (JRJenkins)* 2-8-2 CRutter(1) (spd over 3f)........hd **9**
Siberian Mystic *(31) (PGMurphy)* 2-7-11 (7)ow2 RWaterfield(10) (leggy: scope: bkwd: a outpcd)........½ **10**
480[8] Digwana (IRE) *(27) (TMJones)* 2-8-5 ow2 RPerham(5) (dwlt: sn rdn along & outpcd)........1½ **11**
570[8] Skelton Countess (IRE) *(21) (RHollinshead)* 2-7-9 (5)ow2 AGarth(9) (racd wd: a bhd)........½ **12**

7/2 Clan Chief, Pride of Whalley (IRE) (op 9/4), **9/2** Mrs McBadger (op 5/2), **5/1** Badger Bay (IRE), **8/1** Credite Risque, **10/1** HOTLIPS HOULIHAN (8/1-12/1), **12/1** Lady Dignity (IRE) (op 8/1), **14/1** Fortuitious (IRE), **16/1** Masbro Bird, **20/1** Siberian Mystic, **33/1** Digwana (IRE), Skelton Countess (IRE), CSF £60.12 TOTE £11.80: £3.10 £2.00 £1.30 (£49.50) Trio £100.90 OWNER Mr Harry Ormesher (NEWMARKET) BRED P. Young 12 Rn 60.9 secs (2.90) SF: -/-/-/-/-/-/-/-/-/-/-/-
OFFICIAL EXPLANATION Siberian Mystic: the jockey reported that the filly, who is temperamental and has been difficult to train to stalls, had missed the break and then hung in behind two tiring runners.

783

WARWICK CASTLE MAIDEN LIMITED STKS (0-70) (3-Y.O) (Class E) £3,348.00 (£999.00: £477.00: £108.00: £108.00)
7f Stalls: Low GOING minus 0.50 sec per fur (F) 8-00 (8-01)

552[6] **Speedybird (IRE) (60)***(73+) (BJMeehan)* 3-8-9 BDoyle(7) (led after 1f: qcknd clr 2f out: unchal)........— **1**
Night Time **(70)***(64)*(Fav)*(RHannon)* 3-9-0 TQuinn(2) (bit bkwd: bhd & rdn along: hmpd 3f out: 6th st: rdn & r.o fnl f)........6 **2**
Second Cello **(60)***(59) (DMorris)* 3-8-9 RPrice(6) (bit bkwd: hld up: hdwy & 4th st: chsd wnr fr bel dist: no imp)........hd **3**
Dusk in Daytona **(65)***(57) (CJames)* 3-8-9 AMcGlone(8) (prom: 2nd st: rdn & wknd ins fnl f)........d.h **4**
547[12] Hard Love **(70)***(57) (SPCWoods)* 3-8-9 WWoods(3) (a.p: 3rd st: rdn wl over 1f out: wknd fnl f)........1 **4**
Super High **(60)***(53) (PHowling)* 3-9-0 RCochrane(9) (prom tl 5th & rdn st: sn btn)........4 **6**
Faith 'n Glory (IRE) **(70)***(36) (RHannon)* 3-8-2 (7) DaneO'Neill(5) (bhd: hmpd & snatched up 3f out: nt rcvr)........5 **7**
645[5] Perfect World **(68)***(37) (BAMcMahon)* 3-9-0 GCarter(4) (s.s: rdn & effrt 2f out: no imp)........1¾ **8**

Nordman Lass **(65)***(3) (MissJacquelineDoyle)* 3-8-9 RPerham(1) (swtg: led 1f: wknd qckly 3f out: t.o)....13 9
Ism **(55)***(7) (MajorWRHern)* 3-9-0 PaulEddery(10) (bkwd: r wd: chsd ldrs 4f: sn wknd: t.o)....hd 10

7/4 Night Time, **13/2** Dusk in Daytona, **7/1** SPEEDYBIRD (IRE), **8/1** Perfect World (6/1-9/1), Hard Love, Super High, Ism, **12/1** Second Cello, **14/1** Faith 'n Glory (IRE), **16/1** Nordman Lass, CSF £20.31 TOTE £6.20: £2.70 £1.90 £2.80 (£17.70) Trio £145.00 OWNER Mr A. S. Reid (UPPER LAMBOURN) BRED Beaconhill Enterprises 10 Rn 1m 25.2 (1.00) SF: 40/31/26/24/24/20/3/4/-/-

T/Plpt: £112.90 (86.06 Tckts). T/Qdpt: Not won; £56.40 to Sandown 28/04/95 IM

CARLISLE (R-H)
Friday April 28th (Good, Good to firm patches)
WEATHER: Sunny WIND: Almost nil

784 KESTREL CLAIMING STKS (I) (4-Y.O+) (Class F) £2,689.00 (£754.00: £367.00) **6f 206y** Stalls: High GOING minus 0.47 sec per fur (F) 2-10 (2-10)

627[3] **Allinson's Mate (IRE) (70)***(75) (TDBarron)* 7-9-3 JFortune(4) (lw: trckd ldrs: effrt over 3f out: styd on u.p to ld nr fin)....— 1
672[2] Profit Release (IRE) **(56)***(61) (MJohnston)* 4-8-4 DHolland(6) (led 1f: led over 2f out tl nr fin)....nk 2
636[7] Sweet Supposin (IRE) **(65)***(63)*(Fav)*(KMcAuliffe)* 4-9-3b RCochrane(3) (chsd ldrs: ev ch & hrd rdn 3f out: one pce appr fnl f)....5 3
Once More for Luck (IRE) **(73)***(58) (MrsMReveley)* 4-9-7 KDarley(1) (in tch: effrt over 3f out: sn rdn: nvr nr to chal)....4 4
Daytime Dawn (IRE) *(42) (DMoffatt)* 4-8-6 (3) DarrenMoffatt(5) (unf: in tch: effrt & hung lft 3f out: wandered & nvr rchd ldrs)....1½ 5
534[12] Venture Fourth **(22)***(15) (EJAlston)* 6-8-7 KFallon(8) (led after 1f tl over 2f out: sn wknd)....11 6
Milbank Challenger **(54)** *(WStorey)* 5-8-2 (3) DRMcCabe(2) (bit bkwd: sn bhd)....9 7
578[14] Shropshire Blue **(37)** *(DANolan)* 5-7-12 (5)ow5 CTeague(7) (a in rr)....4 8

9/4 Sweet Supposin (IRE), **3/1** ALLINSON'S MATE (IRE), **7/2** Profit Release (IRE), Once More for Luck (IRE), **10/1** Milbank Challenger (20/1-8/1), **25/1** Venture Fourth, **33/1** Daytime Dawn (IRE), Shropshire Blue, CSF £13.72 TOTE £2.90: £1.30 £1.10 £1.40 (£6.60) OWNER Mr Peter Jones (THIRSK) BRED Gay O'Callaghan 8 Rn 1m 27.1 (1.40) SF: 47/33/35/30/14/-/-/-

785 GOLDEN EAGLE H'CAP (0-85) (3-Y.O+) (Class D) £3,809.00 (£1,154.00: £564.00: £269.00) **7f 214y** Stalls: High GOING minus 0.47 sec per fur (F) 2-45 (2-45)

736[2] **Busy Banana (74)***(92)*(Fav)*(RHannon)* 3-8-3 5x KDarley(14) (lw: mde all: qcknd clr over 2f out: easily)....— 1
642[3] Spanish Verdict **(65)***(73) (DenysSmith)* 8-8-4 (5) CTeague(8) (lw: a.p: styd on appr fnl f: no ch w wnr)....5 2
642[6] Cee-Jay-Ay **(70)***(76) (JBerry)* 8-8-7 (7) PRoberts(12) (s.s: bhd tl hdwy on outside over 2f out: styd on ins fnl f)....1 3
559[5] Veloce (IRE) **(68)***(71) (ABailey)* 7-8-12 FNorton(9) (b: mid div: hdwy over 2f out: kpt on fnl f)....1½ 4
642[13] King of Show (IRE) **(69)***(72) (RAllan)* 4-8-13 CDwyer(13) (sn rr div & drvn along: styd on fnl 2f: eased nr fin)....hd 5
642[8] Self Expression **(55)***(54) (MrsJRRamsden)* 7-7-13 JFanning(7) (hld up & bhd: nt clr run on ins over 3f out tl over 1f out: styd on)....1¾ 6
266[8] My Handy Man **(56)***(54) (RAllan)* 4-8-0 SMaloney(4) (plld hrd: trckd ldrs: effrt over 2f out: no imp)....½ 7
724[5] Princess Maxine (IRE) **(66)***(58) (JJO'Neill)* 6-8-10 JCarroll(15) (lw: chsd ldrs: effrt over 2f out: grad wknd)....3 8
Current Speech (IRE) **(73)***(63) (MHEasterby)* 4-9-3 MBirch(10) (hld up & bhd: sme hdwy 2f out: nvr plcd to chal)....1 9
686[6] Montanelli (FR) **(76)***(60) (KMcAuliffe)* 3-8-5b RCochrane(5) (chsd ldrs tl wknd 3f out)....3 10
702[14] Comeonup **(54)***(37) (JMBradley)* 4-7-12 LCharnock(6) (b: chsd ldrs tl lost pl 3f out)....¾ 11
Gymcrak Flyer **(70)***(49) (GHolmes)* 4-9-0 KFallon(3) (hld up & bhd: sme hdwy whn n.m.r 2f out: n.d)....1¾ 12
439[4] Leif the Lucky (USA) **(84)***(60) (MissSEHall)* 6-10-0 NConnorton(2) (lw: sn trckng ldrs: effrt on outside over 2f out: sn wknd)....1½ 13
597[7] Izza **(68)***(30) (WStorey)* 4-8-9 (3) DRMcCabe(1) (chsd ldrs: drvn along over 3f out: sn wknd)....7 14

7/4 BUSY BANANA, **5/1** Leif the Lucky (USA), **8/1** Spanish Verdict, Self Expression, **11/1** Princess Maxine (IRE), **12/1** Cee-Jay-Ay, Veloce (IRE), Montanelli (FR), **16/1** Gymcrak Flyer, **20/1** Current Speech (IRE), Comeonup, **25/1** My Handy Man, **33/1** King of Show (IRE), Izza, CSF £17.42 CT £131.20 TOTE £2.40: £1.50 £2.00 £2.80 (£11.50) Trio £47.10 OWNER Mr P. D. Savill (MARLBOROUGH) BRED Lingfield Lodge Farm 14 Rn

1m 39.2 (0.20) SF: 48/44/47/42/43/25/25/29/34/16/8/20/31/1

WEIGHT FOR AGE 3yo-15lb

STEWARDS' ENQUIRY Dwyer suspended 8-9/5/95 (failure to ensure best possible placing).

786 MERLIN H'CAP (0-75) (3-Y.O) (Class D) £3,656.90 (£1,107.20: £540.60: £128.65: £128.65) **1m 4f** Stalls: Low GOING minus 0.47 sec per fur (F) 3-15 (3-17)

538⁷ **On a Pedestal (IRE) (52)**_(61) (MrsJRRamsden)_ 3-8-11 RCochrane(3) (lw: hld up: hdwy over 4f out: led over 1f out: hld on wl) — 1

484⁵ Elation **(58)**_(66)_(Fav)_(PFICole)_ 3-9-3b TQuinn(8) (n.m.r after 1f: drvn along ½-wy: hdwy to ld over 2f out: nt qckn ins fnl f) ¾ 2

Bark'n'bite **(51)**_(55)_(Fav)_(MrsMReveley)_ 3-8-10 KDarley(6) (led 1f: chsd ldrs: drvn along & outpcd 3f out: kpt on appr fnl f) 3 3

672⁴ Boundary Express **(50)**_(51) (MJohnston)_ 3-8-9 TWilliams(5) (a chsng ldrs: rdn 4f out: one pce fnl 2f) d.h 4

_592²_ Hard Try **(56)**_(57)_(Fav)_(MJCamacho)_ 3-9-1 LCharnock(4) (led after 1f tl over 2f out: grad wknd) 2 4

572⁴ Kildrummy Castle **(56)**_(51)_(Fav)_(MrsJRRamsden)_ 3-9-1 KFallon(7) (n.m.r after 1f: sn bhd: drvn along ½-wy: sme hdwy 3f out: wknd over 1f out) 5 6

538⁸ Hong Kong Designer **(54)**_(47) (SGNorton)_ 3-8-10 (3) DarrenMoffatt(9) (swtg: bhd & drvn along ½-wy: n.d after) 1½ 7

689³ Spanish Steps (IRE) **(62)**_(50) (MWEasterby)_ 3-9-7 MBirch(2) (trckd ldrs: effrt 3f out: grad wknd) 3½ 8

Caltha **(50)**_(36) (PCalver)_ 3-8-4 (5) NVarley(1) (sn trckng ldrs: rdn 4f out: wknd over 2f out) 1¼ 9

4/1 Kildrummy Castle, Elation, Bark'n'bite, Hard Try (op 5/2), **9/2** ON A PEDESTAL (IRE), **8/1** Spanish Steps (IRE), **12/1** Boundary Express, **20/1** Hong Kong Designer, **33/1** Caltha, CSF 23.11 CT £73.32 TOTE £9.40: £2.00 £1.60 £1.80 (£12.30) Trio £21.00 OWNER Mr Harry Rishworth (THIRSK) BRED Stan Policky 9 Rn 2m 35.1 (4.10) SF: 32/37/26/22/28/22/18/21/7

787 SPARROW HAWK MAIDEN STKS (3-Y.O) (Class D) £3,656.90 (£1,107.20: £540.60: £257.30) **1m 4f** Stalls: Low GOING minus 0.47 sec per fur (F) 3-50 (3-50)

657² **Royal Scimitar (USA) (104)**_(75+)_(Fav)_(PFICole)_ 3-9-0 TQuinn(3) (b.hind: mde all: shkn up & qcknd 5f out: clr 2f out: v.easily) — 1

584⁴ Fearless Venture _(68) (SPCWoods)_ 3-9-0 WWoods(5) (chsd wnr: effrt over 3f out: kpt on) 5 2

Medway (IRE) _(63) (MHTompkins)_ 3-8-9 PRobinson(4) (unf: hdwy ½-wy: effrt & prom over 3f out: kpt on one pce fnl 2f) nk 3

657⁹ Blue Smoke (IRE) _(56) (BAMcMahon)_ 3-9-0 TIves(7) (effrt 4f out: sn rdn: wknd over 2f out) 9 4

641³ Dawn Mission _(54) (MHEasterby)_ 3-9-0 MBirch(2) (trckd ldrs: hung rt tl wknd over 2f out) 1¼ 5

Philmist _(48) (JHetherton)_ 3-8-9 NKennedy(6) (rangy: unf: s.i.s: bhd & pushed along 7f out: n.d) 1 6

Victoria Day _(48) (JWWatts)_ 3-8-9 NConnorton(1) (rangy: scope: bit bkwd: s.i.s: hdwy & pushed along 7f out: lost pl 5f out: sn bhd) s.h 7

1/7 ROYAL SCIMITAR (USA), **10/1** Fearless Venture, **14/1** Medway (IRE), Victoria Day, Dawn Mission, **50/1** Philmist, Blue Smoke (IRE), CSF £3.44 TOTE £1.10: £1.10 £2.60 (£2.80) OWNER Prince Fahd Salman (WHATCOMBE) BRED Newgate Stud Farm Inc 7 Rn

2m 35.4 (4.40) SF: 32/25/20/13/11/5/5

788 BUZZARD MAIDEN STKS (2-Y.O) (Class D) £3,469.10 (£1,050.80: £513.40: £244.70) **5f** Stalls: High GOING: minus 0.47 sec per fur (F) 4-20 (4-22)

617⁶ **Sky Dome (IRE)** _(74t)_(Fav)_(MHTompkins)_ 2-9-0 PRobinson(3) (lw: trckd ldrs: qcknd to ld 1f out: edgd rt & r.o wl: rdn out) — 1

Meeting Point _(67) (MrsMReveley)_ 2-8-9 KDarley(6) (unf: scope: sn outpcd & pushed along: swtchd outside over 1f out: styd on strly: nt rch wnr) ¾ 2

699² Double Point (IRE) _(65) (MBell)_ 2-8-7 (7) GFaulkner(11) (mde most tl over 1f out: kpt on same pce) 2 3

615[4] Ramsey Hope *(64) (CWFairhurst)* 2-9-0 NKennedy(2) (w ldrs: led over 1f out: wnt rt & sn hdd: one pce) ....½ 4
615[8] Royal Rapport *(58) (BAMcMahon)* 2-9-0 TIves(1) (bit bkwd: s.i.s: hdwy ½-wy: kpt on same pce whn sltly hmpd jst ins fnl f) 1¾ 5
595[2] Gagajulu *(51) (PDEvans)* 2-8-9 JFortune(5) (chsd ldrs: styng on one pce whn n.m.r & swtchd 1f out) ....½ 6
523[8] Albert The Bear *(47) (JBerry)* 2-9-0 JCarroll(9) (w ldrs tl rdn & wknd over 1f out) 3 7
684[6] Borana Lodge (USA) *(46) (MrsJRRamsden)* 2-9-0 KFallon(10) (b.off hind: nvr rchd ldrs) ....nk 8
Jackson Park *(43) (MHEasterby)* 2-9-0 MBirch(8) (rangy: scope: s.i.s: nvr wnt pce) 1 9
Village Opera *(30) (GMMoore)* 2-8-9 JFanning(4) (leggy: unf: bkwd: s.s: a bhd) 2½ 10
Kiwud *(29) (GMMoore)* 2-8-9 NConnorton(7) (cmpt: bkwd: s.i.s: a in rr) ....nk 11

7/4 SKY DOME (IRE), **7/2** Double Point (IRE), **5/1** Gagajulu, **11/2** Albert The Bear, **15/2** Ramsey Hope (op 5/1), **10/1** Meeting Point (op 6/1), **12/1** Borana Lodge (USA), **14/1** Royal Rapport (op 9/1), **20/1** Jackson Park, **25/1** Village Opera, **33/1** Kiwud, CSF £22.39 TOTE £2.80: £1.60 £3.20 £1.20 (£17.40) Trio £31.70 OWNER Miss D. J. Merson (NEWMARKET) BRED Andrew Bradley 11 Rn
62.5 secs (2.30) SF: 22/15/13/12/6/-/-/-/-/-/-

789 PEREGRINE FALCON H'CAP (0-65) (3-Y.O+) (Class F) £3,095.00 (£870.00: £425.00) **5f 207y** Stalls: High GOING minus 0.47 sec per fur (F) 4-55 (4-57)

434[18] **Ziggy's Dancer (USA) (64)***(76+) (EJAlston)* 4-9-13 KFallon(13) (w ldrs: led ½-wy: clr over 1f out: r.o strly) ....— 1
688[7] Rich Glow **(44)***(53) (NBycroft)* 4-8-7 SMaloney(8) (hdwy ½-wy: styd on wl u.p fnl f: nt rch wnr) 1¼ 2
701[3] Miss Whittingham (IRE) **(56)***(59)*(Fav)*(JBerry)* 5-9-5 JCarroll(12) (lw: w ldrs: rdn 2f out: kpt on same pce) 2 3
555[4] Michellisa **(52)***(54) (JDBethell)* 4-9-1 KDarley(10) (a chsng ldrs: nt qckn fnl 2f) ....½ 4
594[7] Birchwood Sun **(53)***(55) (MDods)* 5-8-11b(5) VHalliday(9) (bhd & sn drvn along: styd on wl u.p fnl f: nt rch wnr) ....hd 5
646[3] Asterix **(43)***(41) (JMBradley)* 7-8-6v LCharnock(2) (rr div: rdn ½-wy: kpt on) 1¼ 6
559[15] Bogart **(55)***(50) (CWFairhurst)* 4-9-4 RCochrane(6) (in tch: sn drvn along: nvr able chal) 1¼ 7
646[7] Mu-Arrik **(58)***(52) (GROldroyd)* 7-9-7v JFortune(17) (lw: s.i.s: sn in tch: no hdwy fnl 2f) ....½ 8
701[7] Densben **(54)***(45) (DenysSmith)* 11-9-3 DHolland(7) (sn outpcd: sme hdwy 2f out: n.d) 1 9
590[6] Sakharov **(56)***(44) (MJohnston)* 6-9-5 PRobinson(4) (lw: hld up & bhd: sme hdwy ½-wy: n.d) 1 10
Northern Spark **(42)***(29) (MartynWane)* 7-8-5 JFanning(16) (bit bkwd: s.i.s: bhd whn hmpd 2f out) ....½ 11
To Prove a Point **(42)***(28) (JJO'Neill)* 3-7-7 NKennedy(5) (hld up: a in rr) ....½ 12
326[6] Sweet Cheap Pet **(47)***(30) (JJO'Neill)* 3-7-12 FNorton(18) (nvr bttr than mid div) 1 13
702[9] Light Movement (IRE) **(58)***(35) (WSCunningham)* 5-9-7 ACulhane(19) (b.nr fore: in tch: wkng whn hmpd over 1f out) 2 14
701[15] Shotley Again **(32)***(9) (NBycroft)* 5-7-4 (5) NVarley(11) (bit bkwd: sn drvn along: a in rr) ....hd 15
594[2] Cledeschamps **(41)***(7) (MWEllerby)* 6-7-13 (5)ow4 CTeague(15) (led to ½-wy: wknd qckly over 1f out) 2½ 16
Featherstone Lane **(57)***(27) (MissLCSiddall)* 4-9-3v(3) DRMcCabe(3) (racd wd: nvr nr ldrs) ....nk 17
475[7] Uppance **(32)** *(DANolan)* 7-7-6 (3)ow2 DarrenMoffatt(14) (t: w ldrs to ½-wy: wknd qckly) 13 18

LONG HANDICAP To Prove a Point 6-8

4/1 Miss Whittingham (IRE), **7/1** Sakharov, **8/1** ZIGGY'S DANCER (USA), **10/1** Mu-Arrik, **11/1** Asterix, **12/1** Michellisa, Cledeschamps, Densben, **14/1** Rich Glow, Birchwood Sun, Light Movement (IRE), Featherstone Lane, **16/1** Sweet Cheap Pet, Bogart, **20/1** Shotley Again, **33/1** Northern Spark, **50/1** To Prove a Point, Uppance, CSF £111.64 CT £480.41 TOTE £8.70: £2.20 £6.60 £1.40 £1.30 (£201.00) Trio Not won; £447.59 to 3.25 Sandown 29/4/95 OWNER Mr John Patrick Barry (PRESTON) BRED Warren W. Rosenthal 18 Rn
1m 14.5 (2.20) SF: 42/19/25/20/21/7/16/18/11/10/-/-/-/1/-/-/-/-
WEIGHT FOR AGE 3yo-12lb

790 KESTREL CLAIMING STKS (II) (4-Y.O+) (Class F) £2,675.00 (£750.00: £365.00) **6f 206y** Stalls: High GOING minus 0.47 sec per fur (F) 5-25 (5-26)

748[6] **Obsidian Grey (44)***(56) (MissLCSiddall)* 8-8-0 (3) DRMcCabe(5) (hld up: hdwy ½-wy: led over 1f out: sn clr: eased nr fin) ....— 1

535[16] Elle Shaped (IRE) **(69)***(63)*(Fav)*(DNicholls)* 5-9-3 NConnorton(2) (lw: unruly s: trckd ldr: led 3f out tl over 1f out) 3 **2**
672[9] Dundeelin **(35)***(39) (JLEyre)* 4-8-2b RLappin(1) (prom: rdn & hung rt 2f out: nvr able chal) 4 **3**
Karibu (GER) *(44) (MGMeagher)* 4-8-11 JCarroll(8) (chsd ldrs tl outpcd fnl 2f) 1½ **4**
594[14] Kenesha (IRE) **(53)***(29) (DANolan)* 5-7-11 (5) NVarley(6) (b: chsd ldrs tl lost pl over 2f out) 3 **5**
627[9] Nakita **(59)***(25) (CNAllen)* 4-7-13 (5) MBaird(7) (b.hind: s.i.s: a in rr) 2½ **6**
593[9] Operatic Dancer *(31) (RMMcKellar)* 4-8-13 TWilliams(3) (s.s: bhd & pushed along ½-wy: n.d) 1 **7**
593[7] Wali (USA) **(60)** *(VThompson)* 5-8-4 (5) JStack(4) (led to 3f out: sn wknd & bhd) 15 **8**

11/8 Elle Shaped (IRE), **3/1** Nakita, **5/1** Wali (USA), **6/1** OBSIDIAN GREY, **12/1** Dundeelin, **16/1** Karibu (GER), Kenesha (IRE), **50/1** Operatic Dancer, CSF £14.69 TOTE £7.70: £1.40 £1.10 £4.80 (£8.50) OWNER Miss L. C. Siddall (TADCASTER) BRED Oldtown Stud 8 Rn

1m 27.9 (2.20) SF: 25/32/8/13/-/-/-/-

T/Plpt: £8.40 (1,140.06 Tckts). T/Qdpt: £5.90 (5.1 Tckts) WG

SANDOWN (R-H)
Friday April 28th (Good, Good to firm patches)
WEATHER: Fair WIND: Almost nil

791
ALBERT MEDIAN AUCTION MAIDEN STKS (2-Y.O F) (Class D)
£3,647.50 (£1,105.00: £540.00: £257.50)
5f 6y Stalls: Low GOING minus 0.25 sec per fur (GF) 2-00 (2-02)

Flying Squaw *(78t)*(Fav)*(MRChannon)* 2-8-11 RHughes(4) (str: bit bkwd: a.p: rdn over 1f out: led ins fnl f: r.o wl) .....— **1**
Roses In The Snow (IRE) *(76) (JWHills)* 2-8-11 RHills(11) (unf: hld up: rdn over 1f out: r.o wl ins fnl f) .....½ **2**
Bewitching (USA) *(75) (JARToller)* 2-8-11 JWeaver(2) (unf: led tl ins fnl f: unable qckn) .....½ **3**
Beautiful Ballad (IRE) *(72) (BWHills)* 2-8-11 WCarson(5) (b.hind: w'like: bkwd: hld up: shkn up over 1f out: r.o: bttr for r) .....¾ **4**
White Whispers *(65) (BWHills)* 2-8-11 MHills(6) (b.hind: unf: bit bkwd: nvr nr to chal) 2½ **5**
Disallowed (IRE) *(63) (MBell)* 2-8-11 MFenton(12) (leggy: unf: scope: a.p: rdn over 1f out: one pce) .....½ **6**
Honorable Estate (IRE) *(63) (RHannon)* 2-8-11 PatEddery(8) (w'like: hdwy 3f out: shkn up over 1f out: one pce) .....d.h **6**
669[11] Sound Check *(58) (BJMeehan)* 2-8-11 BDoyle(3) (hdwy over 2f out: sn wknd) 1½ **8**
Latin Beauty *(56) (RHannon)* 2-8-4 (7) DaneO'Neill(10) (w'like: bit bkwd: w ldr over 3f) .....¾ **9**
La Modiste *(51) (SDow)* 2-8-11 LDettori(1) (w'like: bkwd: prom over 3f) 1½ **10**
Vera's First (IRE) *(40) (GLewis)* 2-8-11 PaulEddery(7) (neat: bit bkwd: a bhd) 3½ **11**
Wingnut (IRE) *(34) (GLewis)* 2-8-11 SWhitworth(9) (neat: s.s: a bhd) 1¾ **12**

100/30 FLYING SQUAW (2/1-7/2), **5/1** White Whispers (op 5/2), Bewitching (USA) (op 10/1), Disallowed (IRE) (op 3/1), **10/1** Honorable Estate (IRE) (5/1-12/1), Roses In The Snow (IRE), **12/1** Vera's First (IRE) (op 5/1), **20/1** Beautiful Ballad (IRE), **25/1** La Modiste, **33/1** Sound Check, **50/1** Latin Beauty, Wingnut (IRE), CSF £32.16 TOTE £3.90: £1.80 £3.40 £2.20 (£26.40) OWNER Mr Michael Foy (UPPER LAMBOURN) BRED Brook Stud Ltd 12 Rn

62.32 secs (2.52) SF: 33/31/30/27/20/18/18/13/11/6/-/-

792
TUDOR STKS (3-Y.O) (Class C) £4,958.00 (£1,808.00: £884.00: £380.00: £170.00)
1m 14y Stalls: High GOING minus 0.04 sec per fur (G) 2-35 (2-36)

Spectrum (IRE) *(110+)*(Fav)*(PWChapple-Hyam)* 3-9-4 JReid(1) (lw: 5th st: qcknd to ld on bit 2f out: r.o wl) .....— **1**
613* Sanoosea (USA) *(105) (MRStoute)* 3-9-2 WRSwinburn(5) (3rd st: nt clr run over 1f out: swtchd lft: r.o) 1½ **2**
622[3] Stiletto Blade **(110)***(102) (IABalding)* 3-9-4 LDettori(2) (4th st: rdn over 2f out: r.o) 2½ **3**
That Old Feeling (IRE) *(95) (RHannon)* 3-9-2 PatEddery(4) (led over 6f out to 2f out: wknd 1f out) 2½ **4**
*204** Peutetre *(94) (CEBrittain)* 3-9-2 BDoyle(3) (led over 1f: 2nd st: rdn over 2f out: wknd over 1f out) .....½ **5**

11/10 SPECTRUM (IRE), **9/4** Stiletto Blade, **9/2** Sanoosea (USA), **14/1** That Old Feeling (IRE), **25/1** Peutetre, CSF £5.71 TOTE £1.90: £1.30 £2.00 (£2.60) OWNER Lord Weinstock & The Hon Simon Weinstock (MARLBOROUGH) BRED Ballymacoll Stud Farm Ltd. in Ireland 5 Rn

1m 44.3 (5.10) SF: 48/43/40/33/32

793 ATHLONE RATED STKS H'CAP (0-95) (4-Y.O+) (Class B) £7,843.08 (£2,937.72: £1,438.86: £621.30: £280.65: £144.39)
1m 14y Stalls: High GOING minus 0.04 sec per fur (G) 3-05 (3-07)

665⁹ **Mr Martini (IRE) (91)***(101) (CEBrittain)* 5-9-3 MRimmer(2) (6th st: rdn 3f out: led ins fnl f: r.o wl) — 1
Air Commodore (IRE) **(90)***(99) (PFICole)* 4-9-2 CRutter(4) (hdwy over 2f out: ev ch ins fnl f: r.o) nk 2
634⁹ Show Faith (IRE) **(81)***(88) (RHannon)* 5-8-7 PatEddery(5) (3rd st: led over 1f out tl ins fnl f: unable qckn) 1 3
439² Moving Arrow **(92)***(96)*(Fav)*(MissSEHall)* 4-9-4 WRSwinburn(10) (lw: hmpd 7f out: rdn over 3f out: hdwy & n.m.r over 1f out: r.o one pce) 1¾ 4
Wilcuma **(83)***(84) (PJMakin)* 4-8-9 LDettori(3) (4th st: rdn over 2f out: nt clr run over 1f out: one pce) 1½ 5
Shanghai Venture (USA) **(81)***(81) (SPCWoods)* 4-8-0 (7) CWebb(9) (2nd st: led wl over 1f out: sn hdd: wknd fnl f) ¾ 6
714⁷ Master Beveled **(87)***(86) (PDEvans)* 5-8-13 MHills(8) (hdwy 7f out: 5th st: rdn over 3f out: hmpd over 1f out: nt rcvr) s.h 7
Aeroking (USA) **(86)***(80) (GHarwood)* 4-8-12 AClark(7) (led over 6f) 2½ 8
425⁵ Our Rita **(94)***(85) (DrJDScargill)* 6-9-6 DHarrison(1) (a bhd) 1½ 9
Lomas (IRE) **(95)***(47) (MrsHParrott)* 4-9-7 JWeaver(6) (prom 3f) 20 10
LONG HANDICAP Show Faith (IRE) 8-4 Shanghai Venture (USA) 8-6

9/2 Moving Arrow, **5/1** Wilcuma, **11/2** Our Rita, Master Beveled, **13/2** Show Faith (IRE), **7/1** Air Commodore (IRE), **10/1** MR MARTINI (IRE), **11/1** Aeroking (USA), **33/1** Shanghai Venture (USA), **50/1** Lomas (IRE), CSF £68.91 CT £441.97 TOTE £14.00: £3.20 £2.30 £1.60 (£44.50) Trio £133.10 OWNER Parrot Racing (NEWMARKET) BRED Mrs W. Hanson 10 Rn
1m 41.77 (2.57) SF: 72/70/59/67/55/52/57/51/56/18

794 SANDOWN MILE STKS (Gp 2) (4-Y.O+) (Class A) £34,250.00 (£12,743.75: £6,059.38: £2,571.87)
1m 14y Stalls: High GOING minus 0.04 sec per fur (G) 3-40 (3-41)

425³ **Missed Flight (117)***(125)*(Fav)*(CFWall)* 5-9-4 GDuffield(1) (4th st: rdn 2f out: led ins fnl f: r.o wl) — 1
609a² Ridgewood Ben *(118) (JOxx,Ireland)* 4-9-0b JPMurtagh(2) (lw: 3rd st: rdn over 2f out: r.o wl ins fnl f) 1¾ 2
Mutakddim (USA) **(111)***(117) (JHMGosden)* 4-9-0 WCarson(4) (lw: 2nd st: led over 1f out tl ins fnl f: unable qckn) ½ 3
Green Green Desert (FR) **(100)***(113) (MRStoute)* 4-9-0 WRSwinburn(6) (lw: led over 6f) 1¾ 4
425³ Alanees **(110)***(110) (CEBrittain)* 4-9-0 BDoyle(3) (5th st: a bhd) 1¾ 5

7/4 MISSED FLIGHT (op 11/10), **3/1** Green Green Desert (FR) (op 5/1), **7/2** Mutakddim (USA), **9/2** Ridgewood Ben (4/1-6/1), **12/1** Alanees, CSF £8.84 TOTE £2.30: £1.30 £2.00 (£5.00) OWNER Mr Walter Grubmuller (NEWMARKET) BRED Crest Stud Ltd 5 Rn 1m 41.09 (1.89) SF: 80/73/72/68/65

795 GUILDFORD H'CAP (0-85) (4-Y.O+) (Class D) £4,396.50 (£1,332.00: £651.00: £310.50)
2m 78y Stalls: High GOING minus 0.04 sec per fur (G) 4-10 (4-18)

506² **Smuggling (69)***(82)*(Fav)*(RAkehurst)* 4-8-11 LDettori(5) (lw: 7th st: rdn over 3f out: led over 2f out: r.o u.p) — 1
Inchcailloch (IRE) **(52)***(64) (JSKing)* 6-7-12 NCarlisle(18) (lw: hdwy over 2f out: rdn over 1f out: r.o) 1½ 2
632⁵ Lalindi (IRE) **(70)***(79) (DRCElsworth)* 4-8-12 JWilliams(2) (hld up: rdn over 3f out: r.o one pce) 2½ 3
632⁷ Wild Strawberry **(65)***(74) (MissBSanders)* 6-8-8 (3) SSanders(12) (3rd st: rdn over 3f out: one pce) nk 4
661⁴ Polo Kit (IRE) **(79)***(88) (JRFanshawe)* 4-9-7 DHarrison(9) (lw: stdy hdwy on ins over 3f out: rdn over 2f out: one pce) hd 5
741³ Head Turner **(47)***(55) (CPWildman)* 7-7-7 GBardwell(17) (hdwy over 2f out: nvr nrr) nk 6
632⁸ Stoney Valley **(74)***(81) (JRJenkins)* 5-9-6 PatEddery(7) (nvr nr to chal) 1¼ 7
623¹¹ Flight Lieutenant (USA) **(82)***(85) (RHannon)* 6-10-0 JReid(16) (nvr nrr) 4 8
632¹⁰ Chief's Song **(69)***(70) (SDow)* 5-9-1 RHughes(13) (2nd st: led over 3f out to 2f out: sn wknd) 2 9
632⁰ Stalled (IRE) **(54)***(54) (PTWalwyn)* 5-7-7 (7) MHenry(6) (lw: hdwy 11f out: 5th st: wknd over 2f out) 1¼ 10

423[23] High Five (IRE) **(57)***(55) (DAWilson)* 5-8-3 GCarter(10) (6th st: wknd over 2f out).................2½ **11**
Coleridge **(57)***(53) (JJSheehan)* 7-8-3b RPrice(1) (bit bkwd: led 13f)..2 **12**
632[15] Phil's Time **(69)***(64) (TGMills)* 4-8-11b WNewnes(11) (bhd fnl 7f)..nk **13**
Sails Legend **(51)***(45) (MrsMELong)* 4-7-7 NAdams(4) (a bhd)...1 **14**
632[14] Sheltered Cove (IRE) **(58)***(39) (KOCunningham-Brown)* 4-8-0 ow2 BDoyle(15) (b: hdwy over 6f out: wknd over 2f out)...12 **15**
Raahin (USA) **(51)***(17) (SWoodman)* 10-7-11 ow2 WCarson(3) (bhd fnl 7f)...............................15 **16**
Go South **(58)***(26) (JRJenkins)* 11-8-4 DBiggs(14) (a bhd)...hd **17**
582[8] Dakota Girl **(51)** *(GBBalding)* 4-7-2 (5) CHawksley(8) (Withdrawn not under Starter's orders: uns rdr & bolted bef s: rdr inj)... **W**

LONG HANDICAP Sails Legend 7-3 Dakota Girl 7-5

, **4/1** SMUGGLING, **5/1** Stalled (IRE), **6/1** Polo Kit (IRE), **7/1** Stoney Valley, **9/1** Inchcailloch (IRE), **12/1** Lalindi (IRE), Wild Strawberry, **14/1** Head Turner, **16/1** Flight Lieutenant (USA), **20/1** Chief's Song, **25/1** High Five (IRE), Phil's Time, Raahin (USA), **33/1** Sheltered Cove (IRE), **66/1** Go South, **100/1** Sails Legend, Coleridge, CSF £37.15 CT £369.92 TOTE £3.70: £1.40 £2.90 £2.40 £3.00 (£45.00) Trio £222.80 OWNER Mr George Taiano (EPSOM) BRED Lord Howard de Walden 17 Rn

3m 38.39 (8.39) SF: 52/38/49/48/58/29/55/59/44/28/29/27/34/15/9/-/-/-

WEIGHT FOR AGE 4yo-4lb

796

BOW STREET H'CAP (0-90) (3-Y.O+) (Class C) £5,680.00 (£1,720.00: £840.00: £400.00) **5f 6y** Stalls: Low GOING minus 0.25 sec per fur (GF) 4-45 (4-51)

693[2] **Brave Edge (86)***(89)*(Fav)*(RHannon)* 4-9-10 PatEddery(10) (nt clr run 2f out: swtchd lft & hdwy over 1f out: str run fnl f: led last strides)...................................— **1**
Sweet Magic **(74)***(76) (LJHolt)* 4-8-12 JReid(6) (lw: led: rdn over 1f out: hdd last strides)...nk **2**
636[6] Kildee Lad **(74)***(73) (APJones)* 5-8-12 BDoyle(8) (lw: a.p: rdn over 1f out: one pce).................1 **3**
565[4] Name the Tune **(73)***(70) (PHowling)* 4-8-11 PaulEddery(11) (chsd ldr tl ins fnl f: one pce)......¾ **4**
Jobie **(71)***(67) (BWHills)* 5-8-9 MHills(12) (lw: hdwy over 1f out: nvr nrr)................................s.h **5**
507[13] Followmegirls **(60)***(53) (MrsALMKing)* 6-7-12 NAdams(7) (a.p: rdn over 2f out: one pce).........1 **6**
599[2] Sue Me (IRE) **(75)***(66) (WRMuir)* 3-8-2 WCarson(2) (a.p: rdn over 2f out: one pce)................¾ **7**
723* Tenor **(66)***(53) (DNicholls)* 4-8-4 6x AlexGreaves(3) (lw: hmpd over 1f out: nvr nr to chal)...1¼ **8**
Metal Boys **(73)***(60) (MissLCSiddall)* 8-8-11 DHarrison(5) (hld up: rdn 2f out: hmpd over 1f out: one pce)...s.h **9**
693[6] Sir Joey (USA) **(85)***(71) (PGMurphy)* 6-9-4 (5) SDrowne(9) (lw: prom over 2f)..........................hd **10**
Macfarlane **(75)***(59) (MJFetherston-Godley)* 7-8-13 WRSwinburn(4) (a bhd)............................¾ **11**
398[6] Leigh Crofter **(75)***(49) (PDCundell)* 6-8-13b WNewnes(1) (b: a.p: rdn over 2f out: wkng whn hmpd over 1f out)...3 **12**

100/30 BRAVE EDGE, **5/1** Tenor, Sir Joey (USA), **11/1** Kildee Lad, Sweet Magic (op 7/1), Leigh Crofter, **12/1** Name the Tune, **14/1** Followmegirls, Jobie, Sue Me (IRE), **16/1** Macfarlane, **25/1** Metal Boys, CSF £36.29 CT £332.43 TOTE £3.10: £1.60 £2.90 £3.10 (£15.10) Trio £91.50 OWNER Mrs M. Peett (MARLBOROUGH) BRED Mrs G. A. Whent 12 Rn

60.7 secs (0.90) SF: 72/59/56/53/50/36/38/36/43/54/42/32

WEIGHT FOR AGE 3yo-11lb

STEWARDS' ENQUIRY Pat Eddery suspeneded 7-9/5/95 (careless riding).

797

APRIL MAIDEN STKS (3-Y.O F) (Class D) £4,260.00 (£1,290.00: £630.00: £300.00) **1m 2f 7y** Stalls: High GOING minus 0.04 sec per fur (G) 5-20 (5-34)

Pitcroy *(88) (JRFanshawe)* 3-8-11 DHarrison(14) (lw: hdwy over 2f out: rdn over 1f out: led last stride)..— **1**
Dawlah *(88)*(Fav)*(HThomsonJones)* 3-8-11 RHills(2) (bit bkwd: 2nd st: led 2f out: rdn over 1f out: hdd last stride)...s.h **2**
Stage Struck (IRE) *(80) (MRStoute)* 3-8-11 WRSwinburn(13) (hdwy 2f out: r.o one pce)...5 **3**
Wells Whisper (FR) *(75) (GWragg)* 3-8-7 MHills(16) (b.hind: w'like: 7th st: rdn over 2f out: one pce)..¾ **4**
Asterita *(73) (RHannon)* 3-8-11 PatEddery(8) (lw: led 8f)...3½ **5**
Kshessinskaya *(67) (GRimmer)* 3-8-7 MRimmer(12) (w'like: hdwy fnl 2f: nvr nrr)..................1¼ **6**
Elly Fleetfoot (IRE) *(69) (TGMills)* 3-8-11 WNewnes(15) (a bhd)...1½ **7**
Rainelle *(64) (CEBrittain)* 3-8-7 BDoyle(11) (w'like: bit bkwd: 6th st: wknd over 2f out)..¾ **8**
695[4] All The Time *(63) (PFICole)* 3-8-11 RHughes(7) (5th st: wknd 2f out).......................................3 **9**
Trazl (IRE) *(62) (JLDunlop)* 3-8-11 WCarson(1) (a mid div)..nk **10**
Ruby Venture *(62) (SPCWoods)* 3-8-11 MTebbutt(3) (a bhd)..nk **11**
Grey Blade *(54) (IABalding)* 3-8-11 JWeaver(10) (a bhd)..5 **12**

635[16] Lamp of Phoebus (USA) *(49) (JHMGosden)* 3-8-11 LDettori(9) (b: b.hind: a bhd) 3 **13**
Risk a Million *(45) (JRJenkins)* 3-8-11 DBiggs(5) (a bhd) 2½ **14**
Tempting (IRE) *(42) (RHannon)* 3-8-11 JReid(6) (3rd st: wkng whn hmpd over 2f out)............2 **15**
Peripatetic *(MRStoute)* 3-8-11 PaulEddery(4) (Wwithdrawn under Starter's orders: ref to enter stalls) .... **W**

, **11/4** Dawlah, **9/2** All The Time, **11/2** PITCROY, **7/1** Asterita (6/1-10/1), **8/1** Trazl (IRE), **12/1** Rainelle (op 5/1), Wells Whisper (FR) (op 6/1), **14/1** Stage Struck (IRE), **20/1** Lamp of Phoebus (USA), **33/1** Kshessinskaya, Grey Blade, Tempting (IRE), **40/1** Ruby Venture, **50/1** Risk a Million, **66/1** Elly Fleetfoot (IRE), CSF £19.44 TOTE £6.20: £1.70 £1.90 £3.80 (£13.70) OWNER Sir David Wills (NEWMARKET) 15 Rn 2m 9.32 (5.02) SF: 52/52/44/39/37/31/33/28/27/26/26/18/13/9/6/-

T/Jkpt: £7,100.00 (0.88 Tckts); £766.12 to Sandown 29/4/95. T/Plpt: £96.50 (248.81 Tckts). T/Qdpt: £50.90 (2.3 Tckts). AK

LES LANDES (L-H)
Friday April 28th (Good, Good to firm patches)

798a CHANNEL ISLANDS RACING & HUNT CLUB CENTENARY H'CAP (3-Y.O+) £1,100.00 **1m 1f**

Granache (IRE) *(MissAVibert,Jersey)* 6-8-5 VictoriaAppleby ....— **1**
Brown Fairy (USA) *(Jersey)* 7-8-8 CWebb 2 **2**
Wickins *(Jersey)* 5-10-12 AProud 4 **3**
Reality Park *(PDJones)* 4-8-8 ow3 LSuthern 8 **4**

TOTE £3.00 (£6.30) OWNER Lobster Pot Racing 2m 3.0 SF: -/-/-/-

799a SUPPORTERS' H'CAP (3-Y.O+) £720.00 **1m 4f**

Sweet Disorder (IRE) *(CPBillot,Jersey)* 5-9-7 MissSABillot ....— **1**
Riviera Rainbow *(JSOArthur,Jersey)* 7-10-1 MrAWalker 4 **2**
Fortensky (USA) *(CMcCready,Jersey)* 5-10-12 RMcGhin 3 **3**
Northreel *(GAHam)* 4-11-0 ow2 MrGDensley .... **P**

TOTE £3.20 (£4.30) (JERSEY) 2m 54.0 SF: -/-/-/-

800a ON-COURSE BOOKMAKERS' H'CAP (3-Y.O+) £720.00 **1m 110y**

Essex Girl *(CMcCready,Jersey)* 5-10-12 RMcGhin ....— **1**
Time Lapse *(Jersey)* 6-8-13 CWebb ....½ **2**
Screech *(Guernsey)* 5-8-7 ow2 LSuthern 5 **3**
503[12] Chloes Diamond (IRE) *(APJames)* 7-10-0 MissSHiggins (btn further 15½l) **5**

TOTE £2.80: £3.60 (£6.60) OWNER Mrs E. Roberts (JERSEY) 1m 55.0 SF: -/-/-/-

0703a-LONGCHAMP (Paris, France) (R-H)
Monday April 17th (Good to firm)

801a PRIX NOAILLES (Gp 2) (3-Y.O C & F) £34,844.00 **1m 3f** 2-30 (2-30)

Walk on Mix (FR) *(105) (AFabre,France)* 3-9-2 TJarnet (cl up: 2nd st: led 2f out: rdn & r.o wl fnl f)....................— **1**
Solar One (FR) *(JEPease,France)* 3-9-2 CAsmussen (4th st: hdwy to chal 1f out: no ex cl home).................... **2**
Poliglote *(MmeCHead,France)* 3-9-2 FHead (hld up & plld hrd: last st: rdn 2f out: sme hdwy: too much to do)....................2 **3**
Peckinpah's Soul (FR) *(DSmaga,France)* 3-9-2 PMarion (prom: 3rd st: rdn over 2f out: styd on one pce)....................¾ **4**
Farenvaros *(PDemercastel,France)* 3-9-2 OPeslier (5th st: nvr nrr)....................1½ **5**
Sea Gone (USA) *(MmeCHead,France)* 3-9-2 ODoleuze (set gd pce: hdd 2f out: wknd) 10 **6**

P-M 3.70f: 2.00f 1.90f SF: 12.30f OWNER Mr J-L. Lagardere (FRANCE) 6 Rn 2m 18.7 SF: -/-/-/-/-
DS

0704a-SAINT-CLOUD (France) (L-H)
Tuesday April 18th (Good)

802a PRIX PENELOPE (Gp 3) (3-Y.O F)
1m 2f 110y

Muncie (IRE) *(91) (AFabre,France)* 3-9-2 OPeslier ....— 1
Loretta Gianni (FR) *(89) (DSmaga,France)* 3-9-2 GGuignard 1½ 2
Valley of Gold (FR) *(86) (AFabre,France)* 3-9-2 TJarnet 1½ 3
OWNER Mr D. Wildenstein (FRANCE) 2m 21.3 SF: -/-/-

0609a-CURRAGH (Newbridge, Ireland) (R-H)
Saturday April 22nd (Good to soft)

803a LEXUS TETRARCH (Gp 3) (3-Y.O C & F) £16,250.00
7f 3-30 (3-48)

Desert Style (IRE) *(104) (JSBolger,Ireland)* 3-8-6 KJManning (trckd ldr: rdn to ld over 1f out: r.o) ....— 1
Nautical Pet (IRE) *(104) (DKWeld,Ireland)* 3-8-6 PShanahan (hld up in tch: nt clr run tl wl ins fnl f: fin fast) ....hd 2
Burden Of Proof (IRE) *(110)*(Fav)*(CO'Brien,Ireland)* 3-8-12 CRoche (trckd ldrs: hmpd 5f out: ev ch 2f out: r.o) ....s.h 3
Charillus *(103) (JOxx,Ireland)* 3-8-6 MJKinane (led tl over 1f out: r.o) ....hd 4
Sannkaya (IRE) *(98) (JOxx,Ireland)* 3-8-4 ow1 PVGilson (hld up: effrt over 1f out: sn ev ch: no ex nr fin) 1 5
Sir Silver Sox (USA) *(101) (TStack,Ireland)* 3-8-6 WJSupple (hld up in tch: ev ch over 1f out: rdn & no ex ins fnl f) ....s.h 6
7/4 Burden Of Proof (IRE), **4/1** Charillus, Sannkaya (IRE), **5/1** DESERT STYLE (IRE), **12/1** Nautical Pet (IRE), Sir Silver Sox (USA), CSF £45.34: TOTE £5.50: £2.60 £6.90 (£80.50) OWNER Maktoum Al Maktoum (IRELAND) BRED Ovidstown Investments Ltd 6 Rn 1m 29.9 (6.70) SF: -/-/-/-/-/-

804a ATHASI (Listed) (3 & 4-Y.O F) £9,675.00
7f 5-00 (5-20)

Ridgewood Pearl *(101) (JOxx,Ireland)* 3-8-12 JPMurtagh ....— 1
One False Move (IRE) *(80) (CCollins,Ireland)* 4-9-7 PVGilson 7 2
Bawader (USA) *(80) (DKWeld,Ireland)* 3-8-7 MJKinane ....hd 3
CSF £11.91 TOTE £1.60: £1.10 £2.50 £1.70 (£17.00) OWNER Mrs Anne Coughlan BRED S. Coughlan 1m 27.5 (4.30) SF: -/-/- NR

FUCHU (Tokyo, Japan) (L-H)
Saturday April 22nd (Firm)

805a KEIO HAI SPRING CUP (Gp 2) (4-Y.O+) £392,466.00
7f 7-40

Dumaani (USA) *(118) (KMcLaughlin,Dubai)* 4-8-12 RHills ....— 1
Biko Alpha (JPN) *(119) (Japan)* 5-9-0 EOtsuka ....nk 2
Hokuto Vega (JPN) *(118) (Japan)* 5-9-0 NYokoyama ....½ 3
Emperor Jones (USA) *(120) (SbinSuroor)* 5-9-2 MRoberts ....nk 4
Heart Lake *(114) (SbinSuroor)* 4-8-12 YTake ....½ 5
Erin Bird (FR) *(106) (PWChapple-Hyam)* 4-8-10 MEbina (btn more than 4l by wnr).................. 13
5,690y: 1,720y 1,010y 920y (86,670y) OWNER Sheikh Hamdan Al Maktoum (DUBAI) BRED Shadwell Farm Inc 1m 21.3 SF: -/-/-/-/-/-

0801a-LONGCHAMP (Paris, France) (R-H)
Sunday April 23rd (Soft)

806a PRIX DE FONTAINEBLEAU (Gp 3) (3-Y.O C) £26,347.00
1m 1-55 (1-53)

Atticus (USA) *(112?) (MmeCHead,France)* 3-9-2 ODoleuze ....— 1
Petit Poucet *(109?) (NClement,France)* 3-9-2 CAsmussen 1½ 2

Kirdoun (FR) *(105?) (ELellouche,France)* 3-9-2 DBoeuf 2 3

P-M 6.00f: 1.60f 1.10f SF: 14.20f OWNER Mr J. Wertheimer (FRANCE) 1m 43.1 SF: -/-/-

807a PRIX DE LA GROTTE (Gp 3) (3-Y.O F) £26,347.00
1m 2-55 (2-58)

Matiara (USA) *(109) (MmeCHead,France)* 3-9-2 FHead ....— 1
Shaanxi (USA) *(108) (ELellouche,France)* 3-9-2 OPeslier ....nk 2
Carling (FR) *(106) (MmePBarbe,France)* 3-9-2 SGuillot 1 3

P-M: 7.80f: 1.70f 1.10f 1.70f SF: 8.20 OWNER Ecurie Aland (FRANCE) BRED Societe Aland 3 Rn
1m 48.4 SF: -/-/-

808a PRIX GREFFULHE (Gp 2) (3-Y.O C & F) £44,653.00
1m 2f 110y 3-25 (3-28)

Diamond Mix (IRE) *(105) (AFabre,France)* 3-9-2 TJarnet (4th st: hdwy to ld over 1f out: drew clr: eased nr fin: impressive) ....— 1
Angel Falls (FR) *(97) (AFabre,France)* 3-9-2 SGuillot (a.p: 3rd st: rdn over 2f out: outpcd: r.o cl home) 5 2
Denver County (USA) *(95) (JEHammond,France)* 3-9-2 CAsmussen (5th st: hdwy over 2f out: wandered u.p 1f out: kpt on one pce ins fnl f) 1½ 3
488a[2] Tzar Rodney (FR) *(95) (GDoleuze,France)* 3-9-2 ODoleuze (2nd st: effrt to ld over 2f out: hdd over 1f out: one pce) ....nk 4
Tec's Champ (IRE) *(86) (DSmaga,France)* 3-9-2 FHead (hld up: last st: sme late hdwy: nvr trbld ldrs) 6 5
Ghayabik (FR) *(79) (AFabre,France)* 3-9-2 TGillet (set gd pce: hdd over 2f out: wknd) 4 6
Ami Bleu (FR) *(64) (PDemercastel,France)* 3-9-2 OPeslier (prom early: rdn over 3f out: 6th st: sn bhd) 10 7

P-M 1.50f (cpld): 1.10f 1.90f SF: 6.80f OWNER Mr J-L. Lagardere (FRANCE) 7 Rn 2m 21.5
DS

0710a-CAPANNELLE (Rome, Italy) (R-H)
Sunday April 23rd (Good to firm)

809a PREMIO REGINA ELENA (Gp 2) (3-Y.O F) £41,982.00
1m 3-30 (3-33)

Olimpia Dukakis (ITY) *(90) (GBotti,Italy)* 3-8-11 GForte ....— 1
551* Baaderah (IRE) *(88) (LMCumani)* 3-8-11 LDettori 1 2
Love Secret (USA) *(80) (Italy)* 3-8-11 BJovine 4 3

TOTE 15L: 11L 13L 12L (28L) OWNER Scuderia Siba (ITALY) BRED Scuderia Siba in Italy 3 Rn
1m 39.1 SF: -/-/-

0547-LEICESTER (R-H)
Saturday April 29th (Good to firm)
WEATHER: dull WIND: slt across

810 E.B.F WILLOUGHBY MEDIAN AUCTION MAIDEN STKS (2-Y.O) (Class F) £3,106.00 (£928.00: £444.00: £202.00)
5f 2y Stalls: High GOING minus 0.28 sec per fur (GF) 2-00 (2-01)

South Salem (USA) *(65+t)*(Fav)*(DRLoder)* 2-9-0 GCarter(8) (w'like: s.i.s: hld up: rdn ½-wy: str run to ld nr fin) ....— 1
Aussie *(63) (MHTompkins)* 2-9-0 PRobinson(4) (leggy: lt-f: sn outpcd & bhd: hdwy wl over 1f out: ev ch ins fnl f: r.o) ....¾ 2
533[5] Pleasure Time *(62) (CSmith)* 2-9-0 JFortune(5) (led: rdn clr appr fnl f: hdd cl home) ....nk 3
Astral's Chance *(55) (KRBurke)* 2-9-0 MFenton(10) (w'like: bit bkwd: chsd ldr: rdn over 1f out: r.o one pce) 2 4
561[7] Heights of Love *(46) (MSSaunders)* 2-8-9 RPrice(1) (plld hrd: prom: rdn 2f out: r.o one pce) 1½ 5
Key To A Million (IRE) *(43) (RHannon)* 2-8-9 JReid(2) (leggy: lt-f: s.i.s: hld up: styd on appr fnl f: nt trble ldrs) ....¾ 6
Welville *(47) (PJMakin)* 2-9-0 TQuinn(7) (leggy: unf: s.i.s: hdwy ½-wy: rdn & hmpd wl over 1f out: n.d) ....½ 7

Silverdale Knight *(46) (KWHogg)* 2-8-7 (7) ADaly(12) (unf: bkwd: sn outpcd & bhd) ....s.h 8
615 14 Topaglow (IRE) *(40) (PTDalton)* 2-9-0 RCochrane(9) (chsd ldrs: rdn wl over 1f out: sn btn) 2 9
554 3 Ghostly Apparition *(37) (JohnUpson)* 2-9-0 KFallon(6) (chsd ldrs: rdn 2f out: sn wknd) 1 10
Dorspring (IRE) *(26) (CEBrittain)* 2-9-0 MRimmer(3) (cmpt: prom 3f) 3½ 11
Foreman *(13) (WAO'Gorman)* 2-9-0 EmmaO'Gorman(11) (w'like: bit bkwd: chsd ldrs 3f)........4 12

7/4 SOUTH SALEM (USA), **5/1** Welville (7/1-4/1), **15/2** Pleasure Time, **8/1** Foreman (6/1-10/1), Key To A Million (IRE), **12/1** Dorspring (IRE) (op 6/1), **14/1** Aussie, **33/1** Silverdale Knight, Topaglow (IRE), Ghostly Apparition, Astral's Chance, Heights of Love, CSF £22.46 TOTE £1.90: £1.10 £3.40 £2.00 (£17.90) Trio £92.90 OWNER Mrs Virginia KraftPayson (NEWMARKET) BRED Virginia Kraft Payson 12 Rn
63.4 secs (4.90) SF: -/-/-/-/-/-/-/-/-/-/-/-

811 SIX HILLS H'CAP (0-80) (3-Y.O+) (Class D) £4,104.10 (£1,226.80: £587.40: £267.70)
1m 3f 183y Stalls: High GOING minus 0.28 sec per fur (GF) 2-30 (2-31)

Cherrington (70)*(85) (GWragg)* 3-7-13 FNorton(8) (lw: chsd ldrs: 4th st: led over 1f out: edgd lft ins fnl f: rdn out) ....— 1
Midyan Blue (IRE) **(67)***(79) (JMPEustace)* 5-9-3 RCochrane(3) (bit bkwd: led 1f: 2nd st: ev ch over 1f out: unable qckn) 2½ 2
Farringdon Hill **(74)***(84) (MajorWRHern)* 4-9-9b PaulEddery(4) (a.p: 5th st: outpcd 3f out: styd on u.p ins fnl f) 1¼ 3
549 2 Slmaat **(73)***(82) (MrsMReveley)* 4-9-8 TQuinn(13) (hld up in tch: 7th st: rdn over 2f out: styd on same pce appr fnl f) ....¾ 4
653 6 Un Parfum de Femme (IRE) **(69)***(77)*(Fav)*(JPearce)* 4-9-4 GBardwell(9) (hld up: 8th st: hdwy over 3f out: styd on ins fnl f) 1 5
558 8 Faal Mario (USA) **(79)***(84) (MrsJRRamsden)* 4-10-0 KFallon(1) (hld up: styd on appr fnl f: nvr plcd to chal) 1¾ 6
634 3 Benfleet **(78)***(83)*(Fav)*(RWArmstrong)* 4-9-13 RPrice(7) (hld up: hdwy & 6th st: led wl over 1f out: sn rdn & hdd: no ex) ....nk 7
549* Cliburnel News (IRE) **(58)***(59) (ALForbes)* 5-8-8 PRobinson(6) (trckd ldrs: 3rd st: led over 2f out tl over 1f out: sn btn) 3 8
246 2 Stevie's Wonder (IRE) **(58)***(58) (MJRyan)* 5-8-8 GCarter(12) (hld up: n.d) ....½ 9
757 9 Kinoko **(51)***(46) (KWHogg)* 7-7-8 (7)ow3 ADaly(10) (hld up: effrt over 3f out: grad wknd) 1½ 10
584 9 Ismeno **(68)***(59) (SDow)* 4-9-3 DHarrison(5) (hld up: hdwy over 3f out: sn rdn & wknd)............5 11
632 19 Triple Tie (USA) **(70)***(52) (MBlanshard)* 4-9-5 JReid(2) (led after 1f: rdn & hdd over 2f out: wknd over 1f out) 7 12
423 20 Sunderland Echo **(77)***(18) (MrsMReveley)* 6-9-13 JFortune(11) (stumbled bdly s: a wl bhd: t.o) 30 13

9/2 Benfleet, Un Parfum de Femme (IRE), **13/2** Stevie's Wonder (IRE), **7/1** Farringdon Hill (op 14/1), **8/1** Slmaat (op 5/1), **9/1** CHERRINGTON, **10/1** Cliburnel News (IRE), **14/1** Midyan Blue (IRE), **16/1** Faal Mario (USA), Sunderland Echo, Ismeno, **20/1** Triple Tie (USA), **25/1** Kinoko, CSF £117.92 CT £857.70 TOTE £12.60: £2.70 £2.80 £2.50 (£44.80) Trio £206.30 OWNER Sheikh Mohammed (NEWMARKET) BRED Sheikh Mohammed bin Rashid al Maktoum 13 Rn
2m 35.4 (6.60) SF: 18/33/37/35/30/37/36/13/12/-/12/5/-
WEIGHT FOR AGE 3yo-21lb, 4yo-1lb

812 BUTLER H'CAP (0-85) (3-Y.O+) (Class D) £4,205.50 (£1,258.00: £603.00: £275.50)
5f 218y Stalls: High GOING minus 0.28 sec per fur (GF) 3-00 (3-02)

611 4 **The Old Chapel (60)***(66) (BAMcMahon)* 6-8-3b FNorton(11) (mde virtually all: edgd rt fnl f: all out) ....— 1
559 3 Tatika **(70)***(75) (GWragg)* 5-8-6 (7) DGibbs(4) (chsd ldrs: rdn 2f out: r.o wl cl home) ....½ 2
702 11 First Gold **(63)***(66) (JWharton)* 6-8-6 PRobinson(13) (hld up: hdwy 2f out: r.o cl home)...........¾ 3
636 4 Yet More Roses **(70)***(73)*(Fav)*(LadyHerries)* 4-8-13 TIves(15) (b.hind: racd alone far side: rdn over 1f out: kpt on ins fnl f) ....s.h 4
386 8 Macs Maharanee **(76)***(74) (PSFelgate)* 8-9-5 GHind(5) (mid div: rdn over 1f out: r.o ins fnl f) 1¾ 5
567 5 Jigsaw Boy **(65)***(60) (PGMurphy)* 6-8-8 DHarrison(14) (hld up: hdwy over 1f out: no imp fnl f) 1 6
621 10 Gallows Corner (IRE) **(85)***(80) (RHannon)* 3-9-2 JReid(10) (hld up: hdwy 2f out: no ex appr fnl f) ....hd 7
723 10 Cradle Days **(70)***(64) (RCSpicer)* 6-8-13 JO'Reilly(6) (chsd ldrs: rdn over 1f out: no ex).........nk 8
636 9 How's Yer Father **(85)***(74) (RJHodges)* 9-10-0 PaulEddery(9) (outpcd: hdwy over 1f out: nt rch ldrs) 1¾ 9

723[15] Just Bob **(80)***(66) (SEKettlewell)* 6-9-9 JFortune(2) (uns rdr bef s: s.i.s: hld up: nvr nrr) 1¼ **10**
Manor Adventure **(57)***(32) (PTDalton)* 5-7-7 (7) JBramhill(8) (prom: rdn over 1f out: wknd fnl f) 4 **11**
Bezirgan **(50)***(25) (JAkehurst)* 4-7-7 GBardwell(3) (mid div: rdn ½-wy: sn btn) .... nk **12**
646[8] Captain Carat **(62)***(31) (MrsJRRamsden)* 4-8-5 KFallon(7) (chsd ldrs: rdn 2f out: sn btn) 2 **13**
535[4] Sailormaite **(74)***(11) (SRBowring)* 4-9-3 SWebster(1) (chsd ldrs: rdn 2f out: sn wknd & eased) 12 **14**
Aughfad **(71)** *(MrsMMcCourt)* 9-8-7b(7) RStudholme(12) (bkwd: prom to ½-wy) 11 **15**

LONG HANDICAP Bezirgan 7-1

9/4 Yet More Roses, **6/1** Sailormaite, **8/1** Gallows Corner (IRE), **9/1** Captain Carat (op 5/1), Tatika, THE OLD CHAPEL, **12/1** First Gold, Jigsaw Boy, **14/1** How's Yer Father (10/1-16/1), **20/1** Aughfad, **25/1** Macs Maharanee, Just Bob, **33/1** Bezirgan, Manor Adventure, Cradle Days, CSF £84.73 CT £897.05 TOTE £12.80: £3.00 £2.80 £8.20 (£26.50) Trio £103.20 OWNER Mr D. J. Allen (TAMWORTH) BRED Roldvale Ltd 15 Rn 1m 11.7 (1.70) SF: 40/49/40/47/48/34/42/38/48/40/6/-/5/-/-

WEIGHT FOR AGE 3yo-12lb

OFFICIAL EXPLANATION Sailormaite: no explanation could be offered for his poor performance.

813

SAFFRON H'CAP (0-80) (3-Y.O) (Class D) £4,509.70 (£1,351.60: £649.80: £298.90) **1m 8y** Stalls: High GOING minus 0.28 sec per fur (GF) 3-30 (3-31)

Hardy Dancer (74)*(76) (GLMoore)* 3-9-1 BRouse(11) (hld up: hdwy over 2f out: led over 1f out: rdn out) .... — **1**
640[2] Shinerolla **(62)***(63)*(Fav)*(MrsJRRamsden)* 3-8-3 KFallon(13) (s.s: hld up: hdwy over 1f out: r.o u.p nr fin) .... ½ **2**
566[7] Yoush (IRE) **(79)***(76) (MAJarvis)* 3-9-6 PRobinson(12) (chsd ldrs: led 2f out: rdn & hdd over 1f out: unable qckn) 2 **3**
Mihriz (IRE) **(80)***(76) (MajorWRHern)* 3-9-7 PaulEddery(10) (hld up in tch: effrt over 1f out: unable qckn) .... ½ **4**
573[2] Blaze of Song **(63)***(55) (RHannon)* 3-8-4 TQuinn(2) (led stands' side: rdn over 1f out: one pce) 2 **5**
Wandering Minstrel (IRE) **(60)***(48) (JMPEustace)* 3-8-1 GCarter(14) (bit bkwd: prom: rdn over 1f out: r.o one pce) 2 **6**
621[5] Astral Invader (IRE) **(71)***(58) (MSSaunders)* 3-8-12 RPrice(16) (prom: rdn & ev ch 2f out: one pce appr fnl f) .... ½ **7**
618[15] Bellas Gate Boy **(71)***(58) (MissHCKnight)* 3-8-12 BThomson(4) (w ldrs: rdn 2f out: no ex) .... s.h **8**
Mariposa Grove **(56)***(40) (RCurtis)* 3-7-11 GBardwell(5) (bhd & rdn ½-wy: styd on appr fnl f: nrst fin) 1½ **9**
Shining Example **(70)***(53) (PJMakin)* 3-8-11 RPerham(3) (chsd ldrs over 6f) .... ¾ **10**
390[4] Noble Neptune **(60)***(39) (WJMusson)* 3-8-1 GHind(9) (hld up: n.d) 2 **11**
El Don **(67)***(39) (MJRyan)* 3-8-8 DBiggs(18) (bit bkwd: nvr trbld ldrs) 3½ **12**
648[6] Delightful Dancer (IRE) **(62)***(31) (BWHills)* 3-8-3 DHarrison(7) (hld up & plld hrd: rdn over 2f out: sn btn) 1¼ **13**
333[5] Water Hazard (IRE) **(57)***(12) (SDow)* 3-7-12 FNorton(1) (n.d) 7 **14**
Euphyllia **(56)***(7) (BobJones)* 3-7-4 (7)ow4 SLanigan(15) (mid div: effrt over 2f out: sn btn) .... s.h **15**
276[5] Just Lucky (IRE) **(65)***(18) (RWArmstrong)* 3-8-6 JReid(8) (led centre 6f: wknd over 1f out) 1 **16**
Divina Mia **(75)***(27) (JWHills)* 3-8-9 (7) MHenry(6) (mid div: rdn over 2f out: sn wknd) .... nk **17**
384[6] Good so Fa (IRE) **(59)***(11) (CNAllen)* 3-7-9 (5) MBaird(17) (hld up & a bhd) .... nk **18**

LONG HANDICAP Euphyllia 7-5

3/1 Shinerolla, **9/2** Blaze of Song, **9/1** Bellas Gate Boy (14/1-8/1), **10/1** HARDY DANCER, Delightful Dancer (IRE), Shining Example, **12/1** Divina Mia (op 20/1), **14/1** Wandering Minstrel (IRE), Mihriz (IRE), Astral Invader (IRE), **16/1** Yoush (IRE), **20/1** Just Lucky (IRE), El Don, **25/1** Good so Fa (IRE), **33/1** Euphyllia, Noble Neptune, Water Hazard (IRE), Mariposa Grove, CSF £41.13 CT £461.38 TOTE £10.90: £2.30 £1.80 £5.60 £3.50 (£44.50) Trio £189.90 OWNER Mr K. Higson (EPSOM) BRED K. Higson 18Rn 1m 36.7 (1.70) SF: 58/45/58/58/37/30/40/40/22/35/21/21/13/-/-/-/9

814

LEICESTERSHIRE STKS (Listed) (4-Y.O+) (Class A) £12,139.20 (£4,492.80: £2,156.40: £882.00: £351.00: £138.60) **7f 9y** Stalls: High GOING minus 0.28 sec per fur (GF) 4-05 (4-06)

Young Ern (116)*(125) (SDow)* 5-9-6 TQuinn(6) (hld up: hdwy over 2f out: led ins fnl f: comf) .... — **1**
Mistle Cat (USA) **(104)***(116) (SPCWoods)* 5-8-12 WWoods(8) (led: rdn over 1f out: hdd & unable qckn ins fnl f) .... ½ **2**
Hever Golf Rose **(109)***(101) (TJNaughton)* 4-8-11 DHolland(5) (w ldr: ev ch wl over 1f out: sn outpcd) 6 **3**

6598 Branston Abby (IRE) **(105)***(97) (MJohnston)* 6-8-11 JReid(1) (trckd ldrs: outpcd over 2f out: r.o ins fnl f)....1¾ **4**
652* Star Talent (USA) **(110)***(95)*(Fav)*(DRCElsworth)* 4-8-12 PaulEddery(7) (hld up: hdwy over 2f out: no ex appr fnl f)....1½ **5**
6522 Cool Jazz **(105)***(92) (CEBrittain)* 4-8-12 MRimmer(2) (lw: chsd ldrs: rdn over 2f out: sn btn)....1¼ **6**
6658 Band on the Run **(88)***(90) (BAMcMahon)* 8-8-12 JFortune(4) (chsd ldrs: rdn 2f out: sn outpcd)....1 **7**
6656 Moccasin Run (USA) **(103)***(86) (IABalding)* 4-8-12 RCochrane(3) (hld up: a bhd)....1¾ **8**

2/1 Star Talent (USA), **4/1** YOUNG ERN, **7/1** Mistle Cat (USA) (5/1-8/1), **8/1** Moccasin Run (USA), Cool Jazz (op 12/1), **9/1** Hever Golf Rose (5/1-10/1), **11/1** Branston Abby (IRE) (8/1-14/1), **25/1** Band on the Run, CSF £27.59 TOTE £4.10: £1.30 £2.40 £3.10 (£10.60) OWNER Mr M. F. Kentish (EPSOM) BRED M. F. Kentish 8 Rn 1m 21.5 (-1.00) SF: 93/84/69/65/63/60/58/54

815

REDMILE MAIDEN STKS (I) (3-Y.O+) (Class D) £4,137.90 (£914.90: £914.90: £270.30)
1m 1f 218y Stalls: High GOING minus 0.28 sec per fur (GF) 4-40 (4-44)

6782 **In Camera (IRE) (80)***(92)*(Fav)*(MRStoute)* 3-8-6 JReid(10) (hld up: hdwy & 7th st: led over 2f out: sn clr)....— **1**
6705 Horesti *(81) (CEBrittain)* 3-8-6 MRimmer(13) (prom: 6th st: led wl over 2f out: sn hdd & outpcd)....d.h **2**
Roufontaine *(76) (WRMuir)* 4-9-5 DHolland(3) (a.p: 5th st: rdn & ev ch 2f out: sn outpcd)....7 **2**
6737 Saleel (IRE) *(79) (ACStewart)* 3-8-1 (5) MHumphries(12) (bhd: hdwy over 3f out: one pce fnl 2f)....1 **4**
Desert Spring *(79) (PWHarris)* 3-8-6 RCochrane(4) (hld up: 8th st: hdwy over 3f out: sn rdn: styd on same pce)....hd **5**
George Bull *(79) (MajorWRHern)* 3-8-6 PaulEddery(11) (leggy: unf: led 1f: 3rd st: wknd 2f out)....nk **6**
6356 High Patriarch (IRE) *(71) (JLDunlop)* 3-8-6 GCarter(2) (hld up: effrt over 3f out: n.d)....5 **7**
Innocence *(65) (GWragg)* 3-8-1 FNorton(1) (chsd ldr: 2nd st: wknd over 1f out)....nk **8**
Alzoomo (IRE) *(67) (HRACecil)* 3-8-6 AMcGlone(8) (lt-f: prom over 5f)....2 **9**
6735 Turnpole (IRE) *(66) (MrsMReveley)* 4-9-10 JFortune(5) (hld up: a in rr)....nk **10**
Tajar (USA) **(75)***(64) (DMorley)* 3-8-6 BThomson(6) (bit bkwd: chsd ldrs: 4th st: wknd over 2f out)....1¾ **11**
Remaadi Sun *(62) (JHMGosden)* 3-8-6 GHind(9) (b.hind: leggy: scope: hld up: effrt 3f out: sn wknd)....1¼ **12**
Lord Palmerston (USA) *(60) (PFICole)* 3-8-6 TQuinn(7) (swtg: led 9f out tl wl over 2f out: sn wknd)....1¼ **13**

8/13 IN CAMERA (IRE), **7/1** Horesti, **8/1** Alzoomo (IRE) (6/1-10/1), **12/1** High Patriarch (IRE) (7/1-14/1), **14/1** Remaadi Sun (8/1-16/1), **20/1** Lord Palmerston (USA), Tajar (USA), **25/1** Desert Spring, George Bull, **33/1** Innocence, Saleel (IRE), Roufontaine, Turnpole (IRE), CSF IC & R £13.69, IC & H £3.20 TOTE £1.40: £1.10 R £7.80 H £1.60 (IC & R £18.50, IC & H £2.20) Trio £35.50 OWNER Sheikh Mohammed (NEWMARKET) BRED Swettenham Stud 13 Rn
2m 6.6 (3.90) SF: 36/25/38/23/23/23/15/9/11/28/8/6/4
WEIGHT FOR AGE 3yo-18lb

816

REDMILE MAIDEN STKS (II) (3-Y.O+) (Class D) £4,137.90 (£1,237.20: £592.60: £270.30)
1m 1f 218y Stalls: High GOING minus 0.28 sec per fur (GF) 5-10 (5-11)

6732 **Godwin (USA)** *(81)*(Fav)*(HRACecil)* 4-9-5 AMcGlone(8) (chsd ldrs: 5th st: rdn over 1f out: led ins fnl f: r.o)....— **1**
Hagwah (USA) **(80)***(81) (BHanbury)* 3-8-1 PaulEddery(1) (prom: 6th st: rdn & ev ch ins fnl f: kpt on)....nk **2**
Haniya (IRE) *(79) (JLDunlop)* 3-8-1 DHarrison(6) (hld up: hdwy over 2f out: r.o cl home)....1 **3**
Sahil (IRE) *(83) (DMorley)* 3-8-6 BThomson(7) (w'like: scope: chsd ldrs: 3rd st: led over 3f out: hdd & unable qckn ins fnl f)....nk **4**
Persian Saint (IRE) *(80) (DRCElsworth)* 4-9-5 (5) AProcter(10) (led tl over 3f out: wknd over 1f out)....2 **5**
5846 Chahaya Timor (IRE) *(72) (PFICole)* 3-8-6 TQuinn(5) (mid div: 7th st: wknd over 2f out)....5 **6**
Discorsi *(71) (GWragg)* 3-7-13 (7) DGibbs(12) (lt-f: chsd ldr: 2nd st: rdn & wknd 2f out)....¾ **7**
Sayyed Alraqs (USA) *(69) (MAJarvis)* 3-8-6 PRobinson(11) (w'like: prom: 4th st: wknd over 2f out)....1½ **8**

673[3] Sugar Mill *(65) (MrsMReveley)* 5-9-10 JFortune(3) (hld up: effrt over 3f out: n.d)....2 9
Menshaar (USA) *(60) (JHMGosden)* 3-8-6 GHind(2) (w'like: scope: bit bkwd: mid div: rdn 5f out: wknd wl over 2f out)....3½ 10
677[8] Time Leader *(60) (MRStoute)* 3-8-6 DHolland(9) (plld hrd: hld up: hdwy over 3f out: wknd over 2f out)....s.h 11
Shepherds Rest (IRE) *(50) (SMellor)* 3-8-6 TSprake(4) (hld up: swvd lft 3f out: a in rr)....6 12

2/1 GODWIN (USA) (5/4-9/4), **5/2** Hagwah (USA), **7/1** Time Leader, **9/1** Chahaya Timor (IRE), **10/1** Haniya (IRE) (4/1-11/1), **12/1** Discorsi, Sugar Mill (op 88/1), Menshaar (USA) (op 4/1), **16/1** Sayyed Alraqs (USA), **25/1** Persian Saint (IRE), Sahil (IRE), **50/1** Shepherds Rest (IRE), CSF £8.11 TOTE £2.00: £2.00 £1.50 £6.70 (£3.80) Trio Not won; £62.98 to 1/5/95 OWNER Sheikh Mohammed (NEWMARKET) BRED Golden Gate Stud & Henri Mastey 12 Rn

2m 7.2 (4.50) SF: 44/26/24/28/43/17/16/14/28/5/5/-

WEIGHT FOR AGE 3yo-18lb

817

SPRING H'CAP (0-70) (3-Y.O+) (Class E) £3,731.20 (£1,117.60: £536.80: £246.40)
1m 1f 218y Stalls: High GOING minus 0.28 sec per fur (GF) 5-40 (5-42)

Bold Look (56)*(67) (PWHarris)* 4-9-0 DHolland(18) (chsd ldr: 2nd st: rdn over 2f out: styd on to ld last strides)....— 1
Porte Belloch **(41)***(52) (CTNash)* 4-7-13 ATucker(16) (led: rdn over 2f out: hdd cl home)....nk 2
550[13] Rock The Barney (IRE) **(47)***(54) (PBurgoyne)* 6-8-2 (3) DRMcCabe(5) (hld up: hdwy over 2f out: styd on ins fnl f: nt rch ldrs)....2½ 3
*66** South Eastern Fred **(62)***(67) (HJCollingridge)* 4-9-6 MRimmer(8) (chsd ldrs: 3rd st: rdn 2f out: styd on same pce)....1 4
Plinth **(49)***(52) (NAGraham)* 4-8-7 PaulEddery(9) (hld up: hdwy u.p over 2f out: nvr able to chal)....1½ 5
Tony's Fen **(76)***(77) (DRCElsworth)* 6-10-1 (5) AProcter(10) (b.hind: hld up: hdwy over 3f out: nt pce to chal)....¾ 6
485[6] Rushaway **(64)***(65) (RHannon)* 4-9-8 RPerham(19) (hld up in tch: 6th st: rdn over 2f out: sn btn)....s.h 7
592[9] Glitter of Gold **(60)***(61) (SCWilliams)* 4-9-1 (3) DWright(13) (nvr trbld ldrs)....s.h 8
778[6] Parish Walk (IRE) **(43)***(44) (KWHogg)* 4-7-8 (7) ADaly(4) (prom: lost pl ½-wy: styd on appr fnl f)....nk 9
605[3] Mazirah **(56)***(56) (PJMakin)* 4-9-0 TQuinn(6) (hld up: effrt over 3f out: n.d)....nk 10
505[3] Pink Brief (IRE) **(61)***(59) (MJRyan)* 4-9-0 (5) MBaird(15) (s.i.s: hld up: hdwy over 2f out: sn rdn & btn)....1¼ 11
548[9] Export Mondial **(47)***(44) (PBurgoyne)* 5-8-5 BRouse(17) (nvr nrr)....1 12
Inderaputeri **(60)***(56) (MissGayKelleway)* 5-9-4 RCochrane(2) (dwlt: hdwy 6f out: 4th st: wknd 3f out)....½ 13
676[8] Bescaby Boy **(57)***(48)*(Fav)*(JWharton)* 9-9-1 MBirch(7) (prom: 8th st: rdn over 3f out: sn btn) .3 14
Jairzinho (USA) **(65)***(46) (PHayward)* 6-9-9 SRaymont(14) (bkwd: prom: 7th st: rdn & wknd 3f out)....6 15
Cracking Prospect **(53)***(34) (BRMillman)* 4-8-11 JReid(3) (prom over 5f)....s.h 16
Catawampus **(43)** *(CJames)* 4-8-1 ow1 RPrice(12) (a in rr)....25 17
403[8] Telephus **(41)** *(BJMcMath)* 6-7-13 GBardwell(11) (bhd fnl 3f)....hd 18

9/2 Bescaby Boy, **5/1** Tony's Fen, **6/1** South Eastern Fred, **7/1** Pink Brief (IRE), **8/1** Rock The Barney (IRE) (op 16/1), **10/1** Mazirah, **11/1** Cracking Prospect, **12/1** Telephus (op 8/1), **14/1** Inderaputeri, **16/1** Plinth, **20/1** Rushaway, **25/1** BOLD LOOK, Jairzinho (USA), Glitter of Gold, Porte Belloch, **33/1** Export Mondial, Catawampus, Parish Walk (IRE), CSF £507.96 CT £4,856.35 TOTE £28.10: £4.10 £6.50 £3.60 £2.60 (£690.90) Trio Not won; £139.71 to 1/5/95 OWNER The Bold Team (BERKHAMSTED) BRED S. Wingfield Digby 18 Rn

2m 8.3 (5.60) SF: 31/16/18/31/16/41/29/25/8/20/23/8/20/12/10/-/-/-

T/Plpt: £450.30 (31.52 Tckts). T/Qdpt: £45.80 (0.2 Tckts); £49.52 to 1/5/95 CR

0684-RIPON (R-H)
Saturday April 29th (Good to firm)

WEATHER: overcast WIND: mod half bhd

818

ALDBOROUGH (S) STKS (3-Y.O+) (Class F) £2,970.00 (£900.00: £440.00: £210.00)
1m 2f Stalls: High GOING minus 0.54 sec per fur (F) 2-05 (2-09)

569[2] **Tropical Jungle (USA) (55)***(64+)*(Fav)*(PJMakin)* 5-9-10b KDarley(7) (lw: a gng wl: led appr fnl f: qcknd: comf)....— 1

548[11] Bold Mick **(55)***(60) (DJGMurraySmith)* 4-9-7 (3) JTate(11) (swtchd & hdwy over 3f out: r.o fnl f: nrst fin) 2½ **2**
626[5] Spitfire Bridge (IRE) **(52)***(57) (MMcCormack)* 3-8-6 GDuffield(5) (hdwy 4f out: ev ch over 1f out: nt qckn) 2 **3**
628[10] Kirov Protege (IRE) **(46)***(56) (HJCollingridge)* 3-8-10 DaleGibson(6) (bhd: hdwy 4f out: styd on one pce fnl 2f) 3 **4**
Java Red (IRE) *(51) (JGFitzGerald)* 3-8-6 LCharnock(8) (cmpt: scope: hdwy 4f out: sn prom: nt qckn appr fnl f) ....¾ **5**
478[6] Puffy **(34)***(50) (MDods)* 8-9-10b JCarroll(13) (b: s.i.s: gd hdwy to ld over 3f out: hdd over 1f out: sn wknd) ....½ **6**
Cozzi (FR) **(32)***(49) (JMBradley)* 7-9-5 (5) SDrowne(16) (b: a chsng ldrs: one pce fnl 3f) ....½ **7**
643[5] River Wye (IRE) *(44) (JMCarr)* 3-8-6 SMorris(14) (lw: chsd ldrs tl grad lost pl fnl 3f) 3½ **8**
653[5] Awesome Power **(59)***(38) (JWHills)* 9-9-10 AClark(10) (chsd ldrs tl hmpd & lost pl 3f out: no ch after) 3½ **9**
Master Fiddler *(28) (EWeymes)* 5-9-10 DeanMcKeown(12) (mid div & c wd st: n.d) 6 **10**
Mellouise *(22) (DEddy)* 4-9-5 RHills(2) (unf: s.i.s: n.d) ....¾ **11**
578[11] Nord Lys (IRE) **(31)***(26) (FHLee)* 4-9-10 ACulhane(15) (cl up tl wknd over 2f out) ....½ **12**
494[8] Marble **(43)***(17) (MartynWane)* 4-9-5 JFanning(4) (n.d) 2½ **13**
722[12] Blackspot (IRE) **(35)***(3) (FHLee)* 3-8-2bow1 RLappin(18) (chsd ldrs tl wknd 3f out) 9 **14**
Newgate Bubbles *(BWMurray)* 4-8-12 (7) GParkin(3) (s.i.s: a bhd) 6 **15**
117[13] Monkey Boy (IRE) **(40)** *(TTBill)* 4-9-10b NCarlisle(17) (led tl hdd over 3f out: sn wknd) 2 **16**
578[9] Petal's Jarred **(32)** *(WStorey)* 5-9-2 (3) DRMcCabe(1) (s.s: a bhd) ....nk **17**

5/2 TROPICAL JUNGLE (USA) (op 4/1), **9/2** Awesome Power, **13/2** Spitfire Bridge (IRE), **7/1** River Wye (IRE), **8/1** Bold Mick, **9/1** Kirov Protege (IRE), **12/1** Java Red (IRE) (op 6/1), Mellouise, **14/1** Marble, Puffy, **16/1** Master Fiddler, **20/1** Nord Lys (IRE), Monkey Boy (IRE), Petal's Jarred, **33/1** Newgate Bubbles, Cozzi (FR), Blackspot (IRE), CSF £27.40 TOTE £3.10: £1.40 £3.80 £2.30 (£41.80) Trio £49.90 OWNER Mr D. M. Ahier (MARLBOROUGH) BRED Charles Cyzer 17 Rn

2m 6.1 (2.60) SF: 43/39/18/17/12/29/28/5/17/7/1/5/-/-/-/-/-

WEIGHT FOR AGE 3yo-18lb

Bt in 4,400 gns

819 LISHMAN, SIDWELL, CAMPBELL & PRICE MAIDEN AUCTION STKS (2-Y.O F) (Class E) £3,375.50 (£1,022.00: £499.00: £237.50)

5f Stalls: Low GOING minus 0.54 sec per fur (F) 2-35 (2-41)

638[3] **Kunucu (IRE)** *(78?t) (TDBarron)* 2-8-5 KDarley(12) (a.p: rdn 2f out: r.o to ld wl ins fnl f) ....— **1**
638[2] Top Cat (FR) *(69) (EWeymes)* 2-7-11 (5)ow2 AGarth(17) (cl up: led ½-wy tl wl ins fnl f) 1¼ **2**
671[2] Butterwick Belle (IRE) *(63) (RAFahey)* 2-8-0 SMaloney(6) (b: w ldrs: rdn & btn appr fnl f) 2 **3**
570[3] Mystique Smile *(60) (JBerry)* 2-8-2 ow1 JCarroll(14) (led to ½-wy: rdn & btn appr fnl f) 1 **4**
Trickledown *(51) (CWFairhurst)* 2-8-1 JFanning(4) (w'like: w ldrs: rdn & btn appr fnl f) 3 **5**
Mill End Lady *(42) (MWEasterby)* 2-7-9 (7) RuthCoulter(5) (w'like: scope: s.i.s: bhd tl r.o wl fnl 2f) 3 **6**
Derek's Bo *(30) (NBycroft)* 2-7-5 (5) NVarley(1) (neat: scope: cl up tl hung rt & wknd fnl 2f) 2 **7**
Veshca Lady (IRE) *(27) (EWeymes)* 2-7-12 JMarshall(16) (neat: sme hdwy 2f out: nvr nr to chal) 1½ **8**
Canlubang *(26) (MJCamacho)* 2-7-11 LCharnock(10) (unf: nvr nr to chal) ....hd **9**
Babyshooz *(24) (MBrittain)* 2-7-9 JLowe(3) (small: neat: lw: s.i.s: hdwy ½-wy: nvr trbld ldrs) ....d.h **10**
617[3] Miss Waterline *(35)*(Fav)*(PDEvans)* 2-8-6 RHills(9) (in tch: rdn ½-wy: no imp) ....s.h **10**
595[3] Itsinthepost *(29) (MJohnston)* 2-8-2 TWilliams(2) (chsd ldrs tl outpcd fnl 2f) ....½ **12**
Shepherds Dean (IRE) *(12) (PCHaslam)* 2-7-12 DaleGibson(7) (lengthy: a bhd) 4 **13**
Pat's Choice (IRE) *(MHEasterby)* 2-8-2 ow5 GDuffield(11) (leggy: s.i.s: a bhd) 7 **14**
699[6] Harsh Times *(MHEasterby)* 2-7-11 NCarlisle(15) (s.i.s: a bhd) 1¼ **15**
Diminuet *(JWWatts)* 2-8-0 NKennedy(8) (w'like: scope: bit bkwd: a bhd) 3 **16**
Superfrills *(MissLCSiddall)* 2-7-13 (3)ow7 DMcCabe(13) (Withdrawn under Starter's orders: ref to ent stalls) .... **W**

, **7/2** Miss Waterline, **9/2** Butterwick Belle (IRE), **5/1** Top Cat (FR), **11/2** KUNUCU (IRE) (4/1-6/1), **6/1** Mystique Smile, **7/1** Itsinthepost, **14/1** Trickledown, Pat's Choice (IRE), Diminuet, **16/1** Shepherds Dean (IRE), Harsh Times, Veshca Lady (IRE), **25/1** Babyshooz, Mill End Lady, Canlubang, **33/1** Derek's Bo, CSF £38.35 TOTE £8.30: £3.10 £1.80 £2.00 (£14.20) Trio £18.20 OWNER Mr P. D. Savill (THIRSK) BRED Mrs Rita Fitzgerald 16 Rn

58.7 secs (0.70) SF: 32/23/17/14/5/-/-/-/-/-/-/-/-/-/-/-

820

NEW PLAN FURNITURE PRO-AM LADIES' H'CAP (0-70) (3-Y.O+)
(Class E) £3,195.50 (£968.00: £473.00: £225.50)
1m Stalls: High GOING minus 0.54 sec per fur (F) 3-05 (3-05)

568[13] **Tovarich (56)***(63) (DNicholls)* 4-10-2 AlexGreaves(10) (cl up: led wl over 2f out: hld on wl fnl f) — 1
Mr Cube (IRE) **(46)***(52) (JMBradley)* 5-9-6v AmandaSanders(17) (trckd ldrs: chal on bit over 2f out: rdn & nt run on fnl f) ¾ 2
642* Thatched (IRE) **(46)***(48)*(Fav)*(REBarr)* 5-9-6 MrsDKettlewell(3) (hdwy ½-wy: chsng ldrs appr fnl f: kpt on same pce) 1¾ 3
415[10] Murphy's Gold (IRE) **(49)***(49) (RAFahey)* 4-9-4 (5) MrsLFahey(5) (in tch: hdwy ½-wy: rdn over 1f out: styd on one pce) 1¼ 4
Louisville Belle (IRE) **(51)***(44) (MDIUsher)* 6-9-6 (5) MrsAUsher(14) (in tch: kpt on fnl 3f) 3½ 5
642[10] Avishayes (USA) **(49)***(41) (MrsMReveley)* 8-9-4 (5) MissSBainbridge(6) (stdy hdwy fnl 4f: nvr nr to chal) nk 6
672[16] Waterlord (IRE) **(50)***(40) (DNicholls)* 5-9-5 (5)ow1 MissMCarson(15) (chsd ldrs tl over 2f out) nk 7
672[13] Tolls Choice (IRE) **(54)***(45) (MWEasterby)* 6-10-0 RuthCoulter(7) (trckd ldrs: c wd appr st: effrt & ch 3f out: wknd 2f out) s.h 8
598[6] Juice Plus **(33)***(24) (JParkes)* 4-8-2 (5) VictoriaAppleby(11) (w ldrs tl wknd over 3f out) hd 9
472[6] Green's Bid **(55)***(42) (DWChapman)* 5-9-10 (5) MissRClark(1) (racd wd: cl up tl wknd fnl 3f) 2 10
601[11] Talented Ting (IRE) **(68)***(55) (PCHaslam)* 6-10-9 (5) CarolDavison(4) (led tl hdd wl over 2f out: sn wknd) s.h 11
780[13] Hill Farm Katie **(41)***(26) (WMBrisbourne)* 4-9-1 ow1 MissDianaJones(13) (hmpd appr st: n.d) ½ 12
Habeta (USA) **(35)***(19) (JWWatts)* 9-8-9 MrsJCrossley(2) (a bhd) ¾ 13
Clurican (IRE) **(60)***(36) (NTinkler)* 6-10-6 KimTinkler(9) (nd) 4 14
430[20] Rave-on-Hadley (IRE) **(41)***(13) (SWCampion)* 5-8-10 (5)ow4 MrsSJCampion(16) (mid div & rn wd appr st: sn wknd) nk 15
408[3] Bold Habit **(57)***(29) (JPearce)* 10-10-3 MrsLPearce(12) (hdwy 4f out: wknd & eased fnl 2f) 1¾ 16
293[4] Private Fixture (IRE) **(65)***(27) (DMarks)* 4-10-11 MissKMarks(8) (n.d) 5 17

LONG HANDICAP Juice Plus 8-1

4/1 Thatched (IRE), **9/2** Bold Habit, **8/1** TOVARICH, **9/1** Talented Ting (IRE), Louisville Belle (IRE), Avishayes (USA), **10/1** Habeta (USA), **12/1** Tolls Choice (IRE), Green's Bid, **14/1** Private Fixture (IRE), Murphy's Gold (IRE), **16/1** Mr Cube (IRE), Hill Farm Katie, Waterlord (IRE), **20/1** Clurican (IRE), **33/1** Rave-on-Hadley (IRE), Juice Plus, CSF £134.68 CT £557.25 TOTE £11.30: £2.50 £4.30 £1.30 £4.50 (£243.10) Trio £250.30 OWNER Mrs Dyanne Benjamin (THIRSK) BRED Sir John Astor 17 Rn 1m 40.2 (2.50) SF: 25/14/10/11/6/3/2/7/-/4/17/-/-/-/-/-/-

821

C. B. HUTCHINSON MEMORIAL CHALLENGE CUP H'CAP (0-90) (4-Y.O+)
(Class C) £7,002.50 (£2,120.00: £1,035.00: £492.50)
2m Stalls: Centre GOING minus 0.54 sec per fur (F) 3-40 (3-40)

632[16] **Argyle Cavalier (IRE) (59)***(69) (MJohnston)* 5-8-7 JCarroll(2) (hld up: swtchd & effrt over 2f out: hmpd & swtchd ins fnl f: r.o wl: fin 2nd, hd: awrdd r) — 1
Uncle Doug **(52)***(62)*(Fav)*(MrsMReveley)* 4-7-10 JLowe(6) (lw: led 2f: chsd ldrs: swtchd & qcknd to ld over 2f out: hrd rdn & hung rt ins fnl f: all out: fin 1st: disq: plcd 2nd) 2
432[13] Mondragon **(73)***(82) (MrsMReveley)* 5-9-7 DeanMcKeown(8) (hld up: hdwy 2f out: swtchd 1f out: fin wl) ¾ 3
556[3] White Willow **(67)***(76) (MrsMReveley)* 6-9-1v KDarley(10) (led after 2f to 11f out: prom tl outpcd 3f out: styd on wl fnl f) s.h 4
Solomon's Dancer (USA) **(74)***(82) (WWHaigh)* 5-9-8 DaleGibson(3) (bit bkwd: trckd ldrs: led over 3f out tl over 2f out: btn appr fnl f) 1¼ 5
Highflying **(76)***(83) (GMMoore)* 9-9-7 (3) JTate(1) (bit bkwd: hld up: smooth hdwy to chal over 3f out: wknd 2f out) 1¼ 6
Good Hand (USA) **(74)***(80) (JWWatts)* 9-9-8 NConnorton(4) (b: b.hind: effrt ent st: styd on nr fin: nvr able chal) nk 7
*206** Art Form (USA) **(76)***(81) (CACyzer)* 8-9-10 GDuffield(5) (b: hld up: hdwy to chal over 3f out: wknd 2f out) 1¼ 8
558[11] Sarawat **(80)***(60) (DNicholls)* 7-10-0 AlexGreaves(9) (plld hrd: hdwy 12f out: wknd 3f out) 25 9
597[3] Tanah Merah (IRE) **(57)***(22) (EJAlston)* 4-8-1 NCarlisle(7) (plld hrd: led 11f out tl over 3f out: sn wknd) 15 10

3/1 Uncle Doug, **5/1** White Willow, Art Form (USA), **6/1** Good Hand (USA), **7/1** ARGYLE CAVALIER (IRE), **9/1** Mondragon (op 8/1), Sarawat, **14/1** Solomon's Dancer (USA), **20/1** Highflying, Tanah Merah (IRE), CSF £27.64 CT £174.27 TOTE £7.50: £2.00 £1.60 £2.40 (£20.50) Trio £28.50 OWNER E H Jones (Paints) Ltd (MIDDLEHAM) BRED Oldtown Bloodstock Holdings Ltd in Ireland 10 Rn 3m 32.9 (7.90) SF: 13/-/-/-/-/-/-/-/-/-

WEIGHT FOR AGE 4yo-4lb

822 LANGTHORPE RATED STKS H'CAP (0-95) (3-Y.O) (Class B) £8,913.36 (£2,879.76: £1,404.88)
1m 2f Stalls: High GOING minus 0.54 sec per fur (F) 4-15 (4-15)

614* **Murajja (USA) (93)***(101+)*(Fav)*(PTWalwyn)* 3-9-0 RHills(2) (lw: mde all: qcknd 4f out: easily)........— **1**
Eight Sharp (IRE) **(84)***(82) (BWHills)* 3-8-0 (5) JDSmith(3) (plld hrd: effrt over 3f out: rdn & no ch w wnr)........6 **2**
*566*6 Vin St Koola **(88)***(86) (HJCollingridge)* 3-8-9 DaleGibson(1) (plld hrd to st: sn pushed along & outpcd)........nk **3**

2/9 MURAJJA (USA), **5/1** Eight Sharp (IRE), **6/1** Vin St Koola, CSF £1.92 TOTE £1.20 (£1.40) OWNER Mr Hamdan Al Maktoum (LAMBOURN) BRED Shadwell Farm Inc & Shadwell Estate Co Ltd in USA 3 Rn
2m 7.4 (3.90) SF: 24/5/9

823 YORKSHIRE-TYNE TEES TELEVISION H'CAP (0-80) (3-Y.O) (Class D) £4,004.30 (£1,213.40: £593.20: £283.10)
6f Stalls: Low GOING minus 0.54 sec per fur (F) 4-45 (4-46)

The Scythian (58)*(70) (BobJones)* 3-7-13 JFanning(14) (mde most: r.o wl fnl 2f)........— **1**
7234 French Grit (IRE) **(80)***(87) (MDods)* 3-9-7 DaleGibson(6) (hdwy u.p 2f out: r.o nr fin)........2 **2**
6977 Brecongill Lad **(66)***(71) (MissSEHall)* 3-8-7 NConnorton(1) (lw: trckd ldrs: smooth hdwy 2f out: hung rt appr fnl f: nt run on)........¾ **3**
6212 Denbrae (IRE) **(75)***(73) (DJGMurraySmith)* 3-8-13 (3) JTate(2) (chsd ldrs: hung rt most of wy: styd on wl fnl f)........2½ **4**
6744 Stolen Kiss (IRE) **(65)***(62) (MWEasterby)* 3-8-6b LCharnock(9) (chsd ldrs: hmpd appr fnl f: r.o one pce)........nk **5**
5774 Bollin Frank **(60)***(56) (MHEasterby)* 3-8-1 SMaloney(4) (chsd ldrs: hmpd appr fnl f: r.o one pce)........½ **6**
6974 Penny's Wishing **(62)***(58) (JPLeigh)* 3-8-3 DeanMcKeown(7) (nvr plcd to chal)........hd **7**
6743 Brockton Flame **(65)***(54) (JMPEustace)* 3-8-6 RHills(10) (nvr trbld ldrs)........2½ **8**
7012 Russian Heroine **(60)***(46) (MJohnston)* 3-8-1 TWilliams(5) (cl up: hmpd appr fnl f: r.o one pce)........1¼ **9**
Best of All (IRE) **(74)***(58)*(Fav)*(JBerry)* 3-9-1 JCarroll(8) (prom tl outpcd ½-wy: n.d after)........½ **10**
5354 Tee Tee Too (IRE) **(68)***(47) (PCHaslam)* 3-8-4 (5) JStack(11) (lw: w ldrs 4f: btn whn hmpd appr fnl f)........2 **11**
Rymer's Rascal **(64)***(39) (EJAlston)* 3-8-5 NCarlisle(12) (a bhd)........1½ **12**
6742 Arasong **(72)***(31) (EWeymes)* 3-8-13 KDarley(13) (cl up 4f: btn whn hmpd appr fnl f)........6 **13**
*685*5 Thick as Thieves **(72)** *(RonaldThompson)* 3-8-13 GDuffield(15) (Withdrawn not under Starter's orders: veterinary advice)........ **W**

, **7/2** Best of All (IRE), **11/2** Denbrae (IRE), **13/2** French Grit (IRE), **7/1** Russian Heroine, **15/2** Brockton Flame, Arasong, **10/1** Stolen Kiss (IRE), **12/1** Tee Tee Too (IRE), Brecongill Lad, Penny's Wishing, **14/1** Bollin Frank, **16/1** THE SCYTHIAN, **20/1** Rymer's Rascal, CSF £119.96 CT £1,225.46 TOTE £81.60: £14.50 £3.00 £4.10 (£279.50) Trio Not won; £400.85 to Pontefract 1/5/95 OWNER Mr Ian Vogt (NEWMARKET) BRED J. O'Neill 13 Rn
1m 11.2 (1.00) SF: 24/41/25/27/16/10/12/8/-/12/1/-/-/-

824 LEVY BOARD MAIDEN STKS (3-Y.O) (Class D) £3,859.70 (£1,169.60: £571.80: £272.90)
1m 2f Stalls: High GOING minus 0.54 sec per fur (F) 5-20 (5-22)

4352 **Maeterlinck (IRE)** *(83)*(Fav)*(BWHills)* 3-9-0 RHills(9) (a.p: led wl over 1f out: hung rt: r.o)........— **1**
Flame War (USA) *(76) (HRACecil)* 3-8-9 JLowe(7) (lw: a cl up: led over 2f out tl wl over 1f out: hmpd over 1f out: styd on)........1½ **2**
Tilaal (USA) *(80) (EALDunlop)* 3-8-11 (3) JTate(6) (w'like: str: bit bkwd: sn wl bhd: stdy hdwy 3f out: r.o strly nr fin)........½ **3**
6636 Okavango (USA) *(76) (JHMGosden)* 3-9-0 JCarroll(3) (led tl over 2f out: one pce)........2½ **4**
Eau de Cologne *(60) (CWThornton)* 3-9-0 DeanMcKeown(8) (bhd: hdwy 2f out: nvr plcd to chal)........10 **5**
Wurlitzer (USA) *(59) (JHMGosden)* 3-9-0 DaleGibson(5) (w'like: leggy: outpcd & bhd tl sme late hdwy)........¾ **6**
Golden Digger (USA) *(54) (MRStoute)* 3-8-9 KDarley(10) (chsd ldrs tl wknd fnl 3f)........s.h **7**
Prince Equiname *(56) (DEddy)* 3-9-0 JFanning(2) (prom tl rdn & wknd fnl 3f)........1½ **8**
6436 Island Cascade *(11) (DonEnricoIncisa)* 3-8-9 KimTinkler(4) (sn bhd)........25 **9**

539[17] Mr Personality (11) (MrsMReveley) 3-8-7 (7) SCopp(1) (rdn ½-wy: a bhd)....3½ 10
Kralingen **(45)** (NChamberlain) 3-8-9 NConnorton(11) (a bhd)....15 11

13/8 MAETERLINCK (IRE), **7/2** Okavango (USA), **5/1** Flame War (USA), **6/1** Golden Digger (USA), **11/1** Tilaal (USA), Wurlitzer (USA), **25/1** Mr Personality, **33/1** Prince Equiname, Eau de Cologne, **100/1** Island Cascade, Kralingen, CSF £10.04 TOTE £2.60: £1.40 £1.80 £3.30 (£9.40) OWNER Sheikh Mohammed (LAMBOURN) BRED Sean Collins 11 Rn
2m 4.5 (1.00) SF: 47/40/44/40/24/23/18/20/-/-/-

T/Plpt: £396.00 (29.48 Tckts). T/Qdpt: £40.20 (2 Tckts). AA

0791-SANDOWN (R-H)
Saturday April 29th (Good, Good to firm patches)

Other races run under jump racing rules.
WEATHER: overcast WIND: almost nil

825 PIZZA HUT MAIDEN STKS (2-Y.O C & G) (Class D) £4,240.50 (£1,284.00: £627.00: £298.50)
5f 6y Stalls: Low GOING minus 0.31 sec per fur (GF) 2-10 (2-11)

Mubhij (IRE) (89+t)(Fav)(BWHills) 2-8-11 WCarson(10) (str: scope: a.p: led over 1f out: rdn out)....— 1
Bahamian Knight (CAN) (89) (DRLoder) 2-8-11 JWeaver(6) (neat: a.p: led over 2f out tl over 1f out: r.o wl ins fnl f)....hd 2
First Fiddler (87) (WJarvis) 2-8-11 MTebbutt(1) (neat: hld up: rdn over 2f out: r.o ins fnl f)....½ 3
Galapino (83) (CEBrittain) 2-8-11 BDoyle(5) (neat: rdn 3f out: hdwy over 1f out: r.o wl ins fnl f)....1¼ 4
Welsh Mountain (83) (MJHeaton-Ellis) 2-8-11 StephenDavies(7) (w'like: bkwd: led over 2f: unable qckn fnl f)....hd 5
Ca'd'oro (70) (GBBalding) 2-8-11 JWilliams(9) (leggy: dwlt: nvr nr to chal)....4 6
Nikita's Star (IRE) (70) (DJGMurraySmith) 2-8-11 LDettori(8) (w'like: lw: no hdwy fnl 2f)....hd 7
617[14] Arctic Romancer (IRE) (70) (GLewis) 2-8-11 SWhitworth(4) (w ldr over 2f: wknd over 1f out)s.h 8
Forever Noble (IRE) (54) (MRChannon) 2-8-11 RHughes(3) (w'like: bkwd: outpcd)....5 9
Etterby Park (USA) (51) (MDIUsher) 2-8-11 MWigham(11) (neat: s.s: a bhd)....1 10
Mr Speaker (IRE) (44) (CFWall) 2-8-6 (5) LNewton(12) (leggy: bit bkwd: a bhd)....2 11
Freeloader (35) (JWHills) 2-8-11 MHills(2) (neat: a bhd)....3 12

9/4 MUBHIJ (IRE), **3/1** Bahamian Knight (CAN) (op 5/4), **4/1** First Fiddler, **10/1** Forever Noble (IRE) (op 4/1), **12/1** Freeloader, Arctic Romancer (IRE) (10/1-20/1), **16/1** Nikita's Star (IRE), **25/1** Ca'd'oro, **33/1** Galapino, Welsh Mountain, **50/1** Etterby Park (USA), Mr Speaker (IRE), CSF £9.06 TOTE £3.70: £1.40 £1.80 £1.90 (£4.50) Trio £10.10 OWNER Mr Hamdan Al Maktoum (LAMBOURN) BRED Shadwell Estate Company Limited 12 Rn
61.18 secs (1.38) SF: 46/46/44/40/40/27/27/27/11/8/1/-

826 THRESHER CLASSIC TRIAL STKS (Gp 3) (3-Y.O) (Class A) £42,636.00 (£15,973.80: £7,686.90: £3,363.30)
1m 2f 7y Stalls: High GOING minus 0.10 sec per fur (G) 4-00 (4-05)

Pentire (105)(107) (GWragg) 3-8-10 MHills(8) (rdn & hdwy over 1f out: led wl ins fnl f: r.o wl)....— 1
Singspiel (IRE) **(109)**(107) (MRStoute) 3-8-10 WRSwinburn(7) (bit bkwd: 5th st: rdn 2f out: ev ch ins fnl f: r.o)....nk 2
Balliol Boy (104) (HRACecil) 3-8-10 WRyan(3) (led: qcknd wl over 1f out: hdd wl ins fnl f: unable qckn)....1½ 3
663[2] Luso (99) (CEBrittain) 3-8-10 BDoyle(1) (lw: 2nd st: rdn over 3f out: one pce fnl 2f)....3 4
536* Torrential (USA) (99)(Fav)(JHMGosden) 3-8-10 LDettori(4) (b.hind: lw: 6th st: rdn over 2f out: one pce)....nk 5
622* Two O'Clock Jump (IRE) **(90)**(97) (RHannon) 3-8-10 PatEddery(6) (nvr nr to chal)....1 6
Tremplin (USA) (95) (AFabre,France) 3-8-10 TJarnet(2) (unf: scope: 4th st: wknd over 1f out)....1¾ 7
Prince of India (93) (LordHuntingdon) 3-8-10 JWeaver(5) (bit bkwd: 3rd st: rdn over 2f out: wknd fnl f)....1 8

7/4 Torrential (USA), **9/4** Tremplin (USA), **6/1** Two O'Clock Jump (IRE) (op 10/1), **8/1** Singspiel (IRE), **9/1** Balliol Boy (6/1-10/1), **20/1** Luso, **25/1** PENTIRE, **33/1** Prince of India, CSF £179.86 TOTE £25.30: £4.10 £2.10 £2.10 (£68.80) OWNER Mollers Racing (NEWMARKET) BRED Lord Halifax 8 Rn
2m 7.48 (3.18) SF: 61/61/58/53/53/51/49/47

827

T.G.I. FRIDAY'S GORDON RICHARDS STKS (Gp 3) (4-Y.O+) (Class A) £22,020.00 (£8,256.00: £3,978.00: £1,746.00)
1m 2f 7y Stalls: High GOING minus 0.10 sec per fur (G) 4-35 (4-35)

Prince of Andros (USA) (108)*(123) (DRLoder)* 5-8-10 JWeaver(4) (chsd ldr: led 2f out: rdn out) ...— **1**
666[4] Nicolotte **(104)***(120) (GWragg)* 4-8-10 MHills(3) (lw: 3rd st: rdn over 2f out: unable qckn) ...2 **2**
606a[6] Ionio (USA) **(114)***(120) (CEBrittain)* 4-8-10 BDoyle(5) (lw: led 8f: one pce) ...s.h **3**
Blush Rambler (USA) **(115)***(114) (MRStoute)* 5-8-10 WRyan(1) (s.s: 5th st: a bhd) ...3½ **4**
666* Desert Shot **(111)***(109)*(Fav)*(MRStoute)* 5-8-13 WRSwinburn(6) (4th st: rdn over 2f out: no rspnse) ...5 **5**

11/10 Desert Shot, **9/2** Ionio (USA), **5/1** Nicolotte, **6/1** PRINCE OF ANDROS (USA) (4/1-7/1), **8/1** Blush Rambler (USA), CSF £28.94 TOTE £6.60: £2.00 £2.00 (£23.60) OWNER Lucayan Stud (NEWMARKET) BRED Spendthrift Farm 5 Rn 2m 9.69 (5.39) SF: 43/40/40/34/29

828

BEEFEATER RATED STKS H'CAP (0-100) (3-Y.O) (Class B) £7,687.20 (£2,884.80: £1,417.40: £617.00: £283.50: £150.10)
5f 6y Stalls: Low GOING minus 0.31 sec per fur (GF) 5-05 (5-07)

483[7] **Double Quick (IRE) (83)***(95) (MJohnston)* 3-8-4 JWeaver(6) (a.p: led 2f out: rdn out) ...— **1**
621* Katya (IRE) **(89)***(93)*(Fav)*(MRChannon)* 3-8-10 RHughes(7) (lw: hdwy over 1f out: r.o ins fnl f: too much to do) ...2½ **2**
719[2] Lago Di Varano **(101)***(105) (JBerry)* 3-9-8b LDettori(2) (lw: a.p: ev ch 2f out: unable qckn) ...hd **3**
498[6] That Man Again **(84)***(87) (GLewis)* 3-8-0 (5) AWhelan(9) (lw: a.p: rdn over 2f out: one pce) ...hd **4**
483* Portend **(83)***(82) (SRBowring)* 3-7-13 (5) CTeague(8) (hld up: rdn over 2f out: one pce) ...1½ **5**
Musical Season **(93)***(91) (TDBarron)* 3-9-0 MHills(3) (nvr nr to chal) ...nk **6**
681* Cheyenne Spirit **(94)***(87) (BHanbury)* 3-9-1 WRyan(4) (b.off hind: lw: led 3f) ...1½ **7**
Tart and a Half **(85)***(72) (BJMeehan)* 3-8-6 BDoyle(5) (lw: prom 3f) ...2 **8**
692[7] Signs **(99)***(78)*(Fav)*(RHannon)* 3-9-6 PatEddery(1) (outpcd) ...2½ **9**

4/1 Signs, Katya (IRE), **9/2** Cheyenne Spirit, **5/1** Lago Di Varano, **6/1** Portend (op 4/1), **9/1** DOUBLE QUICK (IRE) (6/1-10/1), **20/1** Musical Season, Tart and a Half, That Man Again, CSF £40.83 CT £179.91 TOTE £12.00: £2.90 £1.70 £1.90 (£21.80) Trio £58.20 OWNER The 2nd Middleham Partnership (MIDDLEHAM) 9 Rn 60.9 secs (1.10) SF: 44/42/54/36/31/40/36/21/27

829

COUNTRY CLUB HOTELS H'CAP (0-105) (3-Y.O) (Class B) £12,776.00 (£4,784.00: £2,342.00: £1,010.00: £455.00: £233.00)
1m 14y Stalls: High GOING minus 0.10 sec per fur (G) 5-35 (5-39)

Holtye (IRE) (85)*(96)*(Fav)*(HRACecil)* 3-8-9 PatEddery(13) (bit bkwd: 6th st: hmpd wl over 1f out: swtchd rt: edgd rt & led ins fnl f: drvn out) ...— **1**
694[2] Ihtiram (IRE) **(97)***(108) (JLDunlop)* 3-9-7 WCarson(15) (lw: hdwy & hmpd on ins over 2f out: led 1f out tl ins fnl f: r.o wl) ...s.h **2**
Ela-Aristokrati (IRE) **(96)***(103) (MRStoute)* 3-9-6 WRSwinburn(2) (rdn over 3f out: hdwy over 1f out: r.o) ...2 **3**
659[11] Cim Bom Bom (IRE) **(95)***(97) (MBell)* 3-9-5 MFenton(7) (hdwy over 2f out: ev ch whn carried lft wl over 1f out: one pce: fin 5th, 13/4l: plcd 4th) ... **4**
621[7] Quintus Decimus **(77)***(83) (LordHuntingdon)* 3-7-10 (5) AWhelan(10) (led over 4f out: hung lft wl over 1f out: hdd 1f out: unable qckn: fin 4th, 3/4l: disq: plcd 5th) ... **5**
504[11] Out on a Promise (IRE) **(80)***(82) (GWragg)* 3-8-4 MHills(11) (lw: hdwy over 1f out: nvr nrr) ...hd **6**
536[7] Captain's Day **(90)***(78) (TGMills)* 3-9-0 StephenDavies(8) (lw: bmpd over 6f out: 7th st: wknd over 1f out) ...7 **7**
614[10] Percy Braithwaite (IRE) **(90)***(75) (MJohnston)* 3-9-0 WRyan(14) (lw: nvr nr to chal) ...1¼ **8**
Twilight Patrol **(89)***(65) (RHannon)* 3-8-13 LDettori(3) (b.nr hind: 5th st: wknd over 1f out) ...5 **9**
689* Danegold (IRE) **(70)***(42) (MRChannon)* 3-7-8v NAdams(4) (lw: 4th st: wknd over 1f out) ...1¾ **10**
Te Amo (IRE) **(88)***(60) (RAkehurst)* 3-8-12 JWeaver(9) (3rd st: wknd over 2f out) ...s.h **11**
618[11] Night Dance **(83)***(45) (GLewis)* 3-8-7 SWhitworth(12) (lw: led over 3f: 2nd st: wknd over 2f out) ...5 **12**

662[5] Axeman (IRE) **(95)***(55) (RHannon)* 3-9-5 RHughes(1) (a bhd)....1 **13**
*618** Rockforce **(78)** *(MRChannon)* 3-8-2 CRutter(6) (Withdrawn not under Starter's orders: ref to ent stalls) .... **W**

3/1 HOLTYE (IRE), **7/2** Ihtiram (IRE), **7/1** Ela-Aristokrati (IRE), Quintus Decimus, **10/1** Twilight Patrol, **14/1** Danegold (IRE), **16/1** Te Amo (IRE), Out on a Promise (IRE), Cim Bom Bom (IRE), Axeman (IRE), **25/1** Night Dance, **33/1** Percy Braithwaite (IRE), Captain's Day, CSF £12.88 CT £54.56 TOTE £3.20: £1.70 £1.80 £3.20 (£3.80) Trio £12.20 OWNER Mr K. Abdullah (NEWMARKET) BRED Juddmonte Farms 13 Rn 1m 41.42 (2.22) SF: 63/75/70/66/46/49/45/42/32/9/27/12/22/-

T/Jkpt: Not won; £14,223.48 to Pontefract 1/5/95. T/Plpt: £245.50 (184.17 Tckts). T/Qdpt: £81.40 (4.4 Tckts). AK

0624-WOLVERHAMPTON (L-H)
Saturday April 29th (Standard)
WEATHER: overcast WIND: slight across

830
SARUMAN MAIDEN H'CAP (0-65) (3-Y.O) (Class F) £2,519.00 (£694.00: £329.00)
6f (Fibresand) Stalls: Low GOING: 0.03 sec per fur (STD) 7-00 (7-01)

Shanghai Lil (40)*(48) (MJFetherston-Godley)* 3-7-11 FNorton(6) (sn drvn along in mid div: hdwy to ld ins fnl f: r.o).... — **1**
Frans Lad **(62)***(67) (JBerry)* 3-8-12 (7) PRoberts(7) (bit bkwd: chsd ldrs: rdn to chal 1f out: unable qckn cl home) 1 **2**
587[3] Speedy Snaps Pride **(41)***(45) (PDCundell)* 3-7-5 (7) SLanigan(3) (s.i.s: bhd: rdn ½-wy: r.o wl ins fnl f) ....½ **3**
732[8] Lawnswood Lady **(43)***(37) (RHollinshead)* 3-7-9 (5)ow3 AGarth(1) (bhd & outpcd tl r.o wl appr fnl f)....2½ **4**
551[4] Sharp Holly (IRE) **(53)***(47) (JABennett)* 3-8-10 TSprake(2) (led tl hdd & wknd ins fnl f) 1¼ **5**
648[9] Embezzler **(58)***(50)*(Fav)*(GLewis)* 3-9-1b GCarter(4) (w ldr: rdn & ev ch 2f out: wknd fnl f) ....¾ **6**
394[6] Happy Brave **(38)***(25) (PDCundell)* 3-7-9b NKennedy(9) (spd over 4f)....1¾ **7**
727[6] Kreef **(64)***(42) (RJO'Sullivan)* 3-9-7b WWoods(8) (swtg: chsd ldrs: rdn over 2f out: wknd over 1f out)....3½ **8**
363[5] Jessica's Secret (IRE) **(48)***(20) (ABailey)* 3-8-0 (5)ow3 VHalliday(5) (outpcd: a bhd) 1 **9**

2/1 Embezzler, **5/1** Speedy Snaps Pride, **11/2** Sharp Holly (IRE), **8/1** Kreef (6/1-9/1), **9/1** Jessica's Secret (IRE), Frans Lad (op 6/1), **12/1** SHANGHAI LIL, **16/1** Happy Brave, Lawnswood Lady, CSF £100.43 CT £554.03 TOTE £12.10: £3.10 £1.90 £1.50 (£43.10) Trio £99.20 OWNER Mr M. J. Fetherston-Godley (EAST ILSLEY) BRED Highfield Stud Ltd 9 Rn
1m 16.6 (5.40) SF: 10/29/7/-/9/12/-/4/-

831
STRIDER CLAIMING STKS (3-Y.O+) (Class F) £2,519.00 (£694.00: 29.00)
5f (Fibresand) Stalls: Low GOING: 0.03 sec per fur (STD) 7-30 (7-31)

196[7] **One for Jeannie (64)***(72) (ABailey)* 3-8-0v(5)ow1 VHalliday(8) (chsd ldrs: led wl over 1f out: qcknd clr fnl f) .... — **1**
754[5] Ultra Beet **(83)***(75)*(Fav)*(PCHaslam)* 3-9-1 JFortune(6) (chsd ldrs: effrt over 1f out: r.o ins fnl f)....2½ **2**
629[3] Daily Starshine (IRE) **(59)***(65) (JBerry)* 3-7-13b(7) PFessey(4) (lw: led after 2f tl wl over 1f out: rdn & one pce)....nk **3**
565[11] Little Saboteur **(71)***(50) (PJMakin)* 6-8-13b AClark(1) (b.nr hind: prom tl rdn & one pce appr fnl f)....3½ **4**
Southern Dominion **(55)***(38) (WGMTurner)* 3-7-13 (7)ow3 DScott(7) (swtg: bit bkwd: led 2f: rdn & wknd over 1f out)....4 **5**
392[9] Ho Mei Surprise **(44)***(32) (BPreece)* 3-7-12 (7)ow2 AEddery(3) (outpcd: a bhd)....2 **6**
723[13] Primula Bairn **(62)***(32) (JMackie)* 5-9-1v GCarter(2) (s.s: a bhd & outpcd) ....hd **7**

11/8 Ultra Beet, **4/1** Little Saboteur, **11/2** Primula Bairn, **6/1** ONE FOR JEANNIE, **7/1** Daily Starshine (IRE), **16/1** Southern Dominion, **25/1** Ho Mei Surprise, CSF £14.19 TOTE £5.90: £2.10 £1.90 (£6.00) OWNER Mrs Jean Jones (TARPORLEY) BRED A. Saccomando 7 Rn
62.4 secs (4.40) SF: 18/21/11/7/-/-/-
WEIGHT FOR AGE 3yo-11lb

832
ELROND H'CAP (0-65) (3-Y.O+) (Class F) £2,519.00 (£694.00: £329.00)
7f (Fibresand) Stalls: High GOING: 0.03 sec per fur (STD) 8-00 (8-00)

627[4] **Heathyards Lady (USA) (49)***(55) (RHollinshead)* 4-9-4 GCarter(6) (bhd: hdwy 2f out: led ins fnl f: drvn clr) .... — **1**

731[7] Words of Wisdom (IRE) **(59)***(59) (CACyzer)* 5-10-0 GDuffield(10) (chsd ldrs: 3rd st: rdn & kpt on ins fnl f) 2½ 2
594* Panther (IRE) **(55)***(54)*(Fav)*(JHetherton)* 5-9-10 NKennedy(5) (a.p: 4th & rdn st: ev ch 1f out: one pce) ....½ 3
529[7] Fitzroy Lad **(31)***(24) (RJBaker)* 5-8-0b SRaymont(4) (chsd ldr: 2nd st: led wl over 1f out tl hdd & wknd ins fnl f) 2½ 4
473[7] Tachycardia **(43)***(26) (RJO'Sullivan)* 3-7-12 ow1 DBiggs(3) (led over 5f: wknd appr fnl f) 4 5
524[6] Garlande D'Or **(50)***(32) (JLSpearing)* 3-8-5 GHind(8) (s.i.s: wl bhd tl sme late hdwy) 1 6
*766** Titanium Honda (IRE) **(50)***(23)*(Fav)*(CEBrittain)* 4-9-5 6x BDoyle(2) (bhd & sn pushed along: effrt ½-wy: wknd 2f out) 4 7
627[6] Arawa **(43)***(13) (DMarks)* 5-8-7 (5) MBaird(1) (prom 4f: sn rdn & wknd) 1¼ 8

11/4 Titanium Honda (IRE), Panther (IRE), **4/1** HEATHYARDS LADY (USA), **13/2** Words of Wisdom (IRE), **9/1** Garlande D'Or, **12/1** Tachycardia, Arawa, **25/1** Fitzroy Lad, CSF £27.49 CT £74.59 TOTE £4.10: £1.40 £1.90 £1.30 (£9.00) Trio £16.10 OWNER Mr L. A. Morgan (UPPER LONGDON) BRED S A'Long Farm and Dennis Swartz 8 Rn 1m 30.2 (6.20) SF: 32/36/31/1/-/-/-/-
WEIGHT FOR AGE 3yo-14lb

833 MAIREAD BYTHEWAY BIRTHDAY H'CAP (0-70) (3-Y.O+) (Class E) £3,273.60 (£976.80: £466.40: £211.20)
1m 6f 166y (Fibresand) Stalls: High GOING: 0.03 sec per fur (STD) 8-30 (8-33)

649[12] **Jaraab (51)***(65) (GLewis)* 4-8-13v SWhitworth(12) (lw: hld up: hdwy to ld over 2f out: clr fnl f: eased cl home) ....— 1
582[6] Red Whirlwind **(58)***(68) (RJO'Sullivan)* 5-9-8 WWoods(2) (lw: chsd ldrs: led 3f out: sn hdd: 2nd st: one pce fnl f) 3½ 2
530[6] Premier Dance **(59)***(65) (DHaydnJones)* 8-9-4 (5) SDrowne(6) (lw: a.p: 3rd st: rdn & one pce fnl 2f) 3½ 3
*530** Shakiyr (FR) **(64)***(70)*(Fav)*(RHollinshead)* 4-9-12 LDettori(1) (hld up: hdwy 6f out: 6th st: nvr able to chal) ....hd 4
582[7] Child Star (FR) **(42)***(48) (DMarks)* 6-8-1e(5) MBaird(11) (in tch: effrt 4f out: 5th st: nt rch ldrs) ....nk 5
280[7] Scalp 'em (IRE) **(54)***(57) (PDEvans)* 7-9-4 JFortune(4) (bit bkwd: chsd ldr: led 4f out to 3f out: 4th st: wknd wl over 1f out) 3 6
412[8] Epica **(55)***(52) (ABailey)* 4-9-3b JCarroll(7) (b: led over 10f: wknd qckly) 5 7
649[5] Awestruck **(46)***(37) (BPreece)* 5-8-10 GDuffield(3) (a bhd: t.o) 6 8
582[9] Mint a Million (IRE) **(36)***(5) (MBlanshard)* 4-7-12 FNorton(9) (prom to ½-wy: wknd qckly: t.o) 20 9
514[3] Nothing Doing (IRE) **(35)***(4) (WJMusson)* 6-7-13 NAdams(5) (s.s: hdwy on outside after 5f: lost tch 6f out: t.o: bit slipped) ....hd 10
Sultan's Son **(35)** *(KSBridgwater)* 9-7-6 (7)ow5 MHenry(10) (bkwd: a bhd: rdn ½-wy: no rspnse: t.o) ....s.h 11

6/4 Shakiyr (FR), **7/1** Red Whirlwind, Child Star (FR), **8/1** JARAAB, **9/1** Premier Dance, Scalp 'em (IRE), Nothing Doing (IRE), **10/1** Awestruck, **12/1** Epica, **20/1** Mint a Million (IRE), **33/1** Sultan's Son, CSF £63.39 CT £484.41 TOTE £8.80: £2.00 £3.30 £2.60 (£35.70) Trio £63.00 OWNER Mr S. I. Ross (EPSOM) BRED Shadwell Estate Company Limited 11 Rn
3m 17.8 (113.80) SF: 44/49/46/49/29/38/31/18/-/-/-
WEIGHT FOR AGE 4yo-2lb
OFFICIAL EXPLANATION **Nothing Doing: was unsteerable after the bit went through his mouth.**

834 MORDOR (S) STKS (2-Y.O) (Class G) £2,588.00 (£713.00: £338.00)
5f (Fibresand) Stalls: Low GOING: 0.03 sec per fur (STD) 9-00 (9-01)

770[3] **Nameless** *(53t) (DJSCosgrove)* 2-8-7 JFortune(4) (lw: hld up: led wl over 1f out: sn clr: edgd lft fnl f) ....— 1
561[3] Bites *(31) (GLewis)* 2-8-7 PaulEddery(1) (s.i.s: drvn along ½-wy: kpt on ins fnl f: no ch w wnr)7 2
554[2] Penny Parkes *(32)*(Fav)*(JBerry)* 2-8-12 JCarroll(2) (lw: led: hrd rdn & hdd wl over 1f out: sn outpcd) 1 3

4/7 Penny Parkes, **3/1** NAMELESS, **100/30** Bites, CSF £9.56 TOTE £3.30 (£3.30) OWNER Mr J. C. Wilson (NEWMARKET) BRED J. Ford 3 Rn 63.7 secs (5.70) SF: -/-/-
Bt in 7,600 gns

835 ROHAN H'CAP (0-60) (3-Y.O+) (Class F) £2,560.00 (£760.00: £360.00: £160.00)
1m 1f 79y (Fibresand) Stalls: Low GOING: 0.03 sec per fur (STD) 9-30 (9-32)

Rolling Waters (50)*(60) (JARToller)* 5-9-6 WNewnes(8) (bit bkwd: chsd ldrs: led over 3f out: clr fnl f: easily) ....— 1

472[5] Fiaba **(40)***(48) (MrsNMacauley)* 7-8-3 (7) AmandaSanders(1) (hld up & bhd: hdwy ent st: swtchd lft over 1f out: fin wl)....1 **2**
627[10] Quinzii Martin **(56)***(61) (DHaydnJones)* 7-9-7v(5) SDrowne(7) (hld up: hdwy 4f out: 2nd st: rdn over 1f out: one pce)....1¾ **3**
Big Chance **(34)***(36) (WJMusson)* 6-8-4 GHind(11) (bit bkwd: hld up: hdwy 4f out: 5th st: rdn & one pce fnl f)....2 **4**
472* Eastleigh **(55)***(56)*(Fav)*(RHollinshead)* 6-9-11 LDettori(4) (hld up: hdwy & 6th st: nvr nr to chal)....¾ **5**
624[5] Delgarth Lady **(33)***(30) (JLSpearing)* 4-8-3 DeanMcKeown(9) (hld up: hdwy 4f out: 4th st: wknd wl over 1f out)....2 **6**
409[4] Ju Ju's Girl (IRE) **(34)***(19) (BSmart)* 5-7-11 (7) ADaly(2) (b.hind: chsd ldrs over 6f: sn lost tch)....7 **7**
520[6] Cicerone **(48)***(21) (JLHarris)* 5-9-4 GDuffield(3) (a in rr: t.o)....7 **8**
605[2] Backstabber **(35)***(3) (MissSJWilton)* 5-8-5 SDWilliams(13) (led: hrd rdn & hdd over 3f out: 3rd & btn st: eased)....3 **9**
416[11] Ballyhays (IRE) **(43)***(7) (JAHarris)* 6-8-13 JO'Reilly(10) (lw: s.s: a bhd: t.o)....2½ **10**
605[10] Swynford Flyer **(39)** *(JAHarris)* 6-8-9b PaulEddery(5) (lost pl ½-wy: sn hrd rdn: t.o)....13 **11**
478[10] Brigadore Gold **(32)** *(FHLee)* 5-7-13b(3) DRMcCabe(6) (rdn & lost pl ½-wy: sn bhd: t.o)....2½ **12**
A Badge Too Far (IRE) **(34)** *(LJBarratt)* 5-8-1 (3) SSanders(12) (b: bkwd: a bhd: t.o)....2½ **13**

11/4 Eastleigh, **9/2** Cicerone, **6/1** Swynford Flyer, Backstabber, **8/1** ROLLING WATERS, **10/1** Delgarth Lady, Fiaba, **12/1** Ju Ju's Girl (IRE), **14/1** Quinzii Martin (op 8/1), Big Chance, **16/1** Ballyhays (IRE), **20/1** Brigadore Gold, **33/1** A Badge Too Far (IRE), CSF £87.85 CT £1,040.96 TOTE £10.20: £2.80 £4.20 £3.80 (£27.80) Trio £214.20 OWNER Blandford (WHITSBURY) BRED R. E. Crutchley 13 Rn
2m 4.6 (8.60) SF: 33/21/34/9/29/3/-/-/-/-/-/-/-

T/Plpt: £540.70 (17.61 Tckts). T/Plpt: £59.70 (1.6 Tckts). IM

0746-PONTEFRACT (L-H)
Monday May 1st (Firm)

WEATHER: overcast, warm WIND: slt across

836
EUROPEAN BREEDERS FUND TOTE MAIDEN STKS (2-Y.O) (Class D)
£4,162.50 (£1,260.00: £615.00: £292.50)
5f Stalls: Low GOING minus 0.48 sec per fur (F) 2-45 (2-49)

682[2] **L'Ami Louis (USA)** *(65+)*(Fav)*(JHMGosden)* 2-9-0 LDettori(2) (lw: trckd ldrs: nt clr run over 1f out: squeezed thro to ld wl ins fnl f: easily)....— **1**
684[4] Tadeo *(62) (MRChannon)* 2-9-0 RHughes(6) (led tl hdd wl ins fnl f: no ch w wnr)....1 **2**
Pekay *(62) (JBerry)* 2-9-0 GCarter(7) (w'like: leggy: cl up: rdn 2f out: r.o)....hd **3**
Theatre Magic *(20) (TJEtherington)* 2-9-0 JFortune(4) (str: bit bkwd: chsd ldrs: outpcd ½-wy: no imp after)....13 **4**
Prime Connections *(MPBielby)* 2-9-0 ACulhane(3) (w'like: outpcd & bhd fr ½-wy)....7 **5**
Primo Lad *(WGMTurner)* 2-9-0 GDuffield(5) (w'like: scope: s.s: virtually p.u)....dist **6**

1/3 L'AMI LOUIS (USA) (op 1/2), **8/1** Tadeo, **10/1** Primo Lad (op 6/1), **11/1** Pekay (op 5/1), **33/1** Theatre Magic, **100/1** Prime Connections, CSF £3.31 TOTE £1.30: £1.10 £2.00 (£2.20) OWNER Oak Cliff Foals of 1993 Plus 2, LLC (NEWMARKET) BRED E. A. Cox Jr 6 Rn
64.4 secs (2.90) SF: 14/11/11/-/-/-

OFFICIAL EXPLANATION **Primo Lad: the jockey felt his mount was wrong on the way down to the start and the Vet also stated that the colt had an awkward gait but was fit to race. A representative of the trainer said that there had been no signs of unsoundness at home.**

837
TOTE CREDIT (S) STKS (3-Y.O) (Class G) £2,497.00 (£692.00: £331.00)
1m 4f 8y Stalls: Low GOING minus 0.48 sec per fur (F) 3-15 (3-19)

521[5] **Risky Rose (39)***(53) (RHollinshead)* 3-8-7 LDettori(1) (trckd ldrs: led ins fnl f: styd on)....— **1**
135[9] High Flown (USA) **(60)***(63) (RonaldThompson)* 3-9-5 MBirch(5) (cl up: led over 2f out tl ins fnl f: one pce)....1½ **2**
Nivasha **(44)***(50) (MBell)* 3-8-7 KFallon(2) (in tch tl outpcd 5f out: hdwy over 2f out: n.m.r & r.o one pce)....1 **3**
Africannightingale (IRE) *(53)*(Fav)*(MHTompkins)* 3-8-7 (5) SMulvey(6) (outpcd over 4f out: hdwy u.p 2f out: one pce ins fnl f)....1¼ **4**
654[11] Emnala (IRE) **(48)***(44) (MRChannon)* 3-8-2 (5) JStack(9) (prom: effrt over 3f out: one pce fnl 2f)....3 **5**
477[5] Bitter N Twisted **(36)***(40) (SEKettlewell)* 3-8-7 JFortune(10) (chsd ldrs: rdn 4f out: sn btn)....3 **6**

213[8] Sergio (IRE) **(30)***(42) (MCChapman)* 3-8-5 (7) CMunday(7) (a outpcd & bhd) 2½ 7
468[8] He's Special *(37) (CACyzer)* 3-8-12 GDuffield(4) (led tl hdd & wknd over 2f out) 3½ 8

100/30 Africannightingale (IRE), **7/2** Emnala (IRE), RISKY ROSE, **4/1** Nivasha, **9/1** High Flown (USA), **10/1** He's Special, **16/1** Bitter N Twisted, **33/1** Sergio (IRE), CSF £30.83 TOTE £4.00: £1.30 £2.10 £1.40 (£13.70) Trio £35.20 OWNER Mr M. Johnson (UPPER LONGDON) BRED Miss Sarah Hollinshead 8 Rn
2m 43.8 (9.50) SF: -/10/-/-/-/-/-/-
Bt in 4,400 gns

838

TOTE DUAL FORECAST H'CAP (0-80) (3-Y.O+) (Class D) £6,264.00 (£1,872.00: £896.00: £408.00)
6f Stalls: Low GOING minus 0.48 sec per fur (F) 3-45 (3-48)

611[6] **Castlerea Lad (79)***(82) (RHollinshead)* 6-10-0 LDettori(7) (rr div: hdwy on ins over 1f out: r.o wl to ld wl ins fnl f) ....— 1
674* Chiming In **(73)***(76)*(Fav)*(MrsJRRamsden)* 3-8-11 KFallon(3) (bhd: hdwy on ins to ld 1f out: hung rt & hdd wl ins fnl f) ....hd 2
Jato **(74)***(76) (SCWilliams)* 6-9-9 GHind(5) (b.nr fore: trckd ldrs: chal ins fnl f: nt qckn nr fin) ....nk 3
General Gubbins **(60)***(59) (JHetherton)* 4-8-9 BThomson(10) (in tch: styd on wl fnl f) 1 4
434[17] Two Moves in Front (IRE) **(74)***(70) (JBerry)* 5-9-9 GCarter(12) (bhd & rdn over 2f out: styd on fnl f) 1¼ 5
702[4] Sobering Thoughts **(66)***(62) (JLEyre)* 9-9-1 JFortune(1) (b.hind: s.i.s: sn in tch: effrt 2f out: one pce fnl f) ....hd 6
601[4] Love Legend **(56)***(52) (DWPArbuthnot)* 10-8-5 BDoyle(8) (b: in tch: effrt 2f out: nt pce to chal) ....s.h 7
579[5] Blue Grit **(55)***(48) (MDods)* 9-8-4 WWoods(2) (cl up: led wl over 1f out tl hdd 1f out: sn btn) 1 8
611[11] Benzoe (IRE) **(69)***(59) (MrsJRRamsden)* 5-9-4 SDWilliams(13) (chsd ldrs: shkn up 2f out: r.o one pce) 1 9
Tutu Sixtysix **(52)***(41) (DonEnricoIncisa)* 4-8-1 KimTinkler(11) (hld up & bhd: sme late hdwy) nk 10
702[5] Bella Parkes **(64)***(53) (DNicholls)* 4-8-13b AlexGreaves(6) (lw: led tl hdd wl over 1f out: nt qckn) ....hd 11
526[19] Cafe Solo **(47)***(36) (NBycroft)* 4-7-10 NKennedy(4) (hld up & bhd: nvr nr to chal) ....s.h 12
King Rat (IRE) **(74)***(60) (TJEtherington)* 4-9-9 MBirch(9) (cl up tl rdn & btn appr fnl f) 1¼ 13

5/1 Chiming In, **11/2** CASTLEREA LAD, **6/1** Sobering Thoughts, Blue Grit, **13/2** Bella Parkes, **9/1** Jato, **10/1** Love Legend, **12/1** Two Moves in Front (IRE), **14/1** King Rat (IRE), **20/1** Benzoe (IRE), **25/1** General Gubbins, **33/1** Cafe Solo, Tutu Sixtysix, CSF £31.38 CT £223.05 TOTE £7.20: £2.20 £1.70 £3.10 (£19.50) Trio £97.60 OWNER Mrs Tess Graham (UPPER LONGDON) BRED J. D. Hurd 13 Rn
1m 17.3 (3.00) SF: 33/16/27/10/21/13/3/-/10/-/4/-/11
WEIGHT FOR AGE 3yo-11lb

839

TOTE BOOKMAKERS LIMITED STKS (0-60) (3-Y.O+) (Class F) £3,081.00 (£866.00: £423.00)
1m 4y Stalls: Low GOING minus 0.48 sec per fur (F) 4-15 (4-16)

813[2] **Shinerolla (62)***(69)*(Fav)*(MrsJRRamsden)* 3-8-9 KFallon(5) (trckd ldrs: shkn up to ld ins fnl f: comf) ....— 1
492* Concer Un **(60)***(69) (SCWilliams)* 3-8-11 GHind(13) (lw: trckd ldrs: smooth hdwy to ld 1½f out: hdd ins fnl f: kpt on) 1¼ 2
568[4] Wentbridge Lad (IRE) **(49)***(64) (BAMcMahon)* 5-9-10b LDettori(14) (hdwy over 3f out: chsng ldrs 1f out: r.o) 2½ 3
549[8] Aljawab (USA) **(57)***(59) (JLDunlop)* 4-9-8 BThomson(4) (trckd ldr gng wl: led wl over 1f out: sn hdd & one pce) 1¼ 4
Desert Zone (USA) **(60)***(52) (JLHarris)* 6-9-8 PRobinson(3) (bhd tl styd on wl fnl 2f: nrst fin) 3½ 5
702[7] Johnnie the Joker **(60)***(51) (JPLeigh)* 4-9-8b DeanMcKeown(1) (led tl hdd wl over 1f out: one pce) ....nk 6
676[14] Zanzara (IRE) **(46)***(44) (MrsVAAconley)* 4-9-3 MDeering(10) (bhd tl styd on fnl 3f) 1¼ 7
Durham Drapes **(60)***(42) (MHEasterby)* 4-9-3 MBirch(8) (bhd: hdwy 3f out: nvr nr to chal) 1 8
*587** Three Arch Bridge **(58)***(41) (MJohnston)* 3-8-6b RHills(17) (in tch: effrt 3f out: btn wl over 1f out) 1½ 9
546[15] Dalcross **(47)***(39) (HJCollingridge)* 4-9-3 MRimmer(20) (s.i.s: hdwy 3f out: rdn & btn appr fnl f) ....s.h 10
Gant Bleu (FR) **(45)***(34) (RMWhitaker)* 8-9-8 ACulhane(2) (trckd ldrs tl rdn & wknd 2f out) 5 11

Saint Amigo **(59)***(31) (JLEyre)* 3-8-9 JFortune(15) (bhd: rdn & hdwy ½-wy: wknd wl over 1f out) 1½ **12**
702[15] Awesome Venture **(52)***(28) (MCChapman)* 5-9-1 (7) CMunday(18) (cl up tl wknd fnl 2f) 1¼ **13**
Nobby Barnes **(47)***(28) (DonEnricoIncisa)* 6-9-8 KimTinkler(7) (s.i.s: hdwy ½-wy: wknd 2f out) ....s.h **14**
Sweetlittlemystery **(32)***(23) (EJAlston)* 4-9-3 WWoods(19) (n.d) ....hd **15**
178[7] Dolly Dolittle **(28)***(18) (HJCollingridge)* 4-9-3 DBiggs(11) (a bhd) 2½ **16**
672[10] Reed My Lips (IRE) **(35)***(9) (BPJBaugh)* 4-9-1 (7) PRoberts(16) (b.nr hind: s.i.s: hdwy ½-wy: sn wknd) 7 **17**
Bee Dee Best (IRE) **(37)***(7) (JPSmith)* 4-9-5 (3) CHodgson(12) (in tch tl wknd over 2f out) 1¼ **18**
587[2] Shared Risk **(60)** *(SGNorton)* 3-8-4 (5) JStack(6) (cl up 5½f: sn lost pl) 6 **19**
Steadfast Elite (IRE) **(43)** *(JJO'Neill)* 4-9-3 SDWilliams(9) (b: a bhd: t.o) 20 **20**

9/4 SHINEROLLA, **11/2** Three Arch Bridge, **7/1** Concer Un, Wentbridge Lad (IRE), **15/2** Aljawab (USA), **8/1** Johnnie the Joker (6/1-9/1), **10/1** Durham Drapes, **16/1** Saint Amigo, Desert Zone (USA), **20/1** Shared Risk, **33/1** Dalcross, Zanzara (IRE), Awesome Venture, Gant Bleu (FR), Steadfast Elite (IRE), **50/1** Nobby Barnes, Sweetlittlemystery, Bee Dee Best (IRE), **100/1** Dolly Dolittle, Reed My Lips (IRE), CSF £20.26 TOTE £3.80: £1.80 £3.10 £2.70 (£23.60) Trio £42.20 OWNER Mrs Alison Iles (THIRSK) BRED Lord Vestey 20 Rn

1m 43.9 (1.90) SF: 38/38/46/41/34/33/26/24/10/21/16/-/10/10/5/-/-/-/-/-

WEIGHT FOR AGE 3yo-13lb

840 TOTE MARATHON H'CAP (0-70) (4-Y.O+) (Class E) £4,045.00 (£1,210.00: £580.00: £265.00)

2m 5f 122y Stalls: Centre GOING minus 0.48 sec per fur (F) 4-45 (4-46)

696[6] **Elburg (IRE) (58)***(74) (RPCHoad)* 5-9-6 KFallon(4) (bhd: hdwy u.p 7f out: styd on wl to ld wl ins fnl f: eased twrds fin) ....— **1**
696[8] Brandon Prince (IRE) **(66)***(80) (IABalding)* 7-10-0 LDettori(12) (swtg: hdwy 8f out: hmpd over 2f out: kpt on wl ins fnl f) 2½ **2**
751[3] Kadiri (IRE) **(52)***(66)*(Fav)*(JRBosley)* 4-9-0 GHind(5) (lw: hld up & bhd: hdwy 7f out: led over 3f out tl wknd & hdd wl ins fnl f) ....½ **3**
Grace Card **(45)***(56) (MrsMReveley)* 9-8-7 JFortune(10) (lw: chsd ldrs: rdn to chal over 3f out: one pce) 4 **4**
729[4] Cristal Springs **(35)***(45) (BJMcMath)* 4-7-4 (7) MartinDwyer(11) (in tch: effrt & ev ch 4f out: one pce) 1¾ **5**
751[7] Murphys Way **(41)***(36) (JLEyre)* 6-8-3 RLappin(8) (a.p: led 5f out tl over 3f out: sn wknd) 20 **6**
Wings of Freedom (IRE) **(40)***(24) (JRJenkins)* 7-8-2v DBiggs(7) (bhd: effrt ½-wy: n.d) 15 **7**
649[3] Arc Bright (IRE) **(38)***(20) (RHollinshead)* 5-7-9 (5)ow1 AGarth(13) (lw: cl up: led 8½f out tl hdd 5f out: sn wknd) ....½ **8**
Master of Troy **(58)***(40) (CParker)* 7-9-6v MBirch(15) (mid div: effrt 7f out: sn btn) 1¼ **9**
598[3] Milngavie (IRE) **(40)***(21) (MJohnston)* 5-8-2 PRobinson(3) (prom: hmpd over 8f out: sn wknd) 1 **10**
778[10] Jalore **(40)***(18) (SCoathup)* 6-8-2 TSprake(9) (led 2f: chsd ldrs tl wknd 6f out) 4 **11**
751[13] Mandalay Prince **(31)** *(TKersey)* 11-7-7 NKennedy(6) (b: sn outpcd & bhd: t.o) 20 **12**
One for the Chief **(34)** *(RMWhitaker)* 7-7-7v(3)ow3 DWright(2) (sn outpcd & bhd: t.o) 12 **13**
751[12] Eightandahalf (IRE) **(56)** *(MrsVAAconley)* 6-8-13 (5) JStack(14) (led after 2f tl hdd 8½f out: sn wknd: wl t.o) ....dist **14**

LONG HANDICAP Mandalay Prince 6-12 One for the Chief 7-1

11/4 Kadiri (IRE), **9/2** Grace Card, **7/1** ELBURG (IRE), **9/1** Master of Troy, **10/1** Arc Bright (IRE), Brandon Prince (IRE), Milngavie (IRE), **16/1** Murphys Way, **20/1** Wings of Freedom (IRE), **25/1** Eightandahalf (IRE), **33/1** Cristal Springs, One for the Chief, **100/1** Jalore, **200/1** Mandalay Prince, CSF £65.85 CT £215.81 TOTE £9.10: £2.50 £2.70 £1.70 (£30.40) Trio £62.40 OWNER Mrs Alison Gamble BRED Sheikh Mohammed bin Rashid al Maktoum 14 Rn

4m 49.4 (9.40) SF: 34/40/26/16/5/-/-/-/-/-/-/-/-/-

841 TOTE PLACEPOT LIMITED STKS (0-75) (4-Y.O+) (Class D) £4,110.00 (£1,230.00: £590.00: £270.00)

1m 2f 6y Stalls: Low GOING minus 0.48 sec per fur (F) 5-15 (5-19)

505[4] **Hazard a Guess (IRE) (67)***(85) (MrsJRRamsden)* 5-9-6 KFallon(9) (hld up: effrt over 2f out: r.o to ld wl ins fnl f) ....— **1**
539[7] Zaralaska **(75)***(91) (LMCumani)* 4-9-11 (3) CHodgson(8) (a.p: chal 2f out: edgd rt fnl f: kpt on wl) 1 **2**
Benjamins Law **(52)***(64) (JAPickering)* 4-8-5 DeanMcKeown(6) (led & sn clr: hdd & no ex wl ins fnl f) 2½ **3**

535[21] Braille (IRE) **(65)***(76) (MGMeagher)* 4-9-4 JFortune(12) (hld up: effrt 3f out: styd on u.p: nvr able chal) 1 4
Floating Line **(63)***(74) (PWigham)* 7-9-2 MWigham(7) (chsd ldrs tl wknd fnl 2f) ....s.h 5
Access Carnival (IRE) **(58)***(68) (RBoss)* 4-8-11 LDettori(3) (bhd: hdwy 3f out: rdn & nt pce to chal) ....½ 6
676[3] Hillzah (USA) **(67)***(77) (RBastiman)* 7-9-1 (5) HBastiman(4) (chsd ldrs tl outpcd fnl 2f) ....hd 7
The Lone Dancer **(74)***(83) (KMcAuliffe)* 4-9-8 (5) RPainter(11) (hld up & bhd: c wd & hdwy appr st: nrst fin) ....nk 8
722[4] Spanish Stripper (USA) **(53)***(58) (MCChapman)* 4-7-13 (7) CMunday(5) (chsd ldrs tl wknd over 3f out) 3 9
676[18] Lochore **(47)***(37) (MrsVAAconley)* 5-8-0 DBiggs(1) (prom tl rdn & btn over 2f out) 9 10
Diamond Crown (IRE) **(49)***(39) (MartynWane)* 4-8-2 GHind(14) (n.d) ....s.h 11
Golden Star (IRE) **(48)***(19) (MWEasterby)* 4-7-8 (7) MartinDwyer(13) (chsd ldrs tl wknd 3f out) 12 12
676* Obelos (USA) **(69)***(29)*(Fav)*(MrsJCecil)* 4-9-8 RHills(2) (chsd ldrs tl outpcd over 3f out: fin lame) 7 13
215[6] Atherton Green (IRE) **(58)** *(JAGlover)* 5-8-11b MBirch(10) (lost tch fnl 4f: t.o) 30 14

9/4 Obelos (USA), **3/1** Zaralaska (op 2/1), **13/2** HAZARD A GUESS (IRE), **8/1** Hillzah (USA), **12/1** The Lone Dancer (op 8/1), Access Carnival (IRE), Atherton Green (IRE), **14/1** Floating Line, **25/1** Spanish Stripper (USA), Diamond Crown (IRE), **33/1** Benjamins Law, Golden Star (IRE), Lochore, **50/1** Braille (IRE), CSF £26.19 CT £575.54 TOTE £7.10: £2.40 £1.70 £9.60 (£17.10) Trio not won; £829.04 to Nottingham 02/05/95 OWNER Mrs D. Ridley (THIRSK) BRED A. F. O'Callaghan in Ireland 14 Rn
2m 12.1 (3.80) SF: 37/43/16/28/26/20/29/35/10/-/-/-/-/-

OFFICIAL EXPLANATION **Atherton Green (IRE): was reported to have become overexcited in blinkers for the first time and after going to the start too freely, ran no sort of race.**

T/Jkpt: £16,212.00 (0.3 Tckts) £15,983.89 to Nottingham 2/5/95. T/Plpt: £31.80 (612.95 Tckts). T/Qdpt: £49.20 (3.80 Tckts). AA

0766-SOUTHWELL (L-H)
Monday May 1st (Standard)

WEATHER: fine WIND: slt against

842
WENSLEYDALE H'CAP (0-65) (3-Y.O) (Class F) £2,519.00 (£694.00: £329.00)
6f (Fibresand) Stalls: Low GOING minus 0.08 sec per fur (STD) 2-30 (2-31)

587[W] **Sweet Mate (42)***(47) (SRBowring)* 3-8-0b(5) CTeague(6) (chsd ldrs: rdn & c wd 2f out: led ins fnl f: sn clr) ....— 1
591[2] Aston Manor (IRE) **(58)***(56)*(Fav)*(RHannon)* 3-9-7 KDarley(5) (chsd ldrs: rdn 2f out: slt ld ent fnl f: sn hdd & no ex) 2½ 2
769[5] Charnwood Queen **(38)***(34) (RWArmstrong)* 3-8-1 RPrice(9) (lw: prom: led bel dist tl hdd & nt qckn ins fnl f) ....¾ 3
Kama Simba **(55)***(43) (NACallaghan)* 3-9-4 TIves(8) (leggy: bit bkwd: hld up in rr: rdn & styd on appr fnl f: nvr nrr) 3 4
646[15] Most Uppitty **(56)***(31) (JBerry)* 3-9-5b JCarroll(3) (led after 1f tl hdd & wknd bel dist) 5 5
732[17] Tish **(40)***(14) (ASmith)* 3-8-3 SMaloney(4) (a in rr) ....nk 6
482[8] Prince Rudolf (IRE) **(48)***(21) (MrsNMacauley)* 3-8-11b MFenton(7) (prom tl wknd wl over 1f out) ....nk 7
146[5] Shartel **(36)** *(MJohnston)* 3-7-13 TWilliams(1) (outpcd: a bhd) 4 8
769[11] Benten **(46)** *(DWChapman)* 3-8-9 DeanMcKeown(2) (led 1f: wknd ½-wy: t.o) 8 9

7/4 Aston Manor (IRE), **6/1** SWEET MATE, Charnwood Queen, Kama Simba, Prince Rudolf (IRE), **13/2** Most Uppitty, **14/1** Shartel, **20/1** Benten, **33/1** Tish, CSF £16.90 CT £62.27 TOTE £8.00: £2.00 £1.40 £1.60 (£6.60) Trio £22.30 OWNER Mrs P. A. Barratt (EDWINSTOWE) BRED T. Barratt 9 Rn
1m 18.4 (4.90) SF: 18/27/5/14/2/-/-/-/-

843
LEICESTER CLAIMING STKS (4-Y.O+) (Class F) £2,519.00 (£694.00: £329.00)
1m 4f (Fibresand) Stalls: High GOING minus 0.08 sec per fur (STD) 3-00 (3-00)

771[4] **Palacegate Jo (IRE) (60)***(71) (RHollinshead)* 4-8-8 TIves(7) (hld up: hdwy & 4th st: led over 1f out: rdn out) ....— 1
588[2] El Nido **(59)***(75) (MJCamacho)* 7-9-0 LCharnock(8) (lw: hld up in tch: hdwy to ld over 2f out: hdd over 1f out: one pce) 1¼ 2
516[4] Red Indian **(50)***(48) (WWHaigh)* 9-8-7 DeanMcKeown(3) (hld up: hdwy 3f out: 5th st: rdn & kpt on one pce) 15 3
367[10] Sagasan **(58)***(58) (WRMuir)* 4-9-3 JCarroll(2) (hld up: hdwy 7f out: 2nd st: rdn & wknd 2f out) ....½ 4

329[8] Killing Time **(56)***(41) (MrsNMacauley)* 4-8-5v MFenton(4) (led tl hdd over 2f out: 3rd st: wknd qckly bel dist) 3½ 5
605[8] Kristis Girl **(40)***(20) (DHaydnJones)* 8-8-4 AMackay(1) (prom over 7f: 6th & btn st: t.o) 15 6
729[10] Moled Again *(12) (JRBosley)* 4-8-2 (3) SSanders(6) (swtg: reard s: prom tl wknd over 4f out: t.o) 7 7
Dakota Brave (IRE) **(66)** (Fav)*(JPearce)* 4-8-7 GBardwell(5) (b: bit bkwd: sn drvn along: lost tch & t.o ½-wy: fin lame) 25 8

5/2 Dakota Brave (IRE), **3/1** PALACEGATE JO (IRE), **7/2** El Nido, **7/1** Killing Time, **15/2** Red Indian, **12/1** Sagasan, **25/1** Kristis Girl, **33/1** Moled Again, CSF £13.12 TOTE £4.00: £1.10 £1.30 £1.30 (£5.70) OWNER Palacegate Corporation Ltd (UPPER LONGDON) BRED Brendan and Sheila Powell 8 Rn 2m 44.9 (10.70) SF: 18/22/-/5/-/-/-/-
Palacegate Jo clmd D Chapman £8,000

844 CHEDDAR MEDIAN AUCTION MAIDEN STKS (3-Y.O) (Class F)
£2,519.00 (£694.00: £329.00)
1m (Fibresand) Stalls: Low GOING minus 0.08 sec per fur (STD) 3-30 (3-30)

Quango *(71+)*(Fav)*(JGFitzGerald)* 3-9-0 TIves(6) (w'like: leggy: bit bkwd: hld up: hdwy to ld over 3f out: clr appr fnl f: canter) ....— 1
591[7] Komiamaite *(65) (SRBowring)* 3-8-9b(5) CTeague(5) (s.s: 5th st: hung rt & hdwy 2f out: no imp fnl f) 3 2
592[7] Top Fella (USA) **(58)***(61) (WAO'Gorman)* 3-9-0v EmmaO'Gorman(4) (chsd ldrs: led 5f out tl over 3f out: 2nd st: rdn & one pce fnl 2f) 2 3
628[5] Claireswan (IRE) *(49) (SCWilliams)* 3-9-0 MFenton(3) (prom: 3rd & rdn st: wknd 2f out) 6 4
Halfabob (IRE) *(DHaydnJones)* 3-9-0 AMackay(7) (w'like: str: bkwd: s.s: hdwy ½-wy: 4th st: sn wknd: t.o) 25 5
Donna Fugata (IRE) *(CBBBooth)* 3-8-9 JCarroll(1) (w'like: scope: bkwd: s.i.s: sn chsng ldrs: 6th & wkng st: t.o) 11 6
732[15] Daniel's Lass *(CNAllen)* 3-8-9 MTebbutt(2) (led 3f: wknd over 3f out: t.o) 5 7

2/1 QUANGO, **9/4** Top Fella (USA), **5/1** Claireswan (IRE), **11/2** Komiamaite, **14/1** Donna Fugata (IRE), **16/1** Halfabob (IRE), Daniel's Lass, CSF £12.57 TOTE £2.60: £1.90 £2.50 (£7.10) OWNER Mr L. Milligan (MALTON) BRED Lord Fairhaven 7 Rn 1m 46.8 (7.50) SF: 18/12/8/-/-/-/-

845 BRIE H'CAP (0-70) (3-Y.O+) (Class E) £3,359.40 (£1,003.20: £479.60: £217.80)
1m (Fibresand) Stalls: Low GOING minus 0.08 sec per fur (STD) 4-00 (4-01)

749[16] **Major Mouse (57)***(65) (WWHaigh)* 7-9-3 DaleGibson(10) (lw: hld up: hdwy over 2f out: led appr fnl f: hrd rdn: all out) ....— 1
634[14] A Million Watts **(68)***(75) (LadyHerries)* 4-10-0 TIves(9) (mid div: rdn ½-wy: hdwy & 7th st: jnd wnr over 1f out: unable qckn nr fin) ....½ 2
675[4] Crucis (IRE) **(47)***(51) (BAMcMahon)* 4-8-4 (3) SSanders(5) (chsd ldrs: 4th st: ev ch appr fnl f: one pce) 1¾ 3
624[2] Flashfeet **(54)***(48) (KBishop)* 5-9-0 JWilliams(12) (hdwy ½-wy: 6th st: styd on one pce fnl 2f) 5 4
601[3] Duello **(66)***(53) (MBlanshard)* 4-9-12 StephenDavies(7) (a.p: led 3f out: hdd & 2nd st: wknd over 1f out) 3½ 5
738[10] Scottish Park **(40)***(26) (RWEmery)* 6-8-0 AMackay(11) (lw: hld up: hdwy ½-wy: nt rch ldrs) ....½ 6
478[3] Mary's Case (IRE) **(56)***(39) (MJohnston)* 5-9-2b TWilliams(4) (prom: led over 2f out tl hdd & wknd over 1f out) 1¼ 7
627[2] Indian Serenade **(54)***(29) (PWHarris)* 4-9-0 JCarroll(1) (chsd ldrs to ½-wy: wknd qckly) 4 8
Mohican Brave (IRE) **(61)***(34) (JLHarris)* 5-9-7be SMaloney(8) (a in rr) 1 9
749[2] Queens Consul (IRE) **(62)***(27)*(Fav)*(BSRothwell)* 5-9-8 LCharnock(6) (sn led: hrd rdn & hdd over 3f out: 5th & btn ent st) 4 10
*519** South Forest (IRE) **(65)***(22) (SRBowring)* 4-9-6 (5) CTeague(2) (lw: dwlt: hdwy 4f out: eased whn btn wl over 1f out) 4 11
769[13] Wellsy Lad (USA) **(35)** *(DWChapman)* 8-7-2b(7)ow2 CAdamson(3) (chsd ldr: led over 3f out: hdd & 3rd st: sn lost pl) 1 12
LONG HANDICAP Wellsy Lad (USA) 7-6

9/4 Queens Consul (IRE) (op 4/1), **5/1** Indian Serenade, South Forest (IRE), **11/2** A Million Watts (4/1-6/1), **13/2** Duello, **10/1** MAJOR MOUSE, **12/1** Mary's Case (IRE) (op 8/1), **14/1** Crucis (IRE), **16/1** Flashfeet, **20/1** Wellsy Lad (USA), **25/1** Scottish Park, Mohican Brave (IRE), CSF £66.71 CT £727.09 TOTE £22.20: £4.90 £4.10 £2.10 (£36.40) Trio £449.30 OWNER Mr N. Barber (MALTON) BRED Mrs V. Haigh 12 Rn 1m 45.5 (6.20) SF: 33/43/19/16/21/-/7/-/2/-/-/-

OFFICIAL EXPLANATION Queens Consul (IRE): was reported to have felt lifeless going to post and ran flat during the race. A routine test was ordered.

846 GLOUCESTER (S) STKS (2-Y.O) (Class G) £2,243.00 (£618.00: £293.00)
5f (Fibresand) Stalls: High GOING minus 0.08 sec per fur (STD) 4-30 (4-30)

Moi Canard *(66)*(Fav)*(JBerry)* 2-8-11 JCarroll(3) (neat: lw: s.i.s: hdwy 3f out: sn rdn: led bel dist: clr fnl f: eased nr fin)......— 1
644⁵ Donington Park *(45) (JAHarris)* 2-8-1 (5) PMcCabe(4) (led after 2f to bel dist: sn rdn & outpcd)......5 2
699⁸ Royal Rigger *(29) (CSmith)* 2-8-6 JFanning(2) (led 2f: ev ch tl wknd 2f out)......5 3
638⁵ Baileys Bride (IRE) *(29) (MJohnston)* 2-8-6 TWilliams(1) (early spd: rdn & lost tch ½-wy: sn outpcd)......hd 4

4/7 MOI CANARD, **7/2** Donington Park, **5/1** Baileys Bride (IRE) (7/2-11/2), **8/1** Royal Rigger, CSF £3.07 TOTE £1.40 (£2.20) OWNER Bloy & Hughes (COCKERHAM) BRED Llety Stud 4 Rn
62.6 secs (4.60) SF: 11/-/-/-
Bt in 3,200 gns

847 GOUDA H'CAP (0-65) (3-Y.O F) (Class F) £2,519.00 (£694.00: £329.00)
7f (Fibresand) Stalls: Low GOING minus 0.08 sec per fur (STD) 5-00 (5-02)

*515** **Cloette (63)***(76)*(Fav)*(WAO'Gorman)* 3-9-7 EmmaO'Gorman(8) (lw: led after 2f tl over 2f out: rallied to ld ins fnl f: r.o wl)......— 1
360⁶ Sand Star **(51)***(61) (DHaydnJones)* 3-8-9 AMackay(9) (chsd ldrs: 2nd st: led over 2f out tl ins fnl f: no ex nr fin)......1¼ 2
766⁸ Nuthatch (IRE) **(43)***(42) (MDIUsher)* 3-7-8 (7) CAdamson(5) (bhd & outpcd: sn drvn along: styd on appr fnl f)......5 3
587⁴ Joyful Times **(43)***(36) (MrsNMacauley)* 3-7-8 (7) AmandaSanders(6) (hld up: hdwy fnl 2f: nrst fin)......2½ 4
573⁷ Prudent Pet **(60)***(52) (CWFairhurst)* 3-9-4 JFanning(2) (prom: 3rd st: wknd wl over 1f out).....nk 5
732⁵ Dowdency **(42)***(29) (JAPickering)* 3-8-0 DaleGibson(4) (hld up: effrt & 4th st: rdn 2f out: grad wknd)......2½ 6
576² Woodrising **(55)***(37) (LadyHerries)* 3-8-13 GDuffield(7) (led 1f: 6th & rdn ent st: sn btn)......2 7
546¹¹ Jobber's Fiddle **(58)***(40) (DJSffrenchDavis)* 3-9-2b TIves(3) (led after 1f to 5f out: 5th & rdn st: sn btn)......hd 8
759¹⁹ Longcroft **(43)***(12) (KWHogg)* 3-7-8 (7)ow1 ADaly(1) (dwlt: sn rcvrd to chse ldrs: wknd 3f out: t.o)......5 9

7/4 CLOETTE (5/2-6/4), **4/1** Woodrising, **11/2** Prudent Pet, **8/1** Jobber's Fiddle, Joyful Times, Dowdency, **10/1** Sand Star (7/1-12/1), **14/1** Nuthatch (IRE), **25/1** Longcroft, CSF £19.79 CT £183.68 TOTE £2.00: £1.50 £3.50 £3.10 (£14.40) Trio £66.80 OWNER Mr S. Fustok (NEWMARKET) BRED Deerfield Farm 9 Rn 1m 32.3 (5.50) SF: 36/21/2/-/12/-/-/-/-

T/Plpt: £306.10 (30.66 Tckts). T/Qdpt: Not won; £41.80 to Nottingham 2/5/95. IM

WINDSOR (Fig. 8)
Monday May 1st (Good)
WEATHER: sunny WIND: almost nil

848 TORRISH CLAIMING STKS (3-Y.O+) (Class F) £2,969.00 (£834.00: £407.00)
1m 67y Stalls: High GOING minus 0.32 sec per fur (GF) 5-30 (5-31)

371⁶ **Arndilly (67)***(67) (BJMeehan)* 4-8-13b TQuinn(2) (3rd st: led wl over 1f out: drvn out)......— 1
748⁴ Roseate Lodge **(64)***(62) (KRBurke)* 9-8-13 AClark(13) (7th st: ev ch over 1f out: nt qckn)......2½ 2
Cyrano's Lad (IRE) *(60) (JohnBerry)* 6-9-1 CDwyer(12) (led tl wl over 1f out: r.o)......2 3
Cape Pigeon (USA) **(58)***(58) (LGCottrell)* 10-9-0 NCarlisle(17) (lw: 5th st: r.o one pce fnl 2f)......½ 4
Tykeyvor (IRE) **(74)***(65) (LadyHerries)* 5-9-7 WRyan(8) (b: hdwy 3f out: one pce fnl 2f)......hd 5
563⁶ Gulf Shaadi **(84)***(60)*(Fav)*(GLewis)* 3-8-9 SWhitworth(19) (plld hrd: hdwy & 8th st: one pce fnl 3f)......3 6
Horsetrader *(48) (RHannon)* 3-8-6 RPerham(4) (leggy: bit bkwd: hdwy fnl 2f: nvr nrr)......5 7
624⁹ Ballestro (IRE) **(40)***(49) (JFfitch-Heyes)* 3-8-8 PaulEddery(14) (4th st: wknd 2f out)......½ 8
Formidable Lass *(37) (LGCottrell)* 4-9-0 MFenton(6) (2nd st: wknd over 2f out)......2½ 9
355⁸ Doodies Pool (IRE) **(53)***(36) (GLMoore)* 5-9-0 BRouse(11) (6th st: wknd over 2f out)......½ 10

450[16] Ragazzo (IRE) **(41)***(36) (KOCunningham-Brown)* 5-9-0 WNewnes(9) (a mid div)....................hd 11
39[7] Prince Rodney **(42)***(32) (CJDrewe)* 6-8-7 (5) AWhelan(7) (bit bkwd: sme hdwy 4f out: wknd 2f out)....................1 12
543[9] False Pretences (IRE) **(35)***(25) (BAPearce)* 3-7-9 (5) MBaird(10) (a bhd)....................4 13
543[7] R Dragon **(35)***(23) (MMadgwick)* 3-7-5 (7) IonaWands(18) (lw: a bhd)....................s.h 14
Allimac Nomis *(18) (ICampbell)* 6-9-5 NAdams(3) (bkwd: a bhd)....................7 15
Indian Treasure (IRE) *(13) (DJSCosgrove)* 3-8-1 RPrice(15) (str: bit bkwd: s.s: a bhd)....................s.h 16
149[8] Honest Achiever (IRE) *(APJames)* 4-8-8 FNorton(1) (a bhd)....................6 17
Head For Heaven *(RPCHoad)* 5-9-5 AMcGlone(5) (bit bkwd: s.s: a wl bhd)....................6 18

13/8 Gulf Shaadi, **4/1** Roseate Lodge, **13/2** ARNDILLY, **7/1** Tykeyvor (IRE), **10/1** Cape Pigeon (USA), Cyrano's Lad (IRE), **16/1** Horsetrader, Ragazzo (IRE), Head For Heaven, Doodies Pool (IRE), Prince Rodney, Indian Treasure (IRE), **33/1** Formidable Lass, **50/1** R Dragon, Allimac Nomis, Ballestro (IRE), Honest Achiever (IRE), False Pretences (IRE), CSF £36.64 TOTE £7.40: £2.30 £1.70 £3.00 (£12.60) Trio £148.30 OWNER Mr A. S. Reid (UPPER LAMBOURN) BRED Hilborough Stud Farm Ltd 18 Rn 1m 45.0 (3.40) SF: 38/33/31/29/36/18/6/7/8/7/7/3/-/-/-/-/-/-
WEIGHT FOR AGE 3yo-13lb

849

EUROPEAN BREEDERS FUND BLUE CHARM MAIDEN STKS (2-Y.O) (Class D) £3,891.25 (£1,180.00: £577.50: £276.25)
5f 10y Stalls: High GOING minus 0.32 sec per fur (GF) 6-00 (6-02)

617[8] **Jolis Present** *(65)*(Fav)*(MJRyan)* 2-9-0 WCarson(9) (a.p: hrd rdn & led ins fnl f: r.o)....................— 1
671[4] Princely Sound *(64)*(Fav)*(MBell)* 2-9-0 MFenton(8) (led tl ins fnl f: r.o)....................nk 2
What Fun *(55) (RHannon)* 2-9-0 RHughes(3) (neat: s.s: hdwy 2f out: nt clr run over 1f out: nt rcvr)....................3 3
Ben'a'vachei Boy *(43) (JDBethell)* 2-9-0 WRSwinburn(6) (w'like: a.p: ev ch over 1f out: wknd fnl f)....................3½ 4
Northern Saga (IRE) *(36) (AndrewTurnell)* 2-9-0 NAdams(7) (w'like: bit bkwd: chsd ldrs: one pce fnl 2f)....................2½ 5
Petite Annie *(25) (TGMills)* 2-8-9 AClark(5) (neat: bit bkwd: spd 3f)....................1¾ 6
617[11] Pride of Kashmir *(30) (PWHarris)* 2-9-0 RCochrane(4) (spd 3f)....................hd 7
Young Butt *(20) (JFfitch-Heyes)* 2-9-0 RPrice(2) (b: neat: a bhd)....................3 8
455[7] Red Sky Delight (IRE) *(PButler)* 2-8-4 (5) SDrowne(1) (prom over 2f)....................6 9
Secret Commander *(TJNaughton)* 2-9-0 DHolland(10) (str: bkwd: a bhd: t.o)....................30 10

2/1 JOLIS PRESENT, Princely Sound (6/4-5/2), **6/1** Ben'a'vachei Boy, **7/1** What Fun (op 3/1), **8/1** Pride of Kashmir (op 4/1), **10/1** Petite Annie (8/1-12/1), **16/1** Secret Commander, **33/1** Young Butt, Red Sky Delight (IRE), Northern Saga (IRE), CSF £6.92 TOTE £3.40: £1.10 £1.10 £2.90 (£3.40) Trio £5.30 OWNER Mr D. G. Thomson (NEWMARKET) BRED Mrs M. A. Ryan 10 Rn
62.3 secs (3.30) SF: 17/16/7/-/-/-/-/-/-/-

850

STORACALL H'CAP (0-95) (3-Y.O) (Class C) £5,680.00 (£1,720.00: £840.00: £400.00)
5f 10y Stalls: High GOING: 0.32 sec per fur (G) 6-30 (6-33)

621[13] **Sally Slade (72)***(81) (CACyzer)* 3-8-8 KDarley(11) (hdwy 3f out: led 2f out: all out)....................— 1
Youdontsay **(60)***(64) (RCurtis)* 3-7-3 (7)ow3 SLanigan(7) (gd hdwy over 1f out: ev ch ins fnl f: r.o)....................½ 2
524[13] Tharwa (IRE) **(57)***(63) (NACallaghan)* 3-7-2 (5) MBaird(16) (b.nr fore: b.off hind: led 3f: ev ch ins fnl f: edgd lft: r.o)....................½ 3
681[4] Cats Bottom **(72)***(67)*(Fav)*(DJSCosgrove)* 3-8-8 MRimmer(15) (a.p: nt qckn fnl f)....................3½ 4
681[6] Musica **(80)***(70)*(Fav)*(MRChannon)* 3-9-2 RHughes(5) (hdwy fnl 2f: nvr nrr)....................1½ 5
In Love Again (IRE) **(85)***(73) (MRChannon)* 3-9-0 (7) JDennis(9) (dwlt: gd hdwy fnl 2f: r.o)....................½ 6
Montserrat **(83)***(68) (LGCottrell)* 3-9-5 NCarlisle(1) (nrst fin)....................1 7
621[14] Classic Pet (IRE) **(57)***(41) (CAHorgan)* 3-7-7 NAdams(8) (b: nt clr run over 1f out: nvr nr to chal)....................nk 8
Solo Prize **(75)***(59) (PHowling)* 3-8-11 WNewnes(10) (b.hind: bhd tl r.o fnl f)....................s.h 9
Try to Please (IRE) **(82)***(62) (MJHeaton-Ellis)* 3-9-4 WWoods(2) (nvr trbld ldrs)....................1¼ 10
581[3] Endless Wave **(75)***(50)*(Fav)*(MBell)* 3-8-11 MFenton(13) (prom 3f)....................1¾ 11
621[11] Squire Corrie **(67)***(37)*(Fav)*(LJHolt)* 3-7-12 (5) NVarley(6) (prom 3f)....................1½ 12
Medieval Miss **(72)***(42) (GLewis)* 3-8-8 PaulEddery(12) (w ldr: wknd qckly over 1f out)....................s.h 13
697[9] Just Dissident (IRE) **(64)***(23) (RMWhitaker)* 3-8-0 WCarson(3) (outpcd)....................3½ 14
629[10] Top Pearl **(60)***(6) (NAGraham)* 3-7-10b GBardwell(4) (lw: outpcd)....................4 15
LONG HANDICAP Youdontsay 7-4 Classic Pet (IRE) 7-5

6/1 Cats Bottom, Musica, Squire Corrie, Endless Wave, **8/1** Tharwa (IRE) (6/1-9/1), **9/1** SALLY SLADE, Medieval Miss, **10/1** Just Dissident (IRE), Try to Please (IRE), **14/1** Top Pearl, Montserrat, **20/1** In Love Again (IRE), Solo Prize, **40/1** Youdontsay, Classic Pet (IRE), CSF £278.52 CT £2,733.45 TOTE £21.60: £5.70 £31.40 £4.40 (£272.40) Trio £547.40 OWNER Mr R. M. Cyzer (HORSHAM) BRED C. A. Cyzer 15 Rn 61.2 secs (2.20) SF: 29/12/11/15/18/21/16/-/7/10/-/-/-/-/-

851 DUSTY MILLER H'CAP (0-80) (3-Y.O) (Class D) £3,842.50 (£1,165.00: £570.00: £272.50) **1m 3f 135y** Stalls: High GOING minus 0.32 sec per fur (GF) 7-00 (7-04)

745* **Fujiyama Crest (IRE) (60)***(67+)*(Fav)*(MRStoute)* 3-8-2v(3) 5x JTate(3) (b.nr hind: 5th st: led over 2f out: r.o wl) — 1
647[5] Red Bustaan **(75)***(80) (ACStewart)* 3-9-6 WRSwinburn(6) (lw: hld up: 7th st: ev ch fnl 2f: hrd rdn: r.o) 1½ 2
648[4] Silktail (IRE) **(59)***(63) (JohnBerry)* 3-8-4 GCarter(10) (gd hdwy fnl 2f: nvr nrr) 1 3
453* Iron N Gold **(51)***(52) (SDow)* 3-7-10 ow3 FNorton(1) (hdwy 3f out: ev ch 2f out: hung bdly lft: nt rcvr: fin 5th, 3l: plcd 4th) 4
663[8] Birthday Boy (IRE) **(70)***(70) (RHannon)* 3-9-1 RHughes(8) (6th st: no hdwy fnl 2f: fin 6th, ½l: plcd 5th) 5
717[7] Euro Forum **(55)** *(GLMoore)* 3-8-0 WCarson(7) (wl bhd tl r.o fnl 2f) 4 7
626[2] Last Corner **(58)** *(RHollinshead)* 3-8-3 KDarley(5) (a mid div) 1½ 8
Sorisky **(48)** *(BGubby)* 3-7-7 NCarlisle(14) (led tl over 6f out: 2nd st: wknd 3f out) 4 9
Bobby's Dream **(50)** *(MHTompkins)* 3-7-9 GBardwell(15) (lw: hdwy 5f out: wknd 3f out) hd 10
545[11] Mega Tid **(55)** *(BAPearce)* 3-7-11 (3) SSanders(9) (nvr nr to chal) 1¾ 11
655[4] Vizard (IRE) **(70)** *(MJHeaton-Ellis)* 3-9-1b PaulEddery(11) (3rd st: led over 3f out tl wknd 2f out) 2 12
651[5] Much Too High **(56)** *(TJNaughton)* 3-8-1 AMcGlone(4) (nvr nr ldrs) s.h 13
584[3] Crowned Glory (USA) **(76)** *(PFICole)* 3-9-7 TQuinn(2) (lw: 4th st: wkng whn bmpd 2f out) ½ 14
635[12] China Mail (IRE) **(66)** *(JMPEustace)* 3-8-11 RCochrane(12) (lw: outpcd) s.h 15
618[9] Paper Cloud **(70)** *(CEBrittain)* 3-9-1 BDoyle(16) (led over 6f out tl wknd over 3f out) 2½ 16
651* Poly Road **(55)***(59) (MRChannon)* 3-8-0 CRutter(13) (gd hdwy & veered lft 2f out: r.o wl fnl f: fin 4th, nk: disq, plcd last) 0

LONG HANDICAP Sorisky 7-4

7/2 FUJIYAMA CREST (IRE) (op 2/1), **9/2** Iron N Gold, **7/1** Red Bustaan, Silktail (IRE) (op 9/2), **8/1** Mega Tid, Poly Road (5/1-9/1), Crowned Glory (USA), **9/1** Last Corner (7/1-11/1), **10/1** Birthday Boy (IRE) (8/1-12/1), **12/1** Paper Cloud, **20/1** Bobby's Dream, Much Too High, Vizard (IRE), Euro Forum, **25/1** China Mail (IRE), **33/1** Sorisky, CSF £33.25 CT £170.24 TOTE £4.80: £2.10 £2.00 £2.30 £1.60 (£20.60) Trio £77.00 OWNER Mr Seisuke Hata (NEWMARKET) BRED B. Kennedy 16 Rn 2m 29.5 (3.50) SF: 41/54/37/-/-/-/-/-/-/-/-/-/-/-/-/-

STEWARDS' ENQUIRY Rutter suspended 10-15/5/95 (irresponsible riding).

852 ROBERT WALTERS ASSOCIATES STKS (2-Y.O F) (Class C) £4,660.10 (£1,745.90: £855.45: £369.75: £167.38: £86.42) **5f 10y** Stalls: High GOING minus 0.32 sec per fur (GF) 7-30 (7-35)

650* **Anotheranniversary** *(78)*(Fav)*(GLewis)* 2-8-8 PaulEddery(2) (swvd rt s: w ldrs: led wl over 1f out: pushed out) — 1
Marl *(73) (RAkehurst)* 2-8-4 GCarter(4) (neat: hmpd s: outpcd: rapid hdwy fnl f: r.o) nk 2
Cascadia (IRE) *(72) (PFICole)* 2-8-4 TQuinn(5) (w'like: bdly hmpd s: outpcd: gd hdwy over 1f out: r.o) ½ 3
To The Whire *(71) (GLMoore)* 2-8-4 BRouse(3) (leggy: bdly hmpd twice after s: gd late hdwy: r.o) nk 4
716* Kandavu *(75) (MMcCormack)* 2-8-11 AClark(8) (w ldr: led over 2f out tl wl over 1f out) ¾ 5
Mystery Matthias *(55) (MissBSanders)* 2-8-1 (3) SSanders(1) (neat: bit bkwd: nrst fin) 4 6
725* Sam Coles (USA) *(50) (BJMeehan)* 2-8-8 BDoyle(7) (prom tl wknd fnl f) 3 7
650[3] Gracious Gretclo *(44) (CJHill)* 2-8-8 KDarley(9) (led over 2f) 2 8
Hi Hoh (IRE) *(14) (MBell)* 2-8-4 MFenton(6) (w'like: bkwd: hmpd s: spd over 2f) 8 9

Evens ANOTHERANNIVERSARY, **5/2** Cascadia (IRE), **15/2** Kandavu (4/1-9/1), **9/1** Marl (8/1-14/1), **14/1** Sam Coles (USA) (10/1-16/1), Gracious Gretclo, **16/1** Hi Hoh (IRE), **40/1** Mystery Matthias, To The Whire, CSF £11.41 TOTE £2.10: £1.10 £2.20 £1.50 (£8.90) Trio £10.10 OWNER Mr David Barker (EPSOM) BRED Capt A. L. Smith-Maxwell 9 Rn 61.4 secs (2.40) SF: 25/20/19/18/22/2/-/-/-

853 MAR LODGE MAIDEN STKS (3-Y.O+) (Class D) £3,972.50 (£1,205.00: £590.00: £282.50) **1m 67y** Stalls: High GOING minus 0.32 sec per fur (GF) 8-00 (8-08)

670[6] **Krystallos** *(88)*(Fav)*(RHannon)* 3-8-11 WRSwinburn(3) (4th st: edgd rt 1f out: led wl ins fnl f: r.o) — 1

616[5] Jam N Shadeed (USA) *(88) (PFICole)* 3-8-11 TQuinn(16) (plld hrd: led over 5f out: edgd lft fnl f: hdd wl ins fnl f) ....hd **2**
Arzani (USA) *(82) (DJSCosgrove)* 4-9-10 MRimmer(20) (gd hdwy 2f out: nt qckn fnl f) 3 **3**
621[3] Easy Dollar **(80)***(74) (BGubby)* 3-8-11v RCochrane(13) (3rd st: r.o one pce fnl 2f) 4 **4**
613[3] Carol's Dream (USA) **(74)***(67) (JWHills)* 3-8-11 MHills(18) (lw: 5th st: hmpd over 4f out: one pce fnl 2f) 4 **5**
764[20] Caerle Lad (IRE) *(66) (GHarwood)* 4-9-10 WWoods(19) (6th st: no hdwy fnl 2f) ....½ **6**
Verde Luna *(66) (MHTompkins)* 3-8-11 BRouse(14) (w'like: stdy hdwy fnl f: bttr for r) ....s.h **7**
Restructure (IRE) *(65)*(Fav)*(MrsJCecil)* 3-8-11 PaulEddery(10) (str: scope: lw: hdwy 3f out: rdn 2f out: nt qckn) ....nk **8**
695[15] Lidhama (USA) *(57) (GLewis)* 3-8-6 SWhitworth(8) (nvr nr to chal) 1½ **9**
Step Aloft *(54) (LordHuntingdon)* 3-8-6 JWeaver(9) (unf: scope: hdwy 3f out: wknd 2f out) ..1½ **10**
658[10] Mister Rm *(58) (RGuest)* 3-8-11 MFenton(1) (nvr plcd to chal) ....¾ **11**
715[18] Admiral's Guest (IRE) *(57) (GHarwood)* 3-8-11 AClark(4) (lw: a mid div) ....nk **12**
Senaan *(51) (TThomsonJones)* 3-8-11 WCarson(11) (a mid div) 3 **13**
Addaya (IRE) *(45) (LMCumani)* 3-8-6 KDarley(21) (leggy: a bhd) ....¾ **14**
783[9] Nordman Lass **(65)***(30) (MissJacquelineDoyle)* 3-8-6 RPerham(2) (swtg: bhd fnl 3f) 8 **15**
Shoodah (IRE) *(30) (PHayward)* 4-9-10 SRaymont(15) (outpcd) 2½ **16**
187[12] Indian Fire *(25) (KOCunningham-Brown)* 5-9-10 WNewnes(7) (lw: 7th st: wknd 3f out) 2½ **17**
Kingswood Manor *(6) (MDixon)* 3-8-11 RHughes(17) (t.o) 10 **18**
Shedansar (IRE) *(MDixon)* 3-8-6 (5) AWhelan(5) (t.o) 6 **19**
Green Apache *(TJNaughton)* 3-8-11 GCarter(12) (led tl 2nd st: wknd 4f out: t.o) ....dist **20**

4/1 KRYSTALLOS, Restructure (IRE) (op 2/1), **9/2** Carol's Dream (USA), **6/1** Jam N Shadeed (USA) (9/2-7/1), **7/1** Easy Dollar, **15/2** Addaya (IRE) (5/1-8/1), **8/1** Step Aloft (5/1-9/1), **20/1** Verde Luna, **25/1** Admiral's Guest (IRE), **33/1** Caerle Lad (IRE), Mister Rm, Lidhama (USA), Senaan, Arzani (USA), Nordman Lass, Shoodah (IRE), Indian Fire, Kingswood Manor, Shedansar (IRE), Green Apache, CSF £28.45 TOTE £5.10: £1.80 £2.10 £13.30 (£12.80) Trio £137.20 OWNER Mr Ali Saeed (MARLBOROUGH) BRED Mrs E. Longton 20 Rn

1m 46.4 (4.80) SF: 23/23/30/9/2/14/1/-/-/-/-/-/-/-/-/-/-/-/-/-

WEIGHT FOR AGE 3yo-13lb

T/Plpt: £154.20 (71.41 Tckts). T/Qdpt: Not won; £70.40 to Nottingham 2/5/95. Hn

BATH (L-H)
Tuesday May 2nd (Good, Good to firm patches)

WEATHER: sunny WIND: nil

854

BLATHWAYT MAIDEN STKS (3-Y.O) (Class D) £4,060.00 (£1,225.00: £595.00: £280.00)
1m 2f 46y Stalls: Low GOING minus 0.71 sec per fur (HD) 2-00 (2-04)

Endowment *(76) (MajorWRHern)* 3-9-0 WCarson(15) (gd sort: scope: mde all: clr over 1f out: pushed out) ....— **1**
United Front *(72) (HRACecil)* 3-9-0 WNewnes(9) (w'like: scope: hld up & bhd: hdwy 2f out: r.o fnl f) 2½ **2**
Top Lady (IRE) *(66) (MRStoute)* 3-8-9 WRSwinburn(13) (bkwd: 3rd st: rdn over 1f out: one pce) ....¾ **3**
Volunteer (IRE) *(71) (HRACecil)* 3-9-0 AMcGlone(5) (small: cmpt: 4th st: one pce fnl 2f) ....s.h **4**
616[7] Smolensk (IRE) *(67) (JBerry)* 3-9-0 JCarroll(8) (chsd ldrs: 7th st: no hdwy fnl 2f) 2½ **5**
Stylish Interval *(66) (RJHodges)* 3-8-9 (5) SDrowne(1) (5th st: rdn 3f out: no hdwy fnl 2f) ....½ **6**
654[9] Backview *(64) (BJLlewellyn)* 3-9-0 RPrice(2) (hld up: hdwy on ins 6f out: btn whn hmpd 2f out) 1½ **7**
Royal College (IRE) *(61)*(Fav)*(PFICole)* 3-9-0 CRutter(12) (bit bkwd: prom: 6th & rdn st: wknd 2f out) 2 **8**
Little Shefford *(48) (DJSffrenchDavis)* 3-9-0 PatEddery(11) (dwlt: a bhd) 8 **9**
Harding Brown (USA) *(44) (GHarwood)* 3-9-0 AClark(3) (bkwd: bhd fnl 4f) 2½ **10**
Ambidextrous (IRE) *(35) (CEBrittain)* 3-9-0 BDoyle(6) (w'like: scope: bit bkwd: a bhd) 6 **11**
Hethers Footsteps *(33) (PGMurphy)* 3-8-7 (7) RWaterfield(14) (w'like: bkwd: a bhd) 1¼ **12**
Dick Christian *(BJMeehan)* 3-9-0 RHughes(4) (leggy: lt-f: dwlt: a bhd: t.o) 25 **13**
635[8] Tadjoni *(IABalding)* 3-9-0 RCochrane(7) (prom: 2nd st: ev ch whn p.u lame 2f out: dead) .... **P**

3/1 Royal College (IRE), **7/2** Tadjoni, **11/2** Volunteer (IRE), **6/1** ENDOWMENT, **8/1** Top Lady (IRE), **10/1** Ambidextrous (IRE) (8/1-12/1), **12/1** United Front (op 7/1), **25/1** Harding Brown (USA), Smolensk (IRE), **50/1** Dick Christian, **66/1** Little Shefford, Stylish Interval, **100/1** Hethers Footsteps, Backview, CSF £67.79 TOTE £5.30: £1.90 £4.00 £2.30 (£35.50) Trio £128.80 OWNER Mr Hamdan Al Maktoum (LAMBOURN) BRED Bloomsbury Stud 14 Rn

2m 9.4 (1.70) SF: 29/25/19/24/20/19/17/14/1/-/-/-/-/-

855 SPA (S) STKS (3-Y.O) (Class G) £2,619.00 (£734.00: £357.00)
5f 11y Stalls: Low GOING minus 0.71 sec per fur (HD) 2-30 (2-34)

831[5] **Southern Dominion (55)***(63) (WGMTurner)* 3-8-12 TSprake(14) (mde all: clr over 1f out: rdn out) — **1**
274[5] Nomadic Dancer (IRE) **(52)***(45) (MSSaunders)* 3-8-7 JWilliams(7) (hdwy whn carried lft wl over 1f out: r.o fnl f) 4 **2**
473[8] Deardaw **(43)***(45) (MDIUsher)* 3-8-0 (7) CAdamson(6) (chsd wnr: rdn over 1f out: no imp) s.h **3**
581[4] My Lady Brady **(57)***(49) (GROldroyd)* 3-8-12 RCochrane(17) (a.p: one pce fnl 2f) ½ **4**
Almapa **(58)***(48) (RJHodges)* 3-8-7 (5) SDrowne(10) (bhd tl gd hdwy over 1f out: r.o ins fnl f) .hd **5**
331[8] Colston-C *(48) (CJHill)* 3-8-12 RHughes(11) (a.p: one pce fnl 2f) s.h **6**
629[9] Superbit **(50)***(44) (BAMcMahon)* 3-8-12 FNorton(1) (lw: nvr nr to chal) 1¼ **7**
315[7] Ladybower (IRE) *(37) (LordHuntingdon)* 3-8-0 (7) JWilkinson(12) (lw: nvr trbld ldrs) ¾ **8**
732[12] Fortunes Leap **(60)***(41) (MrsLAMurphy)* 3-8-12 RPrice(13) (n.d) nk **9**
645[4] Mister Raider **(49)***(41)*(Fav)*(SMellor)* 3-8-12 PatEddery(4) (swtg: prom: rdn & wknd 2f out) s.h **10**
Mossalier **(46)***(31) (MartynMeade)* 3-8-7b VSlattery(3) (a bhd) 1½ **11**
732[7] Kencol **(65)***(32) (AGFoster)* 3-8-12 WCarson(8) (b.hind: bhd fnl 2f) 1¼ **12**
426[14] Fiery Footsteps **(58)***(21) (PHowling)* 3-8-0b(7) SLanigan(9) (a bhd) 2 **13**
Smiley Face **(53)***(16) (RJHodges)* 3-8-5 (7) AmandaSanders(16) (s.s: a bhd) 3 **14**
Silent Sky **(45)***(7) (CJHill)* 3-8-7 GBardwell(15) (bkwd: a bhd) 1¼ **15**
Clan Scotia **(48)***(11) (JBerry)* 3-8-12b JCarroll(5) (chsd ldrs tl hung lft wl over 1f out: sn wknd)nk **16**
363[9] Positive Result (IRE) *(6) (RJPrice)* 3-8-7 AClark(2) (a bhd) s.h **17**

2/1 Mister Raider, **6/1** My Lady Brady, **13/2** Kencol, **7/1** Clan Scotia, **14/1** Almapa (op 8/1), Mossalier (10/1-16/1), SOUTHERN DOMINION (10/1-16/1), **16/1** Fiery Footsteps, **20/1** Nomadic Dancer (IRE), Fortunes Leap, Superbit, Ladybower (IRE), Smiley Face, **25/1** Colston-C, **33/1** Deardaw, Silent Sky, Positive Result (IRE), CSF £253.14 TOTE £19.70: £5.00 £3.60 £7.30 (£261.40) Trio Not won; £514.76 to Ascot 03/05/95 OWNER Mr A. Wilkinson (SHERBORNE) BRED A. Wilkinson and J. W. Brown 17 Rn 61.4 secs (0.90) SF: 23/5/5/9/8/8/4/-/1/1/-/-/-/-/-/-/-
Bt in 7,800 gns

856 TRIPLEPRINT H'CAP (0-70) (3-Y.O+) (Class E) £3,285.00 (£990.00: £480.00: £225.00) **5f 11y** Stalls: Low GOING minus 0.71 sec per fur (HD) 3-00 (3-03)

Jucea (61)*(66)*(Fav)*(JLSpearing)* 6-9-7 PatEddery(17) (lw: a.p: led ins fnl f: drvn out) — **1**
583[4] Canovas Heart **(60)***(60) (BobJones)* 6-9-6 RCochrane(7) (a.p: led wl over 1f out tl ins fnl f: nt qckn) 1½ **2**
Winsome Wooster **(65)***(64) (PGMurphy)* 4-9-11 WRSwinburn(10) (rdn & hdwy 2f out: r.o ins fnl f) nk **3**
Raisa Point **(53)***(52) (WRMuir)* 4-8-13 JCarroll(16) (a.p: r.o one pce fnl f) s.h **4**
734* Harry's Coming **(56)***(51) (RJHodges)* 11-8-11 (5) 7x SDrowne(9) (sn rdn along:nvr nr to chal) 1¼ **5**
Ashkernazy (IRE) **(50)***(44) (NEBerry)* 4-8-5 (5) JDSmith(2) (led over 3f: wknd fnl f) ½ **6**
656[7] John O'Dreams **(54)***(47) (MrsALMKing)* 10-8-9 (5) AGarth(4) (b: s.s: nvr nrr) hd **7**
522[16] La Belle Dominique **(65)***(58) (SGKnight)* 3-9-1 WNewnes(14) (dwlt: hld up & bhd: hdwy over 1f out: nvr plcd to chal) s.h **8**
Paley Prince (USA) **(57)***(46) (MDIUsher)* 9-8-10 (7) CAdamson(15) (n.d) 1¼ **9**
Tinker Osmaston **(61)***(49) (MSSaunders)* 4-9-7 JWilliams(5) (bit bkwd: a bhd) nk **10**
734[3] Sison (IRE) **(68)***(53) (KGWingrove)* 5-10-0b JMcLaughlin(11) (b.hind: wnt lft s: a bhd) 1 **11**
La Thuile **(48)***(20) (MDIUsher)* 3-7-12 TSprake(8) (a bhd) 4 **12**
656[9] Kensington Freight **(47)***(19) (JAkehurst)* 3-7-11 GBardwell(6) (a bhd) s.h **13**
629[7] Ivy Lilian (IRE) **(48)***(8) (WMBrisbourne)* 3-7-5 (7) SLanigan(13) (prom over 2f) 4 **14**
Miriam **(57)***(16) (MJFetherston-Godley)* 4-8-10 (7) MartinDwyer(1) (chsd ldrs over 2f) hd **15**
688[11] Purbeck Centenary **(47)***(2) (PHowling)* 5-8-7 AClark(12) (a bhd) 1½ **16**
Shades of Jade **(41)** *(JJBridger)* 7-7-12 (3) SSanders(3) (spd over 2f) 1 **17**

5/1 JUCEA, **6/1** Canovas Heart, **7/1** Winsome Wooster, John O'Dreams, Harry's Coming, **14/1** Miriam, Tinker Osmaston, **16/1** Purbeck Centenary, Paley Prince (USA), Raisa Point, **20/1** Sison (IRE), **25/1** Shades of Jade, Ashkernazy (IRE), Ivy Lilian (IRE), Kensington Freight, **33/1** La Thuile, La Belle Dominique, CSF £33.07 CT £195.09 TOTE £5.90: £2.00 £1.50 £1.80 £4.30 (£16.90) Trio £33.30 OWNER Mr A. A. Campbell (ALCESTER) BRED G. W. Mills and Sons 17 Rn
61.5 secs (1.00) SF: 30/24/28/16/15/8/11/12/10/13/17/-/-/-/-/-/-
WEIGHT FOR AGE 3yo-10lb

857 JACQUELINE COXON BIRTHDAY H'CAP (0-80) (3-Y.O) (Class D) £3,809.75 (£1,148.00: £556.50: £260.75)
1m 2f 46y Stalls: Low GOING minus 0.71 sec per fur (HD) 3-30 (3-33)

618[5] **Kimbridge Knight (IRE) (72)***(80) (PTWalwyn)* 3-9-5v PatEddery(3) (lw: mde all: hrd rdn over 1f out: drvn out) — **1**

618 16 Bob's Ploy **(71)***(78) (RAkehurst)* 3-9-4 BThomson(10) (a.p: 3rd st: rdn 2f out: ev ch 1f out: nt qckn) ....¾ 2
637 8 Lucky Coin **(64)***(61) (CEBrittain)* 3-8-11 BDoyle(2) (swtg: prom: rdn & 4th st: one pce fnl 2f) ...6 3
618 4 No Pattern **(74)***(70) (GLMoore)* 3-9-7v BRouse(5) (lw: hld up & plld hrd: 6th st: rdn over 2f out: no hdwy) ....¾ 4
Paradise Waters **(52)***(47)*(Fav)*(RFJohnsonHoughton)* 3-7-13 FNorton(8) (bit bkwd: nvr nr to chal) 1 5
Pennycairn **(74)***(66) (HRACecil)* 3-9-7 AMcGlone(11) (chsd wnr: 2nd st: wknd 2f out) 1½ 6
647* Himalayan Blue **(67)***(54) (MRChannon)* 3-9-0 RHughes(4) (prom: 5th st: wknd over 2f out) 3½ 7
635 15 Greycoat Boy **(60)***(43) (BJMeehan)* 3-8-7 RCochrane(7) (bit bkwd: a bhd) 2½ 8
630 7 Yubralee (USA) **(68)***(50) (MRStoute)* 3-9-1 WRSwinburn(1) (hld up: 8th st: a bhd) ....½ 9
613 9 Magical Bid (IRE) **(55)***(25) (JMBradley)* 3-8-2 ATucker(9) (plld hrd: rn wd bnd over 4f out: hdwy 3f out: wknd 2f out) 8 10
651 16 Arctic Poppy (USA) **(60)***(19) (IABalding)* 3-8-0 (7) MartinDwyer(6) (b.hind: 7th st: hrd rdn 3f out: sn wknd: t.o) 7 11

3/1 Paradise Waters, **7/2** Bob's Ploy, **9/2** Yubralee (USA), **5/1** KIMBRIDGE KNIGHT (IRE), **7/1** No Pattern, **9/1** Pennycairn, **10/1** Himalayan Blue, **14/1** Lucky Coin (op 7/1), **25/1** Greycoat Boy, Arctic Poppy (USA), **50/1** Magical Bid (IRE), CSF £23.81 CT £222.46 TOTE £5.50: £2.00 £2.30 £2.30 (£14.70) Trio £135.20 OWNER Mrs Roger Waters (LAMBOURN) BRED Tarworth Bloodstock Investments Ltd 11 Rn 2m 7.5 (-0.20) SF: 48/46/29/38/15/34/22/11/18/-/-

858 CORSTON STKS (3-Y.O+) (Class C) £5,271.20 (£1,911.20: £925.60: £388.00: £164.00) **5f 11y** Stalls: Low GOING minus 0.71 sec per fur (HD) 4-00 (4-00)

571 5 **Lucky Parkes (100)***(103)*(Fav)*(JBerry)* 5-9-9 JCarroll(3) (mde all: rdn out) ....— 1
693 5 Crystal Magic **(94)***(93) (RHannon)* 4-9-3 PatEddery(2) (chsd wnr: rdn over 2f out: r.o one pce fnl f) 1¼ 2
Jayannpee **(96)***(104) (IABalding)* 4-10-0 RCochrane(5) (hld up: rdn over 1f out: r.o fnl f) ....s.h 3
633 2 Welton Arsenal **(98)***(92) (MRChannon)* 3-9-0 RHughes(1) (lw: hld up: n.m.r on ins 3f out: wknd fnl f) 2½ 4
Croeso-I-Cymru **(96)***(89) (BAMcMahon)* 4-9-9 WRSwinburn(4) (bit bkwd: prom over 3f) ....¾ 5

2/1 LUCKY PARKES, **5/2** Crystal Magic, **11/4** Welton Arsenal, **11/2** Jayannpee (7/2-6/1), **14/1** Croeso-I-Cymru (op 6/1), CSF £6.95 TOTE £2.60: £1.50 £1.70 (£3.40) OWNER Mr Joseph Heler (COCKERHAM) BRED Joseph Heler 5 Rn 60.6 secs (0.10) SF: 46/36/47/25/32
WEIGHT FOR AGE 3yo-10lb

859 PENSFORD MAIDEN AUCTION STKS (2-Y.O) (Class D) £3,330.50 (£1,004.00: £487.00: £228.50) **5f 11y** Stalls: Low GOING minus 0.71 sec per fur (HD) 4-30 (4-32)

Polly Golightly *(60) (BSmart)* 2-7-11 (3)ow3 SSanders(1) (small: lt-f: a.p: led 2f out: rdn out) ....— 1
671 6 Eights High (USA) *(68) (RHannon)* 2-8-5 WCarson(6) (lw: led over 3f out tl 2f out: hrd rdn, rallied & ev ch ins fnl f: r.o) ....hd 2
Lucky Revenge *(44) (MartynMeade)* 2-7-6 (7)ow2 CTinel(3) (leggy: unf: s.s: hdwy over 1f out: nt trble ldrs) 5 3
436 10 Stealth Attack (IRE) *(46) (JBerry)* 2-8-5 JCarroll(4) (lw: led over 1f: wknd over 1f out) 2 4
Mellors (IRE) *(28) (JARToller)* 2-8-10 PatEddery(7) (w'like: outpcd) 7 5
617 20 Sharp Night *(13) (MSSaunders)* 2-8-7 RPrice(8) (lw: a bhd) 4 6
650 2 Kossolian (Fav)*(BPalling)* 2-7-9 (5)ow3 AWhelan(5) (hung rt: rn v.wd bnd over 3f out: sn bhd) 1½ 7

11/8 Kossolian (op Evens), **11/4** Stealth Attack (IRE), **4/1** Mellors (IRE) (op 6/1), **8/1** Eights High (USA), **25/1** Sharp Night, **33/1** Lucky Revenge, POLLY GOLIGHTLY, CSF £220.42 TOTE £17.40: £3.20 £2.50 (£100.60) OWNER Mr David Sykes (LAMBOURN) BRED Aston Park Stud and T. R. Lock 7 Rn 61.8 secs (1.30) SF: 6/14/-/-/-/-/-

860 EMPIRE H'CAP (0-75) (4-Y.O+ F & M) (Class D) £3,696.00 (£1,113.00: £539.00: £252.00) **1m 3f 144y** Stalls: Low GOING minus 0.71 sec per fur (HD) 5-00 (5-01)

653 2 **Hill Farm Dancer (50)** *(WMBrisbourne)* 4-7-12 (5) AGarth(2) (hld up & bhd: stdy hdwy 6f out: 5th st: led 1f out: r.o wl) ....— 1
Seren Quest **(75)** (Fav)*(RAkehurst)* 5-10-0 WRSwinburn(3) (bit bkwd: hld up: hdwy & 4th st: ev ch 1f out: nt qckn) ....¾ 2

41210 Uncharted Waters **(64)** *(CACyzer)* 4-9-3 PatEddery(9) (prom: lost pl 4f out: hrd rdn over 1f out: styd on wl fnl f) ... 1¾ 3
8172 Porte Belloch **(44)** *(CTNash)* 4-7-11 ow3 ATucker(1) (led: rdn 3f out: hdd 1f out: wknd ins fnl f) ... 1½ 4
4545 Sacred Mirror (IRE) **(54)** *(CEBrittain)* 4-8-7 BDoyle(4) (a.p: 2nd st: nt clr run over 1f out: one pce) ... nk 5
52615 La Belle Shyanne **(40)** *(CJHill)* 4-7-7 GBardwell(7) (hld up & bhd: stdy hdwy 6f out: 6th st: hrd rdn 3f out: one pce) ... 1½ 6
66113 Rumi **(71)** *(CREgerton)* 4-9-5 (5) AProcter(8) (prom: 7th st: rdn over 2f out: eased whn btn ins fnl f) ... 9 7
Jubilee Line **(45)** *(DWPArbuthnot)* 5-7-12 FNorton(5) (a bhd) ... 2½ 8
5458 Homemaker **(40)** *(PGMurphy)* 5-7-7v NAdams(10) (chsd ldr over 6f: 3rd st: rdn & wknd over 2f out) ... 1½ 9
74411 Kala Star **(52)** *(JFfitch-Heyes)* 4-8-5 WCarson(11) (bhd fnl 6f) ... 5 10
2805 Ginka **(51)** *(PJBevan)* 4-8-1v(3) SSanders(6) (a bhd) ... 1¼ 11

LONG HANDICAP Homemaker 7-0 La Belle Shyanne 7-4

5/2 Seren Quest, **9/2** HILL FARM DANCER, **11/2** Sacred Mirror (IRE) (4/1-6/1), **7/1** Porte Belloch (op 4/1), **8/1** Rumi, **9/1** Uncharted Waters, **11/1** La Belle Shyanne, **16/1** Jubilee Line, Kala Star, **25/1** Ginka, **33/1** Homemaker, CSF £15.93 CT £91.28 TOTE £4.70: £1.50 £1.40 £3.70 (£10.90) Trio £47.60 OWNER Mr Dennis Newton (NESSCLIFFE) BRED D. Newton 11 Rn

2m 27.9 (1.20) SF: -/-/-/-/-/-/-/-/-/-/-

T/Plpt: £7,151.80 (1.49 Tckts). T/Qdpt: £85.70 (2 Tckts). KH

0732-NOTTINGHAM (L-H)
Tuesday May 2nd (Good to firm)
WEATHER: fine WIND: slt against

861
MEADOWS (S) STKS (3-Y.O) (Class G) £2,243.00 (£618.00: £293.00)
6f 15y Stalls: High GOING minus 0.21 sec per fur (GF) 2-15 (2-17)

5772 **Hi Rock (52)***(62+) (MJCamacho)* 3-8-7 LCharnock(2) (swtg: hld up in tch: hdwy over 2f out: led bel dist: hrd rdn: all out) ... — 1
62811 Lady Davenport (IRE) **(70)***(68) (RonaldThompson)* 3-8-13 JWeaver(9) (hld up: hdwy & swtchd lft 2f out: str run fnl f: jst failed) ... s.h 2
5812 Noosa (IRE) **(74)***(63)*(Fav)*(MJohnston)* 3-8-13 DHolland(7) (a.p: effrt & rdn 1f out: nt pce to chal) ... 1¾ 3
7482 Six for Luck **(75)***(63)*(Fav)*(JBerry)* 3-9-4b GCarter(10) (b.hind: chsd ldrs: rdn to ld over 2f out: hdd bel dist: r.o one pce) ... 2 4
73210 Red O'Reilly *(53) (MrsNMacauley)* 3-8-12b DaleGibson(6) (chsd ldrs: rdn & bmpd 2f out: kpt on one pce) ... 1½ 5
739W Little Wilma *(45) (APJarvis)* 3-8-4 (3) JTate(8) (swtg: hld up: hdwy wl over 1f out: sn rdn: nt rch ldrs) ... 1¼ 6
Eileen's Guest (IRE) *(34) (RJRWilliams)* 3-8-7 GDuffield(1) (nt grwn: swvd lft s: a bhd) ... 4 7
75813 Undawaterscubadiva *(16) (MPBielby)* 3-8-12 ACulhane(5) (lw: prom: rdn along ½-wy: sn lost tch: t.o) ... 9 8
5818 Il Furetto *(JSKing)* 3-8-12 LDettori(4) (swtg: led tl hdd & wknd over 2f out: t.o) ... 8 9
6756 Lelise (IRE) **(29)** *(APJarvis)* 3-8-7 DHarrison(3) (a in rr: lost tch fnl 2f: t.o) ... 6 10

9/4 Six for Luck, Noosa (IRE), **13/2** Eileen's Guest (IRE) (4/1-7/1), **8/1** Little Wilma (op 5/1), **9/1** HI ROCK, **14/1** Lady Davenport (IRE), **16/1** Il Furetto, **25/1** Red O'Reilly, **33/1** Undawaterscubadiva, Lelise (IRE), CSF £109.49 TOTE £8.90: £1.80 £5.80 £1.10 (£71.00) Trio £35.60 OWNER Filey Hi Flyers (MALTON) BRED B. Nordan 10 Rn 1m 15.9 (4.90) SF: 7/13/8/8/-/-/-/-/-/-

Bt in 3,600 gns. Noosa (IRE) clmd JGraham £6,000

STEWARDS' ENQUIRY Charnock suspended 11-12/5/95 (excessive use of whip).

862
BRADMORE H'CAP (0-70) (3-Y.O+ F & M) (Class E) £3,588.20 (£1,073.60: £514.80: £235.40)
6f 15y Stalls: High GOING minus 0.21 sec per fur (GF) 2-45 (2-46)

60311 **Christian Flight (IRE) (39)***(41) (SGollings)* 6-8-2 MFenton(15) (chsd ldrs: shkn up to ld wl ins fnl f) ... — 1
6896 Le Bal **(43)***(44) (MrsNMacauley)* 3-7-9b DaleGibson(14) (bhd: hdwy stands' side over 1f out: fin wl) ... nk 2
70117 Twice in Bundoran (IRE) **(44)***(42) (PSFelgate)* 4-8-2 (5) PMcCabe(13) (led: rdn & drifted lft 1f out: hdd wl ins fnl f) ... 1¼ 3
Annie Fay (IRE) **(58)***(54) (JLHarris)* 3-8-10 KDarley(10) (a.p: rdn over 1f out: one pce) ... ¾ 4

5228 Secret Miss **(52)***(48)*(Fav)*(APJarvis)* 3-8-1 (3) JTate(11) (in tch: rdn & effrt 2f out: kpt on fnl f: nt pce to chal) ....hd 5
Poyle Jezebelle **(48)***(38+) (MBlanshard)* 4-8-11 StephenDavies(4) (s.s: r.o appr fnl f: nrst fin) 2 6
4999 Pab's Choice **(58)***(47) (MMcCormack)* 4-9-7 GDuffield(9) (bhd: rdn 2f out: r.o ins fnl f) ....½ 7
753* We're Joken **(46)***(32) (JBerry)* 3-7-5 (7) PFessey(6) (b.nr hind: effrt over 2f out: eased whn btn fnl f) 1¼ 8
732* Tael of Silver **(61)***(46) (KRBurke)* 3-8-13 7x DHolland(2) (lw: prom: rdn over 2f out: sn wknd) ....nk 9
Lady Silk **(62)***(45) (JHetherton)* 4-9-11 SWebster(3) (bit bkwd: prom to ½-wy: sn rdn & wknd) ....¾ 10
4818 Kinnegad Kid **(52)***(34) (RIngram)* 6-8-12 (3) DWright(1) (racd centre: in tch 4f) ....½ 11
7019 Angelic Dancer **(46)***(26) (SRBowring)* 4-8-4b(5) CTeague(7) (chsd ldrs over 3f) ....½ 12
7487 Bonny Melody **(56)***(36) (PDEvans)* 4-9-5 JFortune(8) (spd 4f) ....nk 13
7465 Bonita **(55)***(28) (MrsLPiggott)* 3-8-0 (7) VictoriaAppleby(12) (b: b.hind: outpcd: swtchd lft ½-wy: a bhd) 2½ 14
7335 Runs in the Family **(66)***(28) (PGMurphy)* 3-9-4 DHarrison(5) (prom 4f: eased whn btn appr fnl f) 4 15

7/2 Secret Miss, **11/2** We're Joken, Tael of Silver, **6/1** Runs in the Family, **8/1** Bonita (op 5/1), **9/1** Kinnegad Kid, **10/1** Annie Fay (IRE), **12/1** Angelic Dancer (op 8/1), Pab's Choice, **14/1** Twice in Bundoran (IRE) (10/1-16/1), **16/1** Lady Silk, **20/1** Le Bal, CHRISTIAN FLIGHT (IRE), **25/1** Bonny Melody, **33/1** Poyle Jezebelle, CSF £358.03 CT £5,173.21 TOTE £60.10: £14.70 £19.20 £4.30 (£124.90) Trio £225.90 OWNER Mr Derek Holland (LOUTH) BRED Martyn J. McEnery 15 Rn
1m 14.3 (3.30) SF: 23/15/24/25/19/20/29/3/17/27/16/8/18/-/-
WEIGHT FOR AGE 3yo-11lb

863 PORCHESTER MEDIAN AUCTION MAIDEN STKS (2-Y.O) (Class F)
£2,519.00 (£694.00: £329.00)
5f 13y Stalls: High GOING minus 0.21 sec per fur (GF) 3-15 (3-16)

4802 **Dankeston (USA)** *(63+)*(Fav)*(MBell)* 2-9-0 MFenton(3) (lw: s.i.s: sn wnt prom: hrd rdn over 1f out: ld wl ins fnl f: all out) ....— 1
Missile Toe (IRE) *(58) (JEBanks)* 2-9-0 DBiggs(4) (w'like: scope: bit bkwd: unruly s: mde most tl hdd wl ins fnl f) 1¾ 2
8108 Silverdale Knight *(54) (KWHogg)* 2-8-7 (7) ADaly(6) (chsd ldrs: rdn 2f out: kpt on fnl f) 1¼ 3
Copper Bright *(38) (PCHaslam)* 2-9-0 JFortune(2) (cmpt: bkwd: chsd ldrs over 3f: sn rdn & wknd) 5 4
Jaleel *(28) (RHannon)* 2-9-0 RPerham(1) (w'like: dwlt: effrt u.p 2f out: no imp) 3 5
Bobsworthatcaspers *(28) (GLewis)* 2-9-0 PaulEddery(5) (unf: scope: outpcd: a bhd) ....hd 6
Elle Mac *(18) (MPBielby)* 2-8-9 ACulhane(7) (lt-f: bkwd: prom to ½-wy: sn rdn & wknd) 1½ 7

4/11 DANKESTON (USA) (op 8/13), **7/1** Jaleel (op 4/1), **8/1** Bobsworthatcaspers (op 4/1), **16/1** Missile Toe (IRE), **20/1** Silverdale Knight, **33/1** Copper Bright, Elle Mac, CSF £7.12 TOTE £1.30: £1.10 £5.50 (£5.50) OWNER Mr Luciano Gaucci (NEWMARKET) BRED Donald MacRae 7 Rn
62.4 secs (3.70) SF: 19/14/10/-/-/-/-
STEWARDS' ENQUIRY Fenton suspended 11-12/5/95 (excessive use of whip).

864 SUE SANDERS DEB LONG SERVICE H'CAP (0-80) (4-Y.O+) (Class D)
£3,935.10 (£1,174.80: £561.40: £254.70)
1m 1f 213y Stalls: Low GOING minus 0.12 sec per fur (G) 3-45 (3-46)

Clouded Elegance (74)*(83) (LadyHerries)* 5-9-11 KDarley(7) (a.p: 4th st: led over 2f out: rdn & r.o wl) ....— 1
7622 Montone (IRE) **(58)***(65) (KRBurke)* 5-8-6 (3) DRMcCabe(12) (lw: a.p: 2nd st: led 3f out to over 2f out: rallied & ev ch fnl f: no ex cl home) 1 2
6006 Rasayel (USA) **(45)***(49) (PDEvans)* 5-7-10 ow3 JFanning(3) (prom tl lost pl ent st: rallied over 2f out: kpt on nr fin) ....hd 3
Marchman **(50)***(51) (JSKing)* 10-8-1 ow1 GCarter(5) (bit bkwd: hld up: shkn up & hdwy 2f out: eased whn btn nr fin) 3 4
5504 Sadler's Walk **(70)***(70)*(Fav)*(GWragg)* 4-9-7 MHills(2) (swtg: hld up: 5th st: rdn 2f out: kpt on one pce) 1¼ 5
7677 Shuttlecock **(52)***(49) (MrsNMacauley)* 4-7-10 (7) MHenry(1) (bhd: hdwy over 2f out: nvr nrr) 2 6
40611 Bentico **(65)***(62) (MrsNMacauley)* 6-9-2 LDettori(11) (chsd ldrs: 7th st: rdn over 2f out: sn btn) ....hd 7
6539 Midnight Jazz (IRE) **(77)***(71) (WAO'Gorman)* 5-10-0 EmmaO'Gorman(4) (bit bkwd: hld up: rdn 3f out: no imp) 2 8

Bataan (USA) **(75)***(67)* *(MrsJCecil)* 4-9-12 PaulEddery(9) (a bhd)....1¼ 9
817[9] Parish Walk (IRE) **(43)***(34)* *(KWHogg)* 4-7-1 (7) DLockhart(10) (swtg: wnt 3rd st: wknd over 3f out)....½ 10
634[19] Locorotondo (IRE) **(76)***(66)* *(MBell)* 4-9-13 MFenton(8) (b: swtg: led to 3f out: eased whn btn appr fnl f)....½ 11
Scottish Bambi **(72)***(54)* *(RHannon)* 7-9-9 RPerham(6) (bkwd: hld up & bhd: effrt & rdn 3f out: no imp)....5 12

LONG HANDICAP Rasayel (USA) 7-5

6/4 Sadler's Walk, **15/2** Montone (IRE), **8/1** CLOUDED ELEGANCE, Bataan (USA) (op 5/1), Bentico, **12/1** Locorotondo (IRE), Midnight Jazz (IRE), **16/1** Scottish Bambi, **25/1** Parish Walk (IRE), Shuttlecock, **33/1** Rasayel (USA), Marchman, CSF £61.47 CT £1,689.77 TOTE £9.50: £3.30 £2.00 £8.10 (£26.60) Trio £329.80 OWNER Lady Sarah Clutton (LITTLEHAMPTON) BRED M. E. Wates 12 Rn 2m 7.2 (4.70) SF: 61/43/27/29/48/27/40/49/45/12/44/32

865 RADFORD MAIDEN STKS (3-Y.O F) (Class D) £4,374.50 (£1,310.00: £629.00: £288.50) **1m 54y** Stalls: Low GOING minus 0.12 sec per fur (G) 4-15 (4-15)

White Palace *(87)* *(JRFanshawe)* 3-8-11 DHarrison(2) (still unf: hld up: 5th st: shkn up bel dist: qcknd to ld fnl 50y)....— 1
Celtic Fringe *(85)*(Fav)*(HRACecil)* 3-8-11 WRyan(7) (rangy: bit bkwd: hld up: 4th st: led wl over 1f out: rdn & edgf lft: hdd wl ins fnl f)....1 2
695[3] Courageous Dancer (IRE) *(78)* *(BHanbury)* 3-8-11 TIves(5) (a.p: 2nd st: slt ld 2f out: sn hdd: one pce)....3½ 3
Eurolink Mischief *(78)* *(LMCumani)* 3-8-11 KDarley(4) (b.hind: leggy: hld up & bhd: sme hdwy appr fnl f: nvr nrr)....hd 4
616[2] Khamseh *(75)* *(JWWatts)* 3-8-11 LDettori(6) (hld up: 6th st: effrt over 2f out: rdn appr fnl f: no ex)....1½ 5
Makri *(64)* *(MrsJCecil)* 3-8-11 PaulEddery(3) (w'like: scope: prom: 3rd st: eased whn btn over 1f out)....6 6
Western Reel (USA) **(89)***(61)* *(PFICole)* 3-8-11 TQuinn(1) (half reard s: sn led: hdd 2f out & wknd)....1½ 7
Zitziana (IRE) *(22)* *(CEBrittain)* 3-8-11 MRimmer(8) (still unf: stdd s: a bhd: t.o)....20 8

1/2 Celtic Fringe (4/6-11/8), **4/1** Western Reel (USA) (3/1-5/1), **7/1** Courageous Dancer (IRE) (op 4/1), **8/1** Khamseh, **20/1** Makri, Eurolink Mischief, **25/1** WHITE PALACE, **33/1** Zitziana (IRE), CSF £40.85 TOTE £40.20: £6.20 £1.10 £1.30 (£23.00) OWNER Cheveley Park Stud (NEWMARKET) BRED Cheveley Park Stud Ltd 8 Rn 1m 44.1 (4.50) SF: 41/39/32/32/29/18/15/-

866 ATTENBOROUGH H'CAP (0-70) (4-Y.O+) (Class E) £3,902.80 (£1,170.40: £563.20: £259.60) **1m 6f 15y** Stalls: Low GOING minus 0.12 sec (G) 4-45 (4-47)

737[2] **Mizyan (IRE) (60)***(72)*(Fav)*(JEBanks)* 7-9-6 LDettori(2) (lw: a.p: 4th st: rdn to ld ins fnl f: r.o wl)....— 1
649[4] Environmentalist (IRE) **(55)***(66)* *(BJMcMath)* 4-9-0 AMackay(9) (swtg: hld up: hdwy over 4f out: ev ch 1f out: rdn & r.o)....½ 2
696[10] Requested **(53)***(64)* *(PBurgoyne)* 8-8-13 JWeaver(18) (hld up: hdwy over 2f out: fin wl)....nk 3
737* New Inn **(60)***(71)* *(EWeymes)* 4-9-5 5x KDarley(5) (mde most tl rdn & hdd ins fnl f)....½ 4
741[2] Soojama (IRE) **(38)***(43)* *(RMFlower)* 5-7-12 StephenDavies(17) (lw: hld up: gd hdwy bel dist: nvr nrr)....5 5
649[11] Salinger **(33)***(36)* *(JParkes)* 7-7-7 NCarlisle(13) (disp ld: 2nd st: wknd fnl 2f)....2 6
514[5] Royal Citizen (IRE) **(50)***(51)* *(JFBottomley)* 6-8-10 TIves(3) (in tch: hmpd 9f out: hdwy 6f out: rdn & wknd wl over 1f out)....1¼ 7
811[10] Kinoko **(48)***(48)* *(KWHogg)* 7-8-1 (7) ADaly(11) (swtg: r.o over 2f out: nvr nrr)....¾ 8
Shamshadal (IRE) **(59)***(59)* *(JRJenkins)* 5-9-5 DBiggs(16) (mid div tl styd on fnl f)....hd 9
737[12] Swordking (IRE) **(46)***(43)* *(JLHarris)* 6-8-6v PaulEddery(20) (prom: 3rd st: wknd over 2f out)....3 10
589[2] La Menorquina (USA) **(35)***(28)* *(DMarks)* 5-7-4 (5) MBaird(12) (a in rr)....3 11
279[6] All on **(47)***(38)* *(JHetherton)* 4-8-6 NKennedy(14) (swtg: a bhd)....1¾ 12
Marjimel **(52)***(41)* *(JLEyre)* 4-8-11 RLappin(4) (hdwy ½-wy: 6th st: rdn & wknd wl over 2f out)1¾ 13
632[13] Chimborazo **(69)***(58)* *(BJMcMath)* 4-10-0 WWoods(8) (chsd ldrs over 10f: sn lost tch)....½ 14
556[18] Lightning Quest (IRE) **(37)***(24)* *(JSWainwright)* 4-7-10 JFanning(15) (hdwy 7f out: 7th st: wknd over 3f out)....1¾ 15
632[18] Chakalak **(59)***(45)* *(SDow)* 7-9-5 AMartinez(6) (bit bkwd: chsd ldrs over 9f: sn wknd)....¾ 16
751[11] Efaad (IRE) **(59)***(42)* *(JNorton)* 4-9-4 ACulhane(19) (chsd ldrs: 5th st: rdn & wknd 3f out)....2½ 17
161[8] Portolano (FR) **(52)***(35)* *(WClay)* 4-8-11 MWigham(1) (bit bkwd: a bhd)....½ 18
Chez Catalan **(54)***(14)* *(RAkehurst)* 4-8-13 GCarter(10) (bkwd: hdwy ½-wy: wknd 4f out: t.o)....20 19

LONG HANDICAP Salinger 7-4

4/1 MIZYAN (IRE) (op 6/1), **6/1** Environmentalist (IRE) (op 4/1), **7/1** Soojama (IRE), **8/1** New Inn, **9/1** Chez Catalan (op 5/1), **12/1** La Menorquina (USA), **14/1** Swordking (IRE), Salinger, Royal Citizen (IRE), **20/1** All on, Kinoko, Marjimel, Shamshadal (IRE), Chakalak, Chimborazo, **25/1** Portolano (FR), **33/1** Requested, Efaad (IRE), Lightning Quest (IRE), CSF £28.95 CT £667.51 TOTE £4.60: £1.90 £2.40 £2.60 (£16.80) Trio £384.50 OWNER Mr J. A. Bianchi (NEWMARKET) BRED S. Niarchos in Ireland 19 Rn

3m 5.8 (7.30) SF: 54/47/46/52/25/18/33/30/41/25/10/19/22/39/5/27/23/16/-

WEIGHT FOR AGE 4yo-1lb

867

COTMANHAY H'CAP (0-70) (3-Y.O) (Class E) £3,960.00 (£1,188.00: £572.00: £264.00) **1m 54y** Stalls: Low GOING minus 0.12 sec per fur (G) 5-15 (5-16)

521[3] **Don't Forget Ruby (IRE) (43)***(61) (DWPArbuthnot)* 3-7-6 (5) NVarley(11) (a.p: 2nd st: rdn 2f out: led ins fnl f: r.o wl)....— **1**

759* Mac's Taxi **(61)***(73)*(Fav)*(PCHaslam)* 3-8-10 (5) 5x JStack(8) (led: sn clr: shkn up wl over 1f out: hdd ins fnl f)....3 **2**

Nunnery Grove (IRE) **(46)***(53) (TThomsonJones)* 3-8-0 StephenDavies(12) (bit bkwd: hdwy 6f out: 4th st: styd on ins fnl f)....2½ **3**

435[6] Leading Spirit (IRE) **(60)***(64) (CFWall)* 3-9-0 WWoods(3) (hld up: hdwy 2f out: styd on ins fnl f)....1¾ **4**

651[12] Most Welcome News **(47)***(49) (JRJenkins)* 3-8-1 DaleGibson(7) (chsd ldrs: 3rd st: rdn & wknd 2f out)....1¼ **5**

580[6] Deceit the Second **(47)***(45) (GLewis)* 3-8-1 PaulEddery(18) (chsd ldrs: kpt on fnl 2f: nvr nrr)....2 **6**

648[3] Kevasingo **(54)***(47) (SDow)* 3-8-8 GDuffield(17) (lw: hdwy & 6th st: rdn 2f out: no imp)....2½ **7**

Euro Singer **(54)***(46) (RAkehurst)* 3-8-8 GCarter(2) (chsd ldrs: 5th st: one pce fnl 3f)....½ **8**

847[9] Longcroft **(48)***(18) (KWHogg)* 3-7-9 (7)ow6 ADaly(15) (s.s: a bhd)....8 **9**

733[11] Alute (IRE) **(53)***(25) (CEBrittain)* 3-8-7 MRimmer(10) (nvr nr to chal)....2 **10**

Club Elite **(41)***(12) (MJCamacho)* 3-7-9 LCharnock(16) (nvr bttr than mid div)....1 **11**

715[19] Rock Oyster **(60)***(30) (BJMeehan)* 3-9-0 JWeaver(13) (bit bkwd: a in rr)....hd **12**

658[11] Sooty (IRE) **(62)***(25) (HThomsonJones)* 3-9-2 RHills(1) (bit bkwd: mid div tl wknd 3f out)....4 **13**

701[11] Polli Pui **(58)***(18) (PDEvans)* 3-8-12 DHarrison(4) (dwlt: a bhd)....1¼ **14**

*603** Cool Tactician **(67)***(22) (RHollinshead)* 3-9-7 TIves(14) (a in rr)....2½ **15**

Biased View **(47)** *(RThompson)* 3-8-1 TWilliams(5) (a bhd: t.o fnl 3f)....7 **16**

Tilthams **(42)** *(DAWilson)* 3-7-7 (3)ow3 DWright(6) (a bhd: t.o)....10 **17**

LONG HANDICAP Tilthams 7-3

5/2 Mac's Taxi, **7/1** Cool Tactician, **8/1** Leading Spirit (IRE), **9/1** Rock Oyster, **10/1** Deceit the Second (op 16/1), Alute (IRE), Kevasingo, Sooty (IRE), **11/1** Euro Singer (8/1-12/1), **12/1** DON'T FORGET RUBY (IRE) (10/1-16/1), **14/1** Polli Pui (op 33/1), **20/1** Club Elite, Most Welcome News, Nunnery Grove (IRE), **25/1** Biased View, **33/1** Longcroft, Tilthams, CSF £45.89 CT £604.12 TOTE £23.40: £3.60 £1.10 £21.30 £1.30 (£24.20) Trio £180.90 OWNER Mr J. S. Gutkin (COMPTON) BRED Islanmore Stud 17 Rn 1m 44.5 (4.90) SF: 24/36/16/27/12/8/10/9/-/-/-/-/-/-/-/-/-

T/Jkpt: Not won; £26,341.71 to Ascot 3/5/95. T/Plpt: £2,107.00 (7.15 Tckts). T/Qdpt £121.30 (0.2 Tckts); £131.20 to Ascot 3/5/95 IM

ASCOT (R-H)
Wednesday May 3rd (Good to firm)

WEATHER: sunny, hot WIND: almost nil

868

INSULPAK STKS (3-Y.O F) (Class B) £8,191.30 (£3,066.70: £1,500.85: £646.75: £290.88: £148.52) **1m (round)** Stalls: Centre GOING minus 0.20 sec per fur (GF) 2-30 (2-31)

547[2] **A la Carte (IRE) (88)***(102) (JLDunlop)* 3-8-8 JReid(3) (stdy hdwy 2f out: led over 1f out: pushed out)....— **1**

664[2] Tinashaan (IRE) *(99) (JRFanshawe)* 3-8-8 DHarrison(7) (3rd st: led over 2f out tl over 1f out: unable qckn)....1¾ **2**

Phantom Gold *(102)*(Fav)*(LordHuntingdon)* 3-8-13 JWeaver(4) (swtg: 4th st: rdn over 2f out: r.o one pce)....¾ **3**

620[3] Cask *(94) (JHMGosden)* 3-8-13 LDettori(9) (6th st: rdn over 2f out: one pce)....4 **4**

Crystal Cavern (USA) *(92) (RCharlton)* 3-8-13 KDarley(10) (lw: 5th st: nt clr run over 2f out & over 1f out: one pce)....1¼ **5**

Strutting (IRE) *(90) (RHannon)* 3-8-13 PatEddery(1) (hrd rdn over 2f out: nvr nr to chal)....¾ **6**

664[8] Miss Haversham *(84) (CACyzer)* 3-8-8 PaulEddery(5) (2nd st: ev ch over 2f out: wknd over 1f out) .... nk 7
620[5] Shefoog **(91)***(89) (RWArmstrong)* 3-8-13 MJKinane(8) (lw: nt clr run over 2f: swtchd lft: sme hdwy 1f out: sn wknd) .... nk 8
Dom One **(99)***(88) (JBerry)* 3-9-1 JCarroll(6) (lw: a bhd) 1¼ 9
Opera Lover (IRE) **(105)***(72) (MRStoute)* 3-8-13 WRSwinburn(2) (bit bkwd: led over 5f) 7 10

7/2 Phantom Gold, **5/1** Cask (op 3/1), **11/2** Tinashaan (IRE) (op 3/1), **6/1** Strutting (IRE), **13/2** Opera Lover (IRE) (4/1-7/1), **8/1** Shefoog, **10/1** A LA CARTE (IRE) (7/1-12/1), **14/1** Miss Haversham (10/1-20/1), Dom One (8/1-16/1), **20/1** Crystal Cavern (USA), CSF £60.37 TOTE £9.20: £2.30 £2.40 £1.60 (£41.20) Trio £74.20 OWNER Mrs Patrick Darling-Susan Abbott Racing (ARUNDEL) BRED Dene Investments N V 10 Rn 1m 42.63 (3.03) SF: 46/43/46/38/36/34/28/33/32/16

869 INSULPAK SAGARO STKS (Gp 3) (4-Y.O+) (Class A) £25,480.00 (£9,644.00: £4,722.00: £2,154.00)

2m 45y Stalls: High GOING minus 0.20 sec per fur (GF) 3-05 (3-05)

Double Trigger (IRE) (111)*(115)*(Fav)*(MJohnston)* 4-8-12 JWeaver(2) (3rd st: led wl over 1f out to 1f out: led ins fnl f: rdn out) .... — 1
735[3] Poltarf (USA) **(101)***(112)*(Fav)*(HRACecil)* 4-8-9 MJKinane(1) (lw: hdwy over 4f out: 5th st: led 1f out tl ins fnl f: r.o) .... hd 2
610[3] Silence in Court (IRE) **(93)***(110) (BAMcMahon)* 4-8-9 JFortune(9) (4th st: nt clr run over 2f out: swtchd rt & nt clr run over 1f out: r.o one pce) 2 3
610[2] Old Rouvel (USA) **(83)***(108) (DJGMurraySmith)* 4-8-9 KDarley(6) (lw: rdn over 4f out: 6th st: nt clr run on ins wl over 1f out: swtchd lft: one pce) 2½ 4
712[9] Escarpment (USA) **(103)***(104) (PWChapple-Hyam)* 4-8-9 JReid(5) (nt clr run over 3f out: nvr nr to chal) 3½ 5
Admiral's Well (IRE) **(93)***(94) (RAkehurst)* 5-8-12 TQuinn(4) (lw: 2nd st: ev ch wl over 1f out: sn wknd) 10 6
Transom (USA) **(93)***(93) (GHarwood)* 4-8-9 PatEddery(8) (rdn 7f out: led over 4f out tl wl over 1f out: sn wknd) 1½ 7
610* Further Flight **(107)***(93)*(Fav)*(BWHills)* 9-9-1 MHills(7) (rdn over 6f out: hdwy over 4f out: wknd over 2f out) 2½ 8
661[10] Not in Doubt (USA) **(87)***(78) (HCandy)* 6-8-12b WNewnes(3) (led 12f) 12 9

9/2 DOUBLE TRIGGER (IRE), Poltarf (USA), Further Flight (op 3/1), **5/1** Silence in Court (IRE), **11/2** Transom (USA), **9/1** Old Rouvel (USA) (6/1-10/1), **12/1** Admiral's Well (IRE), **16/1** Escarpment (USA), **50/1** Not in Doubt (USA), CSF £22.51 TOTE £5.40: £1.70 £1.60 £1.60 (£11.00) Trio £18.60 OWNER Mr R. W. Huggins (MIDDLEHAM) BRED Dene Investments N V 9 Rn
3m 28.9 (2.40) SF: 69/66/64/62/58/51/47/50/35
WEIGHT FOR AGE 4yo-3lb

870 INSULPAK VICTORIA CUP H'CAP (0-110) (4-Y.O+) (Class B) £19,700.00 (£5,975.00: £2,925.00: £1,400.00)

7f Stalls: Centre GOING minus 0.20 sec per fur (GF) 3-40 (3-43)

714[2] **Jawaal (82)***(93)*(Fav)*(LadyHerries)* 5-8-6 JReid(16) (lw: stdy hdwy 2f out: led 1f out: rdn out) .... — 1
714[9] Royal Hill **(79)***(89) (LordHuntingdon)* 4-8-3 JWeaver(19) (hrd rdn & hdwy over 1f out: r.o wl ins fnl f) .... nk 2
Top Banana **(73)***(77) (HCandy)* 4-7-11 NAdams(15) (hld up: hrd rdn over 1f out: unable qckn) 3 3
Jolto **(69)***(72) (KOCunningham-Brown)* 6-7-2 (5) MBaird(23) (led 6f: one pce) .... nk 4
Kayvee **(97)***(100) (GHarwood)* 6-9-7 WRSwinburn(10) (rdn & hdwy over 1f out: r.o ins fnl f) .... s.h 5
714[11] Indian Fly **(92)***(94) (RHannon)* 4-9-2 RHughes(6) (rdn over 2f out: hdwy & bmpd over 1f out: r.o) .... hd 6
665[2] Classic Sky (IRE) **(100)***(102) (BHanbury)* 4-9-10 WRyan(4) (hld up: rdn over 2f out: r.o ins fnl f) .... nk 7
665[3] Belfry Green (IRE) **(97)***(99) (CAHorgan)* 5-9-7 WWoods(5) (rdn over 2f out: hdwy & bmpd over 1f out: r.o) .... s.h 8
486[8] Tawafij (USA) **(81)***(80) (TDyer)* 6-8-5 StephenDavies(2) (swtg: nvr nr to chal) 1¼ 9
714[14] Roving Minstrel **(87)***(85) (BAMcMahon)* 4-8-11 KDarley(14) (hld up: rdn over 2f out: wkng whn hmpd over 1f out) .... ½ 10
714[5] Czarna (IRE) **(88)***(86) (CEBrittain)* 4-8-12 MRimmer(3) (prom over 5f) .... s.h 11
728* Ertlon **(81)***(77) (CEBrittain)* 5-8-5 6x JQuinn(8) (swtg: a.p: hrd rdn over 1f out: wknd fnl f) .... ½ 12

439[22] Neither Nor **(85)***(79) (DAWilson)* 6-8-9 GCarter(12) (swtg: a mid div)....1 **13**
665[17] Realities (USA) **(99)***(92) (GHarwood)* 5-9-9 MJKinane(22) (a.p: rdn over 1f out: wknd fnl f)....nk **14**
636[3] Fionn de Cool (IRE) **(72)***(63) (RAkehurst)* 4-7-10 GBardwell(21) (rdn over 3f out: hdwy over 1f out: wknd fnl f)....1 **15**
765[8] Bayin (USA) **(69)***(60) (MDIUsher)* 6-7-7 RStreet(18) (b: swtg: nt clr run over 1f out: nvr nrr)....hd **16**
685[2] Rossini Blue **(74)***(65) (ABailey)* 4-7-12 FNorton(13) (swtg: prom over 5f)....hd **17**
Serious **(87)***(77) (LadyHerries)* 5-8-11 TIves(24) (lw: hld up: rdn 2f out: wknd over 1f out)....½ **18**
439[8] Cameron Highland (IRE) **(82)***(71) (PFICole)* 4-8-6 TQuinn(9) (lw: prom over 5f)....hd **19**
No Extras (IRE) **(92)***(81) (GLMoore)* 5-9-2 BRouse(11) (swtg: a bhd)....nk **20**
785[4] Veloce (IRE) **(71)***(53) (ABailey)* 7-7-2 (7)ow2 MartinDwyer(20) (b: bhd fnl 2f)....2 **21**
665[13] New Capricorn (USA) **(95)***(71) (MAJarvis)* 5-9-5 PatEddery(17) (lw: bhd fnl 2f)....3½ **22**
659[5] Hard to Figure **(104)***(73) (RJHodges)* 9-10-0 RCochrane(25) (bhd fnl 2f)....3 **23**
Law Commission **(84)***(49) (DRCElsworth)* 5-8-8 PaulEddery(1) (prom over 4f)....2 **24**
652[4] Masnad (USA) **(100)***(37) (RWArmstrong)* 4-9-10 WCarson(7) (s.s: a bhd)....12 **25**

LONG HANDICAP Veloce (IRE) 7-6 Bayin (USA) 7-4 Jolto 7-4

7/1 JAWAAL, **9/1** Fionn de Cool (IRE), **10/1** Ertlon, Belfry Green (IRE), **12/1** New Capricorn (USA) (10/1-16/1), Czarna (IRE), **14/1** Royal Hill, Classic Sky (IRE), Realities (USA), **16/1** Top Banana, Indian Fly, Kayvee, **20/1** Cameron Highland (IRE), **25/1** Roving Minstrel, Serious, Hard to Figure, Masnad (USA), **33/1** No Extras (IRE), Tawafij (USA), Jolto, **40/1** Law Commission, Neither Nor, **50/1** Veloce (IRE), Bayin (USA), **66/1** Rossini Blue, CSF £94.41 CT £1,411.60 TOTE £7.40: £2.40 £2.40 £3.70 £5.90 (£44.90) Trio £1,202.20 OWNER Mr T.G.Fox (LITTLEHAMPTON) BRED Gainsborough Stud Management Ltd 25 Rn
1m27.03 (0.53) SF: 69/65/53/48/76/70/78/75/56/61/62/53/55/68/39/36/41/53/47/57/29/47/49/25/13

871 GARTER STKS (2-Y.O) (Class B) £6,301.00 (£2,359.00: £1,154.50: £497.50: £223.75: £114.25)
5f Stalls: High GOING minus 0.20 sec per fur (GF) 4-10 (4-12)

570* **Unconditional Love (IRE)** *(91+) (MJohnston)* 2-8-6 DHolland(2) (mde all: rdn over 1f out: r.o wl)....— **1**
424* World Premier *(87) (CEBrittain)* 2-9-1 MRimmer(7) (a.p: ev ch over 1f out: unable qckn)....4 **2**
480* Cabcharge Striker *(83) (MRChannon)* 2-8-11 RHughes(4) (lw: rdn & hdwy over 1f out: one pce)....hd **3**
617* Amaretto Bay (IRE) *(79) (BJMeehan)* 2-9-1 JWeaver(3) (lw: a.p: ev ch over 1f out: sn wknd)....2½ **4**
540* General Rose *(67) (RHannon)* 2-8-11 RPerham(6) (bhd fnl 2f)....2½ **5**
638* My Melody Parkes *(64)*(Fav)*(JBerry)* 2-8-10 JCarroll(1) (spd 3f)....½ **6**
683[3] Kustom Kit (IRE) *(44) (BAMcMahon)* 2-9-1 FNorton(5) (lw: bhd fnl 2f)....8 **7**

15/8 My Melody Parkes, **4/1** World Premier, Cabcharge Striker (op 2/1), **5/1** UNCONDITIONAL LOVE (IRE), **12/1** Amaretto Bay (IRE) (op 8/1), **25/1** General Rose, **33/1** Kustom Kit (IRE), CSF £21.66 TOTE £4.10: £1.70 £3.00 (£9.90) OWNER Mrs H. Conroy (MIDDLEHAM) BRED Rathbarry Stud 7 Rn
61.15 secs (1.65) SF: 46/42/38/34/22/19/-

872 CHOBHAM STKS (4-Y.O+) (Class C) £5,534.40 (£1,790.40: £875.20)
1m (round) Stalls: Centre GOING minus 0.20 sec per fur (GF) 4-40 (4-41)

665[14] **Calling Collect (USA) (97)***(104) (LMCumani)* 6-8-12 PatEddery(1) (2nd st: rdn over 1f out: qcknd & led ins fnl f: r.o wl)....— **1**
666[3] Airport (USA) **(102)***(110)*(Fav)*(JHMGosden)* 4-9-5 LDettori(2) (b.hind: lw: led: rdn over 1f out: hdd ins fnl f: r.o)....½ **2**
425[8] Risk Master **(92)***(96) (CAHorgan)* 6-9-1 PaulEddery(3) (3rd st: rdn over 1f out: unable qckn)....5 **3**

8/13 Airport (USA), **3/1** CALLING COLLECT (USA), **4/1** Risk Master (3/1-9/2), CSF £4.92 TOTE £3.70 (£1.70) OWNER Godolphin (NEWMARKET) BRED B & R Partners 3 Rn
1m 45.23 (5.63) SF: 24/30/16

873 WHITE ROSE H'CAP (0-80) (3-Y.O+) (Class D) £9,105.00 (£2,760.00: £1,350.00: £645.00)
1m (round) Stalls: Centre GOING minus 0.20 sec per fur (GF) 5-15 (5-16)

Deevee (66)*(79) (CJBenstead)* 6-9-3 PRobinson(12) (bit bkwd: hdwy over 1f out: str run fnl f: led wl ins fnl f: r.o wl)....— **1**
486[7] Saifan **(65)***(76) (DMorris)* 6-8-13b(3) CHodgson(3) (lw: hdwy over 1f out: ev ch ins fnl f: unable qckn)....1 **2**

539[5] Tregaron (USA) **(72)***(82) (PCalver)* 4-9-9 MBirch(5) (9th st: hdwy 2f out: led 1f out tl wl ins fnl f: one pce) ....nk 3
731[2] Pistol (IRE) **(58)***(67) (CAHorgan)* 5-8-9 PaulEddery(1) (b.hind: swtchd rt & hdwy over 1f out: r.o wl ins fnl f)....¾ 4
634[5] Uncle Oswald **(77)***(85) (RHannon)* 4-9-7 (7) DaneO'Neill(20) (b: 2nd st: led 2f out to 1f out: one pce)....nk 5
762[5] Sooty Tern **(66)***(73) (JMBradley)* 8-8-12 (5) SDrowne(2) (8th st: rdn over 2f out: r.o one pce fnl f) ....¾ 6
Khayrapour (IRE) **(70)***(76) (BJMeehan)* 5-9-7 PatEddery(25) (bit bkwd: 6th st: rdn over 2f out: one pce) ....½ 7
678[9] Battleship Bruce **(70)***(74) (NACallaghan)* 3-8-8 LDettori(8) (b.hind: nvr nr to chal)....1 8
686[4] Kings Assembly **(70)***(74) (PWHarris)* 3-8-8 RCochrane(23) (nvr nrr) ....s.h 9
Fairy Knight **(71)***(75) (RHannon)* 3-8-9 JReid(22) (a mid div)....s.h 10
728[2] Shepherd Market (IRE) **(59)***(62) (DAWilson)* 4-8-10 GCarter(21) (lw: a mid div) ....½ 11
Zajko (USA) **(70)***(70) (LadyHerries)* 5-9-7 TIves(15) (n.m.r on ins over 1f out: nvr plcd to chal)....1¼ 12
762* Daytona Beach (IRE) **(56)***(56)*(Fav)*(PBurgoyne)* 5-8-7 TQuinn(11) (swtg: 4th st: rdn over 2f out: wknd over 1f out)....nk 13
501[7] Broughtons Turmoil **(52)***(51) (WJMusson)* 6-7-12 (5) PMcCabe(24) (led over 5f out to 2f out: wknd over 1f out)....s.h 14
586[3] Roman Reel (USA) **(64)***(63) (GLMoore)* 4-9-1 BRouse(6) (lw: a mid div) ....nk 15
634[12] Eqtesaad (USA) **(74)***(69) (SCWilliams)* 4-9-11 KDarley(19) (swtg: 3rd st: wknd over 1f out)....1¾ 16
724* Karinska **(54)***(49) (MCChapman)* 5-7-12 (7) CMunday(13) (s.s: nvr nrr)....s.h 17
642[2] Hawwam **(54)***(47) (EJAlston)* 9-8-5 ow1 KFallon(18) (nvr nrr)....¾ 18
Set the Fashion **(74)***(67) (LordHuntingdon)* 6-9-11v JWeaver(16) (a bhd)....½ 19
Court Minstrel **(56)***(47) (LJHolt)* 6-8-7 AMcGlone(17) (bit bkwd: swtg: hdwy & nt clr run over 1f out: eased whn btn fnl f)....1 20
731[3] Confronter **(69)***(58) (SDow)* 6-9-6 RHughes(14) (a bhd)....1 21
Sir Norman Holt (IRE) **(59)***(41) (RJO'Sullivan)* 6-8-10 MRimmer(9) (lw: bhd fnl 3f) 3½ 22
Rupiana (IRE) **(71)***(47) (JRArnold)* 3-8-9 DHarrison(10) (lw: bhd fnl 3f) 3 23
714[4] Knobbleeneeze **(76)***(52) (MRChannon)* 5-9-8v(5) PPMurphy(4) (lw: 7th st: wknd over 2f out) ....hd 24
320[12] Kingchip Boy **(74)***(46) (MJRyan)* 6-9-11v AClark(7) (led over 2f: 5th st: wknd over 2f out)....1¾ 25

7/2 Daytona Beach (IRE), **13/2** Zajko (USA), **10/1** Confronter, **14/1** Shepherd Market (IRE), Kings Assembly, Eqtesaad (USA) (10/1-16/1), Knobbleeneeze, Set the Fashion, **16/1** Pistol (IRE), Tregaron (USA), Fairy Knight, Battleship Bruce, **20/1** Hawwam, DEEVEE, Broughtons Turmoil, Khayrapour (IRE), Karinska, **25/1** Sooty Tern, Kingchip Boy, Uncle Oswald, **33/1** Court Minstrel, Saifan, Rupiana (IRE), Roman Reel (USA), Sir Norman Holt (IRE), CSF £546.63 CT £9,319.13 TOTE £36.40: £6.10 £9.20 £5.40 £3.80 (£145.70) Trio £2,277.90 (0.37 Tckts); £2,021.29 to Salisbury 4/5/95. OWNER Mr D. Turner (EPSOM) BRED Mrs Deborah Paul 25 Rn

1m 42.02 (2.42) SF: 61/58/64/49/67/55/58/43/43/44/44/52/38/33/45/51/31/29/49/29/40/23/16/34/28

WEIGHT FOR AGE 3yo-13lb

T/Jkpt: Not won; £41,641.71 to Salisbury 4/5/95. T/Plpt: £3,221.10 (10.73 Tckts). T/Qdpt: £278.30 (0.6 Tckts); £150.44 to Salisbury 4/5/95. AK

0593-HAMILTON (R-H)
Thursday May 4th (Good, Good to firm patches)
WEATHER: sunny & warm WIND: almost nil

874 EAGLESHAM LIMITED LIMITED STKS (0-50) (4-Y.O+) (Class F) £3,025.00 (£850.00: £415.00) **1m 1f 36y** Stalls: High GOING minus 0.43 sec (F) 2-20 (2-21)

593* **Ivan the Terrible (IRE) (47)***(67) (BEllison)* 7-9-0 NKennedy(7) (b: mde all: qcknd clr over 3f out: styd on wl) ....— 1
738[2] Broughton's Pride (IRE) **(48)***(54)*(Fav)*(JAGlover)* 4-8-3 (3) SSanders(10) (in tch: hdwy on ins 4f out: rdn appr fnl f: nt qckn)....3 2
757[3] Soba Up **(49)***(51) (TJEtherington)* 5-8-6 LCharnock(16) (lw: in tch: hdwy over 2f out: styd on one pce fnl f)....1½ 3
476[5] Gold Desire **(36)***(52) (MBrittain)* 5-8-11 NConnorton(6) (in tch: hdwy u.p over 2f out: nt pce to chal)....2½ 4
676[9] Myfontaine **(48)***(52) (KTIvory)* 8-8-11 GDuffield(11) (lw: styd on wl fnl 4f: nrst fin) ....hd 5
568[W] Friar Street (IRE) **(50)***(49) (EJAlston)* 5-8-11 KFallon(14) (hdwy ½-wy: styd on one pce fnl 2f)....1¼ 6

*601*8 Kissavos **(45)***(46) (CCElsey)* 9-8-11 DHolland(13) (chsd ldrs tl wknd fnl 2f)....2 7
672* Calisar **(44)***(46) (PHowling)* 5-9-0 KDarley(15) (bhd: sme hdwy 3f out: nvr trbld ldrs)....1¾ 8
Thisonesforalice **(38)***(42) (AHarrison)* 7-8-6 (5) JStack(17) (lw: s.i.s: sme late hdwy)....½ 9
550 6 Lord of a Dance **(48)***(42)*(Fav)*(WJHaggas)* 4-8-11 PRobinson(12) (trckd ldrs: effrt over 3f out: sn rdn & grad wknd)....s.h 10
672 20 Lady Highfield **(40)***(36) (MJRyan)* 4-8-6 GCarter(18) (b.hind: chsd ldrs tl wknd 3f out)....¾ 11
*771*6 Fryup Satellite **(34)***(34) (LRLloyd-James)* 4-8-11 DaleGibson(9) (b.hind: lw: effrt u.p ½-wy: n.d)....4 12
776 4 Kilnamartyra Girl **(46)***(18) (JParkes)* 5-7-13 (7) GFaulkner(1) (lw: chsd ldrs to ½-wy: sn wknd)....6 13
Roscommon Joe (IRE) **(34)***(23) (JJO'Neill)* 5-8-11 SMaloney(8) (n.d)....s.h 14
646 13 Killy's Filly **(45)***(17) (JMBradley)* 5-8-1 (5) SDrowne(5) (lw: in tch to ½-wy)....½ 15
818 13 Marble **(43)***(15) (MartynWane)* 4-8-6 AMackay(3) (s.i.s: n.d)....1¼ 16
722 14 Quiet Mission **(40)***(20) (JLEyre)* 4-8-11 RLappin(4) (chsd ldrs to ½-wy: sn bhd)....nk 17
*469*5 Aerial View **(49)***(17) (WGMTurner)* 4-8-8 (3) DRMcCabe(2) (bhd fr ½-wy)....1½ 18

4/1 Lord of a Dance, Broughton's Pride (IRE), **5/1** Soba Up, **10/1** Kilnamartyra Girl, **11/1** IVAN THE TERRIBLE (IRE) (8/1-12/1), **12/1** Myfontaine (op 8/1), **16/1** Friar Street (IRE), Calisar, Thisonesforalice, Kissavos, Killy's Filly, **20/1** Roscommon Joe (IRE), Gold Desire, **50/1** Lady Highfield, Fryup Satellite, Marble, Aerial View, **66/1** Quiet Mission, CSF £52.79 TOTE £7.80: £2.80 £1.30 £2.30 (£31.70) Trio £28.70 OWNER Mrs Jean Stapleton (CONSETT) BRED Stud-On-The-Chart 18 Rn 1m 56.4 (2.10) SF: 46/33/30/31/31/28/25/25/21/21/15/13/-/2/-/-/-/-

875 BELLSHILL CLAIMING STKS (I) (3-Y.O) (Class F) £2,717.00 (£762.00: £371.00)
1m 65y Stalls: High GOING minus 0.43 sec per fur (F) 2-50 (2-57)

*767*6 **Samaka Hara (IRE) (42)***(63) (WSCunningham)* 3-8-7 KDarley(9) (chsd ldrs: hrd drvn over 2f out: styd on to ld ins fnl f)....— 1
786 4 Boundary Express **(53)***(58)*(Fav)*(MJohnston)* 3-8-3b DHolland(11) (chsd ldrs: rdn 3f out: ev ch over 1f out: hung lft: styd on twrds fin)....½ 2
521 14 Okay Baby (IRE) **(47)***(48) (MHTompkins)* 3-8-1 ow1 PRobinson(1) (lw: led tl hdd & wknd ins fnl f)....3½ 3
594 13 Benjarong **(42)***(33) (RMMcKellar)* 3-7-12 DaleGibson(8) (hld up: effrt ½-wy: sn rdn & nvr able to chal)....7 4
593 10 Keith's Pride (IRE) **(33)***(40) (TDyer)* 3-8-6 (3) SSanders(7) (a in tch: rdn & no hdwy fnl 4f)....2 5
Nebrangus (IRE) **(40)***(44) (NBycroft)* 3-8-13 AMackay(2) (hdwy u.p ½-wy: n.d)....hd 6
594 15 Seenthelight **(50)***(33) (DMoffatt)* 3-8-3 (3) DarrenMoffatt(10) (hld up & n.d)....2 7
596 2 Ricana **(47)***(17) (WTKemp)* 3-7-12 JMarshall(6) (chsd ldrs to ½-wy: sn lost pl)....4 8
Ladys Promise *(4) (MartynWane)* 3-7-12 LCharnock(4) (dwlt: a bhd)....7 9
Melissa's Baby *(14) (MissLAPerratt)* 3-9-2 GDuffield(5) (a bhd)....4 10
*647*7 Chaldon Herring **(63)** *(TDBarron)* 3-8-13 JFortune(3) (Withdrawn not under Starter's orders: uns rdr & bolted gng to s).... W

, **7/4** Boundary Express, **3/1** Ricana, **5/1** SAMAKA HARA (IRE), **10/1** Benjarong, Okay Baby (IRE), Seenthelight, **33/1** Keith's Pride (IRE), Melissa's Baby, **50/1** Ladys Promise, Nebrangus (IRE), CSF £13.21 TOTE £5.90: £1.30 £1.00 £3.80 (£4.20) Trio £21.50 OWNER Mr B. L. Cassidy (YARM) BRED The Mount Coote Partnership 10 Rn 1m 48.0 (4.70) SF: 13/8/-/-/-/-/-/-/-/-
Boundary Express clmd E.Alston £3,000.

876 LANSON CHAMPAGNE H'CAP (0-70) (3-Y.O+) (Class E) £4,074.50 (£1,235.00: £604.00: £288.50)
1m 65y Stalls: High GOING minus 0.43 sec per fur (F) 3-20 (3-25)

785 11 **Comeonup (54)***(68) (JMBradley)* 4-8-9 (5) SDrowne(12) (b: prom: led appr fnl f: r.o)....— 1
579 2 Sharp Rebuff **(68)***(77) (PJMakin)* 4-10-0 GDuffield(15) (lw: chsd ldrs: led wl over 2f out tl appr fnl f: no ex)....2½ 2
676 16 King Curan (USA) **(57)***(64) (ABailey)* 4-9-3b AMackay(8) (lw: a.p: effrt 3f out: hrd rdn & r.o one pce fnl 2f)....1¼ 3
*601** Marowins **(44)***(45)*(Fav)*(EJAlston)* 6-8-4 KFallon(10) (effrt over 4f out: styd on: nvr able chal)....3 4
Trooping (IRE) **(60)***(61) (MGMeagher)* 6-9-6 JFortune(6) (hdwy ½-wy: styd on: no imp)....hd 5
579 3 Equerry **(62)***(62) (MJohnston)* 4-9-8 DHolland(1) (lw: bhd tl styd on u.p fnl 3f: nrst fin)....½ 6
780 8 Comanche Companion **(68)***(67) (TJNaughton)* 5-10-0 GCarter(3) (rr div: hdwy 3f out: nvr trbld ldrs)....½ 7

642[11] Never so True **(40)***(36) (MartynWane)* 4-8-0b LCharnock(16) (led tl hdd wl over 2f out: sn btn) 1¼ **8**
593[5] Gospel Song **(50)***(42) (WTKemp)* 3-7-11 JMarshall(14) (chsd ldrs to ½-wy) 2½ **9**
Runrig (IRE) **(42)***(28) (MissLAPerratt)* 5-8-2 JFanning(13) (b: prom to ½-wy) 3 **10**
Moofaji **(66)***(49) (FWatson)* 4-9-12 DeanMcKeown(7) (bhd fr ½-wy) 1¼ **11**
559[6] Ochos Rios (IRE) **(64)***(47) (BSRothwell)* 4-9-5 (5) JStack(2) (n.d) ....½ **12**
749[11] Pendolino (IRE) **(62)***(44) (MBrittain)* 4-9-8b PRobinson(4) (n.d) ....½ **13**
Al Wujud (IRE) **(42)***(23) (TDyer)* 4-7-13 (3) DarrenMoffatt(9) (s.i.s: n.d) ....½ **14**
Evan 'elp Us **(66)***(44) (JLEyre)* 3-8-13b KDarley(11) (chsd ldrs to ½-wy: sn wknd) 1¼ **15**
785[5] King of Show (IRE) **(63)***(36) (RAllan)* 4-9-6 (3) SSanders(5) (mid div tl wknd fr ½-wy) 2½ **16**

11/2 Marowins, **6/1** Sharp Rebuff, King Curan (USA), **7/1** Equerry, Comanche Companion, **9/1** Evan 'elp Us, King of Show (IRE) (6/1-10/1), **11/1** Ochos Rios (IRE) (8/1-12/1), **16/1** Moofaji, Al Wujud (IRE), **20/1** Gospel Song, **25/1** COMEONUP, **33/1** Never so True, **40/1** Runrig (IRE), **50/1** Trooping (IRE), Pendolino (IRE), CSF £159.37 CT £945.50 TOTE £86.90: £8.50 £2.00 £2.20 £2.00 (£131.10) Trio £358.50; £106.04 to Hamilton 5/5/95 OWNER Mr M. B. Carver (CHEPSTOW) BRED P. J. McCalmont 16 Rn 1m 46.9 (3.60) SF: 30/39/26/7/23/24/29/-/-/-/11/9/6/-/-/-
WEIGHT FOR AGE 3yo-13lb

877

I.M.I. YORKSHIRE FITTINGS H'CAP (0-75) (3-Y.O+) (Class D) £4,552.50 (£1,380.00: £675.00: £322.50)
6f 5y Stalls: High GOING minus 0.43 sec per fur (F) 3-50 (3-55)

639[3] **Colway Rake (62)***(71)*(Fav)*(JWWatts)* 4-9-2b NConnorton(10) (w ldr far side: led ins fnl f: r.o) ....— **1**
565[9] Oggi **(61)***(65) (PJMakin)* 4-9-1 GDuffield(15) (lw: led far side tl ins fnl f: no ex) 2 **2**
723[11] Craigie Boy **(61)***(64) (NBycroft)* 5-9-1 SMaloney(17) (lw: chsd ldrs far side: hdwy u.p over 1f out: styd on) ....nk **3**
728[8] Persian Affair (IRE) **(71)***(71) (DHaydnJones)* 4-9-11 AMackay(16) (chsd ldrs far side: hrd rdn 2f out: r.o one pce) 1 **4**
594[5] Millemay **(39)***(35) (PMonteith)* 5-7-7 JMarshall(14) (lw: racd far side: bhd tl hdwy 2f out: nvr able chal) 1½ **5**
611[9] So Intrepid (IRE) **(73)***(66) (JMBradley)* 5-9-8 (5) SDrowne(13) (prom far side tl outpcd fnl 2f) 1¼ **6**
Miss Pigalle **(41)***(29) (MissLAPerratt)* 4-7-9 ow2 DaleGibson(12) (nvr wnt pce far side) 1¼ **7**
594[4] Blow Dry (IRE) **(58)***(46) (MartynWane)* 5-8-12 KDarley(2) (lw: racd stands' side: n.d) ....¾ **8**
832[3] Panther (IRE) **(60)***(47) (JHetherton)* 5-9-0 NKennedy(9) (lw: in tch far side: rdn & no imp fr ½-wy) ....nk **9**
838[5] Two Moves in Front (IRE) **(74)***(59) (JBerry)* 5-10-0 GCarter(11) (racd far side: outpcd after 2f) ....¾ **10**
746* Plum First **(56)***(38) (LRLloyd-James)* 5-8-10 JFortune(4) (b.hind: lw: racd stand's side: n.d) 1 **11**
491[11] Diet **(43)***(23) (MissLAPerratt)* 9-7-11v JFanning(6) (led stands' side: no ch fnl 2f) ....¾ **12**
701[19] Muzz (IRE) **(55)***(14) (RMMcKellar)* 4-8-9 MFenton(3) (a bhd) 8 **13**
594[8] Strathtore Dream (IRE) **(51)***(3) (MissLAPerratt)* 4-8-5 KFallon(5) (rcd stands' side: a bhd) 2½ **14**
701[18] Skiptamaloo **(41)** *(DonEnricoIncisa)* 4-7-9vow2 KimTinkler(8) (hung lft fr ½-wy: n.d) 1 **15**
Oscar the Second (IRE) **(41)** *(CWFairhurst)* 5-7-9 ow2 LCharnock(1) (racd stands' side: a bhd) ....½ **16**
784[8] Shropshire Blue **(42)** *(DANolan)* 5-7-7 (3)ow3 DarrenMoffatt(7) (racd centre: outpcd fr ½-wy) 6 **17**

LONG HANDICAP Miss Pigalle 7-6 Millemay 6-12 Skiptamaloo 7-2 Oscar the Second (IRE) 7-3 Shropshire Blue 7-5

11/2 COLWAY RAKE, **6/1** Plum First, Two Moves in Front (IRE), **13/2** Oggi, **7/1** Craigie Boy, **8/1** Panther (IRE), **10/1** Persian Affair (IRE), **11/1** So Intrepid (IRE), **12/1** Blow Dry (IRE), **20/1** Diet, **25/1** Millemay, **33/1** Miss Pigalle, **50/1** Muzz (IRE), Strathtore Dream (IRE), **66/1** Skiptamaloo, Oscar the Second (IRE), **100/1** Shropshire Blue, CSF £38.69 CT £237.21 TOTE £4.60: £1.10 £2.80 £2.30 £2.20 (£40.50) Trio £67.10 OWNER Mr R. Coleman (RICHMOND) BRED P. D. and Mrs Player 17 Rn 1m 11.6 (1.60) SF: 41/35/34/41/5/36/-/16/17/29/8/-/-/-/-/-/-

878

COATBRIDGE MAIDEN AUCTION STKS (2-Y.O) (Class F) £2,759.00 (£774.00: £377.00) **5f 4y** Stalls: High GOING minus 0.43 sec per fur (F) 4-20 (4-22)

615[2] **Mallia** *(78)*(Fav)*(TDBarron)* 2-8-7 JFortune(4) (lw: disp ld tl led 2f out: drvn along & r.o) ....— **1**
Red River Valley *(72) (DenysSmith)* 2-8-4 ow1 KFallon(6) (w'like: scope: bit bkwd: disp ld 3f: kpt on wl) ....¾ **2**

Gothenberg (IRE) *(64)*(Fav)*(MJohnston)* 2-8-7 DHolland(3) (leggy: scope: b.off hind: chsd ldrs: rdn 2f out: kpt on) 3½ 3
Whispering Dawn *(53) (MRChannon)* 2-8-2 KDarley(5) (w'like: sn outpcd: hdwy u.p 2f out: nvr rch ldrs) 2 4
725³ Crimson And Clover *(44) (MBell)* 2-8-2 MFenton(7) (chsd ldrs tl outpcd fnl 2f) 3 5
615¹¹ Oriole *(48) (NTinkler)* 2-8-7 KimTinkler(1) (s.i.s: hdwy 2f out: styd on) ....nk 6
Sunday Maelstrom (IRE) *(27) (JBerry)* 2-8-2 GCarter(8) (neat: unf: b.off fore: sn outpcd: hung lft 2f out) 5 7
474⁶ Braes'O'Shieldhill *(17) (ABailey)* 2-8-2 FNorton(9) (s.i.s: hdwy & swtchd 2f out: n.d) 3 8
Our Tom's Boy *(KTIvory)* 2-8-3 GDuffield(2) (leggy: unf: dwlt: sn outpcd & wl bhd) 8 9

9/4 MALLIA (op 6/4), Gothenberg (IRE), **4/1** Crimson And Clover, **11/2** Whispering Dawn (7/2-6/1), **8/1** Braes'O'Shieldhill, Our Tom's Boy (6/1-9/1), **10/1** Sunday Maelstrom (IRE) (op 6/1), **16/1** Red River Valley, **33/1** Oriole, CSF £38.73 TOTE £3.40: £1.30 £7.60 £2.40 (£58.50) Trio £135.20; £60.97 to Hamilton 5/5/95 OWNER Mr H. T. Duddin (THIRSK) BRED B. J. McAllister 9 Rn
59.8 secs (1.50) SF: 30/24/16/5/-/-/-/-/-

879 EAST KILBRIDE H'CAP (0-70) (3-Y.O+) (Class E) £4,092.05 (£1,240.40: £606.70: £289.85)
1m 5f 9y Stalls: High GOING minus 0.43 sec per fur (F) 4-50 (4-52)

641* **Embryonic (IRE) (70)***(84)*(Fav)*(RFFisher)* 3-9-2 KFallon(6) (bhd: gd hdwy on ins 4f out: led ins fnl f: r.o) ....— 1
430¹⁵ Mentalasanythin **(53)***(67) (ABailey)* 6-9-5 AMackay(9) (sn prom: led & qcknd wl over 2f out: hdd ins fnl f: kpt on) ....nk 2
530² Broom Isle **(48)***(56) (DBurchell)* 7-9-0 FNorton(10) (a chsng ldrs: ev ch over 3f out: r.o one pce) 5 3
771ᵂ Jarrow **(42)***(48) (MrsAMNaughton)* 4-8-8v JFortune(2) (hdwy on outside 3f out: styd on wl) 1 4
598² Zaaheyah (USA) **(48)***(54) (MDHammond)* 5-9-0 PRobinson(5) (outpcd tl styd on u.p fnl 4f: nrst fin) ....nk 5
661¹⁴ Guards Brigade **(47)***(49) (JHetherton)* 4-8-13 NKennedy(13) (chsd ldrs: one pce fnl 3f) 3 6
568¹² Lord Hastie (USA) **(62)***(61) (CWThornton)* 7-10-0 DeanMcKeown(18) (chsd ldrs: ev ch 4f out: wknd over 2f out) 2½ 7
763⁶ Achilles Heel **(50)***(49) (CNAllen)* 4-9-2 GDuffield(16) (led tl hdd wl over 2f out: grad wknd) ....nk 8
556¹⁶ Sir Dickie Cox (IRE) **(44)***(39) (FHLee)* 4-8-10 ACulhane(3) (effrt whn hmpd over 3f out: n.d) 3½ 9
589⁸ Vaigly Sunthyme **(41)***(35) (JMCarr)* 5-8-7 SMorris(4) (bhd tl sme late hdwy) ....hd 10
687⁴ Flyaway Blues **(57)***(49) (MrsMReveley)* 3-8-3 KDarley(11) (lw: bhd & c wd st: n.d) 1¾ 11
Beekman Street **(48)***(38) (DHaydnJones)* 9-8-9 (5) SDrowne(17) (b: hdwy 5f out: n.d) 2 12
582⁴ Snow Dream **(40)***(28) (MJRyan)* 5-8-6 GCarter(7) (chsd ldrs tl wknd over 3f out) 1¾ 13
534² Rejects Reply **(38)***(24) (WJMusson)* 5-8-1 (3) DRMcCabe(15) (lw: trckd ldrs tl lost pl fnl 4f) 1¼ 14
Deb's Ball **(46)***(29) (DMoffatt)* 9-8-9 (3) DarrenMoffatt(14) (s.i.s: a bhd) 2½ 15
737⁶ Rapporteur (USA) **(58)***(40) (CCElsey)* 9-9-10 DHolland(8) (b: chsd ldrs tl wknd over 3f out) ....½ 16
597⁵ Dawn Rock **(35)***(9) (RMMcKellar)* 4-8-1b DaleGibson(1) (bhd fnl 4f) 7 17
Sealed With a Kiss **(52)***(12) (MBell)* 5-9-4 MFenton(12) (prom tl wknd over 4f out) 11 18

3/1 EMBRYONIC (IRE), **6/1** Achilles Heel, **10/1** Mentalasanythin, Broom Isle (8/1-12/1), Flyaway Blues, **14/1** Snow Dream, Lord Hastie (USA), Rejects Reply, Deb's Ball, **16/1** Zaaheyah (USA), **20/1** Rapporteur (USA), **25/1** Guards Brigade, Sealed With a Kiss, **33/1** Sir Dickie Cox (IRE), **50/1** Beekman Street, Vaigly Sunthyme, Dawn Rock, **100/1** Jarrow, CSF £30.08 CT £248.46 TOTE £3.90: £1.30 £1.90 £2.00 £29.40 (£20.50) Trio £34.90 OWNER Mrs D. Miller (ULVERSTON) BRED Tsarina Stud 18 Rn 2m 49.2 (3.50) SF: 45/48/37/29/35/30/42/30/20/16/10/19/9/5/10/21/-/-
WEIGHT FOR AGE 3yo-20lb

880 BELLSHILL CLAIMING STKS (II) (3-Y.O) (Class F) £2,717.00 (£762.00: £371.00)
1m 65y Stalls: High GOING minus 0.43 sec per fur (F) 5-20 (5-24)

587⁶ **Slytly Beveled (49)***(59) (NPLittmoden)* 3-8-2b(5) TGMcLaughlin(7) (bhd: hdwy & swtchd 3f out: led ins fnl f: hung lft: r.o) ....— 1
Fishy Affair **(45)***(56) (TDyer)* 3-8-9 MFenton(11) (in tch: hdwy to ld over 1f out: hdd & no ex ins fnl f) 2½ 2
Mudlark **(60)***(47)*(Fav)*(JWWatts)* 3-8-7b NConnorton(6) (b: bhd: hdwy 2f out: swtchd 1f out: fin wl) 3½ 3
J C Grey **(40)***(34) (DenysSmith)* 3-8-5 KFallon(1) (chsd ldrs: led wl over 1f out: sn hdd & wknd) 6 4

596[5] Chastleton **(45)***(32) (MRChannon)* 3-8-6 KDarley(9) (bhd: hdwy 4f out: hmpd 1f out: no imp) 1¾ 5
Move With Edes **(64)***(39)*(Fav)*(WGMTurner)* 3-9-3 GDuffield(3) (cl up: led over 4f out tl over 1f out: wknd) 1¾ 6
759[17] Leap Year Baby (IRE) **(43)***(14) (MDHammond)* 3-8-0 DaleGibson(4) (nvr trbld ldrs) 4 7
789[13] Sweet Cheap Pet **(47)***(18) (JJO'Neill)* 3-8-4 FNorton(5) (lw: effrt 4f out: n.d) .... s.h 8
596[3] Sul Fosso **(47)***(17) (JBerry)* 3-8-7 GCarter(10) (led tl hdd & wknd over 4f out) 2½ 9
732[14] Fuzzy *(SEKettlewell)* 3-8-2 (5) JStack(2) (a bhd) 20 10
315[6] Robaty's Law (IRE) *(PMonteith)* 3-8-3 JMarshall(8) (chsd ldrs tl wknd 4f out) 2½ 11

3/1 Move With Edes, Mudlark (9/4-7/2), **6/1** Chastleton, **13/2** Sweet Cheap Pet, **10/1** Sul Fosso, SLYTLY BEVELED, **14/1** Fishy Affair, **16/1** Leap Year Baby (IRE), **20/1** J C Grey, Robaty's Law (IRE), **50/1** Fuzzy, CSF £123.74 TOTE £12.00: £2.20 £3.80 £2.00 (£57.40) Trio £94.20 OWNER Trojan Racing (NEWARK) BRED Gordian Troeller Bloodstock Ltd 11 Rn

1m 47.7 (4.40) SF: 16/13/4/-/-/-/-/-/-/-/-

STEWARDS' ENQUIRY Connorton suspended 13-15/5/95 (irresponsible riding).

T/Plpt: £37.10 (336.7 Tckts). T/Qdpt: £14.70 (3.4 Tckts). AA

SALISBURY (R-H)
Thursday May 4th (Good to firm, Firm patches)

WEATHER: hot WIND: almost nil

881
MORRISTON MAIDEN STKS (I) (3-Y.O) (Class D) £4,077.50 (£1,220.00: £585.00: £267.50)
1m Stalls: High GOING minus 0.53 sec per fur (F) 2-00 (2-03)

Yarn (IRE) *(76) (MRChannon)* 3-8-9 RHughes(10) (hld up: led 1f out: pushed out) .... — 1
Artful Dane (IRE) **(75)***(76)*(Fav)*(MJHeaton-Ellis)* 3-9-0 StephenDavies(12) (led 7f: unable qckn) 2½ 2
Anonym (IRE) *(75) (JLDunlop)* 3-9-0 BThomson(5) (leggy: unf: bit bkwd: hdwy over 2f out: ev ch over 1f out: one pce) .... nk 3
Best of Bold *(74) (RHannon)* 3-9-0 LDettori(6) (a.p: ev ch over 1f out: one pce) .... ½ 4
Arabride *(61)*(Fav)*(JARToller)* 3-8-9 WCarson(3) (leggy: unf: hdwy over 2f out: shkn up over 1f out: rn green: bttr for r) 4 5
715[20] Merit (IRE) *(66) (PFICole)* 3-9-0 TQuinn(9) (rdn over 3f out: nvr nr to chal) .... nk 6
Equasion (IRE) *(59) (GLMoore)* 3-8-9 BRouse(8) (leggy: s.s: hld up: rdn over 3f out: wknd over 2f out) .... ¾ 7
Hazel *(58) (MissGayKelleway)* 3-8-9 RCochrane(1) (leggy: unf: bit bkwd: s.s: a bhd) .... ¾ 8
673[14] Surgiva *(40) (JRArnold)* 3-8-9 CRutter(4) (prom over 5f) 9 9
761[15] Autumn Cover *(43) (RMFlower)* 3-8-9 (5) JDSmith(2) (b: prom over 5f) 1 10
730[10] Return To Brighton *(26) (PCClarke)* 3-8-9 PatEddery(7) (s.s: a bhd: t.o fnl 3f) 6 11

4/1 Artful Dane (IRE) (5/2-9/2), Arabride, **5/1** Best of Bold, **11/2** YARN (IRE) (3/1-6/1), **8/1** Anonym (IRE) (op 4/1), Merit (IRE) (op 4/1), **25/1** Return To Brighton, **33/1** Equasion (IRE), Autumn Cover, Hazel, **50/1** Surgiva, CSF £23.84 TOTE £6.50: £2.10 £1.60 £2.70 (£9.10) Trio £25.90 OWNER Mr D. W. Shepherd (UPPER LAMBOURN) BRED Richard Hutch 11 Rn

1m 44.04 (4.74) SF: 6/6/5/4/-/-/-/-/-/-/-

882
ALMOND APPRENTICE H'CAP (0-70) (3-Y.O+) (Class G) £2,389.00 (£679.00: £337.00) **6f 212y** Stalls: High GOING minus 0.53 sec per fur (F) 2-30 (2-32)

587[9] **Scharnhorst (57)***(51) (SDow)* 3-7-12 (5) ADaly(18) (a.p: led over 2f out: r.o wl) .... — 1
450[15] Greatest **(55)***(47) (RAkehurst)* 4-8-8 (5) RMoogan(13) (lw: led over 4f: hrd rdn: r.o) .... ¾ 2
Vanborough Lad **(53)***(38) (MJBolton)* 6-8-11 GMitchell(12) (lw: hdwy over 2f out: r.o one pce) 3 3
762[13] Shaynes Domain **(45)***(24) (RMFlower)* 4-8-0b(3)ow6 RWaterfield(20) (lw: hdwy 2f out: r.o one pce) .... s.h 4
702[12] Soaking **(62)***(45) (GLMoore)* 5-9-6 LSuthern(16) (lw: hdwy 5f out: one pce fnl 2f) 1 5
766[2] Nautical Jewel **(54)***(36) (MDIUsher)* 3-8-0 CAdamson(15) (b: swtg: hdwy fnl 2f: nvr nrr) .... nk 6
503[4] Finjan **(54)***(36) (AGFoster)* 8-8-12 MHenry(6) (prom over 3f) .... s.h 7
541[6] Pair of Jacks (IRE) **(41)***(12) (DAWilson)* 5-7-6 (7)ow4 RachaelMoody(9) (prom 5f) 3 8
762[20] Indefence (IRE) **(70)***(45) (MRChannon)* 4-9-7 (7) DSweeney(10) (nvr nr to chal) .... s.h 9
731[15] Mutinique **(53)***(26) (BAPearce)* 4-8-4 (7) TField(14) (lw: prom 5f) 1 10
415[6] King Parrot (IRE) **(51)***(24) (LordHuntingdon)* 7-8-4 (5) AimeeCook(11) (lw: prom over 4f) .... s.h 11

648⁷ Double Rush (IRE) **(58)***(30)*(Fav)*(TGMills)* 3-8-1 (3) DToole(8) (lw: a mid div) ....½ **12**
780¹⁸ Glen Miller **(43)***(14) (JWPayne)* 5-8-1v NicolaHowarth(3) (nvr nrr) ....nk **13**
848¹¹ Ragazzo (IRE) **(42)***(9) (KOCunningham-Brown)* 5-7-9b(5)ow1 JWilkinson(1) (nvr nrr) 1½ **14**
*138*⁷ Early Star **(44)***(11) (KBishop)* 6-8-2 DaneO'Neill(17) (a bhd) ....s.h **15**
549¹¹ Allahrakha **(48)***(11) (DRTucker)* 4-8-6 CScally(5) (s.s: a bhd) 2 **16**
648¹² Shot the Sheriff **(62)***(22) (PFICole)* 3-8-1 (7) DavidO'Neill(4) (s.s: a bhd) 1¼ **17**
726¹² Little Hooligan **(47)** *(JAkehurst)* 4-8-5v SLanigan(19) (s.s: a bhd) 3 **18**
*371*⁸ Courting Newmarket **(51)***(3) (MrsAKnight)* 7-8-9 SarahThompson(2) (lw: a bhd) ....½ **19**
*219*⁷ It's so Easy **(53)** *(APJames)* 4-8-11 MartinDwyer(7) (bhd fnl 3f) 2½ **20**

13/2 Double Rush (IRE), **8/1** Greatest, Nautical Jewel, **10/1** Shot the Sheriff, Soaking, **12/1** Courting Newmarket, King Parrot (IRE), SCHARNHORST, **16/1** Pair of Jacks (IRE), Vanborough Lad, **20/1** Glen Miller, Shaynes Domain, Finjan, **25/1** Ragazzo (IRE), Little Hooligan, Indefence (IRE), **33/1** Mutinique, Early Star, **50/1** Allahrakha, It's so Easy, CSF £94.55 CT £1,408.60 TOTE £22.10: £3.50 £1.70 £7.60 £5.00 (£174.50) Trio Not won OWNER Mackenzie Print (EPSOM) BRED M. F. Kentish 20 Rn 1m 28.22 (2.52) SF: 17/25/16/2/23/2/14/-/23/4/2/-/-/-/-/-/-/-/-/-
WEIGHT FOR AGE 3yo-12lb

883 CHEVIOT STKS (3-Y.O+) (Class C) £5,141.00 (£1,919.00: £934.50: £397.50: £173.75: £84.25)
6f Stalls: High GOING minus 0.53 sec per fur (F) 3-00 (3-01)

Shamanic (105)*(102) (RHannon)* 3-8-13 PatEddery(9) (led 1f out: rdn out) ....— **1**
633³ Fire Dome (IRE) **(99)***(105)*(Fav)*(TGMills)* 3-9-3 JReid(8) (lw: hld up: rdn 3f out: n.m.r over 1f out: ev ch 1f out: r.o) ....½ **2**
Far Fetched (IRE) *(92) (LordHuntingdon)* 3-8-6 LDettori(2) (bit bkwd: hld up: ev ch 1f out: unable qckn) ....½ **3**
438⁸ Anniversarypresent **(94)***(96) (GLewis)* 3-8-13b PaulEddery(3) (a.p: ev ch 1f out: one pce) 1¼ **4**
633⁶ Kayrawan (USA) *(94) (HThomsonJones)* 3-8-11 RHills(5) (lw: nt clr run on ins over 2f out: hdwy on ins over 1f out: ev ch 1f out: one pce) ....hd **5**
633⁸ Al Nufooth (IRE) **(100)***(92) (MajorWRHern)* 3-9-3e WCarson(7) (lw: led 5f out to 1f out: eased whn btn ins fnl f) 3 **6**
814⁵ Star Talent (USA) **(110)***(88) (DRCElsworth)* 4-9-9 (5) AProcter(4) (swtg: a bhd) 1¼ **7**
Young Sensation *(38) (BAPearce)* 3-8-7 StephenDavies(6) (bhd fnl 4f) 15 **8**

7/2 Fire Dome (IRE), **9/2** SHAMANIC, Anniversarypresent, **5/1** Al Nufooth (IRE), **7/1** Kayrawan (USA), Star Talent (USA) (op 4/1), **9/1** Far Fetched (IRE) (5/1-10/1), **100/1** Young Sensation, CSF £18.69 TOTE £5.50: £1.70 £1.30 £2.30 (£10.20) Trio £20.10 OWNER Mr Robert Russell (MARLBOROUGH) BRED Aston House Stud Co 8 Rn 1m 13.46 (1.16) SF: 38/41/28/32/30/28/35/-
WEIGHT FOR AGE 3yo-11lb

884 GRAMPIAN H'CAP (0-70) (3-Y.O+) (Class E) £3,470.00 (£1,040.00: £500.00: £230.00) **1m 4f** Stalls: High GOING minus 0.53 sec per fur (F) 3-30 (3-31)

738³ **Credit Squeeze (69)***(85) (RFJohnsonHoughton)* 5-10-0 JQuinn(4) (stdy hdwy over 3f out: led over 1f out: edgd rt ins fnl f: r.o wl) ....— **1**
744³ Mr Browning (USA) **(54)***(68)*(Fav)*(RAkehurst)* 4-8-13b TQuinn(3) (lw: led: hrd rdn over 2f out: hdd over 1f out: 2nd & btn whn hmpd on ins ins fnl f) 1¼ **2**
736⁴ Mutazz (USA) **(65)***(67) (MajorWRHern)* 3-8-5 WCarson(9) (a.p: rdn over 4f out: one pce) 9 **3**
Rocquaine Bay **(45)***(46) (MJBolton)* 8-8-4 AMcGlone(15) (bit bkwd: hdwy over 3f out: r.o one pce) 1¼ **4**
*445*¹¹ Father Dan (IRE) **(49)***(48) (MissGayKelleway)* 6-8-8 SWhitworth(17) (hdwy on ins over 2f out: wknd over 1f out) 1½ **5**
744* Bookcase **(60)***(59) (DRCElsworth)* 8-9-5 5x JWilliams(14) (hdwy 3f out: wknd over 1f out) ....s.h **6**
Queens Contractor **(45)***(40) (SMellor)* 5-7-11b(7) ADaly(16) (prom over 9f) 3 **7**
696⁹ Sight'n Sound **(58)***(49) (DRCElsworth)* 4-9-3 RCochrane(8) (rdn & hdwy 3f out: wknd over 1f out) 3 **8**
668¹⁰ Beautete **(57)***(47) (SDow)* 4-9-2 PatEddery(6) (lw: prom over 9f) ....nk **9**
668¹⁴ Rising Spray **(64)***(53) (CAHorgan)* 4-9-9 PaulEddery(5) (nvr plcd to chal) 1¼ **10**
Gentleman Sid **(40)***(29) (PGMurphy)* 5-7-13 NAdams(2) (nvr nrr) ....s.h **11**
*374*¹³ Pip's Dream **(44)***(31) (MJRyan)* 4-8-3 AClark(7) (prom 9f) 1¼ **12**
Joys First **(47)***(23) (HJCollingridge)* 4-8-6 BThomson(13) (prom over 9f) 8 **13**
544⁵ Share the Secret **(53)***(13) (BHanbury)* 3-7-0 (7) MartinDwyer(19) (lw: bhd fnl 3f) 12 **14**
Princesse Abigail **(38)** *(RMFlower)* 4-7-11 ATucker(18) (bkwd: a bhd) 2½ **15**
*97*⁴ Surprise Guest (IRE) **(67)***(11) (APJames)* 4-9-12 JWeaver(11) (lw: a bhd) 10 **16**
*403*¹⁴ Kingsfold Fountain **(43)** *(MJHaynes)* 4-7-9 (7)ow8 DToole(1) (a bhd) 15 **17**

585[13] Tennyson Bay **(55)** *(RMFlower)* 3-7-2 (7)ow2 SLanigan(12) (plld hrd: bhd fnl 6f) 1¼ **18**
LONG HANDICAP Share the Secret 7-4 Tennyson Bay 6-8

9/2 Mr Browning (USA), **6/1** Mutazz (USA), **13/2** Beautete, **9/1** CREDIT SQUEEZE, **10/1** Sight'n Sound, Bookcase, **12/1** Rocquaine Bay, **14/1** Father Dan (IRE), **20/1** Surprise Guest (IRE), Rising Spray, Share the Secret, **25/1** Pip's Dream, Queens Contractor, **33/1** Joys First, **50/1** Princesse Abigail, Gentleman Sid, Kingsfold Fountain, **66/1** Tennyson Bay, CSF £ 44.11 CT £243.28 TOTE £10.60: £2.90 £1.10 £2.00 £1.80 (£22.80) Trio £48.70 OWNER Mr R. C. Naylor (DIDCOT) BRED Home Stud Ltd 18 Rn 2m 32.62 (0.02) SF: 70/53/33/31/33/44/25/34/32/38/14/16/8/-/-/-/-/-
WEIGHT FOR AGE 3yo-19lb

OFFICIAL EXPLANATION **Rising Spray: the jockey reported that his instructions were to settle the gelding but he ran too freely and stumbled on the bend. He let the gelding regain his momentum and tried to improve at the two-furlong marker. The trainer added that the gelding suffers from a mouth allergy.**

885

LAUDERDALE H'CAP (0-80) (3-Y.O+ F & M) (Class D) £4,012.50 (£1,200.00: £575.00: £262.50) **1m** Stalls: High GOING minus 0.53 sec per fur (F) 4-00 (4-00)

686[3] **Hujjab (USA) (79)***(87)*(Fav)*(JLDunlop)* 3-9-3 WCarson(8) (chsd ldr: led 5f out: pushed out) .... — **1**
731[13] Audrey Grace **(51)***(56)* *(BJMeehan)* 4-8-2 DHarrison(5) (bhd tl hdwy 2f out: r.o wl ins fnl f) 1¾ **2**
481[9] Belleminette (IRE) **(55)***(59)* *(DHaydnJones)* 4-8-6 JReid(9) (plld hrd: hdwy 2f out: r.o ins fnl f) .... hd **3**
694[11] Santa Fan (IRE) **(76)***(80)* *(PFICole)* 3-9-0 TQuinn(4) (hdwy 3f out: ev ch over 1f out: one pce) .... s.h **4**
664[10] Anna-Jane **(65)***(69)* *(RHannon)* 3-8-3 RHills(1) (b.off hind: plld hrd: a.p: ev ch whn hmpd 2f out: rallied ins fnl f) .... nk **5**
724[10] Misty Silks **(76)***(68)* *(MJRyan)* 5-9-13 AClark(11) (prom tl wknd over 1f out) 6 **6**
Linger **(75)***(55)* *(LordHuntingdon)* 3-8-13 LDettori(3) (bit bkwd: plld hrd: bhd fnl 2f) 6 **7**
Peveril Princess **(44)***(23)* *(GBBalding)* 4-7-9 NAdams(10) (swtg: a bhd) .... nk **8**
626[9] Shanuke (IRE) **(56)***(32)* *(JSMoore)* 3-7-1 (7)ow1 MartinDwyer(6) (bhd fnl 2f) 1 **9**
Phylian **(64)***(40)* *(SCWilliams)* 4-9-1 PatEddery(7) (led 3f: wknd over 2f out) .... nk **10**
Any One Line (IRE) **(57)***(5)* *(JAkehurst)* 3-7-9 ow2 JQuinn(2) (a bhd: t.o) 13 **11**
LONG HANDICAP Shanuke (IRE) 7-0 Any One Line (IRE) 7-6

3/1 HUJJAB (USA), **6/1** Phylian (op 4/1), Santa Fan (IRE), **7/1** Misty Silks, **15/2** Anna-Jane, **8/1** Linger (6/1-9/1), **10/1** Belleminette (IRE), **16/1** Audrey Grace, **25/1** Peveril Princess, Any One Line (IRE), **33/1** Shanuke (IRE), CSF £42.83 CT £383.79 TOTE £2.80: £1.80 £3.10 £2.10 (£62.50) Trio £241.60; £279.14 to Newmarket 5/5/95 OWNER Mr Hamdan Al Maktoum (ARUNDEL) BRED North Central Bloodstock 11 Rn 1m 42.37 (3.07) SF: 28/10/13/21/10/22/-/-/-/-/-
WEIGHT FOR AGE 3yo-13lb

886

PENTLAND STKS (3-Y.O) (Class C) £5,313.00 (£1,853.00: £901.50: £382.50) **1m 1f 209y** Stalls: High GOING minus 0.53 sec per fur (F) 4-30 (4-30)

Precede (110)*(94)*(Fav)*(PFICole)* 3-9-0 TQuinn(3) (plld hrd: wnt 2nd 7f out: led over 3f out: drvn out) .... — **1**
622[4] Dahik **(100)***(86)* *(MajorWRHern)* 3-9-0 WCarson(6) (swtg: led over 8f out tl over 3f out: ev ch over 1f out: eased whn btn ins fnl f) 5 **2**
Pesce D'Aprile *(72)* *(JLDunlop)* 3-8-11 BThomson(2) (unf: scope: bit bkwd: hld up: rdn 4f out: wknd over 1f out) 7 **3**
715[14] En Vacances (IRE) *(55)* *(AGFoster)* 3-8-2 DHarrison(1) (led over 1f: rdn 4f out: sn bhd) 5 **4**

1/2 PRECEDE (op 4/5), **11/4** Dahik (op 7/4), **7/1** Pesce D'Aprile, **100/1** En Vacances (IRE), CSF £2.10 TOTE £1.50 (£1.70) OWNER Mr Anthony Speelman (WHATCOMBE) BRED Filletts Farm Stud and Darley Stud Management 4 Rn 2m 8.07 (3.37) SF: 30/22/8/-

887

SUTHERLAND H'CAP (0-70) (3-Y.O+) (Class E) £3,626.00 (£1,088.00: £524.00: £242.00)
6f Stalls: High GOING minus 0.53 sec per fur (F) 5-00 (5-02)

Thatcherella (61)*(72)* *(MajorDNChappell)* 4-9-7 BThomson(12) (a.p: led over 1f out: all out) .... — **1**
780* Dawalib (USA) **(57)***(68)* *(DHaydnJones)* 5-9-3 6x TQuinn(3) (chsd ldrs: ev ch over 1f out: r.o wl) .... s.h **2**
629[2] Half Tone **(45)***(44)* *(RMFlower)* 3-7-1b(7)ow1 SLanigan(11) (a.p: ev ch over 1f out: wknd ins fnl f) 4 **3**
832[2] Words of Wisdom (IRE) **(50)***(48)* *(CACyzer)* 5-8-10 PatEddery(16) (hld up: hdwy over 2f out: styd on fnl f) 1 **4**

765[11] Face the Future **(67)***(61) (LJHolt)* 6-9-13 JReid(17) (hdwy over 2f out: one pce appr fnl f) 1¼ **5**
731[9] Friendly Brave (USA) **(65)***(59) (TGMills)* 5-9-11b JWeaver(4) (lw: led over 4f) ....hd **6**
765[2] Ahjay **(40)***(33)*(Fav)*(DAWilson)* 5-8-0 JQuinn(2) (nvr nr to chal) ....nk **7**
Perfect Brave **(56)***(41) (DRCElsworth)* 4-9-2 JWilliams(13) (s.i.s: nrst fin) 3 **8**
726[7] Halbert **(47)***(31) (MRChannon)* 6-8-0 (7) DSweeney(8) (swtg: prom over 3f) ....½ **9**
567[4] Great Hall **(60)***(43) (PDCundell)* 6-9-6 WNewnes(14) (nvr nrr) ....nk **10**
541[3] Waverley Star **(45)***(27) (KOCunningham-Brown)* 10-8-5 LDettori(15) (swtg: chsd ldrs over 3f) ....nk **11**
656[4] Grey Charmer (IRE) **(55)***(33) (CJames)* 6-9-1 SWhitworth(5) (chsd ldrs over 3f) 1½ **12**
Mislemani (IRE) **(53)***(30) (AGNewcombe)* 5-8-8 (5) DGriffiths(10) (a bhd) ....nk **13**
Duty Sergeant (IRE) **(43)***(7) (PMitchell)* 6-7-10 (7)ow10 DToole(7) (a bhd) 1¼ **14**
175[8] Clancy's Express **(35)***(6) (GBBalding)* 4-7-2 (7) MartinDwyer(18) (a bhd) 1 **15**
637[10] Poor Printer (IRE) **(38)***(4) (JAkehurst)* 4-7-12 CRutter(1) (lw: a bhd) 2 **16**
Slivovitz **(64)***(27) (MJHeaton-Ellis)* 5-9-10b StephenDavies(6) (spd over 3f) 1 **17**
316[11] Crocodile Rock **(44)***(5) (MJHeaton-Ellis)* 3-7-7b NAdams(9) (dwlt: a bhd) 1 **18**

LONG HANDICAP Duty Sergeant (IRE) 7-6 Crocodile Rock 6-7

5/1 Ahjay, **11/2** Dawalib (USA), **13/2** THATCHERELLA, **15/2** Great Hall, **9/1** Face the Future, **10/1** Grey Charmer (IRE), Slivovitz, Words of Wisdom (IRE), **14/1** Waverley Star, **16/1** Half Tone, Perfect Brave, **25/1** Mislemani (IRE), Friendly Brave (USA), **33/1** Halbert, Clancy's Express, Crocodile Rock, **50/1** Poor Printer (IRE), Duty Sergeant (IRE), CSF £41.82 CT £522.14 TOTE £13.70: £3.50 £1.90 £3.70 £2.30 (£48.60) Trio £400.20 OWNER Mr J. H. Widdows (WHITSBURY) BRED M. L. Page 18 Rn 1m 13.73 (1.43) SF: 42/38/3/18/31/29/3/11/1/13/-/3/-/-/-/-/-/-

WEIGHT FOR AGE 3yo-11lb

888

MORRISTON MAIDEN STKS (II) (3-Y.O) (Class D) £4,045.00 (£1,210.00: £580.00: £265.00)
1m Stalls: High GOING minus 0.53 sec per fur (F) 5-30 (5-31)

Mary's Way (GR) *(84) (RCharlton)* 3-8-9 JWeaver(4) (leggy: scope: hld up in rr: gd hdwy wl over 1f out: led ins fnl f: r.o wl) ....— **1**
Azdihaar (USA) **(95)***(80)*(Fav)*(JLDunlop)* 3-8-9 WCarson(10) (a.p: led 3f out tl ins fnl f) 2 **2**
Suvalu (USA) *(78) (PFICole)* 3-9-0 TQuinn(2) (hld up: ev ch 2f out: one pce) 3½ **3**
630[8] Edan Heights *(70) (SDow)* 3-9-0 BThomson(5) (hld up: hdwy over 2f out: nttrbl ldrs) 4 **4**
695[5] Mighty Squaw *(64) (MissGayKelleway)* 3-8-9 RCochrane(6) (prom 6f) ....nk **5**
Just for a Reason *(66) (DJGMurraySmith)* 3-8-9 (5) RPainter(1) (nvr nr to chal) 1½ **6**
Brockton Light *(58) (MRChannon)* 3-8-9 RHughes(3) (w'like: bit bkwd: s.s: nvr nr ldrs) 1½ **7**
Victoria's Secret (IRE) **(78)***(56) (DRCElsworth)* 3-8-9 WNewnes(9) (bit bkwd: s.i.s: hmpd over 3f out: a bhd) 1¼ **8**
630[9] Ironic (IRE) *(59) (RHannon)* 3-9-0 PatEddery(8) (lw: prom over 5f) ....¾ **9**
Born to Please (IRE) *(57) (PWHarris)* 3-9-0 PaulEddery(11) (bit bkwd: rdn 4f out: sn bhd)...1¼ **10**
637[9] Rumpelstiltskin *(39) (MartynMeade)* 3-8-7 (7) CTinel(7) (bit bkwd: led 5f: btn whn swtchd & hung lft wl over 1f out: t.o) 9 **11**

10/11 Azdihaar (USA) (5/4-4/5), **9/2** Mighty Squaw, **11/2** Suvalu (USA) (3/1-6/1), **9/1** MARY'S WAY (GR) (6/1-10/1), **10/1** Ironic (IRE), **16/1** Brockton Light, Victoria's Secret (IRE), **20/1** Edan Heights, **25/1** Born to Please (IRE), **100/1** Just for a Reason, Rumpelstiltskin, CSF £18.07 TOTE £10.40: £2.20 £1.10 £2.50 (£6.80) Trio £11.20 OWNER Mrs Alexandra Chandris (BECKHAMPTON) BRED Queensway EPE 11 Rn 1m 41.61 (2.31) SF: 28/24/22/14/8/10/2/-/3/1/-

T/Jkpt: Not won; £53,014.96 to Hamilton 5/5/95. T/Plpt: £42.80 (415.02 Tckts). T/Qdpt: £20.00 (13.95 Tckts). AK

0830-WOLVERHAMPTON (L-H)
Thursday May 4th (Standard)

WEATHER: fine & sunny WIND: slt bhd

889

SLOANE MAIDEN AUCTION STKS (2-Y.O) (Class F) £2,519.00(£694.00: £329.00)
5f (Fibresand) Stalls: Low GOING: 0.11 sec per fur (SLW) 2-10 (2-11)

574[2] **Afisiak** *(59)*(Fav)*(MJohnston)* 2-8-0 TWilliams(5) (mde all: shkn up appr fnl f: r.o wl) ....— **1**
671[7] U-No-Harry (IRE) *(60) (RHollinshead)* 2-8-0 (5) AGarth(2) (chsd wnr: ev ch 1f out: rdn & unable qckn fnl f) 1¼ **2**
Lila Pedigo (IRE) *(39) (JBerry)* 2-7-7 (7) PFessey(1) (lt-f: unf: chsd ldrs over 3f: sn outpcd) 5 **3**
Simon Harold *(25) (WRMuir)* 2-8-5 JCarroll(4) (lt-f: s.s: effrt u.p ½-wy: no imp) 6 **4**
February *(15) (MRChannon)* 2-7-9 (5) PPMurphy(3) (lt-f: unf: sn outpcd: a bhd) 1½ **5**

13/8 AFISIAK (11/10-7/4), **2/1** U-No-Harry (IRE) (op 4/1), **7/2** February (op 6/4), **9/2** Simon Harold, **8/1** Lila Pedigo (IRE) (5/1-10/1), CSF £5.78 TOTE £2.10: £1.90 £4.20 (£2.80) OWNER Mr D. Crossland (MIDDLEHAM) BRED Mrs R. J. Mitchell 5 Rn 63.6 secs (5.60) SF: -/1/-/-/-

890 GROSVENOR CLAIMING STKS (3-Y.O+) (Class F) £2,519.00 (£694.00: £329.00) **6f** Stalls: Low GOING: 0.11 sec per fur (G) 2-40 (2-40)

*366*6 **Walk the Beat (63)***(62) (MartynMeade)* 5-9-1 VSlattery(1) (b: swtg: hdwy ½-wy: led ent fnl f: sn clr: v.easily)......— 1
*591*3 Casper's Risk **(57)***(54) (DNicholls)* 3-7-13b(5) NVarley(4) (outpcd: hdwy over 2f out: rdn & kpt on fnl f: no ch w wnr)......3 2
*603*5 Pacific Spirit **(45)***(50) (MTate)* 5-8-11 (3) JTate(2) (bit bkwd: wl bhd & outpcd tl r.o strly appr fnl f)......1¼ 3
702 13 Tyrone Flyer **(48)***(55) (GFierro)* 6-9-7 MWigham(6) (slt ld after 1f tl over 3f out: sn hrd rdn & wknd over 1f out)......¾ 4
732 2 Dark Shot (IRE) **(70)***(45)*(Fav)*(JBerry)* 3-8-10v JCarroll(5) (lw: led over 3f out: rdn & hdd 1f out: sn btn)......3½ 5
*624*12 Millridge (IRE) **(25)** *(RLee)* 4-8-6 TWilliams(3) (b: led 1f: wknd qckly ½-wy: t.o)......20 6

8/11 Dark Shot (IRE) (Evens-4/6), **100/30** WALK THE BEAT, **4/1** Casper's Risk (3/1-9/2), **12/1** Tyrone Flyer (op 8/1), **20/1** Pacific Spirit, **25/1** Millridge (IRE), CSF £16.25 TOTE £8.40: £5.60 £2.40 (£21.80) OWNER The Country Life Partnership (MALMESBURY) BRED R. B. Warren 6 Rn
1m 15.9 (4.70) SF: 43/24/31/36/15/-
WEIGHT FOR AGE 3yo-11lb

OFFICIAL EXPLANATION **Dark Shot: the trainer reported that the colt, who appears to be a bit ungenuine, was unable to dominate which he likes to do and a routine test was ordered.**

891 JOHN WILMAN H'CAP (0-70) (3-Y.O F) (Class E) £3,102.00 (£924.00: £440.00: £198.00) **6f (Fibresand)** Stalls: Low GOING: 0.11 sec per fur (SLW) 3-10 (3-10)

862 8 **We're Joken (46)***(50)*(Fav)*(JBerry)* 3-8-3 JCarroll(6) (b.nr hind: lw: mde all: clr over 1f out: unchal)......— 1
*591*6 Jersey Belle **(44)***(41) (PJMakin)* 3-8-1 NCarlisle(2) (swtg: dwlt: hdwy ½-wy: kpt on u.p ins fnl f: nvr nrr)......2½ 2
753 8 Poly Laureon (IRE) **(60)***(57) (RHollinshead)* 3-9-3 TIves(5) (prom: rdn 2f out: kpt on ins fnl f)s.h 3
*831** One for Jeannie **(71)***(68)*(Fav)*(ABailey)* 3-9-9v(5) 7x VHalliday(3) (chsd ldrs: rdn 2f out: kpt on one pce)......s.h 4
867* Don't Forget Ruby (IRE) **(47)***(41) (DWPArbuthnot)* 3-7-13 (5) 7x NVarley(4) (b.hind: in rr: rdn along over 2f out: no imp)......1 5
*830*5 Sharp Holly (IRE) **(53)***(46) (JABennett)* 3-8-5v(5) CTeague(1) (chsd wnr: rdn 2f out: wknd ins fnl f)......½ 6

5/2 WE'RE JOKEN, One for Jeannie (2/1-3/1), **7/2** Don't Forget Ruby (IRE), **8/1** Poly Laureon (IRE), **9/1** Jersey Belle (op 5/1), **10/1** Sharp Holly (IRE), CSF £20.22 TOTE £3.20: £1.70 £3.20 (£33.40) OWNER Mr J. K. M. Oliver (COCKERHAM) BRED James Thom and Sons 6 Rn
1m 16.7 (5.50) SF: 21/12/28/39/12/17

892 PORTMAN H'CAP (0-60) (3-Y.O+) (Class F) £2,519.00 (£694.00: £329.00) **5f (Fibresand)** Stalls: Low GOING: 0.11 sec per fur (SLW) 3-40 (3-43)

*769*7 **The Real Whizzbang (IRE) (40)***(45+)*(Fav)*(PSFelgate)* 4-8-4b(5) PMcCabe(11) (a.p: led wl over 1f out: sn clr: eased nr fin)......— 1
753 4 Lugana Vision **(43)***(42) (GFierro)* 3-8-2v GHind(9) (swtg: outpcd & bhd: gd hdwy 2f out: fin wl) 2 2
Flashing Sabre **(60)***(58) (JBerry)* 3-9-5 JCarroll(6) (a.p: rdn & one pce appr fnl f)......nk 3
734 7 Grey Toppa **(43)***(36) (NPLittmoden)* 4-8-12 RPrice(4) (b: mid div tl r.o ins fnl f)......1½ 4
Miami Banker **(40)***(26) (WRMuir)* 9-8-9b WWoods(7) (bkwd: swtg: led tl wknd wl over 1f out)...2 5
Disco Boy **(57)***(39) (BAMcMahon)* 5-9-12 TIves(3) (bit bkwd: prom: hrd rdn ½-wy: wknd over 1f out)......1¼ 6
*602*5 Rocky Two **(59)***(38) (PHowling)* 4-9-7b(7) DebbieBiggs(1) (outpcd tl sme late hdwy)......1 7
*625*5 Farndale **(47)***(26) (RonaldThompson)* 8-8-11 (5) VHalliday(2) (outpcd: a in rr)......hd 8
*831*6 Ho Mei Surprise **(44)***(19) (BPreece)* 3-7-10 (7) AEddery(8) (swtg: a bhd & outpcd)......1¼ 9
*247*4 Tommy Tempest **(35)***(2) (REPeacock)* 6-8-1b(3) DWright(12) (bit bkwd: spd 3f: sn lost tch)...2½ 10
734 8 Lucy's Gold **(36)***(3) (MJRyan)* 4-8-0 (5) MBaird(13) (outpcd)......hd 11

9/4 THE REAL WHIZZBANG (IRE), **11/2** Flashing Sabre, **6/1** Disco Boy, **7/1** Lugana Vision, Tommy Tempest (10/1-6/1), **8/1** Farndale, **14/1** Rocky Two (op 8/1), Miami Banker (10/1-20/1), **16/1** Grey Toppa, Lucy's Gold, **20/1** Ho Mei Surprise, CSF £18.87 CT £75.67 TOTE £2.40: £1.90 £3.10 £3.10 (£18.20) Trio £58.30 OWNER Mr S. J. Beard (MELTON MOWBRAY) BRED Drumconrath Stud 11 Rn 63.0 secs (5.00) SF: 18/5/21/9/-/12/11/-/-/-/- WEIGHT FOR AGE 3yo-10lb

893

MANCHESTER (S) STKS (3-Y.O) (Class F) £2,519.00 (£694.00: £329.00)
1m 4f (Fibresand) Stalls: High GOING: 0.11 sec per fur (SLW) 4-10 (4-12)

521⁹ **Absolute Folly (57)***(54)*(Fav)*(JBerry)* 3-8-11 JCarroll(4) (mde all: rdn over 1f out: styd on strly) .... — 1
Ranger Sloane **(45)***(51) (GFierro)* 3-8-11 MWigham(1) (chsd wnr: 2nd st: rdn bel dist: kpt on fnl f: no ch w wnr) 2½ 2
485¹⁵ Boundless (IRE) **(49)***(46) (BJMeehan)* 3-8-6 TWilliams(3) (a.p: 3rd & rdn st: kpt on same pce) .... hd 3
339⁹ Something Speedy (IRE) **(45)***(50) (PJBevan)* 3-8-11 NCarlisle(2) (bhd: hdwy over 3f out: 6th st: styd on ins fnl f) .... nk 4
444⁸ Two Way Stretch **(32)***(44) (GLMoore)* 3-8-1 (5) AWhelan(6) (chsd ldrs: rdn along 3f out: 5th st: one pce) 1¼ 5
Anchor Crown *(36) (KGWingrove)* 3-8-6 JMcLaughlin(8) (lt-f: unf: swtg: s.s: a in rr) 6 6
736⁷ Cranbrook Kate **(53)***(26) (JMackie)* 3-8-1 (5) CTeague(7) (chsd ldrs tl 5th & btn st: t.o) 7 7
544⁶ Kings of Canvey Is **(35)***(26) (JWhite)* 3-8-6 RPrice(5) (swtg: in tch tl wknd over 3f out: t.o) .... ½ 8
773¹¹ Granny's Legacy **(35)***(25) (JDBethell)* 3-8-6 NRodgers(9) (a wl bhd: t.o) .... ½ 9
388⁴ Chadleigh Walk (IRE) **(40)***(29)*(Fav)*(RHollinshead)* 3-8-11 TIves(10) (b: b.hind: prom: 4th & rdn ent st: sn btn: t.o) .... nk 10

3/1 ABSOLUTE FOLLY, Chadleigh Walk (IRE), **9/2** Something Speedy (IRE), **6/1** Two Way Stretch, **7/1** Boundless (IRE), **10/1** Anchor Crown (op 6/1), **12/1** Ranger Sloane, Kings of Canvey Is (op 6/1), **20/1** Granny's Legacy, Cranbrook Kate, CSF £38.34 TOTE £4.50: £1.90 £4.50 £5.20 (£31.50) OWNER Mr P.T.Chandler (COCKERHAM) BRED M.Yiapatos 10 Rn 2m 47.8 (16.80) SF: -/-/-/-/-/-/-
Bt in 4,800 gns.

OFFICIAL EXPLANATION **Chadleigh Walk: the jockey reported that the colt, who was running over a longer distance, became very tired at halfway and was unable to quicken thereafter.**

894

BERKELEY H'CAP (0-60) (3-Y.O+) (Class F) £2,560.00 (£760.00: £360.00: £160.00) **1m 4f (Fibresand)** Stalls: High GOING: 0.11 sec (SLW) 4-40 (4-40)

Pistols At Dawn (USA) (48)*(62) (BJMeehan)* 5-9-2 JCarroll(5) (chsd ldr: led over 2f out: hrd rdn fnl f: hld on) .... — 1
771² Ijab (CAN) **(35)***(49)*(Fav)*(JParkes)* 5-8-3b GBardwell(7) (led tl over 2f out: 2nd st: rdn & rallied fnl f: jst failed) .... hd 2
412⁴ Charlie Bigtime **(50)***(55) (DTThom)* 5-9-1 (3) DWright(6) (hld up: hdwy 6f out: 3rd st: nt rch ldrs) 7 3
72⁴ Frome Lad **(58)***(60) (WGMTurner)* 3-8-2 (5) PMcCabe(3) (bkwd: bhd: hdwy 4f out: 4th st: kpt on ins fnl f) 1¾ 4
676¹⁷ Augustan **(56)***(42) (SGollings)* 4-9-7 (3) JTate(1) (chsd ldrs: 5th & outpcd ent st: sn btn) 12 5
Ajdar **(48)***(34) (PAKelleway)* 4-9-2v MWigham(8) (hld up & bhd: nvr nrr) .... nk 6
776⁶ Asmarina **(42)***(24) (SRBowring)* 5-8-5 (5) CTeague(9) (hld up: hdwy 5f out: 6th & btn st) 3 7
Verro (USA) **(28)***(7) (KBishop)* 8-7-5e(5)ow3 NVarley(2) (lw: prom: rdn ½-wy: sn lost tch) .... hd 8
757¹⁰ In the Money (IRE) **(60)***(26) (RHollinshead)* 6-10-0 TIves(4) (chsd ldrs over 8f: sn rdn & wknd: t.o) 12 9

LONG HANDICAP Verro (USA) 7-1

9/4 Ijab (CAN), **3/1** Charlie Bigtime, **6/1** In the Money (IRE), Asmarina (op 4/1), **7/1** PISTOLS AT DAWN (USA) (5/1-8/1), **9/1** Augustan, **12/1** Ajdar, **14/1** Frome Lad, **33/1** Verro (USA), CSF £23.54 CT £54.83 TOTE £11.20: £3.30 £1.40 £1.90 (£15.40) Trio £23.40 OWNER Mr G. Howard-Spink (UPPER LAMBOURN) BRED North Ridge Farm 9 Rn 2m 41.4 (10.40) SF: 40/27/33/19/20/12/2/-/4
WEIGHT FOR AGE 3yo-19lb

STEWARDS' ENQUIRY Bardwell suspended 13-15/5/95 (excessive use of whip).
T/Plpt: £142.90 (46.55 Tckts). T/Qdpt: £48.10 (0.5 tckts). £32.50 to Hamilton 5/5/95. IM

0705a-EVRY (France) (R-H)
Monday April 24th (Soft)

895a

PRIX SERVANNE (Listed) (3-Y.O+) £16,766.00
5f 110y

Wessam Prince *(108) (CLaffon-Parias,France)* 4-9-4 WRSwinburn .... — 1
441⁵ Daring Destiny *(101) (KRBurke)* 4-9-1 JTate 1½ 2
608a³ Poplar Bluff (IRE) *(104) (AFabre,France)* 3-8-8 OPeslier .... hd 3

P-M 4.80.f: 1.70f 2.10f 1.50f (16.50f) OWNER Maktoum Al Maktoum BRED F.Fabre 68.5 secs

0806a-LONGCHAMP (Paris, France) (R-H)
Thursday April 27th (Heavy)

896a PRIX D'HEDOUVILLE (Gp 3) (4-Y.O+) £26,347.00
1m 4f

703a* **Tot Ou Tard (IRE)** *(116) (SWattel,France)* 5-8-9 ESaint-Martin ....— 1
Grioun (FR) *(109) (DSepulchre,France)* 4-8-7 ow1 ODoleuze 4 2
L'ile Tudy (IRE) *(109) (MmeMBollack-Badel,France)* 5-8-8 ABadel ....¾ 3
Close Conflict (USA) *(115) (PWChapple-Hyam)* 4-9-6 JReid (btn 10¼l by wnr) 6
SF: 121.30f P-M 6.80f: 3.00f 5.90f OWNER Ecurie Kura BRED M.Kura 2m 51.8 SF: -/-/-/-

0895a-EVRY (France) (R-H)
Friday April 28th (Soft)

897a PRIX CORRIDA (Gp 3) (4-Y.O+ F & M) £26,347.00
1m 2f 110y

Hollywood Dream (GER) *(117) (UOstmann,Germany)* 4-9-2 CAsmussen ....— 1
704a2 Agathe (USA) *(117) (AFabre,France)* 4-9-2 OPeslier ....s.h 2
607a10 Truly a Dream (IRE) *(119) (RCollet,France)* 4-9-4 WMongil ....s.nk 3
6317 Girl From Ipanema *(108) (PFICole)* 4-8-11 TJarnet (btn approx further 2¼l) 6
P-M 4.30f: 1.60f 1.10f 2.90f (6.00f) OWNER Gestut Ittlingen 2m 23.1 (13.10) SF: -/-/-/-

0896a-LONGCHAMP (Paris, France) (R-H)
Sunday April 30th (Heavy)

898a PRIX GANAY (Gp 1) (4-Y.O+ C & F) £59,880.00
1m 2f 110y

607a2 **Pelder (IRE)** *(125) (PAKelleway)* 5-9-2 LDettori (hld up: 6th st: smooth prog to ld 1f out: sn clr: eased cl hme.) ....— 1
607a7 Alderbrook *(120) (MrsJCecil)* 6-9-2 PaulEddery (5th early: cl 3rd st: rdn to ld 1½f out: hdd 1f out: styd on one pce.) 3 2
Richard of York *(118) (AFabre,France)* 5-9-2 SGuillot (4th early: 5th st: sn rdn and outpcd: r.o wl fnl f.) 1½ 3
607a* Freedom Cry *(117) (AFabre,France)* 4-9-2 OPeslier (sn ld: set gd pce tl hdd 1½f out: grad wknd) ....¾ 4
Hernando (FR) *(116) (JEHammond,France)* 5-9-2 CAsmussen (hld up: rdn 2f out: hung & one pce fnl f) ....¾ 5
Partipral (USA) *(115) (MDelcher,Spain)* 6-9-2 GMosse (hld up: outpcd early in st: sme late prog.) ....½ 6
607a3 Tuesday's Special (USA) *(113) (AFabre,France)* 5-9-2 TJarnet (7th early: styd on fnl f.) 1½ 7
7124 Right Win (IRE) *(101) (RHannon)* 5-9-2 PatEddery (a.p. 2nd st: rdn 2½f out: wknd qkly) 8 8
607a9 Marildo (FR) *(96) (DSmaga,France)* 8-9-2 GGuignard (prom early: 4th & btn st.) 3 9
607a5 Millkom *(88) (J-CRouget,France)* 4-9-2 J-RDubosc (m.n.s.) 5 10

P-M 13.90f: 4.90f 8.20f 5.00f (123.90f) OWNER Mr Osvaldo Pedroni (NEWMARKET) 10 Rn
2m 20.7 SF: -/-/-/-/-/-/-/-/-/-

899a PRIX VANTEAUX (Gp 3) (3-Y.O F) £26,347.00
1m 1f

Secret Quest *(95?) (PBary,France)* 3-9-2 DBoeuf ....— 1
Marble Falls (IRE) *(91?) (ELellouche,France)* 3-9-2 LDettori 2½ 2
Nimble Mind (USA) *(85?) (MmeCHead,France)* 3-9-2 FHead 3 3
P-M 3.00f:1.80f 2.00f (9.50f) OWNER Mrs A. O'Reilly 2m 7.7 SF: -/-/-

0809a-CAPANNELLE (Rome, Italy) (R-H)
Sunday April 30th (Good)

900a PREMIO PARIOLI (Gp 1) (3-Y.O C & F) £59,024.00
1m

6772 **Prince Arthur (IRE)** *(107) (PWChapple-Hyam)* 3-9-2 JReid ....— 1

Thomire *(104) (PMazzoni,Italy)* 3-9-2 BJovine 1½ 2
Robins (IRE) *(103) (AColella,Italy)* 3-9-2 VMezzatesta ....½ 3
504* El Supremo (USA) *(99) (DRLoder)* 3-9-2 JWeaver (btn approx 4l) 5
622[10] Albinor (IRE) *(79) (JLDunlop)* 3-9-2 WCarson (btn approx further 14l) 11
713[3] Moon King (IRE) *(69) (RHannon)* 3-9-2 WRSwinburn (btn approx 19l).... 13

TOTE 32L:19L 43L 24L (501L) OWNER Mr M. Tabor (MARLBOROUGH) BRED Mrs J. Costelloe 6 Rn 1m 38.5 SF: -/-/-/-/-/-

SAN SIRO (Milan, Italy) (R-H)
Sunday April 30th (Heavy)

901a
PREMIO CERTOSA (Listed) (3-Y.O+) £20,094.00
5f

Imprevedibile (IRE) *(114) (PCeriotti,Italy)* 5-8-13 AParravani ....— 1
Late Parade (IRE) *(112) (PLodigiani,Italy)* 4-8-13 ACorniani ....¾ 2
Starry Typhoon *(104) (RosannaTurri,Italy)* 5-8-13 SDettori 2½ 3
608a[4] Imperial Bailiwick (IRE) *(89) (MDIUsher)* 4-8-10 JWilliams 3¾ 4

TOTE 27L:13L12L(19L) 61.0 secs SF: -/-/-/-

COLOGNE (Germany) (R-H)
Sunday April 30th (Soft)

902a
BEHR MEMORIAL (Listed) (3-Y.O) £6,049.00
1m

Ermbold (GER) *(92) (BSchutz,Germany)* 3-9-0 THellier ....— 1
Neapolitano (GER) *(95) (RPrinzinger,Germany)* 3-9-4 PSchiergen ....½ 2
Standman *(86) (ALowe,Germany)* 3-9-4 AHelfenbein 4½ 3
Queen's Ransom (IRE) *(72) (PWChapple-Hyam)* 3-8-9 BThomson (btn approx 10l).... 6

TOTE 30DM: 21DM 23DM (184DM)

0874-HAMILTON (R-H)
Friday May 5th (Good to firm, Good patches)
WEATHER: Fine & sunny WIND: almost nil

903
EUROPEAN BREEDERS FUND LOCH STRIVEN MEDIAN AUCTION MAIDEN STKS (2-Y.O F) (Class F) £2,736.00 (£828.00: £404.00: £192.00)
5f 4y Stalls: High GOING minus 0.48 sec per fur (F) 2-15 (2-16)

La Volta *(76+) (JGFitzGerald)* 2-8-11 TIves(6) (neat: scope: a cl up: led ½-wy: r.o wl fnl f) ....— 1
669[5] Whittle Rock *(71)*(Fav)*(EJAlston)* 2-8-11 KFallon(2) (w ldrs: rdn after 2f: one pce) 1½ 2
Corniche Quest (IRE) *(62) (MRChannon)* 2-8-11 RHughes(1) (neat: leggy: wnt lft s: cl up: outpcd ½-wy: swtchd & r.o wl fnl f) 3 3
Rose of Siberia (USA) *(54) (MBell)* 2-8-11 MFenton(3) (w'like: leggy: sn disp ld: bmpd after 2f: sn outpcd: styd on fnl f)....2½ 4
Mouna El Arab *(46)*(Fav)*(JBerry)* 2-8-11 JCarroll(4) (neat: cl up: ev ch 2f out: sn rdn & btn: eased fnl f) 2½ 5
540[3] Miss Offset *(36) (MJohnston)* 2-8-11 TWilliams(5) (w ldrs: bmpd after 2f: grad lost pl) 3 6

5/2 Whittle Rock, Mouna El Arab, **3/1** Rose of Siberia (USA) (2/1-100/30), **5/1** LA VOLTA, **6/1** Corniche Quest (IRE), **16/1** Miss Offset, CSF £17.80 TOTE £7.60: £2.90 £2.50 (£27.20) OWNER Mr J. G. FitzGerald (MALTON) BRED K. G. Bridges 6 Rn 60.7 secs (2.40) SF: 15/10/1/-/-/-

904
FIRTH OF CLYDE H'CAP (0-70) (3-Y.O) (Class E) £3,863.90 (£1,170.20: £571.60: £272.30)
5f 4y Stalls: High GOING minus 0.48 sec per fur (F) 2-45 (2-47)

772[5] **La Suquet (68)***(74) (MRChannon)* 3-9-7 RHughes(1) (chsd ldrs: led ent fnl f: r.o wl)....— 1

Ninety-Five **(64)***(70)*(Fav)*(JGFitzGerald)* 3-9-3 TIves(3) (prom: rdn to disp ld appr fnl f: r.o) ....hd **2**
823[9] Russian Heroine **(60)***(58) (MJohnston)* 3-8-13 TWilliams(11) (mde most: rdn along appr fnl f: sn hdd & no ex) 2½ **3**
Mister Westsound **(49)***(46) (MissLAPerratt)* 3-8-2 NConnorton(9) (chsd ldrs: rdn ½-wy: r.o same pce fnl f) ....hd **4**
Carol Again **(45)***(42) (NBycroft)* 3-7-12 JQuinn(7) (in tch: hdwy & rdn over 2f out: styd on fnl f) ....hd **5**
754[4] Absolutely Fabulus **(49)***(43) (JLSpearing)* 3-7-13 (3) DarrenMoffatt(6) (cl up: rdn ½-wy: r.o one pce appr fnl f) 1 **6**
734[6] Oneineverycolour **(50)***(34) (PDEvans)* 3-8-3 FNorton(10) (bhd & outpcd: nvr trbld ldrs) 3 **7**
348[9] Precious Times **(45)***(24) (MGMeagher)* 3-7-12 AMackay(4) (prom: sn rdn along: wknd wl over 1f out) 1¾ **8**
594[11] Sunday Mail Too (IRE) **(51)***(27) (MissLAPerratt)* 3-8-4 GDuffield(2) (in tch: rdn ½-wy: grad wknd) ....¾ **9**
685[8] Another Nightmare (IRE) **(56)***(13) (RMMcKellar)* 3-8-9 SWhitworth(5) (s.i.s: sn in tch: rdn & wknd wl over 1f out) 6 **10**
Tannerrun (IRE) **(65)***(16) (JBerry)* 3-9-4e JCarroll(8) (disp ld: rdn ½-wy: wknd qckly wl over 1f out) 2 **11**

3/1 Ninety-Five, **9/2** Russian Heroine (3/1-5/1), **5/1** Absolutely Fabulus, **6/1** LA SUQUET (op 4/1), **8/1** Tannerrun (IRE), **11/1** Sunday Mail Too (IRE), **12/1** Mister Westsound, **16/1** Oneineverycolour, Another Nightmare (IRE), **50/1** Precious Times, **66/1** Carol Again, CSF £22.57 CT £80.57 TOTE £5.50: £1.60 £1.70 £1.80 (£8.40) Trio £11.70 OWNER Mr Brian Buckley (UPPER LAMBOURN) BRED Rockhouse Farms Ltd 11 Rn
60.2 secs (1.90) SF: 32/28/16/4/-/1/-/-/-/-/-

905

BOLLINGER CHAMPAGNE CHALLENGE SERIES GENTLEMENS' H'CAP (0-70) (3-Y.O+) (Class F) £2,775.00 (£840.00: £410.00: £195.00)
1m 3f 16y Stalls: High GOING minus 0.48 sec per fur (F) 3-20 (3-20)

245[5] **Moonlight Calypso (41)***(53) (EJAlston)* 4-10-7 (4) MrPBlane(2) (hld up & bhd: stdy hdwy 3f out: led appr fnl f: styd on) ....— **1**
537[7] Sedvicta **(50)***(62) (MrsMReveley)* 3-9-12 (4) MrSRutherford(6) (led 3f: w ldrs: disp ld appr fnl f: styd on) ....hd **2**
879[2] Mentalasanythin **(53)***(61) (ABailey)* 6-11-5 (4) MrJDelahunt(3) (trckd ldrs: outpcd 4f out: hdwy on bit fnl 2f: nrst fin) 3 **3**
778[2] Daily Sport Girl **(37)***(43) (BJLlewellyn)* 6-10-7 MrJLLlewellyn(1) (cl up: led wl over 2f out: hdd appr fnl f: one pce) 1¼ **4**
*626** Vintage Taittinger (IRE) **(41)***(44)*(Fav)*(MBell)* 3-9-7 MrDParker(9) (in tch: hdwy & ev ch 2f out: no ex) 1¾ **5**
Supertop **(58)***(61) (LLungo)* 7-12-0 MrSSwiers(5) (hld up & bhd: hdwy over 2f out: styd on fnl f) ....½ **6**
Sylvan Celebration **(30)***(28) (MissLAPerratt)* 4-9-10 (4) MrLDonnelly(10) (in tch: rdn ent st: r.o same pce fnl 2f) 3 **7**
597[4] Monkey Wench (IRE) **(52)***(47) (JBerry)* 4-11-8v MrRHale(13) (chsd ldrs: dsptd ld 2f out: rdn & no ex fnl f) 2½ **8**
598* The Premier Expres **(50)***(39) (FJO'Mahony)* 5-11-2 (4) MrVLukaniuk(11) (bhd: rdn over 3f out: nvr rch ldrs) 4 **9**
672[P] Hi Penny **(40)***(19) (KTIvory)* 4-10-6 (4) MrDMarshall(12) (a bhd) 7 **10**
Dots Dee **(31)***(2) (JMBradley)* 6-10-1 MrRJohnson(7) (led after 3f tl hdd wl over 2f out: sn wknd) 5 **11**
778[9] Port Sunlight (IRE) **(56)***(22) (PDEvans)* 7-11-8b(4) MrWMcLaughlin(8) (chsd ldrs: rdn & wknd 3f out) 4 **12**
476[2] Doubling Dice **(46)** *(RAllan)* 4-10-12 (4)ow11 MrARobson(4) (hld up & a bhd) 4 **13**
LONG HANDICAP Vintage Taittinger (IRE) 9-6

9/4 Vintage Taittinger (IRE), **3/1** The Premier Expres, **8/1** Daily Sport Girl, Mentalasanythin (4/1-9/1), **9/1** Monkey Wench (IRE), **10/1** Supertop, Sedvicta, **11/1** Dots Dee, **20/1** Doubling Dice, **33/1** Hi Penny, MOONLIGHT CALYPSO, Port Sunlight (IRE), **100/1** Sylvan Celebration, CSF £312.88 CT £2,642.68 TOTE £39.30: £6.90 £3.60 £3.10 (£120.90) Trio £605.40; £545.72 to Newmarket 06/05/95 OWNER Mr R. Smalley (PRESTON) BRED R. Smalley 13 Rn
2m 25.6 (6.60) SF: 37/28/45/27/10/45/12/31/23/3/-/6/-
WEIGHT FOR AGE 3yo-18lb

906

LOCH GOIL LIMITED STKS (0-65) (4-Y.O+) (Class F) £2,717.00(£762.00: £371.00)
5f 4y Stalls: High GOING minus 0.48 sec per fur (F) 3-55 (3-57)

646[5] **Cool Edge (IRE) (65)***(67)*(Fav)*(MHTompkins)* 4-8-11 PRobinson(6) (trckd ldrs: led appr fnl f: rdn & r.o wl) ....— **1**

639[10] My Cherrywell **(55)***(54) (LRLloyd-James)* 5-8-9 JFortune(2) (cl up: rdn 2f out: swtchd to chal ent fnl f: r.o one pce)....3½ 2
790[5] Kenesha (IRE) **(53)***(48) (DANolan)* 5-8-6 JQuinn(8) (trckd ldrs: rdn 2f out: r.o same pce)....1 3
Miss Vaxette **(65)***(43) (MBrittain)* 6-8-6 GBardwell(3) (bhd: sn rdn along: styd on fnl f: nrst fin)....1½ 4
Evening Falls **(65)***(38) (JLSpearing)* 4-8-6 DeanMcKeown(4) (w ldrs: rdn & ev ch wl over 1f out: no ex)....1½ 5
688[9] Gondo **(63)***(41) (EJAlston)* 8-8-11v KFallon(1) (chsd ldrs: rdn 2f out: one pce)....¾ 6
789[3] Miss Whittingham (IRE) **(56)***(33) (JBerry)* 5-8-6v JCarroll(7) (ev ch tl rdn & btn wl over 1f out)....1 7
688[3] Leading Princess (IRE) **(44)***(29) (MissLAPerratt)* 4-8-6b GDuffield(5) (led tl rdn & hdd appr fnl f: sn btn)....1 8

7/4 COOL EDGE (IRE), **5/2** Miss Whittingham (IRE), **6/1** Evening Falls (op 4/1), **8/1** Gondo, **12/1** Miss Vaxette (8/1-16/1), My Cherrywell, **20/1** Leading Princess (IRE), **50/1** Kenesha (IRE), CSF £19.86 TOTE £2.40: £1.10 £3.00 £7.30 (£18.50) OWNER Mr Henry Chan (NEWMARKET) BRED Hollybank Breeders 8 Rn 59.9 secs (1.60) SF: 28/15/9/4/-/2/-/-

907

PLUMB CENTER H'CAP (0-80) (3-Y.O) (Class D) £5,015.50 (£1,519.00: £742.00: £353.50)
1m 65y Stalls: High GOING minus 0.48 sec per fur (F) 4-30 (4-31)

739* **Ma Petite Anglaise (75)***(80) (WJarvis)* 3-9-0 (7) MHenry(4) (bhd & sn rdn along: gd hdwy to ld appr fnl f: r.o wl)....— 1
585[5] Northern Fan (IRE) **(74)***(72)*(Fav)*(ACStewart)* 3-9-6 SWhitworth(6) (in tch: rdn to ld wl over 1f out: sn hdd & one pce)....3½ 2
647[14] Eden's Star (IRE) **(64)***(56) (MHTompkins)* 3-8-10 PRobinson(2) (plld hrd: disp ld tl led 2f out: sn hdd: one pce)....3½ 3
630[6] Equity's Darling (IRE) **(66)***(51) (MBell)* 3-8-12 MFenton(1) (in tch: rdn & ev ch over 2f out: no ex)....3½ 4
745[8] Jackatack (IRE) **(57)***(41) (MRChannon)* 3-7-12 (5) PPMurphy(5) (mde most tl rdn & hdd 2f out: no ex)....nk 5
Intendant **(62)***(40) (JGFitzGerald)* 3-8-5 (3) DRMcCabe(3) (prom: rdn & ev ch wl over 1f out: one pce)....3 6
674[8] Cabcharge Blue **(75)***(52) (TJNaughton)* 3-9-7 GCarter(8) (plld hrd: prom: rdn 3f out: sn outpcd)....¾ 7
686[5] Rock Foundation **(70)***(43) (PCHaslam)* 3-9-2 TWilliams(7) (cl up: rdn & ev ch 2f out: sn wknd)....2 8

9/4 Northern Fan (IRE), **11/4** MA PETITE ANGLAISE, **8/1** Equity's Darling (IRE), Cabcharge Blue (op 5/1), **9/1** Eden's Star (IRE) (6/1-10/1), Jackatack (IRE), **12/1** Intendant, Rock Foundation (op 8/1), CSF £8.98 CT £42.19 TOTE £3.00: £1.10 £1.80 £2.70 (£2.40) OWNER Mr K. P. Seow (NEWMARKET) BRED R. P. Williams 8 Rn 1m 47.3 (4.00) SF: 29/21/5/-/-/-/1/-

908

HOLY LOCH RATING RELATED MAIDEN STKS (3-Y.O) (Class F) £2,843.00 (£798.00: £389.00)
1m 65y Stalls: High GOING minus 0.48 sec per fur (F) 5-00 (5-01)

733[13] **Voila Premiere (IRE) (58)***(66) (MHTompkins)* 3-9-0 PRobinson(8) (hld up & bhd: hdwy & rdn wl over 2f out: led ins fnl f: styd on)....— 1
538[11] Green Land (BEL) **(60)***(57) (SCWilliams)* 3-8-9 KFallon(11) (a cl up: rdn & dsptd ld appr fnl f: styd on)....2 2
759[4] Our Robert **(60)***(62) (JGFitzGerald)* 3-9-0 TIves(2) (chsd ldrs: led wl over 1f out: hdd ins fnl f: no ex)....hd 3
524[9] Miss Felixstowe (USA) **(54)***(47) (MrsMReveley)* 3-8-9 GCarter(4) (hld up: rdn & hdwy over 3f out: styd on: nt pce to chal)....5 4
745[2] Carnbrea Belle (IRE) **(57)***(43)*(Fav)*(MBell)* 3-8-9 MFenton(6) (chsd ldrs: rdn & ev ch wl over 2f out: one pce)....2 5
599[3] Ganador **(57)***(36) (JBerry)* 3-8-9 JCarroll(3) (led: qcknd over 3f out: hdd wl over 1f out: sn btn)....4 6
613[10] Northern Charmer **(54)***(37) (MGMeagher)* 3-9-0 JFortune(5) (in tch: rdn over 3f out: no ex)....2 7
Ace Chapel (IRE) **(46)***(32) (CCElsey)* 3-9-0 MBirch(7) (hld up & bhd: rdn wl over 3f out: no imp)....2½ 8
789[12] To Prove a Point **(29)***(31) (JJO'Neill)* 3-9-0 NKennedy(1) (s.i.s: a in rr)....½ 9
449[3] Sobeloved **(56)***(23) (MRChannon)* 3-9-0 RHughes(9) (chsd ldrs: rdn wl over 3f out: sn lost pl)....4 10
Wychwood-Palace **(60)** *(HJCollingridge)* 3-8-9 JQuinn(10) (prom tl rdn & wknd 3f out: sn wl in rr).... 11

2/1 Cambrea Belle (IRE), **4/1** VOILA PREMIERE (IRE) (op 12/1), **5/1** Our Robert (6/1-4/1), Green Land (BEL), **15/2** Sobeloved, **8/1** Wychwood-Palace, **16/1** Miss Felixstowe (USA), **20/1** Ace Chapel (IRE), Ganador, **50/1** To Prove a Point, Northern Charmer, CSF £25.03 TOTE £10.70: £3.30 £2.60 £2.00 (£16.50) Trio £64.90 OWNER Mr B. W. Gaule (NEWMARKET) BRED Mrs W. Hanson 11 Rn
1m 47.9 (4.60) SF: 22/13/18/3/-/-/-/-/-/-/-

909 LEVY BOARD H'CAP (0-70) (3-Y.O+) (Class E) £3,209.80 (£972.40: £475.20: £226.60)

1m 1f 36y Stalls: High GOING minus 0.48 sec per fur (F) 5-35 (5-36)

774[3] **Nigel's Lad (IRE) (75)***(81)*(Fav)*(PCHaslam)* 3-8-13 (5) 5x JStack(9) (a cl up: led 3f out: rdn & styd on wl appr fnl f) — 1
785[7] My Handy Man **(56)***(59) (RAllan)* 4-9-0 SMaloney(2) (hld up & bhd: gd hdwy 3f out: ev ch tl one pce appr fnl f) 2 2
876[3] King Curan (USA) **(57)***(59) (ABailey)* 4-9-1b AMackay(10) (hld up: hdwy & ev ch over 1f out: no ex) ½ 3
820[13] Habeta (USA) **(35)***(31) (JWWatts)* 9-7-7 NKennedy(8) (hld up: styd on fnl 2f: nrst fin) 3 4
874[4] Gold Desire **(36)***(31) (MBrittain)* 5-7-8 GBardwell(4) (hld up: rdn & ev ch over 2f out: nt qckn) ¾ 5
874[8] Calisar **(44)***(32) (PHowling)* 5-8-2 PRobinson(3) (chsd ldrs: ev ch 2f out: sn rdn & outpcd) 4 6
738[6] Queens Stroller (IRE) **(59)***(45) (CCElsey)* 4-9-3 MBirch(13) (lost pl & bhd after 2f: hdwy over 2f out: no imp) 1½ 7
546[8] My Lifetime Lady (IRE) **(44)***(24) (KTIvory)* 4-8-2 ow2 GDuffield(1) (w ldrs: ev ch tl rdn & wknd over 2f out) 2 8
749[7] Yoxall Lodge **(63)***(42) (HJCollingridge)* 5-9-7 JQuinn(6) (prom: rdn 3f out: sn btn) 2 9
774[10] Hamilton Silk **(58)***(31) (MGMeagher)* 3-8-1 MFenton(14) (chsd ldrs tl lost pl appr st: rdn 3f out: grad wknd: nvr rchd ldrs) 3 10
157[6] Faynaz **(35)***(8) (RMMcKellar)* 9-7-0 (7) PFessey(7) (led tl hdd 3f out: sn wknd) nk 11

LONG HANDICAP Faynaz 7-5

3/1 NIGEL'S LAD (IRE), **4/1** Yoxall Lodge (op 6/1), **6/1** Queens Stroller (IRE), King Curan (USA) (op 4/1), **13/2** Gold Desire, **10/1** Calisar, **12/1** Habeta (USA), **14/1** My Handy Man, Hamilton Silk, **33/1** My Lifetime Lady (IRE), **50/1** Faynaz, CSF £41.14 CT £222.24 TOTE £2.70: £1.60 £4.90 £2.10 (£59.10) Trio £113.20 OWNER Mr N. C. Dunnington (MIDDLEHAM) BRED Nikita Investments 11 Rn
1m 57.9 (3.60) SF: 33/26/26/-/-/-/12/-/9/-/-
WEIGHT FOR AGE 3yo-15lb

T/Jkpt: Not won; £82,426.54 to Newmarket 6/5/95. T/Plpt: £727.60 (22.18 Tckts). T/Qdpt: £113.60 (0.5 Tckts); £153.55 to Newmarket 6/5/95 GB

0677-NEWMARKET (R-H)
Friday May 5th (Good)
WEATHER: Sunny & hot WIND: Almost nil

910 NGK SPARK PLUGS ARLINGTON MAIDEN AUCTION STKS (2-Y.O) (Class E) £5,344.50 (£1,596.00: £763.00: £346.50)

5f (Rowley) Stalls: Centre GOING minus 0.28 sec per fur (GF) 2-00 (2-00)

810[12] **Foreman** *(81) (WAO'Gorman)* 2-8-7 EmmaO'Gorman(3) (trckd ldrs: swtchd & effrt 2f out: rdn to ld ins fnl f) — 1
669[4] Capture The Moment *(78)*(Fav)*(RJRWilliams)* 2-8-10 WRyan(1) (cl up: led 2f out tl ins fnl f: no ex) 1¾ 2
716[2] Lussuria (IRE) *(78) (BJMeehan)* 2-8-10 LDettori(4) (dsptd ld 3f: kpt on fnl f) hd 3
Magic Imp (IRE) *(70) (WJMusson)* 2-7-11 (5) PMcCabe(5) (lt-f: s.i.s: hdwy 2f out: styd on wl nr fin) hd 4
Delaunay (IRE) *(79) (RHannon)* 2-8-8 (7) MarkDenaro(6) (w'like: leggy: bhd: shkn up over 1f out: styd on twrds fin) 1¼ 5
615[15] Dancing Lottie (IRE) *(62) (PAKelleway)* 2-7-9 (7) AdelleGibbons(7) (plld hrd: swtchd & hdwy 2f out: sn btn) 1¼ 6
690[11] Current Leader *(63) (RHannon)* 2-8-7 KDarley(8) (lw: chsd ldrs: rdn 2f out: sn btn) 1¼ 7
782[2] Badger Bay (IRE) *(57) (JohnBerry)* 2-8-2 DaleGibson(2) (lw: slt ld 3f: grad wknd) hd 8

15/8 Capture The Moment, **3/1** Lussuria (IRE), **7/2** Badger Bay (IRE), **7/1** Current Leader, **14/1** FOREMAN (10/1-16/1), **20/1** Dancing Lottie (IRE), Delaunay (IRE), **25/1** Magic Imp (IRE), CSF £38.53 TOTE £20.90: £2.80 £1.20 £1.30 (£31.80) OWNER Times of Wigan (NEWMARKET) BRED J. R. Wills 8 Rn
61.11 secs (2.41) SF: 27/24/24/16/25/8/9/3

911

LONDON EVENING STANDARD H'CAP (0-90) (3-Y.O) (Class C)
£6,108.00 (£1,824.00: £872.00: £396.00)
1m (Rowley) Stalls: Centre GOING minus 0.28 sec per fur (GF) 2-35 (2-36)

Brave Revival (89)*(96) (MRStoute)* 3-9-7 WRSwinburn(3) (h.d.w: led after 1f tl ins fnl f: rallied to ld post) .....— **1**
722* Nordic Doll (IRE) **(72)***(79)*(Fav)*(BWHills)* 3-8-4 MHills(2) (a.p: hdwy to chal over 1f out: led ins fnl f: hung lft: r.o: jst ct) .....s.h **2**
777[6] Mr Christie **(68)***(66) (MissLCSiddall)* 3-8-0 ow1 DHarrison(4) (bhd: effrt 3f out: styd on: nt pce to chal) 4 **3**
538[10] Mr Frosty **(65)***(60) (WJarvis)* 3-7-11 WCarson(5) (led 1f: cl up tl rdn & btn appr fnl f) 2 **4**
637* Atlaal (USA) **(83)***(73)*(Fav)*(HThomsonJones)* 3-9-1 RHills(1) (lw: hld up: effrt 2f out: sn btn) 2½ **5**
635[13] Maplestead (IRE) **(65)***(54) (CEBrittain)* 3-7-11 DaleGibson(6) (wnt rt s: sn rcvrd: cl up: rdn over 2f out: sn wknd) .....nk **6**

5/2 Nordic Doll (IRE) (6/4-11/4), Atlaal (USA), **7/2** Mr Frosty, **6/1** BRAVE REVIVAL (9/2-7/1), **12/1** Maplestead (IRE), **25/1** Mr Christie, CSF £18.73 TOTE £5.80: £2.20 £1.80 (£12.80) OWNER Cheveley Park Stud (NEWMARKET) BRED Cheveley Park Stud Ltd 6 Rn
1m 38.7 (1.70) SF: 64/47/34/28/41/22

912

MADAGANS NEWMARKET STKS (Listed) (3-Y.O C) (Class A)
£13,192.00 (£4,552.00: £2,176.00: £880.00)
1m 2f (Rowley) Stalls: Centre GOING minus 0.28 sec per fur (GF) 3-05 (3-05)

619* **Presenting (111)***(112+)*(Fav)*(JHMGosden)* 3-8-11 LDettori(3) (lw: trckd ldrs: led wl over 3f out: pushed along & r.o wl) .....— **1**
657[4] Anchor Clever *(91) (PAKelleway)* 3-8-8 JWeaver(1) (lw: racd alone centre: outpcd 2f out: styd on fnl f: no ch w wnr) 11 **2**
622[7] Sotoboy (IRE) **(104)***(90) (PWHarris)* 3-8-8 RCochrane(2) (trckd ldrs: effrt over 3f out: sn chsng wnr: btn appr fnl f) .....¾ **3**
670* Solar Flight *(71) (BWHills)* 3-8-8 PatEddery(4) (swtchd rt after s: led tl hdd wl over 3f out: sn outpcd) 12 **4**

1/2 PRESENTING, **4/1** Solar Flight, **6/1** Sotoboy (IRE) (op 4/1), **25/1** Anchor Clever, CSF £7.66 TOTE £1.40: (£5.00) OWNER Mr George Strawbridge (NEWMARKET) BRED George Strawbridge 4 Rn
2m 2.12 (-0.48) SF: 77/56/55/36

913

MADAGANS JOCKEY CLUB STKS (Gp 2) (4-Y.O+) (Class A)
£32,589.00 (£12,051.00: £5,775.50: £2,352.50: £926.25: £355.75)
1m 4f (Rowley) Stalls: High GOING minus 0.28 sec per fur (GF) 3-40 (3-41)

Only Royale (IRE) (119)*(123) (LMCumani)* 6-8-11 LDettori(5) (lw: b.nr fore: hld up: swtchd 3f out: qcknd to ld ins fnl f: r.o) .....— **1**
Tikkanen (USA) *(126)*(Fav)*(JEPease,France)* 4-9-0 CAsmussen(3) (lw: trckd ldrs: led over 2f out tl ins fnl f: r.o) .....nk **2**
Time Star (USA) **(111)***(122) (PFICole)* 4-9-0 TQuinn(7) (h.d.w: cl up: chal 3f out: nt qckn appr fnl f) 2½ **3**
Sacrament **(115)***(120) (MRStoute)* 4-8-12 WRSwinburn(6) (lw: led tl hdd over 2f out: one pce) .....½ **4**
631[4] Alriffa **(116)***(114) (RHannon)* 4-8-9b PatEddery(2) (lw: hld up: hdwy to chal 3f out: sn rdn: wknd 2f out) 1¾ **5**
666[7] Garden of Heaven (USA) **(105)***(109) (CEBrittain)* 6-8-9 MJKinane(1) (bhd: effrt over 3f out: no imp) 4 **6**
712[10] Wayne County (IRE) **(84)***(72t) (GFierro)* 5-8-9v MWigham(4) (cl up tl wknd fnl 2f) .....½ **7**

2/1 Tikkanen (USA), **7/2** Sacrament, **4/1** ONLY ROYALE (IRE), **13/2** Alriffa, **7/1** Time Star (USA), **25/1** Garden of Heaven (USA), **100/1** Wayne County (IRE), CSF £11.01 TOTE £5.50: £2.40 £1.80 (£3.80) OWNER Mr Frank Stronach (NEWMARKET) BRED Barronstown Stud 7 Rn
2m 31.26 (1.96) SF: 60/63/59/57/51/46/45

914

MARCH H'CAP (0-100) (3-Y.O) (Class C) £14,620.00 (£4,360.00: £2,080.00: £940.00)
7f (Rowley) Stalls: High GOING minus 0.28 sec per fur (GF) 4-15 (4-16)

Royal Rebuke (80)*(89) (RCharlton)* 3-8-6 PatEddery(3) (in tch: hdwy u.p 2f out: led appr fnl f: r.o wl) .....— **1**

694[4] Lipizzaner (IRE) **(88)***(90)*(Fav)*(BWHills)* 3-9-0 MJKinane(2) (b.off fore: s.i.s: hdwy 3f out: ev ch over 1f out: no ex) 3 **2**
697* Pelleman **(75)***(75) (RBoss)* 3-8-1 WCarson(8) (swtg: chsd ldrs: chal over 2f out: nt qckn fnl f) ....¾ **3**
662[2] Noble Kingdom **(87)***(85) (RAkehurst)* 3-8-13 TQuinn(6) (cl up: chal 3f out: rdn & btn appr fnl f) 1¼ **4**
662[10] Tiler (IRE) **(86)***(80) (MJohnston)* 3-8-12 DHolland(11) (led tl hdd & wknd appr fnl f) 1¾ **5**
720[5] Impulsive Air (IRE) **(95)***(88) (EWeymes)* 3-9-7 DHarrison(7) (outpcd tl styd on u.p fnl 2f) ....hd **6**
775[5] Mister Fire Eyes (IRE) **(84)***(75) (CEBrittain)* 3-8-10 MRimmer(4) (in tch: drvn along over 2f out: one pce) 1¼ **7**
Zilayah (USA) **(82)***(66) (MRStoute)* 3-8-8 ow2 WRSwinburn(1) (hld up & bhd: effrt over 2f out: no imp) 2 **8**
552[4] River Keen (IRE) **(75)***(38) (RWArmstrong)* 3-8-1 RPrice(9) (prom over 4f) 10 **9**

4/1 Lipizzaner (IRE) (3/1-9/2), **5/1** ROYAL REBUKE, **11/2** Zilayah (USA) (4/1-6/1), Noble Kingdom, **6/1** Pelleman, **8/1** Tiler (IRE), **12/1** River Keen (IRE) (op 8/1), Mister Fire Eyes (IRE) (8/1-14/1), **33/1** Impulsive Air (IRE), CSF £22.61 CT £105.22 TOTE £6.50: £1.80 £1.60 £1.60 (£13.20) Trio £45.80 OWNER Mrs M. Bryce-Smith (BECKHAMPTON) BRED David Allan 9 Rn
1m 24.38 (0.68) SF: 59/60/45/55/50/58/45/36/8

915 PORTLAND LODGE MAIDEN STKS (3-Y.O F) (Class D) £5,162.50 (£1,540.00: £735.00: £332.50)
7f (Rowley) Stalls: Centre GOING minus 0.28 sec per fur (GF) 4-50 (4-51)

Moonlight Saunter (USA) *(77)*(Fav)*(EALDunlop)* 3-8-11 WRSwinburn(3) (lw: swtg: trckd ldrs gng wl: led wl over 1f out: rdn & r.o) ....— **1**
Lucky Soph (USA) *(75) (BWHills)* 3-8-11 RHills(5) (hld up: hdwy over 2f out: styd on wl) ....¾ **2**
Bibliotheque (USA) *(75) (JHMGosden)* 3-8-11 LDettori(2) (w'like: scope: b: dwlt: sn in tch: effrt over 2f out: r.o twrds fin) ....hd **3**
By The Bay *(72) (BWHills)* 3-8-11 MHills(7) (lt-f: leggy: trckd ldrs: hdwy & ev ch over 1f out: rdn & no ex) 1¼ **4**
Feinte *(72) (WJarvis)* 3-8-11 JReid(6) (in tch: outpcd 2f out: styd on wl nr fin) ....nk **5**
My First Romance *(70) (MAJarvis)* 3-8-11 WWoods(8) (w'like: bkwd: led over 5f: grad wknd) ....½ **6**
Bouche Bee (USA) *(70) (LMCumani)* 3-8-11 JWeaver(4) (w'like: scope: bhd: hdwy 2f out: nvr able to chal) ....hd **7**
Lady Nash *(59) (CEBrittain)* 3-8-11 MRimmer(1) (gd sort: bkwd: chsd ldrs 5f: wknd) 5 **8**

5/2 MOONLIGHT SAUNTER (USA) (6/4-11/4), **3/1** Bibliotheque (USA), **7/2** Lady Nash, **11/1** By The Bay (7/1-12/1), **12/1** Bouche Bee (USA) (4/1-14/1), Feinte (op 8/1), **14/1** Lucky Soph (USA) (7/1-16/1), **33/1** My First Romance, CSF £29.67 TOTE £2.70: £1.40 £2.30 £1.30 (£18.00) OWNER Maktoum Al Maktoum (NEWMARKET) BRED Gainsborough Farm Inc 8 Rn
1m 26.69 (2.99) SF: 37/35/35/32/32/30/30/19

916 NEWMARKET CHALLENGE WHIP MAIDEN STKS (3-Y.O) (Class G)
1m (Rowley) Stalls: Centre GOING minus 0.28 sec per fur (GF) 5-20 (5-20)

670[8] **Catercap (IRE)** *(75t)*(Fav)*(JHMGosden)* 3-9-0 LDettori(1) (lw: mde all: qcknd over 2f out: rdn & r.o wl) ....— **1**
Niggle *(68t) (HThomsonJones)* 3-8-9 RHills(2) (gd sort: hld up: effrt over 2f out: ev ch 1f out: eased whn btn twrds fin) 1¼ **2**

30/100 CATERCAP (IRE), **5/2** Niggle (6/4-11/4), TOTE £1.20: OWNER Sheikh Mohammed (NEWMARKET) BRED Upstream Ltd 2 Rn
1m 40.05 (3.05) SF: 44/37

T/Plpt: £8.20 (2,379.22 Tckts). T/Qdpt: £5.10 (28.3 Tckts). AA

0910-NEWMARKET (R-H)
Saturday May 6th (Good to firm)
WEATHER: sunny & hot WIND: almost nil

917 MAYER PARRY STKS (3-Y.O) (Class C) £5,326.40 (£1,838.40: £879.20: £356.00)
1m 4f (Rowley) Stalls: High GOING minus 0.30 sec per fur (GF) 1-55 (1-56)

691* **Tamure (IRE)** *(96)*(Fav)*(JHMGosden)* 3-8-13 LDettori(4) (lw: b.hind: hld up: hdwy to ld over 1f out: rdn & r.o) ....— **1**

657* Sebastian *(95) (HRACecil)* 3-8-13 WRyan(3) (lw: trckd ldrs: led wl over 2f out: sn rdn: hdd over 2f out: r.o) 1 **2**
711[8] Great Crusader **(102)***(88) (CACyzer)* 3-8-13 JWeaver(2) (led: shkn up & qcknd 5f out: hdd wl over 2f out: sn outpcd) 5 **3**
619[6] Korambi **(90)***(83) (CEBrittain)* 3-8-11 BDoyle(1) (chsd ldr: chal 5f out: outpcd fnl 2½f) 2 **4**

4/5 TAMURE (IRE), **5/4** Sebastian, **20/1** Great Crusader, **50/1** Korambi, CSF £1.99 TOTE £1.60: (£1.10) OWNER Sheikh Mohammed (NEWMARKET) BRED Sheikh Mohammed bin Rashid al Maktoum 4 Rn 2m 33.5 (4.20) SF: 45/44/37/32

918 TORCH MOTOR POLICIES AT LLOYDS RATED STKS H'CAP (0-100)

(4-Y.O+) (Class B) £9,976.80 (£3,691.20: £1,770.60: £723.00: £286.50: £111.90)
1m 2f (Rowley) Stalls: Centre GOING minus 0.30 sec per fur (GF) 2-30 (2-30)

Burooj (91)*(103) (DMorley)* 5-8-12 WCarson(2) (lw: swtg: a.p: led 2f out: pushed out) ....— **1**
Taufan's Melody **(97)***(109) (LadyHerries)* 4-9-4 TIves(7) (hld up: effrt over 1f out: r.o wl: nrst fin) ....nk **2**
623[15] Statajack (IRE) **(86)***(96) (DRCElsworth)* 7-8-7b TQuinn(10) (hld up & bhd: smooth hdwy to chal 1f out: sn rdn & no ex) ....¾ **3**
631[8] Old Hickory (IRE) **(100)***(110) (LMCumani)* 4-9-7b LDettori(8) (led tl hdd 2f out: one pce) ....nk **4**
714[13] Embankment (IRE) **(86)***(92) (RHannon)* 5-8-7 JReid(6) (trckd ldrs: effrt & ev ch 2f out: r.o one pce) 2½ **5**
Sherman (IRE) **(92)***(95) (HThomsonJones)* 4-8-13b RHills(1) (bit bkwd: hld up: effrt over 2f out: rdn & no imp) 2 **6**
793[7] Master Beveled **(87)***(89) (PDEvans)* 5-8-5 (3) SSanders(9) (plld hrd: effrt 3f out: n.d) ....½ **7**
634[6] Sue's Artiste **(86)***(88) (BWHills)* 4-8-7 MHills(3) (mid div: hdwy 3f out: btn appr fnl f) ....s.h **8**
634* Special Dawn (IRE) **(86)***(86)*(Fav)*(JLDunlop)* 5-8-7 PatEddery(5) (lw: hld up: hdwy over 2f out: sn hrd drvn: btn appr fnl f) 1¼ **9**
714[17] Geisway (CAN) **(90)***(88) (NJHWalker)* 5-8-11 RCochrane(4) (lw: cl up tl wknd fnl 2½f) 1¼ **10**
LONG HANDICAP Statajack (IRE) 8-4 Sue's Artiste 8-5 Special Dawn (IRE) 8-3

7/2 Special Dawn (IRE) (3/1-9/2), **5/1** Old Hickory (IRE), BUROOJ, **13/2** Master Beveled (9/2-7/1), **8/1** Sue's Artiste, Sherman (IRE), **10/1** Taufan's Melody (8/1-12/1), **12/1** Embankment (IRE), **20/1** Statajack (IRE), Geisway (CAN), CSF £48.38 CT £816.79 TOTE £3.60: £1.40 £4.40 £5.90 (£41.60) Trio £255.50 OWNER Mr Hamdan Al Maktoum (NEWMARKET) BRED Shadwell Estate Company Limited 10 Rn 2m 3.97 (1.37) SF: 61/67/54/68/50/53/47/46/44/46

919 SPRING MAIDEN STKS (2-Y.O) (Class D) £4,889.50 (£1,456.00: £693.00:

£311.50) **5f (Rowley)** Stalls: Centre GOING minus 0.30 sec per fur (GF)3-00 (3-00)

Lucky Lionel (USA) *(78+) (RHannon)* 2-9-0 KDarley(4) (gd sort: s.i.s: hld up: stdy hdwy ½-wy: led 1f out: r.o wl) ....— **1**
682[6] Oberons Boy (IRE) *(74) (BJMeehan)* 2-9-0 PatEddery(2) (cl up: ev ch 1f out: kpt on wl) 1¼ **2**
617[7] Tropical Dance (USA) *(69) (MrsJCecil)* 2-8-9 JReid(5) (lw: dsptd ld tl hdd 1f out: kpt on) ....s.h **3**
Double Diamond (IRE) *(70) (MJohnston)* 2-9-0 DHolland(6) (w'like: leggy: disp ld 4f: grad wknd) 1¼ **4**
Alpine *(51) (PFICole)* 2-9-0 TQuinn(3) (cmpt: scope: bkwd: chsd ldrs tl wknd wl over 1f out) 6 **5**
Indian Bluff *(31)*(Fav)*(CNWilliams)* 2-9-0 RCochrane(1) (gd sort: dwlt: plld hrd & sn prom: effrt 2f out: sn btn) 6 **6**

11/4 Indian Bluff (op 9/2), **4/1** Double Diamond (IRE), Tropical Dance (USA) (op 5/2), **9/2** Alpine (3/1-5/1), **6/1** LUCKY LIONEL (USA) (4/1-7/1), **13/2** Oberons Boy (IRE), CSF £37.42 TOTE £5.80: £2.30 £2.20 (£19.80) OWNER Lucayan Stud (MARLBOROUGH) BRED Richard & Mrs Kaster 6 Rn 60.16 secs (1.46) SF: 48/44/39/40/21/1

920 MADAGANS 2000 GUINEAS STKS (Gp 1) (3-Y.O C & F) (Class A)

£117,912.00 (£43,608.00: £20,904.00: £8,520.00: £3,360.00: £1,296.00)
1m (Rowley) Stalls: Low GOING minus 0.30 sec per fur (GF) 3-40 (3-41)

706a* **Pennekamp (USA)** *(131+) (AFabre,France)* 3-9-0 TJarnet(11) (h.d.w: hld up & bhd: hdwy over 2f out: qcknd to ld ins fnl f: r.o) ....— **1**
713* Celtic Swing **(130)***(131)*(Fav)*(LadyHerries)* 3-9-0 KDarley(7) (lw: s.i.s: sn trckng ldrs: led over 2f out & qcknd: hdd ins fnl f: r.o wl) ....hd **2**

713^{2} Bahri (USA) **(125)***(127) (JLDunlop)* 3-9-0 WCarson(1) (lw: hld up & bhd: gd hdwy 2f out: chsng ldrs 1f out: nt qckn) 2 **3**
Pipe Major (IRE) **(110)***(123) (PCHaslam)* 3-9-0 JWeaver(8) (h.d.w: cl up: led 3f out tl over 2f out: kpt on wl) 2 **4**
680^{3} Nwaamis (USA) *(121) (JLDunlop)* 3-9-0 RHills(5) (plld hrd: chsd ldrs: outpcd over 2f out: n.m.r appr fnl f: kpt on u.p) ....¾ **5**
667* Diffident (FR) *(115) (AFabre,France)* 3-9-0 MJKinane(4) (lw: in tch: effrt over 2f out: rdn & no imp) 3 **6**
680* Painter's Row (IRE) **(117)***(110) (PWChapple-Hyam)* 3-9-0 JReid(9) (in tch: effrt over 2f out: no imp) 2½ **7**
680^{4} Chilly Billy **(116)***(109) (MrsJRRamsden)* 3-9-0 KFallon(6) (unruly s: dwlt: hld up & bhd: effrt 3f out: nvr able to chal) ....½ **8**
667^{10} Silca Blanka (IRE) **(109)***(102) (MRChannon)* 3-9-0 RHughes(2) (disp ld tl hdd 3f out: sn wknd) 3½ **9**
616* Zeb (IRE) **(100)***(100) (BAMcMahon)* 3-9-0 TIves(3) (disp ld tl wknd 3f out) 1¼ **10**
Green Perfume (USA) **(121)***(93) (PFICole)* 3-9-0 TQuinn(10) (lw: plld hrd: in tch: wkng whn hmpd over 2f out) 3½ **11**

4/5 Celtic Swing, **9/2** PENNEKAMP (USA), **6/1** Diffident (FR), **14/1** Painter's Row (IRE), Bahri (USA), **25/1** Green Perfume (USA), **33/1** Chilly Billy, **40/1** Nwaamis (USA), **50/1** Pipe Major (IRE), **100/1** Zeb (IRE), **200/1** Silca Blanka (IRE), CSF £7.70 TOTE £5.40: £1.70 £1.20 £2.10 (£3.70) Trio £11.30 OWNER Sheikh Mohammed (FRANCE) BRED Mrs M. O. Bryant in USA 11 Rn
1m 35.16 (-1.84) SF: 94/94/90/86/84/78/73/72/65/63/56

921

DUBAI RACING CLUB PALACE HOUSE STKS (Gp 3) (3-Y.O+) (Class A) £23,807.00 (£8,813.00: £4,231.50: £1,732.50: £691.25: £274.75)
5f (Rowley) Stalls: Low GOING minus 0.30 sec per fur (GF) 4-15 (4-24)

612* **Mind Games (115)***(119) (JBerry)* 3-8-5 JCarroll(13) (a.p: edgd lft over 1f out: led ins fnl f: r.o) ....— **1**
571^{9} Eveningperformance **(97)***(110) (HCandy)* 4-8-9 WNewnes(11) (led tl hdd ins fnl f: kpt on) 1 **2**
Owington **(124)***(118)*(Fav)*(GWragg)* 4-9-6 MHills(4) (h.d.w: bit bkwd: in tch: nt clr run over 1f out & swtchd: nt qckn wl ins fnl f) ....½ **3**
612^{3} Millstream (USA) **(109)***(109) (MJohnston)* 3-8-2 DHolland(1) (a chsng ldrs: led wl over 1f out: r.o) ....nk **4**
700* El Yasaf (IRE) **(106)***(103) (GFierro)* 7-8-12 MWigham(5) (lw: pushed along ½-wy: styd on fnl f: nrst fin) 1¾ **5**
Piccolo **(113)***(110) (MRChannon)* 4-9-6 RHughes(14) (h.d.w: effrt & hmpd over 1f out: r.o one pce) ....nk **6**
612^{2} Wavian **(104)***(99) (RCharlton)* 3-8-2 DHarrison(7) (lw: effrt ½-wy: hmpd over 1f out: styd on twrds fin) 1 **7**
Raah Algharb (USA) **(110)***(105) (MRStoute)* 3-8-8 WRSwinburn(9) (lw: s.i.s: styd on fnl f: nrst fin) ....hd **8**
700^{2} Mistertopogigo (IRE) **(116)***(98) (WSCunningham)* 5-8-12 KDarley(10) (b.off hind: chsd ldrs: hrd rdn & outpcd over 1f out: no imp after) ....hd **9**
692^{8} Loyalize (USA) **(109)***(91) (DRLoder)* 3-7-13 GCarter(6) (in tch: btn whn hmpd over 1f out) ...1¼ **10**
719^{7} Bunty Boo **(106)***(86) (RHannon)* 6-8-9 MJKinane(12) (lw: chsd ldrs over 3f: btn whn hmpd over 1f out) 1½ **11**
659^{4} Tajannub (USA) **(106)***(86) (RWArmstrong)* 3-8-2 WCarson(2) (outpcd fnl 2f) 1 **12**
571^{2} Blue Siren **(113)***(80) (IABalding)* 4-8-9 LDettori(3) (prom over 3f: sn wknd) 1 **13**
659^{9} Windmachine (SWE) *(42) (RHarris)* 4-8-9 PatEddery(8) (chsd ldrs 3f: wknd qckly) 12 **14**

11/4 Owington, **4/1** MIND GAMES (3/1-9/2), **5/1** Mistertopogigo (IRE), **7/1** Blue Siren, **12/1** Millstream (USA), **16/1** Raah Algharb (USA), Wavian, **20/1** El Yasaf (IRE), Tajannub (USA), **25/1** Loyalize (USA), **33/1** Bunty Boo, Eveningperformance, Piccolo, Windmachine (SWE), CSF £111.59 TOTE £3.30: £1.80 £7.40 £1.70 (£102.20) Trio £225.70 OWNER Mr Robert Hughes (COCKERHAM) BRED Mrs V. E. Hughes 14 Rn 58.15 secs (-0.55) SF: 74/75/83/64/68/75/54/60/63/46/51/41/45/7
WEIGHT FOR AGE 3yo-10lb

922

LADBROKES H'CAP (0-95) (3-Y.O+) (Class C) £24,075.00 (£7,200.00: £3,450.00: £1,575.00)
6f (Rowley) Stalls: Centre GOING minus 0.30 sec per fur (GF) 4-45 (4-54)

665^{16} **Saseedo (USA) (84)***(94) (WAO'Gorman)* 5-9-3 EmmaO'Gorman(17) (swtg: hdwy over 2f out: r.o wl to ld cl home) ....— **1**
789* Ziggy's Dancer (USA) **(71)***(81) (EJAlston)* 4-8-4 KFallon(16) (lw: trckd ldrs: led over 1f out: r.o: jst ct) ....s.h **2**

796 10 Sir Joey (USA) **(83)***(88) (PGMurphy)* 6-8-11 (5) SDrowne(10) (swtg: gd hdwy 2f out: swtchd appr fnl f: r.o)....2 3
Elfland (IRE) **(77)***(81) (LadyHerries)* 4-8-10 KDarley(8) (in tch: rdn ½-wy: no imp)....s.h 4
Astrac (IRE) **(89)***(90) (RAkehurst)* 4-9-5 (3) SSanders(9) (lw: w ldr: led over 2f out tl over 1f out: no ex)....1¼ 5
702 16 Orthorhombus **(64)***(62) (DJSCosgrove)* 6-7-11b CRutter(21) (swtg: bhd tl r.o fnl f)....1¼ 6
796 5 Jobie **(70)***(64)*(Fav)*(BWHills)* 5-8-3 MHills(2) (lw: mid div: hdwy 2f out: nvr able chal)....1¼ 7
611 5 Chinour (IRE) **(67)***(59) (EJAlston)* 7-8-0 ow2 PRobinson(4) (swtg: s.i.s: styd on fnl 2f: nrst fin)....s.h 8
611 12 Selhurstpark Flyer (IRE) **(88)***(81) (JBerry)* 4-9-7e JCarroll(14) (trckd ldrs: btn whn hmpd over 1f out)....½ 9
Celestial Key (USA) **(93)***(85) (MJohnston)* 5-9-12 DHolland(19) (lw: led tl hdd & wknd over 2f out)....nk 10
723 6 Saddlehome (USA) **(76)***(68) (TDBarron)* 6-8-9 LDettori(20) (trckd ldrs: effrt 2f out: sn btn)....s.h 11
765 4 Moujeeb (USA) **(61)***(52) (PatMitchell)* 5-7-8v NKennedy(15) (lw: drvn along & n.m.r ½-wy: eased whn btn fnl f)....nk 12
665 15 Be Warned **(82)***(71) (NACallaghan)* 4-9-1 PatEddery(12) (nvr trbld ldrs)....1 13
636 13 Invocation **(67)***(55) (AMoore)* 8-7-9 (5) AWhelan(13) (b.nr hind: nvr trbld ldrs)....s.h 14
765 12 Samsolom **(67)***(52) (PHowling)* 7-8-0 ow1 RPrice(1) (n.d)....1 15
Master of Passion **(84)***(70) (JMPEustace)* 6-9-3 MJKinane(3) (nvr nr to chal)....hd 16
693 3 Mister Jolson **(86)***(70) (RJHodges)* 6-9-5 RCochrane(11) (in tch: effrt 2f out: sn btn)....½ 17
765 9 Make Time **(72)***(55) (JPearce)* 3-7-8 GBardwell(6) (n.d)....½ 18
636* Gone Savage **(65)***(45) (WJMusson)* 7-7-12 WCarson(5) (cl up tl wknd appr fnl f)....1 19
765* Teetotaller (IRE) **(70)***(49) (GBBalding)* 4-8-3 JWilliams(7) (n.d)....½ 20
486 10 Serious Option (IRE) **(80)***(59) (PFICole)* 4-8-13b TQuinn(18) (prom 3f: sn rdn & btn)....hd 21

7/1 Jobie, **9/1** Mister Jolson, **10/1** Gone Savage, Be Warned, Saddlehome (USA), **12/1** Ziggy's Dancer (USA), Teetotaller (IRE), Chinour (IRE), **14/1** Astrac (IRE), Celestial Key (USA), Elfland (IRE), Make Time, **16/1** Selhurstpark Flyer (IRE), Sir Joey (USA), **20/1** SASEEDO (USA), Master of Passion, Moujeeb (USA), Invocation, Serious Option (IRE), **25/1** Samsolom, **40/1** Orthorhombus, CSF £240.13 CT £3,590.32 TOTE £36.30: £5.80 £2.40 £4.60 £7.90 (£248.30) Trio £2,328.90; £984.08 to Newmarket 07/05/95 OWNER Mr S. Fustok (NEWMARKET) BRED Audley Farm Incorporated 21 Rn
1m 11.26 (-0.04) SF: 77/64/71/64/73/45/47/42/64/68/51/35/54/38/35/53/53/27/28/32/42
WEIGHT FOR AGE 3yo-11lb

923
CHIPPENHAM PARK STKS (4-Y.O+) (Class C) £5,276.80 (£1,820.80: £870.40: £352.00) **1m 2f (Rowley)** Stalls: Centre GOING minus 0.30 sec (GF) 5-20 (5-22)

Baron Ferdinand (103)*(112+) (RCharlton)* 5-9-0 PatEddery(2) (b: hld up: smooth hdwy to ld wl over 1f out: rdn & r.o)....— 1
750* Florid (USA) **(107)***(111)*(Fav)*(HRACecil)* 4-9-5 WRyan(1) (lw: led tl hdd wl over 1f out: r.o one pce)....4 2
Brier Creek (USA) **(108)***(108) (JHMGosden)* 6-9-4 LDettori(3) (lw: trckd ldr: effrt 3f out: r.o one pce)....¾ 3
Mercadier *(91t) (CEBrittain)* 4-8-10 MJKinane(4) (trckd ldrs tl outpcd 4f out: n.d after)....6 4

6/5 Florid (USA), **2/1** BARON FERDINAND (6/4-9/4), **4/1** Brier Creek (USA), **14/1** Mercadier, CSF £4.39 TOTE £3.10: (£2.00) OWNER Lady Rothschild (BECKHAMPTON) BRED Exors of the late Mrs D. M. de Rothschild 4 Rn
2m 4.62 (2.02) SF: 57/56/53/36
T/Jkpt: £57,666.30 (1.78 Tckts). T/Plpt: £530.90 (84.11 Tckts). T/Qdpt: £72.60 (7.7 Tckts). AA

0718-THIRSK (L-H)
Saturday May 6th (Good to firm, Firm Patches)
WEATHER: Fine & Sunny WIND: Almost nil

924
MILLGATE MAIDEN STKS (3-Y.O) (Class D) £4,205.50 (£1,258.00: £603.00: £275.50) **7f** Stalls: High GOING minus 0.36 sec per fur (F) 2-20 (2-20)

677 6 **Rug** *(81) (GWragg)* 3-9-0 PaulEddery(1) (lw: trckd ldrs: led wl over 1f out: drvn out)....— 1
715 3 Pinzon (USA) *(76)*(Fav)*(PWChapple-Hyam)* 3-9-0 BThomson(4) (chsd ldrs: effrt 3f out: ev ch over 1f out: unable qckn)....2 2

616[3] Dosses Dan (IRE) *(74) (BWHills)* 3-8-9 (5) JDSmith(7) (prom: drvn along 3f out: styd on fnl f: nvr able to chal) 1¼ 3
Statistician *(73) (JohnBerry)* 3-9-0 MFenton(8) (rangy: scope: led tl wl over 1f out: kpt on one pce)....nk 4
758[2] Dr Caligari (IRE) *(66) (JBerry)* 3-9-0 SDWilliams(6) (trckd ldr: chal over 2f out: edgd rt & wknd over 1f out) 3 5
758[11] Highfield Fizz *(59) (CWFairhurst)* 3-8-9 JFanning(3) (sn in tch: effrt over 2f out: sn wknd)....¾ 6
591[5] Shazanni (IRE) *(48) (JGFitzGerald)* 3-8-9 JFortune(5) (a in rr)....5 7
758[6] Cupronickel (IRE) *(32) (JWWatts)* 3-8-9 NConnorton(2) (sn outpcd & bhd)....7 8

4/5 Pinzon (USA) (op 1/2), **7/2** RUG, **5/1** Dosses Dan (IRE), **14/1** Dr Caligari (IRE), **25/1** Statistician, **33/1** Cupronickel (IRE), **66/1** Highfield Fizz, Shazanni (IRE), CSF £6.15 TOTE £4.60: £1.40 £1.10 £1.50 (£2.30) OWNER Lord Hartington (NEWMARKET) BRED Side Hill Stud and B. Haggas 8 Rn
1m 25.8 (3.10) SF: 31/26/24/23/16/9/-/-

925

E.B.F. MARKET PLACE MEDIAN AUCTION MAIDEN STKS (2-Y.O)
(Class F) £3,590.00 (£1,070.00: £510.00: £230.00)
5f Stalls: Low GOING minus 0.36 sec per fur (F) 2-50 (2-57)

Hoh Majestic (IRE) *(68+)*(Fav)*(MBell)* 2-9-0 MFenton(3) (neat: lw: mde virtually all: r.o strly appr fnl f: sn clr) ....— 1
671[8] Lucky Bea *(52) (MWEasterby)* 2-9-0 LCharnock(4) (dwlt s: sn chsg ldrs: kpt on u.p appr fnl f: no ch w wnr) 5 2
Fancy Clancy *(34) (MissLCSiddall)* 2-8-9 AMcGlone(2) (neat: unf: s.i.s: sn outpcd & rn green: hdwy over 1f out: styd on)....4 3
Eccentric Dancer *(25) (MPBielby)* 2-8-9 ACulhane(7) (cmpt: bit bkwd: s.s: wl bhd tl styd on fnl f)....3 4
Time To Fly *(28) (BWMurray)* 2-9-0 DeanMcKeown(1) (cmpt: unf: sn w ldrs: outpcd ½-wy: sn wknd)....½ 5
595[6] Supergal *(15) (MWEasterby)* 2-8-9 MBirch(9) (sn wl outpcd: some hdwy & hung bdly lft over 1f out: eased whn bit slipped) 2½ 6
Marketeer Magic *(18)*(Fav)*(JBerry)* 2-9-0 SDWilliams(8) (cmpt: s.i.s: a outpcd)....½ 7
Poppy My Love *(13) (BJMcMath)* 2-8-9 AMackay(5) (small: unruly s: sn w ldrs: edgd lft & wknd qckly wl over 1f out) ....s.h 8
Lac Dessert (USA) *(DRLoder)* 2-8-9 MTebbutt(6) (Withdrawn not under Starters' orders: broke out of stalls) .... **W**

9/4 Marketeer Magic, HOH MAJESTIC (IRE), **7/2** Poppy My Love, **5/1** Lucky Bea, **10/1** Supergal, **12/1** Time To Fly, **16/1** Eccentric Dancer, **20/1** Fancy Clancy, CSF £14.87 TOTE £2.60: £1.40 £1.30 £5.10 (£11.70) Trio £94.30; £55.83 to Newmarket 07/04/95 OWNER Mr D. F. Allport (NEWMARKET) BRED Ballinacurra Stud 8 Rn 60.1 secs (2.90) SF: 18/2/-/-/-/-/-/-
OFFICIAL EXPLANATION **Supergal: the bit slipped through her mouth and her jockey could not ride her out.**

926

BUSINESS FURNITURE CENTRE H'CAP (0-80) (3-Y.O+) (Class D)
£4,340.70 (£1,299.60: £623.80: £285.90)
5f Stalls: High GOING minus 0.36 sec per fur (F) 3-20 (3-25)

639[6] **My Abbey (55)***(59) (EJAlston)* 6-8-5 AMackay(18) (mde virtually all stands side: edgd lft u.p fnl f: styd on)....— 1
656[3] Spender **(69)***(70) (PWHarris)* 6-9-5 GDuffield(15) (lw: hdwy ½-wy: styd on wl u.p fnl f: nt rch wnr) 1 2
Lady Sheriff **(45)***(41) (MWEasterby)* 4-7-9bow1 LCharnock(2) (chsd ldrs far side: kpt on wl fnl f)....1¼ 3
723[3] Ned's Bonanza **(69)***(63)*(Fav)*(MDods)* 6-9-5 SWhitworth(13) (hdwy ½-wy: styd on fnl f: nt rch ldrs)....¾ 4
789[17] Featherstone Lane **(55)***(49) (MissLCSiddall)* 4-8-2v(3) DRMcCabe(12) (hdwy over 1f out: styd on twrds fin) ....s.h 5
796[8] Tenor **(66)***(56) (DNicholls)* 4-9-2 AlexGreaves(7) (swtchd rt s: sn prom: effrt 2f out: kpt on same pce)....1¼ 6
507[16] The Fed **(57)***(45) (RMWhitaker)* 5-8-7v ACulhane(20) (a chsng ldrs: one pce fnl 2f)....¾ 7
Call to the Bar (IRE) **(74)***(62) (MDods)* 6-9-10 DaleGibson(19) (chsd ldrs tl wknd over 1f out) ....s.h 8
688[2] Miss Siham (IRE) **(45)***(28) (DNicholls)* 6-7-2 (7)ow2 SLanigan(3) (led far side tl wknd over 1f out) 1 9
646[9] Sir Tasker **(59)***(43) (JLHarris)* 7-8-9 PaulEddery(17) (lw: chsd ldrs tl wknd over 1f out)....hd 10

723[5] Croft Imperial **(68)***(50) (MJohnston)* 8-9-4 TWilliams(4) (chsd ldrs far side tl wknd 2f out) ...¾ **11**
812[10] Just Bob **(78)***(60) (SEKettlewell)* 6-9-9 (5) JStack(8) (s.i.s: a in rr)...s.h **12**
688[8] Nineacres **(53)***(34) (DNicholls)* 4-7-12 (5) NVarley(11) (swtchd rt s: in tch 3f) ...hd **13**
674[10] Dominelle **(53)***(34) (MHEasterby)* 3-7-7 NCarlisle(6) (spd centre 3f) ...s.h **14**
Knayton Lass **(70)***(50) (MWEasterby)* 4-9-6 MBirch(9) (gd spd centre 3f: sn wknd)...½ **15**
784[7] Milbank Challenger **(50)***(27) (WStorey)* 5-8-0 JFanning(16) (a outpcd) ...¾ **16**
524[17] Double Glow **(57)***(33) (NBycroft)* 3-7-11 JQuinn(10) (a rr div)...½ **17**
754[8] High Ranking **(76)***(47) (MHEasterby)* 3-9-2 SMaloney(1) (w ldrs far side to ½-wy) ...1½ **18**
High Domain (IRE) **(76)***(43) (TDBarron)* 4-9-5 (7) JennyBenson(14) (bit bkwd: spd to ½-wy: sn bhd)...1¼ **19**
639[7] Lord Sky **(68)***(22) (ABailey)* 4-8-13v(5) VHalliday(5) (b: in tch to ½-wy: sn lost pl) ...4 **20**
LONG HANDICAP Dominelle 7-3 Miss Siham (IRE) 7-6

5/1 Ned's Bonanza, **11/2** Spender, **6/1** Sir Tasker, **13/2** Tenor, **9/1** Croft Imperial, **10/1** Miss Siham (IRE), **12/1** Lord Sky, **14/1** MY ABBEY, The Fed, **16/1** Dominelle, Call to the Bar (IRE), High Ranking, **20/1** Nineacres, **25/1** High Domain (IRE), Just Bob, Knayton Lass, Featherstone Lane, **33/1** Milbank Challenger, Lady Sheriff, Double Glow, CSF £94.52 CT £2,359.70 TOTE £17.20: £3.70 £1.30 £9.60 £1.70 (£58.90) Trio Not won £966.45 to Newmarket 07/04/95 OWNER Abbey Racing (PRESTON) BRED Stetchworth Park Stud Ltd 20 Rn
58.8 secs (1.60) SF: 31/42/13/35/21/28/17/34/-/15/22/32/6/-/22/-/-/9/15/-
WEIGHT FOR AGE 3yo-10lb

927 THIRSK HUNT CUP H'CAP (0-90) (3-Y.O+) (Class C) £12,597.75

(£3,762.00: £1,798.50: £816.75)
1m Stalls: Low GOING minus 0.36 sec per fur (F) 3-55 (3-58)

724[9] **Pride of Pendle (66)***(76) (DNicholls)* 6-8-8 AlexGreaves(8) (hld up: hdwy on ins over 2f out: r.o wl u.p to ld nr fin) ...— **1**
845[10] Queens Consul (IRE) **(76)***(85) (BSRothwell)* 5-8-13 (5) JStack(1) (led: rdn over 2f out: hdd nr fin) ...½ **2**
665[4] Castel Rosselo **(84)***(90)*(Fav)*(BJMcMath)* 5-9-12 AMackay(9) (lw: bhd: stmbld appr st: gd hdwy on ins 2f out: ev ch 1f out: nt qckn)...1½ **3**
724[4] Celestial Choir **(78)***(81) (JLEyre)* 5-9-6 GDuffield(6) (dwlt s: bhd tl styd on u.p fnl 2f: nt rch ldrs)...1¾ **4**
784* Allinson's Mate (IRE) **(72)***(74) (TDBarron)* 7-9-0 JFortune(4) (lw: s.i.s: hdwy over 3f out: styd on same pce fnl 2f)...½ **5**
702[3] Sycamore Lodge (IRE) **(67)***(68)*(Fav)*(PCalver)* 4-8-9 GHind(2) (sn chsng ldrs: rdn over 2f out: one pce) ...½ **6**
784[2] Profit Release (IRE) **(58)***(53) (MJohnston)* 4-8-0b TWilliams(3) (chsd ldrs: rdn over 2f out: wknd over 1f out)...3 **7**
785[2] Spanish Verdict **(66)***(51) (DenysSmith)* 8-8-3 (5) CTeague(13) (lw: racd wd: chsd ldrs: outpcd over 2f out: n.d after)...5 **8**
766[9] Lancashire Life (IRE) **(53)***(36) (EJAlston)* 4-7-9 ow1 JQuinn(5) (prom tl lost pl over 3f out: hung lft: n.d after) ...hd **9**
679[7] Seckar Vale (USA) **(88)***(69) (JHanson)* 3-9-3 ACulhane(12) (hld up: sme hdwy whn n.m.r over 1f out: n.d) ...1½ **10**
728[9] Robsera (IRE) **(80)***(61) (GLewis)* 4-9-8 PaulEddery(7) (in tch: drvn along over 3f out: sn lost pl)...hd **11**
559* Sandmoor Chambray **(76)***(54) (MHEasterby)* 4-9-4b MBirch(10) (chsd ldrs tl wknd over 2f out)...1¾ **12**
839[11] Gant Bleu (FR) **(53)***(21) (RMWhitaker)* 8-7-4 (5)ow2 NVarley(11) (s.i.s: a in rr)...4 **13**
LONG HANDICAP Gant Bleu (FR) 7-1

5/1 Castel Rosselo, Sycamore Lodge (IRE), **6/1** Celestial Choir, **13/2** Sandmoor Chambray, Spanish Verdict, **8/1** PRIDE OF PENDLE, Robsera (IRE), **10/1** Queens Consul (IRE), **12/1** Allinson's Mate (IRE), **14/1** Profit Release (IRE), **16/1** Seckar Vale (USA), **25/1** Lancashire Life (IRE), **33/1** Gant Bleu (FR), CSF £85.03 CT £414.29 TOTE £10.70: £2.80 £3.80 £2.60 (£39.20) Trio £125.60 OWNER Mrs Linda Miller (THIRSK) BRED James Simpson 13 Rn
1m 36.8 (1.20) SF: 50/59/64/55/48/42/27/25/10/30/35/28/-
WEIGHT FOR AGE 3yo-13lb

928 VICTORY IN EUROPE H'CAP (0-90) (3-Y.O+) (Class C) £5,744.00

(£1,712.00: £816.00: £368.00)
7f Stalls: Low GOING minus 0.36 sec per fur (F) 4-30 (4-30)

724[6] **Willshe Gan (47)***(55) (DenysSmith)* 5-7-13 JQuinn(6) (trckd ldr: led over 2f out: jst hld on)...— **1**
535[6] Pine Ridge Lad (IRE) **(53)***(61) (JLEyre)* 5-8-5 JFanning(3) (hld up: hmpd 5f out: drvn along 3f out: styd on wl & swtchd ins fnl f: jst failed) ...hd **2**

686² Barrel of Hope **(78)***(86) (JLEyre)* 3-9-4 JFortune(8) (led: hrd rdn & hdd over 2f out: wandered: kpt on wl twrds fin)....hd **3**
812² Tatika **(72)***(78)*(Fav)*(GWragg)* 5-9-10 PaulEddery(5) (lw: trckd ldrs: effrt on ins 2f out: nt clr run & hmpd ins fnl f: nt rcvr)....½ **4**
714¹⁸ Perilous Plight **(70)***(75) (WRMuir)* 4-9-8 BThomson(2) (hld up: hmpd bnd 5f out: styd on fnl 2f: n.m.r: nvr nr ldrs)....¾ **5**
Pharazini **(70)***(73) (MJCamacho)* 4-9-8 LCharnock(4) (bit bkwd: hld up & bhd: styd on appr fnl f: nvr nr to chal)....¾ **6**
*845*⁷ Mary's Case (IRE) **(56)***(59) (MJohnston)* 5-8-8b TWilliams(1) (hmpd after 1½f: effrt 2f out: kpt on u.p: nvr able chal)....s.h **7**
Superoo **(65)***(68) (MrsPSly)* 9-9-3 MBirch(7) (trckd ldrs: effrt on outside 2f out: nvr rchd ldrs)....s.h **8**

13/8 Tatika (op 5/2), **4/1** Barrel of Hope, **9/2** WILLSHE GAN, **7/1** Pine Ridge Lad (IRE), Superoo, **17/2** Perilous Plight, **12/1** Mary's Case (IRE), **20/1** Pharazini, CSF £34.76 CT £127.23 TOTE £4.40: £2.10 £2.20 £1.10 (£12.10) OWNER Mr H. Hewitson (BISHOP AUCKLAND) BRED H. Alexander and R. E. Sangster 8 Rn 1m 26.4 (3.70) SF: 10/16/29/33/30/28/14/23

WEIGHT FOR AGE 3yo-12lb

929

SPRING MAIDEN STKS (3-Y.O+) (Class D) £4,239.30 (£1,268.40: £608.20: £278.10) **1m 4f** Stalls: High GOING minus 0.36 sec per fur (F) 5-00 (5-01)

663⁷ **Nine Barrow Down (IRE)** *(80)*(Fav)*(HRACecil)* 3-8-5 AMcGlone(8) (lw: sn trckng ldrs: rdn 2f out: wandered & styd on to ld nr fin)....— **1**
Embracing *(75) (MRStoute)* 3-8-0 JQuinn(3) (hld up: stdy hdwy over 2f out: shkn up & r.o wl ins fnl f: jst failed)....nk **2**
663¹³ Snow Valley *(79) (LMCumani)* 3-8-3 (3)ow1 CHodgson(9) (lw: led after 1f: drvn clr over 3f out: hdd wl ins fnl f)....½ **3**
610⁵ Dato Star (IRE) *(79) (JMJefferson)* 4-9-10 JFortune(11) (chsd ldrs: rdn & outpcd 2f out: nt qckn ins fnl f)....hd **4**
584⁸ Sharazi (USA) *(72) (DJSCosgrove)* 4-9-3 (7) DGibbs(1) (chsd ldrs: outpcd over 2f out: hrd rdn: kpt on one pce)....5 **5**
Shrewd Alibi *(63) (IABalding)* 4-9-10 SO'Gorman(4) (bit bkwd: led 1f: chsd ldrs tl outpcd fnl 3f)....7 **6**
Our Main Man *(60) (RMWhitaker)* 5-9-10 ACulhane(2) (outpcd & pushed along 6f out: n.d)....2½ **7**
787⁵ Dawn Mission *(40) (MHEasterby)* 3-8-5 MBirch(7) (hld up: rn wd bnd over 8f out: sn prom: rdn & wknd 3f out: eased)....15 **8**
698⁷ Kraton Garden (USA) *(24) (WJarvis)* 3-8-5 MTebbutt(6) (sn outpcd & bhd: rn wd bnd over 8f out)....12 **9**
Black Ice Boy (IRE) **(43)***(23) (RBastiman)* 4-9-5 (5) HBastiman(5) (sn bhd)....s.h **10**
Wassl's Guest (IRE) *(16) (RFMarvin)* 4-9-5 FNorton(10) (bkwd: sn bhd & pushed along)....1½ **11**

Evens NINE BARROW DOWN (IRE), **100/30** Dato Star (IRE), **6/1** Embracing (op 4/1), **9/1** Snow Valley, **12/1** Dawn Mission, **14/1** Kraton Garden (USA), Sharazi (USA) (op 33/1), **20/1** Shrewd Alibi, **33/1** Our Main Man, **50/1** Black Ice Boy (IRE), **100/1** Wassl's Guest (IRE), CSF £8.59 TOTE £2.60: £1.40 £1.80 £2.10 (£4.50) Trio £10.10 OWNER Hill Top (NEWMARKET) BRED Barronstown Stud and Ron Con Ltd 11 Rn 2m 32.7 (2.70) SF: 43/38/42/61/54/45/42/3/-/5/-

WEIGHT FOR AGE 3yo-19lb

T/Plpt: £60.40 (183.3 Tckts). T/Qdpt: £47.60 (1.2 Tckts). WG

0917-NEWMARKET (R-H)
Sunday May 7th (Good to firm)

WEATHER: fine & sunny WIND: fresh half against

930

LORDS TAVERNERS SUNDAY EXPRESS STKS (3-Y.O) (Class C) £5,720.00 (£2,120.00: £1,020.00: £420.00: £170.00: £70.00) **7f (Rowley)** Stalls: Centre GOING minus 0.37 sec per fur (F) 2-00 (2-00)

713⁴ **Peace Envoy (109)***(100) (HRACecil)* 3-9-1 WRyan(4) (lw: a.p: slt ld over 1f out: hdd ins fnl f: rallied to ld nr fin)....— **1**
Desert Courier *(99) (MRStoute)* 3-9-1 WRSwinburn(6) (lw: hld up: hdwy 2f out: ev ch wl ins fnl f: r.o)....nk **2**
695* Tarhhib *(94)*(Fav)*(JHMGosden)* 3-8-10 WCarson(5) (hld up: hdwy 2f out: led ins fnl f: ct nr fin)....s.h **3**
658* Magnificent Devil (USA) *(88) (JWWatts)* 3-9-1 BThomson(1) (led over 5f: rdn & wknd appr fnl f)....5 **4**

Pearl Venture **(93)***(79) (SPCWoods)* 3-8-10 WWoods(7) (hld up & bhd: effrt bel dist: no imp)........1½ **5**
Warning Shot *(68) (MartynMeade)* 3-9-1 JReid(3) (lw: chsd ldrs over 4f: sn outpcd)........7 **6**
715[4] Office Hours *(58) (CACyzer)* 3-8-9 KDarley(2) (w ldr tl wknd wl over 1f out)........2 **7**

5/2 Tarhhib, **11/4** PEACE ENVOY, **9/2** Desert Courier (2/1-5/1), Magnificent Devil (USA) (7/1-4/1), **20/1** Office Hours, **25/1** Pearl Venture, Warning Shot, CSF £13.00 TOTE £3.40: £2.10 £2.40 (£5.10) OWNER Mr K. Abdullah (NEWMARKET) BRED Juddmonte Farms 7 Rn
1m 24.82 (1.12) SF: 55/54/49/43/34/23/13

931 LADBROKE FIRST SUNDAY H'CAP (0-105) (4-Y.O+) (Class B)
£18,468.00 (£6,912.00: £3,381.00: £1,455.00: £652.50: £331.50)
1m 4f (Rowley) Stalls: Centre GOING minus 0.37 sec per fur (F) 2-30 (2-34)

668* **Parthian Springs (94)***(110)*(Fav)*(JHMGosden)* 4-9-11 LDettori(2) (lw: chsd ldrs: shkn up to ld bel dist: rdn out)........— **1**
634[2] Blushing Flame (USA) **(87)***(101) (MRStoute)* 4-9-4 WRSwinburn(10) (lw: chsd ldrs: hrd drvn over 1f out: styd on)........1¼ **2**
Beauchamp Hero **(97)***(111) (JLDunlop)* 5-10-0 JReid(3) (hld up: hdwy over 2f out: rdn & styd on ins fnl f)........s.h **3**
Marsoom (CAN) **(96)***(109) (BHanbury)* 4-9-13 JWeaver(1) (b: b.hind: led 9f: hrd rdn & wknd fnl f)........1 **4**
623[13] Bit on the Side (IRE) **(73)***(83) (WJMusson)* 6-7-13 (5) PMcCabe(5) (hld up & bhd: hdwy & wnt rt appr fnl f: fin strly)........2½ **5**
Arctic Thunder (USA) **(89)***(95) (LadyHerries)* 4-9-6 KDarley(4) (b: prom: led 3f out tl hdd bel dist: wknd fnl f)........2½ **6**
661[8] Microlite (USA) **(68)***(71) (MDHammond)* 4-7-13v WCarson(7) (swtg: nvr trbld ldrs)........2½ **7**
661* Tudor Island **(77)***(78) (CEBrittain)* 6-8-8 MRimmer(12) (lw: prom: rdn 4f out: btn over 2f out) 1½ **8**
623* Wishing (USA) **(89)***(85) (RAkehurst)* 4-9-6 GCarter(9) (lw: hld up: effrt u.p over 3f out: no imp)........3½ **9**
623[7] Endless Light (USA) **(87)***(80) (PFICole)* 4-9-4 TQuinn(6) (a bhd)........2½ **10**
Highbrook (USA) **(79)***(67) (MHTompkins)* 7-8-10 PRobinson(13) (b: stdd s: hld up: a bhd)...3½ **11**
439[14] Rainbow Walk (IRE) **(82)** *(JGMO'Shea)* 5-8-8v(5) JStack(8) (Withdrawn not under Starter's orders: bolted bef s)........**W**

, **11/4** PARTHIAN SPRINGS, **100/30** Blushing Flame (USA), **6/1** Wishing (USA), **10/1** Marsoom (CAN), Arctic Thunder (USA), Tudor Island, **12/1** Endless Light (USA), **16/1** Beauchamp Hero, **20/1** Bit on the Side (IRE), **25/1** Microlite (USA), **40/1** Highbrook (USA), CSF £11.47 CT £109.25 TOTE £3.20: £1.60 £1.50 £4.70 (£4.70) Trio £39.80 OWNER Hesmonds Stud (NEWMARKET) BRED Hesmonds Stud Ltd 11 Rn 2m 30.16 (0.86) SF: 73/64/74/72/46/58/34/41/48/43/30/-

932 MADAGANS PRETTY POLLY STKS (Listed) (3-Y.O F) (Class A)
£12,106.40 (£4,517.60: £2,198.80: £934.00: £407.00: £196.20)
1m 2f (Rowley) Stalls: Low GOING minus 0.37 sec per fur (F) 3-05 (3-05)

620[13] **Musetta (IRE) (106)***(101) (CEBrittain)* 3-8-11 BDoyle(1) (lw: mde all: qcknd clr 2f out: hld on wl)........— **1**
Fanjica (IRE) *(97) (JLDunlop)* 3-8-8 TQuinn(7) (leggy: lt-f: hld up: hdwy wl over 1f out: fin wl)........¾ **2**
Llia *(91) (JLDunlop)* 3-8-8 WCarson(8) (chsd ldrs: rdn 2f out: kpt on one pce)........3½ **3**
Watch the Clock **(107)***(90) (DRLoder)* 3-8-8 JWeaver(5) (hld up: hdwy 3f out: rdn wl over 1f out: one pce)........1 **4**
Alessia **(85)***(89) (BWHills)* 3-8-8 MHills(4) (lw: hld up: hdwy over 2f out: nt pce to chal)........½ **5**
660[4] Germane **(107)***(89)*(Fav)*(MBell)* 3-9-1 MFenton(2) (hld up & prom: rdn 2f out: sn outpcd)........4 **6**
Alfaaselah (GER) **(97)***(76) (MRStoute)* 3-8-8 MJKinane(3) (lw: prom over 7f: sn lost tch)........4 **7**
Circa **(104)***(67) (WJarvis)* 3-8-13 LDettori(6) (chsd wnr tl wknd over 2f out: t.o)........9 **8**

11/4 Germane, **9/2** Alessia, Watch the Clock, **6/1** Llia, **8/1** Alfaaselah (GER) (6/1-9/1), **12/1** Fanjica (IRE), Circa, **14/1** MUSETTA (IRE), CSF £134.27 TOTE £21.80: £3.10 £2.40 £2.00 (£38.40) OWNER Mr B. H. Voak (NEWMARKET) BRED Gainsborough Stud Management Ltd 8 Rn
2m 3.67 (1.07) SF: 57/53/47/46/45/45/32/23

933 MADAGANS 1000 GUINEAS STKS (Gp 1) (3-Y.O F) (Class A)
£110,791.00 (£40,969.00: £19,634.50: £7,997.50: £3,148.75: £1,209.25)
1m (Rowley) Stalls: Low GOING minus 0.37 sec per fur (F) 3-45 (3-49)

667[2] **Harayir (USA) (118)***(118) (MajorWRHern)* 3-9-0 RHills(2) (a gng wl: led over 1f out: r.o wl)........— **1**

692* Aqaarid (USA) **(111)***(115)*(Fav)*(JLDunlop)* 3-9-0 WCarson(13) (lw: hld up: hdwy 2f out: kpt on strly ins fnl f) 1½ 2
Moonshell (IRE) *(114)* *(SbinSuroor)* 3-9-0 LDettori(6) (h.d.w: a.p: rdn 3f out: styd on wl fnl f) ....¾ 3
692[2] Hoh Magic **(117)***(110)* *(MBell)* 3-9-0 MHills(15) (chsd ldrs: kpt on u.p fnl f) 2 4
660[2] Epagris *(109)* *(HRACecil)* 3-9-0 WRyan(1) (lw: led tl hdd over 1f out: kpt on one pce) ....½ 5
705a* Macoumba (USA) *(106)* *(MmeCHead,France)* 3-9-0 FHead(10) (leggy: lt-f: bhd: effrt, hmpd & snatched up over 2f out: swtchd & r.o strly fnl f) 1½ 6
692[5] Gay Gallanta (USA) **(116)***(105)* *(MRStoute)* 3-9-0 WRSwinburn(11) (lw: hld up: effrt 2f out: sn rdn & outpcd) ....s.h 7
660* Myself **(115)***(103)* *(PWChapple-Hyam)* 3-9-0 JReid(14) (lw: b.hind: mid div: effrt 3f out: no real imp) 1 8
620[7] Bring on the Choir **(90)***(103)* *(RBoss)* 3-9-0 KDarley(4) (lw: prom over 6f: sn rdn & outpcd) ....s.h 9
692[3] Autumn Affair **(106)***(102)* *(CEBrittain)* 3-9-0 BDoyle(9) (hld up & bhd: hdwy 3f out: sn rdn: no imp) ....¾ 10
Queenfisher **(103)***(101)* *(RHannon)* 3-9-0 BRouse(3) (h.d.w: plld hrd: hld up: a bhd) ....½ 11
620[9] Menas Gold **(97)***(100)* *(SDow)* 3-9-0 TQuinn(5) (chsd ldrs over 5f) ....nk 12
620[4] Fleet Hill (IRE) **(102)***(97)* *(MRChannon)* 3-9-0 RHughes(12) (hld up in rr: effrt 3f out: sn outpcd) 1½ 13
692[4] All Time Great **(103)***(89)* *(LMCumani)* 3-9-0 JWeaver(7) (lw: a in rr) 4 14

3/1 Aqaarid (USA), **5/1** HARAYIR (USA) (7/2-11/2), Moonshell (IRE), **13/2** Macoumba (USA), **8/1** Epagris, Myself, **10/1** Gay Gallanta (USA), **16/1** Hoh Magic, **40/1** Autumn Affair, All Time Great, **100/1** Fleet Hill (IRE), **150/1** Bring on the Choir, Queenfisher, **200/1** Menas Gold, CSF £18.31 TOTE £8.10: £2.80 £2.00 £2.10 (£10.00) Trio £32.50 OWNER Mr Hamdan Al Maktoum (LAMBOURN) BRED Shadwell Farm Inc in USA 14 Rn
1m 36.72 (-0.28) SF: 71/68/67/63/62/59/58/56/56/55/54/53/50/42

934

R. L. DAVISON RATED STKS H'CAP (0-110) (4-Y.O+) (Class B)
£9,294.90 (£3,479.10: £1,702.05: £732.75: £328.88: £167.32)
6f (Rowley) Stalls: Centre GOING minus 0.37 sec per fur (F) 4-20 (4-22)

Master Planner (96)*(106)* *(CACyzer)* 6-8-11 KDarley(10) (a.p: led over 1f out: rdn & r.o wl) ....— 1
571[6] Alzianah **(92)***(101)* *(JDBethell)* 4-8-7 WCarson(11) (a.p: ev ch over 1f out: rdn & r.o strly nr fin) ....½ 2
659[6] Welsh Mist **(94)***(97)* *(RBoss)* 4-8-9 WRyan(1) (led tl rdn & hdd over 1f out: one pce) 2 3
659[3] Montendre **(106)***(109)* *(MMcCormack)* 8-9-7 JReid(4) (lw: hld up: hdwy over 1f out: nrst fin) .hd 4
611* Domulla **(92)***(92)*(Fav)*(RAkehurst)* 5-8-7 LDettori(7) (b.off fore: chsd ldrs: sn rdn along: kpt on fnl f: nt pce to chal) 1 5
700[4] Snipe Hall **(92)***(92)* *(TRWatson)* 4-8-7 DeanMcKeown(3) (b.hind: outpcd & bhd tl r.o appr fnl f) ....nk 6
719[6] Lord Olivier (IRE) **(95)***(95)* *(WJarvis)* 5-8-5 (5) NVarley(2) (chsd ldrs: effrt over 2f out: sn rdn: btn over 1f out) ....s.h 7
659[7] Double Blue **(104)***(100)*(Fav)*(MJohnston)* 6-9-5 JWeaver(8) (lw: w ldr over 3f: sn wknd) 1¼ 8
Pinkerton's Pal **(95)***(91)* *(CEBrittain)* 4-8-10 MRimmer(6) (lw: a in rr) ....s.h 9
693[11] Darren Boy (IRE) **(92)***(81)* *(PFICole)* 4-8-7 TQuinn(5) (a in rr) 2½ 10
LONG HANDICAP Domulla 8-5 Darren Boy (IRE) 8-5

9/2 Domulla, Double Blue, **11/2** Montendre, **15/2** Alzianah, Welsh Mist, **9/1** MASTER PLANNER, Lord Olivier (IRE), **10/1** Snipe Hall (7/1-12/1), **12/1** Darren Boy (IRE), **16/1** Pinkerton's Pal, CSF £67.93 CT £484.20 TOTE £12.00: £3.00 £2.00 £2.50 (£63.00) Trio £118.30 OWNER Mr R. M. Cyzer (HORSHAM) BRED C. A. Cyzer 10 Rn 1m 10.73 (-0.57) SF: 73/68/64/76/59/59/62/67/58/48

935

SUNDAY EXPRESS BEST FOR SPORT SERIES (QUALIFIER) H'CAP (0-80) (3-Y.O+) (Class D) £5,832.50 (£1,760.00: £855.00: £402.50)
1m 2f (Rowley) Stalls: Centre GOING minus 0.37 sec per fur (F) 4-50 (4-54)

445[2] **Herr Trigger (53)***(66)* *(DrJDScargill)* 4-8-1b MFenton(2) (a.p: led 2f out tl ins fnl f: rallied u.p to ld cl home) ....— 1
Sovereign Page (USA) **(75)***(88)* *(BHanbury)* 6-9-9 RHughes(10) (b: hld up: hdwy over 2f out: led ins fnl f: hdd & no ex nr fin) ....hd 2
Access Adventurer (IRE) **(66)***(74)* *(RBoss)* 4-9-0 WRyan(9) (led over 7f out to 3f out: kpt on u.p fnl f) 3 3
550[2] Superluminal **(72)***(78)* *(GRimmer)* 4-9-6 MRimmer(7) (lw: chsd ldrs: hrd drvn over 2f out: styd on) 1¼ 4

El Bailador (IRE) **(60)**_(66) (JDBethell)_ 4-8-8 RHills(11) (hdwy 3f out: rdn & kpt on ins fnl f)....nk 5

668[3] Sharp Falcon (IRE) **(71)**_(77)_(Fav)_(JWharton)_ 4-9-5 JReid(3) (bhd: hdwy 2f out: rdn & r.o ins fnl f)....s.h 6

634[8] No Speeches (IRE) **(60)**_(65) (CACyzer)_ 4-8-8 TQuinn(17) (hdwy over 2f out: nt trbld ldrs)....nk 7

623[4] Chatham Island **(65)**_(68) (CEBrittain)_ 7-8-13 BDoyle(15) (chsd ldrs: one pce fnl 2f)....1½ 8

851[3] Silktail (IRE) **(61)**_(62) (JohnBerry)_ 3-7-7 NKennedy(1) (a.p: led 3f out to 2f out: wknd appr fnl f)....1¼ 9

_414_[2] Tu Opes **(68)**_(65) (JLHarris)_ 4-9-2 DaleGibson(6) (bhd tl styd on fnl 2f: nvr nrr)....2 10

668[16] Silver Hunter (USA) **(75)**_(70) (GCBravery)_ 4-9-9 MHills(13) (led over 2f: wknd 3f out)....1½ 11

Rival Bid (USA) **(66)**_(61) (MAJarvis)_ 7-9-0 LDettori(5) (nvr bttr than mid div)....nk 12

744[4] Shabanaz **(65)**_(56) (WRMuir)_ 10-8-13 JWeaver(8) (a in rr)....2 13

764[18] Elpida (USA) **(62)**_(52) (JPearce)_ 3-7-8 GBardwell(19) (a in rr)....¾ 14

749[5] Safey Ana (USA) **(68)**_(57) (BHanbury)_ 4-9-2 KDarley(14) (b: b.hind: prom over 7f)....½ 15

668[17] Kaafih Homm (IRE) **(62)**_(48) (NACallaghan)_ 4-8-10 BThomson(20) (b.hind: hld up: in tch tl lost pl 2f out)....2 16

738[14] Ayunli **(57)**_(37) (SCWilliams)_ 4-8-2 (3) DWright(4) (prom 6f)....4 17

Eben Al Habeeb (IRE) **(80)**_(57) (MajorWRHern)_ 4-10-0 WCarson(16) (chsd ldrs over 6f: sn lost tch)....2 18

Lowawatha **(72)**_(9) (DMorris)_ 7-9-6 RPrice(18) (bkwd: hdwy ½-wy: rdn over 3f out: sn wknd: t.o)....25 19

756[6] College Night (IRE) **(74)** _(JohnBerry)_ 3-8-6 CDwyer(12) (prom over 6f: wknd qckly: t.o: p.u over 1f out).... P

LONG HANDICAP Silktail (IRE) 7-5

9/2 Sharp Falcon (IRE), **15/2** Chatham Island, Superluminal, **10/1** Eben Al Habeeb (IRE) (14/1-8/1), Rival Bid (USA), Silktail (IRE), **12/1** HERR TRIGGER, **14/1** Safey Ana (USA) (10/1-16/1), No Speeches (IRE) (10/1-16/1), **16/1** Tu Opes, Lowawatha, Shabanaz, Elpida (USA), **20/1** College Night (IRE), Kaafih Homm (IRE), Sovereign Page (USA), **25/1** El Bailador (IRE), Silver Hunter (USA), Access Adventurer (IRE), Ayunli, CSF £225.32 CT £5,262.37 TOTE £14.00: £2.60 £6.60 £7.60 £2.50 (£547.60) Trio: Not won; £2,395.04 to Newcastle 8/5/95 OWNER The Inn Crowd (NEWMARKET) BRED Johnathan Crisp 20 Rn

2m 2.35 (-0.25) SF: 58/80/66/70/58/69/57/60/38/57/62/53/48/28/49/40/29/49/1/-

WEIGHT FOR AGE 3yo-16lb

936

MADAGANS COMPANY SERVICES MAIDEN STKS (3-Y.O) (Class D) £5,085.00 (£1,530.00: £740.00: £345.00)
1m (Rowley) Stalls: Centre GOING minus 0.37 sec per fur (F) 5-25 (5-27)

715[2] **Abu Simbel (USA)** _(89+)_(Fav)_(JHMGosden)_ 3-9-0 LDettori(1) (lw: b.hind: mde most: qcknd clr 3f out: unchal)....— 1

Triquetti (IRE) _(87) (LMCumani)_ 3-9-0 JWeaver(4) (w'like: scope: dwlt: hdwy over 2f out: kpt on fnl f: no ch w wnr)....1¼ 2

Jandeel (IRE) _(84) (ACStewart)_ 3-9-0 MJKinane(6) (gd sort: b.hind: a.p: rdn whn pce qcknd 3f out: styd on)....1¼ 3

637[2] Banadam (USA) _(81) (BHanbury)_ 3-9-0 WRyan(2) (lw: b.hind: hld up & bhd: rdn over 2f out: no imp)....1½ 4

730[8] Nero Kris _(71) (PAKelleway)_ 3-9-0 MWigham(5) (chsd wnr: rdn over 3f out: sn lost tch)....5 5

6/4 ABU SIMBEL (USA), **5/2** Jandeel (IRE), **10/3** Banadam (USA), **6/1** Triquetti (IRE), **33/1** Nero Kris, CSF £9.27 TOTE £2.20: £1.30 £2.00 (£4.60) OWNER Sheikh Mohammed (NEWMARKET) BRED Eaglestone Farm Inc 5 Rn 1m 38.92 (1.92) SF: 48/46/43/40/30

T/Jkpt: Not won; £9,754.38 to Newcastle 8/5/95. T/Plpt: £476.40 (82.55 Tckts). T/Qdpt: £353.80 (2.1 Tckts). IM

0881-SALISBURY (R-H)
Sunday May 7th (Good to firm, Firm patches)

Race 2: Flip start & hand-timed
WEATHER: sunny WIND: slt against

937

WOODFORD MAIDEN STKS (3-Y.O) (Class D) £4,370.00 (£1,310.00: £630.00: £290.00) **6f** Stalls: High GOING minus 0.49 sec per fur (F) 2-15 (2.-18)

547[7] **Christmas Kiss (82)**_(85) (RHannon)_ 3-8-2 (7) DaneO'Neill(4) (a.p: led wl over 1f out: r.o wl)....— 1

637[3] Silver Sting **(80)***(82) (IABalding)* 3-9-0 RCochrane(3) (led over 4f: nt qckn ins fnl f) 3 **2**
Dark Menace **(52)***(77) (SMellor)* 3-9-0 TSprake(14) (hdwy fnl 2f: r.o) 1¾ **3**
677[4] Samwar **(85)***(74)*(Fav)*(BWHills)* 3-9-0 DHolland(7) (hld up & bhd: hdwy over 3f out: ev ch over 1f out: wknd fnl f) 1¼ **4**
752[2] Intiaash (IRE) *(62) (PTWalwyn)* 3-8-9 DHarrison(5) (a.p: rdn & ev ch over 2f out: wknd over 1f out) 2½ **5**
715[8] Dawsha (IRE) *(62) (SDow)* 3-8-2 (7) ADaly(15) (bhd tl hdwy over 1f out: nvr nrr) ....s.h **6**
With Intent *(58) (CJames)* 3-9-0 AMcGlone(1) (unf: prom over 3f) 3½ **7**
Bella Coola *(50) (CAHorgan)* 3-8-9 AClark(13) (n.d) 1 **8**
658[12] Mousehole *(51) (RGuest)* 3-9-0 GHind(11) (lw: bhd fnl 3f) 1¾ **9**
670[9] Raayaat (USA) *(50) (ACStewart)* 3-9-0 SWhitworth(6) (lw: s.i.s: a bhd) ....nk **10**
695[18] Pacific Overture *(44) (CRBarwell)* 3-8-9 JWilliams(8) (bhd fnl 2f) ....nk **11**
730[6] Zuno Flyer (USA) *(44) (GLewis)* 3-8-9 (5) AWhelan(2) (a bhd) 1¾ **12**
Vaporize *(31) (DMHyde)* 3-9-0 WNewnes(12) (unf: scope: dwlt: a bhd) 5 **13**
742[10] Logie Pert Lad **(30)***(28) (JJBridger)* 3-8-11 (3) SSanders(9) (lw: prom over 3f) 1¼ **14**
Silver Academy (IRE) *(24) (MissGayKelleway)* 3-9-0 GDuffield(10) (dwlt: a bhd) 1¼ **15**

7/4 Samwar, **4/1** Silver Sting, Intiaash (IRE), **8/1** CHRISTMAS KISS, **12/1** Raayaat (USA) (op 7/1), **20/1** Dawsha (IRE), **25/1** Zuno Flyer (USA), **33/1** Bella Coola, Silver Academy (IRE), **50/1** With Intent, Dark Menace, Vaporize, Mousehole, **66/1** Pacific Overture, **100/1** Logie Pert Lad, CSF £36.62 TOTE £9.20; £2.10 £1.90 £7.00 (£13.20) Trio £286.10. £161.20 to Newcastle 8/5/95 OWNER Mr Peter Pritchard (MARLBOROUGH) BRED Tarworth Bloodstock Investments Ltd 15 Rn
1m 15.09 (2.79) SF: 16/13/8/5/-/-/-/-/-/-/-/-/-/-/-

938

SMITH & WILLIAMSON H'CAP (0-90) (4-Y.O+) (Class C) £5,995.00 (£1,810.00: £880.00: £415.00) **1m 6f** GOING minus 0.49 sec per fur (F) 2-50 (2.-51)

632[3] **Blaze Away (USA) (79)***(92) (IABalding)* 4-9-5 RCochrane(4) (lw: swtg: hld up: stdy hdwy over 4f out: chal over 1f out: r.o to ld last 50y) ....— **1**
668[4] Pride of May (IRE) **(63)***(76) (RHannon)* 4-8-3b DHolland(11) (led: rdn over 2f out: hdd last 50y: r.o) ....nk **2**
737[5] Wings Cove **(74)***(87) (LadyHerries)* 5-8-8 (7) JO'Dwyer(1) (a.p: ev ch fnl f: r.o) ....s.h **3**
763[5] Shadow Leader **(76)***(87) (MissAJWhitfield)* 4-9-2 DHarrison(2) (lw: hld up: hdwy over 4f out: nt clr run over 2f out & over 1f out: nt qckn) 1¾ **4**
795[3] Lalindi (IRE) **(70)***(74) (DRCElsworth)* 4-8-10 JWilliams(6) (prom tl wknd wl over 1f out) 6 **5**
737[7] La Spezia **(57)***(58) (MBlanshard)* 5-7-12 ow1 StephenDavies(7) (swtg: hld up & bhd: hdwy 4f out: wknd over 1f out) 1¾ **6**
Iron Gent (USA) **(77)***(77) (PJHobbs)* 4-9-3 AMcGlone(3) (chsd ldrs tl wknd over 2f out) 1¼ **7**
Tamarpour (USA) **(63)***(63) (MCPipe)* 8-8-4 TSprake(5) (a bhd) ....nk **8**
795[9] Chief's Song **(65)***(65) (SDow)* 5-7-13 (7) ADaly(13) (lw: bhd fnl 4f) ....hd **9**
584* Mokhtar (IRE) **(84)***(83)*(Fav)*(JLDunlop)* 4-9-10 GDuffield(9) (lw: hld up: stdy hdwy over 4f out: wknd over 2f out) ....¾ **10**
795[11] High Five (IRE) **(54)***(47) (DAWilson)* 5-7-9 JQuinn(10) (lw: a bhd) 5 **11**
152[7] Jonjas Chudleigh **(70)***(53) (WGMTurner)* 8-8-6 (5) SDrowne(12) (prom: rdn & wknd over 5f out: t.o) 9 **12**
668[8] Walsham Whisper (IRE) **(75)***(50) (JWharton)* 4-9-1 AClark(8) (lw: a bhd: t.o) 7 **13**

9/2 Mokhtar (IRE), **5/1** BLAZE AWAY (USA), **6/1** Lalindi (IRE), **7/1** Wings Cove, **8/1** Shadow Leader, **9/1** Pride of May (IRE), **12/1** Walsham Whisper (IRE), **14/1** Chief's Song, Iron Gent (USA), **16/1** Tamarpour (USA), La Spezia, **20/1** High Five (IRE), **33/1** Jonjas Chudleigh, CSF £46.61 CT £292.34 TOTE £5.80: £1.80 £2.40 £2.80 (£15.30) Trio £74.40 OWNER Mr Paul Mellon (KINGSCLERE) BRED Paul Mellon 13 Rn 3m 1.2 (3.00) SF: 48/32/44/43/30/15/33/20/22/39/4/10/6
WEIGHT FOR AGE 4yo-1lb

939

GIBBS-MEW RATED STKS H'CAP (0-100) (3-Y.O) (Class B) £8,030.50 (£2,999.50: £1,462.25: £623.75: £274.38: £134.62) **6f** Stalls: High GOING minus 0.49 sec per fur (F) 3-25 (3.-27)

621[9] **Bold Effort (FR) (81)***(88) (KOCunningham-Brown)* 3-7-6 (5) MBaird(8) (mde virtually all: r.o wl) ....— **1**
585* Hakiki (IRE) **(86)***(86) (PTWalwyn)* 3-8-2 DHolland(2) (w wnr: ev ch over 1f out: nt qckn) 2½ **2**
681[2] Kabil **(87)***(78)*(Fav)*(HThomsonJones)* 3-8-3 NCarlisle(7) (lw: bhd tl hdwy & nt clr run 2f out: r.o one pce fnl f) 3½ **3**
Ffynone (IRE) **(88)***(69) (RHannon)* 3-8-4 ow1 RCochrane(10) (a.p: no hdwy fnl 2f) 3½ **4**
667[12] The Jotter **(98)***(76) (WJarvis)* 3-9-0 AMcGlone(5) (rdn over 2f out: no hdwy) 1¼ **5**
694[14] Sylvandra **(89)***(65) (PGMurphy)* 3-8-5 ow1 JWilliams(6) (nvr nrr) ....½ **6**

Bajan Rose **(89)***(57) (MBlanshard)* 3-8-5 StephenDavies(9) (prom: hrd rdn 2f out: sn wknd) 3½ 7
621[4] Star Tulip **(91)***(52) (JLDunlop)* 3-8-7 GDuffield(1) (lw: stmbld s: sn rcvrd: rdn over 2f out: wkng whn hung rt over 1f out) 2½ 8
Jibereen **(96)***(46) (GLewis)* 3-8-12 SWhitworth(3) (bkwd: a bhd) 4 9
618[7] Duffertoes **(86)***(28) (MJRyan)* 3-8-2 ow5 AClark(4) (prom over 3f) 1¼ 10

LONG HANDICAP Bold Effort (FR) 7-4

7/2 Kabil, **9/2** Hakiki (IRE) (op 3/1), Star Tulip, **7/1** Ffynone (IRE), **8/1** The Jotter, **10/1** Bajan Rose, Jibereen, Duffertoes, **20/1** BOLD EFFORT (FR), **25/1** Sylvandra, CSF £100.01 CT £361.15 TOTE £20.10: £3.20 £1.10 £2.50 (£54.50) Trio £122.00 OWNER Mr A. J. Richards (STOCKBRIDGE) BRED Ewar Stud Farm 10 Rn 1m 13.26 (0.96) SF: 29/27/19/10/17/6/-/-/-/-

940

SALISBURY STKS (2-Y.O) (Class C) £4,735.00 (£1,765.00: £857.50: £362.50: £156.25: £73.75)
5f Stalls: High GOING minus 0.49 sec per fur (F) 4-00 (4.-04)

436[2] **Ortolan** *(98+) (RHannon)* 2-8-4 (7) DaneO'Neill(6) (chsd ldr: led over 1f out: rdn out) ....— 1
781* Passion For Life *(85)*(Fav)*(GLewis)* 2-9-0 SWhitworth(3) (led over 3f: one pce) 5 2
725* Satellite Star (IRE) *(66) (MRChannon)* 2-8-6 CRutter(2) (prom: rdn over 2f out: wknd over 1f out) 3½ 3
Castan (IRE) *(67) (JLDunlop)* 2-8-8 GDuffield(1) (w'like: nvr nr to chal) ....nk 4
Rumba Rhythm (CAN) *(56) (JWHills)* 2-8-3 DHolland(4) (w'like: no hdwy fnl 2f) 1¾ 5
Al's Alibi *(42) (WRMuir)* 2-8-8 DHarrison(5) (w'like: rdn over 2f out: sn bhd) 6 6

Evens Passion For Life, **4/1** ORTOLAN, **11/2** Rumba Rhythm (CAN), **6/1** Satellite Star (IRE), **7/1** Castan (IRE) (op 4/1), **14/1** Al's Alibi (op 8/1), CSF £8.70 TOTE £6.50: £2.90 £1.10 (£2.90) OWNER Mr J. A. Lazzari (MARLBOROUGH) BRED Filletts Farm Stud 6 Rn
60.77 secs (0.77) SF: 42/29/10/11/-/-

941

WILTON H'CAP (0-100) (3-Y.O) (Class C) £5,507.50 (£1,660.00: £805.00: £377.50)
1m 1f 209y Stalls: High GOING minus 0.49 sec per fur (F) 4-35 (4-37)

630[4] **Francfurter (74)***(80)*(Fav)*(RCharlton)* 3-8-2 TSprake(3) (hld up: swtchd lft & hdwy over 2f out: rdn to ld last strides) ....— 1
618[2] At Liberty (IRE) **(80)***(86) (RHannon)* 3-8-1 (7) DaneO'Neill(6) (hld up: hdwy 2f out: led over 1f out: hdd last strides) ....s.h 2
673* Al Safeer (IRE) **(83)***(88) (JWHills)* 3-8-11 DHolland(4) (chsd ldr: led over 3f out tl over 1f out: hrd rdn: r.o wl) ....¾ 3
647[9] Silently **(76)***(72) (IABalding)* 3-8-4 ow1 RCochrane(5) (lw: led: rdn 5f out: hdd over 3f out: wknd fnl f) 5 4
675* Beauchamp Jazz **(93)***(83) (JLDunlop)* 3-9-7 GDuffield(2) (hld up & plld hrd: hdwy over 2f out: wknd over 1f out) 4 5
764[8] Braydon Forest **(73)***(57) (CJDrewe)* 3-8-1 NCarlisle(1) (lw: rdn over 4f out: a bhd) 4 6
614[5] New Century (USA) **(90)***(68) (HRACecil)* 3-9-4 AMcGlone(7) (plld hrd: prom: ev ch 2f out: sn wknd) 3½ 7

7/4 FRANCFURTER, **100/30** New Century (USA), **5/1** Beauchamp Jazz, **6/1** At Liberty (IRE), **13/2** Silently, **9/1** Al Safeer (IRE), **20/1** Braydon Forest, CSF £12.39 TOTE £3.00: £2.10 £2.20 (£11.80) OWNER Cliveden Stud (BECKHAMPTON) BRED Cliveden Stud Ltd 7 Rn
2m 7.87 (3.17) SF: 23/29/31/15/26/-/11

942

WINCANTON MAIDEN STKS (3-Y.O) (Class D) £4,337.50 (£1,300.00: £625.00: £287.50) **1m 4f** Stalls: High GOING minus 0.49 sec per fur (F) 5-10 (5.-14)

635[2] **Istidaad (USA) (105)***(88)*(Fav)*(ACStewart)* 3-9-0 SWhitworth(8) (plld hrd: a.p: chsd ldr over 6f out: led over 2f out: all out) ....— 1
Pedraza *(88) (HRACecil)* 3-9-0 AMcGlone(7) (led: clr 7f out: hdd over 2f out: hrd rdn fnl f: r.o wl) ....nk 2
691[5] Cypress Avenue (IRE) *(82) (RHannon)* 3-9-0 DHolland(6) (rdn & hdwy over 4f out: swtchd lft over 2f out: r.o one pce) 4 3
Rosie Sweetheart (IRE) *(67) (HRACecil)* 3-8-9 WNewnes(2) (bit bkwd: plld hrd: prom tl wknd 3f out) 8 4
715[12] High Commotion (IRE) *(67) (DRCElsworth)* 3-8-9 JWilliams(5) (prom tl wknd over 2f out) ....s.h 5
National Grid *(65) (RJRWilliams)* 3-9-0 GDuffield(10) (nvr nr ldrs) 5 6
Hanifa *(60) (MissGayKelleway)* 3-8-9 StephenDavies(11) (unf: rdn over 3f out: sn bhd) ....nk 7
Niknaks Nephew *(64) (MissAJWhitfield)* 3-9-0 DHarrison(12) (lt-f: unf: a bhd) ....nk 8

854[10] Harding Brown (USA) *(61) (GHarwood)* 3-9-0 AClark(13) (bit bkwd: chsd ldr 6f: wknd 3f out)....2½ **9**
Kyrenia Times *(51) (PMitchell)* 3-8-11 (3) SSanders(9) (leggy: s.s: a bhd: t.o fnl 6f)....7 **10**
Barnaby Willow **(50)***(45) (MJRyan)* 3-8-9 (5) MBaird(4) (a.p: t.o fnl 6f)....5 **11**
764[13] Pending *(IABalding)* 3-9-0 RCochrane(1) (lw: bhd tl p.u 7f out: lame).... **P**

8/11 ISTIDAAD (USA), **11/2** Pedraza, **6/1** Cypress Avenue (IRE) (4/1-7/1), **8/1** Pending, **9/1** Rosie Sweetheart (IRE), **14/1** High Commotion (IRE), **33/1** National Grid, Harding Brown (USA), **40/1** Hanifa, **50/1** Kyrenia Times, **66/1** Niknaks Nephew, Barnaby Willow, CSF £6.15 TOTE £1.60: £1.10 £2.30 £2.00 (£4.90) Trio £9.20 OWNER Mr Hamdan Al Maktoum(NEWMARKET) BRED Shadwell Farm Inc and Shadwell Estate Co Ltd 12 Rn 2m 34.03 (1.43) SF: 51/51/45/30/30/28/23/27/24/14/8

T/Plpt: £59.40 (228.45 Tckts). T/Qdpt: £11.10 (18.60 Tckts). KH

0436-DONCASTER (L-H)
Monday May 8th (Good to firm)
WEATHER: overcast WIND: mod across

943
WISETON MAIDEN AUCTION STKS (2-Y.O) (Class E) £3,582.00 (£1,071.00: £513.00: £234.00)
5f Stalls: High GOING minus 0.18 sec per fur (GF) 2-20 (2-21)

760[5] **Eastern Prophets** *(64)*(Fav)*(GLewis)* 2-8-4 WCarson(8) (a cl up: chal 1½f out: rdn to ld nr fin)....— **1**
Erupt *(63) (GBBalding)* 2-8-5 ow1 JWilliams(1) (lengthy: unf: s.i.s: gd hdwy ½-wy: led 1½f out: r.o: jst ct)....nk **2**
819[8] Veshca Lady (IRE) *(39) (EWeymes)* 2-7-10 TWilliams(10) (outpcd tl hdwy over 1f out: r.o)....5 **3**
Bearnaise (IRE) *(38) (RHannon)* 2-7-10 JQuinn(2) (small: str: bit bkwd: chsd ldrs: led 2f out: hung rt: sn hdd & btn)....nk **4**
Napoleon's Return *(43) (AGFoster)* 2-8-1 GHind(5) (cmpt: chsd ldrs: chal 2f out: btn appr fnl f)....hd **5**
Imprimis (IRE) *(28) (CNAllen)* 2-7-3 (7) KarenMarkham(4) (small: lt-f: s.i.s: nrst fin)....3 **6**
699[3] Patrington Park *(33) (MWEasterby)* 2-8-1 LCharnock(9) (cl up: wandered u.p fnl 2f: wknd)....s.h **7**
Brockville Bairn *(31) (MrsASwinbank)* 2-8-1 JMarshall(7) (leggy: scope: dwlt: n.d)....½ **8**
Mels Baby (IRE) *(30) (JLEyre)* 2-8-1 RLappin(12) (leggy: lt-f: spd 3f: btn whn hmpd 1f out)....½ **9**
650[9] Swifty Nifty (IRE) *(17) (JBerry)* 2-8-0 ow1 BDoyle(6) (led 3f: hung lft & hmpd: sn wknd)....3½ **10**
Down The Yard *(MCChapman)* 2-7-7 (3) DWright(3) (w'like: bkwd: s.s: a bhd)....5 **11**
Double Vintage (IRE) *(MCChapman)* 2-7-11 (7) CMunday(11) (bkwd: s.s: a t.o)....30 **12**

7/4 EASTERN PROPHETS (5/2-13/8), **9/2** Bearnaise (IRE), **5/1** Erupt, **11/2** Patrington Park, **7/1** Swifty Nifty (IRE), **16/1** Napoleon's Return, Mels Baby (IRE), Veshca Lady (IRE), **20/1** Imprimis (IRE), **33/1** Brockville Bairn, Down The Yard, Double Vintage (IRE), CSF £11.90 TOTE £2.00: £1.40 £2.40 £4.40 (£8.70) Trio £174.50 OWNER Mrs J. M. Purches (EPSOM) BRED Miss K. Zavon 12 Rn 61.58 secs (3.18) SF: 20/19/-/-/-/-/-/-/-/-/-/-
STEWARDS' ENQUIRY J.Quinn suspended 17-20/5/95 (careless riding).

944
BAWTRY CLAIMING STKS (4-Y.O+) (Class E) £3,260.25 (£972.00: £463.50: £209.25) **5f** Stalls: High GOING minus 0.18 sec per fur (GF) 2-50 (2-51)

723[14] **Fangio (78)***(86) (WGMTurner)* 6-8-7 (5) PMcCabe(5) (mde all: hng lft: clr over 1f out: styd on)— **1**
723[8] King Rambo **(61)***(79) (RHollinshead)* 4-9-0 WRyan(3) (sn bhd: hdwy over 1f out: fin wl)....2½ **2**
693[12] Lord High Admiral (CAN) **(92)***(71)*(Fav)*(MJHeaton-Ellis)* 7-9-0 GDuffield(2) (lw: hung lft: cl up tl hmpd & swtchd ½-wy: rdn & no imp after)....2½ **3**
746[6] Sigama (USA) **(56)***(53) (DNicholls)* 9-8-2 JQuinn(1) (cl up 3f: grad wknd)....1¾ **4**
188[6] Another Episode (IRE) **(79)***(53) (JBerry)* 6-9-4 DeanMcKeown(4) (dwlt: a wl bhd)....5 **5**

Evens Lord High Admiral (CAN), **5/2** FANGIO, **6/1** Another Episode (IRE), **7/1** Sigama (USA), **12/1** King Rambo, CSF £22.68 TOTE £3.80: £2.20 £3.60 (£26.00) OWNER Mr Malcolm Heygate-Browne (SHERBORNE) BRED Melbury Park Stud 5 Rn 61.13 secs (2.73) SF: 35/29/21/3/3
STEWARDS' ENQUIRY McCabe suspended 17/5/95 (excessive use of whip).

945
CARR HILL STKS (3-Y.O) (Class C) £5,673.60 (£1,961.60: £940.80: £384.00)
1m (round) Stalls: High GOING minus 0.36 sec per fur (F) 3-20 (3-20)

667[6] **Sonic Boy (108)***(104) (RFJohnsonHoughton)* 3-9-2 JQuinn(3) (mde all: hld on gamely)....— **1**

715* Lyrikos (USA) *(103)*(Fav)*(HRACecil)* 3-9-2 WRyan(2) (lw: b.nr fore: hld up: effrt over 2f out: ev ch ins fnl f: kpt on) ....nk **2**
792³ Stiletto Blade **(103)***(100)* *(IABalding)* 3-9-4 RCochrane(4) (cl up: hrd rdn & outpcd over 1f out: styd on towards fin) 2½ **3**
Muhab (USA) **(108)***(102)* *(PTWalwyn)* 3-9-6 WCarson(1) (trckd ldrs: hdwy to chal over 1f out: eased whn btn wl ins fnl f) ....nk **4**

5/4 Lyrikos (USA), **100/30** SONIC BOY, **7/2** Muhab (USA), **5/1** Stiletto Blade, CSF £7.29 TOTE £5.10: (£3.30) OWNER Mr Anthony Pye-Jeary (DIDCOT) BRED E. R. W. Stanley and New England Stud Farm Ltd 4 Rn 1m 40.96 (4.66) SF: 23/22/19/21

STEWARDS' ENQUIRY Carson suspended 17-19/5/95 (failing to secure best possible place).

946 V.E. ANNIVERSARY HOLIDAY H'CAP (0-90) (3-Y.O+) (Class C) £5,952.00 (£1,776.00: £848.00: £384.00)

1m (round) Stalls: High GOING minus 0.36 sec per fur (F) 3-55 (3-55)

Billy Bushwacker (82)*(91+)*(Fav)*(MrsMReveley)* 4-9-10 RCochrane(5) (h.d.w: hld up: nt clr run 2f out: eased & swtchd: str run to ld wl ins fnl f) ....— **1**
662⁹ Fame Again **(73)***(79)* *(MrsJRRamsden)* 3-8-2 BDoyle(6) (hld up: led over 2f out: sn qcknd clr: hdd wl ins fnl f: r.o) 1¾ **2**
864⁸ Midnight Jazz (IRE) **(77)***(73)* *(WAO'Gorman)* 5-9-5 EmmaO'Gorman(1) (lw: trckd ldrs: n.m.r 2f out tl over 1f out: r.o) 5 **3**
848* Arndilly **(72)***(65)* *(BJMeehan)* 4-9-0b 5x KFallon(3) (lw: in tch: rdn 3f out: hdwy over 1f out: one pce fnl f) 1¼ **4**
728⁵ Dom Pennion **(66)***(57)* *(RGuest)* 4-8-8 GHind(2) (in tch: effrt over 2f out: btn over 1f out) 1 **5**
Dalu (IRE) **(67)***(53)* *(MJCamacho)* 4-8-9 LCharnock(4) (led after 1f tl hdd over 2f out: sn outpcd) 2½ **6**
Astral Weeks (IRE) **(80)***(52)* *(RHannon)* 4-9-8 WRyan(7) (led 1f: cl up tl wknd wl over 1f out) 7 **7**

7/2 BILLY BUSHWACKER, **5/1** Fame Again, Dom Pennion, **11/2** Midnight Jazz (IRE), **6/1** Arndilly, **7/1** Dalu (IRE), Astral Weeks (IRE), CSF £18.83 TOTE £3.00: £2.10 £2.60 (£8.90) OWNER Mr T. S. Child (SALTBURN) BRED Trevor S. Child 7 Rn 1m 41.2 (4.90) SF: 28/3/10/2/-/-/-

WEIGHT FOR AGE 3yo-13lb

947 INTAKE H'CAP (0-80) (3-Y.O) (Class D) £4,002.70 (£1,195.60: £571.80: £259.90)

1m 6f 132y Stalls: Low GOING minus 0.36 sec per fur (F) 4-25 (4-28)

655⁶ **Doddington Flyer (62)***(68)* *(RHollinshead)* 3-7-13 (5) AGarth(10) (hld up: hdwy to ld 2f out: hung lft: r.o) ....— **1**
851⁷ Euro Forum **(55)***(59)* *(GLMoore)* 3-7-4 (7) MartinDwyer(2) (hld up & bhd: hdwy on ins whn nt clr run over 2f out: swtchd over 1f out: r.o wl) 2 **2**
816⁶ Chahaya Timor (IRE) **(69)***(70)* *(PFICole)* 3-8-11 RCochrane(5) (mid div: hdwy & ev ch over 2f out: nt qckn) 2½ **3**
857⁸ Greycoat Boy **(62)***(60)* *(BJMeehan)* 3-8-4 ow2 KFallon(12) (in tch: hdwy appr st: chsng ldrs 2f out: r.o one pce) ....¾ **4**
655* Toy Princess (USA) **(72)***(72)* *(CEBrittain)* 3-9-0 BDoyle(9) (cl up: led 3f out to 2f out: one pce) ....s.h **5**
786³ Bark'n'bite **(51)***(46)* *(MrsMReveley)* 3-7-7 LCharnock(7) (chsd ldrs: rdn & one pce fnl 3f) 5 **6**
626³ Mr Mactavish **(74)***(68)* *(MrsJCecil)* 3-9-2 GDuffield(1) (cl up tl wknd fnl 2f) ....nk **7**
787⁴ Blue Smoke (IRE) **(64)***(58)* *(BAMcMahon)* 3-8-6 DeanMcKeown(8) (hld up & bhd: nvr nr to chal) ....nk **8**
575* Slapy Dam **(53)***(45)*(Fav)*(MrsJRRamsden)* 3-7-9 ow1 JQuinn(3) (lw: hld up & bhd: effrt 3f out: n.d) 1¼ **9**
537⁴ Maysann **(59)***(51)* *(JLDunlop)* 3-8-1b WCarson(4) (trckd ldrs: effrt 3f out: n.m.r & eased) 1 **10**
525² Al Corniche (IRE) **(54)***(39)* *(KOCunningham-Brown)* 3-7-7 (3)ow3 DWright(6) (led tl hdd 3f out: wknd) 3½ **11**
*376** Warluskee **(79)***(45)* *(MJohnston)* 3-9-7 WRyan(11) (rdn & lost tch over 4f out) 20 **12**

LONG HANDICAP Al Corniche (IRE) 7-2

4/1 Slapy Dam, **11/2** Toy Princess (USA), **6/1** Maysann, Bark'n'bite, **7/1** Chahaya Timor (IRE), Warluskee, **9/1** Mr Mactavish, **10/1** DODDINGTON FLYER, **14/1** Euro Forum, **16/1** Blue Smoke (IRE), Al Corniche (IRE), **20/1** Greycoat Boy, CSF £134.92 CT £967.56 TOTE £14.40: £3.40 £6.40 £3.10 (£188.70) Trio £320.70 OWNER Mr J. F. Bower (UPPER LONGDON) BRED Worksop Manor Stud Farm 12 Rn 3m 9.52 (5.92) SF: 29/20/31/21/33/7/29/19/6/12/-/6

948
MAY DAY HOLIDAY LIMITED STKS (0-65) (3-Y.O) (Class F)
£3,158.00 (£944.00: £452.00: £206.00)
1m 2f 60y Stalls: Low GOING minus 0.36 sec per fur (F) 4-55 (4-57)

813[5] **Blaze of Song (63)***(67) (RHannon)* 3-8-11 WRyan(3) (trckd ldrs: hdwy to ld 1f out: hrd rdn & r.o gamely) — 1
647[6] Advance East **(64)***(67) (MrsJRRamsden)* 3-8-11 KFallon(6) (hld up: effrt over 3f out: hdwy to chal 1f out: r.o u.p: jst failed) s.h 2
Hydrofoil **(65)***(60) (BWHills)* 3-8-1 (5) JDSmith(4) (cl up: led over 3f out tl hdd 1f out: kpt on one pce) 1½ 3
844[3] Top Fella (USA) **(60)***(60) (WAO'Gorman)* 3-8-11b EmmaO'Gorman(2) (hld up: hdwy on ins 3f out: hmpd & swtchd 2f out: no imp) 3 4
689[4] Court Joker (IRE) **(65)***(60) (MHTompkins)* 3-8-11 PRobinson(7) (lw: hld up: effrt & nt clr run 3f out: one pce after) s.h 5
774* Dont Shoot Fairies **(69)***(54)*(Fav)*(CEBrittain)* 3-8-13 BDoyle(9) (lw: jnd ldrs 6f out: outpcd fnl 2f) 5 6
Tirolette (IRE) **(56)***(46) (RJRWilliams)* 3-8-6 RCochrane(5) (lw: smooth hdwy & prom 4f out: wknd fnl 2f) ½ 7
648[14] Dance of Joy **(62)***(35) (JLDunlop)* 3-8-6 WCarson(8) (led tl hdd over 3f out: wknd over 2f out) 7 8
748[13] Never Time (IRE) **(47)***(37) (MrsVAAconley)* 3-8-11 TWilliams(1) (bhd: effrt over 4f out: sn btn) 2 9

3/1 Dont Shoot Fairies, **7/2** Advance East (5/2-4/1), **4/1** Dance of Joy, BLAZE OF SONG, **6/1** Court Joker (IRE), **9/1** Hydrofoil, **12/1** Top Fella (USA), **16/1** Tirolette (IRE), **50/1** Never Time (IRE), CSF £19.16 TOTE £5.80: £1.60 £2.20 £3.10 (£11.90) Trio £66.10 OWNER Mr D. Boocock (MARLBOROUGH) BRED D. G. Mason 9 Rn 2m 11.84 (4.84) SF: 29/29/22/22/22/16/8/-/-

949
COAL MINER H'CAP (0-85) (3-Y.O+) (Class D) £3,984.75
(£1,188.00: £566.50: £255.75)
6f Stalls: High GOING minus 0.36 sec per fur (F) 5-25 (5-25)

812[13] **Captain Carat (59)***(66)*(Fav)*(MrsJRRamsden)* 4-8-4 KFallon(6) (lw: bhd: hdwy 2f out: r.o u.p to ld wl ins fnl f) — 1
345[3] Croft Pool **(74)***(80) (JAGlover)* 4-9-5 PRobinson(9) (hld up: qcknd to ld over 1f out: hdd wl ins fnl f: r.o) nk 2
790[2] Elle Shaped (IRE) **(66)***(64) (DNicholls)* 5-8-11 RCochrane(4) (led tl hdd over 1f out: no ex) 3 3
838[6] Sobering Thoughts **(66)***(60) (JLEyre)* 9-8-11 GDuffield(5) (b.hind: chsd ldrs tl rdn & btn over 1f out) 1½ 4
838* Castlerea Lad **(86)***(80)*(Fav)*(RHollinshead)* 6-10-3 7x WRyan(7) (lw: hld up & bhd: effrt over 2f out: nvr rch ldrs) s.h 5
812[5] Macs Maharanee **(75)***(68)*(Fav)*(PSFelgate)* 8-9-6 GHind(8) (lw: prom tl outpcd appr fnl f) nk 6
765[3] Napoleon Star (IRE) **(73)***(58)*(Fav)*(MSSaunders)* 4-9-4 DeanMcKeown(3) (in tch tl outpcd fnl 2f) 3 7
636[5] Bryan Robson (USA) **(68)***(52) (GBBalding)* 4-8-13 JWilliams(2) (in tch: effrt ½-wy: sn btn) ½ 8
583[6] Judgement Call **(51)***(24) (PHowling)* 8-7-10 JQuinn(1) (b: cl up 4f: sn lost pl) 4 9

5/1 CAPTAIN CARAT, Napoleon Star (IRE), Macs Maharanee, Castlerea Lad, **11/2** Bryan Robson (USA), **6/1** Croft Pool, **13/2** Sobering Thoughts, **10/1** Elle Shaped (IRE), **16/1** Judgement Call, CSF £34.52 CT £270.41 TOTE £6.60: £1.70 £1.90 £2.30 (£17.70) Trio £60.80 OWNER Mr Colin Webster (THIRSK) BRED Lt-Col J. H. Scott 9 Rn 1m 13.31 (2.31) SF: 41/55/39/35/55/43/33/27/-
OFFICIAL EXPLANATION Captain Carat: his improved running was put down to his preference for a flat track

T/Plpt: £4,310.70 (1.55 Tckts). T/Qdpt: Not won; £134.45 to Doncaster 9/5/95. AA

0610-HAYDOCK (L-H)
Monday May 8th (Good to firm)
WEATHER: dull WIND: fresh against

950
TAPSTER'S MOSS MAIDEN STKS (3-Y.O F) (Class D) £3,915.50
(£1,184.00: £577.00: £273.50)
1m 2f 120y Stalls: High GOING: nil sec per fur (G) 2-00 (2-05)

777[2] **Tillandsia (IRE)** *(86)*(Fav)*(DRLoder)* 3-8-11 JWeaver(7) (lw: mde all: qcknd clr 2f out: v.easily) — 1

Top Shop *(82) (HRACecil)* 3-8-11 AMcGlone(2) (w'like: leggy: bit bkwd: a.p: 3rd st: chsd wnr fnl 2f: no imp) 2½ 2
Hatta Breeze *(78) (MAJarvis)* 3-8-11 PRobinson(4) (chsd ldrs: 5th st: n.m.r over 2f out: kpt on fnl f) 3 3
Zuiena (USA) *(70) (PFICole)* 3-8-11 MFenton(6) (h.d.w: lost pl ½-wy: rdn over 3f out: styd on)5 4
Lavender (IRE) *(69) (LMCumani)* 3-8-8 (3) CHodgson(1) (w'like: scope: dwlt: bhd tl hdwy 3f out: nt rch ldrs) ....¾ 5
797[11] Ruby Venture *(67) (SPCWoods)* 3-8-11 WWoods(10) (bit bkwd: prom: 2nd st: wknd over 2f out) 1¼ 6
Nickitoto *(66) (JLDunlop)* 3-8-11 BThomson(3) (lt-f: unf: a in rr) ....¾ 7
779[3] Cyphell (IRE) *(64) (MRStoute)* 3-8-11 KBradshaw(9) (chsd ldrs: 6th st: wknd over 2f out) 1 8
Alaraby (IRE) *(64) (IABalding)* 3-8-11 WNewnes(5) (nt grwn: a in rr) ....½ 9
Autumn Wings (FR) *(61) (BWHills)* 3-8-11 MHills(8) (still unf: s.s: hdwy & 4th st: wknd over 2f out) 2 10

4/5 TILLANDSIA (IRE), **11/2** Top Shop (op 7/2), **7/1** Cyphell (IRE) (6/1-9/1), **10/1** Zuiena (USA), Autumn Wings (FR), **12/1** Nickitoto (8/1-14/1), **14/1** Alaraby (IRE), **16/1** Lavender (IRE), **25/1** Hatta Breeze, Ruby Venture, CSF £6.84 TOTE £1.60: £1.10 £1.50 £6.00 (£2.90) Trio £91.70 OWNER Sheikh Mohammed (NEWMARKET) BRED Sheikh Mohammed bin Rashid al Maktoum 10 Rn
2m 17.29 (5.79) SF: 52/48/44/36/35/33/32/30/30/27

951

E.B.F. GALLOWS HALL MAIDEN STKS (2-Y.O) (Class D) £4,065.00 (£1,230.00: £600.00: £285.00)
5f Stalls: High GOING: nil sec per fur (G) 2-30 (2-30)

Dovebrace *(98t?) (ABailey)* 2-9-0 MWigham(5) (leggy: s.s: bhd & nt clr run ½-wy: hdwy bel dist: rdn to ld wl ins fnl f) ....— 1
669[2] Hear The Music (IRE) *(87)*(Fav)*(BWHills)* 2-8-9 MHills(3) (hld up: hdwy 2f out: led ins fnl f: sn hdd: no ex) 2 2
Prince Aslia *(84) (MJohnston)* 2-9-0 JWeaver(6) (w'like: leggy: bit bkwd: a.p: led ½-wy tl hdd & wknd ins fnl f) 2½ 3
684[2] Scathebury *(61) (SPCWoods)* 2-9-0 WWoods(2) (lw: prom over 3f) 7 4
788[7] Albert The Bear *(60) (JBerry)* 2-9-0 JCarroll(1) (prom tl rdn & outpcd wl over 1f out) ....½ 5
716[4] Mono Lady (IRE) *(32) (DHaydnJones)* 2-8-9 AMackay(4) (led to ½-wy: wknd over 1f out: t.o) 7 6

4/7 Hear The Music (IRE), **4/1** Prince Aslia (3/1-9/2), **11/2** Scathebury, **12/1** Albert The Bear, **14/1** Mono Lady (IRE), **25/1** DOVEBRACE, CSF £41.03 TOTE £32.60: £5.10 £1.10 (£17.20) OWNER Mr David Jones (TARPORLEY) BRED Mrs M. Christian 6 Rn 62.45 secs (3.45) SF: 40/29/26/3/2/-

952

LODGE LANE STKS (3-Y.O) (Class C) £4,910.40 (£1,790.40: £875.20: £376.00: £168.00)
5f Stalls: High GOING: nil sec per fur (G) 3-00 (3-00)

Warning Star (102)*(101) (BWHills)* 3-9-3 MHills(4) (hld up: swtchd lft wl over 1f out: qcknd to ld ins fnl f: sn clr) ....— 1
612[4] Hinton Rock (IRE) **(99)***(90)*(Fav)*(MBell)* 3-9-0 MFenton(5) (lw: led: rdn over 1f out: hdd ins fnl f: one pce) 2½ 2
719[3] Don't Worry Me (IRE) **(100)***(91) (FHLee)* 3-9-3 PRobinson(3) (lw: stumbled s: sn prom: ev ch 1f out: rdn & unable qckn fnl f) ....¾ 3
823[W] Thick as Thieves **(72)***(88) (RonaldThompson)* 3-9-2 JWeaver(1) (lw: outpcd: a bhd) ....½ 4
Ginger Tree (USA) *(75) (PWChapple-Hyam)* 3-8-11 BThomson(2) (rangy: bit bkwd: spd 3f: sn rdn & wknd) 2½ 5

7/4 Hinton Rock (IRE), **10/3** Don't Worry Me (IRE), **7/2** WARNING STAR, **4/1** Ginger Tree (USA), **20/1** Thick as Thieves, CSF £9.12 TOTE £4.70: £2.00 £1.30 (£4.80) OWNER Mr Stephen Crown (LAMBOURN) BRED Snailwell Stud Co Ltd 5 Rn 62.45 secs (3.45) SF: 43/32/33/30/17
OFFICIAL EXPLANATION Ginger Tree(USA): was found to be distressed after the race

953

HAYDOCK PARK SPRING TROPHY H'CAP (0-110) (Listed) (3-Y.O+) (Class A) £12,045.20 (£4,506.80: £2,203.40: £947.00: £423.50: £214.10)
7f 30y Stalls: Low GOING: nil sec per fur (G) 3-30 (3-31)

814[8] **Moccasin Run (USA) (100)***(106) (IABalding)* 4-8-13 MHills(8) (lw: mde all: qcknd over 2f out: hrd rdn fnl f: hld on gamely) ....— 1
652[3] Storiths (IRE) **(108)***(114) (JWWatts)* 5-9-7b BThomson(2) (b: lw: hld up: 4th st: swtchd rt over 1f out: shkn up to chal ins fnl f: no ex cl home) ....hd 2

8294 Cim Bom Bom (IRE) **(96)***(97)*(Fav)*(MBell)* 3-7-11 ow1 AMackay(4) (lw: hld up: 5th st: rdn & r.o wl ins fnl f) 1½ 3
719* Venture Capitalist **(100)***(102) (DNicholls)* 6-8-13 AlexGreaves(5) (lw: stdd s: hld up: n.m.r 2f out: rdn & r.o wl ins fnl f) .... nk 4
En Attendant (FR) **(103)***(101) (BHanbury)* 7-9-2 TIves(3) (bkwd: dwlt: hld up & bhd: hdwy on ins over 2f out: sn rdn: nvr able to chal) 1½ 5
8147 Band on the Run **(94)***(92) (BAMcMahon)* 8-8-7 JCarroll(6) (lw: prom: 3rd st: hrd rdn & wandered 2f out: sn btn) .... hd 6
63615 Zifta (USA) **(94)***(85) (SCWilliams)* 4-8-7 MFenton(7) (chsd wnr: 2nd st: rdn & wknd over 2f out) 3 7
Miss Sacha (IRE) **(106)***(92) (DRLoder)* 4-9-5 JWeaver(1) (b: bit bkwd: hld up: 6th st: rdn over 2f out: sn btn) 2½ 8

LONG HANDICAP Band on the Run 8-1 Zifta (USA) 7-1

3/1 Cim Bom Bom (IRE) (op 2/1), **100/30** Miss Sacha (IRE), **5/1** Venture Capitalist, Storiths (IRE), **17/2** MOCCASIN RUN (USA), En Attendant (FR), **12/1** Band on the Run (10/1-16/1), **33/1** Zifta (USA), CSF £45.39 CT £141.29 TOTE £9.60: £2.00 £1.50 £1.80 (£15.60) OWNER Mr George Strawbridge (KINGSCLERE) BRED Jayeff B Stables 8 Rn

1m 32.23 (4.93) SF: 41/49/20/37/36/27/20/27
WEIGHT FOR AGE 3yo-12lb

954 CLIFTON CASINO CLUB V.E. DAY CELEBRATION H'CAP (0-85) (4-Y.O+) (Class D) £3,835.75 (£1,156.00: £560.50: £262.75)

1m 6f Stalls: Low GOING: nil sec per fur (G) 4-05 (4-05)

74112 **Seize the Day (IRE) (55)***(69) (CDBroad)* 7-8-6 MFenton(6) (hld up & bhd: hdwy over 3f out: shkn up to ld ins fnl f: r.o wl) .... — 1
63212 Paradise Navy **(71)***(83) (CREgerton)* 6-9-3b(5) AProcter(8) (swtg: chsd ldr: 2nd st: led 3f out tl ins fnl f: nt qckn) 1½ 2
7373 Cuango (IRE) **(76)***(85)*(Fav)*(RHollinshead)* 4-9-12 TIves(5) (lw: hld up & bhd: 6th st: hdwy over 2f out: kpt on one pce fnl f) 2½ 3
58216 Zahid (USA) **(48)***(53) (BobJones)* 4-7-12 AMackay(1) (lw: led 1f: chsd ldrs: 5th st: one pce fnl 3f) 4 4
8116 Faal Mario (USA) **(76)***(80) (MrsJRRamsden)* 4-9-12 JWeaver(4) (lw: hld up: styd on fnl 2f: nvr nrr) .... ½ 5
8215 Solomon's Dancer (USA) **(74)***(74) (WWHaigh)* 5-9-11 DaleGibson(3) (lw: prom: led 6f out tl hdd 3f out: sn rdn & wknd) 3½ 6
Provence **(73)***(73) (LLungo)* 8-9-10b WNewnes(2) (rdn to ld after 1f: hdd 6f out: 3rd st: sn lost tch) .... ½ 7
*186*13 Mhemeanles **(55)***(26) (CaptJWilson)* 5-8-6 SDWilliams(7) (bkwd: hld up: hdwy & 4th st: wknd 3f out: t.o) 25 8

3/1 Cuango (IRE), **100/30** Solomon's Dancer (USA), **7/2** Faal Mario (USA), **15/2** Provence, **8/1** SEIZE THE DAY (IRE), **10/1** Paradise Navy, **16/1** Zahid (USA), **33/1** Mhemeanles, CSF £69.87 CT £255.83 TOTE £8.80: £2.00 £2.60 £1.20 (£35.70) OWNER Veterans of Trelleborgs (WESTBURY-ON-SEVE) 8 Rn

3m 5.7 (7.50) SF: 49/63/64/32/59/54/53/6
WEIGHT FOR AGE 4yo-1lb

OFFICIAL EXPLANATION Seize The Day(IRE): regarding the improvement shown, the trainer reported that the gelding had been unsuited by the sharp track and the fitting of a visor on his last run.

955 DERBYSHIRE HILL MAIDEN STKS (3-Y.O) (Class D) £3,993.50 (£1,208.00: £589.00: £279.50) 7f 30y

Stalls: Low GOING: nil sec per fur (G) 4-35 (4-35)

Ten Past Six *(82)*(Fav)*(BWHills)* 3-9-0 MHills(10) (bit bkwd: hld up in tch: 4th st: hdwy to ld bel dist: rdn & hld on wl) .... — 1
Silvicolous (USA) *(81) (PWChapple-Hyam)* 3-9-0 BThomson(4) (h.d.w: bit bkwd: hld up: 6th st: nt clr run 2f out: swtchd rt: str run fnl f: jst failed) .... nk 2
6164 Houghton Venture (USA) *(74) (SPCWoods)* 3-9-0 WWoods(2) (chsd ldrs: 3rd st: led over 2f out to bel dist: sn rdn & btn) 3½ 3
7779 Carlito Brigante *(71) (MrsJRRamsden)* 3-9-0 JWeaver(1) (hld up: hdwy over 2f out: nt rch ldrs) 1 4
Young Benson *(67) (BAMcMahon)* 3-9-0 TIves(3) (chsd ldrs: 5th st: one pce fnl 2f) 1¾ 5
African-Pard (IRE) **(74)***(62) (DHaydnJones)* 3-9-0 AMackay(5) (bkwd: plld hrd: led tl hdd & 2nd st: wknd 2f out: eased whn btn) 2½ 6
6585 Bedouin Invader *(60) (MRStoute)* 3-9-0 KBradshaw(7) (bit bkwd: hld up & bhd: nvr plcd to chal) 1 7
7525 It's Academic *(47) (MrsJRRamsden)* 3-8-9 SDWilliams(8) (mid div: rdn along over 2f out: no ex) 3½ 8

Dragon Rose *(46) (TPTate)* 3-9-0 WNewnes(6) (w'like: str: bkwd: s.s: a bhd)........................2½ 9
772[2] Cemaes Bay **(70)***(45) (JBerry)* 3-9-0 JCarroll(9) (lw: chsd ldr tl led ent st: hdd over 2f out: wknd bel dist)........................½ 10

15/8 TEN PAST SIX, **7/2** Houghton Venture (USA), **11/2** Cemaes Bay, **13/2** Silvicolous (USA), **7/1** Bedouin Invader, **14/1** It's Academic, **16/1** African-Pard (IRE), **20/1** Carlito Brigante, **25/1** Dragon Rose, **33/1** Young Benson, CSF £14.59 TOTE £2.90: £1.30 £2.30 £1.50 (£10.50) Trio £25.20 OWNER Mr J. Hanson (LAMBOURN) BRED T. D. Holland-Martin 10 Rn
1m 32.52 (5.22) SF: 39/38/31/28/24/19/17/4/3/2

956

BOTANY BAY H'CAP (0-90) (3-Y.O+) (Class C) £5,368.00 (£1,624.00: £792.00: £376.00) **1m 3f 200y** Stalls: High GOING: nil sec per fur (G) 5-05 (5-05)

757[6] **Slasher Jack (IRE) (78)***(93) (SGNorton)* 4-9-12 JWeaver(3) (drppd rr & 4th st: effrt & rdn 3f out: led ins fnl f: hung lft: all out)........................— 1
Swallows Dream (IRE) **(80)***(95)*(Fav)*(JLDunlop)* 4-10-0 BThomson(1) (bit bkwd: hld up: 3rd st: rdn over 2f out: led bel dist tl ins fnl f)........................nk 2
623[12] Beauman **(72)***(77) (PDEvans)* 5-9-6 TIves(4) (led after 1f tl hdd bel dist: outpcd fnl f)........................7 3
661[15] Chimanimani **(73)***(78) (NTinkler)* 4-9-7 WWoods(2) (led 1f: 2nd st: disp ld over 2f out: wknd appr fnl f)........................nk 4

6/4 Swallows Dream (IRE), **5/2** SLASHER JACK (IRE), **7/2** Beauman, **6/1** Chimanimani, CSF £5.98 TOTE £3.00: (£2.80) OWNER Mr T. C. Chiang (BARNSLEY) BRED Ardenode Stud Ltd in Ireland 4 Rn
2m 36.72 (8.72) SF: 51/53/35/36

T/Plpt: £8.50 (1,071.7 Tckts). T/Qdpt: £13.40 (8.9 Tckts). IM

0760-KEMPTON (R-H)
Monday May 8th (Good to firm, Rnd Course. Firm back st)
WEATHER: warm WIND: almost nil

957

RHINE MAIDEN STKS (3-Y.O F) (Class D) £4,474.50 (£1,356.00: £663.00: £316.50) **1m (Jubilee)** Stalls: High GOING minus 0.35 sec per fur (F) 2-10 (2-11)

Blue Zulu (IRE) *(88) (JRFanshawe)* 3-8-11 DHarrison(9) (rdn & hdwy 2f out: led over 1f out: r.o wl)........................— 1
664[4] Avignon (IRE) *(82) (PWChapple-Hyam)* 3-8-11 JReid(8) (2nd st: led over 2f out tl over 1f out: unable qckn)........................3 2
Tranquillity *(81) (LordHuntingdon)* 3-8-11 WRSwinburn(13) (4th st: ev ch over 1f out: one pce)........................nk 3
Almizaj *(78) (HThomsonJones)* 3-8-11 RHills(1) (hdwy over 4f out: 5th st: nt clr run over 1f out: r.o)........................1¾ 4
664[5] Vena (IRE) **(95)***(75) (JLDunlop)* 3-8-11 PaulEddery(6) (hdwy on ins over 3f out: 6th st: rdn over 2f out: one pce)........................1½ 5
Barford Sovereign *(71) (JRFanshawe)* 3-8-11 RHughes(7) (swtg: led over 5f: ev ch over 1f out: sn wknd)........................2 6
Nightscene (IRE) *(64) (TGMills)* 3-8-11 AClark(4) (3rd st: wknd 2f out)........................3½ 7
779[10] Sadler's Pearl *(60) (BJMeehan)* 3-8-11 MRimmer(11) (a bhd)........................2 8
Rozalina Lady *(57) (NAGraham)* 3-8-11 StephenDavies(5) (hmpd over 4f out: bhd fnl 3f)........................1½ 9
Vezelay (USA) *(54) (JHMGosden)* 3-8-11 LDettori(12) (unf: scope: a bhd)........................1¼ 10
Supreme (USA) *(46) (IABalding)* 3-8-11 SO'Gorman(2) (w'like: scope: bit bkwd: bhd fnl 2f)....4 11
695[2] Farani (Fav)*(RCharlton)* 3-8-11 TQuinn(3) (3rd whn p.u over 4f out: dead)........................ P

Evens Farani, **5/1** Vena (IRE), **11/2** Avignon (IRE) (4/1-6/1), **9/1** Vezelay (USA) (6/1-10/1), **14/1** BLUE ZULU (IRE), Tranquillity, **20/1** Supreme (USA), **33/1** Almizaj, Nightscene (IRE), **50/1** Barford Sovereign, **66/1** Sadler's Pearl, Rozalina Lady, CSF £83.33 TOTE £16.00: £2.40 £1.80 £2.20 (£33.20) Trio £212.70 OWNER T & J Vestey (NEWMARKET) BRED A. Watkins 12 Rn
1m 38.92 (1.92) SF: 47/41/40/37/34/30/23/19/16/13/5/-

958

PEGASUS STKS (4-Y.O+) (Class C) £4,901.60 (£1,834.40: £897.20: £386.00: £173.00: £87.80)
1m 6f 92y Stalls: High GOING minus 0.35 sec per fur (F) 2-40 (2-41)

Cuff Link (IRE) (106)*(111+) (MajorWRHern)* 5-9-8 PaulEddery(1) (lw: 4th st: led 2f out: pushed out)........................— 1
Misbelief **(102)***(100) (JRFanshawe)* 5-8-13 DHarrison(4) (5th st: rdn & hdwy over 2f out: r.o one pce)........................1½ 2

735[6] Blue Judge (IRE) **(100)***(97) (RThompson)* 5-8-10 LDettori(7) (led 12f: one pce) ....¾ 3
735[4] Castle Courageous **(106)***(110)*(Fav)*(LadyHerries)* 8-9-10 JReid(3) (chsd ldr: ev ch 2f out: one pce) ....hd 4
English Invader *(103) (RAkehurst)* 4-9-5 TQuinn(6) (lw: 3rd st: wknd 2f out) 3 5
Nawar (FR) *(88) (JRJenkins)* 5-9-0 RHills(5) (6th st: a bhd) 8 6
Miss Gruntled *(51) (DJSffrenchDavis)* 4-8-4 RPrice(2) (bhd fnl 4f) 25 7

7/4 Castle Courageous, **2/1** Misbelief, **7/2** CUFF LINK (IRE), **8/1** Blue Judge (IRE), **20/1** English Invader, **33/1** Nawar (FR), **100/1** Miss Gruntled, CSF £10.25 TOTE £4.40: £2.30 £2.00 (£5.90) OWNER Lord Weinstock & The Hon Simon Weinstock (LAMBOURN) BRED Ballymacoll Stud Farm Ltd 7 Rn 3m 10.78 (7.78) SF: 36/25/22/35/27/13/-
WEIGHT FOR AGE 4yo-1lb

959

V E DAY STKS (3-Y.O F) (Class C) £4,924.80 (£1,843.20: £901.60: £388.00: £174.00: £88.40) **6f** Stalls: High GOING minus 0.35 sec per fur (F) 3-10 (3-11)

633[4] **Overbrook (90)***(91)*(Fav)*(IABalding)* 3-8-12 LDettori(3) (lw: hld up: led over 1f out: rdn out) ....— 1
633[7] Al Rawda (FR) **(96)***(90) (HRACecil)* 3-8-12 WRSwinburn(5) (hdwy 2f out: ev ch 1f out: r.o) ....½ 2
743[2] Prima Cominna **(87)***(78) (MBell)* 3-8-10 TQuinn(4) (lw: hld up: rdn 2f out: nt clr run over 1f out: r.o one pce) 3½ 3
660[8] Paris Babe **(95)***(75) (DMorris)* 3-8-8 DHarrison(6) (hdwy & n.m.r on ins over 1f out: r.o one pce) ....½ 4
563[11] Nagnagnag (IRE) **(90)***(78) (SDow)* 3-9-0 PaulEddery(1) (lw: chsd ldr: ev ch over 1f out: sn wknd) 1 5
Veuve Hoornaert (IRE) **(90)***(66) (RHannon)* 3-8-10 JReid(2) (led over 4f) 3 6

5/2 OVERBROOK, **7/2** Paris Babe, **4/1** Veuve Hoornaert (IRE), **9/2** Al Rawda (FR), **6/1** Prima Cominna, **14/1** Nagnagnag (IRE), CSF £12.59 TOTE £2.60: £1.60 £2.40 (£6.20) OWNER Sir William Purves (KINGSCLERE) BRED I. A. Balding 6 Rn 1m 12.58 (1.28) SF: 49/48/36/33/36/24

960

JUBILEE H'CAP (0-105) (4-Y.O+) (Class B) £21,105.00 (£6,390.00: £3,120.00: £1,485.00) **1m (Jubilee)** Stalls: High GOING minus 0.35 sec per fur (F) 3-40 (3-41)

665[10] **Desert Green (FR) (85)***(98) (RHannon)* 6-9-4 RPerham(9) (nt clr run & swtchd lft over 2f out: gd hdwy over 1f out: led ins fnl f: r.o wl) ....— 1
Hunters of Brora (IRE) **(82)***(89) (JDBethell)* 5-9-1 RHills(5) (rdn over 4f out: hdwy 2f out: led over 1f out tl ins fnl f: unable qckn) 3 2
793* Mr Martini (IRE) **(95)***(101) (CEBrittain)* 5-10-0 MRimmer(11) (lw: 6th st: rdn over 2f out: r.o one pce) ....¾ 3
439[21] Knave's Ash (USA) **(88)***(93) (MRStoute)* 4-9-7 JReid(7) (b.nr hind: lw: hdwy 2f out: ev ch 1f out: one pce) ....s.h 4
714[3] Gadge **(73)***(77) (DMorris)* 4-8-6 RPrice(10) (4th st: ev ch over 1f out: wknd fnl f) ....¾ 5
Weaver Bird **(78)***(79) (HCandy)* 5-8-11 AClark(8) (hdwy on ins over 2f out: wknd fnl f) 1½ 6
793[2] Air Commodore (IRE) **(93)***(93)*(Fav)*(PFICole)* 4-9-12 TQuinn(1) (2nd st: led 2f out to over 1f out: wknd fnl f) ....nk 7
665[11] Caleman **(86)***(72) (RBoss)* 6-9-5 LDettori(6) (led 6f: wknd fnl f) 7 8
714[16] Pay Homage **(86)***(72) (IABalding)* 7-9-5 SO'Gorman(4) (lw: 3rd st: wknd over 2f out) ....nk 9
665[18] Top Guide (USA) **(87)***(73) (EALDunlop)* 4-9-6 WRSwinburn(2) (b: lw: 5th st: wknd over 1f out) ....hd 10
714[19] Brave Patriarch (IRE) **(82)***(60) (JLDunlop)* 4-9-1 PaulEddery(3) (a bhd) 4 11

3/1 Air Commodore (IRE), **6/1** Caleman, **7/1** DESERT GREEN (FR) (6/1-9/1), Gadge, **9/1** Mr Martini (IRE) (6/1-10/1), **11/1** Knave's Ash (USA) (7/1-12/1), **12/1** Weaver Bird, Hunters of Brora (IRE), Pay Homage, Top Guide (USA), **20/1** Brave Patriarch (IRE), CSF £77.52 CT £691.59 TOTE £7.10: £2.20 £3.00 £2.80 (£49.40) Trio £146.90 OWNER Mr Mana Al Maktoum (MARLBOROUGH) BRED Gainsborough Stud Management 11 Rn 1m 37.75 (0.75) SF: 74/65/77/69/53/55/69/48/48/49/36

961

LADBROKE 'CHANGING FACES' H'CAP (0-80) (3-Y.O+) (Class D) £4,318.50 (£1,308.00: £639.00: £304.50) **1m 4f** Stalls: High GOING minus 0.35 sec per fur (F) 4-10 (4-11)

763[2] **Dancing Sensation (USA) (56)***(68)*(Fav)*(RAkehurst)* 8-8-5 LDettori(2) (6th st: led over 1f out: sn clr: r.o wl) ....— 1
668[6] Artic Courier **(76)***(85) (DJSCosgrove)* 4-9-4 (7) DGibbs(6) (swtg: 5th st: hmpd over 2f out & over 1f out: r.o wl ins fnl f) 2½ 2
763* Roisin Clover **(67)***(75)*(Fav)*(SDow)* 4-9-2 TQuinn(5) (lw: hdwy over 2f out: hrd rdn over 1f out: unable qckn) ....nk 3

795[4] Wild Strawberry **(64)***(71) (MissBSanders)* 6-8-13 JReid(4) (3rd st: ev ch 2f out: one pce).......¾ **4**
634[15] Proton **(73)***(80) (RAkehurst)* 5-9-8 AClark(7) (lw: 4th st: nt clr run over 1f out: r.o ins fnl f).....s.h **5**
Mowlaie **(79)***(81) (JDBethell)* 4-10-0 RHills(3) (lw: led over 10f) 4 **6**
728[3] Canary Falcon **(63)***(38) (RJO'Sullivan)* 4-8-12 StephenDavies(1) (lw: 2nd st: wkng whn hmpd over 2f out) 20 **7**

100/30 DANCING SENSATION (USA) (op 2/1), Roisin Clover, **4/1** Proton, **5/1** Wild Strawberry, **8/1** Artic Courier, **14/1** Mowlaie, **16/1** Canary Falcon, CSF £24.40 TOTE £3.00: £1.70 £2.80 (£12.50) OWNER Chelgate Public Relations Ltd (EPSOM) BRED Martin W. Bach and Chris Vonderlohe 7 Rn
2m 32.79 (2.59) SF: 45/62/52/48/57/58/15

962

ROTHMANS ROYALS NORTH SOUTH CHALLENGE SERIES H'CAP (0-90) (3-Y.O) (Class C) £6,937.50 (£2,100.00: £1,025.00: £487.50)
1m 1f (round) Stalls: High GOING minus 0.35 sec per fur (F) 4-40 (4-42)

813* **Hardy Dancer (79)***(85)*(Fav)*(GLMoore)* 3-8-12 BRouse(11) (lw: 6th st: led over 1f out: r.o wl)— **1**
813[4] Mihriz (IRE) **(80)***(83) (MajorWRHern)* 3-8-13 RHills(6) (lw: 5th st: nt clr run & swtchd lft over 2f out: hrd rdn over 1f out: unable qckn fnl f).....1¾ **2**
Sherqy (IRE) **(80)***(81) (JLDunlop)* 3-8-13 PaulEddery(5) (7th st: nt clr run over 2f out: hdwy over 1f out: r.o wl ins fnl f).....1 **3**
775[4] The Stager (IRE) **(75)***(73) (JRJenkins)* 3-8-8 LDettori(10) (lw: led over 7f: wknd fnl f).....1¾ **4**
724[3] Donna Viola **(74)***(68) (CFWall)* 3-8-7 NCarlisle(4) (lw: 3rd st: rdn over 2f out: wknd fnl f).....2 **5**
730* Stone Ridge (IRE) **(88)***(77) (RHannon)* 3-9-7 RHughes(7) (4th st: nt clr run on ins over 1f out: nt rcvr).....3 **6**
618[12] Snowy Petrel (IRE) **(82)***(68) (JLDunlop)* 3-9-1 WRSwinburn(8) (2nd st: wknd over 1f out) 2 **7**
614[4] Tribal Peace (IRE) **(67)***(44) (BGubby)* 3-8-0 ow1 DHarrison(3) (lw: bhd fnl 4f) 4 **8**
694[12] Bobanlyn (IRE) **(74)***(31) (DMorris)* 3-8-7 StephenDavies(1) (bhd fnl 4f) 12 **9**

5/2 HARDY DANCER, **9/2** Mihriz (IRE), **11/2** Donna Viola, **8/1** Tribal Peace (IRE), The Stager (IRE) (6/1-9/1), **10/1** Stone Ridge (IRE), **12/1** Sherqy (IRE), **14/1** Bobanlyn (IRE), **16/1** Snowy Petrel (IRE), CSF £13.09 CT £99.25 TOTE £2.90: £1.50 £1.60 £2.30 (£5.00) Trio £23.70 OWNER Mr K. Higson (EPSOM) BRED K. Higson 9 Rn 1m 51.76 (1.76) SF: 52/50/48/40/35/44/35/11/-

963

'SPORTING BEARS' MAIDEN STKS (3-Y.O C & G) (Class D) £4,318.50 (£1,308.00: £639.00: £304.50)
1m (Jubilee) Stalls: High GOING minus 0.35 sec per fur (F) 5-10 (5-11)

670[2] **Tertium (IRE)** *(88+)*(Fav)*(PWChapple-Hyam)* 3-8-11 JReid(2) (lw: 2nd st: led over 2f out: pushed out).....— **1**
Primo Lara *(81) (PWHarris)* 3-8-11 WRSwinburn(5) (lw: led over 5f: unable qckn) 3½ **2**
Kilcoran Bay *(79) (IABalding)* 3-8-11 LDettori(3) (w'like: bit bkwd: 5th st: rdn over 2f out: one pce) 1¼ **3**
777[3] Sharpical *(74) (JRFanshawe)* 3-8-11 DHarrison(6) (7th st: rdn & hdwy over 1f out: r.o one pce) 2½ **4**
853[4] Easy Dollar **(80)***(64) (BGubby)* 3-8-11 PaulEddery(7) (3rd st: wknd over 1f out).....5 **5**
742[6] Anegre (IRE) **(60)***(58) (LJHolt)* 3-8-11 MRimmer(4) (lw: plld hrd: 4th st: wknd 2f out) 3 **6**
Magnate's Point *(57) (PWHarris)* 3-8-11 AClark(9) (plld hrd: 6th st: wknd over 2f out) .....s.h **7**
Western Country *(27) (SMellor)* 3-8-11 NCarlisle(8) (w'like: lw: a bhd).....15 **8**
761[14] Napoleon's Law *(RHannon)* 3-8-11 RHughes(1) (hung bdly lft & virtually rn out over 3f out: t.o) .....dist **9**

5/4 TERTIUM (IRE), **4/1** Magnate's Point, **7/1** Easy Dollar, **8/1** Sharpical, **10/1** Kilcoran Bay, **16/1** Napoleon's Law, Primo Lara, **33/1** Anegre (IRE), **66/1** Western Country, CSF £19.02 TOTE £1.70: £1.10 £3.90 £1.60 (£12.90) Trio £60.90 OWNER Mrs C. A. Waters (MARLBOROUGH) BRED Mrs C. A. Waters 9 Rn 1m 39.6 (2.60) SF: 40/33/31/26/16/10/9/-/-
T/Plpt: £235.10 (119.81 Tckts). T/Qdpt: £55.00 (3.35 Tckts). AK

0638-NEWCASTLE (L-H)
Monday May 8th (Good, Good to firm patches becoming Good to soft)

WEATHER: overcast WIND: slt half against

964

BIG DIPPER MAIDEN AUCTION STKS (2-Y.O) (Class F) £2,274.00 (£639.00: £312.00) **5f** Stalls: High GOING minus 0.08 sec per fur (G) 2-25 (2-25)

671[9] **Blessingindisguise** *(58t) (MWEasterby)* 2-8-10 MBirch(2) (trckd ldrs: shkn up to ld over 1f out: r.o strly).....— **1**

Silent Soprano *(43) (DenysSmith)* 2-8-5 DHolland(3) (cmpt: dwlt: sn chsng ldrs: styd on same pce fnl f) 3 **2**
Shafir (IRE) *(43) (JBerry)* 2-7-12 (7) PFessey(1) (leggy: unf: led over 3f out tl over 1f out: wknd nr fin) ....s.h **3**
Bit of Bother (IRE) *(41) (TDBarron)* 2-8-6 JFortune(9) (lengthy: unf: dwlt: sn chsng ldrs: outpcd & rn green ½-wy: styd on wl ins fnl f) 1 **4**
Homeland *(26) (CWThornton)* 2-8-10 ACulhane(7) (neat: sn outpcd & pushed along: sme hdwy over 1f out: n.d) 6 **5**
Stoleamarch *(16)*(Fav)*(MrsMReveley)* 2-8-6 KDarley(8) (neat: unf: prom early: outpcd ½-wy: n.d) 1¾ **6**
819[14] Pat's Choice (IRE) *(6) (MHEasterby)* 2-8-5 SMaloney(4) (sn wl outpcd & bhd) 3 **7**
Wydale *(MWEllerby)* 2-8-6 SMorris(5) (unf: wl outpcd & bhd fr ½-wy) 2 **8**
755[6] Dispol Sapphire *(MrsVAAconley)* 2-8-1 MDeering(6) (led over 1f: sn lost pl & wl bhd) 12 **9**

11/4 Stoleamarch, **3/1** Shafir (IRE), **9/2** Bit of Bother (IRE), **6/1** Silent Soprano, BLESSINGINDISGUISE, **10/1** Homeland, **12/1** Pat's Choice (IRE) (op 7/1), **33/1** Wydale, **50/1** Dispol Sapphire, CSF £39.52 TOTE £7.90: £1.80 £1.70 £1.50 (£21.90) Trio £24.40 OWNER Mr A. G. Black (SHERIFF HUTTON) BRED Mrs A. Meller 9 Rn 63.57 secs (5.17) SF: 2/-/-/-/-/-/-/-/-

965 LUCKY DIP CLAIMING STKS (3-Y.O+) (Class F) £2,326.50 (£654.00: £319.50)
7f Stalls: High GOING minus 0.08 sec per fur (G) 2-55 (2-57)

Broctune Gold (65)*(64)*(Fav)*(MrsMReveley)* 4-9-4 KDarley(14) (lw: mde all: drvn clr over 1f out: unchal) ....— **1**
Mbulwa **(52)***(56) (SEKettlewell)* 9-9-4b JFortune(6) (trckd ldrs: kpt on fnl f: no ch w wnr) 3½ **2**
789[5] Birchwood Sun **(51)***(58)*(Fav)*(MDods)* 5-9-1b(7) SCopp(11) (effrt & swtchd centre over 2f out: kpt on u.p: nvr trbld ldrs) 1 **3**
790* Obsidian Grey **(52)***(51) (MissLCSiddall)* 8-8-13 (3) DRMcCabe(5) (chsd ldrs: edgd lft & one pce fnl f) ....½ **4**
548[2] Beware of Agents **(61)***(45) (MJohnston)* 6-9-2 DHolland(1) (lw: chsd ldrs: rdn 2f out: sn wknd) 2½ **5**
559[13] Ashdren **(59)***(44) (AHarrison)* 8-8-13 (5) JStack(2) (lw: chsd ldrs tl wknd over 1f out) 1¼ **6**
642[9] Sharp N' Smooth **(51)***(36) (WTKemp)* 8-8-12b MBirch(9) (hld up: effrt over 2f out: nvr nr ldrs) 1 **7**
748[5] Perfect Bertie (IRE) **(54)***(36) (MrsJRRamsden)* 3-8-3 SMaloney(7) (lw: in tch: effrt & hung lft ½-wy: no imp) 1 **8**
785[14] Izza **(59)***(29) (WStorey)* 4-8-13 NConnorton(10) (s.i.s: sn prom: rdn & wknd over 2f out) 2½ **9**
Lancaster Bomber *(22) (DMoffatt)* 3-7-8 (3) DarrenMoffatt(12) (unf: bhd: effrt & hung lft over 2f out: n.d) 1 **10**
The Right Time **(45)***(5) (JParkes)* 10-8-7 (5) LNewton(13) (b: s.s: a wl bhd) 9 **11**
748[11] Drum Sergeant **(38)***(3) (JParkes)* 8-8-12b MDeering(8) (s.s: a bhd) 1 **12**
776[10] Sottises (IRE) **(28)** *(PTDalton)* 4-8-9b ACulhane(4) (chsd ldrs: rdn ½-wy: sn lost pl) 15 **13**
Sheroot *(DMoffatt)* 3-8-12 NKennedy(3) (lengthy: unf: s.s: swvd bdly lft after 1f: virtually p.u) ....dist **14**

5/1 BROCTUNE GOLD, Birchwood Sun, **11/2** Perfect Bertie (IRE), **6/1** Beware of Agents, Ashdren, **8/1** Obsidian Grey, Sharp N' Smooth, **16/1** Mbulwa, Izza, **20/1** Lancaster Bomber, **50/1** The Right Time, Drum Sergeant, Sottises (IRE), Sheroot, CSF £74.14 TOTE £4.60: £2.30 £4.40 £2.60 (£46.80) Trio £246.80 OWNER Mrs M. B. Thwaites (SALTBURN) BRED A. J. Poulton (Epping) Ltd 14 Rn 1m 29.34 (5.04) SF: 36/28/30/23/17/16/8/-/1/-/-/-/-/-
WEIGHT FOR AGE 3yo-12lb
Perfect Bertie(IRE) clmd WB Imison £3,500

966 HELTER SKELTER H'CAP (0-70) (3-Y.O) (Class E) £2,431.50 (£684.00: £334.50)
6f Stalls: High GOING minus 0.08 sec per fur (G) 3-25 (3-29)

Bollin Harry (53)*(63) (MHEasterby)* 3-8-4 MBirch(2) (w ldrs: led centre over 2f out: styd on strly fnl f) ....— **1**
722[3] Statius **(64)***(71) (TDBarron)* 3-9-1 JFortune(16) (trckd ldrs: disp ld over 2f out: nt qckn fnl f) .1¼ **2**
733[3] The Kings Ransom **(54)***(50)*(Fav)*(MrsJRRamsden)* 3-8-5 DHolland(10) (prom: rdn & outpcd ½-wy: styd on fnl f) 4 **3**
823[5] Stolen Kiss (IRE) **(64)***(60) (MWEasterby)* 3-8-8 (7) GParkin(5) (a chsng ldrs: kpt on same pce appr fnl f) ....hd **4**
Another Time **(55)***(50) (MissSEHall)* 3-8-6 NConnorton(20) (bit bkwd: in tch: styd on fnl f: nvr nr to chal) ....nk **5**

Ramborette **(55)***(45) (DenysSmith)* 3-8-3 (3) DarrenMoffatt(17) (led: hung lft & hdd over 2f out: kpt on same pce) 2 **6**
Celebration Cake (IRE) **(60)***(48) (MissLAPerratt)* 3-8-11 SMorris(19) (in tch: effrt ½-wy: kpt on: nvr nr to chal) ....½ **7**
722[7] Nafta **(60)***(48) (SEKettlewell)* 3-8-6 (5) JStack(8) (racd far side: chsd ldrs tl grad wknd fnl 2f) ....s.h **8**
823[7] Penny's Wishing **(62)***(47) (JPLeigh)* 3-8-6 (7) SCopp(6) (chsd ldrs tl wknd 2f out) 1¼ **9**
842[7] Prince Rudolf (IRE) **(51)***(36) (MrsNMacauley)* 3-7-9b(7) AmandaSanders(1) (racd far side: nvr nr ldrs) ....s.h **10**
904[9] Sunday Mail Too (IRE) **(51)***(26) (MissLAPerratt)* 3-8-2v MDeering(12) (chsd ldrs tl wknd over 1f out) 3½ **11**
862[4] Annie Fay (IRE) **(58)***(30) (JLHarris)* 3-8-9 KDarley(15) (in tch tl wknd over 2f out) 1¼ **12**
753[2] Mr Slick **(53)***(22) (WStorey)* 3-8-1 (3) DRMcCabe(9) (b.hind: sn wl outpcd & bhd: sme hdwy over 1f out: n.d) 1¼ **13**
Blue Lugana **(50)***(18) (NBycroft)* 3-8-1 SMaloney(18) (a wl outpcd) ....hd **14**
862[2] Le Bal **(43)***(11) (MrsNMacauley)* 3-7-8b NKennedy(4) (racd far side: in tch to ½-wy) ....nk **15**
759[14] Prime Property (IRE) **(51)***(18) (MWEasterby)* 3-8-2 ow1 ACulhane(14) (s.s: a in rr) ....d.h **15**
758[9] Alltime Dancer (IRE) **(60)***(27) (MrsJRRamsden)* 3-8-4 (7) TFinn(13) (a wl outpcd) ....hd **17**
398[13] Saltz (IRE) **(70)***(28) (PTDalton)* 3-9-0 (7) GMitchell(7) (chsd ldrs tl wknd over 2f out) 3½ **18**
732[16] Chosen Man **(42)** *(MWEllerby)* 3-7-7 ClaireBalding(11) (sn bhd: hung lft fr ½-wy) 4 **19**
LONG HANDICAP Chosen Man 7-0

7/2 The Kings Ransom (op 6/1), **11/2** Statius, **8/1** Annie Fay (IRE), Another Time, **9/1** Mr Slick, Prime Property (IRE), **10/1** Ramborette, Penny's Wishing, **12/1** Stolen Kiss (IRE), **14/1** Blue Lugana, **16/1** Le Bal, BOLLIN HARRY, Nafta, **25/1** Sunday Mail Too (IRE), Celebration Cake (IRE), Alltime Dancer (IRE), **33/1** Prince Rudolf (IRE), Chosen Man, **50/1** Saltz (IRE), CSF £110.33 CT £367.91 TOTE £42.00: £5.40 £1.90 £1.40 £3.90 (£183.60) Trio £411.80 OWNER Sir Neil Westbrook (MALTON) BRED Sir Neil and Lady Westbrook 19 Rn
1m 14.95 (3.45) SF: 34/43/22/32/22/17/20/20/19/8/-/2/-/-/-/-/-/-/-

967 BANK HOLIDAY H'CAP (0-85) (3-Y.O+) (Class D) £3,538.60 (£1,070.80: £522.40: £248.20) **1m 4f 93y** Stalls: Low GOING minus 0.08 sec per fur (G) 4-00 (4-02)

Blue Blazer (71)*(82)*(Fav)*(BHanbury)* 5-9-2 (5) JStack(1) (hld up & bhd: smooth hdwy over 2f out: qcknd to ld 1f out: pushed out & hld on wl) ....— **1**
757[4] Southern Power (IRE) **(78)***(89) (MrsMReveley)* 4-10-0 KDarley(3) (b.nr hind: trckd ldrs: squeezed thro & chal 1f out: nt qckn nr fin) ....hd **2**
Latvian **(67)***(73) (RAllan)* 8-9-3 NConnorton(6) (chsd ldrs: effrt over 2f out: r.o same pce appr fnl f) 3½ **3**
811[13] Sunderland Echo **(77)***(82) (MrsMReveley)* 6-9-6 (7) SCopp(2) (plld hrd: led after 2f to 5f out: drvn along over 3f out: one pce appr fnl f) 1¼ **4**
864[6] Shuttlecock **(52)***(53) (MrsNMacauley)* 4-8-2 ACulhane(4) (plld hrd: trckd ldrs: drvn along & outpcd 4f out: one pce) 3 **5**
556[10] Thaleros **(62)***(62) (GMMoore)* 5-8-12 JFortune(5) (led 2f: led 5f out to 1f out: sn wknd) ....¾ **6**
757[8] Sallyoreally (IRE) **(57)***(44) (WStorey)* 4-8-4 (3) DRMcCabe(7) (hld up: effrt & swtchd ins over 2f out: n.m.r & wknd over 1f out: eased) 10 **7**

7/4 BLUE BLAZER, **11/4** Southern Power (IRE), **5/1** Sunderland Echo, **6/1** Latvian, **7/1** Sallyoreally (IRE) (op 25/1), **8/1** Thaleros, **16/1** Shuttlecock, CSF £7.50 TOTE £2.40: £1.80 £1.70 (£4.10) OWNER McHalapar Syndicate (NEWMARKET) BRED Oak Bloodstock Ltd 7 Rn
2m 47.42 (8.92) SF: 43/50/34/43/14/23/5

968 CATERPILLAR MAIDEN STKS (3-Y.O+) (Class D) £3,707.60 (£1,122.80: £548.40: £261.20) **1m 2f 32y** Stalls: Low GOING minus 0.08 sec per fur (G) 4-30 (4-36)

Diaghilef (IRE) (102)*(80)*(Fav)*(MJohnston)* 3-8-8 DHolland(8) (lw: trckd ldrs: led 2f out: sn qcknd clr: easily) ....— **1**
Munaadee (USA) *(74) (EALDunlop)* 3-8-3 (5) JStack(5) (b.hind: trckd ldrs: swtchd rt 2f out: r.o: no ch w wnr: improve) 4 **2**
764[15] Dahlenburg (IRE) *(61) (JHMGosden)* 3-8-8 JFortune(6) (chsd ldrs: effrt 3f out: one pce) 8 **3**
747[9] Mill Thyme *(50) (MrsMReveley)* 3-7-10 (7) DDenby(2) (led to 2f out: wknd over 1f out) 4 **4**
815[10] Turnpole (IRE) *(53) (MrsMReveley)* 4-9-10 KDarley(3) (dwlt: hld up & bhd: stdy hdwy over 2f out: nvr plcd to chal) 1 **5**
Royal York *(47) (MissSEHall)* 3-8-3 NConnorton(7) (bit bkwd: hld up: stdy hdwy 2f out: nvr plcd to chal) ....½ **6**

750[4] Young Steven *(49) (WTKemp)* 4-9-10 MBirch(1) (plld hrd: trckd ldrs tl wknd 2f out) 2½ 7
Pitter Patter *(36) (MrsNMacauley)* 3-8-3 ACulhane(9) (hld up & bhd: gd hdwy on outside & prom 5f out: wknd 2f out) 5 8
816[10] Menshaar (USA) *(37) (JHMGosden)* 3-8-5 (3) DRMcCabe(10) (bit bkwd: bhd: drvn along 5f out: n.d) 2 9
Freckles Kelly *(31) (MHEasterby)* 3-8-3 SMaloney(4) (plld hrd: trckd ldrs tl lost pl 4f out).......¾ 10

10/11 DIAGHILEF (IRE), **4/1** Dahlenburg (IRE), **6/1** Munaadee (USA), **17/2** Royal York, **10/1** Menshaar (USA), **20/1** Turnpole (IRE), **25/1** Pitter Patter, **33/1** Freckles Kelly, Mill Thyme, **40/1** Young Steven, CSF £7.47 TOTE £1.70: £1.10 £1.50 £1.80 (£4.90) Trio £5.30 OWNER Mr C. C. Buckley (MIDDLEHAM) BRED Rathasker Stud 10 Rn 2m 14.05 (7.35) SF: 29/23/10/-/18/-/14/-/-/-
WEIGHT FOR AGE 3yo-16lb

969

ROUNDABOUT H'CAP (0-75) (3-Y.O) (Class D) £3,724.50 (£1,128.00: £551.00: £262.50) **1m** Stalls: Low GOING minus 0.08 sec per fur (G) 5-00 (5-06)

759[5] **Vindaloo (45)***(54) (JLHarris)* 3-7-8 (7) PFessey(7) (lw: chsd ldr: led 2f out: styd on wl)...........— 1
839[9] Three Arch Bridge **(58)***(64) (MJohnston)* 3-9-0b DHolland(8) (chsd ldrs: rdn & hung bdly lft 2f out: kpt on same pce ins fnl f).............1½ 2
876[9] Gospel Song **(50)***(55) (WTKemp)* 3-8-3 (3) DRMcCabe(11) (mid div: hdwy over 2f out: styd on u.p fnl f: nvr trbld ldrs) ....nk 3
759[15] Tinklers Folly **(46)***(47) (DenysSmith)* 3-7-13 (3) DarrenMoffatt(1) (led to 2f out: styd on one pce fnl f) 2 4
786[8] Spanish Steps (IRE) **(62)***(53) (MWEasterby)* 3-9-4 SMaloney(9) (chsd ldrs: rdn over 2f out: one pce) 5 5
759[8] Simand **(53)***(43) (EWeymes)* 3-8-9 NKennedy(13) (bhd tl styd on fnl 2f: nvr nr ldrs)................½ 6
Ring of Vision (IRE) **(50)***(37)*(Fav)*(MrsMReveley)* 3-8-6 KDarley(10) (sn pushed along: hmpd & lost pl 5f out: sme hdwy 2f out: n.d).............1½ 7
758[10] Farfields Prince **(57)***(40) (DNicholls)* 3-8-13 NConnorton(6) (trckd ldrs tl wknd over 2f out: n.m.r over 1f out: eased).............2 8
Cumbrian Minstrel **(65)***(48) (MHEasterby)* 3-9-7 MBirch(12) (hld up & bhd: hdwy on ins over 3f out: n.m.r 2f out & 1f out: n.d).............hd 9
773[8] Kings Vision **(60)***(42) (BSRothwell)* 3-8-11 (5) JStack(4) (t: nvr bttr than mid div) ....¾ 10
Belinda Blue **(56)** *(RAFahey)* 3-8-12 ACulhane(2) (b.hind: stdd s: hld up & plld hrd: rapid hdwy & prom 5f out: wknd qckly 3f out: t.o).............20 11
875[W] Chaldon Herring **(63)** *(TDBarron)* 3-9-5 JFortune(3) (hld up & plld hrd: mid div: eased over 2f out: p.u ins fnl f: lame)............. P

3/1 Ring of Vision (IRE) (op 5/1), **11/2** Chaldon Herring, **7/1** Simand, VINDALOO, **8/1** Three Arch Bridge, **9/1** Spanish Steps (IRE), Tinklers Folly, Farfields Prince, **12/1** Cumbrian Minstrel, **14/1** Kings Vision, **20/1** Gospel Song, Belinda Blue, CSF £61.82 CT £989.74 TOTE £4.80: £1.40 £3.30 £5.00 (£15.80) Trio £54.00 OWNER Mr J. D. Abell (MELTON MOWBRAY) BRED Green Park Investments Ltd 12 Rn 1m 45.89 (6.89) SF: 11/21/12/4/10/-/-/-/5/-/-/-

T/Jkpt: Not won; £15,700.26 to Chester 9/5/95. T/Plpt: £55.50 (197.69 Tckts). T/Qdpt: £10.40 (7.85 Tckts). WG

0778-WARWICK (L-H)

Monday May 8th (Firm, Good to firm patches)

WEATHER: fair WIND: mod across

970

E.B.F. PRIMROSE MAIDEN STKS (2-Y.O F) (Class D) £3,752.50 (£1,120.00: £535.00: £242.50) **5f** Stalls: Low GOING minus 0.39 sec per fur (F) 2-15 (2-16)

716[3] **Windswept (IRE)** *(81) (DJSffrenchDavis)* 2-8-11 MTebbutt(4) (led: rdn 2f out: drvn out).......— 1
Mystic Tempo (USA) *(79) (PWChapple-Hyam)* 2-8-4 (7) RHavlin(5) (small: unf: lw: prom: hrd rdn & outpcd 2f out: rallied fnl f: r.o wl).............½ 2
669[8] Limerick Princess (IRE) *(73)*(Fav)*(JBerry)* 2-8-11 GCarter(8) (w wnr: rn green & ev ch over 1f out: nt qckn) 2 3
Our Worley (IRE) *(63) (APJarvis)* 2-8-11 TSprake(1) (lengthy: bit bkwd: hld up: swtchd lft over 1f out: one pce).............3 4
791[12] Wingnut (IRE) *(47) (GLewis)* 2-8-11 SWhitworth(2) (bit bkwd: s.i.s: bhd fnl 2f) 5 5
Cashtal Lace *(SGKnight)* 2-8-6 (5) SDrowne(6) (unf: bkwd: prom: rdn over 2f out: wknd qckly: t.o).............20 6

6/4 Limerick Princess (IRE), **11/4** Mystic Tempo (USA), **100/30** WINDSWEPT (IRE), **8/1** Our Worley (IRE), **12/1** Wingnut (IRE), **33/1** Cashtal Lace, CSF £12.03 TOTE £4.20: £1.60 £1.70 (£6.70) OWNER Miss Henrietta Senn (UPPER LAMBOURN) BRED Mrs A. T. Doyle 6 Rn
60.2 secs (2.20) SF: 25/23/17/7/-/-

971

STONELEIGH PARK POLO CLUB H'CAP (0-80) (3-Y.O) (Class D) £4,273.10 (£1,278.80: £613.40: £280.70)
7f Stalls: Low GOING minus 0.39 sec per fur (F) 2-45 (2-47)

621[12] **Maiandros (GR) (80)***(90) (RCharlton)* 3-9-7 SWhitworth(1) (hld up: rdn & 6th st: hdwy 2f out: edgd rt & led ins fnl f: r.o wl) — 1
624[7] Fairelaine **(60)***(66) (APJarvis)* 3-8-1 TSprake(10) (chsd ldrs: rdn over 3f out: 5th st: r.o wl ins fnl f) 1¾ 2
*443** Indrapura (IRE) **(66)***(70)*(Fav)*(PFICole)* 3-8-7b CRutter(8) (led: clr 5f out: hrd rdn over 1f out: hdd ins fnl f) ¾ 3
Dancing Heart **(69)***(72) (BJMeehan)* 3-8-10 MTebbutt(7) (chsd ldr: 2nd st: rdn 2f out: ev ch 1f out: nt qckn) ½ 4
722[8] Blasted **(60)***(63) (RHannon)* 3-8-1 SRaymont(6) (hld up: 4th st: rdn & ev ch 1f out: nt qckn) nk 5
674[9] Delight of Dawn **(75)***(75) (KTIvory)* 3-8-9 (7) CScally(9) (b.hind: hld up: 7th st: hdwy on ins & hung lft over 1f out: nt clr run: one pce fnl f) 1 6
*300** Irie Mon (IRE) **(62)***(62) (JWHills)* 3-7-10 (7) MHenry(11) (3rd st: ev ch over 1f out: wknd ins fnl f) s.h 7
Nosirrah **(60)***(54) (CAHorgan)* 3-7-10 (5) NVarley(4) (9th st: a bhd) 2½ 8
Anistop **(58)***(46) (RAkehurst)* 3-7-13 ow2 GCarter(2) (a bhd) 1¾ 9
648[18] Can't Say (IRE) **(56)***(29) (JMBradley)* 3-7-4 (7)ow4 SLanigan(3) (a bhd) 6 10
648[16] Anna Bannanna **(64)***(40) (MCPipe)* 3-8-5 GBardwell(5) (8th st: a bhd) ½ 11

LONG HANDICAP Can't Say (IRE) 6-9

4/1 Indrapura (IRE), **9/2** Irie Mon (IRE) (op 7/1), **11/2** MAIANDROS (GR), **7/1** Anistop, **8/1** Anna Bannanna, **9/1** Blasted, **10/1** Delight of Dawn, Dancing Heart, **12/1** Fairelaine, **20/1** Nosirrah, **33/1** Can't Say (IRE), CSF £63.08 CT £268.08 TOTE £6.50: £2.80 £4.80 £1.60 (£98.90) Trio £83.90 OWNER Ippotour A (BECKHAMPTON) BRED Ippotour S A 11 Rn
1m 25.4 (1.20) SF: 58/34/38/40/31/43/30/22/14/-/8

972

STILL MATERIALS HANDLING LIMITED STKS (0-60) (4-Y.O+) (Class F) £2,796.20 (£773.20: £368.60)
6f Stalls: Low GOING minus 0.39 sec per fur (F) 3-15 (3-17)

877[11] **Plum First (60)***(64) (LRLloyd-James)* 5-8-4 (7) KimberleyHart(1) (b.hind: 3rd st: rdn to ld ins fnl f: r.o wl) — 1
726* Aragrove **(58)***(64)*(Fav)*(JWPayne)* 5-9-0b MTebbutt(8) (b: 7th st: hdwy, hrd rdn & edgd rt over 1f out: hung bdly rt ins fnl f: r.o wl) 1¼ 2
656[5] Petraco (IRE) **(55)***(59) (NASmith)* 7-8-11 DBiggs(7) (w ldr: led 2f out: hdd ins fnl f) ½ 3
739[8] Bold Cyrano (IRE) **(55)***(55) (BPalling)* 4-8-11 TSprake(3) (hld up: 5th st: rdn over 1f out: r.o one pce) 1½ 4
839[18] Bee Dee Best (IRE) **(37)***(55) (JPSmith)* 4-8-11 GCarter(5) (hld up & bhd: hdwy on ins & 6th st: r.o one pce fnl f) nk 5
887[10] Great Hall **(60)***(54) (PDCundell)* 6-8-6b(5) DGriffiths(2) (s.s: 8th st: hdwy 2f out: carried rt over 1f out: bdly hmpd ins fnl f: nt rcvr) hd 6
748* Brookhead Lady **(59)***(50) (PDEvans)* 4-8-6 (3) SSanders(4) (led 4f: wknd fnl f) ¾ 7
887[9] Halbert **(42)***(48) (MRChannon)* 6-8-4 (7) DSweeney(9) (9th st: hdwy 2f out: carried rt over 1f out: hmpd ins fnl f: one pce) 1½ 8
656[6] Windrush Boy **(58)***(44) (JRBosley)* 5-8-11 CRutter(10) (4th st: wknd over 1f out) 1½ 9
Calling (USA) **(49)***(40) (WMBrisbourne)* 4-8-6 (5) SDrowne(6) (bit bkwd: a bhd) 1¾ 10

3/1 Aragrove, **4/1** Brookhead Lady, **9/2** Great Hall, **11/2** Petraco (IRE), **6/1** PLUM FIRST, **8/1** Windrush Boy, **12/1** Bold Cyrano (IRE), **20/1** Bee Dee Best (IRE), Halbert, **25/1** Calling (USA), CSF £24.58 TOTE £7.00: £2.50 £1.60 £2.40 (£13.20) Trio £24.60 OWNER Mr J. B. Slatcher (MALTON) BRED Limestone Stud 10 Rn 1m 13.2 (1.20) SF: 46/46/41/37/37/36/32/30/26/22

STEWARDS' ENQUIRY Tebbutt suspended 17-18/5/95 (careless riding).

973

GLOBE INSURANCE MAIDEN STKS (3-Y.O+) (Class D) £4,002.70 (£1,195.60: £571.80: £259.90)
1m Stalls: Low GOING minus 0.39 sec per fur (F) 3-45 (3-53)

853[2] **Jam N Shadeed (USA)** *(77)*(Fav)*(PFICole)* 3-8-11 CRutter(3) (w ldr: led 5f out: qcknd clr over 3f out: hrd rdn 3f out: jst hld on) — 1
715[15] Proud Image *(76) (APJarvis)* 3-8-11 TSprake(6) (wnt 2nd st: hrd rdn over 1f out: r.o wl ins fnl f) nk 2
Manabar *(76) (DMorley)* 3-8-11 MTebbutt(2) (nt clr run 3f out: 5th st: hdwy whn hung lft over 1f out: r.o wl cl home) hd 3
394[5] Adilov *(68) (JRFanshawe)* 3-8-6 (5) NVarley(1) (hld up: 6th st: hdwy 2f out: one pce fnl f) 4 4

French Ginger *(57) (IABalding)* 4-9-0 (5) DGriffiths(4) (w'like: lw: hld up: 4th st: wknd wl over 1f out)....3 5
Torch Dancer (IRE) *(54) (MRStoute)* 4-9-10 GCarter(5) (lengthy: s.s: rdn 4f out: last st: a bhd)....4 6
Rubadub *(46) (JMBradley)* 4-9-0 (5) SDrowne(7) (set slow pce 3f: 3rd st: wknd 2f out)....1½ 7

13/8 JAM N SHADEED (USA), **2/1** Manabar, **4/1** Torch Dancer (IRE), **9/1** French Ginger (8/1-12/1), **12/1** Adilov, **25/1** Proud Image, **33/1** Rubadub, CSF £30.66 TOTE £2.20: £1.50 £4.50 (£23.40) OWNER Mr Thomas Liang (WHATCOMBE) BRED James Wigan 7 Rn
1m 40.3 (3.30) SF: 30/29/29/21/23/20/12
WEIGHT FOR AGE 3yo-13lb

974

ALEX LAWRIE H'CAP (0-80) (3-Y.O) (Class D) £4,104.10 (£1,226.80: £587.40: £267.70) **1m 4f 115y** Stalls: Low GOING minus 0.39 sec per fur (F) 4-15 (4-17)

Celeric (75)*(87) (DMorley)* 3-9-7 MTebbutt(12) (hld up: hdwy 5f out: led over 3f out: r.o wl)....— 1
851⁰ Poly Road **(55)***(66) (MRChannon)* 3-8-1 FNorton(8) (dwlt: hdwy 5f out: rdn & 3rd st: chsd wnr wl over 1f out: r.o)....1 2
745¹¹ Hi-Aud **(58)***(64) (JAkehurst)* 3-8-1 (3) SSanders(4) (hld up & bhd: hdwy 6f out: 2nd st: hrd rdn & swtchd rt over 1f out: one pce)....3½ 3
717² Courbaril **(61)***(60) (SDow)* 3-8-7 GCarter(3) (hld up: hrd rdn 4f out: 4th st: wknd 2f out)....6 4
*894*⁴ Frome Lad **(58)***(54) (WGMTurner)* 3-7-11 (7) ADaly(6) (hld up: gd hdwy 6f out: 5th st: wknd 2f out)....1¾ 5
773² Just Fizzy **(47)***(33) (JWharton)* 3-7-2 (5) MBaird(2) (plld hrd: a.p: led 5f out tl over 3f out: 6th & wknd st)....8 6
618¹⁰ John Lee Hooker **(70)***(56) (DWPArbuthnot)* 3-8-11 (5) NVarley(7) (bhd fnl 6f)....hd 7
745¹² My Mum Said **(62)***(42) (LadyHerries)* 3-8-1b(7)ow2 JO'Dwyer(9) (led: clr 9f out: hdd 5f out: wknd 2f out)....3½ 8
786² Elation **(62)***(42) (PFICole)* 3-8-8 CRutter(1) (lw: 4th st: wknd 2f out)....1¼ 9
651² Matamoros **(70)***(47)*(Fav)*(JLDunlop)* 3-9-2 SWhitworth(5) (lw: hdwy 6f out: wknd over 3f out)....2½ 10
647¹³ Million Dancer **(70)***(46) (MCPipe)* 3-9-2b TSprake(10) (lw: prom tl rdn & wknd 6f out)....nk 11
651¹⁴ Little Secret (IRE) **(57)** *(TMJones)* 3-7-10 (7)ow10 DToole(11) (chsd ldrs tl wknd 5f out: t.o)...dist 12

11/10 Matamoros, **7/1** Courbaril, **8/1** Poly Road (op 5/1), CELERIC (op 5/1), Elation, John Lee Hooker, **12/1** Million Dancer, **16/1** Just Fizzy, Hi-Aud, **20/1** Frome Lad, My Mum Said, **33/1** Little Secret (IRE), CSF £73.27 CT £947.62 TOTE £12.20: £3.10 £1.70 £3.70 (£30.00) Trio £259.60; £182.84 to Chester 09/05/95 OWNER Mr Christopher Spence (NEWMARKET) BRED Chieveley Manor Enterprises 12 Rn 2m 40.5 (3.00) SF: 55/34/32/28/22/1/24/10/10/15/14/-

975

PARTCO H'CAP (0-70) (4-Y.O+) (Class E) £3,874.50 (£1,161.00:£558.00: £256.50) **1m 2f 169y** Stalls: Low GOING minus 0.39 sec per fur (F) 4-45 (4-46)

738⁴ **Haroldon (IRE) (56)***(67) (BPalling)* 6-9-1 TSprake(9) (4th st: led over 1f out: comf)....— 1
864³ Rasayel (USA) **(40)***(47) (PDEvans)* 5-7-13 FNorton(11) (hdwy over 5f out: 2nd st: ev ch over 1f out: one pce)....3 2
762¹⁰ Anlace **(54)***(56) (SMellor)* 6-8-13 MWigham(7) (hdwy 5f out: 5th st: edgd lft over 1f out: r.o one pce)....3 3
634¹⁶ Roi de la Mer (IRE) **(65)***(65) (JAkehurst)* 4-9-10 SWhitworth(3) (led: rdn & hdd over 1f out: wknd ins fnl f)....1¼ 4
Masuri Kabisa (USA) **(37)***(34) (HJCollingridge)* 4-7-3 (7)ow3 SLanigan(4) (wl bhd tl gd hdwy 3f out: r.o ins fnl f)....hd 5
Mister O'Grady (IRE) **(48)***(48)*(Fav)*(RAkehurst)* 4-8-7 GCarter(2) (no hdwy fnl 2f)....hd 6
731¹⁰ Araboybill **(60)***(60) (MartynMeade)* 4-9-5 VSlattery(1) (prom: rdn 4f out: 6th st: no hdwy)......s.h 7
Thatchmaster (IRE) **(57)***(44) (CAHorgan)* 4-8-11 (5) NVarley(8) (plld hrd: chsd ldr tl 3rd st: wknd 2f out)....9 8
634ᵁ Prenonamoss **(65)***(44) (DWPArbuthnot)* 7-9-10v MTebbutt(5) (b.hind: bhd fnl 3f)....5 9
653⁸ Tony's Mist **(66)***(43) (JMBradley)* 5-9-6 (5) SDrowne(6) (a bhd)....1½ 10
762⁴ Lady Reema **(41)***(9) (MissAJWhitfield)* 4-8-0 CRutter(10) (a bhd: t.o)....6 11
LONG HANDICAP Masuri Kabisa (USA) 7-5

7/4 Mister O'Grady (IRE), **9/2** Rasayel (USA), **8/1** Anlace, Lady Reema, **9/1** Roi de la Mer (IRE), HAROLDON (IRE), **10/1** Prenonamoss, **14/1** Araboybill, **16/1** Tony's Mist, Thatchmaster (IRE), **20/1** Masuri Kabisa (USA), CSF £49.97 CT £320.72 TOTE £13.70: £3.50 £2.00 £2.50 (£29.00) Trio £35.80 OWNER Lamb Brook Associates (COWBRIDGE) BRED Owen Bourke in Ireland 11 Rn
2m 16.8 (3.30) SF: 43/23/32/41/10/24/36/20/20/19/-

976 LEVY BOARD APPRENTICE H'CAP (0-70) (3-Y.O+) (Class G) £2,385.50 (£678.00: £336.50)
1m Stalls: Low GOING minus 0.39 sec per fur (F) 5-15 (5-16)

526[10] **Aitch N'Bee (58)***(63) (LadyHerries)* 12-8-9 (7) PDoe(7) (hld up: 8th st: hdwy on ins 2f out: led wl ins fnl f: r.o wl)........— 1
627[5] Court Nap (IRE) **(54)***(57) (SMellor)* 3-7-10 (3) ADaly(9) (4th st: hung rt over 2f out: ev ch ins fnl f: r.o)........1 2
820[2] Mr Cube (IRE) **(49)***(52)*(Fav)*(JMBradley)* 5-8-4v(3) RWaterfield(10) (hdwy & 5th st: ev ch ins fnl f: r.o)........s.h 3
766[4] Keys Seminar **(49)***(51) (JohnBerry)* 3-7-1b(7)ow1 RMullen(12) (led 6f out: rn wd ent st: clr whn hung lft over 1f out: hdd wl ins fnl f)........s.h 4
526[4] Chairmans Choice **(46)***(45) (APJarvis)* 5-7-13 (5) BHunter(8) (hld up: 7th st: hdwy over 1f out: r.o wl ins fnl f)........1¾ 5
790[6] Nakita **(57)***(55) (CNAllen)* 4-8-8 (7) KarenMarkham(3) (b.hind: s.s: hdwy fnl 2f: nt rch ldrs)........½ 6
817[12] Export Mondial **(42)***(38) (PBurgoyne)* 5-8-0 MHenry(11) (2nd st: wknd over 1f out)........1 7
651[10] Specialize **(55)***(44) (KRBurke)* 3-7-7 (7)ow7 SO'Shea(4) (6th st: no hdwy fnl f)........nk 8
752[6] Sweet Pavlova (USA) **(67)***(62)*(Fav)*(PFICole)* 3-8-5 (7) DavidO'Neill(1) (b.hind: led 2f: 3rd st: wknd fnl f)........½ 9
Honest Woman **(37)***(31) (NEBerry)* 4-7-4 (5) JBramhill(2) (bhd: 9th st: hdwy & nt clr run over 1f out: n.d)........nk 10
335[8] Personimus **(35)***(28) (CaptJWilson)* 5-7-2 (5) BHalligan(5) (a bhd)........½ 11
Harvest Rose **(55)***(46) (OO'Neill)* 6-8-8 (5) AimeeCook(13) (a bhd)........1¼ 12
Mohawk Trail **(70)***(35) (GLewis)* 6-9-9 (5) ALakeman(6) (lw: a wl bhd: t.o)........13 13
LONG HANDICAP Specialize 7-4 Personimus 7-1 Keys Seminar 7-5

4/1 Sweet Pavlova (USA), Mr Cube (IRE), **6/1** Chairmans Choice, Mohawk Trail, **8/1** Keys Seminar, **10/1** Court Nap (IRE), **11/1** Export Mondial, **12/1** Harvest Rose, **14/1** AITCH N'BEE, Nakita, **20/1** Honest Woman, **25/1** Specialize, **33/1** Personimus, CSF £141.27 CT £616.76 TOTE £13.40: £4.50 £2.70 £2.10 (£64.60) Trio £78.40 OWNER Lady Herries (LITTLEHAMPTON) BRED Liam Ward 13 Rn
1m 39.4 (2.40) SF: 44/25/33/19/26/36/19/12/30/12/9/27/16
WEIGHT FOR AGE 3yo-13lb
T/Plpt: £97.00 (69.36 Tckts). T/Qdpt: £20.80 (4.2 Tckts). KH

CHESTER (L-H)
Tuesday May 9th (Good to firm)
WEATHER: dry & dull WIND: fresh against

977 LILY AGNES STKS (2-Y.O) (Class B) £6,797.20 (£2,534.80: £1,232.40: £522.00: £226.00: £107.60)
5f 16y Stalls: Low GOING minus 0.23 sec per fur (GF) 2-10 (2-12)

849[3] **What Fun** *(69+)*(Fav)*(RHannon)* 2-8-10 MJKinane(5) (lw: a.p: led over 1f out: sn clr: easily)........— 1
Il Doria (IRE) *(50) (JBerry)* 2-8-2 JCarroll(3) (lt-f: unf: dwlt: hdwy over 2f out: hmpd & checked ent st: kpt on fnl f: no ch w wnr)........3½ 2
782* Hotlips Houlihan *(42) (RJRWilliams)* 2-8-5 DBiggs(6) (a.p: ev ch over 1f out: one pce)........3½ 3
Elmswood (USA) *(28) (PWChapple-Hyam)* 2-8-4 ow2 BThomson(4) (neat: s.s: hdwy fnl 2f: nvr nrr)........3½ 4
Le Sport *(20) (DNicholls)* 2-8-7 RCochrane(2) (leggy: lt-f: outpcd)........4 5
Secret Voucher *(5) (BAMcMahon)* 2-8-7 TQuinn(1) (lt-f: unf: bit bkwd: chsd ldrs: led ½-wy tl over 1f out: wknd qckly)........5 6
699* Just Lady *(WGMTurner)* 2-8-5 PMcCabe(7) (led: racd v.wd & hdd ½-wy: sn bhd)........8 7

2/1 WHAT FUN, **4/1** Il Doria (IRE), **9/2** Elmswood (USA) (op 5/2), **5/1** Just Lady, **7/1** Hotlips Houlihan, **16/1** Secret Voucher, **20/1** Le Sport, CSF £9.62 TOTE £3.10: £1.70 £1.90 (£4.80) OWNER Noodles Racing (MARLBOROUGH) BRED R. B. Stokes 7 Rn
62.92 secs (2.92) SF: 27/8/-/-/-/-/-

978 CHRISTLETON MAIDEN STKS (3-Y.O) (Class D) £8,503.50 (£2,568.00: £1,249.00: £589.50)
1m 2f 75y Stalls: High GOING minus 0.23 sec per fur (GF) 2-40 (2-41)

677[5] **Royal Solo (IRE)** *(91) (PWChapple-Hyam)* 3-9-0 BThomson(6) (hld up: hdwy 4f out: 3rd st: swtchd rt: rdn to ld wl ins fnl f)........— 1
663[4] Sanmartino (IRE) *(90) (BWHills)* 3-9-0 MHills(4) (lw: led 5f: 2nd st: rdn & ev ch wl ins fnl f: no ex cl home)........¾ 2

6355 Main Offender *(87) (HRACecil)* 3-9-0 WRyan(11) (lw: a.p: led over 5f out tl wl ins fnl f)........1¼ 3
6354 Mackook (USA) *(79)*(Fav)*(MRStoute)* 3-9-0 WRSwinburn(1) (lw: a.p: rdn over 2f out: 4th st: edgd lft fnl f: no imp)........5 4
7303 Berkeley Bounder (USA) **(79)***(76) (PFICole)* 3-9-0 TQuinn(2) (chsd ldrs: 6th & rdn st: one pce)........2½ 5
6918 Heath Robinson (IRE) *(76) (JHMGosden)* 3-9-0 LDettori(7) (b: b.hind: bit bkwd: hld up: rdn over 2f out: kpt on one pce)........s.h 6
Hoh Express *(68) (IABalding)* 3-9-0 RCochrane(5) (h.d.w: bit bkwd: hld up: hdwy over 4f out: 5th st: sn rdn & wknd)........5 7
76412 Istabraq (IRE) *(66) (JHMGosden)* 3-9-0 WCarson(10) (b.hind: bit bkwd: a bhd)........1¼ 8
7619 Baddi Quest *(66) (BHanbury)* 3-9-0 PaulEddery(9) (bit bkwd: a in rr)........hd 9
85411 Ambidextrous (IRE) *(62) (CEBrittain)* 3-9-0 MJKinane(8) (bit bkwd: prom to ½-wy: grad lost tch)........2½ 10
42811 Roscommon Lad (IRE) **(42)** *(RHollinshead)* 3-9-0 JReid(3) (s.s: a bhd & t.o)........dist 11

5/2 Mackook (USA), **4/1** Sanmartino (IRE), **5/1** Main Offender, Hoh Express, **7/1** ROYAL SOLO (IRE) (op 4/1), **11/1** Istabraq (IRE), Heath Robinson (IRE), **20/1** Berkeley Bounder (USA), Baddi Quest, **25/1** Ambidextrous (IRE), **100/1** Roscommon Lad (IRE), CSF £34.92 TOTE £10.60: £2.70 £1.70 £2.30 (£18.30) Trio £54.80 OWNER Mr R. E. Sangster (MARLBOROUGH) BRED Littleton Stud and Camas Park Stud 11 Rn 2m 12.15 (3.45) SF: 53/52/49/41/38/38/30/28/28/24/-

979 DALHAM CHESTER VASE STKS (Gp 3) (3-Y.O) (Class A) £29,250.00 (£10,935.00: £5,242.50: £2,272.50)
1m 4f 66y Stalls: Low GOING minus 0.23 sec per fur (GF) 3-10 (3-12)

8264 **Luso (102)***(103) (CEBrittain)* 3-8-10 MJKinane(1) (lw: a.p: 3rd st: led ins fnl f: all out)........— 1
Court of Honour (IRE) *(107) (PWChapple-Hyam)* 3-9-0 JReid(2) (h.d.w: bit bkwd: hld up: hdwy over 3f out: 2nd st: ev ch fnl f: r.o wl)........hd 2
*564** Maralinga (IRE) **(92)***(102) (MBell)* 3-8-10 MFenton(5) (led tl hdd ins fnl f: unable qckn cl home)........¾ 3
8262 Singspiel (IRE) **(109)***(97)*(Fav)*(MRStoute)* 3-8-10 WRSwinburn(4) (hld up & bhd: effrt & 6th st: nvr nr to chal)........4 4
7115 Stiffelio (IRE) **(102)***(96) (RHannon)* 3-8-10 LDettori(3) (s.i.s: bhd: hdwy 3f out: 5th st: nt rch ldrs)........¾ 5
787* Royal Scimitar (USA) **(104)***(95) (PFICole)* 3-8-10 TQuinn(6) (lw: b.hind: prom: 4th & rdn st: hmpd bel dist: nt rcvr)........¾ 6
7157 Northern Law *(BWHills)* 3-8-10 MHills(7) (bit bkwd: chsd ldrs over 8f: wknd qckly: 7th & t.o ent st)........dist 7

Evens Singspiel (IRE), **7/2** Court of Honour (IRE), **9/2** Royal Scimitar (USA), **11/1** LUSO, **14/1** Stiffelio (IRE), **16/1** Maralinga (IRE), **33/1** Northern Law, CSF £45.63 TOTE £13.60: £4.20 £2.00 (£25.50) OWNER Mr Saeed Manana (NEWMARKET) BRED Saeed Manana 7 Rn
2m 38.38 (1.78) SF: 65/69/64/59/58/57/-

980 TOTE CREDIT TROPHY H'CAP (0-100) (3-Y.O) (Class C) £18,147.50 (£5,480.00: £2,665.00: £1,257.50)
7f 122y Stalls: Low GOING minus 0.23 sec per fur (GF) 3-40 (3-41)

758* **Classicy (80)***(86+)*(Fav)*(MRStoute)* 3-8-3 WCarson(2) (a.p: 3rd st: rdn to ld ins fnl f: hld on)........— 1
6943 Bedivere (USA) **(83)***(88) (PWChapple-Hyam)* 3-8-6 JReid(10) (lw: hld up: hdwy 3f out: 6th st: r.o u.p fnl f: jst failed)........nk 2
5049 Emirates Express **(79)***(80) (JWHills)* 3-8-2 RHills(4) (chsd ldr: 2nd st: led jst ins fnl f: sn hdd: one pce)........2 3
6784 Dance Band (USA) **(92)***(88) (BHanbury)* 3-9-1 WRSwinburn(1) (led tl hdd & wknd ins fnl f: kpt on one pce)........2½ 4
6949 Shifting Moon **(77)***(72) (IABalding)* 3-8-0 PaulEddery(6) (bit bkwd: chsd ldrs: pushed along ½-wy: kpt on ins fnl f)........½ 5
686* Bettergeton **(77)***(67) (PJBevan)* 3-7-11 (3) SSanders(11) (chsd ldrs tl 5th & rdn st: sn btn).....2½ 6
5722 Lyford Law (IRE) **(82)***(71) (JHMGosden)* 3-8-5 LDettori(5) (b: b.hind: chsd ldrs: 4th st: rdn & one pce appr fnl f)........s.h 7
8584 Welton Arsenal **(98)***(86) (MRChannon)* 3-9-7 RHughes(9) (hld up in rr: swtchd ins & effrt ent st: no imp)........½ 8
6147 Tidal Reach (USA) **(70)***(57) (ABailey)* 3-7-7 GBardwell(8) (s.i.s: a bhd)........½ 9
6375 Floridante (USA) **(74)***(61) (PFICole)* 3-7-11 CRutter(12) (hld up: effrt ½-wy: wknd over 2f out)nk 10
*527** Heathyards Magic (IRE) **(70)***(55) (RHollinshead)* 3-7-7 NCarlisle(3) (a bhd)........1 11
Flamboro **(70)***(42) (JDBethell)* 3-7-7 JQuinn(7) (a rr div: t.o)........6 12
LONG HANDICAP Tidal Reach (USA) 7-3 Heathyards Magic (IRE) 7-2 Flamboro 7-4

3/1 CLASSICY, **5/1** Dance Band (USA), Lyford Law (IRE), **6/1** Bedivere (USA), **10/1** Floridante (USA), **11/1** Bettergeton, **12/1** Emirates Express, **16/1** Shifting Moon, Welton Arsenal, **20/1** Tidal Reach (USA), Heathyards Magic (IRE), **33/1** Flamboro, CSF £20.64 CT £176.43 TOTE £2.90: £1.60 £2.10 £2.40 (£8.70) Trio £34.60 OWNER Maktoum Al Maktoum (NEWMARKET) BRED S. P. and Major B. P. Hornung 12 Rn 1m 33.63 (1.93) SF: 48/50/42/50/34/29/33/48/19/23/17/4

981

WALKER SMITH & WAY H'CAP (0-90) (4-Y.O+) (Class C) £10,502.00 (£3,176.00: £1,548.00: £734.00)
1m 2f 75y Stalls: High GOING minus 0.23 sec per fur (GF) 4-10 (4-11)

653* **Son of Sharp Shot (IRE) (80)***(90) (JLDunlop)* 5-9-11 PaulEddery(2) (lw: hld up: hdwy 3f out: 4th st: led ins fnl f: all out) — 1
864[5] Sadler's Walk **(70)***(80) (GWragg)* 4-9-1 MHills(4) (lw: chsd ldrs: 5th st: ev ch ins fnl f: r.o) s.h 2
634[11] Laxford Bridge **(80)***(90) (PWHarris)* 4-9-11 WRSwinburn(1) (a.p: led ent st tl ins fnl f: rallied gamely u.p cl home) hd 3
935[2] Sovereign Page (USA) **(75)***(84)*(Fav)*(BHanbury)* 6-9-6 RHughes(5) (hld up: hdwy & 6th st: rdn & unable qckn fnl f) ¾ 4
Lesley's Fashion **(66)***(72) (DJSffrenchDavis)* 4-8-11 TQuinn(8) (hld up & bhd: hdwy 3f out: kpt on fnl f: unable chal) 1¼ 5
811[7] Benfleet **(78)***(82) (RWArmstrong)* 4-9-9 LDettori(6) (hld up & bhd: r.o u.p fnl 2f: nvr nrr) 1¼ 6
Desert Power **(67)***(63) (MartynMeade)* 6-8-12 RPrice(3) (bit bkwd: led tl hdd & 2nd st: wknd over 1f out) 5 7
776[2] Killick **(49)***(44) (ABailey)* 7-7-8 GBardwell(7) (lw: hld up in tch: hdwy 4f out: 3rd st: wknd & eased appr fnl f) ¾ 8
764[2] Quandary (USA) **(83)***(78) (HRACecil)* 4-10-0 WRyan(10) (plld hrd: chsd ldrs over 6f) nk 9
Racing Brenda **(55)***(11) (BAMcMahon)* 4-8-0 FNorton(9) (a bhd: t.o) 25 10

100/30 Sovereign Page (USA), **4/1** SON OF SHARP SHOT (IRE), **9/2** Quandary (USA), **6/1** Killick, Benfleet, **13/2** Sadler's Walk, **9/1** Laxford Bridge, **25/1** Desert Power, Lesley's Fashion, Racing Brenda, CSF £29.78 CT £199.94 TOTE £4.10: £1.80 £2.70 £2.80 (£19.40) Trio £65.40 OWNER Windflower Overseas Holdings Inc (ARUNDEL) BRED Windflower Overseas 10 Rn 2m 11.58 (2.88) SF: 68/58/68/62/50/60/41/22/56/-

982

PRINCE OF WALES H'CAP (0-100) (3-Y.O) (Class C) £7,148.00 (£2,144.00: £1,032.00: £476.00) **5f 16y** Stalls: Low GOING minus 0.23 sec (GF) 4-40 (4-42)

483[2] **Total Stranger (74)***(84) (MrsLPiggott)* 3-8-12 WRyan(4) (mde all: clr ent fnl f: jst hld on) — 1
674[5] Golden Lady (IRE) **(80)***(90) (RHannon)* 3-9-4 MJKinane(6) (lw: a.p: rdn over 1f out: str run fnl f: jst failed) s.h 2
The Happy Fox (IRE) **(76)***(78) (BAMcMahon)* 3-9-0 JFortune(2) (bkwd: chsd ldrs: rdn & one pce fnl f) 2½ 3
828[8] Tart and a Half **(83)***(83) (BJMeehan)* 3-9-7 TQuinn(1) (a.p: swtchd rt over 1f out: kpt on) ½ 4
697[5] Rasas (IRE) **(74)***(74)*(Fav)*(HThomsonJones)* 3-8-12 RHills(3) (lw: hld up: effrt 2f out: nt pce to chal) s.h 5
891[4] One for Jeannie **(66)***(64) (ABailey)* 3-8-4 FNorton(5) (s.i.s: hdwy & nt clr run ent st: wknd fnl f) ¾ 6
904* La Suquet **(73)***(55) (MRChannon)* 3-8-6 (5) 7x PPMurphy(8) (outpcd: a bhd) 5 7
850* Sally Slade **(79)***(52) (CACyzer)* 3-9-3 7x JReid(7) (lw: outpcd & bhd: eased whn btn appr fnl f) 3 8

9/4 Rasas (IRE), **5/1** TOTAL STRANGER, Tart and a Half, **11/2** Sally Slade, **6/1** Golden Lady (IRE), **8/1** La Suquet, **10/1** One for Jeannie, **12/1** The Happy Fox (IRE), CSF £33.54 CT £315.74 TOTE £5.20: £1.40 £2.10 £2.90 (£16.70) OWNER Total Asset Ltd BRED J. K. Bloodstock Ltd 8 Rn 61.25 secs (1.25) SF: 56/62/50/55/46/36/27/24

T/Jkpt: £22,016.30 (0.1 Tckts); £27,908.10 to Chester 10/5/95. T/Plpt: £424.40 (75.59 Tckts). T/Qdpt: £46.60 (9.8 Tckts). IM

0943-DONCASTER (L-H)
Tuesday May 9th (Good to firm, Firm patches)
WEATHER: Cloudy WIND: Almost nil

983

CHUKYO (S) STKS (2-Y.O) (Class F) £3,002.00 (£896.00: £428.00: £194.00)
5f Stalls: High GOING minus 0.41 sec per fur (F) 6-00 (6-01)

740* **Arvzees (IRE)** *(69)*(Fav)*(MRChannon)* 2-9-4 KDarley(8) (chsd ldrs: nt clr run over 1f out: styd on wl to ld wl ins fnl f: drvn out) — 1

8343 Penny Parkes (59) (JBerry) 2-8-13 JCarroll(4) (b.hind: w ldrs: rdn over 1f out: sn led: edgd lft: kpt on) 1½ 2
April's Joy (52) (JNorton) 2-8-6 ACulhane(3) (small: lt-f: hdwy to chse ldrs ½-wy: ev ch over 1f out: unable qckn) ....s.h 3
Fiddles Delight (52) (MRChannon) 2-7-13 (7) DSweeney(2) (leggy: unf: sn outpcd: hdwy over 1f out: styd on wl towards fin) ....hd 4
7706 Snitch (54) (CSmith) 2-8-11 WWoods(7) (rdn & edgd lft over 1f out: sn hdd: no ex fnl f) 1 5
9256 Supergal (29) (MWEasterby) 2-8-6 LCharnock(1) (sn wl outpcd & drvn along) 6 6
7554 Power Dee (21) (MWEasterby) 2-8-6b MBirch(5) (chsd ldrs tl lost pl ½-wy) 2½ 7
Miss Hotshot (RBastiman) 2-8-6 DeanMcKeown(6) (leggy: bkwd: unruly: s.s: rn green & a bhd) 15 8

6/4 ARVZEES (IRE), **2/1** Penny Parkes, **13/2** Supergal, **9/1** Miss Hotshot, **12/1** Fiddles Delight, **14/1** Power Dee, **20/1** Snitch, April's Joy, CSF £5.08 TOTE £2.30: £1.30 £1.30 £4.90 (£1.80) OWNER . Albion Investments (UPPER LAMBOURN) BRED Topazio Est Vaduz 8 Rn
61.52 secs (3.12) SF: 15/5/-/-/-/-/-/-
Bt in 7,000 gns

984

SAPPORO H'CAP (0-75) (3-Y.O+) (Class D) £4,408.30 (£1,320.40: £634.20: £291.10) **7f** Stalls: High GOING minus 0.41 sec per fur (F) 6-30 (6-31)

7806 **Fleet Cadet (45)**(54) (NAGraham) 4-8-1b PaulEddery(15) (sn trckng ldrs: led over 2f out: hrd rdn: all out) ....— 1
7897 Bogart **(55)**(63) (CWFairhurst) 4-8-11 RCochrane(4) (swtchd rt after 2f: hdwy ½-wy: ev ch fnl f: r.o) ....nk 2
5636 Set Table (USA) **(72)**(74)(Fav)(JHMGosden) 6-10-0v LDettori(6) (lw: swtchd rt after 2f: effrt 2f out: kpt on wl) 2½ 3
83913 Awesome Venture **(52)**(51) (MCChapman) 5-8-1 (7) CMunday(18) (led stands side tl over 2f out: kpt on one pce) 1 4
7802 Aquado **(48)**(42) (ALForbes) 6-8-4 JQuinn(7) (lw: swtchd rt after 2f: trckd ldrs gng wl: ev ch 2f out: edgd lft & wknd fnl f) 2 5
1609 Kindergarten Boy (IRE) **(63)**(56) (RBoss) 4-9-5 JCarroll(8) (lw: swtchd rt after 2f: in tch: effrt over 2f out: one pce appr fnl f) ....s.h 6
31311 Rafter-J **(56)**(47) (JAHarris) 4-8-12 KFallon(10) (s.s: bhd tl styd on u.p fnl 2f) ....¾ 7
7494 Admirals Flame (IRE) **(63)**(52) (CFWall) 4-9-5 GDuffield(2) (lw: racd far side: hld up: hdwy over 2f out: nt qckn appr fnl f) ....¾ 8
5837 Coalisland **(40)**(16) (RIngram) 5-7-5v(5)ow3 NVarley(14) (w ldrs: rdn 3f out: sn wknd) 4 9
Robellion **(68)**(47) (DWPArbuthnot) 4-9-10 JWeaver(5) (racd far side: chsd ldr tl wknd 2f out) ....s.h 10
8128 Cradle Days **(67)**(43) (RCSpicer) 6-9-9 JO'Reilly(3) (led far side: wkng whn hung bdly rt over 1f out) 1 11
6753 Shaffishayes **(64)**(35) (MrsMReveley) 3-8-8 KDarley(1) (chsd ldrs far side: wkng whn hmpd 1f out: eased) 1½ 12
4934 The Happy Loon (IRE) **(60)**(31) (DenysSmith) 4-9-2 MBirch(16) (w ldrs tl wknd over 2f out) ....nk 13
7026 Peacefull Reply (USA) **(51)**(18) (FHLee) 5-8-7 ACulhane(9) (chsd ldrs: effrt 3f out: sn wknd) 1¾ 14
4798 Pegs **(48)**(8) (CWThornton) 4-8-4 DeanMcKeown(13) (bhd & drvn along ½-wy: n.d) 2½ 15
75916 Bad News **(57)**(13) (GFierro) 3-7-8 (7)ow2 ADaly(11) (in tch to ½-wy: sn lost pl) ....½ 16
Master M-E-N (IRE) **(60)**(17) (NMBabbage) 3-7-11v(7) SallySandes(17) (lw: chsd ldrs 4f: sn wknd) ....s.h 17
Out of the Mist **(40)** (JAPickering) 4-7-10 NCarlisle(12) (chsd ldrs 4f: sn lost pl) ....hd 18
LONG HANDICAP Coalisland 7-5

100/30 Set Table (USA), **4/1** Admirals Flame (IRE) (tchd 6/1), **9/2** Aquado, **8/1** Shaffishayes, **14/1** FLEET CADET, Peacefull Reply (USA), Kindergarten Boy (IRE), Bogart, **16/1** The Happy Loon (IRE), Robellion, **20/1** Bad News, Rafter-J, Pegs, **33/1** Cradle Days, Coalisland, Master M-E-N (IRE), **40/1** Awesome Venture, **50/1** Out of the Mist, CSF £193.55 CT £751.48 TOTE £27.80: £4.30 £3.60 £1.70 £7.80 (£211.90) Trio £428.90 OWNER Sir John Swaine (NEWMARKET) BRED R. D. Hollingsworth 18 Rn 1m 25.43 (2.03) SF: 28/37/48/25/16/30/21/26/-/21/17/-/5/-/-/-/-/-
WEIGHT FOR AGE 3yo-12lb

985

TOKYO LIMITED STKS (0-80) (3-Y.O) (Class D) £5,526.50 (£1,652.00: £791.00: £360.50) **6f** Stalls: High GOING minus 0.41 sec per fur (F) 7-00 (7-01)

8232 **French Grit (IRE) (80)**(91)(Fav)(MDods) 3-8-11 JWeaver(3) (lw: hld up: hdwy ½-wy: led over 1f out: hung bdly rt: rdn out) ....— 1
Maydaan (IRE) **(80)**(82) (BHanbury) 3-8-6 WRyan(5) (hld up: effrt & n.m.r 2f out: chsd wnr fnl f: nt qckn) 1½ 2

662[4] Jawlaat (USA) **(80)***(77)*(Fav)*(JLDunlop)* 3-8-6 WCarson(9) (swtg: mde most tl hdd over 1f out: kpt on same pce)....1¾ **3**
Banner (USA) **(77)***(73) (BWHills)* 3-8-6 MHills(2) (in tch on outside: effrt ½-wy: sn rdn & no imp)....1½ **4**
674[6] Fantasy Racing (IRE) **(78)***(69) (MRChannon)* 3-8-6 KDarley(8) (lw: trckd ldrs: n.m.r 2f out: grad wknd)....1½ **5**
850[4] Cats Bottom **(72)***(69) (DJSCosgrove)* 3-8-6 MRimmer(7) (s.i.s: bhd: styd on appr fnl f)....s.h **6**
742* Prolific Lady (IRE) **(75)***(64) (MBrittain)* 3-8-9 RCochrane(4) (chsd ldrs: pushed along ½-wy: sn outpcd)....3 **7**
Corio **(77)***(65) (MissSEHall)* 3-8-11 NConnorton(11) (s.i.s: bhd: sme hdwy over 2f out: nvr nr ldrs)....½ **8**
585[2] Midnight Spell **(80)***(52) (MrsJCecil)* 3-8-6 PaulEddery(10) (w ldrs: rdn over 2f out: hung rt & sn wknd)....3 **9**
621[6] Fata (IRE) **(76)***(57) (PTWalwyn)* 3-9-0 LDettori(6) (chsd ldrs tl wknd over 2f out: eased)....1 **10**
Petomi **(80)***(45) (SirMarkPrescott)* 3-8-6 GDuffield(1) (chsd ldrs: drvn along ½-wy: sn lost pl)1½ **11**

4/1 FRENCH GRIT (IRE) (op 7/1), Jawlaat (USA), **9/2** Midnight Spell, **8/1** Petomi, **17/2** Fata (IRE), Banner (USA), **10/1** Maydaan (IRE), **12/1** Fantasy Racing (IRE), **14/1** Cats Bottom, **16/1** Prolific Lady (IRE), Corio, CSF £42.17 TOTE £5.50: £2.00 £5.10 £1.40 (£44.70) Trio £65.20 OWNER Mr Michael Wilson (DARLINGTON) BRED Miss Aisling O'Connell 11 Rn

1m 12.25 (1.25) SF: 43/34/29/25/21/21/16/17/4/9/-

986

NAKAYAMA H'CAP (0-75) (3-Y.O+) (Class D) £3,949.00 (£1,177.00: £561.00: £253.00)
1m 4f Stalls: Low GOING minus 0.41 sec per fur (F) 7-30 (7-31)

495[3] **Dvorak (IRE) (63)***(73) (BJMcMath)* 4-9-8 AMackay(3) (effrt over 3f out: styd on wl u.p appr fnl f: led ins fnl f)....— **1**
778[3] Preston Guild (IRE) **(50)***(57) (ALForbes)* 5-8-9 JWeaver(2) (lw: b: trckd ldrs: led over 2f out: hdd & no ex ins fnl f)....2 **2**
312[2] Fearless Wonder **(60)***(63)*(Fav)*(MrsMReveley)* 4-9-5b KDarley(5) (hld up: effrt & hrd rdn 3f out: kpt on appr fnl f: nvr nr to chal)....3 **3**
860* Hill Farm Dancer **(55)***(58)*(Fav)*(WMBrisbourne)* 4-8-9 (5) 5x AGarth(6) (hld up: drvn along 4f out: edgd lft & one pce fnl 2f)....½ **4**
851[15] China Mail (IRE) **(67)***(68) (JMPEustace)* 3-8-7 ow1 RCochrane(7) (chsd ldrs: rdn & outpcd 3f out: kpt on fnl f)....¾ **5**
879[9] Sir Dickie Cox (IRE) **(44)***(36) (FHLee)* 4-8-3 ACulhane(1) (led tl over 2f out: wknd over 1f out)7 **6**
894[5] Augustan **(56)***(39) (SGollings)* 4-8-10 (5) JStack(9) (hdwy & pushed along ½-wy: rdn 3f out: sn wknd)....7 **7**
762[3] Progression **(65)***(45) (PCHaslam)* 4-9-10 TWilliams(4) (lw: chsd ldrs: rdn 4f out: lost pl over 2f out)....2½ **8**
403[13] General Chase **(45)***(13) (ICampbell)* 5-8-4v DaleGibson(8) (drvn along 5f out: sn bhd)....9 **9**

4/1 Hill Farm Dancer, Fearless Wonder, **9/2** Preston Guild (IRE), DVORAK (IRE), Progression, **12/1** Augustan, **16/1** General Chase, China Mail (IRE), **25/1** Sir Dickie Cox (IRE), CSF £23.75 CT £79.58 TOTE £5.70: £1.80 £1.80 £1.50 (£12.40) Trio £14.40 OWNER Mr Ron Dawson (NEWMARKET) BRED Sheikh Mohammed bin Rashid al Maktoum 9 Rn

2m 34.05 (3.45) SF: 50/34/40/35/26/13/16/22/-
WEIGHT FOR AGE 3yo-19lb

987

FUKUSHIMA MAIDEN STKS (3-Y.O+) (Class D) £4,239.30 (£1,268.40: £608.20: £278.10)
1m (straight) Stalls: High GOING minus 0.41 sec per fur (F) 8-00 (8-01)

663[5] **Mezaan (IRE)** *(84+)*(Fav)*(MRStoute)* 3-8-11 WRSwinburn(5) (lw: trckd ldrs: led over 3f out: styd on u.p fnl 2f)....— **1**
Bakers' Gate (USA) *(82+) (JHMGosden)* 3-8-11 LDettori(4) (w'like: scope: trckd ldrs: effrt over 2f out: nt qckn ins fnl f: improve)....1 **2**
Posing (IRE) *(71) (JRFanshawe)* 3-8-6 DHarrison(10) (in tch: effrt over 2f out: styd on fnl f)...3 **3**
Zygo (USA) *(76) (WJarvis)* 3-8-11 KDarley(7) (bit bkwd: mde most tl over 3f out: r.o same pce appr fnl f)....hd **4**
613[2] Amrak Ajeeb (IRE) *(73) (BHanbury)* 3-8-11 WRyan(1) (lw: swvd lft s: sn chsng ldrs: kpt on same pce appr fnl f)....1½ **5**
841[9] Spanish Stripper (USA) **(53)***(69) (MCChapman)* 4-9-3 (7) CMunday(6) (swtg: a chsng ldrs: drvn along ½-wy: kpt on: nvr able to chal)....1¾ **6**
715[9] Western Fame (USA) *(66) (JLDunlop)* 3-8-11 WCarson(8) (lw: hld up & plld hrd: outpcd & pushed along ½-wy: hmpd over 2f out: nvr nr ldrs)....1¾ **7**
394[4] Daleria *(47) (MissJFCraze)* 4-9-5 SWebster(11) (lw: outpcd & drvn along over 3f out: n.d)....7 **8**

853[3] Arzani (USA) *(52) (DJSCosgrove)* 4-9-10 MRimmer(2) (bit bkwd: swtg: s.i.s: sn chsng ldrs: wknd over 2f out) ....s.h 9
Amnesty Bay *(47) (JRFanshawe)* 3-8-1 (5) NVarley(9) (unf: dwlt: sn chsng ldrs: drvn along ½-wy: sn bhd) ....hd 10
White Knowle *(7) (PTDalton)* 5-9-5 LCharnock(3) (w ldrs tl wknd qckly 3f out: sn bhd: t.o) 20 11

10/11 MEZAAN (IRE), **4/1** Bakers' Gate (USA) (11/4-9/2), **6/1** Amrak Ajeeb (IRE), **7/1** Western Fame (USA), **10/1** Zygo (USA), **12/1** Posing (IRE), Arzani (USA), **20/1** Amnesty Bay, **33/1** Daleria, **50/1** Spanish Stripper (USA), White Knowle, CSF £6.22 TOTE £2.10: £1.20 £1.80 £4.20 (£3.10) Trio £34.20 OWNER Mr Mana Al Maktoum (NEWMARKET) BRED Barronstown Stud and Ron Con Ltd. 11 Rn
1m 38.53 (2.03) SF: 41/39/28/33/30/39/23/17/22/4/-
WEIGHT FOR AGE 3yo-13lb

988

HANSHIN H'CAP (0-70) (3-Y.O+) (Class E) £4,273.10 (£1,278.80: £613.40: £280.70) **1m 2f 60y** Stalls: Low GOING minus 0.41 sec per fur (F) 8-30 (8-35)

738[8] **Larn Fort (50)***(60) (CWFairhurst)* 5-8-13v RCochrane(4) (in tch: effrt on ins & nt clr run 2f out: swtchd & r.o wl u.p to ld post) ....— 1
470[2] Zacaroon **(62)***(72) (LordHuntingdon)* 4-9-11 LDettori(17) (in tch: effrt 3f out: led 1f out tl nr fin) ....hd 2
Alabang **(50)***(58)*(Fav)*(MJCamacho)* 4-8-13 LCharnock(13) (lw: trckd ldrs gng wl: shkn up to ld over 1f out: hdd 1f out: no ex) 1½ 3
841[4] Braille (IRE) **(65)***(72) (MGMeagher)* 4-10-0 JFortune(9) (mid div: hdwy & n.m.r 2f out: nt clr run: styd on ins fnl f) ....hd 4
Barford Lad **(64)***(71) (JRFanshawe)* 8-9-13 DHarrison(18) (hld up: effrt over 2f out: styd on appr fnl f: nt rch ldrs) ....nk 5
818[4] Kirov Protege (IRE) **(48)***(52) (HJCollingridge)* 3-7-9 ow2 JQuinn(14) (s.s: bhd tl styd on wl fnl 2f: nrst fin) ....nk 6
676[2] Kalou **(55)***(61) (CWCElsey)* 4-9-4v TIves(8) (chsd ldr: led over 2f out tl over 1f out: one pce) s.h 7
771[8] Modest Hope (USA) **(48)***(53) (BRichmond)* 8-8-11 JWeaver(2) (lw: s.i.s: hld up & bhd: swtchd outside & styd on over 1f out: nt rch ldrs) ....¾ 8
Colorful Ambition **(62)***(63) (MrsASwinbank)* 5-9-11 NConnorton(3) (bhd: stdy hdwy 2f out: nvr plcd to chal) 3 9
749[9] Move Smartly (IRE) **(55)***(53) (FHLee)* 5-9-4 KDarley(11) (chsd ldrs tl wknd appr fnl f: eased towards fin) 1½ 10
Danus Rex (IRE) **(53)***(49) (CASmith)* 3-7-9 (5)ow2 AGarth(6) (a in rr) ....nk 11
841[3] Benjamins Law **(52)***(47) (JAPickering)* 4-9-1 DeanMcKeown(5) (led to 4f out: wknd 2f out) 2 12
745[9] Kristal Breeze **(53)***(44) (WRMuir)* 3-8-0 WCarson(12) (a bhd) 2½ 13
545[10] Ivanhoe **(30)***(19) (JRArnold)* 4-7-7 RStreet(7) (chsd ldrs tl lost pl over 3f out) 1 14
820[11] Talented Ting (IRE) **(65)***(52) (PCHaslam)* 6-10-0 TWilliams(15) (lw: trckd ldr: led 4f out tl over 2f out: sn lost pl) 1½ 15
748[12] Amlak (USA) **(34)***(19) (TKersey)* 6-7-11 NKennedy(19) (prom: rdn 4f out: sn lost pl) 1½ 16
Kanat Lee (IRE) **(45)***(29) (DonEnricoIncisa)* 4-8-8 KimTinkler(10) (s.i.s: a in rr) ....hd 17
874[2] Broughton's Pride (IRE) **(51)***(21) (JAGlover)* 4-8-9 (5) CTeague(16) (mid div: effrt on outside 3f out: sn wknd & eased) 9 18
Lady Confess **(30)** *(JohnUpson)* 5-7-2b(5) MBaird(1) (Withdawn not under Starter's orders: v.unruly & uns rdr in paddock: jockey sltly inj) .... W

LONG HANDICAP Kirov Protege (IRE) 7-6 Lady Confess 7-1

, **3/1** Alabang (10/1-11/4), **8/1** Zacaroon, Broughton's Pride (IRE), Barford Lad, Kalou, **10/1** Braille (IRE), LARN FORT, **12/1** Benjamins Law, **14/1** Modest Hope (USA), Kirov Protege (IRE), Kristal Breeze, Talented Ting (IRE), **16/1** Move Smartly (IRE), Colorful Ambition, **20/1** Danus Rex (IRE), **40/1** Ivanhoe, Kanat Lee (IRE), **100/1** Amlak (USA), CSF £92.76 CT £286.78 TOTE £11.50: £2.10 £1.60 £1.80 £3.90 (£21.60) Trio £230.90 OWNER A P Development Products (NE) Ltd (MIDDLEHAM) BRED Robert T. Cartwright 18 Rn
2m 9.85 (2.85) SF: 42/54/40/54/53/18/43/35/45/35/15/29/10/1/34/1/11/3/-
WEIGHT FOR AGE 3yo-16lb
T/Plpt: £19.00 (876.67 Tckts). T/Qdpt: £20.90 (9.75 Tckts). WG

AYR (L-H)
Wednesday May 10th (Good to firm)

WEATHER: overcast & cool WIND: almost nil

989

GREIG MIDDLETON STOCKBROKERS LIMITED STKS (0-65) (3-Y.O) (Class F) £2,801.00 (£848.00: £414.00: £197.00) **1m** Stalls: Low GOING minus 0.32 sec per fur (GF) 1-55 (1-57)

640[4] **Persian Fayre (65)***(79) (JBerry)* 3-8-12 JFortune(4) (lw: trckd ldr: led 1½f out: rdn & styd on strly) ....— 1

7222 Takeshi (IRE) **(65)***(68)*(Fav)*(EALDunlop)* 3-8-7 PaulEddery(1) (lw: led: qcknd over 2f out: hdd 1½f out: no ex) 3 **2**
Music Maker **(65)***(68)* *(SirMarkPrescott)* 3-8-7 GDuffield(6) (prom: effrt 3f out: one pce) ....hd **3**
7748 Grate British (IRE) **(62)***(72)* *(EWeymes)* 3-8-12 KDarley(2) (trckd ldrs: effrt over 2f out: r.o one pce) ....½ **4**
6649 Jurassic Sue **(65)***(65)* *(BWHills)* 3-8-2 (5) JDSmith(7) (lw: effrt over 3f out: rdn & no imp) 1 **5**
Teejay'n'aitch (IRE) **(54)***(63)* *(JSGoldie)* 3-8-12 GBardwell(5) (outpcd & bhd appr st: n.d) 3½ **6**
7587 Hutchies Lady **(54)***(42)* *(RMMcKellar)* 3-8-7 DHarrison(3) (b.off hind: in tch to st: sn wknd) 8 **7**

85/40 Takeshi (IRE), **9/4** Music Maker, **5/2** Jurassic Sue (op 6/4), **8/1** PERSIAN FAYRE, **14/1** Grate British (IRE), **16/1** Teejay'n'aitch (IRE), **50/1** Hutchies Lady, CSF £24.79 TOTE £8.40: £2.60 £1.30 (£8.00) OWNER Mr Murray Grubb (COCKERHAM) BRED Aramstone Stud Co 7 Rn
1m 41.03 (4.23) SF: 27/16/16/20/13/11/-

990 BLUE CHIP PEP CLAIMING MAIDEN STKS (3-Y.O+) (Class F)
£2,840.00 (£860.00: £420.00: £200.00)
1m 2f Stalls: Low GOING minus 0.32 sec per fur (GF) 2-25 (2-28)

59111 **Bulsara (50)***(53)* *(CWFairhurst)* 3-8-3 PaulEddery(11) (trckd ldrs: led 2f out: r.o wl) ....— **1**
8249 Island Cascade *(44)* *(DonEnricoIncisa)* 3-8-0 KimTinkler(5) (s.i.s: hdwy 3f out: hung lft: styd on wl towards fin) 4 **2**
8768 Never so True **(40)***(36)* *(MartynWane)* 4-8-10v JFortune(6) (led after 1f tl hdd 2f out: one pce) 1 **3**
72210 Upex le Gold Too **(50)***(40)* *(MrsASwinbank)* 3-7-13 SMaloney(10) (in tch: effrt 3f out: one pce)½ **4**
9089 To Prove a Point **(29)***(39)* *(JJO'Neill)* 3-7-13 NKennedy(3) (bhd tl styd on wl fnl 2f) ....½ **5**
59211 Chita Rivera **(51)***(37)*(Fav)*(PJMakin)* 4-9-2v KDarley(1) (a.p: effrt 3f out: no rspnse) 2 **6**
5785 Funny Rose **(23)***(30)* *(PMonteith)* 5-8-9 JMarshall(7) (prom: hmpd ent st: no imp after) ....s.h **7**
81810 Master Fiddler **(33)***(32)* *(EWeymes)* 5-9-5 DeanMcKeown(8) (led 1f: chsd ldrs tl bdly hmpd ent st: n.d after) 5 **8**
8755 Keith's Pride (IRE) **(33)***(23)* *(TDyer)* 3-8-3 DHarrison(12) (cl up tl wknd over 2f out) 6 **9**
75814 Thrushwood *(12)* *(NChamberlain)* 3-7-6 (5)ow3 NVarley(2) (bhd fnl 3f) 1¼ **10**
8807 Leap Year Baby (IRE) **(41)***(6)* *(MDHammond)* 3-7-9 DaleGibson(13) (in tch to st: sn wknd) 4 **11**
7845 Daytime Dawn (IRE) *(DMoffatt)* 4-9-4 (3) DarrenMoffatt(9) (cl up tl stumbled bdly ent st: nt rcvr) 30 **12**
6417 Solor Dancer **(27)** *(CBBBooth)* 3-8-5v MBirch(4) (bhd fnl 6f) 5 **13**

5/2 Chita Rivera, **7/1** BULSARA, Upex le Gold Too, **8/1** Master Fiddler, **9/1** Leap Year Baby (IRE), Funny Rose, **10/1** Never so True, **14/1** Keith's Pride (IRE), **20/1** Daytime Dawn (IRE), To Prove a Point, **50/1** Solor Dancer, Island Cascade, **100/1** Thrushwood, CSF £222.86 TOTE £6.80: £2.30 £57.70 £3.50 (£125.50) Trio Not won; £362.57 to Chester 11/05/95 OWNER Twinacre Nurseries Ltd (MIDDLEHAM) BRED P. and Mrs Blacker 13 Rn 2m 10.2 (5.60) SF: 18/9/17/5/4/18/11/13/-/-/-/-/-
WEIGHT FOR AGE 3yo-16lb

OFFICIAL EXPLANATION Island Cascade: was reported to have hung badly left

991 GREIG MIDDLETON STOCKBROKERS CUP H'CAP (0-70) (3-Y.O+) (Class E) £4,279.50 (£1,296.00: £633.00: £301.50)
1m 2f 192y Stalls: Low GOING minus 0.32 sec per fur (GF) 2-55 (2-57)

Keep Battling (35)*(44)* *(JSGoldie)* 5-7-7 GBardwell(5) (a in tch: qcknd to ld appr fnl f: r.o) ...— **1**
67615 Drummer Hicks **(51)***(58)* *(EWeymes)* 6-8-9 DeanMcKeown(10) (led: qcknd ent st: hdd appr fnl f: no ex) 1¼ **2**
77112 Bardia **(36)***(42)* *(DonEnricoIncisa)* 5-7-8 ow1 KimTinkler(4) (hld up & bhd: rdn 3f out: r.o towards fin) ....nk **3**
2293 Imperial Bid (FR) **(55)***(61)* *(DenysSmith)* 7-8-13 MBirch(7) (hld up: effrt 3f out: squeezed thro appr fnl f: styd on wl) ....½ **4**
9058 Monkey Wench (IRE) **(52)***(56)* *(JBerry)* 4-8-10v JFortune(6) (cl up: rdn 3f out: grad wknd fnl 2f) 1½ **5**
7763 Samsonesque **(66)***(70)*(Fav)*(JRFanshawe)* 4-9-10 DHarrison(8) (lw: prom: effrt ent st: sn rdn & one pce) ....hd **6**
27112 Sunday News'n'echo (USA) **(57)***(60)* *(WStorey)* 4-9-1 PaulEddery(2) (chsd ldrs tl outpcd 3f out: btn whn hmpd over 1f out) ....¾ **7**
87414 Roscommon Joe (IRE) **(35)***(34)* *(JJO'Neill)* 5-7-7 NKennedy(3) (hdwy 7f out: btn whn hmpd over 1f out) 2½ **8**
7639 Children's Choice (IRE) **(64)***(60)*(Fav)*(PJMcBride)* 4-9-8 KDarley(1) (b.off hind: sn chsng ldrs: rdn ent st: wknd wl over 1f out) 2 **9**

876[11] Moofaji **(66)***(57) (FWatson)* 4-9-10 NConnorton(11) (lost tch fnl 3f)....3½ **10**
My Kerry Dancer (USA) **(70)***(55) (JJO'Neill)* 5-10-0 GDuffield(9) (lost tch appr st)....4 **11**
LONG HANDICAP Roscommon Joe (IRE) 7-6 Bardia 7-2 Keep Battling 7-4

7/2 Samsonesque, Children's Choice (IRE), **4/1** KEEP BATTLING, **5/1** Drummer Hicks, **11/1** Monkey Wench (IRE), Imperial Bid (FR), **12/1** Sunday News'n'echo (USA), **16/1** My Kerry Dancer (USA), **20/1** Moofaji, **33/1** Roscommon Joe (IRE), **66/1** Bardia, CSF £23.27 CT £1,044.90 TOTE £6.60: £2.00 £1.80 £8.00 (£19.60) Trio £350.40; £128.33 to Chester 11/05/95 OWNER Mr J. S. Goldie (KILMARNOCK) BRED Mrs E. Campbell 11 Rn

2m 20.06 (3.86) SF: 25/39/23/42/37/51/41/15/41/38/36

992

GREIG MIDDLETON PRIVATE CLIENT AMATEUR H'CAP (0-60) (3-Y.O+) (Class F) £2,970.00 (£900.00: £440.00: £210.00)
7f Stalls: Low GOING minus 0.48 sec per fur (F) 3-25 (3-26)

419[16] **Royal Comedian (42)***(47) (BWMurray)* 6-11-1 MissAElsey(3) (mde all: clr 2f out: kpt on wl)....— **1**
876[14] Al Wujud (IRE) **(42)***(45) (TDyer)* 4-11-1 MrsAFarrell(13) (cl up: rdn 3f out: styd on strly fnl f)....¾ **2**
877[7] Miss Pigalle **(38)***(33) (MissLAPerratt)* 4-10-7b(4) MrLDonnelly(10) (a chsng ldrs: kpt on fnl 2f)....3½ **3**
820[7] Waterlord (IRE) **(47)***(35) (DNicholls)* 5-11-6 MissAHarwood(12) (chsd ldrs: one pce fnl 3f)....3 **4**
789[15] Shotley Again **(27)***(13) (NBycroft)* 5-10-0 MissPRobson(1) (lw: prom: one pce fnl 3f)....1 **5**
877[5] Millemay **(30)***(16) (PMonteith)* 5-10-3 MrDParker(11) (in tch: effrt & nt clr run over 2f out: swtchd & styd on one pce)....nk **6**
759[7] Malzoom **(33)***(18) (SEKettlewell)* 3-9-8 MrsDKettlewell(4) (in tch: effrt & n.m.r 2f out: no imp)....nk **7**
876[10] Runrig (IRE) **(42)***(26) (MissLAPerratt)* 5-11-1 MissLPerratt(5) (b: s.i.s: sn wl bhd: hdwy 2f out: fin wl)....nk **8**
824[11] Kralingen **(45)***(23) (NChamberlain)* 3-10-2 (4) MissCMetcalfe(7) (wl bhd tl sme late hdwy)....2½ **9**
790[7] Operatic Dancer **(35)***(13) (RMMcKellar)* 4-10-8 MrRHale(8) (chsd ldrs to st: sn wknd)....nk **10**
642[4] Desiderata **(55)***(14)*(Fav)*(BWHills)* 4-12-0 MrsMCowdrey(6) (n.m.r & sn bhd: c wd st: nvr able to chal)....8 **11**
766[10] Wild Adventure **(30)** *(DWChapman)* 6-9-13 (4) MissRClark(15) (a outpcd & bhd)....3 **12**
875[4] Benjarong **(42)** *(RMMcKellar)* 3-9-10 (7) MrMMcGoldrick(14) (chsd ldrs tl wknd fnl 3f)....2 **13**
766[11] Scent of Power **(34)** *(MartynWane)* 5-10-3 (4) MrRDGreen(9) (sddle slipped & uns rdr appr fnl f).... **U**

2/1 Desiderata, **5/1** Waterlord (IRE), **6/1** Millemay, **9/1** Shotley Again, **10/1** Malzoom, **12/1** Al Wujud (IRE), **14/1** Runrig (IRE), **16/1** Miss Pigalle, ROYAL COMEDIAN, **20/1** Scent of Power, **25/1** Benjarong, **33/1** Wild Adventure, **50/1** Operatic Dancer, **100/1** Kralingen, CSF £177.61 CT £2,821.30 TOTE £18.20: £3.40 £2.30 £2.90 (£94.30) Trio £225.30; £126.94 to Chester 11/05/95 OWNER Fir Trading Ltd (MALTON) BRED Miss N. A. Harrod 14 Rn

1m 27.94 (3.94) SF: 40/38/26/28/6/9/-/19/4/6/7/-/-/-
WEIGHT FOR AGE 3yo-12lb

993

ST VINCENT HIGH INCOME STKS (2-Y.O) (Class D) £4,045.50 (£1,224.00: £597.00: £283.50) **5f** Stalls: High GOING minus 0.32 sec per fur (GF) 3-55 (3-56)

819* **Kunucu (IRE)** *(87) (TDBarron)* 2-8-13 KDarley(5) (a cl up: r.o u.p to ld wl ins fnl f)....— **1**
Larghetto (IRE) *(84) (JBerry)* 2-8-12 JFortune(4) (leggy: scope: s.i.s: in tch: hdwy to ld over 1f out: hdd & no ex wl ins fnl f)....½ **2**
871[3] Cabcharge Striker *(84)*(Fav)*(MRChannon)* 2-9-2 PaulEddery(3) (lw: disp ld tl led ½-wy: hdd over 1f out: kpt on one pce)....1¼ **3**
788[4] Ramsey Hope *(79) (CWFairhurst)* 2-8-12 NKennedy(2) (disp ld to ½-wy: sn drvn along: nt qckn appr fnl f)....nk **4**
490* Precious Girl *(78) (DMoffatt)* 2-8-8 (3) DarrenMoffatt(1) (hld up: hdwy & ev ch over 1f out: nt qckn)....s.h **5**

Evens Cabcharge Striker, **7/4** KUNUCU (IRE), **6/1** Larghetto (IRE) (9/2-7/1), **8/1** Ramsey Hope, **11/1** Precious Girl (8/1-12/1), CSF £11.79 TOTE £3.60: £1.90 £3.40 (£6.30) OWNER Mr P. D. Savill (THIRSK) BRED Mrs Rita Fitzgerald 5 Rn 59.18 secs (2.18) SF: 32/29/29/24/23

994

GREIG MIDDLETON H'CAP (0-70) (3-Y.O+) (Class E) £3,452.50 (£1,045.00: £510.00: £242.50)
5f Stalls: High GOING minus 0.32 sec per fur (GF) 4-25 (4-25)

789[2] **Rich Glow (47)***(53) (NBycroft)* 4-8-7 SMaloney(2) (bhd: swtchd & gd hdwy over 2f out: led wl ins fnl f: drvn out)....— **1**

723² Broadstairs Beauty (IRE) **(68)**_(74)_(Fav)_(SRBowring)_ 5-10-0b SDWilliams(5) (b: b.hind: lw: led tl hdd wl ins fnl f: rallied) ....s.h **2**
926¹³ Nineacres **(53)**_(52)_ _(DNicholls)_ 4-8-8b⁽⁵⁾ NVarley(6) (in tch: hdwy 2f out: styd on) 2 **3**
856* Jucea **(68)**_(63)_ _(JLSpearing)_ 6-10-0 7x KDarley(1) (lw: a chsng ldrs: rdn ½-wy: nt qckn fnl f) .1½ **4**
838¹⁰ Tutu Sixtysix **(52)**_(43)_ _(DonEnricoIncisa)_ 4-8-12v KimTinkler(9) (lw: s.i.s: swtchd & hdwy 2f out: nvr nrr) 1 **5**
701⁴ Kalar **(43)**_(30)_ _(DWChapman)_ 6-8-3b ACulhane(10) (cl up tl wknd appr fnl f) 1¼ **6**
753⁹ Sonderise **(49)**_(35)_ _(NTinkler)_ 6-8-9 PaulEddery(7) (in tch tl outpcd fnl 2f) ....½ **7**
877¹² Diet **(43)**_(26)_ _(MissLAPerratt)_ 9-8-3v NConnorton(8) (early spd: outpcd fr ½-wy) ....¾ **8**
789¹⁸ Uppance **(33)**_(5)_ _(DANolan)_ 7-7-4 ⁽³⁾ NKennedy(3) (squeezed out after s: a bhd) 3½ **9**
906⁸ Leading Princess (IRE) **(44)**_(16)_ _(MissLAPerratt)_ 4-8-4b GDuffield(4) (prom to ½-wy) ....hd **10**

LONG HANDICAP Uppance 6-13

11/4 Broadstairs Beauty (IRE), **3/1** Jucea, **5/1** Nineacres, **6/1** Kalar, **7/1** Sonderise, **8/1** Leading Princess (IRE), **9/1** RICH GLOW, **20/1** Diet, Tutu Sixtysix, **50/1** Uppance, CSF £34.96 CT £132.99 TOTE £15.20: £2.90 £1.90 £3.50 (£31.80) Trio £103.40 OWNER Mr M. J. Bateson (BRANDSBY) BRED P. Young 10 Rn 58.73 secs (1.73) SF: 34/55/33/44/24/11/16/7/-/-

T/Plpt: £737.20 (12.25 Tckts); T/Qdpt: Not won £72.90 to Chester 11/5/95. AA

0977-CHESTER (L-H)
Wednesday May 10th (Good to firm)

WEATHER: dull WIND: almost nil

995

CHESHIRE REGIMENT H'CAP (0-95) (3-Y.O) (Class C) £8,552.00 (£2,576.00: £1,248.00: £584.00)
1m 4f 66y Stalls: Low GOING minus 0.32 sec per fur (GF) 2-10 (2-11)

657¹¹ **Astrolabe (75)**_(83)_ _(BWHills)_ 3-8-6b MHills(5) (mde all: hrd rdn fnl f: hld on gamely) ....— **1**
717* Monarch **(74)**_(82)_ _(PFICole)_ 3-8-5 TQuinn(4) (b.hind: plld hrd: hld up: drvn along 3f out: 5th st: ev ch fnl f: r.o) ....hd **2**
811* Cherrington **(78)**_(85)_(Fav)_(GWragg)_ 3-8-9 MJKinane(6) (lw: chsd wnr: 2nd st: ev ch ins fnl f: unable qckn) 1 **3**
851* Fujiyama Crest (IRE) **(68)**_(73)_ _(MRStoute)_ 3-7-13v 5x WCarson(1) (b.nr hind: a.p: 4th & hrd drvn ent st: kpt on one pce) 1¼ **4**
773* Tonka **(71)**_(73)_ _(DJGMurraySmith)_ 3-7-13 ⁽³⁾ow1 SSanders(8) (hld up & bhd: hdwy 3f out: kpt on fnl f) 1¼ **5**
_564⁵_ Bardon Hill Boy (IRE) **(74)**_(76)_ _(BHanbury)_ 3-8-0 ⁽⁵⁾ JStack(3) (hld up: hdwy on outside over 3f out: 6th & rdn st: no imp) 1¼ **6**
774² Komreyev Dancer **(72)**_(65)_ _(ABailey)_ 3-8-3 GCarter(9) (chsd ldrs: wnt 3rd st: wknd wl over 1f out) 7 **7**
_599*_ Chadleigh Lane (USA) **(62)**_(29)_ _(RHollinshead)_ 3-7-7 NCarlisle(2) (s.i.s: hld up & bhd: nvr plcd to chal: t.o) 20 **8**
Time for Action (IRE) **(90)**_(31)_ _(MHTompkins)_ 3-9-7 PRobinson(7) (nt grwn: bit bkwd: hld up & bhd: effrt 4f out: wknd ent st: sn t.o: sddle slipped) 20 **9**

LONG HANDICAP Chadleigh Lane (USA) 7-4

11/4 Cherrington, **3/1** Monarch, **7/2** Fujiyama Crest (IRE), **8/1** Komreyev Dancer, **12/1** Tonka, **14/1** ASTROLABE, **20/1** Bardon Hill Boy (IRE), **25/1** Chadleigh Lane (USA), Time for Action (IRE), CSF £50.56 CT £135.76 TOTE £18.00: £3.10 £1.50 £1.50 (£36.50) Trio £26.20 OWNER Mr R. D. Hollingsworth (LAMBOURN) BRED R. D. Hollingsworth 9 Rn
2m 39.76 (3.16) SF: 46/45/48/36/36/39/28/-/-

996

EVELYN DELVES BROUGHTON MAIDEN STKS (2-Y.O) (Class D) £7,112.50 (£2,140.00: £1,035.00: £482.50)
5f 16y Stalls: Low GOING minus 0.32 sec per fur (GF) 2-40 (2-42)

683² **Night Parade (USA)** _(98+)_(Fav)_(PWChapple-Hyam)_ 2-8-11 JReid(2) (lw: mde all: shkn up ent fnl f: r.o strly) ....— **1**
562² Repertory _(89)_(Fav)_(MRChannon)_ 2-8-11 RHughes(4) (chsd wnr: rdn wl over 1f out: no imp) 3 **2**
Sualtach (IRE) _(73)_ _(RHollinshead)_ 2-8-11 LDettori(1) (w'like: scope: bkwd: chsd ldrs: pushed along 2f out: sn outpcd) 5 **3**
615ᵂ Just Rory _(54)_ _(EJAlston)_ 2-8-11b KFallon(5) (s.s: hdwy over 2f out: nvr nr ldrs) 6 **4**
Haute Cuisine _(46)_ _(JBerry)_ 2-8-11 JCarroll(3) (w'like: bkwd: chsd ldrs: hrd drvn ½-wy: sn lost tch) 2½ **5**

11/8 NIGHT PARADE (USA) (10/11-6/4), Repertory, **11/2** Haute Cuisine (7/2-6/1), **10/1** Sualtach (IRE), **40/1** Just Rory, CSF £3.54 TOTE £2.10: £1.30 £1.60 (£2.00) OWNER Mr R. E. Sangster (MARLBOROUGH) BRED Swettenham Stud 5 Rn 61.24 secs (1.24) SF: 48/39/23/4/-

997

SHADWELL STUD CHESHIRE OAKS STKS (Listed) (3-Y.O F) (Class A)
£24,790.00 (£7,420.00: £3,560.00: £1,630.00)
1m 3f 79y Stalls: Low GOING minus 0.32 sec per fur (GF) 3-10 (3-12)

Dance a Dream (102)(97) (MRStoute) 3-8-9 WRSwinburn(2) (chsd ldr to ½-wy: pushed along & 2nd st: styd on to ld ins fnl f).......— 1
881* Yarn (IRE) (96) (MRChannon) 3-8-9 RHughes(6) (hld up: hdwy 4f out: 3rd st: rdn to ld 1f out: sn hdd & no ex).......¾ 2
Najmat Alshemaal (IRE) (93) (MajorWRHern) 3-8-9 MJKinane(4) (still unf: s.s: hdwy over 3f out: 4th st: rdn & kpt on fnl f).......2 3
Snowtown (IRE) **(108)**(88)(Fav)(PWChapple-Hyam) 3-8-9 JReid(7) (led tl rdn & hdd 1f out: wknd fnl f).......3½ 4
Bint Zamayem (IRE) (83) (BWHills) 3-8-9 PatEddery(5) (hld up: rdn 6f out: 6th st: nvr nr ldrs).......4 5
698* Bambara **(64)**(83) (CEBrittain) 3-8-9 LDettori(1) (lw: chsd ldrs: drvn along over 4f out: 5th & btn st).......s.h 6
797⁴ Wells Whisper (FR) (66) (GWragg) 3-8-9 MHills(3) (prom tl wknd over 2f out).......12 7

2/1 Snowtown (IRE), **3/1** DANCE A DREAM, **6/1** Najmat Alshemaal (IRE), Wells Whisper (FR), **8/1** Bint Zamayem (IRE), **11/1** Yarn (IRE) (8/1-12/1), **16/1** Bambara, CSF £29.32 TOTE £3.90: £2.20 £4.10 (£28.80) OWNER Cheveley Park Stud (NEWMARKET) BRED Cheveley Park Stud Ltd 7 Rn
2m 25.07 (1.07) SF: 61/60/57/52/47/47/30

998

LADBROKE CHESTER CUP H'CAP (4-Y.O+) (Class B) £29,325.00
(£8,850.00: £4,300.00: £2,025.00)
2m 2f 147y Stalls: High GOING minus 0.32 sec per fur (GF) 3-40 (3-41)

661⁵ **Top Cees (72)**(87+) (MrsJRRamsden) 5-8-8 KFallon(15) (lw: hld up: hdwy 6f out: 4th st: led over 1f out: sn clr: readily).......— 1
632⁹ Harlestone Brook **(82)**(93) (JLDunlop) 5-9-4 WCarson(8) (hld up: hdwy 7f out: 3rd & rdn st: styd on).......5 2
735⁵ The Flying Phantom **(90)**(100) (MHTompkins) 4-9-8 PRobinson(1) (a.p: 2nd st: ev ch over 1f out: rdn & r.o wl).......½ 3
New Reputation **(86)**(96) (BWHills) 4-9-4b MHills(9) (led tl hdd over 1f out: rdn & no ex fnl f).......hd 4
821* Argyle Cavalier (IRE) **(61)**(71) (MJohnston) 5-7-11 JFanning(18) (hld up: hdwy over 4f out: styd on wl appr fnl f: nvr nrr).......hd 5
Jack Button (IRE) **(88)**(96) (BobJones) 6-9-10 MJKinane(14) (hld up & bhd: styd on fnl 3f: nvr nrr).......2 6
821³ Mondragon **(73)**(81) (MrsMReveley) 5-8-9 RCochrane(13) (hdwy over 5f out: styd on appr fnl f: nvr able to chal).......nk 7
751² Noufari (FR) **(75)**(81) (RHollinshead) 4-8-7 PatEddery(6) (bhd: styd on u.p fnl 3f: nvr nrr).......2 8
661³ Well Beloved **(81)**(85)(Fav)(HRACecil) 4-8-13v WRyan(7) (lw: mid div: drvn along 5f out: no imp).......2½ 9
632* Always Aloof (USA) **(92)**(96) (MRStoute) 4-9-10 WRSwinburn(5) (prom: rdn 3f out: 6th & btn st).......¾ 10
632² Moonlight Quest **(73)**(76) (BHanbury) 7-8-9 TIves(12) (b.off hind: nvr trbld ldrs).......nk 11
661² Thunderheart **(77)**(79) (LMCumani) 4-8-9 LDettori(17) (chsd ldrs: rdn over 3f out: 5th st: wknd appr fnl f).......1¾ 12
Star Player **(78)**(76) (RJBaker) 9-9-0 JWeaver(4) (a in rr).......5 13
Shujan (USA) **(77)**(74) (RAkehurst) 6-8-13 GCarter(3) (lw: hld up & a bhd).......¾ 14
Pridwell **(57)**(53) (MCPipe) 5-7-7 NCarlisle(10) (hdwy ½-wy: wknd 5f out).......1 15
696³ Bardolph (USA) **(77)**(73) (PFICole) 8-8-13 TQuinn(11) (lw: hld up in tch: rdn 4f out: sn lost tch: eased whn btn).......s.h 16
Welshman **(71)**(61) (MBlanshard) 9-8-7 JQuinn(16) (prom 14f: sn lost tch: t.o).......7 17
820¹⁴ Clurican (IRE) **(59)**(21) (NTinkler) 6-7-9 ow2 LCharnock(2) (chsd ldrs 12f: sn wknd: t.o).......30 18

LONG HANDICAP Clurican (IRE) 7-6

6/1 Well Beloved, **7/1** Always Aloof (USA), **15/2** Harlestone Brook, **8/1** TOP CEES, **9/1** Thunderheart, **12/1** Pridwell, Mondragon, Moonlight Quest, New Reputation, Argyle Cavalier (IRE), **14/1** Shujan (USA), Bardolph (USA), **16/1** Noufari (FR), Star Player, **20/1** The Flying Phantom, Jack Button (IRE), Welshman, **100/1** Clurican (IRE), CSF £68.33 CT £1,102.66 TOTE £12.00: £2.60 £2.30 £6.50 £4.70 (£27.10) Trio £1,662.50 OWNER Mr P. A. Leonard (THIRSK) BRED Pendley Farm 18 Rn 4m 3.35 SF: 45/51/54/50/29/54/39/35/39/50/34/33/34/32/11/31/19/-
WEIGHT FOR AGE 4yo-4lb

999 BOODLE & DUNTHORNE DIAMOND H'CAP (0-90) (3-Y.O) (Class C) £10,710.00 (£3,240.00: £1,580.00: £750.00)
6f 18y Stalls: Low GOING minus 0.32 sec per fur (GF) 4-10 (4-11)

621[8] **Go Hever Golf (82)**(97+)(Fav)*(TJNaughton)* 3-9-7 GCarter(2) (b.hind: mde all: wl clr 2f out: unchal) ....— **1**
733[10] Bolshoi (IRE) **(70)**(72) *(JBerry)* 3-8-9b JCarroll(4) (hld up: hdwy over 2f out: r.o fnl f: no ch w wnr) 5 **2**
Q Factor **(73)**(72) *(DHaydnJones)* 3-8-12 TQuinn(3) (a.p: hrd rdn over 1f out: r.o one pce)...1¼ **3**
772* Fairy Wind (IRE) **(70)**(68) *(NACallaghan)* 3-8-9 LDettori(8) (hdwy ½-wy: rdn over 1f out: one pce) ....nk **4**
823[12] Rymer's Rascal **(64)**(59) *(EJAlston)* 3-8-3 JQuinn(1) (chsd ldrs: effrt ent st: wknd appr fnl f) 1¼ **5**
823[4] Denbrae (IRE) **(75)**(62) *(DJGMurraySmith)* 3-9-0 JWeaver(12) (rdn over 2f out: nvr nr to chal) 3 **6**
Masafah (USA) **(78)**(59) *(HThomsonJones)* 3-9-3 RHills(7) (mid div tl wknd wl over 1f out) 2 **7**
775[7] Flight Soundly (IRE) **(76)**(57) *(MRStoute)* 3-9-1 WRSwinburn(11) (s.s: a in rr) ....s.h **8**
850[9] Solo Prize **(75)**(51) *(PHowling)* 3-9-0 WNewnes(5) (a outpcd & bhd) 2 **9**
867[15] Cool Tactician **(67)**(27) *(RHollinshead)* 3-8-6 WRyan(6) (outpcd: a bhd: t.o) 6 **10**
823* The Scythian **(64)**(11) *(BobJones)* 3-8-3 JFanning(10) (chsd ldrs tl rdn & wknd 2f out: t.o) 5 **11**
674[12] Crystal Loop **(68)**(10) *(ABailey)* 3-8-2 (5) VHalliday(9) (prom tl rdn & wknd over 2f out: t.o) 1¾ **12**

100/30 GO HEVER GOLF, **7/2** Fairy Wind (IRE), **5/1** The Scythian, **9/1** Denbrae (IRE), Flight Soundly (IRE), **10/1** Bolshoi (IRE), **14/1** Cool Tactician, Masafah (USA), **20/1** Q Factor, Crystal Loop, **25/1** Solo Prize, Rymer's Rascal, CSF £34.41 CT £525.24 TOTE £3.40: £1.80 £2.60 £4.70 (£21.00) Trio £113.10 OWNER Hever Racing Club (EPSOM) BRED Ronald Popely 12 Rn
1m 14.27 (0.97) SF: 65/40/40/36/27/30/27/25/19/-/-/-

1000 SEFTON MAIDEN STKS (3-Y.O F) (Class D) £7,158.00 (£2,154.00: £1,042.00: £486.00)
7f 2y Stalls: Low GOING minus 0.32 sec per fur (GF) 4-40 (4-43)

664[3] **Dream Ticket (USA)** (78+)(Fav)*(MRStoute)* 3-8-11 WRSwinburn(4) (chsd ldrs: 2nd st: led ins fnl f: drvn out) ....— **1**
Nawaasi (75) *(HThomsonJones)* 3-8-11 RHills(9) (unf: scope: bit bkwd: s.s: hdwy ½-wy: 3rd st: no ex fnl f) 1¼ **2**
761[5] Shift Again (IRE) (73) *(WJarvis)* 3-8-11 JReid(1) (chsd ldrs: 4th & rdn st: kpt on ins fnl f) 1 **3**
697[12] Hey Up Dolly (IRE) **(68)**(73) *(JBerry)* 3-8-11 JCarroll(7) (chsd ldr: led over 2f out tl ins fnl f: one pce) ....hd **4**
Fresh Fruit Daily (72) *(PAKelleway)* 3-8-11 JWeaver(5) (dwlt: sn pushed along: hdwy 2f out: nvr nrr) ....nk **5**
Coryana Dancer (IRE) (72) *(RHollinshead)* 3-8-11 TIves(3) (lt-f: unf: s.s: sn rcvrd to chse ldrs: 6th & rdn st: no ex appr fnl f) ....s.h **6**
Anam **(80)**(56) *(PTWalwyn)* 3-8-11 WCarson(10) (lw: nvr gng pce of ldrs: a bhd: t.o) 7 **7**
752[7] Just Whistle (55) *(CWThornton)* 3-8-11 RCochrane(11) (bkwd: hmpd after 1f: a bhd: t.o) ....nk **8**
Shining Candle (USA) (51) *(BHanbury)* 3-8-11 WRyan(2) (bit bkwd: led over 4f: 3rd & wkng st: t.o) 1¾ **9**
830[9] Jessica's Secret (IRE) **(42)**(50) *(ABailey)* 3-8-11b FNorton(12) (a bhd: t.o) ....¾ **10**
758[4] Skedaddle (46) *(JGFitzGerald)* 3-8-11 DHolland(6) (lw: hmpd after 2f: a bhd: t.o) 1½ **11**
779[12] Pinkerton Polka (35) *(CEBrittain)* 3-8-11 LDettori(8) (bit bkwd: a bhd: t.o) 5 **12**

6/5 DREAM TICKET (USA), **9/2** Fresh Fruit Daily (3/1-5/1), **6/1** Anam, **7/1** Nawaasi, **9/1** Shift Again (IRE), **16/1** Pinkerton Polka, **20/1** Skedaddle, Shining Candle (USA), **25/1** Hey Up Dolly (IRE), Coryana Dancer (IRE), **50/1** Jessica's Secret (IRE), Just Whistle, CSF £10.99 TOTE £1.90: £1.10 £2.20 £3.40 (£7.40) Trio £34.20 OWNER Maktoum Al Maktoum (NEWMARKET) BRED Gainsborough Farm Inc 12 Rn 1m 27.17 (1.97) SF: 46/43/41/41/40/40/24/23/19/18/14/3

T/Jkpt: £35,459.00 (0.39 Tckts); £30,464.78 to Chester 11/5/95. T/Plpt: £101.70 (386.66 Tckts).T/Qdpt £80.40 (6.8 Tckts). IM

0802a-SAINT-CLOUD (France) (L-H)
Monday May 1st (Good to soft)

1001a PRIX DE BARBEVILLE (Gp 3) (4-Y.O+) £26,347.00 (£9,581.00: £4,790.00: £2,395.00) **1m 7f 110y** 2-20 (2-19)

607a[6] **Nononito (FR)** *(116) (JLesbordes,France)* 4-8-9 GMosse ....— 1
The Little Thief (FR) *(119) (EDanel,France)* 4-8-13 AJunk 1½ 2
Always Earnest (USA) *(113) (MmeMBollack-Badel,France)* 7-8-11 ABadel 1½ 3

P-M 6.10f: 2.00f 2.10f 1.40f (32.50f) OWNER P. Sebagh 11 Rn 3m 49.0 SF: -/-/-

1002a PRIX DU MUGUET (Gp 2) (4-Y.O+) £35,928.00 (£14,371.00: £7,186.00: £3,593.00) **1m** 3-25 (3-27)

607a[4] **Green Tune (USA)** *(129) (MmeCHead,France)* 4-9-4 ODoleuze (a cl up: smooth hdwy to ld 2f out: qknd clr: easily) ....— 1
609a* Bin Ajwaad (IRE) *(116) (BHanbury)* 5-8-11 PatEddery (hld up: 5th st: prog to chal wnr 1½f out: unable qkn) 3 2
Kaldounevees(FR) *(110) (JEHammond,France)* 4-8-11 CAsmussen (7th st: r.o fnl f: nvr plcd to chal) 3 3
609a[6] Port Lucaya *(107) (DRLoder)* 5-9-4 JWeaver (4th & rdn st: r.o u.p fnl f) 5 4
Moonlight Dance (USA) *(104) (AFabre,France)* 4-9-1 OPeslier (6th st: rdn over 2f out: outpcd) ....hd 5
Scandinavian (FR) *(92) (NPelat,France)* 4-8-11 GGuignard (prom early: hrd rdn over 2f out: wknd) 4 6
Dernier Empereur (USA) *(91) (AFabre,France)* 5-9-4 SGuillot (hld up: a bhd) 4 7
Simply Tricky (USA) *(81) (MmeCHead,France)* 4-8-11 RLibert (led tl hdd 2f out: sn wknd) ..1½ 8

P-M 2.20f;1.10f 1.10f 1.10f (3.50) OWNER Mr J. Wertheimer (FRANCE) BRED Wertheimer & Frere in USA 8 Rn 1m 48.1 SF: -/-/-/-/-/-/-/-

0901a-SAN SIRO (Milan, Italy) (R-H)
Monday May 1st (Good to soft)

1003a PREMIO BORMIO (2-Y.O) **5f** 1-55 (1-55)

Coyote Bluff(IRE) *(PWChapple-Hyam)* 2-9-0 JReid ....— 1
Montenidoli(IRE) *(Italy)* 2-9-0 OFrancera ....¾ 2
Golden Lucky(USA) *(Italy)* 2-9-0 MEsposito ....½ 3

Tote 17L;13L 22L (46L) OWNER Mr P. W. Chapple-Hyam (MARLBOROUGH) 6 Rn 61.9 secs

1004a PREMIO AMBROSIANO (Gp 3) (4-Y.O+) £22,269.00 (£10,473.00: £5,910.00: £1,347.00) **1m 2f** 3-40 (3-58)

425[6] **Penny Drops** *(115) (LordHuntingdon)* 6-8-6 DHarrison ....— 1
Zohar (GER) *(117) (UOstmann,Germany)* 6-8-9 JReid ....¾ 2
New Herald *(117) (MCiciarelli,Italy)* 6-8-9 LSorrentino ....hd 3

Tote 36L; 16L 14L 20L (40L) OWNER Mr Stanley Sharp (WEST ILSLEY) BRED T. M. Saud 8 Rn 2m 7.9 SF: -/-/-

0897a-EVRY (France) (R-H)
Wednesday May 3rd (Soft)

1005a PRIX DU TREMBLAY (4-Y.O) £21,557.00 **1m 2f** 3-20 (3-21)

Befuto (FR) *(104) (MmeMBollack-Badel,France)* 4-9-2 ABadel ....— 1
El Shitane(FR) *(96) (France)* 4-8-12 GGuignard 2½ 2
Walter Willy (IRE) *(99) (France)* 4-9-2 CAsmussen ....½ 3
631[5] Cedez le Passage (FR) *(94) (CEBrittain)* 4-8-12 FSanchez ....¾ 4

P-M 12.60f; 2.50f 2.30f 1.40f (56.00) 12 Rn 2m 10.28 (7.28) SF: -/-/-/-

CHURCHILL DOWNS (Louisville, USA) (L-H)
Saturday May 6th (Fast)

1006a KENTUCKY DERBY (Gp 1) (3-Y.O C & F) £453,461.00 (£92,949.00: £44,871.00: £22,436.00) **1m 2f** 10-31 (10-33)

Thunder Gulch(USA) *(124) (DWLukas,USA)* 3-9-0 GStevens ....— 1
Tejano Run (USA) *(120) (KMcPeek,USA)* 3-9-0 JBailey 2¼ 2
Timber Country (USA) *(120) (DWLukas,USA)* 3-9-0 PDay ....hd 3
679[3] Eltish (USA) *(116) (HRACecil)* 3-9-0 EDelahoussaye (btn approx 4l) 6
667[3] Citadeed (USA) *(109) (PWChapple-Hyam)* 3-9-0 EMaple (btn approx 7½l) 9

, , , , , P-M £51.00 PL(1-2) £24.20 £10.20 SHOW(1-2-3) £12.20 £6.80 £3.80 SF £480.00 OWNER Mr M. Tabor BRED P.Brant 19 Rn
2m 1.2 SF: -/-/-/-/-

0898a-LONGCHAMP (Paris, France) (R-H)
Sunday May 7th (Good)

1007a PRIX DE GUICHE (Gp 3) (3-Y.O C) £26,347.00 (£9,581.00: £4,790.00: £2,395.00) **1m 1f** 3-00 (3-01)

Valanour(IRE) *(100?) (AdeRoyerDupre,France)* 3-9-2 GMosse ....— 1
Housamix (FR) *(98?) (AFabre,France)* 3-9-2 TJarnet 1 2
East of Heaven(IRE) *(94?) (AFabre,France)* 3-9-2 SGuillot 2½ 3

P-M 2.10f; 1.50f 1.50f (7.10f) OWNER Aga Khan BRED H.H.Aga Khan Farms S.C. 6 Rn 1m 55.6

1008a PRIX HOCQUART (Gp 2) (3-Y.O+ C & F) £45,892.00 (£18,204.00: £8,719.00: £3,593.00) **1m 4f** 3-30 (3-29)

Rifapour (IRE) *(110) (AdeRoyerDupre,France)* 3-9-2 GMosse (7th st: rapid hdwy fnl f: led cl home) ....— 1
801a[3] Poliglote *(110) (MmeCHead,France)* 3-9-2 ODoleuze (plld hrd: chsd ldr tl led over 1f out: hdd nr fin) ....hd 2
El Tenor(FR) *(105) (ASpanu,France)* 3-9-2 FSanchez (5th st: r.o fnl f) 4 3
Copent Garden(IRE) *(104) (AFabre,France)* 3-9-2 TJarnet (4th st: rdn & outpcd 2f out: r.o)...¾ 4
Highest Cafe (FR) *(102) (PBary,France)* 3-9-2 OPeslier (hld up in rr: fin wl: nvr nrr).......1½ 5
801a[4] Peckinpah's Soul (FR) *(102) (DSmaga,France)* 3-9-2 PMarion (mid div: rdn 2f out: nvr able to chal) ....nse 6
Fifty Four(USA) *(100) (MmeCHead,France)* 3-9-2 RLibert (ld tl over 1f out: wknd) 1 7
Double Eclipse (IRE) *(99) (MJohnston)* 3-9-2 CAsmussen (prom to st: sn rdn & btn) ....¾ 8
Hawk's Castle *(AFabre,France)* 3-9-2 SGuillot (fell 5f out: dead)....... F

P-M 4.40f ;1.90f 1.20f 2.50f (5.60) OWNER Aga Khan 9 Rn 2m 29.3 SF: -/-/-/-/-/-/-/-

DUSSELDORF (Germany) (R-H)
Sunday May 7th (Good)

1009a ARAG-PREIS (Gp 2) (3-Y.O F) £49,383.00 (£19,753.00: £9,877.00: £4,938.00) **1m** 4-05 (4-18)

Tryphosa (IRE) *(108) (AWohler,Germany)* 3-8-9 ABoschert ....— 1
S'Il Vous Plait(GER) *(107) (AWohler,Germany)* 3-8-9 AStarke ....¾ 2
Centaine *(105) (HRemmert,Germany)* 3-8-9 KWoodburn ....¾ 3
620* Subya *(104) (JLDunlop)* 3-8-9 PaulEddery ....½ 4
Kill the Crab (IRE) *(99) (WNeuroth,Norway)* 3-8-9 MLarsen 2½ 5
White On Red(GER) *(94) (BSchutz,Germany)* 3-8-9 THellier 2½ 6
Thara(GER) *(92) (FrauEMader,Germany)* 3-8-9 LMader 1 7
Anna Domani(FR) *(91) (JKappel,Germany)* 3-8-9 PBloomfield ....¾ 8
Rockafaba(GER) *(88) (HRemmert,Germany)* 3-8-9 ESchindler 1½ 9

Tote 80DM; 24MD 34DM 18DM (SF760) OWNER Gestut Burg Eberstein BRED H. Volz in Ireland 16 Rn
1m 37.78 SF: -/-/-/-/-/-/-/-/-

1003a-SAN SIRO (Milan, Italy) (R-H)
Sunday May 7th (Firm)

1010a PREMIO EMANUELE FILIBERTO (Listed) (3-Y.O) £20,094.00 (£8,842.00: £4,823.00: £2,411.00) **1m 2f** 3-40 (4-09)

720* **Moments of Fortune (USA)** *(101) (BHanbury)* 3-9-2 TIves .... — 1
Seattle John (USA) *(101) (GBotti,Italy)* 3-9-2 MBotti .... nk 2
Ice and Glacial (IRE) *(98) (GBotti,Italy)* 3-9-2 LSorrentino 1½ 3
Steady Ready Go (IRE) *(98) (LMCumani)* 3-9-3 FJovine .... ¾ 4

Tote 20L;15L 41L (130L) OWNER Mr Abdullah Ali (NEWMARKET) BRED Mrs Hardie Scott 7 Rn
2m 3.3 SF: -/-/-/-

0725-BRIGHTON (L-H)
Thursday May 11th (Firm)
WEATHER: overcast WIND: str half behind

1011 E.B.F. ST ANN'S WELLS MAIDEN STKS (2-Y.O) (Class D) £3,655.00 (£1,090.00: £520.00: £235.00)
5f 59y Stalls: Low GOING minus 0.66 sec per fur (HD) 2-20 (2-21)

910³ **Lussuria (IRE)** *(79) (BJMeehan)* 2-8-9 DHarrison(4) (3rd st: rdn over 2f out: ev ch ins fnl f: r.o wl: fin 2nd, s.h: awrdd r) .... — 1
781³ Bath Knight *(71) (DJSffrenchDavis)* 2-9-0 JWilliams(3) (b.hind: hmpd s: 4th st: rdn over 1f out: unable qckn: fin 3rd, 2½l: plcd 2nd) 2
690² Caricature (IRE) *(66)(Fav)(GLewis)* 2-9-0 PaulEddery(1) (5th st: bdly hmpd on ins over 1f out: nt rcvr: fin 4th, 1 3/4l: plcd 3rd) 3
788³ Double Point (IRE) *(74) (MBell)* 2-8-7 (7) GFaulkner(5) (wnt lft s: mde virtually all: edgd lft over 1f out: pushed out: fin 1st: disq: plcd 4th) 4
791⁹ Latin Beauty *(50) (RHannon)* 2-8-2 (7) DaneO'Neill(6) (2nd st: wknd over 2f out) 3½ 5
Jemsilverthorn (IRE) *(34) (JJBridger)* 2-8-11 (3) SSanders(2) (unf: 6th st: a bhd) 7 6

4/11 Caricature (IRE), **13/2** Double Point (IRE) (op 7/2), **7/1** LUSSURIA (IRE) (op 4/1), **14/1** Latin Beauty (7/1-16/1), **33/1** Bath Knight, **66/1** Jemsilverthorn (IRE), CSF £104.23 TOTE £10.20: £2.70 £3.50 (£47.50) OWNER Mr Mario Lanfranchi (UPPER LAMBOURN) BRED Blandford Bloodstock 6 Rn
61.7 secs (1.70) SF: 9/6/1/14/-/-
STEWARDS' ENQUIRY Faulkner susp 20-25/5/95 (irresponsible, careless & improper riding).

1012 HOLLINGBURY CLAIMING STKS (3-Y.O) (Class F) £2,519.00 (£694.00: £329.00)
6f 209y Stalls: Low GOING minus 0.66 sec per fur (HD) 2-50 (3-04)

739⁴ **Emphatic Candidate (IRE) (76)***(71)*(Fav)*(RAkehurst)* 3-8-10 (3) SSanders(9) (b: lw: 2nd st: led over 1f out: all out) .... — 1
515⁷ Nyali Beach (IRE) **(60)***(58) (BJMeehan)* 3-8-0 PaulEddery(13) (5th st: hrd rdn & wandered over 1f out: r.o wl ins fnl f) .... s.h 2
518¹² Sapphire Son (IRE) **(48)***(66) (CNWilliams)* 3-8-11v RCochrane(6) (led over 5f: unable qckn) 1¼ 3
Cedar Girl **(54)***(51) (RJHodges)* 3-7-5 (7) AmandaSanders(12) (uns rdr & bolted bef s: 3rd st: one pce fnl 2f) .... ¾ 4
521¹⁹ Green Green Ruby **(33)***(49) (GLMoore)* 3-7-12v(5) AWhelan(7) (6th st: rdn over 2f out: one pce) 3 5
855¹¹ Mossalier **(46)***(44) (MartynMeade)* 3-7-8 (7)ow1 CTinel(8) (nvr nr to chal) 1¼ 6
580⁵ Ilustre (IRE) **(50)***(56) (LJHolt)* 3-8-13 AMcGlone(11) (lw: 4th st: wknd over 1f out) .... hd 7
521¹⁷ Fly the Eagle **(40)***(44) (DJSffrenchDavis)* 3-8-3b DHarrison(4) (t: nvr nrr) 1 8
848⁷ Horsetrader *(50) (RHannon)* 3-9-3 RPerham(5) (lw: a mid div) 3½ 9
521¹⁵ Danny's Gift **(24)***(23) (MissAJWhitfield)* 3-7-5 (7) CAdamson(3) (bhd fnl 5f) 3½ 10
444¹² More Bills (IRE) **(40)***(24) (AMoore)* 3-8-3 CandyMorris(2) (a bhd) 1¾ 11
332⁷ Margaret Modes *(31) (CACyzer)* 3-8-12 JWeaver(10) (a bhd) .... ¾ 12
591¹² Little Tyson (IRE) *(8) (JJBridger)* 3-8-3 AClark(1) (a bhd) 6 13

2/1 EMPHATIC CANDIDATE (IRE), **11/4** Sapphire Son (IRE), **7/1** Nyali Beach (IRE), **10/1** Cedar Girl (6/1-12/1), Mossalier (6/1-12/1), **14/1** Margaret Modes, Ilustre (IRE) (op 8/1), Horsetrader (op 8/1), **25/1** More Bills (IRE), **33/1** Danny's Gift, **50/1** Fly the Eagle, Green Green Ruby, Little Tyson (IRE), CSF £16.24 TOTE £2.30: £1.70 £1.80 £1.80 (£6.80) Trio £10.10 OWNER Modacom Ltd T/A E M P (EPSOM) BRED Thoroughbred Trust 13 Rn
1m 20.6 (0.60) SF: 33/20/28/13/11/6/18/6/12/-/-/-/-
STEWARDS' ENQUIRY S.Sanders susp 20/5/95 (excessive use of whip).

1013

BRIGHTON FESTIVAL H'CAP (0-75) (3-Y.O+) (Class D) £3,935.10 (£1,174.80: £561.40: £254.70)
6f 209y Stalls: Low GOING minus 0.66 sec per fur (HD) 3-20 (3-26)

877[4] **Persian Affair (IRE) (67)***(76) (DHaydnJones)* 4-9-12 DHarrison(9) (lw: 5th st: led & edgd lft over 1f out: rdn out) .... — 1
728[4] Walnut Burl (IRE) **(57)***(63) (LJHolt)* 5-9-2 AMcGlone(8) (hdwy over 1f out: r.o wl ins fnl f) 1½ 2
731[5] Pirates Gold (IRE) **(49)***(50) (JWhite)* 5-8-8 WWoods(2) (lw: 6th st: rdn & nt clr run 2f out: r.o wl fnl f) 2 3
838[7] Love Legend **(56)***(56) (DWPArbuthnot)* 10-9-1 MTebbutt(3) (b: hdwy over 1f out: r.o wl ins fnl f) .... ½ 4
727* Tafahhus **(70)***(69)*(Fav)*(RWArmstrong)* 3-9-3 RHills(10) (4th st: led over 3f out to over 1f out: wknd fnl f) .... nk 5
728[7] Top Pet (IRE) **(64)***(59) (RAkehurst)* 5-9-9 AClark(4) (lw: nt clr run over 1f out: nvr nr to chal)...2 6
882[14] Ragazzo (IRE) **(41)***(33) (KOCunningham-Brown)* 5-7-9b(5) NVarley(6) (outpcd) 1 7
817[13] Inderaputeri **(58)***(47) (MissGayKelleway)* 5-9-3v RCochrane(11) (a bhd) 1½ 8
882[8] Pair of Jacks (IRE) **(37)***(24) (DAWilson)* 5-7-10 JQuinn(5) (lw: led 2f: 2nd st: wknd over 2f out) .... ¾ 9
All the Joys **(49)***(29) (CACyzer)* 4-8-8 JWeaver(1) (led 5f out tl over 3f out: wknd over 2f out) 3 10
541[2] Apollo Red **(53)***(15) (AMoore)* 6-8-12 CandyMorris(7) (b.off hind: 3rd st: wknd 3f out) 8 11

11/4 Tafahhus, **4/1** Walnut Burl (IRE), **6/1** Top Pet (IRE), **15/2** PERSIAN AFFAIR (IRE) (5/1-8/1), **10/1** Inderaputeri, **11/1** Pair of Jacks (IRE), **14/1** Pirates Gold (IRE) (20/1-12/1), Apollo Red, **16/1** Love Legend, **20/1** All the Joys, **33/1** Ragazzo (IRE), CSF £34.78 CT £375.43 TOTE £9.50: £2.50 £1.40 £4.50 (£56.40) Trio £86.50 OWNER Mrs M. O'Donnell (PONTYPRIDD) BRED Barronstown Bloodstock Ltd. in Ireland 11 Rn 1m 20.2 (0.20) SF: 50/37/24/30/31/33/7/21/-/3/-
WEIGHT FOR AGE 3yo-12lb

1014

JIM TAYLOR MEMORIAL H'CAP (0-70) (4-Y.O+) (Class E) £3,159.20 (£941.60: £448.80: £202.40)
1m 3f 196y Stalls: High GOING minus 0.66 sec per fur (HD) 3-50 (3-54)

*178** **Carpathian (50)***(63) (LordHuntingdon)* 4-8-8 JWilliams(4) (lw: 6th st: shkn up over 1f out: led ins fnl f: r.o wl) .... — 1
860[3] Uncharted Waters **(64)***(74) (CACyzer)* 4-9-8 PaulEddery(1) (led to ins fnl f: unable qckn).....2½ 2
445[3] Prince Danzig (IRE) **(52)***(61)*(Fav)*(DJGMurraySmith)* 4-8-10 JWeaver(8) (lw: hrd rdn over 2f out: hdwy over 1f out: r.o ins fnl f) .... nk 3
884[5] Father Dan (IRE) **(49)***(58) (MissGayKelleway)* 6-8-7 BRouse(2) (lw: 2nd st: rdn over 2f out: one pce) .... s.h 4
778* Total Joy (IRE) **(65)***(74) (PFICole)* 4-9-9 RCochrane(6) (5th st: hrd rdn over 2f out: ev ch over 1f out: one pce) .... ½ 5
729* Pharamineux **(70)***(72) (RAkehurst)* 9-10-0 RHughes(3) (lw: 4th st: wknd over 1f out) 5 6
352[7] Lord Wellington (IRE) **(37)***(34) (JRJenkins)* 4-7-4 (5)ow2 NVarley(9) (lw: 3rd st: wknd 2f out) ..1¾ 7
744[2] Bag of Tricks (IRE) **(58)***(40) (SDow)* 5-9-2 DHarrison(5) (lw: s.s: a bhd) 13 8
Legal Train **(54)** *(AHide)* 4-8-12 WWoods(7) (3rd whn stumbled & fell over 3f out: dead) .... F
LONG HANDICAP Lord Wellington (IRE) 7-4

9/4 Prince Danzig (IRE) (3/1-2/1), **9/2** CARPATHIAN, Pharamineux, **8/1** Total Joy (IRE), **9/1** Bag of Tricks (IRE), **10/1** Father Dan (IRE) (8/1-12/1), **12/1** Uncharted Waters (op 8/1), **20/1** Legal Train, **50/1** Lord Wellington (IRE), CSF £47.59 CT £133.61 TOTE £6.30: £1.90 £2.70 £1.30 (£42.50) Trio £16.60 OWNER The Queen (WEST ILSLEY) BRED Sheikh Mohammed bin Rashid al Maktoum 9 Rn 2m 32.7 (3.70) SF: 17/28/15/12/28/26/-/-/-

1015

VARDEAN MAIDEN STKS (3-Y.O) (Class D) £3,698.50 (£1,102.00: £525.00: £236.50)
1m 1f 209y Stalls: High GOING minus 0.66 sec per fur (HD) 4-20 (4-30)

824[4] **Okavango (USA) (79)***(88)*(Fav)*(JHMGosden)* 3-9-0v GHind(1) (mde all: clr over 1f out: easily) .... — 1
779[5] Built for Comfort (IRE) *(69) (RHannon)* 3-8-9 RPerham(4) (chsd wnr: rdn 3f out: wknd over 1f out) 9 2
854[8] Royal College (IRE) *(71) (PFICole)* 3-9-0 RCochrane(3) (b: b.hind: lw: bhd fnl 4f) 1½ 3
Late Mail (USA) *(70) (JMPEustace)* 3-9-0 MTebbutt(2) (bhd fnl 4f) .... ½ 4

8/13 OKAVANGO (USA), **3/1** Built for Comfort (IRE), **4/1** Royal College (IRE), **25/1** Late Mail (USA), CSF £2.81 TOTE £1.50: (£1.80) OWNER Sheikh Mohammed (NEWMARKET) BRED Cardiff Stud Farm 4 Rn 2m (2.00) SF: 27/8/10/9

1016
LIONEL BEECROFT HALF CENTURY MAIDEN H'CAP (0-70) (3-Y.O+)
(Class E) £3,531.00 (£1,056.00: £506.00: £231.00)
5f 213y Stalls: Low GOING minus 0.66 sec per fur (HD) 4-50 (4-56)

541[5] **Dahiyah (USA) (53)***(67) (GLMoore)* 4-8-6v(5) AWhelan(3) (lw: led 4f out: clr over 2f out: r.o wl)........— **1**
693[8] Eagle Day (USA) **(70)***(76) (DRCElsworth)* 4-9-9b(5) AProcter(15) (lw: 5th st: rdn over 2f out: r.o one pce)........3 **2**
502[15] Taylord **(70)***(73) (RHannon)* 3-8-10 (7) DaneO'Neill(4) (2nd st: rdn over 2f out: one pce)........1¼ **3**
765[5] Dashing Dancer (IRE) **(56)***(57)*(Fav)*(RAkehurst)* 4-8-11 (3) SSanders(6) (lw: 4th st: rdn over 2f out: one pce)........½ **4**
813[13] Delightful Dancer (IRE) **(59)***(58) (BWHills)* 3-8-1 (5) JDSmith(9) (nvr nr to chal)........¾ **5**
645[7] Kellaire Girl (IRE) **(48)***(47) (GLewis)* 3-7-2 (7) CAdamson(14) (lw: nvr nrr)........nk **6**
855[10] Mister Raider **(54)***(44) (SMellor)* 3-7-8b(7)ow5 ADaly(1) (lw: prom over 2f)........1¼ **7**
473[4] Woolverstone Hall (IRE) **(60)***(50) (DJGMurraySmith)* 3-8-7 JWeaver(8) (a mid div)........1¾ **8**
733[8] Cedar Dancer **(51)***(36) (RJHodges)* 3-7-5 (7)ow5 JoHunnam(13) (outpcd)........s.h **9**
853[17] Indian Fire **(37)***(22) (KOCunningham-Brown)* 5-7-4 (5)ow2 NVarley(10) (lw: outpcd)........1¼ **10**
727[2] Cork Street Girl (IRE) **(62)***(48) (BJMeehan)* 3-8-9 PaulEddery(2) (led 2f: 3rd st: wknd over 1f out)........nk **11**
586[13] Arrasas Lady **(35)***(10) (JELong)* 5-7-0 (7) MartinDwyer(11) (a bhd)........4 **12**
830[8] Kreef **(55)***(30) (RJO'Sullivan)* 3-8-2 AClark(5) (6th st: wknd over 2f out)........s.h **13**
218[5] Stipple **(35)***(7) (SWoodman)* 4-7-0 (7) DLockhart(12) (lw: a bhd)........1¼ **14**
580[7] Black Shadow **(48)***(13) (PJMcBride)* 3-7-9 ow2 JQuinn(7) (outpcd)........1¾ **15**
Ginza Lights (IRE) **(60)** *(KCBailey)* 4-9-4 RHughes(16) (s.s: a bhd)........20 **16**

LONG HANDICAP Arrasas Lady 6-10 Stipple 7-5 Black Shadow 7-3 Indian Fire 7-1

9/2 Dashing Dancer (IRE), **6/1** Cork Street Girl (IRE), Taylord (3/1-13/2), Woolverstone Hall (IRE) (10/1-5/1), **7/1** Kellaire Girl (IRE) (op 16/1), **8/1** Eagle Day (USA) (op 9/2), **12/1** Mister Raider, Delightful Dancer (IRE), Kreef, DAHIYAH (USA), **14/1** Cedar Dancer (12/1-20/1), **25/1** Black Shadow, Stipple, Ginza Lights (IRE), **33/1** Arrasas Lady, Indian Fire, CSF £108.06 CT £597.75 TOTE £20.00: £4.10 £2.40 £2.50 £1.60 (£145.70) Trio £457.20, £135.25 to Lingfield 12/05/95 OWNER Mr Bryan Pennick (EPSOM) BRED Foxfield 16 Rn

67.6 secs (0.20 under best) (-0.80) SF: 50/59/45/40/30/19/16/22/8/5/20/-/2/-/-/-
WEIGHT FOR AGE 3yo-11lb
T/Plpt: £374.00 (22.78 Tckts). T/Qdpt: £129.40 (2.25 Tckts). AK

0995-CHESTER (L-H)
Thursday May 11th (Good to firm)
WEATHER: Dry & Cloudy WIND: Slight Behind

1017
E.B.F. SCEPTRE MAIDEN STKS (2-Y.O F) (Class D) £7,021.50
(£2,112.00: £1,021.00: £475.50) **5f 16y** GOING minus 0.08 sec per fur (G) 2-10 (2-10)

819[4] **Mystique Smile** *(76) (JBerry)* 2-8-11 JCarroll(2) (lw: mde all: wl clr ½-wy: unchal)........— **1**
Branston Danni *(63) (MrsJRRamsden)* 2-8-11 KFallon(3) (small: lt-f: bhd & outpcd: hdwy over 1f out: fin wl)........4 **2**
791[6] Honorable Estate (IRE) *(62) (RHannon)* 2-8-11 PatEddery(1) (bit bkwd: sn drvn along: chsd ldrs: no imp fnl 2f)........nk **3**
791[3] Bewitching (USA) *(61) (JARToller)* 2-8-11 MHills(8) (dwlt: hdwy on outside 2f out: nvr able to chal)........½ **4**
Like A Hawk (USA) *(61)*(Fav)*(PFICole)* 2-8-11 TQuinn(4) (lt-f: bit bkwd: chsd ldrs over 3f: sn lost pl: rdn & rallied fnl f)........s.h **5**
782[10] Siberian Mystic *(42) (PGMurphy)* 2-8-11 RWaterfield(6) (bit bkwd: outpcd: a in rr)........6 **6**
782[12] Skelton Countess (IRE) *(41) (RHollinshead)* 2-8-11 LDettori(5) (lw: hdwy to chse wnr ½-wy: wknd qckly appr fnl f)........nk **7**
782[8] Credite Risque *(28) (MMcCormack)* 2-8-11 WRyan(7) (chsd ldrs 3f: sn outpcd)........4 **8**

2/1 Like A Hawk (USA), **3/1** Honorable Estate (IRE) (op 2/1), **4/1** Bewitching (USA), **6/1** MYSTIQUE SMILE, **10/1** Branston Danni, **20/1** Credite Risque, **25/1** Skelton Countess (IRE), **33/1** Siberian Mystic, CSF £54.14 TOTE £7.00: £1.50 £2.00 £1.10 (£41.50) OWNER C H Newton Jnr Ltd (COCKERHAM) BRED James Thom and Sons 8 Rn 62.89 secs (2.89) SF: 41/28/27/26/26/7/6/-

1018
BNFL INTERNATIONAL DEE STKS (Listed) (3-Y.O) (Class A)
£24,595.00 (£7,360.00: £3,530.00: £1,615.00)
1m 2f 75y GOING minus 0.08 sec per fur (G) 2-40 (2-41)

826* **Pentire (110)***(110) (GWragg)* 3-8-13 MHills(5) (lw: hld up: hdwy 3f out: 3rd st: led ins fnl f: rdn out)........— **1**

792[2] Sanoosea (USA) **(102)***(103) (MRStoute)* 3-8-8 WRSwinburn(3) (wnt 2nd 7f out: hrd rdn & ev ch 1f out: no ex)....1¼ 2
822* Murajja (USA) **(106)***(103)*(Fav)*(PTWalwyn)* 3-8-8 WCarson(4) (lw: led tl rdn & hdd ins fnl f: unable qckn)....nk 3
713[5] Rambrino **(106)***(98) (PWChapple-Hyam)* 3-8-8 JReid(2) (lw: prom: rdn & 4th st: one pce fnl 2f)....3 4
679[6] Heathyards Rock **(95)***(96) (RHollinshead)* 3-8-8 TIves(1) (hld up in rr: outpcd over 2f out: 5th & btn st)....1¼ 5

2/1 Murajja (USA), **9/4** PENTIRE, **3/1** Sanoosea (USA), **11/2** Rambrino, **14/1** Heathyards Rock (op 33/1), CSF £8.71 TOTE £3.30: £1.70 £1.70 (£4.50) OWNER Mollers Racing (NEWMARKET) BRED Lord Halifax 5 Rn 2m 11.78 (3.08) SF: 67/60/60/55/53

1019 THOMAS A. HIGGINS & CO RATED STKS H'CAP (0-100) (4-Y.O+) (Class B) £9,168.40 (£3,415.60: £1,657.80: £699.00: £299.50: £139.70) **5f 16y** GOING minus 0.08 sec per fur (G) 3-10 (3-10)

693[13] **Ashtina (88)***(93) (RJHodges)* 10-8-13 PatEddery(5) (chsd ldr: rdn to ld 1f out: sn clr: r.o) ....— 1
858[3] Jayannpee **(96)***(98)*(Fav)*(IABalding)* 4-9-7 LDettori(1) (lw: chsd ldrs: rdn wl over 1f out: kpt on fnl f: no ch w wnr)....1 2
723[7] Magic Pearl **(80)***(76) (EJAlston)* 5-8-5 ow1 KFallon(4) (bhd: hdwy on ins 2f out: swtchd rt appr fnl f: r.o wl)....1½ 3
Barossa Valley (IRE) **(79)***(75) (PWChapple-Hyam)* 4-8-4 BThomson(8) (bkwd: racd wd: r.o appr fnl f: nvr nrr)....½ 4
Tuscan Dawn **(88)***(78) (JBerry)* 5-8-13 JCarroll(2) (bit bkwd: led 4f: wknd fnl f)....1¾ 5
693* Royale Figurine (IRE) **(93)***(83) (MJFetherston-Godley)* 4-9-4 WRSwinburn(6) (lw: bhd: effrt u.p wl over 1f out: no imp)....s.h 6
Insider Trader **(83)***(67) (RJRWilliams)* 4-8-8b TQuinn(3) (b: bkwd: in tch tl wknd & eased ent fnl f)....1¾ 7
Encore M'Lady (IRE) **(84)***(67) (FHLee)* 4-8-9 TIves(7) (lw: spd 3f)....½ 8
926[20] Lord Sky **(79)***(43) (ABailey)* 4-8-4b MHills(9) (b: spd to ½-wy: sn outpcd)....6 9
LONG HANDICAP Barossa Valley (IRE) 8-3 Magic Pearl 7-12 Lord Sky 7-7

11/4 Jayannpee, **7/2** Royale Figurine (IRE), **6/1** Barossa Valley (IRE) (op 4/1), Tuscan Dawn, **7/1** Encore M'Lady (IRE), Insider Trader, **10/1** ASHTINA, **14/1** Magic Pearl, **33/1** Lord Sky, CSF £37.09 CT £362.50 TOTE £11.40: £2.30 £1.80 £3.90 (£13.40) Trio £83.90 OWNER Ms S. A. Joyner (SOMERTON) BRED D. R. and Mrs Fairbairn 9 Rn 62.24secs (2.24) SF: 53/58/36/35/38/43/27/27/3

1020 ORMONDE STKS (Gp 3) (4-Y.O+) (Class A) £28,170.00(£10,521.00: £5,035.50: £2,173.50)**1m 5f 89y** GOING minus 0.08 sec per fur (G) 3-40 (3-41)

712[7] **Zilzal Zamaan (USA) (109)***(120) (MRStoute)* 4-8-11 WRSwinburn(1) (led 8f out: clr ent st: styd on strly)....— 1
712[3] Shambo **(111)***(122) (CEBrittain)* 8-9-0 BDoyle(3) (lw: bhd: pushed along 7f out: chsd wnr & 2nd st: styd on fnl f)....1¼ 2
712[2] Broadway Flyer (USA) **(115)***(104)*(Fav)*(JWHills)* 4-9-0 MHills(4) (chsd ldr: 3rd st: sn rdn & outpcd)....15 3
712[5] Linney Head (USA) **(108)** *(JHMGosden)* 4-9-0 LDettori(2) (led 5f: drppd rr 5f out: 4th & t.o st)....dist 4

8/11 Broadway Flyer (USA), **4/1** Shambo, **9/2** ZILZAL ZAMAAN (USA) (3/1-5/1), **11/2** Linney Head (USA), CSF £18.23 TOTE £4.50: (£9.90) OWNER Mr Mana Al Maktoum (NEWMARKET) BRED Gainsborough Farm Inc in USA 4 Rn 2m 52.47 (2.47) SF: 75/77/59/-

OFFICIAL EXPLANATION **Broadway Flyer (USA): no explanation offered.**

1021 WYNN H'CAP (0-90) (4-Y.O+) (Class C) £8,916.00 (£2,688.00: £1,304.00: £612.00) **7f 122y** GOING minus 0.08 sec per fur (G) 4-10 (4-13)

887[2] **Dawalib (USA) (59)***(69+)*(Fav)*(DHaydnJones)* 5-8-0 WCarson(13) (chsd ldrs: 4th st: led 200y out: all out)....— 1
862[7] Pab's Choice **(58)***(66) (MMcCormack)* 4-7-6 (7) MHenry(6) (chsd ldrs: gd hdwy fnl f: fin wl).....¾ 2
870[17] Rossini Blue **(74)***(82) (ABailey)* 4-9-1 FNorton(8) (bhd: hdwy on ins over 2f out: fin wl)....s.h 3
611[3] Highborn (IRE) **(83)***(91) (PSFelgate)* 6-9-10 WRyan(16) (lw: dwlt: hdwy 3f out: 7th st: kpt on ins fnl f)....hd 4
728[11] Shikari's Son **(87)***(95) (JWhite)* 8-10-0 TQuinn(11) (chsd ldrs: rdn & r.o wl fnl f)....hd 5
873[6] Sooty Tern **(64)***(71) (JMBradley)* 8-8-0 (5) SDrowne(17) (chsd ldrs: 3rd st: rdn & no ex fnl f) ...nk 6
785[3] Cee-Jay-Ay **(70)***(76) (JBerry)* 8-8-11 JCarroll(10) (dwlt: wl bhd tl gd hdwy fnl f)....½ 7
949[3] Elle Shaped (IRE) **(66)***(72) (DNicholls)* 5-8-7 LDettori(1) (lw: led tl ins fnl f: sn rdn & wknd)....nk 8

927* Pride of Pendle **(72)***(77) (DNicholls)* 6-8-13 6x AlexGreaves(9) (hdwy & n.m.r ent st: nvr able to chal) .....nk **9**
563[3] Sagebrush Roller **(86)***(90) (JWWatts)* 7-9-13 WRSwinburn(4) (hld up & bhd: hdwy ent st: eased whn btn fnl f) .....nk **10**
870[21] Veloce (IRE) **(67)***(69) (ABailey)* 7-8-3 (5) VHalliday(12) (b: nvr nrr) 1 **11**
890* Walk the Beat **(68)***(67) (MartynMeade)* 5-8-9 6x VSlattery(3) (b: mid div tl rdn & wknd over 1f out) 1½ **12**
714[10] Chickawicka (IRE) **(85)***(83) (MCPipe)* 4-9-12b PatEddery(15) (prom: 5th & rdn st: outpcd appr fnl f) .....½ **13**
439[15] Promise Fulfilled (USA) **(83)***(78) (SGNorton)* 4-9-10 KFallon(5) (a in rr) 1¼ **14**
337[6] Twin Creeks **(60)***(54) (MDHammond)* 4-7-12 (3) DWright(2) (prom: 2nd st: wknd wl over 1f out) .....¾ **15**
862[11] Kinnegad Kid **(52)***(38) (RIngram)* 6-7-7 GBardwell(14) (lw: outpcd: a bhd) 3½ **16**
Indiahra **(60)***(39) (RHollinshead)* 4-7-10 (5) AGarth(18) (bit bkwd: s.i.s: hdwy ½-wy: 6th st: eased whn btn appr fnl f) 3½ **17**

3/1 DAWALIB (USA) (op 5/1), **6/1** Sagebrush Roller, **7/1** Elle Shaped (IRE), **10/1** Highborn (IRE), Chickawicka (IRE), **11/1** Pride of Pendle (8/1-12/1), Cee-Jay-Ay, **14/1** Sooty Tern, **16/1** Shikari's Son, Twin Creeks, **20/1** Pab's Choice, Veloce (IRE), Walk the Beat, Kinnegad Kid, **25/1** Promise Fulfilled (USA), Rossini Blue, **33/1** Indiahra, CSF £61.82 CT £1,238.64 TOTE £3.80: £1.30 £8.50 £5.00 £2.50 (£141.10) Trio £2,926.10; £1,112.77 to Lingfield 12/05/95 OWNER Jack Brown (Bookmaker) Ltd (PONTYPRIDD) BRED Hilary J. Boone Jnr 17 Rn

1m 34.8 (3.10) SF: 45/42/58/67/71/47/52/48/53/66/45/43/59/54/30/14/15

1022 EATON H'CAP (0-80) (3-Y.O+) (Class D) £7,564.00 (£2,272.00: £1,096.00: £508.00) **1m 4f 66y** GOING minus 0.08 sec per fur (G) 4-40 (4-41)

981[8] **Killick (49)***(62) (ABailey)* 7-7-13 GBardwell(8) (mde all: qcknd 5f out: clr fnl 2f) .....— **1**
833[4] Shakiyr (FR) **(61)***(71) (RHollinshead)* 4-8-11 LDettori(12) (hld up in tch: hdwy & 3rd st: rdn & kpt on fnl f) 2½ **2**
623[9] General Mouktar **(74)***(82) (MCPipe)* 5-9-10b PatEddery(2) (chsd wnr: 2nd & rdn st: kpt on same pce) 1¼ **3**
668[12] Lookingforarainbow (IRE) **(73)***(81) (BobJones)* 7-9-9 MWigham(11) (hld up & bhd: hdwy over 2f out: 5th st: fin wl) .....nk **4**
778[4] Mad Militant (IRE) **(65)***(70)*(Fav)*(ALForbes)* 6-9-1 WRyan(1) (hld up: effrt 4f out: 6th st: rdn & one pce fnl f) 2½ **5**
494* Barti-Ddu **(60)***(64) (SCWilliams)* 4-8-7 (3) DWright(6) (prom: rdn over 2f out: 4th st: wknd over 1f out) .....¾ **6**
995[7] Komreyev Dancer **(73)***(74) (ABailey)* 3-8-4 ow1 MHills(10) (hld up: hdwy ½-wy: rdn ent st: sn btn) 1½ **7**
647[8] Dr Edgar **(67)***(64) (GWragg)* 3-7-12 FNorton(9) (sn pushed along: a bhd: btn whn hmpd over 1f out) 3½ **8**
811[4] Slmaat **(73)***(69) (MrsMReveley)* 4-9-9 JReid(4) (a in rr) .....¾ **9**
Mamnoon (USA) **(77)***(57) (WClay)* 4-9-13b JCarroll(5) (s.i.s: a bhd: lost tch 5f out: t.o) 12 **10**
956[4] Chimanimani **(73)***(52) (NTinkler)* 4-9-9 WCarson(3) (chsd ldrs: rdn 3f out: sn wknd: t.o) 1 **11**

7/2 Mad Militant (IRE), **9/2** Shakiyr (FR), **13/2** Slmaat, General Mouktar, **8/1** KILLICK, Lookingforarainbow (IRE), **9/1** Barti-Ddu, **12/1** Komreyev Dancer, Dr Edgar, **14/1** Chimanimani, **25/1** Mamnoon (USA), CSF £43.30 CT £232.98 TOTE £9.60: £2.40 £1.70 £2.40 (£20.50) Trio £32.80 OWNER Esprit de Corps Racing (TARPORLEY) BRED Juddmonte Farms 11 Rn

2m 41.93 (5.33) SF: 44/53/64/63/52/46/37/27/51/39/34

WEIGHT FOR AGE 3yo-19lb

T/Jpt: £37,507.80 (0.10 Tckts) £47,545.12 to Lingfield 12/05/95. T/Plpt: £578.70 (58.01 Tckts). T/Qdpt: £157.90 (4.85 Tckts). IM

0903-HAMILTON (R-H)
Thursday May 11th (Good to firm, Good Patches)
WEATHER: overcast & cool WIND: almost nil

1023 DANNY KANES AMATEUR H'CAP (0-65) (3-Y.O+) (Class F) £2,814.00(£852.00: £416.00: £198.00) **5f 4y** Stalls: Low GOING minus 0.50 sec per fur (F) 6-30 (6-33)

994[8] **Diet (43)***(49) (MissLAPerratt)* 9-10-6v(4) MrLDonnelly(3) (chsd ldrs: styd on to ld wl ins fnl f) .....— **1**
823[11] Tee Tee Too (IRE) **(65)***(67) (PCHaslam)* 3-11-8 MrsDKettlewell(10) (lw: swtchd rt after s: hdwy ½-wy: r.o fnl f) 1¼ **2**
994[6] Kalar **(43)***(44) (DWChapman)* 6-10-6b(4) MissRClark(1) (lw: led: hung rt most of wy: hdd & no ex wl ins fnl f) .....nk **3**

926[9] Miss Siham (IRE) **(42)***(40)*(Fav)*(DNicholls)* 6-10-9 MissAHarwood(2) (chsd ldrs: ev ch over 1f out: hung rt & nt qckn)....1 **4**
994[4] Jucea **(68)***(63) (JLSpearing)* 6-12-3 (4) 7x MissCSpearing(4) (s.i.s: hdwy ½-wy: nvr able to chal)....1 **5**
789[8] Mu-Arrik **(56)***(50) (GROldroyd)* 7-11-2v(7) MissABycroft(13) (swtchd lft after s: effrt ½-wy: nvr rchd ldrs)....nk **6**
906[3] Kenesha (IRE) **(43)***(33) (DANolan)* 5-10-10 MrRHale(7) (prom over 3f)....1¼ **7**
475[11] Serious Hurry **(50)***(36) (RMMcKellar)* 7-10-10 (7) MrMMcGoldrick(14) (spd far side over 3f: eased whn btn)....1¼ **8**
685[11] Supreme Desire **(35)***(20) (GROldroyd)* 7-9-12 (4) MrSWalker(15) (racd far side: n.d)....nk **9**
726[13] The Noble Oak (IRE) **(55)***(33) (MJBolton)* 7-11-1 (7) DrJNaylor(12) (prom tl wknd fnl 2f)....2 **10**
135[7] Magic Leader (IRE) **(45)***(17) (TTClement)* 3-9-12 (4) MrVLukaniuk(8) (b: s.i.s: n.d)....2 **11**
726[5] Distant Dynasty **(51)***(22) (BAPearce)* 5-10-11 (7) MrRBlyth(6) (b: unruly s: s.i.s: a bhd)....nk **12**
Younger Days (IRE) **(47)***(17) (MartynWane)* 4-11-0 MissPRobson(9) (rdn ½-wy: no imp)....nk **13**
Shakiri **(26)** *(RMMcKellar)* 6-9-0 (7) MissLBradburne(5) (wnt rt after s: sn t.o)....dist **14**

LONG HANDICAP Shakiri 9-5

7/2 Miss Siham (IRE), **5/1** Distant Dynasty, **6/1** Jucea, Tee Tee Too (IRE), **7/1** Kenesha (IRE), **12/1** Kalar, **14/1** DIET, Mu-Arrik, **20/1** The Noble Oak (IRE), Younger Days (IRE), **25/1** Magic Leader (IRE), Supreme Desire, **33/1** Serious Hurry, **100/1** Shakiri, CSF £88.90 CT £957.41 TOTE £12.50: £3.00 £3.00 £3.20 (£92.50) Trio £199.20; £56.13 to 13/05/95 OWNER Mrs M. S. J. Clydesdale (AYR) BRED Rowcliffe Stud 14 Rn 61.1 secs (2.80) SF: 31/39/26/22/45/32/15/18/2/15/-/4/-/-

WEIGHT FOR AGE 3yo-10lb

1024

ARCHIBALD ARROL'S 80/- MAIDEN AUCTION STKS (2-Y.O) (Class F) £2,619.00 (£734.00: £357.00) **5f 4y** Stalls: Low GOING minus 0.50 sec per fur (F) 7-00 (7-01)

878[3] **Gothenberg (IRE)** *(64+) (MJohnston)* 2-8-10 DHolland(1) (mde all: rdn clr 2f out: pushed out)....— **1**
878[6] Oriole *(51) (NTinkler)* 2-8-10 KimTinkler(2) (a chsng wnr: rdn ½-wy: one pce)....4 **2**
Abbott of Whalley *(46) (JBerry)* 2-8-10 SDWilliams(4) (w'like: leggy: sn chsg ldrs: rdn ½-wy: no imp)....1¾ **3**
810[2] Aussie *(38)*(Fav)*(MHTompkins)* 2-8-10 PRobinson(5) (unruly s: prom: sn drvn along: wl outpcd fr ½-wy)....2½ **4**
Rozel Bay *(JLSpearing)* 2-7-12b(3) DarrenMoffatt(3) (unf: s.s: a t.o)....14 **5**

4/5 Aussie, **7/4** GOTHENBERG (IRE), **5/1** Abbott of Whalley, **25/1** Rozel Bay, **33/1** Oriole, CSF £27.36 TOTE £3.20: £1.20 £11.10 (£53.00) OWNER Brian Yeardley Continental Ltd (MIDDLEHAM) BRED Brownstown Stud Farm 5 Rn 60.6 secs (2.30) SF: 14/1/-/-/-

OFFICIAL EXPLANATION Aussie: the jockey reported the horse had boiled over in the stalls.

1025

CARLSBERG-TETLEY H'CAP (0-75) (4-Y.O+) (Class D) £3,828.80 (£1,159.40: £566.20: £269.60) **1m 5f 9y** Stalls: High GOING minus 0.50 sec per fur (F) 7-30 (7-30)

Noyan (43)*(58) (LLungo)* 5-8-5 KDarley(6) (lw: b: hdwy & prom 8f out: rdn over 2f out: led jst ins fnl f: r.o)....— **1**
905[3] Mentalasanythin **(53)***(67)*(Fav)*(ABailey)* 6-9-1 AMackay(5) (lw: hdwy to trck ldrs 8f out: effrt appr fnl f: r.o: nt pce of wnr)....¾ **2**
879[6] Guards Brigade **(47)***(57) (JHetherton)* 4-8-9 NKennedy(3) (led tl hdd & no ex jst ins fnl f)....3½ **3**
Weaver George (IRE) **(34)***(39) (JAHellens)* 5-7-7 (3)ow2 DarrenMoffatt(7) (prom tl lost pl 8f out: hdwy 5f out: one pce fnl 2f)....2 **4**
534[14] Don't Cry **(31)***(36) (DonEnricoIncisa)* 7-7-7 KimTinkler(4) (sn wl bhd: hdwy over 2f out: nvr able to chal)....2 **5**
879[5] Zaaheyah (USA) **(48)***(47) (MDHammond)* 5-8-10 PRobinson(8) (cl up tl outpcd fnl 3f)....5 **6**
Pomorie (IRE) **(66)***(65) (JWPayne)* 4-10-0 DHolland(1) (hdwy & prom 8f out: rdn over 3f out: sn btn)....hd **7**
905[7] Sylvan Celebration **(31)***(15) (MissLAPerratt)* 4-7-0 (7) PFessey(2) (in tch tl outpcd fnl 3f)....12 **8**

LONG HANDICAP Don't Cry 6-10 Sylvan Celebration 7-6

6/4 Mentalasanythin, **9/4** NOYAN, **5/1** Pomorie (IRE), **8/1** Weaver George (IRE), **12/1** Guards Brigade (op 8/1), **14/1** Zaaheyah (USA), **20/1** Sylvan Celebration, **50/1** Don't Cry, CSF £6.10 CT £28.84 TOTE £3.60: £1.80 £1.20 £2.20 (£3.00) OWNER Mr C. H. McGhie (CARRUTHERSTOWN) BRED Oakgrove Stud 8 Rn 2m 49.9 (4.20) SF: 26/35/25/7/4/15/33/-

1026

CALDER'S 70/- MEDIAN AUCTION MAIDEN STKS (3-Y.O) (Class F) £2,661.00 (£746.00: £363.00) **1m 4f 17y** Stalls: High GOING minus 0.50 sec (F) 8-00 (8-01)

687[2] **Westminster (IRE) (62)***(71) (MHTompkins)* 3-9-0v PRobinson(5) (hld up: hdwy on bit 4f out: rdn to ld wl ins fnl f: all out)....— **1**

641² Toraja *(71)*(Fav)*(JLDunlop)* 3-9-0 KDarley(4) (trckd ldrs gng wl: led over 2f out: swvd lft: qcknd appr fnl f: hdd wl ins fnl f: rallied) ....hd 2
641⁴ Jackmanii **(47)***(55)* *(WTKemp)* 3-9-0 KFallon(3) (lw: led tl hdd over 2f out: sn outpcd) 12 3
787⁶ Philmist *(50)* *(JHetherton)* 3-8-9 NKennedy(2) (prom tl outpcd fnl 2f) ....hd 4
773⁵ Kindred Greeting *(48)* *(DMorris)* 3-9-0b RPrice(1) (chsd ldrs: rdn 4f out: sn wknd) 5 5

1/2 Toraja, **7/4** WESTMINSTER (IRE), **16/1** Jackmanii, **20/1** Philmist, **50/1** Kindred Greeting, CSF £3.05 TOTE £3.60: £1.20 £1.10 (£1.30) OWNER Mr John Bull (NEWMARKET) BRED Ballymacarney Stud 5 Rn
2m 39.1 (7.10) SF: 14/14/-/-/-

1027

KIRKSTYLE INN H'CAP (0-70) (4-Y.O+) (Class E) £3,598.75 (£1,090.00: £532.50: £253.75) **1m 65y** Stalls: High GOING minus 0.50 sec per fur (F) 8-30 (8-31)

909³ **King Curan (USA) (57)***(65)*(Fav)*(ABailey)* 4-9-6b AMackay(1) (in tch: effrt 4f out: led appr fnl f: r.o u.p) ....— 1
839⁴ Aljawab (USA) **(57)***(62)* *(JLDunlop)* 4-9-6 KDarley(10) (hld up: effrt & n.m.r 2f out: r.o towards fin) 1½ 2
731* Mr Rough **(62)***(67)* *(DMorris)* 4-9-11 RPrice(5) (lw: a.p: led over 2f out tl over 1f out: hung lft & nt qckn) ....s.h 3
839¹⁴ Nobby Barnes **(47)***(49)* *(DonEnricoIncisa)* 6-8-10 KimTinkler(3) (sn bhd: hdwy 4f out: no ex ins fnl f) 1½ 4
882³ Vanborough Lad **(53)***(54)* *(MJBolton)* 6-9-2 PRobinson(7) (lw: hld up: stdy hdwy 4f out: effrt 2f out: one pce) ....¾ 5
876⁴ Marowins **(44)***(45)* *(EJAlston)* 6-8-7 KFallon(2) (bhd: hdwy 3f out: kpt on one pce fnl f) ....s.h 6
835⁹ Backstabber **(33)***(26)* *(MissSJWilton)* 5-7-7 (3)ow1 DarrenMoffatt(6) (prom tl wknd over 2f out) 3½ 7
817⁸ Glitter of Gold **(58)***(48)* *(SCWilliams)* 4-9-7 DHolland(4) (trckd ldr: chal over 2f out: sn rdn & no ex) 1¾ 8
874⁹ Thisonesforalice **(38)***(19)* *(AHarrison)* 7-8-1 RLappin(9) (lw: in tch: rdn 4f out: grad wknd) 5 9
992⁴ Waterlord (IRE) **(47)***(27)* *(DNicholls)* 5-8-3 (7) SCopp(8) (led tl hdd over 2f out: sn wknd) ....nk 10
780¹⁵ Lawnswood Junior **(58)***(15)* *(JLSpearing)* 8-9-7 SDWilliams(11) (a bhd) 12 11

4/1 KING CURAN (USA), **9/2** Vanborough Lad, **5/1** Mr Rough, **11/2** Aljawab (USA) (4/1-6/1), **8/1** Marowins, Glitter of Gold (op 12/1), **14/1** Nobby Barnes, Waterlord (IRE), Thisonesforalice, **33/1** Backstabber, Lawnswood Junior, CSF £24.57 CT £100.56 TOTE £5.10: £1.60 £2.90 £2.10 (£7.80) Trio £21.00 OWNER Mrs M. O'Donnell (TARPORLEY) BRED Executive Bloodstock & Adstock Manor Stud 11 Rn
1m 47.4 (4.10) SF: 25/22/27/9/14/5/-/8/-/-/-

1028

TETLEY BITTER LIMITED STKS (0-60) (3-Y.O) (Class F) £2,745.00 (£770.00: £375.00) **1m 1f 36y** Stalls: High GOING minus 0.50 sec per fur (F) 9-00 (9-01)

969³ **Gospel Song (50)***(65)* *(WTKemp)* 3-8-11b KFallon(1) (led & clr to ½-wy: hdd wl over 1f out: led ins fnl f: styd on u.p) ....— 1
839² Concer Un **(60)***(66)*(Fav)*(SCWilliams)* 3-8-13 KDarley(6) (lw: hld up: hdwy 5f out: led wl over 1f out: hrd drvn: hdd & no ex ins fnl f) ....¾ 2
969² Three Arch Bridge **(58)***(56)* *(MJohnston)* 3-8-8b DHolland(5) (trckd ldrs: rdn over 2f out: n.m.r over 1f out: one pce) 2½ 3
880* Slytly Beveled **(49)***(63)* *(NPLittmoden)* 3-8-12b(5) TGMcLaughlin(4) (lw: bhd: effrt ½-wy: sn chsng ldrs: one pce appr fnl f) 1¼ 4
875* Samaka Hara (IRE) **(42)***(59)* *(WSCunningham)* 3-9-1 AMackay(3) (lw: chsd ldr tl wknd fnl 2f) 1¼ 5
180⁴ Rose Chime (IRE) **(59)***(43)* *(MJohnston)* 3-8-6 TWilliams(2) (prom tl rdn & wknd over 2f out) ..4 6

Evens Concer Un, **5/2** Three Arch Bridge, **7/1** Rose Chime (IRE), **9/1** Samaka Hara (IRE), **12/1** GOSPEL SONG (op 8/1), **14/1** Slytly Beveled, CSF £24.47 TOTE £10.20: £3.70 £1.10 (£12.90) OWNER Drakemyre Racing (DUNS) BRED Miss Elizabeth Streatfeild 6 Rn
1m 58.4 (4.10) SF: 21/22/12/19/15/-
T/Plpt: £60.20 (189.36 Tckts). T/Qdpt: £3.60 (26.8 Tckts). AA

0842-SOUTHWELL (L-H)
Thursday May 11th (Standard)

WEATHER: overcast WIND: mod across

1029

MAGNOLIA H'CAP (0-65) (3-Y.O+) (Class F) £3,199.40 (£888.40:£426.20) **1m 4f (Fibresand)** Stalls: Low GOING minus 0.02 sec per fur (STD) 2-00 (2-04)

833¹⁰ **Nothing Doing (IRE) (34)***(44)* *(WJMusson)* 6-7-11 ow1 TWilliams(8) (hld up: 4th st: led wl ins fnl f: rdn out) ....— 1

676⁴ Sommersby (IRE) **(51)***(61) (ACStewart)* 4-9-0 SWhitworth(6) (lw: hld up & bhd: hdwy on ins 5f out: led over 2f out tl wl ins fnl f) ....½ 2
*894** Pistols At Dawn (USA) **(53)***(59) (BJMeehan)* 5-9-2 5x GCarter(5) (6th st: ev ch over 1f out: one pce) 3 3
988⁸ Modest Hope (USA) **(46)***(52) (BRichmond)* 8-8-4 (5) CTeague(4) (hld up & bhd: hdwy & 8th st: r.o one pce fnl f) ....s.h 4
506⁶ Absalom's Pillar **(64)***(70) (JHetherton)* 5-9-13 NCarlisle(9) (a.p: led over 3f out tl over 2f out: wknd fnl f) ....½ 5
*221*⁵ Tiger Shoot **(63)***(67+) (DTThom)* 8-9-7 (5) LNewton(14) (bit bkwd: hld up & bhd: stdy hdwy fnl 2f: nvr plcd to chal) 1 6
*843** Palacegate Jo (IRE) **(63)***(66) (DWChapman)* 4-9-12 5x DeanMcKeown(12) (nvr nr to chal) ....¾ 7
*624*¹¹ Our Bessie **(40)***(42) (DMarks)* 4-7-12e(5) MBaird(13) (plld hrd: stdy hdwy 7f out: 2nd st: wknd over 1f out) 1 8
Wordsmith (IRE) **(50)***(32) (JLHarris)* 5-8-13 GDuffield(15) (bit bkwd: bhd fnl 3f) 15 9
*894*³ Charlie Bigtime **(50)***(32) (DTThom)* 5-8-13 AMackay(2) (sn rdn along: a bhd) ....hd 10
*835** Rolling Waters **(55)***(34)*(Fav)*(JARToller)* 5-9-4 WNewnes(16) (led over 8f: 3rd st: wknd wl over 1f out) 2½ 11
654² Recovery Lad (IRE) **(51)***(27) (KRBurke)* 3-7-9 ow2 DaleGibson(1) (bhd fnl 5f) ....¾ 12
Goodbye Millie **(39)***(10) (JLEyre)* 5-8-2 JFanning(10) (sn pushed along & outpcd) 5 13
*771*⁹ Sea Spouse **(52)***(21) (MBlanshard)* 4-8-8 (7) SMcCarthy(3) (plld hrd: prom tl n.m.r on ins & 7th st: sn wknd) 1¼ 14
Fred's Delight (IRE) **(45)** *(MJHeaton-Ellis)* 4-8-8b StephenDavies(11) (prom to 9th & wkng st: t.o) 15 15
Lixos **(47)** *(JEBanks)* 4-8-10 DBiggs(7) (Withdrawn not under Starter's orders: ref ent stalls) .... W

LONG HANDICAP Recovery Lad (IRE) 7-6

, **9/2** Rolling Waters, **6/1** Pistols At Dawn (USA), Sommersby (IRE), Modest Hope (USA), **10/1** Recovery Lad (IRE), **11/1** Palacegate Jo (IRE), Charlie Bigtime, **12/1** Tiger Shoot, **14/1** Absalom's Pillar, **16/1** Sea Spouse, **20/1** NOTHING DOING (IRE), **25/1** Our Bessie, Wordsmith (IRE), Fred's Delight (IRE), Goodbye Millie, CSF £121.20 CT £645.07 TOTE £36.00: £8.10 £1.40 £3.70 (£66.50) Trio £179.60, £204.93 to Lingfield 12/05/95 OWNER Broughton Bloodstock (NEWMARKET) BRED Cleaboy Stud 15 Rn 2m 43.6 (9.40) SF: 23/40/38/31/49/46/45/21/11/11/13/-/-/-/-/-

WEIGHT FOR AGE 3yo-19lb

STEWARDS' ENQUIRY Tiger Shoot banned 30 days. Thom fined £1000. Newton susp. 7 days under Rule 151.

1030 CAMELLIA CLAIMING STKS (3-Y.O) (Class F) £2,519.00 (£694.00: £329.00) 1m (Fibresand) Stalls: Low GOING minus 0.02 sec per fur (STD) 2-30 (2-32)

*767** **Legally Delicious (67)***(68)*(Fav)*(BJMcMath)* 3-8-0 AMackay(13) (hld up: led over 2f out: all out) ....— 1
848⁶ Gulf Shaadi **(82)***(87) (GLewis)* 3-9-5 SWhitworth(9) (hld up & bhd: hdwy over 3f out: 3rd st: ev ch fnl f: r.o) ....hd 2
818⁵ Java Red (IRE) *(57) (JGFitzGerald)* 3-8-9 MBirch(14) (prom: 8th st: r.o one pce fnl 2f) 10 3
648¹¹ Red River Rose (IRE) **(50)***(49) (NPLittmoden)* 3-8-1b(5)ow2 TGMcLaughlin(7) (s.s: hdwy & 5th st: one pce fnl 2f) 1¼ 4
*844*² Komiamaite *(44) (SRBowring)* 3-8-2b(5) CTeague(6) (s.i.s: wl bhd tl hdwy over 3f out: nt rch ldrs) 4 5
867¹¹ Club Elite **(59)***(33) (MJCamacho)* 3-8-0 JFanning(11) (prom tl wknd over 2f out) 2 6
654⁴ Star Fighter **(55)***(37) (WAO'Gorman)* 3-8-10v EmmaO'Gorman(1) (hld up: 7th st: wknd over 2f out) 3 7
736⁶ Simply Simon **(40)***(27) (KRBurke)* 3-8-5v GCarter(5) (4th st: wknd 2f out) 2½ 8
576⁵ Lucky Peg **(46)** *(FJO'Mahony)* 3-7-12 TWilliams(12) (a.p: led over 3f out: hdd & 2nd st: sn wknd) 10 9
*771*¹¹ Mrs Tigger **(50)***(1) (RWArmstrong)* 3-8-2b RPrice(2) (swtg: sn rdn along: bhd fnl 4f) 1½ 10
*842*⁶ Tish **(35)** *(ASmith)* 3-7-12 ow2 SMaloney(8) (led over 4f: 6th & wkng st) 1½ 11
521¹⁰ Pendine **(35)** *(SCWilliams)* 3-7-3 (7) RMullen(4) (prom over 3f) 3½ 12
654⁷ Darius The Great (IRE) *(DMarks)* 3-8-6 (5) MBaird(3) (lw: bhd fnl 3f) 6 13

11/8 LEGALLY DELICIOUS, **3/1** Gulf Shaadi, **6/1** Star Fighter, **13/2** Komiamaite, **10/1** Club Elite, **12/1** Java Red (IRE), **20/1** Red River Rose (IRE), Lucky Peg, **25/1** Mrs Tigger, **33/1** Simply Simon, Tish, Pendine, Darius The Great (IRE), CSF £6.81 TOTE £2.40: £1.60 £1.50 £3.10 (£3.20) Trio £6.30 OWNER Mr Ron Dawson (NEWMARKET) BRED E. Landi 13 Rn

1m 44.7 (5.40) SF: 33/52/22/14/9/-/2/-/-/-/-/-/-

Legally Delicious clmd MJHall £4,000

OFFICIAL EXPLANATION Komiamaite: the jockey thought something might be amiss, as the horse was never travelling.

1031 TULIP MAIDEN AUCTION STKS (2-Y.O) (Class F) £2,519.00 (£694.00: £329.00)
5f (Fibresand) Stalls: High GOING minus 0.29 sec per fur (FST) 3-00 (3-01)

Born A Lady *(49) (NPLittmoden)* 2-7-10 NCarlisle(9) (lt-f: unf: hdwy 2f out: swtchd lft over 1f out: hrd rdn to ld last strides) ....— **1**
863² Missile Toe (IRE) *(59)*(Fav)*(JEBanks)* 2-8-6 DBiggs(4) (lw: a.p: led over 1f out: edgd rt ins fnl f: hdd last strides) ....hd **2**
*889*³ Lila Pedigo (IRE) *(43) (JBerry)* 2-8-0 GCarter(5) (sn chsng ldrs: r.o one pce fnl f) 3 **3**
*604*³ Tymeera *(39) (BPalling)* 2-7-12 ow1 TSprake(7) (b: w ldrs: one pce appr fnl f).......½ **4**
810⁴ Astral's Chance *(43) (KRBurke)* 2-8-5 JFortune(6) (led: edgd rt & hdd over 1f out: wknd fnl f) 1 **5**
819⁹ Canlubang *(25) (MJCamacho)* 2-7-12 DaleGibson(2) (rdn over 2f out: no hdwy).......3½ **6**
Cupla Focail *(7) (WRMuir)* 2-7-5 (5) MBaird(1) (lt-f: unf: outpcd) 5 **7**
595⁴ Margi Boo *(2) (GMMoore)* 2-7-13 JFanning(8) (rdn over 3f out: bhd fnl 2f).......2½ **8**
Princess Renata (IRE) *(DTThom)* 2-7-13 AMackay(3) (cmpt: bkwd: s.s: outpcd).......3½ **9**

10/11 Missile Toe (IRE), **7/2** Astral's Chance, **6/1** Lila Pedigo (IRE) (op 4/1), **12/1** Tymeera (8/1-14/1), **14/1** Canlubang, Margi Boo, **16/1** Princess Renata (IRE), **20/1** Cupla Focail, BORN A LADY, CSF £40.16 TOTE £23.90: £2.10 £1.60 £2.10 (£28.80) Trio £60.70 OWNER Mr D. Voivodich (NEWARK) BRED T. Barratt 9 Rn 61.4 secs (3.40) SF: -/10/-/-/-/-/-/-/-

1032 FREESIA H'CAP (0-65) (3-Y.O+ F & M) (Class F) £2,519.00 (£694.00: £329.00)
5f (Fibresand) Stalls: High GOING minus 0.29 sec per fur (FST) 3-30 (3-31)

772⁸ **Sing With the Band (60)***(66) (BAMcMahon)* 4-9-10 JFortune(7) (lw: a.p: rdn to ld 2f out: edgd rt fnl f: all out).......— **1**
906² My Cherrywell **(48)***(54) (LRLloyd-James)* 5-8-12 TWilliams(6) (chsd ldrs: ev ch fnl f: r.o) ....hd **2**
*842*⁵ Most Uppitty **(56)***(57) (JBerry)* 3-8-10b GCarter(5) (a.p: ev ch 1f out: nt qckn) 1½ **3**
524² Portelet **(55)***(43)*(Fav)*(RJRWilliams)* 3-8-9 GDuffield(3) (lw: a.p: ev ch over 1f out: wknd ins fnl f) 4 **4**
639⁹ Bells of Longwick **(64)***(50) (WWHaigh)* 6-10-0 DaleGibson(9) (outpcd: hdwy over 1f out: nvr nr to chal) ....¾ **5**
685⁷ Sunshine Belle **(45)***(28) (GMMoore)* 3-7-13 JFanning(8) (a.p: no hdwy fnl 2f) ....¾ **6**
*274*³ Merrie le Bow **(52)***(26) (PatMitchell)* 3-8-6 MRimmer(14) (outpcd: nvr nrr).......3 **7**
855⁴ My Lady Brady **(62)***(35) (MBrittain)* 3-9-2 SWhitworth(2) (lw: prom over 3f) ....nk **8**
*842*³ Charnwood Queen **(41)***(11) (RWArmstrong)* 3-7-2 (7)ow2 SLanigan(12) (s.s: outpcd).......nk **9**
754³ Nadwaty (IRE) **(55)***(24) (MCChapman)* 3-8-2b(7) CMunday(11) (led tl hdd 2f out: grad wknd)...1 **10**
862¹² Angelic Dancer **(42)***(7) (SRBowring)* 4-8-1b(5) CTeague(13) (chsd ldrs 3f) 1¼ **11**
*892*¹¹ Lucy's Gold **(36)** *(MJRyan)* 4-7-9 (5) MBaird(10) (sn outpcd: t.o) 15 **12**
541¹³ Grecian Garden **(29)** *(RCSpicer)* 4-7-7b JO'Reilly(4) (outpcd: t.o).......4 **13**

LONG HANDICAP Charnwood Queen 7-6

9/2 Portelet, **6/1** My Cherrywell, Nadwaty (IRE), **7/1** SING WITH THE BAND, Most Uppitty, **8/1** Angelic Dancer, Charnwood Queen, **10/1** My Lady Brady, **12/1** Merrie le Bow, **14/1** Bells of Longwick, **20/1** Sunshine Belle, Lucy's Gold, **25/1** Grecian Garden, CSF £49.08 CT £289.56 TOTE £4.30: £1.80 £2.60 £3.40 (£15.10) Trio £85.70 OWNER Mr D. J. Allen (TAMWORTH) BRED D. J. Allen 13 Rn

60.0 secs (2.00) SF: 49/37/30/16/33/1/-/8/-/-/-/-/-

WEIGHT FOR AGE 3yo-10lb

1033 BEGONIA (S) STKS (3-Y.O+) (Class G) £2,243.00 (£618.00:£293.00)
6f (Fibresand) Stalls: Low GOING minus 0.02 sec per fur (STD) 4-00 (4-02)

*625*² **Sea Devil (66)***(73) (MJCamacho)* 9-9-10 MBirch(9) (4th st: edgd lft 1f out: r.o to ld wl ins fnl f).......— **1**
732⁴ Rupert's Princess (IRE) **(50)***(59) (MJHeaton-Ellis)* 3-8-3b StephenDavies(5) (2nd st: ev ch ins fnl f: nt qckn).......1½ **2**
904³ Russian Heroine **(62)***(59)*(Fav)*(MJohnston)* 3-8-3 DeanMcKeown(6) (led: rdn 2f out: hdd wl ins fnl f) ....hd **3**
*842** Sweet Mate **(42)***(63) (SRBowring)* 3-8-8b(5) CTeague(10) (hld up: nt clr run & swtchd 2f out: sn rdn: r.o one pce fnl f) 2 **4**
674⁷ Noor El Houdah (IRE) **(59)***(56) (JBerry)* 3-8-8 GCarter(11) (7th st: one pce fnl 2f).......1 **5**
*892*⁸ Farndale **(47)***(42) (RonaldThompson)* 8-9-5 WNewnes(13) (hdwy & 6th st: wknd over 1f out) 5 **6**
*832*⁸ Arawa **(38)***(27) (DMarks)* 5-8-9 (5) MBaird(4) (3rd st: wknd 2f out).......4 **7**
867¹⁴ Polli Pui **(50)***(27) (PDEvans)* 3-8-3 SMaloney(8) (nvr trbld ldrs).......s.h **8**
Sizzling Romp **(73)***(23) (DTThom)* 3-8-0 (3) DRMcCabe(12) (a bhd) 1½ **9**
855⁷ Superbit **(47)***(27) (BAMcMahon)* 3-8-8 JFortune(2) (prom: rdn & 5th st: wknd 2f out) ....nk **10**
Noble Spirit (IRE) **(60)***(16) (MrsAMNaughton)* 4-9-5v AMercer(7) (a bhd) 4 **11**

733[4] Code of Silence **(47)**(13) (BPalling) 3-8-8v TSprake(1) (prom 3f) 1¼ **12**
813[16] Just Lucky (IRE) **(65)** (RWArmstrong) 3-8-8 RPrice(3) (b: uns rdr s) .... **U**

3/1 Russian Heroine, **100/30** Noor El Houdah (IRE), **5/1** SEA DEVIL (op 3/1), **6/1** Sweet Mate, **10/1** Sizzling Romp, **11/1** Just Lucky (IRE), **12/1** Rupert's Princess (IRE), Code of Silence, **14/1** Superbit, Polli Pui, Farndale (10/1-16/1), **20/1** Arawa, **33/1** Noble Spirit (IRE), CSF £66.77 TOTE £4.00: £2.60 £4.00 £1.50 (£36.30) Trio £89.40 OWNER Mr A. N. Goacher (MALTON) BRED A. L. Goacher and E. G. Noble 13 Rn 1m 18.0 (4.50) SF: 48/23/23/27/20/17/2/-/-/-/-/-
WEIGHT FOR AGE 3yo-11lb
Bt in 4,800 gns

1034 PETUNIA H'CAP (0-70) (3-Y.O+) (Class E) £3,388.00 (£1,012.00: £484.00: £220.00)
7f (Fibresand) Stalls: Low GOING minus 0.02 sec per fur (STD) 4-30 (4-35)

767[3] **No Submission (USA) (65)**(71) (DWChapman) 9-9-9b DeanMcKeown(15) (gd hdwy over 1f out: led ins fnl f: sn clr) ....— **1**
845[12] Wellsy Lad (USA) **(35)**(34) (DWChapman) 8-7-7 NCarlisle(9) (2nd st: led over 2f out tl wl over 1f out: r.o one pce fnl f) 3 **2**
672[6] Corona Gold **(40)**(38) (JGFitzGerald) 5-7-12 SMaloney(7) (4th st: led wl over 1f out tl ins fnl f) ....½ **3**
*768** Mixed Mood **(60)**(58) (BPalling) 3-8-6 TSprake(13) (5th st: ev ch over 1f out: one pce) ....s.h **4**
89[14] World Traveller **(70)**(67) (WAO'Gorman) 4-10-0b EmmaO'Gorman(6) (7th st: r.o ins fnl f) ....nk **5**
783[8] Perfect World **(64)**(60) (BAMcMahon) 3-8-10 GCarter(14) (lw: s.i.s: hdwy & edgd lft over 1f out: nvr nrr) ....½ **6**
Rosevear (IRE) **(50)**(44) (SMellor) 3-7-10 DaleGibson(12) (bit bkwd: nrst fin) 1 **7**
830[2] Frans Lad **(64)**(57) (JBerry) 3-8-3 (7) PRoberts(16) (3rd st: ev ch over 1f out: wknd fnl f) ....nk **8**
769[3] Farmer Jock **(47)**(33) (MrsNMacauley) 13-8-0 (5)ow6 CTeague(5) (b: hld up & bhd: hung rt ent st: nt clr run over 1f out: nt rch ldrs) ....nk **9**
789[16] Cledeschamps **(39)**(27) (MWEllerby) 6-7-11 ClaireBalding(11) (6th st: ev ch over 1f out: wknd fnl f) 2 **10**
848[12] Prince Rodney **(35)**(21) (CJDrewe) 6-7-2 (5) MBaird(10) (b: a bhd) ....¾ **11**
832[7] Titanium Honda (IRE) **(48)**(30) (CEBrittain) 4-8-6 ow1 MRimmer(4) (chsd ldrs: wknd over 1f out) 1½ **12**
867[2] Mac's Taxi **(61)**(43)(Fav)(PCHaslam) 3-8-2 (5) JStack(3) (led tl over 2f out: grad wknd) ....nk **13**
730[4] Crystal Gift **(66)**(45) (PFICole) 3-8-12 JFortune(8) (bhd fnl 2f) 1¼ **14**
862[10] Lady Silk **(68)** (JHetherton) 4-9-12 SWebster(1) (sn rdn: a bhd: t.o) 25 **15**
*518** Exclusive Assembly **(56)** (APJames) 3-8-2 StephenDavies(2) (prom: rdn 4f out: wknd 3f out: t.o) 7 **16**

LONG HANDICAP Wellsy Lad (USA) 7-2 Prince Rodney 7-6

9/4 Mac's Taxi, **5/1** Exclusive Assembly, **9/1** Frans Lad (op 6/1), NO SUBMISSION (USA), Crystal Gift, **10/1** Wellsy Lad (USA), **11/1** Titanium Honda (IRE) (8/1-12/1), **12/1** Perfect World (op 8/1), Mixed Mood, **16/1** World Traveller, Lady Silk, **20/1** Farmer Jock, Corona Gold, Cledeschamps, **25/1** Rosevear (IRE), **33/1** Prince Rodney, CSF £101.07 CT £1,657.30 TOTE £20.10: £2.40 £4.60 £3.00 £4.80 (£72.10) Trio £230.00, £259.23 to Lingfield 12/05/95 OWNER Mr T. S. Redman (YORK) BRED Mr. Francis X. Weber 16 Rn 1m 31.6 (4.80) SF: 53/16/20/28/49/30/14/27/15/9/3/12/13/15/-/-
WEIGHT FOR AGE 3yo-12lb
T/Plpt: £149.00 (60.51 Tckts). T/Qdpt: £61.20 (4.3 Tckts). KH

0772-BEVERLEY (R-H)
Friday May 12th (Good to firm)
WEATHER: cloudy WIND: almost nil

1035 LUND CLAIMING STKS (2-Y.O) (Class F) £2,798.00 (£778.00: £187.00: £187.00)
5f Stalls: Centre GOING minus 0.39 sec per fur (F) 2-30 (2-31)

755* **Monsieur Culsyth** (60) (JBerry) 2-8-10 GCarter(2) (chsd ldrs: effrt 2f out: carried lft fnl f: led post) ....— **1**
781[2] Swiss Valley Lady (57) (WGMTurner) 2-8-7 TSprake(3) (led: hung bdly lft u.p over 1f out: jst ct) ....s.h **2**
943[6] Imprimis (IRE) (44) (CNAllen) 2-7-11 (5) MBaird(7) (swvd lft s: bhd tl swtchd rt & styd on wl fnl f: nt rch ldrs) 2½ **3**
Grimstone Girl (45) (MWEasterby) 2-8-3 SMaloney(8) (cmpt: bit bkwd: unruly s: swvd rt s: sn chsng ldrs: kpt on fnl 2f) ....d.h **3**
644* Orange And Blue (46)(Fav)(MAJarvis) 2-8-4c MHills(4) (blind nr eye: eyecover: chsd ldrs: effrt ½-wy: carried sltly lft & no ex fnl f) ....hd **5**
574[4] Abduction (45) (EWeymes) 2-8-10 GHind(9) (outpcd & drvn along over 3f out: hdwy over 1f out: nvr nr ldrs) 2 **6**

810[10] Ghostly Apparition *(37) (JohnUpson)* 2-8-0 (5) CTeague(1) (w wnr: hung lft 2f out: wnt rt & wknd over 1f out) 1 7
755[3] Exactly (IRE) *(33) (MJohnston)* 2-8-1 TWilliams(6) (wl outpcd & sn drvn along: styd on u.p appr fnl f) ....s.h 8
Cottage Prince (IRE) *(30) (JJQuinn)* 2-8-11 MBirch(5) (str: cmpt: bit bkwd: dwlt: outpcd fr ½-wy) 4 9

6/4 Orange And Blue (op Evens), **2/1** Swiss Valley Lady, **9/2** MONSIEUR CULSYTH, **12/1** Imprimis (IRE), Abduction, **14/1** Exactly (IRE), **20/1** Grimstone Girl, Ghostly Apparition, Cottage Prince (IRE), CSF £14.76 TOTE £4.60: £1.40 £1.30 GG £2.50 I £1.30 (£6.70) Trio 3-4-7 £23.40, 3-4-8 £23.80 OWNER Forsyth Cully Racing (COCKERHAM) BRED J. Forsyth 9 Rn

65.4 secs (3.90) SF: 2/-/-/-/-/-/-/-/-

1036 DON & RAYMOND GIBBON MEMORIAL H'CAP (0-70) (4-Y.O+) (Class E)

£3,470.00 (£1,040.00: £500.00: £230.00)
2m 35y Stalls: Centre GOING minus 0.39 sec per fur (F) 3-00 (3-00)

741* **Rolling the Bones (USA) (41)***(52)*(Fav)*(PSFelgate)* 6-8-6 AMackay(3) (hdwy to ld 10f out: hdd 5f out: led wl over 1f out: styd on u.p) ....— 1
Vain Prince **(42)***(52) (NTinkler)* 8-8-7 GCarter(6) (chsd ldrs: effrt 3f out: styd on u.p fnl f: nt rch wnr) 1 2
Hullbank **(63)***(73) (WWHaigh)* 5-10-0 DaleGibson(5) (b: trckd ldrs: effrt 5f out: styd on u.p appr fnl f) ....hd 3
840[6] Murphys Way **(40)***(49) (JLEyre)* 6-8-5 RLappin(1) (chsd ldrs: led 5f out tl wl over 1f out: one pce) 1 4
Bahrain Queen (IRE) **(29)***(33) (CSmith)* 7-7-3 (5) MBaird(7) (b: bit bkwd: led 2f: outpcd & pushed along 9f out: sn lost pl: kpt on fnl 2f: n.d) 5 5
Cavina **(50)***(53) (NAGraham)* 5-9-1 WRyan(2) (hld up: hdwy ½-wy: effrt 3f out: wknd wl over 1f out) 1¼ 6
Brusque (USA) **(28)***(6) (DonEnricoIncisa)* 11-7-7 KimTinkler(4) (led after 2f to 10f out: outpcd & lost pl 7f out: grad wknd: eased) 25 7

LONG HANDICAP Brusque (USA) 7-2

11/10 ROLLING THE BONES (USA), **9/2** Hullbank, Cavina, **8/1** Vain Prince, Murphys Way, **25/1** Bahrain Queen (IRE), **33/1** Brusque (USA), CSF £9.66 TOTE £1.80: £1.20 £2.40 (£4.20) OWNER Mr M. F. Hyman (MELTON MOWBRAY) BRED Holtsinger Incorporated 7 Rn

3m 38.7 (8.20) SF: 23/23/44/20/4/24/-

1037 HUMBERSIDE APPRENTICE H'CAP (0-70) (4-Y.O+) (Class F)

£2,903.00 (£808.00: £389.00)
1m 100y Stalls: High GOING minus 0.39 sec per fur (F) 3-30 (3-31)

30[12] **Chantry Bellini (37)***(45) (MrsSMAustin)* 6-7-12b DarrenMoffatt(13) (b: chsd ldrs: styd on u.p to ld ins fnl f) ....— 1
820[4] Murphy's Gold (IRE) **(48)***(53) (RAFahey)* 4-8-4 (5) CTeague(4) (stdd s: hld up & bhd: gd hdwy on ins 2f out: r.o wl u.p towards fin: too much to do) 1¾ 2
749[15] Calder King **(61)***(65) (JLEyre)* 4-9-5b(3) NVarley(15) (chsd ldrs: led over 1f out tl ins fnl f: nt qckn) ....nk 3
820[8] Tolls Choice (IRE) **(51)***(55) (MWEasterby)* 6-8-7 (5) RuthCoulter(8) (stdd s: plld hrd: hdwy to trck ldrs 5f out: outpcd 3f out: kpt on u.p appr fnl f) ....nk 4
Mary Macblain **(37)***(38) (JLHarris)* 6-7-12 DWright(7) (s.s: bhd tl kpt on u.p fnl 2f) 1¼ 5
820[3] Thatched (IRE) **(46)***(45)*(Fav)*(REBarr)* 5-8-2 (5) PFessey(3) (mid div: hdwy on outside 3f out: kpt on: nvr rchd ldrs) 1¼ 6
94[4] Polonez Prima **(67)***(66) (JLSpearing)* 8-9-9 (5) ADaly(6) (chsd ldrs: effrt over 2f out: one pce) ....s.h 7
672[19] Greek Gold (IRE) **(46)***(43) (DNicholls)* 6-8-2 (5)ow2 SCopp(14) (led tl edgd lft & hdd over 1f out: sn wknd) ....hd 8
526[7] Maurangi **(57)***(55) (BWMurray)* 4-8-13 (5) GParkin(11) (trckd ldrs: effrt over 2f out: grad wknd) ....nk 9
820[9] Juice Plus **(32)***(28) (JParkes)* 4-7-2 (5) CAdamson(9) (in tch tl outpcd 3f out: n.d after) 1 10
753[7] East Barns (IRE) **(45)***(35) (SGollings)* 7-8-6 JTate(5) (mid div: outpcd 3f out: n.d after) 3 11
Touch Above **(50)***(36) (TDBarron)* 9-8-6 (5) KimberleyHart(10) (in tch tl outpcd 3f out: sn wknd) 2½ 12
676[12] Muzrak (CAN) **(60)***(41) (MDHammond)* 4-9-2 (5) CarolDavison(1) (s.i.s: a bhd) 2½ 13
Flair Lady **(57)***(25) (WGMTurner)* 4-8-11 (7) DScott(12) (chsd ldrs tl wknd over 2f out) 7 14
334[9] Charlotte Penny **(32)** *(NPLittmoden)* 4-7-2 (5) MBaird(2) (a bhd) 4 15

LONG HANDICAP Juice Plus 7-2 Charlotte Penny 7-1

4/1 Thatched (IRE), **7/1** East Barns (IRE), Maurangi, **15/2** Murphy's Gold (IRE), **9/1** Calder King, **10/1** Greek Gold (IRE), Touch Above, Polonez Prima, Tolls Choice (IRE), **14/1** Flair Lady, Mary Macblain, **25/1** Juice Plus, Muzrak (CAN), **33/1** CHANTRY BELLINI, Charlotte Penny, CSF £252.83 CT £2,218.46 TOTE £52.00: £9.70 £1.80 £4.10 (£277.00) Trio £396.80; £447.21 to Lingfield 13/5/95 OWNER Mrs J. J. KirkScott (MALTON) BRED J. Heyworth 15 Rn
1m 46.6 (2.60) SF: 27/35/47/37/20/27/48/25/37/10/17/18/23/7/-

1038 EVERINGHAM MEDIAN AUCTION MAIDEN STKS (3-Y.O) (Class E) £3,208.50 (£963.00: £464.00: £214.50)
1m 1f 207y Stalls: High GOING minus 0.39 sec per fur (F) 4-00 (4-00)

816[4] **Sahil (IRE)** *(88)*(Fav)*(DMorley)* 3-9-0 WCarson(7) (lw: sn led: edgd lft & styd on wl fnl f: drvn out)......— 1
815[4] Saleel (IRE) *(88) (ACStewart)* 3-9-0 WRSwinburn(5) (chsd wnr: chal 2f out: hard rdn: nt qckn nr fin)......hd 2
618[6] Dont Forget Curtis (IRE) **(79)***(78) (JRFanshawe)* 3-9-0 DHarrison(2) (lw: unruly in stalls: trckd ldrs: effrt & outpcd over 3f out: wknd wl over 1f out)......6 3
816[8] Sayyed Alraqs (USA) *(69) (MAJarvis)* 3-9-0 GCarter(6) (dwlt: bhd: lost tch 5f out: kpt on fnl 2f: n.d)......6 4
747[3] Invest Wisely *(65) (JMPEustace)* 3-9-0 MTebbutt(3) (sn outpcd: lost tch 5f out)......2½ 5
Aconorace *(57) (RAFahey)* 3-9-0 ACulhane(1) (leggy: unf: bit bkwd: sn outpcd: lost tch 5f out)......5 6
853[5] Carol's Dream (USA) **(74)***(51) (JWHills)* 3-9-0 MHills(4) (led early: chsd ldrs: effrt & hung lft 3f out: sn wknd & eased)......3½ 7

2/1 SAHIL (IRE), **5/2** Dont Forget Curtis (IRE), **9/2** Carol's Dream (USA), **11/2** Saleel (IRE), **8/1** Invest Wisely, **12/1** Sayyed Alraqs (USA), **33/1** Aconorace, CSF £12.92 TOTE £2.70: £1.60 £2.90 (£4.80) OWNER Mr Hamdan Al Maktoum (NEWMARKET) BRED Peter Savill 7 Rn
2m 6.2 (3.70) SF: 37/37/27/18/14/6/-

1039 SETTRINGTON H'CAP (0-70) (3-Y.O+) (Class E) £3,120.75 (£936.00: £450.50: £207.75)
1m 3f 216y Stalls: High GOING minus 0.39 sec per fur (F) 4-30 (4-30)

568[10] **Ho-Joe (IRE) (43)***(55) (JMCarr)* 5-8-8 SMorris(9) (b: trckd ldrs: led & hung rt over 1f out: drvn out)......— 1
757[7] Merry Mermaid **(45)***(55) (JFBottomley)* 5-8-10 ACulhane(12) (trckd ldrs: styd on u.p appr fnl f: nt qckn ins fnl f)......1¼ 2
833[6] Scalp 'em (IRE) **(40)***(50)*(Fav)*(PDEvans)* 7-8-5 JFortune(8) (led tl over 6f out: rdn & outpcd over 2f out: styd on fnl f)......½ 3
744[9] Kimberley Boy **(58)***(64) (MBrittain)* 5-9-9 SWhitworth(7) (stdd s: hld up & plld hrd: hdwy to ld over 6f out: hdd & sltly hmpd over 1f out: grad wknd)......3 4
866[13] Marjimel **(52)***(54) (JLEyre)* 4-9-3 RLappin(10) (in tch: effrt over 3f out: nt rch ldrs)......2½ 5
841[5] Floating Line **(63)***(65)*(Fav)*(PWigham)* 7-10-0 MWigham(1) (trckd ldrs: effrt over 2f out: wknd over 1f out)......nk 6
Abalene **(42)***(42) (TWDonnelly)* 6-8-7 SDWilliams(4) (prom: effrt 3f out: grad wknd)......1¼ 7
Bold Top **(49)***(46) (BSRothwell)* 3-7-4 (5)ow2 NVarley(11) (in tch: outpcd 3f out: kpt on fnl f)......¾ 8
295[10] Ozzie Jones **(44)***(34) (MCChapman)* 4-8-2 (7) CMunday(5) (hld up: a bhd)......7 9
384[9] Brownlows **(50)***(38) (MPBielby)* 3-7-7 (3) DarrenMoffatt(3) (s.i.s: a bhd)......1¼ 10
Ellastyle (IRE) **(33)***(3) (MissLCSiddall)* 4-7-12 DaleGibson(6) (a in rr: lost tch 3f out)......14 11
LONG HANDICAP Bold Top 7-6

7/2 Floating Line (op 9/4), Scalp 'em (IRE), **6/1** HO-JOE (IRE) (10/1-5/1), **7/1** Merry Mermaid, Kimberley Boy, **10/1** Ozzie Jones, **11/1** Abalene (op 7/1), **12/1** Marjimel, **16/1** Bold Top, Ellastyle (IRE), **25/1** Brownlows, CSF £46.03 CT £157.45 TOTE £4.70: £2.00 £2.70 £1.30 (£34.90) Trio £38.90 OWNER Mr S. Ho (MALTON) BRED Mrs C. L. Weld 11 Rn
2m 37.7 (6.20) SF: 22/22/17/31/21/32/9/-/1/-/-
WEIGHT FOR AGE 3yo-19lb

1040 HOUGHTON MAIDEN STKS (3-Y.O) (Class D) £3,788.50 (£1,138.00: £549.00: £254.50) 5f Stalls: Centre GOING minus 0.39 sec per fur (F) 5-00 (5-02)

Three Stops (USA) *(68)*(Fav)*(MRStoute)* 3-9-0 WRSwinburn(8) (lw: led to 2f out: led over 1f out: r.o u.p)......— 1
772[4] Never Such Bliss *(61) (JDBethell)* 3-8-9 TIves(3) (s.i.s: outpcd & bhd: hdwy over 1f out: squeezed thro ins fnl f: fin wl)......½ 2
Never Say so **(48)***(57) (CSmith)* 3-8-9 JFortune(11) (chsd ldrs: outpcd & n.m.r ½-wy: styd on fnl f)......1½ 3

Millesime (IRE) *(61) (BHanbury)* 3-9-0 WRyan(6) (leggy: s.i.s: hdwy ½-wy: sn prom: kpt on same pce fnl f) ....s.h 4
*768*2 Mamma's Due *(56) (JBerry)* 3-8-9 GCarter(7) (in tch: effrt ½-wy: kpt on same pce: nvr nr to chal)....s.h 5
758 12 Samsung Lovelylady (IRE) *(55) (EWeymes)* 3-8-9 GHind(10) (w ldrs tl wknd fnl f) ....nk 6
739 2 Lorelei Lee (IRE) *(51) (JohnBerry)* 3-8-2 (7) GFaulkner(4) (sn outpcd: hdwy ½-wy: kpt on: nvr nr to chal) 1¼ 7
772 9 Surprise Mission *(52) (RMWhitaker)* 3-9-0 ACulhane(5) (w ldr: slt ld 2f out: hung rt & sn hdd: wkng whn sltly hmpd ins fnl f) 1¼ 8
Takeapull **(55)***(36) (JBalding)* 3-8-7 (7) JEdmunds(2) (bit bkwd: s.i.s: a wl bhd)....5 9
924 7 Shazanni (IRE) *(6) (JGFitzGerald)* 3-8-2 (7) FLynch(1) (b: sn wl outpcd) 8 10

8/11 THREE STOPS (USA), **5/1** Millesime (IRE), **9/1** Never Such Bliss, Surprise Mission, Lorelei Lee (IRE), **14/1** Mamma's Due, **25/1** Samsung Lovelylady (IRE), Never Say so, **33/1** Takeapull, Shazanni (IRE), CSF £8.93 TOTE £1.70: £1.10 £2.30 £5.50 (£5.30) Trio £48.40 OWNER Maktoum Al Maktoum (NEWMARKET) BRED Swettenham Stud, J. Jones Jnr et al 10 Rn
63.4 secs (1.90) SF: 36/29/25/29/24/23/19/20/4/-
T/Plpt: £68.00 (174.16 Tckts). T/Qdpt: £47.10 (1.4 Tckts). WG

0784-CARLISLE (R-H)
Friday May 12th (Firm, Hard patches)
WEATHER: showers WIND: almost nil

1041

E.B.F. CALDEW MAIDEN STKS (2-Y.O) (Class D) £4,084.50(£1,236.00: £603.00: £286.50) **5f** Stalls: High GOING minus 0.69 sec per fur (HD) 2-40 (2-41)

836 2 **Tadeo** *(62)*(Fav)*(MRChannon)* 2-9-0 RHughes(4) (lw: mde all: rdn over 1f out: r.o: eased nr fin)....— 1
Evening Chime (USA) *(56) (MrsJRRamsden)* 2-9-0 KFallon(2) (w'like: leggy: scope: trckd wnr: effrt 2f out: wknd ins fnl f)....1¾ 2
Laurel Crown (IRE) *(28) (JBerry)* 2-9-0 JCarroll(1) (w'like: bit bkwd: s.i.s: nvr wnt pce) 9 3
Domoor *(5) (MJohnston)* 2-9-0 DHolland(3) (w'like: scope: bit bkwd: a outpcd & bhd)....7 4

6/4 TADEO, **13/8** Evening Chime (USA), **4/1** Domoor, **5/1** Laurel Crown (IRE) (op 3/1), CSF £4.37 TOTE £2.10 (£1.90) OWNER Mr J. R. Good (UPPER LAMBOURN) BRED J. R. and Mrs P. Good 4 Rn
61.5 secs (1.30) SF: 21/15/-/-

1042

IRTHING LIMITED STKS (0-60) (3-Y.O+) (Class F) £2,759.00 (£774.00: £377.00) **5f** Stalls: Low GOING minus 0.69 sec per fur (HD) 3-10 (3-14)

726 4 **Giggleswick Girl (54)***(56) (MRChannon)* 4-9-0 RHughes(6) (in tch: qcknd to ld ins fnl f: r.o) ....— 1
1023 7 Kenesha (IRE) **(43)***(54) (DANolan)* 5-9-0 KFallon(8) (mde most tl hdd ins fnl f: kpt on) ....½ 2
862* Christian Flight (IRE) **(39)***(52) (SGollings)* 6-8-12 (5) JStack(2) (lw: racd wd: a cl up: nt qckn fnl f)....1¾ 3
796 6 Followmegirls **(58)***(49)*(Fav)*(MrsALMKing)* 6-9-0 DHolland(1) (unruly s: hdwy 2f out: styd on one pce ins fnl f)....s.h 4
701 13 The Institute Boy **(44)***(47) (MissJFCraze)* 5-9-5v SWebster(5) (lw: chsd ldrs: effrt ½-wy: btn over 1f out)....2 5
*892*4 Grey Toppa **(58)***(34) (NPLittmoden)* 4-9-0 RPrice(9) (b: chsd ldrs over 3f: sn wknd) 2½ 6
856 14 Ivy Lilian (IRE) **(48)***(34) (WMBrisbourne)* 3-7-13 (5) AGarth(7) (spd to ½-wy: sn outpcd) ....hd 7
*892*3 Flashing Sabre **(60)***(26) (JBerry)* 3-8-9 JCarroll(3) (cl up over 3f: wknd) 4 8
*877*16 Oscar the Second (IRE) **(35)** *(CWFairhurst)* 5-9-5 KDarley(10) (Withdrawn not under Starter's orders: bolted gng to s).... W
First Option **(60)** *(RBastiman)* 5-9-0 (5) HBastiman(4) (Withdrawn not under Starter's orders: ref to ent stalls).... W

5/2 Followmegirls, **4/1** GIGGLESWICK GIRL, **5/1** Flashing Sabre, **9/1** First Option, Christian Flight (IRE), **10/1** Grey Toppa, **14/1** Kenesha (IRE), **20/1** The Institute Boy, **25/1** Ivy Lilian (IRE), CSF £38.18 TOTE £3.50: £1.60 £3.80 £1.10 (£25.40) Trio £12.70 OWNER Mr M. Bishop (UPPER LAMBOURN) BRED B. Minty 8 Rn 60.4 secs (0.20) SF: 38/36/34/31/29/16/6/-/-/-
WEIGHT FOR AGE 3yo-10lb

1043

BORDER ESK H'CAP (0-70) (3-Y.O+) (Class E) £3,181.20(£963.60: £470.80: £224.40) **5f 207y** Stalls: Low GOING minus 0.69 sec per fur (HD) 3-40 (3-45)

966 3 **The Kings Ransom (55)***(61+)*(Fav)*(MrsJRRamsden)* 3-8-6vow1 KFallon(6) (trckd ldrs: qcknd to ld 1f out: sn clr)....— 1

789[11] Northern Spark **(42)***(42) (MartynWane)* 7-8-4 RPrice(2) (bhd tl styd on wl fnl f: no ch w wnr) 2½ 2
753[10] Brisas **(42)***(40) (CWFairhurst)* 8-8-4v JFanning(4) (disp ld tl hdd & no ex 1f out) 1 3
949[4] Sobering Thoughts **(66)***(60) (JLEyre)* 9-10-0 KDarley(7) (b.hind: disp ld tl rdn & wknd 1f out) 1½ 4
789[9] Densben **(51)***(40) (DenysSmith)* 11-8-13 RHughes(5) (bhd: sme hdwy 2f out: no imp) 1¾ 5
Lady-Bo-K **(64)***(50) (CaptJWilson)* 4-9-5 (7) PBowe(8) (b: s.i.s: effrt over 2f out: no imp) 1 6
297[8] Hello Hobson's (IRE) **(50)***(32) (RBastiman)* 5-8-12 DeanMcKeown(3) (spd 4f) 1½ 7
Gymcrak Tycoon **(53)***(28) (GHolmes)* 6-8-10 (5) JStack(1) (a bhd) 2½ 8

6/4 THE KINGS RANSOM, **100/30** Sobering Thoughts, **6/1** Densben, **7/1** Brisas, **10/1** Northern Spark, **14/1** Lady-Bo-K, Gymcrak Tycoon, **50/1** Hello Hobson's (IRE), CSF £15.38 CT £73.37 TOTE £2.40: £1.20 £1.50 £1.60 (£10.70) OWNER Mr M. J. Simmonds (THIRSK) BRED M. J. Simmonds 8 Rn

1m 12.6 (0.30) SF: 30/22/20/40/20/30/12/8
WEIGHT FOR AGE 3yo-11lb

1044

DERWENT CLAIMING STKS (3-Y.O+) (Class F) £2,801.00 (£786.00: £383.00) **6f 206y** Stalls: Low GOING minus 0.69 sec per fur (HD) 4-10 (4-12)

927[7] **Profit Release (IRE) (58)***(52)*(Fav)*(MJohnston)* 4-8-11b DHolland(4) (mde all: sn clr: wknd nr fin) ....— 1
965[4] Obsidian Grey **(52)***(52) (MissLCSiddall)* 8-8-9 (3) DRMcCabe(7) (a chsng wnr: kpt on wl nr fin) ....½ 2
877[8] Blow Dry (IRE) **(58)***(53) (MartynWane)* 5-9-4 KDarley(5) (hld up & bhd: hdwy over 2f out: rdn & no imp appr fnl f) 2 3
753[6] My Godson **(45)***(41) (FJO'Mahony)* 5-8-4 (7) BPeel(9) (chsd ldrs tl lost pl ent st: styd on again fnl f) 2½ 4
965[3] Birchwood Sun **(51)***(47) (MDods)* 5-8-13b(5) VHalliday(2) (lw: outpcd & bhd tl sme late hdwy) nk 5
839[17] Reed My Lips (IRE) **(35)***(41) (BPJBaugh)* 4-8-12 RPrice(8) (prom tl outpcd fnl 2f) ....s.h 6
906[7] Miss Whittingham (IRE) **(55)***(38) (JBerry)* 5-8-13 JCarroll(6) (effrt ent st: sn rdn & btn) 1¾ 7
Orchard Gold **(44)***(36) (FJYardley)* 4-9-2 RHughes(3) (dwlt: wnt prom appr st: wknd 2fout) 2 8
965[5] Beware of Agents **(61)***(28) (MJohnston)* 6-9-0 DeanMcKeown(1) (outpcd appr st: n.d after) 2½ 9

5/2 PROFIT RELEASE (IRE), **9/2** Birchwood Sun, **11/2** Blow Dry (IRE), Miss Whittingham (IRE), **6/1** Obsidian Grey, **8/1** Beware of Agents, **12/1** My Godson, **33/1** Orchard Gold, **100/1** Reed My Lips (IRE), CSF £16.48 TOTE £3.40: £1.10 £1.70 £2.10 (£8.90) Trio £36.90 OWNER G R Bailey Ltd (Baileys Horse Feeds) (MIDDLEHAM) BRED Moyglare Stud Farm Ltd 9 Rn

1m 27.6 (1.90) SF: 19/19/20/8/14/8/5/3/-

OFFICIAL EXPLANATION **Orchard Gold: the jockey stated that the horse lost his action inside the final furlong.**

1045

EAMONT H'CAP (0-70) (3-Y.O) (Class E) £3,152.60 (£954.80: £466.40: £222.20) **7f 214y** Stalls: Low GOING minus 0.69 sec per fur (HD) 4-40 (4-42)

576[4] **Indian Rhapsody (40)***(47) (MRChannon)* 3-7-10v NCarlisle(5) (plld hrd: hdwy over 2f out: chal ins fnl f: led post) ....— 1
980[11] Heathyards Magic (IRE) **(65)***(72)*(Fav)*(RHollinshead)* 3-9-7 KDarley(3) (trckd ldr: led wl over 1f out: rdn & put hd in air: jst ct) ....s.h 2
880[2] Fishy Affair **(45)***(45) (TDyer)* 3-8-1 JFanning(4) (hld up: hdwy over 2f out: one pce appr fnl f) 3½ 3
842[9] Benten **(44)***(34) (DWChapman)* 3-7-9 (5)ow2 AGarth(2) (led tl wl over 1f out: sn btn) 4 4
759[13] Pash **(45)***(17) (CWCElsey)* 3-8-1v NKennedy(1) (chsd ldrs tl rdn & btn 2f out) 10 5

13/8 Heathyards Magic (IRE), **5/2** Fishy Affair, **4/1** INDIAN RHAPSODY, Pash, **50/1** Benten, CSF £10.17 TOTE £3.50: £1.50 £1.30 (£2.50) OWNER Mr J. R. Good (UPPER LAMBOURN) BRED Mrs P. Good 5 Rn 1m 43.7 (4.70) SF: -/25/-/-/-

1046

EDEN H'CAP (0-70) (3-Y.O+) (Class E) £3,152.60 (£954.80:£466.40: £222.20) **1m 6f 32y** Stalls: High GOING minus 0.69 sec per fur (HD) 5-10 (5-10)

840[8] **Arc Bright (IRE) (35)***(42) (RHollinshead)* 5-8-6 (5) AGarth(1) (hld up: qcknd to ld over 4f out: hdd wl over 1f out: rallied fnl f to ld cl home) ....— 1
494[5] Persuasive **(48)***(55)*(Fav)*(MrsMReveley)* 8-9-10 KDarley(4) (hld up: hdwy u.p over 3f out: led gng wl wl over 1f out: rdn & fnd nil whn hdd ins fnl f) ....nk 2
Lord Advocate **(30)***(25) (DANolan)* 7-8-1b(5)ow3 VHalliday(2) (chsd ldrs: outpcd 3f out: no imp after) 8 3

866 15 Lightning Quest (IRE) **(37)***(35) (JSWainwright)* 4-8-12 DeanMcKeown(3) (lw: in tch: rdn to chal over 6f out: one pce fnl 3f)....hd 4
418 11 Rubislaw **(47)***(37) (CWFairhurst)* 3-8-2 JMarshall(6) (led 2f: lost pl 4f out: n.d after)....7 5
534 4 Arian Spirit (IRE) **(33)***(21) (JLEyre)* 4-8-8 JFanning(5) (led after 2f tl over 4f out: sn outpcd).1¾ 6

7/4 Persuasive, **2/1** ARC BRIGHT (IRE), **9/2** Arian Spirit (IRE), **6/1** Lightning Quest (IRE), **20/1** Rubislaw, Lord Advocate, CSF £5.65 TOTE £3.40: £1.20 £1.60 (£2.40) OWNER Mr J. E. Bigg (UPPER LONGDON) BRED Tsarina Stud 6 Rn 3m 6.4 (6.40) SF: 8/21/-/-/-/-
WEIGHT FOR AGE 3yo-21lb, 4yo-1lb
T/Plpt: £19.40 (347.28 Tckts). T/Qdpt: £9.70 (2.5 Tckts). AA

0560-LINGFIELD (L-H)
Friday May 12th (Turf Good to firm, AWT Standard)
WEATHER: drizzle WIND: almost nil

1047
STEVE WOOD MEMORIAL MAIDEN STKS (2-Y.O) (Class D) £3,360.50 (£998.00: £473.00: £210.50)
5f Stalls: High GOING minus 0.35 sec per fur (F) 2-20 (2-21)

852 4 **To The Whire** *(79) (GLMoore)* 2-8-9 BRouse(5) (a.p: rdn over 1f out: led ins fnl f: r.o wl) ....— 1
825 5 Welsh Mountain *(84)*(Fav)*(MJHeaton-Ellis)* 2-9-0 StephenDavies(8) (a.p: led over 2f out tl ins fnl f: r.o)....hd 2
849 6 Petite Annie *(75) (TGMills)* 2-8-9 JReid(6) (a.p: rdn 2f out: unable qckn ins fnl f)....1¼ 3
436 8 Oriel Lad *(75) (KRBurke)* 2-9-0 TQuinn(9) (lw: a.p: rdn 2f out: one pce)....1½ 4
682 5 Red Nose (IRE) *(74) (MHTompkins)* 2-9-0 PRobinson(10) (led over 2f: wknd over 1f out)....nk 5
852 6 Mystery Matthias *(65) (MissBSanders)* 2-8-6 (3) SSanders(1) (a.p: rdn over 2f out: wknd fnl f)....1¼ 6
Hurricane Horn (IRE) *(65) (WRMuir)* 2-9-0 JWeaver(4) (neat: a bhd)....1½ 7
863 6 Bobsworthatcaspers *(65) (GLewis)* 2-9-0 PaulEddery(3) (lw: a bhd)....s.h 8
Multi Franchise *(63) (BGubby)* 2-9-0 JQuinn(7) (str: bit bkwd: s.s: a bhd)....¾ 9

11/8 Welsh Mountain, **5/2** TO THE WHIRE, **9/2** Red Nose (IRE) (6/1-4/1), **14/1** Mystery Matthias (8/1-16/1), **16/1** Oriel Lad, Bobsworthatcaspers, **20/1** Hurricane Horn (IRE), Petite Annie, **33/1** Multi Franchise, CSF £6.30 TOTE £3.30: £1.10 £1.20 £4.40 (£2.60) Trio £27.80 OWNER Mr K. Higson (EPSOM) BRED Lord Rotherwick 9 Rn 59.98 secs (2.98) SF: 12/17/8/8/7/-/-/-/-

1048
BOLLINGER CHAMPAGNE CHALLENGE SERIES GENTLEMENS' H'CAP (0-70) (3-Y.O+) (Class F) £2,972.60 (£823.60: £393.80)
1m 2f Stalls: Low GOING minus 0.35 sec per fur (F) 2-50 (2-52)

738 5 **Bajan (IRE) (52)***(69)*(Fav)*(LadyHerries)* 4-10-8 (4) MrPPritchard-Gordon(6) (lw: led over 7f out: clr over 2f out: r.o wl)....— 1
864 2 Montone (IRE) **(58)***(65) (KRBurke)* 5-11-0 (4) MrMMannish(8) (led over 1f: 5th st: chsd wnr over 2f out: unable qckn)....6 2
586 4 Shaarid (USA) **(67)***(66)*(Fav)*(IABalding)* 7-11-9 (4) MrABalding(9) (swtchd lft over 2f out: hdwy over 1f out: r.o wl ins fnl f)....5 3
873 15 Roman Reel (USA) **(64)***(63) (GLMoore)* 4-11-6 (4) MrKGoble(13) (lw: hdwy over 4f out: 6th st: hrd rdn over 2f out: unable qckn)....½ 4
905 11 Dots Dee **(36)***(30) (JMBradley)* 6-9-6 (4)ow3 MrRBarrett(3) (lw: hdwy 7f out: 2nd st: rdn over 2f out: wknd over 1f out)....1¼ 5
778 5 Air Command (BAR) **(40)***(35) (CTNash)* 5-9-10 (4) MrPPhillips(16) (nvr nr to chal)....1¼ 6
729 8 Starlight Flyer **(35)***(21) (JELong)* 8-9-5b(4)ow2 MrTWaters(2) (b: no hdwy fnl 3f)....4 7
818 7 Cozzi (FR) **(33)***(15) (JMBradley)* 7-9-3 (4) MrVLukaniuk(14) (a mid div)....4 8
630 12 Ela Palikari Mou (IRE) **(42)***(19) (RAkehurst)* 4-10-2 MrTMcCarthy(5) (lw: a mid div)....3 9
Swan Flyer **(33)***(8) (JJSheehan)* 4-9-3 (4) MrPClose(15) (s.s: a bhd)....1½ 10
Overpower **(61)***(24) (MHTompkins)* 11-11-3 (4)ow11 MrMJenkins(4) (a bhd)....½ 11
584 11 Catempo (IRE) **(53)***(26) (SDow)* 5-10-13 MrTCuff(10) (prom over 4f)....nk 12
812 12 Bezirgan **(40)** *(JAkehurst)* 4-9-10 (4) MrCAppleby(11) (3rd st: wknd 3f out)....20 13
Todd (USA) **(68)***(9) (PMitchell)* 4-12-0 MrRTeal(12) (b.nr hind: lw: bhd fnl 4f)....nk 14
851 11 Mega Tid **(60)** *(BAPearce)* 3-10-0 (4)ow5 MrRBlyth(1) (sddle slipped: led over 8f out tl over 7f out: 4th st: wknd 3f out)....13 15

LONG HANDICAP Dots Dee 9-5 Swan Flyer 9-4 Starlight Flyer 8-13 Cozzi (FR) 9-6
5/1 BAJAN (IRE), Shaarid (USA), **11/2** Montone (IRE), Roman Reel (USA), **13/2** Mega Tid (9/1-6/1), **14/1** Overpower, **16/1** Cozzi (FR), Dots Dee, **20/1** Todd (USA), Ela Palikari Mou (IRE), **25/1** Air Command (BAR), Catempo (IRE), **33/1** Bezirgan, **50/1** Swan Flyer, Starlight Flyer, CSF £29.85 CT £131.65 TOTE £4.30: £2.10 £1.80 £2.10 (£9.10) Trio £7.50 OWNER Mr Tim Sinclair (LITTLEHAMPTON) BRED Rathbarry Stud 15 Rn 2m 9.45 (6.45) SF: 43/39/40/37/4/9/-/-/-/-/-/-/-/-/-
WEIGHT FOR AGE 3yo-16lb

1049

UNITED HOUSE H'CAP (0-80) (4-Y.O+) (Class D) £3,935.10(£1,174.80: £561.40: £254.70) **1m (Equitrack)** Stalls: High GOING minus 0.35 sec per fur (FS) 3-20 (3-22)

731[14] **Whatever's Right (IRE) (57)***(65) (MDIUsher)* 6-8-6 TQuinn(7) (lw: a.p: led over 1f out: rdn out) ....— 1
845[8] Indian Serenade **(54)***(57) (PWHarris)* 4-8-3 GDuffield(9) (lw: hdwy over 2f out: rdn over 1f out: r.o one pce) 2½ 2
762[6] Hatta Sunshine (USA) **(51)***(49) (AMoore)* 5-7-11 (3) SSanders(4) (b.hind: lw: a.p: led 2f out tl over 1f out: one pce) 2½ 3
928[5] Perilous Plight **(75)***(72) (WRMuir)* 4-9-10 JWeaver(5) (lw: hdwy over 2f out: hrd rdn over 1f out: r.o one pce) ....½ 4
887[14] Duty Sergeant (IRE) **(44)***(36) (PMitchell)* 6-7-7 GBardwell(11) (s.s: rdn thrght: hdwy over 1f out: nvr nrr) 2½ 5
882[5] Soaking **(70)***(60) (GLMoore)* 5-9-5 BRouse(3) (led 6f: wknd over 1f out) 1 6
401[3] Spencer's Revenge **(74)***(63)*(Fav)*(LordHuntingdon)* 6-9-9 LDettori(10) (lw: hdwy over 3f out: rdn over 2f out: wknd 1f out) ....¾ 7
542[9] Maid Welcome **(60)***(45) (MrsNMacauley)* 8-8-2v(7) AmandaSanders(8) (prom over 4f) 2 8
731[11] Dragon Bold (IRE) **(47)***(30) (LJHolt)* 4-7-10b CAvery(2) (bhd fnl 3f) ....¾ 9
780[17] Zahran (IRE) **(56)***(37) (JMBradley)* 4-8-0 (5) SDrowne(6) (b: lw: bhd fnl 4f) 1¼ 10
634[21] El Atrevido (FR) **(68)***(39) (NJHWalker)* 5-9-3 RCochrane(1) (lw: a bhd) 5 11

LONG HANDICAP Duty Sergeant (IRE) 6-9

7/2 Spencer's Revenge, **4/1** Perilous Plight, **8/1** Hatta Sunshine (USA), Soaking (6/1-9/1), El Atrevido (FR), **9/1** Zahran (IRE) (14/1-8/1), Indian Serenade, WHATEVER'S RIGHT (IRE), **10/1** Maid Welcome, **33/1** Dragon Bold (IRE), **66/1** Duty Sergeant (IRE), CSF £79.08 CT £615.50 TOTE £12.10: £3.40 £3.70 £2.90 (£75.30) Trio £184.00 OWNER Mr M. S. C. Thurgood (SWINDON) BRED Rockville House Stud 11 Rn 1m 38.49 (2.09) SF: 40/32/24/47/11/35/38/20/5/12/14

1050

MAXIMS H'CAP (0-70) (3-Y.O+) (Class E) £3,502.40 (£1,047.20: £501.60: £228.80) **5f** Stalls: High GOING minus 0.35 sec per fur (F) 3-50 (3-56)

Hickory Blue (64)*(74) (MrsNMacauley)* 5-9-13b JWeaver(1) (mde all: clr over 2f out: drvn out) ....— 1
583* Bashful Brave **(58)***(62)*(Fav)*(JWPayne)* 4-9-7 MRimmer(13) (lw: a.p: rdn over 1f out: unable qckn) 2 2
850[3] Tharwa (IRE) **(57)***(56) (NACallaghan)* 3-8-10 LDettori(4) (b.nr fore: b.off hind: a.p: rdn over 2f out: one pce) 1½ 3
972[9] Windrush Boy **(58)***(55) (JRBosley)* 5-9-7 JReid(11) (rdn & hdwy over 1f out: r.o) ....½ 4
887[3] Half Tone **(44)***(37) (RMFlower)* 3-7-4b(7) SLanigan(8) (hdwy over 1f out: r.o) 1¼ 5
656[8] Tee-Emm **(43)***(35) (PHowling)* 5-8-6 JQuinn(3) (a.p: rdn over 2f out: wknd fnl f) ....nk 6
856[4] Raisa Point **(53)***(42) (WRMuir)* 4-9-2 TQuinn(9) (hld up: rdn over 2f out: wknd over 1f out) 1 7
Lorins Gold **(39)***(28) (AndrewTurnell)* 5-8-2b BDoyle(7) (b.nr hind: a.p: rdn over 2f out: wknd fnl f) ....hd 8
856[10] Tinker Osmaston **(61)***(49) (MSSaunders)* 4-9-10 JWilliams(5) (outpcd) ....nk 9
Night Asset **(52)***(37) (JO'Donoghue)* 6-8-10 (5) PMcCabe(6) (outpcd) 1 10
Trina **(35)***(10) (DLWilliams)* 4-7-5 (7)ow5 AmandaSanders(16) (outpcd) 1½ 11
765[15] Red Admiral **(58)***(33) (PCHaslam)* 5-9-0 (7) NicolaHowarth(2) (b.hind: spd over 2f) 1½ 12
Tomal **(59)***(28) (RIngram)* 3-8-12 AMcGlone(12) (a bhd) 2 13
856[13] Kensington Freight **(47)***(8) (JAkehurst)* 3-7-11 (3) SSanders(14) (lw: bhd fnl 2f) 2½ 14
507[19] Baton Bleu **(34)** *(PHowling)* 4-7-11 GBardwell(10) (lw: a bhd) 8 15
739[9] Sandra Dee (IRE) **(60)** *(BAPearce)* 3-8-13 StephenDavies(15) (Withdrawn not under Starter's orders: lame) .... W

3/1 Bashful Brave, **4/1** Tharwa (IRE), **5/1** Half Tone, **7/1** Raisa Point (op 7/2), **10/1** HICKORY BLUE, **14/1** Windrush Boy, Tomal, Red Admiral, **16/1** Tee-Emm, Tinker Osmaston, **20/1** Lorins Gold, **25/1** Kensington Freight, **33/1** Night Asset, Baton Bleu, **66/1** Trina, CSF £40.17 CT £136.23 TOTE £13.20: £2.40 £2.10 £1.90 (£43.60) Trio £56.10 OWNER Mrs Christine Griffin (MELTON MOWBRAY) BRED A. and Mrs Griffin 15 Rn

58.35 secs (1.35) SF: 56/44/28/37/9/17/24/10/31/19/-/15/-/-/-/-
WEIGHT FOR AGE 3yo-10lb

1051

MCCALL GROUP STKS (3-Y.O+) (Class D) £5,588.00 (£1,664.00:£792.00: £356.00) **7f 140y** Stalls: High GOING minus 0.35 sec per fur (F) 4-20 (4-21)

730[2] **Bernard Seven (IRE) (82)***(83) (SPCWoods)* 3-8-7 LDettori(3) (lw: chsd ldr: led over 2f out: hung lft fnl f: drvn out) ....— 1
677[3] Bin Rosie *(82)*(Fav)*(DRLoder)* 3-8-7 JWeaver(2) (lw: a.p: ev ch & hung lft fnl 2f: r.o) ....½ 2
887[6] Friendly Brave (USA) **(60)***(67) (TGMills)* 5-9-6b TQuinn(4) (lw: led 5f) 7 3

Robin Island *(61) (RHannon)* 3-8-7 JReid(1) (bhd fnl 5f)..........3 **4**
Twice Knightly *(34) (JRJenkins)* 4-9-6 DBiggs(5) (lw: a bhd)..........13 **5**

4/11 Bin Rosie, **7/2** BERNARD SEVEN (IRE) (op 9/4), **12/1** Robin Island (op 8/1), **25/1** Friendly Brave (USA), **40/1** Twice Knightly, CSF £5.01 TOTE £4.70: £1.40 £1.10 (£1.60) OWNER Mr Bernard Butt (NEWMARKET) BRED Bobby Donworth and Honora Corridan 5 Rn

1m 32.25 (4.25) SF: 15/14/12/-/-
WEIGHT FOR AGE 3yo-13lb

1052 INFONET LIMITED STKS (0-70) (3-Y.O+) (Class E) £3,330.80(£994.40: £475.20: £215.60) 7f 140y Stalls: High GOING minus 0.35 sec per fur (F) 4-50 (4-52)

618[8] **Greenwich Again (66)***(77) (TGMills)* 3-8-11 JReid(5) (hld up: nt clr run over 2f out: hrd rdn over 1f out: led last strides)..........— **1**
Nashaat (USA) **(64)***(74) (NJHWalker)* 7-9-3 (5) RPainter(3) (hld up: rdn over 1f out: led ins fnl f: hdd last strides)..........nk **2**
813[7] Astral Invader (IRE) **(70)***(74) (MSSaunders)* 3-8-9 JWilliams(1) (lw: hdwy over 2f out: ev ch ins fnl f: r.o)..........nk **3**
648[13] Risky Romeo **(68)***(71) (GCBravery)* 3-8-9 RCochrane(6) (s.s: stdy hdwy & nt clr run over 1f out: r.o wl ins fnl f)..........1¼ **4**
Piquant **(69)***(70) (LordHuntingdon)* 8-9-8 LDettori(2) (bit bkwd: hld up: rdn over 3f out: led 2f out tl ins fnl f: sn wknd)..........¾ **5**
870[4] Jolto **(66)***(65)*(Fav)*(KOCunningham-Brown)* 6-9-8 JWeaver(4) (a.p: led 4f out to 2f out: wknd fnl f)..........2 **6**
Absolutely Fayre **(70)***(65) (RAkehurst)* 4-9-8 TQuinn(8) (lw: a.p: rdn over 2f out: wkng whn hmpd over 1f out)..........hd **7**
634[17] Folly Finnesse **(69)***(59) (BRMillman)* 4-8-12 (5) AWhelan(10) (sme hdwy 2f out: wknd fnl f)..........¾ **8**
636[17] Peter Rowley **(65)***(55) (RHannon)* 4-9-1 (7) DaneO'Neill(9) (led over 3f: wknd 2f out)..........4 **9**
East Sheen **(70)***(47) (CJBenstead)* 3-8-5 ow1 BRouse(7) (bhd fnl 2f)..........1¾ **10**

15/8 Jolto, **7/2** GREENWICH AGAIN, **6/1** Absolutely Fayre, Piquant (op 7/2), **10/1** Risky Romeo (op 6/1), Astral Invader (IRE), **14/1** East Sheen, Folly Finnesse, **25/1** Peter Rowley, Nashaat (USA), CSF £73.61 TOTE £5.90: £2.00 £3.90 £2.40 (£97.40) Trio £259.70 OWNER John Humphreys (Turf Accountants) Ltd (EPSOM) BRED T. G. Mills Ltd 10 Rn

1m 31.36 (3.36) SF: 28/38/25/22/34/29/29/23/19/-
WEIGHT FOR AGE 3yo-13lb

T/Jkpt: Not won; £69,876.37 to Worcester 13/5/95. T/Plpt: £164.00 (133.96 Tckts). T/Qdpt: £97.90 (0.2 Tckts); £105.92 to Lingfield 13/5/95. AK

0854-BATH (L-H)
Saturday May 13th (Firm)
WEATHER: fair WIND: moderate across

1053 CHAPEL FARM MAIDEN STKS (3-Y.O F) (Class D) £3,991.75(£1,204.00: £584.50: £274.75) 1m 5y Stalls: Low GOING minus 0.56 sec per fur (F) 2-10 (2-13)

547[3] **Cap And Gown (IRE)** *(78)*(Fav)*(PFICole)* 3-8-11 JCarroll(4) (lw: 4th st: led wl over 1f out: drvn out)..........— **1**
Jalfrezi *(78) (JARToller)* 3-8-11 JWeaver(11) (unf: bit bkwd: hdwy over 2f out: r.o wl ins fnl f)hd **2**
865[6] Makri *(66) (MrsJCecil)* 3-8-11 PaulEddery(12) (2nd st: led over 2f out tl wl over 1f out: unable qckn)..........6 **3**
695[12] Indescent Blue *(63) (DWPArbuthnot)* 3-8-11 RPrice(10) (lw: 3rd st: ev ch wl over 1f out: sn wknd)..........1¼ **4**
797[15] Tempting (IRE) *(63) (RHannon)* 3-8-4 (7) DaneO'Neill(6) (lw: 6th st: one pce fnl 2f)..........nk **5**
Great Tern *(58) (NMBabbage)* 3-8-11 BDoyle(3) (unf: 5th st: wknd 2f out)..........2½ **6**
Flammant Rose (IRE) *(50) (MartynMeade)* 3-8-11 VSlattery(5) (leggy: s.s: nvr nrr)..........4 **7**
888[5] Mighty Squaw *(49) (MissGayKelleway)* 3-8-11 GDuffield(7) (led over 5f)..........½ **8**
Bold Sally *(44) (MrsSDWilliams)* 3-8-11 JWilliams(2) (str: bkwd: s.s: a bhd)..........2½ **9**
Treasure Keay *(32) (PJMakin)* 3-8-11 RPerham(9) (bhd fnl 3f)..........6 **10**
888[7] Brockton Light *(30) (MRChannon)* 3-8-11 RHughes(8) (bit bkwd: s.s: bhd fnl 2f)..........¾ **11**
635[20] Blazing Miracle *(25) (BRMillman)* 3-8-11 AMackay(1) (a bhd)..........2½ **12**

8/11 CAP AND GOWN (IRE), **9/2** Makri, **7/1** Jalfrezi (8/1-14/1), **10/1** Mighty Squaw (op 6/1), **16/1** Brockton Light, **20/1** Tempting (IRE), **25/1** Treasure Keay, Indescent Blue, **33/1** Bold Sally, **66/1** Great Tern, Flammant Rose (IRE), **100/1** Blazing Miracle, CSF £6.93 TOTE £1.60: £1.10 £1.60 £1.90 (£4.90) Trio £5.90 OWNER Sheikh Mohammed (WHATCOMBE) BRED Sheikh Mohammed bin Rashid al Maktoum 12 Rn 1m 40.4 (1.90) SF: 31/31/19/16/16/11/3/2/-/-/-/-

1054 TATTERSALLS MAIDEN AUCTION STKS (2-Y.O) (Class E) £3,246.00 (£978.00: £474.00: £222.00)
5f 11y Stalls: Low GOING minus 0.56 sec per fur (F) 2-40 (2-43)

760[2] **Sonic Mail** *(65)*(Fav)*(KMcAuliffe)* 2-8-6 RCochrane(7) (a.p: led over 1f out: edgd lft: rdn out) — 1
859[2] Eights High (USA) *(62)* *(RHannon)* 2-7-13 (7)ow1 DaneO'Neill(11) (b.off hind: led over 3f out tl over 2f out: ev ch ins fnl f: unable qckn) ¾ 2
859[3] Lucky Revenge *(43)* *(MartynMeade)* 2-7-5 (7)ow1 CTinel(10) (hdwy over 1f out: r.o) 3½ 3
Polish Bear (IRE) *(37)* *(BJMeehan)* 2-8-3 BDoyle(13) (neat: a.p: one pce fnl 2f) 3½ 4
Dande Flyer *(39)* *(DWPArbuthnot)* 2-8-7 RPrice(12) (b.hind: neat: bit bkwd: a.p: led over 2f out tl over 1f out: sn wknd) ¾ 5
Nina From Pasadena *(25)* *(CJames)* 2-7-12 DaleGibson(4) (neat: nvr nr to chal) 1½ 6
903[3] Corniche Quest (IRE) *(23)* *(MRChannon)* 2-8-0 PaulEddery(8) (prom over 2f) 1½ 7
Ivory's Grab Hire *(9)* *(KTIvory)* 2-8-2 GDuffield(3) (leggy: s.s: a bhd) 5 8
Croeso Cynnes *(BPalling)* 2-7-12 ow1 TSprake(1) (neat: bit bkwd: led over 1f: wknd over 2f out) 1¼ 9
782[7] Masbro Bird *(BRMillman)* 2-7-11 AMackay(9) (a bhd) s.h 10
Members Welcome (IRE) *(PGMurphy)* 2-8-2 JCarroll(5) (neat: bit bkwd: a bhd) 1½ 11
Midnight Cookie *(RJHodges)* 2-8-1 (5) SDrowne(2) (neat: s.s: a bhd) 6 12

13/8 SONIC MAIL, **7/2** Corniche Quest (IRE), **9/2** Eights High (USA) (op 3/1), **10/1** Dande Flyer (6/1-12/1), Polish Bear (IRE) (8/1-12/1), **12/1** Croeso Cynnes (20/1-33/1), **20/1** Lucky Revenge, Masbro Bird, **25/1** Midnight Cookie, **33/1** Ivory's Grab Hire, Members Welcome (IRE), Nina From Pasadena, CSF £9.88 TOTE £2.80: £1.20 £2.20 £5.00 (£6.40) Trio £21.40 OWNER Folly Road Racing Partners 1995 (LAMBOURN) BRED Stud-On-The-Chart 12 Rn
62.5 secs (2.00) SF: 13/10/-/-/-/-/-/-/-/-/-/-

1055 RADSTOCK STKS (3-Y.O+) (Class C) £5,661.80 (£1,818.80:£879.40)
5f 11y Stalls: Low GOING minus 0.56 sec per fur (F) 3-10 (3-10)

858* **Lucky Parkes (100)***(101)*(Fav)*(JBerry)* 5-9-9 JCarroll(2) (lw: mde all: shkn up 2f out: r.o wl) — 1
982[4] Tart and a Half **(83)***(88)* *(BJMeehan)* 3-8-5 BDoyle(1) (chsd wnr: rdn thrght: unable qckn fnl 2f) 1½ 2
858[2] Crystal Magic **(94)***(87)* *(RHannon)* 4-8-8 (7) DaneO'Neill(3) (lw: hld up: rdn 2f out: one pce) nk 3

4/6 LUCKY PARKES, **6/4** Crystal Magic, **9/1** Tart and a Half, CSF £4.58 TOTE £1.40 (£2.60) OWNER Mr Joseph Heler (COCKERHAM) BRED Joseph Heler 3 Rn 61.8 secs (1.30) SF: 39/16/25
WEIGHT FOR AGE 3yo-10lb

1056 SOMERSET STKS (4-Y.O+) (Class C) £5,272.00 (£1,832.00: £886.00: £370.00)
1m 3f 144y Stalls: Low GOING minus 0.56 sec per fur (F) 3-40 (3-41)

913[5] **Alriffa (116)***(100+)*(Fav)*(RHannon)* 4-9-2 RHughes(3) (chsd ldr: led 7f out: easily) — 1
958[5] English Invader *(97)* *(RAkehurst)* 4-9-6 BThomson(1) (lw: 2nd st: rdn over 3f out: no imp) 5 2
Spot Prize (USA) **(111)***(81)* *(IABalding)* 4-8-7 RCochrane(4) (lw: 4th st: no hdwy fnl 3f) 2 3
Classical Star *(RJHodges)* 6-8-3 (7) AmandaSanders(2) (led over 4f: 3rd st: wknd over 3f out: t.o) dist 4

4/7 ALRIFFA, **9/4** Spot Prize (USA), **11/2** English Invader, **66/1** Classical Star, CSF £3.92 TOTE £1.60 (£2.50) OWNER Sheikh Essa Bin Mubarak (MARLBOROUGH) BRED Patrick Eddery Ltd 4 Rn
2m 25.9 (0.40 under best) (-0.80) SF: 61/58/42/-

1057 ROMAN CITY H'CAP (0-90) (3-Y.O+) (Class C) £5,881.00(£1,768.00: £854.00: £397.00) **5f 11y** Stalls: Low GOING minus 0.56 sec per fur (F) 4-10 (4-11)

693[14] **Ann's Pearl (IRE) (75)***(81)* *(JWHills)* 4-9-1 BThomson(7) (mde virtually all: all out) — 1
856[3] Winsome Wooster **(65)***(71)* *(PGMurphy)* 4-8-5 JCarroll(8) (a.p: rdn over 1f out: r.o wl ins fnl f) s.h 2
565* Nordico Princess **(71)***(69)*(Fav)*(MBrittain)* 4-8-11 RCochrane(1) (w wnr: ev ch 1f out: unable qckn) 2½ 3
765[14] Domicksky **(65)***(63)* *(MRChannon)* 7-8-5 PaulEddery(2) (lw: hdwy over 3f out: one pce fnl 2f) s.h 4
949[7] Napoleon Star (IRE) **(72)***(70)* *(MSSaunders)* 4-8-12 RPrice(15) (lw: hdwy over 1f out: r.o) s.h 5
796[3] Kildee Lad **(74)***(71)* *(APJones)* 5-9-0 BDoyle(12) (lw: s.s: hdwy over 1f out: r.o) nk 6
1016[2] Eagle Day (USA) **(70)***(67)* *(DRCElsworth)* 4-8-10b JWilliams(9) (hdwy over 1f out: r.o) s.h 7

812[9] How's Yer Father **(84)***(80) (RJHodges)* 9-9-5 (5) SDrowne(13) (hdwy over 1f out: nvr nrr) ......s.h **8**
856[9] Paley Prince (USA) **(55)***(47) (MDIUsher)* 9-7-2 (7) CAdamson(10) (nvr nr to chal) 1½ **9**
734[5] Random **(58)***(49) (CJames)* 4-7-12 DaleGibson(14) (lw: nvr nrr) ....hd **10**
Seaside Minstrel **(59)***(46) (DLWilliams)* 7-7-13 AMackay(6) (a bhd) 1¼ **11**
856[7] John O'Dreams **(55)***(37) (MrsALMKing)* 10-7-4 (5)ow2 NVarley(4) (b: bhd fnl 2f)............................1 **12**
856[15] Miriam **(55)***(30) (MJFetherston-Godley)* 4-7-2 (7) MartinDwyer(3) (bhd fnl 2f)..............................3 **13**
856[8] La Belle Dominique **(66)***(37) (SGKnight)* 3-7-3 (7)ow3 SLanigan(5) (lw: spd over 3f) ....nk **14**

LONG HANDICAP John O'Dreams 7-6

4/1 Nordico Princess, **6/1** Winsome Wooster, Kildee Lad, **13/2** Eagle Day (USA) (10/1-6/1), **9/1** Domicksky, La Belle Dominique, **10/1** John O'Dreams, **12/1** Napoleon Star (IRE), **14/1** How's Yer Father (10/1-16/1), **25/1** Random, ANN'S PEARL (IRE), **33/1** Paley Prince (USA), Miriam, Seaside Minstrel, CSF £155.34 CT £666.13 TOTE £26.00: £7.00 £2.10 £2.10 (£66.20) OWNER Mrs Paul Levinson (LAMBOURN) BRED R. G. Percival 14 Rn

61.7 secs (1.20) SF: 33/23/21/15/22/23/19/32/-/1/-/-/-/-

WEIGHT FOR AGE 3yo-10lb

1058

BATH FESTIVAL H'CAP (0-70) (4-Y.O+) (Class E) £3,421.50 (£1,032.00: £501.00: £235.50)
2m 1f 34y Stalls: Low GOING minus 0.56 sec per fur (F) 4-40 (4-43)

795[2] **Inchcailloch (IRE) (55)***(67)*(Fav)*(JSKing)* 6-9-0 PaulEddery(6) (lw: hdwy over 2f out: led ins fnl f: rdn out) ....— **1**
French Ivy (USA) **(51)***(63) (FMurphy)* 8-8-10 TSprake(20) (hdwy 5f out: 5th st: led over 1f out to ins fnl f: unable qckn) ....½ **2**
432[12] Flashman **(38)***(42) (BJLlewellyn)* 5-7-11 ow4 TWilliams(1) (a.p: led 4f out tl over 1f out: one pce) 4 **3**
696[5] Tarthooth (IRE) **(65)***(71) (CJBenstead)* 4-9-7 JWilliams(7) (lw: hdwy 9f out: 3rd st: one pce fnl 3f)..2½ **4**
866[5] Soojama (IRE) **(38)***(42) (RMFlower)* 5-7-11 FNorton(18) (s.s: hdwy 8f out: r.o one pce fnl 2f) 1¼ **5**
795[12] Coleridge **(50)***(54) (JJSheehan)* 7-8-9b RPrice(5) (2nd st: wknd 2f out) ....s.h **6**
795[15] Sheltered Cove (IRE) **(50)***(52) (KOCunningham-Brown)* 4-8-6 JWeaver(12) (b: lw: nvr nrr) ..2½ **7**
Sarazar (USA) **(50)***(51) (RAkehurst)* 6-8-9 BThomson(9) (lw: nvr nr to chal)..........................¾ **8**
840[2] Brandon Prince (IRE) **(69)***(69) (IABalding)* 7-10-0 RCochrane(3) (a mid div) 1¾ **9**
649[9] Lajadhal (FR) **(34)***(26) (KBishop)* 6-7-0 (7) BHalligan(2) (prom 11f) 8 **10**
374[4] Regal Pursuit (IRE) **(57)***(49) (CAHorgan)* 4-8-13b DaleGibson(17) (nvr nrr)...........................nk **11**
506[14] Wannaplantatree **(62)***(53) (GHYardley)* 4-8-13 (5) DGriffiths(16) (prom 13f)............................½ **12**
741[14] Secret Assignment (USA) **(37)***(26) (RCurtis)* 5-7-7 (3)ow2 DWright(15) (t: nvr nrr).....................hd **13**
Rumpus (IRE) **(51)***(42) (MrsLAMurphy)* 5-8-5 (5) SDrowne(8) (hdwy 5f out: wknd over 2f out) ....½ **14**
741[4] By Arrangement (IRE) **(37)***(22) (SWoodman)* 6-7-10 AMackay(13) (a bhd) 6 **15**
Nornax Lad (USA) **(65)***(49) (MartynMeade)* 7-9-10 VSlattery(4) (4th st: wknd over 2f out) 1½ **16**
884[15] Princesse Abigail **(39)***(2) (RMFlower)* 4-7-2 (7)ow2 SLanigan(14) (a bhd).................................20 **17**
A Suitable Girl **(39)** *(DLWilliams)* 4-7-4 (5)ow2 NVarley(11) (bhd fnl 6f)..3 **18**
266[7] Art Deco Lady **(54)***(15) (NMBabbage)* 4-8-10 BDoyle(10) (lw: prom over 12f) 1 **19**
201[6] Super Assignation (IRE) **(46)** *(MissGayKelleway)* 4-8-2 ow1 GDuffield(19) (lw: led 13f: 6th st: wknd over 3f out: t.o) 20 **20**

LONG HANDICAP Princesse Abigail 7-1 A Suitable Girl 6-12 Lajadhal (FR) 6-7

3/1 INCHCAILLOCH (IRE), **5/1** Soojama (IRE), **11/2** Tarthooth (IRE), **7/1** Sarazar (USA) (op 4/1), **15/2** Brandon Prince (IRE), **8/1** Sheltered Cove (IRE), **10/1** By Arrangement (IRE), **20/1** Rumpus (IRE), Regal Pursuit (IRE), Super Assignation (IRE), **25/1** Wannaplantatree, **33/1** Nornax Lad (USA), Flashman, French Ivy (USA), **40/1** Coleridge, **50/1** Art Deco Lady, **66/1** Princesse Abigail, A Suitable Girl, Secret Assignment (USA), Lajadhal (FR), CSF £96.43 CT £2,642.16 TOTE £3.80: £1.30 £13.90 £4.20 £1.60 (£221.30) Trio Not won; £1010.04 to Windsor 15/5/95 OWNER Mr F. J. Carter (SWINDON) BRED Hascombe and Valiant Studs 20 Rn

3m 47.4 (6.40) SF: 27/23/2/28/2/14/9/11/29/-/6/10/-/2/-/9/-/-/-/-

WEIGHT FOR AGE 4yo-3lb

T/Plpt: £5.90 (1,666.21 Tkts). T/Qdpt: £29.90 (9.7 Tckts). AK

1035-BEVERLEY (R-H)
Saturday May 13th (Good to firm)

WEATHER: fine but cloudy WIND: moderate half against

1059

KIPLINGCOTE (S) STKS (3-Y.O) (Class F) £2,903.00 (£808.00:£389.00)
1m 1f 207y GOING minus 0.47 sec per fur (F) 2-20 (2-20)

Charm Dancer *(73) (JWharton)* 3-8-9 JQuinn(4) (cmpt: hld up: gd hdwy on ins & nt clr run 2f out: r.o wl u.p to ld ins fnl f)...— **1**

773[4] Gentle Irony **(50)***(77) (PJMakin)* 3-9-2 KDarley(2) (hld up: hdwy over 2f out: led over 1f out tl ins fnl f: unable qckn)....1¾ **2**
*893** Absolute Folly **(53)***(66)*(Fav)*(JBerry)* 3-9-0 GCarter(10) (led after 1f tl over 1f out: one pce)....6 **3**
837* Risky Rose **(48)***(60) (RHollinshead)* 3-8-9 ACulhane(1) (hld up: effrt & hmpd over 3f out: styd on fnl 2f: nvr nr to chal)....½ **4**
837[2] High Flown (USA) **(58)***(58) (RonaldThompson)* 3-9-0 MBirch(3) (in tch: effrt on outside 3f out: sn wknd)....4 **5**
Our Rainbow *(53) (MrsSMAustin)* 3-8-9 JMarshall(7) (b: chsd ldrs: n.m.r & lost pl over 3f out: n.d after)....hd **6**
990[4] Upex le Gold Too **(50)***(58) (MrsASwinbank)* 3-9-0 SMaloney(5) (chsd ldrs: rdn over 2f out: sn wknd)....hd **7**
893[6] Anchor Crown *(53) (KGWingrove)* 3-8-6 (3) DRMcCabe(9) (dwlt: hld up: a bhd)....hd **8**
773[6] Cuillin Caper *(50) (TRWatson)* 3-8-9 DeanMcKeown(8) (bit bkwd: led 1f: chsd ldrs tl wknd qckly wl over 1f out)....2 **9**
548[17] Corina's Glow **(30)***(17) (MissJFCraze)* 3-8-9 SWebster(6) (chsd ldrs: sn drvn along: lost pl over 3f out: sn bhd)....20 **10**

11/4 Absolute Folly, **3/1** High Flown (USA) (op 5/1), **4/1** Gentle Irony (3/1-9/2), **5/1** Risky Rose, **8/1** Cuillin Caper, **12/1** Upex le Gold Too, **16/1** CHARM DANCER, Anchor Crown, **25/1** Our Rainbow, **33/1** Corina's Glow, CSF £78.35 TOTE £29.20: £4.50 £1.60 £1.30 (£49.30) Trio £90.50 OWNER Mr G. W. Turner (MELTON MOWBRAY) BRED G. W. and Mrs Turner 10 Rn
2m 6.6 (4.10) SF: 23/27/16/10/8/3/8/3/-/-
Sold MPipe 9,800 gns

1060

HYPAC H'CAP (0-70) (3-Y.O) (Class E) £4,432.00 (£1,336.00: £648.00: £304.00)
7f 100y GOING minus 0.47 sec per fur (F) 2-50 (2-51)

759[6] **Euro Sceptic (IRE) (41)***(48) (MHEasterby)* 3-8-2b SMaloney(7) (led to 6f out: led over 1f out: edgd lft u.p: jst hld on)....— **1**
1028[3] Three Arch Bridge **(56)***(63)*(Fav)*(MJohnston)* 3-9-3b DHolland(8) (chsd ldrs: chal over 1f out: edgd rt & sltly hmpd ins fnl f: nt qckn nr fin)....hd **2**
724[7] Grey Again **(54)***(60) (SRBowring)* 3-8-10b(5) CTeague(9) (effrt over 2f out: styd on wl fnl f)....nk **3**
Khan **(59)***(63) (CWThornton)* 3-9-6 DeanMcKeown(11) (hmpd s: bhd tl styd on wl fnl 2f: nt rch ldrs)....1¼ **4**
759[3] Pc's Cruiser (IRE) **(54)***(56) (MCChapman)* 3-8-8b(7) CMunday(10) (wnt rt s: chsd ldrs: ev ch over 1f out: kpt on same pce)....½ **5**
992[7] Malzoom **(33)***(29) (SEKettlewell)* 3-7-8 NKennedy(4) (bhd: hdwy 2f out: wknd ins fnl f)....3 **6**
Borrowby **(50)***(46) (MWEasterby)* 3-8-11b LCharnock(6) (led 6f out: hung lft & hdd over 1f out: wknd fnl f)....s.h **7**
Rushen Raider **(60)***(55) (KWHogg)* 3-9-0 (7) ADaly(5) (unruly s: plld hrd: trckd ldrs tl wknd over 1f out)....½ **8**
624[8] Studio Thirty **(48)***(34) (RHollinshead)* 3-8-9 GCarter(2) (s.s: a bhd)....4 **9**
409[7] Fairy's Son **(38)***(18) (DNicholls)* 3-7-13 JQuinn(12) (sltly hmpd s: plld hrd: sn trckng ldrs: wknd over 2f out)....3 **10**
Tabard Garden **(46)***(23) (DNicholls)* 3-8-7 AlexGreaves(3) (mid div: effrt over 2f out: sn wknd)....1½ **11**
754[11] Pemley **(54)***(9) (RMWhitaker)* 3-9-1 ACulhane(1) (a bhd)....10 **12**

100/30 Three Arch Bridge, **9/2** Grey Again, **6/1** Fairy's Son, Pc's Cruiser (IRE), **13/2** EURO SCEPTIC (IRE), **12/1** Khan, **14/1** Pemley, Borrowby, **16/1** Rushen Raider, Malzoom, Tabard Garden, Studio Thirty, CSF £28.69 CT £102.96 TOTE £6.80: £2.00 £1.60 £2.40 (£11.70) Trio £9.50 OWNER Mr C. H. Stevens (MALTON) BRED Martyn J. McEnery 12 Rn
1m 33.5 (1.50) SF: 33/48/45/48/41/14/31/40/19/3/8/-

1061

ROTHMANS ROYAL NORTH SOUTH CHALLENGE SERIES H'CAP (0-85) (3-Y.O+) (Class D) £4,250.00 (£1,280.00: £620.00: £290.00)
1m 100y GOING minus 0.47 sec per fur (F) 3-20 (3-21)

876[6] **Equerry (60)***(71) (MJohnston)* 4-8-6 KDarley(9) (chsd ldrs: drvn along over 3f out: styd on to ld ins fnl f)....— **1**
774[9] Kemo Sabo **(72)***(81) (MrsJRRamsden)* 3-8-5 KFallon(7) (led 6f out: clr 3f out: hdd & no ex ins fnl f)....1 **2**
928[8] Superoo **(65)***(68) (MrsPSly)* 9-8-11 MBirch(4) (trckd ldrs: effrt over 2f out: kpt on u.p)....3 **3**
817[4] South Eastern Fred **(62)***(64)*(Fav)*(HJCollingridge)* 4-8-8 JQuinn(3) (trckd ldrs: effrt & outpcd over 2f out: styd on)....¾ **4**
839[5] Desert Zone (USA) **(60)***(60) (JLHarris)* 6-8-6 PRobinson(8) (bhd: effrt u.p 3f out: nvr nr ldrs)....1¼ **5**

873[17] Karinska **(56)***(54) (MCChapman)* 5-7-9 (7)ow2 CMunday(6) (reluctant to go to s: s.i.s: bhd: hdwy on wd outside 3f out: kpt on: nvr nr ldrs)....hd **6**
922[6] Orthorhombus **(63)***(58) (DJSCosgrove)* 6-8-9 JFortune(11) (led to 6f out: sn drvn along: lost pl over 2f out)....2½ **7**
928[2] Pine Ridge Lad (IRE) **(54)***(48) (JLEyre)* 5-8-0 JFanning(10) (hld up: effrt & outpcd over 3f out: n.d after)....½ **8**
928[6] Pharazini **(70)***(61) (MJCamacho)* 4-9-2 LCharnock(5) (dwlt s: hld up & plld hrd: effrt 3f out: sn wknd)....1¾ **9**
749* Western General **(82)***(69) (MissSEHall)* 4-9-9 (5) JStack(1) (hld up & bhd: effrt on outside 3f out: hung rt: n.d)....1¾ **10**
793[6] Shanghai Venture (USA) **(79)** *(SPCWoods)* 4-9-4 (7) CWebb(2) (ref to r: virtually t.n.p)....dist **11**

4/1 South Eastern Fred, **5/1** Western General, **11/2** Kemo Sabo, **13/2** Pine Ridge Lad (IRE), **7/1** EQUERRY, **8/1** Shanghai Venture (USA), **11/1** Karinska, **12/1** Orthorhombus, Superoo, **14/1** Pharazini, Desert Zone (USA), CSF £44.71 CT £425.91 TOTE £6.60: £2.30 £3.30 £3.90 (£28.20) Trio £366.10 OWNER Mr J. R. Good (MIDDLEHAM) BRED J. R. and Mrs P. Good 11 Rn

1m 45.0 (1.00) SF: 43/40/40/36/32/26/30/20/33/41/-

WEIGHT FOR AGE 3yo-13lb

1062 YORKSHIRE-TYNE TEES TELEVISION STKS (3-Y.O) (Class D)

£4,023.40 (£1,112.40: £530.20)
1m 3f 216y GOING minus 0.47 sec per fur (F) 3-50 (3-50)

663[3] **Prussian Blue (USA)** *(83)*(Fav)*(HRACecil)* 3-8-12 AMcGlone(2) (led: pushed along 5f out: styd on wl u.p fnl 2f: hld on wl towards fin)....— **1**
619[3] Warning Order **(100)***(89) (JLDunlop)* 3-9-4 KDarley(1) (swvd lft s: hld up gng wl: smooth hdwy to chal over 1f out: sn rdn: nt qckn nr fin)....hd **2**
797[8] Rainelle *(71) (CEBrittain)* 3-8-7 MBirch(3) (sn w wnr: drvn along over 2f out: rn green & wknd over 1f out)....5 **3**

8/13 PRUSSIAN BLUE (USA), **7/4** Warning Order, **9/1** Rainelle, CSF £1.93 TOTE £1.50 (£1.20) OWNER Mr L. Marinopoulos (NEWMARKET) BRED E. A. Cox Jnr 3 Rn

2m 38.8 (7.30) SF: 13/19/1

1063 E.B.F. RIDINGS MEDIAN AUCTION MAIDEN STKS (2-Y.O) (Class E)

£3,626.00 (£1,088.00: £524.00: £242.00)
5f GOING minus 0.47 sec per fur (F) 4-20 (4-21)

951[3] **Prince Aslia** *(84+)*(Fav) *(MJohnston)* 2-9-0 DHolland(6) (mde all: clr ½-wy: jst hld on)....— *1*
810[7] Welville *(84) (PJMakin)* 2-9-0 AMcGlone(10) (chsd wnr: rdn & hung rt ins fnl f: styd on strly towards fin)....hd **2**
788[2] Meeting Point *(63) (MrsMReveley)* 2-8-9 KDarley(1) (chsd wnr: drvn along ½-wy: sn wl outpcd)....5 **3**
Northern Clan *(45) (MWEasterby)* 2-9-0 LCharnock(5) (leggy: unf: rn green & sn drvn along: wandered: hdwy ½-wy: nvr nr ldrs)....7 **4**
Eric's Bett *(34) (MrsSMAustin)* 2-9-0 JMarshall(4) (unf: bit bkwd: b: unruly: s.s: a outpcd)....3½ **5**
Imp Express (IRE) *(33) (GMMoore)* 2-9-0 MTebbutt(8) (lengthy: bit bkwd: s.i.s: nvr wnt pce)....nk **6**
Propolis Power (IRE) *(32) (MWEasterby)* 2-8-7 (7) RuthCoulter(7) (bkwd: a outpcd)....½ **7**
Phantom Dancer (IRE) *(12) (JBerry)* 2-9-0 GCarter(3) (str: lengthy: s.i.s: a wl bhd)....6 **8**

5/4 PRINCE ASLIA, **2/1** Meeting Point, **7/1** Welville, **8/1** Phantom Dancer (IRE), **14/1** Northern Clan, Imp Express (IRE), **33/1** Propolis Power (IRE), Eric's Bett, CSF £10.73 TOTE £2.40: £1.10 £1.60 £1.60 (£5.30) Trio £2.40 OWNER Mrs R. J. Daniels (MIDDLEHAM) BRED Mrs A. H. Daniels 8 Rn

64.1 secs (2.60) SF: 19/19/-/-/-/-/-/-

1064 WILLIAM HILL H'CAP (0-80) (3-Y.O+) (Class D) £4,206.00(£1,263.00: £609.00: £282.00) **1m 1f 207y** GOING minus 0.47 sec per fur (F) 4-50 (4-50)

841* **Hazard a Guess (IRE) (72)***(83)*(Fav)*(MrsJRRamsden)* 5-9-8 KFallon(6) (lw: stdd s: hld up: hdwy to trck ldrs & n.m.r over 2f out: swtchd ins & qcknd to ld over 1f out: sn clr: readily)....— **1**
986[7] Augustan **(56)***(61) (SGollings)* 4-8-6v DHolland(5) (chsd ldrs: drvn along over 5f out: outpcd 2f out: kpt on fnl f)....3½ **2**
967[2] Southern Power (IRE) **(78)***(83) (MrsMReveley)* 4-10-0v KDarley(2) (b.nr hind: sn trckng ldrs: led over 3f out: edgd lft & hdd over 1f out: kpt on)....s.h **3**
Hawkish (USA) **(45)***(48) (DMorley)* 6-7-9 JQuinn(1) (a.p: ev ch 3f out: nt qckn appr fnl f)....1½ **4**

839[8] Durham Drapes **(60)***(62) (MHEasterby)* 4-8-10 MBirch(7) (hld up: drvn along over 3f out: kpt on u.p fnl 2f: nvr nr to chal)....½ 5
874[3] Soba Up **(49)***(45) (TJEtherington)* 5-7-13 LCharnock(3) (chsd ldrs: drvn along & outpcd over 3f out: edgd lft: sn wknd)....4 6
876[5] Trooping (IRE) **(59)***(52) (MGMeagher)* 6-8-9 JFortune(4) (led tl over 3f out: wknd 2f out)......1½ 7

2/1 HAZARD A GUESS (IRE), **11/4** Southern Power (IRE), **7/1** Durham Drapes, Hawkish (USA), Soba Up, **10/1** Trooping (IRE), **12/1** Augustan, CSF £22.12 TOTE £3.10: £2.20 £3.20 (£31.00) OWNER Mrs D. Ridley (THIRSK) BRED A. F. O'Callaghan in Ireland 7 Rn
2m 6.3 (3.80) SF: 37/15/37/2/16/-/6
T/Plpt: £38.80 (297.61 Tckts). T/Qdpt: £44.20 (7.15 Tckts). WG

1047-LINGFIELD (L-H)
Saturday May 13th (Firm)
WEATHER: fine & sunny WIND: almost nil

1065 EUROPHARM GROUP MAIDEN STKS (I) (3-Y.O+) (Class D) £3,968.90 (£1,185.20: £566.60: £257.30)
7f Stalls: High GOING minus 0.19 sec per fur (GF) 1-30 (1-33)

Fakih (USA) *(88)*(Fav)*(ACStewart)* 3-8-12 WCarson(3) (a.p: led ins fnl f: r.o wl)....— 1
Mubariz (IRE) *(85) (EALDunlop)* 3-8-12 LDettori(10) (w'like: scope: a.p: led over 1f out tl ins fnl f)....1½ 2
Ramsdens (IRE) *(82) (WJHaggas)* 3-8-12 MHills(7) (w ldr: r.o one pce fnl 2f)....1¼ 3
Red Rita (IRE) **(90)***(71)*(Fav)*(WRMuir)* 4-9-5 TQuinn(11) (led tl wknd over 1f out)....2½ 4
584[5] Tadellal (IRE) *(60) (MDixon)* 4-9-2 (3) SSanders(6) (no hdwy fnl 2f)....5 5
Brass Tacks *(58) (RHannon)* 3-8-7 PatEddery(8) (nvr nr to chal)....½ 6
Run-Do-Run *(56) (HJCollingridge)* 3-8-7 MRimmer(2) (nvr nrr)....1¼ 7
Chinese Viking *(61) (GLMoore)* 3-8-12 BRouse(1) (w'like: scope: nrst fin)....s.h 8
853[9] Lidhama (USA) *(55) (GLewis)* 3-8-7 SWhitworth(4) (wl bhd tl r.o fnl f)....nk 9
H'Ani *(48) (MrsLPiggott)* 3-8-0 (7) VictoriaAppleby(9) (prom 3f)....3 10
779[14] Midnight Mass *(32) (AGFoster)* 3-8-8b(5)ow6 RPainter(5) (a bhd)....7 11

7/2 FAKIH (USA), Red Rita (IRE), **9/2** Brass Tacks (3/1-5/1), **11/2** Mubariz (IRE) (7/2-6/1), **10/1** Ramsdens (IRE) (op 6/1), **14/1** H'Ani (20/1-40/1), **20/1** Run-Do-Run, **25/1** Chinese Viking, Tadellal (IRE), **33/1** Lidhama (USA), **50/1** Midnight Mass, CSF £20.15 TOTE £3.50: £1.40 £2.00 £3.00 (£10.10) Trio £33.30 OWNER Mr Hamdan Al Maktoum (NEWMARKET) BRED Shadwell Farm 11 Rn
1m 23.99 (3.39) SF: 38/35/32/33/22/8/6/11/5/-/-
WEIGHT FOR AGE 3yo-12lb

1066 CRAWLEY WARREN CHARTWELL STKS (Listed) (3-Y.O+ F) (Class A) £12,622.50 (£3,780.00: £1,815.00: £832.50)
7f Stalls: High GOING minus 0.19 sec per fur (GF) 2-00 (2-00)

895a[2] **Daring Destiny (96)***(103) (KRBurke)* 4-9-3 JTate(4) (lw: hld up: qcknd to ld ins fnl f: r.o)......— 1
828[7] Cheyenne Spirit **(94)***(98) (BHanbury)* 3-8-5 WRyan(1) (led tl ins fnl f)....2 2
829[9] Twilight Patrol **(88)***(92) (RHannon)* 3-8-5 PatEddery(3) (in rr tl rdn & hdwy 2f out: nt rch ldrs)....3 3
933[11] Queenfisher **(103)***(89)*(Fav)*(RHannon)* 3-8-5 BRouse(5) (chsd ldr tl hung lft & wknd over 1f out)....1 4
620[12] Regal Fanfare (IRE) **(103)***(78) (JWHills)* 3-8-6 ow1 MHills(2) (prom 4f)....5 5

13/8 Queenfisher, **15/8** DARING DESTINY, **11/2** Cheyenne Spirit, **8/1** Regal Fanfare (IRE) (7/1-12/1), **10/1** Twilight Patrol (8/1-12/1), CSF £10.60 TOTE £2.70: £1.40 £2.90 (£5.30) OWNER Mrs Ann Wright (WANTAGE) BRED Mrs Ann E. M. Wright 5 Rn 1m 23.99 (3.39) SF: 43/26/20/17/6
WEIGHT FOR AGE 3yo-12lb

1067 CHAMPAGNE RUINART OAKS TRIAL STKS (Listed) (3-Y.O F) (Class A) £12,285.50 (£4,448.00: £2,149.00: £895.00: £372.50)
1m 3f 106y Stalls: Low GOING minus 0.19 sec per fur (GF) 2-30 (2-31)

797[5] **Asterita (79)***(92) (RHannon)* 3-8-8 PatEddery(4) (2nd st: led over 2f out: all out)....— 1
557* Bunting **(94)***(91) (JHMGosden)* 3-8-8 LDettori(3) (lw: led tl over 2f out: rallied over 1f out: n.m.r fnl f: r.o)....¾ 2
797[6] Kshessinskaya *(91) (CEBrittain)* 3-8-8 MRimmer(5) (lost pl & 4th st: styd on fnl 2f)....hd 3
797* Pitcroy *(90)*(Fav)*(JRFanshawe)* 3-8-8 DHarrison(2) (hdwy & 3rd st: rn wd: ev ch 2f out: nt qckn fnl f)....nk 4

747[8] Last Spin **(65)***(49) (JRJenkins)* 3-8-8 TQuinn(1) (5th st: wknd over 3f out: t.o)........................30 5

11/10 Pitcroy, **2/1** Bunting (op 11/10), **6/1** ASTERITA, **10/1** Kshessinskaya, **40/1** Last Spin, CSF £16.55 TOTE £5.70: £1.80 £1.10 (£4.30) OWNER Mr B. E. Nielsen (MARLBOROUGH) BRED Grange Stud (UK) 5 Rn 2m 28.54 (6.54) SF: 32/31/31/30/-

1068 TRIPLEPRINT DERBY TRIAL STKS (Gp 3) (3-Y.O) (Class A)

£30,820.00 (£11,380.00: £5,440.00: £2,200.00: £850.00: £310.00)
1m 3f 106y Stalls: Low GOING minus 0.19 sec per fur (GF) 3-00 (3-01)

679* **Munwar (116)***(106)*(Fav)*(PTWalwyn)* 3-8-7 WCarson(2) (mde all: shkn up 1f out: r.o)..........— 1
764* Riyadian *(106) (PFICole)* 3-8-7 TQuinn(3) (lw: 3rd st: rdn fnl 2f: r.o ins fnl f)..........................hd 2
815* In Camera (IRE) **(86)***(104) (MRStoute)* 3-8-7 LDettori(4) (5th st: r.o one pce fnl 2f)...............1¼ 3
826[3] Balliol Boy *(103) (HRACecil)* 3-8-7 WRyan(5) (lw: 2nd st: rdn 2f out: r.o one pce)..................½ 4
619[2] Commoner (USA) **(101)***(94) (RHannon)* 3-8-7 PatEddery(7) (4th st: wknd 2f out).....................7 5
536[5] Lancer (USA) **(94)***(80) (MBell)* 3-8-7 MFenton(1) (6th st: wknd 3f out)....................................10 6
713[6] Henry Koehler **(100)***(70) (CEBrittain)* 3-8-7 MRimmer(6) (7th st: wknd over 3f out)..................7 7

5/6 MUNWAR, **7/2** Balliol Boy (9/4-4/1), **15/2** In Camera (IRE), **8/1** Riyadian, Commoner (USA), **40/1** Lancer (USA), Henry Koehler, CSF £7.96 TOTE £1.80: £1.40 £3.10 (£4.10) OWNER Mr Hamdan Al Maktoum (LAMBOURN) BRED W. and R. Barnett Ltd 7 Rn
2m 25.37 (3.37) SF: 56/56/54/53/44/30/20

1069 JAMES CAPEL RATED STKS H'CAP (0-95) (3-Y.O) (Class B)

£8,133.40 (£3,010.60: £1,445.30: £591.50: £235.75: £93.45)
7f Stalls: High GOING minus 0.19 sec per fur (GF) 3-30 (3-31)

775* **Shahid (88)***(94)*(Fav)*(JLDunlop)* 3-9-0 WCarson(1) (chsd ldrs gng wl: led ins fnl f: comf).....— 1
Muchtarak (IRE) **(82)***(85) (CJBenstead)* 3-8-8 BRouse(4) (hld up: hdwy 2f out: r.o fnl f: nvr nr to chal)..1¼ 2
939* Bold Effort (FR) **(87)***(87) (KOCunningham-Brown)* 3-8-8 (5) MBaird(3) (lw: led: rdn over 1f out: hdd ins fnl f: one pce)..1½ 3
829[13] Axeman (IRE) **(89)***(86+) (RHannon)* 3-9-1 PatEddery(6) (broke wl: sn settled in rr: hdwy over 1f out: r.o)..1¼ 4
542[2] Chewit **(82)***(75) (AMoore)* 3-8-8 CandyMorris(5) (dwlt: sn rcvrd: plld hrd: prom tl rdn & wknd 1f out)..1¾ 5
765[16] Landlord **(81)***(67) (JARToller)* 3-8-7 WNewnes(7) (prom: rdn over 2f out: sn wknd)..................3 6
829[7] Captain's Day **(85)***(66) (TGMills)* 3-8-11 StephenDavies(8) (chsd ldrs: rdn & wknd 2f out).......2 7
Masruf (IRE) **(95)***(60) (TThomsonJones)* 3-9-7 SWhitworth(2) (bit bkwd: rdn over 3f out: a bhd)..7 8

LONG HANDICAP Landlord 8-6

8/11 SHAHID, **13/2** Bold Effort (FR), **15/2** Axeman (IRE), **10/1** Chewit (8/1-12/1), **14/1** Muchtarak (IRE), Landlord (10/1-16/1), Masruf (IRE), **20/1** Captain's Day, CSF £11.38 CT £39.48 TOTE £1.50: £1.20 £2.20 £1.60 (£6.50) OWNER Mr Hamdan Al Maktoum (ARUNDEL) BRED Somerhall Bloodstock Ltd and Lord Chelsea 8 Rn 1m 23.03 (2.43) SF: 52/43/45/44/33/25/24/18

1070 OCS LADIES' H'CAP (0-80) (3-Y.O+) (Class E) £3,416.60(£1,020.80: £488.40: £222.20) 7f Stalls: High GOING minus 0.19 sec per fur (GF) 4-00 (4-01)

262[5] **Moon Strike (FR) (70)***(82) (WJarvis)* 5-10-7 (4) MissIFoustok(11) (lw: hld up: hdwy 2f out: led over 1f out: r.o)..— 1
873[14] Broughtons Turmoil **(49)***(61) (WJMusson)* 6-9-4 MissEJJones(13) (b: a.p: led over 3f out: hdd over 1f out: ev ch ins fnl f: r.o)..s.h 2
646[17] Tiddy Oggie **(45)***(48) (NAGraham)* 4-9-0 MrsLPearce(16) (lw: bhd: hdwy & edgd lft over 1f out: one pce)..4 3
984[10] Robellion **(68)***(68) (DWPArbuthnot)* 4-10-9 MrsDArbuthnot(1) (a.p: ev ch 2f out: rdn over 1f out: one pce)..1¼ 4
780[4] Pusey Street Boy **(56)***(52)*(Fav)*(JRBosley)* 8-9-11 MrsSBosley(15) (bhd: rdn 4f out: nvr nrr)..1¾ 5
439[20] Second Chance (IRE) **(80)***(74) (PMitchell)* 5-11-3 (4) MissHMitchell(10) (nvr nrr).....................¾ 6
Helios **(77)***(68) (NJHWalker)* 7-11-4 MrsMCowdrey(8) (a mid div)..1½ 7
738[11] Breezed Well **(52)***(36) (BRCambidge)* 9-9-7 ow7 MrsHNoonan(6) (nvr nrr)..............................hd 8
972[6] Great Hall **(59)***(49) (PDCundell)* 6-10-0b MrsDKettlewell(12) (bhd: rdn over 2f out: hdwy fnl f: nvr nrr)..hd 9
726[7] Lift Boy (USA) **(45)***(32) (AMoore)* 6-8-10 (4) MrsJMoore(14) (prom 4f)..................................1½ 10
873[24] Knobbleeneeze **(75)***(62) (MRChannon)* 5-11-2v MissJWinter(9) (chsd ldrs: rdn & wknd over 1f out)..hd 11
331[5] Waders Dream (IRE) **(49)***(33) (PatMitchell)* 6-9-4b MissDianaJones(3) (a bhd)......................1¼ 12

Ben Gunn **(72)***(55) (PTWalwyn)* 3-10-1 MarchionesBlandford(5) (prom over 4f)....................½ **13**
882[20] It's so Easy **(46)***(22) (APJames)* 4-9-1 MissCHyde(7) (prom to ½-wy)....................3 **14**
Top Tycoon (IRE) **(45)***(21) (JJBridger)* 4-8-10 (4) MissJLSmith(2) (prom 3f)....................hd **15**
820[5] Louisville Belle (IRE) **(50)***(25) (MDIUsher)* 6-9-5 MrsAUsher(4) (led over 3f: sn wknd)....................hd **16**

LONG HANDICAP Tiddy Oggie 8-13 Lift Boy (USA) 8-11 Breezed Well 8-12

9/2 Pusey Street Boy, **5/1** Helios (7/1-9/2), **15/2** MOON STRIKE (FR), **8/1** Great Hall, Ben Gunn, Knobbleeneeze, **10/1** Broughtons Turmoil, **12/1** Louisville Belle (IRE), **14/1** Tiddy Oggie, Second Chance (IRE), **16/1** Robellion, **20/1** Lift Boy (USA), **25/1** Top Tycoon (IRE), Breezed Well, **33/1** It's so Easy, Waders Dream (IRE), CSF £80.12 CT £961.35 TOTE £8.30: £2.90 £2.20 £3.40 £3.30 (£62.80) Trio £564.50 OWNER Mr A. Foustok (NEWMARKET) BRED Haras de Manneville in France
16 Rn 1m 24.74 (4.14) SF: 54/33/20/40/24/46/40/8/21/4/34/5/15/-/-/-

WEIGHT FOR AGE 3yo-12lb

1071 A A APPOINTMENTS H'CAP (0-80) (3-Y.O+) (Class D) £4,378.00(£1,309.00: £627.00: £286.00) 6f Stalls: High GOING minus 0.19 sec per fur (GF) 4-30 (4-32)

765[7] **Paddy's Rice (49)***(55) (LJHolt)* 4-8-1 DHarrison(10) (mid div: hdwy 2f out: swtchd rt over 1f out: led ins fnl f: r.o wl)....................— **1**
922[12] Moujeeb (USA) **(60)***(62) (PatMitchell)* 5-8-12v LDettori(1) (lw: hld up: swtchd rt 4f out: hdwy over 1f out: ev ch ins fnl f: unable qckn)....................1½ **2**
726[2] Another Jade **(63)***(64)*(Fav)*(APJarvis)* 5-9-1 TQuinn(9) (a.p: led ins fnl f: sn hdd: one pce).....½ **3**
728[6] Crystal Heights (FR) **(65)***(65) (RJO'Sullivan)* 7-9-3 MRimmer(13) (chsd ldrs: rdn over 1f out: ev ch ins fnl f: one pce)....................nk **4**
636[2] La Petite Fusee **(65)***(64) (RJO'Sullivan)* 4-9-3 AClark(8) (b.hind: lw: led: hdd ins fnl f: one pce)....................½ **5**
922[14] Invocation **(65)***(57) (AMoore)* 8-8-12 (5) AWhelan(5) (b.nr hind: chsd ldrs: rdn over 1f out: one pce)....................2½ **6**
726[9] Bright Paragon (IRE) **(45)***(29) (HJCollingridge)* 6-7-11 NCarlisle(3) (nvr nrr)....................3 **7**
765[6] Efra **(73)***(54) (RHannon)* 6-9-4 (7) MarkDenaro(11) (nvr nrr)....................1¼ **8**
Pride of Hayling (IRE) **(47)***(26) (PRHedger)* 4-7-13 CAvery(2) (lw: mid div tl rdn & wknd over 2f out)....................¾ **9**
743[3] Anzio (IRE) **(68)***(45) (BAPearce)* 4-9-6 MHills(7) (b: prom 4f)....................½ **10**
563[12] Deeply Vale (IRE) **(76)***(48) (GLMoore)* 4-10-0 BRouse(4) (chsd ldrs 4f)....................2 **11**
192[10] Riskie Things **(60)***(27) (JSMoore)* 4-8-12 NAdams(12) (bhd fnl 3f)....................2 **12**
856[17] Shades of Jade **(41)***(7) (JJBridger)* 7-7-0 (7) IonaWands(6) (prom over 3f)....................nk **13**

LONG HANDICAP Shades of Jade 7-3

3/1 Another Jade, **9/2** La Petite Fusee (op 3/1), **5/1** PADDY'S RICE, Moujeeb (USA), **6/1** Efra, **12/1** Crystal Heights (FR) (op 8/1), Invocation, **14/1** Bright Paragon (IRE), **20/1** Anzio (IRE), Deeply Vale (IRE), **25/1** Riskie Things, **33/1** Pride of Hayling (IRE), Shades of Jade, CSF £31.20 CT £83.72 TOTE £6.90: £1.90 £1.90 £1.70 (£16.00) Trio £43.60 OWNER Mrs R. G. Wellman (BASINGSTOKE) BRED Mrs H. Lawson 13 Rn 1m 11.34 (2.34) SF: 36/43/45/46/45/38/10/35/7/26/29/8/-

1072 EUROPHARM GROUP MAIDEN STKS (II) (3-Y.O+) (Class D) £3,968.90 (£1,185.20: £566.60: £257.30) 7f Stalls: High GOING minus 0.19 sec per fur (GF) 5-00 (5-01)

Decorated Hero *(80)*(Fav)*(JHMGosden)* 3-8-12 LDettori(4) (w'like: bit bkwd: dwlt: sn chsd ldrs: rdn over 2f out: led ins fnl f: r.o)....................— **1**
637[6] Roderick Hudson *(79) (JARToller)* 3-8-12 WNewnes(3) (led: rdn over 1f out: hdd ins fnl f: r.o)....................nk **2**
930[7] Office Hours *(74) (CACyzer)* 3-8-12 TQuinn(2) (a.p: rdn over 1f out: one pce)....................2½ **3**
502[12] Express Routing *(60) (RAkehurst)* 3-8-9 (3) SSanders(1) (chsd ldrs: rdn over 2f out: one pce) .6 **4**
Zatopek *(59) (RHannon)* 3-8-12 PatEddery(6) (dwlt: rdn over 4f out: hdwy 2f out: eased whn btn fnl f)....................nk **5**
881[10] Autumn Cover *(59) (RMFlower)* 3-8-7 (5) JDSmith(8) (b: mid div: rdn over 3f out: one pce fnl 2f)....................nk **6**
Fern's Governor *(48) (WJMusson)* 3-8-7 GHind(7) (unf: bhd: rdn 3f out: nvr nrr)....................2½ **7**
637[11] Jimbo *(39) (JRJenkins)* 4-9-10 DBiggs(5) (bhd fnl 3f)....................6 **8**
635[21] Burnt Sienna (IRE) *(32) (JSMoore)* 3-8-7 DHarrison(11) (prom tl rdn & wknd over 2f out).......1 **9**
853[13] Senaan *(32) (TThomsonJones)* 3-8-12 WCarson(10) (a bhd)....................2 **10**

15/8 DECORATED HERO (11/10-2/1), **5/2** Office Hours (4/1-9/4), **5/1** Zatopek, **7/1** Roderick Hudson (5/1-10/1), **12/1** Senaan, **20/1** Fern's Governor, **25/1** Express Routing, **50/1** Autumn Cover, Jimbo, Burnt Sienna (IRE), CSF £14.25 TOTE £2.00: £1.60 £1.90 £1.40 (£6.90) Trio £6.10 OWNER Mr Herbert Allen (NEWMARKET) BRED Reg Griffin and Jim McGrath 10 Rn

1m 22.99 (2.39) SF: 50/49/44/30/29/29/18/21/2/2

WEIGHT FOR AGE 3yo-12lb

T/Plpt: £49.90 (483.85 Tckts). T/Qdpt: £29.30 (19.3 Tckts). Hn

0889-WOLVERHAMPTON (L-H)
Saturday May 13th (Standard)
WIND: fresh half against

1073 E.B.F. E. G. CONSULTING MEDIAN AUCTION MAIDEN STKS (2-Y.O) (Class F) £2,847.00 (£787.00: £375.00)
5f (Fibresand) Stalls: Low GOING: 0.21 sec per fur (SLW) 7-00 (7-00)

Doubleyoubeay *(61) (JBerry)* 2-9-0 JCarroll(5) (w'like: leggy: bit bkwd: w ldr: rdn to ld 1f out: edgd lft fnl f: r.o)....— 1
889² U-No-Harry (IRE) *(61)*(Fav)*(RHollinshead)* 2-9-0 TIves(3) (slt ld 4f: rdn & rallied whn carried lft ins fnl f)....hd 2
Colour Counsellor *(56) (KMcAuliffe)* 2-8-11 (3) JTate(1) (lt-f: bit bkwd: dwlt: bhd & wl outpcd tl r.o strly fnl f)....1½ 3
Cool Caper *(52) (AGFoster)* 2-8-9 (5) RPainter(4) (small: lt-f: unf: outpcd: a bhd)....1¼ 4
983⁴ Fiddles Delight *(12) (MRChannon)* 2-8-9 RHughes(2) (chsd ldrs: rdn 2f out: wknd rapidly appr fnl f)....11 5

4/5 U-No-Harry (IRE), **7/2** Fiddles Delight, **4/1** DOUBLEYOUBEAY (op 9/4), **10/1** Colour Counsellor (op 6/1), **33/1** Cool Caper, CSF £7.36 TOTE £5.00: £2.20 £1.10 (£3.90) OWNER Mr A. S. Hill (COCKERHAM) BRED Mrs J. M. Berry 5 Rn
65.9 secs (7.90) SF: -/-/-/-/-

1074 BETA HEAT TREATMENT SUPERFAST NITRIDING CLAIMING STKS (3-Y.O+) (Class F) £2,519.00 (£694.00: £329.00)
1m 1f 79y (Fibresand) Stalls: High GOING: 0.21 sec per fur (SLW) 7-30 (7-31)

Reported (IRE) (82)*(75) (BPreece)* 6-9-5 JWeaver(13) (bit bkwd: hdwy 5f out: led 3f out: sn clr: rdn & drifted lft fnl f: held on wl)....— 1
839³ Wentbridge Lad (IRE) **(78)***(80)*(Fav)*(BAMcMahon)* 5-9-11b GCarter(5) (b: hld up: hdwy & nt clr run 4f out: 4th st: rdn & styd on fnl f)....¾ 2
835² Fiaba **(43)***(49) (MrsNMacauley)* 7-8-1 (7) AmandaSanders(8) (lw: hld up: hdwy 4f out: 3rd st: styd on one pce)....8 3
672³ Pop to Stans **(47)***(59) (JPearce)* 6-8-12 (7) ElizabethTurner(7) (hld up: hdwy over 2f out: 6th st: kpt on fnl f: nvr nrr)....¾ 4
843⁶ Kristis Girl **(40)***(47) (DHaydnJones)* 8-8-12v AMackay(4) (led 7f out to 3f out: 2nd & rdn st: sn btn)....3 5
Nordross *(36) (RTJuckes)* 7-8-3v(5) SDrowne(11) (dwlt: rdn 6f out: styd on fnl 2f: nvr nrr)....4 6
584¹⁰ Trapeze *(39) (CLPopham)* 4-9-4b(3) DRMcCabe(12) (led over 2f: 5th & wkng st)....6 7
Turrill House *(28) (WJMusson)* 3-7-10 (5) PMcCabe(2) (lt-f: s.s: a in rr)....3½ 8
905¹² Port Sunlight (IRE) **(40)***(22) (PDEvans)* 7-8-10 (3) JTate(10) (b: prom 6f: sn rdn & wknd)....1¼ 9
Love of the North (IRE) **(40)***(24) (RTJuckes)* 4-8-10 (5) AGarth(6) (bkwd: chsd ldrs: rdn along ½-wy: sn lost pl)....s.h 10
Tony's Delight (IRE) *(6) (CREgerton)* 7-9-1 RHughes(9) (chsd ldrs over 6f: eased whn btn appr fnl f)....11 11
T'Niel **(30)** *(GFierro)* 4-8-10 MWigham(1) (a in rr: t.o)....10 12
Lord Frederick *(MissSJWilton)* 3-8-10 SDWilliams(3) (w'like: leggy: a bhd: t.o)....5 13

13/8 Wentbridge Lad (IRE), **4/1** Fiaba, **6/1** REPORTED (IRE), **7/1** Pop to Stans, **10/1** Tony's Delight (IRE), **12/1** Port Sunlight (IRE) (op 8/1), **16/1** Trapeze, Kristis Girl, **20/1** Nordross, Turrill House, **25/1** Lord Frederick, T'Niel, **33/1** Love of the North (IRE), CSF £17.01 TOTE £7.20: £2.30 £1.60 £2.20 (£6.70) Trio £11.30 OWNER Mr M. Ephgrave (TELFORD) BRED John Byrne 13 Rn
2m 4.8 (8.80) SF: 44/49/18/28/16/5/8/-/-/-/-/-/-
WEIGHT FOR AGE 3yo-15lb

OFFICIAL EXPLANATION Tony's Delight (IRE): the jockey reported that the horse was hanging so badly that he was unable to ride him out.

1075 UES BRIGHT BAR H'CAP (0-70) (4-Y.O+) (Class E) £3,210.00(£960.00: £460.00: £210.00) **1m 6f 166y (Fibresand)** Stalls: Low GOING: 0.21 sec per fur (SLW) 8-00 (8-00)

*833** **Jaraab (58)***(75+)*(Fav)*(GLewis)* 4-9-7v SWhitworth(10) (lw: hld up: stdy hdwy 5f out: 2nd st: led wl over 1f out: canter)....— 1
866¹⁰ Swordking (IRE) **(42)***(57) (JLHarris)* 6-8-7 PaulEddery(9) (a.p: led over 4f out tl wl over 1f out: no ch w wnr)....1¾ 2
833³ Premier Dance **(59)***(63) (DHaydnJones)* 8-9-5 (5) SDrowne(1) (hdwy over 3f out: 3rd st: rdn & no imp)....10 3
866¹⁴ Chimborazo **(64)***(64) (BJMcMath)* 4-9-13 AMackay(7) (chsd ldrs: led 6f out tl over 4f out: 4th & btn st)....4 4

*588*6 Turfmans Vision **(34)***(30) (RHollinshead)* 5-7-8 (5)ow1 AGarth(3) (hld up: hdwy 8f out: 5th & btn st) 2½ 5
*227*10 Dormston Boyo **(31)** *(KWhite)* 5-7-7 (3)ow1 DWright(2) (prom: led over 6f out: sn hdd: wknd over 3f out: poor 6th st: t.o) ....dist 6
778W Spice and Sugar **(34)** *(BRCambidge)* 5-7-13 TWilliams(4) (a bhd: t.o) 10 7
884 16 Surprise Guest (IRE) **(65)** *(APJames)* 4-10-0 FNorton(5) (lw: lost pl ½-wy: t.o) 1½ 8
Laabas **(40)** *(JELong)* 12-7-12 (7) TField(8) (b: bkwd: drppd rr ½-wy: sn t.o) 11 9
*588** Nigelschinapalace **(45)** *(MissSJWilton)* 6-8-3 (7) GFaulkner(6) (b: led tl hdd & wknd over 6f out: t.o) ....dist 10

10/11 JARAAB, **5/1** Swordking (IRE), **6/1** Premier Dance, **8/1** Nigelschinapalace (op 5/1), **11/1** Chimborazo, **25/1** Surprise Guest (IRE), **33/1** Dormston Boyo, Spice and Sugar, Laabas, Turfmans Vision, CSF £5.87 CT £14.73 TOTE £2.10: £1.20 £1.50 £1.40 (£3.90) Trio £4.10 OWNER Mr S. I. Ross (EPSOM) BRED Shadwell Estate Company Limited 10 Rn 3m 20.8 (13.40) SF: 50/34/40/39/7
WEIGHT FOR AGE 4yo-2lb

1076 GOODYEAR H'CAP (0-70) (3-Y.O+) (Class E) £3,288.00 (£984.00:£472.00: £216.00) 6f (Fibresand) Stalls: Low GOING: 0.21 sec per fur (SLW) 8-30 (8-31)

812* **The Old Chapel (68)***(76) (BAMcMahon)* 6-9-12b FNorton(5) (lw: led tl ins fnl f: rallied u.p to ld cl home) ....— 1
890 4 Tyrone Flyer **(51)***(58) (GFierro)* 6-8-9 MWigham(4) (a.p: shkn up to ld ins fnl f: hdd & no ex nr fin) ....½ 2
*892*6 Disco Boy **(57)***(56) (BAMcMahon)* 5-9-1b TIves(9) (chsd ldrs: kpt on ins fnl f: nt pce to chal)....3 3
*769*2 Efficacy **(42)***(39) (APJarvis)* 4-7-7 (7)ow1 BHunter(10) (s.i.s: hdwy on ins ent st: nt rch ldrs).....hd 4
*769*6 Gate of Heaven **(35)***(25) (JohnBerry)* 5-7-7 NKennedy(3) (rdr lost irons s: bhd & outpcd tl r.o wl fnl f) 3 5
*769** At the Savoy (IRE) **(61)***(47)*(Fav)*(TDBarron)* 4-8-12b(7) KimberleyHart(7) (chsd ldrs: rdn 2f out: wknd appr fnl f) 1½ 6
*237*6 Pageboy **(67)***(53) (PCHaslam)* 6-9-11 JWeaver(2) (bit bkwd: outpcd: a bhd) ....nk 7
748 8 Make the Break **(40)***(19) (SCoathup)* 4-7-12b TWilliams(11) (chsd ldrs: hrd rdn ½-wy: sn bhd) 2½ 8
*892*7 Rocky Two **(57)***(20) (PHowling)* 4-9-1b PaulEddery(6) (spd 4f: sn lost tch) 6 9
*847*2 Sand Star **(54)** *(DHaydnJones)* 3-8-1 AMackay(1) (outpcd: a bhd: t.o) 11 10
LONG HANDICAP Gate of Heaven 6-12

11/4 At the Savoy (IRE), **9/2** THE OLD CHAPEL, **11/2** Pageboy, Sand Star, **7/1** Disco Boy, **8/1** Efficacy, **10/1** Tyrone Flyer (op 16/1), **14/1** Make the Break, **16/1** Rocky Two, **33/1** Gate of Heaven, CSF £46.20 CT £289.38 TOTE £3.70: £2.20 £3.00 £2.60 (£37.60) Trio £214.40 OWNER Mr D. J. Allen (TAMWORTH) BRED Roldvale Ltd 10 Rn 1m 16.4 (5.20) SF: 54/36/34/17/3/25/31/-/-/-
WEIGHT FOR AGE 3yo-11lb

1077 LIFTING GEAR & TOOL HIRE (S) STKS (2-Y.O) (Class G) £2,245.00(£620.00: £295.00) 6f (Fibresand) Stalls: Low GOING: 0.21 sec per fur (SLW) 9-00 (9-02)

Subfusk *(61) (WGMTurner)* 2-8-2 (5) PMcCabe(3) (cmpt: hdwy 4f out: led 2f out: sn clr: eased cl home) ....— 1
*846** Moi Canard *(66)*(Fav)*(JBerry)* 2-9-3 JCarroll(2) (lw: outpcd: sn bhd: swtchd outside & hdwy over 3f out: hrd rdn fnl f: kpt on) 1¾ 2
740 2 Mustaffa (IRE) *(48) (MRChannon)* 2-8-12 RHughes(1) (hdwy 3f out: rdn bel dist: no imp).......5 3
Euskara *(42) (MDIUsher)* 2-8-7 RStreet(7) (cmpt: bkwd: chsd ldrs: rdn & wknd over 1f out)...½ 4
*770** Shanoora (IRE) *(45) (BPalling)* 2-8-12v TSprake(5) (chsd ldrs over 4f: sn rdn & outpcd).........½ 5
*834** Nameless *(44) (DJSCosgrove)* 2-8-5 (7) DGibbs(8) (lw: led 4f: sn rdn: wknd fnl f) ....½ 6
474 4 In A Tizzy *(38) (PCHaslam)* 2-8-7 JWeaver(6) (gd spd to ½-wy: sn rdn & wknd) ....nk 7
Swangrove (IRE) *(MartynMeade)* 2-8-7 VSlattery(4) (small: bkwd: prom over 3f: wknd qckly: t.o) ....dist 8

3/1 Moi Canard, **4/1** Nameless, In A Tizzy (3/1-5/1), **9/2** Shanoora (IRE), **11/2** Mustaffa (IRE) (4/1-6/1), **8/1** SUBFUSK, **16/1** Euskara, **33/1** Swangrove (IRE), CSF £31.22 TOTE £20.10: £2.90 £1.30 £1.70 (£28.80) OWNER Mrs J. M. Sexton (SHERBORNE) BRED A. J. Sexton 8 Rn
1m 18.3 (7.10) SF: 11/16/-/-/-/-/-/-
Bt in 5,600 gns

1078 CASTLE HILL CASINO APPRENTICE H'CAP (0-70) (3-Y.O+) (Class F) £2,550.00 (£725.00: £360.00) 1m 100y (Fibresand) Stalls: High GOING: 0.21 sec per fur (SLW) 9-30 (9-30)

*520*8 **Whitelock Quest (33)***(45) (NEBerry)* 7-8-9 AdelleGibbons(3) (hld up & bhd: hdwy on outside over 3f out: r.o to ld cl home) ....— 1

762[16] Captain Marmalade **(48)***(59)*(Fav)*(DTThom)* 6-9-10 GMilligan(7) (lw: hld up: gd hdwy to ld 3f out: rdn & caught nr fin) ....½ **2**
Sparkling Roberta **(37)***(35) (MDIUsher)* 4-8-13 AimeeCook(8) (bit bkwd: chsd ldrs: 3rd st: one pce fnl 2f) 7 **3**
1048[7] Starlight Flyer **(25)***(15) (JELong)* 8-7-10b(5) TField(1) (b: bit bkwd: prom: 4th & rdn st: one pce) 4 **4**
624[4] Olivia Val **(21)***(7) (AGNewcombe)* 5-7-11 BHalligan(4) (chsd ldrs: 6th & outpcd st) 2½ **5**
Marsh Arab **(48)***(7) (JBalding)* 4-9-10 JEdmunds(6) (b: bkwd: plld hrd: prom to ½-wy: t.o) 14 **6**
883[8] Young Sensation **(50)***(5) (BAPearce)* 3-8-13 JWilkinson(2) (swtg: led over 5f: 5th st wknd qckly: t.o) 2 **7**
Dance on Sixpence **(47)** *(JHPeacock)* 7-9-9b DDenby(5) (bit bkwd: chsd ldrs over 4f: sn rdn & wknd: t.o) 11 **8**

9/4 Captain Marmalade (7/4-11/4), **100/30** WHITELOCK QUEST, **9/2** Olivia Val, **11/2** Dance on Sixpence, **6/1** Sparkling Roberta, **16/1** Young Sensation, **20/1** Marsh Arab, Starlight Flyer, CSF £11.00 CT £36.71 TOTE £5.50: £1.50 £1.50 £1.30 (£7.50) OWNER Mr B. Beale (UPPER LAMBOURN) BRED Patrick Eddery Ltd 8 Rn
1m 52.9 (8.90) SF: 26/40/16/-/-/-/-/-
WEIGHT FOR AGE 3yo-13lb
T/Plpt: £14.00 (721.52 Tckts). T/Qdpt: £18.00 (4.4 Tckts). IM

REDCAR (L-H)
Monday May 15th (Firm)
WEATHER: sunny, cool WIND: slt across

1079 HUNTCLIFFE H'CAP (0-80) (3-Y.O+ F & M) (Class D) £3,762.50 (£1,130.00: £545.00: £252.50) 7f Stalls: Centre GOING minus 0.38 sec per fur (F) 2-15 (2-15)

953[7] **Zifta (USA) (74)***(85)*(Fav)*(SCWilliams)* 4-10-0 AMackay(1) (mde all: qcknd 2f out: r.o wl) ....— **1**
928* Willshe Gan **(49)***(28)*(Fav)*(DenysSmith)* 5-8-3 JQuinn(4) (lw: trckd wnr: effrt over 2f out: r.o one pce) 3½ **2**
838[12] Cafe Solo **(43)***(19) (NBycroft)* 4-7-11 NKennedy(2) (hld up: effrt ½-wy: styd on towards fin) .1½ **3**
906[4] Miss Vaxette **(62)***(38) (MBrittain)* 6-9-2 GCarter(5) (trckd ldrs: rdn & nt qckn fnl 2½f) ....s.h **4**
724[11] Ballard Ring (IRE) **(62)***(36) (JSWainwright)* 4-9-2 KFallon(3) (trckd ldrs: effrt over 2f out: sn rdn & btn) ....½ **5**

6/4 ZIFTA (USA), Willshe Gan, **13/2** Cafe Solo, **8/1** Miss Vaxette, **10/1** Ballard Ring (IRE), CSF £4.13 TOTE £2.60: £1.60 £1.20 (£1.90) OWNER Mr Ron Dawson (NEWMARKET) BRED Darley Stud Management 5 Rn
1m 24.9 (2.90) SF: 44/-/-/6/6

1080 KILTON CLAIMING STKS (3-Y.O+) (Class F) £3,113.00 (£868.00: £419.00) 6f Stalls: Centre GOING: 0.00 sec per fur (G) 2-45 (2-46)

965* **Broctune Gold (65)***(66+)*(Fav)*(MrsMReveley)* 4-8-12 (7) GParkin(13) (a.p stands' side: led 2f out: r.o) ....— **1**
848[3] Cyrano's Lad (IRE) *(65) (JohnBerry)* 6-9-7 CDwyer(6) (lw: trckd ldrs centre: effrt over 2f out: kpt on u.p) 1¼ **2**
Flashy's Son **(66)***(65) (GMMoore)* 7-9-11 MTebbutt(12) (b: a.p stands' side: kpt on fnl f) 1½ **3**
625[6] Top Show (IRE) **(65)***(54) (KWHogg)* 4-8-8 (7) ADaly(11) (chsd ldrs stands' side: outpcd over 2f out: kpt on fnl f) ....nk **4**
926[8] Call to the Bar (IRE) **(73)***(58) (MDods)* 6-9-8 WRyan(3) (racd far side: prom: effrt ½-wy: nt qckn appr fnl f) 1¼ **5**
862[13] Bonny Melody **(50)***(39) (PDEvans)* 4-7-11 (7) AmandaSanders(8) (cl up centre: led ½-wy: hdd 2f out: grad wknd) ....s.h **6**
734[2] Best Kept Secret **(74)***(56) (JBerry)* 4-9-7 GCarter(9) (outpcd stands' side tl styd on fnl 2f) ....hd **7**
926[16] Milbank Challenger **(46)***(40) (WStorey)* 5-8-11 JFanning(5) (nvr wnt pce) 2½ **8**
880[4] J C Grey **(40)***(40) (DenysSmith)* 3-8-4 ow2 KFallon(14) (racd stands' side: n.d) ....½ **9**
861[2] Lady Davenport (IRE) **(65)***(37) (RonaldThompson)* 3-8-5 ow2 JWeaver(10) (a outpcd & bhd) .1½ **10**
685[13] Pete Afrique (IRE) **(78)***(46) (MWEasterby)* 4-9-4 (7) RuthCoulter(7) (b: led centre 3f: wknd) 1 **11**
880[8] Sweet Cheap Pet **(40)***(26) (JJO'Neill)* 3-7-9b LCharnock(1) (racd far side: sn bhd) ....hd **12**
348[3] Sense of Priority **(62)***(34) (MHEasterby)* 6-9-1 KDarley(2) (cl up far side to ½-wy: wknd) ....½ **13**
877[15] Skiptamaloo **(31)***(24) (DonEnricoIncisa)* 4-8-6v KimTinkler(4) (racd far side: a outpcd & bhd)..½ **14**

11/4 BROCTUNE GOLD, **9/2** Best Kept Secret, **5/1** Call to the Bar (IRE), **11/2** Lady Davenport (IRE), **6/1** Sense of Priority, **7/1** Flashy's Son, **8/1** Cyrano's Lad (IRE), **20/1** Pete Afrique (IRE), **33/1** Top Show (IRE), J C Grey, **50/1** Milbank Challenger, Sweet Cheap Pet, Bonny Melody, **100/1** Skiptamaloo, CSF £26.11 TOTE £3.90: £1.70 £2.20 £3.20 (£23.90) Trio £107.50 OWNER Mrs M. B. Thwaites (SALTBURN) BRED A. J. Poulton (Epping) Ltd 14 Rn
1m 11.5 (2.20) SF: 39/38/38/27/31/12/29/13/2/-/19/-/7/-
WEIGHT FOR AGE 3yo-11lb

1081

KISS AND CUDDLE LADIES' H'CAP (0-70) (3-Y.O+) (Class E)£3,143.50 (£943.00: £454.00: £209.50) **1m** Stalls: Centre GOING: 0.00 sec per fur (G) 3-15 (3-16)

1037⁴ **Tolls Choice (IRE) (51)**(61) (MWEasterby) 6-8-6 (7) RuthCoulter(8) (stdd s: hdwy 3f out: led appr fnl f: r.o) — 1
1074³ Fiaba **(42)**(49) (MrsNMacauley) 7-7-11 (7) AmandaSanders(6) (lw: in tch: styd on fnl 2f: nt pce of wnr) 1¾ 2
820* Tovarich **(61)**(61)(Fav)(DNicholls) 4-9-9 AlexGreaves(5) (a.p: effrt over 2f out: rdn & one pce) 3½ 3
1027⁴ Nobby Barnes **(47)**(46) (DonEnricoIncisa) 6-8-9 KimTinkler(4) (hld up: effrt 3f out: rdn & one pce fnl 2f) nk 4
762¹⁷ Tanseeq **(66)**(64) (HThomsonJones) 4-9-7b(7) CatherineCooper(2) (lw: led & sn clr: hdd & wknd appr fnl f) ½ 5
820⁶ Avishayes (USA) **(47)**(42) (MrsMReveley) 8-8-9 CandyMorris(1) (hld up: effrt over 2f out: sn rdn & btn) 1¼ 6
835¹² Brigadore Gold **(35)**(24) (FHLee) 5-7-4 (7)ow4 JoHunnam(3) (chsd ldrs over 5f: wknd) 1 7
976³ Mr Cube (IRE) **(49)**(30) (JMBradley) 5-8-4v(7) KimberleyHart(9) (prom tl wknd fnl 2½f) 6 8
965⁹ Izza **(59)**(26) (WStorey) 4-9-7 ClaireBalding(7) (outpcd & bhd fr ½-wy) 7 9

LONG HANDICAP Brigadore Gold 7-1

3/1 Tovarich, **7/2** Mr Cube (IRE), **9/2** Avishayes (USA), **5/1** Nobby Barnes, **7/1** TOLLS CHOICE (IRE), **17/2** Fiaba, **9/1** Tanseeq, **20/1** Izza, **33/1** Brigadore Gold, CSF £60.75 CT£199.50 TOTE £11.10: £2.20 £2.50 £1.50 (£35.20) Trio £91.90 OWNER Mr T. A. Hughes (SHERIFF HUTTON) BRED John Irish 9 Rn 1m 38.6 (3.60) SF: 28/16/28/13/-/-/-/3/-

1082

AYTON MEDIAN AUCTION MAIDEN STKS (2-Y.O) (Class F) £2,882.00 (£802.00: £386.00) **5f** Stalls: Centre GOING: 0.00 sec per fur (G) 3-45 (3-45)

810³ **Pleasure Time** (71)(Fav)(CSmith) 2-9-0 KDarley(5) (lw: mde all: hung lft fnl 2f: jst hld on) — 1
788⁶ Gagajulu (66) (PDEvans) 2-8-9 TIves(3) (chsd ldrs: effrt 2f out: styd on wl towards fin) s.h 2
925² Lucky Bea (63) (MWEasterby) 2-9-0 LCharnock(4) (chsd wnr: rdn after 2f: outpcd fnl 2f) 2½ 3
925⁷ Marketeer Magic (62) (JBerry) 2-9-0 GCarter(1) (sn pushed along: hdwy 2f out: no imp) nk 4
Sovitaka (IRE) (47) (MHEasterby) 2-8-9 MBirch(2) (neat: unf: bkwd: a outpcd & bhd) 3 5

10/11 PLEASURE TIME, **7/2** Gagajulu, **4/1** Lucky Bea, **7/1** Marketeer Magic (op 4/1), **8/1** Sovitaka (IRE) (op 5/1), CSF £4.78 TOTE £2.10: £1.20 £2.40 (£3.40) OWNER The Temple Bruers (WELLINGORE) BRED John David Abell 5 Rn 59.4 secs (2.70) SF: 19/14/11/10/-

1083

MACKINLAY MEMORIAL H'CAP (0-70) (3-Y.O) (Class E) £3,663.50(£1,103.00: £534.00: £249.50) **1m 2f** Stalls: Low GOING: 0.00 sec per fur (G) 4-15 (4-16)

492³ **Toshiba Talk (IRE) (49)**(54) (BEllison) 3-8-0 NKennedy(5) (chsd ldrs: led over 2f out: hung rt u.p: all out) — 1
Drumochter **(50)**(55) (DMorley) 3-8-1 GCarter(3) (bhd: nt clr run & swtchd 3f out: r.o wl towards fin) s.h 2
857⁵ Paradise Waters **(50)**(54) (RFJohnsonHoughton) 3-8-1 ATucker(13) (lw: pushed along & hdwy appr st: rdn to chal 2f out: bmpd over 1f out: btn whn hmpd cl home) ¾ 3
626⁶ Beau Matelot **(58)**(62) (JDBethell) 3-8-9 TIves(1) (hdwy 4f out: nt clr run 2f out: swtchd & kpt on appr fnl f) s.h 4
774⁵ Harry Browne (IRE) **(56)**(56) (MrsJRRamsden) 3-8-7 KFallon(6) (lw: bhd: hdwy on ins 4f out: nt clr run & swtchd 2f out: nrst fin) 2 5
830⁶ Embezzler **(56)**(56) (GLewis) 3-8-7 WRyan(7) (lw: bhd: hdwy 4f out: nvr trbld ldrs) s.h 6
786⁹ Caltha **(45)**(45) (PCalver) 3-7-5 (5) NVarley(9) (in tch: hdwy & ev ch over 1f out: wknd) ½ 7
773³ Durgams First (IRE) **(59)**(55) (MrsMReveley) 3-8-10 KDarley(4) (lw: bhd: effrt 4f out: no imp) 2 8
651¹¹ Gulf Bay **(42)**(38) (MBell) 3-7-0v(7) RMullen(8) (in tch: effrt 3f out: outpcd fnl 2f) nk 9
Castletown Count **(52)**(45) (KWHogg) 3-7-10 (7) ADaly(10) (bhd & rdn ent st: n.d) 2 10
698³ Mansur (IRE) **(70)**(59)(Fav)(DRLoder) 3-9-7v JWeaver(11) (lw: plld hrd: cl up: led 4f out tl over 2f out: wknd) 2½ 11
641⁵ Battery Boy **(52)**(25) (CWCElsey) 3-8-3 LCharnock(12) (chsd ldrs tl wknd fnl 3f) 10 12
576⁶ Miss Tri Colour **(45)** (FHLee) 3-7-7 (3)ow3 DarrenMoffatt(2) (led tl hdd & wknd 4f out: t.o) 30 13

LONG HANDICAP Gulf Bay 7-3 Miss Tri Colour 7-5

5/2 Mansur (IRE), **7/2** Paradise Waters, **4/1** Harry Browne (IRE), **8/1** Drumochter, **10/1** Durgams First (IRE), **12/1** TOSHIBA TALK (IRE), **14/1** Embezzler, Battery Boy, **20/1** Beau Matelot, **33/1** Castletown Count, Gulf Bay, **50/1** Caltha, **66/1** Miss Tri Colour, CSF £99.74 CT £377.93 TOTE £31.80: £5.50 £2.10 £2.10 (£63.90) Trio £81.10 OWNER Toshiba (UK) Ltd (CONSETT) BRED Dr F. J. Healy 13 Rn 2m 6.2 (3.70) SF: 24/25/24/32/26/26/15/25/8/15/29/-/-

STEWARDS' ENQUIRY Kennedy suspended 24-25/5/95 (careless riding).

1084 TEES H'CAP (0-80) (4-Y.O+) (Class D) £3,762.50 (£1,130.00: £545.00: £252.50)
2m 4y Stalls: Low GOING: 0.00 sec per fur (G) 4-45 (4-45)

7378 **Moshaajir (USA) (66)**_(76) (CSmith)_ 5-9-0 (5) JStack(1) (lw: hld up: hdwy gng wl 4f out: led over 2f out: r.o) .....— 1
8217 Good Hand (USA) **(73)**_(83)_(Fav)_(JWWatts)_ 9-9-12 MBirch(3) (b: b.hind: jnd ldr ½-wy: led over 3f out tl over 2f out: rallied ins fnl f: nt qckn cl home).....nk 2
Dominant Serenade **(43)**_(48) (MDHammond)_ 6-7-7 (3)ow3 DarrenMoffatt(5) (a.p: effrt 3f out: nt qckn appr fnl f).....1½ 3
7419 Limosa **(52)**_(49) (RFJohnsonHoughton)_ 4-8-2 ATucker(4) (led tl hdd over 3f out: wknd over 2f out) 11 4
Commanche Creek **(47)** _(JAHellens)_ 5-8-0v NKennedy(2) (outpcd & lost tch ent st).....dist 5

LONG HANDICAP Dominant Serenade 7-2

7/4 Good Hand (USA), **9/4** MOSHAAJIR (USA), **100/30** Dominant Serenade, **7/2** Limosa, **33/1** Commanche Creek, CSF £6.61 TOTE £4.50: £1.60 £1.10 (£3.60) OWNER Mr Steve Macdonald (WELLINGORE) BRED Katalpa Farm 5 Rn 3m 33.3 (8.30) SF: 34/41/6/4/-
WEIGHT FOR AGE 4yo-3lb

1085 DANBY MAIDEN STKS (3-Y.O) (Class D) £4,204.50 (£1,266.00:£613.00: £286.50)
1m 2f Stalls: Low GOING: 0.00 sec per fur (G) 5-15 (5-16)

8542 **United Front** _(76)_(Fav)_(HRACecil)_ 3-9-0 WRyan(5) (mde most: rdn over 2f out: styd on wl).— 1
Hakika (USA) _(69) (DMorley)_ 3-8-9 MTebbutt(1) (lw: trckd ldrs: qcknd to chal over 2f out: no ex ins fnl f).....1 2
9246 Highfield Fizz _(57) (CWFairhurst)_ 3-8-9 TIves(2) (in tch: kpt on fnl 2f: no imp).....8 3
Quilling **(75)**_(58) (MDods)_ 3-9-0 SWebster(6) (plld hrd: w wnr tl wknd over 2f out).....2½ 4
Deauville Dancer (IRE) _(55) (DNicholls)_ 3-9-0 AlexGreaves(3) (prom to st: sn outpcd).....1½ 5
9684 Mill Thyme _(49) (MrsMReveley)_ 3-8-9 KDarley(8) (lw: outpcd ½-wy: n.d).....½ 6
Gunnerdale _(37) (DenysSmith)_ 3-8-9 KFallon(4) (w'like: bit bkwd: in tch to st: sn rdn & wknd).....8 7
7777 Beauchief _(26) (RFMarvin)_ 3-9-0 AProud(9) (a bhd).....10 8

4/11 UNITED FRONT, **100/30** Hakika (USA), **20/1** Highfield Fizz, Quilling, Mill Thyme, **25/1** Gunnerdale, **33/1** Deauville Dancer (IRE), Beauchief, CSF £2.36 TOTE £1.50: £1.10 £1.10 £1.80 (£1.80) Trio £4.70 OWNER Prince Fahd Salman (NEWMARKET) BRED Brook Stud Ltd 8 Rn
2m 7.0 (4.50) SF: 31/24/12/13/10/4/-/-
T/Plpt: £74.50 (166.07 Tckts). T/Qdpt: £37.80 (1.1 Tckts). AA

1029-SOUTHWELL (L-H)
Monday May 15th (Standard)
WEATHER: overcast WIND: slt half bhd

1086 ITALY H'CAP (0-65) (4-Y.O+) (Class F) £2,519.00 (£694.00: £329.00)
2m (Fibresand) Stalls: High GOING minus 0.08 sec per fur (STD) 2-30 (2-32)

86611 **La Menorquina (USA) (43)**_(56) (DMarks)_ 5-8-7 JFortune(10) (hld up: hdwy 9f out: styd on wl u.p to ld over 1f out: readily).....— 1
_1075*_ Jaraab **(62)**_(72)_(Fav)_(GLewis)_ 4-9-9v 4x SWhitworth(5) (trckd ldrs: effrt & ev ch over 3f out: nt qckn fnl f).....3 2
7415 Who's the Best (IRE) **(34)**_(43) (APJarvis)_ 5-7-9 (3) DWright(8) (chsd ldrs: led 3f out tl over 1f out: one pce).....1½ 3
1036* Rolling the Bones (USA) **(36)**_(35) (PSFelgate)_ 6-8-0 ow1 4x GHind(15) (lw: hld up: stdy hdwy 6f out: ev ch 3f out: sn rdn: wknd over 1f out).....9 4
87913 Snow Dream **(37)**_(35) (MJRyan)_ 5-7-10 (5) MBaird(11) (chsd ldrs: chal 3f out: wknd over 1f out) 2 5
_10293_ Pistols At Dawn (USA) **(54)**_(50) (BJMeehan)_ 5-9-4b BDoyle(12) (lw: trckd ldrs: led after 5f to 3f out: wknd over 1f out).....2 6
79510 Stalled (IRE) **(60)**_(52) (PTWalwyn)_ 5-9-10 RCochrane(1) (hld up: stdy hdwy 5f out: effrt over 2f out: eased whn btn fnl f).....4 7
8608 Jubilee Line **(40)**_(12) (DWPArbuthnot)_ 5-8-4 RPrice(6) (hdwy u.p on wd outside 6f out: sn lost pl) 20 8
Desert Force (IRE) **(45)**_(16) (GFierro)_ 6-8-9 MWigham(7) (sn drvn along: wl bhd fnl 5f).....s.h 9
_5148_ Sassiver (USA) **(38)**_(5) (PAKelleway)_ 5-8-2 DaleGibson(4) (mid div: sn drvn along: lost pl 5f out).....4 10
8797 Lord Hastie (USA) **(56)**_(23) (CWThornton)_ 7-9-6 DeanMcKeown(9) (led 5f: chsd ldrs tl lost pl 4f out) .....nk 11

295[12] Electrolyte **(49)***(13) (BPalling)* 5-8-13 TSprake(3) (b: sn drvn along & bhd)....3 **12**
96[9] Premier Blues (FR) **(32)** *(RJRWilliams)* 5-7-10b NCarlisle(14) (in tch tl wknd 5f out)....3 **13**
Rye Hill Queen (IRE) **(35)** *(RAFahey)* 5-7-13b SMaloney(13) (b.off hind: s.i.s: wl bhd: t.o 6f out)....12 **14**

5/4 Jaraab, **4/1** Rolling the Bones (USA), **8/1** Stalled (IRE), **10/1** LA MENORQUINA (USA), **12/1** Lord Hastie (USA) (20/1-10/1), **14/1** Pistols At Dawn (USA) (op 7/1), Snow Dream, **16/1** Desert Force (IRE), **20/1** Who's the Best (IRE), Sassiver (USA), **33/1** Jubilee Line, Electrolyte, Premier Blues (FR), Rye Hill Queen (IRE), CSF £23.43 CT £246.14 TOTE £12.90: £2.00 £1.60 £3.30 (£16.00)Trio £39.70 OWNER Mr Joe Arden (UPPER LAMBOURN) BRED R. L. Elam 14 Rn
3m 44.9 (18.90) SF: -/-/-/-/-/-/-/-/-/-/-/-/-/-
WEIGHT FOR AGE 4yo-3lb

1087 SPAIN CLAIMING STKS (3-Y.O+) (Class F) £2,519.00 (£694.00: £329.00)
7f (Fibresand) Stalls: Low GOING minus 0.08 sec per fur (STD) 3-00 (3-05)

780[7] **Berge (IRE) (74)***(84)*(Fav)*(WAO'Gorman)* 4-9-4b EmmaO'Gorman(4) (lw: chsd ldrs: styd on to ld over 1f out: drvn out)....— **1**
1076[2] Tyrone Flyer **(51)***(73) (GFierro)* 6-8-9 (5) CTeague(10) (trckd ldr: led ½-wy tl over 1f out: kpt on)....3 **2**
Pytchley Night *(68) (DMorris)* 8-8-10 JCarroll(9) (lw: b: trckd ldrs: kpt on same pce appr fnl f)....½ **3**
Mezzoramio *(60) (SirMarkPrescott)* 3-8-4 GDuffield(11) (bit bkwd: b: chsd ldrs: sn drvn along: outpcd ½-wy: hung lft & kpt on fnl f)....6 **4**
1074[5] Kristis Girl **(40)***(51) (DHaydnJones)* 8-8-4v(5) SDrowne(5) (s.i.s: rdn thrght: bhd tl kpt on appr fnl f)....1 **5**
767[4] What a Nightmare (IRE) **(63)***(54) (JAGlover)* 3-7-11b(3) SSanders(7) (chsd ldrs tl wknd over 2f out)....hd **6**
235[3] Medland (IRE) **(52)***(40) (BJMcMath)* 5-8-10 RCochrane(3) (hld up & bhd: some hdwy over 2f out: eased whn btn over 1f out)....5 **7**
Melodic Drive **(43)***(40) (JAGlover)* 5-9-2 SDWilliams(6) (s.i.s: a in rr)....3 **8**
746[9] Monsieur Petong **(40)***(28) (JParkes)* 4-8-3 (7) CAdamson(2) (a in rr: rn wd ent st)....2½ **9**
767[2] Northern Celadon (IRE) **(69)***(26) (MJHeaton-Ellis)* 4-9-6 SWhitworth(1) (lw: hld up: effrt & n.m.r 2f out: eased)....5 **10**
790[8] Wali (USA) **(67)***(7) (VThompson)* 5-8-10 JFortune(12) (chsd ldrs tl lost pl & c wd ½-wy)....4 **11**
861[6] Little Wilma *(APJarvis)* 3-7-7 (3)ow3 DWright(8) (unruly s: led to ½-wy: sn lost pl)....10 **12**

2/1 BERGE (IRE), **3/1** Pytchley Night (op 6/1), **8/1** Northern Celadon (IRE) (op 4/1), **9/1** Melodic Drive, Medland (IRE) (7/1-12/1), **10/1** Mezzoramio (op 6/1), **11/1** Tyrone Flyer, **14/1** What a Nightmare (IRE) (op 7/1), **20/1** Little Wilma, **25/1** Wali (USA), **33/1** Monsieur Petong, Kristis Girl, CSF £24.90 TOTE £3.30: £1.60 £3.40 £1.50 (£19.10) Trio £45.70 OWNER Mr S. Fustok (NEWMARKET) BRED S. Fustok 12 Rn
1m 31.3 (4.50) SF: 44/33/28/8/11/2/-/-/-/-/-/-
WEIGHT FOR AGE 3yo-12lb

OFFICIAL EXPLANATION **Northern Celadon (IRE): because he was outpaced early and unable to dominate, the colt was never travelling. His trainer confirmed that he may now want a longer trip.**

1088 FRANCE H'CAP (0-70) (3-Y.O+) (Class E) £3,445.20 (£1,029.60:£492.80: £224.40)
1m (Fibresand) Stalls: Low GOING minus 0.08 sec per fur (STD) 3-30 (3-33)

783[6] **Super High (60)***(69) (PHowling)* 3-8-5 RCochrane(9) (trckd ldrs: plld hrd: led over 1f out: rdn out)....— **1**
676[6] Douce Maison (IRE) **(55)***(62) (APJarvis)* 4-8-10 (3) JTate(5) (unruly s: chsd ldrs: nt qckn ins fnl f)....1 **2**
845[4] Flashfeet **(53)***(56) (KBishop)* 5-8-11 MWigham(12) (hdwy to ch ldrs ½-wy: kpt on same pce appr fnl f)....2 **3**
785[6] Self Expression **(59)***(59)*(Fav)*(MrsJRRamsden)* 7-9-3 SDWilliams(14) (dwlt: bhd: effrt on outside over 2f out: sn outpcd: styd on fnl f)....1¾ **4**
839[7] Zanzara (IRE) **(50)***(49) (MrsVAAconley)* 4-8-8 TWilliams(10) (chsd ldrs tl wl outpcd & lost pl ½-wy: kpt on wl u.p fnl 2f)....hd **5**
Caddy's First **(55)***(53) (SMellor)* 3-8-0 DaleGibson(6) (lw: trckd ldrs: led over 4f out tl over 1f out: grad wknd)....½ **6**
1034[5] World Traveller **(70)***(66) (WAO'Gorman)* 4-10-0b EmmaO'Gorman(3) (lw: bhd: effrt & n.m.r 2f out: kpt on: nvr rchd ldrs)....1¼ **7**
987[6] Spanish Stripper (USA) **(43)***(33) (MCChapman)* 4-7-8 (7)ow4 CMunday(1) (swtg: a chsng ldrs: one pce fnl 2f)....¾ **8**
835[3] Quinzii Martin **(56)***(34) (DHaydnJones)* 7-8-9v(5) SDrowne(11) (bhd & drvn along ½-wy: n.d)....8 **9**

1034[3] Corona Gold **(40)***(16) (JGFitzGerald)* 5-7-12 SMaloney(15) (s.i.s: prom whn bmpd 5f out: effrt & n.m.r 2f out: sn wknd) 1 **10**
976[4] Keys Seminar **(50)***(19) (JohnBerry)* 3-7-6b(3)ow2 DWright(13) (s.i.s: a bhd) 2½ **11**
605[5] La Residence **(47)***(11) (MrsNMacauley)* 4-8-2 (3) SSanders(2) (led tl over 4f out: wknd over 2f out) 3½ **12**
992[5] Shotley Again **(39)** *(NBycroft)* 5-7-4 (7)ow4 SLanigan(8) (prom early: lost pl over 4f out: hmpd over 1f out) ....hd **13**
874[11] Lady Highfield **(38)** *(MJRyan)* 4-7-5 (5) MBaird(4) (b.hind: chsd ldrs: drvn along over 4f out: lost pl over 2f out) 1½ **14**
820[10] Green's Bid **(58)***(17) (DWChapman)* 5-9-2 ACulhane(7) (chsd ldrs tl lost pl over 2f out) 1¼ **15**

LONG HANDICAP Shotley Again 7-6 Keys Seminar 7-0

4/1 Self Expression (3/1-5/1), **7/1** Corona Gold, **8/1** Douce Maison (IRE), SUPER HIGH, Quinzii Martin, **10/1** Spanish Stripper (USA), World Traveller (op 6/1), Keys Seminar, **12/1** Flashfeet, La Residence, **14/1** Green's Bid, **16/1** Shotley Again, Zanzara (IRE), **20/1** Caddy's First, **33/1** Lady Highfield, CSF £71.43 CT £722.91 TOTE £11.00: £2.80 £3.20 £4.50 (£56.10) Trio £454.50; £512.17 to York 16/5/95 OWNER Mrs J. M. Khan (NEWMARKET) BRED Nam Seng Yong 15 Rn
1m 45.4 (6.10) SF: 23/29/23/26/16/7/33/-/1/-/-/-/-/-/-
WEIGHT FOR AGE 3yo-13lb

1089 SWEDEN MAIDEN AUCTION STKS (2-Y.O) (Class F) £2,846.60 (£787.60: £375.80) **5f (Fibresand)** Stalls: High GOING minus 0.40 sec (FST) 4-00 (4-03)

Amy Leigh (IRE) *(70+) (CaptJWilson)* 2-7-13 AMackay(5) (cmpt: bit bkwd: dwlt: sn rcvrd: led ½-wy: rdn clr fnl f: eased nr fin) ....— **1**
903[6] Miss Offset *(62) (MJohnston)* 2-8-1 TWilliams(2) (a chsng ldrs: kpt on fnl 2f: no ch w wnr) 3 **2**
Weetman's Weigh (IRE) *(65) (RHollinshead)* 2-8-7 RCochrane(9) (leggy: sn outpcd: styd on fnl 2f: nvr nr to chal) 1 **3**
782[6] Pride of Whalley (IRE) *(51)*(Fav)*(JBerry)* 2-8-2 JCarroll(4) (led to ½-wy: wknd over1f out) 3 **4**
846[2] Donington Park *(39) (JAHarris)* 2-7-12 DaleGibson(6) (a chsg ldrs: sn drvn along: no imp fr ½-wy) 2½ **5**
Times of Times (IRE) *(36) (DJSCosgrove)* 2-7-13 JQuinn(7) (neat: unf: unruly s: s.s: hdwy & ev ch ½-wy: rdn & wknd wl over 1f out) 1 **6**
Havana Heights (IRE) *(27) (RWEmery)* 2-7-9 (3) DWright(1) (cmpt: bit bkwd: unruly: s.s: wl bhd tl sme late hdwy) 2½ **7**
910[6] Dancing Lottie (IRE) *(28) (PAKelleway)* 2-7-6 (7) AdelleGibbons(3) (chsd ldrs tl rdn & wknd 2f out) ....hd **8**
819[7] Derek's Bo *(27) (NBycroft)* 2-7-13 ow1 SMaloney(10) (chsd ldrs tl wknd ½-wy) ....hd **9**
943[11] Down The Yard *(25) (MCChapman)* 2-7-8 (7)ow4 CMunday(8) (dwlt: a outpcd & bhd) ....nk **10**

11/4 Pride of Whalley (IRE) (2/1-7/2), **4/1** Miss Offset, Times of Times (IRE), **11/2** Dancing Lottie (IRE) (op 5/2), **7/1** Weetman's Weigh (IRE), Derek's Bo, **8/1** Donington Park, **12/1** AMY LEIGH (IRE), **16/1** Down The Yard, **20/1** Havana Heights (IRE), CSF £64.13 TOTE £25.30: £2.10 £1.50 £2.30 (£146.00) Trio £105.80 OWNER Mr J. P. Hacking (PRESTON) BRED S. W. D. McIlveen 10 Rn
59.9 secs (1.90) SF: 18/10/13/-/-/-/-/-/-/-
STEWARDS' ENQUIRY Mark Johnston fined £80 under Rule 149(iii)(horse carried wrong number-cloth).

1090 DENMARK (S) STKS (2-Y.O) (Class G) £2,243.00 (£618.00: £293.00) **5f (Fibresand)** Stalls: High GOING minus 0.40 sec per fur (FST) 4-30 (4-30)

770[2] **Gi La High** *(58)*(Fav)*(JBerry)* 2-8-11 JCarroll(4) (lw: led to ½-wy: styd on u.p to ld ins fnl f: jst hld on) ....— **1**
Chik's Secret *(52) (BPalling)* 2-8-6 TSprake(5) (bit bkwd: sn outpcd: hdwy 2f out: styd on wl u.p ins fnl f) ....nk **2**
Boffy (IRE) *(44) (BPJBaugh)* 2-8-11 ACulhane(1) (small: bit bkwd: w ldr gng wl: led ½-wy: edged rt u.p over 1f out: wknd & hdd ins fnl f) 4 **3**
878[9] Our Tom's Boy *(38) (KTIvory)* 2-8-11 GDuffield(2) (chsd ldrs: sn rdn: lost pl 2f out) 2 **4**
834[2] Bites *(32) (GLewis)* 2-8-6 GHind(7) (chsd ldrs: rdn & outpcd ½-wy: n.d after) ....nk **5**
Alpheton Prince *(8) (RWEmery)* 2-8-11 BDoyle(6) (cmpt: s.s: a outpcd & wl bhd) 9 **6**
Waitingforwalnuts (IRE) *(CASmith)* 2-8-7 ow1 MWigham(3) (neat: s.s: edged lft & lost pl 3f out: eased) 1 **7**

4/5 GI LA HIGH (4/7-10/11), **4/1** Boffy (IRE) (op 16/1), **8/1** Bites (op 4/1), Our Tom's Boy, **10/1** Chik's Secret (op 6/1), Waitingforwalnuts (IRE), **20/1** Alpheton Prince, CSF £9.78 TOTE £1.60: £1.30 £7.00 (£13.40) OWNER Mr Basheer Kielany (COCKERHAM) BRED J. H. Heath 7 Rn
60.7 secs (2.70) SF: 16/10/2/-/-/-/-
No bid

1091 GERMANY H'CAP (0-65) (3-Y.O+) (Class F) £2,519.00 (£694.00: £329.00) **1m 3f (Fibresand)** Stalls: Low GOING minus 0.40 sec per fur (FST) 5-00 (5-04)

*517*2 **Mr Bean (56)***(67)*(Fav)*(KRBurke)* 5-9-9 (3) JTate(14) (hld up: wnt prom ½-wy: led over 2f out: rdn & r.o wl) ....— **1**
558 12 Sushi Bar (IRE) **(55)***(64) (MrsMReveley)* 4-9-11 DHolland(7) (lw: hld up: hdwy on outside 6f out: effrt 3f out: styd on fnl f) 1½ **2**
*470*3 Brave Spy **(56)***(61) (CACyzer)* 4-9-12 GDuffield(12) (a.p: rdn 3f out: hung lft: kpt on one pce appr fnl f) 3 **3**
*445*8 Camden's Ransom (USA) **(58)***(60) (HGRowsell)* 8-10-0 BDoyle(11) (a chsng ldrs: kpt on one pce fnl 2f) 1¾ **4**
841 10 Lochore **(54)***(56) (MrsVAAconley)* 5-9-10 MDeering(13) (bhd: effrt on outside 3f out: kpt on: nvr nr ldrs) ....hd **5**
Armston **(55)***(57) (JWharton)* 3-8-7 JQuinn(10) (mid div: effrt 4f out: kpt on fnl 2f: nvr rch ldrs) ....d.h **5**
*1029*7 Palacegate Jo (IRE) **(56)***(57) (DWChapman)* 4-9-12 DeanMcKeown(6) (bhd: hdwy over 3f out: styd on: nvr nr to chal) ....½ **7**
783 10 Ism **(55)***(50) (MajorWRHern)* 3-8-7 TSprake(2) (chsd ldrs: drvn along over 3f out: wknd over 1f out) 4 **8**
Merchant House (IRE) **(37)***(29) (GFierro)* 7-8-2 (5) CTeague(8) (chsd ldrs: led 5f out tl over 2f out: sn lost pl) 2½ **9**
*330*10 Lexus (IRE) **(39)***(25) (RJRWilliams)* 7-8-9b GHind(5) (led to 5f out: wknd over 2f out) 4 **10**
*845*6 Scottish Park **(38)***(18) (RWEmery)* 6-8-8 TWilliams(1) (bhd & sn drvn along: sme hdwy 5f out: wknd 3f out) 4 **11**
750 3 Moneghetti **(47)***(21) (RHollinshead)* 4-9-3 RCochrane(4) (prom tl rdn & lost pl over 5f out: sn bhd) 4 **12**
Arctic Diamond **(55)** *(CREgerton)* 4-9-6b(5) AProcter(3) (bhd & drvn along ½-wy: sn lost tch) 20 **13**
882 15 Early Star **(44)** *(KBishop)* 6-9-0 AMackay(9) (bhd & sn drvn along: lost tch 5f out) 14 **14**

3/1 MR BEAN, **9/2** Brave Spy, **7/1** Palacegate Jo (IRE) (5/1-8/1), **9/1** Sushi Bar (IRE), Camden's Ransom (USA), **11/1** Ism (7/1-12/1), **12/1** Arctic Diamond, **14/1** Early Star, Lexus (IRE), **16/1** Merchant House (IRE), Lochore, Moneghetti, Armston, Scottish Park, CSF £31.73 CT £119.16 TOTE £3.40: £1.60 £2.00 £1.90 (£13.20) Trio £22.20 OWNER Mr Brendan Toner (WANTAGE) BRED M. L. Page 14 Rn 2m 30.4 (8.90) SF: 41/38/35/34/30/13/31/6/3/-/-/-/-/-
WEIGHT FOR AGE 3yo-18lb
T/Plpt: £121.10 (101.73 Tckts). T/Qdpt: £39.60 (0.1 Tckts), £48.24 to York 16/5/95. WG

0848-WINDSOR (Fig. 8)
Monday May 15th (Good to firm, Good st)
WEATHER: fair WIND: almost nil

1092 SLOANE STREET CLAIMING STKS (3 & 4-Y.O) (Class F) £3,039.00 (£854.00: £417.00) **1m 67y** Stalls: High GOING minus 0.51 sec per fur (F) 6-00 (6-02)

946 4 **Arndilly (69)***(63)*(Fav)*(BJMeehan)* 4-9-0b TQuinn(5) (2nd st: led 1f out: rdn clr) ....— **1**
663 11 Komodo (USA) **(68)***(65) (DRCElsworth)* 3-8-11 PatEddery(3) (lw: led to 1f out: nt qckn) 4 **2**
729 9 Thames Side **(42)***(54) (MMadgwick)* 4-9-1 MFenton(15) (7th st: lost pl 3f out: hdwy over 1f out: r.o) 1¼ **3**
*395*6 Owdbetts (IRE) **(73)***(56) (GLMoore)* 3-8-5 BRouse(17) (plld hrd: 3rd st: hrd rdn over 2f out: one pce) ....½ **4**
984 7 Rafter-J **(56)***(49) (JAHarris)* 4-9-0 PaulEddery(19) (hdwy fnl 2f: nvr nrr) 1½ **5**
*157*9 Miss Mah-Jong **(60)***(46) (JWhite)* 4-8-12 CAvery(10) (dwlt: nrst fin) ....½ **6**
*387*6 Pillow Talk (IRE) **(59)***(44) (KRBurke)* 4-8-11 RHughes(6) (lw: 6th st: no hdwy fnl 2f) ....½ **7**
Bushehr (IRE) *(52) (JWHills)* 3-8-6 MHills(12) (bit bkwd: nvr nr to chal) ....hd **8**
*1030*8 Simply Simon **(40)***(42) (KRBurke)* 3-7-8 (7) SO'Shea(21) (5th st: wknd over 2f out) 2½ **9**
887 15 Clancy's Express **(35)***(42) (GBBalding)* 4-8-7 (7) DaneO'Neill(8) (lw: nvr trbld ldrs) ....nk **10**
848 8 Ballestro (IRE) **(40)***(42) (JFfitch-Heyes)* 3-8-5b NAdams(13) (nvr bttr than mid div) 1¾ **11**
976 6 Nakita **(57)***(32) (CNAllen)* 4-8-2 (7) KarenMarkham(11) (b.hind: a bhd) ....½ **12**
*470*5 General Shirley (IRE) **(55)***(30) (PRHedger)* 4-8-13v MPerrett(14) (8th st: wknd 3f out) 3 **13**
761 13 Dixit Dominus *(29) (GBBalding)* 4-9-3 JWilliams(7) (a bhd) 3 **14**
Broughtons Bird (IRE) *(18) (WJMusson)* 4-8-5 (5) PMcCabe(20) (bit bkwd: s.s: a bhd) 2 **15**
Northern Spruce (IRE) *(25) (MissJacquelineDoyle)* 3-8-7 ow1 JReid(18) (w'like: s.s: a bhd) 1 **16**
848 16 Indian Treasure (IRE) *(DJSCosgrove)* 3-8-2 ow1 RPrice(9) (t.o) 7 **17**
*405*7 Marjorie's Orchid **(47)** *(MJHeaton-Ellis)* 4-8-12 AClark(2) (9th & wd st: wknd 4f out: t.o) 3 **18**

567⁷ Clarion Call (IRE) **(65)** *(GThorner)* 4-8-11b(5) TGMcLaughlin(16) (4th st: wknd over 3f out: t.o) 2½ **19**
*512*⁶ Portland Way **(40)** *(APJarvis)* 3-8-4 DHarrison(1) (t.o) 1½ **20**
Ruthy's Romance *(AGNewcombe)* 4-8-5 (5)ow1 DGriffiths(4) (rn v.wd st: t.o fnl 4f) ....dist **21**

5/2 ARNDILLY, **11/2** Komodo (USA), Owdbetts (IRE) (4/1-6/1), **9/1** Rafter-J, Pillow Talk (IRE), **10/1** Nakita, **12/1** Bushehr (IRE), General Shirley (IRE) (op 8/1), **16/1** Miss Mah-Jong, **20/1** Dixit Dominus, **25/1** Clarion Call (IRE), Broughtons Bird (IRE), **33/1** Ballestro (IRE), Marjorie's Orchid, Northern Spruce (IRE), **50/1** Simply Simon, Indian Treasure (IRE), Clancy's Express, Thames Side, Portland Way, Ruthy's Romance, CSF £17.86 TOTE £3.50: £1.90 £2.40 £8.60 (£8.90) Trio £83.10 OWNER Mr A. S. Reid (UPPER LAMBOURN) BRED Hilborough Stud Farm Ltd 21 Rn

1m 45.1 (3.50) SF: 23/12/14/3/9/6/4/-/-/2/-/-/-/-/-/-/-/-/-/-/-
WEIGHT FOR AGE 3yo-13lb

1093 READING UNIVERSITY TURF CLUB H'CAP (0-70) (3-Y.O) (Class E) £3,324.20 (£1,007.60: £492.80: £235.40)

1m 3f 135y Stalls: High GOING minus 0.51 sec per fur (F) 6-25 (6-35)

*509*² **Darling Clover (54)***(64) (DMorley)* 3-8-5 MFenton(8) (led 3f: 2nd st: led ins fnl f: r.o wl) ....— **1**
884³ Mutazz (USA) **(62)***(71) (MajorWRHern)* 3-8-13 WCarson(18) (lw: led after 3f tl ins fnl f: r.o) ....¾ **2**
974² Poly Road **(55)***(62)*(Fav)*(MRChannon)* 3-8-6 FNorton(15) (s.s: hdwy fnl 2f: nvr nrr) 1¾ **3**
974³ Hi-Aud **(58)***(63) (JAkehurst)* 3-8-9 SWhitworth(12) (hdwy & 6th st: ev ch 2f out: one pce) 1 **4**
867⁴ Leading Spirit (IRE) **(59)***(60) (CFWall)* 3-8-10 LDettori(2) (lw: hdwy over 3f out: hrd rdn 2f out: one pce) 3 **5**
453² Rocky Forum **(54)***(55) (GLMoore)* 3-8-5 RPerham(17) (5th st: no hdwy fnl 2f) ....nk **6**
*624*³ Marchant Ming (IRE) **(57)***(56) (MAJarvis)* 3-8-8 PRobinson(6) (hdwy over 3f out: wknd over 1f out) 1½ **7**
664¹¹ Bellateena **(55)***(52) (HJCollingridge)* 3-8-6 MRimmer(19) (3rd st: wknd 2f out) 1¼ **8**
851⁵ Birthday Boy (IRE) **(68)***(64) (RHannon)* 3-9-5 PatEddery(7) (lw: nvr plcd to chal) ....nk **9**
764¹¹ Pedaltothemetal (IRE) **(56)***(52) (PMitchell)* 3-8-2 (5) AWhelan(20) (8th st: wknd 3f out) ....s.h **10**
762¹⁸ Santella Boy (USA) **(60)***(56) (GHarwood)* 3-8-11 AClark(11) (lw: 7th st: rdn over 3f out: sn wknd) ....hd **11**
947⁹ Slapy Dam **(52)***(48) (MrsJRRamsden)* 3-8-3 DHarrison(3) (nvr nr to chal) ....nk **12**
538ᵂ Labibeh (USA) **(70)***(65) (JLDunlop)* 3-9-7 WNewnes(16) (bit bkwd: hdwy on ins 6f out: swtchd outside 3f out: nt rch ldrs) ....nk **13**
974⁹ Elation **(62)***(56) (PFICole)* 3-8-13b TQuinn(13) (lw: nvr nr ldrs) ....¾ **14**
851¹² Vizard (IRE) **(66)***(58) (MJHeaton-Ellis)* 3-9-3b PaulEddery(4) (s.s: wl bhd tl hdwy 4f out: hrd rdn 3f out: no ex) 2 **15**
Negative Equity **(59)***(47) (KRBurke)* 3-8-10 RHughes(14) (lw: outpcd) 2½ **16**
762¹⁴ Nanton Point (USA) **(56)***(43) (LadyHerries)* 3-8-7 ow1 JReid(5) (4th st: wknd 4f out) ....½ **17**
813⁹ Mariposa Grove **(55)***(36) (RCurtis)* 3-8-3 (3) SSanders(10) (lw: mid div whn stumbled after 2f: bhd after) 5 **18**
654¹⁰ Pewter Lass **(52)***(30) (MBlanshard)* 3-8-0 (3)ow2 DMcCabe(9) (a bhd) ....nk **19**
292* Fen Terrier **(55)** *(WJHaggas)* 3-8-6 MHills(1) (Withdrawn not under Starter's orders: ref to ent stalls) .... **W**

4/1 Poly Road, **9/2** Birthday Boy (IRE), **8/1** Slapy Dam (6/1-10/1), Mutazz (USA), Leading Spirit (IRE) (6/1-9/1), **12/1** Nanton Point (USA), Hi-Aud, **14/1** Elation, Mariposa Grove, Rocky Forum, **16/1** DARLING CLOVER, **20/1** Marchant Ming (IRE), Labibeh (USA), Pedaltothemetal (IRE), Santella Boy (USA), **25/1** Pewter Lass, Vizard (IRE), **33/1** Negative Equity, Bellateena, CSF £138.31 CT £506.50 TOTE £28.50: £4.80 £1.80 £1.60 £2.50 (£114.20) Trio £87.30 OWNER Mr K. Craddock (NEWMARKET) BRED Astalon Ltd 19 Rn

2m 29.3 (3.30) SF: 27/34/25/26/23/18/19/15/27/15/19/11/28/19/21/10/6/-/-/-
OFFICIAL EXPLANATION Birthday Boy (IRE): encountered traffic problems throughout.

1094 LADBROKES H'CAP (0-80) (3-Y.O) (Class D) £4,102.50 (£1,245.00: £610.00: £292.50)

5f 217y Stalls: High GOING minus 0.33 sec per fur (GF) 6-55 (7-05)

850² **Youdontsay (62)***(70) (RCurtis)* 3-7-10 (7) SLanigan(21) (lw: a.p: led wl over 1f out: r.o wl) ....— **1**
966² Statius **(64)***(67)*(Fav)*(TDBarron)* 3-8-5 JFortune(12) (lw: a.p: ev ch 1f out: no imp) 2 **2**
752⁴ Lough Erne **(68)***(67) (CFWall)* 3-8-9 NCarlisle(9) (gd hdwy fnl 2f: r.o) 1¼ **3**
Sally Weld **(65)***(64) (CJBenstead)* 3-8-6 BRouse(25) (a.p: led over 2f out tl wl over 1f out: nt qckn) ....nk **4**
796⁷ Sue Me (IRE) **(73)***(70) (WRMuir)* 3-9-0 JWeaver(14) (hdwy over 1f out: r.o ins fnl f) ....½ **5**
733⁹ La Bossette (IRE) **(52)***(45) (JRArnold)* 3-7-2b(5) MBaird(19) (s.s: hrd rdn & hdwy over 1f out: r.o ins fnl f) 1½ **6**

637[4] Forzair **(76)***(68) (MMcCormack)* 3-9-3 PatEddery(22) (led over 3f: hrd rdn over 1f out: nt qckn)....nk **7**
862[5] Secret Miss **(56)***(40) (APJarvis)* 3-7-4 (7)ow4 BHunter(24) (lw: no hdwy fnl 2f)....1½ **8**
662[6] Singing Rock (IRE) **(70)***(56) (RHannon)* 3-8-11 LDettori(26) (lw: nvr nr to chal)....¾ **9**
Grand Chapeau (IRE) **(70)***(56) (RHannon)* 3-8-4 (7) DaneO'Neill(16) (spd over 4f)....hd **10**
733[12] Blushing Grenadier (IRE) **(56)***(35) (MJFetherston-Godley)* 3-7-11 FNorton(7) (nvr nr ldrs)....2½ **11**
742[2] Jo Maximus **(72)***(51) (SDow)* 3-8-13 TQuinn(17) (prom over 3f)....nk **12**
850[13] Medieval Miss **(69)***(42) (GLewis)* 3-8-10 PaulEddery(10) (nt pce to chal)....2 **13**
Seventeens Lucky **(70)***(43) (BobJones)* 3-8-11 MRimmer(15) (no imp)....s.h **14**
862[9] Tael of Silver **(65)***(36) (KRBurke)* 3-7-13 (7) SO'Shea(20) (spd over 4f)....¾ **15**
850[11] Endless Wave **(71)***(41) (MBell)* 3-8-12 MFenton(4) (nvr trbld ldrs)....nk **16**
823[8] Brockton Flame **(64)***(34) (JMPEustace)* 3-8-5 MHills(11) (spd 4f)....hd **17**
Prime Match (IRE) **(80)***(50) (PWHarris)* 3-9-7 PRobinson(5) (prom over 4f)....s.h **18**
Crowded Avenue **(52)***(19) (PJMakin)* 3-7-7 NAdams(27) (nvr on terms)....1 **19**
853[15] Nordman Lass **(60)***(20) (MissJacquelineDoyle)* 3-7-12 (3)ow2 SSanders(8) (swtg: a bhd)....2 **20**
Star of Gold **(70)***(31) (CREgerton)* 3-8-11 BThomson(13) (a bhd)....nk **21**
658[6] Mutabassim (IRE) **(73)***(29) (ACStewart)* 3-9-0 WCarson(6) (lw: bhd fnl 2f)....2 **22**
761[11] Hot Snap **(70)***(24) (CFWall)* 3-8-6 (5) LNewton(23) (prom 4f)....¾ **23**
855[3] Deardaw **(54)** *(MDIUsher)* 3-7-2 (7)ow2 CAdamson(3) (bhd fnl 2f: t.o)....5 **24**

LONG HANDICAP Secret Miss 7-6 Deardaw 7-3

11/2 Statius, **8/1** Forzair, Mutabassim (IRE), **9/1** Singing Rock (IRE), **10/1** YOUDONTSAY, **12/1** Secret Miss (8/1-14/1), **14/1** Brockton Flame, Sue Me (IRE), Medieval Miss, Jo Maximus, **16/1** Tael of Silver, Blushing Grenadier (IRE), Prime Match (IRE), **20/1** Hot Snap, Star of Gold, Crowded Avenue, Sally Weld, Endless Wave, **25/1** Lough Erne, Seventeens Lucky, Deardaw, **33/1** Nordman Lass, La Bossette (IRE), Grand Chapeau (IRE), CSF £69.26 CT £1,297.08 TOTE £10.50: £2.40 £2.20 £7.20 £13.00 (£23.40) Trio £1,604.40 OWNER Mr T. W. Nicholls (CARSHALTON) BRED Mrs and Exors of the late Col F. R. Hue-Williams 24 Rn

1m 11.8 (1.30) SF: 42/39/39/36/42/17/40/12/28/28/7/23/14/15/8/13/6/22/-/-/3/1/-/-

1095

BONUSPRINT LIMITED STKS (0-75) (4-Y.O+) (Class D) £3,631.25 (£1,100.00: £537.50: £256.25)
1m 2f 7y Stalls: High GOING minus 0.51 sec per fur (F) 7-25 (7-28)

817[6] **Tony's Fen (75)***(83) (DRCElsworth)* 6-9-0 TQuinn(9) (b.hind: 5th st: hrd rdn fnl 2f: led wl ins fnl f: r.o wl)....— **1**
Ball Gown **(69)***(77) (DTThom)* 5-8-6 (3) DRMcCabe(5) (8th st: hdwy 3f out: led over 1f out tl wl ins fnl f: r.o)....½ **2**
320[8] Ultimate Warrior **(70)***(78) (CACyzer)* 5-9-2 JReid(8) (led: qcknd clr 5f out: hdd over 1f out: one pce)....4 **3**
Majboor Yafooz (USA) **(65)***(73) (JRBosley)* 5-9-0 LDettori(7) (3rd st: one pce fnl 2f)....2 **4**
935[19] Lowawatha **(72)***(72) (DMorris)* 7-9-0 RPrice(6) (4th st: wknd 2f out)....nk **5**
864[12] Scottish Bambi **(70)***(64) (RHannon)* 7-9-0 RPerham(4) (lw: 7th st: rdn 3f out: no imp)....5 **6**
841[8] The Lone Dancer **(74)***(59)*(Fav)*(KMcAuliffe)* 4-9-0 JWeaver(1) (6th st: wknd over 2f out)....3½ **7**
817[15] Jairzinho (USA) **(60)***(35) (PHayward)* 6-9-0 SRaymont(3) (2nd st: wknd over 4f out: t.o fnl 3f)....15 **8**

2/1 The Lone Dancer, **11/4** Ball Gown, **4/1** TONY'S FEN (op 5/2), **11/2** Lowawatha, **8/1** Scottish Bambi, **10/1** Majboor Yafooz (USA), **12/1** Ultimate Warrior, **33/1** Jairzinho (USA), CSF £16.21 TOTE £3.70: £1.30 £1.90 £2.90 (£7.00) Trio £33.10 OWNER The Executive (WHITCOMBE) BRED Stackallan Stud 8 Rn 2m 7.0 (2.10) SF: 41/35/36/31/30/22/17/-

1096

JIM O'CONNELL COMING HOME CONDITIONS STKS (2-Y.O) (Class C) £4,656.57 (£1,699.70: £832.35: £359.25: £162.13)
5f 10y Stalls: High GOING minus 0.33 sec per fur (GF) 7-55 (7-55)

562* **Whicksey Perry** *(85)*(Fav)*(JBerry)* 2-9-3 JCarroll(2) (lw: w ldr: led over 2f out: all out)....— **1**
Ice Pick (IRE) *(75) (RHannon)* 2-8-8 PatEddery(4) (neat: bit bkwd: rdn along: sltly hmpd over 1f out: r.o wl ins fnl f)....nk **2**
760[9] Dancing Jack *(76) (JJBridger)* 2-8-8 (3) SSanders(5) (lw: led over 2f: ev ch 1f out: nt qckn)....¾ **3**
910* Foreman *(75) (WAO'Gorman)* 2-8-13 EmmaO'Gorman(1) (sn w ldrs: ev ch over 1f out: one pce)....¾ **4**
Charterhouse Xpres *(70) (MMcCormack)* 2-8-8 JReid(3) (neat: bit bkwd: chsd ldrs: nt qckn fnl f)....hd **5**

4/6 WHICKSEY PERRY, **3/1** Foreman, **9/2** Ice Pick (IRE) (op 3/1), **16/1** Charterhouse Xpres, **50/1** Dancing Jack, CSF £3.99 TOTE £1.90: £1.10 £1.60 (£2.50) OWNER Mr J. Henderson (COCKERHAM) BRED D. H. Jones 5 Rn 62.4 secs (3.40) SF: 17/7/8/7/2

1097

GREEN PARK MEDIAN AUCTION MAIDEN STKS (3-Y.O) (Class E)
£3,395.70 (£1,029.60: £503.80: £240.90)
1m 2f 7y Stalls: High GOING minus 0.51 sec per fur (F) 8-25 (8-28)

813[3] **Yoush (IRE) (79)***(86) (MAJarvis)* 3-9-0 PRobinson(15) (lw: 5th st: led ins fnl f: r.o wl)...........— **1**
747[2] Heboob Alshemaal (IRE) *(79)*(Fav)*(JHMGosden)* 3-8-9 LDettori(16) (4th st: led over 1f out tl ins fnl f)...........1½ **2**
657[10] Vaugrenier (IRE) **(84)***(80) (RHannon)* 3-9-0 PatEddery(13) (9th st: styd on fnl 3f: nvr nrr)...........2½ **3**
Meghdoot **(73)***(75) (HJCollingridge)* 3-8-9 JQuinn(3) (hdwy fnl 3f: nrst fin)...........s.h **4**
764[4] Zidac *(79) (PJMakin)* 3-9-0 RPerham(18) (lw: led after 3f tl over 1f out: wknd ins fnl f)...........nk **5**
Ataxia *(68) (HRACecil)* 3-8-9 WNewnes(11) (w'like: scope: wl bhd tl r.o fnl f)...........4 **6**
Swivel *(62) (JRFanshawe)* 3-8-9 DHarrison(6) (lw: hdwy over 2f out: wknd over 1f out)...........3½ **7**
815[6] George Bull *(66) (MajorWRHern)* 3-9-0 PaulEddery(9) (lw: nvr nr to chal)...........¾ **8**
Shooter **(74)***(60) (PFICole)* 3-9-0 TQuinn(22) (nvr nr to chal)...........3½ **9**
797[7] Elly Fleetfoot (IRE) *(54) (TGMills)* 3-8-9 JCarroll(4) (lw: nvr trbld ldrs)...........¾ **10**
854[4] Volunteer (IRE) *(59) (HRACecil)* 3-9-0 AMcGlone(8) (lw: hdwy over 3f out: hrd rdn & wknd 2f out)...........s.h **11**
942[7] Hanifa *(52) (MissGayKelleway)* 3-8-9 BRouse(12) (10th st: a mid div)...........1½ **12**
670[4] Prophets Honour *(56) (CACyzer)* 3-9-0 JWeaver(21) (2nd st: rdn over 3f out: sn wknd)...........nk **13**
Hadabet *(56) (MissJacquelineDoyle)* 3-9-0 RHughes(17) (outpcd)...........hd **14**
677[9] City Run (USA) *(54) (DJSCosgrove)* 3-9-0 MRimmer(5) (lw: n.d)...........1½ **15**
673[10] My Boy Josh *(54) (RGuest)* 3-9-0 MFenton(10) (n.d)...........s.h **16**
Debutante Days *(48) (ACStewart)* 3-8-4 (5) MHumphries(14) (w'like: a bhd)...........nk **17**
816[12] Shepherds Rest (IRE) *(52) (SMellor)* 3-9-0 MWigham(7) (a bhd)...........½ **18**
745[10] Alka International **(46)***(52) (JWhite)* 3-8-9 (5) SDrowne(1) (8th st: wknd over 3f out)...........hd **19**
973[2] Proud Image *(49) (APJarvis)* 3-9-0 BThomson(19) (3rd st: wknd over 3f out)...........2 **20**
Quillon Rose *(43) (CFWall)* 3-8-4 (5) LNewton(20) (7th st: wknd qckly 2f out)...........½ **21**
813[8] Bellas Gate Boy **(68)***(44) (MissHCKnight)* 3-9-0b JReid(2) (lw: led 3f: 6th st: wknd over 3f out)...........2½ **22**

4/1 Heboob Alshemaal (IRE), **9/2** Prophets Honour, **5/1** Zidac, **7/1** Volunteer (IRE) (6/1-10/1), Vaugrenier (IRE) (5/1-8/1), **10/1** YOUSH (IRE) (5/1-11/1), **12/1** Swivel (op 7/1), **14/1** George Bull (8/1-16/1), **16/1** Shooter, Ataxia, Proud Image, **25/1** Elly Fleetfoot (IRE), **33/1** Hanifa, Bellas Gate Boy, **50/1** Meghdoot, My Boy Josh, Hadabet, Shepherds Rest (IRE), Alka International, City Run (USA), Quillon Rose, Debutante Days, CSF £51.93 TOTE £10.50: £2.90 £2.10 £2.80 (£18.40) Trio £62.80 OWNER Sheikh Ahmed Al Maktoum (NEWMARKET) BRED Dictum Enterprises Ltd 22 Rn
2m 6.8 (1.90) SF: 42/35/36/31/35/24/18/22/16/10/15/8/12/12/10/10/4/8/8/5/-/-

T/Jkpt: Not won; £90,564.29 to York 16/5/95. T/Plpt: £20.10 (1,253.79 Tckts). T/Qdpt: £10.60 (9.25 Tckts). Hn

YORK (L-H)
Tuesday May 16th (Good to firm, Good patches)
WEATHER: overcast, cool WIND: mod half behind

1098

E.B.F. ZETLAND MAIDEN STKS (2-Y.O F) (Class D) £5,162.50(£1,540.00: £735.00: £332.50) **5f** Stalls: High GOING minus 0.12 sec per fur (G) 2-00 (2-01)

919[3] **Tropical Dance (USA)** *(85)*(Fav)*(MrsJCecil)* 2-8-11 JReid(5) (mde all: drvn out)...........— **1**
High Cut *(82) (IABalding)* 2-8-11 LDettori(2) (rangy: unf: a.p: rdn 2f out: hdwy & ev ch 1f out: nt qckn cl home)...........1 **2**
Desert Tiger *(79)*(Fav)*(MJohnston)* 2-8-11 WRSwinburn(6) (neat: in tch: outpcd ½-wy: hung lft: hdwy over 1f out: r.o towards fin)...........1 **3**
791[2] Roses In The Snow (IRE) *(75)*(Fav)*(JWHills)* 2-8-11 RHills(1) (cl up tl rdn & btn appr fnl f)...........1 **4**
Queen's Insignia (USA) *(71) (PFICole)* 2-8-11 TQuinn(4) (leggy: dwlt: sn drvn along: styd on towards fin)...........1¼ **5**
Amanita *(60)*(Fav)*(JWWatts)* 2-8-11 MJKinane(7) (w'like: rn green: sn pushed along: nvr trbld ldrs)...........3½ **6**
Oatey *(55) (MrsJRRamsden)* 2-8-11 KFallon(8) (cmpt: s.i.s: a outpcd & bhd)...........1½ **7**
Rothley Imp (IRE) *(30) (JWharton)* 2-8-11 KDarley(3) (leggy: unf: gd spd 2f: wknd qckly)...........8 **8**

4/1 TROPICAL DANCE (USA), Desert Tiger, Roses In The Snow (IRE), Amanita, **11/2** High Cut, **8/1** Oatey (op 12/1), **9/1** Queen's Insignia (USA), **16/1** Rothley Imp (IRE), CSF £25.69 TOTE £6.60: £1.70 £1.80 £1.70 (£26.20) OWNER Mr George Ward (NEWMARKET) BRED Charles T Wilson Jr. 8 Rn
59.99 secs (2.99) SF: 33/30/27/23/19/8/3/-

1099 SOTHEBY'S SLEDMERE CONDITIONS STKS (3-Y.O) (Class C)
£4,931.20 (£1,820.80: £870.40: £352.00: £136.00: £49.60)
1m 5f 194y Stalls: Low GOING minus 0.12 sec per fur (G) 2-35 (2-39)

711⁴ **Stelvio** *(98+)*(Fav)*(HRACecil)* 3-8-13 MJKinane(1) (lw: a gng wl: led 2f out: pushed along & r.o strly) ....— **1**
942³ Cypress Avenue (IRE) *(90) (RHannon)* 3-8-11 PatEddery(3) (trckd ldrs: chal over 3f out: one pce fnl 2f) 5 **2**
691⁴ Candle Smile (USA) *(89) (MRStoute)* 3-8-11 WRSwinburn(7) (led: hung lft fnl 4f: hdd 2f out: one pce) 1 **3**
717⁴ Lord Jim (IRE) **(80)***(91) (MissGayKelleway)* 3-8-13 RCochrane(5) (sn outpcd: bhd tl styd on fnl 3f: nrst fin) ....½ **4**
917³ Great Crusader **(100)***(90) (CACyzer)* 3-8-13 JWeaver(6) (effrt ent st: jnd ldrs 3f out: hung lft: sn rdn & btn) ....nk **5**
756* Wot-If-We (IRE) **(98)***(89) (TGMills)* 3-9-1 JCarroll(4) (lw: a bhd: lost tch fnl 4f).......3 **6**
657⁶ Torch Vert (IRE) *(67) (BWHills)* 3-8-11 MHills(2) (cl up tl wknd 4f out) 15 **7**

13/8 STELVIO, **3/1** Candle Smile (USA), **11/2** Wot-If-We (IRE), **7/1** Cypress Avenue (IRE), **10/1** Great Crusader, **20/1** Lord Jim (IRE), Torch Vert (IRE), CSF £11.79 TOTE £2.30: £1.40 £2.90 (£10.30) OWNER Sheikh Mohammed (NEWMARKET) BRED Hesmonds Stud Ltd 7 Rn
2m 57.69 (4.09) SF: 64/56/55/57/56/55/33

1100 PAUL CADDICK AND MACGAY SPRINT TROPHY RATED STKS H'CAP
(0-105) (3-Y.O+) (Class B) £11,802.00 (£4,368.00: £2,096.50:£857.50: £341.25: £134.75) **6f** Stalls: High GOING minus 0.12 sec per fur (G) 3-05 (3-07)

953⁴ **Venture Capitalist (100)***(110) (DNicholls)* 6-9-3 AlexGreaves(8) (lw: bhd: hdwy 2f out: led ins fnl f: hld on gamely) ....— **1**
814⁴ Branston Abby (IRE) **(104)***(114) (MJohnston)* 6-9-7 JReid(2) (hdwy over 2f out: r.o u.p to disp ld wl ins fnl f: kpt on) ....s.h **2**
934* Master Planner **(102)***(105) (CACyzer)* 6-9-5 KDarley(7) (lw: a chsng ldrs: kpt on wl u.p fnl f) 2½ **3**
Roger the Butler (IRE) **(99)***(101) (MBell)* 5-9-2 MFenton(9) (lw: led tl hdd & no ex ins fnl f) .....½ **4**
922¹⁰ Celestial Key (USA) **(90)***(89) (MJohnston)* 5-8-7 DHolland(13) (chsd ldrs: rdn over 2f out: r.o one pce) 1¼ **5**
659¹⁰ Amron **(92)***(88) (JBerry)* 8-8-9 NCarlisle(3) (s.i.s: hdwy 2f out: nvr trbld ldrs) 1 **6**
719⁴ Monaassib (IRE) **(96)***(91)*(Fav)*(EALDunlop)* 4-8-13 WRSwinburn(10) (prom: effrt ½-wy: eased whn btn ins fnl f) ....½ **7**
934⁶ Snipe Hall **(92)***(82) (TRWatson)* 4-8-9 DeanMcKeown(11) (b.hind: hung lft thrght: n.d: fin lame) 1¾ **8**
700⁶ Call Me I'm Blue (IRE) **(95)***(84) (NTinkler)* 5-8-12 MTebbutt(4) (cl up: rdn 2f out: grad wknd)..½ **9**
652⁵ Palacegate Touch **(92)***(75) (JBerry)* 5-8-9v JCarroll(5) (cl up tl rdn & wknd appr fnl f) 2 **10**
934⁷ Lord Olivier (IRE) **(93)***(74) (WJarvis)* 5-8-5 (5) NVarley(6) (chsd ldrs tl wknd fnl 2f) 1 **11**
870²³ Hard to Figure **(104)***(81) (RJHodges)* 9-9-7 RCochrane(1) (dwlt: a outpcd & bhd).......1½ **12**
Sheila's Secret (IRE) **(98)***(69) (TGMills)* 5-9-1 GCarter(12) (b.hind: a outpcd & bhd) 2 **13**

5/1 Monaassib (IRE), **6/1** Master Planner, **7/1** Celestial Key (USA), Roger the Butler (IRE), **15/2** VENTURE CAPITALIST, **8/1** Lord Olivier (IRE), Palacegate Touch, **11/1** Hard to Figure, Branston Abby (IRE), Snipe Hall, **16/1** Amron, **20/1** Sheila's Secret (IRE), **25/1** Call Me I'm Blue (IRE), CSF £84.42 CT £492.19 TOTE £9.70: £2.70 £3.00 £2.60 (£45.80) Trio £72.50 OWNER Mr W. G. Swiers (THIRSK) BRED Brook Bloodstock Plc 13 Rn
1m 11.51 (1.91) SF: 63/67/58/54/42/41/44/35/37/28/27/34/22
OFFICIAL EXPLANATION **Monaassib (IRE): hung left, thus preventing his jockey from riding him out to the line. A routine test was ordered.**

1101 TATTERSALLS MUSIDORA STKS (Gp 3) (3-Y.O F) (Class A)
£22,141.00 (£7,966.00: £3,808.00: £1,540.00: £595.00)
1m 2f 85y Stalls: Low GOING minus 0.12 sec per fur (G) 3-40 (3-42)

Pure Grain (109)*(113)*(Fav)*(MRStoute)* 3-8-10 JReid(2) (lw: trckd ldrs: led on bit wl over 2f out: edgd rt: r.o u.p fnl f) ....— **1**
Caramba *(110) (RHannon)* 3-8-8 PatEddery(4) (hld up: gd hdwy over 3f out: chal over 1f out: edgd rt: nt qckn towards fin) 1 **2**
932* Musetta (IRE) **(110)***(97) (CEBrittain)* 3-8-8 BDoyle(3) (cl up: chal ent st: led 4f out tl wl over 2f out: sn outpcd) 6 **3**
Sparrowhawk (IRE) *(91) (BWHills)* 3-8-8 MHills(1) (lw: led tl hdd 4f out: outpcd whn hmpd wl over 2f out: sn wknd) 4 **4**

932[6] Germane **(105)***(70) (MBell)* 3-8-10 MFenton(5) (chsd ldrs tl rdn & wknd over 3f out)..............15 5

Evens PURE GRAIN, **3/1** Musetta (IRE), **5/1** Caramba (4/1-6/1), **8/1** Germane (6/1-9/1), **16/1** Sparrowhawk (IRE), CSF £5.78 TOTE £1.90: £1.20 £2.00 (£3.50) OWNER Mr R. Barnett (NEWMARKET) BRED W. and R. Barnett Ltd 5 Rn 2m 11.59 (4.09) SF: 53/50/37/31/10

1102 ROYAL BRITISH LEGION INSURANCE SERVICES H'CAP (0-90) (4-Y.O+)

(Class C) £7,635.00 (£2,280.00: £1,090.00: £495.00)
1m 3f 195y Stalls: Low GOING minus 0.12 sec per fur (G) 4-10 (4-11)

931[6] **Arctic Thunder (USA) (89)***(101) (LadyHerries)* 4-10-0 KDarley(3) (b: hld up & bhd: hdwy 4f out: rdn to ld over 1f out: r.o wl)........— 1
967* Blue Blazer **(76)***(85) (BHanbury)* 5-8-10 (5) 5x JStack(9) (hld up: hdwy 4f out: chal over 2f out: kpt on same pce)........2½ 2
816* Godwin (USA) **(78)***(87) (HRACecil)* 4-9-3 MJKinane(7) (lw: led tl hdd over 6f out: led over 2f out tl over 1f out: one pce)........hd 3
931[10] Endless Light (USA) **(84)***(89) (PFICole)* 4-9-9 TQuinn(8) (in tch: hdwy over 3f out: sn chsng ldrs: one pce fnl 2f)........2½ 4
884* Credit Squeeze **(74)***(79)*(Fav)*(RFJohnsonHoughton)* 5-8-13 JQuinn(2) (b: hld up: stdy hdwy over 3f out: rdn & edgd lft over 2f out: nt pce to chal)........nk 5
931[11] Highbrook (USA) **(74)***(77) (MHTompkins)* 7-8-13 PRobinson(5) (hld up: sme hdwy 4f out: nvr nr to chal)........1¼ 6
757[2] George Dillingham **(85)***(77) (DenysSmith)* 5-9-10v JCarroll(6) (plld hrd: cl up: led over 6f out tl over 2f out: wknd)........8 7
Chantry Beath **(62)***(46) (CWThornton)* 4-8-1 AMackay(1) (a bhd)........6 8
935[3] Access Adventurer (IRE) **(66)***(49) (RBoss)* 4-8-5 WRyan(4) (lw: chsd ldrs tl wknd 3f out).....1¼ 9
738[13] Gallardini (IRE) **(60)***(25) (BSRothwell)* 6-7-8 (5) NVarley(10) (cl up tl wknd qckly over 4f out)..13 10

7/2 Credit Squeeze, **4/1** Godwin (USA), **9/2** ARCTIC THUNDER (USA) (op 3/1), **11/2** Access Adventurer (IRE), **7/1** Blue Blazer, George Dillingham, **10/1** Endless Light (USA), **16/1** Chantry Beath, **33/1** Highbrook (USA), **50/1** Gallardini (IRE), CSF £34.05 CT £125.34 TOTE £5.60: £2.00 £2.30 £1.60 (£29.20) Trio £26.30 OWNER Mr P. D. Savill (LITTLEHAMPTON) BRED H and Y Bloodstock 10 Rn 2m 31.03 (4.03) SF: 75/59/61/63/53/51/51/20/23/-

1103 FITZWILLIAM RATED STKS H'CAP (0-100) (3-Y.O) (Class B)

£8,096.50 (£2,993.50: £1,434.25: £583.75: £229.38: £87.62)
1m 2f 85y Stalls: Low GOING minus 0.12 sec per fur (G) 4-40 (4-41)

886[2] **Dahik (100)***(109) (MajorWRHern)* 3-9-7 WCarson(6) (hld up & bhd: effrt 3f out: hdwy over 1f out: str run to ld last strides)........— 1
979[3] Maralinga (IRE) **(92)***(101) (MBell)* 3-8-13 MFenton(7) (led: rdn over 2f out: r.o: jst ct)............s.h 2
Romios (IRE) **(86)***(90) (PFICole)* 3-8-2 (5) CTeague(4) (b.nr fore: bhd: c wd st: hdwy & swvd rt 3f out: sn prom: one pce appr fnl f)........3 3
619[8] Taipan (IRE) **(92)***(93) (JLDunlop)* 3-8-13 TQuinn(2) (a.p: outpcd 4f out: styd on wl fnl f) 2 4
694[6] Myrtle Quest **(86)***(86)*(Fav)*(RCharlton)* 3-8-7 PatEddery(5) (lw: hld up: effrt 3f out: hrd rdn & hung lft 2f out: sn btn)........1 5
Greenspan (IRE) **(86)***(84) (WRMuir)* 3-8-7 JWeaver(3) (chsd ldrs tl wknd fnl 3f)..................1¼ 6
822[2] Eight Sharp (IRE) **(86)***(79) (BWHills)* 3-8-7 MHills(1) (cl up tl wknd fnl 2f)........3 7
LONG HANDICAP Romios (IRE) 7-13 Greenspan (IRE) 8-6 Eight Sharp (IRE) 8-5

2/1 Myrtle Quest, **9/4** Maralinga (IRE) (10/11-5/2), **7/2** Taipan (IRE), **6/1** DAHIK, **14/1** Eight Sharp (IRE), **16/1** Greenspan (IRE), **20/1** Romios (IRE), CSF £19.62 TOTE £4.40: £1.80 £2.00 (£5.90) OWNER Mr Hamdan Al Maktoum (LAMBOURN) BRED Shadwell Estate Company Limited 7 Rn 2m 11.14 (3.64) SF: 67/59/48/51/44/42/37

T/Jkpt: £45,991.60 (2.58 Tckts). T/Plpt: £24.50 (1,634.32 Tckts). T/Qdpt: £97.70 (0.2 Tckts); £105.86 to York 17/5/95 AA

1098-YORK (L-H)

Wednesday May 17th (Good, Good to firm patches becoming Good)

WEATHER: overcast WIND: slt against

1104 DALTON CONDITIONS STKS (2-Y.O) (Class B) £6,898.50

(£2,551.50: £1,223.25: £498.75: £196.88: £76.12)
6f Stalls: High GOING: 0.16 sec per fur (G) 2-00 (2-01)

951* **Dovebrace** *(92) (ABailey)* 2-8-13 MWigham(2) (bhd & outpcd: swtchd rt & hdwy bel dist: r.o strly to ld cl home)........— 1

682* Lucayan Prince (USA) *(91)*(Fav)*(DRLoder)* 2-8-13 JWeaver(4) (lw: a.p: led over 2f out: hrd rdn over 1f out: swvd lft ins fnl f: hdd nr fin) ....½ 2
Belzao *(81) (MRChannon)* 2-8-8 RHughes(1) (w'like: cmpt: a.p: ev ch 1f out: rdn & hld whn impeded ins fnl f)....1¾ 3
Corporal Nym (USA) *(78) (PFICole)* 2-8-8 PatEddery(5) (lengthy: unf: led tl over 2f out: rdn & one pce fnl f) 1 4
871² World Premier *(81) (CEBrittain)* 2-9-1 MRimmer(6) (prom: rdn over 2f out: sn btn)....1½ 5
718* Safio *(68) (CSmith)* 2-9-1 JFortune(3) (a bhd: outpcd fr ½-wy) 5 6

10/11 Lucayan Prince (USA), **4/1** DOVEBRACE, **6/1** World Premier (op 4/1), **13/2** Corporal Nym (USA), **7/1** Belzao, **14/1** Safio, CSF £8.36 TOTE £5.20: £2.30 £1.40 (£2.80) OWNER Mr David Jones (TARPORLEY) BRED Mrs M. Christian 6 Rn 1m 15.12 (5.52) SF: 32/31/21/18/21/8
STEWARDS' ENQUIRY Hughes susp 26-27/5/95 (incorrect use of whip).

1105 YORKSHIRE-TYNE TEES TELEVISION MIDDLETON STKS (3-Y.O F)
(Class C) £5,024.00 (£1,856.00: £888.00: £360.00: £140.00: £52.00)
1m 2f 85y Stalls: Low GOING: 0.16 sec per fur (G) 2-35 (2-37)

Ludgate (USA) (88)*(99) (RJRWilliams)* 3-9-1 GDuffield(6) (bit bkwd: hld up: 4th st: led over 2f out: rdn & styd on wl) ....— 1
932⁴ Watch the Clock **(103)***(97) (DRLoder)* 3-9-1 JWeaver(5) (led 1f: 2nd st: led 3f out tl over 2f out: rdn & no ex fnl f) 1½ 2
797² Dawlah *(87)*(Fav)*(HThomsonJones)* 3-8-9 RHills(3) (chsd ldrs: 3rd st: ev ch 3f out: kpt on one pce)....2½ 3
857³ Lucky Coin *(73) (CEBrittain)* 3-8-9 BDoyle(7) (s.s: led after 1f to 3f out: sn rdn: grad wknd) 9 4
Jadwal (USA) *(69) (DMorley)* 3-8-11 MHills(4) (b.nr hind: hld up: 5th st: lost tch over 2f out) 4 5
698² True Bird (IRE) *(61) (JDBethell)* 3-8-9 JCarroll(1) (outpcd & drvn along ½-wy: 7th st: a bhd)3½ 6
888* Mary's Way (GR) *(43) (RCharlton)* 3-8-11 PatEddery(2) (lw: hld up & bhd: 6th st: wknd over 2f out: eased whn btn: t.o) 13 7

7/4 Dawlah, **9/4** Mary's Way (GR), **4/1** Watch the Clock, **8/1** Jadwal (USA), **14/1** True Bird (IRE), **16/1** LUDGATE (USA), **25/1** Lucky Coin, CSF £72.05 TOTE £28.70: £6.10 £2.20 (£42.90) OWNER Lord Matthews (NEWMARKET) BRED Waverton Stud 7 Rn
2m 13.74 (6.24) SF: 63/61/51/37/33/25/7

1106 HOMEOWNERS SPRINT H'CAP (0-105) (3-Y.O+) (Class B) £15,270.00
(£4,560.00: £2,180.00: £990.00)
5f Stalls: Low GOING: 0.16 sec per fur (G) 3-05 (3-06)

796* **Brave Edge (90)***(98+)*(Fav)*(RHannon)* 4-9-7 PatEddery(8) (lw: hld up: hdwy & nt clr run 2f out: r.o wl to ld ins fnl f) ....— 1
922¹¹ Saddlehome (USA) **(75)***(78) (TDBarron)* 6-8-6 JFortune(6) (swtg: hld up: hdwy ½-wy: ev ch ins fnl f: unable qckn)....1½ 2
796⁴ Name the Tune **(72)***(74) (PHowling)* 4-8-3 PaulEddery(1) (lw: led early: led 2f out tl ins fnl f)....½ 3
796¹¹ Macfarlane **(73)***(67) (MJFetherston-Godley)* 7-8-4 FNorton(4) (hdwy ½-wy: rdn & kpt on ins fnl f)....2½ 4
949² Croft Pool **(74)***(64) (JAGlover)* 4-8-5v PRobinson(9) (chsd ldrs: outpcd & rdn 2f out: one pce)1¼ 5
922³ Sir Joey (USA) **(84)***(70) (PGMurphy)* 6-8-10 (5) SDrowne(5) (in tch: effrt 2f out: kpt on fnl f)....1 6
441¹⁰ Palacegate Jack (IRE) **(95)***(75) (JBerry)* 4-9-12 MJKinane(7) (hdwy ½-wy: rdn over 1f out: nt pce to chal)....2 7
926¹¹ Croft Imperial **(67)***(44) (MJohnston)* 8-7-5b(7) BHalligan(3) (dwlt: nvr nrr)....1 8
Princess Oberon (IRE) **(82)***(56) (MBell)* 5-8-13 MFenton(10) (nvr nr ldrs) ....¾ 9
1019⁵ Tuscan Dawn **(88)***(60) (JBerry)* 5-9-5 JCarroll(2) (reard s: sn led: hdd 2f out: wknd qckly) ....¾ 10
685³ Gorinsky (IRE) **(97)***(64) (JBerry)* 7-10-0 GCarter(12) (chsd ldrs stands' side 3f: sn outpcd) 1½ 11
926² Spender **(71)***(34) (PWHarris)* 6-8-2 DHarrison(11) (s.s: a bhd)....1¼ 12
944³ Lord High Admiral (CAN) **(92)***(51) (MJHeaton-Ellis)* 7-9-9 RPerham(14) (chsd ldr stands' side over 3f)....1¼ 13
1019⁷ Insider Trader **(83)***(39) (RJRWilliams)* 4-9-0b GDuffield(13) (b: led stands' side: lost tch 2f out)....1 14
1019³ Magic Pearl **(73)***(28) (EJAlston)* 5-8-4 JFanning(15) (dwlt: racd stands' side: nvr gng pce of ldrs)....nk 15
Allwight Then (IRE) **(78)***(33) (FHLee)* 4-8-9 TIves(16) (hld up stands' side: a in rr)....hd 16

9/2 BRAVE EDGE, **7/1** Saddlehome (USA), Magic Pearl, Croft Pool, **9/1** Sir Joey (USA), **10/1** Insider Trader, **12/1** Spender, Tuscan Dawn, Palacegate Jack (IRE), **14/1** Princess Oberon (IRE), Macfarlane, Name the Tune, **20/1** Lord High Admiral (CAN), Gorinsky (IRE), **25/1** Croft Imperial, Allwight Then (IRE), CSF £37.07 CT £391.25 TOTE £4.70: £1.70 £2.40 £3.10 £2.60 (£25.10) Trio £145.70 OWNER Mrs M. Peett (MARLBOROUGH) BRED Mrs G. A. Whent 16 Rn
60.73 secs (3.73) SF: 54/34/30/23/20/26/31/-/12/16/20/-/7/-/-/-

1107

HOMEOWNERS DANTE STKS (Gp 2) (3-Y.O) (Class A) £63,931.00(£23,967.30: £11,546.15: £5,065.55) **1m 2f 85y** Stalls: Low GOING: 0.16 sec per fur (G)-40 (3-43)

Classic Cliche (IRE) *(119) (SbinSuroor)* 3-8-11 WRSwinburn(8) (h.d.w: chsd ldrs: 4th st: led over 2f out: hrd rdn fnl f: hld on gamely) — 1
Annus Mirabilis (FR) **(115)***(118) (MRStoute)* 3-8-11 MJKinane(6) (lw: hld up & bhd: 8th st: hdwy over 2f out: ev ch fnl f: r.o) ½ 2
912* Presenting **(111)***(112)*(Fav)*(JHMGosden)* 3-8-11 LDettori(4) (lw: hld up: 6th st: rdn & hdwy 3f out: kpt on one pce) 4 3
920⁴ Pipe Major (IRE) **(110)***(111) (PCHaslam)* 3-8-11 JWeaver(3) (lw: led 8f out tl over 2f out: sn rdn: kpt on same pce) ¾ 4
438* Juyush (USA) **(115)***(106) (BWHills)* 3-8-11 RHills(2) (led over 2f: 2nd st: rdn & wknd over 2f out) 3½ 5
Salmon Ladder (USA) *(103) (PFICole)* 3-8-11 PatEddery(1) (b.nr hind: prom: 3rd st: rdn over 4f out: wknd fnl 2f) 1½ 6
955* Ten Past Six *(101) (BWHills)* 3-8-11 MHills(7) (hld up: 7th st: rdn over 3f out: no imp) 1¼ 7
945³ Stiletto Blade **(110)***(100) (IABalding)* 3-8-11 RCochrane(5) (hld up: 5th st: effrt on ins over 3f out: sn rdn & wknd) ¾ 8

11/8 Presenting, **9/2** Pipe Major (IRE), **5/1** Salmon Ladder (USA) (op 3/1), **13/2** Annus Mirabilis (FR), **9/1** CLASSIC CLICHE (IRE), **12/1** Juyush (USA), **25/1** Ten Past Six, Stiletto Blade, CSF £59.28 TOTE £11.00: £2.10 £2.00 £1.10 (£33.90) OWNER Godolphin (NEWMARKET) BRED Lord Victor Matthews in Ireland 8 Rn 2m 10.63 (3.13) SF: 85/84/78/77/72/69/67/66

1108

HAMBLETON RATED STKS H'CAP (0-110) (Listed) (4-Y.O+) (Class A) £12,884.80 (£4,763.20: £2,281.60: £928.00: £364.00:£138.40) **7f 202y** Stalls: Low GOING: 0.16 sec per fur (G) 4-10 (4-11)

870* **Jawaal (94)***(108+)*(Fav)*(LadyHerries)* 5-8-7 JReid(3) (hld up in tch: 4th st: led over 2f out: qcknd over 1f out: sn clr: readily) — 1
870⁵ Kayvee **(97)***(105) (GHarwood)* 6-8-10 WRSwinburn(7) (lw: hld up & bhd: effrt over 2f out: styd on ins fnl f) 3 2
934⁹ Pinkerton's Pal **(95)***(102) (CEBrittain)* 4-8-8 BDoyle(6) (chsd ldrs: 6th st: rdn over 2f out: styd on towards fin) nk 3
953² Storiths (IRE) **(108)***(115) (JWWatts)* 5-9-7b BThomson(8) (b: hld up: hdwy over 2f out: rdn & one pce fnl f) s.h 4
714¹⁵ Dance Turn **(100)***(103) (RWArmstrong)* 4-8-13 RHills(2) (mde most tl over 2f out: sn wknd) 2 5
Patto (USA) **(95)***(94) (WJHaggas)* 4-8-8 LDettori(5) (lw: prom: 3rd st: chal over 2f out: wknd bel dist) 2 6
870¹⁰ Roving Minstrel **(94)***(92) (BAMcMahon)* 4-8-7 FNorton(1) (hld up: effrt 2f out: nvr nr to chal) ¾ 7
712⁶ Cotteir Chief (IRE) **(107)***(103) (MCPipe)* 4-9-6 PatEddery(10) (lw: prom: 5th st: rdn & outpcd fnl f) ¾ 8
714⁶ Mellottie **(95)***(83) (MrsMReveley)* 10-8-8 KDarley(9) (hld up & bhd: reminders 3f out: no imp) 4 9
953* Moccasin Run (USA) **(100)***(87) (IABalding)* 4-8-13 MHills(4) (w ldr: 2nd st: wknd over 2f out) nk 10

LONG HANDICAP Jawaal 8-2 Roving Minstrel 7-13

7/2 JAWAAL, **5/1** Kayvee, **7/1** Cotteir Chief (IRE), Storiths (IRE), Moccasin Run (USA), Mellottie, **9/1** Dance Turn, Patto (USA), **12/1** Pinkerton's Pal, **25/1** Roving Minstrel, CSF £20.65 CT £174.30 TOTE £3.90: £1.90 £1.80 £2.90 (£8.20) Trio £44.80 OWNER Mr T. G. Fox (LITTLEHAMPTON) BRED Gainsborough Stud Management Ltd 10 Rn 1m38.91(2.91) SF: 75/72/69/82/70/61/59/70/50/54

1109

WILKINSON MEMORIAL H'CAP (0-90) (4-Y.O+) (Class C) £7,765.00(£2,320.00: £1,110.00: £505.00) **1m 5f 194y** Stalls: Low GOING: 0.16 sec per fur (G)4-40 (4-45)

811² **Midyan Blue (IRE) (70)***(82) (JMPEustace)* 5-8-10 RCochrane(4) (led over 5f: 3rd st: styd on u.p to ld wl ins fnl f) — 1
Foundry Lane **(79)***(90)*(Fav)*(MrsMReveley)* 4-9-5 KDarley(13) (h.d.w: chsd ldrs: 4th st: led over 1f out tl wl ins fnl f) ½ 2
954³ Cuango (IRE) **(76)***(84) (RHollinshead)* 4-9-2 WRyan(6) (hld up & bhd: styd on wl fnl 2f: nvr nrr) 3 3

8212 Uncle Doug **(56)**_(61) (MrsMReveley)_ 4-7-10 ow2 JFanning(8) (chsd ldrs: 7th st: led over 3f out tl over 1f out: wknd ins fnl f).....½ **4**
Halkopous **(85)**_(92) (MHTompkins)_ 9-9-11v PRobinson(11) (hld up: shkn up & effrt 3f out: nvr nr to chal).....nk **5**
8798 Achilles Heel **(53)**_(56) (CNAllen)_ 4-7-2 (5) MBaird(10) (lw: hld up & bhd: styd on appr fnl f: rdn & edgd lft: nvr nrr).....3½ **6**
63211 Well Arranged (IRE) **(79)**_(73) (RAkehurst)_ 4-9-5 LDettori(2) (chsd ldrs: 5th st: outpcd 3f out: sn btn).....8 **7**
7958 Flight Lieutenant (USA) **(79)**_(71) (RHannon)_ 6-9-5 JReid(7) (hld up: effrt ent st: no imp).....2 **8**
8219 Sarawat **(77)**_(68) (DNicholls)_ 7-9-3 AlexGreaves(12) (dwlt: hdwy & 6th st: wknd over 3f out) .nk **9**
86616 Chakalak **(54)**_(45) (SDow)_ 7-7-8 GBardwell(3) (sn pushed along: chsd ldrs 8f: sn lost tch) ...s.h **10**
6104 Charity Crusader **(88)**_(73) (PWChapple-Hyam)_ 4-9-7 (7) RHavlin(1) (s.s: a in rr: t.o).....5 **11**
757* Pharly Dancer **(59)**_(39) (WWHaigh)_ 6-7-13 DaleGibson(5) (lw: led over 8f out tl over 3f out: wknd qckly: t.o).....5 **12**

LONG HANDICAP Achilles Heel 7-4

4/1 Foundry Lane (6/1-7/2), **9/2** Uncle Doug, **13/2** Well Arranged (IRE), **7/1** Flight Lieutenant (USA), **15/2** MIDYAN BLUE (IRE), **8/1** Pharly Dancer, **9/1** Charity Crusader, **10/1** Cuango (IRE), **14/1** Chakalak, **16/1** Halkopous, **20/1** Achilles Heel, Sarawat, CSF £37.79 CT £282.18 TOTE £11.20: £3.70 £1.10 £3.40 (£25.00) Trio £99.10 OWNER Mr Keith Palmer (NEWMARKET) BRED Ballykisteen Stud Ltd 12 Rn 3m 1.05 (7.45) SF: 65/73/67/44/75/39/56/54/51/28/56/22

T/Jkpt: Not won; £12,785.56 to York 18/5/95. T/Plpt: £114.30 (377.54 Tckts). T/Qdpt: £19.00 (28.9 Tckts). IM

1001a-SAINT-CLOUD (France) (L-H)
Monday May 8th (Good)

1110a PRIX CLEOPATRE (Gp 3) (3-Y.O F) £26,347.00 (£9,581.00: £4,790.00: £2,395.00) **1m 2f 110y** 2-20 (-)

802a3 **Valley of Gold (FR)** _(100) (AFabre,France)_ 3-8-9 TJarnet .....— **1**
802a2 Loretta Gianni (FR) _(98) (DSmaga,France)_ 3-8-9 GGuignard 1½ **2**
Privity (USA) _(96) (PBary,France)_ 3-8-9 DBoeuf 1 **3**

P-M 2.60F: 1.30F 1.20F (6.80F) OWNER Sheikh Mohammed (FRANCE) 3 Rn 2m 20.2 SF: -/-/-

1010a-SAN SIRO (Milan, Italy) (R-H)
Wednesday May 10th (Good)

1111a PREMIO ALICE FREY MAIDEN (2-Y.O F) £4,186.00 (£2,010.00: £1,005.00) **5f** 1-55 (-)

Infiel _(GBotti,Italy)_ 2-9-0 EBotti .....— **1**
Lasco Blu Velvet (ITY) _(Italy)_ 2-9-0 MEsposito 2¼ **2**
Greek Icon _(JLDunlop)_ 2-9-0 GForte 1¾ **3**

Tote 30L: 22L 46L (168L) OWNER Scuderia dei Cherubini (ITALY) 7 Rn 60.5 secs SF: -/-/-

1007a-LONGCHAMP (Paris, France) (R-H)
Thursday May 11th (Good)

1112a PRIX DE SAINT-GEORGES (Gp 3) (3-Y.O+) £26,347.00 (£9,581.00: £4,790.00: £2,395.00) **5f** 4-15 (4-12)

608a* **Struggler** _(112) (CLaffon-Parias,France)_ 3-8-5 FSanchez .....— **1**
Spain Lane (USA) _(111) (AFabre,France)_ 4-9-5 TJarnet 1½ **2**
Way West (FR) _(108) (MmeCHead,France)_ 5-9-2 ODoleuze .....s.nk **3**
Millyant _(106) (RGuest)_ 5-9-3 CAsmussen .....¾ **4**

P-M 2.40F: 1.30F 1.30F (5.60F) OWNER Mr Abdullah Ali 7 Rn 58.2 secs (3.20) SF: -/-/-/-

0707a-LEOPARDSTOWN (Dublin, Ireland) (L-H)
Saturday May 13th (Good to firm)

1113a DERRINSTOWN STUD DERBY TRIAL (Gp 3) (3-Y.O) £27,000.00 (£7,600.00: £3,600.00: £1,200.00) **1m 2f** 4-00 (4-02)

709a* **Humbel (USA)** _(107) (DKWeld,Ireland)_ 3-8-11 MJKinane .....— **1**

Shemaran (IRE) *(107) (JOxx,Ireland)* 3-8-11 JPMurtagh ....nk 2
Johansson (USA) *(101) (JOxx,Ireland)* 3-8-11 PVGilson 3½ 3
CSF £6.02 TOTE £4.40: £1.20 £1.10 £2.60 (£2.00) OWNER Dr Michael Smurfit BRED A. E. Paulson 8 Rn
2m 6.3 (2.30) SF: -/-/-

1111a-SAN SIRO (Milan, Italy) (R-H)
Saturday May 13th (Heavy)

1114a COPPA D'ORO DI MILANO (Gp 3) (4-Y.O+) £29,346.00 (£13,459.00: £7,502.00: £3,751.00) 1m 7f
3-15 (3-22)

735* **Khamaseen** *(113) (JLDunlop)* 4-8-11 JReid ....— 1
Michel Georges *(111) (JForesi,France)* 7-8-11 OPeslier ....½ 2
Ibiano (IRE) *(105) (FGang,Germany)* 6-8-11 LSorrentino 5½ 3
Tote 15L: 12L 13L (20L) OWNER Prince A. A. Faisal (ARUNDEL) BRED Nawara Stud Co Ltd 7 Rn
3m 22.6 SF: -/-/-

1112a-LONGCHAMP (Paris, France) (R-H)
Sunday May 14th (Soft)

1115a PRIX LUPIN (Gp 1) (3-Y.O C & F) £57,401.00 (£22,814.00: £11,042.00: £4,790.00) 1m 2f 110y
1-50 (1-59)

679² **Flemensfirth (USA)** *(110) (JHMGosden)* 3-9-2 LDettori (trckd ldr: led over 1f out: r.o wl fnl f) ....— 1
801a² Solar One (FR) *(109) (JEPease,France)* 3-9-2 CAsmussen (led tl hdd over 1f out: rallied: no ex cl home) 1 2
808a² Angel Falls (FR) *(108) (AFabre,France)* 3-9-2 TJarnet (4th st: rdn & outpcd 2f out: r.o fnl f) ....nk 3
Beau Temps *(107) (MmeCHead,France)* 3-9-2 FHead (hld up: rdn over 2f out: no imp) ....¾ 4
Leeds (IRE) *(105) (HVandePoele,France)* 3-9-2 OPeslier (3rd tl wknd over 1f out) 1½ 5
Nicosie (USA) *(97) (JEHammond,France)* 3-9-2 WMongil (dwlt: a bhd: btn st) 5 6

P-M 2.70F: 1.30F 1.10F (9.80F) OWNER Sheikh Mohammed (NEWMARKET) BRED Mill Ridge Farm Ltd in USA 6 Rn
2m 17.2 SF: -/-/-/-/-/-

1116a DUBAI POULE D'ESSAI DES POULICHES (Gp 1) (3-Y.O F) £119,760.00 (£47,904.00: £23,952.00: £11,976.00) 1m
3-00 (3-07)

807a* **Matiara (USA)** *(115) (MmeCHead,France)* 3-9-2 FHead (a.p: barged out 2f out: sn led: hrd rdn & jst hld on) ....— 1
807a³ Carling (FR) *(115) (MmePBarbe,France)* 3-9-2 TThulliez (trckd ldrs: 5th st: rapid hdwy fnl f: jst failed) ....nse 2
807a² Shaanxi (USA) *(111) (ELellouche,France)* 3-9-2 OPeslier (hmpd s: gd hdwy 2f out: r.o wl nr fin) 2 3
705a² Smolensk (USA) *(107) (AFabre,France)* 3-9-2 TJarnet (bhd early: chal on outside st: r.o) 2 4
Collecta (FR) *(106) (JEHammond,France)* 3-9-2 ESaint-Martin (hld up: last st: hdwy 2f out: wknd cl home) ....nk 5
Ghostly (IRE) *(103) (PBary,France)* 3-9-2 DBoeuf (hld up: hdwy over 1f out: one pce) 1½ 6
Vadlamixa (FR) *(100) (AFabre,France)* 3-9-2 SGuillot (plld hrd in rr early: hmpd twice st: one pce) 1½ 7
933⁴ Hoh Magic *(97) (MBell)* 3-9-2 MFenton (mid div: no hdwy st) 1½ 8
Tirolling (IRE) *(97) (JForesi,France)* 3-9-2 FSanchez (led tl over 1f out: wknd) ....s.nk 9
705a⁴ Tereshkova (USA) *(95) (AFabre,France)* 3-9-2 TGillet (mid div: 8th st: bdly hmpd: nt rcvr) ....¾ 10
Fairy Path (USA) *(95) (DSmaga,France)* 3-9-2 PatEddery (s.s: a bhd) ....nk 11
Deceive *(93) (SbinSuroor)* 3-9-2 LDettori (hmpd s: nvr nr to chal) ....¾ 12
Piquetnol (USA) *(92) (JEHammond,France)* 3-9-2 CAsmussen (chsd ldr: 2nd st: bdly hmpd 2f out: sn wknd) ....¾ 13
Nuriva (USA) *(90) (SbinSuroor)* 3-9-2 MJKinane (s.s: mid div: styd on one pce) ....¾ 14
705a³ Take Liberties *(89) (AFabre,France)* 3-9-2 PaulEddery (a.p. 3rd st: wknd qckly over 1f out) ..¾ 15
Chrysalu *(84) (NClement,France)* 3-9-2 GMosse (mid div: hdwy over 1f out: sn hmpd: nt rcvr) 2½ 16

P-M 3.60F: 1.50F 2.50F 1.70F (18.50F) OWNER Ecurie Aland (FRANCE) BRED Societe Aland 16 Rn
1m 42.4 SF: -/-/-/-/-/-/-/-/-/-/-/-/-/-/-/-

1117a DUBAI POULE D'ESSAI DES POULAINS (Gp 1) (3-Y.O C) £119,760.00 (£47,904.00: £23,952.00: £11,976.00) **1m** 3-35 (0-34)

	Vettori (IRE) *(115) (SbinSuroor)* 3-9-2 LDettori (a.p: led 1f out: rdn out)	—	1
806a*	Atticus (USA) *(115) (MmeCHead,France)* 3-9-2 ODoleuze (led to 1f out: r.o)	s.nk	2
806a2	Petit Poucet *(111) (NClement,France)* 3-9-2 CAsmussen (hld up: effrt over 1f out: styd on one pce)	2	3
	Lyphard's Honour (FR) *(106) (AFabre,France)* 3-9-2 TJarnet (mid div: hdwy 2f out: one pce fnl f)	2½	4
706a2	Bene Erit (USA) *(98) (CLaffon-Parias,France)* 3-9-2 FHead (nvr plcd to chal)	4	5
	General Monash (USA) *(97) (PWChapple-Hyam)* 3-9-2 JReid (a bhd)	s.nk	6
706a3	Viva Nureyev (USA) *(77) (AFabre,France)* 3-9-2 SGuillot (trckd ldr: hrd rdn st: sn wknd)	10	7
801a6	Sea Gone (USA) *(65) (MmeCHead,France)* 3-9-2 RLibert (nvr wnt pce: last st: t.o)	6	8

P-M 5.50F: 1.50F 1.10F 1.30F (12.20F) OWNER Maktoum Al Maktoum / Godolphin (NEWMARKET) BRED Sheikh Mohammed bin Rashid al Maktoum 8 Rn 1m 40.4 SF: -/-/-/-/-/-/-/-

0900a-CAPANNELLE (Rome, Italy) (R-H)
Sunday May 14th (Heavy)

1118a PREMIO PRESIDENTE DELLA REPUBBLICA (Gp 1) (4-Y.O+) £52,722.00 (£25,994.00: £15,018.00: £7,509.00) **1m 2f** 3-30 (3-37)

	Flagbird (USA) *(118) (SbinSuroor)* 4-8-13 KDarley	—	1
	Del Deya (IRE) *(116) (JHMGosden)* 5-8-13 JCarroll	1½	2
	Firing Line (IRE) *(115) (CMarinelli,Italy)* 6-9-2 JWeaver	2	3
710a*	Lear White (USA) *(114) (FBrogi,Italy)* 4-9-2 JCaro	¾	4
606a2	Volochine (IRE) *(106) (RCollet,France)* 4-9-2 GGuignard	5	5
	Rubhahunish (IRE) *(101) (ARenzoni,Italy)* 4-9-2 SLandi	3	6
	Torrismondo (USA) *(101) (RTibiletti,Italy)* 4-9-2 BDoyle	½	7
	Bemont Park (ITY) *(97) (RBrogi,Italy)* 4-8-13 GBietolini	nk	8
	Dark Street (IRE) *(94) (LCamici,Italy)* 5-9-2 FJovine	4	9
	Sugarland Express (IRE) *(91) (OPessi,Italy)* 4-9-2 AParravani	2	10

Tote 94L: 26L 18L 22L (210L) OWNER Godolphin (NEWMARKET) BRED W. S. Farish in USA 10 Rn 2m 5.6 SF: -/-/-/-/-/-/-/-/-/-

1119a PREMIO MELTON-MEMORIAL TUDINI (Gp 2) (3-Y.O+) £42,730.00 (£19,833.00: £11,121.00: £5,560.00) **6f** 4-30 (4-42)

8143	**Hever Golf Rose** *(116) (TJNaughton)* 4-9-0 JWeaver	—	1
	Fred Bongusto (IRE) *(115) (RBrogi,Italy)* 4-9-3 BJovine	1½	2
	Ashoka *(108) (FGnesi,Italy)* 4-9-3 JCaro	2½	3
901a*	Imprevedibile (IRE) *(106) (PCeriotti,Italy)* 5-9-3 AParravani	1	4
4412	Sharp Prod (USA) *(89) (LordHuntingdon)* 5-9-3 KDarley (btn approx 10l)		11

Tote 53L: 31L 59L 29L (1243L) OWNER Mr M. P. Hanson (EPSOM) BRED Ronald Popely 14 Rn 1m 10.8 SF: -/-/-/-/-

0805a-FUCHU (Tokyo, Japan) (L-H)
Sunday May 14th (Firm)

1120a YASUDA KINEN (Gp 1) (4-Y.O+) £670,840.00 (£263,056.00: £163,561.00: £89,692.00) **1m** 7-35 (7-35)

805a5	**Heart Lake** *(123) (SbinSuroor)* 4-9-0 YTake	—	1
	Sakura Chitose O (JPN) *(123) (KSakai,Japan)* 5-9-0 FKojima	nse	2
	Taiki Blizzard (USA) *(121) (KFujisawa,Japan)* 4-9-0 YOkabe	¾	3
805a13	Erin Bird (FR) *(108) (PWChapple-Hyam)* 4-8-9 SEbina (btn approx further 4l)		8

Tote 1030Y: 270Y 160Y 340Y (2410Y) OWNER Godolphin (NEWMARKET) BRED Sheikh Mohammed bin Rashid al Maktoum 18 Rn

1m 33.2 SF: -/-/-/-

0902a-COLOGNE (Germany) (R-H)
Sunday May 14th (Good)

1121a MEHL-MULHENS RENNEN (Gp 2) (3-Y.O C & F) £78,189.00 (£31,687.00: £15,638.00: £8,230.00) **1m** 3-40 (3-54)

Manzoni (GER) *(111) (AWohler,Germany)* 3-9-2 TMundry ....— 1
680² Montjoy (USA) *(107) (PFICole)* 3-9-2 TQuinn 2 2
A Magicman (FR) *(106) (HSteguweit,Germany)* 3-9-2 NGrant ....½ 3
826⁶ Two O'Clock Jump (IRE) *(105) (RHannon)* 3-9-2 RHughes ....¾ 4
Tajawall (USA) *(102) (AWohler,Germany)* 3-9-2 WRSwinburn 1½ 5
Devil River Peek (USA) *(101) (BSchutz,Germany)* 3-9-2 ASuborics ....nk 6
Sinyar *(99) (BSchutz,Germany)* 3-9-2 WRyan ....¾ 7
Tristano *(98) (ALowe,Germany)* 3-9-2 AHelfenbein ....½ 8
Siberian Grey *(97) (CSprengel,Germany)* 3-9-2 MO'Reilly ....¾ 9
662* Iblis (IRE) *(GWragg)* 3-9-2 MHills (btn more than 7l)................. 11

Tote 556DM: 74DM 17DM 113DM (2204DM) OWNER Gestut Hof Heidendom 15 Rn
1m 33.71 SF: -/-/-/-/-/-/-/-/-/-

MUNICH (Germany) (L-H)
Sunday May 14th (Good)

1122a GROSSER DALLMYR-PREIS VON DEUTSCHLAND (Gp 2) (3-Y.O) £60,494.00 (£23,868.00: £12,346.00: £6,173.00) **1m 3f** 3-30 (3-39)

O'Connor (IRE) *(104) (AWohler,Germany)* 3-9-2 ABoschert ....— 1
Lecroix (GER) *(99) (MHofer,Germany)* 3-9-2 ManfredHofer (fin 3rd, hd: plcd 2nd) ....hd 2
Chadayed (USA) *(96) (Germany)* 3-9-2 PSchiergen (fin 4th, 2½l; plcd 3rd) 2½ 3
756² Dreamer (USA) *(103) (PFICole)* 3-9-2 JFortune (fin 2nd, 2l: disq: plcd 4th) 2 4
711* Posidonas *(PFICole)* 3-9-2 AClark (btn approx 12l) 8

Tote 32DM: 13DM 14DM 13DM (141DM) 10 Rn 2m 22.9 SF: -/-/-/-/-

0937-SALISBURY (R-H)
Thursday May 18th (Good, Good to soft patches)
WEATHER: Fine WIND: Slight, against

1123 WARMINSTER MAIDEN STKS (2-Y.O) (Class D) £3,652.00 (£1,096.00: £528.00: £244.00)
5f Stalls: High GOING minus 0.05 sec per fur (G) 2-10 (2-10)

996² **Repertory** *(85+)*(Fav)*(MRChannon)* 2-9-0 RHughes(7) (a gng wl: led on bit over 1f out: easily) ....— 1
Autobabble (IRE) *(79) (RHannon)* 2-9-0 RPerham(9) (w'like: a.p: rdn over 2f out: swtchd lft over 1f out: r.o) 2 2
Therhea (IRE) *(78) (BRMillman)* 2-9-0 JWilliams(4) (w'like: hdwy over 1f out: swtchd rt & r.o ins fnl f) ....nk 3
910⁵ Delaunay (IRE) *(72) (RHannon)* 2-9-0 JReid(8) (led over 3f: wknd ins fnl f) 1¾ 4
Nellie North *(59) (MrsMMcCourt)* 2-8-2 (7) RStudholme(2) (lt-f: prom over 3f) 2½ 5
Laughing Buccaneer *(54) (BJMeehan)* 2-9-0 WNewnes(6) (cmpt: outpcd) 3 6
Meranti *(52) (LJHolt)* 2-9-0 AMcGlone(5) (neat: outpcd) ....¾ 7
1011⁶ Jemsilverthorn (IRE) *(50) (JJBridger)* 2-8-11b(3) SSanders(3) (w ldr over 2f: wknd fnl 2f) ....¾ 8
Rawi *(CJBenstead)* 2-9-0 BRouse(1) (cmpt: bit bkwd: swvd bdly lft s: v reluctant to r: sddle slipped: p.u over 3f out) .... P

4/7 REPERTORY, **4/1** Delaunay (IRE), **12/1** Therhea (IRE) (op 7/1), Rawi (op 7/1), **16/1** Laughing Buccaneer, **20/1** Autobabble (IRE), **33/1** Nellie North, Meranti, **50/1** Jemsilverthorn (IRE), CSF £12.92 TOTE £1.50: £1.10 £5.10 £3.20 (£16.00) Trio £54.60 OWNER Mr Chris Scott (UPPER LAMBOURN) BRED W. H. Joyce 9 Rn 63.93 secs (3.93) SF: 29/23/22/16/3/-/-/-/-

1124 DRUIDS H'CAP (0-70) (3-Y.O) (Class E) £3,730.00 (£1,120.00: £540.00: £250.00)
1m Stalls: High GOING minus 0.05 sec per fur (G) 2-45 (2-46)

948* **Blaze of Song (68)***(84)*(Fav)*(RHannon)* 3-9-8 5x JReid(15) (lw: a.p: led wl over 1f out: sn clr: easily) ....— 1

829[10] Danegold (IRE) **(67)***(67) (MRChannon)* 3-9-7v RHughes(1) (hld up & bhd: hdwy fnl 2f: nt trble wnr) 8 **2**
867[7] Kevasingo **(53)***(52) (SDow)* 3-8-7 BThomson(11) (a.p: led 3f out tl wl over 1f out: one pce)....½ **3**
779[8] Care And Comfort **(62)***(60) (GWragg)* 3-9-2 FNorton(18) (a.p: swtchd lft over 2f out: one pce) ....½ **4**
648[5] Soviet Bride (IRE) **(54)***(46) (EALDunlop)* 3-8-5 (3) JTate(13) (b.hind: prom tl wknd over 2f out) .3 **5**
766[3] Faustino **(55)***(46) (PFICole)* 3-8-9 CRutter(3) (lw: hdwy over 3f out: one pce fnl 2f)....½ **6**
971[8] Nosirrah **(60)***(47) (CAHorgan)* 3-9-0 TWilliams(2) (hld up & bhd: nrst fin) 2 **7**
Fattash (USA) **(65)***(51) (CJBenstead)* 3-9-5 BRouse(5) (bit bkwd: nvr nr to chal) ....¾ **8**
850[8] Classic Pet (IRE) **(52)***(37) (CAHorgan)* 3-8-6 NAdams(6) (b: plld hrd: bhd tl r.o fnl 2f: nvr nrr)....½ **9**
777[5] Alerting **(64)***(48) (IABalding)* 3-9-4 SO'Gorman(12) (lw: prom 5f) ....hd **10**
857[11] Arctic Poppy (USA) **(55)***(38) (IABalding)* 3-8-4 (5) DGriffiths(4) (lw: n.d) ....½ **11**
908[10] Sobeloved **(54)***(37) (MRChannon)* 3-8-8 AClark(7) (n.d) ....hd **12**
Suile Mor **(60)***(41) (BRMillman)* 3-9-0 DHolland(10) (bkwd: mid div: rdn 4f out: bhd fnl f) 1 **13**
733[15] Bowden Rose **(56)***(35) (MBlanshard)* 3-8-10 TSprake(9) (prom over 5f) 1¼ **14**
715[21] Thomas Crown (IRE) **(60)***(34) (NJHWalker)* 3-9-0 RPerham(8) (bhd fnl 3f) 2½ **15**
854[6] Stylish Interval **(66)***(34) (RJHodges)* 3-9-1 (5) SDrowne(16) (rdn 4f out: sn bhd) 3 **16**
882[6] Nautical Jewel **(53)***(1) (MDIUsher)* 3-8-7 RPrice(14) (led: rdn & hdd 3f out: wknd qckly: t.o) ..10 **17**
761[10] Sporting Risk **(60)***(4) (PWHarris)* 3-9-0 GDuffield(17) (prom: wkng whn hmpd over 3f out: t.o) 2 **18**

5/1 BLAZE OF SONG, **10/1** Nautical Jewel, **11/1** Soviet Bride (IRE), Sporting Risk, **12/1** Faustino (op 8/1), Suile Mor, **14/1** Danegold (IRE), Stylish Interval, Kevasingo, Alerting, Care And Comfort, **16/1** Fattash (USA), Sobeloved, Thomas Crown (IRE), **25/1** Nosirrah, Bowden Rose, **33/1** Arctic Poppy (USA), Classic Pet (IRE), CSF £65.57 CT £837.67 TOTE £3.30: £1.30 £2.30 £2.50 £4.40 (£18.50) Trio £60.80 OWNER Mr D. Boocock (MARLBOROUGH) BRED D. G. Mason 18 Rn
1m 44.72 (5.42) SF: 48/31/16/24/10/10/11/15/1/12/2/1/5/-/-/-/-/-

1125 REDENHAM CLAIMING STKS (3-Y.O) (Class F) £3,029.00 (£844.00:£407.00)
6f 212y Stalls: High GOING minus 0.05 sec per fur (G) 3-15 (3-17)

855[5] **Almapa (53)***(68) (RJHodges)* 3-8-6 (5) SDrowne(20) (n.m.r over 2f out: gd hdwy over 1f out: str run to ld last stride) ....— **1**
1012[3] Sapphire Son (IRE) **(48)***(68) (CNWilliams)* 3-8-8v(3) JTate(13) (led: clr over 1f out: ct last stride) ....s.h **2**
963[6] Anegre (IRE) **(60)***(69) (LJHolt)* 3-8-13 MPerrett(14) (a.p: r.o wl ins fnl f) ....½ **3**
727[3] Assumpsit (IRE) **(65)***(59) (SDow)* 3-8-11v GDuffield(16) (plld hrd: a.p: one pce fnl 2f)....3½ **4**
893[5] Two Way Stretch *(43) (GLMoore)* 3-7-9 (5)ow4 AWhelan(17) (nvr nrr) ....nk **5**
1012[2] Nyali Beach (IRE) **(60)***(46)(Fav)(BJMeehan)* 3-8-2 CRutter(4) (chsd ldr stands' side: led over 1f out: r.o one pce) 1½ **6**
971[5] Blasted **(60)***(53) (RHannon)* 3-8-11 JReid(3) (led stands' side over 5f) ....½ **7**
Steepholme *(46) (BRMillman)* 3-8-8 DHolland(15) (unf: nvr nr to chal)....2 **8**
855[2] Nomadic Dancer (IRE) **(52)***(43) (MSSaunders)* 3-8-8 JWilliams(11) (prom over 5f) 1¼ **9**
1072[9] Burnt Sienna (IRE) *(35) (JSMoore)* 3-8-1 NAdams(1) (racd stands' side: bhd fnl 2f)....½ **10**
987[10] Amnesty Bay *(37) (JRFanshawe)* 3-8-4 SWhitworth(6) (prom over 5f) ....½ **11**
867[17] Tilthams **(35)***(30) (DAWilson)* 3-8-1 NGwilliams(19) (n.d) 1½ **12**
Rock Rambler *(45) (LadyHerries)* 3-9-3 WNewnes(18) (neat: s.s: a bhd)....½ **13**
Damocles *(42) (IABalding)* 3-9-3 SO'Gorman(5) (prom over 4f) 1½ **14**
Dazzle Me *(26) (RJBaker)* 3-8-6 SRaymont(7) (a bhd) 2 **15**
1012[9] Horsetrader *(37) (RHannon)* 3-9-3 RPerham(2) (racd stands' side: a bhd) ....hd **16**
Chase the Melody *(28) (MJHeaton-Ellis)* 3-9-3 BThomson(9) (lw: a bhd)....4 **17**
937[15] Silver Academy (IRE) *(19) (MissGayKelleway)* 3-8-9 BRouse(12) (prom over 5f) ....nk **18**
856[12] La Thuile **(44)***(6) (MDIUsher)* 3-8-2 AMcGlone(10) (a bhd)....2½ **19**
848[14] R Dragon **(35)***(2) (MMadgwick)* 3-8-4vow2 AClark(8) (prom over 4f) 2 **20**

3/1 Nyali Beach (IRE), **6/1** Sapphire Son (IRE), **13/2** Blasted, **8/1** Assumpsit (IRE), **12/1** ALMAPA, Nomadic Dancer (IRE), **14/1** Rock Rambler, Damocles, Anegre (IRE), **16/1** Two Way Stretch, Amnesty Bay, **20/1** Horsetrader, **33/1** Chase the Melody, Steepholme, Silver Academy (IRE), La Thuile, **50/1** Tilthams, Dazzle Me, Burnt Sienna (IRE), R Dragon, CSF £80.75 TOTE £18.70: £5.00 £1.90 £8.50 (£36.90) Trio £279.10 OWNER Mr P. Slade (SOMERTON) BRED Miss M. Carrington-Smith 20 Rn 1m 30.74 (5.04) SF: 33/33/34/24/8/11/18/11/8/-/2/-/10/7/-/2/-/-/-/-

1126 TRYON H'CAP (0-80) (3-Y.O+) (Class D) £4,402.50 (£1,320.00:£635.00: £292.50)
6f 212y Stalls: High GOING minus 0.05 sec per fur (G) 3-45 (3-48)

887[7] **Ahjay (45)***(50) (DAWilson)* 5-7-7 NAdams(5) (hdwy 3f out: led ins fnl f: r.o) ....— **1**
450[10] Mr Nevermind (IRE) **(64)***(67) (GLMoore)* 5-8-12 BRouse(19) (a.p: ev ch ins fnl f: r.o) 1 **2**

Pharsical **(59)***(60) (MRChannon)* 4-8-7 ow1 JReid(18) (led: clr over 1f out: hdd ins fnl f) ....nk 3
862[6] Poyle Jezebelle **(46)***(47) (MBlanshard)* 4-7-8 GBardwell(17) (chsd ldrs: hrd rdn 3f out: r.o ins fnl f) ....½ 4
882[9] Indefence (IRE) **(65)***(65) (MRChannon)* 4-8-13 RHughes(3) (hdwy over 1f out: r.o) ....½ 5
873[20] Court Minstrel **(55)***(54) (LJHolt)* 6-8-3 AMcGlone(4) (s.s: gd hdwy 2f out: swtchd rt over 1f out: nt rch ldrs) ....½ 6
870[15] Fionn de Cool (IRE) **(72)***(69) (RAkehurst)* 4-9-3 (3) SSanders(12) (nvr nr to chal) ....¾ 7
749[6] Unprejudice **(66)***(61) (GRimmer)* 4-9-0 MRimmer(7) (lw: hrd rdn & no hdwy fnl 2f) ....¾ 8
887[13] Mislemani (IRE) **(54)***(48) (AGNewcombe)* 5-8-2 ow1 RPrice(8) (n.d) ....hd 9
922[21] Serious Option (IRE) **(75)***(69) (PFICole)* 4-9-9 BThomson(10) (chsd ldr tl wknd over 2f out) ....½ 10
636[8] Chili Heights **(60)***(53) (GBBalding)* 5-8-8 TSprake(1) (b.hind: dwlt: nvr nr ldrs) ....nk 11
946[7] Astral Weeks (IRE) **(80)***(65) (RHannon)* 4-9-7 (7) DaneO'Neill(16) (bhd fnl 2f) 3½ 12
1052[3] Astral Invader (IRE) **(70)***(54)*(Fav)*(MSSaunders)* 3-8-7 JWilliams(13) (prom over 4f) ....nk 13
Face Up **(58)***(34) (BJMeehan)* 8-8-6 ow1 WNewnes(14) (lw: a bhd) 3 14
High Typha **(56)***(33) (MRChannon)* 4-8-4 CRutter(15) (lw: dwlt: a bhd) ....nk 15
817[16] Cracking Prospect **(52)***(26) (BRMillman)* 4-7-9 (5)ow2 AWhelan(6) (a bhd) ....nk 16
731[6] Dia Georgy **(50)***(23) (RGuest)* 4-7-12 AMackay(11) (prom over 4f) 1¼ 17
780[11] Nabjelsedr **(56)***(29) (AGNewcombe)* 5-8-1 (3) DWright(2) (b.hind: a bhd) ....hd 18
975[8] Thatchmaster (IRE) **(57)***(9) (CAHorgan)* 4-8-5v TWilliams(9) (prom over 3f: t.o) 9 19

LONG HANDICAP Ahjay 7-5

5/1 Astral Invader (IRE), **13/2** Fionn de Cool (IRE), **8/1** Poyle Jezebelle, **9/1** Court Minstrel, **10/1** AHJAY, **12/1** Unprejudice, Mr Nevermind (IRE), **14/1** High Typha, Dia Georgy, **16/1** Chili Heights, **20/1** Indefence (IRE), Pharsical, Astral Weeks (IRE), **25/1** Face Up, Serious Option (IRE), Cracking Prospect, **33/1** Mislemani (IRE), Nabjelsedr, Thatchmaster (IRE), CSF £116.56 CT £2,137.57 TOTE £12.50: £2.80 £2.30 £5.00 £2.50 (£72.10) Trio £163.80 OWNER B. R. A. T. S (EPSOM) BRED Robert J. Thomas 19 Rn 1m 30.68 (4.98) SF: 17/34/27/14/32/21/36/28/15/36/20/32/10/1

WEIGHT FOR AGE 3yo-11lb

1127

DURNFORD CONDITIONS STKS (3-Y.O) (Class C) £4,967.00 (£1,853.00: £901.50: £382.50: £166.25: £79.75)
1m 4f Stalls: High GOING minus 0.05 sec per fur (G) 4-20 (4-20)

917[2] **Sebastian** *(107)*(Fav)*(HRACecil)* 3-8-12 AMcGlone(5) (chsd ldr: led over 3f out: sn clr: rdn out) ....— 1
711[3] Nash Terrace (IRE) *(94) (RCharlton)* 3-8-12 JReid(2) (hld up in rr: hdwy 4f out: chsd wnr over 2f out: no imp) 10 2
663* Burning (USA) *(87) (GHarwood)* 3-8-12 BThomson(6) (lw: plld hrd: a.p: one pce fnl 3f) 5 3
Iridal *(73) (HRACecil)* 3-8-7 WNewnes(1) (unf: scope: led: rdn & hdd over 3f out: wknd over 1f out) 7 4
619[10] Tira Heights (USA) **(102)***(72) (RWArmstrong)* 3-8-12 RPrice(7) (plld hrd: rdn 4f out: sn bhd) ...4 5
854* Endowment *(72) (MajorWRHern)* 3-8-12 AClark(3) (rdn over 4f out: sn bhd) ....½ 6

4/5 SEBASTIAN (op 5/4), **3/1** Burning (USA), **5/1** Nash Terrace (IRE) (op 5/2), **11/1** Endowment (6/1-12/1), **33/1** Iridal, Tira Heights (USA), CSF £5.05 TOTE £1.60: £1.10 £3.00 (£3.50) OWNER Lord Howard de Walden (NEWMARKET) BRED Lord Howard de Walden 6 Rn

2m 34.13 (1.53) SF: 83/70/63/49/48/48

1128

NETHERHAMPTON MAIDEN STKS (3-Y.O+ F & M) (Class D) £4,402.50 (£1,320.00: £635.00: £292.50)
1m 1f 209y Stalls: High GOING minus 0.05 sec per fur (G) 4-50 (4-52)

Senorita Dinero (USA) *(82) (MRStoute)* 3-8-6 DHolland(10) (plld hrd: lost pl 4f out: gd hdwy over 1f out: hung rt: led ins fnl f: r.o) ....— 1
Gloriana **(71)***(81) (LadyHerries)* 3-8-7 ow1 JReid(14) (led: rdn over 1f out: hdd ins fnl f: r.o) ....¾ 2
865[4] Eurolink Mischief *(78)*(Fav)*(LMCumani)* 3-8-4 (3)ow1 CHodgson(5) (b.hind: hld up: stdy hdwy over 3f out: sn rdn: r.o ins fnl f) 1¾ 3
Wathbat Mtoto *(76) (LMCumani)* 3-7-13 (7) JoHunnam(12) (w'like: scope: s.s: hdwy over 2f out: edgd rt over 1f out: r.o one pce fnl f) 1 4
Prague Spring *(74) (GRimmer)* 3-8-6 MRimmer(15) (bkwd: a.p: rdn 3f out: one pce fnl 2f)...1½ 5
695[6] Academy Life *(71) (PFICole)* 3-8-6 CRutter(17) (a.p: ev ch over 1f out: wknd ins fnl f) 1¾ 6
Dancing Destiny *(67) (JRFanshawe)* 3-8-6 SWhitworth(7) (nvr nr to chal) 2½ 7
Bird in Blue (IRE) **(65)***(65) (RHannon)* 3-7-13 (7) EGreehy(13) (nvr nrr) 1¼ 8
797[12] Grey Blade *(65) (IABalding)* 3-8-6 SO'Gorman(11) (nvr nrr) ....s.h 9
957[7] Nightscene (IRE) *(59) (TGMills)* 3-8-6 WNewnes(9) (prom: rdn & wknd over 2f out) 3½ 10
372[3] Silver Rondo (USA) *(59) (LordHuntingdon)* 3-8-6 RPerham(1) (chsd ldrs tl wknd over 2f out) ....hd 11

885[8] Peveril Princess **(40)***(57) (GBBalding)* 4-9-7 JWilliams(16) (a bhd) 1¼ **12**
Cafe Glace *(44) (RAkehurst)* 3-8-3 (3) SSanders(4) (bhd fnl 3f) 8 **13**
815[2] Roufontaine *(43) (WRMuir)* 4-9-7 RHughes(3) (lw: prom tl wknd 2f out) 1 **14**
Ahla *(38) (RWArmstrong)* 3-8-6 RPrice(2) (w'like: scope: bit bkwd: a bhd) 3 **15**
Saucy Maid (IRE) *(37) (MajorDNChappell)* 4-9-7 BThomson(8) (bit bkwd: bhd fnl 3f) ....½ **16**
Nita's Choice *(AGNewcombe)* 5-9-2 (5) DGriffiths(6) (prom 5f: t.o) 30 **17**

3/1 Eurolink Mischief (9/4-7/2), **13/2** Gloriana (14/1-6/1), **8/1** SENORITA DINERO (USA) (op 5/1), Saucy Maid (IRE) (op 12/1), Roufontaine, Academy Life (5/1-9/1), **9/1** Dancing Destiny (7/1-11/1), **20/1** Ahla, **25/1** Nightscene (IRE), Silver Rondo (USA), **33/1** Bird in Blue (IRE), Grey Blade, Wathbat Mtoto, Prague Spring, Cafe Glace, **50/1** Peveril Princess, Nita's Choice, CSF £54.74 TOTE £11.30: £2.80 £1.90 £1.30 (£18.20) Trio £29.40 OWNER Mr A. Al Khalifa (NEWMARKET) BRED Sheikh Rashid Bin Mohammed Al-Khalifa et al 17 Rn

2m 10.84 (6.14) SF: 38/37/34/32/30/27/23/21/21/15/15/28/-/14/-/8/-

WEIGHT FOR AGE 3yo-15lb

T/Plpt: £86.20 (125.93 Tckts). T/Qdpt: £39.70 (1.8 Tckts). KH

1104-YORK (L-H)
Thursday May 18th (Good)

WEATHER: Fine but cloudy WIND: Fresh, ½, against

1129

MICHAEL SEELY MEMORIAL GLASGOW CONDITIONS STKS (3-Y.O C & G) (Class B) £8,319.25 (£3,013.00: £1,456.50: £607.50: £253.75)
1m 2f 85y Stalls: Low GOING minus 0.07 sec per fur (G) 2-00 (2-01)

917* **Tamure (IRE)** *(111)*(Fav)*(JHMGosden)* 3-9-2 LDettori(2) (lw: b.hind: hld up: effrt over 3f out: nt clr run & swtchd outside over 2f out: hung lft: r.o wl to ld ins fnl f) ....— **1**
635* Minds Music (USA) *(107) (HRACecil)* 3-8-12 WRyan(1) (lw: hld up: effrt 4f out: rdn to ld over 1f out: hdd ins fnl f: nt qckn towards fin) ....nk **2**
945* Sonic Boy **(108)***(106) (RFJohnsonHoughton)* 3-9-1 PatEddery(4) (led tl over 1f out: kpt on same pce ins fnl f) 2½ **3**
764[3] Kutta *(95) (RWArmstrong)* 3-8-10 MHills(3) (lw: sn chsng ldrs: effrt over 3f out: kpt on same pce fnl 2f) 3½ **4**
720[3] Sayeh (IRE) **(98)***(88) (HThomsonJones)* 3-8-10 RHills(5) (lw: trckd ldr: chal 3f out: wknd 2f out: eased ins fnl f) 5 **5**

5/4 TAMURE (IRE), **5/2** Minds Music (USA), **11/2** Sonic Boy, **6/1** Sayeh (IRE), **12/1** Kutta, CSF £4.55 TOTE £2.20: £1.20 £1.50 (£1.80) OWNER Sheikh Mohammed (NEWMARKET) BRED Sheikh Mohammed bin Rashid al Maktoum 5 Rn 2m 11.58 (4.08) SF: 63/59/58/47/40

1130

LAMBSON - KNIGHT AIR H'CAP (0-95) (3-Y.O) (Class C) £7,960.00 (£2,380.00: £1,140.00: £520.00)
7f 202y Stalls: Low GOING minus 0.07 sec per fur (G) 2-35 (2-36)

980* **Classicy** **(85)***(96+)*(Fav)*(MRStoute)* 3-9-1 5x WRSwinburn(4) (trckd ldrs gng wl: qcknd to ld over 1f out: drvn out: readily) ....— **1**
839* Shinerolla **(66)***(74) (MrsJRRamsden)* 3-7-10 JFanning(7) (hld up & bhd: plld hrd: hmpd 5f out: gd hdwy & nt clr run 2f out: r.o wl towards fin) 1½ **2**
829[5] Quintus Decimus **(77)***(85) (LordHuntingdon)* 3-8-7 MJKinane(8) (hdwy over 3f out: n.m.r 2f out: hung lft & styd on wl ins fnl f) ....hd **3**
936* Abu Simbel (USA) **(91)***(98) (JHMGosden)* 3-9-7 LDettori(12) (b.hind: w ldrs: led 3f out tl over 1f out: kpt on same pce) ....½ **4**
775[6] Neverending (USA) **(85)***(91) (HRACecil)* 3-9-1 WRyan(11) (b.off hind: hld up & bhd: hdwy on outside 3f out: edgd lft & kpt on same pce fnl f) ....nk **5**
829[6] Out on a Promise (IRE) **(79)***(77) (GWragg)* 3-8-9 MHills(5) (lw: bhd whn hmpd 5f out: hdwy on outside 3f out: hung lft & wknd fnl f) 4 **6**
614[3] Clifton Fox **(81)***(76) (JAGlover)* 3-8-11 PatEddery(6) (mde most to 3f out: wknd appr fnl f) ...1½ **7**
Sticks and Stones (IRE) **(85)***(78) (MrsJCecil)* 3-9-1 PaulEddery(13) (bit bkwd: chsd ldrs: chal 3f out: wknd wl over 1f out) 1 **8**
Elite Justice **(70)***(58) (PFICole)* 3-7-9 (5) NVarley(10) (chsd ldrs: outpcd over 3f out: wknd over 2f out) 2½ **9**
678[3] Sheer Danzig (IRE) **(78)***(64) (RWArmstrong)* 3-8-8 RHills(1) (lw: chsd ldrs tl wknd over 2f out) ....¾ **10**
775[2] Rokeby Bowl **(77)***(58) (IABalding)* 3-8-7 KDarley(3) (plld hrd: hmpd & lost pl 5f out: kpt on fnl 3f: n.d) 2½ **11**
971* Maiandros (GR) **(85)***(62) (RCharlton)* 3-9-1 5x JWeaver(2) (lw: plld hrd: trckd ldrs tl lost pl over 5f out: n.d after) 2 **12**
686[7] In Good Faith **(82)***(56) (JJQuinn)* 3-8-12 MBirch(9) (in tch: effrt over 3f out: grad wknd) 1¾ **13**

5/2 CLASSICY, **11/2** Shinerolla, **6/1** Sheer Danzig (IRE), **15/2** Quintus Decimus, **8/1** Out on a Promise (IRE), **10/1** Abu Simbel (USA), **12/1** Clifton Fox, **14/1** Neverending (USA), Sticks and Stones (IRE), Maiandros (GR), **16/1** Rokeby Bowl, **20/1** In Good Faith, **33/1** Elite Justice, CSF £17.64 CT £90.65 TOTE £3.20: £2.10 £2.00 £2.50 (£8.00) Trio £48.70 OWNER Maktoum Al Maktoum (NEWMARKET) BRED S. P. and Major B. P. Hornung 13 Rn
1m 38.61 (2.61) SF: 66/44/55/68/61/47/46/48/28/34/28/32/26

1131 WILLIAM HILL STKS H'CAP (0-105) (3-Y.O) (Class B) £18,762.50 (£5,600.00: £2,675.00: £1,212.50) **6f 214y** Stalls: High GOING minus 0.07 sec per fur (G) 3-05 (3-06)

883⁴ **Anniversarypresent (93)***(100) (GLewis)* 3-9-2b PaulEddery(11) (lw: bhd: gd hdwy over 2f out: n.m.r: styd on wl u.p to ld nr fin) — **1**
914² Lipizzaner (IRE) **(90)***(95) (BWHills)* 3-8-13 MJKinane(9) (lw: chsd ldrs: led ins fnl f: hdd nr fin) ¾ **2**
914* Royal Rebuke **(88)***(93)*(Fav)*(RCharlton)* 3-8-11 PatEddery(1) (trckd ldrs: led over 2f out tl ins fnl f: no ex) s.h **3**
980⁸ Welton Arsenal **(98)***(102) (MRChannon)* 3-9-7 MHills(8) (hld up gng wl: chal 1f out: nt qckn towards fin) ½ **4**
946² Fame Again **(73)***(76) (MrsJRRamsden)* 3-7-10 LCharnock(6) (lw: hld up: stdy hdwy ½-wy: ev ch fnl f: r.o same pce) nk **5**
838² Chiming In **(75)***(65) (MrsJRRamsden)* 3-7-12 JFanning(2) (swtg: bhd whn sltly hmpd over 4f out: hmpd 2f out: kpt on: nvr nr ldrs) 6 **6**
914⁵ Tiler (IRE) **(84)***(72) (MJohnston)* 3-8-7 JWeaver(3) (chsd ldrs tl wknd over 2f out) ½ **7**
914⁶ Impulsive Air (IRE) **(93)***(73) (EWeymes)* 3-9-2 KDarley(10) (lw: chsd ldrs: effrt ½-wy: ev ch tl wknd appr fnl f) 3½ **8**
622⁸ Magna Carta **(92)***(72) (MRStoute)* 3-9-1 WRSwinburn(12) (bit bkwd: trckd ldrs tl lost pl ½-wy) hd **9**
914⁷ Mister Fire Eyes (IRE) **(83)***(61) (CEBrittain)* 3-8-6 BDoyle(5) (lw: chsd ldrs: effrt & swtchd lft over 2f out: grad wknd) 1 **10**
999* Go Hever Golf **(91)***(23) (TJNaughton)* 3-9-0 9x GCarter(7) (b.hind: led tl over 2f out: sn lost pl & eased) 20 **11**
630* Fawj (USA) **(80)***(5) (RWArmstrong)* 3-8-3 RHills(4) (prom: effrt u.p ½-wy: sn lost pl & eased) 3 **12**

5/2 Royal Rebuke, **4/1** Go Hever Golf, **5/1** Fame Again, **8/1** Lipizzaner (IRE), **10/1** Magna Carta, **12/1** Fawj (USA), **14/1** ANNIVERSARYPRESENT, Tiler (IRE), Mister Fire Eyes (IRE), Chiming In, **25/1** Welton Arsenal, **33/1** Impulsive Air (IRE), CSF £116.24 CT £345.74 TOTE £14.80: £2.60 £2.40 £1.50 (£54.00) Trio £57.90 OWNER Mr David Barker (EPSOM) BRED James Underwood 12 Rn
1m 24.31 (2.81) SF: 60/55/53/62/36/25/32/33/32/21/-/-

1132 YORKSHIRE CUP STKS (Gp 2) (4-Y.O+) (Class A) £51,963.00 (£19,167.00: £9,146.00: £3,680.00: £1,402.50: £491.50) **1m 5f 194y** Stalls: Low GOING minus 0.07 sec per fur (G) 3-40 (3-40)

Moonax (IRE) *(125+)*(Fav)*(SbinSuroor)* 4-9-0 PatEddery(1) (h.d.w: trckd ldrs: stdy hdwy over 3f out: led over 2f out: drvn along & r.o strly) — **1**
931* Parthian Springs **(94)***(119) (JHMGosden)* 4-8-9 LDettori(6) (lw: led tl over 2f out: kpt on wl fnl f) 1¼ **2**
1020² Shambo **(111)***(118) (CEBrittain)* 8-8-9 BDoyle(3) (lw: bhd: effrt 4f out: sn outpcd: styd on fnl 2f: nvr able to chal) nk **3**
869* Double Trigger (IRE) **(111)***(118) (MJohnston)* 4-8-9 JWeaver(4) (trckd ldrs: drvn along & outpcd over 3f out: hung lft: styd on ins fnl f) nk **4**
869⁸ Further Flight **(107)***(114) (BWHills)* 9-8-9 MHills(8) (b.hind: hld up: drvn along & outpcd over 4f out: n.d after) 3½ **5**
696* Bold Gait **(102)***(112) (JRFanshawe)* 4-8-9 DHarrison(2) (lw: hld up: effrt 3f out: sn rdn: wknd wl over 1f out) 1¼ **6**
631² Golden Ball (IRE) **(105)***(110) (MRStoute)* 4-8-9 WRSwinburn(7) (lw: trckd ldrs: chal over 3f out: wknd 2f out: eased) 2 **7**

11/4 MOONAX (IRE), **3/1** Double Trigger (IRE), **7/2** Parthian Springs, **6/1** Bold Gait, **8/1** Shambo, **10/1** Golden Ball (IRE), **12/1** Further Flight, CSF £12.35 TOTE £2.90: £1.90 £2.50 (£6.60) OWNER Godolphin (NEWMARKET) BRED Liscannor Stud Ltd in Ireland 7 Rn
2m 58.89 (5.29) SF: 62/56/55/55/51/49/47

1133 DUKE OF YORK STKS (Gp 3) (3-Y.O+) (Class A) £22,242.00 (£8,322.60: £3,996.30: £1,739.10) **6f** Stalls: High GOING minus 0.07 sec per fur (G) 4-10 (4-11)

659* **Lake Coniston (IRE) (120)***(128)*(Fav)*(GLewis)* 4-9-4 PatEddery(4) (lw: mde all: shkn up over 2f out: r.o strly) — **1**

So Factual (USA) *(116) (SbinSuroor)* 5-9-0 LDettori(2) (trckd wnr: effrt 2f out: kpt on wl u.p fnl f) 3 **2**
1100[2] Branston Abby (IRE) **(104)***(104) (MJohnston)* 6-8-11 JWeaver(7) (prom: rdn & outpcd ½-wy: styd on fnl f) 3½ **3**
920[8] Chilly Billy **(116)***(113) (MrsJRRamsden)* 3-8-10 KFallon(5) (lw: stdd s: hld up & plld hrd: effrt over 1f out: hung lft: kpt on towards fin) ....s.h **4**
920[10] Zeb (IRE) **(100)***(101) (BAMcMahon)* 3-8-4 JFortune(1) (lw: s.i.s: sn chsng ldrs: rdn over 2f out: wknd over 1f out) 2 **5**
921[8] Raah Algharb (USA) **(110)***(91) (MRStoute)* 3-8-10 WRSwinburn(6) (bit bkwd: trckd ldrs: plld hrd: wknd 2f out: eased) 6 **6**
Princely Hush (IRE) **(116)***(82) (MBell)* 3-8-10 MFenton(3) (bit bkwd: chsd ldrs: outpcd over 2f out: sn lost pl) 3½ **7**

8/11 LAKE CONISTON (IRE), **7/2** So Factual (USA), **13/2** Chilly Billy, **12/1** Branston Abby (IRE), **14/1** Raah Algharb (USA), Princely Hush (IRE), **33/1** Zeb (IRE), CSF £3.93 TOTE £1.80: £1.30 £2.00 (£2.10) OWNER Highclere Thoroughbred Racing Ltd (EPSOM) BRED J. P. McManus 7 Rn
1m 11.52 (1.92) SF: 69/57/45/44/32/22/13
WEIGHT FOR AGE 3yo-10lb

1134 E.B.F. YORKSHIRE MAIDEN STKS (2-Y.O) (Class D) £5,952.00(£1,776.00: £848.00: £384.00) 6f Stalls: High GOING minus 0.07 sec per fur (G) 4-40 (4-41)

Allied Forces (USA) *(96+)*(Fav)*(HRACecil)* 2-9-0 WRyan(6) (gd sort: chsd ldrs: led over 1f out: rn green: drvn out) ....— **1**
825[2] Bahamian Knight (CAN) *(89)*(Fav)*(DRLoder)* 2-9-0 JWeaver(8) (chsd ldrs: shkn up over 1f out: no ch w wnr) 2½ **2**
Brilliant Red *(88) (PFICole)* 2-9-0 MJKinane(7) (lengthy: unf: mde most tl over 1f out: kpt on same pce) ....½ **3**
996[3] Sualtach (IRE) *(81) (RHollinshead)* 2-9-0 LDettori(11) (lw: trckd ldrs: chal ½-wy: wknd fnl f) 2½ **4**
Mawwal (USA) *(81) (RWArmstrong)* 2-9-0 RHills(9) (leggy: lt-f: s.i.s: sn chsng ldrs: rn green 2f out: kpt on wl towards fin) ....hd **5**
Pleasant Surprise *(73) (MJohnston)* 2-9-0 WRSwinburn(10) (leggy: lt-f: unf: sn wl outpcd: rn green: sme hdwy over 1f out: n.d) 3 **6**
Vola Via (USA) *(69) (IABalding)* 2-9-0 MHills(5) (w'like: cmpt: bit bkwd: chsd ldrs: hung lft ½-wy: wknd 2f out) 1½ **7**
Take A Left *(58) (MrsJRRamsden)* 2-9-0 KFallon(3) (str: cmpt: bkwd: s.s: bhd: sme hdwy 2f out: n.d) 4 **8**
Duo Master *(56) (MrsMReveley)* 2-9-0 KDarley(12) (w'like: bit bkwd: trckd ldrs tl grad wknd fnl 2f) 1 **9**
Reef Raider *(32) (NTinkler)* 2-9-0 PatEddery(1) (w'like: lengthy: s.s: hung bdly lft & sn wl bhd) 9 **10**
Mybotye *(30) (GROldroyd)* 2-9-0 MMcAndrew(4) (gd sort: bit bkwd: chsd ldrs: edgd lft & grad wknd fnl 2f) ....½ **11**
Swish *(26) (NTinkler)* 2-9-0 MBirch(2) (w'like: scope: bkwd: sn outpcd & rn green: a bhd) ...1½ **12**

9/4 ALLIED FORCES (USA), Bahamian Knight (CAN), **15/2** Brilliant Red, **8/1** Vola Via (USA), Mawwal (USA), Pleasant Surprise, **12/1** Sualtach (IRE), **14/1** Take A Left, Duo Master, **25/1** Reef Raider, Swish, **33/1** Mybotye, CSF £8.88 TOTE £3.00: £1.60 £1.50 £2.30 (£3.20) Trio £7.20 OWNER Buckram Oak Holdings (NEWMARKET) BRED Buckram Oak Farm 12 Rn
1m 13.8 (4.20) SF: 33/26/25/18/18/10/6/-/-/-/-/-

1135 LEVY BOARD SEVENTH RACE RATED STKS H'CAP (0-105) (4-Y.O+) (Class B) £8,183.50 (£3,026.50: £1,450.75: £591.25: £233.13: £89.87) **1m 2f 85y** Stalls: Low GOING minus 0.07 sec per fur (G) 5-10 (5-11)

918[6] **Sherman (IRE) (92)***(106) (HThomsonJones)* 4-8-10b RHills(3) (chsd ldrs: led over 1f out: edgd lft u.p: drvn out) ....— **1**
931[4] Marsoom (CAN) **(96)***(110) (BHanbury)* 4-9-0 WRSwinburn(6) (b.hind: trckd ldrs: led over 3f out: hung lft & hdd over 1f out: styd on towards fin) ....nk **2**
1102* Arctic Thunder (USA) **(92)***(99)*(Fav)*(LadyHerries)* 4-8-10 3x KDarley(8) (b: hld up gng wl: effrt 3f out: outpcd over 1f out) 4 **3**
Mr Confusion (IRE) **(89)***(94) (MissSEHall)* 7-8-2 (5) JStack(4) (bhd: hdwy over 4f out: outpcd 3f out: kpt on appr fnl f) 1½ **4**
918[2] Taufan's Melody **(99)***(100) (LadyHerries)* 4-9-3 TIves(7) (lw: hld up: effrt on outside 3f out: hung lft: nvr nr ldrs) 2½ **5**
Barbaroja **(99)***(93) (JGFitzGerald)* 4-9-3b KFallon(9) (sn drvn along: in tch: outpcd over 3f out: kpt on fnl f) 5 **6**

872² Airport (USA) **(102)***(89) (JHMGosden)* 4-9-6 LDettori(10) (b.hind: chsd ldrs: rdn over 3f out: wandered & sn wknd)....4 **7**
913⁶ Garden of Heaven (USA) **(103)***(88) (CEBrittain)* 6-9-7 MJKinane(5) (bhd: effrt 4f out: wknd over 2f out)....1½ **8**
918⁴ Old Hickory (IRE) **(100)***(85) (LMCumani)* 4-9-4 JWeaver(2) (led early: led 8f out tl over 3f out: sn wknd)....nk **9**
Ringmaster (IRE) **(89)***(58) (MHTompkins)* 4-8-7 PRobinson(1) (sn led: hdd 8f out: lost pl over 3f out: eased)....10 **10**

LONG HANDICAP Mr Confusion (IRE) 8-6 Ringmaster (IRE) 8-3

9/4 Arctic Thunder (USA), **5/1** Airport (USA), Marsoom (CAN), Taufan's Melody, **8/1** Old Hickory (IRE), **9/1** Mr Confusion (IRE), SHERMAN (IRE), **14/1** Garden of Heaven (USA), **20/1** Ringmaster (IRE), **33/1** Barbaroja, CSF £53.22 CT £127.40 TOTE £19.10: £3.00 £1.60 £1.70 (£52.90) Trio £43.10 OWNER Mrs H. T. Jones (NEWMARKET) BRED Mrs H. T. Jones 10 Rn

2m 9.35 (1.85) SF: 75/79/68/63/69/62/58/57/54/27

T/Jkpt: £6,483.40 (3.19 Tckts). T/Plpt: £6.60 (5,792.22 Tckts). T/Qdpt: £4.80 (67.2 Tckts). WG

0711-NEWBURY (L-H)
Friday May 19th (Good)
WEATHER: fair WIND: almost nil

1136 CONNELL WILSON MAIDEN STKS (3-Y.O) (Class D) £4,662.50 (£1,400.00: £675.00: £312.50)**1m (straight)** Stalls: Centre GOING minus 0.20 (GF) 2-05 (2-08)

978⁷ **Hoh Express** *(87) (IABalding)* 3-9-0 KDarley(13) (rdn over 2f out: hdwy over 1f out: led wl ins fnl f: r.o wl)....— **1**
853⁸ Restructure (IRE) *(86) (MrsJCecil)* 3-9-0 PaulEddery(8) (a.p: led over 3f out: hrd rdn over 1f out: hdd wl ins fnl f: r.o)....nk **2**
987² Bakers' Gate (USA) *(83)*(Fav)*(JHMGosden)* 3-9-0 LDettori(10) (a.p: rdn over 2f out: ev ch ins fnl f: unable qckn)....1½ **3**
Nashotah *(78) (JRFanshawe)* 3-8-9 DHarrison(14) (leggy: rdn 3f out: hdwy over 1f out: r.o: rn green)....hd **4**
Major Change *(83) (RHannon)* 3-8-7 (7) DaneO'Neill(17) (bit bkwd: a.p: rdn over 2f out: one pce)....s.h **5**
Latching (IRE) *(75) (RFJohnsonHoughton)* 3-8-9 PatEddery(4) (a.p: rdn over 2f out: wknd fnl f)....1½ **6**
Sejaal (IRE) *(74) (JLDunlop)* 3-9-0 RHills(6) (leggy: scope: hld up: rdn over 2f out: wknd fnl f)3 **7**
715¹⁰ Arcatura *(71) (CJames)* 3-9-0 WNewnes(19) (hdwy fnl 2f: nvr nrr)....1½ **8**
Red Morning *(66) (DRCElsworth)* 3-8-4 (5) SDrowne(11) (b: w'like: a mid div)....nk **9**
Masaafaat (USA) *(65) (MRStoute)* 3-8-9 DHolland(9) (leggy: hld up: shkn up over 2f out: nvr plcd to chal)....hd **10**
695¹¹ Lobana (IRE) *(61) (JWHills)* 3-8-9 JWeaver(5) (a mid div)....2 **11**
Dr Frances (IRE) *(57) (CCElsey)* 3-8-9 CRutter(2) (leggy: s.s: nvr nrr)....2 **12**
Laudation (IRE) *(61) (GBBalding)* 3-9-0 JWilliams(15) (unf: scope: nvr nrr)....½ **13**
Early Peace (IRE) *(60) (RHannon)* 3-9-0 RPerham(16) (cmpt: prom over 5f)....¾ **14**
Toat Chieftain *(55) (GHarwood)* 3-9-0 MPerrett(3) (nvr nrr)....2½ **15**
Twice Purple (IRE) *(54) (BJMeehan)* 3-9-0 AClark(20) (bit bkwd: hdwy 4f out: wknd over 2f out)....½ **16**
881⁷ Equasion (IRE) *(48) (GLMoore)* 3-8-9 BRouse(1) (s.s: a bhd)....nk **17**
Petra's Star *(42) (MJHeaton-Ellis)* 3-8-9 GCarter(7) (hld up: rdn over 2f out: sn wknd)....3 **18**
Salamander King *(46) (PWChapple-Hyam)* 3-9-0 JReid(12) (leggy: scope: bit bkwd: s.s: a bhd)....½ **19**
691¹⁵ Peatsville (IRE) *(46) (MRChannon)* 3-9-0 RHughes(18) (a bhd)....hd **20**
Fire Blast *(40) (LMCumani)* 3-8-11 (3) CHodgson(21) (led over 4f)....3 **21**

11/10 Bakers' Gate (USA), **5/1** Latching (IRE), **13/2** HOH EXPRESS, **9/1** Salamander King (op 4/1), **10/1** Masaafaat (USA) (op 6/1), **12/1** Nashotah (op 6/1), **14/1** Sejaal (IRE), **16/1** Restructure (IRE), Fire Blast, **20/1** Major Change, Lobana (IRE), **33/1** Early Peace (IRE), Toat Chieftain, **50/1** Red Morning, Dr Frances (IRE), Laudation (IRE), Equasion (IRE), Petra's Star, Arcatura, Peatsville (IRE), Twice Purple (IRE), CSF £112.52 TOTE £6.60: £1.90 £7.00 £1.10 (£97.40) Trio £46.60 OWNER HOH Supply Ltd (KINGSCLERE) BRED Mrs M. Upsdell 21 Rn

1m 40.16 (3.16) SF: 40/39/36/31/36/28/27/24/19/18/14/10/14/13/8/7/1/-/-/-/-

1137 HIGHCLERE STUD CONDITIONS STKS (2-Y.O F) (Class C) £4,648.00 (£1,732.00: £841.00: £355.00: £152.50: £71.50) **5f 34y** Stalls: Centre GOING minus 0.20 sec per fur (GF) 2-40 (2-40)

852² **Marl** *(103+) (RAkehurst)* 2-8-8 LDettori(5) (hld up: qcknd & led over 1f out: r.o wl)....— **1**

940[3] Satellite Star (IRE) *(84) (MRChannon)* 2-8-8 RHughes(3) (lw: rdn over 2f out: hdwy over 1f out: r.o one pce) 6 2
871* Unconditional Love (IRE) *(90)*(Fav)*(MJohnston)* 2-9-1 DHolland(2) (lw: led over 3f: one pce) ....nk 3
951[2] Hear The Music (IRE) *(74) (BWHills)* 2-8-8 RHills(4) (lw: chsd ldr: ev ch wl over 1f out: sn wknd) 3 4
Queen's Music (USA) *(69) (PFICole)* 2-8-5 CRutter(1) (b.nr hind: leggy: s.s: a bhd) ....¾ 5
852[5] Kandavu *(70) (MMcCormack)* 2-8-11 AClark(7) (spd over 3f) 1½ 6
Pigeon Hole *(61) (RHannon)* 2-8-5 PatEddery(6) (unf: scope: outpcd) 1 7

7/4 Unconditional Love (IRE), **3/1** Hear The Music (IRE), **4/1** MARL, **9/2** Pigeon Hole, **16/1** Queen's Music (USA), **33/1** Satellite Star (IRE), Kandavu, CSF £73.91 TOTE £4.30: £2.00 £4.70 (£94.20) OWNER Sir Eric Parker (EPSOM) BRED Sir Eric Parker 7 Rn
61.98 secs (1.68) SF: 48/29/35/19/14/15/6

1138 WOODHAY CONDITIONS STKS (3-Y.O) (Class B) £8,202.40 (£3,061.60: £1,490.80: £634.00: £277.00: £134.20)
6f 8y Stalls: Centre GOING minus 0.20 sec per fur (GF) 3-10 (3-11)

633* **Sergeyev (IRE) (99)***(106+) (RHannon)* 3-9-5 RHughes(8) (lw: stdd s: stdy hdwy on bit over 1f out: led ins fnl f: pushed out) ....— 1
809a[2] Baaderah (IRE) **(100)***(97) (LMCumani)* 3-8-12 LDettori(5) (lw: w ldr: led over 2f out tl ins fnl f: unable qckn) ....¾ 2
959* Overbrook **(90)***(90) (IABalding)* 3-8-12 PatEddery(6) (led over 3f: one pce) 2½ 3
959[6] Veuve Hoornaert (IRE) **(90)***(82) (RHannon)* 3-8-6 GCarter(10) (rdn over 2f out: hdwy fnl f: nvr nrr) 1 4
920[9] Silca Blanka (IRE) **(105)***(93) (MRChannon)* 3-9-4 KDarley(7) (hld up: rdn 3f out: wknd wl over 1f out) ....nk 5
Great Bear **(104)***(88) (RFJohnsonHoughton)* 3-8-13 JReid(4) (hld up: rdn 3f out: wknd over 2f out) ....s.h 6
622[9] Bahith (USA) **(96)***(88) (HThomsonJones)* 3-8-13 NCarlisle(9) (lw: hld up: rdn 3f out: wknd over 2f out) ....s.h 7
930[3] Tarhhib *(80)*(Fav)*(JHMGosden)* 3-8-8 RHills(2) (a.p: rdn over 1f out: sn wknd) 1 8
952[2] Hinton Rock (IRE) **(101)***(80) (MBell)* 3-8-12 JWeaver(1) (lw: a.p: rdn over 2f out: wknd fnl f) 1½ 9
959[5] Nagnagnag (IRE) **(90)***(73) (SDow)* 3-8-8 PaulEddery(3) (hld up: rdn 3f out: wknd over 1f out) 1¼ 10

5/4 Tarhhib, **5/1** SERGEYEV (IRE), **11/2** Baaderah (IRE), **6/1** Overbrook, **8/1** Silca Blanka (IRE), **10/1** Hinton Rock (IRE), **20/1** Bahith (USA), **25/1** Great Bear, **33/1** Veuve Hoornaert (IRE), Nagnagnag (IRE), CSF £32.48 TOTE £5.60: £2.10 £1.70 £1.70 (£9.30) Trio £12.60 OWNER Mr B. T. Stewart-Brown (MARLBOROUGH) BRED Hugo Merry and Michael Stanley 10 Rn
1m 13.48 (1.68) SF: 63/54/47/39/50/45/45/37/37/30

1139 VODAFONE GROUP TRIAL STKS (Listed) (3-Y.O F) (Class A) £12,380.00 (£3,740.00: £1,340.00: £1,340.00)
1m 2f 6y Stalls: Low GOING minus 0.20 sec per fur (GF) 3-40 (3-41)

620[10] **Spout (109)***(99) (RCharlton)* 3-8-9 PatEddery(8) (4th st: led over 2f out: rdn out) ....— 1
933[13] Fleet Hill (IRE) **(100)***(100) (MRChannon)* 3-8-12 RHughes(7) (2nd st: ev ch ins fnl f: unable qckn) 1¼ 2
868[6] Strutting (IRE) **(92)***(97) (RHannon)* 3-8-9 JReid(4) (led over 7f: one pce fnl f) ....s.h 3
997[5] Bint Zamayem (IRE) *(97) (BWHills)* 3-8-9 RHills(6) (rdn over 2f out: hdwy over 1f out: r.o wl ins fnl f) ....d.h 3
720[6] Dee-Lady **(89)***(95) (WGMTurner)* 3-8-9 TSprake(3) (b: lw: 5th st: rdn over 2f out: swtchd rt over 1f out: one pce) 1 5
868[3] Phantom Gold **(101)***(95)*(Fav)*(LordHuntingdon)* 3-8-9 JWeaver(1) (3rd st: nt clr run over 2f out: rdn over 1f out: nt clr run ins fnl f: nt rcvr) ....nk 6
933[9] Bring on the Choir **(100)***(84) (RBoss)* 3-8-9 KDarley(5) (6th st: rdn over 3f out: wknd wl over 1f out) 7 7
865* White Palace *(81) (JRFanshawe)* 3-8-9 DHarrison(2) (lw: bhd fnl 2f) 1¾ 8

13/8 Phantom Gold, **9/2** White Palace, SPOUT, **15/2** Bring on the Choir (op 5/1), **11/1** Fleet Hill (IRE) (op 6/1), **14/1** Strutting (IRE) (op 8/1), **25/1** Bint Zamayem (IRE), **33/1** Dee-Lady, CSF £42.37 TOTE £4.90: £1.60 £2.10 BZ £1.30 S £1.30 (£24.20) OWNER Lady Rothschild (BECKHAMPTON) BRED Exors of the late Mrs D. M. de Rothschild 8 Rn
2m 11.16 (8.16) SF: 13/14/11/11/9/9/-/-

1140

MIDGHAM H'CAP (0-90) (3-Y.O+) (Class C) £5,998.00 (£1,804.00: £872.00: £406.00) **1m 4f 5y** Stalls: Low GOING minus 0.20 sec per fur (GF) 4-10 (4-11)

841[2] **Zaralaska (78)***(93+)*(Fav)*(LMCumani)* 4-9-6 LDettori(8) (lw: 5th st: led over 1f out: comf).....— **1**
505* Gone for a Burton (IRE) **(84)***(97) (PJMakin)* 5-9-12 KDarley(7) (lw: hdwy 2f out: r.o ins fnl f)....1¼ **2**
938[6] La Spezia **(53)***(66) (MBlanshard)* 5-7-4 (5) MBaird(6) (rdn over 2f out: hdwy over 1f out: r.o ins fnl f)....hd **3**
Whitechapel (USA) **(86)***(99) (LordHuntingdon)* 7-10-0 JWeaver(3) (3rd st: led over 2f out tl over 1f out: unable qckn)....nk **4**
763[4] Bayrak (USA) **(70)***(80) (MJRyan)* 5-8-12 AClark(1) (lw: w ldr: led over 6f out tl over 2f out: one pce)....2½ **5**
860[2] Seren Quest **(78)***(86) (RAkehurst)* 5-9-6 PatEddery(9) (hdwy on ins 4f out: swtchd rt 3f out: wknd over 1f out)....1 **6**
938[4] Shadow Leader **(77)***(83) (MissAJWhitfield)* 4-9-0 (5) RPainter(4) (6th st: wknd over 1f out) 1½ **7**
764[9] Sea Freedom **(80)***(82) (GBBalding)* 4-9-8 JWilliams(2) (led over 5f: 2nd st: wknd over 3f out)....3 **8**
811[3] Farringdon Hill **(75)***(76) (MajorWRHern)* 4-9-3b PaulEddery(10) (4th st: wknd over 3f out) ......¾ **9**
Persian Elite (IRE) **(77)***(70) (PFICole)* 4-9-5 JReid(12) (bhd fnl 3f)....6 **10**
884[10] Rising Spray **(62)***(47) (CAHorgan)* 4-8-4 RHills(5) (a bhd)....6 **11**

5/2 ZARALASKA, **4/1** Seren Quest, **11/2** Farringdon Hill (8/1-5/1), **8/1** Shadow Leader, **9/1** Bayrak (USA), La Spezia, **10/1** Gone for a Burton (IRE), **12/1** Sea Freedom, Whitechapel (USA), **20/1** Rising Spray, **25/1** Persian Elite (IRE), CSF £28.12 CT £189.96 TOTE £3.20: £1.80 £2.20 £2.60 (£27.00) Trio £63.30 OWNER Fittocks Stud Ltd (NEWMARKET) BRED Fittocks Stud Ltd 11 Rn
2m 33.22 (3.92) SF: 62/66/35/68/49/55/52/51/45/39/16

OFFICIAL EXPLANATION **Persian Elite (IRE): The jockey stated that the horse was difficult to settle and found nothing in the final quarter-mile. The trainer's representative added that a shorter trip would suit.**

1141

MAY H'CAP (0-80) (3-Y.O+) (Class D) £4,471.00 (£1,348.00: £654.00: £307.00) **1m 2f 6y** Stalls: Low GOING minus 0.20 sec per fur (GF) 4-40 (4-44)

Smart Generation (77)*(87) (LordHuntingdon)* 4-9-13 JReid(8) (lw: hdwy over 2f out: led over 1f out: rdn out)....— **1**
Virtual Reality **(73)***(81) (AHide)* 4-9-9 AMcGlone(3) (nt clr run 3f out: swtchd lft over 2f out: hdwy over 1f out: r.o)....1½ **2**
884[6] Bookcase **(58)***(63) (DRCElsworth)* 8-8-8 JWilliams(2) (lw: hdwy on ins over 2f out: r.o one pce)....1¾ **3**
864* Clouded Elegance **(78)***(82) (LadyHerries)* 5-10-0 KDarley(1) (hdwy over 3f out: rdn over 2f out: one pce)....½ **4**
1015* Okavango (USA) **(84)***(80)*(Fav)*(JHMGosden)* 3-9-5v 5x LDettori(9) (led over 8f)....5 **5**
853[6] Caerle Lad (IRE) **(70)***(66) (GHarwood)* 4-9-6 AClark(14) (hdwy 4f out: hrd rdn over 2f out: wknd over 1f out)....nk **6**
817* Bold Look **(63)***(58) (PWHarris)* 4-8-13 DHolland(7) (2nd st: hrd rdn & wandered 2f out: wknd over 1f out)....hd **7**
The French Friar (IRE) **(76)***(69) (GBBalding)* 4-9-12 RHills(4) (4th st: wknd over 1f out) 1¼ **8**
634[20] Windrush Lady **(78)***(69) (MMcCormack)* 5-10-0 MPerrett(12) (lw: 6th st: wknd 3f out)....1¾ **9**
Jarzon Dancer **(50)***(29) (DAWilson)* 7-7-7 (7)ow7 RachaelMoody(6) (b: bit bkwd: nvr nrr)....3 **10**
738[17] Cheveley Dancer (USA) **(43)***(28) (DAWilson)* 7-7-7 NAdams(10) (b: s.s: nvr nrr)....½ **11**
981[5] Lesley's Fashion **(66)***(48) (DJSffrenchDavis)* 4-9-2 PatEddery(5) (a bhd)....1¾ **12**
Koathary (USA) **(70)***(51) (LGCottrell)* 4-9-6 DHarrison(13) (bit bkwd: bhd fnl 2f)....1 **13**
956[3] Beauman **(72)***(49) (PDEvans)* 5-9-8 WNewnes(16) (5th st: wknd 4f out)....2½ **14**
873[4] Pistol (IRE) **(61)***(25) (CAHorgan)* 5-8-11 PaulEddery(17) (b.hind: hdwy over 3f out: wknd over 2f out)....8 **15**
783[4] Dusk in Daytona **(65)***(25) (CJames)* 3-8-0 SRaymont(15) (3rd st: wknd over 3f out)....2½ **16**

LONG HANDICAP Jarzon Dancer 5-12 Cheveley Dancer (USA) 7-4

3/1 Okavango (USA), **6/1** Clouded Elegance (op 7/2), Virtual Reality, **9/1** Bold Look (op 6/1), **10/1** Lesley's Fashion, Pistol (IRE), **12/1** SMART GENERATION, The French Friar (IRE) (op 8/1), **14/1** Caerle Lad (IRE), **16/1** Bookcase, **20/1** Beauman, **25/1** Dusk in Daytona, Windrush Lady, **33/1** Koathary (USA), **50/1** Cheveley Dancer (USA), **100/1** Jarzon Dancer, CSF £79.02 CT £1,077.51 TOTE £19.30: £2.80 £1.90 £4.30 £1.60 (£112.50) Trio £350.60 OWNER Mr George Ward (WEST ILSLEY) BRED Lord Halifax 16 Rn2m 6.12 (3.12) SF: 69/63/45/64/47/48/40/51/51/11/10/30/33/31/7

WEIGHT FOR AGE 3yo-15lb

T/Jkpt: Not won; £6,543.46 to Newbury 20/5/95. T/Plpt: £632.60 (38.05 Tckts). T/Qdpt: £89.40 (2.3 Tckts). AK

0930-**NEWMARKET (R-H)**
Friday May 19th (Good)
WEATHER: overcast, cool WIND: mod half bhd

1142 E.B.F. DITCH MAIDEN STKS (2-Y.O F) (Class D) £4,386.00(£1,308.00: £624.00: £282.00) **6f (Rowley)** Stalls: Centre GOING minus 0.37 sec per fur (F) 2-15 (2-16)

Paloma Bay (IRE) *(78+) (MBell)* 2-8-11 MFenton(7) (leggy: scope: plld hrd: trckd ldrs: rdn to ld ins fnl f) ....— 1
Omara (USA) *(73)*(Fav)*(HRACecil)* 2-8-11 WRyan(6) (w'like: scope: prom: led over 2f out tl hdd & no ex ins fnl f).......1¾ 2
Thrilling Day *(69) (NAGraham)* 2-8-11 WRSwinburn(4) (w'like: scope: hld up: hdwy 2f out: no ex ins fnl f).......1½ 3
Naissant *(67) (CEBrittain)* 2-8-11 GHind(1) (neat: scope: lw: s.s: kpt on fnl 2f: nrst fin) ....¾ 4
Classic Flyer (IRE) *(59) (SCWilliams)* 2-8-11 AMackay(10) (w'like: s.i.s: rdn & hdwy 2f out: nvr rchd ldrs).......3 5
650⁶ Victoria Venture *(58) (SPCWoods)* 2-8-11 TIves(8) (led after 1f tl over 2f out: sn btn) ....s.h 6
Dil Dil *(54) (RHannon)* 2-8-11 RCochrane(9) (lt-f: leggy: trckd ldrs: rdn over 2f out: sn edgd rt & no ex).......1½ 7
Dark Truffle *(54) (MrsJCecil)* 2-8-11 GDuffield(5) (w'like: scope: chsd ldrs tl lost pl over 2f out: n.d after).......hd 8
1054⁴ Polish Bear (IRE) *(40) (BJMeehan)* 2-8-11 BDoyle(3) (lw: led 1f: wknd 2f out: eased whn btn).......5 9

13/8 Omara (USA) (op 4/5), **4/1** PALOMA BAY (IRE), **5/1** Dark Truffle, **6/1** Thrilling Day (op 9/1), **12/1** Dil Dil (op 8/1), **16/1** Polish Bear (IRE), Classic Flyer (IRE), **33/1** Victoria Venture, Naissant, CSF £10.26 TOTE £4.60: £1.90 £1.30 £2.10 (£3.20) Trio £14.30 OWNER Mrs E. A. Harris (NEWMARKET) BRED Watership Down Enterprises 9 Rn 1m 13.05 (1.75) SF: 40/35/31/29/21/21/17/17/4

1143 NGK SPARK PLUGS RATED LIMITED STKS (0-100) (4-Y.O+) (Class B) £8,149.56 (£3,044.04: £1,484.02: £633.10: £278.55: £136.73) **7f (Rowley)** Stalls: Centre GOING minus 0.37 sec per fur (F) 2-50 (2-51)

611⁷ **Madly Sharp (86)***(98+) (JWWatts)* 4-8-1 JFanning(1) (trckd ldrs: led on bit over 1f out: sn shkn up & qcknd clr) ....— 1
870¹⁴ Realities (USA) **(98)***(104) (GHarwood)* 5-8-13 WRSwinburn(12) (lw: hld up & bhd: hdwy 3f out: r.o fnl f: nt trble wnr) 2½ 2
870⁷ Classic Sky (IRE) **(99)***(104) (BHanbury)* 4-9-0 MRimmer(10) (lw: in tch: effrt over 2f out: kpt on fnl f).......½ 3
870¹¹ Czarna (IRE) **(87)***(92) (CEBrittain)* 4-8-2 BDoyle(8) (chsd ldrs: no hdwy fnl 2f) ....hd 4
714¹² Sheppard's Cross **(84)***(89) (PTWalwyn)* 4-7-7 (7) MHenry(2) (prom: led 4f out: hdd over 1f out: sn btn) ....½ 5
946* Billy Bushwacker **(82)***(89)*(Fav)*(MrsMReveley)* 4-8-2 ow2 3x RCochrane(4) (bhd: rdn & hdwy 3f out: nt pce to chal) ....hd 6
922* Saseedo (USA) **(90)***(92) (WAO'Gorman)* 5-8-6 ow1 EmmaO'Gorman(7) (in tch: shkn up over 3f out: nvr rchd ldrs) ....¾ 7
953⁶ Band on the Run **(88)***(85) (BAMcMahon)* 8-8-3b FNorton(3) (prom: rdn over 2f out: sn btn)......2 8
870⁸ Belfry Green (IRE) **(96)***(93) (CAHorgan)* 5-8-11 WRyan(5) (hld up: rdn 2f out: nvr trbld ldrs).......s.h 9
665⁵ Gymcrak Premiere **(90)***(87) (GHolmes)* 7-8-5 GDuffield(9) (hld up: rdn over 2f out: no imp)...hd 10
870²² New Capricorn (USA) **(92)***(82) (MAJarvis)* 5-8-7b MFenton(11) (led 1f: wknd over 1f out).........3 11
870²⁵ Masnad (USA) **(97)***(53) (RWArmstrong)* 4-8-12 RPrice(6) (plld hrd: led after 1f tl hdd 4f out: sn wknd & eased).......15 12

13/8 Billy Bushwacker, **6/1** Realities (USA), **7/1** Belfry Green (IRE), **10/1** MADLY SHARP, **11/1** Saseedo (USA), Sheppard's Cross, Classic Sky (IRE), **14/1** Czarna (IRE), **16/1** Band on the Run, New Capricorn (USA), **20/1** Gymcrak Premiere, **33/1** Masnad (USA), CSF £66.52 CT £625.04 TOTE £9.80: £2.80 £2.60 £3.50 (£40.30) Trio £161.30 OWNER Lord Swaythling (RICHMOND) BRED A. K. Zivanaris 12 Rn 1m 23.33 (-0.37) SF: 60/66/66/54/51/51/54/47/55/49/44/15

1144 MITSUBISHI MT-9 H'CAP (0-80) (3-Y.O+) (Class D) £5,796.00(£1,728.00: £824.00: £372.00) **1m 6f (Rowley)** Stalls: High GOING minus 0.37 sec per fur (F)3-20 (3-22)

866³ **Requested (53)***(66) (PBurgoyne)* 8-7-13 (3) DRMcCabe(6) (hld up & bhd: hdwy over 2f out: r.o wl to ld nr fin).......— 1
661¹¹ Trans Siberia **(78)***(91)*(Fav)*(SPCWoods)* 4-9-13 WRyan(1) (lw: plld hrd: prom: ev ch over 2f out: led 1f out tl hdd & no ex nr fin).......nk 2

661[6] Island Blade (IRE) **(59)***(71) (RAkehurst)* 6-8-5 (3) SSanders(5) (hld up: hdwy over 3f out: r.o fnl f) .... ¾ 3
938[2] Pride of May (IRE) **(65)***(75) (RHannon)* 4-9-0b WRSwinburn(9) (led: rdn over 2f out: hdd 1f out: sn btn) 1½ 4
986* Dvorak (IRE) **(67)***(75) (BJMcMath)* 4-9-2 4x AMackay(8) (a.p: ev ch 2f out: btn appr fnl f)...... 1¾ 5
763[13] Broughtons Formula **(49)***(46) (WJMusson)* 5-7-12 FNorton(7) (bit bkwd: prom: rdn 4f out: btn 2f out) 10 6
811[11] Ismeno **(63)***(60) (SDow)* 4-8-12 GDuffield(10) (lw: in tch: rdn 5f out: sn no ch) .... s.h 7
961[2] Artic Courier **(76)***(69) (DJSCosgrove)* 4-9-11 MRimmer(2) (lw: plld hrd: lost pl after 3f: effrt over 2f out: no imp) 3½ 8
795[7] Stoney Valley **(72)***(60) (JRJenkins)* 5-9-7 DBiggs(3) (hld up: rdn over 3f out: sn btn) 4 9
954[2] Paradise Navy **(71)***(57) (CREgerton)* 6-9-1b(5) AProcter(4) (lw: trckd ldrs: effrt over 2f out: sn wknd) 1¾ 10

9/2 Trans Siberia, **11/2** Pride of May (IRE), **13/2** Island Blade (IRE), **7/1** REQUESTED, Dvorak (IRE), Paradise Navy, **15/2** Artic Courier, **8/1** Stoney Valley, **10/1** Broughtons Formula, **20/1** Ismeno, CSF £37.08 CT £198.71 TOTE £14.50: £3.10 £2.40 £1.90 (£42.50) Trio £112.20 OWNER Mr Brook Alder (WANTAGE) BRED Tommy Stack and Partners 10 Rn

2m 59.99 (3.99) SF: 35/60/40/44/44/15/29/38/29/26

1145 KING CHARLES II STKS (Listed) (3-Y.O) (Class A) £11,826.00 (£4,374.00: £2,097.00: £855.00: £337.50: £130.50)

7f (Rowley) Stalls: Centre GOING minus 0.37 sec per fur (F) 3-50 (3-53)

933[5] **Epagris (111)***(106)*(Fav)*(HRACecil)* 3-8-7 WRyan(4) (lw: set slow pce: qcknd 3f out: pushed out ins fnl f) .... — 1
664* Warning Shadows (IRE) *(103) (CEBrittain)* 3-8-7 BDoyle(2) (lw: hld up: hdwy over 3f out: r.o fnl f: nt trble wnr) 1½ 2
Karayb (IRE) *(98) (DMorley)* 3-8-7 RCochrane(5) (hld up: hdwy 3f out: no ex ins fnl f) 2 3
Night Hero (USA) *(98) (MRStoute)* 3-8-12 WRSwinburn(7) (bit bkwd: prom: outpcd 3f out: r.o appr fnl f) 2 4
945[4] Muhab (USA) **(108)***(94) (PTWalwyn)* 3-8-12 GDuffield(6) (lw: w wnr 4f: sn btn) 2 5
868[8] Shefoog **(91)***(85) (RWArmstrong)* 3-8-7 RPrice(1) (hld up: hdwy over 3f out: sn rdn & no imp) 1¾ 6
883[2] Fire Dome (IRE) **(101)***(76) (TGMills)* 3-8-12 TIves(3) (chsd ldrs: rdn 3f out: sn btn) 6 7

4/6 EPAGRIS, **100/30** Night Hero (USA), **10/1** Warning Shadows (IRE) (op 6/1), Muhab (USA) (op 6/1), **14/1** Fire Dome (IRE), **16/1** Karayb (IRE), **40/1** Shefoog, CSF £8.01 TOTE £1.60: £1.10 £3.40 (£5.60) OWNER Mrs H. G. Cambanis (NEWMARKET) BRED Stilvi Compania Financiera S A 7 Rn

1m 24.98 (1.28) SF: 46/43/38/38/34/25/16

1146 SONIA CONNOLLY MEMORIAL CLAIMING STKS (3-Y.O) (Class E) £3,785.00 (£1,130.00: £540.00: £245.00)

1m (Rowley) Stalls: Centre GOING minus 0.37 sec per fur (F) 4-20 (4-22)

667[11] **Smart Guest (104)***(87+)*(Fav)*(MBell)* 3-9-7 MFenton(3) (trckd ldrs: led on bit over 2f out: easily) .... — 1
847[7] Woodrising **(55)***(57) (LadyHerries)* 3-7-10b GBardwell(2) (lw: chsd ldrs: kpt on u.p fnl 2f: no ch w wnr) 2½ 2
752[8] Miles Away (IRE) **(58)***(51) (JRFanshawe)* 3-8-0 FNorton(8) (rdn & hdwy over 3f out: r.o fnl f)..5 3
780[11] Hong Kong Dollar **(53)***(60) (BJMeehan)* 3-8-9b BDoyle(11) (led over 5f: one pce appr fnl f)....hd 4
Equilibrium **(66)***(54) (JWHills)* 3-8-4 RCochrane(7) (hdwy 3f out: one pce appr fnl f) .... ½ 5
1023[11] Magic Leader (IRE) **(45)***(47) (TTClement)* 3-7-8 (7) SLanigan(10) (bhd: hdwy 4f out: sn rdn: no imp fnl f) 1¾ 6
867[5] Most Welcome News **(45)***(51) (JRJenkins)* 3-8-9 DBiggs(1) (lw: prom: rdn & ev ch 3f out: sn wknd) 2 7
Good (IRE) **(51)***(59) (DTThom)* 3-9-0 (3) DRMcCabe(6) (h.d.w: bhd: rdn 2f out: nvr nr ldrs)....s.h 8
Dismissive (IRE) *(22) (DrJDScargill)* 3-8-1 (7) CDomergue(4) (chsd ldrs 4f: sn rdn & wknd) ...14 9
Keep Quiet **(53)** *(WJMusson)* 3-7-10 AMackay(9) (a bhd) 6 10
Danehill Chief *(20) (MAJarvis)* 3-9-5 GDuffield(5) (wl grwn: s.i.s: hdwy after 2f: wknd 3f out) .... ¾ 11

8/11 SMART GUEST, **11/2** Equilibrium, **10/1** Danehill Chief, **12/1** Keep Quiet, Woodrising (op 8/1), Miles Away (IRE), **16/1** Hong Kong Dollar, **33/1** Good (IRE), Dismissive (IRE), Most Welcome News, Magic Leader (IRE), CSF £10.65 TOTE £1.60: £1.30 £1.80 £4.00 (£3.90) Trio £69.90 OWNER Mrs D. Weatherby (NEWMARKET) BRED Ahmed M. Foustok 11 Rn

1m 38.67 (1.67) SF: 57/27/21/30/24/17/21/29/-/-/-

Smart Guest clmd J McLaughlin £16,000

1147 ASHLEY MAIDEN STKS (3-Y.O) (Class D) £4,542.00 (£1,356.00: £648.00: £294.00)
1m 4f (Rowley) Stalls: High GOING minus 0.37 sec per fur (F) 4-55 (4-58)

Larrocha (IRE) *(80+)*(Fav)*(LMCumani)* 3-8-9 WRSwinburn(6) (gd sort: scope: trckd ldrs: led over 3f out: easily)........— 1
Kymin (IRE) *(76+)* *(LMCumani)* 3-8-2 (7) JoHunnam(11) (b.hind: w'like: bkwd: in tch: plld out & hdwy 3f out: r.o fnl f)........3 2
Eelious (USA) *(77)* *(CEBrittain)* 3-9-0 BDoyle(5) (a.p: rdn & one pce fnl 2f)........3 3
Jellaby Askhir *(74)* *(HRACecil)* 3-9-0 WRyan(10) (wl grwn: in tch: pushed along 5f out: kept on: nt pce to chal)........2 4
Eurolink Shadow *(71+)* *(LMCumani)* 3-8-7 (7) GMitchell(4) (gd sort: bkwd: trckd ldrs: rdn over 2f out: btn appr fnl f)........2½ 5
815[11] Tajar (USA) **(73)***(62)* *(DMorley)* 3-9-0 RCochrane(1) (s.i.s: hld up & bhd: hdwy fnl 2f: nvr nr to chal)........7 6
635[19] Coggle *(57)* *(NAGraham)* 3-8-9 MFenton(8) (chsd ldr: rdn 4f out: sn wknd)........hd 7
Opaque *(61)* *(LMCumani)* 3-8-11 (3) OUrbina(9) (neat: scope: bhd fnl 5f)........¾ 8
968[3] Dahlenburg (IRE) *(60)* *(JHMGosden)* 3-9-0 GHind(7) (led over 8f: wknd appr fnl f)........nk 9
968[9] Menshaar (USA) *(40)* *(JHMGosden)* 3-8-11 (3) DRMcCabe(3) (rdn 6f out: a bhd)........15 10
What's Secreto (USA) *(PAKelleway)* 3-9-0 MWigham(2) (wl grwn: bkwd: s.s: rdn & wandered 7f out: sn bhd: virtually p.u appr fnl f)........dist 11

9/4 LARROCHA (IRE) (op 4/1), **5/2** Jellaby Askhir (op 5/4), **4/1** Tajar (USA) (3/1-9/2), **7/1** Dahlenburg (IRE) (3/1-8/1), **10/1** Eelious (USA) (6/1-14/1), **16/1** Eurolink Shadow, **40/1** Kymin (IRE), Opaque, **50/1** Coggle, Menshaar (USA), What's Secreto (USA), CSF £68.23 TOTE £3.40: £1.30 £6.70 £2.90 (£36.30) Trio £177.60 OWNER Sheikh Mohammed (NEWMARKET) BRED K. and Mrs Prendergast 11 Rn 2m 33.68 (4.38) SF: 35/31/32/29/26/17/12/16/15/-/-

1148 TUDDENHAM LIMITED STKS (0-70) (4-Y.O+) (Class E) £4,815.00 (£1,440.00: £690.00: £315.00)
7f (Rowley) Stalls: Centre GOING minus 0.37 sec per fur (F) 5-25 (5-26)

503[9] **Blockade (USA) (68)***(78)* *(MBell)* 6-8-11 MFenton(8) (t: mde all: rdn & r.o wl fnl f)........— 1
876[2] Sharp Rebuff **(70)***(72)*(Fav)*(PJMakin)* 4-8-11 WRSwinburn(9) (a.p: chsd wnr fnl 2f: no imp).2½ 2
Narbonne **(58)***(62)* *(BJMcMath)* 4-8-6 RCochrane(12) (dwlt: racd alone far side & sn prom: ev ch 2f out: wknd fnl f)........2½ 3
1071[2] Moujeeb (USA) **(60)***(66)* *(PatMitchell)* 5-8-11v JFanning(3) (hdwy over 2f out: no ex fnl f)........nk 4
927[5] Allinson's Mate (IRE) **(70)***(69)* *(TDBarron)* 7-9-0 GDuffield(5) (lw: chsd ldrs: rdn 2f out: kept on same pce)........s.h 5
984[6] Kindergarten Boy (IRE) **(63)***(62)* *(RBoss)* 4-8-11 WRyan(13) (kept on fnl 2f: nvr rchd ldrs) ...1½ 6
Prizefighter **(70)***(62)* *(SGollings)* 4-8-11 FNorton(14) (lw: hdwy 3f out: btn appr fnl f)........hd 7
984[4] Awesome Venture **(45)***(61)* *(MCChapman)* 5-8-4 (7) CMunday(11) (prom: rdn over 2f out: sn wknd)........½ 8
380[5] Frisky Miss (IRE) **(70)***(58)* *(KOCunningham-Brown)* 4-8-6 (3) DRMcCabe(2) (lw: bhd: rdn over 2f out: nvr trbld ldrs)........½ 9
354[7] On Y Va (USA) **(66)***(49)* *(RJRWilliams)* 8-8-6 DBiggs(4) (chsd ldrs 4f)........2½ 10
1061[7] Orthorhombus **(63)***(56)* *(DJSCosgrove)* 6-9-0b MRimmer(1) (sn rdn & bhd)........nk 11
Cheveux Mitchell **(63)***(33)* *(PAKelleway)* 8-8-11 MWigham(10) (w wnr over 4f)........9 12
611[13] Caspian Gold **(60)***(29)* *(CNAllen)* 4-8-11 TIves(7) (prom over 4f)........1¾ 13
Lord Alfie **(49)***(13)* *(BJMeehan)* 6-8-11 BDoyle(6) (b.hind: plld hrd: rdn 3f out: a bhd)........7 14

3/1 Sharp Rebuff, **5/1** Allinson's Mate (IRE), **13/2** BLOCKADE (USA), **8/1** Kindergarten Boy (IRE) (op 5/1), **9/1** Moujeeb (USA), **10/1** On Y Va (USA), Prizefighter, **14/1** Orthorhombus, **20/1** Narbonne, Awesome Venture, Lord Alfie, **25/1** Frisky Miss (IRE), **33/1** Cheveux Mitchell, Caspian Gold, CSF £25.44 TOTE £6.40: £2.40 £1.80 £3.90 (£6.20) Trio £69.80 OWNER Mr A. M. Warrender (NEWMARKET) BRED Patricia C. Warrender 14 Rn
1m 24.72 (1.02) SF: 52/46/36/40/43/36/36/35/32/23/30/7/3/-
T/Plpt: £100.30 (132.44 Tckts). T/Qdpt: £6.60 (19.1 Tckts). Dk

0924-THIRSK (L-H)
Friday May 19th (Good to firm)
WEATHER: sunny WIND: mod ½ bhd

1149 STATION ROAD CLAIMING STKS (4-Y.O+) (Class F) £3,127.80(£865.80: £413.40)
1m 4f Stalls: High GOING minus 0.42 sec per fur (F) 2-00 (2-00)

729[2] **Elementary (76)***(64)*(Fav)*(NJHWalker)* 12-8-7 (5) JStack(2) (mde most: clr appr st: r.o wl) ....— 1

935[13] Shabanaz **(64)***(57) (WRMuir)* 10-8-12 JCarroll(3) (a chsng ldrs: effrt ent st: nt pce to chal)......5 **2**
1014[6] Pharamineux **(70)***(55) (RAkehurst)* 9-8-12 JFortune(9) (lw: trckd ldrs: effrt ent st: one pce) 2 **3**
1039[4] Kimberley Boy **(58)***(53) (MBrittain)* 5-8-12 KFallon(4) (sddle slipped: a chsng ldrs: one pce fnl 3f)......1 **4**
672[11] Greek Night Out (IRE) **(42)***(38) (MrsVAAconley)* 4-8-7 MDeering(1) (chsd ldrs tl hrd rdn & wknd appr st)......8 **5**
673[12] Lawful Love (IRE) *(45) (TWDonnelly)* 5-8-13 (3) JTate(10) (chsd ldrs tl wknd 3f out)......1¼ **6**
1025[5] Don't Cry **(20)***(29) (DonEnricoIncisa)* 7-8-1 KimTinkler(6) (wl bhd tl sme late hdwy)......½ **7**
375[11] Goldenberry **(40)***(16) (JParkes)* 4-8-1 LCharnock(5) (nvr trbld ldrs)......10 **8**
929[11] Wassl's Guest (IRE) *(11) (RFMarvin)* 4-8-11 MTebbutt(8) (a bhd)......11 **9**
818[15] Newgate Bubbles **(22)** *(BWMurray)* 4-8-5 DeanMcKeown(7) (b.hind: disp ld 2f: sn lost pl & wl bhd)......30 **10**

7/4 ELEMENTARY, **5/2** Shabanaz, **11/4** Pharamineux, **15/2** Kimberley Boy, **20/1** Greek Night Out (IRE), **33/1** Wassl's Guest (IRE), Don't Cry, Goldenberry, **50/1** Lawful Love (IRE), Newgate Bubbles, CSF £6.58 TOTE £2.60: £1.20 £1.50 £1.20 (£4.10) Trio £2.40 OWNER Mr Paul Green (WANTAGE) BRED Ballymaglassan Stud 10 Rn 2m 32.6 (2.60) SF: 46/39/37/35/20/27/11/-/-/-

1150 GORDON FOSTER MAIDEN STKS (3-Y.O+) (Class D) £4,205.50

(£1,258.00: £603.00: £275.50)
1m Stalls: Low GOING minus 0.42 sec per fur (F) 2-30 (2-32)

Iktasab *(83) (EALDunlop)* 3-8-12 SWhitworth(7) (bit bkwd: trckd ldrs: led 2f out: r.o)......— **1**
Itab (USA) *(75) (EALDunlop)* 3-8-4 (3) JTate(6) (led tl hdd 2f out: kpt on)......1¾ **2**
Northern Trove (USA) *(79) (GMMoore)* 3-8-12 MTebbutt(2) (str: cmpt: bit bkwd: in tch: hdwy 2f out: kpt on same pce ins fnl f)......½ **3**
955[2] Silvicolous (USA) *(75)*(Fav)*(PWChapple-Hyam)* 3-8-12 BThomson(11) (lw: chsd ldrs: effrt & swtchd 3f out: nt qckn appr fnl f)......2 **4**
Diamond Crown (USA) *(70) (BHanbury)* 3-8-7 (5) JStack(5) (leggy: bhd: hdwy ent st: chsng ldrs & rdn over 1f out: nt qckn)......2½ **5**
657[8] Cross Talk (IRE) *(67) (RHollinshead)* 3-8-9 (3) AGarth(1) (bhd tl styd on wl fnl 3f)......1½ **6**
616[6] Stand Tall *(62) (CWThornton)* 3-8-12 DeanMcKeown(8) (mid div: hdwy 3f out: wknd over 1f out)......2½ **7**
924[4] Statistician *(55) (JohnBerry)* 3-8-12 MBirch(10) (w ldr to st: sn wknd)......3½ **8**
Enchanted Cottage *(51) (MDHammond)* 3-8-12 DaleGibson(3) (a bhd)......1¾ **9**
673[16] Oleron *(46) (JNorton)* 3-8-7 ACulhane(9) (a bhd)......s.h **10**
Sun Mark (IRE) *(39) (MrsSMAustin)* 4-9-10 JMarshall(12) (a bhd)......6 **11**

4/7 Silvicolous (USA), **6/1** Itab (USA), **8/1** Statistician, **9/1** Diamond Crown (USA) (op 6/1), **14/1** Stand Tall, **20/1** IKTASAB, **33/1** Sun Mark (IRE), Northern Trove (USA), **50/1** Enchanted Cottage, Cross Talk (IRE), **66/1** Oleron, CSF £126.91 TOTE £26.40: £3.90 £1.70 £6.50 (£31.90) Trio: Not won; £343.40 to Thirsk 20/5/95. OWNER Maktoum Al Maktoum (NEWMARKET) BRED Floors Farming 11 Rn 1m 37.4 (1.80) SF: 43/35/39/35/30/27/22/15/11/6/11
WEIGHT FOR AGE 3yo-12lb

1151 DICK PEACOCK SPRINT H'CAP (0-75) (3-Y.O+) (Class D) £4,971.00

(£1,488.00: £714.00: £327.00)
6f Stalls: High GOING minus 0.42 sec per fur (F) 3-00 (3-03)

838[9] **Benzoe (IRE) (66)***(77+) (MrsJRRamsden)* 5-9-7 KFallon(15) (lw: hdwy ½-wy: led ins fnl f: sn clr: comf)......— **1**
1094[2] Statius **(64)***(70)*(Fav)*(TDBarron)* 3-8-9 JFortune(17) (chsd ldrs: led over 1f out: hdd & no ch w wnr ins fnl f)......1¾ **2**
926[4] Ned's Bonanza **(68)***(65) (MDods)* 6-9-9 SWhitworth(8) (styd on fnl 2f: hung lft 1f out: nrst fin)......3½ **3**
1021[8] Elle Shaped (IRE) **(66)***(61) (DNicholls)* 5-9-7 AlexGreaves(1) (swtchd rt s: led tl hdd over 1f out: no ex)......¾ **4**
434[21] White Sorrel **(70)***(57) (AHarrison)* 4-9-6 (5) JStack(12) (lw: trckd ldrs: effrt 2f out: nt qckn)......3 **5**
Heart Broken **(52)***(37) (JGFitzGerald)* 5-8-7 LCharnock(16) (bit bkwd: cl up tl rdn & btn appr fnl f)......¾ **6**
823[3] Brecongill Lad **(66)***(51) (MissSEHall)* 3-8-11 NConnorton(11) (prom: effrt over 2f out: rdn & no ex)......s.h **7**
1088[15] Green's Bid **(52)***(30) (DWChapman)* 5-8-7 ACulhane(5) (lw: racd alone far side: no ch fnl 2f)......2½ **8**
952[4] Thick as Thieves **(72)***(46) (RonaldThompson)* 3-9-3 DeanMcKeown(13) (rdn ½-wy: nvr bttr than mid div)......1¾ **9**
93[13] Boursin (IRE) **(72)***(45) (PCalver)* 6-9-13 DaleGibson(10) (chsd ldrs 4f)......hd **10**

640⁷ Euro Rebel **(59)***(30) (MHEasterby)* 3-8-4b MBirch(6) (spd over 3f: sn wknd) ....¾ **11**
838⁴ General Gubbins **(60)***(27) (JHetherton)* 4-9-1 BThomson(9) (nvr wnt pce) 1¾ **12**
926¹⁷ Double Glow **(51)***(16) (NBycroft)* 3-7-10 NKennedy(14) (dwlt: a bhd) ....¾ **13**
Invigilate **(55)***(16) (MartynWane)* 6-8-7 (3) JTate(4) (n.d) 1½ **14**
984⁹ Coalisland **(49)** *(RIngram)* 5-7-13v(5)ow11 PMcCabe(7) (sn bhd) 2 **15**
Matisse **(54)***(9) (JDBethell)* 4-8-9 JCarroll(2) (a bhd) ....nk **16**
994⁵ Tutu Sixtysix **(50)***(1) (DonEnricoIncisa)* 4-8-5v KimTinkler(3) (nvr wnt pce) 1¼ **17**

LONG HANDICAP Coalisland 7-4

3/1 Statius, **6/1** Ned's Bonanza, **7/1** Thick as Thieves, White Sorrel, **8/1** General Gubbins, **9/1** Brecongill Lad, **11/1** Elle Shaped (IRE) (8/1-12/1), **12/1** BENZOE (IRE), Euro Rebel, **20/1** Tutu Sixtysix, Boursin (IRE), Heart Broken, Invigilate, **25/1** Matisse, **33/1** Coalisland, Double Glow, Green's Bid, CSF £50.61 CT £233.82 TOTE £16.80: £2.80 £1.50 £1.70 £2.10 (£22.90) Trio £109.60 OWNER Mr Tony Fawcett (THIRSK) BRED Mrs P. Grubb 17 Rn

1m 10.4 (0.70) SF: 59/42/47/43/39/19/23/12/18/27/2/9/-/-/-/-/-

WEIGHT FOR AGE 3yo-10lb

OFFICIAL EXPLANATION **General Gubbins: the jockey reported that the gelding had given him no feel, and probably acted better on a turning track.**

1152

KILBURN H'CAP (0-80) (3-Y.O+) (Class D) £4,569.70 (£1,366.60:£654.80: £298.90) **5f** Stalls: High GOING minus 0.42 sec per fur (F) 3-30 (3-31)

926³ **Lady Sheriff (44)***(49) (MWEasterby)* 4-7-10b LCharnock(2) (mde all: edgd lft fnl f: r.o) ....— **1**
426⁷ Superpride **(72)***(73) (TDBarron)* 3-9-1 JFortune(12) (a chsng ldrs: kpt on same pce fnl f) 1¼ **2**
701⁶ Shadow Jury **(54)***(55) (DWChapman)* 5-8-6b DeanMcKeown(9) (hdwy ½-wy: nt qckn fnl f) ....hd **3**
906* Cool Edge (IRE) **(68)***(68)*(Fav)*(MHTompkins)* 4-9-6 PRobinson(5) (chsd ldrs: effrt 2f out: kpt on wl) ....hd **4**
926¹⁰ Sir Tasker **(56)***(50) (JLHarris)* 7-8-8 JCarroll(7) (lw: chsd ldrs: nt qckn appr fnl f) 2 **5**
926⁶ Tenor **(65)***(58) (DNicholls)* 4-9-3 AlexGreaves(1) (sn pushed along: styd on fnl 2f: no imp) ....nk **6**
994⁷ Sonderise **(49)***(37) (NTinkler)* 6-8-1v TWilliams(11) (s.i.s: sn drvn along & bhd: sme late hdwy: n.d) 1½ **7**
926¹² Just Bob **(75)***(62) (SEKettlewell)* 6-9-8 (5) JStack(13) (s.s: swtchd lft ½-wy: nvr plcd to chal) ....½ **8**
926¹⁹ High Domain (IRE) **(76)***(62) (TDBarron)* 4-9-7 (7) JennyBenson(4) (lw: sn outpcd & bhd) ....hd **9**
535¹⁴ Rankaidade **(54)***(37) (DonEnricoIncisa)* 4-8-6 KimTinkler(10) (in tch tl outpcd fnl 2f) 1 **10**
926⁷ The Fed **(56)***(35) (RMWhitaker)* 5-8-8 ACulhane(8) (cl up 3f: sn rdn & btn) 1¼ **11**
688¹⁰ Barbezieux **(44)***(7) (MDods)* 8-7-10 DaleGibson(6) (b.nr hind: bhd fr ½-wy) 5 **12**
926* My Abbey **(60)***(22) (EJAlston)* 6-8-12 KFallon(3) (spd over 3f: sn wknd) ....nk **13**

11/4 Cool Edge (IRE), **6/1** My Abbey, **7/1** Just Bob, LADY SHERIFF, Tenor, **9/1** Superpride, The Fed, **10/1** Shadow Jury, Sir Tasker, **11/1** Sonderise, **14/1** Barbezieux, **20/1** High Domain (IRE), **25/1** Rankaidade, CSF £72.69 CT £603.46 TOTE £11.80: £3.10 £2.90 £3.40 (£123.70) Trio £200.20 OWNER Mr E. J. Mangan (SHERIFF HUTTON) BRED Jeremy Green and Sons 13 Rn

58.1 secs (0.90) SF: 29/44/35/48/30/38/17/42/42/17/15/-/2

WEIGHT FOR AGE 3yo-9lb

OFFICIAL EXPLANATION **My Abbey: the jockey stated that the horse lost interest as a result of interference at the start.**

1153

MOWBRAY (S) STKS (I) (3-Y.O+) (Class G) £2,646.20 (£733.20:£350.60) **7f** Stalls: Low GOING minus 0.42 sec per fur (F) 4-00 (4-01)

1060⁸ **Rushen Raider (60)***(51+)*(Fav)*(KWHogg)* 3-8-3 (7) ADaly(1) (chsd ldrs: outpcd ½-wy: hdwy & nt clr run on ins over 1f out: swtchd: styd on wl to ld post) ....— **1**
*766*⁵ Dante's Rubicon (IRE) **(47)***(51) (JDBethell)* 4-9-7 JCarroll(4) (chsd ldrs: effrt u.p over 3f out: led over 1f out: jst ct) ....s.h **2**
927¹³ Gant Bleu (FR) **(40)***(46) (RMWhitaker)* 8-9-7 ACulhane(5) (hld up & plld hrd: smooth hdwy 3f out: ev ch over 1f out: unable qckn) 2 **3**
968¹⁰ Freckles Kelly *(40) (MHEasterby)* 3-8-5 MBirch(6) (led tl over 1f out: one pce) ....¾ **4**
732⁶ Daily Challenger (USA) **(58)***(40) (RonaldThompson)* 3-8-10 DeanMcKeown(3) (hld up: sme hdwy 3f out: nvr nr ldrs) 2 **5**
672¹⁴ Rosina's Folly **(48)***(33) (JLHarris)* 4-8-11 (5) PMcCabe(2) (dwlt: bhd: sme hdwy over 2f out: nvr nr to chal) 1 **6**
1044⁴ My Godson **(45)***(36) (FJO'Mahony)* 5-9-7 TWilliams(8) (chsd ldrs: sn drvn along: outpcd ½-wy: kpt on fnl 2f: n.d) ....¾ **7**
969¹⁰ Kings Vision **(60)***(9) (BSRothwell)* 3-8-5 (5) JStack(9) (t: hld up: bhd & racd wd: drvn along ½-wy: sn lost tch) 12 **8**
1060¹⁰ Fairy's Son **(38)***(3) (DNicholls)* 3-8-10 AlexGreaves(7) (w ldr: reminders 3f out: sn wknd: eased) 2½ **9**
Red Slaney (IRE) **(49)***(3) (RAkehurst)* 4-9-7b BThomson(10) (swtg: chsd ldrs tl rdn & lost pl ½-wy: no rspnse) ....s.h **10**

100/30 RUSHEN RAIDER, **7/2** Red Slaney (IRE) (op 9/4), **9/2** My Godson (op 7/1), **6/1** Kings Vision, **7/1** Dante's Rubicon (IRE), Gant Bleu (FR), **10/1** Daily Challenger (USA), **12/1** Freckles Kelly (op 8/1), **14/1** Rosina's Folly, **16/1** Fairy's Son, CSF £28.36 TOTE £5.80: £2.00 £2.80 £3.80 (£18.10) Trio £75.10 OWNER Exors of the late Mr P J White (ISLE OF MAN) BRED M. H. D. Madden and Partners 10 Rn 1m 26.3 (3.60) SF: 17/28/23/6/6/10/13/-/-/-

WEIGHT FOR AGE 3yo-11lb

No bid

1154 EASINGWOLD RATING RELATED MAIDEN LIMITED STKS (0-70) (3-Y.O) (Class E) £3,275.50 (£976.00: £465.00: £209.50)

1m Stalls: Low GOING minus 0.42 sec per fur (F) 4-30 (4-31)

- 779[4] **Sheama (USA) (69)***(69+) (WJarvis)* 3-8-9 BThomson(2) (lw: trckd ldrs: shkn up & qcknd to ld over 1f out: sn clr: eased nr fin) — 1
- 689[2] Dance King **(66)***(68) (DNicholls)* 3-9-0 AlexGreaves(8) (lw: chsd ldr: effrt over 2f out: kpt on same pce fnl f) 3 2
- 797[10] Trazl (IRE) **(67)***(62)*(Fav)*(JLDunlop)* 3-8-9 JFortune(7) (lw: prom: drvn along over 3f out: styd on appr fnl f) ¾ 3
- Belle of the Ball (IRE) **(70)***(61) (EALDunlop)* 3-8-6 (3) JTate(3) (bit bkwd: led: rdn & hung rt over 1f out: sn hdd: kpt on same pce) s.h 4
- Magical Blues (IRE) **(70)***(50) (KTIvory)* 3-8-9 (5) JStack(4) (hld up: effrt & hung lft over 2f out: eased ins fnl f) 8 5
- 854[5] Smolensk (IRE) **(67)***(48) (JBerry)* 3-9-0 JCarroll(6) (chsd ldrs: drvn along over 3f out: sn lost pl) 1 6
- 772[11] Good Match (IRE) **(60)***(46) (NTinkler)* 3-9-0 KimTinkler(5) (plld hrd: w ldrs tl lost pl after 3f: n.d after) 1¼ 7
- 573[8] Ballard Lady (IRE) **(40)***(41) (JSWainwright)* 3-8-9 DeanMcKeown(1) (dwlt: a in rr) hd 8

2/1 Trazl (IRE), **3/1** SHEAMA (USA), **9/2** Magical Blues (IRE), **6/1** Belle of the Ball (IRE), Smolensk (IRE), **8/1** Dance King, **12/1** Good Match (IRE), **50/1** Ballard Lady (IRE), CSF £26.81 TOTE £3.80: £1.60 £1.80 £1.40 (£10.10) OWNER Mr Mitaab Abdullah (NEWMARKET) BRED White Fox Farm 8 Rn 1m 38.9 (3.30) SF: 25/24/18/17/6/4/2/-

1155 MOWBRAY (S) STKS (II) (3-Y.O+) (Class G) £2,646.20 (£733.20: £350.60)

7f Stalls: Low GOING minus 0.42 sec per fur (F) 5-05 (5-06)

- 1021[11] **Veloce (IRE) (67)***(52)*(Fav)*(ABailey)* 7-9-7v JFortune(9) (b: hld up & bhd: hdwy 3f out: styd on to ld ins fnl f: drvn out) — 1
- 875[3] Okay Baby (IRE) **(44)***(44) (MHTompkins)* 3-8-5 PRobinson(1) (led over 2f: led over 2f out tl ins fnl f: nt qckn) 1¼ 2
- *1030[4]* Red River Rose (IRE) **(45)***(41) (NPLittmoden)* 3-8-1b(5)ow1 TGMcLaughlin(3) (s.s: bhd tl styd on wl appr fnl f: nt rch ldrs) 1½ 3
- Milltown Classic (IRE) *(35) (JParkes)* 3-8-5 MDeering(5) (bhd: swtchd rt & kpt on fnl 2f: nvr rchd ldrs) 2½ 4
- 748[10] Respectable Jones **(40)***(38) (RHollinshead)* 9-9-0 (7) AEddery(8) (hld up: effrt & chsd ldrs over 2f out: wknd over 1f out) 1 5
- Goram's Girl (IRE) **(54)***(25) (MrsASwinbank)* 3-8-5 NConnorton(4) (chsd ldrs: sn drvn along: outpcd & lost pl ½-wy: n.d after) 3½ 6
- Jhan Jeon **(50)***(24) (RAFahey)* 3-8-5 ACulhane(7) (chsd ldrs: effrt over 3f out: edgd rt & wknd over 1f out) nk 7
- 987[11] White Knowle *(18) (PTDalton)* 5-9-2 LCharnock(2) (led over 4f out tl over 2f out: wknd qckly over 1f out) 2½ 8
- 578[15] Jamaica Bridge **(46)***(12) (SGNorton)* 5-9-7 (5) JStack(6) (sn chsng ldrs: hrd rdn & wknd over 2f out: eased) 7 9

8/11 VELOCE (IRE), **9/2** Okay Baby (IRE), **7/1** Red River Rose (IRE), **10/1** Jamaica Bridge, **12/1** Respectable Jones, **14/1** Jhan Jeon, **20/1** Goram's Girl (IRE), Milltown Classic (IRE), **33/1** White Knowle, CSF £5.13 TOTE £1.70: £1.20 £1.10 £2.10 (£2.50) Trio £7.60 OWNER Mr Maximo Gonzalez (TARPORLEY) BRED Miss C. O'Toole 9 Rn

1m 27.0 (115.30 under best) (-116.00) SF: 19/-/-/-/5/-/-/-/-

WEIGHT FOR AGE 3yo-11lb

No bid

1156 HELMSLEY H'CAP (0-85) (4-Y.O+) (Class D) £5,588.00 (£1,664.00: £792.00: £356.00)

2m Stalls: Low GOING minus 0.42 sec per fur (F) 5-35 (5-35)

- 696[2] **Shadirwan (IRE) (72)***(83+)*(Fav)*(RAkehurst)* 4-9-8 BThomson(4) (trckd ldr: shkn up to ld over 2f out: drvn along & styd on strly) — 1

998[5] Argyle Cavalier (IRE) **(61)***(71) (MJohnston)* 5-8-13 JCarroll(1) (hld up: effrt over 3f out: styd on u.p appr fnl f: nt rch wnr)........1½ **2**
998[12] Thunderheart **(77)***(84) (LMCumani)* 4-9-13 KFallon(5) (lw: chsd ldrs: drvn along ½-wy: one pce fnl 3f)........2½ **3**
Chief Minister (IRE) **(68)***(74) (TDyer)* 6-9-6 JFortune(2) (lw: chsd ldrs: pushed along 6f out: one pce fnl 3f)........1¼ **4**
1036[2] Vain Prince **(43)***(43) (NTinkler)* 8-7-9bow1 LCharnock(3) (led tl over 2f out: wknd over 1f out)........5 **5**

13/8 SHADIRWAN (IRE), **3/1** Argyle Cavalier (IRE), **4/1** Thunderheart, Chief Minister (IRE), **12/1** Vain Prince, CSF £6.47 TOTE £2.80: £1.60 £1.50 (£3.30) OWNER Mr Richard Armstrong (EPSOM) BRED His Highness The Aga Khans Studs S.C. 5 Rn 3m 27.4 (4.40) SF: 51/41/52/44/13
WEIGHT FOR AGE 4yo-2lb
T/Plpt: £451.80 (20.6 Tckts). T/Qdpt: £4.60 (13.35 Tckts). AA

1023-HAMILTON (R-H)
Saturday May 20th (Good to firm)
WEATHER: sunny WIND: almost nil

1157 PURE GENIUS APPRENTICE H'CAP (0-70) (3-Y.O+) (Class F)
£2,648.00 (£753.00: £374.00)
5f 4y Stalls: Low GOING minus 0.41 sec per fur (F) 6-20 (6-26)

984[5] **Aquado (48)***(55) (ALForbes)* 6-8-12 DDenby(17) (hld up: hdwy 2f out: rdn to ld wl ins fnl f: r.o)........— **1**
999[12] Crystal Loop **(61)***(67) (ABailey)* 3-8-8 (8) AngelaGallimore(13) (chsd ldrs: led ins fnl f: hdd & no ex cl home)........nk **2**
1023[8] Serious Hurry **(47)***(45) (RMMcKellar)* 7-8-3 (8) NKinnon(16) (led: rdn appr fnl f: sn hdd & no ex)........2½ **3**
831[3] Daily Starshine (IRE) **(60)***(50) (JBerry)* 3-8-9b(6) CLowther(18) (prom: rdn along 2f out: one pce fnl f)........2½ **4**
904[10] Another Nightmare (IRE) **(53)***(42) (RMMcKellar)* 3-8-3 (5) KSked(7) (in tch: hdwy over 2f out: styd on same pce fnl f)........½ **5**
906[6] Gondo **(60)***(41) (EJAlston)* 8-9-7 (3) JEdmunds(15) (hld up: hdwy 2f out: styd on: nvr able to chal)........2½ **6**
926[5] Featherstone Lane **(54)***(32) (MissLCSiddall)* 4-8-10v(8) TSiddall(11) (prom: rdn over 2f out: styd on one pce)........¾ **7**
1042* Giggleswick Girl **(54)***(32) (MRChannon)* 4-8-10 (8) DSweeney(8) (s.i.s: sn rdn along: styd on fnl 2f: nrst fin)........s.h **8**
1042[2] Kenesha (IRE) **(52)***(30) (DANolan)* 5-8-11 (5) RMullen(6) (prom: sn rdn along: no imp fnl 2f) .s.h **9**
268[5] Cheeky Chappy **(38)***(15) (DWChapman)* 4-7-13b(3) JBramhill(4) (cl up stands' side: rdn & one pce fnl f)........nk **10**
1023* Diet **(47)***(21) (MissLAPerratt)* 9-8-11v RWaterfield(12) (mid div: rdn along ½-wy: nvr trbld ldrs) 1 **11**
Pallium (IRE) **(60)***(26) (MrsAMNaughton)* 7-9-5 (5) DLockhart(10) (sn outpcd: a bhd)........2½ **12**
1023[2] Tee Tee Too (IRE) **(66)***(24)*(Fav)*(PCHaslam)* 3-9-1 (6) CarolDavison(3) (prom stands' side tl wknd qckly appr fnl f)........2½ **13**
904[4] Mister Westsound **(47)***(3) (MissLAPerratt)* 3-7-11 (5) JoanneWebster(9) (mid div: rdn & wknd ½-wy)........½ **14**
877[13] Muzz (IRE) **(51)***(2) (RMMcKellar)* 4-8-10 (5) JennyBenson(14) (sn outpcd: n.d)........1¾ **15**
Quick Thinker (IRE) **(53)***(3) (WSCunningham)* 3-8-5 (3) JoHunnam(5) (unruly s: s.i.s: n.d)......nk **16**
880[11] Robaty's Law (IRE) **(47)** *(PMonteith)* 3-7-13 (3) GMacDonald(2) (racd stands' side: rdn ½-wy: sn outpcd)........2½ **17**
My Silversmith (IRE) **(29)** *(PMonteith)* 4-7-4 (3) BHalligan(1) (s.i.s: a bhd)........5 **18**
LONG HANDICAP My Silversmith (IRE) 7-2

11/2 Tee Tee Too (IRE), **7/1** Mister Westsound, Giggleswick Girl, **15/2** Diet (5/1-8/1), **8/1** AQUADO, **10/1** Featherstone Lane, Daily Starshine (IRE), **12/1** Crystal Loop, Kenesha (IRE) (op 8/1), **16/1** Gondo, **20/1** Cheeky Chappy, **25/1** Pallium (IRE), Serious Hurry, Quick Thinker (IRE), **40/1** Muzz (IRE), **50/1** Another Nightmare (IRE), **66/1** Robaty's Law (IRE), My Silversmith (IRE), CSF £92.64 CT £2,093.55 TOTE £8.80: £2.00 £4.20 £13.30 £3.80 (£58.10) Trio £213.00 OWNER Mr K. Nicholls (UTTOXETER) BRED Lord Howard de Walden 18 Rn
59.7 secs (1.40) SF: 38/41/28/24/16/24/15/15/13/-/4/9/-/-/-/-/-/-
WEIGHT FOR AGE 3yo-9lb

1158 TATTERSALLS MAIDEN AUCTION STKS (2-Y.O) (Class E) £3,038.20 (£919.60: £448.80: £213.40) **5f 4y** Stalls: Low GOING minus 0.41 sec per fur (F) 6-50 (6-51)

878[2] **Red River Valley** *(72) (DenysSmith)* 2-7-13 (3) DWright(5) (mde all: rdn & edgd lft fnl f: r.o wl)........— **1**

919[4] Double Diamond (IRE) *(71)*(Fav)*(MJohnston)* 2-8-7 DHolland(3) (cl up: ev ch whn rdn ½-wy: styd on one pce fnl f) 1¾ 2
Marjorie Rose (IRE) *(53) (ABailey)* 2-7-11 GBardwell(1) (chsd ldrs: rdn & outpcd ½-wy: styd on ins fnl f)....2½ 3
964[3] Shafir (IRE) *(36) (JBerry)* 2-7-6 (7) PFessey(6) (swvd bdly rt s: bhd tl styd on strly fnl f)....6 4
Miletrian Refurb (IRE) *(28) (MRChannon)* 2-8-7 AClark(2) (in tch: rdn along ½-wy: sn outpcd)....5 5
996[4] Just Rory *(19) (EJAlston)* 2-8-2b AMackay(4) (trckd ldrs: ev ch tl rdn & wknd qckly wl over 1f out)....1¼ 6

7/4 Double Diamond (IRE), **2/1** RED RIVER VALLEY, **3/1** Marjorie Rose (IRE), **8/1** Shafir (IRE) (op 5/1), Miletrian Refurb (IRE) (op 5/1), **33/1** Just Rory, CSF £6.19 TOTE £3.40: £3.00 £1.80 (£3.10) OWNER Mr Denys Smith (BISHOP AUCKLAND) BRED R. J. Vines 6 Rn

60.5 secs (2.20) SF: 15/14/-/-/-/-

1159 TWO PART POUR CLAIMING STKS (2-Y.O) (Class F) £2,759.00 (£774.00: £377.00) **6f 5y** Stalls: Low GOING minus 0.41 sec per fur (F) 7-20 (7-21)

755[2] **Thorntoun Jewel (IRE)** *(48) (MJohnston)* 2-7-13 TWilliams(7) (chsd ldr: led & edgd lft 1½f out: styd on wl)....— 1
1035[3] Imprimis (IRE) *(44) (CNAllen)* 2-7-8 (5) MBaird(8) (cl up: rdn & ev ch appr fnl f: r.o one pce)....1½ 2
964[5] Homeland *(44) (CWThornton)* 2-8-10 DeanMcKeown(2) (prom: rdn & outpcd ½-wy: styd on one pce fnl f)....4 3
1035* Monsieur Culsyth *(40)*(Fav)*(JBerry)* 2-8-12 JCarroll(4) (mde most: led tl rdn & hung lft appr fnl f: sn hdd & no ex)....2½ 4
1077[3] Mustaffa (IRE) *(14) (MRChannon)* 2-8-2 AClark(6) (cl up: rdn & ev ch whn hmpd & swtchd 1½f out: sn btn)....6 5
Sikosarki (USA) *(2) (WSCunningham)* 2-8-9 GBardwell(5) (rdn along ½-wy: sn outpcd)....7 6
638[6] Annagh *(WTKemp)* 2-7-9 AMackay(3) (sn bhd: nvr wnt pce)....13 7

15/8 Monsieur Culsyth, **3/1** Imprimis (IRE), THORNTOUN JEWEL (IRE), **5/1** Mustaffa (IRE), **16/1** Homeland, **25/1** Sikosarki (USA), **66/1** Annagh, CSF £11.64 TOTE £3.60: £1.80 £2.40 (£7.60) OWNER Mr W. M. Johnstone (MIDDLEHAM) BRED Jamestown House Stud 7 Rn

1m 14.6 (4.60) SF: -/-/-/-/-/-/-
Thorntoun Jewel (IRE) clmd JBalding £5,000

1160 DRAUGHT GUINNESS H'CAP (0-70) (4-Y.O+) (Class E) £3,969.20 (£1,202.60: £587.80: £280.40) **1m 5f 9y** Stalls: High GOING minus 0.41 sec per fur (F) 7-50 (7-50)

1025* **Noyan (48)***(61)*(Fav)*(LLungo)* 5-9-1 KDarley(2) (hld up: hdwy u.p over 3f out: led & edgd lft 2f out: styd on gamely)....— 1
1025[2] Mentalasanythin **(56)***(67) (ABailey)* 6-9-9 AMackay(4) (trckd ldrs: rdn & ev ch over 2f out: chsd wnr fnl f: no imp)....1½ 2
534[8] Mac Rambler **(30)***(41) (NBycroft)* 8-7-6 (5) NVarley(7) (hld up: rdn & outpcd over 3f out: styd on wl ins fnl f: nrst fin)....hd 3
1039[3] Scalp 'em (IRE) **(42)***(52) (PDEvans)* 7-8-9 AClark(10) (trckd ldrs: disp ld 2f out: sn rdn & one pce)....½ 4
811[8] Cliburnel News (IRE) **(57)***(61) (ALForbes)* 5-9-5 (5) AProcter(9) (prom: rdn & one pce fnl 2f)....5 5
1025[3] Guards Brigade **(45)***(47) (JHetherton)* 4-8-12 NKennedy(1) (led tl hdd 2f out: sn btn)....2 6
Bajan Affair **(26)***(22) (MissLCSiddall)* 5-7-2 (5) MBaird(3) (hld up: hdwy over 3f out: rdn & btn appr fnl f)....5 7
1046[4] Lightning Quest (IRE) **(32)***(25) (JSWainwright)* 4-7-13b LCharnock(6) (cl up: rdn over 3f out: grad wknd)....2 8
879[4] Jarrow **(39)***(25) (MrsAMNaughton)* 4-8-6v TWilliams(11) (mid div: rdn ent st: wknd over 2f out)....6 9
874[6] Friar Street (IRE) **(48)***(14) (EJAlston)* 5-9-1 JCarroll(8) (in tch: rdn over 3f out: sn wknd)....16 10
968[7] Young Steven **(50)** *(WTKemp)* 4-9-0 (3) DRMcCabe(5) (w ldrs tl rdn & wknd ½-wy: sn eased)....20 11

7/4 NOYAN, **5/2** Mentalasanythin, **7/1** Scalp 'em (IRE), **8/1** Jarrow, **9/1** Guards Brigade, **14/1** Cliburnel News (IRE), Bajan Affair, **16/1** Lightning Quest (IRE), Friar Street (IRE), **33/1** Young Steven, **50/1** Mac Rambler, CSF £7.05 CT £156.69 TOTE £3.30: £1.70 £1.80 £8.80 (£2.90) Trio £113.30 OWNER Mr C. H. McGhie (CARRUTHERSTOWN) BRED Oakgrove Stud 11 Rn

2m 50.1 (4.40) SF: 41/47/21/32/41/27/2/5/5/-/-

1161 PERFECT PINT (S) H'CAP (0-60) (3-Y.O+) (Class G) £2,731.00 (£766.00: £373.00)
1m 3f 16y Stalls: High GOING minus 0.41 sec per fur (F) 8-20 (8-23)

1046[3] **Lord Advocate (26)***(42) (DANolan)* 7-7-7b(5) NVarley(9) (mde all: rdn & styd on wl fnl 2f) — **1**
991[5] Monkey Wench (IRE) **(48)***(57) (JBerry)* 4-9-6v JCarroll(10) (hld up & bhd: hdwy wl over 3f out: chsd wnr fnl 2f: sn rdn & no imp) 5 **2**
986[2] Preston Guild (IRE) **(52)***(60)*(Fav)*(ALForbes)* 5-9-5 (5) AProcter(6) (a.p: rdn 3f out: r.o one pce) ¾ **3**
909[5] Gold Desire **(34)***(36) (MBrittain)* 5-8-6 GBardwell(11) (bhd: hdwy & styd on fnl 2f: nrst fin) 4 **4**
905[13] Doubling Dice **(35)***(33) (RAllan)* 4-8-7 SMaloney(8) (mid div: rdn & no imp fnl 3f) 2½ **5**
1025[8] Sylvan Celebration **(24)***(19) (MissLAPerratt)* 4-7-10 TWilliams(2) (mid div: styd on fnl f: nvr able to chal) 2 **6**
790[3] Dundeelin **(34)***(27) (JLEyre)* 4-8-6 RLappin(14) (prom: rdn 3f out: grad wknd) 1½ **7**
Tocco Jewel **(23)***(16) (MJRyan)* 5-7-4 (5) MBaird(18) (hld up: hdwy ent st: rdn & one pce fnl 2f) nk **8**
784[6] Venture Fourth **(22)***(12) (EJAlston)* 6-7-1 (7) DLockhart(17) (bhd: rdn ent st: n.d) 2 **9**
Cadeaux Premiere **(32)***(19) (DenysSmith)* 4-8-4 ow2 DeanMcKeown(12) (s.i.s: nvr trbld ldrs) ¾ **10**
Plum Dennis **(37)***(23) (NBycroft)* 4-8-9 AMackay(15) (mid div: rdn over 3f out: nvr able to chal) 1¾ **11**
841[11] Diamond Crown (IRE) **(47)***(30) (MartynWane)* 4-9-5 LCharnock(4) (bhd: hdwy & rdn wl over 2f out: nvr trbld ldrs) 2½ **12**
1026[3] Jackmanii **(47)***(26) (WTKemp)* 3-7-13 (3) DRMcCabe(1) (bhd: rdn ent st: nt rch ldrs) 2½ **13**
954[8] Mhemeanles **(50)***(29) (CaptJWilson)* 5-9-5 (3) DWright(13) (chsd ldrs: rdn over 3f out: eased whn wl btn appr fnl f) s.h **14**
992[12] Wild Adventure **(23)** *(DWChapman)* 6-7-9 NKennedy(16) (trckd ldrs: wknd 3f out: sn eased) 5 **15**
430[21] Alpine Skier (IRE) **(42)***(1) (MrsMReveley)* 4-9-0b KDarley(3) (chsd ldrs: rdn & wknd qckly 3f out) 9 **16**
818[17] Petal's Jarred **(32)** *(WStorey)* 5-7-11 (7) PFessey(7) (a rr div) ½ **17**
672[18] Icanspell **(42)** *(WStorey)* 4-9-0b JFanning(5) (cl up: wknd qckly ent st: sn bhd) 20 **18**

11/4 Preston Guild (IRE), **5/1** Gold Desire, **11/2** Monkey Wench (IRE) (op 7/2), **7/1** Jackmanii, **12/1** Alpine Skier (IRE) (op 7/1), Diamond Crown (IRE), **14/1** Sylvan Celebration, Doubling Dice, **16/1** Cadeaux Premiere, Tocco Jewel, **20/1** Plum Dennis, Venture Fourth, LORD ADVOCATE, Dundeelin, **33/1** Mhemeanles, Icanspell, Petal's Jarred, **66/1** Wild Adventure, CSF £130.59 CT £380.80 TOTE £22.00: £2.10 £1.70 £1.60 £1.50 (£107.40) Trio £31.60) OWNER Mrs J. McFadyen-Murray (WISHAW) BRED London Thoroughbred Services Ltd 18 Rn

2m 24.1 (5.10) SF: 15/30/33/9/6/-/-/-/-/-/-/3/-/2/-/-/-/-
WEIGHT FOR AGE 3yo-17lb
No bid

1162 ARTHUR GUINNESS MAIDEN STKS (3-Y.O+) (Class D) £3,741.40 (£1,133.20: £553.60: £263.80)
1m 4f 17y Stalls: High GOING minus 0.41 sec per fur (F) 8-50 (8-50)

929[2] **Embracing** *(62+)*(Fav)*(MRStoute)* 3-8-1 KDarley(1) (trckd ldrs: drvn to ld wl over 1f out: sn qcknd clr: eased fnl f: easily) — **1**
1038[4] Sayyed Alraqs (USA) *(58) (MAJarvis)* 3-8-6 JCarroll(2) (led 2f: trckd ldr: led over 2f out tl hdd wl over 1f out: nt pce of wnr) 7 **2**
824[8] Prince Equiname *(56) (DEddy)* 3-8-6 JFanning(3) (plld hrd: cl up: led over 3f out: hdd over 2f out: one pce) 1½ **3**
1026[4] Philmist *(50) (JHetherton)* 3-8-1 NKennedy(5) (led after 2f tl hdd & rdn over 3f out: no ex) ½ **4**
Glenrock Dancer (IRE) *(38) (WTKemp)* 3-8-0 (5)ow4 PMcCabe(4) (in tch: rdn ent st: wl outpcd fnl 3f) 9 **5**

1/5 EMBRACING, **4/1** Sayyed Alraqs (USA), **14/1** Prince Equiname, **20/1** Philmist, **50/1** Glenrock Dancer (IRE), CSF £1.82 TOTE £1.50: £1.00 £2.80 (£1.50) OWNER Maktoum Al Maktoum (NEWMARKET) BRED Gainsborough Stud Management Ltd 5 Rn

2m 38.4 (6.40) SF: 13/9/7/1/-

T/Plpt: £48.90 (189.41 Tckts). T/Qdpt: £4.90 (21.6 Tckts).
GB

1065-LINGFIELD (L-H)
Saturday May 20th (Good to firm)
WEATHER: overcast WIND: almost nil

1163 E.B.F. CIDER MAIDEN STKS (2-Y.O) (Class D) £4,045.00 (£1,210.00: £580.00: £265.00) **5f** Stalls: Centre GOING minus 0.20 sec per fur (GF) 6-00 (6-01)

Cayman Kai (IRE) *(78+)*(Fav)*(RHannon)* 2-9-0 PatEddery(2) (str: scope: mde virtually all: pushed out) — **1**
Tarf (USA) *(68) (PTWalwyn)* 2-8-9 RHills(3) (unf: scope: w wnr: ev ch wl over 1f out: unable qckn) 1½ **2**
Hurricane Dancer (IRE) *(63) (SPCWoods)* 2-8-2 (7) CWebb(4) (leggy: dwlt: outpcd: hdwy over 1f out: r.o) 1¾ **3**
1047[6] Mystery Matthias *(59) (MissBSanders)* 2-8-4 (5) AWhelan(1) (hld up: rdn over 3f out: one pce) 1 **4**
No Sympathy *(43) (GLMoore)* 2-8-9 BRouse(6) (neat: bit bkwd: a bhd) 5 **5**
Illegally Yours *(39) (LMontagueHall)* 2-8-9 RPrice(5) (unf: a bhd) 1¼ **6**
Paojiunic (IRE) *(35) (LMCumani)* 2-9-0 LDettori(7) (cmpt: bit bkwd: spd 3f) 3 **7**

11/8 CAYMAN KAI (IRE), **9/4** Tarf (USA), **11/4** Paojiunic (IRE) (op 6/4), **12/1** Mystery Matthias, **33/1** Hurricane Dancer (IRE), No Sympathy, Illegally Yours, CSF £4.88 TOTE £2.60: £1.30 £2.40 (£3.30) OWNER Mr I. A. N. Wight (MARLBOROUGH) BRED Tommy Burns 7 Rn
59.4 secs (2.40) SF: 39/29/24/20/4/-/-

1164 GIN & TONIC (S) H'CAP (0-60) (3-Y.O+) (Class F) £3,426.20 (£953.20: £458.60)
5f Stalls: Centre GOING minus 0.20 sec per fur (GF) 6-30 (6-31)

1070[10] **Lift Boy (USA)** **(42)***(50) (AMoore)* 6-8-10 CandyMorris(11) (a.p: rdn over 1f out: led ins fnl f: drvn out) — **1**
856[5] Harry's Coming **(55)***(62) (RJHodges)* 11-9-4 (5) SDrowne(8) (rdn 3f out: hdwy over 1f out: n.m.r & r.o wl fnl f) nk **2**
1032[6] Sunshine Belle **(45)***(50) (GMMoore)* 3-8-4 NAdams(1) (led: hrd rdn over 1f out: hdd ins fnl f: unable qckn) ½ **3**
1016[7] Mister Raider **(49)***(54) (SMellor)* 3-8-1b(7) ADaly(9) (swtg: hrd rdn over 1f out: hdwy fnl f: r.o wl) hd **4**
972[8] Halbert **(42)***(45) (MRChannon)* 6-8-3 (7) JDennis(2) (hld up: rdn over 2f out: one pce) ¾ **5**
1070[12] Waders Dream (IRE) **(47)***(49) (PatMitchell)* 6-9-1v MFenton(10) (rdn thrght: hdwy over 1f out: one pce ins fnl f) hd **6**
856[16] Purbeck Centenary **(44)***(42) (PHowling)* 5-8-12 RHughes(7) (b: w ldr: hrd rdn & ev ch over 1f out: wknd ins fnl f) 1¼ **7**
1070[15] Top Tycoon (IRE) **(40)***(38) (JJBridger)* 4-8-3 (5) AWhelan(12) (hrd rdn over 1f out: hdwy fnl f: nvr nrr) hd **8**
904[7] Oneineverycolour **(47)***(45) (PDEvans)* 3-7-13 (7) AmandaSanders(13) (nvr nr to chal) hd **9**
Certificate-X **(56)***(49) (MartynMeade)* 4-9-10 VSlattery(15) (bit bkwd: prom 3f) 1½ **10**
1050[4] Windrush Boy **(56)***(47)*(Fav)*(JRBosley)* 5-9-10 JReid(6) (a.p: rdn over 2f out: wknd fnl f) ½ **11**
1032[12] Lucy's Gold **(36)***(26) (MJRyan)* 4-8-4b DBiggs(14) (prom over 3f) nk **12**
1057[9] Paley Prince (USA) **(53)***(38) (MDIUsher)* 9-9-0 (7) CAdamson(3) (sme hdwy 1f out: sn wknd) 1¾ **13**
753[11] Hi Kiki **(48)***(26) (MrsMMcCourt)* 4-9-2b RHills(4) (bhd fnl 2f) 2 **14**
334[8] Europharm Lassie **(41)***(15) (GLMoore)* 4-8-9v BRouse(16) (bit bkwd: spd over 3f: dead) 1¼ **15**

100/30 Windrush Boy (5/1-3/1), **9/2** Harry's Coming, **9/1** Paley Prince (USA) (op 6/1), LIFT BOY (USA), **10/1** Waders Dream (IRE), **12/1** Halbert, Europharm Lassie, Hi Kiki, Mister Raider, **14/1** Purbeck Centenary, **16/1** Oneineverycolour, **20/1** Sunshine Belle, **25/1** Lucy's Gold, Certificate-X, Top Tycoon (IRE), CSF £48.75 CT £731.83 TOTE £11.50: £2.00 £1.80 £6.40 (£25.40) Trio £201.20 OWNER Mr A. Moore (BRIGHTON) BRED Paul & Arnold Bryant in USA 15 Rn
59.82 secs (2.82) SF: 28/40/19/23/23/27/20/16/14/27/25/4/16/4/-
WEIGHT FOR AGE 3yo-9lb
No bid.
STEWARDS' ENQUIRY Daly suspended 29-30/5/95 (excessive use of whip).

1165 OASTWELL WINES H'CAP (0-80) (3-Y.O) (Class D) £4,340.70 (£1,299.60: £623.80: £285.90) **7f** Stalls: Centre GOING minus 0.20 sec per fur (GF) 7-00 (7-01)

971[4] **Dancing Heart** **(69)***(78) (BJMeehan)* 3-9-0 BDoyle(7) (racd far side: led: rdn over 1f out: hdd nr fin: fin 2nd, hd: awrdd r) — **1**

813[6] Wandering Minstrel (IRE) **(60)***(65) (JMPEustace)* 3-8-5 GCarter(1) (lw: racd far side: a.p: rdn over 3f out: hmpd over 1f out: one pce: fin 3rd, 1½l: plcd 2nd) ... **2**
Apollono **(62)***(71) (RAkehurst)* 3-8-7 DHarrison(5) (racd far side: hdwy on ins over 3f out: barged thro over 1f out: led nr fin: fin 1st: disq: plcd 3rd) ... **3**
Balance of Power **(76)***(63) (RAkehurst)* 3-9-7 RHills(6) (racd far side: a.p: rdn over 2f out: wknd over 1f out) ...9 **4**
1052* Greenwich Again **(71)***(54) (TGMills)* 3-9-2 JReid(8) (lw: hld up: rdn over 3f out: one pce) ...¾ **5**
783[3] Second Cello **(65)***(48) (DMorris)* 3-8-10 RPrice(9) (lw: hld up: rdn over 2f out: swtchd lft over 1f out: one pce) ...s.h **6**
300[5] Robo Magic (USA) **(60)***(40) (LMontagueHall)* 3-8-5 JWilliams(4) (racd far side: hld up: rdn over 2f out: sn wknd) ...1½ **7**
813[14] Water Hazard (IRE) **(52)***(30) (SDow)* 3-7-11 NAdams(14) (nvr nrr) ...¾ **8**
Jewel Trader **(58)***(35) (CJBenstead)* 3-8-3 GDuffield(2) (bit bkwd: racd far side: hld up: rdn over 3f out: sn wknd) ...nk **9**
971[3] Indrapura (IRE) **(66)***(42) (PFICole)* 3-8-11 CRutter(10) (prom over 4f) ...nk **10**
733[14] South Sound (IRE) **(61)***(32) (RHannon)* 3-7-13 (7)ow1 DaneO'Neill(3) (lw: racd far side: hld up: rdn over 2f out: sn wknd) ...1¾ **11**
911[2] Nordic Doll (IRE) **(76)***(45)*(Fav)*(BWHills)* 3-9-7 PatEddery(12) (b.hind: lw: hld up: rdn over 3f out: sn wknd) ...1½ **12**
Nordesta (IRE) **(69)***(33) (MRChannon)* 3-9-0 RHughes(13) (lw: s.s: a bhd) ...2 **13**
813[12] El Don **(65)***(23) (MJRyan)* 3-8-10 DBiggs(16) (bhd fnl 3f) ...3 **14**
999[6] Denbrae (IRE) **(73)***(23) (DJGMurraySmith)* 3-9-4 LDettori(15) (bhd fnl 3f) ...3½ **15**
850[15] Top Pearl **(56)***(4) (NAGraham)* 3-8-1 AMcGlone(11) (lw: bhd fnl 4f) ...½ **16**

3/1 Nordic Doll (IRE), **5/1** Greenwich Again, **8/1** Indrapura (IRE), **9/1** Wandering Minstrel (IRE), **10/1** Apollono, Denbrae (IRE), DANCING HEART, **12/1** Nordesta (IRE), **14/1** Balance of Power, **16/1** Second Cello, **25/1** El Don, Robo Magic (USA), **33/1** South Sound (IRE), Water Hazard (IRE), Jewel Trader, Top Pearl, CSF £92.14 CT £844.44 TOTE £13.40: £2.40 £2.70 £2.60 £3.70 (£39.40) Trio £276.30 OWNER Vintage Services Ltd (UPPER LAMBOURN) BRED Vintage Services Ltd 16 Rn
1m 23.47 (2.87) SF: 46/33/39/29/22/16/8/-/3/10/-/13/1/-/-/-
STEWARDS' ENQUIRY Harrison suspended 29-31/5, 1-3/6 & 5/6/95 (irresponsible riding).

1166 S.G.B. / YOUNGMAN H'CAP (0-70) (3-Y.O+) (Class E) £3,817.00 (£1,144.00: £550.00: £253.00) **1m 2f** Stalls: Low GOING minus 0.20 sec per fur (GF) 7-30 (7-33)

817[5] **Plinth (48)***(62+) (NAGraham)* 4-8-9v PatEddery(4) (lw: mde all: clr over 2f out: unchal)...— **1**
744[7] Dutosky **(51)***(61) (RJO'Sullivan)* 5-8-12 DBiggs(2) (chsd wnr: rdn over 2f out: no imp)...2½ **2**
Scenic Dancer **(47)***(57) (AHide)* 7-8-8 JWilliams(1) (bit bkwd: hdwy over 2f out: r.o one pce) hd **3**
1014[3] Prince Danzig (IRE) **(52)***(61) (DJGMurraySmith)* 4-8-13 JWeaver(8) (lw: rdn & hdwy over 2f out: r.o one pce) ...¾ **4**
586* Krayyan Dawn **(50)***(56)*(Fav)*(RAkehurst)* 5-8-11 DHarrison(7) (lw: 7th st: hrd rdn over 2f out: one pce) ...1½ **5**
935[12] Rival Bid (USA) **(64)***(68) (MAJarvis)* 7-9-11 LDettori(5) (swtg: 4th st: one pce fnl 2f) ...1½ **6**
762[12] Brandonhurst **(60)***(63) (LadyHerries)* 5-9-7 TIves(6) (lw: s.s: hdwy & nt clr run over 2f out: r.o one pce) ...nk **7**
651[8] Mo's Main Man (IRE) **(55)***(52) (SDow)* 3-8-1 GDuffield(9) (lw: s.s: nvr nrr)...4 **8**
1029[11] Rolling Waters **(42)***(39) (JARToller)* 5-8-3 GCarter(11) (6th st: wknd over 2f out) ...nk **9**
*496** One Off the Rail (USA) **(44)***(33) (AMoore)* 5-8-0 (5) AWhelan(14) (3rd st: wknd over 2f out)...5 **10**
1027* King Curan (USA) **(61)***(48) (ABailey)* 4-9-8b JReid(13) (lw: bhd fnl 3f) ...¾ **11**
738[U] Mr Devious **(58)***(41) (PJHobbs)* 4-9-5 AMcGlone(3) (lw: bhd fnl 3f)...2½ **12**
975[3] Anlace **(54)***(35) (SMellor)* 6-9-1 MWigham(16) (a bhd) ...1½ **13**
1048[15] Mega Tid **(51)***(31) (BAPearce)* 3-7-11 NCarlisle(12) (a bhd)...nk **14**
981[7] Desert Power **(67)***(46) (MartynMeade)* 6-10-0 RPrice(15) (5th st: wknd 3f out)...¾ **15**
605[6] Red Spectacle (IRE) **(56)***(35) (PCHaslam)* 3-7-9 (7) NicolaHowarth(10) (a bhd)...nk **16**

3/1 Krayyan Dawn, **11/2** Rival Bid (USA), **6/1** Prince Danzig (IRE), **7/1** PLINTH, **8/1** Dutosky, King Curan (USA), **12/1** Anlace, Brandonhurst (op 8/1), **14/1** One Off the Rail (USA), **16/1** Rolling Waters, **20/1** Mr Devious, Desert Power, Mega Tid, **25/1** Mo's Main Man (IRE), Scenic Dancer, Red Spectacle (IRE), CSF £66.47 CT £1,253.26 TOTE £9.80: £2.30 £2.60 £7.60 £2.20 (£51.70) Trio £22.00 OWNER Mr T. H. Chadney (NEWMARKET) BRED Bloomsbury Stud 16 Rn
2m 8.81 (5.81) SF: 31/30/26/30/25/37/32/6/8/2/17/10/4/-/15/-
WEIGHT FOR AGE 3yo-15lb

1167 TEQUILA SUNRISE MAIDEN STKS (3-Y.O+) (Class D) £4,306.90 (£1,289.20: £618.60: £283.30) **1m 1f** Stalls: Low GOING minus 0.20 sec per fur (GF) 8-00 (8-04)

936[2] **Triquetti (IRE)** *(78)*(Fav)*(LMCumani)* 3-8-10 PatEddery(10) (lw: 2nd st: rdn 3f out: led 2f out tl over 1f out: led ins fnl f: r.o wl) ...— **1**

764[6] Moscow Mist (IRE) *(76)*(Fav)*(LadyHerries)* 4-9-10 JWeaver(9) (hdwy over 2f out: led over 1f out tl ins fnl f: unable qckn)....1¼ 2
Lion Tower *(70) (HRACecil)* 3-8-10 WRyan(8) (gd sort: rdn & hdwy over 2f out: one pce fnl f)....3 3
Tragic Hero *(63) (IABalding)* 3-8-10 TIves(7) (bit bkwd: led 7f)....4 4
715[16] Pharly Reef *(63) (IABalding)* 3-8-10 LDettori(12) (3rd st: nt clr run 2f out & over 1f out: nt rcvr)....nk 5
Park Ridge *(63) (TGMills)* 3-8-3 (7) DToole(6) (leggy: unf: nvr nr to chal)....s.h 6
670[W] Farmer's Tern (IRE) *(58) (WJarvis)* 3-8-5 MTebbutt(2) (unf: scope: 6th st: hmpd on ins over 1f out: nt rcvr)....hd 7
Canton Venture *(62) (SPCWoods)* 3-8-3 (7) CWebb(5) (w'like: dwlt: nvr nrr)....½ 8
739[6] I'm Outa Here (IRE) **(73)***(60) (RHannon)* 3-8-10 JReid(3) (nvr nrr)....¾ 9
1072[5] Zatopek *(58) (RHannon)* 3-8-10 RHughes(13) (4th st: rdn over 2f out: eased whn btn fnl f) .1½ 10
Kafani Al Widd (FR) *(55) (MRStoute)* 3-8-10 WRSwinburn(14) (5th st: wknd over 2f out)....1½ 11
957[9] Rozalina Lady *(49) (NAGraham)* 3-8-5 GDuffield(1) (bhd fnl 2f)....½ 12
1056[4] Classical Star *(47) (RJHodges)* 6-9-3 (7) AmandaSanders(4) (bhd fnl 3f)....4 13
Valinco *(38) (SDow)* 4-8-12 (7) ADaly(11) (bhd fnl 6f)....2 14

9/4 TRIQUETTI (IRE), Moscow Mist (IRE), **5/1** Lion Tower (op 3/1), **9/1** Kafani Al Widd (FR), **14/1** Zatopek, **16/1** Pharly Reef, **20/1** I'm Outa Here (IRE), **25/1** Tragic Hero, **33/1** Rozalina Lady, Farmer's Tern (IRE), Canton Venture, **50/1** Park Ridge, Classical Star, Valinco, CSF £7.55 TOTE £2.80: £1.40 £1.70 £2.30 (£3.70) Trio £4.80 OWNER Sheikh Mohammed (NEWMARKET) BRED Dene Investments N V 14 Rn 1m 55.8 (6.50) SF: 20/32/12/5/5/5/-/4/2/-/-/-/3/-
WEIGHT FOR AGE 3yo-14lb

1168 KIR ROYAL MAIDEN STKS (3-Y.O+) (Class D) £4,273.10 (£1,278.80: £613.40: £280.70) 6f Stalls: Centre GOING minus 0.20 sec per fur (GF) 8-30 (8-33)

959[4] **Paris Babe (95)***(78+)*(Fav)*(DMorris)* 3-8-6 LDettori(3) (a.p: led over 1f out: pushed out)....— 1
915[7] Bouche Bee (USA) *(73) (LMCumani)* 3-8-6 JWeaver(2) (lw: hdwy over 2f out: n.m.r & swtchd rt over 1f out: r.o ins fnl f)....1¾ 2
761[3] Takhlid (USA) *(73) (HThomsonJones)* 4-9-7 RHills(10) (lw: a.p: rdn over 3f out: r.o ins fnl f)....2 3
1071[10] Anzio (IRE) **(68)***(70) (BAPearce)* 4-9-7b TIves(13) (b: lw: led 4f: one pce fnl f)....1¼ 4
973[5] French Ginger *(63) (IABalding)* 4-8-11 (5) DGriffiths(8) (lw: nvr nr to chal)....¾ 5
937[4] Samwar **(82)***(66) (BWHills)* 3-8-11 PatEddery(15) (a.p: led 2f out tl over 1f out: wknd fnl f)....¾ 6
742[3] Double Matt (IRE) **(77)***(65) (RHannon)* 3-8-11 JReid(11) (a.p: rdn over 2f out: one pce)....nk 7
695[15] Roka *(59) (RHannon)* 3-7-13 (7) DaneO'Neill(1) (nvr nrr)....½ 8
Frankly Fran *(53) (DWPArbuthnot)* 3-8-6 SWhitworth(5) (w'like: nvr nrr)....2 9
1040[4] Millesime (IRE) *(56) (BHanbury)* 3-8-11 WRyan(7) (lw: hld up: rdn over 2f out: sn wknd)....¾ 10
Try-Haitai (IRE) *(53) (RAkehurst)* 4-9-7 DHarrison(14) (bhd fnl 2f)....1¼ 11
Saltando (IRE) *(52) (PatMitchell)* 4-9-7 MFenton(9) (a bhd)....½ 12
695[17] Amany (IRE) *(31) (GLewis)* 3-8-1 (5) AWhelan(6) (a bhd)....6 13
Royal Sovereign (IRE) *(20) (GLMoore)* 3-8-6 BRouse(12) (b: w'like: a bhd)....4 14
Henry Weston *(18) (PHowling)* 3-8-11 NCarlisle(4) (bhd fnl 2f)....2½ 15

5/2 PARIS BABE (op 4/1), **9/2** Bouche Bee (USA) (11/4-5/1), Takhlid (USA), **11/2** Samwar, **6/1** Double Matt (IRE), **8/1** Millesime (IRE), **16/1** French Ginger, **20/1** Royal Sovereign (IRE), Anzio (IRE), **33/1** Frankly Fran, Roka, Amany (IRE), Try-Haitai (IRE), **50/1** Saltando (IRE), **66/1** Henry Weston, CSF £15.30 TOTE £3.70: £1.30 £2.40 £2.10 (£15.00) Trio £15.20 OWNER Mrs Susan Parry (NEWMARKET) BRED I. W. Parry 15 Rn
1m 10.56 (1.56) SF: 51/46/56/53/46/39/38/32/26/29/36/35/4/-/-
WEIGHT FOR AGE 3yo-10lb
T/Plpt: £68.20 (138.65 Tckts). T/Qdpt: £9.40 (7.9 Tckts). AK

1136-NEWBURY (L-H)
Saturday May 20th (Good to firm)
WEATHER: overcast WIND: almost nil

1169 HATHERDEN MAIDEN STKS (2-Y.O F) (Class D) £3,808.00 (£1,144.00: £552.00: £256.00) 6f 8y Stalls: Centre GOING minus 0.38 sec per fur (F) 2-00 (2-04)

Amazing Bay *(86+) (IABalding)* 2-8-11 LDettori(7) (w'like: scope: a.p: qcknd to ld ins fnl f: r.o)....— 1
Watch Me (IRE) *(83) (RHannon)* 2-8-11 WRSwinburn(6) (unf: led tl ins fnl f: edgd rt: bttr for r)....1 2
Mountain Valley *(77) (PFICole)* 2-8-11 CRutter(1) (leggy: dwlt: sn w ldrs: nt qckn fnl f)....2½ 3

9405 Rumba Rhythm (CAN) *(77) (JWHills)* 2-8-11 RHills(12) (hdwy 2f out: nt qckn fnl f)................hd 4
Yamuna (USA) *(73)*(Fav)*(HRACecil)* 2-8-11 PatEddery(10) (cmpt: dwlt: jnd ldrs 3f out: sn rdn & lost pl: rallied fnl f)..........1¼ 5
Ocean Grove (IRE) *(69) (PWChapple-Hyam)* 2-8-11 JReid(11) (unf: w ldr tl wknd over 1f out)..........1½ 6
8784 Whispering Dawn *(68) (MRChannon)* 2-8-11 RHughes(8) (nrst fin)..........½ 7
Zelaya (IRE) *(68) (CEBrittain)* 2-8-11 BDoyle(2) (lengthy: unf: bit bkwd: dwlt: spd 4f)............hd 8
7915 White Whispers *(67) (BWHills)* 2-8-11 DHarrison(5) (b.hind: bit bkwd: hld up & bhd: nvr nr to chal)..........s.h 9
Myrtle *(64) (RHannon)* 2-8-4 (7) DaneO'Neill(3) (unf: bkwd: s.s: spd 4f)..........1¼ 10
Paris Joelle (IRE) *(62) (MRChannon)* 2-8-6 (5) PPMurphy(9) (leggy: outpcd)..........1 11
Be My Bird *(BJMeehan)* 2-8-11 MFenton(4) (Withdrawn not under Starter's orders).......... W

, **10/11** Yamuna (USA), **7/1** AMAZING BAY (5/1-8/1), Watch Me (IRE) (5/1-8/1), **9/1** Ocean Grove (IRE) (5/1-10/1), **12/1** White Whispers (op 6/1), **20/1** Rumba Rhythm (CAN), Whispering Dawn, **25/1** Mountain Valley, **33/1** Zelaya (IRE), **50/1** Myrtle, Paris Joelle (IRE), CSF £49.41 TOTE £9.10: £2.10 £2.00 £8.50 (£25.20) Trio £33.00 OWNER Mr J. C. Smith (KINGSCLERE) BRED R. G. Percival 11 Rn 1m 14.26 (2.46) SF: 30/27/21/21/17/13/12/12/11/8/6/-

1170 LONDON GOLD CUP RATED STKS H'CAP (0-100) (3-Y.O) (Class B)

£7,996.80 (£2,971.20: £1,435.60: £598.00: £249.00: £109.40)
1m 4f 5y Stalls: Centre GOING minus 0.38 sec per fur (F) 2-30 (2-31)

9174 **Korambi (90)***(89) (CEBrittain)* 3-9-5 BDoyle(3) (lw: 2nd tl led over 3f out: edgd lft 2f out: all out)..........— 1
High Standard **(81)***(79) (MRStoute)* 3-8-10 WRSwinburn(4) (6th st: stdy hdwy 3f out: ev ch fnl f: r.o)..........¾ 2
7116 Grey Shot **(92)***(89) (IABalding)* 3-9-7 LDettori(2) (4th st: ev ch over 1f out: r.o one pce)..........½ 3
9959 Time for Action (IRE) **(90)***(87) (MHTompkins)* 3-9-5 PRobinson(7) (lw: 3rd st: rdn & outpcd 2f out: r.o fnl f)..........½ 4
962* Hardy Dancer **(87)***(80)*(Fav)*(GLMoore)* 3-9-2 BRouse(5) (5th st: ev ch 2f out: wknd ins fnl f)..........2½ 5
10686 Lancer (USA) **(89)***(80) (MBell)* 3-9-4 MFenton(6) (hld up in rr: hdwy on ins over 3f out: sn rdn & btn)..........1¾ 6
8223 Vin St Koola **(85)***(60) (HJCollingridge)* 3-9-0 MRimmer(1) (lw: led tl wknd over 3f out)..........12 7

6/5 Hardy Dancer, **4/1** High Standard, **6/1** Grey Shot, **13/2** Lancer (USA) (9/2-7/1), **12/1** KORAMBI, **14/1** Vin St Koola, **25/1** Time for Action (IRE), CSF £53.07 TOTE £12.00: £3.30 £1.90 (£14.70) OWNER Mr B. H. Voak (NEWMARKET) BRED Stonethorn Stud Farms Ltd 7 Rn
2m 32.62 (3.32) SF: 50/40/50/48/41/41/21

OFFICIAL EXPLANATION Hardy Dancer: the jockey stated the horse did not stay.

1171 QUANTEL ASTON PARK STKS (Listed) (4-Y.O+) (Class A)

£13,160.00 (£3,980.00: £1,940.00: £920.00)
1m 5f 61y Stalls: Centre GOING: 0.00 sec per fur (G) 3-00 (3-01)

8695 **Escarpment (USA) (103)***(115) (PWChapple-Hyam)* 4-8-12 JReid(2) (mde virtually all: all out)..........— 1
Sadler's Image (IRE) **(111)***(117)*(Fav)*(MRStoute)* 4-9-1 WRSwinburn(6) (3rd st: ev ch over 1f out: r.o)..........¾ 2
10204 Linney Head (USA) **(108)***(120) (JHMGosden)* 4-9-4 LDettori(1) (lw: 4th st: rdn over 3f out: styd on fnl 2f)..........nk 3
1056* Alriffa **(114)***(114) (RHannon)* 4-9-1 RHughes(5) (lw: 2nd st: ev ch 2f out: wknd fnl f)..........2 4
9584 Castle Courageous **(106)***(108) (LadyHerries)* 8-9-1 TIves(8) (lw: 5th st: wknd over 2f out).......5 5
9586 Nawar (FR) *(91) (JRJenkins)* 5-8-12 DBiggs(4) (lw: 6th st: wknd 3f out: t.o)..........12 6

7/4 Sadler's Image (IRE), **2/1** Alriffa, **5/1** Linney Head (USA), Castle Courageous, **9/1** ESCARPMENT (USA), **66/1** Nawar (FR), CSF £24.42 TOTE £10.70: £3.00 £1.40 (£11.00) OWNER Godolphin (MARLBOROUGH) 6 Rn 2m 47.26 (1.96) SF: 54/56/59/53/47/30

1172 HEADLEY H'CAP (0-80) (3-Y.O F) (Class D) £4,133.00 (£1,244.00: £602.00:

£281.00) **7f 64y (round)** Stalls: Low GOING minus 0.38 sec per fur (F) 3-30 (3-31)

Forest Cat (IRE) (80)*(87)*(Fav)*(MrsJCecil)* 3-9-7 JReid(7) (b: stdy hdwy over 2f out: swtchd ins over 1f out: qcknd to ld wl ins fnl f)..........— 1
8162 Hagwah (USA) **(77)***(81) (BHanbury)* 3-9-4 TIves(8) (b.off hind: lw: 2nd st: led 4f out to 2f out: r.o ins fnl f)..........1¼ 2
752* Rosebud **(80)***(84) (RHannon)* 3-9-0 (7) DaneO'Neill(14) (3rd st: led 2f out tl wl ins fnl f)..........hd 3

Gypsy Love (USA) **(68)***(66) (PWChapple-Hyam)* 3-8-2 (7)ow4 RHavlin(2) (bit bkwd: hdwy on ins 2f out: nrst fin)......¾ **4**
Green Seed (IRE) **(80)***(82) (JRFanshawe)* 3-9-7 WRSwinburn(3) (hdwy & nt clr run 2f out: r.o wl ins fnl f)......nk **5**
681[5] A Million to One (IRE) **(74)***(76) (MBell)* 3-9-1 MFenton(13) (lw: 6th st: r.o one pce fnl 2f)......s.h **6**
Moody **(67)***(66) (MissGayKelleway)* 3-8-8 PRobinson(4) (plld hrd: 5th st: no hdwy fnl 2f)......1 **7**
971[2] Fairelaine **(61)***(60) (APJarvis)* 3-8-2 TSprake(5) (a mid div: hmpd over 1f out: r.o fnl f)......nk **8**
985[5] Fantasy Racing (IRE) **(76)***(73) (MRChannon)* 3-9-3 RHughes(1) (7th st: one pce fnl 2f)......¾ **9**
742[4] Aoife Alainn (IRE) **(72)***(66) (JWHills)* 3-8-13 RHills(15) (nt clr run on ins 2f out: nt rcvr)......1½ **10**
La Gran Senorita (USA) **(75)***(58) (PFICole)* 3-9-2 PatEddery(9) (led over 3f: wknd qckly fnl f)......5 **11**
761[7] Rookery Girl **(60)***(35) (DMorris)* 3-8-1 RPrice(12) (8th st: wknd 2f out)......3½ **12**
Princess Danielle **(62)***(34) (CCElsey)* 3-8-3 DHarrison(10) (bit bkwd: plld hrd: a bhd)......1¼ **13**
10[5] Tara Colleen (IRE) **(58)***(27) (CAHorgan)* 3-7-13 NAdams(11) (plld hrd: a bhd)......1¾ **14**
873[23] Rupiana (IRE) **(68)***(36) (JRArnold)* 3-8-9 LDettori(6) (4th st: wknd over 2f out)......nk **15**

5/1 FOREST CAT (IRE), **11/2** Hagwah (USA), Rosebud, **9/1** Gypsy Love (USA) (op 14/1), **10/1** Green Seed (IRE), Fairelaine, **12/1** Fantasy Racing (IRE) (op 8/1), **14/1** A Million to One (IRE), La Gran Senorita (USA), **16/1** Moody, Rupiana (IRE), **20/1** Rookery Girl, **25/1** Aoife Alainn (IRE), **33/1** Tara Colleen (IRE), **50/1** Princess Danielle, CSF £30.38 CT £145.09 TOTE £4.90: £2.50 £2.20 £1.90 (£11.20) Trio £11.40 OWNER Mr George Ward (NEWMARKET) BRED Tasia Limited 15 Rn
1m 29.87 (1.37) SF: 58/52/55/37/53/47/37/31/44/37/29/6/5/-/7

1173 FRANK OSGOOD 80TH BIRTHDAY MAIDEN STKS (I) (3-Y.O) (Class D)
£3,899.00 (£1,172.00: £566.00: £263.00)
1m 2f 6y Stalls: Centre GOING minus 0.38 sec per fur (F) 4-00 (4-00)

Danjing (IRE) (98)*(87) (PFICole)* 3-9-0 CRutter(5) (bit bkwd: 6th st: nt clr run 2f out: qcknd over 1f out: r.o to ld last strides)......— **1**
691[11] United Force (IRE) *(87) (PWChapple-Hyam)* 3-9-0 JReid(1) (lw: led: qcknd 2f out: hrd rdn fnl f: hdd fnl strides)......hd **2**
Woodcrest *(80) (HCandy)* 3-8-9 WNewnes(10) (unf: hdwy 3f out: nt clr run over 1f out: r.o fnl f)......1¼ **3**
942[8] Niknaks Nephew *(79) (MissAJWhitfield)* 3-8-9 (5) RPainter(6) (lw: 2nd st: wknd over 1f out)......4 **4**
978[6] Heath Robinson (IRE) *(78) (JHMGosden)* 3-9-0 LDettori(8) (b: b.hind: 7th st: one pce fnl 3f)......nk **5**
Blue And Royal (IRE) *(75) (RHannon)* 3-9-0 RPerham(9) (wl grwn: nrst fin)......2 **6**
881[2] Artful Dane (IRE) **(75)***(72)*(Fav)*(MJHeaton-Ellis)* 3-9-0 PatEddery(3) (lw: 3rd st: rdn over 3f out: wknd 2f out)......1½ **7**
Starofgreatintent (USA) *(64) (JMPEustace)* 3-9-0 RHughes(2) (nvr nr to chal)......5 **8**
Lucky Quest *(64) (NAGraham)* 3-9-0 JWilliams(4) (unf: outpcd)......½ **9**
Cante Chico *(62) (TThomsonJones)* 3-9-0 SWhitworth(11) (lengthy: unf: 5th st: wknd qckly 2f out)......1 **10**
635[9] Stormaway (ITY) *(61) (TGMills)* 3-9-0 GCarter(12) (4th st: wknd over 2f out)......½ **11**
854[9] Little Shefford **(50)***(41) (DJSffrenchDavis)* 3-9-0 DHarrison(7) (plld hrd: a bhd: t.o)......13 **12**

3/1 Artful Dane (IRE), **4/1** Heath Robinson (IRE) (op 5/2), DANJING (IRE) (op 5/2), **9/2** United Force (IRE), **9/1** Stormaway (ITY), **16/1** Woodcrest, Blue And Royal (IRE), **20/1** Cante Chico, **25/1** Lucky Quest, **66/1** Starofgreatintent (USA), Niknaks Nephew, Little Shefford, CSF £20.76 TOTE £5.70: £1.80 £1.90 £4.40 (£16.10) Trio £245.10 OWNER Mrs Linda Gardiner (WHATCOMBE) BRED J. P. McManus 12 Rn
2m 8.9 (5.90) SF: 21/21/14/13/12/9/6/-/-/-/-/-

1174 WINCHESTER H'CAP (0-90) (3-Y.O+) (Class C) £6,076.00 (£1,828.00: £884.00: £412.00) 6f 8y Stalls: Centre GOING minus 0.38 sec per fur (F) 4-30 (4-31)

870[16] **Bayin (USA) (64)***(72) (MDIUsher)* 6-8-2 RStreet(8) (hdwy over 1f out: r.o wl to ld fnl stride)......— **1**
877* Colway Rake **(67)***(75) (JWWatts)* 4-8-5b NConnorton(9) (w ldrs: led 2f out: hdd post)......s.h **2**
887* Thatcherella **(68)***(73) (MajorDNChappell)* 4-8-6 LDettori(1) (hld up: chal over 1f out: nt qckn fnl f)......1¼ **3**
922[16] Master of Passion **(84)***(85) (JMPEustace)* 6-9-5 (3) JTate(6) (a.p: rdn over 2f out: nt qckn)......1¼ **4**
922[7] Jobie **(69)***(68) (BWHills)* 5-8-2 (5) JDSmith(12) (lw: hdwy 2f out: r.o fnl f)......¾ **5**
812[6] Jigsaw Boy **(62)***(61) (PGMurphy)* 6-8-0 GCarter(3) (gd late hdwy: nrst fin)......hd **6**
Sea-Deer **(90)***(89) (LJHolt)* 6-10-0 AMcGlone(16) (bkwd: hdwy over 1f out: r.o ins fnl f)......s.h **7**
870[24] Law Commission **(82)***(79) (DRCElsworth)* 5-9-6 PatEddery(15) (hld up: effrt 2f out: wknd fnl f)......¾ **8**
1019[4] Barossa Valley (IRE) **(78)***(75)*(Fav)*(PWChapple-Hyam)* 4-9-2 JReid(13) (lw: w ldrs tl rdn & wknd 2f out)......s.h **9**

535[8] Tshusick **(80)***(75) (JRFanshawe)* 4-9-4 DHarrison(7) (b.hind: w ldrs: led over 2f out: sn hdd & wknd)....½ **10**
887[5] Face the Future **(64)***(55) (LJHolt)* 6-7-9 (7) IonaWands(4) (nvr nr to chal) 1½ **11**
838[13] King Rat (IRE) **(72)***(61) (TJEtherington)* 4-8-10 TIves(5) (prom 4f)....¾ **12**
922[20] Teetotaller (IRE) **(69)***(55) (GBBalding)* 4-8-7 JWilliams(17) (a bhd)....1¼ **13**
887[17] Slivovitz **(62)***(38) (MJHeaton-Ellis)* 5-8-0v NAdams(10) (lw: led: hdd & wknd qckly over 2f out) 4 **14**
636[10] Champagne Grandy **(70)***(45) (MRChannon)* 5-8-8 RHughes(11) (outpcd) ....nk **15**
796[12] Leigh Crofter **(73)***(8) (PDCundell)* 6-8-11b WNewnes(2) (spd 3f: t.o) 15 **16**

100/30 Barossa Valley (IRE), **9/2** Thatcherella, **9/1** Jobie, **10/1** Tshusick, Colway Rake, **12/1** Law Commission, **14/1** BAYIN (USA), **16/1** Jigsaw Boy, Teetotaller (IRE), Sea-Deer, **20/1** Face the Future, King Rat (IRE), Leigh Crofter, Slivovitz, **25/1** Champagne Grandy, Master of Passion, CSF £138.65 CT £672.72 TOTE £17.50: £2.90 £2.50 £1.50 £7.70 (£88.30) Trio £70.50 OWNER Mr Trevor Barker (SWINDON) 16 Rn 1m13.19 (1.39) SF: 36/39/37/49/32/25/53/43/39/39/19/25/19/2/9

1175

FRANK OSGOOD 80TH BIRTHDAY MAIDEN STKS (II) (3-Y.O) (Class D) £3,899.00 (£1,172.00: £566.00: £263.00)
1m 2f 6y Stalls: Centre GOING minus 0.38 sec per fur (F) 5-00 (5-03)

Mountains of Mist (IRE) *(73)*(Fav)*(RCharlton)* 3-8-9 JReid(6) (lengthy: bit bkwd: 3rd st: led wl over 1f out: rdn ins fnl f: r.o) ....— **1**
Syrian Queen *(73) (HRACecil)* 3-8-9 AMcGlone(8) (w'like: scope: 2nd st: led over 3f out tl wl over 1f out: hrd rdn: r.o)....s.h **2**
Dr Zhivago *(70) (MAJarvis)* 3-9-0 PRobinson(4) (bkwd: led tl over 3f out: r.o one pce)....5 **3**
764[5] Tibetan *(70) (LadyHerries)* 3-9-0 TIves(5) (5th st: rdn over 2f out: r.o one pce)....nk **4**
824[6] Wurlitzer (USA) *(66) (JHMGosden)* 3-9-0 DHarrison(10) (6th st: one pce fnl 3f) 2½ **5**
Indicator *(62) (RHannon)* 3-9-0 WRSwinburn(3) (cmpt: bkwd: 7th st: nvr nr to chal)....2½ **6**
Torreglia (IRE) *(50) (JLDunlop)* 3-8-9 GDuffield(9) (unf: 8th st: nvr trbld ldrs) 4 **7**
Harbour Island *(55) (MRStoute)* 3-8-11 (3) JTate(7) (neat: a bhd)....hd **8**
815[12] Remaadi Sun *(52) (JHMGosden)* 3-9-0 GHind(11) (bit bkwd: 4th st: wknd 3f out) 2 **9**
695[14] Easter Coul (IRE) *(31) (MJFetherston-Godley)* 3-8-9 FNorton(2) (bkwd: a bhd: t.o)....10 **10**
854[13] Dick Christian *(BJMeehan)* 3-9-0 BDoyle(1) (a bhd: t.o) 30 **11**

5/4 MOUNTAINS OF MIST (IRE), **3/1** Tibetan, **7/1** Indicator, **9/1** Syrian Queen (6/1-10/1), **14/1** Wurlitzer (USA), **16/1** Dr Zhivago, Torreglia (IRE), **20/1** Harbour Island, **25/1** Remaadi Sun, **66/1** Easter Coul (IRE), Dick Christian, CSF £13.25 TOTE £2.20: £1.10 £2.20 £2.50 (£9.30) Trio £55.90 OWNER Mr S. S. Niarchos (BECKHAMPTON) BRED S. Niarchos 11 Rn
2m 6.73 (3.73) SF: 33/33/30/30/26/22/10/15/12/-/-
T/Jkpt: Not won; £15,215.17 to Newbury 21/5/95. T/Plpt: £568.30 (49.86 Tckts). T/Qdpt: £44.70 (7.6 Tckts). Hn

1149-THIRSK (L-H)
Saturday May 20th (Firm, Good to firm patches)

WEATHER: cool, sunny periods WIND: almost nil

1176

E.B.F. CARLTON MINIOTT MAIDEN STKS (2-Y.O) (Class D) £3,720.00 (£1,110.00: £530.00: £240.00)
5f Stalls: High GOING minus 0.41 sec per fur (F) 2-15 (2-17)

Sweet Robin (IRE) *(79+) (MJohnston)* 2-8-9 DHolland(1) (leggy: disp ld tl led over 1f out: r.o) ....— **1**
825[3] First Fiddler *(78)*(Fav)*(WJarvis)* 2-9-0 MTebbutt(6) (lw: cl up: hung lft thrght: disp ld ½-wy: nt qckn fnl f)....2 **2**
977[4] Elmswood (USA) *(61) (PWChapple-Hyam)* 2-8-9 BThomson(8) (disp ld to ½-wy: grad wknd)....3½ **3**
Prince of Florence (IRE) *(65) (LMCumani)* 2-9-0 JWeaver(2) (cmpt: s.i.s: hdwy ½-wy: no imp) ....½ **4**
Chamber Music *(57) (JBerry)* 2-8-9 JCarroll(7) (b.hind: leggy: scope: cl up 3f: wknd)....1 **5**
Victoria Sioux *(49) (JWharton)* 2-8-9 KDarley(9) (neat: unf: s.i.s: nvr plcd to chal)....2½ **6**
684[5] Mooncusser *(53) (JGFitzGerald)* 2-9-0 KFallon(10) (s.i.s: nvr trbld ldrs)....hd **7**
925[4] Eccentric Dancer *(39) (MPBielby)* 2-8-9 ACulhane(3) (s.i.s: n.d) 3 **8**
943[9] Mels Baby (IRE) *(44) (JLEyre)* 2-9-0 RLappin(5) (nvr wnt pce)....s.h **9**
Classic Victory *(37) (SCWilliams)* 2-9-0 AMackay(4) (w'like: scope: bit bkwd: chsd ldrs: effrt ½-wy: sn wknd) 2 **10**

4/7 First Fiddler, **11/2** Elmswood (USA), **8/1** Prince of Florence (IRE) (op 5/1), **10/1** SWEET ROBIN (IRE), **12/1** Classic Victory (op 8/1), **14/1** Chamber Music, **16/1** Mooncusser, **25/1** Victoria Sioux, **66/1** Eccentric Dancer, Mels Baby (IRE), CSF £16.69 TOTE £16.50: £2.50 £1.10 £1.50 (£14.70) Trio £11.20 OWNER Sheikh Mohammed (MIDDLEHAM) BRED Sheikh Mohammed bin Rashid al Maktoum 10 Rn 59.3 secs (2.10) SF: 22/21/4/8/-/-/-/-/-/-

1177 SKIPTON CLAIMING STKS (2-Y.O) (Class F) £2,846.00 (£848.00: £404.00: £182.00) 5f Stalls: High GOING minus 0.41 sec per fur (F) 2-45 (2-46)

Standown *(68) (JBerry)* 2-8-7 JCarroll(5) (w'like: scope: lw: chsd ldrs: rdn ½-wy: hdwy over 1f out: hung lft: r.o to ld last stride)......— 1
977[7] Just Lady *(67)*(Fav)*(WGMTurner)* 2-8-1 (5) PMcCabe(2) (lw: led: hung lft most of wy: clr ½-wy: wknd ins fnl f: ct post)......s.h 2
561[4] Never Think Twice *(73) (KTIvory)* 2-8-13 JWeaver(6) (b: lw: chsd ldrs: rdn ½-wy: kpt on nr fin)......nk 3
983* Arvzees (IRE) *(47) (MRChannon)* 2-8-9 KDarley(3) (sn drvn along: chsd ldrs: no imp fr ½-wy)......7 4
Catwalk Girl *(36) (SGNorton)* 2-7-13 AMackay(7) (leggy: s.s: a wl bhd)......nk 5
943[7] Patrington Park *(38) (MWEasterby)* 2-8-4 (7) GParkin(4) (in tch tl outpcd ½-wy)......3 6
Contradictory *(20) (MWEasterby)* 2-8-3 LCharnock(1) (w'like: s.i.s: a bhd)......3 7

2/1 Just Lady, **5/2** Arvzees (IRE) (7/4-11/4), **3/1** STANDOWN, **7/1** Never Think Twice, **12/1** Patrington Park, **25/1** Contradictory, **33/1** Catwalk Girl, CSF £9.06 TOTE £4.20: £2.20 £1.70 (£3.90) OWNER Mr J. Berry (COCKERHAM) BRED Alan Gibson 7 Rn
59.1 secs (1.90) SF: 24/23/29/3/-/-/-

1178 DISHFORTH CONDITIONS STKS (3-Y.O) (Class B) £8,843.55 (£3,236.80: £1,554.90: £637.50: £255.25) 1m Stalls: Low GOING minus 0.41 sec per fur (F) 3-15 (3-15)

829[2] **Ihtiram (IRE) (102)***(110+)*(Fav)*(JLDunlop)* 3-9-2 WCarson(2) (lw: trckd ldrs: led on bit wl over 1f out: shkn up & qcknd: easily)......— 1
1010a[4] Steady Ready Go (IRE) *(101) (LMCumani)* 3-8-13 JWeaver(3) (hld up & bhd: hdwy 3f out: nt pce of wnr fnl f)......3 2
945[2] Lyrikos (USA) *(100) (HRACecil)* 3-8-13 WRyan(6) (b.nr fore: lw: cl up tl outpcd 3f out: nt clr run 2f out: styd on nr fin)......nk 3
*844** Quango *(95) (JGFitzGerald)* 3-8-10 JCarroll(7) (bhd: hdwy over 2f out: nt pce to chal)......1¼ 4
868[5] Crystal Cavern (USA) **(94)***(92) (RCharlton)* 3-8-8 KDarley(5) (lw: led tl hdd wl over 1f out: wknd ins fnl f)......nk 5

8/11 IHTIRAM (IRE) (op 5/4), **5/2** Lyrikos (USA), **13/2** Steady Ready Go (IRE), **10/1** Crystal Cavern (USA), **14/1** Quango, CSF £5.89 TOTE £1.60: £1.10 £2.30 (£5.40) OWNER Mr Hamdan Al Maktoum (ARUNDEL) BRED Kilcarn Stud 5 Rn 1m 37.2 (1.60) SF: 49/40/39/34/31

1179 DIBB LUPTON BROOMHEAD CUP H'CAP (0-95) (4-Y.O+) (Class C) £15,010.00 (£4,480.00: £2,140.00: £970.00) 7f Stalls: Low GOING minus 0.41 sec per fur (F) 3-45 (3-45)

1100[5] **Celestial Key (USA) (90)***(101) (MJohnston)* 5-9-12 DHolland(1) (lw: chsd ldrs: hdwy on ins to ld wl ins fnl f)......— 1
838[3] Jato **(76)***(85) (SCWilliams)* 6-8-12 KDarley(7) (b.nr fore: lw: cl up: rdn to ld ins fnl f: sn hdd: nt qckn nr fin)......¾ 2
493[2] Sarmatian (USA) **(64)***(72) (MDHammond)* 4-8-0 DaleGibson(3) (in tch: n.m.r 2f out: hdwy over 1f out: styd on nr fin)......¾ 3
922[9] Selhurstpark Flyer (IRE) **(85)***(92) (JBerry)* 4-9-7e JCarroll(6) (lw: led tl hdd & no ex ins fnl f)...nk 4
1021[9] Pride of Pendle **(70)***(77) (DNicholls)* 6-8-6 AlexGreaves(4) (lw: in tch: effrt 2f out: n.m.r & nt qckn ins fnl f)......s.h 5
922[8] Chinour (IRE) **(65)***(68) (EJAlston)* 7-7-12 (3) DRMcCabe(9) (lw: hdwy over 2f out: r.o wl)......1¾ 6
927[2] Queens Consul (IRE) **(79)***(80) (BSRothwell)* 5-8-10 (5) JStack(8) (chsd ldrs: effrt 3f out: sn ev ch: wknd 1f out)......1 7
927[4] Celestial Choir **(77)***(77) (JLEyre)* 5-8-13b JFortune(2) (lw: s.i.s: hdwy over 2f out: nt qckn appr fnl f)......nk 8
Hi Nod **(79)***(76) (MJCamacho)* 5-9-1 LCharnock(11) (lw: prom: effrt 3f out: no imp)......1¼ 9
1013* Persian Affair (IRE) **(72)***(69) (DHaydnJones)* 4-8-8 AMackay(5) (bhd & rdn ent st: n.d)......hd 10
1061[8] Pine Ridge Lad (IRE) **(60)***(42) (JLEyre)* 5-7-5 (5)ow3 NVarley(13) (chsd ldrs to st: sn bhd)......5 11
960[4] Knave's Ash (USA) **(89)***(74)*(Fav)*(MRStoute)* 4-9-11 PaulEddery(12) (outpcd & bhd ent st: c wd & hdwy: btn wl over 1f out)......nk 12

877³ Craigie Boy **(61)**_(30) (NBycroft)_ 5-7-11 TWilliams(10) (outpcd appr st: sn bhd).........................7 **13**

LONG HANDICAP Pine Ridge Lad (IRE) 7-4

7/2 Knave's Ash (USA), **6/1** Hi Nod, Jato, **8/1** Persian Affair (IRE), **9/1** CELESTIAL KEY (USA), Celestial Choir, **11/1** Queens Consul (IRE), Chinour (IRE), Pride of Pendle, **14/1** Sarmatian (USA), **16/1** Selhurstpark Flyer (IRE), **20/1** Craigie Boy, **33/1** Pine Ridge Lad (IRE), CSF £60.71 CT £701.75 TOTE £12.60: £4.60 £2.30 £5.00 (£35.50) Trio £333.00 OWNER Mr M. J. Brodrick (MIDDLEHAM) BRED Pillar Stud Inc 13 Rn 1m 23.7 (1.00) SF: 63/47/34/54/39/30/42/39/38/31/4/36/-

1180 ROTHMANS ROYALS NORTH SOUTH CHALLENGE SERIES H'CAP (0-80) (3-Y.O) (Class D) £7,960.00 (£2,380.00: £1,140.00: £520.00)

1m Stalls: Low GOING minus 0.41 sec per fur (F) 4-15 (4-17)

1028* **Gospel Song (60)**_(69) (WTKemp)_ 3-7-11b(5)ow1 PMcCabe(2) (lw: a.p: led wl over 1f out: sn clr)..........................— **1**
1060⁵ Pc's Cruiser (IRE) **(53)**_(58) (MCChapman)_ 3-7-4b(5) NVarley(8) (hdwy 3f out: styd on wl: no ch w wnr)..........................2½ **2**
907⁶ Intendant **(59)**_(64) (JGFitzGerald)_ 3-7-12 (3) DRMcCabe(9) (in tch: hdwy over 2f out: styd on: nt pce to chal)..........................s.h **3**
823⁶ Bollin Frank **(57)**_(57) (MHEasterby)_ 3-7-13 LCharnock(1) (cl up: hmpd appr st: one pce fnl 3f)..........................2½ **4**
966⁵ Another Time **(54)**_(54) (MissSEHall)_ 3-7-10 DaleGibson(12) (styd on fnl 3f: nrst fin)..............s.h **5**
873⁹ Kings Assembly **(68)**_(65) (PWHarris)_ 3-8-10 RCochrane(15) (bhd tl hdwy 2f out: r.o wl nr fin)..........................1¼ **6**
980⁵ Shifting Moon **(75)**_(70)_(Fav)_(IABalding)_ 3-9-3 WRyan(3) (chsd ldrs: hmpd appr st: no imp after)..........................1 **7**
1052⁴ Risky Romeo **(68)**_(63) (GCBravery)_ 3-8-10 BThomson(6) (s.i.s: nrst fin)..........................hd **8**
966¹⁷ Alltime Dancer (IRE) **(55)**_(50) (MrsJRRamsden)_ 3-7-11 JFanning(17) (lw: unruly s: s.i.s: hdwy whn hmpd twice fnl 2f: nrst fin)..........................hd **9**
962⁴ The Stager (IRE) **(75)**_(68) (JRJenkins)_ 3-9-3 WCarson(4) (lw: nvr bttr than mid div)..................1 **10**
971⁶ Delight of Dawn **(74)**_(65) (KTIvory)_ 3-9-2 JWeaver(14) (b.hind: s.i.s: n.d)..........................¾ **11**
999⁵ Rymer's Rascal **(64)**_(49) (EJAlston)_ 3-8-1 (5)ow2 CTeague(7) (lw: led tl wl over 1f out: wknd qckly)..........................2 **12**
1060² Three Arch Bridge **(58)**_(39) (MJohnston)_ 3-8-0b TWilliams(10) (lw: chsd ldrs tl wknd 2f out).....3 **13**
572⁸ Shining Edge **(61)**_(41) (MHEasterby)_ 3-8-3 SMaloney(16) (s.i.s: n.d)..........................¾ **14**
928³ Barrel of Hope **(79)**_(53) (JLEyre)_ 3-9-7 JFortune(5) (in tch to st)..........................3 **15**
857⁷ Himalayan Blue **(67)**_(33) (MRChannon)_ 3-8-9 KDarley(11) (in tch to st)..........................4 **16**
Night Wink (USA) **(77)**_(42) (MRStoute)_ 3-9-5 PaulEddery(13) (lw: cl up tl rdn & wknd qckly over 3f out)..........................nk **17**

4/1 Shifting Moon (op 7/1), **9/2** Night Wink (USA), **7/1** Risky Romeo, **10/1** Another Time, **11/1** The Stager (IRE), **12/1** Kings Assembly, GOSPEL SONG, Intendant, **14/1** Barrel of Hope, Three Arch Bridge, **16/1** Himalayan Blue, Alltime Dancer (IRE), Shining Edge, Delight of Dawn, Rymer's Rascal, **20/1** Bollin Frank, Pc's Cruiser (IRE), CSF £230.37 CT £2,697.25 TOTE £15.40: £4.10 £5.40 £5.00 £6.40 (£190.60) Trio £711.80; £310.81 to Newbury 21/5/95 OWNER Drakemyre Racing (DUNS) BRED Miss Elizabeth Streatfeild 17 Rn

1m 37.8 (2.20) SF: 30/19/25/18/15/26/31/24/11/29/26/10/-/2/14/-/3

1181 D.L.B. CORPORATE FINANCE H'CAP (0-100) (3-Y.O) (Class C) £6,213.50 (£1,853.00: £884.00: £399.50)

5f Stalls: High GOING minus 0.41 sec per fur (F) 4-45 (4-47)

828* **Double Quick (IRE) (90)**_(97)_(Fav)_(MJohnston)_ 3-9-7 JWeaver(3) (cl up: led 2f out: r.o wl)...— **1**
Shashi (IRE) **(75)**_(76) (DMorley)_ 3-8-6 RCochrane(2) (bit bkwd: in tch: hdwy over 1f out: kpt on: nt pce of wnr)..........................1¾ **2**
850¹⁴ Just Dissident (IRE) **(63)**_(63) (RMWhitaker)_ 3-7-8 ow1 DaleGibson(4) (lw: a.p: rdn ½-wy: kpt on: nvr able to chal)..........................s.h **3**
999² Bolshoi (IRE) **(71)**_(71) (JBerry)_ 3-8-2b WCarson(7) (lw: outpcd & bhd: hdwy & swtchd lft over 1f out: styd on)..........................nk **4**
645* Coastal Bluff **(79)**_(74) (TDBarron)_ 3-8-10 JFortune(6) (b.hind: hmpd & stdd s: hld up: hdwy over 1f out: r.o)..........................1¾ **5**
904² Ninety-Five **(68)**_(57) (JGFitzGerald)_ 3-7-13 LCharnock(8) (led 3f: sn rdn & btn)..................1¾ **6**
850⁵ Musica **(78)**_(38) (MRChannon)_ 3-8-9 KDarley(5) (prom tl outpcd fnl 2f)..........................9 **7**
926¹⁸ High Ranking **(74)**_(23) (MHEasterby)_ 3-8-5 MBirch(1) (chsd ldrs over 3f: wknd)..................3½ **8**

LONG HANDICAP Just Dissident (IRE) 7-5

5/2 DOUBLE QUICK (IRE), **7/2** Coastal Bluff, Ninety-Five, **4/1** Bolshoi (IRE), **8/1** Musica, **10/1** Shashi (IRE), **14/1** High Ranking, **16/1** Just Dissident (IRE), CSF £26.87 CT £318.44 TOTE £3.10: £1.60 £2.60 £2.10 (£22.90) OWNER The 2nd Middleham Partnership (MIDDLEHAM) 8 Rn

58.1 secs (0.90) SF: 53/32/19/27/30/13/-/-

1182 ELMIRE MAIDEN STKS (3-Y.O F) (Class D) £3,935.10 (£1,174.80: £561.40: £254.70)
1m 4f Stalls: High GOING minus 0.41 sec per fur (F) 5-15 (5-16)

816³ **Haniya (IRE)** *(81) (JLDunlop)* 3-8-11 WCarson(3) (a.p: rdn to ld 2f out: r.o) ....— **1**
824² Flame War (USA) **(79)***(78) (HRACecil)* 3-8-11 WRyan(1) (lw: trckd ldrs: led 5f out tl hdd 2f out: kpt on wl) 2 **2**
First Amendment (IRE) *(77)*(Fav)*(LMCumani)* 3-8-11 JWeaver(6) (lw: hld up: hdwy appr st: effrt 2f out: r.o one pce) 1¼ **3**
950⁴ Zuiena (USA) *(67) (PFICole)* 3-8-11 JFortune(5) (lw: in tch: hdwy appr st: sn rdn & one pce) .7 **4**
Upper Torrish *(65) (BHanbury)* 3-8-11 RCochrane(7) (w'like: bit bkwd: bhd: rdn appr st: no imp) 1¾ **5**
773⁹ Beyaateh **(38)***(32) (MCChapman)* 3-8-4 (7) CMunday(2) (chsd ldrs: outpcd whn bdly hmpd appr st: sn wl bhd) 25 **6**
Primo Panache **(45)***(16) (MPBielby)* 3-8-11 ACulhane(4) (led tl hdd 5f out: wknd qckly over 3f out) 12 **7**

2/1 First Amendment (IRE), **9/4** HANIYA (IRE), Flame War (USA), **9/1** Zuiena (USA), **14/1** Upper Torrish, **100/1** Beyaateh, Primo Panache, CSF £7.42 TOTE £3.00: £1.70 £1.50 (£3.00) OWNER Mr Hamdan Al Maktoum (ARUNDEL) BRED Shadwell Estate Company Limited 7 Rn
2m 32.7 (2.70) SF: 45/42/41/31/29/-/-
T/Plpt: £631.60 (26.06 Tckts). T/Qdpt: £87.00 (0.1 Tckts); £105.84 to Newbury 21/5/95. AA

1169-NEWBURY (L-H)
Sunday May 21st (Good to firm)
WEATHER: fair WIND: almost nil

1183 MAIL ON SUNDAY CHAMPIONSHIP MILE (QUALIFIER) H'CAP (0-85) (3-Y.O+) (Class D) £8,277.50 (£2,495.00: £1,210.00: £567.50)
1m (straight) Stalls: Centre GOING minus 0.37 sec per fur (F) 2-00 (2-06)

873¹² **Zajko (USA)** **(70)***(80)*(Fav)*(LadyHerries)* 5-9-1 RCochrane(12) (rdn & hdwy 2f out: led ins fnl f: r.o wl) ....— **1**
980¹⁰ Floridante (USA) **(71)***(78) (PFICole)* 3-8-4 ow1 TQuinn(17) (lw: a.p: rdn over 2f out: ev ch ins fnl f: unable qckn) 1¼ **2**
935¹⁵ Safey Ana (USA) **(65)***(71) (BHanbury)* 4-8-10b TIves(16) (a.p: led over 3f out tl over 1f out: one pce) 1 **3**
1052² Nashaat (USA) **(68)***(72) (NJHWalker)* 7-8-8 (5) RPainter(14) (hld up: led over 1f out tl ins fnl f: one pce) 1 **4**
980² Bedivere (USA) **(88)***(91) (PWChapple-Hyam)* 3-9-7 BThomson(15) (lw: a.p: ev ch wl over 1f out: one pce) ....½ **5**
873⁵ Uncle Oswald **(78)***(78) (RHannon)* 4-9-2 (7) DaneO'Neill(20) (hld up: hrd rdn over 1f out: one pce) 1¼ **6**
873⁷ Khayrapour (IRE) **(70)***(69) (BJMeehan)* 5-9-1 BDoyle(6) (lw: a.p: ev ch over 1f out: wknd fnl f) ....nk **7**
Desert Time **(73)***(72) (CAHorgan)* 5-9-4 MPerrett(18) (b.hind: nvr plcd to chal) ....hd **8**
873* Deevee **(73)***(71) (CJBenstead)* 6-9-4 GDuffield(9) (lw: s.s: nvr nrr) ....½ **9**
439⁶ Bagshot **(83)***(79) (RHannon)* 4-10-0 RPerham(22) (a mid div) 1¼ **10**
870³ Top Banana **(74)***(69) (HCandy)* 4-9-5 WNewnes(2) (a mid div) ....nk **11**
975⁹ Prenonamoss **(60)***(55) (DWPArbuthnot)* 7-8-5v MTebbutt(23) (b.hind: nvr nrr) ....s.h **12**
Samba Sharply **(74)***(68) (AHide)* 4-9-5 JWilliams(11) (a mid div) ....nk **13**
873⁸ Battleship Bruce **(68)***(60) (NACallaghan)* 3-8-1 GHind(27) (b.hind: lw: nvr plcd to chal) 1 **14**
749¹² Samah **(67)***(54) (DNicholls)* 5-8-12 CRutter(7) (prom over 5f) 2½ **15**
780¹⁴ Broughton Singer (IRE) **(58)***(45) (WJMusson)* 4-8-3 AMcGlone(8) (a mid div) ....hd **16**
749³ Mo-Addab (IRE) **(74)***(60) (ACStewart)* 5-9-5 RHills(26) (nvr nrr) ....½ **17**
873² Saifan **(70)***(50) (DMorris)* 6-8-12b(3) CHodgson(1) (hld up: rdn over 3f out: wknd over 2f out)...3 **18**
504³ King Balant (IRE) **(75)***(55) (MRStoute)* 3-8-8 WRSwinburn(25) (b.hind: shkn up over 2f out: nvr plcd to chal) ....nk **19**
873¹⁹ Set the Fashion **(71)***(44) (LordHuntingdon)* 6-9-2v DHarrison(5) (sme hdwy over 1f out: sn wknd) 3½ **20**
939¹⁰ Duffertoes **(81)***(53) (MJRyan)* 3-9-0 GCarter(13) (lw: prom over 5f) ....nk **21**
779* Stinging Reply **(80)***(52) (IABalding)* 3-8-13 MHills(4) (led over 4f: wknd over 2f out) ....hd **22**
Make a Stand **(75)***(47) (HCandy)* 4-9-6 NAdams(3) (lw: a bhd) ....s.h **23**
714²⁰ Highland Magic (IRE) **(69)** *(MJFetherston-Godley)* 7-9-0 FNorton(19) (a bhd) 25 **24**
976¹³ Mohawk Trail **(70)** *(GLewis)* 6-8-8 (7) ALakeman(24) (a bhd) 9 **25**

11/2 ZAJKO (USA), **7/1** Bedivere (USA), **8/1** Top Banana, **9/1** King Balant (IRE), **12/1** Deevee, **14/1** Saifan, Stinging Reply, Mo-Addab (IRE), **16/1** Khayrapour (IRE), Bagshot, Set the Fashion, Floridante (USA), **20/1** Uncle Oswald, Samah, **25/1** Broughton Singer (IRE), Battleship Bruce, Prenonamoss, Nashaat (USA), Desert Time, Samba Sharply, **40/1** Mohawk Trail, **50/1** Duffertoes, Make a Stand, Highland Magic (IRE), Safey Ana (USA), CSF £90.49 CT £3,715.80 TOTE £6.90: £2.50 £3.90 £20.00 £7.10 (£85.30) Trio £1,958.70; £2,262.23 to Bath 22/5/95 OWNER Sir Roger Gibbs (LITTLEHAMPTON) BRED Darley Stud Management Company Ltd 25 Rn
1m 37.62 (0.62) SF: 62/48/53/54/61/60/51/54/53/61/51/37/50/30/36/27/42/32/25/26/23/22/29/-/-
WEIGHT FOR AGE 3yo-12lb

OFFICIAL EXPLANATION **Highland Magic: The trainer reported that the gelding broke a blood vessel in the race.**

1184

WATERSHIP DOWN STUD MAIDEN STKS (2-Y.O C & G) (Class D) £5,865.00 (£1,770.00: £860.00: £405.00)
6f 8y Stalls: Centre GOING minus 0.37 sec per fur (F) 2-30 (2-37)

Russian Revival (USA) *(97+)*(Fav)*(PWChapple-Hyam)* 2-8-11 BThomson(4) (w'like: scope: led: rdn over 1f out: hdd ins fnl f: led last stride) — 1
Kahir Almaydan (IRE) *(97) (JLDunlop)* 2-8-11 GCarter(12) (leggy: unf: hdwy over 2f out: rdn over 1f out: led ins fnl f: hdd last stride) s.h 2
Masehaab (IRE) *(86) (JLDunlop)* 2-8-11 RHills(15) (str: scope: bkwd: rdn over 2f out: hdwy over 1f out: r.o: bttr for r) 4 3
Kilvine *(78) (LMCumani)* 2-8-11 WRSwinburn(5) (w'like: scope: bit bkwd: a.p: rdn 2f out: one pce) 3 4
Tagula (IRE) *(78) (IABalding)* 2-8-11 TIves(6) (str: bkwd: hld up: swtchd lft & rdn over 2f out: one pce fnl f) hd 5
Inverlochy *(70) (JLDunlop)* 2-8-11 WNewnes(2) (unf: scope: bit bkwd: rdn over 2f out: hdwy over 1f out: nvr nrr: rn green) 3 6
Gentilhomme *(69) (PFICole)* 2-8-11 TQuinn(7) (leggy: scope: rdn thrght: hdwy 4f out: wknd over 1f out) ½ 7
Munketh (USA) *(67) (JLDunlop)* 2-8-11 GDuffield(13) (leggy: rdn over 2f out: nvr nrr) ¾ 8
The Legions Pride *(65) (JWHills)* 2-8-11 MHills(1) (w'like: scope: bit bkwd: nvr nrr) ¾ 9
760[4] Back By Dawn *(60) (DRCElsworth)* 2-8-11 BDoyle(18) (b.hind: nvr nrr) 2 10
825[6] Ca'd'oro *(59) (GBBalding)* 2-8-11 JWilliams(9) (a mid div) hd 11
1047[9] Multi Franchise *(58) (BGubby)* 2-8-11 AMcGlone(10) (prom over 3f) ½ 12
La Tansani (IRE) *(56) (RHannon)* 2-8-4 (7) DaneO'Neill(8) (w'like: bkwd: prom over 3f) ¾ 13
North Star (IRE) *(54) (RHannon)* 2-8-11 RPerham(17) (neat: prom over 3f) ¾ 14
Master Lynx (USA) *(45) (GLewis)* 2-8-11 SWhitworth(11) (w'like: bkwd: bhd fnl 2f) 3½ 15
Oblomov *(43) (GLewis)* 2-8-11 RCochrane(14) (w'like: scope: a bhd) ½ 16
State Visitor *(42) (RHannon)* 2-8-11 SRaymont(3) (str: scope: bkwd: a bhd) ½ 17
Maygain (IRE) *(29) (MRChannon)* 2-8-11 RHughes(16) (unf: bit bkwd: prom 3f) 5 18

6/5 RUSSIAN REVIVAL (USA), **5/1** Masehaab (IRE), **15/2** Gentilhomme (9/2-8/1), **9/1** Kilvine, **16/1** Tagula (IRE), **20/1** Oblomov, Ca'd'oro, **25/1** State Visitor, Maygain (IRE), Back By Dawn, Inverlochy, Master Lynx (USA), La Tansani (IRE), Kahir Almaydan (IRE), **33/1** North Star (IRE), Multi Franchise, Munketh (USA), The Legions Pride, CSF £34.70 TOTE £2.20: £1.30 £12.40 £2.80 (£77.10) Trio £292.10 OWNER Mr R. E. Sangster (MARLBOROUGH) BRED Swettenham Stud 18 Rn 1m 12.63 (0.83) SF: 53/53/42/34/34/26/25/23/21/16/15/14/12/10/1/-/-/-

1185

CATS CONDITIONS STKS (3-Y.O) (Class C) £5,561.00 (£1,941.00: £945.50: £402.50) **7f 64y (round)** Stalls: Low GOING minus 0.37 sec per fur (F) 3-00 (3-02)

667[5] **Inzar (USA)** **(108)***(104+)*(Fav)*(PFICole)* 3-9-2 TQuinn(1) (3rd st: led 2f out: rdn 1f out: r.o wl) — 1
900a[13] Moon King (IRE) **(110)***(96) (RHannon)* 3-8-12 WRSwinburn(2) (led over 5f: rdn over 1f out: unable qckn) 2 2
826[8] Prince of India **(103)***(103) (LordHuntingdon)* 3-9-6 DHarrison(4) (lw: 4th st: rdn over 1f out: one pce) nk 3
660[6] Dashing Water **(98)***(90) (IABalding)* 3-8-7 MHills(3) (lw: 2nd st: rdn & ev ch 1fout: one pce) hd 4

13/8 INZAR (USA) (Evens-7/4), **7/4** Moon King (IRE), **3/1** Dashing Water, **8/1** Prince of India, CSF £4.64 TOTE £2.10: (£1.90) OWNER Prince Fahd Salman (WHATCOMBE) BRED Newgate Stud Farm Inc in USA 4 Rn 1m 30.72 (2.22) SF: 45/37/44/31

1186

STARLIGHT MAIDEN STKS (3-Y.O) (Class D) £5,735.00(£1,730.00: £840.00: £395.00) **7f 64y (round)** Stalls: Low GOING minus 0.37 sec per fur (F) 3-30 (3-32)

Great Inquest *(85) (JHMGosden)* 3-8-9 RCochrane(2) (scope: s.s: hdwy on ins over 2f out: rdn over 1f out: led nr fin) — 1

Easy Jet (POL) **(70)***(88) (LordHuntingdon)* 3-9-0 DHarrison(16) (2nd st: rdn over 2f out: led ins fnl f: hdd nr fin) ¾ **2**
924[2] Pinzon (USA) *(86)*(Fav)*(PWChapple-Hyam)* 3-9-0 BThomson(15) (led: rdn over 1f out: hdd ins fnl f: one pce) 1¼ **3**
Marocco (USA) *(86) (HRACecil)* 3-9-0 AMcGlone(5) (unf: hdwy over 5f out: 4th st: rdn over 2f out: r.o ins fnl f) s.h **4**
715[6] Desert Harvest *(82)*(Fav)*(RCharlton)* 3-9-0 PaulEddery(3) (lw: hdwy over 5f out: 5th st: rdn over 2f out: one pce) 1½ **5**
Knotally Wood (USA) *(75) (JWHills)* 3-8-9 MHills(11) (unf: nt clr run over 2f out & over 1f out: hdwy fnl f: nvr nrr) 1 **6**
Hugwity *(79) (BHanbury)* 3-9-0 TIves(8) (b.nr hind: lengthy: nvr nr to chal) ½ **7**
Mukhatab *(73)*(Fav)*(HThomsonJones)* 3-9-0 RHills(12) (w'like: scope: hld up: rdn over 2f out: sn wknd) 2½ **8**
Tarawa (IRE) *(73) (NACallaghan)* 3-9-0 GDuffield(18) (w'like: scope: nvr nrr) d.h **8**
Zelda Zonk *(64) (BJMeehan)* 3-8-9 BDoyle(10) (str: scope: bit bkwd: 7th st: rdn over 2f out: wknd over 1f out) 2 **10**
963[5] Easy Dollar **(80)***(63) (BGubby)* 3-9-0v JWilliams(14) (bhd whn stumbled 4f out) 3 **11**
715[24] Yosif (IRE) *(60) (RHannon)* 3-9-0 WRSwinburn(13) (lw: 6th st: wknd over 2f out) 1¼ **12**
Norsong *(60) (RAkehurst)* 3-8-11 (3) SSanders(9) (snatched up over 5f out: bhd fnl 2f) s.h **13**
Karaar *(54) (JHMGosden)* 3-9-0 GHind(1) (b.hind: str: scope: bit bkwd: s.s: a bhd) 2½ **14**
761[8] Backhander (IRE) *(43) (JARToller)* 3-9-0 TQuinn(6) (3rd st: wknd over 2f out) 5 **15**
Truly Madly Deeply *(25) (MrsJRRamsden)* 3-8-9 MWigham(17) (cmpt: bkwd: a wl bhd) 6 **16**

7/2 Desert Harvest, Pinzon (USA), Mukhatab (3/1-5/1), **11/2** Marocco (USA) (op 3/1), **9/1** Karaar (3/1-10/1), **14/1** GREAT INQUEST (op 8/1), Hugwity (op 8/1), **20/1** Backhander (IRE), Knotally Wood (USA), **25/1** Easy Jet (POL), Easy Dollar, Yosif (IRE), Truly Madly Deeply, Zelda Zonk, **33/1** Tarawa (IRE), Norsong, CSF £306.05 TOTE £24.40: £5.50 £6.80 £1.50 (£398.70) Trio £654.60; £636.33 to Bath 22/5/95 OWNER Lord Dalmeny (NEWMARKET) BRED Stanley Estate and Stud Co
16 Rn 1m 29.13 (0.63) SF: 56/59/57/57/53/46/50/44/44/35/34/31/31/25/14/-

1187 JUDDMONTE LOCKINGE STKS (Gp 1) (4-Y.O+) (Class A) £70,210.00 (£26,143.00: £12,446.50: £5,300.50)

1m (straight) Stalls: Centre GOING minus 0.37 sec per fur (F) 4-00 (4-08)

Soviet Line (IRE) (117)*(130+)*(Fav)*(MRStoute)* 5-9-0 WRSwinburn(4) (lw: mde all: rdn over 1f out: r.o wl) — **1**
814* Young Ern **(116)***(126) (SDow)* 5-9-0 TQuinn(5) (lw: a.p: chsd wnr fnl 2f: unable qckn) 2 **2**
794* Missed Flight **(120)***(121) (CFWall)* 5-9-0 GDuffield(3) (lw: stdd s: hld up: rdn 2f out: wknd ins fnl f) 2½ **3**
794[3] Mutakddim (USA) **(111)***(120) (JHMGosden)* 4-9-0 GHind(2) (hld up: rdn 2f out: one pce) ½ **4**
Muhtarram (USA) **(123)***(110) (JHMGosden)* 6-9-0 RHills(1) (lw: chsd wnr 6f) 5 **5**

2/1 SOVIET LINE (IRE), **3/1** Muhtarram (USA), Missed Flight, **7/2** Young Ern, **14/1** Mutakddim (USA), CSF £8.72 TOTE £2.20: £1.50 £2.10 (£4.50) OWNER Maktoum Al Maktoum (NEWMARKET) BRED Cheveley Park Stud Ltd 5 Rn 1m 36.96 (-0.04) SF: 68/64/59/58/48

1188 SUNSET BOULEVARD RATED STKS H'CAP (0-105) (3-Y.O+) (Class B) £9,338.40 (£3,495.60: £1,710.30: £736.50: £330.75: £168.45)

1m 1f Stalls: Low GOING minus 0.37 sec per fur (F) 4-30 (4-35)

829* **Holtye (IRE) (93)***(105)*(Fav)*(HRACecil)* 3-8-0 AMcGlone(4) (lw: 2nd st: led wl over 1f out: edgd lft: rdn out) — **1**
704a[6] Salt Lake **(86)***(97) (PWChapple-Hyam)* 4-8-7 BThomson(8) (led over 7f: hrd drvn fnl f: r.o wl) ¾ **2**
918[5] Embankment (IRE) **(86)***(90) (RHannon)* 5-8-7 TQuinn(7) (lw: 6th st: rdn over 2f out: unable qckn) 4 **3**
Night City **(100)***(103) (LadyHerries)* 4-9-7 RHughes(1) (3rd st: rdn over 2f out: one pce) nk **4**
1010a* Moments of Fortune (USA) **(99)***(99) (BHanbury)* 3-8-6b TIves(6) (4th st: rdn over 3f out: wknd over 2f out) 2 **5**
Green Crusader **(93)***(87) (MRStoute)* 4-9-0v WRSwinburn(3) (a bhd) 3 **6**
872[3] Risk Master **(91)***(85) (CAHorgan)* 6-8-12 RHills(5) (s.s: a bhd) nk **7**
793[10] Lomas (IRE) **(88)***(76) (MrsHParrott)* 4-8-9 VSlattery(2) (5th st: wknd over 3f out) 3 **8**

LONG HANDICAP Embankment (IRE) 8-6

Evens HOLTYE (IRE), **5/1** Moments of Fortune (USA), **11/2** Salt Lake, **8/1** Embankment (IRE) (6/1-10/1), **10/1** Night City (8/1-12/1), Green Crusader (8/1-12/1), **20/1** Risk Master, **50/1** Lomas (IRE), CSF £7.15 CT £27.09 TOTE £1.90: £1.20 £1.40 £1.90 (£4.60) OWNER Mr K. Abdullah (NEWMARKET) BRED Juddmonte Farms 8 Rn 1m49.65 (2.60 under best) (0.45) SF: 50/56/49/62/44/46/44/35
WEIGHT FOR AGE 3yo-14lb

1189 REALLY USEFUL-NORDOFF ROBBINS H'CAP (0-90) (4-Y.O+) (Class C)
£7,522.00 (£2,266.00: £1,098.00: £514.00)
2m Stalls: Low GOING minus 0.37 sec per fur (F) 5-00 (5-02)

795* **Smuggling (74)***(88)*(Fav)*(RAkehurst)* 4-8-13 TQuinn(7) (lw: mde all: hrd rdn 2f out: r.o wl)..— **1**
*469** Maradonna (USA) **(62)***(75) (JWhite)* 6-8-3 GDuffield(6) (4th st: rdn over 3f out: unable qckn fnl f)....1¼ **2**
938⁵ Lalindi (IRE) **(66)***(77) (DRCElsworth)* 4-8-0 (5) SDrowne(1) (lw: rdn over 4f out: hdwy over 1f out: r.o)....1¾ **3**
795⁵ Polo Kit (IRE) **(77)***(88) (JRFanshawe)* 4-9-2v DHarrison(5) (hdwy over 1f out: r.o one pce).....½ **4**
938* Blaze Away (USA) **(81)***(89) (IABalding)* 4-9-6 RCochrane(3) (lw: no hdwy fnl 3f)....2½ **5**
Polish Consul **(68)***(75) (MajorWRHern)* 4-8-7 RHills(4) (2nd st: rdn 3f out: wknd fnl f)....¾ **6**
1058* Inchcailloch (IRE) **(60)***(66) (JSKing)* 6-8-1 PaulEddery(2) (hdwy over 3f out: one pce)....1¾ **7**
795¹⁴ Sails Legend **(54)***(57) (MrsMELong)* 4-7-7 NAdams(9) (gd hdwy over 6f out: 5th st: wknd over 2f out)....3 **8**
Muntafi **(78)***(80) (GHarwood)* 4-9-3 MPerrett(11) (lw: 6th st: wknd 4f out)....¾ **9**
869⁹ Not in Doubt (USA) **(83)***(84) (HCandy)* 6-9-10 WNewnes(12) (lw: 3rd st: wknd 4f out)....1¼ **10**
821⁸ Art Form (USA) **(73)***(68) (CACyzer)* 8-9-0 TIves(8) (b: s.s: hdwy 6f out: wknd over 4f out).......6 **11**

LONG HANDICAP Sails Legend 6-10

2/1 SMUGGLING, **4/1** Blaze Away (USA), **9/2** Inchcailloch (IRE), **6/1** Polo Kit (IRE), **7/1** Lalindi (IRE), **14/1** Art Form (USA), Maradonna (USA), **16/1** Muntafi, **20/1** Polish Consul, Not in Doubt (USA), **100/1** Sails Legend, CSF £30.31 CT £164.66 TOTE £2.70: £1.40 £2.90 £2.50 (£41.80) Trio £110.30 OWNER Mr George Taiano (EPSOM) BRED Lord Howard de Walden 11 Rn
3m 32.39 (5.89) SF: 40/29/29/40/41/27/20/9/32/38/22
WEIGHT FOR AGE 4yo-2lb

T/Jkpt: £11,052.40 (1.38 Tckts). T/Plpt: £49.50 (497.50 Tckts). T/Qdpt: £14.30 (24.15 Tckts). AK

0818-RIPON (R-H)
Sunday May 21st (Good, Good to firm patches)

WEATHER: overcast WIND: slt half bhd

1190 FUN FOR ALL THE FAMILY MAIDEN STKS (2-Y.O) (Class D)
£3,712.50 (£1,125.00: £550.00: £262.50)
6f Stalls: Low GOING minus 0.51 sec per fur (F) 2-15 (2-19)

Jedaal *(77+) (LMCumani)* 2-9-0 KDarley(1) (cmpt: bmpd after s: sn in tch: rdn to ld ins fnl f: hld on wl)....— **1**
Classic Leader *(76+) (SCWilliams)* 2-9-0 AMackay(9) (w'like: scope: s.i.s: hdwy ½-wy: chal wl ins fnl f: nt qckn nr fin)....nk **2**
Percy Park (USA) *(74+) (MJohnston)* 2-9-0 DHolland(2) (w'like: leggy: scope: sn chsng ldrs: led over 1f out tl ins fnl f: kpt on)....1 **3**
819⁵ Trickledown *(65) (CWFairhurst)* 2-8-9 DeanMcKeown(13) (a cl up: nt qckn fnl f)....1¼ **4**
Kingfisher Brave *(62) (SGNorton)* 2-9-0 JFanning(3) (leggy: unf: in tch: outpcd 2f out: styd on ins fnl f)....3 **5**
615⁵ Rapid Liner *(58) (AHarrison)* 2-8-9 (5) JStack(5) (led tl hdd & wknd 2f out)....1¾ **6**
River Tern *(57)*(Fav)*(JBerry)* 2-9-0 JCarroll(6) (leggy: unf: s.i.s: sn rcvrd & cl up: led 2f out tl over 1f out: wknd ins fnl f)....nk **7**
Oversman *(49) (JGFitzGerald)* 2-9-0 KFallon(12) (w'like: bit bkwd: unruly s: bhd tl late hdwy) 3 **8**
810⁹ Topaglow (IRE) *(46) (PTDalton)* 2-9-0 LCharnock(14) (prom 4f)....1 **9**
How Could-I (IRE) *(30) (MHEasterby)* 2-8-9 MBirch(8) (unf: bit bkwd: sn outpcd & bhd)....4 **10**
863⁴ Copper Bright *(32) (PCHaslam)* 2-9-0 JFortune(10) (bit bkwd: in tch 4f)....1¼ **11**
533¹⁴ Euro Express *(31) (MHEasterby)* 2-9-0b SMaloney(7) (sn outpcd & bhd)....nk **12**
863⁷ Elle Mac *(13) (MPBielby)* 2-8-9 ACulhane(4) (s.i.s: a outpcd & bhd)....5 **13**

9/4 River Tern (op 9/2), **3/1** Percy Park (USA), **9/2** JEDAAL, **7/1** Classic Leader, **10/1** Rapid Liner, **12/1** Oversman, **14/1** Trickledown, **20/1** Kingfisher Brave, Euro Express, How Could-I (IRE), **25/1** Topaglow (IRE), **33/1** Copper Bright, Elle Mac, CSF £37.51 TOTE £3.90: £1.80 £2.10 £1.40 (£9.20) Trio £27.40 OWNER Sheikh Ahmed Al Maktoum (NEWMARKET) BRED Sheikh Ahmed bin Rashid al Maktoum 13 Rn
1m 12.3 (2.10) SF: 26/25/23/14/11/7/6/-/-/-/-/-/-

1191 SUNDAY IS FUNDAY AT THE RACES (S) STKS (3-Y.O+) (Class F)
£2,853.00 (£864.00: £422.00: £201.00)
1m Stalls: High GOING minus 0.51 sec per fur (F) 2-45 (2-46)

1030³ **Java Red (IRE)** *(60) (JGFitzGerald)* 3-8-6 KFallon(3) (in tch: rdn over 2f out: hdwy ins fnl f: r.o wl to ld cl home)....— **1**

848² Roseate Lodge **(64)***(64)*(Fav)*(KRBurke)* 9-9-9 AClark(6) (lw: hld up: hdwy over 3f out: led wl over 1f out: hdd & no ex towards fin) ....¾ 2
My Handsome Prince **(37)***(57) (PJBevan)* 3-8-6 NCarlisle(2) (chsd ldrs: ev ch 2f out: r.o one pce) ....¾ 3
1037⁸ Greek Gold (IRE) **(44)***(58) (DNicholls)* 6-9-9 AlexGreaves(5) (lw: sn led: hdd wl over 1f out: one pce) 2 4
1028⁴ Slytly Beveled **(54)***(52) (NPLittmoden)* 3-8-6b(5) TGMcLaughlin(7) (bhd: effrt ½-wy: nt pce to chal) 3 5
*80*⁸ Level Edge **(50)***(47) (MDHammond)* 4-9-4 KDarley(8) (led early: cl up tl rdn & btn over 1f out) ....hd 6
818⁶ Puffy **(34)***(45) (MDods)* 8-9-4b JCarroll(10) (b: s.s: effrt 4f out: no imp) 1 7
Millstock *(33) (APJones)* 5-8-13 JFortune(9) (chsd ldrs tl outpcd fnl 3f) 3½ 8
1083¹⁰ Castletown Count **(52)***(35) (KWHogg)* 3-8-6 DeanMcKeown(1) (rn wd st: sn lost pl) 1½ 9
My Lindianne *(20) (JDooler)* 8-8-13 SWebster(4) (s.i.s: a bhd) 5 10

11/10 Roseate Lodge (op 7/4), **4/1** JAVA RED (IRE), Slytly Beveled, **9/1** Castletown Count, **10/1** Level Edge, **12/1** Greek Gold (IRE), **14/1** Puffy, **33/1** Millstock, My Handsome Prince, My Lindianne, CSF £9.42 TOTE £4.60: £1.50 £1.40 £4.90 (£3.90) Trio £78.60 OWNER Mr J. G. FitzGerald (MALTON) BRED Rathasker Stud 10 Rn 1m 39.9 (2.20) SF: 27/43/24/37/19/26/24/12/2/-
WEIGHT FOR AGE 3yo-12lb
No bid.

1192 SUNDAY EXPRESS BEST FOR SPORT SERIES (QUALIFIER) H'CAP (0-85) (3-Y.O+) (Class D) £5,367.10 (£1,625.80: £794.40: £378.70)
1m 2f Stalls: High GOING minus 0.51 sec per fur (F) 3-15 (3-15)

618ᶠ **Muferr (IRE) (77)***(90)*(Fav)*(LMCumani)* 3-8-6 KDarley(11) (lw: mid div: rdn to ld 2f out: r.o wl) ....— 1
988⁷ Kalou **(55)***(63) (CWCElsey)* 4-7-13v LCharnock(5) (led tl hdd 2f out: kpt on wl) 3 2
981⁴ Sovereign Page (USA) **(77)***(77) (BHanbury)* 6-9-2 (5) JStack(4) (b: in tch: ev ch 2f out: nt qckn) 5 3
1064⁵ Durham Drapes **(59)***(58) (MHEasterby)* 4-8-3 SMaloney(12) (in tch: hdwy 3f out: rdn & one pce appr fnl f) ....½ 4
Essayeffsee **(51)***(50) (MrsMReveley)* 6-7-9 DaleGibson(7) (bhd tl styd on fnl 3f: nrst fin) ....½ 5
1037² Murphy's Gold (IRE) **(51)***(49) (RAFahey)* 4-7-9 ow1 JQuinn(1) (hld up & bhd: hdwy on ins 3f out: rdn & no ex appr fnl f) ....s.h 6
927⁹ Lancashire Life (IRE) **(49)***(40) (EJAlston)* 4-7-7 GBardwell(13) (plld hrd: chsd ldrs tl wknd 2f out) 5 7
864¹¹ Locorotondo (IRE) **(73)***(63) (MBell)* 4-9-3 MFenton(10) (b: prom tl outpcd over 2f out) ....½ 8
*843*³ Red Indian **(51)***(36) (WWHaigh)* 9-7-2 (7)ow2 MartinDwyer(3) (in tch tl rdn & wknd over 3f out) 1½ 9
988¹⁵ Talented Ting (IRE) **(64)***(42) (PCHaslam)* 6-8-8 TWilliams(2) (bhd: rdn 4f out: n.d) 6 10
Desert Fighter **(84)***(22) (DNicholson)* 4-10-0 AClark(6) (chsd ldrs tl wknd 3f out) 25 11
981³ Laxford Bridge **(82)** *(PWHarris)* 4-9-12 DHolland(9) (p.u after 1½f whn sddle slipped) .... P
LONG HANDICAP Red Indian 6-12

3/1 MUFERR (IRE), **7/2** Sovereign Page (USA), **5/1** Laxford Bridge, Murphy's Gold (IRE), **8/1** Locorotondo (IRE) (op 14/1), **10/1** Desert Fighter, **14/1** Durham Drapes, **16/1** Essayeffsee, Kalou, **20/1** Talented Ting (IRE), Red Indian, **25/1** Lancashire Life (IRE), CSF £50.26 CT £171.27 TOTE £4.20: £1.80 £5.20 £1.90 (£42.80) Trio £59.50 OWNER Sheikh Ahmed Al Maktoum (NEWMARKET) BRED Mrs T. V. Ryan 12 Rn 2m 2.8 (-0.70) SF: 55/43/57/38/30/29/20/43/16/22/2/-
WEIGHT FOR AGE 3yo-15lb

1193 RIPON SUNDAY SPRINT CHALLENGE H'CAP (0-90) (3-Y.O+) (Class C) £7,132.50 (£2,160.00: £1,055.00: £502.50)
5f Stalls: Low GOING minus 0.51 sec per fur (F) 3-45 (3-46)

994² **Broadstairs Beauty (IRE) (70)***(77) (SRBowring)* 5-8-5b(5) CTeague(12) (b: b.hind: led tl hdd appr fnl f: rallied to ld nr fin) ....— 1
1106³ Name the Tune **(72)***(79) (PHowling)* 4-8-12 JQuinn(10) (lw: b.hind: trckd ldr: led over 1f out: hdd & no ex cl home) ....hd 2
982* Total Stranger **(79)***(80)*(Fav)*(MrsLPiggott)* 3-8-10 KDarley(9) (chsd ldrs: effrt 2f out: nt qckn fnl f) 1¾ 3
1152⁴ Cool Edge (IRE) **(68)***(69) (MHTompkins)* 4-8-8 PRobinson(8) (chsd ldrs: styd on fnl f: nt pce to chal) ....hd 4
1057⁴ Domicksky **(65)***(65) (MRChannon)* 7-8-5 AClark(13) (hdwy 2f out: styd on towards fin) ....hd 5
723⁹ Beau Venture (USA) **(74)***(70) (FHLee)* 7-8-9 (5) PMcCabe(6) (hdwy ½-wy: kpt on fnl f: nvr trbld ldrs) 1¼ 6
723¹² Stephensons Rocket **(76)***(67) (JBerry)* 4-9-2 JCarroll(4) (lw: b.off hind: effrt ½-wy: styd on: nvr able to chal) 1¾ 7

For the Present **(88)***(79) (TDBarron)* 5-10-0 JFortune(14) (bit bkwd: chsd ldrs over 3f) ....s.h 8
1050* Hickory Blue **(71)***(62) (MrsNMacauley)* 5-8-11b DaleGibson(7) (prom over 3f) ....s.h 9
1057[6] Kildee Lad **(74)***(64) (APJones)* 5-9-0 MFenton(2) (racd stands' side: rdn & outpcd fr ½-wy)..s.h 10
1076[7] Pageboy **(73)***(59) (PCHaslam)* 6-8-13 TWilliams(11) (s.i.s: n.d)..1½ 11
1151[3] Ned's Bonanza **(68)***(51) (MDods)* 6-8-8 KFallon(1) (lw: racd stands' side: no ch fr ½-wy) ....¾ 12
Lepine (IRE) **(75)***(50) (JWWatts)* 4-9-1 NConnorton(3) (swtg: racd stands' side: no ch fr ½-wy) 2½ 13
Here Comes a Star **(76)***(47) (JMCarr)* 7-9-2 SMorris(5) (s.i.s: a bhd) 1¼ 14

9/2 Total Stranger, **5/1** BROADSTAIRS BEAUTY (IRE), **11/2** Name the Tune, **8/1** Hickory Blue, **9/1** Cool Edge (IRE), Domicksky (op 14/1), Ned's Bonanza, **12/1** Kildee Lad, Lepine (IRE), **14/1** Beau Venture (USA), **16/1** For the Present, Pageboy, Stephensons Rocket, **20/1** Here Comes a Star, CSF £34.36 CT £129.31 TOTE £6.20: £2.40 £2.30 £1.80 (£13.40) Trio £27.00 OWNER Mrs Judy Hunt (EDWINSTOWE) BRED Patrick Murnaghan 14 Rn

57.6 secs (0.10 under best) (-0.40) SF: 58/60/52/50/46/51/48/60/43/45/40/32/31/28

WEIGHT FOR AGE 3yo-9lb

1194 MIDDLEHAM TRAINERS ASSOCIATION H'CAP (0-80) (3-Y.O) (Class D)

£4,299.00 (£1,302.00: £636.00: £303.00)

1m 4f 60y Stalls: High GOING minus 0.51 sec per fur (F) 4-15 (4-16)

774[0] **Thaljanah (IRE) (76)***(82) (ACStewart)* 3-9-4 DHolland(2) (swtg: led 8f out: hld on wl fnl f) ....— 1
854[3] Top Lady (IRE) **(67)***(73) (MRStoute)* 3-8-6 (3) JTate(9) (lw: led 1f: chsd ldrs: outpcd & n.m.r 2f out: hdwy ins fnl f: r.o)..hd 2
851[8] Last Corner **(55)***(61) (RHollinshead)* 3-7-11 JQuinn(8) (hld up: hdwy 3f out: chal ins fnl f: r.o)nk 3
485[5] Crespo (IRE) **(73)***(78) (JRFanshawe)* 3-9-1 JCarroll(5) (trckd ldrs: chal 3f out: nt qckn ins fnl f) ....¾ 4
687* Tessajoe **(58)***(62) (MJCamacho)* 3-8-0 LCharnock(3) (lw: trckd ldrs: effrt over 2f out: n.m.r 1f out: styd on one pce)...hd 5
929[3] Snow Valley **(79)***(81)*(Fav)*(LMCumani)* 3-9-7 KDarley(4) (lw: led after 1f tl 8f out: chal 3f out: one pce appr fnl f: btn whn hmpd cl home)..1½ 6
736[5] Lucidity **(62)***(60) (CWThornton)* 3-8-4 DeanMcKeown(6) (swtg: dwlt: hdwy 5f out: rdn & btn appr fnl f) 3½ 7
907[4] Equity's Darling (IRE) **(62)***(53) (MBell)* 3-8-4 MFenton(10) (in tch tl outpcd fnl 2f).....................5 8
643[3] Final Fling **(60)***(50) (JWWatts)* 3-8-2 ow1 NConnorton(7) (bhd: effrt on outside 3f out: sn btn)...s.h 9
Silverdale Count **(51)***(23) (KWHogg)* 3-7-0 (7) DLockhart(1) (wl bhd fnl 4f)..............................15 10

LONG HANDICAP Silverdale Count 7-1

5/2 Snow Valley, **7/2** Tessajoe, **4/1** Top Lady (IRE), **7/1** THALJANAH (IRE), Crespo (IRE), **8/1** Final Fling, **12/1** Lucidity, **14/1** Equity's Darling (IRE), Last Corner, **33/1** Silverdale Count, CSF £36.72 CT £366.44 TOTE £10.50: £2.60 £1.60 £4.10 (£19.70) Trio £66.40 OWNER Mr Hamdan Al Maktoum (NEWMARKET) BRED Abbeville Stud 10 Rn

2m 36.4 (2.40) SF: 46/37/25/42/26/45/24/17/14/-

STEWARDS' ENQUIRY Holland suspended 30-31/5/95 (excessive use of whip).

1195 GO SUNDAY RACING IN YORKSHIRE MAIDEN STKS (3-Y.O) (Class D)

£4,396.50 (£1,332.00: £651.00: £310.50)

1m 1f Stalls: High GOING minus 0.51 sec per fur (F) 4-45 (4-47)

Ellie Ardensky *(88+) (JRFanshawe)* 3-8-4 (5) NVarley(11) (lw: trckd ldrs: led wl over 1f out: r.o) ....— 1
Pilsudski (IRE) *(89) (MRStoute)* 3-9-0 DeanMcKeown(4) (hld up: hdwy 3f out: carried lft 2f out: r.o ins fnl f)..2 2
King's Crown *(88) (EALDunlop)* 3-8-11 (3) JTate(3) (rangy: unf: hdwy 4f out: ev ch 2f out: wandered u.p: nt qckn fnl f)...1 3
865[2] Celtic Fringe *(74)*(Fav)*(HRACecil)* 3-8-9 JCarroll(10) (lw: trckd ldrs: effrt 4f out: one pce) 5 4
824[5] Eau de Cologne *(77) (CWThornton)* 3-9-0 AMackay(5) (hld up & bhd: shkn up 4f out: styd on wl fnl 2f) ....¾ 5
Mountgate **(76)***(77) (MPBielby)* 3-9-0 MFenton(7) (cl up: led over 3f out: hdd wl over 1f out: grad wknd)...hd 6
664[12] Kewaashi (USA) *(67) (LMCumani)* 3-8-9 KDarley(6) (trckd ldrs: effrt over 3f out) 3 7
815[5] Desert Spring *(71) (PWHarris)* 3-9-0 DHolland(8) (prom tl rdn & wknd fnl 2f)............................½ 8
Swandale Flyer *(59) (NBycroft)* 3-9-0 SMaloney(2) (a bhd) 7 9
128[5] Parklife (IRE) *(43) (PCHaslam)* 3-9-0 TWilliams(1) (led tl hdd over 3f out: sn wknd)..9 10

4/5 Celtic Fringe, **5/2** ELLIE ARDENSKY (3/1-2/1), **7/1** Kewaashi (USA), **8/1** Pilsudski (IRE), **14/1** King's Crown, **16/1** Desert Spring, **33/1** Mountgate, Eau de Cologne, **50/1** Swandale Flyer, Parklife (IRE), CSF £23.91 TOTE £3.50: £1.30 £1.80 £2.30 (£21.90) Trio £43.70 OWNER The Snailwell Stud Company Ltd (NEWMARKET) BRED Snailwell Stud Co Ltd 10 Rn
1m 51.1 (0.90) SF: 44/45/44/30/33/33/23/27/15/-
T/Plpt: £200.60 (77.19 Tckts). T/Qdpt: £37.90 (7.7 Tckts). AA

1053-BATH (L-H)
Monday May 22nd (Good to firm)
WEATHER: fine WIND: nil

1196 TIMEFORM DAY AT BATH MEDIAN AUCTION MAIDEN STKS (3-Y.O)
(Class F) £2,967.50 (£830.00: £402.50)
1m 5y Stalls: Low GOING minus 0.61 sec per fur (F) 2-15 (2-19)

1053² **Jalfrezi** *(79)*(Fav)*(JARToller)* 3-8-9 JWeaver(11) (5th st: led wl over 1f out: r.o wl)........— 1
Wild Rita *(77) (WRMuir)* 3-8-9 TQuinn(4) (lengthy: unf: bit bkwd: 4th st: ev ch over 1f out: r.o)........1 2
*768*³ Self Reliance *(76) (MBell)* 3-8-9 MHills(1) (hld up & plld hrd: gd hdwy 3f out: r.o wl ins fnl f)..nk 3
645⁸ Miss Laughter **(46)***(72) (JWHills)* 3-8-2 (7) MHenry(5) (led over 6f: one pce)........2 4
881⁴ Best of Bold *(74) (RHannon)* 3-9-0 JReid(9) (hld up: hdwy 2f out: nvr nr to chal)........1¾ 5
*515*⁸ Norfolk Glory **(44)***(67) (DJGMurraySmith)* 3-9-0 RCochrane(7) (s.i.s: hdwy 3f out: one pce fnl 2f)........3½ 6
Glorious Bid (IRE) *(59) (MartynMeade)* 3-8-2 (7) CTinel(2) (unf: bkwd: dwlt: hdwy 3f out: one pce fnl 2f)........1½ 7
1053⁷ Flammant Rose (IRE) *(39) (MartynMeade)* 3-8-9 VSlattery(10) (3rd st: wknd over 2f out).....10 8
908⁸ Ace Chapel (IRE) **(46)***(43) (CCElsey)* 3-9-0 DHarrison(3) (2nd st: ev ch 2f out: wknd over 1f out)........¾ 9
881³ Anonym (IRE) *(42) (JLDunlop)* 3-9-0 WCarson(12) (prom: 7th whn hung rt & rn wd st: n.d after)........nk 10
Coastguards Haven *(22) (MJBolton)* 3-9-0 CRutter(13) (lengthy: unf: bit bkwd: a bhd: t.o)....10 11
937¹³ Vaporize *(14) (DMHyde)* 3-9-0 WNewnes(8) (a bhd: t.o)........4 12
908¹¹ Wychwood-Palace **(60)***(6) (HJCollingridge)* 3-8-9 MRimmer(6) (hld up: hmpd over 5f out: 6th st: sn wknd: t.o)........1½ 13

4/5 JALFREZI, **3/1** Anonym (IRE) (op 2/1), **6/1** Self Reliance, **13/2** Best of Bold (4/1-7/1), **20/1** Wild Rita, **33/1** Norfolk Glory, Miss Laughter, Wychwood-Palace, **50/1** Ace Chapel (IRE), **100/1** Flammant Rose (IRE), Coastguards Haven, Vaporize, Glorious Bid (IRE), CSF £19.20 TOTE £2.20: £1.40 £3.10 £1.60 (£24.80) Trio £28.90 OWNER Hamthor Ltd (The Rannerdale Trust) (WHITSBURY) BRED Rannerdale Trust 13 Rn 1m 39.9 (1.40) SF: 30/28/27/23/25/18/10/-/-/-/-/-/-

1197 TIMEFORM CARD JUVENILE STKS (2-Y.O) (Class C) £4,677.00
(£1,743.00: £846.50: £357.50: £153.75: £72.25)
5f 11y Stalls: Low GOING minus 0.61 sec per fur (F) 2-45 (2-45)

943* **Eastern Prophets** *(76) (GLewis)* 2-8-11 PaulEddery(6) (mde all: r.o wl)........— 1
1041* Tadeo *(75) (MRChannon)* 2-9-1 RHughes(4) (a.p: hrd rdn & ev ch over 1f out: r.o one pce) 1½ 2
1096² Ice Pick (IRE) *(67)*(Fav)*(RHannon)* 2-8-11 PatEddery(2) (lw: chsd wnr: sn pushed along: hrd rdn 2f out: one pce)........1½ 3
859* Polly Golightly *(62) (BSmart)* 2-8-7 (3) SSanders(5) (chsd ldrs: rdn 3f out: swvd lft over 1f out: one pce)........1 4
Tin Man *(22) (BAMcMahon)* 2-8-8 TQuinn(1) (leggy: wnt lft s: a bhd: t.o)........12 5
1054¹¹ Members Welcome (IRE) *(24) (PGMurphy)* 2-8-4 (7) RWaterfield(3) (prom: hrd rdn over 2f out: sn wknd)........½ 6

4/7 Ice Pick (IRE), **4/1** EASTERN PROPHETS, **13/2** Tadeo (op 4/1), **7/1** Polly Golightly (op 4/1), **33/1** Tin Man, **66/1** Members Welcome (IRE), CSF £25.91 TOTE £5.30: £2.20 £2.20 (£12.90) OWNER Mrs J. M. Purches (EPSOM) BRED Miss K. Zavon 6 Rn
61.0 secs (0.50) SF: 37/36/28/23/-/-

1198 TIMEFORM SILVER TANKARD MAIDEN STKS (3-Y.O+) (Class D)
£4,105.50 (£1,239.00: £602.00: £283.50)
1m 2f 46y Stalls: Low GOING minus 0.61 sec per fur (F) 3-15 (3-19)

Easy Listening (USA) *(89+)*(Fav)*(RCharlton)* 3-8-11 PatEddery(11) (gd sort: scope: hld up: hdwy & 5th st: led over 2f out: rdn over 1f out: comf)........— 1
Paddy's Return (IRE) *(84) (FMurphy)* 3-8-11 RCochrane(15) (hld up: 8th st: hdwy over 2f out: r.o: nt trble wnr)........3 2

8547 Backview *(78) (BJLlewellyn)* 3-8-11 RPrice(13) (3rd st: ev ch over 2f out: one pce) 4 **3**
Sure Care *(72) (CREgerton)* 4-9-2 (5) AProcter(9) (hdwy 3f out: rdn & one pce fnl 2f)....½ **4**
3766 Fabillion *(72) (CASmith)* 3-8-8 (3) AGarth(7) (nvr nr to chal)....3½ **5**
6919 Typhoon Eight (IRE) **(92)***(70) (BWHills)* 3-8-11 MHills(5) (a.p: led over 4f out tl over 2f out: wknd over 1f out)....1¼ **6**
8165 Persian Saint (IRE) **(77)***(62) (DRCElsworth)* 4-9-12 JWilliams(8) (led 6f: 2nd st: wknd over 2f out)....5 **7**
9737 Rubadub *(52) (JMBradley)* 4-9-2 (5) SDrowne(16) (lw: nvr trbld ldrs)....3 **8**
109718 Shepherds Rest (IRE) *(53) (SMellor)* 3-8-4 (7) ADaly(12) (6th st: wknd over 2f out)....3 **9**
10747 Trapeze *(45) (CLPopham)* 4-9-12b JReid(14) (lw: prom 6f)....5 **10**
Commander Glen (IRE) *(42) (MartynMeade)* 3-8-11 VSlattery(6) (prom: hrd rdn 4f out: 7th & wkng st)....1½ **11**
9745 Frome Lad **(55)***(39) (WGMTurner)* 3-8-11 TSprake(4) (plld hrd: 4th st: wknd over 2f out)....2 **12**
Perfect Ending *(30) (CACyzer)* 4-9-12 DHarrison(10) (bit bkwd: a bhd)....6 **13**
113620 Peatsville (IRE) *(27) (MRChannon)* 3-8-12 ow1 RHughes(17) (a bhd)....1¾ **14**
Adjacent Too *(22) (CCElsey)* 3-8-6 CRutter(2) (dwlt: a bhd)....nk **15**
Ziro (IRE) *(24) (PDEvans)* 3-8-11 WNewnes(1) (leggy: b: s.s: a bhd)....1½ **16**
9638 Western Country *(SMellor)* 3-8-11 PaulEddery(3) (t.o fnl 4f)....25 **17**

5/4 EASY LISTENING (USA) (4/5-11/8), **3/1** Typhoon Eight (IRE) (2/1-100/30), **5/1** Persian Saint (IRE), **6/1** Paddy's Return (IRE), **16/1** Frome Lad, **20/1** Ziro (IRE), **25/1** Perfect Ending, **33/1** Sure Care, **50/1** Shepherds Rest (IRE), Trapeze, Fabillion, Backview, Rubadub, Peatsville (IRE), Adjacent Too, Commander Glen (IRE), Western Country, CSF £9.87 TOTE £2.60: £1.50 £1.70 £7.30 (£11.50) Trio £167.90 OWNER Mr K. Abdullah (BECKHAMPTON) BRED Juddmonte Farms
17 Rn 2m 6.6 (0.40 under best) (-1.10) SF: 55/50/44/53/38/36/43/33/19/26/8/5/11/-/-/-/-
WEIGHT FOR AGE 3yo-15lb

1199 TIMEFORM RACEVIEW H'CAP (0-70) (3-Y.O+) (Class E) £3,382.50 (£1,020.00: £495.00: £232.50)
5f 161y Stalls: Low GOING minus 0.61 sec per fur (F) 3-45 (3-48)

10509 **Tinker Osmaston (60)***(68) (MSSaunders)* 4-9-4 JWilliams(10) (lw: gd hdwy over 2f out: hung lft over 1f out: edged lft & led ins fnl f: r.o wl)....— **1**
10505 Half Tone **(47)***(50) (RMFlower)* 3-7-2b(7)ow2 SLanigan(1) (s.s: sn prom: led 2f out: edgd rt & bmpd over 1f out: edged rt & hdd ins fnl f)....1¼ **2**
8772 Oggi **(61)***(61)*(Fav)*(PJMakin)* 4-9-5 JWeaver(7) (a.p: rdn & hung lft over 1f out: ev ch whn n.m.r ins fnl f: nt qckn)....1¾ **3**
105711 Seaside Minstrel **(58)***(53) (DLWilliams)* 7-8-11b(5) DGriffiths(13) (hdwy fnl 2f: nvr nrr)....1½ **4**
10508 Lorins Gold **(38)***(32) (AndrewTurnell)* 5-7-10bow1 ATucker(2) (a.p: led 3f out to 2f out: one pce)....hd **5**
7266 Grand Time **(35)***(29) (CJHill)* 6-7-2b(5) MBaird(9) (hdwy over 1f out: nrst fin)....½ **6**
10124 Cedar Girl **(54)***(41) (RJHodges)* 3-7-9 (7) JoHunnam(4) (no hdwy fnl 2f)....2½ **7**
4207 Havana Miss **(53)***(27) (BPalling)* 3-7-8v(7)ow8 ADaly(5) (nvr trbld ldrs)....1¾ **8**
116410 Certificate-X **(56)***(24) (MartynMeade)* 4-9-0 VSlattery(6) (prom over 2f)....5 **9**
9046 Absolutely Fabulus **(48)***(14) (JLSpearing)* 3-7-10 ow1 WCarson(8) (a bhd)....½ **10**
81211 Manor Adventure **(55)***(20) (PTDalton)* 5-8-13 RCochrane(14) (b: b.hind: s.i.s: a bhd)....¾ **11**
7809 Leguard Express (IRE) **(51)***(15) (OO'Neill)* 7-8-4b(5) SDrowne(3) (prom over 2f)....hd **12**
Dry Point **(70)***(33) (JARToller)* 9-10-0 WNewnes(11) (swtg: a bhd)....nk **13**
86215 Runs in the Family **(62)***(3) (PGMurphy)* 3-8-10b DHarrison(12) (led over 2f)....8 **14**
LONG HANDICAP Half Tone 7-6 Havana Miss 7-2

5/2 Oggi, **7/1** Absolutely Fabulus, Half Tone (5/1-8/1), **8/1** Cedar Girl, Grand Time (6/1-9/1), **10/1** Seaside Minstrel (7/1-12/1), **11/1** Runs in the Family (8/1-12/1), **12/1** Leguard Express (IRE), **14/1** Lorins Gold (8/1-16/1), TINKER OSMASTON (10/1-16/1), Dry Point (op 8/1), **16/1** Manor Adventure, **25/1** Certificate-X, **50/1** Havana Miss, CSF £108.46 CT £306.66 TOTE £34.60: £6.40 £2.70 £1.70 (£119.90) Trio £163.10 OWNER Mrs Denise Saunders (WELLS) BRED Mrs R. D. Peacock 14 Rn
1m 10.0 (0.70) SF: 42/14/35/27/6/3/5/-/-/-/-/-/7/-
WEIGHT FOR AGE 3yo-10lb

1200 TIMEFORM PERSPECTIVE & RATINGS H'CAP (0-80) (3-Y.O+ F & M) (Class D) £3,696.00 (£1,113.00: £539.00: £252.00)
1m 5f 22y Stalls: Low GOING minus 0.61 sec per fur (F) 4-15 (4-16)

9752 **Rasayel (USA) (45)***(55+) (PDEvans)* 5-8-8 TQuinn(2) (hld up & plld hrd: 5th st: hdwy on ins 3f out: led over 1f out: cleverly)....— **1**
9614 Wild Strawberry **(63)***(72)*(Fav)*(MissBSanders)* 6-9-9 (3) SSanders(6) (chsd ldr: led over 8f out: hdd over 1f out: nt qckn)....1¼ **2**
76422 Wizzy Lizzy (IRE) **(49)***(53) (DRCElsworth)* 4-8-12 JWilliams(4) (lw: hld up: 7th st: hdwy over 1f out: r.o one pce fnl f)....3½ **3**

4857 Legendra **(55)***(57) (PGMurphy)* 5-8-11 (7) RWaterfield(3) (b: 4th st: rdn over 2f out: one pce) 1½ 4
764 16 Grandes Oreilles (IRE) **(66)***(67) (NJHWalker)* 3-8-10 RCochrane(1) (3rd st: wknd over 1f out) 1¼ 5
10142 Uncharted Waters **(65)***(66) (CACyzer)* 4-10-0 JReid(5) (led 5f: 2nd st: wknd 2f out) .... hd 6
1058 14 Rumpus (IRE) **(44)***(40) (MrsLAMurphy)* 5-8-2 (5) SDrowne(7) (hdwy & 6th st: wknd over 2f out) 4 7
1058 11 Regal Pursuit (IRE) **(52)***(41) (CAHorgan)* 4-9-1h PaulEddery(8) (hdwy 7f out: wknd 4fout) 6 8

9/4 Wild Strawberry, **11/4** Uncharted Waters, **7/2** RASAYEL (USA), **8/1** Grandes Oreilles (IRE), **12/1** Legendra, Regal Pursuit (IRE) (op 8/1), **16/1** Wizzy Lizzy (IRE), **20/1** Rumpus (IRE), CSF £11.48 CT £98.95 TOTE £4.00: £1.70 £1.40 £1.80 (£5.00) OWNER Pentons Haulage and Cold Storage Ltd (WELSHPOOL) BRED Gainsborough Farm 8 Rn 2m 51.1 (5.40) SF: 13/30/11/15/6/24/-/-
WEIGHT FOR AGE 3yo-19lb

1201 TIMEFORM PHONE SERVICE LIMITED STKS (0-65) (3-Y.O) (Class F)

£2,915.00 (£815.00: £395.00)
5f 11y Stalls: Low GOING minus 0.61 sec per fur (F) 4-45 (4-48)

6456 **Sizzling (59)***(67) (RHannon)* 3-8-11 JReid(5) (lw: a.p: rdn over 1f out: qcknd to ld wl ins fnl f: r.o) .... — 1
855* Southern Dominion **(60)***(67) (WGMTurner)* 3-9-0 TSprake(4) (led tl wl ins fnl f) 1 2
7275 Midnight Break **(60)***(56) (PTWalwyn)* 3-8-6 PatEddery(9) (hld up & bhd: hdwy 2f out: nt clr run over 1f out: squeezed thro ins fnl f: r.o wl) 1 3
1094* Youdontsay **(62)***(56)*(Fav)*(RCurtis)* 3-8-2 (7) SLanigan(10) (wnt rt s: hdwy over 2f out: edgd lft over 1f out: nt qckn) 1 4
1016 11 Cork Street Girl (IRE) **(62)***(52) (BJMeehan)* 3-8-6 DHarrison(12) (prom: rdn 3f out: edgd lft over 1f out: nt qckn) .... s.h 5
1094 19 Crowded Avenue **(52)***(55) (PJMakin)* 3-8-11 JWeaver(1) (hld up: nt clr run 2f out: nvr nr to chal) .... ¾ 6
7332 Magical Manoeuvers **(56)***(53) (BAMcMahon)* 3-8-11 TQuinn(3) (prom: hrd rdn over 2f out: eased whn btn wl ins fnl f) .... ½ 7
6973 Rolling (IRE) **(65)***(45) (BWHills)* 3-8-1 (5) JDSmith(13) (rdn & hdwy 2f out: wknd fnl f) 1 8
7585 Saatchmo **(64)***(48) (JLSpearing)* 3-8-11 PaulEddery(6) (lw: a bhd) .... ¾ 9
10944 Sally Weld **(65)***(42) (CJBenstead)* 3-8-6 BRouse(7) (prom 3f) .... nk 10
1057 14 La Belle Dominique **(63)***(32) (SGKnight)* 3-8-7 ow1 WNewnes(8) (hld up: n.m.r 2f out: sn bhd).. 3 11
984 17 Master M-E-N (IRE) **(56)***(33) (NMBabbage)* 3-8-12vow1 RHughes(2) (prom: hrd rdn over 2f out: sn wknd) 1½ 12
10324 Portelet **(61)***(27) (RJRWilliams)* 3-8-6b WCarson(11) (bmpd s: bhd fnl 2f) .... nk 13

5/2 Youdontsay, **9/2** Rolling (IRE) (3/1-5/1), **6/1** Midnight Break (5/1-15/2), Portelet, **8/1** Southern Dominion, Magical Manoeuvers (6/1-10/1), **9/1** Sally Weld, **14/1** Saatchmo, **16/1** SIZZLING, La Belle Dominique, **20/1** Cork Street Girl (IRE), **50/1** Crowded Avenue, **66/1** Master M-E-N (IRE), CSF £138.81 TOTE £15.90: £3.00 £2.40 £2.40 (£174.00) Trio Not won; £833.80 to Goodwood 23/5/95 OWNER Mrs P. Jubert (MARLBOROUGH) BRED Lord Victor Matthews 13 Rn
61.1 secs (0.60) SF: 35/35/24/24/20/23/21/13/16/10/-/1/-

1202 TIMEFORM BLACK BOOK & RATINGS H'CAP (0-70) (3-Y.O+) (Class E)

£3,577.50 (£1,080.00: £525.00: £247.50)
1m 5y Stalls: Low GOING minus 0.61 sec per fur (F) 5-15 (5-17)

10275 **Vanborough Lad (52)***(54) (MJBolton)* 6-8-13 JReid(5) (lw: 5th st: led ins fnl f: all out) .... — 1
10742 Wentbridge Lad (IRE) **(52)***(54) (PDEvans)* 5-8-13v RHughes(9) (hld up: hdwy over 2f out: r.o wl ins fnl f) .... s.h 2
Dungeon Dancer **(61)***(62) (JAkehurst)* 3-8-10v WNewnes(7) (gd hdwy over 1f out: r.o wl ins fnl f) .... nk 3
5248 Master Millfield (IRE) **(65)***(64)*(Fav)*(CJHill)* 3-9-0 JWeaver(2) (lw: led 1f: led 5f out: hdd ins fnl f) 1¼ 4
5463 Runic Symbol **(42)***(40) (MBlanshard)* 4-8-3 StephenDavies(3) (hdwy over 1f out: nvr nrr) .... nk 5
5349 Noeprob (USA) **(42)***(39) (RJHodges)* 5-7-10 (7) AmandaSanders(6) (hdwy 2f out: one pce fnl f) .... ½ 6
Ring the Chief **(50)***(43) (RAkehurst)* 3-7-10 (3)ow1 SSanders(12) (lw: 3rd st: hrd rdn over 2f out: wknd over 1f out) 1¾ 7
8824 Shaynes Domain **(44)***(31) (RMFlower)* 4-8-0b(5) JDSmith(10) (plld hrd: led 7f out to 5f out: 2nd st: wknd 1f out) 3½ 8
10529 Peter Rowley **(60)***(46) (RHannon)* 4-9-7 PatEddery(8) (nvr nr ldrs) .... ½ 9
62712 Dominion's Dream **(66)***(48) (BSmart)* 3-9-1 MRimmer(1) (4th st: wknd 3f out) 2 10

888[10] Born to Please (IRE) **(60)***(40) (PWHarris)* 3-8-9 RCochrane(15) (n.d)....¾ **11**
1095[8] Jairzinho (USA) **(60)***(32) (PHayward)* 6-9-0 (7) DaneO'Neill(16) (a bhd)....4 **12**
881[9] Surgiva **(49)***(16) (JRArnold)* 3-7-12 ow1 CRutter(18) (s.i.s: a bhd)....2 **13**
Esthal (IRE) **(55)***(7) (ABarrow)* 5-9-2 RPrice(11) (lw: prom 3f)....8 **14**
1125* Almapa **(59)***(9) (RJHodges)* 3-8-3 (5) 6x SDrowne(4) (prom: hrd rdn & 6th st: wknd 3f out)....1 **15**
984* Fleet Cadet **(50)** *(NAGraham)* 4-8-11b PaulEddery(13) (lw: rdn 4f out: a bhd)....1¼ **16**
Legendary Leap **(65)** *(LordHuntingdon)* 5-9-12 DHarrison(14) (prom 4f: t.o)....dist **17**

4/1 Master Millfield (IRE), **11/2** Wentbridge Lad (IRE), **6/1** Fleet Cadet, **7/1** Ring the Chief (op 4/1), Almapa, **8/1** VANBOROUGH LAD, **14/1** Legendary Leap, Peter Rowley, **16/1** Runic Symbol, Shaynes Domain, **20/1** Dominion's Dream, Born to Please (IRE), **25/1** Dungeon Dancer, Noeprob (USA), **50/1** Esthal (IRE), Surgiva, Jairzinho (USA), CSF £51.71 CT £991.42 TOTE £8.50: £2.10 £2.00 £4.80 £1.90 (£16.10) Trio £104.50 OWNER Mr A. R. M. Galbraith (SHREWTON) BRED Small Breeders' Group 17 Rn 1m 39.7 (1.20) SF: 36/36/32/34/22/21/13/13/28/18/10/14/-/-/-/-/-
WEIGHT FOR AGE 3yo-12lb

T/Jkpt: Not won; £5,304.94 to Goodwood 23/5/95. T/Plpt: £317.50 (55.15 Tckts). T/Qdpt: £26.20 (3.4 Tckts). KH

0574-EDINBURGH (R-H)
Monday May 22nd (Good to firm)

Race 6 abandoned due to state of the ground
WEATHER: drizzle WIND: almost nil

1203 PINKIE MAIDEN AUCTION STKS (2-Y.O) (Class F) £2,655.50 (£748.00: £366.50)
5f Stalls: High GOING minus 0.41 sec per fur (F) 6-30 (6-31)

Happy Tycoon (IRE) *(60+)*(Fav)*(MJHeaton-Ellis)* 2-8-7 DHolland(5) (cmpt: lw: mde all: pushed along & kpt on wl)....— **1**
964[4] Bit of Bother (IRE) *(51) (TDBarron)* 2-8-3 ow1 KDarley(8) (chsd ldrs: effrt ½-wy: styd on: nvr able chal)....1¼ **2**
Wee Tinkerbell *(45) (MissLAPerratt)* 2-7-10 DaleGibson(3) (neat: s.s: hdwy over 1f out: fin wl)....hd **3**
964[2] Silent Soprano *(42) (DenysSmith)* 2-7-12 JFanning(4) (a chsng ldrs: nt qckn fnl 2f)....1½ **4**
1090[3] Boffy (IRE) *(47) (BPJBaugh)* 2-8-5 ACulhane(1) (hld up: effrt 2f out: rdn & one pce fnl f)....½ **5**
Katie Komaite *(39) (CaptJWilson)* 2-7-7 (5) NVarley(6) (small: neat: s.i.s: hdwy ½-wy: no imp)....½ **6**
943[10] Swifty Nifty (IRE) *(41) (JBerry)* 2-8-2 NCarlisle(9) (lw: chsd wnr tl wknd over 1f out)....½ **7**
964[8] Wydale *(7) (MWEllerby)* 2-8-0 SMaloney(7) (sn outpcd & wl bhd)....10 **8**
White Emir *(9) (MrsJRRamsden)* 2-8-3 DeanMcKeown(2) (leggy: unf: scope: s.i.s: sn prom: wknd 2f out)....nk **9**

7/4 HAPPY TYCOON (IRE), **7/2** Bit of Bother (IRE), Silent Soprano (5/2-4/1), **8/1** Boffy (IRE), **9/1** Swifty Nifty (IRE) (op 6/1), **10/1** White Emir (5/1-14/1), **16/1** Katie Komaite, **33/1** Wee Tinkerbell, **66/1** Wydale, CSF £8.51 TOTE £3.20: £1.20 £1.80 £4.00 (£7.30) Trio £85.20; £100.13 to 23/5/95 OWNER The Irish Connection (WROUGHTON) BRED R. A. Keogh 9 Rn
60.7 secs (3.00) SF: 6/-/-/-/-/-/-/-/-

1204 LEVENHALL MEDIAN AUCTION MAIDEN STKS (3-Y.O) (Class F) £2,666.00 (£751.00: £368.00)
1m 3f 32y Stalls: High GOING minus 0.41 sec per fur (F) 7-00 (7-02)

Daily Starlight (USA) (60)*(70) (MissGayKelleway)* 3-9-0 MWigham(5) (lw: trckd ldrs: lft in ld ent st: rdn & r.o appr fnl f)....— **1**
772[7] Master Charter *(66)*(Fav)*(MrsJRRamsden)* 3-9-0 KFallon(4) (hld up: hdwy over 2f out: rdn & nt qckn appr fnl f)....2½ **2**
Royal Expression **(60)***(64) (MrsMReveley)* 3-9-0 KDarley(2) (hld up: hdwy 2f out: styd on)....2 **3**
444[2] Mayday Kitty **(39)***(57) (WGMTurner)* 3-8-6 (3) DRMcCabe(1) (lw: hdwy to jn ldrs after 4f: rn wd st: ev ch 2f out: wknd appr fnl f)....1¼ **4**
888[6] Just for a Reason **(61)***(57) (DJGMurraySmith)* 3-9-0 DHolland(7) (lw: led 4f: cl up tl rn wd st: outpcd fnl 2f)....3 **5**
989[6] Teejay'n'aitch (IRE) **(54)***(52) (JSGoldie)* 3-8-7 (7) NKinnon(6) (led 7f out tl rn wd & hdd ent st: wknd fnl 2f)....3½ **6**
884[14] Share the Secret **(47)***(35) (BHanbury)* 3-9-0b JFortune(3) (cl up tl rn wd st: sn wknd)....12 **7**

5/2 Master Charter (6/4-3/1), **7/2** Royal Expression, **4/1** DAILY STARLIGHT (USA), Just for a Reason, **11/2** Mayday Kitty, **7/1** Teejay'n'aitch (IRE), **12/1** Share the Secret, CSF £15.34 TOTE £7.40: £2.30 £3.20 (£10.90) OWNER Mr A. Al-Radi (WHITCOMBE) BRED Robert S. West Jnr 7 Rn
2m 27.4 (7.70) SF: 12/8/6/-/-/-/-

1205 EAST LOTHIAN H'CAP (0-75) (3-Y.O+) (Class D) £4,248.75 (£1,290.00: £632.50: £303.75)

1m 3f 32y Stalls: High GOING minus 0.41 sec per fur (F) 7-30 (7-31)

991[4] **Imperial Bid (FR) (53)**(62) *(DenysSmith)* 7-8-9 KFallon(2) (hld up: hdwy appr st: rdn to ld ins fnl f: r.o)........— **1**
967[3] Latvian **(67)**(75) *(RAllan)* 8-9-9 SMaloney(1) (hld up: effrt & c wd over 3f out: put hd in air: r.o wl fnl f)........¾ **2**
1022* Killick **(55)**(63)(Fav) *(ABailey)* 7-8-11 MWigham(10) (lw: led tl hdd ins fnl f: kpt on same pce).nk **3**
935[10] Tu Opes **(66)**(73) *(JLHarris)* 4-9-8 DaleGibson(11) (chsd ldrs: ev ch 2f out: one pce ins fnl f) nk **4**
909[4] Habeta (USA) **(37)**(41) *(JWWatts)* 9-7-7 NKennedy(7) (lw: hld up: hdwy over 2f out: styd on)2½ **5**
Stormless **(40)**(38) *(PMonteith)* 4-7-10 JFanning(5) (trckd ldrs: disp ld 2 out: wknd appr fnl f)..4 **6**
1161[4] Gold Desire **(37)**(32) *(MBrittain)* 5-7-7 GBardwell(8) (prom tl rdn & wknd over 2f out)........2 **7**
935[11] Silver Hunter (USA) **(72)**(66) *(GCBravery)* 4-10-0 KDarley(3) (lw: cl up tl wknd fnl 2½f)........¾ **8**
1091[5] Lochore **(47)**(36) *(MrsVAAconley)* 5-8-0 (3)ow4 DRMcCabe(9) (prom to st: sn bhd)........½ **9**
988[4] Braille (IRE) **(65)**(56) *(MGMeagher)* 4-9-7 JFortune(6) (effrt & in tch appr st: wknd over 2f out)........1¾ **10**
976[11] Personimus **(37)**(20) *(CaptJWilson)* 5-7-7 NCarlisle(4) (a bhd)........5 **11**

LONG HANDICAP Gold Desire 7-4 Habeta (USA) 7-3 Personimus 6-13

5/2 Killick, **9/2** Braille (IRE), **5/1** Silver Hunter (USA), **7/1** IMPERIAL BID (FR), Tu Opes, Latvian, **9/1** Gold Desire, **16/1** Lochore, Habeta (USA), **33/1** Stormless, Personimus, CSF £55.01 CT £145.33 TOTE £8.10: £3.60 £2.90 £1.50 (£18.60) Trio £19.40 OWNER Lord Durham (BISHOP AUCKLAND) BRED David Grenfell 11 Rn

2m 24.4 (4.70) SF: 28/41/29/39/7/4/-/32/2/22/-

STEWARDS' ENQUIRY Maloney suspended 31/5-3/6/95 (excessive use of whip).

1206 FISHERROW (S) STKS (3-Y.O+) (Class G) £2,613.50 (£736.00: £360.50)

1m 16y Stalls: High GOING minus 0.41 sec per fur (F) 8-00 (8-01)

928[7] **Mary's Case (IRE) (54)**(63)(Fav) *(MJohnston)* 5-9-7b DHolland(2) (chsd ldrs gng wl: chal over 1f out: hrd rdn to ld nr fin)........— **1**
1037[14] Flair Lady **(55)**(58) *(WGMTurner)* 4-8-13 (3) DRMcCabe(7) (led early: led appr st: hrd rdn fnl f: jst ct)........s.h **2**
1044[6] Reed My Lips (IRE) **(35)**(58) *(BPJBaugh)* 4-9-7 ACulhane(9) (lost pl appr st: hdwy 2f out: kpt on u.p)........2½ **3**
990[7] Funny Rose **(23)**(43) *(PMonteith)* 5-8-9 (7) PFessey(4) (bhd: hdwy ent st: rdn 2f out: sn bhd) ...5 **4**
965[7] Sharp N' Smooth **(50)**(47) *(WTKemp)* 8-9-7b KDarley(3) (lw: hld up & bhd: effrt over 2f out: nvr rchd ldrs)........½ **5**
Amnesia (IRE) **(49)**(40) *(MrsSCBradburne)* 4-9-2v NCarlisle(8) (prom tl wknd fnl 2½f)........1 **6**
Prince Songline **(50)**(39) *(MrsASwinbank)* 5-9-7 JMarshall(5) (chsd ldrs tl grad wknd fnl 2f)........3 **7**
790[4] Karibu (GER) (34) *(MGMeagher)* 4-9-7 JFortune(1) (sn led: hdd appr st: rdn & wknd 3f out)2½ **8**
1029[9] Wordsmith (IRE) (24) *(JLHarris)* 5-9-7 KFallon(6) (a outpcd & bhd)........5 **9**

7/4 MARY'S CASE (IRE), **3/1** Sharp N' Smooth, **9/2** Flair Lady, **8/1** Wordsmith (IRE) (op 5/1), **10/1** Karibu (GER), Prince Songline, **16/1** Funny Rose, **20/1** Reed My Lips (IRE), Amnesia (IRE), CSF £10.59 TOTE £2.70: £1.40 £1.60 £2.60 (£6.20) Trio £60.30 OWNER Mr M. Doyle (MIDDLEHAM) BRED Paul Callan 9 Rn

1m 41.9 (3.30) SF: 40/35/35/20/24/17/16/11/1

No bid

Karibu clmd W. Monteith £6,000

1207 MUSSELBURGH HONEST TOUN H'CAP (0-65) (3-Y.O) (Class F) £2,844.50 (£802.00: £393.50)

1m 16y Stalls: High GOING minus 0.41 sec per fur (F) 8-30 (8-31)

759[10] **Champagne N Dreams (53)**(64) *(DNicholls)* 3-9-0 AlexGreaves(6) (trckd ldrs: smooth hdwy to ld appr fnl f: rdn & r.o)........— **1**
1060* Euro Sceptic (IRE) **(43)**(52) *(MHEasterby)* 3-8-4b SMaloney(5) (hdwy & prom appr st: styd on u.p fnl 2f)........1¼ **2**
1028[2] Concer Un **(60)**(68)(Fav) *(SCWilliams)* 3-9-7 KDarley(3) (trckd ldrs: led wl over 1f out: sn hdd & nt qckn)........½ **3**
1028[5] Samaka Hara (IRE) **(56)**(59) *(WSCunningham)* 3-9-0 (3) DRMcCabe(1) (bhd tl styd on wl fnl 3f)........2½ **4**

Legal Issue (IRE) **(58)***(60) (SirMarkPrescott)* 3-9-5 RPerham(7) (h.d.w: bit bkwd: s.i.s: hdwy appr st: chal 2f out: wknd fnl 2f)....nk **5**
969* Vindaloo **(49)***(41) (JLHarris)* 3-8-10 DaleGibson(12) (styd on u.p fnl 3f: nvr rchd ldrs)....5 **6**
969[4] Tinklers Folly **(43)***(34) (DenysSmith)* 3-8-4 JFanning(11) (cl up: led appr st tl wl over 1f out: wknd)....½ **7**
969[6] Simand **(49)***(38) (EWeymes)* 3-8-10 JFortune(4) (bhd tl styd on fnl 2f)....1¼ **8**
875[8] Ricana **(43)***(29) (WTKemp)* 3-8-4 DeanMcKeown(8) (lw: led tl hdd appr st: wknd over 2f out)....1¼ **9**
759[9] Tobago Boy **(40)***(23) (MGMeagher)* 3-7-10 (5) NVarley(9) (a bhd)....1½ **10**
1045[5] Pash **(43)***(10) (CWCElsey)* 3-8-4v NKennedy(10) (bhd fr ½-wy)....8 **11**
473[9] Gilpa Trinkets **(40)** *(DWChapman)* 3-8-1 NCarlisle(2) (plld hrd: slipped ent st: wl bhd after)..12 **12**
887[18] Crocodile Rock **(32)** *(MJHeaton-Ellis)* 3-7-7 GBardwell(13) (in tch tl rdn & wknd appr st)......30 **13**
LONG HANDICAP Crocodile Rock 7-5

2/1 Concer Un, **5/1** Vindaloo, **6/1** Legal Issue (IRE), **13/2** Euro Sceptic (IRE), **8/1** CHAMPAGNE N DREAMS, Tinklers Folly, **10/1** Simand, **14/1** Samaka Hara (IRE), Pash, **16/1** Crocodile Rock, **20/1** Ricana, Tobago Boy, **33/1** Gilpa Trinkets, CSF £63.76 CT £138.58 TOTE £11.20: £2.40 £2.40 £1.90 (£86.90) Trio £102.20 OWNER The Handy Grand Club (THIRSK) BRED S. E. Frater 13 Rn
1m 41.7 (3.10) SF: 34/22/38/29/30/11/4/8/-/-/-/-/-

1208

EAST LOTHIAN DISTRICT COUNCIL H'CAP (0-70) (3-Y.O+) (Class E) £3,243.00 (£984.00: £482.00: £231.00)
7f 15y GOING minus 0.41 sec per fur (F)
- Abandoned -State of Ground

T/Plpt: £14.60 (1,059.03 Tckts). T/Qdpt: £6.20 (9 Tckts). AA

1073-WOLVERHAMPTON (L-H)
Monday May 22nd (Standard)
WEATHER: overcast WIND: almost nil

1209

WOODLAND H'CAP (0-65) (3-Y.O+ F & M) (Class F) £3,098.60 (£859.60: £411.80)
1m 100y (Fibresand) Stalls: Low GOING: 0.13 sec per fur (SLW) 2-30 (2-31)

935[17] **Ayunli (52)***(61) (SCWilliams)* 4-8-12 (3) DWright(10) (lw: chsd ldrs: led over 2f out: rdn out)....— **1**
*832** Heathyards Lady (USA) **(55)***(56)*(Fav)*(RHollinshead)* 4-9-4 TIves(11) (hld up: hdwy over 4f out: 3rd st: chsd wnr 1f out: no imp)....4 **2**
762[9] My Gallery (IRE) **(50)***(51) (ABailey)* 4-8-13 GCarter(9) (w ldr: led over 3f out: rdn & hdd over 2f out: 2nd st: r.o one pce)....hd **3**
1034[7] Rosevear (IRE) **(50)***(47) (SMellor)* 3-8-1 AMcGlone(12) (hld up: hdwy over 1f out: nt rch ldrs)....2½ **4**
1081[2] Fiaba **(43)***(39) (MrsNMacauley)* 7-7-13 (7) AmandaSanders(3) (lw: mid div: effrt & 7th st: nvr able to chal)....nk **5**
Bex Hill **(54)***(39) (DHaydnJones)* 3-8-5 TWilliams(13) (hld up: styd on appr fnl f: nrst fin)....6 **6**
890[3] Pacific Spirit **(45)***(24) (MTate)* 5-8-5 (3) JTate(5) (led 5f: 4th & wkng st)....3 **7**
1076[10] Sand Star **(54)***(31) (DHaydnJones)* 3-8-5 AMackay(2) (chsd ldrs: rdn 3f out: 6th & btn st)....1 **8**
493[7] Mam'zelle Angot **(64)***(38) (MissJFCraze)* 5-9-13 SWebster(7) (b.hind: s.s: a bhd)....1½ **9**
882[10] Mutinique **(40)***(14) (BAPearce)* 4-8-3 GDuffield(6) (chsd ldrs tl rdn & wknd over 3f out)....nk **10**
395[4] Bakers Daughter **(54)***(25) (JRArnold)* 3-8-5 JQuinn(1) (a in rr)....1½ **11**
450[6] Legatee **(65)***(30) (BJMeehan)* 4-10-0b BDoyle(8) (chsd ldrs: 5th & rdn st: sn wknd)....3 **12**
Gwernymynydd **(43)** *(FJordan)* 4-8-6 MFenton(4) (a in rr)....11 **13**

3/1 Heathyards Lady (USA), **6/1** Bakers Daughter, Fiaba, **15/2** AYUNLI, **9/1** My Gallery (IRE), Pacific Spirit, Rosevear (IRE) (6/1-10/1), **11/1** Sand Star (op 7/1), **14/1** Mam'zelle Angot, Legatee (op 8/1), **25/1** Bex Hill, **33/1** Mutinique, Gwernymynydd, CSF £29.96 CT £194.51 TOTE £10.70: £2.00 £2.30 £5.00 (£27.30) Trio £127.30 OWNER Mr I. A. Southcott (NEWMARKET) BRED I. A. Southcott 13 Rn 1m 51.0 (7.00) SF: 43/38/33/17/21/9/6/1/20/-/-/12/-
WEIGHT FOR AGE 3yo-12lb

1210

COPPICE CLAIMING STKS (4-Y.O+) (Class F) £2,519.00 (£694.00: £329.00)
2m 46y (Fibresand) Stalls: Low GOING: 0.13 sec per fur (SLW) 3-00 (3-01)

556[14] **Acrow Line (45)***(49) (DBurchell)* 10-8-7 AMackay(11) (bhd: hdwy u.p over 3f out: 3rd st: led over 1f out: drvn out)....— **1**

304[7] Gunmaker **(30)**(41) (BJLlewellyn) 6-8-3 TWilliams(2) (chsd ldrs: rdn to ld over 4f out: hdd over 1f out: no ex fnl f)....4 **2**
Carfax **(30)**(37) (RPCHoad) 10-8-9 JCarroll(1) (outpcd & bhd: 6th st: styd on appr fnl f: nvr nrr)....10 **3**
Ehtefaal (USA) **(85)**(44)(Fav)(JWhite) 4-9-1b GDuffield(4) (led: hdd over 12f out: led 8f out: rdn & hdd over 4f out: 3rd & wkng st)....1½ **4**
763[15] Saahi (USA) **(47)**(29) (CWeedon) 6-8-8 (5) RPainter(10) (b: mid div: hdwy 8f out: 4th & wkng st)....11 **5**
Chasmarella **(20)**(16) (MrsMELong) 10-7-7 (7) TField(12) (bkwd: chsd ldrs: lost pl 10f out: styd on appr fnl f: n.d)....nk **6**
1091[12] Moneghetti **(47)**(19) (RHollinshead) 4-8-11 WRyan(9) (hld up: hdwy ½-wy: wknd over 3f out)....10 **7**
833[7] Epica **(50)**(4) (ABailey) 4-8-3b FNorton(3) (b: led over 12f out: hdd 8f out: drvn & wknd over 5f out)....7 **8**
843[2] El Nido **(59)** (MJCamacho) 7-9-1 LCharnock(6) (chsd ldrs: rdn over 4f out: sn wknd: poor 5th st: virtually p.u fnl f: fin lame)....25 **9**
516[5] Desert President **(34)** (RPCHoad) 4-8-5 NAdams(5) (bhd fr ½-wy)....13 **10**
1075[9] Laabas **(33)** (JELong) 12-7-12 (3) DWright(8) (b: a in rr)....9 **11**
582[14] Fruitful Affair (IRE) **(40)** (TThomsonJones) 6-7-12 JQuinn(7) (t.o fr ½-wy)....dist **12**

2/1 Ehtefaal (USA), **5/2** El Nido, **5/1** Epica, **7/1** ACROW LINE, **12/1** Fruitful Affair (IRE), **14/1** Saahi (USA), **20/1** Desert President, **33/1** Moneghetti, Chasmarella, Carfax, Laabas, Gunmaker, CSF £180.90 TOTE £5.20: £1.20 £8.80 £16.00 (£62.50) Trio £227.40; £262.66 to Goodwood 23/5/95 OWNER Mr Rhys Thomas Williams (EBBW VALE) BRED W. A. de Vigier and J. Holmes 12 Rn
3m 44.2 SF: 20/12/8/13/-/-/-/-/-/-/-/-
WEIGHT FOR AGE 4yo-2lb

1211 DAILY STAR TOP TIPSTER H'CAP (0-90) (3-Y.O) (Class C) £5,692.00 (£1,696.00: £808.00: £364.00)
1m 1f 79y (Fibresand) Stalls: Low GOING: 0.13 sec per fur (SLW) 3-30 (3-30)

995[6] **Bardon Hill Boy (IRE) (74)**(81) (BHanbury) 3-8-2 (3) JTate(6) (chsd ldrs: led over 2f out: rdn out)....— **1**
1018[5] Heathyards Rock **(90)**(87)(Fav)(RHollinshead) 3-9-7 TIves(7) (hld up: rdn over 4f out: rn wd & 4th st: nt rch wnr)....6 **2**
Dangerous Guest (IRE) **(86)**(83) (SirMarkPrescott) 3-9-3 GDuffield(2) (bit bkwd: chsd ldrs: drvn along over 2f out: 3rd st: no imp appr fnl f)....s.h **3**
1166[14] Mega Tid **(62)**(54) (BAPearce) 3-7-7 NAdams(3) (led: rdn & hdd over 2f out: 2nd st: wknd bel dist)....3 **4**
640[6] Hotspur Street **(73)**(59) (MJohnston) 3-8-4 TWilliams(4) (chsd ldrs: rdn over 3f out: 5th & btn st)....3 **5**
909* Nigel's Lad (IRE) **(80)**(49) (PCHaslam) 3-8-6 (5) JStack(5) (hld up: rdn over 3f out: 7th & btn st)....10 **6**
1022[7] Komreyev Dancer **(83)**(50) (ABailey) 3-8-9 (5) VHalliday(1) (prom: rdn & lost pl over 3f out: 6th & btn st)....1¼ **7**
LONG HANDICAP Mega Tid 7-0

7/4 Heathyards Rock, **2/1** Dangerous Guest (IRE), **4/1** Nigel's Lad (IRE), **7/1** Komreyev Dancer, **8/1** BARDON HILL BOY (IRE) (5/1-10/1), **10/1** Hotspur Street, **50/1** Mega Tid, CSF £23.46 TOTE £11.60: £2.50 £2.00 (£15.70) OWNER The Finsbury Partnership (NEWMARKET) BRED John McNamee in Ireland 7 Rn 2m 2.2 (6.20) SF: 47/53/49/20/25/15/16

1212 E.B.F. ASTON MAIDEN STKS (2-Y.O) (Class D) £3,935.10 (£1,174.80: £561.40: £254.70)
6f (Fibresand) Stalls: Low GOING: 0.13 sec per fur (SLW) 4-00 (4-02)

1011[4] **Double Point (IRE)** (74)(Fav)(MBell) 2-9-0 MFenton(4) (mde all: hrd rdn fnl f: all out)....— **1**
951[4] Scathebury (73) (SPCWoods) 2-9-0 WRyan(8) (lw: chsd wnr: 2nd st: ev ch over 1f out: unable qckn)....½ **2**
480[4] Capilano Princess (61) (DHaydnJones) 2-8-9 AMackay(6) (prom: sn rdn along: 5th st: kpt on ins fnl f)....2½ **3**
684[8] Briganoone (57) (SRBowring) 2-8-9 (5) CTeague(5) (outpcd & bhd: styd on appr fnl f: nrst fin)....3½ **4**
1073[3] Colour Counsellor (56) (KMcAuliffe) 2-8-11 (3) JTate(10) (outpcd ½-wy: styd on appr fnl f)....nk **5**
533[9] Don't Forget Mikie (IRE) (56) (MJHeaton-Ellis) 2-9-0 GCarter(1) (b.hind: prom: lost pl ½-wy: r.o appr fnl f)....d.h **5**
1089[2] Miss Offset (44) (MJohnston) 2-8-9 TWilliams(9) (chsd ldrs: 3rd st: wknd over 1f out)....2½ **7**

671[5] Cinnamon Stick (IRE) *(44) (WJarvis)* 2-9-0 AMcGlone(2) (prom: rdn over 3f out: sn lost tch) ..2 **8**
1073[2] U-No-Harry (IRE) *(41) (RHollinshead)* 2-9-0b TIves(12) (chsd ldrs: 4th & rdn st: wknd over 1f out) 1¼ **9**
970[5] Wingnut (IRE) *(32) (GLewis)* 2-8-9 SWhitworth(11) (prom: 6th & rdn st: sn wknd) 1½ **10**
Miletrian City *(21) (JBerry)* 2-9-0 JCarroll(7) (leggy: scope: prom: rdn ½-wy: grad wknd) 6 **11**
Pulga Circo *(13) (BAMcMahon)* 2-8-9 FNorton(3) (w'like: bkwd: sn outpcd & bhd) 1 **12**

7/4 DOUBLE POINT (IRE), **9/2** Scathebury, **6/1** Capilano Princess (op 9/4), Miletrian City (op 7/2), **8/1** U-No-Harry (IRE), **12/1** Colour Counsellor (op 8/1), Miss Offset (op 7/1), Cinnamon Stick (IRE), Don't Forget Mikie (IRE) (op 8/1), **33/1** Briganoone, **50/1** Wingnut (IRE), Pulga Circo, CSF £11.12 TOTE £2.40: £1.60 £2.90 £6.50 (£16.10) Trio £107.00 OWNER Prince Fahd Salman (NEWMARKET) BRED Newgate Stud Co 12 Rn 1m 17.1 (5.90) SF: 27/26/14/10/9/9/-/-/-/-/-/-

1213 SPINNEY (S) STKS (2-Y.O) (Class G) £2,243.00 (£618.00:£293.00)
6f (Fibresand) Stalls: Low GOING: 0.13 sec per fur (SLW) 4-30 (4-30)

1077[2] **Moi Canard** *(66?)*(Fav)*(JBerry)* 2-9-2 JCarroll(1) (lw: led over 4f out: unchal) ....— **1**
699[10] Merlin's Honour *(43) (PCHaslam)* 2-8-1 (5) JStack(2) (led 5f out: sn hdd: 2nd st: no imp appr fnl f) 5 **2**
508[11] Magic Bird (IRE) *(35) (JLSpearing)* 2-8-6b GHind(6) (led 1f: 3rd & rdn st: no hdwy fnl 2f) 3 **3**
878[8] Braes'O'Shieldhill *(13) (ABailey)* 2-8-6 GCarter(3) (s.s: a outpcd & bhd) 8 **4**
429[7] Iron And Steel *(16) (GLewis)* 2-8-11 SWhitworth(4) (chsd ldrs: 4th & rdn st: sn outpcd) 1 **5**
650[10] Melos *(RonaldThompson)* 2-8-6 TWilliams(5) (sn drvn along: effrt ½-wy: 5th & btn st) 12 **6**

2/5 MOI CANARD, **3/1** Iron And Steel, **10/1** Braes'O'Shieldhill, **20/1** Merlin's Honour, **50/1** Magic Bird (IRE), Melos, CSF £8.77 TOTE £1.30: £1.20 £4.10 (£7.20) OWNER Bloy & Hughes (COCKERHAM) BRED Llety Stud 6 Rn

1m 19.0 (7.80) SF: 4/-/-/-/-/-
No bid

1214 JOHNSON CHOPWELL H'CAP (0-70) (3-Y.O+) (Class E) £3,159.20 (£941.60: £448.80: £202.40)
5f (Fibresand) Stalls: Low GOING: 0.13 sec per fur (SLW) 5-00 (5-00)

944[2] **King Rambo (61)***(70) (RHollinshead)* 4-9-5 WRyan(7) (hld up: hdwy over 1f out: r.o wl to ld nr fin) ....— **1**
1042[5] The Institute Boy **(49)***(58) (MissJFCraze)* 5-8-7v SWebster(10) (lw: chsd ldrs: nt clr run over 1f out: rdn to ld ins fnl f: hdd nr fin) ....hd **2**
*892** The Real Whizzbang (IRE) **(47)***(52)*(Fav)*(PSFelgate)* 4-8-0b(5) PMcCabe(5) (led over 3f out: edgd rt over 1f out: hdd & unable qckn ins fnl f) 1¼ **3**
754[7] Lloc **(59)***(54) (JohnBerry)* 3-8-8 CDwyer(11) (chsd ldrs: rdn over 1f out: outpcd fnl f) 3 **4**
Purple Fling **(70)***(65) (SirMarkPrescott)* 4-10-0 GDuffield(6) (bit bkwd: mid div: drvn along: nvr able to chal) ....hd **5**
*1032** Sing With the Band **(64)***(49) (BAMcMahon)* 4-9-8 FNorton(1) (outpcd & sn drvn along: styd on appr fnl f: nvr trbld ldrs) 3 **6**
1076[5] Gate of Heaven **(37)***(19) (JohnBerry)* 5-7-9 ow2 JQuinn(4) (nvr rchd ldrs) ....½ **7**
602[7] Our Mica **(38)***(16) (LJBarratt)* 5-7-10 ow3 AMackay(8) (sn outpcd & bhd) ....¾ **8**
1033[6] Farndale **(45)***(10) (RonaldThompson)* 8-8-3 TWilliams(9) (a outpcd) 5 **9**
892[5] Miami Banker **(40)***(3) (WRMuir)* 9-7-12b NAdams(2) (led over 1f: rdn & wknd over 1f out) ....¾ **10**
754[9] Statomist **(58)** *(GFierro)* 3-8-7 JCarroll(3) (a outpcd) 7 **11**

LONG HANDICAP Gate of Heaven 6-12 Our Mica 6-11

15/8 The Real Whizzbang (IRE), **7/2** KING RAMBO, **9/2** Sing With the Band (op 3/1), **12/1** The Institute Boy (op 8/1), Lloc, Purple Fling (op 8/1), **14/1** Statomist, **25/1** Gate of Heaven, Farndale, Miami Banker, **33/1** Our Mica, CSF £40.95 CT £92.31 TOTE £4.40: £1.90 £3.70 £1.10 (£35.70) Trio £37.80 OWNER Mr J. D. Graham (UPPER LONGDON) BRED G. Johnson 11 Rn

63.4 secs (5.40) SF: 23/11/5/-/18/2/-/-/-/-/-
WEIGHT FOR AGE 3yo-9lb
T/Plpt: £232.80 (45.46 Tckts). T/Qdpt: £30.60 (1 Tckt). CR

1059-BEVERLEY (R-H)
Tuesday May 23rd (Good to firm becoming Firm)
WEATHER: sunny & warm WIND: almost nil

1215 TIGER INN (S) STKS (2-Y.O) (Class F) £2,756.00 (£766.00:£368.00)
5f Stalls: Centre GOING minus 0.57 sec per fur (F) 2-25 (2-25)

943[3] **Veshca Lady (IRE)** *(54)*(Fav)*(EWeymes)* 2-8-6 KDarley(8) (lw: led to ½-wy: led ins fnl f: styd on u.p) ....— **1**

983[3] April's Joy *(52) (JNorton)* 2-8-6 ACulhane(6) (cl up: led ½-wy tl ins fnl f: styd on u.p) ... ¾ 2
Doug's Folly *(49) (MWEasterby)* 2-8-6 LCharnock(7) (neat: a chsng ldrs: styd on ins fnl f: nt qckn towards fin) ... ¾ 3
Jambo *(43) (MRChannon)* 2-8-6 CRutter(1) (leggy: unf: lw: chsd ldrs: effrt & ch over 1f out: nt qckn) ... 2 4
1063[7] Propolis Power (IRE) *(29) (MWEasterby)* 2-8-11 MBirch(5) (s.i.s: nvr trbld ldrs) ... 6 5
Patrington Boy *(3) (MWEasterby)* 2-8-11 SMaloney(2) (w'like: bkwd: s.i.s: a outpcd & bhd) ... 8 6
Timson *(JPLeigh)* 2-8-11 DeanMcKeown(3) (unf: s.s: rn very green & a wl bhd) ... 10 7
983[2] Penny Parkes *(JBerry)* 2-8-11 JCarroll(4) (Withdrawn not under Starter's orders: lame at s) ... W

, **11/10** VESHCA LADY (IRE) (op Evens), **5/2** Jambo, **4/1** April's Joy, **8/1** Propolis Power (IRE), **12/1** Timson, **20/1** Patrington Boy, Doug's Folly, CSF £6.64 TOTE £1.60: £1.10 £2.30 (£3.90) OWNER Mr J. O'Malley (MIDDLEHAM) BRED A. F. O'Callaghan 7 Rn

63.8 secs (2.30) SF: 9/7/4/-/-/-/-
No bid

1216 WINDMILL INN MAIDEN STKS (3-Y.O) (Class D) £3,788.50 (£1,138.00: £549.00: £254.50)
7f 100y Stalls: High GOING minus 0.57 sec per fur (F) 2-55 (2-55)

Shayim (USA) *(84)*(Fav)*(RWArmstrong)* 3-9-0 RPrice(5) (hld up: hdwy on ins to ld over 2f out: qcknd clr: comf) ... — 1
853[7] Verde Luna *(81) (MHTompkins)* 3-9-0 PRobinson(1) (bhd: hdwy 2f out: styd on wl: no ch w wnr) ... 1½ 2
955[5] Young Benson **(74)***(78) (BAMcMahon)* 3-9-0 TIves(6) (chsd ldrs tl outpcd appr st: styd on again fnl 2f) ... 1½ 3
966[9] Penny's Wishing **(58)***(60) (JPLeigh)* 3-8-9 DeanMcKeown(4) (led tl hdd over 2f out: one pce) .6 4
Golden Tongue (USA) *(57) (EALDunlop)* 3-8-11 (3) JTate(2) (w'like: unruly s: dwlt: gd hdwy appr st: wknd wl over 1f out) ... 3½ 5
937[10] Raayaat (USA) *(57) (ACStewart)* 3-9-0 BThomson(7) (unruly s: chsd ldrs tl wknd over 2f out) ... nk 6

11/10 SHAYIM (USA) (op 4/6), **4/1** Verde Luna, Golden Tongue (USA), **6/1** Young Benson, **10/1** Raayaat (USA) (8/1-12/1), **33/1** Penny's Wishing, CSF £5.84 TOTE £1.70: £1.40 £1.80 (£4.40) OWNER Mr Hamdan Al Maktoum (NEWMARKET) BRED Nicholas M. Lotz and Overbrook Farm 6 Rn

1m 32.0 (0.00) SF: 52/49/46/28/25/25

1217 DAVID SWANNELL RATED STKS MEMORIAL H'CAP (0-95) (3-Y.O+) (Class B) £8,053.65 (£2,927.40: £1,423.70: £603.50: £261.75)
1m 100y Stalls: High GOING minus 0.57 sec per fur (F) 3-25 (3-25)

960[2] **Hunters of Brora (IRE) (85)***(95) (JDBethell)* 5-8-11 TIves(4) (lw: hld up: rdn to ld ins fnl f: r.o) ... — 1
River Board **(87)***(96)*(Fav)*(WJHaggas)* 5-8-13 KDarley(2) (lw: set slow pce: qcknd over 5f out: hdd ins fnl f: no ex) ... ¾ 2
793[4] Moving Arrow **(92)***(95) (MissSEHall)* 4-9-4 NConnorton(1) (hld up: hdwy over 2f out: hung rt & nt qckn appr fnl f) ... 3 3
1021[14] Promise Fulfilled (USA) **(81)***(78) (SGNorton)* 4-8-7 KFallon(5) (trckd ldr tl outpcd fnl 2f) ... 3 4
1108[3] Pinkerton's Pal **(95)***(90) (CEBrittain)* 4-9-7 BDoyle(3) (hld up: effrt over 2f out: sn rdn & btn) 1¼ 5

LONG HANDICAP Promise Fulfilled (USA) 8-4

5/2 River Board, **3/1** HUNTERS OF BRORA (IRE), Moving Arrow, Pinkerton's Pal, **20/1** Promise Fulfilled (USA), CSF £9.88 TOTE £2.60: £1.50 £1.50 (£6.40) OWNER Mr Robert Gibbons (MIDDLEHAM) BRED Gainsborough Stud Management Ltd 5 Rn 1m 45.0 (1.00) SF: 40/41/40/23/35

1218 ANGEL H'CAP (0-80) (3-Y.O F) (Class D) £3,840.50 (£1,154.00: £557.00: £258.50)
1m 1f 207y Stalls: High GOING minus 0.57 sec per fur (F) 3-55 (3-55)

Blue Nile (IRE) (64)*(71) (ACStewart)* 3-9-0 BThomson(8) (s.i.s: hld up: qcknd to ld wl over 1f out: sn clr: comf) ... — 1
957[6] Barford Sovereign **(70)***(71) (JRFanshawe)* 3-9-6 DHarrison(5) (a in tch: styd on fnl 2f: nt pce of wnr) ... 4 2
948[3] Hydrofoil **(60)***(60) (BWHills)* 3-8-10 DHolland(2) (in tch: nt clr run 2f out: swtchd outside & styd on: nvr able to chal) ... ½ 3
955[8] It's Academic **(62)***(60) (MrsJRRamsden)* 3-8-12 KFallon(9) (in tch: n.m.r 2f out: kpt on fnl f) ... 1¼ 4

857[6] Pennycairn **(71)***(67) (HRACecil)* 3-9-7 AMcGlone(1) (prom: led over 3f out tl wl over 1f out: sn btn) 1¼ 5
1060[3] Grey Again **(55)***(47) (SRBowring)* 3-8-0b(5) CTeague(7) (bhd: hdwy over 2f out: no imp) 2½ 6
1093[3] Poly Road **(57)***(47)*(Fav)*(MRChannon)* 3-8-7 CRutter(10) (s.i.s: wl bhd tl styd on fnl 2f) 1 7
Instantaneous **(48)***(38) (MHEasterby)* 3-7-12 LCharnock(3) (lw: cl up: ev ch & rdn 2f out: sn wknd) ....s.h 8
745[5] Western Horizon (USA) **(51)***(39) (CEBrittain)* 3-8-1 JQuinn(4) (chsd ldr tl wknd over 2f out) .1½ 9
133[7] Scylla **(47)** *(PCHaslam)* 3-7-11 TWilliams(6) (led tl hdd & wknd over 3f out) 25 10

11/4 Poly Road, **9/2** Hydrofoil, **6/1** Barford Sovereign, Pennycairn, **8/1** Grey Again, Western Horizon (USA), **9/1** BLUE NILE (IRE), **10/1** It's Academic (op 6/1), **16/1** Instantaneous, **20/1** Scylla, CSF £60.67 CT £256.80 TOTE £14.20: £5.00 £1.70 £1.60 (£41.20) Trio £51.10 OWNER Mr B. H. Farr (NEWMARKET) BRED Ronnie Boland 10 Rn

2m 4.3 (1.80) SF: 38/38/27/27/34/14/14/5/6/-

1219 ROSE & CROWN H'CAP (0-70) (3-Y.O) (Class E) £3,393.75 (£1,020.00: £492.50: £228.75)

1m 3f 216y Stalls: High GOING minus 0.57 sec per fur (F) 4-25 (4-27)

908[2] **Green Land (BEL) (55)***(62) (SCWilliams)* 3-8-10 KDarley(5) (in tch: hdwy to ld ins fnl f: styd on) ....— 1
786[6] Kildrummy Castle **(53)***(58) (MrsJRRamsden)* 3-8-8 KFallon(2) (a.p: rdn to ld appr fnl f: sn hdd: nt qckn) 1¼ 2
635[18] Bowcliffe Court (IRE) **(55)***(59) (BWHills)* 3-8-10 DHolland(11) (bhd tl styd on fnl 3f: nrst fin) ....¾ 3
1026* Westminster (IRE) **(66)***(69)*(Fav)*(MHTompkins)* 3-9-7v PRobinson(3) (hld up: hdwy over 2f out: nt qckn ins fnl f) ....¾ 4
537[6] Coneygree **(40)***(42) (JWharton)* 3-7-9 ow1 JQuinn(12) (led tl hdd appr fnl f: sn btn) ....nk 5
988[11] Danus Rex (IRE) **(50)***(51) (CASmith)* 3-8-2 (3) DRMcCabe(9) (bhd: styd on u.p fnl 3f: nvr rchd ldrs) 1¼ 6
986[5] China Mail (IRE) **(62)***(59) (JMPEustace)* 3-9-3 RCochrane(4) (chsd ldrs: outpcd 3f out: n.d after) 3 7
513[5] Fools of Pride (IRE) **(39)***(33) (RHollinshead)* 3-7-8 ow1 NCarlisle(8) (outpcd & lost pl appr st: sme late hdwy) 2 8
1105[4] Lucky Coin **(63)***(57) (CEBrittain)* 3-9-4 BDoyle(7) (chsd ldrs tl rdn & btn over 1f out) ....¾ 9
948[4] Top Fella (USA) **(58)***(51) (WAO'Gorman)* 3-8-13b EmmaO'Gorman(1) (in tch: effrt 3f out: sn rdn & btn) ....nk 10
444[11] Warrior Lady (IRE) **(38)***(30) (PJMcBride)* 3-7-2 (5) MBaird(6) (a bhd) 1¼ 11
Heavens Above **(50)***(35) (MHEasterby)* 3-8-5 SMaloney(10) (cl up tl wknd fnl 2f) 5 12
525[4] Mim-Lou-and **(41)***(22) (BRMillman)* 3-7-10 ow2 TWilliams(13) (s.i.s: plld hrd: rn wde bnd after 1f: a bhd) 1¾ 13

LONG HANDICAP Warrior Lady (IRE) 7-6

9/2 Westminster (IRE) (op 3/1), **7/1** Kildrummy Castle, Lucky Coin, **15/2** Danus Rex (IRE), **8/1** GREEN LAND (BEL), **9/1** Mim-Lou-and, **10/1** Bowcliffe Court (IRE), China Mail (IRE), Top Fella (USA), **11/1** Heavens Above, **20/1** Coneygree, **25/1** Fools of Pride (IRE), Warrior Lady (IRE), CSF £59.86 CT £518.63 TOTE £9.30: £2.80 £1.90 £5.20 (£44.50) Trio £129.70 OWNER Mrs V. Vilain (NEWMARKET) BRED Patrick Madelein 13 Rn

2m 35.0 (3.50) SF: 24/20/21/31/4/13/21/-/19/13/-/-/-

1220 ROYAL STANDARD STKS (3-Y.O+) (Class C) £4,948.00 (£1,798.00: £874.00: £370.00: £160.00)

5f Stalls: Centre GOING minus 0.57 sec per fur (F) 5-00 (5-00)

922[2] **Ziggy's Dancer (USA) (76)***(100?) (EJAlston)* 4-9-4 KFallon(4) (lw: bhd: gd hdwy to ld ins fnl f: sn clr) ....— 1
700[3] Ya Malak **(100)***(99) (JWPayne)* 4-10-0 BThomson(6) (lw: disp ld tl led over 1f out: hdd & no ex ins fnl f) 3½ 2
1055* Lucky Parkes **(102)***(92)*(Fav)*(JBerry)* 5-9-9 JCarroll(1) (disp ld: rdn 2f out: nt qckn fnl f) ....½ 3
Crofters Ceilidh **(106)***(74) (BAMcMahon)* 3-8-12 KDarley(2) (sltly hmpd s: a outpcd & bhd) 5 4
952[3] Don't Worry Me (IRE) **(100)***(63) (FHLee)* 3-8-10 PRobinson(5) (spd 3f: sn wknd) 3 5

6/4 Lucky Parkes, **5/2** Ya Malak, **4/1** Crofters Ceilidh, **6/1** Don't Worry Me (IRE), **9/1** ZIGGY'S DANCER (USA), CSF £29.28 TOTE £14.40: £2.10 £1.60 (£21.00) OWNER Mr John Patrick Barry (PRESTON) BRED Warren W. Rosenthal 5 Rn 61.0 secs (-0.50) SF: 64/63/56/29/18

WEIGHT FOR AGE 3yo-9lb

T/Plpt: £73.70 (190.15 Tckts). T/Qdpt: £51.10 (1.2 Tckts). AA

GOODWOOD (R-H)
Tuesday May 23rd (Good to firm)
WEATHER: sunny WIND: almost nil

1221
TREHEARNE & NORMAN MAIDEN STKS (3-Y.O) (Class D) £4,127.75 (£910.25: £910.25: £266.75)
1m Stalls: High GOING minus 0.44 sec per fur (F) 2-10 (2-10)

First Island (IRE) *(83) (GWragg)* 3-9-0 MHills(1) (lw: rdn & hdwy over 2f out: led over 1f out: r.o wl)......— **1**
Iktamal (USA) *(78) (EALDunlop)* 3-9-0 WRSwinburn(4) (lw: led over 6f: unable qckn)......2½ **2**
963³ Kilcoran Bay *(78) (IABalding)* 3-9-0 PatEddery(8) (s.s: rdn over 2f out: hdwy over 1f out: r.o)......d.h **2**
Divine Pursuit *(70) (HRACecil)* 3-8-9 WRyan(6) (lw: 5th st: rdn over 2f out: one pce)......1¾ **4**
888⁴ Edan Heights *(72) (SDow)* 3-9-0 StephenDavies(9) (lw: 6th st: rdn over 3f out: one pce)......1½ **5**
915³ Bibliotheque (USA) *(64)*(Fav)*(JHMGosden)* 3-8-9 LDettori(7) (b: lw: 3rd st: rdn over 3f out: wknd over 1f out)......1½ **6**
648¹⁰ Outstayed Welcome **(52)***(55) (MJHaynes)* 3-9-0 DBiggs(5) (bhd fnl 3f)......7 **7**
Almond Rock *(50) (JRFanshawe)* 3-9-0 TQuinn(2) (bit bkwd: 4th st: edgd rt & wknd 2f out).2½ **8**
888⁹ Ironic (IRE) *(40) (RHannon)* 3-9-0 JReid(3) (2nd st: wkng whn hmpd 2f out)......5 **9**

2/1 Bibliotheque (USA), **7/2** Iktamal (USA), **4/1** Kilcoran Bay (3/1-9/2), **5/1** Divine Pursuit (3/1-11/2), **10/1** Almond Rock (op 6/1), **33/1** FIRST ISLAND (IRE), Edan Heights, Ironic (IRE), **50/1** Outstayed Welcome, CSF FI & I £65.12, FI & KB £71.44 TOTE £27.00: £5.80 I £1.20 KB £1.90 (FI & I £36.30, FI & KB £33.40) Trio £223.50 OWNER Mollers Racing (NEWMARKET) BRED Citadel Stud 9 Rn
1m 38.47 (0.87) SF: 53/48/48/40/42/34/25/20/10

1222
CHICHESTER FESTIVAL THEATRE H'CAP (0-100) (3-Y.O) (Class C) £11,452.50 (£3,420.00: £1,635.00: £742.50)
7f Stalls: High GOING minus 0.44 sec per fur (F) 2-40 (2-42)

1069* **Shahid (95)***(105+)*(Fav)*(JLDunlop)* 3-9-7 WCarson(10) (lw: 3rd st: n.m.r over 1f out: qcknd & led ins fnl f: pushed out)......— **1**
980³ Emirates Express **(80)***(87) (JWHills)* 3-7-13 (7) MHenry(11) (led tl ins fnl f: unable qckn)......1½ **2**
973* Jam N Shadeed (USA) **(80)***(84) (PFICole)* 3-8-6 TQuinn(7) (lw: s.s: hdwy on ins over 2f out: nt clr run on ins over 1f out: one pce)......1¼ **3**
937* Christmas Kiss **(82)***(83) (RHannon)* 3-8-1 (7) DaneO'Neill(1) (4th st: rdn over 2f out: one pce)1¼ **4**
829¹¹ Te Amo (IRE) **(85)***(84) (RAkehurst)* 3-8-11 JWeaver(4) (lw: nt clr run 2f out: hdwy over 1f out: r.o one pce)......¾ **5**
694¹³ Chattaroy (IRE) **(86)***(82) (JHMGosden)* 3-8-12 LDettori(3) (lw: rdn & hdwy over 2f out: one pce)......1¼ **6**
Green City **(80)***(72) (RHannon)* 3-8-6 JReid(9) (6th st: no hdwy fnl 2f)......2 **7**
1165* Dancing Heart **(74)***(65) (BJMeehan)* 3-8-0b 5x PaulEddery(8) (2nd st: wknd over 1f out)......nk **8**
999³ Q Factor **(73)***(57) (DHaydnJones)* 3-7-13 AMackay(5) (bhd fnl 3f)......3 **9**
939⁹ Jibereen **(93)***(77) (GLewis)* 3-9-5 SWhitworth(6) (5th st: wknd 3f out)......s.h **10**
1069⁸ Masruf (IRE) **(92)***(68) (TThomsonJones)* 3-9-4 RHills(2) (lw: a bhd)......3½ **11**

5/4 SHAHID (Evens-11/8), **11/2** Emirates Express, **8/1** Dancing Heart, Christmas Kiss, **11/1** Jam N Shadeed (USA) (8/1-12/1), **14/1** Chattaroy (IRE), **16/1** Te Amo (IRE), Q Factor, **25/1** Green City, **33/1** Jibereen, **50/1** Masruf (IRE), CSF £8.38 CT £48.24 TOTE £2.20: £1.40 £1.70 £3.10 (£4.90) Trio £20.10 OWNER Mr Hamdan Al Maktoum (ARUNDEL) BRED Somerhall Bloodstock Ltd and Lord Chelsea 11 Rn
1m 25.62 (1.22) SF: 54/36/33/32/33/31/21/14/6/26/17

1223
E.B.F. CLIVE GRAHAM MAIDEN STKS (2-Y.O) (Class D) £5,744.00 (£1,712.00: £816.00: £368.00)
5f Stalls: Low GOING minus 0.44 sec per fur (F) 3-10 (3-11)

Wisam *(76++)*(Fav)*(RHannon)* 2-9-0 WRSwinburn(4) (cmpt: a.p: led over 2f out: pushed out)......— **1**
940⁴ Castan (IRE) *(66) (JLDunlop)* 2-9-0 WCarson(1) (led over 2f: hung bdly rt fnl 2f: nt rcvr)......3 **2**
Princess Pamgaddy *(60) (JBerry)* 2-8-9 GCarter(2) (leggy: lt-f: bit bkwd: a.p: ev ch whn n.m.r over 1f out: one pce)......nk **3**
617¹² Hever Golf Express *(65) (TJNaughton)* 2-9-0 PatEddery(3) (a.p: ev ch over 1f out: one pce)......hd **4**
Duncombe Hall *(30) (CACyzer)* 2-9-0 JWeaver(7) (neat: bkwd: s.s & hmpd s: a wl bhd)......11 **5**

Reliable Edie *(JFfitch-Heyes)* 2-8-9 LDettori(5) (b: leggy: lt-f: s.s: a wl bhd).....20 6
Mimosa *(LJHolt)* 2-8-9 JReid(6) (str: bit bkwd: swvd bdly rt s & p.u)..... P

4/6 WISAM (op Evens), **6/1** Castan (IRE) (op 4/1), Hever Golf Express (4/1-13/2), **13/2** Princess Pamgaddy (7/2-7/1), **25/1** Duncombe Hall, Mimosa, **33/1** Reliable Edie, CSF £5.07 TOTE £1.80: £1.40 £2.50 (£3.70) OWNER Mr Mohamed Suhail (MARLBOROUGH) BRED GAINSBOROUGH STUD MANAGEMENT LTD 7 Rn 59.31 secs (2.61) SF: 15/5/-/4/-/-/-

1224 WESTMINSTER TAXI INSURANCE PREDOMINATE STKS (Listed) (3-Y.O C & G) (Class A) £22,320.00 (£6,660.00: £3,180.00: £1,440.00)
1m 2f Stalls: High GOING minus 0.44 sec per fur (F) 3-40 (3-42)

1018* **Pentire (113)***(111)*(Fav)*(GWragg)* 3-9-0 MHills(4) (hdwy over 4f out: 4th st: led 1f out: all out).....— 1
942* Istidaad (USA) **(102)***(105) (ACStewart)* 3-8-8 RHills(6) (2nd st: led 2f out to 1f out: ev ch fnl f: r.o wl).....s.h 2
Fahal (USA) **(112)***(107) (DMorley)* 3-8-11 WCarson(5) (3rd st: rdn 2f out: ev ch ins fnl f: r.o) .nk 3
777* Romanzof *(96) (HRACecil)* 3-8-8 MJKinane(2) (lw: led 8f: eased whn btn fnl f).....5 4
679⁵ Wijara (IRE) **(100)***(92) (RHannon)* 3-8-8 RPerham(3) (lw: a bhd).....3 5
815² Horesti *(69) (CEBrittain)* 3-8-8 LDettori(1) (lw: 5th st: wknd over 3f out).....14 6

11/8 PENTIRE (op Evens), **4/1** Fahal (USA), **5/1** Romanzof, **13/2** Istidaad (USA), **15/2** Wijara (IRE), **20/1** Horesti, CSF £9.37 TOTE £2.20: £1.50 £2.50 (£4.90) OWNER Mollers Racing (NEWMARKET) BRED Lord Halifax 6 Rn 2m 5.83 (0.83) SF: 57/51/53/42/38/15

1225 ANNE FRANCES STEVENS MEMORIAL H'CAP (0-100) (4-Y.O+) (Class C) £7,700.00 (£2,300.00: £1,100.00: £500.00)
1m 1f Stalls: High GOING minus 0.44 sec per fur (F) 4-10 (4-12)

960⁹ **Pay Homage (81)***(89) (IABalding)* 7-8-12 MHills(9) (6th st: nt clr run on ins over 2f out: swtchd lft wl over 1f out: led ins fnl f: all out).....— 1
Ham N'Eggs **(86)***(94) (RHannon)* 4-9-3 PatEddery(4) (bit bkwd: 5th st: rdn over 3f out: ev ch fnl f: r.o).....hd 2
793⁵ Wilcuma **(83)***(90)*(Fav)*(PJMakin)* 4-9-0 LDettori(3) (rdn & hdwy over 2f out: r.o ins fnl f).....¾ 3
1095⁵ Lowawatha **(72)***(78) (DMorris)* 7-8-3 AClark(2) (2nd st: led 2f out to ins fnl f: unable qckn) ....hd 4
634¹³ Rory **(80)***(86) (MrsJCecil)* 4-8-6 (5) SMulvey(5) (hdwy & nt clr run over 1f out: r.o ins fnl f).....nk 5
870¹⁸ Serious **(85)***(88) (LadyHerries)* 5-9-2 JReid(1) (swtg: nvr nr to chal).....1¾ 6
1021¹³ Chickawicka (IRE) **(81)***(82) (MCPipe)* 4-8-12v MJKinane(10) (4th st: rdn over 2f out: one pce).1 7
1061¹¹ Shanghai Venture (USA) **(79)***(76) (SPCWoods)* 4-8-10 WRyan(8) (nvr nrr).....2 8
Aljazzaf **(97)***(92) (RAkehurst)* 5-10-0 TQuinn(6) (3rd st: wkng whn n.m.r 2f out).....1¼ 9
Toujours Riviera **(86)***(81) (JPearce)* 5-9-3 GBardwell(11) (lw: led 7f: wknd fnl f).....hd 10
1052⁸ Folly Finnesse **(66)***(48) (BRMillman)* 4-7-11 ow1 AMackay(7) (a bhd).....7 11

3/1 Wilcuma, **11/2** Rory, **13/2** Ham N'Eggs, **7/1** Serious, **15/2** Aljazzaf (9/2-8/1), **11/1** Chickawicka (IRE) (8/1-12/1), **12/1** PAY HOMAGE, Toujours Riviera, **20/1** Shanghai Venture (USA), Lowawatha, **33/1** Folly Finnesse, CSF £77.70 CT £266.79 TOTE £13.10: £3.10 £1.90 £1.60 (£26.20) Trio £54.20 OWNER Miss A. V. Hill (KINGSCLERE) BRED Cheveley Park Stud Ltd 11 Rn 1m 54.54 (3.84) SF: 27/32/28/16/24/26/20/14/30/19/-

1226 SUSSEX COUNTY CRICKET CLUB CLAIMING STKS (2-Y.O) (Class D) £3,687.50 (£1,100.00: £525.00: £237.50)
6f Stalls: Low GOING minus 0.44 sec per fur (F) 4-45 (4-46)

644³ **Takapuna (IRE)** *(67) (RHannon)* 2-8-4 RPerham(6) (lw: hld up: n.m.r over 2f out: rdn wl over 1f out: led ins fnl f: r.o wl).....— 1
1047⁸ Bobsworthatcaspers *(65)*(Fav)*(GLewis)* 2-8-7 PaulEddery(3) (led: hrd rdn over 2f out: hdd ins fnl f: unable qckn).....1¾ 2
*604*⁵ Don't Tell Vicki *(50) (JSMoore)* 2-7-10 (5) NVarley(1) (a.p: rdn 3f out: wknd fnl f).....3½ 3
Dyanko *(59) (MSSaunders)* 2-8-11 ADicks(4) (leggy: lt-f: rdn over 2f out: nvr nr tochal).....nk 4
*1073** Doubleyoubeay *(57) (JBerry)* 2-8-13 GCarter(5) (lw: hld up: hrd rdn over 1f out: wknd fnl f).1½ 5
919⁵ Alpine *(58) (PFICole)* 2-9-2b TQuinn(2) (spd over 3f).....¾ 6
825¹² Freeloader *(21) (JWHills)* 2-8-11 MHills(7) (lw: hld up: rdn over 2f out: sn wknd).....12 7

2/1 Bobsworthatcaspers, **7/2** TAKAPUNA (IRE), **4/1** Doubleyoubeay (11/4-9/2), **5/1** Alpine (5/2-11/2), **8/1** Freeloader, **14/1** Don't Tell Vicki, **33/1** Dyanko, CSF £10.38 TOTE £4.40: £2.30 £1.80 (£5.50) OWNER Mr D. Boocock (MARLBOROUGH) BRED Scarteen Stud 7 Rn 1m 13.29 (3.09) SF: 9/7/-/1/-/-/-

Takapuna (IRE) clmd RA Barber £8,000

1227

COCKED HAT STKS (3-Y.O+) (Class C) £5,203.60 (£1,873.60: £896.80: £364.00: £142.00)
6f Stalls: Low GOING minus 0.44 sec per fur (F) 5-20 (5-21)

959[2] **Al Rawda (FR) (95)***(90) (HRACecil)* 3-8-3 WRyan(4) (lw: hld up: rdn over 2f out: led 1f out: r.o wl) — 1
Everglades (IRE) **(102)***(102) (RCharlton)* 7-10-0 PatEddery(3) (bit bkwd: dwlt: outpcd: hdwy over 2f out: r.o) 1 2
Kassbaan (USA) **(110)***(96)*(Fav)*(SbinSuroor)* 5-9-10 LDettori(5) (lw: a.p: led over 3f out to 1f out: unable qckn) ¾ 3
Marha **(85)***(89) (HThomsonJones)* 3-8-7 RHills(1) (hld up: rdn over 2f out: one pce) nk 4
828[9] Signs **(95)***(88) (RHannon)* 3-8-2 (7) DaneO'Neill(2) (led over 2f: rdn over 2f out: one pce) 1 5

4/5 Kassbaan (USA), **5/2** AL RAWDA (FR), **7/1** Everglades (IRE), **9/1** Signs, **20/1** Marha, CSF £16.36 TOTE £3.00: £1.30 £2.10 (£6.90) OWNER Prince A. A. Faisal (NEWMARKET) BRED Prince Abdul Rahman Faisal in France 5 Rn 1m 10.81 (0.61) SF: 42/64/58/41/40
WEIGHT FOR AGE 3yo-10lb
T/Jkpt: £12,570.70 (0.1 Tckts); £15,934.80 to Goodwood 24/5/95. T/Plpt: £43.70 (666.64 Tckts). T/Qdpt: £5.80 (31.7 Tckts). AK

0798a-LES LANDES (Jersey) (L-H)
Monday May 8th (Good to firm)

1228a

MORGAN GRENFELL JERSEY GUINEAS (3-Y.O+) £900.00 **1m 110y** 3-40 (3-42)

Green's le Sidaner (USA) *(Jersey)* 7-10-7 MrDCuthbert — 1
798a[3] Wickins *(Jersey)* 5-10-7 AMcCabe 2 2
800a* Essex Girl *(Jersey)* 5-10-4 RMcGhin 5 3
Muscat (IRE) *(PDJones)* 8-10-7 MrJCulloty 15 4

Tote £10.40 (£1.90) 4 Rn 1m 47.0 SF: -/-/-/-

1114a-SAN SIRO (Milan, Italy) (R-H)
Wednesday May 17th (Heavy)

1229a

PREMIO FOXY MAIDEN (3-Y.O) £4,186.00 **1m** 3-40 (3-47)

Suranom (IRE) *(LMCumani)* 3-8-10 FJovine — 1
Super Gentle (IRE) *(Italy)* 3-8-10 EBotti 6½ 2
Nimble Boy (USA) *(Italy)* 3-9-0 MTellini 2½ 3

Tote 25L: 15L 15L 55L (40L) OWNER Scuderia Rencati (NEWMARKET) 10 Rn 1m 44.9 SF: -/-/-

CHANTILLY (France) (R-H)
Friday May 19th (Soft)

1230a

PRIX LA FORCE (Gp 3) (3-Y.O) £26,347.00 (£9,581.00: £4,790.00: £2,395.00) **1m 2f** 4-55 (4-50)

808a[4] **Tzar Rodney (FR)** *(104) (GDoleuze,France)* 3-8-11 OPeslier — 1
1008a[4] Copent Garden(IRE) *(104) (AFabre,France)* 3-8-11 TJarnet nse 2
801a[5] Farenvaros *(102) (PDemercastel,France)* 3-8-12 SGuillot 2 3
Vaguely Gay *(102) (MmeCHead,France)* 3-8-12 ODoleuze hd 4

P-M 4.40F: 1.10F 1.10F (SF8.40F) OWNER W. Trichter 4 Rn 2m 12.5 (11.80) SF: -/-/-/-

BADEN-BADEN (Germany) (L-H)
Saturday May 20th (Heavy)

1231a

OLEANDER RENNEN (Gp 3) (4-Y.O+) £30,864.00 (£12,346.00: £6,173.00: £3,292.00)
2m 3-25 (3-29)

Flamingo Paradise *(112) (HBlume,Germany)* 4-8-5 AStarke — 1

Ballet Prince (IRE) *(110) (JEHammond,France)* 5-8-6 CAsmussen 1 2
Flying Dream *(111) (BSchutz,Germany)* 4-8-7 ASuborics 2½ 3

Tote 191DM: 40DM 19DM 25DM (SF 1003DM) 12 Rn 3m 47.48 SF: -/-/-

PIMLICO (Baltimore, USA) (L-H)
Saturday May 20th (Fast)

1232a PREAKNESS STAKES (Gp 1) (3-Y.O) £286,417.00 (£88,128.00: £44,705.00: £22,032.00) **1m 1f 110y** 10-31 (10-31)

1006a[3] **Timber Country (USA)** *(125) (DWLukas,USA)* 3-9-0 PDay ....— 1
Oliver's Twist *(124) (JBoniface,USA)* 3-9-0 ADelgado ....½ 2
1006a* Thunder Gulch(USA) *(124) (DWLukas,USA)* 3-9-0 GStevens ....nk 3

P-M £5.80: PL £4.20 £16.80 SHOW £2.80 £6.40 £3.60 (SF £266.00) OWNER Gainscliffe Racing BRED Lowquest Ltd in USA 11 Rn 1m 54.4 SF: -/-/-

0803a-CURRAGH (Newbridge, Ireland) (R-H)
Sunday May 21st (Good to firm)

1233a WEATHERBYS IRELAND GREENLANDS STAKES (Gp 3) (3-Y.O+) £16,250.00 (£4,750.00: £2,250.00: £750.00) **6f** 3-10 (3-12)

803a[2] **Nautical Pet (IRE)** *(111) (DKWeld,Ireland)* 3-8-8 MJKinane ....— 1
803a* Desert Style (IRE) *(115) (JSBolger,Ireland)* 3-8-12 KJManning ....hd 2
America's Cup (IRE) *(107) (CO'Brien,Ireland)* 3-8-8 NGMcCullagh 1½ 3
Loveyoumillions (IRE) *(100) (MJohnston)* 3-8-8 JReid 2½ 4
934[2] Alzianah *(92) (JDBethell)* 4-9-1 WCarson 2 5

CSF £10.29 Tote £2.20: £1.40 £1.70 £3.50 (£4.90) OWNER Moyglare Stud Farms Ltd 10 Rn 1m 13.0 (2.40) SF: -/-/-/-/-

1234a FIRST NATIONAL BLDG SOCIETY IRISH 2,000 GUINEAS (Gp 1) (3-Y.O C & F) £130,700.00 (£40,000.00: £20,000.00: £8,000.00) **1m** 3-45 (3-53)

792* **Spectrum (IRE)** *(126) (PWChapple-Hyam)* 3-9-0 JReid (trckd ldrs: qcknd to ld 2f out: edgd lft ins fnl f: r.o wl) ....— 1
708a* Adjareli (IRE) *(124) (JOxx,Ireland)* 3-9-0 JPMurtagh (hld up: hdwy to chse wnr over 1f out: r.o u.p) 1 2
920[3] Bahri (USA) *(123) (JLDunlop)* 3-9-0 WCarson (hld up: nt clr run over 2f out: hdwy fnl f: r.o)...½ 3
803a[3] Burden Of Proof (IRE) *(114) (CO'Brien,Ireland)* 3-9-0 CRoche (hld up: hdwy 2f out: nt rch ldrs) 4½ 4
900a* Prince Arthur (IRE) *(113) (PWChapple-Hyam)* 3-9-0 PatEddery (prom tl wknd 2f out) ....½ 5
708a[2] Oscar Schindler (IRE) *(112) (KPrendergast,Ireland)* 3-9-0 WJSupple (a.p. led 3f out to 2f out: wknd) ....½ 6
920[5] Nwaamis (USA) *(112) (JLDunlop)* 3-9-0 MJKinane (hld up: nvr plcd to chal) ....hd 7
Celladonia (IRE) *(109) (JSBolger,Ireland)* 3-9-0 KJManning (hld up: btn over 2f out) 1½ 8
I'm Supposin (IRE) *(89) (KPrendergast,Ireland)* 3-9-0 SCraine (mde most tl hdd 3f out: wknd qckly) 10 9

, , , , , , , , , CSF £29.99 Tote £4.20: £1.80 £1.90 £1.30 (£15.90) OWNER Lord Weinstock & The Hon Simon Weinstock (MARLBOROUGH) BRED Ballymacoll Stud Farm Ltd. in Ireland 9 Rn 1m 40.3 (4.30) SF: -/-/-/-/-/-/-/-/-

1235a TATTERSALLS GOLD CUP (Gp 2) (4-Y.O+) £32,500.00 (£9,500.00: £4,500.00: £1,500.00) **1m 2f** 4-20 (4-21)

827* **Prince of Andros (USA)** *(115) (DRLoder)* 5-8-12 MJKinane (hld up: hdwy to ld ins fnl f: jst hld on) ....— 1
Just Happy (USA) *(117) (MRStoute)* 4-9-1 WCarson (trckd ldrs: prog to ld 2f out: hdd ins fnl f: r.o wl) ....½ 2
Environment Friend *(113) (GRimmer)* 7-8-12 MRimmer (bhd ½-wy: hdwy fnl 2f: r.o wl) 1 3
Double On (IRE) *(109) (PJFlynn,Ireland)* 4-8-9 JReid (a.p. led over 2f out: sn hdd: r.o) ....½ 4

Dancing Sunset (IRE) *(106) (APO'Brien,Ireland)* 4-8-9 CRoche (hld up: styd on u.p 2f out) .1½ 5
Akhiyar (IRE) *(107) (JOxx,Ireland)* 4-8-12 JPMurtagh (hld up: rdn over 2f out: no imp) 1½ 6
State Crystal (IRE) *(103) (APO'Brien,Ireland)* 4-8-9 WRyan (led tl hdd over 2f out: wknd)......½ 7

CSF £19.40 Tote £4.90: £3.30 £4.60 (£9.80) OWNER Lucayan Stud (NEWMARKET) BRED Spendthrift Farm 7 Rn 2m 4.8 (2.50) SF: -/-/-/-/-/-/-

1231a-BADEN-BADEN (Germany) (L-H)
Sunday May 21st (Soft)

1236a BADENER MILE (Gp 3) (3-Y.O+) £30,864.00 (£12,346.00: £6,173.00: £3,292.00) **1m** 3-25 (3-36)

Chato (USA) *(104) (HSteinmetz,Germany)* 3-8-2 AStarke ....— 1
Erminius (GER) *(108) (PRau,Germany)* 4-9-10 TMundry 3 2
Telasco (GER) *(95) (ALowe,Germany)* 5-9-1 AHelfenbein 2 3
1002a⁴ Port Lucaya *(DRLoder)* 5-9-12 JWeaver (btn approx 7l).................... 10

Tote 125DM: 41DM 21DM 65DM (SF 652DM) OWNER Stall Nizza 14 Rn 1m 41.52 SF: -/-/-/-

1229a-SAN SIRO (Milan, Italy) (R-H)
Sunday May 21st (Good to soft)

1237a OAKS D'ITALIA (Gp 1) (3-Y.O F) £86,112.00 (£43,819.00: £25,641.00: £12,820.00) **1m 3f** 3-40 (4-01)

1110a* **Valley of Gold (FR)** *(100) (AFabre,France)* 3-8-11 SGuillot (hld up: hdwy 2f out: led ins fnl f: r.o.wl)....................— 1
809a* Olimpia Dukakis (ITY) *(99) (GBotti,Italy)* 3-8-11 GForte (trckd ldr tl led over 1f out: hdd ins fnl f: r.o)....................1 2
1067² Bunting *(96) (JHMGosden)* 3-8-11 LDettori (led tl over 1f out: r.o one pce)....................1½ 3
932² Fanjica (IRE) *(96) (JLDunlop)* 3-8-11 FJovine (hdwy over 2f out: chal over 1f out: no ex u.p)nk 4
Rosi Zambotti (IRE) *(91) (BGrizzetti,Italy)* 3-8-11 ACarboni 3¼ 5
Leona Satti (IRE) *(86) (GBotti,Italy)* 3-8-11 MBotti 3½ 6
Imco Glaring (IRE) *(86) (PLodigiani,Italy)* 3-8-11 SLandi ....nse 7
Totostar *(79) (MCiciarelli,Italy)* 3-8-11 OFrancera 5 8
Monica Cozzi (ITY) *(76) (RBrogi,Italy)* 3-8-11 LSorrentino 2¼ 9
809a³ Love Secret (USA) *(65) (VZito,Italy)* 3-8-11 MEsposito 7 10
886³ Pesce D'Aprile *(65) (JLDunlop)* 3-8-11 EBotti ....hd 11

Tote 24L: 10L 10L 11L (26L) OWNER Sheikh Mohammed (FRANCE) 11 Rn 2m 19.1

LONGCHAMP (Paris, France) (R-H)
Sunday May 21st (Soft)

1238a PRIX SAINT-ALARY (Gp 1) (3-Y.O F) £61,449.00 (£24,371.00: £11,665.00: £4,790.00) **1m 2f** 3-40 (3-43)

802a* **Muncie (IRE)** *(106) (AFabre,France)* 3-9-2 OPeslier (3rd st: smooth hdwy to ld wl over 1f out: drew clr: impressive)....................— 1
899a² Marble Falls (IRE) *(100) (ELellouche,France)* 3-9-2 GGuignard (hld up: 4th st: hrd rdn 2f out: r.o gamely) 4 2
899a* Secret Quest *(99) (PBary,France)* 3-9-2 DBoeuf (hit hd in stalls: 2nd tl led over 2f out: hdd wl over 1f out: r.o)....................½ 3
Marie de Gloire (FR) *(75) (ASpanu,France)* 3-9-2 SCoerette (led tl hdd over 2f out: wknd qckly)....................15 4
Pourville (USA) *(43) (AFabre,France)* 3-9-2 TJarnet (rdn after 2f: bhd st: t.o) 20 5

P-M 1.30F: 1.10F 1.20F (6.30) OWNER Mr D. Wildenstein (FRANCE) 5 Rn 2m 8.7 SF: -/-/-/-/-

1239a PRIX VICOMTESSE VIGIER (Gp 2) (4-Y.O+) £35,928.00 (£14,371.00: £7,186.00: £3,593.00) **1m 7f 110y** 4-15 (4-13)

1001a² **The Little Thief (FR)** *(118) (EDanel,France)* 4-8-11 AJunk (a.p. rdn to ld over 1f out: r.o wl)....................— 1

1001a* Nononito (FR) *(118) (JLesbordes,France)* 4-8-11 GMosse (trckd wnr: chal over 1f out: r.o)...½ **2**
Epaphos (GER) *(111) (PBary,France)* 5-8-11 DBoeuf (5th st: rdn over 2f out: one pce fnl f)...5 **3**
Petralona (USA) *(107) (AFabre,France)* 4-8-8 TJarnet (4th st: rdn 2f out: one pce)...2 **4**
Infrasonic *(109) (JdeRoualle,France)* 5-8-11 OPeslier (hld up: hdwy 2f out: no ex fnl f)...hd **5**
896a^{2} Grioun (FR) *(101) (DSepulchre,France)* 4-8-8 ODoleuze (led tl hdd over 1f out: wknd qckly)...6 **6**

P-M 3.10F: 1.70F 1.20F (5.10) OWNER Mr George Ohrstrom BRED George L. Ohrstrom in France
6 Rn 3m 29.7 SF: -/-/-/-/-/-

1221-GOODWOOD (R-H)
Wednesday May 24th (St course Good to firm, Rnd Firm)
WEATHER: drizzle WIND: almost nil

1240
FINNBOARD MAIDEN STKS (3-Y.O F) (Class D) £4,199.25
(£1,254.00: £599.50: £272.25)
7f Stalls: High GOING minus 0.34 sec per fur (GF) 2-10 (2-11)

Marguerite Bay (IRE) *(90) (EALDunlop)* 3-8-11 WRSwinburn(6) (unf: bit bkwd: squeezed thro 2f out: hdwy over 1f out: led wl ins fnl f: r.o wl)...— **1**
Sea Thunder *(89)*(Fav)*(IABalding)* 3-8-11 PatEddery(7) (unf: 4th st: led over 2f out tl wl ins fnl f: unable qckn)...½ **2**
442^{13} Summer Retreat (USA) *(83) (JHMGosden)* 3-8-11 LDettori(9) (b.hind: bit bkwd: 5th st: rdn over 3f out: one pce fnl 2f)...2½ **3**
1053^{3} Makri *(81) (MrsJCecil)* 3-8-11 PaulEddery(1) (lw: led over 1f: 2nd st: ev ch over 2f out: hrd rdn over 1f out: one pce)...1 **4**
Ron's Secret *(75) (JWPayne)* 3-8-11 RCochrane(2) (bit bkwd: 6th st: rdn over 3f out: bmpd 2f out: one pce)...2½ **5**
637^{12} Hasaid Lady (IRE) **(74)***(68) (RHannon)* 3-8-4 (7) DaneO'Neill(10) (3rd st: wknd over 1f out)...3 **6**
915^{4} By The Bay *(64) (BWHills)* 3-8-11 MHills(5) (a bhd)...1¾ **7**
752^{9} Barriyah *(60) (HThomsonJones)* 3-8-11 WCarson(8) (lw: plld hrd: led over 5f out tl over 2f out: sn wknd)...2 **8**
Rising River *(28) (SWoodman)* 3-8-11 MFenton(3) (unf: s.s: a bhd)...14 **9**

13/8 Sea Thunder, **9/2** By The Bay (op 5/2), **7/1** MARGUERITE BAY (IRE) (8/1-12/1), **8/1** Summer Retreat (USA) (4/1-9/1), Makri, **10/1** Ron's Secret, **16/1** Hasaid Lady (IRE), **20/1** Barriyah, **33/1** Rising River, CSF £17.55 TOTE £8.90: £1.80 £1.20 £1.70 (£7.90) Trio £16.70 OWNER Maktoum Al Maktoum (NEWMARKET) BRED Gainsborough Stud Management Ltd 9 Rn
1m 27.44 (3.04) SF: 32/31/25/23/17/10/6/2/-

1241
GOODWOOD PARK HOTEL H'CAP (0-100) (3-Y.O+) (Class C)
£7,180.00 (£2,140.00: £1,020.00: £460.00)
6f Stalls: Low GOING minus 0.34 sec per fur (GF) 2-40 (2-40)

949^{5} **Castlerea Lad (82)***(89) (RHollinshead)* 6-9-4 LDettori(6) (hld up: led over 1f out: rdn out)...— **1**
870^{20} No Extras (IRE) **(90)***(90) (GLMoore)* 5-9-12 BRouse(1) (rdn over 2f out: hdwy over 1f out: r.o)...2½ **2**
796^{2} Sweet Magic **(77)***(64)*(Fav)*(LJHolt)* 4-8-13 JReid(3) (plld hrd: a.p: ev ch 1f out: unable qckn)s.h **3**
665^{12} My Best Valentine **(85)***(68) (JWhite)* 5-9-7b FNorton(2) (lw: nt clr run 2f out: hdwy over 1f out: r.o)...1 **4**
828^{4} That Man Again **(84)***(69) (GLewis)* 3-8-5 (5) AWhelan(8) (lw: a.p: led over 2f out tl over 1f out: one pce)...½ **5**
1057^{8} How's Yer Father **(83)***(75) (RJHodges)* 9-9-5 PatEddery(9) (rdn over 2f out: hdwy & hmpd 1f out: nvr nrr)...2 **6**
982^{2} Golden Lady (IRE) **(84)***(82) (RHannon)* 3-8-10 TQuinn(4) (lw: a.p: ev ch wl over 1f out: rdn & fnd nil)...nk **7**
1071^{6} Invocation **(63)***(61) (AMoore)* 8-7-13 TWilliams(7) (b.nr hind: lw: hld up: rdn over 2f out: ev ch over 1f out: wknd fnl f)...¾ **8**
1100^{10} Palacegate Touch **(92)***(79) (JBerry)* 5-10-0b GCarter(5) (lw: led over 3f: wkng whn hmpd on ins 1f out)...2 **9**

9/4 Sweet Magic, **9/2** CASTLEREA LAD, Golden Lady (IRE) (op 7/1), **11/2** How's Yer Father (4/1-6/1), **10/1** That Man Again (op 6/1), **12/1** Palacegate Touch, **20/1** No Extras (IRE), Invocation, **25/1** My Best Valentine, CSF £69.82 CT £225.46 TOTE £5.20: £1.50 £4.10 £1.40 (£72.60) Trio £81.30 OWNER Mrs Tess Graham (UPPER LONGDON) BRED J. D. Hurd 9 Rn
1m 10.67 (0.47) SF: 66/67/54/60/47/51/41/28/52
WEIGHT FOR AGE 3yo-10lb

1242 TRIPLEPRINT LUPE STKS (Listed) (3-Y.O F) (Class A) £18,000.00 (£5,400.00: £2,600.00: £1,200.00)
1m 2f Stalls: High GOING minus 0.34 sec per fur (GF) 3-10 (3-11)

1009a4 **Subya (105)***(103) (JLDunlop)* 3-8-11 WCarson(1) (lw: rdn & hdwy over 2f out: led ins fnl f: r.o wl) — 1
950* Tillandsia (IRE) *(98)*(Fav)*(DRLoder)* 3-8-8 MJKinane(6) (lw: led 2f: led 6f out: qcknd over 4f out: hdd ins fnl f: unable qckn) 1¼ 2
9972 Yarn (IRE) **(100)***(96) (MRChannon)* 3-8-8 RHughes(2) (lw: 3rd st: rdn over 3f out: ev ch over 1f out: one pce) 1 3
10673 Kshessinskaya *(92) (CEBrittain)* 3-8-8 MRimmer(4) (lw: rdn over 3f out: hdwy over 1f out: r.o) 3 4
911* Brave Revival **(94)***(91) (MRStoute)* 3-8-8 WRSwinburn(9) (rdn over 3f out: ev ch over 1f out: wknd fnl f) ½ 5
6206 Mandarina (USA) **(92)***(91) (LMCumani)* 3-8-8 LDettori(8) (lw: 4th st: rdn over 3f out: wknd fnl f) hd 6
957* Blue Zulu (IRE) *(88) (JRFanshawe)* 3-8-8 DHarrison(5) (6th st: hrd rdn 3f out: wknd over 2f out) 1½ 7
9974 Snowtown (IRE) **(107)***(56) (PWChapple-Hyam)* 3-8-8 JReid(7) (bhd fnl 3f) 20 8
10005 Fresh Fruit Daily *(16) (PAKelleway)* 3-8-8 PaulEddery(3) (led 8f out to 6f out: 5th st: wknd 4f out: t.o) 25 9

4/1 Tillandsia (IRE), **11/2** SUBYA, Yarn (IRE), Mandarina (USA), **6/1** Snowtown (IRE), **7/1** Brave Revival, **11/1** Blue Zulu (IRE), **12/1** Kshessinskaya, **25/1** Fresh Fruit Daily, CSF £25.18 TOTE £5.50: £1.90 £1.80 £1.70 (£8.10) Trio £13.60 OWNER Prince A. A. Faisal (ARUNDEL) BRED Nawara Stud Co Ltd 9 Rn
2m 9.31 (4.31) SF: 34/29/27/23/22/22/19/-/-

1243 KINCSEM RATED STKS H'CAP (0-100) (4-Y.O+) (Class B) £9,106.80 (£3,361.20: £1,605.60: £648.00: £249.00: £89.40)
1m 6f Stalls: High GOING minus 0.34 sec per fur (GF) 3-40 (3-41)

9234 **Mercadier (82)***(96) (CEBrittain)* 4-8-4 BDoyle(1) (lw: mde all: sn clr: rdn 3f out: r.o wl) — 1
9319 Wishing (USA) **(89)***(103) (RAkehurst)* 4-8-11 LDettori(5) (lw: chsd wnr: mod 2nd st: rdn over 3f out: r.o wl ins fnl f) nk 2
9313 Beauchamp Hero **(99)***(111)*(Fav)*(JLDunlop)* 5-9-7 JReid(4) (lw: poor 4th st: rdn over 2f out: hdwy over 1f out: r.o: too much to do) 1¾ 3
Saxon Maid **(97)***(103) (LMCumani)* 4-9-5 MJKinane(6) (3rd st: rdn over 3f out: wknd 2f out: one pce) 5 4
11024 Endless Light (USA) **(84)***(88) (PFICole)* 4-8-6 TQuinn(3) (lw: poor 6th st: a bhd) 2 5
11098 Flight Lieutenant (USA) **(82)***(85) (RHannon)* 6-8-4b GCarter(2) (lw: poor 5th st: a bhd) nk 6

LONG HANDICAP Mercadier 8-1 Flight Lieutenant (USA) 8-1

6/4 Beauchamp Hero, **5/2** Saxon Maid, **11/2** Wishing (USA) (7/2-6/1), **7/1** Endless Light (USA), **12/1** Flight Lieutenant (USA), **16/1** MERCADIER, CSF £84.05 TOTE £14.10: £4.10 £1.90 (£33.50) OWNER Sheikh Mohammed (NEWMARKET) BRED Someries Stud 6 Rn
3m 3.57 (4.57) SF: 37/44/52/44/29/26

1244 SOUTHERNPRINT H'CAP (0-80) (3-Y.O+) (Class D) £4,342.25(£1,298.00: £621.50: £283.25) **1m** Stalls: High GOING minus 0.34 sec per fur (GF) 4-10 (4-12)

87325 **Kingchip Boy (72)***(80) (MJRyan)* 6-9-6v AClark(13) (6th st: rdn over 3f out: led ins fnl f: r.o wl) — 1
10697 Captain's Day **(80)***(86) (TGMills)* 3-9-2 JReid(9) (lw: 3rd st: nt clr run over 1f out: r.o wl ins fnl f) 1 2
*1091*11 Scottish Park **(45)***(50) (RWEmery)* 6-7-7 GBardwell(12) (lw: rdn over 5f out: gd hdwy fnl f: r.o wl) nk 3
112619 Thatchmaster (IRE) **(52)***(57) (CAHorgan)* 4-8-0 TWilliams(4) (rdn 3f out: gd hdwy fnl f: r.o wl) s.h 4
*1049** Whatever's Right (IRE) **(60)***(65) (MDIUsher)* 6-8-8 BThomson(7) (swtg: led: hrd rdn over 1f out: hdd ins fnl f: unable qckn) s.h 5
7318 Another Fiddle (IRE) **(66)***(71) (RAkehurst)* 5-9-0 TQuinn(1) (hrd rdn & hdwy over 1f out: nt clr run & snatched up wl ins fnl f: nt rcvr) hd 6
10525 Piquant **(67)***(72)*(Fav)*(LordHuntingdon)* 8-9-1 LDettori(8) (4th st: rdn over 3f out: ev ch 2f out: one pce) d.h 6
11483 Narbonne **(58)***(61) (BJMcMath)* 4-8-6 RCochrane(14) (2nd st: rdn & ev ch over 1f out: one pce) 1 8
*1088*2 Douce Maison (IRE) **(55)***(56) (APJarvis)* 4-8-3 DHarrison(3) (5th st: rdn over 2f out: one pce) 1 9

454[9] Lucky Tucky **(61)***(60) (JRJenkins)* 4-8-9 GCarter(10) (7th st: rdn over 2f out: n.m.r over 1f out: wknd fnl f)....1¼ **10**
Blue Bomber **(80)***(78) (CWeedon)* 4-9-9 (5) RPainter(2) (a bhd)....nk **11**
1015[2] Built for Comfort (IRE) **(69)***(62) (RHannon)* 3-8-5 ow1 PatEddery(6) (bhd fnl 3f)....1¾ **12**
Ballynakelly **(73)***(57) (RAkehurst)* 3-8-6 (3) SSanders(11) (a bhd)....5 **13**
601[10] Across the Bay **(55)***(9) (RWEmery)* 8-8-3b PaulEddery(5) (lw: bhd fnl 4f)....15 **14**
LONG HANDICAP Scottish Park 7-3

4/1 Piquant, **11/2** Whatever's Right (IRE), **6/1** Douce Maison (IRE), **9/1** Another Fiddle (IRE) (6/1-10/1), Narbonne, Built for Comfort (IRE), **10/1** Ballynakelly (6/1-11/1), **12/1** KINGCHIP BOY, Captain's Day, **16/1** Lucky Tucky, **20/1** Scottish Park, **50/1** Blue Bomber, Thatchmaster (IRE), Across the Bay, CSF £132.17 CT £2,554.97 TOTE £12.80: £4.10 £4.30 £9.60 (£66.00) Trio £488.50 OWNER Four Jays Racing Partnership (NEWMARKET) BRED R. M. Scott 14 Rn
1m 39.38 (1.78) SF: 58/52/28/35/43/49/50/39/34/38/56/28/23/-
WEIGHT FOR AGE 3yo-12lb

OFFICIAL EXPLANATION **Built for Comfort (IRE): the jockey stated the filly did not settle for the first three furlongs and, when he asked, there was no response.**

1245 BUSTER HASLAM AND PADDY MORRISSEY CLAIMING STKS (3-Y.O+) (Class E) £3,850.00 (£1,150.00: £550.00: £250.00)

1m 2f Stalls: High GOING minus 0.34 sec per fur (GF) 4-45 (4-45)

763[8] **Trade Wind (71)***(82) (DRCElsworth)* 4-9-9b(5) AProcter(9) (lw: 4th st: hrd rdn over 2f out: led over 1f out: wandered: all out)....— **1**
724[8] Last Laugh (IRE) **(63)***(69)*(Fav)*(RHannon)* 3-8-0 GCarter(3) (lw: rdn over 3f out: hdwy 2f out: r.o wl ins fnl f)....s.h **2**
976[5] Chairmans Choice **(44)***(72) (APJarvis)* 5-9-6 BThomson(6) (lw: led 3f: 2nd st: led over 3f out tl over 1f out: unable qckn)....1 **3**
Irkutsk (USA) *(74) (MCPipe)* 4-9-8 MJKinane(7) (lw: rdn & hdwy over 2f out: nt clr run over 1f out: swtchd rt: nt clr run ins fnl f: swtchd lft: r.o)....½ **4**
1149[4] Kimberley Boy **(56)***(55) (MBrittain)* 5-9-1 RCochrane(8) (led 7f out tl over 3f out: wknd over 1f out)....7 **5**
848[18] Head For Heaven *(51) (RPCHoad)* 5-9-1 RPrice(1) (5th st: wknd over 2f out)....2½ **6**
1083[6] Embezzler **(56)***(48) (GLewis)* 3-8-1 PaulEddery(5) (a bhd)....3 **7**
762[7] Positivo **(67)***(33) (LordHuntingdon)* 4-9-7 LDettori(4) (b.hind: 6th st: wknd over 3f out)....12 **8**
851[9] Sorisky **(45)***(24) (BGubby)* 3-8-3 NCarlisle(2) (3rd st: wknd over 3f out)....4 **9**

5/2 Last Laugh (IRE), **3/1** Positivo, **9/2** Irkutsk (USA), **7/1** TRADE WIND, Embezzler, **15/2** Kimberley Boy, **33/1** Chairmans Choice, **50/1** Sorisky, **66/1** Head For Heaven, CSF £23.29 TOTE £10.70: £2.80 £1.70 £2.90 (£10.60) Trio £61.30 OWNER Mr Ray Richards (WHITCOMBE) BRED Mrs M. H. Hunter 9 Rn 2m 10.18 (5.18) SF: 43/15/33/35/16/12/-/-/-
WEIGHT FOR AGE 3yo-15lb

OFFICIAL EXPLANATION **Positivo: the jockey reported he had lost an iron four furlongs out.**

1246 E.B.F. BOXGROVE MAIDEN STKS (2-Y.O) (Class D) £4,386.00 (£1,308.00: £624.00: £282.00)

6f Stalls: Low GOING: 0.34 sec per fur (G) 5-20 (5-21)

Sea Dane *(98+) (PWHarris)* 2-9-0 MJKinane(8) (w'like: a gng wl: led over 1f out: qcknd: easily)....— **1**
Dashing Blue *(93) (IABalding)* 2-9-0 LDettori(6) (w'like: a.p: ev ch over 1f out: unable qckn)...4 **2**
Goodwood Rocket *(93) (JLDunlop)* 2-9-0 MHills(1) (w'like: scope: lw: hld up: rdn over 3f out: swtchd rt wl over 1f out: r.o one pce)....nk **3**
Chalamont (IRE) *(78)*(Fav)*(PWChapple-Hyam)* 2-8-9 JReid(7) (neat: led over 4f)....3½ **4**
No Cliches *(70) (GLewis)* 2-9-0 SWhitworth(4) (str: scope: hld up: rdn over 2f out: wknd over 1f out)....5 **5**
Seven Crowns (USA) *(65) (TGMills)* 2-9-0 PatEddery(5) (str: scope: hld up: rdn over 2f out: wknd over 1f out)....2 **6**
Get Tough *(64) (SDow)* 2-9-0 StephenDavies(2) (neat: s.s: a bhd)....s.h **7**

5/2 Chalamont (IRE) (op 6/4), **3/1** Dashing Blue, Seven Crowns (USA), **6/1** SEA DANE, **8/1** Goodwood Rocket (4/1-10/1), **33/1** No Cliches, Get Tough, CSF £22.00 TOTE £7.80: £3.30 £2.90 (£15.00) OWNER Carat Gold Connections (BERKHAMSTED) BRED Miss K. Rausing 7 Rn
1m 12.27 (2.07) SF: 40/29/29/14/6/1/-

T/Jkpt: Not won; £29,017.49 to Goodwood 25/5/95. T/Plpt: £3,703.60 (8.67 Tckts). T/Qdpt: Not won; £224.20 to Goodwood 25/5/95. AK

0964-NEWCASTLE (L-H)
Wednesday May 24th (Good, Good to firm patches)
WEATHER: showers WIND: almost nil

1247 CAMPERDOWN MAIDEN STKS (2-Y.O) (Class D) £3,297.50 (£998.00:£487.00: £231.50) **5f** Stalls: High GOING minus 0.27 sec per fur (GF) 6-30 (6-30)

Royal Ceilidh (IRE) *(84+) (DenysSmith)* 2-8-9 JFortune(3) (w'like: bit bkwd: s.i.s: sn rcvrd: rdn to ld ins fnl f: r.o) ....— 1
993² Larghetto (IRE) *(85)*(Fav)*(JBerry)* 2-9-0 JCarroll(1) (lw: trckd ldrs: hung lft fr ½-wy: kpt on one pce fnl f) 1¼ 2
1047² Welsh Mountain *(83) (MJHeaton-Ellis)* 2-9-0 KDarley(6) (led tl hdd & no ex ins fnl f) ....½ 3
Mask Flower (USA) *(74) (MJohnston)* 2-8-9 DHolland(2) (str: scope: bit bkwd: cl up tl wknd ins fnl f) 1½ 4
Creative Account (USA) *(78) (MrsJRRamsden)* 2-9-0 KFallon(4) (w'like: scope: bit bkwd: trckd ldrs: outpcd over 1f out: r.o towards fin) ....nk 5
Alfayza *(44) (JDBethell)* 2-8-9 TIves(5) (neat: cl up tl wknd & hmpd ½-wy) 9 6

5/4 Larghetto (IRE), **5/2** Mask Flower (USA), **3/1** Welsh Mountain, **10/1** Creative Account (USA) (8/1-12/1), **14/1** Alfayza, **16/1** ROYAL CEILIDH (IRE), CSF £37.34 TOTE £16.80: £4.50 £1.30 (£15.30) OWNER Carlton Appointments (Aberdeen) Ltd (BISHOP AUCKLAND) BRED Thomas and Mary Shirley 6 Rn
61.54 secs (3.14) SF: 18/19/17/8/12/-

1248 BURRADON (S) STKS (3-Y.O+) (Class F) £2,801.60 (£787.60: £384.80) **5f** Stalls: High GOING minus 0.27 sec per fur (GF) 7-00 (7-01)

877⁶ **So Intrepid (IRE) (70)***(75) (JMBradley)* 5-9-1 (5) SDrowne(10) (hdwy ½-wy: r.o wl to ld wl ins fnl f) ....— 1
1080³ Flashy's Son **(66)***(71) (GMMoore)* 7-9-6 MTebbutt(7) (b: b.hind: trckd ldrs: led 2f out tl hrd rdn & hdd wl ins fnl f) 1¼ 2
966¹² Annie Fay (IRE) **(56)***(55) (JLHarris)* 3-8-6 DHolland(4) (hdwy 2f out: styd on: nvr able chal) .3½ 3
944⁴ Sigama (USA) **(56)***(54) (DNicholls)* 9-9-11 AlexGreaves(9) (led 3f: grad wknd) 3½ 4
1106¹¹ Gorinsky (IRE) **(97)***(48)*(Fav)*(JBerry)* 7-9-6 JCarroll(11) (chsd ldrs: ev ch 2f out: grad wknd) s.h 5
1080¹³ Sense of Priority **(62)***(42) (MHEasterby)* 6-9-6 KDarley(2) (chsd ldrs: rdn ½-wy: one pce) 2 6
965¹¹ The Right Time **(45)***(37) (JParkes)* 10-9-6 MDeering(12) (b: outpcd & bhd tl styd on fnl 2f) ...1½ 7
China Hand (IRE) **(63)***(29) (MartynWane)* 3-8-11 KFallon(6) (chsd ldrs to ½-wy: sn outpcd) .2½ 8
1042ᵂ First Option **(60)***(28) (RBastiman)* 5-9-1 (5) HBastiman(5) (spd 3f: sn wknd) ....nk 9
1157¹⁷ Robaty's Law (IRE) **(47)** *(PMonteith)* 3-8-11b SDWilliams(3) (s.i.s: n.d) 9 10
Cinders Pet *(MWEllerby)* 4-9-1 SMorris(8) (outpcd & bhd after 2f) 5 11

4/5 Gorinsky (IRE) (tchd 5/4), **4/1** Flashy's Son, **6/1** SO INTREPID (IRE), **10/1** Annie Fay (IRE), **12/1** First Option, Sense of Priority, **16/1** Sigama (USA), **25/1** China Hand (IRE), **33/1** The Right Time, **66/1** Robaty's Law (IRE), Cinders Pet, CSF £31.25 TOTE £7.80: £2.20 £1.50 £1.80 (£11.10) Trio £31.80 OWNER Mr E. A. Hayward (CHEPSTOW) BRED Crest Stud Ltd 11 Rn
59.79 secs (1.39) SF: 57/53/28/36/30/24/19/2/10/-/-
WEIGHT FOR AGE 3yo-9lb
No bid

1249 BRUNSWICK H'CAP (0-85) (3-Y.O) (Class D) £3,842.80(£1,164.40: £569.20: £271.60) **6f** Stalls: High GOING minus 0.27 sec per fur (GF) 7-30 (7-31)

982⁵ **Rasas (IRE) (72)***(77)*(Fav)*(HThomsonJones)* 3-8-13 RHills(7) (lw: trckd ldrs: led 2f out: edgd lft over 1f out: all out) ....— 1
1180¹² Rymer's Rascal **(63)***(67) (EJAlston)* 3-8-4 ow1 KFallon(8) (lw: hld up: smooth hdwy 2f out: hrd rdn & ev ch ins fnl f: r.o) ....s.h 2
Tedburrow **(62)***(60) (MrsAMNaughton)* 3-8-3 ACulhane(12) (bhd: hdwy 2f out: kpt on wl) 2½ 3
966* Bollin Harry **(62)***(59) (MHEasterby)* 3-8-3 JQuinn(2) (trckd ldrs: ev ch 2f out: rdn & nt qckn) ...½ 4
1085⁴ Quilling **(75)***(67) (MDods)* 3-9-2 SWebster(4) (bhd tl styd on wl fnl 2f) 1¾ 5
966⁶ Ramborette **(55)***(45) (DenysSmith)* 3-7-10v JFanning(5) (trckd ldrs: n.m.r over 1f out:sn btn) ..¾ 6
914³ Pelleman **(76)***(48) (RBoss)* 3-9-3 KDarley(1) (chsd ldrs: led over 2f out: sn hdd & wknd) 7 7
823¹³ Arasong **(72)***(43) (EWeymes)* 3-8-13 DeanMcKeown(10) (prom tl outpcd fr ½-wy) ....s.h 8
980¹² Flamboro **(63)***(26) (JDBethell)* 3-8-4 NConnorton(11) (prom over 3f) 3 9
722¹¹ Qualitair Pride **(60)***(23) (JFBottomley)* 3-8-1 LCharnock(9) (lw: prom over 3f: sn rdn& btn) ....nk 10
985¹⁰ Fata (IRE) **(75)***(34) (PTWalwyn)* 3-9-2v DHolland(3) (led tl hdd & wknd over 2f out) 1½ 11
River Garnock **(80)***(29) (JBerry)* 3-9-7 JCarroll(6) (prom 3f: sn bhd) 3½ 12

11/4 RASAS (IRE), **9/2** Pelleman, **5/1** Rymer's Rascal (op 10/1), Bollin Harry, **8/1** River Garnock, **9/1** Fata (IRE), **10/1** Arasong, **14/1** Ramborette, **16/1** Flamboro, Quilling, **20/1** Qualitair Pride, Tedburrow, CSF £18.76 CT £227.16 TOTE £3.60: £1.10 £3.00 £6.50 (£14.50) Trio £174.20 OWNER Mr Hamdan Al Maktoum (NEWMARKET) BRED Shadwell Estate Company Limited 12 Rn
1m 13.73 (2.23) SF: 44/34/27/26/34/12/15/10/-/-/1/-

1250 DINNINGTON H'CAP (0-80) (3-Y.O+) (Class D) £3,775.20 (£1,143.60: £558.80: £266.40) **1m (round)** Stalls: Low GOING minus 0.27 sec per fur (GF) 8-00 (8-03)

749 10 **Somerton Boy (IRE) (67)**_(75) (PCalver)_ 5-9-5 MBirch(12) (trckd ldrs: led over 1f out: r.o u.p)— 1
Coureur **(57)**_(64) (JDBethell)_ 6-8-9 TIves(7) (lw: bhd tl hdwy 2f out: r.o wl towards fin)...........nk 2
1061* Equerry **(67)**_(72) (MJohnston)_ 4-9-5 KDarley(13) (in tch: hdwy over 1f out: r.o) 1 3
1081* Tolls Choice (IRE) **(57)**_(59) (MWEasterby)_ 6-8-9 6x LCharnock(5) (s.i.s: hdwy 3f out: kpt on wl fnl f) 1½ 4
1037 9 Maurangi **(55)**_(57) (BWMurray)_ 4-8-7 JFortune(9) (lw: chsd ldrs: rdn over 2f out: kpt on)........nk 5
739 5 Rasmi (CAN) **(72)**_(74) (ACStewart)_ 4-9-10 RHills(2) (lw: trckd ldrs: effrt 2f out: r.o one pce)..s.h 6
1037 3 Calder King **(62)**_(64) (JLEyre)_ 4-8-9b(5) NVarley(6) (prom: ch appr fnl f: nt qckn)....................hd 7
1021 6 Sooty Tern **(64)**_(65) (JMBradley)_ 8-8-11 (5) SDrowne(10) (chsd ldrs: effrt over 2f out: r.o one pce) ....s.h 8
984 13 The Happy Loon (IRE) **(57)**_(56) (DenysSmith)_ 4-8-9 JQuinn(11) (lw: led tl hdd over 1f out: grad wknd)........................1¼ 9
1021 7 Cee-Jay-Ay **(70)**_(67) (JBerry)_ 8-9-8 JCarroll(3) (s.i.s: hdwy over 2f out: nt clr run fnl f) 1 10
1037 5 Mary Macblain **(44)**_(36) (JLHarris)_ 6-7-7 (3)ow3 DarrenMoffatt(1) (s.i.s: hdwy appr fnl f: n.d) .....¾ 11
1081 4 Nobby Barnes **(46)**_(40) (DonEnricoIncisa)_ 6-7-12 KimTinkler(16) (s.i.s: n.d) ....½ 12
1061 2 Kemo Sabo **(77)**_(64)_(Fav)_(MrsJRRamsden)_ 3-9-3 KFallon(4) (lw: mid div: effrt on ins 3f out: wknd wl over 1f out) 3½ 13
909 2 My Handy Man **(57)**_(39) (RAllan)_ 4-8-9 SMaloney(8) (nvr trbld ldrs)........................2½ 14
1081 3 Tovarich **(61)**_(40) (DNicholls)_ 4-8-13b AlexGreaves(16) (lw: prom tl wknd 3f out) 1¾ 15
1079 3 Cafe Solo **(45)**_(18) (NBycroft)_ 4-7-4 (7)ow2 SLanigan(14) (a rr div) 2 16

LONG HANDICAP Mary Macblain 7-3

7/2 Kemo Sabo, **6/1** Sooty Tern, **7/1** Rasmi (CAN), **8/1** Equerry, **9/1** Tovarich, Cee-Jay-Ay, **10/1** Calder King, **12/1** Mary Macblain, Tolls Choice (IRE), **14/1** Coureur, **16/1** The Happy Loon (IRE), My Handy Man, **20/1** Nobby Barnes, Maurangi, SOMERTON BOY (IRE), Cafe Solo, CSF £269.83 CT £2,207.86 TOTE £74.50: £8.20 £2.70 £2.30 £8.30 (£197.50) Trio £416.20 OWNER Mrs Janis MacPherson (RIPON) BRED Mrs A. Whitehead 16 Rn

1m 43.2 (4.20) SF: 39/28/36/23/21/38/28/29/20/31/-/4/16/3/4/-

WEIGHT FOR AGE 3yo-12lb

1251 DUDLEY LIMITED STKS (0-65) (3-Y.O+) (Class F) £2,763.80 (£776.80: £379.40) **1m 1f 9y** Stalls: Low GOING minus 0.27 sec per fur (GF) 8-30 (8-32)

988 9 **Colorful Ambition (62)**_(68) (MrsASwinbank)_ 5-9-7 NConnorton(9) (hld up & bhd: gd hdwy 2f out: r.o wl to ld cl home)........................— 1
908* Voila Premiere (IRE) **(64)**_(69)_(Fav)_(MHTompkins)_ 3-8-9v PRobinson(7) (lw: sn led: qcknd over 2f out: hdd & no ex towards fin) ....½ 2
1126 5 Indefence (IRE) **(65)**_(65) (MRChannon)_ 4-9-7 JCarroll(5) (a chsng ldrs: ch & hrd rdn 1f out: kpt on) 1¼ 3
1180* Gospel Song **(59)**_(69)_(Fav)_(WTKemp)_ 3-8-11b 2x KDarley(10) (cl up: rdn over 2f out: kpt on appr fnl f) ....hd 4
Magnums Secret **(50)**_(54) (JLEyre)_ 3-8-2 RLappin(3) (hld up: effrt over 2f out: kpt on: nvr able to chal)........................3½ 5
1218 4 It's Academic **(62)**_(52) (MrsJRRamsden)_ 3-8-2 RHills(6) (hld up: effrt over 2f out: hung lft: nvr rchd ldrs)........................1 6
946 6 Dalu (IRE) **(64)**_(49) (MJCamacho)_ 4-9-2 LCharnock(4) (trckd ldrs: rdn & wkng whn hmpd over 1f out) 1¾ 7
876 16 King of Show (IRE) **(65)**_(52) (RAllan)_ 4-9-7 CDwyer(1) (b: effrt 3f out: n.d) 1¼ 8
991 2 Drummer Hicks **(51)**_(50) (EWeymes)_ 6-9-7 DeanMcKeown(11) (led early: cl up tl wknd & hmpd 2f out) ....¾ 9
1079 5 Ballard Ring (IRE) **(62)**_(40) (JSWainwright)_ 4-9-2 JFortune(2) (nvr bttr than mid div)................3 10
785 8 Princess Maxine (IRE) **(63)**_(15) (JJO'Neill)_ 6-8-9 (7) GParkin(8) (prom tl rdn & wknd 3f out)....14 11

3/1 Gospel Song, Voila Premiere (IRE), **5/1** It's Academic, **6/1** Indefence (IRE), **7/1** Dalu (IRE), **8/1** COLORFUL AMBITION, Drummer Hicks, **11/1** Princess Maxine (IRE), **16/1** King of Show (IRE), **20/1** Ballard Ring (IRE), **50/1** Magnums Secret, CSF £35.13 TOTE £14.30: £2.10 £1.80 £1.80 (£91.00) Trio £62.50 OWNER Mr G. A. Swinbank (RICHMOND) BRED Meon Valley Stud 11 Rn

1m 57.24 (4.94) SF: 40/27/37/27/12/10/21/24/22/12/-

WEIGHT FOR AGE 3yo-14lb

1252 SEATON BURN H'CAP (0-70) (3-Y.O+ F & M) (Class E) £3,195.50 (£968.00: £473.00: £225.50) **1m 4f 93y** Stalls: Low GOING minus 0.27 sec (GF) 9-00 (9-04)

991 7 **Sunday News'n'echo (USA) (52)**_(64) (WStorey)_ 4-8-10 JFanning(6) (trckd ldrs: led wl over 2f out: r.o) ....— 1

568[7] Stoproveritate **(39)***(51) (MrsMReveley)* 6-7-11 JQuinn(7) (in tch: hdwy 3f out: sn chsng wnr: kpt on wl towards fin)....hd 2
776* Wonderful Day **(67)***(74)*(Fav)*(SCWilliams)* 4-9-11 KDarley(9) (in tch tl lost pl appr st: hdwy on outside 2f out: r.o u.p)....4 3
931[7] Microlite (USA) **(65)***(71) (MDHammond)* 4-9-9b JCarroll(2) (chsd ldrs: effrt 3f out: one pce) ...nk 4
905* Moonlight Calypso **(46)***(50) (EJAlston)* 4-8-4 ow1 KFallon(10) (bhd: effrt ent st: styd on: nvr able to chal)....1¼ 5
1039[2] Merry Mermaid **(48)***(53) (JFBottomley)* 5-8-6 ACulhane(11) (a.p: effrt 3f out: btn appr fnl f) ...hd 6
1029[13] Goodbye Millie **(43)***(40) (JLEyre)* 5-8-1b RLappin(8) (led tl hdd wl over 2f out: wknd)....6 7
893[9] Granny's Legacy **(57)***(41) (JDBethell)* 3-7-6 (5)ow4 NVarley(4) (a bhd)....7 8
991[3] Bardia **(35)***(23) (DonEnricoIncisa)* 5-7-7 KimTinkler(3) (lw: stdd s: hdwy to jn ldrs after 4f: wknd over 3f out)....nk 9

LONG HANDICAP Granny's Legacy 6-3 Bardia 7-3

5/2 Wonderful Day, **3/1** Moonlight Calypso, **7/2** Stoproveritate, **11/2** Microlite (USA) (4/1-6/1), **9/1** Merry Mermaid, **10/1** SUNDAY NEWS'N'ECHO (USA) (op 6/1), Bardia, **20/1** Goodbye Millie, **50/1** Granny's Legacy, CSF £45.56 CT £108.71 TOTE £24.10: £4.00 £1.80 £1.10 (£25.40) Trio £36.80 OWNER Mr D. C. Batey (CONSETT) BRED Fontainebleau Farm 9 Rn

2m 44.48 (5.98) SF: 36/23/46/43/22/25/12/-/-

WEIGHT FOR AGE 3yo-18lb

OFFICIAL EXPLANATION **Moonlight Calypso: the trainer later reported that the filly had returned lame in front.**

T/Plpt: £502.10 (26.13 Tckts). T/Qdpt: £67.50 (0.4 Tckts). AA

1123-SALISBURY (R-H)

Wednesday May 24th (Good, Good to firm patches becoming Good, Good to soft patches)

WEATHER: overcast & raining WIND: almost nil

1253 WHITEPARISH MAIDEN STKS (2-Y.O F) (Class D) £3,645.50 (£1,094.00: £527.00: £243.50)

6f Stalls: High GOING minus 0.28 sec per fur (GF) 6-15 (6-16)

1017[5] **Like A Hawk (USA)** *(73+)*(Fav)*(PFICole)* 2-8-11 TQuinn(8) (a.p: rdn to ld over 1f out: r.o wl)....— 1
1054[7] Corniche Quest (IRE) *(65) (MRChannon)* 2-8-11 RHughes(1) (a.p: ev ch 1f out: nt qckn)....3 2
1017[3] Honorable Estate (IRE) *(64) (RHannon)* 2-8-11 RPerham(4) (lw: w ldr: ev ch over 1f out: hrd rdn & nt qckn)....½ 3
791[8] Sound Check *(63) (BJMeehan)* 2-8-11 BDoyle(2) (led tl over 1f out: one pce)....hd 4
Secret Pleasure (IRE) *(57) (RHannon)* 2-8-4 (7) DaneO'Neill(3) (neat: hdwy 2f out: r.o ins fnl f)....2½ 5
Risalah *(43) (JLDunlop)* 2-8-11 WCarson(9) (leggy: unf: sn prom: ev ch over 1f out: wknd & eased fnl f)....5 6
Mrs Nevermind *(42) (GLMoore)* 2-8-11 BRouse(5) (neat: dwlt: nrst fin)....½ 7
Madam Marash (IRE) *(31) (AGFoster)* 2-8-11 GHind(6) (cmpt: dwlt: a bhd)....4 8
Willow Dale (IRE) *(26) (DRCElsworth)* 2-8-11 JWilliams(10) (scope: prom 3f)....2 9
Riviere Rouge *(21) (SGKnight)* 2-8-11 WNewnes(7) (neat: bkwd: plld hrd: bhd fnl 3f)....2 10
Petros Pride *(MJBolton)* 2-8-11 CRutter(11) (scope: bkwd: prom over 2f)....25 11

6/4 LIKE A HAWK (USA), **11/4** Risalah (7/4-3/1), **4/1** Honorable Estate (IRE) (3/1-11/2), **12/1** Willow Dale (IRE) (7/1-14/1), **14/1** Corniche Quest (IRE) (10/1-20/1), **16/1** Secret Pleasure (IRE), Sound Check, **33/1** Mrs Nevermind, **50/1** Madam Marash (IRE), **66/1** Riviere Rouge, Petros Pride, CSF £22.01 TOTE £2.40: £1.40 £2.90 £1.50 (£12.20) Trio £11.50 OWNER Mr Brereton Jones (WHATCOMBE) BRED B. C. Jones, A. Clay and M/M G. Lang, Partners 11 Rn

1m 16.48 (4.18) SF: 16/8/7/6/-/-/-/-/-/-/-

1254 SHERBORNE CLAIMING H'CAP (0-60) (3-Y.O+) (Class F) £3,344.00 (£934.00: £452.00) 1m 4f

Stalls: Low GOING minus 0.28 sec per fur (GF) 6-45 (6-51)

444[6] **Royal Rabbit (50)***(58) (GLMoore)* 3-7-9 (5)ow2 AWhelan(12) (gd hdwy over 1f out: r.o to ld cl home)....— 1
Ela Man Howa **(54)***(64) (RAkehurst)* 4-9-8 TQuinn(4) (hdwy 3f out: led ins fnl f tl ct nr fin) .....nk 2
975[11] Lady Reema **(36)***(45) (MissAJWhitfield)* 4-8-4 DHarrison(10) (hdwy 4f out: led over 1f out tl ins fnl f)....¾ 3
1030[7] Star Fighter **(53)***(58) (WAO'Gorman)* 3-8-3 GHind(8) (nrst fin)....2½ 4
811[9] Stevie's Wonder (IRE) **(56)***(61) (MJRyan)* 5-9-10 GCarter(9) (a.p: led over 4f out tl over 1f out: edgd rt: nt qckn)....nk 5
766[12] Il Fratello **(35)***(37) (NACallaghan)* 4-8-3 GDuffield(1) (nvr nrr)....2½ 6

Saafi (IRE) **(59)***(59) (RJBaker)* 4-9-13 WNewnes(16) (bolted bef s: wl bhd tl r.o fnl 2f)..........1¼ 7
864[4] Marchman **(49)***(46) (JSKing)* 10-9-3 PaulEddery(7) (nvr nr to chal)..........2½ 8
Maraady (USA) **(32)***(28) (GPEnright)* 6-8-0 NAdams(20) (nvr nr ldrs)..........hd 9
356[2] Royal Circus **(42)***(38) (JGMO'Shea)* 6-8-10 BDoyle(19) (prom 8f)..........hd 10
521[18] Don't Mean a Thing (IRE) **(48)***(41) (RHannon)* 3-7-12 GBardwell(13) (w ldrs tl wknd 3f out) .2½ 11
884[4] Rocquaine Bay **(44)***(37)*(Fav)*(MJBolton)* 8-8-12 AMcGlone(3) (a bhd)..........nk 12
1128[12] Peveril Princess **(40)***(26) (GBBalding)* 4-8-8 JWilliams(2) (nvr w ldrs)..........5 13
860[6] La Belle Shyanne **(37)***(20) (CJHill)* 4-8-5 NCarlisle(11) (hdwy over 2f out: wknd qckly over 1f out)..........2 14
Persian Smoke **(44)***(25) (AHide)* 4-8-5 (7) MHenry(15) (plld hrd: wknd 4f out)..........1¾ 15
Foremma **(30)***(2) (PRHedger)* 4-7-12 CAvery(5) (w ldrs tl wknd qckly over 3f out)..........7 16
741[6] Captain Starlight (IRE) **(42)***(3) (RAkehurst)* 4-8-10 ow1 RHughes(6) (led tl wknd over 4f out).....7 17
971[11] Anna Bannanna **(59)***(19) (MCPipe)* 3-8-6 (3) JTate(14) (in tch tl wknd 3f out)..........2 18
654[6] Roadsweeper (FR) **(55)***(13) (KOCunningham-Brown)* 3-8-5b AClark(18) (plld hrd: prom tl wknd 4f out)..........1½ 19

5/1 Rocquaine Bay, **7/1** Captain Starlight (IRE), **15/2** Ela Man Howa, **8/1** Stevie's Wonder (IRE), **10/1** Royal Circus, La Belle Shyanne, Marchman, **12/1** Anna Bannanna, **16/1** Peveril Princess, **20/1** Persian Smoke, **25/1** ROYAL RABBIT, Don't Mean a Thing (IRE), **33/1** Saafi (IRE), Star Fighter, Il Fratello, Foremma, Lady Reema, Maraady (USA), Roadsweeper (FR), CSF £176.34 CT £5,460.82 TOTE £48.10: £7.50 £2.10 £5.10 £6.50 (£346.10) Trio not won; £607.22 to 26/5/95 OWNER Mr K. Higson (EPSOM) BRED K. Higson 19 Rn

2m 39.47 (6.87) SF: 19/43/24/19/40/16/38/25/7/17/2/16/5/-/4/-/-/-/-
WEIGHT FOR AGE 3yo-18lb

1255 BOLLINGER CHAMPAGNE CHALLENGE SERIES GENTLEMENS' H'CAP (0-70) (3-Y.O+) (Class F) £3,184.00 (£952.00: £456.00: £208.00)

6f 212y Stalls: High GOING minus 0.28 sec per fur (GF) 7-15 (7-26)

1049[7] **Spencer's Revenge (63)***(74) (LordHuntingdon)* 6-12-0 MrJDurkan(10) (stdy hdwy 3f out: led wl ins fnl f: r.o wl)..........— 1
1202[8] Shaynes Domain **(44)***(53) (RMFlower)* 4-10-9b MrTMcCarthy(2) (a.p: led wl over 1f out tl wl ins fnl f: r.o)..........¾ 2
1088[6] Caddy's First **(55)***(51) (SMellor)* 3-10-9 MrPPritchard-Gordon(1) (w ldrs: led 4f out tl wl over 1f out: one pce)..........6 3
1126* Ahjay **(48)***(38)*(Fav)*(DAWilson)* 5-10-13 5x MrTCuff(3) (a.p: hrd rdn 2f out: nt qckn)..........2½ 4
1126[11] Chili Heights **(60)***(47) (GBBalding)* 5-11-7v(4) MrABalding(4) (hdwy 2f out: nvr nr to chal)......1¼ 5
780[16] Goody Four Shoes **(42)***(25) (AGNewcombe)* 7-10-7 MrMRimell(9) (nrst fin)..........1½ 6
848[10] Doodies Pool (IRE) **(52)***(34) (GLMoore)* 5-10-13 (4) MrKGoble(16) (prom tl wknd over 1f out)..½ 7
1048[2] Montone (IRE) **(60)***(39) (KRBurke)* 5-11-7 (4) MrMMannish(6) (nvr nr ldrs)..........1¼ 8
Sky Diver **(41)***(9) (BJLlewellyn)* 4-10-6 MrJLLlewellyn(12) (spd 5f)..........5 9
Jewel Thief **(35)***(2) (GBBalding)* 5-10-0 MrRJohnson(14) (a bhd)..........nk 10
422[10] Bite the Bullet **(30)** *(AJChamberlain)* 4-9-5 (4) MrYMehmet(8) (a wl bhd)..........2 11
1013[9] Pair of Jacks (IRE) **(34)** *(DAWilson)* 5-9-9 (4) MrVLukaniuk(11) (led after 1f to 4f out: wknd 3f out)..........1¾ 12
142[3] Sharp Imp **(37)** *(RMFlower)* 5-9-12 (4) MrJO'Brien(13) (a bhd)..........1¾ 13
240[4] Glowing Account (IRE) **(55)** *(JWMullins)* 4-11-6 MrEBailey(5) (led 1f: wknd 4f out: t.o)..........20 14
560[6] Scissor Ridge **(50)** *(JJBridger)* 3-10-0b(4) MrPPhillips(15) (spd over 3f: wknd qckly: t.o)..........3 15

9/4 Ahjay, **7/1** Chili Heights, Montone (IRE), **8/1** SPENCER'S REVENGE (op 9/2), **10/1** Caddy's First, Shaynes Domain, **11/1** Sharp Imp, **16/1** Goody Four Shoes, Pair of Jacks (IRE), **20/1** Jewel Thief, Scissor Ridge, **33/1** Glowing Account (IRE), Doodies Pool (IRE), Sky Diver, **50/1** Bite the Bullet, CSF £80.12 CT £746.48 TOTE £9.10: £3.10 £4.20 £3.20 (£66.00) Trio £238.80 OWNER Mr A. S. Reid (WEST ILSLEY) BRED Lord Crawshaw 15 Rn

1m 32.02 (6.32) SF: 42/21/8/6/15/-/2/7/-/-/-/-/-/-/-
WEIGHT FOR AGE 3yo-11lb

1256 WINCHESTER CONDITIONS STKS (4-Y.O+) (Class D) £3,632.50 (£1,090.00: £525.00: £242.50)

1m 1f 209y Stalls: High GOING minus 0.28 sec per fur (GF) 7-45 (7-50)

848[5] **Tykeyvor (IRE) (72)***(76) (LadyHerries)* 5-8-11 GDuffield(5) (hdwy 6f out: led over 4f out: drvn clr over 1f out)..........— 1
935[4] Superluminal **(71)***(72)*(Fav)*(GRimmer)* 4-9-3 MRimmer(3) (jnd wnr 4f out: ev ch 2f out: sn rdn & wknd)..........6 2
471[3] Ginger Jim **(49)***(64) (PRHedger)* 4-8-11v CAvery(1) (a.p: r.o one pce fnl 2f)..........1¾ 3
764[21] Great Expectations (FR) *(61) (KOCunningham-Brown)* 4-8-11 AClark(6) (led tl over 4f out: one pce)..........1½ 4

817[7] Rushaway **(62)**(60) (RHannon) 4-8-11 RPerham(2) (hdwy & hrd rdn 4f out: wknd over 2f out) ....½ 5
1140[11] Rising Spray **(62)**(58) (CAHorgan) 4-8-11 PaulEddery(4) (s.s: bhd most of wy) 1¾ 6

8/15 Superluminal (op 4/5), **7/2** TYKEYVOR (IRE), **7/1** Rushaway (op 9/2), **16/1** Rising Spray, **20/1** Great Expectations (FR), **33/1** Ginger Jim, CSF £5.67 TOTE £4.00: £1.80 £1.30 (£2.30) OWNER Seymour Bloodstock (UK) Ltd (LITTLEHAMPTON) BRED H. Key 6 Rn

2m 10.46 (5.76) SF: 28/24/16/13/12/10

1257

ROMSEY H'CAP (0-70) (3-Y.O+) (Class E) £3,392.00 (£1,016.00: £488.00: £224.00) **5f** Stalls: High GOING minus 0.28 sec per fur (GF) 8-15 (8-17)

999[4] **Fairy Wind (IRE) (70)**(83+)(Fav)(NACallaghan) 3-9-8 LDettori(2) (mde all: qcknd 1f out: easily) ....— 1
887[8] Perfect Brave **(53)**(58) (DRCElsworth) 4-9-0 JWilliams(1) (s.s: hdwy over 2f out: chsd wnr fnl f: no imp) 2½ 2
765[10] Patsy Grimes **(63)**(55) (LJHolt) 5-9-10 AMcGlone(4) (rdn over 2f out: hdwy over 1f out: nrst fin) 4 3
856[6] Ashkernazy (IRE) **(48)**(40) (NEBerry) 4-8-4 (5) JDSmith(8) (a.p: ev ch over 1f out: nt qckn) ....hd 4
726[3] Halliard **(61)**(50) (TMJones) 4-9-8 RPerham(13) (sn w ldrs: ev ch over 1f out: wknd ins fnl f) 1 5
1023[10] The Noble Oak (IRE) **(53)**(41) (MJBolton) 7-9-0 JReid(10) (prom over 3f) ....hd 6
1016[15] Black Shadow **(42)**(28) (PJMcBride) 3-7-8b GBardwell(3) (prom tl rdn & wknd wl over 1f out) ....¾ 7
1199[6] Grand Time **(35)**(15) (CJHill) 6-7-10b NCarlisle(11) (no hdwy fnl 2f) 2 8
Jess Rebec **(50)**(18) (DJSffrenchDavis) 7-8-11 NAdams(6) (bhd most of wy) 3½ 9
937[14] Logie Pert Lad **(41)**(6) (JJBridger) 3-7-0 (7) IonaWands(5) (outpcd) 1 10
541[4] Billy Cruncheon **(56)**(13) (MCPipe) 4-9-3 TQuinn(12) (prom tl rdn & wknd over 2f out) 2½ 11
853[20] Green Apache **(41)** (TJNaughton) 3-7-7 RStreet(9) (hung bdly rt over 1f out: a bhd) 4 12
Admirals Realm **(58)**(2) (AGNewcombe) 6-9-0 (5) DGriffiths(7) (a bhd) ....hd 13

LONG HANDICAP Green Apache 6-8 Logie Pert Lad 6-10

100/30 FAIRY WIND (IRE), **9/2** Perfect Brave (op 7/1), **6/1** Patsy Grimes, Halliard (op 4/1), **9/1** Grand Time, **10/1** Billy Cruncheon, **14/1** Admirals Realm, Ashkernazy (IRE) (8/1-16/1), **16/1** The Noble Oak (IRE), **25/1** Jess Rebec, **33/1** Black Shadow, **66/1** Green Apache, Logie Pert Lad, CSF £17.26 CT £77.70 TOTE £2.50: £1.50 £1.80 £2.80 (£6.90) Trio £23.00 OWNER Mr N. A. Callaghan (NEWMARKET) BRED Ron Con Ltd 13 Rn 61.58 secs (1.58) SF: 56/40/37/22/32/23/1/-/-/-/-/-/-

WEIGHT FOR AGE 3yo-9lb

1258

LANDFORD MAIDEN STKS (3-Y.O) (Class D) £4,077.50 (£1,220.00: £585.00: £267.50) **6f 212y** Stalls: High GOING minus 0.28 sec per fur (GF) 8-45 (8-46)

761[2] **Storm Bid (USA)** (86+)(Fav)(EALDunlop) 3-8-11 (3) JTate(10) (led 4f out: qcknd clr 2f out: easily) ....— 1
761[W] Godmersham Park (75) (MJHeaton-Ellis) 3-9-0 JReid(5) (a.p: chsd wnr fnl 2f: no imp) 5 2
1136[14] Early Peace (IRE) (74) (RHannon) 3-9-0 RPerham(11) (dwlt: hdwy over 2f out: r.o ins fnl f: nvr nrr) ....hd 3
Triple Tricks (IRE) (64) (WJHaggas) 3-8-9 LDettori(9) (led 3f: rdn over 2f out: one pce) 2½ 4
Action Jackson **(75)**(68) (GRimmer) 3-9-0 MRimmer(1) (hdwy 3f out: one pce fnl 2f) ....nk 5
Eurolink the Rebel (USA) (67) (RAkehurst) 3-8-11 (3) SSanders(7) (a mid div: effrt 2f out: r.o one pce) ....nk 6
881[8] Hazel (59) (MissGayKelleway) 3-8-9 StephenDavies(2) (chsd ldrs: hrd rdn 2f out: one pce) 1¼ 7
Sovereigns Parade (57) (LJHolt) 3-9-0 AMcGlone(13) (str: scope: bkwd: s.s: gd hdwy fnl f) ...3 8
742[8] She Said No (47) (LordHuntingdon) 3-8-9 DHarrison(12) (outpcd) 2½ 9
Hever Golf Star (48) (TJNaughton) 3-9-0 GCarter(4) (a bhd) 1¾ 10
1065[8] Chinese Viking (44) (GLMoore) 3-9-0 BRouse(6) (w ldrs early: sn lost pl) 1¾ 11
937[8] Bella Coola (33) (CAHorgan) 3-8-9 AClark(8) (a bhd) 2½ 12
Rainbow Tiara (33) (MRStoute) 3-8-9 PaulEddery(3) (mid div tl wknd over 2f out) ....hd 13

13/8 STORM BID (USA), **3/1** Triple Tricks (IRE), **5/1** Godmersham Park, **8/1** Rainbow Tiara, **12/1** Eurolink the Rebel (USA) (8/1-14/1), **20/1** Early Peace (IRE), **33/1** Action Jackson, Sovereigns Parade, She Said No, Hazel, Chinese Viking, **50/1** Bella Coola, Hever Golf Star, CSF £10.10 TOTE £2.50: £1.10 £1.80 £4.80 (£6.40) Trio £31.00 OWNER Maktoum Al Maktoum (NEWMARKET) BRED Continental Thoroughbreds Inc and Skymarc Farm Inc 13 Rn

1m 30.48 (4.78) SF: 21/10/9/-/3/2/-/-/-/-/-/-/-

T/Plpt: £73.80 (163.45 Tckts). T/Qdpt: £18.10 (3.4 Tckts). Hn

1240-**GOODWOOD (R-H)**
Thursday May 25th (St Good to firm, Rnd Firm)
WEATHER: Overcast with sunny spells WIND: slt half against

1259 ROYAL SUSSEX REGIMENT CONDITIONS STKS (2-Y.O F) (Class C)
£4,710.00 (£1,740.00: £832.50: £337.50: £131.25: £48.75)
6f Stalls: Low GOING minus 0.31 sec per fur (GF) 2-10 (2-11)

791* **Flying Squaw** *(94+) (MRChannon)* 2-8-10 RHughes(6) (lw: hld up: shkn up to ld 1f out: pushed out)......— 1
852* Anotheranniversary *(92)*(Fav)*(GLewis)* 2-8-12 PaulEddery(2) (b.hind: hld up: led over 1f out: sn hdd: unable qckn)......1½ 2
1047* To The Whire *(81) (GLMoore)* 2-8-10 BRouse(3) (plld hrd: w ldr: led 3f out tl over 1f out: one pce)......3½ 3
970* Windswept (IRE) *(67) (DJSffrenchDavis)* 2-8-10 NAdams(4) (prom 3f)......5 4
*1077** Subfusk *(60) (WGMTurner)* 2-8-3 (5) PMcCabe(5) (spd over 4f)......2 5
1011* Lussuria (IRE) *(43) (BJMeehan)* 2-8-10 PatEddery(1) (led 3f)......7 6

7/4 Anotheranniversary, **2/1** FLYING SQUAW, **11/2** To The Whire (11/4-6/1), **8/1** Subfusk, **12/1** Lussuria (IRE) (op 7/1), **16/1** Windswept (IRE), CSF £5.53 TOTE £2.80: £1.60 £1.50 (£2.20) OWNER Mr Michael Foy (UPPER LAMBOURN) BRED Brook Stud Ltd 6 Rn
1m 12.07 (1.87) SF: 42/40/29/15/8/-

1260 BOOKER FOODSERVICE H'CAP (0-100) (4-Y.O+) (Class C) £7,115.00(£2,120.00: £1,010.00: £455.00) **1m 4f** Stalls: Low GOING minus 0.31 sec (GF) 2-40 (2-41)

981* **Son of Sharp Shot (IRE) (83)***(96+)*(Fav)*(JLDunlop)* 5-9-5 PatEddery(6) (lw: rdn over 4f out: swtchd rt 3f out: hdwy over 2f out: stdd over 1f out: led ins fnl f: comf)......— 1
935⁶ Sharp Falcon (IRE) **(71)***(82) (JWharton)* 4-8-7 JReid(7) (lw: 6th st: hmpd on ins 3f out: hdwy over 1f out: r.o ins fnl f)......1¾ 2
961⁵ Proton **(73)***(84) (RAkehurst)* 5-8-9 TQuinn(5) (lw: 3rd st: hrd rdn over 3f out: r.o ins fnl f)......s.h 3
913⁷ Wayne County (IRE) **(92)***(102) (GFierro)* 5-10-0b LDettori(3) (swtg: 5th st: led 2f out tl ins fnl f: unable qckn)......¾ 4
Dormy Three **(73)***(77) (RJHodges)* 5-8-9 JWilliams(2) (led 10f: wknd fnl f)......4 5
Museum (IRE) **(80)***(81) (HCandy)* 4-9-2 WNewnes(4) (4th st: wknd over 3f out)......2½ 6
New Albion (USA) **(73)***(73) (NJHenderson)* 4-8-9 PaulEddery(1) (2nd st: rdn over 3f out: wknd over 1f out)......1 7

13/8 SON OF SHARP SHOT (IRE), **5/2** Proton, **7/2** Sharp Falcon (IRE), **12/1** Wayne County (IRE) (8/1-14/1), **14/1** Museum (IRE), **25/1** New Albion (USA), **33/1** Dormy Three, CSF £7.11 TOTE £2.10: £1.50 £1.90 (£3.30) OWNER Windflower Overseas Holdings Inc (ARUNDEL) BRED Windflower Overseas 7 Rn 2m 37.28 (5.28) SF: 44/30/32/50/25/29/21
STEWARDS' ENQUIRY Eddery susp. 3, 5-6/6/95 (careless riding).

1261 KIDSONS IMPEY TROPHY H'CAP (0-90) (4-Y.O+) (Class C)
£7,960.00 (£2,380.00: £1,140.00: £520.00)
7f Stalls: High GOING minus 0.31 sec per fur (GF) 3-10 (3-13)

383⁷ **Silent Expression (70)***(78) (BJMeehan)* 5-8-11 PatEddery(9) (2nd st: led over 2f out: drvn out)......— 1
873¹¹ Shepherd Market (IRE) **(59)***(66) (DAWilson)* 4-8-0 GCarter(13) (lw: 6th st: rdn & ev ch over 2f out: r.o ins fnl f)......nk 2
1070⁷ Helios **(77)***(82) (NJHWalker)* 7-9-4 RCochrane(12) (rdn over 2f out: hdwy over 1f out: r.o)...1¼ 3
1021⁵ Shikari's Son **(87)***(90) (JWhite)* 8-10-0 TQuinn(8) (rdn & hdwy over 1f out: r.o one pce)......½ 4
1037⁷ Polonez Prima **(65)***(68) (JLSpearing)* 8-8-6 PaulEddery(7) (lw: s.s: nt clr run on ins 2f out: swtchd lft & hdwy over 1f out: r.o wl ins fnl f)......nk 5
1052⁶ Jolto **(69)***(69) (KOCunningham-Brown)* 6-8-5 (5) CTeague(10) (hdwy over 2f out: hrd rdn over 1f out: one pce)......1 6
960⁸ Caleman **(81)***(77)*(Fav)*(RBoss)* 6-9-8 LDettori(11) (led over 4f: wknd over 1f out)......2 7
1013² Walnut Burl (IRE) **(58)***(54) (LJHolt)* 5-7-13 AMcGlone(3) (nvr nr to chal)......s.h 8
1071¹¹ Deeply Vale (IRE) **(73)***(66) (GLMoore)* 4-9-0 BRouse(4) (lw: nvr plcd to chal)......1 9
1021² Pab's Choice **(58)***(49) (MMcCormack)* 4-7-13 RStreet(14) (5th st: wknd over 1f out)......1¼ 10
249⁷ Blurred Image (IRE) **(81)***(71) (MissGayKelleway)* 4-9-8 DHarrison(2) (lw: a bhd)......nk 11
887⁴ Words of Wisdom (IRE) **(54)***(39) (CACyzer)* 5-7-9 ow2 JQuinn(6) (3rd st: wknd over 2f out) ...1¼ 12
1021³ Rossini Blue **(74)***(29) (ABailey)* 4-8-10 (5) VHalliday(1) (4th st: wknd over 2f out)......14 13
1079* Zifta (USA) **(81)***(11) (SCWilliams)* 4-9-8 7x AMackay(5) (7th st: wknd over 3f out)......11 14
LONG HANDICAP Words of Wisdom (IRE) 7-2

11/2 Caleman, **7/1** Zifta (USA) (5/1-8/1), SILENT EXPRESSION, **9/1** Pab's Choice, Shepherd Market (IRE), Jolto, **10/1** Shikari's Son, Walnut Burl (IRE), **12/1** Helios, Rossini Blue (8/1-14/1), **20/1** Polonez Prima, **25/1** Deeply Vale (IRE), Words of Wisdom (IRE), **33/1** Blurred Image (IRE), CSF £61.84 CT £677.70 TOTE £5.30: £2.20 £3.50 £4.10 (£45.30) Trio £209.70 OWNER Mr A. S. Reid (UPPER LAMBOURN) BRED J. B. H. Stevens 14 Rn

1m 26.67 (2.27) SF: 43/31/47/55/33/34/42/19/31/14/36/4/-/-

1262 FESTIVAL STKS (Listed) (4-Y.O+) (Class A) £13,840.00 (£4,120.00: £1,960.00: £880.00) **1m 2f** Stalls: High GOING minus 0.31 sec per fur (GF) 3-40 (3-40)

923* **Baron Ferdinand (108)**(123)(Fav)(RCharlton) 5-8-12 PatEddery(3) (b: lw: 4th st: shkn up to ld 1f out: comf)........— **1**
827[3] Ionio (USA) **(114)**(120) (CEBrittain) 4-8-12 MRoberts(2) (lw: led 9f: unable qckn)........2 **2**
Belle Argentine (FR) (105) (SbinSuroor) 4-8-10 LDettori(4) (3rd st: rdn over 2f out: wknd over 1f out)........8 **3**
Bearall (IRE) **(105)**(99) (RHannon) 4-8-10 BRouse(1) (2nd st: wknd over 2f out)........4 **4**

10/11 BARON FERDINAND, **5/2** Ionio (USA), **100/30** Belle Argentine (FR) (7/4-7/2), **25/1** Bearall (IRE), CSF £3.31 TOTE £1.90: (£1.80) OWNER Lady Rothschild (BECKHAMPTON) BRED Exors of the late Mrs D. M. de Rothschild 4 Rn 2m 9.15 (4.15) SF: 39/36/21/15

1263 GOODWOOD HOUSE CLAIMING STKS (3-Y.O) (Class D) £4,056.25 (£1,210.00: £577.50: £130.63: £130.63) **6f** Stalls: Low GOING minus 0.31 sec per fur (GF) 4-10 (4-10)

1172[9] **Fantasy Racing (IRE) (76)**(71)(Fav)(MRChannon) 3-8-5 PatEddery(9) (hld up: rdn 2f out: led ins fnl f: r.o wl)........— **1**
985[7] Prolific Lady (IRE) **(75)**(67) (MBrittain) 3-8-6 RCochrane(8) (a.p: led over 1f out tl ins fnl f: unable qckn)........2 **2**
1125[4] Assumpsit (IRE) **(65)**(60) (SDow) 3-8-3v GDuffield(2) (hld up: rdn over 2f out: r.o one pce)........1¼ **3**
1016[6] Kellaire Girl (IRE) **(46)**(54) (GLewis) 3-7-11 JQuinn(1) (hld up: swtchd rt 3f out: rdn over 2f out: r.o one pce)........nk **4**
939[6] Sylvandra **(85)**(63) (PGMurphy) 3-8-6 JWilliams(3) (rdn over 2f out: hdwy over 1f out: r.o)...d.h **4**
1012* Emphatic Candidate (IRE) **(73)**(59) (RAkehurst) 3-8-1 (3) SSanders(6) (b: lw: a.p: led over 3f out tl over 2f out: one pce)........¾ **6**
1033[5] Noor El Houdah (IRE) **(59)**(53) (JBerry) 3-7-13v GCarter(7) (lw: a.p: led over 2f out tl over 1f out: one pce)........nk **7**
1201[5] Cork Street Girl (IRE) **(62)**(41) (BJMeehan) 3-7-11 TWilliams(5) (led over 2f)........3½ **8**
Halleluja Time (33) (RHannon) 3-8-2 SRaymont(4) (a bhd)........5 **9**

2/1 FANTASY RACING (IRE), **7/2** Sylvandra, **6/1** Emphatic Candidate (IRE) (7/2-7/1), **8/1** Kellaire Girl (IRE) (op 25/1), Prolific Lady (IRE), Noor El Houdah (IRE) (6/1-9/1), **14/1** Cork Street Girl (IRE) (7/1-16/1), **16/1** Assumpsit (IRE), **33/1** Halleluja Time, CSF £17.58 TOTE £3.20: £1.40 £2.00 £3.20 (£8.70) Trio £45.80 OWNER Aldridge Racing Ltd (UPPER LAMBOURN) BRED Barronstown Stud and Ron Con Ltd 9 Rn 1m 11.61 (1.41) SF: 43/39/32/26/35/31/25/13/5

1264 SIS LIVE ACTION MAIDEN STKS (3-Y.O) (Class D) £3,913.25 (£1,166.00: £555.50: £250.25) **1m 1f** Stalls: High GOING minus 0.31 sec (GF) 4-45 (4-46)

Rahy Zoman (USA) (85)(Fav)(JRFanshawe) 3-9-0 DHarrison(4) (hdwy over 2f out: plld out wl over 1f out: led ins fnl f: r.o wl)........— **1**
1128[3] Eurolink Mischief (78)(Fav)(LMCumani) 3-8-9 LDettori(7) (b.hind: 2nd st: rdn over 2f out: ev ch ins fnl f: unable qckn)........1¼ **2**
Game Ploy (POL) **(73)**(83) (FMurphy) 3-9-0 RCochrane(6) (6th st: rdn over 3f out: ev ch over 1f out: r.o one pce)........s.h **3**
1097[5] Zidac (81) (PJMakin) 3-9-0 PatEddery(2) (led: rdn wl over 1f out: hdd ins fnl f: one pce)........¾ **4**
Caisson (73) (RHannon) 3-8-9 RHughes(8) (3rd st: rdn over 2f out: one pce)........1¾ **5**
Bella Sedona (61) (LadyHerries) 3-8-9 JReid(5) (lw: 5th st: wknd over 2f out)........7 **6**
Dantean (61) (GHarwood) 3-9-0 AClark(1) (str: bit bkwd: a bhd)........3 **7**
1136[15] Toat Chieftain (48) (GHarwood) 3-9-0 MPerrett(3) (bit bkwd: 4th st: wknd over 3f out)........7 **8**

3/1 RAHY ZOMAN (USA) (2/1-100/30), Eurolink Mischief, **7/2** Zidac, **6/1** Bella Sedona (8/1-12/1), **13/2** Game Ploy (POL) (12/1-6/1), **10/1** Dantean (5/1-11/1), **16/1** Caisson, **50/1** Toat Chieftain, CSF £12.04 TOTE £4.00: £1.40 £1.30 £2.20 (£4.10) OWNER Mr Khalifa Nasser (NEWMARKET) BRED Carmine Carcieri 8 Rn

1m 56.96 (6.26) SF: 18/11/16/14/6/-/-/-

1265

LEVIN DOWN APPRENTICE H'CAP (0-70) (3-Y.O+) (Class E)
£3,582.50 (£1,085.00: £530.00: £252.50)
5f Stalls: Low GOING minus 0.31 sec per fur (GF) 5-20 (5-22)

*769*12 **Mazzarello (IRE) (35)**(38) (RCurtis) 5-7-7v MBaird(15) (a.p: hrd rdn over 1f out: led ins fnl f: r.o wl) ...— 1
1071 3 Another Jade **(63)**(66) (APJarvis) 5-9-2 (5) BHunter(7) (a.p: rdn over 1f out: ev ch ins fnl f: r.o) ...hd 2
1199 2 Half Tone **(44)**(46)(Fav)(RMFlower) 3-7-4b(3) SLanigan(10) (led tl ins fnl f: r.o) ...hd 3
1164 13 Paley Prince (USA) **(53)**(53) (MDIUsher) 9-8-8 (3) CAdamson(14) (hdwy over 1f out: r.o ins fnl f) ...¾ 4
1193 5 Domicksky **(65)**(64) (MRChannon) 7-9-9 PPMurphy(8) (swtg: hrd rdn & hdwy over 1f out: r.o) ...nk 5
949 9 Judgement Call **(49)**(48) (PHowling) 8-8-2 (5) DebbieBiggs(9) (b: a.p: rdn over 1f out: unable qckn) ...hd 6
982 6 One for Jeannie **(65)**(62) (ABailey) 3-9-0v VHalliday(11) (rdn over 3f out: hdwy over 1f out: r.o) ...½ 7
1057 7 Eagle Day (USA) **(70)**(63) (DRCElsworth) 4-10-0b AProcter(1) (hdwy over 1f out: nvr nrr) ...1¼ 8
1050 11 Trina **(35)**(23) (DLWilliams) 4-7-4 (3) MartinDwyer(3) (nvr nr to chal) ...1¾ 9
1050 6 Tee-Emm **(42)**(25) (PHowling) 5-8-0 ow2 JDSmith(2) (b.hind: spd over 2f) ...¾ 10
1071 13 Shades of Jade **(35)**(15) (JJBridger) 7-7-2 (5) IonaWands(5) (prom over 2f) ...1½ 11
*1214*11 Statomist **(58)**(32) (GFierro) 3-8-7 PMcCabe(13) (swtg: outpcd) ...2 12
*1078*7 Young Sensation **(47)**(15) (BAPearce) 3-7-3 (7)ow3 TField(4) (swtg: stumbled s: bhd fnl 2f) ...1 13

LONG HANDICAP Mazzarello (IRE) 7-1 Trina 7-0

100/30 Half Tone, **5/1** Another Jade, Domicksky, **6/1** Eagle Day (USA), **7/1** One for Jeannie, **10/1** Tee-Emm, **12/1** Judgement Call (8/1-14/1), Shades of Jade, **14/1** Paley Prince (USA), **33/1** Statomist, **40/1** MAZZARELLO (IRE), **66/1** Trina, Young Sensation, CSF £214.71 CT £789.17 TOTE £80.10: £9.60 £2.00 £1.40 (£196.00) Trio £293.20 OWNER Mr D. W. Hoskyns (CARSHALTON) BRED Thomas Naughton 13 Rn 58.65 secs (1.95) SF: 17/45/16/32/43/27/32/42/2/4/-/2/-
WEIGHT FOR AGE 3yo-9lb

T/Jkpt: £1,121.90 (35.71 Tckts). T/ Plpt: £23.30 (1,144.73 Tckts). T/Qdpt: £67.80 (4.7 Tckts). AK

1247-NEWCASTLE (L-H)
Thursday May 25th (Good)

WEATHER: Sunny spells WIND: Fresh across

1266

ANNITSFORD CLAIMING STKS (2-Y.O) (Class F) £2,700.80 (£758.80: £370.40)
6f Stalls: High GOING minus 0.09 sec per fur (G) 2-25 (2-27)

615 17 **Russian Rascal (IRE)** (54) (MHEasterby) 2-8-5 MBirch(1) (mde virtually all: rdn & hld on wl nr fin) ...— 1
1024 3 Abbott of Whalley (55)(Fav)(JBerry) 2-8-7 JCarroll(6) (trckd ldrs: hdwy u.p 1f out: kpt on towards fin) ...nk 2
1177 7 Contradictory (47) (MWEasterby) 2-8-2 LCharnock(5) (dwlt: reminders after 2½f: hdwy over 1f out: nt qckn ins fnl f) ...1¼ 3
1035 3 Grimstone Girl (43) (MWEasterby) 2-8-2 SMaloney(3) (sn trckng ldrs: effrt 2f out: one pce) .1½ 4
1035 5 Abduction (29) (EWeymes) 2-8-7v KDarley(4) (lw: cl up: rdn ½-wy: wknd wl over 1f out) ...7 5
964 6 Stoleamarch (MrsMReveley) 2-7-10 (7) DDenby(2) (outpcd & bhd fr ½-wy) ...30 6

2/1 Abbott of Whalley, **5/2** Grimstone Girl, **3/1** Stoleamarch, **5/1** Abduction, **10/1** RUSSIAN RASCAL (IRE), **16/1** Contradictory, CSF £30.18 TOTE £11.00: £2.60 £1.50 (£16.70) OWNER Mr C. H. Stevens (MALTON) BRED R. M. Fox 6 Rn 1m 16.57 (5.07) SF: 13/14/6/2/-/-

1267

CRAMLINGTON CONDITIONS STKS (2-Y.O) (Class D) £3,333.60 (£1,009.80: £493.40: £235.20) **5f** Stalls: High GOING minus 0.09 sec per fur (G) 2-55 (2-56)

1024* **Gothenberg (IRE)** (82+) (MJohnston) 2-9-1 DHolland(6) (lw: hld up: hdwy to ld ins fnl f: r.o wl) ...— 1
964* Blessingindisguise (76) (MWEasterby) 2-9-1 MBirch(3) (chsd ldrs: rdn to ld 1f out: sn hdd: kpt on) ...1¾ 2
1134 9 Duo Master (66) (MrsMReveley) 2-8-11 KDarley(8) (lw: s.i.s: hld up & bhd: stdy late hdwy: promising) ...2 3
1035 2 Swiss Valley Lady (65) (WGMTurner) 2-8-10 TSprake(2) (led tl hdd 1f out: no ex) ...hd 4
1082* Pleasure Time (70) (CSmith) 2-8-10 (5) JStack(1) (cl up: ev ch over 1f out: no ex) ...s.h 5
993 3 Cabcharge Striker (69) (MRChannon) 2-9-1 PRobinson(5) (lw: chsd ldrs: effrt 2f out: btn appr fnl f) ...hd 6

925* Hoh Majestic (IRE) *(64)*(Fav)*(MBell)* 2-9-1 MFenton(9) (cl up tl wknd over 1f out)................1¾ 7
993[5] Precious Girl *(57) (DMoffatt)* 2-8-7 (3) DarrenMoffatt(4) (chsd ldrs tl wknd appr fnl f)................½ 8

6/4 Hoh Majestic (IRE), **4/1** GOTHENBERG (IRE), **5/1** Cabcharge Striker, **7/1** Duo Master, **9/1** Blessingindisguise, **10/1** Precious Girl, **14/1** Swiss Valley Lady, Pleasure Time, CSF £36.71 TOTE £4.60: £1.80 £2.90 £2.80 (£20.40) Trio £41.90 OWNER Brian Yeardley Continental Ltd (MIDDLEHAM) BRED Brownstown Stud Farm 8 Rn 61.82 secs (3.42) SF: 34/28/18/17/22/21/16/9

OFFICIAL EXPLANATION Duo Master: the trainer later reported that the colt had injured a knee and was lame on returning.

1268 MALT HOUSE VINTNERS H'CAP (0-80) (3-Y.O+) (Class D) £3,690.70 (£1,117.60: £545.80: £259.90)

2m 19y Stalls: High GOING minus 0.09 sec per fur (G) 3-25 (3-26)

1084[2] **Good Hand (USA) (73)***(84) (JWWatts)* 9-9-9 NConnorton(5) (b: b.hind: lw: a.p: swtchd over 2f out: r.o to ld wl ins fnl f)..— 1
821[6] Highflying **(75)***(85) (GMMoore)* 9-9-8 (3) JTate(4) (lw: hld up: hdwy 7f out: rdn to ld ins fnl f: sn hdd: kpt on)..¾ 2
Bedevil (USA) **(73)***(81) (MrsJCecil)* 5-9-9 JCarroll(6) (led tl hdd ins fnl f: kpt on same pce) ...2½ 3
1160* Noyan **(53)***(53)*(Fav)*(LLungo)* 5-8-3 5x KDarley(7) (lw: b: hdwy 7f out: outpcd appr st: styd on fnl 2f: no imp)..8 4
Cumbrian Rhapsody **(70)***(67) (MHEasterby)* 5-9-6 MBirch(2) (trckd ldrs: ev ch 3f out: grad wknd fnl 2f)..2½ 5
Leap in the Dark (IRE) **(43)***(38) (MissLCSiddall)* 6-7-7 NCarlisle(9) (b: hld up: effrt over 3f out: nvr nr to chal)..2½ 6
954[7] Provence **(66)***(61) (LLungo)* 8-9-2 KFallon(1) (b: cl up tl wknd fnl 3½f)..nk 7
Balzino (USA) **(56)***(48) (NTinkler)* 6-8-6 KimTinkler(3) (a bhd)..2½ 8

LONG HANDICAP Leap in the Dark (IRE) 7-6

15/8 Noyan, **3/1** Highflying, **4/1** GOOD HAND (USA), **11/2** Bedevil (USA), **9/1** Cumbrian Rhapsody, **14/1** Provence, Balzino (USA), **33/1** Leap in the Dark (IRE), CSF £16.50 CT £61.50 TOTE £4.70: £1.50 £1.80 £2.00 (£5.80) Trio £12.60 OWNER Mrs M. M. Haggas (RICHMOND) BRED Tauner Dunlap, Jr. and Brereton C. Jones 8 Rn 3m 36.72 (11.22) SF: 45/46/42/14/28/-/22/9

1269 CHEF'S LARDER H'CAP (0-85) (3-Y.O) (Class D) £3,656.90 (£1,107.20: £540.60: £257.30)

1m (round) Stalls: Low GOING minus 0.09 sec per fur (G) 3-55 (3-56)

1211[6] **Nigel's Lad (IRE) (81)***(93) (PCHaslam)* 3-9-7 JFortune(5) (cl up: led over 2f out: r.o wl).......— 1
911[5] Atlaal (USA) **(79)***(85)*(Fav)*(HThomsonJones)* 3-9-5 RHills(6) (hld up & bhd: effrt over 2f out: swtchd twice: r.o: too much to do)..3 2
969[5] Spanish Steps (IRE) **(59)***(64) (MWEasterby)* 3-7-13b LCharnock(4) (led tl hdd over 2f out: hung rt: one pce)..¾ 3
1060[4] Khan **(59)***(62) (CWThornton)* 3-7-13 JFanning(2) (bhd: rdn ent st: hdwy 2f out: n.m.r 1f out: kpt on)..1 4
969[9] Cumbrian Minstrel **(62)***(59) (MHEasterby)* 3-8-2b SMaloney(1) (cl up tl wknd over 2f out).........3 5
989[4] Grate British (IRE) **(63)***(39) (EWeymes)* 3-8-3 ow1 KDarley(3) (prom tl outpcd ent st: sn btn) ..10 6

2/1 Atlaal (USA), **5/2** Khan, **6/1** NIGEL'S LAD (IRE), Cumbrian Minstrel, **13/2** Spanish Steps (IRE), **7/1** Grate British (IRE), CSF £18.09 TOTE £9.10: £2.00 £2.20 (£5.70) OWNER Mr N. C. Dunnington (MIDDLEHAM) BRED Nikita Investments 6 Rn 1m 44.05 (5.05) SF: 47/39/18/16/13/-

1270 TYNEMOUTH MAIDEN STKS (3-Y.O) (Class D) £3,623.10 (£1,096.80: £535.40: £254.70) **1m 2f 32y** Stalls: Low GOING minus 0.09 sec per fur (G) 4-25 (4-29)

936[3] **Jandeel (IRE)** *(84)*(Fav)*(ACStewart)* 3-9-0 SWhitworth(10) (b.hind: sn prom: led over 2f out: rdn & r.o)..— 1
Anna of Brunswick *(77) (HRACecil)* 3-8-9 WRyan(4) (leggy: unf: hld up: c wd & effrt ent st: chsd wnr fnl 2f: r.o)..1½ 2
High Pyrenees *(72) (RAllan)* 3-9-0 SMaloney(2) (w'like: unruly in paddock: trckd ldrs: styd on wl fnl f)..6 3
950[5] Lavender (IRE) *(67) (LMCumani)* 3-8-9 KDarley(9) (hdwy after 3f: led over 3f out tl over 2f out: one pce)..s.h 4
Nashwanah *(62) (HThomsonJones)* 3-8-9 RHills(11) (unf: cl up tl outpcd fnl 2f)....................3 5
911[3] Mr Christie **(66)***(65) (MissLCSiddall)* 3-9-0 JFortune(1) (led tl hdd over 3f out: grad lost pl)...1½ 6
1038[6] Aconorace *(63) (RAFahey)* 3-9-0 ACulhane(5) (hld up & bhd: shkn up 3f out: sme late hdwy)..1¼ 7
428[9] Homecrest *(59) (MrsAMNaughton)* 3-9-0 AMercer(3) (effrt 3f out: rdn & no imp)..................2½ 8
Legal Brief *(28) (JSWainwright)* 3-9-0 DeanMcKeown(6) (nvr trbld ldrs)................................20 9

Warrgem *(13) (BEllison)* 3-8-9 TIves(7) (leggy: s.s: n.d) 6 10
Cashmirie *(JLEyre)* 3-8-9 RLappin(8) (Withdrawn not under Starter's orders: ref to ent stalls) .... W

10/11 JANDEEL (IRE), **7/2** Anna of Brunswick, **13/2** Nashwanah, **7/1** Lavender (IRE), **14/1** Mr Christie, **33/1** Homecrest, **66/1** Legal Brief, High Pyrenees, **100/1** Aconorace, Warrgem, CSF £4.36 TOTE £2.10: £1.10 £9.10 (£2.10) Trio £185.30 OWNER Sheikh Ahmed Al Maktoum (NEWMARKET) BRED Biddestone Stud 10 Rn 2m 12.88 (6.18) SF: 43/36/31/26/21/24/22/18/-/-/-

1271

WHITLEY BAY H'CAP (0-75) (3-Y.O+) (Class D) £3,775.20 (£1,143.60: £558.80: £266.40) **5f** Stalls: High GOING minus 0.09 sec per fur (G) 5-00 (5-01)

862³ **Twice in Bundoran (IRE) (44)***(55) (PSFelgate)* 4-7-9 (3) DWright(3) (trckd ldrs: led over 1f out: qcknd) .... — 1
Miss Aragon **(51)***(54) (MissLCSiddall)* 7-8-2 (3) DMcCabe(11) (prom stands' side: hdwy over 1f out: r.o) 2½ 2
994* Rich Glow **(50)***(50)*(Fav)*(NBycroft)* 4-8-4 SMaloney(10) (prom stands' side: edgd lft fnl f: kpt on) 1 3
1152⁶ Tenor **(65)***(63) (DNicholls)* 4-9-5 AlexGreaves(1) (hld up: effrt 2f out: styd on towards fin) .... ½ 4
1023³ Kalar **(43)***(40) (DWChapman)* 6-7-11b NCarlisle(4) (cl up tl rdn & btn appr fnl f) .... ½ 5
Tino Tere **(64)***(55) (JBalding)* 6-8-11 (7) JEdmunds(5) (led tl hdd appr fnl f: sn btn) 1¾ 6
796⁹ Metal Boys **(70)***(59) (MissLCSiddall)* 8-9-10 JFortune(8) (bhd tl r.o fnl f) .... ¾ 7
611² Barato **(67)***(48) (MrsJRRamsden)* 4-9-7 MFenton(2) (b.hind: s.i.s: hdwy ½-wy: nvr nr to chal) 2½ 8
1151* Benzoe (IRE) **(73)***(48)*(Fav)*(MrsJRRamsden)* 5-9-13 7x KFallon(6) (lw: reard s: sme hdwy whn hmpd & snatched up over 1f out: nvr plcd to chal) 1¾ 9
926¹⁵ Knayton Lass **(67)***(36) (MWEasterby)* 4-9-7 MBirch(9) (spd 3f: sn wknd) 1¾ 10
1081⁹ Izza **(49)***(9) (WStorey)* 4-8-3 JFanning(7) (s.i.s: a bhd) 3 11

3/1 Benzoe (IRE) (op 2/1), Rich Glow, **9/2** Tenor, **7/1** Barato, **14/1** TWICE IN BUNDORAN (IRE), Kalar, Knayton Lass, **16/1** Miss Aragon, Metal Boys, **33/1** Tino Tere, Izza, CSF £185.10 CT £768.33 TOTE £20.20: £2.90 £4.20 £1.30 (£162.50) Trio £258.90 OWNER Wild Racing (MELTON MOWBRAY) BRED Golden Vale Stud 11 Rn 60.64 secs (2.24) SF: 37/36/32/45/22/37/41/30/30/18

T/Plpt: £209.80 (56.12 Tckts). T/Qdpt: £19.70 (5.5 Tckts). AA

1011-BRIGHTON (L-H)
Friday May 26th (Firm)

WEATHER: sunny WIND: almost nil

1272

VICTORIA GARDENS (S) STKS (2-Y.O) (Class G) £2,243.00 (£618.00: £293.00) **5f 213y** Stalls: Low GOING minus 0.54 sec per fur (F) 2-10 (2-11)

1226³ **Don't Tell Vicki** *(48) (JSMoore)* 2-8-1 (5) NVarley(5) (lw: 3rd st: led over 2f out: wandered wl over 1f out: rdn out) .... — 1
725⁶ Caveat Emptor (IRE) *(44) (SDow)* 2-8-11 StephenDavies(3) (led over 3f: ev ch over 1f out: unable qckn) 3½ 2
1159² Imprimis (IRE) *(32)*(Fav)*(CNAllen)* 2-8-6 JQuinn(1) (lw: 5th st: rdn over 2f out: one pce) 2½ 3
740³ Solva Mist *(31) (LJHolt)* 2-8-6 CAvery(2) (4th st: rdn over 2f out: one pce) .... ½ 4
1077⁴ Euskara *(23) (MDIUsher)* 2-8-6 RStreet(4) (2nd st: wknd 2f out) 3 5
849⁹ Red Sky Delight (IRE) *(PButler)* 2-8-1 (5) AWhelan(6) (6th st: wknd 2f out) 9 6

6/5 Imprimis (IRE), **4/1** DON'T TELL VICKI, Caveat Emptor (IRE), **9/1** Solva Mist (5/1-10/1), **10/1** Euskara (9/2-12/1), **33/1** Red Sky Delight (IRE), CSF £17.62 TOTE £2.90: £1.50 (£12.40) OWNER Mrs Victoria Goodman (ANDOVER) BRED Highfield Stud Ltd 6 Rn 1m 11.3 (2.90) SF: 4/-/-/-/-/-
No bid

1273

OLD STEINE MAIDEN STKS (3-Y.O+) (Class D) £3,630.90 (£1,081.20: £514.60: £231.30) **1m 1f 209y** Stalls: High GOING minus 0.54 sec per fur (F) 2-40 (2-41)

1128⁴ **Wathbat Mtoto** *(76)*(Fav)*(LMCumani)* 3-8-4 JQuinn(3) (3rd st: rdn over 2f out: led over 1f out: r.o wl) .... — 1
978⁵ Berkeley Bounder (USA) **(79)***(75) (PFICole)* 3-8-9 TQuinn(1) (lw: led over 8f: unable qckn)..3½ 2
552⁵ Empower (IRE) *(75) (RHannon)* 3-8-9 PatEddery(5) (w ldr: rdn over 2f out: ev ch over 1f out: one pce) .... nk 3
1053¹¹ Brockton Light *(51) (MRChannon)* 3-8-4v CRutter(4) (4th st: wknd over 2f out) 12 4
Guest Alliance (IRE) **(58)***(56) (AMoore)* 3-8-9 CandyMorris(2) (lw: 5th st: wknd 3f out) .... s.h 5

8/15 WATHBAT MTOTO, **4/1** Empower (IRE) (op 5/2), **9/2** Berkeley Bounder (USA) (op 9/4), **40/1** Brockton Light, **50/1** Guest Alliance (IRE), CSF £3.14 TOTE £1.40: £1.20 £1.10 (£1.90) OWNER Sheikh Ahmed Al Maktoum (NEWMARKET) BRED Sheikh Ahmed bin Rashid al Maktoum 5 Rn

2m 1.2 (3.20) SF: 17/16/16/-/-

1274

A.R. DENNIS BOOKMAKERS MAY H'CAP (0-70) (3-Y.O+ F & M) (Class E) £3,502.40 (£1,047.20: £501.60: £228.80)
7f 214y Stalls: Low GOING minus 0.54 sec per fur (F) 3-10 (3-10)

Elite Racing (61)*(72) (PFICole)* 3-8-8 TQuinn(3) (5th st: rdn 2f out: led ins fnl f: r.o wl) ....— 1
Life's Too Short (IRE) **(47)***(57) (JEBanks)* 4-8-6 JQuinn(10) (bit bkwd: led tl ins fnl f: r.o)........¾ 2
1206² Flair Lady **(55)***(59) (WGMTurner)* 4-8-9 (5) PMcCabe(6) (4th st: rdn over 2f out: unable qckn) ..3 3
1093¹⁰ Pedaltothemetal (IRE) **(56)***(56) (PMitchell)* 3-8-3 SO'Gorman(11) (b.hind: lw: 6th st: rdn over 2f out: one pce) 1¾ 4
Tout de Val **(35)***(34) (KBishop)* 6-7-8 NAdams(9) (lw: swvd lft s: hdwy over 1f out: nvr nrr).....½ 5
727⁴ Polly Garter **(60)***(57)*(Fav)*(RHannon)* 3-8-7 PatEddery(5) (outpcd: gd hdwy over 1f out: one pce) 1¼ 6
320⁷ Myjinka **(34)***(29) (JO'Donoghue)* 5-7-0b(7) IonaWands(1) (bit bkwd: 2nd st: wknd wl over 1f out) ....¾ 7
1048¹³ Bezirgan **(36)***(27) (JAkehurst)* 4-7-4 (5)ow2 NVarley(8) (outpcd) ....¾ 8
1092* Arndilly **(74)***(64) (BJMeehan)* 4-10-0b(5) 5x MBaird(4) (3rd st: hrd rdn over 2f out: sn wknd) ...1¾ 9
1126¹⁵ High Typha **(56)***(45) (MRChannon)* 4-9-1 CRutter(2) (a bhd)........nk 10

LONG HANDICAP Bezirgan 7-6 Myjinka 7-5

100/30 Polly Garter, **9/2** Life's Too Short (IRE), **11/2** Flair Lady, **6/1** Arndilly (72/-13/2), **8/1** ELITE RACING (5/1-9/1), Myjinka, **9/1** High Typha, **20/1** Pedaltothemetal (IRE), Tout de Val, **33/1** Bezirgan, CSF £40.25 CT £195.28 TOTE £6.60: £1.20 £2.90 £2.50 (£26.80) Trio £58.10 OWNER Elite Racing Club (WHATCOMBE) BRED R. J. McAlpine 10 Rn

1m 34.6 (2.40) SF: 21/18/20/5/-/6/-/-/25/6
WEIGHT FOR AGE 3yo-12lb

1275

GRAND PARADE MEDIAN AUCTION MAIDEN STKS (3-Y.O) (Class E) £3,044.80 (£906.40: £431.20: £193.60)
1m 3f 196y Stalls: High GOING minus 0.54 sec per fur (F) 3-40 (3-41)

1097³ **Vaugrenier (IRE) (84)***(86) (RHannon)* 3-9-0 PatEddery(1) (mde all: r.o wl) ....— 1
1147² Kymin (IRE) *(76)*(Fav)*(LMCumani)* 3-8-9 TQuinn(4) (b.hind: chsd wnr 11f out: rdn over 5f out: unable qckn fnl 3f) 3½ 2
797¹⁴ Risk a Million *(JRJenkins)* 3-8-9 DBiggs(2) (lw: t.o fnl 5f) ....dist 3
764²³ Paddy's Storm *(RMFlower)* 3-8-9 (5) JDSmith(3) (t.o fnl 5f) ....dist 4

4/6 Kymin (IRE), **5/4** VAUGRENIER (IRE), **66/1** Risk a Million, **100/1** Paddy's Storm, CSF £2.28 TOTE £2.60 (£1.10) OWNER Mr Ivan Twigden (MARLBOROUGH) BRED Michael Doyle 4 Rn

2m 29.9 (0.90) SF: 49/39/-/-

1276

DOME H'CAP (0-70) (3-Y.O+) (Class E) £3,245.00 (£968.00: £462.00: £209.00)
5f 213y Stalls: Low GOING minus 0.54 sec per fur (F) 4-10 (4-11)

1013⁵ **Tafahhus (68)***(76) (RWArmstrong)* 3-9-2 WCarson(10) (4th st: led over 1f out: r.o wl)........— 1
1050¹⁰ Night Asset **(50)***(53) (JO'Donoghue)* 6-8-3 (5) PMcCabe(3) (gd hdwy over 1f out: r.o wl ins fnl f) 1¾ 2
1157⁸ Giggleswick Girl **(54)***(48) (MRChannon)* 4-8-12 AClark(5) (lw: hdwy & nt clr run wl over 1f out: r.o one pce) 3½ 3
922¹⁵ Samsolom **(63)***(53) (PHowling)* 7-9-7 JQuinn(8) (hdwy over 1f out: r.o one pce) 1½ 4
1071⁴ Crystal Heights (FR) **(64)***(54) (RJO'Sullivan)* 7-9-8 MRimmer(11) (b: 6th st: one pce fnl 2f) ..s.h 5
102⁹ As Such (IRE) **(55)***(37) (NACallaghan)* 4-8-13b TQuinn(4) (bit bkwd: swtg: nvr nr to chal) 3 6
1013¹¹ Apollo Red **(53)***(35) (AMoore)* 6-8-11 CandyMorris(7) (b.off hind: swtg: 5th st: wknd over 2f out) ....hd 7
447² Das Island **(56)***(35) (JRJenkins)* 3-8-4 DBiggs(1) (led over 4f) ....¾ 8
1016* Dahiyah (USA) **(63)***(36)*(Fav)*(GLMoore)* 4-9-2v(5) AWhelan(9) (3rd st: rdn 3f out: nt clr run on ins over 1f out: nt rcvr) 2½ 9
507¹⁸ Tiheros **(65)***(34) (RHannon)* 3-8-13 PatEddery(2) (lw: 2nd st: ev ch over 1f out: sn wknd) 1½ 10

2/1 Dahiyah (USA), **3/1** TAFAHHUS, **7/1** Giggleswick Girl, **8/1** Crystal Heights (FR), **10/1** Tiheros (6/1-11/1), **11/1** Das Island (8/1-12/1), **12/1** Samsolom, **14/1** Apollo Red (10/1-16/1), As Such (IRE) (10/1-16/1), **33/1** Night Asset, CSF £77.02 CT £602.17 TOTE £2.60: £1.30 £3.90 £1.90 (£49.90) Trio £140.60 OWNER Mr Hamdan Al Maktoum (NEWMARKET) BRED Shadwell Estate Company Limited 10 Rn

68.7 secs (0.30) SF: 49/36/31/36/37/20/18/8/19/7
WEIGHT FOR AGE 3yo-10lb

1277 BRIGHTON CENTRE H'CAP (0-85) (3-Y.O) (Class D) £4,074.00 (£1,212.00: £576.00: £258.00) **5f 59y** Stalls: Low GOING minus 0.54 sec per fur (F) 4-40 (4-40)

1181[7] **Musica (78)***(84) (MRChannon)* 3-9-1v TQuinn(5) (4th st: rdn 2f out: led ins fnl f: r.o wl)..........— 1
1181[2] Shashi (IRE) **(75)***(81)*(Fav)*(DMorley)* 3-8-12 WCarson(1) (5th st: rdn over 2f out: hdwy over 1f out: r.o wl ins fnl f)..........hd 2
1201[13] Portelet **(61)***(62) (RJRWilliams)* 3-7-12 DBiggs(2) (lw: 3rd st: nt clr run on ins over 1f out: swtchd rt: r.o one pce)..........1½ 3
1055[2] Tart and a Half **(84)***(80) (BJMeehan)* 3-9-7b PatEddery(3) (lw: led tl ins fnl f: sn wknd)..........1¾ 4
1069[5] Chewit **(82)***(60) (AMoore)* 3-9-5 CandyMorris(4) (2nd st: ev ch over 1f out: wknd fnl f)..........6 5

Evens Shashi (IRE), **5/2** Tart and a Half, **5/1** Chewit (5/2-11/2), **12/1** Portelet (op 6/1), MUSICA (op 5/1), CSF £23.72 TOTE £15.70: £4.20 £1.10 (£6.40) OWNER Mr Jonathan Knight (UPPER LAMBOURN) BRED Cheveley Park Stud Ltd 5 Rn 61.3 secs (1.30) SF: 31/28/9/27/7

T/Plpt: £176.50 (45.28 Tckts). T/Qdpt: £51.80 (0.3 Tckts); £49.00 to Haydock 27/5/95. AK

0950-HAYDOCK (L-H)
Friday May 26th (Good)
WEATHER: overcast WIND: str half bhd

1278 PARKSIDE MAIDEN AUCTION STKS (2-Y.O) (Class D) £3,566.25 (£1,080.00: £527.50: £251.25) **5f** Stalls: High GOING minus 0.10 sec per fur (G) 2-00 (2-01)

791[4] **Beautiful Ballad (IRE)** *(76)*(Fav)*(BWHills)* 2-7-12 AMcGlone(11) (b.hind: mde virtually all: shkn up & r.o wl fnl f)..........— 1
910[2] Capture The Moment *(73) (RJRWilliams)* 2-8-2 ow1 MRoberts(4) (w wnr tl rdn & no ex ins fnl f)..........1¾ 2
Power Game *(69) (JBerry)* 2-8-6 JCarroll(3) (w'like: leggy: hdwy bel dist: kpt on wl fnl f)..........3 3
1063[4] Northern Clan *(64) (MWEasterby)* 2-8-3 LCharnock(12) (bit bkwd: chsd ldrs: rdn over 1f out: nt pce to chal)..........½ 4
Arc of The Diver (IRE) *(66) (JBerry)* 2-8-9 KDarley(9) (unf: scope: bit bkwd: r.o appr fnl f: nvr nrr)..........1¼ 5
Bold Times *(59) (PDEvans)* 2-8-3 DHolland(8) (small: s.i.s: sn chsng ldrs: no hdwy fnl f)......nk 6
690[13] Bozeman (IRE) *(61) (RHannon)* 2-8-6 LDettori(5) (disp ld 3f: rdn over 1f out: sn btn)..........nk 7
Sizzling Symphony *(46) (RAFahey)* 2-8-3 ACulhane(6) (leggy: lt-f: drvn along ½-wy: a outpcd)..........4 8
436[12] Magical Midnight *(40) (NTinkler)* 2-7-12 KimTinkler(7) (outpcd: a bhd)..........hd 9
943[8] Brockville Bairn *(40) (MrsASwinbank)* 2-8-3 JMarshall(2) (spd on outside 3f)..........1½ 10
Scenicris (IRE) *(32) (RHollinshead)* 2-7-9 (3) DWright(1) (neat: bkwd: s.s: outpcd: a bhd)........1 11
Seeking Destiny (IRE) *(34) (MrsMMcCourt)* 2-8-9 WNewnes(10) (lt-f: bkwd: dwlt: a outpcd & bhd)..........3 12

4/5 BEAUTIFUL BALLAD (IRE) (op 6/4), **9/2** Capture The Moment (3/1-5/1), **8/1** Power Game (op 9/2), **10/1** Bozeman (IRE) (op 6/1), **12/1** Arc of The Diver (IRE) (op 6/1), Northern Clan (op 6/1), **16/1** Seeking Destiny (IRE), Scenicris (IRE), **20/1** Bold Times, **33/1** Brockville Bairn, Sizzling Symphony, Magical Midnight, CSF £6.08 TOTE £2.10: £1.10 £1.50 £1.90 (£2.40) Trio £6.80 OWNER K. Al-Said (LAMBOURN) BRED T. J. Rooney 12 Rn
61.72 secs (2.72) SF: 29/26/22/17/19/12/14/-/-/-/-/-

1279 SILVERDALE APPRENTICE H'CAP (0-70) (3-Y.O) (Class E) £3,371.25 (£1,020.00: £497.50: £236.25) **6f** Stalls: High GOING minus 0.10 sec per fur (G) 2-30 (2-32)

759[2] **Showery (62)***(79+) (JWWatts)* 3-9-0 CTeague(7) (a.p: led ent fnl f: sn clr: eased nr fin)......— 1
1157[2] Crystal Loop **(61)***(65)*(Fav)*(ABailey)* 3-8-13 VHalliday(8) (a w ldrs: led wl over 1f out: sn rdn: hdd ent fnl f: one pce)..........5 2
722[5] Spara Tir **(59)***(61) (BobJones)* 3-8-11 GParkin(12) (a.p: led over 2f out: sn hdd: one pce)......¾ 3
1154[7] Good Match (IRE) **(60)***(58) (NTinkler)* 3-8-12 MarkDenaro(1) (gd hdwy over 1f out: fin wl).....1½ 4
1034[4] Mixed Mood **(50)***(45) (BPalling)* 3-8-2 MHumphries(2) (chsd ldrs: kpt on one pce appr fnl f)....1 5
999[10] Cool Tactician **(61)***(55) (RHollinshead)* 3-8-8 (5) AEddery(9) (chsd ldrs: rdn bel dist: r.o one pce)..........nk 6
1034[8] Frans Lad **(62)***(56) (JBerry)* 3-9-0v PRoberts(11) (led over 3f: sn rdn: one pce)..........s.h 7
999[9] Solo Prize **(69)***(55) (PHowling)* 3-9-7 RPainter(13) (outpcd)..........3 8
1060[7] Borrowby **(50)***(27) (MWEasterby)* 3-7-13b(3) PFessey(10) (sn chsg ldrs: rdn & wknd wl over 1f out)..........3½ 9

875[7] Seenthelight **(45)***(17) (DMoffatt)* 3-7-4v(7) RMullen(6) (bhd: rdn & swvd lft 2f out: no imp)......1¾ **10**
966[14] Blue Lugana **(49)***(16) (NBycroft)* 3-8-1 ow2 DGriffiths(14) (nvr nr to chal)......1 **11**
1094[6] La Bossette (IRE) **(52)***(8) (JRArnold)* 3-8-4b PPMurphy(3) (lw: chsd ldrs: rdn 2f out: sn lost tch)......5 **12**
1164[9] Oneineverycolour **(47)***(1) (PDEvans)* 3-7-13 AmandaSanders(4) (chsd ldrs 4f: sn wknd)......¾ **13**
1033[2] Rupert's Princess (IRE) **(53)** *(MJHeaton-Ellis)* 3-7-12b(7) JFowle(5) (dwlt: a bhd & utpcd)......4 **14**

7/2 Crystal Loop, **4/1** SHOWERY, **8/1** Spara Tir, Borrowby (6/1-9/1), **10/1** Cool Tactician, **11/1** Rupert's Princess (IRE), **12/1** Mixed Mood, Frans Lad, **14/1** Solo Prize, La Bossette (IRE), **16/1** Good Match (IRE), Oneineverycolour, **20/1** Seenthelight, Blue Lugana, CSF £19.01 CT £102.52 TOTE £3.60: £1.60 £2.10 £3.20 (£5.20) Trio £32.80 OWNER Lord Derby (RICHMOND) BRED Stanley Estate and Stud Co 14 Rn 1m 14.51 (2.81) SF: 51/37/33/30/17/27/28/27/-/-/-/-/-/-

1280 COAL PRODUCTS PHURNACITE H'CAP (0-90) (4-Y.O+) (Class C)

£5,654.00 (£1,712.00: £836.00: £398.00)
1m 30y Stalls: Low GOING minus 0.10 sec per fur (G) 3-00 (3-01)

642[5] **Up in Flames (IRE) (63)***(77+) (MDHammond)* 4-8-5 JCarroll(8) (lw: hld up: hdwy 3f out: shkn up to ld 2f out: sn clr)......— **1**
1021* Dawalib (USA) **(64)***(70)*(Fav)*(DHaydnJones)* 5-8-6 DHolland(10) (lw: chsd ldrs: 5th st: ev ch 2f out: rdn & one pce)......4 **2**
793[3] Show Faith (IRE) **(82)***(88) (RHannon)* 5-9-10 KDarley(2) (hld up: 6th st: hdwy bel dist: kpt on towards fin)......nk **3**
Dancing Heights (IRE) **(78)***(83) (IABalding)* 4-9-6 WRyan(9) (bit bkwd: hld up: hdwy over 2f out: rdn & r.o ins fnl f)......s.h **4**
960[5] Gadge **(73)***(76) (DMorris)* 4-9-1 RPrice(1) (prom: 4th st: rdn over 1f out: nvr able to chal)......1½ **5**
960[10] Top Guide (USA) **(82)***(81) (EALDunlop)* 4-9-7 (3) JTate(7) (b: hld up: styd on appr fnl f: nvr nrr)......1¾ **6**
927[8] Spanish Verdict **(65)***(61) (DenysSmith)* 8-8-2 (5) CTeague(6) (lw: prom: 2nd st: racd centre: rdn 3f out: wknd bel dist)......1½ **7**
918[7] Master Beveled **(86)***(75) (PDEvans)* 5-9-9 (5) JStack(11) (hld up & bhd: effrt & rdn 3f out: no imp)......3½ **8**
1148* Blockade (USA) **(73)***(52) (MBell)* 6-9-1 5x MHills(4) (t: led tl hdd & wknd 2f out)......5 **9**
873[3] Tregaron (USA) **(76)***(52) (PCalver)* 4-9-4 MBirch(3) (lw: s.i.s: effrt & nt clr run 3f out: no imp)1¾ **10**
1088[7] World Traveller **(62)***(28) (WAO'Gorman)* 4-8-4v LDettori(5) (prom: 3rd st: rdn & wandered 3f out: sn wknd & eased)......5 **11**

7/2 Dawalib (USA), **5/1** Tregaron (USA), **13/2** Show Faith (IRE), **15/2** Gadge, **8/1** Blockade (USA), **9/1** Master Beveled, **10/1** Top Guide (USA), UP IN FLAMES (IRE), World Traveller, **14/1** Dancing Heights (IRE), Spanish Verdict, CSF £44.77 CT £232.51 TOTE £29.30: £4.90 £1.70 £2.20 (£40.30) Trio £166.50 OWNER Mr Mark Kilner (MIDDLEHAM) BRED Mrs D. Hutch 11 Rn
1m 45.37 (4.97) SF: 33/26/44/39/32/37/17/31/8/8/-

1281 SPINAL INJURIES ASSOCIATION RATED STKS H'CAP (0-95) (3-Y.O)

(Class B) £8,062.50 (£2,812.50: £1,368.75: £581.25)
1m 6f Stalls: Low GOING minus 0.10 sec per fur (G) 3-30 (3-30)

851[2] **Red Bustaan (77)***(83)*(Fav)*(ACStewart)* 3-8-6 MRoberts(2) (lw: hld up: 3rd st: shkn up over 2f out: led over 1f out: cheekily)......— **1**
1170[3] Grey Shot **(92)***(98) (IABalding)* 3-9-7 LDettori(4) (dropped rr 8f out: 4th st: hdwy to ld over 3f out: hdd bel dist: rallied u.p cl home)......nk **2**
995* Astrolabe **(78)***(73) (BWHills)* 3-8-7b MHills(1) (lw: led tl over 3f out: rdn & ev ch tl wknd wl over 1f out)......9 **3**
717[8] Sarasota Storm **(80)** *(MBell)* 3-8-9 JCarroll(3) (lw: chsd ldr 9f out: 2nd st: wknd 3f out: t.o)..dist **4**

6/4 RED BUSTAAN, **13/8** Astrolabe, **3/1** Grey Shot, **10/1** Sarasota Storm, CSF £5.92 TOTE £2.20 (£3.30) OWNER Sheikh Ahmed Al Maktoum (NEWMARKET) BRED Mrs Willa Harford 4 Rn
3m 6.59 (8.39) SF: 36/51/26/-

1282 AGECROFT (S) STKS (2-Y.O) (Class G) £2,598.00 (£728.00: £354.00)

5f Stalls: High GOING minus 0.10 sec per fur (G) 4-00 (4-02)

Lunar Mist *(50) (MartynMeade)* 2-8-6 VSlattery(2) (cmpt: bit bkwd: swvd lft s: sn bhd & outpcd: hdwy to ld 1f out: rdn & r.o wl)......— **1**
1215[3] Doug's Folly *(50)*(Fav)*(MWEasterby)* 2-8-6 LDettori(6) (a.p: slt ld over 1f out: sn hdd: rallied u.p cl home)......hd **2**
Pathaze *(40) (NBycroft)* 2-8-6 SMaloney(4) (scope: bkwd: s.s: hdwy over 1f out: nvr nrr)......3 **3**

1215[2] April's Joy *(27) (JNorton)* 2-8-6 ACulhane(5) (chsd ldrs: rdn bel dist: one pce) 4 4
Distinct (IRE) *(21) (JBerry)* 2-8-11 JCarroll(3) (w'like: leggy: bit bkwd: bhd: rdn ½-wy: nvr nr to chal) 3½ 5
1089[7] Havana Heights (IRE) *(16) (RWEmery)* 2-8-3 (3) DWright(8) (a bhd & outpcd) ....s.h 6
983[5] Snitch *(20) (CSmith)* 2-8-11 KDarley(1) (w ldr over 3f: sn wknd) ....nk 7
903[5] Mouna El Arab *(9) (JBerry)* 2-8-6 SDWilliams(7) (b.nr hind: led tl hdd & wknd ent fnl f: eased) 2 8

7/4 Doug's Folly (9/4-6/4), **7/2** Distinct (IRE) (op 2/1), **4/1** April's Joy, **11/2** Mouna El Arab, **9/1** LUNAR MIST (op 20/1), Snitch, **25/1** Havana Heights (IRE), Pathaze, CSF £25.46 TOTE £17.10: £2.80 £1.10 £4.30 (£13.20) OWNER Ladyswood Racing Club (MALMESBURY) BRED T. Barratt 8 Rn 62.52 secs (3.52) SF: 23/23/13/-/-/-/-/-
Bt in 3,700 gns

1283 LITTLETON MAIDEN STKS (3-Y.O F) (Class D) £3,896.00 (£1,178.00: £574.00: £272.00) **1m 3f 200y** Stalls: Low GOING minus 0.10 sec per fur (G) 4-30 (4-31)

950[2] **Top Shop** *(80)*(Fav)*(HRACecil)* 3-8-11 WRyan(3) (lw: stdd s: sn chsng ldrs: 3rd st: led over 2f out: clr ent fnl f: pushed out nr fin) ....— 1
Lucayan Sunshine (USA) *(78) (LadyHerries)* 3-8-11 KDarley(5) (w'like: leggy: hld up: 5th st: hdwy u.p 2f out: styd on wl fnl f) 1½ 2
1097[7] Swivel *(70) (JRFanshawe)* 3-8-11 JCarroll(4) (hld up: 4th st: r.o one pce fnl 2f) 6 3
Cephista *(68) (PTWalwyn)* 3-8-11 DHolland(1) (lw: led over 9f: wknd over 1f out) 1½ 4
797[W] Peripatetic *(66) (MRStoute)* 3-8-11 PaulEddery(6) (hld up & bhd: 6th st: nvr plcd to chal) 1¼ 5
1062[3] Rainelle *(66) (CEBrittain)* 3-8-11 MRoberts(2) (chsd ldr: 2nd st: rdn 3f out: sn wknd) ....hd 6

30/100 TOP SHOP, **10/1** Swivel, Rainelle, **14/1** Lucayan Sunshine (USA), Cephista, Peripatetic, CSF £5.75 TOTE £1.30: £1.10 £2.90 (£5.00) OWNER Cliveden Stud (NEWMARKET) BRED Cliveden Stud 6 Rn 2m 41.54 (13.54) SF: -/-/-/-/-/-

1284 BICKERSHAW STKS (3-Y.O+) (Class C) £5,148.40 (£1,878.40: £919.20: £396.00: £178.00) **7f 30y** Stalls: Low GOING minus 0.10 sec per fur (G) 5-00 (5-02)

814[2] **Mistle Cat (USA)** **(104)***(117)*(Fav)*(SPCWoods)* 5-9-10 WRyan(1) (mde all: clr over 1f out: comf) ....— 1
710a[2] Fraam **(109)***(113) (EALDunlop)* 6-9-12 PaulEddery(2) (b: lw: a.p: 3rd st: chsd wnr fnl 2f: no imp) 2½ 2
814[6] Cool Jazz **(100)***(100) (CEBrittain)* 4-9-2 MRoberts(4) (lw: hld up: 4th st: rdn & hung lft 3f out: kpt on ins fnl f) 1½ 3
Carranita (IRE) **(101)***(98) (BPalling)* 5-9-7 JCarroll(3) (bit bkwd: chsd wnr: 2nd st: wknd wl over 1f out) 3 4
1108[4] Storiths (IRE) **(109)***(96) (JWWatts)* 5-9-7b BThomson(5) (lw: b.hind: s.i.s: hld up & bhd: 5th st: rdn over 2f out: no imp) 1 5

15/8 MISTLE CAT (USA), **9/4** Fraam, **11/4** Storiths (IRE), **8/1** Cool Jazz, **12/1** Carranita (IRE) (op 8/1), CSF £6.18 TOTE £2.50: £1.30 £1.20 (£2.10) OWNER Mr P. K. L. Chu (NEWMARKET) BRED Henry H. Fitzgibbon & Overbrook Farm 5 Rn 1m 31.12 (3.82) SF: 56/52/39/37/35
T/Plpt: £16.70 (878.79 Tckts). T/Qdpt: £12.60 (7.75 Tckts) IM

0861-NOTTINGHAM (L-H)
Friday May 26th (Good to firm, Firm patches)
WEATHER: overcast WIND: moderate against

1285 ARNOLD (S) H'CAP (0-60) (3-Y.O+) (Class G) £2,243.00 (£618.00: £293.00) **1m 1f 213y** Stalls: High GOING minus 0.37 sec per fur (F) 2-20 (2-24)

Indian Jockey **(52)***(65+) (PJMcBride)* 3-9-0 AMackay(12) (bit bkwd: hdwy & 6th st: led over 2f out: clr 1f out: easily) ....— 1
1161[12] Diamond Crown (IRE) **(47)***(50) (MartynWane)* 4-9-10 KFallon(16) (hdwy 2f out: swtchd rt 1f out: r.o: no ch w wnr) 6 2
258[7] Presto Boy **(48)***(51) (MBell)* 3-8-10 MFenton(3) (lw: hdwy 2f out: r.o ins fnl f) ....nk 3
1048[5] Dots Dee **(25)***(25) (JMBradley)* 6-8-2 GDuffield(4) (hdwy on ins 4f out: nt clr run over 1f out & ins fnl f: r.o) 2 4
990[5] To Prove a Point **(35)***(34) (JJO'Neill)* 3-7-11b NKennedy(17) (led over 2f: 3rd st: led over 3f out tl over 2f out: one pce) ....nk 5
Bronze Runner **(35)***(33) (SMellor)* 11-8-5b(7) ADaly(19) (5th st: no hdwy fnl 2f) ....½ 6
948[9] Never Time (IRE) **(43)***(41) (MrsVAAconley)* 3-8-2 (3) DRMcCabe(5) (8th st: edgd lft ins fnl f: one pce) ....nk 7

5694 Ann Hill (IRE) **(36)**(32) (RHollinshead) 5-8-13 DHarrison(22) (swtg: hdwy 2f out: nt clr run ins fnl f: nt rch ldrs) 1 **8**
9096 Calisar **(42)**(37) (PHowling) 5-9-5 RCochrane(14) (hdwy 4f out: wknd over 1f out) 1 **9**
Sinclair Lad (IRE) **(47)**(41) (RJHodges) 7-9-5b(5) SDrowne(23) (4th st: ev ch whn hung lft 2f out: btn whn nt clr run ins fnl f) ....nk **10**
11498 Goldenberry **(40)**(32) (JParkes) 4-9-3 MDeering(6) (s.s: a bhd) 1½ **11**
11919 Castletown Count **(52)**(42) (KWHogg) 3-8-11 (3) AGarth(21) (7th st: wknd over 1f out) 1 **12**
*835*11 Swynford Flyer **(30)**(20) (JAHarris) 6-8-4 (3) SSanders(2) (hdwy 4f out: wknd 2f out) ....nk **13**
*766*13 Gamzatti **(30)**(19) (CBBBooth) 4-8-7 MTebbutt(11) (bhd fnl 2f) ....nk **14**
11914 Greek Gold (IRE) **(44)**(33)(Fav)(DNicholls) 6-9-7 AlexGreaves(13) (lw: led over 7f out tl over 2f out: wknd over 1f out) ....hd **15**
Mai Pen Rai **(34)**(23) (RJHodges) 7-8-11 TSprake(8) (hdwy 4f out: wknd 2f out) ....nk **16**
11618 Tocco Jewel **(23)**(11) (MJRyan) 5-8-0 GBardwell(10) (a bhd) ....½ **17**
8679 Longcroft **(38)**(10) (KWHogg) 3-7-7 (7) DLockhart(18) (s.s: hung rt after 2f: a bhd) 10 **18**
My Fiore **(30)**(1) (PJBevan) 4-8-7 NCarlisle(7) (bit bkwd: bhd fnl 3f) ....½ **19**
86618 Portolano (FR) **(44)**(10) (WClay) 4-9-7 MWigham(9) (a bhd) 3 **20**
*520*13 Arrogant Boy **(30)** (DWChapman) 6-8-7 DeanMcKeown(20) (bit bkwd: dwlt: a bhd) 2 **21**
*517*6 Tremolante **(30)** (CaptJWilson) 4-8-7 PRobinson(1) (a bhd) ....s.h **22**
Merseyside Man **(32)** (DrJDScargill) 9-8-2v(7) CDomergue(15) (w ldr: 2nd st: wknd over 2f out: t.o) 20 **23**

3/1 Greek Gold (IRE), **6/1** Dots Dee, INDIAN JOCKEY, **12/1** Presto Boy (op 7/1), Sinclair Lad (IRE) (op 6/1), **14/1** Diamond Crown (IRE) (op 8/1), Calisar, Ann Hill (IRE), To Prove a Point, Swynford Flyer, **16/1** Castletown Count, **20/1** Portolano (FR), Tremolante, Longcroft, **25/1** Bronze Runner, Mai Pen Rai, Tocco Jewel, Never Time (IRE), Merseyside Man, **33/1** My Fiore, Arrogant Boy, Goldenberry, Gamzatti, CSF £93.90 CT £941.02 TOTE £7.00: £1.70 £4.90 £2.10 £2.00 (£62.30) Trio £287.20 OWNER Mrs D. Handley (NEWMARKET) BRED John Hayter 23 Rn

2m 7.2 (4.70) SF: 31/31/17/6/-/14/7/13/18/22/13/8/1/-/14/4/-/-/-/-/-/-/-

WEIGHT FOR AGE 3yo-15lb

Sold MPipe 7,500gns

1286 MCEWANS LAGER H'CAP (0-70) (3-Y.O+) (Class E) £3,702.60 (£1,108.80: £532.40: £244.20) **1m 1f 213y** Stalls: High GOING minus 0.37 sec (F) 2-50 (2-51)

103711 **East Barns (IRE) (44)**(52) (SGollings) 7-8-13b FNorton(7) (hld up: 6th st: hrd rdn 2f out: hdwy 1f out: led ins fnl f: all out) ....— **1**
10835 Harry Browne (IRE) **(56)**(64)(Fav)(MrsJRRamsden) 3-8-10 KFallon(5) (hld up: 8th st: hdwy 3f out: swtchd rt over 1f out: ev ch ins fnl f: r.o) ....nk **2**
*1078*3 Sparkling Roberta **(43)**(47) (MDIUsher) 4-8-5 (7) CAdamson(6) (2nd st: led over 1f out tl ins fnl f) 2½ **3**
Course Fishing **(42)**(38) (BAMcMahon) 4-8-11 GDuffield(4) (led tl wknd over 1f out) 5 **4**
7446 Art Tatum **(52)**(47) (RHannon) 4-9-7 RHills(1) (4th st: rdn over 3f out: wknd 2f out) ....nk **5**
101310 All the Joys **(49)**(44) (CACyzer) 4-9-4 RCochrane(8) (hld up: 7th st: bhd fnl 2f) ....hd **6**
Ruddigore **(60)**(52) (RHannon) 3-9-0 GCarter(3) (plld hrd: 3rd st: swtchd rt over 2f out: hmpd over 1f out: sn wknd) 1¾ **7**
*1034** No Submission (USA) **(47)**(38) (DWChapman) 9-9-2 DeanMcKeown(2) (lw: s.i.s: nvr gng wl: a bhd) ....½ **8**
9734 Adilov **(70)**(57) (JRFanshawe) 3-9-10 DHarrison(9) (5th st: rdn over 3f out: wknd over 2f out) 2½ **9**

7/2 Harry Browne (IRE), **9/2** Art Tatum (op 7/1), **11/2** Sparkling Roberta, **6/1** Adilov (op 4/1), Ruddigore (op 7/2), **8/1** No Submission (USA), **11/1** EAST BARNS (IRE), **12/1** All the Joys, **33/1** Course Fishing, CSF £45.50 CT £214.52 TOTE £25.50: £2.50 £1.80 £1.60 (£28.70) Trio £62.90 OWNER Northern Bloodstock Racing (LOUTH) BRED P. J. Mulhall 9 Rn

2m 7.3 (4.80) SF: 29/26/24/15/24/21/14/15/19

WEIGHT FOR AGE 3yo-15lb

1287 E.B.F. MAIDEN STKS (2-Y.O F) (Class D) £3,622.50 (£1,080.00:£515.00: £232.50) **6f 15y** Stalls: High GOING minus 0.37 sec per fur (F) 3-20 (3-22)

8192 **Top Cat (FR)** (69) (EWeymes) 2-8-11 DeanMcKeown(3) (dwlt: led after 1f: clr over 1f out: drvn out) ....— **1**
Honest Guest (IRE) (68) (MHTompkins) 2-8-11 PRobinson(6) (unf: a.p: chsd wnr fnl 2f: r.o wl) ....½ **2**
7916 Disallowed (IRE) (55)(Fav)(MBell) 2-8-11 MFenton(1) (outpcd: r.o fnl f: n.d) 5 **3**
11426 Victoria Venture (53) (SPCWoods) 2-8-11 TIves(5) (no hdwy fnl 2f) ....¾ **4**
8106 Key To A Million (IRE) (49) (RHannon) 2-8-11 GCarter(2) (prom: edgd lft over 2f out: wknd wl over 1f out) 1½ **5**

570[6] Lady Eclat *(45) (JAGlover)* 2-8-11 RCochrane(4) (led 1f: wknd over 2f out)....1½ 6
Welsh Melody *(31) (KRBurke)* 2-8-11 ATucker(7) (small: lengthy: unf: bhd fnl 3f)....5 7

6/4 Disallowed (IRE), **9/4** TOP CAT (FR), **6/1** Honest Guest (IRE), Key To A Million (IRE) (op 7/2), **9/1** Victoria Venture (op 5/1), **25/1** Lady Eclat, **50/1** Welsh Melody, CSF £14.99 TOTE £2.40: £1.80 £3.90 (£14.80) OWNER Mrs A. Birkett (MIDDLEHAM) BRED Major C. R. and Mrs Philipson 7 Rn
1m 14.5 (3.50) SF: 16/15/2/-/-/-/-

1288

RADCLIFFE CLAIMING STKS (2-Y.O) (Class F) £2,519.00 (£694.00: £329.00)
6f 15y Stalls: High GOING minus 0.37 sec per fur (F) 3-50 (3-53)

1177[4] **Arvzees (IRE)** *(69) (MRChannon)* 2-8-12 DHarrison(2) (hld up: hdwy 2f out: swtchd lft & led over 1f out: pushed out)....— 1
1054[8] Ivory's Grab Hire *(55) (KTIvory)* 2-8-8 GDuffield(1) (a.p: led 2f out tl over 1f out: one pce)....4 2
Miss Impulse *(41) (JWharton)* 2-8-1 AMackay(4) (unf: bkwd: dwlt: sn rcvd: ev ch 2f out: one pce)....2½ 3
1090[2] Chik's Secret *(40)*(Fav)*(BPalling)* 2-8-11 TSprake(3) (nvr nr to chal)....4 4
Mazoski *(37) (PCHaslam)* 2-8-13 JFortune(7) (lengthy: bkwd: led 4f)....2 5
1082[4] Marketeer Magic *(32)*(Fav)*(JBerry)* 2-8-12 GCarter(6) (w ldr: rdn & n.m.r wl over 1f out: sn wknd)....1½ 6
782[9] Fortuitious (IRE) *(5) (JRJenkins)* 2-8-8v(3) SSanders(5) (prom: rdn 3f out: sn wknd)....10 7

3/1 Chik's Secret, Marketeer Magic, **4/1** ARVZEES (IRE) (op 2/1), **9/2** Mazoski (op 5/2), **10/1** Ivory's Grab Hire, **16/1** Miss Impulse, **20/1** Fortuitious (IRE), CSF £34.41 TOTE £2.40: £3.10 £4.50 (£27.70) OWNER . Albion Investments (UPPER LAMBOURN) BRED Topazio Est Vaduz 7 Rn
1m 15.8 (4.80) SF: -/-/-/-/-/-/-

1289

GEDLING H'CAP (0-80) (3-Y.O) (Class D) £4,036.50 (£1,206.00: £577.00: £262.50)
1m 6f 15y Stalls: High GOING minus 0.37 sec per fur (F) 4-20 (4-21)

974* **Celeric (79)***(87)*(Fav)*(DMorley)* 3-9-7 RHills(8) (hld up: 4th st: led over 1f out: drvn out)....— 1
947[4] Greycoat Boy **(60)***(66) (BJMeehan)* 3-8-2 DHarrison(9) (lw: chsd ldr: rdn & ev ch 2f out: r.o ins fnl f)....1½ 2
908[5] Carnbrea Belle (IRE) **(58)***(64) (MBell)* 3-8-0 JFanning(7) (hld up: 8th st: hdwy over 2f out: swtchd rt over 1f out: r.o one pce)....nk 3
947* Doddington Flyer **(66)***(70) (RHollinshead)* 3-8-5 (3) AGarth(10) (hld up: 5th st: hdwy 3f out: r.o one pce fnl f)....1¾ 4
947[7] Mr Mactavish **(69)***(73) (MrsJCecil)* 3-8-11 GDuffield(1) (led: hdd over 1f out: one pce)....nk 5
1029[12] Recovery Lad (IRE) **(53)***(56) (KRBurke)* 3-7-9 NKennedy(2) (hld up & plld hrd: 6th st: no hdwy fnl 2f)....½ 6
947[11] Al Corniche (IRE) **(51)***(50) (KOCunningham-Brown)* 3-7-7 NCarlisle(5) (lw: hld up: 9th st: hdwy over 3f out: wknd 2f out)....4 7
673[9] Shamekh **(64)***(62) (JEBanks)* 3-8-6 RCochrane(4) (lw: 3rd st: wknd over 2f out)....¾ 8
309[3] Shy Paddy (IRE) **(62)***(53) (KOCunningham-Brown)* 3-8-4b GCarter(3) (bit bkwd: plld hrd: 7th st: a bhd)....6 9

LONG HANDICAP Al Corniche (IRE) 7-2

6/4 CELERIC, **7/2** Doddington Flyer, **9/2** Shamekh, **13/2** Carnbrea Belle (IRE), **11/1** Greycoat Boy, **14/1** Mr Mactavish, **25/1** Shy Paddy (IRE), Al Corniche (IRE), **33/1** Recovery Lad (IRE), CSF £17.70 CT £80.11 TOTE £2.60: £1.40 £1.50 £1.80 (£10.40) Trio £72.20 OWNER Mr Christopher Spence (NEWMARKET) BRED Chieveley Manor Enterprises 9 Rn
3m 3.4 (4.90) SF: 49/28/26/32/35/18/12/24/15

1290

COLWICK MAIDEN APPRENTICE H'CAP (0-70) (3-Y.O+) (Class G)
£2,243.00 (£618.00: £293.00)
1m 54y Stalls: High GOING minus 0.37 sec per fur (F) 4-50 (4-54)

992[U] **Scent of Power (34)***(37) (MartynWane)* 5-7-8 (10)ow3 MSemple(5) (plld hrd: 6th st: led over 1f out: r.o)....— 1
730[5] Domitia (USA) **(62)***(67) (MBell)* 3-8-12 (8) GFaulkner(11) (b: hdwy on ins over 3f out: ev ch fnl 2f: r.o wl)....nk 2
174[3] Opera Fan (IRE) **(60)***(65) (SirMarkPrescott)* 3-9-4 GMitchell(2) (4th st: led over 2f out tl over 1f out: r.o)....hd 3
715[13] Miss Jemmima **(63)***(64) (LordHuntingdon)* 3-8-13 (8) AimeeCook(17) (lw: hdwy 3f out: r.o one pce fnl f)....2 4
867[3] Nunnery Grove (IRE) **(46)***(46)*(Fav)*(TThomsonJones)* 3-8-4 MHenry(14) (7th st: r.o one pce fnl 2f)....½ 5
780[19] Daring Ryde **(41)***(37) (JPSmith)* 4-8-11 ow2 LSuthern(10) (lw: hdwy on ins over 3f out: r.o one pce fnl 2f)....1¼ 6

857[10] Magical Bid (IRE) **(50)***(44) (JMBradley)* 3-8-5 (3) RWaterfield(13) (hdwy 2f out: nt rch ldrs) 2 7
1051[4] Robin Island **(62)***(56) (RHannon)* 3-9-3 (3) DaneO'Neill(4) (lw: rdn over 3f out: nvr trbld ldrs) ....nk 8
839[10] Dalcross **(43)***(35) (HJCollingridge)* 4-8-13 SLanigan(1) (s.i.s: nvr trbld ldrs) 1 9
733[16] The Cape Doctor (IRE) **(56)***(42) (AGFoster)* 3-9-0 MartinDwyer(18) (b: nvr nrr) 3 10
976[10] Honest Woman **(37)***(19) (NEBerry)* 4-8-2 (5) AdelleGibbons(12) (lw: n.d) 1¾ 11
649[15] Mr Moriarty (IRE) **(31)***(10) (SRBowring)* 4-7-12 (3) ADaly(8) (3rd st: wknd over 2f out) 1¾ 12
Highbank **(55)***(34) (MrsMReveley)* 3-8-7 (6) DDenby(19) (lw: a mid div) ....s.h 13
971[10] Can't Say (IRE) **(40)***(18) (JMBradley)* 3-7-12v CAdamson(7) (led over 5f) ....nk 14
1016[9] Cedar Dancer **(46)***(22) (RJHodges)* 3-7-13 (5) JoHunnam(20) (a bhd) 1 15
616[10] Social Register **(60)***(31) (HThomsonJones)* 3-8-10 (8) CatherineCooper(6) (plld hrd: a bhd) 3 16
817[17] Catawampus **(36)***(3) (CJames)* 4-8-1 (5) JWilkinson(3) (a bhd) 1¾ 17
1207[12] Gilpa Trinkets **(40)***(5) (DWChapman)* 3-7-7 (5) JBramhill(16) (plld hrd: 5th st: wknd over 2f out) 1 18
Prim Lass **(55)***(19) (JHetherton)* 4-9-6 (5) ALakeman(15) (2nd st: wknd over 2f out) ....½ 19
843[7] Moled Again **(30)** *(JRBosley)* 4-7-7v(7) DLockhart(9) (Withdrawn not under Starter's orders: uns rdr & bolted bef s) .... W

, **7/2** Nunnery Grove (IRE) (4/1-6/1), **9/2** Opera Fan (IRE) (5/1-65/1), **6/1** Robin Island (op 4/1), **10/1** Domitia (USA) (7/1-11/1), **12/1** Dalcross (op 8/1), Cedar Dancer, Highbank, **14/1** Miss Jemmima, Mr Moriarty (IRE), **16/1** Prim Lass, **20/1** Social Register, Magical Bid (IRE), The Cape Doctor (IRE), SCENT OF POWER, **25/1** Honest Woman, **33/1** Daring Ryde, Gilpa Trinkets, Can't Say (IRE), Catawampus, CSF £206.21 CT £981.05 TOTE £31.70: £4.00 £2.20 £1.70 £3.90 (£239.90) Trio £398.50; £347.99 to Haydock 27/5/95 OWNER Mr James Kennerley (RICHMOND) BRED M. Yiapatos 19 Rn 1m 44.9 (5.30) SF: 6/24/22/21/3/6/1/13/4/-/-/-/-/-/-/-/-/-/-

WEIGHT FOR AGE 3yo-12lb

T/Jkpt: Not won; £3,362.49 to Haydock 27/5/95. T/Plpt: £153.80 (84.61 Tckts). T/Qdpt: £148.40 (0.65 Tckts); £70.23 to Haydock 27/5/95. KH

0836-PONTEFRACT (L-H)
Friday May 26th (Good)

WEATHER: Overcast and cloudy

1291 COURSE BOOKMAKERS CLAIMING STKS (4-Y.O+) (Class F) £3,083.50 (£856.00: £410.50) **1m 4y** Stalls: Low GOING minus 0.39 sec per fur (F) 6-45 (6-47)

1092[5] **Rafter-J (54)***(55) (JAHarris)* 4-8-7 KFallon(10) (bhd: drvn along 5f out: hdwy u.p 3f out: styd on wl to ld nr fin) ....— 1
784[4] Once More for Luck (IRE) **(70)***(58) (MrsMReveley)* 4-8-11 KDarley(2) (lw: trckd ldrs: squeezed thro on ins to ld over 1f out: hdd & no ex towards fin) ....nk 2
*1074** Reported (IRE) **(71)***(50) (BPreece)* 6-8-8 LDettori(3) (a in tch: ev ch 1f out: kpt on same pce) 2½ 3
1191[2] Roseate Lodge **(64)***(46)*(Fav)*(KRBurke)* 9-8-7 ow2 TIves(6) (lw: hld up: hdwy 3f out: n.m.r over 1f out: swtchd & styd on) ....¾ 4
929[7] Our Main Man *(60) (RMWhitaker)* 5-9-7 ACulhane(9) (trckd ldrs: led wl over 1f out: sn hdd: one pce) 1 5
Daawe (USA) **(85)***(42) (MrsVAAconley)* 4-8-11 MDeering(11) (hld up & bhd: styd on fnl 2f: nvr nr ldrs) 4 6
539[15] Brother Barnabas *(34) (CWThornton)* 4-8-7 DeanMcKeown(8) (hld up & bhd: stdy hdwy 3f out: nvr nr to chal) 2 7
1092[12] Nakita **(55)***(26) (CNAllen)* 4-8-0 EJohnson(7) (b.hind: in tch: effrt 3f out: wknd 2f out) ....¾ 8
1191[6] Level Edge **(50)***(22) (MDHammond)* 4-8-1 DaleGibson(13) (chsd ldrs tl rdn & wknd 2f out) ..2½ 9
984[18] Out of the Mist **(36)***(28) (JAPickering)* 4-8-10b NCarlisle(14) (led tl hdd wl over 1f out: sn wknd) 1½ 10
848[17] Honest Achiever (IRE) **(30)** *(APJames)* 4-8-0b FNorton(4) (chsd ldrs to ½-wy: sn wl bhd: t.o)20 11
Kenilworth Ford **(34)** *(FJO'Mahony)* 4-8-6 JFanning(12) (chsd ldrs tl wknd qckly over 3f out: sn bhd: t.o) ....s.h 12
1061[9] Pharazini **(67)** *(MJCamacho)* 4-8-8 LCharnock(1) (s.s: virtually ref to r: t.n.p) .... R
777W Bali Tender *(MWEasterby)* 4-8-8 ow1 MBirch(5) (Withdrawn not under Starter's orders: v.unruly in stalls) .... W

, **11/4** Roseate Lodge (op 5/1), **3/1** Reported (IRE), **9/2** Once More for Luck (IRE), **9/1** Pharazini (op 6/1), RAFTER-J, **10/1** Daawe (USA), **12/1** Nakita, **16/1** Level Edge, **25/1** Our Main Man, **40/1** Honest Achiever (IRE), Kenilworth Ford, Out of the Mist, Brother Barnabas, CSF £47.74 TOTE £17.20: £2.60 £1.60 £1.80 (£37.20) Trio £30.80 OWNER Mr W. Meah (SOUTHWELL) BRED P. K. J. and Mrs Brightwell 13 Rn 1m 46.0 (4.00) SF: 23/26/18/14/28/10/2/-/-/-/-/-/-

Roseate Lodge clmd DMaloney £4,000

1292

NORTHERN RACING SCHOOL H'CAP (0-70) (3-Y.O+) (Class E) £3,552.75 (£1,062.00: £508.50: £231.75)
1m 2f 6y Stalls: Low GOING minus 0.39 sec per fur (F) 7-10 (7-15)

Straw Thatch (46)*(54) (MrsJRRamsden)* 6-8-8 KFallon(5) (lw: hld up: effrt 3f out: styd on to ld ins fnl f: all out) — 1
988* Larn Fort **(54)***(61) (CWFairhurst)* 5-9-2v RCochrane(2) (chsd ldrs: styd on u.p fnl 2f: nt qckn nr fin) ½ 2
988 12 Benjamins Law **(50)***(57) (JAPickering)* 4-8-12 DeanMcKeown(7) (led: clr 7f out: hdd ins fnl f: no ex) hd 3
988 17 Kanat Lee (IRE) **(41)***(47) (DonEnricoIncisa)* 4-8-3 KimTinkler(9) (s.i.s: bhd tl hdwy 3f out: styd on wl ins fnl f: fin wl) ¾ 4
*1029*10 Charlie Bigtime **(49)***(50) (DTThom)* 5-8-11v AMackay(11) (sn drvn along: wnt prom 5f out: outpcd 2f out: kpt on u.p) 3 5
*121*3 Sudden Spin **(43)***(41)*(Fav)*(SGNorton)* 5-8-0 (5)ow3 JStack(6) (hld up gng wl: stdy hdwy 3f out: rdn & outpcd 2f out: kpt on fnl f) nk 6
1064 2 Augustan **(58)***(56) (SGollings)* 4-9-6v DHolland(12) (lw: hld up & bhd: effrt 2f out: kpt on: nvr nr ldrs) 1½ 7
1109 6 Achilles Heel **(50)***(44) (CNAllen)* 4-8-12 TIves(4) (bhd: hdwy on outside 2f out: nvr rchd ldrs) 2½ 8
Master Ofthe House **(62)***(48) (MDHammond)* 9-9-10 JMarshall(1) (hld up & plld hrd: stdy hdwy 3f out: wknd over 1f out) 5 9
Fort Vally **(43)***(18) (BWMurray)* 5-8-5 SMaloney(3) (trckd ldrs: plld hrd: drvn along & lost pl 3f out: sn bhd) 7 10
*349*9 Brackenthwaite **(47)***(21) (LRLloyd-James)* 5-8-2 (7) KimberleyHart(8) (b.hind: chsd ldrs tl lost pl over 5f out) ¾ 11
848 15 Allimac Nomis **(35)** *(ICampbell)* 6-7-11 DaleGibson(10) (trckd ldrs: plld hrd: lost pl 3f out: sn bhd) 10 12

7/2 Sudden Spin, **9/2** Larn Fort, **6/1** Achilles Heel, **7/1** Charlie Bigtime, STRAW THATCH, **8/1** Augustan, Master Ofthe House, **12/1** Benjamins Law, **16/1** Fort Vally, **20/1** Brackenthwaite, **25/1** Kanat Lee (IRE), **33/1** Allimac Nomis, CSF £38.35 CT £351.43 TOTE £17.10: £3.60 £2.00 £3.80 (£30.30) Trio £127.30 OWNER Mr David McKenzie (THIRSK) BRED Sheikh Mohammed bin Rashid al Maktoum 12 Rn 2m 14.8 (6.50) SF: 13/20/16/6/9/-/15/3/7/-/-/-

1293

TOTE STKS (2-Y.O F) (Class C) £4,981.80 (£1,816.80: £888.40: £382.00: £171.00)
6f Stalls: Low GOING minus 0.39 sec per fur (F) 7-35 (7-35)

669* **Incarvillea (USA)** *(90+)*(Fav)*(DRLoder)* 2-8-12 LDettori(4) (lw: led over 2f: shkn up to ld over 1f out: r.o strly: readily) — 1
993* Kunucu (IRE) *(84) (TDBarron)* 2-9-0 KDarley(2) (w wnr: plld hrd: led over 3f out tl over 1f out: eased whn hld) 3 2
1137 2 Satellite Star (IRE) *(69) (MRChannon)* 2-8-8 DHarrison(1) (trckd ldrs: effrt over 2f out: kpt on same pce) 3½ 3
819 3 Butterwick Belle (IRE) *(66) (RAFahey)* 2-8-8 ACulhane(5) (b: chsd ldrs: effrt over 2f out: sn wl outpcd) 1 4
1082 2 Gagajulu *(59) (PDEvans)* 2-8-8 JFortune(3) (trckd ldrs: effrt over 2f out: sn rdn & no imp) 2½ 5

4/5 INCARVILLEA (USA) (op Evens), **11/4** Kunucu (IRE), **4/1** Satellite Star (IRE), **16/1** Butterwick Belle (IRE), **20/1** Gagajulu, CSF £3.42 TOTE £1.70: £1.10 £1.70 (£2.00) OWNER Sheikh Mohammed (NEWMARKET) BRED Darley Stud Management Inc 5 Rn
1m 18.0 (3.70) SF: 17/11/-/-/-

1294

WILLIAM HILL H'CAP (0-80) (3-Y.O) (Class D) £3,915.00 (£1,170.00: £560.00: £255.00) **1m 4y** Stalls: Low GOING minus 0.39 sec per fur (F) 8-05 (8-06)

1130 2 **Shinerolla (66)***(71+)*(Fav)*(MrsJRRamsden)* 3-9-1 KFallon(3) (lw: stdd s: hld up & bhd: stdy hdwy over 3f out: effrt over 1f out: qcknd to ld jst ins fnl f: eased towards fin) — 1
1124 2 Danegold (IRE) **(67)***(70) (MRChannon)* 3-9-2v DHarrison(6) (chsd ldr: rdn & wnt lft over 1f out: kpt on: no ch w wnr) 1 2
Juweilla **(67)***(67) (JWPayne)* 3-9-2 GBardwell(4) (trckd ldr: ev ch & edgd rt u.p over 1f out: kpt on same pce) 1¾ 3
Trumble **(55)***(54) (CWThornton)* 3-8-4 AMackay(1) (led tl jst ins fnl f: one pce) ½ 4
Prince's Feather (IRE) **(72)***(61) (DMorley)* 3-9-7 LDettori(5) (unruly in stalls: hld up & plld hrd: effrt over 2f out: wknd over 1f out) 5 5
995 8 Chadleigh Lane (USA) **(59)***(34) (RHollinshead)* 3-8-8 KDarley(2) (hld up: effrt over 3f out: sn drvn along: wknd wl over 1f out) 7 6

10/11 SHINEROLLA, **11/4** Prince's Feather (IRE), **6/1** Danegold (IRE), **7/1** Juweilla, **14/1** Chadleigh Lane (USA), **33/1** Trumble, CSF £6.79 TOTE £1.90: £1.30 £2.20 (£2.90) OWNER Mrs Alison Iles (THIRSK) BRED Lord Vestey 6 Rn
1m 47.2 (5.20) SF: 19/18/15/2/9/-

1295 NRS LIBRARY H'CAP (0-70) (3-Y.O+) (Class E) £3,699.00 (£1,107.00: £531.00: £243.00) **1m 4f 8y** Stalls: Low GOING minus 0.39 sec per fur (F) 8-35 (8-35)

*37*5 **Admirals Secret (USA)** **(55)***(63) (CFWall)* 6-9-0 NCarlisle(6) (lw: hld up mid div: stdy hdwy over 3f out: led 2f out: drvn out)......— 1
9482 Advance East **(66)***(71)*(Fav)*(MrsJRRamsden)* 3-8-7 KFallon(3) (lw: hld up & bhd: stdy hdwy 3f out: rdn over 1f out: kpt on: nvr able to chal)......2 2
103713 Muzrak (CAN) **(55)***(55) (MDHammond)* 4-9-0 TIves(8) (hld up & bhd: hdwy 3f out: kpt on appr fnl f: nvr nr to chal)......4 3
College Don **(55)***(52) (MPBielby)* 4-9-0 RCochrane(11) (trckd ldrs: plld hrd: one pce fnl 2f).....2 4
11603 Mac Rambler **(34)***(27) (NBycroft)* 8-7-7 NKennedy(10) (s.i.s: hld up & bhd: styd on fnl 2f: nvr nr to chal)......3½ 5
1200* Rasayel (USA) **(50)***(42) (PDEvans)* 5-8-9 5x KDarley(7) (hld up: hdwy 5f out: effrt over 2f out: nvr rchd ldrs)......nk 6
Eid (USA) **(69)***(59) (MrsSJSmith)* 6-10-0 DeanMcKeown(4) (led 2f: chsd ldr tl lost pl 3f out)....2 7
10397 Abalene **(39)***(26) (TWDonnelly)* 6-7-12 JFanning(13) (w ldrs: led over 3f out to 2f out: sn wknd)......1¾ 8
7514 Northern Kingdom (USA) **(48)***(19) (SGNorton)* 6-8-7 JFortune(5) (plld hrd: trckd ldrs: led over 5f out tl over 3f out: sn wknd)......12 9
10154 Late Mail (USA) **(66)***(33) (JMPEustace)* 3-8-7 MTebbutt(2) (a in rr)......3 10
87412 Fryup Satellite **(37)** *(LRLloyd-James)* 4-7-10bow3 MDeering(1) (b: plld hrd: sn in tch: lost pl over 4f out: sn bhd)......6 11
Escape Talk **(34)** *(JDooler)* 8-7-7 GBardwell(12) (sn bhd & drvn along: n.d)......3½ 12
99818 Clurican (IRE) **(50)** *(NTinkler)* 6-8-9b LDettori(9) (led after 2f tl over 5f out: sn lost pl)......4 13

LONG HANDICAP Mac Rambler 7-3 Fryup Satellite 7-3 Escape Talk 6-3

13/8 Advance East, **3/1** Rasayel (USA), **7/1** Northern Kingdom (USA), **10/1** ADMIRALS SECRET (USA), **11/1** Mac Rambler, **14/1** Eid (USA), Clurican (IRE), **16/1** Abalene, Late Mail (USA), **20/1** Muzrak (CAN), **33/1** College Don, **50/1** Fryup Satellite, **100/1** Escape Talk, CSF £26.87 CT £320.91 TOTE £10.40: £2.90 £1.70 £4.30 (£11.70) Trio £71.00 OWNER Mrs C. A. Wall (NEWMARKET) BRED Haras Santa Maria de Araras & Peter M. Brant 13 Rn
2m 37.9 (3.60) SF: 45/35/37/34/9/24/41/8/1/-/-/-/-
WEIGHT FOR AGE 3yo-18lb

1296 FRIENDS OF THE NORTHERN RACING SCHOOL MAIDEN STKS (3-Y.O) (Class D) £3,793.75 (£1,150.00: £562.50: £268.75) **6f** Stalls: Low GOING minus 0.39 sec per fur (F) 9-05 (9-05)

6582 **Twice as Sharp** **(85)***(83)*(Fav)*(PWHarris)* 3-9-0 RCochrane(6) (lw: mde all: drvn out)......— 1
8655 Khamseh **(77)***(78) (JWWatts)* 3-8-9 LDettori(5) (b.hind: a in tch: hdwy over 1f out: styd on wl u.p ins fnl f)......hd 2
9375 Intiaash (IRE) **(77)***(78) (PTWalwyn)* 3-8-9 RHills(2) (lw: a chsng ldrs: effrt & hung lft over 1f out: ev ch ins fnl f: nt qckn towards fin)......s.h 3
Mr Teigh *(76) (KMcAuliffe)* 3-8-11 (3) JTate(4) (a chsng ldrs: kpt on same pce appr fnl f)......2½ 4
Firm Contract (IRE) *(60) (CNAllen)* 3-9-0 TIves(7) (chsd ldrs tl wknd over 2f out)......6 5
9557 Bedouin Invader **(76)***(59) (MRStoute)* 3-9-0 DHolland(11) (lw: in tch: rdn over 2f out: no imp)......nk 6
Pumice *(53) (LMCumani)* 3-8-9 KDarley(3) (prom: outpcd & drvn along 2f out: sn wknd)......½ 7
Me Cherokee *(46) (CWThornton)* 3-8-9 DeanMcKeown(8) (w'like: scope: leggy: dwlt s: bhd tl kpt on appr fnl f)......2½ 8
7583 Harry's Treat *(46) (JLEyre)* 3-8-9 JFortune(12) (prom tl lost pl over 2f out)......hd 9
10947 Forzair **(76)***(38) (MMcCormack)* 3-9-0 KFallon(10) (effrt u.p over 2f out: sn wknd)......5 10
Handsome Squaw *(27) (BWMurray)* 3-8-9 SMaloney(1) (bkwd: b: a in rr)......2 11
*844*6 Donna Fugata (IRE) *(25) (CBBBooth)* 3-8-9 MBirch(9) (sn pushed along: in tch tl lost pl ½-wy: sn bhd)......¾ 12
Irish Angel (IRE) **(48)** *(CSmith)* 3-8-4 (5) JStack(13) (b.hind: swvd rt s: prom over 3f: sn lost pl)......12 13

11/4 TWICE AS SHARP, **7/2** Pumice, **4/1** Intiaash (IRE), **6/1** Khamseh, **9/1** Forzair, **10/1** Bedouin Invader, Mr Teigh, **14/1** Firm Contract (IRE), **16/1** Harry's Treat, **50/1** Me Cherokee, Handsome Squaw, Donna Fugata (IRE), Irish Angel (IRE), CSF £20.54 TOTE £3.40: £1.10 £2.80 £2.20 (£14.20) Trio £9.30 OWNER Formula Twelve (BERKHAMSTED) BRED R. and A. Craddock 13 Rn
1m 16.5 (2.20) SF: 38/33/33/31/15/14/8/1/1/-/-/-/-

T/Plpt: £11.60 (1,461.41 Tckts). T/Qdpt: £2.50 (34.95 Tckts). WG

0983-**DONCASTER (L-H)**
Saturday May 27th (Good)
WEATHER: sunny periods and warm WIND: fresh against

1297 RACING SCHOOLS FURNITURE FACTORS LTD APPRENTICE H'CAP (0-70) (4-Y.O+) (Class F) £2,785.00 (£850.00: £420.00: £205.00)
7f Stalls: High GOING minus 0.13 sec per fur (G) 2-20 (2-20)

Glowing Jade (65)(79)(Fav)*(MissGayKelleway)* 5-9-9 RPainter(3) (trckd ldrs: led on bit over 2f out: hung rt: styd on)......— 1
927[6] Sycamore Lodge (IRE) **(65)***(78) (PCalver)* 4-9-9 AGarth(6) (hdwy ½-wy: ev ch 2f out: carried rt: kpt on towards fin)......½ 2
874[13] Kilnamartyra Girl **(42)***(39) (JParkes)* 5-7-6 (8) DLockhart(9) (effrt & hung lft ½-wy: racd alone far side: styd on: no imp)......7 3
839[6] Johnnie the Joker **(57)***(54) (JPLeigh)* 4-8-11b(4) GMitchell(5) (chsd ldrs: one pce fnl 2½f)......hd 4
1076[6] At the Savoy (IRE) **(46)***(38) (TDBarron)* 4-8-0b(4) KimberleyHart(13) (effrt stands' side ½-wy: nvr rchd ldrs)......2 5
976* Aitch N'Bee **(60)***(46) (LadyHerries)* 12-8-10 (8) RSmith(7) (racd stands' side: sn pushed along: n.d)......2½ 6
1043[5] Densben **(49)***(32) (DenysSmith)* 11-8-7 CTeague(4) (a chsng ldrs: no imp)......1½ 7
Canny Lad **(36)***(17) (MPBielby)* 5-7-4v(4)ow1 SLanigan(12) (cl up 3f: sn bhd: styd on again fnl f)......nk 8
972* Plum First **(60)***(42) (LRLloyd-James)* 5-9-4 SMulvey(10) (b.hind: nvr wnt pce)......s.h 9
877[9] Panther (IRE) **(60)***(39) (JHetherton)* 5-9-0 (4) ALakeman(15) (racd stands' side: nvr trbld ldrs)......1¼ 10
1157* Aquado **(56)***(34) (ALForbes)* 6-8-10 (4) DDenby(1) (cl up: led ½-wy tl over 2f out: sn wknd)......½ 11
1034[12] Titanium Honda (IRE) **(41)***(15) (CEBrittain)* 4-7-9 (4)ow1 JWilkinson(8) (chsd ldrs over 4f)......1¼ 12
1088[13] Shotley Again **(35)***(7) (NBycroft)* 5-7-7 MBaird(11) (n.d)......1¼ 13
1080* Broctune Gold **(68)***(39) (MrsMReveley)* 4-9-12 SCopp(2) (led to ½-wy: sn rdn & btn)......¾ 14
992[2] Al Wujud (IRE) **(44)** *(TDyer)* 4-8-2 SSanders(14) (Withdrawn not under Starter's orders)...... W

LONG HANDICAP Shotley Again 6-10 Canny Lad 7-4

5/1 GLOWING JADE (op 8/1), **11/2** Broctune Gold, Sycamore Lodge (IRE), **6/1** Aquado, **9/1** At the Savoy (IRE), **10/1** Aitch N'Bee, Johnnie the Joker, **12/1** Kilnamartyra Girl, Plum First, **14/1** Panther (IRE), Titanium Honda (IRE), Densben, **20/1** Canny Lad, **25/1** Shotley Again, CSF £33.85 CT £303.39 TOTE £6.40: £1.90 £2.20 £3.90 (£7.60) Trio £115.90 OWNER Mr Brian Eastick (WHITCOMBE) BRED F. C. T. Wilson 14 Rn 1m 26.29 (2.89) SF: 61/60/21/36/20/28/14/-/24/21/16/-/-/21

1298 E.B.F. ZETLAND MAIDEN STKS (2-Y.O) (Class D) £4,581.00 (£1,368.00: £654.00: £297.00) **6f** Stalls: High GOING minus 0.13 sec per fur (G) 2-55 (2-55)

Mushahid (USA) *(89+?) (JLDunlop)* 2-9-0 WRyan(3) (gd sort: s.i.s: r.o to ld ins fnl f)......— 1
Arajaan (USA) *(85)*(Fav)*(BHanbury)* 2-9-0 MRimmer(5) (cmpt: lw: trckd ldrs: rdn to ld jst ins fnl f: sn hdd: no ex)......1½ 2
825[4] Galapino *(84) (CEBrittain)* 2-9-0 RCochrane(6) (hld up: stdy hdwy & swtchd over 1f out: r.o: nvr plcd to chal)......nk 3
1011[3] Caricature (IRE) *(76)*(Fav)*(GLewis)* 2-9-0 SWhitworth(4) (led: qcknd ½-wy: hdd & no ex jst ins fnl f)......3 4
Swing Mania (IRE) *(39) (SGNorton)* 2-8-9 KDarley(2) (neat: unf: spd to ½-wy: hung lft & sn wknd)......12 5
Kuwam (IRE) *(42) (JBerry)* 2-9-0 SDWilliams(1) (w'like: leggy: scope: outpcd fr ½-wy)......1 6

9/4 Caricature (IRE), Arajaan (USA), **9/2** Galapino, **5/1** MUSHAHID (USA) (3/1-11/2), **7/1** Kuwam (IRE) (op 9/2), **12/1** Swing Mania (IRE) (op 8/1), CSF £16.34 TOTE £5.40: £2.40 £1.80 (£7.90) OWNER Mr Hamdan Al Maktoum (ARUNDEL) BRED Courtney and Congleton 6 Rn
1m 15.07 (4.07) SF: 31/27/26/18/-/-

1299 MERLIN LAND ROVER H'CAP (0-100) (3-Y.O+) (Class C) £7,635.00 (£2,280.00: £1,090.00: £495.00) **7f** Stalls: High GOING minus 0.13 sec per fur (G) 3-25 (3-26)

922[4] **Elfland (IRE) (77)***(88)*(Fav)*(LadyHerries)* 4-8-12 KDarley(2) (lw: b: a.p: led 2f out: r.o wl)......— 1
870[9] Tawafij (USA) **(80)***(84) (TDyer)* 6-9-1 JFortune(10) (lw: hld up & bhd: swtchd & hdwy 2f out: r.o: no ch w wnr)......3 2
927[3] Castel Rosselo **(84)***(88) (BJMcMath)* 5-9-5 AMackay(8) (hdwy 2f out: styd on: nt pce to chal)nk 3
1179* Celestial Key (USA) **(93)***(94) (MJohnston)* 5-10-0 TWilliams(6) (lw: chsd ldrs: led over 2f out: sn hdd & one pce)......1¼ 4
1131[5] Fame Again **(73)***(73) (MrsJRRamsden)* 3-7-11 JFanning(12) (lw: hld up & bhd: nt clr run over 2f out tl ins fnl f: fin fast)......nk 5

812³ First Gold **(63)***(62) (JWharton)* 6-7-12 SMaloney(7) (lw: effrt 3f out: styd on: no imp) ....½ 6
1130⁸ Sticks and Stones (IRE) **(83)***(82) (MrsJCecil)* 3-8-7 RCochrane(3) (cl up: chal 3f out: wknd fnl 2f: eased fnl f) ....hd 7
928⁴ Tatika **(72)***(67) (GWragg)* 5-8-7 WRyan(5) (cl up tl outpcd over 2f out: sn btn) 1½ 8
1179³ Sarmatian (USA) **(64)***(59) (MDHammond)* 4-7-13 DaleGibson(9) (chsd ldrs tl wknd over 2f out) ....hd 9
1021¹⁰ Sagebrush Roller **(85)***(77) (JWWatts)* 7-9-6 NConnorton(4) (lw: hld up & bhd: effrt 3f out: no imp) 1¼ 10
1131¹⁰ Mister Fire Eyes (IRE) **(80)***(70) (CEBrittain)* 3-8-4 DHarrison(11) (lw: led tl hdd & wknd over 2f out) ....¾ 11
Petite-D-Argent **(78)***(41) (TDyer)* 6-8-10 (3) SSanders(1) (racd alone far side: prom tl rdn & wknd wl over 2f out) 12 12

100/30 ELFLAND (IRE), **9/2** Fame Again, **5/1** Celestial Key (USA), **8/1** Castel Rosselo, Tatika, Sticks and Stones (IRE), Sagebrush Roller, **10/1** Tawafij (USA), **11/1** Sarmatian (USA), **16/1** First Gold, **20/1** Mister Fire Eyes (IRE), **33/1** Petite-D-Argent, CSF £38.02 CT £242.00 TOTE £4.60: £1.90 £4.40 £3.10 (£34.70) Trio £74.90 OWNER Mr Michael Broke (LITTLEHAMPTON) BRED A. Tarry 12 Rn 1m 27.05 (3.65) SF: 42/38/42/48/16/16/25/21/13/31/13/-

WEIGHT FOR AGE 3yo-11lb

1300 HAREWOOD RATED STKS H'CAP (0-95) (4-Y.O+) (Class B) £8,107.00 (£3,013.00: £1,456.50: £607.50: £253.75: £112.25)

2m 110y Stalls: Low GOING minus 0.13 sec per fur (G) 3-55 (3-57)

1144² **Trans Siberia (80)***(91)*(Fav)*(SPCWoods)* 4-8-9 WRyan(6) (a.p: disp ld 3f out: styd on gamely to ld cl home) ....— 1
998⁴ New Reputation **(87)***(98) (BWHills)* 4-9-2b KDarley(2) (lw: trckd ldrs: disp ld 3f out: hrd rdn: no ex towards fin) ....hd 2
998⁸ Noufari (FR) **(75)***(85) (RHollinshead)* 4-8-4 DHarrison(5) (hld up: effrt appr st: disp ld 2f out: wknd towards fin) ....½ 3
1109* Midyan Blue (IRE) **(74)***(75) (JMPEustace)* 5-8-5 RCochrane(3) (lw: chsd ldr: chal 6f out: wknd fnl 3f) 10 4
1109⁵ Halkopous **(85)***(85) (MHTompkins)* 9-8-11v(5) SMulvey(1) (lw: dwlt: rdn 6f out: sn lost tch) ......½ 5
Tethys (USA) **(92)***(83) (JLEyre)* 4-9-7 JFortune(4) (led tl hdd 3f out: wknd) 10 6

LONG HANDICAP Noufari (FR) 8-2

13/8 TRANS SIBERIA, **9/4** New Reputation, **4/1** Midyan Blue (IRE), **6/1** Halkopous, **9/1** Tethys (USA), **12/1** Noufari (FR), CSF £6.05 TOTE £2.40: £1.70 £1.80 (£3.20) OWNER Mr H. Laska (NEWMARKET) BRED I. A. Southcott 6 Rn 3m 38.68 (9.68) SF: 37/44/31/23/33/29

WEIGHT FOR AGE 4yo-2lb

1301 DONCASTER SUNDAY MARKET CONDITIONS STKS (3-Y.O) (Class B) £8,397.00 (£3,123.00: £1,511.50: £632.50: £266.25: £119.75)

1m 2f 60y Stalls: Low GOING minus 0.13 sec per fur (G) 4-25 (4-26)

Don Corleone (113)*(113) (RCharlton)* 3-9-5 DHarrison(6) (lw: hld up: hdwy to disp ld over 2f out: styd on wl cl home) ....— 1
1129² Minds Music (USA) *(107)*(Fav)*(HRACecil)* 3-8-13 WRyan(2) (lw: cl up: disp ld over 2f out tl over 1f out: rallied to disp ld wl ins fnl f: kpt on) ....s.h 2
Traikey (IRE) *(106) (JEBanks)* 3-8-13 RCochrane(5) (lw: trckd ldrs: disp ld over 2f out: no ex ins fnl f) ....¾ 3
Alanar (USA) *(94) (PFICole)* 3-9-3 JFortune(3) (b: prom tl outpcd fnl 2½f) 10 4
Wakeel (USA) **(97)***(85) (EALDunlop)* 3-8-13 KDarley(1) (bhd: drvn along 4f out: no imp) 3½ 5
963* Tertium (IRE) *(80) (PWChapple-Hyam)* 3-8-13 RHavlin(4) (lw: led tl hdd & wknd over 2f out) .3 6

8/11 Minds Music (USA) (op Evens), **11/4** Traikey (IRE), **11/2** DON CORLEONE, **11/1** Tertium (IRE), **12/1** Alanar (USA) (op 8/1), **14/1** Wakeel (USA), CSF £10.65 TOTE £6.80: £2.80 £1.10 (£4.00) OWNER Mr Wafic Said (BECKHAMPTON) BRED Ridgecourt Stud 6 Rn

2m 9.5 (2.50) SF: 73/67/66/54/45/40

1302 RIFLE BUTTS MEDIAN AUCTION MAIDEN STKS (3-Y.O) (Class E) £3,172.50 (£945.00: £450.00: £202.50)

5f Stalls: High GOING minus 0.13 sec per fur (G) 4-55 (4-56)

1040⁸ **Surprise Mission** *(69) (RMWhitaker)* 3-9-0 ACulhane(2) (lw: in tch: effrt 2f out: r.o to ld wl ins fnl f) ....— 1
772⁶ Premium Gift *(62)*(Fav)*(CBBBooth)* 3-8-9 MBirch(1) (lw: led: clr ½-wy: rdn 1f out: hdd & no ex towards fin) ....½ 2
937⁹ Mousehole **(52)***(66) (RGuest)* 3-9-0 KDarley(6) (chsd ldrs: ev ch 1f out: nt qckn) ....½ 3

1040³ Never Say so **(59)**(32) (CSmith) 3-8-9 JFortune(7) (prom: outpcd ½-wy: no imp after) 9 **4**
966¹⁸ Saltz (IRE) **(64)**(31) (PTDalton) 3-9-0 LCharnock(5) (chsd ldr over 3f) 2 **5**
Super Look (25) (TJEtherington) 3-8-9 RCochrane(4) (w'like: scope: bkwd: wnt rt & s.s: wl bhd tl styd on fnl f) ....nk **6**
1033⁹ Sizzling Romp **(70)**(20) (DTThom) 3-8-6 (3) DRMcCabe(8) (nvr trbld ldrs) 1½ **7**
Cinders Chance (MWEllerby) 3-8-9 SMorris(3) (wnt rt s: a outpcd & wl bhd) 15 **8**

15/8 Premium Gift, **4/1** Never Say so (op 5/2), **9/2** SURPRISE MISSION (3/1-5/1), **7/1** Mousehole, Super Look, **15/2** Sizzling Romp, **10/1** Saltz (IRE), **25/1** Cinders Chance, CSF £13.73 TOTE £6.70: £2.30 £1.30 £2.10 (£8.30) OWNER Mr D. R. Brotherton (LEEDS) BRED D. R. Brotherton 8 Rn
61.43 secs (3.03) SF: 34/27/31/-/-/-/-/-

1303

ROSEHILL H'CAP (0-85) (3-Y.O+) (Class D) £4,425.00 (£1,320.00: £630.00: £285.00) **1m 4f** Stalls: Low GOING minus 0.13 sec per fur (G) 5-25 (5-25)

935⁸ **Chatham Island (64)**(77) (CEBrittain) 7-8-7 RCochrane(4) (mde all: qcknd ent st: sn clr: styd on strly) ....— **1**
956² Swallows Dream (IRE) **(82)**(90)(Fav)(JLDunlop) 4-9-11 KDarley(6) (lw: hld up & bhd: hdwy ent st: sn rdn: styd on fnl f: no ch w wnr) 4 **2**
1102² Blue Blazer **(78)**(84) (BHanbury) 5-9-2 (5) JStack(1) (in tch: hdwy ent st: sn pushed along: styd on one pce) 1½ **3**
756⁵ Manful **(82)**(87) (JHetherton) 3-8-7 NKennedy(2) (in tch tl outpcd ent st: styd on fnl f) ....¾ **4**
1022⁴ Lookingforarainbow (IRE) **(73)**(76) (BobJones) 7-9-2 MWigham(3) (lw: trckd ldrs: wnt 2nd appr st: outpcd fnl 3f) 1¼ **5**
815⁸ Innocence **(68)**(71) (GWragg) 3-7-7 NCarlisle(5) (lw: chsd wnr tl outpcd appr st: no imp after) ....nk **6**
1064* Hazard a Guess (IRE) **(79)**(78) (MrsJRRamsden) 5-9-8 KFallon(7) (lw: hld up & bhd: effrt 4f out: n.d) 2½ **7**

11/4 Swallows Dream (IRE), **7/2** Hazard a Guess (IRE), **4/1** Blue Blazer, Lookingforarainbow (IRE), **13/2** CHATHAM ISLAND, **7/1** Innocence, **20/1** Manful, CSF £24.42 TOTE £8.40: £3.00 £1.60 (£13.00) OWNER Mr B. H. Voak (NEWMARKET) BRED G. C. Hughes 7 Rn
2m 34.97 (4.37) SF: 52/65/59/44/51/28/53
WEIGHT FOR AGE 3yo-18lb

T/Plpt: £42.50 (488.26 Tckts). T/Qdpt: £10.70 (16.65 Tckts). AA

1278-HAYDOCK (L-H)
Saturday May 27th (Good to soft)
WEATHER: dry & overcast WIND: fresh half behind

1304

BE FRIENDLY H'CAP (0-90) (3-Y.O+) (Class C) £5,706.00 (£1,728.00: £844.00: £402.00) **5f** Stalls: High GOING minus 0.02 sec per fur (G) 2-00 (2-01)

1106¹³ **Lord High Admiral (CAN) (86)**(95) (MJHeaton-Ellis) 7-10-0v MRoberts(15) (swtg: lw: mde all stands' side: clr appr fnl f: r.o) ....— **1**
1193² Name the Tune **(76)**(77)(Fav)(PHowling) 4-9-4b PaulEddery(1) (b.hind: lw: racd far side: chsd ldrs: rdn & kpt on wl ins fnl f) 2½ **2**
I'm Your Lady **(74)**(75) (BAMcMahon) 4-8-11 (5) PMcCabe(13) (bit bkwd: chsd wnr stands' side: rdn & no ex ins fnl f) ....s.h **3**
856² Canovas Heart **(61)**(58) (BobJones) 6-8-3 GDuffield(5) (led far side tl ins fnl f) 1¼ **4**
434¹⁴ Ansellman **(75)**(67) (JBerry) 5-9-3 JCarroll(16) (bit bkwd: chsd ldrs stands' side: no hdwy fnl 2f) 1½ **5**
1106⁸ Croft Imperial **(65)**(56) (MJohnston) 8-8-7 JWeaver(12) (hld up stands' side: r.o ins fnl f: nrst fin) ....nk **6**
1193⁶ Beau Venture (USA) **(72)**(58) (FHLee) 7-9-0 RLappin(11) (chsd ldrs: rdn over 1f out: nvr able chal) 1½ **7**
1265⁷ One for Jeannie **(67)**(50) (ABailey) 3-8-0vow2 GCarter(2) (s.i.s: hdwy 2f out: kpt on fnl f) ....nk **8**
1214* King Rambo **(73)**(54) (RHollinshead) 4-9-1 7x TIves(17) (drvn along stands' side: nvr rchd ldrs) 1¼ **9**
1019⁹ Lord Sky **(65)**(46) (ABailey) 4-8-2b(5) VHalliday(3) (prom far side: rdn 2f out: sn btn) ....hd **10**
1152⁷ Sonderise **(51)**(30) (NTinkler) 6-7-7 KimTinkler(10) (chsd ldrs stands' side over 3f: sn lost tch: b.b.v) ....½ **11**
1157³ Serious Hurry **(51)**(30) (RMMcKellar) 7-7-0 (7) PFessey(8) (racd centre: prom over 3f) ....hd **12**
1157⁶ Gondo **(58)**(33) (EJAlston) 8-8-0 PRobinson(4) (a in rr) 1¼ **13**
1199⁴ Seaside Minstrel **(58)**(32) (DLWilliams) 7-7-7b(7) MartinDwyer(14) (lw: nvr nr ldrs) ....nk **14**
1106⁴ Macfarlane **(71)**(41) (MJFetherston-Godley) 7-8-13 FNorton(6) (dwlt: sn rdn along: a in rr) 1¼ **15**

Rhythmic Dancer **(72)***(38) (JLSpearing)* 7-9-0 DeanMcKeown(7) (bkwd: unruly s: a bhd).....1¼ **16**
1057* Ann's Pearl (IRE) **(80)***(21) (JWHills)* 4-9-8 RHills(9) (spd 3f: sn wknd & t.o)..............................8 **17**
LONG HANDICAP Sonderise 7-3 Serious Hurry 7-3

13/2 Name the Tune, **8/1** Macfarlane, **9/1** Ann's Pearl (IRE), Canovas Heart, Beau Venture (USA), **10/1** Gondo, LORD HIGH ADMIRAL (CAN), **12/1** Ansellman, Seaside Minstrel, Croft Imperial, **14/1** King Rambo, One for Jeannie, **16/1** I'm Your Lady, **33/1** Sonderise, Lord Sky, Rhythmic Dancer, Serious Hurry, CSF £68.59 CT £938.85 TOTE £10.30: £2.70 £2.00 £4.00 £2.10 (£22.50) Trio £330.40 OWNER Mr E. J. G. Young (WROUGHTON) BRED Windfields Farm 17 Rn
60.91 secs (1.91) SF: 78/60/58/41/50/39/41/24/37/29/13/13/16/15/24/21/4
WEIGHT FOR AGE 3yo-9lb
OFFICIAL EXPLANATION Sonderise: bled from the nose.

1305 SANDY LANE RATED STKS H'CAP (0-110) (Listed) (3-Y.O) (Class A) £12,393.20 (£4,638.80: £2,269.40: £977.00: £438.50: £223.10)
6f Stalls: High GOING minus 0.02 sec per fur (G) 2-30 (2-31)

939⁸ **Star Tulip (91)***(97) (JLDunlop)* 3-8-7 GDuffield(9) (a.p: led over 2f out: rdn & r.o strly)..........— **1**
633⁵ Lennox Lewis **(95)***(98) (APJarvis)* 3-8-11 MRoberts(5) (lw: hdwy over 2f out: ev ch dist: r.o one pce)..........1¼ **2**
1133⁵ Zeb (IRE) **(100)***(96) (BAMcMahon)* 3-9-2v TIves(8) (lw: s.i.s: hdwy u.p 2f out: kpt on ins fnl f)..........2½ **3**
1233a⁴ Loveyoumillions (IRE) **(96)***(90)*(Fav)*(MJohnston)* 3-8-12 JWeaver(7) (lw: a.p: effrt & ev ch over 1f out: unable qckn)..........¾ **4**
921¹⁰ Loyalize (USA) **(105)***(96) (DRLoder)* 3-9-7 GCarter(6) (lw: chsd ldrs: swtchd stands' side: swtchd lft bel dist: nvr nr to chal)..........1¼ **5**
1066² Cheyenne Spirit **(93)***(70) (BHanbury)* 3-8-9 RHills(4) (led tl hdd over 2f out: wknd appr fnl f)..........5 **6**
828² Katya (IRE) **(91)***(68) (MRChannon)* 3-8-7 PaulEddery(2) (rdn & effrt 2f out: no imp)..............nk **7**
939⁵ The Jotter **(95)***(68) (WJarvis)* 3-8-11 JCarroll(1) (outpcd)..........1¼ **8**
Fajjoura (IRE) **(91)***(62) (JEBanks)* 3-8-7 JQuinn(3) (bit bkwd: prom 4f: sn wknd)..........¾ **9**
LONG HANDICAP Star Tulip 8-6 Katya (IRE) 8-6 Fajjoura (IRE) 8-6

2/1 Loveyoumillions (IRE), **11/2** Katya (IRE) (4/1-6/1), **6/1** Cheyenne Spirit (op 4/1), **13/2** Loyalize (USA), **7/1** Lennox Lewis, **15/2** Zeb (IRE), **8/1** STAR TULIP, **14/1** The Jotter, **20/1** Fajjoura (IRE), CSF £59.76 CT £404.22 TOTE £11.60: £1.80 £2.50 £2.50 (£40.00) Trio £235.40 OWNER Mr Nicholas Jones (ARUNDEL) BRED Nicholas M. H. Jones 9 Rn
1m 13.61 (1.91) SF: 64/65/63/57/63/37/35/35/29

1306 TOTE CREDIT SILVER BOWL H'CAP (0-110) (3-Y.O) (Class B) £17,668.75 (£5,350.00: £2,612.50: £1,243.75)
1m 30y Stalls: Low GOING minus 0.02 sec per fur (G) 3-00 (3-01)

1129³ **Sonic Boy (104)***(113) (RFJohnsonHoughton)* 3-9-7 JQuinn(7) (lw: mde all: drvn clr wl over 1f out: unchal)..........— **1**
662⁷ Sue's Return **(87)***(84) (APJarvis)* 3-8-4 MRoberts(1) (lw: hld up: hdwy u.p 2f out: r.o ins fnl f)..6 **2**
694* Crumpton Hill (IRE) **(85)***(80)*(Fav)*(NAGraham)* 3-8-2 PaulEddery(8) (hld up: 4th st: effrt bel dist: no imp)..........1¼ **3**
987* Mezaan (IRE) **(87)***(82) (MRStoute)* 3-8-4 RHills(4) (prom: 3rd st: rdn 2f out: one pce)...........s.h **4**
907* Ma Petite Anglaise **(82)***(73) (WJarvis)* 3-7-6 (7) MHenry(5) (chsd ldrs: 6th st: one pce fnl 3f)..1¾ **5**
1066³ Twilight Patrol **(88)***(78) (RHannon)* 3-8-5 GCarter(3) (b.nr fore: hld up & bhd: effrt u.p over 2f out: no imp)..........½ **6**
Shandine (USA) **(99)***(79) (RCharlton)* 3-9-2 JWeaver(2) (s.s: a bhd)..........5 **7**
1131⁸ Impulsive Air (IRE) **(89)***(30) (EWeymes)* 3-8-6 KFallon(6) (lw: prom to ½-wy: sn lost pl: t.o) ..20 **8**
953³ Cim Bom Bom (IRE) **(95)***(33) (MBell)* 3-8-12 MFenton(9) (lw: chsd wnr: 2nd st: rdn 3f out: sn wknd: t.o)..........1¾ **9**

7/4 Crumpton Hill (IRE), **4/1** Mezaan (IRE), **13/2** Cim Bom Bom (IRE), **8/1** Shandine (USA), **9/1** SONIC BOY, **10/1** Ma Petite Anglaise, **14/1** Sue's Return, Twilight Patrol, **25/1** Impulsive Air (IRE), CSF £106.45 CT £290.90 TOTE £9.30: £2.00 £2.60 £1.40 (£55.00) Trio £93.50 OWNER Mr Anthony Pye-Jeary (DIDCOT) BRED E. R. W. Stanley and New England Stud Farm Ltd 9 Rn
1m 45.32 (4.92) SF: 54/25/21/23/14/19/20/-/-

1307 E.B.F. ST HELENS MAIDEN STKS (2-Y.O F) (Class D) £4,143.00 (£1,254.00: £612.00: £291.00)
5f Stalls: High GOING minus 0.02 sec per fur (G) 3-30 (3-30)

1098³ **Desert Tiger** *(79)*(Fav)*(MJohnston)* 2-8-11 MRoberts(1) (lw: mde all: rdn & hung lft fnl f: jst hld on)..........— **1**

1158[3] Marjorie Rose (IRE) *(79) (ABailey)* 2-8-11 GCarter(3) (hld up & bhd: swtchd lft appr fnl f: swtchd lft dist: jst failed) ....hd 2
Amaniy (USA) *(73) (HThomsonJones)* 2-8-11 RHills(2) (neat: s.i.s: hdwy & ev ch 200y out: rdn & unable qckn) 1¾ 3
Exceedingly *(69) (WJarvis)* 2-8-11 AMcGlone(4) (lt-f: bkwd: plld hrd: chsd wnr 4f: sn outpcd) 1¼ 4

5/6 DESERT TIGER (5/4-4/5), **2/1** Amaniy (USA) (op 5/4), **8/1** Marjorie Rose (IRE), Exceedingly, CSF £6.38 TOTE £1.70 (£3.70) OWNER Maktoum Al Maktoum (MIDDLEHAM) BRED Gainsborough Stud Management Ltd 4 Rn 62.9 secs (3.90) SF: 28/28/22/18

1308

ECCLES MAIDEN STKS (3-Y.O) (Class D) £4,032.50 (£1,220.00: £595.00: £282.50) **1m 2f 120y** Stalls: Low GOING minus 0.02 sec per fur (G) 4-00 (4-01)

978[2] **Sanmartino (IRE)** *(86)*(Fav)*(BWHills)* 3-9-0 PaulEddery(6) (lw: a.p: 4th st: led over 3f out: rdn over 1f out: r.o wl) ....— 1
Hadeyya Ramzeyah *(84) (ACStewart)* 3-9-0 MRoberts(7) (wl grwn: b: s.i.s: 5th st: hdwy 3f out: rdn & rn green fnl f: r.o) 1½ 2
779[2] Incha *(71) (HThomsonJones)* 3-8-9 RHills(1) (lw: a.p: 3rd st: chsd wnr fr 3f out: rdn & wknd fnl f) 5 3
1162[3] Prince Equiname *(72) (DEddy)* 3-9-0 MFenton(3) (hld up & bhd: 6th st: effrt over 2f out: nt rch ldrs) 3 4
691[14] Zalament **(68)***(44) (APJarvis)* 3-8-9 GDuffield(5) (hld up & bhd: 7th st: nvr nr ldrs) 15 5
1000[6] Coryana Dancer (IRE) *(40) (RHollinshead)* 3-8-9 TIves(2) (led after 2f tl hdd over 3f out: sn outpcd) 2½ 6
Irshad *(36) (PTWalwyn)* 3-9-0 JWeaver(4) (h.d.w: bkwd: led 2f: 2nd st: eased whn btn wl over 2f out: t.o) 6 7

4/5 SANMARTINO (IRE) (tchd Evens), **3/1** Incha, **6/1** Hadeyya Ramzeyah, **10/1** Coryana Dancer (IRE), **12/1** Irshad, **25/1** Zalament, Prince Equiname, CSF £6.51 TOTE £2.00: £1.40 £2.10 (£4.60) OWNER Mr K. Abdullah (LAMBOURN) BRED Juddmonte Farms 7 Rn
2m 20.03 (8.53) SF: 32/30/17/18/-/-/-

1309

SHEVINGTON MAIDEN STKS (3-Y.O+) (Class D) £3,974.00 (£1,202.00: £586.00: £278.00) **7f 30y** Stalls: Low GOING minus 0.02 sec per fur (G) 4-30 (4-30)

936[4] **Banadam (USA) (78)***(82) (BHanbury)* 3-8-13 TIves(3) (lw: a.p: 2nd st: led bel dist: rdn out) ....— 1
1168[3] Takhlid (USA) *(78) (HThomsonJones)* 4-9-10 RHills(7) (lw: led to bel dist: rdn & one pce fnl f) 2 2
Empty Quarter *(57) (JHMGosden)* 3-8-13 AMcGlone(4) (str: cmpt: bit bkwd: chsd ldrs: 4th st: one pce fnl 2f) 9 3
1000[8] Just Whistle *(39) (CWThornton)* 3-8-8 DeanMcKeown(1) (bkwd: prom: 3rd st: rdn & wknd over 2f out) 6 4
Hand of Straw (IRE) *(39) (JWWatts)* 3-8-13 GDuffield(5) (rangy: bit bkwd: chsd ldrs: 5th st: outpcd over 2f out: sn btn) 2 5
Gold Sand *(37)*(Fav)*(JHMGosden)* 3-8-13 JCarroll(8) (b: gd sort: bkwd: hld up: 6th st: hdwy over 3f out: wknd over 2f out) 1¼ 6
Street Lady **(40)***(11) (ABailey)* 5-9-5 GCarter(6) (bit bkwd: dwlt: a bhd: t.o) 9 7
955[9] Dragon Rose *(11) (TPTate)* 3-8-13 PRobinson(2) (bkwd: a bhd: t.o) 2½ 8

2/1 Gold Sand, **7/2** Takhlid (USA), BANADAM (USA), **11/2** Empty Quarter (4/1-6/1), **10/1** Hand of Straw (IRE), **25/1** Street Lady, **33/1** Just Whistle, **50/1** Dragon Rose, CSF £14.65 TOTE £4.20: £1.30 £1.20 £2.60 (£3.90) Trio £12.40 OWNER Mr Saeed Suhail (NEWMARKET) BRED Delsol Farm 8 Rn 1m 33.23 (5.93) SF: 29/36/4/-/-/-/-/-
WEIGHT FOR AGE 3yo-11lb

1310

FORMBY H'CAP (0-80) (4-Y.O+) (Class D) £4,279.50 (£1,296.00: £633.00: £301.50) **1m 6f** Stalls: Low GOING minus 0.02 sec per fur (G) 5-05 (5-05)

1084* **Moshaajir (USA) (69)***(81) (CSmith)* 5-9-5 GDuffield(4) (lw: mde most 9f: 2nd st: led 2f out: rdn & styd on) ....— 1
1252* Sunday News'n'echo (USA) **(55)***(66) (WStorey)* 4-8-0 (5) 3x PMcCabe(7) (a.p: led 5f out to 2f out: rallied u.p fnl f) ....¾ 2
1102[6] Highbrook (USA) **(72)***(80)*(Fav)*(MHTompkins)* 7-9-8 PRobinson(8) (lw: hld up & bhd: 8th st: styd on wl fnl 2f: nt rch ldrs) 2½ 3
1086[11] Lord Hastie (USA) **(50)***(54) (CWThornton)* 7-8-0 JQuinn(6) (hld up: 5th st: hdwy over 3f out: nt rch ldrs) 3½ 4

1109[3] Cuango (IRE) **(76)***(80) (RHollinshead)* 4-9-12 TIves(5) (lw: hld up: outpcd & 6th st: effrt u.p 2f out: no imp)....½ **5**
954* Seize the Day (IRE) **(62)***(59) (CDBroad)* 7-8-12 MFenton(2) (hld up & bhd: 7th st: effrt & rdn 3f out: no imp)....6 **6**
1058[16] Nornax Lad (USA) **(60)***(48) (MartynMeade)* 7-8-10 VSlattery(1) (w wnr: 3rd st: wknd over 3f out)....8 **7**
1109[9] Sarawat **(71)***(53) (DNicholls)* 7-9-7 AlexGreaves(3) (lw: plld hrd: chsd ldrs: 4th st: wknd 3f out)....5 **8**

100/30 Highbrook (USA) (9/2-3/1), **4/1** Cuango (IRE), **9/2** Sunday News'n'echo (USA), **5/1** MOSHAAJIR (USA), Seize the Day (IRE), **11/1** Lord Hastie (USA) (16/1-10/1), **14/1** Nornax Lad (USA), Sarawat, CSF £25.95 CT £77.18 TOTE £5.50: £1.80 £1.80 £1.90 (£12.90) OWNER Mr Steve Macdonald (WELLINGORE) BRED Katalpa Farm 8 Rn 3m 9.92 (11.72) SF: 36/21/35/9/35/14/3/8
T/Jkpt: Not won; £11,820.17 to Sandown 29/5/95. T/Plpt: £77.50 (305.7 Tckts). T/Qdpt: £4.40 (76 Tckts). IM

0957-KEMPTON (R-H)
Saturday May 27th (Good to firm, Good for last 3f on Rnd Course)

WEATHER: Warm WIND: slt bhd

1311 NEW ENGLAND CONDITIONS STKS (2-Y.O) (Class C) £4,981.80 (£1,816.80: £888.40: £382.00: £171.00)
6f Stalls: Low GOING minus 0.53 sec per fur (F) 2-10 (2-11)

836* **L'Ami Louis (USA)** *(86) (JHMGosden)* 2-9-0 LDettori(3) (lw: hld up: rdn over 2f out: led ins fnl f: r.o wl)....— **1**
919[2] Oberons Boy (IRE) *(82) (BJMeehan)* 2-8-10 PatEddery(1) (led: rdn over 2f out: hdd ins fnl f: r.o)....hd **2**
1104[4] Corporal Nym (USA) *(78)*(Fav)*(PFICole)* 2-8-10 TQuinn(5) (lw: hld up: ev ch 1f out: unable qckn)....1½ **3**
King of The East (IRE) *(54) (MRStoute)* 2-8-10 WRSwinburn(4) (w'like: bit bkwd: chsd ldr 4f: lame)....9 **4**
Awafeh *(52) (JWPayne)* 2-8-10 BThomson(2) (leggy: scope: bhd fnl 2f)....¾ **5**

7/4 Corporal Nym (USA), **2/1** King of The East (IRE), **5/2** L'AMI LOUIS (USA) (5/4-11/4), **8/1** Oberons Boy (IRE) (5/1-10/1), **20/1** Awafeh, CSF £18.14 TOTE £2.20: £1.50 £1.60 (£4.60) OWNER Oak Cliff Foals of 1993 Plus 2, LLC (NEWMARKET) BRED E. A. Cox Jr 5 Rn
1m 11.52 (0.22) SF: 50/46/42/18/16

1312 CALIFORNIAN MAIDEN STKS (3-Y.O) (Class D) £4,221.00 (£1,278.00: £624.00: £297.00) 1m (Jubilee) Stalls: High GOING minus 0.53 sec per fur (F) 2-40 (2-42)

1136[2] **Restructure (IRE)** *(94+)*(Fav)*(MrsJCecil)* 3-9-0 PatEddery(5) (lw: 3rd st: qcknd & led over 2f out: clr over 1f out: comf)....— **1**
695[8] Proud Destiny *(79) (MRStoute)* 3-8-9 WRSwinburn(9) (5th st: chsd wnr over 1f out: no imp)..5 **2**
761[4] Mokuti *(82) (GWragg)* 3-9-0 MHills(6) (rdn over 6f out: gd hdwy over 1f out: r.o wl fnl f)....1¼ **3**
963[2] Primo Lara **(80)***(75) (PWHarris)* 3-9-0 GHind(7) (lw: led 5f out to 2f out: wknd over 1f out)....3½ **4**
White Heat *(66) (MJHeaton-Ellis)* 3-8-9 StephenDavies(4) (led 3f: 2nd st: wknd over 2f out)..2 **5**
Cuba *(66) (MRStoute)* 3-8-11 (3) JTate(2) (nvr plcd to chal)....2½ **6**
Contract Venture (IRE) *(65) (WJarvis)* 3-9-0 BThomson(3) (b.nr hind: 4th st: wknd 2f out)....½ **7**
Mighty Marston *(59) (LadyHerries)* 3-9-0 TQuinn(1) (6th st: wknd over 2f out)....3 **8**
677[10] Bergholt *(45) (GLMoore)* 3-9-0 AClark(8) (b.off hind: lw: a bhd)....7 **9**

5/4 RESTRUCTURE (IRE), **3/1** Mokuti (2/1-100/30), **6/1** Proud Destiny, Primo Lara, **20/1** White Heat, **33/1** Cuba, Contract Venture (IRE), Mighty Marston, **50/1** Bergholt, CSF £8.68 TOTE £1.90: £1.10 £1.90 £1.20 (£7.10) Trio £5.80 OWNER Mr Martin Myers (NEWMARKET) BRED J. H. Stone 9 Rn 1m 38.23 (1.23) SF: 42/27/30/23/14/14/13/7/-
OFFICIAL EXPLANATION **Cuba: the jockey stated that the horse had been fractious in the stalls and was told to educate him. He added that Cuba would appreciate a longer trip and easier ground, and had pulled up a little sore.**

1313 CRAWLEY WARREN H'CAP (0-95) (4-Y.O+) (Class C) £10,162.50 (£3,075.00: £1,500.00: £712.50) 2m Stalls: High GOING minus 0.53 sec per fur (F) 3-10 (3-10)

610[6] **Latahaab (USA) (80)***(96)*(Fav)*(RAkehurst)* 4-9-10 TQuinn(6) (lw: chsd ldr: led 6f out: rdn over 2f out: r.o wl)....— **1**

1189³ Lalindi (IRE) **(66)***(79) (DRCElsworth)* 4-8-10 PatEddery(3) (rdn over 4f out: 2nd st: hrd rdn over 1f out: unable qckn) 3½ 2
1156² Argyle Cavalier (IRE) **(62)***(67) (MJohnston)* 5-8-8 MHills(5) (rdn over 6f out: 3rd st: wknd over 1f out) 8 3
1189⁵ Blaze Away (USA) **(80)***(81) (IABalding)* 4-9-10 LDettori(4) (lw: 4th st: wknd over 2f out) 4 4
763³ Durshan (USA) **(53)***(43) (JRJenkins)* 6-7-13 DBiggs(7) (lw: bhd fnl 4f) 11 5
582¹³ Lunar Risk **(47)***(36) (MissBSanders)* 5-7-7 NAdams(1) (lw: hdwy over 3f out: 5th st: wknd over 2f out) ....½ 6
998¹³ Star Player **(75)***(52) (RJBaker)* 9-9-7 WRSwinburn(2) (lw: led 10f: wknd over 4f out) 12 7

9/4 LATAHAAB (USA), **4/1** Lalindi (IRE), **9/2** Argyle Cavalier (IRE), Blaze Away (USA), **10/1** Durshan (USA), Star Player, **33/1** Lunar Risk, CSF £10.36 TOTE £3.30: £1.80 £1.50 (£6.50) OWNER Ascot Racing Partnership (EPSOM) BRED Gainsborough Farm Inc 7 Rn
3m 26.53 (0.88 under best) (2.13) SF: 56/39/29/41/5/-/14
WEIGHT FOR AGE 4yo-2lb

1314

BROKING H'CAP (0-90) (3-Y.O+) (Class C) £5,628.00 (£1,704.00: £832.00: £396.00) **1m 2f (Jubilee)** Stalls: High GOING minus 0.53 sec (F) 3-40 (3-41)

857² **Bob's Ploy (77)***(91+)*(Fav)*(RAkehurst)* 3-8-4 ow1 BThomson(9) (2nd st: led over 2f out: comf) ....— 1
981⁶ Benfleet **(77)***(88) (RWArmstrong)* 4-9-5 LDettori(1) (4th st: rdn over 2f out: chsd wnr over 1f out: no imp) 2½ 2
My Learned Friend **(71)***(82) (AHide)* 4-8-13 JWilliams(2) (bit bkwd: 6th st: shkn up over 1f out: r.o ins fnl f) ....nk 3
918³ Statajack (IRE) **(86)***(96) (DRCElsworth)* 7-10-0b TQuinn(4) (hdwy over 1f out: r.o) ....s.h 4
987⁹ Arzani (USA) **(70)***(78) (DJSCosgrove)* 4-8-12 MHills(5) (lw: 5th st: rdn over 2f out: one pce) 1¾ 5
1192ᴾ Laxford Bridge **(82)***(90) (PWHarris)* 4-9-10 WRSwinburn(7) (lw: led over 3f: 3rd st: rdn over 2f out: one pce) ....hd 6
986⁸ Progression **(62)***(67) (PCHaslam)* 4-8-1 (3) JTate(6) (nvr nr to chal) 1½ 7
764¹⁹ I Recall (IRE) **(65)***(46) (PHayward)* 4-8-7 RStreet(3) (bhd fnl 6f) 15 8
Raven's Roost (IRE) **(56)***(32) (MajorDNChappell)* 4-7-12 ow3 StephenDavies(8) (led over 6f out tl over 2f out: sn wknd) 1¼ 9

9/4 BOB'S PLOY, **4/1** Laxford Bridge, **11/2** Benfleet, Raven's Roost (IRE), **6/1** Statajack (IRE), **16/1** Progression, **20/1** Arzani (USA), My Learned Friend, **25/1** I Recall (IRE), CSF £14.05 CT £175.08 TOTE £2.70: £1.30 £2.10 £3.30 (£6.20) Trio £99.60 OWNER Mr Kevin Reddington (EPSOM) BRED Hyde Stud 9 Rn
2m 2.8 (0.30) SF: 43/55/49/63/45/57/34/13/-
WEIGHT FOR AGE 3yo-15lb

1315

CRAWLEY WARREN HERON STKS (Listed) (3-Y.O) (Class A) £14,312.50 (£4,300.00: £2,075.00: £962.50) **1m (Jubilee)** Stalls: Low GOING minus 0.53 sec per fur (F) 4-10 (4-10)

930* **Peace Envoy (109)***(111) (HRACecil)* 3-8-12 PatEddery(3) (4th st: shkn up to ld over 1f out: hung rt ins fnl f: r.o wl) ....— 1
1178* Ihtiram (IRE) **(102)***(108)*(Fav)*(JLDunlop)* 3-8-12 TQuinn(4) (lw: s.s: 5th st: hdwy over 1f out: ev ch whn hit rail & n.m.r ins fnl f: nt rcvr) 1¾ 2
Royal Philosopher **(107)***(104) (KMcAuliffe)* 3-8-12 JTate(5) (led 5f: led 2f out to over 1f out: one pce) 2 3
792⁴ That Old Feeling (IRE) **(98)***(98) (RHannon)* 3-8-12 LDettori(1) (lw: 3rd st: rdn over 2f out: sn wknd) 3 4
1139⁵ Dee-Lady **(89)***(90) (WGMTurner)* 3-8-7 MHills(2) (2nd st: led 3f out to 2f out: wkng whn n.m.r over 1f out) 1¼ 5

8/11 Ihtiram (IRE), **2/1** PEACE ENVOY (6/4-9/4), **11/1** That Old Feeling (IRE) (8/1-12/1), **12/1** Royal Philosopher (7/1-14/1), **20/1** Dee-Lady, CSF £3.77 TOTE £2.40: £1.30 £1.10 (£1.20) OWNER Mr K. Abdullah (NEWMARKET) BRED Juddmonte Farms 5 Rn 1m 38.25 (1.25) SF: 40/37/33/27/19

1316

UNDERWRITING H'CAP (0-95) (3-Y.O+) (Class C) £5,602.00 (£1,696.00: £828.00: £394.00) **6f** Stalls: High GOING minus 0.53 sec per fur (F) 4-40 (4-40)

693⁴ **Humbert's Landing (IRE) (90)***(97)*(Fav)*(PFICole)* 4-9-13 TQuinn(3) (a.p: rdn over 2f out: led ins fnl f: all out) ....— 1
Actual Fact (USA) **(80)***(87) (GHarwood)* 3-8-7 PatEddery(5) (hdwy over 2f out: hrd rdn fnl f: r.o wl) ....s.h 2
922¹⁷ Mister Jolson **(86)***(91) (RJHodges)* 6-9-4 (5) SDrowne(4) (hld up: led over 1f out tl ins fnl f: unable qckn) ....¾ 3

1186[11] Easy Dollar **(79)***(82) (BGubby)* 3-8-6vow1 JWilliams(8) (lw: hdwy over 1f out: r.o ins fnl f)........nk 4
1021[4] Highborn (IRE) **(83)***(84) (PSFelgate)* 6-9-6 GHind(2) (a.p: led wl over 1f out: sn hdd: one pce)1¼ 5
1143[7] Saseedo (USA) **(90)***(89) (WAO'Gorman)* 5-9-13 EmmaO'Gorman(10) (lw: hdwy over 1f out: nvr nrr).....................½ 6
1174[7] Sea-Deer **(90)***(87) (LJHolt)* 6-9-13 MPerrett(1) (bit bkwd: nvr plcd to chal).....................¾ 7
1151[4] Elle Shaped (IRE) **(64)***(51) (DNicholls)* 5-8-1 StephenDavies(9) (led over 4f).....................4 8
Gilt Throne **(75)***(51) (MHTompkins)* 8-8-5 (7) JGotobed(7) (lw: a bhd).....................4 9
Rock Symphony **(91)***(62) (WJHaggas)* 5-10-0 MHills(6) (lw: chsd ldr 4f).....................2 10

5/2 HUMBERT'S LANDING (IRE), **5/1** Actual Fact (USA) (4/1-6/1), Highborn (IRE), **13/2** Elle Shaped (IRE), Sea-Deer, **8/1** Saseedo (USA), **11/1** Mister Jolson, **14/1** Rock Symphony, **20/1** Easy Dollar, **33/1** Gilt Throne, CSF £15.40 CT £109.54 TOTE £3.00: £1.80 £1.90 £2.60 (£5.00) Trio £31.50 OWNER Lord Donoughmore (WHATCOMBE) BRED Rathbarry Stud 10 Rn
1m 11.44 (0.14) SF: 64/44/58/39/51/56/54/18/18/29
WEIGHT FOR AGE 3yo-10lb

OFFICIAL EXPLANATION **Sea-Deer: the jockey reported that the gelding blew up a furlong out and could not have finished any closer.**

T/Plpt: £7.20 (2,982.12 Tckts). T/Qdpt: £3.80 (13.85 Tckts). AK

1163-LINGFIELD (L-H)
Saturday May 27th (Turf Good to firm, AWT Standard)
WEATHER: fair WIND: almost nil

1317
HALL MAIDEN APPRENTICE STKS (3-Y.O) (Class F) £2,634.00 (£749.00: £372.00) **1m 2f** Stalls: Centre GOING minus 0.62 sec per fur (F) 6-10 (6-13)

937[6] **Dawsha (IRE) (70)***(71)*(Fav)*(SDow)* 3-8-3 (3) ADaly(5) (a.p: 3rd st: led ins fnl f: pushed out)..— 1
Rising Dough (IRE) **(83)***(73) (GLMoore)* 3-8-3 (8) CarolineHovington(2) (led tl hdd ins fnl f: unable qckn).....................2 2
1167[7] Farmer's Tern (IRE) *(61) (WJarvis)* 3-8-6 GMilligan(11) (chsd ldr: 2nd st: rdn over 2f out: one pce).....................4 3
1167[8] Canton Venture *(61) (SPCWoods)* 3-8-8 (3) CWebb(4) (chsd ldrs: 4th st: sn rdn: one pce fnl 2f).....................3½ 4
942[10] Kyrenia Times *(53) (PMitchell)* 3-8-6 (5) DavidO'Neill(1) (s.i.s: nvr nrr).....................5 5
689[5] Harvey White (IRE) **(65)***(52) (JPearce)* 3-8-8 (3) ElizabethTurner(9) (nvr nrr).....................¾ 6
Sound Trick (USA) *(45) (GCBravery)* 3-8-6 GFaulkner(7) (6th st: rdn 3f out: no hdwy).....................¾ 7
739[11] Colt D'Or **(47)***(50) (JWhite)* 3-8-3 (8) CCarver(6) (bhd fnl 5f).....................½ 8
1198[11] Commander Glen (IRE) *(48) (MartynMeade)* 3-8-6 (5) CDomergue(8) (a bhd).....................¾ 9
144[10] Fosters Top *(29) (JFfitch-Heyes)* 3-8-11 RMoogan(10) (prom: 5th st: sn wknd).....................12 10
Morning Master *(5) (RMFlower)* 3-8-11 CScudder(3) (w'like: bit bkwd: dwlt: a bhd).....................15 11

7/4 DAWSHA (IRE), **3/1** Farmer's Tern (IRE), **4/1** Rising Dough (IRE) (3/1-9/2), **9/1** Harvey White (IRE) (6/1-10/1), **12/1** Canton Venture (op 5/1), Sound Trick (USA) (5/1-14/1), **20/1** Kyrenia Times, Morning Master, **50/1** Commander Glen (IRE), Fosters Top, Colt D'Or, CSF £9.28 TOTE £2.50: £1.30 £1.60 £1.70 (£3.50) Trio £2.70 OWNER Mrs J. M. A. Churston (EPSOM) BRED Newgate Stud Co 11 Rn
2m 8.48 (5.48) SF: -/2/-/-/-/-/-/-/-/-/-
STEWARDS' ENQUIRY Moogan susp. 5/6/95 (unnecessary use of whip).

1318
E.B.F. LINGFIELD MAIDEN STKS (2-Y.O) (Class D) £3,915.00 (£1,170.00: £560.00: £255.00) **6f** Stalls: Centre GOING minus 0.62 sec per fur (F) 6-40 (6-41)

1134[2] **Bahamian Knight (CAN)** *(88+)*(Fav)*(DRLoder)* 2-9-0 LDettori(10) (a.p: led over 3f out: comf).....................— 1
Rabican (IRE) *(79) (GCBravery)* 2-9-0 MHills(7) (leggy: hdwy 3f out: rdn 2f out: r.o one pce).....................3½ 2
Nilgiri Hills (IRE) *(75) (JLDunlop)* 2-9-0 BThomson(4) (unf: a.p: ev ch 2f out: sn rdn: one pce).....................1¼ 3
Proud Monk *(73) (GLMoore)* 2-9-0 BRouse(5) (w'like: bit bkwd: hld up: hdwy & n.m.r over 2f out: rdn over 1f out: r.o).....................1 4
Brother Roy *(65) (TGMills)* 2-9-0 StephenDavies(2) (w'like: bit bkwd: chsd ldrs: rdn over 2f out: one pce).....................3 5
Arch Angel (IRE) *(58) (DJSffrenchDavis)* 2-8-9 NAdams(3) (leggy: unf: nvr nrr).....................½ 6
849[8] Young Butt *(59) (JFfitch-Heyes)* 2-8-11 (3) DarrenMoffatt(9) (prom: rdn & edgd lft over 2f out: ev ch 2f out: wknd wl over 1f out).....................1¾ 7
690[9] Two Socks *(53) (MMcCormack)* 2-9-0 AClark(1) (prom: ev ch 2f out: wknd wl over 1f out)......2 8
1123[P] Rawi *(44) (CJBenstead)* 2-9-0 DBiggs(8) (prom: wkng whn n.m.r over 2f out: sn faded).....................3½ 9

Hadadabble *(36) (PatMitchell)* 2-8-9 SO'Gorman(6) (w'like: bit bkwd: led: hdd over 3f out: wknd over 2f out)....1¼ 10
1169W Be My Bird *(29) (BJMeehan)* 2-8-9 RPerham(11) (w'like: bit bkwd: prom 2f)....2½ 11

1/3 BAHAMIAN KNIGHT (CAN), **15/2** Nilgiri Hills (IRE) (5/1-8/1), **10/1** Brother Roy, **14/1** Rabican (IRE) (op 8/1), **16/1** Two Socks, **20/1** Rawi, Arch Angel (IRE), **25/1** Hadadabble, Be My Bird, **33/1** Proud Monk, Young Butt, CSF £8.52 TOTE £1.40: £1.20 £3.80 £1.80 (£7.80) Trio £10.10 OWNER Lucayan Stud (NEWMARKET) BRED Donald F. Prowse & Don A. McIntosh 11 Rn

1m 10.54 (1.54) SF: 23/14/10/8/-/-/-/-/-/-/-

1319 PATIO (S) H'CAP (0-60) (3-Y.O+) (Class G) £2,646.20 (£733.20: £350.60)
2m (Equitrack) Stalls: Centre GOING minus 0.75 sec per fur (FST) 7-10 (7-12)

654[5] **Hever Golf Lady (46)***(52+)*(Fav)*(TJNaughton)* 3-8-3 StephenDavies(12) (hld up: hdwy 4f out: led over 1f out: comf)....— 1
469[4] Call Me Albi (IRE) **(47)***(49) (GLMoore)* 4-9-10 AClark(2) (chsd ldrs: rdn over 1f out: r.o one pce)....4 2
Teoroma **(30)***(31) (DrJDScargill)* 5-8-2 (7) CDomergue(1) (in rr: hdwy over 2f out: r.o fnl f: nvr nrr)....1¼ 3
1204[4] Mayday Kitty **(39)***(40) (WGMTurner)* 3-7-10 NAdams(4) (chsd ldrs: led over 3f out: hdd over 1f out: one pce)....hd 4
1210[8] Epica **(50)***(51) (ABailey)* 4-9-13b LDettori(14) (mid div: hdwy over 4f out: rdn 2f out: one pce)hd 5
879[14] Rejects Reply **(34)***(35) (WJMusson)* 5-8-13 BThomson(7) (hld up: hdwy 6f out: rdn 2f out: one pce)....s.h 6
744[8] Glow Forum **(30)***(27) (GLMoore)* 4-8-7 RPerham(10) (chsd ldrs: rdn 2f out: wknd over 1f out)....4 7
329[10] Cone Lane **(24)***(7) (BGubby)* 9-7-12 (5) AWhelan(9) (prom: led 10f out: hdd 6f out: rdn over 2f out: sn wknd)....14 8
729[6] Ragtime Song **(27)** *(AMoore)* 6-8-6 SO'Gorman(6) (prom: led 6f out tl over 3f out: wknd over 2f out)....11 9
Strath Kitten **(32)***(2) (WJMusson)* 4-8-9 MTebbutt(3) (prom 9f)....1¾ 10
1210[3] Carfax **(30)** *(RPCHoad)* 10-8-6b(3) JTate(5) (reluctant to r: a wl bhd: t.o)....5 11
545[12] Rosscoyne **(30)** *(JFfitch-Heyes)* 5-8-9 DBiggs(8) (bhd fnl 7f: t.o)....10 12
Deliffin **(44)** (Fav)*(RMFlower)* 9-9-9 JWeaver(13) (led 6f: t.o)....dist 13
Choir Master (CAN) **(49)** *(AMoore)* 8-10-0 CandyMorris(11) (mid div: hdwy 8f out: wknd 3f: t.o whn p.u ins fnl f).... P

5/1 HEVER GOLF LADY, Deliffin, **11/2** Mayday Kitty, **13/2** Epica, **8/1** Call Me Albi (IRE), Carfax, **9/1** Rejects Reply (6/1-10/1), **12/1** Glow Forum, **16/1** Strath Kitten, **20/1** Ragtime Song, Teoroma, **25/1** Cone Lane, Rosscoyne, **33/1** Choir Master (CAN), CSF £43.77 CT £692.52 TOTE £5.30: £1.70 £2.40 £6.10 (£13.40) Trio £113.70 OWNER Mrs E. Jackman (EPSOM) BRED M. M. Allen 14 Rn

3m 27.48 (3.98) SF: 11/28/12/-/30/16/6/-/-/-/-/-/-/-

WEIGHT FOR AGE 3yo-22lb, 4yo-2lb

Bt in 6,200 gns

1320 KING POST LIMITED STKS (0-70) (3-Y.O+) (Class E) £3,044.80 (£906.40: £431.20: £193.60)
1m 2f (Equitrack) Stalls: Centre GOING minus 0.75 sec per fur (FST) 7-40 (7-40)

655[7] **Persian Conquest (IRE) (70)***(69+)*(Fav)*(RIngram)* 3-8-9b JWeaver(3) (mde all: clr over 1f out: comf)....— 1
1126[17] Dia Georgy **(47)***(59) (RGuest)* 4-9-8 MFenton(2) (hld up: hdwy over 2f out: rdn over 1f out: one pce)....5 2
1211[4] Mega Tid **(55)***(58) (BAPearce)* 3-8-9 NAdams(1) (hld up: hdwy 2f out: rdn over 1f out: one pce)....2 3
818[3] Spitfire Bridge (IRE) **(52)***(48) (MMcCormack)* 3-8-7 BThomson(5) (chsd wnr: rdn 2f out: wknd over 1f out)....5 4
Yo Kiri-B **(51)***(33) (JFfitch-Heyes)* 4-9-0 (3) DarrenMoffatt(6) (a.p: rdn over 2f out: sn wknd)....6 5
1245[8] Positivo **(70)***(37) (LordHuntingdon)* 4-9-8v LDettori(7) (hld up: rdn over 4f out: sme hdwy 3f out: wknd over 2f out)....½ 6
818[9] Awesome Power **(65)***(5) (JWHills)* 9-9-8 AClark(4) (hld up: wknd over 3f out)....20 7

Evens PERSIAN CONQUEST (IRE), **9/2** Positivo, **5/1** Awesome Power, **10/1** Mega Tid (op 6/1), Spitfire Bridge (IRE) (7/1-12/1), **16/1** Dia Georgy, **20/1** Yo Kiri-B, CSF £15.11 TOTE £2.10: £1.80 £5.20 (£19.10) OWNER Mrs A. V. Cappuccini (EPSOM) BRED Louis A. Walshe 7 Rn

2m 6.06 (3.06) SF: 10/15/-/-/-/-/-

WEIGHT FOR AGE 3yo-15lb

1321
RICHARD PURKIS BIRTHDAY CELEBRATION H'CAP (0-70) (3-Y.O+) (Class E) £3,245.00 (£968.00: £462.00: £209.00)
5f Stalls: Centre GOING minus 0.62 sec per fur (F) 8-10 (8-11)

972² **Aragrove (60)***(71) (JWPayne)* 5-9-7b MTebbutt(1) (swtg: hld up far side: hdwy over 1f out: led ins fnl f: sn clr: comf)......— 1
1148⁴ Moujeeb (USA) **(61)***(64)*(Fav)*(PatMitchell)* 5-9-8v LDettori(3) (outpcd: c stands' side & rdn 3f out: styd on fnl f)......2½ 2
1057¹³ Miriam **(53)***(54) (MJFetherston-Godley)* 4-9-0 MRoberts(5) (racd far side: led tl hdd ins fnl f: one pce)......¾ 3
831⁴ Little Saboteur **(63)***(60) (PJMakin)* 6-9-10b MHills(2) (chsd ldr far side: rdn over 1f out: one pce)......1¼ 4
1164⁵ Halbert **(42)***(32) (MRChannon)* 6-7-12 (5) PPMurphy(7) (racd centre: chsd ldrs: rdn over 1f out: one pce)......2 5
1164* Lift Boy (USA) **(45)***(30) (AMoore)* 6-8-6 CandyMorris(9) (racd centre: chsd ldrs: rdn ½-wy: no hdwy)......1½ 6
1265¹¹ Shades of Jade **(40)***(19) (JJBridger)* 7-7-10 (5)ow5 AWhelan(8) (racd centre: prom: rdn 2f out: wknd fnl f)......½ 7
1164⁷ Purbeck Centenary **(42)***(15) (PHowling)* 5-8-3 DBiggs(6) (racd centre: chsd ldr: rdn 2f out: wknd over 1f out)......3½ 8
541¹⁰ Splash of Salt (IRE) **(53)** *(TJNaughton)* 5-9-0 StephenDavies(4) (racd centre: a outpcd)......8 9

13/8 Moujeeb (USA), **5/2** ARAGROVE, **15/2** Miriam, Little Saboteur, **8/1** Lift Boy (USA) (5/1-9/1), **12/1** Purbeck Centenary, Shades of Jade, **14/1** Halbert (10/1-16/1), **25/1** Splash of Salt (IRE), CSF £7.48 CT £25.93 TOTE £4.40: £1.90 £1.40 £1.60 (£3.30) Trio £14.30 OWNER Mr Dennis Purkiss (NEWMARKET) BRED Mrs J. R. Hine and Miss J. Bunting 9 Rn
56.81 secs (-0.19) SF: 54/47/37/43/15/13/2/-/-

1322
GABLE H'CAP (0-80) (3-Y.O) (Class D) £4,205.50 (£1,258.00: £603.00: £275.50)
1m 2f Stalls: Centre GOING minus 0.62 sec per fur (F) 8-40 (8-50)

324³ **Grand Selection (IRE) (67)***(69)*(Fav)*(MBell)* 3-8-8 MFenton(12) (chsd ldr: led 7f out: rdn over 1f out: r.o wl)......— 1
867⁸ Euro Singer **(55)***(54) (RAkehurst)* 3-7-7 (3)ow1 DarrenMoffatt(11) (mid div: 6th st: rdn over 2f out: r.o ins fnl f)......1¼ 2
626⁴ Elpidos **(66)***(66) (CEBrittain)* 3-8-7 MRoberts(2) (led 3f: chsd wnr: 2nd st: rdn over 1f out: r.o)s.h 3
1124³ Kevasingo **(56)***(51) (SDow)* 3-7-11 ow3 StephenDavies(3) (chsd ldrs: 4th st: rdn over 1f out: one pce)......1 4
777⁴ Ahaalee (USA) **(65)***(62) (EALDunlop)* 3-8-3 (3) JTate(1) (chsd ldrs: 3rd st: rdn 2f out: one pce)¾ 5
618¹⁴ Orchidarma **(66)***(60) (RJRWilliams)* 3-8-7 DBiggs(6) (5th st: rdn over 2f out: one pce)......2 6
1103³ Romios (IRE) **(86)***(72) (PFICole)* 3-9-6 (7) DavidO'Neill(5) (mid div: 7th st: rdn 2f out: no hdwy)......5 7
1124⁸ Fattash (USA) **(62)***(48) (CJBenstead)* 3-7-12 (5) AWhelan(7) (nvr nrr)......s.h 8
957⁸ Sadler's Pearl **(61)***(41) (BJMeehan)* 3-8-2 ow1 AClark(10) (hdwy over 5f out: 8th st: rdn & wknd over 2f out)......3 9
566⁸ Amboyna Burl (IRE) **(57)***(20) (DAWilson)* 3-7-12 ow5 NGwilliams(8) (dwlt: a bhd)......8 10
1124⁷ Nosirrah **(57)***(21) (CAHorgan)* 3-7-12 NAdams(9) (dwlt: a bhd)......2½ 11
1125¹² Tilthams **(61)***(8) (DAWilson)* 3-7-9 (7)ow9 RachaelMoody(13) (a bhd)......5 12

LONG HANDICAP Amboyna Burl (IRE) 7-5 Tilthams 6-1

3/1 GRAND SELECTION (IRE) (tchd 9/2), **4/1** Euro Singer, Elpidos (op 8/1), **9/2** Kevasingo (3/1-5/1), **5/1** Romios (IRE) (tchd 8/1), **8/1** Ahaalee (USA), **12/1** Orchidarma, **25/1** Fattash (USA), **33/1** Sadler's Pearl, Nosirrah, **50/1** Amboyna Burl (IRE), **66/1** Tilthams, CSF £16.43 CT £48.03 TOTE £3.90: £1.70 £1.50 £2.00 (£17.20) Trio £20.10 OWNER Mr M. B. Hawtin (NEWMARKET) BRED Mount Coote Stud in Ireland 12 Rn 2m 8.23 (5.23) SF: 2/-/-/-/-/-/5/-/-/-/-/-

T/Plpt: £10.20 (958.24 Tckts). T/Qdpt: £17.00 (5.4 Tckts). SM

0970-WARWICK (L-H)
Saturday May 27th (Good)
WEATHER: overcast, rain at times WIND: mod half bhd

1323
SEVERN TRENT WATER AMATEUR H'CAP (0-70) (3-Y.O+) (Class G) £3,116.60 (£867.60: £417.80)
1m Stalls: Low GOING minus 0.25 sec per fur (GF) 6-20 (6-22)

361⁴ **Polly Peculiar (50)***(59) (BSmart)* 4-9-12 (5) MissVMarshall(1) (bhd: plld out & rapid hdwy appr fnl f: led nr fin)......— 1

1202² Wentbridge Lad (IRE) **(52)***(57)*(Fav)*(PDEvans)* 5-10-0 (5) MrWMcLaughlin(7) (in tch: hdwy & 6th st: r.o fnl f) 2 **2**
1061³ Superoo **(65)***(70) (MrsPSly)* 9-10-13 (5) MissLAllan(12) (prom: 3rd st: led 1f out tl hdd & no ex nr fin) ....s.h **3**
1048⁶ Air Command (BAR) **(50)***(39) (CTNash)* 5-9-12 (5)ow13 MrPPhillips(11) (chsd ldrs: 5th st: kpt on appr fnl f) 1¼ **4**
1070⁸ Breezed Well **(44)***(45) (BRCambidge)* 9-9-6 (5)ow1 MrsHNoonan(6) (in tch: kpt on wl appr fnl f: nrst fin) ....nk **5**
1245³ Chairmans Choice **(44)***(45) (APJarvis)* 5-9-6 (5) MrsEBurke(23) (led 7f) ....nk **6**
1070⁵ Pusey Street Boy **(55)***(50) (JRBosley)* 8-10-8 MrsSBosley(3) (t: lw: chsd ldrs tl n.m.r & lost pl over 3f out) 3 **7**
1166¹³ Anlace **(49)***(44) (SMellor)* 6-9-11 (5) MissEJoyce(4) (nvr nrr) ....hd **8**
965² Mbulwa **(54)***(46) (SEKettlewell)* 9-10-7b MrsDKettlewell(18) (prom: 4th st: wknd over 1f out) 1¾ **9**
*1209*⁷ Pacific Spirit **(39)***(30) (MTate)* 5-9-1 (5) MrRThornton(2) (bhd tl r.o fnl 3f) ....nk **10**
972¹⁰ Calling (USA) **(47)***(37) (WMBrisbourne)* 4-10-0 MissDianaJones(21) (prom: 2nd st: sn wknd) ½ **11**
Bill Moon **(36)***(24) (DTThom)* 9-9-3 MissJFeilden(8) (in tch: effrt & 7th st: no imp) ....¾ **12**
762¹⁵ Lady Lacey **(50)***(32) (GBBalding)* 8-9-12v(5) MissKGreaney(22) (bhd fnl 3f) 3 **13**
*364*⁹ Sweet Trentino (IRE) **(68)***(48) (MTate)* 4-11-2 (5) MrsHNeedham(10) (lw: n.d) 1¼ **14**
976² Court Nap (IRE) **(54)***(24) (SMellor)* 3-9-9 MrTCuff(19) (chsd ldrs 5f) 5 **15**
1070³ Tiddy Oggie **(44)***(13) (NAGraham)* 4-9-11 MrsLPearce(5) (lw: a bhd) ....½ **16**
738²² Bresil (USA) **(53)***(2) (KRBurke)* 6-10-1 (5)ow13 MrsHSweeting(16) (lw: a bhd) 3½ **17**
1148¹⁴ Lord Alfie **(49)***(7) (BJMeehan)* 6-10-2 MissJAllison(9) (b.hind: bhd fnl 4f) 1¾ **18**
*1088*⁴ Self Expression **(55)***(10) (MrsJRRamsden)* 7-10-3 (5) MissFHaynes(20) (lw: a bhd) 1¾ **19**
*402*⁷ Storm Bidder **(39)** *(BGubby)* 4-9-1v(5) MrsMBusby(13) (w ldr 4f: sn wknd) 20 **20**
*1049*² Indian Serenade **(47)** *(PWHarris)* 4-10-0 MissAElsey(14) (hmpd & uns rdr s) .... **U**
*307*⁵ Fighter Squadron **(57)** *(REPeacock)* 6-10-5v(5) MrsCPeacock(15) (jinked lft & uns rdr s) .... **U**

9/2 Wentbridge Lad (IRE), **6/1** Chairmans Choice, **8/1** Court Nap (IRE), Tiddy Oggie (6/1-9/1), **10/1** Self Expression, Pusey Street Boy, **12/1** Mbulwa, Indian Serenade (op 8/1), **16/1** Superoo, POLLY PECULIAR, Anlace, Lady Lacey, **20/1** Bill Moon, Sweet Trentino (IRE), **25/1** Breezed Well, Lord Alfie, Pacific Spirit, **33/1** Fighter Squadron, Air Command (BAR), Storm Bidder, Calling (USA), **50/1** Bresil (USA), CSF £90.71 CT £1,139.23 TOTE £40.70: £7.10 £1.70 £3.40 £2.60 (£103.00) Trio £360.10; £405.84 to 29/5/95 OWNER Mr B. Smart (LAMBOURN) BRED Aston Park Stud 22 Rn
1m 41.5 (4.50) SF: 47/45/58/27/33/33/38/32/34/18/25/12/20/36/-/1/-/-/-/-/-/-
WEIGHT FOR AGE 3yo-12lb

1324 ALVIS VEHICLES H'CAP (0-80) (3-Y.O+) (Class D) £3,833.70 (£1,143.60: £545.80: £246.90) **1m 2f 169y** Stalls: Low GOING minus 0.25 sec per fur (GF) 6-50 (6-51)

874⁵ **Myfontaine (48)***(58+) (KTIvory)* 8-7-13 GBardwell(6) (lw: hld up: hdwy & 6th st: led 2f out: sn clr: eased ins fnl f) ....— **1**
975* Haroldon (IRE) **(66)***(70) (BPalling)* 6-9-3 TSprake(5) (b: in tch: lost pl over 3f out: plld out & styd on wl fnl 2f) 4 **2**
935¹⁶ Kaafih Homm (IRE) **(55)***(55)*(Fav)*(NACallaghan)* 4-8-6 PaulEddery(3) (lw: b.hind: hld up: hdwy & 5th st: rdn & nt qckn appr fnl f) 3 **3**
986⁴ Hill Farm Dancer **(54)***(53) (WMBrisbourne)* 4-8-2 (3) AGarth(4) (lw: hdwy 7f out: 3rd st: no ex appr fnl f) ....nk **4**
1140¹⁰ Persian Elite (IRE) **(77)***(70) (PFICole)* 4-10-0 TQuinn(7) (chsd ldrs: rdn & 2nd st: wknd fnl f) ...4 **5**
738⁷ Telopea **(75)***(61) (HCandy)* 4-9-12 WNewnes(9) (led 8f) 5 **6**
744⁵ Jemima Puddleduck **(54)***(40) (DWPArbuthnot)* 4-8-5 JWilliams(8) (b.hind: chsd ldr: rdn 4f out: wknd 3f out) ....hd **7**
935⁷ No Speeches (IRE) **(59)***(37) (CACyzer)* 4-8-7 (3) DRMcCabe(2) (rdn & hdwy 5f out: 4th st: sn wknd) 5 **8**
Radio Caroline **(45)** *(MTate)* 7-7-5 (5)ow3 NVarley(1) (bkwd: plld hrd: prom 4f: sn t.o) ....dist **9**
LONG HANDICAP Radio Caroline 5-13

9/2 Kaafih Homm (IRE), **5/1** Jemima Puddleduck, No Speeches (IRE), **6/1** MYFONTAINE (op 4/1), Hill Farm Dancer, Haroldon (IRE), **8/1** Telopea, **10/1** Persian Elite (IRE), **66/1** Radio Caroline, CSF £38.20 CT £160.24 TOTE £6.30: £2.00 £3.20 £1.50 (£25.00) Trio £37.50 OWNER Mr K. T. Ivory (RADLETT) BRED Farmleigh Partners 9 Rn 2m 18.5 (5.00) SF: 26/38/23/21/38/29/8/5/-

1325 HOUSEHOLD DIVISION MEMORIAL CLAIMING STKS (3-Y.O) (Class F) £2,745.80 (£758.80: £361.40) **1m 2f 169y** Stalls: Low GOING minus 0.25 sec per fur (GF) 7-20 (7-21)

1059² **Gentle Irony (59)***(70) (PJMakin)* 3-7-10 (3) SSanders(3) (trckd ldrs: 2nd st: led on bit over 1f out: rdn clr fnl f) ....— **1**
687⁵ What's the Verdict (IRE) **(75)***(81) (MJohnston)* 3-9-0 TWilliams(5) (plld hrd: led after 1f tl edgd rt & hdd over 1f out: no ex) 3 **2**

1012[12] Margaret Modes *(66) (CACyzer)* 3-8-1 (3) DRMcCabe(1) (bhd: last st: styd on fnl 2f) 3 **3**
Salfrill (IRE) *(64) (MrsPSly)* 3-8-4 ACulhane(2) (led 1f: 3rd st: r.o one pce fnl 2f)..................1¼ **4**
851[14] Crowned Glory (USA) **(73)***(45)*(Fav)*(PFICole)* 3-9-0 TQuinn(4) (prom: 4th st: sn wknd).........20 **5**

6/4 Crowned Glory (USA), **2/1** GENTLE IRONY, **11/4** What's the Verdict (IRE), **25/1** Margaret Modes, **33/1** Salfrill (IRE), CSF £7.06 TOTE £3.20: £1.60 £1.10 (£3.50) OWNER Mrs J. M. West (MARLBOROUGH) BRED Red House Stud 5 Rn 2m 22.2 (8.70) SF: 1/12/-/-/-
Gentle Irony clmd JAllison £5000

OFFICIAL EXPLANATION Crowned Glory (USA): the trainer stated that the horse has a wind problem and has to have his tongue tied down.

1326

GROSVENOR CAREER SERVICES MAIDEN STKS (3-Y.O+) (Class D)
£4,036.50 (£1,206.00: £577.00: £262.50)
7f Stalls: Low GOING minus 0.25 sec per fur (GF) 7-50 (7-53)

695[9] **Brave Princess** *(75) (MAJarvis)* 3-8-8 PRobinson(2) (lw: prom: 2nd st: led 2f out: rdn out) ..— **1**
Bargash *(79) (PDEvans)* 3-8-10 (3) SSanders(3) (hld up: hdwy & 5th st: ev ch over 1f out: edgd lft & nt qckn) ....½ **2**
924[3] Dosses Dan (IRE) **(81)***(65)*(Fav)*(BWHills)* 3-8-13 TQuinn(9) (trckd ldrs: shkn up & 4th st: one pce)........6 **3**
1065[10] H'Ani *(46) (MrsLPiggott)* 3-8-1 (7) VictoriaAppleby(5) (chsd ldrs over 3f) 6 **4**
1168[13] Amany (IRE) *(38) (GLewis)* 3-8-8 PaulEddery(7) (dwlt: bhd tl r.o fnl 2f) 3½ **5**
Valetta *(35) (BJMeehan)* 4-9-5 TWilliams(4) (unf: scope: chsd ldrs: rdn & 6th st: no rspnse)1½ **6**
Christian Warrior **(25)***(39) (REPeacock)* 6-9-10 TSprake(1) (prom: led over 3f out: hdd & wknd 2f out)........nk **7**
1044[8] Orchard Gold **(44)***(21) (FJYardley)* 4-9-10 JWilliams(8) (led over 3f: 3rd st: sn wknd) 8 **8**
Charlie Charlie *(5) (RMFlower)* 4-9-5 (5) JDSmith(6) (swtg: a bhd) 7 **9**

1/3 Dosses Dan (IRE) (op 4/6), **4/1** BRAVE PRINCESS (op 2/1), **20/1** Amany (IRE), Valetta, **50/1** H'Ani, Bargash, Orchard Gold, **100/1** Christian Warrior, **500/1** Charlie Charlie, CSF £111.00 TOTE £4.10: £1.40 £4.30 £1.10 (£107.50) Trio £4.90 OWNER Sheikh Ahmed Al Maktoum (NEWMARKET) BRED Sheikh Ahmed bin Rashid al Maktoum 9 Rn 1m 29.0 (4.80) SF: 16/20/6/-/-/-/-/-/-
WEIGHT FOR AGE 3yo-11lb

1327

BRINK UK MEDIAN AUCTION MAIDEN STKS (2-Y.O) (Class E)
£3,318.75 (£990.00: £472.50: £213.75)
5f Stalls: Low GOING minus 0.25 sec per fur (GF) 8-20 (8-28)

825[8] **Arctic Romancer (IRE)** *(76)*(Fav)*(GLewis)* 2-9-0 PaulEddery(1) (mde all: hung rt tl 2f out: pushed out)........— **1**
Duralock Fencer *(68) (PGMurphy)* 2-8-7 (7) RWaterfield(4) (leggy: unf: hdwy over 2f out: r.o fnl f) 2½ **2**
1011[2] Bath Knight *(46) (DJSffrenchDavis)* 2-9-0 JWilliams(6) (w wnr over 3f: sn rdn & found nil)......7 **3**
Morning Surprise *(38) (APJarvis)* 2-8-9 JMHunter(5) (neat: s.i.s: r.o fnl 2f: n.d) ....¾ **4**
Mister Sean (IRE) *(37) (JWPayne)* 2-9-0 GBardwell(8) (w'like: scope: bkwd: nvr nr to chal)....2 **5**
Vax New Way *(JLSpearing)* 2-9-0 AMackay(3) (lt-f: unf: dwlt: sn bhd) 12 **6**
Mindrace *(KTIvory)* 2-9-0 PRobinson(7) (unruly & uns rdr stalls)........ **W**
849[4] Ben'a'vachei Boy *(JDBethell)* 2-9-0 TQuinn(2) (ref to enter stalls)........ **W**

11/8 ARCTIC ROMANCER (IRE), **6/1** Bath Knight (op 3/1), **16/1** Morning Surprise, Vax New Way, Mister Sean (IRE), **33/1** Duralock Fencer, CSF £14.68 TOTE £1.60: £1.40 £4.00 (£10.80) OWNER Mr A. Al Khalifa (EPSOM) BRED Peter Phelan 6 Rn 61.7 secs (3.70) SF: 15/7/-/-/-/-/-/-

1328

JOBSON JAMES H'CAP (0-70) (3-Y.O+) (Class E) £3,669.75 (£1,098.00: £526.50: £240.75) **1m 6f 194y** Stalls: Low GOING minus 0.25 sec per fur (GF) 8-50 (8-56)

1086[5] **Snow Dream (37)***(47) (MJRyan)* 5-7-11 (5) MBaird(4) (lw: hld up: hdwy 6f out: led over 3f out: rdn & hld on wl fnl 2f)........— **1**
1058[6] Coleridge **(45)***(55) (JJSheehan)* 7-8-7b(3) DRMcCabe(7) (chsd ldrs: 6th st: styd on wl appr fnl f) ....½ **2**
938[8] Tamarpour (USA) **(58)***(67) (MCPipe)* 8-9-9 AMcGlone(9) (b.nr fore: hld up: hdwy 2f out: r.o wl fnl f)........s.h **3**
840[3] Kadiri (IRE) **(59)***(67) (JRBosley)* 4-9-9 GBardwell(11) (sn rdn & bhd: rapid hdwy & 5th st: ev ch over 1f out: kpt on one pce) 1¼ **4**
1075[3] Premier Dance **(44)***(52)*(Fav)*(DHaydnJones)* 8-8-9 TQuinn(6) (prom: 2nd st: ev ch over 1f out: one pce) ....hd **5**
1084[4] Limosa **(47)***(49) (RFJohnsonHoughton)* 4-8-11 JWilliams(1) (lw: prom: rdn 6f out: 4th st: sn btn)........6 **6**

1046* Arc Bright (IRE) **(39)***(35) (RHollinshead)* 5-8-1 (3) AGarth(12) (prom: led 5f out tl over 3f out: rdn & 3rd st: sn btn)....5 **7**
696[7] Romalito **(55)***(48) (MBlanshard)* 5-9-6v TSprake(14) (trckd ldrs tl 7th & btn st)....2½ **8**
967[5] Shuttlecock **(49)***(33) (MrsNMacauley)* 4-8-13 ACulhane(8) (nvr nr to chal)....9 **9**
778[7] Hillswick **(38)***(18) (JSKing)* 4-7-11 (5) NVarley(13) (prom tl 8th & wkng st)....3½ **10**
Deerlet **(59)***(34) (KCBailey)* 4-9-4 (5) JDSmith(15) (swtg: in tch: rn wd 10f out: wknd 4f out)....5 **11**
592[13] The Chairman (IRE) **(64)***(6) (FJordan)* 4-10-0 TWall(2) (lw: led over 10f: sn wknd)....30 **12**
1036[6] Cavina **(45)** *(NAGraham)* 5-8-10 PaulEddery(10) (lw: wl bhd fnl 6f)....3 **13**
Eretan (IRE) **(62)** *(TThomsonJones)* 4-9-12 AMackay(3) (a bhd: broke leg & p.u over 1f out: dead).... **P**
Bee Beat **(50)** *(AJChamberlain)* 7-8-8 (7) MartinDwyer(5) (lw: ref to race: t.n.p).... **R**

11/2 Premier Dance, **6/1** Arc Bright (IRE) (op 4/1), Tamarpour (USA), **13/2** Kadiri (IRE) (4/1-7/1), **7/1** Limosa, **9/1** Cavina, **10/1** SNOW DREAM (8/1-12/1), **14/1** Coleridge, Romalito, **16/1** Bee Beat, Deerlet, **20/1** Shuttlecock, **25/1** Eretan (IRE), **33/1** Hillswick, The Chairman (IRE), CSF £133.23 CT £839.42 TOTE £10.90: £3.00 £3.00 £2.70 (£52.30) Trio £117.20 OWNER Mr P. E. Axon (NEWMARKET) BRED Stud-On-The-Chart 15 Rn 3m 17.9 (8.90) SF: 21/29/41/40/26/22/9/22/6/-/7/-/-/-/-
WEIGHT FOR AGE 4yo-1lb
T/Plpt: £120.80 (78.76 Tckts). T/Qdpt: £19.10 (4.5 Tckts). Dk

1209-WOLVERHAMPTON (L-H)
Saturday May 27th (Standard)
WEATHER: rain early, fine later WIND: fresh across

1329 HEADINGLEY MAIDEN H'CAP (0-70) (3-Y.O+) (Class E) £3,158.00 (£944.00: £452.00: £206.00)
1m 1f 79y (Fibresand) Stalls: Low GOING: 0.13 sec per fur (SLW) 7-00 (7-01)

1027[2] **Aljawab (USA) (57)***(71+)*(Fav)*(JLDunlop)* 4-9-10 GCarter(9) (hld up: hdwy over 5f out: led 2f out: easily)....— **1**
1030[5] Komiamaite **(60)***(64) (SRBowring)* 3-8-8b(5) CTeague(8) (plld hrd: prom: 3rd st: r.o one pce fnl f)....6 **2**
Scale the Summit **(50)***(50) (SirMarkPrescott)* 3-8-3 GDuffield(6) (bit bkwd: led after 2f: hdd 2f out: 2nd st: one pce)....2½ **3**
845[3] Crucis (IRE) **(48)***(32) (BAMcMahon)* 4-9-1 TIves(1) (led 2f: 4th & wkng st)....9 **4**
908[7] Northern Charmer **(49)***(30) (MGMeagher)* 3-8-2 FNorton(7) (lw: sn rdn along: prom: wknd over 3f out: 6th & btn st)....2 **5**
935[9] Silktail (IRE) **(44)***(22) (JohnBerry)* 3-7-11 JQuinn(4) (b: rdn & hdwy over 3f out: 5th & wkng st)....1½ **6**
273[9] Elite Number (USA) **(42)** *(MJCamacho)* 3-7-9 LCharnock(5) (prom tl wknd qckly 3f out: t.o).15 **7**

Evens ALJAWAB (USA), **3/1** Silktail (IRE), **6/1** Komiamaite, Crucis (IRE), **8/1** Scale the Summit, **16/1** Elite Number (USA), **25/1** Northern Charmer, CSF £8.28 CT £32.78 TOTE £1.90: £1.10 £3.10 (£4.40) Trio £10.30 OWNER Mr S. Khaled (ARUNDEL) BRED Mandysland Farm 7 Rn
2m 3.6 (7.60) SF: 53/32/18/14/-/-/-
WEIGHT FOR AGE 3yo-14lb

1330 TRENT BRIDGE CLAIMING STKS (3-Y.O) (Class F) £2,243.00 (£618.00: £293.00)
1m 100y (Fibresand) Stalls: Low GOING: 0.13 sec per fur (SLW) 7-30 (7-31)

1030[2] **Gulf Shaadi (82)***(87+)*(Fav)*(GLewis)* 3-9-2 SWhitworth(2) (lw: hld up & plld hrd: hdwy 6f out: led over 2f out: sn clr: v.easily)....— **1**
1146[4] Hong Kong Dollar **(53)***(64) (BJMeehan)* 3-8-8b DHarrison(8) (led over 6f: 2nd st: no ch w wnr)8 **2**
*1030** Legally Delicious **(67)***(60) (DWChapman)* 3-8-5 DeanMcKeown(5) (a.p: 3rd st: one pce)....½ **3**
1030[6] Club Elite **(52)***(46) (MJCamacho)* 3-7-9 LCharnock(3) (chsd ldr over 5f: 4th st: one pce)....2 **4**
681[9] Montague Dawson (IRE) **(73)***(50) (MrsNMacauley)* 3-8-11 (5) SDrowne(9) (bhd: rdn 5f out: 5th st: no hdwy)....9 **5**
Irchester Lass **(45)***(25) (SRBowring)* 3-7-11 JQuinn(1) (prom: rdn over 4f out: wknd over 3f out: 6th & btn st)....3 **6**
72[8] Zesti **(54)***(31) (TTClement)* 3-8-6 GHind(6) (b: swtg: a bhd)....2 **7**
Campaspe *(3) (JGFitzGerald)* 3-8-7 KFallon(7) (lengthy: unf: bkwd: sn rdn along: a bhd: t.o)15 **8**
893[10] Chadleigh Walk (IRE) **(38)** *(RHollinshead)* 3-7-12 (7)ow1 AEddery(4) (lw: a in rr: t.o)....½ **9**

8/11 GULF SHAADI, **7/2** Legally Delicious, **7/1** Montague Dawson (IRE), **12/1** Hong Kong Dollar (op 8/1), **20/1** Club Elite, Irchester Lass, Campaspe, Chadleigh Walk (IRE), **25/1** Zesti, CSF £11.08 TOTE £1.50: £1.20 £1.90 £1.10 (£5.50) Trio £4.30 OWNER Laurel (Leisure) Ltd (EPSOM) BRED Sheikh Mohammed bin Rashid al Maktoum 9 Rn 1m 50.9 (6.90) SF: 45/22/18/4/8/-/-/-/-

1331 EDGBASTON H'CAP (0-65) (3-Y.O+) (Class F) £2,243.00 (£618.00: £293.00)
5f (Fibresand) Stalls: Low GOING: 0.13 sec per fur (SLW) 8-00 (8-02)

1080⁶ **Bonny Melody (30)***(40) (PDEvans)* 4-7-5 (7) AmandaSanders(10) (a.p: 3rd st: hung lft 1f out: qcknd to ld cl home) — **1**
688⁵ Chadwell Hall **(58)***(66)*(Fav)*(SRBowring)* 4-9-7b(5) CTeague(5) (b.off hind: led tl hdd cl home) ½ **2**
1157⁷ Featherstone Lane **(60)***(67) (MissLCSiddall)* 4-9-9v(5) PMcCabe(3) (s.s: gd hdwy fnl f: fin wl) ½ **3**
1214² The Institute Boy **(49)***(53) (MissJFCraze)* 5-9-3v SWebster(1) (lw: w ldr: 2nd st: ev ch 1f out: nt qckn) 1 **4**
1032² My Cherrywell **(51)***(52) (LRLloyd-James)* 5-9-5v JFortune(7) (gd late hdwy: nvr nrr) ¾ **5**
891³ Poly Laureon (IRE) **(60)***(60) (RHollinshead)* 3-9-5 TIves(11) (chsd ldrs: 5th st: no hdwy) ½ **6**
1151⁸ Green's Bid **(56)***(51) (DWChapman)* 5-9-10 DeanMcKeown(6) (lw: a bhd) 1½ **7**
1042⁷ Ivy Lilian (IRE) **(43)***(38) (WMBrisbourne)* 3-7-9 (7) SLanigan(9) (prom: 4th st: wknd over 1f out) s.h **8**
1032³ Most Uppitty **(56)***(50) (JBerry)* 3-8-8b(7) PRoberts(2) (a bhd) hd **9**
1201² Southern Dominion **(52)***(38) (WGMTurner)* 3-8-11 DHarrison(4) (chsd ldrs: 6th st: eased whn btn fnl f) 2½ **10**

5/2 Chadwell Hall, **3/1** Southern Dominion, **11/2** My Cherrywell, **6/1** The Institute Boy, **7/1** Most Uppitty, **8/1** Poly Laureon (IRE), **12/1** Featherstone Lane, BONNY MELODY, **16/1** Green's Bid, **25/1** Ivy Lilian (IRE), CSF £44.75 CT £362.91 TOTE £19.10: £3.30 £1.70 £5.50 (£111.80) Trio £158.80 OWNER Mrs E. A. Dawson (WELSHPOOL) BRED Mrs M. Watt 10 Rn

64.0 secs (6.00) SF: -/-/-/-/-/-/-/-/-/-
WEIGHT FOR AGE 3yo-9lb

1332 OVAL H'CAP (0-70) (4-Y.O+) (Class E) £2,976.00 (£888.00: £424.00: £192.00)
1m 4f (Fibresand) Stalls: Low GOING: 0.13 sec per fur (SLW) 8-30 (8-30)

1029² **Sommersby (IRE) (56)***(70+) (ACStewart)* 4-9-7 SWhitworth(11) (b: hld up & bhd: hdwy over 5f out: led 2f out: qcknd clr: v.easily) — **1**
1166⁹ Rolling Waters **(54)***(65) (JARToller)* 5-9-5 WNewnes(7) (hld up: hdwy over 5f out: 2nd st: ev ch wl over 1f out: one pce) 2 **2**
*1091** Mr Bean **(62)***(67) (KRBurke)* 5-9-8 (5) SDrowne(2) (lw: chsd ldr: led 5f out tl 2f out: 3rd st: one pce) 5 **3**
1022⁶ Barti-Ddu **(59)***(61) (SCWilliams)* 4-9-7 (3) DWright(4) (lw: prom: 4th st: one pce) 2 **4**
1029⁸ Our Bessie **(33)***(33) (DMarks)* 4-7-12e FNorton(6) (prom: rdn over 5f out: lost pl 4f out: styd on fnl 2f) 1¾ **5**
1029⁵ Absalom's Pillar **(63)***(63) (JMackie)* 5-10-0 GCarter(10) (wl bhd 5f out: hdwy & 6th st: n.d) s.h **6**
1160⁴ Scalp 'em (IRE) **(50)***(35) (PDEvans)* 7-9-1 JFortune(5) (s.s: sn rcvrd: rdn & wknd 5f out) 11 **7**
1205³ Killick **(55)***(37)*(Fav)*(ABailey)* 7-9-6 MWigham(1) (led 7f: 5th & wkng st) 2½ **8**
1149⁵ Greek Night Out (IRE) **(40)***(21) (MrsVAAconley)* 4-8-5 MDeering(8) (a bhd) ½ **9**
389⁵ Winn's Pride (IRE) **(50)***(28) (RHollinshead)* 4-9-1 TIves(9) (lw: a bhd) 2½ **10**
Lady Tjonger **(44)** *(DrJDScargill)* 4-8-9 GHind(3) (bit bkwd: bhd: rdn 7f out: t.o fnl 4f) dist **11**

5/2 Killick (4/1-2/1), **4/1** SOMMERSBY (IRE), **11/2** Mr Bean, **7/1** Barti-Ddu, Scalp 'em (IRE), **10/1** Rolling Waters, Our Bessie, Winn's Pride (IRE), **12/1** Absalom's Pillar, **20/1** Lady Tjonger, **25/1** Greek Night Out (IRE), CSF £44.56 CT £213.00 TOTE £4.60: £2.00 £3.60 £2.10 (£71.90) Trio £31.30 OWNER Mr Frank Nastasi (NEWMARKET) BRED Campbell Stud 11 Rn

2m 43.1 (12.10) SF: 36/31/33/27/-/29/1/3/-/-/-

1333 FOLEY STEEL (S) STKS (2-Y.O) (Class G) £2,610.00 (£630.00)
6f (Fibresand) Stalls: Low GOING: 0.13 sec per fur (SLW) 9-00 (9-00)

1031³ **Lila Pedigo (IRE)** *(19+)*(Fav)*(JBerry)* 2-8-7 GCarter(1) (lw: chsd ldr: 2nd st: led wl over 1f out: v.easily) — **1**
1213³ Magic Bird (IRE) *(6) (JLSpearing)* 2-8-7b GHind(2) (led over 4f: no ch w wnr) 5 **2**

1/5 LILA PEDIGO (IRE), **7/2** Magic Bird (IRE), TOTE £1.20 OWNER Mr J. Nixon (COCKERHAM) BRED Miss Corona O'Brien 2 Rn

1m 19.8 (8.60) SF: -/-
No bid

1334 LINDLEY PLANT H'CAP (0-65) (3-Y.O+) (Class F) £2,415.00 (£665.00: £315.00)
7f (Fibresand) Stalls: Low GOING: 0.13 sec per fur (SLW) 9-30 (9-32)

769⁸ **Souperficial (56)***(69)*(Fav)*(JAGlover)* 4-9-10v JFortune(1) (hld up & bhd: hdwy 4f out: 3rd st: led wl over 1f out: sn clr: hung lft: r.o wl) — **1**

1087[6] What a Nightmare (IRE) **(59)***(61) (JAGlover)* 3-9-2b TIves(10) (plld hrd: a.p: led 4f out tl wl over 1f out: one pce) 5 2
1034[9] Farmer Jock **(41)***(42) (MrsNMacauley)* 13-8-4 (5) CTeague(11) (hld up & bhd: gd hdwy 3f out: 2nd st: ev ch wl over 1f out: one pce) ....hd 3
601[13] Letsbeonestaboutit **(52)***(47) (MissGayKelleway)* 9-9-6v MWigham(12) (hdwy over 1f out: r.o ins fnl f) 3 4
1088[10] Corona Gold **(40)***(30) (JGFitzGerald)* 5-8-8 KFallon(2) (lw: prom: 6th st: no hdwy) 2 5
1070[14] It's so Easy **(42)***(23) (APJames)* 4-8-10 FNorton(3) (lw: prom: 7th & wkng st) 4 6
1199[12] Leguard Express (IRE) **(37)***(11) (OO'Neill)* 7-8-5b ow1 VSlattery(7) (lw: prom: rdn 3f out: 5th & wkng st: eased whn btn ins fnl f) 2½ 7
648[19] Prince Pellinore **(54)***(25) (JohnBerry)* 3-8-11 CDwyer(8) (a bhd) 2 8
283[7] Mr Lowry **(48)***(15) (LJBarratt)* 3-8-5 LCharnock(5) (a bhd) 1½ 9
594[16] Cronk's Courage **(41)***(4) (MGMeagher)* 9-8-4v(5) VHalliday(6) (led 3f: 4th st: eased whn btn fnl f) 1¾ 10
992* Royal Comedian **(36)** *(BWMurray)* 6-8-4 JQuinn(4) (hrd rdn 5f out: bhd fnl 3f) 3½ 11
1126[14] Face Up **(57)***(8) (BJMeehan)* 8-9-11 DHarrison(9) (lw: a bhd) 2 12

7/2 SOUPERFICIAL, **4/1** Leguard Express (IRE), **5/1** Royal Comedian (op 3/1), **6/1** What a Nightmare (IRE), **8/1** Corona Gold, **10/1** Letsbeonestaboutit, **12/1** Farmer Jock (op 8/1), **14/1** It's so Easy, Face Up, Cronk's Courage, **16/1** Mr Lowry, **33/1** Prince Pellinore, CSF £25.56 CT £219.40 TOTE £4.80: £2.10 £2.20 £3.20 (£8.00) Trio £177.50; £82.51 to 29/5/95 OWNER Mr M. G. Ridley (WORKSOP) BRED C. L. Loyd 12 Rn 1m 30.9 (6.90) SF: 37/18/10/15/-/-/-/-/-/-/-/-
WEIGHT FOR AGE 3yo-11lb

T/Plpt: £14.70 (636.5 Tckts). T/Qdpt: £10.10 (6.8 Tckts). KH

CHEPSTOW (L-H)
Monday May 29th (Good, Good to soft patches)

WEATHER: sunny WIND: fresh half against

1335 ST BRIDES H'CAP (0-80) (3-Y.O+ F & M) (Class D) £4,060.00 (£1,225.00: £595.00: £280.00) **6f 16y** Stalls: High GOING: 0.05 sec per fur (G) 2-00 (2-04)

1174[3] **Thatcherella (69)***(76) (MajorDNChappell)* 4-9-10 JReid(2) (a.p: slt ld over 1f out: r.o wl ins fnl f) ....— 1
1070[16] Louisville Belle (IRE) **(46)***(48) (MDIUsher)* 6-7-8 (7) CAdamson(1) (outpcd & bhd to ½-wy: styd on wl ins fnl f: nrst fin) 2 2
1126[3] Pharsical **(60)***(62) (MRChannon)* 4-9-1 RHughes(6) (led tl over 1f out: no ex) ....s.h 3
985[2] Maydaan (IRE) **(80)***(78)*(Fav)*(BHanbury)* 3-9-11 WRyan(4) (chsd ldrs: ev ch over 1f out: one pce fnl f) 1½ 4
1199* Tinker Osmaston **(67)***(65) (MSSaunders)* 4-9-8 7x NAdams(3) (lw: in rr: hdwy ½-wy: rdn 2f out: unable qckn) ....s.h 5
563[5] Prima Silk **(73)***(57) (MJRyan)* 4-10-0 DBiggs(9) (trckd ldrs: rdn 2f out: one pce) 5 6
1148[9] Frisky Miss (IRE) **(67)***(51) (KOCunningham-Brown)* 4-9-8 MRimmer(8) (chsd ldrs: rdn over 1f out: sn btn) ....nk 7
1222[7] Green City **(80)***(48) (RHannon)* 3-9-4 (7) MarkDenaro(5) (in tch whn stumbled over 4f out: sltly hmpd 3f out: nt rcvr) 6 8
Ithkurni (USA) **(39)** *(PHayward)* 6-7-8 ow1 EJohnson(7) (in tch whn broke leg & p.u 3f out: dead) .... P

LONG HANDICAP Ithkurni (USA) 6-10

2/1 Maydaan (IRE), **7/2** THATCHERELLA, **11/2** Pharsical, **13/2** Green City, **8/1** Prima Silk (op 5/1), **9/1** Tinker Osmaston (op 6/1), **14/1** Frisky Miss (IRE), **33/1** Louisville Belle (IRE), **66/1** Ithkurni (USA), CSF £80.03 CT £566.48 TOTE £3.80: £1.50 £4.00 £1.70 (£85.10) Trio £68.30 OWNER Mr J. H. Widdows (WHITSBURY) BRED M. L. Page 9 Rn 1m 12.6 (3.60) SF: 59/31/45/51/48/40/34/21/-
WEIGHT FOR AGE 3yo-10lb

1336 ST FAGANS (S) STKS (2-Y.O) (Class G) £2,437.00 (£682.00: £331.00) **6f 16y** Stalls: High GOING: 0.05 sec per fur (G) 2-30 (2-32)

1169[7] **Whispering Dawn** *(64+)*(Fav)*(MRChannon)* 2-8-1 (5) PPMurphy(1) (cl up gng wl: led 2f out: sn clr: rdn out) ....— 1
Natatari (IRE) *(54) (MCPipe)* 2-8-6 JReid(5) (w'like: scope: slt ld 4f: sn rdn: kpt on one pce) 4 2
1077[5] Shanoora (IRE) *(57) (BPalling)* 2-8-11 TSprake(4) (cl up: rdn & ev ch 2f out: kpt on one pce)½ 3
Spanish Luck *(44) (JWHills)* 2-7-13 (7) MHenry(2) (cmpt: scope: sn cl up: ev ch over 2f out: unable qckn: eased whn btn fnl f) 3 4
Red Time *(36) (MSSaunders)* 2-8-11 ADicks(7) (leggy: unf: swvd bdly lft s: wl bhd tl r.o fnl 2f: nrst fin) 5 5

782[11] Digwana (IRE) *(36) (TMJones)* 2-8-11 MRimmer(6) (chsd ldrs: rdn & hung lft over 2f out: sn wknd) ....hd 6
Public Acclaim *(23) (MBlanshard)* 2-8-6 WRyan(3) (w'like: bit bkwd: s.i.s: nvr nr ldrs) 3 7
970[6] Cashtal Lace *(SGKnight)* 2-8-3 (3) SSanders(8) (chsd ldrs over 2f: wl bhd fnl 2f: t.o) 15 8

Evens WHISPERING DAWN, **5/2** Natatarl (IRE), **7/1** Shanoora (IRE), **12/1** Spanish Luck (op 5/1), **14/1** Public Acclaim (op 6/1), **33/1** Red Time, **50/1** Digwana (IRE), Cashtal Lace, CSF £3.69 TOTE £1.70: £1.10 £1.10 £1.60 (£1.50) OWNER Mr W. H. Ponsonby (UPPER LAMBOURN) BRED R. Barber 8 Rn 1m 14.6 (5.60) SF: 17/7/10/-/-/-/-/-
Bt in 11,500 gns

1337 ST BRIAVELS MAIDEN STKS (3-Y.O+) (Class D) £3,923.50 (£1,183.00: £574.00: £269.50) **1m 14y** Stalls: High GOING: 0.05 sec per fur (G) 3-00 (3-03)

695[7] **Lovely Lyca** *(81) (JWHills)* 3-8-0 (7) MHenry(9) (trckd ldrs: led wl over 2f out to 1f out: r.o u.p to ld last strides) ....— 1
Aldevonie *(81) (HRACecil)* 3-8-7 WRyan(7) (scope: s.s: hdwy over 2f out: r.o wl ins fnl f: jst failed) ....hd 2
1186[3] Pinzon (USA) **(83)***(86)*(Fav)*(PWChapple-Hyam)* 3-8-12 JReid(5) (lw: trckd ldrs gng wl: led 1f out: sn rdn: no ex & hdd last strides) ....s.h 3
My Gina *(67) (MRStoute)* 3-8-7 KBradshaw(12) (w'like: bit bkwd: chsd ldrs: outpcd over 2f out: kpt on fnl f) 7 4
Mukallad (IRE) *(68) (MajorWRHern)* 3-8-12 TSprake(8) (w'like: trckd ldrs: led over 3f out tl wl over 2f out: unable qckn) 2 5
937[11] Pacific Overture *(58) (CRBarwell)* 3-8-10 ow3 RHughes(3) (hld up: shkn up over 1f out: nvr nr to chal) 2½ 6
Julia's Freebee *(50) (TMJones)* 4-9-5 MRimmer(10) (bit bkwd: in tch: rdn 3f out: kpt on) 4 7
888[11] Rumpelstiltskin *(53) (MartynMeade)* 3-8-12 VSlattery(6) (prom to ½-wy) 1¼ 8
1128[13] Cafe Glace *(44) (RAkehurst)* 3-8-4 (3) SSanders(1) (cl up to ½-wy: grad wknd) 2 9
1053[9] Bold Sally *(37) (MrsSDWilliams)* 3-8-7 SO'Gorman(2) (led tl over 3f out: wknd) 3½ 10
881[11] Return To Brighton *(30) (PCClarke)* 3-8-7 NAdams(4) (a bhd) 3½ 11
853[16] Shoodah (IRE) *(PHayward)* 4-9-7 (3) CHodgson(11) (bhd fnl 3f: t.o) 20 12

7/4 Pinzon (USA), **100/30** Aldevonie (op 2/1), **9/2** My Gina, **13/2** LOVELY LYCA (op 4/1), **8/1** Mukallad (IRE) (op 4/1), **33/1** Cafe Glace, **66/1** Julia's Freebee, Rumpelstiltskin, Bold Sally, **100/1** Pacific Overture, Return To Brighton, Shoodah (IRE), CSF £25.09 TOTE £10.00: £2.20 £1.60 £1.20 (£20.90) Trio £6.30 OWNER The Losers Owners Group (LAMBOURN) BRED Stowell Hill Ltd 12 Rn 1m 37.0 (4.50) SF: 46/46/51/32/33/23/27/18/9/2/-/-
WEIGHT FOR AGE 3yo-12lb

1338 ST JOHN LIMITED STKS (0-75) (3-Y.O+) (Class D) £3,741.50 (£1,127.00: £546.00: £255.50) **1m 14y** Stalls: High GOING: 0.05 sec per fur (G) 3-30 (3-32)

1124* **Blaze of Song** **(82)***(88)*(Fav)*(RHannon)* 3-9-0 JReid(2) (plld hrd early: trckd ldrs: chal 1f out: hrd rdn to ld wl ins fnl f) ....— 1
1070[11] Knobbleeneeze **(74)***(83) (MRChannon)* 5-9-8v RHughes(4) (trckd ldr gng wl: led tl wl ins fnl f: r.o) ....nk 2
504[17] Daffaq **(73)***(78) (PTWalwyn)* 3-8-10 WRyan(3) (led: pushed along over 2f out: rdn & hdd 1f out: one pce) 2½ 3
1172[6] A Million to One (IRE) **(74)***(73) (MBell)* 3-8-1 (7)ow3 GFaulkner(1) (lw: hld up: plld out 2f out: rdn & hung lft over 1f out: one pce) ....½ 4

8/15 BLAZE OF SONG (op 4/5), **4/1** A Million to One (IRE) (op 5/2), **13/2** Knobbleeneeze, **7/1** Daffaq (op 9/2), CSF £4.13 TOTE £1.50 (£2.80) OWNER Mr D. Boocock (MARLBOROUGH) BRED D. G. Mason 4 Rn 1m 37.4 (4.90) SF: 50/57/40/35
WEIGHT FOR AGE 3yo-12lb

1339 ST ARVANS MAIDEN STKS (3-Y.O+) (Class D) £3,900.75 (£1,176.00: £570.50: £267.75) **1m 4f 23y** Stalls: Low GOING: 0.05 sec per fur (G) 4-00 (4-04)

Song of Tara (IRE) *(79++) (PWChapple-Hyam)* 3-8-8 JReid(1) (w'like: scope: chsd ldrs: wnt 2nd over 3f out: led on bit 2f out: shkn up: sn clr: impressive) ....— 1
886[4] En Vacances (IRE) *(65) (AGFoster)* 3-8-3 TSprake(2) (led 2f: chsd ldrs: outpcd over 2f out: rallied u.p fnl f) 7 2
978[3] Main Offender **(89)***(69)*(Fav)*(HRACecil)* 3-8-8 WRyan(6) (led after 2f: rdn over 2f out: sn hdd: one pce) ....¾ 3
853[10] Step Aloft *(63) (LordHuntingdon)* 3-8-0 (3) SSanders(4) (mid div: hdwy over 2f out: one pce fnl f) ....nk 4

978[9] Baddi Quest *(68) (BHanbury)* 3-8-8 MRimmer(8) (a.p: trckd ldr 6f out tl over 3f out: hrd rdn: one pce) ....nk 5
929[6] Shrewd Alibi *(61) (IABalding)* 4-9-12 SO'Gorman(10) (mid div: rdn 3f out: no hdwy) 5 6
1175[6] Indicator *(55) (RHannon)* 3-8-9 ow1 RHughes(11) (hld up mid div: gd hdwy over 5f out: no imp fnl 3f) 5 7
Young Clifford (USA) *(48) (FJordan)* 4-9-12 TWall(7) (bit bkwd: chsd ldrs tl rdn & wknd over 2f out) 5 8
Riverbank Red *(43) (PCClarke)* 4-9-0 (7) IonaWands(3) (bhd tl sme late hdwy) ....hd 9
Yahmi (IRE) *(15) (JABOld)* 5-9-9 (3) CHodgson(5) (lost tch 5f out: t.o) 25 10
Silent Sovereign *(PCClarke)* 6-9-12b NAdams(9) (a bhd: t.o fnl 6f) 25 11

8/13 Main Offender (op Evens), **4/1** SONG OF TARA (IRE) (op 7/4), **7/1** Indicator, **20/1** Step Aloft, Shrewd Alibi, **25/1** Baddi Quest, Young Clifford (USA), **40/1** En Vacances (IRE), Yahmi (IRE), **100/1** Riverbank Red, Silent Sovereign, CSF £113.03 TOTE £3.40: £1.40 £3.90 £1.10 (£58.90) Trio £22.80 OWNER Dr A. J. F. O'Reilly (MARLBOROUGH) BRED Kilcarn Stud 11 Rn

2m 39.3 (8.00) SF: 43/29/33/27/32/43/19/30/25/-/-

WEIGHT FOR AGE 3yo-18lb

1340

ST ATHAN H'CAP (0-80) (3-Y.O+) (Class D) £3,787.00 (£1,141.00: £553.00: £259.00) **1m 4f 23y** Stalls: Low GOING: 0.05 sec per fur (G) 4-30 (4-33)

1140[5] **Bayrak (USA) (69)***(84) (MJRyan)* 5-9-10 RHughes(4) (led 3f: 2nd st: led over 4f out: clr over 1f out: eased ins fnl f: cheekily) ....— 1
763[7] Exemption **(65)***(79) (HCandy)* 4-9-6 GeorginaFrost(7) (trckd ldrs: 3rd st: chsd wnr over 3f out: kpt on u.p fnl f: no ch w wnr) ....¾ 2
763[12] Wildfire (SWI) **(57)***(51) (RAkehurst)* 4-8-12 WRyan(6) (hld up: 5th st: rdn over 3f out: kpt on one pce) 15 3
1166[15] Desert Power **(63)***(57) (MartynMeade)* 6-9-4 VSlattery(2) (cl up: led after 3f tl over 4f out: rdn & one pce fnl 2f) ....hd 4
River Island (USA) **(60)***(52) (JABOld)* 7-9-1 TSprake(5) (s.i.s: bhd: lost tch 5f out: styd on again fnl 2f: nvr nr ldrs) 1½ 5
950[6] Ruby Venture **(64)***(53) (SPCWoods)* 3-7-12 (3) SSanders(3) (lw: hld up in rr: outpcd ½-wy: hdwy & cl 6th st: wknd over 2f out) 2 6
783[2] Night Time **(70)***(40)*(Fav)*(RHannon)* 3-8-7 JReid(1) (lw: trckd ldrs: 4th st: rdn & wknd 4f out: eased whn btn) 15 7

2/1 Night Time (op 7/2), **7/2** BAYRAK (USA) (5/2-4/1), **9/2** Wildfire (SWI) (op 11/4), **6/1** Exemption (op 4/1), **13/2** Ruby Venture, **14/1** River Island (USA), **16/1** Desert Power, CSF £22.23 TOTE £3.80: £2.10 £2.30 (£11.20) OWNER Mr A. S. Reid (NEWMARKET) BRED Swettenham Stud 7 Rn

2m 39.5 (8.20) SF: 58/53/25/31/26/9/-

WEIGHT FOR AGE 3yo-18lb

OFFICIAL EXPLANATION **Night Time: the jockey stated that the colt had gurgled two furlongs out and may have wind problems.**

T/Plpt: £10.10 (596.48 Tckts). T/Qdpt: £3.00 (20.5 Tckts). RL

1297-DONCASTER (L-H)
Monday May 29th (Good)

WEATHER: overcast WIND: str against

1341

E.B.F. VYNER MAIDEN STKS (2-Y.O) (Class D) £3,655.00 (£1,090.00: £520.00: £235.00) **5f** Stalls: High GOING: 0.07 sec per fur (G) 2-15 (2-17)

Red Stream (USA) *(67+) (MRStoute)* 2-8-9 RHills(5) (lt-f: unf: hld up: swtchd lft over 1f out: qcknd to ld wl ins fnl f) ....— 1
1041[2] Evening Chime (USA) *(70) (MrsJRRamsden)* 2-9-0 KFallon(3) (lw: a.p: led ent fnl f tl hdd nr fin) ....¾ 2
760[3] Centurion *(63)*(Fav)*(RHannon)* 2-9-0 PatEddery(6) (lw: led tl appr fnl f: sn rdn: no ex) 2 3
Midnight Escape *(60) (CFWall)* 2-9-0 NCarlisle(4) (unf: scope: bit bkwd: dwlt: sn chsng ldrs: outpcd over 1f out: rallied u.p ins fnl f) 1 4
Haysong (IRE) *(23) (JPLeigh)* 2-8-6 (3) JTate(2) (leggy: lt-f: swvd lft s: a bhd & outpcd) 10 5
Distinctly Red (IRE) *(JBerry)* 2-9-0 GCarter(1) (lt-f: hmpd s: a bhd & outpcd: t.o) 15 6

5/4 Centurion, **3/1** RED STREAM (USA) (op 2/1), **4/1** Evening Chime (USA), **13/2** Distinctly Red (IRE) (op 4/1), **8/1** Midnight Escape, **20/1** Haysong (IRE), CSF £14.93 TOTE £4.10: £2.00 £2.50 (£10.40) OWNER Mr Saeed Suhail (NEWMARKET) BRED C. Clay, M. Clay, C. Clay, B. Clay III et al 6 Rn

62.99 secs (4.59) SF: 22/25/18/15/-/-

1342 SHADWELL STUD SERIES APPRENTICE H'CAP (0-70) (3-Y.O+) (Class E) £3,103.20 (£939.60: £458.80: £218.40)
5f Stalls: High GOING: 0.07 sec per fur (G) 2-50 (2-51)

*107*9 **Super Rocky (60)***(65)*(Fav)*(RBastiman)* 6-9-8 HBastiman(7) (swtg: led tl appr fnl f: rallied u.p to ld cl home) — 1
966 4 Stolen Kiss (IRE) **(63)***(68) (MWEasterby)* 3-9-2b GParkin(2) (a.p: led appr fnl f: shkn up & hdd nr fin) s.h 2
*1032*10 Nadwaty (IRE) **(54)***(56) (MCChapman)* 3-8-7 CMunday(3) (swtg: chsd ldrs: rdn over 1f out: kpt on nr fin) 1 3
Murray's Mazda (IRE) **(48)***(46) (JLEyre)* 6-8-5 (5) GMacDonald(4) (bit bkwd: dwlt: r.o appr fnl f: nvr nrr) 1¼ 4
Taffeta Silk (USA) **(64)***(62) (WJarvis)* 4-9-12 MHumphries(5) (s.i.s: sn chsng ldrs: rdn 2f out: kpt on same pce fnl f) s.h 5
645 8 Honey Trader **(66)***(56) (JBerry)* 3-9-5 PRoberts(1) (in tch: rdn over 2f out: no imp) 2½ 6
Coney Hills **(34)***(21) (NBycroft)* 4-7-10 NVarley(9) (bit bkwd: a outpcd & bhd) ¾ 7
Kabcast **(57)***(33) (DWChapman)* 10-9-5b DarrenMoffatt(6) (bkwd: swtg: chsd ldrs: rdn ½-wy: sn lost pl) 3½ 8

3/1 SUPER ROCKY, **7/2** Stolen Kiss (IRE), **5/1** Taffeta Silk (USA) (op 3/1), **6/1** Nadwaty (IRE), **7/1** Honey Trader, **9/1** Murray's Mazda (IRE), **12/1** Kabcast (op 8/1), **14/1** Coney Hills, CSF £13.19 CT £52.31 TOTE £3.90: £1.60 £1.40 £2.40 (£5.60) Trio £25.80 OWNER Mr I. B. Barker (WETHERBY) BRED J. Berry 8 Rn 63.27 secs (4.87) SF: 29/23/11/10/26/11/-/-
WEIGHT FOR AGE 3yo-9lb

1343 OWLERTON STADIUM SHEFFIELD CONDITIONS STKS (2-Y.O) (Class C) £4,840.50 (£1,789.50: £857.25: £348.75: £136.88: £52.12)
6f Stalls: High GOING: 0.07 sec per fur (G) 3-20 (3-20)

810* **South Salem (USA)** *(76+)*(Fav)*(DRLoder)* 2-8-11 GCarter(2) (lw: hld up: shkn up & qcknd to ld ins fnl f: r.o wl) — 1
1197* Eastern Prophets *(79) (GLewis)* 2-9-5 PatEddery(1) (lw: a.p: led wl over 1f out tl ins fnl f: one pce) 2 2
1104 6 Safio *(70) (CSmith)* 2-9-0 (3) JTate(3) (s.i.s: swtchd lft & hdwy over 1f out: outpcd fnl f) 2½ 3
684* Montrestar *(49) (PDEvans)* 2-9-1 RHills(4) (led over 4f: rdn & outpcd appr fnl f) 7 4
825 10 Etterby Park (USA) *(39) (MDIUsher)* 2-8-11 RCochrane(5) (bit bkwd: prom: rdn 2f out: sn btn) 2½ 5
871 7 Kustom Kit (IRE) *(41) (BAMcMahon)* 2-9-1 KFallon(6) (lw: chsd ldrs: rdn ½-wy: sn lost tch) ¾ 6

Evens SOUTH SALEM (USA), **15/8** Eastern Prophets, **7/1** Montrestar, **10/1** Safio (op 6/1), Kustom Kit (IRE), **25/1** Etterby Park (USA), CSF £3.51 TOTE £1.90: £1.10 £1.70 (£1.60) OWNER Mrs Virginia KraftPayson (NEWMARKET) BRED Virginia Kraft Payson 6 Rn
1m 16.22 (5.22) SF: 29/32/23/2/-/-

1344 ST LEGER CLUB SOCIETY DRAW H'CAP (0-80) (3-Y.O+) (Class D) £4,503.00 (£1,344.00: £642.00: £291.00)
1m (round) Stalls: Low GOING: 0.07 sec per fur (G) 3-50 (3-52)

980 6 **Bettergeton (75)***(85) (PJBevan)* 3-9-0 NCarlisle(3) (chsd ldrs: 6th st: qcknd to ld over 1f out: sn clr: rdn out) — 1
1183 7 Khayrapour (IRE) **(68)***(76)*(Fav)*(BJMeehan)* 5-9-5 PatEddery(6) (lw: s.s: hdwy on ins & n.m.r 3f out: swtchd rt & hmpd over 1f out: str run fnl f: unlucky) 1 2
546 2 Just Harry **(64)***(66) (MJRyan)* 4-9-1 RCochrane(13) (hld up: hdwy over 2f out: kpt on u.p fnl f) 3 3
1126 4 Poyle Jezebelle **(46)***(48) (MBlanshard)* 4-7-11 GBardwell(10) (swtg: hdwy 3f out: sn rdn: styd on fnl f) hd 4
988 10 Move Smartly (IRE) **(53)***(53) (FHLee)* 5-8-4 GCarter(11) (hld up: hdwy over 2f out: one pce appr fnl f) 1 5
*1033*4 Sweet Mate **(57)***(51) (SRBowring)* 3-7-7b(3)ow3 DarrenMoffatt(5) (swtg: chsd ldrs: 5th st: wknd over 1f out) 1¼ 6
749 14 Halmanerror **(61)***(56) (MrsJRRamsden)* 5-8-12 KFallon(1) (hld up in tch: 7th st: sn rdn: r.o wl ins fnl f) 1 7
Buster **(47)***(41) (MrsBarbaraWaring)* 7-7-7 (5) NVarley(2) (bit bkwd: prom: 4th st: wknd over 2f out) ½ 8
Parliament Piece **(73)***(64) (MrsMReveley)* 9-9-3 (7) GParkin(9) (bit bkwd: prom: 3rd st: wknd wl over 1f out) 1¾ 9
1172 4 Gypsy Love (USA) **(70)***(59)*(Fav)*(PWChapple-Hyam)* 3-8-2 (7)ow2 RHavlin(7) (bhd: effrt u.p 4f out: no imp) s.h 10

1148[8] Awesome Venture **(51)***(41) (MCChapman)* 5-7-9 (7) CMunday(14) (led & sn clr: hdd over 1f out: wknd qckly)....½ **11**
Ooh Ah Cantona **(60)***(50) (JLEyre)* 4-8-11 RLappin(4) (chsd ldr: 2nd st: wknd wl over 1f out)....s.h **12**
Petonellajill **(57)***(47) (JGMO'Shea)* 5-8-5 (3) JTate(8) (bit bkwd: a in rr)....s.h **13**
946[3] Midnight Jazz (IRE) **(72)***(44) (WAO'Gorman)* 5-9-9 EmmaO'Gorman(12) (lw: s.s: bhd: rdn 4f out: no imp: t.o)....9 **14**

LONG HANDICAP Sweet Mate 6-12

7/2 Khayrapour (IRE) (9/2-3/1), Gypsy Love (USA), **13/2** Just Harry, **8/1** Poyle Jezebelle, Midnight Jazz (IRE), Halmanerror, **10/1** BETTERGETON, **16/1** Parliament Piece, Move Smartly (IRE), Awesome Venture, **20/1** Sweet Mate, Ooh Ah Cantona, **25/1** Petonellajill, **50/1** Buster, CSF £46.14 CT £237.84 TOTE £12.30: £3.10 £1.20 £2.00 (£50.90) Trio £76.20 OWNER Mr Derek Boulton (UTTOXETER) BRED R. and Mrs Healy-Fenton 14 Rn
1m 41.21 (4.91) SF: 53/56/46/28/33/19/36/21/44/27/21/30/27/24
WEIGHT FOR AGE 3yo-12lb

1345 GRESLEY STKS (3-Y.O+) (Class C) £5,679.60 (£2,049.60: £984.80: £404.00: £162.00) 1m (round) Stalls: High GOING: 0.07 sec per fur (G) 4-20 (4-22)

1221* **First Island (IRE)** *(110) (GWragg)* 3-8-8 RCochrane(5) (lw: hld up: swtchd outside 3f out: led over 1f out: drvn clr)....— **1**
853* Krystallos *(104) (RHannon)* 3-8-8 PatEddery(1) (a.p: ev ch over 1f out: unable qckn fnl f)....3 **2**
1107[5] Juyush (USA) **(112)***(106)*(Fav)*(BWHills)* 3-8-12 RHills(2) (stumbled s: sn led: rdn & hdd over 1f out: sn btn)....1¼ **3**
Zamalek (USA) **(102)***(90) (HRACecil)* 3-8-8 AMcGlone(6) (h.d.w: bit bkwd: prom tl wknd over 1f out: improve)....6 **4**
1135[6] Barbaroja **(97)***(63) (JGFitzGerald)* 4-9-9b KFallon(4) (sn bhd: lost tch 3f out: t.o)....15 **5**
Mytilene (IRE) *(JHMGosden)* 4-9-0 GHind(3) (Withdrawn not under Starter's orders: unruly & uns rdr leaving paddock).... **W**

6/4 Juyush (USA), **11/4** FIRST ISLAND (IRE) (op 5/1), **4/1** Zamalek (USA), **7/1** Krystallos, **20/1** Barbaroja, CSF £15.28 TOTE £4.20: £1.60 £1.90 (£6.40) OWNER Mollers Racing (NEWMARKET) BRED Citadel Stud 5 Rn
1m 41.21 (4.91) SF: 50/44/46/30/15/-
WEIGHT FOR AGE 3yo-12lb

1346 YORKSHIRE STAND MAIDEN STKS (3-Y.O F) (Class D) £4,070.30 (£1,216.40: £582.20: £265.10) 1m 2f 60y Stalls: Low GOING: 0.07 sec per fur (G) 4-50 (4-53)

1105[3] **Dawlah (92)***(100) (HThomsonJones)* 3-8-11 RHills(6) (swtg: chsd ldr: 2nd st: led over 2f out: shkn up & qcknd fnl f)....— **1**
868[2] Tinashaan (IRE) *(99)*(Fav)*(JRFanshawe)* 3-8-6 (5) NVarley(3) (plld hrd: hld up: 6th st: hdwy 3f out: ev ch ins fnl f: r.o)....¾ **2**
Dorothea Brooke (IRE) *(98) (PWHarris)* 3-8-11 GHind(7) (a.p: 5th st: effrt & ev ch 1f out: unable qckn)....nk **3**
Jambia *(88) (HRACecil)* 3-8-11 AMcGlone(8) (led tl over 2f out: rdn & wknd over 1f out)....7 **4**
950[3] Hatta Breeze *(64)*(Fav)*(MAJarvis)* 3-8-11 PatEddery(2) (swtg: hld up: 4th st: rdn 3f out: sn lost pl: t.o)....15 **5**
Bella Vitessa (IRE) *(53) (JWHills)* 3-8-11 RCochrane(4) (small: lt-f: bkwd: a in rr: t.o)....7 **6**
Deep Divide *(52) (EALDunlop)* 3-8-8 (3) JTate(1) (swtg: hld up: hdwy & 3rd st: wknd over 2f out: t.o)....¾ **7**
968[8] Pitter Patter *(MrsNMacauley)* 3-8-11 ACulhane(5) (s.s: a wl bhd: t.o)....dist **8**

5/2 Tinashaan (IRE), Hatta Breeze, **7/2** DAWLAH, **4/1** Jambia, **12/1** Bella Vitessa (IRE), Deep Divide, **16/1** Dorothea Brooke (IRE), **50/1** Pitter Patter, CSF £13.00 TOTE £4.10: £1.60 £1.40 £3.10 (£3.70) OWNER Mr Hamdan Al Maktoum (NEWMARKET) BRED Shadwell Estate Company Limited 8 Rn
2m 11.32 (4.32) SF: 67/66/65/55/31/20/19/-

1347 ARSKEY H'CAP (0-70) (3-Y.O+ F & M) (Class E) £3,947.50 (£1,180.00: £565.00: £257.50) 1m 4f Stalls: Low GOING: 0.07 sec per fur (G) 5-20 (5-21)

1095[2] **Ball Gown (69)***(77) (DTThom)* 5-9-10 (3) DRMcCabe(5) (hld up: 5th st: effrt & n.m.r over 1f out: str run fnl f: led cl home)....— **1**
635[11] Turquoise Sea (USA) **(70)***(78) (JLDunlop)* 3-8-10 PatEddery(8) (led: hrd rdn appr fnl f: ct nr fin)....nk **2**
566[4] Inchkeith **(61)***(68) (GWragg)* 3-8-1 AMcGlone(6) (lw: chsd ldr: 2nd st: ev ch ins fnl f: no ex cl home)....¾ **3**

786* On a Pedestal (IRE) **(56)***(59) (MrsJRRamsden)* 3-7-5 (5) NVarley(2) (chsd ldrs: 4th st: rdn over 1f out: one pce) 3 4
1218* Blue Nile (IRE) **(69)***(71)*(Fav)*(ACStewart)* 3-8-4 (5) 5x MHumphries(3) (hld up & bhd: hdwy & 6th st: effrt over 1f out: nt pce to chal) ....¾ 5
Quivira **(56)***(58) (TTClement)* 4-9-0 RHills(7) (swtg: hld up & bhd: nvr nr to chal) ....hd 6
975 5 Masuri Kabisa (USA) **(38)***(34) (HJCollingridge)* 4-7-3 (7)ow3 SLanigan(4) (bit bkwd: chsd ldrs: 3rd st: rdn over 2f out: sn btn) 2 7
839 16 Dolly Dolittle **(36)***(14) (HJCollingridge)* 4-7-8 ow1 GBardwell(1) (plld hrd: hld up: lost tch fnl 3f: t.o) 15 8

LONG HANDICAP Masuri Kabisa (USA) 7-4 Dolly Dolittle 7-0

2/1 Blue Nile (IRE), **4/1** On a Pedestal (IRE), Turquoise Sea (USA), **5/1** BALL GOWN, **9/1** Inchkeith (op 6/1), **10/1** Quivira, Masuri Kabisa (USA), **25/1** Dolly Dolittle, CSF £25.06 CT £162.96 TOTE £5.40: £1.90 £1.50 £2.10 (£17.90) Trio £44.10 OWNER Mr C. V. Lines (NEWMARKET) BRED J. M. Greetham 8 Rn
2m 40.6 (10.00) SF: 54/37/27/18/30/35/11/-
WEIGHT FOR AGE 3yo-18lb

T/Plpt: £29.30 (326.46 Tckts). T/Qdpt: £23.70 (5.4 Tckts). IM

0810-LEICESTER (R-H)
Monday May 29th (Good to firm)
WEATHER: overcast, heavy rain bef race 7 WIND: mod bhd

1348 LIONESS MAIDEN STKS (2-Y.O F) (Class D) £3,682.05 (£1,100.40: £526.70: £239.85) 5f 218y Stalls: Low GOING minus 0.60 sec per fur (F) 2-20 (2-21)

Solar Crystal (IRE) *(73+)*(Fav)*(HRACecil)* 2-8-11 WNewnes(2) (scope: chsd ldrs: led appr fnl f: rdn out) ....— 1
791 10 La Modiste *(70) (SDow)* 2-8-11 StephenDavies(6) (w ldr tl led 3f out: hdd 2f out: no ex ins fnl f) 1¼ 2
Singoalla (IRE) *(69) (JLDunlop)* 2-8-11 GDuffield(7) (leggy: unf: prom: led 2f out tl hdd & no ex appr fnl f) ....hd 3
Pendley Rose *(68) (PWHarris)* 2-8-11 JFortune(3) (unf: bkwd: chsd ldrs: ev ch over 1f out: kpt on) ....½ 4
Fag End (IRE) *(60) (MHTompkins)* 2-8-11 RDorans(8) (leggy: chsd ldrs: shkn up & wandered over 2f out: ev ch over 1f out: sn btn) 3 5
Pacific Grove *(55) (PFICole)* 2-8-11 TQuinn(1) (lt-f: unf: lw: led 3f: eased whn btn ins fnl f) 2 6
Herald Angel (IRE) *(25) (MHTompkins)* 2-8-6 (5) SMulvey(4) (cmpt: bit bkwd: s.i.s: a wl bhd) 11 7
Flash In The Pan (IRE) *(24) (MBell)* 2-8-11 JFanning(9) (lengthy: scope: sn pushed along: in tch 4f) ....½ 8
Miss Carottene *(20) (MJRyan)* 2-8-11 AClark(5) (w'like: scope: bit bkwd: dwlt: a bhd) 1½ 9

9/4 SOLAR CRYSTAL (IRE) (op 5/4), **7/2** Pacific Grove, **9/2** Pendley Rose, **15/2** Flash In The Pan (IRE), **10/1** Singoalla (IRE) (op 6/1), **14/1** La Modiste, **16/1** Fag End (IRE), **20/1** Miss Carottene, **25/1** Herald Angel (IRE), CSF £28.66 TOTE £2.50: £1.50 £3.70 £2.20 (£11.50) Trio £64.80; £42.01 to Leicester 30/5/95 OWNER Mr Michael Poland (NEWMARKET) BRED Michael Poland 9 Rn
1m 11.7 (1.70) SF: 21/18/17/16/8/3/-/-/-

1349 TIGERS APPRENTICE H'CAP (0-65) (4-Y.O+) (Class F) £2,826.80 (£794.80: £388.40) 1m 3f 183y Stalls: Low GOING minus 0.60 sec per fur (F) 2-55 (2-57)

1160 5 **Cliburnel News (IRE) (55)***(67) (ALForbes)* 5-8-13 (5) DDenby(2) (chsd ldrs: 5th st: led over 2f out: clr over 1f out: comf) ....— 1
884 12 Pip's Dream **(37)***(42) (MJRyan)* 4-7-11 (3) NicolaHowarth(3) (led & sn clr: hdd & no ex over 2f out) 5 2
550 12 Platini (IRE) **(55)***(54) (GBBalding)* 4-9-4v RPainter(6) (rdn & hdwy over 2f out: kpt on) 5 3
Thrower **(48)***(43) (WMBrisbourne)* 4-8-8 (3) MartinDwyer(5) (lw: hdwy over 4f out: one pce fnl 2f) 2½ 4
1086 7 Stalled (IRE) **(52)***(43) (PTWalwyn)* 5-8-8 (7)ow2 LJames(10) (lw: hld up & plld hrd: effrt 4f out: nvr rchd ldrs) 1½ 5
1144 4 Pride of May (IRE) **(65)***(56)*(Fav)*(RHannon)* 4-9-7b(7) EGreehy(1) (lw: chsd ldrs: 4th st: btn over 2f out) 1¾ 6
46 9 Springtime Affair **(44)***(34) (JWMullins)* 4-8-4 (3) DaneO'Neill(4) (hdwy 4f out: wknd 2f out) ....¾ 7
Belgran (USA) **(51)***(14) (WMBrisbourne)* 6-9-0 DGriffiths(7) (bkwd: chsd ldrs 8f) 20 8
Nordic Crown (IRE) **(54)***(11) (MCPipe)* 4-9-3b DGibbs(8) (prom: 3rd st: wknd 3f out) 4 9
Safe Secret **(46)** *(RBrotherton)* 4-8-6 (3) SLanigan(9) (bit bkwd: plld hrd: sn prom: 2nd st: sn wknd) ....dist 10

9/4 Pride of May (IRE), **3/1** Stalled (IRE), **11/2** CLIBURNEL NEWS (IRE), **6/1** Nordic Crown (IRE), **12/1** Safe Secret, **14/1** Pip's Dream, **16/1** Platini (IRE), **20/1** Belgran (USA), Thrower, **25/1** Springtime Affair, CSF £69.51 CT £1,052.73 TOTE £5.40: £1.40 £3.30 £3.20 (£17.60) Trio £162.40 OWNER Target Racing (UTTOXETER) BRED St Simon Foundation 10 Rn
2m 34.6 (5.80) SF: 17/-/4/-/-/6/-/-/-/-

1350 ANSTEY (S) H'CAP (0-60) (3-Y.O+) (Class G) £3,071.80 (£854.80: £411.40)
1m 1f 218y Stalls: Low GOING minus 0.60 sec per fur (F) 3-25 (3-40)

*1088*14 **Lady Highfield (35)***(43) (MJRyan)* 4-8-9 AClark(5) (b.hind: trckd ldrs: 7th st: led over 1f out: sn clr: pushed out) — **1**
1254 6 Il Fratello **(35)***(41) (NACallaghan)* 4-8-9 GDuffield(6) (prom: led 3f out tl over 1f out: one pce) 1¼ **2**
*628*7 Centaur Express **(40)***(40) (ALForbes)* 3-7-10 (3)ow6 AGarth(11) (bhd tl hdwy 3f out: r.o fnl f) ...nk **3**
818 2 Bold Mick **(49)***(53) (DJGMurraySmith)* 4-9-9 AMackay(15) (hdwy 2f out: r.o wl fnl f: nrst fin) 1 **4**
1285 4 Dots Dee **(25)***(28)*(Fav)*(JMBradley)* 6-7-10 (3) DWright(12) (b: s.i.s: hld up & bhd: nvr plcd to chal) nk **5**
1153 6 Rosina's Folly **(42)***(45) (JLHarris)* 4-8-11 (5) SDrowne(16) (chsd ldrs: 9th st: rdn 2f out: no imp) ½ **6**
1092 10 Clancy's Express **(35)***(38) (GBBalding)* 4-8-2 (7) DaneO'Neill(4) (hdwy 5f out: one pce fnl 2f) .hd **7**
1285 17 Tocco Jewel **(26)***(20) (MJRyan)* 5-7-7 (7)ow6 NicolaHowarth(14) (bhd: hdwy 5f out: wknd over 1f out) 1¾ **8**
1125 5 Two Way Stretch **(42)***(36) (GLMoore)* 3-7-10 (5)ow3 AWhelan(13) (in tch: pushed along over 4f out: no imp appr fnl f) 2 **9**
*833*9 Mint a Million (IRE) **(31)***(27) (MBlanshard)* 4-8-5 StephenDavies(1) (hld up & bhd: effrt over 3f out: sn btn & eased) nk **10**
1083 9 Gulf Bay **(38)***(28) (MBell)* 3-7-11vow1 JFanning(18) (plld hrd: nvr nr to chal) 3 **11**
1146 6 Magic Leader (IRE) **(39)***(29) (TTClement)* 3-7-5 (7) SLanigan(8) (b: prom: 6th st: wknd 3f out) ¾ **12**
860 4 Porte Belloch **(43)***(33)*(Fav)*(CTNash)* 4-9-3 TQuinn(3) (dwlt: led after 1f to 3f out: sn wknd) ..nk **13**
Mutawali (IRE) **(39)***(28) (RJBaker)* 5-8-13 JWilliams(17) (in tch 8f) hd **14**
Amaam Amaam **(50)***(39) (WJMusson)* 5-9-5 (5) PMcCabe(10) (in tch 5f) ½ **15**
Dream Missy **(31)***(19) (JRBosley)* 4-8-5 CRutter(19) (lw: chsd ldrs: 5th st: sn wknd) nk **16**
1207 10 Tobago Boy **(40)***(24) (MGMeagher)* 3-7-13 FNorton(7) (lw: led 1f: 4th st: wknd over 3f out) 2½ **17**
*399*7 Delmour **(25)***(4) (WMBrisbourne)* 4-7-6 (7) MartinDwyer(2) (lw: chsd ldrs: 8th st: sn wknd).....3½ **18**
*592*4 Midlin **(35)***(12) (JLHarris)* 5-8-9 SDWilliams(9) (chsd ldrs: 3rd st: wknd & eased 2f out) 1¼ **19**

LONG HANDICAP Centaur Express 7-3

4/1 Porte Belloch, Dots Dee, **6/1** Bold Mick, **10/1** Il Fratello, **11/1** Mint a Million (IRE), **12/1** Two Way Stretch, Tobago Boy, **14/1** Clancy's Express, Gulf Bay, Mutawali (IRE), **20/1** LADY HIGHFIELD, Magic Leader (IRE), Amaam Amaam, Midlin, **25/1** Centaur Express, **33/1** Rosina's Folly, Tocco Jewel, Dream Missy, **40/1** Delmour, CSF £209.04 CT £4,563.36 TOTE £37.50: £5.10 £2.50 £3.80 £1.60 (£173.30) Trio Not won; £511.41 to Leicester 30/5/95 OWNER Miss J. Nicholls (NEWMARKET) BRED Mrs E. S. Bradley 19 Rn 2m 9.0 (6.30) SF: -/-/-/10/-/2/-/-/-/-/-/-/-/-/-/-/-/-/-
WEIGHT FOR AGE 3yo-15lb
No bid. Il Fratello clmd BBeale £6,500.

1351 ROTHMANS ROYALS NORTH SOUTH CHALLENGE SERIES H'CAP (0-85) (3-Y.O+) (Class D) £4,464.00 (£1,332.00: £636.00: £288.00)
1m 8y Stalls: Low GOING minus 0.60 sec per fur (F) 3-55 (4-07)

1130 7 **Clifton Fox (80)***(90) (JAGlover)* 3-9-0 SDWilliams(4) (mde virtually all: hld on wl ins fnl f) ....— **1**
960 6 Weaver Bird **(77)***(86) (HCandy)* 5-9-9 WNewnes(6) (hld up: hdwy 2f out: ev ch fnl f: no ex nr fin) nk **2**
1130 6 Out on a Promise (IRE) **(76)***(85) (GWragg)* 3-8-10 FNorton(12) (lw: chsd ldrs: ev ch ins fnl f: unable qckn cl home) hd **3**
864 7 Bentico **(62)***(65) (MrsNMacauley)* 6-8-8b JFortune(3) (hld up: hdwy & ev ch 2f out: no ex appr fnl f) 3 **4**
981 10 Racing Brenda **(52)***(51) (BAMcMahon)* 4-7-12 JFanning(7) (lw: prom: no hdwy fnl 2f) 2 **5**
1183 2 Floridante (USA) **(75)***(74)*(Fav)*(PFICole)* 3-8-9 TQuinn(10) (lw: trckd ldrs: no ex appr fnl f)....hd **6**
*1049*10 Zahran (IRE) **(65)***(54) (JMBradley)* 4-8-6 (5) SDrowne(1) (chsd ldrs 5f) 5 **7**
885 6 Misty Silks **(75)***(58) (MJRyan)* 5-9-7 AClark(5) (hld up: hdwy 3f out: eased whn btn appr fnl f) 3 **8**
1126 12 Astral Weeks (IRE) **(78)***(60) (RHannon)* 4-9-3 (7) DaneO'Neill(2) (hld up: rdn over 2f out: no imp) ½ **9**
653 10 Conic Hill (IRE) **(69)***(51) (RJBaker)* 4-9-1b JWilliams(8) (lw: w wnr over 4f) nk **10**
1061 5 Desert Zone (USA) **(57)***(35) (JLHarris)* 6-8-3 GDuffield(9) (prom 5f) 1¾ **11**

1291* Rafter-J **(58)***(36) (JAHarris)* 4-8-4 5x AMackay(11) (rdn 3f out: sn bhd) ....hd **12**
10818 Mr Cube (IRE) **(51)***(19) (JMBradley)* 5-7-8v(3)ow2 DWright(13) (plld hrd: trckd ldrs 6f: sn rdn & btn) 4 **13**

5/2 Floridante (USA), **9/2** Out on a Promise (IRE), **6/1** Weaver Bird, **7/1** Misty Silks, **8/1** CLIFTON FOX, **10/1** Rafter-J, **14/1** Bentico, **16/1** Desert Zone (USA), **20/1** Zahran (IRE), Astral Weeks (IRE), Conic Hill (IRE), Mr Cube (IRE), **33/1** Racing Brenda, CSF £54.69 CT £228.20 TOTE £10.90: £2.00 £2.70 £2.30 (£38.00) Trio £46.40 OWNER P and S Partnership (WORKSOP) BRED Crest Stud Ltd
13 Rn 1m 33.8 (0.60 under best) (-1.20) SF: 60/68/55/47/33/44/36/40/42/33/17/18/1
WEIGHT FOR AGE 3yo-12lb

1352 LOUGHBOROUGH CLAIMING STKS (2-Y.O) (Class F) £2,720.60 (£751.60: £357.80) 5f 218y Stalls: Low GOING minus 0.60 sec per fur (F) 4-25 (4-27)

12129 **U-No-Harry (IRE)** *(66) (RHollinshead)* 2-8-4 (3) AGarth(3) (led 1f: led over 1f out: rdn out) ....— **1**
12262 Bobsworthatcaspers *(60)*(Fav)*(GLewis)* 2-8-0 (5) AWhelan(4) (lw: trckd ldrs: rdn over 2f out: r.o ins fnl f) 1½ **2**
*1213** Moi Canard *(65) (JBerry)* 2-8-11 SDWilliams(5) (led after 1f tl over 1f out: no ex fnl f) ....½ **3**
Simply Silly (IRE) *(30) (RThompson)* 2-8-0 StephenDavies(1) (w'like: lengthy: swvd lft s: a bhd) 9 **4**
Ultra Barley *(37) (PCHaslam)* 2-8-13 JFortune(2) (unf: scope: dwlt: sn chsng ldrs: btn whn eased ins fnl f) 2 **5**

4/5 Bobsworthatcaspers (op 5/4), **9/4** Moi Canard, **6/1** U-NO-HARRY (IRE), **8/1** Ultra Barley, **20/1** Simply Silly (IRE), CSF £11.57 TOTE £8.90: £3.20 £1.10 (£8.80) OWNER Mr D. Coppenhall (UPPER LONGDON) BRED A. J. Poulton (Epping) Ltd 5 Rn 1m 13.7 (3.70) SF: -/-/-/-/-

1353 MARKET BOSWORTH MEDIAN AUCTION MAIDEN STKS (3-Y.O) (Class F) £2,972.60 (£823.60: £393.80) 1m 8y Stalls: Low GOING minus 0.60 sec per fur (F) 4-55 (4-57)

11365 **Major Change** *(82+) (RHannon)* 3-8-7 (7) DaneO'Neill(3) (mde all: qcknd 3f out: comf) ....— **1**
5853 Secret Spring (FR) *(81)*(Fav)*(RCharlton)* 3-9-0 SRaymont(8) (hld up: hdwy 3f out: ev ch fnl f: nt qckn) ....¾ **2**
11962 Wild Rita *(60) (WRMuir)* 3-8-9 TQuinn(6) (prom: ev ch over 2f out: rdn & one pce appr fnl f) ..8 **3**
Bell Contractors (IRE) *(62) (CDBroad)* 3-9-0 AMackay(2) (prom: rdn & ev ch 3f out: sn outpcd) 1¼ **4**
109720 Proud Image **(68)***(62) (APJarvis)* 3-9-0 GDuffield(9) (lw: chsd ldrs over 5f) ....nk **5**
129014 Can't Say (IRE) **(40)***(55) (JMBradley)* 3-8-9v(5) SDrowne(5) (in tch: no hdwy fnl 3f) 3½ **6**
113612 Dr Frances (IRE) *(47) (CCElsey)* 3-8-9 CRutter(1) (wl bhd tl r.o fnl 2f) 1½ **7**
Claudia Habibi (IRE) *(45) (CCElsey)* 3-8-9 WNewnes(4) (hld up: hdwy 4f out: wknd wl over 1f out) 1 **8**
113613 Laudation (IRE) *(38) (GBBalding)* 3-9-0 JWilliams(7) (prom 4f) 6 **9**
74710 Call Me Flash **(52)***(26) (MrsPSly)* 3-9-0 AClark(10) (swtg: plld hrd: bhd fnl 3f) 6 **10**

15/8 Secret Spring (FR), **2/1** MAJOR CHANGE (6/4-9/4), **5/2** Wild Rita, **12/1** Proud Image, **16/1** Laudation (IRE), **20/1** Dr Frances (IRE), **40/1** Call Me Flash, **50/1** Can't Say (IRE), Claudia Habibi (IRE), Bell Contractors (IRE), CSF £6.31 TOTE £2.80: £1.60 £1.30 £1.10 (£3.40) Trio £1.30 OWNER Mrs C. J. Powell (MARLBOROUGH) BRED Shanbally House Stud 10 Rn
1m 36.7 (1.70) SF: 30/29/8/10/10/3/-/-/-/-

1354 GROBY H'CAP (0-85) (3-Y.O+) (Class D) £4,340.70 (£1,299.60: £623.80: £285.90) 5f 218y Stalls: Low GOING minus 0.40 sec per fur (F) 5-25 (5-27)

Join the Clan (84)*(91) (MrsNMacauley)* 6-9-9 (5) SDrowne(8) (hdwy 2f out: led ins fnl f: rdn out) ....— **1**
11065 Croft Pool **(78)***(84) (JAGlover)* 4-9-8 TQuinn(7) (a.p: ev ch 1f out: r.o) ....nk **2**
11746 Jigsaw Boy **(61)***(61) (PGMurphy)* 6-7-12 (7) RWaterfield(1) (lw: hdwy wl over 1f out: nrst fin) 2½ **3**
11744 Master of Passion **(83)***(81) (JMPEustace)* 6-9-13 MTebbutt(13) (chsd ldrs: rdn & edgd rt over 2f out: led over 1f out tl ins fnl f: sn btn) ....½ **4**
9496 Macs Maharanee **(73)***(69) (PSFelgate)* 8-8-12 (5) PMcCabe(9) (hld up: rdn 3f out: kpt on fnl f: nrst fin) 1 **5**
*1076** The Old Chapel **(65)***(60)*(Fav)*(BAMcMahon)* 6-8-9b FNorton(12) (led over 4f) ....nk **6**
949* Captain Carat **(65)***(58) (MrsJRRamsden)* 4-8-9 SDWilliams(10) (prom: ev ch over 2f out: wknd fnl f: eased nr fin) ....½ **7**
109421 Star of Gold **(67)***(59) (CREgerton)* 3-8-1 CRutter(4) (rdn over 2f out: nvr rchd ldrs) ....½ **8**
Pyramus (USA) **(75)***(63) (MrsLPiggott)* 4-8-12 (7) GMilligan(2) (b: prom 4f: sn rdn & btn) 1½ **9**

1193[11] Pageboy **(71)***(59) (PCHaslam)* 6-9-1 JFortune(14) (prom over 3f: sn rdn & btn) ....s.h **10**
1174[14] Slivovitz **(60)***(47) (MJHeaton-Ellis)* 5-8-4b StephenDavies(5) (prom over 4f)............................nk **11**
949[8] Bryan Robson (USA) **(67)***(43) (GBBalding)* 4-8-11 JWilliams(6) (bhd fnl 2f)..............................4 **12**
1070[9] Great Hall **(57)***(20) (PDCundell)* 6-8-1 AMackay(11) (a bhd) 5 **13**
Malibu Man **(63)** *(SMellor)* 3-7-8 (3)ow4 DWright(3) (a bhd: t.o fnl 3f).. **14**

LONG HANDICAP Malibu Man 7-5

9/2 The Old Chapel, **13/2** Captain Carat, **7/1** Croft Pool, Great Hall, Macs Maharanee, **8/1** Jigsaw Boy, Master of Passion, **10/1** Pageboy, **12/1** Slivovitz, **14/1** Star of Gold, JOIN THE CLAN, **20/1** Pyramus (USA), Bryan Robson (USA), **33/1** Malibu Man, CSF £109.39 CT £787.71 TOTE £22.40: £5.40 £2.00 £3.40 (£72.70) Trio £431.80; £36.49 to Leicester 30/5/95 OWNER Mr J. Redden (MELTON MOWBRAY) BRED John Redden Farms 14 Rn

1m 10.9 (0.90) SF: 65/58/35/55/43/34/32/23/37/33/21/17/-/-

WEIGHT FOR AGE 3yo-10lb

T/Plpt: £201.30 (32.41 Tckts). T/Qdpt: £25.80 (1.9 Tckts). Dk

1079-REDCAR (L-H)
Monday May 29th (Good)

WEATHER: overcast, showers WIND: fresh across

1355 LADY TAVERNERS (S) STKS (3-Y.O+) (Class G) £2,775.00 (£775.00: £375.00)
7f Stalls: Centre GOING minus 0.50 sec per fur (F) 2-10 (2-13)

1155* **Veloce (IRE) (66)***(69)*(Fav)*(ABailey)* 7-9-10 SMaloney(14) (b: bhd: hdwy over 2f out: r.o to ld wl ins fnl f)...— **1**
1080[7] Best Kept Secret **(71)***(65) (JBerry)* 4-9-0 (7) PFessey(15) (in tch: hdwy to ld over 1f out: hdd wl ins fnl f: r.o) ....nk **2**
Winter Scout (USA) **(64)***(65) (MrsMReveley)* 7-9-7 KDarley(13) (effrt 3f out: chal over 1f out: kpt on)..nk **3**
748[3] Kid Ory **(63)***(60) (PCalver)* 4-9-7 MBirch(3) (lw: a.p: ev ch 2f out: no ex fnl f)...........................2 **4**
965[6] Ashdren **(58)***(56) (AHarrison)* 8-9-2 (5) JStack(16) (lw: in tch: effrt & ch 2f out: nt qckn).............2 **5**
1044[5] Birchwood Sun **(56)***(50) (MDods)* 5-9-2b(5) VHalliday(10) (chsd ldrs: led ½-wy to over 1f out: wknd)..2½ **6**
1153[3] Gant Bleu (FR) **(43)***(49) (RMWhitaker)* 8-9-7 ACulhane(11) (hld up: effrt over 2f out: sn rdn & no ex)..½ **7**
1080[4] Top Show (IRE) **(60)***(49) (KWHogg)* 4-9-7 DaleGibson(9) (chsd ldrs: ev ch 2f out: wknd ins fnl f)..s.h **8**
1153[8] Kings Vision **(47)***(45) (BSRothwell)* 3-8-10b MFenton(12) (cl up 4f: sn wknd)...........................1½ **9**
759[11] Red Hot Risk **(55)***(41) (MDods)* 3-8-10v LCharnock(1) (n.d)..2 **10**
Bitch **(51)***(33) (DNicholls)* 3-8-5 NConnorton(5) (bhd fr ½-wy)..1 **11**
1080[14] Skiptamaloo **(31)***(30) (DonEnricoIncisa)* 4-9-2v KimTinkler(8) (n.d)...................................1¼ **12**
1044[2] Obsidian Grey **(54)***(36) (MissLCSiddall)* 8-9-3 (7) TSiddall(6) (led to ½-wy: sn wknd)..............1¼ **13**
Monkey Face **(40)***(26) (JHetherton)* 4-9-2 JQuinn(2) (bit bkwd: b.hind: cl up 4f) ....¾ **14**
1044[9] Beware of Agents **(54)***(25) (MJohnston)* 6-9-7 DeanMcKeown(4) (effrt ½-wy: sn btn) 2½ **15**
Halls Burn *(2) (JSGoldie)* 7-9-7 TWilliams(7) (a bhd) 10 **16**
350[7] Kitty Waterjet **(30)** *(BEllison)* 3-8-5 NKennedy(17) (a bhd)...13 **17**

100/30 VELOCE (IRE), **6/1** Best Kept Secret, **7/1** Kid Ory, **8/1** Winter Scout (USA) (op 5/1), Ashdren, Top Show (IRE), **12/1** Birchwood Sun (op 8/1), Halls Burn (33/1-50/1), **14/1** Beware of Agents, Gant Bleu (FR), **16/1** Obsidian Grey, **25/1** Red Hot Risk, Bitch, **33/1** Kings Vision, **66/1** Skiptamaloo, **100/1** Monkey Face, Kitty Waterjet, CSF £23.86 TOTE £4.30: £2.00 £2.40 £2.70 (£13.90) Trio £38.80 OWNER Mr Maximo Gonzalez (TARPORLEY) BRED Miss C. O'Toole 17 Rn

1m 23.0 (1.00) SF: 53/49/49/44/40/34/33/33/18/14/6/14/20/10/9/-/-

WEIGHT FOR AGE 3yo-11lb

No bid

1356 IDEAL HOMES MAIDEN AUCTION STKS (2-Y.O) (Class E) £3,276.75 (£984.00: £474.50: £219.75) 5f Stalls: Centre GOING minus 0.50 sec per fur (F) 2-40 (2-44)

1203[9] **White Emir** *(60+) (MrsJRRamsden)* 2-8-2 MFenton(6) (w ldr: led ½-wy: r.o wl)....................— **1**
1089[4] Pride of Whalley (IRE) *(51) (JBerry)* 2-7-8 (7) PFessey(8) (lw: hdwy ½-wy: styd on wl: nvr able chal) 2½ **2**
Tabriz *(41) (JDBethell)* 2-7-11 TWilliams(7) (leggy: scope: s.i.s: hdwy ½-wy: nt qckn fnl f)..2 **3**
Camionneur (IRE) *(47) (MHEasterby)* 2-8-6 SMaloney(10) (w'like: scope: s.i.s: hdwy 2f out: styd on wl u.p) ....¾ **4**
1278[4] Northern Clan *(38)*(Fav)*(MWEasterby)* 2-8-2 LCharnock(4) (hdwy ½-wy: rdn & no imp).......1¾ **5**

Klipspinger (23) (BSRothwell) 2-7-11 JMarshall(9) (cmpt: scope: sn drvn along: in tch: no hdwy fr ½-wy) 3 6
Turbo North (32) (MDods) 2-8-6 DaleGibson(11) (lt-f: unf: s.i.s: nvr trbld ldrs) ....hd 7
Sandblaster (21) (MissJFCraze) 2-7-11 NKennedy(5) (unf: dwlt: a in rr div) ....½ 8
Chillam (13) (JPLeigh) 2-8-3 ow1 DeanMcKeown(3) (w'like: slt ld to ½-wy: sn wknd) 4 9
Taurean Fire (11) (MrsMReveley) 2-8-3 ow1 KDarley(12) (leggy: outpcd fr ½-wy) ....¾ 10
1190⁶ Rapid Liner (12)(Fav)(AHarrison) 2-8-1 (5) JStack(2) (lw: sn drvn along: bhd fr ½-wy) 1 11
Supreme Scholar (BWMurray) 2-7-11 JQuinn(1) (unf: unruly s: dwlt: t.o) 25 12

4/1 Rapid Liner, Northern Clan, **5/1** Chillam, Pride of Whalley (IRE), **8/1** Taurean Fire, **10/1** Camionneur (IRE), **12/1** WHITE EMIR (op 6/1), **14/1** Sandblaster (op 25/1), **20/1** Turbo North, Tabriz, **25/1** Klipspinger, **33/1** Supreme Scholar, CSF £68.41 TOTE £13.90: £2.90 £1.90 £5.30 (£28.80) Trio £136.30; £134.36 to Redcar 30/5/95 OWNER Mrs D. Ridley (THIRSK) BRED G. Dickinson 12 Rn
58.4 secs (1.70) SF: 13/4/-/-/-/-/-/-/-/-/-/-

1357 ZETLAND GOLD CUP H'CAP (0-105) (3-Y.O+) (Class B) £14,507.50 (£4,360.00: £2,105.00: £977.50) **1m 2f** Stalls: Low GOING minus 0.50 sec (F) 3-10 (3-11)

Penny a Day (IRE) (94)(106) (MrsMReveley) 5-9-10 KDarley(6) (hld up: hdwy 3f out: chal over 1f out: r.o u.p to ld cl home) ....— 1
1141² Virtual Reality **(76)**(88)(Fav)(AHide) 4-8-6 DaleGibson(2) (trckd ldrs: smooth hdwy 2f out: led ins fnl f: no ex & hdd cl home) ....hd 2
918* Burooj **(94)**(104) (DMorley) 5-9-10 MFenton(5) (trckd ldrs: led over 2f out: hung lft: hdd ins fnl f: nt qckn) 1¼ 3
1211* Bardon Hill Boy (IRE) **(78)**(87) (BHanbury) 3-7-2 (5) 6x MBaird(3) (prom whn n.m.r appr st: hit rail ent st & lost pl: hdwy 2f out: r.o) ....nk 4
634¹⁰ Country Lover **(85)**(86) (LordHuntingdon) 4-9-1 DeanMcKeown(8) (lw: hld up & bhd: hdwy 3f out: no imp) 5 5
1179⁵ Pride of Pendle **(70)**(71) (DNicholls) 6-8-0 LCharnock(4) (hld up: hdwy 3f out: hmpd 2f out: r.o one pce) ....nk 6
1135⁴ Mr Confusion (IRE) **(88)**(88) (MissSEHall) 7-8-13 (5) JStack(7) (effrt appr st: outpcd 4f out: styd on fnl f) ....nk 7
1179⁷ Queens Consul (IRE) **(78)**(78) (BSRothwell) 5-8-8 MBirch(9) (disp ld tl hdd over 2f out: wknd) ....s.h 8
634⁴ Secret Aly (CAN) **(70)**(62) (CEBrittain) 5-8-0 JQuinn(10) (lw: chsd ldr tl wknd over 2f out) 5 9
961⁶ Mowlaie **(77)**(63) (JDBethell) 4-8-7 TWilliams(1) (disp ld tl hdd over 2f out: hmpd & sn lost pl) 4 10

LONG HANDICAP Bardon Hill Boy (IRE) 7-0

3/1 Virtual Reality, **4/1** Burooj, **11/2** Country Lover, **13/2** Bardon Hill Boy (IRE), Mr Confusion (IRE), **8/1** Secret Aly (CAN), **9/1** PENNY A DAY (IRE), **14/1** Pride of Pendle, **25/1** Queens Consul (IRE), Mowlaie, CSF £35.62 CT £116.17 TOTE £7.70: £2.60 £1.10 £2.20 (£16.40) Trio £25.90 OWNER Mr J. R. Good (SALTBURN) BRED Mrs Noeleen Roche 10 Rn
2m 4.0 (1.50) SF: 54/36/52/20/34/19/36/26/10/11
WEIGHT FOR AGE 3yo-15lb
STEWARDS' ENQUIRY Charnock susp. 7-12/6/95 (irresponsible riding).

1358 ROYAL AIR FORCE LEEMING AIR FAIR DAY 1995 H'CAP (0-70) (3-Y.O) (Class E) £3,484.75 (£1,048.00: £506.50: £235.75) **1m 2f** Stalls: Low GOING minus 0.50 sec per fur (F) 3-45 (3-48)

969⁷ **Ring of Vision (IRE) (47)**(52) (MrsMReveley) 3-8-8 KDarley(2) (a.p: squeezed thro to ld ins fnl f: r.o wl) ....— 1
1083² Drumochter **(54)**(56)(Fav)(DMorley) 3-9-1 MFenton(5) (hld up: gd hdwy over 3f out: ev ch whn sltly hmpd over 1f out: r.o one pce) 2 2
1180¹⁴ Shining Edge **(57)**(57) (MHEasterby) 3-9-4 MBirch(10) (led tl hdd & no ex ins fnl f) 1 3
1285¹⁸ Longcroft **(38)**(32) (KWHogg) 3-7-8 (5) MBaird(14) (styd on fnl 4f: nrst fin) 4 4
1083⁴ Beau Matelot **(60)**(51) (JDBethell) 3-9-7 TWilliams(4) (cl up: wkng whn sltly hmpd over 1f out) 1½ 5
1083* Toshiba Talk (IRE) **(53)**(35) (BEllison) 3-9-0 NKennedy(15) (nvr nr to chal) 6 6
990* Bulsara **(55)**(36) (CWFairhurst) 3-8-11 (5) JStack(6) (chsd ldrs: effrt over 3f out: no imp) ....¾ 7
1180⁹ Alltime Dancer (IRE) **(54)**(30) (MrsJRRamsden) 3-8-8 (7) TFinn(9) (in tch: no hdwy fnl 4f) 3 8
966¹⁵ Prime Property (IRE) **(45)**(18) (MWEasterby) 3-8-6 LCharnock(11) (nvr trbld ldrs) 1½ 9
1154⁸ Ballard Lady (IRE) **(43)**(12) (JSWainwright) 3-8-4 ow3 DeanMcKeown(1) (n.d) 1 10
Coast Along (IRE) **(35)**(4) (CWThornton) 3-7-10 JMarshall(7) (n.d) 2 11
990² Island Cascade **(45)**(10) (DonEnricoIncisa) 3-8-6 KimTinkler(13) (lost tch fnl 4f) 2 12
924⁸ Cupronickel (IRE) **(58)**(18) (JWWatts) 3-9-5 NConnorton(3) (lw: a bhd) 3½ 13
1040¹⁰ Shazanni (IRE) **(56)**(5) (JGFitzGerald) 3-9-3 SMaloney(8) (b: prom to st) 7 14
Dance Motion **(51)** (TJEtherington) 3-8-12 DaleGibson(12) (lost tch 4f out: t.o) 20 15

6/4 Drumochter (3/1-11/8), **6/1** RING OF VISION (IRE), **7/1** Toshiba Talk (IRE), **8/1** Bulsara, **9/1** Beau Matelot, **10/1** Alltime Dancer (IRE), **12/1** Prime Property (IRE), **14/1** Shining Edge, Shazanni (IRE), Island Cascade, **20/1** Coast Along (IRE), Cupronickel (IRE), Dance Motion, **33/1** Ballard Lady (IRE), Longcroft, CSF £17.26 CT £131.11 TOTE £7.90: £2.10 £1.50 £3.40 (£9.50) Trio £161.00 OWNER Mr P. D. Savill (SALTBURN) BRED Amberush Investments 15 Rn
2m 6.8 (4.30) SF: 18/22/23/-/17/1/2/-/-/-/-/-/-/-/-

1359 PARK HOTEL REDCAR H'CAP (0-70) (3-Y.O+) (Class E) £3,208.50 (£963.00: £464.00: £214.50)
1m 6f 19y Stalls: Low GOING minus 0.50 sec per fur (F) 4-15 (4-17)

1156[5] **Vain Prince (41)***(52) (NTinkler)* 8-8-3 LCharnock(9) (a.p: led over 2f out: r.o) ....— **1**
1039* Ho-Joe (IRE) **(49)***(58) (JMCarr)* 5-8-11 SMorris(1) (lw: b.hind: trckd ldrs: swtchd & effrt over 2f out: ev ch 1f out: nt qckn) 1½ **2**
423[19] Hit the Canvas (USA) **(66)***(73)*(Fav)*(MrsMReveley)* 4-10-0 KDarley(2) (chsd ldrs: effrt over 3f out: one pce) 2½ **3**
1025[4] Weaver George (IRE) **(32)***(37) (JAHellens)* 5-7-8 ow1 DaleGibson(4) (cl up: led ent st tl over 2f out: one pce) ....hd **4**
1149[7] Don't Cry **(31)***(37) (DonEnricoIncisa)* 7-7-7 KimTinkler(6) (bhd: hdwy 4f out: nvr rch ldrs) ....½ **5**
1102[8] Chantry Beath **(60)***(65) (CWThornton)* 4-9-8 DeanMcKeown(7) (bhd: effrt 4f out: no imp) ....¾ **6**
1160[7] Bajan Affair **(31)***(32) (MissLCSiddall)* 5-7-2 (5) MBaird(8) (prom: outpcd 4f out: n.d after) 3½ **7**
1295[12] Escape Talk **(32)***(15) (JDooler)* 8-7-8 ow1 JQuinn(5) (nvr trbld ldrs) 15 **8**
569[6] Persian Linnet **(45)** *(MrsMReveley)* 4-8-7 MFenton(3) (t: led tl hdd & wknd qckly ent st: t.o) ....dist **9**

LONG HANDICAP Don't Cry 7-1 Bajan Affair 6-12 Escape Talk 6-6 Weaver George (IRE) 7-6

2/1 Hit the Canvas (USA), **4/1** Ho-Joe (IRE), **9/2** VAIN PRINCE, **5/1** Chantry Beath, **6/1** Weaver George (IRE), **12/1** Persian Linnet, **16/1** Don't Cry, **33/1** Bajan Affair, **100/1** Escape Talk, CSF £22.18 CT £42.94 TOTE £5.20: £1.70 £1.60 £1.50 (£19.80) Trio £15.70 OWNER Mr A. C. Findlay (MALTON) BRED Lodge Park Stud 9 Rn 3m 5.0 (7.00) SF: 11/17/32/-/-/24/-/-/-

1360 YARM WINDOWS MEDIAN AUCTION MAIDEN STKS (3-Y.O) (Class D) £3,762.50 (£1,130.00: £545.00: £252.50)
6f Stalls: Centre GOING minus 0.50 sec per fur (F) 4-45 (4-46)

1094[18] **Prime Match (IRE) (76)***(86) (PWHarris)* 3-9-0 MFenton(5) (hld up: hdwy on bit to ld ins fnl f: hung lft: qcknd) ....— **1**
1168[2] Bouche Bee (USA) *(76)*(Fav)*(LMCumani)* 3-8-6 (3) OUrbina(2) (b.hind: mde most tl hdd ins fnl f: one pce) 2 **2**
Just Like Me *(72) (RGuest)* 3-8-9 JQuinn(4) (a chsng ldrs: nt qckn appr fnl f) 1¼ **3**
772[3] Roy Boy **(72)***(73) (MrsMReveley)* 3-9-0 KDarley(1) (cl up: effrt 2f out: rdn & nt r.o) 1½ **4**
1040[5] Mamma's Due **(59)***(64) (JBerry)* 3-8-9 MBirch(7) (w ldrs tl wknd wl over 1f out) 1¾ **5**
Young Ben (IRE) *(47) (JSWainwright)* 3-9-0 DeanMcKeown(3) (cmpt: outpcd & bhd fr ½-wy) 8 **6**
880[10] Fuzzy *(31) (SEKettlewell)* 3-8-9 (5) JStack(6) (prom tl rdn & wknd ½-wy) 6 **7**

11/10 Bouche Bee (USA), **11/4** Roy Boy, **4/1** PRIME MATCH (IRE), **10/1** Just Like Me, Mamma's Due, **100/1** Young Ben (IRE), Fuzzy, CSF £8.58 TOTE £5.90: £2.40 £1.10 (£4.60) OWNER T. Tring Ensemble (BERKHAMSTED) BRED Pendley Farm 7 Rn 1m 10.1 (0.80) SF: 44/34/30/31/22/5/-
T/Plpt: £25.30 (399.86 Tckts). T/Qdpt: £4.50 (£19.45 Tckts). AA

0825-SANDOWN (R-H)
Monday May 29th (St Good to firm, Rnd Good, Good to firm patches)
WEATHER: sunny spells WIND: slt half against

1361 E.B.F. MAIDEN STKS (2-Y.O F) (Class D) £4,123.50 (£1,248.00: £609.00: £289.50) **5f 6y** Stalls: Low GOING minus 0.18 sec per fur (GF) 2-00 (2-02)

Blue Duster (USA) *(91+)*(Fav)*(DRLoder)* 2-8-11 MJKinane(9) (str: a.p: led 2f out: rdn fnl f: r.o wl) ....— **1**
Dance Sequence (USA) *(87) (MRStoute)* 2-8-11 WRSwinburn(8) (unf: hdwy over 2f out: chsd wnr over 1f out: unable qckn) 1¼ **2**
Wollstonecraft (IRE) *(79) (JHMGosden)* 2-8-11 LDettori(4) (unf: scope: plld hrd: led over 2f: one pce) 2½ **3**
Agnella (IRE) *(77) (GLMoore)* 2-8-11 SWhitworth(5) (w'like: hld up: rdn over 2f out: one pce fnl f) ....¾ **4**

Stop Play (IRE) *(74) (MHTompkins)* 2-8-11 PRobinson(2) (w'like: bit bkwd: hdwy over 3f out: 4th whn stumbled over 2f out: wknd fnl f)....¾ 5
1047[3] Petite Annie *(70) (TGMills)* 2-8-11 JCarroll(1) (a.p: led over 2f out: sn hdd: wknd fnl f)....1¼ 6
Uoni *(64) (CEBrittain)* 2-8-11 MRoberts(6) (leggy: unf: bhd fnl 3f)....2 7
Intisab *(64) (RWArmstrong)* 2-8-11 WCarson(3) (w'like: bit bkwd: a bhd)....hd 8
Windi Imp (IRE) *(35) (BJMeehan)* 2-8-11 JWeaver(7) (neat: bit bkwd: spd over 2f)....9 9

8/11 BLUE DUSTER (USA), **4/1** Dance Sequence (USA) (op 9/4), **8/1** Intisab (6/1-9/1), **9/1** Wollstonecraft (IRE) (9/2-10/1), **14/1** Petite Annie (10/1-16/1), **16/1** Agnella (IRE), **25/1** Uoni, Windi Imp (IRE), **33/1** Stop Play (IRE), CSF £4.54 TOTE £1.90: £1.20 £1.50 £2.30 (£2.70) Trio £6.40
OWNER Sheikh Mohammed (NEWMARKET) BRED Darley Stud Management Inc 9 Rn
62.52 secs (2.72) SF: 35/31/23/21/18/14/8/8/-

1362

BONUSPOST H'CAP (0-100) (3-Y.O+ F & M) (Class C) £10,357.50 (£3,135.00: £1,530.00: £727.50) **7f 16y** Stalls: High GOING: 0.03 sec per fur (G) 2-35 (2-35)

1172* **Forest Cat (IRE) (86)***(96) (MrsJCecil)* 3-9-5 LDettori(2) (b: hdwy over 2f out: n.m.r on ins over 1f out: led wl ins fnl f: rdn out)....— 1
876[7] Comanche Companion **(65)***(74) (TJNaughton)* 5-8-4 (5) JDSmith(5) (2nd st: led over 2f out: hrd rdn over 1f out: edgd rt: hdd wl ins fnl f: r.o)....nk 2
1172[5] Green Seed (IRE) **(80)***(84)*(Fav)*(JRFanshawe)* 3-8-13 WRSwinburn(8) (rdn & hdwy over 1f out: r.o one pce)....2½ 3
870[13] Neither Nor **(84)***(87) (DAWilson)* 6-10-0 TIves(9) (lw: 5th st: rdn over 2f out: one pce)....hd 4
Doctor's Glory (USA) **(85)***(86) (RHannon)* 3-9-4 JWeaver(7) (led 1f: 3rd st: ev ch 2f out: one pce)....1 5
939[4] Ffynone (IRE) **(85)***(77) (RHannon)* 3-9-4 MJKinane(3) (lw: 6th st: rdn over 2f out: one pce)....4 6
620[11] Karayib (USA) **(86)***(76) (JLDunlop)* 3-9-5v WCarson(4) (plld hrd: led 6f out tl over 2f out: sn wknd)....¾ 7
662[8] Iltimas (USA) **(88)***(78) (PTWalwyn)* 3-9-7 MHills(1) (a bhd)....nk 8
914[8] Zilayah (USA) **(80)***(66) (MRStoute)* 3-8-13 PRobinson(6) (4th st: wknd over 2f out)....1½ 9

7/4 Green Seed (IRE), **2/1** FOREST CAT (IRE), **6/1** Karayib (USA) (8/1-5/1), **12/1** Ffynone (IRE), **14/1** Neither Nor, Comanche Companion (op 8/1), Zilayah (USA) (op 8/1), **20/1** Doctor's Glory (USA), Iltimas (USA), CSF £27.89 CT £52.18 TOTE £2.50: £1.10 £2.60 £1.50 (£19.10) Trio £12.10
OWNER Mr George Ward (NEWMARKET) BRED Tasia Limited 9 Rn
1m 29.94 (3.34) SF: 67/56/55/69/57/48/47/49/37
WEIGHT FOR AGE 3yo-11lb

1363

BONUSPRINT HENRY II STKS (Gp 3) (4-Y.O+) (Class A) £25,500.00 (£9,590.00: £4,645.00: £2,065.00)
2m 78y Stalls: High GOING: 0.03 sec per fur (G) 3-05 (3-07)

1132[4] **Double Trigger (IRE) (111)***(118+)*(Fav)*(MJohnston)* 4-8-13 JWeaver(5) (lw: 3rd st: led over 2f out: clr 1f out: r.o wl)....— 1
869[4] Old Rouvel (USA) **(96)***(109) (DJGMurraySmith)* 4-8-10 MJKinane(4) (lw: rdn over 3f out: hdwy 2f out: r.o one pce)....6 2
1171[3] Linney Head (USA) **(112)***(112) (JHMGosden)* 4-8-13 LDettori(1) (lw: chsd ldr 14f: one pce)..nk 3
998[3] The Flying Phantom **(91)***(108) (MHTompkins)* 4-8-10 PRobinson(2) (lw: led 14f: one pce)....¾ 4
1132[5] Further Flight **(107)***(105) (BWHills)* 9-9-1 MHills(7) (b.hind: 6th st: nvr nr to chal)....6 5
958* Cuff Link (IRE) **(108)***(97) (MajorWRHern)* 5-8-12 PaulEddery(3) (lw: 5th st: wknd over 2f out)....5 6
Cayumanque (CHI) *(92) (SbinSuroor)* 6-8-12 WRSwinburn(6) (4th st: wknd 3f out)....6 7

5/4 DOUBLE TRIGGER (IRE), **11/4** Cuff Link (IRE), **9/2** Linney Head (USA), **8/1** Cayumanque (CHI), **14/1** Old Rouvel (USA), Further Flight (op 8/1), **25/1** The Flying Phantom, CSF £17.16 TOTE £2.30: £1.30 £5.00 (£12.30) OWNER Mr R. W. Huggins (MIDDLEHAM) BRED Dene Investments N V 7 Rn
3m 33.01 (3.01) SF: 86/77/80/76/75/67/62
WEIGHT FOR AGE 4yo-2lb

1364

TRIPLEPRINT TEMPLE STKS (Gp 2) (3-Y.O+) (Class A) £38,075.00 (£14,210.00: £6,792.50: £2,922.50) **5f 6y** Stalls: Low GOING minus 0.18 sec (GF) 3-40 (3-41)

921* **Mind Games (117)***(121+)*(Fav)*(JBerry)* 3-8-8 JCarroll(2) (lw: chsd ldr: led on bit over 2f out: clr over 1f out: easily)....— 1
921[4] Millstream (USA) **(109)***(109) (MJohnston)* 3-8-5 MJKinane(1) (led over 2f: unable qckn)....3 2
921[3] Owington **(124)***(111) (GWragg)* 4-9-10 PaulEddery(3) (lw: hld up: rdn over 2f out: one pce).2½ 3
1133[6] Raah Algharb (USA) **(110)***(104) (MRStoute)* 3-8-12 WRSwinburn(5) (hld up: shkn up over 1f out: one pce)....1 4

921[5] El Yasaf (IRE) **(106)***(99) (GFierro)* 7-9-3 LDettori(4) (lw: hld up: rdn over 2f out: one pce).......½ 5

10/11 MIND GAMES, **13/8** Owington, **7/1** Millstream (USA), **16/1** El Yasaf (IRE), **25/1** Raah Algharb (USA), CSF £7.09 TOTE £1.70: £1.30 £2.30 (£3.40) OWNER Mr Robert Hughes (COCKERHAM) BRED Mrs V. E. Hughes 5 Rn
60.1 secs (0.30) SF: 73/61/72/56/60
WEIGHT FOR AGE 3yo-9lb

1365

BONUSFILM WHITSUN CUP RATED STKS H'CAP (0-105) (3-Y.O+) (Class B) £14,998.50 (£5,611.50: £2,743.25: £1,178.75: £526.88: £266.12) **1m 14y** Stalls: High GOING: 0.03 sec per fur (G) 4-10 (4-11)

1108[5] **Dance Turn (99)***(108) (RWArmstrong)* 4-9-3 MHills(4) (swtg: mde all: drvn out) ....— 1
1143[4] Czarna (IRE) **(89)***(97) (CEBrittain)* 4-8-7 MRoberts(1) (lw: 4th st: ev ch fnl 3f: unable qckn wl ins fnl f)......½ 2
1145[4] Night Hero (USA) **(98)***(103)*(Fav)*(MRStoute)* 3-8-4 LDettori(5) (6th st: nt clr run & swtchd lft over 1f out: r.o one pce)......1½ 3
Thabit (USA) **(89)***(91) (PTWalwyn)* 4-8-7 WCarson(8) (lw: 3rd st: nt clr run on ins over 2f out: rdn over 1f out: one pce)......1¾ 4
960* Desert Green (FR) **(95)***(94) (RHannon)* 6-8-13 RPerham(7) (b.off fore: lw: hdwy over 2f out: rdn over 1f out: one pce)......1¼ 5
953[5] En Attendant (FR) **(103)***(96) (BHanbury)* 7-9-7 TIves(6) (lw: a bhd)......3 6
Lap of Luxury **(102)***(90) (WJarvis)* 6-9-6 BThomson(3) (5th st: ev ch 2f out: wknd over 1f out)......2½ 7
665[19] Waikiki Beach (USA) **(97)***(77) (GLMoore)* 4-9-1 BRouse(2) (lw: 2nd st: wknd wl over 1f out) ...4 8

LONG HANDICAP Thabit (USA) 8-1 Czarna (IRE) 8-5

2/1 Night Hero (USA) (11/8-9/4), **100/30** DANCE TURN, Desert Green (FR), **5/1** Czarna (IRE), **10/1** Lap of Luxury, **14/1** En Attendant (FR), **16/1** Thabit (USA), **33/1** Waikiki Beach (USA), CSF £19.92 CT £38.09 TOTE £4.10: £1.50 £1.80 £1.10 (£10.60) OWNER Mr George Ward (NEWMARKET) BRED Marquess of Hartington and the Earl of Halifax 8 Rn
1m 42.36 (3.16) SF: 72/61/55/55/58/60/54/41
WEIGHT FOR AGE 3yo-12lb

1366

FAMILY DAY OUT H'CAP (0-80) (3-Y.O) (Class D) £4,416.00 (£1,338.00: £654.00: £312.00) **7f 16y** Stalls: High GOING: 0.03 sec per fur (G) 4-45 (4-46)

882* **Scharnhorst (63)***(70) (SDow)* 3-8-4 MRoberts(2) (lw: mde all: rdn out) ......— 1
640[3] Hawa Al Nasamaat (USA) **(75)***(79) (EALDunlop)* 3-9-2 WRSwinburn(1) (lw: 4th st: rdn over 1f out: unable qckn)......1¼ 2
1125[2] Sapphire Son (IRE) **(59)***(62) (CNWilliams)* 3-8-0v PaulEddery(7) (lw: 3rd st: hrd rdn over 1f out: one pce)......½ 3
753[3] Crimson Shower **(57)***(50) (JRFanshawe)* 3-7-12 ow4 WCarson(11) (mid div whn snatched up on ins over 4f out: hdwy over 1f out: nvr nrr)......2½ 4
813[10] Shining Example **(69)***(66) (PJMakin)* 3-8-10 MHills(4) (2nd st: wknd over 1f out)......hd 5
1094[9] Singing Rock (IRE) **(67)***(64) (RHannon)* 3-8-8 MJKinane(15) (lw: hdwy over 1f out: nvr nrr)..s.h 6
*168** Almuhtaram **(72)***(63) (MissGayKelleway)* 3-8-13 MWigham(6) (swtg: bit bkwd: nvr nr to chal)......2½ 7
681[3] Peggy Spencer **(59)***(50) (CWThornton)* 3-8-0 RStreet(9) (7th st: wknd over 1f out) ......s.h 8
980[7] Lyford Law (IRE) **(80)***(65) (JHMGosden)* 3-9-7 LDettori(3) (b: 5th st: wknd over 1f out)......3 9
1172[14] Tara Colleen (IRE) **(53)***(37) (CAHorgan)* 3-7-8 EJohnson(10) (a mid div) ......nk 10
1052[10] East Sheen **(65)***(45) (CJBenstead)* 3-8-6 BRouse(14) (nvr nrr)......1¾ 11
1180[11] Delight of Dawn **(72)***(52) (KTIvory)* 3-8-13 JWeaver(13) (b.hind: s.s: a bhd) ......s.h 12
1165[3] Apollono **(67)***(44)*(Fav)*(RAkehurst)* 3-8-8 BThomson(8) (hdwy over 2f out: hrd rdn over 1f out: sn wknd)......1¼ 13
1072[6] Autumn Cover **(59)***(33) (RMFlower)* 3-8-0 DBiggs(16) (b: a bhd) 1¼ 14
1172[7] Moody **(67)***(35) (MissGayKelleway)* 3-8-8 PRobinson(5) (lw: 6th st: wknd over 2f out)......2½ 15
1322[10] Amboyna Burl (IRE) **(57)** *(DAWilson)* 3-7-12 ow5 NGwilliams(12) (lw: s.s: a bhd)......12 16

LONG HANDICAP Amboyna Burl (IRE) 7-5

100/30 Apollono, **5/1** Hawa Al Nasamaat (USA) (7/1-9/2), **6/1** Crimson Shower, **7/1** SCHARNHORST, **8/1** Sapphire Son (IRE), **10/1** Peggy Spencer, **12/1** Lyford Law (IRE) (op 8/1), **14/1** Shining Example, Moody, **16/1** Delight of Dawn, Autumn Cover, **20/1** Almuhtaram, Singing Rock (IRE), **33/1** East Sheen, Tara Colleen (IRE), **66/1** Amboyna Burl (IRE), CSF £43.30 CT £277.25 TOTE £9.20: £1.90 £1.80 £1.80 £1.60 (£21.90) Trio £65.90 OWNER Mackenzie Print (EPSOM) BRED M. F. Kentish 16 Rn 1m 31.11 (4.51) SF: 39/48/31/19/35/33/32/19/34/6/14/21/13/2/4/-

1367

BANK HOLIDAY H'CAP (0-80) (4-Y.O+) (Class D) £4,279.50 (£1,296.00: £633.00: £301.50) **1m 2f 7y** Stalls: High GOING: 0.03 sec per fur (G) 5-15 (5-20)

1166[2] **Dutosky (52)***(65) (RJO'Sullivan)* 5-8-2 DBiggs(4) (lw: 6th st: led over 1f out: drvn out) ......— 1

1141[3] Bookcase **(59)***(69)*(Fav)*(DRCElsworth)* 8-8-9 WRSwinburn(12) (hdwy over 1f out: r.o)...........2 2
1141[13] Koathary (USA) **(65)***(74) (LGCottrell)* 4-9-1 LDettori(3) (lw: 3rd st: led over 2f out tl over 1f out: unable qckn)....................nk 3
318[8] Tondres (USA) **(71)***(79) (RIngram)* 4-9-7b MRoberts(5) (rdn 3f out: hdwy over 1f out: r.o)........1 4
1052[7] Absolutely Fayre **(68)***(75) (RAkehurst)* 4-9-4 BThomson(8) (lw: hdwy over 2f out: hrd rdn over 1f out: one pce)....................½ 5
Fieldridge **(78)***(84) (CPEBrooks)* 6-10-0 MHills(1) (lw: 5th st: ev ch over 1f out: wknd fnl f).....½ 6
1065[5] Tadellal (IRE) **(62)***(63) (MDixon)* 4-8-12 TIves(11) (lw: s.s: hdwy over 8f out: led over 4f out to over 2f out: sn wknd)....................3 7
1141[6] Caerle Lad (IRE) **(68)***(69) (GHarwood)* 4-9-4 WCarson(10) (4th st: wknd over 1f out)............½ 8
991[6] Samsonesque **(64)***(61) (JRFanshawe)* 4-9-0v JCarroll(2) (lw: bhd fnl 2f)..............2 9
Quest Again **(65)***(58) (DWPArbuthnot)* 4-9-1 SWhitworth(7) (lw: hdwy 3f out: wknd over 2f out)....................2½ 10
1091[4] Camden's Ransom (USA) **(60)***(53) (HGRowsell)* 8-8-10 JWeaver(9) (led over 5f: 2nd st: wknd over 2f out)....................½ 11

7/2 Bookcase, **9/2** Absolutely Fayre (op 3/1), **11/2** DUTOSKY, **6/1** Fieldridge, **15/2** Samsonesque, **8/1** Caerle Lad (IRE), **10/1** Tadellal (IRE), **12/1** Camden's Ransom (USA), **14/1** Quest Again, Koathary (USA), **25/1** Tondres (USA), CSF £25.42 CT £243.91 TOTE £6.10: £2.00 £1.30 £4.90 (£6.40) Trio £194.40 OWNER Mr D. A. Johnson (BOGNOR REGIS) BRED Lord Victor Matthews 11 Rn
2m 9.55 (5.25) SF: 47/51/56/61/57/66/45/51/43/40/35

T/Jkpt: £1,404.60 (13.31 Tckts). T/Plpt: £14.50 (2,273 Tckts). T/Qdpt: £7.30 (41.85 Tckts). AK

1348-LEICESTER (R-H)
Tuesday May 30th (Good to firm)
WEATHER: overcast WIND: nil

1368 TOTE CREDIT H'CAP (0-70) (3-Y.O+) (Class E) £3,416.60 (£1,020.80: £488.40: £222.20) **1m 1f 218y** Stalls: High GOING minus 0.30 sec per fur (GF) 2-30 (2-49)

763[10] **Allesca (55)***(64) (MDIUsher)* 5-8-6 (7) CAdamson(9) (hld up & bhd: rdn & hdwy over 2f out: str run to ld cl home)....................— 1
1064[4] Hawkish (USA) **(44)***(53) (DMorley)* 6-8-2 GCarter(7) (bit bkwd: dwlt: hdwy over 3f out: led wl ins fnl f: ct nr fin)....................nk 2
1292[7] Augustan **(58)***(65) (SGollings)* 4-9-2v JWeaver(15) (lw: hld up & bhd: hdwy u.p over 2f out: r.o wl fnl f)....................1 3
1014[4] Father Dan (IRE) **(47)***(52) (MissGayKelleway)* 6-8-5 PRobinson(3) (lw: chsd ldrs: 6th & rdn st: kpt on ins fnl f)....................1½ 4
817[3] Rock The Barney (IRE) **(48)***(52) (PBurgoyne)* 6-8-3 (3) JTate(2) (hld up & bhd: hdwy on outside 3f out: nrst fin)....................s.h 5
984[8] Admirals Flame (IRE) **(60)***(64) (CFWall)* 4-9-4 GDuffield(10) (b: lw: led & sn wl clr: wknd qckly & hdd wl ins fnl f)....................nk 6
1029[14] Sea Spouse **(45)***(44) (MBlanshard)* 4-8-3 StephenDavies(14) (chsd ldr: 2nd st: rdn 2f out: sn wknd)....................3 7
935[5] El Bailador (IRE) **(60)***(54) (JDBethell)* 4-9-4 RHills(11) (lw: nvr plcd to chal)..............3 8
1093[9] Birthday Boy (IRE) **(66)***(56)*(Fav)*(RHannon)* 3-8-9 TQuinn(16) (lw: chsd ldrs: 3rd st: wknd over 2f out)....................3 9
988[18] Broughton's Pride (IRE) **(50)***(33) (JAGlover)* 4-8-8 SDWilliams(13) (in tch: rdn along over 3f out: sn wknd)....................4 10
1060[9] Studio Thirty **(50)***(33) (RHollinshead)* 3-7-7 NCarlisle(5) (dwlt: a bhd)..............nk 11
Al Jinn **(44)***(26) (RCurtis)* 4-8-2 JQuinn(1) (bkwd: a bhd)..............nk 12
726[10] Rustic League (IRE) **(39)** *(DBurchell)* 4-7-11 ow2 AMackay(4) (lw: plld hrd: sn bhd: t.o)..........20 13
873[16] Eqtesaad (USA) **(70)***(18) (SCWilliams)* 4-10-0 WRSwinburn(8) (lw: chsd ldrs: 4th st: rdn 3f out: sn btn: t.o)....................1½ 14
780[20] Persian Heritage **(38)** *(AJChamberlain)* 4-7-3v(7) MartinDwyer(12) (b: bit bkwd: 5th st: wknd over 3f out: t.o)....................dist 15
942[11] Barnaby Willow **(50)** *(MJRyan)* 3-7-2 (5) MBaird(6) (Withdrawn not under Starter's orders: loose bef s).................... W

LONG HANDICAP Studio Thirty 7-0 Barnaby Willow 7-4

, **7/2** Birthday Boy (IRE), **5/1** Rock The Barney (IRE), **7/1** Father Dan (IRE), **9/1** El Bailador (IRE) (op 6/1), Eqtesaad (USA), **10/1** Admirals Flame (IRE), Hawkish (USA), **14/1** Broughton's Pride (IRE), **16/1** Augustan, **25/1** ALLESCA, Al Jinn, Rustic League (IRE), **33/1** Sea Spouse, **50/1** Persian Heritage, Studio Thirty, CSF £227.97 CT £3,694.64 TOTE £17.40: £3.50 £2.50 £3.00 (£92.00) Trio £243.70 OWNER Miss D. G. Kerr (SWINDON) BRED Mrs E. M. Gauvain 15 Rn
2m 9.9 (7.20) SF: 16/5/17/4/4/16/-/6/-/-/-/-/-/-/-
WEIGHT FOR AGE 3yo-15lb

1369

TOTE EACH WAY (S) STKS (2-Y.O) (Class G) £2,556.60 (£707.60: £337.80)
5f 218y Stalls: High GOING minus 0.30 sec per fur (GF) 3-00 (3-15)

Deerly *(67+) (DMorris)* 2-8-6 JWeaver(2) (lt-f: mde all: clr appr fnl f: unchal) ....— 1
*1090*5 Bites *(48) (GLewis)* 2-8-6 PaulEddery(5) (hld up: effrt to chse wnr over 1f out: outpcd fnl f) 7 2
12724 Solva Mist *(44) (LJHolt)* 2-8-7 ow1 JReid(1) (w wnr: rdn wl over 1f out: sn wknd)....................1½ 3
*1212*8 Cinnamon Stick (IRE) *(39)(Fav)(WJarvis)* 2-8-11 MHills(7) (prom: rdn 2f out: sn lost pl)..........4 4
1184 18 Maygain (IRE) *(20) (MRChannon)* 2-8-11 RHughes(6) (lw: s.s: bhd: rdn over 2f out: no imp)..7 5
Kai's Lady (IRE) *(SWCampion)* 2-8-6 NCarlisle(4) (unf: bkwd: s.s: a bhd & outpcd: t.o) 20 6

2/1 Cinnamon Stick (IRE), **11/4** Maygain (IRE), **4/1** DEERLY, Bites, **10/1** Solva Mist, **25/1** Kai's Lady (IRE), CSF £18.54 TOTE £4.90: £3.50 £1.70 (£8.10) OWNER D & L Racing (NEWMARKET) BRED Stetchworth Park Stud Ltd 6 Rn 1m 15.7 (5.70) SF: -/-/-/-/-/-
Bt in 10,000 gns

1370

TOTE PLACEPOT CONDITIONS STKS (3-Y.O) (Class C) £5,395.20 (£1,996.80: £958.40: £392.00: £156.00: £61.60)
7f 9y Stalls: High GOING minus 0.30 sec per fur (GF) 3-30 (3-35)

Star of Zilzal (USA) *(99) (MRStoute)* 3-8-13 WRSwinburn(4) (h.d.w: dwlt: hld up & bhd: hdwy 2f out: hung rt over 1f out: shkn up to ld wl ins fnl f)...................................— 1
1224 4 Romanzof *(96)(Fav)(HRACecil)* 3-8-13 WRyan(2) (lw: led tl hdd wl ins fnl f)..........................1½ 2
1185 4 Dashing Water **(95)***(87) (IABalding)* 3-8-8 PatEddery(1) (lw: a.p: rdn over 1f out: nt pce to chal)...1¾ 3
1138 6 Great Bear **(102)***(85) (RFJohnsonHoughton)* 3-8-13 JReid(3) (hld up: pushed along 3f out: nvr trbld ldrs) 3 4
883 5 Kayrawan (USA) **(91)***(81) (HThomsonJones)* 3-8-13 RHills(5) (swtg: hld up in tch: rdn & edgd rt 2f out: sn wknd) 1½ 5
1121a 11 Iblis (IRE) **(94)***(77) (GWragg)* 3-9-3 MHills(6) (lw: prom: rdn over 2f out: sn btn)....................3½ 6

9/4 Romanzof, **11/4** Iblis (IRE), **7/2** STAR OF ZILZAL (USA), **6/1** Great Bear, **13/2** Dashing Water, **11/1** Kayrawan (USA) (8/1-12/1), CSF £11.55 TOTE £3.30: £2.00 £2.30 (£4.20) OWNER Mr Mana Al Maktoum (NEWMARKET) BRED Gainsborough Farm Inc 6 Rn 1m 27.4 (4.90) SF: 14/11/2/-/-/-

1371

WOODHOUSE EAVES CLAIMING STKS (3-Y.O) (Class F) £2,997.80 (£830.80: £397.40) **1m 8y** Stalls: High GOING minus 0.30 sec per fur (GF) 4-00 (4-00)

1207 6 **Vindaloo (49)***(59) (JLHarris)* 3-8-8 PaulEddery(2) (lw: hld up in tch: hdwy 2f out: shkn up to ld wl ins fnl f) ....— 1
974 6 Just Fizzy **(45)***(51) (JWharton)* 3-7-12 (5) MBaird(4) (led over 4f out tl wl ins fnl f)...................1½ 2
1202 10 Dominion's Dream **(66)***(52) (BSmart)* 3-8-6 (3) SSanders(3) (a.p: ev ch over 1f out: unable qckn)...2½ 3
1196 5 Best of Bold *(66)(Fav)(RHannon)* 3-9-10 JReid(7) (chsd ldrs: ev ch 2f out: sn rdn: one pce)..¾ 4
1097 19 Alka International **(46)***(42) (JWhite)* 3-8-11 (5) SDrowne(6) (chsd ldrs: rdn 3f out: kpt on one pce)...8 5
*847*4 Joyful Times **(45)***(24) (MrsNMacauley)* 3-7-10 (7) AmandaSanders(9) (nvr nr to chal) 2½ 6
1125 3 Anegre (IRE) **(60)***(40) (LJHolt)* 3-9-10 MPerrett(10) (chsd ldrs: rdn over 2f out: sn outpcd) ...2½ 7
1125 8 Steepholme *(24) (BRMillman)* 3-8-11 JCarroll(11) (nvr trbld ldrs)...1½ 8
1245 9 Sorisky **(45)***(19) (BGubby)* 3-8-12v NCarlisle(8) (led over 3f: wknd over 2f out) 3 9
773 7 Bretton Princess **(36)***(11) (RHollinshead)* 3-8-5 WRyan(12) (spd over 4f) ....nk 10
1092 16 Northern Spruce (IRE) *(19) (MissJacquelineDoyle)* 3-9-6 RHughes(1) (bit bkwd: dwlt: effrt ½-wy: wknd over 2f out: t.o)..3½ 11
758 15 Charlie-Don't Surf *(22) (RThompson)* 3-9-10 GDuffield(5) (bkwd: s.s: a wl bhd: t.o) ....¾ 12
861 5 Red O'Reilly **(46)***(8) (MrsNMacauley)* 3-8-12b JWeaver(13) (s.s: a bhd & outpcd: t.o) 1 13

2/1 Best of Bold, **6/1** Dominion's Dream, Anegre (IRE), **7/1** Just Fizzy, VINDALOO, **12/1** Steepholme, **14/1** Joyful Times, **20/1** Red O'Reilly, **25/1** Alka International, Bretton Princess, **33/1** Sorisky, **50/1** Northern Spruce (IRE), Charlie-Don't Surf, CSF £51.17 TOTE £5.80: £1.90 £1.50 £3.00 (£13.60) Trio £35.40 OWNER Mr J. D. Abell (MELTON MOWBRAY) BRED Green Park Investments Ltd 13 Rn 1m 38.7 (3.70) SF: 29/21/22/36/12/-/10/-/-/-/-/-/-
Dominion's Dream clmd CBarnes £7,000; Just Fizzy clmd CBarnes £4,000

1372

TOTE DUAL FORECAST H'CAP (0-70) (3-Y.O) (Class E) £3,817.00 (£1,144.00: £550.00: £253.00) **1m 3f 183y** Stalls: High GOING minus 0.30 sec (GF) 4-30 (4-33)

1219* **Green Land (BEL) (59)***(69) (SCWilliams)* 3-9-1 4x WRSwinburn(1) (b.nr fore: hld up: 7th st: led over 1f out: sn drvn clr) ....— 1

1083³ Paradise Waters **(52)***(58)*(Fav)*(RFJohnsonHoughton)* 3-8-8 JReid(8) (led 2f: led over 2f out tl over 1f out: no ex fnl f)....3 **2**
1194³ Last Corner **(56)***(59)* *(RHollinshead)* 3-8-12 WRyan(4) (chsd ldrs: 6th st: rdn 3f out: kpt on ins fnl f)....2 **3**
745¹³ First Bite (IRE) **(59)***(61)* *(JLDunlop)* 3-9-1 JWeaver(5) (hld up: hdwy over 2f out: rdn & styd on fnl f)....1¼ **4**
1022⁸ Dr Edgar **(62)***(60)* *(GWragg)* 3-9-4 MHills(10) (lw: a.p: 5th st: ev ch 2f out: rdn & wknd appr fnl f)....3 **5**
851¹⁰ Bobby's Dream **(46)***(37)* *(MHTompkins)* 3-8-2 PRobinson(6) (bit bkwd: hld up: hdwy over 2f out: nt trble ldrs)....5 **6**
1097¹⁰ Elly Fleetfoot (IRE) **(65)***(55)* *(TGMills)* 3-9-7 JCarroll(3) (chsd ldrs: 4th st: rdn over 2f out: sn btn)....½ **7**
1097¹⁴ Hadabet **(63)***(52)* *(MissJacquelineDoyle)* 3-9-5 RHughes(11) (bit bkwd: nvr nr ldrs)....1 **8**
867⁶ Deceit the Second **(45)***(33)* *(GLewis)* 3-8-1 NAdams(14) (effrt 3f out: sn rdn: nt pce to chal)...¾ **9**
1093* Darling Clover **(60)***(47)* *(DMorley)* 3-9-2 MTebbutt(2) (led after 2f tl over 2f out: rdn & wknd) ..½ **10**
1093W Fen Terrier **(55)***(42)* *(WJHaggas)* 3-8-11 RMcGhin(12) (bit bkwd: w ldrs: 2nd st: rdn 3f out: sn lost tch)....nk **11**
Rock Group **(60)***(36)* *(JPearce)* 3-9-2 GBardwell(9) (a bhd: t.o)....8 **12**
1093¹⁸ Mariposa Grove **(50)***(25)* *(RCurtis)* 3-8-6 GDuffield(7) (a bhd: t.o)....½ **13**
Silver Bird (IRE) **(37)** *(MJRyan)* 3-7-2 (5) MBaird(13) (swtg: bhd fr ½-wy: t.o fnl 3f)....dist **14**

LONG HANDICAP Silver Bird (IRE) 7-5

9/2 Paradise Waters, **5/1** Last Corner, **11/2** GREEN LAND (BEL), **8/1** Fen Terrier (op 12/1), **9/1** Darling Clover (op 6/1), **10/1** First Bite (IRE), **12/1** Dr Edgar, **14/1** Deceit the Second, **16/1** Mariposa Grove, **20/1** Elly Fleetfoot (IRE), Rock Group, Bobby's Dream, **25/1** Hadabet, **50/1** Silver Bird (IRE), CSF £28.35 CT £121.58 TOTE £4.50: £2.10 £1.90 £2.00 (£11.10) Trio £12.70 OWNER Mrs V. Vilain (NEWMARKET) BRED Patrick Madelein 14 Rn

2m 35.6 (6.80) SF: 30/19/20/22/21/-/16/13/-/8/3/-/-/-

1373 TOTE CONDITIONS STKS (3-Y.O) (Class C) £5,256.00 (£1,944.00: £932.00: £380.00: £150.00: £58.00)
5f 218y Stalls: High GOING minus 0.30 sec per fur (GF) 5-00 (5-01)

Stylish Ways (IRE) **(85)***(99)* *(GWragg)* 3-9-1 MHills(3) (hld up: qcknd to ld ins fnl f: readily)....— **1**
1131⁴ Welton Arsenal **(98)***(97)* *(MRChannon)* 3-9-3 RHughes(6) (lw: hld up: str chal fnl f: nt pce of wnr)....1½ **2**
1168* Paris Babe **(92)***(89)* *(DMorris)* 3-8-10 JWeaver(1) (a.p: ev ch ins fnl f: unable qckn)....nk **3**
Espartero (IRE) *(93)*(Fav)*(SirMarkPrescott)* 3-9-1 GDuffield(4) (bit bkwd: reard s: sn prom: ev ch ent fnl f: unable qckn)....nk **4**
Painted Desert **(104)***(84)*(Fav)*(RCharlton)* 3-8-10 PatEddery(2) (swtg: led tl hdd & outpcd ins fnl f)....1½ **5**
1138⁴ Veuve Hoornaert (IRE) **(89)***(78)* *(RHannon)* 3-8-8 GCarter(5) (dwlt: a bhd: rdn over 2f out: sn outpcd)....1½ **6**

5/2 Espartero (IRE) (7/2-2/1), Painted Desert, **4/1** Welton Arsenal, **7/1** Veuve Hoornaert (IRE) (op 9/2), **8/1** Paris Babe, **10/1** STYLISH WAYS (IRE), CSF £43.37 TOTE £13.90: £3.30 £2.10 (£19.50) OWNER Mollers Racing (NEWMARKET) BRED Mrs C. L. Weld 6 Rn

1m 12.9 (2.90) SF: 33/31/23/27/18/12
T/Plpt: £412.90 (30.95 Tckts). T/Qdpt: £24.20 (3.95 Tckts). IM

1355-REDCAR (L-H)
Tuesday May 30th (Firm)
WEATHER: sunny periods, warm WIND: slt across

1374 BILLINGHAM CONDITIONS STKS (3-Y.O+) (Class D) £3,684.50 (£1,106.00: £533.00: £246.50) 7f (st) Stalls: Centre GOING minus 0.60 sec (F) 2-15 (2-15)

Verzen (IRE) *(92)*(Fav)*(DRLoder)* 3-8-5 LDettori(1) (lw: trckd ldrs: led wl over 1f out: shkn up & r.o)....— **1**
1178⁴ Quango *(87)* *(JGFitzGerald)* 3-8-9 KFallon(4) (trckd ldrs: effrt 2f out: r.o: nt pce of wnr)....4 **2**
984² Bogart **(59)***(73)* *(CWFairhurst)* 4-9-6 RCochrane(3) (lw: hld up: effrt over 2f out: no imp)....6 **3**
959³ Prima Cominna **(87)***(70)* *(MBell)* 3-8-6 MFenton(2) (led tl hdd & wknd wl over 1f out)....hd **4**

4/5 VERZEN (IRE), **2/1** Quango, **9/2** Prima Cominna, **33/1** Bogart, CSF £2.70 TOTE £1.80 (£1.40) OWNER Mr Saeed Manana (NEWMARKET) BRED Sheikh Mohammed bin Rashid al Maktoum 4 Rn

1m 22.6 SF: 32/27/24/10
WEIGHT FOR AGE 3yo-11lb

1375

E.B.F. MEDIAN AUCTION MAIDEN STKS (2-Y.O F) (Class E)
£3,257.25 (£978.00: £471.50: £218.25)
6f Stalls: Centre GOING minus 0.60 sec per fur (F) 2-45 (2-47)

1098[6] **Amanita** *(75)*(Fav)*(JWWatts)* 2-8-11 LDettori(1) (lw: b.hind: chsd ldrs: effrt over 2f out: r.o to ld cl home)......— 1
React *(75) (WJarvis)* 2-8-11 KDarley(2) (w'like: scope: lw: trckd ldr: led ½-wy: rdn ins fnl f: no ex nr fin)......s.h 2
Stately *(72) (SirMarkPrescott)* 2-8-11 RPerham(5) (neat: scope: bit bkwd: b.hind: sn drvn along: hdwy 2f out: kpt on wl)......1¼ 3
819[12] Itsinthepost *(66) (MJohnston)* 2-8-11 TWilliams(4) (chsd ldrs: rdn over 2f out: r.o one pce)......2 4
Merrily *(50) (MissSEHall)* 2-8-11 NConnorton(8) (b.hind: neat: dwlt: hdwy ½-wy: no imp appr fnl f)......6 5
Impromptu Melody (IRE) *(46) (BSRothwell)* 2-8-11 MFenton(7) (b.nr hind: leggy: unf: led to ½-wy: sn wknd)......1¾ 6

11/10 AMANITA, **7/4** React, **12/1** Merrily, **14/1** Stately (7/1-16/1), Impromptu Melody (IRE), **16/1** Itsinthepost, CSF £3.25 TOTE £2.20: £1.70 £1.50 (£1.90) OWNER Sheikh Mohammed (RICHMOND) BRED Sheikh Mohammed bin Rashid al Maktoum 6 Rn 1m 11.7 (2.40) SF: 11/11/8/2/-/-

1376

JAMESON IRISH WHISKEY SPRINT H'CAP (0-90) (3-Y.O+) (Class C)
£5,842.00 (£1,756.00: £848.00: £394.00)
5f Stalls: Centre GOING minus 0.60 sec per fur (F) 3-15 (3-16)

1152[3] **Shadow Jury (54)***(59) (DWChapman)* 5-8-2b LCharnock(8) (led after 1½f: r.o wl)......— 1
1106[16] Allwight Then (IRE) **(74)***(73) (FHLee)* 4-9-8 TIves(5) (a cl up: effrt 2f out: nt qckn fnl f)......1¾ 2
1193[14] Here Comes a Star **(76)***(75) (JMCarr)* 7-9-10 KDarley(9) (hdwy 2f out: styd on: nvr able to chal)......hd 3
Palo Blanco **(76)***(70) (TDBarron)* 4-9-10 JFortune(6) (bit bkwd: in tch: kpt on fnl f: nvr plcd to chal)......1½ 4
1257* Fairy Wind (IRE) **(77)***(70)*(Fav)*(NACallaghan)* 3-9-2 7x LDettori(2) (b.hind: chsd ldrs: effrt 2f out: wknd ins fnl f)......½ 5
1152[10] Rankaidade **(51)***(38) (DonEnricoIncisa)* 4-7-13 KimTinkler(1) (outpcd ½-wy: n.d after)......1¾ 6
1057[3] Nordico Princess **(71)***(58) (MBrittain)* 4-9-5 RCochrane(3) (led 1½f: cl up tl wknd over 1f out)......hd 7
1152[8] Just Bob **(72)***(36) (SEKettlewell)* 6-9-1b(5) JStack(4) (lw: s.s: a wl bhd)......7 8

8/11 Fairy Wind (IRE), **6/1** Just Bob, **13/2** SHADOW JURY, **7/1** Nordico Princess, **10/1** Palo Blanco, **12/1** Allwight Then (IRE) (16/1-10/1), **16/1** Here Comes a Star, **25/1** Rankaidade, CSF £72.09 CT £1,100.51 TOTE £7.40: £1.60 £2.60 £3.00 (£71.00) Trio £133.60 OWNER Mrs Jeanne Chapman (YORK) BRED J. S. Bell 8 Rn 58.0 secs (1.30) SF: 13/27/29/24/15/-/12/-
WEIGHT FOR AGE 3yo-9lb

1377

REDCAR MAIDEN AMATEUR H'CAP (0-60) (3-Y.O+) (Class F)
£3,113.00 (£868.00: £419.00)
6f Stalls: Centre GOING minus 0.60 sec per fur (F) 3-45 (3-48)

1088[8] **Spanish Stripper (USA) (53)***(69) (MCChapman)* 4-11-5 (7) MrMMackley(15) (swtg: chsd ldrs: led over 1f out: r.o wl)......— 1
879[11] Flyaway Blues **(52)***(59)*(Fav)*(MrsMReveley)* 3-10-10b(5) MrSRutherford(13) (dwlt: r.o fnl 2f: nrst fin)......3½ 2
753[12] Henry the Hawk **(41)***(44) (MDods)* 4-10-7 (7) MissEMaude(8) (cl up: nt qckn fnl f)......1¼ 3
1214[7] Gate of Heaven **(20)***(21) (JohnBerry)* 5-9-2 (5) MrVLukaniuk(16) (lw: racd stands' side: chsd ldrs: one pce appr fnl f)......1 4
1195[10] Parklife (IRE) **(40)***(39) (PCHaslam)* 3-9-10 (7) MissAArmitage(9) (s.s: hdwy 2f out: styd on wl) ½ 5
992[3] Miss Pigalle **(36)***(29) (MissLAPerratt)* 4-10-4b(5) MrLDonnelly(14) (lw: racd stands' side: in tch: wknd ins fnl f)......2½ 6
1080[9] J C Grey **(40)***(32) (DenysSmith)* 3-9-12 (5) MissMCarson(1) (led tl hdd & wknd over 1f out)......hd 7
813[15] Euphyllia **(50)***(42) (BobJones)* 3-10-8 (5) MissDJJones(5) (drvn along ½-wy: nvr rchd ldrs)......nk 8
966[8] Nafta **(56)***(46) (SEKettlewell)* 3-11-5b MrsDKettlewell(6) (lw: bhd: hdwy u.p ½-wy: n.d)......¾ 9
Kilernan **(43)***(29) (TDBarron)* 4-11-2 MrsAFarrell(4) (swtg: nvr wnt pce)......1½ 10
1157[10] Cheeky Chappy **(36)***(22) (DWChapman)* 4-10-4 (5) MissRClark(3) (cl up tl wknd wl over 1f out)......s.h 11
Aquiletta **(47)***(22) (CBBBooth)* 5-11-6 MrTCuff(7) (chsd ldrs over 3f: sn lost pl)......4 12
Tarn Lane (IRE) **(45)***(11) (JPearce)* 3-10-8 MrsLPearce(10) (prom: wkng whn hmpd 1f out)......3½ 13

1023[13] Younger Days (IRE) **(42)***(4) (MartynWane)* 4-10-10 (5) MrRDGreen(2) (prom 4f)....................1¼ 14
304[11] Seraphic **(55)***(7) (BRCambidge)* 4-12-0 MrJCambidge(11) (sn bhd)..4 15
1016[5] Delightful Dancer (IRE) **(57)** *(BWHills)* 3-10-13b(7) MrCBHills(12) (lw: chsd ldrs tl sddle slipped & uns rdr 1f out).. U

5/1 Flyaway Blues, **6/1** Tarn Lane (IRE) (op 4/1), Delightful Dancer (IRE), **13/2** Miss Pigalle, **10/1** Nafta, **11/1** Euphyllia, **12/1** Aquiletta, SPANISH STRIPPER (USA), Gate of Heaven, **14/1** Parklife (IRE), **20/1** Cheeky Chappy, Henry the Hawk, Kilernan, J C Grey, **25/1** Younger Days (IRE), Seraphic, CSF £70.69 CT £1,116.63 TOTE £14.10: £2.30 £2.10 £5.60 £2.80 (£59.90) Trio £458.70 OWNER Mr Tony Satchell (MARKET RASEN) BRED Edward A. Seltzer Irrevocable Trust et al 16 Rn

1m 12.3 (3.00) SF: 42/22/17/-/2/2/-/5/9/2/-/-/-/-/-/-

WEIGHT FOR AGE 3yo-10lb

STEWARDS' ENQUIRY Lukaniuk susp. 8-11/6/95 (excessive use of whip).

1378 DORMANSTOWN H'CAP (0-70) (3-Y.O+) (Class E) £3,416.50 (£1,027.00: £496.00: £230.50) **1m 1f** Stalls: Low GOING minus 0.60 sec per fur (F) 4-15 (4-16)

1251* **Colorful Ambition (67)***(70)*(Fav)*(MrsASwinbank)* 5-10-0 5x NConnorton(9) (lw: hld up: hdwy 3f out: r.o to ld nr fin)..— 1
1192[5] Essayeffsee **(49)***(52) (MrsMReveley)* 6-8-10 KDarley(2) (lw: b.nr hind: trckd ldrs: rdn to ld ins fnl f: r.o: jst ct)...hd 2
1037[12] Touch Above **(50)***(53) (TDBarron)* 9-8-11 JFortune(5) (set slow pce: qcknd 4f out: hdd 1f out: r.o)..s.h 3
1205[11] Personimus **(36)***(35) (CaptJWilson)* 5-7-8 (3)ow4 DWright(6) (a cl up: led 1f out: sn hdd: kpt on wl)..hd 4
568[5] North Ardar **(51)***(51) (MrsMReveley)* 5-8-5 (7) SCopp(8) (swtg: hld up: effrt 3f out: n.m.r: kpt on one pce fnl f)...1¼ 5
1037[6] Thatched (IRE) **(46)***(44) (REBarr)* 5-8-7 SWebster(4) (hld up: hdwy & ev ch appr fnl f: sn rdn & btn)...1¼ 6
1081[6] Avishayes (USA) **(45)***(43) (MrsMReveley)* 8-8-6b JFanning(1) (lw: hld up & bhd: rdn 3f out: sme late hdwy)...nk 7
Beaumont (IRE) **(67)***(64) (JPearce)* 5-9-9 (5) JStack(3) (hld up: effrt on ins 3f out: no imp)......hd 8
1150[9] Enchanted Cottage **(48)***(40) (MDHammond)* 3-7-9 DaleGibson(10) (effrt 4f out: no imp)..........3 9
1085[5] Deauville Dancer (IRE) **(62)***(52) (DNicholls)* 3-8-9 AlexGreaves(7) (effrt & hung lft over 2f out: n.d)..1¼ 10

LONG HANDICAP Personimus 7-4

9/4 COLORFUL AMBITION (7/2-2/1), **4/1** Essayeffsee, **6/1** Beaumont (IRE), Avishayes (USA) (op 4/1), North Ardar, **8/1** Thatched (IRE), **9/1** Touch Above, **12/1** Deauville Dancer (IRE), **25/1** Enchanted Cottage, **66/1** Personimus, CSF £12.44 CT £66.90 TOTE £3.90: £1.50 £1.30 £1.80 (£7.50) Trio £14.30 OWNER Mr G. A. Swinbank (RICHMOND) BRED Meon Valley Stud 10 Rn

1m 53.9 (4.90) SF: 19/1/2/-/-/-/-/13/-/-

WEIGHT FOR AGE 3yo-14lb

STEWARDS' ENQUIRY Wright susp. 8-12/6/95 (excessive use of whip).

OFFICIAL EXPLANATION Deauville Dancer (IRE): the jockey reported that the gelding had hung so badly, she was unable to ride him out.

1379 SKELTON MAIDEN H'CAP (0-60) (3-Y.O) (Class F) £3,050.00 (£850.00: £410.00) **1m 6f 19y** Stalls: Low GOING minus 0.60 sec per fur (F) 4-45 (4-51)

1219[6] **Danus Rex (IRE) (50)***(63) (CASmith)* 3-8-11 TIves(15) (in tch: hdwy to ld over 1f out: r.o wl)— 1
1093[15] Vizard (IRE) **(60)***(69) (MJHeaton-Ellis)* 3-9-7b JFortune(7) (hld up: smooth hdwy to chal 2f out: one pce fnl f)...4 2
1219[2] Kildrummy Castle **(53)***(58)*(Fav)*(MrsJRRamsden)* 3-9-0 KFallon(8) (chsd ldrs: drvn along 4f out: one pce)...3½ 3
1088[11] Keys Seminar **(48)***(50) (JohnBerry)* 3-8-9 CDwyer(5) (chsd ldrs: one pce fnl 3f).......................2 4
528[3] Remontant (IRE) **(45)***(47) (RHollinshead)* 3-8-6 RCochrane(4) (styd on fnl 3f: nvr nrr) ....s.h 5
837[3] Nivasha **(44)***(44) (MBell)* 3-8-5 MFenton(11) (trckd ldrs: led wl over 2f out tl wl over 1f out: sn btn)..2 6
905[2] Sedvicta **(53)***(50) (MrsMReveley)* 3-8-7 (7) GParkin(2) (outpcd & bhd tl styd on fnl 3f)..............3 7
1289[2] Greycoat Boy **(60)***(55) (BJMeehan)* 3-9-7 TWilliams(14) (w ldr: drvn along over 4f out: wknd 3f out)..1¼ 8
1219[5] Coneygree **(39)***(33) (JWharton)* 3-8-0 JFanning(10) (led tl hdd & wknd wl over 2f out)............1 9
947[6] Bark'n'bite **(48)***(36) (MrsMReveley)* 3-8-9 KDarley(1) (chsd ldrs: drvn along ent st: sn outpcd) 5 10
525[5] Tommyknocker (IRE) **(38)***(25) (JRJenkins)* 3-7-13 DaleGibson(6) (n.d)..............................1¼ 11
1046[5] Rubislaw **(40)***(22) (CWFairhurst)* 3-8-1 LCharnock(9) (rn wd paddock bnd: n.d).......................4 12
1039[8] Bold Top **(46)***(27) (BSRothwell)* 3-8-2v(5) JStack(13) (chsd ldrs: chal over 4f out: wknd 3f out)..¾ 13
818[14] Blackspot (IRE) **(32)** *(FHLee)* 3-7-7b NKennedy(3) (a bhd: t.o) 20 14

Sharmoor **(50)** *(MissLCSiddall)* 3-8-11 GHind(12) (a bhd: t.o) ....dist **15**
LONG HANDICAP Blackspot (IRE) 7-3

11/4 Kildrummy Castle, **5/1** Sedvicta, Bark'n'bite, **11/2** Greycoat Boy, **9/1** DANUS REX (IRE), **11/1** Coneygree (8/1-12/1), **12/1** Nivasha, Tommyknocker (IRE), **14/1** Remontant (IRE), **25/1** Sharmoor, Keys Seminar, Bold Top, **33/1** Vizard (IRE), Blackspot (IRE), Rubislaw, CSF £246.06 CT £949.58 TOTE £10.10: £2.40 £5.90 £1.70 (£198.20) Trio £308.60 OWNER Bowling Green Garage (Powick) Ltd (HANLEY SWAN) BRED T. J. Hurley 15 Rn 3m 2.4 (4.40) SF: 24/30/19/11/8/5/11/16/-/-/-/-/-/-/-

1380

KIRKLEATHAM RATING RELATED MAIDEN LIMITED STKS (0-70) (3-Y.O+) (Class E) £3,234.50 (£971.00: £468.00: £216.50)
7f Stalls: Centre GOING minus 0.60 sec per fur (F) 5-15 (5-20)

1183[3] **Safey Ana (USA) (68)***(75) (BHanbury)* 4-9-2b(5) JStack(1) (b: b.hind: swtg: mde all: clr 3f out: all out) ....— **1**
1094[22] Mutabassim (IRE) **(70)***(74) (ACStewart)* 3-8-10 SWhitworth(6) (trckd ldrs: rdn to chal ins fnl f: no ex towards fin) ....nk **2**
1151[7] Brecongill Lad **(65)***(70) (MissSEHall)* 3-8-10b NConnorton(3) (plld hrd: effrt 2f out: rdn & nt qckn fnl f) 2 **3**
Moneefa **(64)***(61)*(Fav)*(HRACecil)* 4-9-2 AMcGlone(10) (chsd ldrs: effrt over 2f out: nvr able to chal) 1½ **4**
1249[5] Quilling **(69)***(66) (MDods)* 3-8-10 SWebster(2) (chsd ldrs: rdn 3f out: one pce) ....nk **5**
1151[2] Statius **(69)***(65) (TDBarron)* 3-8-10 JFortune(7) (chsd ldrs: rdn over 2f out: nt r.o) ....nk **6**
989[5] Jurassic Sue **(62)***(56) (BWHills)* 3-8-5 RCochrane(9) (lw: spd 4f: sn wknd) 1¾ **7**
1040[7] Lorelei Lee (IRE) **(69)***(54) (JohnBerry)* 3-8-5 KFallon(4) (nvr trbld ldrs) 1 **8**
963[7] Magnate's Point **(70)***(53) (PWHarris)* 3-8-10 MFenton(8) (effrt ½-wy: sn btn) 2½ **9**
Full Gloss **(60)***(19) (MrsMReveley)* 3-8-10 KDarley(5) (outpcd & bhd fnl 3f) 15 **10**

7/2 Moneefa, **9/2** Statius, **5/1** Mutabassim (IRE), **7/1** Lorelei Lee (IRE), Magnate's Point (5/1-8/1), **8/1** Quilling, SAFEY ANA (USA), **10/1** Jurassic Sue, Brecongill Lad, **25/1** Full Gloss, CSF £47.56 TOTE £7.20: £1.90 £2.70 £3.30 (£19.90) Trio £436.50 OWNER The Optimists Racing Partnership (NEWMARKET) BRED Robert N. Clay 10 Rn 1m 23.0 (1.00) SF: 42/30/26/28/22/21/12/10/9/-
WEIGHT FOR AGE 3yo-11lb

T/Plpt: £373.10 (23.76 Tckts). T/Qdpt: Not won; £97.40 to Newbury 31/5/95. AA

1361-SANDOWN (R-H)
Tuesday May 30th (Good becoming Soft)

WEATHER: heavy rain WIND: almost nil

1381

BONIO CLAIMING STKS (3-Y.O+) (Class E) £3,192.50 (£965.00:£470.00: £222.50)
1m 14y Stalls: High GOING: 0.20 sec per fur (G) 6-25 (6-29)

857[9] **Yubralee (USA) (66)***(78) (MRStoute)* 3-8-8 ow1 WRSwinburn(2) (lw: 2nd st: led over 1f out: rdn out) ....— **1**
1092[2] Komodo (USA) **(68)***(75)*(Fav)*(DRCElsworth)* 3-8-12 MRoberts(7) (3rd st: hrd rdn over 2f out: unable qckn) 4 **2**
1044* Profit Release (IRE) **(56)***(59) (MJohnston)* 4-8-11b JReid(8) (led over 6f: one pce) 1¾ **3**
1126[10] Serious Option (IRE) **(72)***(71) (PFICole)* 4-9-10b TQuinn(4) (5th st: hrd rdn 3f out: one pce) ..hd **4**
1013[6] Top Pet (IRE) **(62)***(57)*(Fav)*(RAkehurst)* 5-9-3 LDettori(9) (4th st: hrd rdn over 3f out: wknd over 1f out) 4 **5**
1012[5] Green Green Ruby **(40)***(51) (GLMoore)* 3-7-10 (5)ow1 AWhelan(11) (nvr nr to chal) ....½ **6**
544[7] Elmer's Tune **(43)***(40) (RHannon)* 3-8-5 RPerham(5) (a bhd) 8 **7**
1146[3] Miles Away (IRE) **(52)***(21) (JRFanshawe)* 3-8-0 FNorton(1) (6th st: wknd over 3f out) 7 **8**
1092[15] Broughtons Bird (IRE) *(WJMusson)* 4-8-5 (5) PMcCabe(10) (lw: a bhd) 13 **9**
346[12] Esperer **(28)** *(JO'Donoghue)* 5-8-10 (3) DRMcCabe(6) (a wl bhd) 7 **10**

7/2 Komodo (USA), Top Pet (IRE) (op 9/4), **4/1** YUBRALEE (USA) (3/1-9/2), Profit Release (IRE) (3/1-9/2), **10/1** Serious Option (IRE) (op 6/1), Miles Away (IRE), **33/1** Green Green Ruby, Broughtons Bird (IRE), **50/1** Elmer's Tune, **66/1** Esperer, CSF £16.50 TOTE £5.30: £1.90 £1.20 £1.40 (£7.40) Trio £8.40 OWNER Mr Saeed Suhail (NEWMARKET) BRED Gainsborough Farm Inc 10 Rn 1m 45.23 (6.03) SF: 48/45/41/53/39/21/10/-/-/-
WEIGHT FOR AGE 3yo-12lb
Yubralee (USA) clmd DRichmond £10,000

1382

SHAPES H'CAP (0-80) (3-Y.O) (Class D) £4,318.50 (£1,308.00: £639.00: £304.50)
1m 3f 91y Stalls: High GOING: 0.20 sec per fur (G) 6-55 (7-00)

857* **Kimbridge Knight (IRE) (79)***(83)*(Fav)*(PTWalwyn)* 3-9-7v PatEddery(7) (mde all: all out) ....— **1**

7647 Polydamas (78)(82) (MRStoute) 3-9-6 WRSwinburn(11) (3rd st: rdn over 2f out: r.o ins fnl f)....hd 2
7454 Flight Master (62)(66) (PJMakin) 3-8-1 (3) SSanders(4) (lw: hdwy over 2f out: hrd rdn over 1f out: r.o wl ins fnl f: sddle slipped)....s.h 3
10936 Rocky Forum (52)(53) (GLMoore) 3-7-8 JQuinn(2) (hdwy on ins, ins 2f out: nt clr run ins fnl f: nt rcvr)....1¾ 4
85116 Paper Cloud (68)(61) (CEBrittain) 3-8-10 MRoberts(8) (2nd st: rdn over 3f out: wknd over 1f out)....6 5
9747 John Lee Hooker (67)(58) (DWPArbuthnot) 3-8-9 TQuinn(3) (5th st: wknd over 2f out)....1¼ 6
9414 Silently (73)(62) (IABalding) 3-9-1 LDettori(5) (lw: hdwy over 1f out: sn wknd)....1¼ 7
6472 Elfin Laughter (75)(60) (RHannon) 3-9-3 MJKinane(9) (lw: nvr nrr)....3 8
10383 Dont Forget Curtis (IRE) (76)(56) (JRFanshawe) 3-8-13 (5) NVarley(10) (4th st: wknd over 2f out)....3½ 9
7872 Fearless Venture (73)(34) (SPCWoods) 3-9-1 JReid(12) (lw: a bhd)....14 10
9429 Harding Brown (USA) (60) (GHarwood) 3-8-2 ow1 AClark(6) (lw: 6th st: wknd over 3f out)....20 11

9/4 KIMBRIDGE KNIGHT (IRE), **3/1** Elfin Laughter, **5/1** Polydamas, **9/1** Silently, **10/1** John Lee Hooker (14/1-8/1), **12/1** Flight Master (op 8/1), Dont Forget Curtis (IRE), **16/1** Fearless Venture, **20/1** Rocky Forum, Paper Cloud, **33/1** Harding Brown (USA), CSF £14.28 CT £106.88 TOTE £3.40: £1.80 £2.00 £2.10 (£9.70) Trio £51.70 OWNER Mrs Roger Waters (LAMBOURN) BRED Tarworth Bloodstock Investments Ltd 11 Rn 2m 32.54 (10.84) SF: 45/44/28/15/23/20/24/22/18/-/-

1383 PRIME MAIDEN STKS (3-Y.O+) (Class D) £3,858.75 (£1,170.00: £572.50: £273.75) 1m 2f 7y Stalls: High GOING: 0.20 sec per fur (G) 7-25 (7-44)

12212 **Kilcoran Bay** (84)(Fav)(IABalding) 3-8-11 PatEddery(12) (5th st: rdn over 3f out: led ins fnl f: r.o wl)....— 1
11753 Dr Zhivago (84) (MAJarvis) 3-8-11 PRobinson(4) (3rd st: led over 2f out tl ins fnl f: unable qckn)....nk 2
Yarrow (IRE) (80) (JHMGosden) 3-8-11 LDettori(5) (unf: scope: bit bkwd: 4th st: ev ch 1f out: one pce)....2 3
11475 Eurolink Shadow (76) (LMCumani) 3-8-11 JWeaver(8) (rdn over 2f out: hdwy over 1f out: nvr nrr)....3 4
9873 Posing (IRE) (70) (JRFanshawe) 3-8-6 JReid(10) (led over 2f: led over 4f out tl over 2f out: wknd fnl f)....hd 5
117311 Stormaway (ITY) (64) (TGMills) 3-8-11 JCarroll(15) (lw: rdn over 3f out: hdwy over 1f out: wknd fnl f)....7 6
Vlaanderen (IRE) (59) (MRStoute) 3-8-6 MJKinane(3) (str: bit bkwd: nvr nr to chal)....s.h 7
Fast Forward Fred (62) (LMontagueHall) 4-9-12 StephenDavies(2) (prom 5f)....1¼ 8
118612 Yosif (IRE) (58) (RHannon) 3-8-11 WRSwinburn(16) (lw: a bhd)....2½ 9
100012 Pinkerton Polka (52) (CEBrittain) 3-8-6 JQuinn(1) (lw: hdwy over 2f out: wknd over 1f out)....½ 10
63517 Red Dragon (55) (GWragg) 3-8-11 MHills(7) (sme hdwy over 2f out: wknd over 1f out)....1½ 11
Mont d'Or (USA) (JO'Donoghue) 5-9-12 MPerrett(6) (bit bkwd: led over 7f out tl over 4f out: 2nd st: wknd 3f out).... 12
Monrush (IRE) (SDow) 4-9-9 (3) SSanders(14) (6th st: wknd over 3f out).... 13
109221 Ruthy's Romance (AGNewcombe) 4-9-2 (5) DGriffiths(9) (Withdrawn not under Starter's orders: jockey inj).... W
Balasara (IRE) (76) (DRCElsworth) 5-9-12 MRoberts(13) (Withdrawn not under Starter's orders: ref to ent stalls).... W

2/1 KILCORAN BAY, **5/1** Posing (IRE), **11/2** Yarrow (IRE) (4/1-6/1), **8/1** Eurolink Shadow (6/1-10/1), Dr Zhivago (op 4/1), **10/1** Vlaanderen (IRE) (4/1-12/1), **14/1** Red Dragon, **25/1** Stormaway (ITY), **33/1** Yosif (IRE), Pinkerton Polka, **66/1** Mont d'Or (USA), Monrush (IRE), Fast Forward Fred, CSF £15.90 TOTE £2.90: £1.50 £1.80 £2.30 (£8.20) Trio £12.20 OWNER Mr Nigel Harris (KINGSCLERE) BRED Crest Stud Ltd 13 Rn 2m 15.58 (11.28) SF: 22/22/18/14/8/2/-/15/-/-/-/-/-
WEIGHT FOR AGE 3yo-15lb

1384 WINALOT NATIONAL STKS (Listed) (2-Y.O) (Class A) £10,406.25 (£3,150.00: £1,537.50: £731.25) 5f 6y Stalls: Low GOING: 0.20 sec per fur (G) 7-55 (8-12)

8714 **Amaretto Bay (IRE)** (91) (BJMeehan) 2-9-1 MJKinane(6) (a.p: led 1f out: hrd rdn: r.o wl)....— 1
1163* Cayman Kai (IRE) (89)(Fav)(RHannon) 2-9-1 PatEddery(2) (lw: hld up: led over 1f out: sn hdd: unable qckn wl ins fnl f)....¾ 2
1096* Whicksey Perry (84) (JBerry) 2-9-3 JCarroll(4) (lw: a.p: led over 2f out tl over 1f out: wknd ins fnl f)....2 3
11424 Naissant (73) (CEBrittain) 2-8-7 MRoberts(3) (s.s: hdwy over 2f out: r.o one pce)....½ 4
10963 Dancing Jack (55) (JJBridger) 2-8-12 SSanders(1) (lw: led over 2f: wknd over 1f out)....7 5
9773 Hotlips Houlihan (45) (RJRWilliams) 2-8-7 DBiggs(5) (bhd fnl 2f)....1¾ 6

Evens Cayman Kai (IRE), **100/30** Naissant, **4/1** Whicksey Perry (op 5/2), **10/1** AMARETTO BAY (IRE) (8/1-14/1), **25/1** Dancing Jack, Hotlips Houlihan, CSF £19.49 TOTE £10.00: £2.30 £1.60 (£6.10) OWNER The Harlequin Partnership (UPPER LAMBOURN) BRED Gay O'Callaghan 6 Rn
63.54 secs (3.74) SF: 49/47/42/31/13/3

1385 SPILLERS BRIGADIER GERARD STKS (Gp 3) (4-Y.O+) (Class A)
£21,840.00 (£8,187.00: £3,943.50: £1,729.50)
1m 2f 7y Stalls: High GOING: 0.20 sec per fur (G) 8-25 (8-37)

1171[4] **Alriffa (111)**_(115) (RHannon)_ 4-8-10 PatEddery(2) (lw: led 8f out: drvn out)......— 1
1235a[2] Just Happy (USA) **(115)**_(117)_(Fav)_(MRStoute)_ 4-9-1 WRSwinburn(6) (swtg: led 9f out to 8f out: 3rd st: rdn over 2f out: ev ch ins fnl f: unable qckn)......1¾ 2
827[2] Nicolotte **(109)**_(112) (GWragg)_ 4-8-10 MHills(3) (lw: 4th st: rdn over 2f out: ev ch ins fnl f: one pce)......hd 3
1260[4] Wayne County (IRE) **(92)**_(110) (GFierro)_ 5-8-10b LDettori(5) (hdwy over 2f out: hrd rdn over 1f out: one pce)......1½ 4
La Confederation **(116)**_(96)_(Fav)_(DRLoder)_ 4-8-12 MJKinane(7) (5th st: rdn over 2f out: wknd over 1f out)......10 5
1135[8] Garden of Heaven (USA) **(101)**_(94) (CEBrittain)_ 6-8-10 MRoberts(4) (lw: 6th st: wknd over 3f out)......s.h 6
Midnight Legend **(109)** _(LMCumani)_ 4-8-10 JWeaver(1) (led 1f: 2nd st: jinked & uns rdr over 3f out)...... U

9/4 Just Happy (USA), La Confederation, **4/1** Nicolotte, **11/2** ALRIFFA, **13/2** Midnight Legend, **12/1** Garden of Heaven (USA) (op 20/1), **66/1** Wayne County (IRE), CSF £18.28 TOTE £5.60: £2.70 £2.00 (£6.20) OWNER Sheikh Essa Bin Mubarak (MARLBOROUGH) BRED Patrick Eddery Ltd 7 Rn
2m 12.15 (7.85) SF: 48/50/45/43/29/27/-

1386 BETA H'CAP (0-80) (3-Y.O+) (Class D) £4,221.00 (£1,278.00: £624.00: £297.00)
1m 6f Stalls: High GOING: 0.20 sec per fur (G) 8-55 (9-02)

1162* **Embracing (74)**_(85)_(Fav)_(MRStoute)_ 3-8-4 KDarley(6) (5th st: led over 2f out: rdn out)......— 1
1144* Requested **(57)**_(66) (PBurgoyne)_ 8-8-4 (3) DRMcCabe(8) (rdn over 3f out: hdwy over 1f out: unable qckn fnl f)......2 2
947[2] Euro Forum **(63)**_(71) (GLMoore)_ 3-7-2 (5) MBaird(7) (led over 12f out tl over 6f out: led over 4f out to 3f out: ev ch over 1f out: one pce)......nk 3
1022[3] General Mouktar **(74)**_(80) (MCPipe)_ 5-9-10v MRoberts(3) (lw: 2nd st: led 3f out tl over 2f out: ev ch over 1f out: one pce)......2 4
1156[3] Thunderheart **(75)**_(77) (LMCumani)_ 4-9-11 LDettori(10) (led over 1f: lost pl 6f out: rallied over 2f out: wknd fnl f)......3½ 5
661[12] Simafar (IRE) **(74)**_(75) (NAGraham)_ 4-9-10 WRSwinburn(5) (3rd st: wknd over 1f out)......¾ 6
1144[9] Stoney Valley **(67)**_(64) (JRJenkins)_ 5-9-3 PatEddery(9) (hdwy over 2f out: eased whn btn ins fnl f)......3½ 7
1149[3] Pharamineux **(66)**_(56) (RAkehurst)_ 9-9-2 TQuinn(11) (lw: 6th st: wknd over 2f out)......6 8
866[19] Chez Catalan **(50)**_(35) (RAkehurst)_ 4-8-0 JQuinn(2) (led over 6f out tl over 4f out: 4th st: wknd over 3f out)......5 9

LONG HANDICAP Euro Forum 7-0

2/1 EMBRACING, **5/1** Requested, Thunderheart, **13/2** General Mouktar, **8/1** Euro Forum, Stoney Valley (5/1-10/1), **12/1** Chez Catalan, Pharamineux (6/1-14/1), **14/1** Simafar (IRE), CSF £12.91 CT £63.75 TOTE £3.00: £1.80 £1.80 £1.70 (£7.10) Trio £14.80 OWNER Maktoum Al Maktoum (NEWMARKET) BRED Gainsborough Stud Management Ltd 9 Rn 3m 22.6 (27.90) SF: -/-/-/-/-/-/-/-/-
WEIGHT FOR AGE 3yo-20lb

T/Jkpt: Not won; £6,067.54 to Newbury 31/5/95. T/Plpt: £12.60 (2,015.74 Tckts). T/Qdpt: £4.00 (53.3 Tckts). AK

1110a-SAINT-CLOUD (France) (L-H)
Tuesday May 23rd (Good)

1387a PRIX JEAN DE CHAUDENAY (Gp 2) (4-Y.O+) £35,928.00
(£14,371.00: £7,186.00: £3,593.00) **1m 4f** 3-40 (3-49)

Sunshack _(117) (AFabre,France)_ 4-9-2 TJarnet (3rd st: rdn & hdwy over 1f out: r.o to ld ins fnl f)......— 1
Sand Reef _(112) (MmeCHead,France)_ 4-8-12 ODoleuze (trckd ldr: led after ½-wy tl ins fnl f: r.o)......¾ 2
898a[6] Partipral (USA) _(115) (ELellouche,France)_ 6-9-2 DBoeuf (hld up: 8th st: rdn & styd on fnl f)......¾ 3

703a2 Danseur Landais *(111) (JLesbordes,France)* 4-8-12 GMosse (hld up: 7th st: sn rdn: r.o u.p: nvr nrr) ....nk 4
Scribano *(111) (GBotti,Italy)* 5-8-12 EBotti (4th st: r.o one pce fnl 2f) ....hd 5
607a8 Suave Tern (USA) *(110) (JEHammond,France)* 4-8-12 WMongil (hld up: 6th st: hdwy 2f out: one pce fnl f) ....¾ 6
1005a3 Walter Willy (IRE) *(109) (JEHammond,France)* 4-8-12 CAsmussen (ld tl hdd after ½-wy: 2nd st: r.o one pce fnl f) ....½ 7
489a3 Matarun (IRE) *(108) (HVandePoele,France)* 7-8-12 OPeslier (prom early: 5th st: sn wknd) 1 8

P-M 2.10F: 1.10F 1.30F 1.40F (4.00) OWNER Mr K. Abdullah (FRANCE) BRED Juddmonte Farms 8 Rn
2m 42.3 (13.00) SF: -/-/-/-/-/-/-/-

1236a-BADEN-BADEN (Germany) (L-H)
Wednesday May 24th (Good)

1388a PREIS DER HOTELLERIE BADEN-BADEN (Listed) (3-Y.O) £16,461.00 (£6,584.00: £4,115.00: £2,469.00) **1m 1f** 2-10 (2-11)

900a5 **El Supremo (USA)** *(74) (DRLoder)* 3-8-9 JWeaver ....— 1
Green's Wootton (USA) *(73) (WFigge,Germany)* 3-8-8 PPiatkowski ....nk 2
Don't Go Crazy (USA) *(71) (AWohler,Germany)* 3-8-7 ABoschert ....hd 3

Tote 18DM: 13DM 32DM 22DM (SF 374DM) OWNER Mr Wafic Said (NEWMARKET) BRED Miss K. Rausing 7 Rn
1m 54.43 SF: -/-/-

1238a-LONGCHAMP (Paris, France) (R-H)
Thursday May 25th (Good)

1389a PRIX DU PALAIS-ROYAL (Gp 3) (3-Y.O+) £26,347.00 (£9,581.00: £4,790.00: £2,395.00) **7f** 3-30 (3-31)

Cherokee Rose (IRE) *(117) (JEHammond,France)* 4-9-1 CAsmussen ....— 1
Sayyedati *(117) (CEBrittain)* 5-9-1 WRSwinburn ....hd 2
895a3 Poplar Bluff (IRE) *(116) (AFabre,France)* 3-8-7 OPeslier 1½ 3

P-M 6.80F: 2.20F 2.00F (39.40F) OWNER Sheikh Mohammed BRED Sheikh Mohammed 5 Rn
1m 25.9 SF: -/-/-

1233a-CURRAGH (Newbridge, Ireland) (R-H)
Saturday May 27th (Good becoming Soft)

1390a AIRLIE/COOLMORE IRISH 1,000 GUINEAS (Gp 1) (3-Y.O F) £84,250.00 (£28,750.00: £13,750.00: £4,750.00) **1m** 3-50 (3-51)

804a* **Ridgewood Pearl** *(118) (JOxx,Ireland)* 3-9-0 CRoche (a cl up: led 2f out: sn clr: rdn & r.o wl) ....— 1
11452 Warning Shadows (IRE) *(110) (CEBrittain)* 3-9-0 MJKinane (hld up: hdwy 2f out: r.o up ins fnl f) 4 2
707a* Khaytada (IRE) *(108) (JOxx,Ireland)* 3-9-0 JPMurtagh (ld tl hdd by wnr: r.o) 1 3
1116a6 Ghostly (IRE) *(105) (PBary,France)* 3-9-0 CAsmussen (hld up: r.o fnl 2f: nvr nrr) 1½ 4
933* Harayir (USA) *(102)(Fav)(MajorWRHern)* 3-9-0 WCarson (hld up: rdn & chsd wnr 2f out: wknd u.p fnl f) 1½ 5
11392 Fleet Hill (IRE) *(96) (MRChannon)* 3-9-0 CRutter (trckd ldrs: rdn over 2f out: wknd) 3 6
707a2 Mediation (IRE) *(93) (JOxx,Ireland)* 3-9-0 PVGilson (hld up: hdwy st: rdn 2f out: sn btn) 1½ 7
Park Charger *(91) (APO'Brien,Ireland)* 3-9-0 SCraine (trckd ldrs: rdn over 2f out: wknd) 1 8
Taibhseach (USA) *(90) (JSBolger,Ireland)* 3-9-0 JAHeffernan (prom tl rdn & wknd over 2f out) ....¾ 9
Ailleacht (USA) *(70) (JSBolger,Ireland)* 3-9-0 KJManning (hld up: hdwy ½-wy: bhd fnl 2f) 10 10

11/10f Harayir (USA), **9/4** RIDGEWOOD PEARL, **8/1** Khaytada (IRE), **9/1** Warning Shadows (IRE), **14/1** Ghostly (IRE), **16/1** Mediation (IRE), **20/1** Fleet Hill (IRE), **25/1** Park Charger, **50/1** Taibhseach (USA), Ailleacht (USA), Tote £3.20: £1.60 £2.20 £2.30 (£10.70) OWNER Mrs Anne Coughlan BRED S. Coughlan 10 Rn
1m 43.9 (7.90) SF: -/-/-/-/-/-/-/-/-/-

1118a-CAPANNELLE (Rome, Italy) (R-H)
Saturday May 27th (Good to firm)

1391a CRITERIUM DI ROMA (Listed) (2-Y.O) £17,730.00 (£7,801.00: £4,255.00: £2,128.00) **5f 110y** 2-00 (2-03)

Try My Segnor *(OPessi,Italy)* 2-8-11 JacquelineFreda (fin 2nd, 2l: awrdd r) ....— 1
683* Dungeon Master (IRE) *(MRChannon)* 2-8-11 JReid (fin 1st: disq: plcd 2nd) 2
Gransvelt (IRE) *(APeraino,Italy)* 2-8-11 JCaro 1 3

Tote 192L: 34L 13L (140L) OWNER Gerecon Italia 7 Rn 66.3 secs SF: -/-/-

1392a PREMIO ELLINGTON (Gp 2) (4-Y.O+) £41,529.00 (£18,932.00: £10,520.00: £5,260.00) **1m 4f** 3-30 (3-39)

Laroche (GER) *(121) (HJentzsch,Germany)* 4-9-0 PSchiergen (mde all: r.o wl) ....— 1
631* Captain Horatius (IRE) *(114) (JLDunlop)* 6-8-9 JReid (hld up: hdwy & 2nd st: rdn 2f out: r.o) 1¼ 2
Guado d'Annibale (IRE) *(114) (ARenzoni,Italy)* 6-8-9 EBotti (hld up: hdwy & 4th st: r.o up) ....s.nk 3
Puerto Escondido (USA) *(107) (OPessi,Italy)* 4-8-9 JacquelineFreda (hld up: nvr plcd to chal) 5 4
Mr Richard (IRE) *(107) (Italy)* 5-8-9 MPasquale (trckd ldr: 3rd st: no ex fnl 2f) ....½ 5
1118a6 Rubhahunish (IRE) *(97) (ARenzoni,Italy)* 4-8-9 SLandi (rdn st: sn btn) 7 6
1118a3 Firing Line (IRE) *(Italy)* 6-8-9 VMezzatesta (wknd qckly 2f out: p.u: lame) .... P

Tote 37L: 21L 13L (25L) OWNER Gestut Ittlingen BRED Gestut Hof Ittlingen in Germany 7 Rn
2m 26.4 SF: -/-/-/-/-/-/-

1388a-BADEN-BADEN (Germany) (L-H)
Friday May 26th (Soft)

1393a BENAZET-RENNEN (Gp 3) (3-Y.O+) £30,864.00 (£12,346.00: £6,173.00: £3,292.00) **6f** 3-25 (3-31)

895a* **Wessam Prince** *(117) (CLaffon-Parias,France)* 4-9-6 WRSwinburn ....— 1
Glenlivet (SWE) *(116) (LKelp,Sweden)* 7-9-6 KWoodburn ....½ 2
921 6 Piccolo *(114) (MRChannon)* 4-9-6 JReid ....¾ 3
1119a* Hever Golf Rose *(110) (TJNaughton)* 5-9-2 JWeaver ....s.h 4
1133 3 Branston Abby (IRE) *(108) (MJohnston)* 6-9-2 TWilliams (btn approx 2½l) 6
921 11 Bunty Boo *(105) (RHannon)* 6-9-2 RPerham (btn approx 4l) 7

Tote 32DM: 16DM 42DM 18DM (SF 1198DM) OWNER Maktoum Al Maktoum BRED F.Fabre 11 Rn
1m 12.07 SF: -/-/-/-/-/-

1389a-LONGCHAMP (Paris, France) (R-H)
Sunday May 28th (Good)

1394a PRIX D'ISPAHAN (Gp 1) (4-Y.O+ C & F) £59,880.00 (£23,952.00: £11,976.00: £5,988.00) **1m 1f** 2-35 (2-39)

1002a* **Green Tune (USA)** *(125) (MmeCHead,France)* 4-9-2 ODoleuze (trckd ldr: rdn to ld 2f out: hdd 1f out: rallied to ld cl home) ....— 1
898a* Pelder (IRE) *(125) (PAKelleway)* 5-9-2 PatEddery (4th st: hdwy to ld 1f out: r.o: hdd nr fin) ....s.h 2
898a9 Marildo (FR) *(121) (DSmaga,France)* 8-9-2 GGuignard (3rd st: rdn over 2f out: one pce) 2½ 3
Thames (FR) *(117) (LAudon,France)* 4-9-2 FHead (5th st: rdn 2f out: one pce) 2 4
897a2 Agathe (USA) *(114) (AFabre,France)* 4-8-13 OPeslier (7th & rdn st: sme late hdwy) ....nse 5
1118a* Flagbird (USA) *(113) (SbinSuroor)* 4-8-13 CAsmussen (hld up: last st: rdn 2f out: one pce)...½ 6
1002a7 Dernier Empereur (USA) *(115) (AFabre,France)* 5-9-2 TJarnet (6th st: rdn 2f out: styd on) ....½ 7
1002a8 Simply Tricky (USA) *(104) (MmeCHead,France)* 4-9-2 NGuesdon (ld to 2f out) 6 8
1118a2 Del Deya (IRE) *(84) (JHMGosden)* 5-8-13 LDettori (dwlt: 8th st: sn rdn & btn) 10 9

P-M 2.60F: 1.10F 1.30F 2.30F (2.60F) OWNER Mr J. Wertheimer (FRANCE) BRED Wertheimer & Frere in USA 9 Rn 1m 53.7 SF: -/-/-/-/-/-/-/-/-

1391a-CAPANNELLE (Rome, Italy) (R-H)
Sunday May 28th (Good to firm)

1395a
PREMIO ALESSANDRO PERRONE (Listed) (2-Y.O F) £17,730.00 (£7,801.00: £4,255.00: £2,128.00) **5f 110y** 1-30 (1-31)

Pappa Reale *(RBrogi,Italy)* 2-8-11 GBietolini .... — 1
Bella Michela (IRE) *(MSalles,Italy)* 2-8-11 LFicuciello 1½ 2
Golden Rosy (ITY) *(GFratini,Italy)* 2-8-11 VMezzatesta 1½ 3
1017* Mystique Smile *(JBerry)* 2-8-11 JCarroll (btn 11½l) 7

Tote 32L; 19L 55L (190L) 7 Rn 66.2 secs SF: -/-/-/-

1396a
DERBY ITALIANO (Gp 1) (3-Y.O C & F) £234,439.00 (£126,972.00: £76,242.00: £38,121.00) **1m 4f** 4-05 (4-17)

979* **Luso** *(107) (CEBrittain)* 3-9-2 MJKinane (6th st: led over 2f out: sn clr: r.o wl) .... — 1
979² Court of Honour (IRE) *(105) (PWChapple-Hyam)* 3-9-2 JReid (a.p: 5th st: r.o wl fnl f) 1½ 2
886* Precede *(104) (PFICole)* 3-9-2 TQuinn (a.p: 4th st: chal 2f out: one pce) .... ½ 3
1068⁴ Balliol Boy *(104) (HRACecil)* 3-9-2 WRyan (7th st: chal 2f out: no ex fnl f) .... nk 4
Tarhelm (IRE) *(104) (GColleo,Italy)* 3-9-2 MLattore (9th st: hdwy to chal over 2f out: one pce fnl f) .... hd 5
1010a³ Ice and Glacial (IRE) *(103) (GBotti,Italy)* 3-9-2 EBotti (hdwy st: nrst fin) .... ¾ 6
Oxford Line (IRE) *(103) (FBrogi,Italy)* 3-9-2 JCaro (hdwy fnl 3f: nvr plcd to chal) .... s.h 7
1010a² Seattle John (USA) *(103) (GBotti,Italy)* 3-9-2 GForte (r.o fnl 3f: nvr plcd to chal) .... s.nk 8
912² Anchor Clever *(96) (PAKelleway)* 3-9-2 MWigham (trckd ldr: 2nd st: sn wknd) 5 9
979⁶ Royal Scimitar (USA) *(95) (PFICole)* 3-9-2 JCarroll (ld tl over 2f out: wknd) .... ½ 10
900a² Thomire *(91) (PMazzoni,Italy)* 3-9-2 BJovine (a bhd) 3 11
Popolare (IRE) *(65) (LCamici,Italy)* 3-9-2 MPasquale (prom tl wknd st) 20 12

Tote 57L: 17L 16L 17L (58L) OWNER Mr Saeed Manana (NEWMARKET) BRED Saeed Manana 12 Rn 2m 25.7 SF: -/-/-/-/-/-/-/-/-/-/-/-

1397a
PREMIO W.W.F. (Listed) (4-Y.O+) £17,730.00 (£7,801.00: £4,255.00: £2,128.00) **7f** 5-30 (5-30)

1143³ **Classic Sky (IRE)** *(101) (BHanbury)* 4-8-7 WRyan .... — 1
Beat of Drums *(98) (GBotti,Italy)* 4-8-7 EBotti 1½ 2
Power of Polly (USA) *(94) (OPessi,Italy)* 5-8-7 JacquelineFreda 1½ 3

Tote 28L: 15L 23L 35L (134L) OWNER Mr Saeed Suhail (NEWMARKET) 11 Rn 1m 22.2 SF: -/-/-

1393a-BADEN-BADEN (Germany) (L-H)
Sunday May 28th (Soft)

1398a
GROSSER PREIS DER WIRTSCHAFT (Gp 2) (4-Y.O+) £65,844.00 (£26,749.00: £12,346.00: £6,996.00) **1m 3f** 3-25 (3-31)

898a⁴ **Freedom Cry** *(122) (AFabre,France)* 4-9-4 SGuillot (hdwy 3f out: qcknd to ld ins fnl f: r.o wl) .... — 1
898a² Alderbrook *(123) (MrsJCecil)* 6-9-6 PaulEddery (hdwy 3f out: chal 1f out: r.o) .... ¾ 2
Lando (GER) *(122) (HJentzsch,Germany)* 5-9-6 ATylicki (hld up in rr: gd hdwy to chal 1f out: wknd ins fnl f) .... ½ 3
Aratikos (GER) *(114) (HBlume,Germany)* 4-9-0 OSchick (trckd ldr tl led 5f out: hdd ins fnl f: one pce) 1¼ 4
Kornado *(116) (Germany)* 5-9-4 MRimmer (a.p: 2nd st: one pce fnl f) 1½ 5
Monsun (GER) *(105) (Germany)* 5-9-6 PSchiergen (prom: rdn over 2f out: sn btn) 9 6
Bad Bertrich (IRE) *(92) (Germany)* 4-9-4 AHelfenbein (mid div: wknd st) 8 7
Embarcadero (GER) *(70) (Germany)* 7-9-0 SEccles (led to 5f out: wknd qckly) 12 8
Theophanu (USA) *(Germany)* 4-8-12 KWoodburn (t.o fr ½-wy) 48 9

Tote 53DM: 22DM 23DM 21DM (238DM) OWNER Mr D. Wildenstein (FRANCE) BRED Dayton Ltd 9 Rn 2m 22.17 SF: -/-/-/-/-/-/-/-/-

0739-FOLKESTONE (R-H)
Wednesday May 31st (Good to firm)
WEATHER: overcast WIND: almost nil

1399 TATTERSALLS MAIDEN AUCTION STKS (2-Y.O) (Class E) £3,130.60 (£932.80: £444.40: £200.20)
5f Stalls: Centre GOING minus 0.50 sec per fur (F) 2-15 (2-16)

1223[4] **Hever Golf Express** *(78+) (TJNaughton)* 2-8-9 PaulEddery(1) (mde all: rdn out)........— 1
1163[3] Hurricane Dancer (IRE) *(62) (SPCWoods)* 2-7-8 (5) NVarley(2) (lw: rdn thrght: hdwy fnl f: r.o)........1¾ 2
859[5] Mellors (IRE) *(68) (JARToller)* 2-8-10 JWeaver(6) (lw: a.p: ev ch 2f out: unable qckn)........1¾ 3
Veesey *(55) (JohnBerry)* 2-8-1 ow1 MFenton(3) (neat: bit bkwd: w wnr: ev ch 2f out: wknd 1f out)........¾ 4
1123[2] Autobabble (IRE) *(57)*(Fav)*(RHannon)* 2-8-6 PatEddery(4) (lw: rdn over 3f out: nvr nr to chal)........1½ 5
1031[9] Princess Renata (IRE) *(45) (DTThom)* 2-7-12 AMackay(5) (bit bkwd: hld up: rdn over 2f out: wknd fnl f)........1¼ 6

11/10 Autobabble (IRE), **9/4** HEVER GOLF EXPRESS, **100/30** Hurricane Dancer (IRE) (2/1-7/2), **20/1** Mellors (IRE), **33/1** Veesey, **66/1** Princess Renata (IRE), CSF £9.38 TOTE £4.00: £1.30 £1.50 (£6.80) OWNER Hever Racing Club II (EPSOM) BRED S. Tindall and Stowell Hill Ltd 6 Rn
61.2 secs (2.60) SF: 12/-/2/-/-/-

1400 BREDE H'CAP (0-70) (3-Y.O+) (Class E) £3,216.40 (£959.20: £457.60: £206.80)
5f Stalls: Centre GOING minus 0.50 sec per fur (F) 2-45 (2-52)

1050[2] **Bashful Brave (60)***(62)*(Fav)*(JWPayne)* 4-9-12 MRimmer(5) (lw: a.p: led 2f out: rdn out)........— 1
452[5] Texas Cowgirl (IRE) **(45)***(46) (HVanderdussen,Belgium)* 5-8-11 PascalVandekeere(6) (lw: hld up: ev ch fnl 2f: r.o)........nk 2
832[5] Tachycardia **(45)***(43) (RJO'Sullivan)* 3-7-13 (3)ow3 SSanders(4) (a.p: hrd rdn over 1f out: r.o) .hd 3
*1331** Bonny Melody **(50)***(50) (PDEvans)* 4-8-9 (7) 7x AmandaSanders(2) (hld up: hrd rdn over 1f out: r.o wl ins fnl f)........hd 4
1201* Sizzling **(66)***(58) (RHannon)* 3-9-9 7x JReid(7) (lw: rdn 3f out: hdwy over 1f out: nvr nrr)........2½ 5
1265[10] Tee-Emm **(40)***(30) (PHowling)* 5-8-6 JQuinn(1) (led 3f: wknd over 1f out)........¾ 6
856[11] Sison (IRE) **(62)***(48) (KGWingrove)* 5-9-9 (5) PMcCabe(3) (a bhd)........1¼ 7
1023[12] Distant Dynasty **(50)***(26) (BAPearce)* 5-9-2 StephenDavies(8) (bhd fnl 2f)........3 8
1076[9] Rocky Two **(60)***(20) (PHowling)* 4-9-5b(7) DebbieBiggs(9) (bhd fnl 3f)........5 9

9/4 BASHFUL BRAVE, **5/2** Sizzling, **5/1** Texas Cowgirl (IRE), **14/1** Tee-Emm, **16/1** Bonny Melody, Tachycardia, Sison (IRE), Distant Dynasty, **25/1** Rocky Two, CSF £12.34 CT £115.97 TOTE £2.70: £1.40 £3.20 £1.90 (£17.70) Trio £64.70 OWNER Mrs G. M. Hay (NEWMARKET) BRED Mrs G. M. Hay 9 Rn
60.2 secs (1.60) SF: 44/28/16/32/31/12/30/8/2
WEIGHT FOR AGE 3yo-9lb

1401 LYMPNE LIMITED STKS (0-50) (3-Y.O+) (Class F) £2,519.00 (£694.00: £329.00)
1m 4f Stalls: Low GOING minus 0.50 sec per fur (F) 3-15 (3-16)

1166[5] **Krayyan Dawn (49)***(52)*(Fav)*(RAkehurst)* 5-10-0 TQuinn(1) (lw: 3rd st: led on bit ins fnl f: hrd hld)........— 1
1292[5] Charlie Bigtime **(49)***(50) (DTThom)* 5-9-12v AMackay(4) (2nd st: led over 1f out tl ins fnl f: r.o)s.h 2
403[11] Ikhtiraa (USA) **(49)***(43) (RJO'Sullivan)* 5-9-10 AClark(7) (swtg: chsd ldr: led over 5f out tl over 1f out: unable qckn)........4 3
1254* Royal Rabbit **(48)***(43)*(Fav)*(GLMoore)* 3-8-3 (5) AWhelan(8) (hdwy over 3f out: 4th st: wknd over 1f out)........1½ 4
626[8] Fair Ella (IRE) **(40)***(25) (JFfitch-Heyes)* 3-7-12 (3) DWright(5) (lw: hld up: rdn over 3f out: wknd over 2f out: 6th st)........8 5
1196[9] Ace Chapel (IRE) **(46)***(30) (CCElsey)* 3-8-6 JWeaver(9) (led over 6f: wknd over 3f out: 5th st)hd 6
Scud Missile (IRE) **(49)***(29)*(Fav)*(GFJohnsonHoughton)* 4-9-5 (5) LNewton(2) (lw: a bhd)........½ 7
91[10] Perdition (IRE) **(49)** *(KRBurke)* 5-9-5v ATucker(3) (s.s: a bhd)........25 8
1051[5] Twice Knightly **(46)** *(JRJenkins)* 4-9-10 DBiggs(6) (prom over 6f)........14 9

3/1 KRAYYAN DAWN, Scud Missile (IRE) (op 9/2), Royal Rabbit, **5/1** Ikhtiraa (USA), **8/1** Charlie Bigtime, **16/1** Twice Knightly, **20/1** Perdition (IRE), **33/1** Fair Ella (IRE), Ace Chapel (IRE), CSF £25.56 TOTE £3.70: £1.70 £1.30 £2.60 (£13.50) Trio £13.80 OWNER Mr R. E. Greatorex (EPSOM) BRED R. Voorspuy 9 Rn
2m 39.6 (8.40) SF: 20/18/11/-/-/-/-/-/-
WEIGHT FOR AGE 3yo-18lb

1402
GLOVER INSURANCE SERVICES CHALLENGE CUP H'CAP (0-70) (3-Y.O+) (Class E) £3,416.60 (£1,020.80: £488.40: £222.20)
1m 1f 149y Stalls: Low GOING minus 0.50 sec per fur (F) 3-45 (3-46)

1141[15] **Pistol (IRE) (59)***(64) (CAHorgan)* 5-9-7 PaulEddery(2) (hdwy over 3f out: 6th st: rdn over 1f out: led ins fnl f: r.o wl)......— 1
948[6] Dont Shoot Fairies **(68)***(72) (CEBrittain)* 3-9-1 BDoyle(13) (lw: 5th st: rdn over 1f out: one pce)¾ 2
873[13] Daytona Beach (IRE) **(62)***(65) (PBurgoyne)* 5-9-3 (7) DebbieBiggs(3) (lw: led tl ins fnl f: one pce)......nk 3
1166* Plinth **(56)***(55)*(Fav)*(NAGraham)* 4-9-4v PatEddery(4) (rdn 3f out: 3rd st: hrd rdn over 1f out: btn whn hmpd ins fnl f)......2½ 4
975[6] Mister O'Grady (IRE) **(46)***(44) (RAkehurst)* 4-8-8b TQuinn(6) (2nd st: hrd rdn over 1f out: btn whn bdly hmpd ins fnl f)......½ 5
Riva Rock **(33)***(30) (TPMcGovern)* 5-7-9 ow1 JQuinn(5) (nvr nr to chal)......nk 6
1049[5] Duty Sergeant (IRE) **(32)***(26) (PMitchell)* 6-7-8 GBardwell(7) (nvr nrr)......2½ 7
Bronze Maquette (IRE) **(42)***(35) (RJO'Sullivan)* 5-8-4 AClark(11) (lw: stdy hdwy over 3f out: 4th st: btn whn squeezed out 1f out)......nk 8
885[2] Audrey Grace **(51)***(33) (BJMeehan)* 4-8-13 JWeaver(9) (hdwy 4f out: wknd over 2f out)......7 9
1124[4] Care And Comfort **(62)***(43) (GWragg)* 3-8-9 MRimmer(10) (lw: bhd fnl 3f)......hd 10
845[2] A Million Watts **(58)***(31) (LadyHerries)* 4-9-6 TIves(1) (bhd fnl 4f)......5 11
Blanchland **(60)***(27) (KTIvory)* 6-9-1 (7) CScally(12) (bhd fnl 5f)......4 12

5/2 Plinth (7/2-9/4), **11/2** Bronze Maquette (IRE), **13/2** A Million Watts, **7/1** Audrey Grace, **8/1** Mister O'Grady (IRE), PISTOL (IRE), **11/1** Daytona Beach (IRE), **12/1** Care And Comfort, **14/1** Dont Shoot Fairies, **20/1** Blanchland, **33/1** Duty Sergeant (IRE), **66/1** Riva Rock, CSF £104.15 CT £1,129.83 TOTE £10.70: £3.20 £4.10 £4.60 (£35.70) Trio £75.00 OWNER Mrs B. Sumner (BILLINGBEAR) BRED David Brogan 12 Rn 2m 1.6 (3.90) SF: 32/25/33/23/12/-/-/3/1/-/-/-
WEIGHT FOR AGE 3yo-15lb

1403
SELLINDGE CLAIMING STKS (I) (3-Y.O+) (Class F) £2,519.00 (£694.00: £329.00)
1m 1f 149y Stalls: Low GOING minus 0.50 sec per fur (F) 4-15 (4-19)

1149[2] **Shabanaz (68)***(72)*(Fav)*(WRMuir)* 10-9-8 StephenDavies(3) (stdy hdwy over 3f out: 4th st: rdn over 1f out: led ins fnl f: r.o wl)......— 1
1092[7] Pillow Talk (IRE) **(54)***(63) (KRBurke)* 4-9-3v TQuinn(5) (lw: 2nd st: hrd rdn over 1f out: ev ch ins fnl f: unable qckn)......2½ 2
1219[13] Mim-Lou-and **(39)***(69) (BRMillman)* 3-8-9 JWilliams(1) (2nd st: hrd rdn over 1f out: ev ch ins fnl f: one pce)......¾ 3
1245[7] Embezzler **(55)***(56) (GLewis)* 3-7-10b(5)ow2 AWhelan(4) (lw: led: sn clr: hrd rdn over 1f out: hdd ins fnl f: sn wknd)......1½ 4
546[12] Assignment **(52)***(40) (JFfitch-Heyes)* 9-9-0 DBiggs(6) (b.off hind: lw: mod 5th st: nvr nr to chal)......10 5
1048[10] Swan Flyer **(28)***(47) (JJSheehan)* 4-9-7 VSmith(8) (nvr nrr)......s.h 6
288[10] Side Bar **(28)***(22) (KGWingrove)* 5-8-11 (5) PMcCabe(7) (chsd ldr over 3f: mod 6th st)......12 7
King Etzel (IRE) *(9) (JEBanks)* 3-8-5 JQuinn(2) (lw: w'like: a bhd)......10 8

10/11 SHABANAZ, **3/1** Embezzler (2/1-7/2), **9/2** Pillow Talk (IRE), **11/1** King Etzel (IRE) (14/1-8/1), **20/1** Assignment, **33/1** Side Bar, Mim-Lou-and, **50/1** Swan Flyer, CSF £5.54 TOTE £1.80: £1.30 £1.20 £1.90 (£4.50) OWNER Fayzad Thoroughbred Ltd (LAMBOURN) BRED The Overbury Stud 8 Rn 2m 3.7 (6.00) SF: 16/7/-/-/-/-/-/-
WEIGHT FOR AGE 3yo-15lb

1404
SELLINDGE CLAIMING STKS (II) (3-Y.O+) (Class F) £2,519.00 (£694.00: £329.00)
1m 1f 149y Stalls: Low GOING minus 0.50 sec per fur (F) 4-45 (4-46)

672[5] **Guesstimation (USA) (57)***(63) (JPearce)* 6-9-8 GBardwell(7) (rdn & hdwy over 1f out: led wl ins fnl f: drvn out)......— 1
988[6] Kirov Protege (IRE) **(47)***(63) (HJCollingridge)* 3-8-7 MRimmer(5) (lw: 4th st: hrd rdn over 1f out: ev ch ins fnl f: r.o)......nk 2
1245[6] Head For Heaven *(62) (RPCHoad)* 5-9-8 RPrice(6) (2nd st: led 2f out tl wl ins fnl f: unable qckn)......hd 3
1092[3] Thames Side **(56)***(57) (MMadgwick)* 4-9-8 MFenton(8) (rdn over 3f out: hdwy over 1f out: one pce)......3½ 4
1092[4] Owdbetts (IRE) **(67)***(51)*(Fav)*(GLMoore)* 3-8-6 BRouse(4) (hdwy over 3f out: 3rd st: wknd over 1f out)......3 5
Kipini **(42)***(37) (HVanderdussen,Belgium)* 6-8-9 PascalVandekeere(2) (led 4f: 5th st: wknd over 1f out)......¾ 6

Aconitum (USA) *(46) (JMBradley)* 7-9-1 (5) SDrowne(3) (6th st: wknd 2f out)........................1½ 7
1016 14 Stipple **(30)***(39) (SWoodman)* 4-8-13 TIves(1) (lw: led over 5f out to 2f out: wknd over 1f out) ....s.h 8

7/4 Owdbetts (IRE), **3/1** GUESSTIMATION (USA) (op 7/4), **4/1** Kirov Protege (IRE), **9/2** Thames Side, **20/1** Kipini, Aconitum (USA), **25/1** Head For Heaven, **33/1** Stipple, CSF £14.64 TOTE £3.50: £1.60 £1.30 £2.80 (£8.10) OWNER Quintet Partnership (NEWMARKET) BRED Oak Crest Farm 8 Rn 2m 5.5 (7.80) SF: 2/-/1/-/-/-/-/-
WEIGHT FOR AGE 3yo-15lb

1405 SMEETHE MEDIAN AUCTION MAIDEN STKS (3-Y.O) (Class F) £2,519.00 (£694.00: £329.00)
6f 189y Stalls: Low GOING minus 0.50 sec per fur (F) 5-15 (5-18)

697 10 **Shen Yang (USA) (75)***(77)*(Fav)*(GLMoore)* 3-9-0 BRouse(3) (lw: mde all: clr 5f out: unchal)..— 1
739 3 Mo's Star **(64)***(58) (SDow)* 3-8-2 (7) ADaly(5) (3rd st: chsd wnr over 1f out: no imp) 6 2
670 10 Md Thompson *(52) (SCWilliams)* 3-8-6 (3) DWright(6) (4th st: one pce fnl 2f)..........................2½ 3
1168 10 Millesime (IRE) *(55) (BHanbury)* 3-9-0 MRimmer(1) (lw: 2nd st: one pce fnl 2f) 1 4
Misty Melody **(62)***(42) (RAkehurst)* 3-8-9 TQuinn(7) (6th st: one pce fnl 2f) 3½ 5
Time Is Money (IRE) **(61)***(42) (MHTompkins)* 3-9-0 PRobinson(4) (5th st: wknd 2f out) 2 6
1146 11 Danehill Chief *(MAJarvis)* 3-9-0 PaulEddery(2) (bhd fnl 5f)...25 7

5/2 SHEN YANG (USA), **11/4** Mo's Star (2/1-3/1), **7/2** Millesime (IRE) (3/1-9/2), **6/1** Misty Melody (op 3/1), **10/1** Danehill Chief (op 6/1), **11/1** Time Is Money (IRE) (op 6/1), **25/1** Md Thompson, CSF £9.29 TOTE £3.00: £1.90 £2.30 (£3.60) OWNER Mr Peter Higson (EPSOM) BRED Dorothy Price, Jackie W. Ramos and Ken Hickson 7 Rn 1m 22.9 (1.30) SF: 41/22/16/19/6/6/-

T/Plpt: £128.80 (108.99 Tckts). T/Qdpt: £20.00 (4.9 Tckts). AK

1183-NEWBURY (L-H)
Wednesday May 31st (Good)
WEATHER: showers WIND: almost nil

1406 E.B.F BOXFORD MAIDEN STKS (2-Y.O) (Class D) £3,376.00 (£1,018.00: £494.00: £232.00)
5f 34y Stalls: Centre GOING minus 0.21 sec per fur (GF) 6-30 (6-31)

Royal Applause *(91+) (BWHills)* 2-9-0 WRSwinburn(4) (lengthy: scope: led over 1f: led over 1f out: pushed out)..— 1
Rambling Bear *(80) (MBlanshard)* 2-9-0 StephenDavies(2) (w'like: plld hrd: led over 3f out tl over 1f out: r.o one pce) 3½ 2
1104 3 Belzao *(80)*(Fav)*(MRChannon)* 2-9-0 RHughes(3) (lw: hld up: rdn wl over 1f out: one pce)..s.h 3
1047 4 Oriel Lad *(68) (KRBurke)* 2-9-0 LDettori(5) (prom: rdn 2f out: wknd over 1f out) 4 4
Spotted Eagle *(61) (RHannon)* 2-9-0 PatEddery(1) (cmpt: prom: rdn over 2f out: sn wknd).....2 5

4/7 Belzao, **5/2** ROYAL APPLAUSE, **9/1** Spotted Eagle (op 4/1), **14/1** Rambling Bear (10/1-16/1), **20/1** Oriel Lad, CSF £24.70 TOTE £3.90: £1.70 £3.30 (£24.60) OWNER Maktoum Al Maktoum (LAMBOURN) BRED Gainsborough Stud Management Ltd 5 Rn 63.96 secs (3.66) SF: 28/17/17/5

1407 BASINGSTOKE CLAIMING STKS (3-Y.O) (Class E) £3,044.50 (£916.00: £443.00: £206.50) **1m 4f 5y** Stalls: Centre GOING minus 0.21 sec per fur (GF) 7-00 (7-01)

1245 2 **Last Laugh (IRE) (63)***(56) (RHannon)* 3-8-8 PatEddery(8) (lw: hld up & bhd: last st: swtchd rt & hdwy over 2f out: rdn & edged lft over 1f out: led ins fnl f: r.o wl) ....— 1
1093 16 Negative Equity **(52)***(62) (KRBurke)* 3-9-1v LDettori(3) (led tl rdn & hdd ins fnl f).......................¾ 2
974 11 Million Dancer **(66)***(55) (MCPipe)* 3-8-12 MRoberts(5) (lw: hld up: 6th st: hdwy 4f out: rdn & ev ch 2f out: nt qckn fnl f)..3 3
885 9 Shanuke (IRE) **(47)***(40) (JSMoore)* 3-8-1 (5)ow1 SDrowne(1) (lw: 5th st: rdn over 4f out: wknd over 2f out)..6 4
995 5 Tonka **(68)***(44)*(Fav)*(DJGMurraySmith)* 3-8-13 JWeaver(2) (lw: hld up & plld hrd: hdwy to jn ldr 8f out: 2nd st: rdn & wknd over 2f out)..3 5
Premazing **(40)***(38) (JPearce)* 3-8-11 RHills(7) (4th st: wknd over 2f out) 3 6
1175 11 Dick Christian *(15) (BJMeehan)* 3-8-8 BDoyle(6) (3rd st: rdn & wknd over 3f out)...................15 7
907 5 Jackatack (IRE) **(52)***(17) (MRChannon)* 3-8-10 RHughes(4) (lw: hld up: 7th st: rdn over 3f out: no rspnse)...s.h 8

5/4 Tonka, **13/8** LAST LAUGH (IRE), **9/1** Million Dancer, **14/1** Negative Equity (op 8/1), **20/1** Jackatack (IRE), **33/1** Shanuke (IRE), **50/1** Premazing, Dick Christian, CSF £20.55 TOTE £2.50: £1.30 £1.80 £1.30 (£12.20) OWNER Mr St J O'Connell (MARLBOROUGH) BRED Brigitte Wolff in Ireland 8 Rn 2m 35.81 (6.51) SF: 33/39/32/17/21/15/-/-

Last Laugh (IRE) clmd CBarnes £10,000; Tonka clmd JCarrington £10,000.

1408 HERMITAGE CONDITIONS STKS (4-Y.O+) (Class C) £5,067.20

(£1,884.80: £912.40: £382.00: £161.00: £72.60)
1m 2f 6y Stalls: Centre GOING minus 0.21 sec per fur (GF) 7-30 (7-31)

Capias (USA) (109)*(105) (JHMGosden)* 4-8-12 LDettori(5) (lw: hld up: 4th st: n.m.r wl over 1f out: rdn to ld wl ins fnl f) .... — 1
923[2] Florid (USA) **(107)***(111) (HRACecil)* 4-9-5 WRyan(4) (lw: led: rdn & qcknd over 2f out: hdd wl ins fnl f) .... ½ 2
Wind in Her Hair (IRE) **(114)***(101) (JWHills)* 4-8-13 RHills(2) (lw: 2nd st: ev ch over 1f out: nt qckn) 2½ 3
794[4] Green Green Desert (FR) **(106)***(91)*(Fav)*(MRStoute)* 4-8-11 WRSwinburn(6) (hld up: 5th st: stdy hdwy over 3f out: hrd rdn & wknd over 1f out) 5 4
1056[3] Spot Prize (USA) **(106)***(82) (IABalding)* 4-8-6 MHills(7) (3rd st: wknd over 2f out) 2½ 5
Rainfest (FR) *(82) (RCharlton)* 4-8-7 PatEddery(3) (lw: hld up: 7th st: rdn 3f out: hung lft 2f out: n.d) .... ½ 6
Darkwood Bay (USA) **(86)***(83) (DRCElsworth)* 4-8-11 JWilliams(1) (bkwd: hld up: 6th st: bhd fnl 3f) 2 7

2/1 Green Green Desert (FR), **4/1** Florid (USA), **9/2** Wind in Her Hair (IRE) (op 3/1), **5/1** Rainfest (FR), **9/1** CAPIAS (USA) (op 5/1), Spot Prize (USA) (op 6/1), **33/1** Darkwood Bay (USA), CSF £40.10 TOTE £10.70: £3.10 £2.70 (£20.10) OWNER Sheikh Mohammed (NEWMARKET) BRED Overbrook Farm 7 Rn 2m 7.32 (4.32) SF: 44/50/40/30/21/21/22

1409 COOPERS & LYBRAND H'CAP (0-90) (4-Y.O+) (Class C) £5,767.50

(£1,740.00: £845.00: £397.50)
7f 64y (round) Stalls: Centre GOING minus 0.21 sec per fur (GF) 8-00 (8-00)

1261[2] **Shepherd Market (IRE) (59)***(66) (DAWilson)* 4-8-1 GCarter(5) (lw: mde all: pushed out) .... — 1
1126[7] Fionn de Cool (IRE) **(70)***(72) (RAkehurst)* 4-8-12 RHills(1) (lw: 5th st: chsd wnr over 2f out: no imp) 2½ 2
1143[8] Band on the Run **(86)***(82) (BAMcMahon)* 8-10-0 LDettori(6) (3rd st: rdn over 2f out: r.o one pce) 2½ 3
1183[10] Bagshot **(81)***(76) (RHannon)* 4-9-2 (7) MarkDenaro(2) (lw: 7th st: hdwy on ins over 2f out: n.m.r over 1f out: one pce) .... nk 4
946[5] Dom Pennion **(60)***(55) (RGuest)* 4-8-2 MRoberts(4) (8th st: hdwy over 1f out: styd on ins fnl f) .... hd 5
1183[8] Desert Time **(73)***(59)*(Fav)*(CAHorgan)* 5-9-1 MPerrett(7) (stdd s: last st: nvr plcd to chal) 4 6
1225[6] Serious **(85)***(70) (LadyHerries)* 5-9-13 JReid(8) (lw: plld hrd: 4th st: wknd 2f out) .... ½ 7
1174[5] Jobie **(67)***(52) (BWHills)* 5-8-9 MHills(10) (plld hrd: 9th st: rdn over 2f out: sn bhd) .... hd 8
870[19] Cameron Highland (IRE) **(80)***(61) (PFICole)* 4-9-8 TQuinn(9) (lw: 6th st: wknd over 2f out) 2 9
Tom Morgan **(82)***(56) (PTWalwyn)* 4-9-10 PatEddery(3) (lw: plld hrd: 2nd st: rdn over 2f out: wknd over 1f out) 3 10

4/1 Desert Time (3/1-9/2), **11/2** SHEPHERD MARKET (IRE), **6/1** Bagshot, **8/1** Fionn de Cool (IRE) (op 5/1), Tom Morgan, Jobie, Serious (op 9/2), **10/1** Band on the Run, **14/1** Cameron Highland (IRE), Dom Pennion, CSF £44.12 CT £387.73 TOTE £6.60: £2.00 £3.50 £2.70 (£42.90) Trio £110.40 OWNER Mr T. S. M. S. Riley-Smith (EPSOM) BRED S. Niarchos 10 Rn
1m 30.43 (1.93) SF: 33/39/49/43/22/26/37/19/28/23

1410 KENNETH ROBERTSON H'CAP (0-80) (3-Y.O+) (Class D) £3,795.00

(£1,140.00: £550.00: £255.00)
1m 5f 61y Stalls: Centre GOING minus 0.21 sec per fur (GF) 8-30 (8-31)

423[9] **Johns Act (USA) (66)***(79) (DHaydnJones)* 5-9-3 JReid(5) (mde all: qcknd 2f out: r.o wl) .... — 1
961* Dancing Sensation (USA) **(62)***(69) (RAkehurst)* 8-8-13 LDettori(7) (3rd st: chsd wnr over 1f out: no imp) 5 2
931[5] Bit on the Side (IRE) **(72)***(77)*(Fav)*(WJMusson)* 6-9-9 PatEddery(11) (2nd st: rdn over 2f out: one pce) 1¾ 3
1095* Tony's Fen **(75)***(79) (DRCElsworth)* 6-9-12 MRoberts(6) (lw: b.hind: plld hrd: 5th st: hrd rdn over 2f out: one pce) .... ¾ 4
1038[5] Invest Wisely **(70)***(72) (JMPEustace)* 3-8-2 PRobinson(9) (rdn 3f out: sme late hdwy) 1½ 5

1014[5] Total Joy (IRE) **(63)***(65) (PFICole)* 4-9-0 TQuinn(1) (plld hrd: 6th st: no hdwy fnl 2f)................hd **6**
811[5] Un Parfum de Femme (IRE) **(67)***(67) (JPearce)* 4-9-4 GBardwell(10) (hld up: 7th st: rdn over 2f out: no hdwy)..........1½ **7**
938[11] High Five (IRE) **(52)***(46) (DAWilson)* 5-8-3 GCarter(2) (a bhd)..........5 **8**
1140[8] Sea Freedom **(77)***(71) (GBBalding)* 4-10-0 JWilliams(4) (a bhd)..........s.h **9**
Brumon (IRE) **(64)***(56) (DWPArbuthnot)* 4-9-1 SWhitworth(8) (s.i.s: hdwy after 3f: 4th st: rdn over 3f out: wknd over 2f out)..........1½ **10**
1140[3] La Spezia **(55)** *(MBlanshard)* 5-8-6 StephenDavies(3) (a bhd: t.o whn p.u over 3f out: dead).......... **P**

15/8 Bit on the Side (IRE), **4/1** Dancing Sensation (USA), **6/1** La Spezia, **7/1** Tony's Fen, **14/1** Total Joy (IRE) (10/1-16/1), JOHNS ACT (USA) (10/1-16/1), Un Parfum de Femme (IRE) (10/1-16/1), **16/1** High Five (IRE), **20/1** Sea Freedom, Invest Wisely, **50/1** Brumon (IRE), CSF £64.89 CT £142.05 TOTE £15.30: £3.40 £1.80 £1.30 (£33.50) Trio £28.50 OWNER Jack Brown (Bookmaker) Ltd (PONTYPRIDD) BRED Galloping Acres Farm 11 Rn
2m 56.06 (10.76) SF: 21/11/19/21/-/7/9/-/13/-/-
WEIGHT FOR AGE 3yo-19lb

1411 BURGHCLERE H'CAP (0-80) (3-Y.O+) (Class D) £4,367.00 (£1,316.00: £638.00: £299.00) **6f 8y** Stalls: Centre GOING minus 0.21 sec per fur (GF) 9-00 (9-05)

1199[3] **Oggi (61)***(65) (PJMakin)* 4-8-9b LDettori(6) (lw: a.p: led over 1f out: r.o wl)..........— **1**
1304[15] Macfarlane **(71)***(70) (MJFetherston-Godley)* 7-9-5 MRoberts(12) (lw: hdwy 2f out: r.o ins fnl f)..........2 **2**
1070[4] Robellion **(66)***(65) (DWPArbuthnot)* 4-9-0 TQuinn(10) (lw: a.p: ev ch over 1f out: nt qckn)....s.h **3**
1057[2] Winsome Wooster **(69)***(64) (PGMurphy)* 4-8-12 (5) SDrowne(8) (lw: prom: lost pl over 3f out: rallied over 1f out: r.o one pce fnl f)..........1¼ **4**
1214[5] Purple Fling **(72)***(67) (SirMarkPrescott)* 4-9-6 GDuffield(15) (lw: led stands' side: r.o one pce fnl f)..........s.h **5**
887[12] Grey Charmer (IRE) **(54)***(48) (CJames)* 6-8-2 CRutter(3) (hdwy fnl f: r.o)..........½ **6**
1174[8] Law Commission **(80)***(74) (DRCElsworth)* 5-9-9 (5) AProcter(7) (lw: rdn 3f out: no hdwy fnl f)..........s.h **7**
1057[5] Napoleon Star (IRE) **(72)***(65) (MSSaunders)* 4-9-6 RPrice(14) (hdwy 3f out: one pce fnl f).....nk **8**
1265[5] Domicksky **(64)***(57) (MRChannon)* 7-8-12 RHughes(13) (lw: nvr nr to chal)..........s.h **9**
922[19] Gone Savage **(65)***(56) (WJMusson)* 7-8-8 (5) PMcCabe(9) (lw: hld up: hdwy & swtchd lft over 2f out: wknd ins fnl f)..........½ **10**
733* Media Express **(70)***(54)*(Fav)*(TGMills)* 3-8-8 JReid(11) (lw: led over 4f)..........3 **11**
1174[11] Face the Future **(62)***(42) (LJHolt)* 6-8-10 MPerrett(2) (prom over 4f)..........1½ **12**
1094[10] Grand Chapeau (IRE) **(67)***(45) (RHannon)* 3-8-5 PatEddery(5) (lw: prom over 4f)..........¾ **13**
1174* Bayin (USA) **(69)***(33) (MDIUsher)* 6-9-3 RStreet(16) (lw: s.s: hdwy over 2f out: wknd over 1f out)..........5 **14**
Green Golightly (USA) **(70)***(28) (DAWilson)* 4-9-4 NGwilliams(1) (prom 3f)..........2½ **15**
812[15] Aughfad **(71)** *(MrsMMcCourt)* 9-9-5b BThomson(4) (spd 2f: t.o whn virtually p.u wl over 1f out)..........dist **16**

6/1 Media Express, **13/2** Domicksky, **15/2** OGGI, **9/1** Winsome Wooster, Bayin (USA), **10/1** Macfarlane (8/1-14/1), Purple Fling (12/1-8/1), **12/1** Law Commission, Robellion (op 8/1), **14/1** Face the Future, **20/1** Gone Savage, Napoleon Star (IRE), Green Golightly (USA), **25/1** Grey Charmer (IRE), **33/1** Grand Chapeau (IRE), Aughfad, CSF £73.90 CT £813.30 TOTE £5.40: £1.60 £2.00 £3.10 £2.00 (£31.40) Trio £201.40 OWNER Skyline Racing Ltd (MARLBOROUGH) BRED H. D. and M. J. Gee 16 Rn 1m 14.45 (2.65) SF: 39/44/39/38/41/22/48/39/31/30/18/16/9/7/2/-
WEIGHT FOR AGE 3yo-10lb

T/Jkpt: Not won; £13,909.13 to Brighton 1/6/95. T/Plpt: £164.40 (133.13 Tckts). T/Qdpt: £160.90 (6.5 Tckts). KH

1190-RIPON (R-H)
Wednesday May 31st (Good to firm)
WEATHER: sunny WIND: almost nil

1412 RIPON THORPE PREBEND TRUST APPEAL CLAIMING STKS (3-Y.O) (Class F) £2,775.00 (£840.00: £410.00: £195.00) **1m** Stalls: High GOING minus 0.24 sec per fur (GF) 6-45 (6-45)

1180[3] **Intendant (62)***(69)*(Fav)*(JGFitzGerald)* 3-9-1 KFallon(7) (mid div: hdwy over 2f out: hrd rdn ins fnl f to ld nr fin)..........— **1**
1191[3] My Handsome Prince **(43)***(57) (PJBevan)* 3-8-3 TWilliams(4) (chsd ldrs: led 1½f out: r.o: jst ct)..........s.h **2**

1092[8] Bushehr (IRE) *(63) (JWHills)* 3-8-4 (7) MHenry(11) (mid div: hdwy on outside 3f out: rdn & one pce appr fnl f)....¾ **3**
1083[7] Caltha **(43)***(40) (PCalver)* 3-7-5 (5) NVarley(3) (led tl hdd 1½f out: no ex)....4 **4**
1355[9] Kings Vision **(47)***(41) (BSRothwell)* 3-8-1b LCharnock(1) (cl up tl rdn & btn appr fnl f)....2 **5**
640[8] Cool Steel (IRE) **(53)***(49) (MissSEHall)* 3-8-9v NConnorton(8) (prom: effrt over 3f out: no imp)....nk **6**
1290[13] Highbank **(55)***(45) (MrsMReveley)* 3-8-5 KDarley(12) (rdn ½-wy: nvr nrr) ....s.h **7**
1155[3] Red River Rose (IRE) **(45)***(32) (NPLittmoden)* 3-7-10b NCarlisle(6) (drvn along 3f out: nvr trbld ldrs) 1¾ **8**
1218[10] Scylla **(47)***(42) (PCHaslam)* 3-8-3 (7) JulieLemin(9) (chsd ldrs tl wknd fnl 3f)....2 **9**
1270[9] Legal Brief *(27) (JSWainwright)* 3-8-5 DeanMcKeown(2) (a bhd) 5 **10**
773[13] Malsisio **(27)** *(SGNorton)* 3-7-11 ow1 JFanning(5) (prom: effrt over 3f out: wknd wl over 2f out) 13 **11**

9/4 INTENDANT, **5/1** Red River Rose (IRE), **11/2** Caltha, **6/1** Bushehr (IRE) (op 4/1), **15/2** Highbank, **8/1** Cool Steel (IRE), My Handsome Prince, **16/1** Kings Vision, Scylla, **25/1** Malsisio, **50/1** Legal Brief, CSF £21.47 TOTE £3.20: £1.60 £2.10 £2.10 (£13.90) Trio £28.90 OWNER Marquesa de Moratalla (MALTON) BRED Mrs M. Chaworth Musters 11 Rn

1m 41.1 (3.40) SF: 45/33/39/16/17/25/21/8/18/3/-

STEWARDS' ENQUIRY Fallon susp. 9-13/6/95 (excessive use of whip).

1413 LISHMAN, SIDWELL, CAMPBELL AND PRICE MAIDEN STKS (2-Y.O) (Class D) £3,538.00 (£1,063.00: £513.00: £238.00)

5f Stalls: Low GOING minus 0.24 sec per fur (GF) 7-15 (7-15)

1134[8] **Take A Left** *(81) (MrsJRRamsden)* 2-9-0 KFallon(6) (lw: a.p: rdn to ld ins fnl f: r.o)....— **1**
970[3] Limerick Princess (IRE) *(73) (JBerry)* 2-8-9 JCarroll(4) (led tl hdd & no ex ins fnl f) 1 **2**
1176[4] Prince of Florence (IRE) *(65)*(Fav)*(LMCumani)* 2-9-0 KDarley(9) (lw: chsd ldrs: outpcd 2f out: kpt on fnl f)....4 **3**
Mystic Times *(58) (MissSEHall)* 2-8-9 NConnorton(11) (small: unf: b.hind: chsd ldrs tl rdn & btn over 1f out)....¾ **4**
1063[6] Imp Express (IRE) *(62) (GMMoore)* 2-9-0 MTebbutt(3) (lw: chsd ldrs: rdn & no hdwy fnl 2f) ....hd **5**
Willisa *(46) (JDBethell)* 2-8-9 WCarson(8) (leggy: scope: bit bkwd: chsd ldrs 3f: grad wknd)3½ **6**
1190[11] Copper Bright *(47) (PCHaslam)* 2-9-0 JFortune(2) (nvr nr ldrs) 1¼ **7**
Westcourt Magic *(47) (MWEasterby)* 2-9-0 MBirch(10) (cmpt: in tch to ½-wy: eased whn btn)....hd **8**
Flood's Fancy *(40) (MrsJRRamsden)* 2-8-9 SDWilliams(1) (neat: bit bkwd: scope: s.i.s: n.d) .½ **9**
788[10] Village Opera *(32) (GMMoore)* 2-8-9 JFanning(7) (s.i.s: n.d)....2½ **10**
Sonya Marie *(GPKelly)* 2-8-9 ACulhane(5) (bkwd: s.s: t.o) 20 **11**

8/13 Prince of Florence (IRE), **9/2** Limerick Princess (IRE), **7/1** TAKE A LEFT (op 4/1), **10/1** Willisa (op 6/1), **16/1** Imp Express (IRE), **20/1** Mystic Times, Copper Bright, Westcourt Magic, Flood's Fancy, **25/1** Sonya Marie, **33/1** Village Opera, CSF £40.60 TOTE £8.60: £1.60 £1.30 £1.20 (£16.40) Trio £3.00 OWNER Mr Bernard Hathaway (THIRSK) BRED P. Meadows 11 Rn

59.4 secs (1.40) SF: 54/46/38/31/35/19/20/20/13/5/-

1414 TOUCHE ROSS H'CAP (0-70) (3-Y.O) (Class E) £3,215.00 (£965.00: £465.00: £215.00)

6f Stalls: Low GOING minus 0.24 sec per fur (GF) 7-45 (7-46)

999[11] **The Scythian (64)***(72) (BobJones)* 3-9-1 JFanning(2) (lw: disp ld tl led 2f out: r.o)....— **1**
Special-K **(57)***(62) (EWeymes)* 3-8-8 JFortune(13) (in tch: hdwy over 1f out: r.o towards fin)....1¼ **2**
1279* Showery **(62)***(66)*(Fav)*(JWWatts)* 3-8-8 (5) CTeague(7) (lw: b.hind: disp ld tl outpcd over 1f out: rallied ins fnl f: no ex towards fin)....hd **3**
1094[11] Blushing Grenadier (IRE) **(51)***(50) (MJFetherston-Godley)* 3-8-2 FNorton(1) (in tch: hdwy u.p 2f out: one pce ins fnl f)....2 **4**
1094[3] Lough Erne **(70)***(69) (CFWall)* 3-9-7 NCarlisle(6) (lw: hdwy ½-wy: styd on: nvr able chal)....hd **5**
966[15] Le Bal **(46)***(43) (MrsNMacauley)* 3-7-11b DaleGibson(3) (s.i.s: bhd: pushed along tl styd on wl fnl f) ....¾ **6**
832[6] Garlande D'Or **(50)***(36) (JLSpearing)* 3-8-1 GHind(4) (chsd ldrs tl rdn & btn wl over 1f out)......4 **7**
1249[3] Tedburrow **(62)***(44) (MrsAMNaughton)* 3-8-13 ACulhane(11) (prom tl rdn & wknd wl over 1f out) 1¾ **8**
904[5] Carol Again **(43)***(24) (NBycroft)* 3-7-8 NKennedy(12) (nvr trbld ldrs) ....s.h **9**
768[4] Westcourt Princess **(50)***(25) (MWEasterby)* 3-8-1b WCarson(8) (prom over 3f: grad wknd) ...2½ **10**
861* Hi Rock **(57)***(25) (MJCamacho)* 3-8-8 LCharnock(9) (chsd ldrs tl wknd over 1f out)....2½ **11**

1033[3] Russian Heroine **(58)***(19) (MJohnston)* 3-8-9 DeanMcKeown(5) (lw: prom 3f: sn lost pl).......2½ **12**
646[18] Fairy Fay (IRE) **(55)***(8) (BJMcMath)* 3-8-6 EJohnson(14) (lw: b.hind: sn outpcd)......................3 **13**
1136[21] Fire Blast **(69)***(6) (LMCumani)* 3-9-6 KDarley(15) (sn outpcd & bhd)..6 **14**
965[8] Perfect Bertie (IRE) **(54)** *(GROldroyd)* 3-8-5 MBirch(10) (s.s: a wl bhd: eased fr ½-wy).......dist **15**

6/5 Showery, **6/1** Lough Erne, **8/1** Fire Blast (op 5/1), **10/1** THE SCYTHIAN, **12/1** Tedburrow, Blushing Grenadier (IRE) (16/1-10/1), **14/1** Hi Rock, **16/1** Russian Heroine, Westcourt Princess, Carol Again, **20/1** Le Bal, Special-K, Fairy Fay (IRE), Perfect Bertie (IRE), **25/1** Garlande D'Or, CSF £193.34 CT £385.90 TOTE £13.30: £2.90 £4.70 £1.40 (£229.80) Trio £234.90 OWNER Mr Ian Vogt (NEWMARKET) BRED J. O'Neill 15 Rn 1m 12.6 (2.40) SF: 45/35/39/23/42/16/9/17/-/-/-/-/-/-/-

OFFICIAL EXPLANATION Perfect Bertie (IRE): the jockey reported that the horse had felt all wrong and the trainer added that the three-year-old has suffered from back problems.
OFFICIAL EXPLANATION: The Scythian: the jockey explained that the gelding had become over-excited before the start of his previous race at Chester and had received a bump leaving the stalls.

1415 AMEC CIVIL ENGINEERING H'CAP (0-85) (3-Y.O+) (Class D)

£4,500.00 (£1,350.00: £650.00: £300.00)
1m Stalls: High GOING minus 0.24 sec per fur (GF) 8-15 (8-15)

1051* **Bernard Seven (IRE) (82)***(94+) (SPCWoods)* 3-8-13b KDarley(10) (lw: trckd ldrs: led 2f out: r.o wl)........— **1**
927[12] Sandmoor Chambray **(74)***(76) (MHEasterby)* 4-9-3b MBirch(2) (cl up: led 3f out to 2f out: one pce)........5 **2**
885* Hujjab (USA) **(84)***(86)*(Fav)*(JLDunlop)* 3-9-1 WCarson(1) (lw: a.p: effrt over 2f out: styd on towards fin)........s.h **3**
1261[5] Polonez Prima **(65)***(66) (JLSpearing)* 8-8-8 DeanMcKeown(4) (bhd: effrt & n.m.r 2f out: styd on wl towards fin)........nk **4**
*845** Major Mouse **(51)***(51) (WWHaigh)* 7-7-8 DaleGibson(6) (in tch: effrt 3f out: styd on: no imp) ..½ **5**
1250[4] Tolls Choice (IRE) **(58)***(55) (MWEasterby)* 6-8-1 LCharnock(9) (lw: trckd ldrs: effrt 3f out: one pce)........1½ **6**
Forever Diamonds **(85)***(81) (MHEasterby)* 8-10-0 JCarroll(3) (hld up: nt clr run 2f out: nvr plcd to chal)........¾ **7**
Jubran (USA) **(70)***(65) (MJohnston)* 9-8-10 (3) AGarth(5) (bit bkwd: led tl hdd 3f out: grad wknd)........½ **8**
1061[10] Western General **(80)***(72) (MissSEHall)* 4-9-9 NConnorton(7) (hld up: hdwy on ins 3f out: nt clr run: n.d)........1½ **9**
955[4] Carlito Brigante **(75)***(57) (MrsJRRamsden)* 3-8-6 KFallon(8) (lw: plld hrd: sn bhd)....................5 **10**

13/8 Hujjab (USA), **11/2** BERNARD SEVEN (IRE), **6/1** Polonez Prima, **7/1** Carlito Brigante, Western General, **9/1** Major Mouse, **10/1** Tolls Choice (IRE), **11/1** Sandmoor Chambray, **14/1** Forever Diamonds, **16/1** Jubran (USA), CSF £63.99 CT £133.74 TOTE £5.70: £1.90 £4.10 £1.30 (£43.60) Trio £42.60 OWNER Mr Bernard Butt (NEWMARKET) BRED Bobby Donworth and Honora Corridan 10 Rn 1m 38.9 (1.20) SF: 66/60/58/50/35/39/65/49/56/29

WEIGHT FOR AGE 3yo-12lb
STEWARDS' ENQUIRY Garth susp. 11-12/6/95 (excessive use of whip).

1416 ST MARYGATE H'CAP (0-75) (4-Y.O+) (Class D) £3,828.80 (£1,159.40: £566.20: £269.60) **2m** Stalls: Low GOING minus 0.24 sec per fur (GF) 8-45 (8-45)

1268[2] **Highflying (75)***(89) (GMMoore)* 9-9-11 (3) JTate(7) (mde all: shkn up & qcknd 3f out: r.o wl).— **1**
998[11] Moonlight Quest **(70)***(81) (BHanbury)* 7-9-2 (7) PBowe(5) (lw: chsd ldrs: outpcd 3f out: styd on fnl f)........3 **2**
1109[4] Uncle Doug **(55)***(64)*(Fav)*(MrsMReveley)* 4-8-6 KDarley(2) (lw: trckd wnr: effrt over 2f out: rdn & one pce)........2½ **3**
751[5] Ambuscade (USA) **(51)***(57) (EJAlston)* 9-8-4 ow1 KFallon(1) (bhd: styd on fnl 3f: nvr able chal)........2 **4**
1252[4] Microlite (USA) **(65)***(69) (MDHammond)* 4-9-2 JCarroll(6) (effrt ent st: no imp fnl 3f)............2½ **5**
Sharkashka (IRE) **(69)***(72) (MHEasterby)* 5-9-8 MBirch(3) (prom tl wknd fnl 3f)......................1½ **6**
1268* Good Hand (USA) **(79)***(81) (JWWatts)* 9-10-4 5x NConnorton(4) (lw: b: b.hind: lost pl appr st: n.d after)........1 **7**

9/4 Uncle Doug, **11/4** HIGHFLYING, **7/2** Moonlight Quest, **11/2** Good Hand (USA), **9/1** Microlite (USA), **14/1** Ambuscade (USA), **20/1** Sharkashka (IRE), CSF £12.40 TOTE £4.00: £2.30 £2.00 (£8.40) OWNER Mr B. Batey (MIDDLEHAM) BRED Juddmonte Farms 7 Rn

3m 33.5 (8.50) SF: 52/44/25/20/30/35/44
WEIGHT FOR AGE 4yo-2lb

1417 ST AGNESGATE MAIDEN STKS (3-Y.O+) (Class D) £3,754.05 (£1,136.40: £554.70: £263.85) **1m 2f** Stalls: High GOING minus 0.24 sec per fur (GF) 9-15 (9-17)

Segovia *(70+)*(Fav)*(HRACecil)* 3-8-4 AMcGlone(6) (w'like: str: lw: hld up: gd hdwy to ld 3f out: hdd 2f out: rallied to ld cl home)......— 1
1085[2] Hakika (USA) *(70) (DMorley)* 3-8-4 WCarson(5) (lw: hld up: hdwy to ld 2f out: rdn ins fnl f: hdd & no ex towards fin)......hd 2
1173[5] Heath Robinson (IRE) **(82)***(69) (JHMGosden)* 3-8-9 JCarroll(7) (b: b.hind: prom: effrt 3f out: kpt on: nt pce to chal)......3½ 3
1175[9] Remaadi Sun *(63) (JHMGosden)* 3-8-9 GHind(9) (b.hind: led tl hdd 3f out: one pce)......4 4
Punch **(54)***(56) (NTinkler)* 3-8-9 MBirch(4) (cl up tl grad wknd fnl 3f)......4 5
So Amazing **(62)***(47) (MissSEHall)* 3-8-4 NConnorton(8) (b: plld v.hrd: sn stdd & bhd: n.d after)......2½ 6
816[9] Sugar Mill *(50) (MrsMReveley)* 5-9-10 KDarley(1) (hld up & bhd: nvr plcd to chal)......1¾ 7
Zusha *(21) (SGNorton)* 4-9-5 JFanning(3) (w'like: chsd ldrs tl wknd over 3f out)......15 8
816[7] Discorsi *(GWragg)* 3-8-9 FNorton(2) (Withdrawn not under Starter's orders: unruly in stalls) .. W

5/4 SEGOVIA, **85/40** Hakika (USA), **11/2** Heath Robinson (IRE), **8/1** Discorsi, **9/1** Sugar Mill (20/1-8/1), **14/1** Remaadi Sun, **16/1** So Amazing, **25/1** Zusha, **33/1** Punch, CSF £4.34 TOTE £2.70: £1.20 £1.10 £1.10 (£2.20) Trio £1.80 OWNER Mr K. Abdullah (NEWMARKET) BRED Juddmonte Farms 8 Rn
2m 8.7 (5.20) SF: 28/28/27/21/14/5/23/-/-
WEIGHT FOR AGE 3yo-15lb
T/Plpt: £7.70 (2,185.65 Tckts). T/Qdpt: £6.10 (14.4 Tckts). AA

0989-AYR (L-H)
Thursday June 1st (Good to firm)
WEATHER: sunny WIND: slt against

1418 E.B.F. PICKWICK HOTEL MAIDEN STKS (2-Y.O) (Class D) £4,143.00 (£1,254.00: £612.00: £291.00) **6f** Stalls: High GOING minus 0.49 sec per fur (F) 6-45 (6-48)

Double Oscar (IRE) *(68) (MJohnston)* 2-9-0 DHolland(1) (w'like: str: lw: cl up: shkn up over 2f out: led wl over 1f out: styd on wl)......— 1
Classic Lover (IRE) *(58) (BJMcMath)* 2-8-9 AMackay(3) (w'like: leggy: scope: outpcd & bhd after 2f: styd on strly fnl f)......1¾ 2
836[3] Pekay *(63)*(Fav)*(JBerry)* 2-9-0 JCarroll(4) (led over 4f: kpt on one pce) ......hd 3
Larrylukeathugh *(60) (JJO'Neill)* 2-9-0 KFallon(2) (lengthy: unf: lw: cl up tl wknd 1f out)......1¼ 4

11/10 Pekay (op Evens), **9/4** Classic Lover (IRE), **3/1** DOUBLE OSCAR (IRE), **50/1** Larrylukeathugh, CSF £8.77 TOTE £4.00 (£7.90) OWNER Mr R. W. Huggins (MIDDLEHAM) BRED Tasia Limited 4 Rn
1m 15.77 (5.97) SF: -/-/-/-

1419 ANNFIELD HOTEL MAIDEN H'CAP (0-70) (3-Y.O+) (Class E) £3,113.00 (£944.00: £462.00: £221.00) **5f** Stalls: High GOING minus 0.49 sec per fur (F) 7-15 (7-15)

1201[6] **Crowded Avenue (48)***(55)*(Fav)*(PJMakin)* 3-8-13 JWeaver(2) (lw: stdd s: smooth hdwy 2f out: led jst ins fnl f: shkn up & r.o)......— 1
1181[3] Just Dissident (IRE) **(63)***(64) (RMWhitaker)* 3-10-0 ACulhane(1) (chsd ldrs: led 1½f out: hdd & nt qckn ins fnl f)......2 2
1377[3] Henry the Hawk **(41)***(30) (MDods)* 4-8-7 (7) GParkin(6) (lw: outpcd & bhd tl styd on wl fnl 2f) .3½ 3
1000[10] Jessica's Secret (IRE) **(42)***(22) (ABailey)* 3-8-7b LCharnock(9) (outpcd & bhd tl styd on u.p fnl f)......3 4
555[8] Bajan Frontier (IRE) **(50)***(29) (FHLee)* 3-9-1 MBirch(3) (lw: b.hind: led tl hdd & wknd 1½f out)......nk 5
1342[7] Coney Hills **(34)***(7) (NBycroft)* 4-8-7 AlexGreaves(7) (plld hrd early: outpcd & bhd after 2f: n.d after)......1¾ 6
1040[6] Samsung Lovelylady (IRE) **(58)***(26) (EWeymes)* 3-9-9 JFortune(5) (cl up over 3f: sn wknd) .1½ 7
1042[8] Flashing Sabre **(55)***(11) (JBerry)* 3-9-6 JCarroll(8) (chsd ldrs: rdn ½-wy: sn wknd)......4 8

5/2 CROWDED AVENUE, **3/1** Just Dissident (IRE), **11/2** Samsung Lovelylady (IRE), **9/1** Henry the Hawk, **10/1** Bajan Frontier (IRE) (7/1-12/1), **12/1** Jessica's Secret (IRE) (op 8/1), Flashing Sabre (op 7/1), **14/1** Coney Hills, CSF £9.45 CT £45.50 TOTE £2.70: £1.20 £1.10 £2.40 (£4.40) Trio £12.10 OWNER Mr T. W. Wellard (MARLBOROUGH) BRED The Duke of Marlborough 8 Rn
59.61 secs (2.61) SF: 28/37/11/-/2/-/-/-
WEIGHT FOR AGE 3yo-8lb

1420 BURNS MONUMENT HOTEL CLAIMING STKS (3-Y.O+) (Class F)
£2,762.00 (£836.00: £408.00: £194.00)
1m 5f 13y Stalls: Low GOING minus 0.49 sec per fur (F) 7-45 (7-45)

1358[4] **Longcroft (38)***(55) (KWHogg)* 3-7-10 ow1 AMackay(6) (lw: a.p: rdn to ld ins fnl f: styd on strly)........................— 1
Shareoftheaction **(60)***(59) (MrsAMNaughton)* 4-9-5 JFortune(1) (lw: led 1f: cl up: led over 2f out tl ins fnl f: no ex)........................2½ 2
1161[2] Monkey Wench (IRE) **(48)***(57)*(Fav)*(JBerry)* 4-9-6v JCarroll(7) (lw: hld up: smooth hdwy to chal over 2f out: rdn & nt r.o appr fnl f)........................2½ 3
1206[8] Karibu (GER) *(56) (PMonteith)* 4-9-9 SDWilliams(5) (hld up: hdwy 3f out: nvr rchd ldrs).......3½ 4
1268[8] Balzino (USA) **(56)***(53) (NTinkler)* 6-9-9 KimTinkler(3) (lw: wl bhd: hdwy over 3f out: edgd lft u.p 2f out: n.d)........................1¾ 5
Nicky's Feelings *(29) (TDyer)* 3-7-11 JFanning(2) (plld hrd & jnd ldrs after 3f: led over 3f out tl over 2f out: sn wknd)........................13 6
Kincardine Bridge (USA) *(MrsSCBradburne)* 6-9-3 KFallon(4) (led after 1f tl over 3f out: sn wknd)........................dist 7

11/10 Monkey Wench (IRE), **4/1** LONGCROFT, Balzino (USA), **6/1** Shareoftheaction, **33/1** Karibu (GER), Nicky's Feelings, **100/1** Kincardine Bridge (USA), CSF £24.03 TOTE £5.60: £1.60 £2.00 (£13.30) OWNER Exors of the late Mr P J White (ISLE OF MAN) 7 Rn 2m 55.2 (10.40)
WEIGHT FOR AGE 3yo-17lb
Monkey Wench (IRE) clmd DGoodfellow £7,000

1421 BELLEISLE HOTEL H'CAP (0-80) (3-Y.O+) (Class D) £4,221.00
(£1,278.00: £624.00: £297.00)
7f Stalls: Low GOING minus 0.49 sec per fur (F) 8-15 (8-15)

780[5] **Don Pepe (67)***(71) (RBoss)* 4-9-3 JWeaver(2) (lw: in tch: swtchd & hdwy over 1f out: r.o to ld nr fin)........................— 1
1297[2] Sycamore Lodge (IRE) **(65)***(69)*(Fav)*(PCalver)* 4-9-1 MBirch(4) (lw: hld up & bhd: hdwy over 2f out: nt clr run over 1f out: r.o wl nr fin)........................hd 2
1297[W] Al Wujud (IRE) **(46)***(48) (TDyer)* 4-7-10 ow2 JFanning(11) (lw: a cl up: slt ld ins fnl f: hdd & no ex nr fin)........................s.h 3
780[3] Reverand Thickness **(73)***(76) (SCWilliams)* 4-9-6 (3) DWright(3) (lw: led tl hdd ins fnl f: kpt on u.p)........................nk 4
1250[9] The Happy Loon (IRE) **(57)***(57) (DenysSmith)* 4-8-7 JCarroll(6) (a chsng ldrs: kpt on same pce fnl 2f)........................1½ 5
1381[3] Profit Release (IRE) **(56)***(53) (MJohnston)* 4-8-6b DHolland(12) (lw: w ldrs tl wknd ins fnl f)......1 6
1044[3] Blow Dry (IRE) **(56)***(52) (MartynWane)* 5-8-6 ACulhane(5) (hld up & bhd: hdwy 2f out: nvr able to chal)........................½ 7
1148[5] Allinson's Mate (IRE) **(70)***(65) (TDBarron)* 7-9-6 JFortune(10) (lw: nvr bttr than mid div).........½ 8
1179[6] Chinour (IRE) **(65)***(54) (EJAlston)* 7-9-1 KFallon(8) (lw: s.i.s: c wd & effrt ent st: no imp).......2½ 9
877[10] Two Moves in Front (IRE) **(72)***(60) (JBerry)* 5-9-8 DeanMcKeown(9) (in tch tl outpcd fnl 2f)....¾ 10
984[14] Peacefull Reply (USA) **(48)***(33) (FHLee)* 5-7-12 NKennedy(1) (cl up tl wknd wl over 1f out)..1¼ 11
1261[13] Rossini Blue **(74)***(52) (ABailey)* 4-9-10 KDarley(7) (bhd: c wd & effrt 3f out: n.d)........................3 12

11/4 Sycamore Lodge (IRE), **5/1** Chinour (IRE), **6/1** Reverand Thickness, **8/1** Al Wujud (IRE), **10/1** DON PEPE (7/1-12/1), Rossini Blue, Blow Dry (IRE), Allinson's Mate (IRE), **12/1** Profit Release (IRE), **16/1** Two Moves in Front (IRE), **20/1** The Happy Loon (IRE), **25/1** Peacefull Reply (USA), CSF £37.81 CT £222.87 TOTE £9.00: £3.10 £2.30 £1.60 (£16.70) Trio £76.50 OWNER Mrs Elaine Aird (NEWMARKET) BRED Patrick Eddery Ltd 12 Rn
1m 27.44 (3.44) SF: 21/19/-/26/7/3/2/15/4/10/-/2

1422 HANSEL VILLAGE (S) STKS (3-Y.O+) (Class F) £2,840.00 (£860.00: £420.00:
£200.00) **1m 2f** Stalls: Low GOING minus 0.49 sec per fur (F) 8-45 (8-46)

Askern (65)*(71) (GMMoore)* 4-9-12 JCarroll(7) (sn cl up: led over 2f out: r.o u.p)........................— 1
818* Tropical Jungle (USA) **(55)***(61)*(Fav)*(PJMakin)* 5-9-5b KDarley(5) (hld up: hdwy 7f out: ev ch appr fnl f: kpt on)........................1¾ 2
1285[2] Diamond Crown (IRE) **(44)***(58) (MartynWane)* 4-9-5 KFallon(9) (bhd tl hdwy 3f out: styd on strly: nrst fin)........................2 3
1270[7] Aconorace *(52) (RAFahey)* 3-8-6 ACulhane(1) (stdd s: effrt on ins over 3f out: rdn & nt pce to chal)........................3½ 4
990[8] Master Fiddler **(33)***(49) (EWeymes)* 5-9-5 DeanMcKeown(6) (lw: led over 7f out tl over 2f out: sn outpcd)........................2 5
1206[6] Amnesia (IRE) **(49)***(43) (MrsSCBradburne)* 4-9-7v NKennedy(4) (nvr trbld ldrs)........................5 6

1155[6] Goram's Girl (IRE) **(44)***(33) (MrsASwinbank)* 3-8-1 JMarshall(2) (lw: led 2½f: chsd ldrs tl wknd over 2f out) 2 7
839[15] Sweetlittlemystery **(32)***(30) (EJAlston)* 4-9-0 JFortune(3) (chsd ldrs tl outpcd fnl 3f) 1¾ 8
Cymbalo *(JSGoldie)* 4-9-5 AMcGlone(8) (bkwd: s.i.s: t.o) ....dist 9

5/6 Tropical Jungle (USA) (Evens-11/10), **7/2** Diamond Crown (IRE) (11/4-9/2), **7/1** ASKERN, **8/1** Aconorace, **10/1** Cymbalo, **14/1** Master Fiddler, **20/1** Goram's Girl (IRE), **33/1** Sweetlittlemystery, **50/1** Amnesia (IRE), CSF £13.85 TOTE £7.60: £2.10 £1.10 £1.90 (£6.20) Trio £3.30 OWNER Mr John Robson (MIDDLEHAM) BRED Highclere Stud Ltd 9 Rn 2m 10.84 (6.24) SF: 28/18/15/-/6
WEIGHT FOR AGE 3yo-13lb
Sold M. O'Donnell 7,400 gns.

1423 NORTH PARK HOTEL H'CAP (0-70) (3-Y.O) (Class E) £3,217.00 (£976.00: £478.00: £229.00)
1m Stalls: Low GOING minus 0.49 sec per fur (F) 9-15 (9-16)

966[7] **Celebration Cake (IRE) (56)***(61) (MissLAPerratt)* 3-8-8 MBirch(1) (chsd ldrs: led 2½f out: hrd rdn & hld on wl) ....— 1
1045* Indian Rhapsody **(44)***(48) (MRChannon)* 3-7-10 LCharnock(6) (lw: prom: hmpd over 2f out: styd on wl towards fin) ....nk 2
1207* Champagne N Dreams **(59)***(63)*(Fav)*(DNicholls)* 3-8-11 6x AlexGreaves(4) (lw: hld up: hdwy 2f out: ch ins fnl f: hrd rdn & nt qckn) ....nk 3
1204[6] Teejay'n'aitch (IRE) **(54)***(55) (JSGoldie)* 3-8-6 AMcGlone(5) (in tch: effrt over 2f out: sn ev ch: no ex wl ins fnl f) 1½ 4
1045[3] Fishy Affair **(45)***(30) (TDyer)* 3-7-11 JFanning(3) (plld hrd: led & sn wl clr: hdd 2½f out: sn btn) 8 5

8/11 Champagne N Dreams, **4/1** Indian Rhapsody, **11/2** CELEBRATION CAKE (IRE), **6/1** Teejay'n'aitch (IRE), **10/1** Fishy Affair (op 6/1), CSF £24.90 TOTE £8.80: £2.30 £1.90 (£9.10) OWNER Lightbody of Hamilton Ltd (AYR) BRED John Davison 5 Rn 1m 42.21 (5.41) SF: 3/-/5/-/-

T/Plpt: £163.90 (68.15 Tckts). T/Qdpt: £23.90 (2 Tckts). AA

1272-BRIGHTON (L-H)
Thursday June 1st (Firm)
WEATHER: overcast WIND: slt half against

1424 E.B.F. FRESHFIELD MEDIAN AUCTION MAIDEN STKS (2-Y.O) (Class E) £3,754.10 (£987.60: £470.30)
5f 213y Stalls: Low GOING minus 0.35 sec per fur (F) 2-10 (2-11)

669[9] **Cyrillic** *(67)*(Fav)*(PAKelleway)* 2-8-9 MWigham(4) (lw: 3rd st: led over 1f out: rdn out) ....— 1
436[11] Vanishing Point *(69) (GLewis)* 2-9-0 PaulEddery(3) (outpcd: 4th st: rapid hdwy ins fnl f: fin wl) 1¼ 2
1123[6] Laughing Buccaneer *(67) (BJMeehan)* 2-9-0 BDoyle(1) (lw: 2nd st: led over 2f out tl over 1f out: ev ch whn edgd lft ins fnl f: unable qckn) ....½ 3
782[4] Mrs McBadger *(BSmart)* 2-8-9 RPerham(2) (lw: led over 3f: ev ch 1f out: cl 3rd whn bdly hmpd on ins & uns rdr ins fnl f) .... U

6/4 CYRILLIC (4/5-13/8), **9/4** Mrs McBadger, **5/2** Laughing Buccaneer, **10/1** Vanishing Point (3/1-12/1), CSF £11.07 TOTE £2.00 (£4.60) OWNER Chancery Bourse Inv Stud) (NEWMARKET) BRED Brick Kiln Stud and Lariston Apartments Ltd 4 Rn 1m 11.8 (3.40) SF: 15/17/15/-

1425 SHOREHAM MAIDEN STKS (3-Y.O) (Class D) £3,799.90 (£1,133.20: £540.60: £244.30) **6f 209y** Stalls: Low GOING minus 0.35 sec per fur (F) 2-40 (2-41)

Aldaneh (75)*(75) (RHannon)* 3-8-9 JReid(3) (lw: 3rd st: hrd rdn over 1f out: led nr fin) ....— 1
1072[2] Roderick Hudson **(83)***(79)*(Fav)*(JARToller)* 3-9-0 WNewnes(2) (lw: 2nd st: led over 1f out: rdn: hdd nr fin) ....nk 2
1072[3] Office Hours **(78)***(70) (CACyzer)* 3-9-0 TQuinn(1) (lw: led over 5f: eased whn btn ins fnl f) 4 3
1240[9] Rising River *(19) (SWoodman)* 3-8-9 MFenton(4) (4th: a bhd) 20 4

8/11 Roderick Hudson (4/6-Evens), **5/2** ALDANEH, **100/30** Office Hours (5/2-4/1), **66/1** Rising River, CSF £4.67 TOTE £3.10 (£1.60) OWNER Sheikh Essa Bin Mubarak (MARLBOROUGH) BRED M. B. Small 4 Rn
1m 21.5 (1.50) SF: 45/49/40/-

1426 FLANAGAN AND ALLEN H'CAP (0-60) (3-Y.O+) (Class F) £3,401.00 (£946.00: £455.00) 7f 214y Stalls: Low GOING minus 0.35 sec per fur (F) 3-10 (3-10)

882[2] **Greatest (59)**(71)(Fav)*(RAkehurst)* 4-9-13 RPerham(2) (mde virtually all: hrd rdn over 1f out: r.o wl)........— 1
1323[6] Chairmans Choice **(44)***(50) (APJarvis)* 5-8-12 JMHunter(3) (hdwy 5f out: 2nd st: hrd rdn & ev ch over 1f out: unable qckn)........3 2
1126[9] Mislemani (IRE) **(52)***(57) (AGNewcombe)* 5-9-6 RPrice(15) (hdwy over 2f out: hrd rdn over 1f out: r.o one pce)........½ 3
1202[6] Noeprob (USA) **(42)***(47) (RJHodges)* 5-8-10 TSprake(10) (rdn over 2f out: hdwy over 1f out: r.o one pce)........s.h 4
1155[5] Respectable Jones **(40)***(44) (RHollinshead)* 9-8-8b MWigham(8) (lw: mid div whn hmpd over 4f out: hdwy over 2f out: nt clr run & swtchd rt ins fnl f: one pce)........½ 5
501[5] Zinbaq **(33)***(25) (CJBenstead)* 9-8-1 CRutter(4) (lw: 4th st: wknd over 1f out)........6 6
1013[4] Love Legend **(54)***(43) (DWPArbuthnot)* 10-9-8 MTebbutt(5) (b: rdn 2f out: nvr nr to chal) 1¼ 7
1274[7] Myjinka **(32)***(18) (JO'Donoghue)* 5-8-0b NCarlisle(9) (5th st: wknd wl over 1f out)........1½ 8
1013[3] Pirates Gold (IRE) **(48)***(27) (JWhite)* 5-9-2 FNorton(12) (lw: 6th st: wknd over 2f out)........3½ 9
1155[2] Okay Baby (IRE) **(44)***(23) (MHTompkins)* 3-8-1 SRaymont(1) (5th whn hmpd over 4f out: bhd fnl 3f)........d.h 9
546[9] Oozlem (IRE) **(42)***(15) (RMFlower)* 6-8-10b ATucker(7) (s.s: hdwy 3f out: wknd over 2f out) 3 11
1125[10] Burnt Sienna (IRE) **(44)***(17) (JSMoore)* 3-8-1 NAdams(11) (lw: a bhd)........nk 12
1263[4] Kellaire Girl (IRE) **(46)***(16) (GLewis)* 3-8-3 DaleGibson(14) (lw: bhd fnl 5f) 1¼ 13
739[12] Starsport (IRE) **(54)***(18) (DJSffrenchDavis)* 4-9-8b SO'Gorman(6) (lw: 3rd st: wknd over 2f out)........3 14

7/2 GREATEST, **5/1** Kellaire Girl (IRE), **11/2** Chairmans Choice, **8/1** Noeprob (USA), Mislemani (IRE), **10/1** Love Legend, Pirates Gold (IRE), **11/1** Okay Baby (IRE), **14/1** Oozlem (IRE), **25/1** Respectable Jones, Myjinka, Zinbaq, **33/1** Burnt Sienna (IRE), **40/1** Starsport (IRE), CSF £22.79 CT £137.23 TOTE £3.60: £2.20 £2.70 £3.20 (£10.30) Trio £77.80 OWNER Invoshire Ltd (EPSOM) BRED Bloomsbury Stud 14 Rn 1m 34.7 (2.50) SF: 53/32/39/29/26/7/25/-/9/-/-/-/-/-
WEIGHT FOR AGE 3yo-11lb
STEWARDS' ENQUIRY Hunter susp. 10-12/6/95 (excessive & incorrect use of whip).

1427 SEAFORD (S) H'CAP (0-60) (3-Y.O+) (Class G) £2,243.00 (£618.00: £293.00) 1m 3f 196y Stalls: High GOING minus 0.35 sec per fur (F) 3-40 (3-41)

Duggan (25)*(28) (PDEvans)* 8-7-9 (7) AmandaSanders(8) (4th st: hrd rdn over 1f out: led last stride)........— 1
1285[3] Presto Boy **(48)***(51)*(Fav)*(MBell)* 3-8-9 MFenton(10) (hdwy over 4f out: 6th st: led over 1f out: hrd rdn: hdd last stride)........s.h 2
1319[4] Mayday Kitty **(40)***(42) (WGMTurner)* 3-7-8 (7)ow1 ADaly(6) (lw: 3rd st: led 3f out tl over 1f out: hrd rdn & ev ch ins fnl f: r.o) ....nk 3
1285[8] Ann Hill (IRE) **(36)***(35) (RHollinshead)* 5-8-13 WRyan(12) (rdn & hdwy 2f out: unable qckn ins fnl f)........3 4
Drimard (IRE) **(32)***(29) (KMcAuliffe)* 4-8-6 (3) JTate(7) (lost pl 8f out: r.o one pce fnl 2f) 1½ 5
1125[16] Horsetrader **(51)***(47) (RHannon)* 3-8-5 (7) DaneO'Neill(4) (lw: rdn 3f out: hdwy over 1f out: nvr nrr)........¾ 6
416[12] Sharp Gazelle **(44)***(36) (BSmart)* 5-9-0 (7) MartinDwyer(1) (lw: hdwy 8f out: 5th st: ev ch 2f out: wknd over 1f out)........2½ 7
143[5] Mediator **(42)***(26) (AMoore)* 6-9-5v WNewnes(2) (led 9f)........6 8
893[3] Boundless (IRE) **(41)***(25) (BJMeehan)* 3-8-2b BDoyle(11) (bhd fnl 2f)........hd 9
1319[2] Call Me Albi (IRE) **(51)***(30) (GLMoore)* 4-9-7v(7) LSuthern(3) (lw: 2nd st: wknd over 2f out) ...3½ 10
1319[9] Ragtime Song **(27)***(5) (AMoore)* 6-8-4 CandyMorris(5) (lw: bhd fnl 3f) ....¾ 11
861[10] Lelise (IRE) **(35)** *(APJarvis)* 3-7-3 (7)ow3 SLanigan(9) (s.i.s: a bhd: t.o) ....dist 12
LONG HANDICAP Lelise (IRE) 6-9

11/4 Presto Boy, **7/2** Call Me Albi (IRE), **9/2** Mayday Kitty, **6/1** Boundless (IRE) (4/1-13/2), **13/2** Ann Hill (IRE), **10/1** Horsetrader (8/1-14/1), **16/1** Mediator, **20/1** Sharp Gazelle, **33/1** DUGGAN, **40/1** Lelise (IRE), Ragtime Song, **50/1** Drimard (IRE), CSF £118.76 CT £468.36 TOTE £28.20: £5.70 £1.40 £1.20 (£182.00) Trio £215.80 OWNER Mr Colin Booth (WELSHPOOL) BRED M. Sinclair and J. Fisher 12 Rn 2m 32.2 (3.20) SF: 18/25/16/25/19/21/26/16/-/20/-/-
WEIGHT FOR AGE 3yo-16lb
No bid

1428 REGENCY MEDIAN AUCTION MAIDEN STKS (3-Y.O) (Class F) £2,519.00 (£694.00: £329.00) 7f 214y Stalls: Low GOING minus 0.35 sec (F) 4-10 (4-10)

1000[3] **Shift Again (IRE) (72)***(73)*(Fav)*(WJarvis)* 3-8-9 JReid(4) (4th st: led over 2f out: drvn out) ...— 1

Light Fantastic *(72) (RCharlton)* 3-8-9 WRyan(6) (unf: gd hdwy over 2f out: ev ch fnl 2f: unable qckn wl ins fnl f) ....¾ 2
1240[5] Ron's Secret *(62) (JWPayne)* 3-8-9 PRobinson(7) (5th st: rdn over 2f out: one pce) 5 3
1196[3] Self Reliance **(76)***(59) (MBell)* 3-8-9 MFenton(3) (3rd st: nt clr run over 2f out: ne pce) 1½ 4
1125[6] Nyali Beach (IRE) **(56)***(32) (BJMeehan)* 3-8-9 BDoyle(5) (6th st: wknd 2f out) 13 5
1092[20] Portland Way **(40)***(25) (APJarvis)* 3-9-0 TQuinn(1) (lw: led 2f: led over 4f out tl over 2f out: sn wknd) 6 6
1030[10] Mrs Tigger **(46)***(20) (RWArmstrong)* 3-8-9b RPrice(2) (lw: led 6f out tl over 4f out: 2nd st: wknd over 2f out) ....nk 7

13/8 SHIFT AGAIN (IRE), **7/4** Light Fantastic, **5/1** Ron's Secret, Self Reliance (op 5/2), **12/1** Nyali Beach (IRE) (8/1-14/1), **50/1** Portland Way, Mrs Tigger, CSF £5.04 TOTE £2.20: £1.90 £1.90 (£3.30) OWNER Buckram Oak Holdings (NEWMARKET) BRED Buckram Thoroughbred Enterprises Inc 7 Rn
1m 34.6 (2.40) SF: 38/37/27/24/-/-/-

1429 CLAYTON H'CAP (0-70) (3-Y.O+) (Class E) £3,245.00 (£968.00: £462.00: £209.00)
5f 213y Stalls: Low GOING minus 0.35 sec per fur (F) 4-40 (4-40)

1276[2] **Night Asset (50)***(57) (JO'Donoghue)* 6-8-9 (5) PMcCabe(7) (hdwy 2f out: hrd rdn & edgd lft over 1f out: led last strides) ....— 1
1265[2] Another Jade **(63)***(69) (APJarvis)* 5-9-13 TQuinn(8) (lw: 6th st: led over 2f out: rdn & hdd last strides) ....nk 2
1276* Tafahhus **(75)***(73)*(Fav)*(RWArmstrong)* 3-10-2 7x WCarson(2) (lw: 5th st: ev ch over 1f out: eased whn btn ins fnl f) 3 3
1276[4] Samsolom **(63)***(61) (PHowling)* 7-9-13 PaulEddery(5) (lw: 3rd st: rdn over 1f out: one pce) ..s.h 4
1261[12] Words of Wisdom (IRE) **(47)***(37) (CACyzer)* 5-8-11 JReid(1) (4th st: nt clr run 2f out: sn wknd)3 5
1276[9] Dahiyah (USA) **(63)***(45) (GLMoore)* 4-9-8v(5) AWhelan(6) (lw: a bhd) 3 6
541[8] Tyrian Purple (IRE) **(58)***(35) (TJNaughton)* 7-9-8b GCarter(3) (led over 3f) 2 7
1199[7] Cedar Girl **(54)***(28) (RJHodges)* 3-8-9 BDoyle(4) (2nd st: wknd 3f out) 1 8

9/4 Tafahhus, **7/2** NIGHT ASSET, Another Jade, **13/2** Dahiyah (USA), **12/1** Samsolom (op 8/1), **14/1** Words of Wisdom (IRE), **16/1** Tyrian Purple (IRE), **25/1** Cedar Girl, CSF £14.90 CT £28.78 TOTE £3.90: £2.10 £1.80 £1.30 (£7.60) OWNER Mr Roy Bays (REIGATE) 8 Rn
69.5 secs (1.10) SF: 47/59/54/51/27/35/25/9
WEIGHT FOR AGE 3yo-9lb
T/Jkpt: £17,401.60 (0.2 Tckts); £19,607.54 to Catterick 2/5/95. T/Plpt: £53.60 (215.84 Tckts). T/Qdpt: £5.70 (17.9 Tckts). AK

1041-CARLISLE (R-H)
Thursday June 1st (Good, Good to firm patches)
WEATHER: sunny WIND: fresh half against

1430 TUCK SHOP CLAIMING STKS (3-Y.O) (Class F) £2,703.00 (£758.00: £369.00)
1m 4f Stalls: Low GOING minus 0.55 sec per fur (F) 2-20 (2-20)

1083[8] **Durgams First (IRE) (57)***(68)*(Fav)*(MrsMReveley)* 3-8-13 KDarley(5) (hld up: hdwy over 3f out: led over 1f out: hung rt u.p: all out) ....— 1
1161[13] Jackmanii **(42)***(60) (WTKemp)* 3-8-5 KFallon(7) (effrt over 3f out: ev ch over 1f out: styd on u.p: nt qckn nr fin) ....nk 2
1059[3] Absolute Folly **(53)***(62) (JBerry)* 3-8-13 JCarroll(6) (led tl over 1f out: one pce) 4 3
1059[5] High Flown (USA) **(51)***(58) (RonaldThompson)* 3-8-9 JWeaver(2) (chsd ldrs: ev ch 2f out: one pce) ....hd 4
837[4] Africannightingale (IRE) *(36) (MHTompkins)* 3-8-2 (5) SMulvey(1) (chsd ldr: drvn along 5f out: wknd over 2f out: eased) 15 5
875[9] Ladys Promise *(26) (MartynWane)* 3-7-12 LCharnock(3) (lost pl over 4f out: sn bhd) 1¼ 6
1270[10] Warrgem *(10) (BEllison)* 3-8-2 NKennedy(4) (chsd ldrs: drvn along ½-wy: lost pl over 4f out: sn wl bhd) 15 7

2/1 DURGAMS FIRST (IRE), **100/30** Absolute Folly, **4/1** Africannightingale (IRE), **5/1** High Flown (USA), **13/2** Jackmanii, **33/1** Warrgem, **50/1** Ladys Promise, CSF £13.72 TOTE £2.70: £1.40 £2.60 (£14.90) OWNER The Mary Reveley Racing Club (SALTBURN) BRED William McGladdery in Ireland 7 Rn
2m 35.9 (4.90) SF: 12/4/6/2/-/-/-

1431 GOLD MARK MAIDEN STKS (3-Y.O+ F & M) (Class D) £3,589.30 (£1,086.40: £530.20: £252.10) **7f 214y** Stalls: High GOING minus 0.55 sec (F) 2-50 (2-51)

Varvarka *(78+) (JWWatts)* 3-8-9 JWeaver(1) (lengthy: unf: trckd ldrs: smooth hdwy 3f out: led over 1f out: r.o strly) ....— 1

915[5] Feinte *(72)*(Fav)*(WJarvis)* 3-8-9 KDarley(2) (hld up: hdwy 4f out: ev ch & rdn 2f out: nt qckn fnl f)....3 2
Thatcher's Era (IRE) *(69)* *(TDBarron)* 3-8-9 JFortune(3) (chsd ldr: pushed along 4f out: led over 2f out tl over 1f out: one pce)....1¾ 3
824[7] Golden Digger (USA) *(60)* *(MRStoute)* 3-8-9 DeanMcKeown(5) (hld up & plld hrd: stdd 6f out: hdwy over 3f out: rdn & wknd 2f out)....4 4
1085[7] Gunnerdale *(30)* *(DenysSmith)* 3-8-9 KFallon(4) (led tl over 2f out: sn wknd)....15 5

5/6 Feinte, **100/30** Golden Digger (USA), **7/2** VARVARKA, **14/1** Thatcher's Era (IRE), **25/1** Gunnerdale, CSF £6.62 TOTE £3.60: £2.70 £1.10 (£2.50) OWNER Sheikh Mohammed (RICHMOND) BRED Sheikh Mohammed bin Rashid al Maktoum 5 Rn 1m 41.6 (2.60) SF: 18/12/9/-/-

1432 BOOKER CASH & CARRY H'CAP (0-70) (3-Y.O+) (Class E) £3,166.90 (£959.20: £468.60: £223.30) **7f 214y** Stalls: High GOING minus 0.55 sec (F) 3-20 (3-26)

1192[7] **Lancashire Life (IRE) (45)***(58)* *(EJAlston)* 4-8-6 JCarroll(3) (mde virtually all: clr over 1f out: drvn out)....— 1
1280[7] Spanish Verdict **(65)***(68)* *(DenysSmith)* 8-9-12 JFortune(4) (lw: chsd ldrs: effrt over 2f out: kpt on: no ch w wnr)....5 2
1037* Chantry Bellini **(42)***(44)* *(MrsSMAustin)* 6-8-3b JFanning(1) (b: b.hind: chsd ldr: disp ld over 3f out: sn rdn: one pce fnl 2f)....¾ 3
Pine Essence (USA) **(63)***(60)* *(MrsMReveley)* 4-9-10 KDarley(2) (bit bkwd: chsd ldrs: effrt 3f out: one pce)....2 4
1291[4] Roseate Lodge **(64)***(59)* *(NBycroft)* 9-9-6 (5) JStack(6) (lw: hld up & bhd: hdwy on outside over 2f out: nvr nr ldrs)....1¼ 5
1286[2] Harry Browne (IRE) **(55)***(47)*(Fav)*(MrsJRRamsden)* 3-8-5v KFallon(8) (hld up: effrt 3f out: sn rdn: nvr nr to chal)....1¼ 6
1250[7] Calder King **(62)***(48)* *(JLEyre)* 4-9-4 (5) NVarley(5) (dwlt: hdwy 3f out: sn rdn: grad wknd)....3 7
Wild Prospect **(40)** *(BSRothwell)* 7-8-1 LCharnock(7) (chsd ldrs tl lost pl ½-wy: sn bhd & eased)....20 8

13/8 Harry Browne (IRE), **9/2** Spanish Verdict, **11/2** Chantry Bellini, **13/2** Calder King, **15/2** Roseate Lodge, **8/1** Pine Essence (USA), **16/1** LANCASHIRE LIFE (IRE), **20/1** Wild Prospect, CSF £81.00 CT £413.52 TOTE £10.20: £2.20 £1.90 £1.40 (£24.60) OWNER Mrs Doreen Lawrence (PRESTON) BRED William Flood 8 Rn 1m 39.9 (0.90) SF: 31/41/17/33/32/9/21/-
WEIGHT FOR AGE 3yo-11lb

1433 MALT HOUSE VINTNERS H'CAP (0-70) (3-Y.O+) (Class E) £3,295.60 (£998.80: £488.40: £233.20) **6f 206y** Stalls: High GOING minus 0.55 sec (F) 3-50 (3-55)

1043[2] **Northern Spark (42)***(50)* *(MartynWane)* 7-8-0 JFanning(6) (w ldr: led over 1f out: styd on wl)....— 1
1297[3] Kilnamartyra Girl **(42)***(49)* *(JParkes)* 5-8-0 LCharnock(3) (prom: outpcd over 2f out: styd on wl ins fnl f: nt rch wnr)....¾ 2
491[6] Cavers Yangous **(67)***(72)* *(MJohnston)* 4-9-11 DHolland(9) (mde most tl over 1f out: kpt on one pce)....1 3
1355[13] Obsidian Grey **(54)***(55)* *(MissLCSiddall)* 8-8-9 (3) DRMcCabe(10) (a.p: kpt on same pce fnl 2f)....2 4
1043* The Kings Ransom **(61)***(62)*(Fav)*(MrsJRRamsden)* 3-8-9v KFallon(8) (bhd: effrt 3f out: ev ch & rdn over 1f out: wknd fnl f)....½ 5
1297[11] Aquado **(56)***(52)* *(ALForbes)* 6-9-0 JWeaver(4) (lw: chsd ldrs: effrt over 2f out: one pce)....2 6
1021[15] Twin Creeks **(55)***(49)* *(MDHammond)* 4-8-8 (5) JStack(2) (in tch: effrt on outside over 2f out: kpt on: nvr rchd ldrs)....1 7
909[11] Faynaz **(35)***(26)* *(RMMcKellar)* 9-7-0 (7) DLockhart(7) (b: dwlt: wl bhd tl sme late hdwy)....1¼ 8
776[9] Suedoro **(41)***(28)* *(RMMcKellar)* 5-7-6 (7) PFessey(5) (b.hind: prom tl wknd over 2f out)....1¾ 9
1151[16] Matisse **(50)***(35)* *(JDBethell)* 4-8-8b JCarroll(1) (bit bkwd: prom tl wknd over 2f out)....1¼ 10
861[3] Noosa (IRE) **(63)***(43)* *(DMoffatt)* 3-8-8 (3) DarrenMoffatt(12) (hld up & bhd: effrt 3f out: sn wknd)....3 11
875[6] Nebrangus (IRE) **(48)***(22)* *(NBycroft)* 3-7-5 (5)ow3 NVarley(11) (s.i.s: a bhd)....1¼ 12
297[7] Cheerful Groom (IRE) **(50)***(24)* *(JMackie)* 4-8-3 (5) CTeague(13) (chsd ldrs tl lost pl over 2f out)....1¼ 13

LONG HANDICAP Faynaz 7-0 Nebrangus (IRE) 7-2

7/4 The Kings Ransom, **7/1** Aquado, **8/1** NORTHERN SPARK, Noosa (IRE), **10/1** Kilnamartyra Girl, Cavers Yangous, **12/1** Twin Creeks, Cheerful Groom (IRE), **14/1** Obsidian Grey, **20/1** Suedoro, Matisse, **33/1** Nebrangus (IRE), **50/1** Faynaz, CSF £80.84 CT £746.95 TOTE £10.90: £2.80 £3.20 £2.10 (£61.20) Trio £341.40 OWNER Mr Jonathan Hill (RICHMOND) BRED I. Thoday 13 Rn
1m 27.6 SF: 13/11/34/16/12/13/9/-/-/-/-/-/-
WEIGHT FOR AGE 3yo-10lb

1434 CHEF'S LARDER LIMITED STKS (0-55) (3-Y.O+) (Class F) £2,983.00 (£838.00: £409.00) **5f** Stalls: High GOING minus 0.55 sec per fur (F) 4-20 (4-25)

1276³ **Giggleswick Girl (54)***(59)*(Fav)*(MRChannon)* 4-9-3 DHolland(4) (hld up: gd hdwy over 1f out: r.o wl to ld ins fnl f: readily) ....— **1**
972³ Petraco (IRE) **(55)***(55) (NASmith)* 7-9-0 (5) NVarley(6) (mde most tl hdd & no ex ins fnl f) 1¾ **2**
1331⁴ The Institute Boy **(44)***(49) (MissJFCraze)* 5-9-5v SWebster(8) (hdwy on outside 2f out: kpt on same pce fnl f: nvr rchd ldrs) 2 **3**
1151⁶ Heart Broken **(49)***(44) (JGFitzGerald)* 5-9-0 KFallon(5) (in tch: effrt 2f out: kpt on: nvr rchd ldrs) ....hd **4**
1331⁶ Poly Laureon (IRE) **(50)***(36) (RHollinshead)* 3-8-6 KDarley(9) (rr div: drvn along ½-wy: styd on: nvr nr to chal) 2½ **5**
1249⁶ Ramborette **(55)***(34) (DenysSmith)* 3-8-6v JFortune(2) (in tch: effrt over 2f out: one pce) ....½ **6**
1271² Miss Aragon **(51)***(29) (MissLCSiddall)* 7-8-11 (3) DRMcCabe(12) (lw: in tch: rdn 2f out: no imp) 1½ **7**
1157⁵ Another Nightmare (IRE) **(51)***(29) (RMMcKellar)* 3-8-6 JWeaver(13) (w ldr tl wknd over 1f out) ....hd **8**
Mokaite **(45)***(25) (MABarnes)* 4-8-7 (7) PFessey(7) (s.s: bhd tl sme late hdwy) 1¼ **9**
1043⁸ Gymcrak Tycoon **(51)***(30) (GHolmes)* 6-9-0 (5) JStack(3) (b: b.off hind: chsd ldrs tl wknd 2f out) ....hd **10**
789¹⁴ Light Movement (IRE) **(53)***(29) (WSCunningham)* 5-9-5v DeanMcKeown(1) (b.nr fore: chsd ldrs tl wknd 2f out) ....nk **11**
1080¹² Sweet Cheap Pet **(40)***(11) (JJO'Neill)* 3-8-6b JFanning(11) (bhd whn hmpd over 3f out: n.d) 4 **12**
1023⁹ Supreme Desire **(32)***(9) (GROldroyd)* 7-9-0 LCharnock(10) (a in rr: sn drvn along) ....½ **13**

3/1 GIGGLESWICK GIRL, **4/1** Miss Aragon, **11/2** Light Movement (IRE), **15/2** Petraco (IRE), **10/1** Ramborette, Poly Laureon (IRE), Another Nightmare (IRE), **12/1** Heart Broken, **16/1** The Institute Boy, Gymcrak Tycoon, **20/1** Mokaite, **25/1** Sweet Cheap Pet, Supreme Desire, CSF £26.74 TOTE £2.80: £2.00 £2.80 £4.30 (£13.70) Trio £45.90 OWNER Mr M. Bishop (UPPER LAMBOURN) BRED B. Minty 13 Rn 61.1 secs (0.90) SF: 41/37/31/26/10/8/11/3/7/12/11/-/-

WEIGHT FOR AGE 3yo-8lb

STEWARDS' ENQUIRY Holland & Fallon fined £200 under Rule 162(iv)(leaving track before weighed-in sign).

1435 FAMILY CHOICE H'CAP (0-70) (4-Y.O+) (Class E) £3,109.70 (£941.60: £459.80: £218.90) **1m 6f 32y** Stalls: Low GOING minus 0.55 sec per fur (F) 4-50 (4-50)

841⁷ **Hillzah (USA) (66)***(75) (RBastiman)* 7-9-9 (5) HBastiman(6) (s.i.s: hld up & bhd: hdwy & swtchd outside over 2f out: hrd rdn & hung rt over 1f out: styd on to ld wl ins fnl f) ..— **1**
1161* Lord Advocate **(34)***(41) (DANolan)* 7-7-5b(5)ow1 NVarley(1) (lw: trckd ldrs: led over 3f out: sn clr: hdd & no ex ins fnl f) 1 **2**
1046² Persuasive **(51)***(53)*(Fav)*(MrsMReveley)* 8-8-13 KDarley(3) (hld up & bhd: hdwy 5f out: kpt on u.p fnl 2f: nvr able chal) 5 **3**
1349* Cliburnel News (IRE) **(55)***(54) (ALForbes)* 5-8-10 (7) DDenby(9) (b: a chsng ldrs: effrt u.p 3f out: kpt on one pce) 2½ **4**
1328⁷ Arc Bright (IRE) **(39)***(27) (RHollinshead)* 5-7-12 (3) AGarth(10) (lw: led to 10f out: drvn along 5f out: wknd over 3f out) 10 **5**
Great Oration (IRE) **(40)***(26) (FWatson)* 6-8-2 NConnorton(11) (bit bkwd: in tch: effrt u.p 3f out: sn wknd) 2 **6**
1160⁸ Lightning Quest (IRE) **(33)***(13) (JSWainwright)* 4-7-9bow2 LCharnock(4) (in tch: rdn & prom over 3f out: sn lost pl) 3½ **7**
879¹⁵ Deb's Ball **(43)***(19) (DMoffatt)* 9-8-2 (3) DarrenMoffatt(5) (lw: bhd: drvn along 5f out: n.d) 5 **8**
19³ Strictly Personal (USA) **(66)***(42) (MABarnes)* 5-9-9 (5) JStack(2) (chsd ldr: led 10f out tl over 3f out: sn wknd) ....½ **9**
1161¹¹ Plum Dennis **(33)** *(NBycroft)* 4-7-6 (3)ow1 DWright(8) (prom early: drvn along 7f out: sn bhd) 15 **10**
1160¹¹ Young Steven **(43)** *(WTKemp)* 4-8-5 MBirch(7) (prom 5f: sn bhd: t.o) ....dist **11**

LONG HANDICAP Lightning Quest (IRE) 7-3

6/4 Persuasive, **4/1** Cliburnel News (IRE), **11/2** Arc Bright (IRE) (4/1-6/1), **8/1** Lord Advocate, **10/1** HILLZAH (USA), **14/1** Great Oration (IRE), Deb's Ball, **16/1** Strictly Personal (USA), **20/1** Plum Dennis, **25/1** Lightning Quest (IRE), **33/1** Young Steven, CSF £84.28 CT £173.56 TOTE £11.40: £3.40 £2.30 £1.30 (£61.80) Trio £52.20 OWNER Mrs P. Churm (WETHERBY) BRED Helen M. Polinger, Benjamin Polinger et al 11 Rn 3m 4.9 (4.90) SF: 20/-/-/-/-/-/-/-/-/-/-

STEWARDS' ENQUIRY Bastiman susp. 11-12/6/96 (excessive use of whip).

T/Plpt: £254.30 (45.12 Tckts). T/Qdpt: £77.10 (0.2 Tckts); £83.36 to Catterick 2/6/95 WG

1418-**AYR (L-H)**
Friday June 2nd (Good to firm)
WEATHER: sunny periods WIND: almost nil

1436
CROSSHILL RATING RELATED MAIDEN LIMITED STKS (0-70) (3-Y.O) (Class E) £2,931.00 (£888.00: £434.00: £207.00)
1m 2f Stalls: Low GOING minus 0.24 sec per fur (GF) 2-00 (2-00)

1195[5] **Eau de Cologne (70)**_(77)_(Fav)_(CWThornton)_ 3-9-0 DeanMcKeown(3) (trckd ldrs: led over 1f out: styd on wl) — **1**
1147[9] Dahlenburg (IRE) **(67)**_(74) (JHMGosden)_ 3-9-0v LDettori(5) (cl up: led wl over 2f out: hdd over 1f out: kpt on one pce) 1¾ **2**
1154[2] Dance King **(70)**_(70) (DNicholls)_ 3-9-0 AlexGreaves(1) (a.p: chal over 1f out: wknd fnl f) 2½ **3**
1358[12] Island Cascade **(45)**_(62) (DonEnricoIncisa)_ 3-8-9 KimTinkler(2) (s.i.s: bhd tl sme late hdwy) 1¾ **4**
1254[19] Roadsweeper (FR) **(55)**_(63) (KOCunningham-Brown)_ 3-9-0v JWeaver(4) (led tl hdd wl over 2f out: sn outpcd) 2½ **5**

6/5 EAU DE COLOGNE, **5/2** Dahlenburg (IRE) (6/4-11/4), Dance King, **40/1** Island Cascade, **50/1** Roadsweeper (FR), CSF £4.19 TOTE £2.40: £1.30 £1.50 (£2.70) OWNER Mr Guy Reed (MIDDLEHAM) BRED G. Reed 5 Rn 2m 9.5 (4.90) SF: 46/43/39/31/32

1437
TORRANYARD H'CAP (0-80) (3-Y.O+) (Class D) £4,162.50 (£1,260.00: £615.00: £292.50) **1m 2f** Stalls: Low GOING minus 0.24 sec per fur (GF) 2-30 (2-30)

991* **Keep Battling (38)**_(48) (JSGoldie)_ 5-8-3 AMcGlone(6) (hld up: qcknd to ld wl ins fnl f: jst hld on) — **1**
1160[2] Mentalasanythin **(57)**_(67)_(Fav)_(ABailey)_ 6-9-8 AMackay(2) (lw: hld up: effrt & n.m.r over 1f out: r.o wl towards fin) s.h **2**
1192[2] Kalou **(59)**_(67) (CWCElsey)_ 4-9-10v LDettori(1) (cl up: led 1½f out: edgd lft: hdd & no ex wl ins fnl f) 1¼ **3**
1292* Straw Thatch **(51)**_(57) (MrsJRRamsden)_ 6-9-2 5x KFallon(3) (hld up: pushed along appr st: hdwy over 1f out: nvr able to chal) 1¼ **4**
1205* Imperial Bid (FR) **(58)**_(58) (DenysSmith)_ 7-9-9 5x JFortune(4) (chsd ldrs tl rdn & btn over 1f out) 4 **5**
1160[6] Guards Brigade **(42)**_(38) (JHetherton)_ 4-8-7 NKennedy(5) (led tl hdd, wknd & hmpd 1½f out) 2½ **6**

100/30 Mentalasanythin, **7/2** KEEP BATTLING, Straw Thatch, **4/1** Kalou, **6/1** Imperial Bid (FR), **14/1** Guards Brigade, CSF £13.87 TOTE £4.00: £1.50 £2.50 (£5.30) OWNER Mr J. S. Goldie (KILMARNOCK) BRED Mrs E. Campbell 6 Rn 2m 8.78 (4.18) SF: 41/60/60/50/51/31

1438
KILMACOLM H'CAP (0-70) (4-Y.O+) (Class E) £3,087.00 (£936.00: £458.00: £219.00) **1m** Stalls: Low GOING minus 0.24 sec per fur (GF) 3-00 (3-00)

1166[11] **King Curan (USA) (60)**_(65)_(Fav)_(ABailey)_ 4-9-9b AMackay(2) (hld up: hdwy over 1f out: str run to ld nr fin) — **1**
1027[3] Mr Rough **(62)**_(67)_(Fav)_(DMorris)_ 4-9-11 JWeaver(4) (lw: set slow pce: qcknd over 2f out: r.o: jst ct) hd **2**
1206[5] Sharp N' Smooth **(50)**_(52) (WTKemp)_ 8-8-13b LDettori(1) (hld up: hdwy on ins 3f out: nt qckn fnl f) 1½ **3**
1192[6] Murphy's Gold (IRE) **(50)**_(50)_(Fav)_(RAFahey)_ 4-8-13 ACulhane(3) (lw: trckd ldrs: plld hrd: effrt 2f out: nt pce to chal) ¾ **4**
1377[6] Miss Pigalle **(36)**_(35) (MissLAPerratt)_ 4-7-13b NKennedy(7) (lw: hld up: oupcd 2f out: styd on towards fin) ½ **5**
1250[12] Nobby Barnes **(46)**_(45) (DonEnricoIncisa)_ 6-8-9 KimTinkler(8) (lw: s.i.s: hld up & bhd: n.m.r over 1f out: nvr nr to chal) hd **6**
1250[14] My Handy Man **(57)**_(53) (RAllan)_ 4-9-6 JFortune(9) (prom tl rdn & btn appr fnl f) 1¾ **7**
877[14] Strathtore Dream (IRE) **(46)**_(38) (MissLAPerratt)_ 4-8-9 NConnorton(10) (cl up: chal over 2f out: wknd over 1f out) 2 **8**
_1033_[11] Noble Spirit (IRE) **(46)**_(28) (MrsAMNaughton)_ 4-8-9v AMercer(6) (trckd ldrs: plld hrd: outpcd 2f out) 5 **9**

7/2 KING CURAN (USA), Mr Rough, Murphy's Gold (IRE), **10/1** Nobby Barnes, My Handy Man, **12/1** Sharp N' Smooth (op 8/1), **16/1** Miss Pigalle, **25/1** Strathtore Dream (IRE), **66/1** Noble Spirit (IRE), CSF £13.42 CT £84.61 TOTE £6.90: £1.90 £2.00 £1.90 (£7.40) Trio £16.80 OWNER Mrs M. O'Donnell (TARPORLEY) BRED Executive Bloodstock & Adstock Manor Stud 9 Rn
1m 42.86 (6.06) SF: 32/34/19/17/2/12/20/5/-

1439 CAIRNRYAN MAIDEN STKS (3-Y.O+) (Class D) £3,647.50 (£1,105.00: £540.00: £257.50) 1m 5f 13y Stalls: Low GOING minus 0.24 sec per fur (GF) 3-30 (3-30)

1270[3] **High Pyrenees** *(80) (RAllan)* 3-8-7 JWeaver(2) (hld up & bhd: hdwy 3f out: rdn to ld wl ins fnl f).....— **1**
1175[5] Wurlitzer (USA) *(79)*(Fav)*(JHMGosden)* 3-8-7 LDettori(7) (hld up: hdwy to ld wl over 1f out: no ex wl ins fnl f).....½ **2**
747[4] Junior Ben (IRE) **(78)***(72) (JBerry)* 3-8-7 JFortune(3) (mde most tl hdd wl over 1f out: one pce).....6 **3**
1291[5] Our Main Man *(62) (RMWhitaker)* 5-9-10 ACulhane(5) (trckd ldrs: chal over 3f out: wknd 2f out: fin 5th, 3½l: plcd 4th)..... **4**
1256[4] Great Expectations (FR) *(56) (KOCunningham-Brown)* 4-9-10 AMcGlone(6) (lw: w ldr tl wknd over 3f out: fin 6th, 5l: plcd 5th)..... **5**
1162[4] Philmist **(54)***(46) (JHetherton)* 3-8-2 NKennedy(4) (outpcd appr st: no imp after).....3½ **7**
1105[6] True Bird (IRE) *(61) (JDBethell)* 3-8-2 NConnorton(1) (hld up: effrt ent st: n.m.r over 2f out: one pce: fin 4th, 5l: disq: plcd last)..... **0**

10/11 Wurlitzer (USA), **4/1** True Bird (IRE), **5/1** HIGH PYRENEES, **6/1** Junior Ben (IRE), **20/1** Our Main Man, **33/1** Great Expectations (FR), **50/1** Philmist, CSF £9.59 TOTE £5.50: £1.50 £1.60 (£2.80) OWNER Mr J. Stephenson (CORNHILL-ON-TWEED) BRED Sheikh Mohammed bin Rashid al Maktoum 7 Rn 2m 51.8 (7.00) SF: 29/28/21/-/-/-/-

WEIGHT FOR AGE 3yo-17lb

STEWARDS' ENQUIRY Connorton susp. 11-12/6/95 (failure to weigh-in).

1440 FENWICK MEDIAN AUCTION MAIDEN STKS (2-Y.O) (Class E) £2,996.00 (£908.00: £444.00: £212.00) 6f Stalls: High GOING minus 0.24 sec(GF) 4-00 (4-02)

Persian Secret (FR) *(84+)*(Fav)*(JWWatts)* 2-8-9 LDettori(1) (neat: trckd ldrs gng wl: led 2f out: shkn up & qcknd).....— **1**
993[4] Ramsey Hope *(84) (CWFairhurst)* 2-9-0 NKennedy(4) (a.p: kpt on wl fnl f).....1¾ **2**
863[3] Silverdale Knight *(84) (KWHogg)* 2-9-0 JWeaver(3) (hld up & bhd: qcknd to chal wl over 1f out: wknd ins fnl f).....hd **3**
1024[2] Oriole *(79) (NTinkler)* 2-9-0 KimTinkler(7) (led 3f: kpt on one pce).....2 **4**
Globe Runner *(63) (JJO'Neill)* 2-9-0 KFallon(5) (cmpt: s.i.s: sn in tch: nt clr run 2f out: one pce after).....6 **5**
1203[4] Silent Soprano *(54) (DenysSmith)* 2-8-9 JFortune(2) (lw: cl up: led 3f out to 2f out: wknd) ...1¼ **6**
878[7] Sunday Maelstrom (IRE) *(38) (JBerry)* 2-8-9 SDWilliams(6) (chsd ldrs tl wknd & n.m.r 2f out).....6 **7**

13/8 PERSIAN SECRET (FR), **100/30** Ramsey Hope (5/2-4/1), **9/2** Silverdale Knight, **11/1** Silent Soprano (6/1-12/1), **12/1** Oriole, **14/1** Globe Runner, **25/1** Sunday Maelstrom (IRE), CSF £6.50 TOTE £2.10: £1.10 £2.40 (£4.50) OWNER Sheikh Mohammed (RICHMOND) BRED Darley Stud Management Co Ltd 7 Rn 1m 14.09 (4.29) SF: 11/11/11/6/-/-/-

1441 BALLANTRAE H'CAP (0-80) (3-Y.O+) (Class D) £3,745.00 (£1,135.00: £555.00: £265.00) 6f Stalls: High GOING minus 0.24 sec per fur (GF) 4-30 (4-32)

1271[8] **Barato (67)***(74)*(Fav)*(MrsJRRamsden)* 4-9-4 KFallon(7) (b.nr hind: bhd: hdwy ½-wy: led over 1f out: rdn & r.o).....— **1**
1193[13] Lepine (IRE) **(73)***(75) (JWWatts)* 4-9-10 LDettori(4) (lw: trckd ldrs: chal 2f out: kpt on u.p fnl f).....1¾ **2**
1248[2] Flashy's Son **(66)***(68) (GMMoore)* 7-8-12 (5) JStack(6) (lw: b: b.hind: chsd ldrs: effrt 2f out: kpt on fnl f).....hd **3**
1193[12] Ned's Bonanza **(67)***(69)*(Fav)*(MDods)* 6-9-4 JWeaver(8) (hld up & bhd: gd hdwy 2f out: no ex ins fnl f).....hd **4**
1157[12] Pallium (IRE) **(58)***(52) (MrsAMNaughton)* 7-8-9 JFortune(9) (outpcd & bhd tl sme late hdwy)..3 **5**
1151[10] Boursin (IRE) **(71)***(64) (PCalver)* 6-9-8 NConnorton(5) (cl up: led 2f out: sn hdd & wknd)........½ **6**
1157[11] Diet **(47)***(38) (MissLAPerratt)* 9-7-12v JFanning(1) (led 4f: hung lft & sn wknd).....¾ **7**
1151[17] Tutu Sixtysix **(49)***(39) (DonEnricoIncisa)* 4-8-0 KimTinkler(2) (nvr wnt pce).....nk **8**
563[9] Garnock Valley **(73)***(61) (JBerry)* 5-9-10 DeanMcKeown(3) (chsd ldrs 4f).....½ **9**
1250[16] Cafe Solo **(42)***(30) (NBycroft)* 4-7-7 NKennedy(10) (a outpcd & bhd).....s.h **10**

LONG HANDICAP Cafe Solo 7-6

7/2 BARATO, Ned's Bonanza, **5/1** Lepine (IRE), **11/2** Flashy's Son, **7/1** Garnock Valley, **8/1** Boursin (IRE), **20/1** Tutu Sixtysix, Diet, **25/1** Pallium (IRE), Cafe Solo, CSF £20.05 CT £83.47 TOTE £4.20: £2.80 £3.20 £1.50 (£9.20) Trio £18.40 OWNER Mr David Young (THIRSK) BRED J. Carr and Miss L. Charlton 10 Rn 1m 12.61 (2.81) SF: 50/51/44/45/28/40/14/15/37/6

T/Plpt: £14.60 (688.92 Tckts). T/Qdpt: £12.90 (2.85 Tckts). AA

1196-**BATH (L-H)**
Friday June 2nd (Good)
Race 4 stalls 1-10 opened 0.5 second late.
WEATHER: fair WIND: mod across

1442
GRITTLETON RATING RELATED MAIDEN LIMITED STKS (0-65) (3-Y.O F) (Class F) £2,792.50 (£780.00: £377.50)
1m 2f 46y Stalls: Low GOING minus 0.53 sec per fur (F) 6-35 (6-36)

783[4] **Hard Love (65)**(66) (SPCWoods) 3-8-4 (7) CWebb(1) (plld hrd: chsd ldr 8f out: 2nd st: led 2f out: edgd lft: hdd 1f out: led last strides)........— 1
976[9] Sweet Pavlova (USA) **(64)**(66) (PFICole) 3-8-11 TQuinn(2) (hld up: 4th st: hdwy over 2f out: led 1f out: hdd last strides)........hd 2
1154[3] Trazl (IRE) **(64)**(64)(Fav)(JLDunlop) 3-8-11 WCarson(5) (lw: 3rd st: ev ch whn nt clr run on ins wl over 1f out: nt rcvr)........1¼ 3
1172[8] Fairelaine **(60)**(61) (APJarvis) 3-8-11 BThomson(7) (5th st: hdwy over 2f out: ev ch wl over 1f out: one pce)........1¾ 4
988[13] Kristal Breeze **(48)**(55) (WRMuir) 3-8-11 RHughes(4) (lw: 6th st: no hdwy fnl 2f)........4 5
1128[9] Grey Blade **(60)**(51) (IABalding) 3-8-11 MHills(6) (b.nr hind: led tl hdd & n.m.r 2f out: sn wknd)........2½ 6
1128[8] Bird in Blue (IRE) **(62)**(45) (RHannon) 3-8-11 PatEddery(3) (lw: last st: a in rr)........4 7

13/8 Trazl (IRE), **4/1** Fairelaine, **9/2** Sweet Pavlova (USA), **13/2** HARD LOVE, Bird in Blue (IRE), **14/1** Grey Blade, **33/1** Kristal Breeze, CSF £32.18 TOTE £8.00: £2.20 £1.90 (£13.10) OWNER Mr Arashan Ali (NEWMARKET) BRED W. L. Caley 7 Rn 2m 10.8 (3.10) SF: 26/26/24/21/15/11/5

1443
E.B.F. SWAINSWICK MAIDEN STKS (2-Y.O F) (Class D) £4,406.00 (£1,328.00: £644.00: £302.00)
5f 161y Stalls: Low GOING minus 0.53 sec per fur (F) 7-05 (7-05)

Home Shopping (81+) (KMcAuliffe) 2-8-8 (3) JTate(5) (lt-f: mde all: clr over 2f out: easily)........— 1
Invigorating (70) (RHannon) 2-8-11 TQuinn(4) (unf: dwlt: hdwy 3f out: chsd wnr over 2f out: no imp)........4 2
Shining Cloud (69) (LGCottrell) 2-8-11 NCarlisle(3) (lengthy: scope: plld hrd: a.p: swtchd rt over 2f out: sn outpcd: r.o wl fnl f)........nk 3
951[6] Mono Lady (IRE) (50) (DHaydnJones) 2-8-11 JReid(2) (prom 3f)........7 4
Fro (47) (JFfitch-Heyes) 2-8-11 RPrice(7) (leggy: bit bkwd: slipped 4f out: rdn 3f out: sn bhd)........¾ 5
Film Buff (43)(Fav)(BWHills) 2-8-11 MHills(6) (w'like: bkwd: prom 3f)........1½ 6
Emei Shan (38) (PGMurphy) 2-8-4 (7) RWaterfield(9) (neat: rdn 3f out: a bhd)........1¾ 7
Queen Emma (IRE) (19) (JSMoore) 2-8-11 RHughes(1) (w'like: bit bkwd: w wnr 3f: wknd qckly)........7 8

7/4 Film Buff, **15/8** Invigorating, **8/1** Mono Lady (IRE), **10/1** Shining Cloud, HOME SHOPPING, **16/1** Queen Emma (IRE), **33/1** Emei Shan, Fro, CSF £27.12 TOTE £13.60: £2.30 £1.60 £1.60 (£10.50) Trio £88.90 OWNER Mr Peter Barclay (LAMBOURN) BRED Bridge End Bloodstock 8 Rn
1m 12.7 (3.40) SF: 9/-/-/-/-/-/-/-

1444
FRIDAY EVENING H'CAP (0-75) (4-Y.O+) (Class D) £3,969.00 (£1,197.00: £581.00: £273.00)
2m 1f 34y Stalls: Low GOING minus 0.53 sec per fur (F) 7-35 (7-35)

1189[7] **Inchcailloch (IRE) (58)**(67)(Fav)(JSKing) 6-8-12 PaulEddery(2) (lw: hld up & bhd: stdy hdwy 6f out: 7th st: rdn to ld ins fnl f: r.o wl)........— 1
1058[2] French Ivy (USA) **(55)**(64) (FMurphy) 8-8-9 TSprake(14) (b: hld up & plld hrd: hdwy 6f out: 6th st: led 1f out tl ins fnl f)........½ 2
1144[10] Paradise Navy **(70)**(77) (CREgerton) 6-9-10 RHughes(5) (a.p: led 5f out: clr over 2f out: hdd 1f out: nt qckn)........2 3
1328[3] Tamarpour (USA) **(58)**(62)(Fav)(MCPipe) 8-8-12 JReid(10) (lw: b.nr fore: hld up & bhd: hdwy & 8th st: hung lft 1f out: one pce)........3 4
738[18] Allmosa **(57)**(55) (TJNaughton) 6-8-11 PatEddery(7) (swtg: hld up & bhd: hdwy fnl 2f: nvr nrr)........6 5
998[16] Bardolph (USA) **(74)**(69) (PFICole) 8-10-0 TQuinn(9) (lw: 3rd st: wknd over 2f out)........3½ 6
1058[8] Sarazar (USA) **(47)**(40) (RAkehurst) 6-8-1 CRutter(12) (lw: rdn 8f out: hdwy 6f out: 4th st: wknd over 2f out)........2½ 7
582[11] Access Sun **(41)**(31) (JSKing) 8-7-4 (5)ow2 NVarley(13) (led over 12f: 2nd st: wknd over 2f out)........½ 8

1189[11] Art Form (USA) **(68)***(55) (CACyzer)* 8-9-8 WCarson(4) (lw: hdwy 9f out: rdn 7f out: 5th st: wknd over 2f out) 6 **9**
Turret **(70)***(48) (RBrotherton)* 4-9-9 JWilliams(3) (a bhd: t.o) 9 **10**
1058[10] Lajadhal (FR) **(42)***(17) (KBishop)* 6-7-3 (7)ow3 SLanigan(11) (prom 11f: t.o) ....nk **11**
295[13] Surcoat **(39)***(11) (RJBaker)* 8-7-7 NCarlisle(1) (plld hrd: prom 13f: t.o) 6 **12**
240[7] Lady Valensina (IRE) **(64)***(31) (BJLlewellyn)* 4-9-3 RPrice(6) (a bhd: t.o fnl 2f) 6 **13**
1086[3] Who's the Best (IRE) **(41)***(5) (APJarvis)* 5-7-6 (3)ow2 DWright(8) (prom 12f: t.o) ....¾ **14**

LONG HANDICAP Lajadhal (FR) 6-2 Who's the Best (IRE) 6-13

4/1 INCHCAILLOCH (IRE), Tamarpour (USA) (3/1-9/2), **13/2** Allmosa (9/2-7/1), **7/1** Bardolph (USA), French Ivy (USA), Sarazar (USA), **12/1** Art Form (USA), **14/1** Paradise Navy, **25/1** Access Sun, **33/1** Turret, Who's the Best (IRE), Surcoat, **50/1** Lady Valensina (IRE), **100/1** Lajadhal (FR), CSF £29.86 CT £328.90 TOTE £4.70: £2.00 £3.00 £3.70 (£14.30) Trio £100.50 OWNER Mr F. J. Carter (SWINDON) BRED Hascombe and Valiant Studs 14 Rn

3m 46.7 (5.70) SF: 44/41/54/39/32/46/17/8/32/24/-/-/7/-

WEIGHT FOR AGE 4yo-1lb

1445 HAYMAKING CLAIMING STKS (3-Y.O) (Class F) £3,020.00 (£845.00: £410.00)
5f 11y Stalls: Low GOING minus 0.53 sec per fur (F) 8-05 (8-05)

1033[10] **Superbit (50)***(64) (BAMcMahon)* 3-8-7 FNorton(16) (a.p: led ins fnl f: r.o wl) ....— **1**
1263* Fantasy Racing (IRE) **(75)***(71)*(Fav)*(MRChannon)* 3-9-2 RHughes(13) (lw: a.p: rdn & r.o wl ins fnl f) ....¾ **2**
1331[10] Southern Dominion **(60)***(75) (WGMTurner)* 3-9-0 (7) ADaly(15) (lw: led: edgd rt over 1f out: hdd ins fnl f) ....nk **3**
855[6] Colston-C **(50)***(68) (CJHill)* 3-9-2 JReid(12) (a.p: r.o one pce fnl f) ....½ **4**
1033[12] Code of Silence **(47)***(51) (BPalling)* 3-8-5 TSprake(7) (lw: hdwy over 1f out: r.o) 2 **5**
522[14] Name That Tune *(49) (CJHill)* 3-8-6 NCarlisle(14) (lw: hld up: no hdwy fnl 2f) ....¾ **6**
1125[9] Nomadic Dancer (IRE) **(50)***(51) (MSSaunders)* 3-8-12 JWilliams(1) (nvr nr to chal) 1¼ **7**
1290[15] Cedar Dancer **(46)***(39) (RJHodges)* 3-8-0 BDoyle(5) (nvr trbld ldrs) ....nk **8**
1257[10] Logie Pert Lad **(30)***(36) (JJBridger)* 3-8-6 (3) SSanders(4) (a outpcd) 3½ **9**
1125[14] Damocles **(54)***(30) (IABalding)* 3-8-7 PatEddery(8) (n.d) 1½ **10**
Miltak *(28) (PJMakin)* 3-8-6 WNewnes(10) (a bhd) ....nk **11**
1276[10] Tiheros **(65)***(42) (RHannon)* 3-9-0b(7) DaneO'Neill(3) (lw: a bhd) ....nk **12**
1032[8] My Lady Brady **(53)***(25) (MBrittain)* 3-8-6 SWhitworth(17) (spd 3f) ....½ **13**
473[5] Abbey House **(50)***(9) (RGuest)* 3-7-11b(5) AWhelan(6) (a bhd) 4 **14**
855[17] Positive Result (IRE) *(10) (RJPrice)* 3-8-4 StephenDavies(11) (bhd fnl 2f) ....s.h **15**
861[9] Il Furetto *(6) (JSKing)* 3-8-6 (5) NVarley(9) (swtg: a bhd) 3½ **16**
Warm Hearted (USA) *(RIngram)* 3-8-13 NGwilliams(2) (lt-f: bit bkwd: unruly s: reard & uns rdr stalls) .... **U**

15/8 Fantasy Racing (IRE) (op 5/4), **6/1** Southern Dominion, **8/1** Damocles, Tiheros (op 5/1), Warm Hearted (USA), **10/1** Nomadic Dancer (IRE), Colston-C (tchd 20/1), **12/1** My Lady Brady (op 7/1), **14/1** Abbey House, **25/1** Code of Silence, **33/1** Cedar Dancer, Name That Tune, SUPERBIT, **50/1** Miltak, Positive Result (IRE), **66/1** Il Furetto, Logie Pert Lad, CSF £95.54 TOTE £76.80: £13.40 £1.80 (£111.40) Trio £246.40 OWNER Mr Neville Smith (TAMWORTH) BRED A. D. Bottomley 17 Rn

63.2 secs (2.70) SF: 5/12/16/9/-/-/-/-/-/-/-/-/-/-/-/-/-

Code of Silence clmd GCharlesJones £2,000; Abbey House clmd R Guest £3,000

1446 HAMSWELL MAIDEN STKS (3-Y.O+) (Class D) £3,832.50 (£1,155.00: £560.00: £262.50) **1m 5y** Stalls: Low GOING minus 0.53 sec per fur (F) 8-35 (8-37)

957[3] **Tranquillity (85)***(71)*(Fav)*(LordHuntingdon)* 3-8-5 TQuinn(7) (3rd st: led over 2f out: rdn out) ....— **1**
955[6] African-Pard (IRE) **(74)***(73) (DHaydnJones)* 3-8-10 JReid(12) (5th st: hdwy 3f out: ev ch 2f out: r.o one pce) 1½ **2**
1168[5] French Ginger *(66) (IABalding)* 4-9-2 MHills(11) (hdwy 2f out: r.o ins fnl f) 1¼ **3**
1198[3] Backview *(67) (BJLlewellyn)* 3-8-10 RPrice(10) (4th st: hrd rdn 3f out: one pce fnl 2f) 1¾ **4**
Shahrani *(67) (MCPipe)* 3-8-10 RHughes(6) (hld up: 6th st: r.o one pce fnl 2f) ....hd **5**
Indian Temple **(43)***(61) (MSSaunders)* 4-9-7 JWilliams(1) (nvr nr to chal) 3 **6**
627[7] Sherblu **(40)***(53) (JFfitch-Heyes)* 4-9-7 PaulEddery(5) (chsd ldr: led over 4f out tl over 2f out: sn wknd) 4 **7**
1167[6] Park Ridge *(50) (TGMills)* 3-8-3 (7) DToole(2) (a bhd) 1¼ **8**
1167[5] Pharly Reef *(50) (IABalding)* 3-8-10 PatEddery(8) (led over 3f: 2nd st: wknd over 2f out) ....nk **9**
1196[11] Coastguards Haven *(40) (MJBolton)* 3-8-10 CRutter(4) (lw: 7th st: bhd fnl 3f) 5 **10**
1167[13] Classical Star *(37) (RJHodges)* 6-9-0 (7) AmandaSanders(3) (b: a bhd) 1½ **11**
Dickyvearncombe *(FMurphy)* 3-8-10 TSprake(9) (Withdrawn not under Starters' orders: unruly s: ref to ent stalls) .... **W**

10/11 TRANQUILLITY, **100/30** Pharly Reef, **8/1** French Ginger, **10/1** Backview, African-Pard (IRE), **14/1** Park Ridge (op 8/1), **25/1** Dickyvearncombe, **33/1** Shahrani, **50/1** Indian Temple, **66/1** Sherblu, Coastguards Haven, Classical Star, CSF £10.94 TOTE £1.80: £1.40 £1.60 £2.70 (£9.40) Trio £14.60 OWNER Lord Carnarvon (WEST ILSLEY) BRED Highclere Stud Ltd 11 Rn
1m 40.6 (2.10) SF: 31/33/37/27/27/32/24/10/10/-/8/-
WEIGHT FOR AGE 3yo-11lb

1447

END OF THE DAY H'CAP (0-70) (3-Y.O) (Class E) £3,441.00 (£1,038.00: £504.00: £237.00) **1m 5y** Stalls: Low GOING minus 0.53 sec per fur (F) 9-05 (9-06)

1294[2] **Danegold (IRE) (67)***(72+) (MRChannon)* 3-9-7v RHughes(5) (lw: s.s: gd hdwy 2f out: led 1f out: easily) ....— 1
1202[4] Master Millfield (IRE) **(65)***(64)*(Fav)*(CJHill)* 3-9-5 JReid(11) (5th st: hdwy to ld over 2f out: hdd 1f out: no ch w wnr) 3 2
1165[11] South Sound (IRE) **(57)***(54) (RHannon)* 3-8-4 (7) DaneO'Neill(8) (lw: hdwy 2f out: r.o fnl f) 1 3
1130[9] Elite Justice **(67)***(63) (PFICole)* 3-9-7 TQuinn(4) (lw: 4th st: hrd rdn over 2f out: one pce) ....½ 4
624[6] Old Swinford (IRE) **(65)***(56) (BJMeehan)* 3-9-5 BDoyle(2) (9th st: plld out 2f out: r.o fnl f) 2½ 5
1124[13] Suile Mor **(60)***(50) (BRMillman)* 3-8-9 (5) AWhelan(10) (8th st: no hdwy fnl 2f) ....nk 6
1255[15] Scissor Ridge **(50)***(40) (JJBridger)* 3-8-1 (3) SSanders(3) (led over 5f) ....hd 7
1196[6] Norfolk Glory **(44)***(32) (DJGMurraySmith)* 3-7-7 (5) NVarley(6) (6th st: wknd over 2f out) 1¼ 8
1202[3] Dungeon Dancer **(61)***(41) (JAkehurst)* 3-9-1v WNewnes(1) (3rd st: wknd over 2f out) 4 9
1173[12] Little Shefford **(50)***(26) (DJSffrenchDavis)* 3-8-4 PaulEddery(7) (a bhd) 2 10
1196[4] Miss Laughter **(46)***(21) (JWHills)* 3-7-7 (7) MHenry(12) (2nd st: wknd over 2f out) ....½ 11
1172[15] Rupiana (IRE) **(63)***(12) (JRArnold)* 3-9-3 BThomson(9) (7th st: wknd qckly over 2f out: t.o) ...13 12

11/4 Master Millfield (IRE), **7/2** Dungeon Dancer (5/2-4/1), **9/2** DANEGOLD (IRE) (3/1-5/1), Miss Laughter (3/1-5/1), **8/1** Elite Justice, **14/1** Old Swinford (IRE) (8/1-16/1), **16/1** Rupiana (IRE), Norfolk Glory, **20/1** South Sound (IRE), Suile Mor, **50/1** Scissor Ridge, Little Shefford, CSF £17.67 CT £214.98 TOTE £4.10: £1.50 £1.90 £8.60 (£9.90) Trio £275.80 OWNER The Dream Team (UPPER LAMBOURN) BRED Barronstown Stud and Ron Con Ltd 12 Rn
1m 40.9 (2.40) SF: 43/35/25/34/27/21/11/3/12/-/-/-

T/Plpt: £139.00 (117.72 Tckts), T/Qdpt: £5.40 (19.25 Tckts). KH

0753-CATTERICK (L-H)
Friday June 2nd (Good)
WEATHER: overcast WIND: slt half against

1448

STAPLETON MAIDEN AUCTION STKS (2-Y.O F) (Class F) £2,882.00 (£802.00: £386.00) **5f** Stalls: Low GOING: 0.27 sec per fur (G) 2-20 (2-21)

1158[4] **Shafir (IRE)** *(67)*(Fav)*(JBerry)* 2-8-2 JCarroll(3) (s.i.s: sn chsng ldrs: nt clr run ½-wy: swtchd rt 2f out: r.o u.p to ld jst ins fnl f: sn clr) ....— 1
910[8] Badger Bay (IRE) *(56) (JohnBerry)* 2-8-2 JQuinn(2) (swtg: chsd ldrs: rdn & hmpd 2f out & over 1f out: kpt on same pce) 3½ 2
740[6] Touch of Fantasy *(49) (JohnBerry)* 2-7-12 TWilliams(4) (mde most: hung lft ½-wy: hdd jst ins fnl f: kpt on) ....¾ 3
1203[6] Katie Komaite *(49) (CaptJWilson)* 2-8-2 MFenton(1) (w ldr: wknd 1f out: hmpd ins fnl f) 1½ 4
943[4] Bearnaise (IRE) *(48) (RHannon)* 2-8-2 KDarley(7) (sn outpcd: effrt ½-wy: no imp whn sltly hmpd over 1f out) ....s.h 5
1203[3] Wee Tinkerbell *(40) (MissLAPerratt)* 2-7-12 DaleGibson(5) (chsd ldrs: rdn ½-wy: wknd over 1f out) 1½ 6
Madam Pigtails *(24) (PJMcBride)* 2-7-12 GBardwell(6) (unf: s.i.s: a outpcd & sn drvn along) ..5 7
Contract Bridge (IRE) *(CWThornton)* 2-8-2 LCharnock(8) (cmpt: bit bkwd: s.s: a & bhd) 10 8

2/1 SHAFIR (IRE), **3/1** Bearnaise (IRE) (op 2/1), **4/1** Badger Bay (IRE), **11/2** Wee Tinkerbell (4/1-6/1), **8/1** Madam Pigtails, **14/1** Contract Bridge (IRE), Katie Komaite, **33/1** Touch of Fantasy, CSF £10.64 TOTE £3.20: £1.50 £1.10 £13.80 (£5.00) OWNER Mr Norman Jackson (COCKERHAM) BRED Dene Investments N V 8 Rn
63.1 secs (5.60) SF: 11/-/-/-/-/-/-/-

1449

CROFT (S) STKS (4-Y.O+) (Class G) £2,434.00 (£674.00: £322.00) **1m 7f 177y** Stalls: Low GOING: 0.27 sec per fur (G) 2-50 (2-51)

Reach for Glory (47)*(43)*(Fav)*(WGMTurner)* 6-8-10 (5) PMcCabe(4) (lw: chsd ldrs: drvn along 5f out: kpt on wl u.p to ld over 1f out: eased towards fin) ....— 1
649[14] Naawy **(27)***(43) (CSmith)* 5-9-1 MFenton(1) (led tl over 1f out: one pce) ....½ 2
840[11] Jalore **(30)***(41) (SCoathup)* 6-9-1 TWilliams(7) (hld up & bhd: reminders 6f out: kpt on one pce fnl 4f) 1¾ 3

840[5] Cristal Springs **(36)***(35) (BJMcMath)* 4-8-9 EJohnson(8) (chsd ldrs: disp ld 7f out tl over 2f out: one pce) 1¼ 4
514[12] Bud's Bet (IRE) *(36) (WWHaigh)* 7-9-1 DaleGibson(5) (hld up: effrt 4f out: rdn 2f out: hung lft: wknd fnl f) 3½ 5
Plain Sailing (FR) *(23) (MartynMeade)* 5-9-1 VSlattery(6) (trckd ldrs: rdn & lost pl over 5f out: sn bhd) 13 6
Easy D'Or **(43)***(20) (MrsASwinbank)* 4-9-0 JMarshall(2) (s.s: hld up & plld hrd: rdn & lost tch 5f out) 3 7
1075[5] Turfmans Vision **(28)** *(RHollinshead)* 5-9-1 KDarley(3) (hdwy & prom over 4f out: lost pl & p.u over 3f out: lame) .... P

7/4 REACH FOR GLORY, **3/1** Cristal Springs, **9/2** Easy D'Or (op 3/1), **5/1** Bud's Bet (IRE), **12/1** Turfmans Vision, **14/1** Naawy, **20/1** Plain Sailing (FR), Jalore, CSF £24.07 TOTE £2.60: £1.20 £2.40 £2.30 (£13.40) OWNER Mr O. J. Stokes (SHERBORNE) BRED Ridgecourt Stud 8 Rn

3m 38.2 (17.20) SF: 35/35/33/26/28/15/11/-
WEIGHT FOR AGE 4yo-1lb
No bid.

1450 WENSLEY SPRINT H'CAP (0-80) (3-Y.O) (Class D) £4,077.50 (£1,220.00: £585.00: £267.50)
5f Stalls: Low GOING: 0.27 sec per fur (G) 3-20 (3-21)

1249[4] **Bollin Harry (62)***(72+)*(Fav)*(MHEasterby)* 3-8-7 MBirch(4) (lw: mde virtually all: styd on strly u.p fnl 2f) ....— 1
1181[6] Ninety-Five **(67)***(69) (JGFitzGerald)* 3-8-12 DHolland(7) (sn chsng ldrs: ev ch over 1f out: kpt on same pce) 2½ 2
754[6] Able Sheriff **(51)***(47) (MWEasterby)* 3-7-10b GBardwell(1) (chsd ldrs: ev ch & rdn over 1f out: unable qckn) 2 3
982[3] The Happy Fox (IRE) **(76)***(71) (BAMcMahon)* 3-9-7 KDarley(9) (chsd ldrs: rdn & outpcd ½-wy: kpt on fnl f) ....hd 4
1214[4] Lloc **(59)***(53) (JohnBerry)* 3-8-4 MFenton(6) (swvd lft s: cl up 3f: grad wknd) ....½ 5
966[11] Sunday Mail Too (IRE) **(51)***(36) (MissLAPerratt)* 3-7-10 ow3 DaleGibson(3) (sn outpcd: styd on fnl 2f: n.d) 1¾ 6
754[2] C-Yer-Simmie (IRE) **(61)***(46) (RHollinshead)* 3-8-3 (3) AGarth(2) (w ldrs tl wknd over 1f out) 1 7
Petova (IRE) **(52)***(29) (MJCamacho)* 3-7-11 LCharnock(8) (swtg: a outpcd & bhd) 2½ 8
*284** Hannah's Usher **(75)***(46) (PCHaslam)* 3-9-6 TWilliams(5) (sltly hmpd s: a in rr: eased fnl f) ..1¾ 9

LONG HANDICAP Sunday Mail Too (IRE) 7-4

3/1 BOLLIN HARRY, **7/2** Hannah's Usher, **9/2** The Happy Fox (IRE), **6/1** Ninety-Five, **7/1** C-Yer-Simmie (IRE), **8/1** Able Sheriff, **12/1** Lloc, **16/1** Petova (IRE), **25/1** Sunday Mail Too (IRE), CSF £20.73 CT £121.25 TOTE £4.10: £1.80 £2.30 £1.50 (£19.70) Trio £92.70 OWNER Sir Neil Westbrook (MALTON) BRED Sir Neil and Lady Westbrook 9 Rn

61.4 secs (3.90) SF: 44/41/19/43/25/8/18/1/18

1451 PEN HILL CLAIMING STKS (3-Y.O+) (Class F) £2,840.00 (£790.00: £380.00)
5f Stalls: Low GOING: 0.27 sec per fur (G) 3-50 (3-54)

1106[7] **Palacegate Jack (IRE) (93)***(90)*(Fav)*(JBerry)* 4-9-12 JCarroll(4) (w ldr: led 2f out: r.o wl u.p fnl f: readily) ....— 1
944* Fangio **(80)***(82) (WGMTurner)* 6-9-3 (5) PMcCabe(5) (lw: chsd ldrs: sn drvn along: ev ch over 1f out: unable qckn) 1¼ 2
1304[16] Rhythmic Dancer **(72)***(62) (JLSpearing)* 7-8-12 JQuinn(2) (swtg: unruly s: dwlt: sn chsng ldrs: kpt on same pce appr fnl f) 3 3
1248[4] Sigama (USA) **(56)***(49) (DNicholls)* 9-8-3 (7) RuthCoulter(3) (lw: led: hung rt: hdd 2f out: sn wknd) 3½ 4
Marjorie's Memory (IRE) **(78)***(37) (MJHeaton-Ellis)* 4-9-3 KDarley(1) (chsd ldrs: rdn ½-wy: wknd over 1f out: eased) 6 5

Evens PALACEGATE JACK (IRE), **15/8** Fangio, **11/2** Marjorie's Memory (IRE), **11/1** Sigama (USA), **20/1** Rhythmic Dancer, CSF £3.28 TOTE £1.70: £1.10 £1.90 (£1.80) OWNER Palacegate Corporation Ltd (COCKERHAM) BRED Brendan and Sheila Powell 5 Rn

61.9 secs (4.40) SF: 53/45/25/12/-

1452 MUKER RATING RELATED MAIDEN LIMITED STKS (0-60) (3-Y.O+) (Class F) £3,029.00 (£844.00: £407.00)
1m 3f 214y Stalls: Low GOING: 0.27 sec per fur (G) 4-20 (4-28)

1218[3] **Hydrofoil (60)***(67)*(Fav)*(BWHills)* 3-8-3 DHolland(11) (led after 2f: shkn up 3f out: edgd lft over 1f out: drvn out) ....— 1

1289[3] Carnbrea Belle (IRE) **(58)***(65) (MBell)* 3-8-3 MFenton(3) (chsd ldrs: outpcd over 3f out: kpt on u.p fnl 2f: no imp) 1½ **2**
1093[7] Marchant Ming (IRE) **(52)***(69) (MAJarvis)* 3-8-8b PRobinson(8) (lw: hld up: hdwy over 3f out: rdn 2f out: hung lft & nt r.o) 1 **3**
1204[3] Royal Expression **(60)***(66) (MrsMReveley)* 3-8-8 KDarley(2) (a chsng ldrs: ev ch over 2f out: kpt on one pce) 2 **4**
189[2] Inn At the Top **(60)***(63) (JNorton)* 3-8-8 DaleGibson(7) (hmpd & lost pl 8f out: kpt on fnl 3f: n.d) 2½ **5**
347[3] Song of Years (IRE) **(60)***(48) (JWHills)* 4-9-5 RHills(9) (swtg: hld up: effrt over 3f out: fnd nil: eased over 1f out) 7 **6**
1329[6] Silktail (IRE) **(59)***(42) (JohnBerry)* 3-8-3 JQuinn(5) (prom: hmpd 8f out: effrt over 3f out: sn wl outpcd) 5 **7**
1039[11] Ellastyle (IRE) **(28)***(36) (MissLCSiddall)* 4-9-0 (5) PMcCabe(6) (sn wl bhd: t.o 2f out: kpt on towards fin) 4 **8**
1192[4] Durham Drapes **(57)***(34) (MHEasterby)* 4-9-5 MBirch(10) (trckd ldrs: effrt over 3f out: wknd 2f out: eased) 2 **9**
Riva-Deva **(25)** *(SCoathup)* 3-8-8 TWilliams(1) (led 2f: lost pl over 4f out: sn t.o) ....dist **10**
1085[6] Mill Thyme **(59)** *(MrsMReveley)* 3-7-10 (7) DDenby(4) (Withdrawn not under Starter's orders: ref to ent stalls) .... **W**

2/1 HYDROFOIL, **7/2** Song of Years (IRE), **5/1** Carnbrea Belle (IRE), **11/2** Silktail (IRE), **6/1** Royal Expression, **10/1** Marchant Ming (IRE), Durham Drapes, **14/1** Inn At the Top, **20/1** Mill Thyme, **50/1** Riva-Deva, Ellastyle (IRE), CSF £13.65 TOTE £2.80: £1.60 £1.60 £1.70 (£7.20) Trio £38.30 OWNER Mr R. D. Hollingsworth (LAMBOURN) BRED R. D. Hollingsworth 10 Rn
2m 41.2 (10.20) SF: -/-/-/-/-/-/-/-/-/-
WEIGHT FOR AGE 3yo-16lb

1453 GRINTON H'CAP (0-70) (3-Y.O) (Class E) £3,470.00 (£1,040.00:£500.00: £230.00)
5f 212y Stalls: High GOING: 0.27 sec per fur (G) 4-50 (4-56)

*891** **We're Joken (52)***(57)*(Fav)*(JBerry)* 3-8-8 JCarroll(2) (b.nr hind: led 2f: led over 2f out: sn clr: hld on wl towards fin) ....— **1**
1342[2] Stolen Kiss (IRE) **(63)***(66) (MWEasterby)* 3-8-12v(7) GParkin(1) (lw: w ldr: led 4f out: hung rt & hdd over 3f out: rn wd: hung lft & wandered: nt qckn ins fnl f) ....¾ **2**
1065[6] Brass Tacks **(65)***(64) (RHannon)* 3-9-7 KDarley(5) (s.i.s: wl bhd: hdwy & swtchd outside over 1f out: styd on u.p) 1½ **3**
1207[9] Ricana **(43)***(40) (WTKemp)* 3-7-10 (3) DarrenMoffatt(6) (sn outpcd: sme hdwy whn hmpd 1f out: nt rch ldrs) ....¾ **4**
1257[7] Black Shadow **(42)***(36) (PJMcBride)* 3-7-12b GBardwell(7) (in tch: effrt ½-wy: kpt on one pce fnl 2f) 1 **5**
Sweet Water (IRE) **(58)***(50) (DJSCosgrove)* 3-8-9 (5) PMcCabe(3) (s.i.s: hdwy over 2f out: edgd lft u.p 1f out: n.d) 1 **6**
1040[2] Never Such Bliss **(64)***(50) (JDBethell)* 3-9-6 MFenton(4) (in tch: rdn & outpcd over 2f out: n.d after) 2 **7**
1290[18] Gilpa Trinkets **(40)***(16) (DWChapman)* 3-7-10 LCharnock(8) (w ldrs: led over 3f out: hdd & wknd over 2f out) 4 **8**

5/2 WE'RE JOKEN, **3/1** Stolen Kiss (IRE), **7/2** Brass Tacks, Never Such Bliss, **12/1** Sweet Water (IRE), **14/1** Black Shadow, **16/1** Ricana, **33/1** Gilpa Trinkets, CSF £10.63 CT £24.18 TOTE £3.50: £1.30 £1.80 £1.10 (£4.10) OWNER Mr J. K. M. Oliver (COCKERHAM) BRED James Thom and Sons 8 Rn
1m 16.1 (5.60) SF: 36/45/43/19/15/29/29/-

T/Jkpt: £265.20 (98.57 Tckts). T/Plpt: £16.40 (838.71 Tckts). T/Qdpt: £7.90: (23.3 Tckts). WG

1329-WOLVERHAMPTON (L-H)
Friday June 2nd (Standard)
WEATHER: overcast WIND: slt half across

1454 PEVERIL HOMES MAIDEN STKS (2-Y.O) (Class D) £3,559.85 (£1,062.80: £507.90: £230.45) 6f (Fibre) Stalls: Low GOING minus 0.03 sec (STD) 2-10 (2-11)

562[3] **Worldwide Elsie (USA)** *(68) (PAKelleway)* 2-8-6 (3) JTate(6) (chsd ldr: 2nd st: rdn to ld ins fnl f: r.o) ....— **1**
1212[2] Scathebury *(73)*(Fav)*(SPCWoods)* 2-9-0 WRyan(5) (lw: led: rdn over 1f out: hdd wl ins fnl f: r.o) ....s.h **2**
480[7] Ebony Boy *(64) (JWharton)* 2-9-0 JWilliams(4) (bit bkwd: chsd ldrs: 4th st: styd on same pce appr fnl f) 3½ **3**

Ned Al Sheeba *(59)*(Fav)*(WJHaggas)* 2-9-0 MHills(7) (leggy: lt-f: s.i.s: hdwy 3f out: 3rd & rdn st: wknd bel dist)........1¾ 4
*1089*3 Weetman's Weigh (IRE) *(56) (RHollinshead)* 2-9-0 TIves(3) (chsd ldrs: outpcd ½-wy: styd on appr fnl f)........1¼ 5
*1212*3 Capilano Princess *(47) (DHaydnJones)* 2-8-9 PaulEddery(9) (prom: rdn ½-wy: 5th st: sn wknd)........1¼ 6
*1212*4 Briganoone *(52) (SRBowring)* 2-8-9 (5) CTeague(8) (mid div: effrt & 6th st: wknd over 1f out) hd 7
11767 Mooncusser *(51) (JGFitzGerald)* 2-9-0 MWigham(1) (prom: sn drvn along: 7th & wkng st) ....½ 8
Four Weddings (USA) *(44) (MBell)* 2-9-0 GDuffield(10) (unf: s.i.s: a in rr)........2½ 9
9515 Albert The Bear *(23) (JBerry)* 2-9-0 GCarter(2) (hld up: drvn along ½-wy: grad lost tch)........8 10

2/1 Ned Al Sheeba (tchd 5/4), Scathebury (5/2-9/2), **4/1** WORLDWIDE ELSIE (USA) (5/2-9/2), **12/1** Capilano Princess (op 11/2), Weetman's Weigh (IRE) (op 8/1), **14/1** Four Weddings (USA) (op 6/1), **20/1** Briganoone, **25/1** Ebony Boy, Albert The Bear, **50/1** Mooncusser, CSF £12.50 TOTE £5.90: £4.30 £1.20 £8.40 (£4.30) Trio £116.70 OWNER Mr Ron Dawson (NEWMARKET) BRED Lantern Hill Farm and Dr. M. G. Marenchic 10 Rn 1m 15.3 (4.10) SF: 33/38/29/24/21/12/17/16/9/-

1455 GROUPER CLAIMING STKS (3-Y.O+) (Class F) £2,519.00 (£694.00: £329.00)
1m 4f (Fibresand) Stalls: Low GOING minus 0.03 sec per fur (STD) 2-40 (2-41)

*1086*6 **Pistols At Dawn (USA) (50)***(59)*(Fav)*(BJMeehan)* 5-9-12 BDoyle(5) (hld up: hdwy 6f out: led over 2f out: pushed clr appr fnl f: sn eased)........— 1
*1332*11 Lady Tjonger **(44)***(33) (DrJDScargill)* 4-8-6 (3) JTate(2) (chsd ldr: plld hrd: led over 8f out: hdd over 2f out: 2nd st: sn outpcd)........7 2
*1074*10 Love of the North (IRE) **(30)***(33) (RTJuckes)* 4-8-9 (5) SDrowne(1) (led over 3f: ev ch wl over 2f out: 3rd & rdn st: sn wknd)........3½ 3
Baroski **(45)***(33) (JLHarris)* 4-9-3 GDuffield(3) (bkwd: trckd ldrs: rdn 7f out: 4th & btn st)........2½ 4
Courage-Mon-Brave *(15) (RPCHoad)* 7-9-0 JWilliams(4) (bkwd: b: hld up: t.o & 5th st) 11 5

2/5 PISTOLS AT DAWN (USA), **3/1** Lady Tjonger, **11/1** Love of the North (IRE) (8/1-12/1), **25/1** Baroski, **33/1** Courage-Mon-Brave, CSF £2.05 TOTE £1.40: £1.10 £1.40 (£1.30) OWNER Mr G. Howard-Spink (UPPER LAMBOURN) BRED North Ridge Farm 5 Rn 2m 45.2 (14.20) SF: 33/7/7/7

1456 ANGEL H'CAP (0-65) (3-Y.O+) (Class F) £3,098.60 (£859.60: £411.80)
6f Stalls: Low GOING minus 0.03 sec per fur (G) 3-10 (3-14)

*1076*4 **Efficacy (40)***(47) (APJarvis)* 4-8-3 (3) DWright(8) (lw: hld up: hdwy ½-wy: 2nd st: led 1f out: rdn out)........— 1
*1331*7 Green's Bid **(56)***(62) (DWChapman)* 5-9-5 (3) DRMcCabe(2) (lw: mid div: 7th st: r.o u.p ins fnl f)........½ 2
*892*9 Ho Mei Surprise **(40)***(45) (BPreece)* 3-7-11 NAdams(13) (hld up: hdwy & 4th st: ev ch fnl f: r.o)........nk 3
109413 Medieval Miss **(65)***(68)*(Fav)*(GLewis)* 3-9-8b PaulEddery(6) (led: rdn & hdd 1f out: no ex) ......¾ 4
12553 Caddy's First **(54)***(56) (SMellor)* 3-8-11 MWigham(11) (prom: 5th st: styd on u.p ins fnl f) ....½ 5
*1076*3 Disco Boy **(56)***(54) (BAMcMahon)* 5-9-8b TIves(5) (chsd ldrs: 3rd & rdn st: no ex appr fnl f)..1¼ 6
10426 Grey Toppa **(41)***(37) (NPLittmoden)* 4-8-7 BDoyle(10) (b: n.d)........¾ 7
*1334*3 Farmer Jock **(41)***(36) (MrsNMacauley)* 13-8-2b(5) CTeague(9) (b: chsd ldrs: rdn ½-wy: rn wd ent st: no imp)........nk 8
*830** Shanghai Lil **(44)***(35) (MJFetherston-Godley)* 3-8-1 FNorton(1) (s.i.s: a in rr)........1½ 9
Unison **(37)***(27) (CRBarwell)* 4-8-3 NCarlisle(7) (nvr trbld ldrs)........½ 10
13097 Street Lady **(41)***(25) (ABailey)* 5-8-2 (5)ow1 VHalliday(12) (swtg: unruly stalls: dwlt: a in rr) 1¾ 11
*1214*3 The Real Whizzbang (IRE) **(47)***(23) (PSFelgate)* 4-8-13 GHind(3) (mid div: drvn along ½-wy: wknd wl over 1f out)........3½ 12
*139*2 Fairey Firefly **(58)***(21) (MJCamacho)* 4-9-7 (3) JTate(4) (bit bkwd: s.i.s: sn prom: outpcd ½-wy) 5 13

4/1 Medieval Miss, **6/1** Disco Boy, EFFICACY (op 4/1), **7/1** The Real Whizzbang (IRE), **8/1** Shanghai Lil (op 5/1), **10/1** Fairey Firefly, **12/1** Caddy's First, **14/1** Unison (op 33/1), **16/1** Farmer Jock, **20/1** Grey Toppa, Street Lady, Green's Bid, **40/1** Ho Mei Surprise, CSF £101.66 CT £3,916.47 TOTE £6.30: £2.10 £7.30 £8.10 (£51.70) Trio not won; £402.93 to Newmarket 3/6/95 OWNER Mrs Ann Jarvis (ASTON UPTHORPE) BRED Hever Castle Stud Farm Ltd 13 Rn
1m 16.2 (5.00) SF: 19/34/8/31/19/26/9/8/-/-/-/-/-
WEIGHT FOR AGE 3yo-9lb

1457 STAR H'CAP (0-65) (3-Y.O+) (Class F) £2,519.00 (£694.00: £329.00)
7f (Fibresand) Stalls: Low GOING minus 0.03 sec per fur (STD) 3-40 (3-43)

*1088*3 **Flashfeet (53)***(53) (KBishop)* 5-9-8 JWilliams(6) (outpcd & bhd: hdwy & 3rd st: rdn & edged rt over 1f out: led ins fnl f: r.o)........— 1

1323[10] Pacific Spirit **(45)***(42) (MTate)* 5-8-11 (3) DWright(11) (outpcd & bhd: gd hdwy 3f out: 8th st: r.o ins fnl f)....1½ **2**
830[3] Speedy Snaps Pride **(41)***(37) (PDCundell)* 3-8-0 RPrice(10) (outpcd & bhd: hdwy & 5th st: nt clr run over 1f out: r.o)....nk **3**
1218[6] Grey Again **(57)***(52) (SRBowring)* 3-8-11b(5) CTeague(7) (s.i.s: outpcd & bhd: hdwy & 6th st: nt clr run over 1f out: nt rcvr)....½ **4**
1209[3] My Gallery (IRE) **(50)***(41)*(Fav)*(ABailey)* 4-9-5b MWigham(12) (chsd ldr: led 4f out: edgd rt over 1f out: hdd & unable qckn ins fnl f)....1¾ **5**
1033[7] Arawa **(36)***(24) (DMarks)* 5-8-5e GDuffield(4) (prom: drvn along 4f out: 7th st: nvr able to chal)....1¼ **6**
701[14] Fyne Song **(42)***(30) (WJMusson)* 3-8-1 GHind(9) (mid div: rdn 4f out: 4th st: btn over 1f out)s.h **7**
1081[7] Brigadore Gold **(26)** *(FHLee)* 5-7-9b NCarlisle(2) (led 3f: 2nd & wkng st)....6 **8**
1088[12] La Residence **(47)***(19) (MrsNMacauley)* 4-8-13 (3) SSanders(3) (chsd ldrs: drvn along over 3f out: wknd over 2f out)....¾ **9**
358[4] Soba Guest (IRE) **(46)***(18) (RTJuckes)* 6-9-1 TIves(5) (prom: drvn along 4f out: wknd wl over 2f out)....hd **10**
992[11] Desiderata **(55)***(11) (BWHills)* 4-9-10 MHills(8) (chsd ldrs: drvn along ½-wy: wknd over 2f out)....7 **11**
1209[6] Bex Hill **(54)** *(DHaydnJones)* 3-8-13 PaulEddery(1) (sn outpcd & bhd)....5 **12**

3/1 My Gallery (IRE) (op 5/1), **7/2** Desiderata (5/2-4/1), **6/1** Grey Again, **7/1** FLASHFEET (5/1-15/2), **8/1** Speedy Snaps Pride, **10/1** Bex Hill, **14/1** Brigadore Gold, **16/1** Fyne Song, Pacific Spirit, **20/1** Arawa, La Residence, **33/1** Soba Guest (IRE), CSF £102.95 CT £842.06 TOTE £7.30: £2.10 £3.90 £2.30 (£81.80) Trio £258.70 OWNER Mr P. D. Purdy (BRIDGWATER) BRED Littleton Stud 12 Rn
1m 31.7 (7.70) SF: 17/6/-/6/5/-/-/-/-/-/-/-
WEIGHT FOR AGE 3yo-10lb

1458 LION (S) STKS (3-Y.O+) (Class G) £2,243.00 (£618.00: £293.00)
1m 1f 79y (Fibresand) Stalls: Low GOING minus 0.03 sec per fur (STD) 4-10 (4-12)

1291[3] **Reported (IRE) (80)***(78)*(Fav)*(BPreece)* 6-9-11 WRyan(4) (chsd ldrs: 2nd st: led over 1f out: all out)....— **1**
Katy's Lad **(55)***(73) (BAMcMahon)* 8-9-3b(3) SSanders(6) (lw: prom: led 6f out: hdd over 1f out: sn hrd rdn: r.o)....s.h **2**
1087[4] Mezzoramio *(54) (KAMorgan)* 3-8-8 PaulEddery(3) (b: led over 1f: 3rd & rdn st: sn wknd)....11 **3**
1074[8] Turrill House *(34) (WJMusson)* 3-8-0 (3) DRMcCabe(7) (sn outpcd & bhd: poor 6th st: n.d)......9 **4**
1087[7] Medland (IRE) **(52)***(27) (BJMcMath)* 5-9-11 VSmith(5) (led 8f out: hdd 6f out: rdn over 3f out: 4th & wkng st)....10 **5**
596[6] Lady Kuynder *(6) (DrJDScargill)* 3-8-0 (3) DWright(8) (prom: drvn along over 4f out: grad wknd: poor 5th st)....6 **6**
1285[14] Gamzatti **(26)** *(CBBBooth)* 4-9-1 MTebbutt(2) (t.o fnl 7f)....4 **7**
Albeit **(36)** *(MFBarraclough)* 5-9-1 JWilliams(1) (sn outpcd & bhd: t.o)....13 **8**

4/9 REPORTED (IRE), **5/1** Mezzoramio, **11/2** Katy's Lad, **12/1** Medland (IRE) (op 8/1), **20/1** Lady Kuynder, **25/1** Turrill House, Albeit, **33/1** Gamzatti, CSF £4.25 TOTE £1.50: £1.10 £1.10 £1.70 (£3.10) OWNER Mr M. Ephgrave (TELFORD) BRED John Byrne 8 Rn
2m 2.8 (6.80) SF: 48/43/12/-/-/-/-/-
WEIGHT FOR AGE 3yo-12lb
No bid.

1459 CLOWN H'CAP (0-65) (3-Y.O+) (Class F) £3,322.10 (£993.80: £476.40: £217.70)
1m 100y (Fibresand) Stalls: Low GOING minus 0.03 sec per fur (STD) 4-40 (4-42)

1320[2] **Dia Georgy (47)***(51) (RGuest)* 4-8-13 GHind(8) (chsd ldrs: led over 2f out: all out)....— **1**
1194[8] Equity's Darling (IRE) **(58)***(62) (MBell)* 3-8-13 GDuffield(9) (hld up: hdwy over 4f out: 3rd st: ev ch ins fnl f: r.o)....s.h **2**
1034[2] Wellsy Lad (USA) **(37)***(39) (DWChapman)* 8-8-0 (3)ow1 DRMcCabe(6) (lw: hld up: hdwy over 3f out: r.o)....½ **3**
1368[11] Studio Thirty **(48)***(35) (RHollinshead)* 3-7-10 (7)ow5 AEddery(11) (outpcd & bhd: hdwy over 1f out: nrst fin)....6 **4**
1290[12] Mr Moriarty (IRE) **(31)***(21) (SRBowring)* 4-7-11 ClaireBalding(7) (prom: outpcd over 2f out: 6th st: no imp)....¾ **5**
1034[16] Exclusive Assembly **(56)***(45) (APJames)* 3-8-11 FNorton(2) (chsd ldrs: 2nd st: wknd over 1f out)....¾ **6**
*1209**** Ayunli **(58)***(34)*(Fav)*(SCWilliams)* 4-9-7 (3) 6x DWright(1) (lw: trckd ldrs: rdn over 3f out: 7th & btn st)....7 **7**
1286[4] Course Fishing **(42)***(17) (BAMcMahon)* 4-8-8 GCarter(10) (led 6f: 5th & wkng st)....½ **8**
1292[11] Brackenthwaite **(62)***(32) (LRLloyd-James)* 5-9-7 (7) KimberleyHart(4) (b.hind: a outpcd & bhd)2½ **9**

1285[23] Merseyside Man **(42)** *(DrJDScargill)* 9-8-1v(7)ow10 CDomergue(3) (sn outpcd & bhd) 8 **10**
1324[9] Radio Caroline **(31)** *(MTate)* 7-7-4 (7)ow4 SLanigan(5) (bit bkwd: s.i.s: outpcd fr ½-wy) 20 **11**

LONG HANDICAP Radio Caroline 7-0

5/4 Ayunli, **7/2** DIA GEORGY (5/2-4/1), **7/1** Wellsy Lad (USA), **8/1** Course Fishing, **10/1** Equity's Darling (IRE), Exclusive Assembly, **14/1** Brackenthwaite, **20/1** Mr Moriarty (IRE), **33/1** Studio Thirty, Merseyside Man, **50/1** Radio Caroline, CSF £37.97 CT £221.99 TOTE £6.00: £2.20 £2.70 £1.10 (£26.60) Trio £37.70 OWNER Mrs Deborah Crowley (NEWMARKET) BRED Stuart Powell 11 Rn

1m 51.8 (7.80) SF: 21/21/9/-/-/4/4/-/2/-/-

WEIGHT FOR AGE 3yo-11lb

T/Plpt: £27.30 (292.23 Tckts). T/Qdpt: £25.90 (1.2 Tckts). CR

1436-AYR (L-H)
Saturday June 3rd (Good to firm)

WEATHER: overcast, showers WIND: slt half bhd

1460 E.B.F. OCHILTREE MAIDEN STKS (2-Y.O) (Class D) £4,065.00 (£1,230.00: £600.00: £285.00) 5f Stalls: High GOING minus 0.11 sec per fur (G) 2-25 (2-26)

Zalotti (IRE) *(83+) (TJEtherington)* 2-8-9 KDarley(1) (w'like: str: scope: mde all: shkn up & r.o wl appr fnl f) ....— **1**
1247[4] Mask Flower (USA) *(73) (MJohnston)* 2-8-9 DHolland(6) (lw: chsd wnr: effrt 1½f out: nt pce to chal) 3 **2**
1176[3] Elmswood (USA) *(72) (PWChapple-Hyam)* 2-8-2 (7) RHavlin(3) (lw: hld up: effrt & outpcd ½-wy: styd on wl fnl f) ....nk **3**
1041[3] Laurel Crown (IRE) *(72) (JBerry)* 2-8-7 (7) PRoberts(5) (squeezed out & lost pl after 1f: hdwy over 1f out: nvr able to chal) 1¾ **4**
1307[2] Marjorie Rose (IRE) *(51)*(Fav)*(ABailey)* 2-8-9 MWigham(2) (lw: trckd ldrs tl rdn & wknd over 1f out) 5 **5**
Termon *(41) (MissLAPerratt)* 2-8-9 NConnorton(4) (neat: scope: bit bkwd: s.i.s: a outpcd & bhd) 3 **6**

15/8 Marjorie Rose (IRE), **5/2** Mask Flower (USA) (7/4-11/4), **4/1** ZALOTTI (IRE), **5/1** Elmswood (USA) (op 3/1), **40/1** Laurel Crown (IRE), **100/1** Termon, CSF £12.41 TOTE £5.60: £2.70 £1.40 (£7.10) OWNER Mr P. D. Savill (MALTON) BRED Peter Savill 6 Rn

60.74 secs (3.74) SF: 37/27/26/26/5/-

1461 KILWINNING H'CAP (0-70) (3-Y.O+) (Class E) £2,983.00 (£904.00: £442.00: £211.00) 5f Stalls: High GOING minus 0.11 sec per fur (G) 2-55 (2-56)

1271[3] **Rich Glow (50)***(53) (NBycroft)* 4-8-12 KDarley(7) (in tch: hdwy over 1f out: r.o to ld post).....— **1**
1304[6] Croft Imperial **(63)***(66) (MJohnston)* 8-9-11 DHolland(10) (chsd ldrs: rdn to ld ins fnl f: edgd lft: hrd rdn & jst ct)............s.h **2**
1441[4] Ned's Bonanza **(66)***(64) (MDods)* 6-10-0 MWigham(5) (hld up: hdwy over 1f out: nt qckn wl ins fnl f) 1½ **3**
1441[7] Diet **(46)***(41) (MissLAPerratt)* 9-8-8v NConnorton(1) (prom: outpcd fr 2f out: kpt on towards fin)............1 **4**
1271[4] Tenor **(64)***(59)*(Fav)*(DNicholls)* 4-9-12 PRobinson(4) (lw: trckd ldrs: effrt over 1f out: hrd rdn & nt qckn)............hd **5**
1342* Super Rocky **(60)***(54) (RBastiman)* 6-9-3 (5) HBastiman(3) (cl up: led ½-wy tl ins fnl f: no ex) .hd **6**
1304[12] Serious Hurry **(50)***(37) (RMMcKellar)* 7-8-5 (7)ow3 NKinnon(6) (led to ½-wy: grad wknd).........1¼ **7**
1157[14] Mister Westsound **(46)***(35) (MissLAPerratt)* 3-8-0 DaleGibson(2) (outpcd & bhd: hdwy over 1f out: n.m.r & no imp)............nk **8**
1450[6] Sunday Mail Too (IRE) **(45)***(32) (MissLAPerratt)* 3-7-13 NKennedy(8) (s.i.s: nvr wnt pce).......¾ **9**

7/2 Tenor, **4/1** RICH GLOW, **9/2** Super Rocky, **5/1** Croft Imperial, **11/2** Ned's Bonanza, **20/1** Diet, **25/1** Serious Hurry, Mister Westsound, **33/1** Sunday Mail Too (IRE), CSF £20.86 CT £84.23 TOTE £3.10: £1.10 £1.50 £2.50 (£7.40) Trio £6.20 OWNER Mr M. J. Bateson (BRANDSBY) BRED P. Young 9 Rn

60.37 secs (3.37) SF: 46/59/57/34/52/47/30/20/17

WEIGHT FOR AGE 3yo-8lb

1462 HIGH SPEED PRODUCTION H'CAP (0-85) (3-Y.O+) (Class D) £4,065.00 (£1,230.00: £600.00: £285.00) 1m 5f 13y Stalls: Low GOING minus 0.11 sec per fur (G) 3-25 (3-25)

1310[3] **Highbrook (USA) (72)***(80)*(Fav)*(MHTompkins)* 7-9-3 PRobinson(3) (lw: hld up: effrt 2f out: led ins fnl f: r.o) ....— **1**

1205² Latvian **(68)***(75) (RAllan)* 8-8-13 AMackay(2) (prom: effrt 3f out: swtchd over 1f out: r.o towards fin) 1¼ **2**
1359³ Hit the Canvas (USA) **(66)***(72) (MrsMReveley)* 4-8-11b KDarley(4) (lw: led 2f: cl up: chal ent st: sn rdn: nt qckn ins fnl f) ....nk **3**
1102⁷ George Dillingham **(83)***(89) (DenysSmith)* 5-10-0 DHolland(1) (led after 2f: qcknd appr st: hdd & no ex ins fnl f) ....hd **4**

7/4 HIGHBROOK (USA), **3/1** Latvian, Hit the Canvas (USA) (2/1-10/1), **4/1** George Dillingham, CSF £6.36 TOTE £2.30 (£3.30) OWNER Mr Nick Cook (NEWMARKET) BRED Larry Stewart in USA 4 Rn 2m 53.31 (8.51) SF: 39/34/31/48

1463

KILBIRNIE CLAIMING STKS (3-Y.O) (Class E) £3,009.00 (£912.00: £446.00: £213.00)
1m 2f Stalls: Low GOING minus 0.11 sec per fur (G) 3-55 (3-59)

1325² **What's the Verdict (IRE) (75)***(73)*(Fav)*(MJohnston)* 3-9-7 PRobinson(2) (mde all: put hd in air & kpt on wl fnl 3f) ....— **1**
1207⁸ Simand **(45)***(50) (EWeymes)* 3-8-8 KDarley(6) (a chsng wnr: rdn 3f out: one pce) 6 **2**
880³ Mudlark **(55)***(51) (JWWatts)* 3-8-11b NConnorton(3) (a chsng ldrs: effrt over 3f out: nt r.o) 1½ **3**
1026⁵ Kindred Greeting **(41)***(43) (DMorris)* 3-8-7b DHolland(4) (bhd: sme hdwy 2f out: nvr trbld ldrs) 2½ **4**
Salduba *(24) (TDyer)* 3-8-1 (5) CTeague(5) (nvr trbld ldrs) 11 **5**
965¹⁰ Lancaster Bomber *(18) (DMoffatt)* 3-8-1 (3) DarrenMoffatt(1) (prom tl outpcd ent st) 2½ **6**

6/4 WHAT'S THE VERDICT (IRE), **9/4** Mudlark, **3/1** Simand, **20/1** Kindred Greeting, Lancaster Bomber, **50/1** Salduba, CSF £5.77 TOTE £1.90: £1.80 £1.70 (£3.30) OWNER Mr R. W. Huggins (MIDDLEHAM) BRED Islanmore Stud 6 Rn 2m 12.19 (7.59) SF: 42/19/20/12/-/-

1464

LOGANSWELL MAIDEN STKS (3-Y.O+) (Class D) £3,680.00 (£1,115.00: £545.00: £260.00)
1m Stalls: Low GOING minus 0.11 sec per fur (G) 4-25 (4-38)

1150⁴ **Silvicolous (USA) (82)***(83)*(Fav)*(PWChapple-Hyam)* 3-8-3 (7) RHavlin(3) (cl up: slt ld 3f out: r.o) ....— **1**
1216² Verde Luna *(75)*(Fav)*(MHTompkins)* 3-8-10 PRobinson(2) (chsd ldrs: styd on fnl 2f: nt pce to chal) 4 **2**
1150⁵ Diamond Crown (USA) *(70) (BHanbury)* 3-8-10 KDarley(6) (lw: led: hung bdly rt appr st: hdd 3f out: grad wknd fnl 2f) 2½ **3**
1270⁸ Homecrest *(50) (MrsAMNaughton)* 3-8-10 AMercer(5) (chsd ldrs: no imp fnl 3f) 10 **4**
Pipers Glen **(55)***(32) (CParker)* 3-8-10 SDWilliams(1) (outpcd appr st: n.d after) 9 **5**
Kirkie Cross *(RMMcKellar)* 3-8-5 AMackay(4) (leggy: bkwd: s.s: a t.o) ....dist **6**
990¹² Daytime Dawn (IRE) *(DMoffatt)* 4-9-7 DHolland(7) (Withdrawn not under Starter's orders: unruly s: uns rdr & bolted twice) .... **W**

7/4 SILVICOLOUS (USA) (6/4-9/4), Verde Luna (5/4-2/1), **5/2** Diamond Crown (USA), **33/1** Homecrest, Kirkie Cross, Daytime Dawn (IRE), **50/1** Pipers Glen, CSF £4.84 TOTE £2.20: £1.50 £1.60 (£2.30) OWNER Mr R. E. Sangster (MARLBOROUGH) BRED Swettenham Stud and Partners 6 Rn 1m 40.75 (3.95) SF: 42/34/29/9/-/-/-
WEIGHT FOR AGE 3yo-11lb

1465

NORRIS AND KAREN WEDDING CELEBRATION H'CAP (0-70) (3-Y.O) (Class E) £3,165.00 (£960.00: £470.00: £225.00)
7f Stalls: Low GOING minus 0.11 sec per fur (G) 4-55 (5-02)

613⁸ **Nordic Breeze (IRE) (60)***(71) (ABailey)* 3-9-7 MWigham(6) (lw: hld up: shkn up ent st: qcknd to ld ins fnl f: r.o) ....— **1**
1377² Flyaway Blues **(52)***(60)*(Fav)*(MrsMReveley)* 3-8-13b KDarley(8) (s.i.s: hdwy 2f out: r.o towards fin) 1¼ **2**
1423* Celebration Cake (IRE) **(62)***(67) (MissLAPerratt)* 3-9-9 6x NConnorton(4) (trckd ldrs: led over 1f out: hdd & no ex ins fnl f) 1¼ **3**
1180¹³ Three Arch Bridge **(56)***(57) (MJohnston)* 3-9-3b DHolland(10) (chsd ldrs: slt ld 2f out: hdd over 1f out: one pce) 2 **4**
1423³ Champagne N Dreams **(58)***(58) (DNicholls)* 3-8-12 (7) SCopp(3) (hld up: hdwy on ins to chal 2f out: rdn & nt qckn appr fnl f) ....nk **5**
1153* Rushen Raider **(58)***(58) (KWHogg)* 3-9-5 PRobinson(2) (chsd ldrs: outpcd over 2f out: no imp after) ....s.h **6**
1060⁶ Malzoom **(32)***(23) (SEKettlewell)* 3-7-7 NKennedy(5) (prom tl wknd fnl 2f) 4 **7**

1294[4] Trumble **(52)***(40) (CWThornton)* 3-8-13 AMackay(11) (prom tl outpcd fnl 2½f) 1¼ 8
990[11] Leap Year Baby (IRE) **(34)***(19) (MDHammond)* 3-7-9bow2 DaleGibson(1) (led tl hdd & wknd 2f out) ....nk 9
904[11] Tannerrun (IRE) **(60)***(44) (JBerry)* 3-9-0e(7) PRoberts(7) (plld hrd: cl up tl wknd wl over 1f out) 1¼ 10
1423[5] Fishy Affair **(45)***(21) (TDyer)* 3-8-1 (5) CTeague(12) (stdd s: a bhd) 3½ 11
LONG HANDICAP Leap Year Baby (IRE) 7-0 Malzoom 7-5

5/2 Flyaway Blues, **11/4** Champagne N Dreams, **5/1** NORDIC BREEZE (IRE) (op 8/1), **9/1** Rushen Raider, **10/1** Three Arch Bridge, Celebration Cake (IRE) (op 5/1), Trumble, **14/1** Malzoom (12/1-20/1), **16/1** Fishy Affair, **25/1** Tannerrun (IRE), **33/1** Leap Year Baby (IRE), CSF £18.53 CT £117.19 TOTE £20.20: £4.00 £1.20 £5.60 (£35.10) Trio £118.20 OWNER Mr Malcolm Jones (TARPORLEY) BRED P. F. N. Fanning 11 Rn

1m 28.97 (4.97) SF: 37/26/33/23/24/24/-/6/-/10/-

T/Plpt: £60.50 (123.57 Tckts). T/Qdpt: £11.90 (8.15 Tckts). AA

1448-CATTERICK (L-H)
Saturday June 3rd (Good, Good to Soft patches)
WEATHER: overcast WIND: slt across

1466 BEDALE (S) STKS (2-Y.O) (Class G) £2,602.00 (£722.00: £346.00)
5f 212y Stalls: Low GOING: 0.24 sec per fur (G) 2-15 (2-16)

*1333** **Lila Pedigo (IRE)** *(62)*(Fav)*(JBerry)* 2-8-12 JCarroll(8) (mde all: styd on u.p fnl 2f: all out) ....— 1
1177[5] Catwalk Girl *(55) (SGNorton)* 2-8-6 KFallon(6) (a chsng ldrs: hrd rdn & styd on fnl f) ....½ 2
1082[5] Sovitaka (IRE) *(48) (MHEasterby)* 2-8-6 DeanMcKeown(9) (cl up tl lost pl ½-wy: hdwy 2f out: kpt on u.p) 2½ 3
1176[9] Mels Baby (IRE) *(52) (JLEyre)* 2-8-11 RLappin(4) (chsd ldrs: kpt on one pce fnl 2f) ....nk 4
Kratz (IRE) *(50) (BSRothwell)* 2-8-6 (5) JStack(2) (neat: unf: dwlt: bhd tl styd on fnl 2f) 1 5
770[4] Brogans Brush *(45) (CWFairhurst)* 2-8-11 JFanning(5) (sn outpcd & drvn along: n.d) 1¾ 6
1369[5] Maygain (IRE) *(43) (MRChannon)* 2-8-6 (5) PPMurphy(1) (in tch: effrt over 2f out: sn wknd & eased) ....½ 7
1031[6] Canlubang *(20) (MJCamacho)* 2-8-6v LCharnock(3) (sn chsng ldrs: wknd 2f out) 7 8
Ticka Ticka Timing *(BWMurray)* 2-8-4 (7) GParkin(7) (small: s.i.s: sn wl bhd: t.o ½-wy) 11 9

5/4 LILA PEDIGO (IRE), **9/2** Sovitaka (IRE), **5/1** Maygain (IRE), **11/2** Catwalk Girl, **9/1** Mels Baby (IRE), **11/1** Kratz (IRE), **12/1** Brogans Brush, Canlubang, **16/1** Ticka Ticka Timing, CSF £10.30 TOTE £1.80: £1.30 £1.80 £1.90 (£7.00) Trio £21.60 OWNER Mr J. Nixon (COCKERHAM) BRED Miss Corona O'Brien 9 Rn 1m 16.7 (6.20) SF: 30/23/16/20/18/13/11/-/-

No bid.

1467 GAINFORD MEDIAN AUCTION MAIDEN STKS (3-Y.O) (Class E) £3,054.00 (£912.00: £436.00: £198.00)
7f Stalls: High GOING: 0.24 sec per fur (G) 2-45 (2-46)

853[11] **Mister Rm (69)***(71) (RGuest)* 3-9-0 KFallon(3) (hld up: effrt over 2f out: r.o u.p to ld ins fnl f: drvn out) ....— 1
924[5] Dr Caligari (IRE) **(74)***(68) (JBerry)* 3-9-0 JCarroll(5) (trckd ldr: led 2f out tl ins fnl f: nt qckn) 1½ 2
Boldina Bay **(78)***(51)*(Fav)*(MJohnston)* 3-8-9 DeanMcKeown(1) (sn drvn along: rdn & lost pl over 3f out: wandered u.p: no imp) 5 3
783[7] Faith 'n Glory (IRE) **(70)***(47) (RHannon)* 3-8-9 SWhitworth(4) (led to 2f out: wknd over 1f out) 2 4
1296[12] Donna Fugata (IRE) *(1) (CBBBooth)* 3-8-9 ACulhane(2) (trckd ldrs tl lost pl ½-wy: sn bhd)...20 5

Evens Boldina Bay, **3/1** Faith 'n Glory (IRE), **7/2** Dr Caligari (IRE), **9/1** MISTER RM, **33/1** Donna Fugata (IRE), CSF £34.95 TOTE £12.00: £3.50 £ 1.30 (£25.10) OWNER R.M. Partnership Architectural Consultan (NEWMARKET) BRED Major and Mrs R. B. Kennard 5 Rn

1m 29.9 (6.70) SF: 38/35/18/14/-

1468 ROTHMANS ROYALS NORTH SOUTH CHALLENGE SERIES H'CAP (0-85) (3-Y.O+) (Class D) £4,503.00 (£1,344.00: £642.00: £291.00)
7f Stalls: Low GOING: 0.24 sec per fur (G) 3-15 (3-18)

1061[6] **Karinska (54)***(62) (MCChapman)* 5-7-11 (7) CMunday(12) (s.i.s: bhd & drvn along: hdwy ½-wy: styd on wl to ld towards fin) ....— 1
1079[2] Willshe Gan **(49)***(55) (DenysSmith)* 5-7-13 JQuinn(2) (lw: trckd ldrs gng wl: led over 2f out: sn clr: hdd nr fin) 1 2

1179[8] Celestial Choir **(76)**_(78) (JLEyre)_ 5-9-12 RLappin(1) (bhd: hdwy & n.m.r over 1f out: styd on wl towards fin)....1¾ 3
1179[9] Hi Nod **(78)**_(75) (MJCamacho)_ 5-10-0 LCharnock(7) (s.i.s: bhd & pushed along: hdwy ½-wy: effrt 2f out: kpt on same pce)....2 4
1292[9] Master Ofthe House **(61)**_(57) (MDHammond)_ 9-8-11 JMarshall(3) (hld up: hdwy 2f out: styd on towards fin)....½ 5
_378_[13] Phase One (IRE) **(51)**_(43) (JLEyre)_ 5-8-1 ow1 TGMcLaughlin(5) (swtg: hld up & bhd: sme hdwy 2f out: nvr nr ldrs)....1½ 6
1323[9] Mbulwa **(53)**_(45) (SEKettlewell)_ 9-8-3bow1 JCarroll(6) (chsd ldrs: effrt & bmpd 2f out: sn outpcd)....s.h 7
1344[11] Awesome Venture **(51)**_(40) (MCChapman)_ 5-8-1 JFanning(4) (led tl over 2f out: sn lost pl) ..1½ 8
1174[12] King Rat (IRE) **(70)**_(56) (TJEtherington)_ 4-9-1 (5) JStack(11) (chsd ldrs tl wknd 2f out)....1½ 9
1338[2] Knobbleeneeze **(74)**_(59)_(Fav)_(MRChannon)_ 5-9-5v(5) PPMurphy(10) (chsd ldrs: effrt & hung rt 2f out: sn btn)....hd 10
Cumbrian Waltzer **(77)**_(56) (MHEasterby)_ 10-9-13 DeanMcKeown(9) (hld up: bhd fr ½-wy).....3 11

3/1 Knobbleeneeze, **5/1** Celestial Choir, Willshe Gan, **11/2** Hi Nod (4/1-6/1), **10/1** KARINSKA, Mbulwa, **12/1** King Rat (IRE), **14/1** Cumbrian Waltzer, **16/1** Master Ofthe House, **20/1** Awesome Venture, Phase One (IRE), CSF £56.56 CT £255.99 TOTE £13.90: £3.20 £1.60 £1.60 (£25.20) Trio £47.30 OWNER Mr Geoff Whiting (MARKET RASEN) BRED Sheikh Mohammed bin Rashid al Maktoum 11 Rn 1m 28.5 (5.30) SF: 39/32/55/52/34/20/22/17/33/36/33

1469 YORKSHIRE-TYNE TEES TELEVISION LIMITED STKS (0-60) (3-Y.O+) (Class F) £2,966.00 (£826.00: £398.00)

7f Stalls: Low GOING: 0.24 sec per fur (G) 3-45 (3-47)

1414[12] **Russian Heroine (58)**_(62) (MJohnston)_ 3-8-6 TWilliams(6) (chsd ldrs: led over 1f out: styd on u.p)....— 1
1274[6] Polly Garter **(60)**_(56) (RHannon)_ 3-8-6 SWhitworth(3) (s.i.s: hdwy ½-wy: hrd rdn: styd on appr fnl f: nt rch wnr)....2½ 2
1207[5] Legal Issue (IRE) **(58)**_(58)_(Fav)_(SirMarkPrescott)_ 3-8-11 KFallon(9) (lw: trckd ldrs: ev ch & rdn 2f out: nt qckn)....1½ 3
1297[4] Johnnie the Joker **(55)**_(54) (JPLeigh)_ 4-9-7b DeanMcKeown(10) (trckd ldr: led 3f out tl over 1f out: one pce)....1¾ 4
_767_[8] Second Colours (USA) **(59)**_(48) (MrsMReveley)_ 5-9-9 LCharnock(7) (lw: hld up & bhd: hdwy ½-wy: effrt 2f out: wknd over 1f out)....3½ 5
_1087_[2] Tyrone Flyer **(55)**_(43) (GFierro)_ 6-9-2 (5) RPainter(4) (led to 3f out: wknd over 1f out)....1¼ 6
_354_[9] Dauntless Fort **(50)**_(27) (MrsVAAconley)_ 4-8-11 (5) JStack(5) (chsd ldrs tl wknd over 2f out).....5 7
1180[2] Pc's Cruiser (IRE) **(56)**_(30) (MCChapman)_ 3-8-8b(7) CMunday(8) (s.i.s: bhd & drvn along: sme hdwy 2f out: n.d)....2½ 8
1291[12] Kenilworth Ford **(34)**_(3) (FJO'Mahony)_ 4-9-2 JFanning(11) (prom early: sn bhd)....8 9
746[11] Rennyholme **(20)**_(6) (MWEllerby)_ 4-9-7 SMorris(12) (prom early: sn bhd)....½ 10
1153[2] Dante's Rubicon (IRE) **(47)**_(5) (JDBethell)_ 4-9-7 JCarroll(2) (chsd ldrs tl hung rt & lost pl over 2f out)....¾ 11

7/4 Legal Issue (IRE), **11/2** Polly Garter, Pc's Cruiser (IRE), **13/2** Johnnie the Joker, **8/1** RUSSIAN HEROINE, Tyrone Flyer, Second Colours (USA), **12/1** Dante's Rubicon (IRE), **33/1** Dauntless Fort, Kenilworth Ford, **66/1** Rennyholme, CSF £51.92 TOTE £11.10: £2.50 £2.20 £1.60 (£19.40) Trio £10.90 OWNER The Knavesmire Partnership (MIDDLEHAM) BRED D. R. Botterill 11 Rn 1m 29.6 (6.40) SF: 34/28/30/36/30/25/9/2/-/-/-
WEIGHT FOR AGE 3yo-10lb

1470 WILLIAM EDWIN NEESHAM MEMORIAL H'CAP (0-70) (4-Y.O+) (Class E) £3,184.00 (£952.00: £456.00: £208.00)

1m 7f 177y Stalls: Low GOING: 0.24 sec per fur (G) 4-15 (4-16)

1328* **Snow Dream (41)**_(57) (MJRyan)_ 5-7-8 (5) MBaird(6) (chsd ldrs: pushed along 6f out: led over 1f out: wnt rt: drvn out)....— 1
1310* Moshaajir (USA) **(74)**_(89) (CSmith)_ 5-9-13 (5) JStack(4) (hld up: stdy hdwy 5f out: ev ch & rdn 2f out: styd on towards fin)....1½ 2
1295[9] Northern Kingdom (USA) **(43)**_(56) (SGNorton)_ 6-8-1 JFanning(3) (led tl over 1f out: kpt on u.p)....1½ 3
737[4] Memorable **(43)**_(47) (JHetherton)_ 4-8-0 TWilliams(5) (chsd ldr: reminders 8f out: sn hrd drvn: lost pl over 3f out: n.d after)....9 4
_1086_[2] Jaraab **(46)**_(49) (GLewis)_ 4-8-3v SWhitworth(1) (hld up: stdy hdwy 5f out: effrt over 3f out: edgd rt u.p & wknd 2f out)....1 5
866* Mizyan (IRE) **(63)**_(61)_(Fav)_(JEBanks)_ 7-9-7 JQuinn(2) (hld up: drvn along & lost pl 7f out: bhd fnl 5f)....5 6

9/4 Mizyan (IRE), **7/2** Moshaajir (USA), Jaraab, **5/1** SNOW DREAM, **13/2** Memorable, **10/1** Northern Kingdom (USA), CSF £21.20 TOTE £4.70: £1.60 £2.70 (£8.10) OWNER Mr P. E. Axon (NEWMARKET) BRED Stud-On-The-Chart 6 Rn 3m 39.4 (18.40) SF: 8/40/7/-/-/12

WEIGHT FOR AGE 4yo-1lb

1471 ALDBROUGH RATING RELATED MAIDEN LIMITED STKS (0-60) (3-Y.O+) (Class F) £2,966.00 (£826.00: £398.00)

5f 212y Stalls: High GOING: 0.24 sec per fur (G) 4-45 (4-46)

1216[4] **Penny's Wishing (58)***(69) (JPLeigh)* 3-8-6 DeanMcKeown(5) (mde all: styd on u.p fnl 2f) ...— 1
1302[3] Mousehole **(63)***(67) (RGuest)* 3-8-11 JCarroll(1) (s.i.s: bhd & drvn along: c wd ent st: sn hrd drvn: kpt on fnl f) 2½ 2
758[8] Ligurian (USA) **(60)***(62) (JWWatts)* 3-8-6b KFallon(3) (chsd ldrs: drvn along over 3f out: styd on same pce appr fnl f) ....nk 3
746[2] Nite-Owl Dancer **(58)***(56) (JAHarris)* 3-8-6 JO'Reilly(7) (lw: chsd ldrs tl wknd over 1f out) 2 4
1180[4] Bollin Frank **(56)***(56)*(Fav)*(MHEasterby)* 3-8-11b LCharnock(6) (chsd ldrs: rdn 3f out: wknd over 1f out) 2 5
1157[16] Quick Thinker (IRE) **(49)***(37) (WSCunningham)* 3-8-11b RPrice(2) (b: chsd ldrs: rdn over 3f out: sn lost pl) 7 6
867[16] Biased View **(42)***(2) (RThompson)* 3-8-6 (5) JStack(4) (sn outpcd: rdn & swvd lft 3f out: sn wl bhd) 13 7

2/1 Bollin Frank (op 7/2), **11/4** Mousehole, **5/1** PENNY'S WISHING, Ligurian (USA), Nite-Owl Dancer, **16/1** Quick Thinker (IRE), **33/1** Biased View, CSF £18.89 TOTE £7.60: £2.00 £2.50 (£6.90) OWNER Mr K. Pennington (GAINSBOROUGH) BRED Clive Tomkins 7 Rn

1m 17.2 (6.70) SF: 17/15/10/4/4/-/-

T/Plpt: £143.60 (50.13 Tckts). T/Qdpt: £10.40 (6 Tckts). WG

1311-KEMPTON (R-H)
Saturday June 3rd (Good)

WEATHER: overcast WIND: almost nil

1472 AMBITION APPRENTICE H'CAP (0-75) (3-Y.O+) (Class E) £3,598.75 (£1,090.00: £532.50: £253.75) 1m (Jub) Stalls: High GOING minus 0.16 sec (GF) 6-30 (6-32)

1250[8] **Sooty Tern (63)***(73) (JMBradley)* 8-9-11 SDrowne(5) (mde all: clr 1f out: r.o wl) ....— 1
1097[22] Bellas Gate Boy **(62)***(66) (GLewis)* 3-8-13 AWhelan(16) (lw: 3rd st: chsd wnr over 1f out: unable qckn) 3 2
1323[13] Lady Lacey **(48)***(49) (GBBalding)* 8-8-5v(5) IonaWands(6) (rdn over 2f out: hdwy over 1f out: r.o) 1½ 3
1202[5] Runic Symbol **(42)***(37) (MBlanshard)* 4-7-13 (5)ow1 RWaterfield(4) (hld up: rdn over 2f out: one pce) 2½ 4
1426[11] Oozlem (IRE) **(42)***(38) (RMFlower)* 6-8-4b JDSmith(13) (s.s: rdn over 4f out: hdwy over 1f out: r.o wl ins fnl f) ....s.h 5
1286[6] All the Joys **(43)***(36) (CACyzer)* 4-8-5 PMcCabe(11) (2nd st: hrd rdn over 2f out: wknd fnl f) 1¼ 6
975[4] Roi de la Mer (IRE) **(63)***(54)*(Fav)*(JAkehurst)* 4-9-11 AProcter(14) (4th st: wknd over 1f out) 1¼ 7
882[11] King Parrot (IRE) **(50)***(39) (LordHuntingdon)* 7-8-7 (5) JWilkinson(7) (lw: 6th st: rdn over 2f out: wknd fnl f) ....¾ 8
885[5] Anna-Jane **(65)***(53) (RHannon)* 3-8-11 (5) DaneO'Neill(15) (lw: a mid div) ....¾ 9
1126[18] Nabjelsedr **(50)***(36) (AGNewcombe)* 5-8-12 SMulvey(3) (b.hind: nvr nrr) ....¾ 10
1202[9] Peter Rowley **(58)***(43) (RHannon)* 4-9-3 (3) MarkDenaro(8) (lw: nvr nrr) ....¾ 11
988[14] Ivanhoe **(32)***(15) (JRArnold)* 4-7-3 (5)ow1 SLanigan(2) (prom over 4f) ....nk 12
1165[8] Water Hazard (IRE) **(48)***(29) (SDow)* 3-7-8 (5)ow1 ADaly(9) (bhd fnl 3f) 1 13
321[12] Malingerer **(32)***(11) (DAWilson)* 4-7-3 (5)ow1 MartinDwyer(1) (bhd fnl 3f) 1 14
738[21] Ripsnorter (IRE) **(54)***(29) (JABennett)* 6-9-2 NVarley(10) (b.off hind: lw: s.s: hdwy over 3f out: wknd over 2f out) 2½ 15
1225[11] Folly Finnesse **(60)***(32) (BRMillman)* 4-9-5 (3) DGibbs(12) (3rd st: wknd over 2f out) 1¾ 16

LONG HANDICAP Malingerer 7-3 Ivanhoe 7-1

3/1 Roi de la Mer (IRE) (5/1-8/1), **5/1** Anna-Jane, **7/1** Runic Symbol (op 4/1), **8/1** Bellas Gate Boy, **9/1** Lady Lacey, SOOTY TERN (6/1-10/1), **11/1** All the Joys (8/1-12/1), **12/1** King Parrot (IRE) (8/1-14/1), **14/1** Oozlem (IRE) (8/1-16/1), **16/1** Ripsnorter (IRE), Peter Rowley, Folly Finnesse, **20/1** Nabjelsedr, Water Hazard (IRE), **33/1** Malingerer, Ivanhoe, CSF £83.06 CT £634.07 TOTE £9.40: £2.40 £2.20 £1.90 £2.00 (£28.10) Trio £85.10 OWNER Mr J. M. Bradley (CHEPSTOW) BRED Sheikh Mohammed bin Rashid al Maktoum 16 Rn

1m 40.64 (3.64) SF: 58/40/34/22/23/21/39/24/27/21/28/-/3/-/14/17

WEIGHT FOR AGE 3yo-11lb

1473

KEMPTON EXHIBITION CENTRE MAIDEN STKS (3-Y.O F) (Class D)
£3,753.00 (£1,134.00: £552.00: £261.00)
1m 1f (round) Stalls: Low GOING minus 0.16 sec per fur (GF) 7-00 (7-03)

9575 **Vena (IRE) (81)***(87) (JLDunlop)* 3-8-11 WCarson(11) (3rd st: hrd rdn over 1f out: led wl ins fnl f: r.o wl) — **1**
11722 Hagwah (USA) **(79)***(87)*(Fav)*(BHanbury)* 3-8-11 WRyan(6) (led 7f out: hrd rdn over 1f out: hdd wl ins fnl f: r.o) nk **2**
Rosy Hue (IRE) *(81) (RCharlton)* 3-8-11 JWeaver(4) (lw: 6th st: rdn over 2f out: r.o one pce) 3 **3**
11366 Latching (IRE) **(82)***(78) (RFJohnsonHoughton)* 3-8-11 JReid(7) (lw: 4th st: rdn over 2f out: one pce) 2 **4**
9162 Niggle *(75) (HThomsonJones)* 3-8-11 PaulEddery(12) (lw: 5th st: hrd rdn over 1f out: one pce) 1¼ **5**
Shining Dancer *(72) (MRStoute)* 3-8-11 WRSwinburn(2) (7th st: rdn 2f out: one pce) 2 **6**
11369 Red Morning *(68) (DRCElsworth)* 3-8-11 MRoberts(8) (lw: nvr nr to chal) 2 **7**
112810 Nightscene (IRE) *(68) (TGMills)* 3-8-11 JWilliams(3) (plld hrd: nvr nrr) nk **8**
Spread The Word *(61) (LGCottrell)* 3-8-11 MFenton(9) (unf: scope: lw: a bhd) 4 **9**
Rockusa *(41) (LadyHerries)* 3-8-11 WNewnes(10) (lw: a bhd) 11 **10**
95710 Vezelay (USA) *(25) (JHMGosden)* 3-8-11 LDettori(1) (led 2f: 2nd st: wknd over 2f out) 9 **11**
Cahita *(11) (TJNaughton)* 3-8-11 StephenDavies(5) (neat: a bhd) 8 **12**

11/8 Hagwah (USA), **4/1** Latching (IRE), **11/2** VENA (IRE) (4/1-6/1), **10/1** Rosy Hue (IRE) (op 6/1), **11/1** Shining Dancer (7/1-12/1), **12/1** Niggle, Red Morning, Vezelay (USA) (op 4/1), **20/1** Rockusa, **33/1** Nightscene (IRE), **50/1** Spread The Word, Cahita, CSF £13.92 TOTE £7.20: £1.50 £1.30 £4.10 (£5.90) Trio £42.80 OWNER Skyline Racing Ltd (ARUNDEL) BRED J. Throsby 12 Rn
1m 53.82 (3.82) SF: 48/48/42/39/36/33/29/29/22/2/-/-

1474

CHANNEL ONE H'CAP (0-90) (3-Y.O) (Class C) £5,784.00
(£1,752.00: £856.00: £408.00)
7f (round) Stalls: High GOING minus 0.16 sec per fur (GF) 7-30 (7-32)

12226 **Chattaroy (IRE) (83)***(91) (JHMGosden)* 3-9-0 LDettori(1) (swtg: hdwy on ins over 2f out: led over 1f out: r.o wl) — **1**
9804 Dance Band (USA) **(90)***(94)*(Fav)*(BHanbury)* 3-9-7 JReid(7) (swtg: 3rd st: rdn over 1f out: unable qckn) 1¾ **2**
12224 Christmas Kiss **(82)***(81) (RHannon)* 3-8-13 WRSwinburn(2) (5th st: rdn over 2f out: one pce) .2 **3**
9306 Warning Shot **(83)***(82) (MartynMeade)* 3-9-0 VSlattery(8) (4th st: rdn over 2f out: nt clr run over 1f out: one pce) hd **4**
10007 Anam **(80)***(76) (PTWalwyn)* 3-8-11 WCarson(10) (lw: nvr plcd to chal) 1½ **5**
116512 Nordic Doll (IRE) **(75)***(66) (BWHills)* 3-8-6 MHills(12) (lw: 6th st: rdn & n.m.r 2f out: wknd fnl f) 2 **6**
Melasus (IRE) **(79)***(69) (DWPArbuthnot)* 3-8-10 TQuinn(4) (b: lw: led over 5f) ½ **7**
7753 Pengamon **(90)***(78) (HJCollingridge)* 3-9-7 MRimmer(3) (2nd st: ev ch over 1f out: sn wknd) ..1 **8**
Bon Luck (IRE) **(70)***(58) (RAkehurst)* 3-7-12 (3) SSanders(5) (w'like: lw: a bhd) s.h **9**
11865 Desert Harvest **(80)***(63) (RCharlton)* 3-8-11 JWeaver(9) (lw: s.s: a bhd) 2 **10**
12634 Sylvandra **(79)***(61) (PGMurphy)* 3-8-10 JWilliams(6) (bhd fnl 3f) ½ **11**

4/1 Dance Band (USA), **5/1** Desert Harvest (7/2-11/2), **7/1** Christmas Kiss (5/1-15/2), **15/2** Nordic Doll (IRE), **9/1** Bon Luck (IRE) (5/1-10/1), CHATTAROY (IRE), Pengamon, Sylvandra, **11/1** Melasus (IRE), **12/1** Anam, **25/1** Warning Shot, CSF £42.86 CT £247.93 TOTE £10.50: £3.10 £1.70 £2.50 (£19.00) Trio £20.30 OWNER Sheikh Mohammed (NEWMARKET) BRED Sheikh Mohammed bin Rashid al Maktoum 11 Rn 1m 25.92 (1.42) SF: 68/71/58/59/53/43/46/55/35/40/38

1475

RING & BRYMER ACHILLES STKS (Listed) (3-Y.O+) (Class A)
£11,394.00 (£4,266.00: £2,088.00: £900.00: £405.00: £207.00)
5f Stalls: High GOING minus 0.16 sec per fur (GF) 8-00 (8-03)

12202 **Ya Malak (100)***(107) (JWPayne)* 4-9-2 BThomson(10) (lw: chsd ldr: led 1f out: rdn out) — **1**
9212 Eveningperformance **(108)***(100)*(Fav)*(HCandy)* 4-9-1 WNewnes(8) (led 4f: unable qckn) 2 **2**
10196 Royale Figurine (IRE) **(93)***(95) (MJFetherston-Godley)* 4-8-11 WRSwinburn(6) (lw: hld up: rdn over 2f out: r.o ins fnl f) hd **3**
Easy Option (IRE) *(99) (SbinSuroor)* 3-8-7 LDettori(7) (lw: a.p: rdn over 1f out: r.o one pce) hd **4**
11389 Hinton Rock (IRE) **(99)***(87) (MBell)* 3-8-8 MFenton(5) (lw: nvr nr to chal) 4 **5**
Loch Patrick **(101)***(83) (LJHolt)* 5-9-2 AMcGlone(3) (outpcd: nvr nrr) 1¼ **6**
952* Warning Star **(108)***(77) (BWHills)* 3-8-3 MHills(4) (outpcd) nk **7**

1055[3] Crystal Magic **(92)***(73) (RHannon)* 4-8-11b JReid(1) (lw: bhd fnl 2f) 1¼ 8
665[21] Hello Mister **(100)***(67) (JO'Donoghue)* 4-9-2 PMcCabe(2) (a bhd) 3½ 9
921[14] Windmachine (SWE) *(34) (RHarris)* 4-9-1 JWeaver(9) (b: lw: bhd fnl 2f) 10 10

13/8 Eveningperformance (11/10-7/4), **9/4** Easy Option (IRE), **11/2** Warning Star (op 7/2), **12/1** Loch Patrick (7/1-14/1), **16/1** Royale Figurine (IRE), YA MALAK, **25/1** Hinton Rock (IRE), Crystal Magic, **33/1** Hello Mister, Windmachine (SWE), CSF £40.31 TOTE £17.90: £2.20 £1.30 £2.50 (£12.10) Trio £90.00 OWNER Mr G. Jabre (NEWMARKET) BRED Mrs R. B. Kennard 10 Rn

58.87 secs (1.07) SF: 90/83/78/74/62/66/52/56/50/17

WEIGHT FOR AGE 3yo-8lb

1476 WATERLOO MAIDEN STKS (3-Y.O) (Class D) £3,928.50 (£1,188.00: £579.00: £274.50) 7f (Jubilee) Stalls: High GOING minus 0.16 sec per fur (GF) 8-30 (8-34)

987[5] **Amrak Ajeeb (IRE) (78)***(85)*(Fav)*(BHanbury)* 3-9-0 MRimmer(4) (b: lw: 3rd st: hrd rdn over 1f out: led ins fnl f: r.o wl) ....— 1
Supreme Thought *(72) (LGCottrell)* 3-8-9 MFenton(6) (led tl ins fnl f: unable qckn) 3½ 2
Direct Dial (USA) *(61) (JARToller)* 3-9-0 WNewnes(17) (leggy: rdn 4f out: hdwy & n.m.r on ins over 1f out: r.o) 7 3
1240[4] Makri **(70)***(56) (MrsJCecil)* 3-8-9 PaulEddery(9) (2nd st: wknd over 1f out) ....s.h 4
Cutpurse Moll *(56) (JRFanshawe)* 3-8-4 (5) NVarley(2) (bit bkwd: 5th st: wknd over 2f out) ....hd 5
937[7] With Intent *(57) (CJames)* 3-9-0 AMcGlone(12) (lw: nvr nr to chal) 1¾ 6
Never Explain (IRE) **(86)***(51)*(Fav)*(JLDunlop)* 3-8-9 WCarson(11) (bit bkwd: nvr nrr) ....nk 7
1136[16] Twice Purple (IRE) *(56) (BJMeehan)* 3-9-0 BDoyle(13) (lost pl over 4f out: one pce fnl 2f) ....hd 8
Another Batchworth *(51) (SMellor)* 3-8-2 (7) ADaly(5) (a mid div) ....hd 9
585[10] Jovie King (IRE) *(54) (PMitchell)* 3-9-0 SO'Gorman(15) (bhd fnl 5f) ....¾ 10
1168[8] Roka *(48) (RHannon)* 3-8-9 JReid(7) (lw: 6th st: wknd over 2f out) ....nk 11
Crown of Love (USA) *(48) (MRStoute)* 3-8-9 WRSwinburn(1) (b.nr hind: bhd fnl 2f) ....hd 12
Jameel Asmar *(51) (CREgerton)* 3-9-0 CRutter(3) (bit bkwd: a bhd) 1 13
Last Ambition (IRE) *(43) (CREgerton)* 3-8-9 BThomson(14) (b.off fore: unf: 4th st: wknd over 2f out) 1 14
1136[18] Petra's Star *(39) (MJHeaton-Ellis)* 3-8-9 StephenDavies(10) (a bhd) 1¾ 15

7/2 AMRAK AJEEB (IRE), Never Explain (IRE), **4/1** Makri, **6/1** Crown of Love (USA) (3/1-13/2), **14/1** Cutpurse Moll (8/1-16/1), Supreme Thought, Roka (op 8/1), **16/1** Jameel Asmar, **20/1** Direct Dial (USA), Petra's Star, **25/1** Last Ambition (IRE), **50/1** Jovie King (IRE), Another Batchworth, With Intent, Twice Purple (IRE), CSF £48.51 TOTE £7.70: £2.40 £3.90 £4.70 (£32.20) Trio £304.50 OWNER Mr A. Merza (NEWMARKET) BRED Ovidstown Investments Ltd 15 Rn

1m 26.55 (2.35) SF: 61/48/37/32/32/33/27/32/27/30/24/24/27/19/15

1477 BLACKBIRD H'CAP (0-80) (3-Y.O+) (Class D) £3,714.00 (£1,122.00: £546.00: £258.00) 1m 4f Stalls: High GOING minus 0.16 sec per fur (GF) 9-00 (9-02)

1194[4] **Crespo (IRE) (73)***(85+)*(Fav)*(JRFanshawe)* 3-8-9 LDettori(6) (lw: 2nd st: led 2f out: r.o wl) ..— 1
884[2] Mr Browning (USA) **(58)***(68) (RAkehurst)* 4-8-10b TQuinn(7) (led 10f: unable qckn) 1½ 2
1141[8] The French Friar (IRE) **(74)***(82) (GBBalding)* 4-9-12 MWigham(10) (lw: 3rd st: rdn over 2f out: one pce) 1½ 3
1260[5] Dormy Three **(71)***(77) (RJHodges)* 5-9-9 JWilliams(1) (hdwy over 1f out: r.o) 1¾ 4
430[3] Teen Jay **(74)***(78) (SESherwood)* 5-9-12 MFenton(8) (lw: rdn over 3f out: hdwy over 1f out: r.o one pce) 1½ 5
623[8] Pembridge Place **(76)***(75) (JLDunlop)* 4-10-0 WCarson(5) (b.nr fore: lw: bdly hmpd on ins over 4f out: 6th st: eased whn btn over 1f out) 3½ 6
1245* Trade Wind **(73)***(70) (DRCElsworth)* 4-9-6b(5) AProcter(4) (lw: 4th st: wknd over 2f out) 1¼ 7
668[20] Dusty Point (IRE) **(66)***(63) (JPearce)* 5-9-4 GBardwell(2) (a bhd) ....nk 8
1014[8] Bag of Tricks (IRE) **(56)***(48) (SDow)* 5-8-8 MRoberts(9) (hdwy 6f out: 5th st: wknd over 2f out) 4 9
771[5] Risky Tu **(52)** *(PAKelleway)* 4-7-11 (7) AdelleGibbons(3) (lw: hdwy 9f out: wknd over 3f out: t.o) ....dist 10

100/30 CRESPO (IRE), **7/2** Mr Browning (USA), Pembridge Place, **8/1** The French Friar (IRE), **9/1** Trade Wind (6/1-10/1), **12/1** Bag of Tricks (IRE) (6/1-14/1), **14/1** Teen Jay, **20/1** Dormy Three, **25/1** Dusty Point (IRE), Risky Tu, CSF £14.36 CT £74.67 TOTE £5.00: £1.90 £2.00 £2.70 (£6.80) Trio £39.20 OWNER Sheikh Mohammed (NEWMARKET) BRED Darley Stud Management Co Ltd 10 Rn

2m 34.73 (4.53) SF: 51/50/64/59/60/57/52/45/30/-

WEIGHT FOR AGE 3yo-16lb

T/Plpt: £46.60 (356.37 Tckts). T/Qdpt: £37.30 (1.95 Tckts). AK

1317-LINGFIELD (L-H)
Saturday June 3rd (Good)
WEATHER: raining WIND: almost nil

1478 BET WITH THE TOTE H'CAP (0-100) (3-Y.O) (Class C) £5,900.00 (£1,760.00: £840.00: £380.00)
1m 2f Stalls: Low GOING minus 0.38 sec per fur (F) 2-00 (2-00)

941² **At Liberty (IRE) (82)***(86) (RHannon)* 3-8-10 RPerham(3) (hdwy & 3rd st: led ins fnl f: all out)..........— 1
1322* Grand Selection (IRE) **(72)***(76) (MBell)* 3-8-0 MFenton(6) (2nd tl led over 2f out: hdd ins fnl f: r.o)..........s.h 2
930⁵ Pearl Venture **(93)***(83) (SPCWoods)* 3-9-7 TQuinn(2) (hdwy & 5th st: one pce fnl 2f)..........9 3
1141⁵ Okavango (USA) **(84)***(70) (JHMGosden)* 3-8-12v GHind(1) (lw: led tl wknd over 2f out)..........2½ 4
962² Mihriz (IRE) **(84)***(65) (MajorWRHern)* 3-8-12 TSprake(8) (4th st: wknd 3f out)..........3 5
1306² Sue's Return **(88)***(58) (APJarvis)* 3-9-2 MRoberts(5) (8th st: a bhd)..........7 6
1085* United Front **(80)***(26)*(Fav)*(HRACecil)* 3-8-8 AMcGlone(4) (prom tl wknd & 6th st: t.o)..........15 7
1038* Sahil (IRE) **(85)***(25) (DMorley)* 3-8-13 GBardwell(7) (prom tl wknd & 7th st: t.o)..........3½ 8

11/4 United Front, **5/1** Grand Selection (IRE), Mihriz (IRE), **6/1** Sahil (IRE) (op 4/1), **7/1** AT LIBERTY (IRE), **10/1** Sue's Return (op 6/1), Okavango (USA), **16/1** Pearl Venture, CSF £36.91 CT £464.59 TOTE £9.80: £2.10 £1.70 £3.60 (£16.70) OWNER Mr Bruce Adams (MARLBOROUGH) BRED Pegasus Farm 8 Rn 2m 7.56 (4.56) SF: 27/17/24/11/6/-/-/-

1479 TOTE BOOKMAKERS CONDITIONS STKS (4-Y.O+) (Class B) £8,037.45 (£2,896.20: £1,388.10: £565.50: £222.75)
1m 3f 106y Stalls: Low GOING minus 0.38 sec per fur (F) 2-30 (2-30)

750² **Waiting (100)***(109) (PFICole)* 4-8-11 TQuinn(5) (lw: 4th st: led over 1f out: r.o wl)..........— 1
1135² Marsoom (CAN) **(99)***(111) (BHanbury)* 4-9-1 MRimmer(2) (2nd tl led over 5f out: hdd over 1f out: r.o)..........1¾ 2
1132⁷ Golden Ball (IRE) **(105)***(103)*(Fav)*(MRStoute)* 4-8-12 WCarson(3) (3rd st: nt clr run over 2f out: swtchd rt over 1f out: nt qckn)..........3½ 3
1056² English Invader *(97) (RAkehurst)* 4-9-3 RPerham(4) (2nd st: wknd over 2f out)..........8 4
1171⁶ Nawar (FR) *(84) (JRJenkins)* 5-8-13 MRoberts(1) (led tl wknd over 5f out: 5th st)..........6 5

5/4 Golden Ball (IRE) (op Evens), **13/8** Marsoom (CAN), **5/1** WAITING, **10/1** English Invader, **66/1** Nawar (FR), CSF £12.74 TOTE £5.70: £2.00 £1.70 (£6.10) OWNER Prince Fahd Salman (WHATCOMBE) BRED Newgate Stud Co 5 Rn 2m 28.02 (6.02) SF: 23/25/17/11/-

1480 TOTE CREDIT LEISURE STKS (Listed) (3-Y.O+) (Class A) £14,184.00 (£5,256.00: £2,528.00: £1,040.00: £420.00: £172.00)
6f Stalls: Centre GOING minus 0.38 sec per fur (F) 3-00 (3-01)

1100⁴ **Roger the Butler (IRE) (99)***(111) (MBell)* 5-9-0 MFenton(8) (mde virtually all: r.o wl)..........— 1
Fard (IRE) **(117)***(118) (DMorley)* 3-9-1 WCarson(9) (a.p: ev ch 1f out: r.o)..........1¼ 2
1284³ Cool Jazz **(100)***(107) (CEBrittain)* 4-9-0 MRoberts(2) (racd alone far side: ev ch fnl 2f: r.o)....hd 3
1138³ Overbrook **(97)***(86) (IABalding)* 3-8-0 SO'Gorman(7) (prom tl wknd fnl f)..........6 4
1100³ Master Planner **(102)***(87) (CACyzer)* 6-9-0 DBiggs(5) (rdn along: nvr nr to chal)..........1½ 5
1393a⁷ Bunty Boo **(105)***(80) (RHannon)* 6-8-9 RPerham(6) (gd spd over 4f)..........¾ 6
921⁷ Wavian **(104)***(72)*(Fav)*(RCharlton)* 3-8-5 TQuinn(3) (lw: rdn & sme hdwy over 3f out: wknd 2f out)..........5 7
883* Shamanic **(105)***(71) (RHannon)* 3-8-5 GHind(4) (in tch tl wknd over 2f out)..........nk 8
1227* Al Rawda (FR) **(95)***(26) (HRACecil)* 3-8-0 AMcGlone(1) (a bhd: t.o)..........15 9

9/2 Wavian, **5/1** Fard (IRE), **11/2** Al Rawda (FR), **6/1** ROGER THE BUTLER (IRE), **7/1** Bunty Boo, **8/1** Master Planner, Cool Jazz, **9/1** Overbrook, **11/1** Shamanic (8/1-12/1), CSF £33.73 TOTE £7.40: £2.00 £2.30 £1.70 (£17.00) Trio £68.10 OWNER Mr M. B. Hawtin (NEWMARKET) BRED Gaberson Ltd in Ireland 9 Rn 69.81 secs (0.81) SF: 54/52/50/20/30/23/6/5/-
WEIGHT FOR AGE 3yo-9lb

1481 SMUGGLERS MAIDEN AUCTION STKS (2-Y.O) (Class D) £3,682.05 (£1,100.40: £526.70: £239.85)
5f Stalls: Centre GOING minus 0.38 sec per fur (F) 3-30 (3-34)

1278² **Capture The Moment** *(78)*(Fav)*(RJRWilliams)* 2-7-13 DBiggs(10) (mde virtually all stands' side: all out)..........— 1

Essentialselection *(82) (WJHaggas)* 2-8-5 MRoberts(3) (w'like: scope: racd far side: hdwy over 1f out: swtchd lft & r.o ins fnl f) ....½ 2
Rowlandsons Charm (IRE) *(69) (GLMoore)* 2-7-10 FNorton(1) (scope: racd far side: a.p: nt qckn ins fnl f) 1½ 3
1253[5] Secret Pleasure (IRE) *(72) (RHannon)* 2-8-0 AMcGlone(4) (racd far side: a.p: nt qckn fnl f) ....s.h 4
1288[2] Ivory's Grab Hire *(72) (KTIvory)* 2-8-2 GBardwell(2) (racd far side: w ldrs tl wknd ins fnl f) ....¾ 5
1123[7] Meranti *(74) (LJHolt)* 2-8-5 MFenton(6) (racd far side: gd spd 4f) ....nk 6
1327[W] Ben'a'vachei Boy *(62) (JDBethell)* 2-8-4 WCarson(8) (racd stands' side: w wnr tl wknd fnl f) 3½ 7
1123[8] Jemsilverthorn (IRE) *(55) (JJBridger)* 2-8-0 (3) SSanders(9) (racd stands' side: spd 3f) 2 8
1054[6] Nina From Pasadena *(47) (CJames)* 2-7-12 ow1 CRutter(11) (racd stands' side: a bhd) ....½ 9
Reclaimed *(34) (JSMoore)* 2-7-6 (5) NVarley(7) (scope: racd stands' side: a bhd) 4 10
Dragonjoy *(7) (LJHolt)* 2-8-2 CAvery(5) (bkwd: s.s: a t.o) 10 11

13/8 CAPTURE THE MOMENT (5/4-2/1), **11/4** Ben'a'vachei Boy (4/1-5/2), **4/1** Secret Pleasure (IRE) (3/1-9/2), **9/1** Essentialselection (6/1-10/1), **12/1** Ivory's Grab Hire (8/1-14/1), **16/1** Nina From Pasadena, **25/1** Rowlandsons Charm (IRE), Meranti, **33/1** Reclaimed, **50/1** Dragonjoy, **66/1** Jemsilverthorn (IRE), CSF £16.69 TOTE £2.40: £1.30 £2.70 £2.10 (£12.20) Trio £172.00 OWNER The Really Keen Partnership (NEWMARKET) BRED Terry Minahan 11 Rn
58.87 secs (1.87) SF: 19/23/10/13/13/15/3/-/-/-/-

1482 FERRENDONS CONDITIONS STKS (4-Y.O+) (Class C) £5,013.20 (£1,803.20: £861.60: £348.00: £134.00)
7f 140y Stalls: Centre GOING minus 0.38 sec per fur (F) 4-00 (4-01)

1080[2] **Cyrano's Lad (IRE)** *(90) (JohnBerry)* 6-8-10 CDwyer(2) (w ldr: led over 2f out: all out) ....— 1
897a[6] Girl From Ipanema **(104)***(90)*(Fav)*(PFICole)* 4-8-11 TQuinn(5) (hld up: hdwy over 2f out: ev ch & hrd rdn fnl f: r.o) ....nk 2
666[6] Jafeica (IRE) **(96)***(95) (RHannon)* 4-9-7 MRoberts(3) (a.p: ev ch over 1f out: nt qckn) 2½ 3
Reprehend **(100)***(86) (RHannon)* 4-8-11 (7) DaneO'Neill(1) (led tl wknd over 2f out) 3 4
1100* Venture Capitalist **(105)***(90) (DNicholls)* 6-9-12 AlexGreaves(4) (plld hrd: ev ch over 2f out: sn wknd) 1¾ 5

6/5 Girl From Ipanema (Evens-5/4), **3/1** Jafeica (IRE), **10/3** Venture Capitalist, **15/2** Reprehend (6/1-9/1), **33/1** CYRANO'S LAD (IRE), CSF £68.22 TOTE £17.80: £2.20 £1.60 (£13.70) OWNER Mr M. M. Foulger (NEWMARKET) BRED J. C. Condon 5 Rn 1m 31.75 (3.75) SF: 20/20/25/16/20

1483 MEDWAY H'CAP (0-70) (3-Y.O+) (Class E) £3,588.20 (£1,073.60: £514.80: £235.40) 6f
Stalls: Centre GOING minus 0.38 sec per fur (F) 4-30 (4-32)

1071[5] **La Petite Fusee (64)***(72) (RJO'Sullivan)* 4-9-9 StephenDavies(11) (mde all: r.o wl) ....— 1
1016[4] Dashing Dancer (IRE) **(55)***(58) (RAkehurst)* 4-9-0 TQuinn(12) (trckd wnr: ev ch fnl 2f: r.o) 2 2
1265[3] Half Tone **(48)***(46) (RMFlower)* 3-7-12b DBiggs(1) (led far side: ev ch 1f out: nt qckn) 1¾ 3
1050[3] Tharwa (IRE) **(57)***(44)*(Fav)*(NACallaghan)* 3-8-7b MRoberts(9) (a.p: no hdwy fnl 2f) 4 4
1071* Paddy's Rice **(55)***(40) (LJHolt)* 4-9-0 MPerrett(7) (hdwy over 1f out: nvr nrr) ....¾ 5
1199[14] Runs in the Family **(59)***(40) (PGMurphy)* 3-8-9 MFenton(3) (chsd ldr far side tl wknd over 1f out) 1½ 6
1164[8] Top Tycoon (IRE) **(44)***(11) (JJBridger)* 4-8-0 (3)ow6 SSanders(2) (in tch tl wknd 2f out) 3 7
1199[13] Dry Point **(69)***(42) (JARToller)* 9-10-0 MRimmer(6) (hdwy 3f out: wknd over 1f out) ....hd 8
1326[7] Christian Warrior **(40)***(10) (REPeacock)* 6-7-6 (7) CAdamson(10) (spd over 2f) 1¼ 9
1164[2] Harry's Coming **(57)***(19) (RJHodges)* 11-8-11 (5) SDrowne(8) (a bhd) 3 10
1126[13] Astral Invader (IRE) **(68)***(22) (MSSaunders)* 3-9-4 NAdams(5) (in tch tl wknd over 2f out) 3 11
1071[7] Bright Paragon (IRE) **(44)** *(HJCollingridge)* 6-8-3v GBardwell(4) (in tch tl wknd over 2f out) 3 12

4/1 Tharwa (IRE) (5/1-3/1), **9/2** LA PETITE FUSEE, **5/1** Dashing Dancer (IRE) (4/1-6/1), **11/2** Paddy's Rice, **10/1** Half Tone (op 6/1), Harry's Coming, Dry Point, **12/1** Astral Invader (IRE) (8/1-14/1), **16/1** Bright Paragon (IRE), **20/1** Runs in the Family, **33/1** Top Tycoon (IRE), **50/1** Christian Warrior, CSF £25.86 CT £197.25 TOTE £6.40: £2.60 £2.20 £3.20 (£13.50) Trio £58.80 OWNER Skampcargo Racing Partnership (BOGNOR REGIS) BRED H. Powis 12 Rn
1m 10.35 (1.35) SF: 54/40/19/17/22/13/-/24/-/1/-/-
WEIGHT FOR AGE 3yo-9lb

T/Plpt: £191.70 (96 Tckts). T/Qdpt: £24.40 (5.85 Tckts). Hn

1142-NEWMARKET (R-H)
Saturday June 3rd (Good becoming Good to soft)
WEATHER: rain WIND: mod half bhd

1484 SUBARU CELEBRITY H'CAP (0-60) (4-Y.O+) (Class F) £3,517.50 (£1,065.00: £520.00: £247.50)
1m (Rowley) Stalls: Low GOING minus 0.39 sec per fur (F) 2-10 (2-11)

1048[11] **Overpower (50)***(58+) (MHTompkins)* 11-11-4 SSmithEccles(9) (hld up: hdwy over 2f out: led ins fnl f: eased nr fin) — 1
*1329** Aljawab (USA) **(57)***(64)*(Fav)*(JLDunlop)* 4-11-11 BillSmith(10) (lw: a.p: led over 1f out: hdd ins fnl f: unable qckn) nk 2
838[8] Blue Grit **(53)***(60) (MDods)* 9-11-7 SCKnight(7) (trckd ldrs: rdn & ev ch over 1f out: kpt on) hd 3
1378[7] Avishayes (USA) **(45)***(50) (MrsMReveley)* 8-10-13 RJBeggan(5) (hld up: hdwy u.p over 1f out: nt rch ldrs) 1¼ 4
1323[8] Anlace **(48)***(50) (SMellor)* 6-11-2 GThorner(6) (chsd ldrs: outpcd over 2f out: styd on u.p ins fnl f) 1¼ 5
1351[11] Desert Zone (USA) **(57)***(56) (JLHarris)* 6-11-11 CBrown(4) (prom: hrd rdn over 1f out: styd on same pce) 1½ 6
1078[2] Captain Marmalade **(45)***(42) (DTThom)* 6-10-13 JohnnyKingSumHo(8) (lw: prom: sn lost pl: rdn 3f out: styd on ins fnl f: n.d) 1¼ 7
1402[12] Blanchland **(60)***(53) (KTIvory)* 6-12-0 RChampion(2) (lw: chsd ldrs: rdn & ev ch over 2f out: wknd over 1f out) 2 8
1334[4] Letsbeonestaboutit **(51)***(41) (MissGayKelleway)* 9-11-5v HDavies(11) (led over 4f: led over 2f out: hdd & wknd over 1f out) 1¼ 9
909[7] Queens Stroller (IRE) **(57)***(42) (CCElsey)* 4-11-11 PeterScudamore(12) (chsd ldrs: rdn 2f out: sn wknd) 2½ 10
Magication **(42)***(23) (CNAllen)* 5-10-10 WHood(1) (bit bkwd: b: hld up: outpcd fnl 2f) 2 11
874[7] Kissavos **(45)***(26) (CCElsey)* 9-10-13 RStill(3) (chsd ldrs: led over 3f out: hdd over 2f out: sn wknd) nk 12

7/4 Aljawab (USA), **6/1** Queens Stroller (IRE), **7/1** Avishayes (USA), Captain Marmalade, **10/1** OVERPOWER, **11/1** Blue Grit (8/1-12/1), **14/1** Letsbeonestaboutit, **16/1** Anlace, **20/1** Desert Zone (USA), **25/1** Magication, Kissavos, **33/1** Blanchland, CSF £26.70 CT £188.53 TOTE £12.20: £2.50 £1.30 £3.20 (£19.00) Trio £110.40 OWNER Mr M. P. Bowring (NEWMARKET) BRED Barronstown Stud 12 Rn 1m 42.57 (5.57) SF: 40/46/42/32/32/38/24/35/23/24/5/8

1485 E.B.F SUNLEY BUILDS MAIDEN STKS (2-Y.O) (Class D) £4,854.00 (£1,452.00: £696.00: £318.00)
6f (Rowley) Stalls: Low GOING minus 0.39 sec per fur (F) 2-40 (2-41)

1184[5] **Tagula (IRE)** *(88) (IABalding)* 2-9-0 MHills(2) (chsd ldrs: rdn to ld over 1f out: r.o wl) — 1
Tumbleweed Ridge *(75) (BJMeehan)* 2-9-0 PaulEddery(5) (leggy: scope: led: rdn & hdd over 1f out: sn outpcd) 5 2
Modern Day (USA) *(74)*(Fav)*(HRACecil)* 2-9-0 WRyan(4) (gd sort: bhd: drvn along ½-wy: hdwy over 2f out: r.o) hd 3
1134[5] Mawwal (USA) *(65) (RWArmstrong)* 2-9-0 RHills(3) (chsd ldrs: rdn 2f out: wknd appr fnl f) 3½ 4
Lionel Edwards (IRE) *(64) (PFICole)* 2-9-0 JReid(8) (cmpt: bit bkwd: nvr trbld ldrs) nk 5
Shaha *(56) (RHannon)* 2-9-0 WRSwinburn(7) (neat: prom over 3f) 3 6
Resounder (USA) *(54) (JHMGosden)* 2-9-0 LDettori(10) (w'like: scope: hld up: hdwy ½-wy: wknd fnl f) ¾ 7
617[10] The Imps (IRE) *(48) (BWHills)* 2-9-0 BThomson(1) (lw: chsd ldr over 3f: grad lost pl) 2½ 8
Gympie *(38) (JHMGosden)* 2-9-0 TIves(6) (neat: scope: s.i.s: a outpcd) 3½ 9
Dubai College (IRE) *(32) (CEBrittain)* 2-9-0 BDoyle(9) (gd sort: bkwd: outpcd fr ½-wy) 2½ 10

11/4 Modern Day (USA) (2/1-3/1), **3/1** Mawwal (USA), **4/1** Resounder (USA) (op 5/2), **7/1** Tumbleweed Ridge (10/1-6/1), **8/1** Shaha (op 5/1), **14/1** TAGULA (IRE) (12/1-20/1), **20/1** Lionel Edwards (IRE), **25/1** The Imps (IRE), **33/1** Gympie, Dubai College (IRE), CSF £97.32 TOTE £13.90: £3.00 £1.50 £1.50 (£77.00) Trio £63.80 OWNER Robert & Elizabeth Hitchins (KINGSCLERE) BRED Sean and Patrick Twomey 10 Rn 1m 14.02 (2.72) SF: 28/15/14/5/4/-/-/-/-/-

1486 BRADSTOCK HAMILTON MAIDEN STKS (3-Y.O) (Class D) £4,542.00 (£1,356.00: £648.00: £294.00) **1m (Rowley)** Stalls: Low GOING minus 0.39 sec (F) 3-10 (3-13)

1051[2] **Bin Rosie** *(94+) (DRLoder)* 3-8-11 (3) DRMcCabe(5) (chsd ldrs: led over 1f out: edgd lft ins fnl f: r.o wl) — 1

1309[3] Empty Quarter *(84) (JHMGosden)* 3-9-0 WRSwinburn(8) (led over 1f: ev ch over 1f out: sn outpcd)....5 **2**
Bend Wavy (IRE) *(84) (LMCumani)* 3-8-11 (3) CHodgson(6) (w'like: hld up: hdwy 4f out: r.o ins fnl f)....hd **3**
11867 Hugwity *(79) (BHanbury)* 3-9-0 TIves(10) (b: b.hind: hld up in tch: rdn 2f out: r.o one pce)...2½ **4**
1186[4] Marocco (USA) *(74)*(Fav)*(HRACecil)* 3-9-0 WRyan(11) (lw: chsd ldrs: led 4f out: hdd over 1f out: sn btn)....2½ **5**
Top Skipper (IRE) *(73) (BHanbury)* 3-8-11 (3) JTate(3) (hld up: nvr plcd to chal)....½ **6**
Moon Over Awir (IRE) *(65) (LMCumani)* 3-8-2 (7) GMitchell(7) (leggy: scope: nvr nrr)....1¼ **7**
Snow Queen (USA) *(39) (JHMGosden)* 3-8-9 LDettori(1) (w'like: scope: prom 5f)....13 **8**
Dancing Sioux *(44) (RJRWilliams)* 3-9-0 GDuffield(9) (b: bit bkwd: chsd ldrs over 4f)....s.h **9**
1173[8] Starofgreatintent (USA) *(44) (JMPEustace)* 3-9-0 MTebbutt(2) (cmpt: hld up: n.d)....s.h **10**
Sharp Consul (IRE) *(44) (HCandy)* 3-9-0 WNewnes(4) (lw: prom: led over 6f out: hdd 4f out: wknd over 2f out)....s.h **11**
Errant *(42) (JHMGosden)* 3-9-0 RHills(12) (w'like: b.nr fore: s.s: effrt ½-wy: sn lost tch)....1¼ **12**

7/4 Marocco (USA), **100/30** BIN ROSIE, **4/1** Snow Queen (USA) (3/1-9/2), **10/1** Empty Quarter (8/1-14/1), **12/1** Dancing Sioux, **14/1** Hugwity (op 7/1), Errant (op 8/1), **20/1** Moon Over Awir (IRE), **25/1** Bend Wavy (IRE), **33/1** Top Skipper (IRE), **40/1** Starofgreatintent (USA), Sharp Consul (IRE), CSF £35.75 TOTE £3.70: £1.40 £2.50 £7.60 (£20.60) Trio £235.50 OWNER Mr Wafic Said (NEWMARKET) BRED Addison Racing Ltd Inc 12 Rn 1m 39.35 (2.35) SF: 39/29/29/24/19/18/10/-/-/-/-/-

1487 CORAL SPRINT H'CAP (0-105) (3-Y.O) (Class B) £23,490.00 (£7,020.00: £3,360.00: £1,530.00)

6f (Rowley) Stalls: Centre GOING minus 0.19 sec per fur (GF) 3-40 (3-43)

754* **Perryston View (81)***(88)*(Fav)*(PCalver)* 3-8-3v MBirch(14) (chsd ldr: led 3f out: rdn out)....— **1**
1069[3] Bold Effort (FR) **(87)***(93) (KOCunningham-Brown)* 3-8-9 TIves(13) (lw: led: hdd ½-wy: rdn over 1f out: r.o)....½ **2**
985* French Grit (IRE) **(86)***(91) (MDods)* 3-8-8 JWeaver(10) (lw: hld up: hdwy over 1f out: fin wl)..nk **3**
1181[5] Coastal Bluff **(81)***(83) (TDBarron)* 3-8-3 ow2 JFortune(6) (b.hind: hdwy & edgd lft over 1f out: r.o)....½ **4**
850[7] Montserrat **(80)***(80) (LGCottrell)* 3-8-2 NCarlisle(9) (hld up: hdwy over 1f out: r.o: nrst fin)....1¼ **5**
1172[3] Rosebud **(82)***(81) (RHannon)* 3-8-4 MHills(16) (chsd ldrs: rdn 2f out: no imp)....½ **6**
1040* Three Stops (USA) **(80)***(79) (MRStoute)* 3-8-2 WRyan(2) (chsd ldrs: rdn over 1f out: no ex fnl f)....s.h **7**
743* Emerging Market **(94)***(89) (JLDunlop)* 3-9-2 JReid(7) (hld up: hdwy over 1f out: r.o: nvr nrr)....1¼ **8**
1181[4] Bolshoi (IRE) **(71)***(66) (JBerry)* 3-7-0b(7) PFessey(3) (hld up: hdwy over 1f out: nt rch ldrs)....s.h **9**
1305[2] Lennox Lewis **(99)***(94) (APJarvis)* 3-9-7 BThomson(1) (hld up: hdwy 2f out: bmpd over 1f out: nvr able to chal)....nk **10**
1373[2] Welton Arsenal **(98)***(92) (MRChannon)* 3-9-6 RHughes(4) (s.i.s: hld up: rdn over 1f out: no imp)....nk **11**
985[6] Cats Bottom **(73)***(65) (DJSCosgrove)* 3-7-6 (3)ow2 DWright(15) (s.i.s: effrt ½-wy: n.d)....s.h **12**
939[2] Hakiki (IRE) **(87)***(80) (PTWalwyn)* 3-8-9 WRSwinburn(11) (chsd ldrs: rdn 2f out: wknd over 1f out)....hd **13**
1277[4] Tart and a Half **(83)***(72) (BJMeehan)* 3-8-5 BDoyle(8) (chsd ldrs 4f)....1¾ **14**
Elite Hope (USA) **(87)***(74) (CREgerton)* 3-8-9 PaulEddery(12) (prom 4f)....¾ **15**
1094[5] Sue Me (IRE) **(75)***(54) (WRMuir)* 3-7-4 (7)ow4 SLanigan(17) (prom 4f)....1¼ **16**
1069[2] Muchtarak (IRE) **(85)***(50)*(Fav)*(CJBenstead)* 3-8-7 RHills(5) (lw: sn outpcd & bhd)....7 **17**

LONG HANDICAP Cats Bottom 7-6

5/1 PERRYSTON VIEW, Muchtarak (IRE), **6/1** Three Stops (USA), **9/1** Coastal Bluff, Rosebud, **10/1** Lennox Lewis, Welton Arsenal, French Grit (IRE), **14/1** Emerging Market, Hakiki (IRE), **16/1** Bold Effort (FR), Sue Me (IRE), **20/1** Bolshoi (IRE), **25/1** Cats Bottom, Tart and a Half, **40/1** Elite Hope (USA), Montserrat, CSF £82.84 CT £733.97 TOTE £6.70: £2.10 £6.00 £2.30 £2.40 (£127.00) Trio £477.00 OWNER Mrs Janis MacPherson (RIPON) BRED Mrs V. E. Hughes 17 Rn
1m 12.55 (1.25) SF: 54/59/57/49/46/47/45/55/32/60/58/31/46/38/40/20/16

1488 HAMBRO GROUP CHARLOTTE STKS (Listed) (3-Y.O+ F & M) (Class A) £12,452.40 (£4,611.60: £2,215.80: £909.00: £364.50: £146.70)

6f (Rowley) Stalls: Low GOING minus 0.19 sec per fur (GF) 4-15 (4-16)

1138[2] **Baaderah (IRE) (102)***(108) (LMCumani)* 3-8-7 LDettori(10) (lw: prom far side: led 2f out: jst hld on)....— **1**
1393a[6] Branston Abby (IRE) **(108)***(111) (MJohnston)* 6-9-6 JReid(4) (hld up stands' side: hdwy over 1f out: edgd rt fnl f: r.o wl)....nk **2**
659[2] Triple Joy **(98)***(103) (SirMarkPrescott)* 4-9-2 GDuffield(5) (chsd ldrs stands' side: ev ch over 1f out: unable qckn)....1½ **3**

Tanami **(115)**(102)(Fav)(DRLoder) 3-8-7 GCarter(2) (w ldr stands' side: led over 2f out: sn hdd: no ex fnl f)....½ **4**
1305[7] Katya (IRE) **(90)**(97) (MRChannon) 3-8-7 RHughes(8) (prom far side: rdn over 2f out: no imp)2 **5**
921[12] Tajannub (USA) **(104)**(99) (RWArmstrong) 3-8-13 RHills(7) (led far side 4f: wknd fnl f)....1¼ **6**
660[5] With the Fairies **(99)**(89) (RHannon) 3-8-8 ow1 WRSwinburn(9) (chsd ldrs far side 4f)....1½ **7**
1220[4] Crofters Ceilidh **(106)**(79) (BAMcMahon) 3-8-7 JFortune(1) (led stands' side over 3f)....4 **8**
858[5] Croeso-I-Cymru **(94)**(68) (BAMcMahon) 4-9-2 JWeaver(6) (hld up: outpcd fnl 2f)....4 **9**

11/4 Tanami (op 11/8), **3/1** BAADERAH (IRE), **4/1** Branston Abby (IRE), **9/2** Triple Joy, **7/1** With the Fairies, **16/1** Tajannub (USA), **25/1** Crofters Ceilidh, **33/1** Croeso-I-Cymru, **50/1** Katya (IRE), CSF £14.71 TOTE £3.90: £1.50 £1.60 £1.50 (£11.40) Trio £12.30 OWNER Sheikh Ahmed Al Maktoum (NEWMARKET) BRED Sheikh Ahmed bin Rashid al Maktoum 9 Rn

1m 12.64 (1.34) SF: 57/69/61/51/46/48/38/28/26

WEIGHT FOR AGE 3yo-9lb

1489 NGK SPARK PLUGS H'CAP (0-100) (3-Y.O+) (Class C) £5,900.00 (£1,760.00: £840.00: £380.00) 5f (Rowley) Stalls: Low GOING minus 0.19 sec (GF) 4-45 (4-47)

1106[9] **Princess Oberon (IRE) (80)**(87) (MBell) 5-9-1 MHills(10) (led: hdd over 3f out: led over 2f out: r.o wl)....— **1**
Saint Express **(90)**(95) (MrsMReveley) 5-9-11 JFortune(2) (chsd ldrs: outpcd over 1f out: r.o ins fnl f)....¾ **2**
1321[2] Moujeeb (USA) **(65)**(60) (PatMitchell) 5-8-0vow2 BDoyle(6) (bhd: rdn ½-wy: r.o ins fnl f)....2½ **3**
1304[2] Name the Tune **(77)**(72)(Fav)(PHowling) 4-8-12 PaulEddery(3) (b.hind: prom: rdn to chse wnr over 1f out: unable qckn)....½ **4**
Magic Orb **(78)**(73) (JLHarris) 5-8-13 LDettori(5) (s.i.s: bhd: rdn ½-wy: nvr able to chal)....hd **5**
1100[9] Call Me I'm Blue (IRE) **(93)**(87) (NTinkler) 5-10-0 MTebbutt(7) (lw: mid div: rdn over 2f out: nvr able to chal)....hd **6**
1106[14] Insider Trader **(80)**(70) (RJRWilliams) 4-9-1b GDuffield(8) (b: w ldrs: led 3f out: sn hdd: wknd fnl f)....1¼ **7**
1193[3] Total Stranger **(79)**(58) (MrsLPiggott) 3-8-6 WRyan(9) (lw: led over 3f out: sn hdd: eased whn btn fnl f)....3½ **8**
1271[7] Metal Boys **(67)**(45) (MissLCSiddall) 8-7-13 (3) DRMcCabe(1) (racd alone stands' side: a outpcd)....nk **9**
Seigneurial **(90)** (GHarwood) 3-9-3 AClark(4) (lw: unruly stalls: virtually t.n.p)....dist **10**

7/2 Name the Tune, **5/1** Total Stranger, **6/1** PRINCESS OBERON (IRE), **7/1** Moujeeb (USA) (10/1-6/1), **15/2** Call Me I'm Blue (IRE) (6/1-9/1), Metal Boys, **8/1** Insider Trader, **10/1** Seigneurial, Magic Orb, **14/1** Saint Express, CSF £78.86 CT £556.02 TOTE £7.70: £2.70 £4.60 £2.20 (£61.60) Trio £370.30 OWNER Mr R. P. B. Michaelson (NEWMARKET) BRED E. O'Gorman 10 Rn

59.74 secs (1.04) SF: 66/74/39/51/52/66/49/29/24/-

WEIGHT FOR AGE 3yo-8lb

1490 MILTON PARK STUD MAIDEN STKS (3-Y.O) (Class D) £4,425.00 (£1,320.00: £630.00: £285.00) 1m 6f (Rowley) Stalls: High GOING minus 0.19 sec per fur (GF) 5-20 (5-21)

942[2] **Pedraza** (93)(Fav)(HRACecil) 3-9-0 WRyan(2) (chsd ldrs: led 3f out: clr over 1f out: rdn out)....— **1**
657[3] General Assembly (IRE) (92) (HRACecil) 3-9-0 JReid(8) (b.off hind: hld up: nt clr run 3f out: hdwy & swtchd lft 2f out: r.o)....1 **2**
1128[15] Ahla (79) (RWArmstrong) 3-8-9 RHills(9) (chsd ldrs tl rdn & wknd over 1f out)....7 **3**
Crystal Blade (81) (IABalding) 3-9-0 LDettori(4) (chsd ldrs: rdn over 2f out: wknd bel dist)....2½ **4**
1147[3] Eelious (USA) (75) (CEBrittain) 3-9-0 BDoyle(7) (lw: led: hdd 3f out: grad wknd)....5 **5**
1147[8] Opaque (58) (LMCumani) 3-8-11 (3) OUrbina(5) (hld up: rdn 5f out: sn lost tch)....15 **6**
1322[6] Orchidarma **(66)**(55) (RJRWilliams) 3-9-0 GDuffield(1) (hld up: outpcd over 5f out: sn bhd)....3 **7**
1264[7] Dantean (32) (GHarwood) 3-9-0 AClark(3) (lw: s.i.s: hld up: rdn & wknd over 3f out: virtually p.u ins fnl f)....20 **8**
979[7] Northern Law (31) (BWHills) 3-9-0 JWeaver(6) (chsd ldrs: ev ch 3f out: grad wknd)....½ **9**

7/4 PEDRAZA (op Evens), **9/4** General Assembly (IRE), **7/2** Crystal Blade, **13/2** Eelious (USA), **20/1** Northern Law, **33/1** Ahla, Orchidarma, Dantean, Opaque, CSF £6.00 TOTE £2.60: £1.40 £1.10 £5.30 (£2.50) Trio £117.50 OWNER Sheikh Mohammed (NEWMARKET) BRED P. J. and Mrs Sands 9 Rn 3m 1.36 (5.36) SF: 53/52/39/41/35/18/15/-/-

T/Jkpt: Not won; £7,667.61 to Leicester 5/6/95. T/Plpt: £347.00 (101.82 Tckts). T/Qdpt: £49.80 (4.7 Tckts). CR

1157-**HAMILTON (R-H)**

Monday June 5th (Firm, Good to firm patches)

False rail on home turn forcing runners wide in straight
WEATHER: overcast, light rain Race 6 WIND: almost nil

1491

OUDENAARDE H'CAP (0-70) (3-Y.O+) (Class E) £3,758.60 (£1,137.80: £555.40: £264.20)
1m 1f 36y Stalls: High GOING minus 0.48 sec per fur (F) 2-30 (2-31)

1192[10] **Talented Ting (IRE) (60)**_(70) (PCHaslam)_ 6-9-10v JWeaver(2) (mde all: qcknd 3f out: r.o wl fnl f) — 1
1378[2] Essayeffsee **(49)**_(54)_(Fav)_(MrsMReveley)_ 6-8-13 KDarley(5) (lw: b.nr hind: trckd wnr: effrt 3f out: nt qckn fnl f) 3 2
493* Scaraben **(52)**_(55) (SEKettlewell)_ 7-9-2 JCarroll(4) (lw: a.p: rdn 3f out: one pce fnl f) 1¼ 3
1422[6] Amnesia (IRE) **(42)**_(42) (MrsSCBradburne)_ 4-8-6 PRobinson(3) (chsd ldrs tl wknd appr fnl f) 1¾ 4
1323[2] Wentbridge Lad (IRE) **(54)**_(53) (PDEvans)_ 5-9-1v(3) SSanders(1) (hld up: hdwy ½-wy: rdn & btn over 1f out) ½ 5

2/1 Essayeffsee, **9/4** TALENTED TING (IRE), **5/2** Wentbridge Lad (IRE), **8/1** Scaraben (op 4/1), **50/1** Amnesia (IRE), CSF £6.45 TOTE £3.00: £1.50 £1.10 (£3.40) OWNER Mr Martin Wickens (MIDDLEHAM) BRED R. A. Keogh 5 Rn
2m 0.3 SF: 19/3/4/-/2

1492

RAPID RACELINE CONDITIONS STKS (2-Y.O) (Class C) £5,409.43 (£1,751.38: £857.19) **6f 5y** Stalls: Low GOING minus 0.48 sec per fur (F) 3-00 (3-01)

1293[3] **Satellite Star (IRE)** _(84)_(Fav)_(MRChannon)_ 2-8-5 KDarley(3) (disp ld tl led over 2f out: hrd rdn ins fnl f: kpt on wl) — 1
1278[3] Power Game _(88) (JBerry)_ 2-8-10 JCarroll(1) (outpcd after 2f: hdwy u.p to disp ld ins fnl f: no ex towards fin) ½ 2
1158* Red River Valley _(71) (DenysSmith)_ 2-8-12 JWeaver(2) (lw: disp ld over 3f: rdn & btn appr fnl f) 7 3

11/8 SATELLITE STAR (IRE) (Evens-6/4), **6/4** Red River Valley, **11/4** Power Game, CSF £4.52 TOTE £2.40: (£2.30) OWNER Express Newspapers Plc (UPPER LAMBOURN) BRED Rathasker Stud 3 Rn
1m 12.8 (2.80) SF: 10/14/-

1493

HEADLAM FLOORING H'CAP (0-70) (3-Y.O+) (Class E) £2,482.63 (£2,482.63: £563.50: £268.25)
6f 5y Stalls: Low GOING minus 0.48 sec per fur (F) 3-30 (3-32)

1355[6] **Birchwood Sun (54)**_(64) (MDods)_ 5-9-6b JWeaver(4) (sn outpcd & bhd: hdwy 2f out: styd on wl fnl f) — 1
1433[9] **Suedoro (41)**_(51) (RMMcKellar)_ 5-8-0 (7) PFessey(7) (b.off hind: mde most: hrd rdn fnl f: kpt on wl) d.h 1
789[10] Sakharov **(54)**_(64)_(Fav)_(MJohnston)_ 6-9-6 KDarley(5) (chsd ldrs: ev ch ins fnl f: nt qckn nr fin) s.h 3
1461[4] Diet **(46)**_(54) (MissLAPerratt)_ 9-8-12v NConnorton(6) (disp ld tl no ex ins fnl f) ¾ 4
1021[17] Indiahra **(58)**_(58) (RHollinshead)_ 4-9-10 JCarroll(2) (s.i.s: nvr rchd ldrs) 3 5
1023[6] Mu-Arrik **(54)**_(52) (GROldroyd)_ 7-9-6v KFallon(3) (lw: in tch tl rdn & btn appr fnl f) ¾ 6
1342[4] Murray's Mazda (IRE) **(48)**_(44) (JLEyre)_ 6-8-11 (3) SSanders(1) (cl up tl wknd appr fnl f) ¾ 7
Valley of Time (FR) **(30)** _(DANolan)_ 7-7-5 (5)ow3 NVarley(8) (w ldrs over 4f: wknd) 15 8

LONG HANDICAP Valley of Time (FR) 7-5

100/30 Sakharov, **9/2** BIRCHWOOD SUN, Diet, **5/1** Murray's Mazda (IRE), Mu-Arrik, **12/1** Indiahra, SUEDORO, **66/1** Valley of Time (FR), CSF BS,S £22.90 S,BS £28.54 CT BS,S,SA £83.34 S,BS,SA £92.89 TOTE BS £2.90 S £8.70: BS £1.50 S £1.90 £1.70 (£39.10) OWNER Mr A. G. Watson (DARLINGTON)/Mr Ray Vardy (LESMAHAGOW) BRED The Hall Stud Ltd 8 Rn
1m 11.6 (1.60) SF: 40/-/40/30/34/28/20/-

STEWARDS' ENQUIRY Fessey susp. 14/6 & Connorton susp. 14-16/6/95 (using whip above shoulder height).

1494

E.B.F. MANDORA MEDIAN AUCTION MAIDEN STKS (2-Y.O) (Class F) £2,736.00 (£828.00: £404.00: £192.00)
5f 4y Stalls: Low GOING minus 0.48 sec per fur (F) 4-00 (4-04)

1440[3] **Silverdale Knight** _(78+) (KWHogg)_ 2-9-0 JWeaver(2) (lw: mde all: styd on strly appr fnl f) — 1

1082³ Lucky Bea *(62) (MWEasterby)* 2-9-0 KDarley(3) (wnt rt s: sn chsng ldrs: effrt 2f out: no ex fnl f)....5 **2**
Craignairn *(54)*(Fav)*(JBerry)* 2-9-0 JCarroll(1) (leggy: unf: chsd wnr: rdn ½-wy: wknd wl over 1f out)....2½ **3**
Dancing Dot (IRE) *(30) (MissLAPerratt)* 2-8-9 NConnorton(4) (bkwd: unruly s: dwlt: a wl bhd) 6 **4**

Evens Craignairn, **6/4** SILVERDALE KNIGHT, **5/1** Lucky Bea (op 3/1), **33/1** Dancing Dot (IRE), CSF £7.72 TOTE £2.80: (£4.20) OWNER Exors of the late Mr P J White (ISLE OF MAN) BRED Auldyn Stud Ltd 4 Rn 61.5 secs (3.20) SF: 5/-/-/-

1495 RAMILLES RATING RELATED MAIDEN LIMITED STKS (0-65) (3-Y.O) (Class F) £3,028.00 (£742.00) **1m 3f 16y** Stalls: High GOING minus 0.48 sec per fur (F) 4-30 (4-30)

1162² **Sayyed Alraqs (USA) (65)***(69?) (MAJarvis)* 3-9-0 PRobinson(2) (lw: mde all: shkn up & kpt on strly appr fnl f)....— **1**
1150⁶ Cross Talk (IRE) **(65)***(55)*(Fav)*(RHollinshead)* 3-9-0 KDarley(1) (trckd wnr: rdn & wandered bdly over 1f out: sn btn)....10 **2**

8/11 Cross Talk (IRE), **6/5** SAYYED ALRAQS (USA) (Evens-5/4), TOTE £1.60 OWNER Sheikh Ahmed Al Maktoum (NEWMARKET) BRED Audley Farm Inc 2 Rn 2m 23.6 (4.60) SF: 28/14

1496 BLENHEIM H'CAP (0-70) (4-Y.O+) (Class E) £3,741.05 (£1,132.40: £552.70: £262.85) **1m 5f 9y** Stalls: High GOING minus 0.48 sec per fur (F) 5-00 (5-00)

1435² **Lord Advocate (33)***(43)*(Fav)*(DANolan)* 7-7-6b(5) NVarley(5) (lw: mde all: styd on wl fnl 3f)..— **1**
1254¹⁰ Royal Circus **(38)***(46) (JGMO'Shea)* 6-8-2 NConnorton(2) (chsd wnr: one pce fnl 2f)....2 **2**
1359⁶ Chantry Beath **(60)***(61) (CWThornton)* 4-9-10 DeanMcKeown(6) (trckd ldrs: effrt 3f out: nt pce to chal)....5 **3**
1046⁶ Arian Spirit (IRE) **(32)***(30) (JLEyre)* 4-7-7 (3)ow2 DarrenMoffatt(3) (lw: dwlt: sn in tch: outpcd 4f out: no imp after)....1¼ **4**
879¹⁰ Vaigly Sunthyme **(34)***(27) (JMCarr)* 5-7-12 NKennedy(7) (hld up: effrt over 3f out: n.d)....6 **5**
1295⁶ Rasayel (USA) **(51)***(40) (PDEvans)* 5-8-12 (3) SSanders(4) (lw: trckd ldrs: effrt over 3f out: wknd over 2f out)....2½ **6**

7/4 LORD ADVOCATE, **3/1** Rasayel (USA), **9/2** Royal Circus, Chantry Beath, **10/1** Vaigly Sunthyme, **14/1** Arian Spirit (IRE), CSF £9.46 TOTE £1.70: £1.40 £2.00 (£5.30) OWNER Mrs J. McFadyen-Murray (WISHAW) BRED London Thoroughbred Services Ltd 6 Rn
2m 49.0 (3.30) SF: 20/23/38/7/4/17
T/Plpt: £69.00 (108.45 Tckts). T/Qdpt: Not won; £22.00 to Pontefract 6/5/95. AA

1368-LEICESTER (R-H)
Monday June 5th (Good)
WEATHER: overcast WIND: almost nil

1497 E.B.F. WOLVEY MAIDEN STKS (2-Y.O F) (Class D) £4,092.00 (£1,221.00: £583.00: £264.00) **5f 2y** Stalls: High GOING minus 0.20 sec (GF) 2-45 (2-46)

Applaud (USA) *(96+)*(Fav)*(DRLoder)* 2-8-11 LDettori(1) (gd sort: bit bkwd: a.p: led bel dist: edgd rt & qcknd clr fnl f: impressive)....— **1**
1123⁵ Nellie North *(80) (MrsMMcCourt)* 2-8-4 (7) RStudholme(2) (lw: w ldrs: ev ch over 1f out: one pce)....5 **2**
1348⁶ Pacific Grove *(75) (PFICole)* 2-8-11 TQuinn(5) (lw: plld hrd: hld up: rdn ½-wy: kpt on ins fnl f: nvr nrr)....1½ **3**
1169² Watch Me (IRE) *(74)*(Fav)*(RHannon)* 2-8-11 WRSwinburn(8) (led tl wl over 1f out: rdn & one pce fnl f)....½ **4**
1142² Omara (USA) *(71) (HRACecil)* 2-8-11 WRyan(7) (a.p: led wl over 1f out: sn hdd: btn whn n.m.r ent fnl f)....¾ **5**
Priddy Fair *(67) (RBoss)* 2-8-11 GDuffield(3) (leggy: bit bkwd: bhd: rdn 2f out: sn outpcd) ...1½ **6**
Ichor *(41) (HThomsonJones)* 2-8-11 RHills(4) (lt-f: unf: s.s: rdn & effrt ½-wy: no imp: t.o) 8 **7**
925⁸ Poppy My Love *(30) (BJMcMath)* 2-8-11 AMackay(6) (dwlt: sn chsng ldrs: rdn & wknd fr ½-wy: t.o)....3½ **8**

2/1 APPLAUD (USA), Watch Me (IRE), **9/4** Omara (USA), **10/1** Ichor, **25/1** Pacific Grove, **33/1** Priddy Fair, **40/1** Nellie North, **50/1** Poppy My Love, CSF £52.59 TOTE £3.30: £1.10 £4.90 £2.80 (£69.50) OWNER Mr Faisal Salman (NEWMARKET) BRED Claiborne Farm and The Gamely Corporation 8 Rn 62.3 secs (3.80) SF: 15/-/-/-/-/-/-/-

1498

OLD DALBY H'CAP (0-70) (3-Y.O) (Class E) £3,817.00 (£1,144.00: £550.00: £253.00) **1m 1f 218y** Stalls: High GOING minus 0.20 sec per fur (GF) 3-15 (3-16)

1180[6] **Kings Assembly (67)***(74) (PWHarris)* 3-9-7 MFenton(4) (chsd ldrs: 5th st: hrd rdn to ld cl home) — 1
745[7] Wet Patch (IRE) **(55)***(62) (RHannon)* 3-8-9 RHughes(1) (hld up: hdwy 3f out: led over 1f out tl ct nr fin) hd 2
948[7] Tirolette (IRE) **(53)***(57) (RJRWilliams)* 3-8-7 RCochrane(13) (hld up: hdwy over 2f out: rdn & hung rt: r.o fnl f) 1½ 3
1183[14] Battleship Bruce **(66)***(64)*(Fav)*(NACallaghan)* 3-9-6 LDettori(6) (b.hind: hld up: hdwy on ins over 3f out: sn rdn: one pce appr fnl f) 4 4
573[5] Rambo Waltzer **(56)***(53) (SGNorton)* 3-8-10 MTebbutt(14) (prom: 2nd st: led over 2f out tl over 1f out: one pce) ½ 5
1322[2] Euro Singer **(57)***(51) (RAkehurst)* 3-8-11 TQuinn(19) (lw: led over 7f: rdn & wknd fnl f) 2 6
1146[8] Good (IRE) **(51)***(37) (DTThom)* 3-8-2 (3) DRMcCabe(9) (styd on fnl 2f: nvr nrr) 5 7
1308[5] Zalament **(62)***(47) (APJarvis)* 3-9-2 BThomson(3) (in tch: 7th st: rdn & wknd over 1f out) ½ 8
1290[7] Magical Bid (IRE) **(48)***(33) (JMBradley)* 3-8-2 JQuinn(17) (lw: nvr nrr) hd 9
1221[7] Outstayed Welcome **(52)***(35) (MJHaynes)* 3-8-6 RHills(15) (b.hind: nvr nr to chal) 1½ 10
1322[4] Kevasingo **(56)***(34) (SDow)* 3-8-10 StephenDavies(16) (prom: 4th st: wknd over 2f out) 3 11
937[12] Zuno Flyer (USA) **(60)***(37) (GLewis)* 3-9-0 WRyan(7) (lw: a bhd) ½ 12
1269[4] Khan **(57)***(29) (CWThornton)* 3-8-11 AMackay(12) (lw: a bhd) 3 13
1322[11] Nosirrah **(52)***(19) (CAHorgan)* 3-8-6 TWilliams(2) (lw: b.off hind: a in rr) 3 14
948[8] Dance of Joy **(58)***(25) (JLDunlop)* 3-8-12 WCarson(11) (chsd ldrs: 6th st: wkng whn hmpd over 2f out) ½ 15
673[13] Laal (USA) **(55)***(15) (EALDunlop)* 3-8-9 WRSwinburn(10) (disp ld: 3rd st: wknd over 2f out) 4 16
1124[16] Stylish Interval **(62)***(20) (RJHodges)* 3-8-11 (5) SDrowne(18) (a in rr) 1½ 17
745[6] Pioneer Princess **(51)***(4) (MJRyan)* 3-8-5 DBiggs(8) (chsd ldrs 6f: wknd qckly) 3 18
372[8] Callonescy (IRE) **(52)***(4) (CEBrittain)* 3-8-6 BDoyle(5) (swtg: bit bkwd: rdn & effrt 4f out: wknd over 2f out) ½ 19

4/1 Battleship Bruce, **9/2** Euro Singer, **7/1** KINGS ASSEMBLY, **10/1** Wet Patch (IRE), Khan, **12/1** Zuno Flyer (USA), Kevasingo (op 8/1), **14/1** Laal (USA) (10/1-16/1), Tirolette (IRE), Dance of Joy (op 7/1), Callonescy (IRE), **16/1** Rambo Waltzer, **20/1** Zalament, Pioneer Princess, **25/1** Good (IRE), Magical Bid (IRE), **33/1** Nosirrah, Stylish Interval, Outstayed Welcome, CSF £78.43 CT £904.41 TOTE £9.00: £2.20 £2.80 £5.80 £1.80 (£42.50) Trio £769.50 OWNER The Everhopefuls I (BERKHAMSTED) BRED Benham Stud 19 Rn

2m 9.1 (6.40) SF: 37/25/20/27/16/14/-/10/-/-/-/-/-/-/-/-/-/-/-

1499

HICKLING (S) H'CAP (0-60) (3-Y.O+) (Class G) £3,430.20 (£957.20: £462.60) **5f 218y** Stalls: High GOING minus 0.20 sec per fur (GF) 3-45 (3-46)

1434[2] **Petraco (IRE) (55)***(68)*(Fav)*(NASmith)* 7-9-9 LDettori(11) (lw: chsd ldrs: rdn over 2f out: led ins fnl f: all out) — 1
1051[3] Friendly Brave (USA) **(60)***(73) (TGMills)* 5-9-7 (7) JCornally(13) (led: hrd rdn over 1f out: hdd ins fnl f: rallied nr fin) hd 2
1087[8] Melodic Drive **(56)***(55) (JAGlover)* 5-9-10b SDWilliams(14) (a.p: ev ch over 1f out: outpcd fnl f) 5 3
Old Comrades **(52)***(48) (TDBarron)* 8-9-6 JFortune(16) (a.p: rdn over 2f out: edgd rt & one pce fnl f) 1¼ 4
1291[10] Out of the Mist **(36)***(29) (JAPickering)* 4-8-4b JQuinn(15) (lw: prom: ev ch 2f out: rdn & wknd appr fnl f) 1 5
1248[7] The Right Time **(45)***(38) (JParkes)* 10-8-13 GCarter(12) (lw: b: hdwy fnl 2f: nrst fin) hd 6
891[2] Jersey Belle **(44)***(35) (PJMakin)* 3-8-3 NCarlisle(19) (nvr trbld ldrs) ¾ 7
972[4] Bold Cyrano (IRE) **(52)***(41) (BPalling)* 4-9-6 TSprake(18) (nvr nr to chal) ¾ 8
1297[12] Titanium Honda (IRE) **(37)***(25) (CEBrittain)* 4-8-5 BDoyle(7) (racd stands' side: sme late hdwy: nvr nrr) ½ 9
1164[6] Waders Dream (IRE) **(46)***(34) (PatMitchell)* 6-9-0v MFenton(17) (chsd ldrs 4f: sn wknd) hd 10
965[12] Drum Sergeant **(35)***(21) (JParkes)* 8-8-0b(3) DRMcCabe(21) (s.s: nvr nr ldrs) ½ 11
1255[6] Goody Four Shoes **(41)***(25) (AGNewcombe)* 7-8-4 (5)ow2 DGriffiths(8) (chsd ldrs over 4f) hd 12
1276[6] As Such (IRE) **(55)***(39) (NACallaghan)* 4-9-9 GDuffield(9) (a in rr) ¾ 13
1094[20] Nordman Lass **(54)***(29) (MissJacquelineDoyle)* 3-8-13 RHughes(5) (swtg: a in rr) 3½ 14
789[6] Asterix **(42)***(16) (JMBradley)* 7-8-5v(5) SDrowne(3) (b: a bhd) nk 15
594[3] Abigails Boy (HOL) **(40)***(10) (DrJDScargill)* 6-8-5 (3) DWright(22) (effrt 3f out: sn rdn: no imp) 1¼ 16

1151[15] Coalisland **(35)***(5) (RIngram)* 5-8-3b AMcGlone(10) (in tch to ½-wy) ....nk **17**
1456[7] Grey Toppa **(53)***(9) (NPLittmoden)* 4-9-2 (5) CTeague(4) (lw: b: racd stands' side: bhd fnl 3f: t.o) 5 **18**
1153[10] Red Slaney (IRE) **(44)** *(RAkehurst)* 4-8-12 TQuinn(1) (racd stands' side: a bhd: t.o) 2 **19**
1164[12] Lucy's Gold **(34)** *(MJRyan)* 4-8-2 DBiggs(6) (racd stands' side: bhd fr ½-wy: t.o) 6 **20**

5/1 PETRACO (IRE), **13/2** Asterix, **8/1** Friendly Brave (USA), Bold Cyrano (IRE), **9/1** Red Slaney (IRE), **10/1** Abigails Boy (HOL), **12/1** Old Comrades (op 8/1), As Such (IRE), **14/1** Goody Four Shoes, Jersey Belle, Waders Dream (IRE), Melodic Drive, Grey Toppa (op 25/1), **16/1** Titanium Honda (IRE), The Right Time, **25/1** Out of the Mist, Nordman Lass, **33/1** Coalisland, Drum Sergeant, Lucy's Gold, CSF £48.95 CT £516.55 TOTE £4.00: £1.60 £2.60 £4.30 £3.70 (£27.40) Trio £146.70 OWNER Mr P. L. Williams (UPTON SNODSBURY) BRED Mrs M. Beaumont 20 Rn
1m 12.8 (2.80) SF: 50/55/37/30/11/20/8/23/7/16/3/7/21/2/-/-/-/-/-/-
WEIGHT FOR AGE 3yo-9lb
Petraco(IRE) sold BGover 8,700 gns. Friendly Brave (USA) clmd IWicks £6,500

1500 COSSINGTON MERCEDES 'SPRINTER' CONDITIONS STKS (3-Y.O F) (Class C) £5,534.40 (£2,049.60: £984.80: £404.00: £162.00: £65.20)
7f 9y Stalls: High GOING minus 0.20 sec per fur (GF) 4-15 (4-16)

1145[3] **Karayb (IRE) (97)***(95)*(Fav)*(DMorley)* 3-9-0 WCarson(1) (lw: mde all: qcknd over 1f out: r.o wl) ....— **1**
883[3] Far Fetched (IRE) **(89)***(92) (LordHuntingdon)* 3-9-0 LDettori(2) (hld up: effrt & rdn over 2f out: ev ch fnl f: unable qckn) 1½ **2**
Private Line (USA) *(90) (HRACecil)* 3-9-0 WRyan(4) (chsd ldrs: effrt 2f out: rdn appr fnl f: nvr able to chal) ....¾ **3**
915* Moonlight Saunter (USA) **(90)***(88) (EALDunlop)* 3-9-0 WRSwinburn(3) (b: lw: chsd wnr: rdn bel dist: one pce) 1 **4**
1139[7] Bring on the Choir **(90)***(85) (RBoss)* 3-8-12 RHills(8) (lw: hld up: kpt on ins fnl f: nvr nrr) ....nk **5**
1053* Cap And Gown (IRE) *(76) (PFICole)* 3-9-0 TQuinn(7) (chsd ldrs: rdn 2f out: sn outpcd: eased ins fnl f) 5 **6**
915[8] Lady Nash *(72) (CEBrittain)* 3-8-10 BDoyle(6) (dwlt: plld hrd: bhd fnl 2f) ....s.h **7**

Evens KARAYB (IRE), **4/1** Far Fetched (IRE), **11/2** Bring on the Choir, **8/1** Private Line (USA), Moonlight Saunter (USA) (6/1-9/1), **10/1** Cap And Gown (IRE) (7/1-11/1), **20/1** Lady Nash, CSF £5.92 TOTE £2.40: £1.20 £2.40 (£4.90) OWNER Mr Hamdan Al Maktoum (NEWMARKET) BRED Shadwell Estate Company Limited in Ireland 7 Rn 1m 26.4 (3.90) SF: 35/32/30/28/25/16/12

1501 SWANNINGTON CLAIMING STKS (3-Y.O+) (Class F) £3,224.60 (£895.60: £429.80)
1m 8y Stalls: High GOING minus 0.20 sec per fur (GF) 4-45 (4-47)

1290[6] **Daring Ryde (39)***(63) (JPSmith)* 4-9-7 GCarter(6) (lw: hld up & bhd: rdn & hdwy over 2f out: styd on to ld cl home) ....— **1**
1351[7] Zahran (IRE) **(65)***(55)*(Fav)*(JMBradley)* 4-8-8 (5) SDrowne(7) (b: a.p: led over 2f out: hrd rdn & ct nr fin) ....hd **2**
Heighth of Fame *(50) (SChristian)* 4-9-1 WRyan(4) (bit bkwd: hdwy 3f out: sn rdn: hung rt appr fnl f: one pce) 3½ **3**
1128[17] Nita's Choice *(37) (AGNewcombe)* 5-8-4 (5)ow3 DGriffiths(5) (bit bkwd: chsd ldrs: lost pl 3f out: rdn & drifted lft: r.o wl ins fnl f) 1¾ **4**
1297[8] Canny Lad **(32)***(42) (MPBielby)* 5-8-13v RCochrane(3) (s.i.s: hdwy over 2f out: wknd fnl f) 1¼ **5**
1209[10] Mutinique **(51)***(27) (BAPearce)* 4-8-3 (3) DRMcCabe(8) (hld up: effrt over 2f out: eased whn btn fnl f) 4 **6**
1350[18] Delmour **(25)***(29) (WMBrisbourne)* 4-8-4 (7) MartinDwyer(2) (chsd ldrs: rdn over 3f out: sn btn) 1½ **7**
Flash Arrow *(17) (JParkes)* 5-8-11 MDeering(1) (t: prom over 5f: sn wknd: t.o) 6 **8**
1323[18] Lord Alfie **(44)** *(BJMeehan)* 6-8-11b BDoyle(9) (plld hrd: led & sn clr: rdn & wknd 3f out: sn hdd: t.o) 30 **9**
1371[12] Charlie-Don't Surf *(RThompson)* 3-9-2 NAdams(10) (lw: a bhd: t.o fr ½-wy) 25 **10**

13/8 Zahran (IRE), **5/1** DARING RYDE, Mutinique, **6/1** Lord Alfie (op 4/1), **10/1** Canny Lad, Heighth of Fame, **14/1** Flash Arrow, **33/1** Nita's Choice, **50/1** Delmour, Charlie-Don't Surf, CSF £12.91 TOTE £5.60: £1.90 £1.40 £2.00 (£5.50) Trio £14.00 OWNER Mrs Linda Barrett (RUGELEY) BRED Manor Grange Stud Co Ltd 10 Rn 1m 40.7 (5.70) SF: 29/21/16/3/8/-/-/-/-/-
WEIGHT FOR AGE 3yo-11lb

1502 LADBROKE H'CAP (0-70) (4-Y.O+) (Class E) £3,302.20 (£985.60: £470.80: £213.40)
1m 3f 183y Stalls: High GOING minus 0.20 sec per fur (GF) 5-15 (5-16)

1254[5] **Stevie's Wonder (IRE) (54)***(61) (MJRyan)* 5-8-12 GCarter(3) (hld up: 4th st: str chal fnl f: led cl home) — 1
1368[4] Father Dan (IRE) **(47)***(54) (MissGayKelleway)* 6-8-0 (5) SDrowne(4) (hld up: 5th st: led over 2f out: hrd rdn & ct fnl strides) nk 2
1144[6] Broughtons Formula **(45)***(48) (WJMusson)* 5-8-0 (3) DRMcCabe(1) (hld up: hdwy over 2f out: styd on ins fnl f) 2½ 3
1295[4] College Don **(53)***(55) (MPBielby)* 4-8-11 RCochrane(9) (led tl over 2f out: wknd appr fnl f) ¾ 4
166[10] Jean de Florette (USA) **(40)***(42) (JohnBerry)* 4-7-12 JQuinn(8) (bit bkwd: chsd ldrs tl lost pl ½-wy: hdwy u.p 2f out: styd on fnl f) hd 5
1303* Chatham Island **(71)***(72)*(Fav)*(CEBrittain)* 7-10-1 BDoyle(6) (lw: w ldr: 2nd st: rdn over 3f out: wknd wl over 1f out) ½ 6
Minnesota Viking **(67)***(67) (LadyHerries)* 4-9-4 (7) PDoe(2) (bkwd: hld up: 6th st: drifted lft fnl 2f: grad wknd) 1¼ 7
841[6] Access Carnival (IRE) **(57)***(42) (RBoss)* 4-9-1 WRyan(5) (a in rr: t.o) 11 8
1141[7] Bold Look **(61)***(42) (PWHarris)* 4-9-5b GDuffield(7) (chsd ldrs: 3rd st: rdn & wknd over 2f out: t.o) 2½ 9

4/1 Chatham Island, **9/2** Father Dan (IRE), **11/2** Broughtons Formula, **6/1** Bold Look, Access Carnival (IRE), STEVIE'S WONDER (IRE), **7/1** Minnesota Viking, **9/1** College Don, **40/1** Jean de Florette (USA), CSF £32.20 CT £145.47 TOTE £5.80: £1.70 £1.90 £2.30 (£13.30) Trio £24.20 OWNER Newmarket Consortium (NEWMARKET) BRED Ovidstown Investments Ltd in Ireland 9 Rn
2m 34.8 (6.00) SF: 40/33/27/34/21/51/46/21/21
T/Jkpt: £8,690.00 (0.29 Tckts); £8,690.03 to Pontefract 6/5/95. T/Plpt: £99.50 (176.08 Tckts). T/Qdpt: £19.40 (2 Tckts). IM

1176-THIRSK (L-H)
Monday June 5th (Good)
WEATHER: overcast WIND: almost nil

1503 PICKERING (S) STKS (2-Y.O F) (Class F) £3,132.00 (£936.00: £448.00: £204.00)
6f Stalls: High GOING: 0.03 sec per fur (G) 6-45 (6-48)

My Kind *(56) (JBerry)* 2-8-9 SDWilliams(1) (leggy: sltly hmpd s: hdwy to chse ldrs ½-wy: led over 1f out: hung lft: drvn out) — 1
1215[4] Jambo *(53) (MRChannon)* 2-8-9 JFortune(8) (led after 2f tl over 1f out: kpt on wl towards fin) 1 2
1288[3] Miss Impulse *(43) (JWharton)* 2-8-9 AMackay(7) (chsd ldrs: ev ch over 1f out: one pce) 4 3
1190[10] How Could-I (IRE) *(33) (MHEasterby)* 2-8-9 MBirch(4) (sn outpcd & pushed along: hdwy & hung lft 2f out: kpt on) 3½ 4
1356[6] Klipspinger *(29) (BSRothwell)* 2-8-4 (5) JStack(6) (led 2f: hung lft & wknd 2f out) 1½ 5
Esther Louise *(19) (MWEasterby)* 2-8-2 (7) RuthCoulter(10) (leggy: unf: b.nr fore: hmpd s: wl bhd tl sme late hdwy) 4 6
1266[4] Grimstone Girl *(MWEasterby)* 2-8-9 LCharnock(9) (swvd rt s: chsd ldrs: rdn ½-wy: sn lost pl) 7 7
1356[12] Supreme Scholar *(BWMurray)* 2-8-4 (7)ow2 GParkin(3) (b.hind: w ldrs: hung bdly lft ½-wy: sn lost pl) 3½ 8
Chilly Looks *(MWEasterby)* 2-8-9 SMaloney(5) (leggy: s.s: a wl bhd) 1½ 9
1259[5] Subfusk (Fav)*(WGMTurner)* 2-8-9 (5) PMcCabe(2) (lw: swvd lft s: chsd ldrs: rdn & hung lft ½-wy: wknd over 1f out: eased) ¾ 10

5/4 Subfusk, **11/2** MY KIND, Grimstone Girl, **6/1** Jambo, **10/1** Miss Impulse, **12/1** How Could-I (IRE), **14/1** Chilly Looks, Klipspinger, **33/1** Esther Louise, **50/1** Supreme Scholar, CSF £37.70 TOTE £8.00: £2.50 £1.60 £1.90 (£25.60) Trio £41.70 OWNER Mr John Hulme (COCKERHAM) BRED Bearstone Stud 10 Rn
1m 15.7 (6.00) SF: 12/9/-/-/-/-/-/-/-/-
No bid.
OFFICIAL EXPLANATION **Subfusk: had hung badly left throughout and a routine test was ordered.**

1504 BEDALE LIMITED STKS (0-70) (3-Y.O) (Class E) £3,143.25 (£936.00: £445.50: £200.25) **7f** Stalls: Low GOING: 0.03 sec per fur (G) 7-15 (7-16)

1000[4] **Hey Up Dolly (IRE) (70)***(71) (JBerry)* 3-8-6 JCarroll(1) (hld up: hdwy & swtchd rt over 2f out: led 1f out: drvn out) — 1

1094[14] Seventeens Lucky **(67)***(73) (BobJones)* 3-8-11 NConnorton(5) (chsd ldrs: effrt ½-wy: led over 1f out: sn hdd & nt qckn)........1½ 2
1045[2] Heathyards Magic (IRE) **(69)***(72) (RHollinshead)* 3-9-0 WRSwinburn(7) (trckd ldrs: effrt 3f out: rdn & kpt on one pce over 1f out)........1½ 3
Break the Rules **(70)***(62)*(Fav)*(MrsMReveley)* 3-8-11 KDarley(2) (trckd ldrs: outpcd & lost pl over 3f out: swtchd & hmpd 1f out: kpt on: nvr nr to chal)........3 4
1312[7] Contract Venture (IRE) **(69)***(61) (WJarvis)* 3-8-11 JWeaver(6) (hld up & bhd: hdwy 2f out: styd on fin: nvr plcd to chal)........½ 5
1154[4] Belle of the Ball (IRE) **(68)***(47) (EALDunlop)* 3-8-3 (3) JTate(3) (led tl over 1f out: sn wknd)........4 6
1147[6] Tajar (USA) **(68)***(51) (DMorley)* 3-8-11 WCarson(4) (chsd ldr tl wknd over 1f out: eased)........nk 7

2/1 Break the Rules, **5/1** Belle of the Ball (IRE) (op 3/1), HEY UP DOLLY (IRE), **11/2** Tajar (USA) (op 7/2), **6/1** Heathyards Magic (IRE), **7/1** Seventeens Lucky, **9/1** Contract Venture (IRE), CSF £36.07 TOTE £6.30: £3.60 £2.70 (£36.20) OWNER Mr A. Barry (COCKERHAM) BRED Mrs J. M. Berry 7 Rn 1m 27.9 (5.20) SF: 31/33/32/22/21/7/11

1505 BUSINESS FURNITURE CENTRE (HOLDINGS) H'CAP (0-80) (3-Y.O+) (Class D) £3,806.00 (£1,133.00: £539.00: £242.00) **1m 4f** Stalls: Low GOING: 0.03 sec per fur (G) 7-45 (7-45)

1303[5] **Lookingforarainbow (IRE) (72)***(83) (BobJones)* 7-10-0 MWigham(7) (hld up: hdwy & swtchd outside over 1f out: styd on wl to ld ins fnl f)........— 1
1340* Bayrak (USA) **(74)***(83) (MJRyan)* 5-10-2 5x JWeaver(6) (lw: trckd ldrs: effrt 3f out: led wl over 1f out: hdd & nt qckn ins fnl f)........1¼ 2
1128* Senorita Dinero (USA) **(76)***(81)*(Fav)*(MRStoute)* 3-9-2 WRSwinburn(4) (trckd ldr: effrt 3f out: rdn & edgd rt over 1f out: kpt on same pce)........3 3
771* Mr Towser **(63)***(68) (WWHaigh)* 4-9-2 (3) JTate(3) (lw: trckd ldrs: rdn & outpcd over 3f out: kpt on appr fnl f)........nk 4
1283[3] Swivel **(68)***(73) (JRFanshawe)* 3-8-8 JCarroll(1) (chsd ldrs: drvn along & outpcd over 3f out: hdwy on ins & rdn 2f out: nt clr run & swtchd: styd on towards fin)........s.h 5
Persian Soldier **(44)***(40) (EJAlston)* 8-8-0 ow1 PRobinson(5) (sn drvn along: led tl wl over 1f out: sn wknd)........6 6
1022[2] Shakiyr (FR) **(63)***(48) (RHollinshead)* 4-9-5 KDarley(2) (bhd & pushed along 7f out: sn rdn: wl outpcd)........9 7

11/8 Senorita Dinero (USA), **3/1** Bayrak (USA) (op 9/2), **7/1** Shakiyr (FR), **8/1** LOOKINGFORARAINBOW (IRE), Swivel, Mr Towser, **16/1** Persian Soldier, CSF £31.40 TOTE £7.80: £2.00 £2.10 (£12.80) OWNER Mr B. M. Saumtally (NEWMARKET) BRED Red Sox Associates 7 Rn 2m 37.7 (7.70) SF: 63/63/45/48/37/20/28
WEIGHT FOR AGE 3yo-16lb

1506 SALTERSGATE H'CAP (0-70) (3-Y.O+) (Class E) £3,947.50 (£1,180.00: £565.00: £257.50) **1m** Stalls: Low GOING: 0.03 sec per fur (G) 8-15 (8-16)

1027[6] **Marowins (43)***(53) (EJAlston)* 6-8-4 ow1 KFallon(10) (lw: sn outpcd & drvn along: hdwy on outside over 2f out: styd on wl to ld wl ins fnl f)........— 1
1344[3] Just Harry **(64)***(74)*(Fav)*(MJRyan)* 4-9-11 WRSwinburn(3) (lw: hld up: hdwy over 2f out: swtchd ins & led over 1f out: hdd & nt qckn nr fin)........nk 2
1432[7] Calder King **(61)***(65) (JLEyre)* 4-9-8b SDWilliams(8) (rr div: hdwy over 2f out: edgd lft & styd on same pce fnl f)........3 3
1279[9] Borrowby **(47)***(50) (MWEasterby)* 3-7-11b LCharnock(4) (led after 1f tl over 1f out: one pce)...½ 4
1378[6] Thatched (IRE) **(46)***(48) (REBarr)* 5-8-7 SWebster(6) (hld up: effrt over 2f out: n.m.r: styd on fnl f)........¾ 5
1205[4] Tu Opes **(66)***(67) (JLHarris)* 4-9-10v(3) SSanders(11) (trckd ldrs: effrt over 2f out: one pce)....nk 6
1351[4] Bentico **(62)***(63) (MrsNMacauley)* 6-9-9b JWeaver(9) (lw: hld up: sn bhd: styd on fnl 2f: nvr rchd ldrs)........s.h 7
1202* Vanborough Lad **(55)***(51) (MJBolton)* 6-9-2 PRobinson(5) (lw: hdwy ½-wy: effrt over 2f out: grad wknd)........2½ 8
Leave it to Lib **(55)***(46) (PCalver)* 8-8-13 (3) JTate(7) (lw: led 1f: chsd ldrs tl wknd over 1f out)2½ 9
1299[6] First Gold **(62)***(50) (JWharton)* 6-9-9 KDarley(13) (hld up & bhd: hdwy & nt clr run 2f out: nvr nr ldrs)........1½ 10
1355[7] Gant Bleu (FR) **(43)***(30) (RMWhitaker)* 8-8-4 ACulhane(1) (hld up & bhd: hdwy on ins 2f out: nvr nr ldrs)........¾ 11
969[8] Farfields Prince **(53)***(40) (DNicholls)* 3-8-3 NConnorton(2) (sn drvn along: chsd ldrs tl lost pl 2f out)........hd 12
1432[8] Wild Prospect **(40)***(17) (BSRothwell)* 7-8-1 SMaloney(12) (chsd ldrs tl wknd over 2f out)........5 13
1219[12] Heavens Above **(45)***(6) (MHEasterby)* 3-7-9 NCarlisle(14) (swtg: chsd ldrs tl lost pl ½-wy: sn bhd)........8 14

5/2 Just Harry (op 5/1), **6/1** Vanborough Lad (op 4/1), **9/1** First Gold, Bentico (op 6/1), Thatched (IRE), MAROWINS, **10/1** Calder King, **12/1** Tu Opes, **14/1** Leave it to Lib, Gant Bleu (FR) (10/1-16/1), **16/1** Borrowby, Farfields Prince, Heavens Above, **33/1** Wild Prospect, CSF £32.85 CT £227.74 TOTE £12.30: £3.60 £1.30 £4.00 (£18.90) Trio £97.90 OWNER Whitehills Racing Syndicate (PRESTON) BRED W. M. Lidsey 14 Rn 1m 41.6 (6.00) SF: 29/50/41/15/24/43/39/27/22/26/6/5/-/-

WEIGHT FOR AGE 3yo-11lb

1507

SPROXTON MAIDEN STKS (3-Y.O+) (Class D) £3,806.00 (£1,133.00: £539.00: £242.00) **1m** Stalls: Low GOING: 0.03 sec per fur (G) 8-45 (8-46)

973³ **Manabar** *(78)*(Fav)*(DMorley)* 3-8-12 WCarson(4) (trckd ldr: plld hrd: smooth hdwy over 2f out: led on bit over 1f out: drvn along: eased nr fin) — 1
1337⁴ My Gina *(71) (MRStoute)* 3-8-4 (3) JTate(3) (chsd ldrs: effrt over 3f out: styd on wl fnl f) 1¼ 2
955³ Houghton Venture (USA) *(64) (SPCWoods)* 3-8-12 KDarley(2) (chsd ldrs: drvn along ½-wy: outpcd fnl 3f) 6 3
1216⁵ Golden Tongue (USA) *(62) (EALDunlop)* 3-8-12 WRSwinburn(1) (led: rdn over 2f out: hdd over 1f out: hung lft & sn wknd) ¾ 4
Ihtimaam (FR) *(60) (MrsASwinbank)* 3-8-12 NConnorton(5) (b: b.hind: unruly s: dwlt: kpt on fnl 2f: n.m.r ins fnl f) 1 5

11/10 MANABAR (Evens-10/11), **9/4** Houghton Venture (USA), **9/2** My Gina, **15/2** Golden Tongue (USA), **33/1** Ihtimaam (FR), CSF £6.04 TOTE £1.80: £1.20 £2.10 (£3.40) OWNER Mr Hamdan Al Maktoum (NEWMARKET) BRED P. J. and Mrs Sands 5 Rn 1m 42.3 (6.70) SF: 30/23/16/14/12

1508

LEEMING BAR H'CAP (0-75) (3-Y.O+) (Class D) £4,235.00 (£1,265.00: £605.00: £275.00) **5f** Stalls: High GOING: 0.03 sec per fur (G) 9-15 (9-17)

1152* **Lady Sheriff (51)***(62+) (MWEasterby)* 4-8-8b LCharnock(3) (lw: chsd ldrs: led over 1f out: r.o wl) — 1
Miss Movie World **(61)***(64) (MDHammond)* 6-8-13 (5) JStack(12) (swvd rt s: sn chsng ldrs: ev ch over 1f out: unable qckn) 2½ 2
1152² Superpride **(73)***(71)*(Fav)*(TDBarron)* 3-9-8 JFortune(13) (sltly hmpd s: bhd: hdwy ½-wy: swtchd lft & kpt on wl appr fnl f: nt rch ldrs) 1½ 3
1271⁵ Kalar **(42)***(40) (DWChapman)* 6-7-13b NCarlisle(10) (lw: unruly in stalls: led: hdd over 1f out: kpt on) hd 4
734⁴ Baileys Sunset (IRE) **(62)***(59) (MJohnston)* 3-8-11 DHolland(11) (chsd ldrs: effrt 2f out: kpt on same pce) nk 5
1152⁹ High Domain (IRE) **(71)***(68) (TDBarron)* 4-9-7 (7) KimberleyHart(7) (a in tch: kpt on wl fnl f) hd 6
1461⁵ Tenor **(64)***(59) (DNicholls)* 4-9-7 AlexGreaves(4) (hld up & bhd: kpt on wl fnl 2f) ½ 7
1179¹³ Craigie Boy **(61)***(50) (NBycroft)* 5-9-4b DeanMcKeown(9) (lw: s.i.s: bhd tl kpt on fnl 2f) 1¾ 8
1193⁹ Hickory Blue **(71)***(51) (MrsNMacauley)* 5-10-0v JWeaver(2) (racd far side: chsd ldrs 3f: sn wknd & eased) 3 9
1257⁶ The Noble Oak (IRE) **(50)***(27) (MJBolton)* 7-8-7 PRobinson(6) (b.off hind: chsd ldrs 3f: sn lost pl) ¾ 10
1152⁵ Sir Tasker **(54)***(30) (JLHarris)* 7-8-8 (3) SSanders(8) (lw: unruly in stalls: chsd ldrs tl lost pl ½-wy) nk 11
1271⁶ Tino Tere **(61)***(28) (JBalding)* 6-8-11 (7) JEdmunds(1) (bit bkwd: racd far side: gd spd to ½-wy: sn bhd) 3 12
*16*⁶ Florac (IRE) **(36)** *(JBalding)* 5-7-7 ClaireBalding(5) (outpcd fr ½-wy) 3 13

LONG HANDICAP Florac (IRE) 7-6

2/1 Superpride, **7/1** LADY SHERIFF, Baileys Sunset (IRE), **8/1** Hickory Blue, **9/1** Tenor, Craigie Boy, **11/1** Sir Tasker, **14/1** Kalar, **16/1** The Noble Oak (IRE), **20/1** High Domain (IRE), Miss Movie World, Tino Tere, **33/1** Florac (IRE), CSF £125.48 CT £353.24 TOTE £6.60: £2.60 £3.30 £1.80 (£173.60) Trio £66.70 OWNER Mr E. J. Mangan (SHERIFF HUTTON) BRED Jeremy Green and Sons 13 Rn 60.1 secs (2.90) SF: 45/47/46/23/34/51/42/33/34/10/13/11/-

WEIGHT FOR AGE 3yo-8lb

T/Plpt: £273.50 (55.19 Tckts). T/Qdpt: £50.90 (0.75 Tckts); £17.23 to Pontefract 6/5/95. WG

1092-WINDSOR (Fig. 8)
Monday June 5th (Good)

WEATHER: sunny WIND: almost nil

1509

SCHOLTES (S) STKS (3-Y.O+) (Class G) £2,687.50 (£750.00: £362.50) **1m 67y** Stalls: High GOING minus 0.35 sec per fur (F) 6-30 (6-30)

848⁴ **Cape Pigeon (USA) (58)***(63)*(Fav)*(LGCottrell)* 10-9-7v LDettori(12) (lw: 2nd st: led over 3f out: r.o) — 1

845[5] Duello **(64)***(58) (MBlanshard)* 4-9-7 StephenDavies(3) (wl bhd tl hdwy over 2f out: r.o: nt rch ldr)....2½ 2
1404* Guesstimation (USA) **(57)***(58) (JPearce)* 6-9-12 GBardwell(7) (hdwy fnl 2f: nvr nrr)....2½ 3
1255[7] Doodies Pool (IRE) **(49)***(53) (GLMoore)* 5-9-7 BRouse(11) (lw: 7th st: jnd wnr 3f out: one pce fnl 2f)....hd 4
880[6] Move With Edes **(62)***(46) (WGMTurner)* 3-8-10 AClark(8) (6th st: r.o one pce fnl 2f)....4 5
1320[4] Spitfire Bridge (IRE) **(46)***(41) (MMcCormack)* 3-8-10 MPerrett(4) (8th st: rdn 3f out: one pce)2½ 6
Vanroy **(58)***(41) (JRJenkins)* 11-9-7v TQuinn(1) (hdwy fnl 2f: r.o)....hd 7
Morocco (IRE) **(55)***(35) (MRChannon)* 6-9-7 RHughes(5) (bit bkwd: nvr nr to chal)....3 8
1255[14] Glowing Account (IRE) **(48)***(32) (JWMullins)* 4-9-7b JWilliams(14) (lw: 4th st: wknd over 2f out)....1½ 9
1337[7] Julia's Freebee *(9) (TMJones)* 4-9-2 RPerham(10) (3rd st: wknd over 2f out)....9 10
Flash Appeal *(RGuest)* 4-8-11 (5) AWhelan(6) (lw: 5th st: wknd 2f out)....5 11
408[11] Smart Teacher (USA) **(50)** *(KRBurke)* 5-9-7 MFenton(2) (led tl wknd over 3f out)....5 12
1381[9] Broughtons Bird (IRE) *(WJMusson)* 4-9-2 SWhitworth(9) (a bhd)....1¼ 13
1146[10] Keep Quiet **(50)** *(WJMusson)* 3-8-5 GHind(13) (lw: a bhd)....1¼ 14

3/1 CAPE PIGEON (USA) (2/1-100/30), **7/2** Duello, **6/1** Guesstimation (USA), Move With Edes, **8/1** Vanroy, Morocco (IRE), **10/1** Spitfire Bridge (IRE), Smart Teacher (USA), **14/1** Doodies Pool (IRE), Keep Quiet, **16/1** Glowing Account (IRE), **20/1** Julia's Freebee, **33/1** Broughtons Bird (IRE), Flash Appeal, CSF £16.37 TOTE £3.20: £1.50 £1.70 £2.90 (£6.90) Trio £6.60 OWNER Mr E. J. S. Gadsden (CULLOMPTON) BRED Ashwood Thoroughbreds, Inc. 14 Rn

1m 45.5 (3.90) SF: 38/33/33/28/10/5/16/10/7/-/-/-/-/-

WEIGHT FOR AGE 3yo-11lb

No bid.

1510 ARISTON BUILT IN LIMITED STKS (0-65) (3-Y.O+) (Class F)

£4,016.00 (£1,208.00: £584.00: £272.00)
5f 217y Stalls: High GOING minus 0.35 sec per fur (F) 7-00 (7-01)

1257[3] **Patsy Grimes (61)***(67) (LJHolt)* 5-9-2 AMcGlone(13) (hdwy 2f out: r.o to ld wl ins fnl f)....— 1
1335[5] Tinker Osmaston **(65)***(69) (MSSaunders)* 4-9-5 JWilliams(6) (hld up: hdwy 2f out: ev ch ins fnl f: r.o)....½ 2
1429[2] Another Jade **(65)***(69) (APJarvis)* 5-9-5 BThomson(9) (lw: a.p: led wl over 1f out tl wl ins fnl f)....s.h 3
1276[5] Crystal Heights (FR) **(63)***(67) (RJO'Sullivan)* 7-9-10 RCochrane(4) (hdwy 2f out: r.o ins fnl f)....2½ 4
1411[9] Domicksky **(64)***(59) (MRChannon)* 7-9-7 RHughes(1) (lw: w ldr: led over 3f out tl wl over 1f out)....2 5
39[3] Spectacle Jim **(49)***(52) (JO'Donoghue)* 6-9-7b MPerrett(11) (bit bkwd: nvr nr to chal)....2½ 6
Maybe Today **(61)***(43) (BRMillman)* 3-8-7 MFenton(5) (no hdwy fnl 2f)....1½ 7
636[14] Madurai **(65)***(42) (JLDunlop)* 4-9-2 TQuinn(14) (led over 2f: hung bdly lft: sn wknd)....nk 8
1043[6] Lady-Bo-K **(62)***(15) (CaptJWilson)* 4-9-2 RHills(12) (spd 4f: t.o)....10 9
1411* Oggi **(62)***(23)*(Fav)*(PJMakin)* 4-9-10b LDettori(3) (prom over 3f: t.o)....nk 10
1354[14] Malibu Man **(57)***(12) (SMellor)* 3-8-5 (7) ADaly(7) (lw: bhd most of wy: t.o)....3 11
1257[13] Admirals Realm **(57)** *(AGNewcombe)* 6-9-7 AClark(8) (bhd fnl 4f: t.o)....7 12

3/1 Oggi (op 2/1), **100/30** Madurai, **4/1** Another Jade, **11/2** PATSY GRIMES (7/2-6/1), **7/1** Domicksky, **9/1** Tinker Osmaston (6/1-10/1), **14/1** Lady-Bo-K, **16/1** Crystal Heights (FR), Spectacle Jim, **20/1** Maybe Today, Admirals Realm, **33/1** Malibu Man, CSF £56.79 TOTE £7.30: £2.00 £2.30 £1.60 (£61.10) Trio £77.60 OWNER Mr J. K. Grimes (BASINGSTOKE) BRED J. C. Fox 12 Rn

1m 12.5 (2.00) SF: 42/44/44/42/34/27/9/17/-/-/-/-

WEIGHT FOR AGE 3yo-9lb

1511 ARISTON CONDITIONS STKS (2-Y.O) (Class D) £5,312.50

(£1,600.00: £775.00: £362.50)
5f 10y Stalls: High GOING minus 0.35 sec per fur (F) 7-30 (7-32)

1176[2] **First Fiddler** *(78)*(Fav)*(WJarvis)* 2-8-11 BThomson(12) (w ldr: led over 2f out: edgd lft: drvn out)....— 1
Crocodile Shoes *(76) (RHannon)* 2-8-11 RHughes(11) (a.p: r.o ins fnl f)....¾ 2
1054* Sonic Mail *(78) (KMcAuliffe)* 2-9-3 RCochrane(7) (a.p: ev ch over 1f out: nt qckn)....1¼ 3
1134[7] Vola Via (USA) *(71) (IABalding)* 2-8-11 LDettori(3) (mid div: swtchd rt over 1f out: r.o ins fnl f)....nk 4
1223[P] Mimosa *(64) (LJHolt)* 2-8-6 MFenton(4) (lw: dwlt: nrst fin)....½ 5
1184[13] La Tansani (IRE) *(65) (RHannon)* 2-8-4 (7) DaneO'Neill(9) (bit bkwd: hdwy over 1f out: r.o) ..1¼ 6
1137[5] Queen's Music (USA) *(56) (PFICole)* 2-8-6 TQuinn(6) (b.nr hind: lw: nvr nr to chal)....1¼ 7
*1089** Amy Leigh (IRE) *(49) (CaptJWilson)* 2-8-10 RHills(10) (led over 2f)....3½ 8
1384[6] Hotlips Houlihan *(49) (RJRWilliams)* 2-8-10 DBiggs(2) (spd 3f)....hd 9

1096[5] Charterhouse Xpres *(47) (MMcCormack)* 2-8-11 AClark(5) (spd 3f)....1 **10**
Fairy Prince (IRE) *(18) (MrsALMKing)* 2-8-8 (3) AGarth(8) (w'like: bit bkwd: a bhd: t.o)....9 **11**
Ed's Folly (IRE) *(SDow)* 2-8-11 StephenDavies(1) (str: bit bkwd: s.s: a bhd: t.o)....7 **12**

15/8 FIRST FIDDLER, **7/2** Vola Via (USA), **4/1** Sonic Mail, **5/1** Queen's Music (USA) (3/1-11/2), **14/1** Crocodile Shoes, Amy Leigh (IRE), **16/1** Hotlips Houlihan, **20/1** Ed's Folly (IRE), La Tansani (IRE), Charterhouse Xpres, **25/1** Mimosa, **33/1** Fairy Prince (IRE), CSF £30.33 TOTE £2.80: £1.40 £2.10 £1.70 (£17.00) Trio £35.70 OWNER The First Fiddler Partnership (NEWMARKET) BRED Cheveley Park Stud Ltd 12 Rn 61.4 secs (2.40) SF: 26/24/26/19/12/13/4/-/-/-/-/-

1512 INDESIT H'CAP (0-70) (3-Y.O) (Class E) £4,849.50 (£1,461.00: £708.00: £331.50) **1m 67y** Stalls: High GOING minus 0.35 sec per fur (F) 8-00 (8-02)

1124[10] **Alerting (60)***(68) (IABalding)* 3-8-11 LDettori(13) (hdwy 3f out: led over 1f out: r.o wl)....— **1**
1165[2] Wandering Minstrel (IRE) **(63)***(68)*(Fav)*(JMPEustace)* 3-9-0 RCochrane(14) (lw: 7th st: led over 2f out tl over 1f out: r.o)....1¾ **2**
1323[15] Court Nap (IRE) **(54)***(57) (SMellor)* 3-8-5 RPerham(11) (lw: hdwy fnl 2f: nvr nrr)....¾ **3**
1274[4] Pedaltothemetal (IRE) **(49)***(45) (PMitchell)* 3-8-0 SO'Gorman(5) (b.hind: nrst fin)....4 **4**
813[11] Noble Neptune **(57)***(51) (WJMusson)* 3-8-8 GHind(6) (hdwy fnl 2f: r.o)....¾ **5**
1065[7] Run-Do-Run **(63)***(55) (HJCollingridge)* 3-9-0 RHughes(12) (lw: hdwy over 1f out: r.o ins fnl f)....1 **6**
651[13] Oakbury (IRE) **(67)***(58) (RHannon)* 3-9-4 SRaymont(17) (nvr nr to chal)....¾ **7**
1124[18] Sporting Risk **(57)***(45) (PWHarris)* 3-8-8 GDuffield(15) (lw: nvr trbld ldrs)....1½ **8**
1124[12] Sobeloved **(50)***(37) (MRChannon)* 3-8-1 CRutter(1) (nvr nr ldrs)....½ **9**
971[9] Anistop **(54)***(40) (RAkehurst)* 3-8-5 TQuinn(18) (b.off hind: 4th st: wknd over 2f out)....½ **10**
Lees Please (IRE) **(60)***(42) (KOCunningham-Brown)* 3-8-11 SWhitworth(16) (5th st: wknd 2f out)....2 **11**
730[7] Silks and Studs **(59)***(39) (JWhite)* 3-8-5 (5) SDrowne(10) (lw: 6th st: wknd over 2f out)....1 **12**
1165[9] Jewel Trader **(58)***(36) (CJBenstead)* 3-8-9 JWilliams(4) (outpcd)....1¼ **13**
Saltis (IRE) **(58)***(34) (DWPArbuthnot)* 3-8-9 BThomson(7) (lw: b.hind: 8th st: wknd 3f out)....¾ **14**
867[12] Rock Oyster **(55)***(31) (BJMeehan)* 3-8-6 BDoyle(19) (3rd st: led 4f out tl wknd over 2f out)....hd **15**
1366[10] Tara Colleen (IRE) **(53)***(16) (CAHorgan)* 3-8-4 EJohnson(21) (plld hrd: led tl wknd 4f out)....7 **16**
Just-Mana-Mou (IRE) **(57)***(15) (GLewis)* 3-8-3 (5) AWhelan(20) (2nd st: wknd 3f out)....2½ **17**
1072[10] Senaan **(54)***(6) (TThomsonJones)* 3-8-5 RHills(2) (sn bhd)....3 **18**
1124[9] Classic Pet (IRE) **(50)***(1) (CAHorgan)* 3-8-1 NAdams(3) (b: hdwy 4f out: wknd 3f out)....nk **19**
1154[5] Magical Blues (IRE) **(70)***(18) (KTIvory)* 3-9-7b MTebbutt(8) (b: s.s: reluctant to r: a bhd)....2 **20**

7/2 Wandering Minstrel (IRE), **7/1** Noble Neptune, **9/1** ALERTING, Anistop, **12/1** Classic Pet (IRE), Magical Blues (IRE), Pedaltothemetal (IRE), Rock Oyster (op 7/1), Oakbury (IRE) (op 8/1), **14/1** Court Nap (IRE) (10/1-16/1), Lees Please (IRE), Just-Mana-Mou (IRE), Saltis (IRE), **16/1** Sporting Risk, Run-Do-Run, **20/1** Senaan, Silks and Studs, Tara Colleen (IRE), Sobeloved, **25/1** Jewel Trader, CSF £45.81 CT £448.39 TOTE £10.30: £2.60 £1.50 £5.90 £3.30 (£10.20) Trio £91.20 OWNER Mr G. M. Smart (KINGSCLERE) BRED Mrs D. O. Joly 20 Rn
1m 46.7 (5.10) SF: 18/18/7/-/1/5/8/-/-/-/-/-/-/-/-/-/-/-/-/-

1513 ONANDONANDON H'CAP (0-60) (3-Y.O+) (Class F) £3,350.00 (£1,010.00: £490.00: £230.00) **1m 3f 135y** Stalls: High GOING minus 0.35 sec (F) 8-30 (8-33)

1093[4] **Hi-Aud (58)***(72+) (JAkehurst)* 3-8-12 TQuinn(4) (6th st: led wl over 1f out: r.o wl)....— **1**
1347[6] Quivira **(56)***(65) (TTClement)* 4-9-12 RHills(10) (5th st: ev ch over 1f out: nt qckn)....4 **2**
1166[3] Scenic Dancer **(48)***(56)*(Fav)*(AHide)* 7-9-4 JWilliams(2) (dwlt: gd hdwy fnl 2f: nvr nrr)....¾ **3**
1328[R] Bee Beat **(43)***(49) (AJChamberlain)* 7-8-6 (7) MartinDwyer(6) (lw: s.s: gd hdwy over 2f out: nrst fin)....¾ **4**
Casual Water (IRE) **(48)***(50) (AGNewcombe)* 4-9-4 RHughes(20) (led 6f out tl wl over 1f out)....3½ **5**
1350[4] Bold Mick **(49)***(41) (DJGMurraySmith)* 4-9-5 LDettori(13) (hdwy 3f out: one pce fnl 2f)....7 **6**
1254[7] Saafi (IRE) **(54)***(46) (RJBaker)* 4-9-10 BPowell(3) (4th st: one pce fnl 3f)....nk **7**
1285[10] Sinclair Lad (IRE) **(45)***(34) (RJHodges)* 7-8-10b(5) SDrowne(14) (lw: 7th st: hdwy 3f out: wknd over 1f out)....1¾ **8**
1202[11] Born to Please (IRE) **(56)***(44) (PWHarris)* 3-8-10 RCochrane(19) (lw: nvr nr to chal)....½ **9**
Supreme Star (USA) **(51)***(38) (PRHedger)* 4-9-7 StephenDavies(11) (a mid div)....1 **10**
843[4] Sagasan **(58)***(43) (WRMuir)* 4-10-0 AMcGlone(16) (b: lw: nvr trbld ldrs)....1¾ **11**
1254[17] Captain Starlight (IRE) **(39)***(20) (RAkehurst)* 4-8-9 BThomson(18) (nvr bttr than mid div)....2½ **12**
1349[3] Platini (IRE) **(55)***(36) (GBBalding)* 4-9-6v(5) RPainter(17) (nvr nr ldrs)....½ **13**
1349[10] Safe Secret **(46)***(25) (RBrotherton)* 4-9-2 RPrice(7) (plld hrd: bhd fnl 2f)....1½ **14**
1200[3] Wizzy Lizzy (IRE) **(46)***(23) (DRCElsworth)* 4-8-11 (5) AWhelan(15) (lw: a bhd)....1 **15**
Bird Island **(56)***(32) (JWhite)* 4-9-12 GDuffield(8) (lw: 3rd st: wknd 3f out)....1 **16**
Pulmicort **(55)***(24) (PBurgoyne)* 5-9-11v BRouse(1) (lw: led to 6f out: 2nd st: wknd 4f out)....5 **17**

1141 11 Cheveley Dancer (USA) **(38)***(5) (DAWilson)* 7-8-8 NAdams(5) (b: a bhd) 1¼ **18**
848 9 Formidable Lass **(40)** *(LGCottrell)* 4-8-10 MFenton(12) (lw: bhd fnl 2f)....5 **19**
Vladivostok **(47)** *(RLee)* 5-9-3 MPerrett(9) (b: s.s: a bhd: t.o) 15 **20**

7/2 Scenic Dancer, **5/1** Casual Water (IRE), **11/2** Bold Mick, **7/1** HI-AUD, **10/1** Wizzy Lizzy (IRE), **12/1** Quivira, Captain Starlight (IRE) (8/1-14/1), **14/1** Platini (IRE), **16/1** Born to Please (IRE), Sinclair Lad (IRE), **20/1** Sagasan, Saafi (IRE), Supreme Star (USA), Safe Secret, Bird Island, **25/1** Bee Beat, Pulmicort, Cheveley Dancer (USA), Vladivostok, **33/1** Formidable Lass, CSF £96.49 CT £334.43 TOTE £7.50: £2.10 £4.70 £1.50 £3.90 (£39.70) Trio £43.40 OWNER Mr A. G. Speake (LAMBOURN) BRED A. G. Speake 20 Rn 2m 29.8 (3.80) SF: 18/27/18/11/12/3/8/-/-/-/5/-/-/-/-/-/-
WEIGHT FOR AGE 3yo-16lb

1514 NEW WORLD MEDIAN AUCTION MAIDEN STKS (3-Y.O) (Class E)
£4,159.00 (£1,252.00: £606.00: £283.00)
1m 2f 7y Stalls: High GOING minus 0.35 sec per fur (F) 9-00 (9-07)

Beyond Doubt *(78+)*(Fav)*(LordHuntingdon)* 3-8-9 LDettori(17) (lw: hdwy 2f out: qcknd to ld ins fnl f: r.o) ....— **1**
1097 4 Meghdoot **(73)***(76) (HJCollingridge)* 3-8-9 JQuinn(10) (7th st: led over 2f out tl ins fnl f)....1¼ **2**
1218 2 Barford Sovereign **(70)***(75) (JRFanshawe)* 3-8-9 RHills(20) (6th st: r.o one pce fnl 2f) ....½ **3**
1264 4 Zidac **(75)***(77) (PJMakin)* 3-9-0 TQuinn(21) (led tl over 2f out: one pce)....2 **4**
941 6 Braydon Forest **(67)***(66) (CJDrewe)* 3-9-0 RCochrane(11) (5th st: no hdwy fnl 2f)....7 **5**
Ottavio Farnese *(62) (AHide)* 3-9-0 AMcGlone(5) (w'like: scope: bit bkwd: wl bhd tl stdy hdwy fnl 3f) 2½ **6**
Dazzler *(61) (MarkCampion)* 3-9-0 CAvery(16) (str: nrst fin)....nk **7**
Nessun Doro *(61) (SMellor)* 3-9-0 RPerham(14) (nvr nrr)....d.h **7**
1097 8 George Bull *(59) (MajorWRHern)* 3-9-0 PaulEddery(7) (lw: nvr plcd to chal)....1½ **9**
1196 10 Anonym (IRE) *(59) (JLDunlop)* 3-9-0 BThomson(1) (hdwy 4f out: ev ch 2f out: sn wknd) ....hd **10**
Painted Hall (USA) *(56) (JARToller)* 3-9-0 WNewnes(13) (wl grwn: bkwd: nvr nr ldrs)....1¾ **11**
Memory's Music *(55) (IABalding)* 3-9-0 SO'Gorman(19) (4th st: wknd 3f out) 1 **12**
Nobby North *(50) (LordHuntingdon)* 3-8-7 (7) AimeeCook(2) (str: bit bkwd: wl bhd tl r.o fnl 2f)....3 **13**
Ardleigh Prince *(46) (GLMoore)* 3-9-0 SWhitworth(6) (leggy: nvr nrr)....2½ **14**
Solazzi (FR) *(38) (LGCottrell)* 3-8-9 MFenton(8) (leggy: bit bkwd: a bhd)....2 **15**
1173 4 Niknaks Nephew *(28) (MissAJWhitfield)* 3-8-9 (5) RPainter(9) (outpcd) 9 **16**
1353 9 Laudation (IRE) *(27) (GBBalding)* 3-9-0 JWilliams(3) (lw: a bhd)....½ **17**
Chalky Dancer *(27) (HJCollingridge)* 3-9-0 RPrice(12) (unf: outpcd) ....½ **18**
Sirius (IRE) *(20) (CWeedon)* 3-9-0 MPerrett(18) (2nd st: wknd 4f out) 4 **19**
316 12 Brooke Wood *(10) (MissBSanders)* 3-8-9 StephenDavies(4) (3rd st: wknd 4f out)....3½ **20**
Mans Passion **(50)***(14) (JWhite)* 3-9-0 GDuffield(15) (bit bkwd: a bhd)....½ **21**

13/8 BEYOND DOUBT, **3/1** Meghdoot, **6/1** Zidac (4/1-7/1), **7/1** Barford Sovereign, **9/1** Niknaks Nephew (op 20/1), Anonym (IRE) (7/1-12/1), **16/1** George Bull, **20/1** Painted Hall (USA), **33/1** Braydon Forest, Memory's Music, **50/1** Nessun Doro, Dazzler, Nobby North, Ardleigh Prince, Solazzi (FR), Ottavio Farnese, Laudation (IRE), Chalky Dancer, Sirius (IRE), Brooke Wood, Mans Passion, CSF £7.81 TOTE £2.60: £1.50 £2.00 £2.40 (£4.60) Trio £7.30 OWNER The Queen (WEST ILSLEY) BRED The Queen 21 Rn 2m 9.5 (4.60) SF: 14/12/11/13/2/-/-/-/-/-/-/-/-/-/-/-/-/-/-/-/-

T/Plpt: £13.40 (1,448.91 Tckts). T/Qdpt: £2.20 (37.3 Tckts). Hn

1424-BRIGHTON (L-H)
Tuesday June 6th (Good to firm)
WEATHER: overcast WIND: almost nil

1515 MOULSECOOMB MEDIAN AUCTION MAIDEN STKS (3-Y.O) (Class E)
£3,130.60 (£932.80: £444.40: £200.20)
5f 213y Stalls: Low GOING minus 0.51 sec per fur (F) 2-30 (2-31)

1094 12 **Jo Maximus (70)***(76) (SDow)* 3-9-0 StephenDavies(2) (mde all: rdn out) ....— **1**
High Priest *(74) (LMCumani)* 3-8-11 (3) OUrbina(5) (bit bkwd: hdwy over 1f out: one pce)....¾ **2**
1150 8 Statistician *(69) (JohnBerry)* 3-9-0 MFenton(8) (2nd st: ev ch over 1f out: one pce)....1¾ **3**
Tonys Gift **(73)***(60) (RHannon)* 3-8-9 RHughes(3) (neat: 3rd st: ev ch over 1f out: wknd fnl f)....1¾ **4**
Al Baha *(58)*(Fav)*(HRACecil)* 3-8-9 AMcGlone(4) (lw: 4th st: rdn over 2f out: one pce) ....¾ **5**
1258 11 Chinese Viking *(55) (GLMoore)* 3-9-0 BRouse(1) (6th st: wknd over 1f out)....3 **6**
1186 13 Norsong *(45) (RAkehurst)* 3-9-0 TQuinn(6) (a bhd)....3½ **7**
Vengan **(51)***(8) (DHaydnJones)* 3-8-9 AMackay(7) (5th st: wknd over 3f out) 12 **8**

7/4 Al Baha, **4/1** Statistician (op 5/2), **5/1** JO MAXIMUS (41/1-11/2), Tonys Gift, **10/1** High Priest (6/1-11/1), **20/1** Norsong, **33/1** Chinese Viking, Vengan, CSF £44.16 TOTE £5.60: £1.60 £3.60 £1.40 (£22.00) OWNER Mr John Kelly (EPSOM) BRED Capt A. L. Smith-Maxwell 8 Rn
69.7 secs (1.30) SF: 35/33/28/19/17/14/4/-

1516 PEACEHAVEN APPRENTICE H'CAP (0-60) (3-Y.O+) (Class F)£2,616.50 (£744.00: £369.50) 6f 209y Stalls: Low GOING minus 0.51 sec per fur (F) 3-00 (3-01)

1335[3] **Pharsical (60)***(71) (MRChannon)* 4-9-6 (8) DSweeney(5) (w ldr: led 5f out: clr over 2f out: pushed out)........— 1
1499[15] Asterix **(42)***(49) (JMBradley)* 7-8-10v RWaterfield(13) (rdn over 2f out: hdwy over 1f out: r.o ins fnl f)........1¾ 2
1426[9] Pirates Gold (IRE) **(48)***(51) (JWhite)* 5-9-2 JWilkinson(7) (lw: 5th st: rdn 2f out: unable qckn)1¾ 3
1426[8] Myjinka **(28)***(29) (JO'Donoghue)* 5-7-10b PDoe(8) (4th st: rdn over 2f out: one pce)........¾ 4
1261[8] Walnut Burl (IRE) **(57)***(57)*(Fav)*(LJHolt)* 5-9-8 (3) IonaWands(1) (rdn 3f out: hdwy over 1f out: nvr nrr)........½ 5
1088[9] Quinzii Martin **(52)***(51) (DHaydnJones)* 7-8-12 (8) AnthonyBond(4) (lw: rdn over 2f out: hdwy over 1f out: nvr nrr)........½ 6
1274[10] High Typha **(51)***(47) (MRChannon)* 4-9-2 (3) JDennis(11) (nvr nrr)........1½ 7
1291[8] Nakita **(50)***(45) (CNAllen)* 4-8-10 (8) KarenMarkham(10) (b.hind: lw: nvr nrr)........nk 8
1353[6] Can't Say (IRE) **(35)***(24) (JMBradley)* 3-7-2v(5) RMullen(6) (3rd st: rdn over 2f out: sn wknd).2½ 9
342[7] Saxon Heir (IRE) **(44)***(29) (JohnBerry)* 3-8-2b GFaulkner(9) (6th st: wknd over 2f out)........1¾ 10
1400[8] Distant Dynasty **(50)***(30) (BAPearce)* 5-8-13 (5) TField(12) (led 2f: 2nd st: wknd wl over 1f out) 2 11
1323[11] Calling (USA) **(44)***(24) (WMBrisbourne)* 4-8-12 VictoriaAppleby(2) (lw: a bhd)........nk 12
1125[15] Dazzle Me **(35)** *(RJBaker)* 3-7-7 JBramhill(3) (7th st: wkng whn hmpd on ins over 1f out).....10 13

LONG HANDICAP Dazzle Me 7-6

6/4 Walnut Burl (IRE) (5/4-2/1), **4/1** PHARSICAL (3/1-9/2), **10/1** Pirates Gold (IRE) (op 6/12), Myjinka (6/1-11/1), Asterix (7/1-12/1), High Typha (7/1-11/1), **16/1** Can't Say (IRE), **20/1** Nakita, Quinzii Martin, Distant Dynasty, **25/1** Saxon Heir (IRE), Calling (USA), **33/1** Dazzle Me, CSF £42.62 CT £353.27 TOTE £3.90: £2.00 £4.50 £2.40 (£24.80) Trio £38.40 OWNER Mr John Sunley (UPPER LAMBOURN) BRED Sunley Stud 13 Rn 1m 22.8 (2.80) SF: 26/4/6/-/12/6/2/-/-/-/-/-/-
WEIGHT FOR AGE 3yo-10lb

1517 BRIGHTON MILE CHALLENGE TROPHY H'CAP (0-80) (3-Y.O+) (Class D) £4,464.00 (£1,332.00: £636.00: £288.00) 7f 214y Stalls: High GOING minus 0.51 sec per fur (F) 3-30 (3-31)

1472* **Sooty Tern (63)***(73)*(Fav)*(JMBradley)* 8-8-8 (5) SDrowne(4) (led 3f: 2nd st: led over 2f out: rdn over 1f out: r.o wl)........— 1
873[21] Confronter **(68)***(78) (SDow)* 6-9-4 PRobinson(1) (lw: 5th st: rdn over 1f out: r.o wl ins fnl f)...s.h 2
1244[6] Piquant **(67)***(71) (LordHuntingdon)* 8-8-12 (5) AWhelan(5) (6th st: nt clr run over 2f out & over 1f out: r.o ins fnl f)........3 3
1179[10] Persian Affair (IRE) **(71)***(70) (DHaydnJones)* 4-9-7 AMackay(7) (lw: 4th st: ev ch wl over 1f out: unable qckn)........2½ 4
1049[4] Perilous Plight **(69)***(63) (WRMuir)* 4-9-2 (3) SSanders(6) (b: lw: hdwy 3f out: ev ch wl over 1f out: wknd fnl f)........2½ 5
1251[3] Indefence (IRE) **(63)***(51) (MRChannon)* 4-8-13 RHughes(8) (hdwy over 1f out: sn wknd)........3 6
1165[5] Greenwich Again **(71)***(55) (TGMills)* 3-8-10 GCarter(3) (bhd fnl 5f)........1¾ 7
1261[11] Blurred Image (IRE) **(78)***(57) (MissGayKelleway)* 4-10-0 DHarrison(9) (lw: hdwy 3f out: wknd 2f out)........2½ 8
373[9] The Little Ferret **(66)***(38) (GLMoore)* 5-9-2 BRouse(2) (lw: 3rd st: wknd over 2f out)........3½ 9
Dontforget Insight (IRE) **(76)***(44) (PFICole)* 4-9-12 TQuinn(10) (led 5f out tl over 2f out: wknd)2 10

9/4 SOOTY TERN, **9/2** Piquant, **13/2** Confronter, Greenwich Again, **9/1** Dontforget Insight (IRE), Indefence (IRE), **10/1** Persian Affair (IRE) (op 6/1), Perilous Plight (op 6/1), **14/1** The Little Ferret, **25/1** Blurred Image (IRE), CSF £17.52 CT £58.57 TOTE £2.80: £1.20 £1.80 £1.90 (£11.00) Trio £19.10 OWNER Mr J. M. Bradley (CHEPSTOW) BRED Sheikh Mohammed bin Rashid al Maktoum 10 Rn 1m 34.6 (2.40) SF: 23/28/21/20/13/1/-/7/-/-
WEIGHT FOR AGE 3yo-11lb

1518 LEVY BOARD H'CAP (0-70) (3-Y.O+) (Class E) £3,187.80 (£950.40: £453.20: £204.60) 1m 3f 196y Stalls: High GOING minus 0.51 sec per fur (F) 4-00 (4-04)

1166[10] **One Off the Rail (USA) (39)***(52) (AMoore)* 5-8-4 CandyMorris(8) (lw: 3rd st: led 3f out: rdn out)........— 1
1166[4] Prince Danzig (IRE) **(52)***(64) (DJGMurraySmith)* 4-9-3 DHarrison(5) (lw: rdn over 5f out: 4th st: chsd wnr over 2f out: r.o)........½ 2

1402[7] Duty Sergeant (IRE) **(32)***(38) (PMitchell)* 6-7-11 GBardwell(10) (rdn & hdwy 5f out: 6th st: unable qckn fnl 2f) 5 **3**
1254[2] Ela Man Howa **(56)***(58)*(Fav)*(RAkehurst)* 4-9-7 TQuinn(4) (lw: rdn over 3f out: hdwy over 2f out: one pce) 2½ **4**
1402* Pistol (IRE) **(64)***(62) (CAHorgan)* 5-10-1 5x PaulEddery(3) (rdn over 3f out: hdwy 2f out: wknd fnl f) 3½ **5**
1200[6] Uncharted Waters **(63)***(60) (CACyzer)* 4-10-0 GDuffield(2) (nvr nr to chal) ....¾ **6**
884[9] Beautete **(53)***(47) (SDow)* 4-9-4 RHughes(6) (lw: hdwy over 4f out: 5th st: wknd over 3f out)1¾ **7**
1382[11] Harding Brown (USA) **(59)***(53) (GHarwood)* 3-8-8 AClark(9) (2nd st: wknd over 2f out)....½ **8**
799a* Sweet Disorder (IRE) **(37)***(22) (DRGandolfo)* 5-8-2 AMcGlone(1) (led 9f) 6 **9**
Shamrock Dancer (IRE) **(30)** *(RJBaker)* 5-7-9 NCarlisle(7) (lw: bhd fnl 6f) 15 **10**

9/4 Ela Man Howa, **7/2** Prince Danzig (IRE) (5/2-4/1), **4/1** Sweet Disorder (IRE) (tchd 6/1), **6/1** Pistol (IRE) (3/1-13/2), **7/1** Uncharted Waters (5/1-8/1), **10/1** Beautete, **16/1** ONE OFF THE RAIL (USA), **20/1** Duty Sergeant (IRE), **33/1** Harding Brown (USA), **66/1** Shamrock Dancer (IRE), CSF £70.28 CT £1,059.24 TOTE £21.60: £4.20 £1.60 £4.40 (£45.90) Trio £115.70 OWNER Mr K. Higson (BRIGHTON) BRED Parrish Hill Farm 10 Rn 2m 31.3 (2.30) SF: 19/31/5/25/29/27/14/4/-/-
WEIGHT FOR AGE 3yo-16lb

1519 HOVE CLAIMING STKS (3-Y.O+) (Class E) £3,187.80 (£950.40: £453.20: £204.60) **1m 1f 209y** Stalls: Low GOING minus 0.51 sec per fur (F) 4-30 (4-34)

1403* **Shabanaz (68)***(66)*(Fav)*(WRMuir)* 10-9-6 StephenDavies(6) (5th st: rdn over 2f out: led ins fnl f: r.o wl) ....— **1**
1484* Overpower **(50)***(60) (MHTompkins)* 11-9-2 PRobinson(1) (stdy hdwy 2f out: ev ch ins fnl f: unable qckn) 1½ **2**
1404[4] Thames Side **(56)***(57) (MMadgwick)* 4-9-1 MFenton(10) (6th st: rdn over 2f out: one pce ins fnl f) 1 **3**
1166[6] Rival Bid (USA) **(62)***(68) (MAJarvis)* 7-9-12 MTebbutt(7) (lw: hdwy over 3f out: led over 2f out tl ins fnl f: one pce) ....s.h **4**
1198[8] Rubadub *(51) (JMBradley)* 4-8-6 (5) SDrowne(2) (hdwy over 1f out: one pce) 1½ **5**
1320[7] Awesome Power **(52)***(56) (JWHills)* 9-9-4 AClark(4) (led over 5f out tl over 2f out: ev ch ins fnl f: sn wknd) ....¾ **6**
Tirollac (IRE) **(45)***(59) (LGCottrell)* 3-8-8 NCarlisle(8) (nvr nr to chal) ....½ **7**
1381[6] Green Green Ruby **(40)***(48) (GLMoore)* 3-7-12 CRutter(3) (no hdwy fnl 2f) ....hd **8**
443[9] Lanesra Breeze **(35)***(48) (TJNaughton)* 3-7-12 (3)ow2 SSanders(5) (4th st: hrd rdn over 2f out: wknd fnl f) ....¾ **9**
1381[7] Elmer's Tune **(43)***(42) (RHannon)* 3-8-1 SRaymont(9) (2nd st: wknd over 2f out) 5 **10**
1295[10] Late Mail (USA) **(60)***(42) (JMPEustace)* 3-8-1 GCarter(11) (led over 4f: 3rd st: wknd over 2f out) ....nk **11**

9/4 SHABANAZ, **5/2** Rival Bid (USA), **4/1** Overpower, **15/2** Late Mail (USA) (5/1-8/1), **10/1** Thames Side (7/1-12/1), **14/1** Green Green Ruby, Awesome Power (8/1-16/1), **25/1** Rubadub, **33/1** Tirollac (IRE), Lanesra Breeze, Elmer's Tune, CSF £12.13 TOTE £2.50: £1.10 £1.50 £4.60 (£4.90) Trio £10.90 OWNER Fayzad Thoroughbred Ltd (LAMBOURN) BRED The Overbury Stud 11 Rn
2m 5.1 (7.10) SF: 4/-/-/6/-/-/-/-/-/-/-
WEIGHT FOR AGE 3yo-13lb

1520 BEVENDEAN MAIDEN STKS (3-Y.O+) (Class D) £3,732.30 (£1,112.40: £530.20: £239.10) **6f 209y** Stalls: Low GOING minus 0.51 sec per fur (F) 5-00 (5-01)

1150[2] **Itab (USA)** *(62+)*(Fav)*(EALDunlop)* 3-8-6 RHills(1) (b.nr hind: mde all: shkn up over 1f out: easily) ....— **1**
1258[8] Sovereigns Parade *(56) (LJHolt)* 3-8-11 AMcGlone(4) (lw: 3rd st: chsd wnr over 2f out: unable qckn) 5 **2**
1168[11] Try-Haitai (IRE) *(47) (RAkehurst)* 4-9-7 TQuinn(3) (lw: 4th st: wknd over 3f out) 3½ **3**
1326[6] Valetta *(34) (BJMeehan)* 4-9-2 DHarrison(2) (2nd st: wknd over 2f out) 3½ **4**

1/12 ITAB (USA), **12/1** Sovereigns Parade (op 7/1), **25/1** Try-Haitai (IRE), **33/1** Valetta, CSF £1.83 TOTE £1.10: (£1.50) OWNER Mr Hamdan Al Maktoum (NEWMARKET) BRED Shadwell Farm Inc and Shadwell Estate Co Ltd 4 Rn 1m 23.3 (3.30) SF: 7/1/2/-
WEIGHT FOR AGE 3yo-10lb

1521 KEMP TOWN H'CAP (0-70) (3-Y.O) (Class E) £3,073.40 (£915.20: £435.60: £195.80) **5f 59y** Stalls: Low GOING minus 0.51 sec per fur (F) 5-30 (5-30)

1400[3] **Tachycardia (42)***(59)*(Fav)*(RJO'Sullivan)* 3-8-0 (3) SSanders(3) (mde all: hrd rdn over 1f out: r.o wl) ....— **1**

1277[3] Portelet **(60)***(62) (RJRWilliams)* 3-9-7 GDuffield(5) (3rd st: hrd rdn over 1f out: unable qckn) 5 2
966[10] Prince Rudolf (IRE) **(47)***(47) (MrsNMacauley)* 3-8-1b(7) AmandaSanders(6) (5th st: rdn over 2f out: one pce) ....½ 3
855[13] Fiery Footsteps **(52)***(42) (PHowling)* 3-8-13v PaulEddery(2) (b.hind: lw: 2nd st: wknd over 2f out) 3½ 4
1050[W] Sandra Dee (IRE) **(60)***(35) (BAPearce)* 3-9-2 (5) AWhelan(4) (lw: outpcd: nvr nrr) 5 5
1146[9] Dismissive (IRE) **(42)***(14) (DrJDScargill)* 3-8-3 MFenton(7) (a bhd) ....¾ 6
Giggleswick Gossip **(49)***(19) (MRChannon)* 3-8-10 RHughes(1) (6th st: wknd over 3f out) ....¾ 7
1331[8] Ivy Lilian (IRE) **(43)***(8) (WMBrisbourne)* 3-7-11 (7) SLanigan(8) (lw: 4th st: wknd over 2f out) 1½ 8

6/4 TACHYCARDIA, **9/4** Portelet, **11/2** Prince Rudolf (IRE), **7/1** Giggleswick Gossip (5/1-8/1), **20/1** Sandra Dee (IRE), **25/1** Fiery Footsteps, **33/1** Dismissive (IRE), Ivy Lilian (IRE), CSF £5.01 CT £11.25 TOTE £2.90: £1.10 £1.00 £1.90 (£2.90) OWNER Mr J. Bury (BOGNOR REGIS) BRED Patrick Eddery Ltd 8 Rn 62.1 secs (2.10) SF: 7/10/-/-/-/-/-/-

T/Plpt: £51.50 (292.81 Tckts). T/Qdpt: £13.30 (11.05 Tckts). AK

1291-PONTEFRACT (L-H)
Tuesday June 6th (Good)

WEATHER: sunny WIND: slt bhd

1522

PONTEFRACT SERIES MAIDEN APPRENTICE STKS (3-Y.O) (Class F) £2,706.00 (£766.00: £378.00)
6f Stalls: Low GOING minus 0.39 sec per fur (F) 2-45 (2-48)

865[3] **Courageous Dancer (IRE)** *(80)*(Fav)*(BHanbury)* 3-8-6 JO'Dwyer(4) (lw: bhd: hdwy over 1f out: str run to ld nr fin) ....— 1
752[3] Allyana (IRE) *(79) (IABalding)* 3-8-6 MartinDwyer(1) (led tl ct cl home) ....½ 2
St Valery *(74) (CREgerton)* 3-8-6 MHenry(2) (leggy: a chsng ldrs: one pce fnl 2f) 1¾ 3
1296[3] Intiaash (IRE) **(77)***(70) (PTWalwyn)* 3-8-3 (3) AEddery(6) (chsd ldrs: hung lft over 1f out: nt r.o) 1½ 4
1258[9] She Said No *(54) (LordHuntingdon)* 3-8-1 (5) AimeeCook(3) (bhd: effrt ½-wy: no imp) 6 5
937[3] Dark Menace **(76)***(46) (SMellor)* 3-8-11 ADaly(5) (prom 4f) 5 6
1059[7] Upex le Gold Too **(45)***(35) (LRLloyd-James)* 3-8-11 KimberleyHart(7) (chsd ldrs over 3f) 4 7
1296[11] Handsome Squaw *(BWMurray)* 3-8-3 (5)ow2 CScudder(8) (Withdrawn not under Starter's orders) .... W

7/4 COURAGEOUS DANCER (IRE), **11/4** Allyana (IRE), Intiaash (IRE), **11/2** Dark Menace, **16/1** St Valery, **33/1** She Said No, **50/1** Handsome Squaw, **100/1** Upex le Gold Too, CSF £6.83 TOTE £2.70: £1.90 £1.30 (£3.00) OWNER Mr Abdullah Ali (NEWMARKET) BRED Gainsborough Stud Management Ltd 7 Rn 1m 16.8 (2.50) SF: 26/25/20/16/-/-/-

1523

GROVE (S) H'CAP (0-60) (3-Y.O+) (Class G) £2,875.00 (£800.00: £385.00)
1m 4y Stalls: Low GOING minus 0.39 sec per fur (F) 3-15 (3-17)

1074[4] **Pop to Stans (46)***(54) (JPearce)* 6-8-12 (7) ElizabethTurner(16) (lw: bhd: c wd & hdwy ent st: r.o wl to ld cl home) ....— 1
1323[19] Self Expression **(53)***(60)*(Fav)*(MrsJRRamsden)* 7-9-12 KFallon(13) (lw: bhd: gd hdwy over 1f out: led wl ins fnl f: hdd & no ex nr fin) ....½ 2
672[8] Resolute Bay **(42)***(47) (RMWhitaker)* 9-9-1 ACulhane(9) (drvn along & hdwy 3f out: led ins fnl f: hdd & no ex wl ins fnl f) 1¼ 3
1191[7] Puffy **(34)***(33) (MDods)* 8-8-7v JCarroll(5) (b: s.i.s: c wd & hdwy ent st: nrst fin) 3 4
1153[7] My Godson **(45)***(43) (FJO'Mahony)* 5-9-4 SDWilliams(3) (a chsng ldrs: rdn 2f out: r.o one pce) ....s.h 5
1155[4] Milltown Classic (IRE) **(39)***(35) (JParkes)* 3-8-1 MDeering(12) (hdwy 3f out: rdn & one pce appr fnl f) 1¼ 6
1291[9] Level Edge **(47)***(41) (MDHammond)* 4-9-6 DaleGibson(2) (prom: effrt 3f out: styd on one pce) ....¾ 7
1332[9] Greek Night Out (IRE) **(35)***(29) (MrsVAAconley)* 4-8-8 TWilliams(11) (nvr nr to chal) ....nk 8
1206[9] Wordsmith (IRE) **(45)***(38) (JLHarris)* 5-9-4 RCochrane(15) (lw: s.i.s: rdn 3f out: styd on fnl f) ....½ 9
1206[3] Reed My Lips (IRE) **(38)***(30) (BPJBaugh)* 4-8-11 RPrice(19) (jnd ldrs ½-wy: wknd ins fnl f) ....½ 10
1290* Scent of Power **(37)***(29) (MartynWane)* 5-8-10 KDarley(10) (sn chsng ldrs: led over 2f out tl ins fnl f: sn btn) ....hd 11
1274[3] Flair Lady **(50)***(40) (WGMTurner)* 4-9-4 (5) PMcCabe(18) (prom tl wknd fnl 2f) ....¾ 12
835[4] Big Chance **(33)***(21) (WJMusson)* 6-8-6 SWhitworth(14) (stdd s: n.d) 1 13

1153[5] Daily Challenger (USA) **(50)**(*32*) (*RonaldThompson*) 3-8-12 DeanMcKeown(7) (chsd ldrs 6f)..3 **14**
Little Blackfoot **(34)**(*14*) (*JLHarris*) 7-8-2 (5) CTeague(17) (n.d) 1¼ **15**
1244[14] Across the Bay **(48)**(*28*) (*RWEmery*) 8-9-7b LDettori(4) (chsd ldrs tl wknd over 2f out)....s.h **16**
1161[7] Dundeelin **(33)**(*10*) (*JLEyre*) 4-8-6 RLappin(8) (trckd ldrs tl rdn & btn wl over 1f out) 1½ **17**
1412[5] Kings Vision **(47)**(*12*) (*BSRothwell*) 3-8-9b LCharnock(1) (t: hdwy ½-wy: no imp)....6 **18**
548[12] Bold Aristocrat (IRE) **(47)**(*9*) (*RHollinshead*) 4-9-6 WRyan(6) (lw: led tl hdd & wknd over 2f out) 1½ **19**

4/1 Self Expression, **5/1** Scent of Power, **8/1** Big Chance, **9/1** Flair Lady, **12/1** Reed My Lips (IRE), POP TO STANS, Puffy, **14/1** Resolute Bay (10/1-16/1), Milltown Classic (IRE), **16/1** Kings Vision, Dundeelin, **20/1** Level Edge, My Godson, Daily Challenger (USA), Wordsmith (IRE), Across the Bay, Greek Night Out (IRE), Bold Aristocrat (IRE), **33/1** Little Blackfoot, CSF £62.21 CT £665.76 TOTE £12.70: £2.50 £1.60 £15.80 £3.30 (£32.00) Trio £221.40 OWNER Mr A. J. Thompson (NEWMARKET) BRED Lincoln Collins 19 Rn 1m 46.8 (4.80) SF: 20/26/13/-/9/-/7/-/4/-/-/6/-/-/-/-/-/-/-
WEIGHT FOR AGE 3yo-11lb
No bid.

1524

KALAMAZOO G.M.S. SECURITY TICKET H'CAP (0-90) (3-Y.O) (Class C) £6,056.00 (£1,808.00: £864.00: £392.00)
1m 2f 6y Stalls: Low GOING minus 0.39 sec per fur (F) 3-45 (3-48)

1130[11] **Rokeby Bowl (76)**(*89*) (*IABalding*) 3-8-12 LDettori(5) (hdwy 4f out: led jst ins fnl f: r.o)....— **1**
1294* Shinerolla **(71)**(*82*)(Fav)(*MrsJRRamsden*) 3-8-7 KFallon(6) (lw: hld up & bhd: stdy hdwy 3f out: led wl over 1f out: hdd jst ins fnl f: r.o) 1½ **2**
962[3] Sherqy (IRE) **(82)**(*83*) (*JLDunlop*) 3-9-4 WCarson(8) (lw: hdwy ½-wy: ch 2f out: r.o ne pce) 6 **3**
829[8] Percy Braithwaite (IRE) **(85)**(*83*) (*MJohnston*) 3-9-7 DHolland(9) (lw: chsd ldrs: led 4f out tl wl over 1f out: sn outpcd) 1¾ **4**
1358[3] Shining Edge **(57)**(*52*) (*MHEasterby*) 3-7-7 JQuinn(3) (chsd ldrs tl outpcd fnl 2f)....1¾ **5**
929* Nine Barrow Down (IRE) **(80)**(*72*) (*HRACecil*) 3-9-2 WRyan(2) (a.p: rdn 4f out: outpcd fnl 2f)2½ **6**
1103[6] Greenspan (IRE) **(83)**(*51*) (*WRMuir*) 3-9-5 MHills(4) (prom tl wknd 2f out) 15 **7**
1150[7] Stand Tall **(64)** (*CWThornton*) 3-8-0 TWilliams(7) (sn pushed along: in tch: hdwy 4f out: wknd wl over 1f out) 20 **8**
1180[17] Night Wink (USA) **(73)**(*2*) (*MRStoute*) 3-8-9v WRSwinburn(1) (led & sn clr: hdd 4f out: btn whn hmpd over 3f out)....4 **9**

7/4 Shinerolla, **4/1** Nine Barrow Down (IRE), **5/1** Sherqy (IRE), **9/1** Greenspan (IRE), **10/1** ROKEBY BOWL, **11/1** Shining Edge (8/1-14/1), **12/1** Night Wink (USA), Stand Tall, **25/1** Percy Braithwaite (IRE), CSF £27.42 CT £93.59 TOTE £10.70: £2.70 £1.30 £1.60 (£13.70) Trio £13.10 OWNER Mr Paul Mellon (KINGSCLERE) BRED Paul Mellon 9 Rn 2m 11.7 (3.40) SF: 40/33/34/34/3/23/2/-/-

1525

E.B.F. THORNE MAIDEN STKS (2-Y.O F) (Class D) £4,162.50 (£1,260.00: £615.00: £292.50) **6f** Stalls: Low GOING minus 0.39 sec per fur (F) 4-15 (4-22)

970[2] **Mystic Tempo (USA)** (*79*)(Fav)(*PWChapple-Hyam*) 2-8-11 JReid(2) (lw: mde all: edgd rt & r.o u.p fnl f) ....— **1**
Amoeba (IRE) (*77*) (*JBerry*) 2-8-11 JCarroll(8) (w'like: chsd ldrs: rdn to chal ins fnl f: kpt on) .¾ **2**
1063[3] Meeting Point (*69*) (*MrsMReveley*) 2-8-11 KDarley(6) (cl up: rdn 2f out: kpt on one pce)....3 **3**
Maid For Baileys (IRE) (*66*) (*MJohnston*) 2-8-11 DHolland(4) (leggy: scope: in tch: sn pushed along: kpt on fnl f) 1¼ **4**
Gladys Althorpe (IRE) (*66*) (*JLEyre*) 2-8-11 RLappin(1) (leggy: unf: unruly s: chsd ldrs over 4f)....s.h **5**
Satin Secret (IRE) (*61*) (*JMPEustace*) 2-8-11 RCochrane(9) (leggy: unf: s.i.s: nvr nr to chal)1¾ **6**
1190[4] Trickledown (*40*) (*CWFairhurst*) 2-8-11 JFortune(3) (uns rdr & bolted gng to s: cl up tl wknd wl over 1f out)....8 **7**
Society Girl (*10*) (*CWThornton*) 2-8-11 DeanMcKeown(5) (cmpt: b.hind: dwlt: hung lft: a outpcd & bhd) 11 **8**
Auriga (*IABalding*) 2-8-11 LDettori(7) (Withdrawn not under Starter's orders) .... **W**

2/1 MYSTIC TEMPO (USA), **4/1** Meeting Point, **9/2** Satin Secret (IRE) (8/1-7/2), **5/1** Auriga, **15/2** Amoeba (IRE), **8/1** Trickledown, **12/1** Maid For Baileys (IRE) (op 7/1), **50/1** Gladys Althorpe (IRE), Society Girl, CSF £12.97 TOTE £2.30: £1.10 £2.40 £1.30 (£9.30) Trio £8.50 OWNER Mr R. E. Sangster (MARLBOROUGH) BRED Swetteham Stud and Ben Sangster 8 Rn
1m 18.2 (3.90) SF: 13/11/3/-/-/-/-/-

1526

ROPERGATE MAIDEN STKS (3-Y.O) (Class D) £3,728.75 (£1,130.00: £552.50: £263.75) **1m 2f 6y** Stalls: Low GOING minus 0.39 sec per fur (F) 4-45 (4-48)

1129[4] **Kutta (93)**(*86*) (*RWArmstrong*) 3-9-0 WCarson(16) (lw: chsd ldrs: outpcd 3f out: r.o u.p to ld jst ins fnl f: styd on) ....— **1**

1173[2] United Force (IRE) **(90)***(82) (PWChapple-Hyam)* 3-9-0 JReid(13) (lw: led tl hdd jst ins fnl f: kpt on) 2½ **2**
1175[2] Syrian Queen *(72)*(Fav)*(HRACecil)* 3-8-9 WRyan(12) (lw: chsd ldrs: chal 3f out: wknd 1f out) 3 **3**
950[9] Alaraby (IRE) *(66) (IABalding)* 3-8-9 KDarley(5) (hdwy over 3f out: styd on fnl f) 4 **4**
1173[9] Lucky Quest *(70) (NAGraham)* 3-9-0 DHolland(3) (styd on fnl 3f: nrst fin) ....½ **5**
1173[10] Cante Chico *(68) (TThomsonJones)* 3-9-0 SWhitworth(1) (chsd ldrs tl outpcd over 3f out: kpt on fnl f) 1½ **6**
1173[3] Woodcrest *(62) (HCandy)* 3-8-9 WNewnes(9) (bhd: rdn & nt clr run over 3f out: sme hdwy whn nt clr run over 1f out: n.d) ....nk **7**
Pretoria Dancer *(67) (JHMGosden)* 3-9-0 LDettori(6) (w'like: str: bkwd: in tch: shkn up over 3f out: styd on) ....hd **8**
1150[10] Oleron *(61) (JNorton)* 3-8-9 ACulhane(4) (nvr bttr than mid div) ....¾ **9**
Young Vic *(60) (GWragg)* 3-8-9 MHills(2) (rangy: unf: bit bkwd: outpcd & bhd tl styd on fnl 3f) ....½ **10**
Reaganesque (USA) *(64) (EALDunlop)* 3-9-0 WRSwinburn(10) (leggy: hld up & bhd: nvr plcd to chal) ....¾ **11**
1198[5] Fabillion *(54) (CASmith)* 3-9-0 MWigham(15) (hld up & bhd: n.d) 6 **12**
Hala Halina *(47) (JEBanks)* 3-8-9 RCochrane(14) (lengthy: scope: bkwd: trckd ldrs: effrt 3f out: sn wknd) 1¼ **13**
Wassl Street (IRE) *(44) (JHMGosden)* 3-9-0 JCarroll(7) (rangy: bit bkwd: pushed along ½-wy: n.d) 5 **14**
Pharr *(27) (CEBrittain)* 3-8-9 BDoyle(8) (cmpt: bkwd: a bhd) 8 **15**
978[11] Roscommon Lad (IRE) **(42)***(20) (RHollinshead)* 3-9-0 TIves(11) (chsd ldrs: sn drvn along: wknd 4f out) 7 **16**

13/8 Syrian Queen, **9/4** KUTTA, **6/1** Woodcrest (4/1-7/1), **7/1** United Force (IRE) (op 9/2), **10/1** Hala Halina (6/1-12/1), **12/1** Pretoria Dancer, **14/1** Young Vic, **16/1** Reaganesque (USA), **20/1** Wassl Street (IRE), Alaraby (IRE), **25/1** Pharr, **33/1** Fabillion, Cante Chico, **50/1** Lucky Quest, **100/1** Oleron, Roscommon Lad (IRE), CSF £21.99 TOTE £3.50: £1.60 £2.00 £1.20 (£11.20) Trio £7.10 OWNER Mr Hamdan Al Maktoum (NEWMARKET) BRED Shadwell Estate Company Limited 16 Rn
2m 14.6 (6.30) SF: 20/16/6/-/4/2/-/1/-/-/-/-/-/-/-/-

1527 IRONBRIDGE H'CAP (0-80) (3-Y.O) (Class D) £4,110.00 (£1,230.00: £590.00: £270.00) **1m 4f 8y** Stalls: Low GOING minus 0.39 sec per fur (F) 5-15 (5-20)

1402[2] **Dont Shoot Fairies (68)***(75) (CEBrittain)* 3-8-11 BDoyle(9) (mde all: hld on wl fnl 2f) ....— **1**
1295[2] Advance East **(70)***(76)*(Fav)*(MrsJRRamsden)* 3-8-13 KFallon(10) (lw: hld up: hdwy 4f out: rdn to chal 1f out: nt qckn) 1 **2**
647[3] Kristal's Paradise (IRE) **(74)***(79) (JLDunlop)* 3-9-3 WCarson(7) (cl up tl outpcd over 2f out: styd on ins fnl f: nt clr run towards fin) ....nk **3**
Beauchamp Jade **(74)***(79) (HCandy)* 3-9-3 WNewnes(5) (hld up: hdwy & prom 4f out: outpcd ent st: styd on towards fin) ....s.h **4**
655[2] Executive Design **(78)***(81) (MrsMReveley)* 3-9-7 KDarley(6) (lw: in tch: hdwy 4f out: chal over 1f out: wknd ins fnl f) 1½ **5**
1372[3] Last Corner **(56)***(57) (RHollinshead)* 3-7-13 LCharnock(4) (hld up: effrt 3f out: styd on wl: nt pce to chal) 1½ **6**
1194[7] Lucidity **(58)***(59) (CWThornton)* 3-8-1 JQuinn(1) (prom tl outpcd fnl 2½f) ....½ **7**
1289[8] Shamekh **(61)***(59) (JEBanks)* 3-8-4 ow1 RCochrane(2) (hld up & bhd: outpcd over 3f out: n.d) 1½ **8**
1379* Danus Rex (IRE) **(53)***(52) (CASmith)* 3-7-10 5x DaleGibson(8) (chsd ldrs tl outpcd fnl 3f) ....s.h **9**
1329[2] Komiamaite **(63)***(32) (SRBowring)* 3-8-1b(5)ow3 CTeague(3) (chsd ldrs tl wknd 3f out: t.o) 20 **10**

7/2 Advance East, **9/2** Danus Rex (IRE), **5/1** Beauchamp Jade (8/1-12/1), **11/2** Executive Design, Kristal's Paradise (IRE), **9/1** Last Corner, **11/1** DONT SHOOT FAIRIES, **12/1** Lucidity, **25/1** Shamekh, Komiamaite, CSF £47.91 CT £217.15 TOTE £9.10: £3.20 £1.40 £2.10 (£36.90) Trio £23.70 OWNER Mrs Celia Miller (NEWMARKET) BRED Mrs Celia Miller 10 Rn
2m 42.4 (8.10) SF: 14/15/18/18/20/-/-/-/-/-
T/Jkpt: Not won; £15,746.05 to Warwick 7/6/95. T/Plpt: £9.50 (2,328.12 Tckts). T/Qdpt: £2.50 (77.25 Tckts). AA

1215-BEVERLEY (R-H)
Wednesday June 7th (Good becoming Good to soft)
WEATHER: showers WIND: slt half against

1528 PASTURE MASTERS H'CAP (0-70) (3-Y.O+) (Class E) £3,510.75 (£1,056.00: £510.50: £237.75) **7f 100y** Stalls: High GOING minus 0.19 sec (GF) 6-30 (6-30)

1207[2] **Euro Sceptic (IRE) (45)***(52)*(Fav)*(MHEasterby)* 3-7-11b SMaloney(8) (trckd ldrs: led 1½f out: rdn & r.o) ....— **1**

876[12] Ochos Rios (IRE) **(62)***(67) (BSRothwell)* 4-9-5 (5) JStack(10) (lw: hld up & bhd: effrt & n.m.r over 3f out: hdwy over 1f out: r.o) ....¾ **2**
1351[5] Racing Brenda **(52)***(57) (BAMcMahon)* 4-9-0 FNorton(11) (lw: trckd ldrs: hdwy & ev ch 1f out: nt qckn towards fin) ....nk **3**
762[8] Buddy's Friend (IRE) **(58)***(60) (RJRWilliams)* 7-9-6 TIves(5) (hdwy 3f out: ch appr fnl f: one pce) 1¼ **4**
876[15] Evan 'elp Us **(66)***(68) (JLEyre)* 3-9-4b JFortune(7) (bhd tl styd on fnl 2f: nrst fin) ....s.h **5**
1206* Mary's Case (IRE) **(54)***(55) (MJohnston)* 5-9-2b DHolland(4) (hld up: swtchd outside & effrt 2f out: no imp) ....½ **6**
749[13] Sea-Ayr (IRE) **(48)***(44) (MrsSMAustin)* 5-8-10 JMarshall(6) (lw: b: hld up & bhd: effrt over 2f out: rdn & nvr able to chal) 2½ **7**
1421[5] The Happy Loon (IRE) **(55)***(44) (DenysSmith)* 4-9-3 JWeaver(9) (led tl hdd & wknd 1½f out) ..3 **8**
1251[10] Ballard Ring (IRE) **(57)***(39) (JSWainwright)* 4-9-5b DeanMcKeown(3) (effrt ent st: no imp) 3½ **9**
1499[11] Drum Sergeant **(35)** *(JParkes)* 8-7-11v MDeering(2) (cl up tl wknd over 2f out) 11 **10**
1045[4] Benten **(41)** *(DWChapman)* 3-7-7 NKennedy(1) (w ldr: sddle slipped appr st: sn lost pl) 30 **11**

LONG HANDICAP Benten 7-5

4/1 EURO SCEPTIC (IRE), **9/2** Sea-Ayr (IRE), **5/1** The Happy Loon (IRE), **7/1** Racing Brenda, **8/1** Buddy's Friend (IRE), Mary's Case (IRE), **10/1** Ochos Rios (IRE), Evan 'elp Us, **25/1** Ballard Ring (IRE), **33/1** Drum Sergeant, Benten, CSF £39.35 CT £243.60 TOTE £3.70: £1.40 £3.30 £2.30 (£36.40) Trio £176.20 OWNER Mr C. H. Stevens (MALTON) BRED Martyn J. McEnery 11 Rn
1m 34.0 (2.00) SF: 24/49/39/42/40/37/26/26/21/-/-
WEIGHT FOR AGE 3yo-10lb

1529 WOODMANSEY H'CAP (0-60) (3-Y.O+) (Class F) £3,135.50 (£944.00: £457.00: £213.50) **1m 3f 216y** Stalls: High GOING minus 0.19 sec per fur (GF) 7-00 (7-02)

1219[3] **Bowcliffe Court (IRE) (55)***(68)*(Fav)*(BWHills)* 3-8-7 DHolland(10) (hld up: hdwy on outside appr st: led over 1f out: r.o wl) ....— **1**
Kintavi **(34)***(40) (TWDonnelly)* 5-8-2 JFanning(12) (hld up: hdwy 6f out: led 3f out tl over 1f out: no ex) 5 **2**
1372* Green Land (BEL) **(64)***(69) (SCWilliams)* 3-9-2 5x KDarley(13) (b.nr fore: lw: a chsng ldrs: one pce fnl 2½f) 1¼ **3**
751[6] Aljadeer (USA) **(45)***(50) (MWEasterby)* 6-8-13b TIves(3) (lw: hld up: effrt 3f out: styd on: nvr able to chal) ....s.h **4**
1377[10] Kilernan **(43)***(45) (TDBarron)* 4-8-11 JFortune(11) (in tch: hdwy to chse ldrs ent st: sn rdn & one pce) 2 **5**
1254[4] Star Fighter **(51)***(52) (WAO'Gorman)* 3-8-3 GHind(6) (in tch: effrt appr st: no imp) ....¾ **6**
1368[3] Augustan **(56)***(53) (SGollings)* 4-9-10v JWeaver(5) (chsd ldrs: led over 5f out to 3f out: sn wknd) 3 **7**
776[5] Missus Murhill (IRE) **(39)***(33) (NTinkler)* 4-8-7 KimTinkler(1) (s.i.s: a bhd) 2½ **8**
1093[17] Nanton Point (USA) **(50)***(42) (LadyHerries)* 3-7-9b(7) ShonaCrombie(9) (bhd tl sme late hdwy) 1½ **9**
1064[6] Soba Up **(47)***(39) (TJEtherington)* 5-9-1b ACulhane(7) (trckd ldrs: effrt 3f out: rdn & no rspnse) ....s.h **10**
1292[10] Fort Vally **(43)***(33) (BWMurray)* 5-8-4 (7)ow1 GParkin(15) (rdn 3f out: nvr trbld ldrs) ....nk **11**
1252[6] Merry Mermaid **(46)***(35) (JFBottomley)* 5-9-0 KFallon(8) (lw: pushed along 6f out: n.d) 1½ **12**
Swiss Mountain **(33)***(10) (PJBevan)* 5-8-1 NCarlisle(2) (cl up: chal over 5f out: wknd over 3f out) 9 **13**
1039[5] Marjimel **(47)***(19) (JLEyre)* 4-9-1 RLappin(4) (a rr div) 3½ **14**
860[11] Ginka **(44)** *(PJBevan)* 4-8-5b(7) DDenby(14) (led tl hdd over 5f out: sn lost pl) 30 **15**

5/2 BOWCLIFFE COURT (IRE), **7/2** Green Land (BEL), **11/2** Aljadeer (USA), **10/1** Merry Mermaid, Star Fighter, Augustan, **12/1** Soba Up, **14/1** Missus Murhill (IRE), **16/1** Nanton Point (USA), **20/1** Fort Vally, Marjimel, **25/1** Kilernan, **33/1** Kintavi, Swiss Mountain, Ginka, CSF £80.03 CT £284.54 TOTE £4.00: £1.80 £11.60 £1.80 (£603.50) Trio £287.50; £324.03 to Beverley 8/6/95 OWNER Mr J. Hanson (LAMBOURN) BRED Crest Stud Ltd 15 Rn 2m 41.6 (10.10) SF: 8/-/9/6/1/-/9/-/-/-/-/-/-/-/-
WEIGHT FOR AGE 3yo-16lb

1530 HILARY NEEDLER TROPHY CONDITIONS STKS (2-Y.O F) (Class B) £9,064.00 (£3,376.00: £1,638.00: £690.00: £295.00: £137.00) **5f** Stalls: Centre GOING minus 0.19 sec per fur (GF) 7-30 (7-30)

1287* **Top Cat (FR)** *(77) (EWeymes)* 2-8-12 DeanMcKeown(1) (lw: sn w ldr: led appr fnl f: all out) ....— **1**
1278* Beautiful Ballad (IRE) *(76) (BWHills)* 2-8-12 DHolland(6) (lw: b.hind: mde most tl hdd appr fnl f: rallied towards fin) ....nk **2**
1163[2] Tarf (USA) *(72) (PTWalwyn)* 2-8-8 WCarson(3) (chsd ldrs: swtchd over 1f out: wandered u.p: styd on towards fin) ....hd **3**

1293[2] Kunucu (IRE) *(71) (TDBarron)* 2-8-12 KDarley(4) (hld up: effrt 2f out: styd on: nvr able to chal)....1½ 4
1341* Red Stream (USA) *(61)*(Fav)*(MRStoute)* 2-8-12 WRSwinburn(5) (lw: hld up: rdn ½-wy: no imp)....3 5
1247* Royal Ceilidh (IRE) *(49) (DenysSmith)* 2-8-12 JFortune(2) (lw: hld up: effrt ½-wy: sn btn)....4 6

13/8 Red Stream (USA), **4/1** Tarf (USA), **5/1** Kunucu (IRE), **11/2** Beautiful Ballad (IRE), **13/2** Royal Ceilidh (IRE), **7/1** TOP CAT (FR) (op 12/1), CSF £39.83 TOTE £8.60: £3.30 £2.90 (£16.70) OWNER Mrs A. Birkett (MIDDLEHAM) BRED Major C. R. and Mrs Philipson 6 Rn

66.8 secs (5.30) SF: -/-/-/-/-/-

1531 DERBY WEEK H'CAP (0-80) (4-Y.O+) (Class D) £3,788.50 (£1,138.00: £549.00: £254.50) 1m 100y Stalls: High GOING minus 0.19 sec per fur (GF) 8-00 (8-00)

1250[2] **Coureur (61)***(71)*(Fav)*(JDBethell)* 6-8-9 TIves(6) (lw: hld up: qcknd to ld appr fnl f: r.o)....— 1
1324[3] Kaafih Homm (IRE) **(53)***(58) (NACallaghan)* 4-8-1 WCarson(1) (lw: b.hind: a.p: hdwy whn nt clr run over 1f out: swtchd & r.o)....2½ 2
1523[2] Self Expression **(53)***(58) (MrsJRRamsden)* 7-8-1 BDoyle(7) (hld up & bhd: hdwy 2f out: nt clr run over 1f out: swtchd & r.o)....nk 3
1415[6] Tolls Choice (IRE) **(57)***(54) (MWEasterby)* 6-8-5 KDarley(5) (trckd ldrs: nt clr run 2f out: nt rcvr)....4 4
652[7] Weather Break **(80)***(74) (HCandy)* 4-10-0 WNewnes(4) (led tl hdd & wknd appr fnl f)....1½ 5
1244[3] Scottish Park **(45)***(30) (RWEmery)* 6-7-7 GBardwell(3) (drvn along 5f out: n.d)....5 6
776[8] Ikis Girl **(49)***(32) (SGollings)* 4-7-11v FNorton(2) (chsd ldrs tl wknd over 2f out)....1¼ 7

LONG HANDICAP Scottish Park 7-2

9/4 COUREUR, **3/1** Kaafih Homm (IRE), **4/1** Self Expression, **6/1** Tolls Choice (IRE), Scottish Park, **10/1** Weather Break, **25/1** Ikis Girl, CSF £9.35 TOTE £3.20: £1.60 £1.80 (£3.80) OWNER Mr Robert Gibbons (MIDDLEHAM) BRED Gainsborough Stud Management Ltd 7 Rn

1m 50.1 (6.10) SF: 6/-/-/-/9/-/-

1532 COTTINGHAM RATING RELATED MAIDEN LIMITED STKS (0-70) (3-Y.O) (Class E) £3,072.00 (£921.00: £443.00: £204.00) 1m 100y Stalls: High GOING minus 0.19 sec per fur (GF) 8-30 (8-30)

1380[8] **Lorelei Lee (IRE) (69)***(67) (JohnBerry)* 3-8-9 KFallon(2) (a.p: swtchd over 1f out: led wl ins fnl f: drvn out)....— 1
1380[7] Jurassic Sue **(62)***(66) (BWHills)* 3-8-9v DHolland(4) (lw: trckd ldrs: led over 1f out: hung lft: hung bdly rt ins fnl f: sn hdd: kpt on)....nk 2
1366[5] Shining Example **(69)***(67)*(Fav)*(PJMakin)* 3-9-0 WRSwinburn(5) (lw: disp ld tl led 3f out: hdd over 1f out: btn whn bdly hmpd ins fnl f)....2½ 3
1270[6] Mr Christie **(66)***(55) (MissLCSiddall)* 3-9-0 WNewnes(1) (lw: effrt 3f out: styd on: nvr able to chal)....6 4
1167[4] Tragic Hero **(70)***(48) (IABalding)* 3-9-0 KDarley(6) (lw: disp ld tl rdn & wknd 3f out)....4 5
Diamond Market **(60)***(35) (RHollinshead)* 3-9-0 TIves(3) (bhd & rdn ent st: n.d)....7 6

6/4 Shining Example, **9/4** Tragic Hero, **5/1** Jurassic Sue, **6/1** LORELEI LEE (IRE), **9/1** Mr Christie, **25/1** Diamond Market, CSF £32.23 TOTE £7.30: £2.00 £2.30 (£15.00) OWNER Mr L. C. Wadey (NEWMARKET) BRED Sheikh Mohammed bin Rashid al Maktoum 6 Rn

1m 52.3 (8.30) SF: -/-/-/-/-/-

1533 WELTON MAIDEN STKS (3-Y.O+) (Class D) £3,788.50 (£1,138.00: £549.00: £254.50) 7f 100y Stalls: High GOING minus 0.19 sec per fur (GF) 9-00 (9-01)

1467[3] **Boldina Bay (78)***(76) (MJohnston)* 3-8-6 JWeaver(10) (bhd: pushed thro & hdwy over 2f out: r.o wl to ld post)....— 1
1136[10] Masaafaat (USA) *(76)*(Fav)*(MRStoute)* 3-8-6 WCarson(4) (b: a.p: led ins fnl f: sn pushed along: nt qckn nr fin: ct post)....s.h 2
915[2] Lucky Soph (USA) *(72) (BWHills)* 3-8-6 DHolland(8) (b.hind: led: hung lft fnl 2f: hdd ins fnl f: no ex)....2 3
1446[3] French Ginger *(68) (IABalding)* 4-9-2 WNewnes(7) (lw: hdwy 3f out: kpt on: nt pce to chal).1½ 4
1216[3] Young Benson **(72)***(71) (BAMcMahon)* 3-8-11 JFortune(11) (a chsng ldrs: effrt 3f out: r.o one pce)....1¼ 5
1309[5] Hand of Straw (IRE) *(69) (JWWatts)* 3-8-11 NConnorton(9) (chsd ldrs tl grad wknd fnl 2f)....¾ 6
1264[6] Bella Sedona *(63) (LadyHerries)* 3-8-6 KDarley(3) (chsd ldrs: ev ch over 2f out: wknd over 1f out)....½ 7
1312[8] Mighty Marston *(66) (LadyHerries)* 3-8-11 TIves(5) (in tch: outpcd ent st: n.m.r over 1f out: styd on one pce)....1 8

1296[8] Me Cherokee *(54) (CWThornton)* 3-8-6 DeanMcKeown(12) (nvr trbld ldrs)....3 9
Moonlight Air *(53) (JLSpearing)* 4-9-2 KFallon(6) (unf: bhd & bmpd over 2f out: n.d)....¾ 10
1291[7] Brother Barnabas *(51) (CWThornton)* 4-9-7 NCarlisle(13) (in tch: one pce fnl 3f)....3 11
1296[9] Harry's Treat *(41) (JLEyre)* 3-8-6 RLappin(1) (a rr div)....2½ 12
Readyspex *(18) (RDEWoodhouse)* 5-9-7 SMaloney(2) (a bhd)....13 13

2/1 Masaafaat (USA), **7/2** Lucky Soph (USA) (2/1-4/1), **5/1** French Ginger, **13/2** BOLDINA BAY, **10/1** Young Benson, Bella Sedona, **16/1** Harry's Treat, **20/1** Mighty Marston, Hand of Straw (IRE), **25/1** Moonlight Air, Me Cherokee, **33/1** Brother Barnabas, Readyspex, CSF £20.76 TOTE £6.10: £1.70 £1.60 £1.50 (£7.90) Trio £7.00 OWNER Greenland Park Ltd (MIDDLEHAM) BRED Laharna Ltd 13 Rn
1m 38.6 (6.60) SF: -/-/-/-/-/-/-/-/-/-/-/-/-
WEIGHT FOR AGE 3yo-10lb

T/Plpt: £429.70 (31.81 Tckts). T/Qdpt: £26.40 (5 Tckts). AA

1399-FOLKESTONE (R-H)
Wednesday June 7th (Good)
WEATHER: overcast WIND: almost nil

1534 PEDLINGE AMATEUR LIMITED STKS (0-70) (3-Y.O+) (Class F)
£3,098.60 (£859.60: £411.80)
6f 189y Stalls: Low GOING minus 0.15 sec per fur (GF) 6-15 (6-17)

Chief of Staff (64)*(75+) (JPearce)* 6-11-0 MrsLPearce(1) (hdwy over 2f out: led 1f out: r.o wl)....— 1
1126[2] Mr Nevermind (IRE) **(66)***(70)*(Fav)*(GLMoore)* 5-10-9 (5) MrKGoble(3) (hdwy over 3f out: hrd rdn over 1f out: unable qckn fnl f)....2 2
448[5] Never so Rite (IRE) **(50)***(63) (DWPArbuthnot)* 3-9-13 MrsDArbuthnot(5) (6th st: rdn over 1f out: one pce)....1 3
1381[5] Top Pet (IRE) **(62)***(66) (RAkehurst)* 5-11-0 MrTMcCarthy(9) (a.p: led over 2f out to 1f out: sn wknd)....1 4
1405[2] Mo's Star **(64)***(59) (SDow)* 3-9-13 MrTCuff(6) (hld up: hrd rdn over 1f out: one pce)....¾ 5
1209[12] Legatee **(62)***(58) (BJMeehan)* 4-10-9 MissJAllison(11) (lost pl 5f out: r.o one pce fnl 2f)....nk 6
1377* Spanish Stripper (USA) **(53)***(65) (MCChapman)* 4-10-11 (5) MrMMackley(2) (hdwy over 3f out: rdn over 1f out: one pce)....s.h 7
784[3] Sweet Supposin (IRE) **(61)***(67) (KMcAuliffe)* 4-11-6b MrJDurkan(7) (3rd st: ev ch over 1f out: sn wknd)....1 8
905[10] Hi Penny **(33)***(50) (KTIvory)* 4-10-4b(5) MrDMarshall(13) (4th st: wknd over 1f out)....2½ 9
1323[U] Fighter Squadron **(57)***(51) (REPeacock)* 6-10-9b(5) MrsCPeacock(12) (bhd fnl 5f)....1¾ 10
1273[5] Guest Alliance (IRE) **(58)***(44) (AMoore)* 3-9-13 (5) MrsJMoore(8) (lw: prom over 2f)....3 11
1148[11] Orthorhombus **(61)***(39) (DJSCosgrove)* 6-10-11b(5) MissOCosgrove(4) (a bhd)....3 12
1071[12] Riskie Things **(53)***(30) (JSMoore)* 4-10-4 (5) MrsSMoore(14) (lw: led over 4f: 2nd st: wknd 2f out)....1 13
Hedgehog **(25)***(9) (JO'Donoghue)* 5-10-4 (5) MrsTEustance(10) (a bhd)....9 14

9/4 Mr Nevermind (IRE), **4/1** Mo's Star (3/1-5/1), **11/2** Top Pet (IRE), **6/1** CHIEF OF STAFF (op 7/2), **8/1** Spanish Stripper (USA) (6/1-10/1), **14/1** Sweet Supposin (IRE) (8/1-16/1), **20/1** Legatee, Orthorhombus, **25/1** Never so Rite (IRE), **33/1** Fighter Squadron, Guest Alliance (IRE), Hi Penny, Riskie Things, **50/1** Hedgehog, CSF £19.32 TOTE £5.00: £2.10 £1.60 £3.80 (£6.60) Trio £60.30 OWNER The Exclusive Partnership (NEWMARKET) BRED Lord Halifax 14 Rn
1m 26.2 (4.60) SF: 57/52/35/48/31/40/47/49/32/33/16/21/12/-
WEIGHT FOR AGE 3yo-10lb

1535 ROBERT FLEMING MARINE H'CAP (0-65) (3-Y.O+) (Class F) £3,224.60 (£895.60: £429.80) **2m 93y** Stalls: Low GOING minus 0.15 sec per fur (GF) 6-45 (6-46)

1058[5] **Soojama (IRE) (36)***(47)*(Fav)*(RMFlower)* 5-8-7 DBiggs(10) (hdwy over 2f out: 5th st: hrd rdn over 1f out: led ins fnl f: r.o wl)....— 1
851[13] Much Too High **(52)***(63) (TJNaughton)* 3-8-3 AMcGlone(6) (hdwy 6f out: 4th st: hrd rdn over 1f out: r.o ins fnl f)....½ 2
1470[5] Jaraab **(46)***(55) (GLewis)* 4-9-2v SWhitworth(12) (lw: a.p: led 3f out: hrd rdn over 1f out: hdd ins fnl f: unable qckn)....1¾ 3
*1086** La Menorquina (USA) **(31)***(37) (DMarks)* 5-7-11 (5) PPMurphy(11) (hdwy over 1f out: nvr nrr)..3 4
1109[10] Chakalak **(48)***(54) (SDow)* 7-9-5 RHughes(3) (lw: nvr nr to chal)....s.h 5
1058[15] By Arrangement (IRE) **(34)***(37) (SWoodman)* 6-8-5 GDuffield(1) (hdwy 12f out: led over 5f out to 3f out: 2nd st: wknd over 1f out)....2½ 6
884[11] Gentleman Sid **(33)***(35) (PGMurphy)* 5-8-4 NAdams(8) (lw: rdn over 7f out: hdwy over 5f out: wknd over 2f out)....2 7

1328[6] Limosa **(42)***(43) (RFJohnsonHoughton)* 4-8-12b AClark(4) (lw: 3rd st: wknd over 1f out) ....¾ **8**
1086[4] Rolling the Bones (USA) **(44)***(44) (PSFelgate)* 6-9-1 AMackay(14) (6th st: wknd 2f out)........1¼ **9**
Qaffal (USA) **(44)***(19) (RTPhillips)* 5-9-1 RPerham(9) (b: a bhd)..25 **10**
374[5] Sure Pride (USA) **(43)***(11) (AMoore)* 7-9-0 CandyMorris(7) (b: a bhd).......................................7 **11**
1328[11] Deerlet **(54)***(21) (KCBailey)* 4-9-5b(5) JDSmith(16) (chsd ldr: led 7f out tl over 5f out: sn wknd)1¾ **12**
1254[16] Foremma **(26)** *(PRHedger)* 4-7-10 ow1 CAvery(2) (bhd fnl 5f)..10 **13**
1058[17] Princesse Abigail **(25)** *(RMFlower)* 4-7-2b(7) MartinDwyer(5) (led over 9f: t.o fnl 5f) ....dist **14**
Yengema **(35)** *(RCSpicer)* 4-8-5b JO'Reilly(15) (prom over 9f: t.o fnl 5f) ....dist **15**

3/1 SOOJAMA (IRE), **9/2** Rolling the Bones (USA), **7/1** By Arrangement (IRE), La Menorquina (USA) (5/1-8/1), **8/1** Limosa (op 5/1), **10/1** Jaraab, **12/1** Deerlet, Much Too High, **14/1** Chakalak, **16/1** Gentleman Sid, **33/1** Sure Pride (USA), **50/1** Qaffal (USA), Foremma, Princesse Abigail, Yengema, CSF £37.41 CT £298.03 TOTE £5.00: £1.90 £4.40 £3.60 (£60.90) Trio £81.70 OWNER Mr N. G. Castleton (JEVINGTON) BRED E. and Mrs Hanley 15 Rn
3m 40.7 (9.70) SF: 41/37/48/31/48/31/29/36/38/13/5/14/-/-/-
WEIGHT FOR AGE 3yo-20lb, 4yo-1lb

1536 E.B.F. HYTHE MAIDEN STKS (2-Y.O F) (Class D) £3,850.00 (£1,150.00: £550.00: £250.00) 6f Stalls: Low GOING minus 0.15 sec per fur (GF) 7-15 (7-17)

1361[4] **Agnella (IRE)** *(88)*(Fav)*(GLMoore)* 2-8-11 SWhitworth(8) (lw: hld up: led wl over 1f out: shkn up & qcknd: comf)..— **1**
Ciserano (IRE) *(72) (MRChannon)* 2-8-11 RHughes(10) (unf: bit bkwd: hld up: rdn over 2f out: swtchd rt: r.o one pce)..6 **2**
669[7] Green Bentley (IRE) *(71) (RHannon)* 2-8-11 RPerham(3) (a.p: led over 2f out tl wl over 1f out: one pce) ....½ **3**
Natural Key *(68) (SirMarkPrescott)* 2-8-11 GDuffield(1) (neat: bit bkwd: led over 3f: one pce).1 **4**
791[11] Vera's First (IRE) *(67) (GLewis)* 2-8-6 (5) AWhelan(7) (rdn over 3f out: swtchd rt & hdwy over 1f out: one pce) ....nk **5**
Primelta *(63) (RAkehurst)* 2-8-11 CRutter(6) (unf: bit bkwd: s.s: hdwy over 1f out: one pce) 1½ **6**
Gentle Friend *(57) (JLDunlop)* 2-8-11 AMcGlone(2) (unf: bit bkwd: outpcd: nvr nrr).............2½ **7**
Fairy Highlands (IRE) *(52) (SCWilliams)* 2-8-11 MRimmer(4) (unf: bit bkwd: prom over 4f)..1¾ **8**
508[7] Apartments Abroad *(49) (KMcAuliffe)* 2-8-8 (3) JTate(5) (a bhd) 1¼ **9**
1348[9] Miss Carottene *(35) (MJRyan)* 2-8-11 AClark(9) (outpcd)...5 **10**

11/10 AGNELLA (IRE) (8/11-6/5), **100/30** Ciserano (IRE) (8/1-3/1), **6/1** Green Bentley (IRE) (3/1-7/1), **8/1** Fairy Highlands (IRE) (op 14/1), **10/1** Gentle Friend (8/1-123/1), **14/1** Natural Key (6/1-20/1), **16/1** Apartments Abroad, **20/1** Primelta, **25/1** Vera's First (IRE), **33/1** Miss Carottene, CSF £5.96 TOTE £2.10: £1.30 £1.10 £2.30 (£5.00) Trio £6.00 OWNER Mr Bryan Pennick (EPSOM) BRED A. Steigenberger 10 Rn 1m 14.1 (2.40) SF: 35/19/18/15/14/10/4/-/-/-

1537 ROSS & CO (SOLICITORS) H'CAP (0-85) (3-Y.O+) (Class D) £4,425.00 (£1,320.00: £630.00: £285.00) 6f Stalls: Low GOING minus 0.15 sec per fur (GF) 7-45 (7-47)

1321* **Aragrove (67)***(72) (JWPayne)* 5-8-13b MTebbutt(2) (b: led 4f out: rdn out) ....— **1**
1241[6] How's Yer Father **(82)***(86) (RJHodges)* 9-10-0 RHughes(1) (hrd rdn 2f out: hdwy on ins over 1f out: r.o wl ins fnl f) ....nk **2**
1411[12] Face the Future **(62)***(65) (LJHolt)* 6-8-8 AMcGlone(3) (hld up: rdn over 1f out: r.o ins fnl f) .....½ **3**
1201[4] Youdontsay **(70)***(70) (RCurtis)* 3-8-0 (7) SLanigan(4) (lw: hdwy & nt clr run over 1f out: swtchd rt: unable qckn) 1 **4**
1241[5] That Man Again **(83)***(75)*(Fav)*(GLewis)* 3-9-1b(5) AWhelan(5) (lw: a.p: ev ch over 1f out: wknd ins fnl f) 3 **5**
1261[9] Deeply Vale (IRE) **(71)***(50) (GLMoore)* 4-9-3 BRouse(6) (a.p: rdn over 2f out: eased whn btn fnl f)..5 **6**
1193[10] Kildee Lad **(73)***(47) (APJones)* 5-9-5 AClark(10) (lw: hld up: rdn over 2f out: wknd over 1f out)2 **7**
1071[8] Efra **(72)***(45) (RHannon)* 6-9-4 SRaymont(11) (lw: outpcd)...nk **8**
23[5] Rambold **(70)***(38) (NEBerry)* 4-9-2 RPerham(9) (prom 4f)...1¾ **9**
984[11] Cradle Days **(65)***(31) (RCSpicer)* 6-8-11 JO'Reilly(8) (led 2f: wknd 2f out).............................¾ **10**
565[7] Myasha (USA) **(78)***(33) (AlexVanderhaeghen,Belgium)* 6-9-10 MServranckx(7) (b.off hind: lw: bhd fnl 3f) 4 **11**

7/2 That Man Again, **9/2** ARAGROVE, **6/1** Youdontsay (op 4/1), **13/2** Deeply Vale (IRE), **8/1** Efra, Face the Future (op 14/1), **9/1** Kildee Lad, **10/1** How's Yer Father (7/1-11/1), **16/1** Rambold, **20/1** Myasha (USA), **33/1** Cradle Days, CSF £46.03 CT £324.42 TOTE £4.10: £2.30 £3.40 £1.70 (£19.90) Trio £58.10 OWNER Mr Dennis Purkiss (NEWMARKET) BRED Mrs J. R. Hine and Miss J. Bunting 11 Rn 1m 12.8 (1.10) SF: 54/68/47/43/48/32/29/27/20/13/15
WEIGHT FOR AGE 3yo-9lb

1538 HASTINGS (S) STKS (3-Y.O+) (Class G) £2,780.60 (£771.60: £369.80)
5f Stalls: Low GOING minus 0.15 sec per fur (GF) 8-15 (8-17)

1168⁴ **Anzio (IRE) (72)***(61) (BAPearce)* 4-9-3b SWhitworth(6) (b: lw: a.p: led over 2f out to 1f out: hrd rdn: led nr fin)......— 1
1164¹¹ Windrush Boy **(56)***(60) (JRBosley)* 5-9-3 RPerham(7) (hld up: led 1f out: hrd rdn: hdd nr fin)......nk 2
1434* Giggleswick Girl **(52)***(58)*(Fav)*(MRChannon)* 4-9-5 RHughes(3) (lw: dwlt: hdwy & n.m.r over 1f out: hrd rdn: r.o one pce)......1¼ 3
Jade City *(56) (AlexVanderhaeghen,Belgium)* 5-9-3 MServranckx(5) (hdwy & nt clr run 2f out: nt clr run over 1f out: r.o ins fnl f)......s.h 4
1057¹⁰ Random **(55)***(48) (CJames)* 4-8-12 AMcGlone(9) (lw: hdwy & n.m.r over 1f out: ev ch 1f out: one pce)......1 5
1071⁹ Pride of Hayling (IRE) **(42)***(47) (PRHedger)* 4-8-12 StephenDavies(11) (lw: hdwy over 1f out: ev ch 1f out: one pce)......hd 6
1263⁹ Halleluja Time *(36) (RHannon)* 3-8-9 TQuinn(2) (lw: prom 3f)......5 7
1321⁷ Shades of Jade **(31)***(19) (JJBridger)* 7-8-5 ⁽⁷⁾ ADaly(12) (led over 2f: wknd 1f out)......4 8
1191⁸ Millstock *(18) (APJones)* 5-8-12 AClark(1) (a bhd)......hd 9
*892*¹⁰ Tommy Tempest **(33)***(15) (REPeacock)* 6-9-3 GDuffield(8) (bhd fnl 2f)......2½ 10

6/5 Giggleswick Girl, **2/1** ANZIO (IRE), **7/1** Windrush Boy (4/1-8/1), Random, **16/1** Jade City, Halleluja Time, **20/1** Shades of Jade, **25/1** Pride of Hayling (IRE), **33/1** Tommy Tempest, **50/1** Millstock, CSF £17.51 TOTE £3.30: £1.30 £2.60 £1.10 (£14.80) Trio £4.80 OWNER Mr Richard Gray (LIMPSFIELD) BRED Rathduff Stud 10 Rn 61.2 secs (2.60) SF: 53/52/50/48/40/39/20/11/10/7
WEIGHT FOR AGE 3yo-8lb
No bid

1539 DEAL H'CAP (0-70) (3-Y.O+ F & M) (Class E) £3,531.00 (£1,056.00: £506.00: £231.00)
1m 1f 149y Stalls: Low GOING minus 0.15 sec per fur (GF) 8-45 (8-47)

1367* **Dutosky (57)***(66)*(Fav)*(RJO'Sullivan)* 5-9-8 5x DBiggs(3) (lw: rdn 5f out: hdwy over 2f out: 4th st: led 1f out: drvn out)......— 1
1472¹⁴ Malingerer **(33)***(37) (DAWilson)* 4-7-12 ow5 AMackay(8) (gd hdwy over 1f out: str run fnl f: fin wl)......hd 2
*1320*⁵ Yo Kiri-B **(51)***(55) (JFfitch-Heyes)* 4-9-2 GDuffield(6) (lw: 3rd st: led over 1f out: sn hdd: unable qckn)......3 3
1349² Pip's Dream **(38)***(38) (MJRyan)* 4-8-3 ow1 AClark(9) (lw: 2nd st: ev ch over 1f out: sn wknd)..1½ 4
1324⁷ Jemima Puddleduck **(52)***(52) (DWPArbuthnot)* 4-9-3 SWhitworth(12) (b.hind: lw: led 8f)......1 5
885¹⁰ Phylian **(60)***(60) (SCWilliams)* 4-9-11 MRimmer(1) (hdwy 3f out: 6th st: rdn over 2f out: one pce)......s.h 6
Aqua Rigia (IRE) **(46)***(43) (HCandy)* 3-7-12 NAdams(4) (nvr nrr)......1½ 7
1167¹⁴ Valinco **(49)***(35) (SDow)* 4-9-0 StephenDavies(10) (lw: dwlt: nvr nrr)......7 8
1274* Elite Racing **(64)***(48) (PFICole)* 3-9-2 TQuinn(7) (lw: 5th st: wknd over 1f out)......1 9
1498¹⁸ Pioneer Princess **(51)***(34) (MJRyan)* 3-7-12 ⁽⁵⁾ MBaird(11) (prom over 4f)......¾ 10
1244¹² Built for Comfort (IRE) **(65)***(39) (RHannon)* 3-9-3 RHughes(5) (lw: hld up: hrd rdn over 2f out: sn wknd)......5 11
1472⁶ All the Joys **(43)***(17) (CACyzer)* 4-8-8 AMcGlone(2) (hdwy over 3f out: wknd over 2f out)......nk 12
LONG HANDICAP Malingerer 7-6

15/8 DUTOSKY, **3/1** Elite Racing, **4/1** Jemima Puddleduck, **8/1** Pip's Dream, **12/1** Built for Comfort (IRE) (8/1-14/1), **14/1** Aqua Rigia (IRE) (10/1-16/1), **16/1** All the Joys, **20/1** Pioneer Princess, Phylian, **33/1** Yo Kiri-B, Valinco, **50/1** Malingerer, CSF £76.87 CT £2,309.98 TOTE £3.50: £1.40 £14.90 £6.90 (£364.00) Trio not won; £392.74 to 8/6/95 OWNER Mr D. A. Johnson (BOGNOR REGIS) BRED Lord Victor Matthews 12 Rn 2m 4.7 (7.00) SF: 36/7/25/8/22/30/-/5/5/-/-/-
WEIGHT FOR AGE 3yo-13lb

T/Plpt: £40.00 (332.46 Tckts). T/Qdpt: £8.80 (6.8 Tckts). AK

1323-WARWICK (L-H)
Wednesday June 7th (Good)
WEATHER: fine WIND: mod across

1540 KENILWORTH MAIDEN AUCTION STKS (2-Y.O) (Class E) £4,110.00 (£1,230.00: £590.00: £270.00) **6f** Stalls: Low GOING minus 0.30 sec per fur (GF) 2-30 (2-35)

1054⁹ **Croeso Cynnes** *(75) (BPalling)* 2-7-13 ow2 TSprake(2) (hdwy on ins to ld wl over 2f out: clr over 1f out: drvn out)......— 1

Silver Harrow *(81) (SirMarkPrescott)* 2-8-10 GDuffield(13) (cmpt: 6th st: hdwy on ins over 1f out: r.o ins fnl f)....2½ 2
1253[4] Sound Check *(66) (BJMeehan)* 2-8-0 BDoyle(14) (led over 1f: 5th st: r.o one pce fnl f)....2 3
718[5] Sharp Monty *(68) (RHollinshead)* 2-8-5 GCarter(11) (led over 4f out tl wl over 2f out: rn wd & 4th st: one pce fnl 2f)....1 4
1031[2] Missile Toe (IRE) *(65) (JEBanks)* 2-8-5 JQuinn(6) (hdwy over 1f out: nt rch ldrs)....1¼ 5
716[5] Evidence In Chief *(62)*(Fav)*(PFICole)* 2-8-4 ow2 TQuinn(5) (hdwy on ins fnl f: nvr nrr)....hd 6
682[7] Incapol *(65) (MJRyan)* 2-8-5 DBiggs(15) (bit bkwd: 2nd st: wknd over 1f out)....s.h 7
615[10] Anshan's Deity *(63) (CWFairhurst)* 2-8-5 RCochrane(4) (s.i.s: nvr nr to chal)....½ 8
1098[8] Rothley Imp (IRE) *(60) (JWharton)* 2-8-2 GBardwell(10) (prom: 7th & wkng st)....hd 9
1017[6] Siberian Mystic *(57) (PGMurphy)* 2-7-12 (7)ow5 RWaterfield(8) (a bhd)....nk 10
788[5] Royal Rapport *(62) (BAMcMahon)* 2-8-7 FNorton(1) (s.i.s: sn pushed along: a bhd)....1 11
1293[5] Gagajulu *(50) (PDEvans)* 2-7-5 (7)ow1 AmandaSanders(3) (3rd st: wknd wl over 1f out)....½ 12
1272[3] Imprimis (IRE) *(50) (CNAllen)* 2-7-6 (5) MBaird(9) (a bhd)....s.h 13
Sphinx Levelv (IRE) *(APJarvis)* 2-8-2 (3) DWright(12) (leggy: lt-f: bit bkwd: s.s: bhd whn rn v.wd ent st: t.o whn p.u 1f out).... P

9/4 Evidence In Chief, **13/2** Missile Toe (IRE), **7/1** Sound Check (5/1-8/1), **9/1** Sharp Monty, **10/1** Royal Rapport, **11/1** Silver Harrow (op 5/1), Gagajulu (7/1-12/1), **16/1** CROESO CYNNES, Imprimis (IRE), **20/1** Incapol, **25/1** Anshan's Deity, Sphinx Levelv (IRE), **33/1** Rothley Imp (IRE), Siberian Mystic, CSF £164.01 TOTE £25.10: £3.00 £4.40 £2.20 (£139.80) Trio £201.30 OWNER Davies and Bridgeman (COWBRIDGE) BRED Taplin, Lee and Cain Ltd 14 Rn
1m 15.9 (3.90) SF: 8/14/-/1/-/-/-/-/-/-/-/-/-/-

1541 CHEF'S LARDER LIMITED STKS (0-60) (3-Y.O+) (Class F) £3,476.60 (£967.60: £465.80) 7f Stalls: Low GOING minus 0.30 sec per fur (GF) 3-00 (3-05)

1244[5] **Whatever's Right (IRE) (60)***(73) (MDIUsher)* 6-9-6 TQuinn(18) (led over 1f: led 3f out: clr over 1f out: rdn out)....— 1
1469[3] Legal Issue (IRE) **(58)***(59) (SirMarkPrescott)* 3-8-7 GDuffield(19) (lw: 5th st: r.o fnl f: no ch w wnr)....5 2
1172[13] Princess Danielle **(60)***(50) (CCElsey)* 3-8-2 CRutter(13) (hdwy & 7th st: r.o ins fnl f)....1½ 3
1165[7] Robo Magic (USA) **(58)***(58) (LMontagueHall)* 3-8-10 StephenDavies(16) (led over 5f out to 3f out: 2nd st: one pce fnl 2f)....nk 4
Marrowfat Lady (IRE) **(58)***(49) (BRMillman)* 4-8-12 JWilliams(4) (8th st: r.o one pce fnl 2f)....nk 5
1354[13] Great Hall **(57)***(53) (PDCundell)* 6-8-12b(5) DGriffiths(9) (b.hind: hdwy over 1f out: nvr nrr)....nk 6
1469* Russian Heroine **(58)***(47) (MJohnston)* 3-8-5 3x TWilliams(1) (2nd st: wknd ins fnl f)....1¾ 7
971[7] Irie Mon (IRE) **(60)***(48)*(Fav)*(JWHills)* 3-8-3 (7) MHenry(10) (nvr nr to chal)....2 8
1202[15] Almapa **(59)***(42) (RJHodges)* 3-8-5 (5) SDrowne(5) (lw: 6th st: wknd over 1f out)....2½ 9
1124[14] Bowden Rose **(52)***(33) (MBlanshard)* 3-8-2b FNorton(12) (hdwy 4f out: prom whn rn v.wd ent st: nt rcvr)....nk 10
882[19] Courting Newmarket **(49)***(36) (MrsAKnight)* 7-8-10 (7) SophieMitchell(15) (prom over 3f)....¾ 11
1280[11] World Traveller **(57)***(34) (WAO'Gorman)* 4-9-6b EmmaO'Gorman(7) (s.i.s: hdwy whn rn wd over 2f out: sn bhd)....2½ 12
Miss Iron Heart (USA) **(55)***(22) (DJSCosgrove)* 3-8-2 JQuinn(6) (bit bkwd: a bhd)....1½ 13
1279[5] Mixed Mood **(47)***(25) (BPalling)* 3-8-5 TSprake(8) (a bhd)....nk 14
587[8] Vaslav Nijinsky **(57)***(11) (GRimmer)* 3-8-7 MRimmer(2) (prom over 3f)....7 15
1330[2] Hong Kong Dollar **(53)***(3) (BJMeehan)* 3-8-7b BDoyle(14) (4th st: wknd wl over 1f out)....3½ 16
862[14] Bonita **(55)** *(MrsLPiggott)* 3-8-2 GCarter(3) (Withdrawn not under Starter's orders: lame at s) .. W

5/1 Irie Mon (IRE), **11/2** WHATEVER'S RIGHT (IRE), Russian Heroine (op 7/2), **13/2** Legal Issue (IRE), **10/1** Almapa, **12/1** World Traveller, Great Hall, Hong Kong Dollar, **16/1** Vaslav Nijinsky, **20/1** Robo Magic (USA), Marrowfat Lady (IRE), Bonita, Mixed Mood, **33/1** Miss Iron Heart (USA), Bowden Rose, Courting Newmarket, Princess Danielle, CSF £38.25 TOTE £6.60: £2.50 £2.20 £6.10 (£19.80) Trio not won; £471.95 to Beverley 8/6/95 OWNER Mr M. S. C. Thurgood (SWINDON) BRED Rockville House Stud 16 Rn 1m 25.5 (1.30) SF: 53/29/20/28/29/33/17/18/12/3/16/14/-/-/-/-
WEIGHT FOR AGE 3yo-10lb

1542 M.H.V. H'CAP (0-70) (3-Y.O+) (Class E) £3,523.50 (£1,053.00: £504.00: £229.50) 1m Stalls: Low GOING minus 0.30 sec per fur (GF) 3-30 (3-32)

1148[2] **Sharp Rebuff (69)***(79) (PJMakin)* 4-10-0 RCochrane(12) (b.nr fore: lw: 4th st: edgd lft & led ins fnl f: r.o wl)....— 1
1506[2] Just Harry **(64)***(71)*(Fav)*(MJRyan)* 4-9-4 (5) MBaird(5) (plld hrd: 2nd st: led 2f out: edgd rt 1f out: hdd ins fnl f)....1½ 2
1351[13] Mr Cube (IRE) **(49)***(56) (JMBradley)* 5-8-1v(7) AmandaSanders(3) (hld up: 7th st: hdwy 2f out: ev ch 1f out: fnd nil)....s.h 3
1167[10] Zatopek **(65)***(66) (RHannon)* 3-8-13 JReid(11) (a.p: led 3f out to 2f out: one pce)....3 4

1061[4] South Eastern Fred **(60)**_(61) (HJCollingridge)_ 4-9-5 MRimmer(7) (5th st: one pce fnl 2f).......s.h 5
820[17] Private Fixture (IRE) **(60)**_(58) (DMarks)_ 4-9-2 (3) DRMcCabe(2) (nvr nr to chal).......................1¼ 6
1244[10] Lucky Tucky **(58)**_(56) (JRJenkins)_ 4-9-3 GCarter(10) (hdwy over 1f out: nvr nrr) ....hd 7
1285[16] Mai Pen Rai **(34)**_(31) (RJHodges)_ 7-7-7 NCarlisle(4) (bkwd: 6th st & n.m.r on ins st: no hdwy fnl 2f)...¾ 8
1274[2] Life's Too Short (IRE) **(48)**_(43) (JEBanks)_ 4-8-7 JQuinn(8) (prom over 3f) ....¾ 9
1274[5] Tout de Val **(35)**_(12) (KBishop)_ 6-7-8 NAdams(9) (bkwd: a bhd) 9 10
_406_[9] Lady Williams (IRE) **(64)**_(33) (LordHuntingdon)_ 4-9-9 BThomson(6) (led 5f: 3rd st: wknd 2f out)...4 11
1183[25] Mohawk Trail **(62)**_(30) (GLewis)_ 6-9-2 (5) AWhelan(1) (lw: dwlt: a bhd) ....¾ 12

LONG HANDICAP Mai Pen Rai 7-3

7/2 Just Harry, **9/2** SHARP REBUFF, **5/1** South Eastern Fred, **13/2** Life's Too Short (IRE), **7/1** Zatopek, **8/1** Lucky Tucky, **11/1** Lady Williams (IRE), **14/1** Mohawk Trail, **16/1** Mr Cube (IRE), **25/1** Private Fixture (IRE), **33/1** Tout de Val, Mai Pen Rai, CSF £20.38 CT £214.95 TOTE £6.60: £2.00 £1.80 £6.30 (£7.50) Trio £76.30 OWNER Mr D. M. Ahier (MARLBOROUGH) BRED Farmers Hill and Fitzroy Studs 12 Rn 1m 40.4 (3.40) SF: 52/44/29/28/34/31/29/4/16/-/6/3

WEIGHT FOR AGE 3yo-11lb

1543

MIDSUMMER H'CAP (0-80) (3-Y.O+) (Class D) £3,867.50 (£1,154.00: £551.00: £249.50)
1m 2f 169y Stalls: Low GOING minus 0.30 sec per fur (GF) 4-00 (4-01)

1324* **Myfontaine (55)**_(65)_(Fav)_(KTIvory)_ 8-8-3 GBardwell(6) (sn pushed along in rr: hdwy & 6th st: led over 1f out: drvn out)......................................— 1
1324[2] Haroldon (IRE) **(66)**_(75) (BPalling)_ 6-9-0 TSprake(8) (b: hdwy & 5th st: ev ch over 1f out: r.o wl)......................................½ 2
1225[8] Shanghai Venture (USA) **(75)**_(74) (SPCWoods)_ 4-9-9 BThomson(4) (plld hrd: chsd ldr 7f out: 2nd st: led 2f out tl over 1f out: wknd fnl f)..............................7 3
1292[2] Larn Fort **(57)**_(54) (CWFairhurst)_ 5-8-5v ow1 RCochrane(1) (hld up: hdwy 5f out: 3rd st: one pce fnl 2f)......................................nk 4
1095[6] Scottish Bambi **(66)**_(61) (RHannon)_ 7-9-0 JReid(1) (led over 8f: wknd over 1f out)................2½ 5
Peaches Polly **(62)**_(53) (GRimmer)_ 5-8-10 MRimmer(9) (bit bkwd: prom: rdn over 6f out: 4th & wkng st)......................................2½ 6
1260[6] Museum (IRE) **(77)**_(61) (HCandy)_ 4-9-11 WNewnes(10) (prom tl 7th & wkng st) 5 7
817[11] Pink Brief (IRE) **(60)**_(42) (MJRyan)_ 4-8-3 (5) MBaird(3) (a bhd)......................................¾ 8
1188[8] Lomas (IRE) **(80)**_(54) (MrsHParrott)_ 4-10-0 VSlattery(7) (chsd ldr over 3f: hrd rdn & wknd 4f out)......................................6 9
Lucayan Cay (IRE) **(79)** _(MrsJPitman)_ 4-9-13 TQuinn(5) (bkwd: prom: rdn 7f out: wknd qckly over 4f out: t.o whn p.u 1f out) .... P

9/4 MYFONTAINE, **6/1** Haroldon (IRE), **7/1** Shanghai Venture (USA) (op 12/1), Larn Fort, Museum (IRE), **10/1** Scottish Bambi, **12/1** Peaches Polly (op 8/1), Pink Brief (IRE), **14/1** Lucayan Cay (IRE), **33/1** Lomas (IRE), CSF £15.21 CT £73.99 TOTE £3.30: £1.50 £2.50 £2.10 (£10.00) Trio £17.30 OWNER Mr K. T. Ivory (RADLETT) BRED Farmleigh Partners 10 Rn

2m 18.2 (4.70) SF: 28/38/37/17/24/16/24/5/17/-

1544

DERBY THIS WEEKEND CONDITIONS STKS (3 & 4-Y.O) (Class D) £4,002.70 (£1,195.60: £571.80: £259.90)
6f Stalls: Low GOING minus 0.30 sec per fur (GF) 4-30 (4-31)

1183[11] **Top Banana (73)**_(89+) (HCandy)_ 4-9-4 WNewnes(6) (lw: chsd ldr: 2nd st: rdn to ld over 1f out: r.o wl)......................................— 1
1240[2] Sea Thunder _(76)_(Fav)_(IABalding)_ 3-8-5 ow1 RCochrane(3) (3rd st: rdn & swtchd rt wl over 1f out: no imp) 3 2
1374[4] Prima Cominna **(87)**_(75) (MBell)_ 3-8-10 JCarroll(2) (led over 4f: one pce)............................2½ 3
Shamrock Fair (IRE) **(74)**_(70) (LordHuntingdon)_ 3-8-10 JWilliams(5) (s.i.s: 6th st: nvr trbld ldrs) 2 4
747* Worldnews Extra (USA) _(74) (PFICole)_ 3-9-1 TQuinn(1) (lw: prom: rdn over 3f out: 5th st: no hdwy fnl 2f) ....½ 5
742[7] Anita's Contessa (IRE) _(62) (BPalling)_ 3-8-4 TSprake(7) (4th st: wknd over 1f out) ....hd 6
Jalwa (USA) **(80)** _(KTIvory)_ 3-8-1 (3) SSanders(4) (last st: a bhd: t.o)......................................25 7

1/2 Sea Thunder, **11/2** Prima Cominna (4/1-6/1), **15/2** Worldnews Extra (USA), **8/1** TOP BANANA, **9/1** Shamrock Fair (IRE) (op 6/1), **20/1** Jalwa (USA), **33/1** Anita's Contessa (IRE), CSF £13.14 TOTE £8.30: £2.40 £1.40 (£4.30) OWNER Exors of the late Mrs C E Gross (WANTAGE) BRED Dunchurch Lodge Stud Co 7 Rn 1m 14.2 (2.20) SF: 47/25/24/19/23/11/-

WEIGHT FOR AGE 3yo-9lb

1545 QUEEN BESS CLAIMING APPRENTICE STKS (3-Y.O+) (Class F)
£3,073.40 (£852.40: £408.20)
6f Stalls: Low GOING minus 0.30 sec per fur (GF) 5-00 (5-03)

1483 10 **Harry's Coming (57)***(56) (RJHodges)* 11-8-8 DGriffiths(5) (lw: 7th st: hdwy to ld & edgd lft over 1f out: edgd lft ins fnl f: r.o) — **1**
1248* So Intrepid (IRE) **(70)***(63)*(Fav)*(JMBradley)* 5-9-2 AmandaSanders(1) (hld up: hdwy & 6th st: n.m.r over 1f out: swtchd rt: edgd lft & r.o wl ins fnl f) nk **2**
1355 2 Best Kept Secret **(71)***(68) (JBerry)* 4-9-8 PRoberts(8) (lw: led 1f: 2nd st: led 2f out: hdd over 1f out: r.o) nk **3**
1199 8 Havana Miss **(40)***(49) (BPalling)* 3-7-7 (3) MHenry(6) (4th st: ev ch over 1f out: nt qckn) ¾ **4**
1164 4 Mister Raider **(50)***(54) (SMellor)* 3-8-4b(3) ADaly(4) (lw: 5th st: ev ch over 1f out: one pce) 2½ **5**
603 13 Rinus Manor (IRE) **(40)***(53) (DMcCain)* 4-8-11 (5) CLowther(7) (swtg: led 5f out to 2f out: wknd fnl f) nk **6**
1433 4 Obsidian Grey **(54)***(46) (MissLCSiddall)* 8-8-5 (7) TSiddall(2) (hdwy on ins over 2f out: nt rch ldrs) 1¼ **7**
1501 6 Mutinique **(51)***(38) (BAPearce)* 4-8-0 (7) TField(10) (3rd st: wknd over 1f out) 1 **8**
848 13 False Pretences (IRE) **(35)***(41) (BAPearce)* 3-7-12 (5) JWilkinson(9) (bhd fnl 3f) ¾ **9**
468 9 Tapping Feet **(41)** *(DMHyde)* 3-7-1 (7) DLockhart(3) (a bhd: t.o fnl 3f) 12 **10**

5/4 So Intrepid (IRE), **11/4** Best Kept Secret, **5/1** HARRY'S COMING, **10/1** Obsidian Grey, **14/1** Mister Raider, **16/1** Mutinique, **33/1** Havana Miss, **50/1** False Pretences (IRE), Tapping Feet, **66/1** Rinus Manor (IRE), CSF £11.16 TOTE £5.40: £1.50 £1.30 £1.10 (£4.70) Trio £2.50 OWNER The Gardens Entertainments Ltd (SOMERTON) BRED T. E. Herring 10 Rn
1m 15.6 (3.60) SF: 19/26/31/3/8/16/9/1/-/-
WEIGHT FOR AGE 3yo-9lb

1546 PRINCE RUPERT MAIDEN H'CAP (0-75) (3-Y.O+) (Class D)
£4,036.50 (£1,206.00: £577.00: £262.50)
5f Stalls: Low GOING minus 0.30 sec per fur (GF) 5-30 (5-33)

1201 3 **Midnight Break (57)***(59)*(Fav)*(PTWalwyn)* 3-8-10 RCochrane(11) (hld up: nt clr run over 2f out: hdwy over 1f out: hrd rdn to ld ins fnl f: r.o wl) — **1**
1094 8 Secret Miss **(50)***(48) (APJarvis)* 3-8-0 (3) DWright(8) (lw: dwlt: hdwy over 1f out: hrd rdn & r.o wl ins fnl f) 1¼ **2**
646 12 Saxon King (IRE) **(42)***(38) (MDIUsher)* 5-8-3 RStreet(2) (b.hind: led 4f out tl ins fnl f) ½ **3**
1445 4 Colston-C **(50)***(44) (CJHill)* 3-8-3v JQuinn(9) (a.p: r.o one pce fnl f) ¾ **4**
1050 7 Raisa Point **(53)***(31) (WRMuir)* 4-9-0 JCarroll(6) (led 1f: wknd over 1f out) 5 **5**
1072 4 Express Routing **(60)***(38) (RAkehurst)* 3-8-10 (3) SSanders(5) (nvr nrr) hd **6**
1302 7 Sizzling Romp **(63)***(40) (DTThom)* 3-8-13 (3) DRMcCabe(7) (w ldrs: nt clr run over 1f out: sn wknd) nk **7**
Indian Lament **(49)***(18) (RJHodges)* 4-8-5 (5) SDrowne(13) (bit bkwd: bhd fnl 2f) 2½ **8**
1265 9 Trina **(36)** *(DLWilliams)* 4-7-11 ow4 TWilliams(3) (hmpd 3f out: a bhd) nk **9**
855 12 Kencol **(55)***(17) (AGFoster)* 3-8-8b TSprake(4) (b.hind: prom 3f) 1¾ **10**
1342 6 Honey Trader **(66)***(15) (JBerry)* 3-8-12 (7) PRoberts(1) (prom over 3f) 4 **11**
772 U Come on Winn **(40)** *(MissSJWilton)* 3-7-2b(5) MBaird(10) (bit bkwd: bolted bef s: reluctant to r: a t.o) 30 **12**

LONG HANDICAP Trina 7-3 Come on Winn 7-2

11/4 MIDNIGHT BREAK (2/1-3/1), **5/1** Colston-C (6/1-4/1), **6/1** Secret Miss, **7/1** Raisa Point, **8/1** Saxon King (IRE) (op 5/1), Express Routing (op 4/1), Honey Trader (5/1-9/1), **14/1** Sizzling Romp (10/1-16/1), **16/1** Kencol, **25/1** Indian Lament, **33/1** Trina, Come on Winn, CSF £19.73 CT £110.89 TOTE £3.70: £1.70 £2.10 £3.20 (£25.50) Trio £44.70 OWNER Major & Mrs Kennard and Partners (LAMBOURN) BRED Mrs R. B. Kennard 12 Rn 60.2 secs (2.20) SF: 33/22/20/18/13/12/14/-/-/-/-/-
WEIGHT FOR AGE 3yo-8lb

T/Jkpt: Not won; £23,713.26 to Southwell 8/6/95. T/Plpt: £71.70 (277.54 Tckts). T/Qdpt: £3.50 (24.15 Tckts). KH

YARMOUTH (L-H)
Wednesday June 7th (Good)
WEATHER: fine WIND: mod bhd

1547 SUFFOLK MAIDEN STKS (3-Y.O) (Class D) £4,070.30 (£1,216.40: £582.20: £265.10) **1m 3y** Stalls: High GOING minus 0.44 sec per fur (F) 2-15 (2-16)

1186 8 **Mukhatab** *(81) (HThomsonJones)* 3-9-0 RHills(4) (plld hrd: a in tch: led over 1f out: drvn out) — **1**

1218[5] Pennycairn **(67)***(75) (HRACecil)* 3-8-9 WRyan(3) (led tl over 1f out: hrd rdn & ev ch ins fnl f: r.o)...nk 2
1312[3] Mokuti *(70)*(Fav)*(GWragg)* 3-9-0 MHills(2) (trckd ldr: rdn ½-wy: btn 2f out)...5 3
1317[3] Farmer's Tern (IRE) *(61) (WJarvis)* 3-8-9 MTebbutt(1) (hld up: nvr able to chal)...2 4
1317[7] Sound Trick (USA) *(61) (GCBravery)* 3-8-9 KDarley(5) (trckd ldr over 4f)...nk 5
1486[6] Top Skipper (IRE) *(58) (BHanbury)* 3-8-11 [3] JTate(7) (bhd fr over 4f out)...4 6
Seyouf (USA) *(54) (JHMGosden)* 3-9-0 GHind(6) (leggy: unf: b: plld hrd in rr: wl bhd fnl f)...2 7

9/4 Mokuti, **3/1** Pennycairn, **4/1** MUKHATAB, **5/1** Seyouf (USA), **14/1** Top Skipper (IRE), **16/1** Farmer's Tern (IRE), **40/1** Sound Trick (USA), CSF £14.52 TOTE £4.80: £2.60 £2.20 (£22.80) OWNER Mr Hamdan Al Maktoum (NEWMARKET) BRED Shadwell Estate Company Limited 7 Rn
1m 37.0 (1.70) SF: 45/39/34/25/25/22/18

1548 FLEGGS (S) H'CAP (0-60) (3-Y.O+) (Class G) £2,691.00 (£746.00: £357.00)
1m 3y Stalls: High GOING minus 0.44 sec per fur (F) 2-45 (2-47)

835[10] **Ballyhays (IRE) (44)***(50+) (JAHarris)* 6-8-13 [5] PMcCabe(5) (chsd ldr: led wl over 1f out: pushed out)...— 1
1426[9] Okay Baby (IRE) **(44)***(48) (MHTompkins)* 3-8-7 PRobinson(3) (hld up: hdwy 2f out: r.o fnl f: nvr rchd wnr)...1¼ 2
1161[16] Alpine Skier (IRE) **(37)***(40) (MrsMReveley)* 4-8-11 KDarley(8) (led tl wl over 1f out: kpt on one pce)...nk 3
Today Tonite **(45)***(47) (JPearce)* 3-8-8 RHills(9) (nt grwn: chsd ldrs: styd on one pce fnl 2f) ...½ 4
1285[9] Calisar **(40)***(40)*(Fav)*(PHowling)* 5-9-0 MRoberts(2) (effrt over 2f out: kpt on one pce fnl f) 1 5
545[13] Grand Salt (IRE) **(50)***(50) (MJHaynes)* 4-9-10 WRyan(1) (t: in rr tl hdwy over 1f out: nrst fin)...s.h 6
1146[7] Most Welcome News **(45)***(42) (JRJenkins)* 3-8-8 DaleGibson(7) (chsd ldrs over 5f)...1½ 7
1028[6] Rose Chime (IRE) **(53)***(50) (JLHarris)* 3-9-2 PaulEddery(6) (trckd ldr tl rdn & wknd over 2f out)...hd 8
1350[8] Tocco Jewel **(26)***(15) (MJRyan)* 5-7-7 [(7)ow7] NicolaHowarth(10) (a in rr)...nk 9
1484[11] Magication **(42)***(34) (CNAllen)* 5-9-2 GHind(4) (a bhd)...2 10
LONG HANDICAP Tocco Jewel 7-4

7/2 Calisar, **5/1** Okay Baby (IRE), **11/2** Magication, **7/1** Alpine Skier (IRE), **15/2** Rose Chime (IRE), **8/1** Most Welcome News, **9/1** Tocco Jewel (10/1-16/1), **10/1** Today Tonite, **20/1** Grand Salt (IRE), BALLYHAYS (IRE), CSF £108.20 CT £702.86 TOTE £18.30: £3.60 £1.20 £2.80 (£50.80) Trio £113.00 OWNER Mrs Annette Harris (SOUTHWELL) BRED James M. Egan 10 Rn
1m 39.2 (3.90) SF: 21/8/11/7/11/21/2/10/-/5
WEIGHT FOR AGE 3yo-11lb
No bid

1549 ROYAL ANGLIAN REGIMENT MEDIAN AUCTION MAIDEN STKS (3-Y.O F) (Class E) £3,114.00 (£927.00: £441.00: £198.00)
7f 3y Stalls: Low GOING minus 0.44 sec per fur (F) 3-15 (3-16)

1360[2] **Bouche Bee (USA)** *(76)*(Fav)*(LMCumani)* 3-8-11 KDarley(1) (hld up: plld out over 2f out: led wl over 1f out: pushed clr: comf)...— 1
Brown Eyed Girl **(70)***(65) (RHannon)* 3-8-11 PatEddery(2) (nt grwn: in tch: hrd rdn to go 2nd ins fnl f: no ch w wnr)...5 2
1240[7] By The Bay *(60) (BWHills)* 3-8-11 MHills(4) (led after 1f tl wl over 1f out: sn wknd)...2 3
Pass Mark *(53) (JRFanshawe)* 3-8-11 DHarrison(3) (pushed along 3f out: nvr able to chal)....3 4
My Brave Girl *(45) (HRACecil)* 3-8-11 WRyan(6) (lt-f: s.i.s: a in rr)...3½ 5
1032[7] Merrie le Bow **(52)***(40) (PatMitchell)* 3-8-11 MFenton(5) (led 1f: trckd ldr tl wknd 3f out)........2½ 6

11/8 BOUCHE BEE (USA), **4/1** My Brave Girl (op 2/1), **9/2** Pass Mark, **11/2** Brown Eyed Girl, **8/1** By The Bay (op 5/1), **33/1** Merrie le Bow, CSF £8.42 TOTE £2.90: £1.40 £1.70 (£5.40) OWNER Miss Gatto Roissard (NEWMARKET) BRED Jones Kamur Partnership 6 Rn
1m 24.0 (1.20) SF: 45/34/29/22/14/9

1550 RADIO NORFOLK H'CAP (0-80) (3-Y.O) (Class D) £3,867.50 (£1,154.00: £551.00: £249.50) **6f 3y** Stalls: Low GOING minus 0.44 sec per fur (F) 3-45 (3-45)

999[7] **Masafah (USA) (76)***(83) (HThomsonJones)* 3-9-6 RHills(1) (hld up: squeezed thro appr fnl f: led 100y out: r.o)...— 1
982[8] Sally Slade **(77)***(81) (CACyzer)* 3-9-7 MRoberts(7) (bhd tl hdwy 2f out: rdn & hung lft ins fnl f: r.o)...1¼ 2
1248[3] Annie Fay (IRE) **(55)***(57) (JLHarris)* 3-7-13 RPrice(4) (led to 100y out: r.o one pce)...¾ 3
922[18] Make Time **(70)***(66) (JPearce)* 3-9-0 PatEddery(3) (lw: chsd ldrs: ev ch appr fnl f: one pce)...2 4

1277² Shashi (IRE) **(77)***(71)*(Fav)*(DMorley)* 3-9-7 WCarson(5) (chsd ldrs: ev ch appr fnl f: btn whn sltly hmpd ins fnl f) ....¾ 5
1405⁶ Time Is Money (IRE) **(61)***(55)* *(MHTompkins)* 3-8-5 PRobinson(6) (trckd ldr: ev ch appr fnl f: sn wknd) ....hd 6
1201⁸ Rolling (IRE) **(63)***(49)* *(BWHills)* 3-8-7 MHills(2) (chsd ldrs: nt clr run over 2f out & appr fnl f: one pce fnl f) 3 7
1360⁴ Roy Boy **(72)***(57)* *(MrsMReveley)* 3-9-2b KDarley(10) (lw: hdwy over 2f out: wknd over 1f out) ....nk 8
1279⁸ Solo Prize **(65)***(40)* *(PHowling)* 3-8-9 PaulEddery(9) (b.hind: a outpcd) 4 9
1276⁸ Das Island **(53)***(17)* *(JRJenkins)* 3-7-11 DaleGibson(8) (spd to ½-wy) 4 10
Fair Attraction **(53)** *(AHide)* 3-7-6 (5)ow3 NVarley(11) (a outpcd) 7 11

9/4 Shashi (IRE) (op 7/2), **9/2** Make Time, **5/1** Roy Boy, **8/1** Rolling (IRE), **10/1** Sally Slade, Annie Fay (IRE), **11/1** Solo Prize (8/1-12/1), **12/1** MASAFAH (USA), **16/1** Fair Attraction, Das Island, **33/1** Time Is Money (IRE), CSF £118.41 CT £1,144.19 TOTE £12.70: £2.40 £2.70 £3.60 (£56.10) Trio £277.10 OWNER Mr Hamdan Al Maktoum (NEWMARKET) BRED Shadwell Farm Inc 11 Rn
1m 11.3 (0.70) SF: 57/55/31/40/45/29/23/31/14/-/-

1551 E.B.F. BRECKLAND MAIDEN STKS (2-Y.O) (Class D) £4,620.00 (£1,380.00: £660.00: £300.00) 6f 3y Stalls: Low GOING minus 0.44 sec per fur (F) 4-15 (4-22)

Rio Duvida *(85+)*(Fav)*(DRLoder)* 2-9-0 PatEddery(1) (leggy: unf: scope: hld up: led 2f out: rdn clr 1f out: qcknd ins fnl f) ....— 1
Unsold *(77)* *(JRFanshawe)* 2-9-0 DHarrison(8) (cmpt: bit bkwd: outpcd early: hdwy over 3f out: r.o one pce fr over 1f out) 3 2
Sovereign's Crown (USA) *(76)* *(JHMGosden)* 2-9-0 GHind(5) (lt-f: dwlt: hdwy over 2f out: kpt on one pce fnl f) ....nk 3
Atraf *(71)* *(DMorley)* 2-9-0 WCarson(4) (lt-f: led 4f: wknd fnl f) 2 4
Inchrory *(70)* *(HRACecil)* 2-9-0 WRyan(7) (cmpt: hld up: hdwy over 2f out: nvr able to chal) ..½ 5
Even Top (IRE) *(69)* *(MHTompkins)* 2-9-0 PRobinson(2) (lengthy: scope: a outpcd) ....nk 6
Truancy *(62)* *(MBell)* 2-9-0 MFenton(3) (leggy: unf: chsd ldrs over 3f) 2½ 7
Emperegrine (USA) *(54)* *(CFWall)* 2-9-0 MRoberts(6) (unf : bit bkwd: trckd ldr over 3f out: sn wknd) 3 8

8/11 RIO DUVIDA, **7/2** Atraf, **6/1** Inchrory (4/1-7/1), **8/1** Sovereign's Crown (USA) (op 53/1), **14/1** Unsold (6/1-16/1), Truancy (op 8/1), **33/1** Even Top (IRE), **40/1** Emperegrine (USA), CSF £12.55 TOTE £1.70: £1.10 £4.00 £2.30 (£19.60) OWNER Lady Harrison (NEWMARKET) BRED Limestone Stud 8 Rn
1m 11.9 (1.30) SF: 41/33/32/27/26/25/18/10

1552 RIVER YARE LIMITED STKS (0-60) (4-Y.O+) (Class F) £2,745.80 (£758.80: £361.40) 1m 6f 17y Stalls: Low GOING minus 0.44 sec per fur (F) 4-45 (4-47)

751⁸ **Upper Mount Clair (60)***(69)* *(CEBrittain)* 5-8-8 MRoberts(3) (3rd st: led over 4f out: clr 3f out: eased ins fnl f) ....— 1
1310² Sunday News'n'echo (USA) **(58)***(66)*(Fav)*(WStorey)* 4-8-3 (5) PMcCabe(7) (4th st: chsd wnr fnl 4f: no imp) 2½ 2
1313⁵ Durshan (USA) **(50)***(60)* *(JRJenkins)* 6-8-11 DaleGibson(6) (6th st: hrd rdn over 2f out: nvr able to chal) 8 3
1444⁵ Allmosa **(57)***(46)* *(TJNaughton)* 6-8-6 PatEddery(5) (last st: no imp) 8 4
*1332*⁴ Barti-Ddu **(56)***(45)* *(SCWilliams)* 4-9-1 KDarley(1) (lw: 5th st: btn 3f out) 9 5
*1075*² Swordking (IRE) **(42)***(35)* *(JLHarris)* 6-8-13 PaulEddery(2) (led 3f: led 6f out tl over 4f out: wknd 3f out) 7 6
*370*⁴ Bures (IRE) **(60)** *(MHTompkins)* 4-8-6v(5) SMulvey(4) (led after 3f to 6f out: 2nd st: wknd over 3f out: sn t.o: virtually p.u) ....dist 7

15/8 Sunday News'n'echo (USA), **5/2** Allmosa (op 6/1), **5/1** UPPER MOUNT CLAIR, **6/1** Bures (IRE) (op 7/2), **12/1** Barti-Ddu, **14/1** Durshan (USA) (op 6/1), Swordking (IRE), CSF £14.38 TOTE £4.10: £2.20 £1.60 (£5.40) OWNER Mr C. E. Brittain (NEWMARKET) BRED J. Ward Hill 7 Rn
3m 2.3 (4.30) SF: 33/30/24/10/9/-/-

1553 HEYDON HALL APPRENTICE H'CAP (0-70) (3-Y.O+) (Class G) £2,329.50 (£662.00: £328.50) 1m 2f 21y Stalls: Low GOING minus 0.44 sec per fur (F) 5-15 (5-15)

1371* **Vindaloo (53)***(66)*(Fav)*(JLHarris)* 3-7-13 5x PFessey(1) (hld up: 5th & carried wd st: squeezed thro 2f out: led 1f out: r.o) ....— 1
1192⁸ Locorotondo (IRE) **(69)***(80)* *(MBell)* 4-9-6 (8) GFaulkner(6) (3rd st: led 2f out to 1f out: unable qckn) 1¼ 2

1368² Hawkish (USA) **(44)***(53) (DMorley)* 6-8-3 GMitchell(5) (hld up: last st: styd on one pce fnl 2f)....1¼ **3**
1314⁷ Progression **(59)***(60) (PCHaslam)* 4-9-1 (3) NicolaHowarth(3) (hdwy on ins & 4th st: ev ch 2f out: one pce)....5 **4**
1286³ Sparkling Roberta **(42)***(38) (MDIUsher)* 4-7-12 (3) CAdamson(4) (2nd st: led 4f out to 2f out: sn wknd)....3 **5**
1290⁸ Robin Island **(60)***(51) (RHannon)* 3-8-3 (3) DaneO'Neill(2) (led 6f: wl bhd fnl 3f)....3½ **6**

11/4 VINDALOO, **3/1** Locorotondo (IRE), Hawkish (USA) (op 2/1), **5/1** Sparkling Roberta, **13/2** Robin Island, **11/1** Progression (op 5/1), CSF £11.01 TOTE £3.60: £2.10 £1.70 (£4.40) OWNER Mr J. D. Abell (MELTON MOWBRAY) BRED Green Park Investments Ltd 6 Rn
2m 9.6 (5.20) SF: 8/35/8/15/-/-
WEIGHT FOR AGE 3yo-13lb
STEWARDS' ENQUIRY Howarth susp. 16-21/6/95 (irresponsible riding).

T/Plpt: £195.50 (63.14 Tckts). T/Qdpt: £17.20 (4 Tckts). RC

1528-BEVERLEY (R-H)
Thursday June 8th (Good to Soft)
WEATHER: overcast WIND: fresh half against

1554 ETTON MAIDEN STKS (3-Y.O+) (Class D) £3,684.50 (£1,106.00: £533.00: £246.50) 1m 100y Stalls: High GOING minus 0.05 sec per fur (G) 2-15 (2-16)

553⁵ **Blisland** *(88+) (RCharlton)* 3-8-10 RCochrane(4) (hld up: hdwy & nt clr run over 2f out: swtchd lft: led over 1f out: sn rdn clr)....— **1**
1312² Proud Destiny *(70) (MRStoute)* 3-8-5 DHolland(5) (trckd ldrs: effrt 3f out: sn rdn & hmpd: kpt on u.p: no ch w wnr)....7 **2**
1221⁴ Divine Pursuit *(69)*(Fav)*(HRACecil)* 3-8-5 WRyan(3) (w ldr: led over 2f out tl over 1f out: one pce)....nk **3**
1000¹¹ Skedaddle *(56) (JGFitzGerald)* 3-8-5 KFallon(6) (sn outpcd: bhd & drvn along: kpt on fnl 2f: n.d)....7 **4**
544² Yet Again *(55) (BHanbury)* 3-8-5 (5) JStack(2) (unruly in stalls: s.s: sn in tch: effrt over 3f out: hung rt: n.d)....3 **5**
1125¹³ Rock Rambler *(50) (LadyHerries)* 3-8-10 KDarley(7) (mde most tl over 2f out: sn wknd)....3 **6**
1291ᵂ Bali Tender *(36) (MWEasterby)* 4-9-7 MBirch(1) (unruly s: swvd lft s: sn chsng ldrs: lost pl over 2f out: sn bhd & eased)....7 **7**

11/8 Divine Pursuit, **2/1** Proud Destiny, **3/1** BLISLAND, **14/1** Yet Again, **16/1** Skedaddle, Rock Rambler, **50/1** Bali Tender, CSF £9.70 TOTE £4.30: £2.20 £1.40 (£6.60) OWNER Mr K. Abdullah (BECKHAMPTON) BRED Juddmonte Farms 7 Rn 1m 49.5 (5.50) SF: 23/5/4/-/-/-/-
WEIGHT FOR AGE 3yo-11lb
STEWARDS' ENQUIRY Cochrane susp. 17 & 19-20/6/95 (careless riding).

1555 HURN CLAIMING STKS (4-Y.O+) (Class F) £2,798.00 (£778.00: £374.00) 1m 3f 216y Stalls: High GOING minus 0.05 sec per fur (G) 2-45 (2-46)

1149* **Elementary (76)***(67+)*(Fav)*(NJHWalker)* 12-8-5 (5) JStack(4) (lw: sn trckng ldr: led 7f out: styd on wl fnl 3f: clr over 1f out)....— **1**
1252⁷ Goodbye Millie **(33)***(42) (JLEyre)* 5-8-1v RLappin(9) (chsd ldrs: wnt 2nd over 3f out: sn rdn & one pce)....12 **2**
1245⁵ Kimberley Boy **(55)***(42) (MBrittain)* 5-8-6 RCochrane(7) (hld up & plld hrd: hdwy to trck ldrs ½-wy: wnt 2nd over 1f out: one pce)....3½ **3**
*1086*¹³ Premier Blues (FR) **(25)***(35) (RJRWilliams)* 5-8-1b DBiggs(1) (trckd ldrs: effrt over 3f out: kpt on fnl 2f: nvr able to chal)....2 **4**
Among Islands *(43) (MrsMReveley)* 4-8-13 KDarley(5) (hld up & bhd: effrt 4f out: sn rdn & no imp)....3 **5**
Jungle Rites (IRE) *(43) (JGFitzGerald)* 7-9-4 KFallon(2) (hld up: effrt 4f out: styd on fnl f: n.d)....3½ **6**
1149⁶ Lawful Love (IRE) *(27) (TWDonnelly)* 5-8-10 SDWilliams(8) (led to 7f out: wknd over 3f out)..6 **7**
67⁹ Scorched Air **(60)** *(JGMO'Shea)* 5-7-10 (7) MHenry(3) (bit bkwd: sn bhd: t.o 5f out: eased)....15 **8**
Vayello **(43)** *(CSmith)* 4-8-0v DaleGibson(6) (plld hrd: trckd ldrs tl wknd 5f out: sn bhd & eased)....2½ **9**

8/11 ELEMENTARY, **5/1** Kimberley Boy, **7/1** Jungle Rites (IRE), **8/1** Scorched Air, **10/1** Among Islands, **12/1** Goodbye Millie, **16/1** Vayello, **25/1** Premier Blues (FR), **33/1** Lawful Love (IRE), CSF £11.73 TOTE £2.00: £1.60 £2.30 £1.60 (£9.80) Trio £17.00 OWNER Mr Paul Green (WANTAGE) BRED Ballymaglassan Stud 9 Rn 2m 41.2 (9.70) SF: 19/-/-/-/-/-/-/-/-

1556
GRP MASSEY TWO YEAR OLD TROPHY CONDITIONS STKS (2-Y.O C & G) (Class B) £7,918.20 (£2,953.80: £1,436.90: £609.50: £264.75: £126.85)
5f Stalls: Centre GOING minus 0.05 sec per fur (G) 3-15 (3-15)

1343[2] **Eastern Prophets** *(86) (GLewis)* 2-9-1 PaulEddery(4) (mde all: styd on wl u.p fnl f) ....— **1**
1267[2] Blessingindisguise *(76) (MWEasterby)* 2-8-9 MBirch(6) (chsd wnr: rdn to chal 1f out: nt qckn ins fnl f) 1¼ **2**
1413* Take A Left *(70) (MrsJRRamsden)* 2-8-13 KFallon(5) (lw: trckd ldrs: outpcd ½-wy: rdn over 1f out: kpt on same pce).............3 **3**
788* Sky Dome (IRE) *(35) (MHTompkins)* 2-8-13 PRobinson(3) (sn outpcd & pushed along: hung rt & racd wd: nvr wnt pce).............11 **4**
533* Playmaker *(34)*(Fav)*(JBerry)* 2-8-13 JCarroll(1) (lw: swvd lft s: racd wd: chsd ldrs: rdn & edgd lft ½-wy: sn btn).............nk **5**
1494* Silverdale Knight *(17) (KWHogg)* 2-8-9 KDarley(2) (racd wd & sn outpcd: bhd fr ½-wy) 4 **6**

7/4 Playmaker (Evens-2/1), **5/2** EASTERN PROPHETS, **9/2** Blessingindisguise, **5/1** Take A Left, **8/1** Sky Dome (IRE), **16/1** Silverdale Knight, CSF £13.47 TOTE £3.30: £1.60 £2.40 (£8.50) OWNER Mrs J. M. Purches (EPSOM) BRED Miss K. Zavon 6 Rn 65.4 secs (3.90) SF: 34/24/18/-/-/-
OFFICIAL EXPLANATION **Playmaker: the jockey reported that the colt went too freely to post and showed no enthusiasm in the race.**

1557
TOUCH ABOVE H'CAP (0-70) (3-Y.O+) (Class E) £3,345.00 (£1,005.00: £485.00: £225.00) **1m 1f 207y** Stalls: High GOING minus 0.05 sec per fur (G) 3-45 (3-47)

1368* **Allesca (60)***(63) (MDIUsher)* 5-9-5 (7) 5x CAdamson(7) (b: hld up & bhd: hdwy on outside 3f out: r.o wl fnl f: led post).............— **1**
866[12] All on **(42)***(45) (JHetherton)* 4-8-8 NKennedy(4) (trckd ldrs: styd on to ld jst ins fnl f: jst ct)....s.h **2**
1150[11] Sun Mark (IRE) **(58)***(60) (MrsSMAustin)* 4-9-10 JMarshall(8) (b: trckd ldrs: nt clr run 2f out: swtchd lft & styd on strly ins fnl f).............½ **3**
1378[3] Touch Above **(50)***(51) (TDBarron)* 9-9-2 JFortune(6) (led tl jst ins fnl f: no ex).............¾ **4**
1192[9] Red Indian **(40)***(35) (WWHaigh)* 9-8-6 DaleGibson(3) (hld up: effrt over 3f out: kpt on one pce fnl 2f: nvr nr to chal).............3½ **5**
1292[4] Kanat Lee (IRE) **(41)***(31) (DonEnricoIncisa)* 4-8-7 KimTinkler(1) (hld up: hdwy on outside over 4f out: effrt u.p 3f out: sn wknd).............3½ **6**
1437[4] Straw Thatch **(49)***(33)*(Fav)*(MrsJRRamsden)* 6-9-1 KFallon(2) (lw: hld up: effrt over 3f out: sn rdn & hung lft: no imp).............3½ **7**
1285[11] Goldenberry **(30)***(14) (JParkes)* 4-7-7 (3) DarrenMoffatt(5) (hld up & plld hrd: effrt on ins over 2f out: sn wknd).............nk **8**

5/2 Straw Thatch, **3/1** ALLESCA, **4/1** Touch Above, **9/2** Kanat Lee (IRE), **12/1** Red Indian, All on, **20/1** Sun Mark (IRE), **25/1** Goldenberry, CSF £33.21 CT £551.56 TOTE £5.00: £2.30 £4.40 £4.40 (£82.40) OWNER Miss D. G. Kerr (SWINDON) BRED Mrs E. M. Gauvain 8 Rn
2m 12.4 (9.90) SF: 14/-/11/2/-/-/-/-

1558
110TH YEAR OF THE WATT MEMORIAL H'CAP (0-90) (3-Y.O+) (Class C) £5,605.00 (£1,690.00: £820.00: £385.00)
1m 3f 216y Stalls: High GOING minus 0.05 sec per fur (G) 4-15 (4-15)

668[5] **Riparius (USA) (76)***(85) (HCandy)* 4-9-4b WNewnes(4) (lw: mde all: sn clr: styd on u.p fnl 2f).............— **1**
1252[3] Wonderful Day **(67)***(76) (SCWilliams)* 4-8-9 JFortune(6) (trckd ldrs: effrt over 2f out: styd on fnl f: nt qckn nr fin) ....nk **2**
1303[7] Hazard a Guess (IRE) **(78)***(85) (MrsJRRamsden)* 5-9-6 KFallon(8) (hld up: effrt & n.m.r over 3f out: sn drvn along: styng on wl whn nt clr run ins fnl f: r.o strly towards fin) 1½ **3**
1303[4] Manful **(81)***(87) (JHetherton)* 3-8-7 NKennedy(11) (chsd ldrs: pushed along 5f out: n.m.r on ins fr 2f out: styd on same pce fnl f) ....¾ **4**
Star Rage (IRE) **(77)***(82) (MJohnston)* 5-9-5 DHolland(10) (trckd ldrs: effrt & ev ch over 1f out: edgd rt & wknd fnl f) ....½ **5**
1135[10] Ringmaster (IRE) **(85)***(89) (MHTompkins)* 4-9-13 PRobinson(9) (hld up: hdwy & in tch 5f out: effrt & hung rt 2f out: wknd over 1f out).............1 **6**
1141[4] Clouded Elegance **(78)***(74)*(Fav)*(LadyHerries)* 5-9-6 KDarley(5) (lw: chsd ldr: effrt over 3f out: wkng whn n.m.r 2f out).............6 **7**
918[10] Geisway (CAN) **(86)***(80) (NJHWalker)* 5-10-0 RCochrane(7) (mid div: effrt over 3f out: sn rdn: n.d) 1¼ **8**
Jabaroot (IRE) **(84)***(73) (MRStoute)* 4-9-12 WRyan(3) (prom: pushed along 4f out: sn lost pl).............3½ **9**

1416[6] Sharkashka (IRE) **(69)***(54) (MHEasterby)* 5-8-11 MBirch(1) (bhd: drvn along & outpcd 4f out: n.d) 3½ **10**
954[6] Solomon's Dancer (USA) **(70)***(52) (WWHaigh)* 5-8-12 DaleGibson(2) (lw: hld up & bhd: effrt & rdn 4f out: n.d) 1¾ **11**

5/2 Clouded Elegance, **9/2** RIPARIUS (USA), **11/2** Wonderful Day, **7/1** Hazard a Guess (IRE), **8/1** Solomon's Dancer (USA) (6/1-9/1), Ringmaster (IRE), Jabaroot (IRE), **12/1** Manful, **14/1** Star Rage (IRE), **16/1** Geisway (CAN), **33/1** Sharkashka (IRE), CSF £30.66 CT £164.84 TOTE £5.70: £1.80 £2.40 £3.80 (£16.70) Trio £99.30 OWNER Mrs David Blackburn (WANTAGE) BRED Rogers Trust 11 Rn 2m 39.9 (8.40) SF: 40/31/40/26/37/44/29/35/28/9/7
WEIGHT FOR AGE 3yo-16lb

1559 FIGHAM MAIDEN APPRENTICE H'CAP (0-75) (3-Y.O+) (Class G) £2,305.00 (£655.00: £325.00) 5f Stalls: Centre GOING minus 0.05 sec per fur (G) 4-45 (4-45)

1419[3] **Henry the Hawk (41)***(54) (MDods)* 4-9-4 CWebb(8) (trckd ldrs: led on ins over 1f out: sn pushed clr) ....— **1**
1471[4] Nite-Owl Dancer **(58)***(52)*(Fav)*(JAHarris)* 3-9-13 AEddery(7) (w ldrs: led ½-wy tl over 1f out: kpt on same pce) 6 **2**
1321[5] Halbert **(41)***(31) (MRChannon)* 6-8-13 (5) DSweeney(3) (mde most to ½-wy: kpt on same pce over 1f out) 1¼ **3**
1248[8] China Hand (IRE) **(56)***(44) (MartynWane)* 3-9-11 MSemple(1) (chsd ldrs: hung bdly rt fr ½-wy: no imp appr fnl f) ....½ **4**
1302[4] Never Say so **(59)***(46) (CSmith)* 3-10-0 CScudder(6) (in tch: rdn & outpcd ½-wy: kpt on: n.d) nk **5**
1040[9] Takeapull **(55)***(33) (JBalding)* 3-9-10 JEdmunds(2) (bit bkwd: sn outpcd: edgd rt -wy: n.d) 3 **6**
Northern Grey **(55)***(33) (JBerry)* 3-9-10 CLowther(4) (bit bkwd: w ldrs tl wknd 2f out) ....s.h **7**
842[8] Shartel **(31)** *(MJohnston)* 3-8-0b BHalligan(5) (s.i.s: a outpcd & bhd) 4 **8**
1465[11] Fishy Affair **(45)** *(TDyer)* 3-8-9b(5) RMullen(9) (s.s: a wl bhd) 8 **9**

3/1 Nite-Owl Dancer, **5/1** HENRY THE HAWK, Halbert, **11/2** Northern Grey, Never Say so, **6/1** Fishy Affair, **14/1** Takeapull, **16/1** Shartel, **20/1** China Hand (IRE), CSF £20.08 CT £73.12 TOTE £4.40: £1.40 £1.40 £1.70 (£7.00) Trio £11.20 OWNER Mr S. Barras (DARLINGTON) BRED Mrs Celia Miller 9 Rn 66.6 secs (5.10) SF: 18/8/-/-/2/-/-/-/-
WEIGHT FOR AGE 3yo-8lb
T/Plpt: £79.80 (187.77 Tckts). T/Qdpt: £26.20 (4.95 Tckts). WG

1017-CHESTER (L-H)
Thursday June 8th (Good)

WEATHER: overcast WIND: str against

1560 PEEPING TOM H'CAP (0-90) (3-Y.O+) (Class C) £7,165.00 (£2,170.00: £1,060.00: £505.00) 7f 2y Stalls: Low GOING minus 0.37 sec per fur (F) 6-45 (6-47)

1174[15] **Champagne Grandy (67)***(74) (MRChannon)* 5-9-1 RHughes(1) (a.p: 2nd st: led over 1f out: rdn & r.o wl) ....— **1**
1280[2] Dawalib (USA) **(64)***(69)*(Fav)*(DHaydnJones)* 5-8-12 TQuinn(4) (lw: hld up: 4th st: chsd wnr fnl f: r.o) ....¾ **2**
1409* Shepherd Market (IRE) **(67)***(70) (DAWilson)* 4-9-1 6x GCarter(7) (lw: a.p: 3rd st: rdn & unable qckn fnl f) 1 **3**
1217[4] Promise Fulfilled (USA) **(75)***(78) (SGNorton)* 4-9-9b KFallon(5) (hld up & bhd: effrt & 6th st: r.o wl ins fnl f) ....s.h **4**
Bold Angel **(73)***(75) (MHEasterby)* 8-9-7 SMaloney(3) (bkwd: hld up & bhd: hdwy on ins & 5th st: kpt on towards fin) ....½ **5**
1250[10] Cee-Jay-Ay **(68)***(63) (JBerry)* 8-9-2 JCarroll(2) (dwlt: hdwy ½-wy: 7th st: nvr nr to chal) 3 **6**
567[8] Little Ibnr **(65)***(59) (PDEvans)* 4-8-13 WCarson(8) (lw: led tl hdd over 1f out: sn rdn: wknd qckly fnl f) ....nk **7**
1179[2] Jato **(76)** *(SCWilliams)* 6-9-10 JFortune(6) (hld up: hdwy ½-wy: lost pl ent st: sn t.o) ....dist **8**

7/2 Dawalib (USA), **4/1** Jato, **5/1** Cee-Jay-Ay, Shepherd Market (IRE), **8/1** Promise Fulfilled (USA), Little Ibnr, **9/1** Bold Angel (6/1-10/1), **10/1** CHAMPAGNE GRANDY, CSF £42.52 CT £180.34 TOTE £12.90: £2.50 £1.40 £2.30 (£26.10) OWNER Grandy Girls (UPPER LAMBOURN) BRED J. B. and Mrs N. G. Stafford 8 Rn 1m 26.96 (1.76) SF: 53/48/49/57/54/42/38/-

1561 RABBIT CATCHER H'CAP (0-80) (3-Y.O+) (Class D) £4,788.00 (£1,449.00: £707.00: £336.00) 1m 2f 75y Stalls: High GOING minus 0.37 sec (F) 7-15 (7-15)

1285* **Indian Jockey (63)***(69+)*(Fav)*(MCPipe)* 3-8-4 MRoberts(1) (hld up gng wl: 2nd st: led bel dist: pushed out) ....— **1**

1126[8] Unprejudice **(64)***(69) (GRimmer)* 4-9-4 MRimmer(6) (hld up & bhd: stdy hdwy over 4f out: 5th st: styd on wl ins fnl f) ....½ **2**
1355* Veloce (IRE) **(71)***(67) (ABailey)* 7-9-11 5x MWigham(5) (b: hld up & bhd: 6th st: hdwy on ins over 1f out: nvr nrr) 6 **3**
1415[8] Jubran (USA) **(70)***(65) (MJohnston)* 9-9-10 DHolland(4) (bkwd: led after 2f to 4f out: rdn & 3rd st: outpcd appr fnl f) ....½ **4**
1154* Sheama (USA) **(72)***(67) (WJarvis)* 3-8-13 BThomson(2) (hld up: 4th st: sn rdn & outpcd) ....s.h **5**
Kings Cay (IRE) **(74)***(64) (THCaldwell)* 4-9-9 (5) JStack(3) (bit bkwd: led 2f: led 4f out to bel dist: sn wknd) 3½ **6**

5/6 INDIAN JOCKEY (5/4-4/5), **4/1** Sheama (USA), **7/1** Jubran (USA), **15/2** Veloce (IRE), **9/1** Unprejudice, **14/1** Kings Cay (IRE), CSF £8.51 TOTE £1.90: £1.60 £3.40 (£10.80) OWNER 0336 405200 Racing (WELLINGTON) BRED John Hayter 6 Rn 2m 13.47 (4.77) SF: 33/46/44/42/31/41
WEIGHT FOR AGE 3yo-13lb

1562 TARRAGON MAIDEN STKS (2-Y.O) (Class D) £4,084.50 (£1,236.00: £603.00: £286.50) **5f 16y** Stalls: Low GOING minus 0.37 sec per fur (F) 7-45 (7-48)

903[2] **Whittle Rock** *(73) (EJAlston)* 2-8-9 KFallon(1) (chsd ldr: led ½-wy: clr appr fnl f: unchal) ....— **1**
859[4] Stealth Attack (IRE) *(65) (JBerry)* 2-9-0 JCarroll(3) (lw: outpcd & bhd: kpt on u.p appr fnl f: no ch w wnr) 5 **2**
1298[2] Arajaan (USA) *(62)*(Fav)*(BHanbury)* 2-9-0 WCarson(4) (lw: sn outpcd & bhd: hrd rdn & effrt over 1f out: no imp) 1 **3**
1203[5] Boffy (IRE) *(60) (BPJBaugh)* 2-9-0 ACulhane(2) (slt ld to ½-wy: wknd appr fnl f) 1 **4**
1158[5] Miletrian Refurb (IRE) *(46) (MRChannon)* 2-9-0 RHughes(5) (bit bkwd: s.i.s: a outpcd & bhd) 5 **5**

2/5 Arajaan (USA), **4/1** WHITTLE ROCK, **8/1** Stealth Attack (IRE), **16/1** Miletrian Refurb (IRE), **20/1** Boffy (IRE), CSF £27.35 TOTE £4.10: £1.60 £2.10 (£10.80) OWNER Bay Horse Racing Syndicate (PRESTON) BRED J. Needham 5 Rn 62.48 secs (2.48) SF: 32/24/21/19/5

1563 BIRD LIME STKS (4-Y.O+) (Class C) £6,248.00 (£2,018.00: £984.00) **1m 4f 66y** Stalls: Low GOING minus 0.37 sec per fur (F) 8-15 (8-15)

1479[2] **Marsoom (CAN) (99)***(110)*(Fav)*(BHanbury)* 4-9-5 MRimmer(1) (b: b.hind: lw: chsd ldr: 2nd st: shkn up over 1f out: led ins fnl f: r.o) ....— **1**
Double Dagger **(93)***(110) (HRACecil)* 4-9-7 WRyan(3) (bit bkwd: led tl hdd & no ex ins fnl f) 1¾ **2**
958[2] Misbelief **(102)** *(JRFanshawe)* 5-8-12 DHarrison(2) (hld up & bhd: pushed along 4f out: sn outpcd: 3rd & t.o ent st) ....dist **3**

5/4 MARSOOM (CAN), **13/8** Misbelief, **3/1** Double Dagger, CSF £4.30 TOTE £2.40 (£2.90) OWNER Mr Hilal Salem (NEWMARKET) BRED Calumet Farm, Black Chip Stable, Wotton House Farm 3 Rn 2m 47.3 (10.70) SF: 7/7/-

1564 FLASH IN THE PAN CLAIMING STKS (3-Y.O) (Class E) £3,493.00 (£1,054.00: £512.00: £241.00) **6f 18y** Stalls: Low GOING minus 0.37 sec per fur (F) 8-45 (8-46)

1445[2] **Fantasy Racing (IRE) (75)***(71)*(Fav)*(MRChannon)* 3-8-9 RHughes(2) (a.p: rdn bel dist: led ins fnl f: r.o wl) ....— **1**
1304[8] One for Jeannie **(64)***(60) (ABailey)* 3-8-1v GCarter(3) (led over 4f out to bel dist: rdn to ld ins fnl f: sn hdd: one pce) 1 **2**
831[2] Ultra Beet **(66)***(67) (PCHaslam)* 3-8-8 JFortune(1) (led over 1f: led bel dist tl ins fnl f) ....nk **3**
1453* We're Joken **(52)***(49) (JBerry)* 3-8-11 JCarroll(7) (b.nr hind: a.p: ev ch whn n.m.r ent fnl f: eased whn btn) 8 **4**
1434[5] Poly Laureon (IRE) **(50)***(35) (RHollinshead)* 3-8-3 WRyan(6) (bhd: effrt over 2f out: wknd appr fnl f) 2 **5**
1371[10] Bretton Princess **(36)***(17) (RHollinshead)* 3-7-10 ow1 AMackay(4) (a bhd & outpcd) 4 **6**
1263[2] Prolific Lady (IRE) **(73)***(20) (MBrittain)* 3-8-11 KFallon(8) (chsd ldrs: rdn ½-wy: wknd wl over 1f out) 5 **7**
Oh Dearie Me *(JGMO'Shea)* 3-8-7 VSlattery(5) (unf: scope: bkwd: s.s: a bhd & outpcd: t.o) 7 **8**

7/4 FANTASY RACING (IRE), **2/1** One for Jeannie, **11/2** Ultra Beet, **13/2** We're Joken, **8/1** Prolific Lady (IRE), **14/1** Poly Laureon (IRE), **25/1** Bretton Princess, Oh Dearie Me, CSF £6.05 TOTE £2.90: £1.40 £1.40 £1.70 (£3.20) OWNER Aldridge Racing Ltd (UPPER LAMBOURN) BRED Barronstown Stud and Ron Con Ltd 8 Rn 1m 14.98 (1.68) SF: 40/29/36/18/4/-/-/-

1565 DOGE OF VENICE H'CAP (0-70) (3-Y.O+) (Class E) £3,551.50 (£1,072.00: £521.00: £245.50) **5f 16y** Stalls: Low GOING minus 0.37 sec per fur (F) 9-15 (9-17)

1316[8] **Elle Shaped (IRE) (63)***(75)*(Fav)*(DNicholls)* 5-9-7 AlexGreaves(2) (lw: a.p: rdn to ld 1f out: sn clr: eased nr fin)......— 1
1151[5] White Sorrel **(66)***(69) (AHarrison)* 4-9-5 (5) JStack(3) (chsd ldrs: kpt on ins fnl f: no ch w wnr)...3 2
1411[2] Macfarlane **(70)***(69) (MJFetherston-Godley)* 7-10-0 MRoberts(11) (hdwy ent st: r.o wl ins fnl f: nrst fin)......1 3
Breakfast Creek **(66)***(58) (JBerry)* 3-9-2 JCarroll(1) (bit bkwd: led 1f: ev ch fnl f: sn outpcd)..2½ 4
1456[12] The Real Whizzbang (IRE) **(44)***(35) (PSFelgate)* 4-8-2b AMackay(7) (lw: led after 1f to 1f out: wknd ins fnl f)......nk 5
1334[10] Cronk's Courage **(50)***(36) (MGMeagher)* 9-8-8v JFortune(5) (bhd tl r.o appr fnl f: nvr nrr)......1½ 6
1400[4] Bonny Melody **(43)***(28) (PDEvans)* 4-7-8 (7) AmandaSanders(12) (hdwy over 1f out: nvr nrr)..nk 7
1304[13] Gondo **(55)***(40) (EJAlston)* 8-8-13v DHolland(4) (effrt ent st: nvr nr to chal)......hd 8
1304[9] King Rambo **(66)***(50) (RHollinshead)* 4-9-10 WRyan(10) (nvr trbld ldrs)......hd 9
1304[10] Lord Sky **(61)***(33) (ABailey)* 4-9-0b(5) VHalliday(13) (swtg: chsd ldrs 3f: sn lost tch)......4 10
1279[2] Crystal Loop **(65)***(37) (ABailey)* 3-9-1 GCarter(9) (lw: prom 3f: wknd qckly bel dist)......s.h 11
1214[8] Our Mica **(36)** *(LJBarratt)* 5-7-8vow1 WHawksley(8) (dwlt: outpcd: a bhd)......3 12
1331[3] Featherstone Lane **(52)***(9) (MissLCSiddall)* 4-8-5v(5) PMcCabe(6) (s.s: a outpcd & bhd)......1½ 13

LONG HANDICAP Our Mica 6-11

4/1 ELLE SHAPED (IRE), **5/1** Gondo, **6/1** Crystal Loop, **13/2** Macfarlane, **8/1** White Sorrel, **10/1** Breakfast Creek, **12/1** Featherstone Lane, King Rambo (op 8/1), **14/1** Bonny Melody (op 8/1), The Real Whizzbang (IRE) (op 8/1), **20/1** Lord Sky, **33/1** Our Mica, Cronk's Courage, CSF £34.48 CT £188.13 TOTE £4.00: £2.00 £3.10 £2.70 (£21.00) Trio £50.20 OWNER Simple Technology UK Ltd (THIRSK) BRED Dan Daly 13 Rn 61.61 secs (1.61) SF: 57/51/51/32/17/18/10/22/32/15/11/-/-

WEIGHT FOR AGE 3yo-8lb

T/Plpt: £98.40 (171.33 Tckts). T/Qdpt: £19.40 (13 Tckts). IM

1086-SOUTHWELL (L-H)
Thursday June 8th (Standard)

1566 LION H'CAP (0-65) (3-Y.O+) (Class F) £2,519.00 (£694.00: £329.00) **5f (Fibresand)** Stalls: Low GOING minus 0.56 sec per fur (FST) 2-00 (2-02)

1304[4] **Canovas Heart (49)***(59)*(Fav)*(BobJones)* 6-8-12 GDuffield(1) (lw: a.p: led ins fnl f: drvn out)— 1
1331[2] Chadwell Hall **(60)***(66) (SRBowring)* 4-9-4b(5) CTeague(4) (b.off hind: led tl ins fnl f)......1¼ 2
1360[5] Mamma's Due **(59)***(63) (JBerry)* 3-9-0 GCarter(13) (lw: chsd ldrs: r.o wl ins fnl f)......½ 3
1214[6] Sing With the Band **(63)***(67) (BAMcMahon)* 4-9-9 (3) SSanders(10) (lw: a.p: r.o ins fnl f)......hd 4
1489[3] Moujeeb (USA) **(60)***(62) (PatMitchell)* 5-9-9v JWeaver(9) (lw: s.i.s: hdwy 2f out: r.o ins fnl f) ...¾ 5
1434[3] The Institute Boy **(51)***(51) (MissJFCraze)* 5-9-0v SWebster(8) (a.p: no ex fnl f)......½ 6
1342[3] Nadwaty (IRE) **(55)***(42) (MCChapman)* 3-8-3 (7) CMunday(3) (prom over 3f)......4 7
1257[8] Grand Time **(37)***(21) (CJHill)* 6-8-0b JQuinn(6) (nvr nr to chal)......1 8
1450[5] Lloc **(56)***(31) (JohnBerry)* 3-8-4 (7) GFaulkner(14) (b: spd 3f)......3 9
1456[4] Medieval Miss **(65)***(39) (GLewis)* 3-9-6b SWhitworth(15) (bhd fnl 2f)......nk 10
Gorodenka Boy **(42)***(7) (MrsJJordan)* 5-8-5 ow5 AMorris(11) (bit bkwd: s.i.s: a bhd)......1 11
746[10] Kangra Valley **(57)***(21) (TRWatson)* 4-9-6 DeanMcKeown(7) (a bhd)......2 12
1342[8] Kabcast **(49)***(13) (DWChapman)* 10-8-12b ACulhane(5) (lw: a bhd)......hd 13
Swallowdale **(50)***(13) (CFWall)* 3-8-5 NCarlisle(2) (bit bkwd: prom over 2f)......hd 14
1151[13] Double Glow **(45)** *(NBycroft)* 3-8-0 TWilliams(12) (s.s: a bhd)......6 15

5/2 CANOVAS HEART, **9/2** Moujeeb (USA), **13/2** Chadwell Hall, **8/1** Sing With the Band, **9/1** Medieval Miss (6/1-10/1), **12/1** The Institute Boy, Grand Time, **14/1** Nadwaty (IRE), Mamma's Due, **20/1** Lloc, **25/1** Swallowdale, Double Glow, **33/1** Kabcast, Kangra Valley, **50/1** Gorodenka Boy, CSF £19.63 CT £187.44 TOTE £3.40: £1.80 £2.30 £2.80 (£10.80) Trio £87.50 OWNER Print Finisher Club and Osborne Controls (NEWMARKET) BRED M. J. Hall 15 Rn

58.4 secs (0.40) SF: 42/49/38/50/45/34/17/4/6/14/-/4/-/-/-

WEIGHT FOR AGE 3yo-8lb

1567 R-BEE CHILDRENS WEAR CLAIMING STKS (4-Y.O+) (Class F) £2,846.60 (£787.60: £375.80) **2m (Fibresand)** Stalls: Low GOING minus 0.26 sec per fur (FST) 2-30 (2-31)

1427[5] **Drimard (IRE) (32)***(51) (KMcAuliffe)* 4-8-6 (3) JTate(1) (lw: hld up: hdwy 7f out: 4th st: styd on to ld cl home: all out)......— 1
*1210** Acrow Line **(45)***(49)*(Fav)*(DBurchell)* 10-8-8 RPrice(6) (lw: sn pushed along: hdwy 7f out: led 3f out: hrd rdn & hdd cl home)......s.h 2
1444[14] Who's the Best (IRE) **(34)***(48) (APJarvis)* 5-8-5 (5) NVarley(10) (lw: hld up: hdwy 6f out: 3rd st: r.o one pce fnl 2f)......3 3

1210[2] Gunmaker **(35)***(32)* *(BJLlewellyn)* 6-8-8b TWilliams(3) (sn prom: led 8f out to 3f out: 2nd st: wknd qckly over 1f out)....14 4
136[3] Tuscania **(33)** *(JWharton)* 5-8-1 JQuinn(8) (b: hld up: hdwy 8f out: wknd 4f out: 5th st: t.o)...25 5
1404[7] Aconitum (USA) *(JMBradley)* 7-8-3 (5) SDrowne(7) (prom 12f: t.o)....15 6
1075[10] Nigelschinapalace **(40)** *(MissSJWilton)* 6-7-13 (7) GFaulkner(2) (b: prom: rdn 6f out: wknd over 4f out: poor 6th st: t.o)....4 7
Waterloo Belle *(MrsNMacauley)* 4-7-11 (7) AmandaSanders(9) (t.o fnl 6f)....dist 8
1455[4] Baroski **(45)** *(JLHarris)* 4-8-11 GDuffield(5) (drppd rr & rdn 8f out: t.o fnl 6f)....10 9
1420[2] Shareoftheaction **(68)** *(MrsAMNaughton)* 4-8-9be JWeaver(4) (led 8f: wknd 6f out: t.o whn p.u & dismntd over 2f out).... P

7/4 Acrow Line, **11/4** Shareoftheaction, **6/1** Who's the Best (IRE), **8/1** Gunmaker, Tuscania, **12/1** Nigelschinapalace (9/1-14/1), **20/1** Aconitum (USA), **25/1** DRIMARD (IRE), **33/1** Waterloo Belle, Baroski, CSF £67.81 TOTE £29.20: £7.30 £1.10 £1.70 (£21.30) Trio £158.80 OWNER Mrs Hannah McAuliffe (LAMBOURN) BRED Airlie Stud 10 Rn 3m 49.5 (23.50) SF: -/-/-/-/-/-/-/-/-/-

WEIGHT FOR AGE 4yo-1lb

OFFICIAL EXPLANATION **Shareoftheaction: the jockey stated that the horse had lost his action and choked.**

1568

TOTE CREDIT MAIDEN H'CAP (0-70) (3-Y.O+) (Class E) £3,588.20 (£1,073.60: £514.80: £235.40)
1m (Fibresand) Stalls: Low GOING minus 0.26 sec per fur (FST) 3-00 (3-04)

1219[10] **Top Fella (USA) (56)***(58)* *(WAO'Gorman)* 3-8-9v ow1 EmmaO'Gorman(5) (sn prom: 3rd st: led over 2f out tl ins fnl f: fin 2nd, 3l: awrdd r)....— 1
1124[17] Nautical Jewel **(56)***(53)* *(MDIUsher)* 3-8-9 RPrice(4) (hdwy & 6th st: r.o one pce fnl f: fin 3rd, 3l: plcd 2nd).... 2
1378[4] Personimus **(33)***(21)* *(CaptJWilson)* 5-7-11 ow3 JFanning(8) (lw: 2nd st: ev ch 2f out: wknd over 1f out: fin 4th, 3l: plcd 3rd).... 3
1160[10] Friar Street (IRE) **(43)***(31)* *(EJAlston)* 5-8-7 JWeaver(10) (led over 5f: wknd over 1f out: fin 5th, 1 3/4l: plcd 4th).... 4
1380[4] Moneefa **(64)***(46)* *(HRACecil)* 4-10-0 AMcGlone(6) (lw: 4th st: wknd over 1f out)....3 6
1459[5] Mr Moriarty (IRE) **(31)***(8)* *(SRBowring)* 4-7-9 ClaireBalding(12) (b.nr hind: no hdwy fnl 3f)....2½ 7
1353[5] Proud Image **(68)***(41)* *(APJarvis)* 3-9-4 (3) JTate(7) (lw: prom: 5th & wkng st)....2 8
1290[3] Opera Fan (IRE) **(58)***(30)*(Fav)*(SirMarkPrescott)* 3-8-11 GDuffield(2) (prom early: bhd fnl 3f)....nk 9
390[7] Lunar Prince **(35)***(3)* *(TTClement)* 5-7-13 AMackay(11) (bhd fnl 2f)....2 10
1330[4] Club Elite **(40)***(4)* *(MJCamacho)* 3-7-7v GBardwell(13) (lw: a bhd)....2 11
1072[8] Jimbo **(50)** *(JRJenkins)* 4-9-0 CRutter(1) (lw: prom 3f: t.o fnl 3f)....14 12
Ocean Park **(60)***(69)* *(LadyHerries)* 4-9-10 DeanMcKeown(14) (gd hdwy over 2f out: hung lft: led ins fnl f: r.o wl: fin 1st: disq: plcd last (prohibited substance (isoxsuprine) found in urine)).... 0

11/4 Opera Fan (IRE), **9/2** Moneefa, **5/1** TOP FELLA (USA), **7/1** Nautical Jewel, **8/1** Personimus, Ocean Park, **10/1** Proud Image, **12/1** Friar Street (IRE) (8/1-14/1), Mr Moriarty (IRE) (op 8/1), **16/1** Club Elite, **33/1** Jimbo, Lunar Prince, CSF £49.29 CT £278.84 TOTE £15.90: £5.20 £1.40 £3.40 (£22.60) Trio £77.80 OWNER Mr T. Mohan (NEWMARKET) BRED Mrs Walter Wickes Jnr 12 Rn 1m 46.2 (6.90) SF: -/-/-/-/-/-/-/-/-/-/-/18

WEIGHT FOR AGE 3yo-11lb

1569

LANGLEYS INSURANCE CLAIMS DEPARTMENT H'CAP (0-60) (3-Y.O) (Class F) £3,300.20 (£917.20: £440.60)
1m (Fibresand) Stalls: Low GOING minus 0.26 sec per fur (FST) 3-30 (3-35)

1091[8] **Ism (51)***(62)* *(MajorWRHern)* 3-9-0b TSprake(10) (hld up: hdwy 4f out: 4th st: led over 1f out: r.o wl)....— 1
1207[4] Samaka Hara (IRE) **(42)***(43)*(Fav)*(WSCunningham)* 3-8-2 (3) DRMcCabe(7) (lw: led over 2f: lost pl & 5th st: rallied fnl f)....5 2
1216[6] Raayaat (USA) **(58)***(59)* *(ACStewart)* 3-9-7b SWhitworth(14) (lw: 2nd st: led over 2f out tl over 1f out: one pce)....hd 3
1329[3] Scale the Summit **(47)***(40)* *(SirMarkPrescott)* 3-8-10 GDuffield(4) (hdwy & 6th st: one pce fnl 2f)....4 4
1459[2] Equity's Darling (IRE) **(58)***(33)*(Fav)*(MBell)* 3-9-7 MFenton(6) (nvr nr ldrs)....9 5
1344[6] Sweet Mate **(52)***(25)* *(SRBowring)* 3-8-10b(5) CTeague(8) (prom: hung rt & 3rd st: wknd 2f out)....¾ 6
339[7] Runforaction (IRE) **(42)***(15)* *(BSRothwell)* 3-8-5 JQuinn(1) (n.d)....nk 7
847[3] Nuthatch (IRE) **(40)***(5)* *(MDIUsher)* 3-8-3 RPrice(13) (lw: led over 5f out tl over 2f out: wknd qckly)....4 8

839[19] Shared Risk **(55)***(2) (SGNorton)* 3-9-1 (3) JTate(9) (prom: 7th & wkng st)....9 **9**
1334[8] Prince Pellinore **(49)** *(JohnBerry)* 3-8-12 CDwyer(3) (a bhd)....nk **10**
1371[13] Red O'Reilly **(46)** *(MrsNMacauley)* 3-8-4v(5) SDrowne(5) (lw: s.i.s: a bhd)....4 **11**
1433[12] Nebrangus (IRE) **(40)** *(NBycroft)* 3-8-3 AMackay(12) (rdn 5f out: sn bhd: t.o)....10 **12**
1412[4] Caltha **(43)** *(PCalver)* 3-8-6 ACulhane(2) (bhd fnl 4f: t.o)....4 **13**

3/1 Samaka Hara (IRE), Equity's Darling (IRE), **5/1** Sweet Mate, **8/1** Nuthatch (IRE), Scale the Summit, Raayaat (USA) (op 5/1), **12/1** Shared Risk, **14/1** Runforaction (IRE), ISM, Caltha, **20/1** Red O'Reilly, Prince Pellinore, **25/1** Nebrangus (IRE), CSF £61.10 CT £358.38 TOTE £22.50: £3.90 £1.90 £3.90 (£95.70) Trio £191.00 OWNER Mrs W. R. Hern (LAMBOURN) BRED Mrs R. D. Peacock 13 Rn 1m 45.6 (6.30) SF: 15/-/12/-/-/-/-/-/-/-/-/-/-

1570 BEEFEATER GIN (S) STKS (2-Y.O) (Class G) £2,601.40 (£720.40: £344.20)
6f (Fibresand) Stalls: Low GOING minus 0.26 sec per fur (FST) 4-00 (4-01)

1266[2] **Abbott of Whalley** *(57)*(Fav)*(JBerry)* 2-8-11 GCarter(3) (2nd st: led over 2f out: clr over 1f out: jst hld on)....— **1**
State Approval *(57) (APJarvis)* 2-8-8 (3) JTate(8) (neat: dwlt: wl bhd tl gd hdwy wl over 1f out: fin wl)....hd **2**
1212[12] Pulga Circo *(38) (BAMcMahon)* 2-8-3 (3) SSanders(4) (4th st: one pce fnl 2f)....5 **3**
1215[7] Timson *(38) (JPLeigh)* 2-8-11 SWhitworth(7) (wl bhd tl gd hdwy over 1f out: no ex fnl f)....2 **4**
1282[4] April's Joy *(20) (JNorton)* 2-8-6 ACulhane(1) (led over 3f: sn wknd)....5 **5**
1089[10] Down The Yard *(4) (MCChapman)* 2-7-13 (7) CMunday(6) (s.i.s: 6th st: a bhd)....6 **6**
1090[4] Our Tom's Boy *(2) (KTIvory)* 2-8-11 GDuffield(2) (3rd & rdn st: wknd 2f out)....2½ **7**
1215* Veshca Lady (IRE) *(EWeymes)* 2-8-12 TWilliams(5) (prom: 5th & wkng st)....dist **8**

10/11 ABBOTT OF WHALLEY, **5/2** Veshca Lady (IRE) (2/1-3/1), **4/1** April's Joy (5/2-9/2), **10/1** State Approval (7/1-12/1), **12/1** Our Tom's Boy, **20/1** Pulga Circo, **33/1** Timson, **50/1** Down The Yard, CSF £11.85 TOTE £1.60: £1.30 £1.60 £3.10 (£8.00) OWNER Swan At Whalley Racing Club Ltd (COCKERHAM) BRED P. Dowson 8 Rn No bid 1m 20.2 (6.70) SF: -/-/-/-/-/-/-/-
OFFICIAL EXPLANATION **Veshca Lady (IRE): the jockey reported that the filly could not handle the surface.**

1571 CHEETAH H'CAP (0-65) (3-Y.O+) (Class F) £2,519.00 (£694.00: £329.00)
7f (Fibresand) Stalls: Low GOING minus 0.26 sec per fur (FST) 4-30 (4-35)

1334[2] **What a Nightmare (IRE) (59)***(68) (JAGlover)* 3-9-0b TIves(10) (swtg: led 5f out tl over 3f out: 2nd st: rallied to ld wl ins fnl f)....— **1**
Night in a Million **(62)***(68) (MrsJCecil)* 4-9-8 (5) AWhelan(5) (bhd tl gd hdwy on ins over 1f out: fin wl)....1¼ **2**
1433[6] Aquado **(51)***(57)*(Fav)*(ALForbes)* 6-9-2 JQuinn(8) (hdwy & 5th st: r.o ins fnl f)....nk **3**
1155[9] Jamaica Bridge **(60)***(64) (SGNorton)* 5-9-8 (3) JTate(15) (swtg: a.p: led over 3f out: clr over 1f out: wknd & hdd wl ins fnl f)....½ **4**
1154[6] Smolensk (IRE) **(63)***(67) (JBerry)* 3-9-4b SDWilliams(13) (dwlt: hdwy 3f out: r.o ins fnl f)....d.h **4**
1459[3] Wellsy Lad (USA) **(36)***(38) (DWChapman)* 8-8-1 NCarlisle(2) (nv nr to chal)....1¼ **6**
1456[8] Farmer Jock **(41)***(41) (MrsNMacauley)* 13-8-1 (5) CTeague(14) (b: hdwy & c stands side 2f out: nvr nrr)....½ **7**
1330[3] Legally Delicious **(65)***(59) (DWChapman)* 3-9-3 (3) SSanders(11) (nvr trbld ldrs)....3 **8**
1429[5] Words of Wisdom (IRE) **(60)***(53) (CACyzer)* 5-9-11 JWeaver(3) (hdwy & 6th st: wknd over 1f out)....hd **9**
1377[8] Euphyllia **(50)***(38) (BobJones)* 3-8-5 GDuffield(7) (7th st: wknd over 1f out)....2½ **10**
1469[7] Dauntless Fort **(38)***(22) (MrsVAAconley)* 4-8-3 TWilliams(1) (bhd fnl 3f)....1½ **11**
Aldwick Colonnade **(53)***(37) (MDIUsher)* 8-9-4 RPrice(12) (b.off hind: outpcd)....hd **12**
1330[6] Irchester Lass **(45)***(24) (SRBowring)* 3-8-0b JFanning(6) (3rd st: wknd wl over 1f out)....2 **13**
1471* Penny's Wishing **(62)***(9) (JPLeigh)* 3-9-3 6x DeanMcKeown(9) (led 2f: 4th & wkng st: t.o)....14 **14**
1034[10] Cledeschamps **(37)** *(MWEllerby)* 6-8-2 ClaireBalding(4) (a bhd)....1¾ **15**

7/2 Aquado, **11/2** Words of Wisdom (IRE), **6/1** WHAT A NIGHTMARE (IRE), **7/1** Wellsy Lad (USA), **8/1** Legally Delicious (5/1-9/1), **9/1** Penny's Wishing (5/1-10/1), **10/1** Night in a Million (6/1-12/1), **12/1** Euphyllia, **14/1** Smolensk (IRE) (op 8/1), **16/1** Jamaica Bridge, **20/1** Farmer Jock, Aldwick Colonnade, Irchester Lass, **25/1** Dauntless Fort, Cledeschamps, CSF £66.47 CT £229.16 TOTE £5.40: £1.90 £3.90 £1.40 (£33.20) Trio £57.60 OWNER Bassetlaw Bloodstock Agency Ltd (WORKSOP) BRED Carrigbeg Stud Co Ltd 15 Rn 1m 33.0 (6.20) SF: 13/23/12/19/12/-/-/4/8/-/-/-/-/-/-
WEIGHT FOR AGE 3yo-10lb

T/Jkpt: Not won; £32,705.77 to Epsom 9/6/95. T/Plpt: £146.10 (113.65 Tckts). T/Qdpt: £39.70 (1.8 Tckts). KH

1230a-CHANTILLY (France) (R-H)
Thursday June 1st (Good)

1572a PRIX DU GROS-CHENE (Gp 2) (3-Y.O+) £35,928.00 (£14,371.00: £7,186.00: £3,593.00) **5f (straight)** 2-25 (2-29)

1112a⁴ **Millyant** *(116) (RGuest)* 4-8-13 CAsmussen (a.p: rdn to ld 1f out: jst hld on)........................— 1
920⁶ Diffident (FR) *(117) (AFabre,France)* 3-8-6 TJarnet (mid div: hdwy over 1f out: str run fnl f: jst failed)........................nse 2
1112a* Struggler *(118) (CLaffon-Parias,France)* 3-8-9 FSanchez (racd centre: rdn 2f out: r.o)...........¾ 3
700⁵ Palacegate Episode (IRE) *(109) (JBerry)* 5-8-13 GHind (broke wl: led to 1f out: wknd).........1½ 4
1112a² Spain Lane (USA) *(104) (AFabre,France)* 4-8-13 SGuillot (hld up: rdn ½-wy: nvr plcd to chal)........................1½ 5
Dairine's Delight (IRE) *(92) (MCunningham,Ireland)* 5-8-9 PShanahan (s.s: one pce fnl 2f) .2½ 6
Great Deeds *(90) (MRChannon)* 4-8-9 RHughes (dwlt: outpcd tl r.o fnl f)........................½ 7
1112a³ Way West (FR) *(97) (MmeCHead,France)* 5-9-2 FHead (outpcd early: r.o u.p fnl f) ....s.nk 8
Key of Luck (USA) *(91) (MmeCHead,France)* 4-8-13 WRSwinburn (sn rr: m.n.s) ....¾ 9
Doree (USA) *(73) (MmeCHead,France)* 3-8-6 ODoleuze (a outpcd) 6 10
Risky *(68) (RHannon)* 4-8-9 PatEddery (prom tl wknd 2f out.)........................hd 11

P-M: 10.90F: 2.70F 1.40F 1.70F (5.40F) OWNER Mr C. J. Mills (NEWMARKET) BRED Jim and Mrs Strange 11 Rn 57.8 secs SF: -/-/-/-/-/-/-/-/-/-/-

1394a-LONGCHAMP (Paris, France) (R-H)
Saturday June 3rd (Good)

1573a PRIX DE LA JONCHERE (Gp 3) (3-Y.O C & G) £26,347.00 (£9,581.00: £4,790.00: £2,395.00) **1m** 2-50 (2-46)

Gold and Steel (FR) *(110) (J-CRouget,France)* 3-8-11 J-RDubosc ....— 1
Bashaayeash (IRE) *(107) (CLaffon-Parias,France)* 3-8-11 FHead 1½ 2
806a³ Kirdoun (FR) *(107) (ELellouche,France)* 3-8-11 DBoeuf ....s.nk 3
1121a⁴ Two O'Clock Jump (IRE) *(106) (RHannon)* 3-8-11 GMosse ....½ 4

P-M: 7.60F: 3.70F 2.20F (SF 42.10) BRED G.Rollain 7 Rn 1m 39.6 SF: -/-/-/-

1572a-CHANTILLY (France) (R-H)
Sunday June 4th (Good)

1574a LES EMIRATES ARABES UNIS PRIX DU JOCKEY-CLUB (Gp 1) (3-Y.O C & F) £299,401.00 (£119,760.00: £59,880.00: £29,940.00: £14,970.00) **1m 4f** 3-15 (3-17)

920² **Celtic Swing** *(121) (LadyHerries)* 3-9-2 KDarley (a.p: rdn to ld over 1f out: r.o wl u.p) ....— 1
1008a² Poliglote *(120) (MmeCHead,France)* 3-9-2 FHead (plld early: wnt 2nd after 3f: led over 2f out tl over 1f out: r.o gamely)........................½ 2
Winged Love (IRE) *(120) (AFabre,France)* 3-9-2 OPeslier (mid div: 6th st: r.o fnl f: fin wl)....s.h 3
1107* Classic Cliche (IRE) *(118) (SbinSuroor)* 3-9-2 WRSwinburn (prom early: 5th & outpcd st: r.o fnl f)........................2 4
1115a* Flemensfirth (USA) *(118) (JHMGosden)* 3-9-2 LDettori (s.s: hmpd & bhd 10f out: hdwy st: nt rch ldrs) ....s.h 5
808a* Diamond Mix (IRE) *(115) (AFabre,France)* 3-9-2 TJarnet (hmpd & bhd 10f out: hdwy st: nvr plcd to chal) 2 6
Affidavit (USA) *(114) (AFabre,France)* 3-9-2 MJKinane (8th st: effrt 2f out: wknd fnl f) ....½ 7
1008a* Rifapour (IRE) *(110) (AdeRoyerDupre,France)* 3-9-2 GMosse (a rr: effrt 2f out: no imp) 3 8
801a* Walk on Mix (FR) *(105) (AFabre,France)* 3-9-2 SGuillot (7th st: wknd over 1f out)..................4 9
679⁴ Indian Light *(104) (JLDunlop)* 3-9-2 PatEddery (prom tl 4th & rdn st: sn btn) 1 10
1068⁵ Commoner (USA) *(103) (RHannon)* 3-9-2 JReid (led tl over 2f out: wknd qckly)....................½ 11

P-M: 2.00F: 1.80F 2.30F 5.30F (17.30F) OWNER Mr P. D. Savill (LITTLEHAMPTON) BRED Lavinia Duchess of Norfolk 11 Rn 2m 32.8 (6.40) SF: -/-/-/-/-/-/-/-/-/-/-

1575a PRIX JEAN PRAT (Gp 1) (3-Y.O C & F) £47,904.00 (£19,162.00: £9,581.00: £4,790.00) **1m 1f** 4-40 (4-45)

826⁵ **Torrential (USA)** *(118) (JHMGosden)* 3-9-2 LDettori (3rd tl rdn & outpcd 2f out: r.o u.p to ld cl home)........................— 1

1107[2] Annus Mirabilis (FR) *(118) (MRStoute)* 3-9-2 MJKinane (5th st: rdn over 2f out: str chal fnl f: jst failed)....nse 2
Labeeb *(118) (CLaffon-Parias,France)* 3-9-2 WRSwinburn (4th st: hdwy to ld over 1f out: hdd cl home)....s.nk 3
Bobinski *(117) (AFabre,France)* 3-9-2 TJarnet (hld up in rr: 6th st: n.m.r 2f out: swtchd rt 1f out: r.o)....nk 4
1115a[5] Leeds (IRE) *(115) (HVandePoele,France)* 3-9-2 OPeslier (hld up in rr: rdn 2f out: no ex)....1 5
1007a* Valanour(IRE) *(114) (AdeRoyerDupre,France)* 3-9-2 GMosse (a.p: 2nd st: ev ch 1f out: no ex)....½ 6
Dalidjan (IRE) *(104) (AdeRoyerDupre,France)* 3-9-2 PCoppin (led tl over 1f out: wknd)....6 7

P-M: 3.60F: 4.20F 2.50F (SF 46.70F) OWNER Sheikh Mohammed (NEWMARKET) BRED Peter M. Brant 7 Rn 1m 55.9 (8.70) SF: -/-/-/-/-/-/-

1576a PRIX DE SANDRINGHAM (Gp 3) (3-Y.O F) £26,347.00 (£9,581.00: £4,790.00: £2,395.00) **1m** 5-15 (5-14)

1116a[4] **Smolensk (USA)** *(110) (AFabre,France)* 3-8-11 TJarnet ....— 1
Hexane (FR) *(107) (PBary,France)* 3-8-11 DBoeuf 1½ 2
Palafairia (FR) *(106) (AFabre,France)* 3-8-11 SGuillot ....¾ 3
1116a[5] Collecta (FR) *(105) (JEHammond,France)* 3-8-11 CAsmussen ....s.h 4

P-M: 1.50F: 1.10F 1.30F (SF 9.70F) OWNER Mr Paul de Moussac (FRANCE) 4 Rn 1m 45.5 (10.90)

1237a-SAN SIRO (Milan, Italy) (R-H)
Sunday June 4th

1577a PREMIO EMILIO TURATI (Gp 2) (3-Y.O+) £38,298.00 (£17,730.00: £9,929.00: £4,965.00) **1m** 4-40 (5-25)

704a[3] **Les Boyer** *(121) (GBotti,Italy)* 4-9-3 EBotti (hld up: 4th st: hdwy to ld 1f out: comf) ....— 1
Lavinia Fontana (IRE) *(110) (JLDunlop)* 6-9-0 JWeaver (led to 1f out: no ex) 4¼ 2
New Herald (IRE) *(108) (MCiciarelli,Italy)* 6-9-3 LSorrentino (hld up: 6th st: nvr plcd to chal)....2¼ 3
Lake Storm (IRE) *(107) (GBotti,Italy)* 4-9-3 MBotti ....½ 4
1118a[4] Lear White (USA) *(104) (Italy)* 4-9-3 JCaro 1½ 5
710a[3] Golden Bechett (IRE) *(92) (Italy)* 5-9-3 VMezzatesta 6 6
Watani (USA) *(62) (Italy)* 4-9-3 MEsposito 15 7

Tote 25L: 15L 19L 25L (37L) (ITALY) BRED Bishop's Down Farm 7 Rn 1m 42.1 SF: -/-/-/-/-/-/-

1466-CATTERICK (L-H)
Friday June 9th (Good, Good to firm patches)
WEATHER: overcast WIND: mod half against

1578 SCOTCH CORNER H'CAP (0-70) (3-Y.O+) (Class E) £3,418.00 (£1,024.00: £492.00: £226.00) **1m 3f 214y** Stalls: Low GOING minus 0.22 sec (GF) 2-20 (2-21)

1295* **Admirals Secret (USA)** **(62)***(71) (CFWall)* 6-9-4 (5) LNewton(6) (lw: hld up: smooth hdwy 4f out: rdn & hung lft 2f out: led jst ins fnl f: drvn out) ....— 1
1322[5] Ahaalee (USA) **(64)***(70) (EALDunlop)* 3-8-9 JWeaver(3) (led: rdn 2f out: hdd jst ins fnl f: unable qckn)....2 2
866[4] New Inn **(59)***(65)*(Fav)*(EWeymes)* 4-9-6 DaleGibson(5) (a chsng ldrs: kpt on same pce appr fnl f) ....nk 3
1292[6] Sudden Spin **(40)***(44) (SGNorton)* 5-8-1 JFanning(9) (sn trckg ldrs: ev ch 2f out: one pce)....1¼ 4
Miroswaki (USA) **(63)***(59) (GFierro)* 5-9-10 MWigham(7) (trckd ldrs: drvn along & outpcd 5f out: n.d after)....6 5
Red Beacon **(33)***(28) (JLGoulding)* 8-7-1 (7)ow1 PFessey(1) (b: chsd ldrs tl wknd 5f out)....s.h 6
1433[10] Matisse **(50)***(44) (JDBethell)* 4-8-11 GDuffield(4) (dwlt: hld up: outpcd 5f out: sn bhd)....2 7
1308[4] Prince Equiname **(69)***(57) (DEddy)* 3-9-0 NConnorton(10) (trckd ldrs: effrt over 4f out: sn wknd)....4 8
Demokos (FR) **(32)***(11) (WLBarker)* 10-7-7 NKennedy(2) (chsd ldrs tl lost pl 6f out: sn bhd) 7 9

LONG HANDICAP Red Beacon 7-0 Demokos (FR) 7-3

9/4 New Inn, **5/2** ADMIRALS SECRET (USA), **7/2** Sudden Spin, **9/2** Ahaalee (USA) (op 3/1), **8/1** Miroswaki (USA), Prince Equiname, **20/1** Matisse, **33/1** Demokos (FR), **50/1** Red Beacon, CSF £15.58 CT £28.42 TOTE £2.70: £1.10 £1.30 £1.70 (£5.70) Trio £7.00 OWNER B.R.A.T.S (NEWMARKET) BRED Haras Santa Maria de Araras & Peter M. Brant 9 Rn

2m 38.7 (7.70) SF: 39/22/33/12/27/-/12/9/-

WEIGHT FOR AGE 3yo-16lb

1579 E.B.F. MAIDEN STKS (2-Y.O F) (Class D) £3,720.00 (£1,110.00:£530.00: £240.00)
5f Stalls: Low GOING minus 0.22 sec per fur (GF) 2-50 (2-51)

1413[2] **Limerick Princess (IRE)** *(73) (JBerry)* 2-8-11 JCarroll(5) (mde all: clr ½-wy: rdn 2f out: jst hld on) — 1
819[16] Diminuet *(73) (JWWatts)* 2-8-11 JFanning(4) (s.i.s: bhd: hdwy ½-wy: styd on wl u.p fnl f: jst failed) s.h 2
Elfin Queen (IRE) *(70) (MJohnston)* 2-8-11 JWeaver(1) (neat: bit bkwd: s.i.s: hdwy ½-wy: shkn up over 1f out: kpt on wl) 1 3
Just Ice *(68) (SirMarkPrescott)* 2-8-11 GDuffield(7) (neat: bit bkwd: swvd rt s: chsd ldrs: rdn & rn green over 1f out: kpt on) ½ 4
1361[5] Stop Play (IRE) *(66)*(Fav)*(MHTompkins)* 2-8-11 PRobinson(8) (prom: drvn along & outpcd ½-wy: kpt on fnl f: nt rch ldrs) ¾ 5
1247[6] Alfayza *(58) (JDBethell)* 2-8-11 JFortune(6) (sn outpcd & pushed along: nvr nr ldrs) 2½ 6
1413[4] Mystic Times *(58) (MissSEHall)* 2-8-11 NConnorton(3) (in tch: outpcd ½-wy: grad wknd) s.h 7
1375[6] Impromptu Melody (IRE) *(52) (BSRothwell)* 2-8-6 (5) JStack(2) (chsd wnr tl wknd over 1f out) 1¾ 8
Katy-Q (IRE) *(49) (PCalver)* 2-8-11 MBirch(9) (w'like: bit bkwd: s.i.s: a outpcd & bhd) 1 9

4/6 Stop Play (IRE), **3/1** LIMERICK PRINCESS (IRE), **11/2** Elfin Queen (IRE), **12/1** Just Ice, **14/1** Mystic Times, Katy-Q (IRE) (op 8/1), **20/1** Diminuet, **25/1** Impromptu Melody (IRE), Alfayza, CSF £56.59 TOTE £4.60: £1.10 £8.80 £2.30 (£125.40) Trio £55.10 OWNER Mr Thomas Doherty (COCKERHAM) BRED Thomas Doherty 9 Rn 62.0 secs (4.50) SF: 1/1/-/-/-/-/-/-/-

1580 JERVAULX H'CAP (0-65) (3-Y.O) (Class F) £2,945.00 (£820.00: £395.00)
5f Stalls: Low GOING minus 0.22 sec per fur (GF) 3-20 (3-20)

892[2] **Lugana Vision (47)***(55) (GFierro)* 3-8-0b(3) DRMcCabe(4) (outpcd & drvn along ½-wy: hdwy over 1f out: hrd rdn to ld last strides) — 1
Stuffed **(50)***(58) (MWEasterby)* 3-8-6 JWeaver(2) (lw: trckd ldrs: effrt ½-wy: rdn to ld jst ins fnl f: jst ct) hd 2
1157[4] Daily Starshine (IRE) **(57)***(60) (JBerry)* 3-8-13b JCarroll(1) (b: led tl jst ins fnl f: no ex) 1½ 3
1157[13] Tee Tee Too (IRE) **(65)***(49) (PCHaslam)* 3-9-7 JFortune(9) (sn outpcd & bhd: hdwy on outside 2f out: wknd appr fnl f) 6 4
1450* Bollin Harry **(69)***(48)*(Fav)*(MHEasterby)* 3-9-11 7x MBirch(8) (lw: in tch: hung bdly lft ½-wy: n.d after) 1½ 5
1450[7] C-Yer-Simmie (IRE) **(61)***(40) (RHollinshead)* 3-9-0 (3) AGarth(6) (chsd ldr tl wknd over 1f out) hd 6
1508[5] Baileys Sunset (IRE) **(62)***(38) (MJohnston)* 3-9-4 PRobinson(7) (in tch: outpcd ½-wy: n.d) ¾ 7
392[10] Jet Classic **(50)***(22) (MissJFCraze)* 3-8-6 SWebster(3) (b.hind: chsd ldrs: edgd lft u.p & wknd over 1f out) 1¼ 8
1164[3] Sunshine Belle **(46)** *(GMMoore)* 3-8-2 JFanning(5) (chsd ldrs: drvn along ½-wy: sn lost pl) 7 9
1302[8] Cinders Chance **(37)** *(MWEllerby)* 3-7-7 ClaireBalding(10) (swvd rt s: a outpcd & bhd) ½ 10

LONG HANDICAP Cinders Chance 7-5

7/4 Bollin Harry, **9/4** Stuffed, **8/1** LUGANA VISION, Sunshine Belle, **9/1** Daily Starshine (IRE), **10/1** C-Yer-Simmie (IRE), Tee Tee Too (IRE), **11/1** Baileys Sunset (IRE) (op 6/1), **33/1** Jet Classic, Cinders Chance, CSF £28.15 CT £162.22 TOTE £10.50: £3.00 £1.80 £2.10 (£30.60) Trio £23.30 OWNER Old School House Racing Ltd (HEDNESFORD) BRED Mrs L. N. Kibble 10 Rn

59.8 secs (2.30) SF: 29/32/34/23/22/14/12/-/-/-

1581 SCORTON CLAIMING STKS (3-Y.O) (Class F) £2,798.00 (£778.00: £374.00)
1m 5f 175y Stalls: Low GOING minus 0.22 sec per fur (GF) 3-55 (3-55)

1059[4] **Risky Rose (47)***(57) (RHollinshead)* 3-7-13 (3) AGarth(8) (hld up gng wl: stdy hdwy over 3f out: led 2f out: rdn out) — 1
1289[6] Recovery Lad (IRE) **(51)***(69) (KRBurke)* 3-8-12 (3) DRMcCabe(2) (chsd ldrs: outpcd over 3f out: hdwy 2f out: hung lft & styd on fnl f: nt rch wnr) ½ 2
1430* Durgams First (IRE) **(57)***(69) (MrsMReveley)* 3-8-10 (7) GParkin(9) (lw: hld up: effrt on ins & bdly hmpd over 4f out: hdwy on ins & ev ch 2f out: kpt on same pce) 1¾ 3
1358[11] Coast Along (IRE) **(35)***(48) (CWThornton)* 3-8-1 AMackay(5) (chsd ldrs: reminders 8f out: sn drvn along: led over 2f out: sn hdd & wknd) 5 4
1427[3] Mayday Kitty **(49)***(47) (WGMTurner)* 3-7-13 (5) PMcCabe(7) (lw: trckd ldrs: rdn & outpcd over 3f out: hung lft: wknd fnl 2f) 3 5

1325* Gentle Irony **(59)***(47)*(Fav)*(BJMeehan)* 3-8-6 JWeaver(1) (lw: trckd ldrs: effrt & hmpd over 3f out: sn rdn: hung lft over 1f out: sn wknd) 2 **6**
1430³ Absolute Folly **(53)***(47) (JBerry)* 3-8-13 JCarroll(4) (led tl over 2f out: wkng whn hmpd wl over 1f out) 6 **7**
1252⁸ Granny's Legacy **(27)***(12) (JDBethell)* 3-7-11 ow1 TWilliams(6) (chsd ldrs: pushed along 7f out: lost pl over 4f out: eased & sn bhd) 15 **8**
Hancock *(33) (JHetherton)* 3-9-3 MBirch(3) (dwlt: a bhd: t.o 5f out) ....¾ **9**

6/4 Gentle Irony (op 9/4), **9/2** Durgams First (IRE) (op 9/4), **6/1** Recovery Lad (IRE), Mayday Kitty, **8/1** Coast Along (IRE), Absolute Folly, **9/1** RISKY ROSE, **20/1** Hancock, **33/1** Granny's Legacy, CSF £61.19 TOTE £9.60: £2.10 £2.10 £1.90 (£36.80) Trio £86.00 OWNER Mr M. Johnson (UPPER LONGDON) BRED Miss Sarah Hollinshead 9 Rn 3m 5.3 (10.10) SF: 13/25/25/4/3/3/3/-/-

1582 LESLIE PETCH H'CAP (0-70) (3-Y.O+) (Class E) £3,262.00 (£976.00: £468.00: £214.00)

5f 212y Stalls: High GOING minus 0.22 sec per fur (GF) 4-30 (4-30)

1434⁴ **Heart Broken (49)***(54) (JGFitzGerald)* 5-8-7 JWeaver(7) (sn bhd: gd hdwy 2f out: r.o wl u.p to ld post) ....— **1**
1043⁷ Hello Hobson's (IRE) **(46)***(51) (RBastiman)* 5-8-4 DeanMcKeown(8) (hld up & bhd: gd hdwy over 2f out: edgd lft & led jst ins fnl f: jst ct) ....s.h **2**
1179¹¹ Pine Ridge Lad (IRE) **(54)***(54) (JLEyre)* 5-8-12 SDWilliams(3) (a in tch: sn drvn along: kpt on same pce fnl 2f) 1¾ **3**
926¹⁴ Dominelle **(48)***(43) (MHEasterby)* 3-7-11 ow1 SMaloney(2) (w ldrs: led 4f out: sn hdd: led 3f out tl jst ins fnl f: one pce) 1½ **4**
1080¹¹ Pete Afrique (IRE) **(70)***(55) (MWEasterby)* 4-10-0 MBirch(5) (b: led 2f: c wd ent st: wknd over 1f out) 4 **5**
Formidable Liz **(62)***(43) (MDHammond)* 5-9-6 DaleGibson(6) (hld up & bhd: kpt on fnl 2f: nvr nr ldrs) 1½ **6**
1469⁶ Tyrone Flyer **(55)***(34) (GFierro)* 6-8-13 MWigham(10) (chsd ldrs: sn drvn: wknd over 1f out) ..¾ **7**
1450³ Able Sheriff **(51)***(30) (MWEasterby)* 3-7-7b(7) RuthCoulter(9) (chsd ldrs tl wknd 2f out) ....s.h **8**
1484³ Blue Grit **(53)***(31)*(Fav)*(MDods)* 9-8-11 JFortune(4) (lw: bhd: hdwy 3f out: sn wknd) ....nk **9**
Lochon **(63)***(39) (WLBarker)* 4-9-7 AlexGreaves(1) (s.i.s: sn chsng ldrs: led over 3f out: sn hdd: wknd over 2f out) ....¾ **10**

2/1 Blue Grit, **11/2** HEART BROKEN, **7/1** Able Sheriff, Dominelle, **8/1** Pine Ridge Lad (IRE), **9/1** Tyrone Flyer (op 6/1), **10/1** Lochon, **12/1** Pete Afrique (IRE), **16/1** Formidable Liz, **33/1** Hello Hobson's (IRE), CSF £128.59 CT £1,315.04 TOTE £4.80: £1.50 £5.60 £2.50 (£61.40) Trio £252.50 OWNER Mr J. G. FitzGerald (MALTON) BRED J. H. Burbidge 10 Rn
1m 13.6 (3.10) SF: 30/27/30/10/31/19/10/-/7/15
WEIGHT FOR AGE 3yo-9lb

1583 ELLERY HILL RATING RELATED MAIDEN APPRENTICE LIMITED STKS (0-60) (3-Y.O+) (Class F) £2,599.00 (£739.00: £367.00)

7f Stalls: Low GOING minus 0.22 sec per fur (GF) 5-00 (5-00)

1251⁶ **It's Academic (60)***(55)*(Fav)*(MrsJRRamsden)* 3-8-7 SBuckley(7) (hld up: hdwy ½-wy: styd on wl to ld jst ns fnl f) ....— **1**
908⁶ Ganador **(53)***(48) (JBerry)* 3-8-7 CLowther(1) (led tl jst ins fnl f: nt qckn) 3 **2**
1290¹⁹ Prim Lass **(53)***(45) (JHetherton)* 4-9-3 CWebb(2) (a chsng ldrs: kpt on same pce u.p fnl 2f) .1½ **3**
*842*⁴ Kama Simba **(55)***(47) (NACallaghan)* 3-8-7 (5) MDavies(8) (swtg: bhd: hdwy & hung lft over 2f out: kpt on fnl f: nvr nrr) 1¼ **4**
1279⁴ Good Match (IRE) **(58)***(33) (NTinkler)* 3-8-12 AEddery(5) (chsd ldrs: drvn along ½-wy: sn lost pl) 6 **5**
990³ Never so True **(37)***(25) (MartynWane)* 4-9-3 MSemple(6) (lost pl ½-wy: sn bhd: kpt on fnl f: n.d) 1½ **6**
1092⁹ Simply Simon **(40)***(22) (KRBurke)* 3-8-7 (5) SO'Shea(4) (chsd ldrs over 3f: sn lost pl) 3½ **7**
1251⁵ Magnums Secret **(50)***(12) (JLEyre)* 3-8-7 GMacDonald(3) (sn drvn along: chsd ldrs to ½-wy: sn wl outpcd) 2 **8**
1559⁸ Shartel **(31)** *(MJohnston)* 3-8-7b(5) KSked(9) (b: racd wd: prom to ½-wy: sn wl bhd) 20 **9**

2/1 IT'S ACADEMIC (11/4-7/4), **5/2** Good Match (IRE), **5/1** Magnums Secret, **11/2** Ganador, **7/1** Kama Simba, **12/1** Prim Lass, **14/1** Simply Simon, **16/1** Never so True, **25/1** Shartel, CSF £14.75 TOTE £3.70: £1.30 £1.80 £2.80 (£10.20) Trio £70.50 OWNER Mr J. R. Chester (THIRSK) BRED W. H. F. Carson 9 Rn 1m 27.8 (4.60) SF: 19/12/19/11/-/-/-/-/-
WEIGHT FOR AGE 3yo-10lb

T/Plpt: £122.40 (88.18 Tckts). T/Qdpt: £39.60 (0.5 Tckts); £26.80 to Epsom 10/6/95. WG

EPSOM (L-H)
Friday June 9th (Good to firm, Good fnl 5f)
WEATHER: fair WIND: almost nil

1584 VODATA CONDITIONS STKS (2-Y.O C & G) (Class B) £9,251.62 (£3,373.50: £1,649.25: £708.75: £316.88) **5f** Stalls: High GOING minus 0.31 sec(GF) 2-10 (2-10)

1063* **Prince Aslia** *(101) (MJohnston)* 2-8-9 DHolland(3) (w ldrs: led over 2f out: r.o wl) ....— 1
1197² Tadeo *(99) (MRChannon)* 2-8-11 RHughes(5) (lw: a.p: chsd wnr fnl f: no imp) 1¼ 2
1384² Cayman Kai (IRE) *(91)*(Fav)*(RHannon)* 2-8-11 PatEddery(2) (lw: w ldrs: rdn & hung lft over 2f out: one pce) 2½ 3
940² Passion For Life *(87) (GLewis)* 2-8-11 PaulEddery(4) (led over 2f: wknd fnl f) 1¼ 4
683⁴ Gwespyr *(74) (JBerry)* 2-8-11 GCarter(1) (lw: s.i.s: a wl bhd) 4 5

5/4 Cayman Kai (IRE), **100/30** PRINCE ASLIA, **7/2** Passion For Life, **8/1** Tadeo (op 4/1), **20/1** Gwespyr, CSF £21.90 TOTE £4.30: £1.80 £2.70 (£18.00) OWNER Mrs R. J. Daniels (MIDDLEHAM) BRED Mrs A. H. Daniels 5 Rn 55.02 secs (0.18 under 2y best) (0.52) SF: 56/54/46/42/29

1585 VODAPAGE RATED STKS H'CAP (0-105) (4-Y.O+) (Class B) £21,363.30 (£7,994.70: £3,909.85: £1,681.75: £753.38: £382.02) **1m 4f 10y** Stalls: Low GOING minus 0.31 sec per fur (GF) 2-45 (2-46)

1243³ **Beauchamp Hero (100)***(112) (JLDunlop)* 5-8-9 JReid(2) (4th st: led over 2f out: drvn out) ...— 1
1479* Waiting **(103)***(112) (PFICole)* 4-8-12 3x TQuinn(4) (hdwy 6f out: 3rd st: ev ch fnl 2f: r.o) 2 2
1243⁴ Saxon Maid **(97)***(104) (LMCumani)* 4-8-6 ow2 TJarnet(5) (7th st: hdwy over 2f out: rdn over 1f out: r.o) ....nk 3
Source of Light **(104)***(110) (RCharlton)* 6-8-13 PatEddery(7) (8th st: gd hdwy 2f out: wknd ins fnl f) 2½ 4
1243² Wishing (USA) **(92)***(93) (RAkehurst)* 4-8-1 PaulEddery(3) (lw: led tl wknd over 2f out) 3½ 5
1357* Penny a Day (IRE) **(97)***(97)*(Fav)*(MrsMReveley)* 5-8-6 3x KDarley(8) (5th st: wknd 2f out) ......½ 6
1385⁶ Garden of Heaven (USA) **(101)***(100) (CEBrittain)* 6-8-10 BDoyle(6) (lw: 6th st: nvr nr to chal) ¾ 7
1262⁴ Bearall (IRE) **(105)***(95) (RHannon)* 4-9-0 BRouse(1) (2nd st: wknd over 2f out) 7 8

5/2 Penny a Day (IRE), **7/2** BEAUCHAMP HERO, **11/2** Wishing (USA), **13/2** Saxon Maid, **7/1** Source of Light, Waiting, **20/1** Garden of Heaven (USA), **50/1** Bearall (IRE), CSF £24.55 CT £130.97 TOTE £4.30: £1.50 £1.90 £1.80 (£11.40) OWNER Mr E. Penser (ARUNDEL) BRED E. Penser 8 Rn 2m 37.28 (2.28) SF: 55/55/47/53/36/40/43/38

1586 VODAFONE DIOMED STKS (Gp 3) (3-Y.O+) (Class A) £28,400.00 (£10,732.50: £5,241.25: £2,376.25) **1m 114y** Stalls: Low GOING minus 0.31 sec per fur (GF) 3-15 (3-16)

960³ **Mr Martini (IRE) (96)***(108) (CEBrittain)* 5-9-4 MRoberts(4) (lw: 2nd st: led 2f out: drvn out) ..— 1
720² Be Mindful **(102)***(106) (JRFanshawe)* 3-8-6 DHarrison(3) (7th st: hdwy 2f out: n.m.r ins fnl f: r.o) 1¼ 2
1236a* Chato (USA) *(HSteinmetz,Germany)* 3-8-9 AStarke(6) (neat: 4th st: ev ch fnl 2f: edgd lft: r.o: fin 2nd, d.h: disq: plcd 3rd) 3
1306* Sonic Boy **(114)** (Fav)*(RFJohnsonHoughton)* 3-8-6 JQuinn(7) (led 7f out to 2f out: r.o ins fnl f) ....hd 4
1185³ Prince of India **(103)** *(LordHuntingdon)* 3-8-6 LDettori(2) (lw: 6th st: bdly hmpd over 2f out: nt rcvr) 3½ 5
1187² Young Ern **(117)** *(SDow)* 5-9-7 TQuinn(1) (5th st: nt clr run over 1f out: bdly hmpd ins fnl f: nt rcvr) 3½ 6
1315³ Royal Philosopher **(105)** *(KMcAuliffe)* 3-8-6 JTate(5) (3rd st: hmpd over 2f out: nt rcvr) 14 7

11/8 Sonic Boy, **6/4** Young Ern, **12/1** Prince of India, **16/1** Royal Philosopher, Be Mindful, **25/1** Chato (USA), MR MARTINI (IRE), CSF £259.99 TOTE £19.70: £3.50 £5.70 (£18.60) OWNER Parrot Racing (NEWMARKET) BRED Mrs W. Hanson 7 Rn 1m 42.51 (0.51) SF: 71/57/-/-/-/-/-
WEIGHT FOR AGE 3yo-12lb
STEWARDS' ENQUIRY Starke susp. 19-23/6/95 (careless riding).

1587 VODAFONE OAKS STKS (Gp 1) (3-Y.O F) (Class A) £147,800.00 (£55,300.00: £26,550.00: £11,550.00) **1m 4f 10y** Stalls: Low GOING minus 0.31 sec per fur (GF) 4-00 (4-04)

933³ **Moonshell (IRE)** *(116) (SbinSuroor)* 3-9-0 LDettori(9) (lw: 3rd st: led over 2f out: r.o wl) ....— 1

997* Dance a Dream **(102)**_(114) (MRStoute)_ 3-9-0 WRSwinburn(10) (lw: 2nd st: ev ch fnl 2f: r.o) 1¼ 2
1101* Pure Grain **(115)**_(113) (MRStoute)_ 3-9-0 JReid(8) (hdwy & 5th st: ev ch over 1f out: nt qckn) .¾ 3
1101³ Musetta (IRE) **(108)**_(109) (CEBrittain)_ 3-9-0 MRoberts(7) (led tl over 2f out: one pce) 3½ 4
1067* Asterita **(96)**_(105) (RHannon)_ 3-9-0 PatEddery(6) (lw: rdn 8f out: 9th st: nrst fin) 2½ 5
933² Aqaarid (USA) **(118)**_(103)_(Fav)_(JLDunlop)_ 3-9-0 WCarson(1) (4th st: wknd over 2f out) 1¾ 6
1139³ Bint Zamayem (IRE) **(97)**_(86) (BWHills)_ 3-9-0 MHills(2) (6th st: nvr nr ldrs)....13 7
1242⁴ Kshessinskaya _(79) (CEBrittain)_ 3-9-0 KDarley(5) (lw: prom tl wknd & 8th st)....5 8
1067⁵ Last Spin **(65)**_(75) (JRJenkins)_ 3-9-0 TQuinn(3) (swtg: sn bhd: 10th st)....3½ 9
1237a³ Bunting **(104)**_(69) (JHMGosden)_ 3-9-0v MJKinane(4) (lw: prom 6f: sn hrd rdn: 7th & btn st) 4 10

6/4 Aqaarid (USA), **3/1** MOONSHELL (IRE), **7/2** Pure Grain, **14/1** Dance a Dream, **20/1** Asterita, **25/1** Bint Zamayem (IRE), Bunting, **33/1** Kshessinskaya, Musetta (IRE), **200/1** Last Spin, CSF £37.55 TOTE £3.70: £1.80 £2.00 £1.80 (£12.60) Trio £25.70 OWNER Maktoum Al Maktoum / Godolphin (NEWMARKET) BRED Sheikh Mohammed bin Rashid al Maktoum in Ireland 10 Rn
2m 35.44 (0.44) SF: 72/70/69/65/61/59/42/35/31/25

OFFICIAL EXPLANATION **Aqaarid (USA): the jockey stated that the filly did not act on the firm ground.**

1588 VODAC VICTRESS STKS (Listed) (3-Y.O+ F & M) (Class A)

£17,425.00 (£5,275.00: £2,575.00: £1,225.00)
1m 114y Stalls: Low GOING minus 0.31 sec per fur (GF) 4-35 (4-38)

1362⁴ **Neither Nor (84)**_(101) (DAWilson)_ 6-9-6 GCarter(7) (lw: 9th st: nt clr run 2f out: rapid hdwy 1f out: qcknd to ld nr fin)....— 1
1242⁵ Brave Revival **(94)**_(99)_(Fav)_(MRStoute)_ 3-8-8 JReid(6) (lw: led 4f out tl cl home)....1 2
Brief Glimpse (IRE) **(98)**_(98)_(Fav)_(MajorDNChappell)_ 3-8-8 BThomson(9) (lost pl & 7th st: hdwy over 2f out: ev ch over 1f out: nt qckn)....¾ 3
933¹² Menas Gold **(97)**_(94) (SDow)_ 3-8-8 MRoberts(5) (8th st: nrst fin)....2 4
620⁸ Hiwaya **(106)**_(96) (HThomsonJones)_ 3-8-11 RHills(3) (lw: 4th st: ev ch 2f out: sn wknd) ....nk 5
1482² Girl From Ipanema **(104)**_(94) (PFICole)_ 4-9-9 TQuinn(8) (lw: 3rd st: wknd 2f out)....1½ 6
1362⁷ Karayib (USA) **(86)**_(87) (JLDunlop)_ 3-8-8 WCarson(4) (led over 4f: 2nd st: wknd over 2f out)....1¾ 7
933¹⁴ All Time Great **(95)**_(85) (LMCumani)_ 3-8-8 PatEddery(1) (6th st: wknd over 2f out)....1¼ 8
1186* Great Inquest _(85) (JHMGosden)_ 3-8-8 LDettori(2) (lw: 5th st: wkng whn n.m.r over 1f out) .s.h 9

9/2 Brave Revival, Brief Glimpse (IRE), **11/2** Hiwaya, All Time Great, **6/1** Great Inquest, **13/2** Girl From Ipanema, **7/1** Menas Gold, **20/1** Karayib (USA), NEITHER NOR, CSF £99.28 TOTE £14.60: £2.70 £1.90 £1.80 (£53.50) Trio £163.40 OWNER Mr T. S. M. S. Riley-Smith (EPSOM) BRED D. Tylden-Wright 9 Rn 1m 43.34 (1.34) SF: 65/51/50/46/48/58/39/37/37
WEIGHT FOR AGE 3yo-12lb

1589 VODACOM H'CAP (0-100) (3-Y.O) (Class C) £17,993.75 (£5,450.00: £2,662.50: £1,268.75) 1m 2f 18y Stalls: Low GOING minus 0.31 sec per fur (GF) 5-10 (5-11)

1097* **Yoush (IRE) (82)**_(87) (MAJarvis)_ 3-8-13 TJarnet(4) (5th st: led over 1f out: r.o wl)....— 1
1478² Grand Selection (IRE) **(72)**_(76) (MBell)_ 3-8-3 MFenton(3) (4th st: ev ch fnl f: r.o)....¾ 2
1170⁵ Hardy Dancer **(87)**_(90) (GLMoore)_ 3-9-4 BRouse(5) (8th st: swtchd rt over 2f out: hdwy over 1f out: r.o)....½ 3
1478* At Liberty (IRE) **(86)**_(89) (RHannon)_ 3-8-10 (7) 4x DaneO'Neill(2) (7th st: r.o one pce fnl 2f)....hd 4
1317* Dawsha (IRE) **(75)**_(75) (SDow)_ 3-8-6 MJKinane(8) (6th st: hrd rdn 2f out: r.o one pce) 1¾ 5
1314* Bob's Ploy **(85)**_(84)_(Fav)_(RAkehurst)_ 3-9-2 BThomson(1) (hmpd after 1f & after 4f: 11th st: gd hdwy fnl 2f: nrst fin)....¾ 6
756⁴ Sea Victor **(84)**_(82) (JHMGosden)_ 3-9-1 LDettori(10) (10th st: nrst fin)....nk 7
1357⁴ Bardon Hill Boy (IRE) **(74)**_(72) (BHanbury)_ 3-8-5 MHills(11) (2nd st: led 3f out tl wknd over 1f out)....nk 8
1382² Polydamas **(78)**_(74) (MRStoute)_ 3-8-9 WRSwinburn(7) (3rd st: wknd 2f out)....1¼ 9
_1330*_ Gulf Shaadi **(83)**_(60) (GLewis)_ 3-9-0 PaulEddery(9) (9th st: a bhd: t.o)....12 10
756³ Raased **(90)**_(59) (JLDunlop)_ 3-9-7 WCarson(6) (led tl wknd 3f out: t.o)....5 11

2/1 Bob's Ploy, **9/2** Bardon Hill Boy (IRE), **7/1** Polydamas, **8/1** Grand Selection (IRE) (6/1-9/1), YOUSH (IRE), **10/1** At Liberty (IRE), **14/1** Dawsha (IRE), Sea Victor, Hardy Dancer, Raased, **25/1** Gulf Shaadi, CSF £67.90 CT £817.29 TOTE £11.10: £2.80 £2.70 £3.20 (£48.40) Trio £216.80 OWNER Sheikh Ahmed Al Maktoum (NEWMARKET) BRED Dictum Enterprises Ltd 11 Rn
2m 6.01 (2.01) SF: 56/45/59/58/44/53/51/41/43/29/28

T/Jkpt: Not won; £72,114.57 to Epsom 10/6/95. T/Plpt: £1,881.80 (20.66 Tckts). T/Qdpt: £207.00 (2.9 Tckts). Hn

1259-**GOODWOOD (R-H)**
Friday June 9th (Rnd Good to firm, St Good)
WEATHER: overcast WIND: almost nil

1590 BBC SOUTH TODAY (S) STKS (2-Y.O) (Class E) £3,882.50 (£1,160.00: £555.00: £252.50) **5f** GOING minus 0.24 sec per fur (GF) 6-40 (6-42)

1278[7] **Bozeman (IRE)** *(61) (RHannon)* 2-8-11 PatEddery(2) (lw: chsd ldrs: rdn 2f out: led 1f out: r.o wl)........— **1**
1361[6] Petite Annie *(56)*(Fav)*(TGMills)* 2-8-6 JReid(13) (lw: dwlt: sn chsng ldrs: hdwy over 1f out: ev ch ins fnl f: r.o)........s.h **2**
760[8] Sporting Fantasy *(57) (MRChannon)* 2-8-11 RHughes(14) (lw: a.p: led 3f out: hdd 1f out: ev ch & rdn fnl f: unable qckn)........1¼ **3**
Trible Pet *(48) (BGubby)* 2-8-1 (5) AWhelan(7) (neat: dwlt: bhd: gd hdwy fnl f: fin wl)........1¼ **4**
1369[3] Solva Mist *(48) (LJHolt)* 2-8-6 CAvery(11) (chsd ldrs: rdn 2f out: one pce)........s.h **5**
1481[5] Ivory's Grab Hire *(50) (KTIvory)* 2-8-11 GBardwell(4) (nvr nrr)........1 **6**
1481[8] Jemsilverthorn (IRE) *(45) (JJBridger)* 2-8-4 (7) ADaly(5) (chsd ldrs: rdn over 2f out: one pce)........1½ **7**
Golden Silver *(40) (JSMoore)* 2-8-1 (5) SDrowne(3) (unf: bit bkwd: nvr nrr)........s.h **8**
1272[2] Caveat Emptor (IRE) *(41) (SDow)* 2-8-11 StephenDavies(10) (led 2f: rdn over 2f out: sn wknd)........1¼ **9**
1503[7] Grimstone Girl *(35) (MWEasterby)* 2-8-6b RCochrane(12) (b: spd over 3f)........hd **10**
1327[3] Bath Knight *(36) (DJSffrenchDavis)* 2-8-11v TQuinn(6) (prom to ½-wy)........1¼ **11**
725[7] Mandy's Risk *(35) (TMJones)* 2-8-11 RPerham(9) (bit bkwd: prom 3f)........½ **12**
1272[6] Red Sky Delight (IRE) *(18) (PButler)* 2-8-6 NCarlisle(1) (a bhd)........3½ **13**

10/11 Petite Annie (6/4-5/6), **11/2** BOZEMAN (IRE), **13/2** Sporting Fantasy (op 4/1), **12/1** Grimstone Girl, **14/1** Ivory's Grab Hire (10/1-16/1), Caveat Emptor (IRE) (10/1-16/1), **16/1** Bath Knight, **33/1** Golden Silver, Trible Pet, **50/1** Jemsilverthorn (IRE), Solva Mist, Mandy's Risk, Red Sky Delight (IRE), CSF £10.35 TOTE £6.20: £1.90 £1.40 £2.10 (£4.90) Trio £9.60 OWNER Lord Carnarvon (MARLBOROUGH) BRED Don Kelly 13 Rn 60.52 secs (3.82) SF: 9/4/5/-/-/-/-/-/-/-/-/-/-
No bid

1591 BBC RADIO SOLENT H'CAP (0-80) (3-Y.O) (Class D) £4,378.00 (£1,309.00: £627.00: £286.00)
1m 2f Stalls: Low GOING minus 0.24 sec per fur (GF) 7-10 (7-12)

873[10] **Fairy Knight (69)***(77)*(Fav)*(RHannon)* 3-8-12 JReid(6) (hld up: 4th st: hdwy over 2f out: rdn 1f out: led nr fin)........— **1**
962[5] Donna Viola **(72)***(80) (CFWall)* 3-9-1 NCarlisle(4) (a.p: 2nd st: led 2f out tl hdd nr fin)........nk **2**
High Flying Adored (IRE) **(78)***(83) (JLDunlop)* 3-9-7 PatEddery(1) (5th st: hdwy over 2f out: rdn over 1f out: one pce)........1¾ **3**
1447[9] Dungeon Dancer **(63)***(65) (JAkehurst)* 3-8-6v TQuinn(2) (led to 2f out: one pce)........1½ **4**
697[11] Shady Deed (USA) **(70)***(72) (JWHills)* 3-8-13 MHills(7) (6th st: rdn over 2f out: one pce)........½ **5**
1322[8] Fattash (USA) **(57)***(55) (CJBenstead)* 3-8-0b WCarson(5) (b: 3rd st: rdn over 3f out: wknd over 2f out)........2½ **6**
1290[4] Miss Jemmima **(62)***(48) (LordHuntingdon)* 3-8-5 DHarrison(3) (a bhd)........7 **7**

9/4 FAIRY KNIGHT, **9/2** Donna Viola, **5/1** High Flying Adored (IRE), **6/1** Dungeon Dancer, **13/2** Miss Jemmima (op 4/1), **10/1** Fattash (USA), **16/1** Shady Deed (USA), CSF £11.27 TOTE £3.40: £2.30 £2.60 (£6.10) OWNER P & S Lever Partners (MARLBOROUGH) BRED Peter McCalmont 7 Rn 2m 11.32 (6.32) SF: 27/30/33/15/22/5/-

1592 E.B.F. BBC RADIO BERKSHIRE MAIDEN STKS (2-Y.O) (Class D) £4,503.00 (£1,344.00: £642.00: £291.00)
6f Stalls: Low GOING: minus 0.24 sec per fur (GF) 7-35 (7-40)

Depreciate *(72?) (CJames)* 2-9-0 RCochrane(5) (neat: lw: a.p: led 4f out to 2f out: led 1f out: hrd rdn fnl f: r.o)........— **1**
683[5] Navigate (USA) *(72) (RHannon)* 2-9-0 PatEddery(1) (lw: chsd ldrs: led 2f out to 1f out: hrd rdn fnl f: r.o)........hd **2**
Al Shafa *(69) (JLDunlop)* 2-9-0 TQuinn(4) (neat: bhd: rdn ½-wy: r.o fnl f)........1 **3**
High Priority (IRE) *(60) (MRChannon)* 2-9-0 RHughes(7) (str: scope: bit bkwd: chsd ldrs: ev ch 2f out: wknd over 1f out)........3½ **4**
1246[3] Goodwood Rocket *(59)*(Fav)*(JLDunlop)* 2-9-0 WCarson(2) (lw: led 2f: rdn & lost pl 3f out: r.o one pce fnl f)........nk **5**
1246[7] Get Tough *(50) (SDow)* 2-9-0 StephenDavies(3) (chsd ldrs tl rdn & wknd over 2f out)........3½ **6**

Coastguards Hero *(MDIUsher)* 2-9-0 DHarrison(6) (Withdrawn not under Starter's orders: inj at s)........ W

6/4 Goodwood Rocket, **2/1** High Priority (IRE), **100/30** Navigate (USA), **10/1** Al Shafa, **25/1** Get Tough, **33/1** DEPRECIATE, Coastguards Hero, CSF £124.89 TOTE £28.50: £7.20 £1.90 (£81.60) OWNER Mr V. R. Bedley (NEWBURY) BRED V. R. Bedley 6 Rn
1m 12.61 (2.41) SF: 44/44/41/32/31/22/-

1593 THREE KEYS H'CAP (0-90) (3-Y.O+) (Class C) £6,368.00 (£1,904.00: £912.00: £416.00)
1m Stalls: Low GOING minus 0.24 sec per fur (GF) 8-05 (8-08)

1409[6] **Desert Time (73)***(79+)*(Fav)*(CAHorgan)* 5-9-6 MPerrett(6) (hld up: 5th st: smooth hdwy 2f out: led wl ins fnl f: comf)........— 1
829[12] Night Dance **(77)***(82) (GLewis)* 3-8-13 SWhitworth(1) (2nd st: led over 2f out: hrd rdn & hdd wl ins fnl f)........¾ 2
1261[3] Helios **(77)***(81) (NJHWalker)* 7-9-10 RCochrane(2) (led tl over 2f out: hrd rdn over 1f out: r.o)s.h 3
1415[4] Polonez Prima **(65)***(62) (JLSpearing)* 8-8-12 PaulEddery(4) (6th st: hdwy over 2f out: rdn & one pce fnl 2f)........3½ 4
1244[11] Blue Bomber **(77)***(68) (CWeedon)* 4-9-5 (5) RPainter(3) (3rd st: rdn over 2f out: sn wknd)........3 5
Glitterazzi **(69)***(30) (LMontagueHall)* 4-9-2 StephenDavies(5) (hdwy 5f out: 4th st: sn wknd) .15 6

5/2 DESERT TIME, **3/1** Night Dance (op 5/1), Polonez Prima, **7/2** Helios, **10/1** Blue Bomber, **33/1** Glitterazzi, CSF £9.86 TOTE £2.90: £1.70 £2.40 (£7.30) OWNER Spoof Racing (BILLINGBEAR) BRED Mrs Amanda Skiffington 6 Rn 1m 40.39 (2.79) SF: 56/48/58/39/45/7
WEIGHT FOR AGE 3yo-11lb

1594 NICK GIRDLER CLAIMING STKS (4-Y.O+) (Class E) £3,785.00 (£1,130.00: £540.00: £245.00) 1m 4f Stalls: Low GOING minus 0.24 sec (GF) 8-35 (8-37)

1386[8] **Pharamineux (66)***(73) (RAkehurst)* 9-8-7 TQuinn(7) (lw: hld up: 7th st: hdwy 3f out: led 2f out: r.o)........— 1
1245[4] Irkutsk (USA) **(67)***(78)*(Fav)*(MCPipe)* 4-8-13 MRoberts(10) (3rd st: rdn over 1f out: ev ch ins fnl f: r.o)........½ 2
1256[3] Ginger Jim **(52)***(76) (PRHedger)* 4-8-11 CAvery(8) (4th st: rdn & edgd lft over 1f out: ev ch ins fnl f: r.o)........s.h 3
1477[7] Trade Wind **(73)***(80) (DRCElsworth)* 4-9-2b(5) AProcter(3) (b: lw: 6th st: rdn 3f out: one pce fnl 2f)........5 4
Captain Scarlet (IRE) **(78)***(65) (BJMeehan)* 4-8-11v BDoyle(2) (b: bit bkwd: 2nd st: led 3f out to 2f out: wknd over 1f out)........3½ 5
1349[6] Pride of May (IRE) **(65)***(64) (RHannon)* 4-9-1b PatEddery(5) (b: led 9f: wknd over 1f out)........4 6
1350[10] Mint a Million (IRE) **(31)***(48) (MBlanshard)* 4-8-4 (5) MBaird(6) (a bhd)........7 7
1319[8] Cone Lane **(30)***(32) (BGubby)* 9-8-1 (5) AWhelan(9) (b: 5th st: wknd 3f out)........10 8
1210[5] Saahi (USA) **(35)***(29) (CWeedon)* 6-8-7v(5)ow1 RPainter(1) (racd wd: prom 7f)........6 9

3/1 Irkutsk (USA), **100/30** PHARAMINEUX, **7/2** Captain Scarlet (IRE), **4/1** Pride of May (IRE), **15/2** Trade Wind, **25/1** Ginger Jim, Mint a Million (IRE), **40/1** Cone Lane, Saahi (USA), CSF £12.88 TOTE £4.20: £1.70 £1.40 £2.10 (£6.10) Trio £32.80 OWNER Mr K. R. Snellings (EPSOM) BRED J.L.C.Pearce 9 Rn 2m 37.12 (5.12) SF: 39/44/42/46/31/30/14/-/-

1595 SANDI JONES H'CAP (0-75) (3-Y.O+) (Class D) £4,235.00 (£1,265.00: £605.00: £275.00)
5f Stalls: Low GOING minus 0.24 sec per fur (GF) 9-05 (9-08)

1265* **Mazzarello (IRE) (39)***(44) (RCurtis)* 5-7-4v(5) MBaird(9) (mde all: rdn fnl f: r.o wl)........— 1
1508* Lady Sheriff **(58)***(62)*(Fav)*(MWEasterby)* 4-9-0b 7x RCochrane(7) (b: a.p: rdn & ev ch ins fnl f: r.o)........nk 2
1214[10] Miami Banker **(40)***(42) (WRMuir)* 9-7-10b GBardwell(2) (b: a.p: hrd rdn fnl f: one pce)........¾ 3
1023[5] Jucea **(66)***(65) (JLSpearing)* 6-9-8 PaulEddery(6) (mid div: hdwy 2f out: rdn over 1f out: one pce)........¾ 4
1265[6] Judgement Call **(47)***(46) (PHowling)* 8-8-3 NCarlisle(3) (chsd ldrs: rdn over 1f out: one pce) s.h 5
1265[8] Eagle Day (USA) **(68)***(66) (DRCElsworth)* 4-9-10b MRoberts(8) (b: sn rdn along: hdwy 2f out: rdn & one pce fnl f)........½ 6
Bold Gem **(57)***(50) (BJMeehan)* 4-8-13b BDoyle(4) (b: hdwy over 1f out: hung lft ins fnl f: eased whn btn)........1½ 7
1510[5] Domicksky **(64)***(56) (MRChannon)* 7-9-6 RHughes(5) (nvr nrr)........hd 8
1257[5] Halliard **(60)***(50) (TMJones)* 4-9-2 RPerham(1) (dwlt: hdwy 2f out: n.m.r over 1f out: sn wknd)........¾ 9

1538[8] Shades of Jade **(46)***(19) (JJBridger)* 7-7-9 (7)ow9 ADaly(10) (spd 3f) 2½ **10**

LONG HANDICAP Shades of Jade 7-1

2/1 Lady Sheriff, **7/2** Domicksky, **6/1** Eagle Day (USA), **8/1** Jucea, **10/1** MAZZARELLO (IRE), **11/1** Judgement Call (8/1-12/1), **12/1** Halliard (op 8/1), **14/1** Bold Gem, **33/1** Miami Banker, Shades of Jade, CSF £29.14 CT £587.85 TOTE £10.90: £2.70 £1.40 £5.80 (£16.40) Trio £771.30 OWNER Mr D. W. Hoskyns (CARSHALTON) BRED Thomas Naughton 10 Rn

58.58 secs (1.88) SF: 26/44/24/47/28/48/32/38/32/1

T/Plpt: £124.00 (120.61 Tckts). T/Qdpt: £28.70 (5.4 Tckts). SM

1304-HAYDOCK (L-H)

Friday June 9th (Good to soft)

WEATHER: bright & dry WIND: fresh half against

1596 RED ROSE AMATEUR H'CAP (0-70) (3-Y.O+) (Class G) £2,864.00 (£804.00: £392.00) 1m 2f 120y Stalls: High GOING minus 0.31 sec per fur (GF) 6-55 (6-57)

1437[2] **Mentalasanythin (55)***(67)*(Fav)*(ABailey)* 6-11-2 MrsJCrossley(2) (hld up: gd hdwy 2f out: str run to ld cl home) ....— **1**

430[12] Gold Blade **(42)***(50) (JPearce)* 6-10-3 MrsLPearce(17) (hld up in tch: hdwy to ld ins fnl f: wknd & ct nr fin) 2½ **2**

1323[4] Air Command (BAR) **(50)***(55) (CTNash)* 5-10-7 (4) MrPPhillips(6) (hld up: hdwy 2f out: r.o wl ins fnl f) 2 **3**

844[4] Claireswan (IRE) **(53)***(57) (SCWilliams)* 3-9-9 (4) MissKWright(7) (in tch: rdn & kpt on appr fnl f) ....½ **4**

Tremendisto **(51)***(55) (CaptJWilson)* 5-10-12 MrsGRees(20) (bit bkwd: a.p: 2nd st: led over 3f out tl hdd & wknd ins fnl) ....s.h **5**

Nordic Mine (IRE) **(45)***(48) (PJHobbs)* 5-10-2 (4) MrsSHobbs(16) (bit bkwd: hdwy over 2f out: nrst fin) ....¾ **6**

1141[14] Beauman **(67)***(69) (PDEvans)* 5-11-10 (4) MrWMcLaughlin(5) (hld up: hdwy over 2f out: nt trble ldrs) ....½ **7**

1323[14] Sweet Trentino (IRE) **(65)***(66) (MTate)* 4-11-8 (4) MrsHNeedham(13) (chsd ldrs: 6th st: wknd over 1f out) 1¼ **8**

1083[12] Battery Boy **(47)***(46) (CWCElsey)* 3-9-7b MissAElsey(10) (led tl over 3f out: wknd appr fnl f) 1¼ **9**

No Comebacks **(59)***(57) (EJAlston)* 7-11-6 MrsAFarrell(12) (bkwd: hld up: effrt on ins over 2f out: wknd appr fnl f) ....½ **10**

Ice Magic **(32)***(26) (FJYardley)* 8-9-3 (4) MissSYardley(18) (bkwd: a bhd) 2½ **11**

1092[14] Dixit Dominus **(54)***(48) (GBBalding)* 4-10-11 (4) MissKGreaney(3) (nvr bttr than mid div).........nk **12**

Bowcliffe **(63)***(56) (JTGifford)* 4-11-10 MrRJohnson(1) (bit bkwd: prom: 4th st: wknd over 2f out) ....¾ **13**

1285[12] Castletown Count **(59)***(27) (KWHogg)* 3-10-1 (4)ow12 MrKDrewry(4) (a bhd: t.o).................8 **14**

1523[18] Kings Vision **(47)***(18) (BSRothwell)* 3-9-3b(4) MissAlexMcCabe(11) (t: chsd ldrs: 7th st: wknd over 3f out: t.o) 6 **15**

1436[2] Dahlenburg (IRE) **(67)***(38) (JHMGosden)* 3-10-13v MrJDurkan(9) (a bhd: rdn over 3f out: no rspnse: t.o) ....½ **16**

Record Lover (IRE) **(46)***(16) (MCChapman)* 5-10-3 (4) MrMMackley(19) (chsd ldrs: 6th st: wknd 3f out) ....s.h **17**

821[10] Tanah Merah (IRE) **(51)***(20) (EJAlston)* 4-10-8 (4) MrPBlane(15) (dwlt: a bhd: t.o).................¾ **18**

1434[9] Mokaite **(45)** *(MABarnes)* 4-10-2 (4) MrsMKendall(8) (prom: 3rd st: wknd over 3f out: t.o) 20 **19**

LONG HANDICAP Ice Magic 9-4 Battery Boy 9-6 Castletown Count 9-5

7/2 MENTALASANYTHIN, **6/1** Dahlenburg (IRE) (op 4/1), **13/2** Gold Blade, **15/2** Beauman, **9/1** No Comebacks, Bowcliffe, **12/1** Tanah Merah (IRE), **14/1** Air Command (BAR), **16/1** Battery Boy, Tremendisto, Dixit Dominus, **20/1** Mokaite, Claireswan (IRE), **25/1** Nordic Mine (IRE), Sweet Trentino (IRE), Ice Magic, Record Lover (IRE), Castletown Count, **33/1** Kings Vision, CSF £29.21 CT £291.02 TOTE £4.00: £1.40 £1.50 £2.90 £6.50 (£8.80) Trio £36.20 OWNER Mrs M. O'Donnell (TARPORLEY) BRED R. B. Warren 19 Rn

2m 18.54 (7.04) SF: 49/32/37/24/37/30/51/48/13/39/8/30/38/-/-/5/-/2/-

WEIGHT FOR AGE 3yo-15lb

1597 E.B.F. WEAVER MAIDEN STKS (2-Y.O) (Class D) £4,416.00 (£1,338.00: £654.00: £312.00) 6f Stalls: High GOING minus 0.31 sec per fur (GF) 7-25 (7-28)

819[10] **Miss Waterline** *(80?) (PDEvans)* 2-8-9 JFortune(14) (mde all: rdn over 1f out: r.o gamely) ..— **1**

Bollin Dorothy *(75) (MHEasterby)* 2-8-9 MBirch(3) (leggy: unf: a.p: rdn & ev ch over 1f out: no ex fnl f) 2 **2**

Shontaine *(74) (MJohnston)* 2-9-0 DHolland(8) (w'like: scope: s.i.s: hdwy 2f out: nt rch ldrs) 2 **3**

1184⁶ Inverlochy *(72)*(Fav)*(JLDunlop)* 2-9-0 WRyan(15) (hld up: hdwy 2f out: kpt on u.p ins fnl f)......1 **4**
Bellator *(67) (GBBalding)* 2-9-0 JWilliams(6) (w'like: scope: hdwy over 1f out: nvr nrr).........1¾ **5**
West Austria (IRE) *(66) (JBerry)* 2-9-0 JCarroll(10) (lt-f: unf: hdwy wl over 1f out: nvr nrr)......½ **6**
1176¹⁰ Classic Victory *(65) (SCWilliams)* 2-9-0 AMackay(11) (prom: rdn over 1f out: sn wknd) ....hd **7**
Steal 'Em *(60) (ABailey)* 2-8-9 MWigham(12) (w'like: bkwd: nvr nrr)....................................s.h **8**
Cumbrian Maestro *(65) (MHEasterby)* 2-9-0 SMaloney(1) (leggy: nvr trbld ldrs) ....nk **9**
Serif (USA) *(59) (JHMGosden)* 2-9-0 GHind(5) (lt-f: s.s: hdwy on outside ½-wy: wknd over 1f out)..2 **10**
977⁵ Le Sport *(59) (DNicholls)* 2-9-0 AlexGreaves(7) (a in rr) ....hd **11**
Give Me A Ring (IRE) *(58) (CWThornton)* 2-9-0 DeanMcKeown(4) (w'like: leggy: s.s: a outpcd)...nk **12**
Oisin An Oir (IRE) *(52) (JBerry)* 2-8-7 (7) PRoberts(13) (lt-f: chsd ldrs 4f: sn wknd)................2¼ **13**
Maysimp (IRE) *(38) (BPJBaugh)* 2-8-9 ACulhane(9) (leggy: lt-f: s.s: a bhd & outpcd)...........3½ **14**
1134¹² Swish *(41) (NTinkler)* 2-9-0 TIves(2) (spd over 3f) ....½ **15**

11/8 Inverlochy (6/4-Evens), **5/1** Serif (USA), **6/1** West Austria (IRE), **9/1** MISS WATERLINE, **10/1** Shontaine, **12/1** Steal 'Em, **16/1** Classic Victory, Oisin An Oir (IRE), **20/1** Bollin Dorothy, Give Me A Ring (IRE), Le Sport, **33/1** Cumbrian Maestro, Bellator, Maysimp (IRE), Swish, CSF £167.23 TOTE £10.30: £2.20 £4.70 £3.50 (£184.30) Trio £299.50 OWNER Mr M. W. Lawrence (WELSHPOOL) BRED P. A. Hurst 15 Rn 1m 16.46 (4.76) SF: 4/-/-/-/-/-/-/-/-/-/-/-/-/-/-

1598 'CATALYST' H'CAP (0-70) (3-Y.O) (Class E) £3,355.00 (£1,015.00: £495.00: £235.00) **1m 30y** Stalls: Low GOING minus 0.31 sec per fur (GF) 7-55 (7-56)

1358¹⁰ **Ballard Lady (IRE) (40)***(46) (JSWainwright)* 3-7-11 SMaloney(1) (bhd: hdwy on outside 2f out: led appr fnl f: sn clr)..— **1**
772¹⁰ Frontiersman **(54)***(53) (JWWatts)* 3-8-11 JCarroll(7) (hld up: 6th st: hdwy over 2f out: ev ch over 1f out: rdn & one pce fnl f) 3½ **2**
1279⁶ Cool Tactician **(59)***(57) (RHollinshead)* 3-9-2 TIves(3) (chsd ldrs: 4th st: ev ch over 1f out: unable qckn)...¾ **3**
1423² Indian Rhapsody **(44)***(41)*(Fav)*(MRChannon)* 3-8-1 CRutter(6) (s.i.s: hdwy & nt clr run over 2f out: swtchd rt & hmpd ent fnl f: nt rcvr)...hd **4**
1465⁶ Rushen Raider **(58)***(55) (KWHogg)* 3-9-1 MTebbutt(5) (bhd: hdwy on outside fnl 2f: nvr nrr).s.h **5**
1097²¹ Quillon Rose **(42)***(34) (CFWall)* 3-7-13 ow1 AMcGlone(10) (prom: 3rd st: led 2f out tl hdd & wknd appr fnl f) 2 **6**
689⁷ Percy Parrot **(45)***(38) (RMWhitaker)* 3-8-2 DaleGibson(9) (chsd ldrs: 5th st: rdn & wknd wl over 1f out) ....hd **7**
1309⁴ Just Whistle **(52)***(44) (CWThornton)* 3-8-9 DeanMcKeown(2) (led 6f: rdn & wknd over 1f out) ....¾ **8**
1308⁷ Irshad **(64)***(46) (PTWalwyn)* 3-9-7 JWeaver(8) (prom: 2nd st: rdn 2f out: n.m.r & eased appr fnl f) 5 **9**
992⁹ Kralingen **(40)** *(NChamberlain)* 3-7-11 JFanning(11) (bit bkwd: a bhd: t.o).........................dist **10**
673¹¹ Bollin Sophie **(52)** *(MHEasterby)* 3-8-9 MBirch(4) (dwlt: a bhd: t.o) 6 **11**

11/4 Indian Rhapsody, **7/2** Frontiersman, **7/1** Just Whistle, Rushen Raider, Irshad, **8/1** Cool Tactician, **11/1** Quillon Rose, **14/1** Bollin Sophie, **16/1** Percy Parrot, **25/1** BALLARD LADY (IRE), **33/1** Kralingen, CSF £108.73 CT £724.70 TOTE £61.60: £8.40 £2.10 £2.30 (£235.10) Trio £410.50 OWNER Mr J. H. Pickard (MALTON) BRED Airlie Stud 11 Rn
1m 44.87 (4.47) SF: 14/21/25/9/23/2/6/12/14/-/-

1599 DARESBURY H'CAP (0-80) (3-Y.O+) (Class D) £3,993.50 (£1,208.00: £589.00: £279.50) **6f** Stalls: High GOING minus 0.31 sec per fur (GF) 8-25 (8-26)

812¹⁴ **Sailormaite (72)***(79) (SRBowring)* 4-9-8 SWebster(9) (a.p: led ins fnl f: rdn out)...................— **1**
1354³ Jigsaw Boy **(61)***(63) (PGMurphy)* 6-8-4 (7) RWaterfield(10) (bhd: hdwy over 1f out: fin wl) 1¾ **2**
1174¹³ Teetotaller (IRE) **(68)***(70) (GBBalding)* 4-9-4 JWilliams(6) (hld up: hdwy over 1f out: rdn & r.o wl fnl f) ....hd **3**
1468¹¹ Cumbrian Waltzer **(77)***(75) (MHEasterby)* 10-9-13 MBirch(7) (bit bkwd: hld up & bhd: r.o fnl 2f: nvr nrr)...1½ **4**
1441¹⁰ Cafe Solo **(43)***(40) (NBycroft)* 4-7-7b NKennedy(13) (b: racd stands' side: hdwy over 1f out: nrst fin)..nk **5**
1304⁵ Ansellman **(73)***(67)*(Fav)*(JBerry)* 5-9-9 JCarroll(12) (a.p: rdn over 1f out: one pce) 1¼ **6**
1461² Croft Imperial **(63)***(56)*(Fav)*(MJohnston)* 8-8-13 DHolland(1) (prom tl rdn & wknd ent fnl f) ....nk **7**
1354⁶ The Old Chapel **(65)***(54) (BAMcMahon)* 6-9-1b FNorton(4) (b: lw: mde most tl hdd & wknd ins fnl f)...1½ **8**
1433¹³ Cheerful Groom (IRE) **(50)***(39) (JMackie)* 4-8-0 GHind(5) (effrt u.p over 1f out: no imp) ....s.h **9**
1354⁷ Captain Carat **(65)***(54) (MrsJRRamsden)* 4-9-1 JWeaver(2) (plld hrd: hld up: hdwy 2f out: hrd rdn appr fnl f: sn btn) ....hd **10**

1032[5] Bells of Longwick **(64)**(51) *(WWHaigh)* 6-9-0 DaleGibson(11) (lw: sn rdn along: a in rr) ....½ 11
1376[3] Here Comes a Star **(76)**(61) *(JMCarr)* 7-9-12 ACulhane(8) (lw: hdwy 2f out: rdn & wknd appr fnl f) ....¾ 12
1174[16] Leigh Crofter **(72)**(56) *(PDCundell)* 6-9-3b(5) DGriffiths(3) (b: prom: effrt & nt clr run over 1f out: sn btn) ....½ 13

LONG HANDICAP Cafe Solo 7-3

11/2 Croft Imperial, Ansellman, **6/1** Jigsaw Boy, Captain Carat (op 4/1), **8/1** SAILORMAITE, The Old Chapel, **10/1** Teetotaller (IRE), Here Comes a Star, **14/1** Cafe Solo, Bells of Longwick, **16/1** Cumbrian Waltzer, Leigh Crofter, **33/1** Cheerful Groom (IRE), CSF £54.48 CT £455.21 TOTE £9.80: £3.00 £1.90 £2.90 (£23.30) Trio £89.60 OWNER Mr S. R. Bowring (EDWINSTOWE) BRED S. R. Bowring 13 Rn 1m 14.67 (2.97) SF: 39/23/30/35/-/27/16/14/-/14/11/21/16

1600 WINWICK MAIDEN STKS (3-Y.O+) (Class D) £3,857.00 (£1,166.00: £568.00: £269.00) 1m 6f Stalls: Low GOING minus 0.31 sec per fur (GF) 8-55 (8-56)

698[4] **Tonnerre** (81) *(CWFairhurst)* 3-8-8 DeanMcKeown(4) (lw: a.p: 3rd st: led 2f out: rdn & edgd lft fnl f: r.o wl) ....— 1
1270[2] Anna of Brunswick (74)(Fav) *(HRACecil)* 3-8-3 WRyan(7) (hld up & bhd: 6th st: hdwy over 2f out: ev ch 1f out: one pce) 1½ 2
1026[2] Toraja (76) *(JLDunlop)* 3-8-8 JWeaver(1) (hld up: 7th st: hdwy over 2f out: styd on fnl f) 2½ 3
1175[4] Tibetan (75) *(LadyHerries)* 3-8-8 TIves(8) (lw: s.i.s: sn chsng ldrs: 5th st: effrt wl over 1f out: nt pce to chal) 1 4
1189[6] Polish Consul **(67)**(70) *(MajorWRHern)* 4-9-12 MBirch(3) (chsd ldrs: 2nd st: led over 2f out: sn hdd & wknd) 5 5
1198[16] Ziro (IRE) (64) *(PDEvans)* 3-8-8v JFortune(5) (bkwd: led tl hdd & wknd over 2f out) 5 6
Telmo (IRE) (61) *(HRACecil)* 3-8-8 AMcGlone(2) (b: nice c: bkwd: dwlt: hld up: hdwy ½-wy: 4th st: wknd over 2f out) 2½ 7
Great Easeby (IRE) (57) *(WStorey)* 5-9-12 JFanning(6) (bkwd: chsd ldrs: rdn ½-wy: sn lost tch) 3½ 8

8/11 Anna of Brunswick, **4/1** Tibetan, **9/2** Toraja (op 3/1), **10/1** Polish Consul, **12/1** Telmo (IRE), **25/1** TONNERRE, **33/1** Great Easeby (IRE), **50/1** Ziro (IRE), CSF £44.91 TOTE £34.40: £3.70 £1.20 £1.30 (£28.70) Trio £32.20 OWNER Twinacre Nurseries Ltd (MIDDLEHAM) BRED Mrs Amanda Skiffington 8 Rn 3m 3.72 (5.52) SF: 38/31/33/32/45/21/18/32

WEIGHT FOR AGE 3yo-18lb

1601 MATTHEW PEACOCK H'CAP (0-80) (3-Y.O) (Class D) £3,818.00 (£1,154.00: £562.00: £266.00) 1m 6f Stalls: Low GOING minus 0.31 sec per fur (GF) 9-25 (9-26)

1382[4] **Rocky Forum (52)**(59)(Fav) *(GLMoore)* 3-7-12 FNorton(3) (lw: a.p: 3rd st: rdn wl over 1f out: styd on to ld fnl 100y) ....— 1
1093[2] Mutazz (USA) **(66)**(70)(Fav) *(MajorWRHern)* 3-8-12 JCarroll(1) (lw: led tl rdn & hdd wl ins fnl f) 2½ 2
1091[5] Armston **(55)**(57) *(JWharton)* 3-8-1 JFanning(6) (lw: chsd ldr most of wy: 2nd st: rdn over 2f out: one pce) 2 3
484[2] Arctic Charmer (USA) **(75)**(60) *(JLDunlop)* 3-9-7b WRyan(2) (b: lw: hld up in tch: 4th st: rdn over 3f out: sn lost tch: t.o) 15 4
1273[4] Brockton Light **(55)**(28) *(MRChannon)* 3-8-1 CRutter(4) (s.i.s: a in rr: 5th st: t.o) 10 5
774[7] Penbola (IRE) **(55)**(27) *(MHEasterby)* 3-8-1 SMaloney(5) (a bhd: lost tch 6f out: 6th st: t.o)....¾ 6

9/4 ROCKY FORUM, Mutazz (USA), **7/2** Arctic Charmer (USA), **8/1** Penbola (IRE), Brockton Light, **9/1** Armston (op 6/1), CSF £7.69 TOTE £3.00: £1.90 £1.50 (£2.70) OWNER The Forum Ltd (EPSOM) BRED Forum Bloodstock Ltd 6 Rn 3m 4.75 (6.55) SF: 23/34/21/24/-/-

T/Plpt: £599.00 (29.71 Tckts). T/Qdpt: £48.90 (4.2 Tckts). IM

1341-DONCASTER (L-H)
Saturday June 10th (Good, Good to firm patches)
WEATHER: overcast WIND: almost nil

1602 ST JOHN AMBULANCE MAIDEN STKS (3-Y.O+) (Class D) £3,766.10 (£1,122.80: £535.40: £241.70) 5f Stalls: High GOING minus 0.20 sec per fur (GF) 2-20 (2-21)

1302[2] **Premium Gift (60)**(71) *(CBBBooth)* 3-8-8 JFortune(8) (lw: trckd ldrs: rdn to ld ins fnl f: drvn out) ....— 1
1419[2] Just Dissident (IRE) **(63)**(74) *(RMWhitaker)* 3-8-13 ACulhane(2) (lw: a.p: chal ins fnl f: kpt on) ....½ 2

1201[11] La Belle Dominique **(60)***(65) (SGKnight)* 3-8-8 WNewnes(6) (led tl ins fnl f: kpt on same pce)....1¼ **3**
1360[3] Just Like Me *(65)*(Fav)*(RGuest)* 3-8-8 JQuinn(3) (s.i.s: stdy hdwy ½-wy: rdn & nt qckn appr fnl f)....s.h **4**
Diebiedale *(64) (RBoss)* 3-8-8 MRimmer(5) (in tch: kpt on wl nr fin)....nk **5**
Chief's Lady *(60) (GFierro)* 3-8-8 MWigham(10) (s.i.s: hdwy ½-wy: nvr rchd ldrs)....1¼ **6**
1296[4] Mr Teigh **(76)***(61) (KMcAuliffe)* 3-8-10 (3) JTate(4) (chsd ldrs tl rdn & wknd appr fnl f)....1¼ **7**
Toasted *(53) (WJarvis)* 3-8-8 TIves(7) (outpcd fr ½-wy)....1 **8**
1515[4] Tonys Gift **(73)***(52) (RHannon)* 3-8-8 RPerham(9) (lw: outpcd fnl 2f)....½ **9**
1302[6] Super Look *(42) (TJEtherington)* 3-8-8 DeanMcKeown(1) (dwlt: n.d)....3 **10**

3/1 Just Like Me, **4/1** Just Dissident (IRE), Mr Teigh, **5/1** PREMIUM GIFT, **11/2** Tonys Gift, **9/1** Toasted, **14/1** Diebiedale, **16/1** La Belle Dominique, Super Look, **33/1** Chief's Lady, CSF £26.16 TOTE £6.20: £2.00 £1.90 £5.90 (£12.10) Trio £296.50; £50.12 to Epsom 11/6/95 OWNER Mr A. Lyons (FLAXTON) BRED A. Lyons 10 Rn 60.14 secs (1.74) SF: 46/49/40/40/39/35/36/28/27/17

1603

KNOWSLEY H'CAP (0-75) (3-Y.O+) (Class D) £6,368.00 (£1,904.00: £912.00: £416.00) **7f** Stalls: High GOING minus 0.20 sec per fur (GF) 2-50 (2-50)

1421[8] **Allinson's Mate (IRE) (68)***(77) (TDBarron)* 7-9-9b JFortune(7) (lw: trckd ldrs: rdn to ld ins fnl f: r.o)....— **1**
1457[4] Grey Again **(54)***(61) (SRBowring)* 3-7-13b TWilliams(3) (in tch: effrt over 2f out: chal ins fnl f: nt qckn nr fin)....1 **2**
909[9] Yoxall Lodge **(59)***(66) (HJCollingridge)* 5-9-0 JQuinn(8) (lw: led: qcknd 3f out: hdd ins fnl f: kpt on)....hd **3**
1297* Glowing Jade **(72)***(76)*(Fav)*(MissGayKelleway)* 5-9-8 (5) RPainter(4) (hld up: effrt over 2f out: r.o: nt pce to chal)....1 **4**
1250[13] Kemo Sabo **(73)***(73) (MrsJRRamsden)* 3-9-4 DHarrison(5) (s.i.s: hld up & bhd: effrt over 2f out: nvr nr to chal)....2 **5**
1250* Somerton Boy (IRE) **(72)***(71) (PCalver)* 5-9-13 SMaloney(1) (lw: w ldrs pllng hrd: rdn over 2f out: sn outpcd)....hd **6**
*1334** Souperficial **(55)***(51) (JAGlover)* 4-8-10v TIves(6) (hld up: effrt 3f out: no imp)....1½ **7**
1469[11] Dante's Rubicon (IRE) **(50)***(42) (JDBethell)* 4-8-2 (3)ow3 JTate(2) (trckd ldrs tl outpcd fnl 2f)....nk **8**

7/4 Glowing Jade, **3/1** Souperficial, **5/1** Kemo Sabo, **13/2** Somerton Boy (IRE), **8/1** ALLINSON'S MATE (IRE), **9/1** Grey Again, **14/1** Yoxall Lodge, **20/1** Dante's Rubicon (IRE), CSF £71.21 CT £913.12 TOTE £10.90: £2.50 £2.00 £3.30 (£57.20) OWNER Mr Peter Jones (THIRSK) BRED Gay O'Callaghan 8 Rn 1m 27.32 (3.92) SF: 43/17/32/42/29/37/17/8

WEIGHT FOR AGE 3yo-10lb

1604

INOVAR H'CAP (0-80) (4-Y.O+ F & M) (Class D) £5,952.00 (£1,776.00: £848.00: £384.00) **6f** Stalls: High GOING minus 0.20 sec per fur (GF) 3-20 (3-20)

1335[6] **Prima Silk (70)***(76) (MJRyan)* 4-9-6 TIves(9) (in tch: hdwy to ld over 1f out: r.o)....— **1**
1489[5] Magic Orb **(77)***(81) (JLHarris)* 5-9-13 JQuinn(4) (lw: in tch: hdwy to chal ins fnl f: nt qckn nr fin)....¾ **2**
1354[5] Macs Maharanee **(72)***(73)*(Fav)*(PSFelgate)* 8-9-8 JFanning(10) (disp ld: led over 2f out tl over 1f out: no ex)....1 **3**
1261* Silent Expression **(74)***(74) (BJMeehan)* 5-9-10 DHarrison(1) (disp ld tl wknd ins fnl f)....½ **4**
1376[4] Palo Blanco **(75)***(71) (TDBarron)* 4-9-11 JFortune(5) (lw: hld up: hdwy ½-wy: rdn & hung lft 2f out: nt qckn)....1½ **5**
*93** Nordan Raider **(72)***(60) (MJCamacho)* 7-9-8 DeanMcKeown(3) (stdd s: effrt ½-wy: no imp)....3 **6**
1304[3] I'm Your Lady **(75)***(59) (BAMcMahon)* 4-9-4 (7) MartinDwyer(6) (disp ld over 3f: grad wknd)....1½ **7**
1376[6] Rankaidade **(47)***(27) (DonEnricoIncisa)* 4-7-11 KimTinkler(7) (prom 4f: sn wknd)....1½ **8**
1434[7] Miss Aragon **(51)***(15) (MissLCSiddall)* 7-8-1 NCarlisle(2) (lw: in tch: effrt over 2f out: sn wknd)....6 **9**
1299[12] Petite-D-Argent **(78)***(39) (TDyer)* 6-10-0 StephenDavies(8) (disp ld over 3f: wknd)....1¼ **10**

7/2 Macs Maharanee, **4/1** Silent Expression, **9/2** Palo Blanco, **6/1** I'm Your Lady, **7/1** Nordan Raider, **8/1** PRIMA SILK, **10/1** Magic Orb, Miss Aragon, **20/1** Rankaidade, **33/1** Petite-D-Argent, CSF £79.43 CT £305.26 TOTE £14.40: £2.80 £2.90 £1.80 (£42.20) Trio £179.20 OWNER Three Ply Racing (NEWMARKET) BRED R. M. Scott 10 Rn

1m 13.06 (2.06) SF: 58/63/55/56/53/42/41/9/-/21

1605 STONES BITTER H'CAP (0-100) (3-Y.O) (Class C) £7,700.00 £2,300.00: £1,100.00: £500.00)

1m (round) Stalls: High GOING minus 0.20 sec per fur (GF) 4-15 (4-15)

1351[6] **Floridante (USA) (72)***(80) (PFICole)* 3-7-9 JQuinn(5) (lw: trckd ldrs: led over 2f out: qcknd clr: jst hld on)........— 1
1136* Hoh Express **(95)***(102) (IABalding)* 3-9-4 WNewnes(1) (lw: hld up & bhd: effrt 3f out: r.o wl fnl f: jst failed)........½ 2
1351[3] Out on a Promise (IRE) **(79)***(82)*(Fav)*(GWragg)* 3-8-2 NCarlisle(6) (lw: a.p: styd on fnl 2f: nt pce to chal)........2 3
1415[10] Carlito Brigante **(70)***(70) (MrsJRRamsden)* 3-7-7 NKennedy(2) (trckd ldrs: stdy hdwy over 3f out: one pce fnl 2f)........1½ 4
1180[15] Barrel of Hope **(77)***(69) (JLEyre)* 3-8-0 RLappin(7) (cl up: led 3f out: sn hdd: grad wknd)........4 5
1315[4] That Old Feeling (IRE) **(98)***(87) (RHannon)* 3-9-7 RPerham(3) (effrt 3f out: n.d)........1¾ 6
504[18] Last Roundup **(91)***(70) (CWThornton)* 3-9-0 DeanMcKeown(4) (led to 3f out: sn wknd)........5 7

5/2 Out on a Promise (IRE), **3/1** FLORIDANTE (USA), Hoh Express, **13/2** That Old Feeling (IRE), **9/1** Carlito Brigante, **10/1** Barrel of Hope, **16/1** Last Roundup, CSF £12.14 TOTE £3.50: £2.00 £2.00 (£5.60) OWNER Lord Donoughmore (WHATCOMBE) BRED John Hettinger 7 Rn

1m 39.45 (3.15) SF: 31/53/33/21/20/38/21

1606 WHITBY CLAIMING STKS (3-Y.O+) (Class E) £3,687.50 (£1,100.00: £525.00: £237.50) 1m 4f

Stalls: High GOING minus 0.20 sec per fur (GF) 4-45 (4-45)

1325[5] **Crowned Glory (USA) (65)***(70)*(Fav)*(PFICole)* 3-8-5 JFortune(2) (trckd ldr: led over 3f out: pushed clr 2f out: eased nr fin)........— 1
Fret (USA) *(67) (JSWainwright)* 5-9-5 DeanMcKeown(4) (lw: trckd ldrs: effrt 3f out: styd on: nvr able to chal)........¾ 2
1420[5] Balzino (USA) **(53)***(58) (NTinkler)* 6-9-3 KimTinkler(1) (bhd: hdwy 4f out: hung lft u.p 2f out: no imp)........5 3
1093[19] Pewter Lass **(45)***(19) (MBlanshard)* 3-7-9 JQuinn(3) (led tl over 3f out: sn outpcd)........25 4

10/11 CROWNED GLORY (USA), **9/4** Balzino (USA), **9/2** Fret (USA), **9/1** Pewter Lass, CSF £4.93 TOTE £1.70 (£2.70) OWNER Prince Fahd Salman (WHATCOMBE) BRED Charles Armstrong 4 Rn

2m 38.65 (8.05) SF: 21/34/25/-

WEIGHT FOR AGE 3yo-16lb

1607 GREAT YORKSHIRE GOLD H'CAP (0-70) (4-Y.O+) (Class E) £3,850.00 (£1,150.00: £550.00: £250.00)

2m 110y Stalls: Low GOING minus 0.20 sec per fur (GF) 5-20 (5-21)

1058[4] **Tarthooth (IRE) (62)***(73)*(Fav)*(CJBenstead)* 4-9-9 WNewnes(11) (trckd ldrs: led 3f out: r.o: eased wl ins fnl f)........— 1
1210[12] Fruitful Affair (IRE) **(40)***(49) (TThomsonJones)* 6-8-2 StephenDavies(10) (hld up & bhd: hdwy 4f out: styd on wl fnl f: no ch w wnr)........2 2
1058[3] Flashman **(37)***(46) (BJLlewellyn)* 5-7-13 TWilliams(8) (a cl up: led 4f out to 3f out: one pce)...½ 3
1328[4] Kadiri (IRE) **(59)***(67) (JRBosley)* 4-9-6 GBardwell(3) (outpcd 9f out: bhd tl r.o fnl 2f)........¾ 4
1156[4] Chief Minister (IRE) **(66)***(73) (TDyer)* 6-10-0 JFortune(6) (in tch: effrt over 3f out: sn rdn: styd on fnl f)........½ 5
1470* Snow Dream **(47)***(54) (MJRyan)* 5-8-4 (5) MBaird(4) (a.p: effrt 3f out: one pce)........½ 6
1310[4] Lord Hastie (USA) **(47)***(53) (CWThornton)* 7-8-9 DeanMcKeown(5) (hld up & bhd: hdwy over 3f out: effrt & hung lft 2f out: no imp after)........1 7
1328[8] Romalito **(48)***(50) (MBlanshard)* 5-8-10 JQuinn(7) (hld up: hdwy appr st: wknd fnl 3f)........4 8
929[10] Black Ice Boy (IRE) **(43)***(26) (RBastiman)* 4-8-4 ACulhane(2) (chsd ldrs tl wknd fnl 4f: t.o)....20 9
1319[3] Teoroma **(31)***(7) (DrJDScargill)* 5-7-7 NKennedy(9) (plld hrd: racd wd: prom to st: sn wl bhd: t.o)........7 10
Yaakum **(50)***(22) (SEKettlewell)* 6-8-9 (3) JTate(1) (led to 4f out: sn wknd: t.o)........4 11

LONG HANDICAP Teoroma 7-4

4/1 TARTHOOTH (IRE), **9/2** Chief Minister (IRE), Snow Dream (op 3/1), Kadiri (IRE), **6/1** Flashman, **8/1** Lord Hastie (USA), **12/1** Romalito, **14/1** Fruitful Affair (IRE), **16/1** Teoroma, **20/1** Black Ice Boy (IRE), Yaakum, CSF £56.88 CT £311.71 TOTE £4.40: £1.90 £5.10 £1.90 (£39.10) Trio £92.50 OWNER Mr Hamdan Al Maktoum (EPSOM) BRED Glen Barrow Farm 11 Rn

3m 39.17 (10.17) SF: 43/20/17/37/44/25/24/21/-/-/-

WEIGHT FOR AGE 4yo-1lb

T/Plpt: £1,132.00 (10.4 Tckts). T/Qdpt: £78.70 (2.2 Tckts). AA

1584-EPSOM (L-H)
Saturday June 10th (Good to firm becoming Firm)
WEATHER: dull WIND: almost nil

1608 VODATA WOODCOTE STKS (Listed) (2-Y.O) (Class A) £13,810.00 (£4,180.00: £2,040.00: £970.00)
6f Stalls: Low GOING minus 0.45 sec per fur (F) 2-00 (2-01)

1267* **Gothenberg (IRE)** *(92+) (MJohnston)* 2-9-0 DHolland(3) (4th st: led ins fnl f: r.o wl) ....— **1**
1104⁵ World Premier *(87) (CEBrittain)* 2-9-2 BDoyle(6) (3rd st: led over 2f out tl ins fnl f: r.o).........2½ **2**
*1212** Double Point (IRE) *(79) (MBell)* 2-9-0 MFenton(5) (2nd st: led over 3f out tl over 2f out: wknd fnl f) 2½ **3**
919* Lucky Lionel (USA) *(71)*(Fav)*(RHannon)* 2-9-0 MJKinane(4) (lw: 6th st: nvr nr to chal) 3 **4**
1399* Hever Golf Express *(64) (TJNaughton)* 2-8-11 PatEddery(2) (led over 2f) 1¼ **5**
849* Jolis Present *(58) (MJRyan)* 2-9-0 WCarson(1) (5th st: a bhd) 3½ **6**

11/8 Lucky Lionel (USA), **9/4** GOTHENBERG (IRE), **7/1** Hever Golf Express, **9/1** World Premier, **11/1** Jolis Present, **16/1** Double Point (IRE), CSF £18.41 TOTE £3.10: £1.70 £3.90 (£15.20) OWNER Brian Yeardley Continental Ltd (MIDDLEHAM) BRED Brownstown Stud Farm 6 Rn
69.38 secs (1.38) SF: 39/34/26/18/11/5

OFFICIAL EXPLANATION Lucky Lionel (USA): the jockey and trainer both stated that the colt did not act on the track.

1609 VODAFONE CORONATION CUP STKS (Gp 1) (4-Y.O+) (Class A) £92,520.00 (£34,309.75: £16,217.38: £6,777.87)
1m 4f 10y Stalls: Low GOING minus 0.45 sec per fur (F) 2-35 (2-36)

1387a* **Sunshack** *(126) (AFabre,France)* 4-9-0 PatEddery(2) (led 2f: 5th st: led over 1f out: hrd rdn: r.o wl) ....— **1**
913* Only Royale (IRE) **(119)***(123) (LMCumani)* 6-8-11 LDettori(7) (b.nr fore: 6th st: hdwy 2f out: ev ch fnl f: r.o).........hd **2**
913³ Time Star (USA) **(117)***(125) (PFICole)* 4-9-0 TQuinn(5) (led 8f out tl over 1f out: r.o one pce) 1 **3**
913² Tikkanen (USA) *(122)*(Fav)*(JEPease,France)* 4-9-0 CAsmussen(3) (lw: last st: hdwy 2f out: nvr nr to chal) 2 **4**
Carnegie (IRE) *(120) (AFabre,France)* 4-9-0 TJarnet(1) (lw: 4th st: rdn 3f out: one pce fnl 2f).........1½ **5**
1262² Ionio (USA) **(114)***(111) (CEBrittain)* 4-9-0 MRoberts(6) (lw: led after 2f to 8f out: 3rd st: wknd over 2f out).........7 **6**
1235a³ Environment Friend **(115)***(109) (GRimmer)* 7-9-0 MJKinane(4) (lw: 2nd st: wknd over 2f out) 1½ **7**

5/2 Tikkanen (USA), **11/4** Only Royale (IRE), Carnegie (IRE), **10/1** SUNSHACK, **11/1** Time Star (USA), **16/1** Environment Friend, **33/1** Ionio (USA), CSF £33.63 TOTE £8.60: £3.10 £2.30 (£16.20) OWNER Mr K. Abdullah (FRANCE) BRED Juddmonte Farms 7 Rn
2m 35.85 (0.85) SF: 58/55/57/54/52/43/41

1610 VODAC RATED STKS H'CAP (0-105) (4-Y.O+) (Class B) £21,200.90 (£7,933.10: £3,879.05: £1,667.75: £746.38: £377.82)
1m 2f 18y Stalls: Low GOING minus 0.45 sec per fur (F) 3-05 (3-06)

1357³ **Burooj (95)***(106)*(Fav)*(DMorley)* 5-8-5 WCarson(10) (7th st: plld out 2f out: qcknd to ld 1f out: r.o wl) ....— **1**
1225⁹ Aljazzaf **(95)***(104)*(Fav)*(RAkehurst)* 5-8-5 TQuinn(4) (lw: 2nd st: led over 3f out to 1f out: r.o) 1 **2**
Mystic Hill **(90)***(98) (RCharlton)* 4-7-11 (3) SSanders(1) (6th st: nt clr run 2f out: swtchd rt: r.o wl fnl f) 1 **3**
1188³ Embankment (IRE) **(90)***(97) (RHannon)* 5-8-0 MRoberts(6) (4th st: nt clr run 2f out & 1f out: nt rcvr) ....½ **4**
1005a⁴ Cedez le Passage (FR) **(100)***(104) (CEBrittain)* 4-8-10 TJarnet(9) (3rd st: one pce fnl 2f) 1¾ **5**
Saibot (USA) **(95)***(98) (DKWeld,Ireland)* 6-8-5 ow1 MJKinane(7) (lw: 8th st: nrst fin) ....½ **6**
1108⁸ Cotteir Chief (IRE) **(104)***(107) (MCPipe)* 4-9-0 PatEddery(2) (last st: nvr nrr)..........hd **7**
1135* Sherman (IRE) **(96)***(97)*(Fav)*(HThomsonJones)* 4-8-6b RHills(8) (5th st: wknd over 2f out) 1½ **8**
634¹⁸ Zermatt (IRE) **(90)***(78) (MDIUsher)* 5-8-0 RPrice(5) (led tl hdd & wknd over 3f out) 8 **9**
LONG HANDICAP Embankment (IRE) 7-10 Mystic Hill 7-9 Zermatt (IRE) 6-4

4/1 BUROOJ, Aljazzaf, Sherman (IRE), **6/1** Cotteir Chief (IRE), Saibot (USA), **10/1** Mystic Hill, Embankment (IRE), **33/1** Cedez le Passage (FR), **100/1** Zermatt (IRE), CSF £18.15 CT £124.93 TOTE £3.10: £1.40 £1.80 £2.40 (£8.10) Trio £26.00 OWNER Mr Hamdan Al Maktoum (NEWMARKET) BRED Shadwell Estate Company Limited 9 Rn 2m 7.05 (3.05) SF: 29/27/21/20/27/21/30/20/1

1611

VODAFONE DERBY STKS (Gp 1) (3-Y.O C & F) (Class A)
£504,500.00 (£190,000.00: £92,250.00: £41,250.00)
1m 4f 10y Stalls: Low GOING minus 0.45 sec per fur (F) 3-50 (3-54)

Lammtarra (USA) *(123) (SbinSuroor)* 3-9-0 WRSwinburn(7) (lw: hdwy & 8th st: str run fnl 2f: led cl home) — **1**
1129* Tamure (IRE) **(111)***(122) (JHMGosden)* 3-9-0 LDettori(13) (3rd st: led ins fnl f tl hdd nr fin) 1 **2**
1107³ Presenting **(115)***(121) (JHMGosden)* 3-9-0 CAsmussen(2) (5th st: hrd rdn fnl 2f: r.o ins fnl f) ¾ **3**
1224³ Fahal (USA) **(112)***(119) (DMorley)* 3-9-0 RHills(12) (led 4f out tl ins fnl f) 1¼ **4**
1396a² Court of Honour (IRE) **(109)***(119) (PWChapple-Hyam)* 3-9-0 BThomson(15) (led over 4f out: sn hdd: 2nd st: r.o one pce) s.h **5**
1117a* Vettori (IRE) *(115) (SbinSuroor)* 3-9-0 RCochrane(9) (11th st: nrst fin) 3 **6**
1068² Riyadian **(111)***(115) (PFICole)* 3-9-0 TQuinn(8) (lw: 4th st: wknd 2f out) hd **7**
1113a* Humbel (USA) *(114) (DKWeld,Ireland)* 3-9-0 MJKinane(6) (12th st: hdwy 3f out: one pce fnl 2f) nk **8**
1068* Munwar **(116)***(105) (PTWalwyn)* 3-9-0 WCarson(3) (7th st: wknd over 2f out) 7 **9**
1107⁶ Salmon Ladder (USA) **(104)***(97) (PFICole)* 3-9-0 KDarley(1) (lw: hmpd & lost pl after 3f: 13th st) 6 **10**
920* Pennekamp (USA) *(96)*(Fav)*(AFabre,France)* 3-9-0 TJarnet(5) (lw: 9th st: rdn 3f out: no rspnse: fin lame) 1 **11**
1170* Korambi **(93)***(81) (CEBrittain)* 3-9-0 MRoberts(14) (lw: prom 6f: 14th st) 11 **12**
1234a* Spectrum (IRE) *(81) (PWChapple-Hyam)* 3-9-0 JReid(4) (lw: 10th st: a bhd: lame) nk **13**
1338³ Daffaq **(73)***(80) (PTWalwyn)* 3-9-0 BRouse(11) (lw: led 1f: 15th st: broke leg: dead) nk **14**
1103² Maralinga (IRE) **(98)***(54) (MBell)* 3-9-0 MFenton(10) (led after 1f tl over 4f out: 6th st: t.o) 20 **15**

11/8 Pennekamp (USA), **5/1** Spectrum (IRE) (7/2-11/2), **8/1** Munwar, **9/1** Tamure (IRE), **12/1** Presenting, **14/1** LAMMTARRA (USA), **16/1** Riyadian, **20/1** Vettori (IRE), **25/1** Humbel (USA), **50/1** Fahal (USA), Salmon Ladder (USA), **66/1** Court of Honour (IRE), **150/1** Korambi, **200/1** Maralinga (IRE), **500/1** Daffaq, CSF £116.16 TOTE £13.40: £2.90 £1.90 £2.70 (£49.70) Trio £129.80 OWNER Mr Saeed Maktoum Al Maktoum (NEWMARKET) BRED Gainsborough Farm Inc. in USA 15 Rn
2m 32.31 (1.00 under best) (-2.69) SF: 81/80/79/77/77/73/73/72/63/55/54/39/39/38/12
OFFICIAL EXPLANATION **Pennekamp (USA): the jockey reported that the colt appeared to lose his action at the three-furlong pole, and believed him to have gone lame.**

1612

PAKNET 'TOTE DIRECT' APPRENTICE H'CAP (0-90) (4-Y.O+) (Class C) £10,747.50 (£3,255.00: £1,590.00: £757.50)
1m 4f 10y Stalls: Low GOING minus 0.45 sec per fur (F) 4-30 (4-39)

762¹¹ **Global Dancer (63)***(78) (SDow)* 4-8-5 (3) ADaly(14) (mde all: r.o wl) — **1**
1144⁸ Artic Courier **(76)***(86) (DJSCosgrove)* 4-9-7 DGibbs(11) (7th st: hdwy fnl 2f: r.o) 4 **2**
1314² Benfleet **(78)***(87) (RWArmstrong)* 4-9-9 SLanigan(12) (lw: wl bhd tl gd hdwy fnl 3f) ¾ **3**
1410⁴ Tony's Fen **(74)***(83) (DRCElsworth)* 6-9-2 (3) AProcter(7) (b.hind: hdwy 2f out: rdn over 1f out: one pce) hd **4**
1109¹¹ Charity Crusader **(82)***(90) (PWChapple-Hyam)* 4-9-10b(3) RHavlin(9) (2nd st: wknd over 1f out) hd **5**
1347* Ball Gown **(73)***(79) (DTThom)* 5-9-4 DRMcCabe(5) (rdn over 2f out: hdwy over 1f out: r.o) 1¾ **6**
1243⁶ Flight Lieutenant (USA) **(74)***(80) (RHannon)* 6-9-2 (3) DaneO'Neill(8) (lw: nvr nrr) nk **7**
1367⁴ Tondres (USA) **(71)***(72) (RIngram)* 4-9-2b SDrowne(10) (4th st: wknd 2f out) 3½ **8**
1410² Dancing Sensation (USA) **(65)***(64) (RAkehurst)* 8-8-7 (3) SSanders(6) (6th st: hdwy over 2f out: wknd over 1f out) 1¼ **9**
Sheriff **(62)***(53) (JWHills)* 4-8-4 (3) MHenry(4) (nvr nr ldrs) 6 **10**
1048* Bajan (IRE) **(62)***(50)*(Fav)*(LadyHerries)* 4-8-4 (3) JO'Dwyer(13) (b.hind: 3rd st: wknd 2f out) 2½ **11**
1243⁵ Endless Light (USA) **(80)***(67) (PFICole)* 4-9-4 (7) DavidO'Neill(2) (5th st: wknd 3f out) 1 **12**
1313⁶ Lunar Risk **(48)***(30) (MissBSanders)* 5-7-3 (4) CarolineHovington(3) (a bhd) 3½ **13**
*1075*⁸ Surprise Guest (IRE) **(58)***(40) (APJames)* 4-8-3 CTeague(1) (lw: bhd fnl 6f) nk **14**

LONG HANDICAP Lunar Risk 6-12

4/1 Bajan (IRE) (3/1-9/2), **9/2** Dancing Sensation (USA), **5/1** Ball Gown, **15/2** Benfleet, **8/1** Tony's Fen, **10/1** Tondres (USA), **12/1** Endless Light (USA), **14/1** Flight Lieutenant (USA), **16/1** Artic Courier, Charity Crusader, **20/1** Sheriff, GLOBAL DANCER, **50/1** Lunar Risk, Surprise Guest (IRE), CSF £276.85 CT £2,369.58 TOTE £40.40: £7.20 £5.00 £3.00 (£296.40) Trio £509.50 OWNER Cornish Arms-Charmandean Investments Plc (EPSOM) BRED C. J. R. Trotter 14 Rn
2m 34.76 (-0.24) SF: 59/67/68/64/71/60/61/53/45/34/31/48/11/21

1613 VODACOM CONDITIONS STKS (3-Y.O) (Class B) £12,752.00 (£3,464.00: £3,464.00: £980.00: £440.00)
7f Stalls: Low GOING minus 0.45 sec per fur (F) 5-00 (5-06)

1138⁵ **Silca Blanka (IRE) (103)**_(104) (MRChannon)_ 3-9-1 KDarley(1) (3rd st: led over 1f out: drvn out) ....— 1
920¹¹ Green Perfume (USA) **(121)**_(105)_(Fav)_(PFICole)_ 3-9-5 TQuinn(5) (5th st: hdwy over 2f out: rdn over 1f out: nt qckn fnl f) 1¼ 2
1227⁵ Signs **(93)**_(95) (RHannon)_ 3-8-9 MRoberts(2) (led tl over 1f out: kpt on wl) ....d.h 2
1146* Smart Guest **(98)**_(98) (JAHarris)_ 3-9-5 MFenton(3) (lw: 2nd st: ev ch 2f out: wknd fnl f) 3 4
1370⁴ Great Bear **(97)**_(86) (RFJohnsonHoughton)_ 3-8-12b JReid(4) (lw: 4th st: wknd 2f out) 2½ 5

5/4 Green Perfume (USA) (op 4/5), **5/2** SILCA BLANKA (IRE), **7/1** Great Bear, **8/1** Smart Guest, **10/1** Signs, CSF £2.75 SB & GP, £9.67 SB & S TOTE £3.10: £1.50 £0.70 GP £1.00 S (£0.90 SB & GP, £4.90 SB & S) OWNER Mr P. D. Savill (UPPER LAMBOURN) BRED Luzi S P A in Ireland 5 Rn
1m 22.42 (2.12) SF: 34/35/25/28/16

1614 VODAPAGE H'CAP (0-100) (3-Y.O+) (Class C) £17,668.75 (£5,350.00: £2,612.50: £1,243.75) **6f** Stalls: Low GOING minus 0.45 sec per fur (F) 5-30 (5-33)

1106² **Saddlehome (USA) (77)**_(82) (TDBarron)_ 6-8-12 KDarley(6) (hdwy 2f out: hrd rdn fnl f: led cl home) ....— 1
1335* Thatcherella **(75)**_(79)_(Fav)_(MajorDNChappell)_ 4-8-10 BThomson(3) (led: clr over 1f out: hdd nr fin) ....nk 2
1261⁴ Shikari's Son **(87)**_(87) (JWhite)_ 8-9-8 MFenton(7) (gd hdwy fnl 2f: nvr nrr) 1½ 3
1316¹⁰ Rock Symphony **(91)**_(88) (WJHaggas)_ 5-9-12 JReid(8) (lw: hdwy over 2f out: rdn over 1f out: r.o) 1¼ 4
1241⁴ My Best Valentine **(85)**_(81) (JWhite)_ 5-9-6b FNorton(11) (lw: 8th st: styd on fnl 2f) ....½ 5
1508⁸ Craigie Boy **(61)**_(56) (NBycroft)_ 5-7-10b AMackay(14) (2nd st: wknd over 1f out) ....nk 6
1411¹⁰ Gone Savage **(63)**_(56) (WJMusson)_ 7-7-12 AMcGlone(2) (7th st: no hdwy fnl 2f) ....¾ 7
934⁵ Domulla **(90)**_(79) (RAkehurst)_ 5-9-11 TQuinn(9) (6th st: wknd 2f out) 1¼ 8
1354* Join the Clan **(89)**_(75) (MrsNMacauley)_ 6-9-10 MRoberts(4) (plld hrd: 5th st: wknd 2f out) 1¼ 9
1174² Colway Rake **(71)**_(57) (JWWatts)_ 4-8-6b WCarson(1) (lw: 4th st: wknd 2f out) ....s.h 10
1241² No Extras (IRE) **(91)**_(77) (GLMoore)_ 5-9-12 BRouse(10) (a bhd) ....s.h 11
1316³ Mister Jolson **(86)**_(67) (RJHodges)_ 6-9-2 (5) SDrowne(13) (a bhd) 2 12
743⁴ Coffee 'n Cream **(85)**_(55) (RHannon)_ 3-8-11 MJKinane(15) (9th st: wknd 3f out) 4 13
1550⁹ Solo Prize **(71)**_(30) (PHowling)_ 3-7-4b(7)ow4 SLanigan(5) (3rd st: wknd 3f out) 2½ 14
1411¹⁵ Green Golightly (USA) **(70)** _(DAWilson)_ 4-8-5 NGwilliams(12) (p.u 4f out: lame) .... P

LONG HANDICAP Solo Prize 7-5

4/1 Thatcherella, **11/2** Join the Clan, **6/1** Colway Rake, **7/1** SADDLEHOME (USA), **8/1** Domulla, **9/1** Shikari's Son, **10/1** No Extras (IRE), Mister Jolson, **11/1** Coffee 'n Cream, **16/1** My Best Valentine, **20/1** Gone Savage, Rock Symphony, Craigie Boy, **33/1** Green Golightly (USA), **40/1** Solo Prize, CSF £36.42 CT £247.97 TOTE £7.80: £2.50 £2.20 £3.30 (£18.00) Trio £75.80 OWNER Mr Kevin Shaw (THIRSK) BRED Saddle Home Farm in USA 15 Rn
69.15 secs (1.15) SF: 40/37/45/46/39/14/14/37/33/15/35/25/4/-/-
WEIGHT FOR AGE 3yo-9lb

T/Jkpt: Not won; £128,203.69 to Epsom 11/6/95. T/Plpt: £528.60 (139.99 Tckts). T/Qdpt: £97.50 (9.15 Tckts). Hn

1596-HAYDOCK (L-H)
Saturday June 10th (Good)
WEATHER: overcast WIND: slt half against

1615 HALSALL MAIDEN STKS (3-Y.O) (Class D) £3,935.00 (£1,190.00: £580.00: £275.00) **1m 30y** Stalls: Low GOING: minus 0.18 sec per fur (GF) 2-10 (2-11)

Hamsaat (IRE) _(88+)_(Fav)_(BHanbury)_ 3-8-9 WRyan(9) (w'like: leggy: b: s.i.s: hld up: 6th st: hdwy 3f out: led bel dist: r.o wl) ....— 1
1101⁴ Sparrowhawk (IRE) **(95)**_(83) (BWHills)_ 3-8-9 JWeaver(8) (chsd ldr: 2nd st: ev ch over 1f out: one pce) 2½ 2
1186¹⁴ Karaar _(83) (JHMGosden)_ 3-9-0 GHind(7) (bit bkwd: dwlt: hld up: 7th st: rdn wl over 1f out: kpt on ins fnl f) 2½ 3
Monument _(80) (RCharlton)_ 3-9-0 TSprake(4) (lengthy: bit bkwd: chsd ldrs: 4th st: shkn up 2f out: nt pce to chal) 1½ 4
1150³ Northern Trove (USA) _(74) (GMMoore)_ 3-9-0 MTebbutt(1) (led tl hdd bel dist: wknd fnl f) 3 5

777[8] Mithraic (IRE) *(67) (JWWatts)* 3-9-0 NConnorton(5) (hld up: effrt 3f out: nvr trbld ldrs) 3½ 6
Barranak (IRE) *(62) (MrsMMcCourt)* 3-9-0 PRobinson(2) (w'like: str: bkwd: chsd ldrs: 3rd st: wknd 2f out) 3 7
1308[6] Coryana Dancer (IRE) *(29) (RHollinshead)* 3-8-9 PaulEddery(3) (lw: s.s: a bhd: t.o fnl 3f) 14 8
Tryph *(19) (JBerry)* 3-8-9 JCarroll(6) (b.hind: 5th st: lost tch 3f out: t.o) 5 9

2/1 HAMSAAT (IRE), **9/4** Sparrowhawk (IRE) (op 6/4), **5/1** Northern Trove (USA), **8/1** Monument, **10/1** Karaar, **12/1** Coryana Dancer (IRE) (op 8/1), **16/1** Mithraic (IRE), **25/1** Tryph, **33/1** Barranak (IRE), CSF £7.05 TOTE £3.50: £1.40 £1.30 £3.20 (£3.60) Trio £21.20 OWNER Mr Hamdan Al Maktoum (NEWMARKET) BRED The Mount Coote Partnership 9 Rn

1m 43.42 (3.02) SF: 49/44/44/41/35/28/23/-/-

1616 SUNDAY EXPRESS BEST FOR SPORT SERIES (QUALIFIER) H'CAP (0-85) (3-Y.O+) (Class D) £3,675.00 (£1,110.00: £540.00: £255.00)
1m 2f 120y Stalls: High GOING minus 0.18 sec per fur (GF) 2-40 (2-40)

1314[3] **My Learned Friend (71)***(83) (AHide)* 4-9-0 JWilliams(1) (hld up: 4th st: hdwy to chal bel dist: rdn to ld wl ins fnl f) ....— 1
1378[*] Colorful Ambition **(68)***(80) (MrsASwinbank)* 5-8-11 NConnorton(3) (chsd ldrs: 5th st: led over 2f out tl wl ins fnl f) ....nk 2
1415[9] Western General **(79)***(88) (MissSEHall)* 4-9-8 PRobinson(6) (hld up: 6th st: hdwy over 2f out: sn ev ch: rdn & one pce fnl f) 2 3
563[8] Adolescence (IRE) **(81)***(89) (KMcAuliffe)* 5-9-10 MTebbutt(5) (bit bkwd: hdwy on ins over 2f out: rdn & one pce ins fnl f) ....hd 4
Redstella (USA) **(72)***(75) (RMWhitaker)* 6-9-1 DaleGibson(2) (bkwd: led 1f: 3rd st: rdn & outpcd 3f out: styd on u.p fnl f) 3½ 5
1141[9] Windrush Lady **(73)***(76) (MMcCormack)* 5-9-2 MPerrett(8) (lw: a.p: 2nd st: wknd wl over 1f out) ....s.h 6
1128[2] Gloriana **(75)***(70) (LadyHerries)* 3-8-3 WRyan(9) (led after 1f tl hdd over 2f out: sn btn) 5 7
1378[8] Beaumont (IRE) **(66)***(61)*(Fav)*(JPearce)* 5-8-9 JWeaver(4) (hld up & bhd: effrt & hrd drvn 3f out: no imp) ....nk 8
Colway Rock (USA) **(78)***(65) (JWWatts)* 5-9-7 GDuffield(7) (bit bkwd: hld up: effrt on outside 3f out: no imp: t.o) 5 9

4/1 Beaumont (IRE), **9/2** Gloriana, Colorful Ambition, **5/1** MY LEARNED FRIEND, **8/1** Western General, **9/1** Windrush Lady, **12/1** Colway Rock (USA), **20/1** Redstella (USA), Adolescence (IRE), CSF £24.73 CT £153.41 TOTE £4.70: £1.60 £1.80 £3.60 (£9.70) Trio £39.90 OWNER Mrs J. Roberts (NEWMARKET) BRED A. D. G. Oldrey 9 Rn

2m 14.0 (2.50) SF: 65/62/70/71/57/58/37/43/47
WEIGHT FOR AGE 3yo-15lb

1617 ROTHMANS ROYALS NORTH SOUTH CHALLENGE SERIES H'CAP (0-100) (3-Y.O+) (Class C) £7,103.00 (£2,144.00: £1,042.00: £491.00)
1m 30y Stalls: Low GOING minus 0.18 sec per fur (GF) 3-15 (3-16)

1299[4] **Celestial Key (USA) (93)***(103) (MJohnston)* 5-10-0 PRobinson(4) (lw: hld up: hdwy over 2f out: led ins fnl f: drvn out) ....— 1
1183[13] Samba Sharply **(73)***(81) (AHide)* 4-8-8 JWilliams(2) (hld up: 4th st: chal 1f out: unable qckn towards fin) 1¼ 2
1409[3] Band on the Run **(86)***(91) (BAMcMahon)* 8-9-7 JWeaver(5) (lw: a.p: 3rd st: led over 2f out tl ins fnl f) 1½ 3
1415[2] Sandmoor Chambray **(74)***(77) (MHEasterby)* 4-8-9b MBirch(1) (lw: led tl hdd over 2f out: rdn & ev ch fnl f: unable qckn) ....¾ 4
1415[7] Forever Diamonds **(85)***(88) (MHEasterby)* 8-9-6 JCarroll(12) (hld up: hdwy on ins over 2f out: nt clr run bel dist: kpt on) ....hd 5
1143[10] Gymcrak Premiere **(87)***(89) (GHolmes)* 7-9-8 GDuffield(7) (b.nr hind: hld up & bhd: rdn 3f out: kpt on appr fnl f) ....nk 6
1468[3] Celestial Choir **(76)***(78)*(Fav)*(JLEyre)* 5-8-11 SDWilliams(10) (hld up in rr: r.o appr fnl f: nvr nrr) ....s.h 7
785[13] Leif the Lucky (USA) **(81)***(82) (MissSEHall)* 6-9-2 NConnorton(8) (hld up: 6th st: wknd bel dist) ....¾ 8
1280[8] Master Beveled **(84)***(78) (PDEvans)* 5-9-5 PaulEddery(11) (lw: hdwy & 2nd st: wknd wl over 1f out) 3½ 9
1326[*] Brave Princess **(72)***(65) (MAJarvis)* 3-7-10 DaleGibson(6) (chsd ldrs: 5th st: wknd over 2f out) ....½ 10
1130[13] In Good Faith **(78)***(69) (JJQuinn)* 3-8-2 ow1 GHind(3) (a bhd) ....½ 11
1351[8] Misty Silks **(74)***(40) (MJRyan)* 5-8-9 AClark(9) (a in rr: t.o) 13 12

5/1 Celestial Choir, **11/2** Samba Sharply, **6/1** Band on the Run, **13/2** Leif the Lucky (USA), **8/1** Sandmoor Chambray, Brave Princess, **9/1** CELESTIAL KEY (USA), Master Beveled, **10/1** Misty Silks, **12/1** Forever Diamonds, **14/1** Gymcrak Premiere, **20/1** In Good Faith, CSF £58.35 CT £303.80 TOTE £13.00: £4.00 £3.30 £2.20 (£56.40) Trio £215.20 OWNER Mr M. J. Brodrick (MIDDLEHAM) BRED Pillar Stud Inc 12 Rn 1m 43.11 (2.71) SF: 70/48/58/44/55/56/45/49/45/21/25/7
WEIGHT FOR AGE 3yo-11lb

1618 FIRSTEEL GROUP JOHN OF GAUNT STKS (Listed) (3-Y.O+) (Class A) £14,070.00 (£4,260.00: £2,080.00: £990.00)
7f 30y Stalls: Low GOING minus 0.18 sec per fur (GF) 4-10 (4-14)

1187[4] **Mutakddim (USA) (111)***(114) (JHMGosden)* 4-8-12 GHind(8) (hld up gng wl: 5th st: led appr fnl f: r.o) ....— 1
1284[4] Carranita (IRE) **(101)***(108) (BPalling)* 5-8-7 TSprake(2) (a.p: 3rd st: led wl over 1f out tl appr fnl f: rallied cl home) ....nk 2
1227[2] Everglades (IRE) **(105)***(108) (RCharlton)* 7-8-12 PaulEddery(6) (lw: hld up: 6th st: hdwy wl over 1f out: r.o) 2½ 3
1185* Inzar (USA) **(108)***(104) (PFICole)* 3-8-2 AClark(5) (hld up: 4th st: ev ch 2f out: rdn & one pce fnl f) 1½ 4
1488[2] Branston Abby (IRE) **(107)***(98) (MJohnston)* 6-8-12 JWeaver(4) (hld up: effrt & rdn 2f out: nvr plcd to chal) 3 5
1482[3] Jafeica (IRE) **(96)***(86) (RHannon)* 4-8-12 JCarroll(3) (lw: 2nd st: led over 2f out: sn hdd: rdn & btn appr fnl f) 5 6
1108[10] Moccasin Run (USA) **(102)***(83) (IABalding)* 4-9-3b MHills(1) (led: sn wl clr: wknd & hdd over 2f out: sn bhd) 4 7
1108* Jawaal **(102)***(71)*(Fav)*(LadyHerries)* 5-9-3 WRyan(7) (lw: unruly s: s.s: a bhd) 5 8

11/4 Jawaal, **3/1** MUTAKDDIM (USA), **9/2** Branston Abby (IRE), **5/1** Inzar (USA), **11/2** Everglades (IRE), **10/1** Carranita (IRE), **20/1** Moccasin Run (USA), **25/1** Jafeica (IRE), CSF £30.02 TOTE £3.60: £1.30 £3.60 £1.50 (£48.80) OWNER Mr Hamdan Al Maktoum (NEWMARKET) BRED Deer Lawn Farm, Carloss and Lamont in USA 8 Rn 1m 28.39 (1.09) SF: 69/63/63/49/53/41/38/26
WEIGHT FOR AGE 3yo-10lb
STEWARDS' ENQUIRY Sprake susp. 19 & 23/6/95 (excessive use of whip).

1619 DOUGLAS RATED STKS H'CAP (0-95) (3-Y.O) (Class B) £7,937.70 (£2,964.30: £1,444.65: £615.75: £270.38: £132.22)
1m 2f 120y Stalls: High GOING minus 0.18 sec per fur (GF) 4-40 (4-40)

1322[7] **Romios (IRE) (83)***(90) (PFICole)* 3-8-5 CRutter(2) (lw: hld up & bhd: 6th st: hdwy on outside 2f out: str run to ld cl home) ....— 1
1103[4] Taipan (IRE) **(89)***(96) (JLDunlop)* 3-8-11 JWeaver(7) (lw: dwlt: led after 1f: sn hdd: 2nd st: led over 2f out: hrd rdn & ct nr fin) ....nk 2
941* Francfurter **(78)***(81)*(Fav)*(RCharlton)* 3-8-0 TSprake(3) (lw: hld up: 5th st: hdwy 2f out: ev ch over 1f out: unable qckn) 2½ 3
1299[7] Sticks and Stones (IRE) **(82)***(83) (MrsJCecil)* 3-8-4 PaulEddery(6) (lw: a.p: 3rd st: ev ch 1f out: rdn & outpcd nr fin) 1 4
1351* Clifton Fox **(84)***(78) (JAGlover)* 3-8-6 MBirch(1) (led 1f: 4th st: rdn 3f out: sn btn) 5 5
775[8] Made in Heaven **(83)***(57) (JWHills)* 3-8-5 MHills(5) (led after 2f: sn clr: wknd & hdd over 2f out: t.o) 13 6
1211[2] Heathyards Rock **(95)***(61) (RHollinshead)* 3-9-3 WRyan(4) (hld up & bhd: 7th st: lost tch over 2f out: t.o) 5 7

LONG HANDICAP Francfurter 7-13

11/4 Francfurter, **7/2** Taipan (IRE), Clifton Fox, **6/1** Sticks and Stones (IRE), **7/1** ROMIOS (IRE), **8/1** Heathyards Rock, **14/1** Made in Heaven, CSF £29.83 TOTE £14.40: £3.50 £2.20 (£23.30) OWNER Mr C. Shiacolas (WHATCOMBE) BRED Gay O'Callaghan in Ireland 7 Rn
2m 13.72 (2.22) SF: 59/65/50/52/47/26/30

1620 E.B.F. LEYLAND MAIDEN STKS (2-Y.O) (Class D) £4,162.50 (£1,260.00: £615.00: £292.50) **5f** Stalls: High GOING minus 0.18 sec per fur (GF) 5-15 (5-16)

Blue Iris *(74) (MAJarvis)* 2-8-9 PRobinson(8) (lt-f: unf: mde all stands' side: hrd drvn fnl f: r.o wl) ....— 1
Bollin Joanne *(70) (MHEasterby)* 2-8-9 MBirch(7) (lt-f: a.p: effrt appr fnl f: unable qckn) 1¼ 2
1341[2] Evening Chime (USA) *(75) (MrsJRRamsden)* 2-9-0 JWeaver(2) (lw: chsd ldrs: effrt over 1f out: kpt on u.p) ....hd 3
1246[2] Dashing Blue *(72) (IABalding)* 2-9-0 WRyan(3) (bit bkwd: chsd ldrs: hdwy & ev ch ent fnl f: rdn & no ex) 1 4

Domino Flyer *(52) (MrsASwinbank)* 2-9-0 NConnorton(9) (w'like: hld up: n.m.r ½-wy: r.o appr fnl f: nvr nrr)....6 5
Ron's Gem *(46) (WWHaigh)* 2-9-0 DaleGibson(6) (lt-f: unf: s.s: a bhd & outpcd)....2 6
Sepoy (IRE) *(45) (CWThornton)* 2-9-0 MTebbutt(4) (b: leggy: lt-f: lw: chsd ldrs over 3f)....nk 7
1247² Larghetto (IRE) *(34)*(Fav)*(JBerry)* 2-9-0b JCarroll(5) (lw: plld hrd: spd 3f)....3½ 8
Islay Brown (IRE) *(21) (CWCElsey)* 2-8-9 GDuffield(1) (w'like: bkwd: s.s: a bhd & outpcd) ..2½ 9

11/4 Larghetto (IRE), **3/1** Dashing Blue (op 2/1), **4/1** Bollin Joanne (6/1-7/2), **5/1** Evening Chime (USA) (op 3/1), **6/1** BLUE IRIS, **20/1** Islay Brown (IRE), **25/1** Sepoy (IRE), **33/1** Domino Flyer, Ron's Gem, CSF £28.48 TOTE £7.70: £2.00 £1.60 £1.70 (£12.00) Trio £36.00 OWNER Mr M. A. Jarvis (NEWMARKET) BRED North Cheshire Trading and Storage Ltd 9 Rn
61.51 secs (2.51) SF: 36/32/37/34/14/8/7/-/-

1621

PENNY LANE H'CAP (0-90) (4-Y.O+) (Class C) £5,784.00 (£1,752.00: £856.00: £408.00)
1m 6f Stalls: Low GOING minus 0.18 sec per fur (GF) 5-45 (5-45)

506³ **Purple Splash (78)***(90) (PJMakin)* 5-9-3b AClark(8) (hld up & bhd: 7th st: hdwy on ins 2f out: styd on to ld ins fnl f)....— 1
Dover Patrol (IRE) **(89)***(100) (HRACecil)* 5-10-0 WRyan(4) (b: bit bkwd: chsd ldrs: 4th st: rdn & kpt on wl towards fin)....1¼ 2
1300⁴ Midyan Blue (IRE) **(72)***(82) (JMPEustace)* 5-8-11 MTebbutt(1) (led tl hdd over 2f out: ev ch 1f out: one pce)....nk 3
1303² Swallows Dream (IRE) **(83)***(92)*(Fav)*(JLDunlop)* 4-9-8 JWeaver(5) (chsd ldr: 2nd st: led over 2f out tl hdd & no ex ins fnl f)....¾ 4
956* Slasher Jack (IRE) **(81)***(88) (SGNorton)* 4-9-6 PRobinson(6) (hld up: 6th st: hdwy 3f out: sn rdn: kpt on one pce)....2½ 5
1268⁵ Cumbrian Rhapsody **(67)***(56) (MHEasterby)* 5-8-6 MBirch(3) (lw: hdwy ½-wy: 3rd st: rdn 2f out: sn wknd: t.o)....15 6
Robingo (IRE) **(87)***(71) (MrsLAMurphy)* 6-9-12b DaleGibson(7) (bit bkwd: hld up: 5th st: wknd over 2f out: t.o)....5 7
821⁴ White Willow **(67)** *(MrsMReveley)* 6-8-6v NConnorton(2) (uns rdr over 9f out).... U

4/1 Swallows Dream (IRE), **9/2** Midyan Blue (IRE), Cumbrian Rhapsody, **5/1** Dover Patrol (IRE), **11/2** Slasher Jack (IRE), White Willow, **12/1** PURPLE SPLASH, **20/1** Robingo (IRE), CSF £64.97 CT £284.67 TOTE £16.30: £2.90 £2.10 £1.80 (£39.70) OWNER Mr Christopher Walford (MARLBOROUGH) BRED W. and R. Barnett Ltd 8 Rn 3m 4.07 (5.87) SF: 54/64/46/56/52/20/35/-

T/Plpt: £303.40 (58.69 Tckts). T/Qdpt: £67.10 (2.15 Tckts). IM

1484-NEWMARKET (R-H)
Saturday June 10th (Good)

WEATHER: fine WIND: nil

1622

NEWMARKET LADIES DERBY AMATEUR H'CAP (0-60) (4-Y.O+) (Class F) £5,049.00 (£1,512.00: £726.00: £333.00)
1m 4f (July) Stalls: High GOING minus 0.40 sec per fur (F) 6-40 (6-46)

1513⁵ **Casual Water (IRE) (48)***(56) (AGNewcombe)* 4-10-4 (5) MissFBurke(7) (mid div: hdwy over 2f out: led over 1f out: pushed out)....— 1
Katie's Kid **(30)***(33) (MJAhern)* 5-9-0 (5) MissEFolkes(9) (b: hdwy ½-wy: led over 3f out tl over 1f out: one pce)....3½ 2
1349⁵ Stalled (IRE) **(50)***(52) (PTWalwyn)* 5-10-6 (5) MarchionesBlandford(22) (a.p: disp ld over 3f out tl over 1f out: wknd fnl f)....1¼ 3
*1332*⁵ Our Bessie **(46)***(48) (DMarks)* 4-10-7 MissKMarks(3) (hdwy fnl 3f: nrst fin)....hd 4
1529⁷ Augustan **(60)***(58) (SGollings)* 4-11-2 (5) MrsJMGollings(13) (s.i.s: styd on fnl 3f: nrst fin)....2½ 5
Sophism (USA) **(51)***(49)*(Fav)*(MCPipe)* 6-10-12 MissAHarwood(18) (hdwy over 2f out: rdn & btn wl over 1f out)....hd 6
*1319*⁶ Rejects Reply **(34)***(31) (WJMusson)* 5-9-9 MrsLPearce(20) (bhd to ½-wy: hdwy fnl 2f: hung lft fnl f: n.d)....¾ 7
*588*⁴ Kalakate **(45)***(33) (JJBridger)* 10-10-1 (5)ow7 MissMBridger(16) (b: bhd tl sme hdwy fnl 3f).....1¾ 8
1403⁶ Swan Flyer **(28)***(23) (JJSheehan)* 4-8-12 (5) MissEJJones(12) (swtg: bhd early: n.d)....s.h 9
1254¹⁵ Persian Smoke **(40)***(31) (AHide)* 4-10-1 MissLHide(21) (lw: s.s: a bhd)....2½ 10
1401² Charlie Bigtime **(49)***(35) (DTThom)* 5-10-10v MissDianaJones(11) (in tch tl over 2f out)....4 11
*409*³ Sian Wyn **(33)***(15) (KRBurke)* 5-9-3 (5)ow3 MrsEBurke(2) (in tch 9f)....½ 12
884⁷ Queens Contractor **(40)***(24) (SMellor)* 5-9-10 (5) MissEJoyce(19) (in tch tl over 2f out)....1 13

1323[17] Bresil (USA) **(41)***(22) (KRBurke)* 6-9-11 (5)ow1 MrsHSweeting(10) (a bhd) 1¼ **14**
Workingforpeanuts (IRE) **(30)***(9) (CASmith)* 5-9-0v(5) MrsDSmith(4) (prom over 9f) 2½ **15**
1254[9] Maraady (USA) **(28)***(3) (GPEnright)* 6-8-12 (5) MrsMEnright(6) (b: a bhd) 3 **16**
1141[10] Jarzon Dancer **(38)***(12) (DAWilson)* 7-9-13 MrsDKettlewell(5) (b: prom tl over 2f out) ....½ **17**
1350[7] Clancy's Express **(33)***(2) (GBBalding)* 4-9-3 (5) MissSarah-JaneDurman(1) (prom 9f) 4 **18**
The Oil Baron **(27)** *(RPCHoad)* 9-8-11 (5) MissLMcIntosh(8) (a bhd: t.o) 4 **19**
402[3] Don't Drop Bombs (USA) **(32)** *(DTThom)* 6-9-7v MissJFeilden(14) (led tl over 3f out: hrd rdn & wknd 2f out) 1¾ **20**
1328[12] The Chairman (IRE) **(57)** *(FJordan)* 4-11-4 MrsCWonnacott(15) (trckd ldr 7f: t.o) 15 **21**

9/4 Sophism (USA) (7/2-2/1), **7/2** Charlie Bigtime, **7/1** Rejects Reply, Stalled (IRE) (op 12/1), **10/1** Don't Drop Bombs (USA), **14/1** CASUAL WATER (IRE), **16/1** Our Bessie, **20/1** Jarzon Dancer, Clancy's Express, **25/1** Swan Flyer, Augustan, Queens Contractor, Kalakate, Sian Wyn, **33/1** Persian Smoke, The Chairman (IRE), Bresil (USA), **50/1** Katie's Kid, The Oil Baron, Workingforpeanuts (IRE), Maraady (USA), CSF £531.61 TOTE £19.40: £3.10 £11.50 £2.10 £4.00 (£532.70) Trio £351.20; £346.32 to 12/6/95 OWNER Mr John Davies (BARNSTAPLE) BRED Dunderry Stud 21 Rn 2m 35.34 (6.64) SF: 44/21/40/36/46/37/19/21/11/19/23/3/12/10/-/-/-/-/-/-/-

1623

CECIL BOYD ROCHFORT MAIDEN STKS (4-Y.O+) (Class D) £4,152.00 (£1,236.00: £588.00: £264.00)
2m 24y (July) Stalls: High GOING minus 0.40 sec per fur (F) 7-10 (7-12)

Anglesey Sea View *(73) (ABailey)* 6-8-9 LDettori(2) (w'like: hld up: hdwy wl over 2f out: led wl over 1f out: all out) ....— **1**
1410[9] Sea Freedom **(77)***(78) (GBBalding)* 4-8-13 JWilliams(7) (lw: trckd ldr 5f out: outpcd over 2f out: r.o appr fnl f: jst failed) ....hd **2**
1339[6] Shrewd Alibi *(78) (IABalding)* 4-8-13 MHills(4) (prom tl outpcd over 2f out: hrd rdn & rallied fnl f: fin wl) ....nk **3**
1268[3] Bedevil (USA) **(73)***(75)*(Fav)*(MrsJCecil)* 5-9-0 PaulEddery(6) (b: led tl wl over 1f out: one pce)3 **4**
929[5] Sharazi (USA) *(72) (DJSCosgrove)* 4-8-13 MRimmer(5) (lw: hrd rdn 3f out: no ch fnl 2f)....2½ **5**
1350[15] Amaam Amaam **(44)***(47) (WJMusson)* 5-9-0 RCochrane(1) (plld early: wl bhd fnl 3f: t.o) 25 **6**

10/11 Bedevil (USA), **11/4** ANGLESEY SEA VIEW, **4/1** Sea Freedom, **8/1** Sharazi (USA) (op 5/1), **10/1** Shrewd Alibi (op 6/1), **33/1** Amaam Amaam, CSF £14.24 TOTE £3.30: £1.30 £2.10 (£9.30) OWNER Mrs P.Hewitt (TARPORLEY) BRED J.A.Hewitt 6 Rn 3m 33.05 (10.05) SF: 14/18/18/16/12/-
WEIGHT FOR AGE 4yo-1lb

1624

NGK SPARK PLUGS H'CAP (0-80) (3-Y.O) (Class D) £6,316.00 (£1,888.00: £904.00: £412.00)
6f (July) Stalls: Low GOING minus 0.40 sec per fur (F) 7-40 (7-41)

1380[3] **Brecongill Lad (65)***(75) (MissSEHall)* 3-8-6b NConnorton(2) (lw: mde all: drvn out) ....— **1**
985[3] Jawlaat (USA) **(76)***(77)*(Fav)*(JLDunlop)* 3-9-3 WCarson(3) (trckd wnr: hrd rdn 2f out: r.o one pce) 3½ **2**
1249[2] Rymer's Rascal **(67)***(67) (EJAlston)* 3-8-8 PRobinson(7) (plld hrd in rr: hdwy 2f out: one pce ins fnl f) ....nk **3**
1487[12] Cats Bottom **(69)***(64) (DJSCosgrove)* 3-8-10 MRimmer(1) (a in tch: styd on one pce u.p fnl 2f) 1¾ **4**
*847** Cloette **(69)***(60) (WAO'Gorman)* 3-8-10 EmmaO'Gorman(8) (in tch tl outpcd over 2f out: sme hdwy fnl f) 1½ **5**
1376[5] Fairy Wind (IRE) **(80)***(67) (NACallaghan)* 3-9-7 LDettori(10) (b:hind: hld up: hdwy over 2f out: hung lft over 1f out: hrd rdn & one pce) 1¾ **6**
1429[3] Tafahhus **(76)***(60) (RWArmstrong)* 3-9-3 RHills(5) (hdwy over 2f out: wknd over 1f out) 1 **7**
1258[4] Triple Tricks (IRE) **(72)***(56) (WJHaggas)* 3-8-13 MHills(6) (lw: a outpcd) ....hd **8**
1070[13] Ben Gunn **(72)***(52) (PTWalwyn)* 3-8-13 PatEddery(9) (a outpcd) 1¼ **9**
Snow Foot **(53)***(32) (PCHaslam)* 3-7-1 (7)ow1 RMullen(4) (spd 3f) ....nk **10**

2/1 Jawlaat (USA) (op 7/2), **5/1** Rymer's Rascal, **11/2** Fairy Wind (IRE), **6/1** Cloette, **7/1** Ben Gunn, BRECONGILL LAD, Tafahhus, **10/1** Triple Tricks (IRE), **12/1** Cats Bottom, **33/1** Snow Foot, CSF £23.87 CT £78.31 TOTE £11.30: £2.40 £1.70 £2.30 (£17.10) Trio £32.40 OWNER Three Horse Shoes Partnership (MIDDLEHAM) BRED Miss S. E. Hall 10 Rn
1m 12.89 (1.39) SF: 38/40/30/27/23/30/23/19/15/-

1625

WALTER EARL (S) STKS (3-Y.O) (Class E) £4,386.00 (£1,308.00: £624.00: £282.00) **1m (July)** Stalls: Low GOING minus 0.40 sec per fur (F) 8-10 (8-12)

1125[11] **Amnesty Bay** *(57) (JRFanshawe)* 3-8-6 DHarrison(8) (trckd ldr: led jst over 2f out: drvn out) ....— **1**

1447[5] Old Swinford (IRE) **(65)***(52)*(Fav)*(BJMeehan)* 3-8-6 BDoyle(6) (lw: a.p: ev ch 2f out: one pce) 2½ **2**
319[6] La Fille de Cirque *(51) (RJRWilliams)* 3-8-6 DBiggs(1) (lw: styod on one pce fr over 1f out: nvr nrr) ....½ **3**
Rose of Cadence **(65)***(45) (PFICole)* 3-8-6 PatEddery(7) (bkwd: led wl over 5f) 3 **4**
Try Omnipotent *(46) (CNAllen)* 3-8-11 TIves(4) (leggy: in tch 5f) 2 **5**
Sastrugi (IRE) *(38) (SPCWoods)* 3-8-11 WRyan(2) (b.nr fore: unf: sn rdn along: a bhd) 4 **6**
Mill Dancer (IRE) *(32) (EJAlston)* 3-8-6 PRobinson(9) (neat: lw: plld hrd: bhd fnl 3f) ....½ **7**
1092[17] Indian Treasure (IRE) *(14) (DJSCosgrove)* 3-8-6 MRimmer(3) (bhd fnl 3f) 9 **8**
1512[20] Magical Blues (IRE) **(70)** *(KTIvory)* 3-8-11 MTebbutt(5) (ref to r: t.n.p) .... **R**

9/4 Old Swinford (IRE), **7/2** Rose of Cadence (op 2/1), **11/2** Sastrugi (IRE), **7/1** Magical Blues (IRE) (10/1-6/1), Try Omnipotent (12/1-5/1), **10/1** La Fille de Cirque (op 6/1), AMNESTY BAY (op 6/1), **16/1** Mill Dancer (IRE), **40/1** Indian Treasure (IRE), CSF £32.13 TOTE £15.10: £3.60 £1.30 £3.30 (£20.00) Trio £50.80 OWNER Cheveley Park Stud (NEWMARKET) BRED Cheveley Park Stud Ltd 9 Rn
1m 41.52 (3.82) SF: 20/15/14/8/9/1/-/-/-
No bid

1626 BILLECART-SALMON CHAMPAGNE H'CAP (0-90) (3-Y.O+) (Class C) £7,570.00 (£2,260.00: £1,080.00: £490.00)
1m (July) Stalls: Low GOING minus 0.40 sec per fur (F) 8-40 (8-42)

1344[2] **Khayrapour (IRE) (74)***(92+)*(Fav)*(BJMeehan)* 5-8-13b PatEddery(9) (hld up: gd hdwy over 1f out: led appr fnl f: drvn clr: r.o wl) ....— **1**
1183[9] Deevee **(72)***(80) (CJBenstead)* 6-8-11 PRobinson(5) (lw: hld up in rr: hdwy fnl 2f: wnt 2nd wl ins fnl f) 5 **2**
1183[18] Saifan **(66)***(73) (DMorris)* 6-8-5b AClark(3) (lw: hdwy over 2f out: ev ch appr fnl f: hrd rdn: one pce) ....nk **3**
1225[3] Wilcuma **(83)***(87) (PJMakin)* 4-9-8 LDettori(2) (hld up mid div: styd on one pce fnl 2f) 1½ **4**
1183[4] Nashaat (USA) **(69)***(72) (NJHWalker)* 7-8-8 RCochrane(1) (in tch: one pce fnl 2f) ....½ **5**
873[18] Hawwam **(54)***(56) (EJAlston)* 9-7-7 GBardwell(6) (effrt over 2f out: wknd fr over 1f out) ....¾ **6**
1225[5] Rory **(80)***(77) (MrsJCecil)* 4-9-5 PaulEddery(12) (lw: a.p: ev ch over 1f out: sn wknd) 2½ **7**
1280[9] Blockade (USA) **(72)***(67) (MBell)* 6-8-11 MFenton(10) (t: led tl over 1f out) ....¾ **8**
1217[3] Moving Arrow **(89)***(83) (MissSEHall)* 4-10-0 NConnorton(4) (lw: trckd ldrs over 5f) ....¾ **9**
1299[3] Castel Rosselo **(85)***(75) (BJMcMath)* 5-9-10 AMackay(7) (s.i.s: a bhd) 1¾ **10**
785[12] Gymcrak Flyer **(69)***(59) (GHolmes)* 4-8-8 GCarter(11) (b.hind: trckd ldr tl wknd 2f out) ....hd **11**
1170[7] Vin St Koola **(78)***(61) (HJCollingridge)* 3-8-6 MRimmer(8) (prom tl rdn & btn 3f out) 3½ **12**
LONG HANDICAP Hawwam 7-5

7/2 KHAYRAPOUR (IRE), **4/1** Wilcuma, **9/2** Rory, **5/1** Saifan (op 8/1), **8/1** Blockade (USA) (op 12/1), **9/1** Moving Arrow (6/1-10/1), **10/1** Nashaat (USA) (op 6/1), Castel Rosselo, **12/1** Deevee (op 8/1), **25/1** Hawwam, Gymcrak Flyer, **33/1** Vin St Koola, CSF £46.53 CT £204.99 TOTE £5.60: £2.00 £4.40 £2.20 (£34.30) Trio £176.40 OWNER Miss J. Semple (UPPER LAMBOURN) BRED His Highness The Aga Khans Stud S.C. 12 Rn
1m 38.4 (0.70) SF: 58/46/39/53/38/22/43/33/49/41/25/16
WEIGHT FOR AGE 3yo-11lb

1627 FRANK BUTTERS MAIDEN STKS (2-Y.O F) (Class D) £4,503.00 (£1,344.00: £642.00: £291.00)
6f (July) Stalls: Low GOING minus 0.40 sec per fur (F) 9-05 (9-08)

Maid For The Hills *(+t)*(Fav)*(DRLoder)* 2-8-11 PatEddery(6) (leggy: scope: mde all: rdn out) ....— **1**
Darling Flame (USA) *(JHMGosden)* 2-8-11 LDettori(4) (lt-f: scope: a.p: hdwy over 1f out: no ex cl home) ....¾ **2**
Frezeliere *(JLDunlop)* 2-8-11 WRyan(5) (w'like: leggy: s.s: gd hdwy over 2f out: one pce fnl f) 2½ **3**
Galine *(WAO'Gorman)* 2-8-11 EmmaO'Gorman(2) (cmpt: bkwd: chsd ldrs: one pce fnl 2f) 1¼ **4**
Leith Academy (USA) *(BWHills)* 2-8-11 MHills(9) (neat: s.s: n.d) 2½ **5**
Arlington Lady *(NACallaghan)* 2-8-11 MRoberts(1) (b.nr hind: w'like: prom over 3f) 3 **6**
Tasliya (USA) *(JLDunlop)* 2-8-11 WCarson(3) (w'like: in tch over 3f) 1¾ **7**
Nottonitejosephine *(RBoss)* 2-8-11 MRimmer(7) (cmpt: scope: a outpcd) 1¾ **8**

8/15 MAID FOR THE HILLS (op 4/5), **4/1** Darling Flame (USA), **9/2** Tasliya (USA), **10/1** Galine, **14/1** Leith Academy (USA) (op 6/1), **16/1** Arlington Lady, **25/1** Frezeliere, **33/1** Nottonitejosephine, CSF £4.21 TOTE £1.70: £1.30 £1.30 £3.10 (£4.21) Trio £18.10 OWNER Mr Chris Brasher (NEWMARKET) BRED Mrs Mary Taylor 8 Rn
1m 15.44 (3.94) SF: 9/7/-/-/-/-/-/-

T/Plpt: £464.20 (25.7 Tckts). T/Qdpt: £9.00 (15.85 Tckts). RC

1454-WOLVERHAMPTON (L-H)
Saturday June 10th (Standard)
WEATHER: drizzling WIND: almost nil

1628 PEVERIL SECURITIES H'CAP (0-60) (3-Y.O) (Class F) £2,519.00 (£694.00: £329.00)
1m 6f 166y (Fibresand) Stalls: Low GOING: 0.03 sec per fur (STD) 7-00 (7-04)

1198 12 **Frome Lad (55)***(61) (WGMTurner)* 3-9-5 TSprake(6) (mde all: r.o wl)...— 1
947 10 Maysann **(57)***(61) (JLDunlop)* 3-9-7b GDuffield(9) (b: hld up: hdwy over 3f out: 5th st: r.o ins fnl f)...1½ 2
905 5 Vintage Taittinger (IRE) **(47)***(49)*(Fav)*(MBell)* 3-8-11 JCarroll(1) (a.p: 2nd st: one pce)...2½ 3
1097 16 My Boy Josh **(55)***(56) (RGuest)* 3-9-5 GHind(4) (prom: lost pl & 7th st: rallied ins fnl f)...½ 4
1401 4 Royal Rabbit **(50)***(50) (GLMoore)* 3-8-9 (5) AWhelan(8) (hld up: hdwy 4f out: 4th st: one pce)...1 5
1322 9 Sadler's Pearl **(55)***(51) (BJMeehan)* 3-9-5 SWhitworth(7) (prom: 3rd & rdn st: wknd over 1f out)...3½ 6
1219 11 Warrior Lady (IRE) **(36)***(28) (PJMcBride)* 3-8-0 ow1 RPrice(12) (prom: rdn over 3f out: 6th & wkng st)...3 7
893 4 Something Speedy (IRE) **(45)***(28) (PJBevan)* 3-8-9 NCarlisle(3) (a bhd)...9 8
1379 5 Remontant (IRE) **(44)***(26) (RHollinshead)* 3-8-5 (3) AGarth(5) (s.i.s: hdwy over 4f out: wknd over 3f out)...1½ 9
1289 9 Shy Paddy (IRE) **(53)***(22) (KOCunningham-Brown)* 3-9-3 NAdams(11) (hld up: hdwy 5f out: wknd over 2f out: t.o)...12 10
1198 15 Adjacent Too **(42)***(6) (CCElsey)* 3-8-6 CRutter(2) (b: prom tl rdn & wknd over 5f out: t.o)...4 11
1198 14 Peatsville (IRE) **(48)***(7) (MRChannon)* 3-8-7 (5) PPMurphy(10) (chsd ldr: rdn 4f out: wknd 3f out: t.o)...5 12

9/4 Vintage Taittinger (IRE), **4/1** My Boy Josh (op 10/1), **5/1** Royal Rabbit, **7/1** Maysann (op 4/1), **8/1** Remontant (IRE), **10/1** Something Speedy (IRE) (op 4/1), **14/1** FROME LAD, **16/1** Warrior Lady (IRE), Sadler's Pearl, Shy Paddy (IRE), Peatsville (IRE), **25/1** Adjacent Too, CSF £110.51 CT £285.53 TOTE £26.70: £4.90 £3.20 £1.50 (£64.00) Trio £73.80 OWNER Mr C. C. Lowe (SHERBORNE) BRED C. C. Lowe and J. W. F. Lowe 12 Rn 3m 24.6 (17.20) SF: 16/16/4/11/5/6/-/-/-/-/-/-

1629 RYDER CONTRACT HIRE CLAIMING STKS (3-Y.O+) (Class F) £2,519.00 (£694.00: £329.00)
7f (Fibresand) Stalls: Low GOING: 0.03 sec per fur (STD) 7-30 (7-44)

1491 5 **Wentbridge Lad (IRE) (78)***(82)*(Fav)*(PDEvans)* 5-9-5 (3) SSanders(7) (hdwy over 3f out: 2nd st: rdn over 1f out: led ins fnl f: r.o wl)...— 1
579 10 Four of Spades **(70)***(69) (WSCunningham)* 4-9-2b JCarroll(1) (lw: led tl ins fnl f)...3 2
1034 6 Perfect World **(63)***(57) (BAMcMahon)* 3-8-2 DaleGibson(2) (prom: 3rd st: rdn over 1f out: one pce)...3½ 3
728 10 Rocky Waters (USA) **(76)***(54) (GLMoore)* 6-8-11 (5) AWhelan(6) (hld up: 4th & rdn st: wknd over 1f out)...3 4
1484 9 Letsbeonestaboutit **(50)***(43) (MissGayKelleway)* 9-8-8v MWigham(4) (outpcd: last st: a bhd) 1½ 5
417 6 Dream Carrier (IRE) **(65)***(38) (JGMO'Shea)* 7-8-3 (7) AmandaSanders(5) (prom over 3f: 5th & wkng st)...3 6
1294 6 Chadleigh Lane (USA) **(67)** *(RHollinshead)* 3-8-12 GDuffield(3) (Withdrawn not under Starter's orders: unruly s)... W

, **6/4** WENTBRIDGE LAD (IRE), **3/1** Four of Spades, **6/1** Dream Carrier (IRE) (5/1-8/1), Rocky Waters (USA) (op 7/2), **7/1** Perfect World (op 4/1), **14/1** Letsbeonestaboutit (op 8/1), CSF £5.86 TOTE £2.60: £1.70 £1.70 (£3.30) OWNER Mr John Pugh (WELSHPOOL) BRED Peter Doyle 6 Rn
1m 29.8 (5.80) SF: 40/27/5/12/1/-/-
WEIGHT FOR AGE 3yo-10lb

1630 CAVENDISH RACING MAIDEN H'CAP (0-70) (3-Y.O+) (Class E) £3,445.20 (£1,029.60: £492.80: £224.40)
7f (Fibresand) GOING: 0.03 sec per fur (STD) 8-00 (8-08)

1210 7 **Moneghetti (31)***(42) (RHollinshead)* 4-7-7 NCarlisle(10) (hld up: hdwy over 4f out: led 2f out: rdn out)...— 1
1426 3 Mislemani (IRE) **(46)***(54) (AGNewcombe)* 5-8-8 RPrice(2) (prom: 4th st: r.o ins fnl f)...1¼ 2
1456 5 Caddy's First **(53)***(54) (SMellor)* 3-8-5 DaleGibson(4) (lw: a.p: led over 4f out to 2f out: 2nd st: one pce fnl f)...3 3
1456 10 Unison **(32)***(24) (CRBarwell)* 4-7-8v NAdams(8) (hld up: hdwy & 6th st: one pce)...4 4

835[6] Delgarth Lady **(31)***(21) (JLSpearing)* 4-7-7b NKennedy(5) (bhd tl hdwy 2f out: nt rch ldrs).......¾ 5
1326[2] Bargash **(50)***(31)*(Fav)*(PDEvans)* 3-7-13 (3) SSanders(1) (lw: dwlt: hdwy over 3f out: 5th & wkng st)....................4 6
1053[8] Mighty Squaw **(63)***(41) (MissGayKelleway)* 3-9-1 MWigham(7) (prom: rdn & wknd over 3f out)....................1½ 7
1421[12] Rossini Blue **(66)***(30) (ABailey)* 4-9-9b(5) VHalliday(9) (prom: led over 5f out tl over 4f out: 3rd & wkng st)....................6 8
1155[7] Jhan Jeon **(44)** *(RAFahey)* 3-7-10 TWilliams(6) (led over 1f: bhd fnl 3f: t.o)....................dist 9

LONG HANDICAP Moneghetti 7-6

5/4 Bargash (op 2/1), **3/1** Rossini Blue, **11/2** Caddy's First (4/1-6/1), **7/1** Mislemani (IRE) (op 4/1), **8/1** Mighty Squaw, **12/1** Delgarth Lady (op 8/1), **14/1** Jhan Jeon (op 8/1), **20/1** Unison, **25/1** MONEGHETTI, CSF £186.38 CT £1,028.36 TOTE £50.40: £4.50 £1.70 £1.40 (£452.90) Trio £66.30; £84.07 to 12/6/95 OWNER Mr Philip Harvey (UPPER LONGDON) BRED P. G. Harvey 9 Rn
1m 30.4 (6.40) SF: 6/18/8/-/-/-/-/-/-
WEIGHT FOR AGE 3yo-10lb

1631 EDMUND BIRTHDAY APPRENTICE H'CAP (0-70) (Class F) £2,550.00 (£725.00: £360.00) 1m 1f 79y (Fibresand) GOING: 0.03 sec per fur (STD) 8-30 (8-30)

*1459** **Dia Georgy (49)***(59) (RGuest)* 4-8-7 CWebb(1) (chsd ldr 4f: 3rd st: led ins fnl f: r.o wl)........— 1
1402[3] Daytona Beach (IRE) **(60)***(69) (PBurgoyne)* 5-9-4 DebbieBiggs(5) (led tl ins fnl f: r.o)............½ 2
1458[5] Medland (IRE) **(50)***(57) (BJMcMath)* 5-8-8 RMoogan(4) (hld up: chsd ldr over 5f out: rdn 3f out: 2nd st: r.o one pce)....................1¼ 3
1250[3] Equerry **(60)***(64)*(Fav)*(MJohnston)* 4-8-13 (5) KSked(6) (lost pl over 3f out: 5th st: one pce)....................1½ 4
1297[6] Aitch N'Bee **(70)***(74) (LadyHerries)* 12-9-9 (5) JMcAuley(2) (hld up: hdwy 4f out: 4th st: one pce)....................½ 5

7/4 Equerry, **9/4** Daytona Beach (IRE), **11/4** DIA GEORGY, **4/1** Aitch N'Bee, **12/1** Medland (IRE) (op 6/1), CSF £9.70 TOTE £4.00: £2.70 £1.30 (£3.60) OWNER Mrs Deborah Crowley (NEWMARKET) BRED Stuart Powell 5 Rn
2m 4.6 (8.60) SF: 21/31/19/26/36

1632 U.E.S. BRIGHT BAR (S) STKS (2-Y.O) (Class G) £2,243.00 (£618.00: £293.00) 6f (Fibresand) Stalls: Low GOING: 0.03 sec per fur (STD) 9-00 (9-02)

1212[7] **Miss Offset** *(67)*(Fav)*(MJohnston)* 2-8-6b TWilliams(4) (mde all: clr over 1f out: r.o wl)........— 1
1077[6] Nameless *(53) (DJSCosgrove)* 2-8-11 JFortune(7) (s.i.s: sn prom: wnt 2nd st: no ch w wnr) ..7 2
644[4] Red Simba *(51) (JBerry)* 2-8-11 JCarroll(1) (bit bkwd: prom: 3rd st: one pce)....................1 3
644[6] Rowhome *(21) (MRChannon)* 2-8-11 CRutter(3) (chsd ldrs: 6th & wkng st)....................11 4
1333[2] Magic Bird (IRE) *(14) (JLSpearing)* 2-8-6 GHind(6) (prom tl 4th & wkng st)....................1 5
Ginger Glint *(15) (MJHeaton-Ellis)* 2-8-11 StephenDavies(5) (small: prom: 5th & wkng st)...1½ 6
Chris's Governor *(13) (RHollinshead)* 2-8-8b(3) AGarth(2) (leggy: w'like: s.s: a bhd)...............½ 7

5/2 MISS OFFSET (3/1-2/1), **3/1** Red Simba (op 7/4), **7/2** Nameless (3/1-5/1), **9/2** Ginger Glint (4/1-6/1), **12/1** Rowhome (op 6/1), Chris's Governor (op 5/1), **16/1** Magic Bird (IRE), CSF £11.21 TOTE £3.40: £1.60 £2.80 (£5.10) OWNER Hertford Offset Ltd (MIDDLEHAM) BRED J. Coombes and E. Henshaw 7 Rn
1m 16.5 (5.30) SF: 20/6/4/-/-/-/-
Bt in 6,000 gns

1633 BREASTPLATE H'CAP (0-70) (3-Y.O+) (Class E) £3,374.00 (£1,007.00: £481.00: £218.00) 6f (Fibresand) Stalls: Low GOING: 0.03 sec per fur (STD) 9-30 (9-34)

1456* **Efficacy (43)***(50) (APJarvis)* 4-7-9 (7) AmandaSanders(4) (a.p: led over 3f out: r.o wl)..........— 1
1202[7] Ring the Chief **(51)***(56) (RAkehurst)* 3-7-12 (3)ow2 SSanders(8) (lw: hld up: 6th & c wd st: hdwy over 1f out: r.o wl ins fnl f)....................s.h 2
1457[5] My Gallery (IRE) **(50)***(54) (ABailey)* 4-8-4b(5) VHalliday(2) (a.p: 3rd st: r.o one pce fnl f)....................1¼ 3
1456[3] Ho Mei Surprise **(43)***(39) (BPreece)* 3-7-7 NAdams(5) (lw: hdwy 3f out: 4th st: one pce)....................3 4
1263[7] Noor El Houdah (IRE) **(54)***(42) (JBerry)* 3-8-4 JCarroll(6) (led over 2f: 2nd st: wknd over 1f out)....................3 5
1335[7] Frisky Miss (IRE) **(61)***(48) (KOCunningham-Brown)* 4-9-6 GDuffield(9) (lw: prom: 5th & wkng st)....................s.h 6
344[2] Present Situation **(69)***(51)*(Fav)*(LordHuntingdon)* 4-10-0 JWeaver(3) (prom tl wknd over 2f out)....................2 7
Ganeshaya **(36)** *(JLSpearing)* 6-7-9 NCarlisle(1) (Withdrawn not under Starter's orders: ref ent stalls)....................W

LONG HANDICAP Ho Mei Surprise 7-4

5/2 Present Situation, **7/2** My Gallery (IRE), **4/1** EFFICACY (3/1-9/2), **5/1** Ring the Chief (op 3/1), **13/2** Noor El Houdah (IRE) (op 4/1), **14/1** Frisky Miss (IRE), **16/1** Ho Mei Surprise, CSF £21.99 CT £67.68 TOTE £4.80: £1.90 £3.50 (£16.50) Trio £59.20 OWNER Mrs Ann Jarvis (ASTON UPTHORPE) BRED Hever Castle Stud Farm Ltd 7 Rn 1m 15.3 (4.10) SF: 32/29/36/12/15/30/33/-
WEIGHT FOR AGE 3yo-9lb
T/Plpt: £167.00 (41.24 Tckts). T/Qdpt: £54.40 (0.5 Tckts); £36.80 to Epsom 11/6/95. KH

1608-EPSOM (L-H)
Sunday June 11th (Good to firm)
WEATHER: drizzle, heavy rain last 3 WIND: almost nil

1634
ASTEC MEDIAN AUCTION CONDITIONS STKS (2-Y.O) (Class C)
£6,272.00 (£2,348.00: £1,149.00: £495.00: £222.50: £113.50)
6f Stalls: Low GOING minus 0.39 sec per fur (F) 2-00 (2-01)

1267[6] **Cabcharge Striker** *(81)*(Fav)*(MRChannon)* 2-8-11 RHughes(5) (lw: 5th st: led ins fnl f: pushed out) — 1
1327* Arctic Romancer (IRE) *(80) (GLewis)* 2-8-11 PaulEddery(7) (2nd tl led over 2f out: hrd rdn & hdd ins fnl f: r.o) ½ 2
1424* Cyrillic *(68) (PAKelleway)* 2-8-6 JWeaver(2) (4th st: r.o one pce fnl 2f) 2½ 3
1259[3] To The Whire *(71) (GLMoore)* 2-8-10 BRouse(6) (swtg: 6th st: rdn over 2f out: r.o one pce) ½ 4
1163[4] Mystery Matthias *(60) (MissBSanders)* 2-8-6 MRoberts(3) (led over 3f) 2½ 5
*1031** Born A Lady *(55) (NPLittmoden)* 2-8-6 TGMcLaughlin(1) (lw: last st: a bhd) 2 6
871[5] General Rose *(52) (RHannon)* 2-8-11 JReid(4) (lw: 3rd st: wknd 3f out) 3 7

5/2 CABCHARGE STRIKER (7/4-11/4), **3/1** To The Whire, **9/2** Arctic Romancer (IRE), **6/1** General Rose (9/2-7/1), **8/1** Cyrillic, **16/1** Born A Lady, **20/1** Mystery Matthias, CSF £12.39 TOTE £3.40: £2.60 £2.80 (£4.70) OWNER Computer Cab Racing Club (UPPER LAMBOURN) BRED J. K. Keegan 7 Rn 1m 10.75 (2.75) SF: 22/21/9/12/1/-/-

1635
TALKLAND LADY RIDERS CONDITIONS AMATEUR STKS (4-Y.O+) (Class C) £6,742.50 (£2,040.00: £995.00: £472.50)
1m 4f 10y Stalls: Low GOING minus 0.39 sec per fur (F) 2-35 (2-37)

Amancio (USA) (84)*(86)*(Fav)*(GHarwood)* 4-10-12 MissAHarwood(2) (lw: 5th st: led ins fnl f: pushed out) — 1
1200[2] Wild Strawberry **(64)***(73) (MissBSanders)* 6-10-6 MissDianaJones(3) (6th st: hdwy 3f out: chsd wnr fnl 2f) 5 2
1332[3] Mr Bean **(38)***(75) (KRBurke)* 5-10-11 (5) MrsEBurke(7) (3rd st: r.o one pce fnl 2f) 6 3
1102[5] Credit Squeeze **(73)***(71) (RFJohnsonHoughton)* 5-10-13 MissEJohnsonHoughton(1) (b: lw: 5th st: rdn over 2f out: no hdwy) ¾ 4
991[9] Children's Choice (IRE) **(62)***(69) (PJMcBride)* 4-10-12 MrsDKettlewell(6) (2nd st: led 3f out: sn hdd & wknd) 1¼ 5
1622[20] Don't Drop Bombs (USA) **(32)***(39) (DTThom)* 6-10-9v MissJFeilden(5) (lw: led tl wknd 3f out: t.o) 20 6

2/1 AMANCIO (USA), **9/4** Credit Squeeze (11/8-5/2), **4/1** Wild Strawberry, **9/1** Children's Choice (IRE), **14/1** Mr Bean (10/1-16/1), **25/1** Don't Drop Bombs (USA), CSF £8.88 TOTE £2.80: £1.80 £1.70 (£4.60) OWNER Mr Paul Locke (PULBOROUGH) BRED Hill'N Dale Farm 6 Rn
2m 38.93 (3.93) SF: 67/54/56/52/50/20

1636
MARTIN DAWES CONDITIONS STKS (3-Y.O+) (Class B) £12,216.50 (£4,454.00: £2,177.00: £935.00: £417.50)
1m 2f 18y Stalls: Low GOING minus 0.39 sec per fur (F) 3-10 (3-10)

829[3] **Ela-Aristokrati (IRE) (97)***(103+)*(Fav)*(MRStoute)* 3-8-4 MHills(1) (lw: 3rd st: led over 2f out: comf) — 1
979[5] Stiffelio (IRE) **(100)***(99) (RHannon)* 3-8-7 ow1 JReid(4) (lw: 2nd st: r.o one pce fnl 2f) 4 2
1408[5] Spot Prize (USA) **(106)***(89) (IABalding)* 4-8-10 WRyan(3) (lw: led tl over 2f out: r.o one pce) nk 3
968* Diaghilef (IRE) **(102)***(95) (MJohnston)* 3-8-4 DHolland(5) (5th st: one pce fnl 2f) ½ 4
1103* Dahik **(106)***(99) (MajorWRHern)* 3-8-12 WCarson(2) (lw: 4th st: wknd over 1f out) 2½ 5

5/4 ELA-ARISTOKRATI (IRE) (4/5-6/4), **3/1** Dahik, **4/1** Diaghilef (IRE), **7/1** Stiffelio (IRE), **12/1** Spot Prize (USA) (op 8/1), CSF £8.85 TOTE £2.30: £1.50 £1.70 (£6.00) OWNER Mr Andreas Michael (NEWMARKET) BRED M. Ervine 5 Rn 2m 6.79 (2.79) SF: 35/31/34/27/31
WEIGHT FOR AGE 3yo-13lb

1637 VODAFONE 'DASH' RATED STKS H'CAP (0-105) (Listed) (3-Y.O+)
(Class A) £24,322.40 (£9,101.60: £4,450.80: £1,914.00: £857.00: £434.20)
5f Stalls: High GOING minus 0.39 sec per fur (F) 3-40 (3-41)

1181* **Double Quick (IRE) (97)***(103) (MJohnston)* 3-8-3 ow1 JWeaver(3) (a.p: hrd rdn fnl 2f: r.o to ld cl home)......— **1**
1220[5] Don't Worry Me (IRE) **(98)***(105) (FHLee)* 3-8-4 PaulEddery(7) (led: hrd rdn & edgd lft over 1f out: hdd nr fin)......hd **2**
693[7] Allthruthenight (IRE) **(86)***(90) (LJHolt)* 6-8-0 WCarson(2) (swtg: gd hdwy fnl 2f: nvr nrr)......¾ **3**
1106* Brave Edge **(99)***(97)*(Fav)*(RHannon)* 4-8-13 RHughes(9) (a.p: hrd rdn over 1f out: nt qckn)....2 **4**
1489[7] Insider Trader **(86)***(74) (RJRWilliams)* 4-8-0b DBiggs(6) (b: gd spd over 3f)......3 **5**
1019[2] Jayannpee **(98)***(86) (IABalding)* 4-8-12 WRyan(5) (nvr nr to chal)......hd **6**
1019* Ashtina **(93)***(75) (RJHodges)* 10-8-7 JQuinn(8) (spd over 2f)......2 **7**
1277* Musica **(87)***(57) (MRChannon)* 3-7-7v GBardwell(4) (a bhd)......3½ **8**
1106[10] Tuscan Dawn **(87)***(52) (JBerry)* 5-8-1 ow1 GHind(1) (s.s: a bhd)......1¼ **9**
1475[10] Windmachine (SWE) **(100)***(44) (RHarris)* 4-9-0b TQuinn(10) (b: lw: bhd fnl 3f)......7 **10**
LONG HANDICAP Allthruthenight (IRE) 7-10 Tuscan Dawn 7-13 Insider Trader 7-5 Musica 7-1

5/2 Brave Edge, **3/1** DOUBLE QUICK (IRE), **6/1** Ashtina, Jayannpee, **13/2** Allthruthenight (IRE), **12/1** Tuscan Dawn, **16/1** Windmachine (SWE), **20/1** Don't Worry Me (IRE), Musica, Insider Trader, CSF £54.11 CT £326.33 TOTE £4.20: £1.70 £4.40 £1.70 (£47.10) Trio £196.80 OWNER The 2nd Middleham Partnership (MIDDLEHAM) 10 Rn 53.86 secs (-0.64) SF: 64/66/59/66/43/55/44/18/21/13
WEIGHT FOR AGE 3yo-8lb

1638 MAIL ON SUNDAY CHAMPIONSHIP MILE SERIES (QUALIFIER) H'CAP
(0-90) (3-Y.O+) (Class C) £14,265.00 (£4,320.00: £2,110.00: £1,005.00)
1m 114y Stalls: Low GOING minus 0.15 sec per fur (GF) 4-10 (4-11)

1280* **Up in Flames (IRE) (70)***(81) (MDHammond)* 4-8-10 WCarson(12) (5th st: led over 1f out: r.o wl)......— **1**
1447* Danegold (IRE) **(73)***(83)*(Fav)*(MRChannon)* 3-8-1v CRutter(7) (in rr tl gd hdwy over 1f out: r.o wl)......½ **2**
1560[3] Shepherd Market (IRE) **(66)***(70) (DAWilson)* 4-8-6 GCarter(2) (led over 4f out tl hmpd & hdd wl over 1f out: r.o)......3½ **3**
1070[6] Second Chance (IRE) **(80)***(84) (PMitchell)* 5-9-3 (3) SSanders(9) (lw: led 4f: 2nd st: led & edgd lft wl over 1f out: sn hdd: one pce: fin 3rd, d.h: disq: plcd 4th)...... **4**
1357[6] Pride of Pendle **(69)***(72) (DNicholls)* 6-8-9 AlexGreaves(5) (hdwy on ins 2f out: nt clr run 1f out: swtchd rt: r.o)......nk **5**
1261[10] Pab's Choice **(58)***(58) (MMcCormack)* 4-7-5 (7) MHenry(8) (7th st: no hdwy fnl 2f)......1¾ **6**
1357[8] Queens Consul (IRE) **(76)***(73) (BSRothwell)* 5-8-11 (5) JStack(11) (4th st: wknd 2f out)......1¼ **7**
396[8] Legal Fiction **(67)***(60) (MJohnston)* 4-8-7 DHolland(6) (lw: 6th st: wknd 2f out)......2½ **8**
927[11] Robsera (IRE) **(77)***(69) (GLewis)* 4-9-3 PaulEddery(13) (3rd st: wknd over 2f out)......½ **9**
1362[2] Comanche Companion **(69)***(56) (TJNaughton)* 5-8-9 JWeaver(10) (a bhd)......2½ **10**
Stately Home (IRE) **(65)***(41) (BRMillman)* 4-8-5 GBardwell(3) (a bhd)......6 **11**
1244* Kingchip Boy **(75)***(49) (MJRyan)* 6-9-1v AClark(4) (a bhd)......¾ **12**
1225* Pay Homage **(84)***(47) (IABalding)* 7-9-10 MHills(14) (t.o fnl 2f)......6 **13**

4/1 Danegold (IRE), **11/2** Comanche Companion, **6/1** UP IN FLAMES (IRE), **7/1** Robsera (IRE), **8/1** Shepherd Market (IRE), Pride of Pendle, Kingchip Boy, **9/1** Pay Homage, **12/1** Legal Fiction, **14/1** Second Chance (IRE), Queens Consul (IRE), **16/1** Pab's Choice, **33/1** Stately Home (IRE), CSF £32.02 CT £189.17 TOTE £4.90: £2.00 £1.70 £3.00 (£12.70) Trio £40.60 OWNER Mr Mark Kilner (MIDDLEHAM) BRED Mrs D. Hutch 13 Rn
1m 44.61 (2.61) SF: 56/46/45/59/47/33/48/35/44/31/16/24/22
WEIGHT FOR AGE 3yo-12lb

1639 VODACALL TOKYO TROPHY H'CAP (0-95) (3-Y.O) (Class C)
£17,831.25 (£5,400.00: £2,637.50: £1,256.25)
7f Stalls: Low GOING minus 0.15 sec per fur (GF) 4-40 (4-42)

1138[10] **Nagnagnag (IRE) (87)***(92) (SDow)* 3-9-0 MRoberts(2) (lost pl & 7th st: hdwy on ins 2f out: led ins fnl f: r.o wl)......— **1**
1222[2] Emirates Express **(83)***(87) (JWHills)* 3-8-3 (7) MHenry(14) (led tl ins fnl f: r.o)......½ **2**
694[8] Midwich Cuckoo **(82)***(80) (PTWalwyn)* 3-8-9 MHills(8) (hdwy over 1f out: r.o ins fnl f)......2½ **3**
1564* Fantasy Racing (IRE) **(79)***(76) (MRChannon)* 3-8-1 (5) 4x PPMurphy(9) (lw: brought wd st: r.o one pce fnl 2f)......½ **4**
1447[2] Master Millfield (IRE) **(66)***(61) (CJHill)* 3-7-7 JQuinn(10) (gd hdwy over 1f out: nt rch ldrs)......¾ **5**
1165[4] Balance of Power **(76)***(71) (RAkehurst)* 3-8-0 (3) SSanders(7) (6th st: r.o one pce fnl 2f)......s.h **6**
1305[4] Loveyoumillions (IRE) **(94)***(85) (MJohnston)* 3-9-7b JWeaver(1) (3rd st: wknd over 1f out)......2 **7**

1178[5] Crystal Cavern (USA) **(92)***(76) (RCharlton)* 3-9-5 TQuinn(4) (lw: 5th st: wknd 2f out) 3 **8**
1130[5] Neverending (USA) **(85)***(65) (HRACecil)* 3-8-12 WRyan(13) (b.off hind: nvr nr to chal) 1¾ **9**
1405* Shen Yang (USA) **(82)***(56) (GLMoore)* 3-8-9 BRouse(6) (lw: 2nd st: wknd over 2f out) 2½ **10**
1366[2] Hawa Al Nasamaat (USA) **(77)***(45)*(Fav)*(EALDunlop)* 3-8-4 PaulEddery(11) (lw: a bhd) 2½ **11**
907[7] Cabcharge Blue **(72)***(11) (TJNaughton)* 3-7-13 AMcGlone(12) (s.s: a bhd: t.o)........................13 **12**

LONG HANDICAP Master Millfield (IRE) 7-6

9/2 Hawa Al Nasamaat (USA), **11/2** Neverending (USA), **6/1** Emirates Express, Master Millfield (IRE), **7/1** Loveyoumillions (IRE), **9/1** Shen Yang (USA), Balance of Power, **10/1** Fantasy Racing (IRE), **12/1** Midwich Cuckoo, Cabcharge Blue, **14/1** Crystal Cavern (USA) (10/1-16/1), **16/1** NAG-NAGNAG (IRE), CSF £109.63 CT £1,119.08 TOTE £14.80: £2.70 £2.10 £6.20 (£54.40) Trio £219.70 OWNER Sir Clement Freud (EPSOM) BRED Rathasker Stud 12 Rn

1m 23.15 (2.85) SF: 50/45/38/34/19/29/43/34/23/14/3/-

T/Jkpt: £95,694.30 (1.38 Tckts). T/Plpt: £187.20 (178.14 Tckts). T/Qdpt: £37.40 (10.5 Tckts). Hn

1285-NOTTINGHAM (L-H)
Monday June 12th (Good to firm, Firm patches)

WEATHER: dull WIND: mod half bhd

1640 PRINTERS RACEDAY (S) STKS (2-Y.O) (Class G) £2,243.00 (£618.00: £293.00)

5f 13y Stalls: High GOING minus 0.23 sec per fur (GF) 2-30 (2-30)

1278[6] **Bold Times** *(59) (PDEvans)* 2-8-11 PaulEddery(3) (a.p: rdn to ld appr fnl f: r.o wl) ....— **1**
1485[8] The Imps (IRE) *(54)*(Fav)*(BWHills)* 2-8-11 BThomson(7) (hld up: effrt & swtchd lft ent fnl f: rdn & r.o)..1½ **2**
1212[10] Wingnut (IRE) *(48) (GLewis)* 2-8-6 SWhitworth(6) (b.nr hind: a.p: led over 2f out tl appr fnl f: unable qckn)..½ **3**
684[3] Don't Tell Anyone *(52) (JBerry)* 2-8-11 JCarroll(4) (w ldrs: shkn up over 1f out: one pce).......nk **4**
1448[3] Touch of Fantasy *(36) (JohnBerry)* 2-8-3 (3) JTate(5) (led to ½-wy: rdn along wl over 1f out: sn outpcd)..3½ **5**
1159[5] Mustaffa (IRE) *(36) (MRChannon)* 2-8-6 (5) PPMurphy(1) (hld up: effrt 2f out: eased whn btn appr fnl f)..1½ **6**
Plausilium *(20) (WGMTurner)* 2-8-11 GDuffield(2) (w'like: str: bkwd: s.s: a wl bhd & outpcd) ..5 **7**

3/1 The Imps (IRE), **7/2** Don't Tell Anyone (6/4-9/2), **4/1** Wingnut (IRE) (8/1-7/2), **5/1** BOLD TIMES (5/2-11/2), **9/1** Plausilium (7/2-10/1), **10/1** Touch of Fantasy (op 6/1), **12/1** Mustaffa (IRE) (op 6/1), CSF £18.59 TOTE £5.70: £2.70 £2.60 (£10.00) OWNER Mr J. Hardman (WELSHPOOL) BRED Mrs P. E. Bell 7 Rn

62.1 secs (3.40) SF: 19/14/8/12/-/-/-

No bid

1641 FERAG UK H'CAP (0-80) (3-Y.O) (Class D) £3,935.10 (£1,174.80: £561.40: £254.70)

5f 13y Stalls: High GOING minus 0.23 sec per fur (GF) 3-00 (3-01)

1302* **Surprise Mission (66)***(73) (RMWhitaker)* 3-8-7 ACulhane(3) (lw: hld up gng wl: qcknd to ld over 1f out: readily)..— **1**
719[5] Karina Heights (USA) **(77)***(79)*(Fav)*(JWWatts)* 3-9-4 JReid(4) (a.p: ev ch appr fnl f: sn rdn & one pce)..1½ **2**
891[6] Sharp Holly (IRE) **(61)***(51) (JABennett)* 3-8-2 JCarroll(5) (bhd & outpcd tl styd on ins fnl f) 4 **3**
754[10] Swan At Whalley **(70)***(56) (MartynWane)* 3-8-11 BThomson(1) (racd centre: slt ld tl hdd & wknd over 1f out)..1 **4**
1602[7] Mr Teigh **(76)***(56) (KMcAuliffe)* 3-9-0b(3) JTate(2) (w ldrs 3f: sn rdn & outpcd)...........................2 **5**
Sound the Trumpet (IRE) **(80)***(44) (MrsJRRamsden)* 3-9-7 DHarrison(6) (h.d.w: bkwd: a bhd: rdn 2f out: no imp)..5 **6**

15/8 Karina Heights (USA), **5/2** SURPRISE MISSION, **11/2** Mr Teigh (4/1-6/1), **13/2** Swan At Whalley, **8/1** Sound the Trumpet (IRE), **14/1** Sharp Holly (IRE) (8/1-16/1), CSF £7.11 TOTE £3.60: £1.70 £1.40 (£2.30) OWNER Mr D. R. Brotherton (LEEDS) BRED D. R. Brotherton 6 Rn

60.4 secs (1.70) SF: 43/49/21/26/26/14

1642 E.B.F. NOTTINGHAM EVENING POST MAIDEN STKS (2-Y.O) (Class D) £3,590.00 (£1,070.00: £510.00: £230.00)

5f 13y Stalls: High GOING minus 0.23 sec per fur (GF) 3-30 (3-31)

Rambo Delight *(67+) (JLEyre)* 2-9-0 RLappin(6) (cmpt: bkwd: disp ld: drvn to ld 1f out: r.o wl)..— **1**
1418[3] Pekay *(62)*(Fav)*(JBerry)* 2-9-0 JCarroll(1) (a.p: hrd rdn appr fnl f: kpt on: no ch w wnr)........1½ **2**
836[4] Theatre Magic *(37) (TJEtherington)* 2-9-0 KDarley(3) (slt ld over 3f: wknd appr fnl f)...............8 **3**

Soul of Honour (FR) *(34) (MrsJRRamsden)* 2-9-0 SMaloney(4) (w'like: bit bkwd: s.s: swtchd stands' side: a bhd & outpcd)....1 4
Opening Chorus *(31) (MrsJRRamsden)* 2-9-0 DHarrison(2) (cmpt: bkwd: dwlt: sn drvn along to chse ldrs: swtchd lft & effrt over 1f out: no imp)....1 5
1336[4] Spanish Luck *(20) (JWHills)* 2-8-9 BThomson(5) (a bhd & outpcd)....1¾ 6

8/11 Pekay (tchd 11/10), **11/2** RAMBO DELIGHT, **6/1** Opening Chorus (2/1-7/1), **9/1** Theatre Magic (6/1-10/1), **14/1** Spanish Luck, **16/1** Soul of Honour (FR), CSF £9.49 TOTE £7.70: £1.90 £1.20 (£3.60) OWNER C H & D W Stephenson Ltd (HAMBLETON) BRED C. Stephenson 6 Rn
61.4 secs (2.70) SF: 33/28/3/-/-/-

1643

SUN CHEMICAL H'CAP (0-70) (3-Y.O+) (Class E) £3,473.80 (£1,038.40: £497.20: £226.60) **1m 6f 15y** Stalls: Low GOING minus 0.23 sec per fur (GF) 4-00 (4-02)

1435[5] **Arc Bright (IRE) (37)***(49) (RHollinshead)* 5-7-7 (7)ow1 MHenry(6) (lw: mde all: clr 2f out: rdn & hld on gamely)....— 1
1452[5] Inn At the Top **(52)***(65) (JNorton)* 3-7-11 DaleGibson(5) (chsd ldrs: hdwy 2f out: hrd rdn & kpt on nr fin)....s.h 2
1529[2] Kintavi **(34)***(45) (TWDonnelly)* 5-7-11 CRutter(13) (hld up: hdwy centre over 3f out: rdn & styd on ins fnl f)....2 3
1435[4] Cliburnel News (IRE) **(61)***(66) (ALForbes)* 5-9-3 (7) DDenby(8) (hld up: hdwy 6f out: 5th st: kpt on one pce fnl 2f)....5 4
1552[6] Swordking (IRE) **(42)***(46) (JLHarris)* 6-8-5v PaulEddery(2) (lw: hld up: effrt 3f out: hrd rdn over 2f out: one pce)....1¼ 5
Tommy Cooper **(46)***(48) (MrsBarbaraWaring)* 4-8-4 (5) SDrowne(10) (bit bkwd: chsd ldrs: 3rd st: wknd wl over 1f out)....1½ 6
1432[6] Harry Browne (IRE) **(56)***(58) (MrsJRRamsden)* 3-8-1 SMaloney(4) (lw: hld up & bhd: hdwy on ins 3f out: sn rdn: nt rch ldrs)....nk 7
1368[12] Al Jinn **(39)***(40) (RCurtis)* 4-8-2 AMorris(9) (chsd wnr: 2nd st: wknd over 2f out)....nk 8
1359* Vain Prince **(45)***(46)*(Fav)*(NTinkler)* 8-8-8 GDuffield(12) (lw: chsd ldrs: 6th st: lost tch wl over 2f out)....nk 9
1349[4] Thrower **(47)***(47) (WMBrisbourne)* 4-8-5 (5) DGriffiths(11) (mid div tl wknd 3f out)....1 10
1268[6] Leap in the Dark (IRE) **(39)***(35) (MissLCSiddall)* 6-8-2 ow1 DHarrison(7) (lw: reard s: a in rr)..2½ 11
986[3] Fearless Wonder **(59)***(47) (MrsMReveley)* 4-9-8b KDarley(3) (lw: a bhd: rdn 3f out: t.o)....8 12
1513[4] Bee Beat **(43)** *(AJChamberlain)* 7-7-13 (7) MartinDwyer(1) (b: w.r.s: ref to r: t.n.p).... R

11/2 Vain Prince (4/1-6/1), **6/1** Fearless Wonder, Swordking (IRE), **7/1** Harry Browne (IRE), Kintavi, **8/1** Cliburnel News (IRE), **10/1** Inn At the Top, **11/1** ARC BRIGHT (IRE), **12/1** Bee Beat (op 8/1), **14/1** Tommy Cooper, **16/1** Leap in the Dark (IRE), **20/1** Thrower, **25/1** Al Jinn, CSF £109.83 CT £762.16 TOTE £12.80: £4.40 £2.40 £2.50 (£77.80) Trio £169.30 OWNER Mr J. E. Bigg (UPPER LONGDON) BRED Tsarina Stud 13 Rn 3m 5.1 (6.60) SF: 30/28/26/47/27/29/21/21/27/28/16/28/-
WEIGHT FOR AGE 3yo-18lb
STEWARDS' ENQUIRY Gibson susp. 23-24/6/95 (incorrect use of whip).

1644

HARLAND SIMON H'CAP (0-70) (3-Y.O+) (Class E) £3,273.60 (£976.80: £466.40: £211.20) **1m 54y** Stalls: Low GOING minus 0.23 sec per fur (GF) 4-30 (4-32)

1469[5] **Second Colours (USA) (57)***(66) (MrsMReveley)* 5-9-6 KDarley(2) (lw: hld up: 4th st: hrd drvn over 1f out: str run to ld cl home)....— 1
1323[U] Indian Serenade **(47)***(56) (PWHarris)* 4-8-5 (5) JStack(1) (led tl ct nr fin)....hd 2
1381* Yubralee (USA) **(72)***(79)*(Fav)*(MCPipe)* 3-9-10 JReid(5) (chsd ldr: 2nd st: rdn over 1f out: nvr able to chal)....1 3
1426[4] Noeprob (USA) **(42)***(48) (RJHodges)* 5-8-0 (5)ow1 SDrowne(4) (lw: chsd ldrs: 5th st: outpcd over 2f out: rallied appr fnl f: fin wl)....s.h 4
1542[3] Mr Cube (IRE) **(46)***(53) (JMBradley)* 5-8-2v(7) AmandaSanders(6) (hdwy 2f out: sn hrd rdn: kpt on ins fnl f)....s.h 5
1506[7] Bentico **(61)***(65) (MrsNMacauley)* 6-9-10 SWhitworth(9) (lw: chsd ldrs: 3rd st: hrd rdn wl over 1f out: one pce)....1¼ 6
839[12] Saint Amigo **(58)***(57) (JLEyre)* 3-8-10v RLappin(3) (dwlt: effrt over 2f out: nvr trbld ldrs)....2½ 7
Mr Butch **(65)***(26) (RCurtis)* 5-10-0 AMorris(8) (bit bkwd: hld up: effrt & c wd ent st: sn rdn: wknd over 2f out: t.o)....20 8
411[3] Mazilla **(58)***(16) (ALForbes)* 3-8-10 SDWilliams(7) (bit bkwd: chsd ldrs: 6th st: sn t.o)....1½ 9

5/2 Yubralee (USA), **5/1** SECOND COLOURS (USA), **11/2** Indian Serenade, Bentico (4/1-6/1), **8/1** Saint Amigo, Mr Cube (IRE), **10/1** Noeprob (USA), **12/1** Mazilla (op 8/1), **20/1** Mr Butch, CSF £31.04 CT £77.44 TOTE £5.50: £2.20 £1.20 £1.50 (£12.20) Trio £11.10 OWNER Mr P. D. Savill (SALTBURN) BRED Dinnaken Farm in USA 9 Rn 1m 45.6 (6.00) SF: 26/16/28/8/13/25/6/-/-
WEIGHT FOR AGE 3yo-11lb

1645 MILES 33 APPRENTICES' APPRENTICE LIMITED STKS (0-50) (3-Y.O+) (Class F) £3,552.20 (£989.20: £476.60)
1m 1f 213y Stalls: Low GOING minus 0.23 sec per fur (GF) 5-00 (5-02)

1553* **Vindaloo (55)***(69) (JLHarris)* 3-8-9 (5) PFessey(16) (lw: hdwy ½-wy: 4th st: led over 2f out: drvn clr fnl f)......— 1
1484[5] Anlace **(48)***(50) (SMellor)* 6-8-9b(5) ADaly(15) (hld up mid div: hdwy over 2f out: r.o u.p fnl f: no ch w wnr)......4 2
1513[8] Sinclair Lad (IRE) **(45)***(53) (RJHodges)* 7-9-2b(3) SDrowne(5) (lw: hld up: hdwy 3f out: chsd wnr over 2f out: one pce fnl f)......¾ 3
1328[9] Shuttlecock **(44)***(54) (MrsNMacauley)* 4-9-4 (5) MHenry(3) (chsd ldrs: 5th st: rdn & wnt lft over 2f out: kpt on one pce)......2 4
1358* Ring of Vision (IRE) **(53)***(52)*(Fav)*(MrsMReveley)* 3-8-3 (5) GParkin(8) (hld up: outpcd 5f out: styd on appr fnl f)......hd 5
1529[14] Marjimel **(47)***(37) (JLEyre)* 4-8-9 (5) DGriffiths(10) (hld up: hdwy & 7th st: rdn over 2f out: sn btn)......5 6
1427[2] Presto Boy **(52)***(42) (MBell)* 3-8-1 (5) GFaulkner(11) (lw: bhd: gd hdwy & 6th st: nt rch ldrs)....nk 7
1166[16] Red Spectacle (IRE) **(48)***(42) (PCHaslam)* 3-8-3 (5) NicolaHowarth(2) (in tch tl wknd over 2f out)......¾ 8
976[8] Specialize **(45)***(38) (KRBurke)* 3-7-13 (7) SO'Shea(4) (hld up in tch: effrt & n.m.r over 3f out: sn btn)......1¾ 9
1350[3] Centaur Express **(37)***(34) (ALForbes)* 3-8-1 (5) DDenby(9) (b.nr hind: effrt 3f out: rdn & wknd wl over 1f out)......2 10
Them Times (IRE) **(23)***(27) (FJordan)* 6-8-9 (5) RHavlin(1) (bit bkwd: led 2f: 2nd st: wknd over 2f out)......1¼ 11
1209[5] Fiaba **(45)***(25) (MrsNMacauley)* 7-8-9 (5) AmandaSanders(13) (lw: a in rr)......1¼ 12
1060[11] Tabard Garden **(43)***(17) (DNicholls)* 3-7-10 (5) RuthCoulter(17) (hld up: effrt 3f out: wknd over 2f out)......5 13
1422[3] Diamond Crown (IRE) **(50)***(18) (MartynWane)* 4-9-5 JTate(14) (a bhd)......2½ 14
1204[7] Share the Secret **(42)***(1) (BHanbury)* 3-8-3 (3) JStack(6) (led after 2f: sn wl clr: wknd & hdd over 2f out: t.o)......11 15
1471[7] Biased View **(35)** *(RThompson)* 3-8-3 (3) LNewton(7) (prom: 3rd st: wknd 3f out: t.o)......15 16
835[13] A Badge Too Far (IRE) **(30)** *(LJBarratt)* 5-8-9v(5) VHalliday(12) (b: lost pl ½-wy: t.o)......dist 17

2/1 Ring of Vision (IRE) (tchd 3/1), **5/1** VINDALOO, **7/1** Presto Boy, **8/1** Anlace, Centaur Express (op 20/1), **10/1** Share the Secret (5/1-12/1), Diamond Crown (IRE) (6/1-12/1), **14/1** Sinclair Lad (IRE) (8/1-16/1), **16/1** Red Spectacle (IRE), **20/1** Fiaba, A Badge Too Far (IRE), Marjimel, **25/1** Tabard Garden, Them Times (IRE), Shuttlecock, Specialize, **33/1** Biased View, CSF £49.91 TOTE £3.40: £1.80 £2.10 £4.80 (£17.00) Trio £92.50 OWNER Mr J. D. Abell (MELTON MOWBRAY) BRED Green Park Investments Ltd 17 Rn 2m 8.0 (5.50) SF: 35/29/32/33/18/16/8/8/4/-/6/4/-/-/-/-/-
WEIGHT FOR AGE 3yo-13lb
TPlpt: £111.80 (102.37 Tckts). T/Qdpt: Not won; £41.90 to Salisbury 13/6/95. IM

1522-PONTEFRACT (L-H)
Monday June 12th (Good)
WEATHER: overcast WIND: fresh across

1646 JUNE MAIDEN AUCTION STKS (I) (2-Y.O) (Class F) £2,717.00 (£762.00: £371.00)
5f Stalls: Low GOING minus 0.24 sec per fur (GF) 2-45 (2-47)

1134[11] **Mybotye** *(61+) (GROldroyd)* 2-8-4 RHills(1) (lw: trckd ldrs: hung lft 2f out: swtchd & qcknd to ld 1f out: r.o)......— 1
Some Horse (IRE) *(58) (MGMeagher)* 2-8-7 JFortune(3) (tall: unf: b: s.i.s: sn in tch: rdn over 2f out: r.o fnl f)......1¾ 2
889[5] February *(49) (MRChannon)* 2-8-3 ow1 AClark(10) (chsd ldrs: ev ch over 1f out: nt qckn)......1¼ 3
1017[7] Skelton Countess (IRE) *(40) (RHollinshead)* 2-7-13 FNorton(8) (plld hrd: hdwy 2f out: styd on)2 4
1336[5] Red Time *(34) (MSSaunders)* 2-8-4 NAdams(4) (a in tch: rdn over 2f out: no imp)......3½ 5
Quinta Boy *(33)*(Fav)*(JBerry)* 2-8-7 GCarter(5) (leggy: unf: led tl hdd & wknd 1f out)......1¼ 6
819[10] Babyshooz *(22) (MBrittain)* 2-7-13 GBardwell(2) (dwlt: a bhd)......¾ 7
1356[8] Sandblaster *(6) (MissJFCraze)* 2-7-13 JFanning(7) (hld up: outpcd fr ½-wy)......5 8
1266[5] Abduction *(3) (EWeymes)* 2-8-7 GHind(9) (effrt ½-wy: no imp)......3½ 9
1203[8] Wydale *(MWEllerby)* 2-8-1 (5)ow2 CTeague(6) (spd 3f: wknd qckly)......9 10

6/4 Quinta Boy, **11/4** MYBOTYE, **7/1** February, **9/1** Abduction, **10/1** Red Time, **16/1** Sandblaster, Skelton Countess (IRE), **20/1** Babyshooz, Some Horse (IRE), **50/1** Wydale, CSF £49.38 TOTE £4.60: £1.20 £3.30 £2.40 (£31.70) Trio £59.70 OWNER Mr Anthony Moroney (YORK) BRED R. S. A. Urquhart 10 Rn 65.4 secs (3.90) SF: 8/5/-/-/-/-/-/-/-/-

1647

DEWSBURY (S) STKS (3-Y.O+) (Class G) £2,644.00 (£734.00: £352.00)
1m 2f 6y Stalls: Low GOING minus 0.24 sec per fur (GF) 3-15 (3-18)

1161[14] **Mhemeanles (43)***(59) (CaptJWilson)* 5-9-4 JFortune(10) (lw: a.p: led wl over 1f out: sn hdd: styd on u.p to ld wl ins fnl f) ....— 1
1350* Lady Highfield **(38)***(60)*(Fav)*(MJRyan)* 4-9-5 AClark(5) (lw: b.hind: mid div: hdwy 4f out: led wl over 1f out tl wl ins fnl f).......nk 2
1285[7] Never Time (IRE) **(41)***(43) (MrsVAAconley)* 3-8-5 MDeering(2) (hdwy over 3f out: styd on: nrst fin) 10 3
874[18] Aerial View **(39)***(42) (WGMTurner)* 4-9-4 TSprake(13) (led 2f: led over 4f out tl wl over 1f out: one pce) ....hd 4
1350[6] Rosina's Folly **(40)***(35)*(Fav)*(JLHarris)* 4-8-13 TIves(14) (prom: effrt 3f out: no imp) 1½ 5
1523[8] Greek Night Out (IRE) **(35)***(27) (MrsVAAconley)* 4-8-13 TWilliams(11) (led after 2f tl over 4f out: hrd drvn & grad wknd) 5 6
1290[10] The Cape Doctor (IRE) **(52)***(29)*(Fav)*(AGFoster)* 3-8-5 DHolland(9) (lw: sn chsng ldrs: rdn & wknd 2f out) 1¾ 7
Leedons Park **(55)***(21) (MWEasterby)* 3-8-5 MBirch(6) (nvr nrr) 5 8
Bex Boy (IRE) *(16) (MWEasterby)* 4-9-4 MWigham(4) (a rr div) 3½ 9
1458[7] Gamzatti **(23)***(10) (CBBBooth)* 4-8-13 GCarter(8) (chsd ldrs tl wknd over 3f out) ....¾ 10
1379[15] Sharmoor **(40)***(9) (MissLCSiddall)* 3-8-0 FNorton(12) (n.d) ....½ 11
1084[5] Commanche Creek **(40)***(6) (JAHellens)* 5-9-4v JWeaver(3) (a bhd) 5 12
1059[9] Cuillin Caper *(TRWatson)* 3-8-0 JQuinn(1) (in tch tl rdn & wknd 6f out: t.o) 20 13
1469[10] Rennyholme **(20)** *(MWEllerby)* 4-9-4 SMorris(7) (cl up 3f: sn bhd: t.o) 6 14

5/1 The Cape Doctor (IRE), Lady Highfield, Rosina's Folly, **6/1** Never Time (IRE), Greek Night Out (IRE) (9/2-8/1), **8/1** Commanche Creek, **16/1** Leedons Park, Aerial View, Cuillin Caper, **20/1** MHEMEANLES, Sharmoor, **33/1** Bex Boy (IRE), Gamzatti, Rennyholme, CSF £111.98 TOTE £21.60: £5.40 £1.90 £2.60 (£51.40) Trio £274.40 OWNER Mr Frank Nicholls (PRESTON) BRED Miss J. Chaplin 14 Rn 2m 14.4 (6.10) SF: 36/37/7/19/12/4/-/-/-/-/-/-/-/-
WEIGHT FOR AGE 3yo-13lb
Bt in 3,300 gns
STEWARDS' ENQUIRY Fortune susp. 21-24/6/95 (excessive use of whip).

1648

HEY GROUP H'CAP (0-90) (3-Y.O+) (Class C) £7,440.00 (£2,220.00: £1,060.00: £480.00) **6f** Stalls: Low GOING minus 0.24 sec per fur (GF) 3-45 (3-46)

1433[3] **Cavers Yangous (67)***(73) (MJohnston)* 4-8-5 DHolland(9) (lw: a chsng ldrs: rdn over 2f out: styd on to ld wl ins fnl f) ....— 1
1354[2] Croft Pool **(81)***(86) (JAGlover)* 4-9-5 TIves(7) (a.p: rdn to ld ins fnl f: hdd wl ins fnl f: kpt on) ..nk 2
1296* Twice as Sharp **(83)***(83)*(Fav)*(PWHarris)* 3-8-12 RCochrane(5) (b: trckd ldrs gng wl: led over 2f out tl ins fn f: no ex) 2 3
1411[8] Napoleon Star (IRE) **(71)***(68) (MSSaunders)* 4-8-9 NAdams(8) (bhd: hdwy wl over 1f out: nvr able to chal) 1¼ 4
1241* Castlerea Lad **(90)***(83) (RHollinshead)* 6-10-0 LDettori(10) (lw: in tch: rdn 2f out: no imp) 1½ 5
922[13] Be Warned **(80)***(70) (NACallaghan)* 4-8-11 (7) AEddery(4) (lw: bhd tl r.o ins fnl f) 1 6
1131[6] Chiming In **(75)***(64) (MrsJRRamsden)* 3-8-4 JFortune(6) (bhd: plld wd wl over 1f out: nvr nr to chal) ....nk 7
1354[9] Pyramus (USA) **(74)***(54) (MrsLPiggott)* 4-8-5b(7) GMilligan(3) (b: chsd ldrs 4f) 3½ 8
1421[10] Two Moves in Front (IRE) **(70)***(45) (JBerry)* 5-8-8b GCarter(2) (s.i.s: sn in tch: outpcd fnl 2½f) 1¾ 9
1019[8] Encore M'Lady (IRE) **(81)***(53) (FHLee)* 4-9-5 JWeaver(1) (bit bkwd: led tl hdd over 2f out: sn wknd) 1 10

9/2 Twice as Sharp, **11/2** Chiming In, Castlerea Lad, **6/1** Croft Pool, **13/2** CAVERS YANGOUS, Be Warned, **8/1** Two Moves in Front (IRE), **10/1** Encore M'Lady (IRE), **14/1** Napoleon Star (IRE), **16/1** Pyramus (USA), CSF £43.52 CT £179.33 TOTE £6.80: £2.20 £2.20 £1.80 (£25.10) Trio £23.60 OWNER Mr F. Leithead (MIDDLEHAM) BRED Frank Leithead 10 Rn
1m 16.5 (2.20) SF: 41/54/42/36/51/38/23/22/13/21
WEIGHT FOR AGE 3yo-9lb
STEWARDS' ENQUIRY Ives susp. 23-24/6/95 (incorrect use of whip).

1649

BOROUGH H'CAP (0-70) (3-Y.O+) (Class E) £3,552.75 (£1,062.00: £508.50: £231.75)
1m 4y Stalls: Low GOING minus 0.24 sec per fur (GF) 4-15 (4-17)

1432[3] **Chantry Bellini (42)***(49) (MrsSMAustin)* 6-8-5b(3) DarrenMoffatt(15) (cl up: led over 2f out: qcknd clr over 1f out: kpt on) ....— 1

1250[11] Mary Macblain **(37)***(43) (JLHarris)* 6-8-3 DHolland(3) (mid div: effrt over 2f out: r.o wl towards fin) ....½ 2
1438[6] Nobby Barnes **(43)***(47) (DonEnricoIncisa)* 6-8-9 KimTinkler(7) (s.i.s: hld up & bhd: hdwy on outside 2f out: r.o towards fin)....1¼ 3
1412* Intendant **(62)***(65) (JGFitzGerald)* 3-9-3 JWeaver(12) (led 2f: chsd ldrs: outpcd 2f out: styd on ins fnl f) ....½ 4
1344[4] Poyle Jezebelle **(46)***(48) (MBlanshard)* 4-8-12 JQuinn(10) (a.p: effrt & ch 2f out: nt qckn fnl f) ....nk 5
1250[5] Maurangi **(54)***(55) (BWMurray)* 4-9-6 LDettori(8) (mid div: effrt over 2f out: r.o one pce) ....½ 6
579[9] Just Flamenco **(50)***(48) (MJRyan)* 4-9-2 AClark(6) (plld hrd: styd on fnl 2f: nvr able to chal) .1¼ 7
1459[4] Studio Thirty **(42)***(39) (RHollinshead)* 3-7-11 ow1 FNorton(11) (bhd: sn drvn along: styd on fnl 2f)....hd 8
1531[3] Self Expression **(53)***(51)*(Fav)*(MrsJRRamsden)* 7-9-5 GCarter(5) (s.i.s: hld up & bhd: nt clr run over 1f out: n.d) ....s.h 9
1291[2] Once More for Luck (IRE) **(62)***(59)*(Fav)*(MrsMReveley)* 4-10-0 RCochrane(9) (hld up & bhd: n.m.r ½-wy: n.d) ....½ 10
1207[11] Pash **(41)***(37) (CWCElsey)* 3-7-10 NKennedy(4) (cl up tl wknd 2f out) ....½ 11
1271[11] Izza **(42)***(18) (WStorey)* 4-8-8v JFanning(13) (chsd ldr tl wknd appr st)....10 12
1033[U] Just Lucky (IRE) **(59)***(35) (RWArmstrong)* 3-9-0 RPrice(1) (in tch 5f) ....nk 13
Rood Music **(59)***(25) (MGMeagher)* 4-9-11 JFortune(14) (cl up: led after 2f tl over 2f out: wknd qckly)....5 14
1290[16] Social Register **(55)***(11) (HThomsonJones)* 3-8-10 RHills(2) (chsd ldrs tl rdn & wknd qckly over 2f out) 5 15

5/1 Self Expression, Once More for Luck (IRE), **11/2** Maurangi, **6/1** Intendant, **9/1** Poyle Jezebelle, **10/1** Izza, **12/1** CHANTRY BELLINI, **14/1** Just Flamenco, Social Register, Nobby Barnes, Mary Macblain, **20/1** Just Lucky (IRE), Studio Thirty, **33/1** Pash, Rood Music, CSF £161.70 CT £2,171.08 TOTE £15.30: £4.10 £4.90 £4.80 (£105.00) Trio £312.40 OWNER Mrs J. J. KirkScott (MALTON) BRED J. Heyworth 15 Rn 1m 46.5 (4.50) SF: 30/24/28/35/29/36/29/9/32/40/7/-/5/6/-
WEIGHT FOR AGE 3yo-11lb

1650 YOUNGSTERS CONDITIONS STKS (2-Y.O) (Class D) £3,533.75 (£1,070.00: £522.50: £248.75)
6f Stalls: Low GOING minus 0.24 sec per fur (GF) 4-45 (4-45)

1440* **Persian Secret (FR)** *(86+)*(Fav)*(JWWatts)* 2-8-11 LDettori(2) (lw: trckd ldr: led wl over 1f out: pushed along & r.o wl)....— 1
718[2] The Frisky Farmer *(73) (WGMTurner)* 2-9-0 TSprake(4) (lw: chsd ldrs: rdn over 2f out: kpt on: no ch w wnr) 6 2
1369* Deerly *(61) (DMorris)* 2-8-9 JWeaver(1) (led tl hdd wl over 1f out: wknd ins fnl f)....2½ 3
1336* Whispering Dawn *(55) (MRChannon)* 2-8-9 RHughes(3) (hld up: effrt ½-wy: hrd rdn & btn over 1f out: eased ins fnl f)....2½ 4

8/11 PERSIAN SECRET (FR), **4/1** Whispering Dawn, **5/1** Deerly, **7/1** The Frisky Farmer (op 4/1), CSF £5.12 TOTE £1.60 (£3.00) OWNER Sheikh Mohammed (RICHMOND) BRED Darley Stud Management Co Ltd 4 Rn 1m 17.2 (2.90) SF: 37/24/12/6
STEWARDS' ENQUIRY Hughes fined £250 (weighing in 3lb heavy).

1651 BATLEY H'CAP (0-70) (3-Y.O+) (Class E) £3,406.50 (£1,017.00: £486.00: £220.50)
1m 2f 6y Stalls: Low GOING minus 0.24 sec per fur (GF) 5-15 (5-17)

1358[8] **Alltime Dancer (IRE) (50)***(61)*(Fav)*(MrsJRRamsden)* 3-7-13 GCarter(11) (lw: rr div: rdn 4f out: hdwy 2f out: r.o to ld wl ins fnl f)....— 1
1252[9] Bardia **(31)***(42) (DonEnricoIncisa)* 5-7-7 KimTinkler(4) (s.i.s: bhd tl hdwy 4f out: ev ch ins fnl f: kpt on fnl f)....hd 2
545[17] Able Choice (IRE) **(48)***(58) (RWArmstrong)* 5-8-10 RPrice(5) (chsd ldrs: rdn to ld over 1f out: hdd & no ex wl ins fnl f) ....¾ 3
1539[6] Phylian **(60)***(66) (SCWilliams)* 4-9-8 TIves(6) (in tch: hdwy over 2f out: styd on one pce fnl f)....2½ 4
876[13] Pendolino (IRE) **(55)***(60) (MBrittain)* 4-9-3 MWigham(2) (a chsng ldrs: one pce fnl 2f)....¾ 5
1244[8] Narbonne **(57)***(60) (BJMcMath)* 4-9-5 RCochrane(7) (cl up: led over 2f out tl over 1f out: sn btn) 1¼ 6
1088[5] Zanzara (IRE) **(44)***(42) (MrsVAAconley)* 4-8-6 MBirch(8) (chsd ldrs tl rdn & btn wl over 1f out)....3 7
1437[5] Imperial Bid (FR) **(56)***(54) (DenysSmith)* 7-9-4 JWeaver(9) (lw: bhd: hdwy 2f out: btn appr fnl f) ....hd 8
1205[10] Braille (IRE) **(64)***(61) (MGMeagher)* 4-9-12 JFortune(1) (lw: effrt over 3f out: n.d) ....s.h 9
967[7] Sallyoreally (IRE) **(53)***(41) (WStorey)* 4-9-1 JFanning(10) (a bhd) 6 10

1292³ Benjamins Law **(52)***(39) (JAPickering)* 4-9-0 DeanMcKeown(3) (lw: led tl hdd over 2f out: sn wknd) ¾ 11

LONG HANDICAP Bardia 7-6

5/2 ALLTIME DANCER (IRE), **11/2** Narbonne (4/1-6/1), **6/1** Phylian, **7/1** Benjamins Law, **15/2** Imperial Bid (FR), **8/1** Braille (IRE), **12/1** Sallyoreally (IRE), **14/1** Bardia, **16/1** Zanzara (IRE), Able Choice (IRE), **33/1** Pendolino (IRE), CSF £35.14 CT £438.32 TOTE £4.00: £2.00 £3.80 £4.30 (£42.40) Trio £166.40 OWNER Mr Colin Webster (THIRSK) BRED K. and Mrs Prendergast 11 Rn

2m 13.4 (5.10) SF: 26/20/36/44/38/38/20/32/39/19/17

WEIGHT FOR AGE 3yo-13lb

1652 JUNE MAIDEN AUCTION STKS (II) (2-Y.O) (Class F) £2,717.00(£762.00: £371.00) **5f** Stalls: Low GOING minus 0.24 sec per fur (GF) 5-45 (6-00)

Benny Glow *(74+) (MrsJRRamsden)* 2-8-7 JFortune(6) (rangy: hdwy over 2f out: r.o to ld wl ins fnl f) — 1
910⁴ Magic Imp (IRE) *(60)*(Fav)*(WJMusson)* 2-7-13 GCarter(4) (w ldrs: led 2f out tl wl ins fnl f) 1¾ 2
1282³ Pathaze *(58) (NBycroft)* 2-7-13 JFanning(2) (chsd ldrs: chal 1f out: wknd towards fin) ¾ 3
943⁵ Napoleon's Return *(52) (AGFoster)* 2-8-4 JWeaver(8) (unruly paddock: led 3f: one pce) 3½ 4
Nkapen Rocks (SPA) *(51) (CaptJWilson)* 2-8-7 GHind(5) (w'like: leggy: scope: dwlt: rn green: bhd tl styd on fnl f) 1¼ 5
1399⁶ Princess Renata (IRE) *(43) (DTThom)* 2-8-2 FNorton(10) (in tch: effrt 2f out: nvr trbld ldrs) ¾ 6
1448² Badger Bay (IRE) *(42) (JohnBerry)* 2-8-2 JQuinn(1) (in tch: effrt ½-wy: no imp) ½ 7
Good To Talk *(38) (MHEasterby)* 2-8-5 ow1 MBirch(3) (w'like: bkwd: chsd ldrs over 3f) 1¾ 8
Needle Knot (IRE) *(32) (MJohnston)* 2-8-4 DHolland(7) (rangy: s.s: a bhd) 2 9
Rushcutter Bay *(TTClement)* 2-8-4 DeanMcKeown(9) (uns rdr & bolted leaving paddock) W

2/1 Magic Imp (IRE), **6/1** Napoleon's Return (op 4/1), Needle Knot (IRE), Badger Bay (IRE) (op 4/1), **10/1** Nkapen Rocks (SPA) (5/1-12/1), **11/1** Pathaze, **14/1** Princess Renata (IRE) (op 33/1), Good To Talk (op 8/1), **16/1** BENNY GLOW, **66/1** Rushcutter Bay, CSF £44.55 TOTE £19.50: £3.90 £1.30 £3.00 (£32.50) Trio £121.30 OWNER Mr Ronald Thorburn (THIRSK) BRED D. H. Jones 9 Rn

65.1 secs (3.60) SF: 15/1/-/-/-/-/-/-/-

T/Jkpt: Not won; £3,635.11 to Salisbury 13/6/95. T/Plpt: £4,903.70 (3.14 Tckts). T/Qdpt: Not won; £142.60 to Salisbury 13/6/95. AA

1540-WARWICK (L-H)
Monday June 12th (Good to firm)
WEATHER: overcast WIND: mod half against

1653 E.B.F. ROYAL MAIDEN STKS (2-Y.O F) (Class D) £3,785.00 (£1,130.00: £540.00: £245.00) **5f** Stalls: Low GOING minus 0.07 sec per fur (G) 6-15 (6-15)

Baize *(82+) (RFJohnsonHoughton)* 2-8-11 JReid(4) (w'like: s.i.s: sn prom: led wl over 1f out: pushed clr: easily) — 1
Splicing *(69)*(Fav)*(JRFanshawe)* 2-8-11 DHarrison(2) (leggy: w'like: dwlt: hdwy over 2f out: rdn over 1f out: chsd wnr fnl f: no imp) 4 2
Volare *(60) (MCPipe)* 2-8-8 (3) DRMcCabe(1) (unf: s.s: hdwy over 1f out: r.o) 3 3
1253⁹ Willow Dale (IRE) *(59) (DRCElsworth)* 2-8-11 WCarson(3) (bhd tl hdwy 2f out: one pce fnl f) hd 4
1223³ Princess Pamgaddy *(58) (JBerry)* 2-8-11 JCarroll(6) (a.p: no hdwy fnl 2f) nk 5
669¹⁰ Mystic Dawn *(49) (SDow)* 2-8-11 WRyan(5) (led over 3f: wknd 1f out) 3 6
1307⁴ Exceedingly *(30) (WJarvis)* 2-8-11 AMcGlone(9) (spd 3f) 6 7
Clincher Club *(29) (MJohnston)* 2-8-11 TWilliams(8) (leggy: lt-f: prom: rdn over 2f out: sn wknd) nk 8
508¹³ Zuno Princess (IRE) *(GLewis)* 2-8-11 SWhitworth(7) (bkwd: dwlt: outpcd: t.o) 13 9

100/30 Splicing, **7/2** Princess Pamgaddy (op 7/4), **11/2** BAIZE, Clincher Club (op 5/2), Exceedingly, **7/1** Volare (8/1-14/1), **20/1** Mystic Dawn, Willow Dale (IRE), **33/1** Zuno Princess (IRE), CSF £22.81 TOTE £5.80: £3.90 £1.10 £1.90 (£10.00) Trio £109.90 OWNER Lady Rothschild (DIDCOT) BRED Exors of the late Mrs D. M. de Rothschild 9 Rn 60.6 secs (2.60) SF: 45/32/23/22/21/12/-/-/-

1654 WARWICK FESTIVAL CLAIMING STKS (3-Y.O) (Class F) £3,149.00 (£874.00: £419.00) **7f** Stalls: Low GOING minus 0.07 sec per fur (G) 6-45 (6-47)

1338⁴ **A Million to One (IRE) (72)***(79)*(Fav)*(MBell)* 3-8-10 MFenton(6) (4th st: led wl over 1f out: pushed out) — 1

1366[12] Delight of Dawn **(69)***(75) (KTIvory)* 3-8-3 (7) CScally(8) (b.hind: s.s: hdwy & 5th st: hung lft over 1f out: chsd wnr fnl f: no imp) 1¾ 2
1263[6] Emphatic Candidate (IRE) **(71)***(69) (RAkehurst)* 3-8-10 (3) SSanders(2) (lw: 3rd st: led 2f out: sn hdd: one pce) 4 3
1381[2] Komodo (USA) **(68)***(68) (DRCElsworth)* 3-9-2 (5) AProcter(3) (lw: led 5f: sn wknd) 4 4
1445[5] Code of Silence **(47)***(55) (GFHCharles-Jones)* 3-8-4 (5) PMcCabe(4) (lost pl 5f out: rdn over 3f out: 7th st: n.d) ....½ 5
1366[3] Sapphire Son (IRE) **(60)***(51) (CNWilliams)* 3-9-1v WRyan(1) (w ldr: 2nd st: ev ch 2f out: wknd over 1f out) 4 6
1403[4] Embezzler **(52)***(31) (GLewis)* 3-8-1b WCarson(5) (plld hrd: hung rt over 3f out: rn wd & lost pl: last st) 3 7
861[7] Eileen's Guest (IRE) **(45)***(13) (RJRWilliams)* 3-8-2 DBiggs(7) (6th st: bhd fnl 2f) 8 8

6/4 A MILLION TO ONE (IRE), **7/2** Sapphire Son (IRE), **5/1** Emphatic Candidate (IRE) (op 3/1), **13/2** Embezzler, **7/1** Komodo (USA), **10/1** Delight of Dawn (op 6/1), **25/1** Code of Silence, Eileen's Guest (IRE), CSF £16.64 TOTE £2.60: £1.10 £3.60 £1.80 (£10.50) OWNER Mrs E. A. Harris (NEWMARKET) BRED Gay O'Callaghan 8 Rn 1m 27.5 (3.30) SF: 50/46/40/39/26/22/2/-

1655

F.A.SIMMS H'CAP (0-80) (3-Y.O+) (Class D) £3,914.20 (£1,081.20: £514.60)
1m 4f 115y Stalls: Low GOING minus 0.07 sec per fur (G) 7-15 (7-15)

1260[2] **Sharp Falcon (IRE) (72)***(81)*(Fav)*(JWharton)* 4-9-10 JReid(1) (trckd ldr: 2nd st: led over 1f out: rdn out) ....— 1
1144[7] Ismeno **(58)***(65) (SDow)* 4-8-10 WRyan(2) (led tl hdd over 1f out: nt qckn) 1¼ 2
280[6] Lone Risk **(50)***(47) (CNAllen)* 4-8-2 GBardwell(3) (lw: hld up: effrt & 3rd st: rdn over 2f out: wknd over 1f out) 8 3

4/11 SHARP FALCON (IRE), **9/2** Ismeno (op 2/1), **11/2** Lone Risk, CSF £2.13 TOTE £1.40 (£1.50) OWNER Mr G. W. Mills (MELTON MOWBRAY) BRED T. Monaghan 3 Rn
2m 49.1 (11.60) SF: 30/14/-

1656

HAZY DAYS RATING RELATED MAIDEN LIMITED STKS (0-70) (3-Y.O+) (Class E) £3,260.25 (£972.00: £463.50: £209.25)
1m 4f 115y Stalls: Low GOING minus 0.07 sec per fur (G) 7-45 (7-46)

1093[13] **Labibeh (USA) (67)***(70)*(Fav)*(JLDunlop)* 3-8-4 WCarson(5) (mde all: rdn & swished tail 4f out: edgd rt ins fnl f: r.o wl) ....— 1
1446[4] Backview **(69)***(70) (BJLlewellyn)* 3-8-9 RPrice(2) (chsd wnr: hrd rdn & 3rd st: r.o one pce fnl f) 4 2
722[6] Fresh Look (IRE) **(59)***(65) (RFJohnsonHoughton)* 3-8-4 DHarrison(3) (hld up: hdwy 7f out: wnt 2nd st: no imp) ....nk 3
1339[5] Baddi Quest **(70)***(66) (BHanbury)* 3-8-9 MRimmer(4) (4th st: one pce fnl 2f) 3 4
730[9] Alpine Storm (IRE) **(47)***(35) (MDIUsher)* 3-7-11 (7) CAdamson(1) (prom tl wknd 4f out: 5th & t.o st) 20 5
1317[8] Colt D'Or **(47)***(38) (JWhite)* 3-8-9 MFenton(6) (rdn 6f out: lost tch 4f out: 6th & t.o st) 1½ 6

11/10 LABIBEH (USA) (4/5-5/4), **2/1** Baddi Quest, **9/2** Backview (4/1-6/1), **9/1** Fresh Look (IRE) (op 5/1), **40/1** Alpine Storm (IRE), Colt D'Or, CSF £6.35 TOTE £1.70: £1.40 £2.00 (£4.70) OWNER Mr Hamdan Al Maktoum (ARUNDEL) BRED Shadwell Farm Estate Co Ltd and Shadwell Farm Inc 6 Rn 2m 45.7 (8.20) SF: 32/32/27/28/-/-

1657

'NURSERY WOOD' H'CAP (0-70) (3-Y.O+) (Class E) £3,465.00 (£1,035.00: £495.00: £225.00)
2m 20y Stalls: Low GOING minus 0.07 sec per fur (G) 8-15 (8-15)

1313[2] **Lalindi (IRE) (70)***(80)*(Fav)*(DRCElsworth)* 4-9-9 (5) AProcter(7) (led after 2f: rdn over 1f out: r.o wl) ....— 1
1535* Soojama (IRE) **(40)***(50)*(Fav)*(RMFlower)* 5-7-13 4x DBiggs(6) (dwlt: hdwy 6f out: 3rd st: hrd rdn over 1f out: ev ch fnl f: r.o) ....nk 2
1535[7] Gentleman Sid **(37)***(41) (PGMurphy)* 5-7-10 ow3 DaleGibson(5) (prom: rdn 4f out: 2nd st: ev ch wl over 1f out: one pce) 2½ 3
1058[13] Secret Assignment (USA) **(34)***(33) (RCurtis)* 5-7-7 GBardwell(2) (hld up: hdwy over 3f out: 5th st: n.d) 8 4
884[13] Joys First **(42)***(40) (HJCollingridge)* 4-8-0 JQuinn(1) (hld up in rr: hdwy over 5f out: 4th st: wknd over 2f out) 1½ 5
1328[2] Coleridge **(47)***(25) (JJSheehan)* 7-8-3b(3) DRMcCabe(4) (hld up: rdn over 5f out: wknd over 4f out: poor 6th st: t.o) 20 6

1407[4] Shanuke (IRE) **(57)***(19) (JSMoore)* 3-7-5 (5)ow3 NVarley(3) (lw: led 2f: rdn 10f out: wknd 5f out: t.o)....13 **7**

LONG HANDICAP Secret Assignment (USA) 7-3 Gentleman Sid 7-6 Shanuke (IRE) 7-0

2/1 LALINDI (IRE), Soojama (IRE), **5/2** Coleridge, **12/1** Joys First, **16/1** Shanuke (IRE), **20/1** Gentleman Sid, **33/1** Secret Assignment (USA), CSF £6.39 TOTE £2.80: £1.90 £1.60 (£3.20) OWNER White Horse Racing Ltd (WHITCOMBE) BRED Hascombe and Valiant Studs 7 Rn

3m 36.5 (10.50) SF: 55/26/17/9/15/1/-

WEIGHT FOR AGE 3yo-20lb, 4yo-1lb

1658

GALLOWS HILL H'CAP (0-70) (3-Y.O+) (Class E) £3,289.50 (£981.00: £468.00: £211.50) **1m 2f 169y** Stalls: Low GOING minus 0.07 sec per fur (G) 8-45 (8-45)

1543* **Myfontaine (60)***(65) (KTIvory)* 8-10-1 5x GBardwell(2) (lw: hld up: hdwy & 4th st: led wl over 1f out: rdn out)....— **1**
1128[7] Dancing Destiny **(67)***(71)*(Fav)*(JRFanshawe)* 3-9-7 DHarrison(8) (hld up: hdwy to ld over 2f out: hdd wl over 1f out: nt qckn)....1 **2**
1091[10] Lexus (IRE) **(36)***(29) (RJRWilliams)* 7-8-5 DBiggs(1) (5th st: r.o one pce fnl 2f)....7 **3**
1198[9] Shepherds Rest (IRE) **(53)***(46) (SMellor)* 3-8-0 (7) ADaly(3) (plld hrd: hdwy & 6th st: hmpd on ins wl over 1f out: swtchd rt: r.o fnl f)....nk **4**
1353[4] Bell Contractors (IRE) **(65)***(54) (CDBroad)* 3-9-2 (3) DRMcCabe(7) (hld up & bhd: last st: hdwy whn nt clr run & hmpd over 1f out: n.d)....2½ **5**
1444[13] Lady Valensina (IRE) **(54)***(36) (BJLlewellyn)* 4-9-9 RPrice(4) (chsd ldrs tl 3rd st: wknd wl over 1f out)....5 **6**
1332[2] Rolling Waters **(38)***(14) (JARToller)* 5-8-7 TWilliams(6) (prom: 7th & wkng st)....3½ **7**
1350[13] Porte Belloch **(41)***(13) (CTNash)* 4-8-10 RPerham(5) (led tl hdd & 2nd st: wknd 2f out)....3 **8**

15/8 Dancing Destiny, **2/1** MYFONTAINE (6/4-9/4), **4/1** Rolling Waters, **8/1** Porte Belloch, **12/1** Lexus (IRE), **16/1** Lady Valensina (IRE), **20/1** Bell Contractors (IRE), **33/1** Shepherds Rest (IRE), CSF £6.31 CT £31.73 TOTE £2.60: £1.30 £1.60 £2.10 (£3.30) OWNER Mr K. T. Ivory (RADLETT) BRED Farmleigh Partners 8 Rn

2m 21.2 (7.70) SF: 49/40/13/15/23/20/-/-

WEIGHT FOR AGE 3yo-15lb

T/Plpt: £16.00 (595.39 Tckts). T/Qdpt: £3.60 (9.6 Tckts). KH

1509-WINDSOR (Fig. 8)
Monday June 12th (Good)

WEATHER: overcast WIND: fresh half against

1659

CANCER RESEARCH CAMPAIGN & BRITISH EQUESTRIAN OLYMPIC FUND CLAIMING STKS (3-Y.O+) (Class F) £2,932.50 (£885.00: £430.00: £202.50) **1m 3f 135y** Stalls: High GOING minus 0.31 sec per fur (GF) 6-30 (6-31)

1372[7] **Elly Fleetfoot (IRE) (58)***(59) (TGMills)* 3-7-11 AMackay(5) (lw: hld up: rdn over 2f out: led over 1f out: hrd rdn: r.o wl)....— **1**
1519* Shabanaz **(68)***(62)*(Fav)*(WRMuir)* 10-9-4 StephenDavies(7) (4th st: led over 2f out tl over 1f out: edgd lft & ev ch fnl f: unable qckn nr fin)....1½ **2**
1436[5] Roadsweeper (FR) **(46)***(59) (KOCunningham-Brown)* 3-8-3 MRoberts(4) (lw: led 4f: 2nd st: led 4f out tl over 2f out: one pce)....3 **3**
Castoret **(73)***(61) (JWHills)* 9-9-7 MHills(2) (bit bkwd: 6th st: rdn over 2f out: onepce)....s.h **4**
1202[14] Esthal (IRE) **(48)***(50) (ABarrow)* 5-9-1v JWilliams(9) (5th st: wknd over 2f out)....3½ **5**
586[11] Brown Carpet **(27)***(51) (CAHorgan)* 8-9-2b MPerrett(1) (stdy hdwy over 2f out: wknd over 1f out)....nk **6**
1513[17] Pulmicort **(55)***(49) (PBurgoyne)* 5-9-5 BRouse(12) (lw: n.m.r on ins over 4f out: nvr nr to chal)....3½ **7**
Dragon Green *(50) (JWhite)* 4-9-7 MTebbutt(10) (bit bkwd: plld hrd: 3rd st: wknd 3f out)....nk **8**
1325[4] Salfrill (IRE) *(43) (MrsPSly)* 3-8-0 NCarlisle(3) (bhd fnl 3f)....2 **9**
Rain Warrior *(47) (MissAJWhitfield)* 5-9-7 WNewnes(6) (s.s: a bhd)....½ **10**
1371[11] Northern Spruce (IRE) *(40) (MissJacquelineDoyle)* 3-8-5 PRobinson(8) (lw: a bhd)....5 **11**
1427[11] Ragtime Song **(20)***(12) (AMoore)* 6-9-0v CandyMorris(11) (led over 7f out to 4f out: sn wknd) 15 **12**

11/8 Shabanaz (Evens-6/4), **3/1** Castoret, **5/1** ELLY FLEETFOOT (IRE) (4/1-6/1), **12/1** Rain Warrior (8/1-33/1), **14/1** Roadsweeper (FR) (12/1-20/1), **25/1** Pulmicort, **33/1** Dragon Green, Brown Carpet, Salfrill (IRE), **50/1** Esthal (IRE), Northern Spruce (IRE), Ragtime Song, CSF £11.31 TOTE £6.60: £1.80 £1.40 £2.00 (£6.70) Trio £36.50 OWNER Dr Susan Barnes (EPSOM) BRED B. Barnes, Dr S. Barnes, Brick Kiln Stud & V. D'Ha 12 Rn 2m 31.2 (5.20) SF: 23/42/23/41/30/31/29/30/7/27/4/-

WEIGHT FOR AGE 3yo-16lb

Elly Fleetfoot (IRE) clmd AReid £7,000

1660 OPUS TECHNOLOGY H'CAP (0-70) (3-Y.O F) (Class E) £3,766.00 (£1,138.00: £554.00: £262.00)
5f 217y Stalls: High GOING minus 0.31 sec per fur (GF) 7-00 (7-02)

1094 17 **Brockton Flame (62)***(68) (JMPEustace)* 3-9-0 MHills(2) (hdwy over 2f out: led over 1f out: drvn out) — 1
1414 5 Lough Erne **(69)***(72) (CFWall)* 3-9-7 NCarlisle(9) (swtchd rt s: nt clr run 2f out: swtchd lft & hdwy over 1f out: unable qckn) 1¼ 2
1032 9 Charnwood Queen **(46)***(40) (RWArmstrong)* 3-7-5 (7)ow5 SLanigan(10) (a.p: led over 2f out tl over 1f out: one pce) 1½ 3
1258 12 Bella Coola **(52)***(49) (CAHorgan)* 3-8-4 CRutter(3) (hdwy 2f out: rdn over 1f out: one pce) ¾ 4
1566 7 Nadwaty (IRE) **(53)***(45) (MCChapman)* 3-7-12 (7) CMunday(6) (a.p: ev ch over 1f out: sn wknd) 1¾ 5
1165 6 Second Cello **(64)***(56) (DMorris)* 3-9-2 StephenDavies(14) (a.p: ev ch over 1f out: wknd fnl f) s.h 6
1453 3 Brass Tacks **(65)***(54) (RHannon)* 3-9-3 GeorginaFrost(15) (lw: hmpd over 1f out: nvr nr to chal) 1 7
1201 10 Sally Weld **(64)***(53) (CJBenstead)* 3-9-2 BRouse(8) (a.p: ev ch over 1f out: sn wknd) s.h 8
1512 19 Classic Pet (IRE) **(50)***(37) (CAHorgan)* 3-8-2 NAdams(18) (stdd s: stdy hdwy & nt clr run over 1f out: swtchd rt: eased ins fnl f) ¾ 9
1279 12 La Bossette (IRE) **(49)***(34) (JRArnold)* 3-8-1b MRoberts(13) (nvr nrr) ¾ 10
733 6 The Mestral **(41)***(25) (MJRyan)* 3-7-2 (5) MBaird(7) (hdwy over 2f out: wknd over 1f out) nk 11
1546 2 Secret Miss **(50)***(31) (APJarvis)* 3-8-2 PRobinson(11) (lw: hld up: rdn over 2f out: wknd over 1f out) 1¼ 12
1521* Tachycardia **(51)***(32)*(Fav)*(RJO'Sullivan)* 3-8-3 7x AClark(16) (led over 3f) s.h 13
1165 13 Nordesta (IRE) **(67)***(40) (MRChannon)* 3-9-5 RHughes(12) (lw: bhd fnl 3f) 3 14
697 8 Blue Sioux **(65)***(31) (JWharton)* 3-9-3 JWilliams(5) (spd 4f) 2½ 15
1053 10 Treasure Keay **(58)***(17) (PJMakin)* 3-8-10 LDettori(17) (bhd fnl 3f) 2½ 16

LONG HANDICAP Charnwood Queen 7-4

7/2 Tachycardia, **6/1** Lough Erne, Secret Miss, **15/2** Brass Tacks (5/1-8/1), **8/1** The Mestral, **12/1** Sally Weld (op 8/1), Second Cello, Treasure Keay, **14/1** La Bossette (IRE) (8/1-16/1), **16/1** Classic Pet (IRE), Nordesta (IRE), **20/1** Blue Sioux, BROCKTON FLAME, Nadwaty (IRE), **25/1** Charnwood Queen, **33/1** Bella Coola, CSF £137.13 CT £2,805.07 TOTE £32.30: £4.20 £2.10 £11.50 £13.40 (£142.80) Trio £474.70 OWNER Mrs D. A. La Trobe (NEWMARKET) BRED J. B. and Mrs N. G. Stafford 16 Rn 1m 13.2 (2.70) SF: 34/38/6/15/11/22/20/19/3/-/-/-/-/6/-/-

1661 SUNLEY H'CAP (0-80) (3-Y.O+) (Class D) £4,500.00 (£1,350.00:£650.00: £300.00)
1m 2f 7y Stalls: High GOING minus 0.31 sec per fur (GF) 7-30 (7-33)

668 9 **Northern Union (CAN) (78)***(88) (MAJarvis)* 4-10-0 PRobinson(12) (hdwy over 1f out: hrd rdn & led nr fin) — 1
1183 6 Uncle Oswald **(76)***(86) (RHannon)* 4-9-5 (7) DaneO'Neill(2) (3rd st: rdn over 2f out: led wl ins fnl f: hdd nr fin) nk 2
678 6 Soldier's Leap (FR) **(71)***(80) (CEBrittain)* 3-8-8v MRoberts(4) (led: rdn over 2f out: hdd wl ins fnl f: r.o) s.h 3
Country Star (IRE) **(73)***(76) (HCandy)* 4-9-9 WNewnes(3) (stdy hdwy over 1f out: nvr plcd to chal) 4 4
1472 3 Lady Lacey **(48)***(50) (GBBalding)* 8-7-5v(7) IonaWands(8) (hrd rdn & hdwy over 2f out: one pce) ½ 5
1472 2 Bellas Gate Boy **(65)***(57) (GLewis)* 3-7-11 (5)ow2 AWhelan(5) (lw: 6th st: wknd over 1f out) 5 6
1225 4 Lowawatha **(72)***(49) (DMorris)* 7-9-8 AClark(11) (5th st: wknd over 2f out) 11 7
1260 7 New Albion (USA) **(71)***(45) (NJHenderson)* 4-9-7 PaulEddery(6) (lw: hdwy over 3f out: wknd over 2f out) 2 8
1273* Wathbat Mtoto **(80)***(51)*(Fav)*(LMCumani)* 3-9-3 LDettori(9) (2nd st: rdn 3f out: wknd over 2f out: lame) 1¾ 9
1367 6 Fieldridge **(76)***(46) (CPEBrooks)* 6-9-12 PatEddery(10) (4th st: wknd over 3f out) ½ 10
1183 23 Make a Stand **(70)***(37) (HCandy)* 4-9-6 NAdams(7) (lw: a bhd) 1¾ 11
678 7 Yacht **(75)***(18) (BWHills)* 3-8-12v MHills(1) (bhd fnl 6f: t.o) 15 12

2/1 Wathbat Mtoto, **11/2** Fieldridge, **6/1** Uncle Oswald (op 7/2), **7/1** Soldier's Leap (FR), **8/1** Lowawatha (op 5/1), **9/1** Bellas Gate Boy (4/1-10/1), **14/1** New Albion (USA) (12/1-20/1), **16/1** Yacht, NORTHERN UNION (CAN), **20/1** Country Star (IRE), Lady Lacey, **50/1** Make a Stand, CSF £105.70 CT £684.30 TOTE £17.80: £3.40 £2.20 £2.30 (£66.10) Trio £72.30 OWNER Mrs Anita Green (NEWMARKET) BRED Kinghaven Farms Ltd in Canada 12 Rn
2m 7.1 (2.20) SF: 69/67/48/57/31/25/30/26/19/27/18/-
WEIGHT FOR AGE 3yo-13lb

1662

DRAGONFLY MAIDEN STKS (2-Y.O) (Class E) £3,696.25 (£1,120.00: £547.50: £261.25) **5f 217y** Stalls: High GOING minus 0.31 sec per fur (GF) 8-00 (8-03)

Regiment (IRE) *(87+) (RHannon)* 2-8-8 KDarley(10) (leggy: scope: bit bkwd: hdwy over 1f out: led ins fnl f: rn green)........ — 1
1481² Essentialselection *(82) (WJHaggas)* 2-8-7 MRoberts(14) (led tl ins fnl f: unable qckn) 1½ 2
Stronz (IRE) *(71) (RAkehurst)* 2-8-7 LDettori(9) (leggy: bit bkwd: hld up: rdn over 2f out: one pce) 4 3
1169³ Mountain Valley *(65) (PFICole)* 2-8-2 CRutter(3) (lw: rdn & hdwy 2f out: one pce fnl f)........½ 4
Urgent Swift *(63) (APJarvis)* 2-8-3 StephenDavies(11) (w'like: nvr nr to chal)........1¼ 5
523³ Thai Morning *(67) (PWHarris)* 2-8-8 PatEddery(5) (a.p: rdn over 2f out: wknd fnl f) ....nk 6
1481¹¹ Dragonjoy *(50) (LJHolt)* 2-8-2 CAvery(8) (lw: prom over 3f)........4 7
White Ensign (IRE) *(54) (RHannon)* 2-8-8 ow2 BThomson(12) (str: bkwd: prom over 2f: wkng whn hmpd over 2f out) ....s.h 8
943² Erupt *(49)*(Fav)*(GBBalding)* 2-8-5 JWilliams(2) (a.p: ev ch over 1f out: sn wknd)........1½ 9
Laser Life Star *(36) (CNWilliams)* 2-8-1 ow4 PRobinson(6) (b.off hind: leggy: unf: hld up: rdn over 2f out: wknd wl over 1f out) 1¾ 10
1184¹⁶ Oblomov *(42) (GLewis)* 2-8-7 PaulEddery(1) (bhd fnl 2f)........1¾ 11
1318⁸ Two Socks *(36) (MMcCormack)* 2-8-5 AClark(4) (bhd fnl 2f) 1¼ 12
943¹² Double Vintage (IRE) *(35) (MCChapman)* 2-7-11 (7) CMunday(7) (bhd fnl 3f)........hd 13
Victory Commander *(TJNaughton)* 2-8-7 MHills(13) (unf: bit bkwd: bhd fnl 4f: t.o)........15 14

9/4 Erupt, **4/1** Thai Morning (3/1-5/1), Essentialselection (5/2-9/2), **7/1** REGIMENT (IRE), Mountain Valley (2/1-8/1), **9/1** Stronz (IRE) (6/1-10/1), **16/1** Laser Life Star, **20/1** Urgent Swift, White Ensign (IRE), Victory Commander, **25/1** Oblomov, **33/1** Two Socks, **50/1** Double Vintage (IRE), Dragonjoy, CSF £37.12 TOTE £10.70: £2.60 £1.60 £2.20 (£25.70) Trio £51.30 OWNER Highclere Thoroughbred Racing Ltd (MARLBOROUGH) BRED N. Browne 14 Rn

1m 14.1 (3.60) SF: 17/12/1/-/-/-/-/-/-/-/-/-/-/-

1663

KINGFISHER H'CAP (0-70) (3-Y.O+) (Class E) £3,629.50 (£1,096.00: £533.00: £251.50) **1m 67y** Stalls: High GOING minus 0.31 sec per fur (GF) 8-30 (8-35)

1468* **Karinska (59)***(66) (MCChapman)* 5-8-12 (7) CMunday(13) (lw: 7th st: rdn over 2f out: led ins fnl f: r.o wl)........— 1
1368⁷ Sea Spouse **(41)***(47) (MBlanshard)* 4-8-1 MRoberts(3) (led: rdn over 1f out: hdd ins fnl f: r.o) ....½ 2
1514⁵ Braydon Forest **(67)***(71) (CJDrewe)* 3-9-2 BThomson(6) (lw: 6th st: rdn over 3f out: r.o ins fnl f)........1¼ 3
158⁷ Lady Sabina **(38)***(40) (WJMusson)* 5-7-12 ow1 CRutter(14) (hdwy over 1f out: hrd rdn: r.o) ......½ 4
1049³ Hatta Sunshine (USA) **(42)***(39) (AMoore)* 5-7-11 (5)ow4 AWhelan(1) (lw: 5th st: ev ch over 1f out: wknd ins fnl f) ....¾ 5
1509⁷ Vanroy **(58)***(57) (JRJenkins)* 11-9-4v LDettori(2) (nvr nr to chal) 1¼ 6
1438² Mr Rough **(64)***(60)*(Fav)*(DMorris)* 4-9-10 StephenDavies(7) (lw: 3rd st: rdn over 2f out: wknd fnl f) 1½ 7
815¹³ Lord Palmerston (USA) **(65)***(59) (PFICole)* 3-9-0 RHughes(12) (4th st: wknd 3f out) 1¼ 8
1366⁶ Singing Rock (IRE) **(65)***(56) (RHannon)* 3-8-7 (7) DaneO'Neill(10) (a bhd) 1¼ 9
1513¹⁴ Safe Secret **(40)***(27) (RBrotherton)* 4-8-0 AMackay(4) (bhd fnl 2f)........2 10
1016¹³ Kreef **(50)***(32) (RJO'Sullivan)* 3-7-8 (5) MBaird(9) (2nd st: wknd over 1f out) 2½ 11
1209⁴ Rosevear (IRE) **(50)***(19) (SMellor)* 3-7-13 NCarlisle(5) (a bhd)........7 12
1244¹³ Ballynakelly **(70)***(20) (RAkehurst)* 3-9-5 AClark(11) (lw: a bhd) 10 13
Diaco **(58)** *(JWHills)* 10-9-4 KDarley(8) (Withdrawn not under Starter's orders: ref to ent stalls) W

, **7/2** Mr Rough, **13/2** KARINSKA, Singing Rock (IRE), Hatta Sunshine (USA), **8/1** Braydon Forest, **10/1** Ballynakelly (6/1-11/1), **11/1** Vanroy, Lord Palmerston (USA) (8/1-12/1), **12/1** Sea Spouse, **25/1** Lady Sabina, Rosevear (IRE), Safe Secret, Kreef, CSF £69.49 CT £489.34 TOTE £6.50: £2.30 £3.40 £2.50 (£53.00) Trio £399.70 OWNER Mr Geoff Whiting (MARKET RASEN) BRED Sheikh Mohammed bin Rashid al Maktoum 13 Rn

1m 46.6 (5.00) SF: 29/10/23/3/2/20/23/11/8/-/-/-/-
WEIGHT FOR AGE 3yo-11lb

1664

ROBIN LIMITED LIMITED STKS (0-55) (3-Y.O+) (Class F) £3,095.00 (£935.00: £455.00: £215.00) **1m 67y** Stalls: High GOING minus 0.31 sec (GF) 9-00 (9-01)

1366⁴ **Crimson Shower (55)***(63) (JRFanshawe)* 3-8-5 LDettori(13) (3rd st: led on bit over 1f out: shkn up: comf)........— 1
1512³ Court Nap (IRE) **(54)***(64) (SMellor)* 3-8-10 MWigham(5) (4th st: led over 2f out tl over 1f out: unable qckn)........2 2

1256[6] Rising Spray **(55)***(64) (CAHorgan)* 4-9-7 PaulEddery(11) (lw: s.s: rdn & hdwy over 1f out: r.o) ....nk 3
1498[2] Wet Patch (IRE) **(55)***(63)*(Fav)*(RHannon)* 3-8-10 MRoberts(4) (lw: 5th st: rdn 4f out: one pce)½ 4
1512[4] Pedaltothemetal (IRE) **(49)***(57) (PMitchell)* 3-8-5 SO'Gorman(1) (2nd st: ev ch over 1f out: one pce) ....½ 5
*1569** Ism **(55)***(63) (MajorWRHern)* 3-8-12b TSprake(10) (lw: dwlt: hdwy over 3f out: hrd rdn over 1f out: one pce) ....nk 6
847[8] Jobber's Fiddle **(54)***(55) (DJSffrenchDavis)* 3-7-12 (7) JBramhill(6) (hdwy 3f out: rdn over 1f out: one pce) ....¾ 7
1509[8] Morocco (IRE) **(55)***(57) (MRChannon)* 6-9-7 RHughes(2) (hrd rdn & hdwy over 1f out: wknd ins fnl f) 1½ 8
1330[7] Zesti **(48)***(56) (TTClement)* 3-8-10 PRobinson(9) (hdwy over 2f out: wknd over 1f out) ....½ 9
1457[3] Speedy Snaps Pride **(54)***(51) (PDCundell)* 3-8-10 WNewnes(14) (6th st: wknd over 3f out)..2½ 10
1426[7] Love Legend **(52)***(50) (DWPArbuthnot)* 10-9-7 PatEddery(12) (led 6f) ....½ 11
1314[9] Raven's Roost (IRE) **(53)***(45) (MajorDNChappell)* 4-9-7 BThomson(3) (hdwy over 2f out: wknd over 1f out) 2½ 12
885[3] Belleminette (IRE) **(55)***(35) (DHaydnJones)* 4-9-2 AMackay(8) (s.s: a bhd) 2½ 13
481[7] Fabriana **(49)***(26) (TJNaughton)* 5-9-2 MHills(7) (a bhd) 5 14

100/30 Wet Patch (IRE), **7/2** CRIMSON SHOWER, **5/1** Ism (7/2-11/2), **6/1** Court Nap (IRE), **8/1** Raven's Roost (IRE), **9/1** Rising Spray (7/1-12/1), **10/1** Belleminette (IRE) (8/1-12/1), **16/1** Love Legend, Fabriana, Speedy Snaps Pride, **20/1** Pedaltothemetal (IRE), Morocco (IRE), **25/1** Jobber's Fiddle, **33/1** Zesti, CSF £27.44 TOTE £5.00: £2.30 £3.20 £2.20 (£21.30) Trio £230.00 OWNER Mrs David Russell (NEWMARKET) BRED Mrs John Trotter 14 Rn

1m 47.1 (5.50) SF: 12/13/24/12/6/12/4/17/5/-/10/5/-/-

WEIGHT FOR AGE 3yo-11lb

T/Plpt: £882.90 (21.55 Tckts). T/Qdpt: Not won; £118.40 to Salisbury 13/6/95. AK

1374-REDCAR (L-H)
Tuesday June 13th (Good to firm)

WEATHER: overcast WIND: mod half against

1665 HARTLEPOOL (S) STKS (2-Y.O) (Class F) £2,987.00 (£832.00: £401.00)
7f Stalls: Centre GOING minus 0.38 sec per fur (F) 2-45 (2-47)

615[12] **Traceability** *(69+) (JBerry)* 2-8-11 JCarroll(4) (hdwy over 2f out: rdn to ld over 1f out: sn clr) ....— 1
1466[5] Kratz (IRE) *(60) (BSRothwell)* 2-8-11 MFenton(7) (hdwy over 2f out: r.o: nrst fin) 4 2
1466[2] Catwalk Girl *(53) (SGNorton)* 2-8-6 JFortune(10) (in tch: styd on u.p fnl 2f: nvr able to chal) ....¾ 3
1352* U-No-Harry (IRE) *(60)*(Fav)*(RHollinshead)* 2-8-12 (3) AGarth(13) (lw: led tl hdd & wknd over 1f out) ....¾ 4
1466[3] Sovitaka (IRE) *(50) (MHEasterby)* 2-8-6 MBirch(8) (w ldrs tl wknd fnl 2½f) ....½ 5
1466[4] Mels Baby (IRE) *(55) (JLEyre)* 2-8-11 RLappin(12) (lw: a in tch: no hdwy fnl 2f) ....hd 6
699[9] Ned's Contessa (IRE) *(48) (MDods)* 2-8-6 DaleGibson(1) (dwlt: bhd tl styd on fnl 2f) 1 7
1503[9] Chilly Looks *(45) (MWEasterby)* 2-8-6 LCharnock(6) (s.s: sme late hdwy) 1¼ 8
788[9] Jackson Park *(49) (MHEasterby)* 2-8-11 SMaloney(2) (nvr wnt pce) ....½ 9
1266[6] Stoleamarch *(42) (MrsMReveley)* 2-8-11 KDarley(14) (a bhd) 3 10
1466[9] Ticka Ticka Timing *(42) (BWMurray)* 2-8-4b(7) GParkin(11) (in tch to ½-wy) ....d.h 10
846[4] Baileys Bride (IRE) *(31) (MJohnston)* 2-8-6 DHolland(3) (cl up: hung rt ½-wy: sn wknd) 2½ 12
1466[6] Brogans Brush *(28) (CWFairhurst)* 2-8-11v JFanning(9) (w ldrs over 4f: wknd rapidly) 3½ 13
Society Sue (IRE) *(5) (RonaldThompson)* 2-8-6 AMackay(5) (leggy: dwlt: wnt rt after s: wl bhd fnl 3f) 8 14

7/4 U-No-Harry (IRE), **7/2** Catwalk Girl, **9/2** TRACEABILITY (5/2-5/1), **7/1** Sovitaka (IRE), **8/1** Kratz (IRE), **10/1** Mels Baby (IRE), **12/1** Stoleamarch (op 8/1), **14/1** Jackson Park, **16/1** Ned's Contessa (IRE), Brogans Brush, **20/1** Baileys Bride (IRE), **25/1** Chilly Looks, Society Sue (IRE), **50/1** Ticka Ticka Timing, CSF £46.76 TOTE £6.90: £2.40 £2.70 £1.90 (£42.10) Trio £90.70 OWNER Mr J. Clayton (COCKERHAM) BRED J. S. A. and Mrs Shorthouse 14 Rn

1m 28.5 (6.50) SF: 4/-/-/-/-/-/-/-/-/-/-/-/-/-

Bt in 6,200gns

1666 EVENING GAZETTE H'CAP (0-70) (3-Y.O+) (Class E) £3,756.00 (£1,128.00: £544.00: £252.00) **1m** Stalls: Centre GOING minus 0.38 sec per fur (F) 3-15 (3-17)

1491[3] **Scaraben (52)***(64) (SEKettlewell)* 7-8-13 JCarroll(8) (hdwy 3f out: rdn to ld 1f out: r.o wl) ....— 1

1528[6] Mary's Case (IRE) **(54)**(64) *(MJohnston)* 5-9-1b DHolland(1) (hld up: hdwy 2f out: styd on u.p: nt pce of wnr)....1 **2**
1465[2] Flyaway Blues **(55)**(60)(Fav)*(MrsMReveley)* 3-8-5b KDarley(4) (trckd ldrs: led 2f out to 1f out: no ex u.p)....2½ **3**
1344[12] Ooh Ah Cantona **(56)**(59) *(JLEyre)* 4-9-3 RLappin(7) (a chsng ldrs: one pce fnl 2f)....1¼ **4**
1415[5] Major Mouse **(50)**(50) *(WWHaigh)* 7-8-11 DaleGibson(6) (lw: in tch: effrt over 2f out: one pce)....1¼ **5**
1037[10] Juice Plus **(32)**(29) *(JParkes)* 4-7-0 (7) CAdamson(10) (disp ld 5f: grad wknd)....1¾ **6**
Mca Below the Line **(63)**(59) *(WLBarker)* 7-9-5v(5) VHalliday(3) (disp ld centre tl hdd & wknd 2f out)....hd **7**
1269[5] Cumbrian Minstrel **(58)**(54) *(MHEasterby)* 3-8-8 MBirch(9) (prom tl rdn & wknd fnl 2½f)....nk **8**
1484[4] Avishayes (USA) **(43)**(39) *(MrsMReveley)* 8-7-11 (7) DDenby(11) (racd stands' side: led ½-wy tl hdd & wknd 2f out)....hd **9**
1380[10] Full Gloss **(60)**(54) *(MrsMReveley)* 3-8-3 (7) SCopp(2) (bit bkwd: effrt 3f out: rdn & n.d)....1 **10**
1529[11] Fort Vally **(42)**(32) *(BWMurray)* 5-7-10 (7) MartinDwyer(5) (hrd rdn & bhd fnl 3f)....1¾ **11**
King Chestnut **(52)**(39) *(MDods)* 4-8-13 JFortune(12) (n.d)....1½ **12**
1433* Northern Spark **(46)**(32) *(MartynWane)* 7-8-7 JFanning(13) (led stands' side to ½-wy: sn wknd)....¾ **13**

LONG HANDICAP Juice Plus 7-2

9/4 Flyaway Blues, **6/1** Northern Spark, **13/2** Avishayes (USA), **7/1** Major Mouse, **9/1** Cumbrian Minstrel, Mary's Case (IRE), **10/1** Mca Below the Line, SCARABEN, King Chestnut, **16/1** Fort Vally, **25/1** Full Gloss, Ooh Ah Cantona, **33/1** Juice Plus, CSF £97.88 CT £257.19 TOTE £15.80: £4.20 £2.90 £1.30 (£53.80) Trio £64.20 OWNER Mr J. Tennant (MIDDLEHAM) BRED Burton Agnes Stud Co Ltd 13 Rn 1m 38.7 (3.70) SF: 27/27/12/22/13/-/22/6/2/6/-/2/-

WEIGHT FOR AGE 3yo-11lb

1667 SUNDERLAND CLAIMING STKS (3-Y.O+) (Class F) £2,735.00 (£760.00: £365.00)

2m 4y Stalls: Low GOING minus 0.38 sec per fur (F) 3-45 (3-45)

223[4] **Brodessa (59)**(57+)(Fav)*(MrsMReveley)* 9-9-9 KDarley(2) (lw: hld up: hdwy 7f out: led 3f out: pushed along & styd on wl)....— **1**
1496[4] Arian Spirit (IRE) **(30)**(44) *(JLEyre)* 4-9-0 JFortune(5) (lw: a chsng ldrs: effrt 4f out: kpt on: no ch w wnr)....5 **2**
1219[8] Fools of Pride (IRE) **(33)**(44) *(RHollinshead)* 3-7-11 NCarlisle(1) (hdwy appr st: styd on: n.d)..2 **3**
1449[2] Naawy **(32)**(41) *(CSmith)* 5-9-7 MFenton(10) (lw: chsd ldrs: rdn appr st: one pce)....7 **4**
1359[5] Don't Cry **(25)**(29) *(DonEnricoIncisa)* 7-8-10 KimTinkler(7) (bhd: effrt 4f out: n.d)....1 **5**
1430[4] High Flown (USA) **(49)**(39) *(RonaldThompson)* 3-8-6v DeanMcKeown(8) (led tl hdd 3f out: sn wknd)....6 **6**
1581[4] Coast Along (IRE) **(30)**(31) *(CWThornton)* 3-7-12 AMackay(9) (hdwy 7f out: wknd fnl 4f)....½ **7**
1452[8] Ellastyle (IRE) **(28)**(21) *(MissLCSiddall)* 4-8-10 DHarrison(3) (n.d)....2½ **8**
1449[7] Easy D'Or **(35)**(28) *(MrsASwinbank)* 4-9-5 NConnorton(4) (hmpd 11f out: a bhd)....2½ **9**
1430[7] Warrgem *(BEllison)* 3-7-13 NKennedy(6) (prom to st: sn bhd: t.o)....dist **10**

4/5 BRODESSA, **8/1** Arian Spirit (IRE), Naawy, Coast Along (IRE), **9/1** High Flown (USA), **10/1** Fools of Pride (IRE), **14/1** Don't Cry, Ellastyle (IRE), **20/1** Easy D'Or, **100/1** Warrgem, CSF £8.97 TOTE £1.70: £1.20 £2.00 £2.90 (£7.80) Trio £36.60 OWNER Mr R. W. S. Jevon (SALTBURN) BRED B. Fairs 10 Rn 3m 31.5 (6.50) SF: 46/32/13/30/18/8/-/9/16/-

WEIGHT FOR AGE 3yo-20lb, 4yo-1lb

1668 FAIRFIELD INDUSTRIES H'CAP (0-70) (3-Y.O+) (Class E)

£3,652.00 (£1,096.00: £528.00: £244.00)
6f Stalls: Centre GOING minus 0.38 sec per fur (F) 4-15 (4-17)

1499[3] **Melodic Drive (56)**(66) *(JAGlover)* 5-9-4b SDWilliams(10) (prom: rdn over 2f out: r.o to ld cl home)....— **1**
1344[7] Halmanerror **(59)**(68)(Fav)*(MrsJRRamsden)* 5-9-7 MHills(11) (lw: trckd ldrs: smooth hdwy to ld 1f out: rdn & no ex wl ins fnl f)....½ **2**
1355[4] Kid Ory **(60)**(61) *(PCalver)* 4-9-8 MBirch(9) (lw: a chsng ldrs: kpt on same pce fnl 2f)....3 **3**
1468[2] Willshe Gan **(52)**(53) *(DenysSmith)* 5-9-0 JQuinn(3) (lw: trckd ldrs: outpcd 2f out: kpt on fnl f)....s.h **4**
1565* Elle Shaped (IRE) **(70)**(64) *(DNicholls)* 5-10-4 7x AlexGreaves(7) (led centre tl rdn & btn appr fnl f)....2½ **5**
1151[11] Euro Rebel **(55)**(48) *(MHEasterby)* 3-8-8 SMaloney(13) (styd on u.p fnl 2f: n.d)....nk **6**
1043[4] Sobering Thoughts **(61)**(53) *(JLEyre)* 9-9-9 JFortune(1) (racd alone far side: led tl hdd & wknd 1f out)....½ **7**
1441[8] Tutu Sixtysix **(45)**(35) *(DonEnricoIncisa)* 4-8-7v KimTinkler(12) (hld up & bhd: rdn over 2f out: no imp)....¾ **8**

7467 Desert Invader (IRE) **(62)***(50) (DWChapman)* 4-9-10 DeanMcKeown(8) (hdwy ½-wy: ev ch over 1f out: sn btn) ½ 9
14413 Flashy's Son **(66)***(46) (GMMoore)* 7-10-0 JCarroll(6) (b: b.hind: trckd ldrs: effrt over 2f out: wknd over 1f out) 3 10
14196 Coney Hills **(33)***(7) (NBycroft)* 4-7-4 (5)ow2 NVarley(5) (nvr wnt pce) 1½ 11
14935 Indiahra **(58)***(32) (RHollinshead)* 4-9-6 TIves(2) (s.s: nt rcvr) 1 12
Oriental Air (IRE) **(55)***(21) (EWeymes)* 4-9-3v KDarley(4) (cl up over 4f) 3 13

LONG HANDICAP Coney Hills 7-4

7/2 Halmanerror, **9/2** Elle Shaped (IRE) (op 3/1), **11/2** Flashy's Son, **6/1** Willshe Gan, **7/1** Sobering Thoughts, **10/1** Kid Ory, **14/1** Indiahra, **16/1** Euro Rebel, MELODIC DRIVE, Desert Invader (IRE), **20/1** Oriental Air (IRE), **25/1** Tutu Sixtysix, **33/1** Coney Hills, CSF £70.51 CT £561.62 TOTE £23.60: £6.50 £2.20 £2.80 (£77.80) Trio £275.70 OWNER Mrs C. M. Stevens (WORKSOP) BRED C. M. Stevens 13 Rn 1m 12.5 (3.20) SF: 42/44/37/29/40/15/29/11/26/22/-/8/-

WEIGHT FOR AGE 3yo-9lb

1669 NEWCASTLE UNITED H'CAP (0-65) (3-Y.O) (Class F) £3,281.00 (£916.00: £443.00) **1m 2f** Stalls: Low GOING minus 0.38 sec per fur (F) 4-45 (4-50)

9686 **Royal York (62)***(71)*(Fav)*(MissSEHall)* 3-9-7 NConnorton(9) (in tch: sn pushed along: styd on u.p fnl 2f to ld cl home) — 1
13587 Bulsara **(51)***(60) (CWFairhurst)* 3-8-10 PaulEddery(1) (a.p: led over 1f out: no ex towards fin)nk 2
137913 Bold Top **(38)***(45) (BSRothwell)* 3-7-8v(3) DarrenMoffatt(14) (bhd & carried wd ent st: sn rdn: styd on wl fnl 2f: hung lft) 1 3
14127 Highbank **(49)***(56) (MrsMReveley)* 3-8-8 DeanMcKeown(13) (hld up & bhd: ran wd st: hdwy over 2f out: r.o) hd 4
12188 Instantaneous **(44)***(49) (MHEasterby)* 3-8-3 SMaloney(8) (lw: chsd ldrs: led 3f out tl over 1f out: sn btn) 1 5
7453 Acquittal (IRE) **(59)***(62)*(Fav)*(JRFanshawe)* 3-9-4 DHarrison(4) (lw: chsd ldrs tl grad wknd fnl 3f) 1½ 6
13586 Toshiba Talk (IRE) **(50)***(47) (BEllison)* 3-8-9 NKennedy(5) (cl up: led over 3f out: hdd 3f out: grad wknd) 3½ 7
141410 Westcourt Princess **(45)***(41) (MWEasterby)* 3-8-4 JFanning(12) (hdwy on outside 3f out: btn wl over 1f out) 1 8
Lindisfarne Lady **(45)***(40) (MrsMReveley)* 3-8-4 KDarley(7) (lw: bhd: effrt 4f out: hung lft & no imp) ½ 9
12855 To Prove a Point **(37)***(26) (JJO'Neill)* 3-7-10bow3 AMackay(17) (mid div: effrt 4f out: no imp) .1¾ 10
135510 Red Hot Risk **(51)***(40) (MDods)* 3-8-10v DaleGibson(2) (s.s: carried wd appr st: n.d) 2 11
152811 Benten **(39)***(13) (DWChapman)* 3-7-12 NCarlisle(16) (bhd: gd hdwy 3f out: wknd fnl 2f) 9 12
135511 Bitch **(49)***(18) (DNicholls)* 3-8-8 GDuffield(6) (led tl hdd & wknd over 3f out) 3½ 13
137810 Deauville Dancer (IRE) **(60)***(26) (DNicholls)* 3-9-5 AlexGreaves(10) (cl up tl wknd 4f out) 1½ 14
13777 J C Grey **(40)** *(DenysSmith)* 3-7-13 JQuinn(11) (prom: ev ch 3f out: wknd qckly fnl 2f) 4 15
13297 Elite Number (USA) **(50)** *(MJCamacho)* 3-8-9 LCharnock(3) (Withdrawn not under Starter's orders: inj leg at start) W

LONG HANDICAP To Prove a Point 7-6

11/4 ROYAL YORK, Acquittal (IRE), **9/1** Instantaneous (6/1-10/1), **10/1** Bulsara, To Prove a Point, Toshiba Talk (IRE), **12/1** Deauville Dancer (IRE) (op 8/1), Lindisfarne Lady, **20/1** Highbank, Red Hot Risk, **25/1** Bold Top, **33/1** Benten, Westcourt Princess, J C Grey, Bitch, CSF £30.44 CT £532.80 TOTE £4.00: £2.30 £2.80 £17.50 (£22.20) Trio £424.50 OWNER Mr Robert Ogden (MIDDLEHAM) BRED Robert Ogden 15 Rn 2m 7.7 (5.20) SF: 32/21/6/17/10/23/8/2/1/-/1/-/-/-/-

1670 MIDDLESBROUGH FOOTBALL CLUB MEDIAN AUCTION MAIDEN STKS (2-Y.O) (Class D) £3,780.50 (£1,139.00: £552.00: £258.50) **6f** Stalls: Centre GOING minus 0.38 sec per fur (F) 5-15 (5-22)

13182 **Rabican (IRE)** *(85) (GCBravery)* 2-9-0 MHills(5) (lw: a.p: led over 1f out: r.o wl) — 1
Pharmacy *(75+) (JWWatts)* 2-8-9 NConnorton(9) (w'like: scope: mde most tl hdd over 1f out: kpt on) 1¾ 2
Staffin *(75+) (JRFanshawe)* 2-8-9 DHarrison(8) (lt-f: unf: hdwy 2f out: r.o towards fin) nk 3
Too Hasty *(77+) (MHEasterby)* 2-9-0 MBirch(16) (leggy: dwlt: plld hrd: styd on fnl 2f) 1 4
11903 Percy Park (USA) *(75)*(Fav)*(MJohnston)* 2-9-0 DHolland(1) (lw: disp ld to ½-wy: wknd appr fnl f) ¾ 5
15253 Meeting Point *(69) (MrsMReveley)* 2-8-9 KDarley(6) (trckd ldrs: nt qckn fnl 2f) ½ 6
13564 Camionneur (IRE) *(67) (MHEasterby)* 2-9-0 SMaloney(17) (bit bkwd: effrt & wandered over 2f out: nvr rchd ldrs) 2½ 7
14139 Flood's Fancy *(59) (MrsJRRamsden)* 2-8-9 JFortune(11) (prom tl lost pl ½-wy: sme late hdwy) 1 8
14184 Larrylukeathugh *(63) (JJO'Neill)* 2-9-0 TIves(7) (in tch: shkn up 3f out: nt qckn) ½ 9
12788 Sizzling Symphony *(56) (RAFahey)* 2-9-0 ACulhane(12) (bhd tl sme late hdwy) 2½ 10

1134[10] Reef Raider *(54) (NTinkler)* 2-9-0 KimTinkler(15) (s.i.s: hung lft fr ½-wy: n.d) ....¾ 11
1375[3] Stately *(43) (SirMarkPrescott)* 2-8-9 GDuffield(19) (b.hind: spd over 3f: wknd qckly) 2½ 12
The Wad *(47) (MWEasterby)* 2-9-0 LCharnock(4) (unf: bkwd: a bhd) ....s.h 13
Ginger Hodgers *(39) (RMWhitaker)* 2-8-9 DeanMcKeown(14) (lengthy: bkwd: outpcd fr ½-wy) 1¼ 14
1356[7] Turbo North *(36) (MDods)* 2-9-0 DaleGibson(10) (a bhd) 3 15
1278[10] Brockville Bairn *(31) (MrsASwinbank)* 2-9-0 JMarshall(18) (plld hrd: spd 4f) 2 16
Petrefuz (IRE) *(29) (EWeymes)* 2-9-0 NRodgers(3) (cmpt: bit bkwd: s.i.s: a outpcd) ....¾ 17
Noble Colours *(25) (JBerry)* 2-9-0 JCarroll(2) (unf: prom over 3f: sn rdn & wknd) 1¼ 18

Evens Percy Park (USA), **5/1** Stately, Pharmacy (op 5/2), **13/2** RABICAN (IRE), **10/1** Staffin (8/1-14/1), **14/1** Meeting Point, **20/1** Noble Colours, **25/1** Too Hasty, **33/1** Flood's Fancy, Larrylukeathugh, **50/1** Ginger Hodgers, Camionneur (IRE), Sizzling Symphony, Turbo North, **66/1** Reef Raider, Brockville Bairn, **100/1** Petrefuz (IRE), The Wad, CSF £40.66 TOTE £7.40: £2.50 £1.50 £5.20 (£25.90) Trio £96.00 OWNER Mr Michael Hwang (NEWMARKET) BRED Charles O'Connor 18 Rn 1m 13.5 (4.20) SF: 24/14/14/16/14/8/6/-/2/-/-/-/-/-/-/-/-/-

T/Plpt: £381.30 (43.2 Tckts). T/Qdpt: £61.80 (1 Tckt). AA

1253-SALISBURY (R-H)
Tuesday June 13th (Good to firm, Good patches)
WEATHER: overcast WIND: almost nil

1671 EDDIE REAVEY MAIDEN AUCTION STKS (2-Y.O F) (Class E)
£3,226.50 (£972.00: £471.00: £220.50)
6f Stalls: High GOING minus 0.44 sec per fur (F) 2-30 (2-32)

1253[3] **Honorable Estate (IRE)** *(68) (RHannon)* 2-8-7 PatEddery(11) (lw: led 5f out: hrd rdn over 1f out: jst hld on) ....— 1
1348[3] Singoalla (IRE) *(68)*(Fav)*(JLDunlop)* 2-8-7 WCarson(5) (hld up: swtchd lft over 2f out: hdwy over 1f out: r.o wl) ....s.h 2
1253[2] Corniche Quest (IRE) *(59) (MRChannon)* 2-8-8 ow1 RHughes(8) (w ldrs: ev ch over 1f out: unable qckn) 3½ 3
1098[5] Queen's Insignia (USA) *(57) (PFICole)* 2-8-7 TQuinn(3) (led 1f: ev ch 2f out: one pce) ....½ 4
1318[11] Be My Bird *(56) (BJMeehan)* 2-8-7 BDoyle(4) (bit bkwd: hld up: hdwy over 1f out: r.o) ....nk 5
Brave Maisie (IRE) *(42) (MMcCormack)* 2-8-3 AClark(10) (leggy: s.s: nvr nrr) 4 6
436[9] Lady of The Mist (IRE) *(41) (JSMoore)* 2-8-3 AMcGlone(6) (a bhd) ....nk 7
Domettes (IRE) *(41) (RHannon)* 2-8-4 ow1 RPerham(1) (neat: bit bkwd: s.s: a bhd) ....hd 8
1253[8] Madam Marash (IRE) *(30) (AGFoster)* 2-8-3 TSprake(7) (bhd fnl 2f) 4 9
Just Another High (IRE) *(23) (DrJDScargill)* 2-8-7 BThomson(2) (w'like: a bhd) 4 10

6/4 Singoalla (IRE), **11/4** Queen's Insignia (USA) (2/1-3/1), **9/2** Corniche Quest (IRE) (4/1-6/1), **6/1** HONORABLE ESTATE (IRE) (op 4/1), **20/1** Just Another High (IRE), **25/1** Brave Maisie (IRE), Lady of The Mist (IRE), Domettes (IRE), **33/1** Madam Marash (IRE), Be My Bird, CSF £15.23 TOTE £6.10: £1.40 £1.50 £1.40 (£6.30) Trio £4.30 OWNER Mr R. A. Bernard (MARLBOROUGH) BRED James W. Ryan 10 Rn 1m 16.12 (3.82) SF: 5/5/-/-/-/-/-/-/-/-

1672 BISHOPSTONE CONDITIONS STKS (3-Y.O) (Class C) £5,007.50
(£1,820.00: £885.00: £375.00: £162.50)
1m 6f Stalls: High GOING minus 0.44 sec per fur (F) 3-00 (3-00)

1396a[9] **Anchor Clever** *(93) (PAKelleway)* 3-8-10 JReid(5) (hld up: swtchd lft over 2f out: hdwy to ld over 1f out: edgd rt: r.o wl) ....— 1
1281[2] Grey Shot **(97)***(96) (IABalding)* 3-9-2 LDettori(6) (led after 2f: hdd over 1f out: nt qckn) 2½ 2
1099[4] Lord Jim (IRE) **(96)***(95) (MissGayKelleway)* 3-9-2 RCochrane(2) (led 2f: ev ch over 1f out: nt qckn) ....¾ 3
1490[2] General Assembly (IRE) *(88)*(Fav)*(HRACecil)* 3-8-10 WRyan(3) (b.off hind: hld up: rdn & hung rt over 2f out: one pce) ....¾ 4
1173* Danjing (IRE) **(93)***(94) (PFICole)* 3-9-2 TQuinn(1) (a.p: rdn over 2f out: one pce) ....¾ 5
619[9] Twilight Sleep (USA) **(95)** *(LordHuntingdon)* 3-9-2 JWeaver(4) (lw: bhd fnl 5f: t.o whn p.u over 3f out) .... P

4/7 General Assembly (IRE), **5/1** Grey Shot (4/1-6/1), **11/2** Danjing (IRE) (3/1-6/1), **11/1** ANCHOR CLEVER (5/1-12/1), **20/1** Twilight Sleep (USA), **25/1** Lord Jim (IRE), CSF £56.20 TOTE £11.20: £2.50 £1.90 (£21.70) OWNER Mr Osvaldo Pedroni (NEWMARKET) BRED Highclere Stud Ltd 6 Rn 3m 1.68 (3.48) SF: 41/44/43/36/42/-

OFFICIAL EXPLANATION **Twilight Sleep, the jockey reported that the colt lost his action and he thought there was something wrong.**

1673

DEVERILL H'CAP (0-90) (3-Y.O+) (Class C) £5,572.50 (£1,680.00: £815.00: £382.50) **6f** Stalls: High GOING minus 0.44 sec per fur (F) 3-30 (3-31)

1560* **Champagne Grandy (74)***(79) (MRChannon)* 5-9-5 7x RHughes(6) (lw: hld up: hrd rdn & hdwy over 1f out: led wl ins fnl f: r.o wl) ....— **1**
1483[8] Dry Point **(67)***(72) (JARToller)* 9-8-12 WNewnes(5) (hld up: hdwy over 1f out: ev ch ins fnl f: r.o) ....hd **2**
1106[6] Sir Joey (USA) **(83)***(86) (PGMurphy)* 6-9-9 (5) SDrowne(9) (lw: hld up: stdy hdwy to ld on bit 1f out: hdd wl ins fnl f) ....½ **3**
1222[9] Q Factor **(73)***(72) (DHaydnJones)* 3-8-9 TQuinn(10) (lw: a.p: led over 1f out: sn hdd: one pce) 1½ **4**
Lynton Lad **(90)***(89) (CPEBrooks)* 3-9-12 BThomson(11) (a.p: nt clr run over 1f out: nt qckn fnl f) ....hd **5**
1411[6] Grey Charmer (IRE) **(52)***(50) (CJames)* 6-7-11 CRutter(1) (s.s: hdwy fnl f: nrst fin) ....nk **6**
906[5] Evening Falls **(62)***(51) (JLSpearing)* 4-8-7 MRoberts(2) (s.s: nvr nrr) 3½ **7**
Norling (IRE) **(59)***(44) (KOCunningham-Brown)* 5-8-4 JWeaver(4) (led over 2f: wknd over 1f out) 1½ **8**
1362[6] Ffynone (IRE) **(80)***(65)*(Fav)*(RHannon)* 3-9-2b LDettori(7) (lw: led over 3f out tl over 1f out: wknd) ....s.h **9**
Agwa **(78)***(60) (RJO'Sullivan)* 6-9-9 RCochrane(3) (spd over 4f) 1¼ **10**
1335[8] Green City **(75)***(30) (RHannon)* 3-8-11 JReid(8) (a bhd: t.o fnl 2f) 10 **11**

7/2 Ffynone (IRE) (op 7/1), **4/1** Sir Joey (USA), **6/1** CHAMPAGNE GRANDY (9/2-7/1), **15/2** Grey Charmer (IRE), **9/1** Agwa (5/1-10/1), **10/1** Dry Point (8/1-12/1), Lynton Lad, **12/1** Q Factor, **14/1** Green City, **20/1** Norling (IRE), **25/1** Evening Falls, CSF £58.62 CT £245.08 TOTE £5.80: £1.70 £3.30 £1.80 (£40.40) Trio £80.50 OWNER Grandy Girls (UPPER LAMBOURN) BRED J. B. and Mrs N. G. Stafford 11 Rn 1m 14.25 (1.95) SF: 40/33/47/24/41/11/12/5/17/21/-
WEIGHT FOR AGE 3yo-9lb

1674

CITY BOWL H'CAP (0-80) (3-Y.O+ F & M) (Class D) £3,817.50 (£1,140.00: £545.00: £247.50)
1m 4f Stalls: High GOING minus 0.44 sec per fur (F) 4-00 (4-03)

1264[2] **Eurolink Mischief (72)***(85)*(Fav)*(LMCumani)* 3-9-7 LDettori(10) (b.hind: a.p: rdn 3f out: r.o wl to ld last stride) ....— **1**
1372[2] Paradise Waters **(57)***(68) (RFJohnsonHoughton)* 3-8-6 ow2 JReid(8) (led: hrd rdn fnl f: hdd last stride) ....s.h **2**
647[10] Shining High **(78)***(86) (JLDunlop)* 3-9-13 WCarson(6) (unruly s: plld hrd: a.p: one pce fnl 2f)...4 **3**
1254[12] Rocquaine Bay **(40)***(44) (MJBolton)* 8-8-5 AMcGlone(7) (hld up: rdn & hdwy 4f out: one pce fnl 2f) 3 **4**
1518[6] Uncharted Waters **(63)***(61) (CACyzer)* 4-10-0 JWeaver(3) (bhd tl hdwy over 1f out: nvr nrr) 4 **5**
1182[4] Zuiena (USA) **(68)***(66) (PFICole)* 3-9-3 TQuinn(4) (lw: no hdwy fnl 3f) ....½ **6**
1407* Last Laugh (IRE) **(60)***(56) (MCPipe)* 3-8-9 MRoberts(2) (hld up: gd hdwy after 3f: rdn 5f out: wknd over 1f out) 1 **7**
1200[5] Grandes Oreilles (IRE) **(62)***(55) (NJHWalker)* 3-8-11 RCochrane(1) (lw: bhd fnl 3f) 2½ **8**
1539[8] Valinco **(49)***(26) (SDow)* 4-9-0 StephenDavies(5) (prom: rdn 4f out: sn wknd: t.o) 12 **9**
1264[5] Caisson **(66)***(35) (RHannon)* 3-9-1 RHughes(9) (hld up: hdwy 4f out: wknd 3f out: t.o) 6 **10**

7/4 EUROLINK MISCHIEF, **4/1** Paradise Waters, Last Laugh (IRE), **10/1** Shining High, Rocquaine Bay, **12/1** Caisson (op 8/1), Zuiena (USA), **20/1** Uncharted Waters, **25/1** Grandes Oreilles (IRE), **50/1** Valinco, CSF £9.21 CT £50.58 TOTE £2.50: £1.30 £1.90 £2.20 (£5.50) Trio £16.80 OWNER Eurolink Group Plc (NEWMARKET) BRED A. G. Antoniades 10 Rn
2m 35.66 (3.06) SF: 50/33/51/25/42/31/21/20/7/-
WEIGHT FOR AGE 3yo-16lb

1675

LAVERSTOCK MAIDEN STKS (3-Y.O F) (Class D) £4,272.50 (£1,280.00: £615.00: £282.50) **1m** Stalls: High GOING minus 0.44 sec per fur (F) 4-30 (4-33)

865[7] **Western Reel (USA) (85)***(87) (PFICole)* 3-8-11 RHughes(14) (hld up: hdwy over 2f out: led ins fnl f: r.o wl) ....— **1**
881[5] Arabride *(86) (JARToller)* 3-8-11 JWeaver(8) (lw: a.p: led over 2f out tl ins fnl f) ....¾ **2**
1353[3] Wild Rita *(68) (WRMuir)* 3-8-11 LDettori(6) (hld up: hdwy over 1f out: r.o) 9 **3**
957[4] Almizaj **(82)***(61) (HThomsonJones)* 3-8-11 RHills(3) (a.p: rdn over 2f out: one pce) 3½ **4**
1186[10] Zelda Zonk *(59) (BJMeehan)* 3-8-11 BDoyle(12) (prom: rdn over 2f out: one pce) 1 **5**
1186[6] Knotally Wood (USA) *(55) (JWHills)* 3-8-11 PatEddery(9) (plld hrd: prom tl wknd over 2f out) 2 **6**
Accuse (USA) *(51) (PFICole)* 3-8-11 TQuinn(11) (w'like: led over 5f: wknd qckly) 2 **7**

Fragaria *(48) (IABalding)* 3-8-11 RCochrane(2) (w'like: bkwd: hld up: hdwy 3f out: wknd 2f out)....1½ 8
888² Azdihaar (USA) **(90)***(30)*(Fav)*(JLDunlop)* 3-8-11 WCarson(7) (hld up: n.m.r over 2f out: sn wknd: t.o)....9 9
1353⁷ Dr Frances (IRE) *(29) (CCElsey)* 3-8-11 CRutter(5) (reluctant to go to s: a bhd: t.o)....nk 10
Press Again *(26) (PHayward)* 3-8-11 RStreet(10) (unf: plld hrd: a bhd: t.o)....1¼ 11
Siska (USA) *(26) (JLDunlop)* 3-8-11 JReid(4) (leggy: scope: lw: hld up & plld hrd: bhd fnl 2f: t.o)....nk 12
Barbrallen *(21) (DJSffrenchDavis)* 3-8-11 NAdams(1) (s.s: a bhd: t.o)....2½ 13

9/4 Azdihaar (USA), **7/2** WESTERN REEL (USA) (op 6/1), **11/2** Knotally Wood (USA) (4/1-6/1), **6/1** Almizaj, **8/1** Accuse (USA) (op 5/1), **10/1** Wild Rita (6/1-12/1), **12/1** Siska (USA), **14/1** Arabride, **25/1** Fragaria, Zelda Zonk, **40/1** Dr Frances (IRE), **66/1** Barbrallen, **100/1** Press Again, CSF £50.85 TOTE £5.30: £1.70 £3.90 £1.60 (£52.10) Trio £331.50 OWNER Prince Fahd Salman (WHATCOMBE) BRED Newgate Stud Farm Inc 13 Rn 1m 41.44 (2.14) SF: 39/38/20/13/11/7/3/-/-/-/-/-/-

1676 DORSET H'CAP (0-70) (3-Y.O+) (Class E) £3,795.00 (£1,140.00:£550.00: £255.00)
6f 212y Stalls: High GOING minus 0.44 sec per fur (F) 5-00 (5-04)

1261⁶ **Jolto (68)***(77) (KOCunningham-Brown)* 6-10-0 JWeaver(15) (mde virtually all: drvn out)....— 1
1366* Scharnhorst **(69)***(77)*(Fav)*(SDow)* 3-9-5 MRoberts(17) (lw: w wnr: ev ch ins fnl f: r.o)....½ 2
1541* Whatever's Right (IRE) **(66)***(73) (MDIUsher)* 6-9-12 6x TQuinn(4) (a.p: r.o ins fnl f)....½ 3
1126⁶ Court Minstrel **(54)***(55) (LJHolt)* 6-9-0 AMcGlone(16) (a.p: one pce fnl 2f)....2½ 4
1541⁶ Great Hall **(54)***(50) (PDCundell)* 6-8-9b(5) DGriffiths(14) (hld up & bhd: hdwy over 1f out: r.o)...2 5
1255⁵ Chili Heights **(57)***(53) (GBBalding)* 5-9-3v TSprake(10) (b.hind: no hdwy fnl 2f)....s.h 6
1541⁵ Marrowfat Lady (IRE) **(58)***(52) (BRMillman)* 4-9-4 JWilliams(2) (nrst fin)....1 7
1510⁴ Crystal Heights (FR) **(63)***(52) (RJO'Sullivan)* 7-9-9 RCochrane(11) (b: nvr nr to chal)....2 8
1202¹⁶ Fleet Cadet **(50)***(38) (NAGraham)* 4-8-10b PatEddery(13) (lw: n.d)....½ 9
1516⁷ High Typha **(51)***(34) (MRChannon)* 4-8-11 RHughes(20) (nvr nrr)....2½ 10
1599² Jigsaw Boy **(59)***(41) (PGMurphy)* 6-8-12 (7) RWaterfield(6) (lw: nvr nrr)....nk 11
1255¹³ Sharp Imp **(36)***(16) (RMFlower)* 5-7-10 ow1 FNorton(1) (nvr nr ldrs)....½ 12
1499¹² Goody Four Shoes **(39)***(19) (AGNewcombe)* 7-7-13 RPrice(3) (bhd fnl 2f)....nk 13
1446⁶ Indian Temple **(43)***(23) (MSSaunders)* 4-8-3 NAdams(9) (lw: bhd fnl 2f)....s.h 14
1366⁷ Almuhtaram **(69)***(49) (MissGayKelleway)* 3-9-5 MWigham(7) (a bhd)....hd 15
1402⁹ Audrey Grace **(50)***(29) (BJMeehan)* 4-8-10 BDoyle(12) (a bhd)....nk 16
1255² Shaynes Domain **(46)***(11) (RMFlower)* 4-8-6b DBiggs(18) (prom over 4f)....6 17
1414¹⁴ Fire Blast **(60)***(19) (LMCumani)* 3-8-10 LDettori(5) (chsd ldrs: rdn over 2f out: sn wknd)....2½ 18
1337⁶ Pacific Overture **(57)***(12) (CRBarwell)* 3-8-7 WCarson(19) (a bhd: t.o fnl 2f)....2 19

9/2 Scharnhorst, **5/1** Court Minstrel, **15/2** Whatever's Right (IRE), **8/1** Jigsaw Boy, **10/1** Shaynes Domain, **14/1** JOLTO, Fire Blast, Fleet Cadet, **16/1** Pacific Overture, **20/1** Audrey Grace, Chili Heights, Sharp Imp, Great Hall, Crystal Heights (FR), Almuhtaram, **25/1** High Typha, **33/1** Marrowfat Lady (IRE), Goody Four Shoes, Indian Temple, CSF £74.70 CT £481.00 TOTE £14.50: £2.90 £1.50 £2.40 £2.20 (£27.10)Trio £38.60 OWNER Mrs G.M.Gooderham (STOCKBRIDGE) BRED Mrs G. Gooderham 19 Rn 1m 27.65 (1.95) SF: 53/43/49/31/26/29/28/28/14/10/17/-/-/-/15/5/-/-/-

WEIGHT FOR AGE 3yo-10lb

T/Plpt: £126.00 (166.56 Tckts). T/Qdpt: £35.20 (12.20 Tckts). KH

1554-BEVERLEY (R-H)
Wednesday June 14th (Good to firm)
WEATHER: overcast WIND: fresh half against

1677 POLYGON HUMBERSIDE H'CAP (0-70) (3-Y.O+ F & M) (Class E) £3,504.25 (£1,054.00: £509.50: £237.25)
5f Stalls: Centre GOING minus 0.43 sec per fur (F) 2-00 (2-02)

1453² **Stolen Kiss (IRE) (65)***(73) (MWEasterby)* 3-9-4b WCarson(8) (chsd ldr: led jst ins fnl f: jst hld on)....— 1
1271* Twice in Bundoran (IRE) **(52)***(59)*(Fav)*(PSFelgate)* 4-8-10 (3) DWright(11) (lw: sn chsng ldrs: styd on wl fnl f: jst failed)....nk 2
1580* Lugana Vision **(54)***(56) (GFierro)* 3-8-2b(5) 7x JStack(12) (dwlt s: hdwy ½-wy: styd on wl u.p fnl f)....1½ 3
Sandmoor Velvet **(54)***(48) (MHEasterby)* 3-8-7 MBirch(10) (lw: led: clr ½-wy: hdd & wknd jst ins fnl f)....2½ 4
1331⁵ My Cherrywell **(57)***(47) (LRLloyd-James)* 5-9-4 JFortune(7) (b.hind: sn outpcd & pushed along: styd on fnl 2f: nvr nr to chal)....1¼ 5
746⁴ Maid O'Cannie **(67)***(56) (MWEasterby)* 4-10-0 LCharnock(13) (lw: in tch: kpt on wl fnl 2f: nvr nr to chal)....½ 6

1249[8] Arasong **(68)**_(52) (EWeymes)_ 3-9-7 KDarley(2) (sn outpcd & drvn along: styd on fnl 2f: nt rch ldrs) 1½ **7**
_1571[13]_ Irchester Lass **(45)**_(29) (SRBowring)_ 3-7-12b JFanning(14) (chsd ldrs over 3f: grad wknd) ....s.h **8**
1355[12] Skiptamaloo **(32)**_(14) (DonEnricoIncisa)_ 4-7-7b KimTinkler(1) (s.i.s: bhd tl styd on fnl f) ....½ **9**
1565[7] Bonny Melody **(49)**_(29) (PDEvans)_ 4-8-3 (7) AmandaSanders(5) (racd wd in tch tl outpcd fr ½-wy) ....¾ **10**
1453[7] Never Such Bliss **(62)**_(41) (JDBethell)_ 3-9-1 RHughes(4) (sn outpcd: pushed along & bhd) ...hd **11**
1060[12] Pemley **(45)**_(23) (RMWhitaker)_ 3-7-7 (5) NVarley(6) (in tch early: drvn along & lost pl ½-wy) ....½ **12**
1434[13] Supreme Desire **(35)**_(8) (GROldroyd)_ 7-7-10 ow3 AMackay(3) (s.i.s: a bhd) ....½ **13**
656[10] Northgate Raver **(32)** _(RonaldThompson)_ 4-7-0 (7) CAdamson(9) (s.i.s: bhd: rdn & hung bdly lft ½-wy: t.o) 20 **14**

LONG HANDICAP Skiptamaloo 7-6 Supreme Desire 7-1 Northgate Raver 7-0

3/1 Twice in Bundoran (IRE), **4/1** STOLEN KISS (IRE), **7/1** Lugana Vision, **9/1** Never Such Bliss, **10/1** Maid O'Cannie, **12/1** My Cherrywell, Arasong, Bonny Melody, **14/1** Irchester Lass, **20/1** Pemley, Sandmoor Velvet, **25/1** Supreme Desire, **33/1** Skiptamaloo, **50/1** Northgate Raver, CSF £15.92 CT £77.21 TOTE £4.20: £1.80 £1.60 £2.30 (£6.40) Trio £5.40 OWNER R O M Racing (SHERIFF HUTTON) BRED Rathbarry Stud 14 Rn 63.7 secs (2.20) SF: 12/6/-/-/-/3/-/-/-/-/-/-/-/-
WEIGHT FOR AGE 3yo-8lb

1678 T.P. COLMAN PLASTICS CLAIMING STKS (2-Y.O) (Class F)

£2,861.00 (£796.00: £383.00)
5f Stalls: Centre GOING minus 0.43 sec per fur (F) 2-30 (2-32)

1282[2] **Doug's Folly** _(67) (MWEasterby)_ 2-8-5 WCarson(8) (mde all: styd on strly fnl f: drvn out) ....— **1**
1288* Arvzees (IRE) _(67) (MRChannon)_ 2-8-11 ow1 RHughes(11) (chsd wnr: ev ch over 1f out: unable qckn) 1½ **2**
1343[4] Montrestar _(68)_(Fav)_(PDEvans)_ 2-9-0 JFortune(10) (trckd ldrs: effrt 2f out: sn rdn & nt qckn) .1 **3**
Julgarant (IRE) _(49) (MDods)_ 2-8-8 KFallon(3) (leggy: lt-f: hdwy ½-wy: kpt on fnl f: nvr rchd ldrs) 4 **4**
Harriet's Beau _(51) (MWEasterby)_ 2-9-0 MBirch(9) (leggy: unf: in tch tl outpcd over 1f out) 1¼ **5**
1266[3] Contradictory _(40) (MWEasterby)_ 2-8-5 LCharnock(4) (s.i.s: outpcd & bhd: sme hdwy fnl f: n.d) ....¾ **6**
Sea of Blue _(36) (MWEasterby)_ 2-7-8 (7) RuthCoulter(7) (neat: bkwd: s.i.s: bhd: sme hdwy over 1f out: n.d) ....hd **7**
Darerock _(33) (MDods)_ 2-8-10 DaleGibson(5) (unf: bit bkwd: in tch tl wknd ½-wy) 3½ **8**
1503[5] Klipspinger _(20) (BSRothwell)_ 2-7-9 (3) DarrenMoffatt(6) (b: chsd ldrs: hung lft u.p 2f out: sn lost pl) ....nk **9**
Bee Health Boy _(16) (MWEasterby)_ 2-8-10 SMaloney(2) (cmpt: bkwd: s.i.s: swvd lft s: hdwy ½-wy: edgd lft & sn wknd) 5 **10**

2/1 Montrestar, **9/4** DOUG'S FOLLY, **11/4** Arvzees (IRE), **10/1** Contradictory, **12/1** Julgarant (IRE), **14/1** Harriet's Beau, **20/1** Darerock, Klipspinger, **25/1** Sea of Blue, **33/1** Bee Health Boy, CSF £9.73 TOTE £3.90: £1.40 £1.30 £1.10 (£3.50) Trio £1.80 OWNER Mr R. J. McAlpine (SHERIFF HUTTON) BRED R. J. McAlpine and D. O. Pickering 10 Rn 64.6 secs (3.10) SF: 7/7/8/-/-/-/-/-/-/-

1679 ELTHERINGTON H'CAP (0-70) (3-Y.O+) (Class E) £4,536.00

(£1,368.00: £664.00: £312.00)
7f 100y Stalls: High GOING minus 0.43 sec per fur (F) 3-00 (3-00)

1438[4] **Murphy's Gold (IRE) (49)**_(60) (RAFahey)_ 4-8-9 ACulhane(15) (hld up: hdwy on ins 3f out: led jst ins fnl f: hld on wl) ....— **1**
1433[2] Kilnamartyra Girl **(44)**_(54) (JParkes)_ 5-8-4 LCharnock(12) (a chsng ldrs: kpt on u.p fnl f) ....nk **2**
1528* Euro Sceptic (IRE) **(51)**_(59) (MHEasterby)_ 3-8-1b 6x SMaloney(13) (a chsng ldrs: kpt on same pce u.p fnl f) 1 **3**
1432* Lancashire Life (IRE) **(54)**_(49) (EJAlston)_ 4-9-0 JCarroll(2) (lw: led tl hdd & wknd jst ins fnl f) 6 **4**
1583* It's Academic **(60)**_(54)_(Fav)_(MrsJRRamsden)_ 3-8-10 KFallon(9) (hld up: hdwy 3f out: effrt & nt clr run over 1f out: wknd ins fnl f) ....¾ **5**
1354[8] Star of Gold **(63)**_(51) (CREgerton)_ 3-8-13 CRutter(4) (rr div tl kpt on fnl 2f) 2½ **6**
1323[3] Superoo **(67)**_(54) (MrsPSly)_ 9-9-13 MBirch(8) (chsd ldrs tl wknd fnl f) ....½ **7**
_1569[6]_ Sweet Mate **(47)**_(32) (SRBowring)_ 3-7-11 JFanning(7) (bhd: kpt on fnl 3f: n.d) 1 **8**
Henry Will **(35)**_(17) (WLBarker)_ 11-7-6 (3)ow2 DarrenMoffatt(1) (s.s: wl bhd tl styd on fnl 2f) ....½ **9**
1528[2] Ochos Rios (IRE) **(62)**_(44) (BSRothwell)_ 4-9-8 KDarley(6) (lw: prom early: sn bhd: effrt on outside over 2f out: edgd rt & styd on fnl f) 1 **10**
1528[9] Ballard Ring (IRE) **(57)**_(37) (JSWainwright)_ 4-8-10b(7) GParkin(11) (trckd ldrs: effrt 3f out: sn wknd) 1 **11**

1433[7] Twin Creeks **(52)***(26) (MDHammond)* 4-8-7 (5) JStack(5) (hdwy on outside 3f out: sn prom: wknd 2f out)....2½ **12**
1414[7] Garlande D'Or **(48)***(21) (JLSpearing)* 3-7-9 (3) DWright(14) (s.i.s: bhd: sme hdwy over 2f out: sn wknd)....½ **13**
1441[5] Pallium (IRE) **(55)***(21) (MrsAMNaughton)* 7-9-1v JFortune(3) (hld up: racd wd: a in rr)....3½ **14**
Cavatina **(68)***(32) (TWDonnelly)* 5-10-0 SDWilliams(10) (chsd ldrs: effrt & hung rt over 2f out: sn wknd)....1 **15**
1265[12] Statomist **(52)** *(GFierro)* 3-8-2b AMackay(16) (plld hrd: trckd ldrs tl wknd 2f out: sn wl bhd)...25 **16**

9/2 It's Academic, **5/1** Ochos Rios (IRE), **13/2** Euro Sceptic (IRE), **7/1** Star of Gold, **8/1** MURPHY'S GOLD (IRE), **9/1** Kilnamartyra Girl, **10/1** Lancashire Life (IRE), **12/1** Sweet Mate, **14/1** Superoo, **16/1** Twin Creeks, **20/1** Statomist, Pallium (IRE), Cavatina, **25/1** Garlande D'Or, **33/1** Henry Will, Ballard Ring (IRE), CSF £78.53 CT £466.40 TOTE £6.90: £2.00 £2.50 £1.50 £3.50 Trio £46.20 OWNER Mr D. A. Read (MALTON) BRED Anthony Byrne 16 Rn
1m 32.8 (0.80) SF: 50/44/39/39/34/31/44/12/7/34/27/16/1/11/22/-
WEIGHT FOR AGE 3yo-10lb

1680 UNIVERSITY OF HUMBERSIDE H'CAP (0-80) (3-Y.O+) (Class D)
£4,094.00 (£1,232.00: £596.00: £278.00)
1m 1f 207y Stalls: High GOING minus 0.43 sec per fur (F) 3-30 (3-31)

1417[2] **Hakika (USA) (76)***(85)*(Fav)*(DMorley)* 3-10-0 WCarson(7) (led after 1f: qcknd clr over 1f out: jst hld on)....— **1**
1378[5] North Ardar **(50)***(59) (MrsMReveley)* 5-8-8 (7) SCopp(8) (chsd ldrs: styd on u.p fnl 2f: kpt on wl towards fin)....hd **2**
1557[2] All on **(42)***(43) (JHetherton)* 4-8-2 (5) JStack(2) (in tch: kpt on same pce fnl 2f)....5 **3**
1469[4] Johnnie the Joker **(55)***(55) (JPLeigh)* 4-9-6 DeanMcKeown(3) (led 1f: trckd ldrs: sltly hmpd over 1f out: grad wknd)....nk **4**
1205[9] Lochore **(42)***(42) (MrsVAAconley)* 5-8-7 WRyan(5) (chsd ldrs: swtchd over 1f out: one pce).s.h **5**
1557[3] Sun Mark (IRE) **(58)***(55) (MrsSMAustin)* 4-9-9v JMarshall(1) (b: chsd ldrs: rdn & hung rt over 2f out: one pce)....1¾ **6**
1651* Alltime Dancer (IRE) **(55)***(41) (MrsJRRamsden)* 3-8-7 5x KFallon(6) (lw: unruly in stalls: hld up: drvn along & outpcd 3f out: n.d: eased)....7 **7**
984[16] Bad News **(51)***(29) (GFierro)* 3-8-3b GCarter(4) (plld hrd: hld up & bhd: effrt 3f out: sn wknd)...5 **8**

15/8 HAKIKA (USA), **7/2** Alltime Dancer (IRE), **5/1** North Ardar, **13/2** All on, **7/1** Sun Mark (IRE), **12/1** Johnnie the Joker, **20/1** Lochore, Bad News, CSF £11.31 CT £43.40 TOTE £2.90: £1.30 £1.50 £1.60 (£11.20) OWNER Mr Hamdan Al Maktoum (NEWMARKET) BRED Leo Gatto-Roissard 8 Rn
2m 7.9 (5.40) SF: 33/20/4/16/3/16/-/-
WEIGHT FOR AGE 3yo-13lb

1681 ERNEST NORRIS MEMORIAL H'CAP (0-80) (3-Y.O+) (Class D)
£4,068.00 (£1,224.00: £592.00: £276.00)
1m 3f 216y Stalls: High GOING minus 0.43 sec per fur (F) 4-00 (4-00)

1194* **Thaljanah (IRE) (79)***(90)*(Fav)*(ACStewart)* 3-8-13 WCarson(2) (lw: trckd ldrs: outpcd & drvn along over 3f out: led wl over 1f out: wandered: drvn clr)....— **1**
351[7] Exclusion **(43)***(50) (JHetherton)* 6-7-0 (7) CAdamson(5) (led: edgd lft 3f out: hdd wl over 1f out: no ch w wnr)....3 **2**
1436* Eau de Cologne **(70)***(77) (CWThornton)* 3-8-4 DeanMcKeown(6) (hld up: effrt over 3f out: swtchd outside & styd on wl fnl f)....hd **3**
1505[2] Bayrak (USA) **(75)***(79) (MJRyan)* 5-9-11 RHughes(1) (lw: trckd ldr: ev ch & rdn over 2f out: r.o same pce: eased towards fin)....2 **4**
1039[6] Floating Line **(61)***(51) (PWigham)* 7-8-11 GCarter(3) (hld up: effrt over 4f out: wknd over 1f out: eased ins fnl f)....11 **5**
Nouvelle Cuisine **(55)***(4) (GMMoore)* 7-8-0 (5) JStack(4) (hld up: effrt 3f out: sn rdn & wknd) ..30 **6**
LONG HANDICAP Exclusion 7-4

5/4 THALJANAH (IRE), **3/1** Eau de Cologne, Bayrak (USA), **8/1** Floating Line, **16/1** Nouvelle Cuisine, **20/1** Exclusion, CSF £19.95 TOTE £2.20: £1.50 £6.00 (£39.00) OWNER Mr Hamdan Al Maktoum (NEWMARKET) BRED Abbeville Stud 6 Rn
2m 34.9 (3.40) SF: 41/17/28/46/18/-
WEIGHT FOR AGE 3yo-16lb

1682 FIRST CHANCELLOR MAIDEN STKS (3-Y.O+) (Class D) £3,788.50
(£1,138.00: £549.00: £254.50)
1m 3f 216y Stalls: High GOING minus 0.43 sec per fur (F) 4-30 (4-30)

1099[7] **Torch Vert (IRE) (75)***(74) (BWHills)* 3-8-8 WCarson(1) (mde all: edgd lft: hrd rdn & styd on fnl f)....— **1**

1127⁴ Iridal *(72)*(Fav)*(HRACecil)* 3-8-8 WRyan(2) (trckd wnr: chal over 2f out: edgd lft: nt qckn ins fnl f) 1¼ 2
771¹³ Gymcrak Diamond (IRE) **(30)***(58) (GHolmes)* 5-9-10 KFallon(4) (hld up & bhd: effrt & prom over 3f out: eased whn no ch w 1st 2 appr fnl f) 11 3
Chief's Princess **(50)***(19) (GFierro)* 3-8-3v GCarter(5) (plld hrd: trckd ldrs: effrt over 3f out: sn lost pl & bhd) 25 4

4/6 Iridal, **5/4** TORCH VERT (IRE), **20/1** Gymcrak Diamond (IRE), **33/1** Chief's Princess, CSF £2.45 TOTE £2.50 (£1.10) OWNER Mr J. Hanson (LAMBOURN) BRED Pegasus Securities Leasing (Pty) Ltd 4 Rn 2m 37.3 (5.80) SF: 21/19/21/-
WEIGHT FOR AGE 3yo-16lb

1683 OPEN LEARNING INSTITUTE MAIDEN STKS (3-Y.O+) (Class D)
£3,736.50 (£1,122.00: £541.00: £250.50)
7f 100y Stalls: High GOING minus 0.43 sec per fur (F) 5-00 (5-00)

1486⁵ **Marocco (USA)** *(78+)*(Fav)*(HRACecil)* 3-8-11 WRyan(9) (mde all: hung lft & drvn clr over 1f out: pushed out: unchal) ....— 1
987⁸ Daleria *(48) (AHarrison)* 4-8-11 (5) JStack(3) (trckd ldrs: edgd lft & kpt on same pce fnl 2f) 11 2
Gymcrak Jareer (IRE) *(54) (GHolmes)* 3-8-4 (7) RuthCoulter(4) (leggy: chsd wnr: kpt on one pce fnl 2f) ....¾ 3
1533⁹ Me Cherokee *(48) (CWThornton)* 3-8-6 DeanMcKeown(6) (sn chsng ldrs: kpt on one pce fnl 2f) ....hd 4
1360⁶ Young Ben (IRE) *(47) (JSWainwright)* 3-8-11 JFanning(2) (sn outpcd & pushed along: kpt on fnl 2f: n.d) 2½ 5
Bold Revival *(37) (MrsPSly)* 3-8-6 ACulhane(8) (leggy: unf: hld up & plld hrd: hdwy to chse ldrs over 3f out: wknd fnl f) 2½ 6
1533¹⁰ Moonlight Air *(5) (JLSpearing)* 4-9-2 KFallon(1) (sn outpcd & bhd: lost tch ½-wy) 15 7
1554⁷ Bali Tender *(6) (MWEasterby)* 4-9-7 MBirch(5) (hld up: effrt 3f out: sn wknd & eased) 1½ 8

1/3 MAROCCO (USA), **5/1** Me Cherokee, **12/1** Moonlight Air, **20/1** Gymcrak Jareer (IRE), **25/1** Daleria, **33/1** Young Ben (IRE), Bold Revival, **40/1** Bali Tender, CSF £10.33 TOTE £1.20: £1.10 £2.20 £5.20 (£9.60) Trio £71.10 OWNER Sheikh Mohammed (NEWMARKET) BRED W Lazy T Limited 8 Rn 1m 33.8 (1.80) SF: 41/21/17/11/10/-/-/-
WEIGHT FOR AGE 3yo-10lb

T/Jkpt: £5,927.60 (1.69 Tckts). T/Plpt: £28.40 (529.5 Tckts). T/Qdpt: £49.50 (1 Tckt). WG

1491-HAMILTON (R-H)
Wednesday June 14th (Firm)
WEATHER: sunny WIND: almost nil

1684 SCOTTISH EQUITABLE CONDITIONS AMATEUR STKS (3-Y.O+) (Class D)
£5,680.00 (£1,720.00: £840.00: £400.00)
1m 1f 36y Stalls: High GOING minus 0.51 sec per fur (F) 7-00 (7-00)

1270* **Jandeel (IRE)** *(106+) (ACStewart)* 3-10-8 MrVLukaniuk(4) (b.hind: lw: trckd ldr: led over 4f out tl appr fnl f: led cl home) ....— 1
1108⁹ Mellottie **(92)***(100)*(Fav)*(MrsMReveley)* 10-11-0 MrDParker(2) (lw: hld up: led on bit appr fnl f: hdd & no ex cl home) ....hd 2
1464⁶ Kirkie Cross *(42) (RMMcKellar)* 3-9-7 (4) MrsCWilliams(1) (rn wd 7f out: a bhd) 30 3
877¹⁷ Shropshire Blue **(27)** *(DANolan)* 5-10-5 (4) MrAMcPherson(3) (led tl hdd & wknd 4f out: t.o).dist 4

5/6 Mellottie, **Evens** JANDEEL (IRE), **150/1** Kirkie Cross, Shropshire Blue, CSF £2.00 TOTE £2.10 (£1.10) OWNER Sheikh Ahmed Al Maktoum (NEWMARKET) BRED Biddestone Stud 4 Rn
1m 56.7 (2.40) SF: 57/63/-/-
WEIGHT FOR AGE 3yo-12lb

1685 VARDY CONTINENTAL CLASSIC MAIDEN AUCTION STKS (2-Y.O) (Class E) £3,517.50 (£1,065.00: £520.00: £247.50)
6f 5y Stalls: Low GOING minus 0.51 sec per fur (F) 7-25 (7-25)

1440² **Ramsey Hope** *(84) (CWFairhurst)* 2-8-9 NKennedy(5) (lw: mde all: styd on wl fnl f) ....— 1
Flying North (IRE) *(78) (MrsMReveley)* 2-8-8 KDarley(7) (w'like: a.p: chal over 1f out: nt qckn ins fnl f) 1¾ 2
1460⁶ Termon *(75) (MissLAPerratt)* 2-8-5 JFortune(2) (bkwd: s.i.s: hdwy ½-wy: styd on nr fin) ....s.h 3
1448⁶ Wee Tinkerbell *(66) (MissLAPerratt)* 2-7-11 DaleGibson(1) (a.p: ch over 1f out: kpt on one pce) ....½ 4

1492² Power Game (75)(Fav)(JBerry) 2-8-10 JCarroll(4) (lw: chsd ldrs: effrt & ch over 1f out: grad wknd)....1½ 5
Admiral Jones (IRE) (58) (MJohnston) 2-8-9 DHolland(3) (b.hind: w'like: scope: lw: chsd ldrs: rdn 2f out: sn btn)....6 6
Flower Miller (51) (JHanson) 2-8-9 JWeaver(6) (gd sort: dwlt: hdwy ½-wy: ev ch over 1f out: sn wknd)....2½ 7

2/1 Power Game, **9/4** Flower Miller, **9/2** RAMSEY HOPE, **11/2** Flying North (IRE) (7/2-6/1), **13/2** Admiral Jones (IRE) (4/1-7/1), **33/1** Wee Tinkerbell, **50/1** Termon, CSF £26.90 TOTE £6.20: £2.60 £2.20 (£19.00) OWNER Mr C. D. Barber-Lomax (MIDDLEHAM) BRED Norton Grove Stud Ltd 7 Rn
1m 12.4 (2.40) SF: 17/11/8/-/8/-/-

1686 LANGS SUPREME GOLD CUP H'CAP (0-80) (3-Y.O+) (Class D) £7,197.50 (£2,180.00: £1,065.00: £507.50)

1m 5f 9y Stalls: High GOING minus 0.51 sec per fur (F) 7-55 (7-55)

1596* **Mentalasanythin (64)**(75) (ABailey) 6-9-6 5x AMackay(8) (lw: hld up: stdy hdwy 4f out: led ins fnl f: r.o wl)....— 1
1313³ Argyle Cavalier (IRE) **(61)**(71) (MJohnston) 5-9-3 JCarroll(9) (lw: chsd ldrs: led over 2f out tl ins fnl f: r.o)....¾ 2
1295³ Muzrak (CAN) **(54)**(57) (MDHammond) 4-8-10 DaleGibson(2) (lw: prom: effrt & ch over 2f out: one pce)....6 3
1435³ Persuasive **(48)**(50) (MrsMReveley) 8-8-4 KDarley(4) (lw: hld up & bhd: hdwy & ev ch 2f out: rdn & btn appr fnl f)....nk 4
1328⁵ Premier Dance **(44)**(46) (DHaydnJones) 8-7-11 (3) DWright(1) (chsd ldrs: outpcd 2f out: kpt on fnl f)....nk 5
1462² Latvian **(68)**(68)(Fav)(RAllan) 8-9-10 JWeaver(3) (hld up: effrt wd 4f out: no imp)....1¼ 6
1324⁴ Hill Farm Dancer **(53)**(45) (WMBrisbourne) 4-8-2 (7) MartinDwyer(5) (bhd: c wd 5f out: no imp) 7 7
1496* Lord Advocate **(41)**(31) (DANolan) 7-7-6b(5) 5x NVarley(7) (led tl hdd & wknd over 2f out)....1¾ 8
1496² Royal Circus **(38)**(27) (JGMO'Shea) 6-7-3 (5) MBaird(6) (lw: chsd ldr tl wknd fnl 2½f)....1 9

9/2 Latvian, **5/1** Argyle Cavalier (IRE), **11/2** Muzrak (CAN), MENTALASANYTHIN, **6/1** Royal Circus, **7/1** Premier Dance, Persuasive, **8/1** Lord Advocate, **20/1** Hill Farm Dancer, CSF £31.90 CT £146.17 TOTE £4.10: £1.60 £1.40 £3.90 (£19.40) Trio £60.50 OWNER Mrs M. O'Donnell (TARPORLEY) BRED R. B. Warren 9 Rn 2m 45.2 (1.20 under best) (-0.50) SF: 67/63/49/42/38/60/37/23/19

1687 CARLSBERG SCOTTISH HUNT CUP H'CAP (0-85) (3-Y.O+) (Class D) £7,132.50 (£2,160.00: £1,055.00: £502.50)

1m 65y Stalls: High GOING minus 0.51 sec per fur (F) 8-25 (8-26)

1491* **Talented Ting (IRE) (66)**(80) (PCHaslam) 6-9-9 6x JWeaver(7) (mde all: qcknd 2½f out: r.o wl)....— 1
1299⁹ Sarmatian (USA) **(63)**(74) (MDHammond) 4-9-6 DaleGibson(9) (a.p: kpt on fnl 3f: nt pce of wnr)....1½ 2
1437* Keep Battling **(41)**(46) (JSGoldie) 5-7-7 (5) NVarley(11) (hld up: nt clr run 3f out: swtchd & styd on wl fnl 2f)....3 3
1524² Shinerolla **(72)**(76)(Fav)(MrsJRRamsden) 3-9-4 KFallon(6) (hld up & bhd: r.o fnl 2f: too much to do)....½ 4
1421⁹ Chinour (IRE) **(63)**(67) (EJAlston) 7-9-6 DeanMcKeown(8) (hld up & bhd: styd on fnl 3f: nvr rchd ldrs)....s.h 5
1644* Second Colours (USA) **(63)**(67) (MrsMReveley) 5-9-6 6x KDarley(2) (hld up: effrt over 2f out: nrst fin)....d.h 5
1438⁷ My Handy Man **(56)**(49) (RAllan) 4-8-13 SMaloney(12) (prom tl outpcd fnl 2½f)....½ 7
1432⁴ Pine Essence (USA) **(63)**(54) (MrsMReveley) 4-8-13 (7) GParkin(10) (hld up & bhd: effrt over 2f out: nt clr run over 1f out: nvr able to chal)....1¼ 8
1468⁷ Mbulwa **(51)**(30) (SEKettlewell) 9-8-8b JFortune(5) (in tch tl outpcd fnl 2½f)....6 9
1638⁸ Legal Fiction **(67)**(43) (MJohnston) 4-9-10 DHolland(1) (chsd ldrs tl wknd over 2f out)....1¾ 10
989* Persian Fayre **(72)**(46) (JBerry) 3-9-4 JCarroll(3) (plld hrd: sn cl up: wknd 2f out)....1¼ 11
1438* King Curan (USA) **(63)**(33) (ABailey) 4-9-6b AMackay(4) (hld up & bhd: effrt ½-wy: n.d)....1¾ 12

2/1 Shinerolla, **9/2** King Curan (USA), **11/2** TALENTED TING (IRE), **7/1** Keep Battling, **9/1** Second Colours (USA), **10/1** Sarmatian (USA), Persian Fayre, **12/1** Legal Fiction, **14/1** Chinour (IRE) (10/1-16/1), **20/1** Pine Essence (USA), **25/1** My Handy Man, Mbulwa, CSF £60.69 CT £368.28 TOTE £6.10: £2.30 £4.10 £1.90 (£56.70) Trio £79.50 OWNER Mr Martin Wickens (MIDDLEHAM) BRED R. A. Keogh 12 Rn 1m 45.5 (2.20) SF: 45/39/11/30/32/32/24/29/5/18/10/8
WEIGHT FOR AGE 3yo-11lb

OFFICIAL EXPLANATION Shinerolla: the jockey stated that his instructions were to drop the gelding out and come with a run to lead at the furlong pole, but the way the race was run did not allow him to do this.

1688 HAMILTON ADVERTISER (S) STKS (3-Y.O+) (Class F) £2,775.00 (£840.00: £410.00: £195.00) **1m 1f 36y** Stalls: High GOING minus 0.51 sec (F) 8-55 (8-56)

1422* **Askern (65)***(69+)*(Fav)*(DHaydnJones)* 4-9-3 AMackay(5) (lw: a gng wl: led over 3f out: easily) — 1
1404³ Head For Heaven **(49)***(62) (RPCHoad)* 5-8-12 JCarroll(8) (b: a.p: kpt on wl fnl 2f: no ch w wnr) 1¼ 2
1491⁴ Amnesia (IRE) **(34)***(53) (MrsSCBradburne)* 4-8-7 AlexGreaves(4) (chsd ldrs: ev ch over 3f out: wknd over 1f out) 2½ 3
1161⁹ Venture Fourth **(18)***(54) (EJAlston)* 6-8-12 KFallon(7) (bhd: effrt 4f out: sn chsng ldrs: one pce fnl 2f) 1¾ 4
1355¹⁶ Halls Burn *(20) (JSGoldie)* 7-8-6 (7)ow1 NKinnon(6) (led tl over 3f out: hung bdly lft & wknd qckly) 20 5
1422⁹ Cymbalo *(4) (JSGoldie)* 4-8-7 (5) NVarley(3) (swtg: a bhd) 9 6
1422⁷ Goram's Girl (IRE) **(34)** *(MrsASwinbank)* 3-7-9b JMarshall(1) (chsd ldrs tl wknd over 3f out) 12 7
1438³ Sharp N' Smooth **(50)** *(WTKemp)* 8-8-12b JWeaver(2) (lw: hld up: effrt & ev ch whn broke down & p.u over 2f out: dead) P

Evens ASKERN, **5/2** Head For Heaven (op 4/1), **7/2** Sharp N' Smooth, **12/1** Amnesia (IRE), **20/1** Halls Burn, **25/1** Goram's Girl (IRE), **50/1** Venture Fourth, **66/1** Cymbalo, CSF £4.15 TOTE £2.00: £1.10 £1.50 £1.40 (£2.90) OWNER Mrs M. O'Donnell (PONTYPRIDD) BRED Highclere Stud Ltd 8 Rn
1m 57.3 (3.00) SF: 34/27/18/19/-/-/-/-
WEIGHT FOR AGE 3yo-12lb
No bid

1689 TENNENT'S LAGER SPRINT H'CAP (0-75) (3-Y.O+) (Class D) £5,732.00 (£1,736.00: £848.00: £404.00) **5f 4y** Stalls: Low GOING minus 0.51 sec per fur (F) 9-25 (9-27)

1376* **Shadow Jury (58)***(68) (DWChapman)* 5-8-13b LCharnock(13) (led after 1½f: hrd rdn fnl 2f: r.o) — 1
1565¹³ Featherstone Lane **(52)***(60) (MissLCSiddall)* 4-8-7v DeanMcKeown(3) (chsd ldrs: r.o ins fnl f) ½ 2
1297⁹ Plum First **(60)***(60) (LRLloyd-James)* 5-8-8 (7) KimberleyHart(6) (b.hind: lw: in tch: styd on ins fnl f) 2½ 3
1376⁸ Just Bob **(68)***(66)*(Fav)*(SEKettlewell)* 6-9-9 JFortune(1) (lw: s.i.s: bhd: gd hdwy 2f out: nt qckn ins fnl f) ¾ 4
1493⁴ Diet **(45)***(42) (MissLAPerratt)* 9-7-9v(5) NVarley(9) (a in tch: kpt on fnl f) nk 5
1152¹³ My Abbey **(60)***(56) (EJAlston)* 6-9-1 KFallon(5) (cl up: effrt 2f out: nt qckn) ½ 6
1517⁴ Persian Affair (IRE) **(71)***(66) (DHaydnJones)* 4-9-12 AMackay(2) (lw: s.i.s: hdwy 2f out: nrst fin) s.h 7
1538³ Giggleswick Girl **(58)***(49) (MRChannon)* 4-8-13 KDarley(4) (lw: prom: rdn & btn over 1f out) 1¼ 8
1354¹⁰ Pageboy **(67)***(54) (PCHaslam)* 6-9-8 JWeaver(7) (chsd ldrs over 3f) 1¼ 9
1461⁷ Serious Hurry **(44)***(27) (RMMcKellar)* 7-7-6 (7) DLockhart(11) (disp ld 1½f: cl up tl rdn & btn appr fnl f) 1¼ 10
1461³ Ned's Bonanza **(65)***(32) (MDods)* 6-9-6 MWigham(10) (outpcd fr ½-wy) 5 11
1249¹² River Garnock **(75)***(30) (JBerry)* 3-9-8 JCarroll(12) (disp ld 1½f: cl up tl wknd over 1f out) 4 12
1582¹⁰ Lochon **(63)***(15) (WLBarker)* 4-9-4 AlexGreaves(8) (nvr wnt pce) 1 13

4/1 Just Bob, **9/2** Giggleswick Girl, **5/1** SHADOW JURY, **11/2** Ned's Bonanza, **8/1** Pageboy, **10/1** My Abbey, Diet, **11/1** Persian Affair (IRE), **14/1** Plum First, **16/1** Featherstone Lane, **25/1** Serious Hurry, River Garnock, **33/1** Lochon, CSF £79.21 CT £989.48 TOTE £7.20: £2.80 £7.90 £7.00 (£122.40) Trio £527.10 OWNER Mrs Jeanne Chapman (YORK) BRED J. S. Bell 13 Rn
59.0 secs (0.70) SF: 42/34/34/40/16/30/40/23/28/1/6/-/-
WEIGHT FOR AGE 3yo-8lb
T/Plpt: £431.00 (36.52 Tckts). T/Qdpt: £73.10 (1.5 Tckts). AA

1472-KEMPTON (R-H)
Wednesday June 14th (Good to firm)
WEATHER: dull WIND: almost nil

1690 CHANNEL ONE MAIDEN AUCTION STKS (2-Y.O) (Class F) £2,905.00 (£880.00: £430.00: £205.00) **6f** Stalls: Low GOING minus 0.37 sec per fur (F) 6-40 (6-49)

615⁶ **Bedside Mail** *(72+) (JMPEustace)* 2-8-7 RCochrane(13) (stdy hdwy over 2f out: qcknd & led 1f out: comf) — 1
1454⁵ Weetman's Weigh (IRE) *(65) (RHollinshead)* 2-8-7 LDettori(9) (a.p: led over 2f out to 1f out: unable qckn) 2½ 2

Kinnescash (IRE) *(64) (RIngram)* 2-8-7 JReid(2) (unf: s.s: hdwy 2f out: ev ch 1f out: one pce) ....½ 3
1399² Hurricane Dancer (IRE) *(54)*(Fav)*(SPCWoods)* 2-8-2 MRoberts(6) (lw: a.p: rdn over 2f out: one pce) 1¾ 4
1184¹⁰ Back By Dawn *(55) (DRCElsworth)* 2-8-4 JWilliams(8) (b.hind: led over 3f: one pce) ....½ 5
Pharaoh's Joy *(42) (JWPayne)* 2-8-2 GBardwell(4) (cmpt: bkwd: hdwy over 1f out: one pce)..4 6
1570² State Approval *(47) (APJarvis)* 2-8-7 BThomson(5) (nvr nr to chal) ....nk 7
1226⁴ Dyanko *(43) (MSSaunders)* 2-8-3 (5)ow1 SDrowne(11) (prom 2f) 1½ 8
Where's Margaret *(37) (GLewis)* 2-8-2 NAdams(10) (leggy: scope: a.p: ev ch over 1f out: eased whn btn fnl f) ....nk 9
Matthias Mystique *(37) (MissBSanders)* 2-7-13 (3) SSanders(3) (unf: bit bkwd: prom over 3f) hd 10
1163⁶ Illegally Yours *(34) (LMontagueHall)* 2-8-2 StephenDavies(12) (a bhd) 1 11
1481³ Rowlandsons Charm (IRE) *(28)*(Fav)*(GLMoore)* 2-7-13 FNorton(1) (lw: bhd fnl 3f) 1¼ 12
Daring Venture *(23) (MartynMeade)* 2-8-3 ow1 AClark(7) (leggy: hld up: rdn over 2f out: sn wknd) 3 13

7/2 Hurricane Dancer (IRE), Rowlandsons Charm (IRE), **4/1** Back By Dawn (op 5/2), **10/1** Where's Margaret (op 4/1), Pharaoh's Joy, **12/1** State Approval, **14/1** BEDSIDE MAIL (op 8/1), Dyanko, Weetman's Weigh (IRE), Daring Venture, **16/1** Kinnescash (IRE), **33/1** Matthias Mystique, **50/1** Illegally Yours, CSF £181.16 TOTE £26.80: £5.30 £2.10 £6.50 (£86.10) Trio £299.50 OWNER Mr Gary Coull (NEWMARKET) BRED R. G. Percival and Miss S. M. Rhodes 13 Rn

1m 14.91 (3.61) SF: 12/5/4/-/-/-/-/-/-/-/-/-/-

1691 OLYMPUS 20TH ANNIVERSARY MAIDEN STKS (3-Y.O) (Class D)

£3,889.50 (£1,176.00: £573.00: £271.50)
1m 4f Stalls: High GOING minus 0.37 sec per fur (F) 7-05 (7-10)

1490³ **Ahla** *(80) (RWArmstrong)* 3-8-9 RPrice(6) (lw: 2nd st: led over 2f out: clr over 1f out: r.o wl) ....— 1
1273² Berkeley Bounder (USA) **(78)***(82) (PFICole)* 3-9-0 TQuinn(8) (lw: 4th st: rdn over 2f out: wandered over 1f out: unable qckn) 2 2
1198² Paddy's Return (IRE) *(81)*(Fav)*(FMurphy)* 3-9-0 RCochrane(10) (5th st: rdn over 2f out: wandered over 1f out: one pce) ....¾ 3
Topanga *(81) (HRACecil)* 3-9-0 AClark(15) (w'like: scope: rdn & hdwy over 2f out: r.o one pce) ....hd 4
1147⁷ Coggle *(71) (NAGraham)* 3-8-9 MRoberts(5) (hdwy over 4f out: 6th st: wknd over 1f out) 4 5
Claque *(76) (MrsJCecil)* 3-9-0 FNorton(9) (lw: 3rd st: wknd over 2f out) ....hd 6
1173⁶ Blue And Royal (IRE) *(73) (RHannon)* 3-9-0 JReid(11) (lw: nvr nr to chal) 2 7
1346⁶ Bella Vitessa (IRE) *(66) (JWHills)* 3-8-9 MHills(13) (led over 1f: wknd 5f out) 1¾ 8
1473⁹ Spread The Word *(65) (LGCottrell)* 3-8-9 MFenton(7) (lw: led over 10f out tl over 2f out: sn wknd) ....nk 9
Brick Court (IRE) *(64) (RFJohnsonHoughton)* 3-8-9 BThomson(12) (leggy: scope: lw: a bhd).1 10
950⁷ Nickitoto *(64) (JLDunlop)* 3-8-9 LDettori(14) (lw: led over 10f out tl over 2f out: sn wknd) ....s.h 11
Bakheta *(62) (KTIvory)* 3-8-9 MTebbutt(16) (b.hind: bit bkwd: bhd fnl 6f) 1¼ 12
Celestial Fire *(54) (JWhite)* 3-8-9 (5) SDrowne(3) (bhd fnl 3f) 10 13
1317¹¹ Morning Master *(51) (RMFlower)* 3-9-0 SWhitworth(2) (a bhd) 2½ 14
1317⁴ Canton Venture *(47) (SPCWoods)* 3-8-7 (7) CWebb(1) (a bhd) 3 15

5/2 Paddy's Return (IRE), **4/1** AHLA, **6/1** Blue And Royal (IRE), **7/1** Nickitoto, Topanga (op 9/2), **10/1** Berkeley Bounder (USA) (8/1-12/1), **12/1** Claque (op 8/1), **25/1** Bakheta, Canton Venture, **33/1** Coggle, Brick Court (IRE), Bella Vitessa (IRE), **66/1** Celestial Fire, Morning Master, Spread The Word, CSF £41.69 TOTE £3.60: £1.70 £2.60 £1.20 (£13.80) Trio £10.80 OWNER Mr Hamdan Al Maktoum (NEWMARKET) BRED Shadwell Estate Company Limited 15 Rn

2m 34.33 (4.13) SF: 37/39/38/38/28/33/30/23/22/21/21/19/11/8/4

1692 BAA H'CAP (0-70) (3-Y.O+ F & M) (Class E) £3,663.75

(£1,110.00: £542.50: £258.75)
7f (Jubilee) Stalls: High GOING minus 0.37 sec per fur (F) 7-35 (7-37)

1541W **Bonita (55)***(66) (MrsLPiggott)* 3-8-2 (7) VictoriaAppleby(16) (hdwy on ins over 1f out: led nr fin) ....— 1
1472⁹ Anna-Jane **(63)***(73) (RHannon)* 3-9-3 JReid(12) (3rd st: hrd rdn over 1f out: ev ch wl ins fnl f: r.o) ....nk 2
1516* Pharsical **(61)***(71)*(Fav)*(MRChannon)* 4-9-11 MHills(2) (led: hrd rdn over 1f out: hdd nr fin) ...nk 3
1541¹⁰ Bowden Rose **(52)***(61) (MBlanshard)* 3-8-6b StephenDavies(7) (4th st: hrd rdn over 1f out: r.o ins fnl f) ....½ 4
1294⁵ Prince's Feather (IRE) **(70)***(77) (DMorley)* 3-9-10 LDettori(6) (5th st: rdn over 2f out: r.o ins fnl f) ....½ 5

1598[6] Quillon Rose **(41)***(47) (CFWall)* 3-7-9 NCarlisle(11) (swtg: 6th st: rdn over 2f out: cl 5th whn nt clr run wl ins fnl f) ....½ 6
1633[6] Frisky Miss (IRE) **(64)***(70) (KOCunningham-Brown)* 4-10-0 RCochrane(14) (lw: rdn over 2f out: hdwy over 1f out: r.o ins fnl f) ....hd 7
1021[16] Kinnegad Kid **(45)***(49) (RIngram)* 6-8-9 MRoberts(10) (2nd st: wknd over 1f out) ....¾ 8
1172[12] Rookery Girl **(56)***(60) (DMorris)* 3-8-10 RPrice(5) (nvr nrr) ....nk 9
989[2] Takeshi (IRE) **(64)***(66) (EALDunlop)* 3-9-1 (3) JTate(1) (b.hind: 7th st: wknd over 1f out) ....½ 10
1516[8] Nakita **(50)***(50) (CNAllen)* 4-9-0 JWilliams(8) (b.hind: bhd fnl 2f) 1 11
1456[9] Shanghai Lil **(40)***(34) (MJFetherston-Godley)* 3-7-8 GBardwell(17) (a bhd) 2½ 12
1457[7] Fyne Song **(40)***(34) (WJMusson)* 3-7-8 NAdams(9) (a bhd) ....nk 13
1428[7] Mrs Tigger **(43)***(28) (RWArmstrong)* 3-7-4 (7)ow4 SLanigan(13) (a bhd) 2 14
Mo Stopher **(60)** *(RAkehurst)* 3-9-0 TQuinn(15) (bhd fnl 4f: t.o) 15

LONG HANDICAP Mrs Tigger 7-6

7/2 Pharsical, **13/2** Kinnegad Kid, **7/1** Prince's Feather (IRE), Takeshi (IRE), **15/2** Anna-Jane, **12/1** Fyne Song, **14/1** Quillon Rose, **20/1** Mo Stopher, Rookery Girl, Nakita, Shanghai Lil, Frisky Miss (IRE), **25/1** Bowden Rose, **33/1** Mrs Tigger, BONITA, CSF £236.33 CT £993.58 TOTE £30.40: £5.80 £2.30 £1.90 (£103.30) Trio £112.30 OWNER Mr Tony Hirschfeld BRED Mrs S. E. Piggott 15 Rn 1m 26.73 (2.53) SF: 33/40/48/28/44/14/47/26/27/33/27/1/1/-/-

WEIGHT FOR AGE 3yo-10lb

1693

ALLIED DUNBAR H'CAP (0-80) (3-Y.O+) (Class D) £3,663.75 (£1,110.00: £542.50: £258.75) **1m (Jubilee)** Stalls: High GOING minus 0.37 sec per fur (F) 8-05 (8-05)

360[3] **Nordinex (IRE) (70)***(81) (RWArmstrong)* 3-8-7 MHills(4) (lw: 4th st: led 2f out: rdn out) ....— 1
1517[2] Confronter **(68)***(78) (SDow)* 6-9-2 MRoberts(3) (lw: 5th st: rdn over 2f out: r.o wl ins fnl f) ....½ 2
962[7] Snowy Petrel (IRE) **(77)***(83) (JLDunlop)* 3-9-0 LDettori(8) (3rd st: ev ch 2f out: unable qckn) ...2 3
*1320** Persian Conquest (IRE) **(61)***(62) (RIngram)* 3-7-12b NCarlisle(1) (lw: 2nd st: led over 2f out: sn hdd: wknd over 1f out) 2½ 4
1244[6] Another Fiddle (IRE) **(67)***(66)*(Fav)*(RAkehurst)* 5-9-1 JReid(9) (b.off hind: hmpd over 4f out: 6th st: n.m.r 2f out: nvr nr to chal) 1 5
1517[10] Dontforget Insight (IRE) **(76)***(73) (PFICole)* 4-9-10 TQuinn(2) (b.nr hind: hdwy over 1f out: one pce) 1¼ 6
1324[6] Telopea **(72)***(57) (HCandy)* 4-9-6 WNewnes(5) (led over 5f) 6 7
1351[9] Astral Weeks (IRE) **(75)***(48) (RHannon)* 4-9-9 RPerham(7) (6th whn slipped over 4f out: sn wknd) 6 8
1366[14] Autumn Cover **(56)***(28) (RMFlower)* 3-7-7 NAdams(11) (b: a bhd) ....nk 9
1571[2] Night in a Million **(62)***(31) (MrsJCecil)* 4-8-5 (5) AWhelan(10) (a bhd) 1¼ 10

LONG HANDICAP Autumn Cover 7-5

3/1 Another Fiddle (IRE), **100/30** Confronter, **13/2** Night in a Million (op 3/1), **15/2** Snowy Petrel (IRE), Persian Conquest (IRE), **10/1** Telopea, **11/1** NORDINEX (IRE), **20/1** Dontforget Insight (IRE), Astral Weeks (IRE), **40/1** Autumn Cover, CSF £43.56 CT £267.20 TOTE £13.90: £2.70 £1.10 £2.90 (£11.50) Trio £52.90 OWNER Mr R. J. Arculli (NEWMARKET) BRED Howard Kaskel in Ireland 10 Rn 1m 38.97 (1.97) SF: 41/49/43/22/37/44/28/19/-/2

WEIGHT FOR AGE 3yo-11lb

1694

SQUIRE'S 60TH ANNIVERSARY H'CAP (0-70) (3-Y.O+) (Class E) £3,371.25 (£1,020.00: £497.50: £236.25) **1m 4f** Stalls: High GOING minus 0.37 sec per fur (F) 8-35 (8-37)

1513* **Hi-Aud (61)***(74+)*(Fav)*(JAkehurst)* 3-8-5 4x TQuinn(5) (6th st: led over 1f out: r.o wl) ....— 1
1518[3] Duty Sergeant (IRE) **(33)***(42) (PMitchell)* 6-7-7 GBardwell(12) (rdn over 3f out: gd hdwy over 1f out: r.o wl ins fnl f) 3 2
1498[8] Zalament **(58)***(65) (APJarvis)* 3-8-2 MRoberts(1) (lw: 4th st: rdn over 2f out: one pce) 1½ 3
1518* One Off the Rail (USA) **(43)***(50) (AMoore)* 5-8-3 4x CandyMorris(11) (3rd st: led over 2f out tl over 1f out: unable qckn) ....s.h 4
1347[7] Masuri Kabisa (USA) **(35)***(37) (HJCollingridge)* 4-7-9 ow2 JQuinn(10) (lw: hdwy over 2f out: hrd rdn over 1f out: one pce) 2 5
*1029** Nothing Doing (IRE) **(33)***(37) (WJMusson)* 6-7-7 NAdams(3) (rdn & hdwy over 2f out: one pce) ....nk 6
1254[3] Lady Reema **(37)***(41) (MissAJWhitfield)* 4-7-4 (7) SLanigan(7) (hdwy 9f out: 5th st: hrd rdn & hung lft over 1f out: one pce) ....hd 7
1205[8] Silver Hunter (USA) **(68)***(69) (GCBravery)* 4-10-0 MHills(4) (lw: led over 9f) 1¾ 8
1340[3] Wildfire (SWI) **(52)***(44) (RAkehurst)* 4-8-12 AMcGlone(2) (2nd st: wknd over 2f out) 7 9
1622[17] Jarzon Dancer **(40)***(27) (DAWilson)* 7-7-7 (7)ow2 RachaelMoody(6) (b: lw: a bhd) 2½ 10
Brunswick Blue (IRE) **(34)***(4) (RMFlower)* 7-7-8 ow1 NCarlisle(8) (bit bkwd: bhd fnl 6f) 13 11

LONG HANDICAP Duty Sergeant (IRE) 7-3 Masuri Kabisa (USA) 7-6 Brunswick Blue (IRE) 7-2

6/5 HI-AUD, **7/1** Silver Hunter (USA), One Off the Rail (USA), **10/1** Lady Reema, Nothing Doing (IRE), **12/1** Wildfire (SWI) (7/1-14/1), **14/1** Zalament, **16/1** Duty Sergeant (IRE), Masuri Kabisa (USA), **66/1** Jarzon Dancer, Brunswick Blue (IRE), CSF £19.65 CT £171.60 TOTE £2.10: £1.20 £3.20 £3.20 (£20.70) Trio £92.40 OWNER Mr A. G. Speake (LAMBOURN) BRED A. G. Speake 11 Rn 2m 32.69 (2.49) SF: 44/28/35/36/23/23/27/55/30/13/-

WEIGHT FOR AGE 3yo-16lb

1695 JUPITER LIMITED STKS (0-65) (3-Y.O+) (Class F) £2,775.00 (£840.00: £410.00: £195.00) 1m 6f 92y Stalls: High GOING minus 0.37 sec per fur (F) 9-05 (9-06)

1635[2] **Wild Strawberry (64)***(73)*(Fav)*(MissBSanders)* 6-9-2 (3) SSanders(6) (mde all: drvn out)......— **1**
1058[12] Wannaplantatree **(56)***(73) (NMBabbage)* 4-9-5 AClark(4) (hdwy over 3f out: 4th st: rdn over 2f out: chsd wnr over 1f out: r.o)......nk **2**
1382[6] John Lee Hooker **(62)***(74) (DWPArbuthnot)* 3-8-6 BThomson(3) (hdwy over 3f out: 5th st: r.o one pce fnl 2f)......3 **3**
1552[3] Durshan (USA) **(50)***(69) (JRJenkins)* 6-9-10 LDettori(5) (lw: 2nd st: wknd over 1f out)......5 **4**
1410[6] Total Joy (IRE) **(61)***(69) (PFICole)* 4-9-12 TQuinn(1) (b.nr fore: 6th st: nvr nr to chal)......1¼ **5**
1386[3] Euro Forum **(63)***(64) (GLMoore)* 3-8-6 RPerham(8) (lw: 3rd st: rdn over 2f out: eased whn btn over 1f out)......3 **6**
1439[5] Great Expectations (FR) **(59)***(49) (KOCunningham-Brown)* 4-9-10 AMcGlone(7) (lw: bhd fnl 6f)......14 **7**
Any Minute Now (IRE) **(49)***(43) (JAkehurst)* 5-9-10 SWhitworth(2) (lw: prom over 9f)......5 **8**

9/4 WILD STRAWBERRY, **11/4** Euro Forum, **5/1** Durshan (USA), **11/2** Total Joy (IRE), **13/2** John Lee Hooker, **16/1** Any Minute Now (IRE), **25/1** Great Expectations (FR), Wannaplantatree, CSF £43.21 TOTE £3.30: £1.50 £3.60 £1.50 (£41.30) OWNER Copyforce Ltd (EPSOM) BRED Castle Farm Stud 8 Rn 3m 7.97 (1.29 under best) (4.97) SF: 47/47/30/43/43/20/23/17

WEIGHT FOR AGE 3yo-18lb

T/Plpt: £182.40 (116.17 Tckts). T/Qdpt: £12.00 (10.4 Tckts). AK

1547-YARMOUTH (L-H)
Wednesday June 14th (Good)

approx extended dists races 3 -7 due to camera failure.
WEATHER: overcast WIND: fresh half bhd

1696 CHARTER H'CAP (0-70) (3-Y.O) (Class E) £3,359.40 (£1,003.20:£479.60: £217.80) 1m 6f 17y Stalls: Low GOING minus 0.38 sec per fur (F) 2-15 (2-16)

1452[2] **Carnbrea Belle (IRE) (57)***(71)*(Fav)*(MBell)* 3-9-0 MFenton(5) (lw: chsd ldrs: 5th st: led over 2f out: rdn clr: hld on wl)......— **1**
1372[6] Bobby's Dream **(43)***(53) (MHTompkins)* 3-8-0 ow3 PRobinson(13) (hld up: gd hdwy 2f out: rdn appr fnl f: fin wl)......1 **2**
1535[2] Much Too High **(52)***(63) (TJNaughton)* 3-8-9 RPerham(4) (hld up: hdwy 3f out: hrd rdn appr fnl f: kpt on)......1¾ **3**
1379[2] Vizard (IRE) **(64)***(73) (MJHeaton-Ellis)* 3-9-7b PaulEddery(7) (hld up & bhd: hdwy over 2f out: rdn & one pce fnl f)......1¾ **4**
1219[7] China Mail (IRE) **(58)***(64) (JMPEustace)* 3-9-1 RCochrane(1) (settled mid div: 7th st: sn pushed along: wknd wl over 1f out)......3 **5**
1529[6] Star Fighter **(51)***(54) (WAO'Gorman)* 3-8-8 EmmaO'Gorman(10) (s.i.s: sn chsng ldrs: 2nd st: wknd wl over 1f out)......2½ **6**
1498[7] Good (IRE) **(51)***(53) (DTThom)* 3-8-5 (3) DRMcCabe(11) (prom: 6th st: rdn 2f out: grad wknd) .1 **7**
1527[8] Shamekh **(60)***(60) (JEBanks)* 3-9-0 (3) JTate(3) (lw: dwlt: a in rr)......1¾ **8**
1218[9] Western Horizon (USA) **(47)***(42) (CEBrittain)* 3-8-4 MRoberts(9) (lw: prom: 4th st: wknd over 2f out)......4 **9**
655[5] Amercius **(48)***(34) (JEBanks)* 3-8-5 GBardwell(12) (lost pl ½-wy: sn bhd: t.o)......8 **10**
1379[4] Keys Seminar **(47)***(29) (JohnBerry)* 3-8-4 StephenDavies(8) (led 3f: 3rd st: wknd wl over 2f out: t.o)......3½ **11**
1407[2] Negative Equity **(59)***(39) (KRBurke)* 3-9-2v LDettori(2) (led after 3f tl hdd & wknd over 2f out: t.o)......1¾ **12**
1182[6] Beyaateh **(38)***(13) (MCChapman)* 3-7-9 JQuinn(6) (a bhd: t.o)......4 **13**

7/2 CARNBREA BELLE (IRE), **5/1** Negative Equity, **7/1** Much Too High, **15/2** Bobby's Dream, **10/1** Good (IRE) (16/1-9/1), **12/1** Western Horizon (USA) (op 8/1), Vizard (IRE) (op 7/1), China Mail (IRE), **14/1** Amercius, **20/1** Shamekh, Keys Seminar, Star Fighter, **33/1** Beyaateh, CSF £27.65 CT £160.08 TOTE £4.50: £2.00 £1.60 £3.20 (£15.40) Trio £56.40 OWNER Mrs S. M. Crompton (NEWMARKET) BRED Limestone Stud 13 Rn

3m 5.3 (7.30) SF: 28/10/20/30/21/11/10/17/-/-/-/-/-

1697

E.B.F RIVER BURE MEDIAN AUCTION MAIDEN STKS (2-Y.O) (Class E) £3,273.60 (£976.80: £466.40: £211.20)
6f 3y Stalls: Low GOING minus 0.38 sec per fur (F) 2-45 (2-46)

1375[2] **React** *(82+)*(Fav)*(WJarvis)* 2-8-9 LDettori(2) (lw: mde all: clr ent fnl f: readily) ....— 1
Champagne Prince *(74) (PWHarris)* 2-9-0 PatEddery(3) (lt-f: prom tl outpcd ½-wy: rallied appr fnl f: no ch w wnr) 5 2
Carmentalia *(62) (SirMarkPrescott)* 2-8-9 GDuffield(5) (w'like: scope: bit bkwd: a.p: shkn up appr fnl f: nvr nrr) 2½ 3
1551[8] Emperegrine (USA) *(62) (CFWall)* 2-9-0 MRoberts(6) (bhd: effrt & hung lft 3f out: styd on appr fnl f: sn outpcd) 2 4
Toffee *(49) (JRFanshawe)* 2-8-9 DHarrison(4) (leggy: lt-f: dwlt: bhd: drvn along over 2f out: no rspnse) 3 5

8/13 REACT, **5/2** Champagne Prince, **11/1** Toffee (6/1-12/1), **14/1** Carmentalia (op 6/1), **25/1** Emperegrine (USA), CSF £2.44 TOTE £1.40: £1.20 £1.20 (£1.70) OWNER Prince Fahd Salman (NEWMARKET) BRED Newgate Stud Co 5 Rn 1m 13.4 (2.80) SF: 23/15/3/3/-

1698

HOPTON CONDITIONS STKS (3-Y.O+) (Class C) £5,163.20 (£1,908.80: £914.40: £372.00: £146.00: £55.60)
6f 3y Stalls: Low GOING minus 0.38 sec per fur (F) 3-15 (3-16)

1373[3] **Paris Babe (91)***(91) (DMorris)* 3-8-4 RCochrane(2) (hld up: shkn up to chal ent fnl f: r.o to ld wl ins fnl f) ....— 1
1138[7] Bahith (USA) **(96)***(92) (HThomsonJones)* 3-8-9 RHills(6) (led: rdn, drifted lft & hdd nr fin)....1½ 2
Maid for Walking **(105)***(90)*(Fav)*(DRLoder)* 3-8-12 LDettori(4) (still unf: chsd ldrs: reminders over 2f out: kpt on one pce fnl f) 1¾ 3
1258* Storm Bid (USA) *(87) (EALDunlop)* 3-8-6 (3) JTate(3) (w ldr tl rdn & wknd over 1f out) ....s.h 4
1216* Shayim (USA) *(66) (RWArmstrong)* 3-8-9 RPrice(1) (rdn & outpcd over 3f out: sn bhd) 8 5
1365[6] En Attendant (FR) **(100)***(73) (BHanbury)* 7-9-12 TIves(7) (b: s.i.s: a in rr: lost tch ½-wy) ....nk 6
1475[9] Hello Mister **(98)***(68) (JO'Donoghue)* 4-9-12 MFenton(5) (dwlt: a bhd: outpcd fr ½-wy) 2 7

15/8 Maid for Walking (5/4-2/1), **5/1** PARIS BABE (8/1-9/2), Shayim (USA), Storm Bid (USA), **9/1** Bahith (USA), **14/1** En Attendant (FR), **16/1** Hello Mister, CSF £39.19 TOTE £7.90: £2.60 £2.80 (£19.20) OWNER Mrs Susan Parry (NEWMARKET) BRED I. W. Parry 7 Rn
1m 10.9 (0.30) SF: 52/53/51/48/27/43/38
WEIGHT FOR AGE 3yo-9lb

1699

TOLLHOUSE (S) STKS (2-Y.O) (Class G) £2,601.40 (£720.40: £344.20)
6f 3y Stalls: Low GOING minus 0.38 sec per fur (F) 3-45 (3-47)

1318[6] **Arch Angel (IRE)** *(58)*(Fav)*(DJSffrenchDavis)* 2-8-6 NAdams(2) (a.p: rdn & outpcd 2f out: rallied to ld ins fnl f: all out) ....— 1
1590[6] Ivory's Grab Hire *(62) (KTIvory)* 2-8-11 GDuffield(7) (b: hld up: gd hdwy 2f out: led over 1f out tl ins fnl f: r.o) ....nk 2
1570[6] Down The Yard *(56) (MCChapman)* 2-8-3 (3) DRMcCabe(5) (bhd: rdn 2f out: r.o strly ins fnl f) ....nk 3
1540[13] Imprimis (IRE) *(55) (CNAllen)* 2-8-6 JQuinn(1) (s.s: bhd: hdwy wl over 1f out: nvr nrr) ....½ 4
1035[5] Orange And Blue *(59) (MAJarvis)* 2-8-11c PRobinson(6) (lw: chsd ldrs: rdn & edgd rt fnl f: unable qckn) ....½ 5
1503[2] Jambo *(49) (MRChannon)* 2-8-6 MRoberts(3) (led tl over 1f out: sn rdn & btn) 1¾ 6
1369[2] Bites *(42) (JAHarris)* 2-8-6 PaulEddery(8) (prom over 4f) 2½ 7
1327[5] Mister Sean (IRE) *(44) (JWPayne)* 2-8-11 RCochrane(9) (bit bkwd: hld up: hdwy over 2f out: wknd fnl f) 1¼ 8
Cottesloe Beach *(10) (KTIvory)* 2-8-4 (7) CScally(4) (b: lt-f: unf: bit bkwd: a bhd: t.o) 13 9

6/4 ARCH ANGEL (IRE), **9/4** Jambo, **7/1** Ivory's Grab Hire (op 4/1), Orange And Blue, **12/1** Imprimis (IRE) (7/1-14/1), Mister Sean (IRE) (8/1-14/1), **14/1** Bites (10/1-20/1), **50/1** Down The Yard, Cottesloe Beach, CSF £12.69 TOTE £2.80: £1.30 £2.40 £8.30 (£10.90) Trio £169.20 OWNER Mr R. J. Lorenz (UPPER LAMBOURN) BRED Mrs P. Grubb 9 Rn 1m 14.1 (3.50) SF: 11/15/9/8/12/2/-/-/-
No bid

1700

POTTER HEIGHAM H'CAP (0-70) (3-Y.O+) (Class E) £3,159.20 (£941.60: £448.80: £202.40)
6f 3y Stalls: Low GOING minus 0.38 sec per fur (F) 4-15 (4-16)

1050[12] **Red Admiral (56)***(62) (PCHaslam)* 5-9-2 MTebbutt(3) (lw: mde all: rdn appr fnl f: hld on all out) ....— 1

1468[8] Awesome Venture **(48)***(53) (MCChapman)* 5-8-5 (3) DRMcCabe(2) (a.p: outpcd 2f out: rallied & r.o wl fnl f) ....nk 2
1429* Night Asset **(54)***(59)*(Fav)*(JO'Donoghue)* 6-9-0 MFenton(4) (lw: chsd ldrs: effrt over 1f out: rdn & r.o wl fnl f) ....s.h 3
1342[5] Taffeta Silk (USA) **(62)***(66) (WJarvis)* 4-9-8 PatEddery(1) (chsd ldrs: rdn 2f out: kpt on ins fnl f) ....½ 4
1405[4] Millesime (IRE) **(65)***(61) (BHanbury)* 3-9-2 TIves(6) (prom: rdn wl over 1f out: sn outpcd) 3 5
1550[6] Time Is Money (IRE) **(56)***(52) (MHTompkins)* 3-8-7 PRobinson(7) (dropped rr over 2f out: sn rdn: no imp) ....hd 6
1566[5] Moujeeb (USA) **(64)***(56) (PatMitchell)* 5-9-10v LDettori(8) (lw: hld up: hdwy 2f out: hrd rdn & nt qckn fnl f) 1½ 7
1571[7] Farmer Jock **(46)***(6) (MrsNMacauley)* 13-8-1 (5) CTeague(5) (b: lw: racd alone: a bhd: t.o) 12 8

7/4 Night Asset, **7/2** Taffeta Silk (USA), **4/1** Moujeeb (USA) (11/4-9/2), **10/1** RED ADMIRAL, Millesime (IRE), Awesome Venture, **12/1** Time Is Money (IRE), **20/1** Farmer Jock, CSF £91.03 CT £233.78 TOTE £8.80: £1.80 £1.80 £1.70 (£44.10) OWNER Sackville House Racing (MIDDLEHAM) BRED Hesmonds Stud Ltd 8 Rn 1m 12.3 (1.70) SF: 44/35/41/48/34/25/38/-
WEIGHT FOR AGE 3yo-9lb

1701

JOHN HOLDRICH MAIDEN STKS (3-Y.O F) (Class D) £3,968.90 (£1,185.20: £566.60: £257.30)
7f 3y Stalls: Low GOING minus 0.38 sec per fur (F) 4-45 (4-46)

1000[2] **Nawaasi** *(75)*(Fav)*(HThomsonJones)* 3-8-11 RHills(7) (hld up gng wl: qcknd to ld ent fnl f: shkn up: hld on wl) ....— 1
1476[5] Cutpurse Moll *(75) (JRFanshawe)* 3-8-11 DHarrison(2) (mde most to 1f out: rallied u.p cl home) ....hd 2
Western Sal *(74) (WJarvis)* 3-8-11 PRobinson(1) (lt-f: unf: hld up: hdwy wl over 1f out: fin wl) ....nk 3
Crown of Sheba (USA) *(73) (EALDunlop)* 3-8-11 WRSwinburn(6) (lt-f: bit bkwd: hld up: hdwy appr fnl f: r.o wl nr fin) ....nk 4
1549[2] Brown Eyed Girl **(70)***(70) (RHannon)* 3-8-11 RPerham(10) (w ldrs: ev ch 2f out: rdn & no ex fnl f) 1½ 5
985[4] Banner (USA) **(75)***(67) (BWHills)* 3-8-11 PatEddery(11) (bit bkwd: stdd s: hld up: hdwy over 2f out: kpt on u.p fnl f) 1¼ 6
1486[7] Moon Over Awir (IRE) *(65) (LMCumani)* 3-8-4 (7) JoHunnam(3) (prom over 5f: sn rdn & outpcd) ....¾ 7
Lancerette *(56) (NAGraham)* 3-8-11 PaulEddery(9) (leggy: scope: s.s: a in rr) 4 8
Maquina *(55) (JHMGosden)* 3-8-11 LDettori(4) (scope: bkwd: hld up: effrt & reminders 2f out: no imp) ....¾ 9
865[8] Zitziana (IRE) *(46) (CEBrittain)* 3-8-11 BDoyle(8) (disp ld over 4f: sn wknd) 4 10
1473[11] Vezelay (USA) *(44) (JHMGosden)* 3-8-11 GHind(5) (a in rr) ....½ 11

15/8 NAWAASI, **7/2** Banner (USA), **5/1** Maquina (7/2-11/2), **11/2** Crown of Sheba (USA) (4/1-6/1), **7/1** Brown Eyed Girl, **16/1** Cutpurse Moll, **25/1** Moon Over Awir (IRE), Lancerette, **40/1** Western Sal, Zitziana (IRE), **50/1** Vezelay (USA), CSF £30.16 TOTE £2.40: £1.50 £3.50 £6.80 (£33.00) Trio £251.60; £152.40 to Yarmouth 15/6/95 OWNER Mr Hamdan Al Maktoum (NEWMARKET) BRED Hesmonds Stud Ltd 11 Rn 1m 25.1 (2.30) SF: 36/36/35/34/31/28/26/17/16/7/5

1702

HORNING H'CAP (0-70) (3-Y.O F) (Class E) £3,445.20 (£1,029.60: £492.80: £224.40) **1m 2f 21y** Stalls: Low GOING minus 0.38 sec per fur (F) 5-15 (5-16)

1372[11] **Fen Terrier (50)***(62) (WJHaggas)* 3-8-8 RHills(4) (lw: mde all: rdn over 2f out: styd on gamely) ....— 1
1347[3] Inchkeith **(63)***(75) (GWragg)* 3-9-7 PaulEddery(5) (chsd wnr: 2nd st: sustained chal fnl f: jst failed) ....hd 2
1219[9] Lucky Coin **(62)***(70) (CEBrittain)* 3-9-6 BDoyle(3) (chsd ldrs: 3rd st: rdn over 2f out: one pce) 2½ 3
521* Boldly So **(45)***(40)*(Fav)*(WJMusson)* 3-8-3 JQuinn(1) (hld up: 4th st: hrd drvn over 3f out: sn outpcd) 8 4
1581[6] Gentle Irony **(59)***(37) (BJMeehan)* 3-9-3 PatEddery(2) (lw: s.i.s: bhd: 5th st: shkn up 3f out: no imp) 11 5

5/2 Boldly So, **7/2** Gentle Irony, Lucky Coin, FEN TERRIER, **13/2** Inchkeith (5/2-7/1), CSF £20.68 TOTE £4.80: £2.80 £2.20 (£7.60) OWNER Jolly Farmers Racing (NEWMARKET) BRED Racing Thoroughbreds P L C 5 Rn 2m 8.6 (4.20) SF: 29/42/37/7/4

T/Plpt: £293.80 (43.3 Tckts). T/Qdpt: Not won; £34.80 to Yarmouth 15/6/95. IM

1113a-LEOPARDSTOWN (Dublin, Ireland) (L-H) Monday June 5th (Good)

1703a BALLYOGAN STKS (Gp 3) (3-Y.O+) £16,250.00 (£4,750.00: £2,250.00: £750.00) 5f 3-30 (3-40)

1364[2] **Millstream (USA)** *(112)*(Fav)*(MJohnston)* 3-8-12 DHolland ....— 1
921[9] Mistertopogigo (IRE) *(106) (WSCunningham)* 5-9-2 CRoche ....½ 2
Petite Fantasy *(100) (APO'Brien,Ireland)* 3-8-5 JFEgan 1 3
901a[4] Imperial Bailiwick (IRE) *(91) (MDIUsher)* 4-8-13 KJManning (btn approx 4½l) 6

2/1 MILLSTREAM (USA), **11/4** Mistertopogigo (IRE), **8/1** Petite Fantasy, **14/1** Imperial Bailiwick (IRE), Tote £2.30: £1.10 £1.40 £3.00 (£3.00) OWNER Sheikh Mohammed (MIDDLEHAM) BRED Darley Stud Management Co Ltd in USA 9 Rn 58.0 secs (-0.50) SF: -/-/-/- NR

1387a-SAINT-CLOUD (France) (L-H) Monday June 5th (Good)

1704a PRIX DE ROYAUMONT (Gp 3) (3-Y.O F) £26,347.00 (£9,581.00: £4,790.00: £2,395.00) 1m 4f 3-10 (3-06)

Genovefa (USA) *(97) (AFabre,France)* 3-9-2 TJarnet ....— 1
Enquiry (FR) *(97) (MmePBarbe,France)* 3-9-2 TThulliez ....s.h 2
1110a[3] Privity (USA) *(95) (PBary,France)* 3-9-2 DBoeuf (fin 4th, s.h: plcd 3rd) 3
De Puntillas *(95) (Ld'Auria,Italy)* 3-9-2 SDettori (fin 3rd, 3/4l: disq: plcd 4th) 4
932[3] Llia *(92) (JLDunlop)* 3-9-2 CAsmussen (btn approx 2¼l) 5

P-M 2.00F: 1.30F 1.50F (SF 5.20F) OWNER Sheikh Mohammed (FRANCE) BRED C.Robinson 5 Rn 2m 41.9 (12.60) SF: -/-/-/-/-

MULHEIM (Mulheim-Ruhr, Germany) Monday June 5th (Good)

1705a PREIS DER DIANA (Gp 2) (3-Y.O F) £96,708.00 (£38,683.00: £19,753.00: £11,523.00) 1m 3f 4-15 (4-15)

1009a[3] **Centaine** *(106) (HRemmert,Germany)* 3-8-11 KWoodburn (hld up: gd hdwy to ld over 1f out: r.o strly) ....— 1
Tascilla (GER) *(102) (HRemmert,Germany)* 3-8-11 MRimmer (hld up: hdwy 2f out: r.o) 3 2
1009a[8] Anna Domani(FR) *(100) (JKappel,Germany)* 3-8-11 PBloomfield (hdwy 3f out: chal over 1f out: no ex) 1½ 3
Ulanowa (GER) *(97) (FrauEMader,Germany)* 3-8-11 LMader 1¾ 4
Blue Bay (GER) *(94) (Germany)* 3-8-11 ATylicki 2 5
1009a[2] S'Il Vous Plait(GER) *(90) (AWohler,Germany)* 3-8-11 ABoschert 3 6
1009a[6] White On Red(GER) *(86) (BSchutz,Germany)* 3-8-11 THellier 2½ 7
Sandy Hollow *(Germany)* 3-8-11 MRoberts 8
Alyeska (GER) *(Germany)* 3-8-11 DavidEddery 9

Tote 40DM: 21DM 33DM 39DM (SF 398DM) OWNER Frau M & Frau U Stoof BRED Kirtlington Stud Ltd 15 Rn 2m 21.36 SF: -/-/-/-/-/-/-/-/-

1703a-LEOPARDSTOWN (Dublin, Ireland) (L-H) Tuesday June 6th (Good)

1706a BALLYCHORUS STKS (Gp 3) (3-Y.O+) £16,250.00 (£4,750.00: £2,250.00: £750.00) 7f 8-30 (8-32)

1233a[2] **Desert Style (IRE)** *(120) (JSBolger,Ireland)* 3-8-13 KJManning ....— 1
1284* Mistle Cat (USA) *(116)*(Fav)*(SPCWoods)* 5-9-5 WRyan ....hd 2
The Puzzler (IRE) *(114) (MKauntze,Ireland)* 4-9-5 WJO'Connor ....¾ 3
Nijo *(113) (DRLoder)* 4-9-5 LDettori ....nk 4

7/4 Mistle Cat (USA), **9/4** Nijo, **5/1** DESERT STYLE (IRE), **14/1** The Puzzler (IRE), Tote £5.50: £1.70 £1.10 £7.30 (£6.80) OWNER Maktoum Al Maktoum (IRELAND) BRED Ovidstown Investments Ltd 8 Rn 1m 29.6 (4.60) SF: -/-/-/-

TABY (Stockholm, Sweden) (L-H)
Tuesday June 6th (Good)

1707a
IBM PC VARSPRINT (Listed) (4-Y.O+) £25,795.00 (£6,879.00: £5,159.00: £3,439.00) **6f** 7-10 (7-10)

Troon *(100) (RHaugen,Norway)* 5-9-2 MSantos ....— 1
Cajun Cadet *(99) (WNeuroth,Norway)* 4-9-2 NGrant ....½ 2
1393a[4] Hever Golf Rose *(93) (TJNaughton)* 4-8-12 JWeaver ....½ 3
Tote 288.20SKr: 13.40SKr 2.90SKr 4.80SKr (2801.20SKr) OWNER Stall Oak Creek BRED D. Seale
15 Rn 1m 9.1 SF: -/-/-

1390a-CURRAGH (Newbridge, Ireland) (R-H)
Saturday June 10th (Good)

1708a
GALLINULE STKS (Gp 2) (3-Y.O+ C & F) £26,000.00 (£7,600.00: £3,600.00: £1,200.00) **1m 2f** 3-30 (3-30)

1113a[2] **Shemaran (IRE)** *(118)*(Fav)*(JOxx,Ireland)* 3-8-10 JPMurtagh (trckd ldr: disp ld over 3f out: led & qcknd 2f out: r.o strly)........................— 1
1235a* Prince of Andros (USA) *(120) (DRLoder)* 5-9-12 GCarter (hld up: rdn to chse wnr 2f out: r.o wl)........................½ 2
1235a[6] Akhiyar (IRE) *(106) (JOxx,Ireland)* 4-9-7 CRoche (set slw pce: hdd 2f out: rdn & wknd).......5½ 3
1390a[9] Taibhseach (USA) *(99) (JSBolger,Ireland)* 3-8-5 JAHeffernan (trckd ldrs: hdwy to disp ld over 3f out: sn rdn & wknd)........................2½ 4
9/10 SHEMARAN (IRE), **13/8** Prince of Andros (USA), **11/2** Akhiyar (IRE), **11/1** Taibhseach (USA), Tote £1.90: (£1.70) OWNER Aga Khan BRED H.H. Aga Khan Studs S.C. 4 Rn
2m 12.8 (10.50) SF: -/-/-/-

1005a-EVRY (France) (R-H)
Saturday June 10th (Good)

1709a
GRAND PRIX D'EVRY (Gp 2) (4-Y.O+) £41,916.00 (£16,766.00: £8,383.00: £4,192.00) **1m 4f** 3-00 (2-58)

896a* **Tot Ou Tard (IRE)** *(120) (SWattel,France)* 5-8-9 ESaint-Martin (a.p: 3rd st: ld over 1f out: hrd rdn: styd on wl)........................— 1
Solid Illusion (USA) *(120) (PDemercastel,France)* 4-8-9 SGuillot (5th st: prog to chal fnl f: r.o wl)........................hd 2
1387a[6] Suave Tern (USA) *(118) (JEHammond,France)* 4-8-9 WMongil (8th st: rapid hdwy fnl 1½f: fin wl)........................1½ 3
Sunrise Song (FR) *(113) (FDoumen,France)* 4-8-6 FSanchez (a cl up: effrt 2f out: one pce)1½ 4
Rainbow Dancer (FR) *(115) (PBary,France)* 4-8-9 GMosse (3rd tl led over 6f out: hrd rdn 3f out: one pce fnl f)........................1 5
Fanion de Fete (FR) *(114) (JBernard,France)* 4-8-9 FHead (s.i.s: last st: gd hdwy fnl f: fin wl)........................nk 6
1387a[3] Partipral (USA) *(114) (ELellouche,France)* 6-8-9 DBoeuf (hld up: 7th st: rdn & some late hdwy)........................s.h 7
897a[3] Truly a Dream (IRE) *(110) (RCollet,France)* 4-8-9 GGuignard (6th st: fnd nil u.p fnl f) 3 8
1387a[8] Matarun (IRE) *(109) (HVandePoele,France)* 7-8-9 OPeslier (led tl over 6f out: 2nd st: hrd rdn 2f out: wknd)........................1 9
P-M 7.40F: 2.40F 1.40F 3.50F (12.90F) OWNER Ecurie Kura BRED M.Kura 9 Rn 2m 37.83 (8.33)
DS

BELMONT PARK (New York, USA) (L-H)
Saturday June 10th (Fast)

1710a
BELMONT STKS (Gp 1) (3-Y.O) £268,205.00 (£89,410.00: £49,193.00: £26,823.00) **1m 4f** 10-30 (10-33)

1232a[3] **Thunder Gulch(USA)** *(118) (DWLukas,USA)* 3-9-0 GStevens ....— 1
Star Standard (USA) *(115) (NZito,USA)* 3-9-0 JulieKrone 2 2
1006a[9] Citadeed (USA) *(111) (RViolette,USA)* 3-9-0 EMaple 3½ 3
P-M £5.00: PL £3.70 £5.80 SHOW £2.90 £4.30 £4.40 (SF 25.20) OWNER M. Tabor BRED P.Brant
11 Rn 2m 32.02 SF: -/-/-

1574a-CHANTILLY (France) (R-H)
Sunday June 11th (Firm)

1711a PRIX DU CHEMIN DE FER DU NORD (Gp 3) (4-Y.O+) £26,347.00 (£9,581.00: £4,790.00: £2,395.00) **1m** 2-30 (2-28)

1002a3 **Kaldounevees(FR)** *(119) (JEHammond,France)* 4-9-1 CAsmussen .....— 1
1284[2] Fraam *(114) (EALDunlop)* 6-8-11 WRSwinburn .....¾ 2
1394a5 Agathe (USA) *(113) (AFabre,France)* 4-8-11 OPeslier .....nk 3

P-M 2.30F: 1.70F 2.20F (SF 10.20F) OWNER Ecurie Chalhoub BRED D.Cherdo 7 Rn 1m 37.0 (2.40)

1712a PRIX DE DIANE HERMES (Gp 1) (3-Y.O F) £167,665.00 (£67,066.00: £33,533.00: £16,766.00) **1m 2f 110y** 3-50 (3-51)

1116a2 **Carling (FR)** *(115) (MmePBarbe,France)* 3-9-2 TThulliez (a.p: led over 1f out: r.o wl u.p).....— 1
1116a* Matiara (USA) *(115) (MmeCHead,France)* 3-9-2 FHead (6th st: hdwy 2f out: r.o wl fnl f).......nk 2
1009a* Tryphosa (IRE) *(113) (AWohler,Germany)* 3-9-2 ABoschert (hld up: 9th st: r.o wl fnl 2f).........¾ 3
Balanka (IRE) *(113) (AdeRoyerDupre,France)* 3-9-2 GMosse (3rd st: hmpd 2f out: r.o fnl f).s.h 4
1238a* Muncie (IRE) *(113) (AFabre,France)* 3-9-2 OPeslier (5th st: chal over 1f out: one pce) ....hd 5
1116a3 Shaanxi (USA) *(113) (ELellouche,France)* 3-9-2 LDettori (plld early: 7th st: hmpd over 1f out: no ex fnl f) .....s.nk 6
1101[2] Caramba *(112) (RHannon)* 3-9-2 PatEddery (bhd early: hmpd st: r.o wl fnl f: unlucky) ....½ 7
Garden Rose (IRE) *(112) (PBary,France)* 3-9-2 DBoeuf (iron broke after s: hld up & 10th st: r.o wl fnl 3f) .....s.nk 8
1110a2 Loretta Gianni (FR) *(111) (DSmaga,France)* 3-9-2 GGuignard (a bhd: sme late hdwy)..........nk 9
1116a7 Vadlamixa (FR) *(108) (AFabre,France)* 3-9-2 TJarnet (plld early: prom tl led 2f out: hdd & wknd over 1f out) 2 10
Tamise *(105) (AFabre,France)* 3-9-2 SGuillot (led tl 2f out: wknd).....2½ 11
Tibersen *(101) (RCaget,France)* 3-9-2 ODoleuze (a bhd).....2 12

P-M 4.50F: 1.80F 2.30F 5.30F (9.90F) OWNER Ecurie Delbart BRED Ecurie Delbart in France 12 Rn 2m 7.7 (0.70) SF: -/-/-/-/-/-/-/-/-/-/-/-
DS

1121a-COLOGNE (Germany) (R-H)
Sunday June 11th (Soft)

1713a OPPENHEIM-UNION-RENNEN (Gp 2) (3-Y.O) £49,383.00 (£19,753.00: £9,876.00: £4,939.00) **1m 3f** 3-40 (3-46)

1122a2 **Lecroix (GER)** *(104) (MHofer,Germany)* 3-9-2 ManfredHofer (2nd tl led 1f out: r.o wl)..........— 1
Kalimnos *(101) (HBlume,Germany)* 3-9-2 OSchick (led tl hdd by wnr: r.o) 2 2
1122a3 Chadayed (USA) *(100) (HJentzsch,Germany)* 3-9-2 PSchiergen (hdwy & 5th st: r.o fnl 2f) ....½ 3
1121a* Manzoni (GER) *(99) (AWohler,Germany)* 3-9-2 TMundry (hld up: hdwy to chal 2f out: wknd ins fnl f) .....¾ 4
Edler Von Baraga (GER) *(96) (Germany)* 3-9-2 BThomson 2½ 5
1121a3 A Magicman (FR) *(94) (HSteguweit,Germany)* 3-9-2 NGrant 1 6
Ceneketes (GER) *(92) (Germany)* 3-9-2 AHelfenbein 1¼ 7
Assur (GER) *(92) (Germany)* 3-9-2 LHammer-Hansen .....s.h 8
Vilander (GER) *(91) (Germany)* 3-9-2 ABest 1 9
Tote 35DM: 14DM 22DM 20DM (SF 221DM) OWNER Gestut Etzean 11 Rn 2m 19.7

1335-CHEPSTOW (L-H)
Thursday June 15th (Good to firm, Firm patches)
WEATHER: fine WIND: slt across

1714 ORSINO AMATEUR H'CAP (0-70) (3-Y.O+) (Class G) £2,703.00(£758.00: £369.00) **7f 16y** Stalls: High GOING minus 0.64 sec per fur (F) 6-45 (6-53)

1664[11] **Love Legend (52)***(61) (DWPArbuthnot)* 10-10-11 MrsDArbuthnot(16) (lw: a.p: led wl ins fnl f: r.o) .....— 1
1516[2] Asterix **(42)***(50)*(Fav)*(JMBradley)* 7-10-1v MrRJohnson(14) (rdn & hdwy over 2f out: led wl over 1f out tl wl ins fnl f) .....nk 2
*1629** Wentbridge Lad (IRE) **(59)***(64)*(Fav)*(PDEvans)* 5-11-1 (3) 5x MrWMcLaughlin(8) (a.p: led 2f out: sn hdd: r.o one pce) 1½ 3

1534[4] Top Pet (IRE) **(59)***(59) (RAkehurst)* 5-11-4 MrTMcCarthy(20) (lw: a.p: r.o ins fnl f)....2 **4**
1484[12] Kissavos **(43)***(42) (CCElsey)* 9-10-2 MissAElsey(13) (lw: a.p: r.o one pce fnl f)....¾ **5**
1255[10] Jewel Thief **(35)***(34) (GBBalding)* 5-9-3v(5) MissKGreaney(17) (hdwy fnl 2f: r.o)....d.h **5**
1323[12] Bill Moon **(34)***(32) (DTThom)* 9-9-7 MissJFeilden(15) (a.p: no hdwy fnl 2f)....nk **7**
1516[12] Calling (USA) **(44)***(40) (WMBrisbourne)* 4-10-3 MissDianaJones(12) (a.p: no hdwy fnl 2f)....¾ **8**
1534[10] Fighter Squadron **(57)***(50) (REPeacock)* 6-10-11b(5) MrsCPeacock(11) (led 5f)....1½ **9**
1323[7] Pusey Street Boy **(54)***(44) (JRBosley)* 8-10-13 MrsSBosley(6) (t: prom 5f)....1½ **10**
1517[5] Perilous Plight **(69)***(58) (WRMuir)* 4-12-0 MrJDurkan(10) (nvr nrr)....nk **11**
Racing Telegraph **(42)***(31) (JPearce)* 5-10-1 MrsLPearce(1) (prom 5f)....hd **12**
1541[11] Courting Newmarket **(49)***(34) (MrsAKnight)* 7-10-5 (3) MrLJefford(2) (prom over 4f)....1¾ **13**
832[4] Fitzroy Lad **(34)***(14) (RJBaker)* 5-9-2b(5) MissLPope(19) (bhd fnl 2f)....2 **14**
1049[6] Soaking **(61)***(40) (GLMoore)* 5-11-3 (3) MrKGoble(7) (racd alone far side: prom: edgd rt 2f out: sn wknd)....¾ **15**
Magical Belle (IRE) **(45)***(23) (CASmith)* 3-9-5 (3) MrsDSmith(5) (s.s: a bhd)....nk **16**
Pacific Girl (IRE) **(63)***(38) (BPalling)* 3-10-9 (3) MissEJJones(4) (prom over 4f)....1¼ **17**
1483[9] Christian Warrior **(34)***(1) (REPeacock)* 6-9-4 (3) MrVLukaniuk(3) (prom 5f)....3½ **18**
Threshfield (USA) **(53)***(16) (BJCurley)* 9-10-7 (5)ow4 MrCCurley(9) (bhd fnl 2f)....hd **19**
1255[11] Bite the Bullet **(34)** *(AJChamberlain)* 4-9-2 (5) MrYMehmet(18) (b: sn t.o)....2½ **20**

LONG HANDICAP Bill Moon 9-6 Christian Warrior 9-3 Fitzroy Lad 9-4 Bite the Bullet 8-12

5/1 Asterix, Wentbridge Lad (IRE), **13/2** Top Pet (IRE), Pusey Street Boy, **10/1** Perilous Plight, Threshfield (USA) (op 6/1), **12/1** Racing Telegraph (op 8/1), **14/1** Soaking, **16/1** LOVE LEGEND, **20/1** Bill Moon, Kissavos, **25/1** Pacific Girl (IRE), Courting Newmarket, **33/1** Jewel Thief, Fighter Squadron, **40/1** Calling (USA), **50/1** Magical Belle (IRE), Fitzroy Lad, **66/1** Christian Warrior, **100/1** Bite the Bullet, CSF £89.42 CT £434.02 TOTE £18.10: £3.50 £1.70 £1.90 £1.80 (£44.90) Trio £210.10 OWNER Mr George Thompson (COMPTON) BRED Hesmonds Stud Ltd 20 Rn

1m 22.1 (2.10) SF: 40/29/43/38/21/13/11/19/29/23/37/10/13/-/19/-/7/-/-/-

WEIGHT FOR AGE 3yo-10lb

1715 E.B.F MEDIAN AUCTION MAIDEN STKS (2-Y.O) (Class D) £3,670.00 (£1,105.00: £535.00: £250.00)

6f 16y Stalls: High GOING minus 0.64 sec per fur (F) 7-15 (7-19)

Line Dancer *(83) (WJarvis)* 2-9-0 PatEddery(8) (w'like: mde virtually all: drvn out)....— **1**
1134[4] Sualtach (IRE) *(81) (RHollinshead)* 2-9-0 WRyan(6) (a.p: outpcd over 2f out: r.o ins fnl f)....¾ **2**
1485[5] Lionel Edwards (IRE) *(80)*(Fav)*(PFICole)* 2-9-0 TQuinn(2) (lw: prom: rdn & outpcd over 2f out: swtchd rt ins fnl f: r.o)....½ **3**
1540[2] Silver Harrow *(79) (SirMarkPrescott)* 2-9-0 MRoberts(7) (w wnr: ev ch over 1f out: nt qckn) .hd **4**
Warbrook *(78) (IABalding)* 2-9-0 WRSwinburn(4) (cmpt: hdwy fnl f: fin wl)....½ **5**
1318[4] Proud Monk *(72) (GLMoore)* 2-9-0 SWhitworth(1) (no hdwy fnl 2f)....2½ **6**
1511[6] La Tansani (IRE) *(67) (RHannon)* 2-9-0 JReid(5) (prom over 3f)....1¾ **7**
1223[2] Castan (IRE) *(66) (JLDunlop)* 2-9-0 WCarson(3) (prom tl wknd 1f out: eased whn btn)....½ **8**
Fernhill Blaze (IRE) *(MCPipe)* 2-9-0 RHughes(9) (lt-f: s.s: sn t.o)....dist **9**

100/30 Lionel Edwards (IRE), **4/1** Sualtach (IRE), **9/2** LINE DANCER (op 5/2), Silver Harrow (op 7/1), **6/1** Castan (IRE), **12/1** Proud Monk (op 7/1), La Tansani (IRE) (8/1-14/1), **16/1** Warbrook, Fernhill Blaze (IRE), CSF £22.36 TOTE £5.40: £1.80 £1.80 £1.70 (£22.80) Trio £13.70 OWNER Richard Prichard-Jones and Adam Gurney (NEWMARKET) BRED Mrs F. G. Allen 9 Rn

1m 11.4 (2.40) SF: 9/7/6/5/4/-/-/-/-

1716 WELSH BREWERS H'CAP (0-80) (3-Y.O+) (Class D) £4,354.00 (£1,312.00: £636.00: £298.00) **1m 2f 36y** Stalls: High GOING minus 0.64 sec (F) 7-45 (7-46)

1340[2] **Exemption (65)***(78) (HCandy)* 4-9-2 GeorginaFrost(6) (lw: a gng wl: 4th st: led over 1f out: pushed out)....— **1**
*356**** Warm Spell **(73)***(83) (GLMoore)* 5-9-10 SWhitworth(5) (bit bkwd: hld up: 8th st: hdwy on ins over 2f out: r.o wl ins fnl f)....2 **2**
195[8] Noblely (USA) **(65)***(73) (NJHWalker)* 8-9-2 JReid(4) (lw: chsd ldr: 2nd st: led over 2f out tl over 1f out: nt qckn)....1 **3**
1561* Indian Jockey **(68)***(72)*(Fav)*(MCPipe)* 3-8-6 5x MRoberts(2) (lw: plld hrd: 3rd st: rdn over 2f out: ev ch over 1f out: wknd ins fnl f)....3 **4**
1402[5] Mister O'Grady (IRE) **(45)***(48) (RAkehurst)* 4-7-10v JQuinn(1) (lw: led: rdn & hdd over 2f out: wknd over 1f out)....½ **5**
1543[2] Haroldon (IRE) **(66)***(61) (BPalling)* 6-9-3 TSprake(9) (b: hld up: 6th st: pushed along over 3f out: wknd over 2f out)....5 **6**
1346[7] Deep Divide **(72)***(59) (EALDunlop)* 3-8-10 WRSwinburn(3) (hld up: 5th st: hrd rdn 3f out: edgd rt & wknd over 2f out)....5 **7**
975[10] Tony's Mist **(60)***(33) (JMBradley)* 5-8-6 (5) SDrowne(8) (7th st: a bhd)....9 **8**
Duke of Dreams **(53)***(20) (RJBaker)* 5-8-4 RPrice(7) (last st: a in rr)....4 **9**

10/11 Indian Jockey (Evens-11/8), **5/1** EXEMPTION, **6/1** Haroldon (IRE) (4/1-13/2), **10/1** Warm Spell, Noblely (USA), Deep Divide, **11/1** Mister O'Grady (IRE) (7/1-12/1), **40/1** Duke of Dreams, **50/1** Tony's Mist, CSF £50.28 CT £446.11 TOTE £6.40: £1.60 £2.40 £2.10 (£18.40) Trio £58.40 OWNER Mr T. A. F. Frost (WANTAGE) BRED Roan Rocket Partners 9 Rn

2m 7.0 (2.70) SF: 27/32/22/8/-/10/-/-/-

WEIGHT FOR AGE 3yo-13lb

1717 THURSDAY NIGHT MAIDEN STKS (3-Y.O F) (Class D) £3,878.00 (£1,169.00: £567.00: £266.00)

1m 4f 23y Stalls: High GOING minus 0.64 sec per fur (F) 8-15 (8-17)

797³ **Stage Struck (IRE)** *(79)*(Fav)*(MRStoute)* 3-8-11 WRSwinburn(9) (b.nr hind: a.p: led on bit 3f out: edgd rt over 1f out: drvn out) — 1

Danesrath (IRE) *(79) (ACStewart)* 3-8-11 MRoberts(8) (hld up & bhd: 9th st: gd hdwy over 3f out: r.o wl ins fnl f) hd 2

1527⁴ Beauchamp Jade **(74)***(78) (HCandy)* 3-8-11 WNewnes(2) (hld up: 7th st: hdwy over 3f out: ev ch ins fnl f: r.o) ½ 3

942⁴ Rosie Sweetheart (IRE) *(74) (HRACecil)* 3-8-11 WRyan(6) (hld up: 4th st: ev ch over 1f out: one pce) 3½ 4

1339² En Vacances (IRE) **(67)***(66) (AGFoster)* 3-8-11 TSprake(11) (led over 1f: 2nd st: led over 4f out tl over 3f out: wknd ins fnl l) 6 5

1175⁷ Torreglia (IRE) *(62) (JLDunlop)* 3-8-11 TQuinn(5) (nvr nrr) 2½ 6

Bala Monaafis (IRE) *(60) (WRMuir)* 3-8-11 JReid(3) (w'like: scope: 8th st: a bhd) 1½ 7

1337¹⁰ Bold Sally *(51) (MrsSDWilliams)* 3-8-11 JWilliams(10) (lw: a bhd) 7 8

*893*⁸ Kings of Canvey Is **(40)***(39) (JWhite)* 3-8-6 (5) SDrowne(4) (lw: hld up: stdy hdwy 6f out: 6th st: rdn & wknd over 3f out) 9 9

Ack's Again *(13) (BWHills)* 3-8-11 PatEddery(1) (led over 10f out tl over 4f out: wknd qckly 3f out: t.o) 20 10

1270⁵ Nashwanah *(HThomsonJones)* 3-8-11 WCarson(7) (5th st: wknd over 3f out: t.o) 10 11

Evens STAGE STRUCK (IRE), **7/2** Beauchamp Jade, **13/2** Rosie Sweetheart (IRE), **12/1** En Vacances (IRE), Nashwanah, **14/1** Ack's Again, **16/1** Danesrath (IRE), **25/1** Torreglia (IRE), **50/1** Bala Monaafis (IRE), **100/1** Kings of Canvey Is, Bold Sally, CSF £17.65 TOTE £2.40: £1.40 £5.20 £1.60 (£43.10) Trio £27.40 OWNER Lord Weinstock & The Hon Simon Weinstock (NEWMARKET) BRED Ballymacoll Stud Farm Ltd 11 Rn 2m 35.2 (3.90) SF: 20/20/19/15/7/3/1/-/-/-/-

1718 EVENING (S) H'CAP (0-60) (3-Y.O) (Class G) £2,703.00 (£758.00: £369.00)

1m 14y Stalls: High GOING minus 0.64 sec per fur (F) 8-45 (8-49)

1371² **Just Fizzy (47)***(55)*(Fav)*(MCPipe)* 3-8-8 MRoberts(10) (a.p: led over 3f out: rdn clr over 1f out: r.o wl) — 1

1512⁹ Sobeloved **(50)***(51) (MRChannon)* 3-8-11 RHughes(7) (hld up: hdwy over 2f out: r.o ins fnl f) 3½ 2

1541⁸ Irie Mon (IRE) **(60)***(60) (JWHills)* 3-9-7 MHills(1) (a.p: one pce fnl 2f) ½ 3

1201¹² Master M-E-N (IRE) **(52)***(52) (NMBabbage)* 3-8-13v JQuinn(12) (a.p: one pce fnl 2f) s.h 4

1445¹¹ Miltak **(39)***(32) (PJMakin)* 3-7-11 (3)ow1 SSanders(14) (hdwy whn nt clr run & swtchd lft over 1f out: r.o) 3 5

1498⁹ Magical Bid (IRE) **(48)***(39) (JMBradley)* 3-8-4v(5) SDrowne(2) (sn prom: no hdwy fnl 2f) 1½ 6

1404⁵ Owdbetts (IRE) **(55)***(45) (GLMoore)* 3-8-9 (7) DaneO'Neill(8) (lw: hld up: hdwy 3f out: hung lft 2f out: wknd over 1f out) ¾ 7

1499⁷ Jersey Belle **(44)***(30) (PJMakin)* 3-8-5 NCarlisle(4) (nvr trbld ldrs) 2 8

*366*⁹ Gigfy **(47)***(32) (BJLlewellyn)* 3-8-8 RPrice(11) (b: no hdwy fnl 2f) ½ 9

Astrojoy (IRE) **(50)***(34) (LordHuntingdon)* 3-8-11 JReid(13) (prom over 5f) hd 10

1521⁸ Ivy Lilian (IRE) **(44)***(27) (WMBrisbourne)* 3-8-5 ow1 JWilliams(5) (led over 4f: wknd 2f out) hd 11

*1330*⁹ Chadleigh Walk (IRE) **(44)***(26) (RHollinshead)* 3-8-5 WRyan(6) (lw: a bhd) 1 12

651⁷ Pink Petal **(35)***(12) (CJHill)* 3-7-10 NAdams(9) (hld up & plld hrd: hdwy 3f out: wknd 2f out) 2½ 13

1401⁶ Ace Chapel (IRE) **(39)***(16) (CCElsey)* 3-8-0 CRutter(16) (prom 5f) hd 14

1548⁴ Today Tonite **(45)***(12) (JPearce)* 3-8-6 GBardwell(3) (lw: prom: rdn 3f out: wknd 2f out) 5 15

855¹⁵ Silent Sky **(40)** *(CJHill)* 3-7-8 (7) MHenry(15) (a bhd) 4 16

2/1 JUST FIZZY, **7/1** Today Tonite, **8/1** Irie Mon (IRE), **10/1** Owdbetts (IRE), **11/1** Astrojoy (IRE) (8/1-12/1), **12/1** Sobeloved, **16/1** Pink Petal, Jersey Belle, Magical Bid (IRE), **20/1** Ace Chapel (IRE), Silent Sky, **25/1** Gigfy, **33/1** Master M-E-N (IRE), Miltak, Chadleigh Walk (IRE), **50/1** Ivy Lilian (IRE), CSF £25.26 CT £154.32 TOTE £2.60: £1.20 £2.10 £2.10 £5.10 (£13.50) Trio £46.70 OWNER 0336 405200 Racing (WELLINGTON) BRED John Rose 16 Rn

1m 33.3 (0.80) SF: 29/25/34/26/6/13/19/4/6/8/1/-/-/-/-/-

No bid

1719 GOOD NIGHT CLAIMING STKS (3-Y.O) (Class F) £2,967.50 (£830.00: £402.50)
7f 16y Stalls: High GOING minus 0.64 sec per fur (F) 9-15 (9-18)

1541⁷ **Russian Heroine (61)***(72) (MJohnston)* 3-8-4 WRyan(3) (hld up: led over 2f out: r.o wl).......— **1**
1546⁴ Colston-C **(54)***(70) (CJHill)* 3-8-9 JReid(6) (led over 4f: r.o one pce)..3 **2**
1146⁵ Equilibrium **(62)***(56) (JWHills)* 3-8-6 MHills(5) (lw: a.p: one pce fnl 2f)..5 **3**
1263⁸ Cork Street Girl (IRE) **(58)***(45) (BJMeehan)* 3-8-2 MFenton(12) (hdwy 3f out: one pce fnl 2f)..3 **4**
1445¹⁰ Damocles **(50)***(43) (IABalding)* 3-8-4 ow1 TQuinn(10) (a.p: no hdwy fnl 2f)..1½ **5**
1515⁶ Chinese Viking *(50) (GLMoore)* 3-8-11 SWhitworth(9) (rdn 3f out: no hdwy fnl 2f)................nk **6**
1371³ Dominion's Dream **(55)***(40)*(Fav)*(MCPipe)* 3-8-10 MRoberts(4) (prom 5f: eased whn btn 1f out)..4 **7**
1371⁸ Steepholme *(29) (BRMillman)* 3-8-6 WNewnes(8) (s.s: hung lft over 3f out: a bhd)................3 **8**
1405⁵ Misty Melody **(62)***(19) (RAkehurst)* 3-8-0 JQuinn(7) (bhd fnl 3f)..2 **9**
1202¹³ Surgiva **(43)***(14) (JRArnold)* 3-8-2b CRutter(2) (a bhd)..3 **10**
1516¹³ Dazzle Me **(34)** *(RJBaker)* 3-7-5 (7) JBramhill(1) (s.s: a bhd)..7 **11**

3/1 Dominion's Dream, **7/2** RUSSIAN HEROINE, **9/2** Equilibrium, **7/1** Colston-C, **8/1** Misty Melody, **9/1** Cork Street Girl (IRE) (op 6/1), **14/1** Damocles (10/1-16/1), **20/1** Chinese Viking, **25/1** Steepholme, **50/1** Surgiva, **66/1** Dazzle Me, CSF £26.09 TOTE £3.00: £1.50 £2.20 £1.80 (£15.70) Trio £51.90 OWNER The Knavesmire Partnership (MIDDLEHAM) BRED D. R. Botterill 11 Rn
1m 21.3 (1.30) SF: 17/15/1/-/-/-/-/-/-/-/-

T/Plpt: £42.40 (406.43 Tckts). T/Qdpt: £6.40 (14.2 Tckts). KH

1684-HAMILTON (R-H)
Thursday June 15th (Firm)
WEATHER: sunny WIND: almost nil

1720 HIGH PARK MEDIAN AUCTION MAIDEN STKS (3 & & 5-Y.O) (Class F) £2,605.00 (£730.00: £355.00)
1m 3f 16y Stalls: High GOING minus 0.50 sec per fur (F) 2-15 (2-15)

1452⁴ **Royal Expression (57)***(66)*(Fav)*(MrsMReveley)* 3-8-11 KDarley(1) (lw: mde all: comf)........— **1**
1583⁶ Never so True **(37)***(54) (MartynWane)* 4-9-7v JFortune(3) (a chsng wnr: rdn & no imp fnl 2½f)..5 **2**
1059⁶ Our Rainbow **(43)***(52) (MrsSMAustin)* 3-8-6 JMarshall(2) (chsd ldrs: hung lft 2f out: sn btn)..1½ **3**
593⁴ Never So Fit *(47) (RBastiman)* 4-9-7 (5) HBastiman(5) (pushed along over 5f out: a last).........7 **4**

4/11 ROYAL EXPRESSION, **3/1** Never So Fit, **12/1** Never so True (op 7/1), Our Rainbow, CSF £4.90 TOTE £1.10 (£2.60) OWNER Mr P. D. Savill (SALTBURN) BRED K. Panos 4 Rn
2m 25.1 (6.10) SF: 14/17/-/10
WEIGHT FOR AGE 3yo-15lb

1721 STONEFIELD (S) H'CAP (0-60) (3-Y.O+) (Class G) £2,689.00 (£754.00: £367.00)
5f 4y Stalls: Low GOING minus 0.50 sec per fur (F) 2-45 (2-47)

1559³ **Halbert (41)***(55) (MRChannon)* 6-8-11v KDarley(16) (racd far side: mde all: clr 2f out: r.o wl)..— **1**
1689⁵ Diet **(45)***(53) (MissLAPerratt)* 9-9-1v GDuffield(15) (chsd wnr far side: kpt on one pce fnl f)..1¾ **2**
1559* Henry the Hawk **(39)***(42)*(Fav)*(MDods)* 4-8-9 JWeaver(5) (chsd ldrs stands' side: rdn ½-wy: styd on: no imp)..1¾ **3**
1152¹¹ The Fed **(55)***(57) (RMWhitaker)* 5-9-11v ACulhane(2) (chsd ldrs stands' side: kpt on fnl f)......nk **4**
1580³ Daily Starshine (IRE) **(57)***(59) (JBerry)* 3-9-5b JCarroll(7) (led stands' side: hung bdly rt fnl 2f: wknd ins fnl f)..s.h **5**
1043³ Brisas **(40)***(34) (CWFairhurst)* 8-8-10 JFanning(3) (in tch: kpt on fnl 2f: no imp)....................2½ **6**
*1566*¹³ Kabcast **(55)***(47) (DWChapman)* 10-9-11b DeanMcKeown(10) (spd centre tl rdn & btn wl over 1f out)..½ **7**
1023⁴ Miss Siham (IRE) **(41)***(31) (DNicholls)* 6-8-11 AlexGreaves(9) (lw: chsd ldrs: rdn ½-wy: no imp)..¾ **8**
1461⁹ Sunday Mail Too (IRE) **(43)***(33) (MissLAPerratt)* 3-8-5b MBirch(1) (lw: dwlt: n.d)....................s.h **9**
*1030*⁹ Lucky Peg **(43)***(31) (FJO'Mahony)* 3-8-5 ow1 KFallon(11) (nvr nr ldrs)..s.h **10**
1434⁸ Another Nightmare (IRE) **(50)***(38) (RMMcKellar)* 3-8-5 (7)ow1 NKinnon(4) (effrt & hung bdly rt ½-wy: nvr rchd ldrs)..hd **11**
1248⁹ First Option **(58)***(39) (RBastiman)* 5-9-9 (5) HBastiman(14) (a bhd)..2½ **12**

1419[4] Jessica's Secret (IRE) **(37)***(17) (ABailey)* 3-7-13b LCharnock(6) (swtg: s.i.s: n.d).....................½ **13**
1453[8] Gilpa Trinkets **(31)***(4) (DWChapman)* 3-7-7b NKennedy(12) (spd to ½-wy: sn bhd)...................2 **14**
1493[7] Murray's Mazda (IRE) **(46)***(18) (JLEyre)* 6-9-2v JFortune(8) (a bhd) ....nk **15**
1493[8] Valley of Time (FR) **(35)** *(DANolan)* 7-8-0 (5)ow10 VHalliday(17) (b: sn bhd) 1 **16**
1465[9] Leap Year Baby (IRE) **(33)** *(MDHammond)* 3-7-9vow2 DaleGibson(13) (a outpcd & bhd)..........3 **17**

LONG HANDICAP Gilpa Trinkets 7-6 Leap Year Baby (IRE) 7-1

3/1 Henry the Hawk, **6/1** Miss Siham (IRE), **8/1** Diet, Daily Starshine (IRE), **10/1** The Fed, **11/1** Brisas (8/1-12/1), Murray's Mazda (IRE), **16/1** HALBERT, **20/1** Sunday Mail Too (IRE), Jessica's Secret (IRE), **25/1** Another Nightmare (IRE), Lucky Peg, Leap Year Baby (IRE), Gilpa Trinkets, **33/1** Kabcast, First Option, **100/1** Valley of Time (FR), CSF £127.74 CT £452.52 TOTE £10.50: £1.40 £2.20 £2.00 £2.60 (£18.10) Trio £32.50 OWNER The Sun Punters Club (UPPER LAMBOURN) BRED Mr and Mrs J. K. S. Cresswell 17 Rn

59.6 secs (1.30) SF: 31/29/18/33/27/10/23/7/1/-/6/15/-/-/-/-/-

WEIGHT FOR AGE 3yo-8lb

Bt in 4,000gns

1722

E.B.F ALMADA MAIDEN STKS (2-Y.O) (Class D) £4,065.00 (£1,230.00: £600.00: £285.00)
5f 4y Stalls: Low GOING minus 0.50 sec per fur (F) 3-15 (3-15)

1579[4] **Just Ice** *(74) (SirMarkPrescott)* 2-8-9 GDuffield(2) (cl up: led over 1f out: r.o wl)...................— **1**
1579[3] Elfin Queen (IRE) *(69)*(Fav)*(MJohnston)* 2-8-9 JWeaver(3) (lw: led tl hdd over 1f out: kpt on wl)..1½ **2**
1190[7] River Tern *(55) (JBerry)* 2-9-0 JCarroll(5) (cl up tl rdn & btn wl over 1f out)..............................6 **3**
Boundary Bird (IRE) *(7) (MJohnston)* 2-9-0 PRobinson(4) (w'like: leggy: scope: sn outpcd & t.o)..15 **4**
Hamilton Gold *(MartynWane)* 2-8-9 JFortune(1) (unf: scope: stmbld s: sn t.o) 10 **5**

7/4 Elfin Queen (IRE), **2/1** JUST ICE, River Tern, **14/1** Boundary Bird (IRE) (op 8/1), **66/1** Hamilton Gold, CSF £5.68 TOTE £2.50: £1.40 £1.10 (£2.00) OWNER Canary Thoroughbreds (NEWMARKET) BRED Prof Klaus E. Rohde 5 Rn 60.8 secs (2.50) SF: 10/5/-/-/-

1723

P & O CONTAINERS SCOTLAND H'CAP (0-75) (3-Y.O) (Class D) £5,015.50 (£1,519.00: £742.00: £353.50)
6f 5y Stalls: Low GOING minus 0.50 sec per fur (F) 3-45 (3-46)

1564[3] **Ultra Beet (66)***(79) (PCHaslam)* 3-9-3v JWeaver(3) (lw: w ldr: led ½-wy: r.o wl) ....— **1**
1423[4] Teejay'n'aitch (IRE) **(52)***(56) (JSGoldie)* 3-8-3 PRobinson(7) (chsd ldrs: hdwy 2f out: nt qckn fnl f)..3½ **2**
1414[2] Special-K **(61)***(62)*(Fav)*(EWeymes)* 3-8-12 KDarley(2) (chsd ldrs: kpt on fnl f: nvr able chal)..1 **3**
1034[13] Mac's Taxi **(70)***(64) (PCHaslam)* 3-9-7 JFortune(8) (cl up: edgd lft & nt qckn appr fnl f) 2½ **4**
1461[8] Mister Westsound **(43)***(35) (MissLAPerratt)* 3-7-8 DaleGibson(1) (lw: effrt ½-wy: hung rt & no imp)..¾ **5**
1564[2] One for Jeannie **(64)***(56) (ABailey)* 3-9-1v MWigham(4) (lw: in tch: effrt 2f out: hmpd 1f out: no imp)..s.h **6**
1624[3] Rymer's Rascal **(67)***(59) (EJAlston)* 3-9-4 KFallon(9) (hld up: effrt 2f out: sn rdn & btn)..........nk **7**
861[4] Six for Luck **(62)***(43) (JBerry)* 3-8-6 (7) PFessey(10) (b.hind: cl up 4f: sn lost pl) 4 **8**
1465[10] Tannerrun (IRE) **(56)***(2) (JBerry)* 3-8-7e JCarroll(5) (lw: led to ½-wy: wknd qckly) 13 **9**

7/2 Special-K, **4/1** ULTRA BEET, One for Jeannie, **5/1** Rymer's Rascal, **13/2** Mac's Taxi, **8/1** Teejay'n'aitch (IRE), **14/1** Mister Westsound, **16/1** Six for Luck, Tannerrun (IRE), CSF £34.07 CT £113.35 TOTE £6.00: £2.30 £3.00 £1.70 (£64.20) Trio £50.30 OWNER Pet Express Ltd T/A Nutrimix (MIDDLEHAM) BRED Rockhouse Farms Ltd 9 Rn 1m 11.5 (1.50) SF: 37/14/20/22/-/14/17/1/-

1724

COURVOISIER CLASSIC H'CAP (0-60) (3-Y.O+) (Class F) £4,127.15 (£1,251.20: £612.10: £292.55)
1m 65y Stalls: High GOING minus 0.50 sec per fur (F) 4-15 (4-16)

1205[5] **Habeta (USA) (34)***(44) (JWWatts)* 9-8-2 ow1 GDuffield(11) (lw: trckd ldrs: led ins fnl f: drvn out) ....— **1**
1493[3] Sakharov **(54)***(64) (MJohnston)* 6-9-8 PRobinson(8) (hld up & bhd: hdwy on ins 3f out: chal ins fnl f: r.o towards fin)..nk **2**
992[8] Runrig (IRE) **(40)***(47) (MissLAPerratt)* 5-8-8 MBirch(10) (hld up & bhd: hdwy on ins 3f out: styd on wl) 1¾ **3**
Sir Arthur Hobbs **(60)***(67) (JLEyre)* 8-10-0 RLappin(4) (led tl hdd & no ex ins fnl f) ....nk **4**
1687* Talented Ting (IRE) **(66)***(67)*(Fav)*(PCHaslam)* 6-10-6 6x JWeaver(6) (lw: hld up: swtchd & qcknd to chal 2f out: wknd ins fnl f)..3 **5**
1421[7] Blow Dry (IRE) **(54)***(50) (MartynWane)* 5-9-8 JFortune(3) (lw: cl up tl wknd fnl 2f) 2½ **6**

847[5] Prudent Pet **(60)***(51) (CWFairhurst)* 3-9-3 JFanning(7) (bhd: effrt 3f out: no imp) 2½ **7**
1438[5] Miss Pigalle **(34)***(22) (MissLAPerratt)* 4-8-2b DaleGibson(5) (in tch: effrt 3f out: n.d) 1½ **8**
Lehmans Lady **(45)***(33) (MrsMReveley)* 3-8-2 KDarley(1) (prom tl wknd wl over 1f out) ....s.h **9**
1664[8] Morocco (IRE) **(55)***(38) (MRChannon)* 6-9-9 JCarroll(9) (mid div: drvn along 3f out: n.d) 2½ **10**
1433[8] Faynaz **(28)** *(RMMcKellar)* 9-7-3 (7) DLockhart(2) (b: cl up tl wknd 3f out)................................7 **11**

5/4 Talented Ting (IRE), **9/2** Sakharov, **11/2** HABETA (USA), **10/1** Lehmans Lady, **12/1** Sir Arthur Hobbs, **14/1** Blow Dry (IRE), Morocco (IRE), **16/1** Miss Pigalle, **20/1** Prudent Pet, **33/1** Runrig (IRE), Faynaz, CSF £30.10 CT £689.85 TOTE £7.00: £2.40 £1.70 £2.70 (£10.20) Trio £239.90 OWNER Mr R. D. Bickenson (RICHMOND) BRED Spendthrift Farm, Inc 11 Rn

1m 45.6 (2.30) SF: 25/45/28/48/48/31/21/3/3/19/-

WEIGHT FOR AGE 3yo-11lb

1725 HOWLET ROW H'CAP (0-70) (3-Y.O) (Class E) £3,863.90 (£1,170.20: £571.60: £272.30) **1m 3f 16y** Stalls: High GOING minus 0.50 sec per fur (F) 4-45 (4-45)

1204* **Daily Starlight (USA) (66)***(78) (MissGayKelleway)* 3-9-7 MWigham(3) (lw: trckd ldrs: led 2f out: rdn & r.o wl) ....— **1**
1430[2] Jackmanii **(47)***(55) (WTKemp)* 3-8-2b KDarley(7) (led 7f out: qcknd 5f out: hdd 2f out: kpt on wl) 2½ **2**
1417[5] Punch **(60)***(58) (NTinkler)* 3-9-1 MBirch(8) (hld up: hmpd 7f out: hdwy 3f out: btn appr fnl f) 7 **3**
1347[4] On a Pedestal (IRE) **(55)***(50)*(Fav)*(MrsJRRamsden)* 3-8-10 KFallon(6) (lw: hdwy 4f out: swtchd 2f out: nvr nr ldrs) 2½ **4**
1379[6] Nivasha **(41)***(32) (MBell)* 3-7-10 JFanning(1) (trckd ldrs tl wknd fnl 2f) 2½ **5**
Can She Can Can **(49)***(40) (MJohnston)* 3-8-4 PRobinson(4) (led 4f: cl up tl wknd over 2f out) ....nk **6**
The Cottonwool Kid **(50)***(29) (THCaldwell)* 3-8-5 JCarroll(5) (prom tl outpcd fnl 5f)..................8 **7**
1350[17] Tobago Boy **(41)***(16) (MGMeagher)* 3-7-3v(7)ow3 MartinDwyer(2) (a bhd)....................½ **8**

LONG HANDICAP Tobago Boy 7-2

5/2 On a Pedestal (IRE), **100/30** DAILY STARLIGHT (USA), **11/2** Jackmanii, Nivasha (4/1-6/1), **6/1** Punch, Can She Can Can, **16/1** The Cottonwool Kid, **33/1** Tobago Boy, CSF £21.20 CT £97.24 TOTE £4.50: £1.50 £1.20 £3.60 (£7.80) OWNER Mr A. Al-Radi (WHITCOMBE) BRED Robert S. West Jnr 8 Rn

2m 24.9 (5.90) SF: 24/1/4/-/-/-/-/-

T/Plpt: £12.10 (1,056.87 Tckts). T/Qdpt: £59.20 (1.5 Tckts). AA

1406-NEWBURY (L-H)
Thursday June 15th (Good to firm)
WEATHER: warm WIND: almost nil

1726 E.B.F KENNETT MAIDEN STKS (2-Y.O) (Class D) £3,938.00 (£1,184.00: £572.00: £266.00) **6f 8y** Stalls: Centre GOING minus 0.45 sec per fur (F) 2-00 (2-01)

1485[7] **Resounder (USA)** *(88+)*(Fav)*(JHMGosden)* 2-9-0 LDettori(12) (lw: hld up: led over 1f out: qcknd: easily)....................— **1**
Tamnia *(78) (JLDunlop)* 2-8-9 TQuinn(1) (str: bkwd: hld up: rdn over 4f out: ev ch over 1f out: unable qckn)....................1¾ **2**
Zuhair *(81) (MajorWRHern)* 2-9-0 WCarson(3) (str: scope: bit bkwd: a.p: ev ch over 1f out: rn green)....................¾ **3**
Lomberto *(75) (RHannon)* 2-9-0 JReid(13) (w'like: scope: bit bkwd: s.s: rdn over 3f out: hdwy fnl f: r.o: bttr for r) 2½ **4**
Winter Quarters (USA) *(74) (IABalding)* 2-9-0 RCochrane(5) (w'like: scope: bit bkwd: s.s: hdwy 5f out: rdn over 2f out: sn wknd)....................nk **5**
Surtees *(73)*(Fav)*(RCharlton)* 2-9-0 PatEddery(7) (str: scope: a.p: led over 3f out tl over 1f out: wknd fnl f) ....nk **6**
Sketchbook *(72) (GLewis)* 2-9-0 PaulEddery(8) (leggy: led over 2f: wknd over 1f out)............½ **7**
Stellar Line (USA) *(72) (BWHills)* 2-9-0 MHills(2) (leggy: scope: lw: rdn & hdwy 2f out: wknd ins fnl f)....................s.h **8**
1246[5] No Cliches *(61) (GLewis)* 2-9-0 SWhitworth(9) (lw: a bhd)....................4 **9**
Asking For Kings (IRE) *(61) (NACallaghan)* 2-9-0 DHarrison(4) (b.hind: unf: bhd fnl 2f) ....hd **10**
Prince of My Heart *(61) (BWHills)* 2-8-9 (5) JDSmith(11) (leggy: scope: a bhd) ....hd **11**
Just One Bid (IRE) *(57) (BJMeehan)* 2-9-0 BDoyle(10) (leggy: scope: bhd fnl 2f) 1¼ **12**
Vendetta *(39) (IABalding)* 2-8-9 WRyan(6) (unf: bit bkwd: s.s: a bhd) 5 **13**

3/1 RESOUNDER (USA), Surtees, **11/2** Zuhair (4/1-8/1), **6/1** Stellar Line (USA) (3/1-7/1), **7/1** Tamnia (op 4/1), **9/1** Winter Quarters (USA) (5/1-10/1), **10/1** Sketchbook (3/1-12/1), **12/1** Lomberto (op 8/1), **14/1** Vendetta (op 8/1), **25/1** No Cliches, **33/1** Prince of My Heart, Asking For Kings (IRE), **50/1** Just One Bid (IRE), CSF £26.57 TOTE £4.60: £1.70 £4.00 £1.80 (£48.60) Trio £57.00 OWNER Mr Herbert Allen (NEWMARKET) BRED Gainesway Thoroughbreds Ltd 13 Rn

1m 12.95 (1.15) SF: 45/35/38/32/31/30/29/29/18/18/18/14/-

1727 KINGSCLERE CONDITIONS STKS (2-Y.O) (Class C) £5,220.00 (£1,820.00: £885.00: £375.00)
6f 8y Stalls: Centre GOING minus 0.45 sec per fur (F) 2-30 (2-30)

More Royal (USA) *(83+) (IABalding)* 2-8-7 LDettori(4) (leggy: scope: lw: hld up: rdn over 2f out: led wl ins fnl f: r.o wl) — 1
1298* Mushahid (USA) *(88)*(Fav)*(JLDunlop)* 2-8-13 WCarson(1) (led: rdn 2f out: hdd wl ins fnl f: r.o) nk 2
1418* Double Oscar (IRE) *(83) (MJohnston)* 2-8-13 DHolland(2) (lw: w ldr: rdn over 2f out: ev ch & edgd rt ins fnl f: unable qckn) 2 3
1137⁶ Kandavu *(77) (MMcCormack)* 2-8-8 JReid(3) (hld up: rdn over 2f out: 4th & btn whn n.m.r ins fnl f) ½ 4

6/5 Mushahid (USA), **13/8** Double Oscar (IRE), **5/1** MORE ROYAL (USA) (9/4-11/2), **14/1** Kandavu (20/1-33/1), CSF £10.56 TOTE £4.50 (£2.90) OWNER Mr George Strawbridge (KINGSCLERE) BRED Gatesby W. Clay 4 Rn 1m 12.78 (0.98) SF: 40/45/40/34

1728 GEORGE SMITH MEMORIAL RATED STAKES H'CAP (0-100) (3-Y.O+) (Class B) £8,542.00 (£3,178.00: £1,539.00: £645.00: £272.50: £123.50)
7f (straight) Stalls: Centre GOING minus 0.45 sec per fur (F) 3-00 (3-01)

1617* **Celestial Key (USA) (96)***(105)*(Fav)*(MJohnston)* 5-9-3 3x DHolland(9) (rdn over 2f out: hdwy over 1f out: led ins fnl f: r.o wl) — 1
1108⁷ Roving Minstrel **(86)***(92) (BAMcMahon)* 4-8-7 LDettori(5) (lw: a.p: led 1f out tl ins fnl f: unable qckn) 1¼ 2
1397a* Classic Sky (IRE) **(99)***(102)*(Fav)*(BHanbury)* 4-9-6 WRyan(3) (rdn & hdwy 2f out: r.o one pce) 1¼ 3
Croft Valley **(94)***(96) (RAkehurst)* 8-9-1 TQuinn(8) (led 6f: one pce) ¾ 4
1143⁹ Belfry Green (IRE) **(95)***(95) (CAHorgan)* 5-9-2 MPerrett(10) (hdwy over 1f out: r.o) ½ 5
1588* Neither Nor **(86)***(84) (DAWilson)* 6-8-7 3x GCarter(1) (hld up: rdn over 2f out: wknd over 1f out) 1¼ 6
1143¹¹ New Capricorn (USA) **(89)***(87) (MAJarvis)* 5-8-10 MHills(4) (hld up: rdn over 2f out: wknd fnl f) s.h 7
912³ Sotoboy (IRE) **(100)***(92) (PWHarris)* 3-8-11 RCochrane(12) (prom over 4f) 2½ 8
Bide Our Time (USA) **(95)***(85) (JARToller)* 3-8-6 WNewnes(11) (bit bkwd: a bhd) ¾ 9
1306⁷ Shandine (USA) **(96)***(82) (RCharlton)* 3-8-7 PatEddery(7) (a bhd) 2 10
1482⁴ Reprehend **(100)***(83) (RHannon)* 4-9-7 JReid(6) (prom over 3f) 1¼ 11
1365⁸ Waikiki Beach (USA) **(90)***(57) (GLMoore)* 4-8-11 CandyMorris(2) (lw: bhd fnl 2f) 7 12

9/2 CELESTIAL KEY (USA), Classic Sky (IRE), **11/2** Neither Nor, **6/1** Shandine (USA), **10/1** Roving Minstrel, **11/1** Croft Valley (6/1-12/1), **12/1** Belfry Green (IRE), Sotoboy (IRE), **16/1** New Capricorn (USA), Reprehend, **25/1** Bide Our Time (USA), **33/1** Waikiki Beach (USA), CSF £43.88 CT £194.14 TOTE £5.90: £2.30 £3.00 £2.00 (£32.90) Trio £68.50 OWNER Mr M.J.Brodrick (MIDDLEHAM) BRED Pillar Stud Inc 12 Rn 1m 23.84 (0.07 under best) (-0.66) SF: 72/59/69/63/62/51/54/49/42/39/50/24
WEIGHT FOR AGE 3yo-10lb

1729 BALLYMACOLL STUD STKS (Listed) (3-Y.O F) (Class A) £12,445.00 (£3,760.00: £1,830.00: £865.00)
1m 2f 6y Stalls: Low GOING minus 0.45 sec per fur (F) 3-30 (3-31)

1147* **Larrocha (IRE)** *(106++) (LMCumani)* 3-8-9 WRSwinburn(3) (lw: mde all: qcknd over 2f out: sn clr: unchal) — 1
620² Poppy Carew (IRE) **(107)***(98)*(Fav)*(PWHarris)* 3-8-9 RCochrane(2) (lw: hdwy over 2f out: chsd wnr wl over 1f out: no imp) 5 2
1139* Spout **(109)***(101) (RCharlton)* 3-8-12 PatEddery(5) (lw: 5th st: swtchd rt over 2f out: r.o one pce) s.h 3
932⁵ Alessia **(97)***(88) (BWHills)* 3-8-9 MHills(1) (hdwy over 1f out: one pce) 6 4
1242⁸ Snowtown (IRE) **(102)***(80) (PWChapple-Hyam)* 3-8-9 JReid(8) (2nd st: wknd over 1f out) 5 5
1067⁴ Pitcroy **(93)***(77) (JRFanshawe)* 3-8-9 DHarrison(6) (hdwy over 4f out: 4th st: wknd wl over 1f out) 2 6
Miasma (USA) **(101)***(71) (JARToller)* 3-8-9 LDettori(4) (3rd st: wknd over 2f out) 4 7
1242³ Yarn (IRE) **(100)***(50) (MRChannon)* 3-8-9 RHughes(7) (lw: 6th st: wknd over 2f out) 13 8

3/1 Poppy Carew (IRE), **7/2** LARROCHA (IRE), **4/1** Spout (3/1-9/2), Yarn (IRE), **7/1** Pitcroy, **16/1** Miasma (USA), **20/1** Alessia, Snowtown (IRE), CSF £13.70 TOTE £3.20: £1.50 £1.10 £1.70 (£4.90) OWNER Sheikh Mohammed (NEWMARKET) BRED K. and Mrs Prendergast 8 Rn
2m 3.62 (0.62) SF: 52/44/47/34/26/23/17/-

1730 SUMMER H'CAP (0-80) (3-Y.O) (Class D) £3,910.25 (£1,172.00: £563.50: £259.25) **1m 4f 5y** Stalls: Low GOING minus 0.45 sec per fur (F) 4-00 (4-01)

995[2] **Monarch (76)***(87) (PFICole)* 3-9-7 TQuinn(2) (lw: 2nd st: shkn up & led ins fnl f: comf).........— 1
1093[11] Santella Boy (USA) **(53)***(61) (GHarwood)* 3-7-12 JQuinn(3) (led tl ins fnl f: unable qckn).........2½ 2
1514[3] Barford Sovereign **(70)***(75) (JRFanshawe)* 3-9-1 DHarrison(4) (4th st: rdn over 3f out: one pce fnl f).........1¾ 3
1529* Bowcliffe Court (IRE) **(60)***(62)*(Fav)*(BWHills)* 3-8-5 5x DHolland(1) (3rd st: hung lft over 1f out: one pce).........2½ 4
687[3] Salaman (FR) **(70)***(70) (JLDunlop)* 3-9-1 WCarson(5) (6th st: a bhd).........1½ 5
1382[3] Flight Master **(64)***(31) (PJMakin)* 3-8-9 LDettori(6) (lw: 5th st: wknd over 3f out).........25 6

9/4 Bowcliffe Court (IRE) (op 6/4), **5/2** MONARCH, **11/4** Flight Master, **7/1** Barford Sovereign, **9/1** Salaman (FR), **33/1** Santella Boy (USA), CSF £43.33 TOTE £3.20: £1.60 £4.60 (£22.20) OWNER Prince Fahd Salman (WHATCOMBE) BRED Newgate Stud Co 6 Rn

2m 35.05 (5.75) SF: 31/5/19/6/14/-

OFFICIAL EXPLANATION **Flight Master: the horse refused to settle in the early stages and choked two furlongs out.**

1731 BUCKLEBURY MEDIAN AUCTION MAIDEN APPRENTICE STKS (3-Y.O) (Class E) £3,100.00 (£940.00: £460.00: £220.00) **7f (straight)** Stalls: Centre GOING minus 0.45 sec per fur (F) 4-30 (4-32)

1425[2] **Roderick Hudson (83)***(83+)*(Fav)*(JARToller)* 3-9-0 SSanders(2) (lw: mde all: qcknd over 1f out: unchal).........— 1
1258[2] Godmersham Park **(79)***(69) (MJHeaton-Ellis)* 3-8-11 (3) SDrowne(3) (chsd wnr: rdn over 2f out: unable qckn).........6 2
1476[10] Jovie King (IRE) *(60) (PMitchell)* 3-8-9 (5) MHenry(1) (lw: hld up: rdn over 3f out: one pce).........4 3
1469[2] Polly Garter **(57)***(53) (RHannon)* 3-8-4 (5) DaneO'Neill(7) (no hdwy fnl 3f).........¾ 4
In the Zim *(53) (RHannon)* 3-8-2 (7) EGreehy(8) (w'like: bit bkwd: s.s: a bhd).........nk 5
Thehillsarealive (IRE) *(26) (DRCElsworth)* 3-8-11 (3) AProcter(6) (lengthy: bit bkwd: sme hdwy over 2f out: sn wknd).........14 6
1196[12] Vaporize *(1) (DMHyde)* 3-8-9 (5) RHavlin(5) (bhd fnl 2f).........11 7
Bold Charlie *(SMellor)* 3-8-9 (5) ADaly(4) (w'like: bit bkwd: s.s: a wl bhd).........nk 8

4/5 RODERICK HUDSON (Evens-11/10), **5/2** Godmersham Park, **15/2** Polly Garter (5/1-8/1), **10/1** Thehillsarealive (IRE) (6/1-12/1), **20/1** In the Zim, **25/1** Bold Charlie, **40/1** Jovie King (IRE), **66/1** Vaporize, CSF £3.30 TOTE £1.90: £1.10 £1.30 £5.20 (£1.90) OWNER Duke of Devonshire (WHITSBURY) BRED Meon Valley Stud 8 Rn 1m 25.02 (0.52) SF: 55/41/32/25/25/-/-/-

1732 LEVY BOARD H'CAP (0-80) (3-Y.O+) (Class D) £3,894.00 (£1,167.00: £561.00: £258.00) **1m (straight)** Stalls: Centre GOING minus 0.45 sec (F) 5-00 (5-00)

1202[17] **Legendary Leap (65)***(75) (LordHuntingdon)* 5-8-13 TQuinn(4) (chsd ldr: led wl over 1f out: rdn out).........— 1
1383[W] Balasara (IRE) **(76)***(85) (DRCElsworth)* 5-9-5b(5) AProcter(5) (led over 6f: rdn: r.o wl ins fnl f) nk 2
1255[4] Ahjay **(49)***(54) (DAWilson)* 5-7-11 JQuinn(2) (hld up: rdn over 1f out: one pce).........2 3
Whispering Loch (IRE) **(45)***(46) (JAkehurst)* 4-7-7 NAdams(8) (lw: hdwy over 2f out: wknd over 1f out).........2 4
1136[8] Arcatura **(69)***(70) (CJames)* 3-8-6 WNewnes(3) (rdn over 2f out: hdwy over 1f out: nvr nrr) ..s.h 5
1603[4] Glowing Jade **(72)***(73)*(Fav)*(MissGayKelleway)* 5-9-6 LDettori(1) (hld up: rdn over 1f out: sn wknd).........hd 6
Ever so Lyrical **(74)***(61) (PWHarris)* 5-9-8 RCochrane(7) (hdwy over 2f out: wknd over 1f out).........7 7
1383[5] Posing (IRE) **(72)***(54) (JRFanshawe)* 3-8-9 DHarrison(6) (prom over 6f).........2½ 8

LONG HANDICAP Whispering Loch (IRE) 7-2

7/4 Glowing Jade, **7/2** Arcatura, **5/1** Posing (IRE), **11/2** Ever so Lyrical, Ahjay, **8/1** Balasara (IRE), **20/1** LEGENDARY LEAP, **50/1** Whispering Loch (IRE), CSF £155.60 CT £922.49 TOTE £18.90: £2.40 £1.50 £1.90 (£47.70) OWNER Mr D. Tylden-Wright (WEST ILSLEY) BRED D. Tylden-Wright 8 Rn 1m 37.82 (0.82) SF: 52/62/31/23/36/50/38/20

WEIGHT FOR AGE 3yo-11lb

T/Jkpt: £7,100.00 (0.1 Tckts); £4,028.36 to Sandown 16/6/95. T/Plpt: £138.60 (119.98 Tckts). T/Qdpt: £10.40 (11.6 Tckts). AK

1696-**YARMOUTH (L-H)**
Thursday June 15th (Good to soft)
WEATHER: wet & misty WIND: str half bhd

1733
SEA PALLING APPRENTICE H'CAP (0-60) (3-Y.O+) (Class G)
£2,322.50 (£660.00: £327.50)
1m 2f 21y Stalls: Low GOING: 0.12 sec per fur (G) 6-30 (6-31)

1498[3] **Tirolette (IRE) (53)***(62) (RJRWilliams)* 3-8-11b GFaulkner(8) (lw: chsd ldrs: 3rd st: led over 3f out: sn hdd: rallied u.p to ld cl home)........— 1
1350[11] Gulf Bay **(35)***(44) (MBell)* 3-6-13 (8) RMullen(7) (hld up: 4th st: led 3f out tl ct nr fin)........nk 2
119[7] Inovar **(29)***(34) (CBBBooth)* 5-7-9 (5) FLynch(5) (bit bkwd: s.s: 6th st: hdwy 3f out: kpt on u.p appr fnl f: nt pce to chal)........2½ 3
1513[3] Scenic Dancer **(48)***(53)*(Fav)*(AHide)* 7-9-5v AEddery(3) (lw: dwlt: hld up & bhd: 5th st: effrt & rdn over 2f out: no imp)........s.h 4
1557[8] Goldenberry **(30)** *(JParkes)* 4-8-1 VictoriaAppleby(1) (slt ld to ½-wy: 2nd st: wknd 4f out: t.o)........25 5
1498[16] Laal (USA) **(55)***(19) (EALDunlop)* 3-8-13 JWilkinson(4) (lw: w ldr tl led ½-wy: hdd over 3f out: wknd qckly: t.o)........nk 6

LONG HANDICAP Gulf Bay 7-4

6/5 Scenic Dancer, **7/4** TIROLETTE (IRE), **9/1** Laal (USA) (9/2-10/1), **10/1** Gulf Bay (6/1-11/1), **33/1** Goldenberry, Inovar, CSF £15.39 CT £303.65 TOTE £3.20: £1.20 £3.20 (£8.70) OWNER Mr Richard Morris Jr (NEWMARKET) BRED W. J. O'Regan 6 Rn 2m 13.8 (9.40) SF: 30/12/15/34/-/-
WEIGHT FOR AGE 3yo-13lb

1734
REPPS (S) STKS (2-Y.O) (Class G) £2,422.20 (£669.20: £318.60)
7f 3y Stalls: Low GOING: 0.12 sec per fur (G) 7-00 (7-01)

*1632** **Miss Offset** *(67)*(Fav)*(MJohnston)* 2-8-11b DHolland(4) (sn drvn along & outpcd: swtchd rt & hdwy ½-wy: led 2f out: sn clr)........— 1
1272* Don't Tell Vicki *(58) (JSMoore)* 2-8-6 (5) NVarley(7) (led over 3f out to 2f out: rdn & outpcd appr fnl f)........4 2
1570[7] Our Tom's Boy *(54) (KTIvory)* 2-8-4b(7) CScally(1) (b.hind: a.p: rdn over 2f out: kpt on one pce)........1¾ 3
671[11] Comrade Chinnery (IRE) *(48) (JMPEustace)* 2-8-11 RCochrane(3) (bit bkwd: led to ½-wy: rdn 2f out: sn btn)........2½ 4
1288[5] Mazoski *(23) (PCHaslam)* 2-8-11 MTebbutt(5) (lw: s.s: a bhd: t.o)........11 5
1466[7] Maygain (IRE) *(20) (MRChannon)* 2-8-11 FNorton(6) (chsd ldr 4f: sn lost tch: t.o)........1½ 6

6/4 MISS OFFSET, **7/2** Don't Tell Vicki, **6/1** Comrade Chinnery (IRE) (op 3/1), Mazoski (op 16/1), **9/1** Maygain (IRE) (6/1-10/1), **20/1** Our Tom's Boy, CSF £6.27 TOTE £2.50: £1.70 £1.70 (£2.90) OWNER Hertford Offset Ltd (MIDDLEHAM) BRED J. Coombes and E. Henshaw 6 Rn
1m 30.9 (8.10) SF: 10/1/-/-/-/-
No bid

1735
APPLEGATE H'CAP (0-70) (3-Y.O F) (Class E) £3,216.40
(£959.20: £457.60: £206.80)
1m 3y Stalls: Low GOING: 0.12 sec per fur (G) 7-30 (7-32)

1598[4] **Indian Rhapsody (44)***(59)*(Fav)*(MRChannon)* 3-8-0 FNorton(4) (chsd ldrs far side: rdn 2f out: kpt on to ld wl ins fnl f)........— 1
1534[3] Never so Rite (IRE) **(50)***(64) (DWPArbuthnot)* 3-8-3 (3) DRMcCabe(9) (lw: chsd ldrs: rdn to ld ent fnl f: hdd nr fin)........nk 2
1465[4] Three Arch Bridge **(55)***(63) (MJohnston)* 3-8-11b DHolland(10) (hld up: hdwy wl over 1f out: fin wl)........3 3
1473[8] Nightscene (IRE) **(60)***(65) (TGMills)* 3-9-2 RHills(1) (hld up: hdwy to ld 2f out: rdn & hdd ent fnl f: sn btn)........1¾ 4
1294[3] Juweilla **(65)***(67) (JWPayne)* 3-9-7 RCochrane(6) (prom: rdn & swished tail over 2f out: grad wknd)........1¼ 5
1402[10] Care And Comfort **(60)***(60) (GWragg)* 3-9-2 PaulEddery(5) (prom: rdn wl over 1f out: one pce)........1 6
1539[9] Elite Racing **(64)***(56) (PFICole)* 3-9-1 (5) NVarley(2) (prom: lost pl & rdn over 3f out)........4 7
1167[12] Rozalina Lady **(59)***(38) (NAGraham)* 3-9-1 DHarrison(8) (lw: bhd & rdn along ½-wy: no imp)..7 8
1539[10] Pioneer Princess **(52)***(29) (MJRyan)* 3-8-8 ow1 TIves(7) (a in rr)........nk 9
1383[10] Pinkerton Polka **(52)***(29) (CEBrittain)* 3-8-8 BDoyle(3) (lw: mde most to 2f out: wknd qckly)........½ 10

9/4 INDIAN RHAPSODY, **5/1** Juweilla, **11/2** Three Arch Bridge, **6/1** Never so Rite (IRE), **13/2** Elite Racing (4/1-7/1), **10/1** Care And Comfort (6/1-12/1), Nightscene (IRE) (7/1-11/1), **16/1** Pinkerton Polka, **25/1** Rozalina Lady, Pioneer Princess, CSF £16.11 CT £60.98 TOTE £3.40: £1.70 £1.10 £1.50 (£5.10) Trio £18.90 OWNER Mr J. R. Good (UPPER LAMBOURN) BRED Mrs P. Good 10 Rn
1m 42.6 (7.30) SF: 19/24/23/25/27/20/16/-/-/-

1736 AMEC PROCESS AND ENERGY MAIDEN STKS (3-Y.O) (Class D)
£4,036.50 (£1,206.00: £577.00: £262.50)
1m 3y Stalls: Low GOING: 0.12 sec per fur (G) 8-00 (8-03)

761[6] **Quinwood (USA)** *(85) (JHMGosden)* 3-8-9 GHind(3) (hdwy 3f out: shkn up appr fnl f: r.o to ld post)........— 1
Bonne Etoile *(85) (DRLoder)* 3-8-6 (3) DRMcCabe(7) (bkwd: hdwy ½-wy: str chal fnl f: r.o)....hd 2
1068[7] Henry Koehler **(98)***(90)*(Fav)*(CEBrittain)* 3-9-0 BDoyle(2) (lw: a.p: led 3f out: clr over 1f out: rdn & hdd nr fin)........hd 3
Future Act (USA) *(80) (HRACecil)* 3-8-9 AMcGlone(6) (lt-f: bit bkwd: w ldrs centre: rdn over 1f out: one pce)........2½ 4
Tap On Tootsie *(60) (ICampbell)* 3-8-9 DBiggs(1) (wl grwn: bkwd: styd on fnl 2f: nvr nrr)......10 5
1312[4] Primo Lara **(77)***(64) (PWHarris)* 3-9-0 DHolland(13) (racd alone stands' side: mde most for 5f: sn rdn & wknd)........½ 6
Hello Peter (IRE) *(58) (MHTompkins)* 3-8-9 (5) SMulvey(10) (bkwd: nvr nrr)........3 7
The Flying Fiddle *(52) (MHTompkins)* 3-8-9 RDorans(4) (lengthy: bkwd: a in rr)........nk 8
Grooms Gold (IRE) *(55) (PWHarris)* 3-9-0 StephenDavies(12) (bkwd: nvr nr ldrs)........1¼ 9
1526[13] Hala Halina *(42) (JEBanks)* 3-8-9 RCochrane(5) (led centre 5f: sn lost tch)........4 10
Dozen Dirham (USA) *(42) (EALDunlop)* 3-9-0 PaulEddery(8) (b: w'like: str: bkwd: a in rr)....2½ 11
1308[3] Incha *(23)*(Fav)*(HThomsonJones)* 3-8-9 RHills(9) (chsd ldrs centre over 5f: sn wknd: t.o) 7 12

3/1 Incha, Henry Koehler, **7/2** Bonne Etoile (7/4-4/1), **13/2** Future Act (USA) (3/1-7/1), **9/1** QUINWOOD (USA) (6/1-10/1), Primo Lara (op 5/1), **14/1** Hala Halina (op 8/1), Dozen Dirham (USA) (10/1-16/1), **20/1** Grooms Gold (IRE), **33/1** Hello Peter (IRE), The Flying Fiddle, Tap On Tootsie, CSF £42.22 TOTE £18.90: £3.10 £2.20 £1.10 (£22.70) Trio £23.00 OWNER Sheikh Mohammed (NEWMARKET) BRED Darley Stud Management 12 Rn
1m 41.9 (6.60) SF: 35/35/40/30/10/14/8/2/5/-/-/-

1737 SOMERTON CLAIMING STKS (3-Y.O+) (Class F) £2,821.40 (£780.40: £372.20)
2m Stalls: Low GOING: 0.12 sec per fur (G) 8-30 (8-31)

*1319** **Hever Golf Lady (43)***(67)*(Fav)*(TJNaughton)* 3-8-2 StephenDavies(3) (mde all: sn wl clr: rdn fnl f: hld on)........— 1
1581[2] Recovery Lad (IRE) **(51)***(69)*(Fav)*(KRBurke)* 3-8-2v(3) DRMcCabe(4) (chsd ldrs: wnt 2nd 9f out: rdn 4f out: hung lft & styd on fnl f)........1¼ 2
Oh So Handy *(47) (RCurtis)* 7-9-9 MTebbutt(1) (bit bkwd: hld up & bhd: wnt 4th st: rdn over 3f out: no imp)........20 3
Noble Society **(32)***(41) (KGWingrove)* 7-9-4 TIves(5) (b: bkwd: hld up: 3rd st: nvr plcd to chal)........1¼ 4
136[10] Mrs Jogglebury **(35)** *(CSmith)* 4-8-7 (5) NVarley(2) (lw: sn pushed along: chsd wnr 7f: 5th & wknd st: t.o)........dist 5

11/8 HEVER GOLF LADY, Recovery Lad (IRE), **8/1** Oh So Handy, Noble Society, **33/1** Mrs Jogglebury, CSF £3.46 TOTE £2.20: £1.50 £1.10 (£1.30) OWNER Mrs E. Jackman (EPSOM) BRED M. M. Allen 5 Rn
3m 42.7 (19.20) SF: 4/6/4/-/-
WEIGHT FOR AGE 3yo-20lb, 4yo-1lb

1738 STURDEE H'CAP (0-70) (3-Y.O+) (Class E) £3,159.20 (£941.60: £448.80: £202.40)
6f 3y Stalls: Low GOING: 0.12 sec per fur (G) 9-00 (9-02)

1483[4] **Tharwa (IRE) (56)***(64) (NACallaghan)* 3-8-7 DHarrison(6) (b: b.hind: a.p: led over 2f out: hrd rdn fnl f: jst hld on)........— 1
1193[4] Cool Edge (IRE) **(68)***(76)*(Fav)*(MHTompkins)* 4-10-0 PRobinson(5) (lw: hld up: gd hdwy over 1f out: hrd drvn fnl f: fin fast)........s.h 2
1400[7] Sison (IRE) **(60)***(57) (KGWingrove)* 5-9-6 TIves(3) (b.hind: led over 3f: rdn & outpcd appr fnl f)........4 3
1483[12] Bright Paragon (IRE) **(43)***(36) (HJCollingridge)* 6-8-3 ow1 RHills(1) (bhd & outpcd tl styd on appr fnl f)........1¼ 4
1377[12] Aquiletta **(46)***(32) (CBBBooth)* 5-8-6 RCochrane(2) (chsd ldrs: rdn 2f out: no imp)........3 5
1429[4] Samsolom **(60)***(25) (PHowling)* 7-9-6 PaulEddery(4) (a bhd & outpcd: t.o)........8 6
1411[11] Media Express **(70)***(31) (TGMills)* 3-9-0 (7) JCornally(7) (spd to ½-wy: sn lost tch: t.o)........1¼ 7

11/4 Cool Edge (IRE) (2/1-3/1), **4/1** THARWA (IRE), **9/2** Samsolom (3/1-5/1), **5/1** Media Express, **6/1** Aquiletta, **13/2** Bright Paragon (IRE), **20/1** Sison (IRE), CSF £14.60 CT £172.34 TOTE £4.20: £1.70 £2.00 (£5.10) Trio £41.80 OWNER K. Al-Said (NEWMARKET) BRED Charlton Down Stud 7 Rn
1m 15.2 (4.60) SF: 37/58/39/18/14/7/4
WEIGHT FOR AGE 3yo-9lb

T/Plpt: £33.40 (375.29 Tckts). T/Qdpt: £13.60 (6.9 Tckts). IM

1203-EDINBURGH (R-H)
Friday June 16th (Good to firm)
WEATHER: drizzle WIND: almost nil

1739
GUILLANE MAIDEN LIMITED STKS (0-60) (3-Y.O+) (Class F) £2,666.00 (£751.00: £368.00)
5f Stalls: High GOING minus 0.21 sec per fur (GF) 6-55 (6-56)

1279⁷ **Frans Lad (59)***(70) (JBerry)* 3-9-0b JCarroll(10) (in tch: drvn along ½-wy: led ins fnl f: r.o) ....— 1
1580⁹ Sunshine Belle **(46)***(59) (GMMoore)* 3-8-9 JFanning(7) (lw: disp ld tl led 2f out: hdd & no ex ins fnl f) 1¾ 2
1157⁹ Kenesha (IRE) **(50)***(55) (DANolan)* 5-9-2 LCharnock(3) (b: a chsng ldrs: kpt on u.p fnl 2f: b.b.v) 1¼ 3
1419⁷ Samsung Lovelylady (IRE) **(55)***(50) (EWeymes)* 3-8-9v SMaloney(6) (lw: a.p: effrt 2f out: r.o one pce) 1¾ 4
1559⁴ China Hand (IRE) **(56)***(51) (MartynWane)* 3-9-0 TWilliams(9) (disp ld 3f: grad wknd) 1¼ 5
1521² Portelet **(60)***(43)*(Fav)*(RJRWilliams)* 3-8-9 GDuffield(5) (prom tl rdn ½-wy: grad wknd) ....¾ 6
1296¹³ Irish Angel (IRE) **(45)***(41) (CSmith)* 3-8-6 (3) DarrenMoffatt(4) (lw: b.hind: unruly s: s.i.s: n.d) ...¾ 7
994⁹ Uppance **(25)***(30) (DANolan)* 7-8-11b(5) NVarley(11) (in tch: sn drvn along: outpcd fr ½-wy)..3½ 8
1721¹³ Jessica's Secret (IRE) **(37)***(17) (ABailey)* 3-8-2b(7) IGrantham(2) (hmpd s: s.s: nt rcvr) 4 9
1360⁷ Fuzzy **(35)***(14) (SEKettlewell)* 3-8-9b(5) JStack(1) (wl bhd fr ½-wy) 2½ 10

13/8 Portelet, **11/2** FRANS LAD, **6/1** Samsung Lovelylady (IRE), **8/1** China Hand (IRE), Kenesha (IRE), **14/1** Irish Angel (IRE) (10/1-16/1), Fuzzy (25/1-12/1), **16/1** Sunshine Belle, **20/1** Jessica's Secret (IRE), **66/1** Uppance, CSF £74.78 TOTE £7.50: £2.60 £9.50 £4.20 (£78.80) Trio £80.01 OWNER F C M Racing (COCKERHAM) BRED Filletts Farm Stud 10 Rn
60.8 secs (3.10) SF: 27/16/19/7/8/-/-/-/-/-
WEIGHT FOR AGE 3yo-7lb
OFFICIAL EXPLANATION Kenesha (IRE): bled from the nose.

1740
DON'T BLINK (S) STKS (2-Y.O) (Class G) £2,365.00 (£665.00: £325.00)
5f Stalls: High GOING minus 0.21 sec per fur (GF) 7-25 (7-26)

1413⁵ **Imp Express (IRE)** *(64)*(Fav)*(GMMoore)* 2-8-11 JFortune(2) (trckd ldrs: led ½-wy: hung lft: pushed out) ....— 1
1562⁵ Miletrian Refurb (IRE) *(61) (MRChannon)* 2-8-11 KDarley(5) (a.p: kpt on fnl f: nrst fin) 1 2
1503¹⁰ Subfusk *(60) (WGMTurner)* 2-8-4 (7) ADaly(1) (hung lft & racd wd: led to ½-wy: rallied 1f out: kpt on) ....nk 3
1570⁸ Veshca Lady (IRE) *(54) (EWeymes)* 2-8-11 TWilliams(4) (outpcd tl styd on wl fnl f) 1¾ 4
1282⁷ Snitch *(53) (CSmith)* 2-8-6v(5) NVarley(3) (w ldrs tl rdn & btn over 1f out) ....½ 5
1159⁴ Monsieur Culsyth *(29) (JBerry)* 2-9-2 JCarroll(6) (nvr wnt pce) 9 6

Evens IMP EXPRESS (IRE), **7/2** Monsieur Culsyth, **6/1** Miletrian Refurb (IRE) (op 4/1), **7/1** Veshca Lady (IRE), Subfusk, **16/1** Snitch, CSF £7.53 TOTE £2.20: £1.70 £3.60 (£8.50) OWNER Ms Sigrid Walter (MIDDLEHAM) BRED M. Morrin 6 Rn
61.9 secs (4.20) SF: 7/4/3/-/-/-
No bid

1741
SHERATON GRAND CUP H'CAP (0-75) (3-Y.O+) (Class D) £4,232.50 (£1,285.00: £630.00: £302.50)
5f Stalls: High GOING minus 0.21 sec per fur (GF) 7-55 (7-56)

1689⁸ **Giggleswick Girl (58)***(66) (MRChannon)* 4-9-1 KDarley(7) (chsd ldrs: led ½-wy: r.o wl) ....— 1
1689⁴ Just Bob **(68)***(70)*(Fav)*(SEKettlewell)* 6-9-11 JCarroll(2) (lw: s.i.s: hdwy ½-wy: kpt on one pce fnl f) 2 2
1677⁵ My Cherrywell **(57)***(49) (LRLloyd-James)* 5-9-0v TWilliams(5) (lw: b.hind: sn chsng ldrs: rdn ½-wy: kpt on) 3 3
1599⁷ Croft Imperial **(66)***(54) (MJohnston)* 8-9-9 DHolland(3) (a.p: sn drvn along: kpt on fnl f) 1¼ 4
1508² Miss Movie World **(61)***(47)*(Fav)*(MDHammond)* 6-8-13 (5) JStack(6) (lw: led to ½-wy: wknd) ...½ 5
1723* Ultra Beet **(66)***(48) (PCHaslam)* 3-9-2v JFortune(4) (lw: outpcd ½-wy: n.d after) 1¼ 6
1445³ Southern Dominion **(65)***(35) (WGMTurner)* 3-8-8 (7) ADaly(1) (stmbld s: cl up tl wknd 2f out) 4 7

5/2 Just Bob (op 4/1), Miss Movie World, **4/1** Ultra Beet (op 5/2), **9/2** Croft Imperial, **12/1** GIGGLESWICK GIRL, Southern Dominion, **20/1** My Cherrywell, CSF £40.23 TOTE £6.00: £2.20 £1.40 (£5.00) OWNER Mr M. Bishop (UPPER LAMBOURN) BRED B. Minty 7 Rn

60.0 secs (2.30) SF: 42/46/25/30/23/17/4

WEIGHT FOR AGE 3yo-7lb

1742 DICK VET TURF CLUB H'CAP (0-60) (3-Y.O+) (Class F) £2,970.50 (£838.00: £411.50) **1m 16y** Stalls: High GOING minus 0.37 sec per fur (F) 8-25 (8-26)

1724[10] **Morocco (IRE) (55)***(63) (MRChannon)* 6-9-9 KDarley(12) (bhd: hdwy on ins whn nt clr run over 2f out: r.o wl to ld cl home) — 1
1465[7] Malzoom **(38)***(43) (SEKettlewell)* 3-7-5 (5)ow3 NVarley(8) (a cl up: led over 2f out tl ct nr fin) s.h 2
1578[7] Matisse **(46)***(53) (JDBethell)* 4-9-0 KFallon(5) (lw: bhd: effrt & nt clr run 2f out: swtchd over 1f out: fin wl) nk 3
1522[7] Upex le Gold Too **(45)***(50) (LRLloyd-James)* 3-8-3 TWilliams(1) (bhd: hdwy over 2f out: chsng ldrs ins fnl f: nt qckn ins fnl f) 1¼ 4
1506[4] Borrowby **(47)***(52) (MWEasterby)* 3-8-5b LCharnock(11) (lw: led tl hdd over 2f out: hrd rdn & r.o one pce) s.h 5
1724[5] Talented Ting (IRE) **(65)***(65) (PCHaslam)* 6-10-5 5x JFortune(2) (lw: chsd ldrs: rdn over 2f out: one pce) 2½ 6
1528[4] Buddy's Friend (IRE) **(58)***(57)*(Fav)*(RJRWilliams)* 7-9-12 GDuffield(4) (lw: effrt over 3f out: one pce fnl f) nk 7
1453[4] Ricana **(39)***(36) (WTKemp)* 3-7-8 (3) DarrenMoffatt(6) (effrt ½-wy: nvr trbld ldrs) 1¼ 8
1721[16] Valley of Time (FR) **(37)***(18) (DANolan)* 7-7-12 (7)ow12 ADaly(3) (b: prom tl wknd 2f out) 1¾ 9
1464[5] Pipers Glen **(47)***(40) (CParker)* 3-8-5 JCarroll(10) (in tch tl wknd appr fnl f) hd 10
1358[13] Cupronickel (IRE) **(50)***(33) (JWWatts)* 3-8-8b JFanning(7) (sn cl up: rdn 3f out: wknd 2f out) 5 11

LONG HANDICAP Malzoom 7-2

9/4 Buddy's Friend (IRE), **7/2** Talented Ting (IRE), **9/2** Borrowby, **6/1** Ricana, **8/1** MOROCCO (IRE), **20/1** Malzoom, Pipers Glen, Matisse, Cupronickel (IRE), **33/1** Upex le Gold Too, **50/1** Valley of Time (FR), CSF £131.88 CT £2,772.37 TOTE £12.00: £3.40 £5.00 £2.20 (£49.50) Trio £178.80 OWNER Mr Martin Myers (UPPER LAMBOURN) BRED Nikita Investments 11 Rn

1m 43.0 (4.40) SF: 33/3/23/10/12/35/27/-/-/-/-

WEIGHT FOR AGE 3yo-10lb

1743 OCHIL HILLS CLAIMING STKS (4-Y.O+) (Class F) £2,624.00 (£739.00: £362.00) **1m 4f 31y** Stalls: High GOING minus 0.37 sec per fur (F) 8-55 (8-57)

1555[2] **Goodbye Millie (33)***(54)*(Fav)*(JLEyre)* 5-8-6v RLappin(3) (lw: chsd ldr: sn pushed along: led over 3f out: kpt on wl) — 1
1555[3] Kimberley Boy **(55)***(54)*(Fav)*(MBrittain)* 5-8-9 KFallon(4) (bhd: effrt ent s: styd on towards fin) 2 2
569[3] Irish Senor (IRE) **(59)***(53) (JLSpearing)* 4-8-9 KDarley(1) (hdwy appr st: ev ch over 1f out: nt qckn) 1¼ 3
1647[4] Aerial View **(39)***(50) (WGMTurner)* 4-8-4 (7) ADaly(5) (a.p: one pce fnl 3f) 3½ 4
1422[5] Master Fiddler **(33)***(28) (EWeymes)* 5-8-9 GDuffield(1) (led tl hdd over 3f out: sn wknd) 15 5

2/1 GOODBYE MILLIE, Kimberley Boy, **9/4** Irish Senor (IRE), **8/1** Master Fiddler, **14/1** Aerial View, CSF £6.40 TOTE £3.30: £1.50 £1.70 (£3.00) OWNER Mr K. Meynell (HAMBLETON) BRED G. Corbett 5 Rn

2m 38.2 (5.70) SF: 25/25/24/21/-

1744 CASTLE H'CAP (0-70) (3-Y.O+) (Class E) £2,983.00 (£904.00: £442.00: £211.00) **1m 3f 32y** Stalls: High GOING minus 0.37 sec per fur (F) 9-25 (9-25)

1529[8] **Missus Murhill (IRE) (39)***(46) (NTinkler)* 4-8-8 GDuffield(2) (lw: trckd ldrs: led wl over 1f out: hrd rdn nr fin: hld on wl) — 1
1686[8] Lord Advocate **(41)***(48) (DANolan)* 7-8-5b(5) 5x NVarley(4) (cl up: led wl over 2f out tl over 1f out: rallied ins fnl f: jst failed) s.h 2
1251[4] Gospel Song **(67)***(73) (WTKemp)* 3-9-8 KDarley(3) (lw: effrt over 3f out: styd on wl fnl f: nrst fin) 1 3
1686* Mentalasanythin **(64)***(69)*(Fav)*(ABailey)* 6-10-5 5x AMackay(1) (lw: a.p: effrt 3f out: styd on towards fin) ½ 4
1251[9] Drummer Hicks **(51)***(52) (EWeymes)* 6-9-6 DeanMcKeown(6) (led tl hdd wl over 2f out: wknd over 1f out) 2½ 5
1420[3] Monkey Wench (IRE) **(48)***(49) (PMonteith)* 4-9-3 SMaloney(5) (bhd: effrt u.p over 2f out: nvr able to chal) ½ 6

Evens Mentalasanythin, **4/1** Drummer Hicks, **5/1** Gospel Song, **8/1** MISSUS MURHILL (IRE) (9/1-6/1), **9/1** Monkey Wench (IRE) (6/1-10/1), **11/1** Lord Advocate (op 6/1), CSF £69.95 TOTE £5.70: £2.10 £2.70 (£34.40) OWNER Mr S. A. Barningham (MALTON) BRED B. Ryan 6 Rn

2m 24.8 (5.10) SF: 27/29/40/50/33/30

WEIGHT FOR AGE 3yo-14lb

T/Plpt: £3,683.40 (2.8 Tckts). T/Qdpt: £89.90 (0.1 Tckts); £109.44 to Sandown 17/06/95. AA

1590-GOODWOOD (R-H)
Friday June 16th (Good to firm)

WEATHER: overcast WIND: mod against

1745 ABELA AMATEUR H'CAP (0-70) (3-Y.O+) (Class E) £3,200.00 (£950.00: £450.00: £200.00) 1m 1f Stalls: Low GOING minus 0.17 sec per fur (GF) 6-40 (6-41)

1645² **Anlace (48)***(60) (SMellor)* 6-9-11 (5) MissEJoyce(14) (hdwy 3f out: led ins fnl f: r.o wl) — 1
1367⁸ Caerle Lad (IRE) **(64)***(75) (GHarwood)* 4-11-4 MissAHarwood(16) (3rd st: led over 2f out tl ins fnl f: r.o) ¾ 2
1498¹¹ Kevasingo **(56)***(52) (SDow)* 3-9-13 MrTCuff(9) (lw: 2nd st: rdn & ev ch over 2f out: unable qckn) 8 3
1517³ Piquant **(67)***(61) (LordHuntingdon)* 8-11-7 MrsMCowdrey(11) (hdwy 3f out: one pce fnl 2f) 1¼ 4
1635⁶ Don't Drop Bombs (USA) **(32)***(23) (DTThom)* 6-9-0v MissJFeilden(12) (led 7f out tl over 2f out: sn wknd) 2 5
1472⁵ Oozlem (IRE) **(40)***(30) (RMFlower)* 6-9-8b MrRJohnson(10) (s.s: nvr gng wl: hdwy 7f out: 7th st: one pce) ½ 6
1380⁹ Magnate's Point **(65)***(54) (PWHarris)* 3-10-8 MissAElsey(13) (rdn 3f out: nvr nrr) ½ 7
1484⁷ Captain Marmalade **(45)***(31) (DTThom)* 6-9-13 MissDianaJones(17) (wl bhd fnl 5f: hrd rdn 3f out: nvr nr to chal) 1½ 8
1531⁶ Scottish Park **(40)***(24) (RWEmery)* 6-9-8b MissJWinter(1) (4th st: wknd over 2f out) 1¼ 9
1244⁹ Douce Maison (IRE) **(53)***(37) (APJarvis)* 4-10-2 (5) MrsEBurke(2) (swtg: led 2f: 6th st: wknd 3f out) nk 10
729⁵ Remember This (IRE) **(37)***(13) (CACyzer)* 5-9-0 (5)ow5 MissAWilcox(7) (nvr gng wl: a bhd) 1¼ 11
1484⁸ Blanchland **(58)***(35) (KTIvory)* 6-10-7 (5) MissLVollaro(8) (bhd fnl 3f) 2½ 12
1350¹⁶ Dream Missy **(32)***(9) (JRBosley)* 4-9-0 MrsSBosley(15) (lw: 5th st: wknd 3f out) s.h 13
1320³ Mega Tid **(44)***(8) (BAPearce)* 3-9-1 MrsLPearce(6) (prom 3f) 7 14
1255⁸ Montone (IRE) **(58)***(21) (KRBurke)* 5-10-7 (5) MrMMannish(3) (prom 5f: 8th & wkng st) ¾ 15
1548⁶ Grand Salt (IRE) **(50)***(11) (MJHaynes)* 4-10-4 MissYHaynes(5) (t: a bhd) 1 16
1417⁴ Remaadi Sun **(69)***(20)*(Fav)*(JHMGosden)* 3-10-12 MrJDurkan(4) (lw: 9th & rdn st: wl bhd fnl 3f) 6 17

LONG HANDICAP Dream Missy 8-7 Remember This (IRE) 8-12

7/2 Remaadi Sun, **5/1** Caerle Lad (IRE), **6/1** Piquant (9/2-7/1), **10/1** ANLACE (8/1-12/1), **12/1** Douce Maison (IRE) (op 8/1), Oozlem (IRE), Montone (IRE) (op 8/1), **14/1** Kevasingo, Scottish Park, Mega Tid, **16/1** Magnate's Point, Captain Marmalade, **20/1** Blanchland, **25/1** Grand Salt (IRE), **33/1** Don't Drop Bombs (USA), **66/1** Dream Missy, Remember This (IRE), CSF £58.42 CT £662.35 TOTE £13.00: £2.30 £1.70 £4.80 £1.90 (£41.00) Trio £455.30 OWNER The Felix Bowness Partnership (SWINDON) BRED Sheikh Mohammed bin Rashid al Maktoum 17 Rn

1m 57.37 (6.67) SF: 40/55/21/41/3/10/23/11/4/17/-/15/-/-/1/-/-

WEIGHT FOR AGE 3yo-11lb

1746 NSPCC MAIDEN STKS (2-Y.O F) (Class D) £3,200.00 (£950.00:£450.00: £200.00) 6f Stalls: Low GOING minus 0.17 sec per fur (GF) 7-05 (7-06)

Prends Ca (IRE) *(74+) (RHannon)* 2-8-4 (7) DaneO'Neill(3) (unf: a.p: rdn over 1f out: led nr fin) — 1
Scarlet Plume *(73)*(Fav)*(JLDunlop)* 2-8-11 WCarson(8) (scope: swvd rt s: ev ch fnl 2f: r.o) nk 2
1536² Ciserano (IRE) *(73) (MRChannon)* 2-8-11 RHughes(6) (led 4f out: hrd rdn fnl f: hdd nr fin) hd 3
Conquistajade (USA) *(60) (SPCWoods)* 2-8-11 LDettori(7) (leggy: rdn 3f out: no hdwy fnl 2f) .5 4
1348⁴ Pendley Rose *(58) (PWHarris)* 2-8-11 PatEddery(5) (dwlt: spd 4f) ¾ 5
1511⁷ Queen's Music (USA) *(54) (PFICole)* 2-8-11 AClark(2) (b.nr hind: prom n.m.r & swtchd over 3f out: nt rcvr) 1¼ 6
Twice Removed *(48) (SDow)* 2-8-11 StephenDavies(9) (w'like: carried rt s: rdn & a bhd) 2½ 7
1443⁵ Fro *(44) (JFfitch-Heyes)* 2-8-11 MRoberts(1) (led 2f: wknd 3f out) 1½ 8
Latzio *(12) (BAPearce)* 2-8-11 SWhitworth(4) (scope: bhd fnl 2f: t.o) 12 9

Evens Scarlet Plume, **7/2** Pendley Rose, **5/1** Ciserano (IRE), **9/1** Conquistajade (USA) (op 6/1), **11/1** Queen's Music (USA) (8/1-12/1), **33/1** Twice Removed, **40/1** PRENDS CA (IRE), **50/1** Fro, Latzio, CSF £77.65 TOTE £23.90: £3.30 £1.30 £1.60 (£45.70) Trio £69.60 OWNER Mr P. B. Adams (MARLBOROUGH) BRED Sheikh Mohammed Bin Rashid Al Maktoum 9 Rn

1m 13.55 (3.35) SF: 34/33/33/20/18/14/8/4/-

1747 NSPCC H'CAP (0-85) (3-Y.O) (Class D) £3,520.00 (£1,045.00: £495.00: £220.00)
1m 2f Stalls: Low GOING minus 0.17 sec per fur (GF) 7-35 (7-35)

16382 **Danegold (IRE) (73)***(87+)*(Fav)*(MRChannon)* 3-8-10v RHughes(4) (dwlt: hdwy on bit 3f out: led 2f out: comf)......— 1
1337* Lovely Lyca **(78)***(90) (JWHills)* 3-8-8 (7) MHenry(1) (lw: hdwy 3f out: ev ch 2f out: unable qckn)......1¼ 2
15912 Donna Viola **(72)***(68) (CFWall)* 3-8-4 (5) LNewton(2) (lw: 4th st: led 3f out: edgd rt & hdd 2f out: wknd over 1f out: fin 4th, 10l: plcd 3rd)...... 3
14253 Office Hours **(78)***(66) (CACyzer)* 3-9-1 TQuinn(7) (hld up: 6th st: n.m.r over 2f out: one pce: fin 5th, 5l: plcd 4th)...... 4
14153 Hujjab (USA) **(84)***(70) (JLDunlop)* 3-9-7 WCarson(6) (swtg: led 7f: wknd over 2f out: fin 6th, 11/4l: plcd 5th)...... 5
12215 Edan Heights **(69)***(55) (SDow)* 3-8-6 MRoberts(5) (lw: prom over 5f)......s.h 7
11679 I'm Outa Here (IRE) **(66)***(51) (RHannon)* 3-8-3 BDoyle(3) (3rd st: wkng whn hmpd over 2f out)......nk 8
14173 Heath Robinson (IRE) **(78)***(41) (JHMGosden)* 3-9-1 LDettori(8) (2nd st: wkng whn bmpd over 2f out: eased: t.o)......14 9
7175 Better Offer (IRE) **(76)** *(GHarwood)* 3-8-13 MPerrett(9) (lw: 5th st: n.m.r over 2f out: swtchd wl over 1f out: r.o: fin 3rd, ½l: disq: plcd last)...... 0

5/2 DANEGOLD (IRE), **6/1** Donna Viola, **13/2** Hujjab (USA), Edan Heights, **7/1** Lovely Lyca (5/1-15/2), **9/1** Heath Robinson (IRE), **14/1** Office Hours, Better Offer (IRE), **20/1** I'm Outa Here (IRE), CSF £17.74 CT £77.83 TOTE £3.20: £1.30 £2.70 £2.30 (£10.80) Trio £20.40 OWNER The Dream Team (UPPER LAMBOURN) BRED Barronstown Stud and Ron Con Ltd 9 Rn
2m 9.4 (4.40) SF: 46/49/27/25/29/14/10/-/-

1748 NSPCC 'CRY FOR CHILDREN' CLAIMING STKS (3-Y.O) (Class E) £3,200.00 (£950.00: £450.00: £200.00)
1m Stalls: Low GOING minus 0.17 sec per fur (GF) 8-05 (8-07)

12586 **Eurolink the Rebel (USA) (74)***(76+) (RAkehurst)* 3-8-7 LDettori(2) (chsd ldr: led on bit 2f out: rdn clr: comf)......— 1
13172 Rising Dough (IRE) **(79)***(75)*(Fav)*(GLMoore)* 3-8-11 AClark(5) (plld hrd: 4th st: nt clr run 2f out: r.o ins fnl f)......2½ 2
12733 Empower (IRE) **(77)***(75) (RHannon)* 3-9-3 PatEddery(3) (led 6f: unable qckn)......3 3
158910 Gulf Shaadi **(83)***(62) (GLewis)* 3-8-11 SWhitworth(4) (3rd st: wknd wl over 1f out)......3½ 4
14254 Rising River *(SWoodman)* 3-8-6b JQuinn(1) (5th st: wknd over 4f out: t.o)......dist 5

7/4 Rising Dough (IRE), **5/2** EUROLINK THE REBEL (USA), **7/2** Empower (IRE), **9/2** Gulf Shaadi (op 3/1), **33/1** Rising River, CSF £6.76 TOTE £2.60: £1.90 £1.50 (£3.80) OWNER Eurolink Group Plc (EPSOM) BRED Joseph Bryan Jnr 5 Rn 1m 40.52 (2.92) SF: 48/47/47/34/-

1749 GREEN FLAG CLAIMING STKS (4-Y.O+) (Class D) £3,520.00 (£1,045.00: £495.00: £220.00)
1m 4f Stalls: Low GOING minus 0.17 sec per fur (GF) 8-35 (8-36)

16127 **Flight Lieutenant (USA) (74)***(87) (RHannon)* 6-9-8 RHughes(1) (led: sn clr: wknd fnl f: all out)......— 1
1594* Pharamineux **(63)***(72)*(Fav)*(RAkehurst)* 9-8-7 TQuinn(5) (mod 4th st: hdwy 2f out: r.o wl fnl f)......nk 2
15943 Ginger Jim **(52)***(74) (PRHedger)* 4-8-10 CAvery(4) (mod 3rd st: chsd wnr 3f out: r.o ins fnl f) .¾ 3
15942 Irkutsk (USA) **(67)***(70) (MCPipe)* 4-8-12 MRoberts(3) (chsd wnr 9f: one pce)......4 4
Yo-Mate *(63) (JFfitch-Heyes)* 4-9-8 AClark(2) (s.s: a bhd)......13 5

7/4 Pharamineux, **5/2** Irkutsk (USA), **3/1** FLIGHT LIEUTENANT (USA), **6/1** Ginger Jim (4/1-7/1), **40/1** Yo-Mate, CSF £7.89 TOTE £4.10: £2.10 £1.60 (£4.40) OWNER P & S Lever Partners (MARLBOROUGH) BRED Dale Barlage 5 Rn 2m 38.92 (6.92) SF: 47/32/34/30/23

1750 LAING & CRUIKSHANK INVESTMENT MANAGEMENT H'CAP (0-75) (3-Y.O+) (Class D) £3,520.00 (£1,045.00: £495.00: £220.00)
6f Stalls: Low GOING minus 0.17 sec per fur (GF) 9-05 (9-07)

12572 **Perfect Brave (56)***(62)*(Fav)*(DRCElsworth)* 4-8-12 MRoberts(2) (hld up: led 1f out: rdn out)— 1
15103 Another Jade **(66)***(70)*(Fav)*(APJarvis)* 5-9-8 TQuinn(4) (hdwy 3f out: ev ch fnl f: r.o)......¾ 2
1483* La Petite Fusee **(70)***(71) (RJO'Sullivan)* 4-9-12 AClark(6) (dwlt: led 3f out to 1f out: unable qckn)......1 3

1411[13] Grand Chapeau (IRE) **(62)***(59) (RHannon)* 3-8-3 (7) DaneO'Neill(7) (rdn 3f out: no hdwy fnl 2f) 1¾ **4**
1483[3] Half Tone **(48)***(40) (RMFlower)* 3-7-10b JQuinn(3) (led over 4f out to 3f out: wknd over 1f out) 1¾ **5**
541[14] Amber Nectar **(39)***(18) (BAPearce)* 9-7-9 ow2 CAvery(5) (outpcd) 4 **6**
1445[7] Nomadic Dancer (IRE) **(52)***(31) (MSSaunders)* 3-8-0 ow2 StephenDavies(8) (hld up: hrd rdn over 2f out: eased whn btn ins fnl f) ....nk **7**
Gallant Spirit (IRE) **(60)***(1) (RJHodges)* 4-8-9 (7) AmandaSanders(1) (led over 1f: wknd 3f out) 15 **8**

LONG HANDICAP Amber Nectar 7-3

11/4 PERFECT BRAVE, Another Jade, **3/1** La Petite Fusee, **11/2** Half Tone (4/1-6/1), **12/1** Grand Chapeau (IRE), **16/1** Nomadic Dancer (IRE), **20/1** Gallant Spirit (IRE), **50/1** Amber Nectar, CSF £10.16 CT £20.64 TOTE £3.80: £1.30 £1.20 £1.40 (£4.20) OWNER Oh So Brave Partnership (WHITCOMBE) BRED R. J. Vines 8 Rn 1m 12.93 (2.73) SF: 43/51/52/32/13/-/4/-

WEIGHT FOR AGE 3yo-8lb

T/Plpt: £12.00 (1,170.31 Tckts). T/Qdpt £3.10 (39.35 Tckts). LMc

1381-SANDOWN (R-H)
Friday June 16th (St Good to firm, Rnd Good, Good to firm patches)

WEATHER: sunny WIND: almost nil

1751

ROSEMARY MAIDEN STKS (2-Y.O) (Class D) £3,501.25 (£1,060.00: £517.50: £246.25) **5f 6y** Stalls: High GOING minus 0.29 sec (GF) 2-15 (2-21)

Warning Time *(91+)*(Fav)*(BJMeehan)* 2-9-0 BDoyle(6) (w'like: hdwy over 2f out: led ins fnl f: rdn out) ....— **1**
1443[3] Shining Cloud *(81) (LGCottrell)* 2-8-9 LDettori(4) (lw: led over 2f: led over 1f out tl ins fnl f: unable qckn) 1½ **2**
Forest Robin *(78) (RFJohnsonHoughton)* 2-9-0 PatEddery(8) (w'like: scope: lw: w ldr: led over 2f out tl over 1f out: one pce) 2½ **3**
1169[4] Rumba Rhythm (CAN) *(70) (JWHills)* 2-8-9 RHills(7) (lw: a.p: rdn over 2f out: one pce) 1 **4**
Oscar Rose *(43) (LordHuntingdon)* 2-9-0 DHarrison(5) (w'like: bit bkwd: s.i.s: a bhd) 10 **5**
996[5] Haute Cuisine *(38) (JBerry)* 2-9-0 GCarter(1) (lw: bhd fnl 3f) 1¾ **6**
Hoodoo (IRE) *(37) (RHannon)* 2-9-0 RPerham(3) (str: bit bkwd: bhd fnl 3f) ....nk **7**

2/1 WARNING TIME, **7/2** Shining Cloud, **4/1** Rumba Rhythm (CAN) (5/2-9/2), **5/1** Forest Robin (2/1-11/2), **12/1** Haute Cuisine, Hoodoo (IRE), **14/1** Oscar Rose (10/1-16/1), CSF £9.04 TOTE £3.80: £2.10 £1.70 (£5.00) OWNER Mr F. C. T. Wilson (UPPER LAMBOURN) BRED F. C. T. Wilson 7 Rn 61.67 secs (1.87) SF: 43/33/30/22/-/-/-

1752

LOGITECH MOUSE MAIDEN STKS (2-Y.O) (Class D) £3,566.25 (£1,080.00: £527.50: £251.25) **7f 16y** Stalls: High GOING: 0.04 sec per fur (G) 2-50 (2-51)

Pommard (IRE) *(83+)*(Fav)*(JHMGosden)* 2-9-0 LDettori(4) (w'like: rdn & hdwy over 2f out: swtchd lft over 1f out: led ins fnl f: r.o wl) ....— **1**
Detachment (USA) *(81) (PWChapple-Hyam)* 2-9-0 BThomson(2) (w'like: scope: lw: hdwy over 5f out: 6th st: led over 1f out tl ins fnl f: unable qckn: bttr for r) ....¾ **2**
Canons Park *(75) (IABalding)* 2-9-0 MHills(3) (w'like: scope: 4th st: ev ch over 1f out: one pce) 3 **3**
1592[2] Navigate (USA) *(74) (RHannon)* 2-9-0 PatEddery(7) (lw: 2nd st: led over 2f out tl over 1f out: one pce) ....hd **4**
Warning Reef *(72) (MRChannon)* 2-9-0 RHughes(8) (w'like: scope: 5th st: rdn over 2f out: 5th & btn whn nt clr run ins fnl f) 1¼ **5**
Star of Ring (IRE) *(71) (MJHeaton-Ellis)* 2-9-0 StephenDavies(1) (str: bit bkwd: dwlt: nvr nr to chal) ....hd **6**
Minsterbeach *(64) (CEBrittain)* 2-9-0 MRoberts(9) (w'like: scope: led over 4f) 3 **7**
1318[7] Young Butt *(62) (JFfitch-Heyes)* 2-9-0 RCochrane(10) (b: 3rd st: wknd over 2f out) 1¼ **8**
Flying Pennant (IRE) *(60) (RHannon)* 2-9-0 RPerham(5) (w'like: bit bkwd: hld up: rdn over 2f out: sn wknd) ....¾ **9**
Influence Pedler *(54) (GRimmer)* 2-9-0 MRimmer(11) (str: scope: dwlt: a bhd) 2½ **10**
Moylough Rebel *(49) (MrsMELong)* 2-9-0 JWilliams(6) (w'like: scope: bit bkwd: bhd fnl 4f) 2½ **11**

7/4 POMMARD (IRE) (5/2-6/4), **11/4** Detachment (USA), **7/2** Navigate (USA), **8/1** Canons Park, **14/1** Warning Reef (10/1-16/1), **16/1** Star of Ring (IRE), Minsterbeach, **25/1** Flying Pennant (IRE), **33/1** Young Butt, Influence Pedler, Moylough Rebel, CSF £7.45 TOTE £2.70: £1.40 £1.50 £2.90 (£6.20) Trio £19.50 OWNER Sheikh Mohammed (NEWMARKET) BRED Kilfrush Stud Ltd 11 Rn

1m 32.39 (5.79) SF: 35/33/27/26/24/23/16/14/12/6/1

1753

CHEQUERS H'CAP (0-100) (3-Y.O+) (Class C) £7,035.00 (£2,130.00: £1,040.00: £495.00) **1m 2f 7y** Stalls: High GOING: 0.04 sec per fur (G) 3-20 (3-20)

918[9] **Special Dawn (IRE) (82)***(90) (JLDunlop)* 5-9-2 PatEddery(3) (lw: 5th st: hrd rdn over 2f out: led 1f out: r.o wl) ....— 1
694[10] Mentor (GR) **(87)***(90) (RCharlton)* 3-8-9 MHills(3) (3rd st: lost pl over 3f out: rallied & swtchd lft over 1f out: r.o ins fnl f) 3 2
1264* Rahy Zoman (USA) **(83)***(86)*(Fav)*(JRFanshawe)* 3-8-5 DHarrison(4) (4th st: rdn 3f out: ev ch 1f out: unable qckn) ....nk 3
793[8] Aeroking (USA) **(82)***(85) (GHarwood)* 4-9-2 AClark(5) (led 9f: one pce) ....s.h 4
1188[6] Green Crusader **(92)***(92) (MRStoute)* 4-9-12v WRSwinburn(2) (lw: 6th st: nvr nr to chal) 2 5
1478[5] Mihriz (IRE) **(81)***(76) (MajorWRHern)* 3-8-3 RHills(1) (lw: 2nd st: rdn over 2f out: wknd fnl f) 3 6

2/1 Rahy Zoman (USA), **9/4** SPECIAL DAWN (IRE), **9/2** Green Crusader, **11/2** Mihriz (IRE), **10/1** Aeroking (USA), **12/1** Mentor (GR) (op 8/1), CSF £23.23 TOTE £2.60: £1.10 £5.20 (£15.50) OWNER Windflower Overseas Holdings Inc (ARUNDEL) BRED Windflower Overseas 6 Rn

2m 8.32 (4.02) SF: 71/59/55/66/73/45
WEIGHT FOR AGE 3yo-12lb

1754

C. GORDON MEDLEN AND SONIA P. COE MEMORIAL H'CAP (0-90) (3-Y.O+) (Class C) £5,550.00 (£1,680.00: £820.00: £390.00) **7f 16y** Stalls: High GOING: 0.04 sec per fur (G) 3-55 (3-55)

1561[3] **Veloce (IRE) (68)***(77)*(Fav)*(ABailey)* 7-8-13v GCarter(5) (b: hdwy over 2f out: led ins fnl f: r.o wl) ....— 1
1474[9] Bon Luck (IRE) **(70)***(78) (RAkehurst)* 3-8-3 (3) SSanders(10) (lw: rdn & hdwy 2f out: r.o wl ins fnl f) ....½ 2
1145[6] Shefoog **(90)***(95)*(Fav)*(RWArmstrong)* 3-9-12 LDettori(1) (lw: 6th st: led over 1f out tl ins fnl f: unable qckn) 1¼ 3
1543[9] Lomas (IRE) **(80)***(84) (MrsHParrott)* 4-9-4 (7) DaneO'Neill(7) (5th st: lost pl over 3f out: nt clr run wl over 1f out: rallied fnl f: r.o) ....½ 4
1383[9] Yosif (IRE) **(58)***(56) (RHannon)* 3-7-8b JQuinn(3) (hdwy over 1f out: nvr nrr) 2½ 5
1130[12] Maiandros (GR) **(84)***(82) (RCharlton)* 3-9-6 DHarrison(8) (swtg: 3rd st: nt clr run over 2f out: one pce) ....s.h 6
1474[4] Warning Shot **(82)***(71) (MartynMeade)* 3-9-4 VSlattery(2) (4th st: hrd rdn over 2f out: wknd over 1f out) 4 7
1531[5] Weather Break **(80)***(65) (HCandy)* 4-9-11 WNewnes(6) (led over 5f) 2 8
1222[10] Jibereen **(89)***(72) (GLewis)* 3-9-11 PatEddery(9) (2nd st: shkn up over 2f out: wkng whn hmpd on ins over 1f out) ....¾ 9
Daswaki (CAN) **(70)***(36) (GLMoore)* 7-8-8 (7)ow1 LSuthern(4) (b: bit bkwd: a wl bhd) 7 10

4/1 VELOCE (IRE), Shefoog, **5/1** Warning Shot (7/2-11/2), Maiandros (GR), **6/1** Weather Break, **8/1** Jibereen (6/1-10/1), **10/1** Bon Luck (IRE) (7/1-12/1), **16/1** Yosif (IRE), **33/1** Lomas (IRE), Daswaki (CAN), CSF £39.99 CT £153.83 TOTE £4.10: £1.80 £4.20 £1.60 (£45.60) Trio £72.70 OWNER Mr Maximo Gonzalez (TARPORLEY) BRED Miss C. O'Toole 10 Rn

1m 30.23 (3.63) SF: 59/51/68/66/29/55/44/47/45/18
WEIGHT FOR AGE 3yo-9lb

1755

JUNE MAIDEN STKS (3-Y.O) (Class D) £3,891.25 (£1,180.00: £577.50: £276.25) **1m 2f 7y** Stalls: High GOING: 0.04 sec per fur (G) 4-30 (4-33)

1308[2] **Hadeyya Ramzeyah** *(87) (ACStewart)* 3-9-0 MRoberts(7) (b: plld hrd: hdwy over 2f out: led ins fnl f: drvn out) ....— 1
1136[4] Nashotah *(82) (JRFanshawe)* 3-8-9 DHarrison(4) (lw: hdwy over 2f out: r.o wl ins fnl f) ....nk 2
Bequeath *(86) (HRACecil)* 3-9-0 PatEddery(12) (w'like: scope: lw: s.s: hdwy over 7f out: 5th st: rdn over 3f out: led wl over 1f out tl ins fnl f: r.o) ....hd 3
824[3] Tilaal (USA) *(81)*(Fav)*(EALDunlop)* 3-9-0 WRSwinburn(10) (lw: led over 8f: unable qckn) ...3½ 4

Star of Persia (IRE) *(80) (PWHarris)* 3-9-0 AClark(9) (bit bkwd: hdwy over 1f out: r.o)............¾ 5
1312⁶ Cuba **(76)***(76) (MRStoute)* 3-9-0 GCarter(6) (2nd st: wknd over 2f out)..................................2½ 6
1473⁷ Red Morning *(67) (DRCElsworth)* 3-8-9 BDoyle(1) (nvr nrr)..2 7
1346³ Dorothea Brooke (IRE) **(89)***(67) (PWHarris)* 3-8-9 RCochrane(8) (4th st: ev ch over 2f out: wknd over 1f out)...½ 8
1526⁸ Pretoria Dancer *(71) (JHMGosden)* 3-9-0 LDettori(11) (3rd st: wknd over 2f out)...................hd 9
1383¹¹ Red Dragon *(71) (GWragg)* 3-9-0 MHills(3) (hdwy 3f out: wknd over 2f out) ....½ 10
1526⁵ Lucky Quest *(61) (NAGraham)* 3-9-0 JWilliams(5) (a bhd)...6 11
Knave of Diamonds *(59) (RJHodges)* 3-8-9 (5) SDrowne(2) (bit bkwd: 6th st: wknd over 3f out) 1½ 12

9/4 Tilaal (USA), **11/4** HADEYYA RAMZEYAH (2/1-3/1), **4/1** Dorothea Brooke (IRE), **13/2** Nashotah, **15/2** Bequeath, **16/1** Cuba, **20/1** Pretoria Dancer, **33/1** Red Morning, Star of Persia (IRE), Red Dragon, Lucky Quest, **66/1** Knave of Diamonds, CSF £21.18 TOTE £3.80: £1.50 £1.80 £2.40 (£15.20) Trio £31.60 OWNER Sheikh Ahmed Al Maktoum (NEWMARKET) BRED Sheikh Ahmed bin Rashid al Maktoum 12 Rn 2m 11.0 (6.70) SF: 48/43/47/42/41/37/28/28/32/32/22/20

1756 MORE LANE CLAIMING STKS (3-Y.O+) (Class F) £2,866.00 (£868.00: £424.00: £202.00)
5f 6y Stalls: High GOING minus 0.29 sec per fur (GF) 5-00 (5-04)

1304* **Lord High Admiral (CAN) (94)***(84+)*(Fav)*(MJHeaton-Ellis)* 7-9-10v MRoberts(2) (lw: mde all: unchal) ....— 1
1248⁵ Gorinsky (IRE) **(80)***(69) (JBerry)* 7-9-3 GCarter(6) (lw: chsd wnr: rdn 2f out: no imp).............2½ 2
1489⁹ Metal Boys **(67)***(61) (MissLCSiddall)* 8-9-0 DHarrison(3) (no hdwy fnl 2f) 1½ 3
1483² Dashing Dancer (IRE) **(55)***(56) (RAkehurst)* 4-9-3 LDettori(4) (lw: no hdwy fnl 2f) 2½ 4
1545* Harry's Coming **(57)***(42) (RJHodges)* 11-8-6 (5) SDrowne(5) (bhd fnl 2f)..................................2½ 5
1546³ Saxon King (IRE) **(42)***(41) (MDIUsher)* 5-9-0 RStreet(1) (b.hind: lw: s.s: sme hdwy 2f out: wknd over 1f out)...1¼ 6
1323²⁰ Storm Bidder **(34)***(20) (BGubby)* 4-8-7b(5) AWhelan(7) (bhd fnl 3f)...6 7

10/11 LORD HIGH ADMIRAL (CAN) (1/2-Evens), **7/2** Gorinsky (IRE), **5/1** Dashing Dancer (IRE) (12/1-9/2), **8/1** Harry's Coming, **12/1** Metal Boys, **16/1** Saxon King (IRE), **50/1** Storm Bidder, CSF £4.74 TOTE £1.90: £1.10 £2.70 (£3.70) OWNER Mr E. J. G. Young (WROUGHTON) BRED Windfields Farm 7 Rn 60.84 secs (1.04) SF: 66/51/43/38/24/23/2

Lord High Admiral (CAN) clmd MBudden (Elite Racing) £15,000. Saxon King (IRE) clmd MissBSanders £5,000.

1757 ESHER PLACE H'CAP (0-70) (4-Y.O+) (Class E) £3,192.50 (£965.00: £470.00: £222.50) **1m 3f 91y** Stalls: High GOING: 0.04 sec per fur (G) 5-35 (5-36)

1368⁵ **Rock The Barney (IRE) (48)***(59) (PBurgoyne)* 6-8-10 (3) DRMcCabe(11) (lw: rdn & hdwy over 2f out: hrd rdn over 1f out: led nr fin) ....— 1
1612¹³ Lunar Risk **(39)***(49) (MissBSanders)* 5-8-1 (3) SSanders(7) (lw: 2nd st: hrd rdn over 1f out: led ins fnl f: hdd nr fin)...½ 2
1502³ Broughtons Formula **(45)***(55) (WJMusson)* 5-8-10 JQuinn(5) (lw: hdwy on ins 1f out: swtchd lft ins fnl f: r.o wl) ....hd 3
1502² Father Dan (IRE) **(47)***(57) (MissGayKelleway)* 6-8-7 (5) SDrowne(3) (lw: 6th st: rdn over 2f out: r.o ins fnl f)...hd 4
1324⁸ No Speeches (IRE) **(57)***(66) (CACyzer)* 4-9-8 MRimmer(1) (4th st: led wl over 1f out tl ins fnl f: unable qckn)...½ 5
1543⁶ Peaches Polly **(62)***(71) (GRimmer)* 5-9-13 MHills(6) (led 10f: one pce) ....nk 6
1367² Bookcase **(60)***(69)*(Fav)*(DRCElsworth)* 8-9-11 JWilliams(4) (lw: hdwy over 1f out: r.o)...........nk 7
1557* Allesca **(65)***(71) (MDIUsher)* 5-9-9 (7) 5x CAdamson(2) (b: nvr nr to chal)...................................1¾ 8
1349⁸ Belgran (USA) **(45)***(51) (WMBrisbourne)* 6-8-5 (5) DGriffiths(8) (lw: 3rd st: wknd over 1f out) ....nk 9
1410⁸ High Five (IRE) **(48)***(50) (DAWilson)* 5-8-13 GCarter(10) (5th st: wknd over 2f out) 2½ 10
1659⁷ Pulmicort **(55)***(46) (PBurgoyne)* 5-9-6b RCochrane(9) (a bhd) 8 11

100/30 Bookcase, **4/1** Father Dan (IRE), **9/2** Broughtons Formula, **5/1** ROCK THE BARNEY (IRE), **6/1** Allesca, **10/1** No Speeches (IRE) (8/1-12/1), **14/1** Peaches Polly, **16/1** Lunar Risk, **20/1** High Five (IRE), **33/1** Pulmicort, **50/1** Belgran (USA), CSF £73.86 CT £356.45 TOTE £7.60: £1.80 £6.90 £1.90 (£84.30) Trio £276.80 OWNER Mrs Satu Marks (WANTAGE) BRED Mrs Mary Travers 11 Rn 2m 30.89 (9.19) SF: 36/26/32/34/43/48/46/48/28/27/23

T/Jkpt: £3,879.70 (1.83 Tckts). T/Plpt: £68.20 (227.56 Tckts). T/Qdpt £15.90 (8.95 Tckts). AK

1566-**SOUTHWELL (L-H)**
Friday June 16th (Standard)
WEATHER: overcast WIND: mod half bhd

1758
RUBY MEDIAN AUCTION MAIDEN STKS (2-Y.O) (Class F) £2,519.00 (£694.00: £329.00) **5f (Fibresand)** Stalls: High GOING minus 0.40 sec (FST) 2-30 (2-31)

1540[12] **Gagajulu** *(66) (PDEvans)* 2-8-9 GHind(6) (chsd ldr: led wl over 1f out: sn clr: v.easily) ....— 1
1454[3] Ebony Boy *(55)*(Fav)*(JWharton)* 2-9-0 AMackay(4) (lw: s.s: swtchd to r centre: hdwy ½-wy: hrd rdn over 1f out: kpt on) 5 2
Paper Maze *(50) (JAHarris)* 2-8-9 SDWilliams(1) (lt-f: unf: bit bkwd: hdwy 2f out: rdn & r.o ins fnl f) ....s.h 3
1356[9] Chillam *(47) (JPLeigh)* 2-9-0 DeanMcKeown(3) (bit bkwd: led over 3f: sn hrd rdn & btn)......2½ 4
1278[9] Magical Midnight *(34) (NTinkler)* 2-8-9 KimTinkler(2) (chsd ldrs: rdn 2f out: one pce) 2½ 5
Time Clash (IRE) *(28) (BPalling)* 2-8-9 TSprake(8) (unf: scope: outpcd: rdn ½-wy: no imp) .1¾ 6
L A Touch *(19) (JohnBerry)* 2-8-9 CDwyer(7) (w'like: bkwd: s.s: a bhd) 3 7
Lawnswood Captain (IRE) *(RHollinshead)* 2-9-0 TIves(5) (neat: bit bkwd: sn wl outpcd & t.o) 8 8

7/4 Ebony Boy, **100/30** GAGAJULU, **11/2** Time Clash (IRE) (7/2-6/1), **7/1** Chillam, **8/1** Paper Maze, **10/1** Lawnswood Captain (IRE), **14/1** L A Touch, **25/1** Magical Midnight, CSF £9.48 TOTE £4.10: £1.50 £1.40 £2.00 (£4.10) OWNER Mr R. F. F. Mason (WELSHPOOL) BRED Mrs P. E. Bell 8 Rn
60.1 secs (2.10) SF: 24/13/8/5/-/-/-/-

1759
DIAMOND CLAIMING STKS (4-Y.O+) (Class F) £2,519.00 (£694.00: £329.00) **1m 6f (Fibresand)** Stalls: High GOING: 0.03 sec per fur (STD) 3-05 (3-07)

1567[3] **Who's the Best (IRE) (34)***(56) (APJarvis)* 5-8-6 (3) DWright(5) (a gng wl: hld up: hdwy & 3rd st: led bel dist: pushed clr) ....— 1
1332[7] Scalp 'em (IRE) **(45)***(45)*(Fav)*(PDEvans)* 7-8-7 GHind(2) (led tl hdd & wknd bel dist)...............8 2
1449* Reach for Glory **(37)***(44) (WGMTurner)* 6-8-9 TIves(8) (hld up: hdwy 6f out: hrd rdn & 4th st: kpt on one pce).........2½ 3
375[8] Rose of Glenn **(47)***(31) (BPalling)* 4-8-6 TSprake(1) (prom tl outpcd 5f out: 6th st: no imp) 9 4
1198[13] Perfect Ending **(55)***(45) (CACyzer)* 4-9-7 DeanMcKeown(6) (lw: s.s: sn rcvrd to chse ldrs: rdn 5f out: 5th & wknd st).........nk 5
1622[16] Maraady (USA) **(28)***(30) (GPEnright)* 6-8-7v NAdams(9) (b: hdwy ½-wy: 2nd & rdn st: sn wknd).........1 6
1427[4] Ann Hill (IRE) **(29)** *(RHollinshead)* 5-7-11 (3) AGarth(3) (lw: a bhd: t.o).........dist 7
1555[9] Vayello **(43)** *(CSmith)* 4-8-5 DaleGibson(4) (bit bkwd: lost pl after 6f: sn t.o).........20 8

2/1 Scalp 'em (IRE), **5/1** WHO'S THE BEST (IRE), Reach for Glory, **7/1** Rose of Glenn (op 4/1), Perfect Ending, **10/1** Ann Hill (IRE), **14/1** Vayello, **20/1** Maraady (USA), CSF £14.34 TOTE £9.60: £1.50 £1.70 £1.50 (£6.40) Trio £10.80 OWNER Mrs Ann Jarvis (ASTON UPTHORPE) BRED F. Feeney 8 Rn
3m 12.6 (12.90) SF: 25/14/13/-/14/-/-/-

1760
LANGLEY MECHANICAL SERVICES H'CAP (0-65) (3-Y.O+) (Class F) £3,023.00 (£838.00: £401.00)
7f (Fibresand) Stalls: Low GOING: 0.03 sec per fur (STD) 3-35 (3-41)

1571[6] **Wellsy Lad (USA) (37)***(45) (DWChapman)* 8-8-6 DeanMcKeown(9) (lw: w ldr: led 4f out: clr fnl f: comf).........— 1
*1571** What a Nightmare (IRE) **(65)***(65) (JAGlover)* 3-9-11b 6x TIves(8) (w ldrs: 2nd st: rdn over 1f out: one pce).........3½ 2
*1457** Flashfeet **(57)***(56) (KBishop)* 5-9-12 MWigham(4) (s.i.s: effrt & rdn bel dist: r.o wl fnl f).........nk 3
1409[5] Dom Pennion **(59)***(56)*(Fav)*(RGuest)* 4-9-7 (7) CWebb(5) (s.i.s: hdwy ½-wy: rdn 2f out: kpt on).........1¼ 4
1649[7] Just Flamenco **(50)***(46) (MJRyan)* 4-9-5 DBiggs(3) (lw: hdwy & 4th st: hrd rdn 2f out: unable qckn).........nk 5
1516[6] Quinzii Martin **(56)***(51) (DHaydnJones)* 7-9-11 AMackay(11) (chsd ldrs: 6th st: sn rdn: r.o one pce).........nk 6
1371[6] Joyful Times **(41)***(35) (MrsNMacauley)* 3-8-1 ClaireBalding(2) (nvr trbld ldrs).........nk 7
314[7] Swinging Tich **(45)***(34) (ALForbes)* 6-9-0 SDWilliams(10) (b: s.s: a in rr).........2½ 8
1527[10] Komiamaite **(60)***(40) (SRBowring)* 3-9-1b(5) CTeague(7) (chsd ldrs: poor 5th & wkng st)..........4 9
1469[8] Pc's Cruiser (IRE) **(56)***(24) (MCChapman)* 3-9-2 DaleGibson(1) (a bhd: t.o).........5 10
1582[7] Tyrone Flyer **(56)***(20) (GFierro)* 6-9-4b(7) GFaulkner(6) (led 3f: 3rd & rdn st: sn lost tch).........2 11

4/1 Dom Pennion, **6/1** What a Nightmare (IRE), Just Flamenco, **13/2** Flashfeet, **8/1** Pc's Cruiser (IRE), **9/1** Quinzii Martin, **10/1** WELLSY LAD (USA), Tyrone Flyer, **12/1** Komiamaite, Joyful Times (op 8/1), **20/1** Swinging Tich, CSF £64.90 CT £387.48 TOTE £8.90: £2.70 £1.80 £2.80 (£17.40) Trio £38.70 OWNER Mr J. M. Chapman (YORK) BRED Mrs. Helen K. Groves 11 Rn

1m 33.5 (6.70) SF: 17/28/28/28/18/23/-/6/3/-/-
WEIGHT FOR AGE 3yo-9lb

1761

LATHAM (MIDLAND)/CABERBOARD MEDIAN AUCTION MAIDEN STKS (3-Y.O) (Class E) £3,245.00 (£968.00: £462.00: £209.00)
1m (Fibresand) Stalls: Low GOING: 0.03 sec per fur (STD) 4-05 (4-05)

747[5] **Oneoftheoldones (78)***(66)*(Fav)*(SGNorton)* 3-9-0 CDwyer(9) (mde all: rdn over 1f out: kpt on gamely) ....— 1
1514[7] Nessun Doro *(65) (SMellor)* 3-9-0 MWigham(7) (a.p: 2nd st: jnd wnr wl over 1f out: no ex fnl f) ....¾ 2
1353[10] Call Me Flash **(45)***(25) (MrsPSly)* 3-9-0 ACulhane(5) (hld up in tch: 5th & rdn st: sn outpcd)..20 3
1330[8] Campaspe *(19) (JGFitzGerald)* 3-8-9 FNorton(6) (lw: hld up: sme hdwy fnl 2f: nvr nrr)..........hd 4
Rock Scene (IRE) *(18) (RHollinshead)* 3-9-0 TIves(2) (lt-f: unf: dwlt: sn chsng ldrs: 3rd st: wknd 2f out) 3 5
844[5] Halfabob (IRE) *(16) (DHaydnJones)* 3-9-0 AMackay(1) (prom: rdn 3f out: 4th st: sn btn).........1 6
1186[16] Truly Madly Deeply *(1) (MrsJRRamsden)* 3-8-9 TGMcLaughlin(8) (b.off hind: nvr trbld ldrs) ...5 7
300[4] Call Tophorse *(PCHaslam)* 3-9-0 DeanMcKeown(4) (bit bkwd: nvr plcd to chal: t.o)..............8 8
Gifted *(DonEnricoIncisa)* 3-8-9 KimTinkler(3) (dwlt: a bhd: t.o) 8 9

4/5 ONEOFTHEOLDONES, **4/1** Nessun Doro (3/1-9/2), **9/1** Call Tophorse, Truly Madly Deeply (op 4/1), Rock Scene (IRE), **20/1** Halfabob (IRE), Campaspe, Gifted, **25/1** Call Me Flash, CSF £4.99 TOTE £1.80: £1.30 £1.50 £4.90 (£3.40) Trio £40.30 OWNER Mr R. Baker (BARNSLEY) BRED Miss E. Drax 9 Rn 1m 45.6 (6.30) SF: 38/37/-/-/-/-/-/-/-

1762

PEARL (S) H'CAP (0-60) (3-Y.O+) (Class G) £2,243.00 (£618.00: £293.00)
1m (Fibresand) Stalls: Low GOING: 0.03 sec per fur (STD) 4-35 (4-36)

1523[4] **Puffy (40)***(52) (MDods)* 8-9-0v DaleGibson(12) (b: hdwy & 5th st: led ins fnl f: drvn clr) ....— 1
1523[13] Big Chance **(33)***(37)*(Fav)*(WJMusson)* 6-8-7 TIves(7) (a.p: 4th st: rdn over 1f out: kpt on) 4 2
1499[9] Titanium Honda (IRE) **(46)***(49) (CEBrittain)* 4-9-6 EmmaO'Gorman(13) (a.p: led 3f out tl ins fnl f: no ex) ....nk 3
1548[5] Calisar **(37)***(30) (PHowling)* 5-8-8 (3) DWright(14) (hdwy over 2f out: nvr nrr) 5 4
1463[3] Mudlark **(45)***(34)*(Fav)*(JWWatts)* 3-8-9b MWigham(11) (dwlt: hdwy fnl 2f: nvr nrr).......2 5
1568[7] Mr Moriarty (IRE) **(28)***(16) (SRBowring)* 4-8-2b NKennedy(5) (prom: 3rd st: rdn & wknd over 1f out) ....½ 6
254[5] Not for Sale **(35)***(13) (JWharton)* 4-8-4b(5) CTeague(8) (bkwd: s.s: nvr nrr) 5 7
1285[13] Swynford Flyer **(36)***(2) (JAHarris)* 6-8-10 DBiggs(3) (nvr rchd ldrs) 6 8
1458[3] Mezzoramio **(51)***(17) (KAMorgan)* 3-9-1v DeanMcKeown(16) (b: led after 2f: hdd & 2nd st: sn rdn & wknd) ....nk 9
444[14] Death by Chocolate **(48)***(12) (ALForbes)* 3-8-12 SDWilliams(6) (bkwd: a in rr) ....¾ 10
Wesshaun **(27)** *(WGMTurner)* 5-8-1 TSprake(2) (bit bkwd: chsd ldrs 5f: rdn & wknd fnl 2f) ....½ 11
628[3] Torrey Pines (IRE) **(44)***(5) (DHaydnJones)* 3-8-8 AMackay(10) (prom tl 6th & wkng st).........1¼ 12
1571[12] Aldwick Colonnade **(53)***(12) (MDIUsher)* 8-9-13 RPrice(9) (b.off hind: a in rr) ....¾ 13
Reigning Royal **(40)** *(DBurchell)* 4-9-0 FNorton(4) (led 2f: sn lost pl: t.o) 1½ 14
626[7] Hunza Story **(38)** *(NPLittmoden)* 3-8-2 TGMcLaughlin(1) (chsd ldrs to ½-wy: sn wknd: t.o).....3 15
1559[6] Takeapull **(55)** *(JBalding)* 3-8-12 (7) JEdmunds(15) (chsd ldrs 4f: sn lost tch: t.o) 5 16

11/2 Big Chance, Mudlark, **13/2** PUFFY, **8/1** Swynford Flyer, **9/1** Titanium Honda (IRE), **10/1** Calisar, Mezzoramio, **12/1** Torrey Pines (IRE), Hunza Story, **14/1** Death by Chocolate, **16/1** Takeapull, Mr Moriarty (IRE), **20/1** Reigning Royal, Aldwick Colonnade, **25/1** Not for Sale, **33/1** Wesshaun, CSF £42.58 CT £309.49 TOTE £7.50: £1.80 £2.90 £2.40 £2.10 (£28.40) Trio £92.30 OWNER Mr A. G. Watson (DARLINGTON) BRED G. P. Griffin 16 Rn

1m 46.7 (7.40) SF: 27/12/24/5/-/-/-/-/-/-/-/-/-/-/-/-
WEIGHT FOR AGE 3yo-10lb
No bid

1763

EMERALD H'CAP (0-65) (3-Y.O+) (Class F) £2,519.00 (£694.00: £329.00)
5f (Fibresand) Stalls: High GOING minus 0.40 sec per fur (FST) 5-10 (5-10)

1566[4] **Sing With the Band (63)***(71) (BAMcMahon)* 4-9-13 FNorton(12) (led stands' side: rdn to ld over 1f out: edgd lft fnl f: r.o strly) ....— 1
1331[9] Most Uppitty **(54)***(57) (JBerry)* 3-8-4 (7) JoanneWebster(6) (chsd ldrs: rdn 2f out: r.o wl fnl f) 1½ 2

1499[18] Grey Toppa **(39)***(41) (NPLittmoden)* 4-8-3 TGMcLaughlin(11) (chsd ldrs: rdn 2f out: kpt on wl ins fnl f)........½ 3
1510[11] Malibu Man **(57)***(55) (SMellor)* 3-9-0 TSprake(10) (a.p: rdn 1f out: nt pce of ldrs)........1¼ 4
1566[2] Chadwell Hall **(60)***(57)*(Fav)*(SRBowring)* 4-9-5b(5) CTeague(13) (b.off hind: a.p stands' side: rdn & wknd fnl f)........hd 5
1538[10] Tommy Tempest **(33)***(29) (REPeacock)* 6-7-11b DaleGibson(1) (led far side over 3f: wknd fnl f)........½ 6
233[13] Arc Lamp **(50)***(45) (JAGlover)* 9-9-0 SDWilliams(3) (bit bkwd: chsd ldrs: no hdwy fnl f)........hd 7
1599[9] Cheerful Groom (IRE) **(41)***(24) (JMackie)* 4-8-5 EJohnson(5) (in tch over 3f)........4 8
1377[11] Cheeky Chappy **(38)***(15) (DWChapman)* 4-7-9b(7) JBramhill(8) (a bhd)........1¾ 9
1515[8] Vengan **(47)***(22) (DHaydnJones)* 3-8-1 (3) DWright(4) (bit bkwd: early spd: sn lost pl)........¾ 10
1377[14] Younger Days (IRE) **(39)***(9) (MartynWane)* 4-8-3 ow1 ACulhane(2) (lw: chsd ldrs 3f)........1¼ 11
1279[13] Oneineverycolour **(38)***(5) (PDEvans)* 3-7-9 NAdams(7) (a bhd & outpcd)........1 12
1550[3] Annie Fay (IRE) **(55)***(19) (JLHarris)* 3-8-12 RPrice(9) (lw: a in rr: eased over 1f out)........1 13
1546[12] Come on Winn **(37)** *(MissSJWilton)* 3-7-8 ow1 NKennedy(14) (swvd & uns rdr s)........ U

LONG HANDICAP Come on Winn 7-6

2/1 Chadwell Hall (op 3/1), **5/1** Annie Fay (IRE), **7/1** SING WITH THE BAND, **10/1** Arc Lamp, **14/1** Most Uppitty, Cheeky Chappy, Tommy Tempest, **16/1** Vengan, Oneineverycolour, **20/1** Cheerful Groom (IRE), Younger Days (IRE), Grey Toppa, **25/1** Malibu Man, **33/1** Come on Winn, CSF £92.63 CT £1,709.43 TOTE £6.80: £1.80 £4.20 £3.00 (£62.90) Trio £307.70 OWNER Mr D. J. Allen (TAMWORTH) BRED D. J. Allen 14 Rn 59.3 secs (1.30) SF: 54/33/24/31/40/12/28/7/-/-/-/-/-
WEIGHT FOR AGE 3yo-7lb

T/Plpt: £22.30 (355.01 Tckts). T/Qdpt £10.20 (3 Tckts). IM

1129-YORK (L-H)
Friday June 16th (Good to firm, Good patches)
WEATHER: fine WIND: fresh half against

1764
MARKETING WEEK MAIDEN STKS (3-Y.O) (Class D) £4,425.00 (£1,320.00: £630.00: £285.00)
1m 3f 195y Stalls: Low GOING minus 0.32 sec per fur (GF) 2-10 (2-10)

691[12] **Corradini** *(90) (HRACecil)* 3-9-0 WRyan(1) (lw: chsd ldrs: pushed along 5f out: hdwy u.p 2f out: styd on wl to ld ins fnl f)........— 1
1490[4] Crystal Blade **(87)***(85) (IABalding)* 3-9-0 KDarley(5) (led & sn clr: drvn along over 3f out: wknd & hdd ins fnl f)........3½ 2
Honfleur (IRE) *(79)*(Fav)*(PWChapple-Hyam)* 3-8-9 JReid(3) (rangy: scope: lw: pushed along 5f out: drvn along & outpcd over 2f out: styd on fnl f)........1 3
691[6] Taklif (IRE) **(93)***(81) (BWHills)* 3-9-0 WCarson(4) (lw: chsd ldr: effrt over 3f out: sn hrd rdn & hung lft: one pce appr fnl f: saddle slipped & eased towards fin)........2 4
Vanola *(49) (PHowling)* 3-8-9 PaulEddery(2) (dwlt s: a last: drvn along 6f out: sn wl outpcd & lost tch)........20 5

13/8 Honfleur (IRE), **7/4** Taklif (IRE), **3/1** Crystal Blade (op 5/1), **9/1** CORRADINI, **50/1** Vanola, CSF £32.20 TOTE £8.90: £2.30 £1.60 (£10.10) OWNER Mr K. Abdullah (NEWMARKET) BRED Juddmonte Farms 5 Rn 2m 29.3 (2.30) SF: 57/52/46/48/16

OFFICIAL EXPLANATION Taklif (IRE): the jockey stated that the horse had been off the bit a long way out and, after hanging towards the rail, the colt's saddle slipped. Therefore he stopped riding.

1765
WILLIAM HILL STKS H'CAP (0-100) (3-Y.O+) (Class C) £8,025.00 (£2,400.00: £1,150.00: £525.00)
5f Stalls: High GOING minus 0.32 sec per fur (GF) 2-40 (2-41)

1489[2] **Saint Express (94)***(106) (MrsMReveley)* 5-10-0 KDarley(4) (lw: chsd ldr far side: led over 1f out: hld on wl)........— 1
1271[9] Benzoe (IRE) **(77)***(87) (MrsJRRamsden)* 5-8-11 KFallon(2) (reard s: racd far side: gd hdwy over 2f out: r.o u.p fnl f)........½ 2
1668[5] Elle Shaped (IRE) **(70)***(72) (DNicholls)* 5-8-4 7x AlexGreaves(10) (s.i.s: bhd: hdwy over 2f out: r.o wl fnl f)........2½ 3
1489[4] Name the Tune **(76)***(78) (PHowling)* 4-8-10 PaulEddery(6) (b.hind: racd far side: chsd ldrs: rdn over 2f out: kpt on same pce)........hd 4
1316[7] Sea-Deer **(90)***(91)*(Fav)*(LJHolt)* 6-9-10 AMcGlone(1) (in tch far side: rdn & outpcd over 2f out: styd on ins fnl f)........nk 5
1508[9] Hickory Blue **(71)***(71) (MrsNMacauley)* 5-7-12v(7) AmandaSanders(7) (racd centre: sn chsng ldrs: edgd rt ½-wy: nt qckn appr fnl f)........½ 6
1106[15] Magic Pearl **(77)***(76) (EJAlston)* 5-8-11 DHolland(8) (sltly hmpd s: bhd: swtchd lft & hdwy 1f out: styd on)........nk 7

1595² Lady Sheriff **(59)**_(57) (MWEasterby)_ 4-7-7b 7x GBardwell(11) (lw: chsd ldrs stands' side: rdn over 2f out: one pce) ....s.h **8**
1376² Allwight Then (IRE) **(73)**_(69) (FHLee)_ 4-8-7 JWeaver(3) (led far side: hdd over 1f out: sn wknd) ....¾ **9**
1508⁷ Tenor **(64)**_(60) (DNicholls)_ 4-7-12b CRutter(5) (racd far side: sn outpcd & bhd) ....hd **10**
1637⁷ Ashtina **(93)**_(86) (RJHodges)_ 10-9-13 JReid(12) (led stands' side tl wknd over 1f out) ....¾ **11**
1488⁸ Crofters Ceilidh **(96)**_(84) (BAMcMahon)_ 3-9-9 TQuinn(13) (chsd ldrs: rdn 2f out: sn wknd) ...1¾ **12**
1489⁶ Call Me I'm Blue (IRE) **(91)**_(76) (NTinkler)_ 5-9-11b WCarson(9) (swvd lft s: a bhd) ....¾ **13**

LONG HANDICAP Lady Sheriff 6-13

11/2 Sea-Deer, **6/1** Lady Sheriff, **7/1** Allwight Then (IRE), SAINT EXPRESS, **8/1** Elle Shaped (IRE), **9/1** Name the Tune, Call Me I'm Blue (IRE), Benzoe (IRE), **10/1** Tenor, **14/1** Magic Pearl, Ashtina, **20/1** Crofters Ceilidh, **25/1** Hickory Blue, CSF £65.94 CT £479.30 TOTE £7.30: £2.90 £4.60 £3.20 (£63.60) Trio £216.90 OWNER Mr D. S. Hall (SALTBURN) BRED R. M. Whitaker 13 Rn

58.01 secs (1.01) SF: 66/47/32/38/51/31/36/17/29/20/46/37/36

WEIGHT FOR AGE 3yo-7lb

1766

INNOVATIVE MARKETING SPRINT RATED STKS H'CAP (0-100) (3-Y.O+)
(Class B) £13,325.60 (£4,930.40: £2,365.20: £966.00: £383.00: £149.80)
6f Stalls: High GOING minus 0.32 sec per fur (GF) 3-10 (3-10)

1305⁶ **Cheyenne Spirit (91)**_(100) (BHanbury)_ 3-8-4 WCarson(2) (mde all: styd on wl appr fnl f: drvn out) ....— **1**
1066* Daring Destiny **(99)**_(105)_(Fav)_(KRBurke)_ 4-9-3 (3) JTate(10) (swtg: hld up: smooth hdwy over 2f out: ev ch 1f out: nt qckn) 1 **2**
1480⁵ Master Planner **(100)**_(104) (CACyzer)_ 6-9-7 KDarley(6) (lw: chsd ldrs: rdn over 2f out: kpt on wl fnl f) 1 **3**
1489* Princess Oberon (IRE) **(86)**_(89) (MBell)_ 5-8-7 MFenton(9) (a chsng ldrs: kpt on same pce appr fnl f) ....hd **4**
1637⁶ Jayannpee **(98)**_(95) (IABalding)_ 4-9-5 WRyan(3) (s.s: bhd tl styd on fnl 2f) 2½ **5**
1537² How's Yer Father **(86)**_(82) (RJHodges)_ 9-8-7 JReid(7) (hdwy ½-wy: sn drvn along: nvr nr to chal) ....nk **6**
1220* Ziggy's Dancer (USA) **(92)**_(84) (EJAlston)_ 4-8-13 KFallon(8) (lw: hld up: hdwy over 2f out: rdn & wknd over 1f out) 1½ **7**
1614⁸ Domulla **(90)**_(74) (RAkehurst)_ 5-8-11 TQuinn(4) (chsd ldrs: rdn over 2f out: wknd wl over 1f out) 3 **8**
1100⁶ Amron **(89)**_(60) (JBerry)_ 8-8-10 NCarlisle(1) (swtg: s.i.s: a bhd: lost tch ½-wy) 5 **9**
1488⁹ Croeso-I-Cymru **(92)**_(56) (BAMcMahon)_ 4-8-13 JFortune(5) (chsd ldrs tl rdn & lost pl ½-wy) 2½ **10**

LONG HANDICAP How's Yer Father 8-3

5/1 Daring Destiny, **11/2** Ziggy's Dancer (USA), **6/1** Master Planner, Princess Oberon (IRE), **7/1** Domulla, How's Yer Father, **8/1** CHEYENNE SPIRIT, Jayannpee, **10/1** Amron, **16/1** Croeso-I-Cymru, CSF £46.27 CT £239.18 TOTE £10.60: £2.40 £2.00 £2.40 (£28.80) Trio £45.20 OWNER Mr C. Mauritzon (NEWMARKET) BRED J. McGarry 10 Rn

1m 10.7 (1.10) SF: 46/59/58/43/49/36/38/28/14/10

WEIGHT FOR AGE 3yo-8lb

1767

SHEPHERD CONSTRUCTION STKS APPRENTICE H'CAP (0-90) (4-Y.O+)
(Class E) £4,935.00 (£1,470.00: £700.00: £315.00)
1m 3f 195y Stalls: Low GOING minus 0.32 sec per fur (GF) 3-40 (3-40)

1622⁵ **Augustan (60)**_(71) (SGollings)_ 4-8-10 VHalliday(6) (dwlt: drvn along 5f out: hdwy to chse ldr over 2f out: led over 1f out: hld on wl) ....— **1**
1416* Highflying **(78)**_(89)_(Fav)_(GMMoore)_ 9-9-11 (3) ADaly(4) (lw: led: drvn clr over 3f out: hdd over 1f out: kpt on wl) ....nk **2**
1417⁷ Sugar Mill **(62)**_(68) (MrsMReveley)_ 5-8-12 GParkin(3) (trckd ldrs: effrt over 3f out: swtchd outside over 1f out: kpt on same pce) 3½ **3**
1616⁵ Redstella (USA) **(72)**_(69) (RMWhitaker)_ 6-9-8 PRoberts(5) (sn pushed along: chsd ldrs tl lost pl 6f out: edgd lft & styd on fnl 2f) 7 **4**
967⁶ Thaleros **(59)**_(51) (GMMoore)_ 5-8-9 SCopp(7) (chsd ldrs tl wknd over 2f out) 3 **5**
1435⁹ Strictly Personal (USA) **(60)**_(46) (MABarnes)_ 5-8-7 (3) GMitchell(1) (prom tl wknd over 3f out) 5 **6**
1303³ Blue Blazer **(78)**_(54) (BHanbury)_ 5-9-11 (3) PBowe(2) (hld up: hdwy & pushed along 6f out: lost pl over 4f out: sn bhd) 7 **7**

11/8 Highflying, **7/2** Sugar Mill (op 9/4), **4/1** Blue Blazer, **7/1** Redstella (USA), **12/1** Thaleros, **14/1** AUGUSTAN, **20/1** Strictly Personal (USA), CSF £33.06 TOTE £17.40: £4.30 £1.70 (£17.00) OWNER Mr Nilesh Unadkat (LOUTH) BRED Someries Stud 7 Rn

2m 30.12 (3.12) SF: 48/66/45/46/28/23/31

1768 WESTMINSTER TAXI INSURANCE RATED STKS H'CAP (0-95) (4-Y.O+)
(Class C) £7,790.04 (£2,880.36: £1,380.18: £561.90: £220.95: £84.57)
1m 5f 194y Stalls: Low GOING minus 0.32 sec per fur (GF) 4-10 (4-11)

1585⁵ **Wishing (USA) (92)***(105) (RAkehurst)* 4-9-4 TQuinn(6) (lw: mde virtually all: pushed along over 4f out: styd on wl u.p fnl 2f)........— 1
1135³ Arctic Thunder (USA) **(95)***(105)*(Fav)*(LadyHerries)* 4-9-7 KDarley(2) (b: hld up: effrt & chsd wnr over 3f out: kpt on same pce fnl 2f: no imp)........2½ 2
1462⁴ George Dillingham **(83)***(93) (DenysSmith)* 5-8-9 JFortune(1) (hld up: smooth hdwy on outside over 3f out: sn outpcd: n.d after)........½ 3
Lombardic (USA) **(87)***(96) (MrsJCecil)* 4-8-13 JReid(4) (trckd ldrs: effrt over 2f out: r.o same pce)........¾ 4
1313⁴ Blaze Away (USA) **(81)***(89) (IABalding)* 4-8-7 WCarson(7) (trckd ldrs: drvn along & outpcd over 4f out: kpt on fnl 2f)........¾ 5
1300* Trans Siberia **(81)***(87)*(Fav)*(SPCWoods)* 4-8-7 WRyan(3) (dwlt: sn w wnr: drvn along over 3f out: sn outpcd: n.d after)........1¼ 6
1558⁵ Star Rage (IRE) **(81)***(87) (MJohnston)* 5-8-7 DHolland(5) (hld up: hdwy on ins over 2f out: nt clr run over 1f out & ins fnl f: nt rcvr)........¾ 7

LONG HANDICAP Blaze Away (USA) 8-5 Star Rage (IRE) 8-3

9/4 Arctic Thunder (USA), Trans Siberia, **11/2** WISHING (USA), **7/1** Blaze Away (USA), **8/1** Lombardic (USA), George Dillingham, Star Rage (IRE), CSF £18.81 TOTE £7.10: £2.70 £2.30 (£9.40) OWNER Mr A. D. Spence (EPSOM) BRED C. L. Kidder & N. L. Kidder 7 Rn
2m 57.07 (3.47) SF: 57/57/45/48/41/39/39

OFFICIAL EXPLANATION Star Rage (IRE): his jockey was forced to ease because, when wanting to make ground up the rail, he found no room and also caught the heels of Arctic Thunder.

1769 UNIVERSITY OF YORK ATHLETIC UNION CONDITIONS STKS (2-Y.O F)
(Class C) £5,251.50 (£1,674.00: £799.50)
6f Stalls: High GOING minus 0.32 sec per fur (GF) 4-45 (4-45)

1169* **Amazing Bay** *(86)*(Fav)*(IABalding)* 2-9-0 WRyan(2) (lw: trckd ldr: plld hrd: led over 2f out: pushed out: hld on wl towards fin)........— 1
1253* Like A Hawk (USA) *(85) (PFICole)* 2-9-0 TQuinn(1) (dwlt: sn drvn along: hdwy & hrd rdn over 1f out: kpt on wl)........nk 2
1530⁶ Royal Ceilidh (IRE) *(69) (DenysSmith)* 2-9-0 JFortune(3) (led tl over 2f out: wknd 1f out: eased)........6 3

4/7 AMAZING BAY, **2/1** Like A Hawk (USA) (6/4-9/4), **8/1** Royal Ceilidh (IRE) (op 5/1), CSF £1.94 TOTE £1.50 (£1.70) OWNER Mr J. C. Smith (KINGSCLERE) BRED R. G. Percival 3 Rn
1m 13.4 (3.80) SF: 18/17/1

1770 LEVY BOARD MAIDEN STKS (3-Y.O) (Class D) £4,241.80 (£1,174.80: £561.40)
1m 2f 85y Stalls: Low GOING minus 0.32 sec per fur (GF) 5-20 (5-20)

663⁹ **San Pietra (IRE)** *(76) (PWChapple-Hyam)* 3-8-9 JReid(1) (hld up: hdwy 4f out: edgd rt & led over 1f out: drvn out)........— 1
1383³ Yarrow (IRE) *(80)*(Fav)*(JHMGosden)* 3-9-0 GHind(2) (lw: led: hung rt & hdd over 1f out: nt qckn towards fin)........½ 2
1473³ Rosy Hue (IRE) *(54d) (RCharlton)* 3-8-9 JWeaver(3) (trckd ldr: rn wd ent st: sn rdn: ev ch 3f out: sn wknd & eased)........14 3

11/10 Yarrow (IRE) (Evens-6/4), **2/1** Rosy Hue (IRE), **11/4** SAN PIETRA (IRE) (2/1-3/1), CSF £5.53 TOTE £3.20 (£2.50) OWNER Mr R. E. Sangster (MARLBOROUGH) BRED Swettenham Stud 3 Rn
2m 13.57 (6.07) SF: 21/25/-
T/Plpt: £295.30 (77.59 Tckts). T/Qdpt: £12.00 (13.65 Tckts). WG

1442-BATH (L-H)
Saturday June 17th (Good to firm)
WEATHER: cloudy WIND: slt against

1771 JUNE (S) STKS (3 & & 5-Y.O) (Class G) £2,647.00 (£742.00: £361.00)
1m 2f 46y GOING: minus 0.43 sec per fur (F) 2-00 (2-04)

1509⁶ **Spitfire Bridge (IRE) (46)***(60) (MMcCormack)* 3-8-7 BThomson(2) (4th st: led 3f out: clr over 1f out: rdn out)........— 1
1422² Tropical Jungle (USA) **(55)***(60)*(Fav)*(PJMakin)* 5-9-10b TQuinn(10) (6th st: chsd wnr over 1f out: no imp)........3½ 2

1427[7] Sharp Gazelle **(38)***(54) (BSmart)* 5-8-12 (7) ADaly(7) (5th st: r.o one pce fnl 2f) ....s.h **3**
1638[11] Stately Home (IRE) **(65)***(52) (BRMillman)* 4-9-5 JWilliams(18) (hdwy fnl 2f: nvr nrr) 1¾ **4**
1625[5] Try Omnipotent *(45) (CNAllen)* 3-8-7 PRobinson(11) (7th st: no hdwy fnl 2f) 4 **5**
Sharp Spring *(45) (JWhite)* 4-9-5 AClark(15) (no hdwy fnl 2f) ....nk **6**
1446[10] Coastguards Haven *(37) (MJBolton)* 3-8-4 (5)ow2 JDSmith(4) (nvr nr to chal) 5 **7**
1501[2] Zahran (IRE) **(54)***(38) (JMBradley)* 4-9-5 (5) SDrowne(13) (no hdwy fnl 3f) 2½ **8**
Smooth Hound *(32) (MCPipe)* 4-9-5b PaulEddery(14) (led over 9f)..¾ **9**
1125[17] Chase the Melody *(21) (MJHeaton-Ellis)* 3-8-4 (3) SSanders(16) (n.d) 7 **10**
Old Master (IRE) *(19) (RJBaker)* 4-9-5 BPowell(17) (prom 6f)..1¼ **11**
1545[10] Tapping Feet **(41)***(14) (DMHyde)* 3-8-2v NAdams(5) (a bhd)..nk **12**
Wharfedale Music **(42)***(13) (MCPipe)* 4-9-0 RHughes(12) (3rd st: wknd over 2f out) ....½ **13**
1659[5] Esthal (IRE) **(48)***(22) (ABarrow)* 5-9-5v(5) NVarley(8) (2nd st: wknd over 2f out) ....nk **14**
958[7] Miss Gruntled **(47)** *(DJSffrenchDavis)* 4-8-9b(5) RPainter(6) (t.o) 15 **15**
Pats Folly *(FJYardley)* 4-8-7 (7) PRoberts(1) (t.o)..2 **16**
Rita's Sofa **(20)** *(MrsAEJermy)* 4-8-7 (7) PRoberts(3) (bhd fnl 3f: t.o) ....dist **17**

7/4 Tropical Jungle (USA), **7/1** Stately Home (IRE), Zahran (IRE), Try Omnipotent (5/1-8/1), **9/1** Sharp Spring, **12/1** Wharfedale Music (op 8/1), **14/1** SPITFIRE BRIDGE (IRE), Smooth Hound (op 8/1), **16/1** Sharp Gazelle, **25/1** Esthal (IRE), **40/1** Miss Gruntled, Old Master (IRE), **50/1** Chase the Melody, Coastguards Haven, **66/1** Tapping Feet, **100/1** Pats Folly, Rita's Sofa, CSF £36.98 TOTE £11.70: £2.70 £1.40 £5.50 (£8.20) Trio £33.10 OWNER East Manton Racing Stables Ltd (WANTAGE) BRED John Harrington 17 Rn No Time Taken SF: -/-/-/-/-/-/-/-/-/-/-/-/-/-/-/-/-
WEIGHT FOR AGE 3yo-12lb
No bid

1772 PUMP ROOM CONDITIONS STKS (2-Y.O) (Class D) £4,198.00 (£1,264.00: £612.00: £286.00)
5f 11y Stalls: Low GOING minus 0.43 sec per fur (F) 2-30 (2-31)

1592[4] **High Priority (IRE)** *(77) (MRChannon)* 2-8-11 RHughes(2) (hld up: hdwy over 2f out: edgd lft 1f out: led nr fin)..— **1**
1530[3] Tarf (USA) *(72)*(Fav)*(PTWalwyn)* 2-8-6 PRobinson(5) (led: hrd rdn fnl f: hdd nr fin)..............s.h **2**
1177* Standown *(56) (JBerry)* 2-8-8 (7) PRoberts(4) (prom: one pce fnl 2f) 8 **3**
1267[7] Hoh Majestic (IRE) *(51) (MBell)* 2-9-1 TQuinn(3) (prom: rdn over 2f out: sn wknd) 1½ **4**
It's A Ripper *(31) (GLewis)* 2-8-11 PaulEddery(1) (neat: dwlt: outpcd) 5 **5**

11/8 Tarf (USA), **5/2** HIGH PRIORITY (IRE), **5/1** Hoh Majestic (IRE), **6/1** Standown, **12/1** It's A Ripper (op 6/1), CSF £6.01 TOTE £3.60: £1.70 £1.10 (£2.70) OWNER Mrs Eileen Sheehan (UPPER LAMBOURN) BRED Mr and Mrs Dare Wigan 5 Rn 62.1 secs (1.60) SF: 34/29/13/8/-

1773 BONUSPRINT STKS H'CAP (0-80) (4-Y.O+) (Class D) £3,790.25 (£1,142.00: £553.50: £259.25) **2m 1f 34y** Stalls: Low GOING minus 0.43 sec (F) 3-05 (3-05)

1416[2] **Moonlight Quest (70)***(81)*(Fav)*(BHanbury)* 7-10-0 PRobinson(4) (hld up: 3rd st: rdn over 2f out: bmpd & slt ld over 1f out: hdd ins fnl f: r.o wl: fin 2nd, s.h: awrdd r) ....— **1**
1535[5] Chakalak **(45)***(56) (SDow)* 7-7-10 (7) ADaly(1) (chsd ldr: 2nd & rdn st: n.m.r over 1f out: squeezed thro to ld ins fnl f: fin 1st: disq: plcd 2nd) **2**
1444[8] Access Sun **(39)***(48) (JSKing)* 8-7-6 (5)ow4 NVarley(5) (led: sn clr: rdn over 3f out: hdd over 1f out: one pce)..2½ **3**
1518[2] Prince Danzig (IRE) **(57)***(57) (DJGMurraySmith)* 4-9-1 RHughes(3) (hld up in rr: 4th & rdn st: hdwy over 2f out: wknd over 1f out) 9 **4**
1622[6] Sophism (USA) **(49)***(44) (MCPipe)* 6-8-7 JWilliams(2) (hld up: poor 5th st: a bhd)....................5 **5**
LONG HANDICAP Access Sun 7-6

7/4 MOONLIGHT QUEST, **3/1** Sophism (USA), **4/1** Chakalak, **9/2** Prince Danzig (IRE) (op 3/1), **10/1** Access Sun (8/1-12/1), CSF £8.12 TOTE £2.60: £1.30 £1.90 (£4.60) OWNER Mr B. Hanbury (NEWMARKET) BRED Raintree Stud 5 Rn 3m 50.2 (9.20) SF: 39/14/2/15/3
STEWARDS' ENQUIRY Daly susp. 26-29/06/95

1774 CHARLCOMBE MAIDEN AUCTION STKS (2-Y.O) (Class E) £3,187.50 (£960.00: £465.00: £217.50) **5f 11y** Stalls: Low GOING minus 0.43 sec per fur (F) 3-35 (3-40)

863[5] **Jaleel** *(66) (RHannon)* 2-8-6 BThomson(9) (a.p: rdn over 1f out: led ins fnl f: r.o wl) ....— **1**
1460[4] Laurel Crown (IRE) *(60) (JBerry)* 2-8-1 (7) PRoberts(8) (a chsng ldrs: rdn 2f out: r.o wl ins fnl f) 2½ **2**
1197[6] Members Welcome (IRE) *(51) (PGMurphy)* 2-7-10 (7)ow3 RWaterfield(7) (chsd ldrs: rdn 2f out: r.o ins fnl f)..½ **3**
1054[5] Dande Flyer *(56)*(Fav)*(DWPArbuthnot)* 2-8-7 TQuinn(2) (a.p: led over 1f out tl ins fnl f).........½ **4**
Chemcast *(45) (BJMeehan)* 2-8-2 BDoyle(1) (outpcd over 2f out: r.o fnl f) 1¾ **5**

4295 Double Or Bust (36) (RJBaker) 2-7-6 (5)ow2 NVarley(6) (led over 3f: wknd ins fnl f) ¾ 6
Malice Corner (18) (LGCottrell) 2-8-2 PRobinson(10) (cmpt: bhd fnl 2f) 8 7
Dish The Dosh (PGMurphy) 2-7-9 NAdams(4) (lengthy: dwlt: outpcd: t.o) 15 8

9/4 Dande Flyer, **11/4** Laurel Crown (IRE), **4/1** JALEEL, **11/2** Chemcast (4/1-6/1), **11/1** Malice Corner, **20/1** Dish The Dosh, Double Or Bust, **25/1** Members Welcome (IRE), CSF £14.57 TOTE £4.20: £1.40 £1.20 £3.10 (£3.80) Trio £25.10 OWNER Mr Saleh Al Homeizi (MARLBOROUGH) BRED G. S. Shropshire 8 Rn 63.1 secs (2.60) SF: 13/7/-/3/-/-/-/-

1775 BECKFORD TOWER STKS H'CAP (0-85) (3-Y.O+) (Class D) £3,582.25 (£1,078.00: £521.50: £243.25)
1m 5y Stalls: Low GOING minus 0.43 sec per fur (F) 4-10 (4-10)

1610⁹ **Zermatt (IRE) (66)**(75) (MDIUsher) 5-9-7 BThomson(4) (3rd st: rdn over 1f out: led ins fnl f: r.o) — 1
1274⁹ Arndilly **(69)**(77) (BJMeehan) 4-9-10b BDoyle(1) (chsd ldr: 2nd st: led over 1f out tl ins fnl f: r.o) ¾ 2
1693² Confronter **(73)**(72) (SDow) 6-9-7 (7) ADaly(6) (hld up: 6th st: hdwy 2f out: wknd over 1f out: fin 4th, 3½l: plcd 3rd) 3
1517⁶ Indefence (IRE) **(61)**(54) (MRChannon) 4-9-2v RHughes(3) (led over 6f: wknd ins fnl f: fin 5th, 3l: plcd 4th) 4
1447⁴ Elite Justice **(66)**(56)(Fav)(PFICole) 3-8-11b TQuinn(2) (4th st: hmpd over 1f out: sn wknd) 1¾ 6
1676¹⁴ Indian Temple **(43)**(27) (MSSaunders) 4-7-7 (5) NVarley(7) (5th & rdn st: wknd 2f out) 3 7
1593⁴ Polonez Prima **(64)**(70) (JLSpearing) 8-9-5 PaulEddery(5) (hld up: last st: hdwy over 2f out: r.o one pce fnl f: fin 3rd, 1¼l: disq: plcd last) 0

9/4 Elite Justice, **7/2** Confronter (2/1-4/1), **9/2** Indefence (IRE), **5/1** ZERMATT (IRE) (7/2-11/2), **11/2** Polonez Prima, **10/1** Arndilly (op 6/1), **16/1** Indian Temple, CSF £45.95 TOTE £6.00: £2.60 £3.50 (£28.80) OWNER Clairtex Gwent (SWINDON) BRED Ivan W. Allan and K. C. Choo 7 Rn
1m 39.8 (1.30) SF: 57/59/53/35/27/8/51
WEIGHT FOR AGE 3yo-10lb

1776 BEDMINSTER LIMITED STKS (0-60) (3-Y.O) (Class F) £2,915.00 (£815.00: £395.00) **1m 3f 144y** GOING minus 0.43 sec per fur (F) 4-40 (4-43)

1452* **Hydrofoil (59)**(67) (BWHills) 3-8-3 (5) JDSmith(1) (2nd & rdn st: r.o to ld nr fin) — 1
1452³ Marchant Ming (IRE) **(58)**(70) (MAJarvis) 3-8-11b PRobinson(5) (led tl hdd nr fin) nk 2
1694* Hi-Aud **(65)**(59)(Fav)(JAkehurst) 3-8-10 2x TQuinn(3) (hld up: slipped 5f out: 3rd st: rdn over 2f out: one pce) 7 3
1372⁸ Hadabet **(55)**(57) (MissJacquelineDoyle) 3-8-11 BDoyle(7) (hld up: hdwy & 4th st: eased whn btn ins fnl f) 2 4
1286⁷ Ruddigore **(56)**(52) (RHannon) 3-8-11 BThomson(4) (last st: a bhd) 3½ 5
1512¹² Silks and Studs **(55)**(47) (JWhite) 3-8-6 (5) SDrowne(6) (6th & rdn st: wknd 3f out) 4 6
1498¹² Zuno Flyer (USA) **(54)**(13) (GLewis) 3-8-11 NVarley(2) (prom: 5th & wknd st: t.o) 25 7

4/6 Hi-Aud, **100/30** HYDROFOIL, **7/1** Marchant Ming (IRE), **12/1** Ruddigore, **20/1** Zuno Flyer (USA), **33/1** Hadabet, **40/1** Silks and Studs, CSF £23.64 TOTE £4.00: £1.90 £3.10 (£10.40) OWNER Mr R. D. Hollingsworth (LAMBOURN) BRED R. D. Hollingsworth 7 Rn No Time Taken SF: -/3/-/-/-/-/-

1777 TETBURY H'CAP (0-85) (3-Y.O+) (Class D) £4,302.00 (£1,296.00: £628.00: £294.00) **5f 161y** Stalls: Low GOING minus 0.43 sec per fur (F) 5-10 (5-11)

1604⁴ **Silent Expression (74)**(81) (BJMeehan) 5-9-5 BDoyle(7) (a.p: led 3f out: drvn out) — 1
1411³ Robellion **(67)**(73) (DWPArbuthnot) 4-8-12 TQuinn(10) (hld up: hdwy 2f out: ev ch ins fnl f: nt qckn) nk 2
1510² Tinker Osmaston **(66)**(67) (MSSaunders) 4-8-11 JWilliams(4) (bhd: hdwy over 2f out: r.o one pce fnl f) 2 3
1537⁷ Kildee Lad **(71)**(69) (APJones) 5-9-2 AClark(5) (hld up: hdwy 2f out: one pce fnl f) 1 4
1335² Louisville Belle (IRE) **(48)**(44) (MDIUsher) 6-7-0 (7) CAdamson(1) (bhd tl hdwy over 1f out: nrst fin) ¾ 5
1595⁴ Jucea **(65)**(57) (JLSpearing) 6-8-10 PaulEddery(6) (nvr nrr) 1½ 6
1411⁴ Winsome Wooster **(67)**(57)(Fav)(PGMurphy) 4-8-7 (5) SDrowne(3) (w ldrs over 3f) ½ 7
Jade Pet **(83)**(68) (RHannon) 4-9-7 (7) MarkDenaro(9) (nvr nr ldrs) 2 8
1257⁴ Ashkernazy (IRE) **(52)**(32) (NEBerry) 4-7-6 (5)ow4 NVarley(8) (led: rdn & hdd 3f out: wknd over 1f out) nk 9
1304¹⁷ Ann's Pearl (IRE) **(79)**(43) (JWHills) 4-9-10 BThomson(2) (spd over 3f) 7 10
LONG HANDICAP Ashkernazy (IRE) 7-5

7/2 Winsome Wooster (9/2-3/1), **6/1** Kildee Lad, Robellion, **13/2** Tinker Osmaston, **7/1** Jucea, **8/1** SILENT EXPRESSION, **10/1** Ann's Pearl (IRE) (7/1-12/1), **12/1** Jade Pet (8/1-14/1), **14/1** Louisville Belle (IRE), **20/1** Ashkernazy (IRE), CSF £50.25 CT £299.90 TOTE £8.50: £3.10 £2.40 £1.90 (£53.20) Trio £30.10 OWNER Mr A. S. Reid (UPPER LAMBOURN) BRED J. B. H. Stevens 10 Rn
1m 11.2 (1.90) SF: 40/32/26/28/3/16/16/27/-/2

T/Plpt: £171.20 (54.13 Tckts). T/Qdpt: £49.70 (1.45 Tckts). KH

1497-LEICESTER (R-H)
Saturday June 17th (Good, Good to firm patches)
WEATHER: cloudy WIND: mod half bhd

1778 SPORTING GREEN H'CAP (0-80) (3-Y.O) (Class D) £4,306.90 (£1,289.20: £618.60: £283.30) **7f 9y** GOING minus 0.42 sec per fur (F) 6-40 (6-41)

9877 **Western Fame (USA) (72)***(80)*(Fav)*(JLDunlop)* 3-9-1 WCarson(6) (hld up: smooth hdwy to ld over 1f out: drvn clr)— 1
16244 Cats Bottom **(67)***(71) (DJSCosgrove)* 3-8-7 (3) JTate(5) (hld up: hdwy over 2f out: r.o wl fnl f: no ch w wnr)2 2
16395 Master Millfield (IRE) **(65)***(66) (CJHill)* 3-8-1 (7) MHenry(3) (w ldr: led over 2f out tl over 1f out: no ex fnl f)1¼ 3
13669 Lyford Law (IRE) **(77)***(66) (JHMGosden)* 3-9-6 LDettori(1) (b: lw: chsd ldrs: effrt & rdn wl over 1f out: sn btn)5 4
16394 Fantasy Racing (IRE) **(78)***(67) (MRChannon)* 3-9-7 RHughes(2) (hld up: hdwy over 2f out: eased whn btn fnl f)s.h 5
16245 Cloette **(66)***(55) (WAO'Gorman)* 3-8-9 EmmaO'Gorman(11) (lw: prom tl wknd over 1f out)...s.h 6
15335 Young Benson **(72)***(58) (BAMcMahon)* 3-9-1 JFortune(10) (hld up: hdwy u.p 3f out: nt rch ldrs)1¼ 7
15122 Wandering Minstrel (IRE) **(65)***(48) (JMPEustace)* 3-8-8 GCarter(7) (lw: hld up: effrt & ev ch bel dist: sn rdn & btn)1½ 8
Silver Tzar **(76)***(13) (WJHaggas)* 3-9-5 MHills(9) (b.hind: bit bkwd: mde most over 4f: sn wknd: t.o)20 9
1377U Delightful Dancer (IRE) **(57)** *(BWHills)* 3-7-9v(5) MBaird(8) (dwlt: rdn ½-wy: a bhd: t.o)25 10

3/1 WESTERN FAME (USA), **7/2** Wandering Minstrel (IRE), **5/1** Master Millfield (IRE), **13/2** Lyford Law (IRE), Fantasy Racing (IRE), **10/1** Silver Tzar, **12/1** Cloette, **14/1** Cats Bottom, **20/1** Young Benson, Delightful Dancer (IRE), CSF £40.98 CT £186.43 TOTE £4.00: £1.60 £2.10 £2.30 (£19.70) Trio £37.60 OWNER Mr S. Khaled (ARUNDEL) BRED Palides Investments N V 10 Rn
1m 23.3 (0.80) SF: 54/45/40/40/41/29/32/22/-/-

1779 TIPSTERS TABLE MEDIAN AUCTION MAIDEN STKS (2-Y.O) (Class F) £2,947.40 (£816.40: £390.20) **5f 2y** GOING minus 0.42 sec per fur (F) 7-10 (7-12)

Polaris Flight (USA) *(79+)*(Fav)*(PWChapple-Hyam)* 2-9-0 JReid(1) (str: cmpt: b.hind: s.i.s: sn chsng ldrs: hdwy to ld ins fnl f: sn clr)— 1
15514 Atraf *(71) (DMorley)* 2-9-0 WCarson(5) (chsd ldr: led 2f out tl ins fnl f)2½ 2
14972 Nellie North *(53) (MrsMMcCourt)* 2-8-2 (7) RStudholme(6) (led 3f: sn rdn: r.o one pce)4 3
12876 Lady Eclat *(45) (JAGlover)* 2-8-9 SDWilliams(2) (prom tl rdn & outpcd appr fnl f)2½ 4
10178 Credite Risque *(36) (MMcCormack)* 2-8-9 WRyan(7) (outpcd tl effrt on ins 2f out: nt rch ldrs)3 5
11975 Tin Man *(37) (BAMcMahon)* 2-9-0 JFortune(3) (chsd ldrs: rdn 2f out: sn outpcd)1¼ 6
Governors Dream *(13) (MrsNMacauley)* 2-8-6 (3) JTate(4) (w'like: bkwd: s.i.s: a bhd & outpcd)6 7

10/11 POLARIS FLIGHT (USA) (Evens-4/5), **7/4** Atraf, **6/1** Nellie North, **20/1** Lady Eclat, **25/1** Governors Dream, **33/1** Credite Risque, Tin Man, CSF £2.97 TOTE £2.20: £1.40 £1.50 (£2.10) OWNER Mr Richard Kaster (MARLBOROUGH) BRED Bill Van Den Dool 7 Rn
60.9 secs (2.40) SF: 23/15/-/-/-/-/-

1780 LEICESTER MERCURY STKS (Listed) (4-Y.O+) (Class A) £11,826.00 (£4,374.00: £2,097.00: £855.00: £337.50: £130.50) **1m 3f 183y** GOING minus 0.42 sec per fur (F) 7-40 (7-41)

1408* **Capias (USA) (109)***(114)*(Fav)*(JHMGosden)* 4-8-12 LDettori(4) (chsd ldrs: 4th st: shkn up 2f out: styd on to ld nr fin)— 1
Totality *(109) (HRACecil)* 4-8-7 WRyan(2) (hld up: 5th st: hdwy to chal ins fnl f: r.o wl)nk 2
8274 Blush Rambler (USA) **(112)***(113) (MRStoute)* 5-8-12 WRSwinburn(1) (sn led & clr: hrd rdn & ct wl ins fnl f)nk 3

1114a* Khamaseen **(107)***(115) (JLDunlop)* 4-9-4 JReid(5) (hld up: 3rd st: effrt over 2f out: one pce appr fnl f) 3½ 4
Summit **(103)***(91) (MrsJPitman)* 4-8-12 DHolland(3) (bkwd: chsd ldr: 2nd st: wknd 2f out: t.o) 13 5
1385 4 Wayne County (IRE) **(105)** *(GFierro)* 5-8-12 JFortune(6) (s.s: 6th st: hdwy over 3f out: outpcd over 2f out: virtually p.u fnl f: t.o) ....dist 6
Katiniyd (IRE) *(MrsNMacauley)* 4-8-12 JTate(7) (bkwd: dwlt: a bhd: 7th & t.o st: virtually p.u fnl f) ....nk 7

11/8 CAPIAS (USA), **4/1** Totality, Blush Rambler (USA) (3/1-9/2), **9/2** Khamaseen, **12/1** Wayne County (IRE), **16/1** Summit, **40/1** Katiniyd (IRE), CSF £7.28 TOTE £2.00: £1.60 £2.20 (£5.00) OWNER Sheikh Mohammed (NEWMARKET) BRED Overbrook Farm 7 Rn
2m 29.3 (0.50) SF: 60/55/59/61/37/-/-

1781

TELE-ADS MEDIAN AUCTION MAIDEN STKS (2-Y.O) (Class D)
£3,865.35 (£1,156.80: £554.90: £253.95)
5f 218y GOING minus 0.42 sec per fur (F) 8-10 (8-12)

1184 4 **Kilvine** *(78)*(Fav)*(LMCumani)* 2-9-0 WRSwinburn(4) (hld up: hdwy bel dist: shkn up & qcknd to ld ins fnl f) ....— 1
Sibbertoft (IRE) *(70) (PFICole)* 2-8-9 TQuinn(1) (leggy: lt-f: unf: led tl hdd & no ex ins fnl f) 1¼ 2
1454 4 Ned Al Sheeba *(67) (WJHaggas)* 2-9-0 MHills(2) (a.p: effrt appr fnl f: eased whn btn cl home) 3 3
Proper Blue (USA) *(60) (TGMills)* 2-9-0 LDettori(8) (lt-f: hdwy wl over 1f out: nt rch ldrs) 2½ 4
1454 9 Four Weddings (USA) *(49) (MBell)* 2-8-7 (7) GFaulkner(6) (chsd ldrs: r.o one pce fnl 2f) 4 5
Animation *(40) (KMcAuliffe)* 2-8-6 (3) JTate(7) (lt-f: unf: s.s: a in rr) 1¾ 6
Night of Glass *(38) (DMorris)* 2-9-0 JFortune(5) (lt-f: unf: outpcd: a bhd) 2½ 7
1278 12 Seeking Destiny (IRE) *(19) (MrsMMcCourt)* 2-9-0 GCarter(9) (bit bkwd: s.i.s: a in rr) 7 8
Our Albert (IRE) *(14) (JAGlover)* 2-9-0 DeanMcKeown(3) (w'like: str: bkwd: spd to ½-wy: wknd qckly: t.o) ....½ 9

Evens KILVINE, **4/1** Sibbertoft (IRE), **5/1** Ned Al Sheeba, **13/2** Proper Blue (USA), **20/1** Animation, **25/1** Our Albert (IRE), **33/1** Four Weddings (USA), Night of Glass, Seeking Destiny (IRE),CSF £5.50 TOTE £2.00: £1.20 £1.20 £1.70 (£3.30) Trio £3.20 OWNER Sheikh Mohammed (NEWMARKET) BRED Sheikh Mohammed bin Rashid al Maktoum 9 Rn 1m 11.8 (1.80) SF: 37/29/26/19/8/-/-/-/-

1782

SPORTS MERCURY CONDITIONS STKS (3-Y.O) (Class C) £5,256.00
(£1,944.00: £932.00: £380.00: £150.00: £58.00)
1m 3f 183y GOING minus 0.42 sec per fur (F) 8-40 (8-41)

Tenorio (94)*(94) (DRLoder)* 3-8-11 (3) DRMcCabe(4) (led tl hdd over 2f out: rallied gamely u.p to ld cl home) ....— 1
1167* Triquetti (IRE) *(93)*(Fav)*(LMCumani)* 3-9-0 LDettori(6) (hld up: 3rd st: hdwy to ld over 2f out: hrd rdn & hdd nr fin) ....¾ 2
1396a 10 Royal Scimitar (USA) **(100)***(90d)*(Fav)*(PFICole)* 3-9-0 TQuinn(5) (b.hind: hld up: 5th st: hdwy over 3f out: disp ld over 2f out tl appr fnl f: no ex) 2½ 3
1105 5 Jadwal (USA) **(85)***(81) (DMorley)* 3-8-9 WCarson(3) (b.nr hind: chsd wnr: 2nd st: rdn & wknd over 2f out) 3 4
1301 5 Wakeel (USA) **(95)***(83) (EALDunlop)* 3-9-0 WRSwinburn(1) (lw: hld up & bhd: 6th st: effrt over 2f out: no imp) 2 5
1237a 11 Pesce D'Aprile *(69) (JLDunlop)* 3-8-11 JReid(2) (chsd ldrs: 4th st: wknd 2f out) 8 6

7/4 Triquetti (IRE), Royal Scimitar (USA), **6/1** TENORIO, **8/1** Wakeel (USA), **9/1** Jadwal (USA), **16/1** Pesce D'Aprile, CSF £16.41 TOTE £10.20: £3.30 £1.20 (£13.10) OWNER Cuadra Africa (NEWMARKET) BRED Sir Eric Parker 6 Rn 2m 33.8 (5.00) SF: 32/31/28/19/21/7

1783

MERCURY RACE NIGHT H'CAP (0-70) (3-Y.O+ F & M) (Class E)
£3,588.20 (£1,073.60: £514.80: £235.40)
5f 218y GOING minus 0.42 sec per fur (F) 9-10 (9-11)

1546* **Midnight Break (63)***(73)*(Fav)*(PTWalwyn)* 3-9-10 JWeaver(3) (lw: a.p: led 1f out: rdn & r.o wl) ....— 1
1660 11 The Mestral **(41)***(49) (MJRyan)* 3-8-2b WCarson(6) (led to 1f out: hrd rdn & rallied cl home) ....¾ 2
1677 3 Lugana Vision **(52)***(59) (GFierro)* 3-8-10b(3) DRMcCabe(1) (hld up: hdwy to chal ins fnl f: unable qckn nr fin) ....½ 3

1565[11] Crystal Loop **(63)***(62) (ABailey)* 3-9-10 GCarter(8) (prom: hrd rdn over 1f out: kpt on one pce) 3 **4**
503[7] Darakah **(46)***(43) (CJHill)* 8-8-8 (7) MHenry(5) (bkwd: s.i.s: bhd tl r.o ins fnl f) ....¾ **5**
1528[3] Racing Brenda **(52)***(48) (BAMcMahon)* 4-9-7 JFortune(2) (bhd: effrt u.p 2f out: nvr able chal) ....hd **6**
1414[6] Le Bal **(44)***(40) (MrsNMacauley)* 3-8-5b DaleGibson(4) (a bhd & outpcd) ....hd **7**
1476[9] Another Batchworth **(58)***(46) (SMellor)* 3-8-12 (7) ADaly(7) (spd over 4f: sn rdn & wknd) 3 **8**

5/2 MIDNIGHT BREAK, **4/1** Racing Brenda, **9/2** Lugana Vision, **6/1** Crystal Loop, **13/2** The Mestral, **8/1** Le Bal, **16/1** Darakah, Another Batchworth, CSF £18.01 CT £63.14 TOTE £2.30: £1.10 £1.60 £1.70 (£8.00) OWNER Major & Mrs Kennard and Partners (LAMBOURN) BRED Mrs R. B. Kennard 8 Rn
1m 12.7 (2.70) SF: 33/9/19/22/11/16/-/6
WEIGHT FOR AGE 3yo-8lb

T/Plpt: £17.40 (548.62 Tckts). T/Qdpt: £6.70 (11.1 Tckts). IM

1478-LINGFIELD (L-H)
Saturday June 17th (AWT Standard, Turf Good to firm becoming Good)

WEATHER: showers WIND: slt half across

1784 SECRET PARTNERSHIP RATING RELATED MAIDEN LIMITED STKS (0-70) (3-Y.O+) (Class E) £3,073.40 (£915.20: £435.60: £195.80)

2m (Equitrack) Stalls: High GOING minus 0.69 sec per fur (FST) 6-30 (6-30)

1328[13] **Cavina (40)***(65) (NAGraham)* 5-9-5 MRimmer(5) (led after 1f: clr over 2f out: rdn over 1f out: r.o) ....— **1**
Finlaggan **(68)***(61)*(Fav)*(SirMarkPrescott)* 3-8-1 ow1 GDuffield(6) (hld up: hdwy over 5f out: chsd wnr over 3f out: rdn over 1f out: one pce) 4 **2**
1091[3] Brave Spy **(57)***(62) (CACyzer)* 4-9-10 DBiggs(1) (chsd ldrs: rdn over 3f out: one pce) 4 **3**
947[3] Chahaya Timor (IRE) **(68)***(62) (PFICole)* 3-8-5 JQuinn(2) (hld up: hdwy 6f out: rdn 4f out: wknd over 2f out) ....s.h **4**
1535[11] Sure Pride (USA) **(40)***(54) (AMoore)* 7-9-10 CandyMorris(4) (prom tl rdn & wknd over 5f out) 8 **5**
1581[5] Mayday Kitty **(40)***(48) (WGMTurner)* 3-8-0v TSprake(3) (a bhd) ....½ **6**
1628[6] Sadler's Pearl **(51)***(35) (BJMeehan)* 3-7-10 (5)ow1 AWhelan(7) (led 1f: prom tl rdn & wknd 4f out) 13 **7**

5/4 Finlaggan, **2/1** Chahaya Timor (IRE), **7/1** Brave Spy, **12/1** Mayday Kitty (6/1-14/1), **16/1** Sadler's Pearl, **20/1** Sure Pride (USA), CAVINA, CSF £43.73 TOTE £20.10: £4.30 £1.80 (£142.00) OWNER Mr Paul Jacobs (NEWMARKET) BRED Stetchworth Park Stud Ltd 7 Rn
3m 24.03 (0.53) SF: 46/23/43/24/35/10/-
WEIGHT FOR AGE 3yo-19lb

1785 GSP (S) H'CAP (0-60) (3-Y.O+) (Class G) £2,870.20 (£797.20: £382.60)

7f Stalls: High GOING minus 0.40 sec per fur (F) 7-00 (7-07)

1629[2] **Four of Spades (48)***(59)*(Fav)*(WSCunningham)* 4-9-8b AMcGlone(15) (a.p: led over 1f out: sn clr: comf) ....— **1**
Legend Dulac (IRE) **(43)***(46) (JAHarris)* 6-8-12 (5) PMcCabe(13) (led: hdd over 1f out: unable qckn) 3½ **2**
882[13] Glen Miller **(40)***(27) (JWPayne)* 5-9-0v MTebbutt(14) (a.p: rdn 2f out: one pce) 7 **3**
882[7] Finjan **(53)***(34) (AGFoster)* 8-9-13 TSprake(11) (mid div: hdwy over 2f out: rdn over 1f out: one pce) 2½ **4**
1521[5] Sandra Dee (IRE) **(54)***(35) (BAPearce)* 3-9-5 SWhitworth(16) (a.p: rdn over 2f out: one pce) ....s.h **5**
1355[15] Beware of Agents **(49)***(27) (MJohnston)* 6-9-9 NAdams(12) (chsd ldrs: rdn over 2f out: one pce fnl 2f) 1½ **6**
1472[8] King Parrot (IRE) **(46)***(20) (LordHuntingdon)* 7-9-1v(5) AWhelan(9) (prom tl rdn & wknd over 1f out) 1¾ **7**
1509[4] Doodies Pool (IRE) **(51)***(24) (GLMoore)* 5-9-4 (7) LSuthern(6) (rr: hdwy over 1f out: nvr nrr) ....½ **8**
1321[9] Splash of Salt (IRE) **(49)***(16) (TJNaughton)* 5-9-9b DBiggs(10) (prom over 4f) 2½ **9**
1276[7] Apollo Red **(51)***(17) (AMoore)* 6-9-11 CandyMorris(3) (prom over 4f) ....½ **10**
1323[16] Tiddy Oggie **(44)***(7) (NAGraham)* 4-9-4b MRimmer(4) (mid div: rdn over 3f out: wknd 2f out) 1¼ **11**
1499[10] Waders Dream (IRE) **(45)***(3) (PatMitchell)* 6-9-5b SO'Gorman(8) (chsd ldrs 5f) 2 **12**

Ain'tlifelikethat **(40)** *(TJNaughton)* 8-9-0 GBardwell(7) (a bhd)....9 **13**
1403[5] Assignment **(49)** *(JFfitch-Heyes)* 9-9-9 GDuffield(1) (a bhd)....4 **14**
1334[6] It's so Easy **(40)** *(APJames)* 4-8-11 (3) DWright(2) (a bhd)....¾ **15**
1501[9] Lord Alfie **(40)** *(BJMeehan)* 6-9-0b JQuinn(5) (a bhd)....4 **16**

4/1 FOUR OF SPADES (op 6/1), **7/1** King Parrot (IRE), **8/1** Doodies Pool (IRE), Beware of Agents, **9/1** Finjan, **10/1** Tiddy Oggie (7/1-11/1), **12/1** Glen Miller (16/1-25/1), Legend Dulac (IRE), **16/1** Assignment, Apollo Red, Sandra Dee (IRE), **20/1** Waders Dream (IRE), Splash of Salt (IRE), **25/1** Ain'tlifelikethat, It's so Easy, Lord Alfie, CSF £49.33 CT £486.82 TOTE £3.80: £1.30 £2.60 £3.60 £4.80 (£21.00) Trio £325.10 OWNER Mr B. L. Cassidy (YARM) BRED Hesmonds Stud Ltd 16 Rn
1m 23.06 (2.46) SF: 41/28/9/16/8/9/2/6/-/-/-/-/-/-/-/-
WEIGHT FOR AGE 3yo-9lb
No bid

1786

LURCHER MAIDEN STKS (3-Y.O+) (Class D) £4,340.70 (£1,299.60: £623.80: £285.90)
6f Stalls: High GOING minus 0.40 sec per fur (F) 7-30 (7-34)

Penny Dip *(88) (RFJohnsonHoughton)* 3-8-7 JQuinn(12) (w'like: hld up: hdwy over 2f out: led over 1f out: r.o)....— **1**
742[5] Glorious Aragon *(81) (RFJohnsonHoughton)* 3-8-7 AMcGlone(10) (a.p: led wl over 2f out: sn hdd: one pce)....2½ **2**
1522[2] Allyana (IRE) *(72)*(Fav)*(IABalding)* 3-8-7 PaulEddery(1) (racd far side: a.p: rdn over 1f out: one pce)....3½ **3**
1486[9] Dancing Sioux *(73) (RJRWilliams)* 3-8-12 GDuffield(5) (b: racd far side: a.p: rdn over 2f out: one pce)....1½ **4**
1476[2] Supreme Thought *(67) (LGCottrell)* 3-8-7 PRobinson(8) (led over 4f)....nk **5**
Safety Factor (USA) *(63) (GHarwood)* 4-9-6 AClark(4) (racd far side: chsd ldrs: rdn over 2f out: wknd fnl f)....3½ **6**
Marwell Indigo *(61) (JARToller)* 3-8-12 WNewnes(2) (unf: bit bkwd: racd far side: nvr nrr)....¾ **7**
Khatim (USA) *(61) (HThomsonJones)* 3-8-12 MTebbutt(3) (racd far side: sn rdn along & outpcd: nvr nrr)....s.h **8**
Vavona *(56) (LJHolt)* 3-8-7 NAdams(7) (a bhd)....s.h **9**
Mizag (IRE) *(60) (CJBenstead)* 3-8-12 DBiggs(11) (scope: bit bkwd: dwlt: a bhd)....nk **10**
1168[12] Saltando (IRE) *(59) (PatMitchell)* 4-9-6 SO'Gorman(9) (prom to ½-wy)....nk **11**
1520[3] Try-Haitai (IRE) *(46) (RAkehurst)* 4-9-3 (3) SSanders(6) (racd far side: a bhd)....5 **12**
1312[9] Bergholt *(45) (GLMoore)* 3-8-12 SWhitworth(13) (a bhd)....nk **13**

7/4 Allyana (IRE) (5/4-2/1), **2/1** Supreme Thought, **9/1** PENNY DIP (8/1-12/1), **11/1** Vavona, **12/1** Dancing Sioux (op 8/1), **14/1** Glorious Aragon, Khatim (USA), **16/1** Safety Factor (USA), Try-Haitai (IRE), **20/1** Marwell Indigo, Mizag (IRE), Bergholt, **50/1** Saltando (IRE), CSF £127.73 TOTE £10.20: £2.50 £5.40 £1.50 (£25.70) Trio £143.90 OWNER Mr T. D. Holland-Martin (DIDCOT) BRED The Overbury Stud 13 Rn 1m 10.38 (1.38) SF: 37/30/21/22/16/20/10/10/5/9/16/3/-
WEIGHT FOR AGE 3yo-8lb

1787

BONUSPOST H'CAP (0-85) (3-Y.O) (Class D) £4,036.50 (£1,206.00: £577.00: £262.50) **7f** Stalls: High GOING minus 0.40 sec per fur (F) 8-00 (8-01)

1522* **Courageous Dancer (IRE) (76)***(86)*(Fav)*(BHanbury)* 3-8-12 MRimmer(7) (hld up: hdwy over 2f out: led over 1f out: r.o)....— **1**
1366[13] Apollono **(66)***(69) (RAkehurst)* 3-7-13 (3) SSanders(5) (hld up: hdwy 3f out: led over 1f out: sn hdd: one pce)....3 **2**
1474[5] Anam **(79)***(76) (PTWalwyn)* 3-9-1 BThomson(6) (a.p: ev ch over 1f out: sn rdn: one pce)....2½ **3**
1069[6] Landlord **(75)***(72) (JARToller)* 3-8-11 WNewnes(3) (a.p: led over 2f out: hdd over 1f out: one pce)....s.h **4**
1487[17] Muchtarak (IRE) **(85)***(77) (CJBenstead)* 3-9-7 GDuffield(1) (rdn over 2f out: nvr nrr)....2½ **5**
1371[7] Anegre (IRE) **(60)***(51) (LJHolt)* 3-7-10 NAdams(4) (led over 4f)....nk **6**
885[7] Linger **(71)***(55) (LordHuntingdon)* 3-8-2 (5) AWhelan(2) (chsd ldrs over 4f)....3 **7**

9/4 COURAGEOUS DANCER (IRE) (6/4-5/2), **7/2** Apollono (op 6/1), **4/1** Muchtarak (IRE) (5/2-5/1), **9/2** Anam, **8/1** Landlord, Anegre (IRE) (10/1-5/1), **16/1** Linger, CSF £10.61 CT £29.85 TOTE £2.80: £1.90 £2.30 (£5.30) OWNER Mr Abdullah Ali (NEWMARKET) BRED Gainsborough Stud Management Ltd 7 Rn 1m 21.99 (1.39) SF: 45/28/35/31/36/10/14

1788

LORDSWOOD LITHO PRINTING H'CAP (0-70) (3-Y.O+) (Class E) £3,330.80 (£994.40: £475.20: £215.60)
1m 2f Stalls: High GOING minus 0.40 sec per fur (F) 8-30 (8-31)

1622[2] **Katie's Kid (32)***(44) (MJAhern)* 5-7-1 (7) CAdamson(1) (b: a.p: 2nd st: led over 1f out: r.o)....— **1**

1402⁴ Plinth **(55)***(65)*(Fav)*(NAGraham)* 4-9-3v PaulEddery(2) (led: hdd over 1f out: hrd rdn fnl f: one pce)........1¼ 2
1477⁹ Bag of Tricks (IRE) **(54)***(58) (SDow)* 5-9-2 GDuffield(3) (hld up: 5th st: hdwy over 2f out: r.o one pce fnl f)........3½ 3
1542⁵ South Eastern Fred **(58)***(59) (HJCollingridge)* 4-9-6 MRimmer(4) (chsd ldrs: 3rd st: rdn & one pce fnl 2f)........2 4
1317⁶ Harvey White (IRE) **(58)***(58) (JPearce)* 3-8-8 GBardwell(10) (6th st: sn rdn: one pce fnl f)......¾ 5
1512¹⁰ Anistop **(50)***(31) (RAkehurst)* 3-7-11 ⁽³⁾ SSanders(8) (hmpd & pushed wd after 3f: sn bhd).....12 6
811¹² Triple Tie (USA) **(66)***(40) (MBlanshard)* 4-10-0 StephenDavies(6) (bhd fnl 4f)........4 7
1535¹⁴ Princesse Abigail **(31)** *(RMFlower)* 4-7-7b NAdams(9) (4th st: sn wknd)........6 8
390⁸ Dynamis (IRE) **(60)***(22) (KOCunningham-Brown)* 4-9-8 SWhitworth(7) (s.i.s: a bhd)........2 9

LONG HANDICAP Princesse Abigail 6-8

5/2 Plinth, **7/2** Anistop, **4/1** South Eastern Fred, **8/1** Harvey White (IRE), **9/1** Bag of Tricks (IRE), **10/1** KATIE'S KID (6/1-12/1), **20/1** Dynamis (IRE), **25/1** Triple Tie (USA), **50/1** Princesse Abigail, CSF £32.04 CT £208.22 TOTE £8.10: £1.90 £1.40 £1.60 (£15.20) Trio £25.20 OWNER Mrs Susan Harraway BRED Mrs S. J. Harraway 9 Rn 2m 9.03 (6.03) SF: -/21/14/15/2/-/-/-/-
WEIGHT FOR AGE 3yo-12lb

1789 RETRIEVER LIMITED STKS (0-65) (3-Y.O+) (Class F) £2,821.40 (£780.40: £372.20) **1m (Equitrack)** Stalls: High GOING minus 0.69 sec (FST) 9-00 (9-01)

989³ **Music Maker (65)***(62)*(Fav)*(SirMarkPrescott)* 3-8-6 GDuffield(6) (hld up: rdn 4f out: hdwy to chse ldr over 2f out: led over 1f out: r.o)........— 1
1517⁹ The Little Ferret **(60)***(64) (GLMoore)* 5-9-0 ⁽⁷⁾ LSuthern(2) (chsd ldr over 5f: rdn over 1f out: r.o one pce fnl f)........1¾ 2
1571⁹ Words of Wisdom (IRE) **(59)***(63) (CACyzer)* 5-9-7 DBiggs(1) (led: hdd over 1f out: one pce) .hd 3
1631³ Medland (IRE) **(50)***(58) (BJMcMath)* 5-9-2 ⁽⁷⁾ RMoogan(5) (chsd ldrs: rdn 2f out: wknd over 1f out)........3½ 4
1472¹³ Water Hazard (IRE) **(57)***(58) (SDow)* 3-9-1 StephenDavies(7) (nvr nrr)........1¼ 5
1638¹² Kingchip Boy **(55)***(44) (MJRyan)* 6-9-9v AClark(4) (bhd fnl 3f)........6 6
726¹¹ Pat Poindestres **(30)***(13) (BAPearce)* 5-9-2 SWhitworth(3) (a bhd)........12 7

6/5 MUSIC MAKER, **4/1** Kingchip Boy, **5/1** The Little Ferret, **13/2** Words of Wisdom (IRE), **11/1** Medland (IRE), **12/1** Water Hazard (IRE) (8/1-14/1), **50/1** Pat Poindestres, CSF £7.34 TOTE £2.00: £1.40 £3.00 (£5.00) OWNER Cheveley Park Stud (NEWMARKET) BRED Cheveley Park Stud Ltd 7 Rn 1m 38.71 (2.31) SF: 11/23/22/17/7/3/-
WEIGHT FOR AGE 3yo-10lb
T/Plpt: £17.30 (517.52 Tckts). T/Qdpt: £4.70 (25 Tckts). SM

1751-SANDOWN (R-H)
Saturday June 17th (St Good to firm, Rnd Good, Good to firm patches)

WEATHER: rain WIND: almost nil

1790 E.B.F. PORTMAN SQUARE MAIDEN STKS (2-Y.O F) (Class D) £3,436.25 (£1,040.00: £507.50: £241.25) **5f 6y** Stalls: High GOING: minus 0.15 sec per fur (GF) 2-20 (2-20)

Forentia *(81+)*(Fav)*(JRFanshawe)* 2-8-11 DHarrison(2) (w'like: dwlt: hdwy 4f out: chsd ldr over 2f out: rdn over 1f out: led ins fnl f: r.o wl)........— 1
1525² Amoeba (IRE) *(77)*(Fav)*(JBerry)* 2-8-11 JCarroll(4) (led to ins fnl f: unable qckn)........1¼ 2
Moving Up (IRE) *(72) (GLMoore)* 2-8-11 SWhitworth(6) (unf: s.s: outpcd: hdwy over 1f out: r.o wl ins fnl f)........1½ 3
1590⁴ Trible Pet *(60) (BGubby)* 2-8-11 LDettori(5) (prom over 2f)........4 4
Oare Budgie *(54) (PTWalwyn)* 2-8-11 PatEddery(3) (str: scope: a bhd)........1¾ 5
Great Intent *(46) (SPCWoods)* 2-8-11 JReid(1) (leggy: prom over 2f)........2½ 6

9/4 FORENTIA, Amoeba (IRE) (6/4-5/2), **3/1** Oare Budgie, **11/2** Trible Pet (4/1-13/2), **12/1** Great Intent (8/1-14/1), **33/1** Moving Up (IRE), CSF £7.41 TOTE £5.00: £2.10 £1.80 (£5.10) OWNER Mrs Nicolas Kairis (NEWMARKET) BRED Clarents Racing Ltd 6 Rn 63.29 secs (3.49) SF: 25/21/16/4/-/-

1791 BERKELEY SQUARE CLAIMING STKS (3-Y.O) (Class F) £2,749.00 (£832.00: £406.00: £193.00) **1m 2f 7y** Stalls: High GOING minus 0.15 sec (GF) 2-55 (2-56)

1412³ **Bushehr (IRE) (56)***(70) (JWHills)* 3-8-1 ⁽⁷⁾ MHenry(5) (4th st: hrd rdn 1f out: led ins fnl f: r.o wl)—1
1382⁹ Dont Forget Curtis (IRE) **(72)***(72d) (JRFanshawe)* 3-8-11 DHarrison(3) (3rd st: hrd rdn & led over 1f out: hdd ins fnl f: unable qckn)........¾ 2

1146[2] Woodrising **(55)***(59)*(Fav)*(LadyHerries)* 3-8-1 MRoberts(1) (rdn 6f out: 5th st: hrd rdn over 1f out: r.o ins fnl f) 2 3
1490[7] Orchidarma **(64)***(62) (RJRWilliams)* 3-8-4b GDuffield(4) (lw: led over 8f) ....hd 4
1702[5] Gentle Irony **(59)***(55) (BJMeehan)* 3-7-10 (5) MBaird(7) (lw: lost pl 7f out: rallied over 2f out: wknd ins fnl f) 2½ 5
1059* Charm Dancer *(51) (MCPipe)* 3-8-12 JQuinn(6) (6th st: wknd over 1f out) 9 6
1490[8] Dantean *(43) (GHarwood)* 3-8-9b PatEddery(8) (2nd st: wknd over 2f out) 3 7
1325[3] Margaret Modes **(56)** *(CACyzer)* 3-8-0 DBiggs(9) (bhd fnl 7f) 9 8
1458[4] Turrill House *(24) (WJMusson)* 3-7-13 (5) PMcCabe(2) (a bhd) ....d.h 8

3/1 Woodrising, **7/2** Dont Forget Curtis (IRE), **6/1** Charm Dancer, Gentle Irony, **9/1** Margaret Modes, **10/1** Orchidarma (8/1-12/1), **11/1** BUSHEHR (IRE) (7/1-12/1), **14/1** Dantean (10/1-16/1), **50/1** Turrill House, CSF £44.49 TOTE £16.40: £2.50 £1.80 £1.40 (£33.90) (£27.10) OWNER Mr N. N. Browne (LAMBOURN) BRED Peter J. Barry 9 Rn 2m 12.05 (7.75) SF: 31/33/20/23/16/12/4/-/-

1792 JOHNSTONE DOUGLAS H'CAP (0-75) (3-Y.O+) (Class D) £4,260.00 (£1,290.00: £630.00: £300.00) 1m 14y Stalls: High GOING:minus 0.15 sec (GF) 3-30 (3-31)

1357[9] **Secret Aly (CAN) (69)***(80) (CEBrittain)* 5-9-9 MRoberts(1) (lw: 2nd st: led over 3f out: rdn out) ....— 1
1603[3] Yoxall Lodge **(60)***(67) (HJCollingridge)* 5-9-0 JQuinn(3) (led over 4f: ev ch 1f out: nt qckn) 2 2
1446[2] African-Pard (IRE) **(74)***(76) (DHaydnJones)* 3-9-4 JReid(7) (3rd st: rdn over 2f out: one pce) 2½ 3
Wayfarers Way (USA) **(70)***(72) (RHannon)* 4-9-10 WRSwinburn(6) (hdwy over 2f out: hrd rdn over 1f out: one pce) ....s.h 4
961[7] Canary Falcon **(63)***(64) (RJO'Sullivan)* 4-9-3 DBiggs(2) (lw: 6th st: rdn over 3f out: one pce) ..½ 5
1512* Alerting **(66)***(64)*(Fav)*(IABalding)* 3-8-10 LDettori(5) (lw: 5th st: rdn over 2f out: one pce) 1½ 6
1148[6] Kindergarten Boy (IRE) **(60)***(57) (RBoss)* 4-9-0 MRimmer(4) (plld hrd: 4th st: rdn over 2f out: wknd fnl f) ....½ 7

9/4 Alerting (6/4-5/2), **9/2** SECRET ALY (CAN), Yoxall Lodge, **11/2** Kindergarten Boy (IRE), **15/2** African-Pard (IRE) (5/1-8/1), **11/1** Canary Falcon, **20/1** Wayfarers Way (USA), CSF £21.57 TOTE £5.60: £2.50 £2.40 (£15.70) OWNER Mr B. H. Voak (NEWMARKET) BRED Northern Equine Thoroughbred Productions 7 Rn 1m 45.08 (5.88) SF: 48/35/34/40/32/22/25
WEIGHT FOR AGE 3yo-10lb

1793 ROTHMANS ROYALS NORTH SOUTH CHALLENGE SERIES H'CAP (0-95) (3-Y.O) (Class C) £7,165.00 (£2,170.00: £1,060.00: £505.00) 1m 1f Stalls: High GOING:minus 0.15 sec per fur (GF) 4-05 (4-06)

1524* **Rokeby Bowl (84)***(89)*(Fav)*(IABalding)* 3-8-13 (5) DGriffiths(2) (lw: hdwy over 2f out: led ins fnl f: rdn out) ....— 1
1196* Jalfrezi **(80)***(85) (JARToller)* 3-9-0 WNewnes(8) (dwlt: hdwy & nt clr run over 1f out: swtchd lft & r.o wl ins fnl f) ....nk 2
1322[3] Elpidos **(68)***(72) (CEBrittain)* 3-8-2 MRoberts(3) (2nd st: led over 1f out to ins fnl f: unable qckn) ....½ 3
1353* Major Change **(87)***(88) (RHannon)* 3-9-0 (7) DaneO'Neill(9) (rdn over 2f out: hdwy fnl f: r.o wl) 1¼ 4
1183[22] Stinging Reply **(77)***(77) (IABalding)* 3-8-11 PatEddery(4) (lw: 6th st: rdn over 3f out: one pce) ¾ 5
914[9] River Keen (IRE) **(75)***(75) (RWArmstrong)* 3-8-9b JQuinn(6) (lw: rdn over 2f out: hdwy fnl f: r.o) ....hd 6
1306[5] Ma Petite Anglaise **(81)***(77) (WJarvis)* 3-9-1 JReid(1) (3rd st: rdn 3f out: wknd fnl f) 2 7
1478[4] Okavango (USA) **(81)***(77) (JHMGosden)* 3-9-1v LDettori(5) (led over 7f: wknd fnl f) ....s.h 8
1446* Tranquillity **(84)***(74) (LordHuntingdon)* 3-9-4 WRSwinburn(7) (chsd ldr over 4f: 4th st: wknd over 1f out) 3½ 9
1533* Boldina Bay **(78)***(56) (MJohnston)* 3-8-12 JCarroll(10) (5th st: wknd over 3f out) 7 10

9/2 ROKEBY BOWL (5/2-5/1), **5/1** Boldina Bay, **13/2** Ma Petite Anglaise, Jalfrezi, **15/2** Tranquillity (5/1-8/1), **8/1** Okavango (USA), **9/1** Elpidos, **10/1** Major Change, Stinging Reply, **11/1** River Keen (IRE), CSF £32.20 CT £232.96 TOTE £5.20: £1.90 £1.80 £3.80 (£12.10) Trio £38.00 OWNER Mr Paul Mellon (KINGSCLERE) BRED Paul Mellon 10 Rn
1m 56.11 (4.71) SF: 60/56/43/59/48/46/48/48/45/27

1794 TRAFALGAR SQUARE H'CAP (0-80) (3-Y.O+) (Class D) £4,377.00 (£1,326.00: £648.00: £309.00) 1m 6f Stalls: High GOING:minus 0.15 sec per fur (GF) 4-35 (4-38)

1386* **Embracing (79)***(90)*(Fav)*(MRStoute)* 3-8-10 WRSwinburn(3) (6th st: rdn over 3f out: led over 1f out: r.o wl) ....— 1

1386[2] Requested **(58)***(68) (PBurgoyne)* 8-8-3 (3) DRMcCabe(6) (5th st: rdn over 2f out: r.o ins fnl f)....¾ 2
1518[4] Ela Man Howa **(55)***(65) (RAkehurst)* 4-8-3 MRoberts(8) (lw: led over 12f: ev ch ins fnl f: unable qckn)....s.h 3
1310[5] Cuango (IRE) **(73)***(83) (RHollinshead)* 4-9-7 LDettori(10) (rdn over 2f out: hdwy over 1f out: r.o ins fnl f)....½ 4
1410* Johns Act (USA) **(75)***(82) (DHaydnJones)* 5-9-9 JReid(5) (chsd ldr: rdn over 2f out: unable qckn fnl f)....2½ 5
1477[6] Pembridge Place **(76)***(79) (JLDunlop)* 4-9-10 PatEddery(7) (b.nr fore: swtg: 4th st: wknd 2f out)....3½ 6
1383[8] Fast Forward Fred **(60)***(61) (LMontagueHall)* 4-8-8 DHarrison(2) (nvr nr to chal)....1¼ 7
Ivor's Flutter **(78)***(79) (DRCElsworth)* 6-9-7 (5) AProcter(11) (b: a bhd)....½ 8
Run High **(49)***(45) (PMitchell)* 12-7-8 (3)ow4 DWright(9) (bit bkwd: 3rd st: rdn over 2f out: wknd over 1f out)....nk 9
1535[3] Jaraab **(46)***(44) (GLewis)* 4-7-8v JQuinn(1) (lw: bhd fnl 3f)....2½ 10
Tukano (CAN) **(79)***(67) (JRJenkins)* 4-9-13 SWhitworth(4) (lw: a bhd)....8 11

15/8 EMBRACING, **6/1** Pembridge Place, **7/1** Requested, Cuango (IRE), **15/2** Johns Act (USA), **8/1** Ela Man Howa, **10/1** Jaraab, **20/1** Ivor's Flutter, **33/1** Fast Forward Fred, Tukano (CAN), **50/1** Run High, CSF £14.80 CT £79.18 TOTE £2.30: £1.50 £2.70 £2.10 (£7.70) Trio £21.60 OWNER Maktoum Al Maktoum (NEWMARKET) BRED Gainsborough Stud Management Ltd 11 Rn

3m 8.97 (14.27) SF: 15/10/7/25/24/21/3/21/-/-/9

WEIGHT FOR AGE 3yo-17lb

1795 LEICESTER SQUARE CONDITIONS STKS (3-Y.O+) (Class C) £4,901.60 (£1,834.40: £897.20: £386.00: £173.00: £87.80)

5f 6y Stalls: High GOING minus 0.15 sec per fur (GF) 5-05 (5-10)

1475[6] **Loch Patrick (101)***(105) (LJHolt)* 5-9-12 AMcGlone(2) (lw: gd hdwy over 1f out: str run fnl f: led nr fin)....— 1
1220[3] Lucky Parkes **(100)***(98) (JBerry)* 5-9-7 JCarroll(3) (lw: led: hrd rdn fnl f: hdd nr fin)....¾ 2
1480[4] Overbrook **(97)***(91) (IABalding)* 3-8-12 LDettori(4) (lw: hld up: rdn over 2f out: r.o one pce)....1½ 3
Takadou (IRE) **(84)***(97) (MissLCSiddall)* 4-9-12 DHarrison(7) (rdn & hdwy over 1f out: r.o one pce)....nk 4
1475[5] Hinton Rock (IRE) **(96)***(85) (MBell)* 3-8-9 MRoberts(5) (lw: hld up: rdn over 2f out: one pce)...¾ 5
1373[5] Painted Desert **(95)***(77)*(Fav)*(RCharlton)* 3-8-6 PatEddery(1) (chsd ldr over 2f: wknd over 1f out)....1½ 6
1698[7] Hello Mister **(98)***(86) (JO'Donoghue)* 4-9-7 (5) PMcCabe(6) (chsd ldr over 2f out tl ins fnl f: wknd qckly)....1¼ 7

9/4 Painted Desert, **5/2** Lucky Parkes, **9/2** LOCH PATRICK (op 5/2), Overbrook, **7/1** Hinton Rock (IRE), **20/1** Hello Mister, **33/1** Takadou (IRE), CSF £15.64 TOTE £5.10: £2.50 £1.70 (£5.60) OWNER Miss E. M. L. Coller (BASINGSTOKE) BRED Miss E. Coller 7 Rn

61.2 secs (1.40) SF: 74/67/53/66/47/39/55

WEIGHT FOR AGE 3yo-7lb

1796 GROSVENOR SQUARE MAIDEN STKS (3-Y.O) (Class D) £3,680.00 (£1,115.00: £545.00: £260.00)

7f 16y Stalls: High GOING:minus 0.15 sec per fur (GF) 5-40 (5-40)

Hawaash (IRE) *(75) (JRFanshawe)* 3-9-0 DHarrison(3) (w'like: scope: 5th st: rdn over 1f out: str run fnl f: led last stride)....— 1
Touch a Million (USA) *(75) (EALDunlop)* 3-9-0 WRSwinburn(6) (4th st: rdn over 1f out: led last strides: hdd last stride)....s.h 2
Akil (IRE) *(75)*(Fav)*(RWArmstrong)* 3-9-0 MRoberts(4) (2nd st: led over 1f out: hrd rdn: hdd last strides)....s.h 3
Millazure (USA) *(68) (RCharlton)* 3-8-9 PatEddery(5) (unf: scope: s.s: hdwy 6f out: 3rd st: ev ch ins fnl f: one pce)....1 4
1476[3] Direct Dial (USA) *(65) (JARToller)* 3-9-0 JCarroll(1) (led over 5f)....3½ 5
1486[11] Sharp Consul (IRE) *(62) (HCandy)* 3-9-0 WNewnes(8) (plld hrd: hdwy over 1f out: nvr nrr)..1¼ 6
Zaaleff (USA) *(60) (MRStoute)* 3-9-0 AMcGlone(2) (w'like: scope: lw: no hdwy fnl 3f)....¾ 7
1186[15] Backhander (IRE) *(52) (JARToller)* 3-9-0 SWhitworth(7) (hdwy over 2f out: wknd over 1f out)....3½ 8
Yeath (IRE) *(52) (RAkehurst)* 3-8-7 (7) TAshley(10) (uns: s.s: hdwy 4f out: 6th st: wknd over 1f out)....nk 9
1072[7] Fern's Governor *(45) (WJMusson)* 3-8-10 ow1 EGuest(9) (s.s: a bhd)....½ 10

15/8 Akil (IRE) (5/4-2/1), **9/4** Touch a Million (USA) (3/1-2/1), **4/1** Millazure (USA) (5/2-5/1), **9/1** Zaaleff (USA) (4/1-10/1), **12/1** Direct Dial (USA), **14/1** HAWAASH (IRE) (10/1-16/1), **33/1** Yeath (IRE), **50/1** Backhander (IRE), Sharp Consul (IRE), Fern's Governor, CSF £43.77 TOTE £20.90: £3.40 £1.30 £1.60 (£30.70) Trio £30.90 OWNER Mr Butti Mussabah (NEWMARKET) BRED D. J. and Mrs Deer 10 Rn
1m 35.44 (8.84) SF: -/-/-/-/-/-/-/-/-/-

T/Jpt: £7,100.00 (0.1 Tckts); £7,881.13 to 19/6/95. T/Plpt: £55.10 (424.96 Tckts). T/Qdpt: £30.40 (11.2 Tckts). AK

1653-WARWICK (L-H)
Saturday June 17th (Good to firm)
WEATHER: fine WIND: almost nil

1797 FERNDALE APPRENTICE H'CAP (0-70) (3-Y.O+) (Class F) £2,669.00 (£759.00: £377.00) **7f** Stalls: Low GOING minus 0.18 sec per fur (GF) 6-50 (6-50)

1644[5] **Mr Cube (IRE) (49)***(64) (JMBradley)* 5-9-0v(3) RWaterfield(14) (hld up: stdy hdwy over 2f out: led 1f out: sn drew clr: comf) .....— 1
1523[10] Reed My Lips (IRE) **(35)***(43) (BPJBaugh)* 4-8-0 (3) IonaWands(11) (hld up: r.o fnl 2f: nt trble wnr) 3 2
1426[2] Chairmans Choice **(44)***(48) (APJarvis)* 5-8-12 SLanigan(9) (chsd ldrs: unable qckn fnl f) 1¾ 3
1414[4] Blushing Grenadier (IRE) **(50)***(54) (MJFetherston-Godley)* 3-8-9b DaneO'Neill(12) (a.p: r.o one pce fnl 2f) .....hd 4
1545[6] Rinus Manor (IRE) **(40)***(10) (DMcCain)* 4-8-3 (5) CLowther(7) (w ldrs 4f: no ex fnl 2f) 2 5
1714[18] Christian Warrior **(30)** *(REPeacock)* 6-7-12 GMitchell(6) (a.p: led 2f out: hdd & wknd 1f out) .....s.h 6
1542[9] Life's Too Short (IRE) **(47)***(15)*(Fav)*(JEBanks)* 4-8-12 (3) GMilligan(1) (lw: w ldrs: led over 3f out: hdd 2f out: r.o one pce) .....¾ 7
1714[2] Asterix **(44)***(12) (JMBradley)* 7-8-12v PFessey(3) (hld up: effrt 3f out: no real hdwy) .....s.h 8
1334[7] Leguard Express (IRE) **(48)***(11) (OO'Neill)* 7-8-13b(3) AEddery(10) (hld up: rdn over 2f out: unable qckn) 2 9
1426[5] Respectable Jones **(40)** *(RHollinshead)* 9-7-12b(10) FLynch(13) (a.p: in tch 2f out: one pce).2½ 10
1457[8] Brigadore Gold **(29)** *(FHLee)* 5-7-6b(5)ow4 JoHunnam(2) (lw: chsd ldrs 4f: wknd rapidly) 2½ 11
1630[3] Caddy's First **(54)***(5) (SMellor)* 3-8-13 ADaly(4) (spd 4f: sn wknd) .....nk 12
1165[10] Indrapura (IRE) **(65)***(39) (PFICole)* 3-9-0 (10) DavidO'Neill(8) (lw: led over 3f: grad lost pl) 5 13
1459[11] Radio Caroline **(31)** *(MTate)* 7-7-6b(7)ow6 TThomas(5) (lw: s.s: t.o fnl 2f) 3½ 14

LONG HANDICAP Radio Caroline 7-2

4/1 Life's Too Short (IRE), **9/2** Chairmans Choice (op 3/1), Asterix, **8/1** Indrapura (IRE), **9/1** Blushing Grenadier (IRE), **10/1** Leguard Express (IRE) (8/1-12/1), MR CUBE (IRE), **12/1** Caddy's First, **14/1** Respectable Jones, **16/1** Reed My Lips (IRE), Rinus Manor (IRE), **25/1** Brigadore Gold, **66/1** Christian Warrior, Radio Caroline, CSF £148.31 CT £755.23 TOTE £12.50: £3.20 £5.60 £2.10 (£42.30) Trio £193.70 OWNER Mr R. Miles (CHEPSTOW) BRED Lyonstown Stud 14 Rn
1m 28.6 (4.40) SF: 35/14/19/16/-/-/-/-/-/-/-/-/1/-
WEIGHT FOR AGE 3yo-9lb

1798 LAMMAS FIELD MAIDEN AUCTION STKS (2-Y.O) (Class F) £3,048.20 (£845.20: £404.60) **7f** Stalls: Low GOING minus 0.18 sec per fur (GF) 7-20 (7-20)

1540[6] **Evidence In Chief** *(69) (PFICole)* 2-8-2 CRutter(10) (a.p: qcknd to ld 1f out: r.o wl) .....— 1
1540[3] Sound Check *(66) (BJMeehan)* 2-8-2 BDoyle(8) (led over 3f: led again over 2f out: hdd 1f out: unable qckn) 1½ 2
Atlantic Mist *(63) (BRMillman)* 2-8-7 RPerham(11) (scope: hdwy fnl 2f: kpt on fnl f) 3½ 3
1540[8] Anshan's Deity *(60) (CWFairhurst)* 2-8-7 TWilliams(3) (w ldrs tl wknd 2f out: unable qckn) ..1¼ 4
Infantry Dancer *(49) (GCBravery)* 2-7-8 (5) NVarley(9) (dwlt s: hdwy ½-wy: styd on fnl 2f) 1¼ 5
Cry Baby *(56) (KTIvory)* 2-8-1 (7)ow1 CScally(2) (bit bkwd: hld up: kpt on fnl 2f: nvr nrr) .....nk 6
878[5] Crimson And Clover *(51)*(Fav)*(MBell)* 2-8-2 MFenton(4) (chsd ldrs tl rdn & btn 2f out) .....nk 7
716[7] Compensate (IRE) *(48) (MJHaynes)* 2-8-2 FNorton(6) (nvr bttr than mid div) 1¼ 8
Wilfull Lad (IRE) *(44) (MartynMeade)* 2-8-7 VSlattery(5) (w'like: racd mid div: no hdwy fnl 2f) 4 9
1352[4] Simply Silly (IRE) *(13) (RThompson)* 2-7-11 (5) LNewton(1) (w ldrs: led over 3f out: hdd over 2f out: sn rdn & btn) 11 10
Dark Robe *(13) (RWEmery)* 2-7-9 (7) PFessey(7) (scope: outpcd) .....nk 11

2/1 Crimson And Clover, **9/4** EVIDENCE IN CHIEF, **7/2** Sound Check, **9/1** Anshan's Deity, **20/1** Atlantic Mist, Infantry Dancer, Cry Baby, **25/1** Wilfull Lad (IRE), **33/1** Simply Silly (IRE), **40/1** Compensate (IRE), **50/1** Dark Robe, CSF £10.49 TOTE £3.60: £1.50 £1.70 £2.90 (£4.40) Trio £91.40 OWNER Mr Raymond Tooth (WHATCOMBE) BRED N. Abbott 11 Rn
1m 30.02 (5.82) SF: 3/-/-/-/-/-/-/-/-/-/-

1799 ASHORNE (S) H'CAP (0-60) (3-Y.O+) (Class G) £2,243.00 (£618.00: £293.00)
1m 4f 115y Stalls: Low GOING minus 0.18 sec per fur (GF) 7-50 (7-50)

1513[10] **Supreme Star (USA) (46)**_(56) (PRHedger)_ 4-9-3 (5) NVarley(5) (a.p: rdn to ld over 1f out: styd on wl) ....— 1
534[5] Persian Bud (IRE) **(39)**_(48) (JRBosley)_ 7-9-1 CRutter(12) (hld up: r.o wl fnl 2f: nt rch wnr) 1 2
Valiant Toski **(43)**_(50)_(Fav)_(MCPipe)_ 4-9-5 BDoyle(11) (w ldr tl led over 2f out: hdd over 1f out: no ex) 1¼ 3
1200[8] Regal Pursuit (IRE) **(45)**_(52) (CAHorgan)_ 4-9-7v TWilliams(1) (racd mid div: styng on fnl 2f: nt rch ldrs) ....½ 4
1519[5] Rubadub **(44)**_(43)_(Fav)_(JMBradley)_ 4-9-1 (5) SDrowne(4) (b: hld up: effrt 2f out: nt trble ldrs) ...6 5
_227[9]_ King's Shilling (USA) **(52)**_(47) (HOliver)_ 8-9-7v(7) AEddery(6) (a.p: no hdwy fnl 3f) 3 6
_1459[8]_ Course Fishing **(38)**_(33) (BAMcMahon)_ 4-9-0 FNorton(8) (led tl hdd over 2f out: wknd qckly over 1f out) ....nk 7
_1457[10]_ Soba Guest (IRE) **(46)**_(40) (RTJuckes)_ 6-9-8 MFenton(3) (plld hrd: prom tl wknd 3f out).......¾ 8
Early to Rise **(33)**_(10) (MissLCSiddall)_ 5-8-9b DHarrison(7) (chsd ldrs 8f: no ch fnl 2f) 13 9
_304[12]_ Kismetim **(45)**_(21) (FJordan)_ 5-9-0 (7) RHavlin(2) (s.s: hdwy ½-wy: wknd 3f out) ....½ 10
1317[9] Commander Glen (IRE) **(54)**_(24) (MartynMeade)_ 3-9-0b VSlattery(13) (a.p: wknd rapidly over 3f out) 5 11
Caromandoo (IRE) **(47)** _(ABarrow)_ 7-9-9v BPowell(9) (hld up: pushed along ½-wy: no hdwy) 15 12

4/1 Rubadub, Valiant Toski, **5/1** SUPREME STAR (USA), **7/1** Persian Bud (IRE) (op 4/1), **9/1** Regal Pursuit (IRE), **10/1** King's Shilling (USA) (op 6/1), Course Fishing (op 5/1), **12/1** Kismetim, **14/1** Early to Rise, **16/1** Commander Glen (IRE), **25/1** Soba Guest (IRE), **33/1** Caromandoo (IRE), CSF £38.54 CT £143.11 TOTE £4.90: £2.20 £2.00 £2.50 (£20.10) Trio £54.30 OWNER Mr J. J. Whelan (CHICHESTER) BRED Peter M. Brant 12 Rn 2m 48.9 (11.40) SF: 21/13/15/17/8/12/-/5/-/-/-/-
WEIGHT FOR AGE 3yo-16lb
No bid

1800 WARWICK OAKS CONDITIONS STKS (3-Y.O+ F & M) (Class C)
£5,013.20 (£1,803.20: £861.60: £348.00: £134.00)
1m 2f 169y Stalls: Low GOING minus 0.18 sec per fur (GF) 8-20 (8-20)

1478[3] **Pearl Venture (90)**_(98) (SPCWoods)_ 3-8-7 BDoyle(2) (hld up: r.o wl ent st to ld over 1f out: pushed out).......— 1
1195* Ellie Ardensky _(97) (JRFanshawe)_ 3-8-7 DHarrison(5) (hld up bhd: effrt 2f out: r.o wl fnl f: nrst fin) ....½ 2
1346* Dawlah **(92)**_(95) (HThomsonJones)_ 3-8-7 RHills(1) (trckd ldr: led over 2f out: hdd over 1f out: unable qckn).......1½ 3
1616[4] Adolescence (IRE) **(81)**_(87) (KMcAuliffe)_ 5-9-3 MFenton(4) (cl up: effrt ent st: no ex over 1f out) 3 4
1105[2] Watch the Clock **(101)**_(65)_(Fav)_(DRLoder)_ 3-8-11 PatEddery(3) (led tl hdd over 2f out: wknd qckly 1f out).......20 5

Evens Watch the Clock, **5/2** Ellie Ardensky, **11/4** Dawlah, **14/1** PEARL VENTURE (op 8/1), **16/1** Adolescence (IRE), CSF £46.54 TOTE £16.60: £3.30 £1.40 (£21.90) OWNER Dr Frank Chao (NEWMARKET) BRED Dr Frank Chao and High Point Bloodstock Ltd 5 Rn
2m 20.8 (7.30) SF: 23/22/20/26/-
WEIGHT FOR AGE 3yo-14lb

1801 SYD MERCER H'CAP (0-80) (3-Y.O+) (Class D) £3,968.90 (£1,185.20: £566.60: £257.30) **1m 2f 169y** Stalls: Low GOING minus 0.18 sec per fur (GF) 8-50 (8-50)

1645* **Vindaloo (57)**_(65+)_(Fav)_(JLHarris)_ 3-7-7 (7) PFessey(3) (w ldrs: led 2f out: veered bdly rt & hdd over 1f out: sn led again: easily).......— 1
1643[10] Thrower **(47)**_(52) (WMBrisbourne)_ 4-7-11 (7) MartinDwyer(6) (a.p: ev ch 1f out: kpt on) 2 2
_1458*_ Reported (IRE) **(59)**_(64) (BPreece)_ 6-9-2 PatEddery(5) (hld up: effrt over 2f out: r.o fnl f: nrst fin).......nk 3
731[4] Taahhub (IRE) **(48)**_(52) (RJPrice)_ 5-8-5 MFenton(7) (hld up: styd on fnl 2f: nvr nrr).......nk 4
1644[3] Yubralee (USA) **(72)**_(74) (MCPipe)_ 3-9-1 DHarrison(9) (led 8f: lft in ld briefly over 1f out: rdn & wknd) 1¼ 5
1561[2] Unprejudice **(67)**_(66) (GRimmer)_ 4-9-10 RHills(4) (hld up: hdwy over 4f out: r.o one pce) 2½ 6
1382[10] Fearless Venture **(68)**_(59) (SPCWoods)_ 3-8-4 (7) CWebb(2) (chsd ldrs: rdn 2f out: unable qckn).......5 7
1543[5] Scottish Bambi **(62)**_(46) (RHannon)_ 7-9-5 RPerham(8) (prom: in tch over 3f out: sn wknd) 5 8
_133[9]_ Our Bairn **(59)** _(RThompson)_ 3-7-11 (5)ow5 LNewton(1) (chsd ldrs 3f: wknd over 3f out: t.o).......dist 9

5/4 VINDALOO (Evens-6/4), **5/2** Reported (IRE) (op 9/2), **15/2** Yubralee (USA) (5/1-8/1), **8/1** Scottish Bambi, Unprejudice, **25/1** Taahhub (IRE), Fearless Venture, **33/1** Our Bairn, **40/1** Thrower, CSF £39.73 CT £111.53 TOTE £2.50: £1.10 £7.10 £1.60 (£73.30) Trio £183.80 OWNER Mr J. D. Abell (MELTON MOWBRAY) BRED Green Park Investments Ltd 9 Rn

2m 21.4 (7.90) SF: 13/14/26/14/22/28/7/8/-

WEIGHT FOR AGE 3yo-14lb

1802 HENLEY IN ARDEN LIMITED STKS (0-70) (3-Y.O+) (Class E)

£3,465.00 (£1,035.00: £495.00: £225.00)
5f Stalls: Low GOING minus 0.18 sec per fur (GF) 9-20 (9-20)

1545² **So Intrepid (IRE) (69)***(79) (JMBradley)* 5-9-2 (5) SDrowne(3) (chsd ldrs: led over 1f out: r.o wl)........— 1
1411⁵ Purple Fling **(70)***(66)*(Fav)*(SirMarkPrescott)* 4-9-4 PatEddery(4) (lw: hld up bhd: effrt 2f out: ev ch over 1f out: no ex ins fnl f)........3 2
1445* Superbit **(54)***(57) (BAMcMahon)* 3-9-0 FNorton(5) (spd 3f: ev ch over 1f out: unable qckn)......4 3
1094¹⁶ Endless Wave **(68)***(47) (MBell)* 3-8-6 MFenton(2) (a same pl: no ex fnl f)........½ 4
1125¹⁸ Silver Academy (IRE) **(40)***(49) (MissGayKelleway)* 3-8-4v(7) DaneO'Neill(6) (spd 3f: one pce)..1 5
Eluned May **(47)***(31) (RMWhitaker)* 4-8-13 ACulhane(1) (led over 3f: wknd qckly fnl f)........4 6

11/8 Purple Fling, **9/4** SO INTREPID (IRE), **11/4** Endless Wave (2/1-3/1), **8/1** Superbit, **20/1** Eluned May, **33/1** Silver Academy (IRE), CSF £5.93 TOTE £3.80: £2.20 £1.60 (£3.50) OWNER Mr E. A. Hayward (CHEPSTOW) BRED Crest Stud Ltd 6 Rn 59.6 secs (1.60) SF: 62/49/33/23/25/14

WEIGHT FOR AGE 3yo-7lb

T/Plpt: £72.40 (121.81 Tckts). T/Qdpt: £23.70 (3.45 Tckts). P

1764-YORK (L-H)
Saturday June 17th (Good to firm)

WEATHER: overcast WIND: fresh across

1803 LEONARD SAINER E.B.F. MAIDEN STKS (2-Y.O) (Class D)£4,123.50 (£1,248.00: £609.00: £289.50) 6f Stalls: High GOING minus 0.29 sec per fur (GF) 2-15 (2-15)

1184² **Kahir Almaydan (IRE)** *(82+)*(Fav)*(JLDunlop)* 2-9-0 WCarson(3) (plld hrd: mde virtually all: hung lft & qcknd clr appr fnl f: easily)........— 1
House of Riches *(77) (LMCumani)* 2-9-0 JWeaver(2) (w'like: leggy: w wnr: shkn up 2f out: sn no ch)........2 2
Desert Bell (IRE) *(73) (MRStoute)* 2-9-0 MHills(1) (cmpt: s.i.s: sn chsng ldrs: nt qckn appr fnl f)........1¼ 3
Intidab (USA) *(73) (JHMGosden)* 2-9-0 RHills(4) (w'like: s.i.s: sn chsng ldrs: hung lft 2 out: nt qckn)........s.h 4

4/9 KAHIR ALMAYDAN (IRE), **9/2** Desert Bell (IRE) (op 3/1), **6/1** House of Riches, **8/1** Intidab (USA), CSF £3.57 TOTE £1.50 (£2.60) OWNER Mr Mirza Al Sayegh (ARUNDEL) BRED B. Ryan 4 Rn 1m 13.29 (3.69) SF: 22/17/13/13

1804 JACK HANSON & GUY REED MAIDEN STKS (3-Y.O) (Class D)

£4,026.00 (£1,218.00: £594.00: £282.00)
7f 202y Stalls: Low GOING minus 0.29 sec per fur (GF) 2-45 (2-45)

539² **Amanah (USA)** *(83)*(Fav)*(JHMGosden)* 3-8-9 WCarson(2) (led 1f: a gng wl: led appr fnl f: v.cheekily)........— 1
Venice Beach *(86) (BWHills)* 3-9-0 MHills(1) (lw: led after 1f tl over 1f out: r.o: no ch w wnr)1¼ 2
1180⁷ Shifting Moon **(74)***(71) (IABalding)* 3-9-0v WRyan(3) (a chsng ldrs: rdn & hung lft fnl 2½f)........7 3
Ruby Rock *(50) (BWMurray)* 3-8-9 JFortune(4) (unf: scope: wnt rt s: a outpcd & bhd)........8 4

4/11 AMANAH (USA), **11/2** Venice Beach, **6/1** Shifting Moon (op 7/2), **25/1** Ruby Rock, CSF £2.59 TOTE £1.40 (£2.00) OWNER Mr Hamdan Al Maktoum (NEWMARKET) BRED Shadwell Farm Inc 4 Rn 1m 38.96 (2.96) SF: 39/42/27/6

1805 QUEEN MOTHER'S CUP RATED STKS (LADIES) H'CAP (0-105) (3-Y.O+)

(Class B) £10,143.00 (£3,069.00: £1,497.00: £711.00)
1m 3f 195y Stalls: Low GOING minus 0.29 sec per fur (GF) 3-15 (3-15)

1300⁶ **Tethys (USA) (88)***(97) (JLEyre)* 4-10-7 MissDianaJones(2) (mde all: qcknd over 2f out: r.o wl)........— 1
1621⁵ Slasher Jack (IRE) **(80)***(86) (SGNorton)* 4-9-13 MrsLPearce(4) (trckd ldrs: effrt over 3f out: ev ch ins fnl f)........2 2

1635* Amancio (USA) **(84)***(86)*(Fav)*(GHarwood)* 4-10-3 MissAHarwood(1) (swtg: hld up: effrt over 2f out: rdn & nt qckn)....3½ **3**
1636³ Spot Prize (USA) **(95)***(86) (IABalding)* 4-11-0 MissCBall(3) (lw: cl up tl outpcd over 3f out: no ch after)....8 **4**

13/8 Amancio (USA), **7/4** Slasher Jack (IRE), **4/1** TETHYS (USA), **7/1** Spot Prize (USA) (5/1-8/1), CSF £10.23 TOTE £5.00 (£4.00) OWNER Mr M. Gleason (HAMBLETON) BRED Cherry Valley Farm Inc 4 Rn
2m 32.86 (5.86) SF: 55/44/44/44

1806

25TH YEAR OF THE WILLIAM HILL TROPHY H'CAP (0-105) (3-Y.O) (Class B) £38,958.00 (£11,814.00: £5,782.00: £2,766.00)
6f Stalls: High GOING minus 0.29 sec per fur (GF) 3-45 (3-46)

1487² **Bold Effort (FR) (87)***(100) (KOCunningham-Brown)* 3-8-8 TIves(4) (mde most: rdn clr over 1f out: r.o wl)....— **1**
1487⁴ Coastal Bluff **(80)***(84)*(Fav)*(TDBarron)* 3-8-1 ow1 KDarley(2) (b.hind: sn chsng ldrs: effrt 2f out: kpt on: nt pce of wnr)....3 **2**
1373* Stylish Ways (IRE) **(92)***(97+) (GWragg)* 3-8-13 7x MHills(14) (lw: hld up: gd hdwy 2f out: r.o ins fnl f)....s.h **3**
1487³ French Grit (IRE) **(86)***(86) (MDods)* 3-8-7 JWeaver(3) (lw: plld hrd: n.m.r over 3f out: hdwy 2f out: kpt on wl)....1¾ **4**
828⁶ Musical Season **(91)***(90) (TDBarron)* 3-8-12 JFortune(5) (hld up: n.m.r ½-wy: hdwy over 1f out: styd on wl)....nk **5**
1362⁵ Doctor's Glory (USA) **(85)***(81) (RHannon)* 3-8-6 RHills(9) (hld up: effrt ½-wy: no imp fnl 2f)..1¼ **6**
1487⁹ Bolshoi (IRE) **(72)***(68) (JBerry)* 3-7-7b NCarlisle(11) (gd spd over 4f)....s.h **7**
1508³ Superpride **(74)***(66) (MrsMReveley)* 3-7-9 ow1 DaleGibson(1) (chsd ldrs tl wknd over 1f out) .1¼ **8**
1487* Perryston View **(88)***(80) (PCalver)* 3-8-9v 7x MBirch(10) (lw: chsd ldrs over 4f: rdn & wknd) ....nk **9**
1131¹¹ Go Hever Golf **(94)***(81) (TJNaughton)* 3-9-1 GCarter(12) (b.hind: disp ld over 3f: sn rdn & wknd)....2 **10**
1360* Prime Match (IRE) **(83)***(64) (PWHarris)* 3-8-4 7x MFenton(7) (hld up: hmpd over 3f out: n.d)....2 **11**
1487⁸ Emerging Market **(94)***(72) (JLDunlop)* 3-9-1 WRyan(6) (hld up: hmpd over 3f out: no imp after)....1¼ **12**
1305³ Zeb (IRE) **(100)***(75) (BAMcMahon)* 3-9-7 WCarson(15) (drvn along & outpcd most of wy) 1¼ **13**
1487¹¹ Welton Arsenal **(98)***(69) (MRChannon)* 3-9-5 CRutter(13) (hld up & bhd: hmpd over 3f out: n.d after)....1¼ **14**
939⁷ Bajan Rose **(86)** *(MBlanshard)* 3-8-7 StephenDavies(8) (hld up & bhd: hmpd over 3f out: virtually p.u: sddle slipped) ....dist **15**

LONG HANDICAP Bolshoi (IRE) 7-6

4/1 Coastal Bluff, **6/1** Stylish Ways (IRE), **13/2** French Grit (IRE), Perryston View, **8/1** Go Hever Golf, **10/1** Emerging Market, BOLD EFFORT (FR), Superpride, Prime Match (IRE) (8/1-12/1), **12/1** Zeb (IRE), **20/1** Welton Arsenal, **25/1** Doctor's Glory (USA), **33/1** Musical Season, Bolshoi (IRE), Bajan Rose, CSF £50.68 CT £248.21 TOTE £13.00: £3.00 £2.20 £2.60 (£25.30) Trio £56.50 OWNER Mr A. J. Richards (STOCKBRIDGE) BRED Ewar Stud Farm 15 Rn
1m 11.58 (1.98) SF: 39/23/36/25/29/20/7/5/19/20/3/11/14/8/-

1807

DANIEL PRENN RATED STKS H'CAP (0-105) (Listed) (3-Y.O) (Class A) £11,890.80 (£4,154.80: £2,027.40: £867.00)
1m 2f 85y Stalls: Low GOING minus 0.29 sec per fur (GF) 4-15 (4-16)

1374² **Quango (90)***(97) (JGFitzGerald)* 3-8-7 KFallon(4) (lw: hld up: hdwy 4f out: led wl over 1f out: r.o u.p)....— **1**
1636* Ela-Aristokrati (IRE) **(104)***(111)*(Fav)*(MRStoute)* 3-9-7 MHills(1) (lw: trckd ldrs: rdn to ld over 2f out: sn hdd: kpt on u.p)....nk **2**
1129⁵ Sayeh (IRE) **(95)***(94) (HThomsonJones)* 3-8-12 RHills(2) (led tl hdd over 3f out: btn whn hmpd over 2f out)....5 **3**
1345⁴ Zamalek (USA) **(95)***(90) (HRACecil)* 3-8-12b WRyan(3) (cl up: led over 3f out tl over 2f out: hung lft & sn btn)....2½ **4**

LONG HANDICAP Quango 8-5

10/11 Ela-Aristokrati (IRE), **3/1** QUANGO, **9/2** Sayeh (IRE), **11/2** Zamalek (USA), CSF £6.02 TOTE £3.80 (£1.90) OWNER Mr L. Milligan (MALTON) BRED Lord Fairhaven 4 Rn
2m 10.17 (2.67) SF: 47/61/44/40

1808

CADOGAN SILVER SALVER H'CAP (0-90) (3-Y.O+) (Class C) £11,137.50 (£3,375.00: £1,650.00: £787.50)
1m 205y Stalls: Low GOING minus 0.29 sec per fur (GF) 4-45 (4-47)

1638⁵ **Pride of Pendle (69)***(79) (DNicholls)* 6-8-9 AlexGreaves(1) (lw: chsd ldrs: rdn to ld over 1f out: wknd towards fin)....— **1**

1524[4] Percy Braithwaite (IRE) **(82)***(92) (MJohnston)* 3-8-11b DHolland(17) (w ldr: led over 2f out tl over 1f out: r.o towards fin) ....nk **2**
1256* Tykeyvor (IRE) **(74)***(82)*(Fav)*(LadyHerries)* 5-9-0 KDarley(7) (b.hind: trckd ldrs: hdwy & gng wl 3f out: effrt & edgd lft 2f out: kpt on) 1 **3**
1649[6] Maurangi **(56)***(61) (BWMurray)* 4-7-3 (7)ow2 MartinDwyer(4) (sn pushed along: in tch: hdwy & ev ch over 2f out: one pce) ....nk **4**
1280[4] Dancing Heights (IRE) **(78)***(83) (IABalding)* 4-9-4 WRyan(2) (bhd: effrt over 3f out: sn chsng ldrs & hrd rdn: no imp appr fnl f) 1 **5**
1421[2] Sycamore Lodge (IRE) **(70)***(71) (PCalver)* 4-8-5 (5) JStack(5) (in tch: effrt 3f out: no imp whn hmpd over 1f out) 2½ **6**
1468[5] Master Ofthe House **(60)***(60) (MDHammond)* 9-8-0 JMarshall(12) (lw: hdwy ½-wy: one pce fnl 2f) ....¾ **7**
1432[5] Roseate Lodge **(62)***(61) (NBycroft)* 9-8-2 SMaloney(10) (bhd: hdwy 3f out: nvr rchd ldrs) ....nk **8**
1357[5] Country Lover **(82)***(80) (LordHuntingdon)* 4-9-8 JWeaver(16) (bhd: rdn 3f out: nvr rchd ldrs) ....nk **9**
Bold Amusement **(83)***(79) (WSCunningham)* 5-9-9 DeanMcKeown(3) (dwlt: plld hrd: a bhd) 1½ **10**
1596[10] No Comebacks **(58)***(51) (EJAlston)* 7-7-12 AMackay(6) (lw: hld up & bhd: styd on fnl 2f) 1¾ **11**
1183[15] Samah **(65)***(58) (DNicholls)* 5-8-5 NConnorton(8) (set str pce tl hdd over 2f out: sn wknd) ....s.h **12**
767[9] Battle Colours (IRE) **(62)***(48) (DonEnricoIncisa)* 6-8-2 KimTinkler(14) (chsd ldr tl wknd over 3f out) 3½ **13**
1291[6] Daawe (USA) **(82)***(58) (MrsVAAconley)* 4-9-8v KFallon(9) (chsd ldrs: effrt over 3f out: wknd over 2f out) 6 **14**
1617[5] Forever Diamonds **(84)***(15) (MHEasterby)* 8-9-10 MBirch(11) (lost tch fnl 4f: t.o) 25 **15**
*1531** Coureur **(66)** *(JDBethell)* 6-8-6 TIves(15) (Withdrawn not under Starter's orders: inj. at s) .... **W**

9/2 Tykeyvor (IRE), **13/2** Coureur, **7/1** PRIDE OF PENDLE, Country Lover, **8/1** Dancing Heights (IRE), Sycamore Lodge (IRE), Forever Diamonds, **10/1** Percy Braithwaite (IRE) (8/1-12/1), **11/1** Master Ofthe House, **12/1** No Comebacks, **14/1** Samah, **25/1** Roseate Lodge, Maurangi, Daawe (USA), **33/1** Bold Amusement, Battle Colours (IRE), CSF £64.36 CT £245.37 TOTE £7.10: £2.00 £3.00 £2.20 (£28.20) Trio £49.50 OWNER Mrs Linda Miller (THIRSK) BRED James Simpson 15 Rn
1m 49.92 (0.92) SF: 62/64/65/44/66/54/43/44/63/62/34/41/31/41/-/-
WEIGHT FOR AGE 3yo-11lb

1809 MICHAEL SOBELL H'CAP (0-75) (3-Y.O+) (Class D) £7,717.50 (£2,340.00: £1,145.00: £547.50) 6f Stalls: High GOING minus 0.29 sec per fur (GF) 5-15 (5-18)

1421[3] **Al Wujud (IRE) (47)***(56) (TDyer)* 4-8-0 JFanning(3) (swtg: chsd ldrs: led over 1f out: r.o wl) ....— **1**
1421[6] Profit Release (IRE) **(54)***(59) (MJohnston)* 4-8-7b DHolland(18) (racd stands' side: r.o fnl 2f: nrst fin) 1½ **2**
1411[14] Bayin (USA) **(68)***(70) (MDIUsher)* 6-9-7 RStreet(19) (b: dwlt: wl bhd tl hdwy ½-wy: hung lft & kpt on) 1 **3**
1602[2] Just Dissident (IRE) **(66)***(67) (RMWhitaker)* 3-8-11 ACulhane(6) (cl up: led after 2f tl over 1f out: kpt on) ....½ **4**
1599[12] Here Comes a Star **(75)***(75) (JMCarr)* 7-10-0 TIves(20) (effrt stands' side ½-wy: r.o: nvr able chal) ....½ **5**
697[6] South Rock **(74)***(70) (JAGlover)* 3-9-5 DeanMcKeown(7) (chsd ldrs: sn rdn along: outpcd fnl 2f) 1½ **6**
1456[2] Green's Bid **(52)***(46) (DWChapman)* 5-8-5 LCharnock(4) (led 2f: wknd over 2f out) ....½ **7**
1582[6] Formidable Liz **(60)***(53) (MDHammond)* 5-8-13 DaleGibson(2) (in tch: styd on one pce fnl 2f) ....½ **8**
1560[5] Bold Angel **(73)***(63) (MHEasterby)* 8-9-12 MBirch(8) (trckd ldrs: effrt over 2f out: no imp) 1 **9**
1668[2] Halmanerror **(59)***(49)*(Fav)*(MrsJRRamsden)* 5-8-12 KFallon(11) (lw: unruly s: effrt ½-wy: rdn & no imp) ....s.h **10**
1461* Rich Glow **(54)***(42) (NBycroft)* 4-8-7 SMaloney(10) (hdwy ½-wy: sn rdn & btn) ....¾ **11**
1599[5] Cafe Solo **(40)***(27) (NBycroft)* 4-7-7b NKennedy(14) (a bhd) ....½ **12**
1355[5] Ashdren **(57)***(44) (AHarrison)* 8-8-5v(5) JStack(13) (nvr trbld ldrs) ....s.h **13**
1604[9] Miss Aragon **(48)***(32) (MissLCSiddall)* 7-8-1 NCarlisle(5) (in tch tl rdn & wknd over 2f out) 1 **14**
1248[6] Sense of Priority **(57)***(38) (DNicholls)* 6-8-10 AlexGreaves(1) (in tch to ½-wy) 1¼ **15**
1421[4] Reverand Thickness **(73)***(48) (SCWilliams)* 4-9-12 KDarley(15) (sn pushed along: no ch fr ½-wy) 2 **16**
1565[8] Gondo **(52)***(24) (EJAlston)* 8-8-0v(5) CTeague(9) (outpcd fr ½-wy) 1¼ **17**
1604[8] Rankaidade **(44)***(15) (DonEnricoIncisa)* 4-7-11 KimTinkler(16) (prom stands' side 4f) ....½ **18**
1508[11] Sir Tasker **(52)***(9) (JLHarris)* 7-8-5 AMackay(12) (lw: unruly in stalls: in tch over 3f) 5 **19**

3/1 Halmanerror, **15/2** Just Dissident (IRE), **10/1** Rich Glow, Bold Angel, Reverand Thickness, **11/1** South Rock, **12/1** AL WUJUD (IRE), **14/1** Profit Release (IRE), Bayin (USA), Here Comes a Star, Miss Aragon, **16/1** Cafe Solo, Green's Bid, **20/1** Formidable Liz, Gondo, **25/1** Ashdren, Sir Tasker, **33/1** Sense of Priority, Rankaidade, CSF £170.66 CT £2,196.95 TOTE £14.90: £2.70 £2.80 £3.40 £1.90 (£126.70) Trio £379.10 OWNER Mr Mike Flynn (INVERGOWRIE) BRED Shadwell Estate Company Limited 19 Rn 1m 11.81 (2.21) SF: 29/32/43/32/48/35/19/26/36/22/15/-/17/5/11/21/-/-/-
WEIGHT FOR AGE 3yo-8lb
T/Plpt: £273.90 (108.12 Tckts). T/Qdpt: £119.40 (3.2 Tckts). AA

1515-BRIGHTON (L-H)
Monday June 19th (Good to firm)
WEATHER: sunny WIND: mod half against

1810
MONTPELIER (S) STKS (2-Y.O) (Class G) £2,243.00 (£618.00: £293.00)
5f 213y Stalls: Low GOING minus 0.45 sec per fur (F) 2-00 (2-00)

1627[6] **Arlington Lady** *(66+)*(Fav)*(NACallaghan)* 2-8-6 MRoberts(6) (b.hind: 2nd st: led 2f out: rdn over 1f out: r.o) ....— 1
Fenna *(59) (SPCWoods)* 2-7-13 (7) CWebb(4) (w'like: 6th st: hdwy over 2f out: rdn over 1f out: one pce) 2½ 2
1632[2] Nameless *(59) (DJSCosgrove)* 2-8-6 (5) PMcCabe(1) (lw: led 5f out to 2f out: one pce) 2 3
1590[5] Solva Mist *(54) (LJHolt)* 2-8-6 AMcGlone(3) (5th st: hdwy over 1f out: r.o one pce fnl f) ....hd 4
1163[5] No Sympathy *(53) (GLMoore)* 2-8-6 SWhitworth(7) (4th st: rdn 2f out: one pce) ....nk 5
1734[2] Don't Tell Vicki *(36) (JSMoore)* 2-8-6 (5) SDrowne(5) (dwlt: 7th st: rdn over 2f out: a bhd) 8 6
1590[9] Caveat Emptor (IRE) *(34) (SDow)* 2-8-11 StephenDavies(2) (led 1f: 3rd st: wknd 3f out) ....¾ 7

4/5 ARLINGTON LADY (op 5/4), **5/1** Don't Tell Vicki (7/2-11/2), **6/1** No Sympathy (7/2-13/2), **9/1** Nameless (op 5/1), **11/1** Solva Mist (5/1-12/1), **25/1** Caveat Emptor (IRE), **33/1** Fenna, CSF £20.31 TOTE £2.20: £1.20 £6.10 (£33.70) OWNER Mr B. H. McCuaig (NEWMARKET) BRED J. R. Bostock and R. W. Hipkin 7 Rn 1m 11.2 (2.80) SF: 12/5/5/-/-/-/-
No bid

1811
HAILSHAM H'CAP (0-70) (3-Y.O+ F & M) (Class E) £3,330.80 (£994.40: £475.20: £215.60)
7f 214y Stalls: Low GOING minus 0.45 sec per fur (F) 2-30 (2-32)

1735[2] **Never so Rite (IRE) (54)***(65)*(Fav)*(DWPArbuthnot)* 3-8-13 TQuinn(3) (chsd ldrs: 5th st: hdwy 3f out: led over 1f out: r.o) ....— 1
1651[6] Narbonne **(57)***(61) (BJMcMath)* 4-9-12 MTebbutt(5) (led tl over 1f out: one pce) 3½ 2
1660[7] Brass Tacks **(65)***(68) (RHannon)* 3-9-3 (7) DaneO'Neill(1) (a.p: 4th st: rdn over 1f out: one pce) ....nk 3
1676[10] High Typha **(49)***(51) (MRChannon)* 4-9-4v RHughes(4) (dwlt: 4th st: smooth hdwy over 2f out: rdn ins fnl f: one pce) ....½ 4
1660[10] La Bossette (IRE) **(49)***(37) (JRArnold)* 3-8-8 MRoberts(9) (mid div: 6th st: no hdwy fnl 3f) 7 5
1539[3] Yo Kiri-B **(50)***(35) (JFfitch-Heyes)* 4-9-5 PaulEddery(6) (prom: 3rd st: rdn 2f out: wknd over 1f out) 1½ 6
1510[7] Maybe Today **(58)***(43) (BRMillman)* 3-9-3 MFenton(2) (bhd: 10th st: nvr nrr) ....hd 7
1532* Lorelei Lee (IRE) **(65)***(49) (JohnBerry)* 3-9-5 (5) HKYim(7) (9th st: a bhd) ....¾ 8
1735[10] Pinkerton Polka **(52)***(33) (CEBrittain)* 3-8-11 BDoyle(11) (chsd ldr: 2nd st: wknd 2f out) 1½ 9
371[5] Panchellita (USA) **(53)***(30) (GLMoore)* 6-9-8 SWhitworth(8) (8th st: sn wknd) 1¾ 10
976[12] Harvest Rose **(53)***(29) (OO'Neill)* 6-9-8 VSlattery(10) (mid div: 6th st: sn wknd) ....½ 11

7/2 NEVER SO RITE (IRE), **11/2** Narbonne, Brass Tacks (4/1-6/1), **6/1** Yo Kiri-B, **7/1** High Typha, La Bossette (IRE) (8/1-12/1), **8/1** Lorelei Lee (IRE) (5/1-9/1), **14/1** Maybe Today, Panchellita (USA) (7/1-16/1), **33/1** Pinkerton Polka, Harvest Rose, CSF £22.53 CT £95.51 TOTE £4.00: £1.70 £1.70 £1.80 (£8.70) Trio £24.40 OWNER Mr J. S. Gutkin (COMPTON) BRED G. Cashin 11 Rn
1m 35.6 (3.40) SF: 23/29/26/19/-/3/1/7/-/-/-
WEIGHT FOR AGE 3yo-10lb

1812
A R DENNIS BOOKMAKERS JUNE MAIDEN H'CAP (0-70) (3-Y.O) (Class E) £3,502.40 (£1,047.20: £501.60: £228.80)
6f 209y Stalls: Low GOING minus 0.45 sec per fur (F) 3-00 (3-01)

1428[4] **Self Reliance (68)***(77) (MBell)* 3-9-6 MFenton(5) (a.p: 2nd st: led over 2f out: clr over 1f out: r.o wl) ....— 1
1504[2] Seventeens Lucky **(69)***(70)*(Fav)*(BobJones)* 3-9-7 TQuinn(3) (hld up: 7th st: hdwy & hmpd 2f out: squeezed thro 1f out: r.o) 3½ 2
1512[17] Just-Mana-Mou (IRE) **(50)***(49) (GLewis)* 3-8-2 PaulEddery(4) (chsd ldr: 2nd st: rdn & edgd lft 2f out: one pce) 1 3

1124[11] Arctic Poppy (USA) **(50)***(45) (IABalding)* 3-8-2 SO'Gorman(9) (lw: bhd: 10th st: hdwy over 1f out: r.o one pce fnl f) 1¾ 4
1663[11] Kreef **(50)***(41) (RJO'Sullivan)* 3-8-2 DBiggs(8) (4th st: rdn over 2f out: one pce) 1½ 5
1630[7] Mighty Squaw **(63)***(53) (MissGayKelleway)* 3-9-1b SWhitworth(7) (9th st: hrd rdn & hdwy over 1f out: nvr nrr) .... ½ 6
773[10] Asking **(41)***(29) (JABennett)* 3-7-2v(5) MBaird(10) (bhd: 11th st: nvr nrr) .... ¾ 7
1428[5] Nyali Beach (IRE) **(51)***(39) (BJMeehan)* 3-8-3 BDoyle(1) (8th st: hdwy whn n.m.r over 1f out: nt rcvr) .... nk 8
1453[6] Sweet Water (IRE) **(55)***(39) (DJSCosgrove)* 3-8-2 (5) PMcCabe(6) (mid div: 6th st: rdn over 2f out: grad wknd) 1¾ 9
1467[4] Faith 'n Glory (IRE) **(63)***(30) (RHannon)* 3-8-8 (7) DaneO'Neill(11) (lw: prom: 5th st: wknd 2f out) 7 10
1050[14] Kensington Freight **(41)***(7) (JAkehurst)* 3-7-7v NAdams(2) (led over 4f) .... ½ 11

LONG HANDICAP Asking 6-12 Kensington Freight 7-6

7/4 Seventeens Lucky, **4/1** Just-Mana-Mou (IRE), **15/2** SELF RELIANCE (5/1-8/1), **8/1** Mighty Squaw, **9/1** Nyali Beach (IRE), **10/1** Sweet Water (IRE) (7/1-11/1), **11/1** Faith 'n Glory (IRE) (11/2-12/1), **20/1** Arctic Poppy (USA), **33/1** Asking, Kreef, Kensington Freight, CSF £20.26 CT £54.65 TOTE £5.70: £1.70 £1.40 £2.00 (£5.30) Trio £16.50 OWNER Mrs Richard Pilkington (NEWMARKET) BRED Stanley Estate and Stud Co 11 Rn 1m 22.8 (2.80) SF: 31/24/3/-/-/7/-/-/-/-/-

1813 OPERATIC SOCIETY CHALLENGE CUP MEDIAN AUCTION MAIDEN STKS (3 & 4-Y.O) (Class E) £3,044.80 (£906.40: £431.20: £193.60) **1m 3f 196y** Stalls: Low GOING minus 0.45 sec per fur (F) 3-30 (3-32)

1554[5] **Yet Again (59)***(75) (BHanbury)* 3-8-8 PaulEddery(3) (hld up: 3rd st: led 1f out: pushed out) .— 1
1367[10] Quest Again **(61)***(74) (DWPArbuthnot)* 4-9-9 TQuinn(2) (led: rdn over 2f out: hdd 1f out: unable qckn) .... ¾ 2
1358[2] Drumochter **(56)***(66)*(Fav)*(DMorley)* 3-8-8 MFenton(4) (chsd ldr: 2nd st: rdn over 2f out: wknd over 1f out) 6 3
1535[13] Foremma **(20)***(41) (PRHedger)* 4-9-4 CAvery(1) (chsd ldrs: 4th & wkng st: sn bhd) 15 4

11/10 Drumochter (4/6-11/8), **6/4** Quest Again, **100/30** YET AGAIN, **100/1** Foremma, CSF £8.34 TOTE £4.50 (£4.00) OWNER Mr G. G. Grayson (NEWMARKET) BRED Aston Park Stud 4 Rn 2m 33.6 (4.60) SF: 27/41/18/8
WEIGHT FOR AGE 3yo-15lb

1814 LEWES MAIDEN STKS (3-Y.O+) (Class D) £3,766.10 (£1,122.80: £535.40: £241.70) **1m 1f 209y** Stalls: High GOING minus 0.45 sec per fur (F) 4-00 (4-00)

618[3] **State Law (86)***(75+)*(Fav)*(GHarwood)* 3-8-11 AClark(3) (lw: hld up: chsd ldrs 6f out: led on bit over 3f out: clr over 1f out: v.easily) ....— 1
Courtown Boy *(69) (OO'Neill)* 5-9-9 VSlattery(4) (bhd & outpcd 6f out: hdwy 4f out: 3rd st: rdn over 2f out: one pce fnl 2f) 3½ 2
978[10] Ambidextrous (IRE) *(69) (CEBrittain)* 3-8-11 BDoyle(1) (led over 3f: 4th st: rdn & hung lft over 2f out: one pce fnl 2f) .... nk 3
1270[4] Lavender (IRE) *(61) (LMCumani)* 3-8-6 TQuinn(2) (chsd ldr: led over 6f out tl over 3f out: rdn over 1f out: eased whn btn wl ins fnl f) 1¾ 4

1/3 STATE LAW (op 4/7), **11/4** Lavender (IRE) (op 6/4), **12/1** Ambidextrous (IRE) (tchd 20/1), **33/1** Courtown Boy, CSF £7.59 TOTE £1.50 (£11.80) OWNER Mr K. J. Buchanan (PULBOROUGH) BRED K. J. and Mrs Buchanan 4 Rn 2m 2.4 (4.40) SF: 21/27/15/7
WEIGHT FOR AGE 3yo-12lb

1815 PALACE H'CAP (0-80) (3-Y.O+) (Class D) £3,630.90 (£1,081.20: £514.60: £231.30) **5f 213y** Stalls: Low GOING minus 0.45 sec per fur (F) 4-30 (4-30)

1537* **Aragrove (71)***(79)*(Fav)*(JWPayne)* 5-9-7b MTebbutt(2) (hld up gng wl: 3rd st: led over 2f out: rdn over 1f out: drvn out) ....— 1
1648[4] Napoleon Star (IRE) **(71)***(76) (MSSaunders)* 4-9-2 (5) SDrowne(3) (4th st: rdn 2f out: r.o one pce fnl f) 1¼ 2
1515* Jo Maximus **(70)***(74) (SDow)* 3-8-12 StephenDavies(1) (led over 3f: rdn over 1f out: one pce) .... nk 3
1516[3] Pirates Gold (IRE) **(47)***(42) (JWhite)* 5-7-11 FNorton(6) (outpcd: 6th st: hdwy 2f out: hrd rdn over 1f out: one pce) 3½ 4
89[16] Dancing Lawyer **(69)***(47) (BJMeehan)* 4-9-5 BDoyle(4) (5th st: rdn & wknd over 2f out) 6 5
1673[10] Agwa **(78)***(43) (RJO'Sullivan)* 6-10-0 DBiggs(5) (chsd ldr: 2nd st: rdn over 2f out: sn wknd) 5 6

2/1 ARAGROVE (6/4-9/4), **7/2** Jo Maximus, **4/1** Napoleon Star (IRE), **9/2** Pirates Gold (IRE), **6/1** Dancing Lawyer, Agwa (3/1-10/1), CSF £10.74 TOTE £3.00: £2.20 £2.00 (£6.40) OWNER Mr Dennis Purkiss (NEWMARKET) BRED Mrs J. R. Hine and Miss J. Bunting 6 Rn

1m 9.2 (0.80) SF: 54/51/41/17/22/18

WEIGHT FOR AGE 3yo-8lb

T/Plpt: £123.70 (74.33 Tckts). T/Qdpt: £34.30 (2.5 Tckts). SM

1739-EDINBURGH (R-H)
Monday June 19th (Good to firm)

WEATHER: overcast, light rain WIND: mod half against

1816 WIMPEY DREAM HOME APPRENTICE H'CAP (0-60) (3-Y.O+) (Class G) £2,668.00 (£748.00: £364.00)

1m 3f 32y Stalls: High GOING minus 0.45 sec per fur (F) 1-45 (1-45)

1669⁶ **Acquittal (IRE) (59)***(67)*(Fav)*(JRFanshawe)* 3-9-2 (3) NVarley(5) (a.p: pushed along appr st: styd on to ld ins fnl f)......— 1

1724³ Runrig (IRE) **(40)***(46) (MissLAPerratt)* 5-8-9 (5) RHavlin(1) (lw: hld up & bhd: hdwy 7f out: led appr st tl ins fnl f: no ex)......1¼ 2

478⁷ Portite Sophie **(34)***(33) (MBrittain)* 4-8-3 (5) VHalliday(4) (hld up: hdwy over 3f out: one pce appr fnl f)......5 3

1161⁵ Doubling Dice **(32)***(27) (RAllan)* 4-8-1 (5) MHumphries(3) (hld up: c wd st: rdn & nt qckn fnl 2f)......2½ 4

1439⁷ Philmist **(54)***(48) (JHetherton)* 3-8-11 (3) JStack(8) (w ldr: led 6f out tl appr st: grad wknd fnl 2f)......1 5

1557⁴ Touch Above **(50)***(37) (TDBarron)* 9-9-5 (5) KimberleyHart(6) (plld hrd: slt ld tl hdd over 6f out: outpcd ent st: grad lost pl)......5 6

990⁹ Keith's Pride (IRE) **(33)***(17) (TDyer)* 3-7-0 (7) RMullen(2) (chsd ldrs tl outpcd ent st: sn no ch)..2 7

1578⁹ Demokos (FR) **(25)***(9) (WLBarker)* 10-7-13 DarrenMoffatt(7) (prom tl lost pl appr st: n.d after)......s.h 8

5/4 ACQUITTAL (IRE), **11/4** Touch Above, **13/2** Runrig (IRE), **8/1** Philmist, **16/1** Doubling Dice, **20/1** Demokos (FR), **25/1** Keith's Pride (IRE), **33/1** Portite Sophie, CSF £9.23 CT £153.00 TOTE £1.80: £1.20 £1.10 £3.40 (£7.30) OWNER Mr William McGregor (NEWMARKET) BRED M. L. Page 8 Rn

2m 24.3 (4.60) SF: 35/28/15/9/16/19/-/-

WEIGHT FOR AGE 3yo-14lb

1817 WIMPEY HOMES EDINBURGH GOLD CUP H'CAP (0-70) (3-Y.O+) (Class E) £5,764.00 (£1,732.00: £836.00: £388.00)

1m 4f 31y Stalls: High GOING minus 0.45 sec per fur (F) 2-15 (2-15)

1529¹⁰ **Soba Up (45)***(58) (TJEtherington)* 5-8-5 ACulhane(6) (lw: in tch: lost pl appr st: hdwy 2f out: led 1f out: r.o wl)......— 1

1687³ Keep Battling **(41)***(49)*(Fav)*(JSGoldie)* 5-8-1 GBardwell(3) (lw: hld up & bhd: smooth hdwy to ld 2f out: hdd 1f out: no ex)......3½ 2

*1332*⁸ Killick **(55)***(61) (ABailey)* 7-9-1 JFortune(8) (lw: cl up: led 7f out tl hdd 2f out: r.o one pce) 1½ 3

1725* Daily Starlight (USA) **(70)***(75)*(Fav)*(MissGayKelleway)* 3-9-1 4x MWigham(4) (gd hdwy 7f out: sn chsng ldrs: nt qckn fnl 2f)......¾ 4

1561⁴ Jubran (USA) **(68)***(71) (MJohnston)* 9-10-0 JWeaver(10) (hld up: effrt over 3f out: r.o one pce)......2 5

1744² Lord Advocate **(39)***(40) (DANolan)* 7-7-8b(5) NVarley(5) (lw: chsd ldrs: chal appr st: wknd over 1f out)......1¾ 6

1502⁵ Jean de Florette (USA) **(39)***(33) (JohnBerry)* 4-7-13v LCharnock(2) (lw: nvr trbld ldrs)......5 7

1651⁵ Pendolino (IRE) **(55)***(47) (MBrittain)* 4-9-1 GDuffield(1) (lost tch ½-wy: n.d after)......1¼ 8

1470⁴ Memorable **(38)***(29) (JHetherton)* 4-7-12b NKennedy(11) (lw: led tl hdd 7f out: wknd over 3f out)......¾ 9

1725² Jackmanii **(50)***(35) (WTKemp)* 3-7-9bow2 DaleGibson(7) (lw: prom tl wknd over 2f out)......3 10

1251⁸ King of Show (IRE) **(62)***(46) (RAllan)* 4-9-8 CDwyer(9) (a wl bhd)......2½ 11

LONG HANDICAP Jackmanii 7-6

7/2 Daily Starlight (USA) (5/2-4/1), Keep Battling, **11/2** Killick, **8/1** Jackmanii, Jubran (USA) (op 5/1), **9/1** Lord Advocate, **11/1** Memorable, **12/1** Jean de Florette (USA), **20/1** SOBA UP, **25/1** Pendolino (IRE), **33/1** King of Show (IRE), CSF £83.87 CT £410.36 TOTE £32.80: £4.90 £1.40 £1.60 (£67.30) Trio £129.00 OWNER Mrs M. Hills (MALTON) BRED Mrs M. J. Hills 11 Rn

2m 34.8 (2.30) SF: 39/30/42/41/52/21/14/28/10/1/27

WEIGHT FOR AGE 3yo-15lb

1818

HAYRICKS MAIDEN LIMITED STKS (0-60) (3-Y.O) (Class F) £2,736.00 (£828.00: £404.00: £192.00) **7f 15y** Stalls: High GOING minus 0.45 sec per fur (F) 2-45 (2-46)

1541[2] **Legal Issue (IRE) (58)***(65)*(Fav)*(SirMarkPrescott)* 3-9-0 GDuffield(2) (lw: s.i.s: pushed along & sn prom: led wl over 2f out: r.o wl)...— **1**
1207[7] Tinklers Folly **(41)***(58) (DenysSmith)* 3-9-0 KFallon(4) (swtg: bhd: hdwy 3f out: hung rt appr fnl f: nt qckn)...3 **2**
1742[8] Ricana **(39)***(44) (WTKemp)* 3-8-9 JFortune(5) (hdwy 3½f out: sn chsng ldrs: no imp fnl 2f)......4 **3**
1569[3] Raayaat (USA) **(58)***(47) (ACStewart)* 3-9-0b DHolland(8) (cl up: lft in ld ent st: hdd wl over 2f out: rdn & no rspnse)...1 **4**
989[7] Hutchies Lady **(49)***(34) (RMMcKellar)* 3-8-2 (7) PRoberts(6) (s.i.s: nvr trbld ldrs)...3½ **5**
1583[5] Good Match (IRE) **(56)***(32) (NTinkler)* 3-9-0 LCharnock(3) (lw: chsd ldrs tl outpcd over 3f out)...3 **6**
1583[2] Ganador **(53)***(27) (JBerry)* 3-8-2 (7) CLowther(1) (cl up: rn wd st: sn lost pl)...nk **7**
1471[3] Ligurian (USA) **(58)** *(JWWatts)* 3-8-9b JWeaver(7) (led tl rn wd st: sn lost pl)...20 **8**

5/4 LEGAL ISSUE (IRE), **100/30** Ligurian (USA), Raayaat (USA), **8/1** Ganador (op 5/1), **12/1** Good Match (IRE) (7/1-14/1), **25/1** Tinklers Folly, **33/1** Hutchies Lady, Ricana, CSF £27.34 TOTE £2.00: £1.10 £3.50 £3.70 (£27.00) OWNER Cheveley Park Stud (NEWMARKET) BRED Naver Enterprises Ltd 8 Rn
1m 28.2 (2.20) SF: 36/29/15/18/5/3/-/-

1819

HOLYGATE CLAIMING STKS (3-Y.O+) (Class F) £2,801.00 (£848.00: £414.00: £197.00) **7f 15y** Stalls: High GOING minus 0.45 sec per fur (F) 3-15 (3-15)

1785* **Four of Spades (48)***(61)*(Fav)*(WSCunningham)* 4-8-7b(5) JStack(1) (chsd ldrs: led wl over 1f out: pushed out)...— **1**
1721[2] Diet **(45)***(61) (MissLAPerratt)* 9-9-0v GDuffield(3) (lw: chsd ldrs: ev ch 3f out: styd on one pce)...1 **2**
1545[3] Best Kept Secret **(68)***(65) (JBerry)* 4-9-6 JFortune(2) (a.p: effrt 2f out: styd on: nvr able to chal)...1 **3**
1721[9] Sunday Mail Too (IRE) **(43)***(51) (MissLAPerratt)* 3-7-12b LCharnock(5) (led tl hdd wl over 1f out: one pce)...nk **4**
1545[7] Obsidian Grey **(52)***(54) (MissLCSiddall)* 8-8-12 DeanMcKeown(7) (in tch: hdwy u.p 2f out: no imp)...¾ **5**
1206[4] Funny Rose **(23)***(34) (PMonteith)* 5-8-0 (5) NVarley(6) (dwlt: nvr trbld ldrs)...6 **6**
1420[6] Nicky's Feelings *(29) (TDyer)* 3-7-7 (7) RMullen(4) (s.i.s: nvr wnt pce)...4 **7**

6/4 FOUR OF SPADES, **5/2** Best Kept Secret (op 6/4), **11/2** Diet, Obsidian Grey, **25/1** Sunday Mail Too (IRE), **33/1** Funny Rose, **40/1** Nicky's Feelings, CSF £9.03 TOTE £2.60: £1.40 £1.60 (£6.90) OWNER Mr B. L. Cassidy (YARM) BRED Hesmonds Stud Ltd 7 Rn
1m 28.5 (2.50) SF: 31/31/35/12/24/4/-
WEIGHT FOR AGE 3yo-9lb
Four of Spades clmd DNolan £4,000.

1820

WESTHOLME H'CAP (0-70) (3-Y.O+) (Class E) £3,550.00 (£1,075.00: £525.00: £250.00) **1m 16y** Stalls: High GOING minus 0.45 sec per fur (F) 3-45 (3-45)

227[12] **Mighty Kingdom (IRE) (37)***(45) (JohnBerry)* 4-7-7 (5) NVarley(3) (lw: a.p: led wl over 1f out: drvn out)...— **1**
1666[2] Mary's Case (IRE) **(53)***(60)*(Fav)*(MJohnston)* 5-9-0b DHolland(2) (hld up: stdy hdwy ent st: ev ch over 1f out: rdn & nt r.o)...¾ **2**
1724[8] Miss Pigalle **(34)***(40) (MissLAPerratt)* 4-7-9b DaleGibson(7) (a.p: ev ch over 1f out: one pce).nk **3**
594[17] Seconds Away **(40)***(34) (JSGoldie)* 4-8-1 GBardwell(8) (outpcd & lost pl appr st: styd on fnl f: nrst fin)...6 **4**
1666[7] Mca Below the Line **(63)***(55) (WLBarker)* 7-9-5v(5) VHalliday(4) (s.i.s: styd on u.p fnl 3f: n.d)...1¼ **5**
1742[5] Borrowby **(35)***(26) (MWEasterby)* 3-7-10v LCharnock(9) (lw: led tl hdd over 3f out: sn rdn & grad wknd)...½ **6**
1506[9] Leave it to Lib **(53)***(37) (PCalver)* 8-8-9 (5) JStack(5) (lw: cl up: led over 3f out tl wl over 1f out: sn btn)...3½ **7**
1463[5] Salduba **(32)***(15) (TDyer)* 3-7-0 (7) RMullen(1) (chsd ldrs to st: sn wknd)...½ **8**
Storm Leader **(32)***(1) (MBrittain)* 4-7-7 NKennedy(6) (reard s: a bhd)...7 **9**

LONG HANDICAP Storm Leader 7-3

11/8 Mary's Case (IRE), **9/2** Borrowby, **5/1** Leave it to Lib, **10/1** Mca Below the Line, Seconds Away (op 6/1), **12/1** Miss Pigalle, **20/1** MIGHTY KINGDOM (IRE), **40/1** Salduba, Storm Leader, CSF £44.44 CT £324.59 TOTE £29.70: £8.10 £1.10 £2.60 (£41.50) Trio £29.60 OWNER Mr John Purcell (NEWMARKET) BRED Rathasker Stud 9 Rn 1m 42.0 (3.40) SF: 13/28/8/2/23/-/5/-/-

1821 E.B.F MEDIAN AUCTION MAIDEN STKS (2-Y.O F) (Class F)
£2,970.00 (£900.00: £440.00: £210.00)
5f Stalls: High GOING minus 0.30 sec per fur (GF) 4-15 (4-15)

Dancing Rainbow *(71+) (MJCamacho)* 2-8-11 LCharnock(3) (cmpt: lw: mde all: pushed clr appr fnl f: eased towards fin) — 1
Cawdor Lady *(60) (TJEtherington)* 2-8-11 JWeaver(2) (leggy: unf: lw: s.i.s: bhd tl gd hdwy 2f out: no ch w wnr) 3½ 2
1646³ February *(53)*(Fav)*(MRChannon)* 2-8-11 DHolland(5) (lw: chsd wnr 3f: sn rdn & btn) 2 3
1440⁶ Silent Soprano *(44) (DenysSmith)* 2-8-11v JFortune(4) (lw: spd 3f: sn btn) 3 4
Spring Silhouette *(25) (MrsVAAconley)* 2-8-11 KFallon(1) (unf: sn prom: wknd fnl 2f) 6 5

2/1 February, **5/2** DANCING RAINBOW, **11/4** Cawdor Lady (op 7/4), **4/1** Silent Soprano, **25/1** Spring Silhouette, CSF £9.21 TOTE £3.80: £1.80 £1.90 (£6.50) OWNER Mr B. S. Adamson (MALTON) BRED B. S. Adamson 5 Rn 60.4 secs (2.70) SF: 24/13/6/-/-

1822 WIMPEY WELCOME HOME H'CAP (0-70) (3-Y.O) (Class E) £3,178.00 (£964.00: £472.00: £226.00) **5f** Stalls: High GOING minus 0.30 sec per fur (GF) 4-45 (4-46)

1419* **Crowded Avenue (56)***(63+)*(Fav)*(PJMakin)* 3-8-7 JWeaver(2) (hld up: qcknd to ld wl over 1f out: rdn & r.o) — 1
1723⁵ Mister Westsound **(44)***(45) (MissLAPerratt)* 3-7-9vow1 DaleGibson(8) (hld up & bhd: hdwy & ev ch over 1f out: hung rt & hit rail: nt r.o) 1½ 2
1580⁷ Baileys Sunset (IRE) **(60)***(57) (MJohnston)* 3-8-11 DHolland(5) (prom: kpt on fnl f: nvr able to chal) 1½ 3
1641⁴ Swan At Whalley **(70)***(64) (MartynWane)* 3-9-7 JFortune(7) (cl up: led wl over 1f out: sn hdd & no ex) 1 4
*1566*⁹ Lloc **(57)***(50) (JohnBerry)* 3-8-3 (5) NVarley(3) (lw: b: disp ld over 3f: grad wknd) nk 5
1434⁶ Ramborette **(51)***(35) (DenysSmith)* 3-8-2v LCharnock(6) (s.i.s: nvr rchd ldrs) 3 6
Chance Me **(42)***(25) (MJohnston)* 3-7-7 NKennedy(4) (disp ld over 3f: sn lost pl) nk 7
1565⁴ Breakfast Creek **(65)***(37) (JBerry)* 3-8-9 (7) PRoberts(1) (lw: b: w ldrs 3f: sn wknd) 3½ 8
LONG HANDICAP Chance Me 7-5

5/6 CROWDED AVENUE, **4/1** Breakfast Creek, **10/1** Baileys Sunset (IRE) (op 6/1), **12/1** Swan At Whalley, Lloc, Ramborette, **14/1** Chance Me, Mister Westsound, CSF £13.19 CT £72.79 TOTE £1.70: £1.10 £1.70 £3.20 (£21.20) OWNER Mr T. W. Wellard (MARLBOROUGH) BRED The Duke of Marlborough 8 Rn 59.3 secs (1.60) SF: 38/20/32/39/25/10/-/12

T/Plpt: £115.10 (97.43 Tckts). T/Qdpt: £23.10 (2.05 Tckts). AA

1646-PONTEFRACT (L-H)
Monday June 19th (Good to firm)
WEATHER: overcast WIND: slt half bhd

1823 TATTERSALLS MEDIAN AUCTION MAIDEN STKS (2-Y.O F) (Class E)
£3,100.00 (£940.00: £460.00: £220.00)
6f Stalls: Low GOING minus 0.27 sec per fur (GF) 6-45 (6-46)

1348⁵ **Fag End (IRE)** *(70) (MHTompkins)* 2-8-1 PRobinson(6) (chsd ldrs: led over 1f out: styd on wl) — 1
1671³ Corniche Quest (IRE) *(63) (MRChannon)* 2-8-2 KDarley(8) (led tl over 1f out: one pce) 3 2
1646⁴ Skelton Countess (IRE) *(56) (RHollinshead)* 2-7-10 (3) AGarth(3) (lw: hld up: hdwy ½-wy: outpcd over 1f out: styd on ins fnl f) 1½ 3
1497⁶ Priddy Fair *(56) (RBoss)* 2-7-13 AMackay(2) (chsd ldrs: outpcd ½-wy: sn lost pl) hd 4
Posen Gold (IRE) *(57) (PAKelleway)* 2-8-0 (3)ow2 JTate(9) (rangy: chsd ldrs: rdn & outpcd 2f out: kpt on fnl f) nk 5
Yuppy Girl (IRE) *(46) (CaptJWilson)* 2-7-13 SMaloney(5) (leggy: unf: s.i.s: outpcd & rn green ½-wy: sn bhd) 3½ 6
1699³ Down The Yard *(42) (MCChapman)* 2-7-6 (7) JBramhill(7) (sn chsng ldrs: rdn along & outpcd 2f out: kpt on ins fnl f) 1½ 7
1579² Diminuet (Fav)*(JWWatts)* 2-8-1 JFanning(4) (lw: hmpd & dropped rr ½-wy: b.b.v: p.u over 1f out) P

7/4 Diminuet, **7/2** Corniche Quest (IRE), **5/1** Priddy Fair (4/1-6/1), **11/2** FAG END (IRE), **9/1** Posen Gold (IRE), **12/1** Down The Yard, **20/1** Skelton Countess (IRE), **33/1** Yuppy Girl (IRE), CSF £23.70 TOTE £6.20: £2.00 £1.10 £4.90 (£8.30) Trio £38.30 OWNER Mr Michael Keogh (NEWMARKET) BRED St Simon Foundation 8 Rn 1m 18.4 (4.10) SF: 11/4/-/-/-/-/-/-

1824

BEECH (S) STKS (3-Y.O) (Class G) £2,728.00 (£758.00: £364.00)
1m 4y Stalls: Low GOING minus 0.27 sec per fur (GF) 7-15 (7-17)

674[11] **Miss Zanzibar (55)***(64) (RAFahey)* 3-8-9 ACulhane(5) (hld up & bhd: gd hdwy on ins over 2f out: r.o wl to ld ins fnl f: hung lft: sn qcknd clr)........— 1
1465[8] Trumble **(50)***(57) (CWThornton)* 3-9-0 AMackay(8) (w ldr: led 4f out tl ins fnl f: nt pce of wnr)........6 2
1625[7] Mill Dancer (IRE) *(49) (EJAlston)* 3-8-9 KFallon(10) (dwlt s: bhd tl hdwy over 2f out: kpt on wl fnl f)........1½ 3
1509[5] Move With Edes **(52)***(58) (WGMTurner)* 3-9-6 GDuffield(14) (a.p: ev ch over 1f out: one pce)........1¼ 4
818[8] River Wye (IRE) **(50)***(49)*(Fav)*(JMCarr)* 3-9-0 SMorris(3) (a chsng ldrs: rdn 3f out: outpcd fnl 2f)........1½ 5
1669[13] Bitch **(49)***(49) (DNicholls)* 3-9-1 AlexGreaves(9) (in tch: effrt over 2f out: kpt on: nvr nr to chal)........s.h 6
Huish Cross **(64)***(39) (DMorley)* 3-8-9 TIves(1) (s.i.s: hld up & bhd: sme hdwy 2f out: nvr rchd ldrs)........2½ 7
1647[3] Never Time (IRE) **(41)***(39) (MrsVAAconley)* 3-9-0 SMaloney(7) (unruly gng to s: bhd: sme hdwy 4f out: sn hrd drvn & wknd)........2½ 8
1379[12] Rubislaw **(31)***(35) (CWFairhurst)* 3-8-11v(3) JTate(2) (prom tl lost pl over 2f out)........1¾ 9
1669[11] Red Hot Risk **(51)***(38) (MDods)* 3-9-6v SWebster(12) (s.i.s: sme hdwy over 3f out: hung bdly lft over 1f out: nt r.o)........1½ 10
1645[15] Share the Secret **(42)***(25) (BHanbury)* 3-9-0 PRobinson(11) (bhd: sme hdwy 4f out: sn wknd)........3½ 11
1434[12] Sweet Cheap Pet **(35)***(19) (JJO'Neill)* 3-9-1 JFortune(13) (lw: chsd ldrs: rdn 3f out: sn lost pl)........3½ 12
1669[W] Elite Number (USA) **(50)** *(MJCamacho)* 3-8-9 JWeaver(4) (led tl 4f out: lost pl over 2f out: eased & t.o)........30 13
1414[15] Perfect Bertie (IRE) **(50)** *(GROldroyd)* 3-9-0 MBirch(6) (bhd whn rn wd bnd 6f out: hung rt & lost pl 3f out: eased over 1f out: t.o)........7 14

4/1 River Wye (IRE), **9/2** Trumble, **11/2** Move With Edes, Huish Cross (op 7/2), **8/1** MISS ZANZIBAR, **9/1** Bitch (op 20/1), **10/1** Elite Number (USA), **12/1** Never Time (IRE), Share the Secret, **14/1** Perfect Bertie (IRE), **20/1** Red Hot Risk, Sweet Cheap Pet, **25/1** Rubislaw, Mill Dancer (IRE), CSF £46.76 TOTE £12.70: £3.80 £2.30 £9.00 (£29.40) Trio £273.20; £96.23 to 21/6/95 OWNER The Butterwick Race Co (MALTON) BRED A. D. G. Oldrey 14 Rn

1m 46.9 (4.90) SF: 25/18/10/19/10/10/-/-/-/-/-/-/-/-
Bt in 6,200 gns

1825

LANDBRIDGE SHIPPING H'CAP (0-75) (3-Y.O) (Class D) £6,056.00 (£1,808.00: £864.00: £392.00)
1m 2f 6y Stalls: Low GOING minus 0.27 sec per fur (GF) 7-45 (7-48)

1476[13] **Jameel Asmar (63)***(69+) (CREgerton)* 3-8-10 TIves(7) (lw: rn in snatches: a in tch: outpcd over 2f out: styd on to ld ins fnl f: drvn out)........— 1
1382[7] Silently **(69)***(73) (IABalding)* 3-9-2 KDarley(13) (trckd ldrs: led on bit over 2f out: hdd ins fnl f: nt qckn)........1 2
1605[4] Carlito Brigante **(69)***(72) (MrsJRRamsden)* 3-9-2 KFallon(10) (hld up: hdwy over 2f out: styd on appr fnl f: nt rch ldrs)........¾ 3
1801* Vindaloo **(62)***(56)*(Fav)*(JLHarris)* 3-8-2 (7) 5x PFessey(3) (hld up on ins: bdly hmpd & lost pl over 2f out: r.o wl fnl f)........6 4
1194[9] Final Fling **(55)***(46) (JWWatts)* 3-8-2v NConnorton(4) (s.i.s: hld up & plld hrd: bhd tl kpt on fnl 2f)........1½ 5
1495* Sayyed Alraqs (USA) **(72)***(62) (MAJarvis)* 3-9-5 GCarter(12) (trckd ldr: led over 4f tl over 2f out: wknd over 1f out)........1 6
1404[2] Kirov Protege (IRE) **(49)***(35) (HJCollingridge)* 3-7-10 AMackay(5) (hdwy on outside 4f out: sn prom: wknd over 1f out)........2½ 7
468[6] Rubylee **(64)***(50) (KMcAuliffe)* 3-8-8 (3) JTate(2) (swtg: bhd: sme hdwy over 2f out: nvr nr ldrs)........s.h 8
1191* Java Red (IRE) **(60)***(44) (JGFitzGerald)* 3-8-7 JFortune(1) (lw: sn trckg ldrs: outpcd & drvn along over 2f out: n.d after)........¾ 9
1464[2] Verde Luna **(74)***(54) (MHTompkins)* 3-9-7 PRobinson(6) (in tch: effrt over 2f out: wknd over 1f out)........2½ 10
1532[4] Mr Christie **(63)***(20) (MissLCSiddall)* 3-8-10 DeanMcKeown(11) (bhd: rdn over 3f out: sn wknd)........15 11
1598[3] Cool Tactician **(58)** *(RHollinshead)* 3-8-5 DHolland(8) (led tl over 2f out: wknd qckly over 1f out: eased)........25 12

2/1 Vindaloo, **5/1** Sayyed Alraqs (USA), **13/2** Carlito Brigante (op 4/1), **8/1** JAMEEL ASMAR, Verde Luna, **9/1** Silently, **11/1** Kirov Protege (IRE), **12/1** Final Fling, Java Red (IRE) (op 8/1), **20/1** Rubylee, Mr Christie, Cool Tactician, CSF £78.78 CT £457.90 TOTE £12.00: £2.80 £2.70 £2.70 (£77.40) Trio £200.30 OWNER Mr Abdul Rahman Mubarak (CHADDLEWORTH) BRED Kirtlington Stud Ltd 12 Rn 2m 12.3 (4.00) SF: 42/46/45/29/19/35/8/23/17/27/-/-

1826 PONTEFRACT CUP H'CAP (0-70) (4-Y.O+) (Class E) £3,655.00 (£1,090.00: £520.00: £235.00)
2m 1f 216y Stalls: Centre GOING minus 0.27 sec per fur (GF) 8-15 (8-16)

1607³ **Flashman (37)***(52) (BJLlewellyn)* 5-9-0 TWilliams(5) (chsd ldrs: drvn along over 4f out: led over 2f out: clr over 1f out: unchal) ....— 1
1416⁴ Ambuscade (USA) **(47)***(58)*(Fav)*(EJAlston)* 9-9-10 KFallon(8) (lw: bhd: pushed along 5f out: hdwy to chse wnr over 1f out: no imp).......4 2
1470³ Northern Kingdom (USA) **(44)***(53) (SGNorton)* 6-9-7 JFanning(6) (led tl over 2f out: one pce) 2½ 3
1596¹⁷ Record Lover (IRE) **(45)***(54) (MCChapman)* 5-9-5 (3) DRMcCabe(2) (bhd tl styd on u.p fnl 2f) hd 4
1667⁵ Don't Cry **(25)***(33) (DonEnricoIncisa)* 7-8-2 KimTinkler(3) (jnd ldr ½-wy: drvn along & outpcd 3f out: kpt on appr fnl f) 1 5
1531⁷ Ikis Girl **(42)***(49) (SGollings)* 4-9-4 DHolland(4) (hld up: effrt 3f out: kpt on fnl f: nvr nr ldrs) 1¼ 6
Karline Ka (FR) **(44)***(50) (RDickin)* 4-9-6 DeanMcKeown(1) (in tch: effrt over 3f out: sn rdn & wknd wl over 1f out) 1¼ 7
*1567** Drimard (IRE) **(30)***(32) (KMcAuliffe)* 4-8-3 (3) JTate(7) (chsd ldrs: rdn 5f out: wknd 3f out).......5 8

5/2 Ambuscade (USA), **7/2** FLASHMAN, Northern Kingdom (USA), **4/1** Drimard (IRE), **8/1** Karline Ka (FR), **14/1** Don't Cry, **16/1** Ikis Girl, **20/1** Record Lover (IRE), CSF £12.86 CT £30.31 TOTE £3.90: £1.60 £1.30 £1.70 (£6.90) OWNER Mr Colin Simpson (BARGOED) BRED P. Asquith 8 Rn
4m 10.7 (18.70) SF: -/6/1/2/-/-/-/-
WEIGHT FOR AGE 4yo-1lb

1827 CEDAR LIMITED STKS (0-70) (3-Y.O+) (Class E) £3,048.00 (£924.00: £452.00: £216.00)
5f Stalls: Low GOING minus 0.27 sec per fur (GF) 8-45 (8-45)

1604* **Prima Silk (74)***(76)*(Fav)*(MJRyan)* 4-9-2 TIves(10) (chsd ldrs: styd on u.p to ld ins fnl f: all out) ....— 1
1802² Purple Fling **(70)***(78) (SirMarkPrescott)* 4-9-4 GDuffield(7) (chsd ldrs: drvn along ½-wy: led over 1f out: nt qckn nr fin) ....hd 2
1534⁷ Spanish Stripper (USA) **(63)***(70) (MCChapman)* 4-9-4 (3) DRMcCabe(9) (swtg: sn outpcd & bhd: kpt on u.p appr fnl f: nvr nr to chal).......3½ 3
1565⁹ King Rambo **(64)***(66) (RHollinshead)* 4-9-7 GCarter(2) (chsd ldrs tl rdn & wknd over 1f out) .1¼ 4
1741² Just Bob **(68)***(60)*(Fav)*(SEKettlewell)* 6-9-4 JFortune(8) (dwlt: bhd: effrt on outside ½-wy: rdn & no imp over 1f out) ....¾ 5
1042⁴ Followmegirls **(55)***(47) (MrsALMKing)* 6-8-13 MWigham(6) (in tch: outpcd ½-wy: kpt on u.p appr fnl f) 2½ 6
1689³ Plum First **(60)***(54) (LRLloyd-James)* 5-9-0 (7) KimberleyHart(4) (b.hind: chsd ldrs: outpcd ½-wy: n.d after).......nk 7
1080⁵ Call to the Bar (IRE) **(70)***(50) (MDods)* 6-9-4 JWeaver(5) (sn bhd: outpcd ½-wy: n.d).......nk 8
1451⁴ Sigama (USA) **(56)***(48) (DNicholls)* 9-9-7 AlexGreaves(3) (led tl over 1f out: sn wknd).......1½ 9

3/1 PRIMA SILK, Just Bob, **4/1** Purple Fling, **6/1** Call to the Bar (IRE), **8/1** Followmegirls, **10/1** King Rambo, **12/1** Plum First (op 8/1), **16/1** Spanish Stripper (USA), **20/1** Sigama (USA), CSF £15.56 TOTE £4.90: £2.20 £1.60 £3.90 (£6.90) Trio £18.70 OWNER Three Ply Racing (NEWMARKET) BRED R. M. Scott 9 Rn 63.6 secs (2.10) SF: 44/46/38/34/28/15/22/18/16

1828 WALNUT H'CAP (0-70) (3-Y.O+) (Class E) £3,582.00 (£1,071.00:£513.00: £234.00)
6f Stalls: Low GOING minus 0.27 sec per fur (GF) 9-15 (9-16)

1433⁵ **The Kings Ransom (61)***(70) (MrsJRRamsden)* 3-9-0v KFallon(4) (hld up: hdwy on ins ½-wy: rdn to ld over 1f out: hld on towards fin).......— 1
1603⁷ Souperficial **(53)***(62) (JAGlover)* 4-9-0v GDuffield(2) (sn outpcd & bhd: hdwy whn swtchd outside over 2f out: ev ch ins fnl f: no ex nr fin).......hd 2
1809² Profit Release (IRE) **(54)***(59)*(Fav)*(MJohnston)* 4-9-1b DHolland(6) (a chsng ldrs: kpt on wl u.p fnl f).......1¼ 3
1668³ Kid Ory **(60)***(62) (PCalver)* 4-9-7 MBirch(5) (lw: w ldrs: ev ch over 1f out: kpt on one pce) 1¼ 4
1297⁷ Densben **(47)***(49) (DenysSmith)* 11-8-3 (5) CTeague(9) (dwlt: bhd tl kpt on wl u.p appr fnl f: nt rch ldrs).......hd 5

17002 Awesome Venture **(48)***(50) (MCChapman)* 5-8-6 (3) DRMcCabe(13) (a chsng ldrs: kpt on one pce fnl 2f)........s.h **6**
1297 10 Panther (IRE) **(58)***(59) (JHetherton)* 5-9-5 SWebster(15) (hdwy on outside ½-wy: hung lft & kpt on same pce appr fnl f)........hd **7**
1582* Heart Broken **(53)***(52) (JGFitzGerald)* 5-9-0 TIves(11) (lw: hld up: effrt on outside & hmpd 2f out: kpt on fnl f)........¾ **8**
14994 Old Comrades **(49)***(48) (TDBarron)* 8-8-10 JFortune(10) (chsd ldrs: hmpd & lost pl over 2f out: styd on u.p fnl f)........nk **9**
15829 Blue Grit **(53)***(50) (MDods)* 9-9-0v JWeaver(7) (s.i.s: bhd tl sme hdwy 2f out: n.d)........¾ **10**
14689 King Rat (IRE) **(67)***(60) (TJEtherington)* 4-9-9v(5) JStack(1) (led tl over 1f out: wknd)........1¼ **11**
1668 12 Indiahra **(55)***(45) (RHollinshead)* 4-9-2 GCarter(3) (bhd: sme hdwy 2f out: n.d)........1¼ **12**
15823 Pine Ridge Lad (IRE) **(53)***(42) (JLEyre)* 5-9-0 KDarley(16) (bhd: hdwy on outside ½-wy: n.d).½ **13**
1493* Birchwood Sun **(54)***(41) (MDods)* 5-8-10b(5) VHalliday(17) (lw: s.i.s: a bhd)........½ **14**
16038 Dante's Rubicon (IRE) **(46)***(17) (JDBethell)* 4-8-4 (3) JTate(8) (chsd ldrs over 3f: sn lost pl)......6 **15**
15109 Lady-Bo-K **(60)***(30) (CaptJWilson)* 4-9-0 (7) PBowe(14) (chsd ldrs over 3f: sn lost pl)........½ **16**
15713 Aquado **(54)***(20) (ALForbes)* 6-9-1 PRobinson(12) (lw: chsd ldrs tl lost pl over 2f out)........1½ **17**

7/2 Profit Release (IRE) (op 6/1), **7/1** Blue Grit, Heart Broken, **15/2** THE KINGS RANSOM, **10/1** Kid Ory, Birchwood Sun, Souperficial, **11/1** Old Comrades, **12/1** Pine Ridge Lad (IRE), **14/1** Awesome Venture, Aquado, **16/1** King Rat (IRE), Panther (IRE), **20/1** Indiahra, **25/1** Dante's Rubicon (IRE), Lady-Bo-K, Densben, CSF £85.10 CT £292.42 TOTE £9.80: £2.30 £2.10 £1.60 £3.60 (£36.60) Trio £53.80 OWNER Mr M. J. Simmonds (THIRSK) BRED M. J. Simmonds 17 Rn
1m 17.6 (3.30) SF: 33/33/30/33/20/21/30/23/19/21/31/16/13/12/-/1/-
WEIGHT FOR AGE 3yo-8lb

T/Plpt: £305.40 (55.42 Tckts). T/Qdpt: £12.00 (9.7 Tckts). WG

1659-WINDSOR (Fig. 8)
Monday June 19th (Good to firm, Good st)
WEATHER: sunny WIND: almost nil

1829 BOWRING MARSH & MCLENNAN (S) STKS (2-Y.O) (Class F) £3,077.00 (£926.00: £448.00: £209.00)
5f 217y Stalls: High GOING minus 0.56 sec per fur (F) 6-30 (6-32)

16714 **Queen's Insignia (USA)** *(59+)*(Fav)*(PFICole)* 2-8-6 TQuinn(6) (b.off hind: a.p: led 2f out: pushed out)........— **1**
1503* My Kind *(57) (JBerry)* 2-8-11 JCarroll(5) (lw: gd hdwy over 2f out: ev ch over 1f out: no imp)........2½ **2**
15908 Golden Silver *(44) (JSMoore)* 2-8-0 (7)ow1 DaneO'Neill(12) (lost pl 3f out: styd on fnl 2f)........3 **3**
Noon (IRE) *(39) (MHTompkins)* 2-8-1 (5) SMulvey(9) (leggy: lt-f: hdwy over 2f out: rdn over 1f out: nt qckn)........2 **4**
16326 Ginger Glint *(41) (MJHeaton-Ellis)* 2-8-11 MRoberts(10) (w ldr: hung bdly lft over 2f out: wknd over 1f out)........1¼ **5**
15907 Jemsilverthorn (IRE) *(40) (JJBridger)* 2-8-4 (7) ADaly(3) (led 1f: wknd over 1f out)........nk **6**
14437 Emei Shan *(32) (PGMurphy)* 2-7-13 (7) RWaterfield(8) (nvr nrr)........1¼ **7**
1662 12 Two Socks *(32) (MMcCormack)* 2-8-11b JReid(11) (lw: led after 1f tl wknd 2f out)........1¾ **8**
Blakenmor *(25) (RWEmery)* 2-8-8 (3) DWright(7) (unf: bit bkwd: a bhd)........2½ **9**
16999 Cottesloe Beach *(23) (KTIvory)* 2-8-4 (7) CScally(4) (b: outpcd)........¾ **10**
Carmarthen Bay *(20) (RWEmery)* 2-8-11 JWilliams(1) (str: bit bkwd: a bhd)........1¼ **11**
1590 12 Mandy's Risk *(15) (TMJones)* 2-8-11 RPerham(2) (bhd fnl 3f)........1¾ **12**

4/5 QUEEN'S INSIGNIA (USA), **5/2** My Kind, **14/1** Noon (IRE) (5/1-16/1), Two Socks, **16/1** Golden Silver, Ginger Glint, **33/1** Jemsilverthorn (IRE), Emei Shan, **50/1** Blakenmor, Mandy's Risk, **66/1** Cottesloe Beach, Carmarthen Bay, CSF £3.31 TOTE £1.90: £1.20 £1.40 £4.50 (£1.90) Trio £20.30 OWNER Mr W. H. Ponsonby (WHATCOMBE) BRED Stephen E. Johnson and Mrs Johnson 12 Rn
1m 12.7 (2.20) SF: 14/12/-/-/-/-/-/-/-/-/-/-
Bt in 6,400 gns

1830 THAMES VALLEY HOSPICE H'CAP (0-70) (3-Y.O+) (Class E) £3,806.50 (£1,147.00: £556.00: £260.50)
1m 67y Stalls: High GOING minus 0.56 sec per fur (F) 7-00 (7-05)

13686 **Admirals Flame (IRE) (60)***(70+)*(Fav)*(CFWall)* 4-9-7 PatEddery(15) (b: 6th st: led 1f out: qcknd clr)........— **1**
15068 Vanborough Lad **(54)***(59) (MJBolton)* 6-9-1 JReid(11) (7th st: hdwy fnl f: r.o)........2½ **2**
15312 Kaafih Homm (IRE) **(53)***(58) (NACallaghan)* 4-9-0 WCarson(9) (b.hind: lw: hdwy over 3f out: nrst fin)........nk **3**

1509* Cape Pigeon (USA) **(62)***(67) (LGCottrell)* 10-9-9v MFenton(7) (lw: 2nd tl led over 2f out: hdd 1f out: one pce)....s.h **4**
*1631*2 Daytona Beach (IRE) **(63)***(65) (PBurgoyne)* 5-9-3 (7) GParkin(14) (led tl over 2f out: wknd fnl f)....1¼ **5**
1070² Broughtons Turmoil **(53)***(52) (WJMusson)* 6-8-9 (5) PMcCabe(1) (swtg: hdwy fnl 2f: r.o)....1½ **6**
1290⁵ Nunnery Grove (IRE) **(46)***(42) (TThomsonJones)* 3-7-11 JQuinn(13) (4th st: wknd over 2f out)....1½ **7**
1472¹¹ Peter Rowley **(54)***(39) (RHannon)* 4-9-1 RHughes(10) (nvr nrr)....6 **8**
1553⁵ Sparkling Roberta **(39)***(18) (MDIUsher)* 4-7-7 (7) CAdamson(8) (a bhd)....3 **9**
1663² Sea Spouse **(41)***(12) (MBlanshard)* 4-8-2 MRoberts(4) (lw: 3rd st: wknd over 2f out)....4 **10**
1513¹⁶ Bird Island **(50)***(10) (JWhite)* 4-8-6 (5) SDrowne(2) (5th st: hrd rdn & wknd over 1f out)....6 **11**
*85*³ Mediate (IRE) **(56)** *(RHannon)* 3-8-7 RPerham(3) (lw: t.o)....20 **12**
505¹⁴ Birequest **(62)** *(RBoss)* 4-9-9 MRimmer(6) (lw: t.o)....1¾ **13**

7/2 ADMIRALS FLAME (IRE), **5/1** Kaafih Homm (IRE), **7/1** Sparkling Roberta, Daytona Beach (IRE), **9/1** Broughtons Turmoil (11/2-10/1), **10/1** Sea Spouse (7/1-11/1), **12/1** Cape Pigeon (USA), Peter Rowley, Vanborough Lad, **14/1** Nunnery Grove (IRE), **20/1** Mediate (IRE), Birequest, **25/1** Bird Island, CSF £43.42 CT £198.32 TOTE £4.10: £1.90 £4.10 £1.80 (£36.80) Trio £46.50 OWNER Mr Walter Grubmuller (NEWMARKET) BRED A. Tarry 13 Rn

1m 42.7 (1.10) SF: 49/38/37/46/44/31/11/18/-/-/-/-/-

WEIGHT FOR AGE 3yo-10lb

1831 DATASERV H'CAP (0-80) (3-Y.O) (Class D) £5,177.75 (£1,562.00: £758.50: £356.75) **1m 2f 7y** Stalls: High GOING minus 0.56 sec per fur (F) 7-30 (7-32)

1372⁵ **Dr Edgar (58)***(67) (GWragg)* 3-7-13 FNorton(6) (lw: mde all: clr over 2f out: eased fnl f)....— **1**
1591* Fairy Knight **(73)***(80) (RHannon)* 3-9-0 JReid(10) (5th st: styd on fnl 2f: no ch w wnr)....1 **2**
1512¹⁵ Rock Oyster **(53)***(58) (BJMeehan)* 3-7-8 ow1 JQuinn(5) (2nd st: rdn over 2f out: r.o one pce)...¾ **3**
1183¹⁹ King Balant (IRE) **(72)***(75) (MRStoute)* 3-8-13v PaulEddery(11) (s.s: 7th st: hrd rdn over 2f out: r.o one pce)....1¾ **4**
1512¹³ Jewel Trader **(54)***(43) (CJBenstead)* 3-7-9 NCarlisle(9) (3rd st: wknd over 2f out)....9 **5**
1664⁵ Pedaltothemetal (IRE) **(52)***(40) (PMitchell)* 3-7-2 (5) MBaird(8) (b.hind: 4th st: wknd 2f out)....½ **6**
1591⁴ Dungeon Dancer **(61)***(46) (JAkehurst)* 3-8-2v MRoberts(2) (a bhd)....2 **7**
Chicodari **(76)***(60) (SirMarkPrescott)* 3-9-3 CNutter(1) (6th st: wknd 3f out)....1 **8**
1498¹⁴ Nosirrah **(52)***(35) (CAHorgan)* 3-7-7 NAdams(7) (b.off hind: a bhd)....½ **9**
1383* Kilcoran Bay **(80)***(62)*(Fav)*(IABalding)* 3-9-7 PatEddery(3) (bhd fnl 4f)....½ **10**
1407⁵ Tonka **(67)** *(PJMakin)* 3-8-8 TQuinn(4) (plld hrd: 2nd whn hmpd & uns rdr 6f out).... **U**

LONG HANDICAP Rock Oyster 7-5 Nosirrah 7-1 Pedaltothemetal (IRE) 7-2

9/4 Kilcoran Bay, **4/1** King Balant (IRE), Fairy Knight, **10/1** Tonka, DR EDGAR, Dungeon Dancer, **14/1** Pedaltothemetal (IRE), **16/1** Chicodari, **33/1** Nosirrah, Jewel Trader, Rock Oyster, CSF £46.94 CT £1,145.55 TOTE £14.50: £2.60 £1.90 £9.20 (£32.40) Trio £456.90; £19.31 to 21/6/95 OWNER Sir Philip Oppenheimer (NEWMARKET) BRED Hascombe and Valiant Studs 11 Rn

2m 9.9 (5.00) SF: 1/14/-/9/-/-/-/-/-/-/-

OFFICIAL EXPLANATION **Dr Edgar: the horse's improvement was accounted for by the different tactics used this time by the jockey, which seemed to suit him better. Kilcoran Bay: was unsuited by the faster ground.**

1832 TOTE CREDIT SPRINT H'CAP (0-75) (3-Y.O+) (Class D) £6,190.00 (£1,870.00: £910.00: £430.00) **5f 217y** Stalls: High GOING minus 0.56 sec (F) 8-00 (8-04)

1537⁴ **Youdontsay (69)***(79+) (RCurtis)* 3-9-1 RHughes(19) (mde virtually all: drvn clr 2f out: r.o wl)....— **1**
1614⁷ Gone Savage **(62)***(67) (WJMusson)* 7-8-11 (5) PMcCabe(11) (a.p: chsd wnr fnl 2f: r.o)....2 **2**
1510* Patsy Grimes **(64)***(58) (LJHolt)* 5-9-4 AMcGlone(7) (hdwy 2f out: r.o ins fnl f)....4 **3**
1541⁴ Robo Magic (USA) **(58)***(51) (LMontagueHall)* 3-8-4 DHarrison(3) (nrst fin)....nk **4**
1400⁹ Rocky Two **(57)***(46) (PHowling)* 4-8-4b(7) DebbieBiggs(17) (w wnr: wknd fnl f)....1½ **5**
1094¹⁵ Tael of Silver **(62)***(51) (KRBurke)* 3-8-8 MFenton(10) (nvr nr to chal)....hd **6**
1595⁵ Judgement Call **(46)***(35) (PHowling)* 8-8-0 NCarlisle(9) (b: lw: prom over 3f)....s.h **7**
1595⁷ Bold Gem **(57)***(42) (BJMeehan)* 4-8-11 BDoyle(8) (a mid div)....1½ **8**
1673² Dry Point **(67)***(52)*(Fav)*(JARToller)* 9-9-7 WNewnes(15) (reard s: wl bhd tl r.o fnl f)....s.h **9**
*1630*⁶ Bargash **(70)***(54) (PDEvans)* 3-9-2 PaulEddery(5) (lw: nvr nr ldrs)....hd **10**
1537⁹ Rambold **(66)***(46) (NEBerry)* 4-9-1 (5) RPainter(14) (a mid div)....1½ **11**
1483¹¹ Astral Invader (IRE) **(66)***(46) (MSSaunders)* 3-8-12 JWilliams(4) (nrst fin)....s.h **12**
1595⁹ Halliard **(59)***(39) (TMJones)* 4-8-13 RPerham(2) (swtg: nvr trbld ldrs)....hd **13**
1673⁶ Grey Charmer (IRE) **(52)***(28) (CJames)* 6-8-6 CRutter(18) (outpcd)....1½ **14**
1537⁸ Efra **(70)***(38) (RHannon)* 6-9-10 JReid(13) (lw: a wl bhd)....3 **15**
1354¹¹ Slivovitz **(58)***(25) (MJHeaton-Ellis)* 5-8-12b StephenDavies(12) (w ldrs tl wknd 2f out)....nk **16**
1565³ Macfarlane **(72)***(39) (MJFetherston-Godley)* 7-9-12 MRoberts(1) (nvr nr ldrs)....hd **17**

1510[6] Spectacle Jim **(49)***(9) (JO'Donoghue)* 6-7-12b(5) MBaird(20) (s.s: a bhd)................................2½ **18**
1673[8] Norling (IRE) **(59)***(16) (KOCunningham-Brown)* 5-8-13 JQuinn(6) (prom over 3f)..................1¼ **19**
1514[21] Mans Passion **(53)***(1) (JWhite)* 3-7-6 (7)ow6 CCarver(16) (a bhd)..1¼ **20**
LONG HANDICAP Mans Passion 6-9

11/2 Dry Point (4/1-6/1), **13/2** Macfarlane, **7/1** Patsy Grimes, **15/2** YOUDONTSAY, **8/1** Grey Charmer (IRE), **10/1** Spectacle Jim, **12/1** Gone Savage, **14/1** Bargash, Efra (10/1-16/1), **16/1** Slivovitz, Norling (IRE), Judgement Call, **20/1** Astral Invader (IRE), Tael of Silver, Robo Magic (USA), Bold Gem, **25/1** Rambold, Halliard, **33/1** Rocky Two, **66/1** Mans Passion, CSF £97.19 CT £628.39 TOTE £9.00: £2.10 £4.20 £1.90 £5.90 (£326.40) Trio £221.80 OWNER Mr T. W. Nicholls (CARSHALTON) BRED Mrs and Exors of the late Col F. R. Hue-Williams 20 Rn
1m 10.4 (-0.10) SF: 53/49/40/25/28/25/17/24/34/28/28/20/21/10/20/7/21/-/-/-
WEIGHT FOR AGE 3yo-8lb

1833 STEAMSHIP MUTUAL CONDITIONS STKS (2-Y.O F) (Class C)
£5,112.00 (£1,908.00: £929.00: £395.00: £172.50: £83.50)
5f 10y Stalls: High GOING minus 0.56 sec per fur (F) 8-30 (8-39)

1653* **Baize** *(83+)*(Fav)*(RFJohnsonHoughton)* 2-8-13 JReid(8) (lw: trckd ldr: led over 1f out: edgd lft: pushed out)..— **1**
1177[2] Just Lady *(66) (WGMTurner)* 2-8-4 (5) PMcCabe(3) (lw: led over 3f: no ch w wnr)...................4 **2**
1530[2] Beautiful Ballad (IRE) *(66) (BWHills)* 2-8-13 WCarson(5) (lw: a.p: rdn along: r.o one pce fnl 2f)...1½ **3**
1597* Miss Waterline *(62) (PDEvans)* 2-8-13 PaulEddery(7) (spd over 3f)...1 **4**
718[4] Miss Bigwig *(57) (JBerry)* 2-8-13 JCarroll(2) (no hdwy fnl 2f)..1¾ **5**
1443[2] Invigorating *(45) (RHannon)* 2-8-2 (7) DaneO'Neill(1) (nvr nr to chal)......................................2½ **6**
Bouton d'Or *(36) (PHowling)* 2-8-6 JQuinn(4) (unf: a bhd)..1¾ **7**
Heaven Sent (IRE) *(17) (PMitchell)* 2-8-6 MRoberts(6) (neat: bit bkwd: a bhd)..........................6 **8**

Evens BAIZE, **9/4** Beautiful Ballad (IRE), **7/1** Invigorating (6/1-14/1), **14/1** Miss Waterline (7/1-16/1), **16/1** Just Lady, Miss Bigwig, **25/1** Heaven Sent (IRE), **50/1** Bouton d'Or, CSF £16.33 TOTE £2.00: £1.20 £2.80 £1.20 (£19.40) OWNER Lady Rothschild (DIDCOT) BRED Exors of the late Mrs D. M. de Rothschild 8 Rn
60.0 secs (1.00) SF: 33/16/16/12/7/-/-/-

1834 LOWE BELL MEDIAN AUCTION MAIDEN STKS (3-Y.O) (Class E)
£3,419.75 (£1,028.00: £496.50: £230.75)
1m 2f 7y Stalls: High GOING minus 0.56 sec per fur (F) 9-00 (9-07)

1514[11] **Painted Hall (USA)** *(81) (JARToller)* 3-9-0 WNewnes(7) (led tl over 2f out: led ins fnl f: r.o wl)...— **1**
1514[2] Meghdoot **(71)***(74)*(Fav)*(HJCollingridge)* 3-8-9 JQuinn(1) (5th st: led over 2f out tl ins fnl f)..1½ **2**
1625[2] Old Swinford (IRE) **(57)***(68) (BJMeehan)* 3-8-9 BDoyle(5) (4th st: one pce fnl 2f)..................3½ **3**
1124[6] Faustino **(52)***(72) (PFICole)* 3-9-0 CRutter(4) (b.off hind: 2nd st: wknd 2f out)........................¾ **4**
1030[13] Darius The Great (IRE) *(32) (DMarks)* 3-8-9 (5) MBaird(3) (lw: a bhd: 6th st: t.o)......................25 **5**
1204[5] Just for a Reason **(60)***(32) (DJGMurraySmith)* 3-9-0 RHughes(2) (lw: 3rd st: wknd over 3f out: t.o)..nk **6**

1/2 Meghdoot, **11/2** Old Swinford (IRE) (op 7/2), **10/1** Faustino (8/1-14/1), **14/1** PAINTED HALL (USA) (7/1-16/1), **16/1** Just for a Reason, **66/1** Darius The Great (IRE), CSF £19.93 TOTE £19.50: £4.50 £1.10 (£5.90) OWNER Duke of Devonshire (WHITSBURY) BRED Nelson McMakin and Tom Snyder 6 Rn
2m 8.5 (3.60) SF: 28/21/15/19/-/-
T/Jkpt: Not won; £13,520.73 to Ascot 20/6/95. T/Plpt: £27.40 (691.68 Tckts). T/Qdpt: £11.10 (11.05 Tckts). Hn

0868-ASCOT (R-H)
Tuesday June 20th (Good to firm)
WEATHER: dry & muggy WIND: almost nil

1835 QUEEN ANNE STKS (Gp 2) (3-Y.O+) (Class A) £51,030.00
(£19,062.00: £9,126.00: £3,942.00)
1m (straight) Stalls: Centre GOING minus 0.06 sec per fur (G) 2-30 (2-32)

1385[3] **Nicolotte (110)***(128) (GWragg)* 4-9-2 MHills(2) (lw: hld up & bhd: hdwy 2f out to ld over 1f out: rdn out)..— **1**
1706a[4] Nijo **(109)***(124) (DRLoder)* 4-9-2 MJKinane(3) (lw: a.p: effrt & ev ch over 1f out: kpt on u.p towards fin)...2 **2**
1187* Soviet Line (IRE) **(121)***(129)*(Fav)*(MRStoute)* 5-9-7 WRSwinburn(5) (lw: led tl hdd over 1f out: sn hrd rdn & no ex)..s.h **3**

1586[6] Young Ern **(117)***(124) (SDow)* 5-9-2 TQuinn(7) (hld up: rdn ½-wy: swtchd rt & hdwy 2f out: styd on)....hd 4
1389a[2] Sayyedati **(120)***(120) (CEBrittain)* 5-8-13 LDettori(1) (swtg: hld up: nt clr run on ins: swtchd rt appr fnl f: one pce)....½ 5
1365* Dance Turn **(99)***(117) (RWArmstrong)* 4-9-2 JReid(4) (lw: chsd ldrs over 5f: sn rdn & wknd)...3 6
1315* Peace Envoy **(109)***(101) (HRACecil)* 3-8-6 PatEddery(6) (chsd ldrs: rdn over 2f out: wknd wl over 1f out: t.o)....8 7

13/8 Soviet Line (IRE), **2/1** Sayyedati, **6/1** Peace Envoy, **15/2** Young Ern, **16/1** NICOLOTTE, **20/1** Nijo, **50/1** Dance Turn, CSF £196.85 TOTE £15.00: £3.50 £4.10 (£52.70) OWNER Mollers Racing (NEWMARKET) BRED Crescent (UK) Ltd 7 Rn 1m 40.28 (1.08) SF: 85/81/86/81/77/74/48
WEIGHT FOR AGE 3yo-10lb

1836

PRINCE OF WALES'S STKS (Gp 2) (3-Y.O+) (Class A) £57,852.00 (£21,677.10: £10,433.55: £4,567.35) **1m 2f** Stalls: Low GOING minus 0.06 sec (G) 3-05 (3-05)

1187[5] **Muhtarram (USA) (123)***(124) (JHMGosden)* 6-9-8 WCarson(5) (hld up: 5th st: hdwy on ins & squeezed thro over 1f out: led ins fnl f: all out)....— 1
1006a[6] Eltish (USA) **(120)***(122) (HRACecil)* 3-8-8 PatEddery(3) (hld up: 6th st: nt clr run bel dist: hrd rdn & ev ch ins fnl f: r.o wl)....s.h 2
Needle Gun (IRE) **(112)***(117) (CEBrittain)* 5-9-3 MJKinane(6) (bit bkwd: led tl ins fnl f: no ex nr fin)....1½ 3
1385[2] Just Happy (USA) **(115)***(116) (MRStoute)* 4-9-6 WRSwinburn(4) (swtg: a.p: 3rd st: ev ch over 1f out: unable qckn)....2 4
Balanchine (USA) *(110)*(Fav)*(SbinSuroor)* 4-9-5 LDettori(2) (lw: sn chsng ldr: 2nd st: wknd wl over 1f out)....3½ 5
1609[6] Ionio (USA) **(112)***(107) (CEBrittain)* 4-9-3v MRoberts(1) (lw: hld up: effrt & 4th st: wknd over 1f out)....¾ 6

4/5 Balanchine (USA), **4/1** Eltish (USA), **5/1** MUHTARRAM (USA) (7/2-11/2), **13/2** Just Happy (USA), **33/1** Needle Gun (IRE), Ionio (USA), CSF £22.59 TOTE £7.10: £2.90 £1.90 (£9.10) OWNER Mr Hamdan Al Maktoum (NEWMARKET) BRED Cotswold Farm 1985 Ltd. in USA 6 Rn
2m 4.94 (0.64) SF: 97/83/90/89/83/80
WEIGHT FOR AGE 3yo-12lb

1837

ST JAMES'S PALACE STKS (Gp 1) (3-Y.O C & F) (Class A) £124,056.00 (£46,167.30: £21,958.65: £9,328.05)
1m (round) Stalls: Low GOING minus 0.06 sec per fur (G) 3-45 (3-46)

1234a[3] **Bahri (USA) (125)***(126)*(Fav)*(JLDunlop)* 3-9-0 WCarson(7) (swtg: hld up: hdwy ½-wy: 4th st: led on bit wl over 1f out: qcknd clr: comf)....— 1
677* Charnwood Forest (IRE) *(118) (HRACecil)* 3-9-0 JReid(6) (hld up & bhd: 8th st: hdwy fnl 2f: no ch w wnr)....4 2
1611[6] Vettori (IRE) *(118) (SbinSuroor)* 3-9-0 MJKinane(2) (chsd ldrs: 5th st: rdn & one pce appr fnl f)....hd 3
1117a[2] Atticus (USA) *(116) (MmeCHead,France)* 3-9-0 ODoleuze(3) (lw: a.p: 3rd st: rdn & nt clr run over 1f out: one pce)....1 4
1575a[2] Annus Mirabilis (FR) **(119)***(115) (MRStoute)* 3-9-0 PatEddery(9) (swtg: lost pl after 4f: 7th st: outpcd over 2f out: styd on fnl f)....nk 5
1574a[5] Flemensfirth (USA) *(110) (JHMGosden)* 3-9-0 LDettori(1) (lw: prom: 2nd st: wknd bel dist) .2½ 6
1234a[2] Adjareli (IRE) *(109) (JOxx,Ireland)* 3-9-0 JPMurtagh(8) (w'like: scope: lw: hmpd s: hld up & bhd: hdwy & 6th st: sn rdn: no imp)....¾ 7
1370* Star of Zilzal (USA) *(99) (MRStoute)* 3-9-0 WRSwinburn(4) (hld up in rr: 9th st: effrt 2f out: no imp)....5 8
1145[5] Muhab (USA) **(100)***(93) (PTWalwyn)* 3-9-0 RHills(5) (swtg: led tl hdd & wknd wl over 1f out)...3 9

11/4 BAHRI (USA), **5/1** Adjareli (IRE), **6/1** Vettori (IRE), Charnwood Forest (IRE), Annus Mirabilis (FR), **8/1** Star of Zilzal (USA), **10/1** Atticus (USA) (7/1-12/1), **12/1** Flemensfirth (USA), **66/1** Muhab (USA), CSF £18.20 TOTE £3.90: £1.60 £1.80 £1.80 (£11.70)Trio £22.10 OWNER Hamdan Al Maktoum (ARUNDEL) BRED Shadwell Farm Inc 9 Rn
1m 40.15 (0.55) SF: 89/81/81/79/78/73/72/62/56

1838

COVENTRY STKS (Gp 3) (2-Y.O) (Class A) £26,080.00 (£9,874.00: £4,837.00: £2,209.00) **6f** Stalls: Centre GOING minus 0.06 sec per fur (G) 4-20 (4-21)

1406* **Royal Applause** *(110+) (BWHills)* 2-8-12 WRSwinburn(12) (lw: mde all: rdn 2f out: clr fnl f: gamely)....— 1

1184* Russian Revival (USA) *(105)*(Fav)*(PWChapple-Hyam)* 2-8-12 BThomson(7) (lw: chsd wnr: hrd rdn over 1f out: unable qckn) 2 **2**
1343* South Salem (USA) *(104) (DRLoder)* 2-8-12 LDettori(8) (lw: hld up: effrt 2f out: rdn & r.o wl ins fnl f) ....s.h **3**
1485* Tagula (IRE) *(95) (IABalding)* 2-8-12 MHills(2) (hld up: hdwy over 2f out: hrd rdn over 1f out: one pce) 1½ **4**
1104* Dovebrace *(88) (ABailey)* 2-8-12 MWigham(9) (bhd: rdn over 2f out: kpt on appr fnl f) 2½ **5**
1246* Sea Dane *(86) (PWHarris)* 2-8-12 MJKinane(1) (r.o appr fnl f: nvr nrr) ....¾ **6**
1556³ Take A Left *(86) (MrsJRRamsden)* 2-8-12 KFallon(10) (hdwy ½-wy: rdn 2f out: nt rch ldrs)..s.h **7**
1134* Allied Forces (USA) *(75)*(Fav)*(HRACecil)* 2-8-12 WRyan(3) (lw: hld up: hdwy 3f out: rdn & no imp fnl 2f) 4 **8**
977* What Fun *(74) (RHannon)* 2-8-12 CAsmussen(13) (chsd ldrs over 4f) ....nk **9**
1608* Gothenberg (IRE) *(73) (MJohnston)* 2-8-12 DHolland(4) (nvr nr ldrs) ....½ **10**
1670* Rabican (IRE) *(68) (GCBravery)* 2-8-12 RHills(11) (spd 4f) 1¾ **11**
1311² Oberons Boy (IRE) *(63) (BJMeehan)* 2-8-12 PatEddery(5) (lw: chsd ldrs 4f: sn lost tch) 2 **12**
1223* Wisam *(63) (RHannon)* 2-8-12 JReid(6) (spd to ½-wy: sn lost pl) ....s.h **13**

11/4 Allied Forces (USA) (2/1-3/1), Russian Revival (USA), **13/2** ROYAL APPLAUSE, **8/1** South Salem (USA), **10/1** Gothenberg (IRE) (12/1-8/1), **12/1** Sea Dane, Wisam, **14/1** Tagula (IRE) (10/1-16/1), **20/1** Dovebrace, **25/1** What Fun, **33/1** Oberons Boy (IRE), Take A Left, **66/1** Rabican (IRE), CSF £24.15 TOTE £6.80: £1.90 £2.00 £2.40 (£18.30) Trio £47.10 OWNER Maktoum Al Maktoum (LAMBOURN) BRED Gainsborough Stud Management Ltd 13 Rn

1m 15.36 (1.76) SF: 68/63/62/58/52/50/50/39/38/37/32/27/27

1839 BRITANNIA H'CAP (0-105) (3-Y.O C & G) (Class B) £27,352.50 (£8,295.00: £4,060.00: £1,942.50)

1m (straight) Stalls: Centre GOING minus 0.06 sec per fur (G) 4-55 (4-59)

643* **Medaille Militaire (84)***(98+)*(Fav)*(JLDunlop)* 3-8-3 TQuinn(10) (chsd ldrs: rdn over 2f out: str run fnl f to ld nr fin) ....— **1**
941⁵ Beauchamp Jazz **(91)***(105) (JLDunlop)* 3-8-10 CAsmussen(11) (swtg: a.p stands' side: led 2f out tl ct cl home) ....hd **2**
1183⁵ Bedivere (USA) **(88)***(99) (PWChapple-Hyam)* 3-8-7 JReid(20) (lw: a.p far side: rdn & kpt on wl fnl f) 1¼ **3**
Naked Welcome **(90)***(99) (MJFetherston-Godley)* 3-8-9 DHolland(21) (lw: hdwy 3f out far side: kpt on fnl f) 1¼ **4**
1486* Bin Rosie **(90)***(96) (DRLoder)* 3-8-9v KDarley(8) (lw: a.p stands' side: unable qckn appr fnl f) 1¼ **5**
1188* Holtye (IRE) **(102)***(105) (HRACecil)* 3-9-7 PatEddery(19) (hdwy 3f out: kpt on wl u.p fnl f) 1½ **6**
1312* Restructure (IRE) **(94)***(95) (MrsJCecil)* 3-8-13 RHills(31) (lw: w ldrs far side: no hdwy fnl 2f) ...1 **7**
1103⁵ Myrtle Quest **(83)***(80) (RCharlton)* 3-8-2 MRoberts(3) (prom stands' side: led over 2f out tl hdd fnl f: sn outpcd) 2 **8**
1338* Blaze of Song **(82)***(79) (RHannon)* 3-8-1 GCarter(13) (sme late hdwy: nvr nrr) ....nk **9**
1374* Verzen (IRE) **(96)***(90) (DRLoder)* 3-9-1 MJKinane(9) (lw: chsd ldrs stands' side tl wknd fnl 2f) 1¼ **10**
1130¹⁰ Sheer Danzig (IRE) **(76)***(69) (RWArmstrong)* 3-7-9 JQuinn(25) (lw: w ldrs far side to ½-wy: wknd bel dist) ....½ **11**
1345² Krystallos **(93)***(83) (RHannon)* 3-8-5 (7) DaneO'Neill(14) (chsd ldrs stands' side 5f) 1¾ **12**
1747* Danegold (IRE) **(84)***(73) (MRChannon)* 3-7-12v(5) 5x PPMurphy(1) (a in rr) ....nk **13**
1131* Anniversarypresent **(96)***(84) (GLewis)* 3-9-1b PaulEddery(22) (chsd ldrs far side 5f) ....½ **14**
1474* Chattaroy (IRE) **(90)***(77) (JHMGosden)* 3-8-9 LDettori(29) (lw: nvr nr to chal) ....½ **15**
Cadeaux Tryst **(102)***(83) (EALDunlop)* 3-9-7 JWeaver(6) (b: prom stands' side over 5f) 3 **16**
1170⁶ Lancer (USA) **(85)***(66) (MBell)* 3-8-4b MFenton(18) (lw: nvr trbld ldrs) ....nk **17**
1474² Dance Band (USA) **(93)***(71) (BHanbury)* 3-8-12 MRimmer(23) (prom far side over 5f) 1¼ **18**
1130* Classicy **(94)***(71) (MRStoute)* 3-8-13 WRSwinburn(27) (in tch far side: rdn over 2f out: sn btn) ....½ **19**
1299¹¹ Mister Fire Eyes (IRE) **(77)***(53) (CEBrittain)* 3-7-10 FNorton(17) (in tch stands' side over 4f) ....nk **20**
1131² Lipizzaner (IRE) **(91)***(65) (BWHills)* 3-8-10 MHills(12) (m.n.s) 1¼ **21**
1415* Bernard Seven (IRE) **(91)***(61) (SPCWoods)* 3-8-10b WRyan(7) (lw: a in rr) 1¾ **22**
1222³ Jam N Shadeed (USA) **(82)***(52) (PFICole)* 3-8-1 CRutter(4) (lw: unruly s: bhd fr ½-wy) ....nk **23**
1474⁷ Melasus (IRE) **(79)***(49) (DWPArbuthnot)* 3-7-12 GBardwell(15) (b: lw: led stands' side over 5f: sn wknd) ....hd **24**
1301⁶ Tertium (IRE) **(87)***(54) (PWChapple-Hyam)* 3-8-6 BThomson(30) (lw: prom over 5f) 1¼ **25**
1736³ Henry Koehler **(98)***(64) (CEBrittain)* 3-9-3 BDoyle(2) (prom over 4f) ....¾ **26**
1589³ Hardy Dancer **(88)***(53) (GLMoore)* 3-8-7 SWhitworth(28) (lw: a bhd) ....nk **27**
1222¹¹ Masruf (IRE) **(86)***(49) (TThomsonJones)* 3-8-5 WCarson(16) (lw: in rr most of wy) 1¼ **28**

1476* Amrak Ajeeb (IRE) **(84)***(45) (BHanbury)* 3-8-3 NCarlisle(24) (lw: b: bhd fnl 3f)......¾ **29**
1639[2] Emirates Express **(87)***(46) (JWHills)* 3-7-13 (7) MHenry(32) (outpcd)......1 **30**
1613[4] Smart Guest **(96)***(45) (JAHarris)* 3-9-1 RHughes(26) (lw: lost pl ½-wy: t.o)......5 **31**
1593[2] Night Dance **(78)***(22) (GLewis)* 3-7-11 JFanning(5) (bhd fnl 3f)......2½ **32**

4/1 MEDAILLE MILITAIRE, **15/2** Classicy, **10/1** Holtye (IRE), **12/1** Restructure (IRE), Verzen (IRE), **14/1** Chattaroy (IRE), **16/1** Myrtle Quest, Anniversarypresent, Blaze of Song, Bin Rosie, **20/1** Bedivere (USA), Danegold (IRE), Bernard Seven (IRE), **25/1** Sheer Danzig (IRE), Krystallos, Emirates Express, Lipizzaner (IRE), Dance Band (USA), Beauchamp Jazz, **33/1** Amrak Ajeeb (IRE), Tertium (IRE), Lancer (USA), Jam N Shadeed (USA), Melasus (IRE), Masruf (IRE), Night Dance, Hardy Dancer, **50/1** Cadeaux Tryst, Henry Koehler, Naked Welcome, Smart Guest, **66/1** Mister Fire Eyes (IRE), CSF £106.75 CT £1,793.90 TOTE £6.80: £2.40 £8.80 £5.30 £11.30 (£225.80) Trio £623.90 OWNER Mr James Hartnett (ARUNDEL) BRED Fares Stables Ltd 32 Rn 1m 41.17 (1.97)
SF:63/70/64/64/61/70/60/45/44/55/34/48/38/49/42/48/31/36/36/18/30/26/17/14/19/29/18/14/10/11/10

1840

ASCOT STKS H'CAP (0-90) (4-Y.O+) (Class C) £26,328.75 (£7,980.00: £3,902.50: £1,863.75) **2m 4f** Stalls: Low GOING minus 0.06 sec per fur (G) 5-30 (5-35)

998[2] **Harlestone Brook (84)***(102) (JLDunlop)* 5-9-8 MJKinane(7) (hld up: effrt & rdn st: gd hdwy 2f out: led ins fnl f: r.o wl)......— **1**
1444[9] Art Form (USA) **(65)***(80) (CACyzer)* 8-8-3 ow2 DBiggs(12) (lw: hld up: gd hdwy 2f out: fin wl)......1¼ **2**
1189* Smuggling **(79)***(95)*(Fav)*(RAkehurst)* 4-9-1 LDettori(8) (lw: a.p: rdn over 3f out: 2nd st: led bel dist tl wl ins fnl f)......1¾ **3**
1156* Shadirwan (IRE) **(75)***(91) (RAkehurst)* 4-8-11 BThomson(25) (a.p: 3rd st: ev ch ins fnl f: r.o)......hd **4**
1444[3] Paradise Navy **(72)***(86) (CREgerton)* 6-8-10 RHughes(14) (lw: chsd ldrs: 7th st: rdn & one pce appr fnl f)......1¾ **5**
1300[3] Noufari (FR) **(74)***(85) (RHollinshead)* 4-8-10 TIves(2) (wl bhd tl styd on fnl 3f)......3½ **6**
1386[6] Simafar (IRE) **(70)***(81) (NAGraham)* 4-8-6 JReid(19) (lw: mid div: effrt 5f out: nt rch ldrs)......s.h **7**
Imad (USA) **(63)***(71) (JWhite)* 5-8-1 ow1 MFenton(6) (nvr nr to chal)......3 **8**
1416[3] Uncle Doug **(57)***(66) (MrsMReveley)* 4-7-7 NCarlisle(22) (swtg: hdwy ½-wy: 6th st: wknd over 1f out)......hd **9**
1607* Tarthooth (IRE) **(67)***(76) (CJBenstead)* 4-8-3 WCarson(28) (lw: prom: 4th & rdn st: eased whn btn appr fnl f)......nk **10**
1686[2] Argyle Cavalier (IRE) **(62)***(70) (MJohnston)* 5-8-0 ow1 GCarter(20) (nvr nr ldrs)......hd **11**
1479[5] Nawar (FR) **(82)***(90) (JRJenkins)* 5-9-6 DHolland(11) (nvr nrr)......¾ **12**
1607[4] Kadiri (IRE) **(58)***(66) (JRBosley)* 4-7-8 GBardwell(10) (a in rr)......hd **13**
Sweet Glow (FR) **(78)***(85) (MCPipe)* 8-9-2 CAsmussen(18) (lw: nvr nrr)......1¼ **14**
1623[3] Shrewd Alibi **(73)***(80) (IABalding)* 4-8-9 MHills(15) (nvr plcd to chal)......nk **15**
1681[4] Bayrak (USA) **(76)***(82) (MJRyan)* 5-9-0 BDoyle(17) (lw: chsd ldsr: nt clr run 3f out: wknd 2f out)......nk **16**
1313[7] Star Player **(68)***(71) (RJBaker)* 9-8-6 JWeaver(27) (lw: led tl hdd & wknd over 1f out)......4 **17**
1444[4] Tamarpour (USA) **(58)***(60) (MCPipe)* 8-7-10b JQuinn(5) (b.nr fore: lw: a bhd)......1¼ **18**
998* Top Cees **(82)***(84) (MrsJRRamsden)* 5-9-6 KFallon(1) (lw: a bhd)......¾ **19**
998[10] Always Aloof (USA) **(89)***(90) (MRStoute)* 4-9-11 WRSwinburn(24) (bhd most of wy)......nk **20**
1444[6] Bardolph (USA) **(70)***(71) (PFICole)* 8-8-8b TQuinn(4) (swtg: chsd ldrs 16f: sn wknd)......hd **21**
1757[10] High Five (IRE) **(55)***(55) (DAWilson)* 5-7-7 NAdams(3) (b.nr fore: a bhd)......1½ **22**
795[13] Phil's Time **(62)***(62) (TGMills)* 4-7-12b AMackay(23) (a in rr)......hd **23**
1768[7] Star Rage (IRE) **(77)***(71) (MJohnston)* 5-9-1 KDarley(16) (mid div: hdwy ½-wy: 5th st: wknd 2f out)......7 **24**
1657* Lalindi (IRE) **(73)***(66) (DRCElsworth)* 4-8-9 3x PatEddery(21) (a bhd)......1¼ **25**
1552* Upper Mount Clair **(63)***(53) (CEBrittain)* 5-8-1 ow3 MRoberts(9) (a in rr)......nk **26**
1189[2] Maradonna (USA) **(65)** *(JWhite)* 6-8-3 ow1 GDuffield(26) (bhd fr ½-wy)......dist **27**

LONG HANDICAP High Five (IRE) 7-0 Uncle Doug 7-3

9/2 Smuggling, **6/1** HARLESTONE BROOK, **10/1** Shadirwan (IRE), Top Cees, **12/1** Sweet Glow (FR), Tarthooth (IRE), **14/1** Lalindi (IRE), Bardolph (USA), Argyle Cavalier (IRE), Always Aloof (USA), **16/1** Tamarpour (USA), Upper Mount Clair, **20/1** Star Rage (IRE), Maradonna (USA), **25/1** Uncle Doug, Shrewd Alibi, **33/1** Paradise Navy, Bayrak (USA), Star Player, Noufari (FR), Simafar (IRE), **40/1** Kadiri (IRE), Art Form (USA), Imad (USA), **50/1** Phil's Time, **66/1** Nawar (FR), **100/1** High Five (IRE), CSF £220.84 CT £1,130.64 TOTE £8.60: £2.30 £10.50 £1.30 £3.40 (£514.20) Trio £1,263.20 OWNER Mr J.L. Dunlop (ARUNDEL) BRED J. Dunlop 27 Rn 4m25.3(6.30)
SF:77/55/68/64/61/58/54/46/39/49/45/65/39/60/53/57/46/35/59/63/46/30/35/46/39/28/-
WEIGHT FOR AGE 4yo-2lb

T/Jkpt: Not won; £46,790.70 to 21/6/95. T/Plpt: £3,830.00 (25.27 Tckts). T/Qdpt £23.30 (104.6 Tckts). IM

1503-THIRSK (L-H)
Tuesday June 20th (Good to firm)
WEATHER: sunny WIND: slt bhd

1841 PLASTICISERS FILAMENT YARN (S) STKS (2-Y.O) (Class G) £2,713.40 (£752.40: £360.20) **6f** Stalls: High GOING minus 0.43 sec per fur (F) 2-15 (2-16)

1525⁸ **Society Girl** *(67) (CWThornton)* 2-8-6 DeanMcKeown(7) (a cl up: led over 2f out: styd on strly) ....— 1
The Butterwick Kid *(61) (RAFahey)* 2-8-11 ACulhane(8) (leggy: unf: in tch: hdwy 2f out: styd on wl towards fin) 4 2
1652⁹ Needle Knot (IRE) *(59) (MJohnston)* 2-8-11 TWilliams(9) (pushed along thrght: in tch: styd on & hung lft fnl 2f) 1 3
1699⁶ Jambo *(48)*(Fav)*(MRChannon)* 2-8-6 DHarrison(13) (led over 3f: sn rdn & one pce) 2 4
1089⁹ Derek's Bo *(38) (NBycroft)* 2-8-6 SMaloney(3) (chsd ldr tl outpcd fnl 2f) 4 5
819¹⁵ Harsh Times *(31) (MHEasterby)* 2-8-6b MBirch(1) (s.i.s: hdwy 2f out: nvr nrr) 2½ 6
1288⁶ Marketeer Magic *(33) (JBerry)* 2-8-11 JCarroll(5) (in tch & rdn ½-wy: no imp) 1 7
1699⁵ Orange And Blue *(33) (MAJarvis)* 2-8-8c(5) JStack(10) (w ldrs 4f: sn rdn & btn) 1 8
1503⁶ Esther Louise *(21) (MWEasterby)* 2-8-6 GHind(12) (b: nvr trbld ldrs) 1¾ 9
1678⁷ Sea of Blue *(20) (MWEasterby)* 2-7-13 (7) RuthCoulter(4) (bit bkwd: outpcd after 2f) ....nk 10
Ceilidh (IRE) *(24) (PCHaslam)* 2-8-11 JFortune(6) (cmpt: bkwd: s.s: rdn & wl bhd tl sme late hdwy) ....nk 11
1215⁵ Propolis Power (IRE) *(20) (MWEasterby)* 2-8-11 LCharnock(11) (s.i.s: a bhd) 1¾ 12
1646⁷ Babyshooz *(MBrittain)* 2-8-6 NConnorton(2) (prom to ½-wy: wknd qckly) 15 13

5/2 Jambo, **11/4** Orange And Blue, **15/2** Marketeer Magic, **9/1** Needle Knot (IRE), **12/1** Harsh Times, **14/1** The Butterwick Kid, **16/1** Propolis Power (IRE), Ceilidh (IRE), Esther Louise, **20/1** Derek's Bo, **25/1** SOCIETY GIRL, **33/1** Sea of Blue, Babyshooz, CSF £300.43 TOTE £118.10: £10.90 £2.70 £1.90 (£324.90) Trio £172.10 OWNER Mr Guy Reed (MIDDLEHAM) BRED G. Reed
13 Rn 1m 12.2 (2.50) SF: 19/13/11/-/-/-/-/-/-/-/-/-/-
No bid

1842 POLYPROPYLENE FIBRE MEDIAN AUCTION MAIDEN STKS (2-Y.O) (Class F) £3,237.00 (£897.00: £429.00)
7f Stalls: Low GOING minus 0.43 sec per fur (F) 2-50 (2-51)

925ᵂ **Lac Dessert (USA)** *(73) (DRLoder)* 2-8-6 (3) DRMcCabe(13) (neat: unf: a chsng ldrs: rdn 2f out: r.o to ld cl home) ....— 1
1670⁴ Too Hasty *(77) (MHEasterby)* 2-9-0 MBirch(10) (cl up: rdn to ld wl ins fnl f: hdd & no ex towards fin) ....nk 2
1662⁸ White Ensign (IRE) *(76) (RHannon)* 2-9-0 RPerham(8) (led: rdn & rn green over 2f out: hdd & no ex wl ins fnl f) ....¾ 3
1525⁵ Gladys Althorpe (IRE) *(67) (JLEyre)* 2-8-9 RLappin(2) (in tch: hmpd appr st: hdwy 2f out: styd on) 1½ 4
903⁴ Rose of Siberia (USA) *(58)*(Fav)*(MBell)* 2-8-9 JCarroll(11) (outpcd appr st: styd on fnl 2f: n.d) 4 5
1063⁵ Eric's Bett *(62) (MrsSMAustin)* 2-9-0 JMarshall(7) (b: styd on fnl 3f: nvr rchd ldrs) ....½ 6
Aztec Flyer (USA) *(59) (MrsMReveley)* 2-9-0 DeanMcKeown(4) (leggy: unf: s.i.s: nvr plcd to chal) 1¼ 7
Ret Frem (IRE) *(56) (MAJarvis)* 2-9-0 GHind(5) (str: cmpt: bit bkwd: in tch tl grad wknd fnl 3f) 1¼ 8
1440⁴ Oriole *(45) (NTinkler)* 2-9-0 KimTinkler(1) (chsd ldrs tl lost pl appr st: n.d after) 5 9
1356⁵ Northern Clan *(17) (MWEasterby)* 2-9-0 LCharnock(9) (sn bhd) 12 10
Mill House Boy (IRE) *(8) (BSRothwell)* 2-8-9 (5) JStack(6) (cmpt: bit bkwd: dwlt: a bhd) 4 11
1646⁸ Sandblaster *(MissJFCraze)* 2-8-9 SWebster(12) (s.s: rn wd st & virtually p.u: bit slipped) ....dist 12

7/2 Rose of Siberia (USA), **4/1** LAC DESSERT (USA) (op 7/4), Too Hasty, **5/1** Gladys Althorpe (IRE), **8/1** Ret Frem (IRE), **10/1** White Ensign (IRE), **14/1** Northern Clan, **20/1** Oriole, Sandblaster, Aztec Flyer (USA), **25/1** Mill House Boy (IRE), **33/1** Eric's Bett, CSF £20.55 TOTE £2.10: £1.50 £2.10 £2.00 (£9.10) Trio £28.40 OWNER Mrs Virginia KraftPayson (NEWMARKET) BRED Virginia Kraft Payson 12 Rn 1m 27.2 (4.50) SF: 5/9/8/-/-/-/-/-/-/-/-/-

1843 CHARISMA LADIES' H'CAP (0-70) (3-Y.O+) (Class G) £2,758.20 (£765.20: £366.60) **7f** Stalls: Low GOING minus 0.43 sec per fur (F) 3-25 (3-25)

1679⁷ **Superoo (66)***(75) (MrsPSly)* 9-10-13 (7) MissLAllan(5) (in tch: hdwy 3f out: styd on to ld post) ....— 1

1809[7] Green's Bid **(52)***(61) (DWChapman)* 5-10-2 (4) MissRClark(6) (mde most tl ct last stride).......s.h **2**
1334[11] Royal Comedian **(46)***(50) (BWMurray)* 6-9-10 (4) MissADeniel(11) (a chsng ldrs: nt qckn appr fnl f) 2 **3**
1723[4] Mac's Taxi **(70)***(73) (PCHaslam)* 3-11-1 MrsDKettlewell(2) (swtg: chsd ldrs: hdwy u.p 2f out: nvr able chal).......½ **4**
1506[11] Gant Bleu (FR) **(40)***(40) (RMWhitaker)* 8-9-1 (7) MissSBrotherton(3) (stdd s: hdwy 3f out: rdn & nt qckn appr fnl f: sddle slipped) 1½ **5**
1714[7] Bill Moon **(33)***(30) (DTThom)* 9-9-1 MissJFeilden(1) (mid div: effrt ent st: no imp) 1¼ **6**
1534* Chief of Staff **(67)***(63)*(Fav)*(JPearce)* 6-11-7 MrsLPearce(10) (hld up & bhd: edgd rt fnl 2f: nvr plcd to chal) ....½ **7**
1583[3] Prim Lass **(51)***(45) (JHetherton)* 4-10-5 MissJThurlow(7) (in tch tl outpcd fnl 3f).......¾ **8**
6[3] Langtonian **(44)***(29) (JLEyre)* 6-9-12v MissDianaJones(9) (w ldr tl wknd 2f out) 4 **9**
1414[9] Carol Again **(41)***(23) (NBycroft)* 3-8-7 (7) MissABycroft(8) (sn bhd).......1¼ **10**
1523[5] My Godson **(43)***(17) (FJO'Mahony)* 5-9-4 (7) MissAYardley(4) (drvn along over 3f out: n.d) 3½ **11**
1297[5] At the Savoy (IRE) **(44)***(9) (TDBarron)* 4-9-8b(4) MissFHaynes(12) (s.i.s: a bhd) 4 **12**

LONG HANDICAP Carol Again 8-13

11/4 Chief of Staff, **4/1** Mac's Taxi, **6/1** Langtonian, **9/1** Royal Comedian, **10/1** Green's Bid, SUPER-OO, **12/1** Prim Lass, **14/1** Gant Bleu (FR), Bill Moon, My Godson, At the Savoy (IRE), **16/1** Carol Again, CSF £102.59 CT £865.95 TOTE £11.00: £3.40 £4.40 £2.80 (£54.10) Trio £198.70 OWNER Mrs P. Sly (PETERBOROUGH) BRED Irish Thoroughbred Holdings Ltd 12 Rn

1m 27.0 (4.30) SF: 43/29/18/32/8/-/31/13/-/-/-/-

WEIGHT FOR AGE 3yo-9lb

1844 PLASTICISERS 50TH ANNIVERSARY H'CAP (0-80) (4-Y.O+) (Class D) £4,051.00 (£1,207.00: £575.00: £259.00)

1m 4f Stalls: Low GOING minus 0.43 sec per fur (F) 4-00 (4-02)

1680[2] **North Ardar (50)***(60) (MrsMReveley)* 5-7-7 (7) PFessey(3) (hld up: jnd ldrs 5f out: rdn 2f out: r.o to ld cl home).......— **1**
1505[6] Persian Soldier **(45)***(52) (EJAlston)* 8-7-4 (5)ow2 NVarley(4) (s.i.s: hdwy to ld after 1f: pushed along 6f out: r.o: nt qckn towards fin) ....½ **2**
1505* Lookingforarainbow (IRE) **(77)***(82)*(Fav)*(BobJones)* 7-9-13 NConnorton(7) (hld up: hit rails appr st: hdwy 2f out: nt pce to chal).......3 **3**
1502* Stevie's Wonder (IRE) **(58)***(61) (MJRyan)* 5-8-8 JCarroll(2) (chsd ldrs: outpcd appr st: no imp after) 2 **4**
1505[4] Mr Towser **(61)***(59) (WWHaigh)* 4-8-8 (3) JTate(1) (lw: led 1f: trckd ldrs tl outpcd fnl 3f).......3½ **5**
1561[6] Kings Cay (IRE) **(71)***(42) (THCaldwell)* 4-9-2 (5) JStack(6) (bhd: hdwy appr st: sn wknd) 20 **6**
First Bid **(66)***(27) (RMWhitaker)* 8-9-2 ACulhane(5) (bit bkwd: outpcd 6f out: n.d after) 8 **7**

LONG HANDICAP Persian Soldier 7-6

5/2 Lookingforarainbow (IRE), **4/1** NORTH ARDAR, **9/2** Stevie's Wonder (IRE), **6/1** Mr Towser, **15/2** Persian Soldier, **9/1** Kings Cay (IRE), **10/1** First Bid, CSF £29.04 TOTE £4.00: £1.80 £3.60 (£12.20) OWNER Laurel (Leisure) Ltd (SALTBURN) BRED Mrs H.Seddington 7 Rn

2m 32.6 (2.60) SF: 34/26/56/35/33/16/1

1845 FIXSET H'CAP (0-80) (3-Y.O+ F & M) (Class D) £4,421.50 (£1,321.00: £632.00: £287.50)

1m Stalls: Low GOING minus 0.43 sec per fur (F) 4-35 (4-35)

1638[7] **Queens Consul (IRE) (75)***(83) (BSRothwell)* 5-9-5 (5) JStack(3) (dwlt: sn rcvrd & led: clr ent st: rdn & r.o wl).......— **1**
1362[3] Green Seed (IRE) **(80)***(84)*(Fav)*(JRFanshawe)* 3-9-5 DHarrison(2) (lw: hld up: effrt ent st: r.o: nvr able chal).......2 **2**
1663* Karinska **(65)***(68) (MCChapman)* 5-8-11 (3) 6x DRMcCabe(7) (hld up & bhd: n.m.r & swtchd over 2f out: r.o) ....½ **3**
1554[4] Skedaddle **(59)***(61) (JGFitzGerald)* 3-7-12 LCharnock(4) (led early: cl up tl rdn appr st: one pce fnl 3f).......nk **4**
1428* Shift Again (IRE) **(77)***(73) (WJarvis)* 3-9-2 AMcGlone(1) (chsd ldrs: hit rails appr st: rdn, wandered & put hd in air over 2f out: sn btn) 3 **5**
999[8] Flight Soundly (IRE) **(72)***(56) (MRStoute)* 3-8-11 DeanMcKeown(6) (prom tl outpcd fnl 3f) 6 **6**
1425* Aldaneh **(79)***(55) (RHannon)* 3-9-4 RPerham(5) (hld up: effrt appr st: n.d) 4 **7**

5/2 Green Seed (IRE), **100/30** Aldaneh, **5/1** Shift Again (IRE), **11/2** QUEENS CONSUL (IRE), **13/2** Karinska, **8/1** Flight Soundly (IRE) (6/1-9/1), **14/1** Skedaddle, CSF £18.77 TOTE £6.70: £2.60 £1.70 (£7.50) OWNER Miss Heather Davison (MALTON) BRED Mrs Ann Galvin 7 Rn

1m 37.7 (2.10) SF: 50/41/35/18/30/13/12

WEIGHT FOR AGE 3yo-10lb

1846 DURON FIBRE MAIDEN STKS (3-Y.O) (Class D) £4,002.70 (£1,195.60: £571.80: £259.90)
7f Stalls: Low GOING minus 0.43 sec per fur (F) 5-10 (5-13)

1167[11] **Kafani Al Widd (FR)** *(70) (MRStoute)* 3-9-0 DeanMcKeown(1) (mde all: hld on wl) ....— 1
1515[5] Al Baha *(64) (HRACecil)* 3-8-9 AMcGlone(2) (lw: in tch: effrt 2f out: hrd rdn & r.o fnl f) ....nk 2
1467[2] Dr Caligari (IRE) **(72)***(68) (JBerry)* 3-9-0 JCarroll(6) (lw: w wnr: nt qckn ins fnl f) ....¾ 3
Mystic Lure **(74)***(56)*(Fav)*(EALDunlop)* 3-8-6 (3) JTate(7) (b.hind: trckd ldrs: effrt 2f out: nt qckn fnl f)..........3 4
963[9] Napoleon's Law *(47) (RHannon)* 3-9-0 RPerham(8) (rr div: effrt ent st: nvr able chal) 6 5
Self Styled (IRE) *(31) (TDBarron)* 3-9-0 JFortune(9) (rangy: s.i.s: hdwy to jn ldrs appr st: edgd lft & wknd over 2f out)..........7 6
1522[W] Handsome Squaw *(24) (BWMurray)* 3-8-9 SMaloney(5) (b.hind: sn outpcd & bhd)..................1 7
1683[5] Young Ben (IRE) *(29) (JSWainwright)* 3-9-0 LCharnock(4) (chsd ldrs to st: sn lost pl)..........s.h 8
1431[5] Gunnerdale *(22) (DenysSmith)* 3-8-4 (5) CTeague(3) (a outpcd & bhd) ....¾ 9

7/4 Mystic Lure, **7/2** Dr Caligari (IRE), **5/1** Al Baha, KAFANI AL WIDD (FR), **9/1** Napoleon's Law (14/1-8/1), **25/1** Self Styled (IRE), **33/1** Handsome Squaw, Young Ben (IRE), Gunnerdale, CSF £27.59 TOTE £9.60: £2.20 £1.10 £2.00 (£12.50) Trio £11.80 OWNER Maktoum Al Maktoum (NEWMARKET) BRED John Lionel Moore 9 Rn 1m 26.2 (3.50) SF: 21/15/19/7/-/-/-/-/-

1847 HELTA H'CAP (0-70) (3-Y.O) (Class E) £3,634.30 (£1,086.40: £520.20: £237.10)
6f Stalls: High GOING minus 0.43 sec per fur (F) 5-40 (5-41)

1471[2] **Mousehole (63)***(71) (RGuest)* 3-9-0 JCarroll(6) (chsd ldrs: led over 2f out: r.o wl) ....— 1
1580[2] Stuffed **(54)***(58)*(Fav)*(MWEasterby)* 3-8-5 MBirch(12) (lw: chsd ldrs: nt clr run over 2f out: hdwy & ev ch ins fnl f: nt qckn)..........1½ 2
1279[3] Spara Tir **(59)***(62) (BobJones)* 3-8-10 NConnorton(11) (hdwy ½-wy: ev ch appr fnl f: nt qckn)..........½ 3
1380[5] Quilling **(70)***(66) (MDods)* 3-9-7 JFortune(4) (drvn along ½-wy: styd on fnl 2f: nrst fin) 2½ 4
1582[4] Dominelle **(46)***(40) (MHEasterby)* 3-7-11 ow1 SMaloney(9) (in tch: hdwy ½-wy: nt qkcn fnl f) ....½ 5
969[11] Belinda Blue **(51)***(45) (RAFahey)* 3-8-2 ACulhane(10) (lw: bhd: hdwy over 2f out: nt qckn fnl f) ....nk 6
1566[15] Double Glow **(45)***(31) (NBycroft)* 3-7-10b TWilliams(14) (led over 3f: nt qckn) 3 7
1679[5] It's Academic **(60)***(46) (MrsJRRamsden)* 3-8-11 SDWilliams(7) (mid div: hdwy 2f out: nvr able chal)..........hd 8
1669[12] Benten **(42)***(23) (DWChapman)* 3-7-7 NKennedy(1) (racd far side: nvr wnt pce) 1¾ 9
1660[5] Nadwaty (IRE) **(53)***(29) (MCChapman)* 3-8-1 (3) DRMcCabe(3) (rdn ½-wy: nvr bttr than mid div)..........2 10
1450[8] Petova (IRE) **(48)***(8) (MJCamacho)* 3-7-13 LCharnock(13) (a bhd) 6 11
1521[7] Giggleswick Gossip **(45)***(2) (MRChannon)* 3-7-5 (5) NVarley(5) (s.i.s: drvn along & n.d) 1 12
1580[4] Tee Tee Too (IRE) **(62)***(18) (PCHaslam)* 3-8-8b(5) JStack(8) (s.i.s: hdwy & prom after 2f: wknd over 2f out)..........nk 13
1721[14] Gilpa Trinkets **(43)** *(DWChapman)* 3-7-1b(7)ow1 JBramhill(2) (racd far side tl hung rt ½-wy: prom over 3f) 2½ 14

LONG HANDICAP Benten 7-4 Gilpa Trinkets 6-9

9/4 Stuffed, **6/1** MOUSEHOLE, Dominelle, It's Academic, **10/1** Spara Tir, Tee Tee Too (IRE), **14/1** Quilling, Giggleswick Gossip, **16/1** Nadwaty (IRE), Belinda Blue, **20/1** Petova (IRE), **33/1** Benten, Double Glow, Gilpa Trinkets, CSF £20.17 CT £127.24 TOTE £5.30: £1.20 £1.60 £3.00 (£6.50) Trio £21.20 OWNER Mr Albert Linskey & Mrs Janet Kent (NEWMARKET) BRED T. H. Rossiter 14 Rn 1m 10.8 (1.10) SF: 46/33/37/41/15/20/6/21/-/4/-/-/-/-

T/Plpt: £1,151.90 (10.47 Tckts). T/Qdpt: Not won; £89.10 to Ripon 21/6/95. AA

1835-ASCOT (R-H)
Wednesday June 21st (Good to firm)
WEATHER: sunny WIND: almost nil

1848 JERSEY STKS (Gp 3) (3-Y.O) (Class A) £33,950.00 (£12,860.00: £6,305.00: £2,885.00)
7f Stalls: Centre GOING minus 0.20 sec per fur (GF) 2-30 (2-32)

1138* **Sergeyev (IRE) (112)***(113+)*(Fav)*(RHannon)* 3-8-10 RHughes(5) (lw: stdd s: hrd rdn & hdwy over 1f out: led ins fnl f: r.o wl) ....— 1
1222* Shahid **(104)***(110) (JLDunlop)* 3-8-10 WCarson(17) (hld up: led over 1f out tl ins fnl f: unable qckn)..........1¼ 2

1345* First Island (IRE) **(99)***(110) (GWragg)* 3-8-10 MHills(16) (lw: rdn over 4f out: hdwy over 1f out: r.o) ....hd **3**
1618[4] Inzar (USA) **(105)***(110) (PFICole)* 3-8-10 MRoberts(12) (hld up: rdn over 2f out: ev ch 1f out: one pce fnl f) ....s.h **4**
Options Open *(106) (SbinSuroor)* 3-8-10 LDettori(3) (bit bkwd: a.p: led over 2f out tl over 1f out: one pce fnl f) 1¾ **5**
1390a[7] Mediation (IRE) *(107) (JOxx,Ireland)* 3-8-12 JPMurtagh(10) (unf: lw: a.p: rdn over 2f out: ev ch over 1f out: one pce) ....nk **6**
1233a* Nautical Pet (IRE) *(110) (DKWeld,Ireland)* 3-9-4 MJKinane(9) (w'like: nvr nr to chal) 1¼ **7**
1121a[2] Montjoy (USA) **(113)***(103) (PFICole)* 3-9-1 TQuinn(15) (lw: hld up: rdn over 2f out: wknd over 1f out) 1¾ **8**
1486[2] Empty Quarter *(94) (JHMGosden)* 3-8-10 JCarroll(7) (lw: led 1f: ev ch over 2f out: wknd over 1f out) 2 **9**
1117a[3] Petit Poucet *(92) (NClement,France)* 3-9-1 CAsmussen(18) (w'like: nvr nrr) 3 **10**
1145* Epagris **(111)***(83) (HRACecil)* 3-8-12 WRyan(11) (lw: hld up: rdn 2f out: wknd over 1f out) ...2½ **11**
1018[4] Rambrino **(104)***(80) (PWChapple-Hyam)* 3-8-10b JReid(6) (led 6f out tl over 2f out: sn wknd) .½ **12**
1475[7] Warning Star **(104)***(76) (BWHills)* 3-8-7 RHills(14) (hld up: rdn over 2f out: wknd over 1f out) ....nk **13**
1613* Silca Blanka (IRE) **(103)***(82) (MRChannon)* 3-9-1 KDarley(4) (lw: bhd fnl 3f) 1 **14**
1488* Baaderah (IRE) **(104)***(79) (LMCumani)* 3-8-12 PatEddery(13) (lw: prom over 4f) ....hd **15**
930[4] Magnificent Devil (USA) **(95)***(76) (JWWatts)* 3-8-10 BThomson(8) (lw: bhd fnl 2f) ....½ **16**
1116a[12] Deceive *(SbinSuroor)* 3-8-7 RCochrane(2) (Withdrawn not under Starter's orders: injured in paddock) .... **W**

, **5/1** SERGEYEV (IRE), **11/2** Shahid (4/1-6/1), **6/1** Epagris, **8/1** Options Open, First Island (IRE), **11/1** Petit Poucet, **12/1** Montjoy (USA), **14/1** Baaderah (IRE), **16/1** Nautical Pet (IRE), **25/1** Inzar (USA), **33/1** Silca Blanka (IRE), Warning Star, Rambrino, **40/1** Mediation (IRE), **50/1** Magnificent Devil (USA), **66/1** Empty Quarter, CSF £28.46 TOTE £5.60: £1.70 £1.30 £2.70 £7.20 (£8.40) Trio £34.70 OWNER Mr B. T. Stewart-Brown (MARLBOROUGH) BRED Hugo Merry and Michael Stanley
16 Rn 1m 27.12 (0.62) SF: 72/69/69/69/65/66/69/62/53/51/42/39/35/41/38/35/-

1849 QUEEN MARY STKS (Gp 3) (2-Y.O F) (Class A) £25,840.00 (£9,782.00: £4,791.00: £2,187.00)

5f Stalls: Centre GOING minus 0.20 sec per fur (GF) 3-05 (3-07)

1361* **Blue Duster (USA)** *(110+)*(Fav)*(DRLoder)* 2-8-8 MJKinane(10) (hld up: led 1f out: pushed out) ....— **1**
1361[2] Dance Sequence (USA) *(105) (MRStoute)* 2-8-8 WRSwinburn(12) (lw: stdy hdwy over 1f out: hrd rdn: r.o) 1½ **2**
871[6] My Melody Parkes *(96) (JBerry)* 2-8-8 JCarroll(6) (led over 3f: unable qckn) 3 **3**
1137[3] Unconditional Love (IRE) *(89) (MJohnston)* 2-8-8 MRoberts(1) (lw: a.p: rdn over 1f out: one pce) 2 **4**
1098* Tropical Dance (USA) *(88) (MrsJCecil)* 2-8-8 JReid(7) (hld up: rdn over 2f out: one pce) ......nk **5**
1137* Marl *(87) (RAkehurst)* 2-8-8 LDettori(4) (hld up: rdn over 2f out: one pce) ....nk **6**
1176* Sweet Robin (IRE) *(87) (MJohnston)* 2-8-8 DHolland(2) (rdn over 3f out: nvr nr to chal) ....s.h **7**
Sagar Pride (IRE) *(87) (JGBurns,Ireland)* 2-8-8 WCarson(9) (small: lost pl over 3f out: r.o one pce fnl 2f) ....hd **8**
1530* Top Cat (FR) *(86) (EWeymes)* 2-8-8 DeanMcKeown(11) (a.p: led over 1f out: sn hdd & wknd) ....nk **9**
1511[5] Mimosa *(67) (LJHolt)* 2-8-8 MFenton(5) (lw: bhd fnl 2f) 6 **10**
1259[2] Anotheranniversary *(65) (GLewis)* 2-8-8 PaulEddery(8) (lw: a bhd) ....½ **11**
1562* Whittle Rock *(52) (EJAlston)* 2-8-8 KFallon(3) (s.s: a bhd) 4 **12**

7/4 BLUE DUSTER (USA), **15/8** Marl, **13/2** Dance Sequence (USA), **14/1** Unconditional Love (IRE), Sweet Robin (IRE) (10/1-16/1), **16/1** Sagar Pride (IRE), Anotheranniversary, **20/1** Top Cat (FR), **33/1** Tropical Dance (USA), **50/1** My Melody Parkes, **66/1** Whittle Rock, **100/1** Mimosa, CSF £13.44 TOTE £3.30: £1.40 £2.50 £16.40 (£8.70) Trio £335.70 OWNER Sheikh Mohammed (NEWMARKET) BRED Darley Stud Management Inc 12 Rn
60.98 secs (1.48) SF: 51/46/37/30/29/28/28/28/27/8/6/-

1850 CORONATION STKS (Gp 1) (3-Y.O F) (Class A) £119,133.00 (£44,372.65: £21,136.33: £9,013.02)

1m (round) Stalls: High GOING minus 0.20 sec per fur (GF) 3-45 (3-46)

1390a* **Ridgewood Pearl** *(124) (JOxx,Ireland)* 3-9-0 JPMurtagh(8) (b: lengthy: 2nd st: led over 2f out: hrd rdn 1f out: r.o wl) ....— **1**
1576a* Smolensk (USA) *(120) (AFabre,France)* 3-9-0 TJarnet(7) (gd sort: lw: 4th st: hrd rdn over 1f out: unable qckn) 2 **2**

1390a5 Harayir (USA) **(121)**_(117)_(Fav)_(MajorWRHern)_ 3-9-0 WCarson(9) (3rd st: hrd rdn over 1f out: one pce) 1¾ 3
1390a2 Warning Shadows (IRE) _(114) (CEBrittain)_ 3-9-0 MJKinane(10) (lw: 6th st: nt clr run & swtchd lft over 2f out: r.o one pce)....1¼ 4
933⁷ Gay Gallanta (USA) **(116)**_(102) (MRStoute)_ 3-9-0v WRSwinburn(6) (8th st: nvr nr to chal) 6 5
868* A la Carte (IRE) **(100)**_(100) (JLDunlop)_ 3-9-0 PatEddery(5) (10th st: nvr nrr)....1¼ 6
933⁸ Myself **(111)**_(99) (PWChapple-Hyam)_ 3-9-0 JReid(4) (b.hind: 4th whn squeezed out over 6f out: 7th st: wknd over 2f out) ....½ 7
Mamlakah (IRE) **(110)**_(98) (HThomsonJones)_ 3-9-0 RHills(3) (lw: led over 5f)....nk 8
1588³ Brief Glimpse (IRE) **(98)**_(91) (MajorDNChappell)_ 3-9-0 BThomson(1) (9th st: a bhd)....3½ 9
933⁶ Macoumba (USA) _(51) (MmeCHead,France)_ 3-9-0 FHead(2) (5th st: wknd over 2f out)....20 10

15/8 Harayir (USA), **9/2** RIDGEWOOD PEARL, **6/1** Smolensk (USA), Macoumba (USA), **12/1** Myself, Gay Gallanta (USA), **14/1** Warning Shadows (IRE), **16/1** A la Carte (IRE), **25/1** Mamlakah (IRE), **33/1** Brief Glimpse (IRE), CSF £29.02 TOTE £4.90: £1.80 £2.10 £1.50 (£14.40) Trio £10.50 OWNER Mrs Anne Coughlan BRED S. Coughlan 10 Rn

1m 38.58 (0.22 under best) (-1.02) SF: 94/90/87/84/72/70/69/68/61/21

1851 ROYAL HUNT CUP H'CAP (3-Y.O+) (Class B) £49,322.50 (£14,830.00: £7,165.00: £3,332.50) **1m (straight)** Stalls: Centre GOING minus 0.20 sec (GF) 4-20 (4-26)

1143² **Realities (USA) (99)**_(111) (GHarwood)_ 5-9-0 MJKinane(30) (lw: hld up: led 1f out: rdn out) .— 1
Darnay **(109)**_(119) (SbinSuroor)_ 4-9-10 LDettori(29) (hld up: led over 2f out to 1f out: unable qckn)....1¼ 2
870⁶ Indian Fly **(93)**_(100) (RHannon)_ 4-8-8 ow1 RHughes(19) (stdy hdwy over 2f out: rdn over 1f out: one pce) 1 3
1143⁶ Billy Bushwacker **(87)**_(94) (MrsMReveley)_ 4-8-2 KDarley(3) (racd stands' side: rdn & hdwy 2f out: r.o wl ins fnl f)....s.h 4
1108² Kayvee **(98)**_(105) (GHarwood)_ 6-8-13 WRSwinburn(1) (racd stands' side: hdwy & nt clr run wl over 1f out: swtchd rt: swtchd lft 1f out: r.o wl)....hd 5
1626⁹ Moving Arrow **(89)**_(96) (MissSEHall)_ 4-8-4v NConnorton(15) (hdwy over 2f out: hrd rdn over 1f out: one pce) ....hd 6
1217* Hunters of Brora (IRE) **(88)**_(94) (JDBethell)_ 5-8-3 RHills(8) (racd stands' side: rdn & hdwy 2f out: r.o)....½ 7
870² Royal Hill **(85)**_(91) (LordHuntingdon)_ 4-8-0 DHarrison(22) (rdn over 2f out: hdwy over 1f out: r.o) ....s.h 8
1188⁴ Night City **(100)**_(106) (LadyHerries)_ 4-9-1 PaulEddery(2) (swtg: racd stands' side: hld up: rdn over 3f out: r.o ins fnl f)....s.h 9
1179¹² Knave's Ash (USA) **(89)**_(94) (MRStoute)_ 4-8-1 (3) JTate(32) (hdwy over 2f out: hrd rdn over 1f out: one pce)....nk 10
Baydur (IRE) **(82)**_(84) (DKWeld,Ireland)_ 4-7-11 WCarson(5) (lw: racd stands' side: a.p: rdn over 2f out: one pce) 1½ 11
960⁷ Air Commodore (IRE) **(92)**_(93) (PFICole)_ 4-8-7 TQuinn(20) (lw: hld up: hrd rdn over 1f out: sn wknd)....¾ 12
1280³ Show Faith (IRE) **(83)**_(81) (RHannon)_ 5-7-12 ow1 DBiggs(17) (swtg: rdn over 2f out: hdwy over 1f out: one pce)....¾ 13
714* Star Manager (USA) **(83)**_(79) (PFICole)_ 5-7-12 FNorton(21) (swtg: rdn over 3f out: nvr nrr)..1¾ 14
1684² Mellottie **(92)**_(87) (MrsMReveley)_ 10-8-7 DeanMcKeown(10) (lw: racd stands' side: rdn over 2f out: nvr nrr)....nk 15
1225⁷ Chickawicka (IRE) **(79)**_(72) (MCPipe)_ 4-7-8v AMackay(31) (led over 5f)....1 16
1617⁸ Leif the Lucky (USA) **(81)**_(72) (MissSEHall)_ 6-7-5 (5) MBaird(18) (lw: prom 6f)....1¼ 17
918⁸ Sue's Artiste **(83)**_(74) (BWHills)_ 4-7-5 (7) MHenry(16) (hdwy over 3f out: wknd wl over 1f out) ....s.h 18
1365² Czarna (IRE) **(87)**_(77) (CEBrittain)_ 4-8-2 MRoberts(4) (lw: racd stands' side: prom over 6f) ....s.h 19
1225² Ham N'Eggs **(88)**_(75) (RHannon)_ 4-8-3 GCarter(27) (nvr nrr)....1½ 20
1626⁴ Wilcuma **(85)**_(70) (PJMakin)_ 4-7-11 (3)ow2 SSanders(25) (prom over 4f) ....hd 21
1409⁷ Serious **(83)**_(70) (LadyHerries)_ 5-7-12 JQuinn(11) (racd stands' side: hdwy over 3f out: wknd over 2f out)....hd 22
Allez Cyrano (IRE) **(92)**_(78) (MBell)_ 4-8-7 MFenton(9) (bit bkwd: racd stands' side: bhd fnl 2f) ....¾ 23
1617⁶ Gymcrak Premiere **(89)**_(71) (GHolmes)_ 7-8-4 ow2 KFallon(6) (b.hind: racd stands' side: bhd fnl 5f) ....¾ 24
1143* Madly Sharp **(93)**_(75)_(Fav)_(JWWatts)_ 4-8-8 PatEddery(26) (hdwy over 4f out: wknd over 2f out)....1¼ 25
1605² Hoh Express **(95)**_(76) (IABalding)_ 3-8-0 CRutter(14) (lw: bhd fnl 3f)....nk 26
1217² River Board **(88)**_(69) (WJHaggas)_ 5-8-3 MHills(24) (prom 5f)....d.h 26
1365⁷ Lap of Luxury **(102)**_(79) (WJarvis)_ 6-9-3 BThomson(13) (prom stands' side over 5f) 1¾ 28

1618[8] Jawaal **(102)***(79) (LadyHerries)* 5-9-3 RCochrane(7) (racd stands' side: hld up: rdn over 3f out: wknd wl over 1f out) ....hd **29**
665* Governor George (USA) **(103)***(70) (JLDunlop)* 4-9-4 JReid(12) (lw: racd stands' side: bhd fnl 2f) 5 **30**
1593* Desert Time **(80)***(31) (CAHorgan)* 5-7-9 7x DaleGibson(28) (b.hind: prom 6f) 8 **31**
Varsavia (USA) **(90)***(29) (LordHuntingdon)* 4-8-5 JWeaver(23) (lw: bhd fnl 3f: t.o whn virtually p.u over 1f out) 6 **32**

9/1 Madly Sharp, **11/1** REALITIES (USA), **12/1** Desert Time, Governor George (USA), **14/1** Darnay, Baydur (IRE), Royal Hill, Indian Fly, **16/1** Hoh Express, Billy Bushwacker, Jawaal, **20/1** Kayvee, Czarna (IRE), Ham N'Eggs, Air Commodore (IRE), **25/1** Varsavia (USA), Lap of Luxury, Hunters of Brora (IRE), Wilcuma, River Board, **33/1** Night City, Knave's Ash (USA), Serious, Star Manager (USA), Mellottie, **40/1** Moving Arrow, Sue's Artiste, **50/1** Show Faith (IRE), Gymcrak Premiere, Leif the Lucky (USA), Allez Cyrano (IRE), **66/1** Chickawicka (IRE), CSF £151.92 CT £2,025.43 TOTE £12.20: £2.90 £5.20 £4.30 £3.00 (£112.80) Trio £749.40 OWNER Mr Roy Taiano (PULBOROUGH) BRED Kathleen Crompton & Russell B. Jones Jnr 32 Rn 1m 40.08 (0.88)
SF:74/82/63/57/68/59/57/54/69/57/47/56/44/42/50/35/35/37/40/38/33/33/41/34/38/29/32/42/42/33/-/-
WEIGHT FOR AGE 3yo-10lb

1852 QUEEN'S VASE STKS (Gp 3) (3-Y.O) (Class A) £32,150.00
(£12,170.00: £5,960.00: £2,720.00)
2m 45y Stalls: High GOING minus 0.20 sec per fur (GF) 4-55 (4-55)

1099* **Stelvio (106)***(102)*(Fav)*(HRACecil)* 3-8-11 MJKinane(10) (rdn & hdwy over 3f out: 6th st: swtchd lft over 2f out: hrd rdn fnl f: led nr fin) ....— **1**
1008a[8] Double Eclipse (IRE) *(102) (MJohnston)* 3-8-11 JWeaver(9) (2nd st: led over 2f out: hrd rdn fnl f: hdd nr fin) ....nk **2**
1490* Pedraza **(100)***(99) (HRACecil)* 3-8-11 WRyan(7) (7th st: rdn & hdwy over 1f out: one pce) ...2½ **3**
1099[6] Wot-If-We (IRE) **(96)***(99) (TGMills)* 3-8-11 JCarroll(1) (4th st: hrd rdn over 2f out: one pce) ....¾ **4**
1099[5] Great Crusader **(96)***(97) (CACyzer)* 3-8-11 KDarley(11) (rdn over 5f out: 8th st: hdwy over 1f out: one pce) 1½ **5**
1672[2] Grey Shot **(97)***(96) (IABalding)* 3-8-11 RCochrane(6) (led 14f: wknd 1f out) 1¼ **6**
1672* Anchor Clever *(93) (PAKelleway)* 3-8-11 PatEddery(3) (rdn over 5f out: 9th st: nvr nrr)....2½ **7**
1127[2] Nash Terrace (IRE) **(98)***(92) (RCharlton)* 3-8-11 JReid(4) (rdn over 3f out: 5th st: wknd over 1f out) 1¼ **8**
1782* Tenorio **(94)***(90) (DRLoder)* 3-8-11 LDettori(8) (lw: 3rd st: hrd rdn over 2f out: wknd over 1f out) 2 **9**
1672[3] Lord Jim (IRE) **(96)** *(MissGayKelleway)* 3-8-11 WCarson(5) (lw: prom 13f: 10th st: t.o) ....dist **10**
1526[2] United Force (IRE) **(90)** *(PWChapple-Hyam)* 3-8-11 BThomson(2) (bhd fnl 4f: 11th st: t.o) ...25 **11**

7/4 STELVIO, **5/1** Pedraza, Tenorio, **11/2** Double Eclipse (IRE), **15/2** Nash Terrace (IRE), **12/1** Anchor Clever, **16/1** Grey Shot, **20/1** Lord Jim (IRE), **25/1** Great Crusader, **33/1** Wot-If-We (IRE), United Force (IRE), CSF £12.26 TOTE £2.20: £1.10 £2.60 £2.30 (£6.90) Trio £12.30 OWNER Sheikh Mohammed (NEWMARKET) BRED Hesmonds Stud Ltd 11 Rn
3m 28.64 (2.14) SF: 70/70/67/67/65/64/61/60/58/-/-

1853 BESSBOROUGH H'CAP (0-105) (3-Y.O+) (Class B) £26,556.25
(£8,050.00: £3,937.50: £1,881.25)
1m 4f Stalls: High GOING minus 0.20 sec per fur (GF) 5-30 (5-32)

1260* **Son of Sharp Shot (IRE) (90)***(105) (JLDunlop)* 5-8-13 PatEddery(19) (lw: 13th st: swtchd lft & hdwy over 1f out: hrd rdn fnl f: led nr fin) ....— **1**
1140* Zaralaska **(86)***(101)*(Fav)*(LMCumani)* 4-8-9 LDettori(9) (lw: dwlt: hdwy over 3f out: 6th st: led over 1f out: hrd rdn fnl f: hdd nr fin) ....nk **2**
1140[7] Shadow Leader **(77)***(86) (MissAJWhitfield)* 4-8-0 ow3 DHarrison(13) (lw: 10th st: hdwy over 2f out: nt clr rn wl over 1f out: one pce fnl f) 1¾ **3**
1612[3] Benfleet **(78)***(88) (RWArmstrong)* 4-8-1 WCarson(3) (16th st: rdn over 2f out: hdwy over 1f out: r.o wl ins fnl f) 1¾ **4**
1563* Marsoom (CAN) **(99)***(107) (BHanbury)* 4-9-8 TIves(4) (b.hind: 3rd st: led 2f out: sn hdd: wknd fnl f) 1¼ **5**
1585[4] Source of Light **(103)***(111) (RCharlton)* 6-9-12 PaulEddery(16) (18th st: hrd rdn & hdwy over 1f out: r.o one pce) ....hd **6**
1260[3] Proton **(74)***(82) (RAkehurst)* 5-7-11 JQuinn(7) (5th st: hrd rdn 2f out: one pce) ....½ **7**
1135[5] Taufan's Melody **(99)***(106) (LadyHerries)* 4-9-8 RCochrane(10) (19th st: rdn over 2f out: hdwy over 1f out: nvr nrr) ....¾ **8**
1109[2] Foundry Lane **(81)***(86) (MrsMReveley)* 4-8-4 KDarley(11) (lw: 12th st: nvr nr to chal) 1 **9**
623[3] Glide Path (USA) **(96)***(100) (JWHills)* 6-9-5 RHills(1) (7th st: swtchd lft over 2f out: hrd rdn over 1f out: sn wknd) ....¾ **10**

931[2] Blushing Flame (USA) **(90)***(91) (MRStoute)* 4-8-13 WRSwinburn(6) (lw: 11th st: hdwy & hmpd over 1f out: nt rcvr) 2½ **11**
1610[3] Mystic Hill **(90)***(89) (RCharlton)* 4-8-13 WRyan(17) (lw: 14th st: nt clr run 2f out: nvr nrr) 1¾ **12**
1558[3] Hazard a Guess (IRE) **(78)***(76) (MrsJRRamsden)* 5-8-1 DBiggs(2) (s.s: 17th st: nvr nrr) .... ¾ **13**
1140[4] Whitechapel (USA) **(87)***(84) (LordHuntingdon)* 7-8-10 JWeaver(15) (lw: 2nd st: led over 2f out: sn hdd: wknd over 1f out) .... ½ **14**
1141* Smart Generation **(83)***(75) (LordHuntingdon)* 4-8-6 JReid(14) (9th st: hdwy over 2f out: n.m.r wl over 1f out: eased whn btn over 1f out) 3½ **15**
1610[5] Cedez le Passage (FR) **(98)***(87) (CEBrittain)* 4-9-7 BDoyle(20) (lw: 4th st: rdn over 2f out: wknd over 1f out) 2½ **16**
1558* Riparius (USA) **(79)***(61) (HCandy)* 4-8-2b MRoberts(18) (led over 7f) 5 **17**
1661[2] Uncle Oswald **(76)***(52) (RHannon)* 4-7-13 GCarter(12) (8th st: wknd over 2f out) 5 **18**
1558[8] Geisway (CAN) **(82)***(53) (NJHWalker)* 5-8-5v CRutter(5) (hdwy 6f out: wknd over 3f out: 15th st) 3½ **19**

100/30 Zaralaska, **5/1** SON OF SHARP SHOT (IRE), **7/1** Mystic Hill, Blushing Flame (USA), **12/1** Foundry Lane, Whitechapel (USA), **14/1** Smart Generation, Marsoom (CAN), **16/1** Glide Path (USA), Uncle Oswald, Hazard a Guess (IRE), Benfleet, **20/1** Source of Light, Proton, Taufan's Melody, **25/1** Riparius (USA), **33/1** Cedez le Passage (FR), **40/1** Shadow Leader, Geisway (CAN), CSF £23.50 CT £604.40 TOTE £5.00: £1.40 £1.20 £17.70 £3.30 (£9.60) Trio £594.80 OWNER Windflower Overseas Holdings Inc (ARUNDEL) BRED Windflower Overseas 19 Rn

2m 28.71 (-0.79) SF: 88/84/69/71/90/94/65/89/69/83/74/72/59/67/58/70/44/35/36

T/Jkpt: £5,462.20 (12.05 Tckts). T/Plpt: £61.80 (1,807.15 Tckts). T/Qdpt: £12.60 (128.35 Tckts). AK

1640-NOTTINGHAM (L-H)
Wednesday June 21st (Good to firm)
WEATHER: sunny WIND: slt across

1854 BURTON JOYCE (S) H'CAP (0-60) (3-Y.O+) (Class G) £2,243.00 (£618.00: £293.00) **1m 1f 213y** Stalls: Low GOING minus 0.24 sec per fur (GF) 6-30 (6-32)

1647[2] **Lady Highfield (38)***(56+)*(Fav)*(MJRyan)* 4-8-12 AClark(15) (b.hind: 7th st: gd hdwy 3f out: led 2f out: sn clr: easily) .... — **1**
1523* Pop to Stans **(47)***(52) (JPearce)* 6-9-0 (7) ElizabethTurner(13) (lw: 6th st: one pce fnl 2f) 8 **2**
1542[10] Tout de Val **(31)***(35) (KBishop)* 6-8-5 ow1 RPerham(8) (4th st: hrd rdn & kpt on one pce fnl 2f) .... nk **3**
534[15] Demurrer **(38)***(41) (MrsAMNaughton)* 5-8-12 AMercer(3) (a.p: 2nd st: hrd rdn & ev ch 2f out: sn btn) 1 **4**
1463[4] Kindred Greeting **(39)***(41) (DMorris)* 3-8-1b JFanning(1) (a.p: 3rd st: one pce fnl 3f) .... ½ **5**
1645[3] Sinclair Lad (IRE) **(40)***(38) (RJHodges)* 7-8-11b(3) SDrowne(17) (s.i.s: sme hdwy fnl 3f: n.d) 3 **6**
1696[11] Keys Seminar **(47)***(44) (JohnBerry)* 3-8-9b CDwyer(7) (led to 2f out) .... nk **7**
1651[2] Bardia **(30)***(27) (DonEnricoIncisa)* 5-8-4 KimTinkler(4) (wl bhd tl hdwy fnl 3f: nvr nrr) .... hd **8**
1680[8] Bad News **(51)***(47) (GFierro)* 3-8-8 (5) PMcCabe(20) (5th st: wknd over 2f out) .... nk **9**
Formaestre (IRE) **(38)***(32) (RLee)* 5-8-12 MPerrett(14) (b: 9th st: no hdwy fnl 3f) 1¼ **10**
1762[12] Torrey Pines (IRE) **(44)***(37) (DHaydnJones)* 3-8-3 (3) DWright(5) (bhd to st: n.d) 1 **11**
1350[5] Dots Dee **(24)***(16) (JMBradley)* 6-7-5 (7) AmandaSanders(23) (b: a bhd) .... ½ **12**
1377[15] Seraphic **(48)***(38) (BRCambidge)* 4-9-8 NAdams(9) (dwlt: a bhd) 1¼ **13**
1622[14] Bresil (USA) **(33)***(17) (KRBurke)* 6-8-7 ATucker(10) (s.i.s: a bhd) 4 **14**
1285[6] Bronze Runner **(34)***(16) (SMellor)* 11-8-1b(7) ADaly(19) (in tch 7f) 1 **15**
1645[10] Centaur Express **(37)***(19) (ALForbes)* 3-7-10 (3) AGarth(6) (b.hind: dwlt: a bhd) .... hd **16**
1499[20] Lucy's Gold **(33)** *(MJRyan)* 4-8-0 (7)ow3 DGibbs(16) (8th st: sn wknd: t.o) 14 **17**
1666[6] Juice Plus **(27)** *(JParkes)* 4-8-1 NKennedy(22) (prom to ½-wy: t.o) .... ¾ **18**
430[25] Britannia Mills **(35)** *(MCChapman)* 4-8-2 (7) JBramhill(2) (cl up whn sddle slipped after 4f: t.o fnl 3f) .... ½ **19**
Lincoln Treasure (IRE) **(54)***(9) (MCChapman)* 4-9-11 (3) DRMcCabe(18) (swtg: plld hrd early: wl bhd fnl 4f: t.o) 1¼ **20**
1459[9] Brackenthwaite **(42)** *(LRLloyd-James)* 5-9-2b MTebbutt(21) (t.o fnl 4f) .... dist **21**

5/1 LADY HIGHFIELD, **6/1** Sinclair Lad (IRE), **7/1** Dots Dee, **8/1** Bardia, **9/1** Pop to Stans, **10/1** Centaur Express, **14/1** Tout de Val, **16/1** Kindred Greeting, Torrey Pines (IRE), **20/1** Bad News, Bronze Runner, Keys Seminar, Brackenthwaite, Bresil (USA), Juice Plus, Lucy's Gold, **25/1** Demurrer, Formaestre (IRE), Britannia Mills, **33/1** Lincoln Treasure (IRE), Seraphic, CSF £52.10 CT £577.20 TOTE £4.60: £1.20 £2.00 £6.00 £23.60 (£28.30) Trio £172.10 OWNER Miss J. Nicholls (NEWMARKET) BRED Mrs E. S. Bradley 21 Rn

2m 7.8 (5.30) SF: 34/30/13/19/7/16/10/5/13/10/3/-/16/-/-/-/-/-/-/-/-

WEIGHT FOR AGE 3yo-12lb

No bid

1855 SAXONDALE H'CAP (0-70) (4-Y.O+) (Class E) £3,502.40 (£1,047.20: £501.60: £228.80) **1m 54y** Stalls: Low GOING minus 0.24 sec per fur (GF) 7-00 (7-02)

1666[9] **Avishayes (USA) (43)***(54) (MrsMReveley)* 8-8-1 JFanning(3) (lw: hld up: hdwy u.p over 3f out: led appr fnl f: rdn out) ....— 1
1542[2] Just Harry **(67)***(77)*(Fav)*(MJRyan)* 4-9-11 AClark(8) (8th st: gd hdwy over 2f out: carried rt 2f out: led briefly over 1f out: r.o) ....nk 2
1645[4] Shuttlecock **(44)***(48) (MrsNMacauley)* 4-7-13 (3) AGarth(1) (lw: led: rdn & hung rt 2f out: hdd over 1f out: r.o one pce) 3½ 3
1775[0] Polonez Prima **(64)***(67) (JLSpearing)* 8-9-8 AMcGlone(5) (5th st: styd on one pce fnl 3f) ....nk 4
1501* Daring Ryde **(51)***(48) (JPSmith)* 4-8-9 MTebbutt(2) (3rd st: wnt 2nd over 3f out: wknd 2f out)..3 5
1649[3] Nobby Barnes **(43)***(40) (DonEnricoIncisa)* 6-8-1 KimTinkler(10) (s.i.s: 7th st: styd on one pce fnl 3f) ....nk 6
1468[6] Phase One (IRE) **(50)***(46) (JLEyre)* 5-8-8 TGMcLaughlin(12) (6th st: hdwy over 3f out: one pce fr over 2f out) ....hd 7
1499[13] As Such (IRE) **(52)***(33) (NACallaghan)* 4-8-10 GDuffield(6) (a bhd) 8 8
1732[4] Whispering Loch (IRE) **(40)***(17) (JAkehurst)* 4-7-12 NAdams(9) (s.i.s: a wl bhd).......2 9
1745[6] Oozlem (IRE) **(40)***(5) (RMFlower)* 6-7-12b StephenDavies(7) (s.i.s: a wl bhd) 6 10
672[7] Northern Chief **(42)***(5) (MissJFCraze)* 5-8-0 NKennedy(4) (4th st: wknd 3f out) 1¼ 11
520[12] Dragonflight **(39)** *(DHaydnJones)* 4-7-8 (3)ow4 DWright(11) (plld hrd: 2nd st: wknd over 3f out: t.o) 20 12

5/2 Just Harry, **9/2** Daring Ryde, **7/1** Polonez Prima, Whispering Loch (IRE), **8/1** AVISHAYES (USA), **10/1** Shuttlecock, Nobby Barnes, **11/1** Oozlem (IRE), **12/1** Phase One (IRE), **14/1** As Such (IRE), **20/1** Northern Chief, **25/1** Dragonflight, CSF £29.67 CT £199.83 TOTE £9.50: £3.30 £1.40 £3.10 (£13.60) Trio £110.60 OWNER Mr P. Davidson-Brown (SALTBURN) BRED Franklin N. Groves 12 Rn 1m 44.2 (4.60) SF: 21/44/15/34/15/7/13/-/-/-/-/-

1856 E.B.F. MAIDEN STKS (2-Y.O) (Class D) £3,752.50 (£1,120.00: £535.00: £242.50) **6f 15y** Stalls: High GOING minus 0.24 sec per fur (GF) 7-30 (7-33)

1551[7] **Truancy** *(76+) (MBell)* 2-9-0 JFanning(10) (mde all: pushed clr appr fnl f: eased cl home) ...— 1
1184[8] Munketh (USA) *(72) (JLDunlop)* 2-9-0 GDuffield(6) (a in tch: hrd rdn to go 2nd appr fnl f: no ch w wnr) 1½ 2
1551[5] Inchrory *(69)*(Fav)*(HRACecil)* 2-9-0 AMcGlone(4) (a.p: rdn & r.o one pce fnl 2f).......1¼ 3
Brecon *(66) (PFICole)* 2-9-0 TGMcLaughlin(9) (neat: a.p: ev ch 2f out: btn whn rdn & hung lft appr fnl f) 1¼ 4
1511[4] Vola Via (USA) *(59) (IABalding)* 2-9-0 SO'Gorman(5) (prom over 4f) 2½ 5
Akalim *(48) (DMorley)* 2-9-0 MTebbutt(12) (leggy: unf: dwlt: a bhd) 4 6
Bright Diamond *(42) (JRArnold)* 2-8-9 RPerham(8) (leggy: lt-f: a outpcd).......½ 7
Lahik (IRE) *(40) (TThomsonJones)* 2-9-0 StephenDavies(11) (scope: lw: a bhd).......2½ 8
Crackernat (IRE) *(40) (LMCumani)* 2-8-11 (3) CHodgson(7) (cmpt: dwlt: a bhd).......hd 9
1158[2] Double Diamond (IRE) *(40) (MJohnston)* 2-9-0 DHolland(1) (chsd ldrs over 3f).......hd 10
Classic Call (IRE) *(27) (MRStoute)* 2-9-0 AClark(3) (leggy: lt-f: a outpcd) 5 11
Classic Delight (USA) *(18) (BJMcMath)* 2-8-6 (3) DWright(2) (neat: s.i.s: a bhd) 1½ 12

2/1 Inchrory, **11/4** Munketh (USA), **6/1** Vola Via (USA), **7/1** Double Diamond (IRE), **8/1** Brecon, **10/1** Crackernat (IRE), Classic Call (IRE), **14/1** TRUANCY, Lahik (IRE), **16/1** Akalim, **25/1** Bright Diamond, **33/1** Classic Delight (USA), CSF £58.45 TOTE £22.40: £3.30 £2.50 £1.30 (£35.40) Trio £124.00 OWNER Cheveley Park Stud (NEWMARKET) BRED Mrs D. O. Joly 12 Rn
1m 13.6 (2.60) SF: 41/37/34/31/24/13/7/5/5/5/-/-

1857 TATTERSALLS MAIDEN AUCTION STKS (2-Y.O) (Class E) £3,273.60 (£976.80: £466.40: £211.20) **5f 13y** Stalls: High GOING minus 0.24 sec per fur (GF) 8-00 (8-02)

1540[7] **Incapol** *(65) (MJRyan)* 2-8-3 AClark(9) (a.p: led 3f out: pushed out).......— 1
Jubilee Place (IRE) *(59) (TThomsonJones)* 2-7-12 StephenDavies(6) (neat: a.p: ev ch over 1f out: rallied ins fnl f: r.o) ....nk 2
1361[9] Windi Imp (IRE) *(60) (BJMeehan)* 2-7-10 (5) NVarley(11) (lw: outpcd early: rdn & r.o one pce fr over 1f out) ....¾ 3
1642[4] Soul of Honour (FR) *(58) (MrsJRRamsden)* 2-8-9 DeanMcKeown(5) (outpcd: hdwy wl over 1f out: hung lft 1f out: one pce).......3 4
1562[2] Stealth Attack (IRE) *(46) (JBerry)* 2-7-13 (7) PFessey(3) (lw: led 2f: btn whn carried lft 1f out) 3 5
1670[5] Percy Park (USA) *(47) (MJohnston)* 2-8-10 DHolland(10) (broke wl: hld up in tch: rdn ½-wy: sn btn).......1 6

1662² Essentialselection *(43)*(Fav)*(WJHaggas)* 2-8-7 MRoberts(1) (sn rdn along: btn whn carried lft 1f out) ....hd 7
1670⁸ Flood's Fancy *(28) (MrsJRRamsden)* 2-8-1 JFanning(8) (a outpcd) 3 8
1399⁴ Veesey *(14) (JohnBerry)* 2-7-11 (3) DWright(4) (a outpcd) 4 9
Stotfold Boy (IRE) *(12) (RHollinshead)* 2-8-4 (3) AGarth(7) (leggy: scope: s.s: a wl bhd) 3 10

6/4 Essentialselection, **7/4** Percy Park (USA), **8/1** INCAPOL, Stealth Attack (IRE), **9/1** Windi Imp (IRE), **14/1** Jubilee Place (IRE), **16/1** Soul of Honour (FR), Veesey, **25/1** Flood's Fancy, Stotfold Boy (IRE), CSF £109.56 TOTE £5.70: £1.10 £3.60 £3.00 (£102.30) Trio £119.90 OWNER Mr D. Bell (NEWMARKET) BRED Denis Bell 10 Rn 61.2 secs (2.50) SF: 25/19/20/18/6/7/3/-/-/-

1858 SHADWELL STUD SERIES APPRENTICE H'CAP (0-70) (3-Y.O+) (Class F) £3,013.20 (£835.20: £399.60)

1m 6f 15y Stalls: Low GOING minus 0.24 sec per fur (GF) 8-30 (8-31)

1502⁴ **College Don (52)***(64) (MPBielby)* 4-8-10 DRMcCabe(10) (hld up: 7th st: led wl over 1f out: rdn out) ....— 1
1435* Hillzah (USA) **(70)***(79) (RBastiman)* 7-10-0 HBastiman(11) (s.i.s: hld up in rr: 9th st: hdwy 3f out: ev ch 1f out: eased whn btn cl home) 3 2
1643* Arc Bright (IRE) **(41)***(46) (RHollinshead)* 5-7-13 5x AGarth(2) (led tl hdd wl over 2f out: led 2f out tl over 1f out: one pce) 3½ 3
1657² Soojama (IRE) **(39)***(36)*(Fav)*(RMFlower)* 5-7-11 SSanders(9) (hld up: rdn & hdwy 3f out: wknd over 1f out) 7 4
1681² Exclusion **(40)***(37) (JHetherton)* 6-7-12 CAdamson(6) (prom: 3rd st: rdn to ld wl over 2f out: hdd & wknd 2f out) ....s.h 5
1578⁵ Miroswaki (USA) **(61)***(47) (GFierro)* 5-9-2 (3) ADaly(1) (hdwy over 5f out: 4th & hrd rdn st: wknd 3f out) 9 6
*352** Handmaiden **(54)***(34) (AHarrison)* 5-8-12 JStack(8) (hdwy 7f out: 5th st: wknd over 2f out) 6 7
Khalidi (IRE) **(57)***(29) (DRGandolfo)* 6-9-1 SophieMitchell(14) (a wl bhd) 7 8
786⁷ Hong Kong Designer **(52)***(24) (SGNorton)* 3-7-7v NVarley(5) (plld hrd: prom 8f: 8th st: t.o fnl 3f) ....hd 9
1578² Ahaalee (USA) **(66)***(36) (EALDunlop)* 3-8-7 DaneO'Neill(13) (sn w ldr: rdn 6f out: 2nd st: wknd wl over 3f out) 1 10
1612¹⁴ Surprise Guest (IRE) **(53)***(17) (APJames)* 4-8-11 DWright(4) (prom 8f: wknd qckly: t.o) 6 11
1567ᴾ Shareoftheaction **(55)***(13) (MrsAMNaughton)* 4-8-13 SDrowne(7) (6th st: wknd 3f out: t.o) 5 12
1161³ Preston Guild (IRE) **(51)***(6) (ALForbes)* 5-8-9 LNewton(12) (lw: bhd fnl 6f: t.o) 2½ 13
1694¹¹ Brunswick Blue (IRE) **(35)** *(RMFlower)* 7-7-0 (7) RMullen(3) (b: prom 8f: t.o) 1 14

LONG HANDICAP Hong Kong Designer 7-6 Brunswick Blue (IRE) 7-0

3/1 Soojama (IRE), **13/2** Hillzah (USA), Ahaalee (USA), **8/1** Handmaiden, Arc Bright (IRE), **10/1** Exclusion, Preston Guild (IRE), **12/1** Khalidi (IRE), COLLEGE DON, Miroswaki (USA), **14/1** Shareoftheaction, **20/1** Surprise Guest (IRE), Hong Kong Designer, **33/1** Brunswick Blue (IRE), CSF £89.30 CT £625.70 TOTE £12.60: £2.60 £3.00 £2.60 (£28.90) Trio £181.00 OWNER Mr J. F. Coupland (GRIMSBY) BRED Chippenham Lodge Stud 14 Rn

3m 5.0 (6.50) SF: 39/54/21/11/12/22/9/4/-/-/-/-/-/-

WEIGHT FOR AGE 3yo-17lb

1859 KPMG H'CAP (0-70) (3-Y.O) (Class E) £3,588.20 (£1,073.60: £514.80: £235.40)

1m 54y Stalls: Low GOING minus 0.24 sec per fur (GF) 9-00 (9-01)

1541³ **Princess Danielle (52)***(60) (CCElsey)* 3-8-3 CRutter(5) (lw: led 2f: 3rd st: rdn 2f out: led ins fnl f: rdn out) ....— 1
1679⁶ Star of Gold **(63)***(69) (CREgerton)* 3-8-7 (7) MHenry(4) (plld hrd: 2nd st: led 3f out tl ins fnl f: r.o) 1¼ 2
1624⁸ Triple Tricks (IRE) **(69)***(73) (WJHaggas)* 3-9-6 MRoberts(2) (hld up: last st: hdwy over 2f out: rdn & r.o fnl f) 1 3
1380² Mutabassim (IRE) **(70)***(66)*(Fav)*(ACStewart)* 3-9-7 SWhitworth(3) (lw: 4th st: hdwy 2f out: hrd rdn & ev ch appr fnl f: sn btn) 4 4
1412² My Handsome Prince **(49)***(44) (PJBevan)* 3-8-0 NCarlisle(1) (5th st: nvr able to chal) ....nk 5
1676¹⁵ Almuhtaram **(69)***(57) (MissGayKelleway)* 3-9-6 MWigham(7) (6th st: nvr able to chal) 4 6
1512¹⁸ Senaan **(47)***(25) (TThomsonJones)* 3-7-12v StephenDavies(6) (led after 2f to 3f out: wknd 2f out) 5 7

10/11 Mutabassim (IRE), **4/1** My Handsome Prince, **7/1** Triple Tricks (IRE), **8/1** PRINCESS DANIELLE, **10/1** Star of Gold, **11/1** Almuhtaram, **25/1** Senaan, CSF £70.73 TOTE £9.00: £2.90 £3.70 (£14.20) OWNER Mrs Marion Wickham (LAMBOURN) BRED Mrs Wickham 7 Rn

1m 45.5 (5.90) SF: 10/19/23/16/-/7/-

T/Plpt: £4,546.40 (3.08 Tckts). T/Qdpt: Not won; £22.20 to Royal Ascot 22/6/95. RC

1412-**RIPON (R-H)**
Wednesday June 21st (Firm)
WEATHER: sunny WIND: almost nil

1860 RICHMOND CONDITIONS STKS (2-Y.O) (Class C) £4,865.34 (£1,702.54: £832.77: £358.35) **6f** Stalls: Low GOING minus 0.41 sec per fur (F) 2-15 (2-15)

1190* **Jedaal** *(95+)*(Fav)*(LMCumani)* 2-8-12 (3) OUrbina(3) (lw: hld up: qckncd to ld wl over 1f out: sn pushed clr) — 1
1556⁵ Playmaker *(71) (JBerry)* 2-9-1 MBirch(4) (lw: mde most over 4f: hung lft & sn btn) 9 2
1492³ Red River Valley *(67) (DenysSmith)* 2-8-13 LCharnock(1) (w ldrs: hung rt 2f out: r.o one pce) ¾ 3
1642* Rambo Delight *(62) (JLEyre)* 2-9-1 RLappin(2) (lw: w ldrs: edgd rt ½-wy: outpcd fnl 2f) 2½ 4

4/5 JEDAAL, **3/1** Rambo Delight, **100/30** Playmaker, **14/1** Red River Valley, CSF £3.66 TOTE £1.70 (£2.10) OWNER Sheikh Ahmed Al Maktoum (NEWMARKET) BRED Sheikh Ahmed bin Rashid al Maktoum 4 Rn 1m 13.7 (3.50) SF: 16/-/-/-

1861 LEVY BOARD H'CAP (0-80) (3-Y.O+) (Class D) £3,899.00 (£1,181.00: £577.00: £275.00) **1m 4f 60y** Stalls: High GOING minus 0.41 sec per fur (F) 2-50 (2-50)

423⁴ **Ashover (49)***(61) (TDBarron)* 5-8-2 NCarlisle(3) (lw: set slow pce: qcknd ent st: r.o wl fnl 3f) — 1
1578* Admirals Secret (USA) **(67)***(71)*(Fav)*(CFWall)* 6-9-1 (5) LNewton(2) (lw: hld up: hdwy over 4f out: ev ch 2½f out: rdn & nt qckn) 6 2
1844⁶ Kings Cay (IRE) **(71)***(66) (THCaldwell)* 4-9-5 (5) JStack(1) (chsd wnr: ev ch 3f out: sn rdn: outpcd fnl 2f) 7 3
568⁹ Bold Elect **(48)** *(PWigham)* 7-8-1 LCharnock(4) (prom tl wknd over 4f out: sn t.o) dist 4

5/6 Admirals Secret (USA), **9/4** ASHOVER, **5/1** Bold Elect, **12/1** Kings Cay (IRE), CSF £4.39 TOTE £3.30 (£1.90) OWNER Mr Timothy Cox (THIRSK) BRED Bridge End Bloodstock 4 Rn
2m 43.3 (9.30) SF: -/6/1/-

1862 CITY OF RIPON H'CAP (0-95) (3-Y.O) (Class C) £7,100.00 (£2,150.00: £1,050.00: £500.00) **1m** Stalls: High GOING minus 0.41 sec per fur (F) 3-25 (3-25)

1344* **Bettergeton (81)***(90+) (PJBevan)* 3-9-0 NCarlisle(2) (a gng wl: led 2f out: qcknd: comf) — 1
1639⁹ Neverending (USA) **(83)***(90)*(Fav)*(HRACecil)* 3-9-2 AMcGlone(5) (b.off hind: lw: hld up: hdwy 3f out: styd on wl: nt pce of wnr) 1¼ 2
1528⁵ Evan 'elp Us **(65)***(71) (JLEyre)* 3-7-7b(5) NVarley(1) (lw: trckd ldr: rdn over 2f out: one pce) nk 3
1474⁸ Pengamon **(88)***(90) (HJCollingridge)* 3-9-7 MRimmer(3) (s.i.s: hdwy over 3f out: wandered u.p: nvr able chal) 2 4
1808² Percy Braithwaite (IRE) **(82)***(74)*(Fav)*(MJohnston)* 3-9-1b TWilliams(4) (led tl hdd 2f out: sn btn) 5 5

2/1 Neverending (USA), Percy Braithwaite (IRE), **100/30** BETTERGETON, **7/1** Pengamon, **9/1** Evan 'elp Us, CSF £9.94 TOTE £4.20: £1.70 £1.50 (£5.70) OWNER Mr Derek Boulton (UTTOXETER) BRED R. and Mrs Healy-Fenton 5 Rn 1m 39.6 (1.90) SF: 45/45/26/45/29

1863 BEAUMONTS INSURANCE LADIES DERBY H'CAP (0-70) (3-Y.O+) (Class F) £3,360.60 (£1,018.80: £498.40: £238.20)
1m 4f 60y Stalls: High GOING minus 0.41 sec per fur (F) 4-00 (4-01)

1498¹⁰ **Outstayed Welcome (46)***(56) (MJHaynes)* 3-9-4 MrsSBosley(13) (cl up: led 7f out: rdn & hld on wl fnl f) — 1
1529⁵ Kilernan **(39)***(48) (TDBarron)* 4-9-12 MrsAFarrell(7) (lw: led after 1f to 7f out: w wnr after: no ex wl ins fnl f) ½ 2
1622⁴ Our Bessie **(43)***(50) (DMarks)* 4-10-2 MissKMarks(10) (in tch tl lost pl appr st: stdy hdwy over 2f out: r.o wl towards fin) 1½ 3
1359² Ho-Joe (IRE) **(51)***(57) (GHYardley)* 5-10-6 (4) MissAYardley(11) (in tch: effrt 3f out: styd on one pce fnl f) 1¼ 4
1596¹¹ Ice Magic **(29)***(33) (FJYardley)* 8-8-12v(4) MissSYardley(2) (a chsng ldrs: nt qckn fnl 2f) 1¾ 5
1596⁴ Claireswan (IRE) **(52)***(55) (SCWilliams)* 3-9-6 (4) MissKWright(12) (lw: led 1f: a chsng ldrs: one pce fnl 3f) nk 6
1496³ Chantry Beath **(55)***(55) (CWThornton)* 4-11-0 MrsDKettlewell(1) (lw: in tch: one pce fnl 4f) 2½ 7
1596² Gold Blade **(43)***(42)*(Fav)*(JPearce)* 6-10-2 MrsLPearce(8) (bhd: plld wd & hdwy 4f out: rdn & no imp fnl 2f) nk 8

1569[7] Runforaction (IRE) **(42)***(37) (BSRothwell)* 3-8-10 (4) MissAlexMcCabe(3) (lw: effrt 4f out: nvr rchd ldrs) 3½ **9**
1558[10] Sharkashka (IRE) **(62)***(40) (MHEasterby)* 5-11-7 MrsLFahey(4) (lw: in tch tl wknd fnl 3½f) 13 **10**
476[4] Rebeccas Secret (IRE) **(58)***(34) (RFFisher)* 4-11-3 MissFBurke(9) (chsd ldrs tl wknd fnl 4f) .1¾ **11**
Sporting Spirit **(32)** *(GPKelly)* 5-9-1 (4)ow5 MissSBrotherton(6) (bit bkwd: n.d) 4 **12**
1598[10] Kralingen **(50)** *(NChamberlain)* 3-9-8 ow8 MissCMetcalfe(14) (sddle slipped after 3f: a bhd)...25 **13**
Restraint **(40)** *(JJBirkett)* 5-9-9 (4)ow8 MissFBarnes(5) (prom to st: sn bhd) 1 **14**

LONG HANDICAP Sporting Spirit 8-12 Kralingen 8-2

2/1 Gold Blade, **5/1** Chantry Beath, **11/2** Our Bessie, **8/1** Ho-Joe (IRE), **9/1** Claireswan (IRE), **10/1** Kilernan, **11/1** Sharkashka (IRE), **12/1** Rebeccas Secret (IRE), **20/1** OUTSTAYED WELCOME, Runforaction (IRE), **25/1** Ice Magic, **33/1** Sporting Spirit, **50/1** Kralingen, Restraint, CSF £200.22 CT £1,155.45 TOTE £3.90: £6.00 £3.00 £1.80 (£412.90) Trio £209.30 OWNER Mrs B. Bell (EPSOM) BRED Hesmonds Stud Ltd 14 Rn

2m 39.0 (5.00) SF: 37/44/46/53/29/36/51/38/18/36/30/-/-/-

WEIGHT FOR AGE 3yo-15lb

1864

NORTHALLERTON H'CAP (0-80) (3-Y.O+) (Class D) £3,758.60 (£1,137.80: £555.40: £264.20) **5f** Stalls: Low GOING minus 0.41 sec per fur (F) 4-35 (4-37)

1304[7] **Beau Venture (USA) (71)***(80) (FHLee)* 7-9-6 RLappin(7) (prom: hdwy to ld over 1f out: edgd lft: r.o) ....— **1**
1689[2] Featherstone Lane **(50)***(54) (MissLCSiddall)* 4-7-13v TWilliams(1) (lw: sn pushed along: hdwy ½-wy: kpt on fnl f) 1½ **2**
1721[4] The Fed **(55)***(55) (RMWhitaker)* 5-8-4v ACulhane(3) (w ldrs: led ½-wy tl over 1f out: one pce)1¼ **3**
1604[2] Magic Orb **(79)***(71)*(Fav)*(JLHarris)* 5-10-0 PRobinson(6) (chsd ldrs: effrt ½-wy: one pce) 2½ **4**
Indian Crystal **(46)***(33) (MrsMReveley)* 4-7-9 NCarlisle(8) (dwlt: hdwy ½-wy: nvr able chal) ..1½ **5**
1400* Bashful Brave **(61)***(48)*(Fav)*(JWPayne)* 4-8-10 MRimmer(5) (w ldrs tl rdn & btn appr fnl f).....hd **6**
1508[12] Tino Tere **(59)***(44) (JBalding)* 6-8-8 ClaireBalding(4) (slt ld to ½-wy: grad wknd) ....¾ **7**
1271[10] Knayton Lass **(63)***(41) (MWEasterby)* 4-8-12b MBirch(2) (reminders after s: a bhd) 2 **8**

3/1 Bashful Brave, Magic Orb, **7/2** Featherstone Lane, **13/2** The Fed, BEAU VENTURE (USA), **11/1** Indian Crystal, **12/1** Knayton Lass, **20/1** Tino Tere, CSF £28.71 CT £142.21 TOTE £10.90: £3.50 £1.50 £2.10 (£29.70) OWNER Mrs A. L. Stacey (WILMSLOW) BRED Mrs C. Oliver Iselin III 8 Rn

58.8 secs (0.80) SF: 55/29/30/46/8/23/19/16

1865

BEDALE LIMITED STKS (0-65) (4-Y.O+) (Class F) £2,749.00 (£832.00: £406.00: £193.00) **1m 2f** Stalls: High GOING minus 0.41 sec per fur (F) 5-10 (5-10)

1513[2] **Quivira (57)***(66)*(Fav)*(TTClement)* 4-8-7 MRimmer(2) (trckd ldrs: led over 2f out: rdn & hld on wl fnl f) ....— **1**
1767* Augustan **(54)***(71) (SGollings)* 4-8-7 (5) VHalliday(3) (trckd ldrs: chal 3f out: r.o wl) ....hd **2**
1506[6] Tu Opes **(65)***(67)*(Fav)*(JLHarris)* 4-8-12 PRobinson(4) (lw: hld up: effrt over 2f out: edgd rt & nt qckn) 2½ **3**
1616[8] Beaumont (IRE) **(64)***(35) (JPearce)* 5-8-7b(5) JStack(1) (lw: led tl hdd over 2f out: sn btn) 20 **4**

5/2 QUIVIRA, Tu Opes, **11/4** Augustan, **3/1** Beaumont (IRE), CSF £8.54 TOTE £3.50 (£3.00) OWNER Mr Maurice Kirby (NEWMARKET) BRED Sheikh Mohammed bin Rashid al Maktoum 4 Rn

2m 5.6 (2.10) SF: 42/47/43/11

1866

MASHAM MAIDEN STKS (3-Y.O) (Class D) £3,863.90 (£1,170.20: £571.60: £272.30) **1m 2f** Stalls: High GOING minus 0.41 sec per fur (F) 5-40 (5-41)

1195[3] **King's Crown** *(77+)*(Fav)*(EALDunlop)* 3-8-9 (5) JStack(3) (lw: hld up: smooth hdwy to ld 3f out: pushed out fnl f) ....— **1**
1283[4] Cephista *(67) (PTWalwyn)* 3-8-9 MRimmer(2) (led early: chsd ldr: rdn 3f out: kpt on: nt pce of wnr) 3 **2**
1526[6] Cante Chico *(63) (TThomsonJones)* 3-9-0 SWhitworth(1) (prom: effrt ent st: outpcd fnl 2½f) 6 **3**
De-Veers Currie (IRE) *(54) (RFFisher)* 3-8-9 TWilliams(5) (shkn up after s & sn led: hdd 3f out: sn outpcd) 2½ **4**
Cavalier Royal Gem *(PWigham)* 3-8-9 ACulhane(4) (w'like: bkwd: reluctant to r & sn wl t.o: virtually p.u) ....dist **5**

4/11 KING'S CROWN, **5/1** Cephista, **11/2** Cante Chico, **40/1** De-Veers Currie (IRE), **150/1** Cavalier Royal Gem, CSF £2.55 TOTE £1.40: £1.00 £2.20 (£1.90) OWNER Maktoum Al Maktoum (NEWMARKET) BRED Gainsborough Stud Management Ltd 5 Rn 2m 7.4 (3.90) SF: 34/24/20/11/-

T/Plpt: £1,310.80 (5.93 Tckts). T/Qdpt: £792.70 (0.6 Tckts); £428.52 to Ripon 22/6/95. AA

1848-ASCOT (R-H)
Thursday June 22nd (Good to firm)
WEATHER: fine & very warm WIND: almost nil

1867 RIBBLESDALE STKS (Gp 2) (3-Y.O F) (Class A) £55,332.00 (£20,711.10: £9,950.55: £4,336.35) **1m 4f** Stalls: Low GOING minus 0.28 sec (GF) 2-30 (2-30)

1139⁶ **Phantom Gold (100)***(111) (LordHuntingdon)* 3-8-8 LDettori(1) (hld up gng wl: 3rd st: led bel dist: rdn & r.o wl)........— 1
1242² Tillandsia (IRE) **(102)***(109) (DRLoder)* 3-8-8 MJKinane(7) (lw: hld up: effrt & 4th st: swtchd lft appr fnl f: r.o wl)........1¼ 2
1587⁴ Musetta (IRE) **(108)***(106) (CEBrittain)* 3-8-8 MRoberts(4) (lw: led tl hdd bel dist: one pce)....2½ 3
1587² Dance a Dream **(102)***(104)*(Fav)*(MRStoute)* 3-8-8 WRSwinburn(5) (lw: chsd ldr 8f out: 2nd st: rdn & one pce fnl 2f)........1¾ 4
1417* Segovia *(99) (HRACecil)* 3-8-8 PatEddery(6) (hld up: hdwy ½-wy: 5th st: wknd over 1f out) 3½ 5
1139³ Strutting (IRE) **(97)***(99) (RHannon)* 3-8-8 JReid(2) (hld up in rr: rdn & 6th st: n.d)........hd 6
1390a⁶ Fleet Hill (IRE) **(100)***(91) (MRChannon)* 3-8-8 RHughes(3) (s.s: a bhd: 7th st: t.o)........6 7

11/10 Dance a Dream, **5/1** Tillandsia (IRE) (op 3/1), PHANTOM GOLD, **6/1** Segovia (op 4/1), **10/1** Musetta (IRE), **33/1** Strutting (IRE), Fleet Hill (IRE), CSF £26.42 TOTE £5.70: £2.00 £1.80 (£13.20) OWNER The Queen (WEST ILSLEY) BRED The Queen 7 Rn
2m 32.15 (2.65) SF: 53/51/48/46/41/41/33

1868 NORFOLK STKS (Gp 3) (2-Y.O) (Class A) £25,360.00 (£9,598.00: £4,699.00: £2,143.00) **5f** Stalls: Centre GOING minus 0.28 sec per fur (GF) 3-05 (3-06)

1608⁴ **Lucky Lionel (USA)** *(99) (RHannon)* 2-8-12 LDettori(1) (lw: bhd: hdwy over 2f out: led ent fnl f: edgd rt: r.o)........— 1
1584³ Cayman Kai (IRE) *(91) (RHannon)* 2-8-12 PatEddery(9) (lw: w ldr: led ½-wy tl ent fnl f: rdn & no ex)........2½ 2
825* Mubhij (IRE) *(90)*(Fav)*(BWHills)* 2-8-12 WCarson(2) (lw: chsd ldrs: effrt & ev ch 1f out: unable qckn)........nk 3
1511* First Fiddler *(90) (WJarvis)* 2-8-12b BThomson(7) (s.i.s: sn wl bhd & outpcd: hdwy over 1f out: fin wl)........hd 4
1384* Amaretto Bay (IRE) *(74) (BJMeehan)* 2-8-12 MJKinane(4) (nvr nr to chal)........5 5
1384³ Whicksey Perry *(69) (JBerry)* 2-8-12 JCarroll(8) (lw: chsd ldrs: effrt 2f out: wknd appr fnl f)........1½ 6
996* Night Parade (USA) *(63)*(Fav)*(PWChapple-Hyam)* 2-8-12 JReid(3) (prom: ev ch 2f out: wknd over 1f out)........1¾ 7
1556* Eastern Prophets *(62) (GLewis)* 2-8-12 PaulEddery(5) (led to ½-wy: rdn & wknd 2f out)........½ 8
1584* Prince Aslia *(43) (MJohnston)* 2-8-12 DHolland(6) (chsd ldrs: drvn along ½-wy: wknd wl over 1f out)........6 9

9/4 Night Parade (USA), Mubhij (IRE), **6/1** Prince Aslia, **7/1** Eastern Prophets, **11/1** LUCKY LIONEL (USA), **14/1** First Fiddler, Cayman Kai (IRE), Amaretto Bay (IRE), **33/1** Whicksey Perry, CSF £130.60 TOTE £10.10: £2.20 £2.90 £1.20 (£62.70) Trio £64.20 OWNER Mr Antonio Balzarini (MARLBOROUGH) BRED Richard & Mrs Kaster 9 Rn
60.38 secs (0.88) SF: 58/50/49/49/33/28/22/21/2

1869 GOLD CUP STKS (Gp 1) (4-Y.O+) (Class A) £111,750.00 (£41,450.00: £19,600.00: £8,200.00) **2m 4f** Stalls: Low GOING minus 0.28 sec per fur (GF) 3-45 (3-45)

1363* **Double Trigger (IRE) (111)***(125) (MJohnston)* 4-9-0 JWeaver(6) (lw: mde all: drvn clr fnl 2f: unchal)........— 1
1132* Moonax (IRE) **(119)***(121)*(Fav)*(BWHills)* 4-9-0 PatEddery(5) (lw: hld up: hdwy & drvn along 6f out: 2nd st: no imp fnl 2f)........5 2
869⁶ Admiral's Well (IRE) **(90)***(121) (RAkehurst)* 5-9-2 TQuinn(3) (lw: a.p: 3rd & rdn st: styd on wl towards fin)........hd 3
Vintage Crop *(119) (DKWeld,Ireland)* 8-9-2 MJKinane(1) (lw: hld up: hdwy 4f out: 4th st: sn hrd rdn: no imp)........2 4
1363² Old Rouvel (USA) **(96)***(113) (DJGMurraySmith)* 4-9-0 LDettori(7) (chsd ldrs: rdn 5f out: 5th st: sn lost tch)........8 5
1363⁴ The Flying Phantom **(91)***(107) (MHTompkins)* 4-9-0 PRobinson(2) (lw: hld up in rr: 6th & rdn st: t.o fnl 2f)........7 6
1239a* The Little Thief (FR) *(EDanel,France)* 4-9-0 AJunk(4) (chsd ldrs tl broke down & p.u ½-wy: dead)........ P

13/8 Moonax (IRE), **9/4** DOUBLE TRIGGER (IRE) (6/4-5/2), **3/1** Vintage Crop, **11/1** The Little Thief (FR), **14/1** Old Rouvel (USA), **25/1** Admiral's Well (IRE), **40/1** The Flying Phantom, CSF £6.19 TOTE £3.60: £2.00 £1.70 (£2.70) OWNER Mr R. W. Huggins (MIDDLEHAM) BRED Dene Investments N V 7 Rn 4m 20.25 (1.25) SF: 72/68/70/68/60/54/-
WEIGHT FOR AGE 4yo-2lb

1870

CORK AND ORRERY STKS (Gp 3) (3-Y.O+) (Class A) £33,350.00 (£12,630.00: £6,190.00: £2,830.00)
6f Stalls: Centre GOING minus 0.28 sec per fur (GF) 4-20 (4-21)

1133² **So Factual (USA) (114)***(125) (SbinSuroor)* 5-8-13 LDettori(9) (led far side over 2f out: rdn to ld nr fin) — 1
1133* Lake Coniston (IRE) **(125)***(129)*(Fav)*(GLewis)* 4-9-3 PatEddery(4) (led stands' side: clr over 1f out: rdn & drifted rt fnl f: ct cl home) hd 2
1116a¹⁴ Nuriva (USA) **(102)***(114) (SbinSuroor)* 3-8-2 GCarter(3) (dwlt: hdwy 2f out: nvr nrr) 3 3
1393a* Wessam Prince *(110) (CLaffon-Parias,France)* 4-9-3 WRSwinburn(6) (lw: chsd ldrs stands' side: nvr nr to chal) 2½ 4
934³ Welsh Mist **(94)***(105) (RBoss)* 4-8-10 WRyan(2) (chsd ldrs stands' side: rdn 2f out: no imp) ¾ 5
1488⁴ Tanami **(115)***(102) (DRLoder)* 3-8-2 WCarson(8) (prom far side: rdn along over 2f out: sn btn) 1¼ 6
Adjmal (IRE) *(105) (PeterLautner,Germany)* 6-8-13 ABond(5) (nvr trbld ldrs) s.h 7
1766* Cheyenne Spirit **(91)***(94) (BHanbury)* 3-8-2 MRoberts(10) (lw: led far side over 3f: sn rdn & outpcd) 3 8
1480⁸ Shamanic **(100)***(73) (RHannon)* 3-8-5 KDarley(7) (lw: racd far side: sn rdn & outpcd: t.o) 9 9
1480* Roger the Butler (IRE) **(104)***(62) (MBell)* 5-8-13 MFenton(13) (lw: chsd ldrs far side over 3f: sn lost tch: t.o) 4 10
1179⁴ Selhurstpark Flyer (IRE) **(84)***(59) (JBerry)* 4-8-13e JCarroll(1) (eyecover: chsd ldrs stands' side 4f: sn wknd: t.o) 1 11

8/11 Lake Coniston (IRE), **9/2** SO FACTUAL (USA), **8/1** Tanami (6/1-9/1), **10/1** Wessam Prince (7/1-12/1), **14/1** Roger the Butler (IRE), **25/1** Cheyenne Spirit, **33/1** Nuriva (USA), **40/1** Welsh Mist, **50/1** Shamanic, **66/1** Adjmal (IRE), Selhurstpark Flyer (IRE), CSF £7.62 TOTE £6.30: £1.40 £1.30 £8.50 (£3.00) Trio £58.60 OWNER Godolphin (NEWMARKET) BRED Juddmonte Farms Inc 11 Rn
1m 12.99 (-0.61) SF: 84/88/65/69/64/53/64/45/24/21/18
WEIGHT FOR AGE 3yo-8lb

1871

CHESHAM STKS (Listed) (2-Y.O) (Class A) £21,888.00 (£6,624.00: £3,232.00: £1,536.00)
6f Stalls: Centre GOING minus 0.28 sec per fur (GF) 4-55 (4-56)

1608² **World Premier** *(97) (CEBrittain)* 2-9-2 BDoyle(5) (lw: a.p: led over 3f out: hrd drvn fnl f: hld on gamely) — 1
1142* Paloma Bay (IRE) *(87) (MBell)* 2-8-9 MFenton(4) (dwlt: hdwy ½-wy: hrd rdn & ev ch fnl f: unable qckn) 1¼ 2
1318* Bahamian Knight (CAN) *(90)*(Fav)*(DRLoder)* 2-9-0 LDettori(6) (hld up in tch: effrt & shkn up over 1f out: nt pce to chal) ¾ 3
1348² La Modiste *(73) (SDow)* 2-8-7 TQuinn(7) (effrt over 2f out: nvr nr to chal) 3½ 4
1634* Cabcharge Striker *(73) (MRChannon)* 2-9-2 RHughes(1) (swtg: chsd ldrs: hrd drvn 2f out: one pce) 3½ 5
1540⁵ Missile Toe (IRE) *(60) (JEBanks)* 2-8-12 WCarson(3) (lw: led over 2f: sn hrd drvn & outpcd) 3½ 6
671* Kala Sunrise *(52) (CSmith)* 2-8-12 KDarley(2) (lw: hrd rdn over 2f out: a bhd) 3 7
*1454** Worldwide Elsie (USA) *(43) (PAKelleway)* 2-8-9 AMackay(8) (lw: chsd ldrs on outside tl lost tch bel dist) 2 8

6/4 Bahamian Knight (CAN) (4/5-13/8), **2/1** Paloma Bay (IRE), **6/1** WORLD PREMIER, **10/1** Cabcharge Striker, **16/1** Kala Sunrise, **20/1** Missile Toe (IRE), La Modiste, **33/1** Worldwide Elsie (USA), CSF £17.58 TOTE £6.90: £1.80 £1.20 £1.10 (£9.40) OWNER Mrs C. E. Brittain (NEWMARKET) BRED Mrs C. E. Brittain 8 Rn 1m 14.97 (1.37) SF: 59/49/52/35/35/22/14/5

1872

KING GEORGE V H'CAP (0-105) (3-Y.O) (Class B) £26,328.75 (£7,980.00: £3,902.50: £1,863.75)
1m 4f Stalls: Low GOING minus 0.28 sec per fur (GF) 5-30 (5-30)

1636⁴ **Diaghilef (IRE) (99)***(108) (MJohnston)* 3-9-7 DHolland(15) (hld up: rdn 4f out: hdwy 2f out: str run, edgd rt & led fnl stride) — 1
1589⁶ Bob's Ploy **(85)***(94)*(Fav)*(RAkehurst)* 3-8-7 LDettori(13) (hld up: hdwy & 6th st: hrd rdn to ld wl ins fnl f: ct post) hd 2

1730* Monarch **(81)***(88) (PFICole)* 3-8-3 ow1 4x TQuinn(2) (lw: hld up: hdwy on outside ent st: swtchd ins & hdwy over 2f out: swtchd lft fnl f: fin fast) ....½ 3
1589⁴ At Liberty (IRE) **(88)***(96) (RHannon)* 3-8-10 JReid(6) (lw: bhd: rapid hdwy appr fnl f: fin fast)....hd 4
995³ Cherrington **(78)***(86) (GWragg)* 3-8-0 FNorton(1) (a.p: 2nd st: led over 2f out tl ins fnl f)....nk 5
1127³ Burning (USA) **(97)***(103) (GHarwood)* 3-9-5 WRSwinburn(10) (s.i.s: hld up & bhd: hdwy ent st: styng on whn squeezed for room ins fnl f)....1¼ 6
1382* Kimbridge Knight (IRE) **(82)***(83) (PTWalwyn)* 3-8-4v JCarroll(18) (led tl hdd over 2f out: wknd appr fnl f)....3½ 7
1170⁴ Time for Action (IRE) **(89)***(88) (MHTompkins)* 3-8-11 PRobinson(14) (lw: w ldr: 3rd st: rdn & wknd over 1f out) 2 8
1619² Taipan (IRE) **(92)***(85) (JLDunlop)* 3-9-0 JWeaver(16) (chsd ldrs: 5th st: rdn 2f out: wknd over 1f out)....4 9
*1211*³ Dangerous Guest (IRE) **(86)***(79) (SirMarkPrescott)* 3-8-8 GDuffield(17) (lw: chsd ldrs: 4th st: wknd over 1f out) ....nk 10
1289* Celeric **(83)***(73) (DMorley)* 3-8-5 MHills(11) (nvr nrr)....2½ 11
1526* Kutta **(94)***(84) (RWArmstrong)* 3-9-2 WCarson(5) (nvr trbld ldrs)....s.h 12
1062* Prussian Blue (USA) **(95)***(83) (HRACecil)* 3-9-3 WRyan(3) (lw: prom: rdn 4f out: sn wknd) ...1¼ 13
1524⁶ Nine Barrow Down (IRE) **(78)***(66) (HRACecil)* 3-8-0 AMcGlone(19) (b.hind: lw: chsd ldrs tl lost tch 4f out) ....nk 14
824* Maeterlinck (IRE) **(88)***(69) (BWHills)* 3-8-10 MJKinane(9) (lw: a bhd)....5 15
941³ Al Safeer (IRE) **(84)***(62) (JWHills)* 3-8-6 RHills(8) (m.n.s) 2½ 16
1195² Pilsudski (IRE) **(82)***(56) (MRStoute)* 3-8-4 KDarley(20) (b.nr hind: lw: nvr nr ldrs)....2½ 17
1188⁵ Moments of Fortune (USA) **(98)***(71) (BHanbury)* 3-9-6 TIves(4) (a in rr) 1 18
1558⁴ Manful **(80)***(52) (JHetherton)* 3-8-2 NKennedy(7) (a in rr) ....½ 19
1383² Dr Zhivago **(79)***(50) (MAJarvis)* 3-8-1 MRoberts(12) (lw: chsd ldrs 8f: sn wknd) ....¾ 20

10/3 Bob's Ploy, **9/2** Monarch, **9/1** Cherrington, **10/1** Kutta, Pilsudski (IRE), **11/1** Celeric, **12/1** Maeterlinck (IRE), Dangerous Guest (IRE), **16/1** Taipan (IRE), Kimbridge Knight (IRE), Prussian Blue (USA), Dr Zhivago, **20/1** Nine Barrow Down (IRE), Burning (USA), At Liberty (IRE), **25/1** Time for Action (IRE), **33/1** Al Safeer (IRE), Moments of Fortune (USA), **40/1** DIAGHILEF (IRE), **66/1** Manful, CSF £177.36 CT £709.25 TOTE £100.30: £18.20 £1.50 £1.60 £5.70 (£414.70) Trio £376.30 OWNER Mr C. C. Buckley (MIDDLEHAM) BRED Rathasker Stud 20 Rn
2m 30.58 (1.08) SF: 76/62/56/64/54/71/51/56/53/47/41/52/51/34/37/30/24/39/20/18

T/Jkpt: £26,899.10; £34,097.48 to Ascot 23/6/95. T/Plpt: £29.00 (3,205.86 Tckts). T/Qdpt: £3.50 (568.4 Tckts). IM

1860-RIPON (R-H)
Thursday June 22nd (Firm)
WEATHER: sunny & warm WIND: slt against

1873 RIPON TRAVEL 10TH ANNIVERSARY (S) APPRENTICE H'CAP (0-60) (3-Y.O+) (Class F) £3,009.00 (£912.00: £446.00: £213.00)
1m Stalls: High GOING minus 0.42 sec per fur (F) 7-00 (7-01)

1509³ **Guesstimation (USA) (57)***(66) (JPearce)* 6-9-9 (5) ElizabethTurner(11) (hld up: stdy hdwy ½-wy: led appr fnl f: r.o) ....— 1
*1633*³ My Gallery (IRE) **(52)***(58) (ABailey)* 4-9-2 (7) AngelaGallimore(6) (a.p: effrt 2f out: styd on wl) 1¾ 2
1742² Malzoom **(32)***(37)*(Fav)*(SEKettlewell)* 3-7-7 MHenry(10) (lw: led tl hdd over 1f out: kpt on same pce)....½ 3
1531⁴ Tolls Choice (IRE) **(55)***(52) (MWEasterby)* 6-9-9 (3) RuthCoulter(2) (s.i.s: hdwy ½-wy: nvr rchd ldrs) 4 4
1843⁵ Gant Bleu (FR) **(40)***(30) (RMWhitaker)* 8-8-11 GParkin(17) (plld hrd in tch: swtchd & effrt over 2f out: one pce fnl f) 3½ 5
*415*¹¹ Intrepid Fort **(25)***(12) (BWMurray)* 6-7-7 (3) MartinDwyer(16) (hdwy ½-wy: styd on one pce fnl 2f)....1¼ 6
1523⁶ Milltown Classic (IRE) **(37)***(24) (JParkes)* 3-7-12 CAdamson(4) (chsd ldrs: outpcd 4f out: kpt on fnl 2f)....hd 7
*384*⁸ Summer Villa **(45)***(30) (PCHaslam)* 3-8-1 (5) CarolDavison(13) (b: chsd ldrs tl rdn & wknd over 2f out)....1 8
1161¹⁷ Petal's Jarred **(29)***(10) (WStorey)* 5-7-7v(7)ow4 JoanneWebster(1) (dwlt: effrt 4f out: nvr rchd ldrs)....s.h 9
1523³ Resolute Bay **(41)***(24) (RMWhitaker)* 9-8-12 DGriffiths(12) (lw: swtchd & effrt 3f out: n.d) 1 10
1647⁵ Rosina's Folly **(40)***(23) (JLHarris)* 4-8-11 PRoberts(7) (lw: shkn up ½-wy: n.d) ....s.h 11
1797² Reed My Lips (IRE) **(35)***(16) (BPJBaugh)* 4-8-1 (5) IonaWands(3) (effrt over 3f out: nvr able to chal)....¾ 12

1548* Ballyhays (IRE) **(48)***(29) (JAHarris)* 6-9-5 PFessey(8) (c wd & effrt 4f out: no imp) ....s.h **13**
1649 12 Izza **(42)***(17) (WStorey)* 4-8-8v(5) VictoriaAppleby(9) (chsd ldrs to ½-wy) 3 **14**
1644 7 Saint Amigo **(58)***(33) (JLEyre)* 3-9-0 (5) GMacDonald(14) (b.off hind: s.i.s: hdwy on outside 4f out: n.d) ....hd **15**
1679 9 Henry Will **(33)** *(WLBarker)* 11-8-4 MHumphries(5) (b: lw: nvr bttr than mid div) 6 **16**

LONG HANDICAP Malzoom 7-5

9/2 Malzoom, **13/2** Tolls Choice (IRE), **7/1** Resolute Bay, GUESSTIMATION (USA), **8/1** Ballyhays (IRE), Gant Bleu (FR), **9/1** Reed My Lips (IRE), **10/1** Summer Villa, **12/1** Saint Amigo, My Gallery (IRE), **14/1** Milltown Classic (IRE), Rosina's Folly, **20/1** Intrepid Fort, **25/1** Izza, Petal's Jarred, Henry Will, CSF £92.68 CT £396.54 TOTE £5.70: £1.40 £5.40 £1.70 £2.00 (£52.50) Trio £79.70 OWNER Quintet Partnership (NEWMARKET) BRED Oak Crest Farm 16 Rn

1m 40.6 (2.90) SF: 48/40/9/34/12/-/-/2/-/6/5/-/11/-/5/-

WEIGHT FOR AGE 3yo-10lb

No bid.

1874 RIPON TRAVEL- CARIBBEAN CONNECTION MAIDEN STKS (3-Y.O)

(Class D) £3,811.25 (£1,154.00: £563.50: £268.25)

1m GOING minus 0.42 sec per fur (F) 7-30 (7-31)

1507 2 **My Gina** *(72+) (MRStoute)* 3-8-9 RCochrane(3) (mde all: easily) ....— **1**
1507 4 Golden Tongue (USA) *(71) (EALDunlop)* 3-8-11 (3) JTate(2) (trckd wnr: effrt over 2f out: one pce) 3 **2**
1136 7 Sejaal (IRE) *(65)*(Fav)*(JLDunlop)* 3-9-0 DHarrison(1) (swtg: unruly s: hld up: effrt over 3f out: rdn & btn over 2f out) 3 **3**
Tirolean Gold *(20) (MHEasterby)* 3-8-9 MBirch(4) (w'like: bit bkwd: dwlt: hdwy & prom ½-wy: rn green: sn wknd & eased) 20 **4**

10/11 Sejaal (IRE), **11/10** MY GINA, **9/1** Golden Tongue (USA), **33/1** Tirolean Gold, CSF £8.60 TOTE £2.00: (£3.90) OWNER Mr A. Al Khalifa (NEWMARKET) BRED P. T. and Mrs Tellwright 4 Rn

1m 40.9 (3.20) SF: 27/26/20/-

1875 PRICE WATERHOUSE H'CAP (0-80) (3-Y.O+) (Class D) £3,776.15

(£1,143.20: £558.10: £265.55)

1m 2f Stalls: High GOING minus 0.42 sec per fur (F) 8-00 (0-80)

935* **Herr Trigger (57)***(67)*(Fav)*(DrJDScargill)* 4-8-13b RCochrane(7) (trckd ldrs: hdwy on ins to ld ins fnl f: drvn out) ....— **1**
1817 5 Jubran (USA) **(68)***(77) (MJohnston)* 9-9-7 (3) JTate(6) (lw: led: rdn 2f out: hdd ins fnl f: kpt on wl) ....½ **2**
1865* Quivira **(57)***(65) (TTClement)* 4-8-13 MRimmer(4) (chsd ldr: effrt 3f out: kpt on wl fnl f) ....½ **3**
1666 4 Ooh Ah Cantona **(56)***(64) (JLEyre)* 4-8-12 RLappin(5) (lw: hld up & bhd: swtchd & effrt over 2f out: kpt on fnl f) ....½ **4**
1686 3 Muzrak (CAN) **(54)***(60) (MDHammond)* 4-8-10v DaleGibson(3) (hdwy u.p 4f out: outpcd 2f out: hrd rdn & styd on fnl f) ....¾ **5**
1506 3 Calder King **(60)***(61) (JLEyre)* 4-8-11v(5) NVarley(2) (in tch: hdwy & ch over 3f out: wknd over 1f out) 3½ **6**
1651 10 Sallyoreally (IRE) **(53)** *(WStorey)* 4-8-9 JFanning(1) (lw: hld up: hdwy & rn wd st: sn wknd) dist **7**

11/8 HERR TRIGGER, **4/1** Jubran (USA), **5/1** Quivira (3/1-11/2), **6/1** Muzrak (CAN), **9/1** Ooh Ah Cantona, Calder King (op 6/1), **16/1** Sallyoreally (IRE), CSF £7.51 TOTE £2.30: £1.70 £2.30 (£3.60) OWNER The Inn Crowd (NEWMARKET) BRED Johnathan Crisp 7 Rn

2m 5.5 (2.00) SF: 47/57/45/44/40/41/-

1876 NORMAN WELLS MEMORIAL CHALLENGE TROPHY H'CAP (0-95) (3-Y.O)

(Class C) £7,002.50 (£2,120.00: £1,035.00: £492.50)

6f Stalls: Low GOING minus 0.42 sec per fur (F) 8-30 (8-31)

1639 3 **Midwich Cuckoo (82)***(89)*(Fav)*(PTWalwyn)* 3-9-7 RCochrane(5) (lw: bhd & pushed along: hdwy 2f out: r.o to ld wl ins fnl f) ....— **1**
1414* The Scythian **(72)***(76) (BobJones)* 3-8-11 JFanning(3) (lw: cl up: led ½-wy tl wl ins fnl f)........1¼ **2**
850 10 Try to Please (IRE) **(80)***(83) (EALDunlop)* 3-9-2 (3) JTate(6) (a.p: effrt 2f out: hrd rdn & nt qckn fnl f) ....nk **3**
1580 5 Bollin Harry **(70)***(68) (MHEasterby)* 3-8-9 MBirch(1) (led to ½-wy: kpt on one pce) 1¾ **4**
1564 4 We're Joken **(59)***(39) (JBerry)* 3-7-5 (7) PFessey(2) (b.hind: cl up over 3f: sn rdn & btn) 7 **5**
1450 9 Hannah's Usher **(72)***(50) (PCHaslam)* 3-8-6 (5) JStack(4) (prom 4f: sn rdn & btn) ....¾ **6**

11/4 MIDWICH CUCKOO, **10/3** The Scythian, **7/2** Bollin Harry, **4/1** Hannah's Usher, **6/1** We're Joken (op 4/1), **8/1** Try to Please (IRE), CSF £12.07 TOTE £4.10: £2.10 £2.00 (£4.30) OWNER Mrs Henry Keswick (LAMBOURN) BRED Mrs Henry Keswick 6 Rn 1m 12.6 (2.40) SF: 35/22/29/14/-/-

1877 RIPON TRAVEL-LEGER HOLIDAYS MEDIAN AUCTION MAIDEN STKS (2-Y.O) (Class E) £3,131.80 (£948.40: £463.20: £220.60)
5f Stalls: Low GOING minus 0.42 sec per fur (F) 9-00 (9-01)

1536⁴ **Natural Key** *(74) (SirMarkPrescott)* 2-8-9 DHarrison(8) (a cl up: led ins fnl f: r.o) ....—— 1
1699⁸ Mister Sean (IRE) *(77) (JWPayne)* 2-9-0 RCochrane(7) (led tl hdd & no ex ins fnl f) ....½ 2
1597² Bollin Dorothy *(67)*(Fav)*(MHEasterby)* 2-8-9 MBirch(2) (lw: chsd ldrs: hung rt ½-wy: rdn & nt qckn appr fnl f) 1¾ 3
1670⁷ Camionneur (IRE) *(66) (MHEasterby)* 2-9-0 SMaloney(3) (bhd tl stdy hdwy fnl 2f: nrst fin) 1¾ 4
1278⁵ Arc of The Diver (IRE) *(61) (JBerry)* 2-9-0 GHind(9) (chsd ldrs: sn drvn along: no imp fr ½-wy) 1½ 5
1642³ Theatre Magic *(60) (TJEtherington)* 2-9-0 ACulhane(10) (trckd ldrs: effrt 2f out: no rspnse) ..nk 6
925⁵ Time To Fly *(55) (BWMurray)* 2-9-0 MRimmer(4) (chsd ldrs: rdn 2f out: one pce) 1¾ 7
819ᵂ Superfrills *(42) (MissLCSiddall)* 2-8-9 DeanMcKeown(1) (small: neat: unf: dwlt: swtchd rt ½-wy: n.d) 2½ 8
1413⁸ Westcourt Magic *(39) (MWEasterby)* 2-9-0 LCharnock(6) (prom to ½-wy: grad lost pl) 2½ 9
1579⁸ Impromptu Melody (IRE) *(23) (BSRothwell)* 2-8-4 (5) JStack(5) (dwlt: n.d) 3½ 10

6/4 Bollin Dorothy, **5/2** NATURAL KEY, **5/1** Arc of The Diver (IRE), **10/1** Camionneur (IRE), **14/1** Mister Sean (IRE), Theatre Magic, **16/1** Superfrills, Westcourt Magic, **20/1** Time To Fly, Impromptu Melody (IRE), CSF £36.77 TOTE £3.00: £1.40 £2.50 £1.50 (£16.90) Trio £19.00 OWNER Cheveley Park Stud (NEWMARKET) BRED Cheveley Park Stud Ltd 10 Rn
59.9 secs (1.90) SF: 25/28/18/17/12/11/6/-/-/-

1878 THE RIPON TRAVEL NORTH AMERICA TRAVEL SERVICE MAIDEN STKS (3-Y.O+) (Class D) £3,846.35 (£1,164.80: £568.90: £270.95)
1m 4f 60y Stalls: High GOING minus 0.42 sec per fur (F) 9-30 (9-31)

1612² **Artic Courier (77)***(74)*(Fav)*(DJSCosgrove)* 4-9-5 MRimmer(2) (trckd ldrs: effrt 2f out: r.o u.p to ld wl ins fnl f) ....—— 1
Festive Lassie *(68) (TDBarron)* 4-9-0 RCochrane(1) (trckd ldrs: led over 3f out: qcknd 2f out: hdd & no ex towards fin) ....¾ 2
1600⁸ Great Easeby (IRE) *(57) (WStorey)* 5-9-5 JFanning(4) (hld up: hdwy 3½f out: one pce fnl 2f) 12 3
Frank the Swank *(50) (PDEvans)* 4-9-5 GHind(3) (led tl hdd 8½f out: wl outpcd fnl 3½f) 6 4
1683⁸ Bali Tender *(35) (MWEasterby)* 4-9-5 MBirch(5) (plld hrd: led 8½f out tl over 3f out: sn rdn & btn) 11 5

1/2 ARTIC COURIER, **2/1** Festive Lassie, **12/1** Great Easeby (IRE), **33/1** Bali Tender, **50/1** Frank the Swank, CSF £1.91 TOTE £1.80: £1.30 £1.30 (£1.10) OWNER Britam Promotions Ltd (NEWMARKET) BRED Stud-On-The-Chart 5 Rn 2m 42.3 (8.30) SF: 17/11/-/-/-

T/Plpt: £9.60 (1,122.65 Tckts). T/Qdpt: £9.40 (49.85 Tckts). AA

1758-SOUTHWELL (L-H)
Thursday June 22nd (Standard)
WEATHER: sunny & hot WIND: mod half bhd

1879 MOULIN ROUGE MAIDEN AUCTION STKS (2-Y.O) (Class F) £2,519.00 (£694.00: £329.00) **5f (Fibresand)** Stalls: High GOING minus 0.08 sec (STD) 2-15 (2-15)

Jimjareer (IRE) *(50+) (CaptJWilson)* 2-8-7 KFallon(3) (blind off eye: rangy: unf: bit bkwd: s.s: outpcd & drvn along: hdwy & hung lft u.p over 1f out: styd on to ld ins fnl f) ....—— 1
Monkey Zanty (IRE) *(44) (JBerry)* 2-8-2 GHind(4) (small: w ldr: chal over 1f out: nt qckn nr fin) ....nk 2
1758⁴ Chillam *(47) (JPLeigh)* 2-8-7 DeanMcKeown(2) (led tl ins fnl f: nt qckn) ....½ 3
1652ᵂ Rushcutter Bay *(41) (TTClement)* 2-8-0 (7)ow3 DGibbs(5) (b: b.hind: unf: s.s: rn green & hung bdly lft: hdwy over 1f out: nvr nr ldrs) 1 4
Efipetite *(33) (NBycroft)* 2-7-13 SMaloney(1) (cmpt: bkwd: s.i.s: outpcd & bhd: kpt on appr fnl f: n.d) 1 5
1823³ Skelton Countess (IRE) *(4)*(Fav)*(RHollinshead)* 2-7-10 (3) AGarth(6) (chsd ldrs: hmpd ½-wy: sn lost pl & bhd: eased) 9 6

11/8 Skelton Countess (IRE), **9/4** Monkey Zanty (IRE) (op 11/10), **6/1** Chillam, **7/1** JIMJAREER (IRE), **16/1** Efipetite, **20/1** Rushcutter Bay, CSF £21.37 TOTE £9.40: £3.70 £1.60 (£10.80) OWNER Mr J. P. Hacking (PRESTON) BRED Rathbarry Stud 6 Rn 61.5 secs (3.50) SF: 8/2/5/-/-/-

1880 MONTE CARLO CLAIMING STKS (3-Y.O+) (Class F) £2,519.00 (£694.00: £329.00) **1m 3f (Fibresand)** Stalls: Low GOING minus 0.08 sec (STD) 2-50 (2-51)

1578[4] **Sudden Spin (47)***(70) (SGNorton)* 5-9-8 KFallon(9) (trckd ldrs: led over 2f out: styd on wl u.p fnl f) ....— 1
1659[2] Shabanaz **(65)***(67)*(Fav)*(WRMuir)* 10-9-6 RCochrane(11) (lw: chsd ldrs: rdn & outpcd over 2f out: styd on fnl f: nt qckn towards fin) 1 2
673[15] Be My Choice *(57) (MrsJCecil)* 3-8-5 GHind(4) (chsd ldrs: drvn along ½-wy: outpcd over 3f out: kpt on fnl 2f) 6 3
1557[5] Red Indian **(48)***(50) (WWHaigh)* 9-8-10 (3) JTate(5) (trckd ldrs: led over 3f out tl over 2f out: grad wknd) ....¾ 4
1286[8] No Submission (USA) **(72)***(57) (DWChapman)* 9-9-8 DeanMcKeown(2) (lw: led 4f: lost pl over 3f out: styd on fnl f) 1½ 5
1578[8] Prince Equiname **(64)***(59) (DEddy)* 3-8-12 AClark(12) (s.i.s: hdwy ½-wy: outpcd fnl 3f) 1 6
1523[9] Wordsmith (IRE) **(41)***(44) (JLHarris)* 5-8-12 DaleGibson(6) (lw: hdwy ½-wy: hung lft & kpt on fnl 2f: nvr nr to chal) ....¾ 7
1463[2] Simand **(45)***(25) (EWeymes)* 3-7-13 JQuinn(8) (chsd ldr: led 7f out tl over 3f out: sn wknd) ...14 8
1501[5] Canny Lad **(39)***(32) (MPBielby)* 5-9-10 ACulhane(7) (s.i.s: a in rr) 2½ 9
1725[7] The Cottonwool Kid **(50)***(20) (THCaldwell)* 3-8-2 JFanning(3) (sn drvn along: chsd ldrs tl lost pl over 4f out) 3 10
1571[8] Legally Delicious **(63)***(9) (DWChapman)* 3-8-1 NCarlisle(1) (a bhd) 7 11
1761[7] Truly Madly Deeply *(MrsJRRamsden)* 3-7-12 ow1 SMaloney(10) (b.off hind: hld up & plld hrd: a bhd: drvn along 5f out: sn lost tch) 14 12

7/4 Shabanaz, **7/1** SUDDEN SPIN, **8/1** Red Indian (op 5/1), No Submission (USA) (op 5/1), Legally Delicious, **11/1** Simand (op 7/1), **12/1** Be My Choice (op 8/1), Prince Equiname, **14/1** Wordsmith (IRE), **33/1** Canny Lad, The Cottonwool Kid, Truly Madly Deeply, CSF £18.89 TOTE £6.90: £2.40 £1.10 £2.60 (£7.10) Trio £20.80 OWNER Mr Billy Parker (BARNSLEY) BRED The Arrow Farm and Stud 12 Rn 2m 29.9 (8.40) SF: 41/38/14/21/28/16/15/-/3/-/-/-
WEIGHT FOR AGE 3yo-14lb

1881 BORDEAUX H'CAP (0-65) (3-Y.O) (Class F) £2,519.00 (£694.00: £329.00) **1m 4f (Fibresand)** Stalls: High GOING minus 0.08 sec per fur (STD) 3-25 (3-28)

1601[3] **Armston (54)***(64) (JWharton)* 3-9-1 JQuinn(5) (sn bhd: hdwy 7f out: led over 2f out: drvn clr over 1f out: eased nr fin) ....— 1
1628[3] Vintage Taittinger (IRE) **(48)***(50)*(Fav)*(MBell)* 3-8-2 (7) GFaulkner(8) (chsd ldrs: led over 5f out tl over 2f out: kpt on) 6 2
1643[7] Harry Browne (IRE) **(60)***(57) (MrsJRRamsden)* 3-9-7 KFallon(9) (lw: trckd ldrs: effrt u.p over 2f out: kpt on one pce: eased nr fin) 3½ 3
1569[9] Shared Risk **(55)***(52) (SGNorton)* 3-8-13b(3) JTate(10) (sn outpcd: hdwy over 4f out: sn hrd rdn: kpt on fnl 2f: nvr nr to chal) ....nk 4
1628[7] Warrior Lady (IRE) **(32)***(25) (PJMcBride)* 3-7-0 (7) RMullen(6) (led tl over 5f out: wknd over 3f out) 3 5
1628[11] Adjacent Too **(35)***(16) (CCElsey)* 3-7-10vow1 DaleGibson(1) (b: s.i.s: sn drvn along: t.o 7f out: sme hdwy fnl 2f) 8 6
1527[7] Lucidity **(55)***(31) (CWThornton)* 3-9-2 DeanMcKeown(12) (chsd ldrs tl wknd 3f out) 5 7
786[4] Hard Try **(57)***(31) (MJCamacho)* 3-9-4 LCharnock(3) (sn chsng ldrs: outpcd 4f out: sn wknd) 1½ 8
893[2] Ranger Sloane **(46)***(16) (GFierro)* 3-8-4b(3) DMcCabe(7) (chsd ldrs: reminder 8f out: lost pl over 4f out) 3 9
1569[4] Scale the Summit **(45)***(14) (SirMarkPrescott)* 3-8-6 CNutter(13) (chsd ldr: sn drvn along: lost pl over 3f out) ....½ 10
1458[6] Lady Kuynder **(33)***(1) (DrJDScargill)* 3-7-8 ow1 NCarlisle(11) (hld up: plld hrd & a bhd) ....hd 11
1696[12] Negative Equity **(59)***(21) (KRBurke)* 3-9-6 RCochrane(2) (chsd ldrs: reminders 8f out: wknd 4f out) 5 12
1696[13] Beyaateh **(38)** *(MCChapman)* 3-7-6 (7) JBramhill(4) (sn outpcd & bhd) ....¾ 13
LONG HANDICAP Lady Kuynder 7-4 Warrior Lady (IRE) 7-5

9/2 Vintage Taittinger (IRE), **5/1** Scale the Summit, **6/1** Hard Try, Lucidity, Negative Equity (op 4/1), **13/2** Harry Browne (IRE) (op 4/1), **7/1** ARMSTON, **12/1** Ranger Sloane, Shared Risk, **20/1** Warrior Lady (IRE), **25/1** Adjacent Too, **33/1** Lady Kuynder, Beyaateh, CSF £39.98 CT £205.19 TOTE £10.30: £2.80 £2.60 £4.80 (£26.20) Trio £104.60 OWNER Mr J. L. Ashby (MELTON MOWBRAY) BRED Farmers Hill and Fitzroy Studs 13 Rn
2m 46.2 (12.00) SF: 17/3/10/5/-/-/-/-/-/-/-/-/-

1882 TOULOUSE LIMITED STKS (0-70) (3-Y.O+) (Class E) £3,130.60 (£932.80: £444.40: £200.20)
6f (Fibresand) Stalls: Low GOING minus 0.08 sec (STD) 4-00 (4-01)

1827² **Purple Fling (68)***(73) (SirMarkPrescott)* 4-9-5 RCochrane(5) (w ldr: led over 3f out: drvn out: hld on wl) — 1
1648* Cavers Yangous **(67)***(74)*(Fav)*(MJohnston)* 4-9-8 TWilliams(4) (lw: a chsng ldrs: sn drvn along: kpt on wl fnl f) ¾ 2
1321⁴ Little Saboteur **(70)***(66) (PJMakin)* 6-9-3b AClark(9) (b.nr hind: hld up: effrt on outside over 2f out: hdwy over 1f out: styd on wl towards fin) 1 3
*1330*⁵ Montague Dawson (IRE) **(70)***(56) (MrsNMacauley)* 3-9-0b(3) SDrowne(2) (b.hind: sn trckng ldrs: effrt over 2f out: wknd qckly over 1f out) 7 4
955¹⁰ Cemaes Bay **(70)***(46) (JBerry)* 3-8-11 GHind(6) (s.i.s: sn drvn along: outpcd fr ½-wy) 1½ 5
*1763*⁸ Cheerful Groom (IRE) **(41)***(44) (JMackie)* 4-9-5 JQuinn(7) (sn bhd: effrt ½-wy: nvr nr ldrs) ¾ 6
1750⁸ Gallant Spirit (IRE) **(56)***(41) (RJHodges)* 4-8-12 (7) AmandaSanders(8) (sn drvn & outpcd: n.d) 1 7
1165¹⁵ Denbrae (IRE) **(70)***(36) (DJGMurraySmith)* 3-9-3 SWhitworth(1) (in tch early: sn outpcd & pushed along) 4 8
1508⁴ Kalar **(69)***(12) (DWChapman)* 6-9-8 DeanMcKeown(3) (led tl over 3f out: wknd 2f out: eased) 8 9

2/1 Cavers Yangous (6/4-9/4), **9/4** PURPLE FLING, **7/1** Denbrae (IRE) (op 9/2), **10/1** Montague Dawson (IRE), Kalar, **11/1** Cemaes Bay, Little Saboteur (8/1-12/1), **20/1** Gallant Spirit (IRE), **33/1** Cheerful Groom (IRE), CSF £7.11 TOTE £2.40: £1.30 £1.10 £2.70 (£3.40) Trio £7.10 OWNER Cheveley Park Stud (NEWMARKET) BRED Mrs P. Lewis 9 Rn

1m 17.6 (4.10) SF: 41/42/34/16/6/12/9/-/-
WEIGHT FOR AGE 3yo-8lb

1883 CHATEAU LAFITE (S) APPRENTICE H'CAP (0-60) (3-Y.O+) (Class G) £2,270.00 (£645.00: £320.00)
7f (Fibresand) Stalls: Low GOING minus 0.08 sec per fur (STD) 4-35 (4-37)

*1334*⁵ **Corona Gold (38)***(45)*(Fav)*(JGFitzGerald)* 5-8-11 GFaulkner(5) (lw: trckd ldrs: styd on to ld ins fnl f: hld on wl) — 1
1499¹⁶ Abigails Boy (HOL) **(37)***(43) (DrJDScargill)* 6-8-5b(5) CDomergue(6) (mde most tl ins fnl f: kpt on) nk 2
*1760*⁹ Komiamaite **(60)***(57) (SRBowring)* 3-9-10 JEdmunds(13) (in tch on outside: rdn & hung lft over 1f out: kpt on) 4 3
1523¹⁹ Bold Aristocrat (IRE) **(47)***(43) (RHollinshead)* 4-9-1 (5) FLynch(2) (lw: trckd ldr: ev ch over 2f out: one pce appr fnl f) ½ 4
1785⁸ Doodies Pool (IRE) **(42)***(37) (GLMoore)* 5-8-10 (5) CarolineHovington(4) (s.i.s: bhd tl kpt on fnl 2f: nt rch ldrs) ½ 5
1285²¹ Arrogant Boy **(30)***(23) (DWChapman)* 6-8-3 JBramhill(10) (in tch: hrd rdn 2f out: one pce) ¾ 6
1368¹³ Rustic League (IRE) **(33)***(22) (DBurchell)* 4-8-6 JWilkinson(11) (lw: chsd ldrs: hrd rdn 2f out: grad wknd) 2 7
*1569*⁸ Nuthatch (IRE) **(37)***(23) (MDIUsher)* 3-8-1 AimeeCook(12) (chsd ldrs tl wknd 2f out) 1¼ 8
1542⁸ Mai Pen Rai **(25)***(5) (RJHodges)* 7-7-12 JoHunnam(14) (bhd: sme hdwy 2f out: n.d) 2½ 9
1290¹¹ Honest Woman **(33)***(2) (NEBerry)* 4-8-6 AEddery(7) (lw: in tch: hung lft u.p over 1f out: sn wknd) 5 10
1435¹⁰ Plum Dennis **(26)** *(NBycroft)* 4-7-8b(5) GWright(3) (s.i.s: a in rr) 1 11
1469⁹ Kenilworth Ford **(34)** *(FJO'Mahony)* 4-8-7 BHalligan(9) (b: in tch: hrd rdn & lost pl ½-wy: sn bhd) hd 12
*1633*⁵ Noor El Houdah (IRE) **(51)***(11) (JBerry)* 3-9-1 CLowther(1) (chsd ldrs tl wknd qckly over 1f out) 2½ 13
*397*¹⁰ Cobbs Cross **(38)** *(THCaldwell)* 5-8-6 (5) BPeel(8) (sn wl bhd) hd 14

3/1 CORONA GOLD, **5/1** Noor El Houdah (IRE), **6/1** Kenilworth Ford (12/1-5/1), **7/1** Nuthatch (IRE), Doodies Pool (IRE) (op 4/1), **10/1** Honest Woman, Abigails Boy (HOL), Komiamaite, **11/1** Mai Pen Rai, **12/1** Bold Aristocrat (IRE), **16/1** Rustic League (IRE), **20/1** Plum Dennis, Arrogant Boy, **33/1** Cobbs Cross, CSF £36.95 CT £272.94 TOTE £4.10: £2.70 £4.10 £5.80 (£43.90) Trio £226.80 OWNER Mr T. J. Fitzgerald (MALTON) BRED Bishop Wilton Stud 14 Rn

1m 32.3 (5.50) SF: 27/25/30/25/19/5/4
WEIGHT FOR AGE 3yo-9lb
No bid

1884 ST TROPEZ H'CAP (0-65) (3-Y.O+) (Class F) £2,519.00 (£694.00: £329.00)
1m (Fibresand) Stalls: Low GOING minus 0.08 sec per fur (STD) 5-10 (5-14)

1666⁵ **Major Mouse (62)***(67) (WWHaigh)* 7-9-13 DaleGibson(4) (sn pushed along: hdwy on outside over 2f out: led jst ins fnl f: all out) — 1

1760* Wellsy Lad (USA) **(42)***(46) (DWChapman)* 8-8-7 6x DeanMcKeown(7) (unruly s: dwlt: sn trckng ldrs: led over 1f out tl jst ins fnl f) ....nk 2
1630* Moneghetti **(36)***(39) (RHollinshead)* 4-8-1 NCarlisle(5) (lw: chsd ldrs: n.m.r 2f out: swtchd outside: styd on wl ins fnl f) ....½ 3
1250 15 Tovarich **(56)***(58)*(Fav)*(GLewis)* 4-9-7 SWhitworth(2) (b.nr hind: hld up: effrt & nt clr run 2f out: styd on u.p fnl f: hmpd nr fin) ....½ 4
1762* Puffy **(46)***(48) (MDods)* 8-8-11v 6x KFallon(6) (b: s.i.s: sn pushed along: hdwy to chse ldrs ½-wy: nt qckn appr fnl f) ....hd 5
874* Ivan the Terrible (IRE) **(50)***(42) (BEllison)* 7-8-12 (3) DRMcCabe(8) (lw: b: led tl over 4f out: wknd fnl f) 5 6
1517* Sooty Tern **(50)***(42)*(Fav)*(JMBradley)* 8-8-12 (3) SDrowne(3) (w ldr: led over 4f out tl over 1f out: sn wknd) ....nk 7
1571 11 Dauntless Fort **(33)** *(MrsVAAconley)* 4-7-12 TWilliams(1) (sn bhd: sme hdwy over 2f out: sn lost pl & eased) 20 8

11/4 Tovarich (2/1-7/2), Sooty Tern, **5/1** Puffy, **6/1** Ivan the Terrible (IRE), MAJOR MOUSE, **9/1** Moneghetti (op 11/2), Wellsy Lad (USA) (op 6/1), **33/1** Dauntless Fort, CSF £53.45 CT £443.87 TOTE £9.00: £2.30 £3.50 £3.20 (£20.80) OWNER Mr N. Barber (MALTON) BRED Mrs V. Haigh 8 Rn 1m 45.0 (5.70) SF: 47/26/19/38/28/22/22/-

T/Plpt: £66.80 (135.64 Tckts). T/Qdpt: £28.80 (1 Tckt). WG

1704a-SAINT-CLOUD (France) (L-H)
Friday June 16th (Good)

1885a PRIX DU LYS (Gp 3) (3-Y.O) £26,347.00 (£9,581.00: £4,790.00: £2,395.00) 1m 6f
3-10 (3-14)

Swain (IRE) *(109) (AFabre,France)* 3-8-11 TJarnet ....— 1
Madaiyn (IRE) *(106) (AdeRoyerDupre,France)* 3-8-11 GMosse 2½ 2
1008a 6 Peckinpah's Soul (FR) *(106) (DSmaga,France)* 3-8-11 FHead ....½ 3

P-M 1.70F: 1.10F 1.10F (3.40F) OWNER Sheikh Mohammed (FRANCE) BRED Sheikh Mohammed 5 Rn 3m 1.2 SF: -/-/-

DS

1577a-SAN SIRO (Milan, Italy) (R-H)
Saturday June 17th (Soft)

1886a PREMIO AGATA (3-Y.O) £6,107.00 (£2,364.00) 1m
2-25 (2-25)

Axel Munthe (USA) *(80) (Ld'Auria,Italy)* 3-8-6 MLatorre ....— 1
1229a* Suranom (IRE) *(75) (LMCumani)* 3-8-9 SDettori 4¼ 2
Astromar (ITY) *(68) (Italy)* 3-8-11 AMarcialis 4¼ 3

Tote 19L: 13L 14L (19L) OWNER Scuderia Incolinx BRED J. L. P. Investments in USA 5 Rn 1m 40.0

1887a PREMIO PONTIDA MAIDEN (2-Y.O F) £4,925.00 (£1,842.00) 7f
2-50 (2-59)

Colpo Di Scena (IRE) *(MariaSacco,Italy)* 2-8-10 EBotti ....— 1
Candrika *(LMCumani)* 2-8-10 MPasquale ....nse 2
Luana Queen (IRE) *(Italy)* 2-8-10 MBotti ....s.nk 3

Tote 186L: 50L 15L 43L (276L) OWNER Scuderia PMZ BRED Agricola del Parco 12 Rn 1m 31.6

1888a PREMIO CORTENO (3-Y.O+) £6,107.00 1m 2f
4-10 (4-20)

1178 2 **Steady Ready Go (IRE)** *(105) (LMCumani)* 3-8-6 SDettori ....— 1
Tarvisio (IRE) *(99) (Italy)* 8-9-2 MEsposito 2½ 2
Last Quick (USA) *(86) (Italy)* 4-9-2 GForte 8 3

Tote 20L: 13L 14L (22L) OWNER Scuderia Rencati (NEWMARKET) BRED Mount Coote Stud in Ireland 7 Rn 2m 7.4 SF: -/-/-

1886a-SAN SIRO (Milan, Italy) (R-H)
Sunday June 18th (Good to firm)

1889a
PREMIO MEZZAVIA MAIDEN (2-Y.O) £4,186.00
7f 2-50 (2-52)

Semper (IRE) *(LMCumani)* 2-9-0 LDettori ....— 1
Golden Relation (IRE) *(Italy)* 2-9-0 MEsposito 3 2
Selenia (IRE) *(Italy)* 2-8-10 GForte 2¾ 3
Teofilo Stephenson (IRE) *(MarkCampion)* 2-9-0 SLandi 41¼ 10

Tote 18L: 14L 20L 28L (69L) OWNER Scuderia Rencati (NEWMARKET) BRED Freddie Lynch 11 Rn 1m 25.6 SF: -/-/-/-

1890a
GRAN PREMIO DI MILANO (Gp 1) (3-Y.O+ C & F) £130,023.00 (£66,982.00: £39,401.00: £19,700.00) **1m 4f** 4-20 (4-42)

1398a³ **Lando (GER)** *(125) (HJentzsch,Germany)* 5-9-7 MRoberts (hld up: 4th st: gd hdwy to ld 1f out: r.o wl) ....— 1
1020³ Broadway Flyer (USA) *(122) (JWHills)* 4-9-7 MHills (trckd ldr tl led 4f out: hdd 1f out: r.o) 2¼ 2
712* Strategic Choice (USA) *(121) (PFICole)* 4-9-7 TQuinn (3rd st: trckd ldr tl hrd rdn & no ex over 1f out) ....¾ 3
1387a⁵ Scribano *(108) (GBotti,Italy)* 5-9-7 EBotti (hld up in rr: nvr nr to chal) 9½ 4
1363³ Linney Head (USA) *(107) (JHMGosden)* 4-9-7 LDettori (5th st: outpcd fnl 4f) ....¾ 5
1398a⁸ Embarcadero (GER) *(78) (HJentzsch,Germany)* 7-9-7 ATylicki (led tl wknd & hdd 4f out) 22 6
1392a³ Guado d'Annibale (IRE) *(69) (Italy)* 6-9-7 JacquelineFreda (wl bhd fnl 4f) 7 7

Tote 16L: 13L 18L (35L) OWNER Gestut Haus Ittlingen BRED Gestut Hof Ittlingen 7 Rn 2m 24.8

BREMEN (Germany) (R-H)
Sunday June 18th (Soft)

1891a
SUCHARD SPRINT CUP (Listed) (3-Y.O+) £9,876.00 (£3,951.00: £2,016.00: £1,029.00) **6f** 2-35 (2-37)

1707a³ **Hever Golf Rose** *(110) (TJNaughton)* 4-9-2 JWeaver ....— 1
Matula (USA) *(106) (BSchutz,Germany)* 3-8-8 TIves 1½ 2
1488⁵ Katya (IRE) *(97) (MRChannon)* 3-8-2 CRutter 1¼ 3

Tote 18DM: 11DM 18DM 16DM (SF 163DM) OWNER Mr M. P. Hanson (EPSOM) BRED Ronald Popely 9 Rn 1m 18.8 SF: -/-/-

DORTMUND (Germany) (R-H)
Sunday June 18th (Soft)

1892a
GROSSER PREIS DER DORTMUNDER WIRTSCHAFT (Gp 3) (3-Y.O+) £29,835.00 (£11,934.00: £5,967.00: £3,704.00) **1m 1f** 4-00 (4-02)

Ladoni *(107) (HRemmert,Germany)* 3-8-5 KWoodburn ....— 1
Dream For Future (IRE) *(108) (PRemmert,Germany)* 5-9-4 GBocskai ....½ 2
1121a⁶ Devil River Peek (USA) *(102) (BSchutz,Germany)* 3-8-1 StephenDavies ....hd 3
Tote 25DM: 18DM 25DM 34DM (SF 174DM) OWNER Gestut Erlenhof BRED Audley Farms 11 Rn 1m 52.6 SF: -/-/-

1867-ASCOT (R-H)
Friday June 23rd (Firm)
WEATHER: hot WIND: mod bhd

1893
WINDSOR CASTLE STKS (2-Y.O) (Class B) £17,325.90 (£6,488.10: £3,176.55: £1,370.25: £617.63: £316.57)
5f Stalls: High GOING minus 0.18 sec per fur (GF) 2-30 (2-31)

Kuantan (USA) *(109+) (PFICole)* 2-8-11 TQuinn(7) (w'like: leggy: a.p: led 1f out: pushed out) ....— 1

1497* Applaud (USA) *(98)*(Fav)*(DRLoder)* 2-8-8 LDettori(8) (lw: hld up: nt clr run & swtchd lft over 1f out: r.o one pce) 2½ 2
1779* Polaris Flight (USA) *(99) (PWChapple-Hyam)* 2-8-11 JReid(14) (b.hind: rdn & hdwy over 2f out: one pce fnl f) ....¾ 3
1485² Tumbleweed Ridge *(98) (BJMeehan)* 2-8-11 MJKinane(3) (lw: racd stands' side: hld up: rdn over 2f out: r.o one pce) ....nk 4
1584² Tadeo *(99) (MRChannon)* 2-8-13 RHughes(12) (lw: led 4f: one pce) ....nk 5
Shaniko (IRE) *(95) (PWChapple-Hyam)* 2-8-11 BThomson(4) (neat: bit bkwd: racd stands' side: hrd rdn over 2f out: hdwy over 1f out: nvr nrr) ....½ 6
690³ April The Eighth *(95) (BWHills)* 2-8-11 MHills(10) (hld up: rdn over 2f: one pce) ....s.h 7
1343³ Safio *(99) (CSmith)* 2-9-1 JTate(9) (lw: rdn over 2f out: hdwy 1f out: nvr nrr) ....s.h 8
1634² Arctic Romancer (IRE) *(87) (GLewis)* 2-8-11 PaulEddery(6) (hrd rdn & hung lft over 1f out: nvr nrr) 2½ 9
1556² Blessingindisguise *(83) (MWEasterby)* 2-8-11b WCarson(1) (racd stands' side: prom over 3f) 1¼ 10
1579* Limerick Princess (IRE) *(75) (JBerry)* 2-8-8 JCarroll(11) (lw: hld up: rdn over 1f out: sn wknd) 1½ 11
1481* Capture The Moment *(38) (RJRWilliams)* 2-8-8 RHills(2) (racd stands' side: a bhd) 1½ 12
1203* Happy Tycoon (IRE) *(51) (MJHeaton-Ellis)* 2-8-11 WRSwinburn(13) (w ldr over 3f) 7 13
1662¹³ Double Vintage (IRE) *(MCChapman)* 2-8-11 DRMcCabe(5) (s.s: a t.o) ....dist 14

6/4 Applaud (USA), **5/1** Polaris Flight (USA), **11/2** Tumbleweed Ridge, **10/1** Tadeo, **11/1** KUANTAN (USA) (6/1-12/1), April The Eighth, **14/1** Blessingindisguise, **25/1** Shaniko (IRE), Happy Tycoon (IRE), **33/1** Arctic Romancer (IRE), **50/1** Safio, Limerick Princess (IRE), Capture The Moment, **200/1** Double Vintage (IRE), CSF £26.22 TOTE £20.90: £4.40 £2.30 (£16.40) Trio £24.40 OWNER H.R.H. Sultan Ahmad Shah (WHATCOMBE) BRED Dinwiddie Farms Ltd Partnership 14 Rn
61.28 secs (1.78) SF: 51/40/41/40/41/37/37/41/29/25/17/12/-/-

1894 HARDWICKE STKS (Gp 2) (4-Y.O+) (Class A) £64,063.00 (£23,980.90: £11,522.95: £5,023.15)
1m 4f Stalls: High GOING minus 0.18 sec per fur (GF) 3-05 (3-05)

1585* **Beauchamp Hero (100)***(119) (JLDunlop)* 5-8-9 JReid(1) (lw: hdwy over 3f out: 3rd st: led over 1f out: rdn out) ....— 1
1385U Midnight Legend **(109)***(116) (LMCumani)* 4-8-9 LDettori(6) (lw: led over 10f: unable qckn) ...2½ 2
Bal Harbour **(104)***(111) (HRACecil)* 4-8-9 PatEddery(5) (lw: 4th st: hrd rdn over 1f out: one pce) 3½ 3
1020* Zilzal Zamaan (USA) **(110)***(106) (MRStoute)* 4-8-9 WRSwinburn(4) (lw: chsd ldr 3f: 5th st: wknd over 2f out) 3½ 4
1408³ Wind in Her Hair (IRE) **(114)***(102) (JWHills)* 4-8-6 RHills(2) (lw: 6th st: wknd over 2f out) 1¼ 5
1609³ Time Star (USA) **(117)***(104)*(Fav)*(PFICole)* 4-9-0 TQuinn(3) (plld hrd: chsd ldr 9f out: 2nd st: wknd over 2f out) 4 6

9/4 Time Star (USA), **7/2** Midnight Legend, **4/1** Zilzal Zamaan (USA) (op 5/2), **11/2** BEAUCHAMP HERO, Wind in Her Hair (IRE), **10/1** Bal Harbour, CSF £22.93 TOTE £7.30: £2.90 £1.90 (£13.20) OWNER Mr E. Penser (ARUNDEL) BRED E. Penser 6 Rn 2m 29.22 (-0.28) SF: 82/79/74/69/65/67

1895 WOKINGHAM H'CAP (0-110) (3-Y.O+) (Class B) £50,118.75 (£15,075.00: £7,287.50: £3,393.75)
6f Stalls: Centre GOING minus 0.18 sec per fur (GF) 3-45 (3-48)

922⁵ **Astrac (IRE) (89)***(102) (RAkehurst)* 4-8-7 (3) SSanders(16) (a.p: led over 1f out: all out)........— 1
1233a⁵ Alzianah **(96)***(108) (JDBethell)* 4-9-3 MJKinane(2) (racd stands' side: chsd ldr: ev ch wl over 1f out: hrd rdn: r.o) ....nk 2
1637⁴ Brave Edge **(98)***(108) (RHannon)* 4-9-5 PatEddery(3) (racd stands' side: hld up; hrd rdn over 1f out: r.o) ....¾ 3
1482⁵ Venture Capitalist **(105)***(114) (DNicholls)* 6-9-12 AlexGreaves(1) (racd stands' side: hrd rdn & hdwy over 1f out: r.o) ....nk 4
1354⁴ Master of Passion **(83)***(87) (JMPEustace)* 6-8-1 (3) JTate(24) (a.p: led wl over 1f out: sn hdd: unable qckn) 2 5
1648⁵ Castlerea Lad **(90)***(91) (RHollinshead)* 6-8-11 LDettori(12) (rdn 3f out: hdwy over 1f out: nvr nrr) 1 6
1475³ Royale Figurine (IRE) **(93)***(89) (MJFetherston-Godley)* 4-9-0 WRSwinburn(13) (nt clr run over 2f out: hdwy & nt clr run over 1f out: swtchd lft: nvr nrr) 2 7
1765⁵ Sea-Deer **(90)***(83) (LJHolt)* 6-8-11 AMcGlone(7) (lw: racd stands' side: rdn over 2f out: nvr nrr) 1¼ 8
1614³ Shikari's Son **(87)***(80) (JWhite)* 8-8-8 MFenton(8) (lw: racd stands' side: rdn over 2f out: nvr nrr) ....s.h 9

1728[5] Belfry Green (IRE) **(95)***(87) (CAHorgan)* 5-9-2 CAsmussen(10) (dwlt: nt clr run over 1f out: gd hdwy fnl f: r.o wl)....nk **10**
1673[3] Sir Joey (USA) **(83)***(73) (PGMurphy)* 6-8-1 (3) SDrowne(23) (no hdwy fnl 2f)....¾ **11**
1316[6] Saseedo (USA) **(89)***(79) (WAO'Gorman)* 5-8-10 EmmaO'Gorman(30) (rdn 2f out: nvr nrr)....hd **12**
1795[7] Hello Mister **(100)***(90) (JO'Donoghue)* 4-9-2 (5) PMcCabe(27) (lw: bmpd s: hdwy over 2f out: wknd ins fnl f)....d.h **12**
1766[7] Ziggy's Dancer (USA) **(92)***(81) (EJAlston)* 4-8-13 KFallon(14) (hld up: hrd rdn over 1f out: wknd fnl f)....hd **14**
1614[9] Join the Clan **(89)***(78) (MrsNMacauley)* 6-8-10 5x JWeaver(4) (racd stands' side: a mid div)..hd **15**
1614[11] No Extras (IRE) **(91)***(80) (GLMoore)* 5-8-12 SWhitworth(5) (racd stands' side: a mid div)....hd **16**
1488[6] Tajannub (USA) **(104)***(92) (RWArmstrong)* 3-9-3 RHills(15) (prom over 4f)....nk **17**
804a[3] Bawader (USA) **(89)***(76) (DKWeld,Ireland)* 3-8-2b WCarson(19) (lw: bmpd s: mid div whn hmpd over 1f out)....nk **18**
1618[3] Everglades (IRE) **(105)***(88) (RCharlton)* 7-9-12 PaulEddery(18) (lw: hmpd s: nvr nrr)....1¾ **19**
934[10] Darren Boy (IRE) **(88)***(67) (PFICole)* 4-8-9 RHughes(28) (hrd rdn 2f out: nvr nrr)....1½ **20**
1766[3] Master Planner **(102)***(80) (CACyzer)* 6-9-9 MRoberts(22) (lw: prom over 3f)....hd **21**
1143[5] Sheppard's Cross **(84)***(62) (PTWalwyn)* 4-8-5 JCarroll(20) (bhd fnl 2f)....s.h **22**
1614[12] Mister Jolson **(86)***(59) (RJHodges)* 6-8-7 JWilliams(11) (b.nr fore: lw: a bhd)....1¾ **23**
1618[5] Branston Abby (IRE) **(107)***(80) (MJohnston)* 6-10-0 JReid(9) (racd stands' side: bhd fnl 3f)..s.h **24**
1614[4] Rock Symphony **(91)***(64) (WJHaggas)* 5-8-12 MHills(21) (hdwy over 2f out: wknd over 1f out)....nk **25**
1648[10] Encore M'Lady (IRE) **(81)***(52) (FHLee)* 4-7-13b(3) DRMcCabe(6) (racd stands' side: led: clr over 4f out: hdd wl over 1f out: sn wknd)....½ **26**
1614[5] My Best Valentine **(85)***(53) (JWhite)* 5-8-6b FNorton(26) (prom over 4f)....1¼ **27**
1766[9] Amron **(89)***(57) (JBerry)* 8-8-10 NCarlisle(25) (gd spd over 3f)....s.h **28**
1673[5] Lynton Lad **(90)***(54) (CPEBrooks)* 3-8-3 BThomson(29) (hld up: hrd rdn over 2f out: wknd over 1f out)....1¼ **29**
1316* Humbert's Landing (IRE) **(93)***(41)*(Fav)*(PFICole)* 4-9-0 TQuinn(17) (lw: bmpd s: hld up: hrd rdn over 2f out: eased whn btn fnl f: lame)....6 **30**

13/2 Humbert's Landing (IRE), **10/1** Brave Edge (12/1-8/1), **11/1** Bawader (USA), **14/1** ASTRAC (IRE), Master Planner, Rock Symphony (25/1-40/1), **16/1** No Extras (IRE), Saseedo (USA), Sea-Deer, Royale Figurine (IRE), Sir Joey (USA), Sheppard's Cross, Castlerea Lad, **20/1** Alzianah, Everglades (IRE), Belfry Green (IRE), **25/1** Lynton Lad, Master of Passion, Join the Clan, Ziggy's Dancer (USA), **33/1** Branston Abby (IRE), My Best Valentine, Shikari's Son, Mister Jolson, Venture Capitalist, **40/1** Hello Mister, Tajannub (USA), Darren Boy (IRE), **50/1** Amron, **66/1** Encore M'Lady (IRE), CSF £262.31 CT £2,693.81 TOTE £22.40: £5.00 £6.00 £2.50 £5.70 (£255.80) Trio £730.10 OWNER Mr C. J. Titcomb (EPSOM) BRED Miss Aisling O'Connell 30 Rn 1m 13.43 (-0.17)
SF:83/89/89/95/68/72/70/64/61/68/54/60/71/62/59/61/65/49/69/48/61/43/40/61/45/33/34/38/27/22
WEIGHT FOR AGE 3yo-8lb

1896 KING'S STAND STKS (Gp 2) (3-Y.O+) (Class A) £61,354.00 (£22,942.45: £11,003.73: £4,774.82)

5f Stalls: Centre GOING minus 0.18 sec per fur (GF) 4-20 (4-23)

1393a[3] **Piccolo (113)***(129) (MRChannon)* 4-9-6 RHughes(7) (lw: hld up: hrd rdn over 1f out: led ins fnl f: r.o wl)....— **1**
1572a[3] Struggler *(121) (CLaffon-Parias,France)* 3-8-10 WRSwinburn(3) (gd sort: hdwy over 1f out: r.o wl ins fnl f)....1½ **2**
1364* Mind Games **(117)***(120)*(Fav)*(JBerry)* 3-8-10 JCarroll(6) (lw: a.p: rdn over 2f out: led over 1f out tl ins fnl f: unable qckn)....½ **3**
1703a* Millstream (USA) **(109)***(111) (MJohnston)* 3-8-7 MJKinane(8) (lw: a.p: rdn over 2f out: ev ch over 1f out: one pce)....1¾ **4**
1480[2] Fard (IRE) **(117)***(112) (DMorley)* 3-8-13b WCarson(2) (outpcd: hdwy fnl f: r.o wl)....1½ **5**
1475[2] Eveningperformance **(108)***(105) (HCandy)* 4-9-0 WNewnes(5) (lw: led over 3f)....nk **6**
1572a* Millyant **(108)***(96) (RGuest)* 5-9-0 CAsmussen(1) (hld up: rdn over 1f out: sn wknd)....3 **7**
1116a[8] Hoh Magic **(117)***(98) (MBell)* 3-8-10 MHills(4) (a bhd)....hd **8**
1703a[2] Mistertopogigo (IRE) **(113)***(82) (WSCunningham)* 5-9-3b JPMurtagh(9) (b.off hind: hld up: hrd rdn over 1f out: sn wknd)....5 **9**
707a[4] Eva Luna (IRE) *(60) (JSBolger,Ireland)* 3-8-10 KJManning(10) (lt-f: dwlt: rdn over 3f out: bhd fnl 2f)....7 **10**

8/11 Mind Games (4/5-Evens), **8/1** Hoh Magic, **10/1** Eva Luna (IRE), Fard (IRE) (8/1-12/1), **11/1** Millstream (USA) (8/1-12/1), **12/1** Millyant (8/1-14/1), **14/1** Struggler, **20/1** Eveningperformance, Mistertopogigo (IRE), PICCOLO, CSF £238.99 TOTE £31.30: £5.30 £2.80 £1.30 (£238.90) Trio £131.50 OWNER John White and Partners (UPPER LAMBOURN) BRED Stanley Estate and Stud Co 10 Rn 59.67 secs (0.17) SF: 87/72/71/62/63/63/54/49/40/11
WEIGHT FOR AGE 3yo-7lb

1897

KING EDWARD VII STKS (Gp 2) (3-Y.O C & G) (Class A)
£62,832.00 (£23,586.10: £11,388.05: £5,023.85)
1m 4f Stalls: High GOING minus 0.18 sec per fur (GF) 4-55 (4-56)

1224* **Pentire (113)***(119) (GWragg)* 3-8-8 MHills(4) (lw: 5th st: led over 1f out: shkn up: r.o wl) ......— 1
1574a4 Classic Cliche (IRE) **(120)***(119)*(Fav)*(SbinSuroor)* 3-8-11 LDettori(2) (lw: rdn over 3f out: 3rd st: ev ch 1f out: unable qckn) 2½ 2
Kalabo (USA) **(104)***(114) (HRACecil)* 3-8-8 MJKinane(5) (bit bkwd: 4th st: rdn over 2f out: one pce) 1¼ 3
1301* Don Corleone **(113)***(112) (RCharlton)* 3-8-8 DHarrison(8) (lw: 8th st: rdn over 2f out: hdwy over 1f out: nvr nrr) 1¼ 4
12242 Istidaad (USA) **(106)***(110) (ACStewart)* 3-8-8 WCarson(7) (swtg: led over 1f: 2nd st: led over 2f out tl over 1f out: sn wknd) 1½ 5
10683 In Camera (IRE) **(109)***(84) (MRStoute)* 3-8-8 WRSwinburn(6) (lw: 7th st: cl 6th whn sddle slipped over 1f out: nt rcvr) 20 6
427* Inquisitor (USA) **(99)***(76) (JHMGosden)* 3-8-8 PatEddery(3) (led over 10f out tl over 2f out: eased whn btn over 1f out) 6 7
10183 Murajja (USA) **(106)***(72) (PTWalwyn)* 3-8-8 RHills(1) (lw: 6th st: wknd over 2f out) 3 8

2/1 Classic Cliche (IRE), **4/1** PENTIRE, **11/2** Don Corleone, **7/1** Kalabo (USA) (10/1-13/2), **8/1** Istidaad (USA), **10/1** In Camera (IRE) (8/1-12/1), Inquisitor (USA) (7/1-11/1), **20/1** Murajja (USA), CSF £11.92 TOTE £4.00: £1.60 £1.40 £2.10 (£3.70) OWNER Mollers Racing (NEWMARKET) BRED Lord Halifax 8 Rn 2m 28.75 (-0.75) SF: 84/84/79/77/75/49/41/37

1898

QUEEN ALEXANDRA STKS (4-Y.O+) (Class B) £19,845.00
(£7,110.00: £3,480.00: £1,500.00: £675.00)
2m 6f 34y Stalls: High GOING minus 0.18 sec per fur (GF) 5-30 (5-30)

13636 **Cuff Link (IRE) (108)***(105)*(Fav)*(MajorWRHern)* 5-9-4 PaulEddery(7) (lw: 3rd st: led over 1f out: pushed out) ......— 1
16212 Dover Patrol (IRE) **(90)***(100) (HRACecil)* 5-9-0 WRyan(6) (b: chsd ldr: led over 2f out tl over 1f out: unable qckn) 1½ 2
Great Marquess *(86) (NATwiston-Davies)* 8-9-0 WRSwinburn(2) (led over 19f: eased whn btn over 1f out) 20 3
1623* Anglesey Sea View *(ABailey)* 6-8-9 LDettori(3) (a bhd: t.o fnl 4f) ......dist 4
Nahla *(MissJacquelineDoyle)* 5-8-9 RHughes(4) (s.s: a bhd: t.o fnl 6f) ......dist 5

Evens CUFF LINK (IRE), **5/2** Dover Patrol (IRE), **6/1** Anglesey Sea View, **9/1** Great Marquess, **16/1** Nahla, CSF £3.65 TOTE £1.90: £1.40 £1.80 (£2.20) OWNER Lord Weinstock & The Hon Simon Weinstock (LAMBOURN) BRED Ballymacoll Stud Farm Ltd 5 Rn 4m 56.73 (8.73) SF: 58/53/39/-/-

T/Jkpt: Not won; £77,863.49 to Ascot 25/6/95. T/Plpt: £43.30 (1982.99 Tckts). T/Qdpt: £10.30 (110.15 Tckts). AK

1460-AYR (L-H)
Friday June 23rd (Firm)

WEATHER: sunny & warm WIND: almost nil

1899

SEAFIELD MAIDEN AUCTION STKS (2-Y.O) (Class F) £2,676.50 (£754.00: £369.50) **5f** Stalls: Low GOING minus 0.22 sec per fur (GF) 2-20 (2-20)

16523 **Pathaze** *(58)*(Fav)*(NBycroft)* 2-7-12 ow1 SMaloney(2) (lw: cl up: led wl over 1f out: r.o) ......— 1
12032 Bit of Bother (IRE) *(55) (TDBarron)* 2-8-2 GCarter(4) (led 1f: chsd ldrs: rdn ½-wy: r.o one pce) 2½ 2
18213 February *(40) (MRChannon)* 2-8-0 CRutter(3) (s.i.s: effrt ½-wy: rdn & no imp) 4 3
159714 Maysimp (IRE) *(34) (BPJBaugh)* 2-7-11 (3) DWright(5) (b: led after 1f tl over 1f out: wknd) 2 4
18214 Silent Soprano *(23) (DenysSmith)* 2-8-0 LCharnock(6) (prom: rdn 2f out: sn btn) 3½ 5

11/8 PATHAZE (op 5/2), **5/2** Bit of Bother (IRE), **3/1** February, **8/1** Silent Soprano (op 5/1), **12/1** Maysimp (IRE) (op 5/1), CSF £5.20 TOTE £2.80: £1.10 £1.20 (£2.20) OWNER Mr Neville Warriner (BRANDSBY) BRED E. H. Ruddock 5 Rn 60.34 secs (3.34) SF: 7/4/-/-/-

1900

BEN H'CAP (0-80) (4-Y.O+) (Class D) £4,162.50 (£1,260.00: £615.00: £292.50)
5f Stalls: Low GOING minus 0.22 sec per fur (GF) 2-50 (2-55)

180911 **Rich Glow (54)***(61) (NBycroft)* 4-8-8 SMaloney(4) (rdn & hdwy ½-wy: led ins fnl f: r.o) ......— 1

1721* Halbert **(46)***(51)*(Fav)*(MRChannon)* 6-8-0v 7x CRutter(7) (lw: led tl ins fnl f: kpt on) ....¾ **2**
812[4] Yet More Roses **(70)***(69) (LadyHerries)* 4-9-3 (7) JO'Dwyer(6) (b.hind: lw: chsd ldrs: hung lft fnl 2f: r.o one pce) 1¾ **3**
1668[13] Oriental Air (IRE) **(55)***(50) (EWeymes)* 4-8-9v PRobinson(1) (hdwy 2f out: styd on: no imp) ..1¼ **4**
1508[6] High Domain (IRE) **(69)***(62) (TDBarron)* 4-9-6 (3) DWright(5) (in tch: effrt 2f out: nvr able to chal) ....¾ **5**
1739[3] Kenesha (IRE) **(50)***(27) (DANolan)* 5-8-4 LCharnock(3) (b: cl up: sn pushed along: wknd fnl 2f) 5 **6**
1648[9] Two Moves in Front (IRE) **(70)***(43) (JBerry)* 5-9-10b GCarter(8) (swtg: s.i.s: sn drvn along & no imp) 1 **7**
994[10] Leading Princess (IRE) **(43)***(10) (MissLAPerratt)* 4-7-11b JMarshall(2) (swtg: spd 3f: sn lost pl) 2 **8**

3/1 Halbert, **4/1** RICH GLOW, Yet More Roses (op 5/2), **9/2** High Domain (IRE), **10/1** Two Moves in Front (IRE), **12/1** Kenesha (IRE) (op 8/1), **16/1** Oriental Air (IRE), **20/1** Leading Princess (IRE), CSF £14.88 CT £42.12 TOTE £5.40: £2.10 £1.70 £1.40 (£6.80) OWNER Mr M. J. Bateson (BRANDSBY) BRED P. Young 8 Rn 58.73 secs (1.73) SF: 43/33/51/32/44/9/25/-

1901

CUNNING PARK MEDIAN AUCTION MAIDEN STKS (3-Y.O) (Class E) £3,186.00 (£896.00: £438.00)
1m 5f 13y Stalls: Low GOING minus 0.22 sec per fur (GF) 3-25 (3-25)

1442[3] **Trazl (IRE) (63)***(64+)*(Fav)*(JLDunlop)* 3-8-9 GCarter(3) (mde all: qcknd 3f out: pushed out) .— **1**
787[3] Medway (IRE) *(63) (MHTompkins)* 3-8-9 PRobinson(1) (trckd wnr: outpcd 2f out: kpt on wl nr fin) 1¼ **2**
1684[3] Kirkie Cross *(26) (RMMcKellar)* 3-8-6 (3) DWright(2) (chsd ldrs tl outpcd fnl 3f) 30 **3**

2/5 TRAZL (IRE), **2/1** Medway (IRE) (op 5/4), **40/1** Kirkie Cross, CSF £1.47 TOTE £31.40: (£1.10) OWNER Hesmonds Stud (ARUNDEL) BRED Hesmonds Stud Ltd 3 Rn 2m 59.25 (14.45) SF: -/-/-

1902

DALMILLING CLAIMING STKS (3-Y.O+) (Class E) £2,957.00 (£896.00: £438.00: £209.00)
1m Stalls: Low GOING minus 0.22 sec per fur (GF) 4-00 (4-01)

1344[9] **Parliament Piece (70)***(76)*(Fav)*(MrsMReveley)* 9-9-3v(7) GParkin(6) (lw: a gng wl: led 3f out: comf) ....— **1**
1548[2] Okay Baby (IRE) **(44)***(56) (MHTompkins)* 3-8-0 ow1 PRobinson(5) (effrt 3f out: one pce) 2½ **2**
1811[4] High Typha **(49)***(59) (MRChannon)* 4-9-1v CRutter(1) (hld up: swtchd & effrt over 1f out: rdn & nt r.o) 1½ **3**
1819[6] Funny Rose **(23)***(37) (PMonteith)* 5-8-0 (3) DWright(3) (s.i.s: nvr rchd ldrs) 5 **4**
1568[11] Club Elite **(39)***(33) (MJCamacho)* 3-7-8bow1 LCharnock(4) (prom: hdwy to ld ent st: hdd 3f out: sn btn) 2 **5**
1688[5] Halls Burn *(30) (JSGoldie)* 7-8-7v(7) RHavlin(2) (led tl rn wd, hdd & lost pl appr st: n.d after) 7 **6**

5/4 PARLIAMENT PIECE (op 4/5), **13/8** Okay Baby (IRE), **7/2** High Typha, **20/1** Club Elite, Halls Burn, **50/1** Funny Rose, CSF £3.75 TOTE £1.80: £1.40 £1.60 (£1.70) OWNER Mr G. A. Farndon (SALTBURN) BRED Patrick Headon 6 Rn 1m 41.27 (4.47) SF: 44/14/27/5/-/-
WEIGHT FOR AGE 3yo-10lb

1903

E.B.F. MAIDEN STKS (2-Y.O) (Class D) £4,162.50 (£1,260.00: £615.00: £292.50)
7f Stalls: Low GOING minus 0.22 sec per fur (GF) 4-35 (4-37)

Myttons Mistake *(74+) (ABailey)* 2-9-0 LCharnock(6) (unf: scope: trckd ldrs: led on bit over 2f out: shkn up & qcknd appr fnl f) ....— **1**
1752[5] Warning Reef *(72)*(Fav)*(MRChannon)* 2-9-0 CRutter(3) (hld up: n.m.r over 2f out: hdwy over 1f out: r.o u.p) 1 **2**
Double Agent *(71) (MJohnston)* 2-9-0 PRobinson(5) (w'like: str: scope: hld up: effrt 3f out: hdwy over 1f out: nt qckn ins fnl f) ....nk **3**
1662[5] Urgent Swift *(64) (APJarvis)* 2-8-11 (3) DWright(1) (led tl over 2f out: one pce) 3 **4**
Bells of Holland *(55) (BWHills)* 2-8-9 SMaloney(4) (neat: unf: plld v.hrd: effrt 3f out: btn appr fnl f) 2 **5**
Lilburne (IRE) *(48) (JBerry)* 2-9-0 GCarter(2) (leggy: sn w ldr: wknd fnl 2f) 5 **6**

15/8 Warning Reef (4/5-2/1), **2/1** Double Agent, **5/1** MYTTONS MISTAKE, **8/1** Lilburne (IRE) (op 5/1), **10/1** Bells of Holland (op 5/1), **14/1** Urgent Swift, CSF £14.02 TOTE £11.80: £2.80 £1.10 (£13.10) OWNER Mr Gordon Mytton (TARPORLEY) BRED R. S. A. Urquhart 6 Rn
1m 29.65 (5.65) SF: 15/13/12/5/-/-

1904 SNODGRASS APPRENTICE H'CAP (0-70) (3-Y.O) (Class F) £2,666.00 (£751.00: £368.00) **1m** Stalls: Low GOING minus 0.22 sec per fur (GF) 5-05 (5-09)

1533[8] **Mighty Marston (67)***(74) (LadyHerries)* 3-9-4 (3) JO'Dwyer(4) (lw: led over 4f out tl over 3f out: led over 1f out: r.o) — **1**
1465* Nordic Breeze (IRE) **(66)***(72)*(Fav)*(ABailey)* 3-9-6 VHalliday(1) (lw: hld up: effrt & nt clr run over 1f out: swtchd & r.o wl) ¾ **2**
1465[3] Celebration Cake (IRE) **(63)***(67) (MissLAPerratt)* 3-9-3 CTeague(3) (b: lw: hld up: hdwy to chal 4f out: led over 3f out: sn rdn: hdd over 1f out: nt qckn) 1 **3**
1568[8] Proud Image **(64)***(67) (APJarvis)* 3-9-4 DGriffiths(5) (lw: set slow pce over 3f: lost pl ent st: hdwy & ev ch over 1f out: no ex) ½ **4**
1735* Indian Rhapsody **(49)***(49) (MRChannon)* 3-7-12 (5) 5x DSweeney(2) (hld up: smooth hdwy 3f out: effrt wl over 1f out: sn btn) 1½ **5**

7/4 Nordic Breeze (IRE), **15/8** Indian Rhapsody, **9/2** Celebration Cake (IRE), **11/2** Proud Image, **11/1** MIGHTY MARSTON (8/1-12/1), CSF £29.21 TOTE £11.20: £4.10 £1.10 (£15.30) OWNER Lucayan Stud (LITTLEHAMPTON) BRED Red House Stud 5 Rn 1m 43.17 (6.37) SF: 22/20/15/15/-

T/Plpt: £11.80 (429.26 Tckts). T/Qdpt: £8.30 (2.4 Tckts). AA

1745-GOODWOOD (R-H)

Friday June 23rd (Good to firm, Rnd course Firm patches)

WEATHER: sunny WIND: mod half across

1905 FESTIVAL OF SPEED CLASSIC MAIDEN STKS (3-Y.O+) (Class D) £4,207.50 (£1,260.00: £605.00: £277.50) **1m 1f** Stalls: Low GOING minus 0.44 sec per fur (F) 6-40 (6-43)

Alkateb *(88) (MissGayKelleway)* 3-8-12 RCochrane(5) (unf: 4th st: smooth hdwy to ld 1f out: comf) — **1**
981[9] Quandary (USA) **(81)***(77)*(Fav)*(HRACecil)* 4-9-4 AMcGlone(2) (a.p: 2nd st: led over 2f out: hdd 1f out: one pce) 3½ **2**
1339[7] Indicator *(76) (RHannon)* 3-8-12 JReid(7) (led tl over 2f out: one pce) 3 **3**
1675[7] Accuse (USA) *(54) (PFICole)* 3-8-7 MRoberts(8) (6th st: rdn & wknd 2f out) 10 **4**
Mafuta (IRE) *(48) (JJSheehan)* 3-8-2 (5) AWhelan(10) (unf: bit bkwd: 5th st: rdn 3f out: sn wknd) 3 **5**
Raincheck (GB) *(48) (MarkCampion)* 4-9-9 CAvery(6) (w'like: bit bkwd: dwlt: nvr nrr) 3 **6**
Gabriel's Lady *(34) (MarkCampion)* 4-9-4 JWilliams(3) (w'like: bkwd: dwlt: a bhd) 5 **7**
1383[12] Mont d'Or (USA) *(38) (JO'Donoghue)* 5-9-9 MPerrett(1) (bit bkwd: bhd fnl 3f) ¾ **8**
1476[14] Last Ambition (IRE) *(20) (CREgerton)* 3-8-7 JWeaver(4) (3rd st: sn wknd) 7 **9**
Knotty Scot *(11) (JJBridger)* 3-8-0 (7) ADaly(9) (a bhd) 5 **10**

4/6 Quandary (USA), **11/2** Accuse (USA) (4/1-6/1), Indicator (4/1-6/1), **10/1** ALKATEB (6/1-12/1), **16/1** Last Ambition (IRE), **33/1** Mafuta (IRE), Gabriel's Lady, Raincheck (GB), **66/1** Mont d'Or (USA), Knotty Scot, CSF £16.41 TOTE £14.80: £2.20 £1.20 £1.60 (£6.90) Trio £14.30 OWNER Mr Steve May (WHITCOMBE) BRED Greenland Park Stud 10 Rn

1m 55.13 (4.43) SF: 22/22/10/-/-/-/-/-/-/-
WEIGHT FOR AGE 3yo-11lb

1906 CELER ET AUDAX CLAIMING STKS (3-Y.O) (Class E) £3,850.00 (£1,150.00: £550.00: £250.00) **7f** Stalls: Low GOING minus 0.44 sec per fur (F) 7-10 (7-13)

1811[3] **Brass Tacks (65)***(68) (RHannon)* 3-7-13 MRoberts(6) (lw: 6th st: rdn over 2f out: hdwy over 1f out: led wl ins fnl f: r.o) — **1**
1778[5] Fantasy Racing (IRE) **(78)***(76)*(Fav)*(MRChannon)* 3-8-9 ow1 RHughes(3) (3rd st: rdn over 2f out: hdwy over 1f out: ev ch wl ins fnl f: unable qckn) nk **2**
1566[10] Medieval Miss **(63)***(71) (GLewis)* 3-8-3b PaulEddery(2) (led: clr over 1f out: hdd wl ins fnl f: one pce) 1 **3**
1447[7] Scissor Ridge **(43)***(64) (JJBridger)* 3-7-9 (7) ADaly(4) (4th st: rdn 2f out: one pce) 2½ **4**
1550[7] Rolling (IRE) **(60)***(64) (BWHills)* 3-8-6 JWeaver(1) (2nd st: rdn 3f out: one pce fnl 2f) 1¾ **5**
1654[2] Delight of Dawn **(69)***(52) (KTIvory)* 3-7-7 (7) AmandaSanders(8) (dwlt: nvr nrr) 2½ **6**
1785[5] Sandra Dee (IRE) **(54)***(24) (BAPearce)* 3-7-12 (5)ow6 PPMurphy(7) (7th st: sn wknd) 11 **7**
1521[6] Dismissive (IRE) **(37)***(16) (DrJDScargill)* 3-7-11 NCarlisle(5) (a bhd) 3½ **8**
Streetwise Sid **(40)***(10) (TMJones)* 3-8-5 ow3 RPerham(9) (5th st: wkng whn hmpd over 2f out: sn bhd) 5 **9**

2/1 Fantasy Racing (IRE), **5/2** BRASS TACKS, **7/2** Delight of Dawn, **11/2** Rolling (IRE), **10/1** Medieval Miss, **20/1** Scissor Ridge, **25/1** Sandra Dee (IRE), **50/1** Dismissive (IRE), Streetwise Sid, CSF £8.00 TOTE £33.80: £1.40 £1.50 £2.20 (£3.70) Trio £15.80 OWNER Mrs Derek Strauss (MARLBOROUGH) BRED Fulling Mill Farm and Stud 9 Rn 1m 27.42 (3.02) SF: 13/21/16/9/9/-/-/-/-
Brass Tacks clmd A Hill £8,000

1907 LUFTHANSA CARGO H'CAP (0-85) (3-Y.O) (Class D) £5,572.50 (£1,680.00: £815.00: £382.50) **1m** Stalls: Low GOING minus 0.44 sec per fur (F) 7-40 (7-40)

1428³ **Ron's Secret (65)***(76) (JWPayne)* 3-8-6 RCochrane(2) (3rd st: rdn 2f out: led ins fnl f: r.o) ..— 1
651⁴ Crested Knight (IRE) **(62)***(72) (CAHorgan)* 3-8-3 AMcGlone(3) (5th st: rdn & swtchd lft over 1f out: r.o wl fnl f) ....nk 2
1676² Scharnhorst **(69)***(74)*(Fav)*(SDow)* 3-8-10 MRoberts(5) (2nd st: led over 3f out: hdd & edgd rt ins fnl f: one pce) 2½ 3
1619⁴ Sticks and Stones (IRE) **(80)***(80) (MrsJCecil)* 3-9-7b PaulEddery(4) (led: hdd over 3f out: ev ch 1f out: one pce) 2½ 4
1544⁴ Shamrock Fair (IRE) **(74)***(58) (LordHuntingdon)* 3-9-1 JWilliams(1) (4th st: sn wknd) 8 5
1619⁶ Made in Heaven **(80)***(56) (JWHills)* 3-9-7 JWeaver(6) (dwlt: 6th st: rdn over 2f out: a bhd) 4 6

11/8 Scharnhorst, **3/1** Shamrock Fair (IRE) (op 5/1), **4/1** Sticks and Stones (IRE), **6/1** RON'S SECRET, **9/1** Made in Heaven (6/1-10/1), **11/1** Crested Knight (IRE) (8/1-12/1), CSF £54.82 TOTE £5.30: £1.90 £4.50 (£40.80) OWNER Mrs Linda Popely (NEWMARKET) BRED Mrs L. Popely 6 Rn
1m 39.06 (1.46) SF: 40/36/38/44/22/20

1908 WILEY H'CAP (0-80) (4-Y.O+) (Class D) £5,345.00 (£1,610.00: £780.00: £365.00) **1m 2f** Stalls: Low GOING minus 0.44 sec per fur (F) 8-10 (8-10)

1616* **My Learned Friend (75)***(86)*(Fav)*(AHide)* 4-9-9 JWilliams(9) (4th st: rdn over 1f out: led ins fnl f: all out) ....— 1
1757⁷ Bookcase **(60)***(71) (DRCElsworth)* 8-8-8 MRoberts(8) (hld up: 8th st: hdwy 2f out: r.o strly fnl f: jst failed) ....s.h 2
1539* Dutosky **(62)***(70) (RJO'Sullivan)* 5-8-5 (5) AWhelan(2) (5th st: hdwy to ld over 1f out: hdd ins fnl f: one pce) 2 3
634⁷ Red Valerian **(73)***(73) (KMcAuliffe)* 4-9-7b MPerrett(1) (6th st: rdn 2f out: r.o one pce fnl f) 5 4
1502⁷ Minnesota Viking **(65)***(58) (LadyHerries)* 4-8-13 JWeaver(3) (3rd st: rdn over 2f out: wknd over 1f out) 4 5
1745² Caerle Lad (IRE) **(64)***(57) (GHarwood)* 4-8-12 AClark(7) (lw: 2nd st: ev ch 2f out: rdn & wknd over 1f out) ....½ 6
1518⁵ Pistol (IRE) **(62)***(52) (CAHorgan)* 5-8-10 PaulEddery(4) (7th st: rdn over 2f out: a bhd) 1½ 7
1661¹⁰ Fieldridge **(76)***(64) (CPEBrooks)* 6-9-10 RCochrane(5) (led tl wl over 1f out: sn wknd) 1¼ 8

11/4 MY LEARNED FRIEND, **4/1** Caerle Lad (IRE), **9/2** Bookcase, **11/2** Dutosky, **6/1** Minnesota Viking, **13/2** Fieldridge, **9/1** Pistol (IRE), **10/1** Red Valerian, CSF £16.34 CT £61.62 TOTE £3.80: £1.60 £1.60 £2.00 (£13.10) Trio £18.10 OWNER Mrs J. Roberts (NEWMARKET) BRED A. D. G. Oldrey 8 Rn 2m 7.96 (2.96) SF: 48/33/32/35/20/19/14/26

1909 ARGUS CLAIMING STKS (3-Y.O+) (Class E) £3,590.00 (£1,070.00: £510.00: £230.00) **5f** Stalls: Low GOING minus 0.44 sec per fur (F) 8-40 (8-42)

1451² **Fangio (80)***(81) (WGMTurner)* 6-8-9 (5) PMcCabe(1) (mde all: rdn & edgd lft over 1f out: r.o) ....— 1
1451* Palacegate Jack (IRE) **(93)***(82)*(Fav)*(JBerry)* 4-9-7 JCarroll(4) (chsd wnr: rdn over 2f out: one pce) 2 2
1538* Anzio (IRE) **(68)***(70) (BAPearce)* 4-8-10b SWhitworth(5) (chsd ldrs: rdn over 2f out: r.o one pce fnl f) ....nk 3
1537¹⁰ Cradle Days **(62)***(63) (RCSpicer)* 6-8-10b RPerham(3) (sn rdn along: hdwy over 2f out: rdn over 1f out: one pce) 2 4
1445¹² Tiheros **(59)***(61) (RHannon)* 3-8-3 MRoberts(7) (chsd ldrs: rdn 2f out: r.o one pce fnl f) ....¾ 5
1265⁴ Paley Prince (USA) **(53)***(55) (MDIUsher)* 9-8-10 JWilliams(2) (prom: rdn 2f out: wknd over 1f out) 1¾ 6
1445⁹ Logie Pert Lad **(30)***(20) (JJBridger)* 3-7-10 (7) ADaly(6) (bhd fnl 3f) 11 7

4/5 Palacegate Jack (IRE), **100/30** FANGIO (2/1-7/2), **13/2** Anzio (IRE), **8/1** Tiheros (op 14/1), **12/1** Paley Prince (USA), **20/1** Cradle Days, **66/1** Logie Pert Lad, CSF £6.39 TOTE £4.10: £2.00 £1.40 (£2.00) OWNER Mr Malcolm Heygate-Browne (SHERBORNE) BRED Melbury Park Stud 7 Rn
57.78 secs (1.08) SF: 41/42/30/23/14/15/-
WEIGHT FOR AGE 3yo-7lb

1910

SUSSEX CHAMBER OF COMMERCE H'CAP (0-75) (3-Y.O+) (Class D) £4,045.00 (£1,210.00: £580.00: £265.00)
6f Stalls: Low GOING minus 0.44 sec per fur (F) 9-10 (9-10)

1738[6] **Samsolom (60)***(64) (PHowling)* 7-9-2 PaulEddery(3) (hld up: hdwy over 2f out: led over 1f out: r.o) — 1
1483[5] Paddy's Rice **(55)***(56)*(Fav)*(LJHolt)* 4-8-11 JReid(2) (a.p: ev ch over 1f out: rdn & one pce fnl f) 1¼ 2
1517[8] Blurred Image (IRE) **(72)***(71) (MissGayKelleway)* 4-9-7 (7) DaneO'Neill(4) (sltly outpcd: hdwy over 1f out: r.o one pce fnl f) ½ 3
1595* Mazzarello (IRE) **(43)***(32) (RCurtis)* 5-7-8v(5) MBaird(5) (led: rdn over 2f out: hdd over 1f out: wknd fnl f) 4 4
1199[5] Lorins Gold **(37)***(19) (AndrewTurnell)* 5-7-7 NAdams(1) (prom: rdn & ev ch 2f out: wknd over 1f out) 2½ 5

LONG HANDICAP Lorins Gold 7-6

5/4 Paddy's Rice, **9/4** Mazzarello (IRE), **7/2** SAMSOLOM, **13/2** Lorins Gold, **9/1** Blurred Image (IRE), CSF £8.78 TOTE £4.40: £1.90 £1.50 (£3.40) OWNER Mr C. Hammond (NEWMARKET) BRED C. R. Mason 5 Rn
1m 10.78 (0.58) SF: 54/46/61/22/9

T/Plpt: £59.80 (226.32 Tckts). T/Qdpt: £62.60 (2.2 Tckts). SM

1622-NEWMARKET (R-H)
Friday June 23rd (Good to firm)
WEATHER: cloudy WIND: slt half bhd

1911

ANGLIAN RACING CLUB APPRENTICE H'CAP (0-70) (3-Y.O+) (Class E) £2,333.75 £2,333.75 (£530.00: £252.50)
1m (July) Stalls: Low GOING minus 0.35 sec per fur (F) 6-50 (6-51)

1666* **Scaraben (55)***(63) (SEKettlewell)* 7-9-7 5x JStack(3) (hmpd s: gd hdwy over 1f out: hrd rdn to jn ldr line) — 1
1830[3] **Kaafih Homm (IRE) (53)***(61)*(Fav)*(NACallaghan)* 4-9-2 (3) MHenry(8) (b.hind: jnd ldrs over 3f out: hrd rdn to ld wl ins fnl f: jnd line) — 1
1693[9] Autumn Cover **(54)***(61) (RMFlower)* 3-8-10b JDSmith(6) (b: gd hdwy appr fnl f: hrd rdn: fin wl) nk 3
1811[2] Narbonne **(57)***(64) (BJMcMath)* 4-9-9 LNewton(9) (led over 2f out tl wl ins fnl f: hrd rdn: r.o) .hd 4
1568[2] Nautical Jewel **(51)***(57) (MDIUsher)* 3-8-4 (3) CAdamson(2) (wnt rt s: sn led: hdd over 3f out: rallied & ev ch ins fnl f: no ex cl home) ¾ 5
1509[2] Duello **(62)***(65) (MBlanshard)* 4-9-9 (5) RWaterfield(7) (a in tch: one pce fnl 2f) 1½ 6
1745* Anlace **(53)***(54) (SMellor)* 6-9-0 (5) 5x JoHunnam(1) (lw: prom tl wknd over 1f out) ¾ 7
1742[7] Buddy's Friend (IRE) **(57)***(57) (RJRWilliams)* 7-9-2 (7) TracyJohnson(4) (plld early: led over 3f out tl over 2f out: ev ch over 1f out: wkng whn hmpd 1f out) ½ 8
1651[3] Able Choice (IRE) **(48)***(48) (RWArmstrong)* 5-8-9 (5) SLanigan(11) (s.i.s: a bhd) nk 9
1854[2] Pop to Stans **(47)***(19) (JPearce)* 6-8-8 (5) ElizabethTurner(5) (lw: in tch tl wknd appr fnl f) 1¼ 10

9/2 KAAFIH HOMM (IRE), **5/1** SCARABEN, **11/2** Anlace, **8/1** Pop to Stans, Able Choice (IRE), **10/1** Buddy's Friend (IRE), Narbonne (7/1-11/1), **14/1** Autumn Cover (10/1-16/1), Duello, **20/1** Nautical Jewel, CSF S & K H £11.97 KH & S £11.71 CT S, KH & AC £117.16 KH, S & AC £115.24 TOTE S £1.80, KH £2.40: S £1.70, KH £1.70 £3.90 (£6.10) Trio £55.60 OWNER Mr J. Tennant (MIDDLEHAM)/Gallagher Materials Ltd (NEWMARKET) BRED Burton Agnes Stud Co Ltd 10 Rn
1m 40.89 (3.19) SF: 44/42/32/45/28/46/35/38/29/-
WEIGHT FOR AGE 3yo-10lb

1912

ANTEC VIRKON H'CAP (0-95) (3-Y.O+) (Class C) £6,056.00 (£1,808.00: £864.00: £392.00)
1m 4f (July) Stalls: Low GOING minus 0.35 sec per fur (F) 7-20 (7-22)

938[10] **Mokhtar (IRE) (83)***(91) (JLDunlop)* 4-9-5 WCarson(1) (hld up: led over 2f out: pushed out) — 1
1844[3] Lookingforarainbow (IRE) **(77)***(83) (BobJones)* 7-8-13 MWigham(5) (hld up: hdwy 5f out: nt clr run 2f out: ev ch ins fnl f: styd on) 1½ 2
1612[6] Ball Gown **(73)***(76) (DTThom)* 5-8-6 (3) DRMcCabe(3) (hld up: hrd rdn over 2f out: ev ch appr fnl f: one pce) 2 3
1275* Vaugrenier (IRE) **(84)***(82) (RHannon)* 3-8-5 TQuinn(2) (led: clr 8f out: hdd over 3f out: hrd rdn & ev ch 2f out: wknd appr fnl f) 4 4
1408[6] Rainfest (FR) **(90)***(86)*(Fav)*(RCharlton)* 4-9-12 PatEddery(4) (pushed along 7f out: led over 3f out to 2f out: sn wknd) 1½ 5

11/4 Rainfest (FR), **100/30** Vaugrenier (IRE), **7/2** Ball Gown, **4/1** Lookingforarainbow (IRE), **5/1** MOKHTAR (IRE), CSF £21.38 TOTE £3.40: £1.50 £1.50 (£7.00) OWNER Mr Hamdan Al Maktoum (ARUNDEL) BRED Kilcarn Stud 5 Rn 2m 32.12 (3.42) SF: 52/44/37/28/47

WEIGHT FOR AGE 3yo-15lb

1913

NGK SPARK PLUGS MAIDEN STKS (2-Y.O) (Class D) £4,620.00 (£1,380.00: £660.00: £300.00)
6f (July) Stalls: Low GOING minus 0.35 sec per fur (F) 7-50 (7-54)

Mons *(80+) (LMCumani)* 2-9-0 PatEddery(3) (cmpt: a.p: led over 2f out: pushed clr: r.o wl)..— 1
Ramooz (USA) *(72) (BHanbury)* 2-9-0 WCarson(4) (unf: scope: s.i.s: hdwy over 2f out: ev ch appr fnl f: one pce)....3 2
Balpare *(59) (NACallaghan)* 2-8-9 BThomson(7) (leggy: unf: hld up: rdn & hdwy 2f out: kpt on one pce fnl f)....3 3
Arctiid (USA) *(63)*(Fav)*(JHMGosden)* 2-9-0 LDettori(6) (wl grwn: bit bkwd: chsd ldrs: ev ch 2f out: wknd fnl f)....nk 4
Classic Artiste (USA) *(58) (BJMcMath)* 2-8-9 AMackay(2) (leggy: lt-f: led over 3f: wknd appr fnl f)....s.h 5
Esperto *(59) (JPearce)* 2-9-0 GBardwell(5) (neat: a outpcd)....1½ 6
Sign From Heaven *(43) (GRimmer)* 2-9-0 MRimmer(1) (cmpt: spd over 3f)....6 7
Caribbean Expresso (IRE) *(BHanbury)* 2-8-4 (5) JStack(8) (scope: bit bkwd: in tch over 3f)..15 8

11/10 Arctiid (USA) (4/5-11/8), **5/2** MONS, **5/1** Ramooz (USA) (tchd 10/1), **12/1** Sign From Heaven (op 7/1), **20/1** Balpare, Classic Artiste (USA), **25/1** Esperto, **33/1** Caribbean Expresso (IRE), CSF £14.72 TOTE £3.40: £1.20 £1.30 £4.10 (£6.80) OWNER Mrs E. H. Vestey (NEWMARKET) BRED Sir Eric Parker 8 Rn 1m 14.31 (2.81) SF: 30/22/9/13/8/9/-/-

1914

KIDSONS IMPEY CLAIMING STKS (3-Y.O) (Class D) £4,659.00 (£1,392.00: £666.00: £303.00)
1m (July) Stalls: Low GOING minus 0.35 sec per fur (F) 8-20 (8-21)

Emily-Mou (IRE) (78)*(62)*(Fav)*(EALDunlop)* 3-8-5 RHills(9) (a in tch: led 2f out: hrd rdn & hung lft jst ins fnl f: drvn out)....— 1
1258[5] Action Jackson **(75)***(70) (GRimmer)* 3-9-0 MRimmer(7) (hdwy 3f out: r.o fnl f)....½ 2
1719[2] Colston-C **(50)***(70) (CJHill)* 3-8-9 (7) MHenry(1) (led 6f: hmpd jst ins fnl f: nt rcvr)....1 3
816[11] Time Leader **(76)***(71) (MRStoute)* 3-9-4 WRSwinburn(3) (w ldr tl rdn & hung lft 2f out: rallied ins fnl f)....½ 4
733[7] Rosa Bonheur **(58)***(46) (MAJarvis)* 3-7-13 JQuinn(5) (in tch 5f)....3 5
1350[12] Magic Leader (IRE) **(33)***(47) (TTClement)* 3-7-13 (7) SLanigan(6) (s.i.s: a bhd)....3 6
1550[11] Fair Attraction **(48)***(41) (AHide)* 3-8-8 MTebbutt(4) (dwlt: a bhd)....4 7
Watch My Lips *(45) (MHTompkins)* 3-8-9 (5) HKYim(8) (lt-f: dwlt: a bhd)....1¼ 8
1553[6] Robin Island **(55)***(23) (RHannon)* 3-8-6b PatEddery(2) (in tch 5f)....7 9

5/2 EMILY-MOU (IRE) (op 6/4), **3/1** Time Leader (op 9/2), **11/2** Action Jackson, **6/1** Robin Island, **8/1** Colston-C, **10/1** Rosa Bonheur, **20/1** Watch My Lips, **25/1** Fair Attraction, **33/1** Magic Leader (IRE), CSF £15.48 TOTE £3.80: £1.70 £2.20 £2.20 (£11.30) Trio £51.40 OWNER Mrs Alexander Scott (NEWMARKET) BRED W. and R. Barnett Ltd 9 Rn
1m 40.4 (2.70) SF: 34/42/42/43/18/19/13/17/-
Emily-Mou (IRE) clmd B Meehan £8,000

1915

KENTFORD H'CAP (0-95) (3-Y.O+) (Class C) £7,635.00 (£2,280.00: £1,090.00: £495.00) **7f (July)** Stalls: Low GOING minus 0.35 sec per fur (F) 8-50 (8-51)

1549* **Bouche Bee (USA) (80)***(86+)*(Fav)*(LMCumani)* 3-8-5 LDettori(4) (lw: hld up in tch: jnd ldr 2f out: led 1f out: r.o wl)....— 1
1693[6] Dontforget Insight (IRE) **(71)***(75) (PFICole)* 4-8-5 TQuinn(8) (hld up in rr: gd hdwy over 1f out: r.o)....1 2
1482* Cyrano's Lad (IRE) **(90)***(93) (JohnBerry)* 6-9-10 CDwyer(3) (bmpd s: sn w ldr: led 3f out to 1f out: one pce)....½ 3
1409[2] Fionn de Cool (IRE) **(72)***(43) (RAkehurst)* 4-8-6 BThomson(5) (chsd ldrs: outpcd over 2f out: rallied fnl f)....1¼ 4
939[3] Kabil **(85)***(52) (HThomsonJones)* 3-8-10 RHills(2) (lw: chsd ldrs: ev ch 1f out: one pce)....1½ 5
1560[8] Jato **(76)***(41) (SCWilliams)* 6-8-7 (3) DWright(6) (b.nr fore: lw: chsd ldrs: ev ch 1f out: one pce)....1 6
1676* Jolto **(73)***(26) (KOCunningham-Brown)* 6-8-7 5x PatEddery(1) (led 4f: wknd 2f out)....5 7
1754* Veloce (IRE) **(73)***(22) (ABailey)* 7-8-7v 5x GCarter(7) (b: a bhd: pushed along after 3f: no rspnse)....2 8

2/1 BOUCHE BEE (USA), **3/1** Kabil, **9/2** Jolto (3/1-5/1), **6/1** Fionn de Cool (IRE) (9/2-7/1), **7/1** Jato, **8/1** Veloce (IRE), **14/1** Cyrano's Lad (IRE) (10/1-16/1), **25/1** Dontforget Insight (IRE), CSF £41.75 CT £540.94 TOTE £2.90: £1.10 £2.60 £2.50 (£20.60) OWNER Miss Gatto Roissard (NEWMARKET) BRED Jones Kamur Partnership 8 Rn 1m 24.68 (0.28) SF: 58/56/74/24/24/22/7/3
WEIGHT FOR AGE 3yo-9lb

1916 GAZELEY MAIDEN STKS (3-Y.O) (Class D) £4,659.00 (£1,392.00: £666.00: £303.00) **1m 2f (July)** Stalls: Low GOING minus 0.35 sec per fur (F) 9-15 (9-18)

Goonda *(72) (HRACecil)* 3-8-9 WRyan(6) (nt grwn: hld up: hdwy 2f out: hung lft: led 1f out: rdn out)......— 1
1283[5] Peripatetic *(70) (MRStoute)* 3-8-9 RHills(2) (lw: led: hung lft over 2f out: hdd 1f out: one pce)1¼ 2
Officer *(74) (HRACecil)* 3-9-0 PatEddery(3) (wl grwn: hld up: hdwy 5f out: ev ch whn carried lft 2f out: r.o ins fnl f)......½ 3
Sadly Sober (IRE) *(65) (PFICole)* 3-8-9 TQuinn(5) (bit bkwd: trckd ldrs: ev ch 2f out: wknd appr fnl f)......2½ 4
1526[11] Reaganesque (USA) *(64)*(Fav)*(EALDunlop)* 3-9-0 WRSwinburn(1) (hdwy 3f out: ev ch 2f out: sn wknd)......4 5
1755[9] Pretoria Dancer *(46) (JHMGosden)* 3-9-0 LDettori(4) (trckd ldr tl wknd over 3f out)......11 6

5/4 Reaganesque (USA) (6/4-Evens), **3/1** Officer (9/4-4/1), **7/2** GOONDA, **7/1** Sadly Sober (IRE), **12/1** Peripatetic (8/1-14/1), Pretoria Dancer (op 8/1), CSF £35.47 TOTE £5.30: £3.00 £4.20 (£25.30) OWNER Lady Howard de Walden (NEWMARKET) BRED Lord Howard de Walden 6 Rn
2m 7.96 (5.56) SF: 21/19/23/14/13/-
T/Plpt: £190.00 (77.84 Tckts). T/Qdpt: £143.20 (1.25 Tckts). RC

1665-REDCAR (L-H)
Friday June 23rd (Firm, Good to firm patches)
WEATHER: fine WIND: fresh half against

1917 NEWTON CLAIMING STKS (3-Y.O+) (Class F) £2,798.00 (£778.00: £374.00) **1m 2f** Stalls: High GOING minus 0.28 sec per fur (GF) 2-10 (2-14)

1687[8] **Pine Essence (USA) (63)***(54)*(Fav)*(MrsMReveley)* 4-9-3 KDarley(1) (hld up: effrt over 2f out: rdn to ld over 1f out: drvn out)......— 1
1733[2] Gulf Bay **(32)***(39) (MBell)* 3-7-0 (7) RMullen(3) (s.i.s: hld up: effrt & swtchd outside over 2f out: kpt on: nvr able to chal)......1¾ 2
1523[15] Little Blackfoot **(34)***(42) (JLHarris)* 7-8-10v AMackay(5) (led & clr tl over 1f out: one pce)......1½ 3
1854[8] Bardia **(30)***(37) (DonEnricoIncisa)* 5-8-7 KimTinkler(2) (s.i.s: bhd: kpt on u.p fnl f: nvr nr to chal)......1¼ 4
Malindi Bay **(23)***(29) (BJMcMath)* 7-8-3 (7) RMoogan(4) (bit bkwd: chsd ldr: drvn along over 4f out: wknd over 2f out)......7 5

4/6 PINE ESSENCE (USA), **5/2** Gulf Bay (op 6/4), **5/1** Bardia (7/2-6/1), **16/1** Little Blackfoot, **20/1** Malindi Bay, CSF £2.91 TOTE £1.60: £1.10 £1.40 (£1.60) OWNER Dab Hand Racing (SALTBURN) BRED David E. Hager II 5 Rn 2m 7.8 (5.30) SF: 36/9/24/19/11
WEIGHT FOR AGE 3yo-12lb

1918 SUTER H'CAP (0-90) (3-Y.O+) (Class C) £6,037.00 (£1,816.00: £878.00: £409.00) **6f** Stalls: Low GOING minus 0.28 sec per fur (GF) 2-40 (2-40)

1668* **Melodic Drive (61)***(70) (JAGlover)* 5-8-10b 7x DeanMcKeown(4) (trckd ldrs: hdwy to ld over 1f out: drvn along & r.o wl)......— 1
1604[3] Macs Maharanee **(72)***(76) (PSFelgate)* 8-9-7 GHind(6) (lw: trckd ldrs: effrt & ev ch over 2f out: sn rdn: nt qckn fnl f)......2 2
1441[2] Lepine (IRE) **(73)***(70)*(Fav)*(JWWatts)* 4-9-8 GDuffield(5) (swtg: led to ½-wy: outpcd & hung rt over 1f out: kpt on nr fin)......2½ 3
1809[5] Here Comes a Star **(75)***(72) (JMCarr)* 7-9-10 ACulhane(3) (chsd ldrs: effrt over 2f out: ev ch over 1f out: kpt on same pce)......hd 4
1668[4] Willshe Gan **(52)***(45) (DenysSmith)* 5-8-1 JFanning(1) (w ldr: led ½-wy tl over 1f out: kpt on same pce: eased nr fin)......1¼ 5
1641[6] Sound the Trumpet (IRE) **(80)***(49) (MrsJRRamsden)* 3-9-7b NConnorton(2) (trckd ldrs pllng hrd: jnd ldrs ½-wy: sn lost pl & bhd)......9 6

2/1 Lepine (IRE), **7/2** MELODIC DRIVE, Macs Maharanee, **4/1** Here Comes a Star, **7/1** Willshe Gan, **8/1** Sound the Trumpet (IRE), CSF £16.13 TOTE £4.60: £1.60 £2.10 (£5.20) OWNER Mrs C. M. Stevens (WORKSOP) BRED C. M. Stevens 6 Rn 1m 12.0 (2.70) SF: 46/52/46/48/21/17
WEIGHT FOR AGE 3yo-8lb

1919

INGS MAIDEN STKS (2-Y.O) (Class D) £3,598.50 (£1,083.00: £524.00: £244.50)
5f Stalls: Low GOING minus 0.28 sec per fur (GF) 3-10 (3-10)

Krystal Max (IRE) *(78+) (TDBarron)* 2-9-0 DeanMcKeown(7) (cmpt: bit bkwd: dwlt: sn trckng ldrs: shkn up to ld 2f out: drvn out) .... — 1
1670[6] Meeting Point **(69)***(68)*(Fav)*(MrsMReveley)* 2-8-9 KDarley(5) (sn chsng ldrs: swtchd rt 2f out: ev ch 1f out: unable qckn) 1½ 2
1579[9] Katy-Q (IRE) *(60) (PCalver)* 2-8-9 MBirch(2) (a chsng ldrs: hung rt & nt qckn appr fnl f)....... 2½ 3
1722[2] Elfin Queen (IRE) *(56)*(Fav)*(MJohnston)* 2-8-9 TWilliams(6) (led to 2f out: wknd over 1f out) 1¼ 4
1579[6] Alfayza *(48) (JDBethell)* 2-8-9 GDuffield(4) (a outpcd & sn drvn along) 2½ 5
1642[5] Opening Chorus *(52) (MrsJRRamsden)* 2-9-0 NConnorton(3) (trckd ldrs: effrt & hung rt 2f out: sn wknd) .... nk 6
Fergal (USA) *(44) (GMMoore)* 2-8-9 (5) JStack(1) (leggy: bit bkwd: swvd lft s: nvr wnt pce)... 2½ 7

2/1 Elfin Queen (IRE) (6/4-9/4), Meeting Point, **5/1** KRYSTAL MAX (IRE), **11/2** Opening Chorus, **12/1** Alfayza, Katy-Q (IRE), Fergal (USA), CSF £15.84 TOTE £6.50: £1.40 £1.90 (£23.20) OWNER The Oakfield Nurseries Partnership (THIRSK) BRED Baronrath Stud 7 Rn
60.4 secs (3.70) SF: 24/14/6/2/-/-/-

1920

NRS H'CAP (0-80) (3-Y.O) (Class D) £3,866.50 (£1,162.00: £561.00: £260.50)
7f Stalls: Low GOING minus 0.28 sec per fur (GF) 3-40 (3-40)

1639[11] **Hawa Al Nasamaat (USA) (77)***(87)*(Fav)*(EALDunlop)* 3-9-2 (5) JStack(5) (lw: trckd ldrs: shkn up to ld over 2f out: drvn out) .... — 1
1735[3] Three Arch Bridge **(55)***(58) (MJohnston)* 3-7-13b TWilliams(3) (led to ½-wy: kpt on u.p fnl f: no ch w wnr) 3 2
1471[5] Bollin Frank **(55)***(58) (MHEasterby)* 3-7-13 JFanning(4) (w ldr pllng hrd: led ½-wy tl over 2f out: kpt on same pce) .... s.h 3
1249[9] Flamboro **(60)***(43) (JDBethell)* 3-8-4 GDuffield(2) (trckd ldrs: drvn along & wl outpcd fr ½-wy) 9 4
1548[8] Rose Chime (IRE) **(52)***(29) (JLHarris)* 3-7-10 ow2 AMackay(1) (in tch tl lost pl ½-wy: sn bhd) 1¾ 5

5/4 HAWA AL NASAMAAT (USA), **100/30** Three Arch Bridge, **4/1** Bollin Frank, **6/1** Flamboro, **11/1** Rose Chime (IRE), CSF £5.45 TOTE £1.60: £1.40 £1.40 (£2.10) OWNER Maktoum Al Maktoum (NEWMARKET) BRED Bud Boschert's Stables Inc 5 Rn 1m 25.2 (3.20) SF: 57/28/28/13/-

1921

MARSKE CLAIMING STKS (4-Y.O+) (Class E) £3,143.50 (£943.00: £454.00: £209.50) **1m 6f 19y** Stalls: High GOING minus 0.28 sec per fur (GF) 4-10 (4-10)

1667* **Brodessa (59)***(56+)*(Fav)*(MrsMReveley)* 9-8-13 KDarley(6) (led after 1f: shkn up & wnt clr over 1f out: readily) .... — 1
1767[5] Thaleros **(59)***(48) (GMMoore)* 5-8-4 (5) JStack(1) (trckd ldrs: hdwy & ev ch 3f out: sn rdn: kpt on same pce) 3½ 2
894[2] Ijab (CAN) **(26)***(50) (JParkes)* 5-9-1 JFanning(4) (drvn along 5f out: kpt on one pce fnl 3f).... 3½ 3
1643[11] Leap in the Dark (IRE) **(38)***(47) (MissLCSiddall)* 6-9-1 GHind(2) (led 1f: chsd wnr: rdn over 3f out: sn wknd) 2½ 4
1606[2] Fret (USA) **(65)***(46) (JSWainwright)* 5-8-10 (5) NVarley(3) (chsd ldrs: pushed along 5f out: sn outpcd) .... ¾ 5
1606[3] Balzino (USA) **(50)***(40) (NTinkler)* 6-8-9 KimTinkler(5) (hld up & bhd: effrt & hung lft over 3f out: n.d) .... s.h 6

4/7 BRODESSA, **11/2** Thaleros (7/2-6/1), **8/1** Ijab (CAN), Fret (USA), **10/1** Balzino (USA), **25/1** Leap in the Dark (IRE), CSF £4.33 TOTE £1.50: £1.50 £1.40 (£2.40) OWNER Mr R. W. S. Jevon (SALTBURN) BRED B. Fairs 6 Rn 3m 5.9 (7.90) SF: 31/23/25/22/21/15

1922

GRIBDALE RATING RELATED MAIDEN LIMITED STKS (0-70) (3-Y.O) (Class E) £3,029.75 (£908.00: £436.50: £200.75)
1m 3f Stalls: High GOING minus 0.28 sec per fur (GF) 4-40 (4-40)

1784[2] **Finlaggan (68)***(67) (SirMarkPrescott)* 3-8-9 GDuffield(1) (lw: stdd s: hld up: hdwy to ld over 4f out: styd on wl: drvn out) .... — 1
1658[2] Dancing Destiny **(67)***(63)*(Fav)*(JRFanshawe)* 3-8-4 (5) NVarley(3) (chsd ldrs: drvn along & outpcd 5f out: sn rdn: kpt on same pce fnl 2f: no imp) 2½ 2
1452[W] Mill Thyme **(59)***(60) (MrsMReveley)* 3-8-9 KDarley(4) (led tl over 4f out: sn outpcd: rallied over 1f out: kpt on) 2½ 3

1383[6] Stormaway (ITY) **(63)***(61) (TGMills)* 3-9-0 AMackay(2) (hld up: hdwy & ev ch 4f out: rdn & wknd 2f out) 2½ 4

5/4 Dancing Destiny (4/5-11/8), **13/8** FINLAGGAN, **5/1** Stormaway (ITY), **8/1** Mill Thyme, CSF £3.92 TOTE £3.10: (£1.60) OWNER Mrs C. R. Philipson (NEWMARKET) BRED Mrs C. R. Philipson 4 Rn 2m 24.6 (8.90) SF: 8/4/1/2

T/Plpt: £38.00 (147.12 Tckts). T/Qdpt: £20.20 (0.95 Tckts). WG

1893-ASCOT (R-H)
Saturday June 24th (Firm)
WEATHER: overcast WIND: slt half bhd

1923
RITZ CLUB FERN HILL RATED STKS H'CAP (0-105) (Listed) (3-Y.O F) (Class A) £12,486.00 (£4,674.00: £2,287.00: £985.00: £442.50: £225.50)
1m (straight) Stalls: Centre GOING minus 0.26 sec per fur (GF) 2-00 (2-00)

868[4] **Cask (92)***(101)*(Fav)*(JHMGosden)* 3-9-1 LDettori(3) (hld up: hrd rdn over 1f out: led last stride) ....— 1
1131[3] Royal Rebuke **(89)***(98)*(Fav)*(RCharlton)* 3-8-12 PatEddery(9) (a.p: led over 2f out: hrd rdn over 1f out: hdd last stride) ....s.h 2
1675* Western Reel (USA) **(87)***(96)*(Fav)*(PFICole)* 3-8-10 TQuinn(8) (hdwy 2f out: hrd rdn 1f out: r.o wl) ....s.h 3
1242[6] Mandarina (USA) **(94)***(99) (LMCumani)* 3-9-3 WRSwinburn(2) (lw: hdwy over 1f out: hrd rdn: one pce) 2 4
1588[4] Menas Gold **(90)***(90) (SDow)* 3-8-13 MRoberts(1) (hdwy over 3f out: ev ch over 2f out: wknd over 1f out) 2½ 5
957[2] Avignon (IRE) **(85)***(85) (PWChapple-Hyam)* 3-8-8 JReid(6) (lw: chsd ldr: led over 3f out tl over 2f out: wknd over 1f out) ....hd 6
1588[7] Karayib (USA) **(84)***(80) (JLDunlop)* 3-8-7 RHills(5) (led over 4f: wknd over 1f out) 2 7
1500* Karayb (IRE) **(98)***(82)*(Fav)*(DMorley)* 3-9-7 WCarson(7) (hdwy 2f out: wknd over 1f out) 6 8
1500[5] Bring on the Choir **(88)***(54) (RBoss)* 3-8-11v BDoyle(10) (prom over 5f) 9 9
1066[5] Regal Fanfare (IRE) **(93)***(58) (JWHills)* 3-9-2 RCochrane(11) (hdwy over 4f out: wknd over 2f out) ....nk 10

LONG HANDICAP Karayib (USA) 8-6

5/1 CASK, Royal Rebuke, Western Reel (USA), Karayb (IRE), **11/2** Mandarina (USA), **8/1** Menas Gold, **12/1** Avignon (IRE), **16/1** Bring on the Choir, **25/1** Karayib (USA), **33/1** Regal Fanfare (IRE), CSF £27.17 CT £117.11 TOTE £4.60: £1.80 £1.40 £2.10 (£7.90) Trio £18.30 OWNER Lord Hartington (NEWMARKET) 10 Rn 1m 41.34 (2.14) SF: 57/54/52/55/46/41/36/38/10/14

1924
PALAN H'CAP (0-105) (3-Y.O) (Class B) £13,875.00 (£4,200.00: £2,050.00: £975.00) **5f** Stalls: Centre GOING minus 0.26 sec per fur (GF) 2-30 (2-31)

1373[4] **Espartero (IRE) (96)***(102) (SirMarkPrescott)* 3-9-3 PatEddery(1) (lw: racd stands' side: hld up: hrd rdn & edgd rt over 1f out: led last strides) ....— 1
1637* Double Quick (IRE) **(100)***(105)*(Fav)*(MJohnston)* 3-9-7 JWeaver(8) (hld up: ev ch fnl 2f: r.o wl) ....nk 2
1537[5] That Man Again **(81)***(86) (GLewis)* 3-7-11b(5) AWhelan(11) (lw: a.p: led over 1f out: hrd rdn: hdd last strides) ....s.h 3
1624[6] Fairy Wind (IRE) **(77)***(77) (NACallaghan)* 3-7-12 WCarson(10) (b.hind: led over 3f out tl over 1f out: unable qckn wl ins fnl f) 1½ 4
1677* Stolen Kiss (IRE) **(72)***(68) (MWEasterby)* 3-7-7b GBardwell(4) (a.p stands' side: rdn over 2f out: one pce) 1¼ 5
1564[7] Prolific Lady (IRE) **(72)***(68) (MBrittain)* 3-7-7b JQuinn(9) (lw: outpcd tl hdwy fnl f: nvr nrr) ....hd 6
1450[4] The Happy Fox (IRE) **(75)***(59) (BAMcMahon)* 3-7-10 ow1 FNorton(5) (hld up stands' side: rdn 3f out: wknd over 1f out) 3½ 7
1637[8] Musica **(80)***(64) (MRChannon)* 3-8-1v MRoberts(7) (a bhd) ....nk 8
1550[2] Sally Slade **(79)***(59) (CACyzer)* 3-8-0 DBiggs(6) (a bhd stands' side) 1¼ 9
1487[14] Tart and a Half **(81)***(54) (BJMeehan)* 3-8-2 BDoyle(12) (lw: led over 1f: wknd over 2f out) 2 10
1241[7] Golden Lady (IRE) **(84)***(53) (RHannon)* 3-8-5b TQuinn(2) (lw: a bhd stands' side) 1¼ 11
850[6] In Love Again (IRE) **(83)***(41) (MRChannon)* 3-8-4 CRutter(3) (lw: spd stands' side 3f) 3½ 12

LONG HANDICAP Prolific Lady (IRE) 7-6 Stolen Kiss (IRE) 7-4

7/2 Double Quick (IRE), **4/1** ESPARTERO (IRE), **13/2** Fairy Wind (IRE), **8/1** That Man Again, **10/1** Golden Lady (IRE), Sally Slade, **12/1** The Happy Fox (IRE) (8/1-14/1), Musica, **14/1** In Love Again (IRE), **20/1** Stolen Kiss (IRE), Tart and a Half, **33/1** Prolific Lady (IRE), CSF £17.36 CT £98.01 TOTE £4.80: £1.70 £1.60 £2.80 (£4.80) Trio £27.40 OWNER Mr Mario Lanfranchi (NEWMARKET) BRED G. S. Shropshire in Ireland 12 Rn 61.43 secs (1.93) SF: 47/50/31/22/13/13/4/9/4/-/-/-

1925 CHURCHILL CONDITIONS STKS (3-Y.O) (Class B) £9,783.00 (£3,423.00: £1,674.00: £720.00) **1m 4f** Stalls: High GOING minus 0.26 sec (GF) 3-00 (3-00)

1345[3] **Juyush (USA) (107)***(99)*(Fav)*(BWHills)* 3-8-13 WCarson(4) (led over 10f out: pushed out) ..— 1
1062[2] Warning Order **(100)***(92) (JLDunlop)* 3-8-11 LDettori(1) (lw: 2nd st: ev ch over 1f out: unable qckn)....4 2
1636[2] Stiffelio (IRE) **(100)***(84) (RHannon)* 3-8-13 PatEddery(2) (lw: lost pl over 4f out: 4th st: one pce fnl 3f)....7 3
1661[3] Soldier's Leap (FR) **(71)***(77) (CEBrittain)* 3-8-11v MRoberts(3) (led over 1f: rdn over 3f out: 3rd st: wknd over 2f out)....4 4

11/8 JUYUSH (USA) (10/11-6/4), **9/4** Warning Order, **5/2** Stiffelio (IRE), **14/1** Soldier's Leap (FR) (10/1-16/1), CSF £4.46 TOTE £2.10: (£2.30) OWNER Mr Hamdan Al Maktoum (LAMBOURN) BRED Corbin J. Robertson 4 Rn 2m 32.76 (3.26) SF: 55/48/40/33

1926 LADBROKE H'CAP (0-105) (4-Y.O+) (Class B) £18,562.50 (£5,625.00: £2,750.00: £1,312.50) **1m 2f** Stalls: High GOING minus 0.26 sec per fur (GF) 3-35 (3-35)

1188[2] **Salt Lake (94)***(106) (PWChapple-Hyam)* 4-9-6 JReid(10) (lw: led 9f out: hrd rdn over 1f out: r.o wl)....— 1
1610* Burooj **(100)***(110) (DMorley)* 5-9-12 WCarson(8) (hdwy over 1f out: r.o ins fnl f)....1¼ 2
981[2] Sadler's Walk **(72)***(81) (GWragg)* 4-7-12 FNorton(6) (lw: hdwy & nt clr run over 1f out: nt clr run 1f out: fin wl)....½ 3
1135[9] Old Hickory (IRE) **(99)***(108) (LMCumani)* 4-9-11b LDettori(4) (6th st: hrd rdn over 1f out: unable qckn)....nk 4
1357[2] Virtual Reality **(79)***(87) (AHide)* 4-8-5 AMcGlone(5) (lw: nt clr run over 2f out: hdwy & n.m.r over 1f out: r.o one pce)....¾ 5
1626* Khayrapour (IRE) **(84)***(88)*(Fav)*(BJMeehan)* 5-8-10b PatEddery(7) (lw: 5th st: nt clr run over 2f out: hrd rdn over 1f out: one pce)....2 6
1340[4] Desert Power **(67)***(71) (DBurchell)* 6-7-7 GBardwell(12) (lost pl over 5f out: one pce fnl 2f) ...hd 7
1183* Zajko (USA) **(79)***(79) (LadyHerries)* 5-8-5 ow1 RCochrane(3) (lw: hdwy over 1f out: sn wknd) ...2 8
1880[2] Shabanaz **(70)***(69) (WRMuir)* 10-7-3 (7)ow2 MartinDwyer(11) (nvr nr to chal)....hd 9
1314[6] Laxford Bridge **(81)***(79) (PWHarris)* 4-8-7 JWeaver(9) (lw: led 1f: 2nd st: rdn over 2f out: eased whn btn ins fnl f)....1¾ 10
1610[4] Embankment (IRE) **(88)***(84) (RHannon)* 5-9-0 TQuinn(2) (4th st: wknd over 1f out)....1½ 11
1792* Secret Aly (CAN) **(75)***(64) (CEBrittain)* 5-8-1 MRoberts(1) (lw: 3rd st: wkng whn hmpd over 1f out)....4 12
1808* Pride of Pendle **(73)***(62) (DNicholls)* 6-7-13 JQuinn(13) (7th st: wknd over 1f out)....nk 13

LONG HANDICAP Desert Power 6-12

100/30 Khayrapour (IRE), **5/1** Virtual Reality, **13/2** Sadler's Walk, **7/1** Zajko (USA), Burooj, **9/1** SALT LAKE, **11/1** Old Hickory (IRE), **12/1** Embankment (IRE), **14/1** Laxford Bridge, Pride of Pendle, **16/1** Secret Aly (CAN), **40/1** Shabanaz, **100/1** Desert Power, CSF £68.41 CT £408.26 TOTE £14.70: £4.50 £2.60 £2.10 (£26.10) Trio £124.00 OWNER Bloomsbury Stud (MARLBOROUGH) BRED Bloomsbury Stud 13 Rn 2m 7.72 (3.42) SF: 56/60/31/58/37/38/21/29/19/29/34/14/12

1927 FENWOLF MAIDEN STKS (3-Y.O) (Class D) £6,872.50 (£1,547.50: £1,547.50: £482.50) **1m (round)** Stalls: High GOING minus 0.26 sec per fur (GF) 4-10 (4-11)

1675[2] **Arabride** *(83) (JARToller)* 3-8-9 JWeaver(3) (lw: mde all: drvn out)....— 1
Grand du Lac (USA) *(86)*(Fav)*(DRLoder)* 3-9-0 PatEddery(5) (gd sort: 3rd st: hrd rdn over 1f out: unable qckn)....1¼ 2
978[4] Mackook (USA) **(87)***(86) (MRStoute)* 3-9-0 WRSwinburn(2) (2nd st: ev ch over 1f out: one pce)....d.h 2
Drum Battle *(70) (RCharlton)* 3-9-0 TQuinn(4) (unf: scope: s.s: 4th st: a bhd)....8 4
Cavil *(64) (CEBrittain)* 3-9-0 MRoberts(1) (str: scope: bit bkwd: rdn over 4f out: 5th st: wknd 3f out)....3 5

4/5 Grand du Lac (USA) (11/10-8/11), **3/1** ARABRIDE, **5/1** Mackook (USA) (7/2-11/2), **10/1** Drum Battle (4/1-11/1), **12/1** Cavil (6/1-14/1), CSF A GL £2.92, A & M £7.99 TOTE £3.90: £1.50, GL £0.60, M £0.80 (A & GL £1.30, A &M £3.10) OWNER Blandford (WHITSBURY) BRED W. H. F. Carson 5 Rn 1m 41.37 (1.77) SF: 55/58/58/42/36

1928 E.B.F. MAIDEN STKS (2-Y.O F) (Class D) £6,775.00 (£2,050.00: £1,000.00: £475.00) **6f** Stalls: Centre GOING minus 0.26 sec per fur (GF) 4-40 (4-40)

Bint Salsabil (USA) *(84+t) (JLDunlop)* 2-8-11 WCarson(1) (w'like: scope: bit bkwd: lost pl 3f out: rallied over 1f out: led ins fnl f: rdn out)....— 1

Prancing *(81t)*(Fav)*(DRLoder)* 2-8-11 LDettori(4) (str: scope: chsd ldr: led over 1f out tl ins fnl f: unable qckn)....1¼ 2
Marjaana (IRE) *(80t)* *(PTWalwyn)* 2-8-11 RHills(3) (w'like: scope: bit bkwd: s.s: rdn over 3f out: hdwy over 1f out: ev ch ins fnl f: one pce)....nk 3
Needham Star (USA) *(73t)* *(PAKelleway)* 2-8-11 JReid(2) (neat: led over 4f)....2½ 4
Al Shadeedah (USA) *(64t)* *(LMCumani)* 2-8-11 PatEddery(5) (leggy: hld up: rdn over 2f out: wknd over 1f out)....3½ 5

6/4 Prancing (Evens-13/8), **2/1** BINT SALSABIL (USA), **3/1** Al Shadeedah (USA) (tchd 9/2), **14/1** Marjaana (IRE) (7/1-16/1), **20/1** Needham Star (USA), CSF £5.13 TOTE £2.60: £1.40 £1.40 (£1.90) OWNER Mr Hamdan Al Maktoum (ARUNDEL) BRED Shadwell Estate Company Limited 5 Rn
1m 17.76 (4.16) SF: 19/16/15/8/-

1929

LEVY BOARD H'CAP (0-80) (3-Y.O+) (Class D) £7,165.00 (£2,170.00: £1,060.00: £505.00)
2m 45y Stalls: High GOING minus 0.26 sec per fur (GF) 5-10 (5-10)

1444[2] **French Ivy (USA) (59)***(73)* *(FMurphy)* 8-8-10 RCochrane(8) (b: hdwy over 3f out: 6th st: hrd rdn over 1f out: led wl ins fnl f: r.o wl)....— 1
1386[5] Thunderheart **(72)***(85)*(Fav)*(LMCumani)* 4-9-9 LDettori(10) (4th st: led over 1f out tl wl ins fnl f: unable qckn)....1½ 2
1840[5] Paradise Navy **(72)***(85)* *(CREgerton)* 6-9-9 RHughes(4) (bhd whn hmpd over 3f out: hdwy over 1f out: r.o wl)....s.h 3
1695* Wild Strawberry **(62)***(72)* *(MissBSanders)* 6-8-10 (3) SSanders(2) (led over 9f out tl over 1f out: one pce)....2½ 4
1773[2] Chakalak **(47)***(55)* *(SDow)* 7-7-12 FNorton(7) (lw: rdn & hdwy over 5f out: 2nd st: n.m.r over 1f out: swtchd rt: eased whn btn ins fnl f)....2½ 5
1773* Moonlight Quest **(72)***(78)* *(BHanbury)* 7-9-9 JWeaver(11) (nvr nr to chal)....1¾ 6
1794[4] Cuango (IRE) **(73)***(77)* *(RHollinshead)* 4-9-10 PatEddery(12) (hdwy over 5f out: 5th st: wknd over 2f out)....2 7
1444[7] Sarazar (USA) **(42)***(42)* *(RAkehurst)* 6-7-7 JQuinn(1) (lw: rdn over 5f out: 3rd st: wknd over 1f out)....3½ 8
1794[11] Tukano (CAN) **(75)***(70)* *(JRJenkins)* 4-9-12 MRoberts(6) (lw: led over 6f: wknd over 1f out)....5 9
1858[4] Soojama (IRE) **(42)***(36)* *(RMFlower)* 5-7-7 NAdams(5) (hdwy over 3f out: wknd over 2f out)....2 10
1826[4] Record Lover (IRE) **(45)***(9)* *(MCChapman)* 5-7-10 GBardwell(13) (a bhd: t.o)....30 11
995[4] Fujiyama Crest (IRE) **(66)***(5)*(Fav)*(MRStoute)* 3-7-12v WCarson(9) (b.nr hind: bhd whn bdly hmpd on ins over 3f out: nt rcvr: t.o)....25 12

LONG HANDICAP Soojama (IRE) 7-6

5/1 Thunderheart, Fujiyama Crest (IRE) (7/2-11/2), **6/1** Chakalak, **13/2** FRENCH IVY (USA), **7/1** Wild Strawberry, Cuango (IRE), **8/1** Sarazar (USA) (6/1-9/1), **9/1** Paradise Navy, Moonlight Quest (6/1-10/1), **16/1** Soojama (IRE), **33/1** Tukano (CAN), **50/1** Record Lover (IRE), CSF £39.00 CT £277.26 TOTE £7.60: £2.20 £1.90 £3.40 (£28.60) OWNER Mr K. Flood (WELLINGTON) BRED John A. Nerud Revocable Trust 12 Rn 3m 36.67 (10.17) SF: 26/38/38/25/8/31/30/-/23/-/-/-
WEIGHT FOR AGE 3yo-19lb

T/Jkpt: £1,398.20 (7.4 Tckts). T/Plpt: £18.10 (2,973.76 Tckts). T/Qdpt: £7.60 (53.65 Tckts). AK

1899-AYR (L-H)
Saturday June 24th (Firm)

WEATHER: sunny & hot WIND: almost nil

1930

LONGHILL MAIDEN STKS (3-Y.O F) (Class D) £3,860.00 (£1,085.00: £530.00)
1m Stalls: Low GOING minus 0.19 sec per fur (GF) 2-15 (2-15)

1533[3] **Lucky Soph (USA) (73)***(72)*(Fav)*(BWHills)* 3-8-11 MHills(2) (b.hind: qcknd 3f out: unchal)..— 1
1431[3] Thatcher's Era (IRE) *(69)* *(TDBarron)* 3-8-11 KFallon(1) (nvr able to chal)....1¾ 2
Harrken Heights (IRE) *(39)* *(JSGoldie)* 3-8-6 (5) NVarley(3) (b: chsd wnr tl outpcd fnl 3f)....15 3

4/7 LUCKY SOPH (USA), **6/4** Thatcher's Era (IRE), **20/1** Harrken Heights (IRE), CSF £1.70 TOTE £1.30: (£1.10) OWNER Newbyth Stud (LAMBOURN) BRED Mandysland Farm 3 Rn
1m 43.12 (6.32) SF: 16/13/-

1931

ROMAN WARRIOR SHIELD MAIDEN STKS (3-Y.O+) (Class D) £3,647.50 (£1,105.00: £540.00: £257.50)
7f Stalls: Low GOING minus 0.19 sec per fur (GF) 2-45 (2-46)

1296[2] **Khamseh (77)***(88)* *(JWWatts)* 3-8-7 BThomson(4) (trckd ldrs: led 1½f out: r.o)....— 1
1615[2] Sparrowhawk (IRE) **(92)***(82)*(Fav)*(BWHills)* 3-8-7 MHills(2) (led tl hdd 1½f out: one pce)......2½ 2

17616 Halfabob (IRE) *(69) (DHaydnJones)* 3-8-12 AMackay(5) (cl up tl rdn & btn over 2f out)...........8 3
Cavendish Rose *(48) (JBerry)* 4-9-2 JCarroll(1) (lengthy: s.i.s: effrt over 3f out: no imp)..........7 4
16308 Rossini Blue **(70)** *(ABailey)* 4-9-7b LCharnock(3) (s.s: hdwy whn sddle slipped & uns rdr over 2f out).. U

Evens Sparrowhawk (IRE), **5/4** KHAMSEH, **10/1** Rossini Blue (8/1-14/1), **20/1** Cavendish Rose, **50/1** Halfabob (IRE), CSF £2.75 TOTE £2.30: £1.20 £1.10 (£1.10) OWNER Sheikh Mohammed (RICHMOND) BRED Sheikh Mohammed bin Rashid al Maktoum 5 Rn

1m 26.38 (2.38) SF: 48/42/29/17/-
WEIGHT FOR AGE 3yo-9lb

1932 ROTHMANS ROYALS NORTH SOUTH CHALLENGE SERIES H'CAP (0-85) (3-Y.O+) (Class D) £5,628.00 (£1,704.00: £832.00: £396.00)
7f Stalls: Low GOING minus 0.19 sec per fur (GF) 3-15 (3-20)

14684 **Hi Nod (78)***(84) (MJCamacho)* 5-9-7 LCharnock(3) (lw: trckd ldr: r.o u.p to ld wl ins fnl f) .....— 1
1809* Al Wujud (IRE) **(55)***(59) (TDyer)* 4-7-12 JFanning(5) (a.p: effrt & n.m.r over 1f out: r.o nr fin) ...1 2
1421* Don Pepe **(71)***(75)*(Fav)*(RBoss)* 4-9-0 MHills(8) (lw: cl up: led wl over 1f out: sn rdn: hdd & no ex wl ins fnl f)..hd 3
1603* Allinson's Mate (IRE) **(73)***(76) (TDBarron)* 7-9-2b KFallon(7) (hld up: effrt & swtchd 2f out: r.o)..s.h 4
168711 Persian Fayre **(70)***(70) (JBerry)* 3-8-4 JCarroll(4) (bhd: hdwy 3f out: nvr rchd ldrs)................1½ 5
18283 Profit Release (IRE) **(58)***(53) (MJohnston)* 4-8-1b PRobinson(1) (led over 5f: wknd ins fnl f).....2 6
17232 Teejay'n'aitch (IRE) **(62)***(46) (JSGoldie)* 3-7-5 (5)ow3 NVarley(9) (prom: effrt over 2f out: hung lft & grad wknd)..3½ 7
16897 Persian Affair (IRE) **(71)***(58)*(Fav)*(DHaydnJones)* 4-9-0 AMackay(2) (hld up & bhd: effrt on outside 3f out: no imp)...nk 8
43916 General Chaos (IRE) **(87)***(53) (JJO'Neill)* 5-9-11 (5)ow2 ARoche(6) (chsd ldr tl rdn & wknd over 2f out)...8 9

LONG HANDICAP Teejay'n'aitch (IRE) 7-0

4/1 Persian Affair (IRE), Don Pepe, **11/2** Al Wujud (IRE) (7/2-6/1), **6/1** Profit Release (IRE), Allinson's Mate (IRE), **15/2** HI NOD, **12/1** Teejay'n'aitch (IRE), **14/1** Persian Fayre, **33/1** General Chaos (IRE), CSF £43.18 CT £169.13 TOTE £7.80: £2.20 £2.90 £1.10 (£15.00) Trio £12.40 OWNER Mr Brian Nordan (MALTON) BRED B. Nordan 9 Rn

1m 25.9 (1.90) SF: 67/42/58/59/44/36/20/41/36
WEIGHT FOR AGE 3yo-9lb

1933 SUNDAY EXPRESS BEST FOR SPORT SERIES QUALIFIER H'CAP (0-80) (3-Y.O+) (Class D) £4,162.50 (£1,260.00: £615.00: £292.50)
1m 2f Stalls: Low GOING minus 0.19 sec per fur (GF) 3-45 (3-46)

168712 **King Curan (USA) (61)***(70) (ABailey)* 4-9-0b JCarroll(2) (lw: mde all: hld on wl) ....— 1
1688* Askern **(65)***(73) (DHaydnJones)* 4-9-4 AMackay(4) (hld up: hdwy to trck ldr appr st: ev ch & rdn 1f out: kpt on)..½ 2
18172 Keep Battling **(43)***(47)*(Fav)*(JSGoldie)* 5-7-5 (5)ow2 NVarley(3) (lw: hld up: hdwy over 2f out: ev ch 1f out: nt qckn)...1½ 3
135710 Mowlaie **(74)***(73) (JDBethell)* 4-9-13 BThomson(5) (prom tl outpcd fnl 2½f)...............................4 4
13263 Dosses Dan (IRE) **(75)***(60) (BWHills)* 3-9-2 MHills(1) (cl up tl wknd fnl 2½f) 9 5

7/4 Keep Battling, **3/1** Askern, **5/1** Dosses Dan (IRE), **6/1** KING CURAN (USA) (4/1-7/1), **7/1** Mowlaie (5/1-10/1), CSF £20.64 TOTE £9.30: £4.30 £1.60 (£16.50) OWNER Mrs M. O'Donnell (TARPORLEY) BRED Executive Bloodstock & Adstock Manor Stud 5 Rn

2m 9.64 (5.04) SF: 43/46/20/46/21
WEIGHT FOR AGE 3yo-12lb

1934 DOONFOOT LIMITED STKS (0-65) (3-Y.O+) (Class F) £2,655.50 (£748.00: £366.50) **1m 7f** Stalls: Low GOING minus 0.19 sec per fur (GF) 4-15 (4-16)

14623 **Hit the Canvas (USA) (65)***(58)*(Fav)*(MrsMReveley)* 4-9-10v MHills(3) (mde virtually all: styd on u.p fnl 3f)..— 1
99111 My Kerry Dancer (USA) **(65)***(55) (JJO'Neill)* 5-9-12 (5)ow7 ARoche(1) (hld up: styng on whn hmpd ins fnl f: fin 3rd, 3½l: plcd 2nd)... 2
16816 Nouvelle Cuisine **(52)***(51) (GMMoore)* 7-9-0 (5) CTeague(2) (wnt 2nd ½-wy: chal 3½f out: sn rdn & hung lft: one pce fnl f: fin 2nd, 1l: disq: plcd 3rd) 3

2/7 HIT THE CANVAS (USA), **5/1** Nouvelle Cuisine (op 3/1), **9/1** My Kerry Dancer (USA) (op 4/1), CSF £1.82 TOTE £1.20: (£1.20) OWNER Mr P. D. Savill (SALTBURN) BRED Jack Lancaster, George and Keith Lancaster 3 Rn 3m 21.85 (11.75) SF: 32/29/25

1935

BELLEISLE MEDIAN AUCTION MAIDEN STKS (2-Y.O) (Class F) £2,750.00 (£775.00: £380.00) **6f** Stalls: Low GOING minus 0.19 sec per fur (GF) 4-45 (4-48)

1627[5] **Leith Academy (USA)** *(64)*(Fav)*(BWHills)* 2-8-9 MHills(5) (lw: hld up: hdwy to ld 1½f out: rdn & r.o ins fnl f) — **1**
King of Peru *(64) (APJarvis)* 2-9-0 BThomson(6) (w'like: scope: lw: dwlt: hdwy 7f out: chsng wnr ins fnl f: nt qckn) 2 **2**
1494[3] Craignairn *(50) (JBerry)* 2-9-0 JCarroll(4) (chsd ldrs: outpcd ½-wy: styd on u.p fnl f) 5 **3**
1440[5] Globe Runner *(50) (JJO'Neill)* 2-9-0 AMackay(3) (trckd ldrs: ev ch 2f out: sn rdn & nt qckn) .hd **4**
1670[14] Ginger Hodgers *(44) (RMWhitaker)* 2-8-9 ACulhane(7) (led over 3f: sn outpcd) nk **5**
490[7] Saturiba (USA) *(48) (MJohnston)* 2-9-0 PRobinson(1) (cl up: led wl over 2f out tl over 1f out: sn wknd) ½ **6**
Ballykissangel *(29) (NBycroft)* 2-9-0 KFallon(2) (wl grwn: a outpcd & bhd) 7 **7**

15/8 LEITH ACADEMY (USA) (6/1-9/4), **3/1** King of Peru (op 2/1), **5/1** Craignairn, **7/1** Saturiba (USA), **15/2** Ballykissangel, **9/1** Globe Runner, **12/1** Ginger Hodgers (8/1-14/1), CSF £8.02 TOTE £2.40: £1.80 £2.20 (£6.10) OWNER Newbyth Stud (LAMBOURN) BRED Harold Black and Arthur Hancock III 7 Rn
1m 14.89 (5.09) SF: 4/4/-/-/-/-/-

1936

ALLOWAY H'CAP (0-80) (3-Y.O) (Class D) £3,647.50 (£1,105.00: £540.00: £257.50) **5f** Stalls: Low GOING minus 0.19 sec per fur (GF) 5-15 (5-18)

1414[8] **Tedburrow (61)***(62) (MrsAMNaughton)* 3-8-9 KFallon(6) (in tch: n.m.r over 1f out: str run ins fnl f to ld last stride) — **1**
1822[2] Mister Westsound **(45)***(46) (MissLAPerratt)* 3-7-0b(7) BHalligan(3) (in tch: hdwy over 1f out: rdn to ld cl home: jst ct) s.h **2**
1641* Surprise Mission **(73)***(73)*(Fav)*(RMWhitaker)* 3-9-7 ACulhane(2) (b: lw: plld hrd: trckd ldrs: led wl over 1f out tl ct cl home) nk **3**
1677[7] Arasong **(65)***(59) (EWeymes)* 3-8-13 MHills(5) (cl up: rdn & nt qckn fnl 2f) 1¾ **4**
1660[14] Nordesta (IRE) **(60)***(54) (MRChannon)* 3-8-8 BThomson(4) (lw: led over 3f out: sn btn) hd **5**
1279[11] Blue Lugana **(48)***(35) (NBycroft)* 3-7-10bow3 AMackay(7) (lw: dwlt: nvr wnt pce) 1¼ **6**
1822[6] Ramborette **(51)***(35) (DenysSmith)* 3-7-13v JFanning(8) (plld hrd: chsd ldr over 3f) 1¾ **7**
LONG HANDICAP Mister Westsound 7-3 Blue Lugana 7-4

11/10 Surprise Mission, **11/2** Mister Westsound, **6/1** Arasong, **7/1** TEDBURROW, Nordesta (IRE), **14/1** Ramborette, **20/1** Blue Lugana, CSF £40.17 CT £66.02 TOTE £11.80: £3.40 £2.10 (£30.60) OWNER Mr Philip Davies (RICHMOND) BRED Lady Matthews 7 Rn
59.74 secs (2.74) SF: 29/13/40/26/21/2/2

T/Plpt: £10.40 (658.95 Tckts). T/Qdpt: £15.60 (3 Tckts). AA

1784-LINGFIELD (L-H)
Saturday June 24th (Turf Good to firm, Firm patches, AWT Standard)

WEATHER: overcast WIND: slt half across

1937

TAIWAN AMATEUR H'CAP (0-70) (3-Y.O+) (Class F) £3,249.80 (£902.80: £433.40) **1m 3f 106y** Stalls: High GOING minus 0.37 sec per fur (F) 6-35 (6-36)

1622[3] **Stalled (IRE) (48)***(63) (PTWalwyn)* 5-10-4 (5) MarchionesBlandford(3) (hld up: hdwy 6f out: 4th st: led over 1f out: comf) — **1**
1730[2] Santella Boy (USA) **(55)***(65)*(Fav)*(GHarwood)* 3-10-2 MissAHarwood(14) (led tl over 1f out: one pce) 3½ **2**
1714[4] Top Pet (IRE) **(57)***(67) (RAkehurst)* 5-11-4 MrTMcCarthy(6) (3rd st: rdn over 1f out: one pce) hd **3**
13[7] Strat's Legacy **(46)***(46) (DWPArbuthnot)* 8-10-7 MrsDArbuthnot(4) (bit bkwd: 8th st: r.o one pce fnl 2f) 7 **4**
1622[13] Queens Contractor **(35)***(30) (SMellor)* 5-9-5b(5) MissEJoyce(11) (a.p: 2nd st: rdn over 2f out: grad wknd) 4 **5**
Phanan **(40)***(33) (REPeacock)* 9-9-10 (5) MrsCPeacock(7) (b: 7th st: rdn 3f out: no hdwy) 1½ **6**
879[16] Rapporteur (USA) **(53)***(43) (CCElsey)* 9-11-0 MissAElsey(1) (b: in tch tl lost pl after 2f: 9th st: rdn 2f out: r.o one pce fnl f) 1¾ **7**
1784[7] Sadler's Pearl **(48)***(36) (BJMeehan)* 3-9-9b MissJAllison(9) (dwlt: nvr nrr) 1¼ **8**
1518[7] Beautete **(47)***(35) (SDow)* 4-10-8 MrTCuff(8) (5th st: wknd over 2f out) ½ **9**
Aramon **(35)***(22) (MJHaynes)* 5-9-10 MissYHaynes(15) (10th st: sn rdn & no hdwy) ¾ **10**
1745[11] Remember This (IRE) **(32)***(16) (CACyzer)* 5-9-2 (5)ow2 MissAWilcox(2) (a bhd) nk **11**
1401[3] Ikhtiraa (USA) **(46)***(28) (RJO'Sullivan)* 5-10-2 (5) MrKSantana(13) (bhd fnl 4f) 3 **12**

1695[5] Total Joy (IRE) **(60)***(41) (PFICole)* 4-11-7b MrJDurkan(10) (dwlt: sn rcvrd: 6th st: wknd over 2f out) .... ½ **13**
Macedonas **(47)***(28) (GThorner)* 7-10-3 (5) MrKWheate(12) (dwlt: a bhd) .... s.h **14**
1534[9] Hi Penny **(38)** *(KTIvory)* 4-9-8b(5)ow5 MrDMarshall(16) (racd wd: bhd fnl 4f: t.o) 15 **15**
1788* Katie's Kid **(36)** *(MJAhern)* 5-9-6 (5) MissEFolkes(5) (b: prom 7f: t.o) **16**

11/4 Santella Boy (USA), **5/1** STALLED (IRE), **15/2** Katie's Kid (5/1-8/1), **8/1** Top Pet (IRE), Total Joy (IRE) (5/1-9/1), **10/1** Beautete (8/1-12/1), **14/1** Ikhtiraa (USA), **16/1** Strat's Legacy, **20/1** Queens Contractor, Rapporteur (USA), **25/1** Sadler's Pearl, **33/1** Hi Penny, Aramon, Macedonas, Remember This (IRE), **50/1** Phanan, CSF £18.35 CT £103.74 TOTE £6.50: £2.00 £1.40 £1.60 £2.00 (£11.40) Trio £19.90 OWNER Mrs P. T. Walwyn (LAMBOURN) BRED D. Aykroyd 16 Rn
2m 28.65 (6.65) SF: 44/32/48/27/11/14/24/3/16/3/-/9/22/9/-/-
WEIGHT FOR AGE 3yo-14lb

1938

KYOTO MAIDEN AUCTION STKS (2-Y.O) (Class E) £3,473.80 (£1,038.40: £497.20: £226.60) **5f** Stalls: High GOING minus 0.37 sec (F) 7-05 (7-11)

1341[4] **Midnight Escape** (Fav)*(CFWall)* 2-8-6 NCarlisle(15) (mde all: rdn ins fnl f: r.o wl) .... — **1**
1690[9] Where's Margaret *(GLewis)* 2-7-10 (5)ow1 AWhelan(14) (hld up: hdwy & swtchd lft 2f out: rdn & ev ch fnl f: r.o) .... ½ **2**
782[3] Clan Chief *(JRArnold)* 2-8-6 TQuinn(13) (b.off hind: a.p: rdn & ev ch ins fnl f: one pce) 1¼ **3**
1481[6] Meranti *(LJHolt)* 2-8-8 JReid(7) (a.p: ev ch 1f out: one pce) 1¼ **4**
Step On Degas *(SDow)* 2-7-13 JQuinn(10) (w'like: s.s: bhd: rdn over 1f out: r.o strly fnl f) . 1½ **5**
1142[7] Dil Dil *(RHannon)* 2-8-3 RPerham(5) (a.p: ev ch 1f out: wknd ins fnl f) 1½ **6**
1536[10] Miss Carottene *(MJRyan)* 2-8-3b AClark(2) (a mid div) .... ½ **7**
1653[8] Clincher Club *(MJohnston)* 2-8-2 MRoberts(4) (prom over 3f) 3½ **8**
Efficacious (IRE) *(CJBenstead)* 2-8-3 DBiggs(16) (unf: bit bkwd: dwlt: nvr nrr) 1½ **9**
1690[12] Rowlandsons Charm (IRE) *(GLMoore)* 2-7-13 FNorton(6) (a mid div) 1¼ **10**
Pearls of Thought (IRE) *(PTWalwyn)* 2-8-0 AMcGlone(1) (neat: a bhd) 1 **11**
1662[14] Victory Commander *(TJNaughton)* 2-8-8 JWeaver(3) (a bhd) 1 **12**
1253[10] Riviere Rouge *(SGKnight)* 2-7-10 (3) SSanders(8) (prom to ½-wy) .... ½ **13**
Pinocchio Boy (IRE) *(BJMeehan)* 2-8-6 LDettori(12) (w'like: bit bkwd: chsd ldrs to ½-wy) .. 2½ **14**
Another Picea *(KTIvory)* 2-8-1 (7)ow4 CScally(9) (w'like: bit bkwd: s.s: a bhd) 1½ **15**

3/1 MIDNIGHT ESCAPE, **5/1** Pinocchio Boy (IRE), **11/2** Where's Margaret, **6/1** Dil Dil, **15/2** Clan Chief (4/1-8/1), **9/1** Meranti, **14/1** Clincher Club, Rowlandsons Charm (IRE), **16/1** Pearls of Thought (IRE), **20/1** Miss Carottene, **25/1** Efficacious (IRE), **33/1** Victory Commander, Riviere Rouge, Step On Degas, Another Picea, CSF £20.38 TOTE £4.40: £1.80 £2.00 £2.60 (£13.80) Trio £34.10 OWNER Mr Mervyn Ayers (NEWMARKET) BRED M. L. Ayers 15 Rn
59.62 secs (2.62) SF: 14/6/8/6/-/-/-/-/-/-/-/-/-/-/-

1939

BEIJING MAIDEN H'CAP (0-65) (3-Y.O+) (Class F) £3,048.20 (£845.20: £404.60) **1m (Equitrack)** Stalls: High GOING minus 0.65 sec per fur (FST) 7-35 (7-38)

1368[8] **El Bailador (IRE) (58)***(66) (JDBethell)* 4-9-12 JWeaver(3) (hld up: rdn & hdwy 3f out: led ins fnl f: r.o) .... — **1**
1426[13] Kellaire Girl (IRE) **(46)***(51) (GLewis)* 3-7-13 (5) AWhelan(2) (mid div: rdn over 2f out: hdwy over 1f out: r.o fnl f) 1¾ **2**
Ninia (USA) **(48)***(52) (MJohnston)* 3-8-6 JReid(4) (a.p: led over 1f out tl ins fnl f: one pce) .... ½ **3**
1512[14] Saltis (IRE) **(58)***(59) (DWPArbuthnot)* 3-9-2 TQuinn(9) (a.p: led over 2f out tl over 1f out: one pce) 1¼ **4**
1534[11] Guest Alliance (IRE) **(54)***(52) (AMoore)* 3-8-12 CandyMorris(6) (mid div tl rdn & lost pl over 3f out: hrd rdn 2f out: r.o one pce fnl f) 1¾ **5**
1548[7] Most Welcome News **(50)***(47) (JRJenkins)* 3-8-8b MRoberts(7) (prom tl rdn & outpcd over 2f out: kpt on one pce fnl f) .... ½ **6**
1446[9] Pharly Reef **(60)***(55)*(Fav)*(IABalding)* 3-9-4v LDettori(11) (led tl over 2f out: wknd 1f out: eased whn btn) 1 **7**
1402[6] Riva Rock **(32)***(23) (TPMcGovern)* 5-8-0 JQuinn(8) (mid div: rdn 3f out: one pce fnl 2f) 2 **8**
1593[6] Glitterazzi **(60)***(37) (LMontagueHall)* 4-10-0 RPerham(1) (s.s: a bhd) 7 **9**
1353[8] Claudia Habibi (IRE) **(52)***(22) (CCElsey)* 3-8-10 CRutter(12) (bhd fnl 4f) 3½ **10**
Nellyssia (FR) **(65)***(28) (GLMoore)* 3-9-2 (7) LSuthern(5) (a bhd) 2½ **11**

100/30 Pharly Reef (2/1-7/2), **7/2** Ninia (USA), **4/1** EL BAILADOR (IRE) (3/1-9/2), **7/1** Kellaire Girl (IRE), **8/1** Saltis (IRE), **10/1** Riva Rock (8/1-12/1), **12/1** Most Welcome News, **20/1** Nellyssia (FR), **33/1** Glitterazzi, Claudia Habibi (IRE), Guest Alliance (IRE), CSF £30.01 CT £95.16 TOTE £4.70: £1.50 £2.40 £1.60 (£14.70) Trio £20.50 OWNER Mrs John Lee (MIDDLEHAM) BRED Miss Anne Reid 11 Rn
1m 38.76 (2.36) SF: 32/7/8/15/8/3/11/-/3/-/-
WEIGHT FOR AGE 3yo-10lb

1940 SOLSTICE H'CAP (0-60) (3-Y.O+) (Class F) £3,501.80 (£974.80: £469.40)
1m 1f Stalls: High GOING minus 0.37 sec per fur (F) 8-05 (8-07)

1716⁵ **Mister O'Grady (IRE) (42)***(51) (RAkehurst)* 4-8-10 TQuinn(3) (3rd st: led over 1f out: hrd rdn fnl f: r.o) ......— **1**
1254⁸ Marchman **(45)***(53) (JSKing)* 10-8-13 AMcGlone(7) (8th st: hdwy 2f out: hrd rdn fnl f: r.o) ......½ **2**
1792⁷ Kindergarten Boy (IRE) **(58)***(66) (RBoss)* 4-9-12 JWeaver(6) (led tl over 1f out: ev ch fnl f: unable qckn) ......nk **3**
1663⁵ Hatta Sunshine (USA) **(39)***(45) (AMoore)* 5-8-4 (3) SSanders(10) (7th st: hdwy 2f out: rdn over 1f out: one pce) ......¾ **4**
1519⁴ Rival Bid (USA) **(59)***(64)*(Fav)*(MAJarvis)* 7-9-13 LDettori(14) (hld up: 9th st: hdwy 2f out: rdn over 1f out: one pce) 1 **5**
1714¹³ Courting Newmarket **(47)***(48) (MrsAKnight)* 7-8-12 (3) DRMcCabe(4) (4th st: rdn 2f out: one pce) 2 **6**
1656³ Fresh Look (IRE) **(62)***(56) (RFJohnsonHoughton)* 3-9-5 JQuinn(1) (6th st: wknd over 2f out) 4 **7**
1183¹² Prenonamoss **(58)***(52) (DWPArbuthnot)* 7-9-12 JReid(9) (5th st: wknd over 2f out) ......s.h **8**
1472⁷ Roi de la Mer (IRE) **(60)***(52) (JAkehurst)* 4-10-0v RHughes(5) (chsd ldr: 2nd st: wknd 2f out: eased whn btn fnl f) 1 **9**
1855¹⁰ Oozlem (IRE) **(38)***(28) (RMFlower)* 6-8-6v DBiggs(13) (dwlt: a bhd) 1 **10**
Le Sorcier **(58)***(22) (GPEnright)* 3-9-1 MPerrett(11) (dwlt: a bhd) 15 **11**
1499¹⁷ Coalisland **(32)** *(RIngram)* 5-8-0 NAdams(12) (a bhd) ......s.h **12**
Michaelmas Park (IRE) **(55)** *(TMJones)* 4-9-9 RPerham(8) (a bhd: t.o) 20 **13**

2/1 Rival Bid (USA), **5/1** MISTER O'GRADY (IRE), **6/1** Fresh Look (IRE), **15/2** Roi de la Mer (IRE), **10/1** Kindergarten Boy (IRE), Hatta Sunshine (USA), **12/1** Prenonamoss, **14/1** Marchman (10/1-20/1), **16/1** Oozlem (IRE), **33/1** Courting Newmarket, **50/1** Le Sorcier, Coalisland, Michaelmas Park (IRE), CSF £67.01 ct £614.93 tote £5.80: £2.00 £4.50 £3.30 (£42.60) Trio £361.10; £45.79 to 26/6/95 OWNER City Industrial Supplies Ltd (EPSOM) BRED A. Ross 13 Rn
1m 52.76 (0.24 under best) (3.46) SF: 33/35/48/27/46/30/27/34/34/10/-/-/-
WEIGHT FOR AGE 3yo-11lb

1941 HONG KONG LIMITED STKS (0-85) (3-Y.O) (Class D) £3,732.30 (£1,112.40: £530.20: £239.10)
7f Stalls: High GOING minus 0.37 sec per fur (F) 8-35 (8-37)

1754⁶ **Maiandros (GR) (82)***(88) (RCharlton)* 3-9-0 JWeaver(4) (took keen hold: chsd ldrs: led over 1f out: r.o) ......— **1**
1222⁵ Te Amo (IRE) **(84)***(82) (RAkehurst)* 3-8-11 TQuinn(2) (chsd ldr: rdn 2f out: led wl over 1f out: sn hdd: one pce) 1¼ **2**
1244² Captain's Day **(81)***(82)*(Fav)*(TGMills)* 3-8-11 LDettori(1) (hld up: rdn over 1f out: one pce fnl f) ......nk **3**
1639¹⁰ Shen Yang (USA) **(80)***(81) (GLMoore)* 3-8-9 (5) AWhelan(3) (led tl wl over 1f out: wknd fnl f) 1¾ **4**

13/8 Captain's Day, **15/8** Te Amo (IRE), **7/2** MAIANDROS (GR), **6/1** Shen Yang (USA), CSF £9.55 TOTE £4.30: (£4.50) OWNER Ippotour A (BECKHAMPTON) BRED Ippotour S A 4 Rn
1m 22.94 (2.34) SF: 38/32/32/31

1942 SINGAPORE H'CAP (0-70) (3-Y.O+) (Class E) £3,388.00 (£1,012.00: £484.00: £220.00) **5f** Stalls: High GOING minus 0.37 sec per fur (F) 9-05 (9-06)

1400⁶ **Tee-Emm (37)***(45) (PHowling)* 5-8-0 JQuinn(1) (mde all: drvn out) ......— **1**
1660¹³ Tachycardia **(51)***(57) (RJO'Sullivan)* 3-8-4 (3) SSanders(3) (a.p: ev ch over 1f out: hrd rdn fnl f: r.o) ......¾ **2**
1515² High Priest **(68)***(73)*(Fav)*(LMCumani)* 3-9-10 LDettori(4) (chsd ldrs: rdn over 1f out: one pce) ......hd **3**
1738³ Sison (IRE) **(58)***(61) (KGWingrove)* 5-9-4 (3) DRMcCabe(5) (chsd ldrs: outpcd 2f out: rdn & hung lft over 1f out: one pce fnl f) ......¾ **4**
1538² Windrush Boy **(60)***(59) (JRBosley)* 5-9-9 RPerham(8) (rr: hdwy 2f out: rdn over 1f out: one pce) 1¼ **5**
1534¹³ Riskie Things **(48)***(47) (JSMoore)* 4-8-11 NAdams(6) (chsd ldrs: rdn 2f out: n.m.r over 4f out: eased whn btn fnl f) ......s.h **6**
1602³ La Belle Dominique **(58)***(57) (SGKnight)* 3-9-0 VSlattery(7) (a.p: ev ch 1f out: wknd ins fnl f) ......s.h **7**

1566[14] Swallowdale **(46)***(32) (CFWall)* 3-8-2 NCarlisle(2) (prom to ½-wy) 4 **8**

7/4 High Priest (6/4-9/4), **7/2** Tachycardia, **5/1** La Belle Dominique, **11/2** Windrush Boy (4/1-6/1), **10/1** Sison (IRE) (6/1-12/1), **11/1** TEE-EMM (8/1-12/1), **20/1** Swallowdale, **25/1** Riskie Things, CSF £46.57 CT £91.58 TOTE £7.10: £1.60 £1.50 £1.10 (£10.90) OWNER Mr Robert Carey (NEWMARKET) BRED Marquess Townshend 8 Rn 58.84 secs (1.84) SF: 21/26/42/37/35/23/26/1

WEIGHT FOR AGE 3yo-7lb

T/Plpt: £226.90. T/Qdpt: £68.10. SM

1917-REDCAR (L-H)
Saturday June 24th (Firm, Good to firm patches)

WEATHER: drizzle WIND: mod half against

1943 LIVERTON (S) STKS (2-Y.O) (Class G) £2,582.50 (£720.00: £347.50)

7f Stalls: Centre GOING minus 0.02 sec per fur (G) 1-50 (2-02)

1670[10] **Sizzling Symphony** *(72+) (RAFahey)* 2-8-11 SMaloney(6) (lw: hdwy ½-wy: led over 2f out: drvn clr fnl f) ....— **1**

1665[3] Catwalk Girl *(51) (SGNorton)* 2-8-6v GHind(10) (a chsng ldrs: kpt on fnl 2f: no ch w wnr) 7 **2**

1665[8] Chilly Looks *(43) (MWEasterby)* 2-8-6 NKennedy(1) (swvd lft s: swtchd rt after 1f: bhd tl kpt on u.p fnl 2f: nvr nr ldrs) 3½ **3**

1665[9] Jackson Park *(47) (MHEasterby)* 2-8-11 MBirch(12) (sn outpcd: rdn ½-wy: styd on fnl 2f: nvr nr to chal) ....½ **4**

1665[6] Mels Baby (IRE) *(45) (JLEyre)* 2-8-11b RLappin(11) (led after 2f tl over 2f out: grad wknd) ....¾ **5**

1740[4] Veshca Lady (IRE) *(43) (EWeymes)* 2-8-12 TWilliams(7) (chsd ldrs tl wknd over 2f out) 1½ **6**

1841[11] Ceilidh (IRE) *(42) (PCHaslam)* 2-8-4 (7) CarolDavison(4) (bit bkwd: sn bhd: hung bdly lft 2f out: kpt on fnl f: n.d) ....hd **7**

1740[2] Miletrian Refurb (IRE) *(40)*(Fav)*(MRChannon)* 2-8-11 KDarley(5) (chsd ldrs: rdn over 2f out: sn wknd) ....½ **8**

1665[2] Kratz (IRE) *(37) (BSRothwell)* 2-8-4 (7) PFessey(3) (prom: wkng whn wnt rt & bmpd 2f out)..1½ **9**

1540[10] Siberian Mystic *(28) (PGMurphy)* 2-7-13 (7) RWaterfield(2) (prom: ev ch & rdn over 2f out: sn btn) 1¾ **10**

1665[10] Ticka Ticka Timing *(24) (BWMurray)* 2-8-4v(7) GParkin(9) (led 2f: chsd ldrs tl wknd over 2f out) 4 **11**

Totally Different *(21) (JohnBerry)* 2-8-11 CDwyer(8) (leggy: bit bkwd: s.i.s: sn wl outpcd & rdn along) 1¼ **12**

1341[6] Distinctly Red (IRE) *(JBerry)* 2-8-11 DeanMcKeown(13) (sn bhd: t.o ½-wy) 30 **13**

3/1 Miletrian Refurb (IRE), **7/2** Siberian Mystic (8/1-3/1), **5/1** Kratz (IRE), SIZZLING SYMPHONY, **7/1** Catwalk Girl (5/1-8/1), **8/1** Distinctly Red (IRE), **9/1** Veshca Lady (IRE) (op 6/1), **14/1** Mels Baby (IRE), Totally Different, **16/1** Chilly Looks, **20/1** Jackson Park, Ceilidh (IRE), **50/1** Ticka Ticka Timing, CSF £44.86 TOTE £13.30: £3.10 £2.30 £4.10 (£57.10) Trio £224.10; £94.72 to 26/6/95 OWNER Mr J. A. Campbell (MALTON) BRED Sexton Enterprises 13 Rn

1m 28.6 (6.60) SF: 15/-/-/-/-/-/-/-/-/-/-/-/-

No bid.

1944 SURFACHEM LADIES MAIDEN H'CAP (0-70) (3-Y.O+) (Class F) £2,973.00 (£828.00: £399.00)

1m Stalls: Centre GOING minus 0.19 sec per fur (GF) 2-20 (2-25)

736[3] **Kaf (65)***(78+) (JLDunlop)* 3-10-7 MissEJohnsonHoughton(8) (lw: hld up: hdwy ½-wy: led 3f out: drew clr fnl f: easily) ....— **1**

1808[6] Sycamore Lodge (IRE) **(69)***(72)*(Fav)*(PCalver)* 4-11-7 MrsFNeedham(4) (w ldrs: led 4f out to 3f out: hung lft & kpt on same pce appr fnl f) 5 **2**

1666[3] Flyaway Blues **(54)***(57)*(Fav)*(MrsMReveley)* 3-9-10b MrsMCowdrey(7) (lw: hld up: gd hdwy ½-wy: ev ch whn hung bdly lft u.p 2f out: nt qckn appr fnl f) ....hd **3**

1431[4] Golden Digger (USA) **(63)***(46) (MRStoute)* 3-10-1 (4) MrsSEddery(5) (in tch: effrt 3f out: grad wknd) 10 **4**

Promitto **(47)***(27) (MDHammond)* 5-9-13 MissDianaJones(9) (in tch tl outpcd fnl 3f) 1¼ **5**

1412[9] Scylla **(44)***(19) (PCHaslam)* 3-8-7 (7) MissAArmitage(1) (mde most to ½-wy: wknd over 2f out) 2½ **6**

1598[11] Bollin Sophie **(52)***(13) (MHEasterby)* 3-9-4 (4)ow7 MrsLFahey(3) (w ldrs tl rdn & lost pl ½-wy) 3½ **7**

1863[13] Kralingen **(55)***(9) (NChamberlain)* 3-9-7 (4)ow11 MissCMetcalfe(2) (s.i.s: outpcd & bhd fr ½-wy) 1¾ **8**

1533[11] Brother Barnabas **(53)** *(CWThornton)* 4-10-5 MrsDKettlewell(6) (outpcd & bhd fr ½-wy: t.o 2f out) 15 **9**

LONG HANDICAP Kralingen 8-0 Scylla 8-11

5/2 Sycamore Lodge (IRE), Flyaway Blues, **7/2** KAF, **11/2** Golden Digger (USA), **10/1** Promitto, **14/1** Brother Barnabas, **20/1** Scylla, **33/1** Bollin Sophie, **50/1** Kralingen, CSF £12.56 CT £23.34 TOTE £4.70: £1.90 £1.10 (£6.50) Trio £4.20 OWNER Prince A. A. Faisal (ARUNDEL) BRED Nawara Stud Co Ltd 9 Rn
1m 40.0 (5.00) SF: 50/54/29/18/9/-/-/-/-
WEIGHT FOR AGE 3yo-10lb

1945 LEVY BOARD H'CAP (0-70) (3-Y.O) (Class E) £3,393.75 (£1,020.00: £492.50: £228.75)
1m 1f Stalls: Low GOING minus 0.19 sec per fur (GF) 2-50 (2-51)

Striffolino (70)*(77) (TDBarron)* 3-9-7 DeanMcKeown(10) (trckd ldr tl led 2f out: drvn along & r.o wl fnl f)....— 1
1724[7] Prudent Pet **(57)***(61) (CWFairhurst)* 3-8-5 (3) JTate(4) (hld up: stdy hdwy over 3f out: ev ch 2f out: nt qckn fnl f)....1½ 2
1514[10] Anonym (IRE) **(64)***(66)*(Fav)*(JLDunlop)* 3-9-1 WRyan(1) (hld up: effrt & n.m.r over 2f out: nt clr run over 1f out: hmpd ins fnl f)....1½ 3
1669[8] Westcourt Princess **(42)***(44) (MWEasterby)* 3-7-7 NKennedy(6) (plld hrd: led to 2f out: one pce)....s.h 4
1358[5] Beau Matelot **(57)***(58) (JDBethell)* 3-8-8 MFenton(8) (s.i.s: bhd tl styd on u.p fnl 3f)....hd 5
1498[5] Rambo Waltzer **(54)***(51) (SGNorton)* 3-8-5 TWilliams(3) (chsd ldrs: effrt 3f out: sn outpcd)...2½ 6
1669[3] Bold Top **(42)***(36) (BSRothwell)* 3-7-0 (7) PFessey(5) (bhd tl kpt on fnl 3f: nvr nr ldrs)....1½ 7
908[4] Miss Felixstowe (USA) **(52)***(46) (MrsMReveley)* 3-8-3 KDarley(7) (bhd tl kpt on u.p fnl 3f: nvr nr to chal)....hd 8
1524[5] Shining Edge **(55)***(31) (MHEasterby)* 3-8-6 MBirch(9) (in tch: rdn over 3f out: sn lost pl & eased)....10 9
1549[4] Pass Mark **(65)***(37) (JRFanshawe)* 3-9-2 DHarrison(2) (lw: plld hrd: trckd ldrs: drvn along over 3f out: sn lost pl & eased)....2½ 10

LONG HANDICAP Westcourt Princess 7-5 Bold Top 7-5

11/8 Anonym (IRE), **4/1** Pass Mark, **8/1** Shining Edge, Miss Felixstowe (USA), **10/1** STRIFFOLINO, Rambo Waltzer, Beau Matelot, **11/1** Bold Top, **16/1** Prudent Pet, **20/1** Westcourt Princess, CSF £144.30 CT £328.80 TOTE £13.40: £2.70 £4.60 £1.20 (£209.50) Trio £232.50; £199.79 to 26/6/95 OWNER Lady Burnham (THIRSK) BRED Mrs H. Lawson and Lady Eyre 10 Rn
1m 53.9 (4.90) SF: 45/29/34/12/26/19/4/14/-/5

1946 FROSTREE WINDOW SYSTEMS H'CAP (0-90) (3-Y.O+) (Class C) £5,686.00 (£1,708.00: £824.00: £382.00)
1m 2f Stalls: Low GOING minus 0.19 sec per fur (GF) 3-25 (3-25)

1825[4] **Vindaloo (64)***(70) (JLHarris)* 3-7-10 (7) PFessey(5) (lw: trckd ldr: led over 2f out: r.o wl fnl f)....— 1
1524[3] Sherqy (IRE) **(81)***(85)*(Fav)*(JLDunlop)* 3-9-6 WRyan(1) (lw: hld up: n.m.r 3f out: nt clr run whn hung lft & styd on wl fnl f: nt rch wnr)....1¼ 2
1808[W] Coureur **(66)***(70) (JDBethell)* 6-9-3 MFenton(2) (hld up pllng hrd: effrt & nt clr run 2f out: ev ch 1f out: unable qckn)....nk 3
1649[10] Once More for Luck (IRE) **(60)***(61) (MrsMReveley)* 4-8-11 KDarley(4) (hld up: hmpd 6f out: hdwy on ins & nt clr run 3f out: styd on appr fnl f)....1½ 4
Doctor's Remedy **(42)***(38) (MrsJJordan)* 9-7-7b NKennedy(3) (set slow pce: hdd over 2f out: wknd over 1f out)....3 5
1139[8] White Palace **(85)***(79) (JRFanshawe)* 3-9-10 DHarrison(6) (hld up: effrt over 3f out: wknd 2f out)....1¼ 6

LONG HANDICAP Doctor's Remedy 6-1

9/4 Sherqy (IRE), **5/2** VINDALOO, **100/30** Coureur, **11/2** Once More for Luck (IRE), **6/1** White Palace, **50/1** Doctor's Remedy, CSF £8.31 TOTE £3.00: £1.60 £1.60 (£4.30) OWNER Mr J. D. Abell (MELTON MOWBRAY) BRED Green Park Investments Ltd 6 Rn
2m 10.8 (8.30) SF: 7/22/19/10/-/16
WEIGHT FOR AGE 3yo-12lb

1947 BOWS & BELLS MAIDEN STKS (3-Y.O+) (Class D) £3,996.50 (£1,202.00: £581.00: £270.50) **1m** Stalls: Centre GOING minus 0.19 sec (GF) 3-55 (3-55)

Behaviour *(84+)*(Fav)*(MrsJCecil)* 3-8-11 PaulEddery(6) (b: lw: hld up gng wl: qcknd to ld jst ins fnl f: impressive)....— 1
1167[2] Moscow Mist (IRE) *(75)*(Fav)*(LadyHerries)* 4-9-7 KDarley(3) (lw: hld up: hdwy ½-wy: rdn to ld over 1f out: nt pce of wnr)....3 2
1615[5] Northern Trove (USA) *(73) (GMMoore)* 3-8-8 (3) JStack(2) (mde most tl over 1f out: one pce)....2½ 3
1533[6] Hand of Straw (IRE) *(71) (JWWatts)* 3-8-11 NConnorton(4) (chsd ldrs: drvn along & outpcd over 2f out: kpt on fnl f)....1¼ 4

1547[6] Top Skipper (IRE) *(70) (BHanbury)* 3-8-8 (3) JTate(1) (trckd ldrs: effrt & rn green over 2f out: styd on one pce)....s.h **5**
1533[13] Readyspex *(27) (RDEWoodhouse)* 5-9-7 SMaloney(5) (w ldr tl rdn & lost pl 3f out: sn bhd)..20 **6**

11/8 BEHAVIOUR, Moscow Mist (IRE), **7/1** Northern Trove (USA), **14/1** Hand of Straw (IRE), Top Skipper (IRE), **50/1** Readyspex, CSF £3.51 TOTE £2.40: £1.50 £1.10 (£1.50) OWNER Oceanic Ltd (NEWMARKET) BRED Oceanic Development Co Ltd 6 Rn 1m 42.2 (7.20) SF: 6/7/-/-/-/-
WEIGHT FOR AGE 3yo-10lb

1948

STAITHES MAIDEN STKS (3-Y.O+) (Class D) £3,762.50 (£1,130.00: £545.00: £252.50) **1m 6f 19y** Stalls: Low GOING minus 0.19 sec per fur (GF) 4-30 (4-31)

1036[3] **Hullbank (64)***(74) (WWHaigh)* 5-9-4 (3) JTate(4) (lw: hld up: smooth hdwy 8f out: led on bit over 3f out: jst hld on)....— **1**
1283[2] Lucayan Sunshine (USA) *(69)*(Fav)*(LadyHerries)* 3-8-2 ow3 KDarley(7) (hld up: effrt 4f out: styd on u.p appr fnl f: jst failed)....hd **2**
1878[3] Great Easeby (IRE) *(66) (WStorey)* 5-9-4 (3) JStack(2) (racd wd: bhd tl styd on fnl 3f: nvr nr to chal)....7 **3**
1439[3] Junior Ben (IRE) **(72)***(63) (JBerry)* 3-8-4 DeanMcKeown(6) (led after 1f tl over 3f out: hung lft u.p & wknd over 1f out)....2½ **4**
Another Venture (IRE) *(46) (MJohnston)* 5-9-7 TWilliams(3) (s.i.s: sn chsng ldrs: rdn & wknd over 2f out: eased fnl f)....15 **5**
766[14] Nuveen (IRE) **(35)***(34) (MrsJJordan)* 4-9-7b AMorris(1) (led 1f: drvn along & lost pl 8f out: sn bhd)....11 **6**
1417[8] Zusha *(20) (SGNorton)* 4-9-2 DHarrison(5) (chsd ldrs: pushed along 7f out: lost pl over 4f out: sn bhd)....8 **7**

4/9 Lucayan Sunshine (USA), **9/2** HULLBANK, **7/1** Junior Ben (IRE), **16/1** Another Venture (IRE), **20/1** Great Easeby (IRE), **25/1** Zusha, **50/1** Nuveen (IRE), CSF £6.86 TOTE £6.70: £1.80 £1.10 (£1.90) OWNER Mrs P. Gibbon (MALTON) BRED D. Gibbon 7 Rn
3m 5.6 (7.60) SF: 47/25/39/19/19/7/-
WEIGHT FOR AGE 3yo-17lb

1949

UGTHORPE RATING RELATED MAIDEN LIMITED STKS (0-70) (3-Y.O) (Class E) £3,120.75 (£936.00: £450.50: £207.75)
6f Stalls: Centre GOING minus 0.02 sec per fur (G) 5-00 (5-00)

1809[4] **Just Dissident (IRE) (65)***(75)*(Fav)*(RMWhitaker)* 3-9-0 DeanMcKeown(2) (lw: mde all: clr 2f out: wandered: drvn out)....— **1**
1515[3] Statistician **(68)***(73) (JohnBerry)* 3-9-0 TWilliams(4) (sn chsng ldrs: rdn & outpcd ½-wy: styd on fnl f: nt rch wnr)....¾ **2**
1034[14] Crystal Gift **(70)***(64) (PFICole)* 3-9-0 KDarley(1) (sn outpcd & drvn along: swtchd lft & kpt on ins fnl f)....3½ **3**
1700[5] Millesime (IRE) **(63)***(60) (BHanbury)* 3-8-11 (3) JStack(3) (w ldrs: rdn ½-wy: edgd lft & wknd fnl f)....1¼ **4**

6/4 JUST DISSIDENT (IRE), **11/4** Statistician, **3/1** Crystal Gift, **9/2** Millesime (IRE), CSF £5.49 TOTE £2.20: (£2.30) OWNER Mrs C. A. Hodgetts (LEEDS) BRED M. Duffy 4 Rn
1m 14.3 (5.00) SF: 25/23/14/10

T/Plpt: £34.90 (346.28 Tckts). T/Qdpt: £5.10 (15.05 Tckts). WG

1628-WOLVERHAMPTON (L-H)
Saturday June 24th (Standard)
WEATHER: cloudy WIND: mod half against

1950

PATTINGHAM MAIDEN H'CAP (0-65) (3-Y.O+) (Class F) £2,519.00 (£694.00: £329.00) **1m 1f 79y (Fibresand)** Stalls: High GOING: 0.02 sec (STD) 7-00 (7-00)

1649[8] **Studio Thirty (43)***(50) (RHollinshead)* 3-8-1 (7) AEddery(10) (bhd: hdwy 4f out: 5th st: rdn to ld ins fnl f: all out)....— **1**
1568[3] Personimus **(30)***(35) (CaptJWilson)* 5-8-6 GCarter(9) (lw: chsd ldrs: 4th st: str chal fnl f: r.o)....1 **2**
1725[5] Nivasha **(37)***(39)*(Fav)*(MBell)* 3-8-2 MFenton(6) (a.p: led over 3f out tl ins fnl f)....2 **3**
1762[6] Mr Moriarty (IRE) **(25)***(25) (SRBowring)* 4-8-1b StephenDavies(2) (prom: 3rd st: rdn & one pce appr fnl f)....1 **4**
1630[2] Mislemani (IRE) **(48)***(48) (AGNewcombe)* 5-9-10 RPrice(8) (chsd ldrs: effrt & 2nd st: rdn over 1f out: no imp)....s.h **5**

1403[3] Mim-Lou-and **(45)**(35) *(BRMillman)* 3-8-10 JWilliams(11) (lw: hld up mid div: rdn over 2f out: nt rch ldrs) 6 **6**
1883[6] Arrogant Boy **(30)**(17) *(DWChapman)* 6-8-6 DHarrison(3) (chsd ldrs: 6th & wkng st)....1¾ **7**
1457[2] Pacific Spirit **(46)**(12) *(MTate)* 5-9-5 (3) DWright(5) (bhd: effrt over 3f out: no imp: t.o)....12 **8**
518[7] Beecham **(46)**(10) *(PCHaslam)* 3-8-4 (7) NicolaHowarth(12) (bit bkwd: a bhd: t.o)....1¼ **9**
1078[5] Olivia Val **(21)** *(AGNewcombe)* 5-7-4 (7)ow3 SLanigan(4) (hdwy 6f out: wknd 3f out: t.o)....8 **10**
Reeling **(25)** *(PaddyFarrell)* 9-8-1 TSprake(7) (swtg: bkwd: a bhd: t.o)....2 **11**
Skelton Princess (IRE) **(29)** *(PDEvans)* 4-8-5b PaulEddery(1) (led over 5f: wknd qckly: t.o)....¾ **12**

7/2 Nivasha, **4/1** Mislemani (IRE), **6/1** Pacific Spirit, **7/1** Mim-Lou-and, **10/1** Personimus, **12/1** Olivia Val, STUDIO THIRTY, **14/1** Beecham, **20/1** Mr Moriarty (IRE), **25/1** Arrogant Boy, Reeling, Skelton Princess (IRE), CSF £110.82 CT £457.70 TOTE £14.20: £3.50 £1.80 £3.20 (£51.50) Trio £151.70; £128.24 to 26/6/95 OWNER Mr Derek Holder (UPPER LONGDON) BRED A. F. Budge (Equine) Ltd 12 Rn
2m 4.7 (8.70) SF: 20/16/9/6/29/5/-/-/-/-/-/-
WEIGHT FOR AGE 3yo-11lb

1951 EXPRESS & STAR CLAIMING STKS (3-Y.O+) (Class F) £2,519.00 (£694.00: £329.00)
1m 100y (Fibresand) Stalls: High GOING: 0.02 sec per fur (STD) 7-25 (7-30)

1534[8] **Sweet Supposin (IRE) (75)**(84) *(KMcAuliffe)* 4-9-7b DHarrison(4) (dwlt: hdwy ½-wy: led 3f out: sn clr: v.easily)....— **1**
1880[5] No Submission (USA) **(72)**(74) *(DWChapman)* 9-9-5b MFenton(10) (led over 5f out to 3f out: 2nd st: hrd rdn: kpt on one pce)....4 **2**
1534[6] Legatee **(63)**(61) *(BJMeehan)* 4-8-11 BDoyle(11) (chsd ldrs: 4th st: kpt on ins fnl f)....3 **3**
1748[4] Gulf Shaadi **(82)**(66)(Fav)*(GLewis)* 3-8-11 SWhitworth(2) (hdwy 5f out: 3rd & rdn st: no imp)....2½ **4**
1087[10] Northern Celadon (IRE) **(69)**(63) *(MJHeaton-Ellis)* 4-9-7 StephenDavies(6) (b: outpcd after 2f: hdwy & 5th st: styd on u.p: nvr nrr)....1¾ **5**
1771[8] Zahran (IRE) **(54)**(34) *(JMBradley)* 4-8-12 (3) SDrowne(5) (b: nvr trbld ldrs)....12 **6**
1789[4] Medland (IRE) **(50)**(22) *(BJMcMath)* 5-8-4 (7) RMoogan(1) (hdwy ½-wy: 6th & rdn st: nvr nr ldrs)....4 **7**
410[4] Pearl Dawn (IRE) (22) *(NoelChance)* 5-8-9 (5) LNewton(9) (bit bkwd: prom over 5f: wknd qckly)....1¾ **8**
1797[11] Brigadore Gold **(24)**(5) *(FHLee)* 5-8-8b GCarter(12) (led 3f: wknd over 3f out: t.o)....6 **9**
Princethorpe *(BRCambidge)* 8-8-13 RPrice(8) (bit bkwd: dwlt: a bhd: t.o)....6 **10**
1501[4] Nita's Choice *(AGNewcombe)* 5-8-5 (5)ow2 DGriffiths(7) (a bhd: t.o)....4 **11**
1797[14] Radio Caroline **(20)** *(MTate)* 7-8-12b(3) DWright(13) (chsd ldrs over 4f: sn lost tch: t.o)....13 **12**
1422[8] Sweetlittlemystery **(27)** *(EJAlston)* 4-8-1 (5) HKYim(3) (Withdrawn not under Starter's orders: broke out of stall).... **W**

5/4 Gulf Shaadi, **11/2** Legatee (8/1-5/1), **7/1** No Submission (USA) (5/1-8/1), **8/1** SWEET SUPPOSIN (IRE) (5/1-9/1), Northern Celadon (IRE), **12/1** Pearl Dawn (IRE), **16/1** Zahran (IRE), Medland (IRE), **25/1** Princethorpe, **33/1** Brigadore Gold, Nita's Choice, Sweetlittlemystery, **50/1** Radio Caroline, CSF £60.91 TOTE £10.00: £2.70 £1.70 £2.30 (£31.40) Trio £46.50 OWNER Mount Juliet Stud (LAMBOURN) BRED Ballylinch Stud Ltd 12 Rn
1m 51.0 (7.00) SF: 40/30/17/12/19/-/-/-/-/-/-/-
WEIGHT FOR AGE 3yo-10lb
Gulf Shaadi clmd SJBibby.

1952 WEATHERBYS 'NEWCOMERS' SERIES H'CAP (0-70) (3-Y.O) (Class E) £3,102.00 (£924.00: £440.00: £198.00)
1m 100y (Fibresand) Stalls: High GOING: 0.02 sec per fur (STD) 7-55 (7-56)

*1088** **Super High (66)**(77)(Fav)*(PHowling)* 3-9-7 RCochrane(5) (lw: hld up: hdwy to ld over 3f out: drvn out)....— **1**
1824* Miss Zanzibar **(61)**(63) *(RAFahey)* 3-9-2 6x ACulhane(7) (hld up: effrt & 4th st: chsd wnr appr fnl f: no imp)....5 **2**
1571[4] Smolensk (IRE) **(63)**(64) *(JBerry)* 3-9-4 GCarter(4) (s.i.s: sn chsng ldrs: 2nd & rdn st: kpt on one pce)....½ **3**
1504[3] Heathyards Magic (IRE) **(66)**(63) *(RHollinshead)* 3-9-7 DHarrison(1) (bhd: rdn ½-wy: 6th st: nvr nrr)....2 **4**
1745[14] Mega Tid **(55)**(52) *(BAPearce)* 3-8-10 StephenDavies(2) (led 5f: 3rd & rdn st: sn btn)....hd **5**
1547[5] Sound Trick (USA) **(54)**(41) *(GCBravery)* 3-8-9 SWhitworth(3) (hld up: drvn along over 3f out: 6th & btn st)....5 **6**
1719[4] Cork Street Girl (IRE) **(58)**(17) *(BJMeehan)* 3-8-13 PaulEddery(6) (lw: prom to ½-wy: sn hrd drvn: outpcd over 2f out: 7th st: t.o)....15 **7**

5/2 SUPER HIGH, **3/1** Heathyards Magic (IRE), **4/1** Smolensk (IRE), **5/1** Miss Zanzibar, **8/1** Sound Trick (USA) (6/1-10/1), **16/1** Mega Tid, Cork Street Girl (IRE), CSF £14.15 TOTE £4.00: £2.00 £1.90 (£19.00) OWNER Mrs J. M. Khan (NEWMARKET) BRED Nam Seng Yong 7 Rn
1m 53.0 (9.00) SF: 22/8/9/8/-/-/-

1953

DAILY STAR TOP TIPSTER H'CAP (0-90) (3-Y.O+) (Class C)
£6,108.00 (£1,824.00: £872.00: £396.00)
6f (Fibresand) Stalls: Low GOING: 0.02 sec per fur (STD) 8-25 (8-26)

1599* **Sailormaite (82)***(90)*(Fav)*(SRBowring)* 4-9-6 SWebster(10) (hld up: smooth hdwy to jn ldrs 2f out: led ent fnl f: pushed out) — **1**
1241[9] Palacegate Touch **(90)***(93) (JBerry)* 5-9-7v(7) PRoberts(6) (chsd ldrs: rdn over 1f out: r.o ins fnl f) 1¾ **2**
1604[6] Nordan Raider **(78)***(77) (MJCamacho)* 7-9-2 LCharnock(12) (hdwy ½-wy: led over 1f out: sn hdd: swtchd lft ins fnl f: rdn & unable qckn) 1½ **3**
1565[10] Lord Sky **(77)***(76) (ABailey)* 4-9-1 GCarter(7) (chsd ldr: slt ld wl over 1f out: sn hdd: no ex fnl f) hd **4**
1714[3] Wentbridge Lad (IRE) **(82)***(73) (PDEvans)* 5-9-6 RCochrane(4) (hdwy over 2f out: kpt on fnl f: nvr plcd to chal) 3 **5**
1296[10] Forzair **(72)***(60) (MMcCormack)* 3-8-2b BDoyle(8) (hdwy over 2f out: nvr nrr) 1 **6**
985[9] Midnight Spell **(80)***(65) (MrsJCecil)* 3-8-10 PaulEddery(13) (led tl wl over 1f out: eased whn btn fnl f) 1¼ **7**
1668[9] Desert Invader (IRE) **(66)***(48) (DWChapman)* 4-8-4 DeanMcKeown(2) (chsd ldrs to ½-wy: sn outpcd) 1¼ **8**
785[10] Montanelli (FR) **(83)***(63) (KMcAuliffe)* 3-8-10 (3) JTate(11) (bit bkwd: s.i.s: hdwy over 2f out: rdn & wknd appr fnl f) ½ **9**
1605[5] Barrel of Hope **(70)***(50) (JLEyre)* 3-8-0 RLappin(3) (lw: chsd ldrs 4f: sn outpcd) s.h **10**
1409[9] Cameron Highland (IRE) **(77)***(41) (PFICole)* 4-9-1b MFenton(1) (lw: spd over 3f: t.o) 6 **11**
1692[7] Frisky Miss (IRE) **(58)***(1) (KOCunningham-Brown)* 4-7-5 (5) MBaird(5) (lost pl ½-wy: t.o) 8 **12**

5/2 SAILORMAITE, **13/2** Nordan Raider, **7/1** Wentbridge Lad (IRE), **8/1** Barrel of Hope, **9/1** Midnight Spell, **10/1** Frisky Miss (IRE), **11/1** Lord Sky (8/1-12/1), **12/1** Palacegate Touch (op 8/1), Cameron Highland (IRE), **16/1** Montanelli (FR), **20/1** Forzair, **25/1** Desert Invader (IRE), CSF £31.08 CT £165.98 TOTE £4.00: £2.00 £3.10 £2.40 (£36.50) Trio £33.30 OWNER Mr S. R. Bowring (EDWINSTOWE) BRED S. R. Bowring 12 Rn 1m 15.2 (4.00) SF: 50/53/37/36/33/12/17/8/15/2/1/-
WEIGHT FOR AGE 3yo-8lb

1954

C L CONYERS AND SON (S) STKS (2-Y.O) (Class G) £2,243.00 (£618.00: £293.00) **6f (Fibresand)** Stalls: Low GOING: 0.02 sec per fur (STD) 8-55 (9-00)

1740[3] **Subfusk** *(61) (WGMTurner)* 2-8-6 (5) PMcCabe(6) (led over 3f out: clr ent st: unchal) — **1**
1640* Bold Times **(69)***(59)*(Fav)*(PDEvans)* 2-9-2 PaulEddery(9) (chsd ldrs: rdn 2f out: kpt on wl ins fnl f) 2½ **2**
1640[4] Don't Tell Anyone *(38) (JBerry)* 2-8-11 GCarter(7) (chsd ldrs tl outpcd wl over 1f out) 6 **3**
1158[6] Just Rory *(28) (EJAlston)* 2-8-6 (5) HKYim(4) (lw: dwlt: sn chsng ldrs: outpcd over 2f out: sn btn) 4 **4**
Dhulikhel *(18) (DMarks)* 2-8-6 DHarrison(2) (small: bkwd: rdn & hdwy over 2f out: nt rch ldrs) 1¾ **5**
1348[7] Herald Angel (IRE) *(7) (MHTompkins)* 2-8-6 SMulvey(5) (bit bkwd: outpcd fr ½-wy) 4 **6**
1570[4] Timson *(12) (JPLeigh)* 2-8-11 SWhitworth(3) (lw: a outpcd & bhd) hd **7**
Inca Queen *(6) (AGFoster)* 2-8-6 TSprake(8) (leggy: lt-f: bit bkwd: unruly stalls: a bhd & outpcd) nk **8**
1632[7] Chris's Governor *(RHollinshead)* 2-8-8 (3) AGarth(1) (led over 2f: sn drvn along: t.o) 20 **9**

13/8 Bold Times, **9/4** SUBFUSK, **11/2** Don't Tell Anyone, **12/1** Just Rory, **14/1** Dhulikhel (10/1-20/1), Herald Angel (IRE), **20/1** Timson, Inca Queen, Chris's Governor, CSF £6.28 TOTE £3.10: £1.30 £1.50 £1.30 (£2.10) Trio £1.70 OWNER Mrs J. M. Sexton (SHERBORNE) BRED A. J. Sexton 9 Rn
1m 17.8 (6.60) SF: 7/5/-/-/-/-/-/-/-
Bt in 4,500gns

1955

JOHN SANDERS MEMORIAL H'CAP (0-65) (3-Y.O+) (Class F)
£2,519.00 (£694.00: £329.00)
1m 4f (Fibresand) Stalls: High GOING: 0.02 sec per fur (STD) 9-25 (9-26)

1552[5] **Barti-Ddu (52)***(63) (SCWilliams)* 4-8-12 (3) DWright(7) (hld up: hdwy ½-wy: led over 3f out tl appr fnl f: rallied u.p to ld wl ins fnl f) — **1**
*1332** Sommersby (IRE) **(64)***(75)*(Fav)*(MrsNMacauley)* 4-9-13 SWhitworth(10) (hld up: hdwy over 3f out: 3rd st: rdn to ld appr fnl f: hrd rdn & ct wl ins fnl f: rallied cl home) hd **2**

1622[11] Charlie Bigtime **(46)***(57) (DTThom)* 5-8-9 AMackay(9) (a.p: 2nd st: ev ch fnl f: hrd rdn & r.o wl) ....nk 3
*1455** Pistols At Dawn (USA) **(53)***(57) (BJMeehan)* 5-9-2 BDoyle(5) (lw: led after 2f: sn hdd: rdn & 4th st: kpt on same pce) 5 4
1658[7] Rolling Waters **(57)***(57) (JARToller)* 5-9-6 WNewnes(3) (hld up: hdwy over 4f out: 5th st: nt pce to chal) 3 5
1702* Fen Terrier **(58)***(45) (WJHaggas)* 3-8-6 RCochrane(11) (lw: led after 3f tl over 3f out: 6th & btn st) 10 6
1332[10] Winn's Pride (IRE) **(45)***(29) (RHollinshead)* 4-8-8 DHarrison(1) (lw: nvr nr to chal) 2 7
1091[7] Palacegate Jo (IRE) **(56)***(37) (DWChapman)* 4-9-5 DeanMcKeown(8) (lw: prom tl wknd 3f out) 2½ 8
1788[9] Dynamis (IRE) **(39)***(12) (KOCunningham-Brown)* 4-7-11 (5) MBaird(12) (s.s: hdwy 7f out: wknd over 3f out: t.o) 6 9
1881[2] Vintage Taittinger (IRE) **(48)***(14) (MBell)* 3-7-3 (7) RMullen(4) (swtg: chsd ldrs 8f: sn wknd: t.o) 5 10
1655[3] Lone Risk **(63)***(29) (CNAllen)* 4-9-7 (5) PMcCabe(6) (a bhd: t.o) ....s.h 11
352[4] Manolete **(41)** *(JFfitch-Heyes)* 4-8-4 StephenDavies(2) (b: led 2f: wknd over 4f out: t.o)......dist 12

7/4 Sommersby (IRE), **5/1** Pistols At Dawn (USA), **6/1** Fen Terrier, **8/1** Vintage Taittinger (IRE), Charlie Bigtime, **12/1** Rolling Waters (op 8/1), **14/1** BARTI-DDU, **16/1** Palacegate Jo (IRE), Manolete, **20/1** Lone Risk, **25/1** Winn's Pride (IRE), Dynamis (IRE), CSF £39.36 CT £206.54 TOTE £13.10: £3.20 £1.90 £3.20 (£24.90) Trio £55.20 OWNER Miss L. J. Ward (NEWMARKET) BRED Lloyd Bros 12 Rn
2m 43.1 (12.10) SF: 22/34/16/16/16/-/-/-/-/-/-/-
WEIGHT FOR AGE 3yo-15lb

T/Plpt: £163.40 (81.69 Tckts). T/Qdpt: £13.70 (5.75 Tckts). IM

1816-EDINBURGH (R-H)
Monday June 26th (Firm)
WEATHER: sunny WIND: mod across

1956
LINLITHGOW CLAIMING STKS (3-Y.O+) (Class F) £2,708.00 (£763.00: £374.00)
1m 16y Stalls: High GOING minus 0.51 sec per fur (F) 2-30 (2-30)

1902[2] **Okay Baby (IRE) (44)***(51) (MHTompkins)* 3-8-3 PRobinson(1) (lw: mde all: clr after 2f: rdn & hld on wl fnl f) ....— 1
1270[W] Cashmirie *(46) (JLEyre)* 3-7-13 DaleGibson(4) (a.p: effrt over 2f out: styd on wl towards fin) ....nk 2
1847[13] Tee Tee Too (IRE) **(62)***(55) (PCHaslam)* 3-8-8 (3) JStack(5) (chsd ldr: drvn over 2f out: nt qckn fnl f) 1½ 3
1666[2] Mary's Case (IRE) **(55)***(52)*(Fav)*(MJohnston)* 5-9-4b DHolland(2) (hld up & bhd: hdwy 2f out: nvr able to chal) ....nk 4
1669[15] J C Grey **(33)***(44) (DenysSmith)* 3-8-6 KFallon(3) (in tch: effrt 2f out: no imp) 3 5
1649[11] Pash **(38)***(25) (CWFairhurst)* 3-7-11 NKennedy(6) (chsd ldrs: rdn ent st: no imp) 5 6
1873[9] Petal's Jarred **(25)***(11) (WStorey)* 5-8-5v JFanning(7) (s.i.s: rapid hdwy appr st: wknd over 2f out) 6 7
1534[12] Orthorhombus **(60)***(28) (DJSCosgrove)* 6-9-8b MWigham(8) (bhd: effrt ½-wy: n.d) ....nk 8

11/8 Mary's Case (IRE), **3/1** OKAY BABY (IRE), **6/1** Orthorhombus, Tee Tee Too (IRE) (op 4/1), **8/1** Pash, **20/1** J C Grey, **25/1** Cashmirie, **50/1** Petal's Jarred, CSF £55.72 TOTE £3.50: £2.30 £1.60 £3.10 (£192.20) OWNER Mr Michael Keogh (NEWMARKET) BRED St Simon Foundation 8 Rn
1m 41.9 (3.30) SF: 14/9/18/25/7/-/-/1
WEIGHT FOR AGE 3yo-10lb

1957
YVONNE MURRAY M.B.E. H'CAP (0-60) (3-Y.O+) (Class F)
£2,697.50 (£760.00: £372.50)
1m 7f 16y Stalls: High GOING minus 0.51 sec per fur (F) 3-00 (3-00)

1643[9] **Vain Prince (43)***(56) (NTinkler)* 8-9-9b LCharnock(6) (lw: trckd ldrs: led appr st: sn qcknd clr: eased ins fnl f) ....— 1
840[10] Milngavie (IRE) **(35)***(43) (MJohnston)* 5-9-1 DHolland(3) (a.p: styd on fnl 3f: no ch w wnr) 5 2
312[9] Sharp Sensation **(41)***(47) (WLBarker)* 5-9-7 AlexGreaves(1) (lw: hld up & bhd: hdwy 3f out: rdn & btn over 1f out) 2 3
1449[3] Jalore **(30)***(34) (SCoathup)* 6-8-10 DaleGibson(5) (hdwy ½-wy: one pce fnl 3f) 1¾ 4
1667[2] Arian Spirit (IRE) **(32)***(35) (JLEyre)* 4-8-12 SMaloney(10) (lw: sme hdwy 3f out: nvr rchd ldrs) ....½ 5
1744[6] Monkey Wench (IRE) **(44)***(47) (PMonteith)* 4-9-10 PRobinson(8) (effrt appr st: n.d) ....d.h 5

1379[3] Kildrummy Castle **(53)***(48)*(Fav)*(MrsJRRamsden)* 3-9-1 KFallon(7) (lw: chsd ldrs: rdn appr st: wknd over 2f out)....8 **7**
1816[5] Philmist **(54)***(28)* *(JHetherton)* 3-9-2 NKennedy(4) (led tl hdd appr st: sn wknd)....20 **8**
1733[5] Goldenberry **(23)** *(JParkes)* 4-8-3 JFanning(2) (stdd s: n.d)....s.h **9**
1688[3] Amnesia (IRE) **(36)** *(MrsSCBradburne)* 4-8-13 (3) JStack(9) (prom tl wknd 5f out: t.o)....dist **10**

9/4 Kildrummy Castle, **4/1** VAIN PRINCE, **5/1** Arian Spirit (IRE), **7/1** Milngavie (IRE), **8/1** Sharp Sensation, **14/1** Monkey Wench (IRE), Jalore (op 6/1), **16/1** Amnesia (IRE), **25/1** Philmist, **40/1** Goldenberry, CSF £29.37 CT £193.40 TOTE £4.20: £1.50 £2.90 £3.40 (£14.40) Trio £70.30 OWNER Mr A. C. Findlay (MALTON) BRED Lodge Park Stud 10 Rn

3m 17.3 (6.80) SF: 32/19/23/10/11/23/6/-/-/-

WEIGHT FOR AGE 3yo-18lb

1958

MOORFOOT HILLS H'CAP (0-70) (3-Y.O+) (Class E) £3,485.00 (£1,055.00: £515.00: £245.00)
1m 3f 32y Stalls: High GOING minus 0.51 sec per fur (F) 3-30 (3-31)

1817* **Soba Up (50)***(62+)*(Fav)*(TJEtherington)* 5-9-6 5x ACulhane(1) (hld up: stdy hdwy 3f out: led appr fnl f: shkn up & r.o: comf)....— **1**
1027[9] Thisonesforalice **(36)***(46)* *(JSGoldie)* 7-8-3 (3) JStack(3) (led tl hdd appr fnl f: kpt on same pce)....1¼ **2**
1651[8] Imperial Bid (FR) **(54)***(59)* *(DenysSmith)* 7-9-10 KFallon(5) (a.p: effrt over 2f out: nt qckn)....3½ **3**
1647* Mhemeanles **(47)***(49)* *(CaptJWilson)* 5-9-3 PRobinson(2) (b.hind: chsd ldr tl outpcd fnl 2f)...2½ **4**
1816[2] Runrig (IRE) **(42)***(41)* *(MissLAPerratt)* 5-8-5 (7)ow2 RHavlin(4) (lw: hld up: effrt 3f out: sn btn)..nk **5**

13/8 SOBA UP, **7/2** Imperial Bid (FR), **9/2** Runrig (IRE), Mhemeanles, **7/1** Thisonesforalice, CSF £11.01 TOTE £2.00: £1.10 £2.40 (£16.60) OWNER Mrs M. Hills (MALTON) BRED Mrs M. J. Hills 5 Rn

2m 25.8 (6.10) SF: 21/5/18/8/-

1959

CRAIGLEITH CLAIMING STKS (2-Y.O) (Class F) £2,634.50 (£742.00: £363.50)
5f Stalls: High GOING minus 0.51 sec per fur (F) 4-00 (4-00)

523[9] **Everyone Can Dream** *(66+)* *(MJohnston)* 2-8-8 DHolland(6) (lw: mde all: r.o strly fnl 2f)....— **1**
595* Chilibang Bang *(48)*(Fav)*(JBerry)* 2-8-9 JCarroll(5) (sn chsng wnr: pushed along: effrt over 2f out: no imp)....6 **2**
1678[4] Julgarant (IRE) *(45)* *(MDods)* 2-8-10 DaleGibson(1) (a chsng ldrs: rdn & no imp fr ½-wy)....1¼ **3**
Ultra Power *(45)* *(PCHaslam)* 2-8-11 (3) JStack(3) (leggy: bit bkwd: dwlt: hdwy ½-wy: wknd 1f out)....1¼ **4**
788[8] Borana Lodge (USA) *(17)* *(MrsJRRamsden)* 2-8-12 KFallon(2) (sn outpcd & bhd)....8 **5**

11/10 Chilibang Bang, **3/1** EVERYONE CAN DREAM (op 2/1), **9/2** Borana Lodge (USA), **6/1** Julgarant (IRE) (4/1-7/1), **15/2** Ultra Power (4/1-8/1), CSF £6.90 TOTE £3.90: £1.80 £1.10 (£3.20) OWNER Brian Yeardley Continental Ltd (MIDDLEHAM) BRED Kiplingcotes Stud 5 Rn

59.3 secs (1.60) SF: 22/4/1/1/-

Everyone Can Dream clmd PMonteith £6,000

1960

HADDINGTON MEDIAN AUCTION MAIDEN STKS (3-Y.O+) (Class E) £2,905.00 (£880.00: £430.00: £205.00)
1m 4f 31y Stalls: High GOING minus 0.51 sec per fur (F) 4-30 (4-30)

1901[2] **Medway (IRE)** *(72+)*(Fav)*(MHTompkins)* 3-8-9 PRobinson(2) (mde all: pushed clr over 3f out: easily)....— **1**
1097[12] Hanifa *(55)* *(MissGayKelleway)* 3-8-9 MWigham(1) (chsd wnr after 3f: rdn appr st: sn btn)...13 **2**
1162[5] Glenrock Dancer (IRE) *(35)* *(WTKemp)* 3-8-9 KFallon(3) (a outpcd & bhd)....15 **3**
1901[3] Kirkie Cross *(31)* *(RMMcKellar)* 3-8-9 JFanning(4) (chsd ldrs tl wknd fnl 3½f)....3 **4**

8/11 MEDWAY (IRE), **5/4** Hanifa, **25/1** Glenrock Dancer (IRE), **66/1** Kirkie Cross, CSF £1.87 TOTE £1.40: (£1.10) OWNER Miss D. J. Merson (NEWMARKET) BRED Oldtown Stud 4 Rn

2m 40.9 (8.40) SF: 1/-/-/-

1961

FIRTH OF FORTH H'CAP (0-70) (3-Y.O) (Class E) £3,009.00 (£912.00: £446.00: £213.00)
7f 15y Stalls: High GOING minus 0.51 sec per fur (F) 5-00 (5-00)

1719* **Russian Heroine (61)***(76)*(Fav)*(MJohnston)* 3-9-7 DHolland(3) (chsd ldrs: rdn 3f out: led over 2f out: r.o)....— **1**
1818[2] Tinklers Folly **(41)***(49)* *(DenysSmith)* 3-8-1 JFanning(5) (chsd ldrs: led wl over 2f out: sn hdd: one pce)....3 **2**

1533[12] Harry's Treat **(56)***(57) (JLEyre)* 3-9-2 KFallon(2) (lw: outpcd tl styd on fnl 2f: nvr able to chal) .3 **3**
1465[5] Champagne N Dreams **(58)***(56) (DNicholls)* 3-9-4 AlexGreaves(6) (lw: trckd ldrs: effrt over 3f out: sn rdn & nt qckn) 1¾ **4**
1819[4] Sunday Mail Too (IRE) **(41)***(18) (MissLAPerratt)* 3-8-1b LCharnock(4) (lw: plld hrd: led tl hdd wl over 2f out: sn wknd) 9 **5**
1541[13] Miss Iron Heart (USA) **(50)***(19) (DJSCosgrove)* 3-8-10 MWigham(1) (a outpcd & bhd)....3½ **6**

7/4 RUSSIAN HEROINE, **10/3** Tinklers Folly, **7/2** Champagne N Dreams (op 9/4), **9/1** Harry's Treat, Sunday Mail Too (IRE) (op 6/1), **16/1** Miss Iron Heart (USA), CSF £7.17 TOTE £2.60: £1.70 £2.10 (£4.10) OWNER The Knavesmire Partnership (MIDDLEHAM) BRED D. R. Botterill 6 Rn
1m 26.8 (0.80) SF: 54/27/35/34/-/-

T/Plpt: £89.60 (102.96 Tckts). T/Qdpt: £3.30 (9.5 Tckts). AA

1854-NOTTINGHAM (L-H)
Monday June 26th (Good to firm)
WEATHER: fine WIND: mod half bhd

1962 SANDIACRE (S) H'CAP (0-60) (3-Y.O) (Class G) £2,243.00 (£618.00: £293.00)
1m 54y Stalls: Low GOING minus 0.15 sec per fur (GF) 2-45 (2-48)

1583[4] **Kama Simba (53)***(64) (NACallaghan)* 3-9-3 WCarson(2) (hld up: hdwy over 2f out: led bel dist: drvn clr) ....— **1**
1718[6] Magical Bid (IRE) **(44)***(47) (JMBradley)* 3-8-8v JWeaver(8) (hld up: hdwy on outside 3f out: kpt on ins fnl f: no ch w wnr)....4 **2**
1824[14] Perfect Bertie (IRE) **(50)***(47) (GROldroyd)* 3-8-7 (7) GParkin(14) (hld up: hdwy 4f out: kpt on u.p fnl 2f)....3 **3**
1569[13] Caltha **(41)***(34) (PCalver)* 3-8-0 (5) NVarley(19) (prom: 2nd st: led over 3f out tl bel dist: sn rdn: one pce)....2½ **4**
1677[8] Irchester Lass **(41)***(33) (SRBowring)* 3-8-0 (5) CTeague(6) (dwlt: hdwy over 2f out: wknd 1f out)....hd **5**
1718* Just Fizzy **(55)***(46)*(Fav)*(MCPipe)* 3-9-5 MRoberts(3) (prom: 6th st: rdn over 2f out: one pce).½ **6**
1762[15] Hunza Story **(38)***(23) (NPLittmoden)* 3-8-2 TGMcLaughlin(4) (nvr nrr)....3½ **7**
1426[12] Burnt Sienna (IRE) **(39)***(14) (JSMoore)* 3-8-3 NAdams(5) (in tch: effrt & rdn over 2f out: nvr able to chal)....5 **8**
1824[6] Bitch **(41)***(14) (DNicholls)* 3-8-5 CRutter(12) (lw: hdwy u.p over 3f out: nvr nr to chal) 1¼ **9**
1824[2] Trumble **(50)***(19) (CWThornton)* 3-9-0 AMackay(7) (prom: 3rd st: wknd over 2f out) 1¾ **10**
1664[9] Zesti **(48)***(16) (TTClement)* 3-8-12 JQuinn(10) (swtg: nvr nr to chal) ....¾ **11**
1625[3] La Fille de Cirque **(45)***(12) (RJRWilliams)* 3-8-9 DBiggs(9) (nvr nr ldrs) ....nk **12**
1834[3] Old Swinford (IRE) **(57)***(22) (BJMeehan)* 3-9-7 BDoyle(1) (mid div tl outpcd 3f out)....1 **13**
1824[11] Share the Secret **(42)***(5) (BHanbury)* 3-8-3 (3) JTate(20) (b: led over 4f: wknd over 2f out).....1¼ **14**
1372[13] Mariposa Grove **(42)** *(RCurtis)* 3-8-6 GBardwell(13) (a in rr) 5 **15**
1718[12] Chadleigh Walk (IRE) **(40)** *(RHollinshead)* 3-8-4v DHarrison(17) (chsd ldrs: 5th st: wknd 3f out)....1¾ **16**
1719[5] Damocles **(46)** *(IABalding)* 3-8-10 LDettori(11) (chsd ldrs: 7th st: wknd 3f out: eased: t.o) 12 **17**
1512[16] Tara Colleen (IRE) **(46)** *(CAHorgan)* 3-8-10 AClark(18) (a in rr: t.o) 3 **18**
1718[2] Sobeloved **(51)** *(MRChannon)* 3-9-1 RHughes(16) (a in rr: t.o) 1½ **19**
1735[9] Pioneer Princess **(42)** *(MJRyan)* 3-8-6b KDarley(15) (swtg: chsd ldrs: 4th st: sn rdn & lost tch: t.o) 1½ **20**

11/4 Just Fizzy, **8/1** La Fille de Cirque, KAMA SIMBA, **9/1** Sobeloved, **10/1** Old Swinford (IRE), **11/1** Trumble, **12/1** Damocles, **16/1** Bitch, Share the Secret, Pioneer Princess, Tara Colleen (IRE), Magical Bid (IRE), **20/1** Caltha, Zesti, Mariposa Grove, **25/1** Chadleigh Walk (IRE), Perfect Bertie (IRE), Irchester Lass, **33/1** Hunza Story, Burnt Sienna (IRE), CSF £133.32 CT £2,850.12 TOTE £7.80: £2.10 £9.20 £7.80 £5.50 (£112.40) Trio £352.90 OWNER K. Al-Said (NEWMARKET) BRED Charlton Down Stud 20 Rn 1m 45.2 (5.60) SF: 33/16/16/3/2/15/-/-/-/-/-/-/-/-/-/-/-/-/-/-
Bt in 8,800 gns

1963 RIVER TRENT H'CAP (0-60) (3-Y.O+) (Class F) £2,519.00 (£694.00: £329.00)
6f 15y Stalls: High GOING minus 0.15 sec per fur (GF) 3-15 (3-16)

1582[2] **Hello Hobson's (IRE) (49)***(56)*(Fav)*(RBastiman)* 5-9-3 DeanMcKeown(17) (lw: swtchd rt sn after s: led wl over 1f out: hld on)....— **1**
1828[5] Densben **(47)***(53) (DenysSmith)* 11-9-1 WCarson(19) (hld up: hdwy bel dist: fin fast)....nk **2**
1797[8] Asterix **(44)***(49) (JMBradley)* 7-8-9v(3) SDrowne(18) (hld up: hdwy stands' side over 1f out: r.o wl ins fnl f) ....nk **3**
1828[9] Old Comrades **(49)***(51) (TDBarron)* 8-9-3 JFortune(22) (lw: disp ld stands' side: rdn & unable qckn fnl f)....1¼ **4**

1679[8] Sweet Mate **(45)***(45) (SRBowring)* 3-8-0b(5) CTeague(21) (slt ld stands' side over 4f: sn rdn: no ex fnl f)....¾ **5**
1763[9] Cheeky Chappy **(34)***(30) (DWChapman)* 4-8-2 MRoberts(1) (led far side 4f: rdn & one pce fnl f)....1¾ **6**
1832[4] Robo Magic (USA) **(58)***(50) (LMontagueHall)* 3-9-4 DHarrison(16) (chsd ldr over 4f)....1½ **7**
1516[9] Can't Say (IRE) **(37)***(22) (JMBradley)* 3-7-6v(5)ow4 NVarley(20) (spd stands' side over 3f)....1 **8**
1783[3] Lugana Vision **(53)***(41) (GFierro)* 3-8-10 (3) DRMcCabe(13) (racd far side: nvr on terms)....½ **9**
1633[2] Ring the Chief **(49)***(35) (RAkehurst)* 3-8-9 TQuinn(14) (prom: rdn 2f out: eased whn btn fnl f)....¾ **10**
1763[7] Arc Lamp **(43)***(28) (JAGlover)* 9-8-11 LDettori(9) (lw: prom centre 4f)....hd **11**
1763[3] Grey Toppa **(50)***(29) (NPLittmoden)* 4-9-4 TGMcLaughlin(3) (spd far side over 3f)....2½ **12**
1499[5] Out of the Mist **(32)***(11) (JAPickering)* 4-8-0v JQuinn(15) (nvr trbld ldrs)....s.h **13**
1521[3] Prince Rudolf (IRE) **(44)***(19) (MrsNMacauley)* 3-7-11v(7) AmandaSanders(11) (lw: a in rr)....1½ **14**
1828[16] Lady-Bo-K **(60)***(35) (CaptJWilson)* 4-10-0 JWeaver(10) (outpcd)....s.h **15**
1660[9] Classic Pet (IRE) **(47)***(18) (CAHorgan)* 3-8-7 NAdams(7) (outpcd)....1½ **16**
1509[9] Glowing Account (IRE) **(45)***(14) (JWMullins)* 4-8-13b JReid(4) (prom far side over 3f)....½ **17**
1580[8] Jet Classic **(45)***(14) (MissJFCraze)* 3-8-5 SWebster(2) (b.hind: prom far side to ½-wy)....hd **18**
1677[13] Supreme Desire **(27)** *(GROldroyd)* 7-7-9 ow1 AMackay(12) (a bhd)....3½ **19**
1797[6] Christian Warrior **(28)** *(REPeacock)* 6-7-3b(7) CAdamson(5) (a bhd)....¾ **20**
1783[7] Le Bal **(43)** *(MrsNMacauley)* 3-8-0b(3) SSanders(6) (lw: dwlt: a bhd & outpcd: t.o)....8 **21**
1042[W] Oscar the Second (IRE) **(30)** *(CWFairhurst)* 5-7-12 JMarshall(8) (outpcd: t.o)....3 **22**

9/2 HELLO HOBSON'S (IRE) (op 7/1), **7/1** Ring the Chief, Old Comrades, **9/1** Lugana Vision, **10/1** Densben, Asterix, **12/1** Sweet Mate, Classic Pet (IRE), Arc Lamp, **14/1** Robo Magic (USA), **16/1** Can't Say (IRE), Le Bal, **20/1** Grey Toppa, Prince Rudolf (IRE), Lady-Bo-K, Out of the Mist, Glowing Account (IRE), **25/1** Cheeky Chappy, **33/1** Supreme Desire, Christian Warrior, Jet Classic, **50/1** Oscar the Second (IRE), CSF £54.09 CT £430.81 TOTE £5.30: £1.40 £2.60 £4.90 £2.10 (£23.50) Trio £111.50 OWNER High Dividend Racing Club (WETHERBY) 22 Rn
1m 12.2 (1.20) SF: 39/36/32/34/20/13/25/-/16/10/11/12/-/-/18/-/-/-/-/-/-/-
WEIGHT FOR AGE 3yo-8lb

1964

E.B.F. MAIDEN STKS (2-Y.O) (Class D) £4,012.50 (£1,200.00: £575.00: £262.50)
6f 15y Stalls: High GOING minus 0.15 sec per fur (GF) 3-45 (3-45)

1715[2] **Sualtach (IRE) (88)***(87+)*(Fav)*(RHollinshead)* 2-9-0 LDettori(9) (lw: mde all: clr fnl 2f: canter)....— **1**
Gryada *(75) (WJarvis)* 2-8-9 WRyan(8) (lt-f: hld up: hdwy over 1f out: styd on ins fnl f)....2½ **2**
1715[3] Lionel Edwards (IRE) *(78) (PFICole)* 2-9-0 TQuinn(2) (a.p: r.o one pce fnl 2f)....¾ **3**
1176[6] Victoria Sioux *(66) (JWharton)* 2-8-9 JQuinn(7) (lw: prom tl wknd wl over 1f out)....3 **4**
682[4] Deadline Time (IRE) *(61) (MHTompkins)* 2-9-0 KDarley(5) (bit bkwd: chsd ldrs over 3f: sn outpcd)....3½ **5**
Golden Pond (IRE) *(38) (RFJohnsonHoughton)* 2-8-9 JReid(4) (lt-f: unf: prom 4f: rn green: sn wknd: t.o)....7 **6**
1627[7] Tasliya (USA) *(30) (JLDunlop)* 2-8-9 WCarson(6) (a bhd: t.o fnl 2f)....3 **7**
Roc de Fer (IRE) *(14) (WAO'Gorman)* 2-9-0 EmmaO'Gorman(3) (unf: scope: bkwd: gd spd over 3f: wknd qckly: t.o)....8 **8**
Khabar *(9) (DMorley)* 2-9-0 RHills(1) (w'like: scope: bkwd: s.i.s: a bhd: t.o 2f)....2 **9**

9/4 SUALTACH (IRE), **3/1** Golden Pond (IRE), **5/1** Lionel Edwards (IRE) (op 3/1), **6/1** Tasliya (USA) (op 9/4), **8/1** Deadline Time (IRE), **12/1** Khabar (op 8/1), **14/1** Roc de Fer (IRE), **20/1** Gryada, Victoria Sioux, CSF £40.44 TOTE £3.30: £1.90 £4.00 £1.20 (£29.30) Trio £69.70 OWNER Mr Noel Sweeney (UPPER LONGDON) BRED Brownstown Stud 9 Rn 1m 12.9 (1.90) SF: 26/14/17/5/-/-/-

1965

LENTON ABBEY CLAIMING STKS (4-Y.O+) (Class F) £2,519.00 (£694.00: £329.00) **2m 9y** Stalls: Low GOING minus 0.15 sec per fur (GF) 4-15 (4-15)

668[18] **Faugeron (71)***(67)*(Fav)*(RAkehurst)* 6-9-1 TQuinn(2) (hld up: 3rd st: led 3f out: clr appr fnl f: unchal)....— **1**
1759[2] Scalp 'em (IRE) **(40)***(51) (PDEvans)* 7-8-6 AClark(12) (hld up: hdwy ½-wy: 5th st: jnd wnr 3f out: sn rdn: one pce)....7 **2**
1826[5] Don't Cry **(21)***(39) (DonEnricoIncisa)* 7-7-9 KimTinkler(10) (hld up: hdwy ½-wy: styd on u.p fnl 2f: nvr nrr)....¾ **3**
Najeb (USA) **(28)***(38) (PDEvans)* 6-8-0 (3) SSanders(1) (swtg: hld up in tch: rdn 3f out: styd on one pce)....9 **4**
1555[5] Among Islands *(42) (MrsMReveley)* 4-8-13 KDarley(6) (hld up: sme hdwy fnl f: nvr nrr)....6 **5**
Strike-a-Pose *(33) (BJLlewellyn)* 5-8-4 RPrice(3) (prom: 2nd st: wknd wl over 2f out)....nk **6**
1667[4] Naawy **(31)***(35) (CSmith)* 5-8-9 JFortune(8) (led 13f: sn rdn & wknd)....3 **7**

*1567*5 Tuscania **(30)***(13) (JWharton)* 5-7-12 JQuinn(5) (b: swtg: hld up: hdwy & 6th st: wknd 3f out: t.o) 11 **8**
1657 4 Secret Assignment (USA) **(27)***(16) (RCurtis)* 5-8-3 GBardwell(11) (a bhd: t.o) 2 **9**
1799 8 Soba Guest (IRE) **(40)***(15) (RTJuckes)* 6-8-3 MFenton(4) (bhd & rdn along ½-wy: no imp: t.o) 1 **10**
1826 8 Drimard (IRE) **(30)***(13) (KMcAuliffe)* 4-8-9 (3) JTate(7) (chsd ldrs 10f: sn lost tch: t.o) 11 **11**
1555 6 Jungle Rites (IRE) *(20) (JGFitzGerald)* 7-9-7 TIves(9) (bit bkwd: chsd ldrs 4th st: wknd over 3f out: t.o) 2½ **12**

4/7 FAUGERON, **7/1** Scalp 'em (IRE) (op 12/1), **12/1** Jungle Rites (IRE), Among Islands, **16/1** Drimard (IRE), Naawy, Tuscania, **20/1** Secret Assignment (USA), **25/1** Don't Cry, Soba Guest (IRE), Strike-a-Pose, **33/1** Najeb (USA), CSF £6.28 TOTE £1.60: £1.60 £1.70 £5.40 (£3.90) Trio £40.50 OWNER Normandy Development(London) (EPSOM) BRED J. L. C. Pearce 12 Rn

3m 32.4 (8.00) SF: 48/32/20/19/23/14/16/-/-/-/-/1

Faugeron clmd DonEnricoIncisa £7,000

1966 BILBOROUGH H'CAP (0-70) (3-Y.O+) (Class E) £3,502.40 (£1,047.20: £501.60: £228.80) 1m 1f 213y Stalls: Low GOING minus 0.15 sec per fur (GF) 4-45 (4-46)

1372 4 **First Bite (IRE) (58)***(74+)*(Fav)*(JLDunlop)* 3-8-4 WCarson(7) (hld up & bhd: c stands' side over 3f out: led wl over 1f out: sn clr: eased nr fin) ....— **1**
1854 * Lady Highfield **(53)***(61) (MJRyan)* 4-8-11 6x AClark(3) (b.hind: hld up: hdwy to ld far side 2f out: sn clr: no ch w wnr) 5 **2**
1557 6 Kanat Lee (IRE) **(40)***(46) (DonEnricoIncisa)* 4-7-12 KimTinkler(11) (bhd: hdwy over 2f out: fin wl) 1½ **3**
1344 14 Midnight Jazz (IRE) **(70)***(72) (WAO'Gorman)* 5-10-0 EmmaO'Gorman(9) (hld up: hdwy & 5th st: styd on one pce fnl 2f) 2 **4**
1687 5 Second Colours (USA) **(60)***(62) (MrsMReveley)* 5-9-4 KDarley(8) (lw: hld up & bhd: hdwy 3f out: rdn & no imp fnl 2f) ....nk **5**
1651 11 Benjamins Law **(50)***(52) (JAPickering)* 4-8-8 DeanMcKeown(2) (led to 2f out: wknd appr fnl f) ....s.h **6**
*18*10 Salska **(60)***(58) (ALForbes)* 4-8-13 (5) LNewton(4) (nvr plcd to chal) 2½ **7**
1854 9 Bad News **(47)***(44) (GFierro)* 3-7-7 NCarlisle(12) (chsd ldrs: rdn along 3f out: sn btn) ....½ **8**
1506 9 Leave it to Lib **(53)***(47) (PCalver)* 8-8-8 (3) JTate(13) (hld up: hdwy 3f out: ev ch over 2f out: sn wknd) 1¾ **9**
1502 9 Bold Look **(58)***(47) (PWHarris)* 4-9-2 MFenton(10) (chsd ldrs: 6th st: wknd 3f out) 3 **10**
1085 3 Highfield Fizz **(65)***(53) (CWFairhurst)* 3-8-11 TIves(1) (s.i.s: sn wnt prom: 3rd st: wknd over 2f out) ....¾ **11**
1816 6 Touch Above **(50)***(33) (TDBarron)* 9-8-8 JFortune(5) (prom: 4th st: wknd over 2f out) 3 **12**
1403 2 Pillow Talk (IRE) **(54)***(17) (SWCampion)* 4-8-12v JWeaver(14) (wnt 2nd st: wknd 3f out: t.o)..13 **13**
Contrac Countess (IRE) **(39)** *(MPBielby)* 5-7-11v AMackay(6) (b: a bhd: t.o) ....¾ **14**

LONG HANDICAP Bad News 7-5

3/1 FIRST BITE (IRE), **9/2** Lady Highfield, **13/2** Touch Above, **7/1** Second Colours (USA), **8/1** Midnight Jazz (IRE), **10/1** Bold Look, **12/1** Pillow Talk (IRE), **14/1** Highfield Fizz, Leave it to Lib, **16/1** Benjamins Law, **25/1** Kanat Lee (IRE), Bad News, **33/1** Salska, **50/1** Contrac Countess (IRE), CSF £17.16 CT £275.31 TOTE £4.00: £2.30 £1.70 £5.40 (£7.40) Trio £178.00 OWNER Mr Ettore Landi (ARUNDEL) BRED Joseph Crowley 14 Rn 2m 9.3 (6.80) SF: 22/21/6/32/22/12/18/-/7/7/1/-/-/-

WEIGHT FOR AGE 3yo-12lb

1967 RADCLIFFE MAIDEN STKS (3-Y.O+) (Class D) £4,408.30 (£1,320.40: £634.20: £291.10) 1m 54y Stalls: Low GOING minus 0.15 sec per fur (GF) 5-15 (5-15)

1701 4 **Crown of Sheba (USA)** *(73+)*(Fav)*(EALDunlop)* 3-8-6 RHills(5) (hld up gng wl: 3rd st: led over 2f out: sn clr: easily) ....— **1**
Chevalier (USA) *(73) (HRACecil)* 3-8-11 WRyan(2) (w'like: scope: hld up: 4th st: drvn along 4f out: shkn up & r.o ins fnl f) 2½ **2**
Doonyasha *(66) (JLDunlop)* 3-8-6 KDarley(3) (lt-f: bit bkwd: chsd ldr: 2nd st: led over 3f out tl over 2f out: no ex) 1 **3**
1786 11 Saltando (IRE) *(60) (PatMitchell)* 4-9-7 SO'Gorman(4) (swtg: hld up & bhd: 5th st: rdn over 3f out: no imp) 6 **4**
1520 4 Valetta *(41) (BJMeehan)* 4-9-2 GCarter(1) (led tl hdd over 3f out: wknd bel dist) 7 **5**

4/6 CROWN OF SHEBA (USA), **5/2** Chevalier (USA), **5/1** Doonyasha (op 3/1), **50/1** Saltando (IRE), Valetta, CSF £2.60 TOTE £1.60: £1.20 £1.30 (£1.20) OWNER Mr Mana Al Maktoum (NEWMARKET) BRED Gainsborough Farm Inc 5 Rn 1m 48.7 (9.10) SF: -/-/-/-/-

WEIGHT FOR AGE 3yo-10lb

T/Jkpt: £7,100.00 (0.8 Tckts); £372.52 to Yarmouth 27/6/95. T/Plpt: £44.20 (372.01 tckts). T/Qdpt: £7.70 (15.4 Tckts). IM

1797-**WARWICK (L-H)**

Monday June 26th (Firm, Good to firm fnl 8f)

WEATHER: sunny WIND: mod against

1968 RAYNSFORD MAIDEN AUCTION STKS (2-Y.O F) (Class E) £3,406.50 (£1,017.00: £486.00: £220.50)
7f Stalls: Low GOING minus 0.36 sec per fur (F) 6-45 (6-46)

1287[5] **Key To A Million (IRE)** *(73) (RHannon)* 2-8-0 MRoberts(6) (mde all: clr over 1f out: r.o wl)..— 1
1671[2] Singoalla (IRE) *(61)*(Fav)*(JLDunlop)* 2-7-11 WCarson(3) (chsd wnr: 3rd st: rdn 2f out: no imp)....4 2
1671[5] Be My Bird *(61) (BJMeehan)* 2-8-0 BDoyle(1) (4th st: one pce fnl 2f)....1¼ 3
1662[4] Mountain Valley *(65) (PFICole)* 2-8-4 CRutter(4) (3rd st: one pce fnl 2f)....s.h 4
Lady Magic (IRE) *(CASmith)* 2-7-11 JQuinn(5) (leggy: s.s: wnt rt s: last st: eased over 1f out: t.o)....dist 5

4/11 Singoalla (IRE), **5/1** Mountain Valley (op 5/2), **10/1** Be My Bird (op 4/1), KEY TO A MILLION (IRE) (op 5/1), **50/1** Lady Magic (IRE), CSF £14.00 TOTE £6.00: £1.70 £1.10 (£2.60) OWNER Million In Mind Part(4) (MARLBOROUGH) BRED Leo Collins 5 Rn 1m 27.5 (3.30) SF: 17/5/5/9/-

1969 UGLY BRIDGE H'CAP (0-80) (3-Y.O+) (Class D) £4,340.70 (£1,299.60: £623.80: £285.90)
1m Stalls: Low GOING minus 0.36 sec per fur (F) 7-15 (7-15)

1775[2] **Arndilly (70)***(79)*(Fav)*(BJMeehan)* 4-9-5b BDoyle(3) (2nd st: edgd lft wl over 1f out: led wl ins fnl f: edgd lft: r.o)....— 1
Young Duke (IRE) **(66)***(74) (MrsSDWilliams)* 7-9-1 MRimmer(8) (hld up: 6th st: hdwy over 1f out: ev ch ins fnl f: r.o)....nk 2
1845* Queens Consul (IRE) **(81)***(87) (BSRothwell)* 5-10-2 6x JFortune(9) (led tl hdd wl ins fnl f: btn whn hmpd nr fin)....1¼ 3
1560[6] Cee-Jay-Ay **(65)***(67) (JBerry)* 8-8-7 (7) PRoberts(6) (s.s: 8th st: hdwy over 1f out: r.o one pce fnl f)....1¾ 4
1654* A Million to One (IRE) **(72)***(73)*(Fav)*(MBell)* 3-8-11 MFenton(7) (3rd st: one pce appr fnl f)....½ 5
1714* Love Legend **(55)***(53) (DWPArbuthnot)* 10-8-4 RPrice(5) (b: rdn 4f out: 5th st: no hdwy fnl 2f)....1¾ 6
1797* Mr Cube (IRE) **(55)***(51) (JMBradley)* 5-8-1v(3) SDrowne(4) (hld up: 7th st: no hdwy fnl 2f)....¾ 7
1638[9] Robsera (IRE) **(75)***(68) (GLewis)* 4-9-10b SWhitworth(1) (4th st: hrd rdn & wknd 2f out)....1¾ 8
1532[6] Diamond Market **(54)***(29) (RHollinshead)* 3-7-7 NCarlisle(2) (hld up: lost pl over 3f out: sn bhd)....9 9

LONG HANDICAP Diamond Market 7-6

9/2 ARNDILLY, A Million to One (IRE), **5/1** Cee-Jay-Ay, **11/2** Mr Cube (IRE), **6/1** Queens Consul (IRE), **7/1** Robsera (IRE), **12/1** Love Legend, **16/1** Young Duke (IRE), **33/1** Diamond Market, CSF £59.00 CT £383.42 TOTE £3.70: £1.60 £5.50 £2.40 (£138.60) Trio £77.90 OWNER Mr A. S. Reid (UPPER LAMBOURN) BRED Hilborough Stud Farm Ltd 9 Rn
1m 38.9 (1.90) SF: 54/49/62/42/38/28/26/43/-
WEIGHT FOR AGE 3yo-10lb

1970 BLACKBRAKE PLANTATION MAIDEN H'CAP (0-60) (3-Y.O+) (Class F) £3,249.80 (£902.80: £433.40)
1m 4f 115y Stalls: Low GOING minus 0.36 sec per fur (F) 7-45 (7-45)

1643[3] **Kintavi (36)***(46) (TWDonnelly)* 5-9-2 CRutter(9) (hld up: hdwy over 4f out: 3rd st: hrd rdn to ld over 1f out: r.o wl)....— 1
1694[5] Masuri Kabisa (USA) **(32)***(39) (HJCollingridge)* 4-8-12 JQuinn(3) (lw: hdwy & 4th st: r.o one pce fnl f)....2 2
1591[6] Fattash (USA) **(52)***(59) (CJBenstead)* 3-9-2b WCarson(6) (hld up: 8th st: hdwy on ins 2f out: r.o wl cl home)....nk 3
1645[7] Presto Boy **(48)***(55) (MBell)* 3-8-12 MFenton(7) (hrd rdn over 3f out: hdwy & 7th st: r.o wl ins fnl f)....nk 4
954[4] Zahid (USA) **(44)***(50) (KRBurke)* 4-9-10 RCochrane(13) (sn prom: led 6f out tl over 1f out: one pce)....nk 5
1834[4] Faustino **(52)***(57) (PFICole)* 3-9-2 JFortune(4) (hld up: hdwy 4f out: 5th st: one pce fnl 2f)....1 6
1776[5] Ruddigore **(51)***(55) (RHannon)* 3-9-1 BThomson(2) (lw: 2nd st: ev ch over 1f out: wknd ins fnl f)....¾ 7
1567[4] Gunmaker **(30)***(32) (BJLlewellyn)* 6-8-10b RPrice(10) (s.i.s: sn prom: rdn 6f out: 6th & wkng st)....2 8
Viceroy Ruler **(44)***(38) (JRJenkins)* 4-9-10 MRoberts(8) (rdn 6f out: a bhd)....6 9

9485 Court Joker (IRE) **(58)***(48)*(Fav)*(MHTompkins)* 3-9-3v(5) HKYim(11) (lw: plld hrd: led over 6f: wknd 4f out) ... 3 **10**
3685 Lawbuster (IRE) **(49)***(7) (MJWilkinson)* 3-8-13 SWhitworth(1) (a bhd: t.o) ... 25 **11**
14426 Grey Blade **(55)***(10) (IABalding)* 3-9-5 KDarley(5) (prom 12f: t.o) ... 2½ **12**
15392 Malingerer **(37)** *(DAWilson)* 4-9-3 GCarter(12) (rdn 6f out: sn bhd: t.o) ... 1¼ **13**

4/1 Court Joker (IRE), **13/2** Presto Boy, **7/1** KINTAVI, **8/1** Faustino, Malingerer (6/1-9/1), **9/1** Ruddigore, **10/1** Masuri Kabisa (USA), Grey Blade (op 6/1), **11/1** Zahid (USA) (8/1-12/1), Fattash (USA), **20/1** Gunmaker, Lawbuster (IRE), Viceroy Ruler, CSF £72.03 CT £691.23 TOTE £7.00: £2.50 £3.50 £2.10 (£36.80) Trio £243.00 OWNER Mr S. Taberner (SWADLINCOTE) BRED S. Taberner 13 Rn
2m 44.6 (7.10) SF: 27/20/24/20/31/22/20/13/19/13/-/-/-
WEIGHT FOR AGE 3yo-16lb

1971 GAVESTON (S) STKS (3-Y.O+) (Class G) £2,243.00 (£618.00: £293.00)
1m 2f 169y Stalls: Low GOING minus 0.36 sec per fur (F) 8-15 (8-18)

18317 **Dungeon Dancer (61)***(66)*(Fav)*(JAkehurst)* 3-8-7v BThomson(11) (hdwy over 3f out: rdn to ld 2f out: r.o wl) ... — **1**
17168 Tony's Mist **(52)***(64) (JMBradley)* 5-9-4 (3) SDrowne(3) (hld up: 7th st: hdwy & swtchd rt 2f out: edgd lft 1f out: r.o fnl f) ... 1½ **2**
17712 Tropical Jungle (USA) **(55)***(61)*(Fav)*(PJMakin)* 5-9-12b KDarley(12) (lw: hld up: hdwy 4f out: 4th st: one pce fnl 2f) ... 5 **3**
Jehol *(53) (NMBabbage)* 9-9-0 (7) SallySandes(2) (2nd st: wknd over 1f out) ... 2 **4**
16586 Lady Valensina (IRE) **(46)***(48) (BJLlewellyn)* 4-9-2 RPrice(1) (lw: led: rdn 3f out: hdd 2f out: sn wknd) ... s.h **5**
15013 Heighth of Fame **(45)***(40) (SChristian)* 4-9-7 RCochrane(8) (nvr trbld ldrs) ... 9 **6**
12559 Sky Diver **(41)***(38) (BJLlewellyn)* 4-9-7 SWhitworth(6) (5th & hmpd st: wknd 2f out) ... 1 **7**
39412 Danson *(33) (THCaldwell)* 4-9-7 JFortune(4) (lw: a bhd) ... 3½ **8**
17997 Course Fishing **(33)***(30) (BAMcMahon)* 4-9-7 FNorton(9) (prom: sddle slipped 6f out: 6th & wkng st) ... 2 **9**
15678 Waterloo Belle *(12) (MrsNMacauley)* 4-8-13b(3) SSanders(5) (lw: a bhd) ... 9 **10**
Amber Lily *(JMBradley)* 3-8-2 JQuinn(7) (prom over 6f: t.o) ... 12 **11**
17618 Call Tophorse *(PCHaslam)* 3-8-0 (7) NicolaHowarth(10) (prom 6f: t.o) ... 10 **12**

2/1 DUNGEON DANCER (6/4-9/4), Tropical Jungle (USA), **11/2** Heighth of Fame, **10/1** Tony's Mist (8/1-12/1), Lady Valensina (IRE) (7/1-12/1), **14/1** Jehol, **16/1** Call Tophorse, **20/1** Course Fishing, **33/1** Sky Diver, Danson, Waterloo Belle, Amber Lily, CSF £22.76 TOTE £3.30: £1.20 £3.80 £1.80 (£31.30) Trio £8.20 OWNER The Persian War Partnership (LAMBOURN) BRED M. Houlston 12 Rn
2m 20.9 (7.40) SF: 9/21/18/10/5/-/-/-/-/-/-/-
WEIGHT FOR AGE 3yo-14lb
No bid

1972 ROTHWELL H'CAP (0-70) (3-Y.O+ F & M) (Class E) £3,903.75 (£1,170.00: £562.50: £258.75)
5f Stalls: Low GOING minus 0.36 sec per fur (F) 8-45 (8-48)

18326 **Tael of Silver (62)***(71+) (KRBurke)* 3-9-10 MFenton(3) (hld up: swtchd rt over 2f out: gd hdwy over 1f out: edgd lft fnl f: r.o wl to ld cl home) ... — **1**
6298 Wasblest **(55)***(62) (MJohnston)* 3-9-3 KDarley(2) (a.p: led over 1f out: edgd lft ins fnl f: hdd cl home) ... ½ **2**
13213 Miriam **(53)***(51)*(Fav)*(MJFetherston-Godley)* 4-9-8 MRoberts(6) (lw: wnt lft s: sn prom: led over 2f out tl over 1f out: one pce) ... 3 **3**
16025 Diebiedale **(57)***(53) (RBoss)* 3-9-5 MRimmer(10) (hdwy over 2f out: hrd rdn over 1f out: one pce) ... ½ **4**
16772 Twice in Bundoran (IRE) **(55)***(50) (PSFelgate)* 4-9-7 (3) DWright(7) (a.p: one pce fnl 2f) ... ½ **5**
16026 Chief's Lady **(55)***(43) (GFierro)* 3-9-0 (3) SSanders(4) (nvr nr to chal) ... 2 **6**
15385 Random **(53)***(41) (CJames)* 4-9-8 CRutter(8) (lw: stumbled over 2f out: no hdwy) ... hd **7**
167916 Statomist **(47)***(31) (GFierro)* 3-8-9b StephenDavies(1) (no hdwy fnl 2f) ... 1¼ **8**
17779 Ashkernazy (IRE) **(45)***(18) (NEBerry)* 4-8-9 (5) JDSmith(9) (lw: wnt lft s: a bhd) ... 3½ **9**
17215 Daily Starshine (IRE) **(56)***(28) (JBerry)* 3-8-11b(7) PFessey(5) (hmpd s: a bhd) ... nk **10**
18026 Eluned May **(47)***(12) (RMWhitaker)* 4-9-2 DeanMcKeown(11) (lw: led over 2f: wknd wl over 1f out) ... 2 **11**

7/2 Miriam, **4/1** Twice in Bundoran (IRE), **11/2** Diebiedale, **8/1** Random, Wasblest, **9/1** Daily Starshine (IRE), **12/1** Ashkernazy (IRE) (op 20/1), Eluned May (8/1-14/1), **16/1** Chief's Lady, TAEL OF SILVER, **33/1** Statomist, CSF £125.84 CT £504.61 TOTE £42.60: £7.40 £1.90 £1.80 (£98.10) Trio £34.50 OWNER Mrs Elaine Burke (WANTAGE) BRED Mrs V. O'Brien 11 Rn
61.3 secs (3.30) SF: 21/12/8/3/7/-/-/-/-/-/-
WEIGHT FOR AGE 3yo-7lb

1973

STONELEIGH H'CAP (0-80) (3-Y.O+) (Class D) £3,833.70 (£1,143.60: £545.80: £246.90) **1m 6f 194y** Stalls: Low GOING minus 0.36 sec per fur (F) 9-15 (9-19)

1730[5] **Salaman (FR)** **(67)***(79+)*(Fav)*(JLDunlop)* 3-8-5 WCarson(6) (lw: hld up: hdwy on ins 5f out: 5th st: rdn to ld wl over 1f out: r.o wl)......— 1
1281[3] Astrolabe **(78)***(88) (BWHills)* 3-9-2b BThomson(3) (chsd ldr: 2nd st: ev ch over 1f out: nt qckn)......1½ 2
1025[7] Pomorie (IRE) **(63)***(72) (JWPayne)* 4-9-5 RCochrane(5) (lw: hld up: stumbled 10f out: hdwy 4f out: 3rd st: ev ch 2f out: r.o one pce fnl f)......1½ 3
346[9] Ibsen **(68)***(74) (RAkehurst)* 7-9-7 (3) SSanders(4) (lw: hld up: 6th st: hdwy 2f out: one pce fnl f)......2½ 4
1643[6] Tommy Cooper **(42)***(48) (MrsBarbaraWaring)* 4-7-9 (3) DWright(7) (hld up & bhd: hdwy 6f out: hrd rdn & 4th st: one pce fnl 2f)......hd 5
1339[8] Young Clifford (USA) **(64)***(67) (FJordan)* 4-9-6 MFenton(2) (dropped rr 5f out: last st)......3 6
1858[6] Miroswaki (USA) **(61)***(62) (GFierro)* 5-9-3 StephenDavies(1) (led: clr 9f out: hdd wl over 1f out: eased whn btn ins fnl f)......2 7

7/4 SALAMAN (FR), **15/8** Astrolabe, **9/2** Ibsen, **10/1** Tommy Cooper, **11/1** Pomorie (IRE) (8/1-12/1), **20/1** Miroswaki (USA), **33/1** Young Clifford (USA), CSF £5.30 TOTE £2.20: £1.50 £1.60 (£2.30) OWNER Lady Cohen (ARUNDEL) BRED Ridgecourt Stud 7 Rn

3m 18.8 (9.80) SF: 11/20/22/24/-/17/12
WEIGHT FOR AGE 3yo-18lb
T/Plpt: £20.10 (624.19 Tckts0. T/Qdpt: £12.80 (7.75 Tckts). KH

1829-WINDSOR (Fig. 8)
Monday June 26th (Good to firm)

WEATHER: fine WIND: nil

1974

QUEEN CHARLOTTE'S HOSPITAL (S) H'CAP (0-60) (3-Y.O+) (Class G) £2,801.00 (£786.00: £383.00) **1m 2f 7y** Stalls: High GOING minus 0.67 sec (HD) 6-30 (6-31)

1854[15] **Bronze Runner** **(34)***(45) (SMellor)* 11-8-5b TSprake(5) (hdwy 2f out: led ins fnl f: drvn out)..— 1
1694[7] Lady Reema **(36)***(46) (MissAJWhitfield)* 4-8-7 DHarrison(4) (hdwy 4f out: led 2f out tl ins fnl f)......½ 2
1663[4] Lady Sabina **(37)***(46) (WJMusson)* 5-8-3 (5) PMcCabe(13) (lw: hdwy 2f out: ev ch ins fnl f: nt qckn)......½ 3
1644[4] Noeprob (USA) **(41)***(46)*(Fav)*(RJHodges)* 5-8-12 PatEddery(8) (swtg: 7th st: ev ch 2f out: wknd fnl f)......3 4
1555[4] Premier Blues (FR) **(29)***(31) (RJRWilliams)* 5-8-0bow1 DBiggs(21) (swtg: led to 2f out: one pce)......1¼ 5
1622[18] Clancy's Express **(25)***(27) (GBBalding)* 4-7-5 (5) NVarley(10) (lw: 4th st: one pce fnl 2f)......nk 6
880[5] Chastleton **(42)***(40) (MRChannon)* 3-8-1 CandyMorris(15) (nvr nrr)......2½ 7
1664[7] Jobber's Fiddle **(48)***(45) (DJSffrenchDavis)* 3-8-0 (7) JBramhill(19) (nrst fin)......¾ 8
Shelter **(31)***(27) (JohnBerry)* 8-8-2 ow1 GHind(7) (nvr nr to chal)......nk 9
1659[6] Brown Carpet **(27)***(22) (CAHorgan)* 8-7-12b NAdams(16) (hdwy fnl f: r.o)......1 10
1519[3] Thames Side **(48)***(42) (MMadgwick)* 4-9-5 AMcGlone(3) (5th st: wknd 3f out)......nk 11
1762[4] Calisar **(39)***(33) (PHowling)* 5-8-7 (3) DWright(20) (nvr trbld ldrs)......½ 12
1813[4] Foremma **(24)***(16) (PRHedger)* 4-7-9vow2 CAvery(11) (swtg: 2nd st: wknd over 3f out)......s.h 13
1519[8] Green Green Ruby **(43)***(30) (GLMoore)* 3-7-11v(5)ow3 AWhelan(22) (6th st: wknd over 3f out)..2 14
White Flash **(55)***(41) (DRCElsworth)* 4-9-7 (5) AProcter(2) (in tch 4f)......2½ 15
1745[12] Blanchland **(54)***(40) (KTIvory)* 6-9-11b MTebbutt(1) (mid div: rdn & wknd over 2f out)......nk 16
1645[11] Them Times (IRE) **(26)***(8) (FJordan)* 6-7-4 (7)ow3 SLanigan(14) (3rd st: wknd 4f out)......¾ 17
1674[9] Valinco **(42)***(23) (SDow)* 4-8-13 AMartinez(9) (lw: mid div: wknd 3f out)......2½ 18
1519[6] Awesome Power **(50)***(24) (JWHills)* 9-9-7 MHills(6) (nvr nr ldrs)......4 19
453[10] Stoneham Girl **(34)** *(PButler)* 3-7-2 (5) MBaird(18) (t.o)......15 20
1519[10] Elmer's Tune **(43)** *(RHannon)* 3-8-2 ow4 SRaymont(12) (t.o)......2 21
1659[11] Northern Spruce (IRE) **(40)** *(MissJacquelineDoyle)* 3-7-6 (7) MartinDwyer(17) (rdr lost irons sn after s: a t.o)......dist 22

LONG HANDICAP Stoneham Girl 7-6 Foremma 7-5

9/4 Noeprob (USA), **13/2** Thames Side, **8/1** Lady Sabina, **10/1** Clancy's Express, **12/1** Lady Reema (8/1-14/1), Brown Carpet, Calisar, **14/1** Chastleton, **16/1** Shelter, Blanchland, Awesome Power, **20/1** Jobber's Fiddle, Green Green Ruby, **25/1** BRONZE RUNNER, White Flash, Elmer's Tune, Northern Spruce (IRE), **33/1** Valinco, Foremma, Stoneham Girl, Premier Blues (FR), Them Times (IRE), CSF £305.25 CT £2,404.07 TOTE £45.50: £6.30 £3.80 £1.60 £1.60 (£559.70) Trio £433.90 OWNER Austin Stroud & Co Ltd (SWINDON) BRED Miss K. Rausing 22 Rn No bid

2m 6.4 (1.50) SF: 25/26/26/26/11/7/8/13/7/2/22/13/-/-/21/20/-/3/4/-/-/-
WEIGHT FOR AGE 3yo-12lb

1975

NAISMITHS H'CAP (0-65) (3-Y.O+) (Class F) £3,874.75 (£1,168.00: £566.50: £265.75) **5f 217y** Stalls: High GOING minus 0.67 sec per fur (HD) 7-00 (7-03)

1777⁵ **Louisville Belle (IRE) (48)***(55) (MDIUsher)* 6-8-4 (7) CAdamson(9) (b: lw: a.p: led 2f out: edgd rt fnl f: r.o) — 1
1499* Petraco (IRE) **(61)***(65) (NASmith)* 7-9-3 (7) JCornally(14) (a.p: ev ch whn hmpd ins fnl f: swtchd lft: r.o) 1¼ 2
1832¹⁸ Spectacle Jim **(49)***(53) (JO'Donoghue)* 6-8-12b MHills(13) (hdwy fnl 2f: nvr nrr) s.h 3
1676⁵ Great Hall **(53)***(56) (PDCundell)* 6-9-2b DHarrison(10) (late hdwy: nrst fin) hd 4
1700⁴ Taffeta Silk (USA) **(62)***(65) (WJarvis)* 4-9-11 PatEddery(15) (w ldrs: ev ch 2f out: nt qckn) hd 5
1499⁸ Bold Cyrano (IRE) **(52)***(52) (BPalling)* 4-9-1 TSprake(11) (lw: a.p: no hdwy fnl 2f) 1¼ 6
1499² Friendly Brave (USA) **(65)***(59) (MissGayKelleway)* 5-9-7 (7) DaneO'Neill(1) (gd spd over 4f) 2 7
1400⁵ Sizzling **(65)***(57) (RHannon)* 3-9-6 JReid(16) (a mid div) 1 8
1508¹⁰ The Noble Oak (IRE) **(47)***(38) (MJBolton)* 7-8-3 (7) AmandaSanders(2) (lw: a mid div) nk 9
1750* Perfect Brave **(60)***(50)*(Fav)*(DRCElsworth)* 4-9-4 (5) AProcter(7) (spd over 3f) nk 10
1050¹³ Tomal **(56)***(43) (RIngram)* 3-8-11 AMcGlone(12) (led 4f) 1¼ 11
Super Serenade **(54)***(40) (GBBalding)* 6-9-3 JWilliams(3) (a bhd) nk 12
1910⁵ Lorins Gold **(36)***(19) (AndrewTurnell)* 5-7-13 NAdams(5) (stumbled s: a bhd) 1 13
*278*⁴ Rotherfield Park (IRE) **(54)***(29) (CSmith)* 3-8-9 GHind(6) (spd 3f) 3 14
*499*⁸ Our Shadee (USA) **(50)***(24) (KTIvory)* 5-8-6v(7) CScally(8) (spd 4f) ½ 15
1700³ Night Asset **(55)** *(JO'Donoghue)* 6-8-13 (5) PMcCabe(4) (bhd tl p.u over 1f out) P

5/1 Perfect Brave, **11/2** Taffeta Silk (USA) (4/1-6/1), **13/2** Night Asset, **7/1** Sizzling, **8/1** Petraco (IRE), **9/1** Friendly Brave (USA), **10/1** Great Hall, **14/1** Spectacle Jim, LOUISVILLE BELLE (IRE) (10/1-16/1), Our Shadee (USA), **16/1** Lorins Gold, **20/1** Bold Cyrano (IRE), Tomal, **25/1** The Noble Oak (IRE), Super Serenade, **33/1** Rotherfield Park (IRE), CSF £128.68 CT £1,488.73 TOTE £28.70: £3.80 £1.80 £2.80 £2.30 (£123.70) Trio £237.90 OWNER Mrs M. P. Pearson (SWINDON) BRED Ballydoyle Partnership 16 Rn 1m 12.2 (1.70) SF: 30/40/28/31/40/27/34/24/13/25/10/15/-/-/-/-

WEIGHT FOR AGE 3yo-8lb

1976

RICHARD & JACK WISEMAN TRUST STKS (3-Y.O) (Class C) £6,636.50 (£2,306.50: £1,115.75: £466.25)
1m 2f 7y Stalls: High GOING minus 0.67 sec per fur (HD) 7-30 (7-31)

Red Azalea *(93++)*(Fav)*(SirMarkPrescott)* 3-8-8 LDettori(1) (swtg: 2nd tl led over 5f out: clr fnl 3f: eased fnl f) — 1
1605⁶ That Old Feeling (IRE) **(94)***(96) (RHannon)* 3-9-2 PatEddery(3) (lw: 4th st: effrt on ins whn bdly hmpd over 2f out: swtchd lft: r.o) 3 2
1301⁴ Alanar (USA) **(96)***(96) (PFICole)* 3-9-7 TQuinn(2) (lw: led: hung lft & 2nd st: wknd over 2f out) 3½ 3
Grandinare (USA) *(90) (PWChapple-Hyam)* 3-9-2 JReid(4) (bit bkwd: 3rd st: bdly hmpd over 2f out: nt rcvr) nk 4

5/6 RED AZALEA (Evens-11/10), **7/2** Alanar (USA), **9/2** Grandinare (USA) (3/1-5/1), **5/1** That Old Feeling (IRE), CSF £4.93 TOTE £1.70: (£4.00) OWNER Cheveley Park Stud (NEWMARKET) BRED Cheveley Park Stud Ltd 4 Rn 2m 5.1 (0.20) SF: 38/41/41/35

STEWARDS' ENQUIRY Eddery suspended 15-27/7/95 (careless riding)

1977

E.B.F. DIBB LUPTON BROOMHEAD MEDIAN AUCTION MAIDEN STKS (2-Y.O) (Class D) £4,822.00 (£1,456.00: £708.00: £334.00)
5f 217y Stalls: High GOING minus 0.67 sec per fur (HD) 8-00 (8-07)

1511² **Crocodile Shoes** *(76)*(Fav)*(RHannon)* 2-9-0 PatEddery(12) (mde all: hung lft over 3f out: r.o wl) — 1
1525^W Auriga *(66) (IABalding)* 2-8-9 LDettori(8) (neat: bit bkwd: a.p: ev ch whn hung bdly rt over 1f out: r.o ins fnl f) 1¾ 2
1697⁴ Emperegrine (USA) *(69) (CFWall)* 2-8-9 (5) LNewton(18) (hdwy fnl 2f: nvr nrr) ¾ 3
1497³ Pacific Grove *(60) (PFICole)* 2-8-9 JWeaver(9) (hdwy 2f out: r.o one pce fnl f) 1¾ 4
1652⁴ Napoleon's Return *(57) (AGFoster)* 2-9-0 TSprake(14) (stdy hdwy fnl 2f: r.o) 3 5
Hank-a-chief *(51) (MMcCormack)* 2-9-0 RStreet(10) (neat: s.s: nrst fin) 2 6
1662⁷ Dragonjoy *(50) (LJHolt)* 2-9-0 AMcGlone(20) (nvr nr to chal) ½ 7
Bailiwick *(47) (NAGraham)* 2-9-0 JWilliams(16) (str: bit bkwd: nvr nrr) 1 8
Lunar Gris *(37) (JEBanks)* 2-8-9 AClark(17) (b: str: bit bkwd: s.s: nrst fin) 2 9
Bold Patriot (IRE) *(42) (JWHills)* 2-9-0 MHills(19) (unf: bit bkwd: prom 4f) s.h 10
Little Millie *(34) (PHayward)* 2-8-2 (7) DaneO'Neill(15) (unf: bit bkwd: prom 4f) 1 11
Honestly *(34) (BSmart)* 2-8-9 DHarrison(2) (unf: s.s: spd 3f) s.h 12
Velvet Jones *(38) (PFICole)* 2-9-0 TQuinn(13) (unf: bit bkwd: s.s: sn w ldrs: wknd 2f out) nk 13

	Tarry *(31) (LordHuntingdon)* 2-8-9 JReid(3) (neat: bit bkwd: prom over 3f) 1	**14**
1772[5]	It's A Ripper *(28) (GLewis)* 2-9-0 WNewnes(6) (outpcd) 3	**15**
	Gemolly (IRE) *(21) (MartynMeade)* 2-8-9 VSlattery(5) (leggy: lt-f: outpcd) ....½	**16**
	Half An Inch (IRE) *(26) (BJMeehan)* 2-9-0 DBiggs(7) (str: bkwd: outpcd) ....hd	**17**
1536[7]	Gentle Friend *(17) (JLDunlop)* 2-8-9 WRyan(11) (bhd fnl 2f) 1½	**18**
	New Technique (FR) *(KMcAuliffe)* 2-8-9 MTebbutt(4) (w'like: a bhd: t.o) 20	**19**

5/6 CROCODILE SHOES, **11/2** Bold Patriot (IRE) (12/1-5/1), **7/1** Auriga (5/1-10/1), **9/1** Velvet Jones (op 2/1), **14/1** Pacific Grove, **16/1** Tarry, **20/1** Gentle Friend, Emperegrine (USA), Half An Inch (IRE), **25/1** It's A Ripper, Napoleon's Return, **33/1** Lunar Gris, Bailiwick, **40/1** Gemolly (IRE), New Technique (FR), Hank-a-chief, **50/1** Little Millie, Honestly, **66/1** Dragonjoy, CSF £9.46 TOTE £1.90: £1.20 £2.10 £7.40 (£6.00) Trio £58.80 OWNER Kennet Valley Thoroughbreds (MARLBOROUGH) BRED R. L. M. and Mrs Stillwell 19 Rn 1m 13.2 (2.70) SF: 20/10/13/4/1/-/-/-/-/-/-/-/-/-/-/-/-/-/-

1978

EDWARD SYMMONS & PARTNERS H'CAP (0-70) (3-Y.O) (Class E) £3,783.75 (£1,140.00: £552.50: £258.75)
1m 3f 135y Stalls: High GOING minus 0.67 sec per fur (HD) 8-30 (8-32)

	Dance So Suite (63)*(71) (PFICole)* 3-9-7 TQuinn(4) (3rd st: led ins fnl f: all out) ....—	**1**
1693[4]	Persian Conquest (IRE) **(58)***(65) (RIngram)* 3-9-2b JWeaver(3) (lw: led tl ins fnl f: edgd lft: r.o)½	**2**
1816*	Acquittal (IRE) **(58)***(64) (JRFanshawe)* 3-8-11 (5) NVarley(2) (7th st: hdwy on ins 3f out: styd on one pce) 1¼	**3**
1664[4]	Wet Patch (IRE) **(59)***(63) (RHannon)* 3-9-3 RHughes(10) (6th st: ev ch over 2f out: one pce) ..1	**4**
974[4]	Courbaril **(61)***(60) (SDow)* 3-9-5 LDettori(5) (2nd st: wknd over 2f out) 4	**5**
1513[9]	Born to Please (IRE) **(50)***(39) (PWHarris)* 3-8-8 WNewnes(8) (lw: hmpd 6f out: nt rcvr) 7	**6**
1372[10]	Darling Clover **(57)***(41) (DMorley)* 3-9-1 MTebbutt(1) (5th st: wknd 3f out) 4	**7**
1831[3]	Rock Oyster **(50)***(33) (BJMeehan)* 3-8-8 DHarrison(11) (a bhd) 1½	**8**
853[12]	Admiral's Guest (IRE) **(60)***(29)*(Fav)*(GHarwood)* 3-9-4 AClark(6) (lw: hdwy & 4th st: wknd over 3f out: t.o) 10	**9**
1696[8]	Shamekh **(53)** *(JEBanks)* 3-8-4b(7) DaneO'Neill(9) (b: b.hind: ref to r: t.n.p)	**R**

2/1 Admiral's Guest (IRE), **7/2** Acquittal (IRE), **6/1** Courbaril, **13/2** Wet Patch (IRE) (9/2-7/1), **8/1** Rock Oyster (6/1-9/1), **9/1** Darling Clover, Persian Conquest (IRE) (6/1-10/1), **12/1** DANCE SO SUITE (op 8/1), **14/1** Shamekh, **33/1** Born to Please (IRE), CSF £113.17 CT £428.13 TOTE £14.60: £2.90 £2.50 £1.60 (£80.30) Trio £71.20 OWNER Mr J. S. Gutkin (WHATCOMBE) BRED Genesis Green Stud and Walter Swinburn Ltd 10 Rn 2m 27.6 (1.60) SF: 41/35/34/33/30/9/11/3/-/-

1979

BOOTH WHITE MAIDEN STKS (3-Y.O) (Class D) £4,926.00 (£1,488.00: £724.00: £342.00) **1m 67y** Stalls: High GOING minus 0.67 sec per fur (HD) 9-00 (9-05)

	Felitza (IRE) *(77)*(Fav)*(HRACecil)* 3-8-9 WRyan(6) (lw: rn wd after 1f: 2nd & wd st: led 4f out: r.o wl) ....—	**1**
572[5]	Raise the Stakes **(78)***(80) (IABalding)* 3-9-0 LDettori(14) (lw: led to 4f out: ev ch 1f out: r.o) .1¼	**2**
1796[6]	Sharp Consul (IRE) *(68) (HCandy)* 3-9-0 DBiggs(18) (hdwy over 3f out: nvr nrr) 6	**3**
	Florismart *(60) (JARToller)* 3-9-0 WNewnes(16) (6th st: r.o one pce fnl 2f) 4	**4**
	Letterluna *(55) (DRGandolfo)* 3-8-9 JReid(12) (w'like: 5th st: outpcd) ....s.h	**5**
	Jareer Do (IRE) *(55) (BPalling)* 3-8-9 TSprake(2) (leggy: lt-f: 7th st: no hdwy fnl 2f) ....s.h	**6**
	Reefa's Mill (IRE) **(84)***(51) (JWHills)* 3-9-0 MHills(9) (nvr nr to chal) 5	**7**
1446[8]	Park Ridge *(44) (TGMills)* 3-8-7 (7) DToole(3) (carried wd after 1f: 3rd st: wknd 3f out) 3½	**8**
1675[11]	Press Again *(38) (PHayward)* 3-8-9 RStreet(11) (nvr nr ldrs) ....½	**9**
	Spumante *(42) (RChampion)* 3-9-0 AClark(13) (hdwy 2f out: nvr plcd to chal) ....nk	**10**
1514[7]	Dazzler *(41) (MarkCampion)* 3-8-7 (7) JDoe(20) (outpcd) ....¾	**11**
1549[5]	My Brave Girl *(35) (HRACecil)* 3-8-9 AMcGlone(5) (a bhd) ....nk	**12**
1053[4]	Indescent Blue *(34) (DWPArbuthnot)* 3-8-9 TQuinn(19) (4th st: wknd 4f out) ....¾	**13**
	Arabian Flight *(37) (TTClement)* 3-9-0 AMackay(15) (w'like: b.hind: outpcd) ....¾	**14**
	Wizzard Star *(30) (MJHaynes)* 3-8-9 PatEddery(8) (leggy: unf: a bhd) 1	**15**
1520[2]	Sovereigns Parade *(33) (LJHolt)* 3-9-0 CAvery(1) (lw: a bhd) 1	**16**
	River May *(25) (AndrewTurnell)* 3-8-9 NAdams(17) (leggy: bit bkwd: a bhd) 2	**17**
1691[12]	Bakheta *(20) (KTIvory)* 3-8-9 MTebbutt(10) (b.hind: s.s: a bhd) 2½	**18**

10/11 FELITZA (IRE), **5/1** Raise the Stakes, **9/1** Reefa's Mill (IRE) (5/1-10/1), **12/1** Indescent Blue, Florismart, **14/1** My Brave Girl, Wizzard Star (10/1-16/1), **16/1** Letterluna, Sharp Consul (IRE), **20/1** Sovereigns Parade, **25/1** Spumante, Bakheta, **33/1** Park Ridge, River May, Dazzler, **50/1** Jareer Do (IRE), Arabian Flight, Press Again, CSF £7.78 TOTE £1.80: £1.30 £2.00 £3.40 (£3.90) Trio £14.30 OWNER Sheikh Mohammed (NEWMARKET) BRED Sheikh Mohammed bin Rashid al Maktoum 18 Rn 1m 43.8 (2.20) SF: 18/21/9/1/-/-/-/-/-/-/-/-/-/-/-/-/-/-

T/Plpt: £28.50 (457.59 Tckts). T/Qdpt: £8.30 (8.5 Tckts). Hn

1937-**LINGFIELD (L-H)**

Tuesday June 27th (Good to firm, Firm bk st, AWT Standard)

WEATHER: hot WIND: almost nil

1980 BDO STOY HAYWARD LIMITED STKS (0-70) (3-Y.O+) (Class E) £3,044.80 (£906.40: £431.20: £193.60)

1m (Equitrack) Stalls: High GOING minus 0.60 sec per fur (FST) 2-30 (2-30)

North Reef (IRE) **(70)***(66)*(Fav)*(SirMarkPrescott)* 4-9-5 GDuffield(3) (chsd ldr over 5f out: led 1f out: drvn out)....— 1
1692[8] Kinnegad Kid **(69)***(74) (RIngram)* 6-10-1 JWeaver(4) (lw: hld up: hrd rdn over 1f out: r.o one pce)....1¼ 2
1789[3] Words of Wisdom (IRE) **(59)***(63) (CACyzer)* 5-9-5 DBiggs(2) (a.p: hrd rdn over 1f out: one pce)....s.h 3
1641[5] Mr Teigh **(70)***(62) (KMcAuliffe)* 3-8-6 (3) JTate(1) (lw: hld up: hrd rdn over 1f out: one pce)....½ 4
1714[15] Soaking **(67)***(57) (GLMoore)* 5-9-5 SWhitworth(5) (led 7f: no ex ins fnl f)....2½ 5

4/6 NORTH REEF (IRE) (op Evens), **11/2** Soaking (7/2-6/1), **6/1** Mr Teigh (3/1-13/2), Kinnegad Kid (4/1-13/2), **7/1** Words of Wisdom (IRE), CSF £5.29 TOTE £1.90: £1.30 £1.90 (£3.40) OWNER Mr W. E. Sturt (NEWMARKET) BRED Limestone Stud 5 Rn 1m 38.63 (2.23) SF: 31/39/28/17/22

WEIGHT FOR AGE 3yo-10lb

1981 AMEC BUILDING (S) STKS (2-Y.O) (Class F) £3,174.20 (£881.20: £422.60)

6f Stalls: High GOING minus 0.28 sec per fur (GF) 3-00 (3-04)

1671[8] **Domettes (IRE)** *(63)*(Fav)*(RHannon)* 2-8-6 JReid(4) (lw: a.p: rdn over 3f out: led ins fnl f: r.o wl)....— 1
1841[4] Jambo **(52)***(60) (MRChannon)* 2-8-1 (5) PPMurphy(10) (a.p: led 2f out tl ins fnl f: unable qckn)....1 2
1184[12] Multi Franchise *(63) (BGubby)* 2-8-11v KFallon(5) (rdn over 3f out: hdwy over 1f out: r.o one pce ins fnl f)....¾ 3
1758[6] Time Clash (IRE) *(58) (BPalling)* 2-8-6 TSprake(8) (rdn over 3f out: hdwy over 2f out: r.o one pce ins fnl f)....s.h 4
1662[10] Laser Life Star *(55)*(Fav)*(CNWilliams)* 2-8-6 PRobinson(6) (b.hind: plld hrd: hld up: hrd rdn over 1f out: one pce)....1¼ 5
1829[3] Golden Silver *(50) (JSMoore)* 2-8-0 (7)ow1 DaneO'Neill(2) (led over 2f: ev ch over 1f out: wknd ins fnl f)....2 6
1536[9] Apartments Abroad *(42) (KMcAuliffe)* 2-8-3v(3) JTate(11) (led over 3f out to 2f out: wknd over 1f out)....3 7
The Clan *(40) (AMoore)* 2-8-6 GDuffield(1) (w'like: bit bkwd: outpcd: hdwy over 1f out: wknd fnl f)....¾ 8
1752[8] Young Butt *(44) (JFfitch-Heyes)* 2-8-11 TQuinn(7) (b: lw: bhd fnl 3f)....hd 9
1590[13] Red Sky Delight (IRE) *(35) (PButler)* 2-8-3 (3) SDrowne(9) (a bhd)....1¾ 10
1746[9] Latzio *(5) (BAPearce)* 2-8-6 JWeaver(3) (lw: outpcd)....11 11

4/1 DOMETTES (IRE) (3/1-9/2), Laser Life Star (op 7/1), **5/1** Jambo (3/1-11/2), **11/2** Apartments Abroad, **6/1** Multi Franchise, Young Butt, **8/1** Golden Silver (op 4/1), **16/1** Time Clash (IRE), **20/1** The Clan, **25/1** Latzio, **50/1** Red Sky Delight (IRE), CSF £24.89 TOTE £5.20: £1.80 £2.30 £3.50 (£8.00) Trio £25.70 OWNER . Albion Investments (MARLBOROUGH) BRED Sandville Stud 11 Rn

1m 13.05 (4.05) SF: 10/7/10/5/2/-/-/-/-/-/-

No bid

1982 HENRY STREETER H'CAP (0-80) (3-Y.O) (Class D) £4,070.30 (£1,216.40: £582.20: £265.10)

6f Stalls: High GOING minus 0.28 sec per fur (GF) 3-30 (3-31)

1624[7] **Tafahhus (75)***(85)*(Fav)*(RWArmstrong)* 3-9-7 WCarson(2) (a.p: led 3f out: pushed out)....— 1
1924[6] Prolific Lady (IRE) **(71)***(78) (MBrittain)* 3-9-3b KFallon(9) (lw: hld up: chsd wnr fnl 2f: unable qckn)....1¼ 2
850[12] Squire Corrie **(64)***(61) (LJHolt)* 3-8-10 JReid(6) (hld up: rdn over 2f out: one pce)....3½ 3
1641[3] Sharp Holly (IRE) **(58)***(55) (JABennett)* 3-8-4 BDoyle(3) (lw: hdwy over 2f out: rdn over 1f out: one pce)....nk 4
1660[8] Sally Weld **(62)***(55) (CJBenstead)* 3-8-8 PRobinson(7) (a.p: rdn over 2f out: wknd over 1f out)....1¼ 5
Royal Carlton (IRE) **(73)***(58) (RAkehurst)* 3-9-5 TQuinn(4) (lw: nvr plcd to chal)....3 6
1522[6] Dark Menace **(68)***(52) (SMellor)* 3-9-0 TSprake(8) (hld up: rdn over 2f out: wknd over 1f out)....nk 7
Almasi (IRE) **(67)***(48) (CFWall)* 3-8-8 (5) LNewton(1) (dwlt: a bhd)....1¼ 8

1786[4] Dancing Sioux **(72)***(52) (RJRWilliams)* 3-9-4 GDuffield(5) (b: lw: led 3f)....½ 9

100/30 TAFAHHUS, **7/2** Prolific Lady (IRE), **5/1** Squire Corrie, **11/2** Sally Weld, **8/1** Dancing Sioux (op 9/2), **9/1** Royal Carlton (IRE) (9/2-10/1), Dark Menace, **14/1** Almasi (IRE) (10/1-16/1), **20/1** Sharp Holly (IRE), CSF £15.15 CT £52.89 TOTE £2.30: £1.30 £1.60 £4.00 (£3.70) Trio £23.30 OWNER Mr Hamdan Al Maktoum (NEWMARKET) BRED Shadwell Estate Company Limited 9 Rn
1m 10.44 (1.44) SF: 60/53/36/30/30/33/27/23/27

1983

WOODLANDS ELECTRICAL SERVICES MAIDEN STKS (3-Y.O) (Class D) £3,766.10 (£1,122.80: £535.40: £241.70)
1m 2f Stalls: Low GOING minus 0.28 sec per fur (GF) 4-00 (4-02)

1182[2] **Flame War (USA) (79)***(79)*(Fav)*(HRACecil)* 3-8-9 WRyan(3) (lw: chsd ldr: led over 2f out: rdn out)....— 1
Temora (IRE) *(76) (HRACecil)* 3-8-9 PatEddery(5) (unf: scope: 5th st: chsd wnr over 1f out: unable qckn)....2 2
1346[5] Hatta Breeze **(77)***(65) (MAJarvis)* 3-8-9 PRobinson(7) (led over 7f: eased whn btn ins fnl f)....7 3
Ewar Imperial *(67) (CEBrittain)* 3-9-0 BDoyle(8) (bkwd: 3rd st: rdn over 2f out: wknd over 1f out)....1½ 4
38[6] See You Again *(64) (RHannon)* 3-9-0 RPerham(2) (4th st: wknd over 1f out)....1¾ 5
Dixiemelody *(62) (RHannon)* 3-9-0 JReid(4) (a bhd)....1¾ 6
1514[14] Ardleigh Prince *(42) (GLMoore)* 3-9-0 SWhitworth(6) (6th st: wknd 3f out)....12 7
1731[8] Bold Charlie *(2) (SMellor)* 3-9-0 MWigham(1) (s.s: a bhd: t.o)....25 8

5/6 FLAME WAR (USA), **11/4** Temora (IRE) (op 7/4), **4/1** Hatta Breeze (op 5/2), **20/1** Ewar Imperial, Dixiemelody, **25/1** See You Again, **50/1** Ardleigh Prince, Bold Charlie, CSF £3.70 TOTE £1.90: £1.30 £1.10 £1.20 (£2.20) OWNER Mr L. Marinopoulos (NEWMARKET) BRED David E. Hagar II and Dunchurch Lodge Stud 8 Rn 2m 6.58 (3.58) SF: 42/39/28/30/27/25/5/-

1984

PAPER CAPER H'CAP (0-80) (3-Y.O F) (Class D) £3,698.50 (£1,102.00: £525.00: £236.50)
1m 3f 106y Stalls: High GOING minus 0.28 sec per fur (GF) 4-30 (4-30)

1591[3] **High Flying Adored (IRE) (77)***(93)*(Fav)*(JLDunlop)* 3-9-7 PatEddery(2) (5th st: led over 1f out: comf)....— 1
1442[2] Sweet Pavlova (USA) **(64)***(75) (PFICole)* 3-8-8 TQuinn(6) (6th st: n.m.r over 1f out: r.o one pce)....3½ 2
1791[6] Charm Dancer **(52)***(62) (MCPipe)* 3-7-10 NCarlisle(4) (led 9f out tl over 1f out: one pce)....½ 3
1659* Elly Fleetfoot (IRE) **(65)***(73) (BJMeehan)* 3-8-9 BDoyle(5) (lw: led over 2f: 2nd st: hrd rdn over 1f out: one pce)....1¾ 4
1733* Tirolette (IRE) **(56)***(58) (RJRWilliams)* 3-8-0b DBiggs(3) (4th st: wknd over 3f out)....4 5
1616[7] Gloriana **(73)***(73) (LadyHerries)* 3-9-3 JReid(7) (lw: 3rd st: wknd over 2f out)....1¾ 6

Evens HIGH FLYING ADORED (IRE), **4/1** Sweet Pavlova (USA), **6/1** Tirolette (IRE), **8/1** Gloriana (op 5/1), Elly Fleetfoot (IRE) (5/1-9/1), **9/1** Charm Dancer, CSF £5.57 TOTE £1.90: £1.10 £1.80 (£2.20) OWNER Mr Anthony Pye-Jeary (ARUNDEL) BRED Airlie Stud and Myrina Holdings S A 6 Rn 2m 25.63 (3.63) SF: 57/39/26/37/22/37

1985

VENNER SHIPLEY APPRENTICE H'CAP (0-70) (3-Y.O+) (Class E) £2,890.75 (£886.00: £440.50: £217.75)
1m 2f Stalls: Low GOING minus 0.28 sec per fur (GF) 5-00 (5-01)

1937[5] **Queens Contractor (35)***(46) (SMellor)* 5-8-7b CarolineHovington(2) (mde all: clr over 1f out: r.o wl)....— 1
1368[9] Birthday Boy (IRE) **(63)***(70)*(Fav)*(RHannon)* 3-9-9 EGreehy(3) (4th st: chsd wnr wl over 1f out: no imp)....2½ 2
1775[6] Elite Justice **(64)***(65) (PFICole)* 3-9-10 DavidO'Neill(1) (lw: 3rd st: 4th whn bdly hmpd on ins wl over 1f out: nt rcvr)....4 3
1658[3] Lexus (IRE) **(31)***(31) (RJRWilliams)* 7-8-3b RMullen(4) (lw: chsd wnr: edgd lft wl over 1f out: sn wknd)....hd 4

11/8 Birthday Boy (IRE), **9/4** Elite Justice, **3/1** Lexus (IRE), **10/1** QUEENS CONTRACTOR (op 6/1), CSF £21.94 TOTE £7.20: (£6.70) OWNER Laurie Butters & Partners (SWINDON) BRED Home Stud Ltd 4 Rn 2m 9.03 (6.03) SF: 21/33/28/6
WEIGHT FOR AGE 3yo-12lb

T/Plpt: £88.50 (134.38 Tckts). T/Qdpt: £40.60 (1.2 Tckts). AK

1733-**YARMOUTH (L-H)**
Tuesday June 27th (Firm)
WEATHER: sunny WIND: v.str bhd

1986 TOTE DUAL FORECAST H'CAP (0-70) (3-Y.O) (Class E) £3,359.40 (£1,003.20: £479.60: £217.80)
1m 6f 17y Stalls: Low GOING minus 0.59 sec per fur (F) 2-15 (2-15)

1529[9] **Nanton Point (USA) (44)**(*57*) (*LadyHerries*) 3-7-9 JQuinn(1) (chsd ldrs: 6th st: swtchd rt to ld over 2f out: drvn out) ....— 1
1505[5] Swivel **(66)**(*75*) (*JRFanshawe*) 3-9-3 DHarrison(4) (hld up & bhd: hdwy 3f out: styd on wl ins fnl f) 3½ 2
1702[3] Lucky Coin **(62)**(*69*) (*CEBrittain*) 3-8-13 MRoberts(6) (lw: a.p: 3rd st: ev ch over 2f out: one pce) 1½ 3
1656* Labibeh (USA) **(70)**(*66*) (*JLDunlop*) 3-9-7 RHills(7) (hld up: hdwy 6f out: 4th st: hmpd & wknd over 2f out) 10 4
1696[5] China Mail (IRE) **(55)**(*48*) (*JMPEustace*) 3-8-6 ow1 RCochrane(2) (led 4f: 2nd st: led over 3f out tl over 2f out: sn wknd) 1¾ 5
1527[6] Last Corner **(55)**(*46*) (*RHollinshead*) 3-8-6 KDarley(9) (hld up: 5th st: effrt 3f out: sn rdn: no imp) 2½ 6
1776* Hydrofoil **(59)**(*43*)(Fav)(*BWHills*) 3-8-10 DHolland(5) (led 10f out tl over 3f out: sn rdn & wknd)6 7
Quillwork (USA) **(67)**(*46*) (*MrsJCecil*) 3-9-4 MHills(8) (b.off hind: lw: hld up: rdn along over 3f out: no rspnse) 5 8
1858[10] Ahaalee (USA) **(66)** (*EALDunlop*) 3-9-3 GBardwell(3) (Withdrawn not under Starter's orders: spread plate at s) .... W

15/8 Hydrofoil, **4/1** Last Corner, Swivel, **9/2** Labibeh (USA), **7/1** China Mail (IRE), **10/1** Lucky Coin, **14/1** Ahaalee (USA), **20/1** NANTON POINT (USA), **25/1** Quillwork (USA), CSF £95.79 CT £795.25 TOTE £34.30: £5.70 £1.50 £1.40 (£289.40) Trio £119.60 OWNER Mr L. G. Lazarus (LITTLEHAMPTON) BRED Newgate Stud Farm Inc 8 Rn 3m 2.2 (4.20) SF: 11/29/23/20/2/-/-/-/-
STEWARDS' ENQUIRY Quinn suspended 15-25/7/95 (careless riding).

1987 TOTE CREDIT MAIDEN STKS (3-Y.O) (Class D) £3,833.70 (£1,143.60: £545.80: £246.90)
1m 6f 17y Stalls: Low GOING minus 0.59 sec per fur (F) 2-45 (2-45)

1490[5] **Eelious (USA) (82)**(*82*) (*CEBrittain*) 3-9-0 MRoberts(4) (hld up: 5th st: rdn to ld bel dist: r.o gamely) ....— 1
1083[11] Mansur (IRE) **(66)**(*81*) (*DRLoder*) 3-9-0 KDarley(2) (a.p: 3rd st: led over 2f out to bel dist: kpt on u.p ins fnl f) 1¼ 2
1691[4] Topanga (*75*) (*HRACecil*) 3-9-0 AMcGlone(8) (hdwy ½-wy: 2nd st: rdn 2f out: sn outpcd).......5 3
1099[2] Cypress Avenue (IRE) **(97)**(*72*)(Fav)(*RHannon*) 3-9-0 DHolland(3) (hdwy to ld 7f out: hdd over 2f out: sn btn) 3 4
Kriva (*63*) (*RJRWilliams*) 3-8-9 RHills(7) (bit bkwd: hld up & bhd: hdwy over 3f out: nt trble ldrs) 3 5
1383[7] Vlaanderen (IRE) (*60*) (*MRStoute*) 3-8-9 MHills(1) (led to ½-wy: lost pl & 6th st: n.d after) 3 6
1691[6] Claque **(72)**(*54*) (*MrsJCecil*) 3-9-0 FNorton(6) (prom tl 4th & wkng st: sn bhd: t.o) 9 7
1764[5] Vanola (*48*) (*PHowling*) 3-8-9 RCochrane(5) (dwlt: a bhd: t.o fnl 2f) 1 8

8/11 Cypress Avenue (IRE) (Evens-11/10), **4/1** Topanga, **9/1** Vlaanderen (IRE) (5/1-10/1), **10/1** EELIOUS (USA), **16/1** Mansur (IRE), Claque, **50/1** Kriva, Vanola, CSF £120.69 TOTE £7.60: £1.40 £2.40 £1.10 (£41.20) OWNER The Dayspring Company Ltd (NEWMARKET) BRED J. Jones Jnr, S. Fahlgren, et al 8 Rn 3m 2.9 (4.90) SF: 25/24/18/15/6/3/-/-

1988 TOTE BOOKMAKERS H'CAP (0-80) (3-Y.O+) (Class D) £4,152.00 (£1,236.00: £588.00: £264.00) **1m 2f 21y** Stalls: Low GOING minus 0.59 sec (F) 3-15 (3-15)

1505[3] **Senorita Dinero (USA) (74)**(*84*)(Fav)(*MRStoute*) 3-9-5 DHolland(1) (chsd ldr: 2nd st: led 3f out: drvn clr appr fnl f) ....— 1
1793[3] Elpidos **(69)**(*74*) (*CEBrittain*) 3-9-0 RCochrane(4) (chsd ldrs: 3rd st: hrd rdn bel dist: kpt on) 3 2
1183[17] Mo-Addab (IRE) **(71)**(*75*) (*ACStewart*) 5-10-0 MRoberts(3) (hld up: outpcd & 6th st: hdwy 3f out: rdn over 1f out: one pce) 1 3
Wellsian (USA) **(75)**(*77*) (*LMCumani*) 3-9-6 OUrbina(2) (bit bkwd: hld up: 5th st: rdn over 2f out: kpt on same pce) 1¼ 4
1644[6] Bentico **(59)**(*53*) (*MrsNMacauley*) 6-9-2 DeanMcKeown(6) (lw: chsd ldrs: 4th st: wknd 2f out) ....hd 6

1826[6] Ikis Girl **(42)**(30) (SGollings) 4-7-13 FNorton(7) (lw: led: sn clr: hdd 3f out: wknd)....3½ 7
1591[5] Shady Deed (USA) **(67)**(61) (JWHills) 3-8-12 MHills(5) (dwlt: 7th st: effrt 3f out: sn rdn: no imp: fin 5th btn 5l: disq).... D

9/4 SENORITA DINERO (USA), **4/1** Elpidos, Mo-Addab (IRE), **5/1** Wellsian (USA) (op 3/1), **7/1** Bentico, **8/1** Shady Deed (USA), **40/1** Ikis Girl, CSF £10.98 TOTE £2.50: £1.70 £1.90 (£3.80) OWNER Mr A. Al Khalifa (NEWMARKET) BRED Sheikh Rashid Bin Mohammed Al-Khalifa et al 7 Rn
2m 6.7 (2.30) SF: 37/27/40/30/18/-/14
WEIGHT FOR AGE 3yo-12lb
STEWARDS' ENQUIRY Hills susp. 6-8/7/95 & 10-16/7/95 under Rule 171 (iii) (causing intentional interference).

1989 TOTE PLACEPOT (S) STKS (2-Y.O) (Class G) £2,556.60 (£707.60: £337.80)
5f 43y Stalls: Low GOING minus 0.59 sec per fur (F) 3-45 (3-45)

1640[2] **The Imps (IRE) (65)**(58)(Fav)(BWHills) 2-8-11 BThomson(6) (lw: a.p: rdn to chal ent fnl f: kpt on to ld cl home)....— 1
1810[3] Nameless (57) (DJSCosgrove) 2-8-6 (5) PMcCabe(1) (lw: led tl ct nr fin)....nk 2
1699[2] Ivory's Grab Hire **(63)**(51) (KTIvory) 2-8-11 GBardwell(2) (chsd ldrs: outpcd & rdn 2f out: rallied u.p fnl f)....2 3
1089[8] Dancing Lottie (IRE) (46) (PAKelleway) 2-8-6 RCochrane(4) (lw: s.i.s: sn chsng ldrs: r.o u.p ins fnl f)....hd 4
1823[7] Down The Yard **(57)**(46) (MCChapman) 2-8-3 (3) DRMcCabe(3) (dwlt: sn rdn along: r.o ins fnl f: nvr nrr)....d.h 4
1699[4] Imprimis (IRE) **(56)**(30) (CNAllen) 2-8-6v JQuinn(5) (spd to ½-wy: sn rdn & outpcd)....5 6
Twice Two (IRE) (6) (MHTompkins) 2-8-1 (5) HKYim(7) (lt-f: unf: a bhd & outpcd: t.o)....8 7

6/4 THE IMPS (IRE), **3/1** Ivory's Grab Hire, **6/1** Dancing Lottie (IRE), **7/1** Nameless, **15/2** Imprimis (IRE), **8/1** Twice Two (IRE) (op 4/1), **12/1** Down The Yard (op 8/1), CSF £12.65 TOTE £2.20: £2.00 £2.00 (£6.10) OWNER Lady Parker (LAMBOURN) BRED Mountarmstrong Stud 7 Rn
61.6 secs (1.30) SF: 24/23/17/12/12/-/-
Bt in 4,500 gns

1990 TOTE PLACE ONLY MAIDEN STKS (3-Y.O F) (Class D) £4,205.50 (£1,258.00: £603.00: £275.50)
1m 3y Stalls: Low GOING minus 0.59 sec per fur (F) 4-15 (4-15)

1736[2] **Bonne Etoile** (89)(Fav)(DRLoder) 3-8-8 (3) DRMcCabe(5) (chsd ldrs: rdn over 1f out: r.o strly to ld nr fin)....— 1
Goalwah (88) (HThomsonJones) 3-8-11 RHills(7) (unf: scope: a.p: led 3f out: hrd rdn & ct cl home)....¾ 2
997[7] Wells Whisper (FR) (82) (GWragg) 3-8-11b MHills(10) (a.p: rdn over 2f out: kpt on same pce)3 3
1221[6] Bibliotheque (USA) (70) (JHMGosden) 3-8-11 GHind(4) (b: b.hind: s.i.s: rdn along ½-wy: nvr able to chal)....6 4
Rival Queen (IRE) (62) (HRACecil) 3-8-11 AMcGlone(2) (chsd ldrs: rdn 2f out: r.o one pce)...4 5
1500[7] Lady Nash (54) (CEBrittain) 3-8-11 MRoberts(6) (led to 3f out: eased whn btn over 1f out).....4 6
1736[8] The Flying Fiddle (53) (MHTompkins) 3-8-6 (5) HKYim(3) (bit bkwd: a in rr)....nk 7
1701[7] Moon Over Awir (IRE) (53) (LMCumani) 3-8-11 OUrbina(1) (chsd ldrs 5f: sn rdn & lost pl)....hd 8
Sari Marais (53) (MrsJCecil) 3-8-11 FNorton(8) (w'like: leggy: bit bkwd: s.s: a in rr)....s.h 9
Mystoski (47) (MHTompkins) 3-8-11 SMulvey(9) (still unf: drppd rr over 3f out: t.o)....3 10

11/8 BONNE ETOILE, **7/2** Goalwah, **6/1** Wells Whisper (FR), **13/2** Bibliotheque (USA), **7/1** Rival Queen (IRE) (9/2-8/1), **14/1** Moon Over Awir (IRE), **20/1** Lady Nash, Sari Marais, **50/1** The Flying Fiddle, Mystoski, CSF £7.06 TOTE £2.00: £1.10 £1.60 £1.40 (£4.30) Trio £10.30 OWNER Miss D. F. Fleming (NEWMARKET) BRED Kirtlington Stud Ltd 10 Rn
1m 34.6 (-0.70) SF: 53/52/46/34/26/18/17/17/17/11

1991 TOTE TRIO H'CAP (0-70) (3-Y.O+) (Class E) £3,531.00 (£1,056.00: £506.00: £231.00) **7f 3y** Stalls: Low GOING minus 0.59 sec per fur (F) 4-45 (4-46)

Keston Pond (IRE) (63)(84) (DAWilson) 5-10-0 GCarter(3) (bit bkwd: hld up: hdwy 3f out: r.o u.p to ld wl ins fnl f)....— 1
1828[6] Awesome Venture **(49)**(68) (MCChapman) 5-8-11v(3) DRMcCabe(7) (led: sn clr: rdn over 1f out: wknd & hdd nr fin)....¾ 2
1911* Kaafih Homm (IRE) **(53)**(65)(Fav)(NACallaghan) 4-9-4 RCochrane(4) (b.hind: bhd: hdwy over 2f out: kpt on: nvr nr to chal)....3 3
1542[7] Lucky Tucky **(56)**(61) (JRJenkins) 4-9-7v DHolland(2) (chsd ldr 5f: rdn & wknd appr fnl f)......3½ 4
1760[5] Just Flamenco **(48)**(47) (MJRyan) 4-8-13 AClark(6) (chsd ldrs: no hdwy fnl 2f)....2½ 5

1785[3] Glen Miller **(39)***(33) (JWPayne)* 5-8-4v GBardwell(11) (lw: chsd ldrs: rdn over 2f out: sn btn)....2 **6**
1762[3] Titanium Honda (IRE) **(33)***(24) (CEBrittain)* 4-7-12 MRoberts(8) (chsd ldrs over 5f) 1¼ **7**
1692[5] Prince's Feather (IRE) **(70)***(57) (DMorley)* 3-9-12b MHills(9) (hld up: effrt & rdn over 2f out: no imp) 2 **8**
1548[10] Magication **(39)***(20) (CNAllen)* 5-8-4 JQuinn(1) (a in rr) 2½ **9**
1426[6] Zinbaq **(30)** *(CJBenstead)* 9-7-9 AMackay(10) (s.s: a bhd: t.o)..6 **10**
1676[17] Shaynes Domain **(44)** *(RMFlower)* 4-8-9b GHind(5) (lw: lost tch 3f out: t.o)..............................5 **11**

11/8 Kaafih Homm (IRE) (op 5/2), **5/1** Lucky Tucky, **6/1** Prince's Feather (IRE) (9/2-7/1), **7/1** Titanium Honda (IRE), Awesome Venture, **12/1** Shaynes Domain, Glen Miller (op 8/1), Just Flamenco, **14/1** KESTON POND (IRE), **20/1** Magication, Zinbaq, CSF £112.98 CT £208.21 TOTE £15.90: £3.00 £2.50 £1.50 (£54.50) Trio £75.20 OWNER Mr T. S. M. S. Riley-Smith (EPSOM) BRED John Harrington in Ireland 11 Rn 1m 22.4 (-0.40) SF: 66/50/47/43/29/15/6/30/2/-/-

WEIGHT FOR AGE 3yo-9lb

T/Jkpt: Not Won; £6,476.94 to Carlisle 28/6/95: T/Plpt £97.10 (193.83 Tckts). T/Qdpt £5.80 (13.3 Tckts). IM

1430-CARLISLE (R-H)
Wednesday June 28th (Firm, Hard patches)

WEATHER: sunny, v.hot WIND: slt bhd

1992 E.B.F. SILLOTH MAIDEN STKS (2-Y.O) (Class D) £4,221.00 (£1,278.00: £624.00: £297.00) **5f 207y** Stalls: High GOING minus 0.70 sec per fur (HD) 2-15 (2-15)

1685[2] **Flying North (IRE)** *(76) (MrsMReveley)* 2-9-0 KDarley(2) (a.p: rdn to ld wl ins fnl f).............— **1**
1318[3] Nilgiri Hills (IRE) *(75)*(Fav)*(JLDunlop)* 2-9-0 JWeaver(6) (lw: hld up: hdwy ½-wy: led 1f out: hdd & no ex wl ins fnl f) ....½ **2**
1540[4] Sharp Monty *(69) (RHollinshead)* 2-9-0 TIves(3) (lw: led to 1f out: kpt on same pce)...............2 **3**
1454[8] Mooncusser *(56) (JGFitzGerald)* 2-9-0 KFallon(1) (in tch: hdwy & ch over 1f out: sn rdn & btn)..5 **4**
1298[6] Kuwam (IRE) *(24) (JBerry)* 2-9-0 JCarroll(5) (cl up tl rdn & wknd 2f out) 12 **5**

4/9 Nilgiri Hills (IRE), **9/2** FLYING NORTH (IRE), **6/1** Sharp Monty, **14/1** Kuwam (IRE) (8/1-16/1), **25/1** Mooncusser, CSF £6.91 TOTE £3.50: £1.50 £1.10 (£1.90) OWNER Dr Glyn Meredith (SALTBURN) BRED P. Henley 5 Rn 1m 13.4 (1.10) SF: 27/26/20/7/-

1993 WIGTON (S) STKS (3-Y.O+) (Class G) £2,563.00 (£718.00: £349.00) **5f 207y** Stalls: High GOING minus 0.70 sec per fur (HD) 2-45 (2-47)

1797[10] **Respectable Jones (40)***(50) (RHollinshead)* 9-9-7b MWigham(11) (bhd: hdwy over 2f out: led wl ins fnl f: jst hld on) ....— **1**
1546[9] Trina **(28)***(45) (DLWilliams)* 4-9-2 AMackay(6) (lw: led tl wl ins fnl f: rallied cl home).............s.h **2**
1819[3] Best Kept Secret **(68)***(49)*(Fav)*(JBerry)* 4-9-7 JCarroll(12) (a chsng ldrs: chal ins fnl f: nt qckn nr fin)..nk **3**
1809[15] Sense of Priority **(53)***(45) (DNicholls)* 6-9-7 AlexGreaves(3) (in tch: styd on fnl 2f: nrst fin) ...1½ **4**
1963[22] Oscar the Second (IRE) **(30)***(44) (CWFairhurst)* 5-9-7 JWeaver(7) (s.i.s: wl bhd tl styd on wl fnl 2f) ....½ **5**
1873[15] Saint Amigo **(55)***(42) (JLEyre)* 3-8-13 JFortune(4) (prom: rdn over 2f out: no imp) ....½ **6**
1721[10] Lucky Peg **(39)***(32) (FJO'Mahony)* 3-8-8 KFallon(10) (prom tl grad wknd fnl 2f).......................2 **7**
1819[5] Obsidian Grey **(52)***(39) (MissLCSiddall)* 8-9-12 DeanMcKeown(2) (prom tl wknd fnl 2f) 1 **8**
972[7] Brookhead Lady **(59)***(32) (PDEvans)* 4-9-7 KDarley(13) (b.nr fore: bhd: hdwy on ins ½-wy: hmpd wl over 1f out: one pce after) ....¾ **9**
1739[10] Fuzzy **(30)** *(SEKettlewell)* 3-8-13 NRodgers(1) (rdn & hung lft over 2f out: n.d) 12 **10**
West Farm Boy **(45)** *(JJO'Neill)* 3-8-13 GDuffield(5) (cl up over 3f: sn wknd).........................1¼ **11**
1580[10] Cinders Chance **(30)** *(MWEllerby)* 3-8-8 SMorris(8) (chsd ldrs over 3f: sn bhd).....................15 **12**

5/4 Best Kept Secret, **4/1** Brookhead Lady, **6/1** Sense of Priority, **10/1** Obsidian Grey, Saint Amigo (8/1-12/1), **14/1** RESPECTABLE JONES, **20/1** Lucky Peg, **33/1** Oscar the Second (IRE), West Farm Boy, **50/1** Trina, Fuzzy, **66/1** Cinders Chance, CSF £402.95 TOTE £14.20: £4.00 £7.80 £1.40 (£193.60) Trio £436.50 OWNER Miss Sarah Hollinshead (UPPER LONGDON) BRED E. and Mrs Weinstein 12 Rn 1m 13.8 (1.50) SF: 28/23/27/23/22/12/2/17/10/-/-/-

WEIGHT FOR AGE 3yo-8lb

no bid

1994 TENNENTS H'CAP (0-80) (3-Y.O+) (Class D) £3,589.30 (£1,086.40: £530.20: £252.10) **6f 206y** Stalls: High GOING minus 0.70 sec per fur (HD) 3-15 (3-17)

1828[13] **Pine Ridge Lad (IRE) (53)***(62) (JLEyre)* 5-8-8 JFortune(1) (sn led: hdd over 1f out: led ins fnl f: all out)..— **1**

1882^{2} Cavers Yangous **(72)***(81) (MJohnston)* 4-9-13 DHolland(3) (led early: cl up: led over 1f out tl ins fnl f: rallied nr fin)....s.h **2**
1724^{2} Sakharov **(55)***(64)*(Fav)*(MJohnston)* 6-8-10 PRobinson(5) (a.p: effrt over 1f out: styd on nr fin)....s.h **3**
1828^{2} Souperficial **(53)***(43)*(Fav)*(JAGlover)* 4-8-8v KDarley(4) (lw: in tch: rdn over 2f out: no imp)......8 **4**
1714^{8} Calling (USA) **(40)***(14) (WMBrisbourne)* 4-7-2 $^{(7)}$ MartinDwyer(2) (dwlt: nvr trbld ldrs)...............7 **5**

2/1 Souperficial, Sakharov, **3/1** Cavers Yangous, **7/1** PINE RIDGE LAD (IRE), **20/1** Calling (USA), CSF £24.79 TOTE £7.40: £2.50 £1.50 (£23.70) OWNER Whitestonecliffe Racing Partnership (HAMBLETON) BRED Whitechurch Stud in Ireland 5 Rn 1m 25.9 (0.20) SF: 34/53/36/15/-

1995 TENNENT'S LAGER CARLISLE BELL H'CAP (0-80) (3-Y.O+) (Class D)

£4,792.60 (£1,451.80: £709.40: £338.20)
7f 214y Stalls: High GOING minus 0.70 sec per fur (HD) 3-45 (3-50)

1808^{7} **Master Ofthe House (58)***(69) (MDHammond)* 9-9-1 JMarshall(13) (hld up: hdwy on ins over 2f out: led wl ins fnl f: all out)....— **1**
1432^{2} Spanish Verdict **(65)***(76) (DenysSmith)* 8-9-8 KFallon(12) (chsd ldrs: disp ld wl over 1f out tl wl ins fnl f: rallied nr fin)....s.h **2**
1506^{5} Thatched (IRE) **(44)***(55) (REBarr)* 5-7-8 $^{(7)}$ PFessey(1) (lw: trckd ldrs: disp ld wl over 1f out tl wl ins fnl f: r.o)....s.h **3**
1855* Avishayes (USA) **(48)***(54) (MrsMReveley)* 8-8-5 ^{5x} JFanning(10) (hld up & bhd: hdwy whn nt clr run over 1f out: swtchd & nt rcvr)....2½ **4**
1830* Admirals Flame (IRE) **(65)***(68)*(Fav)*(CFWall)* 4-9-8 ^{5x} GDuffield(8) (b: hld up & bhd: hdwy 3f out: ch & rdn over 1f out: nt qckn)....1¼ **5**
1649^{2} Mary Macblain **(39)***(37) (JLHarris)* 6-7-10 AMackay(11) (styd on fnl 3f: nvr rchd ldrs)............2½ **6**
594^{17} Seconds Away **(41)***(38) (JSGoldie)* 4-7-12 ^{ow1} LCharnock(9) (led early: chsd ldrs: led 2f out tl wl over 1f out: wknd)....hd **7**
1251^{11} Princess Maxine (IRE) **(60)***(55) (JJO'Neill)* 6-8-10 $^{(7)}$ GParkin(4) (bhd: hdwy 2f out: n.m.r & no imp)....1½ **8**
1148^{7} Prizefighter **(67)***(59) (JLEyre)* 4-9-10 JFortune(5) (in tch tl outpcd fnl 2f)................................1¾ **9**
1374^{3} Bogart **(59)***(47) (CWFairhurst)* 4-9-2 DeanMcKeown(6) (lw: a rr div)..2 **10**
1626^{11} Gymcrak Flyer **(66)***(53) (GHolmes)* 4-9-6 $^{(3)}$ JStack(7) (b.hind: lw: bhd: c wd over 2f out: no imp)....½ **11**
1953^{5} Wentbridge Lad (IRE) **(58)***(44) (PDEvans)* 5-9-1 KDarley(2) (b.off hind: lw: prom tl wknd fnl 2½f)....½ **12**
1742^{4} Upex le Gold Too **(47)***(27) (LRLloyd-James)* 3-7-1 $^{(7)ow1}$ MartinDwyer(3) (b: sn led: hdd & wknd 2f out)....2½ **13**

LONG HANDICAP Upex le Gold Too 7-5

6/4 Admirals Flame (IRE), **15/2** Spanish Verdict, **8/1** MASTER OFTHE HOUSE, **9/1** Avishayes (USA), **10/1** Thatched (IRE), Mary Macblain, Wentbridge Lad (IRE), **14/1** Bogart, Gymcrak Flyer, **16/1** Prizefighter, **20/1** Seconds Away, Princess Maxine (IRE), **33/1** Upex le Gold Too, CSF £67.11 CT £571.36 TOTE £8.60: £2.20 £2.90 £4.10 (£21.20) Trio £298.00 OWNER Allerton Racing Club (MIDDLEHAM) BRED Lord Victor Matthews 13 Rn

1m 38.2 (-0.80) SF: 51/58/37/36/50/19/20/37/41/29/35/26/-
WEIGHT FOR AGE 3yo-10lb

1996 C.G. TRUCK H'CAP (0-70) (3-Y.O+) (Class E) £3,152.60 (£954.80: £466.40:

£222.20) **5f 207y** Stalls: High GOING minus 0.70 sec per fur (HD) 4-15 (4-18)

1828^{14} **Birchwood Sun (54)***(66) (MDods)* 5-9-5b JWeaver(8) (sn outpcd & bhd: hdwy on ins over 1f out: r.o to ld wl ins fnl f)....— **1**
1828^{8} Heart Broken **(53)***(64)*(Fav)*(JGFitzGerald)* 5-9-4 KFallon(7) (lw: in tch: hdwy on ins to ld 2f out: sn rdn: nt qckn nr fin)....½ **2**
1721^{6} Brisas **(39)***(44) (CWFairhurst)* 8-8-4 JFanning(1) (a.p: hdwy 2f out: kpt on fnl f) 2 **3**
1013^{7} Ragazzo (IRE) **(37)***(42) (JSWainwright)* 5-8-2 LCharnock(4) (led after 2f to 2f out: r.o one pce)....s.h **4**
1668^{8} Tutu Sixtysix **(42)***(44) (DonEnricoIncisa)* 4-8-7v KimTinkler(3) (hld up: nt clr run 2f out: r.o fnl f)....1 **5**
1493* Suedoro **(41)***(40) (RMMcKellar)* 5-7-13 $^{(7)}$ PFessey(6) (b.off hind: hdwy 2f out: nvr able chal)1¼ **6**
1434^{10} Gymcrak Tycoon **(49)***(47) (GHolmes)* 6-8-11 $^{(3)}$ JStack(5) (cl up tl wknd appr fnl f) ....½ **7**
1827^{7} Plum First **(60)***(58) (LRLloyd-James)* 5-9-4 $^{(7)}$ KimberleyHart(11) (b: b.hind: led 2f: chsd ldrs tl wknd over 1f out)....s.h **8**
1864^{5} Indian Crystal **(46)***(25) (MrsMReveley)* 4-8-11 KDarley(10) (s.i.s: sn rcvrd to chse ldrs: wknd fnl 2f)....7 **9**
129^{9} Dance and Sing (IRE) **(33)** *(DLWilliams)* 5-7-12 AMackay(2) (s.i.s: n.d)................................13 **10**
1668^{7} Sobering Thoughts **(61)** *(JLEyre)* 9-9-12 GDuffield(9) (Withdrawn not under Starter's orders: lame at s)....**W**

5/2 Heart Broken, **5/1** BIRCHWOOD SUN, **11/2** Suedoro, Plum First, **7/1** Indian Crystal, **8/1** Tutu Sixtysix, **14/1** Ragazzo (IRE), Brisas, **16/1** Gymcrak Tycoon, **33/1** Dance and Sing (IRE), CSF £17.69 CT £153.70 TOTE £6.70: £1.70 £1.50 £3.20 (£8.30) Trio £28.50 OWNER Mr A. G. Watson (DARLINGTON) BRED The Hall Stud Ltd 10 Rn 1m 12.6 (0.30) SF: 42/40/20/18/20/16/23/34/1/-/-

1997 WETHERAL RATING RELATED MAIDEN LIMITED STKS (0-60) (3-Y.O+) (Class F) £2,689.00 (£754.00: £367.00)
1m 6f 32y Stalls: Low GOING minus 0.70 sec per fur (HD) 4-45 (4-46)

1091[2] **Sushi Bar (IRE) (58)***(63) (MrsMReveley)* 4-9-10 KDarley(3) (hld up: hdwy 4f out: led jst ins fnl f: styd on)....— 1
1628[2] Maysann **(57)***(62) (JLDunlop)* 3-8-7b GDuffield(1) (carried wd bnd after 2½f: sn rcvrd to ld: hdd ins fnl f: no ex)....1¼ 2
1725[3] Punch **(59)***(58) (NTinkler)* 3-8-7 MBirch(5) (lw: trckd ldrs: chal over 2f out: rdn & one pce)....3½ 3
1696[3] Much Too High **(53)***(51)*(Fav)*(TJNaughton)* 3-8-7 JWeaver(6) (b: led tl rn wd bnd after 2½f: sn hdd: chsd ldrs tl rdn & wknd wl over 1f out)....6 4
991[8] Roscommon Joe (IRE) **(28)***(40) (JJO'Neill)* 5-9-10 (5)ow5 ARoche(2) (hld up: rdn 3f out: no imp)10 5
1578[6] Red Beacon **(28)***(31) (JLGoulding)* 8-9-3 (7) PFessey(4) (b: cl up whn carried wd after 2½f: rdn & wknd 3f out)....8 6

15/8 Much Too High, **11/4** Maysann, **3/1** Punch, **4/1** SUSHI BAR (IRE), **10/1** Roscommon Joe (IRE) (op 33/1), **66/1** Red Beacon, CSF £15.05 TOTE £4.10: £1.60 £1.60 (£5.30) OWNER Mr P. D. Savill (SALTBURN) BRED Scarteen Stud 6 Rn 3m 5.2 (5.20) SF: 25/7/3/-/2/-
WEIGHT FOR AGE 3yo-17lb

1998 BURGH BARONY RACES GENTLEMAN RIDERS LIMITED STKS (0-60) (3-Y.O+) (Class F) £2,703.00 (£758.00: £369.00)
1m 4f Stalls: Low GOING minus 0.70 sec per fur (HD) 5-15 (5-16)

1696* **Carnbrea Belle (IRE) (60)***(68)*(Fav)*(MBell)* 3-9-11 (4) MrRWakley(6) (lw: trckd ldrs: qcknd to ld over 1f out: sn clr)....— 1
1934[3] Nouvelle Cuisine **(52)***(55) (GMMoore)* 7-11-0 MrSSwiers(3) (cl up: led 4f out & qcknd: hdd over 1f out: sn outpcd)....8 2
1435[7] Lightning Quest (IRE) **(27)***(52) (JSWainwright)* 4-11-1b(4) MrKGreen(2) (chsd ldrs after 4f tl outpcd fnl 2f)....6 3
1596[3] Air Command (BAR) **(49)***(51) (CTNash)* 5-11-1 (4) MrPPhillips(7) (plld hrd: led to 4f out: sn outpcd)....1¼ 4
1921[6] Balzino (USA) **(50)***(50) (NTinkler)* 6-11-1 (4) MrLSpink(5) (hld up: effrt over 3f out: no imp)......¾ 5
Musical March **(30)** *(EWeymes)* 4-10-10 (4) MrJWeymes(4) (sddle slipped after 3f: virt p.u) .dist 6

10/11 CARNBREA BELLE (IRE), **5/2** Nouvelle Cuisine, **7/1** Air Command (BAR), **12/1** Lightning Quest (IRE), **14/1** Balzino (USA) (16/1-25/1), **20/1** Musical March, CSF £3.52 TOTE £2.00: £1.30 £1.80 (£1.70) OWNER Mrs S. M. Crompton (NEWMARKET) BRED Limestone Stud 6 Rn
2m 37.4 (6.40) SF: 17/19/16/15/14/-
WEIGHT FOR AGE 3yo-15lb

T/Jkpt: Not won; £14,471.80 to Carlisle 29/6/95. T/Plpt: £46.90 (313.51 Tckts). T/Qdpt: £33.90 (1.2 Tckts). AA

1560-CHESTER (L-H)
Wednesday June 28th (Good to firm)

WEATHER: sunny, hot WIND: slt half bhd

1999 TARVIN CLAIMING STKS (3-Y.O+) (Class D) £4,172.00 (£1,256.00: £608.00: £284.00) **1m 2f 75y** Stalls: High GOING minus 0.62 sec per fur (F) 6-30 (6-30)

1458[2] **Katy's Lad (60)***(77) (BAMcMahon)* 8-9-0b JFortune(2) (hld up: wnt 2nd 3f out: led ent st: drvn clr)....— 1
157[7] Lunar Mission (IRE) **(78)***(77) (JMPEustace)* 4-9-5 RCochrane(3) (bit bkwd: hld up: hdwy 3f out: 3rd & rdn st: kpt on: no ch w wnr)....3½ 2
1612[12] Endless Light (USA) **(78)***(76)*(Fav)*(PFICole)* 4-9-10 CRutter(4) (chsd ldr: led over 4f out: hdd & 2nd st: sn btn)....3½ 3
1349[9] Nordic Crown (IRE) **(49)***(45) (MCPipe)* 4-8-7v BDoyle(1) (led tl over 4f out: wknd qckly: 4th & btn st)....9 4
1743[2] Kimberley Boy **(47)***(42) (MBrittain)* 5-8-13 DHolland(5) (lw: reard & lost ground s: effrt over 3f out: 5th & rdn st: no imp)....6 5

13/8 Endless Light (USA), **5/2** KATY'S LAD, **5/1** Lunar Mission (IRE), **6/1** Nordic Crown (IRE), **11/1** Kimberley Boy, CSF £12.59 TOTE £2.30: £1.10 £2.90 (£8.70) OWNER Mr J. W. Butler (TAMWORTH) BRED Peter Doyle 5 Rn 2m 10.42 (1.72) SF: 36/36/35/4/1

2000

FARNDON MAIDEN STKS (2-Y.O) (Class D) £3,415.00 (£1,030.00: £500.00: £235.00) **5f 16y** Stalls: Low GOING minus 0.62 sec per fur (F) 7-00 (7-02)

1307³ **Amaniy (USA)** *(73)*(Fav)*(HThomsonJones)* 2-8-9 RHills(5) (lw: hld up: hdwy ent st: rdn to ld ins fnl 100y) ....— 1
1877² Mister Sean (IRE) *(76) (JWPayne)* 2-9-0 RCochrane(3) (led: clr ½-wy: rdn, wknd & hdd wl ins fnl f) ....½ 2
1779³ Nellie North *(71) (MrsMMcCourt)* 2-8-9 PRobinson(1) (lw: s.i.s: hdwy 2f out: rdn & ev ch ins fnl f: unable qckn) ....s.h 3
1562⁴ Boffy (IRE) *(70) (BPJBaugh)* 2-9-0 ACulhane(6) (swtg: hld up: hdwy 2f out: rdn & btn whn n.m.r nr fin) 2 4
Princess Efisio *(37) (BAMcMahon)* 2-8-9 FNorton(2) (small: bkwd: s.s: a outpcd: t.o) 9 5
1841⁵ Derek's Bo *(29) (NBycroft)* 2-8-9 AlexGreaves(4) (spd 3f: sn rdn & outpcd: t.o) 2½ 6

5/4 AMANIY (USA) (Evens-11/8), **5/2** Mister Sean (IRE), **100/30** Nellie North, **16/1** Boffy (IRE), **20/1** Princess Efisio, **25/1** Derek's Bo, CSF £4.53 TOTE £2.30: £1.50 £1.70 (£2.60) OWNER Mr Hamdan Al Maktoum (NEWMARKET) BRED Shadwell Farm Inc 6 Rn 61.58 secs (1.58) SF: 16/19/14/13/-/-

2001

HOLT RATED STKS H'CAP (0-95) (3-Y.O+) (Class B) £7,886.60 (£2,929.40: £1,414.70: £588.50: £244.25: £106.55) **6f 18y** Stalls: Low GOING minus 0.62 sec per fur (F) 7-30 (7-30)

1108⁶ **Patto (USA)** **(92)***(102) (WJHaggas)* 4-9-7 RCochrane(3) (hld up & bhd: gd hdwy 2f out: led jst ins fnl f: all out) ....— 1
1895¹⁴ Ziggy's Dancer (USA) **(88)***(97) (EJAlston)* 4-9-3 KFallon(1) (hld up & bhd: gd hdwy appr fnl f: fin wl) ....½ 2
1777* Silent Expression **(79)***(88) (BJMeehan)* 5-8-8 BDoyle(8) (a.p: rdn to ld over 1f out: hdd ins fnl f: rallied nr fin) ....s.h 3
*1953*² Palacegate Touch **(90)***(89) (JBerry)* 5-9-5v JCarroll(5) (led tl over 1f out: no ex fnl f) 3½ 4
1765³ Elle Shaped (IRE) **(78)***(77)*(Fav)*(DNicholls)* 5-8-7 AlexGreaves(4) (hdwy over 2f out: rdn appr fnl f: nt pce to chal) ....nk 5
1604⁷ I'm Your Lady **(78)***(73) (BAMcMahon)* 4-8-7 JFortune(7) (prom tl rdn & wknd appr fnl f) 1¼ 6
1316⁵ Highborn (IRE) **(83)***(75) (PSFelgate)* 6-8-12 GHind(9) (lw: s.i.s: a outpcd & bhd) 1¼ 7
1673* Champagne Grandy **(78)***(63)*(Fav)*(MRChannon)* 5-8-7 DHolland(2) (prom tl wknd over 1f out) 2½ 8
*386*³ Bold Street (IRE) **(78)***(59) (ABailey)* 5-8-4b(3) DWright(6) (b: swtg: bit bkwd: a outpcd & in rr) 1¾ 9
1500⁴ Moonlight Saunter (USA) **(90)***(63) (EALDunlop)* 3-8-11 RHills(10) (s.s: effrt on outside ½-wy: no imp) 3 10

LONG HANDICAP I'm Your Lady 8-3 Champagne Grandy 8-6 Bold Street (IRE) 8-4 Elle Shaped (IRE) 8-1

9/2 Elle Shaped (IRE), Champagne Grandy, **13/2** Palacegate Touch, Silent Expression, **7/1** PATTO (USA), Highborn (IRE), Ziggy's Dancer (USA), Moonlight Saunter (USA), **12/1** Bold Street (IRE), **16/1** I'm Your Lady, CSF £54.23 CT £311.99 TOTE £8.90: £3.00 £2.10 £2.50 (£25.50) Trio £82.70 OWNER Mr B. Haggas (NEWMARKET) BRED Laura Leigh Partners L. P. in USA 10 Rn
1m 13.45 (0.15) SF: 52/47/38/39/27/23/25/13/9/5
WEIGHT FOR AGE 3yo-8lb

2002

KIDSONS IMPEY H'CAP (0-80) (3-Y.O+) (Class D) £5,530.00 (£1,660.00: £800.00: £370.00) **1m 4f 66y** Stalls: Low GOING minus 0.62 sec per fur (F) 8-00 (8-02)

1958* **Soba Up** **(50)***(65)*(Fav)*(TJEtherington)* 5-8-7 5x ACulhane(8) (lw: hld up: hdwy over 3f out: 2nd st: rdn to ld ins fnl f: all out) ....— 1
1817³ Killick **(55)***(70) (ABailey)* 7-8-12 JCarroll(6) (lw: led tl ins fnl f: rallied u.p cl home) ....s.h 2
1875² Jubran (USA) **(68)***(71) (MJohnston)* 9-9-11 RCochrane(4) (lw: chsd ldrs: hrd rdn & 4th st: nvr able to chal) 9 3
1801³ Reported (IRE) **(59)***(58) (BPreece)* 6-9-2 JWeaver(7) (prom: 3rd & outpcd ent st: sn btn) 3 4
1801² Thrower **(48)***(43) (WMBrisbourne)* 4-7-12 (7) MartinDwyer(1) (bhd: effrt over 3f out: 6th st: nt rch ldrs) 3½ 5
1596⁸ Sweet Trentino (IRE) **(62)***(49) (MTate)* 4-9-5 RHills(2) (chsd ldrs: 5th & hrd rdn st: sn btn) 6 6
1861³ Kings Cay (IRE) **(71)***(56) (THCaldwell)* 4-10-0 TIves(3) (chsd ldr 4f: wknd over 2f out) 1¾ 7
1801⁴ Taahhub (IRE) **(48)***(22) (RJPrice)* 5-8-5 MFenton(9) (a bhd: t.o) 8 8
1502⁶ Chatham Island **(70)***(41) (CEBrittain)* 7-9-13 BDoyle(5) (a in rr: t.o) 2½ 9
1844² Persian Soldier **(43)** *(EJAlston)* 8-8-0 ow1 PRobinson(10) (reluctant to r: sn t.o: p.u after 4f) .... P

11/4 SOBA UP (2/1-3/1), **4/1** Killick, **5/1** Jubran (USA), **13/2** Reported (IRE), **15/2** Chatham Island, **8/1** Persian Soldier, **12/1** Thrower, **20/1** Taahhub (IRE), **25/1** Kings Cay (IRE), **33/1** Sweet Trentino (IRE), CSF £13.68 CT £47.66 TOTE £3.30: £1.50 £1.60 £1.60 (£5.90) Trio £11.00 OWNER Mrs M. Hills (MALTON) BRED Mrs M. J. Hills 10 Rn 2m 35.9 (-0.70) SF: 47/52/53/40/25/31/38/4/23/-

2003

MIDSUMMER H'CAP (0-80) (3-Y.O) (Class D) £5,020.00 (£1,510.00: £730.00: £340.00) **7f 2y** Stalls: Low GOING minus 0.62 sec per fur (F) 8-30 (8-31)

1961* **Russian Heroine (67)***(78)*(Fav)*(MJohnston)* 3-8-10 6x DHolland(1) (mde all: clr ent fnl f: hrd rdn & jst hld on) — **1**
1904² Nordic Breeze (IRE) **(66)***(77) (ABailey)* 3-8-9 JFortune(3) (hld up: hdwy 3f out: 2nd st: str chal wl ins fnl f: jst failed) s.h **2**
1207³ Concer Un **(61)***(61) (SCWilliams)* 3-8-1 (3) DWright(7) (hld up in rr: 6th st: rdn & r.o ins fnl f) 5 **3**
1812* Self Reliance **(74)***(68) (MBell)* 3-9-3 6x MFenton(2) (chsd ldrs: wnt 2nd 3f out: 3rd st: sn rdn & outpcd) 2½ **4**
1520* Itab (USA) **(78)***(63) (EALDunlop)* 3-9-7 RHills(4) (a.p: 5th & rdn st: sn wknd) 4 **5**
1825¹² Cool Tactician **(58)***(37) (RHollinshead)* 3-8-1 FNorton(5) (hdwy ½-wy: 4th st: wknd over 1f out) 2½ **6**
1504* Hey Up Dolly (IRE) **(70)***(38) (JBerry)* 3-8-13 JCarroll(8) (hld up: effrt over 2f out: nvr nr to chal) 5 **7**
1778⁹ Silver Tzar **(76)** *(WJHaggas)* 3-9-5 RCochrane(6) (b.hind: chsd wnr 4f: wknd qckly: t.o) 20 **8**

11/4 RUSSIAN HEROINE, **7/2** Nordic Breeze (IRE), Itab (USA), **13/2** Self Reliance, Hey Up Dolly (IRE), **8/1** Concer Un, **12/1** Silver Tzar, **16/1** Cool Tactician, CSF £13.08 CT £64.22 TOTE £3.60: £1.70 £1.30 £2.30 (£5.20) OWNER The Knavesmire Partnership (MIDDLEHAM) BRED D. R. Botterill 8 Rn 1m 25.68 (0.48) SF: 43/42/26/33/28/2/3/-

2004

BROXTON MAIDEN STKS (3-Y.O) (Class D) £4,172.00 (£1,256.00: £608.00: £284.00) **1m 5f 89y** Stalls: Low GOING minus 0.62 sec per fur (F) 9-00 (9-00)

1764² **Crystal Blade (87)***(70)*(Fav)*(IABalding)* 3-9-0 GHind(1) (lw: mde all: qcknd clr over 1f out: canter) — **1**
1495² Cross Talk (IRE) **(65)***(66) (RHollinshead)* 3-9-0 TIves(2) (lw: hld up & bhd: hdwy 3f out: 2nd st: no imp) 3 **2**
1264³ Game Ploy (POL) **(75)***(61) (FMurphy)* 3-9-0 RCochrane(4) (chsd wnr 5f: 3rd & rdn st: sn outpcd) 5 **3**
787⁷ Victoria Day *(26) (JWWatts)* 3-8-9 JCarroll(3) (bit bkwd: s.i.s: sn chsng ldrs: rdn & lost tch 6f out: 4th & t.o st) 25 **4**
*1880*¹⁰ The Cottonwool Kid **(45)***(29) (THCaldwell)* 3-9-0 FNorton(5) (chsd wnr over 8f: wknd qckly: 5th & t.o st) 1¼ **5**

4/6 CRYSTAL BLADE, **2/1** Game Ploy (POL), **8/1** Cross Talk (IRE), **10/1** Victoria Day, **40/1** The Cottonwool Kid, CSF £6.39 TOTE £1.60: £1.30 £2.80 (£4.70) OWNER Godolphin (KINGSCLERE) BRED Littleton Stud 5 Rn 2m 54.11 (4.11) SF: 26/22/17/-/-

T/Plpt: £24.90 (599.52 Tckts). T/Qdpt: £14.60 (18.55 Tckts). IM

1690-KEMPTON (R-H)
Wednesday June 28th (Good to firm, Firm patches)

WEATHER: sunny, hot WIND: breezy

2005

E.B.F. MAIDEN STKS (2-Y.O) (Class D) £4,279.50 (£1,296.00: £633.00: £301.50) **7f (Jubilee)** Stalls: High GOING minus 0.76 sec per fur (HD) 6-40 (6-43)

1752³ **Canons Park** *(72+) (IABalding)* 2-9-0 MHills(2) (mde all: clr 2f out: comf) — **1**
1184⁷ Gentilhomme *(69) (PFICole)* 2-9-0 TQuinn(6) (lw: rdn over 3f out: 3rd st: chsd wnr over 1f out: r.o) 1¼ **2**
Beauchamp King *(58)*(Fav)*(JLDunlop)* 2-9-0 LDettori(1) (unf: scope: bit bkwd: chsd wnr: ev ch whn hung bdly rt over 2f out: unable qckn) 5 **3**
Sandy Floss (IRE) *(46) (HRACecil)* 2-9-0 WRyan(9) (gd sort: bit bkwd: rdn over 4f out: mod 4th st: one pce fnl 3f) 5 **4**
Roman Gold (IRE) *(23) (RHannon)* 2-9-0 PatEddery(8) (str: scope: a wl bhd) 10 **5**
Nabhaan (IRE) *(23) (DMorley)* 2-9-0 WCarson(3) (leggy: scope: bit bkwd: poor 6th st: a bhd) s.h **6**
Shamand (USA) *(17) (BJMeehan)* 2-9-0 AClark(7) (cmpt: bit bkwd: poor 5th st: a bhd) 3 **7**
Red Raja *(PMitchell)* 2-9-0 GCarter(4) (leggy: unf: bit bkwd: s.s: t.o whn p.u 6f out: lame) **P**

3/1 Beauchamp King (9/4-7/2), **7/2** CANONS PARK (7/4-4/1), **4/1** Sandy Floss (IRE) (9/4-9/2), **5/1** Gentilhomme (op 3/1), **6/1** Roman Gold (IRE) (4/1-13/2), **12/1** Nabhaan (IRE) (6/1-16/1), **14/1** Shamand (USA) (10/1-16/1), **33/1** Red Raja, CSF £19.86 TOTE £3.70: £1.30 £1.70 £1.70 (£8.10) Trio £8.30 OWNER Mr G. M. Smart (KINGSCLERE) BRED Mrs E. Roberts 8 Rn
1m 24.78 (0.58) SF: 29/26/15/3/-/-/-/-

2006

SUN LIFE OF CANADA CONDITIONS STKS (3-Y.O F) (Class C)
£4,878.40 (£1,825.60: £892.80: £384.00: £172.00: £87.20)
1m (Jubilee) Stalls: High GOING minus 0.76 sec per fur (HD) 7-10 (7-11)

1500³ **Private Line (USA)** *(103) (HRACecil)* 3-8-12 PatEddery(4) (lw: led over 5f: hrd rdn & led ins fnl f: r.o wl) — **1**
1804* Amanah (USA) *(102)*(Fav)*(JHMGosden)* 3-8-12 WCarson(6) (lw: 3rd st: led over 2f out tl ins fnl f: r.o) nk **2**
1242⁷ Blue Zulu (IRE) **(93)***(94) (JRFanshawe)* 3-8-12 DHarrison(5) (rdn over 3f out: 5th st: unable qckn fnl 2f) 4 **3**
1066⁴ Queenfisher **(103)***(90) (RHannon)* 3-8-10 RHughes(8) (hdwy on ins over 2f out: hrd rdn over 1f out: one pce) 1¼ **4**
1315⁵ Dee-Lady **(93)***(84) (WGMTurner)* 3-8-7 (5) PMcCabe(7) (4th st: rdn over 2f out: wknd fnl f) 4 **5**
1240* Marguerite Bay (IRE) *(74) (EALDunlop)* 3-8-12 WRyan(3) (6th st: wknd over 2f out) 5 **6**
Skip to Somerfield **(76)***(72) (KMcAuliffe)* 3-8-7 (3) JTate(2) (lw: bhd fnl 4f) s.h **7**
1431* Varvarka *(34) (JWWatts)* 3-8-12 LDettori(1) (lw: 2nd st: wknd over 2f out) 20 **8**

10/11 Amanah (USA), **5/1** Varvarka, **13/2** Queenfisher (5/1-8/1), **15/2** Blue Zulu (IRE) (5/1-8/1), **8/1** PRIVATE LINE (USA) (op 9/2), Marguerite Bay (IRE), **12/1** Dee-Lady, **33/1** Skip to Somerfield, CSF £16.83 TOTE £7.40: £2.40 £1.20 £2.20 (£8.20) OWNER Mr K. Abdullah (NEWMARKET) BRED Juddmonte Farms in USA 8 Rn 1m 35.39 (0.52 under best) (-1.61) SF: 50/49/41/37/31/21/19/-

2007

TAYLOR WALKER H'CAP (0-70) (3-Y.O+) (Class E) £3,761.25 (£1,140.00: £557.50: £266.25) **1m 4f** Stalls: High GOING minus 0.76 sec (HD) 7-40 (7-41)

1757* **Rock The Barney (IRE)** **(52)***(65) (PBurgoyne)* 6-8-8 (3) DRMcCabe(15) (lw: hdwy over 2f out: n.m.r over 1f out: led ins fnl f: r.o wl) — **1**
1477⁴ Dormy Three **(69)***(80) (RJHodges)* 5-10-0 JWilliams(14) (lw: hdwy over 3f out: 6th st: led 1f out tl ins fnl f: unable qckn) 1½ **2**
1799* Supreme Star (USA) **(51)***(60) (PRHedger)* 4-8-5 (5) NVarley(12) (lw: hdwy over 2f out: nt clr run wl over 1f out: hrd rdn: r.o) 1½ **3**
*367*⁴ Wottashambles **(39)***(46) (LMontagueHall)* 4-7-12 ow2 StephenDavies(16) (led over 4f out to 1f out: sn wknd) hd **4**
1674⁴ Rocquaine Bay **(37)***(46) (MJBolton)* 8-7-10 JQuinn(11) (rdn over 3f out: hdwy over 1f out: r.o) hd **5**
*137*⁶ Santana Lady (IRE) **(65)***(69) (MJHeaton-Ellis)* 6-9-10 GCarter(10) (b: led over 7f: 2nd st: ev ch over 1f out: wknd fnl f) 3½ **6**
1757⁵ No Speeches (IRE) **(59)***(61) (CACyzer)* 4-9-4 DHarrison(4) (nvr nrr) 1¾ **7**
1477⁸ Dusty Point (IRE) **(63)***(61) (JPearce)* 5-9-8 MHills(2) (nvr nrr) 2½ **8**
1695⁴ Durshan (USA) **(50)***(47) (JRJenkins)* 6-8-9 PatEddery(13) (3rd st: wknd over 1f out) ¾ **9**
1367⁵ Absolutely Fayre **(67)***(63) (RAkehurst)* 4-9-12 TQuinn(1) (lw: hdwy 9f out: rdn over 3f out: 4th st: wkng whn squeezed out tl over 1f out) 1¼ **10**
1655² Ismeno **(56)***(52) (SDow)* 4-9-1 WRyan(7) (5th st: wknd over 1f out) s.h **11**
1757² Lunar Risk **(43)***(33) (MissBSanders)* 5-7-13 (3)ow1 SSanders(5) (lw: bhd fnl 4f) 3½ **12**
1658⁴ Shepherds Rest (IRE) **(49)***(13) (SMellor)* 3-7-0 (7) CAdamson(3) (hdwy over 4f out: rn v.wd bnd & wknd over 3f out) 20 **13**
1661¹¹ Make a Stand **(65)***(28) (HCandy)* 4-9-10 WNewnes(8) (lw: bhd fnl 4f) ¾ **14**
Greenback (BEL) **(56)***(17)*(Fav)*(PJHobbs)* 4-9-1 LDettori(6) (hdwy 9f out: wknd 4f out) 2 **15**
LONG HANDICAP Shepherds Rest (IRE) 7-5

11/4 Greenback (BEL) (2/1-10/3), **7/1** Absolutely Fayre (9/2-15/2), **8/1** ROCK THE BARNEY (IRE), **10/1** Ismeno (8/1-12/1), Durshan (USA) (7/1-11/1), Lunar Risk, **12/1** Rocquaine Bay, No Speeches (IRE), Supreme Star (USA), **14/1** Dormy Three, **16/1** Dusty Point (IRE), **20/1** Shepherds Rest (IRE), Santana Lady (IRE), **33/1** Wottashambles, Make a Stand, CSF £108.18 CT £1,227.64 TOTE £7.30: £2.10 £3.90 £3.60 (£49.30) Trio £295.60 OWNER Mrs Satu Marks (WANTAGE) BRED Mrs Mary Travers 15 Rn 2m 30.78 (0.58) SF: 32/47/27/13/13/36/28/28/14/30/19/-/-/-/-
WEIGHT FOR AGE 3yo-15lb

2008

GALA STKS (Listed) (3-Y.O+) (Class A) £12,510.00 (£3,780.00: £1,840.00: £870.00) **1m 2f (Jubilee)** Stalls: High GOING minus 0.76 sec (HD) 8-10 (8-10)

Revere (IRE) **(111)***(121) (PFICole)* 5-9-10 TQuinn(7) (b: bit bkwd: mde all: qcknd 3f out: r.o wl) — **1**

631[3] Young Buster (IRE) **(113)***(116)*(Fav)*(GWragg)* 7-9-7 MHills(5) (lw: 6th st: nt clr run over 2f out: swtchd lft wl over 1f out: r.o ins fnl f) 1½ 2
1315[2] Ihtiram (IRE) **(108)***(112)*(Fav)*(JLDunlop)* 3-8-6 WCarson(2) (lw: 5th st: rdn over 2f out: unable qckn) ....½ 3
1408[2] Florid (USA) **(111)***(112) (HRACecil)* 4-9-4 WRyan(6) (lw: chsd wnr: rdn over 2f out: one pce)hd 4
1586[2] Be Mindful **(101)***(107) (JRFanshawe)* 3-8-6 DHarrison(3) (3rd st: rdn over 2f out: one pce) 3 5
Frustration **(104)***(89) (LadyHerries)* 4-8-13 JReid(1) (bit bkwd: 4th st: wknd over 2f out) 8 6
Pursuit of Glory **(75)***(71) (CACyzer)* 4-8-13 PatEddery(4) (swtg: a bhd) 11 7

5/2 Young Buster (IRE), Ihtiram (IRE), **9/2** Florid (USA), **7/1** Be Mindful, **8/1** Frustration, **12/1** REVERE (IRE) (op 8/1), **33/1** Pursuit of Glory, CSF £38.27 TOTE £13.10: £3.50 £2.10 (£16.50) OWNER Prince Fahd Salman (WHATCOMBE) BRED Newgate Stud Co 7 Rn

2m 0.14 (-2.36) SF: 65/60/44/56/39/33/15
WEIGHT FOR AGE 3yo-12lb

2009

'1812' OVERTURE H'CAP (0-80) (3-Y.O+) (Class D) £4,221.00 (£1,278.00: £624.00: £297.00) **6f** Stalls: High GOING minus 0.76 sec per fur (HD) 8-40 (8-41)

1832[9] **Dry Point (69)***(74) (JARToller)* 9-9-10 WNewnes(5) (lw: rdn over 4f out: hdwy 2f out: led last stride) ....— 1
1832* Youdontsay **(75)***(80)*(Fav)*(RCurtis)* 3-9-8 6x RHughes(6) (lw: w ldr: led over 2f out: hrd rdn ins fnl f: hdd last stride) ....s.h 2
1756[4] Dashing Dancer (IRE) **(57)***(62) (RAkehurst)* 4-8-12 TQuinn(4) (lw: hld up: rdn over 2f out: r.o ins fnl f) ....hd 3
1673[4] Q Factor **(72)***(76) (DHaydnJones)* 3-9-5 WCarson(3) (lw: hld up: rdn over 2f out: r.o ins fnl f) nk 4
1537[3] Face the Future **(63)***(66) (LJHolt)* 6-8-11 (7) IonaWands(2) (hdwy over 1f out: r.o one pce) ....½ 5
1909[3] Anzio (IRE) **(68)***(61) (BAPearce)* 4-9-9b SWhitworth(1) (b: lw: led over 3f: wknd over 1f out) .3½ 6
1777[7] Winsome Wooster **(66)***(51) (PGMurphy)* 4-9-7 LDettori(8) (hld up: rdn over 2f out: wknd over 1f out) 3 7

9/4 Youdontsay, **5/1** DRY POINT (7/2-11/2), Dashing Dancer (IRE), Winsome Wooster, **8/1** Face the Future, Q Factor, **12/1** Anzio (IRE), CSF £15.40 CT £49.32 TOTE £6.50: £3.40 £1.90 (£6.50) OWNER Lady Sophia Morrison (WHITSBURY) BRED Cheveley Park Stud Ltd 7 Rn

1m 10.19 (-1.11) SF: 59/57/47/53/51/46/36
WEIGHT FOR AGE 3yo-8lb

2010

CHANNEL ONE H'CAP (0-80) (3-Y.O+) (Class D) £4,260.00 (£1,290.00: £630.00: £300.00)
7f (round) Stalls: High GOING minus 0.76 sec per fur (HD) 9-10 (9-12)

1953[11] **Cameron Highland (IRE) (77)***(85) (PFICole)* 4-9-11 TQuinn(11) (lw: led over 1f: 2nd st: led over 2f out tl over 1f out: led ins fnl f: r.o wl) ....— 1
1560[2] Dawalib (USA) **(65)***(72)*(Fav)*(DHaydnJones)* 5-8-13 WCarson(10) (lw: 3rd st: led over 1f out tl ins fnl f: r.o) ....½ 2
1815[5] Dancing Lawyer **(69)***(74) (BJMeehan)* 4-9-3 RHughes(13) (4th st: hrd rdn over 1f out: unable qckn ins fnl f) ....¾ 3
1754[2] Bon Luck (IRE) **(72)***(77) (RAkehurst)* 3-8-8 (3) SSanders(12) (lw: hdwy over 2f out: hrd rdn over 1f out: r.o ins fnl f) ....nk 4
1676[4] Court Minstrel **(54)***(58) (LJHolt)* 6-8-2 AMcGlone(8) (hdwy over 1f out: r.o one pce) ....nk 5
191[2] Mullitover **(63)***(64) (MJHeaton-Ellis)* 5-8-11 JReid(9) (hmpd over 4f out: nt clr run over 2f out: hdwy over 1f out: r.o one pce) 1¼ 6
1750[3] La Petite Fusee **(70)***(69) (RJO'Sullivan)* 4-9-4 AClark(7) (b.hind: hdwy over 1f out: nvr nrr) ....¾ 7
1664[2] Court Nap (IRE) **(55)***(50) (SMellor)* 3-7-1 (7) CAdamson(5) (lw: nvr nrr) 2 8
313[8] Waldo **(67)***(53) (LordHuntingdon)* 4-9-1v DHarrison(3) (lw: nvr nr to chal) 4 9
1792[4] Wayfarers Way (USA) **(69)***(53) (RHannon)* 4-9-3 LDettori(4) (lw: 6th st: wknd over 1f out) ....½ 10
1299[8] Tatika **(71)***(51) (GWragg)* 5-9-5b MHills(6) (hdwy over 4f out: wknd over 2f out) 1¾ 11
Lucky Lucaya (USA) **(69)***(47) (LadyHerries)* 3-8-8 PatEddery(2) (led over 5f out tl over 2f out: eased whn btn over 1f out) 1¼ 12
1537[6] Deeply Vale (IRE) **(66)***(38) (GLMoore)* 4-9-0 SWhitworth(1) (5th st: wknd 2f out) 2½ 13

3/1 Dawalib (USA), **5/1** Bon Luck (IRE), **8/1** Dancing Lawyer, Court Minstrel, Tatika, **9/1** Wayfarers Way (USA), Lucky Lucaya (USA) (6/1-10/1), **10/1** La Petite Fusee, **14/1** Mullitover (10/1-16/1), **16/1** Court Nap (IRE), Deeply Vale (IRE), **20/1** CAMERON HIGHLAND (IRE), **25/1** Waldo, CSF £80.65 CT £505.59 TOTE £27.30: £5.30 £1.50 £2.10 (£80.10) Trio £165.00 OWNER H.R.H. Sultan Ahmad Shah (WHATCOMBE) BRED Peter McCalmont 13 Rn

1m 23.83 (0.99 under best) (-0.67) SF: 54/41/43/37/27/33/38/10/22/22/20/7/7
WEIGHT FOR AGE 3yo-9lb
T/Plpt: £68.60 (307.54 Tckts). T/Qdpt: £40.10 (6.6 Tckts). AK

1671-**SALISBURY (R-H)**

Wednesday June 28th (Firm, Good to firm fnl 3f)

WEATHER: sunny, hot WIND: mod half against

2011 E.B.F. WEYHILL MAIDEN STKS (2-Y.O F) (Class D) £3,977.00 (£1,196.00: £578.00: £269.00) **5f** Stalls: High GOING minus 0.59 sec per fur (F) 2-00 (2-01)

1653[4] **Willow Dale (IRE)** *(74) (DRCElsworth)* 2-8-11 TQuinn(6) (a.p: rdn over 2f out: led over 1f out: r.o wl) — 1
1536[5] Vera's First (IRE) *(72) (GLewis)* 2-8-6 (5) AWhelan(3) (chsd ldr: rdn over 2f out: ev ch fnl f: r.o) ¾ 2
Dramatic Entry (IRE) *(71) (JARToller)* 2-8-11b WNewnes(5) (unf: led: qcknd over 2f out: hdd over 1f out: r.o) nk 3
1653[2] Splicing *(61)*(Fav)*(JRFanshawe)* 2-8-11 DHarrison(4) (hld up & plld hrd: hdwy 2f out: one pce fnl f) 3 4
Music Mistress (IRE) *(48) (RHannon)* 2-8-11 PatEddery(1) (small: neat: hld up: no hdwy fnl 2f) 4 5
Sunset Harbour (IRE) *(48) (DAWilson)* 2-8-11 NGwilliams(7) (lengthy: unf: bkwd: no hdwy fnl 2f) hd 6
Willie Rushton *(43) (GLMoore)* 2-8-11 SWhitworth(2) (b.hind: lt-f: hld up: rdn & wknd wl over 1f out) 1½ 7

4/9 Splicing, **11/2** Music Mistress (IRE), **7/1** WILLOW DALE (IRE), **14/1** Dramatic Entry (IRE) (op 8/1), **16/1** Sunset Harbour (IRE), **20/1** Vera's First (IRE), **33/1** Willie Rushton, CSF £96.24 TOTE £9.20: £2.30 £4.30 (£44.00) OWNER Michael Jackson Bloodstock Ltd (WHITCOMBE) BRED Shunya Seki 7 Rn 61.79 secs (1.79) SF: 18/16/15/5/-/-/-

2012 HERBERT AND GWEN BLAGRAVE MEMORIAL RATED STKS H'CAP (0-95) (4-Y.O+) (Class B) £7,847.42 (£2,854.30: £1,389.65: £590.75: £257.88) **1m 4f** Stalls: High GOING minus 0.59 sec per fur (F) 2-30 (2-30)

Seasonal Splendour (IRE) (83)*(95) (MCPipe)* 5-8-12 DBiggs(1) (hld up: hdwy 3f out: led over 1f out: rdn out) — 1
1102[3] Godwin (USA) **(80)***(91) (HRACecil)* 4-8-9 WRyan(3) (lw: chsd ldr: led 3f out tl over 1f out: r.o) ¾ 2
1621[4] Swallows Dream (IRE) **(83)***(91)*(Fav)*(JLDunlop)* 4-8-12 WCarson(5) (lw: led 9f: one pce fnl f) 2½ 3
1612[5] Charity Crusader **(82)***(70) (PWChapple-Hyam)* 4-8-11b JReid(2) (a bhd) 15 4
Acting Brave **(92)***(68) (GHarwood)* 4-9-7 PatEddery(4) (lw: bhd fnl 5f: t.o) 9 5

2/1 Swallows Dream (IRE), **7/2** Godwin (USA) (5/2-4/1), **4/1** Charity Crusader, Acting Brave, **7/1** SEASONAL SPLENDOUR (IRE), CSF £27.01 TOTE £8.20: £3.00 £2.00 (£12.80) OWNER Mr D. A. Johnson (WELLINGTON) BRED B. Kennedy 5 Rn 2m 32.88 (0.28) SF: 48/44/44/23/21

2013 ALDERHOLT SPRINT H'CAP (0-85) (3-Y.O+) (Class D) £3,632.50 (£1,090.00: £525.00: £242.50) **5f** Stalls: High GOING minus 0.59 sec per fur (F) 3-00 (3-00)

1474[3] **Christmas Kiss (82)***(87)*(Fav)*(RHannon)* 3-9-3 (7) DaneO'Neill(4) (led over 2f: led 1f out: rdn out) — 1
1595[8] Domicksky **(61)***(65) (MRChannon)* 7-8-10 RHughes(5) (w wnr: hrd rdn & ev ch over 1f out: r.o) nk 2
1815* Aragrove **(78)***(80) (JWPayne)* 5-9-13b 7x MTebbutt(1) (swtg: plld hrd: hdwy to ld over 2f out: hdd 1f out: nt qckn) ¾ 3
1972[2] Wasblest **(55)***(56) (MJohnston)* 3-7-11 JQuinn(2) (lw: hld up: hdwy 2f out: one pce fnl f) nk 4
1614[P] Green Golightly (USA) **(70)***(39) (DAWilson)* 4-9-5 GCarter(3) (lw: sn outpcd) 10 5

9/4 CHRISTMAS KISS (3/1-2/1), **5/2** Aragrove (7/4-11/4), **11/4** Wasblest, **9/2** Domicksky, **25/1** Green Golightly (USA), CSF £10.92 TOTE £3.50: £1.70 £1.40 (£4.10) OWNER Mr Peter Pritchard (MARLBOROUGH) BRED Tarworth Bloodstock Investments Ltd 5 Rn
59.93 secs (-0.07) SF: 60/45/60/29/19
WEIGHT FOR AGE 3yo-7lb

2014 GIBBS MEW BIBURY CUP H'CAP (0-95) (3-Y.O) (Class C) £5,702.50 (£1,720.00: £835.00: £392.50) **1m 4f** Stalls: High GOING minus 0.59 sec (F) 3-30 (3-31)

1514* **Beyond Doubt (79)***(83+)*(Fav)*(LordHuntingdon)* 3-8-12 LDettori(3) (lw: chsd ldr: led over 3f out: shkn up over 1f out: pushed out) — 1

1182* Haniya (IRE) **(83)***(86) (JLDunlop)* 3-9-2 WCarson(2) (led over 8f: unable qckn fnl f)................¾ 2
1753[2] Mentor (GR) **(88)***(90) (RCharlton)* 3-9-7 DHarrison(1) (lw: hld up: rdn 4f out: hdwy over 2f out: ev ch over 1f out: one pce)..1 3
1544[5] Worldnews Extra (USA) **(83)** *(PFICole)* 3-9-2 TQuinn(4) (b: b.hind: rdn 3f out: sn lost tch: virtually p.u fnl f)..dist 4

4/6 BEYOND DOUBT (op 11/8), **9/4** Haniya (IRE), **15/2** Mentor (GR), **11/1** Worldnews Extra (USA) (op 7/1), CSF £2.52 TOTE £1.70: (£1.40) OWNER The Queen (WEST ILSLEY) BRED The Queen 4 Rn
2m 37.19 (4.59) SF: 21/24/28/-

2015 MARGADALE CONDITIONS STKS (3-Y.O) (Class C) £5,406.00 (£1,886.00: £918.00: £390.00) **6f 212y** Stalls: High GOING minus 0.59 sec (F) 4-00 (4-01)

1185[2] **Moon King (IRE) (107)***(89)*(Fav)*(RHannon)* 3-8-12 PatEddery(1) (lw: hld up: pushed along over 3f out: hdwy 2f out: led over 1f out: edgd rt: all out)....................................— 1
Done Well (USA) **(98)***(93) (EALDunlop)* 3-9-2 LDettori(2) (h.d.w: chsd ldr: rdn over 1f out: ev ch whn edgd rt ins fnl f: r.o wl)..s.h 2
Varnishing Day (IRE) *(87) (PWChapple-Hyam)* 3-9-0 JReid(3) (lw: s.i.s: sn prom: rdn 2f out: r.o one pce fnl f)..1½ 3
1683* Marocco (USA) **(82)***(76) (HRACecil)* 3-9-0 WRyan(4) (lw: led over 5f: wkng whn hmpd ins fnl f)..5 4

5/4 MOON KING (IRE), **9/4** Varnishing Day (IRE), **9/2** Done Well (USA), **5/1** Marocco (USA), CSF £6.28 TOTE £1.80 (£3.90) OWNER Mr Mohamed Suhail (MARLBOROUGH) BRED Gainsborough Stud Management Ltd 4 Rn
1m 25.38 (0.25 under best) (-0.32) SF: 52/56/50/39

2016 MARTIN CLAIMING STKS (3-Y.O+) (Class F) £3,092.00 (£862.00: £416.00) **1m** Stalls: High GOING minus 0.59 sec per fur (F) 4-30 (4-31)

1125[7] **Blasted (57)***(68+) (RHannon)* 3-9-0 JReid(3) (lw: hld up: hdwy over 2f out: led on bit ins fnl f: comf)..— 1
1714[11] Perilous Plight **(66)***(65) (WRMuir)* 4-9-7 (3) SSanders(12) (b: lw: chsd ldrs: rdn over 1f out: r.o ins fnl f)..1½ 2
1718[4] Master M-E-N (IRE) **(52)***(57) (NMBabbage)* 3-8-8v JQuinn(6) (stumbled s: plld hrd: sn prom: rdn to ld over 2f out: hdd ins fnl f)..1¼ 3
1883[9] Mai Pen Rai **(30)***(46) (RJHodges)* 7-8-7 (3) SDrowne(5) (a.p: rdn over 2f out: one pce)..........1½ 4
1742* Morocco (IRE) **(57)***(53)*(Fav)*(MRChannon)* 6-9-4 RHughes(1) (lw: hld up & bhd: swtchd rt over 3f out: rdn & nt clr run over 1f out: r.o one pce)..s.h 5
1799[11] Commander Glen (IRE) **(46)***(48) (MartynMeade)* 3-8-6b VSlattery(9) (prom tl wknd ins fnl f)..1½ 6
Isshereal (IRE) *(35) (BPalling)* 3-8-1 TSprake(2) (small: lt-f: a bhd)..4 7
546[13] Forbidden Gem **(30)***(16) (SWoodman)* 4-9-4 SWhitworth(7) (swtg: a bhd)..............................13 8
1207[13] Crocodile Rock **(20)***(20) (MJHeaton-Ellis)* 3-9-0v JWilliams(8) (swtg: led over 5f: sn wknd) ...1¼ 9
Scboo *(REPeacock)* 6-9-4 WNewnes(4) (s.s: a bhd: t.o)..10 10
Harvest Dream *(BJMeehan)* 4-9-5 MTebbutt(11) (a bhd: t.o)...3½ 11
1664[12] Raven's Roost (IRE) **(50)** *(MajorDNChappell)* 4-9-10 BThomson(10) (ref to r: t.n.p)................. R

2/1 Morocco (IRE) (op 3/1), **3/1** Perilous Plight, **100/30** BLASTED, **9/1** Master M-E-N (IRE), Raven's Roost (IRE), **20/1** Commander Glen (IRE), **33/1** Mai Pen Rai, Isshereal (IRE), **40/1** Harvest Dream, **50/1** Crocodile Rock, **66/1** Scboo, Forbidden Gem, CSF £13.05 TOTE £4.30: £1.70 £2.10 £1.70 (£7.60) Trio £26.00 OWNER Mr J. A. Filmer-Wilson (MARLBOROUGH) BRED J. S. Bell 12 Rn
1m 41.85 (2.55) SF: 26/33/15/14/21/6/-/-/-/-/-/-
WEIGHT FOR AGE 3yo-10lb

OFFICIAL EXPLANATION **Morocco (IRE): the jockey stated that he had tried to cover his mount up and win by coming between horses, but the gaps never came. The trainer added that the gelding is a bit of a character.**

2017 ALINGTON H'CAP (0-70) (3-Y.O+ F & M) (Class E) £3,392.00 (£1,016.00: £488.00: £224.00) **6f** Stalls: High GOING minus 0.59 sec per fur (F) 5-00 (5-02)

1692[4] **Bowden Rose (52)***(69) (MBlanshard)* 3-8-2b StephenDavies(3) (mde all: clr 3f out: unchal) .— 1
1602[9] Tonys Gift **(62)***(60) (RHannon)* 3-8-5 (7) DaneO'Neill(1) (swtg: hld up: hdwy 2f out: chsd wnr fnl f: no imp)..7 2
1326[5] Amany (IRE) **(49)***(37)*(Fav)*(GLewis)* 3-7-13 JQuinn(5) (s.i.s: sn prom: chsd wnr over 3f out to 1f out: wknd)..4 3
1811[10] Panchellita (USA) **(53)***(40) (GLMoore)* 6-8-11 SWhitworth(7) (hdwy over 1f out: r.o one pce fnl f)..hd 4

1953[12] Frisky Miss (IRE) **(63)***(50) (KOCunningham-Brown)* 4-9-7 AMcGlone(2) (lw: prom tl wknd fnl f) ....hd **5**
1777[3] Tinker Osmaston **(66)***(49) (MSSaunders)* 4-9-10 JWilliams(6) (lw: a bhd)....1¾ **6**
1692[3] Pharsical **(62)** *(MRChannon)* 4-9-6 RHughes(4) (bolted bef s: chsd wnr over 2f: sn btn & eased: t.o) ....dist **7**

7/4 Amany (IRE) (op 4/1), **11/4** Pharsical, **9/2** Tinker Osmaston, **13/2** BOWDEN ROSE, **9/1** Tonys Gift, **14/1** Frisky Miss (IRE), Panchellita (USA), CSF £54.47 TOTE £9.50: £4.30 £2.10 (£40.40) OWNER The Lower Bowden Syndicate (UPPER LAMBOURN) BRED E. A. Badger 7 Rn
1m 11.82 (-0.48) SF: 45/36/13/24/34/33/-
WEIGHT FOR AGE 3yo-8lb

T/Plpt: £2,010.90 (4.64 Tckts). T/Qdpt: £9.90 (10.15 Tckts). KH

1992-CARLISLE (R-H)
Thursday June 29th (Firm, Hard patches)
WEATHER: sunny WIND: slt across

2018
WALTON CLAIMING STKS (3-Y.O+ F & M) (Class F) £2,857.00 (£802.00: £391.00)
5f 207y Stalls: High GOING minus 0.93 sec per fur (HD) 2-15 (2-17)

1906[2] **Fantasy Racing (IRE) (78)***(72)*(Fav)*(MRChannon)* 3-8-13 RHughes(9) (disp ld 2½f: chsd wnr: hrd rdn over 1f out: styd on one pce: fin 2nd, 1 3/4l: awrdd r) ....— **1**
1723[3] Special-K **(60)***(64) (EWeymes)* 3-8-5 GHind(5) (styd on u.p fnl 3f: nrst fin: fin 3rd, hd: plcd 2nd).... **2**
1564[5] Poly Laureon (IRE) **(44)***(51) (RHollinshead)* 3-8-3 KDarley(4) (a.p: effrt 2f out: one pce: fin 4th, 4l: plcd 3rd) **3**
1739[9] Jessica's Secret (IRE) **(34)***(39) (ABailey)* 3-7-10 ow1 WHawksley(6) (s.i.s: hdwy ½-wy: sn rdn & no imp: fin 5th, 1 3/4l: plcd 4th).... **4**
1993[9] Brookhead Lady **(59)***(36) (PDEvans)* 4-8-7 SMaloney(2) (lw: b.nr fore: hmpd after 1f: chsd ldrs tl wknd over 2f out)....2½ **6**
1993[2] Trina **(28)***(30) (DLWilliams)* 4-8-2 (5) NVarley(1) (lw: hmpd & carried wd after 1f: sn drvn along: wknd fr ½-wy) 2 **7**
Rambo's Rumtime *(6) (FWatson)* 3-7-13 JFanning(8) (bit bkwd: s.i.s: a bhd) 9 **8**
1718[11] Ivy Lilian (IRE) **(40)** *(WMBrisbourne)* 3-7-2 (7) MartinDwyer(7) (chsd ldrs tl rdn & wknd ½-wy) 5 **9**
1763[13] Annie Fay (IRE) **(55)***(61) (JLHarris)* 3-7-11 AMackay(3) (mde most: rdn & styd on wl fnl 2f: fin 1st: disq: plcd last: (prohibited substance (dembrexine) found in urine)) **0**

11/10 FANTASY RACING (IRE) (Evens-5/4), **4/1** Special-K, **9/2** Annie Fay (IRE), **10/1** Trina, Brookhead Lady, **25/1** Poly Laureon (IRE), Ivy Lilian (IRE), **33/1** Jessica's Secret (IRE), **50/1** Rambo's Rumtime, CSF £9.47 TOTE £5.70: £1.60 £1.10 £1.20 (£5.30) Trio £3.90 OWNER Aldridge Racing Ltd (UPPER LAMBOURN) BRED Barronstown Stud and Ron Con Ltd 9 Rn
1m 12.4 (0.10) SF: 17/9/-/-/-/-/-/6
WEIGHT FOR AGE 3yo-8lb

2019
CARLISLE RACE CLUB LIMITED STKS (0-60) (3-Y.O+) (Class F)
£2,801.00 (£786.00: £383.00)
7f 214y Stalls: High GOING minus 0.93 sec per fur (HD) 2-45 (2-47)

1966[5] **Second Colours (USA) (60)***(70) (MrsMReveley)* 5-9-11 KDarley(4) (trckd ldrs: efrt 2f out: r.o wl to ld wl ins fnl f) ....— **1**
1818* Legal Issue (IRE) **(58)***(67)*(Fav)*(SirMarkPrescott)* 3-8-13 GDuffield(3) (lw: trckd ldr: led 2f out tl wl ins fnl f: r.o)....nk **2**
1775[4] Indefence (IRE) **(58)***(43) (MRChannon)* 4-9-7v RHughes(2) (led tl hdd 2f out: sn outpcd).......11 **3**

4/6 Legal Issue (IRE), **3/1** SECOND COLOURS (USA), Indefence (IRE) (op 2/1), CSF £5.17 TOTE £3.80: (£1.80) OWNER Mr P. D. Savill (SALTBURN) BRED Dinnaken Farm in USA 3 Rn
1m 39.3 (0.30) SF: 32/19/5
WEIGHT FOR AGE 3yo-10lb

2020
RAYOPHANE H'CAP (0-70) (3-Y.O) (Class E) £3,095.40 (£937.20: £457.60: £217.80) **7f 214y** Stalls: High GOING minus 0.93 sec per fur (HD) 3-15 (3-16)

1939[3] **Ninia (USA) (48)***(58+) (MJohnston)* 3-8-0 PRobinson(7) (a.p: led 2f out: sn qcknd clr: easily) ....— **1**
1679[3] Euro Sceptic (IRE) **(51)***(55)*(Fav)*(MHEasterby)* 3-8-3b SMaloney(6) (a.p: effrt 3f out: styd on: no ch w wnr) 3 **2**

19524 Heathyards Magic (IRE) **(69)***(72) (RHollinshead)* 3-9-7 JWeaver(4) (s.i.s: bhd tl hdwy 2f out: nt clr run & swtchd over 1f out: no imp) ...¾ 3
15689 Opera Fan (IRE) **(60)***(48) (SirMarkPrescott)* 3-8-12 GDuffield(3) (lw: sn outpcd & bhd: hdwy over 2f out: n.d) ...7 4
18479 Benten **(41)***(27) (DWChapman)* 3-7-7 NKennedy(5) (w ldr: led over 2f out: sn hdd & wknd) ...1 5
759 12 Eden Dancer **(60)***(36) (MrsMReveley)* 3-8-12 KDarley(1) (lw: led tl hdd & wknd over 2f out) ...5 6
15969 Battery Boy **(43)***(16) (CWCElsey)* 3-7-2b(7) PFessey(2) (swtg: prom tl wknd 3f out) ...1½ 7

LONG HANDICAP Benten 7-0

5/2 Euro Sceptic (IRE), **7/2** NINIA (USA), Opera Fan (IRE), **11/2** Eden Dancer (4/1-6/1), **7/1** Heathyards Magic (IRE), **12/1** Battery Boy, **50/1** Benten, CSF £11.68 TOTE £5.30: £2.50 £1.90 (£5.20) OWNER Mrs D. R. Schreiber (MIDDLEHAM) BRED Newgate Stud Farm Inc 7 Rn

1m 38.2 (-0.80) SF: 19/16/33/9/-/-/-

2021

RED MILLS IRISH HORSEFEEDS LADY RIDERS' AMATEUR H'CAP (0-65) (3-Y.O+) (Class G) £2,465.00 (£690.00: £335.00)
6f 206y Stalls: High GOING minus 0.93 sec per fur (HD) 3-45 (3-48)

18432 **Green's Bid (48)***(58)*(Fav)*(DWChapman)* 5-10-10 (5) MissRClark(3) (lw: mde most: c wd st: styd on wl fnl f) ...— 1
18557 Phase One (IRE) **(50)***(58) (JLEyre)* 5-11-3 MissDianaJones(10) (b: chsd ldr: disp ld over 2f out: edgd lft & no ex ins fnl f) ...1 2
1679 12 Twin Creeks **(47)***(54) (MDHammond)* 4-11-0 MrsLPearce(1) (chsd ldrs: hung rt fnl f: kpt on wl) ...nk 3
4169 Rad **(54)***(58) (SPCWoods)* 5-11-7 MrsAFarrell(6) (hdwy 3f out: styd on appr fnl f: nvr able to chal) ...1¼ 4
13775 Parklife (IRE) **(40)***(44) (PCHaslam)* 3-9-12 MrsDKettlewell(8) (s.i.s: hdwy ½-wy: n.m.r over 1f out: nvr able to chal) ...hd 5
17248 Miss Pigalle **(34)***(38) (MissLAPerratt)* 4-10-1b MrsSBosley(9) (effrt ½-wy: nt pce to chal) ...s.h 6
1785 13 Ain'tlifelikethat **(40)***(43) (TJNaughton)* 8-10-2b(5) MrsJNaughton(5) (b: dwlt: sn prom: effrt 2f out: wknd 1f out) ...½ 7
51810 Lord Vivienne (IRE) **(43)***(45) (BSRothwell)* 6-10-5 (5) MissAlexMcCabe(4) (cl up tl wknd wl over 1f out) ...½ 8
1724 11 Faynaz **(23)***(18) (RMMcKellar)* 9-8-13 (5) MrsCWilliams(7) (lw: b: nvr trbld ldrs) ...3 9
1742 10 Pipers Glen **(43)***(15) (CParker)* 3-10-1 MissPRobson(11) (outpcd appr st: n.d after) ...10 10
1863 14 Restraint **(32)** *(JJBirkett)* 5-9-8 (5) MissFBarnes(2) (chsd ldrs 4f: sn wknd) ...20 11

3/1 GREEN'S BID (2/1-7/2), **4/1** Parklife (IRE) (op 5/2), **6/1** Twin Creeks, Phase One (IRE) (op 10/1), Miss Pigalle, **10/1** Rad, **12/1** Pipers Glen (op 8/1), **20/1** Faynaz, Ain'tlifelikethat, **100/1** Lord Vivienne (IRE), Restraint, CSF £19.64 CT £90.96 TOTE £4.10: £2.00 £1.80 £1.90 (£8.20) Trio £16.00 OWNER Mr J. M. Chapman (YORK) BRED Stud-On-The-Chart 11 Rn

1m 26.7 (1.00) SF: 40/40/36/40/17/20/25/27/-/-/-
WEIGHT FOR AGE 3yo-9lb

2022

UCB FILMS CUMBERLAND PLATE H'CAP (0-80) (3-Y.O+) (Class D) £6,905.00 (£2,090.00: £1,020.00: £485.00)
1m 4f Stalls: Low GOING minus 0.93 sec per fur (HD) 4-15 (4-17)

Batabanoo (77)*(90)*(Fav)*(MrsMReveley)* 6-10-0 KDarley(3) (sn trckng ldrs: qcknd to chal 5f out: rdn to ld wl ins fnl f) ...— 1
18653 Tu Opes **(65)***(78) (JLHarris)* 4-9-2 PRobinson(2) (led tl hdd wl ins fnl f: kpt on u.p) ...hd 2
1861* Ashover **(54)***(66)*(Fav)*(TDBarron)* 5-8-5 5x JFortune(6) (lw: chsd wnr tl hmpd & lost pl over 4f out: hdwy u.p 3f out: styd on towards fin) ...1 3
16354 Credit Squeeze **(73)***(81) (RFJohnsonHoughton)* 5-9-10 JQuinn(7) (lw: hld up: hdwy over 3f out: rdn & one pce fnl 2f) ...3 4
14165 Microlite (USA) **(60)***(65) (MDHammond)* 4-8-11b JWeaver(1) (w ldrs tl hmpd & lost pl over 4f out: hdwy 3f out: btn whn hmpd over 1f out) ...2 5
16867 Hill Farm Dancer **(51)***(55) (WMBrisbourne)* 4-7-13 (3) AGarth(5) (hld up: effrt appr st: no imp) .¾ 6

9/4 BATABANOO, Ashover, **9/2** Microlite (USA), Credit Squeeze, **9/1** Hill Farm Dancer, **14/1** Tu Opes, CSF £25.60 TOTE £3.00: £1.90 £2.90 (£12.80) OWNER Mr P. D. Savill (SALTBURN) BRED Clover Stud 6 Rn 2m 29.5 (0.80 under best) (-1.50) SF: 48/36/24/39/23/13

2023

CUMREW (S) STKS (2-Y.O) (Class G) £2,465.00 (£690.00: £335.00)
5f Stalls: High GOING minus 0.93 sec per fur (HD) 4-45 (4-47)

145410 **Albert The Bear** *(60) (JBerry)* 2-8-11 JCarroll(5) (disp ld tl led 2f out: hdd over 1f out: rallied to ld cl home) ...— 1

1740* Imp Express (IRE) **(65)**(*66*)(Fav)*(GMMoore)* 2-9-4 JFortune(7) (lw: hld up: hdwy on bit ½-wy: led appr fnl f: sn hrd rdn: no ex towards fin)....nk **2**
1665[4] U-No-Harry (IRE) *(53) (RHollinshead)* 2-9-1 (3) AGarth(3) (disp ld 3f: r.o one pce)....4 **3**
Peters Folly *(40) (JLEyre)* 2-8-1 (5) NVarley(4) (unf: prom 3f: sn outpcd)....nk **4**
1497[8] Poppy My Love *(8) (BJMcMath)* 2-8-6 AMackay(6) (chsd ldrs tl outpcd fnl 2f)....10 **5**
1821[2] Cawdor Lady (Fav)*(TJEtherington)* 2-8-6 JWeaver(2) (unruly s: hung lft most of wy: no ch fr ½-wy)....2½ **6**
983[8] Miss Hotshot *(RBastiman)* 2-8-6 DeanMcKeown(1) (s.i.s: hung lft thrght: wl bhd fr ½-wy)...15 **7**

9/4 Imp Express (IRE), Cawdor Lady, **3/1** U-No-Harry (IRE), **5/1** ALBERT THE BEAR, **12/1** Poppy My Love (op 8/1), **14/1** Peters Folly, **33/1** Miss Hotshot, CSF £16.85 TOTE £7.50: £2.50 £1.90 (£20.50) OWNER Mr Chris Deuters (COCKERHAM) BRED Rockhouse Farms Ltd 7 Rn
60.5 secs (0.30) SF: 15/21/8/-/-/-/-
No bid.

OFFICIAL EXPLANATION **Cawdor Lady: the jockey reported that the filly was hanging throughout the race and was therefore unable to be ridden out.**

2024

CROGLIN H'CAP (0-70) (3-Y.O) (Class E) £3,095.40 (£937.20: £457.60: £217.80)
5f Stalls: High GOING minus 0.93 sec per fur (HD) 5-15 (5-16)

1847[5] **Dominelle (45)***(52) (MHEasterby)* 3-7-13 SMaloney(5) (a.p: styd on to ld wl ins fnl f: hung rt cl home)....— **1**
1936[2] Mister Westsound **(41)***(45)*(Fav)*(MissLAPerratt)* 3-7-9b DaleGibson(6) (s.i.s: hdwy 2f out: btn whn hmpd cl home)....1 **2**
1580[6] C-Yer-Simmie (IRE) **(59)***(63) (RHollinshead)* 3-8-10 (3) AGarth(3) (led tl hdd & no ex wl ins fnl f)....s.h **3**
1822[4] Swan At Whalley **(67)***(63) (MartynWane)* 3-9-7 JFortune(7) (lw: chsd ldrs: hdwy whn hmpd ins fnl f: nt rcvr)....2½ **4**
1739* Frans Lad **(62)***(54) (JBerry)* 3-9-2b JCarroll(4) (in tch: hrd rdn 2f out: no imp)....1 **5**
1721[11] Another Nightmare (IRE) **(47)***(36) (RMMcKellar)* 3-7-8 (7) PFessey(2) (chsd ldrs over 3f)....1 **6**
1739[2] Sunshine Belle **(48)***(8) (GMMoore)* 3-8-2 JFanning(1) (lw: sn drvn along: lost tch fr ½-wy)....9 **7**

9/4 Mister Westsound, **4/1** DOMINELLE, **9/2** Frans Lad, **5/1** Sunshine Belle, **8/1** C-Yer-Simmie (IRE), **9/1** Swan At Whalley, **16/1** Another Nightmare (IRE), CSF £12.66 TOTE £4.60: £2.20 £2.20 (£7.10) OWNER Sandmoor Textiles Co Ltd (MALTON) BRED Gymcrak Thoroughbred Breeding Ltd 7 Rn
60.0 secs (-0.20) SF: 12/5/23/23/14/-/-
T/Jkpt: £20,991.70 (0.6 Tckts); £11,826.36 to Newmarket 30/6/95. T/Plpt: £119.10 (122.9 Tckts).
T/Qdpt: £41.40 (2 Tckts). AA

1726-NEWBURY (L-H)
Thursday June 29th (Firm)

WEATHER: hot WIND: almost nil

2025

CITY INDEX SPREAD BETTING MAIDEN STKS (2-Y.O F) (Class D)
£3,541.50 (£1,062.00: £511.00: £235.50)
6f 8y Stalls: Centre GOING minus 0.50 sec per fur (F) 6-30 (6-32)

1627[2] **Darling Flame (USA)** *(75+)*(Fav)*(JHMGosden)* 2-8-11 LDettori(5) (lw: a.p: led over 1f out: comf)....— **1**
Min Alhawa (USA) *(70) (MajorWRHern)* 2-8-11 WCarson(7) (leggy: w ldr: led over 2f out tl over 1f out: unable qckn)....1¾ **2**
Lyzia (IRE) *(66+) (CEBrittain)* 2-8-11 BDoyle(10) (leggy: lw: a.p: rdn over 1f out: one pce)..1¾ **3**
Ailesbury Hill (USA) *(62+) (PWChapple-Hyam)* 2-8-11 JReid(1) (leggy: scope: lw: hld up: shkn up over 1f out: one pce: bttr for r)....1½ **4**
Rumpipumpy *(56) (LordHuntingdon)* 2-8-11 WRSwinburn(2) (leggy: unf: hld up: rdn over 2f out: one pce)....2 **5**
Hawanafa *(41) (RHannon)* 2-8-11 RPerham(4) (leggy: s.s: nvr nr to chal)....6 **6**
Northern Ballet (IRE) *(40) (RHannon)* 2-8-11 PatEddery(6) (w'like: bit bkwd: bhd fnl 2f)....hd **7**
Eccola *(40) (IABalding)* 2-8-11 WRyan(11) (w'like: bit bkwd: s.s: bhd fnl 2f)....nk **8**
Zdenka *(37) (MBlanshard)* 2-8-11 RCochrane(3) (leggy: unf: a bhd)....1 **9**
1536[6] Primelta *(36) (RAkehurst)* 2-8-11 TQuinn(8) (bhd fnl 2f)....nk **10**
Red Misty (IRE) *(23) (MrsMMcCourt)* 2-8-4 (7) RStudholme(9) (leggy: unf: led over 3f)....5 **11**

Evens DARLING FLAME (USA), **4/1** Min Alhawa (USA), **9/1** Eccola (4/1-10/1), **10/1** Ailesbury Hill (USA) (op 7/2), **12/1** Rumpipumpy, Northern Ballet (IRE) (op 6/1), **16/1** Lyzia (IRE), **20/1** Primelta, **33/1** Hawanafa, **66/1** Zdenka, Red Misty (IRE), CSF £5.63 TOTE £2.10: £1.20 £1.50 £4.20 (£2.80) Trio £13.80 OWNER Sheikh Mohammed (NEWMARKET) BRED Darley Stud Management Inc 11 Rn
1m 11.64 (-0.16) SF: 56/51/47/43/37/22/21/21/18/17/4

2026

COOPERS & LYBRAND H'CAP (0-80) (3-Y.O) (Class D) £4,337.50 (£1,300.00: £625.00: £287.50)
1m 5f 61y Stalls: Low GOING minus 0.50 sec per fur (F) 7-00 (7-02)

1817[4] **Daily Starlight (USA) (72)***(85) (MissGayKelleway)* 3-9-4 MWigham(7) (hdwy over 3f out: led over 1f out: hrd rdn: r.o wl)....— 1
1674* Eurolink Mischief **(75)***(85)*(Fav)*(LMCumani)* 3-9-7 WRSwinburn(3) (b.hind: 4th st: led over 2f out tl over 1f out: unable qckn ins fnl f)....2½ 2
1695[3] John Lee Hooker **(58)***(66) (DWPArbuthnot)* 3-8-4 TQuinn(6) (5th st: nt clr run over 2f out: one pce)....1½ 3
1410[5] Invest Wisely **(68)***(76) (JMPEustace)* 3-9-0 RCochrane(2) (lw: 6th st: rdn 2f out: one pce).....hd 4
1347[2] Turquoise Sea (USA) **(73)***(79) (JLDunlop)* 3-9-5 WCarson(4) (rdn over 4f out: hdwy over 1f out: nvr nrr)....1½ 5
1601* Rocky Forum **(56)***(48) (GLMoore)* 3-8-2 FNorton(1) (3rd st: wknd over 2f out)....12 6
1881[12] Negative Equity **(52)***(40) (KRBurke)* 3-7-5b(7) MHenry(8) (lw: led 11f)....3½ 7
1439[2] Wurlitzer (USA) **(75)***(53) (JHMGosden)* 3-9-7 LDettori(5) (lw: hdwy over 3f out: wknd over 2f out)....8 8
1514[9] George Bull **(70)***(46) (MajorWRHern)* 3-9-2 PatEddery(9) (lw: 2nd st: wknd over 3f out)....2 9

3/1 Eurolink Mischief, **9/2** George Bull, Turquoise Sea (USA), **5/1** Wurlitzer (USA), **10/1** Rocky Forum (6/1-12/1), **11/1** John Lee Hooker, **16/1** DAILY STARLIGHT (USA), Negative Equity, Invest Wisely, CSF £58.27 CT £505.06 TOTE £20.90: £4.00 £1.50 £1.70 (£20.20) Trio £94.60 OWNER Mr A. Al-Radi (WHITCOMBE) BRED Robert S. West Jnr 9 Rn

2m 48.03 (2.73) SF: 46/46/27/37/40/9/1/14/7

2027

KINGSTON SMITH H'CAP (0-80) (3-Y.O+) (Class D) £4,077.50 (£1,220.00: £585.00: £267.50) **5f 34y** Stalls: Centre GOING minus 0.50 sec (F) 7-30 (7-31)

1544* **Top Banana (79)***(90)*(Fav)*(HCandy)* 4-10-0 WNewnes(1) (lw: w ldr: led over 2f out: rdn out)— 1
1738* Tharwa (IRE) **(60)***(66) (NACallaghan)* 3-7-9 (7) MHenry(3) (b: b.hind: lw: hld up: rdn over 2f out: chsd wnr over 1f out: unable qckn)....1½ 2
1864[2] Featherstone Lane **(55)***(59) (MissLCSiddall)* 4-8-4v DHarrison(5) (outpcd: hdwy over 2f out: hrd rdn over 1f out: one pce)....¾ 3
1174[9] Barossa Valley (IRE) **(77)***(73) (PWChapple-Hyam)* 4-9-12b JReid(2) (lw: led over 2f: wknd fnl f)....2½ 4
1750[2] Another Jade **(68)***(62) (APJarvis)* 5-9-3 TQuinn(4) (lw: hld up: rdn over 2f out: wknd fnl f) ......¾ 5

5/2 TOP BANANA, **7/2** Tharwa (IRE), Another Jade, **5/1** Featherstone Lane, Barossa Valley (IRE), CSF £10.06 TOTE £2.50: £1.50 £2.00 (£4.80) OWNER Major M. G. Wyatt (WANTAGE) BRED Dunchurch Lodge Stud Co 5 Rn 60.08 secs (-0.22) SF: 73/42/42/56/45

WEIGHT FOR AGE 3yo-7lb

2028

WIMPEY MINERALS H'CAP (0-80) (3-Y.O+ F & M) (Class D) £4,435.00 (£1,330.00: £640.00: £295.00)
1m 2f 6y Stalls: Low GOING minus 0.50 sec per fur (F) 8-00 (8-04)

1732* **Legendary Leap (70)***(80) (LordHuntingdon)* 5-9-7 DHarrison(3) (lw: 3rd st: led over 2f out: all out)....— 1
1745[10] Douce Maison (IRE) **(50)***(60) (APJarvis)* 4-7-12 (3) DWright(1) (lw: 6th st: hrd rdn over 1f out: r.o wl)....hd 2
Ruby Heights **(49)***(49) (RHannon)* 4-8-0 ow2 BDoyle(7) (hdwy over 6f out: 2nd st: led over 3f out tl over 2f out: unable qckn)....5 3
1473* Vena (IRE) **(80)***(81)*(Fav)*(JLDunlop)* 3-9-5 WCarson(9) (4th st: one pce fnl 3f)....½ 4
1347[5] Blue Nile (IRE) **(70)***(71) (ACStewart)* 3-8-9 WRSwinburn(4) (rdn 3f out: nvr nr to chal) ....hd 5
1788[7] Triple Tie (USA) **(60)***(55) (MBlanshard)* 4-8-11 RCochrane(8) (swtg: 5th st: wknd 2f out)......3½ 6
1808[5] Dancing Heights (IRE) **(77)***(70) (IABalding)* 4-10-0 LDettori(5) (lw: led over 6f: wknd over 1f out)....1¼ 7
1762[13] Aldwick Colonnade **(46)***(39) (MDIUsher)* 8-7-4 (7) CAdamson(2) (a bhd)....nk 8
888[8] Victoria's Secret (IRE) **(75)***(67) (DRCElsworth)* 3-9-0 WNewnes(6) (a bhd) ....nk 9

5/2 Vena (IRE) (7/4-11/4), **4/1** Dancing Heights (IRE), LEGENDARY LEAP, Blue Nile (IRE), **16/1** Ruby Heights, Douce Maison (IRE), **20/1** Victoria's Secret (IRE), **33/1** Triple Tie (USA), **50/1** Aldwick Colonnade, CSF £52.14 CT £768.29 TOTE £5.40: £1.50 £3.70 £3.00 (£33.50) Trio £212.70 OWNER Mr D. Tylden-Wright (WEST ILSLEY) BRED D. Tylden-Wright 9 Rn

2m 5.32 (2.32) SF: 46/26/15/35/25/21/36/5/21

WEIGHT FOR AGE 3yo-12lb

STEWARDS' ENQUIRY Wright suspended 8/7/95 & 10-15/7/95 (excessive use of whip).

2029 GARDNER LEADER CENTENARY CONDITIONS STKS (2-Y.O) (Class C) £4,858.75 (£1,765.00: £857.50: £362.50: £156.25)
6f 8y Stalls: Centre GOING minus 0.50 sec per fur (F) 8-30 (8-30)

1551* **Rio Duvida** *(91+) (DRLoder)* 2-9-0 PatEddery(4) (lw: w ldr: led 3f out: rdn out).....................— 1
1726* Resounder (USA) *(84)*(Fav)*(JHMGosden)* 2-9-0 LDettori(5) (lw: dwlt: hld up: rdn over 1f out: chsd wnr fnl f: unable qckn).....................2½ 2
1727⁴ Kandavu *(78) (MMcCormack)* 2-8-9 JReid(3) (hld up: ev ch over 1f out: one pce)..................½ 3
Norwegian Blue (IRE) *(65) (APJarvis)* 2-8-7 TQuinn(2) (w'like: led 3f: wknd wl over 1f out).....4 4
1752¹¹ Moylough Rebel *(48) (MrsMELong)* 2-8-11 JWilliams(1) (bit bkwd: bhd fnl 3f).........................8 5

10/11 Resounder (USA), **11/10** RIO DUVIDA, **16/1** Kandavu, **40/1** Norwegian Blue (IRE), **100/1** Moylough Rebel, CSF £2.31 TOTE £1.90: £1.10 £1.10 (£1.20) OWNER Lady Harrison (NEWMARKET) BRED Limestone Stud 5 Rn 1m 12.8 (1.00) SF: 43/36/30/17/-

2030 WEATHERPROOF CONDITIONS STKS (3-Y.O+) (Class C) £5,344.00 (£1,864.00: £907.00: £385.00) **1m 7y (round)** Stalls: Low GOING minus 0.50 sec (F) 9-00 (9-17)

761* **Sulb (USA)** *(96)*(Fav)*(ACStewart)* 3-8-8 WCarson(1) (lw: 3rd st: nt clr run on ins over 3f out: led over 1f out: r.o wl).....................— 1
900a¹¹ Albinor (IRE) *(95) (JLDunlop)* 3-8-8 LDettori(3) (lw: led over 6f: ev ch ins fnl f: r.o) ....nk 2
792⁵ Peutetre *(89) (CEBrittain)* 3-8-8 BDoyle(6) (lw: 2nd st: rdn over 2f out: ev ch over 1f out: unable qckn).....................3 3
Prussian Flag **(102)***(85) (RHannon)* 3-8-10 PatEddery(4) (lw: 4th st: rdn over 2f out: ev ch over 1f out: wknd fnl f).....................3 4
1370² Romanzof **(100)** *(HRACecil)* 3-8-8 WRyan(2) (Withdrawn not under Starter's orders: bolted bef s)..................... W
1478⁶ Sue's Return **(88)** *(APJarvis)* 3-8-0 (3) DWright(5) (Withdrawn not under Starter's orders: unruly in stalls)..................... W

4/5 SULB (USA), **5/2** Prussian Flag (2/1-3/1), **9/2** Albinor (IRE), **10/1** Peutetre, CSF £4.36 TOTE £1.50: £1.90 (£3.20) OWNER Mr Hamdan Al Maktoum (NEWMARKET) BRED Allan Mactier 4 Rn 1m 38.7 (2.70) SF: 24/23/17/13/-/-

T/Plpt: £20.10 (800.7 Tckts). T/Qdpt: £11.20 (171.8 Tckts). AK

2011-SALISBURY (R-H)
Thursday June 29th (Firm)

6th race hand started.
WEATHER: sunny & hot WIND: almost nil

2031 NOEL CANNON MEMORIAL TROPHY H'CAP (0-100) (3-Y.O+) (Class C) £5,637.50 (£1,700.00: £825.00: £387.50)
1m Stalls: High GOING minus 0.64 sec per fur (F) 2-00 (2-01)

1351² **Weaver Bird (80)***(89) (HCandy)* 5-8-10 WNewnes(5) (a.p: rdn & chsd ldr over 2f out: r.o to ld last strides).....................— 1
1617² Samba Sharply **(75)***(84) (AHide)* 4-8-5 WWoods(8) (led: qcknd 3f out: hrd rdn & edgd lft fnl f: hdd last strides).....................hd 2
1411⁷ Law Commission **(78)***(83) (DRCElsworth)* 5-8-8 TQuinn(7) (a.p: chsd ldr over 3f out tl over 2f out: one pce fnl f).....................2 3
1851⁵ Kayvee **(98)***(101)*(Fav)*(GHarwood)* 6-10-0 WRSwinburn(6) (lw: hld up: hdwy over 2f out: rdn over 1f out: one pce).....................¾ 4
1851³¹ Desert Time **(79)***(75) (CAHorgan)* 5-8-9 PatEddery(3) (b.hind: hld up: rdn 2f out: no hdwy)..3½ 5
1626² Deevee **(72)***(67) (CJBenstead)* 6-8-2 WCarson(2) (hld up & bhd: rdn 4f out: nvr nr ldrs).........¾ 6
1754⁴ Lomas (IRE) **(79)***(62) (MrsHParrott)* 4-8-2 (7) DaneO'Neill(1) (lw: chsd ldr over 4f: sn bhd).......6 7

9/4 Kayvee, **4/1** WEAVER BIRD, **5/1** Desert Time (4/1-6/1), Deevee, **6/1** Samba Sharply (op 4/1), **11/1** Law Commission (8/1-12/1), **25/1** Lomas (IRE), CSF £24.44 CT £205.36 TOTE £4.00: £2.30 £3.30 (£8.90) OWNER Mrs Henry Candy (WANTAGE) BRED W. and R. Barnett Ltd 7 Rn 1m 38.94 (0.31 under best) (-0.36) SF: 47/42/41/59/33/25/20

2032 SHREWTON RATING RELATED MAIDEN LIMITED STKS (0-65) (3-Y.O) (Class F) £2,945.00 (£820.00: £395.00)
6f 212y Stalls: High GOING minus 0.64 sec per fur (F) 2-30 (2-31)

1660⁶ **Second Cello (61)***(69) (DMorris)* 3-8-9 LDettori(4) (swtg: a.p: led over 2f out: all out)...........— 1

1747[8] I'm Outa Here (IRE) **(64)***(74) (RHannon)* 3-8-7 (7) DaneO'Neill(9) (a.p: hrd rdn & r.o wl ins fnl f) ....hd 2
1787[6] Anegre (IRE) **(57)***(69) (LJHolt)* 3-9-0 JReid(8) (led over 4f: ev ch 1f out: nt qckn) 2 3
727[7] Solianna **(58)***(58) (MRChannon)* 3-8-4 (5) PPMurphy(3) (hld up & plld hrd: rdn wl over 1f out: one pce) 2½ 4
1532[2] Jurassic Sue **(64)***(58)*(Fav)*(BWHills)* 3-8-9v TQuinn(6) (a.p: rdn over 2f out: nt clr run over 1f out: one pce) ....s.h 5
1514[12] Memory's Music **(56)***(58) (IABalding)* 3-9-0 WRyan(2) (lw: hld up & bhd: nvr nr to chal) 2½ 6
1366[11] East Sheen **(60)***(47) (CJBenstead)* 3-8-9 RCochrane(7) (rdn over 3f out: plld out over 2f out: n.d) 2½ 7
1447[11] Miss Laughter **(46)***(46) (JWHills)* 3-8-2 (7) MHenry(5) (swtg: plld hrd: a bhd) ....nk 8
1660[16] Treasure Keay **(52)** *(PJMakin)* 3-8-9 RPerham(1) (rdn over 3f out: sn eased & bhd: t.o) ....dist 9

9/4 Jurassic Sue, **7/2** SECOND CELLO, **7/1** Anegre (IRE) (6/1-9/1), **8/1** Memory's Music, **10/1** Miss Laughter, **12/1** I'm Outa Here (IRE), **14/1** Solianna (10/1-16/1), East Sheen, **20/1** Treasure Keay, CSF £37.54 TOTE £3.50: £1.40 £2.40 £1.90 (£27.80) Trio £67.20 OWNER Mrs Tim Hinde (NEWMARKET) BRED Mrs S. Hinde 9 Rn 1m 27.03 (1.33) SF: 27/32/27/16/16/16/5/4/-

2033 CARNARVON CHALLENGE CUP AMATEUR H'CAP (0-70) (3-Y.O) (Class F) £2,840.00 (£790.00: £380.00)

1m Stalls: High GOING minus 0.64 sec per fur (F) 3-00 (3-02)

1745[3] **Kevasingo (55)***(66) (SDow)* 3-11-4 MrTCuff(7) (mde all: clr over 2f out: unchal) ....— 1
1811* Never so Rite (IRE) **(59)***(60)*(Fav)*(DWPArbuthnot)* 3-11-8 5x MrsDArbuthnot(5) (plld hrd: a.p: chsd wnr over 2f out: no imp) 5 2
1512[8] Sporting Risk **(54)***(53) (PWHarris)* 3-11-3 MissAElsey(1) (hdwy over 1f out: one pce fnl f) 1¼ 3
384[7] Witney-de-Bergerac (IRE) **(60)***(57) (JSMoore)* 3-11-4 (5) MrsSMoore(2) (a.p: one pce fnl 2f) ...¾ 4
1447[3] South Sound (IRE) **(56)***(51) (RHannon)* 3-11-5 MrsDMcHale(9) (lw: hld up & plld hrd: hdwy over 1f out: one pce fnl f) 1¼ 5
1792[6] Alerting **(65)***(52) (IABalding)* 3-12-0 MrsMCowdrey(4) (lw: stdd s: hdwy over 3f out: wknd 2f out) 4 6
1731[3] Jovie King (IRE) **(63)***(47) (PMitchell)* 3-11-12 MrTMcCarthy(6) (lw: nvr trbld ldrs) 1¼ 7
1569[10] Prince Pellinore **(49)***(26) (JohnBerry)* 3-10-12 MrVLukaniuk(8) (plld hrd: w wnr tl wknd over 2f out) 3½ 8
1771[10] Chase the Melody **(33)***(7) (MJHeaton-Ellis)* 3-9-10 MissAHarwood(3) (prom: rdn & wknd 3f out) 1¾ 9

5/2 Never so Rite (IRE), **9/2** KEVASINGO, Alerting (3/1-5/1), South Sound (IRE), **10/1** Jovie King (IRE), **12/1** Sporting Risk, **20/1** Witney-de-Bergerac (IRE), **33/1** Prince Pellinore, **50/1** Chase the Melody, CSF £14.40 CT £100.78 TOTE £5.20: £1.50 £1.60 £4.10 (£4.20) Trio £74.60 OWNER Mr G. Steinberg (EPSOM) BRED Miss Caroline Dickson 9 Rn 1m 43.29 (3.99) SF: 38/32/25/29/23/24/19

2034 CHAMPAGNE CONDITIONS STKS (2-Y.O) (Class B) £8,186.50 (£2,856.50: £1,390.75: £591.25)

6f 212y Stalls: High GOING minus 0.64 sec per fur (F) 3-30 (3-31)

1727* **More Royal (USA)** *(86) (IABalding)* 2-9-0 LDettori(4) (lw: hld up: chsd ldr over 2f out: rdn over 1f out: r.o to ld wl ins fnl f) ....— 1
1752[2] Detachment (USA) *(81)*(Fav)*(PWChapple-Hyam)* 2-8-10 JReid(3) (lw: led tl wl ins fnl f) ....nk 2
1197[3] Ice Pick (IRE) *(58) (RHannon)* 2-8-10 PatEddery(2) (lw: chsd ldr over 4f: wknd wl over 1f out) 10 3
Gallante *(47) (PFICole)* 2-8-10 TQuinn(1) (unf: scope: s.s: wl bhd most of wy) 5 4

8/11 Detachment (USA), **15/8** MORE ROYAL (USA), **9/1** Ice Pick (IRE) (op 6/1), Gallante (op 6/1), CSF £3.65 TOTE £3.00: (£1.70) OWNER Mr George Strawbridge (KINGSCLERE) BRED Gatesby W. Clay 4 Rn 1m 25.97 (0.27) SF: 43/38/15/4

2035 SOUTHAMPTON CLAIMING STKS (2-Y.O) (Class F) £2,882.00 (£802.00: £386.00)

6f 212y Stalls: High GOING minus 0.64 sec per fur (F) 4-00 (4-02)

1169[9] **White Whispers** *(74+)*(Fav)*(BWHills)* 2-8-1 DHarrison(9) (led 5f out: clr over 2f out: eased 1f out: v.easily) ....— 1
1699* Arch Angel (IRE) **(59)***(55) (DJSffrenchDavis)* 2-8-5 NAdams(1) (a.p: chsd wnr fnl 2f: no imp) 10 2
Peterrex *(53) (MRChannon)* 2-8-12 LDettori(10) (cmpt: bit bkwd: a.p: one pce fnl 2f) 4 3
1640[7] Plausilium *(43) (WGMTurner)* 2-8-5 (5) PMcCabe(2) (hrd rdn & lost pl 3f out: n.d after) 3½ 4
1798[8] Compensate (IRE) *(28) (MJHaynes)* 2-7-9 NCarlisle(5) (nvr nr ldrs) ....hd 5
1734[3] Our Tom's Boy **(51)***(33) (KTIvory)* 2-8-4b GBardwell(8) (b: swtg: plld hrd: prom 3f) 1¾ 6
Welsh Owl *(32) (KRBurke)* 2-8-5 MFenton(6) (small: neat: plld hrd: a bhd) ....¾ 7

*1632*4 Rowhome *(25) (MRChannon)* 2-8-6 CRutter(4) (lw: prom tl rdn & wknd 3f out)....................3½ 8
1226 7 Freeloader *(9) (JWHills)* 2-8-6 RHills(3) (led 2f: rdn over 3f out: sn wknd)................................7 9
Ebony T-A-P-S *(5) (JSMoore)* 2-8-0 (3) SDrowne(7) (small: neat: bhd fnl 3f)..........................nk 10

11/10 WHITE WHISPERS, **9/2** Arch Angel (IRE) (op 3/1), **7/1** Peterrex (3/1-8/1), **10/1** Our Tom's Boy, **14/1** Freeloader, **16/1** Rowhome, **20/1** Welsh Owl, Compensate (IRE), **25/1** Plausilium, **33/1** Ebony T-A-P-S, CSF £6.35 TOTE £1.80: £1.20 £1.30 £1.90 (£2.90) Trio £6.10 OWNER Mr Ray Richards (LAMBOURN) BRED Berkshire Equestrian Services Ltd 10 Rn
1m 27.92 (2.22) SF: 10/-/-/-/-/-/-/-/-/-
White Whispers clmd B. Meehan £6,000

2036 HAMPSHIRE CONDITIONS STKS (3-Y.O+) (Class C) £5,037.25 (£1,831.00: £890.50: £377.50: £163.75)
1m 6f GOING minus 0.64 sec per fur (F) 4-30 (4-30)

1563 3 **Misbelief (102)***(104) (JRFanshawe)* 5-9-5 DHarrison(5) (plld hrd: led after 3f: hrd rdn 2f out: all out)...— 1
1563 2 Double Dagger **(97)***(110)*(Fav)*(HRACecil)* 4-9-11 WRyan(3) (lw: hld up: chsd wnr 5f out: hrd rdn over 3f out: ev ch whn edgd rt ins fnl f: r.o)..........................hd 2
1840 21 Bardolph (USA) **(70)***(85) (PFICole)* 8-9-9 TQuinn(2) (lw: prom tl wknd over 3f out)................20 3
King Ubad (USA) *(48) (KOCunningham-Brown)* 6-9-6 GCarter(4) (plld hrd: led 3f: drppd rr 8f out: t.o fnl 6f)...30 4
1905 8 Mont d'Or (USA) *(28) (JO'Donoghue)* 5-9-3 RCochrane(1) (a bhd: t.o fnl 6f)........................15 5

8/13 Double Dagger, **7/4** MISBELIEF, **9/1** Bardolph (USA) (6/1-10/1), **100/1** King Ubad (USA), Mont d'Or (USA), CSF £3.06 TOTE £2.80: £1.20 £1.30 (£1.30) OWNER T & J Vestey (NEWMARKET) BRED The Overbury Stud 5 Rn 3m 0.63 (2.43) SF: 40/46/21/-/-

OFFICIAL EXPLANATION Misbelief: the stewards enquired into the mare's improvement and noted that on her previous run she had finished distressed and, on this occasion, had worn a tongue-strap.

2037 SOMERSET MAIDEN H'CAP (0-65) (3-Y.O+) (Class F) £3,407.00 (£952.00: £461.00) **1m 1f 209y** Stalls: High GOING minus 0.64 sec per fur (F) 5-00 (5-00)

1539 4 **Pip's Dream (35)***(46) (MJRyan)* 4-8-4 AClark(17) (prom: outpcd 5f out: rdn over 3f out: chsd ldr over 2f out: r.o to ld cl home)...— 1
1452 6 Song of Years (IRE) **(55)***(65) (JWHills)* 4-9-10 RHills(18) (swtg: led: clr over 3f out: hdd cl home)...¾ 2
1498 6 Euro Singer **(55)***(60)*(Fav)*(RAkehurst)* 3-8-12 TQuinn(10) (bhd: rdn 5f out: hdwy over 3f out: nt rch ldrs)...3 3
1831 5 Jewel Trader **(54)***(57) (CJBenstead)* 3-8-11 RCochrane(16) (lw: hdwy 3f out: one pce fnl 2f) ..1 4
1970 13 Malingerer **(37)***(36) (DAWilson)* 4-8-3 (3) DRMcCabe(11) (hdwy over 4f out: one pce fnl 2f)......3 5
1126 16 Cracking Prospect **(47)***(44) (BRMillman)* 4-9-2 JWilliams(13) (nvr nrr)..................................1¼ 6
1532 5 Tragic Hero **(65)***(60) (IABalding)* 3-9-8 LDettori(6) (rdn over 6f out: hdwy 3f out: wknd over 1f out)...1¼ 7
1825 8 Rubylee **(64)***(58) (KMcAuliffe)* 3-9-4 (3) JTate(9) (prom over 6f)..nk 8
Missed the Boat (IRE) **(41)***(29) (AGNewcombe)* 5-8-5 (5) DGriffiths(3) (b.hind: hld up & bhd: n.d)...4 9
1775 7 Indian Temple **(35)***(22) (MSSaunders)* 4-8-4 RPrice(15) (bhd fnl 5f)..½ 10
1447 8 Norfolk Glory **(41)***(15) (DJGMurraySmith)* 3-7-12 CRutter(2) (a bhd)..8 11
1654 5 Code of Silence **(47)***(15) (GFHCharles-Jones)* 3-7-13 (5) PMcCabe(14) (lw: chsd ldr over 6f: sn wknd)...4 12
1512 7 Oakbury (IRE) **(64)***(31) (RHannon)* 3-9-0 (7) DaneO'Neill(1) (bhd fnl 5f)..................................hd 13
1978 8 Rock Oyster **(50)***(17) (BJMeehan)* 3-8-7b DHarrison(4) (prom: rdn over 4f out: chsd ldr over 3f out tl over 2f out: sn wknd)...hd 14
1347 8 Dolly Dolittle **(25)** *(HJCollingridge)* 4-7-8 NAdams(8) (a bhd)..2½ 15
1512 6 Run-Do-Run **(60)***(17) (HJCollingridge)* 3-9-3 MRimmer(7) (b.off hind: s.i.s: a bhd)..................4 16
1735 8 Rozalina Lady **(52)***(6) (NAGraham)* 3-8-9 GCarter(12) (prom 4f)..1¾ 17
1447 10 Little Shefford **(45)** *(DJSffrenchDavis)* 3-8-2 NCarlisle(5) (a bhd)..7 18

9/4 Euro Singer, **7/1** Tragic Hero, **8/1** PIP'S DREAM, **9/1** Oakbury (IRE), **10/1** Song of Years (IRE) (op 6/1), **12/1** Malingerer, Rock Oyster (op 6/1), **14/1** Run-Do-Run, **16/1** Rubylee, Indian Temple, **20/1** Norfolk Glory, Code of Silence, Jewel Trader, Missed the Boat (IRE), **25/1** Cracking Prospect, Rozalina Lady, **33/1** Dolly Dolittle, Little Shefford, CSF £87.67 CT £226.59 TOTE £7.80: £1.30 £2.40 £1.70 £4.50 (£54.20) Trio £49.00 OWNER Mr P. E. Axon (NEWMARKET) BRED Stud-On-The-Chart 18 Rn 2m 6.34 (1.64) SF: 25/44/27/24/15/23/27/25/8/1/-/-/-/-/-/-/-/-
WEIGHT FOR AGE 3yo-12lb
T/Plpt: £33.20 (378.03 Tckts). T/Qdpt: £9.80 (13 Tckts). KH

1228a-LES LANDES (Jersey) (L-H)
Friday June 16th (Good to firm)

2038a
HAMBROS BANK SPRINT H'CAP (3-Y.O+) £720.00
5f 110y 7-30 (7-34)

	Newbury Coat *(CPBillot,Jersey)* 5-10-4 MissSABillot	—	1
800a3	Screech *(ZJones,Guernsey)* 5-9-5 BPowell	3	2
	Arkady (IRE) *(CMcCready,Jersey)* 4-9-7 RMcGhin	2	3
1228a4	Muscat (IRE) *(PDJones)* 8-8-9 SNicoll (btn approx 11l)		6

Tote £4.60: £3.00 £5.20 (£8.40) OWNER Lavender Racing Club (JERSEY) 6 Rn 1m 8.1

1709a-EVRY (France) (R-H)
Wednesday June 21st (Good)

2039a
PRIX HAMPTON (Listed) (3-Y.O+) £16,766.00 (£5,748.00: £3,593.00) **5f** 2-35 (2-46)

	Linoise (FR) *(111) (ELeGuen,France)* 3-8-7 OPeslier	—	1
1475*	Ya Malak *(114) (JWPayne)* 4-9-5 GMosse	½	2
1572a4	Palacegate Episode (IRE) *(99) (JBerry)* 5-8-13 GHind	3	3

P-M 7.20F: 1.30F 1.10F 1.10F (9.50F) OWNER M. Ohana BRED Mme R.J.Wattinne 8 Rn
57.62 secs (-0.88) SF: -/-/-

1573a-LONGCHAMP (Paris, France) (R-H)
Thursday June 22nd (Good)

2040a
PRIX DE LA PORTE MAILLOT (Gp 3) (3-Y.O+) £26,347.00 (£9,581.00: £4,790.00) **7f** 3-05 (3-07)

1389a*	**Cherokee Rose (IRE)** *(123) (JEHammond,France)* 4-9-2 CAsmussen	—	1
1573a2	Bashaayeash (IRE) *(117) (CLaffon-Parias,France)* 3-8-7 FHead	2½	2
1389a3	Poplar Bluff (IRE) *(110) (AFabre,France)* 3-8-7 OPeslier	3	3

P-M 2.60F: 1.30F 1.70F (SF 8.90F) OWNER Sheikh Mohammed BRED Sheikh Mohammed 5 Rn
1m 22.3 SF: -/-/-

2039a-EVRY (France) (R-H)
Saturday June 24th (Good to firm)

2041a
LA COUPE (Gp 3) (4-Y.O+) £26,347.00 (£9,581.00: £4,790.00)
1m 2f 3-10 (3-17)

1394a3	**Marildo (FR)** *(123) (DSmaga,France)* 8-9-1 GGuignard	—	1
1262*	Baron Ferdinand *(117) (RCharlton)* 5-8-11 TJarnet	1	2
	Solidoun (FR) *(117) (ELellouche,France)* 4-8-11 OPeslier	s.nk	3

P-M 4.70F: 2.00F 2.70F (SF 21.60F) OWNER Mr D. Smaga BRED Warnerton Farm 6 Rn
2m 1.3 (-1.70) SF: -/-/-

HAMBURG (Germany) (R-H)
Saturday June 24th (Good to firm)

2042a
DEUTSCHER HEROLD-PREIS (Gp 3) (3-Y.O F & M) £35,391.00 (£14,185.00: £7,407.00) **1m 3f** 4-15 (4-18)

	Alpha City (GER) *(104) (HJentzsch,Germany)* 3-8-2 PSchiergen	—	1
	Lost Love (GER) *(100) (Germany)* 3-8-0 ASuborics	1¾	2
	Secret Energy (USA) *(99) (Germany)* 3-8-1 ow1 AStarke	s.h	3

Tote 19DM: 13DM 22DM 16DM (SF 180DM) OWNER Gestut Haus Ittlingen BRED Gestut Hof Ittlingen 8 Rn 2m 24.7 SF: -/-/-

1889a-SAN SIRO (Milan, Italy) (R-H)
Saturday June 24th (Good to firm)

2043a PREMIO PRIMI PASSI (Gp 3) (2-Y.O) £25,484.00 (£11,785.00: £6,596.00) **6f** 3-45 (4-04)

Tarte Aux Pommes (FR) *(JBertranDeBalanda,France)* 2-8-8 TGillet .... — 1
Last Hero (FR) *(BGrizzetti,Italy)* 2-8-11 ACarboni 5¼ 2
1391a* Try My Segnor *(OPessi,Italy)* 2-8-11 JacquelineFreda .... nk 3

Tote 23L: 13L 17L 17L (73L) OWNER F. Hoffet BRED J-P.Francois & S.Videaud 8 Rn 1m 11.1

2040a-LONGCHAMP (Paris, France) (R-H)
Sunday June 25th (Good to firm)

2044a GRAND PRIX DE PARIS (Gp 1) (3-Y.O C & F) £143,713.00 (£57,485.00: £28,742.00: £14,371.00) **1m 2f** 2-15 (2-15)

1575a6 **Valanour(IRE)** *(120) (AdeRoyerDupre,France)* 3-9-2 GMosse (prom: 2nd st: sn led: clr 1f out : r.o wl u.p) .... — 1
9794 Singspiel (IRE) *(120) (MRStoute)* 3-9-2 MJKinane (rr early: 7th st: prog 1½f out: r.o wl) .... nk 2
1574a6 Diamond Mix (IRE) *(119) (AFabre,France)* 3-9-2 TJarnet (3rd st: rdn and chal over 2f out: no ex ins fnl f) .... ½ 3
1575a* Torrential (USA) *(116) (JHMGosden)* 3-9-2 LDettori (5th st: rdn over 2f out: r.o one pce) 1½ 4
1574a2 Poliglote *(114) (MmeCHead,France)* 3-9-2 FHead (led tl hdd by wnr: wknd fnl f) 1½ 5
1573a* Gold and Steel (FR) *(114) (J-CRouget,France)* 3-9-2 J-RDubosc (hld up: rdn 2f out: some late prog) .... s.h 6
Dancing Beggar *(114) (AFabre,France)* 3-9-2 OPeslier (prom early: 4th st: hrd rdn 2f out: fdd) .... nse 7
9207 Painter's Row (IRE) *(112) (PWChapple-Hyam)* 3-9-2 JReid (6th st: no imp fnl 2f) 1 8
1575a5 Leeds (IRE) *(111) (HVandePoele,France)* 3-9-2 ESaint-Martin (m.n.s) .... ½ 9
1575a4 Bobinski *(AFabre,France)* 3-9-2 SGuillot (dwlt: rr when hit rail after 2f: jockey returned inj.) 10

P-M 7.30F: 3.10F 6.30F 2.10F (90.70F) OWNER Aga Khan BRED H.H.Aga Khan Farms S.C. 10 Rn
2m 2.2 SF: -/-/-/-/-/-/-/-/-/-

2045a PRIX DE MALLERET (Gp 2) (3-Y.O F) £35,928.00 (£14,371.00: £7,186.00: £3,593.00) **1m 4f** 3-10 (3-18)

1704a3 **Privity (USA)** *(100) (PBary,France)* 3-8-9 DBoeuf (3rd st: hmpd 2f out: rdn to ld 1f out: drw clr) .... — 1
Ultra Finesse *(97) (MmeCHead,France)* 3-8-9 WRSwinburn (2nd tl led 2f out: hdd 1f out: r.o gamely) 2 2
1704a* Genovefa (USA) *(97) (AFabre,France)* 3-8-9 TJarnet (4th st: rdn over 2f out: r.o fnl f: nrst fin) .... nse 3
Powder Bowl (USA) *(97) (JEPease,France)* 3-8-9 CAsmussen (rr tl st: rdn 2f out: not qckn fnl f) .... nk 4
1704a2 Enquiry (FR) *(97) (MmePBarbe,France)* 3-8-9 TThulliez (5th st: rdn and outpcd 2f out) .... nk 5
Vielle Rose (IRE) *(93) (AdeRoyerDupre,France)* 3-8-9 GMosse (led tl hdd 2f out: wknd) 3 6

P-M 6.70F: 3.10F 3.50F (SF 39.30F) OWNER Mr K. Abdullah BRED Juddmonte Farms 6 Rn
2m 33.2 SF: -/-/-/-/-/-

2042a-HAMBURG (Germany) (R-H)
Sunday June 25th (Good to firm)

2046a IDEE HANSA-PREIS (Gp 2) (4-Y.O+) £57,613.00 (£22,634.00: £12,346.00: £6,173.00) **1m 3f** 3-40 (3-40)

1398a6 **Monsun (GER)** *(122) (HJentzsch,Germany)* 5-9-8 PSchiergen (3rd tl chal over 1f out: squeezed out 1f out: r.o: fin 2nd btn 3/4l awrdd race) .... — 1
Germany (USA) *(119) (BSchutz,Germany)* 4-9-4 THellier (5th st: chal and hung right 1f out: sn led: r.o wl: fin 1st: disq and plcd 2nd.) 2
1392a* Laroche (GER) *(121) (HJentzsch,Germany)* 4-9-8 ATylicki (led tl hdd 1f out: r.o one pce) .... ½ 3
1398a5 Kornado *(116) (ALowe,Germany)* 4-9-6 MRimmer (8th st: r.o fnl 2f: nvr nrr) 2½ 4
Protektor (GER) *(112) (Germany)* 6-9-2 GBocskai (6th st: one pce fnl 2f) .... nk 5

1398a7 Bad Bertrich (IRE) *(115) (Germany)* 4-9-6 AStarke (rr tl st: nvr plcd to chal) ....½ 6
Silent Lake (GER) *(111) (Germany)* 4-9-2 TMundry ....½ 7
Concepcion (GER) *(109) (Germany)* 5-9-2 ABoschert 2 8
1398a4 Aratikos (GER) *(109) (Germany)* 4-9-2 OSchick ....nk 9
Favourite Prince (IRE) *(Germany)* 4-9-2 KWoodburn 10

Tote 18DM: 12DM 22DM 15DM (SF 208DM) OWNER Baron G Von Ullmann BRED Gestut Isarland in Germany 10 Rn
2m 16.2 SF: -/-/-/-/-/-/-/-/-/-

1534-FOLKESTONE (R-H)
Friday June 30th (Firm)
WEATHER: very hot WIND: almost nil

2047 FOLKESTONE-BOULOGNE CROSS CHANNEL (S) STKS (2-Y.O) (Class G) £2,243.00 (£618.00: £293.00)
5f Stalls: Centre GOING minus 0.50 sec per fur (F) 2-10 (2-12)

*1031*4 **Tymeera** *(69) (BPalling)* 2-8-3 (3) SSanders(3) (b: led over 3f out: hrd rdn ins fnl f: r.o wl)....— 1
1590³ Sporting Fantasy *(61)*(Fav)*(MRChannon)* 2-8-6 (5) PPMurphy(1) (led over 1f: hrd rdn over 1f out: unable qckn) 4 2
1288⁷ Fortuitious (IRE) *(52) (JRJenkins)* 2-8-6 WNewnes(4) (lw: hld up: hrd rdn over 1f out: one pce) 1¼ 3
1810⁵ No Sympathy *(44) (GLMoore)* 2-8-6v SWhitworth(2) (lw: s.s: hrd rdn & hdwy over 1f out: wknd fnl f) 2½ 4
1829⁶ Jemsilverthorn (IRE) *(47) (JJBridger)* 2-8-4 (7) ADaly(5) (a.p: hrd rdn over 2f out: wknd 1f out) ....¾ 5
1790⁴ Trible Pet *(42) (BGubby)* 2-8-6 JReid(6) (hld up: rdn over 2f out: wknd over 1f out) ....hd 6
1938¹⁴ Pinocchio Boy (IRE) *(24) (BJMeehan)* 2-8-11 BDoyle(7) (prom over 3f) 7 7

5/4 Sporting Fantasy, **6/4** Trible Pet, **10/1** TYMEERA (6/1-12/1), Pinocchio Boy (IRE) (op 3/1), **11/1** No Sympathy (6/1-12/1), **20/1** Fortuitious (IRE), **33/1** Jemsilverthorn (IRE), CSF £23.13 TOTE £9.60: £3.40 £1.30 (£12.00) OWNER Glenbrook Associates (COWBRIDGE) BRED R. T. Lingwood 7 Rn
61.0 secs (2.40) SF: 9/1/-/-/-/-/-
No bid

2048 STONE STREET H'CAP (0-70) (3-Y.O+) (Class E) £3,073.40 (£915.20: £435.60: £195.80)
5f Stalls: Centre GOING minus 0.50 sec per fur (F) 2-40 (2-41)

1864⁶ **Bashful Brave (61)***(71)*(Fav)*(JWPayne)* 4-9-8 MRimmer(1) (lw: chsd ldr: rdn over 1f out: led ins fnl f: r.o wl) ....— 1
1595³ Miami Banker **(40)***(44) (WRMuir)* 9-7-12b(3) SSanders(4) (swtg: led tl ins fnl f: unable qckn) 2 2
1900² Halbert **(47)***(43) (MRChannon)* 6-8-3v(5) PPMurphy(5) (swtg: hld up: rdn over 1f out: one pce) 2½ 3
1783² The Mestral **(43)***(36) (MJRyan)* 3-7-6b(5) MBaird(6) (outpcd: hdwy over 1f out: nvr nrr) ....¾ 4
1660³ Charnwood Queen **(46)***(25) (RWArmstrong)* 3-8-0 ow1 RPrice(7) (lw: hld up: rdn over 2f out: sn wknd) 4 5
1199¹⁰ Absolutely Fabulus **(46)***(15) (JLSpearing)* 3-8-0 BDoyle(3) (s.s: s bhd) 3½ 6

2/1 BASHFUL BRAVE (6/4-9/4), **9/4** Halbert, **11/2** Charnwood Queen, **6/1** The Mestral, **7/1** Miami Banker (5/1-8/1), **12/1** Absolutely Fabulus (4/1-14/1), CSF £14.56 TOTE £2.90: £2.20 £3.00 (£10.40) OWNER Mrs G. M. Hay (NEWMARKET) BRED Mrs G. M. Hay 6 Rn
59.2 secs (0.60) SF: 53/26/25/11/-/-
WEIGHT FOR AGE 3yo-7lb

2049 HYTHE FESTIVAL WEEK MEDIAN AUCTION MAIDEN STKS (3-Y.O) (Class F) £2,771.00 (£766.00: £365.00)
6f Stalls: Centre GOING minus 0.50 sec per fur (F) 3-10 (3-12)

739⁷ **Sharp 'n Smart (58)***(64)*(Fav)*(BSmart)* 3-8-11 (3) SSanders(6) (w ldr: led over 2f out: hrd rdn over 1f out: r.o wl) ....— 1
1683⁶ Bold Revival *(51) (MrsPSly)* 3-8-9 ACulhane(4) (hld up: hrd rdn over 1f out: r.o one pce) 3 2
Galacia (IRE) *(46) (WGMTurner)* 3-8-4 (5) PMcCabe(1) (lw: a.p: ev ch over 1f out: one pce) 1¾ 3
1786⁷ Marwell Indigo *(43) (JARToller)* 3-9-0 WNewnes(5) (hld up: rdn over 1f out: one pce) 3 4
1476⁶ With Intent *(37) (CJames)* 3-9-0 JWilliams(3) (lw: no hdwy fnl 2f) 2½ 5
1963⁸ Can't Say (IRE) **(33)***(33) (JMBradley)* 3-8-11v(3) SDrowne(2) (led over 3f: wknd over 1f out) .1½ 6
1583⁷ Simply Simon **(40)***(11) (KRBurke)* 3-9-0 MRimmer(7) (bhd fnl 3f) 8 7
1473¹² Cahita *(4) (TJNaughton)* 3-8-9 BDoyle(8) (b: a bhd) ....¾ 8

7/4 SHARP 'N SMART, **4/1** With Intent, **9/2** Galacia (IRE), Marwell Indigo (op 7/4), **20/1** Bold Revival, Cahita, **25/1** Simply Simon, **33/1** Can't Say (IRE), CSF £27.99 TOTE £2.80: £1.20 £4.10 £1.40 (£13.40) OWNER Mr K. H. Burks (LAMBOURN) BRED Aston Park Stud 8 Rn
1m 13.3 (1.60) SF: 35/22/17/14/8/4/-/-

2050 ROMNEY MARSH H'CAP (0-65) (3-Y.O+) (Class F) £2,997.80 (£830.80: £397.40) **1m 4f** Stalls: Low GOING minus 0.50 sec per fur (F) 3-40 (3-40)

1477[2] **Mr Browning (USA) (61)***(74+) (RAkehurst)* 4-9-11b(3) SSanders(3) (led 7f out: clr over 2f out: r.o wl) ....— **1**
1788[3] Bag of Tricks (IRE) **(54)***(58) (SDow)* 5-9-0 (7) ADaly(8) (a.p: chsd wnr fnl 5f: no imp) 7 **2**
1771[4] Stately Home (IRE) **(49)***(52) (BRMillman)* 4-9-2 JWilliams(9) (hdwy over 2f out: 5th st: hrd rdn over 1f out: one pce) ....nk **3**
1694[4] One Off the Rail (USA) **(45)***(43) (AMoore)* 5-8-12 CandyMorris(5) (3rd st: wknd over 1f out) 4 **4**
1674[2] Paradise Waters **(59)***(52)*(Fav)*(RFJohnsonHoughton)* 3-8-11 JReid(4) (lw: lost pl over 9f out: rallied 5f out: 4th st: wknd over 1f out) 4 **5**
1407[6] Premazing **(41)***(23) (JPearce)* 3-7-2 (5) MBaird(7) (nvr nrr) 8 **6**
1048[8] Cozzi (FR) **(29)***(6) (JMBradley)* 7-7-5 (5)ow2 NVarley(6) (bhd fnl 3f) 2½ **7**
Pie Hatch (IRE) **(41)** *(RJO'Sullivan)* 6-8-8b DBiggs(1) (swtg: led 5f: wknd over 3f out: 6th st) 25 **8**
1688[2] Head For Heaven **(46)** *(RPCHoad)* 5-8-13 ACulhane(2) (bhd fnl 4f) 7 **9**

LONG HANDICAP Premazing 7-6

4/5 Paradise Waters, **4/1** MR BROWNING (USA) (op 9/4), **7/1** Bag of Tricks (IRE) (op 4/1), **8/1** One Off the Rail (USA) (5/1-9/1), **10/1** Head For Heaven, **16/1** Stately Home (IRE), **33/1** Cozzi (FR), Pie Hatch (IRE), Premazing, CSF £31.07 CT £366.01 TOTE £4.90: £1.60 £2.00 £2.30 (£15.60) Trio £32.00 OWNER Mrs M. E. O'Shea (EPSOM) BRED Lord Carnarvon 9 Rn
2m 33.8 (2.60) SF: 55/39/33/24/18/-/-/-/-
WEIGHT FOR AGE 3yo-15lb

2051 ARGLES & COURT H'CAP (0-80) (3-Y.O+) (Class D) £3,867.50 (£1,154.00: £551.00: £249.50) **6f 189y** Stalls: Low GOING minus 0.50 sec (F) 4-10 (4-10)

1676[7] **Marrowfat Lady (IRE) (53)***(68) (BRMillman)* 4-7-11 (5)ow1 AWhelan(5) (3rd st: led over 1f out: comf) ....— **1**
1754[8] Weather Break **(75)***(77) (HCandy)* 4-9-10 WNewnes(6) (lw: led over 5f: unable qckn) 6 **2**
1534[2] Mr Nevermind (IRE) **(66)***(65)*(Fav)*(GLMoore)* 5-9-1 SWhitworth(1) (4th st: hrd rdn over 1f out: one pce) 1½ **3**
1855[4] Polonez Prima **(63)***(60) (JLSpearing)* 8-8-12 JReid(4) (lw: 5th st: rdn over 1f out: one pce) ....½ **4**
1543[3] Shanghai Venture (USA) **(73)***(49) (SPCWoods)* 4-9-8v BDoyle(3) (2nd st: wknd over 1f out) 9 **5**
882[12] Double Rush (IRE) **(56)***(16) (TGMills)* 3-7-5b(5) NVarley(2) (lw: 6th st: wknd over 2f out) 7 **6**

13/8 Mr Nevermind (IRE), **7/2** Weather Break, **4/1** Polonez Prima (op 5/2), **5/1** Shanghai Venture (USA), **9/1** MARROWFAT LADY (IRE) (op 6/1), Double Rush (IRE) (6/1-10/1), CSF £38.01 TOTE £9.10: £3.30 £2.20 (£26.10) OWNER Mrs Nerys Dutfield (CULLOMPTON) BRED A. C. McDonnell 6 Rn
1m 22.3 (0.70) SF: 37/46/34/29/18/-
WEIGHT FOR AGE 3yo-9lb

2052 SHEPWAY AMATEUR H'CAP (0-60) (3-Y.O+) (Class G) £2,243.00 (£618.00: £293.00) **1m 1f 149y** Stalls: Low GOING minus 0.50 sec per fur (F) 4-40 (4-41)

1854[12] **Dots Dee (25)***(35)*(Fav)*(JMBradley)* 6-9-0 MrsLPearce(2) (lw: a.p: led 4f out: r.o wl) ....— **1**
1745[15] Montone (IRE) **(57)***(65) (KRBurke)* 5-11-4 MrMMannish(5) (hdwy 3f out: 5th st: chsd wnr over 1f out: nt qckn) 1½ **2**
975[7] Araboybill **(58)***(65) (MPMuggeridge)* 4-11-5 MrEWilliams(10) (hdwy over 1f out: r.o wl) ....nk **3**
1745[5] Don't Drop Bombs (USA) **(28)***(33) (DTThom)* 6-9-3 MissJFeilden(6) (lw: 3rd st: one pce fnl 2f) 1½ **4**
1596[13] Bowcliffe **(60)***(53) (JTGifford)* 4-11-7b MrRJohnson(4) (lw: 2nd st: wknd over 1f out) 7 **5**
1974[9] Shelter **(30)***(22) (JohnBerry)* 8-9-5 MrVLukaniuk(13) (led over 5f: 4th st: wknd over 1f out) ....½ **6**
1799[2] Persian Bud (IRE) **(42)***(30) (JRBosley)* 7-10-3v MrsSBosley(11) (6th st: wknd over 2f out) 2½ **7**
1372[9] Deceit the Second **(40)***(25) (GLewis)* 3-9-3b MissBCraven(9) (prom 6f) 1¾ **8**
1771[3] Sharp Gazelle **(42)***(17) (BSmart)* 5-10-3 MissVMarshall(1) (a bhd) 6 **9**
*497** Barahin (IRE) **(47)***(12) (JJBridger)* 6-10-3 (5) MissMBridger(7) (b: a bhd) 6 **10**
1797[7] Life's Too Short (IRE) **(46)***(9) (JEBanks)* 4-10-7b MrPPritchard-Gordon(3) (bhd fnl 5f) 1¼ **11**
1445[16] Il Furetto **(38)** *(JSKing)* 3-8-10 (5)ow1 MrLBaker(12) (swtg: prom 6f) 12 **12**
1534[14] Hedgehog **(28)** *(JO'Donoghue)* 5-8-12 (5)ow3 MrsTEustance(8) (swtg: s.s: a wl bhd) 6 **13**

LONG HANDICAP Dots Dee 8-13 Il Furetto 8-12

3/1 DOTS DEE, **9/2** Bowcliffe, **5/1** Life's Too Short (IRE), **13/2** Persian Bud (IRE) (4/1-7/1), **7/1** Don't Drop Bombs (USA) (5/1-8/1), **10/1** Barahin (IRE) (6/1-12/1), Montone (IRE) (5/1-12/1), **12/1** Sharp Gazelle (8/1-14/1), **20/1** Araboybill, Deceit the Second, **33/1** Shelter, Il Furetto, Hedgehog, CSF £33.49 CT £480.36 TOTE £4.70: £2.30 £3.50 £5.80 (£23.40) Trio £198.00 OWNER Mr J. M. Kearney (CHEPSTOW) BRED F. Baldwin 13 Rn 2m 3.6 (5.90) SF: 9/39/39/7/27/-/4/-/-/-/-/-/-

WEIGHT FOR AGE 3yo-12lb

T/Plpt: £986.80 (8.5 Tckts). T/Qdpt: £55.50 (1 Tckt). AK

1905-GOODWOOD (R-H)

Friday June 30th (Firm Rnd course, Good to firm St course)

WEATHER: fine WIND: nil

2053

DINAH SERIDAN APPRENTICE H'CAP (0-80) (4-Y.O+) (Class E)
£3,785.00 (£1,130.00: £540.00: £245.00)
7f Stalls: High GOING minus 0.57 sec per fur (F) 6-40 (6-42)

1648[8] **Pyramus (USA) (70)***(76) (MrsLPiggott)* 4-8-13 (5) GMilligan(2) (2nd tl led wl over 1f out: drvn out) — 1
1851[16] Chickawicka (IRE) **(79)***(84) (MCPipe)* 4-9-13v LNewton(4) (led tl wl over 1f out: hrd rdn & rallied fnl f) nk 2
1910[3] Blurred Image (IRE) **(72)***(76)*(Fav)*(MissGayKelleway)* 4-9-3 (3) DaneO'Neill(5) (6th st: hdwy 3f out: rdn over 1f out: r.o ins fnl f) ½ 3
1533[4] French Ginger **(70)***(56) (IABalding)* 4-9-1 (3) DGriffiths(3) (4th st: wknd 2f out) 8 4
Future Options **(67)***(44) (MSSaunders)* 4-9-1 SDrowne(6) (5th st: sme hdwy over 2f out: sn wknd) 4 5
1789[2] The Little Ferret **(65)***(30) (GLMoore)* 5-8-13 CChoi(1) (3rd st: wknd over 2f out) 5 6

5/2 Blurred Image (IRE), **11/4** Chickawicka (IRE), **7/2** French Ginger, **6/1** The Little Ferret (4/1-13/2), **13/2** PYRAMUS (USA), **20/1** Future Options, CSF £22.44 TOTE £5.10: £2.20 £2.10 (£10.60) OWNER Mr Henryk De Kwiatkowski (NEWMARKET) BRED Kennelot Stables Ltd 6 Rn

1m 26.7 (2.30) SF: 29/37/29/9/-/-

2054

ST JOHN AMBULANCE (S) H'CAP (0-60) (3-Y.O+) (Class E)
£3,200.00 (£950.00: £450.00: £200.00)
6f Stalls: High GOING minus 0.57 sec per fur (F) 7-10 (7-12)

1538[6] **Pride of Hayling (IRE) (42)***(52) (PRHedger)* 4-9-7 TQuinn(5) (a.p: led over 1f out: r.o wl) — 1
1445[8] Cedar Dancer **(42)***(48) (RJHodges)* 3-8-13 BDoyle(2) (chsd ldr: hrd rdn over 1f out: r.o ins fnl f) 1½ 2
1321[8] Purbeck Centenary **(40)***(44) (PHowling)* 5-9-5 JReid(4) (led: sn clr: hdd over 1f out: wknd ins fnl f) ¾ 3
1883[8] Nuthatch (IRE) **(37)***(34) (MDIUsher)* 3-8-8v RPrice(3) (wl bhd tl gd hdwy over 1f out: nt rch ldrs) 2½ 4
1750[7] Nomadic Dancer (IRE) **(48)***(41) (MSSaunders)* 3-9-5 JWilliams(10) (hrd rdn & no hdwy fnl 2f) 1½ 5
1942[2] Tachycardia **(51)***(43)*(Fav)*(RJO'Sullivan)* 3-9-5 (3) SSanders(9) (prom tl hrd rdn & wknd over 2f out) ½ 6
1692[12] Shanghai Lil **(36)***(27) (MJFetherston-Godley)* 3-8-7b PatEddery(1) (nvr nr to chal) ½ 7
1785[9] Splash of Salt (IRE) **(45)***(32) (TJNaughton)* 5-9-5b(5) JDSmith(7) (a bhd) 1½ 8
1545[8] Mutinique **(44)***(30) (BAPearce)* 4-9-2 (7) MHenry(8) (jinked & nearly uns rdr s: bhd most of wy) nk 9
1719[6] Chinese Viking **(52)***(25) (GLMoore)* 3-9-9v SWhitworth(6) (a wl bhd) 5 10

9/4 Tachycardia, **4/1** PRIDE OF HAYLING (IRE), **11/2** Shanghai Lil, **9/1** Nomadic Dancer (IRE), **10/1** Purbeck Centenary, **12/1** Cedar Dancer (8/1-14/1), Chinese Viking (op 8/1), **16/1** Mutinique, Nuthatch (IRE), **20/1** Splash of Salt (IRE), CSF £45.19 CT £406.77 TOTE £6.50: £1.90 £3.80 £2.90 (£26.70) Trio £70.50 OWNER Mr Bill Broomfield (CHICHESTER) BRED Ewar Stud Farm International 10 Rn 1m 11.88 (1.68) SF: 34/22/26/8/15/17/1/14/12/-

WEIGHT FOR AGE 3yo-8lb
No bid

2055

SOUTHERN DAILY ECHO H'CAP (0-90) (3-Y.O+) (Class C) £7,375.00
(£2,200.00: £1,050.00: £475.00)
1m 6f Stalls: High GOING minus 0.57 sec per fur (F) 7-40 (7-40)

1794* **Embracing (83)***(99+)*(Fav)*(MRStoute)* 3-8-11 WRSwinburn(1) (4th st: hdwy over 2f out: led over 1f out: easily) — 1

1612* Global Dancer **(70)***(85) (SDow)* 4-8-8 (7) ADaly(4) (led: sn clr: hdd over 1f out: no ch w wnr) ...¾ 2
1386⁴ General Mouktar **(73)***(65) (MCPipe)* 5-9-4v JReid(3) (wnt 2nd st: wknd over 2f out) 20 3
Chris's Lad **(64)***(33) (RJHodges)* 4-8-9 BDoyle(2) (chsd ldr tl 3rd st: wknd over 3f out) 20 4

5/4 EMBRACING, **2/1** Global Dancer, **11/4** General Mouktar, **12/1** Chris's Lad, CSF £4.04 TOTE £2.00 (£2.10) OWNER Maktoum Al Maktoum (NEWMARKET) BRED Gainsborough Stud Management Ltd 4 Rn 3m 0.69 (1.69) SF: 42/45/25/-
WEIGHT FOR AGE 3yo-17lb

2056 WEATHERBYS 'NEWCOMERS' SERIES H'CAP (0-80) (3-Y.O+) (Class D)
£4,378.00 (£1,309.00: £627.00: £286.00)
1m Stalls: High GOING minus 0.57 sec per fur (F) 8-10 (8-11)

1638⁴ **Second Chance (IRE) (80)***(88) (PMitchell)* 5-9-7 (7) MHenry(9) (4th st: rdn over 1f out: r.o to ld last strides) ....— 1
1638¹⁰ Comanche Companion **(67)***(75) (TJNaughton)* 5-8-10 (5) JDSmith(10) (led: edgd lft over 1f out: hdd fnl strides) ....s.h 2
1732⁷ Ever so Lyrical **(74)***(79) (PWHarris)* 5-9-8 WRSwinburn(5) (hdwy 2f out: swtchd 1f out: r.o ins fnl f) 1½ 3
*1789*⁶ Kingchip Boy **(75)***(80) (MJRyan)* 6-9-9v AClark(1) (hdwy 3f out: rdn over 1f out: r.o ins fnl f)..s.h 4
1693⁵ Another Fiddle (IRE) **(66)***(71)*(Fav)*(RAkehurst)* 5-9-0 TQuinn(6) (5th st: hdwy on ins & hrd rdn 2f out: nt qckn fnl f) ....hd 5
Mnemonic **(65)***(60) (HCandy)* 3-8-3 BDoyle(7) (nvr nr to chal) 5 6
1745⁹ Scottish Park **(47)***(32) (RWEmery)* 6-7-4 (5)ow2 NVarley(2) (6th st: wknd over 2f out) 4 7
1873¹³ Ballyhays (IRE) **(50)***(27) (JAHarris)* 6-7-12 ow2 CRutter(4) (3rd st: wknd 3f out) 4 8
1523¹⁶ Across the Bay **(49)***(12) (RWEmery)* 8-7-4b(7)ow4 SLanigan(3) (bhd & rn wd st: no ch after) 6 9
1750⁶ Amber Nectar **(47)***(2) (BAPearce)* 9-7-9 ow2 CAvery(8) (2nd st: wknd 3f out) 5 10
LONG HANDICAP Scottish Park 7-1 Across the Bay 7-6 Amber Nectar 6-5

11/4 Another Fiddle (IRE), **7/2** Comanche Companion, **5/1** Ever so Lyrical, **6/1** Kingchip Boy, **7/1** SECOND CHANCE (IRE), Mnemonic, **16/1** Scottish Park, Ballyhays (IRE), **50/1** Across the Bay, Amber Nectar, CSF £30.65 CT £122.92 TOTE £10.00: £2.70 £1.80 £2.20 (£22.60) Trio £50.30 OWNER Down and Outs Racing BRED Michael G. O'Brien 10 Rn
1m 38.49 (0.89) SF: 56/43/47/48/39/18/-/-/-/-
WEIGHT FOR AGE 3yo-10lb

2057 WEALD AND DOWNLAND MUSEUM CLAIMING STKS (3-Y.O+) (Class E)
£3,720.00 (£1,110.00: £530.00: £240.00)
1m 1f Stalls: High GOING minus 0.57 sec per fur (F) 8-40 (8-40)

1626⁸ **Blockade (USA) (70)***(87) (MBell)* 6-8-13 TQuinn(1) (mde virtually all: all out) ....— 1
1914* Emily-Mou (IRE) **(78)***(86) (BJMeehan)* 3-8-1 CRutter(2) (a 2nd: ev ch fnl 2f: r.o) ....hd 2
1728¹¹ Reprehend **(95)***(88)*(Fav)*(RHannon)* 4-9-7 PatEddery(4) (4th st: hrd rdn over 3f out: hdwy 2f out: wknd fnl f) 4 3
1969* Arndilly **(70)***(73) (BJMeehan)* 4-8-12b BDoyle(3) (3rd st: ev ch over 2f out: hrd rdn & wknd over 1f out) 3½ 4

6/4 Reprehend, **9/4** Arndilly, **4/1** BLOCKADE (USA), **11/2** Emily-Mou (IRE), CSF £18.61 TOTE £5.20 (£10.00) OWNER Mr A. M. Warrender (NEWMARKET) BRED Patricia C. Warrender 4 Rn
1m 54.81 (4.11) SF: 16/4/17/2
WEIGHT FOR AGE 3yo-11lb
Arndilly clmd G.Harwood £12,000

2058 E.B.F. MIDSUMMER MAIDEN STKS (2-Y.O) (Class D) £4,269.00 (£1,272.00: £606.00: £273.00) **6f** Stalls: High GOING minus 0.57 sec per fur (F) 9-10 (9-11)

Kriscliffe *(83) (PTWalwyn)* 2-9-0 JReid(4) (w'like: scope: swvd rt s: hdwy 2f out: led ins fnl f: rdn out) ....— 1
1592³ Al Shafa *(83) (JLDunlop)* 2-9-0 TQuinn(3) (w ldr: bmpd & led over 1f out: hdd ins fnl f: r.o)...hd 2
1838¹² Oberons Boy (IRE) *(82)*(Fav)*(BJMeehan)* 2-9-0 PatEddery(2) (led: edgd rt & hdd over 1f out: hrd rdn & r.o fnl f) ....nk 3
Shock-A-Lot (IRE) *(66) (GLewis)* 2-9-0 SWhitworth(1) (w'like: bit bkwd: spd tl wknd over 1f out) 6 4

6/5 Oberons Boy (IRE) (op 4/5), **13/8** Al Shafa, **9/2** KRISCLIFFE, **12/1** Shock-A-Lot (IRE), CSF £11.26 TOTE £5.10 (£4.20) OWNER Hesmonds Stud (LAMBOURN) BRED Hesmonds Stud Ltd 4 Rn 1m 13.28 (3.08) SF: 8/8/7/-

T/Plpt: £3,038.20 (4.26 Tckts). T/Qdpt: £121.50 (1 Tckt). Hn

1266-NEWCASTLE (L-H)
Friday June 30th (Firm)
WEATHER: overcast WIND: slt half against

2059 TYNE TEES TELEVISION CONDITIONS STKS (2-Y.O) (Class C)
£4,710.00 (£1,710.00: £830.00: £350.00: £150.00)
7f Stalls: Centre GOING minus 0.07 sec per fur (G) 6-15 (6-15)

1727[2] **Mushahid (USA)** *(92+)*(Fav)*(JLDunlop)* 2-9-1 WCarson(5) (lw: swtchd rt s: sn trckng ldr: shkn up to ld over 1f out: styd on wl) ....— 1
1871[5] Cabcharge Striker *(86) (MRChannon)* 2-9-3 RHughes(4) (hld up: hdwy over 2f out: kpt on u.p fnl f: no ch w wnr) 3½ 2
863* Dankeston (USA) *(75) (MBell)* 2-8-11 MFenton(2) (lw: led: rdn 2f out: hung lft: sn hdd: wknd fnl f) 2 3
1665* Traceability *(66) (JBerry)* 2-8-11 JCarroll(1) (trckd ldrs: rdn & outpcd ½-wy: no imp) 4 4
1769[3] Royal Ceilidh (IRE) **(78)***(58) (DenysSmith)* 2-8-10 KFallon(3) (hld up & plld hrd early: effrt over 2f out: sn wknd) 3 5

8/11 MUSHAHID (USA), **7/4** Dankeston (USA), **8/1** Cabcharge Striker, **16/1** Traceability, **25/1** Royal Ceilidh (IRE), CSF £6.73 TOTE £1.70: £1.40 £2.50 (£3.90) OWNER Mr Hamdan Al Maktoum (ARUNDEL) BRED Courtney and Congleton 5 Rn 1m 28.03 (3.73) SF: 49/43/32/23/15

2060 NORTHERN ROCK GOSFORTH PARK CUP H'CAP (0-105) (3-Y.O+) (Class B) £15,530.00 (£4,640.00: £2,220.00: £1,010.00)
5f Stalls: Centre GOING minus 0.07 sec per fur (G) 6-50 (6-52)

1765[4] **Name the Tune (75)***(87) (PHowling)* 4-8-12 PaulEddery(6) (b.hind: trckd ldrs far side: shkn up to ld jst ins fnl f: drvn out) ....— 1
1241[3] Sweet Magic **(78)***(84)*(Fav)*(LJHolt)* 4-9-1 AMcGlone(7) (trckd ldrs far side: led over 1f out: hung rt & hdd ins fnl f) 1¾ 2
1689* Shadow Jury **(64)***(66) (DWChapman)* 5-8-1b LCharnock(12) (led & sn clr stands' side: rdn ½-wy: kpt on wl) 1½ 3
1765[9] Allwight Then (IRE) **(72)***(72) (FHLee)* 4-8-9 WCarson(1) (w ldr far side: kpt on same pce fnl f) ....½ 4
1900* Rich Glow **(60)***(59) (NBycroft)* 4-7-11 7x JQuinn(4) (racd far side: sn outpcd: hdwy over 1f out: styd on towards fin) ....nk 5
1766[4] Princess Oberon (IRE) **(86)***(80) (MBell)* 5-9-9 MFenton(3) (racd far side: sn outpcd: hdwy over 1f out: nvr nr ldrs) 1½ 6
1795[4] Takadou (IRE) **(87)***(80) (MissLCSiddall)* 4-9-10 DHarrison(5) (s.i.s: racd far side: sn outpcd: styd on u.p fnl f: nvr nr to chal) ....nk 7
1637[9] Tuscan Dawn **(83)***(67) (JBerry)* 5-9-6 JCarroll(2) (unruly in stalls: led tl hdd & wknd over 1f out) 3 8
1181[8] High Ranking **(70)***(51) (MHEasterby)* 3-8-0 NCarlisle(8) (chsd ldrs stands' side tl wknd 2f out) ....¾ 9
2001[5] Elle Shaped (IRE) **(72)***(51) (DNicholls)* 5-8-9 AlexGreaves(10) (racd stands' side: sn outpcd: hung lft: a bhd) ....¾ 10
1765[2] Benzoe (IRE) **(82)***(42) (MrsJRRamsden)* 5-9-5 KFallon(11) (unruly in stalls: reard s: s.s: racd stands' side: a bhd) 6 11
1565[2] White Sorrel **(68)***(25) (AHarrison)* 4-8-2 (3) JStack(9) (racd centre: outpcd & bhd fr ½-wy) ....¾ 12

5/2 Sweet Magic, **6/1** Princess Oberon (IRE), **13/2** Benzoe (IRE), **7/1** Takadou (IRE), **8/1** NAME THE TUNE, **10/1** Allwight Then (IRE), Elle Shaped (IRE), **12/1** Rich Glow, White Sorrel, Shadow Jury, **16/1** Tuscan Dawn, **33/1** High Ranking, CSF £29.10 CT £233.80 TOTE £9.90: £2.60 £1.70 £4.60 (£15.70) Trio £139.00 OWNER Mr C. Hammond (NEWMARKET) BRED Derek R. Price 12 Rn
60.45 secs (2.05) SF: 55/52/34/40/27/48/48/35/12/19/10/-
WEIGHT FOR AGE 3yo-7lb

2061 STEPHEN EASTEN DOBSON PEACOCK H'CAP (0-85) (3-Y.O+) (Class D)
£7,497.50 (£2,255.00: £1,090.00: £507.50)
1m (round) Stalls: Low GOING minus 0.18 sec per fur (GF) 7-25 (7-25)

1911* **Scaraben (55)***(68+)*(Fav)*(SEKettlewell)* 7-8-0 (3) JStack(3) (hld up & bhd: gd hdwy over 2f out: hung lft & led jst ins fnl f: sn rdn clr: readily) ....— 1
1932* Hi Nod **(81)***(88) (MJCamacho)* 5-10-1 5x LCharnock(4) (lw: hld up: effrt 3f out: led wl over 1f out tl jst ins fnl f: no ch w wnr) 3 2
1679* Murphy's Gold (IRE) **(52)***(57) (RAFahey)* 4-8-0 JQuinn(5) (plld hrd: led after 1f tl over 1f out: edgd rt & kpt on same pce) 1 3

1969[4] Cee-Jay-Ay **(65)***(70) (JBerry)* 8-8-13 JCarroll(1) (chsd ldrs: rdn over 2f out: kpt on same pce fnl f) ....s.h 4
1631[4] Equerry **(68)***(67) (MJohnston)* 4-9-2 KDarley(2) (led 1f: trckd ldrs: nt clr run on ins fr 2f out: hmpd over 1f out: eased towards fin) 3 5
1344[5] Move Smartly (IRE) **(52)***(50) (FHLee)* 5-8-0 NCarlisle(7) (w ldr: rdn 2f out: grad wknd) ....nk 6
Pleasure Trick (USA) **(64)***(32) (NTinkler)* 4-8-12 KimTinkler(6) (drvn along: lost pl ½-wy: sn bhd) 15 7

11/4 SCARABEN, **4/1** Hi Nod, Murphy's Gold (IRE), **6/1** Cee-Jay-Ay, Equerry, Move Smartly (IRE), **25/1** Pleasure Trick (USA), CSF £13.20 TOTE £3.30: £1.90 £2.20 (£4.00) OWNER Mr J. Tennant (MIDDLEHAM) BRED Burton Agnes Stud Co Ltd 7 Rn 1m 44.12 (5.12) SF: 22/42/11/24/21/4/-

2062

BRANDLING SPONSORS CLUB JOHN OSBORNE H'CAP (0-95) (3-Y.O) (Class C) £6,815.00 (£2,045.00: £985.00: £455.00)
1m 2f 32y Stalls: Low GOING minus 0.18 sec per fur (GF) 7-55 (7-56)

1589[2] **Grand Selection (IRE) (75)***(85)*(Fav)*(MBell)* 3-9-1 MFenton(1) (plld hrd: led 2f: led on bit 3f out: shkn up ins fnl f: drvn out) ....— 1
1793[10] Boldina Bay **(74)***(84) (MJohnston)* 3-9-0 DHolland(3) (trckd ldrs: drvn along & outpcd over 3f out: hdwy over 1f out: styd on towards fin) ....nk 2
1946* Vindaloo **(69)***(77) (JLHarris)* 3-8-2 (7) 5x PFessey(5) (lw: trckd ldrs: effrt over 2f out: styd on same pce appr fnl f) 1¼ 3
1839[13] Danegold (IRE) **(81)***(78) (MRChannon)* 3-9-7v RHughes(2) (hld up & bhd: effrt over 2f out: nvr able to chal: eased towards fin) 7 4
1945* Striffolino **(75)***(69)*(Fav)*(TDBarron)* 3-9-1 5x JFortune(4) (s.i.s: led after 2f to 3f out: wknd over 1f out: eased cl home) 1¾ 5

5/2 GRAND SELECTION (IRE), Striffolino, **11/4** Vindaloo, **7/2** Danegold (IRE), **11/1** Boldina Bay, CSF £21.82 TOTE £3.60: £1.90 £3.30 (£34.20) OWNER Mr M. B. Hawtin (NEWMARKET) BRED Mount Coote Stud in Ireland 5 Rn 2m 12.05 (5.35) SF: 43/42/35/36/27

2063

ROBSON-BROWN ADVERTISING MAIDEN STKS (2-Y.O) (Class D) £5,442.50 (£1,640.00: £795.00: £372.50)
6f Stalls: Centre GOING minus 0.07 sec per fur (G) 8-25 (8-27)

Mazeed (IRE) *(81)*(Fav)*(HThomsonJones)* 2-9-0 RHills(2) (unf: scope: w ldr: led jst ins fnl f: hld on wl towards fin) ....— 1
Bijou d'Inde *(81+) (MJohnston)* 2-9-0 DHolland(3) (tall: mde most tl jst ins fnl f: edgd rt & kpt on wl) ....hd 2
1774[2] Laurel Crown (IRE) **(70)***(70) (JBerry)* 2-9-0 JCarroll(7) (in tch: effrt u.p over 2f out: kpt on same pce: nvr able to chal) 4 3
La Finale *(60) (MHEasterby)* 2-8-9 KDarley(1) (unf: scope: bit bkwd: s.i.s: bhd & rn green: kpt on appr fnl f: nvr nr to chal) 1¾ 4
1597[9] Cumbrian Maestro *(64) (MHEasterby)* 2-9-0 MBirch(6) (in tch: rdn & outpcd over 2f out: n.d after) ....½ 5
Champagne Warrior (IRE) *(43) (MJCamacho)* 2-8-9 LCharnock(5) (rangy: scope: bit bkwd: reard s: a outpcd & bhd) 6 6
1454[2] Scathebury *(35) (SPCWoods)* 2-9-0 WWoods(4) (sn trckng ldrs: rdn over 2f out: wknd qckly) 5 7

7/4 MAZEED (IRE) (11/10-2/1), **2/1** Bijou d'Inde (5/2-6/4), **4/1** Scathebury, **8/1** Laurel Crown (IRE), **14/1** La Finale, **20/1** Cumbrian Maestro, Champagne Warrior (IRE), CSF £5.69 TOTE £3.00: £1.80 £1.80 (£3.30) OWNER Mr Hamdan Al Maktoum (NEWMARKET) BRED Shadwell Estate Company Limited 7 Rn 1m 15.93 (4.43) SF: 31/31/20/10/14/-/-

2064

WILLIAM EDWIN NEESHAM H'CAP (0-75) (4-Y.O+) (Class D) £3,772.50 (£1,140.00: £555.00: £262.50)
1m 2f 32y Stalls: Low GOING minus 0.18 sec per fur (GF) 8-55 (8-58)

1875[4] **Ooh Ah Cantona (54)***(67) (JLEyre)* 4-9-5 RLappin(4) (lw: trckd ldrs: led over 2f out: rdn clr ent fnl f) ....— 1
1557[7] Straw Thatch **(48)***(56) (MrsJRRamsden)* 6-8-13 KFallon(6) (rn in snatches: rr div tl hdwy over 2f out: styd on over 1f out: nt rch wnr) 3 2
1491[2] Essayeffsee **(49)***(55)*(Fav)*(MrsMReveley)* 6-9-0 KDarley(8) (lw: hld up: hdwy to trck ldrs 4f out: n.m.r over 2f out: kpt on same pce) 1½ 3
1855[6] Nobby Barnes **(43)***(47) (DonEnricoIncisa)* 6-8-8 KimTinkler(10) (s.i.s: bhd: gd hdwy & nt clr run 2f out: styd on same pce appr fnl f) 1 4
1875[7] Sallyoreally (IRE) **(47)***(43) (WStorey)* 4-8-5 (7) PFessey(1) (hld up: hdwy & prom ½-wy: n.m.r on ins 2f out: wknd over 1f out) 5 5

17445 Drummer Hicks **(47)***(36) (EWeymes)* 6-8-12 DeanMcKeown(3) (led tl over 2f out: wknd over 1f out) 5 **6**
1744* Missus Murhill (IRE) **(41)***(29) (NTinkler)* 4-8-6 GDuffield(9) (bhd: hdwy on outside to chse ldrs 2f out: sn wknd) ......hd **7**
14373 Kalou **(59)***(41) (CWCElsey)* 4-9-10v LCharnock(7) (chsd ldrs: wkng whn n.m.r over 1f out) 4 **8**
18084 Maurangi **(54)***(25) (BWMurray)* 4-8-12 (7) MartinDwyer(5) (trckd ldrs: drvn along over 3f out: rdn & wknd over 2f out) 7 **9**
19212 Thaleros **(53)***(7) (GMMoore)* 5-9-1b(3) JStack(2) (trckd ldrs: reminders 4f out: sn lost pl & bhd) 11 **10**

7/4 Essayeffsee (op 3/1), **11/2** Maurangi, **6/1** Straw Thatch, **13/2** OOH AH CANTONA, **8/1** Kalou, Drummer Hicks, Missus Murhill (IRE), **14/1** Thaleros, **16/1** Nobby Barnes, **25/1** Sallyoreally (IRE), CSF £45.78 CT £91.56 TOTE £8.10: £2.40 £3.60 £1.50 (£98.00) Trio £32.70 OWNER Mrs Eve Sweetman (HAMBLETON) BRED R. M. Whitaker and E. Wilkinson 10 Rn

2m 11.8 (5.10) SF: 49/38/37/29/25/18/11/23/7/-

T/Plpt: £18.40 (778.06 Tckts). T/Qdpt: £16.10 (11.7 Tckts). WG

1911-NEWMARKET (R-H)
Friday June 30th (Good to firm)
WEATHER: hot WIND: virtually nil

2065
VISION PARK CLAIMING STKS (3-Y.O) (Class D) £3,840.00 (£1,140.00: £540.00: £240.00) **1m 2f (July)** Stalls: High GOING minus 0.46 sec per fur (F) 2-00 (2-01)

196213 **Old Swinford (IRE) (57)***(60) (BJMeehan)* 3-7-12b GBardwell(5) (lw: chsd ldr: led over 3f out: hdd over 2f out: led over 1f out: rdn out) ......— **1**
1606* Crowned Glory (USA) **(65)***(74)*(Fav)*(PFICole)* 3-8-13 TQuinn(6) (lw: hld up: hdwy over 3f out: r.o cl home) ......¾ **2**
17915 Gentle Irony **(52)***(56) (BJMeehan)* 3-7-12b CRutter(2) (chsd ldrs: rdn to ld over 2f out: hdd over 1f out: unable qckn) 1¾ **3**
1791* Bushehr (IRE) **(62)***(71) (JWHills)* 3-8-8 (7) MHenry(1) (trckd ldrs: rdn over 1f out: one pce) 1½ **4**
17914 Orchidarma **(60)***(57) (RJRWilliams)* 3-8-3v GDuffield(7) (led over 1f: no ex appr fnl f) 1 **5**
17315 In the Zim *(58) (RHannon)* 3-8-5 (7) DaneO'Neill(9) (mid div: rdn over 2f out: wknd bel dist) 5 **6**
19146 Magic Leader (IRE) **(33)***(47) (TTClement)* 3-7-10 (7) SLanigan(8) (b: a in rr) 1¼ **7**
17715 Try Omnipotent *(46) (CNAllen)* 3-8-3 PRobinson(3) (mid div: rdn over 4f out: grad lost tch) ...¾ **8**
19148 Watch My Lips *(32) (MHTompkins)* 3-8-8 (5) HKYim(4) (in tch: rdn 5f out: grad wknd: t.o) 15 **9**

11/4 Crowned Glory (USA), **7/2** Bushehr (IRE), Orchidarma, **8/1** OLD SWINFORD (IRE) (6/1-9/1), **9/1** Gentle Irony (6/1-10/1), **10/1** In the Zim, **14/1** Try Omnipotent (8/1-20/1), **50/1** Magic Leader (IRE), Watch My Lips, CSF £27.54 TOTE £8.50: £1.50 £1.50 £2.70 (£8.70) Trio £24.40 OWNER Old Swinford Betting Partnership (UPPER LAMBOURN) BRED Owen Bourke 9 Rn

2m 7.22 (4.82) SF: 8/22/4/19/5/6/-/-/-

2066
MERIVALE MOORE STKS (3-Y.O+ F & M) (Class C) £5,116.80 (£1,891.20: £905.60: £368.00: £144.00: £54.40) **6f (July)** Stalls: High GOING minus 0.46 sec per fur (F) 2-30 (2-31)

12274 **Marha (90)***(100) (HThomsonJones)* 3-8-10 RHills(7) (hld up: hdwy 2f out: led ins fnl f: r.o wl) ......— **1**
13628 Iltimas (USA) **(83)***(95) (PTWalwyn)* 3-8-6 WCarson(4) (led: hdd ins fnl f: r.o) ......nk **2**
1891a3 Katya (IRE) **(92)***(98) (MRChannon)* 3-8-10 RHughes(3) (trckd ldrs: rdn & ev ch ins fnl f: unable qckn nr fin) ......nk **3**
1698* Paris Babe **(93)***(94)*(Fav)*(DMorris)* 3-8-12 RCochrane(8) (hld up: hdwy 2f out: ev ch 1f out: unable qckn) 2½ **4**
16132 Signs **(92)***(80) (RHannon)* 3-7-13 (7) DaneO'Neill(1) (w ldr: rdn & ev ch wl over 1f out: no ex fnl f) 3 **5**
180615 Bajan Rose **(86)***(80) (MBlanshard)* 3-8-10 WRyan(2) (chsd ldrs over 4f) 1¼ **6**
10654 Red Rita (IRE) **(80)***(62) (WRMuir)* 4-8-10 LDettori(6) (chsd ldrs: ev ch wl over 1f out: sn btn) 4 **7**
66520 Queenbird **(90)***(64) (MJRyan)* 4-8-12 AClark(5) (bhd: hdwy over 2f out: wknd over 1f out) ......hd **8**

3/1 Paris Babe, **100/30** Signs, **4/1** Katya (IRE), **6/1** MARHA, **8/1** Iltimas (USA), **10/1** Red Rita (IRE), **16/1** Bajan Rose, Queenbird, CSF £46.39 TOTE £7.40: £2.00 £2.30 £1.80 (£25.40) OWNER Mr Hamdan Al Maktoum (NEWMARKET) BRED Shadwell Estate Company Limited 8 Rn

1m 11.72 (0.22) SF: 53/48/51/47/33/33/23/25

WEIGHT FOR AGE 3yo-8lb

STEWARDS' ENQUIRY Hughes suspended 15-20/7/95 (using whip above shoulder height).

2067 VALOR GOLD STOCKISTS H'CAP (0-85) (3-Y.O) (Class D) £5,952.00 (£1,776.00: £848.00: £384.00)
5f (July) Stalls: High GOING minus 0.46 sec per fur (F) 3-00 (3-00)

1924[4] **Fairy Wind (IRE)** **(77)***(89+)*(Fav)*(NACallaghan)* 3-9-3 LDettori(7) (b.hind: trckd ldrs: led over 1f out: pushed clr: eased nr fin) — 1
1847* Mousehole **(70)***(77)* *(RGuest)* 3-8-10 7x KFallon(1) (sn outpcd: gd hdwy over 1f out: r.o: no ch w wnr) 1½ 2
1924[10] Tart and a Half **(81)***(85)* *(BJMeehan)* 3-9-7b TQuinn(9) (led over 3f: outpcd fnl f) 1 3
1522[4] Intiaash (IRE) **(76)***(72)* *(PTWalwyn)* 3-9-2v WCarson(3) (racd alone far side: spd over 3f) 2½ 4
1822[3] Baileys Sunset (IRE) **(60)***(51)* *(MJohnston)* 3-8-0 PRobinson(6) (dwlt: outpcd: styd on appr fnl f: nrst fin) 1½ 5
1016[3] Taylord **(68)***(58)* *(RHannon)* 3-8-1 (7) DaneO'Neill(4) (nvr rchd ldrs) nk 6
621[15] Stoppes Brow **(70)***(59)* *(GLMoore)* 3-8-10 AClark(8) (a outpcd) nk 7
1094[23] Hot Snap **(68)***(56)* *(CFWall)* 3-8-8 GDuffield(5) (a outpcd) nk 8
1544[3] Prima Cominna **(81)***(65)* *(MBell)* 3-9-7 MFenton(2) (a outpcd) 1½ 9

6/4 FAIRY WIND (IRE), **7/2** Mousehole, **7/1** Prima Cominna (5/1-15/2), **8/1** Baileys Sunset (IRE) (6/1-9/1), **10/1** Taylord (7/1-11/1), Intiaash (IRE), **14/1** Stoppes Brow, **16/1** Tart and a Half, **33/1** Hot Snap, CSF £7.27 CT £54.88 TOTE £2.30: £1.30 £1.40 £2.40 (£4.30) Trio £21.00 OWNER Mr N. A. Callaghan (NEWMARKET) BRED Ron Con Ltd 9 Rn

58.53 secs (-0.47) SF: 70/58/66/53/32/39/40/37/46

2068 TARTAN INTERNATIONAL H'CAP (0-90) (3-Y.O+) (Class C) £7,245.00 (£2,160.00: £1,030.00: £465.00)
1m 2f (July) Stalls: High GOING minus 0.46 sec per fur (F) 3-30 (3-32)

1875* **Herr Trigger (62)***(74+)*(Fav)*(DrJDScargill)* 4-8-5b 5x RCochrane(1) (hld up: hdwy 3f out: led 1f out: r.o strly) — 1
1753[3] Rahy Zoman (USA) **(83)***(87)* *(JRFanshawe)* 3-9-0 DHarrison(5) (hld up: hdwy 2f out: ev ch 1f out: sn outpcd) 5 2
1800[4] Adolescence (IRE) **(81)***(84)* *(KMcAuliffe)* 5-9-10 TQuinn(7) (hld up: hdwy 5f out: ev ch over 1f out: styd on same pce) ½ 3
1693[3] Snowy Petrel (IRE) **(77)***(80)* *(JLDunlop)* 3-8-8 LDettori(9) (prom: rdn & ev ch over 1f out: no ex) s.h 4
1782[5] Wakeel (USA) **(89)***(89)* *(EALDunlop)* 3-9-6 WRSwinburn(6) (chsd ldr: led over 1f out: sn hdd: eased whn btn) 2 5
1757[6] Peaches Polly **(61)***(59)* *(GRimmer)* 5-8-4 MHills(4) (led: hdd & no ex over 1f out) 1¼ 6
1742[6] Talented Ting (IRE) **(70)***(63)* *(PCHaslam)* 6-8-13 MTebbutt(2) (chsd ldrs: rdn over 3f out: sn lost pl) 3 7
1553[2] Locorotondo (IRE) **(69)***(62)* *(MBell)* 4-8-12 MFenton(3) (trckd ldrs: rdn & ev ch 2f out: wknd fnl f) nk 8
1180[8] Risky Romeo **(67)***(57)* *(GCBravery)* 3-7-12 WCarson(8) (hld up: a in rr) 1¾ 9

5/2 HERR TRIGGER, **9/2** Snowy Petrel (IRE) (5/2-5/1), **5/1** Locorotondo (IRE), **11/2** Rahy Zoman (USA), **7/1** Risky Romeo, **10/1** Wakeel (USA), **12/1** Talented Ting (IRE), **20/1** Peaches Polly, **25/1** Adolescence (IRE), CSF £15.75 CT £250.34 TOTE £3.10: £1.20 £1.60 £8.50 (£8.40) Trio £54.20 OWNER The Inn Crowd (NEWMARKET) BRED Johnathan Crisp 9 Rn

2m 4.33 (1.93) SF: 37/38/47/31/40/22/26/25/8
WEIGHT FOR AGE 3yo-12lb

2069 GIRDLESTONE PUMPS H'CAP (0-80) (4-Y.O+) (Class D) £5,692.00 (£1,696.00: £808.00: £364.00)
1m 4f (July) Stalls: High GOING minus 0.46 sec per fur (F) 4-00 (4-03)

1749[2] **Pharamineux (60)***(73)* *(RAkehurst)* 9-8-11 TQuinn(1) (lw: hld up: hdwy over 4f out: led ins fnl f: r.o wl) — 1
Miss Pin Up **(76)***(86)* *(WJHaggas)* 6-9-13 RMcGhin(7) (lw: hld up: hdwy & n.m.r over 1f out: sn ev ch: unable qckn) 2½ 2
1912[2] Lookingforarainbow (IRE) **(77)***(86)*(Fav)*(BobJones)* 7-10-0 MWigham(5) (chsd ldrs: rdn to ld 1f out: sn hdd & no ex) ¾ 3
1655* Sharp Falcon (IRE) **(74)***(79)*(Fav)*(JWharton)* 4-9-11 LDettori(4) (lw: chsd ldr: led over 2f out: sn edgd rt: hdd 1f out: sn btn) 2½ 4
1865[2] Augustan **(63)***(67)* *(SGollings)* 4-8-9 (5) VHalliday(6) (prom: rdn over 3f out: no hdwy fnl 2f) 1 5
1410[7] Un Parfum de Femme (IRE) **(65)***(69)* *(JPearce)* 4-9-2 GBardwell(2) (hld up: effrt over 3f out: one pce fnl 2f) nk 6
1694[8] Silver Hunter (USA) **(64)***(62)* *(GCBravery)* 4-9-1 MHills(3) (led over 9f: grad wknd) 4 7

100/30 Sharp Falcon (IRE), Lookingforarainbow (IRE), **7/2** PHARAMINEUX, **11/2** Augustan, **6/1** Un Parfum de Femme (IRE), **11/1** Miss Pin Up (8/1-12/1), **14/1** Silver Hunter (USA), CSF £33.97 TOTE £3.30: £1.90 £3.20 (£18.10) OWNER Mr K. R. Snellings (EPSOM) BRED J.L.C.Pearce 7 Rn
2m 34.96 (6.26) SF: 18/31/31/24/12/14/7

2070

E.B.F. ST ANDREW'S PARK MAIDEN STKS (2-Y.O) (Class D)
£4,230.00 (£1,260.00: £600.00: £270.00)
6f (July) Stalls: High GOING minus 0.46 sec per fur (F) 4-30 (4-30)

1726³ **Zuhair** *(85+)*(Fav)*(MajorWRHern)* 2-9-0 RHills(2) (mde all: qcknd clr over 1f out: impressive) ....— 1
Villeggiatura *(76) (BWHills)* 2-9-0 WRSwinburn(4) (w'like: trckd ldrs: chsd wnr over 1f out: no imp) 3½ 2
Fikra (USA) *(64) (DMorley)* 2-8-9 RCochrane(6) (lt-f: prom: shkn up over 1f out: nvr able to chal) 2½ 3
1726¹⁰ Asking For Kings (IRE) *(65) (NACallaghan)* 2-9-0 LDettori(1) (b.hind: hld up: nvr plcd to chal) 1½ 4
Cool Fire *(62) (SPCWoods)* 2-9-0 WWoods(5) (leggy: scope: chsd wnr over 3f: wknd fnl f) 1 5

1/2 ZUHAIR, **3/1** Villeggiatura, **8/1** Fikra (USA) (op 5/1), **16/1** Asking For Kings (IRE), Cool Fire, CSF £2.57 TOTE £1.50: £1.20 £1.70 (£2.00) OWNER Mr Hamdan Al Maktoum (LAMBOURN) BRED Shadwell Estate Company Limited 5 Rn 1m 13.39 (1.89) SF: 34/25/13/14/11

T/Jkpt: £23,692.66 (0.4 Tckts); £14,215.60 to Newmarket 1/7/95. T/Plpt: £38.90 (497.92 Tckts). T/Qdpt: £9.80 (11.7 Tckts). CR

1950-WOLVERHAMPTON (L-H)
Friday June 30th (Standard)
WEATHER: hot WIND: almost nil

2071

SILVER BIRCH MAIDEN H'CAP (0-70) (3-Y.O+) (Class E)
£3,388.00 (£1,012.00: £484.00: £220.00)
5f (Fibresand) Stalls: Low GOING: 0.01 sec per fur (STD) 2-20 (2-24)

*232*⁵ **Pursuance (IRE) (56)***(67) (JBalding)* 3-9-0v(7) JEdmunds(4) (led after 1f: hrd rdn over 1f out: drvn out) ....— 1
1963⁶ Cheeky Chappy **(35)***(42) (DWChapman)* 4-8-7b DaleGibson(9) (prom: hrd rdn & 2nd st: r.o one pce fnl f) 1¼ 2
1822⁷ Chance Me **(40)***(44) (MJohnston)* 3-8-5 DHolland(2) (a.p: 3rd st: r.o one pce fnl f) 1 3
1660¹⁵ Blue Sioux **(59)***(55) (JWharton)* 3-9-10 JQuinn(5) (chsd ldrs: 7th st: r.o one pce) 2½ 4
*1763*¹¹ Younger Days (IRE) **(32)***(27) (MartynWane)* 4-8-4 SMaloney(12) (c wd & hdwy over 1f out: nvr nr to chal) ....nk 5
1559⁷ Northern Grey **(51)***(46) (JBerry)* 3-9-2 GCarter(11) (led 1f: 6th st: no imp fnl f) ....s.h 6
1624¹⁰ Snow Foot **(48)***(37)*(Fav)*(PCHaslam)* 3-8-13 JWeaver(10) (lw: hdwy over 1f out: 4th & btn whn wnt lame ins fnl f) 1¾ 7
*1633*⁴ Ho Mei Surprise **(40)***(28) (BPreece)* 3-8-5 NAdams(6) (hdwy 3f out: 4th st: wknd over 1f out)nk 8
1739⁴ Samsung Lovelylady (IRE) **(50)***(33) (EWeymes)* 3-9-1 GHind(3) (lw: prom: 5th st: wknd over 1f out) 1½ 9
*306*ᵂ Pats Delight **(44)***(24) (SCoathup)* 3-8-9 TIves(13) (a bhd) 1 10
*1763*¹⁰ Vengan **(42)***(19) (DHaydnJones)* 3-8-7 AMackay(7) (spd over 2f) 1 11
1546⁷ Sizzling Romp **(58)***(35) (DTThom)* 3-9-9 TGMcLaughlin(8) (b.hind: led 1f out: wknd over 2f out) ....hd 12
1521⁴ Fiery Footsteps **(48)***(5) (PHowling)* 3-8-13b DeanMcKeown(1) (outpcd) 6 13

9/2 Snow Foot, **11/2** Ho Mei Surprise, **6/1** Cheeky Chappy, Samsung Lovelylady (IRE), **7/1** Northern Grey, **8/1** Blue Sioux, Chance Me, **12/1** PURSUANCE (IRE), Fiery Footsteps, **14/1** Sizzling Romp, **25/1** Vengan, Younger Days (IRE), Pats Delight, CSF £82.05 CT £565.62 TOTE £11.40: £1.90 £2.60 £3.90 (£70.30) Trio £182.60 OWNER Spring Hill Stud (DONCASTER) BRED Michael Coogan 13 Rn 63.0 secs (5.00) SF: 21/3/-/9/-/-/-/-/-/-/-/-/-
WEIGHT FOR AGE 3yo-7lb

2072

SYCAMORE CLAIMING STKS (3-Y.O+) (Class F) £2,519.00 (£694.00: £329.00)
1m 4f (Fibresand) Stalls: Low GOING: 0.01 sec per fur (STD) 2-50 (2-51)

Old Provence (95)*(71)*(Fav)*(ICampbell)* 5-9-12 AMackay(7) (hld up & plld hrd: stdy hdwy 6f out: led 4f out: hrd rdn 2f out: all out) ....— 1
*833*⁸ Awestruck **(40)***(62) (BPreece)* 5-9-4b JWeaver(3) (hld up: stdy hdwy 6f out: 2nd st: rdn & ev ch over 1f out: r.o one pce) ....½ 2

1955[8] Palacegate Jo (IRE) **(56)***(63) (DWChapman)* 4-9-7 DeanMcKeown(2) (s.i.s: hld up: 3rd st: r.o one pce fnl f)....1¾ **3**
1920[5] Rose Chime (IRE) **(39)***(39) (JLHarris)* 3-7-9 JQuinn(4) (lw: lost pl 6f out: sme hdwy & 5th st: n.d)....10 **4**
1628[9] Remontant (IRE) **(42)***(42) (RHollinshead)* 3-7-13 JFanning(5) (hld up: sme hdwy & 4th st: n.d)....¾ **5**
1074[6] Nordross **(26)***(15) (JHPeacock)* 7-8-7b DaleGibson(8) (plld hrd: led 5f out tl hrd rdn & hdd 4f out: sn wknd: poor 6th st)....15 **6**
1567[9] Baroski **(30)** *(JLHarris)* 4-9-2 SMaloney(1) (drppd rr 6f out: t.o fnl 4f)....20 **7**
1455[2] Lady Tjonger **(30)** *(DrJDScargill)* 4-8-9 DHolland(6) (plld hrd: led 7f: wknd over 3f out: poor 7th & eased st: t.o)....nk **8**

11/8 OLD PROVENCE, **5/1** Palacegate Jo (IRE), **11/2** Awestruck, **13/2** Remontant (IRE) (4/1-7/1), **7/1** Rose Chime (IRE), Lady Tjonger, **25/1** Baroski, **50/1** Nordross, CSF £9.41 TOTE £1.80: £1.00 £2.50 £2.30 (£6.20) OWNER Mr Ron Dawson (NEWMARKET) BRED Stowell Hill Ltd and A. J. Tree 8 Rn 2m 43.5 (12.50) SF: 29/20/21/-/-/-/-/-
WEIGHT FOR AGE 3yo-15lb

2073

BSD COLOUR COATED STEEL OLDBURY H'CAP (0-70) (3-Y.O+) (Class E) £3,302.20 (£985.60: £470.80: £213.40)
7f (Fibresand) Stalls: Low GOING: 0.01 sec per fur (STD) 3-20 (3-32)

1760[2] **What a Nightmare (IRE) (66)***(73)*(Fav)*(JAGlover)* 3-9-8b TIves(5) (led 1f: led over 2f out: drvn out)....— **1**
1875[6] Calder King **(61)***(66) (JLEyre)* 4-9-9b(3) JTate(7) (hld up: rdn over 3f out: hdwy & 6th st: r.o wl cl home)....¾ **2**
1843[12] At the Savoy (IRE) **(61)***(64) (TDBarron)* 4-9-12 JFortune(8) (lw: chsd ldrs: hrd rdn & wnt 2nd st: ev ch wl over 1f out: nt qckn)....1 **3**
1828[12] Indiahra **(54)***(52) (RHollinshead)* 4-9-5 GCarter(11) (lw: bhd tl hdwy & 8th st: nt rch ldrs)....2 **4**
1760[4] Dom Pennion **(58)***(55) (RGuest)* 4-9-9 GHind(3) (chsd ldrs: 4th st: wknd over 1f out)....¾ **5**
1506[10] First Gold **(60)***(57) (JWharton)* 6-9-11 JQuinn(1) (dwlt: hdwy & 7th st: nt rch ldrs)....s.h **6**
1021[12] Walk the Beat **(63)***(35) (MartynMeade)* 5-10-0 VSlattery(10) (chsd ldrs: 5th st: wknd over 1f out)....11 **7**
1202[12] Jairzinho (USA) **(53)***(22) (PHayward)* 6-8-11 (7) AmandaSanders(9) (a mid div)....1 **8**
1664[6] Ism **(63)***(25) (MajorWRHern)* 3-9-5b JWeaver(12) (plld hrd: led after 1f tl over 2f out: 3rd & wkng st: eased fnl f)....3 **9**
1692[11] Nakita **(57)***(18) (CNAllen)* 4-9-5 (3) DRMcCabe(2) (b.hind: a bhd)....½ **10**
1638[6] Pab's Choice **(60)***(17) (MMcCormack)* 4-9-11 DeanMcKeown(4) (chsd ldrs over 3f)....2 **11**
1760[6] Quinzii Martin **(55)***(5) (DHaydnJones)* 7-9-6v AMackay(6) (sn bhd)....3 **12**

9/4 WHAT A NIGHTMARE (IRE), **4/1** Ism, **7/1** Dom Pennion, **8/1** At the Savoy (IRE), Calder King (6/1-9/1), **9/1** Quinzii Martin (op 6/1), **11/1** Walk the Beat (8/1-12/1), **12/1** Pab's Choice (op 8/1), First Gold (op 8/1), **25/1** Indiahra, Nakita, **50/1** Jairzinho (USA), CSF £21.41 CT £121.68 TOTE £3.50: £1.40 £3.50 £3.30 (£34.10) Trio £66.70 OWNER Bassetlaw Bloodstock Agency Ltd (WORKSOP) BRED Carrigbeg Stud Co Ltd 12 Rn 1m 30.6 (6.60) SF: 29/31/29/17/20/22/-/-/-/-/-/-
WEIGHT FOR AGE 3yo-9lb

OFFICIAL EXPLANATION **Ism: his jockey was unable to ride the colt out at the finish due to him injuring his leg when leaving the stalls.**

2074

OAK H'CAP (0-60) (3-Y.O+) (Class F) £2,519.00 (£694.00: £329.00)
6f (Fibresand) Stalls: Low GOING: 0.01 sec per fur (STD) 3-50 (3-50)

1763[4] **Malibu Man (55)***(64) (SMellor)* 3-9-2 TSprake(8) (a.p: led 2f out: r.o wl)....— **1**
1633* Efficacy **(48)***(56)*(Fav)*(APJarvis)* 4-9-0 (3) DWright(10) (prom: wnt 2nd st: hrd rdn over 1f out: r.o wl ins fnl f)....½ **2**
1963[4] Old Comrades **(50)***(42) (TDBarron)* 8-9-5 JFortune(6) (lw: prom: 4th st: one pce)....6 **3**
1963[12] Grey Toppa **(39)***(25) (NPLittmoden)* 4-8-8 TGMcLaughlin(2) (hdwy & 5th st: nvr nr to chal)....2 **4**
1963[11] Arc Lamp **(49)***(35) (JAGlover)* 9-9-4 DeanMcKeown(5) (led 1f: lost pl 3f out: one pce fnl f)....nk **5**
1828[10] Blue Grit **(53)***(32) (MDods)* 9-9-8 DaleGibson(3) (outpcd)....2½ **6**
1078[6] Marsh Arab **(41)***(16) (JBalding)* 4-8-10 NAdams(9) (b: nvr trbld ldrs)....1½ **7**
1456[6] Disco Boy **(55)***(25) (BAMcMahon)* 5-9-10b TIves(1) (lw: bhd fnl 3f)....1¾ **8**
1763[6] Tommy Tempest **(31)** *(REPeacock)* 6-7-7b(7) CAdamson(7) (led after 1f: hdd 2f out: 3rd & wkng st)....3 **9**
1677[10] Bonny Melody **(35)** *(PDEvans)* 4-7-11b(7) AmandaSanders(4) (6th st: eased whn btn over 1f out)....½ **10**

11/8 Efficacy, **9/2** Old Comrades, **7/1** Blue Grit, Bonny Melody, **9/1** MALIBU MAN, **10/1** Grey Toppa, Disco Boy, **12/1** Tommy Tempest, **14/1** Arc Lamp, **20/1** Marsh Arab, CSF £23.57 CT £65.97 TOTE £15.20: £3.10 £1.50 £2.20 (£21.60) Trio £23.00 OWNER Church Racing Partnership (SWINDON) BRED Mrs M. Chubb 10 Rn 1m 15.7 (4.50) SF: 38/38/24/7/17/14/-/7/-/-

WEIGHT FOR AGE 3yo-8lb

2075 BEECH (S) STKS (2-Y.O) (Class G) £2,340.00 (£645.00: £306.00)
7f (Fibresand) Stalls: Low GOING: 0.01 sec per fur (STD) 4-20 (4-22)

1981[3] **Multi Franchise** *(65) (BGubby)* 2-8-8 (3) JTate(9) (a.p: led 2f out: all out) — **1**
1690[7] State Approval *(64)*(Fav)*(APJarvis)* 2-8-8 (3) DWright(7) (lw: bhd: nt clr run 3f out: hdwy & 5th st: fin wl) ½ **2**
1287[4] Victoria Venture *(59) (SPCWoods)* 2-7-13 (7) CWebb(1) (a.p: 3rd st: ev ch ins fnl f: r.o) hd **3**
1632[3] Red Simba *(60) (JBerry)* 2-8-11 GCarter(8) (led 5f: 2nd st: btn whn edgd rt ins fnl f) 1¾ **4**
1570[3] Pulga Circo *(48) (BAMcMahon)* 2-8-6 DeanMcKeown(10) (c wd & hdwy over 1f out: nt rch ldrs) 3 **5**
1665[5] Sovitaka (IRE) *(47) (MHEasterby)* 2-8-6 SMaloney(5) (lw: prom: rdn over 4f out: wknd 3f out) ½ **6**
1829[10] Cottesloe Beach *(40) (KTIvory)* 2-8-4 (7) CScally(6) (b: prom: 4th st: wknd qckly wl over 1f out) 5 **7**
1632[5] Magic Bird (IRE) *(24) (JLSpearing)* 2-8-6 GHind(3) (a bhd) 5 **8**
1665[7] Ned's Contessa (IRE) *(6) (MDods)* 2-8-6 DaleGibson(4) (prom: rdn 4f out: wknd 3f out) 8 **9**
1054[3] Lucky Revenge *(2)*(Fav)*(MartynMeade)* 2-8-6 VSlattery(2) (prom: rdn over 3f out: wknd over 2f out) 1¾ **10**

7/2 State Approval, Lucky Revenge, **4/1** MULTI FRANCHISE, Victoria Venture (op 2/1), **10/1** Pulga Circo (op 6/1), **14/1** Sovitaka (IRE), Red Simba, **25/1** Ned's Contessa (IRE), **33/1** Magic Bird (IRE), Cottesloe Beach, CSF £17.28 TOTE £5.40: £1.40 £1.50 £2.40 (£16.30) Trio £25.20 OWNER Brian Gubby Ltd (BAGSHOT) BRED B. Gubby 10 Rn 1m 33.2 (9.20) SF: -/-/-/-/-/-/-/-/-/-

No bid

2076 ASH AMATEUR H'CAP (0-60) (3-Y.O+) (Class F) £2,519.00 (£694.00: £329.00)
1m 100y (Fibresand) Stalls: Low GOING: 0.01 sec per fur (STD) 4-50 (4-50)

1027[7] **Backstabber (34)***(44) (MissSJWilton)* 5-10-0 (4) MissEJJones(9) (hdwy 5f out: 3rd st: carried rt ins fnl f: r.o to ld last 50y) — **1**
1854[21] Brackenthwaite **(58)***(67) (LRLloyd-James)* 5-11-7v(7) MrDSpiteri(5) (bhd: hrd rdn & c wd st: hdwy over 1f out: r.o wl ins fnl f) nk **2**
1884[3] Moneghetti **(36)***(44) (RHollinshead)* 4-10-6 MrDParker(10) (hdwy 5f out: led over 1f out: rdn & hung rt ins fl f: hdd last 50y) 1 **3**
1745[8] Captain Marmalade **(51)***(58) (DTThom)* 6-11-7 MissDianaJones(8) (wl bhd tl hdwy & 8th st: r.o wl ins fnl f: n.m.r cl home) s.h **4**
1760[3] Flashfeet **(58)***(64) (KBishop)* 5-11-10 (4) MissAPurdy(7) (lw: hdwy 4f out: 6th st: nt clr run & swtchd lft ins fnl f: r.o) 1 **5**
1762[9] Mezzoramio **(47)***(52) (KAMorgan)* 3-10-3v(4) MrIMcLelland(1) (b: prom: 5th st: one pce fnl f) ½ **6**
1950[7] Arrogant Boy **(30)***(20) (DWChapman)* 6-9-10 (4) MissRClark(12) (led over 5f out tl over 1f out: sn wknd) 8 **7**
*1631** Dia Georgy **(52)***(36)*(Fav)*(RGuest)* 4-11-8 MrTCuff(3) (prom: rdn 4f out: 4th & wkng st) *3* ***8***
Welsh Column **(31)***(11) (MWEckley)* 9-9-11 (4)ow1 MrRBevis(6) (n.d) 1¾ **9**
1630[4] Unison **(28)***(4) (CRBarwell)* 4-9-5v(7) MissLPope(13) (led 1f: 7th & wkng st) 2½ **10**
1937[15] Hi Penny **(37)***(9) (KTIvory)* 4-10-3b(4) MrDMarshall(2) (bhd fnl 6f) 2 **11**
315[12] Caherass Court (IRE) **(49)** *(BPreece)* 4-10-12 (7) MissLBoswell(4) (bhd fnl 5f: t.o) 12 **12**
1963[20] Christian Warrior **(28)** *(REPeacock)* 6-9-5b(7) MrsCPeacock(11) (plld hrd: led after 1f: hdd over 5f out: wknd over 3f out: t.o) 12 **13**

5/4 Dia Georgy, **5/2** Moneghetti, **7/1** Captain Marmalade, **8/1** Flashfeet (op 4/1), **16/1** BACKSTABBER, **20/1** Unison, **25/1** Mezzoramio, Brackenthwaite, Welsh Column, Arrogant Boy, **33/1** Hi Penny, Caherass Court (IRE), Christian Warrior, CSF £319.58 CT £1,217.07 TOTE £24.70: £5.50 £11.00 £1.70 (£101.20) Trio £232.80 OWNER Mr Ken Baker (STOKE-ON-TRENT) BRED Lady Joanna Wellesley 13 Rn 1m 55.3 (11.30) SF: 10/33/10/24/30/8/-/2/-/-/-/-/-

WEIGHT FOR AGE 3yo-10lb

T/Plpt: £177.30 (47.05 Tckts). T/Qdpt: £3.30 (11.5 Tckts). KH

1771-**BATH (L-H)**
Saturday July 1st (Firm)
WEATHER: fine WIND: almost nil

2077 WESTON MAIDEN AUCTION STKS (2-Y.O) (Class E) £3,246.00 (£978.00: £474.00: £222.00) **5f 161y** Stalls: Low GOING minus 0.44 sec (F) 2-20 (2-22)

6507 **Rhumba Dancer** *(80) (RHannon)* 2-8-5 RPerham(2) (hdwy over 2f out: led over 1f out: r.o).— 1
14064 Oriel Lad *(75) (PDEvans)* 2-8-6 GHind(5) (chsd ldr: led over 2f out tl over 1f out)....2 2
18577 Essentialselection **(87)***(72)*(Fav)*(WJHaggas)* 2-8-10 AClark(4) (led tl over 2f out: hrd rdn: one pce)....2½ 3
16629 Erupt *(66) (GBBalding)* 2-8-6 JWilliams(7) (chsd ldrs: rdn & one pce fnl 2f)....¾ 4
Seaford Star (IRE) *(52) (MRChannon)* 2-8-9 ow3 RHughes(3) (unf: scope: prom 4f)....5 5
Kealbra Lady *(MSSaunders)* 2-8-4 ow3 RPrice(1) (unf: spd 2f: wknd & eased over 1f out: t.o)....20 6

5/2 Essentialselection, **100/30** Erupt, Seaford Star (IRE), **4/1** Oriel Lad, **8/1** RHUMBA DANCER, **50/1** Kealbra Lady, CSF £34.37 TOTE £8.50: £2.20 £2.40 (£17.70) OWNER Mr N. Ahamad (MARLBOROUGH) BRED Tarworth Bloodstock Investments Ltd 6 Rn 1m 11.3 (2.00) SF: 25/20/17/11/-/-

2078 CANADA DAY (S) H'CAP (0-60) (3-Y.O+) (Class F) £2,967.50 (£830.00: £402.50) **2m 1f 34y** Stalls: Low GOING minus 0.44 sec per fur (F) 2-50 (2-51)

17594 **Rose of Glenn (47)***(59) (BPalling)* 4-9-8 TSprake(4) (hdwy & 5th st: r.o to ld cl home)....— 1
17733 Access Sun **(38)***(50)*(Fav)*(JSKing)* 8-8-13 RHughes(5) (led: hrd rdn over 2f out: hdd nr fin)...nk 2
17373 Oh So Handy **(35)***(46) (RCurtis)* 7-8-10b WNewnes(3) (hld up in rr: hdwy & 6th st: hrd rdn 2f out: r.o)....½ 3
151315 Wizzy Lizzy (IRE) **(41)***(50) (DRCElsworth)* 4-8-13 (3) SDrowne(9) (4th st: rdn & one pce fnl 2f) 3 4
144411 Lajadhal (FR) **(20)***(26) (KBishop)* 6-7-9 NAdams(1) (3rd st: one pce fnl 3f)....2½ 5
Distant Memory **(43)***(46) (PJHobbs)* 6-9-4b MPerrett(8) (prom 8f: one pce after)....3½ 6
14279 Boundless (IRE) **(38)***(25) (BJMeehan)* 3-7-10bow2 TWilliams(11) (jnd ldr 8f out: 2nd st: wknd 3f out: t.o)....15 7
142710 Call Me Albi (IRE) **(49)***(37) (GLMoore)* 4-9-10 AClark(10) (hdwy 7f out: wknd over 4f out: t.o) ¾ 8
Hard to Get **(21)***(9) (MFBarraclough)* 8-7-3 (7) CAdamson(6) (a bhd: t.o)....½ 9

2/1 Access Sun, **7/2** Wizzy Lizzy (IRE), **13/2** Distant Memory (4/1-7/1), **7/1** ROSE OF GLENN (op 9/2), **8/1** Call Me Albi (IRE) (op 9/2), Oh So Handy, Boundless (IRE) (op 5/1), **50/1** Lajadhal (FR), Hard to Get, CSF £20.83 CT £105.36 TOTE £9.40: £1.90 £1.50 £2.00 (£10.80) Trio £20.00 OWNER Mr K. M. Rideout (COWBRIDGE) BRED Mrs M. J. Dandy 9 Rn
3m 49.4 (8.40) SF: 34/25/21/25/1/21/-/12/-
WEIGHT FOR AGE 3yo-17lb
Bt in 4,200gns

2079 LITTLE SOMERFORD LIMITED STKS (0-70) (3-Y.O+) (Class E) £3,187.50 (£960.00: £465.00: £217.50) **5f 161y** Stalls: Low GOING minus 0.44 sec per fur (F) 3-25 (3-25)

20177 **Pharsical (62)***(75) (MRChannon)* 4-8-10 ow1 RHughes(4) (mde all: r.o wl)....— 1
*1882** Purple Fling **(71)***(79) (SirMarkPrescott)* 4-9-3 RPerham(5) (a 2nd: rdn fnl 2f: r.o)....1½ 2
14098 Jobie **(65)***(72) (BWHills)* 5-9-0 JWilliams(8) (bhd tl gd hdwy over 1f out: nrst fin)....1¼ 3
17772 Robellion **(70)***(65) (DWPArbuthnot)* 4-9-0 SWhitworth(3) (a.p: no hdwy fnl 2f)....2½ 4
18152 Napoleon Star (IRE) **(70)***(65)*(Fav)*(MSSaunders)* 4-9-0 RPrice(1) (a.p: one pce fnl 2f)....nk 5
19096 Paley Prince (USA) **(53)***(56) (MDIUsher)* 9-8-7 (7) CAdamson(7) (nvr nr to chal)....3 6
1802* So Intrepid (IRE) **(70)***(58) (JMBradley)* 5-9-3 (3) SDrowne(6) (outpcd)....1½ 7
1783* Midnight Break **(67)***(53) (PTWalwyn)* 3-8-8 GHind(2) (s.s: a bhd)....d.h 7

10/3 Napoleon Star (IRE), **4/1** Midnight Break (3/1-9/2), **5/1** Purple Fling, **11/2** So Intrepid (IRE) (op 7/2), **13/2** Robellion, **15/2** Jobie, **8/1** PHARSICAL, **40/1** Paley Prince (USA), CSF £43.06 TOTE £9.20: £1.70 £1.80 £2.10 (£23.20) OWNER Mr John Sunley (UPPER LAMBOURN) BRED Sunley Stud 8 Rn 1m 9.9 (0.60) SF: 50/54/47/40/40/31/33/21
WEIGHT FOR AGE 3yo-7lb

2080 ROTHMANS ROYALS NORTH SOUTH CHALLENGE SERIES H'CAP (0-100) (3-Y.O+) (Class C) £6,830.00 (£2,060.00: £1,000.00: £470.00) **1m 5y** Stalls: Low GOING minus 0.44 sec per fur (F) 4-00 (4-01)

185112 **Air Commodore (IRE) (90)***(103)*(Fav)*(PFICole)* 4-9-9 CRutter(4) (3rd st: led on bit over 1f out: easily)....— 1

1775* Zermatt (IRE) **(69)**_(77) (MDIUsher)_ 5-8-2 RPrice(3) (2nd st: led over 2f out tl over 1f out: no ch w wnr)....................2½ **2**
1365⁵ Desert Green (FR) **(95)**_(100) (RHannon)_ 6-10-0 RPerham(2) (dwlt: 5th st: hdwy & rdn 2f out: nvr nr to chal)....................1½ **3**
1753⁴ Aeroking (USA) **(82)**_(85) (GHarwood)_ 4-9-1 AClark(5) (led tl wknd over 2f out)....................1¼ **4**
_1884⁷_ Sooty Tern **(70)**_(70) (JMBradley)_ 8-8-0 (3)ow2 SDrowne(1) (slipped 5f out: 4th st: wknd 2f out)....................½ **5**

9/4 AIR COMMODORE (IRE), **7/2** Zermatt (IRE), Desert Green (FR) (5/2-4/1), Aeroking (USA), **11/2** Sooty Tern, CSF £9.76 TOTE £3.30: £1.10 £2.30 (£6.50) OWNER Mr W. H. Ponsonby (WHATCOMBE) BRED Hillfields Stud 5 Rn 1m 38.2 (0.70 under best) (-0.30) SF: 74/48/71/56/41

2081

CLAVERTON CLAIMING H'CAP (0-70) (3-Y.O+) (Class E) £3,558.00 (£1,074.00: £522.00: £246.00)
1m 5y Stalls: Low GOING minus 0.44 sec per fur (F) 4-35 (4-37)

1974⁴ **Noeprob (USA) (41)**_(51) (RJHodges)_ 5-8-3 StephenDavies(12) (6th st: led ins fnl f: all out).— **1**
_1951⁶_ Zahran (IRE) **(43)**_(53) (JMBradley)_ 4-8-2 (3) SDrowne(5) (hdwy & swtchd rt 2f out: ev ch ins fnl f: r.o)....................hd **2**
1940² Marchman **(47)**_(56)_(Fav)_(JSKing)_ 10-8-9 AClark(4) (gd hdwy & swtchd lft over 1f out: nrst fin)....................½ **3**
_1762⁸_ Swynford Flyer **(32)**_(38) (JAHarris)_ 6-7-1 (7)ow1 CAdamson(7) (4th st: led over 2f out tl wknd ins fnl f)....................¾ **4**
1969⁷ Mr Cube (IRE) **(55)**_(58) (JMBradley)_ 5-8-10v(7) RWaterfield(11) (7th st: hrd rdn & no hdwy fnl 2f)....................2 **5**
2016⁴ Mai Pen Rai **(36)**_(32) (RJHodges)_ 7-7-5 (7)ow5 AmandaSanders(3) (3rd st: wknd over 1f out) 1¼ **6**
1661⁶ Bellas Gate Boy **(62)**_(62)_(Fav)_(GLewis)_ 3-9-1 SWhitworth(13) (hdwy over 2f out: nvr nr to chal)....................½ **7**
1676¹⁹ Pacific Overture **(53)**_(44) (CRBarwell)_ 3-8-6 ow1 JWilliams(10) (nvr nr ldrs)....................4 **8**
1771⁹ Smooth Hound **(42)**_(30) (MCPipe)_ 4-8-4b TSprake(9) (2nd st: wknd over 2f out: hmpd over 1f out)....................1¾ **9**
Colway Prince (IRE) **(40)**_(22) (APJones)_ 7-8-2 NAdams(1) (8th st: nvr nr ldrs)....................3 **10**
1847¹² Giggleswick Gossip **(48)**_(8) (MRChannon)_ 3-7-8 (7)ow8 DSweeney(8) (prom tl wknd & 5th st)...7 **11**
1859⁵ My Handsome Prince **(47)**_(7) (PJBevan)_ 3-8-0 TWilliams(6) (led tl wknd over 2f out: hmpd over 1f out)....................4 **12**

LONG HANDICAP Swynford Flyer 7-2 Mai Pen Rai 7-6

4/1 Bellas Gate Boy, Marchman (3/1-9/2), **5/1** NOEPROB (USA), **6/1** Mr Cube (IRE), **10/1** Zahran (IRE), **11/1** My Handsome Prince, **12/1** Mai Pen Rai, **16/1** Giggleswick Gossip, Smooth Hound, **25/1** Pacific Overture, **33/1** Swynford Flyer, **50/1** Colway Prince (IRE), CSF £48.13 CT £198.15 TOTE £4.80: £1.70 £4.00 £2.50 (£28.30) Trio £50.20 OWNER Mrs P. A. Bradshaw (SOMERTON) BRED Charles Cyzer 12 Rn 1m 40.4 (1.90) SF: 33/35/38/20/40/14/35/17/12/4/-/-

WEIGHT FOR AGE 3yo-9lb

STEWARDS' ENQUIRY Clark suspended 10-11/7/95 (careless riding).

2082

ST JOHN AMBULANCE MAIDEN STKS (3-Y.O+) (Class D) £3,809.75 (£1,148.00: £556.50: £260.75)
1m 3f 144y Stalls: Low GOING minus 0.44 sec per fur (F) 5-05 (5-07)

1526⁷ **Woodcrest** _(88) (HCandy)_ 3-8-6 WNewnes(3) (lw: wnt 2nd st: led on bit 2f out: qcknd clr) ...— **1**
1717⁶ Torreglia (IRE) _(78) (JLDunlop)_ 3-8-6 SWhitworth(5) (7th st: hdwy on ins whn nt clr run over 1f out: nrst fin)....................7 **2**
Signature _(76)_(Fav)_(HRACecil)_ 3-8-6 AClark(7) (scope: 2nd tl led 4f out: hdd 2f out: wknd ins fnl f)....................1½ **3**
1128¹⁶ Saucy Maid (IRE) _(73) (MajorDNChappell)_ 4-9-5 StephenDavies(8) (6th st: nvr nr to chal)....................2½ **4**
Celestial Dollar _(72) (NMBabbage)_ 4-9-10 JWilliams(4) (leggy: unf: scope: led to 4f out: 3rd st: wknd 2f out)....................4 **5**
Sacha Star _(65) (BPalling)_ 5-9-5 TSprake(6) (leggy: lt-f: unf: b: swtg: 8th st: nrst fin)....................1½ **6**
1691⁸ Bella Vitessa (IRE) _(62) (JWHills)_ 3-8-6 NAdams(1) (5th st: wknd 3f out)....................2½ **7**
1878⁴ Frank the Swank _(33) (PDEvans)_ 4-9-10 RPrice(2) (swtg: 4th st: wknd 3f out: t.o)....................25 **8**

7/4 Signature, **9/4** WOODCREST, **6/1** Saucy Maid (IRE), **8/1** Torreglia (IRE) (op 4/1), **20/1** Frank the Swank, Bella Vitessa (IRE), **50/1** Sacha Star, Celestial Dollar, CSF £17.00 TOTE £3.10: £1.20 £1.90 £1.30 (£9.40) OWNER Major M. G. Wyatt (WANTAGE) BRED Dunchurch Lodge Stud Co 8 Rn 2m 34.3 (7.60) SF: 6/-/-/4/3/-/-/-

WEIGHT FOR AGE 3yo-13lb

T/Plpt: £175.80 (54.57 Tckts). T/Qdpt: £19.70 (7 Tckts). Hn

1602-DONCASTER (L-H)
Saturday July 1st (St course Good, Rnd Good to firm)
WEATHER: sunny periods WIND: slt bhd

2083 E.B.F. LONSDALE MAIDEN STKS (2-Y.O F) (Class D) £3,752.50 (£1,120.00: £535.00: £242.50) **7f** Stalls: High GOING minus 0.41 sec per fur (F) 6-20 (6-20)

1670³ **Staffin** *(75) (JRFanshawe)* 2-8-11 DHarrison(5) (lw: hld up: stdy hdwy to ld over 1f out: r.o wl) — 1
1525⁴ Maid For Baileys (IRE) *(67) (MJohnston)* 2-8-11 DHolland(6) (led tl hdd over 1f out: nt qckn) 3½ 2
1627³ Frezeliere *(63)*(Fav)*(JLDunlop)* 2-8-11 WRyan(3) (dwlt: nt clr run & swtchd 2f out: nvr able to chal) 1¾ 3
Grey Galava *(57) (BWHills)* 2-8-11 WRSwinburn(7) (neat: cl up tl rdn & btn appr fnl f) 2½ 4
1620⁹ Islay Brown (IRE) *(52) (CWCElsey)* 2-8-11 LCharnock(4) (in tch: effrt over 2f out: wnt lft & sn outpcd) 2½ 5
Belana *(52) (JWWatts)* 2-8-11 NConnorton(2) (neat: scope: lw: bhd: effrt 3f out: no imp fnl 2f: bmpd wl over 1f out) s.h 6
Peppers (IRE) *(47) (LMCumani)* 2-8-11 LDettori(1) (w'like: unf: prom 5f: btn whn bmpd wl over 1f out) 2 7
Perfect Gift *(38) (PFICole)* 2-8-11 TQuinn(8) (neat: cl up 5f: sn lost pl) 4 8

10/11 Frezeliere (5/4-8/11), **5/1** STAFFIN, **13/2** Perfect Gift, **7/1** Grey Galava, Peppers (IRE) (5/1-8/1), **16/1** Belana, Maid For Baileys (IRE), **66/1** Islay Brown (IRE), CSF £67.17 TOTE £8.10: £1.90 £1.90 £1.30 (£39.00) OWNER Dr Catherine Wills (NEWMARKET) BRED Miss Catherine Wills 8 Rn
1m 25.96 (2.56) SF: 31/23/19/13/8/8/3/-

2084 GO RACING IN YORKSHIRE MAIDEN H'CAP (0-70) (3-Y.O+) (Class E) £3,699.00 (£1,107.00: £531.00: £243.00) **6f** Stalls: High GOING minus 0.41 sec per fur (F) 6-50 (6-50)

1797⁴ **Blushing Grenadier (IRE) (50)***(58) (MJFetherston-Godley)* 3-9-0b WRSwinburn(15) (s.i.s: hdwy ½-wy: led ins fnl f: rdn & r.o wl) — 1
1677⁹ Skiptamaloo **(28)***(34) (DonEnricoIncisa)* 4-7-13b KimTinkler(9) (s.i.s: swtchd & gd hdwy 2f out: ev ch ins fnl f: r.o) ¾ 2
1949⁴ Millesime (IRE) **(60)***(61) (BHanbury)* 3-9-7 (3) JStack(4) (lw: led tl hdd & no ex ins fnl f) 1¾ 3
1677⁴ Sandmoor Velvet **(52)***(50) (MHEasterby)* 3-9-2 WRyan(5) (b: trckd ldrs: hdwy to chal 1f out: sn rdn & btn) 1¼ 4
1649¹⁵ Social Register **(48)***(45) (HThomsonJones)* 3-8-12b NCarlisle(3) (a chsng ldrs: kpt on same pce fnl 2f) nk 5
1847³ Spara Tir **(59)***(51) (BobJones)* 3-9-9 NConnorton(10) (a.p: kpt on one pce fnl 2f) 2 6
1796⁸ Backhander (IRE) **(60)***(51) (JARToller)* 3-9-10 TQuinn(7) (lw: prom tl wl outpcd ½-wy: styd on fnl f) ½ 7
1355¹⁴ Monkey Face **(40)***(24) (JHetherton)* 4-8-11 PRobinson(11) (chsd ldr over 4f) 2½ 8
1668¹¹ Coney Hills **(24)***(8) (NBycroft)* 4-7-9 GBardwell(13) (outpcd ½-wy: bhd tl sme late hdwy) s.h 9
1677¹² Pemley **(40)***(22) (RMWhitaker)* 3-8-4v ACulhane(2) (lw: cl up tl rdn & wknd appr fnl f) ¾ 10
1920³ Bollin Frank **(55)***(37)*(Fav)*(MHEasterby)* 3-9-5 LDettori(14) (a bhd) hd 11
1559⁵ Never Say so **(56)***(31) (CSmith)* 3-9-6 DaleGibson(6) (rdn & wl outpcd fr ½-wy) 2½ 12
*768*⁵ Royal Dome (IRE) **(55)***(27) (MartynWane)* 3-9-5 RHughes(8) (lw: s.i.s: hld up & bhd: effrt ½-wy: n.d) 1 13
1366⁸ Peggy Spencer **(57)***(23)*(Fav)*(CWThornton)* 3-9-7 DeanMcKeown(12) (swtg: cl up stands' side over 3f: wknd qckly) 2½ 14

5/1 Bollin Frank, Peggy Spencer, **11/2** Spara Tir, **6/1** BLUSHING GRENADIER (IRE), **8/1** Backhander (IRE), **10/1** Sandmoor Velvet, Millesime (IRE), **14/1** Social Register, Never Say so, Royal Dome (IRE), **20/1** Coney Hills, **33/1** Skiptamaloo, Pemley, Monkey Face, CSF £159.28 CT £1,761.42 TOTE £6.30: £2.20 £11.80 £3.70 (£471.00) Trio not won; £578.65 to Doncaster 02/07/95 OWNER Ecurie Fags (EAST ILSLEY) BRED James M. Egan 14 Rn
1m 13.21 (2.21) SF: 33/16/36/25/20/26/26/6/-/-/12/6/2/-
WEIGHT FOR AGE 3yo-7lb

2085 SHEFFIELD METAL CLUB CONDITIONS STKS (2-Y.O) (Class D) £3,687.50 (£1,100.00: £525.00: £237.50) **5f** Stalls: High GOING minus 0.41 sec per fur (F) 7-20 (7-21)

718³ **Maggi For Margaret** *(79)*(Fav)*(MRChannon)* 2-8-10 RHughes(8) (lw: mde all: clr ½-wy: kpt on wl) — 1

1634[6] Born A Lady *(73) (NPLittmoden)* 2-8-10 TGMcLaughlin(6) (chsd ldrs: wandered u.p fnl 2f: kpt on) 1¾ **2**
1511[8] Amy Leigh (IRE) *(68) (CaptJWilson)* 2-8-10 JFortune(2) (lw: prom: swtchd ½-wy: hmpd 2f out: styd on wl) 1¾ **3**
*1758** Gagajulu *(65) (PDEvans)* 2-8-10 DHolland(1) (a chsng ldrs: nt qckn fnl 2f) ....¾ **4**
1652* Benny Glow *(66) (MrsJRRamsden)* 2-9-1 KFallon(4) (sme hdwy whn hmpd 2f out: nvr plcd to chal) 1¼ **5**
Literary Society (USA) *(62) (JARToller)* 2-8-11 PRobinson(5) (s.i.s: drvn along thrght: nvr rchd ldrs) ....hd **6**
1096[4] Foreman *(57) (WAO'Gorman)* 2-9-3 EmmaO'Gorman(9) (lw: nvr nr ldr) 3½ **7**
1821* Dancing Rainbow *(42)*(Fav)*(MJCamacho)* 2-8-10 LCharnock(7) (lw: drvn along thrght: wl outpcd fr ½-wy) 2½ **8**
1267[5] Pleasure Time *(41) (CSmith)* 2-9-1 GDuffield(3) (spd to ½-wy: sn rdn & btn) 1¾ **9**

7/2 MAGGI FOR MARGARET, Dancing Rainbow, **4/1** Benny Glow, **5/1** Literary Society (USA), **13/2** Foreman, **9/1** Gagajulu, Pleasure Time (op 6/1), **16/1** Amy Leigh (IRE), **25/1** Born A Lady, CSF £70.50 TOTE £4.20: £1.40 £3.60 £3.70 (£41.90) Trio £177.70 OWNER Mr Michael Foy (UPPER LAMBOURN) BRED Brook Stud Ltd 9 Rn 59.96 secs (1.56) SF: 33/27/22/19/20/16/11/-/-

2086 YORKSHIRE-TYNE TEES TELEVISION MAIDEN STKS (3-Y.O+) (Class D) £4,207.50 (£1,260.00: £605.00: £277.50)

1m 2f 60y Stalls: Low GOING minus 0.41 sec per fur (F) 7-50 (7-50)

1755[5] **Star of Persia (IRE) (79)***(82) (PWHarris)* 3-8-10 GDuffield(3) (s.s: plld hrd: effrt over 3f out: str run fnl f to ld wl ins fnl f) ....— **1**
1770[2] Yarrow (IRE) *(79)*(Fav)*(JHMGosden)* 3-8-10 LDettori(7) (lw: cl up: led & qcknd 4f out: hung lft: no ex ins fnl f) 1¾ **2**
1755[4] Tilaal (USA) *(75) (EALDunlop)* 3-8-10 WRSwinburn(1) (lw: trckd ldrs: chal over 3f out: rdn & one pce fnl 2f) 2½ **3**
1905[4] Accuse (USA) *(55) (PFICole)* 3-8-5 TQuinn(2) (hld up: hdwy to chse ldrs 4f out: rdn & wl outpcd fnl 3f) 10 **4**
1804[4] Ruby Rock *(33) (BWMurray)* 3-8-5 ACulhane(6) (prom tl wl outpcd & hung rt fnl 3½f) 14 **5**
Michelle's Ella (IRE) *(28) (CDBroad)* 3-8-5 AMackay(4) (leggy: unf: dwlt: hld up: effrt 4f out: sn wl bhd) 3 **6**
1947[6] Readyspex *(2) (RDEWoodhouse)* 5-9-7b NConnorton(5) (led tl hdd 4f out: sn wknd & t.o) 20 **7**

11/8 Yarrow (IRE), **7/4** Tilaal (USA), **3/1** STAR OF PERSIA (IRE), **12/1** Accuse (USA), **33/1** Michelle's Ella (IRE), **66/1** Ruby Rock, **100/1** Readyspex, CSF £7.49 TOTE £5.70: £2.20 £1.50 (£4.70) OWNER The Saturday Club (BERKHAMSTED) BRED Mrs Kiki Ward Platt 7 Rn
2m 10.39 (3.39) SF: 35/32/28/8/-/-/-
WEIGHT FOR AGE 3yo-11lb

2087 CASTLE W.M.C. STAYERS H'CAP (0-80) (4-Y.O+) (Class D) £4,002.70 (£1,195.60: £571.80: £259.90)

1m 6f 132y Stalls: Low GOING minus 0.41 sec per fur (F) 8-20 (8-20)

Opus One (54)*(65) (MissSEHall)* 4-7-13 (7) MHenry(2) (swtg: trckd ldrs: led 1½f out: rdn & r.o) ....— **1**
1416[7] Good Hand (USA) **(75)***(85) (JWWatts)* 9-9-13 NConnorton(5) (hld up & bhd: effrt over 4f out: swtchd & hdwy over 2f out: r.o wl towards fin) ....¾ **2**
1607[7] Lord Hastie (USA) **(44)***(54) (CWThornton)* 7-7-10 JQuinn(4) (lw: hld up: stdy hdwy 3f out: effrt over 1f out: styd on one pce) ....hd **3**
1858* College Don **(60)***(68) (MPBielby)* 4-8-9 (3) DRMcCabe(3) (lw: hld up: hdwy 2f out: hrd rdn & n.m.r: styd on) 1¾ **4**
1929[7] Cuango (IRE) **(72)***(79) (RHollinshead)* 4-9-10 WRyan(7) (lw: hld up & bhd: effrt ent st: hung lft & hdwy 3f out: no imp fnl 2f) 1¼ **5**
1929[2] Thunderheart **(73)***(73)*(Fav)*(LMCumani)* 4-9-11 LDettori(1) (lw: mde most tl hdd & wknd 1½f out) 6 **6**
1948* Hullbank **(64)***(64) (WWHaigh)* 5-9-2 DaleGibson(10) (lw: in tch: effrt 3f out: rdn & no imp) ....hd **7**
Amiarge **(41)***(39) (MBrittain)* 5-7-7 GBardwell(9) (lw: hdwy to disp ld ent st: wknd fnl 3f) 1¾ **8**
1607[6] Snow Dream **(45)** *(MJRyan)* 5-7-6 (5) MBaird(6) (cl up tl wknd & eased fnl 2½f) ....dist **9**
Alilisa (USA) **(53)** *(MrsJJordan)* 7-8-5 ACulhane(8) (prom to st: t.o) ....dist **10**

LONG HANDICAP Amiarge 6-10

2/1 Thunderheart, **11/2** Hullbank, **13/2** Cuango (IRE), **7/1** Snow Dream, College Don, **8/1** Lord Hastie (USA), Good Hand (USA), **16/1** OPUS ONE, **50/1** Amiarge, Alilisa (USA), CSF £124.78 CT £1,001.28 TOTE £18.30: £3.80 £3.30 £1.70 (£116.40) Trio £267.30 OWNER Mr Robert Ogden (MIDDLEHAM) BRED R. Ogden 10 Rn 3m 10.09 (6.49) SF: 24/44/13/27/38/32/23/-/-/-

2088

WESTSIDE AND EASTSIDE MAGAZINES H'CAP (0-70) (3-Y.O+ F & M) (Class E) £3,816.00 (£1,143.00: £549.00: £252.00)
7f Stalls: High GOING minus 0.41 sec per fur (F) 8-50 (8-56)

1664[13] **Belleminette (IRE) (51)***(60) (DHaydnJones)* 4-8-11 AMackay(2) (racd far side: hdwy ½-wy: led wl over 1f out: r.o u.p) — 1
1528[7] Sea-Ayr (IRE) **(47)***(53) (MrsSMAustin)* 5-8-4 (3) DarrenMoffatt(6) (b: hdwy far side ½-wy: ev ch over 1f out: nt qckn) 1½ 2
1809[12] Cafe Solo **(40)***(43) (NBycroft)* 4-8-0b NKennedy(17) (racd stands' side: hdwy over 2f out: styd on wl towards fin) 1 3
1932[6] Profit Release (IRE) **(55)***(57)*(Fav)*(MJohnston)* 4-9-1b DHolland(8) (lw: led & clr far side tl hdd wl over 1f out: sn btn) ½ 4
1649[5] Poyle Jezebelle **(45)***(44) (MBlanshard)* 4-8-5 JQuinn(14) (racd stands' side: hdwy 3f out: one pce fnl 2f) 1½ 5
1783[6] Racing Brenda **(52)***(46) (BAMcMahon)* 4-8-12 JFortune(5) (lw: racd far side: chsd ldrs over 4f) 2 6
1988[7] Ikis Girl **(37)***(31) (SGollings)* 4-7-6 (5) MBaird(4) (racd far side: nvr trbld ldrs) s.h 7
1679[2] Kilnamartyra Girl **(46)***(38) (JParkes)* 5-8-6 LCharnock(3) (lw: prom far side: rdn ½-wy: sn outpcd) ¾ 8
1079[4] Miss Vaxette **(62)***(53) (MBrittain)* 6-9-8 GBardwell(7) (lw: racd far side: nvr trbld ldrs) ¾ 9
1598[8] Just Whistle **(50)***(40) (CWThornton)* 3-8-2 GDuffield(10) (outpcd far side ½-wy: n.d) nk 10
1679[11] Ballard Ring (IRE) **(52)***(40) (JSWainwright)* 4-8-12b ACulhane(9) (racd far side: s.i.s: a bhd) ¾ 11
605[4] Enchanteur **(43)***(27) (TJEtherington)* 4-8-0 (3)ow3 DRMcCabe(12) (lw: s.i.s: hdwy stands' side 3f out: n.d) ½ 12
1083[13] Miss Tri Colour **(41)***(12) (FHLee)* 3-7-7v NCarlisle(19) (b: led & clr stands' side tl wknd fnl 2f) 7 13
1812[4] Arctic Poppy (USA) **(46)***(13) (IABalding)* 3-7-5 (7) MartinDwyer(13) (b.off hind: racd stands' side: a outpcd & bhd) 1¾ 14
1679[15] Cavatina **(68)***(32) (TWDonnelly)* 5-10-0 NConnorton(11) (b: racd stands' side: outpcd fr ½-wy) 1¼ 15
1760[7] Joyful Times **(41)** *(MrsNMacauley)* 3-7-7 ClaireBalding(16) (racd stands' side: rdn & bhd fr ½-wy) 4 16
180[8] Anytime Baby **(46)** *(PTDalton)* 3-7-12 JFanning(15) (Withdrawn not under Starter's orders: ref to ent stalls) W

LONG HANDICAP Miss Tri Colour 7-0 Joyful Times 7-4

, **11/4** Profit Release (IRE) (op 9/2), **5/1** Kilnamartyra Girl, **6/1** Poyle Jezebelle, **7/1** Racing Brenda, **8/1** Arctic Poppy (USA), **10/1** BELLEMINETTE (IRE), **11/1** Sea-Ayr (IRE), **12/1** Cafe Solo, **14/1** Miss Vaxette, **16/1** Just Whistle, Joyful Times, Enchanteur, **20/1** Cavatina, Ikis Girl, **25/1** Miss Tri Colour, Ballard Ring (IRE), CSF £124.29 CT £1,261.28 TOTE £21.70: £3.70 £2.40 £3.00 £1.30 (£115.60) Trio £701.00; £345.57 to Doncaster 2/7/95 OWNER Mrs Judy Mihalop (PONTYPRIDD) BRED Kitty's Sister Syndicate 16 Rn 1m 25.63 (2.23) SF: 35/28/18/32/19/21/6/13/28/7/15/2/-/-/7/-/-

WEIGHT FOR AGE 3yo-8lb

T/Plpt: £1,019.70 (14.28 Tckts). T/Qdpt: Not won; £199.90 to Doncaster 2/7/95 AA

1980-LINGFIELD (L-H)
Saturday July 1st (AWT Standard, Turf Good to firm, Firm back st)

WEATHER: sunny WIND: slt half against

2089

ELIZABETH MASSEY APPRENTICE H'CAP (0-70) (3-Y.O+) (Class F) £2,588.50 (£736.00: £365.50) **1m 3f 106y** Stalls: High GOING minus 0.33 sec (GF) 6-10 (6-10)

1974* **Bronze Runner (35)***(46)*(Fav)*(SMellor)* 11-7-12b 5x ADaly(7) (mod 3rd st: hdwy over 2f out: hrd rdn fnl f: led last stride) — 1
1518[8] Harding Brown (USA) **(50)***(61) (GHarwood)* 3-7-9v(6) GayeHarwood(4) (lw: led: rdn wl ins fnl f: hdd last stride) s.h 2
1694[10] Jarzon Dancer **(38)***(36) (DAWilson)* 7-7-5 (10)ow8 RachaelMoody(2) (b: mod 5th st: hdwy over 1f out: one pce) 3½ 3
1817[7] Jean de Florette (USA) **(33)***(38) (JohnBerry)* 4-7-10 SLanigan(1) (hdwy over 1f out: r.o) ½ 4
1367[7] Tadellal (IRE) **(59)***(60) (BAPearce)* 4-9-3 (5) JWilkinson(5) (lw: chsd ldr: hrd rdn over 2f out: wknd 1f out) 3 5
1917[2] Gulf Bay **(43)***(39) (MBell)* 3-6-12 (10)ow1 RMullen(6) (lw: mod 4th st: hdwy over 2f out: wknd over 1f out) 3 6
277[10] Pearly River **(65)***(54) (DrJDScargill)* 4-9-4 (10) CDomergue(3) (mod 6th st: a bhd) 6 7

LONG HANDICAP Gulf Bay 6-11

9/4 BRONZE RUNNER, **5/1** Gulf Bay, **11/2** Jean de Florette (USA), **6/1** Tadellal (IRE), **7/1** Harding Brown (USA), Pearly River (9/2-8/1), **33/1** Jarzon Dancer, CSF £15.07 TOTE £2.50: £1.10 £4.10 (£10.70) OWNER Austin Stroud & Co Ltd (SWINDON) BRED Miss K. Rausing 7 Rn

2m 28.92 (6.92) SF: 9/12/-/1/23/-/17
WEIGHT FOR AGE 3yo-12lb

2090 SHEILA WATSON BIRTHDAY (S) H'CAP (0-60) (3-Y.O+) (Class G) £2,623.80 (£726.80: £347.40)
1m 5f (Equitrack) Stalls: Centre GOING minus 0.65 sec per fur (FST) 6-40 (6-41)

1319⁷ **Glow Forum (26)***(35) (GLMoore)* 4-8-4 MFenton(4) (hdwy over 3f out: chsd ldr over 2f out: led ins fnl f: r.o wl)........— 1
1799³ Valiant Toski **(43)***(50)*(Fav)*(MCPipe)* 4-9-7b BDoyle(2) (lw: led: clr over 3f out: hdd ins fnl f: unable qckn)........1½ 2
894⁸ Verro (USA) **(19)***(20) (KBishop)* 8-7-4e(7) SLanigan(11) (lw: chsd ldr 12f out tl over 2f out: one pce)........5 3
1759⁵ Perfect Ending **(50)***(50) (CACyzer)* 4-10-0 DBiggs(9) (lw: s.s: hdwy over 1f out: nvr nrr)........1¼ 4
1607¹⁰ Teoroma **(31)***(28) (DrJDScargill)* 5-8-2 (7) CDomergue(10) (s.s: nvr nr to chal)........2 5
1594⁸ Cone Lane **(20)***(16) (BGubby)* 9-7-5 (7)ow1 JoHunnam(1) (b: bhd fnl 7f)........hd 6
1427⁶ Horsetrader **(48)***(38) (RHannon)* 3-8-5 (7) DaneO'Neill(6) (no hdwy fnl 4f)........6 7
1622⁷ Rejects Reply **(31)***(20) (WJMusson)* 5-8-9b GHind(8) (hld up: rdn over 3f out: sn wknd)........hd 8
1854³ Tout de Val **(31)***(17) (KBishop)* 6-8-2 (7) ADaly(7) (lw: prom 9f)........2½ 9
1794⁹ Run High **(41)***(17) (PMitchell)* 12-9-5 SO'Gorman(5) (a bhd)........8 10
1514²⁰ Brooke Wood **(33)** *(MissBSanders)* 3-7-8 (3)ow3 DWright(3) (lw: prom 6f: t.o)........dist 11

7/4 Valiant Toski, **11/2** Rejects Reply, **13/2** Horsetrader, **8/1** Tout de Val, **9/1** Teoroma, **10/1** Run High (8/1-12/1), **14/1** GLOW FORUM (10/1-16/1), **16/1** Cone Lane, Perfect Ending, **20/1** Brooke Wood, **33/1** Verro (USA), CSF £37.76 CT £767.69 TOTE £15.30: £3.50 £1.60 £10.00 (£25.20) Trio £246.90 OWNER The Forum Ltd (EPSOM) BRED Forum Bloodstock Ltd 11 Rn

2m 45.8 (3.30) SF: 18/33/3/33/11/-/7/3/-/-/-
WEIGHT FOR AGE 3yo-14lb
No bid.

2091 E.B.F. CRAWLEY MAIDEN STKS (2-Y.O) (Class D) £3,682.05 (£1,100.40: £526.70: £239.85) 5f
Stalls: Low GOING minus 0.33 sec per fur (GF) 7-10 (7-10)

1893⁴ **Tumbleweed Ridge** *(84+)*(Fav)*(BJMeehan)* 2-9-0 BDoyle(3) (lw: hld up: shkn up to ld over 1f out: easily)........— 1
1620⁴ Dashing Blue *(71) (IABalding)* 2-9-0 SO'Gorman(5) (lw: chsd ldr: led over 2f out tl over 1f out: unable qckn)........4 2
Red Acuisle (IRE) *(62) (MBell)* 2-9-0 MFenton(7) (unf: hdwy over 1f out: nvr nrr: bttr for r)........3 3
1833⁸ Heaven Sent (IRE) *(37) (PMitchell)* 2-8-9 RPerham(6) (lw: prom over 2f)........6 4
Grey Legend *(41) (RMFlower)* 2-9-0 AMorris(2) (neat: bit bkwd: a bhd)........½ 5
1384⁵ Dancing Jack *(30) (JJBridger)* 2-8-7 (7) ADaly(4) (lw: led over 2f)........3½ 6
Beeny *(20) (APJarvis)* 2-8-11 (3) DWright(1) (leggy: bit bkwd: a bhd)........3 7

2/5 TUMBLEWEED RIDGE, **9/2** Dashing Blue (5/2-5/1), **8/1** Red Acuisle (IRE) (5/1-10/1), **14/1** Dancing Jack (10/1-16/1), **33/1** Beeny, **50/1** Grey Legend, Heaven Sent (IRE), CSF £2.82 TOTE £1.50: £1.10 £2.10 (£1.90) OWNER The Tumbleweed Partnership (UPPER LAMBOURN) BRED R. A. Dalton 7 Rn

58.18 secs (1.18) SF: 49/36/27/2/6/-/-

OFFICIAL EXPLANATION **Grey Legend: the jockey reported that the gelding had gurgled during the race.**

2092 WIMPEY HOMES H'CAP (0-80) (3-Y.O+) (Class D) £3,630.90 (£1,081.20: £514.60: £231.30)
5f Stalls: Centre GOING minus 0.33 sec per fur (GF) 7-40 (7-41)

1777⁸ **Jade Pet (80)***(87) (RHannon)* 4-9-7 (7) DaneO'Neill(5) (hld up: rdn over 1f out: led nr fin)........— 1
2013⁴ Wasblest **(55)***(61)*(Fav)*(MJohnston)* 3-7-11 TWilliams(7) (chsd ldr: led over 1f out: hrd rdn fnl f: hdd nr fin)........nk 2
1550⁵ Shashi (IRE) **(76)***(82) (DMorley)* 3-9-4 MFenton(3) (hrd rdn & hdwy over 1f out: r.o wl)........s.h 3
1741* Giggleswick Girl **(63)***(67) (MRChannon)* 4-8-11 AClark(6) (lw: s.s: hdwy over 2f out: hrd rdn over 1f out: r.o)........½ 4
1972³ Miriam **(53)***(45) (MJFetherston-Godley)* 4-7-12 (3) SSanders(1) (led over 3f)........4 5
1832⁸ Bold Gem **(55)***(45) (BJMeehan)* 4-8-3 BDoyle(2) (hld up: rdn over 1f out: sn wknd)........½ 6
1942* Tee-Emm **(48)***(32) (PHowling)* 5-7-7 (3)ow3 DWright(4) (b.off hind: hld up: rdn over 2f out: wknd over 1f out)........1 7

LONG HANDICAP Tee-Emm 7-2

100/30 Wasblest, **4/1** Giggleswick Girl, Shashi (IRE), **6/1** JADE PET, **13/2** Miriam, **9/1** Bold Gem, Tee-Emm, CSF £23.81 TOTE £7.00: £2.70 £2.10 (£8.90) OWNER Mr Geoffrey Greenwood (MARLBOROUGH) BRED G.C.Greenwood and P.Crane 7 Rn 58.03 secs (1.03) SF: 65/33/54/45/23/23/10

WEIGHT FOR AGE 3yo-6lb

2093 MANSTON CLAIMING STKS (3-Y.O) (Class F) £3,023.00 (£838.00: £401.00)
7f (Equitrack) Stalls: Low GOING minus 0.65 sec per fur (FST) 8-10 (8-10)

1830 12 **Mediate (IRE) (58)***(69) (RHannon)* 3-8-3 (7) DaneO'Neill(4) (lw: lost pl over 4f out: rallied 3f out: led ins fnl f: r.o wl) ....— 1
1141 16 Dusk in Daytona **(62)***(63) (CJames)* 3-8-5 RPerham(7) (lw: led: hrd rdn over 1f out: hdd ins fnl f: r.o) ....nk 2
*1882*4 Montague Dawson (IRE) **(70)***(66) (MrsNMacauley)* 3-8-7 (3) SDrowne(3) (b.hind: lw: hld up: hrd rdn over 1f out: r.o) 1¼ 3
1812 5 Kreef **(60)***(44) (RJO'Sullivan)* 3-8-0 DBiggs(9) (a.p: rdn over 3f out: wknd over 1f out) 5 4
Endless Fantasy *(52) (CACyzer)* 3-8-9 MFenton(8) (leggy: s.s: hdwy over 1f out: nvr nrr) ....½ 5
1719 3 Equilibrium **(57)***(46)*(Fav)*(JWHills)* 3-8-3 AClark(6) (lw: a.p: rdn over 2f out: wknd over 1f out) ....hd 6
Lore *(39) (RIngram)* 3-8-5 TWilliams(5) (unf: scope: lw: plld hrd: rdn & hdwy over 3f out: wknd over 2f out) 4 7
1906 7 Sandra Dee (IRE) **(54)***(31) (BAPearce)* 3-7-12 (3)ow2 SSanders(1) (lw: bhd fnl 3f) ....½ 8
1812 8 Nyali Beach (IRE) **(50)***(19) (BJMeehan)* 3-7-9b NAdams(2) (chsd ldr 4f) 3½ 9

7/2 Equilibrium, **4/1** Nyali Beach (IRE), **5/1** Dusk in Daytona, **11/2** MEDIATE (IRE), **7/1** Montague Dawson (IRE), **8/1** Kreef (6/1-9/1), **12/1** Endless Fantasy, Sandra Dee (IRE) (op 8/1), **20/1** Lore, CSF £31.16 TOTE £5.20: £1.80 £2.20 £2.00 (£15.50) Trio £39.80 OWNER Mrs S. H. Spencer-Phillips (MARLBOROUGH) BRED Knocktoran Stud 9 Rn 1m 26.18 (3.18) SF: 4/-/1/-/-/-/-/-/-

2094 SAFFRON MEDIAN AUCTION MAIDEN STKS (3-Y.O) (Class F) £2,897.00
(£802.00: £383.00) **1m 1f** Stalls: Low GOING minus 0.33 sec (GF) 8-40 (8-41)

1748 2 **Rising Dough (IRE) (75)***(73)*(Fav)*(GLMoore)* 3-9-0 SWhitworth(1) (mde all: clr over 2f out: eased fnl f) ....— 1
1663 3 Braydon Forest **(67)***(70) (CJDrewe)* 3-9-0 BDoyle(3) (lw: chsd wnr: rdn over 3f out: r.o ins fnl f) 1½ 2
Adonisis *(63) (TTClement)* 3-8-11 (3) DWright(2) (str: bit bkwd: 4th st: rdn over 3f out: unable qckn) 4 3
Forest Mill *(51) (DWPArbuthnot)* 3-8-9 AClark(4) (b.hind: w'like: 3rd st: rdn over 3f out: wknd over 2f out) 4 4

4/7 RISING DOUGH (IRE), **2/1** Braydon Forest, **8/1** Forest Mill, **12/1** Adonisis (op 20/1), CSF £2.27 TOTE £1.60 (£1.60) OWNER Mr Bryan Pennick (EPSOM) BRED David John Brown 4 Rn
1m 54.8 (5.50) SF: 22/19/12/-

T/Plpt: £26.10 (292.73 Tckts). T/Qdpt: £4.10 (15.89 Tckts). AK

2059-NEWCASTLE (L-H)
Saturday July 1st (Firm)
WEATHER: fine WIND: almost nil

2095 E.B.F. MAIDEN STKS (2-Y.O) (Class D) £5,150.00 (£1,550.00: £750.00: £350.00)
5f Stalls: Centre GOING minus 0.39 sec per fur (F) 2-10 (2-12)

1779 2 **Atraf** *(86) (DMorley)* 2-9-0 RHills(1) (w ldrs: led over 1f out: drvn out) ....— 1
1877 3 Bollin Dorothy *(75) (MHEasterby)* 2-8-9 MBirch(3) (w ldrs: nt qckn fnl f) 2 2
Silver Border *(78)*(Fav)*(IABalding)* 2-9-0 KDarley(5) (gd sort: rangy: effrt ½-wy: styd on fnl f: nvr nr to chal) ....½ 3
1670 2 Pharmacy *(69) (JWWatts)* 2-8-9 GDuffield(2) (lw: led tl over 1f out: one pce) 1¼ 4
1017 2 Branston Danni *(63) (MrsJRRamsden)* 2-8-9 KFallon(6) (b.nr hind: sn outpcd: effrt ½-wy: kpt on same pce: wknd towards fin) 2 5
Europex *(67) (MHEasterby)* 2-9-0 SMaloney(4) (leggy: bit bkwd: unruly s: s.i.s: bhd: sme hdwy fnl f: n.d) ....nk 6

15/8 Silver Border, **11/4** Pharmacy, **100/30** Branston Danni, **4/1** ATRAF, **14/1** Bollin Dorothy (op 8/1), **40/1** Europex, CSF £42.10 TOTE £4.10: £2.30 £2.80 (£18.70) OWNER Mr Hamdan Al Maktoum (NEWMARKET) BRED R. T. and Mrs Watson 6 Rn 61.16 secs (2.76) SF: 28/17/20/11/5/9

2096 LADBROKE SPRINT TROPHY H'CAP (0-95) (3-Y.O+) (Class C)
£15,270.00 (£4,560.00: £2,180.00: £990.00)
6f Stalls: Centre GOING minus 0.28 sec per fur (GF) 2-45 (2-48)

1932[2] **Al Wujud (IRE) (53)**(*61*)(Fav)(*TDyer*) 4-7-7 JQuinn(6) (lw: trckd ldrs: effrt over 2f out: styd on wl to ld ins fnl f) — 1
1832[3] Patsy Grimes **(64)**(*70*) (*LJHolt*) 5-8-4 AMcGlone(1) (prom: hdwy 2f out: styd on u.p ins fnl f) ..¾ 2
1996[8] Plum First **(60)**(*66*) (*LRLloyd-James*) 5-8-0b JFanning(5) (b.hind: w ldr: led over 1f out: hdd & nt qckn ins fnl f) hd 3
1441* Barato **(72)**(*76*) (*MrsJRRamsden*) 4-8-12 JFortune(2) (b.nr hind: hdwy over 2f out: styd on same pce fnl f) ½ 4
Sky Music **(77)**(*80*) (*MissSEHall*) 4-8-10 (7) MHenry(12) (trckd ldrs stands' side: r.o wl ins fnl f) ½ 5
1895[25] Rock Symphony **(88)**(*90*) (*WJHaggas*) 5-10-0 RHills(11) (s.i.s: racd stands' side: sn trckng ldrs: r.o fnl f) nk 6
1599[10] Captain Carat **(65)**(*67*) (*MrsJRRamsden*) 4-8-5 KFallon(9) (swtchd rt s: racd stands' side: hdwy 2f out: styd on wl ins fnl f) hd 7
1668[10] Flashy's Son **(65)**(*67*) (*GMMoore*) 7-8-0 (5) AWhelan(13) (b: b.off hind: led stands' side tl over 1f out: wknd ins fnl f) hd 8
1895[6] Castlerea Lad **(88)**(*85*) (*RHollinshead*) 6-10-0 KDarley(4) (lw: hld up: effrt over 2f out: nvr nr to chal) 1¾ 9
1809[3] Bayin (USA) **(68)**(*58*) (*MDIUsher*) 6-8-8 RStreet(10) (s.i.s: bhd stands' side: sme hdwy over 2f out: wknd over 1f out) 2½ 10
1648[2] Croft Pool **(83)**(*71*) (*JAGlover*) 4-9-9 TIves(8) (chsd ldrs: rdn ½-wy: sn lost pl) 1 11
1604[10] Petite-D-Argent **(68)**(*54*) (*TDyer*) 6-8-8 GBardwell(3) (led tl over 1f out: sn wknd) ½ 12
1918[4] Here Comes a Star **(73)**(*54*) (*JMCarr*) 7-8-13 TQuinn(7) (bhd fr ½-wy) 2 13

10/3 AL WUJUD (IRE) (5/1-3/1), **13/2** Castlerea Lad, Barato, **8/1** Bayin (USA), Here Comes a Star, **9/1** Croft Pool, Captain Carat, Patsy Grimes, **10/1** Rock Symphony, **12/1** Sky Music, **16/1** Flashy's Son, **20/1** Plum First, **40/1** Petite-D-Argent, CSF £34.34 CT £504.78 TOTE £4.30: £1.70 £3.20 £9.20 (£20.60) Trio £285.30 OWNER Mr Mike Flynn (INVERGOWRIE) BRED Shadwell Estate Company Limited 13 Rn 1m 12.59 (1.09) SF: 40/49/45/55/59/69/46/46/64/37/50/33/33

2097 WHITLEY BAY HOLIDAY PARK CHIPCHASE STKS (Listed) (3-Y.O+)
(Class A) £11,512.80 (£4,255.20: £2,037.60: £828.00: £324.00: £122.40)
6f Stalls: Centre GOING minus 0.28 sec per fur (GF) 3-20 (3-20)

1895[24] **Branston Abby (IRE) (107)**(*115*) (*MJohnston*) 6-9-0 DHolland(2) (effrt ½-wy: hdwy 2f out: r.o wl to ld jst ins fnl f: hld on wl) — 1
1848[4] Inzar (USA) **(105)**(*115*)(Fav)(*PFICole*) 3-8-8 TQuinn(3) (lw: sltly hmpd s: sn trckng ldrs: effrt 2f out: ev ch ins fnl f: r.o u.p) ½ 2
1488[3] Triple Joy **(98)**(*110*) (*SirMarkPrescott*) 4-8-10 GDuffield(6) (trckd ldr: sltly hmpd 4f out: led over 1f out: kpt on wl) s.h 3
1895[4] Venture Capitalist **(105)**(*107*) (*DNicholls*) 6-9-1 AlexGreaves(1) (lw: dwlt: bhd tl hdwy 2f out: styd on same pce fnl f) 3 4
1480[7] Wavian **(103)**(*102*) (*RCharlton*) 3-8-8 KDarley(4) (chsd ldrs: n.m.r over 1f out: sn wknd) 1¾ 5
1284[5] Storiths (IRE) **(108)**(*91*) (*JWWatts*) 5-9-1b NConnorton(5) (b: s.i.s: a in rr) 4 6
1870[10] Roger the Butler (IRE) **(104)**(*92*) (*MBell*) 5-9-5 JCarroll(7) (b: led: hdd over 1f out: sn wknd) 1¼ 7

15/8 Inzar (USA), **7/2** Triple Joy, **4/1** Venture Capitalist (3/1-9/2), **8/1** Roger the Butler (IRE) (6/1-9/1), **9/1** Storiths (IRE) (op 5/1), BRANSTON ABBY (IRE) (op 6/1), **12/1** Wavian, CSF £25.52 TOTE £10.60: £3.90 £1.70 (£12.70) OWNER Mr J. D. Abell (MIDDLEHAM) BRED John David Abell 7 Rn 1m 11.49 (-0.01) SF: 75/68/70/67/55/51/52
WEIGHT FOR AGE 3yo-7lb

2098 'NEWCASTLE BROWN ALE' NORTHUMBERLAND PLATE H'CAP (3-Y.O+)
(Class B) £50,071.00 (£18,589.00: £8,969.50: £3,722.50: £1,536.25: £661.75)
2m 19y Stalls: Centre GOING minus 0.39 sec per fur (F) 3-55 (3-57)

1132[6] **Bold Gait (105)**(*121*) (*JRFanshawe*) 4-9-10 DHarrison(5) (lw: hld up: hdwy ½-wy: edgd lft appr st: swtchd outside over 2f out: led over 1f out: rdn & r.o strly) — 1
1768[6] Trans Siberia **(83)**(*93*) (*SPCWoods*) 4-8-2 ow2 KDarley(3) (mid div: hdwy 6f out: styd on wl fnl 2f) 4 2
1768[3] George Dillingham **(83)**(*94*) (*DenysSmith*) 5-8-2 JCarroll(4) (in tch: jnd ldrs ½-wy: led over 2f out tl over 1f out: r.o same pce) ¾ 3
1840[6] Noufari (FR) **(74)**(*85*) (*RHollinshead*) 4-7-7 NCarlisle(9) (sn bhd: drvn along 6f out: styd on wl fnl 3f: nt rch ldrs) hd 4

1840^{20} Always Aloof (USA) **(89)***(100) (MRStoute)* 4-8-8 RHills(8) (in tch: hdwy ½-wy: prom whn bdly hmpd & lost pl appr st: hdwy 2f out: styd on wl ins fnl f)....................................nk **5**
1767^{2} Highflying **(78)***(89) (GMMoore)* 9-7-11 JFanning(16) (lw: jnd ldrs ½-wy: sn drvn along: ev ch & hung lft over 2f out: one pce)....................................nk **6**
1313* Latahaab (USA) **(88)***(95)*(Fav)*(RAkehurst)* 4-8-7 TQuinn(10) (lw: led 1f: chsd ldrs: led over 3f out tl over 2f out: sn wknd)....................................3½ **7**
1794^{8} Ivor's Flutter **(78)***(85) (DRCElsworth)* 6-7-11 AMackay(14) (b: bhd: n.m.r appr st: kpt on fnl 2f: nvr nr to chal)....................................s.h **8**
1852^{3} Pedraza **(100)***(107) (HRACecil)* 3-8-2 AMcGlone(2) (lw: plld hrd: trckd ldrs: led 4f out: sn hdd: wknd over 2f out)....................................½ **9**
998^{7} Mondragon **(74)***(76) (MrsMReveley)* 5-7-7 NKennedy(1) (hdwy 6f out: hmpd appr st: nt rcvr)..5 **10**
1840^{24} Star Rage (IRE) **(77)***(75) (MJohnston)* 5-7-3 (7) PFessey(17) (s.i.s: bhd: effrt u.p 4f out: no imp)....................................4 **11**
1840^{4} Shadirwan (IRE) **(75)***(62) (RAkehurst)* 4-7-8 JQuinn(12) (in tch: effrt over 3f out: sn wknd)....................................11 **12**
1869^{6} The Flying Phantom **(96)***(79) (MHTompkins)* 4-9-1 PRobinson(15) (led after 1f to 4f out: wknd over 2f out)....................................3½ **13**
1768^{5} Blaze Away (USA) **(79)***(60) (IABalding)* 4-7-5b(7) MartinDwyer(6) (mid div: drvn along 5f out: sn wknd)....................................2 **14**
1973^{7} Miroswaki (USA) **(76)***(52) (GFierro)* 5-7-6 (3)ow2 DarrenMoffatt(13) (bhd: sme hdwy 6f out: n.m.r appr st: sn wknd)....................................3 **15**
1607^{5} Chief Minister (IRE) **(74)***(52) (TDyer)* 6-7-7 GBardwell(7) (s.i.s: sn drvn along & bhd) ....nk **16**
1805* Tethys (USA) **(94)** *(JLEyre)* 4-8-13 6x JFortune(11) (chsd ldrs: drvn along 6f out: wkng whn bdly hmpd appr st: virtually p.u)....................................dist **17**

LONG HANDICAP Mondragon 7-6 Miroswaki (USA) 6-8 Chief Minister (IRE) 6-11

5/1 Latahaab (USA), **6/1** Pedraza, **13/2** Always Aloof (USA), **7/1** Shadirwan (IRE), Highflying, **12/1** BOLD GAIT, Trans Siberia, **14/1** Tethys (USA), Blaze Away (USA), Star Rage (IRE), **16/1** Mondragon, George Dillingham, **20/1** Noufari (FR), **25/1** The Flying Phantom, Chief Minister (IRE), **33/1** Ivor's Flutter, **100/1** Miroswaki (USA), CSF £143.04 CT £2,125.42 TOTE £15.50: £2.70 £2.80 £3.70 £6.40 (£48.00) Trio £249.20 OWNER Mrs I. Phillips (NEWMARKET) BRED Ian H. Wills 17 Rn

3m 27.36 (1.86) SF: 68/40/41/32/47/36/42/32/37/23/22/9/26/7/-/-/-

WEIGHT FOR AGE 3yo-17lb

2099 JOURNAL 'GOOD MORNING' H'CAP (0-100) (3-Y.O+) (Class C)

£11,550.00 (£3,450.00: £1,650.00: £750.00)
7f Stalls: Centre GOING minus 0.28 sec per fur (GF) 4-30 (4-31)

1299^{2} **Tawafij (USA)** **(82)***(89)*(Fav)*(TDyer)* 6-8-12 JFortune(7) (lw: trckd ldrs: led over 1f out: jst ct: fin 2nd, ½l: awrdd r)....................................— **1**
1806^{12} Emerging Market **(90)***(94) (JLDunlop)* 3-8-12 KDarley(4) (prom: effrt over 2f out: kpt on same pce appr fnl f: fin 3rd, 1½l: plcd 2nd).................................... **2**
1687^{10} Legal Fiction **(63)***(66) (MJohnston)* 4-7-7 JQuinn(2) (a chsng ldrs: hung rt 2f out: styng on same pce whn sltly hmpd over 1f out: fin 4th, 1¼l: plcd 3rd).................................... **3**
1915^{5} Kabil **(83)***(91) (HThomsonJones)* 3-8-5 RHills(8) (lw: hld up & bhd: nt clr run over 2f out: swtchd & squeezed thro over 1f out: r.o wl to ld wl ins fnl f: fin 1st: disq: plcd 4th).................................... **4**
1809^{9} Bold Angel **(71)***(73) (MHEasterby)* 8-8-1 SMaloney(3) (dwlt: sn chsng ldrs: rdn & edgd rt over 2f out: swvd rt 1f out: one pce)....................................¾ **5**
1299^{10} Sagebrush Roller **(84)***(85) (JWWatts)* 7-9-0 GDuffield(1) (bhd & drvn along: swtchd outside & hdwy over 2f out: no imp whn sltly hmpd jst ins fnl f)....................................hd **6**
1870^{11} Selhurstpark Flyer (IRE) **(84)***(77) (JBerry)* 4-9-0e JCarroll(6) (led tl hdd & wknd over 1f out)....................................4 **7**
1698^{6} En Attendant (FR) **(98)***(85) (BHanbury)* 7-10-0 TIves(5) (b: b.hind: dwlt: bhd: hdwy over 2f out: no imp whn hmpd jst ins fnl f)....................................3 **8**

LONG HANDICAP Legal Fiction 7-6

11/4 TAWAFIJ (USA), **4/1** Emerging Market, **9/2** Kabil (6/1-7/2), **6/1** Bold Angel, **13/2** Selhurstpark Flyer (IRE), **7/1** En Attendant (FR), Sagebrush Roller, **20/1** Legal Fiction, CSF £14.37 CT £171.17 TOTE £3.60: £1.40 £1.80 £3.30 (£7.60) OWNER Mr Stephen Laidlaw (INVERGOWRIE) BRED Oxford Stable 8 Rn

1m 25.44 (1.14) SF: -/-/-/53/-/-/-/-

WEIGHT FOR AGE 3yo-8lb

STEWARDS' ENQUIRY R Hills suspended 10-17/7/95 (irresponsible riding).

2100 NORTHUMBRIAN ENVIRONMENTAL MANAGEMENT MAIDEN STKS (3-Y.O+)

(Class D) £6,961.25 (£2,090.00: £1,007.50: £466.25)
1m (round) Stalls: Low GOING minus 0.39 sec per fur (F) 5-00 (5-03)

1796^{2} **Touch a Million (USA)** *(88)*(Fav)*(EALDunlop)* 3-8-12 KDarley(2) (lw: sn pushed along: hdwy on outside over 2f out: styd on wl u.p to ld ins fnl f: all out)....................................— **1**

1732[2] Balasara (IRE) **(80)***(87) (DRCElsworth)* 5-9-7b AProcter(3) (trckd ldrs: effrt & n.m.r 2f out: squeezed thro & ev ch ins fnl f: hrd rdn & edgd lft nr fin)....nk 2
1309[2] Takhlid (USA) **(80)***(84) (HThomsonJones)* 4-9-7 RHills(1) (plld hrd: led tl ins fnl f: wkng whn hmpd cl home)....1½ 3
1804[2] Venice Beach *(76) (BWHills)* 3-8-12 JCarroll(4) (trckd ldrs: rdn over 2f out: wknd over 1f out)....4 4

5/4 TOUCH A MILLION (USA), **3/1** Balasara (IRE), Venice Beach (op 2/1), **9/2** Takhlid (USA), CSF £5.10 TOTE £1.90 (£4.10) OWNER Maktoum Al Maktoum (NEWMARKET) BRED Gainsborough Farm Inc. 4 Rn
1m 43.36 (4.36) SF: 22/30/27/10
WEIGHT FOR AGE 3yo-9lb
STEWARDS' ENQUIRY Procter suspended 10-14/7/95 (careless riding).

2101 SILVER RING CELEBRATION H'CAP (0-85) (3-Y.O+) (Class D)
£6,863.75 (£2,060.00: £992.50: £458.75)
1m 4f 93y Stalls: Low GOING minus 0.39 sec per fur (F) 5-30 (5-31)

1612[4] **Tony's Fen (74)***(83) (DRCElsworth)* 6-9-7 (5) AProcter(4) (b: b.hind: hld up gng wl: smooth hdwy 2f out: shkn up to ld ins fnl f: rdn out)....— 1
2062[3] Vindaloo **(70)***(76) (JLHarris)* 3-8-2 (7) PFessey(5) (hld up: hdwy 3f out: led over 2f out: edgd rt & hdd ins fnl f: kpt on same pce)....2 2
1621[6] Cumbrian Rhapsody **(62)***(66)*(Fav)*(MHEasterby)* 5-9-0 MBirch(1) (hld up: effrt over 2f out: n.m.r: styd on same pce whn n.m.r ins fnl f)....1¾ 3
967[4] Sunderland Echo **(75)***(70) (MrsMReveley)* 6-9-13 KDarley(3) (trckd ldr: plld hrd: led over 3f out: hdd over 2f out: fnl nil)....7 4
1872[19] Manful **(77)***(70) (JHetherton)* 3-9-2 NKennedy(6) (chsd ldrs: drvn along 5f out: wknd over 2f out)....1½ 5
1782[4] Jadwal (USA) **(85)** *(DMorley)* 3-9-10 RHills(2) (led tl over 3f out: wknd 2f out: eased)....dist 6

11/4 Cumbrian Rhapsody, **3/1** Vindaloo, **100/30** Sunderland Echo, **7/2** TONY'S FEN, **4/1** Jadwal (USA), **9/1** Manful, CSF £15.29 TOTE £6.40: £2.50 £1.90 (£11.60) OWNER The Executive (WHITCOMBE) BRED Stackallan Stud 6 Rn
2m 40.81 (2.31) SF: 65/45/48/52/39/-
WEIGHT FOR AGE 3yo-13lb
STEWARDS' ENQUIRY Fessey suspended 10/7/95 (careless riding).

T/Plpt: £535.40 (59.96 Tckts). T/Qdpt: £38.40 (7.7 Tckts). WG

2065-NEWMARKET (R-H)
Saturday July 1st (Good to firm)
WEATHER: cloudy & warm WIND: slt against

2102 GURTEEN CLAIMING STKS (3-Y.O) (Class E) £3,687.50 (£1,100.00: £525.00: £237.50) 1m (July) Stalls: Low GOING minus 0.16 sec per fur (GF) 1-55 (1-56)

1735[6] **Care And Comfort (58)***(67) (GWragg)* 3-8-7 MHills(7) (lw: hld up: hdwy over 2f out: hung lft: rdn to ld ins fnl f: r.o)....— 1
766[15] Colosse **(51)***(56) (MAJarvis)* 3-7-8 (5) NVarley(5) (prom: led over 2f out: hdd ins fnl f: unable qckn)....1½ 2
1718[3] Irie Mon (IRE) **(60)***(60) (JWHills)* 3-8-5 ow1 JWeaver(6) (lw: chsd ldrs: outpcd over 2f out: r.o ins fnl f)....½ 3
1735[7] Elite Racing **(62)***(72) (PFICole)* 3-9-3 WCarson(2) (chsd ldrs: lost pl 2f out: r.o ins fnl f)....nk 4
Prince of Spades *(67) (CACyzer)* 3-8-12 DBiggs(9) (bit bkwd: hld up: hdwy over 3f out: r.o one pce fnl f)....nk 5
1748[3] Empower (IRE) **(77)***(72) (RHannon)* 3-9-8 GCarter(3) (mid div: rdn over 2f out: no imp)....2½ 6
907[8] Rock Foundation **(65)***(53) (PCHaslam)* 3-8-10 MTebbutt(4) (hld up: hdwy over 4f out: hrd rdn over 1f out: sn btn)....3½ 7
1504[5] Contract Venture (IRE) **(65)***(58) (WJarvis)* 3-9-2 LDettori(1) (led over 5f: wknd fnl f)....½ 8
1914[4] Time Leader **(70)***(32)*(Fav)*(MRStoute)* 3-8-12v WRSwinburn(8) (prom: chsd ldr 5f out: wknd qckly over 2f out: t.o)....11 9

2/1 Time Leader, **11/2** Contract Venture (IRE), Irie Mon (IRE), **6/1** Empower (IRE) (op 4/1), **10/1** CARE AND COMFORT, Elite Racing (8/1-12/1), **14/1** Rock Foundation, **20/1** Colosse, **33/1** Prince of Spades, CSF £144.07 TOTE £10.60: £2.10 £9.60 £1.60 (£132.90) Trio £425.80 OWNER Sir Philip Oppenheimer (NEWMARKET) BRED Hascombe and Valiant Studs 9 Rn
1m 42.02 (4.32) SF: 35/24/28/40/35/40/21/26/-
Care and Comfort clmd S. Benney £10,000

2103 DOM RUINART CHAMPAGNE H'CAP (0-90) (3-Y.O) (Class C) £6,316.00 (£1,888.00: £904.00: £412.00)
1m (July) Stalls: Low GOING minus 0.16 sec per fur (GF) 2-30 (2-33)

1306[6] **Twilight Patrol (86)***(96) (RHannon)* 3-8-10 (7) DaneO'Neill(8) (hld up: hdwy over 2f out: led ins fnl f: r.o wl) — 1
1748* Eurolink the Rebel (USA) **(80)***(87) (RAkehurst)* 3-8-11 LDettori(7) (hld up in tch: ev ch 1f out: unable qckn) 1½ 2
1693* Nordinex (IRE) **(75)***(82) (RWArmstrong)* 3-8-6 MHills(9) (hld up: hdwy over 2f out: nt clr run over 1f out: r.o) s.h 3
1839[20] Mister Fire Eyes (IRE) **(75)***(76) (CEBrittain)* 3-8-6v BDoyle(6) (chsd ldr: led 2f out: hdd & unable qckn ins fnl f) 3 4
1605* Floridante (USA) **(77)***(78) (PFICole)* 3-8-8 WCarson(11) (lw: hld up: hdwy u.p 2f out: no ex fnl f) s.h 5
1180[10] The Stager (IRE) **(74)***(75) (JRJenkins)* 3-8-5 JWeaver(5) (lw: led over 6f: no ex fnl f) hd 6
1874* My Gina **(77)***(66)*(Fav)*(MRStoute)* 3-8-8 RCochrane(12) (mid div: rdn 2f out: sn btn) 6 7
250[5] Whackford Squeers **(68)***(55) (CACyzer)* 3-7-13 DBiggs(3) (prom over 6f) ¾ 8
1825[10] Verde Luna **(72)***(57) (MHTompkins)* 3-8-3 SMulvey(13) (prom 6f) 1 9
1474[6] Nordic Doll (IRE) **(74)***(57) (BWHills)* 3-8-0 (5)ow1 JDSmith(10) (hld up: nvr trbld ldrs) ¾ 10
1812[2] Seventeens Lucky **(69)***(48) (BobJones)* 3-8-0 GCarter(4) (in tch: drvn along ½-wy: wknd 2f out: eased) 2½ 11
1281[4] Sarasota Storm **(72)***(49) (MBell)* 3-8-3 MFenton(14) (s.i.s: sn prom: wknd wl over 2f out) ¾ 12
963[4] Sharpical **(73)***(10) (JRFanshawe)* 3-7-13 (5) NVarley(1) (prom to ½-wy: sn t.o) 20 13

9/2 My Gina, **11/2** Eurolink the Rebel (USA) (4/1-6/1), **6/1** Nordinex (IRE), Floridante (USA), **10/1** Seventeens Lucky, Sarasota Storm, **12/1** Verde Luna, **14/1** TWILIGHT PATROL, Sharpical, The Stager (IRE), **16/1** Nordic Doll (IRE), **20/1** Whackford Squeers, **25/1** Mister Fire Eyes (IRE), CSF £83.82 CT £475.19 TOTE £23.00: £6.20 £2.00 £1.90 (£50.30) Trio £236.00 OWNER Cheveley Park Stud (MARLBOROUGH) BRED Cheveley Park Stud Ltd 13 Rn
1m 40.43 (2.73) SF: 60/51/46/40/42/39/30/19/21/21/12/13/-

2104 FRED ARCHER STKS (Listed) (4-Y.O+) (Class A) £11,922.30 (£4,294.80: £2,057.40: £837.00: £328.50)
1m 4f (July) Stalls: High GOING minus 0.16 sec per fur (GF) 3-05 (3-05)

1585[3] **Saxon Maid (97)***(108)*(Fav)*(LMCumani)* 4-8-6 LDettori(4) (chsd ldr: led over 1f out: pushed out) — 1
Magical Retreat (USA) **(96)***(107) (CACyzer)* 5-8-6 DBiggs(2) (chsd ldrs: led over 2f out: hdd over 1f out: unable qckn nr fin) 1 2
1585[2] Waiting **(104)***(111) (PFICole)* 4-8-11 WCarson(3) (lw: hld up & bhd: hdwy to ld over 3f out: hdd over 2f out: edgd lft & no ex fnl f) ¾ 3
1585[7] Garden of Heaven (USA) **(98)***(105) (CEBrittain)* 6-8-11 BDoyle(5) (hld up in tch: rdn over 1f out: eased whn btn) 4 4
Coigach **(106)***(88) (HRACecil)* 4-8-12 WRyan(1) (bit bkwd: led over 8f: grad wknd: t.o) 14 5

13/8 SAXON MAID, **9/4** Waiting, **11/4** Coigach (2/1-3/1), **14/1** Magical Retreat (USA), **16/1** Garden of Heaven (USA), CSF £16.59 TOTE £2.40: £1.10 £2.90 (£15.40) OWNER Sheikh Mohammed (NEWMARKET) BRED Cleaboy Farms Co 5 Rn 2m 34.38 (5.68) SF: 40/39/43/37/20

2105 VAN GEEST CRITERION STKS (Gp 3) (3-Y.O+) (Class A) £23,807.00 (£8,813.00: £4,231.50: £1,732.50: £691.25: £274.75)
7f (July) Stalls: Low GOING minus 0.16 sec per fur (GF) 3-35 (3-37)

1107[4] **Pipe Major (IRE) (121)***(123)*(Fav)*(PCHaslam)* 3-8-8 JWeaver(8) (lw: chsd ldrs: led over 1f out: rdn out) — 1
1586[5] Prince of India **(103)***(122) (LordHuntingdon)* 3-8-8 PatEddery(7) (lw: hld up in tch: rdn & ev ch fnl f: unable qckn nr fin) ½ 2
1806[3] Stylish Ways (IRE) **(96)***(110) (GWragg)* 3-8-8 MHills(6) (lw: hld up & bhd: hdwy over 2f out: r.o: nt rch ldrs) 5 3
1706a[2] Mistle Cat (USA) **(111)***(104) (SPCWoods)* 5-9-2 WWoods(5) (lw: w ldr: led over 4f out: hdd over 1f out: wknd fnl f) 3 4
1848[5] Options Open **(102)***(94) (SbinSuroor)* 3-8-8 LDettori(1) (led over 2f: rdn over 1f out: eased whn btn ins fnl f) 4 5
1837[8] Star of Zilzal (USA) **(104)***(88) (MRStoute)* 3-8-8 WRSwinburn(3) (hld up: rdn over 2f out: no rspnse) 3 6
1586* Mr Martini (IRE) **(103)***(90) (CEBrittain)* 5-9-7 BDoyle(2) (lw: prom: rdn ½-wy: sn lost pl) 1 7

1618* Mutakddim (USA) **(111)***(85) (JHMGosden)* 4-9-2 WCarson(4) (trckd ldrs: rdn ½-wy: wknd over 2f out) ....hd **8**

5/2 PIPE MAJOR (IRE), **4/1** Mistle Cat (USA), **9/2** Mutakddim (USA), **6/1** Options Open, Star of Zilzal (USA), **8/1** Prince of India, **12/1** Stylish Ways (IRE), **20/1** Mr Martini (IRE), CSF £21.41 TOTE £4.00: £1.50 £2.40 £2.30 (£27.70) OWNER Lord Scarsdale (MIDDLEHAM) BRED W. Maxwell Ervine in Ireland 8 Rn 1m 25.0 (0.60) SF: 73/72/60/62/44/38/48/43

WEIGHT FOR AGE 3yo-8lb

2106

EWAR STUD EMPRESS STKS (Listed) (2-Y.O F) (Class A) £9,594.00 (£3,546.00: £1,698.00: £690.00: £270.00: £102.00)
6f (July) Stalls: Low GOING minus 0.16 sec per fur (GF) 4-10 (4-10)

1627* **Maid For The Hills** *(87)*(Fav)*(DRLoder)* 2-8-11 PatEddery(5) (hld up: hdwy over 2f out: rdn to ld wl ins fnl f: r.o) ....— **1**
1650* Persian Secret (FR) **(85)***(86) (JWWatts)* 2-8-11 LDettori(3) (chsd ldr: led over 1f out: sn rdn: hdd & unable qckn wl ins fnl f) ....nk **2**
1697* React *(78) (WJarvis)* 2-8-8 WRSwinburn(2) (led: hdd over 1f out: no ex ins fnl f) 2 **3**
1348* Solar Crystal (IRE) *(76) (HRACecil)* 2-8-11 WRyan(7) (trckd ldrs: rdn over 1f out: no imp) 2 **4**
1634³ Cyrillic *(67) (PAKelleway)* 2-8-8 MWigham(1) (prom: rdn over 2f out: sn lost pl: kpt on ins fnl f) 2 **5**
1384⁴ Naissant *(66) (CEBrittain)* 2-8-8 BDoyle(4) (chsd ldrs over 4f) ....nk **6**
1746* Prends Ca (IRE) *(65) (RHannon)* 2-8-11 JWeaver(6) (prom: rdn 2f out: sn lost tch) 1½ **7**

7/4 MAID FOR THE HILLS, **11/4** React, **100/30** Persian Secret (FR) (5/2-4/1), **7/1** Solar Crystal (IRE), **14/1** Prends Ca (IRE), **20/1** Naissant, **40/1** Cyrillic, CSF £7.57 TOTE £2.50: £1.70 £1.80 (£3.40) OWNER Mr Chris Brasher (NEWMARKET) BRED Mrs Mary Taylor 7 Rn 1m 14.31 (2.81) SF: 43/42/34/32/23/22/21

2107

KRIS MAIDEN STKS (2-Y.O) (Class D) £4,737.00 (£1,416.00: £678.00: £309.00)
7f (July) Stalls: Low GOING minus 0.16 sec per fur (GF) 4-45 (4-47)

Swift Fandango (USA) *(82+) (PFICole)* 2-9-0 RCochrane(6) (b.off hind: wl grwn: s.i.s: sn prom: chsd ldrs: led over 1f out: r.o strly) ....— **1**
1803² House of Riches *(76)*(Fav)*(LMCumani)* 2-9-0 PatEddery(9) (lw: chsd ldrs: led over 4f out: hdd over 1f out: unable qckn) 2½ **2**
Snow Falcon *(75) (MBell)* 2-9-0 MFenton(7) (unf: bit bkwd: a.p: rdn & edgd lft over 1f out: styd on ins fnl f) ....¾ **3**
Henry The Fifth *(63) (CEBrittain)* 2-9-0 BDoyle(3) (neat: chsd ldrs: outpcd appr fnl f) 5 **4**
White Settler *(61) (RHannon)* 2-9-0 MHills(4) (unf: scope: hld up in tch: plld hrd: effrt over 1f out: grad wknd) ....¾ **5**
Samim (USA) *(50) (JLDunlop)* 2-9-0 WCarson(10) (cmpt: prom: rdn ½-wy: sn lost tch) 5 **6**
1913³ Balpare *(43) (NACallaghan)* 2-8-9 GCarter(2) (hld up: nvr plcd to chal) 1 **7**
Again Together *(42) (NACallaghan)* 2-8-9 MTebbutt(8) (lt-f: s.i.s: hld up: bhd whn nt clr run 2f out: nt rch ldrs) ....½ **8**
1893¹⁴ Double Vintage (IRE) *(24) (MCChapman)* 2-8-11 (3) DRMcCabe(5) (led: hdd over 4f out: wknd over 2f out) 10 **9**

5/4 House of Riches (10/11-11/8), **7/2** SWIFT FANDANGO (USA), **9/2** Samim (USA), **14/1** Balpare, **20/1** White Settler, Snow Falcon, Henry The Fifth, **25/1** Again Together, **50/1** Double Vintage (IRE), CSF £7.55 TOTE £5.30: £1.70 £1.20 £3.00 (£4.00) Trio £35.50 OWNER Mr M. Arbib (WHATCOMBE) BRED M. Arbib 9 Rn 1m 28.79 (4.39) SF: 34/28/27/15/13/2/-/-/-

2108

W.I. (SUFFOLK WEST) 75TH ANNIVERSARY APPRENTICE H'CAP (0-70) (3-Y.O+) (Class E) £3,566.25 (£1,080.00: £527.50: £251.25)
7f (July) Stalls: Low GOING minus 0.16 sec per fur (GF) 5-20 (5-21)

1830⁶ **Broughtons Turmoil (52)***(69) (WJMusson)* 6-8-7 (3) JDSmith(8) (b.off fore: prom: led over 1f out: r.o wl) ....— **1**
Rise Up Singing **(60)***(63) (WJMusson)* 7-9-1b(3) PMcCabe(5) (chsd ldr: led over 2f out: hdd over 1f out: sn outpcd) 6 **2**
1975⁴ Great Hall **(53)***(54) (PDCundell)* 6-8-6b(5) DGriffiths(4) (bhd: styd on appr fnl f: nt rch ldrs) 1 **3**
*2271*¹² Mighty Kingdom (IRE) **(40)***(30) (JohnBerry)* 4-7-9 (3) NVarley(3) (prom: sn rdn along: wknd over 2f out) 5 **4**
1714¹⁹ Threshfield (USA) **(49)***(37) (BJCurley)* 9-8-0 (7) DLockhart(2) (prom over 4f) ....¾ **5**
*1980*⁴ Mr Teigh **(70)***(46) (KMcAuliffe)* 3-9-6v SSanders(9) (led over 4f: grad lost pl) 5 **6**
1855⁸ As Such (IRE) **(48)***(19) (NACallaghan)* 4-7-13 (7) MDavies(10) (hld up: a in rr) 2½ **7**
1692* Bonita **(57)***(16) (MrsLPiggott)* 3-8-2 (5) VictoriaAppleby(1) (b: prom 4f) 5 **8**

1778² Cats Bottom **(69)***(15)*(Fav)*(DJSCosgrove)* 3-9-2 (3) LNewton(6) (lw: hld up: hdwy over 3f out: rdn & wknd 2f out) 6 **9**
1827³ Spanish Stripper (USA) **(66)** *(MCChapman)* 4-9-10 DRMcCabe(7) (s.s: a outpcd & bhd) 9 **10**

11/4 Cats Bottom, **5/1** Great Hall, **11/2** Bonita, **13/2** Mighty Kingdom (IRE), **7/1** Rise Up Singing, Spanish Stripper (USA), **15/2** BROUGHTONS TURMOIL, **12/1** Mr Teigh (op 8/1), **16/1** Threshfield (USA), **25/1** As Such (IRE), CSF £57.74 CT £268.63 TOTE £13.80: £3.10 £2.70 £2.10 (£38.80) Trio £80.10 OWNER Broughton & Westwood (NEWMARKET) BRED Tally Ho Stud Co (U.K.) Ltd and Ninevah Ltd 10 Rn 1m 26.93 (2.53) SF: 51/45/36/12/19/20/1/-/-/-
WEIGHT FOR AGE 3yo-8lb

T/Jkpt: Not won; £30,277.69 to Doncaster 2/7/95. T/Plpt: £157.70 (189.02 Tckts). T/Qdpt: £8.90 (32.35 Tckts). CR

1714-CHEPSTOW (L-H)
Sunday July 2nd (Good to firm)
WEATHER: fine WIND: almost nil

2109 WELSH BOOKMAKERS ASSOCIATION H'CAP (0-70) (3-Y.O+) (Class E) £3,226.50 (£972.00: £471.00: £220.50)
1m 4f 23y Stalls: High GOING minus 0.55 sec per fur (F) 2-15 (2-15)

1622* **Casual Water (IRE) (52)***(64)*(Fav)*(AGNewcombe)* 4-8-11 TQuinn(2) (lw: plld hrd: chsd ldr 7f out: 2nd st: led 4f out: rdn 3f out: r.o wl) ....— **1**
2007² Dormy Three **(69)***(77)* *(RJHodges)* 5-10-0 JWilliams(1) (chsd ldr 5f: 3rd st: rdn & chsd wnr fnl 2f: no imp) 3 **2**
1788⁵ Harvey White (IRE) **(54)***(60)* *(JPearce)* 3-8-0 GBardwell(3) (dwlt: hld up: 5th st: hdwy over 3f out: one pce fnl 2f) 1¾ **3**
1863⁴ Ho-Joe (IRE) **(49)***(55)* *(GHYardley)* 5-8-8 RPrice(4) (b.hind: plld hrd: 4th st: hdwy over 4f out: rdn over 3f out: one pce) ....s.h **4**
1686⁹ Royal Circus **(40)***(28)* *(JGMO'Shea)* 6-7-10 (3)ow1 AGarth(6) (led 8f: wknd 3f out) 13 **5**
1643ᴿ Bee Beat **(43)** *(AJChamberlain)* 7-7-9b(7) MartinDwyer(5) (b: ref to r: t.n.p) .... **R**

2/1 CASUAL WATER (IRE), **5/2** Dormy Three, **4/1** Ho-Joe (IRE), **6/1** Harvey White (IRE), **8/1** Royal Circus (6/1-9/1), **20/1** Bee Beat, CSF £7.07 TOTE £2.40: £1.50 £1.80 (£3.00) OWNER Mr John Davies (BARNSTAPLE) BRED Dunderry Stud 6 Rn 2m 38.0 (6.70) SF: 9/22/-/-/-/-
WEIGHT FOR AGE 3yo-13lb

2110 SUNDAY EXPRESS BEST FOR SPORT SERIES (QUALIFIER) H'CAP (0-80) (3-Y.O+) (Class D) £5,655.00 (£1,580.00: £765.00)
1m 2f 36y Stalls: High GOING minus 0.55 sec per fur (F) 2-45 (2-47)

1926⁷ **Desert Power (62)***(72)* *(DBurchell)* 6-9-0 RPrice(3) (hld up: led over 5f out: hrd rdn over 3f out: edgd rt over 1f out: r.o wl) ....— **1**
1716* Exemption **(72)***(78)* *(HCandy)* 4-9-10 GeorginaFrost(4) (lw: led after 3f tl over 5f out: 2nd st: rdn 2f out: no imp) 2½ **2**
1447⁶ Suile Mor **(60)***(32)* *(BRMillman)* 3-7-10 (5)ow3 AWhelan(1) (plld hrd: led 3f: 3rd st: wknd over 3f out) 20 **3**
1717* Stage Struck (IRE) **(80)** (Fav)*(MRStoute)* 3-9-7 PaulEddery(2) (b.nr hind: hld up: last whn stumbled & fell 6f out) .... **F**

5/4 Stage Struck (IRE), **6/4** Exemption, **9/2** DESERT POWER, **16/1** Suile Mor, CSF £10.75 TOTE £5.90: (£4.30) OWNER Mr Rhys Thomas Williams (EBBW VALE) BRED Mrs C. F. Van Straubenzee and R. Mead 4 Rn 2m 8.2 (3.90) SF: 23/29/-/-
WEIGHT FOR AGE 3yo-11lb

2111 PARK CASINO CLUB CONDITIONS STKS (3-Y.O+) (Class C) £5,710.35 (£1,838.10: £891.55) 1m 2f 36y Stalls: High GOING minus 0.55 sec (F) 3-15 (3-17)

1848⁸ **Montjoy (USA) (113)***(111+)*(Fav)*(PFICole)* 3-8-9 TQuinn(3) (hld up: 2nd st: led on bit over 3f out: very easily) ....— **1**
1408⁴ Green Green Desert (FR) **(106)***(104)* *(MRStoute)* 4-9-4 PaulEddery(1) (led over 6f: no ch w wnr) 3½ **2**
1905* Alkateb *(82)* *(MissGayKelleway)* 3-8-9 StephenDavies(4) (hld up: 3rd st: rdn & wknd 3f out) 15 **3**

4/5 MONTJOY (USA) (op Evens), **9/4** Green Green Desert (FR) (6/4-5/2), **7/2** Alkateb, CSF £2.68 TOTE £1.80: (£1.60) OWNER Sir George Meyrick (WHATCOMBE) BRED Anthony M. Warrender 3 Rn 2m 8.0 (3.70) SF: 20/24/-
WEIGHT FOR AGE 3yo-11lb

2112
PAST V PRESENT JOCKEYS CHALLENGE LIMITED H'CAP (0-70) (3-Y.O+) (Class G) £2,342.00 (£662.00: £326.00)
6f 16y Stalls: High GOING minus 0.55 sec per fur (F) 3-45 (3-47)

365[9] **Rocketeer (IRE) (66)***(78) (WRMuir)* 4-11-7b(5) PeterScudamore(5) (a.p: led on bit wl over 1f out: drvn out) — 1
1963[3] Asterix **(47)***(52)*(Fav)*(JMBradley)* 7-10-7v TQuinn(3) (outpcd: hrd rdn & hdwy 2f out: r.o fnl f: nt trble wnr) 2½ 2
1366[15] Moody **(65)***(61) (MissGayKelleway)* 3-10-13 (5) RichardLinley(6) (chsd ldr: led 3f out tl wl over 1f out: wknd ins fnl f) 3½ 3
1756[5] Harry's Coming **(56)***(47) (RJHodges)* 11-10-11 (5) PatMurphy(4) (hdwy 2f out: one pce fnl f) 2 4
1994[5] Calling (USA) **(47)***(17) (WMBrisbourne)* 4-10-2 (5) GayKelleway(2) (outpcd) 8 5
1802[5] Silver Academy (IRE) **(54)***(11) (MissGayKelleway)* 3-10-7v PaulEddery(1) (led 3f: wknd qckly) 5 6

LONG HANDICAP Asterix 10-4 Calling (USA) 10-0 Silver Academy (IRE) 9-7

11/8 Asterix, **11/4** Harry's Coming, **9/2** ROCKETEER (IRE) (op 3/1), **11/1** Moody (op 6/1), **14/1** Silver Academy (IRE), **16/1** Calling (USA), CSF £10.25 TOTE £3.80: £1.70 £1.60 (£4.30) OWNER Mrs J. M. Muir (LAMBOURN) BRED Mrs T. Bracken in Ireland 6 Rn
1m 10.9 (1.90) SF: 60/34/36/29/-/-
WEIGHT FOR AGE 3yo-7lb

2113
SUNDAY MARKET (S) STKS (3-Y.O+) (Class G) £2,647.00 (£742.00: £361.00)
7f 16y Stalls: High GOING minus 0.55 sec per fur (F) 4-20 (4-24)

1980[5] **Soaking (60)***(68) (GLMoore)* 5-9-2 SWhitworth(6) (lw: w ldr: led 4f out: drvn out) — 1
1602[8] Toasted **(62)***(57)*(Fav)*(WJarvis)* 3-8-3 PaulEddery(3) (lw: hld up & plld hrd: chsd wnr fnl 3f: one pce fnl 2f) 2½ 2
1509[10] Julia's Freebee *(44) (TMJones)* 4-8-11 RPerham(1) (a.p: hrd rdn over 3f out: one pce fnl 2f) 6 3
1971[7] Sky Diver **(41)***(46) (BJLlewellyn)* 4-9-2 TWilliams(5) (led 3f: sn hrd rdn: one pce fnl 2f) 1¼ 4
1538[9] Millstock *(27) (APJones)* 5-8-11 NAdams(2) (swtg: dwlt: a bhd) 6 5
Big Tickle (IRE) *(32) (GAHam)* 6-9-2 ADicks(4) (dwlt: plld hrd: bhd fnl 3f) hd 6

5/4 Toasted (op 4/5), **15/8** SOAKING (5/4-2/1), **6/1** Sky Diver (op 10/1), **10/1** Big Tickle (IRE), **14/1** Julia's Freebee, **50/1** Millstock, CSF £4.40 TOTE £3.10: £1.90 £1.50 (£1.90) OWNER Mr K. Higson (EPSOM) BRED David John Brown 6 Rn 1m 21.8 (1.80) SF: 30/11/6/8/-/-
WEIGHT FOR AGE 3yo-8lb
No bid.

2114
SUNDAY MEDIAN AUCTION MAIDEN STKS (2-Y.O F) (Class E) £3,168.00 (£954.00: £462.00: £216.00)
5f 16y Stalls: High GOING minus 0.55 sec per fur (F) 4-50 (4-51)

Defined Feature (IRE) *(73+)*(Fav)*(MRStoute)* 2-8-11 PaulEddery(3) (w'like: rdn over 3f out: hdwy & nt cl run 2f out: r.o wl to ld cl home) — 1
1790[3] Moving Up (IRE) *(72) (GLMoore)* 2-8-11 SWhitworth(2) (a.p: hrd rdn over 2f out: edgd rt & led over 1f out: hdd cl home) nk 2
Fayre Holly (IRE) *(64) (MJHeaton-Ellis)* 2-8-11 TQuinn(4) (lt-f: disp ld: rdn to ld wl over 1f out: sn hdd: nt qckn) 2½ 3
810[5] Heights of Love *(45) (MSSaunders)* 2-8-11 RPrice(1) (disp ld over 3f: wknd 1f out) 6 4

5/4 DEFINED FEATURE (IRE) (op Evens), **13/8** Moving Up (IRE), **5/1** Fayre Holly (IRE), **9/1** Heights of Love, CSF £3.49 TOTE £2.30: (£1.50) OWNER Mr Saeed Suhail (NEWMARKET) BRED Gainsborough Stud Management Ltd 4 Rn 59.9 secs (2.90) SF: -/-/-/-

2115
MADEMOISELLE LADIES AMATEUR H'CAP (0-70) (3-Y.O+) (Class G) £2,591.00 (£726.00: £353.00)
1m 14y Stalls: High GOING minus 0.55 sec per fur (F) 5-20 (5-23)

1048[4] **Roman Reel (USA) (62)***(75) (GLMoore)* 4-10-9 (7) MrsJMoore(1) (led: sn clr: shkn up over 1f out: r.o wl) — 1
1320[6] Positivo **(63)***(72) (LordHuntingdon)* 4-11-3 MissDianaJones(9) (b.hind: hdwy 3f out: chsd wnr fnl f: r.o one pce) 2 2
1323* Polly Peculiar **(56)***(61) (BSmart)* 4-10-5 (5) MissVMarshall(8) (chsd wnr: edgd rt over 1f out: one pce) 2 3
1561[5] Sheama (USA) **(70)***(69) (WJarvis)* 3-10-10 (5) MissIFoustok(11) (chsd wnr: nt clr run & swtchd lft over 1f out: one pce) 3 4
1714[5] Jewel Thief **(33)***(10) (GBBalding)* 5-8-8v(7) MissKGreaney(4) (rdn over 4f out: sn bhd) 11 5

1843[7] Chief of Staff **(67)***(44) (JPearce)* 6-11-7 MrsLPearce(6) (hld up & plld hrd: rdn 3f out: sn wknd)....hd 6
1944* Kaf **(75)***(50)*(Fav)*(JLDunlop)* 3-11-6 MissEJohnsonHoughton(10) (lw: rdn & hdwy 3f out: 4th whn eased ins fnl f: sddle slipped ½-wy)....1 7
1974[6] Clancy's Express **(32)***(7) (GBBalding)* 4-8-7 (7) MissSarah-JaneDurman(2) (lw: bhd fnl 3f)....hd 8
1714[9] Fighter Squadron **(54)***(28) (REPeacock)* 6-10-1b(7) MrsCPeacock(5) (wl bhd fnl 5f)....nk 9
1950[10] Olivia Val **(37)** *(AGNewcombe)* 5-9-0b(5)ow5 MissFBurke(3) (s.s: a bhd)....4 10

LONG HANDICAP Clancy's Express 8-7 Olivia Val 8-3

2/1 Kaf (op 5/4), **7/2** Chief of Staff, **5/1** Polly Peculiar, **8/1** Sheama (USA), **12/1** ROMAN REEL (USA), Positivo, **14/1** Jewel Thief, **20/1** Clancy's Express, **33/1** Fighter Squadron, Olivia Val, CSF £125.88 CT £732.39 TOTE £15.90: £3.90 £2.30 £1.90 (£64.60) Trio £84.90 OWNER Mr K. Higson (EPSOM) BRED Dorothy Price, Jackie W. Ramos & Ken Hickson 10 Rn

1m 35.1 (2.60) SF: 51/48/37/36/-/20/17/-/4/-
WEIGHT FOR AGE 3yo-9lb

T/Plpt: £106.90 (74.38 Tckts). T/Qdpt: £8.00 (13.2 Tckts). KH

2083-DONCASTER (L-H)
Sunday July 2nd (St course Good, Good to firm patches, Rnd Good to firm)

WEATHER: sunny WIND: almost nil

2116 E.B.F. SUNDAY SPECIAL MAIDEN STKS (2-Y.O) (Class D)
£3,452.50 (£1,045.00: £510.00: £242.50)
6f Stalls: High GOING minus 0.29 sec per fur (GF) 2-30 (2-30)

1597[3] **Shontaine** *(74)*(Fav)*(MJohnston)* 2-9-0 DHolland(4) (w ldr: led ½-wy: r.o wl)....— 1
Lucky Rabbit *(70+)*(Fav)*(BWHills)* 2-9-0 MHills(3) (leggy: scope: s.i.s: hdwy ½-wy: sn chsng ldrs: kpt on fnl f)....1½ 2
Royal Mark (IRE) *(67+)* *(JWWatts)* 2-9-0 GDuffield(7) (leggy: lw: cl up: effrt 2f out: r.o one pce)....1 3
Relatively Clever (USA) *(57+)* *(MrsJRRamsden)* 2-9-0 KFallon(5) (w'like: leggy: bit bkwd: outpcd & bhd tl styd on fnl 2f)....4 4
Welcome Royale (IRE) *(46)* *(MHTompkins)* 2-9-0 PRobinson(6) (w'like: lengthy: chsd ldrs 4f)....4 5
Winston *(41)* *(JDBethell)* 2-9-0 TIves(1) (w'like: scope: bit bkwd: sn outpcd & bhd: sme late hdwy)....2 6
1781[6] Animation *(35)* *(KMcAuliffe)* 2-8-9 DHarrison(8) (unruly s: led to ½-wy: sn rdn & wknd)....nk 7
Unihoc Ball *(6)* *(TRWatson)* 2-8-9 DeanMcKeown(2) (w'like: bit bkwd: unruly s: s.i.s: sn outpcd & bhd)....11 8

3/1 SHONTAINE (op 6/4), Lucky Rabbit, **4/1** Welcome Royale (IRE) (op 6/1), **11/2** Royal Mark (IRE) (4/1-6/1), **7/1** Relatively Clever (USA), **16/1** Winston, Animation, **33/1** Unihoc Ball, CSF £11.54 TOTE £2.90: £1.40 £1.30 £1.70 (£2.90) OWNER Mr Paul Dean (MIDDLEHAM) BRED Mark Johnston Racing Ltd 8 Rn 1m 13.85 (2.85) SF: 34/30/27/17/6/1/-/-

2117 MAIL ON SUNDAY MILE (QUALIFIER) H'CAP (0-90) (3-Y.O+) (Class C) £7,360.00 (£2,230.00: £1,090.00: £520.00)
1m (round) Stalls: High GOING minus 0.29 sec per fur (GF) 3-00 (3-01)

1862* **Bettergeton (85)***(98+) (PJBevan)* 3-9-2 NCarlisle(2) (trckd ldrs: led ins fnl f: r.o wl)....— 1
1299[5] Fame Again **(73)***(84)*(Fav)*(MrsJRRamsden)* 3-8-4 KFallon(5) (hld up: stdy hdwy 3f out: effrt & ev ch ins fnl f: no ex)....1¼ 2
1638* Up in Flames (IRE) **(77)***(87)*(Fav)*(MDHammond)* 4-9-3 JCarroll(7) (hld up: effrt 4f out: sn drvn along: styd on wl towards fin)....nk 3
1603[5] Kemo Sabo **(72)***(80) (MrsJRRamsden)* 3-8-3 GCarter(10) (lw: led tl hdd & wknd ins fnl f)....1 4
1851[15] Mellottie **(88)***(93) (MrsMReveley)* 10-9-7 (7) SCopp(11) (hld up & bhd: effrt ½-wy: gd hdwy 2f out: nt qckn appr fnl f)....1½ 5
1617[4] Sandmoor Chambray **(73)***(73) (MHEasterby)* 4-8-13b MBirch(6) (chsd ldr: effrt 2f out: wknd ins fnl f)....2½ 6
1616[3] Western General **(79)***(72) (MissSEHall)* 4-9-5b NConnorton(1) (chsd ldr tl wknd fnl 3f)....3½ 7
1808[15] Forever Diamonds **(84)***(70) (MHEasterby)* 8-9-10 SMaloney(4) (hld up: effrt ½-wy: no imp)..3½ 8
1617[9] Master Beveled **(80)***(63) (PDEvans)* 5-9-3 (3) JStack(8) (bhd: rdn ½-wy: n.d)....1½ 9
1728[7] New Capricorn (USA) **(86)***(68) (MAJarvis)* 5-9-12 MHills(3) (chsd ldrs tl rdn & wknd fnl 3f)....½ 10
1560[4] Promise Fulfilled (USA) **(74)***(48) (SGNorton)* 4-9-0v JFortune(9) (prom 5f)....4 11

4/1 Fame Again, Up in Flames (IRE), **5/1** BETTERGETON, **8/1** Western General, **10/1** Sandmoor Chambray, Kemo Sabo, **12/1** New Capricorn (USA), Promise Fulfilled (USA), Master Beveled, **14/1** Mellottie, Forever Diamonds, CSF £24.65 CT £81.65 TOTE £4.40: £2.00 £2.30 £1.60 (£11.40) Trio £18.50 OWNER Mr Derek Boulton (UTTOXETER) BRED R. and Mrs Healy-Fenton 11 Rn

1m 37.67 (1.37) SF: 62/48/60/44/66/46/45/43/36/41/21

WEIGHT FOR AGE 3yo-9lb

2118

HOME OF SUNDAY RACING H'CAP (0-105) (3-Y.O+) (Class B)
£10,656.60 (£3,989.40: £1,952.20: £841.00: £378.00: £192.80)
1m 2f 60y Stalls: Low GOING minus 0.29 sec per fur (GF) 3-35 (3-35)

1851[10] **Knave's Ash (USA) (88)***(99) (MRStoute)* 4-8-10 (3) JTate(3) (trckd ldrs: led over 2f out: wknd towards fin)........— 1

1793* Rokeby Bowl **(87)***(97)*(Fav)*(IABalding)* 3-8-1 DHarrison(4) (lw: chsd ldrs: outpcd ent st: hdwy over 2f out: sn hrd drvn: styd on wl towards fin)........¾ 2

1872[15] Maeterlinck (IRE) **(86)***(95) (BWHills)* 3-8-0 GCarter(1) (in tch: stdy hdwy 3f out: effrt over 1f out: styd on)........nk 3

1357[7] Mr Confusion (IRE) **(86)***(85) (MissSEHall)* 7-8-4 (7) MHenry(8) (lw: in tch: effrt 3f out: hrd rdn & one pce fnl 2f)........7 4

2069[5] Augustan **(68)***(60) (SGollings)* 4-7-2 (5) MBaird(5) (lw: sn w ldr: led over 3f out tl over 2f out: wknd)........4 5

1616[9] Colway Rock (USA) **(76)***(44) (JWWatts)* 5-8-1 ow1 GDuffield(7) (outpcd & wl bhd fnl 4f)........15 6

Wainwright (USA) **(103)***(49) (JHMGosden)* 6-10-0 GHind(6) (led tl hdd & wknd over 3f out)..15 7

LONG HANDICAP Augustan 7-2

7/4 Rokeby Bowl, **4/1** KNAVE'S ASH (USA) (3/1-9/2), **9/2** Wainwright (USA), **5/1** Mr Confusion (IRE), **11/2** Maeterlinck (IRE), **12/1** Augustan, **20/1** Colway Rock (USA), CSF £11.54 CT £35.24 TOTE £5.40: £2.40 £1.70 (£6.10) OWNER Sheikh Mohammed (NEWMARKET) BRED Farfellow Farms Ltd in USA 7 Rn

2m 7.52 (0.52) SF: 70/57/55/56/31/15/20

WEIGHT FOR AGE 3yo-11lb

2119

'BOBS RETURN' CUP CONDITIONS STKS (3-Y.O+) (Class B)
£7,891.80 (£2,956.20: £1,448.10: £625.50: £282.75: £145.65)
1m 6f 132y Stalls: Low GOING minus 0.29 sec per fur (GF) 4-10 (4-12)

1363[5] **Further Flight (107)***(98)*(Fav)*(BWHills)* 9-9-12 MHills(3) (b.hind: a gng wl: led over 1f out: comf)........— 1

1852[10] Lord Jim (IRE) **(96)***(86) (MissGayKelleway)* 3-8-1 ow1 GDuffield(4) (led 3f: cl up: led 4f out & qcknd: hdd over 1f out: kpt on wl)........1½ 2

1987[4] Cypress Avenue (IRE) **(97)***(86) (RHannon)* 3-8-0 GCarter(7) (hld up: effrt 4f out: rdn to chse ldrs appr fnl f: kpt on wl)........hd 3

2087[4] College Don **(60)***(78) (MPBielby)* 4-9-2 DRMcCabe(8) (lw: led after 3f to 4f out: one pce)........8 4

Djais (FR) *(79) (RTPhillips)* 6-9-5 PRobinson(2) (chsd ldrs: rdn 4f out: outpcd fnl 2½f)........1¾ 5

1171[5] Castle Courageous **(106)***(75) (LadyHerries)* 8-9-12 DHarrison(5) (lw: trckd ldrs tl rdn & wknd 3f out)........10 6

2098[15] Miroswaki (USA) **(56)***(59) (GFierro)* 5-8-13 (3) DMoffat(6) (hdwy to jn ldrs 8f out: rdn & wknd wl over 3f out)........5 7

13/8 FURTHER FLIGHT, **11/4** Castle Courageous (2/1-3/1), **7/2** Cypress Avenue (IRE), **6/1** Lord Jim (IRE), **10/1** Djais (FR), **20/1** College Don, **100/1** Miroswaki (USA), CSF £11.32 TOTE £2.30: £1.40 £2.40 (£6.80) OWNER Mr S. WingfieldDigby (LAMBOURN) BRED S. Wingfield Digby 7 Rn

3m 11.72 (8.12) SF: 43/15/15/23/24/20/4

WEIGHT FOR AGE 3yo-16lb

OFFICIAL EXPLANATION Castle Courageous: the trainer's representative reported that the gelding was unsuited by the slow pace, was unable to quicken and finished sore. A routine test was ordered.

2120

'SEA KING' AIR SEA RESCUE H'CAP (0-90) (3-Y.O+) (Class C)
£5,576.00 (£1,688.00: £824.00: £392.00)
5f Stalls: High GOING minus 0.29 sec per fur (GF) 4-40 (4-42)

1895[15] **Join the Clan (88)***(97) (MrsNMacauley)* 6-9-11 (3) SDrowne(5) (lw: in tch: hdwy 2f out: r.o to ld wl ins fnl f)........— 1

2060[3] Shadow Jury **(64)***(71)*(Fav)*(DWChapman)* 5-8-4b LCharnock(7) (led tl hdd & no ex wl ins fnl f)........½ 2

2060* Name the Tune **(75)***(78) (PHowling)* 4-9-1 7x JQuinn(2) (b.hind: chsd ldrs: effrt & ev ch over 1f out: nt qckn)........1¼ 3

1864* Beau Venture (USA) **(77)***(76) (FHLee)* 7-9-3 RLappin(3) (chsd ldrs: effrt ½-wy: r.o one pce) 1¼ 4

1765[6] Hickory Blue **(69)***(64) (MrsNMacauley)* 5-8-9b GCarter(9) (lw: chsd ldrs tl rdn & btn over 1f out)........1½ 5
1741[4] Croft Imperial **(64)***(55) (MJohnston)* 8-8-4 DHolland(1) (lw: sn outpcd & bhd: swtchd & effrt 2f out: nvr able to chal)........1 6
1641[2] Karina Heights (USA) **(80)***(63) (JWWatts)* 3-9-0 GDuffield(8) (cl up: edgd lft ½-wy: wknd wl over 1f out)........2½ 7
1806[5] Musical Season **(90)***(73) (TDBarron)* 3-9-10 JFortune(6) (lw: s.i.s: swtchd & effrt 2f out: nt clr run & n.d)........s.h 8
1864[3] The Fed **(54)***(37) (RMWhitaker)* 5-7-8 DaleGibson(4) (chsd ldr tl outpcd ½-wy: sn btn)........hd 9

9/2 Shadow Jury, **5/1** Karina Heights (USA), Name the Tune, Musical Season, **7/1** Beau Venture (USA), **9/1** JOIN THE CLAN, **10/1** Croft Imperial, Hickory Blue, The Fed, CSF £46.24 CT £206.70 TOTE £9.40: £2.50 £2.00 £1.70 (£16.50) Trio £23.00 OWNER Mr J. Redden (MELTON MOWBRAY) BRED John Redden Farms 9 Rn 59.37 secs (0.97) SF: 70/44/51/49/37/28/30/40/10

WEIGHT FOR AGE 3yo-6lb

2121 DONCASTER 'SUPER SUNDAY MARKET' CONDITIONS STKS (3-Y.O) (Class C) £5,219.80 (£1,904.80: £932.40: £402.00: £181.00)
1m (straight) Stalls: High GOING minus 0.29 sec per fur (GF) 5-10 (5-10)

1072* **Decorated Hero** *(97+) (JHMGosden)* 3-8-13 GHind(2) (lw: trckd ldrs: led wl over 2f out: pushed along & r.o wl)........— 1
1107[7] Ten Past Six **(95)***(91)*(Fav)*(BWHills)* 3-8-13 MHills(3) (lw: hld up: stdy hdwy ½-wy: chsd wnr fnl 2f: rdn & no imp)........3 2
1728[8] Sotoboy (IRE) **(96)***(92) (PWHarris)* 3-9-3 GDuffield(6) (hld up: effrt 3f out: rdn & no imp)......1½ 3
1150* Iktasab *(88) (EALDunlop)* 3-8-10 (3) JTate(4) (cl up: led ½-wy tl wl over 2f out: sn rdn & btn) .hd 4
1807[4] Zamalek (USA) **(90)***(78) (HRACecil)* 3-8-13b AMcGlone(1) (led to ½-wy: sn rdn & no rspnse)..5 5

2/1 Ten Past Six, **5/2** DECORATED HERO, **4/1** Iktasab, **11/2** Sotoboy (IRE), **7/1** Zamalek (USA), CSF £7.42 TOTE £3.40: £1.80 £1.30 (£2.80) OWNER Mr Herbert Allen (NEWMARKET) BRED Reg Griffin and Jim McGrath 5 Rn 1m 38.41 (1.91) SF: 54/48/49/45/35

£16,381.80 (2.09 Tckts). T/Plpt: £6.80 (4,053.18 Tckts). T/Qdpt: £13.90 (38.25 Tckts). AA

1956-EDINBURGH (R-H)
Monday July 3rd (Good to firm)
WEATHER: sunny WIND: mod against

2122 TARMAC CONSTRUCTION APPRENTICE H'CAP (0-65) (3-Y.O+) (Class F) £3,300.25 (£1,012.00: £503.50: £249.25)
1m 4f 31y Stalls: High GOING minus 0.38 sec per fur (F) 6-15 (6-15)

1427* **Duggan (30)***(40) (PDEvans)* 8-9-0 JoHunnam(6) (bhd: swtchd over 3f out: hung rt: r.o to ld wl ins fnl f)........— 1
1958[2] Thisonesforalice **(36)***(45)*(Fav)*(JSGoldie)* 7-9-1 (5) DLockhart(5) (led after 2f tl appr st: led over 2f out: hdd & nt qckn wl ins fnl f)........¾ 2
1645[8] Red Spectacle (IRE) **(47)***(54) (PCHaslam)* 3-9-4 CarolDavison(3) (led 2f: led appr st tl over 2f out: sn outpcd)........1¾ 3
1858[5] Exclusion **(40)***(36) (JHetherton)* 6-9-10 JEdmunds(2) (lw: cl up tl outpcd fnl 3f)........8 4
1720[2] Never so True **(40)***(33) (MartynWane)* 4-9-10v MSemple(1) (lw: bhd: rdn over 3f out: no imp)2½ 5
1995[13] Upex le Gold Too **(43)***(29) (LRLloyd-James)* 3-8-9 (5) KSked(4) (chsd ldrs tl wknd wl over 2f out)........5 6

15/8 Thisonesforalice, **9/4** Exclusion, **5/1** DUGGAN (3/1-11/2), **8/1** Red Spectacle (IRE), **14/1** Never so True, **16/1** Upex le Gold Too, CSF £13.25 TOTE £4.10: £1.20 £1.30 (£5.00) OWNER Mr Colin Booth (WELSHPOOL) BRED M. Sinclair and J. Fisher 6 Rn 2m 38.8 (6.30) SF: 28/33/29/24/21/4

WEIGHT FOR AGE 3yo-13lb

2123 EAST LOTHIAN DISTRICT COUNCIL H'CAP (0-80) (3-Y.O+) (Class D) £5,602.00 (£1,696.00: £828.00: £394.00)
1m 16y Stalls: High GOING minus 0.38 sec per fur (F) 6-45 (6-46)

1995[3] **Thatched (IRE) (44)***(57)*(Fav)*(REBarr)* 5-7-0 (7) PFessey(4) (bhd: hdwy 3f out: led ins fnl f: r.o)........— 1
1679[4] Lancashire Life (IRE) **(54)***(61) (EJAlston)* 4-8-3 DHolland(8) (led tl hdd & no ex ins fnl f)........3 2
1932[5] Persian Fayre **(67)***(70) (JBerry)* 3-8-7 JFortune(7) (chsd ldr: effrt 3f out: btn over 1f out)........2 3

2002[3] Jubran (USA) **(69)***(72) (MJohnston)* 9-9-1 (3) JTate(1) (lw: chsd ldrs: outpcd over 3f out: no imp after) ....nk 4
1744[3] Gospel Song **(67)***(68) (WTKemp)* 3-8-7b KFallon(2) (outpcd & bhd appr st: sme hdwy u.p 3f out: n.d) ....¾ 5
1995[9] Prizefighter **(67)***(68) (JLEyre)* 4-9-2 KDarley(6) (chsd ldrs: rdn over 3f out: grad wknd) ....s.h 6
1745[4] Piquant **(65)***(62)*(Fav)*(LordHuntingdon)* 8-9-0 JWeaver(3) (lw: wl bhd appr st: rn wd & rdn over 3f out: n.d) 2 7
Nonios (IRE) **(77)***(56) (GMMoore)* 4-9-5 (7) IGrantham(5) (unruly stalls: outpcd appr st: bhd after) 9 8

7/2 THATCHED (IRE), Piquant, **6/1** Prizefighter (8/1-12/1), Jubran (USA), **7/1** Gospel Song, **8/1** Persian Fayre, Lancashire Life (IRE) (5/1-9/1), **20/1** Nonios (IRE), CSF £27.48 CT £185.12 TOTE £5.00: £1.10 £2.70 £2.90 (£24.50) OWNER Mr J. C. Garbutt (MIDDLESBROUGH) BRED D. P. O'Brien 8 Rn
1m 41.2 (2.60) SF: 22/26/26/37/24/33/27/21
WEIGHT FOR AGE 3yo-9lb

2124 WHEATSHEAF CATERING (S) H'CAP (0-60) (3-Y.O+) (Class F) £2,879.00 (£872.00: £426.00: £203.00)
5f Stalls: High GOING minus 0.38 sec per fur (F) 7-15 (7-20)

2048[3] **Halbert (49)***(57) (MRChannon)* 6-9-3v KDarley(9) (mde all: drvn out) ....— 1
1679[14] Pallium (IRE) **(52)***(58) (MrsAMNaughton)* 7-9-6 JWeaver(8) (lw: stdd after s: sn wl bhd: rapid hdwy over 1f out: fin wl) ....½ 2
2067[5] Baileys Sunset (IRE) **(58)***(62)*(Fav)*(MJohnston)* 3-9-6 DHolland(2) (a chsng ldrs: kpt on same pce fnl f) ....¾ 3
Glow of Hope **(30)***(30) (RMMcKellar)* 5-7-5 (7) PFessey(3) (hdwy ½-wy: styd on wl: nrst fin)..1¼ 4
1721[15] Murray's Mazda (IRE) **(44)***(42) (JLEyre)* 6-8-12 KFallon(5) (b.hind: hdwy 2f out styd on wl)....¾ 5
1419[8] Flashing Sabre **(49)***(43) (JBerry)* 3-8-4 (7) PRoberts(13) (b.off hind: racd far side: one pce fnl 2f) 1 6
1827[9] Sigama (USA) **(56)***(47) (DNicholls)* 9-9-10 AlexGreaves(7) (dwlt: nvr trbld ldrs) 1 7
1763[12] Oneineverycolour **(43)***(34) (PDEvans)* 3-7-12 (7) JoHunnam(4) (bhd: hdwy ½-wy: rdn & btn over 1f out) ....s.h 8
1741[3] My Cherrywell **(55)***(40) (LRLloyd-James)* 5-9-9v JFortune(11) (b.hind: racd far side: rdn ½-wy: no imp) 1¾ 9
1961[5] Sunday Mail Too (IRE) **(39)***(22) (MissLAPerratt)* 3-7-8b(7) DLockhart(10) (nvr wnt pce) ....¾ 10
2024[6] Another Nightmare (IRE) **(45)***(17) (RMMcKellar)* 3-8-0 (7) KSked(12) (prom far side to ½-wy)3½ 11
2071[3] Chance Me **(37)***(1) (MJohnston)* 3-7-13 TWilliams(6) (outpcd & bhd fr ½-wy) 2½ 12
2024[7] Sunshine Belle **(48)** *(GMMoore)* 3-8-7b(3) JTate(1) (chsd ldrs tl stumbled & uns rdr ½-wy) .... U

7/2 Baileys Sunset (IRE), **9/2** HALBERT, **6/1** Chance Me, **13/2** My Cherrywell, **10/1** Sigama (USA), Pallium (IRE), **16/1** Sunshine Belle, Murray's Mazda (IRE), **20/1** Another Nightmare (IRE), **25/1** Oneineverycolour, Sunday Mail Too (IRE), Flashing Sabre, **66/1** Glow of Hope, CSF £43.10 CT £157.79 TOTE £3.50: £1.90 £2.60 £1.50 (£21.20) Trio £29.00 OWNER Miss Bridget Coyle (UPPER LAMBOURN) BRED Mr and Mrs J. K. S. Cresswell 13 Rn
59.8 secs (2.10) SF: 33/34/32/6/18/13/23/4/16/-/-/-/-
WEIGHT FOR AGE 3yo-6lb
No bid

2125 TARMAC CONSTRUCTION RATING RELATED MAIDEN LIMITED STKS (0-70) (3-Y.O+) (Class E) £3,035.00 (£920.00: £450.00: £215.00)
1m 16y Stalls: High GOING minus 0.38 sec per fur (F) 7-45 (7-47)

1172[10] **Aoife Alainn (IRE) (70)***(65) (JWHills)* 3-8-7 DHolland(4) (hld up: hdwy over 2f out: swtchd ins & qcknd to ld ins fnl f) ....— 1
1859[3] Triple Tricks (IRE) **(69)***(64)*(Fav)*(WJHaggas)* 3-8-7 KDarley(2) (lw: hld up: nt clr run over 1f out: swtchd & fin wl: too much to do) ....¾ 2
1818[3] Ricana **(39)***(62) (WTKemp)* 3-8-7 KFallon(3) (led early: cl up: led wl over 1f out tl ins fnl f: nt qckn) ....¾ 3
1952[3] Smolensk (IRE) **(63)***(55) (JBerry)* 3-8-12 JFortune(1) (sn led: hdd & wknd wl over 1f out)....6 4

Evens Triple Tricks (IRE), **11/8** AOIFE ALAINN (IRE), **8/1** Smolensk (IRE) (op 9/2), **33/1** Ricana, CSF £2.89 TOTE £2.20: (£1.40) OWNER Mr Garrett Freyne (LAMBOURN) BRED G. J. Freyne 4 Rn
1m 42.8 (4.20) SF: 19/18/16/9

2126 DAILY STAR LIMITED STKS (0-50) (3-Y.O+) (Class F) £2,955.00 (£830.00: £405.00) **1m 3f 32y** Stalls: High GOING minus 0.38 sec per fur (F) 8-15 (8-15)

1817[10] **Jackmanii (46)***(59) (WTKemp)* 3-8-8b KFallon(6) (led 1f: cl up tl outpcd over 3f out: styd on u.p to ld wl ins fnl f) ....— 1

1496[6] Rasayel (USA) **(48)***(55) (PDEvans)* 5-9-3 JFortune(5) (chsd ldrs: hdwy ent st: led ins fnl f: no ex towards fin) ... ¾ 2
2064[3] Essayeffsee **(49)***(58)*(Fav)*(MrsMReveley)* 6-9-6 KDarley(3) (lw: trckd ldrs: rdn over 2f out: ev ch ins fnl f: styd on) ... hd 3
1725[6] Can She Can Can **(46)***(52) (MJohnston)* 3-8-3 DHolland(1) (lw: led after 1f: qcknd over 3f out: hdd ins fnl f: one pce) ... ½ 4
1958[5] Runrig (IRE) **(42)***(49) (MissLAPerratt)* 5-8-8 (7) RHavlin(2) (lw: hld up & bhd: hdwy u.p 2f out: hit rails: no imp) ... 2 5
1645[14] Diamond Crown (IRE) **(47)***(48) (MartynWane)* 4-9-6 JWeaver(4) (lw: bhd: hdwy ent st: wknd 2f out) ... 4 6

6/5 Essayeffsee, **5/1** JACKMANII, **11/2** Can She Can Can, **6/1** Rasayel (USA) (op 4/1), **10/1** Runrig (IRE) (op 6/1), **11/1** Diamond Crown (IRE) (6/1-12/1), CSF £29.10 TOTE £5.40: £3.00 £4.00 (£11.00) OWNER Drakemyre Racing (DUNS) BRED Newmarket Thoroughbred Breeders P L C 6 Rn 2m 26.3 (6.60) SF: 16/24/27/9/18/17
WEIGHT FOR AGE 3yo-12lb

2127 LOTHIAN RACING SYNDICATE H'CAP (0-70) (3-Y.O+) (Class E)
£3,452.50 (£1,045.00: £510.00: £242.50)
1m 7f 16y Stalls: High GOING minus 0.38 sec per fur (F) 8-45 (8-45)

1957* **Vain Prince (47)***(59)*(Fav)*(NTinkler)* 8-8-9b 4x LCharnock(4) (lw: hld up: led on bit over 2f out: rdn clr fnl f) ... — 1
1934* Hit the Canvas (USA) **(65)***(73) (MrsMReveley)* 4-9-13v KDarley(2) (lw: a.p: disp ld over 2f out: r.o one pce) ... 3½ 2
1957[2] Milngavie (IRE) **(35)***(37) (MJohnston)* 5-7-11 TWilliams(3) (lw: led after 5f to 7f out: wl outpcd fnl 2½f) ... 6 3
1998[2] Nouvelle Cuisine **(52)***(51) (GMMoore)* 7-9-0 JWeaver(1) (led tl rn wd & hdd paddock bnd after 5f: led 7f out tl over 2f out: sn btn) ... 2½ 4

5/4 VAIN PRINCE, **11/4** Milngavie (IRE), **3/1** Hit the Canvas (USA) (5/2-4/1), **11/2** Nouvelle Cuisine (4/1-6/1), CSF £5.04 TOTE £2.40: (£2.50) OWNER Mr A. C. Findlay (MALTON) BRED Lodge Park Stud 4 Rn 3m 20.3 (9.80) SF: -/-/-/-

T/Plpt: £314.60 (31.11 Tckts). T/Qdpt: £82.50 (0.5 Tckts). AA

1823-PONTEFRACT (L-H)
Monday July 3rd (Good to firm)
WEATHER: dry & overcast WIND: almost nil

2128 PADDOCK MAIDEN AUCTION STKS (2-Y.O) (Class E) £3,113.00 (£944.00: £462.00: £221.00) **5f** Stalls: Low GOING minus 0.30 sec per fur (GF) 2-45 (2-48)

Anthelia *(64+)*(Fav)*(GWragg)* 2-8-0 FNorton(5) (w'like: chsd ldrs: nt clr run & swtchd outside over 1f out: r.o wl to ld cl home) ... — 1
1938[3] Clan Chief *(67) (JRArnold)* 2-8-4 JWeaver(8) (b.hind: w ldr: led 2f out: clr 1f out: rdn & ct towards fin) ... nk 2
1879[6] Skelton Countess (IRE) **(57)***(56) (RHollinshead)* 2-7-9 (3)ow1 AGarth(10) (hld up: hdwy over 1f out: styd on wl towards fin) ... 1¼ 3
1877[4] Camionneur (IRE) **(68)***(59) (MHEasterby)* 2-8-4 SMaloney(12) (chsd ldrs: wandered u.p over 1f out: kpt on one pce) ... 1¼ 4
Annaberg (IRE) *(51+) (MrsJRRamsden)* 2-8-2 MFenton(1) (unf: scope: bkwd: b.nr hind: s.s: bhd: hdwy on outside 2f out: styd on wl towards fin) ... 2 5
1176[5] Chamber Music *(40) (JBerry)* 2-8-1 LCharnock(2) (led to 2f out: wknd fnl f) ... 3 6
Niteowl Raider (IRE) *(41) (JAHarris)* 2-8-5 WRyan(3) (leggy: unf: chsd ldrs tl wknd over 1f out) ... 1 7
1913[6] Esperto *(38) (JPearce)* 2-8-5 GBardwell(6) (mid div: effrt & hung lft over 1f out: n.d) ... ¾ 8
1665[14] Society Sue (IRE) *(26) (RonaldThompson)* 2-7-11 AMackay(7) (hld up & plld hrd: hdwy ½-wy: effrt u.p 2f out: nvr nr ldrs) ... 1¼ 9
In Paradisum (USA) *(36) (MrsJRRamsden)* 2-8-8 KFallon(4) (rangy: bkwd: s.i.s: a in rr) ... ½ 10
1879[5] Efipetite *(12) (NBycroft)* 2-7-11 NKennedy(9) (s.i.s: a bhd) ... 4 11
Dispol Princess (IRE) *(MrsVAAconley)* 2-7-11 NCarlisle(11) (unf: bkwd: s.i.s: a outpcd) ... 11 12

3/1 ANTHELIA, **100/30** Clan Chief, **5/1** Camionneur (IRE), **11/2** Chamber Music, **8/1** Esperto (6/1-9/1), **10/1** In Paradisum (USA), **20/1** Annaberg (IRE), **25/1** Niteowl Raider (IRE), Skelton Countess (IRE), Efipetite, **33/1** Society Sue (IRE), Dispol Princess (IRE), CSF £13.15 TOTE £3.40: £1.70 £1.70 £4.10 (£6.50) Trio £51.60 OWNER Mrs Claude Lilley (NEWMARKET) BRED Whitsbury Manor Stud 12 Rn 64.6 secs (3.10) SF: 12/15/4/7/-/-/-/-/-/-/-/-

2129 SMEATON (S) H'CAP (0-60) (3-Y.O) (Class G) £2,707.00 (£752.00: £361.00)
1m 4f 8y Stalls: Low GOING minus 0.30 sec per fur (GF) 3-15 (3-20)

Bunker (IRE) (44)(58) (JPearce) 3-9-3 GBardwell(12) (lw: bhd: drvn along 6f out: hdwy u.p 4f out: edgd lft & styd on wl to ld wl ins fnl f) ......— **1**
1667⁶ High Flown (USA) **(44)**(58) (RonaldThompson) 3-8-12 (5) LNewton(1) (trckd ldrs: led over 1f out tl nr fin) ......nk **2**
1667⁷ Coast Along (IRE) **(32)**(43) (CWThornton) 3-8-5 KFallon(6) (s.i.s: hdwy ½-wy: prom 2f out: styd on appr fnl f: nvr nr to chal) 2 **3**
1720³ Our Rainbow **(41)**(47) (MrsSMAustin) 3-8-11 (3) DarrenMoffatt(5) (b: chsd ldrs: led over 2f out tl over 1f out: one pce) 4 **4**
1581* Risky Rose **(47)**(53)(Fav)(RHollinshead) 3-9-6 LDettori(10) (hld up: hdwy 5f out: ev ch over 1f out: sn wknd) ......s.h **5**
1970⁴ Presto Boy **(48)**(47) (MBell) 3-9-7 MFenton(7) (mid div: effrt u.p over 3f out: prom 2f out: sn wknd) 5 **6**
1718⁹ Gigfy **(43)**(41) (BJLlewellyn) 3-9-2 TWilliams(8) (led 1f: led over 3f out tl over 2f out: sn wknd) ......½ **7**
1420* Longcroft **(42)**(35) (KWHogg) 3-9-1 AMackay(3) (s.i.s: bhd & drvn along: styd on fnl 3f: nvr nr ldrs) 4 **8**
1881¹³ Beyaateh **(27)**(16) (MCChapman) 3-8-0 NKennedy(9) (swtg: bhd: sme hdwy on outside 2f out: n.d) 3 **9**
1944⁶ Scylla **(39)**(23) (PCHaslam) 3-8-12 JWeaver(4) (bhd: hdwy u.p over 2f out: sn wknd) 4 **10**
1824¹² Sweet Cheap Pet **(35)**(13) (JJO'Neill) 3-8-8 FNorton(11) (led after 1f: hdd after 2f: led 4f out: sn hdd: wknd & eased wl over 1f out) 4 **11**
1863⁹ Runforaction (IRE) **(37)**(15) (BSRothwell) 3-8-10 LCharnock(2) (led after 1f to 4f out: sn wknd) ......hd **12**

9/4 Risky Rose, **3/1** Presto Boy, **5/1** Longcroft, **7/1** High Flown (USA), Coast Along (IRE), **12/1** BUNKER (IRE) (8/1-14/1), **14/1** Our Rainbow, **20/1** Gigfy, Scylla, **25/1** Runforaction (IRE), Sweet Cheap Pet, **33/1** Beyaateh, CSF £93.95 CT £595.28 TOTE £18.10: £4.00 £2.60 £2.30 (£68.90) Trio £261.70 OWNER Mr Jeff Pearce (NEWMARKET) BRED Bernard Cooke 12 Rn
2m 41.5 (7.20) SF: 32/32/17/21/27/21/15/9/-/-/-/-
Bt in 3,700 gns

2130 ACTIVE BUSINESS SERVICES H'CAP (0-90) (3-Y.O+) (Class C)
£7,115.00 (£2,120.00: £1,010.00: £455.00)
6f Stalls: Low GOING minus 0.30 sec per fur (GF) 3-45 (3-46)

1809¹⁰ **Halmanerror (61)**(69) (MrsJRRamsden) 5-8-11 KFallon(6) (lw: hld up & bhd: effrt ½-wy: styd on u.p: hung lft & led ins fnl f: drvn out) ......— **1**
1994² Cavers Yangous **(72)**(73) (MJohnston) 4-9-8 DHolland(2) (chsd ldrs: n.m.r & styd on same pce ins fnl f) 2½ **2**
1648⁶ Be Warned **(78)**(75)(Fav)(NACallaghan) 4-10-0b PatEddery(7) (trckd ldrs: led over 1f out tl ins fnl f: unable qckn) 1¾ **3**
1809⁸ Formidable Liz **(58)**(51) (MDHammond) 5-8-8 DaleGibson(5) (led: qcknd ½-wy: hdd over 1f out: grad wknd) 1¼ **4**
1864⁴ Magic Orb **(78)**(69) (JLHarris) 5-10-0 LDettori(1) (lw: b: effrt & hmpd over 1f out: nvr nr ldrs) 1 **5**
1915⁶ Jato **(74)**(64) (SCWilliams) 6-9-10 TIves(3) (b.nr fore: chsd ldrs: effrt ½-wy: sltly hmpd over 1f out: sn wknd) ......hd **6**
1380* Safey Ana (USA) **(70)**(52) (BHanbury) 4-9-3b(3) JStack(4) (b: reard s: hdwy on outside ½-wy: rdn & wnt lft over 1f out: sn wknd) 3 **7**

100/30 Be Warned, **7/2** HALMANERROR, **9/2** Cavers Yangous, **11/2** Jato, **6/1** Formidable Liz, Magic Orb, Safey Ana (USA), CSF £19.40 TOTE £5.70: £2.30 £1.60 (£12.80) OWNER Mrs Joan Smith(Lincoln)(THIRSK) BRED Ulceby Vale Stud Ltd 7 Rn 1m 16.7 (2.40) SF: 39/43/45/21/39/34/22

2131 SPINDRIFTER CONDITIONS STKS (2-Y.O) (Class C) £4,660.10
(£1,745.90: £855.45: £369.75: £167.38: £86.42)
6f Stalls: Low GOING minus 0.30 sec per fur (GF) 4-15 (4-15)

1838⁶ **Sea Dane** (97)(Fav)(PWHarris) 2-9-2 JWeaver(6) (lw: trckd ldrs: shkn up to ld over 1f out: drvn out: readily) ......— **1**
1715* Line Dancer (92) (WJarvis) 2-9-2 PatEddery(5) (lw: w ldr: led over 2f out tl over 1f out: kpt on: no ch w wnr) 2 **2**
1267⁸ Precious Girl **(69)**(75) (DMoffatt) 2-8-4 (3) DarrenMoffatt(4) (sn outpcd & bhd: edgd rt & styd on u.p fnl f: nvr nr ldrs) 3 **3**

1685* Ramsey Hope **(73)**_(78) (CWFairhurst)_ 2-9-0 NKennedy(2) (led tl over 2f out: hrd rdn & kpt on same pce) 1½ 4
1177³ Never Think Twice _(71) (KTIvory)_ 2-8-10 MTebbutt(1) (b: chsd ldrs: effrt over 2f out: outpcd over 1f out) 1 5
1556⁶ Silverdale Knight **(75)**_(54) (KWHogg)_ 2-8-12 AMackay(7) (racd wd: outpcd fr ½-wy) 7 6
1964* Sualtach (IRE) **(88)**_(37) (RHollinshead)_ 2-9-2 LDettori(3) (lw: trckd ldrs: effrt over 2f out: rdn & wknd over 1f out: eased) 8 7

11/10 SEA DANE, **5/2** Line Dancer, **3/1** Sualtach (IRE), **20/1** Ramsey Hope, **25/1** Precious Girl, Never Think Twice, Silverdale Knight, CSF £4.39 TOTE £1.90: £1.40 £1.40 (£2.00) OWNER Carat Gold Connections (BERKHAMSTED) BRED Miss K. Rausing 7 Rn
1m 17.2 (2.90) SF: 37/32/15/18/11/-/-

2132

HOUGHTON H'CAP (0-70) (3-Y.O+) (Class E) £3,377.25 (£1,008.00: £481.50: £218.25) **1m 2f 6y** Stalls: Low GOING minus 0.30 sec per fur (GF) 4-45 (4-45)

1825² **Silently (72)**_(82) (IABalding)_ 3-9-13 WRyan(7) (lw: trckd ldrs: qcknd to ld over 1f out: pushed clr: comf) ....— 1
1962* Kama Simba **(58)**_(65)_(Fav)_(NACallaghan)_ 3-8-13 5x PatEddery(5) (lw: hld up: effrt over 3f out: chsd wnr fnl f: no imp) 2 2
1917⁴ Bardia **(31)**_(35) (DonEnricoIncisa)_ 5-7-11 KimTinkler(4) (dwlt: bhd: stdy hdwy 4f out: effrt & outpcd over 1f out: kpt on ins fnl f) 1½ 3
1651⁷ Zanzara (IRE) **(39)**_(41) (MrsVAAconley)_ 4-8-5 MDeering(6) (w ldr: hrd rdn to ld 2f out: sn hdd: one pce) 1¼ 4
Durano **(62)**_(49) (MHEasterby)_ 4-10-0 MBirch(2) (prom: effrt over 3f out: sn wknd) 10 5
1724⁴ Sir Arthur Hobbs **(60)**_(40) (JLEyre)_ 8-9-12 RLappin(3) (b: mde most to 2f out: sn wknd) 4 6
1944⁵ Promitto **(44)**_(22) (MDHammond)_ 5-8-7 (3) JStack(1) (chsd ldrs: rdn over 3f out: wknd 2f out) 1¼ 7

6/4 Kama Simba, **9/4** SILENTLY, **5/1** Sir Arthur Hobbs, **8/1** Bardia, **16/1** Durano, **20/1** Zanzara (IRE), Promitto, CSF £5.83 TOTE £2.70: £1.50 £1.50 (£2.20) OWNER Mr Paul Mellon (KINGSCLE-RE) BRED Paul Mellon 7 Rn 2m 13.4 (5.10) SF: 48/31/12/18/26/17/-
WEIGHT FOR AGE 3yo-11lb

2133

PONTEFRACT SERIES (ROUND 3) MAIDEN APPRENTICE STKS (3-Y.O) (Class E) £2,983.20 (£909.60: £448.80: £218.40)
1m 2f 6y Stalls: Low GOING minus 0.30 sec per fur (GF) 5-15 (5-15)

1831⁸ **Chicodari (72)**_(47)_(Fav)_(SirMarkPrescott)_ 3-8-11 MHenry(3) (mde all: rdn clr over 1f out: hung rt: eased nr fin) ....— 1
1962⁷ Hunza Story **(38)**_(34) (NPLittmoden)_ 3-8-6 CAdamson(2) (dwlt: sn trckng wnr: effrt over 2f out: sn rdn & no imp) 5 2
Panama Hat (IRE) _(15) (PCHaslam)_ 3-8-4 (7) JulieLemin(1) (bit bkwd: chsd ldrs: reminders 5f out: wknd over 3f out) 15 3
1526¹⁶ Roscommon Lad (IRE) **(42)** _(RHollinshead)_ 3-8-8 (3) AEddery(4) (sn bhd & pushed along: t.o 3f out) ....dist 4

2/9 CHICODARI, **6/1** Panama Hat (IRE), **9/1** Hunza Story, **16/1** Roscommon Lad (IRE), CSF £2.99 TOTE £1.30: (£2.40) OWNER Hesmonds Stud (NEWMARKET) BRED Hesmonds Stud Ltd 4 Rn
2m 16.8 (8.50) SF: 8/-/-/-

T/Plpt: £93.30 (155.74 Tckts). T/Qdpt: £4.20 (23.6 Tckts). WG

1974-WINDSOR (Fig. 8)
Monday July 3rd (Good)

WEATHER: overcast WIND: nil

2134

UNION BANK OF SWITZERLAND (S) STKS (3-Y.O+) (Class G) £2,507.00 (£702.00: £341.00) **1m 67y** Stalls: High GOING minus 0.35 sec per fur (F) 6-30 (6-35)

1830⁴ **Cape Pigeon (USA) (62)**_(74)_(Fav)_(LGCottrell)_ 10-9-7v LDettori(2) (lw: mde all: clr 5f out: unchal) ....— 1
1523¹² Flair Lady **(48)**_(54) (WGMTurner)_ 4-8-11 RPerham(4) (3rd st: chsd wnr fnl 4f: no imp) 5 2
1940⁹ Roi de la Mer (IRE) **(57)**_(59) (JAkehurst)_ 4-9-2v GCarter(1) (hdwy over 2f out: r.o fnl f) ....hd 3
1974¹⁵ White Flash **(55)**_(48) (DRCElsworth)_ 4-8-11 MRoberts(6) (nvr nrr) 3 4
1092¹¹ Ballestro (IRE) **(40)**_(52) (JFfitch-Heyes)_ 3-8-7b RPrice(9) (lw: 4th st: one pce fnl 3f) ....½ 5
2016² Perilous Plight **(66)**_(56) (WRMuir)_ 4-9-7 TQuinn(5) (lw: 5th st: hdwy 4f out: hrd rdn 3f out: wknd over 1f out) ....¾ 6

Excelled (IRE) **(30)***(42) (CJDrewe)* 6-8-11 AClark(7) (bit bkwd: nvr nr to chal)..........2 7
1974[22] Northern Spruce (IRE) **(40)***(43) (MissJacquelineDoyle)* 3-8-2 (7)ow2 DaneO'Neill(3) (6th st: wknd over 2f out)..........2 8
Dirty Dancer *(43) (MMadgwick)* 6-9-2 CAvery(10) (lw: a bhd)..........nk 9
Tartan Dancer *(RPCHoad)* 6-9-2 StephenDavies(8) (swtg: 2nd st: wknd over 4f out: virtually p.u 3f out: t.o)..........dist 10

13/8 CAPE PIGEON (USA) (5/4-2/1), **2/1** Perilous Plight, **4/1** Roi de la Mer (IRE), **15/2** Flair Lady, **16/1** White Flash, **25/1** Dirty Dancer, **33/1** Ballestro (IRE), **50/1** Excelled (IRE), **66/1** Northern Spruce (IRE), Tartan Dancer, CSF £14.19 TOTE £2.50: £1.40 £1.60 £1.70 (£8.70) Trio £7.70 OWNER Mr E. J. S. Gadsden (CULLOMPTON) BRED Ashwood Thoroughbreds, Inc. 10 Rn

1m 46.4 (4.80) SF: 30/10/15/4/-/12/-/-/-/-
WEIGHT FOR AGE 3yo-9lb
No bid.

2135 TATTERSALLS MAIDEN AUCTION STKS (2-Y.O) (Class E) £4,484.00 (£1,352.00: £656.00: £308.00)
5f 10y Stalls: High GOING minus 0.35 sec per fur (F) 7-00 (7-07)

1879[4] **Rushcutter Bay** *(63) (TTClement)* 2-8-0 (7)ow5 DGibbs(11) (b.hind: a.p: led over 1f out: r.o wl)..........— 1
1142[9] Polish Bear (IRE) *(59) (BJMeehan)* 2-8-3 BDoyle(13) (a.p: led 2f out: sn hdd: r.o)..........1¾ 2
1652[2] Magic Imp (IRE) *(48) (WJMusson)* 2-7-11 AMackay(3) (wl bhd tl gd hdwy fnl 2f)..........1½ 3
1938[6] Dil Dil *(50)*(Fav)*(RHannon)* 2-8-2 MRoberts(7) (lw: rdn along: a.p: r.o one pce fnl 2f)..........¾ 4
725[4] All She Surveys *(41) (JAkehurst)* 2-8-0 ow2 GCarter(4) (nvr nrr)..........1¾ 5
1774[4] Dande Flyer *(43) (DWPArbuthnot)* 2-8-7 TQuinn(12) (b: b.hind: led over 3f)..........2 6
1938[7] Miss Carottene *(38) (MJRyan)* 2-8-3 AClark(2) (no hdwy fnl 2f)..........½ 7
1627[8] Nottonitejosephine *(28) (RBoss)* 2-7-8 (5) NVarley(8) (outpcd)..........2 8
Soul Risk *(34) (JARToller)* 2-8-7 LDettori(9) (unf: spd 3f)..........½ 9
1424[2] Vanishing Point *(32) (GLewis)* 2-8-7 MHills(5) (s.s: a bhd)..........½ 10
1833[7] Bouton d'Or *(11) (PHowling)* 2-7-12 ow1 GBardwell(6) (bhd fnl 2f)..........3½ 11
Cotytto *(13) (MJFetherston-Godley)* 2-7-13 FNorton(1) (leggy: unf: bit bkwd: s.s: a bhd)......s.h 12
1774[7] Malice Corner *(14) (LGCottrell)* 2-8-3 MFenton(10) (lw: outpcd)..........1 13

7/2 Dil Dil, **4/1** Miss Carottene (7/1-3/1), **5/1** Magic Imp (IRE) (op 5/2), **6/1** Vanishing Point (op 4/1), **9/1** Dande Flyer (7/1-12/1), **11/1** Polish Bear (IRE) (6/1-12/1), **12/1** Soul Risk (op 8/1), Nottonitejosephine, **20/1** All She Surveys, RUSHCUTTER BAY, Bouton d'Or, Cotytto, **33/1** Malice Corner, CSF £211.38 TOTE £17.10: £2.90 £5.30 £1.70 (£111.00) Trio £183.40 OWNER Treasure Seekers Partnership (NEWMARKET) BRED Lloyd Bros 13 Rn

61.4 secs (2.40) SF: 22/18/7/9/-/2/-/-/-/-/-/-/-

2136 JUDITH CHALMERS LADY TAVERNERS CONDITIONS STKS (2-Y.O F) (Class C) £5,344.00 (£1,864.00: £907.00: £385.00)
5f 217y Stalls: High GOING minus 0.35 sec per fur (F) 7-30 (7-31)

1849[5] **Tropical Dance (USA)** **(98)***(84+)*(Fav)*(MrsJCecil)* 2-8-12 JReid(4) (lw: mde all: r.o wl)..........— 1
1790* Forentia *(79) (JRFanshawe)* 2-8-12 DHarrison(3) (a.p: ev ch whn hung bdly lft over 1f out: nt qckn)..........2 2
1823* Fag End (IRE) **(68)***(73) (MHTompkins)* 2-8-10 PRobinson(1) (chsd wnr over 3f: btn whn carried lft over 1f out)..........1½ 3
Kebili (IRE) *(57) (MRStoute)* 2-8-8 WCarson(5) (w'like: bit bkwd: dwlt: swished tail repeatedly: a last)..........5 4

11/10 TROPICAL DANCE (USA) (Evens-6/5), **9/4** Forentia, **9/2** Fag End (IRE), Kebili (IRE) (2/1-5/1), CSF £4.00 TOTE £2.10 (£1.90) OWNER Mr George Ward (NEWMARKET) BRED Charles T Wilson Jr. 4 Rn

1m 12.7 (2.20) SF: -/-/-/-

2137 COOPERS & LYBRAND H'CAP (0-70) (3-Y.O+) (Class E) £3,345.00 (£1,005.00: £485.00: £225.00)
5f 217y Stalls: High GOING minus 0.35 sec per fur (F) 8-00 (8-00)

2108[3] **Great Hall** **(53)***(62) (PDCundell)* 6-9-0b DHarrison(1) (gd hdwy 2f out: led ins fnl f: r.o)..........— 1
1972* Tael of Silver **(66)***(70) (KRBurke)* 3-9-6 7x MFenton(8) (hdwy over 1f out: r.o ins fnl f)..........2 2
1975[6] Bold Cyrano (IRE) **(52)***(55) (BPalling)* 4-8-13 TSprake(4) (lw: hdwy fnl 2f: r.o)..........hd 3
1429[8] Cedar Girl **(49)***(47) (RJHodges)* 3-7-10 (7) AmandaSanders(2) (led: rdn & edgd lft 1f out: hdd & wknd ins fnl f)..........2 4
1975[2] Petraco (IRE) **(61)***(54)*(Fav)*(NASmith)* 7-9-8 LDettori(11) (a.p: rdn & no hdwy fnl 2f)..........2 5
1786[9] Vavona **(56)***(45) (LJHolt)* 3-8-10 JReid(12) (lw: a mid div: rdn 2f out: one pce)..........1½ 6
1797[12] Caddy's First **(52)***(40) (SMellor)* 3-7-13 (7) ADaly(3) (prom over 3f)..........nk 7

1499[14] Nordman Lass **(49)***(32) (MissJacquelineDoyle)* 3-8-3 BDoyle(6) (nvr nr to chal)....................1¾ **8**
1832[5] Rocky Two **(54)***(36) (PHowling)* 4-9-1b MRoberts(10) (spd 4f)....................½ **9**
1257[12] Green Apache **(39)***(17) (TJNaughton)* 3-7-7 NAdams(9) (s.s: a bhd)....................1½ **10**
1832[19] Norling (IRE) **(56)***(33) (KOCunningham-Brown)* 5-9-3 GCarter(5) (spd over 3f)....................½ **11**
2017[5] Frisky Miss (IRE) **(63)***(38) (KOCunningham-Brown)* 4-9-10 AMcGlone(7) (spd over 3f)....................½ **12**

LONG HANDICAP Green Apache 6-10

2/1 Petraco (IRE), **7/2** GREAT HALL, **5/1** Tael of Silver (3/1-11/2), **15/2** Rocky Two (5/1-8/1), **8/1** Vavona (5/1-9/1), **12/1** Frisky Miss (IRE), **14/1** Bold Cyrano (IRE), **20/1** Norling (IRE), Caddy's First, **25/1** Cedar Girl, **33/1** Nordman Lass, **50/1** Green Apache, CSF £21.72 CT £209.22 TOTE £5.40: £1.40 £2.30 £3.70 (£11.20) Trio £93.90 OWNER Miss M. C. Fraser (NEWBURY) BRED Dorothea Viscountess Kelburn 12 Rn 1m 12.6 (2.10) SF: 39/40/32/17/31/15/10/2/13/-/10/15

WEIGHT FOR AGE 3yo-7lb

2138

PIPER CHAMPAGNE AND RAFFLES NIGHTCLUB H'CAP (0-75) (3-Y.O+) (Class D) £3,718.75 (£1,120.00: £542.50: £253.75)
1m 3f 135y Stalls: High GOING minus 0.35 sec per fur (F) 8-30 (8-31)

1716[6] **Haroldon (IRE) (68)***(79) (BPalling)* 6-10-0 TSprake(5) (b: 3rd st: led 2f out: r.o wl)....................— **1**
1776[4] Hadabet **(54)***(60) (MissJacquelineDoyle)* 3-8-1 ow1 BDoyle(6) (lw: 2nd st: led over 2f out: sn hdd: r.o)....................3 **2**
1733[4] Scenic Dancer **(48)***(51) (AHide)* 7-8-8 WWoods(1) (lw: 6th st: hdwy & hrd rdn 2f out: nt rch ldrs)....................3 **3**
676[7] Eden's Close **(61)***(62) (MHTompkins)* 6-9-7 PRobinson(3) (led tl wknd over 2f out)....................1 **4**
1861[2] Admirals Secret (USA) **(67)***(66) (CFWall)* 6-9-8 (5) LNewton(4) (lw: 5th st: wknd 3f out)....................2 **5**
1014* Carpathian **(55)***(47)*(Fav)*(LordHuntingdon)* 4-9-1 LDettori(2) (lw: 4th st: rdn over 3f out: no rspnse)....................5 **6**

Evens Carpathian, **4/1** Scenic Dancer, **6/1** Admirals Secret (USA) (7/2-13/2), **13/2** Hadabet, **12/1** HAROLDON (IRE) (op 5/1), Eden's Close (op 5/1), CSF £72.55 TOTE £14.30: £4.30 £2.20 (£35.90) OWNER Lamb Brook Associates (COWBRIDGE) BRED Owen Bourke in Ireland 6 Rn 2m 31.9 (5.90) SF: 44/12/16/27/31/12

WEIGHT FOR AGE 3yo-13lb

2139

D.B.S. FINANCIAL MANAGEMENT LIMITED STKS (0-65) (3-Y.O+) (Class F) £3,174.50 (£956.00: £463.00: £216.50)
1m 2f 7y Stalls: High GOING minus 0.35 sec per fur (F) 9-00 (9-01)

1875[3] **Quivira (62)***(72) (TTClement)* 4-9-3 MRimmer(7) (lw: 3rd st: led ins fnl f: r.o wl)....................— **1**
1922* Finlaggan **(69)***(71)*(Fav)*(SirMarkPrescott)* 3-8-6 GDuffield(6) (led 2f: 2nd st: led over 2f out tl ins fnl f: r.o)....................½ **2**
988[2] Zacaroon **(65)***(69) (LordHuntingdon)* 4-9-1 LDettori(3) (lw: 4th st: jnd ldr 2f out: ev ch: nt qckn nr fin)....................nk **3**
1658* Myfontaine **(64)***(69) (KTIvory)* 8-9-12 GBardwell(1) (lw: bhd tl hdwy 3f out: nvr nr to chal)....................7 **4**
1219[4] Westminster (IRE) **(65)***(57) (MHTompkins)* 3-8-11 PRobinson(12) (lw: 8th st: nvr trbld ldrs)....................5 **5**
11[5] Mulciber **(61)***(50) (GHarwood)* 7-9-6 MHills(11) (6th st: wknd over 2f out)....................3 **6**
1955[9] Dynamis (IRE) **(60)***(44) (KOCunningham-Brown)* 4-9-3 BDoyle(10) (lw: led after 2f tl wknd over 2f out)....................1¾ **7**
1811[8] Lorelei Lee (IRE) **(65)***(40) (JohnBerry)* 3-8-6 DHarrison(4) (lw: hdwy & 5th st: wknd over 2f out)....................2½ **8**
1658[5] Bell Contractors (IRE) **(60)***(22) (CDBroad)* 3-8-6 (3) DRMcCabe(9) (prom tl wknd & 7th st).....13 **9**
1442[4] Fairelaine **(60)***(9) (APJarvis)* 3-8-1 (3) DWright(2) (lw: a bhd)....................5 **10**
1736[9] Grooms Gold (IRE) **(63)** *(PWHarris)* 3-8-9 AClark(8) (lw: plld hrd: sddle slipped early: t.o)....................dist **11**

9/4 Finlaggan, **11/4** Zacaroon, **9/2** QUIVIRA, **8/1** Myfontaine (5/1-9/1), **11/1** Westminster (IRE) (8/1-12/1), **12/1** Grooms Gold (IRE) (20/1-10/1), **16/1** Fairelaine, Lorelei Lee (IRE), Bell Contractors (IRE), Mulciber, **33/1** Dynamis (IRE), CSF £15.72 TOTE £6.10: £1.70 £1.90 £1.50 (£11.80) Trio £6.80 OWNER Mr Maurice Kirby (NEWMARKET) BRED Sheikh Mohammed bin Rashid al Maktoum 11 Rn 2m 9.0 (4.10) SF: 41/29/38/38/15/19/13/-/-/-/-

WEIGHT FOR AGE 3yo-11lb

T/Jkpt: Not Won; £4,952.49 to Chepstow 4/7/95. T/Plpt: £369.10 (50.94 Tckts). T/Qdpt: Not Won; £78.00 to Chepstow 4/7/95. Hn

2071-WOLVERHAMPTON (L-H)
Monday July 3rd (Standard)
WEATHER: overcast WIND: almost nil

2140 ANSELLS MAIDEN H'CAP (0-65) (3-Y.O+ F & M) (Class F) £2,519.00 (£694.00: £329.00) **1m 100y (Fibresand)** Stalls: Low GOING: 0.22 sec (SLW) 2-30 (2-30)

*1569*5 **Equity's Darling (IRE) (58)***(64)*(Fav)*(MBell)* 3-9-1 GDuffield(7) (lw: hld up: hdwy ½-wy: 4th & rdn st: led ent fnl f: r.o wl) — 1
15225 She Said No **(52)***(55) (LordHuntingdon)* 3-8-9 DHarrison(8) (hld up: hdwy over 3f out: 2nd st: ev ch 1f out: unable qckn) 1¾ 2
166312 Rosevear (IRE) **(50)***(47) (SMellor)* 3-8-7 ow1 MWigham(3) (hld up & bhd: gd hdwy 2f out: fin wl) 2½ 3
169213 Fyne Song **(37)***(32) (WJMusson)* 3-7-8 ow1 JQuinn(11) (chsd ldr: led over 2f out tl hdd 1f out: no ex) 1¼ 4
167616 Audrey Grace **(47)***(33) (BJMeehan)* 4-8-13v BDoyle(2) (s.s: bhd: hdwy fnl 2f: 5th st: nvr nr to chal) 5 5
124910 Qualitair Pride **(55)***(37) (JFBottomley)* 3-8-12 ACulhane(9) (hld up mid div: effrt 3f out: nvr plcd to chal) 2 6
10278 Glitter of Gold **(56)***(37) (SCWilliams)* 4-9-5 (3) DWright(5) (prom 5f: sn rdn & wknd) ½ 7
6589 Distant Princess **(65)***(44) (BWHills)* 3-9-8 JCarroll(6) (chsd ldrs tl 6th & wkng st) 1¼ 8
*1883*10 Honest Woman **(29)***(4) (NEBerry)* 4-7-9b NAdams(10) (led tl over 2f out: 3rd & rdn st: wknd) 2 9
Loving Legacy **(62)***(36) (WJHaggas)* 4-10-0 RCochrane(1) (b.off hind: b.nr fore: bit bkwd: a bhd) ¾ 10
16565 Alpine Storm (IRE) **(47)***(13) (MDIUsher)* 3-8-4 RPrice(4) (lw: swtg: a in rr) 4 11

3/1 EQUITY'S DARLING (IRE), **9/2** She Said No, Distant Princess, **5/1** Loving Legacy, **8/1** Audrey Grace, **10/1** Glitter of Gold, **16/1** Fyne Song, **20/1** Qualitair Pride, Rosevear (IRE), **33/1** Honest Woman, Alpine Storm (IRE), CSF £16.20 CT £205.49 TOTE £3.50: £1.20 £1.50 £5.00 (£6.60) Trio £46.80 OWNER Innlaw Racing (NEWMARKET) BRED Pat Doyle 11 Rn
1m 53.5 (9.50) SF: 27/18/10/-/5/-/9/7/-/8/-
WEIGHT FOR AGE 3yo-9lb

2141 CASTLEMAINE XXXX CLAIMING STKS (I) (3-Y.O+) (Class F) £2,519.00 (£694.00: £329.00)
7f (Fibresand) Stalls: High GOING: 0.22 sec per fur (SLW) 3-00 (3-04)

18732 **My Gallery (IRE) (50)***(58) (ABailey)* 4-8-1 (3) SSanders(10) (hld up: hdwy 3f out: 2nd st: led wl over 1f out: rdn clr) — 1
*1951*3 Legatee **(61)***(56) (BJMeehan)* 4-8-8 BDoyle(3) (a.p: 3rd st: rdn & one pce appr fnl f) 2½ 2
*1953*6 Forzair **(68)***(70) (MMcCormack)* 3-9-1b PaulEddery(4) (led tl hdd wl over 1f out: sn hrd rdn: one pce) ½ 3
16266 Hawwam **(73)***(52)*(Fav)*(EJAlston)* 9-9-1 (5)ow1 AProcter(7) (dwlt: hdwy 4f out: 4th & outpcd ent st: sn btn) 6 4
*1629*6 Dream Carrier (IRE) **(65)***(42) (JGMO'Shea)* 7-8-2 (7) AmandaSanders(8) (hld up: hdwy 3f out: 5th st: kpt on same pce) hd 5
171416 Magical Belle (IRE) **(47)***(19) (CASmith)* 3-7-12 JQuinn(1) (a bhd & outpcd) 9 6
*1761*4 Campaspe *(22) (JGFitzGerald)* 3-8-2 JFanning(6) (swtg: a in r) nk 7
Night Excellence *(29) (BWHills)* 3-9-1 RStreet(5) (h.d.w: bkwd: b.hind: prom tl wknd & 6th st) 2½ 8
*2076*12 Caherass Court (IRE) **(49)** *(BPreece)* 4-8-6 NAdams(11) (chsd ldrs to ½-wy: sn lost tch: t.o) 20 9
160210 Super Look *(TJEtherington)* 3-8-4 JCarroll(9) (lw: dwlt: a wl bhd: t.o) ¾ 10
190510 Knotty Scot *(JJBridger)* 3-7-9 (7)ow2 ADaly(2) (bit bkwd: prom early: sn rdn & lost pl: t.o) ½ 11

5/2 Hawwam (7/4-11/4), **11/4** MY GALLERY (IRE), **9/2** Legatee, **11/2** Forzair, **9/1** Night Excellence (op 5/1), **14/1** Dream Carrier (IRE), **20/1** Magical Belle (IRE), **33/1** Super Look, Caherass Court (IRE), **40/1** Campaspe, Knotty Scot, CSF £15.16 TOTE £3.90: £1.30 £1.90 £1.90 (£5.30) Trio £11.10 OWNER Mr Gordon Mytton (TARPORLEY) BRED East Riding Sack and Paper Co 11 Rn
1m 29.9 (5.90) SF: 37/35/41/31/21/-/-/-/-/-/-
WEIGHT FOR AGE 3yo-8lb

2142 CASTLEMAINE XXXX CLAIMING STKS (II) (3-Y.O+) (Class F) £2,519.00 (£694.00: £329.00) **7f (Fibresand)** Stalls: High GOING: 0.22 sec per fur (SLW) 3-30 (3-30)

*1951** **Sweet Supposin (IRE) (80)***(80+) (KMcAuliffe)* 4-9-7b DHarrison(5) (hdwy to ld over 2f out: sn wl clr: eased fnl f) — 1

1995 12 Wentbridge Lad (IRE) **(82)***(74) (PDEvans)* 5-9-6 (3) SSanders(2) (hdwy 3f out: 3rd st: chsd wnr appr fnl f: no imp) 3½ 2
*1951*2 No Submission (USA) **(68)***(54) (DWChapman)* 9-9-3b DeanMcKeown(8) (lw: s.i.s: r.o fnl 2f: nvr nrr) 6 3
Red Phantom (IRE) *(49) (SMellor)* 3-8-9 MWigham(1) (w'like: bkwd: bhd & outpcd tl r.o appr fnl f) 2½ 4
1963 13 Out of the Mist **(32)***(39) (JAPickering)* 4-8-11b JQuinn(3) (led to ½-wy: 4th & outpcd ent st) 1¾ 5
985 11 Petomi **(75)***(27)*(Fav)*(SirMarkPrescott)* 3-8-10 GDuffield(4) (prom: led ½-wy tl over 2f out: 2nd st: wknd bel dist) 8 6
1818 7 Ganador **(53)***(14) (JBerry)* 3-8-4 JCarroll(6) (swtg: chsd ldrs: 6th & rdn st: sn bhd) 3 7
*1882*3 Little Saboteur **(69)***(5) (PJMakin)* 6-8-12 RCochrane(7) (b.nr hind: in tch over 4f) 4 8
Sabella *(RHarris)* 4-8-10 CDwyer(10) (bkwd: prom tl 5th & btn st) 1¼ 9
Soviet Union *(JJBridger)* 3-8-11 JFanning(9) (leggy: bkwd: s.s: a wl bhd: t.o) 25 10

13/8 Petomi, **3/1** SWEET SUPPOSIN (IRE), **7/2** Wentbridge Lad (IRE), **8/1** Little Saboteur, No Submission (USA), **20/1** Ganador, **33/1** Sabella, Out of the Mist, Soviet Union, **40/1** Red Phantom (IRE), CSF £14.08 TOTE £4.70: £1.70 £1.80 £1.60 (£9.00) Trio £6.10 OWNER Mount Juliet Stud (LAMBOURN) BRED Ballylinch Stud Ltd 10 Rn 1m 30.3 (6.30) SF: 48/42/22/9/7/-/-/-/-/-

WEIGHT FOR AGE 3yo-8lb

Sweet Supposin (IRE) clmd SGough £9,000

2143 CARLSBERG PILSNER MAIDEN AUCTION STKS (2-Y.O) (Class E)

£3,359.40 (£1,003.20: £479.60: £217.80)
6f (Fibresand) Stalls: Low GOING: 0.22 sec per fur (SLW) 4-00 (4-02)

1375 4 **Itsinthepost (66)***(66) (MJohnston)* 2-8-2 PRobinson(11) (swtg: hdwy over 2f out: hmpd & swtchd lft ent fnl f: hrd rdn to ld nr fin) ....— 1
1690 2 Weetman's Weigh (IRE) **(63)***(66) (RHollinshead)* 2-8-3 DHarrison(5) (hld up: hdwy over 2f out: rdn to ld ins fnl f: ct cl home) ....nk 2
1511 10 Charterhouse Xpres *(66) (MMcCormack)* 2-8-7 DeanMcKeown(9) (w ldrs: led ent st tl ins fnl f) 1¾ 3
1540 P Sphinx Levelv (IRE) *(43) (APJarvis)* 2-8-0 (3) DWright(4) (bit bkwd: hdwy 2f out: kpt on fnl f: nvr nr to chal) 7 4
1774 5 Chemcast *(43) (BJMeehan)* 2-8-3 BDoyle(10) (bit bkwd: led over 3f out tl hdd 2f out: rdn & wknd fnl f) ....s.h 5
1790 2 Amoeba (IRE) *(41)*(Fav)*(JBerry)* 2-8-4 ow2 JCarroll(7) (led over 2f: hrd rdn & wknd appr fnl f) ....nk 6
1352 2 Bobsworthatcaspers **(56)***(36) (GLewis)* 2-8-1 ow1 PaulEddery(3) (outpcd: a bhd) 1 7
1448 4 Katie Komaite *(33) (CaptJWilson)* 2-7-13 ow1 JFanning(12) (swtg: gd spd 4f) ....½ 8
1823 4 Priddy Fair *(27) (RBoss)* 2-7-4 (5) NVarley(8) (lw: chsd ldr: rdn & outpcd 2f out) 1 9
The Kastarbids (IRE) *(25) (DMorris)* 2-8-6 ow3 RCochrane(2) (lt-f: s.s: a bhd & outpcd) 4 10
1646 2 Some Horse (IRE) *(21) (MGMeagher)* 2-8-3 JQuinn(1) (b: a bhd & outpcd) 1¼ 11
*1597*8 Steal 'Em *(ABailey)* 2-7-13 (3) SSanders(6) (Withdrawn not under Starter's orders: inj at s) ..... W

, **2/1** Amoeba (IRE), **7/1** Weetman's Weigh (IRE), **8/1** Some Horse (IRE) (6/1-9/1), Bobsworthatcaspers (6/1-9/1), **10/1** Priddy Fair (6/1-12/1), ITSINTHEPOST, Chemcast, **12/1** Sphinx Levelv (IRE), **14/1** The Kastarbids (IRE) (8/1-16/1), **20/1** Charterhouse Xpres, Katie Komaite, CSF £58.37 TOTE £11.90: £2.20 £1.60 £6.40 (£21.00) Trio £218.70 OWNER First Class-Four Seasons (MIDDLEHAM) BRED Roldvale Ltd 11 Rn 1m 17.2 (6.00) SF: 22/22/22/-/-/-/-/-/-/-/-

STEWARDS' ENQUIRY Wright suspended 16-17/7/95 (careless riding).

2144 TETLEY BITTER H'CAP (0-65) (3-Y.O) (Class F) £2,519.00 (£694.00: £329.00)

6f (Fibresand) Stalls: Low GOING: 0.22 sec per fur (SLW) 4-30 (4-30)

1718 8 **Jersey Belle (44)***(56) (PJMakin)* 3-8-7 GDuffield(8) (lw: hdwy over 2f out: rdn to ld ins fnl f: r.o wl) ....— 1
1541 16 Hong Kong Dollar **(53)***(63) (BJMeehan)* 3-9-2b BDoyle(3) (led tl ins fnl f: kpt on u.p nr fin) ......¾ 2
1906 4 Scissor Ridge **(51)***(54) (JJBridger)* 3-8-7 (7) ADaly(6) (a.p: rdn bel dist: unable qckn) 2½ 3
1445 14 Abbey House **(58)***(51) (RGuest)* 3-9-4b(3) SSanders(7) (lw: w ldrs: rdn 2f out: wknd fnl f) 4 4
*2071*8 Ho Mei Surprise **(40)***(27) (BPreece)* 3-8-3 NAdams(5) (hdwy ½-wy: rdn 2f out: nt pce to chal) 2 5
*1763*2 Most Uppitty **(55)***(26)*(Fav)*(JBerry)* 3-9-4 JCarroll(4) (s.i.s: effrt ½-wy: sn rdn along: no imp: t.o) 6 6
*830*4 Lawnswood Lady **(40)***(9) (RHollinshead)* 3-7-10 (7) FLynch(1) (outpcd ½-wy: sn bhd: t.o) ....¾ 7
1483 6 Runs in the Family **(55)***(22) (PGMurphy)* 3-9-4 DHarrison(2) (chsd ldrs: rdn & outpcd 2f out: eased whn btn: t.o) ....¾ 8

11/4 Most Uppitty (5/1-3/1), **7/2** Runs in the Family, **5/1** Abbey House, **11/2** Hong Kong Dollar, **8/1** Scissor Ridge, JERSEY BELLE, **10/1** Ho Mei Surprise, **14/1** Lawnswood Lady (8/1-16/1), CSF £48.12 CT £333.36 TOTE £8.20: £2.00 £2.00 £2.10 (£19.00) OWNER Mr D. A. Poole (MARLBOROUGH) BRED B and Mrs Shelton 8 Rn 1m 16.9 (5.70) SF: 31/38/29/26/2/1/-/-

2145 VANGUARD LIMITED STKS (0-70) (3-Y.O+) (Class E) £3,130.60 (£932.80: £444.40: £200.20) **1m 4f (Fibresand)** Stalls: Low GOING: 0.22 sec(SLW) 5-00 (5-01)

1978[2] **Persian Conquest (IRE) (70)***(84) (RIngram)* 3-8-9b AMcGlone(5) (lw: led tl wl over 1f out: rallied up to ld fnl strides)........— 1
2068[8] Locorotondo (IRE) **(69)***(75) (MBell)* 4-8-6 (7) GFaulkner(9) (hld up: hdwy 4f out: 2nd st: led wl over 1f out tl ct cl home)........hd 2
1955[2] Sommersby (IRE) **(66)***(74) (MrsNMacauley)* 4-9-6 DeanMcKeown(8) (lw: hld up: hdwy 4f out: 3rd st: sn rdn: one pce)........6 3
1955[4] Pistols At Dawn (USA) **(50)***(71) (BJMeehan)* 5-9-8 PaulEddery(1) (chsd ldrs: 4th & rdn st: r.o one pce)........3½ 4
1600[5] Polish Consul **(65)***(66) (MajorWRHern)* 4-9-4 TSprake(3) (prom st: sn rdn along & btn)........1 5
2002[4] Reported (IRE) **(70)***(69) (BPreece)* 6-9-5 (3) SSanders(2) (hld up: hdwy over 3f out: 6th st: nvr nr ldrs)........¾ 6
*1789** Music Maker **(65)***(60)*(Fav)*(SirMarkPrescott)* 3-8-2 GDuffield(7) (lw: hld up: hdwy ½-wy: 5th & btn ent st)........1¾ 7
1659[4] Castoret **(70)***(51) (JWHills)* 9-9-4 DHarrison(6) (bit bkwd: chsd ldrs 8f: sn lost tch: t.o)........9 8
1755[11] Lucky Quest **(67)***(11) (NAGraham)* 3-8-5 JCarroll(4) (prom: rdn 7f out: sn lost tch: t.o)........30 9

9/4 Music Maker, **5/2** Sommersby (IRE), **6/1** PERSIAN CONQUEST (IRE) (4/1-13/2), **15/2** Castoret (9/2-8/1), **8/1** Polish Consul, **10/1** Locorotondo (IRE) (op 6/1), **14/1** Reported (IRE) (10/1-16/1), **20/1** Lucky Quest, **25/1** Pistols At Dawn (USA), CSF £58.49 TOTE £7.30: £2.20 £1.40 £1.50 (£28.20) Trio £45.90 OWNER Mrs A. V. Cappuccini (EPSOM) BRED Louis A. Walshe 9 Rn
2m 41.7 (10.70) SF: 40/44/43/40/35/38/16/20/-
WEIGHT FOR AGE 3yo-13lb

2146 CARLSBERG EXPORT (S) STKS (2-Y.O) (Class G) £2,243.00 (£618.00: £293.00) **5f (Fibresand)** Stalls: Low GOING: 0.22 sec per fur (SLW) 5-30 (5-32)

1989[2] **Nameless (55)***(59) (DJSCosgrove)* 2-8-6 (5) PMcCabe(5) (lw: swtg: mde all: clr over 1f out: unchal)........— 1
2000[4] Boffy (IRE) *(49) (BPJBaugh)* 2-8-11 ACulhane(8) (hld up: hdwy over 2f out: kpt on fnl f: no ch w wnr)........3 2
1640[3] Wingnut (IRE) **(59)***(39) (GLewis)* 2-8-6 SWhitworth(4) (prom: rdn over 1f out: one pce)........1¾ 3
1640[5] Touch of Fantasy **(52)***(38) (JohnBerry)* 2-8-3 (3) SDrowne(10) (chsd ldrs: rdn over 1f out: kpt on ins fnl f)........nk 4
1954[5] Dhulikhel *(35) (DMarks)* 2-8-3 (3) SSanders(1) (chsd ldrs: rdn bel dist: nt pce to chal)........¾ 5
*1570** Abbott of Whalley *(20)*(Fav)*(JBerry)* 2-9-2 JCarroll(2) (lw: spd to ½-wy: sn rdn & wknd)........8 6
1758[7] L A Touch *(5) (JohnBerry)* 2-8-8 ow2 CDwyer(9) (outpcd: a bhd)........1½ 7
1954[4] Just Rory **(52)***(6) (EJAlston)* 2-8-6b(5) HKYim(7) (chsd ldrs 3f: sn rdn & outpcd)........1¼ 8
1090[7] Waitingforwalnuts (IRE) *(CASmith)* 2-8-8 ow2 MWigham(3) (outpcd: a bhd)........¾ 9
1327[4] Morning Surprise *(APJarvis)* 2-8-3 (3) DWright(6) (s.i.s: a wl bhd & outpcd)........¾ 10

5/2 Abbott of Whalley (7/4-11/4), **3/1** NAMELESS, **5/1** Wingnut (IRE) (3/1-11/2), **6/1** Boffy (IRE), **12/1** Just Rory (op 25/1), **14/1** Touch of Fantasy, Morning Surprise (10/1-16/1), **25/1** Waitingforwalnuts (IRE), **33/1** L A Touch, Dhulikhel, CSF £19.60 TOTE £3.70: £1.20 £2.00 £1.80 (£10.80) Trio £15.00 OWNER Mr J. C. Wilson (NEWMARKET) BRED J. Ford 10 Rn
64.2 secs (6.20) SF: 10/-/-/-/-/-/-/-/-/-
No bid.

2147 ANSELLS H'CAP (0-60) (3-Y.O+) (Class F) £3,098.60 (£859.60: £411.80) **1m 6f 166y (Fibresand)** Stalls: High GOING: 0.22 sec per fur (SLW) 6-00 (6-03)

1955[5] **Rolling Waters (55)***(72) (JARToller)* 5-10-0 WNewnes(9) (hld up: hdwy 4f out: 3rd st: led 1f out: sn clr: comf)........— 1
*1881** Armston **(61)***(74) (JWharton)* 3-9-4 JQuinn(7) (hld up: hdwy 5f out: led over 2f out to 1f out: one pce)........4 2
2072[2] Awestruck **(40)***(49) (BPreece)* 5-8-13b GDuffield(8) (s.i.s: hdwy ½-wy: 4th st: sn ev ch: rdn & no imp fnl f)........3½ 3
1643[5] Swordking (IRE) **(41)***(48)*(Fav)*(JLHarris)* 6-9-0 PaulEddery(4) (a.p: led over 3f out tl hdd & 2nd st: sn rdn & btn)........2 4
833[5] Child Star (FR) **(42)***(27) (DMarks)* 6-8-12 (3) SSanders(3) (prom: rdn & outpcd 3f out: 5th & btn st: t.o)........20 5

1596[5] Tremendisto **(49)***(28) (CaptJWilson)* 5-9-8 JFanning(6) (prom tl rdn & wknd over 3f out: t.o) 6 **6**

*1759** Who's the Best (IRE) **(48)***(23) (APJarvis)* 5-9-4 (3) DWright(2) (plld hrd: prom tl wknd 4f out: t.o) 3½ **7**

*1628** Frome Lad **(60)***(32) (WGMTurner)* 3-8-12 (5) PMcCabe(10) (led tl hdd over 3f out: 6th & btn st: t.o) 3 **8**

1622[8] Kalakate **(38)***(7) (JJBridger)* 10-8-11 DeanMcKeown(5) (dropped rr 7f out: sn t.o) 2½ **9**

1527[9] Danus Rex (IRE) **(57)** *(CASmith)* 3-9-0 MWigham(1) (Withdrawn not under Starter's orders: broke out of stalls: jockey inj) .... **W**

, **9/4** Swordking (IRE), **9/2** Frome Lad, **5/1** Armston (op 3/1), **7/1** Tremendisto, Awestruck, **8/1** Who's the Best (IRE), **12/1** Child Star (FR), **14/1** ROLLING WATERS (op 8/1), **20/1** Kalakate, CSF £70.95 CT £373.34 TOTE £20.90: £4.90 £2.80 £1.90 (£39.60) Trio £228.10 OWNER Blandford (WHITSBURY) BRED R. E. Crutchley 9 Rn 3m 22.4 (15.00) SF: 49/35/26/25/4/5/-/-/-/-
WEIGHT FOR AGE 3yo-16lb

T/Plpt: £131.00 (90.2 Tckts). T/Qdpt: Not Won; £68.40 to Chepstow 4/7/95. IM

2109-CHEPSTOW (L-H)
Tuesday July 4th (Good to firm)

WEATHER: overcast WIND: almost nil

2148 BOLLINGER CHAMPAGNE CHALLENGE SERIES AMATEUR H'CAP (0-70) (3-Y.O+) (Class G) £2,367.00 (£662.00: £321.00)

1m 14y Stalls: High GOING minus 0.70 sec per fur (HD) 2-00 (2-07)

2112[2] **Asterix (44)***(61)*(Fav)*(JMBradley)* 7-10-8v MrRJohnson(4) (hld up: hdwy 3f out: led wl over 1f out: sn clr: drvn out) ....— **1**

1940[6] Courting Newmarket **(44)***(41) (MrsAKnight)* 7-10-4 (4) MrLJefford(6) (lw: led 1f: led over 2f out tl wl over 1f out: no ch w wnr) 10 **2**

1749[4] Irkutsk (USA) **(64)***(58)*(Fav)*(MCPipe)* 4-12-0 MrJDurkan(7) (rdn over 5f out: hdwy over 1f out: nt rch ldrs) 1½ **3**

1966[7] Salska **(60)***(54) (ALForbes)* 4-11-6 (4) MrPClinton(5) (wl bhd tl gd hdwy 2f out: one pce fnl f) .s.h **4**

1854[10] Formaestre (IRE) **(35)***(17) (RLee)* 5-9-9 (4) MrKSantana(3) (chsd ldrs 5f) 6 **5**

2076[9] Welsh Column **(30)***(7) (MWEckley)* 9-9-4 (4) MrVLukaniuk(2) (led after 1f: hdd over 2f out: sn wknd) 2½ **6**

1459[6] Exclusive Assembly **(50)***(23) (APJames)* 3-10-5 MrJLLlewellyn(1) (plld hrd: prom: hrd rdn over 3f out: sn wknd) 2 **7**

Mascalls Lady **(41)** *(NBThomson)* 10-10-1 (4)ow12 MrSDavis(8) (sn t.o) 20 **8**

LONG HANDICAP Mascalls Lady 9-5

2/1 ASTERIX, Irkutsk (USA) (6/4-9/4), **5/1** Exclusive Assembly, **7/1** Courting Newmarket, **16/1** Formaestre (IRE), **20/1** Salska, **50/1** Welsh Column, **100/1** Mascalls Lady, CSF £14.30 CT £24.42 TOTE £2.40: £1.10 £1.90 £1.40 (£8.00) OWNER Mr Clifton Hunt (CHEPSTOW) BRED Sexton Enterprises 8 Rn 1m 33.9 (1.40) SF: 43/23/40/36/-/-/-/-
WEIGHT FOR AGE 3yo-9lb

2149 SUMMER (S) STKS (3-Y.O) (Class G) £2,395.00 (£670.00: £325.00)

1m 14y GOING minus 0.70 sec per fur (HD) 2-30 (0-23)

1962[6] **Just Fizzy (55)***(58)*(Fav)*(MCPipe)* 3-9-0 TQuinn(6) (mde all: clr over 1f out: pushed out) .....— **1**

2102[3] Irie Mon (IRE) **(60)***(56)*(Fav)*(JWHills)* 3-8-12 (7) MHenry(8) (w wnr: ev ch over 2f out: no imp) 3½ **2**

1718[5] Miltak **(38)***(43) (PJMakin)* 3-8-6 (3) SSanders(5) (b: hld up: rdn & hdwy 2f out: hung bdly lft over 1f out: one pce) 1¾ **3**

1519[7] Tirollac (IRE) **(45)***(39) (LGCottrell)* 3-8-9 NCarlisle(1) (lw: plld hrd: a.p: one pce fnl 2f) 1¾ **4**

1962[19] Sobeloved **(51)***(43) (MRChannon)* 3-9-0 RHughes(2) (hld up: no hdwy fnl 2f) ....½ **5**

1719[10] Surgiva **(40)***(8) (JRArnold)* 3-8-9 CRutter(3) (a bhd) 15 **6**

1971[11] Amber Lily *(7) (JMBradley)* 3-8-6 (3) SDrowne(4) (plld hrd: prom: rdn 4f out: sn wknd) ....¾ **7**

1962[16] Chadleigh Walk (IRE) **(40)** *(RHollinshead)* 3-9-0v WRyan(7) (a bhd: t.o fnl 4f) 10 **8**

13/8 JUST FIZZY (5/4-2/1), Irie Mon (IRE), **7/1** Tirollac (IRE), Sobeloved (op 7/2), **16/1** Miltak, **33/1** Surgiva, Chadleigh Walk (IRE), **50/1** Amber Lily, CSF £4.49 TOTE £2.50: £1.30 £1.30 £2.00 (£2.20) OWNER 0336 405200 Racing (WELLINGTON) BRED John Rose 8 Rn
1m 33.7 (1.20) SF: 25/23/10/6/10/-/-/-
Just Fizzy sld JHetherton 6,200 gns

2150 STEWARDS TRIAL H'CAP (0-100) (3-Y.O+) (Class C) £5,502.50 (£1,655.00: £800.00: £372.50) **5f 16y** Stalls: High GOING minus 0.70 sec (HD) 3-00 (3-02)

1895[11] **Sir Joey (USA) (84)***(89) (PGMurphy)* 6-8-13 (3) SDrowne(3) (hld up: hrd rdn to ld wl ins fnl f: r.o)........— 1
1599[6] Ansellman **(70)***(75) (JBerry)* 5-8-2 GCarter(6) (w ldrs: led over 2f out: hdd wl ins fnl f)........hd 2
1895[12] Hello Mister **(96)***(90) (JO'Donoghue)* 4-9-9 (5) PMcCabe(1) (lw: stdd s: swtchd rt: gd hdwy over 2f out: one pce fnl f)........3½ 3
1765[11] Ashtina **(91)***(79) (RJHodges)* 10-9-9 TQuinn(4) (led over 2f: hrd rdn over 1f out: one pce)....1¾ 4
2013[2] Domicksky **(61)***(43)*(Fav)*(MRChannon)* 7-7-7 JQuinn(2) (hld up: hrd rdn over 1f out: wknd ins fnl f)........2 5
327[5] Press the Bell **(74)** *(WRMuir)* 5-8-6 MHills(5) (w ldrs: rdn & wknd 2f out: t.o)........20 6

2/1 Domicksky, **5/2** SIR JOEY (USA), **4/1** Hello Mister, **11/2** Ansellman (op 3/1), **6/1** Ashtina (op 4/1), **16/1** Press the Bell, CSF £15.54 TOTE £3.90: £1.70 £2.50 (£17.40) OWNER Mrs A. G. Sims (BRISTOL) BRED William Plescia & Natalie Plescia 6 Rn 57.9 secs (0.90) SF: 23/9/24/13/-/-

2151 NPI MAIDEN STKS (3-Y.O) (Class D) £3,673.25 (£1,106.00: £535.50: £250.25) **1m 2f 36y** Stalls: High GOING minus 0.70 sec per fur (HD) 3-30 (3-33)

Razana (IRE) *(64) (JHMGosden)* 3-8-9 GHind(1) (w'like: b: dwlt: 5th st: hdwy over 3f out: hrd rdn to ld wl ins fnl f: r.o)........— 1
Richelieu (IRE) *(69)*(Fav)*(HRACecil)* 3-9-0 WRyan(5) (w'like: scope: 3rd st: rdn 3f out: ev ch fnl f: r.o)........s.h 2
Harry Welsh (IRE) **(70)***(68) (KMcAuliffe)* 3-9-0 DHarrison(7) (chsd ldr: 2nd st: led over 3f out tl wl ins fnl f)........nk 3
Tappeto *(64) (HCandy)* 3-9-0 WNewnes(2) (w'like: 4th st: one pce fnl 2f)........3 4
362[6] Handson *(45) (BRMillman)* 3-9-0 JWilliams(6) (last st: a bhd)........12 5
1600[6] Ziro (IRE) *(43) (PDEvans)* 3-9-0v PaulEddery(3) (b: plld hrd: led: rdn over 4f out: hdd over 3f out: sn wknd)........1 6

7/4 Richelieu (IRE) (op 4/6), **3/1** Harry Welsh (IRE) (op 11/2), **100/30** RAZANA (IRE) (2/1-7/2), **6/1** Tappeto, **25/1** Ziro (IRE), **50/1** Handson, CSF £8.47 TOTE £4.10: £1.80 £1.50 (£2.40) OWNER Sheikh Mohammed (NEWMARKET) BRED J. G. O'Brien 6 Rn 2m 12.7 (8.40) SF: -/-/-/-/-/-

2152 INDEPENDENCE DAY H'CAP (0-85) (3-Y.O F) (Class D) £3,696.00 (£1,113.00: £539.00: £252.00) **1m 2f 36y** Stalls: High GOING minus 0.70 sec (HD) 4-00 (4-02)

1702[2] **Inchkeith (67)***(76)*(Fav)*(GWragg)* 3-8-6 MHills(1) (lw: led over 3f: 2nd st: led over 1f out: comf)........— 1
1793[5] Stinging Reply **(75)***(81) (IABalding)* 3-9-0 WRyan(4) (swtg: plld hrd: led over 6f out: sn clr: hdd over 1f out: nt qckn)........2 2
885[4] Santa Fan (IRE) **(75)***(79) (PFICole)* 3-8-7 (7) DavidO'Neill(3) (lw: s.s: last st: hdwy 3f out: styd on fnl f)........1½ 3
1500[6] Cap And Gown (IRE) **(82)***(82) (PFICole)* 3-9-7 TQuinn(2) (hld up: 4th st: rdn over 3f out: one pce fnl 2f)........2½ 4
1866[2] Cephista **(66)***(53) (PTWalwyn)* 3-8-5 DHarrison(5) (lw: 3rd st: rdn 4f out: bhd fnl 3f)........8 5

6/4 INCHKEITH, **11/4** Stinging Reply, **7/2** Cap And Gown (IRE), **5/1** Cephista, **14/1** Santa Fan (IRE) (6/1-16/1), CSF £5.80 TOTE £2.60: £1.70 £1.80 (£3.00) OWNER Sir Philip Oppenheimer (NEWMARKET) BRED Hascombe and Valiant Studs 5 Rn 2m 10.3 (6.00) SF: -/-/-/-/-

2153 BREAM CLAIMING STKS (2-Y.O) (Class F) £2,775.00 (£775.00: £375.00) **6f 16y** Stalls: High GOING minus 0.70 sec per fur (HD) 4-30 (4-32)

1877* **Natural Key (70)***(64+)*(Fav)*(SirMarkPrescott)* 2-8-3 GDuffield(5) (mde all: shkn up over 1f out: comf)........— 1
1352[3] Moi Canard **(66)***(65) (JBerry)* 2-8-8 GCarter(4) (lw: chsd wnr: r.o one pce fnl f)........1½ 2
1954[2] Bold Times **(69)***(60) (PDEvans)* 2-8-5 PaulEddery(1) (a.p: hrd rdn over 1f out: nt qckn)........¾ 3
2035[6] Our Tom's Boy **(51)***(54) (KTIvory)* 2-8-4 DHarrison(6) (b: hld up & plld hrd: rdn 2f out: one pce)........2 4
1899[3] February **(55)***(47) (MRChannon)* 2-8-0 CRutter(2) (dwlt: nvr trbld ldrs)........1¼ 5
1774[3] Members Welcome (IRE) **(64)***(51) (PGMurphy)* 2-7-13 (7) RWaterfield(3) (lw: hdwy over 2f out: wknd over 1f out)........½ 6

4/6 NATURAL KEY, **7/2** Bold Times, **7/1** Moi Canard (5/1-8/1), **9/1** Members Welcome (IRE), **12/1** February (op 7/1), **33/1** Our Tom's Boy, CSF £5.95 TOTE £1.60: £1.30 £2.50 (£3.10) OWNER Cheveley Park Stud (NEWMARKET) BRED Cheveley Park Stud Ltd 6 Rn 1m 11.7 (2.70)
Natural Key clmd G. Weeks £10,000

2154

STARS AND STRIPES H'CAP (0-70) (3-Y.O+) (Class E) £3,168.00 (£954.00: £462.00: £216.00)
2m 2f Stalls: High GOING minus 0.70 sec per fur (HD) 5-00 (5-01)

1840 18 **Tamarpour (USA) (55)***(69) (MCPipe)* 8-9-1v AMcGlone(2) (b.hind: hld up: 8th st: hdwy 3f out: rdn to ld 1f out: r.o wl) .... — 1
1826* Flashman **(42)***(53) (BJLlewellyn)* 5-8-2 TWilliams(6) (lw: 3rd st: led over 3f out: hrd rdn 2f out: hdd 1f out: one pce) 3 2
1840 2 Art Form (USA) **(66)***(77)*(Fav)*(CACyzer)* 8-9-12 DBiggs(7) (hld up: rdn 6f out: 6th st: styd on ins fnl f) .... ¾ 3
1410 10 Brumon (IRE) **(60)***(70) (DWPArbuthnot)* 4-9-6b JWilliams(1) (hld up: stdy hdwy on ins 10f out: 4th st: ev ch over 1f out: one pce) .... nk 4
1840 15 Shrewd Alibi **(68)***(78) (IABalding)* 4-10-0 MHills(3) (chsd ldr: 2nd st: led over 4f out tl over 3f out: ev ch 2f out: one pce) .... hd 5
2036 3 Bardolph (USA) **(65)***(73) (PFICole)* 8-9-11 TQuinn(4) (hld up: 5th st: hdwy 3f out: wknd wl over 1f out) 2½ 6
2078 5 Lajadhal (FR) **(33)***(30) (KBishop)* 6-7-7 NAdams(8) (led tl hdd over 4f out: sn wknd: t.o) 13 7
866 9 Shamshadal (IRE) **(52)***(38) (JRJenkins)* 5-8-12 RHughes(5) (prom: 7th st: wknd qckly 4f out: t.o fnl 2f) 12 8

LONG HANDICAP Lajadhal (FR) 6-8

7/4 Art Form (USA), **4/1** Flashman, **9/2** Bardolph (USA), **11/2** TAMARPOUR (USA) (4/1-6/1), **13/2** Shrewd Alibi, **20/1** Shamshadal (IRE), **25/1** Brumon (IRE), **33/1** Lajadhal (FR), CSF £25.78 CT £48.18 TOTE £10.70: £2.50 £1.20 £1.30 (£13.10) OWNER Mrs Alison Farrant (WELLINGTON) BRED H. H. The Aga Khan 8 Rn 4m 0.2 SF: 12/-/20/13/21/16/-/-

T/Jkpt: £380.10 (28.5 Tckts). T/Plpt: £7.00 (2,417.81 Tckts). T/Qdpt: £19.50 (11.6 Tckts). KH

2122-EDINBURGH (R-H)
Tuesday July 4th (Good to firm)

WEATHER: sunny WIND: fresh bhd

2155

BRAIDS CLAIMING STKS (2-Y.O) (Class F) £2,671.00 (£808.00:£394.00: £187.00)
7f 15y Stalls: High GOING minus 0.68 sec per fur (HD) 2-15 (2-18)

1981 2 **Jambo (52)***(54)*(Fav)*(MRChannon)* 2-8-6 (5) PPMurphy(2) (lw: mde all: rdn out fnl f) .... — 1
1943 6 Veshca Lady (IRE) **(55)***(54) (EWeymes)* 2-8-11 KDarley(1) (trckd wnr: chal 2f out: r.o towards fin) .... s.h 2
1943 7 Ceilidh (IRE) *(41) (PCHaslam)* 2-8-6 ow1 JWeaver(3) (hld up: effrt ent st: one pce appr fnl f) ...3 3
1954 3 Don't Tell Anyone **(57)***(14) (JBerry)* 2-8-12 JCarroll(4) (trckd ldrs: effrt over 2f out: sn btn) 15 4

11/10 JAMBO (6/4-Evens), **3/1** Don't Tell Anyone (op 7/4), **4/1** Veshca Lady (IRE), **9/2** Ceilidh (IRE), CSF £5.32 TOTE £1.80: (£2.40) OWNER Mr Ruthven Urquhart (UPPER LAMBOURN) BRED R. S. A. Urquhart 4 Rn 1m 31.6 (5.60) SF: -/-/-/-

2156

GULLANE H'CAP (0-60) (3-Y.O+) (Class F) £3,204.00 (£972.00: £476.00: £228.00)
7f 15y Stalls: High GOING minus 0.68 sec per fur (HD) 2-45 (2-45)

2021 6 **Miss Pigalle (34)***(41) (MissLAPerratt)* 4-8-8b DaleGibson(12) (mid div: hdwy on ins to ld over 1f out: all out) .... — 1
2073 3 At the Savoy (IRE) **(41)***(47)*(Fav)*(TDBarron)* 4-9-1b JFortune(8) (chsd ldrs: outpcd 3f out: hdwy over 1f out: fin wl) .... nk 2
*1883** Corona Gold **(42)***(48) (JGFitzGerald)* 5-9-2 KFallon(9) (in tch: hdwy & ev ch ins fnl f: kpt on) .... nk 3
1995 7 Seconds Away **(37)***(43) (JSGoldie)* 4-8-8 (3) JStack(10) (lw: bhd: hdwy 2f out: r.o towards fin) .... s.h 4
1724 6 Blow Dry (IRE) **(52)***(55) (MartynWane)* 5-9-12 JWeaver(13) (cl up: led 3f out tl over 1f out: no ex) 1¼ 5
1528 8 The Happy Loon (IRE) **(53)***(52) (DenysSmith)* 4-9-13 JCarroll(14) (swtg: chsd ldrs: effrt 3f out: btn appr fnl f) 1¾ 6
1956 4 Mary's Case (IRE) **(54)***(53) (MJohnston)* 5-10-0b DHolland(1) (lw: bhd: hdwy whn hmpd wl over 1f out: nt rcvr) .... hd 7
1854 4 Demurrer **(37)***(32) (MrsAMNaughton)* 5-8-11 AMercer(6) (nvr nrr) 1¾ 8
992 13 Benjarong **(35)***(23) (RMMcKellar)* 3-8-1 TSprake(11) (bhd tl sme late hdwy) 3 9
1843 9 Langtonian **(40)***(25) (JLEyre)* 6-9-0v KDarley(7) (lw: bhd: swtchd wd 2f out: n.d) 1¼ 10
1873 3 Malzoom **(36)***(19) (SEKettlewell)* 3-7-11 (5) NVarley(5) (lw: unruly s: chsd ldrs tl wknd over 2f out) .... ¾ 11

Passion Sunday **(51)***(31) (LRLloyd-James)* 4-9-4v(7) KimberleyHart(4) (b.nr hind: s.i.s: hdwy appr st: wknd 3f out) 1¼ **12**
1996[4] Ragazzo (IRE) **(37)***(12) (JSWainwright)* 5-8-11b LCharnock(2) (led tl hdd 3f out: sn wknd)....2½ **13**
2125[3] Ricana **(39)** *(WTKemp)* 3-8-5b ACulhane(3) (effrt & rn wd st: sn wknd) 6 **14**

4/1 At the Savoy (IRE), **7/1** Malzoom, Corona Gold, **8/1** Mary's Case (IRE), **9/1** Blow Dry (IRE), Ragazzo (IRE), Seconds Away, **11/1** Langtonian, The Happy Loon (IRE), **12/1** Ricana, MISS PIGALLE, **16/1** Demurrer, **33/1** Passion Sunday, **50/1** Benjarong, CSF £58.94 CT £344.98 TOTE £12.20: £5.70 £1.60 £2.90 (£73.10) Trio £173.10 OWNER The Globe Bar Syndicate (AYR) BRED Miss Heather Galbraith 14 Rn 1m 28.0 (2.00) SF: 15/21/22/17/29/26/27/6/-/-/-/5/-/-
WEIGHT FOR AGE 3yo-8lb

2157 LUFTNESS CLAIMING STKS (3-Y.O+) (Class F) £2,703.00 (£758.00: £369.00)
1m 7f 16y Stalls: High GOING minus 0.68 sec per fur (HD) 3-15 (3-16)

1965* **Faugeron (71)***(62)*(Fav)*(NTinkler)* 6-9-12 LCharnock(6) (b: lw: trckd ldrs: rdn appr st: styd on to ld ins fnl f) ....— **1**
1921* Brodessa **(59)***(60) (MrsMReveley)* 9-9-10 KDarley(2) (lw: a.p: led & qcknd over 3f out: hdd ins fnl f: kpt on) ....nk **2**
1957[5] Arian Spirit (IRE) **(32)***(43) (JLEyre)* 4-8-13 JFortune(3) (lw: led 4f: chsd ldrs: one pce fnl 3f)....5 **3**
Daleside **(26)***(35) (AHarrison)* 7-8-13 (3) JStack(5) (hdwy appr st: sn rdn & no imp)....11 **4**
Electric Committee (IRE) *(31) (PMonteith)* 5-9-12 TSprake(4) (led after 4f & qcknd: hdd over 3f out: sn wknd) 13 **5**
1854[13] Seraphic **(42)***(1) (BRCambidge)* 4-8-9 ACulhane(1) (s.s: a bhd) 12 **6**

10/11 FAUGERON, **Evens** Brodessa, **16/1** Arian Spirit (IRE), **25/1** Electric Committee (IRE), **50/1** Seraphic, **100/1** Daleside, CSF £2.17 TOTE £2.00: £1.00 £3.50 (£1.30) OWNER Elite Racing Club (MALTON) BRED J. L. C. Pearce 6 Rn 3m 18.3 (7.80) SF: 17/15/-/-/-/-

2158 VOGRIE PARK (S) STKS (2-Y.O) (Class F) £2,717.00 (£762.00: £371.00)
5f Stalls: High GOING minus 0.68 sec per fur (HD) 3-45 (3-46)

2047[2] **Sporting Fantasy** *(57)*(Fav)*(MRChannon)* 2-8-11 KDarley(4) (lw: mde all: edgd lft fr ½-wy: styd on wl fnl f) ....— **1**
1959[2] Chilibang Bang **(62)***(49) (JBerry)* 2-8-11 JCarroll(3) (cl up tl rdn & btn appr fnl f) 2½ **2**
Distinctly Swingin (IRE) *(42) (MissLAPerratt)* 2-7-13 (7) PFessey(2) (neat: bit bkwd: b: hdwy to chse ldrs after 1f: ev ch over 1f out: wknd ins fnl f)....¾ **3**
755[5] Vales Ales *(35) (RMMcKellar)* 2-8-11 TSprake(1) (spd to ½-wy: sn btn) 3½ **4**

4/7 SPORTING FANTASY, **6/4** Chilibang Bang, **16/1** Distinctly Swingin (IRE), **100/1** Vales Ales, CSF £1.77 TOTE £1.50: (£1.30) OWNER Miss Melanie Hacker (UPPER LAMBOURN) BRED R. P. Williams 4 Rn 60.2 secs (2.50) SF: -/-/-/-
Sporting Fantasy sold JBalding 6,000gns

2159 MUIRFIELD H'CAP (0-80) (3-Y.O+) (Class D) £3,517.50 (£1,065.00: £520.00: £247.50) **1m 3f 32y** Stalls: High GOING minus 0.68 sec per fur (HD) 4-15 (4-16)

1844* **North Ardar (53)***(64) (MrsMReveley)* 5-9-2 (7) SCopp(5) (trckd ldr: led wl over 1f out: r.o u.p) ....— **1**
2002* Soba Up **(56)***(66)*(Fav)*(TJEtherington)* 5-9-12 5x ACulhane(4) (lw: trckd ldrs: hdwy & ev ch 2f out: r.o) 1 **2**
1817[6] Lord Advocate **(38)***(43) (DANolan)* 7-8-3b(5) NVarley(2) (led tl hdd wl over 1f out: sn outpcd) 3½ **3**
1958[3] Imperial Bid (FR) **(54)***(58) (DenysSmith)* 7-9-10 KFallon(3) (lw: hld up: effrt over 3f out: no imp)....nk **4**
1687[9] Mbulwa **(47)***(32) (SEKettlewell)* 9-9-3 JFortune(1) (hld up: shkn up over 2f out: n.d) 13 **5**

11/10 Soba Up, **9/4** NORTH ARDAR, **11/2** Imperial Bid (FR), **7/1** Lord Advocate, **16/1** Mbulwa, CSF £5.03 TOTE £3.40: £1.90 £1.40 (£2.20) OWNER Laurel (Leisure) Ltd (SALTBURN) BRED Mrs H.Seddington 5 Rn 2m 26.1 (6.40) SF: 9/11/-/3/-

2160 RAMBLING RIVER AMATEUR H'CAP (0-60) (3-Y.O+) (Class F) £2,815.00 (£790.00: £385.00) **5f** Stalls: High GOING minus 0.68 sec per fur (HD) 4-45 (4-46)

2124[2] **Pallium (IRE) (52)***(59) (MrsAMNaughton)* 7-11-11 MrsDKettlewell(1) (lw: sn outpcd: hdwy 2f out: hung rt & r.o to ld cl home)....— **1**
1689[10] Serious Hurry **(42)***(47) (RMMcKellar)* 7-10-10 (5) MrsCWilliams(8) (led tl ct cl home) ....¾ **2**
2024[2] Mister Westsound **(47)***(48)*(Fav)*(MissLAPerratt)* 3-11-0b MrsAFarrell(5) (s.i.s: hdwy ½-wy: styd on towards fin)....1¼ **3**

*1566*6 The Institute Boy **(47)***(41) (MissJFCraze)* 5-11-1v(5) MrWWenyon(3) (lw: prom: hdwy & hung rt 2f out: nt qckn fnl f)....2 **4**
19004 Oriental Air (IRE) **(52)***(41) (EWeymes)* 4-11-11 MrJWeymes(4) (lw: prom: rdn ½-wy: no hdwy)....1¾ **5**
212410 Sunday Mail Too (IRE) **(39)***(26) (MissLAPerratt)* 3-10-6b MrsSBosley(2) (s.i.s: nvr trbld ldrs)..½ **6**
17217 Kabcast **(53)***(24) (DWChapman)* 10-11-12b MissRClark(6) (spd over 3f: wknd)....5 **7**

9/4 Mister Westsound, **3/1** PALLIUM (IRE), **9/2** Oriental Air (IRE), **11/2** Kabcast (op 7/2), **13/2** The Institute Boy (4/1-7/1), **16/1** Serious Hurry, Sunday Mail Too (IRE), CSF £38.48 CT £113.46 TOTE £3.90: £3.50 £7.40 (£31.60) OWNER Mr W. J. Kelly (RICHMOND) BRED North Ridge Farm Inc 7 Rn 59.1 secs (1.40) SF: 52/40/35/34/34/13/17
WEIGHT FOR AGE 3yo-6lb

T/Plpt: £128.10 (83.67 Tckts). T/Qdpt: £35.80 (2 Tckts). AA

1578-CATTERICK (L-H)
Wednesday July 5th (Good to firm, Good patches)
WEATHER: overcast - raining WIND: almost nil

2161
QUILL AND INK MEDIAN AUCTION MAIDEN STKS (2-Y.O) (Class F) £2,924.00 (£814.00: £392.00)
7f Stalls: Low GOING minus 0.28 sec per fur (GF) 2-15 (2-18)

18422 **Too Hasty** *(72+)*(Fav)*(MHEasterby)* 2-9-0 MBirch(11) (a.p: rdn to ld ins fnl f: r.o)....— **1**
19923 Sharp Monty **(66)***(69) (RHollinshead)* 2-9-0 JWeaver(2) (led tl hdd & no ex ins fnl f)....1½ **2**
13563 Tabriz *(60) (JDBethell)* 2-8-9 TIves(1) (lw: plld hrd: chsd ldrs: effrt & hung lft over 1f out: nt qckn)....1¾ **3**
Danico *(63) (SCWilliams)* 2-8-11 (3) DWright(3) (lt-f: unf: lw: mid div: hdwy u.p over 1f out: nrst fin)....½ **4**
67112 Bear To Dance *(49) (JohnBerry)* 2-8-9 MFenton(9) (a chsng ldrs: one pce fnl 2½f)....4 **5**
*1212*5 Colour Counsellor *(54) (KMcAuliffe)* 2-8-11 (3) JTate(5) (styd on fnl 2f: nvr rchd ldrs)....nk **6**
16205 Domino Flyer *(53) (MrsASwinbank)* 2-9-0 NConnorton(6) (chsd ldrs tl grad wknd fnl 2f)....½ **7**
18427 Aztec Flyer (USA) *(47) (MrsMReveley)* 2-9-0 DeanMcKeown(7) (nvr bttr than mid div)....2½ **8**
Vague Spirit *(41) (CEBrittain)* 2-9-0 BDoyle(4) (unf: n.d)....2½ **9**
Scenic Air *(34) (EWeymes)* 2-8-9 KDarley(8) (w'like: scope: bit bkwd: dwlt: a bhd)....1 **10**
14942 Lucky Bea **(64)***(38) (MWEasterby)* 2-9-0 LCharnock(10) (reard s: hdwy & prom ent st: sn rdn & wknd)....½ **11**

11/10 TOO HASTY, **7/1** Sharp Monty, Vague Spirit, **8/1** Tabriz (6/1-10/1), **9/1** Colour Counsellor (op 6/1), **12/1** Scenic Air, Danico, **14/1** Lucky Bea (op 8/1), **16/1** Domino Flyer, Aztec Flyer (USA), **50/1** Bear To Dance, CSF £10.56 TOTE £2.30: £1.60 £1.70 £1.90 (£6.20) Trio £10.40 OWNER Mr C. H. Stevens (MALTON) BRED M. H. Easterby 11 Rn 1m 27.6 (4.40) SF: 22/19/10/13/-/4/3/-/-/-/-

2162
XI SQUADRON EAGLES (S) STKS (3-Y.O+) (Class G) £2,623.00 (£728.00: £349.00) **5f 212y** Stalls: High GOING minus 0.28 sec per fur (GF) 2-45 (2-47)

19934 **Sense of Priority** **(53)***(58)*(Fav)*(DNicholls)* 6-9-0 AlexGreaves(4) (lw: trckd ldrs: smooth hdwy to ld 1f out: r.o: comf)....— **1**
17213 Henry the Hawk **(50)***(51) (MDods)* 4-8-11 (3) JStack(2) (hdwy over 2f out: r.o: no ch w wnr) ..2½ **2**
Pakol (IRE) **(56)***(44) (MrsASwinbank)* 6-8-9 NConnorton(6) (led 1½f: cl up: kpt on one pce fnl f)....1 **3**
127910 Seenthelight **(41)***(43) (DMoffatt)* 3-7-13v(3) DarrenMoffatt(1) (lw: in tch: hdwy & hung lft over 1f out: styd on)....nk **4**
*1884*8 Dauntless Fort **(43)***(39) (MrsVAAconley)* 4-8-9v MDeering(7) (led after 1½f tl hdd & wknd 1f out)....1½ **5**
152810 Drum Sergeant **(30)***(37) (JParkes)* 8-9-0b LCharnock(3) (a chsng ldrs: one pce fnl 2f)....2½ **6**
Kajostar *(25) (SWCampion)* 5-8-9 DeanMcKeown(9) (hld up & bhd: rn wd st: sme lte hdwy)2½ **7**
19937 Lucky Peg **(39)***(21) (FJO'Mahony)* 3-8-2b JFanning(11) (dwlt: c wd st: n.d)....1½ **8**
141211 Malsisio **(27)***(18) (SGNorton)* 3-8-2v NCarlisle(5) (lw: b: cl up tl wknd over 2f out)....1¼ **9**
Susan-H *(7) (MissJFCraze)* 3-8-2 NKennedy(10) (b: rn wd appr st: a bhd)....4 **10**
17397 Irish Angel (IRE) **(43)** *(CSmith)* 3-8-1b(3)ow2 JTate(8) (lw: b.hind: sn bhd: t.o)....dist **11**

13/8 SENSE OF PRIORITY, **7/4** Henry the Hawk, **10/1** Irish Angel (IRE), **12/1** Seenthelight (op 8/1), Lucky Peg (op 8/1), Pakol (IRE) (op 8/1), **16/1** Susan-H, Drum Sergeant, **33/1** Dauntless Fort, Malsisio, **66/1** Kajostar, CSF £5.08 TOTE £2.90: £1.10 £1.10 £3.50 (£2.30) Trio £9.20 OWNER Mr S. Schofield (THIRSK) BRED Cheveley Park Stud Ltd 11 Rn 1m 13.7 (3.20) SF: 29/22/15/7/10/8/-/-/-
WEIGHT FOR AGE 3yo-7lb
No bid

2163

EXCALIBUR H'CAP (0-75) (3-Y.O+) (Class D) £3,915.00 (£1,170.00: £560.00: £255.00) **5f** Stalls: Low GOING minus 0.28 sec per fur (GF) 3-15 (3-15)

1765[8] **Lady Sheriff (60)***(68) (MWEasterby)* 4-8-8b(7) RuthCoulter(7) (a cl up: led ins fnl f: kpt on wl) — **1**
2092[2] Wasblest **(55)***(61)*(Fav)*(MJohnston)* 3-8-4 TWilliams(6) (a chsng ldrs: hdwy over 1f out: styd on wl) ¾ **2**
2124* Halbert **(56)***(58) (MRChannon)* 6-8-11v 7x KDarley(5) (lw: a cl up: rdn ½-wy: r.o one pce fnl f) 1¼ **3**
1741[5] Miss Movie World **(62)***(63)*(Fav)*(MDHammond)* 6-9-0 (3) JStack(1) (lw: led tl hdd & wknd ins fnl f) hd **4**
1900[5] High Domain (IRE) **(67)***(59) (TDBarron)* 4-9-8 JFortune(2) (s.i.s: outpcd & bhd tl styd on wl fnl 2f) 3 **5**
1689[6] My Abbey **(59)***(48) (EJAlston)* 6-9-0 JWeaver(4) (swtg: outpcd tl styd on fnl 2f) 1 **6**
1882[9] Kalar **(41)***(27) (DWChapman)* 6-7-10b DaleGibson(9) (gd spd over 3f) ¾ **7**
2120[9] The Fed **(54)***(31) (RMWhitaker)* 5-8-9v ACulhane(3) (sn outpcd & bhd) 3 **8**
1451[5] Marjorie's Memory (IRE) **(73)***(45) (MrsASwinbank)* 4-10-0 NConnorton(10) (nvr wnt pce) 1½ **9**
1582[5] Pete Afrique (IRE) **(65)***(34) (MWEasterby)* 4-9-6 LCharnock(8) (lw: b: sn outpcd & bhd) 1 **10**

4/1 Miss Movie World, Wasblest, **6/1** LADY SHERIFF, **7/1** Halbert, Pete Afrique (IRE), **8/1** My Abbey, High Domain (IRE), **10/1** The Fed, **16/1** Kalar, **33/1** Marjorie's Memory (IRE), CSF £28.86 CT £158.06 TOTE £8.70: £3.00 £1.60 £2.80 (£23.20) Trio £9.00 OWNER Mr E.J.Mangan (SHERIFF HUTTON) BRED Jeremy Green and Sons 10 Rn 60.1 secs (2.60) SF: 32/19/22/27/23/12/-/-/9/-

WEIGHT FOR AGE 3yo-6lb

OFFICIAL EXPLANATION Kalar: bled from the nose

2164

CAN-DO SPANNER MEDIAN AUCTION MAIDEN STKS (3-Y.O F) (Class F) £2,714.00 (£754.00: £362.00)
7f Stalls: Low GOING minus 0.28 sec per fur (GF) 3-45 (3-46)

2032[4] **Solianna (58)***(59) (MRChannon)* 3-8-11 JCarroll(1) (lw: mde all: qcknd clr ent st: jst hld on) — **1**
Agoer *(58)*(Fav)*(CEBrittain)* 3-8-11 BDoyle(2) (swtg: a.p: r.o fnl f: jst failed) nk **2**
1405[3] Md Thompson *(50) (SCWilliams)* 3-8-8 (3) DWright(4) (lw: hld up & bhd: effrt ent st: sme late hdwy) 3½ **3**
Ballindalloch *(39) (TJEtherington)* 3-8-11 KDarley(5) (neat: str: bit bkwd: sn chsng wnr: outpcd fnl 2f) 5 **4**
Don't Look Now **(65)***(34) (DrJDScargill)* 3-8-11 MFenton(3) (prom tl rn wd st: sn btn) 2 **5**

11/4 Agoer, **3/1** Md Thompson, Don't Look Now (op 2/1), **7/2** SOLIANNA (9/4-4/1), **15/2** Ballindalloch (5/1-8/1), CSF £12.37 TOTE £4.10: £1.80 £1.70 (£5.30) OWNER Mrs M. M. Hunt (UPPER LAMBOURN) BRED Mrs M. M. Hunt 5 Rn 1m 26.5 (3.30) SF: 33/32/24/13/8

2165

25 SQUADRON FALCON CLAIMING STKS (3-Y.O+) (Class F) £2,798.00 (£778.00: £374.00) **1m 3f 214y** Stalls: Low GOING minus 0.28 sec (GF) 4-15 (4-15)

2064[10] **Thaleros (50)***(58+) (GMMoore)* 5-9-6 JWeaver(3) (led after 1½f: clr 2f out: styd on wl) — **1**
399[5] Anorak (USA) **(46)***(49) (GMMoore)* 5-8-11v(3) JStack(7) (cl up: rdn over 2f out: one pce) 2 **2**
1999[5] Kimberley Boy **(47)***(49) (MBrittain)* 5-9-2 KFallon(6) (hdwy ½-wy: sn chsng ldrs: kpt on: nt pce to chal) 2 **3**
Skiddaw Samba *(48)*(Fav)*(MrsMReveley)* 6-9-3 KDarley(1) (trckd ldrs: effrt ent st: hrd rdn & one pce) 1½ **4**
1956[7] Petal's Jarred **(25)***(37) (WStorey)* 5-8-7v JFanning(8) (bhd tl styd on fnl 2f) nk **5**
1966[13] Pillow Talk (IRE) **(54)***(41) (SWCampion)* 4-8-8 (7) PFessey(9) (cl up: slipped bdly ent st: wknd over 2f out:) 3 **6**
367[7] Bodantree **(35)***(40) (KRBurke)* 4-9-4v TIves(4) (lw: plld hrd: chsng ldrs whn hmpd 7f out: wknd ent st) 3 **7**
1688[4] Venture Fourth **(21)***(22) (EJAlston)* 6-9-0 JFortune(5) (plld hrd: n.d) 11 **8**
270[8] Royal Addiction (IRE) *(MrsMReveley)* 3-8-0 (7) DDenby(2) (led 1½f: lost pl ½-wy: sn t.o) 25 **9**

85/40 Skiddaw Samba, **11/4** THALEROS, **7/2** Kimberley Boy, **9/1** Anorak (USA), Pillow Talk (IRE) (op 6/1), **14/1** Venture Fourth, **20/1** Bodantree, Petal's Jarred, **25/1** Royal Addiction (IRE), CSF £26.25 TOTE £3.50: £1.80 £2.10 £1.60 (£16.70) Trio £10.10 OWNER Mr M. Gleason (MIDDLEHAM) BRED A. Christodoulou 9 Rn 2m 40.8 (9.80) SF: 18/9/9/8/-/1/-/-/-

WEIGHT FOR AGE 3yo-13lb

2166 CATCH-ALL H'CAP (0-70) (3-Y.O) (Class E) £3,158.00 (£944.00:£452.00: £206.00) **1m 3f 214y** Stalls: Low GOING minus 0.28 sec per fur (GF) 4-45 (4-46)

1194⁵ **Tessajoe (58)***(67) (MJCamacho)* 3-9-0 LCharnock(2) (lw: a.p: qcknd to ld ent st: eased towards fin) .... — 1
1978* Dance So Suite **(67)***(76)*(Fav)*(PFICole)* 3-9-9 4x JFortune(8) (a chsng ldrs: chal over 1f out: edgd lft: styd on u.p towards fin) .... nk 2
1669⁵ Instantaneous **(44)***(51) (MHEasterby)* 3-8-0 SMaloney(7) (a cl up: chal 5f out: disp ld over 2f out: btn whn hmpd cl home) 1 3
1680⁷ Alltime Dancer (IRE) **(53)***(50) (MrsJRRamsden)* 3-8-9b KFallon(4) (hld up: effrt ent st: rdn & no imp) 8 4
1667³ Fools of Pride (IRE) **(37)***(28) (RHollinshead)* 3-7-7 NCarlisle(6) (hdwy 5f out: one pce fnl 3f) 4 5
1379⁹ Coneygree **(37)***(26) (JWharton)* 3-7-7 NKennedy(5) (led tl hdd ent st: sn lost pl) 2 6
1669⁹ Lindisfarne Lady **(41)***(29) (MrsMReveley)* 3-7-11 JFanning(9) (lw: in tch tl outpcd appr st: n.d after) .... ¾ 7
1814³ Ambidextrous (IRE) **(65)***(52) (CEBrittain)* 3-9-7v BDoyle(3) (lw: prom tl outpcd 4f out: slipped ent st: n.d after) .... nk 8
1358⁹ Prime Property (IRE) **(41)***(19) (MWEasterby)* 3-7-8 (3)ow1 DWright(1) (a bhd) 6 9

LONG HANDICAP Fools of Pride (IRE) 7-3 Coneygree 7-5

13/8 Dance So Suite, **7/2** TESSAJOE (5/2-4/1), **13/2** Instantaneous, Alltime Dancer (IRE), **10/1** Ambidextrous (IRE), **12/1** Lindisfarne Lady, **14/1** Prime Property (IRE), **16/1** Coneygree, **33/1** Fools of Pride (IRE), CSF £9.47 CT £32.06 TOTE £3.00: £1.50 £1.30 £1.70 (£2.80) Trio £13.40 OWNER Riley Partnership (MALTON) BRED A. and Mrs Rhodes 9 Rn

2m 38.0 (7.00) SF: 30/39/14/13/-/-/-/15/-

T/Jkpt: £7,100.00 (0.9 Tckts); £457.45 to Salisbury 6/7/95. T/Plpt: £7.80 (1,980.06 Tckts). T/Qdpt: £9.50 (1.5 Tckts). AA

1634-EPSOM (L-H)
Wednesday July 5th (Good to firm, Good last 3f)
WEATHER: fine WIND: almost nil

2167 CHANNEL ONE MAIDEN STKS (3-Y.O F) (Class D) £4,026.00 (£1,218.00: £594.00: £282.00) **1m 2f 18y** Stalls: Low GOING minus 0.36 sec (F) 6-20 (6-21)

1736⁴ **Future Act (USA)** *(91)*(Fav)*(HRACecil)* 3-8-11 WRyan(4) (scope: 4th st: led 2f out: sn clr: rdn out) .... — 1
1755⁸ Dorothea Brooke (IRE) **(87)***(80) (PWHarris)* 3-8-11 RCochrane(2) (swtg: led tl 2f out: no ch w wnr) 7 2
Duchess of Alba *(75) (RCharlton)* 3-8-11 PatEddery(5) (lost pl 5f out: 5th st: gd hdwy 1f out: r.o) 3 3
1812⁶ Mighty Squaw **(58)***(74) (MissGayKelleway)* 3-8-11 MWigham(1) (3rd st: rdn over 3f out: one pce) .... ¾ 4
Special Beat *(68) (PFICole)* 3-8-11 TQuinn(6) (scope: 2nd st: wknd over 2f out) 4 5
1831⁶ Pedaltothemetal (IRE) **(46)***(60) (PMitchell)* 3-8-11 RHughes(3) (a last) 5 6

15/8 FUTURE ACT (USA), **9/4** Duchess of Alba (6/4-5/2), **7/2** Dorothea Brooke (IRE) (op 9/4), **11/2** Special Beat (3/1-6/1), **25/1** Mighty Squaw, **40/1** Pedaltothemetal (IRE), CSF £8.08 TOTE £2.50: £1.60 £2.40 (£3.90) OWNER Buckram Oak Holdings (NEWMARKET) BRED Cabin Creek Farm 6 Rn

2m 4.8 (0.80) SF: 60/49/44/43/37/29

2168 LONDON RACING CLUB H'CAP (0-85) (3-Y.O+) (Class D) £4,026.00 (£1,218.00: £594.00: £282.00) **6f** Stalls: Low GOING minus 0.36 sec (F) 6-50 (6-50)

1982* **Tafahhus (81)***(88)*(Fav)*(RWArmstrong)* 3-9-3 6x WCarson(3) (lw: 2nd st: led over 3f out: pushed out) .... — 1
1815³ Jo Maximus **(69)***(76) (SDow)* 3-7-12 (7) ADaly(7) (led over 2f: ev ch fnl 2f: r.o) .... s.h 2
1910* Samsolom **(64)***(66) (PHowling)* 7-8-7 PaulEddery(1) (4th st: hrd rdn over 1f out: r.o ins fnl f) 2 3
1637³ Allthruthenight (IRE) **(85)***(86) (LJHolt)* 6-10-0 JReid(2) (b.off hind: swtg: 5th st: hdwy over 1f out: nt qckn ins fnl f) .... nk 4
1639⁶ Balance of Power **(75)***(76) (RAkehurst)* 3-8-11 TQuinn(5) (3rd st: hrd rdn over 1f out: one pce) .... s.h 5
1812¹¹ Kensington Freight **(57)***(44) (JAkehurst)* 3-7-7 NAdams(6) (6th st: wknd over 2f out) 5 6
Southern Ridge **(72)***(27) (CAHorgan)* 4-9-1 PatEddery(4) (b.hind: a last: t.o) 12 7

LONG HANDICAP Kensington Freight 5-12

3/1 TAFAHHUS, **7/2** Samsolom, Allthruthenight (IRE), **9/2** Balance of Power, **5/1** Jo Maximus, **20/1** Southern Ridge, **66/1** Kensington Freight, CSF £16.34 TOTE £3.10: £2.20 £2.50 (£7.30) OWNER Mr Hamdan Al Maktoum (NEWMARKET) BRED Shadwell Estate Company Limited 7 Rn

1m 8.91 (0.91) SF: 56/44/41/61/44/12/2
WEIGHT FOR AGE 3yo-7lb

2169

NABS H'CAP (0-95) (3-Y.O+) (Class C) £5,420.00 (£1,640.00: £800.00: £380.00)
7f Stalls: Low GOING minus 0.36 sec per fur (F) 7-20 (7-21)

Fairy Story (IRE) (68)*(78) (RAkehurst)* 5-8-5 (3) SSanders(6) (mde all: drvn out)........— **1**
1895[9] Shikari's Son **(88)***(94) (JWhite)* 8-9-7 (7) DaneO'Neill(3) (5th st: hdwy 2f out: nvr nrr)........1¾ **2**
1839[30] Emirates Express **(84)***(90) (JWHills)* 3-8-9 (7) MHenry(5) (2nd st: ev ch 2f out: no imp)........hd **3**
2010[3] Dancing Lawyer **(67)***(67)*(Fav)*(BJMeehan)* 4-8-7 PatEddery(2) (3rd st: hrd rdn 2f out: nt qckn)........2½ **4**
1593[3] Helios **(76)***(73) (NJHWalker)* 7-9-2 RCochrane(1) (4th st: wknd over 1f out)........1¼ **5**
1915[2] Dontforget Insight (IRE) **(72)***(68) (PFICole)* 4-8-12 TQuinn(7) (7th st: hdwy on ins over 2f out: nvr nr to chal)........¾ **6**
1775[3] Confronter **(72)***(64) (SDow)* 6-8-12 RHughes(4) (6th st: hrd rdn 2f out: no rspnse)........1½ **7**
Premier League (IRE) **(75)***(10) (JJBridger)* 5-8-8 (7) ADaly(8) (dwlt: sn t.o)........25 **8**

7/2 Dancing Lawyer, **4/1** Shikari's Son, **9/2** Dontforget Insight (IRE) (op 3/1), **5/1** Emirates Express, **6/1** Helios, **7/1** Confronter, **12/1** FAIRY STORY (IRE) (8/1-14/1), **40/1** Premier League (IRE), CSF £54.43 CT £247.56 TOTE £17.20: £3.00 £1.70 £1.50 (£58.30) OWNER The Fairy Story Partnership (EPSOM) BRED Deepwood Farm Stud 8 Rn 1m 20.38 (0.08) SF: 60/76/64/49/55/50/46/-
WEIGHT FOR AGE 3yo-8lb

2170

E.B.F. TATTENHAM MAIDEN STKS (2-Y.O) (Class D) £4,026.00 (£1,218.00: £594.00: £282.00)
5f Stalls: High GOING minus 0.36 sec per fur (F) 7-50 (7-51)

1341[3] **Centurion (88)***(81)*(Fav)*(RHannon)* 2-9-0 PatEddery(1) (led over 3f: led ins fnl f: all out)......— **1**
2000[2] Mister Sean (IRE) **(74)***(77) (JWPayne)* 2-9-0 RCochrane(4) (chsd wnr: led over 1f out: wknd & hdd ins fnl f)........1¼ **2**
1497[7] Ichor *(64) (HThomsonJones)* 2-8-9 WRyan(3) (nvr nrr)........2½ **3**
1857[3] Windi Imp (IRE) *(58) (BJMeehan)* 2-8-9 TQuinn(2) (chsd ldrs tl wknd over 1f out)........2 **4**

6/5 CENTURION, **9/4** Mister Sean (IRE), **7/2** Windi Imp (IRE), **12/1** Ichor (7/1-14/1), CSF £3.86 TOTE £1.90: (£1.70) OWNER Mr George Teo (MARLBOROUGH) BRED Roger C. Denton 4 Rn

56.82 secs (2.32) SF: 24/20/7/1
STEWARDS' ENQUIRY Eddery suspended 28/7-3/8/95 (careless riding)

2171

BURGH HEATH CLAIMING STKS (3-Y.O) (Class D) £4,084.50 (£1,236.00: £603.00: £286.50) **1m 114y** Stalls: Low GOING minus 0.36 sec (F) 8-20 (8-24)

2102[4] **Elite Racing (62)***(83) (PFICole)* 3-8-8 WCarson(2) (3rd st: led over 2f out: r.o wl)........— **1**
2057[2] Emily-Mou (IRE) **(70)***(77)*(Fav)*(BJMeehan)* 3-8-6 PatEddery(3) (4th st: hrd rdn fnl 2f: ev ch over 1f out: nt qckn)........2 **2**
1906[3] Medieval Miss **(63)***(64) (GLewis)* 3-8-6b PaulEddery(6) (led tl wknd over 2f out)........7 **3**
2014[4] Worldnews Extra (USA) **(83)***(72) (PFICole)* 3-9-2 TQuinn(4) (rdn along: 5th st: nvr nr to chal)........1¼ **4**
2037[11] Norfolk Glory **(41)***(52) (DJGMurraySmith)* 3-8-6b RCochrane(5) (s.s: 6th st: a bhd)........5 **5**
1317[10] Fosters Top **(35)***(44) (JFfitch-Heyes)* 3-8-5 RPrice(1) (2nd st: wknd 3f out)........4 **6**

10/11 Emily-Mou (IRE), **7/2** ELITE RACING, **11/2** Worldnews Extra (USA) (7/2-6/1), **6/1** Medieval Miss (op 4/1), **33/1** Norfolk Glory, **66/1** Fosters Top, CSF £6.63 TOTE 3.70: £1.60 £1.40 (£2.80) OWNER Elite Racing Club (WHATCOMBE) BRED R. J. McAlpine 6 Rn

1m 42.62 (0.62) SF: 57/51/38/46/26/18

2172

EPSOM AND EWELL H'CAP (0-90) (3-Y.O) (Class C) £5,394.00 (£1,632.00: £796.00: £378.00)
1m 4f 10y Stalls: Low GOING minus 0.36 sec per fur (F) 8-55 (8-56)

1984* **High Flying Adored (IRE) (81)***(88)*(Fav)*(JLDunlop)* 3-9-4 4x PatEddery(3) (3rd st: swtchd rt over 1f out: hrd rdn to ld wl ins fnl f)........— **1**
1912[4] Vaugrenier (IRE) **(81)***(87) (RHannon)* 3-9-4 JReid(2) (lw: 2nd st: led 2f out tl wl ins fnl f)........½ **2**
1978[5] Courbaril **(61)***(67) (SDow)* 3-7-12 JQuinn(4) (4th st: hdwy over 2f out: bmpd over 1f out: r.o)........½ **3**

1681* Thaljanah (IRE) **(84)***(89) (ACStewart)* 3-9-7 WCarson(1) (led tl 2f out: ev ch ins fnl f: nt qckn)........¾ 4

8/11 HIGH FLYING ADORED (IRE) (Evens-11/8), **5/2** Thaljanah (IRE) (7/4-11/4), **11/2** Courbaril (10/1-5/1), **13/2** Vaugrenier (IRE) (3/1-7/1), CSF £5.44 TOTE £2.00: (£4.70) OWNER Mr Anthony Pye-Jeary (ARUNDEL) BRED Airlie Stud and Myrina Holdings S A 4 Rn
2m 39.9 (4.90) SF: 43/42/22/44

T/Plpt: £40.20 (339.44 Tckts). T/Qdpt: £14.80 (9.2 Tckts). Hn

2047-FOLKESTONE (R-H)
Wednesday July 5th (Good, Good to firm patches)
WEATHER: fair WIND: slt half bhd

2173
E.B.F. ROMNEY MARSH MAIDEN STKS (2-Y.O F) (Class D)
£3,622.50 (£1,080.00: £515.00: £232.50)
6f 189y Stalls: High GOING minus 0.43 sec per fur (F) 2-30 (2-30)

1964² **Gryada** *(71+)*(Fav)*(WJarvis)* 2-8-11 WRyan(3) (lw: 5th st: rdn over 1f out: led ins fnl f: r.o wl)........— 1
1169¹⁰ Myrtle *(67) (RHannon)* 2-8-11 JReid(2) (bit bkwd: hdwy over 3f out: 2nd st: led 1f out to ins fnl f: unable qckn)........1¾ 2
Streete Dancer (IRE) *(62+) (PFICole)* 2-8-11 TQuinn(1) (leggy: lt-f: bit bkwd: dwlt: hdwy over 5f out: led over 2f out to 1f out: one pce)........2 3
Martha Quest *(61) (BWHills)* 2-8-11 WCarson(7) (small: dwlt: nvr nr to chal)........½ 4
1968³ Be My Bird **(75)***(57) (BJMeehan)* 2-8-11 DHarrison(6) (rdn thrght: 6th st: no hdwy fnl 2f)......1¾ 5
2011² Vera's First (IRE) *(54) (GLewis)* 2-8-11 PaulEddery(5) (4th st: hrd rdn over 1f out: wknd ins fnl f)........1¼ 6
1790⁵ Oare Budgie *(48) (PTWalwyn)* 2-8-11v DHolland(4) (led over 4f: 3rd st: wknd 2f out)........2½ 7

6/5 GRYADA, **11/4** Streete Dancer (IRE), **5/1** Martha Quest (op 7/4), **9/1** Vera's First (IRE) (6/1-10/1), **16/1** Myrtle, **20/1** Be My Bird, Oare Budgie, CSF £17.60 TOTE £1.90: £1.40 £5.50 (£18.70) OWNER Lord Howard de Walden (NEWMARKET) BRED Lord Howard de Walden 7 Rn
1m 25.2 (3.60) SF: 17/13/8/7/3/-/-

2174
SCHATUNOWSKI BROOKS H'CAP (0-60) (3-Y.O+) (Class F) £3,073.40 (£852.40: £408.20) **1m 1f 149y** Stalls: High GOING minus 0.43 sec (F) 3-00 (3-01)

2052³ **Araboybill (58)***(70) (MPMuggeridge)* 4-9-12b SWhitworth(7) (2nd st: led over 1f out: drvn out)........— 1
2028³ Ruby Heights **(47)***(58)*(Fav)*(RHannon)* 4-9-1 JReid(9) (hdwy over 1f out: shkn up: r.o ins fnl f)........¾ 2
*2076*⁸ Dia Georgy **(47)***(55) (RGuest)* 4-9-1 GHind(1) (lw: rdn over 3f out: 5th st: unable qckn fnl 2f)........2 3
1970⁵ Zahid (USA) **(44)***(50) (KRBurke)* 4-8-12 TQuinn(5) (lw: chsd ldr: led over 2f out tl over 1f out: one pce)........¾ 4
1825⁷ Kirov Protege (IRE) **(46)***(51) (HJCollingridge)* 3-8-3 JQuinn(6) (lw: 4th st: rdn over 1f out: one pce)........½ 5
*1939*⁸ Riva Rock **(32)***(29) (TPMcGovern)* 5-7-9 (5) NVarley(3) (rdn over 3f out: nvr nr to chal)........5 6
873²² Sir Norman Holt (IRE) **(56)***(50) (RJO'Sullivan)* 6-9-10b DBiggs(4) (lw: a bhd)........2 7
1962⁸ Burnt Sienna (IRE) **(39)***(31) (JSMoore)* 3-7-10 NAdams(10) (lw: led 7f: 3rd st: wknd 2f out) 1 8
*1950*⁶ Mim-Lou-and **(45)***(34) (BRMillman)* 3-7-11 (5) AWhelan(8) (hdwy over 3f out: 6th st: wknd 2f out)........2 9
*335*⁷ Saxon Magic **(29)***(1) (JABennett)* 5-7-11v GBardwell(2) (a bhd)........10 10

2/1 Ruby Heights, **4/1** ARABOYBILL, **6/1** Dia Georgy (op 4/1), **13/2** Zahid (USA) (6/1-4/1), **7/1** Sir Norman Holt (IRE), **9/1** Kirov Protege (IRE), **12/1** Mim-Lou-and (8/1-14/1), **16/1** Riva Rock, **40/1** Burnt Sienna (IRE), Saxon Magic, CSF £12.36 CT £32.06 TOTE £6.10: £2.60 £1.20 £2.40 (£9.10) Trio £10.60 OWNER Nigel Gay & Bernard G Barry (NEWBURY) BRED Southdown Stud 10 Rn
2m 3.0 (5.30) SF: 30/18/15/10/-/-/10/-/-/-
WEIGHT FOR AGE 3yo-11lb

2175
SHADDOXHURST H'CAP (0-70) (3-Y.O+) (Class E) £3,073.40
(£915.20: £435.60: £195.80)
1m 4f Stalls: High GOING minus 0.43 sec per fur (F) 3-30 (3-30)

2050³ **Stately Home (IRE) (49)***(62) (BRMillman)* 4-8-12 (5) AWhelan(6) (2nd st: led over 1f out: rdn out)........— 1

2007[11] Ismeno (56)*(67) (SDow)* 4-9-3 (7) ADaly(2) (lw: a.p: led over 4f out tl over 1f out: unable qckn)....1¼ 2
1553[4] Progression (56)*(57)*(Fav)*(PCHaslam)* 4-9-10 SO'Gorman(4) (4th st: one pce fnl 2f)....8 3
1937[12] Ikhtiraa (USA) (40)*(40) (RJO'Sullivan)* 5-8-8b DBiggs(5) (swtg: 3rd st: wknd over 2f out)....½ 4
1858[14] Brunswick Blue (IRE) (25)*(5) (RMFlower)* 7-7-7b GBardwell(3) (b: bhd fnl 7f: 6th st)....15 5
1937[13] Total Joy (IRE) (57)*(18)*(Fav)*(PFICole)* 4-9-11 TQuinn(1) (swtg: 5th st: led over 7f: wknd over 3f out)....11 6

LONG HANDICAP Brunswick Blue (IRE) 7-3

9/4 Progression, Total Joy (IRE), **11/4** STATELY HOME (IRE), **15/2** Ismeno (4/1-8/1), **9/1** Ikhtiraa (USA) (op 4/1), **33/1** Brunswick Blue (IRE), CSF £20.08 TOTE £3.10: £1.50 £2.60 (£12.20) OWNER Mrs Nerys Dutfield (CULLOMPTON) 6 Rn 2m 37.5 (6.30) SF: 26/31/21/4/-/-

2176 HAMSTREET (S) STKS (2-Y.O) (Class G) £2,243.00 (£618.00: £293.00)
5f Stalls: Low GOING minus 0.43 sec per fur (F) 4-00 (4-00)

2146[3] **Wingnut (IRE)** *(49)*(Fav)*(GLewis)* 2-8-6 PaulEddery(2) (lw: mde vitually all: drvn out)....— 1
2011[5] Music Mistress (IRE) *(48) (RHannon)* 2-7-13 (7) DaneO'Neill(3) (s.s: hdwy over 1f out: ev ch ins fnl f: r.o)....nk 2
1989* The Imps (IRE) *(58)*(Fav)*(BWHills)* 2-9-3 DHolland(8) (lw: a.p: rdn over 2f out: ev ch ins fnl f: r.o)....nk 3
2047[4] No Sympathy *(45) (GLMoore)* 2-8-6 SWhitworth(6) (swtg: a.p: rdn over 2f out: r.o ins fnl f)....¾ 4
2047[3] Fortuitious (IRE) *(34) (JRJenkins)* 2-8-6 WNewnes(1) (hld up: rdn over 2f out: unable qckn)3½ 5
1981[6] Golden Silver (53)*(24) (JSMoore)* 2-8-1 (5) NVarley(5) (bhd fnl 3f)....3 6
1954[8] Inca Queen *(8) (AGFoster)* 2-8-6 TSprake(7) (bit bkwd: bhd fnl 3f)....5 7
2035[3] Peterrex *(5) (MRChannon)* 2-8-12 ow1 RHughes(4) (hld up: rdn over 2f out: sn wknd)....2½ 8

3/1 WINGNUT (IRE), The Imps (IRE) (op 2/1), **4/1** Music Mistress (IRE) (3/1-9/2), **9/2** Peterrex (5/2-6/1), **11/2** Golden Silver, **10/1** Fortuitious (IRE), **12/1** No Sympathy, **33/1** Inca Queen, CSF £15.72 TOTE £4.40: £1.30 £2.10 £1.30 (£11.30) OWNER Mr John Manley (EPSOM) BRED George McNulty 8 Rn 60.9 secs (2.30) SF: 11/10/20/7/-/-/-/-
No bid

OFFICIAL EXPLANATION Peterrex: finished sore on the near foreleg

2177 ROSS & CO ANNIVERSARY H'CAP (0-70) (3-Y.O) (Class E) £3,502.40 (£1,047.20: £501.60: £228.80)
1m 7f 92y Stalls: High GOING minus 0.43 sec per fur (F) 4-30 (4-30)

1986* **Nanton Point (USA) (48)***(61+)*(Fav)*(LadyHerries)* 3-8-9 4x JQuinn(5) (a.p: chsd ldr 7f out: led over 3f out: clr over 2f out: v.easily)....— 1
1737* Hever Golf Lady (53)*(60) (TJNaughton)* 3-9-0 StephenDavies(2) (mod 3rd st: chsd wnr wl over 1f out: no imp)....6 2
1970[3] Fattash (USA) (52)*(59) (CJBenstead)* 3-8-13b WCarson(8) (lw: led over 4f: lost pl over 6f out: poor 4th st: r.o one pce fnl 2f)....hd 3
368[7] Dingo Warrior (35)*(38) (JFfitch-Heyes)* 3-7-5 (5)ow3 NVarley(6) (lw: poor 5th st: nvr nr to chal)....nk 4
1922[4] Stormaway (ITY) (60)*(60) (TGMills)* 3-9-0 (7) JCornally(7) (lw: w ldr: led 11f out tl over 3f out: 2nd st: wknd wl over 1f out)....6 5
1771[7] Coastguards Haven (40)*(19) (MJBolton)* 3-8-1 GBardwell(4) (lw: poor 6th st: a bhd)....20 6
1264[8] Toat Chieftain (54)*(20) (GHarwood)* 3-9-1 AClark(1) (bhd fnl 8f)....13 7

LONG HANDICAP Dingo Warrior 7-4

10/11 NANTON POINT (USA) (Evens-4/5), **3/1** Fattash (USA), **7/2** Hever Golf Lady (5/2-9/2), **20/1** Toat Chieftain, Stormaway (ITY), **50/1** Coastguards Haven, **66/1** Dingo Warrior, CSF £4.39 CT £5.58 TOTE £2.20: £1.30 £1.80 (£3.00) OWNER Mr L. G. Lazarus (LITTLEHAMPTON) BRED Newgate Stud Farm Inc 7 Rn 3m 26.3 (9.40) SF: 14/13/12/-/13/-/-

2178 WOODCHURCH H'CAP (0-65) (3-Y.O+) (Class F) £2,997.80 (£830.80: £397.40)
6f 189y Stalls: High GOING minus 0.43 sec per fur (F) 5-00 (5-02)

2051* **Marrowfat Lady (IRE) (58)***(69)*(Fav)*(BRMillman)* 4-9-4 (5) 6x AWhelan(7) (3rd st: led over 1f out: r.o wl)....— 1
1676[8] Crystal Heights (FR) (63)*(69) (RJO'Sullivan)* 7-9-7 (7) MHenry(2) (s.s: gd hdwy over 2f out: 6th st: chsd wnr over 1f out: unable qckn)....2 2
1991[10] Zinbaq (30)*(36) (CJBenstead)* 9-7-9 JQuinn(5) (lw: 5th st: r.o one pce fnl 2f)....hd 3
1778[6] Cloette (63)*(69) (WAO'Gorman)* 3-9-6 GHind(1) (lw: 4th st: hrd rdn over 1f out: one pce)....s.h 4
1515[7] Norsong (54)*(54) (RAkehurst)* 3-8-11 AClark(3) (2nd st: wknd over 1f out)....2½ 5

1663[9] Singing Rock (IRE) **(62)***(62) (RHannon)* 3-9-5 JReid(8) (lw: led over 5f) ....nk **6**
1859[7] Senaan **(42)***(5) (TThomsonJones)* 3-7-13 ow2 StephenDavies(6) (lw: a bhd) 15 **7**
Magical Touch **(45)** *(RMFlower)* 3-8-2 AMorris(4) (ref to ent stalls) .... **W**

10/11 MARROWFAT LADY (IRE) (Evens-11/10), **7/2** Singing Rock (IRE), **11/2** Cloette (4/1-6/1), **10/1** Crystal Heights (FR), Norsong (op 4/1), **20/1** Zinbaq, **33/1** Senaan, CSF £10.16 CT £102.07 TOTE £1.80: £2.10 £2.60 (£6.80) OWNER Mrs Nerys Dutfield (CULLOMPTON) BRED A. C. McDonnell 7 Rn 1m 24.2 (2.60) SF: 39/39/6/31/16/24/-/-
WEIGHT FOR AGE 3yo-8lb

T/Plpt: £10.60 (1,161.84). T/Qdpt: £21.20 (1.7 Tckts). AK

1986-YARMOUTH (L-H)
Wednesday July 5th (Good to firm)
WEATHER: fair WIND: almost nil

2179
GREAT YARMOUTH MERCURY APPRENTICE LIMITED STKS (0-65) (3-Y.O+) (Class G) £2,511.80 (£694.80: £331.40)
5f 43y Stalls: Low GOING minus 0.46 sec per fur (F) 6-30 (6-30)

1936[4] **Arasong (63)***(62) (EWeymes)* 3-7-13 (3) PMcCabe(7) (lw: a.p: led appr fnl f: drvn out) ....— 1
1461[6] Super Rocky **(62)***(68) (RBastiman)* 6-8-13 (3) HBastiman(6) (lw: led tl appr fnl f: hrd rdn & ev ch ins fnl f: r.o) ....¾ 2
2027[2] Tharwa (IRE) **(60)***(59)*(Fav)*(NACallaghan)* 3-8-2 (3) JDSmith(4) (b: b.hind: squeezed out s: hdwy over 1f out: r.o) 1¼ 3
1991[2] Awesome Venture **(49)***(58) (MCChapman)* 5-8-13v DRMcCabe(3) (pressed ldrs: one pce fnl f) 1 4
1832[7] Judgement Call **(45)***(47) (PHowling)* 8-8-6 (7) TThomas(2) (b: chsd ldrs to ½-wy: sn wknd) ...3½ 5
Mitsis **(41)***(46) (RHarris)* 4-8-13 SDrowne(5) (bit bkwd: bhd fr ½-wy) ....nk 6
1568[10] Lunar Prince **(35)***(12) (TTClement)* 5-8-8v(5) PBowe(1) (a outpcd) 11 7

15/8 Tharwa (IRE), **5/2** ARASONG, **4/1** Awesome Venture, **7/1** Super Rocky, **10/1** Judgement Call (7/1-12/1), **20/1** Mitsis, **50/1** Lunar Prince, CSF £17.83 TOTE £3.90: £1.60 £3.60 (£9.30) OWNER Mr T. A. Scothern (MIDDLEHAM) BRED Lord Victor Matthews 7 Rn
61.4 secs (1.10) SF: 30/42/27/32/21/20/-
WEIGHT FOR AGE 3yo-6lb

OFFICIAL EXPLANATION **Awesome Venture: the jockey reported that the horse had gurgled shortly before the line and was subsequently eased**

2180
NORTH NORFOLK NEWS (S) STKS (3-Y.O) (Class G) £2,444.60 (£675.60: £321.80) **7f 3y** Stalls: Low GOING minus 0.46 sec per fur (F) 7-05 (7-05)

1824[4] **Move With Edes (51)***(71) (WGMTurner)* 3-8-12 (7) AEddery(4) (a.p: led over 3f out: pushed clr appr fnl f: r.o wl) ....— 1
1914[5] Rosa Bonheur **(50)***(50)*(Fav)*(MAJarvis)* 3-8-9 LDettori(1) (effrt over 2f out: one pce appr fnl f) 5 2
767[11] Corrievarkie **(57)***(49) (MissGayKelleway)* 3-8-6 (3) SDrowne(2) (hdwy over 2f out: nvr able to chal) ....½ 3
1719[9] Misty Melody **(57)***(19) (RAkehurst)* 3-8-9 DHarrison(5) (w ldrs 4f: hrd rdn & sn wknd) 13 4
1811[5] La Bossette (IRE) **(44)***(12) (JRArnold)* 3-8-4b(5) MBaird(3) (a outpcd: wl bhd fnl 2f) 3 5
Mr Jasper *(MrsNMacauley)* 3-8-7 (7) AmandaSanders(6) (led over 3f: t.o) 15 6

11/8 Rosa Bonheur, **4/1** MOVE WITH EDES (5/2-9/2), **5/1** Corrievarkie, Misty Melody, **13/2** La Bossette (IRE) (4/1-7/1), **25/1** Mr Jasper, CSF £9.60 TOTE £4.20: £1.90 £1.40 (£2.90) OWNER W Ede & Co Partnership (SHERBORNE) BRED Tony J. Smith 6 Rn 1m 25.1 (2.30) SF: 37/16/15/-/-/-
Bt in 5,000gns

2181
EASTERN DAILY PRESS H'CAP (0-75) (3-Y.O+) (Class D) £3,833.70 (£1,143.60: £545.80: £246.90)
1m 3y Stalls: Low GOING minus 0.46 sec per fur (F) 7-35 (7-36)

1626[3] **Saifan (66)***(79) (DMorris)* 6-9-9b LDettori(5) (lw: hld up: hdwy 2f out: led appr fnl f: rdn out) ....— 1
2020* Ninia (USA) **(53)***(65)*(Fav)*(MJohnston)* 3-8-1 5x PRobinson(4) (swtg: a.p: led wl over 1f out tl appr fnl f: unable qckn) ....¾ 2
1845[3] Karinska **(64)***(74) (MCChapman)* 5-9-4 (3) DRMcCabe(6) (hld up: gd hdwy 2f out: r.o fnl f) ....¾ 3
1541[12] World Traveller **(53)***(60) (WAO'Gorman)* 4-8-10b EmmaO'Gorman(7) (plld early: trckd ldrs: outpcd 2f out: rallied ins fnl f) 1½ 4

1991* Keston Pond (IRE) **(68)***(71) (DAWilson)* 5-9-11 5x GCarter(3) (hld up: jnd ldr over 3f out: ev ch over 1f out: wknd fnl f) 2 5
1991[4] Lucky Tucky **(56)***(49) (JRJenkins)* 4-8-13 DHolland(8) (trckd ldrs: rdn over 3f out: btn over 2f out) 5 6
1732[6] Glowing Jade **(71)***(64) (MissGayKelleway)* 5-9-9 (5) RPainter(1) (swtg: in tch tl over 2f out: eased ins fnl f) ....s.h 7
1755[10] Red Dragon **(65)***(58) (GWragg)* 3-8-13 MHills(2) (lw: led over 6f: wknd qckly) ....hd 8

9/4 Ninia (USA), **3/1** SAIFAN, **5/1** Keston Pond (IRE), **13/2** Karinska, **7/1** Glowing Jade (6/1-9/1), Red Dragon (5/1-15/2), **10/1** Lucky Tucky, **25/1** World Traveller, CSF £10.62 CT £38.45 TOTE £4.50: £1.80 £1.30 £2.00 (£5.70) OWNER Ms L. Hawes (NEWMARKET) BRED M. M. Nashar 8 Rn
1m 37.5 (2.20) SF: 45/22/40/26/37/15/30/15
WEIGHT FOR AGE 3yo-9lb

2182 PETER WARE MEMORIAL MAIDEN STKS (2-Y.O) (Class D) £3,622.50 (£1,080.00: £515.00: £232.50)

6f 3y Stalls: Low GOING minus 0.46 sec per fur (F) 8-05 (8-05)

1781[3] **Ned Al Sheeba** *(77+) (WJHaggas)* 2-9-0 MHills(7) (hld up: qcknd 1f out: led wl ins fnl f: pushed out) ....— 1
Laafee *(74) (HThomsonJones)* 2-9-0 RHills(3) (w'like: scope: bit bkwd: sn led: hdd wl ins fnl f: r.o) 1 2
1781[4] Proper Blue (USA) *(72) (TGMills)* 2-9-0 LDettori(4) (hld up: hdwy u.p 2f out: ev ch ins fnl f: r.o one pce) ....¾ 3
1803[3] Desert Bell (IRE) *(72)*(Fav)*(MRStoute)* 2-9-0 WRSwinburn(5) (lw: rdn to chal over 1f out: ev ch ins fnl f: one pce) ....s.h 4
1856[6] Akalim *(63) (DMorley)* 2-9-0 MTebbutt(6) (w ldr over 3f) 3½ 5
Sylva Paradise (IRE) *(60) (CEBrittain)* 2-9-0 WWoods(2) (unf: lw: pressed ldr: ev ch over 1f out: wknd qckly) 1¼ 6
1964[5] Deadline Time (IRE) *(52) (MHTompkins)* 2-9-0 PRobinson(1) (lw: prom over 3f: wknd qckly) .3 7

Evens Desert Bell (IRE), **7/2** Laafee (7/4-4/1), **8/1** Proper Blue (USA), **17/2** NED AL SHEEBA, **12/1** Akalim (8/1-14/1), Deadline Time (IRE), **14/1** Sylva Paradise (IRE), CSF £36.04 TOTE £10.40: £4.80 £2.30 (£16.10) OWNER Sheikh Abdullah Al Quasimi (NEWMARKET) BRED Jeremy Green and Sons 7 Rn
1m 12.3 (1.70) SF: 33/30/28/28/19/16/8

2183 E.B.F. LOWESTOFT JOURNAL MAIDEN STKS (2-Y.O) (Class D) £4,308.00 (£1,284.00: £612.00: £276.00)

7f 3y Stalls: Low GOING minus 0.46 sec per fur (F) 8-40 (8-40)

1142[5] **Classic Flyer (IRE)** *(68+) (SCWilliams)* 2-8-9 AMackay(6) (lw: mde all: cleverly) ....— 1
Bonarelli (IRE) *(72+) (MRStoute)* 2-9-0 WRSwinburn(8) (str: scope: lw: styd on one pce fnl f: no imp) ....½ 2
Acharne *(69) (CEBrittain)* 2-9-0 WWoods(4) (unf: bit bkwd: jnd wnr over 2f out: ev ch over 1f out: no ex) 1¼ 3
Opera *(59+) (WJarvis)* 2-8-9 MHills(5) (unf: hld up: hdwy 2f out: nrst fin) 2 4
1413[3] Prince of Florence (IRE) *(64)*(Fav)*(LMCumani)* 2-9-0 LDettori(7) (lw: trckd ldrs: rdn & unable qckn 1f out: eased cl home) ....nk 5
1964[9] Khabar *(64) (DMorley)* 2-9-0 RHills(1) (in tch 5f) ....hd 6
1047[5] Red Nose (IRE) *(63) (MHTompkins)* 2-9-0 PRobinson(2) (plld hrd in rr: btn over 2f out) ....nk 7
Akansa (IRE) *(38) (MJohnston)* 2-9-0 DHolland(3) (unf: scope: bkwd: w ldrs: rdn 3f out: wknd 2f out) 11 8

9/4 Prince of Florence (IRE), **3/1** CLASSIC FLYER (IRE), **4/1** Bonarelli (IRE) (op 5/2), **6/1** Akansa (IRE), **10/1** Acharne, **12/1** Red Nose (IRE), **16/1** Opera, **20/1** Khabar, CSF £14.88 TOTE £4.30: £1.10 £1.90 £3.50 (£7.90) OWNER Classic Bloodstock Plc (NEWMARKET) BRED Holborn Trust Co 8 Rn
1m 26.2 (3.40) SF: 15/19/16/6/11/11/10/-

2184 75TH ANNIVERSARY H'CAP (0-75) (3-Y.O+) (Class D) £4,191.00 (£1,248.00: £594.00: £267.00)

1m 6f 17y Stalls: Low GOING minus 0.46 sec per fur (F) 9-10 (9-11)

2022[2] **Tu Opes (63)***(75) (JLHarris)* 4-9-9 PRobinson(3) (3rd st: led over 3f out: rdn clr over 1f out: drvn out) ....— 1
1986[2] Swivel **(66)***(75)*(Fav)*(JRFanshawe)* 3-8-11 DHarrison(5) (hld up: 5th st: hdwy over 3f out: ev ch 2f out: one pce) 3 2
1794[3] Ela Man Howa **(56)***(63) (RAkehurst)* 4-9-2 LDettori(6) (hld up: last st: hdwy wl over 2f out: one pce fr wl over 1f out) 1¼ 3

947⁵ Toy Princess (USA) **(70)***(75) (CEBrittain)* 3-9-1 MHills(1) (led 1f: 2nd st: led over 4f out tl over 3f out: wknd wl over 2f out)....1¾ **4**
1929⁹ Tukano (CAN) **(68)***(72) (JRJenkins)* 4-10-0 DHolland(4) (4th st: wknd wl over 3f out)....1½ **5**
1801⁷ Fearless Venture **(62)***(63) (SPCWoods)* 3-8-7 WWoods(7) (6th st: bhd fnl 3f)....2 **6**
1929¹¹ Record Lover (IRE) **(43)***(15) (MCChapman)* 5-8-0 (3)ow1 DRMcCabe(2) (led after 1f to 4f out: t.o)....25 **7**

2/1 Swivel, **5/2** Ela Man Howa, **4/1** TU OPES, **6/1** Toy Princess (USA), **12/1** Tukano (CAN), **16/1** Fearless Venture, **33/1** Record Lover (IRE), CSF £11.77 TOTE £5.80: £2.30 £1.90 (£5.60) OWNER Ms S. Miller (MELTON MOWBRAY) BRED Hamilton Bloodstock (UK) Ltd 7 Rn
3m 3.8 (5.80) SF: 38/23/26/23/35/11/-
WEIGHT FOR AGE 3yo-15lb

T/Plpt: £76.10 (183.44 Tckts). T/Qdpt: £15.80 (5.2 Tckts). RC

2161-CATTERICK (L-H)
Thursday July 6th (Good to firm, Good patches)
Race 6: altered running rail into st.
WEATHER: overcast WIND: fresh half against

2185
SILVER BIRCH (S) STKS (2-Y.O) (Class G) £2,644.00 (£734.00: £352.00)
5f Stalls: Low GOING minus 0.13 sec per fur (G) 2-15 (2-23)

2023³ **U-No-Harry (IRE) (64)***(66) (RHollinshead)* 2-8-13 (3) AGarth(6) (lw: chsd ldrs: led 1½f out: sn clr)....— **1**
1740⁵ Snitch *(45) (CSmith)* 2-8-11v MFenton(3) (led & sn clr: hdd 1½f out: no ex)....5 **2**
1919⁷ Fergal (USA) *(43) (GMMoore)* 2-8-8 (3) JStack(2) (in tch: hdwy 2f out: styd on wl)....½ **3**
1570⁵ April's Joy **(53)***(37) (JNorton)* 2-8-6 ACulhane(7) (a chsng ldrs: rdn & no imp fr ½-wy)....½ **4**
1981⁷ Apartments Abroad *(35) (KMcAuliffe)* 2-8-3v(3) JTate(1) (styd on fr ½-wy: nrst fin)....½ **5**
1678¹⁰ Bee Health Boy *(39) (MWEasterby)* 2-8-11 MBirch(10) (drvn along ½-wy: no imp)....nk **6**
1653⁵ Princess Pamgaddy *(25)*(Fav)*(JBerry)* 2-8-6 JCarroll(11) (sn drvn along: nvr rchd ldrs)....3 **7**
1821⁵ Spring Silhouette *(20) (MrsVAAconley)* 2-8-6 MDeering(13) (swvd rt s: nvr rchd ldrs)....1½ **8**
2023⁴ Peters Folly *(13) (JLEyre)* 2-8-6 JFortune(4) (b.hind: in tch: rdn after 2f: sn wknd)....2 **9**
1590¹⁰ Grimstone Girl **(50)***(4) (MWEasterby)* 2-8-6 LCharnock(8) (b.off hind: outpcd after 2f)....3 **10**
1959³ Julgarant (IRE) *(5) (MDods)* 2-8-11 KFallon(12) (sn outpcd & bhd)....1¼ **11**
2023⁷ Miss Hotshot *(RBastiman)* 2-8-6 DeanMcKeown(9) (sn bhd)....9 **12**
Royal Romance *(GMMoore)* 2-8-6 JWeaver(5) (Withdrawn not under Starter's orders: unruly s: ref to ent stalls).... **W**

7/4 Princess Pamgaddy, **7/2** U-NO-HARRY (IRE), **6/1** Apartments Abroad, **8/1** Peters Folly, **10/1** Fergal (USA), Julgarant (IRE), **12/1** April's Joy, **14/1** Snitch, **20/1** Grimstone Girl, **33/1** Bee Health Boy, **66/1** Spring Silhouette, **100/1** Miss Hotshot, CSF £49.49 TOTE £3.80: £1.50 £5.60 £3.00 (£81.90) Trio £94.40 OWNER Mr D. Coppenhall (UPPER LONGDON) BRED A. J. Poulton (Epping) Ltd 12 Rn 61.1 secs (3.60) SF: 27/6/4/-/-/-/-/-/-/-/-/-
Bt in 4,000 gns

2186
'TURMERIC' H'CAP (0-70) (3-Y.O+) (Class E) £3,340.00 (£1,000.00: £480.00: £220.00)
1m 7f 177y Stalls: Low GOING minus 0.13 sec per fur (G) 2-45 (2-46)

1863² **Kilernan (41)***(53) (TDBarron)* 4-7-13 LCharnock(6) (chsd ldrs: qcknd to ld 5f out: styd on u.p fnl 2f)....— **1**
1873¹⁴ Izza **(35)***(44) (WStorey)* 4-7-0v(7) PFessey(8) (plld hrd: trckd ldrs: led 7f out to 5f out: one pce fnl 2f)....3½ **2**
1386⁹ Chez Catalan **(47)***(55) (RAkehurst)* 4-8-5b TQuinn(2) (lw: trckd ldrs: chal 5f out: slipped ent st: one pce after)....½ **3**
1965³ Don't Cry **(35)***(34) (DonEnricoIncisa)* 7-7-7 KimTinkler(5) (lw: hld up: outpcd ½-wy: styd on fnl 2f: nrst fin)....9 **4**
1578³ New Inn **(60)***(57)*(Fav)*(EWeymes)* 4-9-4 KDarley(9) (lw: led tl hdd 7f out: outpcd 5f out: sn btn)....1½ **5**
1933⁴ Mowlaie **(70)***(64) (JDBethell)* 4-10-0 TIves(1) (prom tl outpcd 5f out: n.d after)....3½ **6**
866⁸ Kinoko **(43)***(26) (KWHogg)* 7-7-12 (3) AGarth(4) (hld up & bhd: effrt 6f out: n.d)....11 **7**
721⁶ Greenfinch (CAN) **(35)** *(MrsAMNaughton)* 4-7-7v NKennedy(7) (prom: reminders ½-wy: wknd over 6f out)....20 **8**
1607¹¹ Yaakum **(43)***(5) (SEKettlewell)* 6-8-1 MFenton(3) (outpcd 6f out: sn wl bhd)....hd **9**
LONG HANDICAP Don't Cry 6-7

13/8 New Inn, **5/2** Chez Catalan, **4/1** KILERNAN, **7/1** Kinoko, **10/1** Mowlaie, **14/1** Yaakum, **25/1** Don't Cry, **33/1** Izza, **50/1** Greenfinch (CAN), CSF £94.05 CT £365.09 TOTE £5.40: £1.40 £6.00 £1.70 (£127.60) Trio £67.70 OWNER Mr J. O. Hall (THIRSK) BRED James Hall 9 Rn
3m 31.1 (10.10) SF: 24/15/26/5/28/35/-/-/-

2187 OLD OAK LIMITED STKS (0-70) (4-Y.O+) (Class E) £3,106.00 (£928.00: £444.00: £202.00) 7f Stalls: Low GOING minus 0.13 sec per fur (G) 3-15 (3-16)

2053* **Pyramus (USA) (70)***(76)*(Fav)*(MrsLPiggott)* 4-8-4 (7) GMilligan(3) (b: hld up: smooth hdwy to ld ent fnl f: r.o) — 1
1426* Greatest **(66)***(75) (RAkehurst)* 4-9-3 TQuinn(4) (lw: w ldr: sn pushed along: slt ld over 2f out: hdd & one pce ent fnl f) 3 2
*1953*3 Nordan Raider **(69)***(64) (MJCamacho)* 7-8-9 LCharnock(2) (lw: trckd ldrs: effrt & slipped ent st: sn hrd drvn: one pce fnl f) 1½ 3
Golden Chip (IRE) **(65)***(59) (JLEyre)* 7-8-11 KDarley(1) (slt ld tl hdd over 2f out: wknd appr fnl f) 3 4

11/8 PYRAMUS (USA), **9/4** Greatest, Nordan Raider, **12/1** Golden Chip (IRE) (op 7/1), CSF £4.63 TOTE £2.30: (£2.70) OWNER Mr Henryk De Kwiatkowski (NEWMARKET) BRED Kennelot Stables Ltd 4 Rn
1m 27.1 (3.90) SF: 38/37/26/21

2188 HAWES CRICKET CLUB 50TH ANNIVERSARY H'CAP (0-75) (3-Y.O) (Class D) £3,882.50 (£1,160.00: £555.00: £252.50) 7f Stalls: Low GOING minus 0.13 sec per fur (G) 3-45 (3-45)

2003* **Russian Heroine (67)***(78)*(Fav)*(MJohnston)* 3-8-13 6x DHolland(5) (lw: cl up: slipped ent st: led 2f out: r.o) — 1
1692 10 Takeshi (IRE) **(61)***(68) (EALDunlop)* 3-8-4 (3) JTate(8) (lw: a chsng ldrs: kpt on fnl 2f: nt pce of wnr) 1¾ 2
2003 3 Concer Un **(61)***(67) (SCWilliams)* 3-8-7 KDarley(2) (lw: bhd tl r.o fnl 2f: nrst fin) ½ 3
1417 6 So Amazing **(62)***(65) (MissSEHall)* 3-8-8 NConnorton(1) (b: trckd ldrs pllng hrd: hmpd 4f out: one pce fnl 2f) 1¼ 4
1920 4 Flamboro **(55)***(55) (JDBethell)* 3-8-1 TWilliams(3) (a.p: effrt & one pce fnl 2½f) 1½ 5
1843 4 Mac's Taxi **(68)***(64) (PCHaslam)* 3-9-0 JWeaver(7) (lw: led tl hdd & wknd 2f out) 1½ 6
1195 6 Mountgate **(72)***(59) (MPBielby)* 3-9-4 TQuinn(6) (lw: hld up: c wd st: sn rdn & btn) 4 7
1846* Kafani Al Widd (FR) **(75)***(54) (MRStoute)* 3-9-7 WRSwinburn(4) (lw: hld up & bhd: rdn over 2f out: n.d) 3½ 8

9/4 RUSSIAN HEROINE, **9/2** Kafani Al Widd (FR) (op 3/1), **5/1** So Amazing, Mac's Taxi, **6/1** Takeshi (IRE), **7/1** Concer Un, **14/1** Mountgate, **20/1** Flamboro, CSF £15.91 CT £76.35 TOTE £3.60: £1.80 £1.50 £1.60 (£23.50) OWNER The Knavesmire Partnership (MIDDLEHAM) BRED D. R. Botterill 8 Rn
1m 26.4 (3.20) SF: 48/38/37/35/25/34/29/24

2189 WEEPING WILLOW RATING RELATED MAIDEN LIMITED STKS (0-65) (3-Y.O) (Class F) £2,714.00 (£754.00: £362.00) 1m 5f 175y Stalls: Low GOING minus 0.13 sec per fur (G) 4-15 (4-15)

2004 2 **Cross Talk (IRE) (65)***(74) (RHollinshead)* 3-9-0 TIves(6) (pushed along 6f out: hdwy whn carried wd st: led 1f out: styd on) — 1
1290 2 Domitia (USA) **(62)***(67) (MBell)* 3-8-9 MFenton(1) (chsd ldr: lft in ld ent st: hdd 1f out: one pce) 2 2
929 8 Dawn Mission **(58)***(49) (MHEasterby)* 3-9-0b MBirch(5) (plld hrd: cl up tl carried wd st: sn btn) 20 3
1039 10 Brownlows **(43)***(43) (MPBielby)* 3-8-9 (5) LNewton(2) (outpcd 5f out: wl bhd after) 5 4
1691 5 Coggle **(65)***(3) (NAGraham)* 3-8-9 KDarley(4) (trckd ldrs: effrt & ev ch whn badly hmpd ent st: nt rcvr) 30 5
1986 W Ahaalee (USA) **(62)** (Fav)*(EALDunlop)* 3-9-0 WRSwinburn(3) (led tl s.u ent st: dead) S

9/4 Ahaalee (USA), **5/2** Domitia (USA), **3/1** Coggle, **4/1** CROSS TALK (IRE), **11/1** Dawn Mission (6/1-14/1), **33/1** Brownlows, CSF £13.99 TOTE £5.00: £2.10 £1.30 (£4.00) OWNER Mr J. E. Bigg (UPPER LONGDON) BRED Juddmonte Farms 6 Rn
3m 7.1 (11.90) SF: 21/14/-/-/-/-

2190 SPREADING CHESTNUT H'CAP (0-70) (3-Y.O) (Class E) £3,106.00 (£928.00: £444.00: £202.00) 5f 212y Stalls: High GOING minus 0.13 sec (G) 4-45 (4-59)

1949 2 **Statistician (66)***(76) (JohnBerry)* 3-9-7 KFallon(2) (mde most: styd on strly fnl f) — 1
1972 4 Diebiedale **(57)***(62) (RBoss)* 3-8-12 JWeaver(4) (disp ld 2f: cl up tl rdn & btn 1f out) 2 2
2137 2 Tael of Silver **(66)***(68)*(Fav)*(KRBurke)* 3-9-7 7x MFenton(3) (lw: hld up: hdwy ent st: rdn & one pce appr fnl f) 1 3

2020[5] Benten **(38)**_(32) (DWChapman)_ 3-7-7b NCarlisle(5) (lw: chsd ldrs: effrt over 2f out: btn appr fnl f) 3 4
1453[5] Black Shadow **(38)**_(19) (PJMcBride)_ 3-7-7b GBardwell(1) (effrt appr st: rdn & btn wl over 1f out) 5 5
LONG HANDICAP Benten 7-3 Black Shadow 7-6

5/6 Tael of Silver (op 5/4), **11/4** Diebiedale, **7/2** STATISTICIAN, **10/1** Benten, **14/1** Black Shadow (op 8/1), CSF £13.33 TOTE £3.70: £1.80 £1.60 £8.10 (£8.10) OWNER Mrs Caroline Berry (NEWMARKET) BRED Mrs Caroline Berry 5 Rn 1m 13.5 (3.00) SF: 52/38/44/8/-

T/Plpt: £163.70 (67.42 Tckts). T/Qdpt: £6.90 (9.4 Tckts). AA

1615-HAYDOCK (L-H)
Thursday July 6th (Good to firm)
WEATHER: cloudy WIND: fresh half against

2191 HALEWOOD APPRENTICE H'CAP (0-70) (3-Y.O+) (Class E) £3,208.75 (£970.00: £472.50: £223.75)
7f 30y Stalls: Low GOING minus 0.39 sec per fur (F) 6-50 (6-52)

2088[3] **Cafe Solo (40)**_(47) (NBycroft)_ 4-7-12b(3) GMitchell(2) (chsd ldrs: 6th st: r.o to ld wl ins fnl f) ....— 1
1819* Four of Spades **(58)**_(64)_(Fav)_(PDEvans)_ 4-9-5 AmandaSanders(8) (hld up: 4th st: shkn up to ld 1f out: ct cl home) ....nk 2
1873[12] Reed My Lips (IRE) **(35)**_(41) (BPJBaugh)_ 4-7-5 (5) IonaWands(5) (bhd: rdn over 3f out: str run fnl f: jst failed) ....nk 3
1904[4] Proud Image **(63)**_(66) (APJarvis)_ 3-8-13 (3) SLanigan(3) (2nd st: ev ch 1f out: rdn & hung lft: unable qckn) 1¼ 4
1302[5] Saltz (IRE) **(57)**_(54) (PTDalton)_ 3-8-5 (5) JBramhill(6) (prom: 3rd st: led over 2f out to 1f out: wknd ins fnl f) 2½ 5
1501[7] Delmour **(32)**_(21) (WMBrisbourne)_ 4-7-4 (3) MartinDwyer(4) (chsd ldrs: 5th st: rdn 3f out: sn btn) 3½ 6
_1951[9]_ Brigadore Gold **(32)**_(20) (FHLee)_ 5-7-7b CAdamson(7) (led tl hdd over 2f out: sn wknd) ....½ 7
1666[10] Full Gloss **(56)**_(13) (MrsMReveley)_ 3-8-9 SCopp(1) (hld up: effrt 3f out: no imp: t.o) 14 8
LONG HANDICAP Delmour 6-6 Brigadore Gold 7-0

5/2 Four of Spades, **11/4** CAFE SOLO, **9/2** Proud Image, **11/2** Reed My Lips (IRE), **13/2** Full Gloss, **20/1** Brigadore Gold, Saltz (IRE), **25/1** Delmour, CSF £9.67 CT £30.81 TOTE £3.70: £1.30 £1.50 £1.60 (£3.40) Trio £4.20 OWNER Mr J. G. White (BRANDSBY) BRED Britton House Stud 8 Rn
1m 31.93 (4.63) SF: 3/20/-/14/2/-/-/-
WEIGHT FOR AGE 3yo-8lb

2192 STEVE DONOGHUE MAIDEN AUCTION STKS (2-Y.O) (Class D) £3,746.50 (£1,132.00: £551.00: £260.50)
6f Stalls: High GOING minus 0.39 sec per fur (F) 7-20 (7-22)

1935[2] **King of Peru** _(75+) (APJarvis)_ 2-8-1 (3)ow2 JTate(4) (hdwy over 2f out: led ent fnl f: rdn clr) ...— 1
1054[2] Eights High (USA) **(84)**_(69) (RHannon)_ 2-7-13 (7)ow1 DaneO'Neill(10) (chsd ldrs: rdn 2f out: styd on one pce) 3½ 2
2063[5] Cumbrian Maestro _(70) (MHEasterby)_ 2-8-7 MBirch(7) (led tl rdn & hdd over 1f out: rallied towards fin) ....hd 3
1746[3] Ciserano (IRE) _(62)_(Fav)_(MRChannon)_ 2-8-5 JCarroll(5) (a.p: jnd ldr 2f out: led over 1f out: sn hdd & outpcd) 2½ 4
1685[3] Termon _(47) (MissLAPerratt)_ 2-8-0 DaleGibson(1) (lw: dwlt: hdwy 2f out: r.o one pce) 3½ 5
1841[3] Needle Knot (IRE) _(47) (MJohnston)_ 2-8-2 TWilliams(6) (prom tl rdn & wknd over 1f out) ....¾ 6
1399[3] Mellors (IRE) _(47) (JARToller)_ 2-8-7 JWeaver(2) (spd over 4f) 2 7
2095[6] Europex _(34) (MHEasterby)_ 2-8-2 SMaloney(3) (prom 4f: eased whn btn over 1f out) 3 8
Sheemore (IRE) _(33) (JDBethell)_ 2-8-5 KFallon(8) (leggy: lt-f: a bhd) 1½ 9
1670[11] Reef Raider _(35) (NTinkler)_ 2-8-7 LCharnock(12) (s.i.s: a bhd & outpcd) ....hd 10
Sedbergh (USA) _(24) (MrsMReveley)_ 2-8-5 KDarley(11) (w'like: leggy: bit bkwd: s.s: a bhd & outpcd) 3½ 11

2/1 Ciserano (IRE) (op 3/1), **3/1** Eights High (USA), **9/2** KING OF PERU, **10/1** Mellors (IRE), **12/1** Needle Knot (IRE), Termon, Sedbergh (USA) (8/1-14/1), **14/1** Cumbrian Maestro, Sheemore (IRE), Europex (10/1-16/1), **33/1** Reef Raider, CSF £19.55 TOTE £5.80: £2.00 £1.80 £2.90 (£8.60) Trio £65.80 OWNER Mr L. Fust (ASTON UPTHORPE) BRED C. R. Black 11 Rn
1m 13.49 (1.79) SF: 32/26/27/19/4/4/4/-/-/-/-

2193 BODYCARE SALON H'CAP (0-80) (3-Y.O) (Class D) £3,673.25 (£1,106.00: £535.50: £250.25) **1m 6f** Stalls: Low GOING minus 0.39 sec per fur (F) 7-50 (7-50)

1527³ **Kristal's Paradise (IRE) (75)***(88) (JLDunlop)* 3-9-4 WCarson(2) (lw: mde virtually all: 2nd st: sn led: rdn over 2f out: styd on strly fnl f) ....— **1**
1527⁵ Executive Design **(77)***(87) (MrsMReveley)* 3-9-6 KDarley(4) (lw: hld up: 5th st: chal & ev ch 2f out: sn rdn: nt qckn).......3 **2**
1973² Astrolabe **(78)***(87) (BWHills)* 3-9-7v JWeaver(6) (hld up & bhd: 7th st: effrt & rdn over 2f out: styd on ins fnl f) ....nk **3**
2026* Daily Starlight (USA) **(72)***(81)*(Fav)*(MissGayKelleway)* 3-9-1 3x MWigham(1) (lw: chsd ldrs: 4th st: rdn over 2f out: btn ent fnl f).......nk **4**
1694³ Zalament **(61)***(58) (APJarvis)* 3-8-1 (3)ow1 JTate(7) (lw: hld up in rr: 6th st: rdn over 2f out: sn outpcd).......10 **5**
1656² Backview **(69)***(65) (BJLlewellyn)* 3-8-12 TWilliams(5) (lw: chsd wnr: led ent st: sn hdd: rdn 3f out: grad wknd) 1 **6**
947⁸ Blue Smoke (IRE) **(61)***(56) (BAMcMahon)* 3-8-4bow1 JFortune(3) (bit bkwd: dwlt: sn chsng ldrs: 3rd & rdn st: wknd over 3f out).......nk **7**

2/1 Daily Starlight (USA) (6/4-9/4), **9/4** KRISTAL'S PARADISE (IRE), **9/2** Executive Design, **5/1** Astrolabe, **12/1** Zalament, **16/1** Backview, **20/1** Blue Smoke (IRE), CSF £12.43 TOTE £3.00: £1.80 £2.80 (£7.70) OWNER Windflower Overseas Holdings Inc (ARUNDEL) BRED Windflower Overseas 7 Rn
3m 4.25 (6.05) SF: 38/37/37/31/8/15/6

2194 FAMOUS GROUSE H'CAP (0-80) (3-Y.O+) (Class D) £3,878.00 (£1,169.00: £567.00: £266.00) **6f** Stalls: High GOING minus 0.39 sec per fur (F) 8-20 (8-20)

1624² **Jawlaat (USA) (77)***(89)*(Fav)*(JLDunlop)* 3-9-4 WCarson(8) (lw: mde all: qcknd clr appr fnl f: comf).......— **1**
2096⁴ Barato **(72)***(79)*(Fav)*(MrsJRRamsden)* 4-9-6 KFallon(7) (b.nr hind: hld up: hdwy bel dist: chsd wnr fnl f: rdn & no imp).......2 **2**
1809¹⁴ Miss Aragon **(46)***(49) (MissLCSiddall)* 7-7-8 NCarlisle(10) (lw: hld up in tch: effrt bel dist: kpt on ins fnl f).......1½ **3**
1832¹⁰ Bargash **(66)***(68) (PDEvans)* 3-8-7 JFortune(5) (lw: s.i.s: hld up & bhd: hdwy & nt clr run wl over 1f out: fin wl).......hd **4**
1687⁵ Chinour (IRE) **(62)***(64) (EJAlston)* 7-8-10 JWeaver(2) (lw: hld up & bhd: hdwy over 1f out: r.o ins fnl f).......nk **5**
1931U Rossini Blue **(70)***(72) (ABailey)* 4-9-4 JCarroll(9) (hld up: effrt u.p 2f out: nt pce to chal).......s.h **6**
1677⁶ Maid O'Cannie **(65)***(60) (MWEasterby)* 4-8-13 LCharnock(3) (chsd ldrs: rdn over 2f out: sn btn) 2½ **7**
2060⁵ Rich Glow **(59)***(54) (NBycroft)* 4-8-7 SMaloney(6) (lw: chsd ldrs: rdn 2f out: wknd bel dist).......hd **8**
1895²⁶ Encore M'Lady (IRE) **(76)***(67) (FHLee)* 4-9-10b TIves(1) (spd over 4f: btn whn n.m.r ent fnl f) 1¼ **9**
1924¹² In Love Again (IRE) **(80)***(31) (MRChannon)* 3-9-7 KDarley(4) (lw: a in rr: outpcd fr ½-wy: t.o).......15 **10**

3/1 JAWLAAT (USA), Barato, **7/1** Rich Glow, **8/1** Chinour (IRE), **9/1** Maid O'Cannie, **11/1** Encore M'Lady (IRE), **12/1** In Love Again (IRE), **14/1** Rossini Blue, Miss Aragon, **16/1** Bargash, CSF £12.03 CT £98.78 TOTE £2.80: £1.70 £1.80 £3.00 (£3.40) Trio £17.10 OWNER Mr Hamdan Al Maktoum (ARUNDEL) BRED Shadwell Farm Inc. in USA 10 Rn
1m 12.65 (0.95) SF: 56/53/23/35/38/46/34/28/41/-
WEIGHT FOR AGE 3yo-7lb

2195 SUMMER (S) STKS (2-Y.O) (Class F) £2,773.00 (£778.00: £379.00) **6f** Stalls: High GOING minus 0.39 sec per fur (F) 8-50 (8-51)

1857⁸ **Flood's Fancy** *(60)*(Fav)*(MrsJRRamsden)* 2-8-6 KFallon(7) (a.p: rdn to ld ins fnl f: all out) ..— **1**
1981* Domettes (IRE) **(60)***(63) (RHannon)* 2-8-4 (7) DaneO'Neill(3) (a.p: led bel dist tl ins fnl f: rdn & nt qckn nr fin) ....¾ **2**
Marmy *(51) (MHEasterby)* 2-8-6 MBirch(11) (scope: dwlt: effrt & swtchd lft over 1f out: rdn & hung lft fnl f: r.o).......2½ **3**
1159³ Homeland *(54) (CWThornton)* 2-8-11 DeanMcKeown(2) (lw: w ldr: ev ch 1f out: rdn & no ex fnl f).......1 **4**
1829⁵ Ginger Glint *(43) (MJHeaton-Ellis)* 2-8-11 KDarley(8) (chsd ldrs: rdn 2f out: no imp) 4 **5**
1943¹¹ Ticka Ticka Timing *(40) (BWMurray)* 2-8-4 (7) GParkin(1) (hdwy wl over 1f out: nvr nr to chal).......1 **6**

1226[5] Doubleyoubeay *(42) (JBerry)* 2-9-2 JCarroll(4) (bit bkwd: mde most tl hdd & wknd over 1f out) 1¼ 7
Song Song Blue (IRE) *(26) (NTinkler)* 2-8-11 LCharnock(5) (lt-f: unf: chsd ldrs 4f: sn lost tch) 4 8
1842[11] Mill House Boy (IRE) *(24) (BSRothwell)* 2-8-11 MFenton(10) (bit bkwd: a in rr) .... ¾ 9

13/8 FLOOD'S FANCY, **9/4** Domettes (IRE), **11/2** Doubleyoubeay, **8/1** Homeland, **9/1** Ginger Glint, **11/1** Song Song Blue (IRE) (8/1-12/1), **12/1** Marmy (op 8/1), **16/1** Mill House Boy (IRE), **25/1** Ticka Ticka Timing, CSF £6.50 TOTE £2.80: £1.60 £1.30 £2.20 (£2.70) Trio £26.80 OWNER Richard Flood Bloodstock Ltd (THIRSK) BRED Downclose Stud 9 Rn 1m 15.4 (3.70) SF: 8/11/-/2/-/-/-/-/-
Sold A. Bailey 7,000 gns

2196

MILES GOSLING FAREWELL H'CAP (0-80) (3-Y.O+) (Class D)
£3,627.75 (£1,092.00: £528.50: £246.75)
1m 3f 200y Stalls: High GOING minus 0.39 sec per fur (F) 9-20 (9-20)

1986[3] **Lucky Coin (62)***(77) (CEBrittain)* 3-8-11 BDoyle(2) (lw: hld up: 4th st: led wl over 1f out: clr fnl f: easily) .... — 1
1303[6] Innocence **(66)***(76) (GWragg)* 3-9-1 PRobinson(5) (led after 1f tl hdd over 4f out: rdn to ld wl over 2f out: sn hdd: one pce) 4 2
2002[2] Killick **(55)***(59)*(Fav)*(ABailey)* 7-9-3 JCarroll(1) (lw: led 1f: 2nd st: led over 4f out tl over 2f out: one pce) 4 3
2101[3] Cumbrian Rhapsody **(62)***(61) (MHEasterby)* 5-9-10 SMaloney(4) (chsd ldrs: 3rd st: rdn over 3f out: wknd fnl 2f) 4 4
1966[3] Kanat Lee (IRE) **(40)***(34) (DonEnricoIncisa)* 4-8-2 KimTinkler(3) (lw: s.i.s: a bhd: 5th st) 4 5

15/8 Killick, **5/2** Cumbrian Rhapsody, **4/1** Innocence, LUCKY COIN, **10/1** Kanat Lee (IRE), CSF £17.90 TOTE £5.70: £2.10 £2.00 (£7.40) OWNER Mrs J. M. Khan (NEWMARKET) BRED Mrs M. Brittain and Mrs J. M. Khan 5 Rn 2m 32.58 (4.58) SF: 34/33/29/31/4
WEIGHT FOR AGE 3yo-13lb
T/Plpt: £28.60 (544.04 Tckts). T/Qdpt: £8.60 (16.4 Tckts). IM

2031-SALISBURY (R-H)
Thursday July 6th (Good to Firm, firm patches)

Race 5: flip start
WEATHER: overcast WIND: nil

2197

CRESTED LARK AMATEUR H'CAP (0-70) (3-Y.O+) (Class F)
£3,029.00 (£844.00: £407.00)
1m 4f Stalls: High GOING minus 0.29 sec per fur (GF) 6-35 (6-35)

*384** **Shaft of Light (70)***(83+) (LordHuntingdon)* 3-11-6 MrJDurkan(2) (lw: led 2f: rdn to ld 4f out: r.o wl) .... — 1
1863[3] Our Bessie **(43)***(52) (DMarks)* 4-10-6 MissKMarks(8) (a.p: ev ch over 2f out: one pce) 3 2
1937* Stalled (IRE) **(54)***(59)*(Fav)*(PTWalwyn)* 5-10-12 (5) MarchionessBlandford(9) (hld up & bhd: hdwy over 2f out: hung rt fnl f: nvr rch ldrs) 3 3
Shirley's Train (USA) **(42)***(39) (PJHobbs)* 6-10-0 (5) MrsSHobbs(10) (led after 2f: hdd 4f out: sn rdn: hung lft & wknd 2f out) 6 4
1937[3] Top Pet (IRE) **(58)***(48) (RAkehurst)* 5-11-7 MrTMcCarthy(4) (prom tl wknd over 2f out) 5 5
1937[8] Sadler's Pearl **(43)***(29) (BJMeehan)* 3-9-7b MissJAllison(6) (hdwy 5f out: wknd over 2f out) .. 3½ 6
1854[14] Bresil (USA) **(39)***(10) (KRBurke)* 6-9-11 (5)ow13 MrsHSweeting(5) (s.s: a wl bhd) 1½ 7
Roxy River **(43)***(23) (JLSpearing)* 6-10-1 (5)ow4 MissCSpearing(1) (plld hrd: prom: stumbled over 6f out: wknd 3f out) .... s.h 8
1716[9] Duke of Dreams **(45)***(26) (RJBaker)* 5-10-3 (5) MissLPope(7) (bhd fnl 5f) 2 9
2148[8] Mascalls Lady **(41)** *(NBThomson)* 10-9-13 (5)ow14 MrSDavis(3) (bhd: rdn 6f out: sn t.o) .... dist 10

2/1 Stalled (IRE), **5/2** SHAFT OF LIGHT, **9/2** Our Bessie, **6/1** Top Pet (IRE), **14/1** Shirley's Train (USA), **20/1** Roxy River, **25/1** Sadler's Pearl, **50/1** Duke of Dreams, **100/1** Bresil (USA), **200/1** Mascalls Lady, CSF £12.89 CT £22.79 TOTE £3.00: £1.60 £1.70 £1.50 (£6.90) Trio £7.60 OWNER The Queen (WEST ILSLEY) BRED The Queen 10 Rn
2m 39.16 (6.56) SF: 65/47/54/34/43/11/5/18/21/-
WEIGHT FOR AGE 3yo-13lb

2198

MYROBELLA MAIDEN AUCTION STKS (2-Y.O) (Class F) £2,952.00 (£822.00: £396.00) **6f** Stalls: High GOING minus 0.29 sec per fur (GF) 7-05 (7-06)

Last Token *(66) (JSMoore)* 2-7-10 (5) NVarley(5) (leggy: unf: a.p: led 2f out: edgd rt over 1f out: r.o wl) .... — 1

1448[5] Bearnaise (IRE) *(57) (RHannon)* 2-7-13 GCarter(4) (a.p: chsd wnr over 1f out: no imp).......2½ 2
1690[3] Kinnescash (IRE) *(62)*(Fav)*(RIngram)* 2-8-7 JReid(11) (led: edgd lft & hdd 2f out: one pce).1¼ 3
1184[9] The Legions Pride *(55) (JWHills)* 2-8-7 DHolland(1) (chsd ldrs: rdn over 2f out: one pce) 2½ 4
1938[11] Pearls of Thought (IRE) *(46) (PTWalwyn)* 2-8-2 DHarrison(13) (a.p: no hdwy fnl 2f) 1½ 5
Little Kenny *(44) (MJFetherston-Godley)* 2-8-2 FNorton(7) (unf: nvr nr to chal).......................¾ 6
Daunting Destiny (BEL) *(42) (RHannon)* 2-8-4 RPerham(12) (w'like: bit bkwd: hdwy 3f out: wknd wl over 1f out) 1½ 7
Move Darling *(36) (CACyzer)* 2-8-2 DBiggs(10) (wl grwn: chsd ldr: rdn over 3f out: sn wknd)1½ 8
Classic Daisy *(33) (MissGayKelleway)* 2-7-13 StephenDavies(3) (unf: bkwd: dwlt: a bhd).....nk 9
1977[7] Dragonjoy *(19) (LJHolt)* 2-8-4 AMcGlone(2) (a bhd) 7 10
1774[8] Dish The Dosh *(8) (PGMurphy)* 2-7-8 (3)ow1 DWright(9) (prom over 3f) 1¼ 11
1938[15] Another Picea *(KTIvory)* 2-8-5 ow1 WNewnes(6) (s.s & wnt lft: a bhd: t.o) 10 12

2/1 Kinnescash (IRE), **7/2** Bearnaise (IRE), **4/1** The Legions Pride, **10/1** Classic Daisy, **12/1** Daunting Destiny (BEL) (op 8/1), Dragonjoy, **16/1** Pearls of Thought (IRE), Little Kenny, Move Darling, **33/1** LAST TOKEN, Dish The Dosh, Another Picea, CSF £142.69 TOTE £46.30: £7.70 £1.70 £1.40 (£98.20) Trio £209.80 OWNER Mr J. S. Moore (EAST GARSTON) BRED J. B. Walker
12 Rn 1m 16.74 (4.44) SF: 3/-/-/-/-/-/-/-/-/-/-/-

2199

FAIR TRIAL H'CAP (0-80) (3-Y.O) (Class D) £4,142.50 (£1,240.00: £595.00: £272.50) **1m** Stalls: High GOING minus 0.29 sec per fur (GF) 7-35 (7-35)

829[W] **Rockforce** **(78)***(85) (MRChannon)* 3-9-7 RHughes(10) (hld up & bhd: rdn & gd hdwy over 1f out: hung rt ins fnl f: led nr fin)..— 1
2033* Kevasingo **(60)***(66)*(Fav)*(SDow)* 3-7-10 (7) 5x ADaly(5) (led: rdn over 2f out: hdd nr fin)............½ 2
1221[8] Almond Rock **(65)***(70) (JRFanshawe)* 3-8-8 DHarrison(2) (plld hrd: a.p: rdn & chsd ldr over 2f out: hung rt over 1f out: r.o)...½ 3
1907* Ron's Secret **(71)***(75) (JWPayne)* 3-9-0 RCochrane(7) (hdwy over 2f out: r.o one pce fnl f) ....¾ 4
857[4] No Pattern **(73)***(67) (GLMoore)* 3-9-2 SWhitworth(11) (hld up & bhd: stdy hdwy fnl 2f: nvr plcd to chal)..5 5
1792[3] African-Pard (IRE) **(73)***(62) (DHaydnJones)* 3-9-2 JReid(4) (plld hrd: prom: rdn 3f out: wknd 2f out)...2½ 6
1904* Mighty Marston **(71)***(55) (LadyHerries)* 3-9-0 PatEddery(6) (hld up: reminder 4f out: bhd fnl 3f) 2½ 7
1663[13] Ballynakelly **(63)***(43) (RAkehurst)* 3-8-6 AClark(1) (prom: rdn over 3f out: sn wknd) 1¾ 8
1787[4] Landlord **(73)***(43) (JARToller)* 3-9-2 WNewnes(3) (chsd ldr over 5f: sn wknd) 5 9
1982[3] Squire Corrie **(64)***(18) (LJHolt)* 3-8-7 AMcGlone(9) (bhd fnl 2f) 8 10
1754[5] Yosif (IRE) **(56)** *(RHannon)* 3-7-13 GCarter(8) (a bhd) 9 11

9/2 Kevasingo, **5/1** Almond Rock, **6/1** ROCKFORCE, Ron's Secret (tchd 7/2), **13/2** Mighty Marston, **9/1** Yosif (IRE), **11/1** African-Pard (IRE), **12/1** No Pattern, Landlord, **20/1** Squire Corrie, **25/1** Ballynakelly, CSF £31.19 CT £133.01 TOTE £6.10: £2.30 £2.30 £1.80 (£12.10) Trio £26.10 OWNER Mr G. Z. Mizel (UPPER LAMBOURN) BRED Guest Leasing and Bloodstock Co 11 Rn
1m 43.17 (3.87) SF: 43/24/28/33/25/20/13/1/1/-/-

2200

E.B.F. QUEENPOT MAIDEN STKS (2-Y.O) (Class D) £4,240.00 (£1,270.00: £610.00: £280.00)
6f 212y Stalls: High GOING minus 0.29 sec per fur (GF) 8-05 (8-06)

1697[2] **Champagne Prince** *(78) (PWHarris)* 2-9-0 PatEddery(7) (mde all: shkn up over 1f out: pushed out)...— 1
1726[4] Lomberto *(75)*(Fav)*(RHannon)* 2-9-0 JReid(1) (a.p: r.o ins fnl f) 1¼ 2
1856[4] Brecon *(72) (PFICole)* 2-9-0 RCochrane(4) (a.p: chsd wnr fnl 2f: nt qckn) 1¼ 3
Flying Green (FR) *(72) (RCharlton)* 2-9-0 DHarrison(6) (lengthy: unf: plld hrd: a.p: r.o one pce fnl 2f) ....hd 4
617[4] Tapintime (USA) *(61) (PFICole)* 2-9-0 TQuinn(8) (chsd wnr tl over 3f out: rdn & wandered over 2f out: sn wknd) 5 5
1592[5] Goodwood Rocket *(59) (JLDunlop)* 2-9-0 WNewnes(5) (prom: chsd wnr over 3f out tl wknd 2f out)..½ 6
Island Victory *(56) (IABalding)* 2-9-0 GHind(2) (w'like: rn green: plld hrd: a bhd)...................1½ 7
Louisiana Purchase *(45) (MrsBarbaraWaring)* 2-9-0 JWilliams(3) (lt-f: unf: hld up & plld hrd: a bhd) 5 8

5/4 Lomberto, **4/1** CHAMPAGNE PRINCE, **9/2** Tapintime (USA) (7/2-11/2), **7/1** Flying Green (FR) (5/1-8/1), **14/1** Goodwood Rocket, Island Victory, **16/1** Brecon, **66/1** Louisiana Purchase, CSF £9.13 TOTE £3.60: £1.10 £1.30 £3.80 (£4.80) OWNER Magnum Force (BERKHAMSTED) BRED Cheveley Park Stud Ltd 8 Rn 1m 30.62 (4.92) SF: 19/16/13/13/2/-/-/-

2201

FELSTEAD LIMITED STKS (0-65) (3-Y.O+) (Class F) £2,840.00 (£790.00: £380.00)
1m 6f GOING minus 0.29 sec per fur (GF) 8-35 (8-36)

1901* **Trazl (IRE) (63)***(75)*(Fav)*(JLDunlop)* 3-8-2 GCarter(2) (hld up: hdwy over 3f out: led ins fnl f: comf) ....— 1
1929⁴ Wild Strawberry **(60)***(73) (MissBSanders)* 6-9-0 (3) SSanders(3) (prom: led over 9f out: clr 6f out: hdd ins fnl f) 1¾ 2
1749³ Ginger Jim **(55)***(75) (PRHedger)* 4-9-6 CAvery(7) (a.p: hrd rdn over 1f out: nt qckn) 1 3
1695² Wannaplantatree **(56)***(63) (NMBabbage)* 4-9-1 AClark(1) (hld up & bhd: hdwy 5f out: wknd 2f out) 6 4
1594⁶ Pride of May (IRE) **(60)***(65) (RHannon)* 4-9-6b JReid(4) (lost pl 7f out: no hdwy fnl 3f) 2½ 5
1978³ Acquittal (IRE) **(63)***(51) (JRFanshawe)* 3-8-0 (5) NVarley(6) (prom: rdn over 4f out: wknd 2f out) 12 6
Chucklestone **(58)***(38) (JSKing)* 12-9-6 TQuinn(8) (bit bkwd: led over 4f: wknd over 4f out: t.o) 12 7
795⁶ Head Turner **(46)***(22) (CPWildman)* 7-9-7 StephenDavies(5) (prom 9f: t.o) 15 8

5/2 TRAZL (IRE), **3/1** Acquittal (IRE), **4/1** Wild Strawberry, **5/1** Wannaplantatree, **11/1** Pride of May (IRE), Ginger Jim, **25/1** Chucklestone, Head Turner, CSF £12.20 TOTE £3.30: £1.70 £1.30 £1.90 (£7.40) OWNER Hesmonds Stud (ARUNDEL) BRED Hesmonds Stud Ltd 8 Rn
3m 4.73 (6.53) SF: 28/41/43/31/33/4/6/-
WEIGHT FOR AGE 3yo-15lb

2202

OWEN TUDOR H'CAP (0-70) (3-Y.O+) (Class E) £3,210.00
(£960.00: £460.00: £210.00)
6f Stalls: High GOING minus 0.29 sec per fur (GF) 9-05 (9-06)

2017* **Bowden Rose (59)***(70)*(Fav)*(MBlanshard)* 3-9-0b 7x StephenDavies(7) (mde all: clr after 2f: rdn over 1f out: r.o wl) ....— 1
1975⁷ Friendly Brave (USA) **(65)***(65) (MissGayKelleway)* 5-9-13 DHolland(8) (chsd wnr: no imp fnl 2f) 4 2
1910² Paddy's Rice **(56)***(55) (LJHolt)* 4-9-4 JReid(4) (hdwy 2f out: r.o ins fnl f) ....½ 3
2009⁷ Winsome Wooster **(66)***(64) (PGMurphy)* 4-9-11 (3) SDrowne(5) (hdwy over 2f out: one pce fnl f) ....½ 4
1975¹³ Lorins Gold **(34)***(30) (AndrewTurnell)* 5-7-10b NAdams(2) (hdwy over 2f out: one pce fnl f) .....¾ 5
1738⁷ Media Express **(68)***(56) (RHannon)* 3-9-2 (7) MarkDenaro(9) (sn outpcd: eased whn no ch ins fnl f) 3 6
1714¹⁷ Pacific Girl (IRE) **(63)***(49) (BPalling)* 3-9-4 TSprake(6) (prom 3f) ....¾ 7
*1980*³ Words of Wisdom (IRE) **(45)***(31) (CACyzer)* 5-8-7 DBiggs(3) (prom: rdn over 2f out: sn wknd) ....s.h 8
1942⁶ Riskie Things **(45)** *(JSMoore)* 4-8-2 (5) NVarley(1) (rdn over 2f out: a bhd: t.o) 15 9

Evens BOWDEN ROSE, **7/2** Paddy's Rice, **9/1** Media Express, **10/1** Words of Wisdom (IRE) (7/1-11/1), **11/1** Friendly Brave (USA) (8/1-12/1), **12/1** Riskie Things (op 7/1), **14/1** Winsome Wooster (op 8/1), **33/1** Lorins Gold, **40/1** Pacific Girl (IRE), CSF £12.61 CT £28.89 TOTE £2.30: £1.50 £2.80 £1.40 (£10.50) Trio £5.00 OWNER The Lower Bowden Syndicate (UPPER LAMBOURN) BRED E. A. Badger 9 Rn 1m 16.0 (3.70) SF: 24/26/16/25/-/10/3/-/-
WEIGHT FOR AGE 3yo-7lb

T/Jkpt: Not won; £5,013.17 to Sandown 7/7/95. T/Plpt: £5.30 (3,165.04 Tckts). T/Qdpt: £4.90 (22.1 Tckts). KH

2179-YARMOUTH (L-H)
Thursday July 6th (Good to firm)

WEATHER: fine WIND: slight against

2203

FRED ARMSTRONG H'CAP (0-70) (3-Y.O+) (Class E) £3,130.60
(£932.80: £444.40: £200.20)
6f 3y Stalls: High GOING minus 0.46 sec per fur (F) 2-00 (2-03)

2179³ **Tharwa (IRE) (60)***(66+)*(Fav)*(NACallaghan)* 3-8-13 LDettori(7) (b: b.hind: hld up: led 2f out: pushed out) ....— 1
2168³ Samsolom **(64)***(69) (PHowling)* 7-9-10 PaulEddery(3) (hld up: gd hdwy appr fnl f: hrd rdn & ev ch ins fnl f: unable qckn cl home) ....nk 2
1975¹⁵ Our Shadee (USA) **(50)***(46) (KTIvory)* 5-8-3v(7) CScally(2) (outpcd early: hdwy 2f out: one pce fnl f) 3½ 3
1602⁴ Just Like Me **(67)***(60) (RGuest)* 3-9-6 WCarson(5) (chsd ldr: ev ch 1f out: no ex) 1 4
1700* Red Admiral **(58)***(33) (PCHaslam)* 5-9-4 MTebbutt(6) (chsd ldrs tl wknd over 2f out) 7 5

1414[13] Fairy Fay (IRE) **(50)***(19) (BJMcMath)* 3-8-3 AMcGlone(4) (b.hind: chsd ldrs: hrd rdn 2f out: wknd appr fnl f:)....2 **6**
2179[4] Awesome Venture **(49)***(18) (MCChapman)* 5-8-6v(3) DRMcCabe(1) (led 4f: wknd qckly)........s.h **7**

9/4 THARWA (IRE) (2/1-3/1), **4/1** Red Admiral, Awesome Venture, **5/1** Samsolom, **8/1** Just Like Me, **14/1** Our Shadee (USA), **16/1** Fairy Fay (IRE), CSF £12.57 TOTE £3.70: £2.10 £3.00 (£8.30) OWNER K. Al-Said (NEWMARKET) BRED Charlton Down Stud 7 Rn
1m 13.6 (3.00) SF: 34/44/21/28/8/-/-
WEIGHT FOR AGE 3yo-7lb

2204 DUNSTON (S) STKS (2-Y.O) (Class G) £2,534.20 (£701.20: £334.60)
6f 3y Stalls: High GOING minus 0.46 sec per fur (F) 2-30 (2-32)

1810[2] **Fenna** *(66) (SPCWoods)* 2-8-6 WWoods(3) (chsd ldrs: led jst over 2f out: pushed out: r.o wl)....— **1**
2070[4] Asking For Kings (IRE) *(63)*(Fav)*(NACallaghan)* 2-8-11 LDettori(9) (b.hind: hld up: nt clr run over 2f out: hdwy 2f out: chsd wnr appr fnl f: sn hrd rdn & unable qckn) 3 **2**
1699[7] Bites **(47)***(47) (JAHarris)* 2-8-6 PaulEddery(8) (in rr tl hdwy 2f out: nvr nrr) 4 **3**
1989[4] Dancing Lottie (IRE) **(46)***(46) (PAKelleway)* 2-8-6 DHarrison(6) (swtg: w ldr over 3f: kpt on one pce)....½ **4**
1989[3] Ivory's Grab Hire **(63)***(44) (KTIvory)* 2-8-11b GDuffield(4) (outpcd & rdn ½-wy: no real hdwy)2½ **5**
1653[7] Exceedingly *(35) (WJarvis)* 2-8-6 WCarson(7) (b: led wl over 3f) 1½ **6**
1954[6] Herald Angel (IRE) *(31) (MHTompkins)* 2-8-6 SMulvey(2) (chsd ldrs 4f) 1¾ **7**
1829[4] Noon (IRE) *(31) (MHTompkins)* 2-8-1 (5) HKYim(1) (in tch tl wknd over 1f out) ....s.h **8**
1989[4] Down The Yard **(54)***(17) (MCChapman)* 2-8-3 (3) DRMcCabe(5) (a outpcd) 5 **9**

6/5 Asking For Kings (IRE) (6/4-Evens), **5/1** FENNA, **11/2** Exceedingly (op 3/1), **6/1** Ivory's Grab Hire, **12/1** Dancing Lottie (IRE) (op 8/1), Down The Yard (8/1-14/1), **14/1** Noon (IRE) (8/1-16/1), **33/1** Herald Angel (IRE), Bites, CSF £11.30 TOTE £5.50: £1.20 £1.60 £3.50 (£5.30) Trio £20.30 OWNER Mr S. P. C. Woods (NEWMARKET) BRED High Point Bloodstock Ltd and Nigel Fenner Fownes 9 Rn
1m 14.6 (4.00) SF: 14/11/-/-/-/-/-/-/-
Bt in 10,000 gns

2205 HEMSBY CONDITIONS STKS (3-Y.O+) (Class C) £5,727.20 (£2,067.20: £993.60: £408.00: £164.00)
7f 3y Stalls: High GOING minus 0.46 sec per fur (F) 3-00 (3-01)

912[4] **Solar Flight** *(90) (BWHills)* 3-8-8 RHills(1) (trckd ldr: led wl over 1f out: pushed out: r.o wl)....— **1**
1839[16] Cadeaux Tryst **(97)***(87) (EALDunlop)* 3-8-8 WRyan(4) (b: hld up: hdwy 2f out: hrd rdn 1f out: r.o one pce) 1¼ **2**
Hedera (USA) *(80) (MRStoute)* 3-8-3 WCarson(5) (h.d.w: n.m.r over 2f out: rdn & hung rt wl over 1f out: styd on one pce) ....¾ **3**
1698[3] Maid for Walking **(105)***(88) (DRLoder)* 3-8-12 LDettori(2) (set stdy pce: led tl wl over 1f out: no ex) ....½ **4**
2105[3] Stylish Ways (IRE) **(96)***(85)*(Fav)*(GWragg)* 3-8-12 PaulEddery(3) (lw: hld up: nt clr run wl over 1f out: nvr able to chal) 1½ **5**

4/6 Stylish Ways (IRE) (Evens-11/10), **4/1** Maid for Walking (5/2-9/2), **6/1** SOLAR FLIGHT, **13/2** Hedera (USA), **12/1** Cadeaux Tryst (7/1-14/1), CSF £49.75 TOTE £7.40: £2.40 £3.40 (£31.20) OWNER Mr K. Abdullah (LAMBOURN) BRED Juddmonte Farms 5 Rn
1m 25.8 (3.00) SF: 36/33/26/34/31

2206 LODDON H'CAP (0-80) (3-Y.O+ F & M) (Class D) £3,968.90 (£1,185.20: £566.60: £257.30) **7f 3y** Stalls: High GOING minus 0.46 sec per fur (F) 3-30 (3-31)

1701[2] **Cutpurse Moll (74)***(77)*(Fav)*(JRFanshawe)* 3-9-0 DHarrison(3) (lw: mde all: hung lft appr fnl f: all out)....— **1**
2032* Second Cello **(67)***(70) (DMorris)* 3-8-7 6x LDettori(4) (swtg: hld up: ev ch wl ins fnl f: unable qckn cl home)....hd **2**
First Veil **(80)***(77) (JRFanshawe)* 5-9-9 (5) NVarley(2) (a.p: rdn 2f out: n.mr appr fnl f: ev ch jst ins fnl f: one pce)....2½ **3**
1918[2] Macs Maharanee **(72)***(66) (PSFelgate)* 8-9-6 GHind(1) (a.p: ev ch 1f out: one pce) 1½ **4**

5/4 CUTPURSE MOLL (Evens-11/8), **15/8** Macs Maharanee, **7/2** Second Cello (5/2-4/1), **14/1** First Veil (op 7/1), CSF £5.30 TOTE £2.30: (£3.10) OWNER Dexa'tex Ltd (NEWMARKET) BRED R. H. Cowell 4 Rn
1m 27.6 (4.80) SF: 21/14/29/18
WEIGHT FOR AGE 3yo-8lb

2207 HIGH STEWARD CLAIMING STKS (3-Y.O+) (Class F) £2,947.40 (£816.40: £390.20) **1m 3y** Stalls: High GOING minus 0.46 sec per fur (F) 4-00 (4-01)

2057* **Blockade (USA) (70)***(80)*(Fav)*(MBell)* 6-9-4 LDettori(3) (t: swtg: mde all: pushed clr: r.o wl) .... — 1
1914[2] Action Jackson **(70)***(75) (GRimmer)* 3-8-9 MRimmer(5) (b: swtg: hld up: hdwy over 2f out: hrd rdn appr fnl f: sn btn) 2½ 2
2032[5] Jurassic Sue **(64)***(63) (BWHills)* 3-8-4v RHills(4) (lw: trckd ldr tl wknd appr fnl f) 3½ 3
2065[5] Orchidarma **(60)***(60) (RGuest)* 3-8-4v GDuffield(2) (hld up: hdwy over 3f out: wknd 2f out) 1½ 4
2056[8] Ballyhays (IRE) **(48)***(34) (JAHarris)* 6-8-8 (3) DRMcCabe(1) (in tch 5f) 12 5

5/6 BLOCKADE (USA) (op 5/4), **5/2** Action Jackson, **11/2** Jurassic Sue, **11/1** Orchidarma, **16/1** Ballyhays (IRE), CSF £3.32 TOTE £1.80: £1.40 £1.60 (£2.20) OWNER Mr A. M. Warrender (NEWMARKET) BRED Patricia C. Warrender 5 Rn 1m 40.2 (4.90) SF: 30/16/4/1/-
WEIGHT FOR AGE 3yo-9lb
Action Jackson clmd BMcMath £10,000

2208 HAPPISBURGH MAIDEN STKS (3-Y.O+) (Class D) £3,935.10 (£1,174.80: £561.40: £254.70) **1m 3f 101y** Stalls: High GOING minus 0.46 sec per fur (F) 4-30 (4-32)

1346[2] **Tinashaan (IRE) (90)***(84+)*(Fav)*(JRFanshawe)* 3-8-5 DHarrison(2) (4th st: led over 2f out: rdn out) .... — 1
Speed to Lead (IRE) *(83) (HRACecil)* 3-8-5 WCarson(8) (hld up: last st: hdwy 3f out: rdn & hung lft 2f out: r.o one pce) 1 2
1682[2] Iridal *(86) (HRACecil)* 3-8-10 WRyan(6) (lw: 3rd st: led 4f out tl over 2f out: one pce) 1½ 3
1717[2] Danesrath (IRE) *(78) (ACStewart)* 3-8-5 PaulEddery(1) (s.i.s: 6th st: hdwy 3f out: hrd rdn & no ex fnl f) 1¾ 4
Racing Hawk (USA) *(69) (HRACecil)* 3-8-10 AMcGlone(3) (lengthy: unf: led to 4f out) 10 5
Big Treat (IRE) *(55) (PAKelleway)* 3-8-10 LDettori(5) (2nd st: wknd over 2f out: eased over 1f out) 10 6
1514[18] Chalky Dancer *(38) (HJCollingridge)* 3-8-10 MRimmer(4) (5th st: wknd over 3f out) 12 7

11/8 TINASHAAN (IRE), **11/4** Danesrath (IRE) (7/4-3/1), **5/1** Iridal (7/2-11/2), **11/2** Speed to Lead (IRE), **12/1** Big Treat (IRE) (8/1-14/1), **20/1** Racing Hawk (USA), **50/1** Chalky Dancer, CSF £9.08 TOTE £2.10: £1.50 £2.40 (£6.40) OWNER Mrs James McAllister (NEWMARKET) BRED Chippenham Lodge Stud 7 Rn 2m 26.5 (3.50) SF: 29/28/31/23/14/-/-

2209 HICKLING LADY RIDERS AMATEUR H'CAP (0-70) (3-Y.O+) (Class G) £2,467.00 (£682.00: £325.00) **1m 2f 21y** Stalls: High GOING minus 0.46 sec per fur (F) 5-00 (5-01)

1612[11] **Bajan (IRE) (62)***(70)*(Fav)*(LadyHerries)* 4-10-13 MrsMCowdrey(3) (lw: trckd ldr tl led 4f out: pushed out) .... — 1
Blaze of Oak (USA) **(70)***(75) (WJHaggas)* 4-11-7 MissDianaJones(6) (led to 4f out: kpt on one pce) 2 2
2052* Dots Dee **(35)***(38) (JMBradley)* 6-9-0 5x MrsLPearce(2) (3rd st: r.o one pce fnl 2f) 1½ 3
1442* Hard Love **(65)***(64) (SPCWoods)* 3-10-5 MissLHide(1) (lw: 4th st: no hdwy fnl 3f) 2 4
1974[16] Blanchland **(54)***(44) (KTIvory)* 6-10-0 (5) MissLVollaro(5) (last st: a bhd) 6 5
1622[9] Swan Flyer **(37)** *(JJSheehan)* 4-8-11 (5)ow2 MissEJJones(4) (s.s: 5th st: sn wl bhd) 25 6
LONG HANDICAP Dots Dee 8-1 Swan Flyer 8-2

7/4 BAJAN (IRE), **11/4** Dots Dee, Hard Love, **6/1** Blaze of Oak (USA), **16/1** Swan Flyer, **20/1** Blanchland, CSF £11.71 TOTE £2.50: £1.60 £1.80 (£7.10) OWNER Mr Tim Sinclair (LITTLEHAMPTON) BRED Rathbarry Stud 6 Rn 2m 8.4 (4.00) SF: 55/60/23/38/29/-
WEIGHT FOR AGE 3yo-11lb
T/Plpt: £163.50 (71.62 Tckts). T/Qdpt: £47.80 (0.25 Tckts). RC

1711a-CHANTILLY (France) (R-H)
Friday June 30th (Firm)

2210a PRIX DU BOIS (Gp 3) (2-Y.O) £26,347.00 (£9,581.00: £4,790.00) **5f (straight)** 2-15 (2-14)

Media Nox *(AFabre,France)* 2-8-8 TJarnet .... — 1
Shining Molly (FR) *(PBary,France)* 2-8-8 OPeslier .... nse 2

Kistena (FR) *(MmeCHead,France)* 2-8-8 GDoleuze 1½ 3

P-M 1.70F: 1.30F 1.40F (SF 3.90F) OWNER Mr K. Abdullah (FRANCE) BRED Juddmonte Farms 6 Rn
58.2 secs SF: -/-/-

1708a-CURRAGH (Newbridge, Ireland) (R-H)
Saturday July 1st (Good)

2211a INDEPENDENT PRETTY POLLY STKS (Gp 2) (3-Y.O+ F & M) £30,000.00 (£10,000.00: £5,000.00: £2,000.00: £1,500.00: £1,000.00) **1m 2f**
4-00 (4-02)

1394a6 **Flagbird (USA)** *(119) (SbinSuroor)* 4-9-13 CAsmussen (cl up: 3rd st: led 2f out: edgd lft & r.o wl fnl f) ....— 1
Russian Snows (IRE) *(111) (JOxx,Ireland)* 3-8-8 MJKinane (hld up: 5th st: chal over 1f out: no ex cl home) ....nk 2
Ballykett Nancy (IRE) *(108) (JSBolger,Ireland)* 4-9-5 KJManning (bhd: hdwy ent st: r.o wl up fnl f) 1½ 3
Royal Ballerina (IRE) *(113) (MKauntze,Ireland)* 5-9-10 WJO'Connor (prom tl rdn & one pce over 1f out) ....nk 4
Alisidora (IRE) *(106) (CO'Brien,Ireland)* 3-8-9 ow1 CRoche 1 5
1235a4 Double On (IRE) *(105) (PJFlynn,Ireland)* 4-9-5 JFEgan ....½ 6
1242* Subya *(105)*(Fav)*(JLDunlop)* 3-8-8 JReid ....hd 7
Tea Service (IRE) *(97) (MKauntze,Ireland)* 3-8-8 PVGilson 5 8
1390a3 Khaytada (IRE) *(96) (JOxx,Ireland)* 3-8-9 ow1 JPMurtagh ....¾ 9
1235a5 Dancing Sunset (IRE) *(90) (APO'Brien,Ireland)* 4-9-5 SCraine 3½ 10

5/2 Subya, **5/1** FLAGBIRD (USA), **6/1** Khaytada (IRE), **8/1** Alisidora (IRE), **10/1** Ballykett Nancy (IRE), Royal Ballerina (IRE), Russian Snows (IRE), **11/1** Double On (IRE), Dancing Sunset (IRE), **25/1** Tea Service (IRE), Tote £6.60: £2.80 £2.20 £2.20 (£30.70) OWNER Godolphin (NEWMARKET) BRED W. S. Farish in USA 10 Rn
2m 7.1 (4.80) SF: -/-/-/-/-/-/-/-/-/-

2046a-HAMBURG (Germany) (R-H)
Saturday July 1st (Good to firm)

2212a HOLSTEN-TROPHY (Gp 3) (3-Y.O+) £49,383.00 (£19,753.00: £9,877.00) **6f**
3-40 (3-40)

1891a* **Hever Golf Rose** *(113+) (TJNaughton)* 4-9-4 PaulEddery ....— 1
Desidera (IRE) *(101) (HBlume,Germany)* 3-8-3 AStarke 1½ 2
1891a2 Matula (USA) *(102) (BSchutz,Germany)* 3-8-7 ASuborics 1¼ 3
17662 Daring Destiny *(KRBurke)* 4-8-9 JTate (btn over 6l) 11

Tote 66DM: 26DM 17DM 27DM (SF 153DM) OWNER Mr M. P. Hanson (EPSOM) BRED Ronald Popely 11 Rn
1m 11.9 SF: -/-/-/-

1885a-SAINT-CLOUD (France) (L-H)
Sunday July 2nd (Soft)

2213a GRAND PRIX DE SAINT-CLOUD (Gp 1) (3-Y.O+) £143,713.00 (£57,485.00: £28,742.00: £14,371.00) **1m 4f**
2-00 (2-01)

16095 **Carnegie (IRE)** *(128) (AFabre,France)* 4-9-8 TJarnet (3rd st: rdn over 2f out: r.o u.p to ld cl home) ....— 1
1396a* Luso *(128) (CEBrittain)* 3-8-9 RCochrane (2nd tl led over 2f out: r.o gamely: hdd cl home) ....s.nk 2
16092 Only Royale (IRE) *(122) (LMCumani)* 6-9-5 GMosse (rr early: 4th st: effrt 2f out: r.o one pce) 2 3
16094 Tikkanen (USA) *(122) (JEPease,France)* 4-9-8 CAsmussen (hld up: hrd rdn & hdwy 2f out: one pce fnl f) 2½ 4
1609* Sunshack *(118) (AFabre,France)* 4-9-8 PatEddery (last st: rdn 2f out: no imp) 3 5
1709a2 Solid Illusion (USA) *(107) (PDemercastel,France)* 4-9-8 DBoeuf (hld up; 6th st: rdn & btn 2f out) 8 6
1709a* Tot Ou Tard (IRE) *(104) (SWattel,France)* 5-9-8 ESaint-Martin (5th st: rdn 2f out: sn btn) 2 7

Citizen Darnet (USA) *(99) (JEPease,France)* 4-9-8 WMessina (led tl hdd 2f out: wknd qckly) .4 8

P-M 2.90F: 1.40F 2.70F 1.90F (18.60F) OWNER Sheikh Mohammed (FRANCE) BRED Swettenham Stud 8 Rn
2m 35.2 (5.90) SF: -/-/-/-/-/-/-/-

2214a PRIX AMANDINE (Listed) (3-Y.O F) £16,766.00 (£5,748.00: £3,593.00) 1m 4-05 (4-20)

1116a[11] **Fairy Path (USA)** *(104) (DSmaga,France)* 3-9-2 FHead .....— 1
1639* Nagnagnag (IRE) *(104) (SDow)* 3-9-2 GMosse .....hd 2
Coco Passion (FR) *(96) (JEHammond,France)* 3-9-2 WMongil 4 3

P-M 5.60F: 3.70F 4.60F 3.60F (55.70F) OWNER Lord Weinstock BRED Ballymacoll Stud Farm Ltd. in USA 8 Rn
1m 47.0 SF: -/-/-

2212a-HAMBURG (Germany) (R-H) Sunday July 2nd (Good to firm)

2215a BMW DEUTSCHES DERBY (Gp 1) (3-Y.O C & F) £202,469.00 (£67,490.00: £40,494.00: £20,247.00) 1m 4f 3-30 (3-36)

All My Dreams (IRE) *(114) (HRemmert,Germany)* 3-9-2 KWoodburn (mid-div: hmpd 4f out: prog to ld 1f out: r.o wl) .....— 1
1713a[4] Manzoni (GER) *(111) (AWohler,Germany)* 3-9-2 ABoschert (a.p: 4th st: chal over 1f out: nt qckn fnl f) 2½ 2
Masterplayer (GER) *(110) (HRemmert,Germany)* 3-9-2 MRimmer (rr tl st: hdwy 2f out: fn wl) .....nk 3
Sir King (GER) *(110) (RSuerland,Germany)* 3-9-2 GBocskai (rr tl hdwy st: nrst fin) .....nk 4
Artan (IRE) *(110) (MRolke,Germany)* 3-9-2 RMorse .....nk 5
Oxalagu (GER) *(102) (BSchutz,Germany)* 3-9-2 ASuborics 6 6
Speedster *(99) (BSchutz,Germany)* 3-9-2 ASchikora 1¾ 7
1713a* Lecroix (GER) *(99) (MHofer,Germany)* 3-9-2 ManfredHofer .....nk 8
1713a[6] A Magicman (FR) *(95) (HSteguweit,Germany)* 3-9-2 NGrant 2½ 9
1713a[9] Vilander (GER) *(87) (HJentzsch,Germany)* 3-9-2 SEccles 6 10
Kulshee Mashee (USA) *(87) (BSchutz,Germany)* 3-9-2 AStarke .....nk 11
1705a* Centaine *(72) (HRemmert,Germany)* 3-8-12 MRoberts 8 12
Mr.Woodman (USA) *(75) (BSchutz,Germany)* 3-9-2 THellier 1 13
Dannec (IRE) *(72) (BSchutz,Germany)* 3-9-2 LHammer-Hansen 2½ 14
Rivero (GER) *(58) (PRau,Germany)* 3-9-2 TMundry 10 15
Kalimnos (GER) *(56) (HBlume,Germany)* 3-9-2 OSchick 2 16
2042a* Alpha City (GER) *(41) (HJentzsch,Germany)* 3-8-12 ATylicki 8 17
1713a[3] Chadayed (USA) *(HJentzsch,Germany)* 3-9-2 PSchiergen (cl up whn hmpd & nearly fell 4f out: p.u) ..... P

Tote 35DM: 19DM 44DM 45DM (SF 735DM) OWNER Stall Rheinwiese BRED J.C.Condon 18 Rn
2m 32.85 SF: -/-/-/-/-/-/-/-/-/-/-/-/-/-/-/-/-/-

2211a-CURRAGH (Newbridge, Ireland) (R-H) Sunday July 2nd (Good to firm)

2216a P. V. DOYLE MEMORIAL RAILWAY STKS (Gp 3) (2-Y.O) £15,000.00 (£5,000.00: £2,500.00) 6f 2-10 (2-10)

Flame of Athens (IRE) *(98) (MJGrassick,Ireland)* 2-8-10 JReid .....— 1
1849[7] Sweet Robin (IRE) *(95) (MJohnston)* 2-8-7 LDettori .....s.h 2
Ribot's Secret (IRE) *(92)*(Fav)*(APO'Brien,Ireland)* 2-8-7 CRoche 1 3
1868[5] Amaretto Bay (IRE) *(88) (BJMeehan)* 2-8-10 BDoyle (btn approx 3¼l) 5

5/2 Ribot's Secret (IRE), **9/2** Sweet Robin (IRE), **5/1** Amaretto Bay (IRE), **8/1** FLAME OF ATHENS (IRE), Tote £7.60: £2.40 £2.40 (£29.60) OWNER Miss P. F. O'Kelly BRED Kilcarn Stud 7 Rn
1m 12.8 (2.20) SF: -/-/-/-

2217a SEA WORLD INTERNATIONAL (Gp 2) (3-Y.O+) £30,000.00 (£10,000.00: £5,000.00: £2,000.00: £1,500.00: £1,000.00) 1m 2-45 (2-50)

1851[2] **Darnay** *(119)*(Fav)*(SbinSuroor)* 4-9-4 LDettori (hld up gng wl: chal to ld 1½f out: readily) .....— 1

1835[6] Dance Turn *(117) (RWArmstrong)* 4-9-4 JReid (disp ld tl hdd by wnr: r.o wl) 1 2
564[3] Off'n'away (IRE) *(116) (DKWeld,Ireland)* 3-8-9 MJKinane (rr early: prog to chal 1½f out: r.o) ....½ 3
1711a[2] Fraam *(114) (EALDunlop)* 6-9-4 WRSwinburn (hld up: prog to chal 2f out: one pce fnl f) 1 4
794[2] Ridgewood Ben *(110) (JOxx,Ireland)* 4-9-4 CRoche (nt rch ldrs) 2 5
Ivory Frontier (IRE) *(109) (JSBolger,Ireland)* 5-9-4 KJManning (ld tl hdd by wnr: wknd qckly) ½ 6
1708a* Shemaran (IRE) *(97) (JOxx,Ireland)* 3-9-1 JPMurtagh (4th ½-way: rdn & btn 2f out: eased fnl f) 9 7

2/1 DARNAY, **5/2** Shemaran (IRE), **9/2** Fraam, **13/2** Ridgewood Ben, **10/1** Off'n'away (IRE), Dance Turn, **16/1** Ivory Frontier (IRE), Tote £2.60: £2.10 £7.80 (£26.10) OWNER Godolphin (NEWMARKET) BRED Sheikh Mohammed bin Rashid al Maktoum 7 Rn 1m 36.4 (0.40) SF: -/-/-/-/-/-/-

2218a BUDWEISER IRISH DERBY (Gp 1) (3-Y.O C & F) £338,350.00 (£120,000.00: £60,000.00: £24,000.00: £18,000.00: £12,000.00) **1m 4f** 4-00 (4-04)

1574a[3] **Winged Love (IRE)** *(123) (AFabre,France)* 3-9-0 OPeslier (3rd st: led 2f out: hdd 1f out: rallied to ld cl hme) ....— 1
Definite Article *(123) (DKWeld,Ireland)* 3-9-0 MJKinane (hld up: 7th st: swtchd to chal 2f out: led 1f out: r.o gamely: ct cl home) ....s.h 2
1837[5] Annus Mirabilis (FR) *(122) (MRStoute)* 3-9-0 WRSwinburn (hld up: hdwy & hmpd st: chal 2f out: r.o gamely) ....¾ 3
1234a[6] Oscar Schindler (IRE) *(121) (KPrendergast,Ireland)* 3-9-0 CRoche (hld up in rr: 8th st: r.o wl fnl 2f: nrst fin) ....¾ 4
1897[2] Classic Cliche (IRE) *(118) (SbinSuroor)* 3-9-0 LDettori (in tch: 5th st: r.o fnl f: nt rch ldrs) 2 5
Damancher *(118) (PMullins,Ireland)* 3-9-0 RHughes (9th st: r.o fnl 1½f: fin wl) ....½ 6
1234a[9] I'm Supposin (IRE) *(114) (KPrendergast,Ireland)* 3-9-0 WJSupple (10th st: r.o fnl 2f) 3 7
1574a* Celtic Swing *(113)*(Fav)*(LadyHerries)* 3-9-0 KDarley (hld up in tch: 4th st: sn rdn & btn) ....nk 8
1611[5] Court of Honour (IRE) *(112) (PWChapple-Hyam)* 3-9-0 JReid (a cl up: 2nd st: sn rdn & wknd) 1 9
1852[2] Double Eclipse (IRE) *(111) (MJohnston)* 3-9-0 JWeaver (a.p: led 4f out tl hdd by wnr: sn wknd) ....½ 10
1611[8] Humbel (USA) *(97) (DKWeld,Ireland)* 3-9-0 PShanahan (mid-div & rdn 5f out: no imp) 11 11
1611[9] Munwar *(93) (PTWalwyn)* 3-9-0 WCarson (led 7f out tl 4f out: sn btn: t.o) 2½ 12
Daraydan (IRE) *(JOxx,Ireland)* 3-9-0 PVGilson (led 5f: sn rdn & btn: t.o) 13

5/4 Celtic Swing, **5/1** Definite Article, WINGED LOVE (IRE), **8/1** Classic Cliche (IRE), **9/1** Annus Mirabilis (FR), Munwar, **16/1** Court of Honour (IRE), **25/1** Humbel (USA), **33/1** Double Eclipse (IRE), Oscar Schindler (IRE), **200/1** Daraydan (IRE), Damancher, **400/1** I'm Supposin (IRE), Tote £6.00: £2.30 £1.50 £4.00 (£13.70) OWNER Sheikh Mohammed (FRANCE) BRED Eric Puerari 13 Rn
2m 30.1 (1.40) SF: -/-/-/-/-/-/-/-/-/-/-/-/-

2219a ANHEUSER BUSCH CURRAGH CUP (Gp 3) (3-Y.O+) £18,000.00 (£6,000.00: £3,000.00: £1,200.00: £900.00: £600.00) **1m 6f** 4-45 (4-47)

1869[4] **Vintage Crop** *(124)*(Fav)*(DKWeld,Ireland)* 8-10-4 MJKinane ....— 1
1780* Capias (USA) *(113) (JHMGosden)* 4-9-8 LDettori ....½ 2
Mohaajir (USA) *(112) (JSBolger,Ireland)* 4-9-8 KJManning 1 3
1113a[3] Johansson (USA) *(112) (JOxx,Ireland)* 3-8-7 CRoche ....hd 4
1780[4] Khamaseen *(115) (JLDunlop)* 4-9-11 WCarson ....nk 5
1171* Escarpment (USA) *(102) (PWChapple-Hyam)* 4-9-8 JReid 9 6

7/4 VINTAGE CROP, **5/2** Capias (USA), **5/1** Escarpment (USA), **7/1** Mohaajir (USA), **8/1** Khamaseen, Tote £2.80: £1.90 £2.10 (£3.10) OWNER Dr Michael Smurfit BRED Bertram & Mrs R. Firestone 7 Rn 3m 0.2 (4.80) SF: -/-/-/-/-/-
NR

1677-BEVERLEY (R-H)
Friday July 7th (Good to firm)
WEATHER: fine WIND: mod half against

2220 FERGUSON FAWSITT ARMS (S) H'CAP (0-60) (3-Y.O+) (Class F) £3,113.00 (£868.00: £419.00) **7f 100y** Stalls: High GOING minus 0.55 sec per fur (F) 6-45 (6-45)

1828[15] **Dante's Rubicon (IRE) (42)***(47) (JDBethell)* 4-9-1 TIves(9) (led over 5f out: clr over 2f out: hung rt: drvn out) ....— 1

1153[4] Freckles Kelly **(37)***(40) (MHEasterby)* 3-8-2 SMaloney(11) (chsd ldrs: rdn to chal 1f out: kpt on same pce)....1 **2**
1902[3] High Typha **(47)***(42)*(Fav)*(MRChannon)* 4-9-6v AClark(5) (in tch: effrt 3f out: kpt on fnl f: nvr nr to chal)....3½ **3**
2084[8] Monkey Face **(40)***(35) (JHetherton)* 4-8-13 MWigham(10) (led tl over 5f out: rdn 3f out: one pce)....s.h **4**
1647[9] Bex Boy (IRE) **(30)***(25) (MWEasterby)* 4-7-10 (7) RuthCoulter(6) (s.i.s: bhd tl hdwy on ins 2f out: styd on towards fin)....s.h **5**
1809[13] Ashdren **(55)***(47) (AHarrison)* 8-9-11 (3) JStack(3) (mid div: effrt u.p over 2f out: hung rt & no imp)....1¼ **6**
1962[5] Irchester Lass **(41)***(31) (SRBowring)* 3-8-1 (5) CTeague(4) (hld up & bhd: effrt on outside 3f out: nvr nr ldrs)....1 **7**
1548[3] Alpine Skier (IRE) **(37)***(25) (MrsMReveley)* 4-8-10 JFortune(2) (lw: hld up: effrt 3f out: sn rdn & no imp)....1¼ **8**
1509[12] Smart Teacher (USA) **(45)***(29) (KRBurke)* 5-9-4v GHind(8) (lw: trckd ldrs: ev ch tl wknd over 2f out)....1½ **9**
1847[11] Petova (IRE) **(40)***(24) (MJCamacho)* 3-8-5 LCharnock(7) (chsd ldrs tl wknd over 2f out)....nk **10**
1963[19] Supreme Desire **(26)***(7) (GROldroyd)* 7-7-13 NKennedy(12) (plld hrd: hmpd & lost pl after 1f: n.d after)....1½ **11**
Golden Fish **(50)***(20) (JLEyre)* 3-8-10 (5) NVarley(1) (bhd: effrt on outside 3f out: sn wknd)....5 **12**

5/2 High Typha, **5/1** Alpine Skier (IRE), Smart Teacher (USA), **6/1** Ashdren, **7/1** Freckles Kelly, **8/1** Irchester Lass, **12/1** DANTE'S RUBICON (IRE), **14/1** Petova (IRE), **16/1** Golden Fish, **20/1** Monkey Face, Supreme Desire, Bex Boy (IRE), CSF £95.52 CT £257.39 TOTE £11.30: £3.00 £2.20 £1.40 (£33.60) Trio £19.00 OWNER The Dante Partnership (MIDDLEHAM) BRED Thomas Corbett 12 Rn
1m 34.0 (2.00) SF: 34/19/29/22/12/34/10/12/16/3/-/-
WEIGHT FOR AGE 3yo-8lb
No bid.

2221 SANDSFIELD GRAVEL MAIDEN STKS (2-Y.O) (Class D) £4,435.00 (£1,330.00: £640.00: £295.00)
5f Stalls: Centre GOING minus 0.55 sec per fur (F) 7-15 (7-15)

1893[7] **April The Eighth** *(81+)*(Fav)*(BWHills)* 2-8-9 (5) JDSmith(8) (b.off hind: trckd ldrs: shkn up to ld over 1f out: edgd lft & drvn out)....— **1**
1460[2] Mask Flower (USA) *(68) (MJohnston)* 2-8-9 DHolland(4) (lw: led tl over 1f out: unable qckn)....2½ **2**
Arrhythmic (IRE) *(68) (MBrittain)* 2-8-9 JQuinn(6) (lengthy: unf: scope: sn trckng ldrs: n.m.r ½-wy: rdn & ev ch 1f out: nt qckn)....s.h **3**
1919[5] Alfayza *(52) (JDBethell)* 2-8-9 JFortune(1) (chsd ldrs: rdn ½-wy: edgd rt & grad wknd)....5 **4**
1678[5] Harriet's Beau *(55) (MWEasterby)* 2-9-0 LCharnock(7) (hld up & bhd: effrt ½-wy: edgd rt & kpt on: nvr nr to chal)....½ **5**
Magic Lake *(47) (WJHaggas)* 2-8-9 TIves(3) (small: lengthy: bkwd: s.i.s: sme hdwy ½-wy: nvr nr ldrs)....1 **6**
1877[8] Superfrills *(25) (MissLCSiddall)* 2-8-9 DeanMcKeown(5) (plld hrd: sn trckng ldrs: effrt & hung lft 2f out: sn wknd)....7 **7**
Gresham Flyer *(1) (BRichmond)* 2-9-0 MFenton(2) (cmpt: bit bkwd: swvd bdly lft s: a wl bhd)....9 **8**
General Equation *(JBalding)* 2-8-7 (7) JEdmunds(9) (lengthy: unf: bkwd: a outpcd: hung bdly lft over 1f out)....nk **9**

8/11 APRIL THE EIGHTH, **7/2** Mask Flower (USA), **13/2** Arrhythmic (IRE), **8/1** Magic Lake (op 5/1), **16/1** Harriet's Beau, **25/1** Alfayza, Superfrills, Gresham Flyer, **33/1** General Equation, CSF £4.27 TOTE £1.90: £1.20 £1.50 £1.80 (£2.30) Trio £7.90 OWNER Mr Michael Siu (LAMBOURN) BRED Miss E. Aldous 9 Rn
64.5 secs (3.00) SF: 7/-/-/-/-/-/-/-/-

2222 WILLIAM JACKSON'S RATED STKS H'CAP (0-85) (4-Y.O+) (Class D) £7,025.00 (£2,120.00: £1,030.00: £485.00)
1m 100y Stalls: High GOING minus 0.55 sec per fur (F) 7-45 (7-45)

2061[3] **Murphy's Gold (IRE) (52)***(61) (RAFahey)* 4-7-11 JQuinn(2) (hld up: hdwy ½-wy: swtchd ins 2f out: styd on wl to ld ins fnl f)....— **1**
1969[3] Queens Consul (IRE) **(79)***(86) (BSRothwell)* 5-9-7 (3) JStack(9) (led: edgd lft over 1f out: hdd wl ins fnl f)....1 **2**
1946[3] Coureur **(67)***(74)*(Fav)*(JDBethell)* 6-8-12 TIves(8) (plld hrd: trckd ldrs: hmpd & lost pl 5f out: styd on u.p fnl 2f)....nk **3**
2061[5] Equerry **(68)***(74) (MJohnston)* 4-8-13 DHolland(5) (chsd ldr: ev ch 1f out: wknd towards fin)....nk **4**

1855² Just Harry **(70)**_(67) (MJRyan)_ 4-8-8 (7) DGibbs(3) (hld up & bhd: sme hdwy over 2f out: nvr nr to chal) 5 **5**
2056⁴ Kingchip Boy **(75)**_(67) (MJRyan)_ 6-9-6v AClark(7) (in tch: outpcd over 3f out: n.d after) 2½ **6**
2052² Montone (IRE) **(57)**_(48) (KRBurke)_ 5-8-2 MFenton(1) (in tch: outpcd over 3f out: sn lost pl) ....½ **7**
1617⁷ Celestial Choir **(75)**_(60) (JLEyre)_ 5-9-6 JFortune(4) (s.i.s: a in rr) 3 **8**
1843* Superoo **(68)**_(52) (MrsPSly)_ 9-8-13 MBirch(6) (chsd ldrs tl wknd 2f out) ....¾ **9**
Gymcrak Tiger (IRE) **(76)**_(60) (GHolmes)_ 5-9-7 GHind(10) (sn wl bhd: t.o ½-wy: kpt on fnl f) ....hd **10**

3/1 Coureur (op 9/2), **6/1** Queens Consul (IRE), Celestial Choir, **7/1** Kingchip Boy, Montone (IRE), Just Harry, **15/2** MURPHY'S GOLD (IRE), Equerry, **12/1** Superoo, **33/1** Gymcrak Tiger (IRE), CSF £50.92 CT £153.61 TOTE £7.80: £1.70 £2.20 £1.70 (£27.00) Trio £21.50 OWNER Mr D. A. Read (MALTON) BRED Anthony Byrne 10 Rn 1m 45.2 (1.20) SF: 26/51/39/39/32/32/13/25/17/25

2223

WELLBEING CONDITIONS STKS (2-Y.O) (Class C) £4,412.50 (£1,600.00: £775.00: £325.00: £137.50)
5f Stalls: Centre GOING minus 0.55 sec per fur (F) 8-15 (8-15)

1903* **Myttons Mistake** _(85) (ABailey)_ 2-8-12 MWigham(1) (hld up: outpcd ½-wy: hdwy over 1f out: r.o wl to ld jst ins fnl f: hld on wl) ....— **1**
1307* Desert Tiger _(79)_(Fav)_(MJohnston)_ 2-8-7 DHolland(4) (sn trckng ldrs: led on bit 2f out: shkn up & styd on ins fnl f: nt qckn towards fin) ....nk **2**
1857* Incapol **(69)**_(66) (MJRyan)_ 2-8-10 AClark(5) (mde most to 2f out: outpcd appr fnl f) 5 **3**
1919* Krystal Max (IRE) _(68) (TDBarron)_ 2-8-12 JFortune(2) (trckd ldrs: effrt u.p over 1f out: edgd rt & kpt on same pce) ....s.h **4**
1893⁸ Safio **(97)**_(62) (CSmith)_ 2-8-11 (3) JStack(3) (disp ld over 1f: edgd lft & wknd 2f out) 2½ **5**

6/4 Desert Tiger, **9/4** Safio, **4/1** Krystal Max (IRE), **11/2** MYTTONS MISTAKE, **10/1** Incapol, CSF £14.05 TOTE £7.00: £2.40 £1.10 (£5.40) OWNER Mr Gordon Mytton (TARPORLEY) BRED R. S. A. Urquhart 5 Rn 64.2 secs (2.70) SF: 10/4/-/-/-

2224

BOLLINGER CHAMPAGNE CHALLENGE SERIES AMATEUR H'CAP (0-70) (3-Y.O+) (Class E) £3,418.00 (£1,024.00: £492.00: £226.00)
1m 3f 216y Stalls: High GOING minus 0.55 sec per fur (F) 8-45 (8-45)

1295⁸ **Abalene (32)**_(49) (TWDonnelly)_ 6-9-12 MrRJohnson(7) (chsd ldrs: rdn along to ld over 3f out: styd on) ....— **1**
2089⁴ Jean de Florette (USA) **(33)**_(43) (JohnBerry)_ 4-9-9 (4) MrVLukaniuk(2) (bhd: effrt on outside & wnt lft over 2f out: kpt on fnl f) 5 **2**
2022⁵ Microlite (USA) **(60)**_(69) (MDHammond)_ 4-11-12b MrCBonner(4) (led 9f out tl over 3f out: kpt on one pce) 1¼ **3**
1998³ Lightning Quest (IRE) **(35)**_(34) (JSWainwright)_ 4-9-11b(4)ow8 MrKGreen(8) (prom early: lost pl 7f out: sn wl bhd: edgd lft & styd on fnl 2f) 1 **4**
2022³ Ashover **(54)**_(61)_(Fav)_(TDBarron)_ 5-11-6 MrPPritchard-Gordon(3) (chsd ldr: drvn along & outpcd 4f out: edgd lft u.p 2f out: sn wknd) ....nk **5**
2165³ Kimberley Boy **(47)**_(49) (MBrittain)_ 5-10-9 (4) MrRWakley(5) (hld up: stdy hdwy 5f out: effrt & edgd lft over 1f out: sn wknd) 3½ **6**
864¹⁰ Parish Walk (IRE) **(40)**_(16) (KWHogg)_ 4-10-2 (4) MrKDrewry(6) (led to 9f out: lost pl 6f out: sn wl bhd) 20 **7**
1439⁴ Our Main Man **(62)**_(37) (RMWhitaker)_ 5-12-0 MrSWhitaker(1) (hld up & bhd: lost tch ½-wy) ...¾ **8**

11/10 Ashover, **9/2** Microlite (USA), **11/2** ABALENE, **13/2** Kimberley Boy, **10/1** Jean de Florette (USA), **14/1** Lightning Quest (IRE), Our Main Man, **25/1** Parish Walk (IRE), CSF £52.89 CT £246.00 TOTE £7.90: £2.30 £2.40 £1.70 (£56.30) OWNER Mr S. Taberner (SWADLINCOTE) BRED Mr S. Taberner 8 Rn 2m 40.6 (9.10) SF: 9/3/29/-/21/9/-/-

2225

SANCTON H'CAP (0-70) (3-Y.O) (Class E) £3,834.00 (£1,152.00: £556.00: £258.00)
1m 1f 207y Stalls: High GOING minus 0.55 sec per fur (F) 9-15 (9-15)

1945⁴ **Westcourt Princess (41)**_(50) (MWEasterby)_ 3-8-2 GBardwell(9) (mde all: styd on wl appr fnl f: unchal) ....— **1**
1945⁷ Bold Top **(39)**_(45) (BSRothwell)_ 3-8-0b JQuinn(1) (a chsng wnr: kpt on same pce appr fnl f) 2 **2**
_1952²_ Miss Zanzibar **(60)**_(63) (RAFahey)_ 3-9-2 (5) JDSmith(8) (hld up & bhd: hdwy over 4f out: effrt 2f out: kpt on same pce) 1¾ **3**

1845[4] Skedaddle **(57)***(60)*(Fav)*(JGFitzGerald)* 3-9-4 DHolland(5) (chsd ldrs: drvn along 6f out: one pce fnl 3f) .... s.h **4**
1945[5] Beau Matelot **(56)***(57)*(Fav)*(JDBethell)* 3-9-3 TIves(2) (in tch: effrt 3f out: one pce) 1¼ **5**
1904[5] Indian Rhapsody **(49)***(34)* *(MRChannon)* 3-8-10 AClark(4) (hld up: hdwy 5f out: effrt over 2f out: sn wknd) 10 **6**
759[18] Foist **(38)***(20)* *(MWEasterby)* 3-7-13 LCharnock(3) (dwlt: a in rr) 1½ **7**
Persistent (IRE) **(57)***(33)* *(MHEasterby)* 3-9-4 MBirch(6) (hld up & bhd: hdwy 4f out: effrt over 2f out: sn wknd) 4 **8**
1761[9] Gifted **(38)***(6)* *(DonEnricoIncisa)* 3-7-13 KimTinkler(7) (hld up: plld hrd & bhd: lost tch 3f out) 5 **9**

7/2 Skedaddle, Beau Matelot, **4/1** Indian Rhapsody, **6/1** Miss Zanzibar, **13/2** Persistent (IRE), **7/1** Bold Top, **8/1** WESTCOURT PRINCESS, **20/1** Foist, **33/1** Gifted, CSF £59.87 CT £333.23 TOTE £9.30: £2.40 £2.60 £2.00 (£43.80) Trio £82.20 OWNER Mr K. Hodgson (SHERIFF HUTTON) BRED Britton House Stud 9 Rn 2m 6.7 (4.20) SF: 10/5/23/20/17/-/-/-/-

T/Plpt: £98.70 (149.67 Tckts). T/Qdpt: Not won; £120.60 to Sandown 8/7/95. WG

1720-**HAMILTON (R-H)**
Friday July 7th (Firm)

WEATHER: sunny WIND: almost nil

2226

LETHEBY & CHRISTOPHER PREMIUM CUVEE LADY RIDERS AMATEUR H'CAP (0-75) (3-Y.O+) (Class F) £2,749.00 (£832.00: £406.00: £193.00)
1m 3f 16y Stalls: High GOING minus 0.55 sec per fur (F) 6-30 (6-36)

1863[8] **Gold Blade (42)***(55)* *(JPearce)* 6-9-9 MrsLPearce(6) (lw: hld up: hdwy 6f out: led 3f out: rdn & r.o wl) .... — **1**
1744[4] Mentalasanythin **(67)***(73)*(Fav)*(ABailey)* 6-10-13 (7) MissHGDudgeon(7) (lw: trckd ldrs: ev ch over 3f out: r.o one pce) 5 **2**
1933[2] Askern **(68)***(71)* *(DHaydnJones)* 4-11-7 MrsJCrossley(1) (unruly gng to s: reluctant to r early: sn wl bhd: hdwy 4f out: r.o) 2 **3**
2159[4] Imperial Bid (FR) **(54)***(54)* *(DenysSmith)* 7-10-3 (4) MissMCarson(2) (hdwy 5f out: one pce fnl 2½f) 1¾ **4**
1863[5] Ice Magic **(37)***(31)* *(FJYardley)* 8-8-11v(7)ow4 MissSYardley(4) (chsd ldrs: one pce fnl 4f) 2 **5**
2159[3] Lord Advocate **(47)***(32)* *(DANolan)* 7-9-7b(7)ow9 MissFBarnes(3) (lw: mde most tl hdd & wknd 3f out) 2½ **6**
2109[5] Royal Circus **(39)***(17)* *(JGMO'Shea)* 6-9-6 MrsSBosley(5) (w ldrs to st: wknd over 3f out) 11 **7**

LONG HANDICAP Ice Magic 8-7

5/2 Mentalasanythin, **3/1** GOLD BLADE, **5/1** Askern (op 5/2), **8/1** Lord Advocate, **10/1** Imperial Bid (FR), Ice Magic, **16/1** Royal Circus, CSF £9.52 TOTE £3.40: £1.60 £2.10 (£3.70) OWNER Mr Jeff Pearce (NEWMARKET) BRED Ballymacoll Stud Co 7 Rn 2m 22.2 (3.20) SF: 40/58/56/39/16/17/2

2227

KAY CASSELLS CLAIMING STKS (3-Y.O+) (Class F) £2,675.00 (£750.00: £365.00) **1m 1f 36y** Stalls: High GOING minus 0.55 sec per fur (F) 7-00 (7-00)

2019* **Second Colours (USA) (60)***(67)*(Fav)*(MrsMReveley)* 5-9-10 KDarley(4) (lw: hld up: shkn up to ld appr fnl f: sn hdd: rallied u.p to ld post) .... — **1**
2132[6] Sir Arthur Hobbs **(60)***(63)* *(JLEyre)* 8-9-6 RLappin(1) (lw: b: hld up: swtchd & qcknd to ld 1f out: r.o) .... s.h **2**
2165[7] Bodantree **(35)***(52)* *(KRBurke)* 4-8-9v(7) MHenry(3) (lw: led tl hdd appr fnl f: sn outpcd) 4 **3**
1817[11] King of Show (IRE) **(54)***(38)* *(RAllan)* 4-8-9b(7) PFessey(2) (b: s.s: sn rcvrd & chsd ldr: rdn & btn 1½f out) 8 **4**

8/13 SECOND COLOURS (USA), **2/1** Sir Arthur Hobbs, **7/1** King of Show (IRE) (op 7/4), **40/1** Bodantree, CSF £2.19 TOTE £1.60: (£1.10) OWNER Mr P. D. Savill (SALTBURN) BRED Dinnaken Farm in USA 4 Rn 1m 57.1 (2.80) SF: 40/36/25/11

2228

LINN VOLVO SAFETY LIMITED STKS (0-55) (3-Y.O+) (Class F) £2,815.00 (£790.00: £385.00)
1m 65y Stalls: Low GOING minus 0.55 sec per fur (F) 7-30 (7-30)

1920[2] **Three Arch Bridge (55)***(63)* *(MJohnston)* 3-8-8b TWilliams(3) (chsd ldrs: led over 2f out: rdn & r.o) .... — **1**
1687[7] My Handy Man **(53)***(63)* *(RAllan)* 4-9-6 JFanning(4) (lw: hld up & bhd: hdwy over 2f out: nt qckn ins fnl f) 1½ **2**

2037² Song of Years (IRE) **(55)***(58)*(Fav)*(JWHills)* 4-8-8 (7) MHenry(5) (swtg: led tl hdd over 2f out: kpt on u.p) ....hd 3
1944³ Flyaway Blues **(54)***(63) (MrsMReveley)* 3-8-11v KDarley(2) (lw: in tch: effrt over 3f out: sn outpcd: styd on u.p fnl f) ....s.h 4
2156¹² Passion Sunday **(51)***(24) (LRLloyd-James)* 4-9-6v KFallon(1) (b.nr hind: prom tl wknd fnl 3f) 20 5

6/4 Song of Years (IRE), **9/4** THREE ARCH BRIDGE, **5/2** Flyaway Blues, **10/1** My Handy Man (8/1-12/1), **50/1** Passion Sunday, CSF £18.34 TOTE £3.60: £1.60 £4.10 (£7.50) OWNER Mr R. N. Pennell (MIDDLEHAM) BRED R. Taylor 5 Rn 1m 45.5 (2.20) SF: 28/37/32/28/-
WEIGHT FOR AGE 3yo-9lb

2229 GLENGOYNE SINGLE HIGHLAND MALT SCOTCH WHISKY H'CAP (0-70) (3-Y.O+) (Class E) £3,863.90 (£1,170.20: £571.60: £272.30)
6f 5y Stalls: Low GOING minus 0.55 sec per fur (F) 8-00 (8-01)

2088⁴ **Profit Release (IRE) (55)***(67) (MJohnston)* 4-8-13b TWilliams(3) (lw: disp ld tl led 2f out: r.o wl) ....— 1
1819² Diet **(47)***(51) (MissLAPerratt)* 9-8-5v JCarroll(5) (disp ld 4f: kpt on wl) 3 2
1963² Densben **(47)***(48) (DenysSmith)* 11-8-5 KFallon(1) (lw: s.i.s: hdwy 2f out: r.o towards fin) 1 3
1996⁶ Suedoro **(41)***(42) (RMMcKellar)* 5-7-6 (7) PFessey(6) (chsd ldrs: ev ch over 1f out: one pce) ....s.h 4
2160⁶ Sunday Mail Too (IRE) **(45)***(42) (MissLAPerratt)* 3-7-7b(3)ow3 DarrenMoffatt(7) (lw: cl up: hung bdly rt most of wy: nt qckn fnl f) ....½ 5
2190³ Tael of Silver **(65)***(61) (KRBurke)* 3-8-9 (7) 6x MHenry(8) (lw: bhd: sme hdwy u.p ½-wy: no imp) 1½ 6
1996* Birchwood Sun **(60)***(53) (MDods)* 5-9-4b 6x NConnorton(9) (sn bhd: sme hdwy 2f out: n.d) 1 7
1932⁸ Persian Affair (IRE) **(68)***(61)*(Fav)*(DHaydnJones)* 4-9-12 AMackay(2) (lw: nvr wnt pce) ....nk 8
2021² Phase One (IRE) **(48)***(35) (JLEyre)* 5-8-6 KDarley(10) (b.nr fore: a outpcd & bhd) 2 9
1996⁹ Indian Crystal **(43)***(12) (MrsMReveley)* 4-8-1v JFanning(4) (dwlt: n.d) 7 10
LONG HANDICAP Sunday Mail Too (IRE) 7-4

9/2 Persian Affair (IRE), **5/1** PROFIT RELEASE (IRE), **11/2** Densben (op 7/2), **6/1** Birchwood Sun, **15/2** Phase One (IRE), **8/1** Tael of Silver, Diet, **10/1** Suedoro (8/1-12/1), **25/1** Indian Crystal, **40/1** Sunday Mail Too (IRE), CSF £39.36 CT £203.73 TOTE £4.20: £1.60 £1.90 £2.70 (£12.80) Trio £18.50 OWNER G R Bailey Ltd (Baileys Horse Feeds) (MIDDLEHAM) BRED Moyglare Stud Farm Ltd 10 Rn 1m 10.9 (0.90) SF: 38/22/19/13/6/25/24/32/6/-
WEIGHT FOR AGE 3yo-7lb

2230 E.B.F. SPH PROPERTY SEARCH MEDIAN AUCTION MAIDEN STKS (2-Y.O) (Class E) £3,403.75 (£1,030.00: £502.50: £238.75)
5f 4y Stalls: Low GOING minus 0.55 sec per fur (F) 8-30 (8-34)

No Monkey Nuts *(66+?) (JBerry)* 2-9-0 JCarroll(2) (w'like: wl grwn: mde all: hung rt thrght: r.o u.p fnl f) ....— 1
2091³ Red Acuisle (IRE) *(61)*(Fav)*(MBell)* 2-9-0 KFallon(3) (chsd wnr: effrt over 1f out: r.o: nt pce of wnr) 1½ 2
2158⁴ Vales Ales *(26) (RMMcKellar)* 2-9-0 TWilliams(4) (chsd ldrs: hrd rdn 2f out: wknd fnl f) 11 3
Lord Cornelious *(DANolan)* 2-9-0 KDarley(1) (cmpt: bkwd: dwlt: a outpcd & bhd) 15 4

2/11 Red Acuisle (IRE), **4/1** NO MONKEY NUTS, **20/1** Lord Cornelious, **40/1** Vales Ales, CSF £5.25 TOTE £3.70: (£1.30) OWNER The Monkey Racing Club Ltd (COCKERHAM) BRED Miss C. Tagart 4 Rn 61.6 secs (3.30) SF: -/-/-/-
STEWARDS' ENQUIRY McKellar fined £150 (Horse arrived at start with girth knotted).

2231 HERALD FOUNDATION FOR WOMENS HEALTH (S) STKS (3-Y.O+) (Class G) £2,423.00 (£678.00: £329.00)
5f 4y Stalls: High GOING minus 0.55 sec per fur (F) 9-00 (9-00)

2096⁸ **Flashy's Son (65)***(66)*(Fav)*(GMMoore)* 7-9-4 KDarley(4) (b: b.hind: trckd ldrs: qcknd to ld ins fnl f: comf) ....— 1
1741⁷ Southern Dominion **(65)***(68) (WGMTurner)* 3-8-11 (7) ADaly(2) (lw: led: hrd rdn 2f out: hdd ins fnl f: kpt on) 1¼ 2
1900⁸ Leading Princess (IRE) **(40)***(53) (MissLAPerratt)* 4-8-13b JFanning(1) (trckd ldrs: effrt over 1f out: hrd rdn & no ex) 1¼ 3
2162² Henry the Hawk **(50)***(52) (MDods)* 4-9-4v KFallon(5) (outpcd ½-wy: styd on u.p: no imp) 1¾ 4
1546¹¹ Honey Trader **(58)***(21) (JBerry)* 3-8-12 JCarroll(3) (s.i.s: hdwy ½-wy: sn wknd) 10 5

4/7 FLASHY'S SON, **4/1** Henry the Hawk, **5/1** Southern Dominion (7/2-11/2), **10/1** Honey Trader, **25/1** Leading Princess (IRE), CSF £3.95 TOTE £1.70: £1.10 £1.70 (£3.10) OWNER Mr K. Lee (MIDDLEHAM) BRED Brian A. Shovelton (North Wales) Ltd 5 Rn 59.3 secs (1.00) SF: 38/34/25/24/-
WEIGHT FOR AGE 3yo-6lb
Bt in 3,200 gns; Southern Dominion clmd JSMorrison £6,000

2232 FLOWERSCENE DOZEN RED ROSES MAIDEN H'CAP (0-65) (3-Y.O+) (Class F) £2,762.00 (£836.00: £408.00: £194.00)

1m 5f 9y Stalls: High GOING minus 0.55 sec per fur (F) 9-30 (9-31)

1863⁶ **Claireswan (IRE) (49)***(62)*(Fav)*(SCWilliams)* 3-9-4 KFallon(5) (lw: mde all: qcknd 4f out: clr 2f out: r.o wl) — 1
2087⁸ Amiarge **(30)***(39) (MBrittain)* 5-8-13 NConnorton(1) (a chsng ldrs: kpt on fnl 3f: no ch w wnr) ..3 2
1379¹⁰ Bark'n'bite **(43)***(51) (MrsMReveley)* 3-8-12 KDarley(2) (chsd ldrs tl outpcd 4f out: styd on fnl f) 1 3
2122⁵ Never so True **(40)***(48) (MartynWane)* 4-9-9v JCarroll(6) (lw: a chsng ldrs: rdn over 3f out: one pce) nk 4
2129³ Coast Along (IRE) **(32)***(39) (CWThornton)* 3-8-1 AMackay(4) (hld up & bhd: effrt 4f out: nt pce to chal) ¾ 5
2126⁵ Runrig (IRE) **(42)***(45) (MissLAPerratt)* 5-9-11 JFanning(3) (lw: hld up & bhd: hdwy 5f out: rdn & wknd 2f out) 3½ 6

2/1 CLAIRESWAN (IRE), **5/2** Bark'n'bite, **3/1** Coast Along (IRE), **13/2** Amiarge, **10/1** Runrig (IRE) (7/1-11/1), **25/1** Never so True, CSF £13.72 TOTE £2.50: £1.70 £3.10 (£12.50) OWNER Mr J. Wright (NEWMARKET) BRED Thomas Bean 6 Rn 2m 54.3 (8.60) SF: 9/-/-/9/-/6
WEIGHT FOR AGE 3yo-14lb

T/Plpt: £125.40 (79.3 Tckts). T/Qdpt: Not won; £75.20 to Sandown 8/7/95. AA

2191-HAYDOCK (L-H)
Friday July 7th (Good to firm)
WEATHER: fine & cloudy WIND: mod half against

2233 JOHNNY OSBORNE CLAIMING STKS (3-Y.O+) (Class E) £2,965.00 (£895.00: £435.00: £205.00)

1m 3f 200y Stalls: High GOING minus 0.24 sec per fur (GF) 2-20 (2-20)

1581³ **Durgams First (IRE) (57)***(72) (MrsMReveley)* 3-8-8 (7) GParkin(1) (lw: hld up: 5th st: hdwy on bit to ld 2f out: comf) — 1
1863* Outstayed Welcome **(49)***(63) (MJHaynes)* 3-8-4 (3) SSanders(2) (b.off hind: a.p: slt ld 4f out tl over 2f out: hrd rdn & unable qckn fnl f) ¾ 2
1612¹⁰ Sheriff **(59)***(56)*(Fav)*(JWHills)* 4-9-8b RHills(3) (a.p: 4th st: jnd ldr 4f out: rdn over 2f out: nt r.o) 7 3
2002ᴾ Persian Soldier **(47)***(13) (EJAlston)* 8-9-6 JFortune(4) (sn drvn along: 2nd st: rdn 4f out: wknd qckly: t.o) 30 4
1917³ Little Blackfoot **(34)** *(JLHarris)* 7-9-0v AMackay(5) (led 8f: sn hrd rdn & wknd: t.o) 10 5
*1074*¹³ Lord Frederick *(MissSJWilton)* 3-8-7 DeanMcKeown(6) (bit bkwd: racd wd: t.o fr ½-wy: 6th st) 15 6

2/1 Sheriff, **9/4** Outstayed Welcome, **11/4** DURGAMS FIRST (IRE), **5/1** Persian Soldier, **20/1** Little Blackfoot, **33/1** Lord Frederick, CSF £9.18 TOTE £3.10: £1.80 £1.60 (£3.10) OWNER The Mary Reveley Racing Club (SALTBURN) BRED William McGladdery in Ireland 6 Rn
2m 34.18 (6.18) SF: 39/30/36/-/-/-
WEIGHT FOR AGE 3yo-13lb

2234 ST. HELENS STAR H'CAP (0-70) (3-Y.O+) (Class E) £3,208.75 (£970.00: £472.50: £223.75)

5f Stalls: High GOING minus 0.24 sec per fur (GF) 2-50 (2-51)

2120² **Shadow Jury (64)***(71)*(Fav)*(DWChapman)* 5-9-8b LCharnock(1) (a.p: led bel dist: rdn out) — 1
1809¹⁹ Sir Tasker **(50)***(55) (JLHarris)* 7-8-8v AMackay(4) (bhd & outpcd tl r.o appr fnl f: no ch w wnr) ½ 2
2027³ Featherstone Lane **(54)***(58) (MissLCSiddall)* 4-8-12v DeanMcKeown(7) (a.p: ev ch over 1f out: sn hrd rdn: no ex) nk 3
1827⁴ King Rambo **(64)***(68) (RHollinshead)* 4-9-8 WRyan(3) (lw: hld up: hdwy u.p wl over 1f out: nt pce to chal) nk 4

1763* Sing With the Band **(56)***(58) (BAMcMahon)* 4-9-0 JFortune(8) (lw: led to bel dist: hrd rdn & outpcd fnl f)....½ 5
2092[4] Giggleswick Girl **(63)***(61) (MRChannon)* 4-9-7 JCarroll(5) (dwlt: sn chsng ldrs: eased whn btn fnl f)....1¼ 6
1827[8] Call to the Bar (IRE) **(67)***(49) (MDods)* 6-9-11 DaleGibson(6) (swtg: chsd ldrs: rdn over 2f out: sn btn)....5 7
1809[17] Gondo **(49)***(31) (EJAlston)* 8-8-0 (7) JoanneWebster(2) (s.i.s: a bhd & outpcd)....hd 8

3/1 SHADOW JURY, **7/2** Sing With the Band, **4/1** Featherstone Lane, **11/2** Giggleswick Girl, **7/1** King Rambo, **14/1** Call to the Bar (IRE), **16/1** Sir Tasker, Gondo, CSF £40.11 CT £173.61 TOTE £3.80: £1.40 £3.60 £1.50 (£27.60) OWNER Mrs Jeanne Chapman (YORK) BRED J. S. Bell 8 Rn
62.7 secs (3.70) SF: 24/8/11/21/11/14/2/-

2235

NORTHWICH RATED STKS H'CAP (0-95) (3-Y.O+) (Class B)
£8,248.81 (£2,999.56: £1,459.78: £619.90: £269.95)
7f 30y Stalls: Low GOING minus 0.24 sec per fur (GF) 3-25 (3-25)

1617[3] **Band on the Run (86)***(95) (BAMcMahon)* 8-8-12 JFortune(4) (lw: chsd ldr: 2nd st: rdn to ld appr fnl f: r.o wl)....— 1
1728[4] Croft Valley **(94)***(97)*(Fav)*(RAkehurst)* 8-9-6 DeanMcKeown(5) (led tl hdd appr fnl f: kpt on one pce)....2½ 2
1217[5] Pinkerton's Pal **(95)***(97) (CEBrittain)* 4-9-7 RHills(2) (lw: chsd ldrs: 3rd st: effrt bel dist: nvr able to chal)....¾ 3
1851[24] Gymcrak Premiere **(84)***(79) (GHolmes)* 7-8-10 WRyan(3) (b.hind: sn bhd & outpcd: 5th st: effrt u.p 2f out: no imp)....3 4
662[3] Otterbourne (IRE) **(86)***(78)*(Fav)*(JHMGosden)* 3-8-4 JCarroll(1) (bit bkwd: bhd: 4th st: hdwy 3f out: wknd bel dist)....1¼ 5

11/4 Croft Valley, Otterbourne (IRE), **3/1** BAND ON THE RUN, **6/1** Pinkerton's Pal, Gymcrak Premiere, CSF £10.32 TOTE £3.00: £1.50 £2.00 (£4.40) OWNER Mr D. J. Allen (TAMWORTH) BRED Mrs J. R. Hine and Miss J. Bunting 5 Rn 1m 29.87 (2.57) SF: 48/50/50/32/23
WEIGHT FOR AGE 3yo-8lb

2236

HEUBACH MAIDEN STKS (3-Y.O) (Class D) £4,268.00 (£1,289.00: £627.00: £296.00) **7f 30y** Stalls: Low GOING minus 0.24 sec per fur (GF) 3-55 (3-57)

658[3] **Alarming** *(75+) (JHMGosden)* 3-8-9 JCarroll(4) (prom: 3rd st: led over 2f out: sn clr: easily)....— 1
1778[7] Young Benson **(69)***(77) (BAMcMahon)* 3-9-0 DeanMcKeown(1) (chsd ldrs: 5th st: hdwy 3f out: hrd rdn & no ex fnl f)....1½ 2
1476[12] Crown of Love (USA) *(68) (MRStoute)* 3-8-9 GHind(9) (hdwy 3f out: styd on u.p fnl f)....1¾ 3
Brave Fighter (USA) *(67) (BHanbury)* 3-8-9 TIves(6) (w'like: scope: bit bkwd: hdwy 3f out: rdn & kpt on ins fnl f)....½ 4
Highspeed (IRE) *(58) (SEKettlewell)* 3-9-0 JFortune(5) (leggy: lt-f: s.i.s: hdwy fnl 2f: nrst fin)....6 5
1221[2] Iktamal (USA) *(58)*(Fav)*(EALDunlop)* 3-8-11 (3) JStack(3) (bit bkwd: led tl rdn & hdd over 2f out: sn btn)....nk 6
1796[5] Direct Dial (USA) *(53) (JARToller)* 3-8-11 (3) SSanders(7) (chsd ldrs: 4th st: wknd over 2f out)2 7
Boston Rock (IRE) *(19) (PWHarris)* 3-9-0 WRyan(13) (b.hind: wl grwn: bkwd: s.s: a bhd: t.o)15 8
Akola Angel *(14) (CREgerton)* 3-8-9 DaleGibson(2) (prom: 2nd st: wknd over 2f out: t.o)....nk 9
Respect A Secret *(10) (SEKettlewell)* 3-8-9 NRodgers(12) (unf: scope: bkwd: chsd ldrs: 6th st: outpcd fnl 2f: t.o)....1¾ 10
Fred Said Right (IRE) *(7) (MJHeaton-Ellis)* 3-9-0 DHarrison(8) (w'like: leggy: hdwy ½-wy: wknd wl over 2f out: t.o)....3½ 11
Four Lane Flyer *(1) (EJAlston)* 3-8-9 AMackay(10) (w'like: bkwd: b: s.s: a bhd: t.o)....nk 12
Nukud (USA) *(6) (HThomsonJones)* 3-9-0b RHills(11) (cmpt: bkwd: s.s: a bhd: t.o)....nk 13

11/10 Iktamal (USA) (11/8-Evens), **7/2** ALARMING, **10/1** Direct Dial (USA), Nukud (USA), **12/1** Young Benson, Crown of Love (USA), Brave Fighter (USA) (op 8/1), **14/1** Boston Rock (IRE), **33/1** Highspeed (IRE), Akola Angel, Fred Said Right (IRE), Four Lane Flyer, Respect A Secret, CSF £43.76 TOTE £3.80: £1.40 £3.40 £3.70 (£42.90) Trio £42.90 OWNER Mr K. Abdullah (NEWMARKET) BRED Juddmonte Farms 13 Rn 1m 31.82 (4.52) SF: 23/25/16/15/6/6/1/-/-/-/-/-/-

2237

PENNINE CONDITIONS STKS (3-Y.O+) (Class C) £5,215.75 (£1,897.00: £923.50: £392.50: £171.25) **6f** Stalls: High GOING minus 0.24 sec per fur (GF) 4-25 (4-26)

1480[3] **Cool Jazz (101)***(98)*(Fav)*(CEBrittain)* 4-9-4 WRyan(1) (lw: a.p: led over 2f out: clr whn veered lft fnl f: unchal)....— 1

1698² Bahith (USA) **(96)***(92) (HThomsonJones)* 3-8-13 RHills(5) (lw: led over 3f: kpt on u.p ins fnl f) 3 **2**
Hindaawee (USA) **(90)***(85) (EALDunlop)* 3-8-8 (3) JStack(3) (bit bkwd: b.hind: stdd s: hdwy ½-wy: rdn over 1f out: sn outpcd) 2 **3**
2001² Ziggy's Dancer (USA) **(85)***(89) (EJAlston)* 4-9-12 JFortune(4) (hld up: effrt 2f out: no imp) ...1¼ **4**
828³ Lago Di Varano **(101)***(81) (JBerry)* 3-9-7b JCarroll(2) (lw: spd to ½-wy: sn rdn & wknd) 4 **5**

15/8 COOL JAZZ, **5/2** Bahith (USA), **9/2** Ziggy's Dancer (USA), **11/2** Lago Di Varano, **7/1** Hindaawee (USA), CSF £6.47 TOTE £2.40: £1.60 £1.40 (£2.40) OWNER Mr Saeed Manana (NEWMARKET) BRED Saeed Manana 5 Rn 1m 15.42 (3.72) SF: 31/18/11/22/7
WEIGHT FOR AGE 3yo-7lb

2238

FRANK WOOTTON H'CAP (0-85) (4-Y.O+) (Class D) £3,673.25 (£1,106.00: £535.50: £250.25)
1m 6f Stalls: Low GOING minus 0.24 sec per fur (GF) 4-55 (4-56)

1767⁷ **Blue Blazer (76)***(88) (BHanbury)* 5-9-11 (3) SSanders(3) (hld up & bhd: 6th st: hdwy over 2f out: styd on to ld ent fnl f: r.o) ....— **1**
1621³ Midyan Blue (IRE) **(72)***(83)*(Fav)*(JMPEustace)* 5-9-10 MTebbutt(9) (led: qcknd wl over 1f out: hdd ent fnl f: kpt on wl u.p) 1 **2**
2087⁵ Cuango (IRE) **(72)***(82) (RHollinshead)* 4-9-10 WRyan(6) (lw: hld up & bhd: 8th st: hdwy 3f out: styd on wl fnl f) 1 **3**
1908⁵ Minnesota Viking **(63)***(69) (LadyHerries)* 4-9-1 DHarrison(1) (lw: a.p: 3rd st: rdn wl over 1f out: one pce) 3 **4**
2098¹¹ Star Rage (IRE) **(75)***(79) (MJohnston)* 5-9-13 RHills(2) (chsd ldrs: 4th st: effrt 3f out: sn ev ch: rdn & outpcd fnl f) 1¼ **5**
1558¹¹ Solomon's Dancer (USA) **(67)***(68) (WWHaigh)* 5-9-5 DaleGibson(7) (swtg: hld up: 5th st: rdn & effrt 3f out: nt pce to chal) 2½ **6**
1022¹¹ Chimanimani **(68)***(58) (NTinkler)* 4-9-6 KimTinkler(8) (chsd ldr: 2nd st: wknd over 2f out: t.o) 10 **7**
2087¹⁰ Alilisa (USA) **(53)***(20) (MrsJJordan)* 7-8-5 AMorris(5) (hld up in rr: 7th st: lost tch 3f out: t.o) 20 **8**

11/4 Midyan Blue (IRE), **7/2** Minnesota Viking, **5/1** Cuango (IRE), **11/2** Star Rage (IRE), **6/1** Solomon's Dancer (USA), **7/1** BLUE BLAZER, **14/1** Chimanimani, **33/1** Alilisa (USA), CSF £25.62 CT £96.39 TOTE £10.10: £2.40 £1.50 £1.30 (£7.70) Trio £17.20 OWNER McHalapar Syndicate (NEWMARKET) BRED Oak Bloodstock Ltd 8 Rn 3m 6.74 (8.54) SF: 45/40/39/26/36/25/15/-

T/Plpt: £16.00 (646.82 tckts). T/Qdpt: £5.60 (16.3 Tckts). IM

1790-SANDOWN (R-H)
Friday July 7th (Good, Good to firm patches st)
WEATHER: hot WIND: almost nil

2239

TIN TIN DAILY NEWS TROPHY H'CAP (0-70) (3-Y.O) (Class E) £3,785.50 (£1,144.00: £557.00: £263.50)
5f 6y Stalls: Low GOING minus 0.08 sec per fur (G) 1-55 (1-57)

1936* **Tedburrow (64)***(73) (MrsAMNaughton)* 3-9-4 LDettori(10) (swtg: hld up: led wl over 1f out: r.o wl) ....— **1**
1822* Crowded Avenue **(64)***(67)*(Fav)*(PJMakin)* 3-9-4 JWeaver(2) (swtg: gd hdwy 2f out: ev ch ins fnl f: unable qckn) 1¾ **2**
1828* The Kings Ransom **(66)***(66) (MrsJRRamsden)* 3-9-6v KFallon(5) (nt clr run over 2f out & over 1f out: hdwy fnl f: r.o wl) 1¼ **3**
1660* Brockton Flame **(67)***(66) (JMPEustace)* 3-9-7 RCochrane(6) (swtg: hdwy over 1f out: r.o ins fnl f) ....nk **4**
1700⁶ Time Is Money (IRE) **(54)***(50) (MHTompkins)* 3-8-3 (5) HKYim(13) (hld up: led 2f out tl wl over 1f out: edgd lft ins fnl f: one pce) ....¾ **5**
1660¹² Secret Miss **(53)***(46) (APJarvis)* 3-8-7 BThomson(3) (swtg: a.p: hrd rdn over 1f out: one pce) .1 **6**
1963¹⁴ Prince Rudolf (IRE) **(44)***(35) (MrsNMacauley)* 3-7-5v(7) AmandaSanders(1) (prom over 2f) .....¾ **7**
1982⁴ Sharp Holly (IRE) **(58)***(44) (JABennett)* 3-8-12 TQuinn(9) (rdn over 2f out: hdwy over 1f out: btn whn bmpd ins fnl f) 1½ **8**
867¹³ Sooty (IRE) **(58)***(41) (HThomsonJones)* 3-8-12 NCarlisle(12) (lw: nvr nr to chal) ....¾ **9**
1936⁵ Nordesta (IRE) **(58)***(26) (MRChannon)* 3-8-12 RHughes(11) (a.p: led over 2f out: sn hdd: wknd over 1f out) 5 **10**
1963¹⁸ Jet Classic **(45)***(5) (MissJFCraze)* 3-7-10 (3) DWright(4) (b.hind: swtg: led over 2f: wknd over 1f out) 2½ **11**
1975¹¹ Tomal **(56)***(15) (RIngram)* 3-8-10 AMcGlone(8) (swtg: prom over 3f) ....nk **12**
1094²⁴ Deardaw **(48)** *(MDIUsher)* 3-7-9 (7) CAdamson(7) (b: prom over 2f) 11 **13**

7/2 Crowded Avenue, **5/1** The Kings Ransom, **11/2** TEDBURROW, **7/1** Brockton Flame, **10/1** Secret Miss, Nordesta (IRE), **16/1** Tomal, **20/1** Time Is Money (IRE), **25/1** Sharp Holly (IRE), Prince Rudolf (IRE), Deardaw, **33/1** Sooty (IRE), **66/1** Jet Classic, CSF £21.68 CT £89.22 TOTE £4.20: £1.70 £1.50 £1.70 (£6.60) Trio £8.20 OWNER Mr Philip Davies (RICHMOND) BRED Lady Matthews 13 Rn 62.74 secs (2.94) SF: 46/40/39/39/23/19/8/17/14/-/-/-/-

2240 SING TAO TROPHY H'CAP (0-95) (3-Y.O) (Class C) £8,832.00 (£2,676.00: £1,308.00: £624.00) 7f 16y Stalls: High GOING minus 0.08 sec (G) 2-30 (2-31)

1839[32] **Night Dance (76)***(85) (GLewis)* 3-8-2 (5) AWhelan(7) (gd hdwy 2f out: led ins fnl f: r.o wl) .....— 1
1931* Khamseh **(80)***(88)*(Fav)*(JWWatts)* 3-8-11 MJKinane(2) (swtg: hdwy over 2f out: hrd rdn over 1f out: ev ch ins fnl f: r.o) ....½ 2
1941[3] Captain's Day **(81)***(86) (TGMills)* 3-8-12 JReid(5) (lw: hdwy over 1f out: r.o ins fnlf) 1½ 3
1920* Hawa Al Nasamaat (USA) **(83)***(87) (EALDunlop)* 3-9-0 WRSwinburn(10) (lw: 4th st: led over 2f out tl ins fnl f: unable qckn)....nk 4
1731* Roderick Hudson **(86)***(90) (JARToller)* 3-9-3 WNewnes(13) (lw: plld hrd: hdwy & n.m.r over 1f out: cl 6th whn nt clr run ins fnl f: r.o)....s.h 5
1839[23] Jam N Shadeed (USA) **(80)***(84) (PFICole)* 3-8-11 TQuinn(8) (lw: 7th st: hrd rdn over 1f out: one pce ins fnl f) ....s.h 6
962[6] Stone Ridge (IRE) **(87)***(90) (RHannon)* 3-9-4 RHughes(1) (hdwy over 1f out: r.o ins fnl f) ......nk 7
1923[9] Bring on the Choir **(84)***(81) (RBoss)* 3-9-1 WWoods(3) (hdwy over 1f out: r.o)....2½ 8
1605[3] Out on a Promise (IRE) **(79)***(76) (GWragg)* 3-8-10b PRobinson(14) (lw: 5th st: wknd over 1f out) ....s.h 9
1876* Midwich Cuckoo **(86)***(78)*(Fav)*(PTWalwyn)* 3-9-3 PatEddery(11) (hdwy & nt clr run on ins over 1f out: nt rcvr)....2½ 10
1588[9] Great Inquest **(86)***(70) (JHMGosden)* 3-9-3 LDettori(6) (nt clr run wl over 1f out: nvr nrr) 3½ 11
1895[29] Lynton Lad **(89)***(71) (CPEBrooks)* 3-9-6 BThomson(12) (2nd st: wknd over 1f out) ....¾ 12
1839[11] Sheer Danzig (IRE) **(73)***(53) (RWArmstrong)* 3-8-4 WCarson(9) (lw: bhd fnl 2f) ....¾ 13
1839[31] Smart Guest **(90)***(67) (JAHarris)* 3-9-7 MFenton(16) (lw: 3rd st: wknd over 1f out) 1½ 14
1648[3] Twice as Sharp **(83)***(57) (PWHarris)* 3-9-0 RCochrane(4) (lw: 6th st: wknd over 1f out) 1¼ 15
1296[6] Bedouin Invader **(74)***(41) (MRStoute)* 3-8-5 DHolland(15) (swtg: led over 4f: wknd 2f out).......3 16

7/1 Midwich Cuckoo, Khamseh, **8/1** Sheer Danzig (IRE), Hawa Al Nasamaat (USA), Great Inquest, Out on a Promise (IRE), **9/1** Roderick Hudson, **14/1** Jam N Shadeed (USA) (10/1-16/1), **16/1** Captain's Day, **20/1** Stone Ridge (IRE), NIGHT DANCE, Twice as Sharp, Bedouin Invader, **33/1** Lynton Lad, Bring on the Choir, **40/1** Smart Guest, CSF £137.19 CT £2,087.41 TOTE £87.40: £11.30 £1.60 £3.50 £1.80 (£289.20) Trio £1,499.40 OWNER Mr G. V. Wright (EPSOM) BRED Miss J. A. Challen 16 Rn 1m 29.02 (2.42) SF: 57/60/58/59/62/56/62/53/48/50/42/43/25/39/29/13

OFFICIAL EXPLANATION **Night Dance: the jockey reported that the colt had missed the break and had to ride his race from the rear.**

2241 ROYAL HONG KONG JOCKEY CLUB TROPHY H'CAP (0-110) (3-Y.O+) (Class B) £45,950.00 (£17,150.00: £8,350.00: £3,550.00: £1,550.00: £750.00) 1m 2f 7y Stalls: High GOING minus 0.08 sec per fur (G) 3-05 (3-08)

1589* **Yoush (IRE) (87)***(105)*(Fav)*(MAJarvis)* 3-8-1 BDoyle(11) (swtg: 9th st: hdwy over 2f out: led over 1f out: r.o wl)....— 1
1926* Salt Lake **(98)***(110) (PWChapple-Hyam)* 4-9-9 4x JReid(4) (lw: led over 8f: unable qckn) 4 2
1805[2] Slasher Jack (IRE) **(80)***(88) (SGNorton)* 4-8-0b(5) HKYim(2) (4th st: hrd rdn & hung rt over 1f out: one pce) 2 3
1851* Realities (USA) **(103)***(110) (GHarwood)* 5-10-0 4x MJKinane(6) (lw: 13th st: hdwy over 1f out: one pce) ....¾ 4
1853[13] Hazard a Guess (IRE) **(79)***(84) (MrsJRRamsden)* 5-8-4 ow1 KFallon(9) (17th st: hrd rdn & hdwy over 1f out: btn whn n.m.r ins fnl f)....½ 5
1558[6] Ringmaster (IRE) **(84)***(90) (MHTompkins)* 4-8-9 PRobinson(5) (lw: 15th st: rdn over 2f out: hdwy over 1f out: nvr nrr)....s.h 6
1926[4] Old Hickory (IRE) **(99)***(105) (LMCumani)* 4-9-10b LDettori(10) (lw: 12th st: hdwy over 2f out: nt clr run over 1f out: one pce)....nk 7
1141[12] Lesley's Fashion **(68)***(72) (DJSffrenchDavis)* 4-7-2 (5) MBaird(7) (8th st: rdn 2f out: sn wknd) 1¼ 8
Silver Groom (IRE) **(68)***(72) (RAkehurst)* 5-7-7 JQuinn(16) (6th st: nt clr run over 1f out & ins fnl f: nt rcvr) ....hd 9
1477[3] The French Friar (IRE) **(74)***(78) (GBBalding)* 4-7-13 AMcGlone(14) (lw: 5th st: wknd over 1f out) ....s.h 10
1661[4] Country Star (IRE) **(73)***(77) (HCandy)* 4-7-12 NAdams(13) (14th st: nvr nr to chal) ....hd 11
1800* Pearl Venture **(94)***(93) (SPCWoods)* 3-8-8 4x WWoods(1) (7th st: wknd over 3f out) 3 12
Unforgiving Minute **(81)***(80) (PWHarris)* 6-8-6 PatEddery(15) (lw: 3rd st: wknd over 2f out) ...hd 13
1853[4] Benfleet **(78)***(76) (RWArmstrong)* 4-8-3 WCarson(17) (lw: 10th st: hdwy over 2f out: bdly hmpd over 1f out: nt rcvr)....½ 14

1851[4] Billy Bushwacker **(87)***(84) (MrsMReveley)* 4-8-12 KDarley(12) (lw: 16th st: nt clr run over 2f out: swtchd lft: a bhd) ....½ 15
1753[5] Green Crusader **(92)***(86) (MRStoute)* 4-9-3v WRSwinburn(8) (11th st: bhd fnl 2f) 2 16
1610[2] Aljazzaf **(97)***(84) (RAkehurst)* 5-9-8 JWeaver(3) (2nd st: wkng whn hmpd over 1f out) 4 17
LONG HANDICAP Silver Groom (IRE) 7-4 Lesley's Fashion 7-3

6/1 YOUSH (IRE), **13/2** Billy Bushwacker, **8/1** Salt Lake, Benfleet, Aljazzaf, **10/1** Country Star (IRE), **11/1** Realities (USA) (8/1-12/1), **12/1** Old Hickory (IRE), **14/1** Silver Groom (IRE), The French Friar (IRE), **16/1** Slasher Jack (IRE), Pearl Venture, **20/1** Green Crusader, Hazard a Guess (IRE), Ringmaster (IRE), **33/1** Unforgiving Minute, **66/1** Lesley's Fashion, CSF £51.78 CT £687.54 TOTE £5.80: £1.60 £2.30 £4.00 £2.80 (£17.50) Trio £115.80 OWNER Sheikh Ahmed Al Maktoum (NEWMARKET) BRED Dictum Enterprises Ltd 17 Rn
2m 6.73 (2.43) SF: 60/76/54/76/50/56/71/38/38/44/43/48/46/42/50/52/50
WEIGHT FOR AGE 3yo-11lb
STEWARDS' ENQUIRY Yim suspended 16-17 July(careless riding)

2242 HSBC CUP CONDITIONS STKS (2-Y.O) (Class C) £6,185.00 (£2,315.00: £1,132.50: £487.50: £218.75: £111.25)
7f 16y Stalls: High GOING minus 0.08 sec per fur (G) 3-35 (3-43)

1287[2] **Honest Guest (IRE)** *(85) (MHTompkins)* 2-8-5 PRobinson(6) (lw: 3rd st: led over 2f out: rdn out) ....— 1
1662* Regiment (IRE) *(87)*(Fav)*(RHannon)* 2-8-10 JReid(7) (lw: 4th st: rdn over 1f out: ev ch ins fnl f: unable qckn) 1¼ 2
Taufan Boy *(80) (PWHarris)* 2-8-10 LDettori(2) (w'like: bit bkwd: s.s: hdwy 2f out: edgd rt over 1f out: one pce) 3 3
1690* Bedside Mail **(68)***(75) (JMPEustace)* 2-8-10 RCochrane(3) (lw: 6th st: rdn over 2f out: edgd rt over 1f out: one pce) 2½ 4
2035* White Whispers **(74)***(63) (BJMeehan)* 2-8-5 BDoyle(8) (plld hrd: 2nd st: led over 3f out tl over 2f out: wkng whn hmpd over 1f out) 3 5
1893[9] Arctic Romancer (IRE) **(88)***(66) (GLewis)* 2-8-10 PatEddery(5) (lw: hdwy 2f out: btn whn n.m.r on ins over 1f out) ....¾ 6
1311[5] Awafeh *(55) (JWPayne)* 2-8-10 BThomson(1) (5th st: wknd over 2f out) 5 7
2075[3] Victoria Venture **(67)***(16) (SPCWoods)* 2-8-5 HKYim(4) (led over 3f: wknd over 2f out) 15 8

9/4 Regiment (IRE), **7/2** HONEST GUEST (IRE) (5/2-4/1), **9/2** White Whispers (3/1-5/1), **7/1** Taufan Boy, Bedside Mail, **8/1** Arctic Romancer (IRE) (11/2-9/1), **33/1** Awafeh, **40/1** Victoria Venture, CSF £11.02 TOTE £4.90: £1.60 £1.20 £1.80 (£4.60) OWNER Mr Ian Lochhead (NEWMARKET) BRED Mount Coote Stud 8 Rn 1m 30.85 (4.25) SF: 35/37/30/25/13/16/5/-
STEWARDS' ENQUIRY Cochrane susp. 22-29/7/95 (careless riding)

2243 SINO GROUP DRAGON TROPHY STKS (Listed) (2-Y.O) (Class A) £11,987.00 (£3,626.00: £1,768.00: £839.00)
5f 6y Stalls: Low GOING minus 0.08 sec per fur (G) 4-05 (4-14)

1443* **Home Shopping** *(93) (KMcAuliffe)* 2-8-10 JTate(5) (hdwy over 1f out: squeezed thro to ld nr fin) ....— 1
1849[11] Anotheranniversary **(90)***(92) (GLewis)* 2-8-10 SWhitworth(4) (b.nr hind: led: rdn over 1f out: hdd nr fin) ....nk 2
1868[3] Mubhij (IRE) *(96)*(Fav)*(BWHills)* 2-9-1 WCarson(3) (lw: hld up: rdn over 1f out: ev ch ins fnl f: unable qckn) ....½ 3
1868[2] Cayman Kai (IRE) **(107)***(95) (RHannon)* 2-9-1 PatEddery(2) (lw: a.p: rdn over 1f out: ev ch ins fnl f: one pce) ....nk 4
2029[4] Norwegian Blue (IRE) *(84) (APJarvis)* 2-8-12 MJKinane(7) (lw: rdn & hdwy over 1f out: one pce) 2½ 5
1893[5] Tadeo **(96)***(85) (MRChannon)* 2-9-1 RHughes(6) (lw: hld up: rdn over 1f out: wknd fnl f) ....½ 6
1849[4] Unconditional Love (IRE) **(99)***(60) (MJohnston)* 2-8-12 DHolland(1) (lw: spd 3f) 7 7

6/4 Mubhij (IRE), **3/1** Cayman Kai (IRE) (2/1-100/30), **4/1** Unconditional Love (IRE), **8/1** HOME SHOPPING, **9/1** Tadeo, **20/1** Anotheranniversary, **25/1** Norwegian Blue (IRE), CSF £107.07 TOTE £11.30: £3.50 £3.90 (£74.60) OWNER Mr Peter Barclay (LAMBOURN) BRED Bridge End Bloodstock 7 Rn 62.55 secs (2.75) SF: 42/41/45/44/33/34/9

2244 SUN HUNG KAI SECURITIES 'GUANGXI' CLAIMING STKS (3-Y.O) (Class E) £3,371.25 (£1,020.00: £497.50: £236.25)
1m 6f Stalls: High GOING minus 0.08 sec per fur (G) 4-35 (4-42)

2026[3] **John Lee Hooker (58)***(73)*(Fav)*(DWPArbuthnot)* 3-9-1 MJKinane(5) (b: b.hind: lw: 5th st: rdn over 3f out: led over 1f out: r.o wl) ....— 1

2065* Old Swinford (IRE) **(57)***(61) (BJMeehan)* 3-8-4 BDoyle(9) (hmpd on ins 3f out: hdwy over 1f out: r.o wl ins fnl f) ....¾ 2
1858⁹ Hong Kong Designer **(46)***(65) (SGNorton)* 3-8-4 (5) HKYim(8) (4th st: hrd rdn 2f out: r.o one pce) 1 3
1490⁹ Northern Law **(70)***(70) (BWHills)* 3-9-3 DHolland(7) (lw: hdwy over 7f out: 3rd st: led over 2f out tl over 1f out: one pce) 2½ 4
1978⁶ Born to Please (IRE) **(50)***(62) (PWHarris)* 3-9-1 WNewnes(3) (lw: nvr nr to chal) 5 5
1986⁵ China Mail (IRE) **(54)***(54) (JMPEustace)* 3-8-11 RCochrane(2) (lw: 2nd st: led over 3f out tl over 2f out: wknd over 1f out) 4 6
2065² Crowned Glory (USA) **(65)***(40) (PFICole)* 3-8-13 TQuinn(1) (lw: 6th st: wknd over 2f out) 14 7
1737² Recovery Lad (IRE) **(54)***(27) (KRBurke)* 3-8-6v(3) JTate(4) (lw: led over 10f) 8 8

13/8 JOHN LEE HOOKER, **11/4** Crowned Glory (USA) (2/1-3/1), **13/2** Recovery Lad (IRE), Old Swinford (IRE) (4/1-7/1), **8/1** China Mail (IRE) (6/1-10/1), **14/1** Northern Law (op 8/1), **20/1** Born to Please (IRE), **33/1** Hong Kong Designer, CSF £12.19 TOTE £3.00: £1.40 £1.90 £3.50 (£11.50) Trio £65.00 OWNER Mr Christopher Wright (COMPTON) BRED Snailwell Stud Co Ltd 8 Rn
3m 4.0 (9.30) SF: 40/28/32/37/29/21/7/-

T/Jkpt: Not won; £13,218.95 to Sandown 8/7/95. T/Plpt: £379.20 (82.38 Tckts). T/Qdpt: £219.70 (1.4 Tckts). AK

1968-WARWICK (L-H)
Friday July 7th (Firm, good to firm final mile)
WEATHER: sunny WIND: mod half bhd

2245 COURTNEY WALSH MAIDEN H'CAP (0-65) (3-Y.O+) (Class F) £3,401.00 (£946.00: £455.00) 1m 2f 169y Stalls: Low GOING minus 0.51 sec (F) 2-10 (2-14)

1971⁹ **Course Fishing (33)***(44) (BAMcMahon)* 4-8-9 FNorton(3) (hld up: stdy hdwy 5f out: 4th st: hung lft over 1f out: led ins fnl f: r.o wl) ....— 1
*1086*⁸ Jubilee Line **(33)***(40) (NEBerry)* 5-8-9 RPerham(6) (chsd ldr: led 4f out: clr over 1f out: hdd ins fnl f) 2½ 2
1529¹³ Swiss Mountain **(28)***(33) (PJBevan)* 5-8-4 GCarter(8) (lw: hdwy 2f out: r.o fnl f: nrst fin) 1¼ 3
2037⁴ Jewel Trader **(48)***(52) (CJBenstead)* 3-8-12 MRimmer(11) (lw: hdwy over 1f out: r.o ins fnl f) 1¼ 4
1791³ Woodrising **(55)***(59) (LadyHerries)* 3-9-5b GDuffield(4) (lw: 7th st: no hdwy fnl 2f) ....s.h 5
1526¹² Fabillion **(64)***(67) (CASmith)* 3-10-0 VSlattery(1) (3rd & rdn st: wknd wl over 1f out) ....nk 6
1776² Marchant Ming (IRE) **(58)***(51)*(Fav)*(MAJarvis)* 3-9-8b MTebbutt(2) (lw: led over 6f: 2nd st: wknd wl over 1f out) 7 7
1940⁷ Fresh Look (IRE) **(59)***(48) (RFJohnsonHoughton)* 3-9-9 StephenDavies(5) (5th & rdn st: wknd 2f out) 2½ 8
2037¹⁰ Indian Temple **(35)***(19) (MSSaunders)* 4-8-11 JWilliams(10) (6th st: wknd 2f out) 3½ 9
1799⁵ Rubadub **(41)***(23) (JMBradley)* 4-9-0 (3) SDrowne(7) (lw: prom tl wknd over 3f out) 1½ 10
1529¹⁵ Ginka **(35)***(3) (PJBevan)* 4-8-11 GBardwell(9) (a bhd: t.o fnl 5f) 9 11

9/4 Marchant Ming (IRE), **5/2** Woodrising, **6/1** Jewel Trader (op 4/1), **8/1** Fresh Look (IRE), Fabillion (op 5/1), **12/1** COURSE FISHING (op 20/1), Indian Temple, **14/1** Rubadub (10/1-16/1), **20/1** Ginka, **25/1** Jubilee Line, **33/1** Swiss Mountain, CSF £235.32 CT £8,386.42 TOTE £14.70: £3.10 £5.70 £10.50 (£175.40) Trio not won; £277.39 to Sandown 8/7/95 OWNER Mr G. D. Bull (TAMWORTH) BRED Hyde Stud 11 Rn
2m 17.8 (4.30) SF: 21/17/10/17/24/32/16/13/-/-/-
WEIGHT FOR AGE 3yo-12lb

2246 JIMMY ADAMS (S) H'CAP (0-60) (3-Y.O+) (Class G) £2,243.00 (£618.00: £293.00) 1m Stalls: Low GOING minus 0.51 sec per fur (F) 2-40 (2-46)

2108⁴ **Mighty Kingdom (IRE) (40)***(48) (JohnBerry)* 4-8-8 (5) NVarley(14) (chsd ldrs: rdn 5f out: r.o wl fnl f: led last strides) ....— 1
1714¹⁰ Pusey Street Boy **(51)***(59) (JRBosley)* 8-9-3 (7) AimeeCook(9) (t: hdwy 2f out: led ins fnl f: hdd last strides) ....s.h 2
2081² Zahran (IRE) **(43)***(50)*(Fav)*(JMBradley)* 4-8-13 (3) SDrowne(6) (b: lw: hdwy over 1f out: r.o wl ins fnl f) ....nk 3
1974⁸ Jobber's Fiddle **(48)***(53) (DJSffrenchDavis)* 3-8-5v(7) JBramhill(3) (4th st: nt clr run on ins over 1f out: r.o one pce fnl f) 1¼ 4
1811⁶ Yo Kiri-B **(48)***(53) (JFfitch-Heyes)* 4-9-7 GDuffield(5) (hld up: hdwy on ins over 3f out: 3rd st: rdn to ld over 1f out: hdd ins fnl f) ....hd 5
*1760*⁸ Swinging Tich **(43)***(47) (ALForbes)* 6-8-11 (5) LNewton(13) (dwlt: hdwy over 1f out: nvr nrr) ....nk 6
1855⁹ Whispering Loch (IRE) **(40)***(44) (JAkehurst)* 4-8-13b GCarter(4) (s.s: hdwy 4f out: nt qckn fnl 2f) ....s.h 7

2052[8] Deceit the Second **(40)***(43) (GLewis)* 3-8-1b(3) DRMcCabe(18) (nvr nr to chal) ....nk **8**
1718[15] Today Tonite **(43)***(44) (JPearce)* 3-8-7 GBardwell(19) (nvr trbld ldrs)....1¼ **9**
1663[10] Safe Secret **(34)***(33) (RBrotherton)* 4-8-2 (5) DGriffiths(2) (5th st: wknd over 1f out)....¾ **10**
2028[8] Aldwick Colonnade **(46)***(44) (MDIUsher)* 8-9-5 RPrice(20) (b: hdwy over 2f out: wknd over 1f out) ....¾ **11**
1783[5] Darakah **(43)***(40) (CJHill)* 8-9-2 RPerham(8) (2nd st: ev ch 2f out: wknd over 1f out) ....½ **12**
1951[11] Nita's Choice **(30)***(26) (AGNewcombe)* 5-7-10 (7) SLanigan(17) (n.d) ....½ **13**
Emma Grimes (IRE) **(40)***(33) (JSMoore)* 4-8-6 (7) DaneO'Neill(7) (bit bkwd: a.p: led 3f out: hdd over 1f out: sn wknd)....1¼ **14**
2054[7] Shanghai Lil **(36)***(29) (MJFetherston-Godley)* 3-8-0 FNorton(10) (a bhd) ....nk **15**
Lucknam Style **(43)***(34) (MrsBarbaraWaring)* 7-9-2 JWilliams(15) (b.hind: a.p: led over 4f out to 3f out: sn wknd)....¾ **16**
672[17] Genesis Four **(36)***(27) (SRBowring)* 5-8-4b(5) CTeague(12) (w ldrs: 6th st: wknd 2f out) ....nk **17**
1956[6] Pash **(38)***(26) (CWFairhurst)* 3-8-2 NKennedy(1) (a bhd) 1½ **18**
1854[7] Keys Seminar **(42)***(13) (JohnBerry)* 3-7-13b(7)ow1 GFaulkner(11) (led over 3f: wknd 3f out) 8 **19**
1078[8] Dance on Sixpence **(47)** *(JHPeacock)* 7-9-1 (5) VHalliday(16) (chsd ldrs 4f: t.o) 11 **20**

5/1 Zahran (IRE), **6/1** Darakah, **7/1** MIGHTY KINGDOM (IRE), **8/1** Pusey Street Boy, **12/1** Keys Seminar, Genesis Four, Whispering Loch (IRE), **14/1** Shanghai Lil, Swinging Tich, Today Tonite, **16/1** Jobber's Fiddle, Yo Kiri-B, Deceit the Second, **25/1** Nita's Choice, Safe Secret, Lucknam Style, Aldwick Colonnade, Pash, Emma Grimes (IRE), Dance on Sixpence, CSF £59.53 CT £278.69 TOTE £7.50: £2.00 £1.70 £1.70 £4.40 (£32.50) Trio £36.70 OWNER Mr John Purcell (NEWMARKET) BRED Rathasker Stud 20 Rn
1m 39.2 (2.20) SF: 33/44/35/29/38/32/29/19/20/18/29/25/11/18/5/19/12/2/-/-
WEIGHT FOR AGE 3yo-9lb
No bid.

2247 EAGLE STAR H'CAP (0-80) (3-Y.O+) (Class D) £4,002.70 (£1,195.60: £571.80: £259.90) **5f** Stalls: Low GOING minus 0.51 sec per fur (F) 3-15 (3-16)

2048* **Bashful Brave (68)***(72) (JWPayne)* 4-9-6 7x MRimmer(8) (a.p: rdn over 1f out: led ins fnl f: r.o) ....— **1**
1942[5] Windrush Boy **(60)***(64) (JRBosley)* 5-8-5 (7) AimeeCook(4) (hld up: outpcd over 2f out: hdwy fnl f: r.o)....hd **2**
2060[4] Allwight Then (IRE) **(72)***(75)*(Fav)*(FHLee)* 4-9-10 GCarter(5) (led tl hdd & jumped bare patch ins fnl f: r.o)....nk **3**
1832[13] Halliard **(58)***(57) (TMJones)* 4-8-10 RPerham(2) (w ldr: rdn & ev ch 2f out: r.o one pce) 1¼ **4**
1924[7] The Happy Fox (IRE) **(72)***(69) (BAMcMahon)* 3-9-4b FNorton(7) (rdn over 2f out: nvr nr to chal)....½ **5**
1057[12] John O'Dreams **(51)***(47) (MrsALMKing)* 10-8-0 (3) AGarth(1) (nvr trbld ldrs) ....nk **6**
1777[6] Jucea **(64)***(54) (JLSpearing)* 6-9-2 GDuffield(3) (s.i.s: a bhd) 2 **7**

2/1 Allwight Then (IRE) (6/4-5/2), **3/1** BASHFUL BRAVE, **4/1** Jucea, **11/2** The Happy Fox (IRE), **10/1** Halliard (8/1-12/1), **12/1** Windrush Boy, **16/1** John O'Dreams, CSF £32.24 CT £79.26 TOTE £4.00: £2.50 £3.80 (£34.40) OWNER Mrs G. M. Hay (NEWMARKET) BRED Mrs G. M. Hay 7 Rn
59.2 secs (1.20) SF: 40/32/43/25/31/15/22
WEIGHT FOR AGE 3yo-6lb

2248 BRIAN LARA H'CAP (0-70) (3-Y.O+) (Class E) £3,318.75 (£990.00: £472.50: £213.75) **1m 6f 194y** Stalls: Low GOING minus 0.51 sec per fur (F) 3-45 (3-45)

2109* **Casual Water (IRE) (57)***(70+) (AGNewcombe)* 4-9-4 (3) 5x DRMcCabe(5) (hld up: hdwy 4f out: 3rd st: rdn to ld over 1f out: sn clr: easily)....— **1**
1840[10] Tarthooth (IRE) **(64)***(73)*(Fav)*(CJBenstead)* 4-10-0 GDuffield(1) (chsd ldr: led 9f out tl over 3f out: led 3f out tl over 1f out: one pce)....3½ **2**
1973[3] Pomorie (IRE) **(63)***(64) (JWPayne)* 4-9-8 (5) AProcter(4) (hld up: rdn 6f out: outpcd & 5th st: r.o one pce fnl f)....8 **3**
1858[11] Surprise Guest (IRE) **(47)***(46) (APJames)* 4-8-11 FNorton(3) (hld up: outpcd & last st: n.d after) 1¾ **4**
1695[6] Euro Forum **(58)***(53) (GLMoore)* 3-8-6 ow1 RPerham(2) (lw: hld up: hdwy 7f out: 4th st: wknd 2f out)....3 **5**
1757[9] Belgran (USA) **(43)***(15) (WMBrisbourne)* 6-8-2 (5)ow2 DGriffiths(6) (b: led 6f: led over 3f out: sn hdd: 2nd st: wknd qckly wl over 1f out: eased fnl f) 20 **6**

11/10 Tarthooth (IRE), **3/1** CASUAL WATER (IRE) (op 2/1), **5/1** Euro Forum, **11/2** Pomorie (IRE) (7/2-6/1), **12/1** Belgran (USA), **16/1** Surprise Guest (IRE), CSF £6.90 TOTE £3.00: £1.60 £1.30 (£2.40) OWNER Mr John Davies (BARNSTAPLE) BRED Dunderry Stud 6 Rn
3m 15.1 (6.10) SF: 33/36/27/9/-/-
WEIGHT FOR AGE 3yo-16lb

2249 CURTLEY AMBROSE CLAIMING STKS (2-Y.O) (Class F) £2,897.00 (£802.00: £383.00) 7f Stalls: Low GOING minus 0.51 sec per fur (F) 4-15 (4-16)

1642[6] **Spanish Luck** *(47) (JWHills)* 2-8-2 GDuffield(3) (sn pushed along: chsd ldr: 2nd st: hrd rdn over 1f out: r.o to ld last stride)......— **1**
1903[5] Bells of Holland *(55)*(Fav)*(BWHills)* 2-8-10 JWilliams(4) (led: sn clr: rdn over 1f out: hdd last stride)......s.h **2**
Saint Rosalina *(42) (CJHill)* 2-8-4ow4 RPrice(1) (leggy: unf: bit bkwd: hld up: 3rd st: hdwy & hung lft over 1f out: r.o one pce)......1½ **3**
Impending Danger *(16) (KSBridgwater)* 2-8-6 (3) SDrowne(2) (w'like: bkwd: s.s: lost tch 3f out: poor 4th st: t.o)......15 **4**

4/6 Bells of Holland, **3/1** SPANISH LUCK, **5/1** Saint Rosalina (op 9/4), **12/1** Impending Danger (op 6/1), CSF £5.27 TOTE £3.80: (£1.80) OWNER Avon Industries Ltd (LAMBOURN) BRED Avon Industries Bath Ltd 4 Rn
1m 29.0 (4.80) SF: -/-/-/-

2250 KEITH SIMMONS RATING RELATED MAIDEN APPRENTICE LIMITED STKS (0-60) (3-Y.O+) (Class F) £2,616.50 (£744.00: £369.50) 1m Stalls: Low GOING minus 0.51 sec per fur (F) 4-45 (4-46)

1914[3] **Colston-C (57)***(66)*(Fav)*(CJHill)* 3-8-12 DToole(4) (mde all: shkn up over 1f out: pushed out)— **1**
2020[4] Opera Fan (IRE) **(60)***(64) (SirMarkPrescott)* 3-8-12 GFaulkner(2) (chsd wnr 4f out: 2nd st: r.o one pce fnl f)......1¼ **2**
1911[5] Nautical Jewel **(50)***(61) (MDIUsher)* 3-8-12 AimeeCook(3) (hld up: last st: hdwy over 1f out: r.o one pce fnl f)......1¼ **3**
1969[9] Diamond Market **(53)***(57t) (RHollinshead)* 3-8-12 AEddery(1) (chsd wnr 4f: 3rd st: r.o one pce fnl f)......hd **4**

11/10 COLSTON-C (Evens-5/4), **9/4** Opera Fan (IRE), **3/1** Nautical Jewel, **16/1** Diamond Market, CSF £3.73 TOTE £2.00: (£1.50) OWNER Mr John Hill (BARNSTAPLE) BRED R. M. Eggo 4 Rn
1m 39.7 (2.70) SF: 27/25/22/22
T/Plpt: £6,986.20 (0.3 Tckts); £6,608.62 to Sandown 8/7/95. T/Qdpt: £15.60 (0.1 Tckts); £19.08 to Sandown 8/7/95. KH

2220-BEVERLEY (R-H)
Saturday July 8th (Good to firm)
WEATHER: fine WIND: fresh half bhd

2251 JUDI MURDEN AND STEVE MASSAM (S) STKS (2-Y.O) (Class F) £2,945.00 (£820.00: £395.00) 7f 100y Stalls: High GOING minus 0.58 sec (F) 2-05 (2-06)

2075[6] **Sovitaka (IRE)** *(54) (MHEasterby)* 2-8-6 MBirch(2) (mde virtually all: styd on wl fnl 2f: drvn out)......— **1**
964[7] Pat's Choice (IRE) *(51) (MHEasterby)* 2-8-6 KFallon(1) (chsd ldrs: sn drvn along: styd on same pce fnl 2f: no ch w wnr)......1½ **2**
1943[9] Kratz (IRE) **(61)***(55)*(Fav)*(BSRothwell)* 2-8-11v MFenton(10) (chsd wnr: effrt 2f out: hung rt: no imp)......nk **3**
Frances Mary *(50+) (CWFairhurst)* 2-8-6 RCochrane(8) (rangy: bhd: effrt on outside over 2f out: kpt on same pce appr fnl f)......nk **4**
1943[3] Chilly Looks **(51)***(45) (MWEasterby)* 2-8-6 LCharnock(4) (swtg: bhd: effrt on ins over 2f out: nvr nr to chal)......2 **5**
Nonconformist (IRE) *(46) (MRChannon)* 2-8-11 RHughes(5) (leggy: hld up: effrt & nt clr run over 2f out: swtchd & no imp)......1¾ **6**
2075[9] Ned's Contessa (IRE) *(39) (MDods)* 2-8-6 DaleGibson(3) (in tch: effrt 3f out: sn outpcd) 1¼ **7**
1190[12] Euro Express *(44) (MHEasterby)* 2-8-11 SMaloney(7) (bhd: sme hdwy over 2f out: n.d) ......s.h **8**
1670[13] The Wad *(31) (MWEasterby)* 2-8-11 AClark(6) (lw: s.i.s: a in rr)......6 **9**
1841[12] Propolis Power (IRE) *(28) (MWEasterby)* 2-8-11 AlexGreaves(11) (prom: effrt u.p 3f out: sn wknd)......1¼ **10**
1841[9] Esther Louise *(MWEasterby)* 2-7-13 (7) RuthCoulter(9) (unruly: chsd ldrs tl wknd qckly ½-wy: sn t.o)......30 **11**

4/1 Kratz (IRE), **9/2** Nonconformist (IRE) (3/1-2/1), **5/1** SOVITAKA (IRE), **6/1** Chilly Looks, **7/1** The Wad, **15/2** Pat's Choice (IRE) (op 12/1), **9/1** Frances Mary, **14/1** Euro Express, **20/1** Ned's Contessa (IRE), Propolis Power (IRE), **25/1** Esther Louise, CSF £44.76 TOTE £7.20: £2.00 £2.30 £1.70 (£24.90) Trio £129.70 OWNER Mr T. H. Bennett (MALTON) BRED Mrs K. Twomey 11 Rn
1m 35.6 (3.60) SF: 7/4/8/3/-/-/-/-/-/-/-
No bid.

2252 JACKSONS BAKERY H'CAP (0-80) (3-Y.O+) (Class D) £4,469.25 (£1,344.00: £649.50: £302.25)
5f Stalls: Centre GOING minus 0.58 sec per fur (F) 2-35 (2-39)

1689[11] **Ned's Bonanza (64)***(71) (MDods)* 6-9-0 AClark(2) (swtchd rt after 1f: bhd tl hdwy on ins ½-wy: styd on wl to ld wl ins fnl f)......— 1
1924[5] Stolen Kiss (IRE) **(69)***(75) (MWEasterby)* 3-8-13b LCharnock(7) (lw: trckd ldrs: led over 1f out: nt qckn cl home)......nk 2
2092[3] Shashi (IRE) **(77)***(79)*(Fav)*(DMorley)* 3-9-7 RCochrane(11) (w ldrs: nt qckn fnl f)......1¼ 3
2120[6] Croft Imperial **(62)***(64) (MJohnston)* 8-8-12 TWilliams(4) (unruly s: chsd ldrs; rdn ½-wy: kpt on same pce appr fnl f)......hd 4
1972[5] Twice in Bundoran (IRE) **(55)***(54) (PSFelgate)* 4-8-2 (3) DRMcCabe(8) (lw: plld hrd: led over 1f out: grad wknd)......1 5
1828[11] King Rat (IRE) **(65)***(62) (TJEtherington)* 4-9-1v MBirch(6) (hdwy ½-wy: kpt on fnl f: nvr nr to chal)......½ 6
1996[5] Tutu Sixtysix **(43)***(38) (DonEnricoIncisa)* 4-7-7v KimTinkler(9) (hdwy ½-wy: effrt & nt clr run over 1f out: nt rcvr)......½ 7
1996[7] Gymcrak Tycoon **(46)***(40) (GHolmes)* 6-7-10 DaleGibson(10) (b: b.hind: prom: wkng whn hmpd over 1f out)......½ 8
2088[9] Miss Vaxette **(60)***(47) (MBrittain)* 6-8-10 SMaloney(5) (s.i.s: a bhd: sn drvn along)......2 9
1756[3] Metal Boys **(67)***(48) (MissLCSiddall)* 8-9-3 RHughes(3) (a bhd)......2 10
1765[7] Magic Pearl **(74)** *(EJAlston)* 5-9-10 KFallon(1) (Withdrawn not under Starter's orders: bolted bef s & unfit to r)...... W

LONG HANDICAP Tutu Sixtysix 7-4

9/4 Shashi (IRE), **3/1** Stolen Kiss (IRE), **5/1** Twice in Bundoran (IRE), **13/2** Croft Imperial, **7/1** NED'S BONANZA, **8/1** Metal Boys, **10/1** Gymcrak Tycoon, **12/1** King Rat (IRE), Miss Vaxette, Tutu Sixtysix, Magic Pearl, CSF £32.24 CT £62.71 TOTE £10.40: £2.40 £2.00 £1.60 (£31.60) Trio £26.00 OWNER Mr Ned Jones (DARLINGTON) BRED D. W. McHarg 10 Rn
61.7 secs (0.20) SF: 48/46/50/41/31/39/15/17/24/25/-
WEIGHT FOR AGE 3yo-6lb

2253 B.B.C. RADIO HUMBERSIDE H'CAP (0-85) (3-Y.O) (Class D) £4,235.25 (£1,272.00: £613.50: £284.25)
1m 100y GOING minus 0.58 sec per fur (F) 3-05 (3-05)

1680* **Hakika (USA) (79)***(88+) (DMorley)* 3-9-4 RCochrane(6) (lw: stdd s: hld up: nt clr run over 2f out: swtchd: qcknd to ld 1f out: pushed clr)......— 1
1698[5] Shayim (USA) **(82)***(84)*(Fav)*(RWArmstrong)* 3-9-7 RPrice(3) (lw: trckd ldr: effrt, ev ch & drvn along over 2f out: kpt on towards fin)......3½ 2
1945[9] Shining Edge **(57)***(56) (MHEasterby)* 3-7-7 (3)ow3 DarrenMoffatt(2) (led tl 1f out: kpt on same pce)......hd 3
1839[17] Lancer (USA) **(81)***(80) (MBell)* 3-9-6 MFenton(1) (hld up: effrt over 2f out: styd on appr fnl f: nvr nr to chal)......1½ 4
1736[6] Primo Lara **(72)***(60) (PWHarris)* 3-8-11 ow2 RHughes(5) (trckd ldrs: effrt over 2f out: outpcd over 1f out)......5 5

LONG HANDICAP Shining Edge 7-5

6/4 Shayim (USA) (9/4-11/8), **13/8** HAKIKA (USA), **9/2** Lancer (USA), **6/1** Primo Lara (op 4/1), **10/1** Shining Edge, CSF £4.76 TOTE £2.30: £1.60 £1.40 (£2.00) OWNER Mr Hamdan Al Maktoum (NEWMARKET) BRED Leo Gatto-Roissard 5 Rn 1m 45.9 (1.90) SF: 37/33/5/29/9

2254 HULL MITSUBISHI CENTRE LADY AMATEUR H'CAP (0-70) (4-Y.O+) (Class F) £2,823.50 (£848.00: £409.00: £189.50)
1m 1f 207y Stalls: High GOING minus 0.58 sec per fur (F) 3-35 (3-35)

2064* **Ooh Ah Cantona (61)***(70)*(Fav)*(JLEyre)* 4-11-7 MrsDKettlewell(6) (lw: trckd ldrs: led wl over 1f out: kpt on u.p fnl f: all out)......— 1
1649[9] Self Expression **(53)***(61) (MrsJRRamsden)* 7-10-6 (7) MissERamsden(8) (lw: bhd whn hmpd 5f out: hdwy on outside over 2f out: hung rt: styd on wl fnl f: jst failed)......½ 2
2021[8] Lord Vivienne (IRE) **(41)***(45) (BSRothwell)* 6-9-8 (7) MissAlexMcCabe(2) (chsd ldrs: led over 2f out: sn hdd & nt qckn)......2½ 3
1666[11] Fort Vally **(36)***(38) (BWMurray)* 5-9-10 MissAElsey(5) (bhd whn hmpd 5f out: styd on fnl 2f: nt rch ldrs)......1¼ 4
1966[12] Touch Above **(47)***(49) (TDBarron)* 9-10-7 MrsAFarrell(3) (in tch: outpcd 5f out: styd on same pce fnl 2f)......s.h 5
1971[2] Tony's Mist **(55)***(54) (JMBradley)* 5-10-11 (4) MissEJJones(4) (chsd ldrs: outpcd wl over 4f out: wknd 3f out)......1¾ 6
2209[3] Dots Dee **(28)***(11) (JMBradley)* 6-9-2 MrsLPearce(7) (plld hrd: led tl over 2f out: sn wknd) 10 7

1863[12] Sporting Spirit **(32)***(1) (GPKelly)* 5-8-13 (7)ow6 MissSBrotherton(9) (in tch tl outpcd over 4f out: sn bhd)..........5 8
1880[9] Canny Lad **(32)** *(MPBielby)* 5-8-13v(7) MissSJudge(1) (hung bdly lft thrght: t.o 3f out)..........15 9

LONG HANDICAP Sporting Spirit 8-13

9/4 OOH AH CANTONA, **11/4** Dots Dee, **4/1** Self Expression, Touch Above, **8/1** Tony's Mist, **16/1** Fort Vally, **20/1** Canny Lad, **25/1** Lord Vivienne (IRE), **33/1** Sporting Spirit, CSF £12.33 CT £171.45 TOTE £3.00: £1.40 £1.80 £6.50 (£9.20) Trio £145.70 OWNER Mrs Eve Sweetman (HAMBLETON) BRED R. M. Whitaker and E. Wilkinson 9 Rn 2m 6.5 (4.00) SF: 52/43/27/20/31/36/-/-/-

2255

MILLERS MILE MAIDEN STKS (3-Y.O) (Class D) £3,684.50 (£1,106.00: £533.00: £246.50)
1m 100y Stalls: High GOING minus 0.58 sec per fur (F) 4-10 (4-10)

1796[3] **Akil (IRE)** *(83)*(Fav)*(RWArmstrong)* 3-9-0 RPrice(1) (lw: trckd ldr: led over 2f out: drvn out) .— 1
1979[7] Reefa's Mill (IRE) **(78)***(78) (JWHills)* 3-9-0 RCochrane(3) (swtg: trckd ldrs: effrt over 2f out: sn rdn & no imp)..........2½ 2
Far Ahead *(76) (MrsVAAconley)* 3-9-0 MDeering(2) (unf: dwlt: sn trckng ldrs: outpcd over 3f out: hdwy on outside 2f out: kpt on one pce)..........1¼ 3
1683[3] Gymcrak Jareer (IRE) *(55) (GHolmes)* 3-8-7 (7) RuthCoulter(4) (led tl over 2f out: wknd over 1f out)..........11 4

30/100 AKIL (IRE), **7/2** Reefa's Mill (IRE), **12/1** Gymcrak Jareer (IRE), **16/1** Far Ahead, CSF £1.93 TOTE £1.30: (£1.20) OWNER Mr Hamdan Al Maktoum (NEWMARKET) BRED Denis Noonan 4 Rn
1m 47.3 (3.30) SF: 21/16/14/-

2256

MARTIN PLENDERLEITH H'CAP (0-70) (3-Y.O+) (Class E) £3,231.25 (£970.00: £467.50: £216.25) **2m 35y** Stalls: Centre GOING minus 0.58 sec (F) 4-45 (4-45)

1973* **Salaman (FR) (72)***(83+)*(Fav)*(JLDunlop)* 3-8-13 RCochrane(4) (lw: hld up: wnt 2nd 6f out: shkn up to ld wl over 1f out: drvn out)..........— 1
Eire Leath-Sceal **(58)***(67) (MBrittain)* 8-9-2 LCharnock(1) (led: pushed along over 3f out: hdd wl over 1f out: kpt on wl)..........2½ 2
1929[6] Moonlight Quest **(70)***(78) (BHanbury)* 7-9-11 (3) JStack(3) (lw: hld up: effrt over 2f out: sn rdn: one pce)..........1 3
2072[7] Baroski **(38)***(39) (JLHarris)* 4-7-7b(3)ow3 DarrenMoffatt(2) (chsd ldr: drvn along 3f out: ev ch & rdn 2f out: wnt rt & sn wknd)..........3½ 4

LONG HANDICAP Baroski 6-11

10/11 SALAMAN (FR) (Evens-4/5), **7/4** Moonlight Quest, **11/2** Eire Leath-Sceal, **16/1** Baroski, CSF £5.47 TOTE £1.80: (£2.50) OWNER Lady Cohen (ARUNDEL) BRED Ridgecourt Stud 4 Rn
3m 45.8 (15.30) SF: -/1/12/-
WEIGHT FOR AGE 3yo-17lb

2257

PETER ADAMSON CONDITIONS STKS (2-Y.O F) (Class D) £3,548.00 (£1,064.00: £512.00: £236.00)
7f 100y Stalls: High GOING minus 0.58 sec per fur (F) 5-20 (5-20)

1842* **Lac Dessert (USA)** *(71+)*(Fav)*(DRLoder)* 2-8-9 (3) DRMcCabe(4) (lw: mde all: pushed along over 2f out: styd on strgly appr fnl f: drvn out)..........— 1
1935* Leith Academy (USA) **(64)***(66) (BWHills)* 2-8-7 (5) JDSmith(3) (trckd wnr: effrt 2f out: hung rt u.p: no imp)..........2½ 2
1678[6] Contradictory *(47) (MWEasterby)* 2-8-8 LCharnock(1) (dwlt: sn chsng ldrs: outpcd fnl 3f).......7 3
1413[11] Sonya Marie *(45) (GPKelly)* 2-8-1 (7) RuthCoulter(2) (bit bkwd: chsd ldr: grad wknd fnl 2f)......¾ 4

10/11 LAC DESSERT (USA) (4/5-Evens), **6/4** Leith Academy (USA), **7/1** Contradictory (10/1-6/1), **25/1** Sonya Marie, CSF £2.52 TOTE £1.60: (£1.10) OWNER Mrs Virginia KraftPayson (NEWMARKET) BRED Virginia Kraft Payson 4 Rn 1m 38.3 (6.30) SF: -/-/-/-

T/Plpt: £16.10 (440.16 Tckts) T/Qdpt: £3.70 (23.8 Tckts). WG

2018-CARLISLE (R-H)
Saturday July 8th (Firm)

WEATHER: overcast WIND: mod half bhd

2258

MACMILLAN NURSES CLAIMING STKS (3-Y.O+) (Class E) £3,023.90 (£915.20: £446.60: £212.30) **6f 206y** Stalls: High GOING minus 0.65 sec (HD) 6-40 (6-41)

2018* **Fantasy Racing (IRE) (76)***(76)*(Fav)*(MRChannon)* 3-8-11 RHughes(2) (lw: trckd ldrs: led on bit wl over 1f out: shkn up & qcknd appr fnl f: eased towards fin)..........— 1

1995⁸ Princess Maxine (IRE) **(56)**_(71) (JJO'Neill)_ 6-8-8 (7) GParkin(1) (lw: effrt u.p ½-wy: ev ch over 1f out: r.o)....nk 2
1962⁹ Bitch **(39)**_(40) (DNicholls)_ 3-7-13 JMarshall(3) (rdn ½-wy: nvr trbld ldrs)....10 3
1742⁹ Valley of Time (FR) **(23)**_(38) (DANolan)_ 7-8-9 KFallon(4) (b: led & sn clr: hdd wl over 1f out: sn btn)....2 4

1/2 FANTASY RACING (IRE), **7/4** Princess Maxine (IRE), **8/1** Bitch, **40/1** Valley of Time (FR), CSF £1.94 TOTE £1.50: (£1.10) OWNER Aldridge Racing Ltd (UPPER LAMBOURN) BRED Barronstown Stud and Ron Con Ltd 4 Rn 1m 26.7 (1.00) SF: 32/35/-/2
WEIGHT FOR AGE 3yo-8lb

2259

'OOH AAH DAILY STAR' MAIDEN AUCTION STKS (2-Y.O) (Class F) £2,647.00 (£742.00: £361.00) **5f 207y** Stalls: High GOING minus 0.65 sec (HD) 7-10 (7-15)

2077² **Oriel Lad (85)**_(75)_(Fav)_(PDEvans)_ 2-8-10v KFallon(4) (lw: trckd ldrs: led 2f out: r.o)....— 1
1842⁹ Oriole **(68)**_(70d) (NTinkler)_ 2-8-10 KimTinkler(6) (led tl hdd 2f out: kpt on one pce)....2 2
Silver Welcome _(52) (MHEasterby)_ 2-8-6 MBirch(1) (w'like: unf: bit bkwd: hld up: hdwy over 2f out: grad lost pl appr fnl f)....5 3
_1525⁷_ Trickledown **(65)** _(CWFairhurst)_ 2-8-5 NConnorton(2) (Withdrawn not under Starter's orders: uns rdr & bolted).... W

Evens ORIEL LAD, **5/2** Trickledown, **7/2** Silver Welcome, **4/1** Oriole, CSF £2.98 TOTE £1.60: (£1.60) OWNER Kendall White & Co Ltd (WELSHPOOL) BRED D. J. Watkins 3 Rn
1m 16.1 (3.80) SF: -/-/-/-

2260

STARBIRD LIMITED STKS (0-75) (3-Y.O+) (Class D) £3,555.50 (£1,076.00: £525.00: £249.50) **5f 207y** Stalls: High GOING minus 0.65 sec per fur (HD) 7-40 (7-42)

2079* **Pharsical (70)**_(79)_(Fav)_(MRChannon)_ 4-9-0 RHughes(3) (mde all: rdn appr fnl f: r.o)....— 1
1648⁷ Chiming In **(74)**_(60) (MrsJRRamsden)_ 3-8-7 KFallon(4) (lw: a chsng wnr: rdn 2f out: no imp)..7 2
2234⁶ Giggleswick Girl **(63)**_(59) (MRChannon)_ 4-8-13 (7) JDennis(2) (stdd s: sn bhd: shkn up 2f out: n.d)....2½ 3
1993⁵ Oscar the Second (IRE) **(30)**_(20) (CWFairhurst)_ 5-9-2 JFortune(1) (in tch to ½-wy: sn wl outpcd)....13 4

4/9 PHARSICAL (op Evens), **7/4** Chiming In (5/4-2/1), **5/1** Giggleswick Girl, **40/1** Oscar the Second (IRE), CSF £2.04 TOTE £1.80: (£1.50) OWNER Mr John Sunley (UPPER LAMBOURN) BRED Sunley Stud 4 Rn 1m 12.2 (-0.10) SF: 46/20/26/-
WEIGHT FOR AGE 3yo-7lb

2261

STARFORM SPRINT H'CAP (0-70) (3-Y.O) (Class E) £3,744.40 (£919.60) **5f** Stalls: High GOING minus 0.65 sec per fur (HD) 8-10 (8-10)

2024* **Dominelle (49)**_(51)_(Fav)_(MHEasterby)_ 3-9-2 SMaloney(1) (mde all: eased ins fnl f: pushed out cl home)....— 1
1936⁶ Blue Lugana **(42)**_(44) (NBycroft)_ 3-8-9b KFallon(2) (lw: chsd wnr: rdn 2f out: r.o towards fin).s.h 2

30/100 DOMINELLE, **9/4** Blue Lugana, TOTE £1.10 OWNER Sandmoor Textiles Co Ltd (MALTON) BRED Gymcrak Thoroughbred Breeding Ltd 2 Rn 62.8 secs (2.60) SF: 6/-

2262

C.F.M. SOUND OF SUMMER MEDIAN AUCTION MAIDEN STKS (3-Y.O) (Class F) £3,028.00 (£742.00) **1m 4f** Stalls: Low GOING minus 0.65 sec per fur (HD) 8-40 (8-40)

2151³ **Harry Welsh (IRE) (70)**_(67)_(Fav)_(KMcAuliffe)_ 3-9-0 JFortune(2) (lw: a gng wl: led ent fnl f: easily)....— 1
1960² Hanifa **(55)**_(60) (MissGayKelleway)_ 3-8-9 KFallon(1) (led tl hdd ent fnl f: no ch w wnr)....1¾ 2

1/6 HARRY WELSH (IRE) (op 2/7), **4/1** Hanifa (op 5/2), TOTE £1.20 OWNER Mr Jorg Vasicek (LAMBOURN) BRED Leo Collins 2 Rn 2m 41.4 (10.40) SF: -/-

2263

RISTORANTE MICHELANGELO H'CAP (0-70) (3-Y.O+) (Class E) £2,995.30 (£906.40: £442.20: £210.10) **1m 4f** Stalls: Low GOING minus 0.65 sec per fur (HD) 9-10 (9-11)

2101² **Vindaloo (71)**_(82)_(Fav)_(JLHarris)_ 3-9-10 MBirch(1) (lw: in tch: rdn over 2f out: led appr fnl f: styd on wl)....— 1

2087* Opus One **(57)***(66)*(Fav)*(MissSEHall)* 4-9-2 (7) MHenry(4) (hld up: effrt over 2f out: kpt on: nt pce of wnr) ... 1¾ **2**
2224[3] Microlite (USA) **(57)***(62) (MDHammond)* 4-9-9b KFallon(2) (led after 1f tl appr fnl f: one pce) ... 2½ **3**
1958[4] Mhemeanles **(46)***(50) (CaptJWilson)* 5-8-12 JFortune(3) (b.hind: led 1f: cl up tl rdn & btn appr fnl f) ... 1 **4**

11/8 VINDALOO, Opus One, **100/30** Microlite (USA), **14/1** Mhemeanles, CSF £3.69 TOTE £2.00: (£2.00) OWNER Mr J. D. Abell (MELTON MOWBRAY) BRED Green Park Investments Ltd 4 Rn
2m 31.9 (0.90) SF: 50/47/43/31
WEIGHT FOR AGE 3yo-13lb

T/Plpt: £4.30 (1,080.21 Tckts). T/Qdpt: £5.40 (3.25 Tckts). AA

2148-CHEPSTOW (L-H)
Saturday July 8th (Good to firm, Good patches)
WEATHER: sunny & hot WIND: nil

2264 E.B.F. MEDIAN AUCTION MAIDEN STKS (2-Y.O) (Class E) £3,533.50 (£1,063.00: £514.00: £239.50)
6f 16y Stalls: High GOING minus 0.51 sec per fur (F) 2-25 (2-29)

859[7] **Kossolian** *(74) (BPalling)* 2-8-9 TSprake(3) (mde all: pushed out) ... — **1**
1913[2] Ramooz (USA) *(76)*(Fav)*(BHanbury)* 2-9-0 MRimmer(5) (lw: chsd wnr: ev ch over 1f out: nt qckn ins fnl f) ... 1¼ **2**
1977[3] Emperegrine (USA) **(73)***(71) (CFWall)* 2-9-0 GDuffield(4) (lw: outpcd: rdn & hdwy 3f out: r.o ins fnl f) ... 1¾ **3**
Kiss Me Again (IRE) *(53) (RHannon)* 2-8-2 (7) DaneO'Neill(1) (neat: bmpd s: a bhd) ... 5 **4**
1592[W] Coastguards Hero *(18) (MDIUsher)* 2-9-0 MWigham(2) (unf: wnt lft s: bhd fnl 3f: t.o) ... 15 **5**

5/6 Ramooz (USA) (Evens-4/5), **11/4** Emperegrine (USA), **5/1** Kiss Me Again (IRE), **6/1** KOSSOLIAN, **25/1** Coastguards Hero, CSF £11.72 TOTE £7.70: £2.20 £1.10 (£3.70) OWNER Mr K. J. Mercer (COWBRIDGE) BRED Cymru Racing Club 5 Rn 1m 11.6 (2.60) SF: 13/15/10/-/-

2265 STARLING MAIDEN STKS (3-Y.O F) (Class D) £3,949.50 (£1,191.00: £578.00: £271.50)
7f 16y Stalls: High GOING minus 0.51 sec per fur (F) 2-55 (2-58)

1554[2] **Proud Destiny** **(73)***(81) (MRStoute)* 3-8-8 (3) JTate(8) (lw: hld up: led wl over 1f out: pushed out) ... — **1**
1701[3] Western Sal *(73)*(Fav)*(WJarvis)* 3-8-11 PRobinson(3) (hld up: rdn over 2f out: chsd wnr over 1f out: no imp) ... 3½ **2**
1979[6] Jareer Do (IRE) *(67) (BPalling)* 3-8-11 TSprake(7) (plld hrd: led over 5f: one pce) ... 2½ **3**
630[2] Summertown (USA) *(65)*(Fav)*(JHMGosden)* 3-8-11 SWhitworth(2) (s.s: hld up: hdwy over 2f out: one pce) ... 1¼ **4**
Joyful (IRE) *(60) (JHMGosden)* 3-8-11 GHind(5) (w'like: dwlt: hld up: rdn over 2f out: no hdwy) ... 2 **5**
Awayil (USA) *(58) (HThomsonJones)* 3-8-11 NCarlisle(4) (plld hrd: prom over 4f) ... ¾ **6**
Radiance (IRE) *(58) (RHannon)* 3-8-4 (7) DaneO'Neill(6) (bit bkwd: chsd ldr 4f: wknd over 2f out) ... s.h **7**

5/2 Summertown (USA), Western Sal, **4/1** PROUD DESTINY, **6/1** Joyful (IRE) (op 9/4), **15/2** Awayil (USA), **10/1** Jareer Do (IRE), **25/1** Radiance (IRE), CSF £14.01 TOTE £4.40: £1.90 £2.40 (£4.80) OWNER Maktoum Al Maktoum (NEWMARKET) BRED Gainsborough Stud Management Ltd 7 Rn
1m 21.9 (1.90) SF: 27/19/13/11/6/4/4

2266 ROTHMANS ROYALS NORTH SOUTH CHALLENGE SERIES H'CAP (0-85) (3-Y.O+) (Class D) £4,224.00 (£1,272.00: £616.00: £288.00)
1m 14y Stalls: High GOING minus 0.51 sec per fur (F) 3-25 (3-28)

Lord Oberon (IRE) **(54)***(61) (JAkehurst)* 7-8-6 SWhitworth(5) (a.p: rdn over 2f out: led wl ins fnl f: all out) ... — **1**
1915[4] Fionn de Cool (IRE) **(71)***(78) (RAkehurst)* 4-9-6 (3) SSanders(4) (prom: rdn over 3f out: hrd rdn & ev ch ins fnl f: r.o) ... s.h **2**
2080[2] Zermatt (IRE) **(69)***(76)*(Fav)*(MDIUsher)* 5-9-7 GDuffield(6) (lw: a.p: ev ch ins fnl f: r.o) ... hd **3**
2080[5] Sooty Tern **(67)***(73) (JMBradley)* 8-9-2 (3) SDrowne(3) (led tl wl ins fnl f) ... nk **4**
2169[6] Dontforget Insight (IRE) **(72)***(76) (PFICole)* 4-9-10 CRutter(8) (lw: b.hind: hld up: hdwy over 2f out: n.m.r & stmbld over 1f out: nt rcvr) ... 1¼ **5**

1474[11] Sylvandra **(73)***(72) (PGMurphy)* 3-8-9 (7) RWaterfield(7) (hld up: nt clr run over 2f out: swtchd lft over 1f out: one pce) 2½ 6
1589[7] Sea Victor **(81)***(66) (JHMGosden)* 3-9-10 GHind(2) (lw: prom: rdn over 3f out: wknd over 2f out) 7 7
1693[7] Telopea **(67)***(22) (HCandy)* 4-9-5b NAdams(1) (bhd fnl 4f: t.o) 15 8

5/2 Zermatt (IRE), **4/1** Sea Victor, **5/1** Fionn de Cool (IRE), **6/1** Sooty Tern, Dontforget Insight (IRE) (op 4/1), **10/1** Telopea, **20/1** Sylvandra, LORD OBERON (IRE), CSF £103.28 CT £306.99 TOTE £23.80: £4.00 £1.60 £1.30 (£154.40) OWNER Mrs John Akehurst (LAMBOURN) BRED H. Ward 8 Rn 1m 32.8 (0.30) SF: 43/60/58/55/58/45/39/4

WEIGHT FOR AGE 3yo-9lb

STEWARDS' ENQUIRY Sanders susp. 17-19/7/95 (excessive use of whip).

2267

CHAFFINCH RATING RELATED MAIDEN LIMITED STKS (0-65) (3-Y.O) (Class F) £2,726.00 (£818.00: £394.00: £182.00)
5f 16y Stalls: High GOING minus 0.51 sec per fur (F) 3-55 (3-59)

2084[3] **Millesime (IRE) (59)***(72)*(Fav)*(BHanbury)* 3-9-0 MRimmer(2) (mde all: rdn & qcknd clr ins fnl f: drvn out) .....— 1
1750[4] Grand Chapeau (IRE) **(60)***(56) (RHannon)* 3-8-7 (7) DaneO'Neill(4) (a.p: hrd rdn over 1f out: r.o ins fnl f: no ch w wnr) 5 2
1942[7] La Belle Dominique **(58)***(47) (SGKnight)* 3-8-9 VSlattery(1) (hld up: hdwy 2f out: chsd wnr wl over 1f out: no imp) 1½ 3
2112[6] Silver Academy (IRE) **(40)***(41) (MissGayKelleway)* 3-9-0b GDuffield(3) (w wnr 3f: wknd over 1f out) 3½ 4

5/4 MILLESIME (IRE), **7/4** Grand Chapeau (IRE), **4/1** La Belle Dominique, **15/2** Silver Academy (IRE), CSF £3.78 TOTE £2.00: (£1.50) OWNER Boxall Asset Management Ltd (NEWMARKET) BRED Killarkin Stud 4 Rn 58.4 secs (1.40) SF: 29/13/4/-

2268

SWALLOW MAIDEN H'CAP (0-65) (3-Y.O+) (Class F) £3,096.50 (£932.00: £451.00: £210.50) **2m 2f** Stalls: High GOING minus 0.51 sec per fur (F) 4-25 (4-27)

1657[3] **Gentleman Sid (35)***(45) (PGMurphy)* 5-8-3 NAdams(12) (lw: a.p: led 5f out: clr 2f out: eased wl ins fnl f) .....— 1
1973[5] Tommy Cooper **(40)***(48) (MrsBarbaraWaring)* 4-8-5v(3) SDrowne(7) (hld up & plld hrd: hdwy 7f out: 5th st: chsd wnr wl over 1f out: no imp) 2½ 2
1840[23] Phil's Time **(57)***(64) (TGMills)* 4-9-4 (7) JCornally(1) (lw: hld up: hdwy over 2f out: styd on fnl f) 1¼ 3
Celcius **(32)***(36) (MCPipe)* 11-8-0b TSprake(5) (hld up & bhd: hdwy 3f out: one pce fnl 2f) 2½ 4
2078[3] Oh So Handy **(37)***(40) (RCurtis)* 7-8-2b(3) JTate(4) (hld up & bhd: stdy hdwy 7f out: 7th st: one pce fnl 2f) 1¼ 5
2090[5] Teoroma **(33)***(25) (DrJDScargill)* 5-7-12 (3)ow8 SSanders(2) (nvr nr to chal) 3½ 6
1997[2] Maysann **(58)***(55)*(Fav)*(JLDunlop)* 3-8-7b GDuffield(11) (hld up: stdy hdwy 8f out: 4th & rdn st: wknd over 2f out) 4 7
1973[6] Young Clifford (USA) **(60)***(56) (FJordan)* 4-9-7 (7) RHavlin(6) (lw: nvr trbld ldrs) 1 8
1696[4] Vizard (IRE) **(63)***(58) (MJHeaton-Ellis)* 3-8-12b GHind(13) (hdwy after 5f: 3rd st: wknd 2f out) ½ 9
1937[10] Aramon **(30)***(22) (MJHaynes)* 5-7-12 NCarlisle(3) (led 5f: 6th st: wknd over 2f out) 4 10
1210[6] Chasmarella **(31)***(16) (MrsMELong)* 10-7-6 (7)ow6 TField(9) (prom tl wknd over 5f out) .....¾ 11
1950[11] Reeling **(31)***(14) (PaddyFarrell)* 9-7-6 (7)ow6 SLanigan(8) (led after 5f: hdd 5f out: 2nd st: wknd 4f out) 2½ 12
2089[3] Jarzon Dancer **(30)** *(DAWilson)* 7-7-5 (7) RachaelMoody(10) (b: lw: sddle slipped after 6f: sn t.o) .....dist 13

LONG HANDICAP Chasmarella 7-2 Teoroma 7-5

11/4 Maysann, **11/2** Vizard (IRE) (op 7/2), **6/1** GENTLEMAN SID, **7/1** Phil's Time (5/1-8/1), Oh So Handy, Celcius (8/1-12/1), **9/1** Tommy Cooper, **10/1** Young Clifford (USA), **12/1** Teoroma (6/1-14/1), Jarzon Dancer (op 6/1), **33/1** Chasmarella, Aramon, **50/1** Reeling, CSF £61.15 CT £369.90 TOTE £9.30: £2.70 £1.70 £2.60 (£34.60) Trio £175.80 OWNER Miss J. Collison (BRISTOL) BRED D. I. Heathcote 13 Rn 4m 0.9 SF: 12/15/31/3/7/-/3/23/6/-/-/-/-

WEIGHT FOR AGE 3yo-19lb

2269

WOODPECKER H'CAP (0-80) (3-Y.O+) (Class D) £3,904.00 (£1,177.00: £571.00: £268.00) **1m 2f 36y** Stalls: High GOING minus 0.51 sec per fur (F) 5-00 (5-02)

1988* **Senorita Dinero (USA) (80)***(92)*(Fav)*(MRStoute)* 3-9-4 (3) JTate(2) (led 1f: 3rd st: led over 2f out tl over 1f out: rallied to ld last strides) .....— 1
1853[18] Uncle Oswald **(76)***(88) (RHannon)* 4-9-7 (7) DaneO'Neill(5) (hld up: 5th st: hdwy to ld over 1f out: hdd last strides) .....s.h 2

Newport Knight **(65)**(66) (RAkehurst) 4-9-0 (3) SSanders(6) (sn chsng ldrs: led over 5f out: hdd & hrd rdn over 2f out: one pce)....7 3

2002[6] Sweet Trentino (IRE) **(57)**(57) (MTate) 4-8-9 NCarlisle(1) (hld up & bhd: last st: nvr trbld ldrs)....nk 4

1250[6] Rasmi (CAN) **(71)**(70) (ACStewart) 4-9-9 SWhitworth(4) (hld up: 4th st: hdwy 4f out: wknd 2f out)....1¼ 5

678[8] Zingibar **(72)**(47) (BWHills) 3-8-13 GDuffield(3) (led after 1f: 2nd st: rdn 3f out: hdd & wknd qckly over 5f out: t.o)....15 6

6/5 SENORITA DINERO (USA), **5/2** Uncle Oswald, **6/1** Newport Knight, **7/1** Zingibar, **9/1** Rasmi (CAN) (op 6/1), **16/1** Sweet Trentino (IRE), CSF £4.74 TOTE £1.90: £1.10 £1.80 (£2.90) OWNER Mr A. Al Khalifa (NEWMARKET) BRED Sheikh Rashid Bin Mohammed Al-Khalifa et al 6 Rn

2m 7.0 (2.70) SF: 42/49/27/18/31/-

WEIGHT FOR AGE 3yo-11lb

T/Plpt: £121.90 (58.03 Tckts). T/Qdpt: £36.70 (1.5 Tckts). KH

2233-HAYDOCK (L-H)
Saturday July 8th (Good to firm)

WEATHER: fine & sunny WIND: slt bhd

2270

SHADWELL STUD SERIES APPRENTICE H'CAP (0-80) (3-Y.O+) (Class E) £3,743.50 (£1,048.00: £509.00)
1m 2f 120y Stalls: High GOING minus 0.45 sec per fur (F) 2-00 (2-00)

1858[2] **Hillzah (USA) (75)**(84) (RBastiman) 7-10-0 HBastiman(4) (led after 3f: sn hdd: 3rd st: led over 2f out: jst hld on)....— 1

2118[5] Augustan **(62)**(71) (SGollings) 4-9-1 VHalliday(2) (lw: led 3f: 2nd st: led wl over 2f out: sn hdd: hrd rdn & rallied cl home)....nk 2

1716[4] Indian Jockey **(68)**(54)(Fav)(MCPipe) 3-8-9 LNewton(1) (hld up: plld hrd: sddle slipped & led 6f out: sn clr: rdn & hdd wl over 2f out: wknd bel dist)....15 3

6/5 Indian Jockey, **9/4** Augustan, **11/4** HILLZAH (USA), CSF £7.09 TOTE £3.00: (£3.30) OWNER Mrs P. Churm (WETHERBY) BRED Helen M. Polinger, Benjamin Polinger et al 3 Rn

2m 19.92 (8.42) SF: 14/1/-

WEIGHT FOR AGE 3yo-12lb

2271

EDWARD SYMMONS & PARTNERS COCK O'THE NORTH H'CAP (0-100) (3-Y.O) (Class C) £5,732.00 (£1,736.00: £848.00: £404.00)
6f Stalls: High GOING minus 0.45 sec per fur (F) 2-30 (2-30)

1870[8] **Cheyenne Spirit (97)**(103)(Fav)(BHanbury) 3-9-7 WRyan(1) (racd centre: mde all: qcknd appr fnl f: r.o wl)....— 1

1876[4] Bollin Harry **(69)**(72) (MHEasterby) 3-7-7 GBardwell(5) (chsd ldrs: effrt u.p wl over 1f out: kpt on towards fin)....1¼ 2

1876[2] The Scythian **(73)**(76) (BobJones) 3-7-11 JFanning(2) (swtg: chsd wnr: ev ch 2f out: rdn & one pce fnl f)....s.h 3

1839[28] Masruf (IRE) **(78)**(71) (TThomsonJones) 3-8-2 RHills(3) (lw: chsd ldrs: rdn 2f out: kpt on one pce)....3½ 4

1982[2] Prolific Lady (IRE) **(74)**(57) (MBrittain) 3-7-12b JQuinn(6) (lw: hld up: hdwy 2f out: sn rdn: nvr nr to chal)....4 5

1806[11] Prime Match (IRE) **(82)**(60)(Fav)(PWHarris) 3-8-6 JWeaver(4) (hld up: hdwy ½-wy: rdn 2f out: nt rch ldrs)....1¾ 6

2066[6] Bajan Rose **(83)**(48) (MBlanshard) 3-8-7 StephenDavies(8) (effrt stands' side over 2f out: no imp)....5 7

1876[3] Try to Please (IRE) **(80)** (EALDunlop) 3-8-1 (3) JStack(7) (swtg: a bhd: eased whn btn 2f out: t.o)....20 8

LONG HANDICAP Bollin Harry 7-6

4/1 CHEYENNE SPIRIT, Prime Match (IRE), **5/1** Prolific Lady (IRE), Try to Please (IRE), **11/2** The Scythian, **6/1** Bollin Harry, **12/1** Masruf (IRE), Bajan Rose, CSF £26.47 CT £120.83 TOTE £4.90: £2.00 £2.30 £1.90 (£16.10) OWNER Mr C. Mauritzon (NEWMARKET) BRED J. McGarry 8 Rn

1m 11.18 (-0.52) SF: 75/44/48/43/29/32/20/-

2272

LANCASHIRE OAKS STKS (Gp 3) (3-Y.O+ F & M) (Class A) £21,400.00 (£8,080.00: £3,940.00: £1,780.00)
1m 3f 200y Stalls: High GOING minus 0.45 sec per fur (F) 3-00 (3-00)

1237a[4] **Fanjica (IRE)** (111) (JLDunlop) 3-8-4 GCarter(4) (chsd ldrs: 3rd st: led over 3f out: sn clr: rdn out)....— 1

1780² Totality **(103)***(109)*(Fav)*(HRACecil)* 4-9-3 WRyan(2) (lw: led 1f: 2nd st: rdn over 1f out: one pce) 1¼ **2**
2104² Magical Retreat (USA) **(96)***(106)* *(CACyzer)* 5-9-3 DBiggs(5) (lw: hld up: 4th st: hdwy 3f out: sn hrd rdn: nt pce to chal) 2½ **3**
Noble Rose (IRE) **(107)***(106)* *(LMCumani)* 4-9-3 JWeaver(3) (bit bkwd: hld up in rr: 5th st: effrt over 2f out: nvr nr to chal) ....nk **4**
2036* Misbelief **(102)***(96)* *(JRFanshawe)* 5-9-3 DHarrison(1) (led after 1f tl over 3f out: rdn & wknd fnl 2f) 7 **5**

6/4 Totality, **15/8** Noble Rose (IRE), **6/1** FANJICA (IRE), **7/1** Misbelief, **9/1** Magical Retreat (USA), CSF £14.79 TOTE £8.50: £2.70 £1.20 (£6.60) OWNER Diamond Thoroughbreds Inc (ARUNDEL) BRED Allevamento Annarosa di V. Schirone 5 Rn 2m 29.74 (1.74) SF: 41/52/49/49/39
WEIGHT FOR AGE 3yo-13lb

2273 ROBERT SICE MEMORIAL JULY TROPHY STKS (Listed) (3-Y.O C & G) (Class A) £12,510.00 (£3,780.00: £1,840.00: £870.00)
1m 3f 200y Stalls: High GOING minus 0.45 sec per fur (F) 3-30 (3-30)

1897⁴ **Don Corleone (113)***(102+)* *(RCharlton)* 3-8-10 DHarrison(4) (lw: hld up & bhd: 4th st: effrt on ins & hmpd over 1f out: checked & swtchd rt: qcknd to ld wl ins fnl f)....— **1**
1574a¹⁰ Indian Light **(102)***(100)* *(JLDunlop)* 3-8-10 JWeaver(3) (lw: chsd ldr: 2nd st: shkn up 3f out: ev ch ins fnl f: unable qckn)....1¼ **2**
1611⁴ Fahal (USA) **(117)***(100)*(Fav)*(DMorley)* 3-8-10 RHills(2) (lw: plld hrd: hld up: 3rd st: rdn to ld over 1f out: hdd & no ex nr fin) ....½ **3**
1925³ Stiffelio (IRE) **(97)***(99)* *(RHannon)* 3-8-10 JReid(1) (lw: led tl rdn & hdd over 1f out: unable qckn)....½ **4**

evens Fahal (USA), **2/1** DON CORLEONE, **9/2** Indian Light, **12/1** Stiffelio (IRE), CSF £9.25 TOTE £2.80: (£5.80) OWNER Mr Wafic Said (BECKHAMPTON) BRED Ridgecourt Stud 4 Rn
2m 30.27 (2.27) SF: 13/11/11/10

2274 197TH YEAR OF THE OLD NEWTON CUP H'CAP (0-110) (3-Y.O+) (Class B) £14,256.25 (£4,300.00: £2,087.50: £981.25)
1m 3f 200y Stalls: High GOING minus 0.45 sec per fur (F) 4-00 (4-02)

1768⁴ **Lombardic (USA) (87)***(97)* *(MrsJCecil)* 4-8-12 JReid(1) (mde all: hrd rdn fnl f: hld on gamely)....— **1**
1872* Diaghilef (IRE) **(104)***(114)*(Fav)*(MJohnston)* 3-9-2 DHolland(8) (a.p: 3rd st: jnd wnr over 2f out: hrd rdn fnl f: r.o) ....nk **2**
1853³ Shadow Leader **(80)***(89)* *(DJSffrenchDavis)* 4-8-5 JWeaver(5) (chsd wnr: 2nd st: rdn & wknd 2f out: rallied u.p wl towards fin) ....¾ **3**
2012* Seasonal Splendour (IRE) **(86)***(95)* *(MCPipe)* 5-8-11 DBiggs(3) (hld up: hdwy over 2f out: styd on ins fnl f) ....hd **4**
1853⁵ Marsoom (CAN) **(99)***(106)* *(BHanbury)* 4-9-10 TIves(4) (b: a.p: 4th st: rdn & n.m.r over 1f out: one pce) 1 **5**
1853⁹ Foundry Lane **(80)***(85)* *(MrsMReveley)* 4-8-5 JFortune(10) (lw: chsd ldrs: 6th st: rdn over 2f out: kpt on one pce)....1¼ **6**
1853⁶ Source of Light **(103)***(102)* *(RCharlton)* 6-10-0 DHarrison(9) (lw: s.s: rdn & hdwy 3f out: eased whn btn over 1f out)....5 **7**
1853¹⁰ Glide Path (USA) **(95)***(92)*(Fav)*(JWHills)* 6-8-13 (7) MHenry(2) (lw: hld up: effrt & 4th st: rdn over 2f out: sn btn) 1 **8**
2068³ Adolescence (IRE) **(80)***(76)* *(KMcAuliffe)* 5-8-5 JCarroll(6) (swtg: bhd: effrt u.p 3f out: wknd 2f out)....¾ **9**
1912* Mokhtar (IRE) **(89)***(80)* *(JLDunlop)* 4-9-0b RHills(7) (hld up in rr: shkn up & effrt over 3f out: no imp) 4 **10**

5/1 Diaghilef (IRE), Glide Path (USA), **6/1** Foundry Lane, **7/1** Seasonal Splendour (IRE), Marsoom (CAN), Mokhtar (IRE), **8/1** Shadow Leader, Source of Light, **10/1** LOMBARDIC (USA), **20/1** Adolescence (IRE), CSF £56.63 CT £388.69 TOTE £10.50: £2.50 £2.40 £2.40 (£32.70) Trio £168.90 OWNER Bonusprint (NEWMARKET) BRED Juddmonte Farms 10 Rn
2m 29.4 (1.40) SF: 50/54/42/48/59/38/55/45/29/33
WEIGHT FOR AGE 3yo-13lb

2275 E.B.F. JULY MAIDEN STKS (2-Y.O F) (Class D) £4,406.00 (£1,328.00: £644.00: £302.00) **6f** Stalls: High GOING minus 0.45 sec per fur (F) 4-30 (4-31)

1726² **Tamnia** *(78+)*(Fav)*(JLDunlop)* 2-8-11 JReid(5) (a.p: led over 2f out: rdn fnl f: r.o wl) ....— **1**
1142³ Thrilling Day *(76+)* *(NAGraham)* 2-8-11 DHolland(1) (w ldrs: ev ch fnl f: no ex cl home)....¾ **2**

1413[6] Willisa *(57) (JDBethell)* 2-8-11 TIves(4) (led over 3f: outpcd appr fnl f)....................7 3
1460[5] Marjorie Rose (IRE) **(82)***(53d) (ABailey)* 2-8-11 GCarter(3) (bhd: effrt 2f out: nt rch ldrs).......1½ 4
Crissem (IRE) *(45) (RHollinshead)* 2-8-11 WRyan(2) (lt-f: gd spd 4f: sn outpcd)....................3 5
2000[5] Princess Efisio *(41) (BAMcMahon)* 2-8-11 FNorton(6) (bit bkwd: a bhd: rdn over 2f out: no rspnse)....................1¾ 6

4/7 TAMNIA, **7/2** Thrilling Day, **9/2** Marjorie Rose (IRE), **11/1** Crissem (IRE), **20/1** Princess Efisio, **25/1** Willisa, CSF £3.49 TOTE £1.60: £1.30 £1.70 (£2.00) OWNER Prince A. A. Faisal (ARUNDEL) BRED Nawara Stud Co Ltd 6 Rn
1m 11.63 (-0.07) SF: 59/57/38/34/26/22

2276 LADBROKE H'CAP (0-65) (3-Y.O+) (Class F) £2,997.00 (£842.00: £411.00)
1m 30y Stalls: Low GOING minus 0.45 sec per fur (F) 5-05 (5-07)

2084[11] **Bollin Frank (53)***(64) (MHEasterby)* 3-9-2 JCarroll(16) (mde all: rdn clr over 2f out: r.o wl)....................— 1
2061[6] Move Smartly (IRE) **(49)***(56) (FHLee)* 5-9-7v RHills(12) (hld up: 5th st: gd hdwy 3f out: rdn over 1f out: one pce)....................2 2
2141[4] Hawwam **(52)***(59) (EJAlston)* 9-9-10 JWeaver(9) (hld up: c wd & hdwy over 2f out: fin wl).....nk 3
1830[2] Vanborough Lad **(55)***(60) (MJBolton)* 6-9-13 JReid(2) (lw: hld up in tch: hdwy over 2f out: nt clr run bel dist: rdn & r.o nr fin)....................¾ 4
2021[3] Twin Creeks **(47)***(51) (MDHammond)* 4-9-5 DHolland(8) (prom: 2nd st: rdn over 1f out: one pce)....................½ 5
2064[4] Nobby Barnes **(41)***(42) (DonEnricoIncisa)* 6-8-13 KimTinkler(7) (hld up & bhd: hdwy 2f out: rdn & kpt on fnl f)....................1½ 6
1724* Habeta (USA) **(36)***(34) (JWWatts)* 9-8-8 NConnorton(3) (hld up: effrt & rdn over 2f out: nvr nrr)....................1¾ 7
1506* Marowins **(47)***(44)*(Fav)*(EJAlston)* 6-9-5 JFortune(11) (s.s: hdwy on outside over 2f out: rdn & hung lft wl over 1f out: nvr nrr)....................nk 8
1855[5] Daring Ryde **(49)***(41) (JPSmith)* 4-9-7 GCarter(6) (hld up: hdwy & hmpd wl over 1f out: sn btn)....................2½ 9
2088[7] Ikis Girl **(35)***(27) (SGollings)* 4-8-7 FNorton(1) (prom: 4th st: wknd over 2f out)....................hd 10
2016[3] Master M-E-N (IRE) **(51)***(42) (NMBabbage)* 3-9-0v JQuinn(4) (chsd ldrs: 7th st: wknd over 2f out)....................nk 11
1472[4] Runic Symbol **(40)***(30) (MBlanshard)* 4-8-12 WRyan(13) (mid div whn bdly hmpd wl over 1f out: nt rcvr)....................¾ 12
2088[8] Kilnamartyra Girl **(45)***(35) (JParkes)* 5-9-3 DHarrison(5) (chsd ldrs over 5f)....................hd 13
1742[3] Matisse **(44)***(29) (JDBethell)* 4-9-2 TIves(15) (nvr trbld ldrs)....................2½ 14
Maple Bay (IRE) **(49)***(34) (ABailey)* 6-9-2 (5) VHalliday(14) (bit bkwd: prom: 6th st: rdn & wknd over 2f out)....................hd 15
1950[2] Personimus **(33)***(2) (CaptJWilson)* 5-8-5 JFanning(10) (prom: 3rd st: rdn 3f out: sn btn)..........8 16

6/1 Marowins, **13/2** Vanborough Lad, **7/1** Habeta (USA), **9/1** Twin Creeks, **11/1** BOLLIN FRANK, **12/1** Matisse, Runic Symbol, Hawwam, Kilnamartyra Girl (8/1-14/1), **14/1** Nobby Barnes, Master M-E-N (IRE), Move Smartly (IRE), Personimus, **16/1** Daring Ryde, **20/1** Maple Bay (IRE), Ikis Girl, CSF £148.33 CT £1716.91 TOTE £13.60: £2.80 £2.70 £3.10 £2.30 (£50.70) Trio £354.80 OWNER Sir Neil Westbrook (MALTON) BRED Sir Neil and Lady Westbrook 16 Rn
1m 43.12 (2.72) SF: 37/38/41/42/33/24/16/26/23/9/15/12/17/11/16/-
WEIGHT FOR AGE 3yo-9lb

T/Plpt: £56.10 (227.27 Tckts). T/Qdpt: £33.10 (5 Tckts). IM

1962-NOTTINGHAM (L-H)
Saturday July 8th (Firm)
WEATHER: sunny WIND: str bhd

2277 NOTTINGHAM EVENING POST MAIDEN AUCTION STKS (2-Y.O) (Class E) £3,287.00 (£912.00: £437.00)
6f 15y Stalls: Centre GOING minus 0.39 sec per fur (F) 6-50 (6-52)

She's My Love *(65+)*(Fav)*(JEBanks)* 2-8-1 JQuinn(2) (leggy: dwlt: hdwy over 2f out: led over 1f out: rdn out)....................— 1
1690[4] Hurricane Dancer (IRE) **(54)***(60) (SPCWoods)* 2-7-10 (5) NVarley(3) (prom: ev ch over 1f out: kpt on)....................1¾ 2
1690[6] Pharaoh's Joy *(60) (JWPayne)* 2-8-1 DHarrison(5) (chsd ldrs: ev ch over 1f out: sn rdn & no ex)....................hd 3
1212[5] Don't Forget Mikie (IRE) *(69) (MJHeaton-Ellis)* 2-8-10 WWoods(4) (led over 4f: no ex).........hd 4
Impetuous Lady (USA) *(58) (WJMusson)* 2-7-12 (3) PMcCabe(1) (unf: prom over 3f out: sn rdn & no imp)....................¾ 5

Manderella *(53) (JAkehurst)* 2-7-11 DaleGibson(7) (unf: sn bhd & pushed along: kpt on fnl 2f) ....½ 6
1662[6] Thai Morning *(60) (PWHarris)* 2-8-10 MFenton(8) (in tch: effrt & n.m.r over 1f out: sn btn) 2 7
Rock Sharp *(56) (RHannon)* 2-8-6 WRyan(9) (w'like: s.i.s: hdwy & ev ch 2f out: sn wknd) ....nk 8
Soviet Sakti (IRE) *(37) (PMitchell)* 2-8-6 RPerham(6) (scope: s.i.s: sn in tch: rdn 2f out: sn wknd) 7 9

3/1 SHE'S MY LOVE, **7/2** Hurricane Dancer (IRE), Thai Morning, **4/1** Pharaoh's Joy, **7/1** Rock Sharp, **11/1** Don't Forget Mikie (IRE), **20/1** Impetuous Lady (USA), **25/1** Soviet Sakti (IRE), **50/1** Manderella, CSF £13.85 TOTE £8.80: £2.00 £2.40 £1.10 (£18.10) Trio £14.10 OWNER Sheik Ahmad Yousuf Al Sabah (NEWMARKET) BRED W. H. Joyce 9 Rn

1m 13.2 (2.20) SF: 22/17/17/26/15/10/17/13/-

2278

JEFF MARSH H'CAP (0-70) (3-Y.O) (Class E) £3,313.60 (£919.60: £440.80)
1m 54y Stalls: Low GOING minus 0.39 sec per fur (F) 7-20 (7-24)

1809[6] **South Rock (70)***(77) (JAGlover)* 3-9-7 DeanMcKeown(5) (trckd ldrs: 6th st: rdn over 2f out: str run to ld ins fnl f) ....— 1
1979[10] Spumante **(64)***(69) (RChampion)* 3-9-1 RCochrane(7) (prom: 4th st: led over 3f out: hdd & no ex ins fnl f) 1¼ 2
1859[2] Star of Gold **(64)***(69)*(Fav)*(CREgerton)* 3-9-1 WCarson(2) (lw: hld up: plld hrd: hdwy & 5th st: n.m.r 1f out: r.o fnl f) ....s.h 3
1812[3] Just-Mana-Mou (IRE) **(50)***(50) (GLewis)* 3-7-10 (5)ow2 AWhelan(4) (bhd: gd hdwy fnl 2f: n.m.r nr fin) 1¼ 4
1862[3] Evan 'elp Us **(65)***(62) (JLEyre)* 3-9-2b WRyan(8) (prom: 2nd st: ev ch 2f out: eased whn btn) 2½ 5
1625* Amnesty Bay **(60)***(56) (JRFanshawe)* 3-8-11 DHarrison(6) (prom: 3rd st: one pce fnl 2f) ....½ 6
1812[7] Asking **(42)***(35) (JABennett)* 3-7-2v(5) MBaird(10) (led over 4f: wknd & edgd rt over 1f out).....1½ 7
1963[21] Le Bal **(45)***(14) (MrsNMacauley)* 3-7-10vow3 DaleGibson(1) (rdn over 3f out: nvr nr to chal)....11 8
1514[17] Laudation (IRE) **(52)***(17) (GBBalding)* 3-7-12 (5) NVarley(3) (a bhd) 3½ 9
1760[10] Pc's Cruiser (IRE) **(56)***(12) (MCChapman)* 3-8-7 MFenton(9) (rdn 4 out: a bhd) 5 10

LONG HANDICAP Le Bal 7-6 Asking 6-11

7/2 Star of Gold, **9/2** SOUTH ROCK, **5/1** Just-Mana-Mou (IRE), **11/2** Evan 'elp Us, Amnesty Bay (4/1-6/1), **12/1** Pc's Cruiser (IRE), **14/1** Spumante (10/1-16/1), Laudation (IRE), **20/1** Le Bal, **33/1** Asking, CSF £56.65 CT £221.70 TOTE £4.70: £1.80 £3.60 £1.30 (£60.10) Trio £54.40 OWNER Mr B. H. Farr (WORKSOP) BRED Worksop Manor Stud Farm 10 Rn

1m 44.9 (5.30) SF: 21/13/13/-/6/-/-/-/-/-

2279

EAST MIDLAND COMMERCIALS MAIDEN H'CAP (0-70) (3-Y.O+) (Class E) £3,765.80 (£1,048.80: £505.40)
1m 1f 213y GOING minus 0.39 sec per fur (F) 7-50 (7-52)

1093[8] **Bellateena (48)***(61) (HJCollingridge)* 3-8-2 JQuinn(3) (chsd ldr: 2nd st: led over 2f out: hld on wl) ....— 1
1038[7] Carol's Dream (USA) **(70)***(82) (JWHills)* 3-9-10 RCochrane(2) (a.p: 3rd st: ev ch over 1f out: unable qckn fnl f) ....½ 2
1974[3] Lady Sabina **(38)***(42) (WJMusson)* 5-8-0 (3) PMcCabe(7) (lw: hdwy 3f out: nvr rchd ldrs)..........5 3
1945[3] Anonym (IRE) **(64)***(67)*(Fav)*(JLDunlop)* 3-9-4 WCarson(10) (prom: 4th st: sn rdn: btn appr fnl f) ....½ 4
1988[D] Shady Deed (USA) **(63)***(50) (JWHills)* 3-9-3 RHills(5) (led: sn clr: hdd over 2f out: sn btn & eased) 10 5
1743[5] Master Fiddler **(33)***(15) (EWeymes)* 5-7-12 FNorton(11) (in tch: effrt 4f out: sn no imp).........3½ 6
2033[7] Jovie King (IRE) **(60)***(39) (PMitchell)* 3-8-7 (7) DaneO'Neill(4) (in tch: rdn over 2f out: sn wknd) 2 7
1791[2] Dont Forget Curtis (IRE) **(70)***(48) (JRFanshawe)* 3-9-10 DHarrison(8) (lw: rdn & hdwy 4f out: wknd 2f out) ....hd 8
1526[9] Oleron **(60)***(38) (JNorton)* 3-9-0 DaleGibson(6) (a bhd) ....hd 9
1431[2] Feinte **(70)***(46) (WJarvis)* 3-9-10 WRyan(1) (s.i.s: stumbled over 5f out: nvr nr to chal) 1¼ 10
2102[2] Colosse **(51)***(14) (MAJarvis)* 3-8-0 (5) NVarley(9) (lw: chsd ldrs tl rdn & wknd over 3f out).........8 11

10/11 Anonym (IRE) (op 6/4), **8/1** Shady Deed (USA), Dont Forget Curtis (IRE), Feinte, **9/1** Colosse, **10/1** Lady Sabina, **11/1** Carol's Dream (USA), **20/1** BELLATEENA, Jovie King (IRE), **25/1** Master Fiddler, **33/1** Oleron, CSF £210.52 CT £2,132.49 TOTE £40.00: £5.30 £2.50 £2.70 (£129.90) Trio not won; £217.32 to Windsor 10/7/95 OWNER Mr N. H. Gardner (NEWMARKET) BRED N. H. Gardner 11 Rn

2m 7.1 (4.60) SF: 19/40/11/25/8/-/-/6/-/4/-

WEIGHT FOR AGE 3yo-11lb

2280 'FAMILY NIGHT' (S) H'CAP (0-60) (3-Y.O+) (Class G) £2,070.00 (£570.00: £270.00) **1m 6f 15y** Stalls: Low GOING minus 0.39 sec per fur (F) 8-20 (8-22)

1607[8] **Romalito (41)***(54) (MBlanshard)* 5-9-1 RCochrane(15) (bhd: plld out & hdwy over 3f out: r.o to ld wl ins fnl f) —- **1**
1921[4] Leap in the Dark (IRE) **(33)***(45) (MissLCSiddall)* 6-8-7 GHind(4) (lw: chsd ldrs: 2nd st: led over 3f out tl hdd & nt qckn wl ins fnl f) ¾ **2**
649[17] Opera Buff (IRE) **(52)***(63) (MCPipe)* 4-9-9v(3) DRMcCabe(14) (a.p: 3rd st: ev ch 3f out: rdn & edgd lft over 1f out: nt r.o) 1 **3**
Star of the Glen **(30)***(37) (SCoathup)* 9-7-13 (5) AWhelan(12) (hdwy & 7th st: one pce fnl 2f) 4 **4**
2090[10] Run High **(42)***(45) (PMitchell)* 12-8-9 (7) DaneO'Neill(9) (lw: bdly hmpd after 3f: kpt on wl fnl 3f: nrst fin) 3 **5**
2129[8] Longcroft **(42)***(43) (KWHogg)* 3-7-10 (5) MBaird(1) (bhd: gd hdwy over 2f out: nrst fin) 2 **6**
1743* Goodbye Millie **(47)***(47)*(Fav)*(JLEyre)* 5-9-7v RLappin(11) (chsd ldrs: 6th st: rdn & no imp fnl 3f) ¾ **7**
2072[5] Remontant (IRE) **(43)***(37) (RHollinshead)* 3-8-2 ow1 DHarrison(2) (lw: bhd: hdwy 3f out: nvr rchd ldrs) 4 **8**
109[8] Prosequendo (USA) **(54)***(44) (GLMoore)* 8-10-0 AClark(8) (b.hind: hdwy 8f out: wknd 4f out) 5 **9**
Green's Seago (USA) **(34)***(20) (JAHarris)* 7-8-8 PRobinson(3) (nvr nr to chal) 3 **10**
1854[20] Lincoln Treasure (IRE) **(49)***(34) (MCChapman)* 4-9-9 MFenton(5) (prom: 4th st: wknd over 2f out) 1¼ **11**
1771[14] Esthal (IRE) **(41)***(20) (ABarrow)* 5-9-1 JQuinn(13) (lw: prom: 5th st: wknd 3f out) 5 **12**
2090[3] Verro (USA) **(25)** *(KBishop)* 8-7-6 (7)ow6 SLanigan(7) (prom 7f) nk **13**
1854[19] Britannia Mills **(35)***(10) (MCChapman)* 4-8-6 (3) PMcCabe(6) (led over 8f: sn wknd) 3 **14**
1881[6] Adjacent Too **(36)***(5) (CCElsey)* 3-7-9 ow2 DaleGibson(10) (in tch 4f) 4 **15**

LONG HANDICAP Adjacent Too 6-13

10/3 Goodbye Millie, **4/1** ROMALITO, **8/1** Leap in the Dark (IRE), Opera Buff (IRE), **9/1** Remontant (IRE), Longcroft, **14/1** Prosequendo (USA), **16/1** Verro (USA), Run High, **20/1** Lincoln Treasure (IRE), Esthal (IRE), **25/1** Star of the Glen, Adjacent Too, **33/1** Green's Seago (USA), Britannia Mills, CSF £34.92 CT £228.66 TOTE £5.10: £2.20 £1.80 £2.90 (£15.70) Trio £59.10 OWNER Mr C. McKenna (UPPER LAMBOURN) BRED The Duke of Marlborough 15 Rn

3m 5.2 (6.70) SF: 32/23/41/15/23/6/25/-/22/-/12/-/-/-/-

WEIGHT FOR AGE 3yo-15lb

No bid.

2281 BBC RADIO NOTTINGHAM CLAIMING STKS (2-Y.O) (Class F) £2,208.00 (£608.00: £288.00) **5f 13y** Stalls: Centre GOING minus 0.39 sec per fur (F) 8-50 (8-51)

2085[4] **Gagajulu (64)***(66) (PDEvans)* 2-8-7 GHind(5) (lw: prom: led 1f out: edgd lft & all out) —- **1**
*1090** Gi La High *(66?) (JBerry)* 2-8-7 JCarroll(4) (w ldr tl led over 1f out: sn hdd: jst failed) s.h **2**
*2146** Nameless **(64)***(55) (DJSCosgrove)* 2-8-4 (3) PMcCabe(1) (lw: led tl hung lft & hdd over 1f out) 3½ **3**
Impington (IRE) *(53)*(Fav)*(MAJarvis)* 2-8-9 PRobinson(3) (lengthy: unf: b.nr hind: dwlt: sn pushed along: nvr able to chal) 1¼ **4**

11/8 Impington (IRE), **9/4** GAGAJULU (op Evens), **7/2** Nameless, **5/1** Gi La High, CSF £11.09 TOTE £3.40: (£4.80) OWNER Mr R. F. F. Mason (WELSHPOOL) BRED Mrs P. E. Bell 4 Rn

60.0 secs (1.30) SF: 36/36/25/23

2282 'FUN FOR ALL AGES' LIMITED STKS (0-55) (3-Y.O) (Class F) £2,208.00 (£608.00: £288.00) **1m 1f 213y** Stalls: Low GOING: minus 0.39 sec per fur (G) 9-20 (9-21)

2138[2] **Hadabet (53)** *(MissJacquelineDoyle)* 3-9-0 JQuinn(1) (lw: chsd ldr: 2nd st: led 4f out: rdn out) —- **1**
1452[7] Silktail (IRE) **(50)** *(JohnBerry)* 3-8-9 PRobinson(4) (hld up: plld out & gd hdwy 2f out: nt rch ldrs) nk **2**
1128[11] Silver Rondo (USA) **(55)** *(LordHuntingdon)* 3-8-9 DHarrison(3) (lw: chsd ldrs: 5th st: rdn over 2f out: sn ev ch: nt qckn fnl f) 1¾ **3**
1970[7] Ruddigore **(48)** *(RHannon)* 3-9-0 RPerham(9) (chsd ldrs tl lost pl 5f out: r.o fnl 3f) 6 **4**
Maziere **(54)** *(MJHeaton-Ellis)* 3-8-9 WWoods(5) (led: sn clr: hdd 4f out: sn btn) 1¼ **5**
2132[2] Kama Simba **(61)** (Fav)*(NACallaghan)* 3-9-2 RCochrane(7) (lw: s.i.s: hdwy over 2f out: nvr rchd ldrs) 5 **6**
*1568** Top Fella (USA) **(53)** *(WAO'Gorman)* 3-9-0v EmmaO'Gorman(2) (prom: 4th st: wknd over 2f out) 2 **7**
1974[7] Chastleton **(38)** *(MRChannon)* 3-8-11 CandyMorris(8) (lw: hdwy: 6th & rn wd st: sn wknd) 1¾ **8**

1813[3] Drumochter **(54)** *(DMorley)* 3-9-0 MFenton(10) (drppd rr 5f out: bhd after)....hd **9**
1645[9] Specialize **(44)** *(KRBurke)* 3-9-0 AClark(6) (hdwy & 3rd st: wknd 3f out)....1¾ **10**

10/3 Kama Simba, **4/1** Drumochter, **13/2** HADABET, **7/1** Silktail (IRE), Silver Rondo (USA), Top Fella (USA), **12/1** Ruddigore, **25/1** Maziere, Chastleton, Specialize, CSF £45.26 TOTE £6.20: £1.50 £2.00 £3.20 (£34.00) Trio £110.40 OWNER The Basics (LAMBOURN) BRED Stetchworth Park Stud Ltd 10 Rn 2m 8.7 (6.20) SF: -/-/-/-/-/-/-/-/-/-

T/Plpt: £1,017.10 (11.72 Tckts). T/Qdpt: £57.70 (1 Tckt). DK

2239-SANDOWN (R-H)
Saturday July 8th (Rnd Good to firm, 5f Good, Good to firm patches)
WEATHER: very hot WIND: almost nil

2283 E.B.F. PADDOCK MAIDEN STKS (2-Y.O) (Class D) £4,260.00 (£1,290.00: £630.00: £300.00) 7f 16y Stalls: High GOING minus 0.17 sec (GF) 2-15 (2-17)

1485[4] **Mawwal (USA)** *(84+) (RWArmstrong)* 2-9-0 WCarson(6) (lw: mde virtually all: comf)....— **1**
Kings Witness (USA) *(76) (WJHaggas)* 2-9-0 KDarley(9) (unf: scope: bkwd: 6th st: chsd wnr over 1f out: no imp)....3½ **2**
Committal (IRE) *(72) (JHMGosden)* 2-9-0 LDettori(10) (str: scope: lw: 2nd st: ev ch over 2f out: one pce)....2 **3**
Night Watch (USA) *(70) (IABalding)* 2-9-0 TQuinn(1) (w'like: scope: bit bkwd: rdn 3f out: hdwy over 1f out: r.o one pce)....¾ **4**
1903[3] Double Agent *(69)*(Fav)*(MJohnston)* 2-9-0 MJKinane(8) (lw: 3rd st: rdn over 2f out: one pce)½ **5**
Labeed (USA) *(61) (MajorWRHern)* 2-9-0 AMcGlone(7) (w'like: scope: bit bkwd: nvr nr to chal)....3½ **6**
Top of The Stack *(59) (RHannon)* 2-9-0 RPerham(4) (str: scope: bit bkwd: rdn 3f out: nvr nrr)....¾ **7**
1715[5] Warbrook *(59) (IABalding)* 2-9-0 WRSwinburn(11) (lw: 5th st: wknd over 2f out)....hd **8**
1903[4] Urgent Swift *(56) (APJarvis)* 2-9-0 BThomson(5) (lw: a bhd)....1¼ **9**
1597[7] Classic Victory *(27) (SCWilliams)* 2-9-0 AMackay(3) (plld hrd: 4th st: wknd over 2f out)....13 **10**
1662[11] Oblomov *(13) (GLewis)* 2-9-0 PatEddery(2) (bhd fnl 5f)....6 **11**

3/1 Double Agent, **7/2** MAWWAL (USA), **5/1** Warbrook, **7/1** Committal (IRE) (op 3/1), **10/1** Night Watch (USA) (7/1-12/1), Kings Witness (USA), **16/1** Labeed (USA), **33/1** Top of The Stack, **40/1** Classic Victory, **50/1** Urgent Swift, Oblomov, CSF £32.23 TOTE £4.10: £1.40 £2.60 £1.80 (£27.50) Trio £38.10 OWNER Mr Hamdan Al Maktoum (NEWMARKET) BRED Shadwell Estate Co., Ltd. and Shadwell Farm Inc. 11 Rn 1m 29.84 (3.24) SF: 47/39/35/33/32/24/22/22/19/-/-

2284 COMMONWEALTH H'CAP (0-85) (3-Y.O+) (Class D) £7,360.00 (£2,230.00: £1,090.00: £520.00) 2m 78y Stalls: High GOING minus 0.17 sec per fur (GF) 2-45 (2-50)

1674[3] **Shining High (76)***(92+) (JLDunlop)* 3-8-5 KDarley(3) (mde all: qcknd over 3f out: r.o wl)....— **1**
1929[3] Paradise Navy **(72)***(83)*(Fav)*(CREgerton)* 6-9-4 PatEddery(4) (swtg: hdwy 8f out: 6th st: rdn over 3f out: chsd wnr over 1f out: no imp)....5 **2**
931[8] Tudor Island **(75)***(86) (CEBrittain)* 6-9-7 BDoyle(2) (lw: chsd wnr 8f out tl over 1f out: one pce)....s.h **3**
1281* Red Bustaan **(84)***(93) (ACStewart)* 3-8-13 MJKinane(7) (swtg: lost pl 6f out: rallied over 2f out: r.o one pce)....1¾ **4**
1794[2] Requested **(59)***(68) (PBurgoyne)* 8-8-5 TQuinn(9) (hdwy over 6f out: 3rd st: rdn over 3f out: one pce)....s.h **5**
1623[2] Sea Freedom **(70)***(79) (GBBalding)* 4-9-2 JWilliams(1) (5th st: one pce fnl 3f)....s.h **6**
1621[7] Robingo (IRE) **(82)***(87) (MrsLAMurphy)* 6-10-0b BThomson(8) (a bhd)....4 **7**
1840[12] Nawar (FR) **(78)***(78) (JRJenkins)* 5-9-10 LDettori(10) (swtg: a bhd)....5 **8**
1929[12] Fujiyama Crest (IRE) **(67)***(53) (MRStoute)* 3-7-10vow1 WCarson(5) (chsd wnr over 8f: 4th st: wknd over 3f out)....14 **9**
1657[6] Coleridge **(47)***(19) (JJSheehan)* 7-7-2b(5) MBaird(6) (prom over 9f)....15 **10**

LONG HANDICAP Coleridge 7-4

4/1 Paradise Navy, **5/1** Red Bustaan, Requested, **6/1** Fujiyama Crest (IRE) (4/1-13/2), **7/1** SHINING HIGH, Tudor Island, **8/1** Sea Freedom (5/1-9/1), **20/1** Nawar (FR), **33/1** Coleridge, **66/1** Robingo (IRE), CSF £31.61 CT £182.28 TOTE £10.80: £2.60 £1.40 £2.60 (£22.60) Trio £89.50 OWNER Mrs Mark Burrell (ARUNDEL) BRED Mrs M. Burrell 10 Rn
3m 36.15 (6.15) SF: 47/55/58/48/40/51/59/50/8/-
WEIGHT FOR AGE 3yo-17lb

2285 ADVANCED MICRO DEVICES SPRINT STKS (Listed) (3-Y.O+) (Class A) £13,875.00 (£4,200.00: £2,050.00: £975.00)
5f 6y Stalls: Low GOING minus 0.29 sec per fur (GF) 3-20 (3-26)

1480[6] **Bunty Boo (101)***(106) (RHannon)* 6-8-12 MJKinane(5) (lw: mde all: drvn out) ......— 1
1765* Saint Express **(101)***(109) (MrsMReveley)* 5-9-3 KDarley(10) (lw: a.p: hrd rdn over 1f out: unable qckn) ......¾ 2
1848[13] Warning Star **(100)***(100) (BWHills)* 3-8-6 WCarson(6) (outpcd: hdwy over 1f out: r.o) 1 3
1487[10] Lennox Lewis **(99)***(102) (APJarvis)* 3-8-11 BDoyle(8) (hld up: rdn over 2f out: r.o one pce)......1 4
1924[2] Double Quick (IRE) **(102)***(100)*(Fav)*(MJohnston)* 3-8-10 LDettori(3) (lw: a.p: ev ch over 1f out: one pce) ......nk 5
1848[16] Magnificent Devil (USA) **(95)***(96) (JWWatts)* 3-8-11 BThomson(7) (lw: hld up: rdn over 3f out: one pce) 1¾ 6
1870[5] Welsh Mist **(94)***(89) (RBoss)* 4-9-2 PatEddery(9) (swtg: spd over 3f) 1¾ 7
1795* Loch Patrick **(106)***(88)*(Fav)*(LJHolt)* 5-9-3 AMcGlone(1) (lw: nt clr run on ins over 2f out: stumbled 2f out: nvr nr to chal) ......¾ 8
2150[3] Hello Mister **(96)***(84) (JO'Donoghue)* 4-9-3 PMcCabe(2) (bhd fnl 2f) 1¼ 9
1572a[7] Great Deeds **(105)***(78) (MRChannon)* 4-9-5 TQuinn(11) (bhd fnl 3f) 2½ 10
1896[9] Mistertopogigo (IRE) **(106)** *(WSCunningham)* 5-9-7 WRSwinburn(4) (Withdrawn not under Starter's orders: lame at s) ...... W

3/1 Double Quick (IRE), Loch Patrick, **13/2** Mistertopogigo (IRE), Saint Express, **7/1** Welsh Mist (op 12/1), **14/1** Warning Star, **16/1** Great Deeds, **20/1** BUNTY BOO, Lennox Lewis, **33/1** Hello Mister, Magnificent Devil (USA), CSF £105.59 TOTE £16.10: £2.80 £2.10 £3.60 (£66.00) Trio £509.10 OWNER Mrs R. C. Mayall (MARLBOROUGH) BRED Mrs J. McMahon 10 Rn
60.0 secs (0.20) SF: 69/72/57/59/57/53/52/51/47/41/-
WEIGHT FOR AGE 3yo-6lb

2286 CORAL-ECLIPSE STKS (Gp 1) (3-Y.O+) (Class A) £154,560.00 (£57,768.00: £27,684.00: £11,988.00)
1m 2f 7y Stalls: High GOING minus 0.17 sec per fur (GF) 4-05 (4-07)

Halling (USA) *(128) (SbinSuroor)* 4-9-7 WRSwinburn(3) (lw: mde all: rdn 2f out: r.o wl) ......— 1
2044a[2] Singspiel (IRE) **(109)***(128) (MRStoute)* 3-8-10 MJKinane(1) (chsd wnr: rdn over 2f out: r.o wl ins fnl f) ......nk 2
606a* Red Bishop (USA) *(123) (SbinSuroor)* 7-9-7 LDettori(7) (swtg: 3rd st: rdn over 2f out: unable qckn) 3 3
1609[7] Environment Friend **(112)***(116) (CEBrittain)* 7-9-7 BDoyle(8) (s.s: 5th st: rdn over 2f out: one pce) 4 4
1836[2] Eltish (USA) **(120)***(116)*(Fav)*(HRACecil)* 3-8-10 PatEddery(6) (swtg: 8th st: nt clr run on ins over 2f out: hmpd on ins over 1f out: nvr nr to chal) ......hd 5
1836* Muhtarram (USA) **(123)***(113) (JHMGosden)* 6-9-7 WCarson(4) (7th st: nt clr run over 2f out: hdwy over 1f out: 4th & btn whn wnt lame & virtually p.u ins fnl f) 2 6
1708a[2] Prince of Andros (USA) **(113)***(109) (DRLoder)* 5-9-7 KDarley(5) (6th st: wknd over 1f out)....2½ 7
1712a[3] Tryphosa (IRE) *(98) (AndreasWoehler)* 3-8-7 ABoschert(2) (unf: scope: 4th st: wknd 2f out) ..5 8

100/30 Eltish (USA), **4/1** Muhtarram (USA), Red Bishop (USA), **9/2** Singspiel (IRE), **7/1** HALLING (USA), **9/1** Prince of Andros (USA), **16/1** Tryphosa (IRE), **25/1** Environment Friend, CSF £34.98 TOTE £7.30: £2.20 £1.40 £1.90 (£12.20) OWNER Godolphin (NEWMARKET) BRED Cyril Humphries 8 Rn
2m 5.32 (1.02) SF: 84/73/79/72/61/69/65/43
WEIGHT FOR AGE 3yo-11lb

2287 SANDOWN RATED STKS H'CAP (0-100) (3-Y.O+) (Class B) £12,381.60 (£4,634.40: £2,267.20: £976.00: £438.00: £222.80)
1m 14y Stalls: High GOING minus 0.17 sec per fur (GF) 4-40 (4-43)

1851[28] **Lap of Luxury (100)***(110) (WJarvis)* 6-9-7 BThomson(6) (lw: hdwy over 2f out: rdn over 1f out: led ins fnl f: r.o wl) ......— 1
1926[6] Khayrapour (IRE) **(86)***(95) (BJMeehan)* 5-8-7b PatEddery(10) (lw: nt clr run over 1f out: hdwy & swtchd lft ins fnl f: r.o wl) ......½ 2
1500[2] Far Fetched (IRE) **(92)***(100) (LordHuntingdon)* 3-8-4 LDettori(8) (lw: 3rd st: rdn over 1f out: ev ch ins fnl f: unable qckn) ......nk 3
1839[2] Beauchamp Jazz **(100)***(107)*(Fav)*(JLDunlop)* 3-8-12 MJKinane(2) (lw: led tl ins fnl f: one pce)½ 4
2030[W] Sue's Return **(88)***(95) (APJarvis)* 3-7-7 (7) CAdamson(7) (6th st: rdn over 1f out: n.m.r on ins ins fnl f: one pce) ......nk 5
2080* Air Commodore (IRE) **(97)***(104)*(Fav)*(PFICole)* 4-9-4 TQuinn(5) (hdwy & nt clr run over 1f out: swtchd lft: r.o one pce) ......hd 6

1926[11] Embankment (IRE) **(86)***(92) (RHannon)* 5-8-7 BDoyle(9) (4th st: rdn over 2f out: ev ch over 1f out: one pce) ....hd 7
1728[3] Classic Sky (IRE) **(99)***(101) (BHanbury)* 4-9-6 WCarson(3) (5th st: nt clr run over 2f out: one pce) 2½ 8
Shot At Love (IRE) **(86)***(87) (CACyzer)* 4-8-7 AMcGlone(1) (2nd st: wknd over 1f out) ....nk 9
LONG HANDICAP Khayrapour (IRE) 8-4 Embankment (IRE) 8-6 Shot At Love (IRE) 8-1

7/2 Air Commodore (IRE), Beauchamp Jazz, **4/1** Khayrapour (IRE) (3/1-9/2), **5/1** Far Fetched (IRE), **6/1** Classic Sky (IRE), **8/1** Embankment (IRE), **14/1** LAP OF LUXURY, **25/1** Sue's Return, **40/1** Shot At Love (IRE), CSF £65.93 CT £296.66 TOTE £16.50: £3.50 £2.00 £1.50 (£30.10) Trio £86.50 OWNER Mr I. C. Hill-Wood (NEWMARKET) BRED Langham Hall Bloodstock 9 Rn
1m 43.4 (4.20) SF: 49/34/30/37/25/43/31/40/26
WEIGHT FOR AGE 3yo-9lb

2288 VICTORIA AMATEUR TURF CLUB H'CAP (0-95) (3-Y.O+) (Class C)
£5,784.00 (£1,752.00: £856.00: £408.00)
5f 6y Stalls: Low GOING minus 0.29 sec per fur (GF) 5-10 (5-15)

1924[3] **That Man Again (83)***(94)*(Fav)*(GLewis)* 3-9-0b PatEddery(8) (lw: mde virtually all: hrd rdn over 1f out: r.o wl) ....— 1
1895[5] Master of Passion **(81)***(84) (JMPEustace)* 6-9-4 MTebbutt(7) (hld up: ev ch over 1f out: unable qckn) 2½ 2
1815[6] Agwa **(74)***(76) (RJO'Sullivan)* 6-8-11 BDoyle(13) (rdn & hdwy over 1f out: r.o) ....½ 3
2130[5] Magic Orb **(78)***(79) (JLHarris)* 5-9-1 LDettori(5) (b: hdwy over 1f out: r.o) ....nk 4
2079[4] Robellion **(69)***(69) (DWPArbuthnot)* 4-8-6v TQuinn(11) (b: hld up: rdn over 2f out: one pce) ....nk 5
1614[10] Colway Rake **(70)***(69) (JWWatts)* 4-8-7 WCarson(9) (lw: a.p: ev ch over 1f out: one pce) ....hd 6
2079[3] Jobie **(65)***(64) (BWHills)* 5-8-2 AMcGlone(1) (swtg: hdwy over 1f out: r.o) ....hd 7
2060[7] Takadou (IRE) **(85)***(79) (MissLCSiddall)* 4-9-8 WRSwinburn(12) (nvr nrr) 1½ 8
1614[2] Thatcherella **(79)***(73) (MajorDNChappell)* 4-9-2 BThomson(10) (a.p: ev ch over 1f out: wknd fnl f) ....hd 9
1673[7] Evening Falls **(58)***(52) (CJames)* 4-7-2 (7) CAdamson(6) (hld up: rdn over 2f out: wknd over 1f out) ....hd 10
1354[12] Bryan Robson (USA) **(64)***(57) (GBBalding)* 4-7-10 (5) PPMurphy(2) (a bhd) ....nk 11
2013[5] Green Golightly (USA) **(65)***(55) (DAWilson)* 4-8-2 NGwilliams(3) (bhd fnl 2f) ....¾ 12
2027[5] Another Jade **(68)***(57) (APJarvis)* 5-8-0 (5) HKYim(4) (lw: hld up: rdn over 2f out: wknd over 1f out) ....nk 13
1895[16] No Extras (IRE) **(89)***(70) (GLMoore)* 5-9-7 (5) CChoi(14) (outpcd) 2½ 14

9/2 THAT MAN AGAIN, **5/1** Thatcherella, **11/2** Magic Orb, **7/1** Takadou (IRE), Jobie, **15/2** Master of Passion, **11/1** Colway Rake (8/1-12/1), **16/1** Another Jade, **20/1** Robellion, Agwa, Bryan Robson (USA), No Extras (IRE), **40/1** Evening Falls, **50/1** Green Golightly (USA), CSF £36.55 CT £571.77 TOTE £4.00: £2.00 £2.80 £4.60 (£18.50) Trio £530.10 OWNER Mr M. Jameson (EPSOM) BRED T. P. Milne and M. Jameson 14 Rn 60.04 secs (0.24) SF: 70/66/58/61/51/51/46/61/55/34/39/37/39/52
WEIGHT FOR AGE 3yo-6lb

2289 SPINAL INJURIES ASSOCIATION H'CAP (0-80) (3-Y.O+) (Class D)
£4,515.00 (£1,365.00: £665.00: £315.00)
1m 3f 91y Stalls: High GOING minus 0.17 sec per fur (GF) 5-40 (5-44)

1908[2] **Bookcase (63)***(73) (DRCElsworth)* 8-9-0 (5) AProcter(4) (lw: hdwy over 1f out: str run fnl f: led last strides) ....— 1
1831[2] Fairy Knight **(74)***(84) (RHannon)* 3-9-4 PatEddery(1) (lw: 2nd st: led over 1f out tl ins fnl f: hrd rdn: r.o) ....hd 2
1612[9] Dancing Sensation (USA) **(64)***(74)*(Fav)*(RAkehurst)* 8-9-6 LDettori(11) (4th st: led over 3f out tl over 1f out: led ins fnl f: hrd rdn: hdd last strides) ....s.h 3
1757[3] Broughtons Formula **(48)***(57) (WJMusson)* 5-8-4 BDoyle(7) (lw: rdn over 2f out: hdwy over 1f out: r.o wl ins fnl f) ....¾ 4
1674[5] Uncharted Waters **(58)***(64) (CACyzer)* 4-9-0b MTebbutt(3) (lw: 5th st: hrd rdn over 2f out: one pce) 1¾ 5
1747[2] Lovely Lyca **(80)***(85) (JWHills)* 3-9-10 JWilliams(5) (lw: 6th st: rdn over 2f out: one pce) 1¼ 6
2002[5] Thrower **(46)***(50) (WMBrisbourne)* 4-7-9 (7) MartinDwyer(9) (lw: led 8f: wknd fnl f) ....nk 7
1757[8] Allesca **(62)***(64) (MDIUsher)* 5-8-11 (7) CAdamson(8) (b: gd hdwy 4f out: 3rd & rn wd st: wknd over 1f out) 1¾ 8
2007* Rock The Barney (IRE) **(56)***(57)*(Fav)*(PBurgoyne)* 6-8-12 TQuinn(2) (lw: hdwy & nt clr run over 1f out: nt clr run & eased whn btn ins last) ....nk 9
1612[8] Tondres (USA) **(70)***(66) (RIngram)* 4-9-12b AMcGlone(12) (lw: bhd fnl 3f) 4 10

9/2 Rock The Barney (IRE) (op 3/1), Dancing Sensation (USA), **11/2** Fairy Knight, Broughtons Formula, **6/1** BOOKCASE, **13/2** Lovely Lyca, **8/1** Uncharted Waters, **10/1** Allesca, **20/1** Tondres (USA), **33/1** Thrower, CSF £37.72 CT £150.76 TOTE £8.90: £2.50 £2.40 £1.50 (£13.40) Trio £21.90 OWNER Adept (80) Ltd (WHITCOMBE) BRED The Sussex Stud 10 Rn

2m 33.23 (11.53) SF: 10/9/11/-/1/10/-/1/-/3

WEIGHT FOR AGE 3yo-12lb

T/Jkpt: Not won; £33,030.80 to Windsor 10/7/95. T/Plpt: £681.50 (91.35 Tckts). T/Qdpt: £238.50 (3.3 Tckts). AK

2140-WOLVERHAMPTON (L-H)
Saturday July 8th (Standard)

WEATHER: sunny WIND: almost nil

2290 TRIBUNE LIMITED STKS (0-55) (4-Y.O+) (Class F) £2,519.00 (£694.00: £329.00) 7f (Fibresand) Stalls: High GOING: 0.26 sec per fur (SLW) 7-00 (7-01)

*2141** **My Gallery (IRE) (50)***(62)*(Fav)*(ABailey)* 4-8-6 (3) SSanders(1) (lw: chsd ldr: led over 2f out: r.o wl) — **1**
2137[12] Frisky Miss (IRE) **(53)***(50) (KOCunningham-Brown)* 4-8-6 JWeaver(5) (a.p: 2nd st: rdn & one pce fnl f) 4 **2**
2073[4] Indiahra **(52)***(45) (RHollinshead)* 4-8-6 GCarter(10) (lw: dwlt: wl bhd: rdn & hdwy 2f out: no imp fnl f) 2 **3**
1760[11] Tyrone Flyer **(54)***(39) (GFierro)* 6-8-4 (7) ADaly(4) (rdr lost iron leaving stalls: plld hrd: led tl hdd over 2f out: 3rd & wknd ent st) 5 **4**
1344[13] Petonellajill **(53)***(30) (JGMO'Shea)* 5-8-6 VSlattery(6) (lw: in tch: 4th & rdn st: wknd over 1f out) 1½ **5**
Window Display **(48)***(33) (MrsNMacauley)* 4-8-4 (7) AmandaSanders(9) (bit bkwd: b: hld up: effrt & 5th st: wknd appr fnl f) 1¼ **6**
Star Performer (IRE) **(55)***(26) (MrsMReveley)* 4-8-11 KDarley(3) (bit bkwd: hld up & bhd: rdn & effrt ½-wy: sn btn) 3 **7**
2073[12] Quinzii Martin **(53)***(9) (DHaydnJones)* 7-9-3 AMackay(8) (nvr nr ldrs: eased over 1f out) 10 **8**
2074[7] Marsh Arab **(37)** *(JBalding)* 4-8-11v NAdams(7) (b: hld up towards rr: lost tch over 2f out: t.o) 9 **9**
Technological Risk **(35)** *(DBurchell)* 4-8-11 RPrice(2) (swtg: prom to ½-wy: t.o) 2 **10**

6/4 MY GALLERY (IRE), **3/1** Indiahra (op 5/1), **7/1** Frisky Miss (IRE), Star Performer (IRE) (op 9/2), **10/1** Petonellajill, **12/1** Tyrone Flyer (op 8/1), Quinzii Martin (op 8/1), **20/1** Window Display, **25/1** Technological Risk, **33/1** Marsh Arab, CSF £13.25 TOTE £2.40: £1.50 £1.90 £1.50 (£8.10) Trio £8.00 OWNER Mr Gordon Mytton (TARPORLEY) BRED East Riding Sack and Paper Co 10 Rn

1m 30.8 (6.80) SF: 35/23/18/12/3/6/-/-/-/-

2291 TIPTON BRIGHT BAR CLAIMING STKS (3-Y.O+) (Class F) £2,519.00 (£694.00: £329.00) 1m 100y (Fibresand) Stalls: Low GOING: 0.26 sec (SLW) 7-30 (7-30)

2142[3] **No Submission (USA) (68)***(76) (DWChapman)* 9-9-5 ACulhane(9) (lw: chsd ldrs: rdn to ld over 2f out: sn jnd: r.o gamely) — **1**
1988[6] Bentico **(73)***(77) (MrsNMacauley)* 6-9-7b JWeaver(13) (hld up: hdwy over 3f out: 2nd st: ev ch wl over 1f out: rdn & no ex wl ins fnl f) ½ **2**
1951[5] Northern Celadon (IRE) **(67)***(60) (MJHeaton-Ellis)* 4-9-7 KDarley(3) (led after 1f: hdd over 2f out: 3rd st: sn wknd) 9 **3**
1969[8] Robsera (IRE) **(72)***(62) (GLewis)* 4-9-9b SWhitworth(10) (prom: drvn & 5th st: grad wknd) s.h **4**
2142[2] Wentbridge Lad (IRE) **(82)***(57)*(Fav)*(PDEvans)* 5-9-6 (3) SSanders(6) (lw: hdwy to chse ldrs ½-wy: 4th & rdn st: sn wknd) 2½ **5**
528[4] David James' Girl **(65)***(41) (ABailey)* 3-8-1 GCarter(11) (chsd ldrs 4f: 6th btn st) 1¾ **6**
Patrice *(27) (MrsLAMurphy)* 4-8-9 GDuffield(2) (bit bkwd: bhd fr ½-wy) 7 **7**
1647[6] Greek Night Out (IRE) **(33)***(19) (MrsVAAconley)* 4-8-8v RPrice(4) (prom tl wknd qckly ½-wy) 3½ **8**
Bold Appeal (IRE) *(22) (PWChapple-Hyam)* 3-8-3 (7)ow2 RHavlin(1) (w'like: s.i.s: sn pushed along: effrt ½-wy: sn btn) 3 **9**
2072[6] Nordross **(26)** *(JHPeacock)* 7-8-0b(5)ow1 VHalliday(12) (swtg: dwlt: a bhd: t.o) 6 **10**
1771[16] Pats Folly **(22)** *(FJYardley)* 4-8-3 (3) SDrowne(7) (led after 1f: prom tl wknd over 3f out: t.o) 11 **11**
Phlirty *(RFJohnsonHoughton)* 3-8-9 TSprake(8) (w'like: bit bkwd: dwlt: a bhd: t.o) ½ **12**
Fair Rose *(JGFitzGerald)* 4-8-5 ow1 DHolland(5) (bit bkwd: prom 3f: t.o) 11 **13**

7/4 Wentbridge Lad (IRE) (op 11/4), **11/2** David James' Girl, **7/1** Bentico (4/1-8/1), Bold Appeal (IRE) (3/1-8/1), **8/1** Northern Celadon (IRE) (tchd 12/1), **9/1** NO SUBMISSION (USA), **10/1** Phlirty, **12/1** Robsera (IRE) (op 8/1), **20/1** Fair Rose, Greek Night Out (IRE), **33/1** Patrice, Pats Folly, **50/1** Nordross, CSF £71.15 TOTE £6.50: £2.10 £1.50 £1.30 (£19.50) Trio £16.30 OWNER Mr T. S. Redman (YORK) BRED Mr. Francis X. Weber 13 Rn 1m 51.9 (7.90) SF: 48/49/32/34/29/4/-/-/-/-/-/-/-

WEIGHT FOR AGE 3yo-9lb

2292

MALCOLM J. TAYLOR H'CAP (0-70) (3-Y.O+) (Class E) £3,502.40 (£1,047.20: £501.60: £228.80)
1m 1f 79y (Fibresand) Stalls: High GOING: 0.26 sec per fur (SLW) 8-00 (8-00)

*894*7 **Asmarina (39)***(48+) (SRBowring)* 5-7-13b StephenDavies(6) (hld up: hdwy 3f out: 4th st: rdn to ld over 1f out: r.o) — 1
*1955*6 Fen Terrier **(55)***(57) (WJHaggas)* 3-8-5 KDarley(4) (chsd ldrs fr ½-wy: rdn to ld 2f out: hdd over 1f out: kpt on one pce) 4 2
*1209*9 Mam'zelle Angot **(63)***(64) (AHarrison)* 5-9-9 TIves(8) (b.hind: hld up in tch: rdn & hdwy 3f out: 2nd st: one pce) ½ 3
*605*7 Shansi (IRE) **(42)***(37) (MDIUsher)* 4-8-2v RStreet(3) (led tl rdn & hdd 2f out: 2nd st: wknd fnl f) 4 4
*2076*2 Brackenthwaite **(60)***(49) (LRLloyd-James)* 5-9-6v TWilliams(9) (hld up: rdn & effrt 3f out: sn btn: poor 6th st) 3 5
2010 9 Waldo **(62)***(45) (LordHuntingdon)* 4-9-8v JWeaver(11) (hld up & bhd: hdwy 4f out: rdn & 5th st: sn btn) 3½ 6
1484 2 Aljawab (USA) **(68)***(31)*(Fav)*(JLDunlop)* 4-10-0 GCarter(5) (lw: hld up: hdwy to chse ldrs ½-wy: btn over 2f out: eased) 12 7
2139 7 Dynamis (IRE) **(34)** *(KOCunningham-Brown)* 4-7-8 NAdams(12) (plld hrd: bhd: effrt ½-wy: sn btn: t.o) 10 8
*1762*2 Big Chance **(34)** *(WJMusson)* 6-7-8 NKennedy(2) (chsd ldr to ½-wy: wknd qckly: t.o) 3 9
1858 12 Shareoftheaction **(57)** *(MrsAMNaughton)* 4-9-0be(3) SDrowne(7) (lost tch ½-wy: t.o) 8 10
1933* King Curan (USA) **(66)** *(ABailey)* 4-9-12b AMackay(1) (chsd ldrs 4f: wknd qckly: t.o) 25 11
1680 5 Lochore **(53)** *(MrsVAAconley)* 5-8-13 ACulhane(13) (a bhd: t.o whn p.u over 4f out) P
*1950** Studio Thirty **(53)** *(RHollinshead)* 3-7-10 (7)ow5 AEddery(10) (reard & uns rdr leaving stalls) U

3/1 Aljawab (USA), **11/2** Fen Terrier, King Curan (USA) (4/1-6/1), **9/1** Waldo, Studio Thirty, **10/1** Brackenthwaite, **12/1** Big Chance, ASMARINA, **14/1** Mam'zelle Angot, **20/1** Lochore, Shareoftheaction, **25/1** Dynamis (IRE), Shansi (IRE), CSF £73.11 CT £859.20 TOTE £22.50: £3.10 £1.90 £7.60 (£38.00) Trio not won; £220.01 to Windsor 10/7/95 OWNER Mr S. R. Bowring (EDWINSTOWE) BRED S. R. Bowring 13 Rn 2m 4.8 (8.80) SF: 30/29/46/19/31/27/13/-/-/-/-/-
WEIGHT FOR AGE 3yo-10lb

OFFICIAL EXPLANATION Aljawab: no explanation offered and routine test was ordered.

2293

LIFTING GEAR & TOOL HIRE H'CAP (0-70) (3-Y.O+) (Class E) £3,359.40 (£1,003.20: £479.60: £217.80)
1m 4f (Fibresand) Stalls: High GOING: 0.26 sec per fur (SLW) 8-30 (8-34)

*2072*3 **Palacegate Jo (IRE) (50)***(59) (DWChapman)* 4-9-2 ACulhane(4) (lw: hld up in tch: led over 3f out: clr 2f out: drvn out) — 1
*1884*4 Tovarich **(56)***(64) (GLewis)* 4-9-8 SWhitworth(2) (swtg: dwlt: hld up towrds rr: rdn & hdwy 3f out: 3rd st: kpt on fnl f) ¾ 2
*1955** Barti-Ddu **(55)***(63)*(Fav)*(SCWilliams)* 4-9-4 (3) JTate(1) (led 4f: drvn along over 3f out: outpcd 2f out: 2nd st: styd on fnl f) hd 3
Kierchem (IRE) **(60)***(63) (RFFisher)* 4-9-12 GDuffield(7) (sn wl bhd: kpt on fr 3f out: 6th st: nvr nrr) 3½ 4
1680 3 All on **(50)***(49) (JHetherton)* 4-9-2 NKennedy(12) (plld hrd: prom: 4th & rdn st: sn btn) 3 5
2007 8 Dusty Point (IRE) **(60)***(58) (JPearce)* 5-9-12 GBardwell(3) (b: sn bhd: kpt on u.p fr over 3f out: nvr nr ldrs) 1 6
1635 5 Children's Choice (IRE) **(60)***(57) (PJMcBride)* 4-9-12 TIves(11) (lw: chsd ldrs: led after 4f: hdd over 4f out: 5th & btn st) 1 7
*1955*7 Winn's Pride (IRE) **(40)***(35) (RHollinshead)* 4-8-6 GCarter(8) (wl bhd: mod late hdwy: n.d) 1¼ 8
1643 12 Fearless Wonder **(56)***(50) (MrsMReveley)* 4-9-1b(7) SCopp(6) (bhd: rmndrs after 3f: no imp) ¾ 9
Grand Applause (IRE) **(57)***(35) (MPMuggeridge)* 5-9-9 TWilliams(10) (bit bkwd: bhd fr ½-wy: t.o) 12 10
1442 5 Kristal Breeze **(48)** *(WRMuir)* 3-7-12 (3) SSanders(9) (prom tl rdn & wknd over 3f out: t.o) 25 11
World Express (IRE) **(62)***(6) (BRMillman)* 5-10-0 DHolland(5) (in tch tl wknd ½-wy: t.o) ½ 12

10/3 Barti-Ddu, **8/1** PALACEGATE JO (IRE) (6/1-9/1), Tovarich (op 5/1), Children's Choice (IRE), All on, Dusty Point (IRE) (op 4/1), **10/1** Grand Applause (IRE), **12/1** Fearless Wonder (op 7/1), World Express (IRE) (op 7/1), **16/1** Winn's Pride (IRE), Kristal Breeze, **40/1** Kierchem (IRE), CSF £63.34 CT £23.59 TOTE £8.10: £3.00 £2.50 £1.60 (£26.90) Trio £12.50 OWNER Mr David Chapman (YORK) BRED Brendan and Sheila Powell 12 Rn
2m 46.0 (15.00) SF: 23/28/27/27/13/22/21/-/14/-/-/-
WEIGHT FOR AGE 3yo-13lb

2294 WOLVERHAMPTON CONFERENCE CLASSIC (S) STKS (2-Y.O) (Class G) £2,243.00 (£618.00: £293.00)
7f (Fibresand) Stalls: High GOING: 0.26 sec per fur (SLW) 9-00 (9-01)

2075[4] **Red Simba (57)***(60+)*(Fav)*(JBerry)* 2-8-11 GCarter(6) (chsd ldr: led over 2f out: sn clr: v.easily)......— 1
1272[5] Euskara *(32) (MDIUsher)* 2-8-6 RStreet(2) (b: bhd: hdwy 3f out: 3rd st: no ch w wnr)......10 2
2153[5] February **(55)***(32) (MRChannon)* 2-8-6 DHolland(1) (led: drvn & hdd over 2f out: 2nd st: sn outpcd)......nk 3
2035[8] Rowhome **(40)***(27) (MRChannon)* 2-8-11 GBardwell(3) (sn rdn & outpcd: hdwy over 2f out: 4th st: one pce)......4 4
1077[7] In A Tizzy *(19) (PCHaslam)* 2-8-6v JWeaver(5) (chsd ldrs: rdn & wknd 3f out: 5th & btn st) ..1½ 5
Lucky Lees (IRE) *(PGMurphy)* 2-8-4 (7) RWaterfield(4) (leggy: lt-f: s.s: a bhd: t.o)......25 6

11/10 RED SIMBA (9/4-Evens), **7/2** February, **4/1** In A Tizzy, **10/1** Euskara (op 5/1), Lucky Lees (IRE) (op 4/1), **12/1** Rowhome, CSF £11.46 TOTE £2.70: £1.40 £2.80 (£8.90) OWNER Mr J. R. Ali (COCKERHAM) BRED John V. Phillips 6 Rn 1m 34.0 (10.00) SF: 1/-/-/-/-/-
Bt in 5,600 gns

2295 BROSELEY H'CAP (0-60) (3-Y.O+) (Class F) £2,519.00 (£694.00: £329.00)
5f (Fibresand) Stalls: Low GOING: 0.26 sec per fur (SLW) 9-30 (9-31)

2074[10] **Bonny Melody (35)***(42) (PDEvans)* 4-8-0 (7) AmandaSanders(12) (in tch: jnd ldrs 2f out: styd on to ld wl ins fnl f)......— 1
*1566** Canovas Heart **(54)***(59)*(Fav)*(BobJones)* 6-9-12 GDuffield(3) (chsd ldrs: led 1f out: hdd & no ex wl ins fnl f)......¾ 2
*2074** Malibu Man **(62)***(63) (SMellor)* 3-10-0 TSprake(10) (dwlt: bhd: rdn & hdwy over 2f out: r.o wl fnl f)......1 3
*2071** Pursuance (IRE) **(61)***(62) (JBalding)* 3-9-6v(7) JEdmunds(4) (a.p: ev ch over 1f out: unable qckn)......hd 4
2124[12] Chance Me **(40)***(39) (MJohnston)* 3-8-6 DHolland(6) (prom: rdn 2f out: r.o same pce)......¾ 5
2071[2] Cheeky Chappy **(37)***(34) (DWChapman)* 4-8-9b ACulhane(11) (led tl rdn & hdd 1f out: sn wknd)......½ 6
507[5] Matthew David **(41)***(29) (SRBowring)* 5-8-13 StephenDavies(7) (b: sn drvn along: nvr nr ldrs).3 7
Super Sonata **(59)***(39) (PDEvans)* 3-9-8b(3) SDrowne(8) (bit bkwd: nvr on terms)......2½ 8
2074[9] Tommy Tempest **(29)** *(REPeacock)* 6-7-12b(3) SSanders(5) (chsd ldrs tl rdn & wknd over 1f out)......4 9
348[5] Pretty Chic **(28)** *(DWChapman)* 6-8-0 NKennedy(2) (bit bkwd: outpcd)......s.h 10
1972[8] Statomist **(45)***(4) (GFierro)* 3-8-4b(7) ADaly(9) (dwlt: a bhd)......2½ 11
2071[10] Pats Delight **(42)** *(SCoathup)* 3-8-8 TWilliams(1) (sn drvn along & outpcd)......2 12

6/4 Canovas Heart, **7/2** Malibu Man, **7/1** Pursuance (IRE), **15/2** Cheeky Chappy, **9/1** Chance Me, **14/1** BONNY MELODY, **16/1** Matthew David, Tommy Tempest, Pretty Chic, Pats Delight, **20/1** Super Sonata, **25/1** Statomist, CSF £37.92 CT £94.55 TOTE £24.90: £4.80 £1.40 (£21.70) Trio £90.90 OWNER Mrs E. A. Dawson (WELSHPOOL) BRED Mrs M. Watt 12 Rn
64.8 secs (6.80) SF: -/-/-/-/-/-/-/-/-/-/-/-
WEIGHT FOR AGE 3yo-6lb

T/Plpt: £87.30 (125.21 Tckts). T/Qdpt: £13.00 (5.2 Tckts). MJ

2077-BATH (L-H)
Monday July 10th (Hard)
WEATHER: cloudy & humid WIND: nil

2296 ORCHARDLEIGH LIMITED STKS (0-60) (3-Y.O) (Class F) £2,775.00 (£775.00: £375.00) **1m 3f 144y** Stalls: Low GOING minus 0.57 sec per fur (F) 2-00 (2-01)

1986[7] **Hydrofoil (56)***(69) (BWHills)* 3-8-4 (5) JDSmith(2) (swtg: 3rd st: rdn over 2f out: hrd rdn to ld post)......— 1
1998* Carnbrea Belle (IRE) **(60)***(69)*(Fav)*(MBell)* 3-8-9 MFenton(3) (chsd ldr 4f out: 2nd & rdn st: led ins fnl f: hdd post)......s.h 2
2282* Hadabet **(53)***(71) (MissJacquelineDoyle)* 3-8-12 2x JQuinn(4) (led: hrd rdn over 1f out: hdd ins fnl f: r.o)......1 3
Saterne Lady **(60)***(50) (PFICole)* 3-8-5 TQuinn(1) (hld up: 4th st: rdn & hmpd over 2f out: sn wknd)......10 4
1939[11] Nellyssia (FR) **(60)***(31) (GLMoore)* 3-8-5 SWhitworth(5) (chsd ldrs 5f out to 4f out: 5th & wkng st)......14 5

5/4 Carnbrea Belle (IRE), **11/4** Hadabet, **3/1** HYDROFOIL (2/1-100/30), **8/1** Saterne Lady (6/1-9/1), **50/1** Nellyssia (FR), CSF £6.79 TOTE £3.70: £1.80 £1.10 (£2.20) OWNER Mr R. D. Hollingsworth (LAMBOURN) BRED R. D. Hollingsworth 5 Rn 2m 28.9 (2.20) SF: 34/34/36/15/-

2297

LIMPLEY STOKE MAIDEN STKS (3-Y.O) (Class D) £4,081.00 (£1,141.00: £553.00) **1m 2f 46y** Stalls: Low GOING minus 0.57 sec per fur (F) 2-30 (2-31)

1931² **Sparrowhawk (IRE) (80)***(88) (BWHills)* 3-8-9 PatEddery(3) (lw: mde all: shkn up & qcknd 3f out: hrd rdn over 1f out: r.o wl).......— 1
1923⁶ Avignon (IRE) **(82)***(86)*(Fav)*(PWChapple-Hyam)* 3-8-9 JReid(1) (trckd wnr: 2nd st: rdn over 2f out: nt qckn ins fnl f).......1 2
2016⁷ Isshereal (IRE) *(74?) (BPalling)* 3-8-9 TSprake(2) (t: hld up: 3rd st: outpcd fnl 3f).......8 3

4/5 Avignon (IRE), **11/10** SPARROWHAWK (IRE), **33/1** Isshereal (IRE), CSF £2.17 TOTE £2.10 (£1.10) OWNER Mr R. E. Sangster (LAMBOURN) BRED Swettenham Stud 3 Rn 2m 15.1 (7.40)

2298

HOBSON'S CHOICE H'CAP (0-80) (3-Y.O+) (Class D) £3,673.25 (£1,106.00: £535.50: £250.25) **1m 2f 46y** Stalls: Low GOING minus 0.57 sec (F) 3-00 (3-01)

2132* **Silently (77)***(89+)*(Fav)*(IABalding)* 3-9-7 5x LDettori(7) (a gng wl: 4th st: qcknd to ld wl ins fnl f).......— 1
1908⁸ Fieldridge **(73)***(82) (CPEBrooks)* 6-10-0 RCochrane(3) (3rd st: led wl over 1f out tl wl ins fnl f).......1¾ 2
1788² Plinth **(56)***(65) (NAGraham)* 4-8-11v PatEddery(4) (led 1f: led 7f out tl wl over 1f out: nt qckn wl ins fnl f).......s.h 3
2139⁶ Mulciber **(61)***(69) (GHarwood)* 7-9-2 TQuinn(1) (hld up: 5th st: rdn & hdwy over 2f out: nt clr run & swtchd lft ins fnl f: nt qckn).......½ 4
1831ᵁ Tonka **(67)***(64) (PJMakin)* 3-8-11 JWeaver(2) (hld up in rr: 6th st: rdn 3f out: sn bhd).......7 5
1127⁶ Endowment **(80)***(54) (MajorWRHern)* 3-9-10 WCarson(5) (led after 1f to 7f out: snatched up bnd 5f out: 2nd st: wknd & eased 3f out).......15 6

15/8 SILENTLY, **7/2** Plinth (op 9/4), **4/1** Endowment, **5/1** Tonka, **10/1** Fieldridge (6/1-11/1), **12/1** Mulciber (8/1-14/1), CSF £16.97 TOTE £2.70: £1.40 £3.40 (£10.20) OWNER Mr Paul Mellon (KINGSCLERE) BRED Paul Mellon 6 Rn 2m 8.0 (0.30) SF: 57/61/44/48/32/22
WEIGHT FOR AGE 3yo-11lb

2299

E.B.F. EVERSHOT MAIDEN STKS (2-Y.O) (Class D) £4,328.00 (£1,304.00: £632.00: £296.00) **5f 161y** Stalls: Low GOING minus 0.57 sec (F) 3-30 (3-32)

1856⁵ **Vola Via (USA) (89)***(75) (IABalding)* 2-9-0 LDettori(5) (a.p: hrd rdn to ld 1f out: r.o wl).......— 1
2011³ Dramatic Entry (IRE) *(69) (JARToller)* 2-8-9b JWeaver(8) (hld up & bhd: gd hdwy over 1f out: ev ch ins fnl f: nt qckn).......½ 2
1715⁶ Proud Monk *(72) (GLMoore)* 2-9-0 SWhitworth(3) (led: hrd rdn 2f out: hdd 1f out: one pce)...½ 3
1406³ Belzao *(64)*(Fav)*(MRChannon)* 2-9-0 RHughes(6) (hld up: hrd rdn & edgd lft over 1f out: one pce).......3 4
Indira *(51) (HCandy)* 2-8-9 WNewnes(7) (small: neat: bkwd: no hdwy fnl 2f).......3 5
2091⁷ Beeny *(47) (APJarvis)* 2-9-0 PatEddery(4) (lw: w ldr over 3f: sn wknd).......3 6
Bluetong *(46) (PTWalwyn)* 2-9-0 RCochrane(2) (w'like: s.i.s: sn prom: rdn 2f out: sn wknd)..nk 7

4/9 Belzao, **5/1** VOLA VIA (USA), **8/1** Dramatic Entry (IRE) (7/1-12/1), **12/1** Bluetong (op 4/1), **20/1** Indira, **25/1** Proud Monk, **50/1** Beeny, CSF £38.51 TOTE £6.90: £2.40 £2.70 (£14.10) OWNER Mr G. M. Smart (KINGSCLERE) BRED Hurstland Farm Inc. 7 Rn 1m 10.8 (1.50) SF: 30/24/27/19/6/2/1

2300

EUROPEAN YOUTH OLYMPICS MAIDEN H'CAP (0-75) (3-Y.O+) (Class D) £3,582.25 (£1,078.00: £521.50: £243.25)
2m 1f 34y Stalls: Low GOING minus 0.57 sec per fur (F) 4-00 (4-01)

1600³ **Toraja (71)***(83)*(Fav)*(JLDunlop)* 3-9-10 WCarson(1) (mde all: qcknd clr 3f out: r.o wl).......— 1
1674⁶ Zuiena (USA) **(62)***(71) (PFICole)* 3-9-1 TQuinn(2) (trckd wnr: 2nd st: rdn over 2f out: one pce)3 2
2078⁴ Wizzy Lizzy (IRE) **(40)***(39) (DRCElsworth)* 4-8-10 PatEddery(4) (3rd & rdn st: wknd over 1f out).......11 3
Tazamisha **(30)** *(MrsJGRetter)* 6-8-0 NAdams(3) (b: bkwd: hld up in rr: rdn 4f out: lost tch & last st: t.o).......dist 4

8/13 TORAJA, **7/2** Zuiena (USA) (2/1-4/1), Wizzy Lizzy (IRE), **50/1** Tazamisha, CSF £2.97 TOTE £1.40 (£1.40) OWNER Mr J. L. Dunlop (ARUNDEL) BRED Hesmonds Stud Ltd 4 Rn
4m 1.6 (20.60) SF: -/-/-/-
WEIGHT FOR AGE 3yo-17lb

2301 SALTFORD APPRENTICE H'CAP (0-65) (3-Y.O+) (Class G) £2,333.00 (£663.00: £329.00) **5f 11y** Stalls: Low GOING minus 0.57 sec per fur (F) 4-30 (4-31)

2079[6] **Paley Prince (USA) (53)***(61) (MDIUsher)* 9-9-1 (5) AimeeCook(4) (b: lw: hld up: hdwy over 2f out: led over 1f out: sn clr) — 1
1975[9] The Noble Oak (IRE) **(47)***(42) (MJBolton)* 7-9-0 GMitchell(2) (hld up: hdwy over 1f out: r.o ins fnl f: no ch w wnr) 4 2
1546[5] Raisa Point **(49)***(43) (WRMuir)* 4-8-6 (10) RPooles(1) (swtg: chsd ldr: edgd rt wl over 1f out: one pce) ½ 3
1951[8] Pearl Dawn (IRE) **(60)***(53) (NoelChance)* 5-9-3 (10) LHagen(5) (swtg: hdwy over 1f out: one pce fnl f) hd 4
2092[5] Miriam **(51)***(44)*(Fav)*(MJFetherston-Godley)* 4-9-4b MartinDwyer(7) (lw: led: sn clr: hdd over 1f out: wknd ins fnl f) hd 5
2112[4] Harry's Coming **(56)***(41) (RJHodges)* 11-9-9 RWaterfield(6) (a bhd) 2½ 6
1545[4] Havana Miss **(40)** *(BPalling)* 3-8-1 GMilligan(8) (chsd ldrs tl wknd over 2f out) 8 7
1783[8] Another Batchworth **(54)** *(SMellor)* 3-9-1 ADaly(3) (Withdrawn not under Starter's orders: inj in paddock) W

3/1 Miriam, **7/2** Harry's Coming, **9/2** PALEY PRINCE (USA), **13/2** Havana Miss, Raisa Point, **7/1** Pearl Dawn (IRE), **10/1** The Noble Oak (IRE), CSF £40.27 CT £260.46 TOTE £4.30: £1.90 £6.90 (£27.70) OWNER . Shirval Partners (SWINDON) BRED Larry Deaton 7 Rn
62.6 secs (2.10) SF: 23/4/5/15/6/3/-/-
WEIGHT FOR AGE 3yo-6lb

T/Plpt: £228.80 (31.9 Tckts). T/Qdpt: £43.80 (1.5 Tckts). KH

2155-EDINBURGH (R-H)
Monday July 10th (Firm)
WEATHER: sunny WIND: fresh across

2302 E.B.F. PRESTONPANS MEDIAN AUCTION MAIDEN STKS (2-Y.O) (Class E) £3,046.25 (£920.00: £447.50: £211.25) **5f** Stalls: Low GOING minus 0.64 sec per fur (F) 2-15 (2-16)

2095[5] **Branston Danni** *(54+)*(Fav)*(MrsJRRamsden)* 2-8-9 KFallon(1) (lw: b.nr hind: cl up: led ½-wy: pushed clr appr fnl f: eased) — 1
1879[2] Monkey Zanty (IRE) *(46) (JBerry)* 2-8-9 JCarroll(2) (lw: a w ldrs: nt qckn appr fnl f) 2½ 2
925[3] Fancy Clancy *(33) (MissLCSiddall)* 2-8-9 DeanMcKeown(5) (lw: led to ½-wy: sn outpcd) 4 3
2128[11] Efipetite *(30) (NBycroft)* 2-8-9 SMaloney(4) (chsd ldrs: outpcd ½-wy: no imp after) 1 4
1440[7] Sunday Maelstrom (IRE) *(JBerry)* 2-8-2 (7) PRoberts(3) (sn outpcd & bhd) 11 5

1/2 BRANSTON DANNI, **11/4** Monkey Zanty (IRE), **9/1** Fancy Clancy, **20/1** Efipetite, **33/1** Sunday Maelstrom (IRE), CSF £2.27 TOTE £1.60: £1.10 £1.10 (£1.40) OWNER Mr J. D. Abell (THIRSK) BRED John David Abell 5 Rn
59.4 secs (1.70) SF: 11/3/-/-/-

2303 LE GARCON D'OR H'CAP (0-60) (3-Y.O+) (Class F) £2,814.00 (£852.00: £416.00: £198.00) **5f** Stalls: Low GOING minus 0.64 sec per fur (F) 2-45 (2-47)

2124[6] **Flashing Sabre (49)***(57) (JBerry)* 3-8-6 (7) PRoberts(2) (mde all stands' side: hld on wl) — 1
2234[2] Sir Tasker **(50)***(58) (JLHarris)* 7-9-6v AMackay(1) (lw: a chsng ldrs stands' side: r.o fnl f: jst failed) hd 2
1936[7] Ramborette **(47)***(54) (DenysSmith)* 3-8-11 KFallon(9) (a chsng ldrs centre: kpt on wl towards fin) nk 3
2163[2] Wasblest **(57)***(60)*(Fav)*(MJohnston)* 3-9-7b DHolland(6) (lw: sn cl up: disp ld ½-wy: nt qckn fnl f) 1¼ 4
2160[4] The Institute Boy **(47)***(47) (MissJFCraze)* 5-9-3v SWebster(5) (lw: outpcd tl sme hdwy 2f out: styd on towards fin) 1 5
2234[3] Featherstone Lane **(54)***(50) (MissLCSiddall)* 4-9-10v DeanMcKeown(8) (lw: hdwy far side ½-wy: sn rdn & btn) 1¼ 6
2231[3] Leading Princess (IRE) **(40)***(35) (MissLAPerratt)* 4-8-5b(5) CTeague(11) (led far side: outpcd fr ½-wy) nk 7
2160* Pallium (IRE) **(59)***(53) (MrsAMNaughton)* 7-9-12 (3) 7x JStack(7) (lw: bhd tl sme late hdwy) hd 8
2160[2] Serious Hurry **(42)***(30) (RMMcKellar)* 7-8-5 (7) NKinnon(3) (spd to ½-wy) 2 9
411[11] Fiveaday **(57)***(45) (BHanbury)* 3-9-7 JCarroll(4) (racd stands' side: nvr wnt pce) s.h 10
2084[4] Sandmoor Velvet **(50)***(27) (MHEasterby)* 3-9-0 MBirch(10) (b: racd far side: outpcd fr ½-wy) 3½ 11

5/2 Wasblest (op 4/1), **11/2** Sir Tasker, **6/1** Pallium (IRE) (op 4/1), **7/1** Featherstone Lane, Sandmoor Velvet, **10/1** Serious Hurry, **11/1** The Institute Boy, **12/1** Fiveaday (op 8/1), **16/1** FLASHING SABRE, **33/1** Leading Princess (IRE), Ramborette, CSF £94.67 CT £2,593.49 TOTE £31.20: £8.60 £3.10 £5.50 (£78.20) Trio £551.00; £395.81 to Newmarket 11/7/95 OWNER Mr Chris Deuters (COCKERHAM) BRED R. Bowers 11 Rn 58.1 secs (0.40) SF: 35/42/32/38/31/34/19/37/14/23/5

WEIGHT FOR AGE 3yo-6lb

2304

DUNBAR CLAIMING STKS (3-Y.O+) (Class F) £2,815.00 (£790.00: £385.00)
7f 15y Stalls: High GOING minus 0.64 sec per fur (F) 3-15 (3-16)

2229² **Diet (47)***(63) (MissLAPerratt)* 9-9-6v JCarroll(6) (lw: mde all: rdn out) — 1
2227⁴ King of Show (IRE) **(54)***(60) (RAllan)* 4-9-1 (5) CTeague(4) (b: prom tl lost pl appr st: swtchd lft & hdwy over 2f out: kpt on towards fin) 1¼ 2
2156¹⁴ Ricana **(39)***(51) (WTKemp)* 3-8-3 SMaloney(1) (a.p: hdwy over 2f out: styd on u.p: nt pce to chal) hd 3
2018⁰ Annie Fay (IRE) **(57)***(53)*(Fav)*(JLHarris)* 3-8-7 AMackay(2) (chsd wnr: rdn 3f out: ne pce) ¾ 4
Thwaab **(45)***(24) (FWatson)* 3-8-12 JFanning(5) (effrt ent st: btn 2f out) 15 5
2258⁴ Valley of Time (FR) **(23)** *(DANolan)* 7-8-6 (5) VHalliday(3) (b: chsd ldrs tl wknd over 2f out) 7 6

4/5 Annie Fay (IRE), **9/4** DIET, **11/1** King of Show (IRE) (op 7/1), **12/1** Ricana, **40/1** Valley of Time (FR), **50/1** Thwaab, CSF £20.50 TOTE £2.90: £1.90 £2.60 (£7.90) OWNER Mrs M. S. J. Clydesdale (AYR) BRED Rowcliffe Stud 6 Rn 1m 28.2 (2.20) SF: 27/24/7/9/-/-

WEIGHT FOR AGE 3yo-8lb

2305

GEORGE BOYD H'CAP (0-65) (3-Y.O+ F & M) (Class F) £2,736.00 (£828.00: £404.00: £192.00)
1m 4f 31y Stalls: High GOING minus 0.64 sec per fur (F) 3-45 (3-46)

2159² **Soba Up (57)***(68+)*(Fav)*(TJEtherington)* 5-10-0 ACulhane(2) (lw: a gng wl: led & qcknd over 2f out: eased) — 1
2126⁴ Can She Can Can **(46)***(55) (MJohnston)* 3-8-4 DHolland(1) (hdwy to chal 8f out: outpcd ent st: no imp after) 1¾ 2
2064⁷ Missus Murhill (IRE) **(38)***(45) (NTinkler)* 4-8-9 MBirch(4) (reard s: sn rcvrd: effrt 3f out: styd on towards fin: nvr plcd to chal) 1½ 3
1696⁹ Western Horizon (USA) **(42)***(49) (CEBrittain)* 3-8-0 LCharnock(3) (led tl hdd over 2f out) s.h 4

Evens SOBA UP, **9/4** Can She Can Can, **5/1** Missus Murhill (IRE), **7/1** Western Horizon (USA) (op 7/2), CSF £3.47 TOTE £2.10 (£2.00) OWNER Mrs M. Hills (MALTON) BRED Mrs M. J. Hills 4 Rn 2m 38.8 (6.30) SF: 21/-/-/-

WEIGHT FOR AGE 3yo-13lb

2306

NEWBATTLE (S) H'CAP (0-60) (3-Y.O+) (Class G) £2,465.00 (£690.00: £335.00)
1m 3f 32y Stalls: High GOING minus 0.64 sec per fur (F) 4-15 (4-16)

1902⁴ **Funny Rose (23)***(36) (PMonteith)* 5-8-11 DHolland(3) (lw: hld up: hdwy 3f out: r.o wl to ld cl home) — 1
1816³ Portite Sophie **(34)***(47) (MBrittain)* 4-9-3 (5) VHalliday(6) (led: qcknd clr appr st: rdn 2f out: hdd & no ex nr fin) nk 2
2126* Jackmanii **(51)***(58)*(Fav)*(WTKemp)* 3-9-13b 5x KFallon(8) (lw: bhd: outpcd & last appr st: r.o fnl 3f: nvr able chal) 4 3
2165⁵ Petal's Jarred **(25)***(25) (WStorey)* 5-8-13v JFanning(1) (hld up: hdwy ent st: sn chsng ldr: rdn & btn 2f out) 5 4
1819⁷ Nicky's Feelings **(35)***(25) (TDyer)* 3-8-4 (7) RMullen(2) (s.i.s: bhd & rn wd paddock bnd & appr st: hdwy 3f out: sn btn) 7 5
*2072*⁴ Rose Chime (IRE) **(47)***(33) (JLHarris)* 3-9-9 AMackay(4) (prom tl wl outpcd fnl 3½f) 2½ 6
Lordan Velvet (IRE) **(48)***(29) (LLungo)* 3-9-5 (5) CTeague(5) (plld hrd: chsd ldrs to st: sn wknd) 3½ 7
1902⁶ Halls Burn **(30)** *(JSGoldie)* 7-9-1 (3) JStack(7) (plld hrd: cl up tl wknd ent st) 9 8

Evens Jackmanii, **6/1** Petal's Jarred, **7/1** FUNNY ROSE, **8/1** Rose Chime (IRE), **10/1** Portite Sophie, **12/1** Lordan Velvet (IRE) (8/1-14/1), **14/1** Nicky's Feelings, **20/1** Halls Burn, CSF £64.00 CT £115.03 TOTE £7.30: £2.20 £1.70 £1.80 (£18.30) OWNER Mr P. Monteith (ROSEWELL) BRED C. Sheehan 8 Rn 2m 27.9 (8.20) SF: -/1/-/-/-/-/-/-

WEIGHT FOR AGE 3yo-12lb

Bt in 3,600 gns

OFFICIAL EXPLANATION **Jackmanii: the jockey reported that the colt was unable to go the fast early pace and did not run on until he was in the straight.**

2307 MILL HILL H'CAP (0-70) (3-Y.O+) (Class E) £3,143.75 (£950.00: £462.50: £218.75)
1m 16y Stalls: High GOING minus 0.64 sec per fur (F) 4-45 (4-45)

2099³ **Legal Fiction (62)***(74) (MJohnston)* 4-9-8 DHolland(5) (lw: a.p: led over 2f out: r.o wl) ....— **1**
2156² At the Savoy (IRE) **(41)***(47)*(Fav)*(TDBarron)* 4-8-1b LCharnock(6) (lw: chsd ldrs tl hmpd & lost pl appr st: hdwy 3f out: nt pce of wnr fnl f).....3 **2**
1995² Spanish Verdict **(68)***(71) (DenysSmith)* 8-10-0 KFallon(4) (lw: bhd: hdwy u.p 3f out: rst fin)..1½ **3**
2156⁸ Demurrer **(37)***(38) (MrsAMNaughton)* 5-7-11 TWilliams(8) (led tl hdd over 2f out: one pce) 1 **4**
2228² My Handy Man **(53)***(52) (RAllan)* 4-8-13 JFanning(1) (hdwy over 2f out: rdn & no imp appr fnl f) 1¼ **5**
2156* Miss Pigalle **(38)***(36) (MissLAPerratt)* 4-7-12b 5x DaleGibson(7) (chsd ldrs tl wknd appr fnl f)...½ **6**
1995⁶ Mary Macblain **(37)***(34) (JLHarris)* 6-7-11 AMackay(3) (lw: bhd: rdn ent st: no imp).................½ **7**
991¹⁰ Moofaji **(60)***(54) (FWatson)* 4-9-6 SMaloney(2) (plld hrd: prom to st: sn lost pl) 1½ **8**

5/2 At the Savoy (IRE), **3/1** Spanish Verdict, **7/2** LEGAL FICTION, **8/1** My Handy Man, **9/1** Mary Macblain, **12/1** Miss Pigalle (op 6/1), **20/1** Demurrer, **40/1** Moofaji, CSF £11.70 CT £24.65 TOTE £4.20: £1.40 £1.10 £1.60 (£8.00) OWNER Mr J. S. Morrison (MIDDLEHAM) BRED Fares Stables Ltd 8 Rn 1m 42.4 (3.80) SF: 17/-/14/-/-/-/-/-
T/Plpt: £30.90 (324.61 Tckts). T/Qdpt: £15.70 (2.6 Tckts). AA

1873-RIPON (R-H)
Monday July 10th (Good to firm, Firm patches)
WEATHER: fine WIND: almost nil

2308 SKELLGATE MAIDEN AUCTION STKS (2-Y.O F) (Class F) £2,801.00 (£848.00: £414.00: £197.00) **5f** Stalls: Centre GOING minus 0.54 sec per fur (F) 7-00 (7-00)

2135⁵ **All She Surveys** *(60) (JAkehurst)* 2-8-5 GCarter(2) (swtg: trckd ldrs: styd on u.p fnl f: led post) .....— **1**
Lia Fail (IRE) *(60) (RHollinshead)* 2-8-5 WRyan(6) (leggy: unf: trckd ldrs: effrt 2f out: r.o to ld wl ins fnl f: jst ct) .....s.h **2**
1857² Jubilee Place (IRE) *(60)*(Fav)*(TThomsonJones)* 2-8-5 SWhitworth(3) (lw: trckd ldrs: led over 1f out tl wl ins fnl f) .....hd **3**
1758³ Paper Maze *(55) (JAHarris)* 2-8-2 PRobinson(1) (bit bkwd: chsd ldrs: rdn ½-wy: kpt on same pce fnl f) .....½ **4**
Rebel County (IRE) *(54) (DJSCosgrove)* 2-8-2 JQuinn(4) (str: cmpt: s.i.s: sn chsng ldrs: outpcd ½-wy: edgd rt & kpt on appr fnl f) .....nk **5**
Hickleton Miss *(51) (MrsMReveley)* 2-8-2 KDarley(8) (led tl over 1f out: wkng whn n.m.r & eased towards fin) 1 **6**
Time For Tea (IRE) *(30) (CACyzer)* 2-8-7 DBiggs(5) (cmpt: bkwd: s.s: a wl bhd).....................8 **7**

5/4 Jubilee Place (IRE), **7/2** Rebel County (IRE) (5/1-3/1), **9/2** Hickleton Miss, **7/1** Paper Maze (op 4/1), Time For Tea (IRE) (op 7/2), **9/1** ALL SHE SURVEYS, **12/1** Lia Fail (IRE) (op 8/1), CSF £94.66 TOTE £7.20: £3.10 £3.70 (£303.40) OWNER Fraser Miller (LAMBOURN) BRED R. G. Percival and Red House Stud 7 Rn 61.0 secs (3.00) SF: -/-/-/-/-/-/-

2309 FISHERGATE (S) STKS (3-Y.O+) (Class F) £2,723.00 (£824.00: £402.00: £191.00)
1m 2f Stalls: High GOING minus 0.54 sec per fur (F) 7-25 (7-26)

2102⁵ **Prince of Spades (60)***(69) (CACyzer)* 3-8-10 DBiggs(7) (trckd ldrs: effrt & swtchd over 2f out: styd on to ld 1f out: drvn out) .....— **1**
1917⁵ Malindi Bay **(23)***(66) (BJMcMath)* 7-9-7 KDarley(1) (led to 1f out: nt pce of wnr).....................2 **2**
1971* Dungeon Dancer **(58)***(66)*(Fav)*(JAkehurst)* 3-8-10v GCarter(6) (hld up: effrt & swtchd over 2f out: sn rdn: kpt on: nvr able to chal) .....hd **3**
185³ Samana Cay **(48)***(41) (DNicholls)* 3-8-5 JFortune(2) (trckd ldrs: effrt 3f out: sn wknd) 12 **4**
Indian Colours *(46) (JNorton)* 4-9-7 JQuinn(5) (unf: bit bkwd: s.s: rn green & lost pl ent st: wandered: nvr nr ldrs) .....nk **5**
Brandon Lane *(45) (RMWhitaker)* 4-9-7 ACulhane(4) (bit bkwd: s.i.s: bhd: effrt 4f out: sn in tch: wknd 2f out) .....¾ **6**
472⁷ Melody Dancer **(50)***(44) (MissJFCraze)* 4-9-2 (5) HKYim(3) (b.hind: trckd ldrs: ev ch tl wknd over 2f out) .....½ **7**

5/6 Dungeon Dancer, **9/4** PRINCE OF SPADES, **6/1** Samana Cay, **9/1** Melody Dancer, **10/1** Indian Colours, **16/1** Brandon Lane, **20/1** Malindi Bay, CSF £38.38 TOTE £3.80: £2.00 £3.20 (£29.60) OWNER Mr Stephen Crown (HORSHAM) BRED S. Crown 7 Rn 2m 10.2 (6.70) SF: -/8/-/-/-/-/-
WEIGHT FOR AGE 3yo-11lb
Bt in 5,600 gns

2310 WEATHERBYS 'NEWCOMERS' SERIES H'CAP (0-70) (3-Y.O+) (Class E)

£3,346.30 (£1,014.40: £496.20: £237.10)
1m Stalls: High GOING minus 0.54 sec per fur (F) 7-55 (7-56)

1797[3] **Chairmans Choice (44)***(55) (APJarvis)* 5-8-2 KDarley(5) (lw: mde all: drvn clr 2f out: jst hld on)......— 1
1994[3] Sakharov **(55)***(66)*(Fav)*(MJohnston)* 6-8-13 PRobinson(11) (lw: trckd ldrs: effrt over 1f out: styd on wl towards fin)......hd 2
2007[7] No Speeches (IRE) **(55)***(63) (CACyzer)* 4-8-13 KFallon(12) (in tch: sn pushed along: hdwy 3f out: kpt on same pce appr fnl f)......1¼ 3
2123* Thatched (IRE) **(53)***(57) (REBarr)* 5-8-6 (5) 6x GParkin(2) (lw: hld up & bhd: gd hdwy over 2f out: styd on fnl f: nt rch ldrs)......2 4
2056[2] Comanche Companion **(70)***(74) (TJNaughton)* 5-9-9 (5) JDSmith(3) (a chsng ldrs: kpt on same pce fnl 2f)......nk 5
2081[4] Swynford Flyer **(36)***(29) (JAHarris)* 6-7-1 (7)ow1 CAdamson(13) (chsd ldrs tl outpcd fnl 3f)......5 6
1824[5] River Wye (IRE) **(45)***(33) (JMCarr)* 3-7-8 NKennedy(8) (in tch: outpcd 3f out: kpt on appr fnl f)3 7
1151[12] General Gubbins **(60)***(43) (JHetherton)* 4-9-4 WRyan(15) (lw: hld up & bhd: styd on fnl 2f: nvr nr ldrs)......2½ 8
2207[5] Ballyhays (IRE) **(46)***(28) (JAHarris)* 6-8-1 (3) PMcCabe(9) (reard s: s.s: bhd: swtchd & sme hdwy 3f out: n.d)......½ 9
1855[11] Northern Chief **(40)***(16) (MissJFCraze)* 5-7-9 (3)ow3 AGarth(14) (chsd ldrs tl wknd 3f out)......1¼ 10
1874[2] Golden Tongue (USA) **(70)***(48) (EALDunlop)* 3-9-2 (3) JTate(7) (in tch: effrt 3f out: sn wknd) ...¾ 11
2084[9] Coney Hills **(37)***(11) (NBycroft)* 4-7-9 ow2 JQuinn(4) (rr div: n.d)......1 12
2056[9] Across the Bay **(40)***(13) (RWEmery)* 8-7-5b(7)ow3 SLanigan(10) (a bhd)......hd 13
2056[7] Scottish Park **(39)***(13) (RWEmery)* 6-7-8 (3) DarrenMoffatt(1) (in tch: outpcd over 3f out: sn lost pl)......¾ 14
2064[5] Sallyoreally (IRE) **(43)***(13) (WStorey)* 4-8-1 JFanning(6) (bhd: effrt on outside over 3f out: sn wknd)......2 15

LONG HANDICAP Swynford Flyer 7-2 Coney Hills 6-10

7/2 Sakharov, **11/2** Comanche Companion, **6/1** Thatched (IRE), **13/2** No Speeches (IRE), **7/1** CHAIRMANS CHOICE, **9/1** Golden Tongue (USA), **12/1** Swynford Flyer, River Wye (IRE), General Gubbins, **16/1** Scottish Park, **20/1** Ballyhays (IRE), Sallyoreally (IRE), **33/1** Northern Chief, Across the Bay, **50/1** Coney Hills, CSF £32.60 CT £163.14 TOTE £8.20: £2.00 £1.70 £3.70 (£12.40) Trio £106.80 OWNER Mrs D. B. Brazier (ASTON UPTHORPE) BRED D. V. Wakefield 15 Rn

1m 38.3 (0.60) SF: 37/48/45/39/56/11/6/25/10/-/21/-/-/-/-
WEIGHT FOR AGE 3yo-9lb

2311 SINGER & FRIEDLANDER H'CAP (0-80) (3-Y.O) (Class D) £5,270.00 (£1,470.00: £710.00)

6f Stalls: Centre GOING minus 0.54 sec per fur (F) 8-25 (8-25)

1249* **Rasas (IRE) (77)***(83) (HThomsonJones)* 3-9-7 WRyan(3) (lw: trckd ldrs: led over 1f out: edgd lft: drvn out)......— 1
1783[4] Crystal Loop **(61)***(60) (ABailey)* 3-8-5 GCarter(2) (led tl over 3f out: n.m.r 1f out: one pce)....2½ 2
1624* Brecongill Lad **(74)***(69)*(Fav)*(MissSEHall)* 3-9-4b NConnorton(1) (plld hrd: w ldr: led over 3f out: hung rt & hdd over 1f out: wknd towards fin)......1½ 3

11/10 Brecongill Lad, **6/5** RASAS (IRE), **4/1** Crystal Loop, CSF £4.98 TOTE £1.80 (£2.90) OWNER Mr Hamdan Al Maktoum (NEWMARKET) BRED Shadwell Estate Company Limited 3 Rn

1m 11.9 (1.70) SF: 35/12/21

2312 BONDGATE H'CAP (0-80) (3-Y.O) (Class D) £4,922.50 (£1,480.00: £715.00: £332.50)

1m 4f 60y Stalls: High GOING minus 0.54 sec per fur (F) 8-55 (8-55)

1669* **Royal York (67)***(76)*(Fav)*(MissSEHall)* 3-9-0 NConnorton(3) (lw: trckd ldrs: led over 2f out: hung rt: drvn out)......— 1
1720* Royal Expression **(57)***(66) (MrsMReveley)* 3-8-4 KDarley(2) (lw: led & qcknd over 6f out: hdd over 2f out: styd on u.p: nt qckn nr fin)......nk 2
1717[4] Rosie Sweetheart (IRE) **(74)***(76) (HRACecil)* 3-9-7 WRyan(4) (hld up: effrt over 3f out: sn outpcd: nvr nr to chal)......5 3
1997[3] Punch **(55)***(52) (NTinkler)* 3-8-2 LCharnock(5) (chsd ldrs: drvn along over 4f out: wknd fnl 2f)......4 4
2101[5] Manful **(72)***(68) (JHetherton)* 3-9-5v NKennedy(1) (led tl over 6f out: hung rt 4f out: sn wknd) ..1 5

7/4 ROYAL YORK, **3/1** Rosie Sweetheart (IRE), **100/30** Royal Expression, **4/1** Manful, **11/1** Punch, CSF £7.55 TOTE £2.40: £1.30 £1.80 (£3.60) OWNER Mr Robert Ogden (MIDDLEHAM) BRED Robert Ogden 5 Rn

2m 37.1 (3.10) SF: 36/26/36/12/28

2313

KIRKGATE MAIDEN STKS (3-Y.O+) (Class D) £3,793.70 (£1,148.60: £560.80: £266.90) **1m** Stalls: High GOING minus 0.54 sec per fur (F) 9-25 (9-25)

15472 **Pennycairn (69)***(78)*(Fav)*(HRACecil)* 3-8-7 WRyan(1) (lw: mde all: clr 2f out: eased towards fin) — **1**
17474 Office Hours **(76)***(69) (CACyzer)* 3-8-12 KFallon(3) (hld up & plld hrd: effrt over 3f out: sn chsng wnr: no imp: eased towards fin) 7 **2**
15075 Ihtimaam (FR) *(61) (MrsASwinbank)* 3-8-12 NConnorton(2) (b: hld up in rr: hung rt 2f out: styd on fnl f: nvr nr ldrs) 4 **3**
Galafron *(43) (JHMGosden)* 3-8-12 JCarroll(4) (dwlt: sn chsng wnr: hung bdly rt fr over 4f out: eased fnl 2f) 9 **4**

4/5 PENNYCAIRN, **11/4** Office Hours, **3/1** Galafron (2/1-4/1), **14/1** Ihtimaam (FR), CSF £3.43 TOTE £1.80 (£2.60) OWNER Sir David Wills (NEWMARKET) BRED Sir David Wills 4 Rn
1m 41.5 (3.80) SF: 10/1/-/-

T/Plpt: £1,188.00 (9.64 Tckts). T/Qdpt: £8.00 (11 Tckts). WG

2134-WINDSOR (Fig. 8)
Monday July 10th (Good to firm)

WEATHER: muggy WIND: nil

2314

'MISS MORLEY'S NURSERY' H'CAP (0-70) (3-Y.O+) (Class E) £3,874.75 (£1,168.00: £566.50: £265.75)
1m 2f 7y Stalls: High GOING minus 0.44 sec per fur (F) 6-45 (6-46)

19915 **Just Flamenco (45)***(54+) (MJRyan)* 4-8-9 WCarson(6) (swtg: stdy hdwy 3f out: led ins fnl f: easily) — **1**
19117 Anlace **(53)***(59) (SMellor)* 6-9-3 MWigham(9) (swtg: hdwy fnl 2f: nvr nrr) 1¾ **2**
20942 Braydon Forest **(67)***(73) (CJDrewe)* 3-9-6 RCochrane(5) (lw: 7th st: ev ch over 1f out: nt qckn) s.h **3**
12115 Hotspur Street **(67)***(72)*(Fav)*(MJohnston)* 3-9-6 JReid(13) (swtg: 3rd st: led over 3f out tl ins fnl f) ½ **4**
19787 Darling Clover **(56)***(61) (DMorley)* 3-8-9 MFenton(11) (nvr nrr) nk **5**
16615 Lady Lacey **(46)***(51) (GBBalding)* 8-8-10v JWilliams(3) (nvr nr to chal) s.h **6**
18546 Sinclair Lad (IRE) **(40)***(42) (RJHodges)* 7-8-1 (3) SDrowne(15) (lw: 5th st: wknd 2f out) 1½ **7**
13407 Night Time **(70)***(68) (RHannon)* 3-9-9 PatEddery(10) (lw: nvr trbld ldrs) 3 **8**
200714 Make a Stand **(57)***(55) (HCandy)* 4-9-7b WNewnes(1) (lw: led tl over 3f out: wknd over 1f out) s.h **9**
20824 Saucy Maid (IRE) **(60)***(55)*(Fav)*(MajorDNChappell)* 4-9-10 BThomson(2) (swtg: nvr nr ldrs) 1½ **10**
19834 Ewar Imperial **(67)***(57) (CEBrittain)* 3-9-6 MRoberts(7) (2nd st: wknd over 2f out) 3 **11**
194011 Le Sorcier **(50)***(35) (GPEnright)* 3-8-3 NAdams(8) (b.hind: lw: a bhd) 3½ **12**
Utrillo (USA) **(45)***(17) (BJCurley)* 6-8-9v LDettori(14) (a bhd) 8 **13**
Legendary Lady **(37)** *(RTPhillips)* 4-8-1 AMcGlone(12) (6th st: wknd 3f out) 10 **14**
22797 Jovie King (IRE) **(60)***(12) (PMitchell)* 3-8-6 (7) MHenry(4) (lw: 4th st: wknd 4f out) 2½ **15**

11/2 Hotspur Street, Saucy Maid (IRE), **15/2** Braydon Forest (9/2-8/1), **8/1** Anlace, Utrillo (USA) (3/1-10/1), **9/1** Ewar Imperial, **10/1** Night Time, Sinclair Lad (IRE), **11/1** Lady Lacey (8/1-12/1), **12/1** Darling Clover (8/1-14/1), JUST FLAMENCO (op 8/1), **20/1** Make a Stand, Jovie King (IRE), **33/1** Legendary Lady, Le Sorcier, CSF £103.20 CT £716.33 TOTE £16.00: £5.20 £2.10 £3.20 (£97.00) Trio £150.20 OWNER Mrs S. M. Martin (NEWMARKET) BRED Mrs L. Martin 15 Rn
2m 7.8 (2.90) SF: 35/40/43/42/31/32/23/38/36/36/27/5/-/-/-
WEIGHT FOR AGE 3yo-11lb

2315

MICHAEL TESTLER CONDITIONS STKS (2-Y.O) (Class D) £5,572.50 (£1,680.00: £815.00: £382.50)
5f 217y Stalls: High GOING minus 0.44 sec per fur (F) 7-10 (7-13)

Lacryma Cristi (IRE) *(91+)*(Fav)*(MrsJCecil)* 2-8-10 PaulEddery(5) (str: scope: bit bkwd: hld up & bhd: hdwy on bit over 2f out: led over 1f out: easily) — **1**
10984 Roses In The Snow (IRE) *(75) (JWHills)* 2-8-5 BThomson(9) (a.p: led over 2f out tl over 1f out: r.o: no ch w wnr) 4 **2**
17265 Winter Quarters (USA) *(67) (IABalding)* 2-8-10 LDettori(3) (lw: prom tl outpcd over 2f out: styd on fnl f) 5 **3**
1938* Midnight Escape **(80)***(73) (CFWall)* 2-9-2 NCarlisle(11) (led over 3f) hd **4**
17267 Sketchbook *(59) (GLewis)* 2-8-10 PatEddery(1) (swtg: spd over 4f) 3 **5**
1540* Croeso Cynnes **(75)***(56) (BPalling)* 2-8-11 TSprake(2) (no hdwy fnl 2f) 1¼ **6**

7606 Daily Risk *(54) (SDow)* 2-8-3 (7) ADaly(8) (swtg: nvr nr to chal) ....½ 7
Samara Song *(52) (RJBaker)* 2-8-10 JWilliams(7) (unf: nvr trbld ldrs) ....¾ 8
Alamein (USA) *(44) (MrsLPiggott)* 2-8-10 RCochrane(4) (b: str: scope: bit bkwd: outpcd) 3 9
Sheilana (IRE) *(36) (TGMills)* 2-8-5 WCarson(6) (lt-f: spd over 3f) 1 10
Midas Gold *(28) (BJMeehan)* 2-8-10 BDoyle(12) (unf: sn bhd) 5 11
Muhandam (IRE) *(26) (MRStoute)* 2-8-10 WRSwinburn(10) (str: scope: lw: wl bhd fnl 3f) ....¾ 12

7/4 LACRYMA CRISTI (IRE), **3/1** Winter Quarters (USA) (5/2-4/1), **7/1** Roses In The Snow (IRE), Sketchbook (4/1-8/1), **8/1** Muhandam (IRE) (op 3/1), **10/1** Croeso Cynnes (op 9/2), **12/1** Midnight Escape (op 6/1), **16/1** Midas Gold, **20/1** Sheilana (IRE), Alamein (USA), **25/1** Daily Risk, **33/1** Samara Song, CSF £16.54 TOTE £3.70: £1.30 £2.10 £1.50 (£14.40) Trio £20.10 OWNER Mr Matthew Oram (NEWMARKET) BRED Mrs J. Costelloe 12 Rn

1m 12.2 (1.70) SF: 34/18/10/16/2/-/-/-/-/-/-/-

2316 PERPETUAL PEP CONDITIONS STKS (3 & 4-Y.O) (Class D) £5,475.00 (£1,650.00: £800.00: £375.00)

1m 2f 7y Stalls: High GOING minus 0.44 sec per fur (F) 7-40 (7-45)

19252 **Warning Order (99)***(88)*(Fav)*(JLDunlop)* 3-9-1 WCarson(10) (6th st: hrd rdn over 1f out: qcknd ins fnl f: led last strides) ....— 1
11987 Persian Saint (IRE) **(75)***(82) (DRCElsworth)* 4-9-6 TQuinn(9) (swtg: led to fnl strides) ....s.h 2
Frozen Sea (USA) *(71) (GPEnright)* 4-9-6 NAdams(5) (hdwy & 7th st: ev ch over 2f out: one pce) 7 3
151413 Nobby North *(70) (LordHuntingdon)* 3-8-2 (7) AimeeCook(1) (hdwy fnl 2f: nvr nrr) ....nk 4
112814 Roufontaine *(65) (WRMuir)* 4-9-1 JWeaver(2) (5th st: ev ch 2f out: one pce) ....nk 5
5858 Zine Lane **(73)***(69) (MajorWRHern)* 3-8-9 PaulEddery(3) (nvr nr to chal) ....¾ 6
58413 Chocolate Charlie *(68) (RCharlton)* 4-9-6 TSprake(6) (s.s: nvr nr ldrs) ....hd 7
Talk Back (IRE) *(70) (MissHCKnight)* 3-9-1 RHughes(8) (w'like: 4th st: wknd over 2f out) 3 8
181210 Faith 'n Glory (IRE) **(56)***(52) (RHannon)* 3-7-13 (7)ow2 DaneO'Neill(7) (lw: 3rd st: wknd qckly over 1f out) 4 9
Carnegie Blue *(AJChamberlain)* 4-9-4bow3 BPowell(4) (b.hind: 2nd st: wknd over 4f out: t.o) ....dist 10

8/11 WARNING ORDER, **4/1** Talk Back (IRE) (6/1-7/2), **10/1** Persian Saint (IRE), **11/1** Zine Lane (7/1-12/1), **12/1** Roufontaine, **20/1** Faith 'n Glory (IRE), **25/1** Nobby North, **33/1** Chocolate Charlie, Frozen Sea (USA), **66/1** Carnegie Blue, CSF £8.97 TOTE £1.60: £1.10 £2.60 £5.70 (£6.60) Trio £151.00 OWNER Mr Ian Cameron (ARUNDEL) BRED Giles W. Pritchard-Gordon 10 Rn

2m 7.1 (2.20) SF: 46/51/40/28/34/27/37/28/10/-

WEIGHT FOR AGE 3yo-11lb

2317 CADOGAN GROUP H'CAP (0-70) (3-Y.O+) (Class E) £3,874.75 (£1,168.00: £566.50: £265.75)

1m 67y Stalls: High GOING minus 0.44 sec per fur (F) 8-10 (8-15)

19403 **Kindergarten Boy (IRE) (59)***(68) (RBoss)* 4-9-9 JWeaver(4) (led 1f: 2nd st: led over 3f out tl wl ins fnl f: led last stride: all out) ....— 1
20108 Court Nap (IRE) **(54)***(63) (SMellor)* 3-8-9 MWigham(15) (lw: 5th st: led wl ins fnl f: ct last stride) ....s.h 2
197512 Super Serenade **(54)***(61) (GBBalding)* 6-9-4 JWilliams(11) (hdwy fnl 2f: nvr nrr) 1 3
Secret Ballad (IRE) **(63)***(70) (JAkehurst)* 3-9-4 TQuinn(8) (b: 4th st: hrd rdn over 2f out: ev ch 1f out: nt qckn) ....hd 4
1664* Crimson Shower **(57)***(63)*(Fav)*(JRFanshawe)* 3-8-12 DHarrison(6) (swtg: hdwy over 2f out: r.o ins fnl f) ....nk 5
15345 Mo's Star **(62)***(68) (SDow)* 3-8-10 (7) ADaly(9) (nrst fin) ....s.h 6
19753 Spectacle Jim **(50)***(53) (JO'Donoghue)* 6-8-11b(3) DRMcCabe(10) (nvr nr to chal) 1½ 7
19116 Duello **(60)***(61) (MBlanshard)* 4-9-10 RCochrane(13) (hdwy fnl 2f: r.o) 1 8
Chieftain's Crown (USA) **(38)***(36) (JWhite)* 4-8-2 RPrice(7) (nvr trbld ldrs) 1½ 9
20334 Witney-de-Bergerac (IRE) **(59)***(56) (JSMoore)* 3-8-9 (5) NVarley(2) (swtg: nvr nr ldrs) 1 10
21085 Threshfield (USA) **(46)***(42) (BJCurley)* 9-8-10 LDettori(3) (swtg: 7th st: wknd 2f out) ....hd 11
20165 Morocco (IRE) **(55)***(51) (MRChannon)* 6-9-5 RHughes(17) (6th st: ev ch & hrd rdn 2f out: sn wknd) ....nk 12
16337 Present Situation **(60)***(50) (LordHuntingdon)* 4-9-5 (5) AWhelan(5) (a bhd) 3 13
20378 Rubylee **(58)***(45) (KMcAuliffe)* 3-8-13v GDuffield(1) (swtg: 8th st: wknd 3f out) 1½ 14
Real Madrid **(37)***(13) (GPEnright)* 4-8-1 NAdams(14) (3rd st: wknd over 3f out) 6 15
12219 Ironic (IRE) **(60)***(33) (RHannon)* 3-9-1 JReid(12) (lw: outpcd) 1¼ 16
16547 Embezzler **(52)***(23) (GLewis)* 3-8-7b PaulEddery(16) (lw: led after 1f tl wknd over 3f out) 1¼ 17

3/1 Crimson Shower, **5/1** KINDERGARTEN BOY (IRE), **7/1** Threshfield (USA) (5/1-8/1), **9/1** Morocco (IRE), **10/1** Present Situation, **11/1** Court Nap (IRE), **12/1** Spectacle Jim, Duello, **14/1** Mo's Star (10/1-16/1), **16/1** Rubylee, Secret Ballad (IRE), Super Serenade, Ironic (IRE), Embezzler, **20/1** Witney-de-Bergerac (IRE), **25/1** Real Madrid, **33/1** Chieftain's Crown (USA), CSF £63.61 CT £802.05 TOTE £7.70: £1.80 £2.20 £5.50 £6.00 (£83.30) Trio £399.40 OWNER Mrs Joan Root (NEWMARKET) BRED Bernard Eivers 17 Rn

1m 45.9 (4.30) SF: 30/16/23/23/16/21/15/23/-/9/4/13/12/-/-/-/-

WEIGHT FOR AGE 3yo-9lb

2318

FRIENDS OF GREAT ORMOND STREET H'CAP (0-70) (3-Y.O) (Class E) £3,738.25 (£1,126.00: £545.50: £255.25)
5f 217y Stalls: High GOING minus 0.44 sec per fur (F) 8-40 (8-44)

1624⁹ **Ben Gunn (67)**(74) (PTWalwyn) 3-9-4 PatEddery(4) (lw: hdwy 2f out: hrd rdn & edgd rt 1f out: led ins fnl f: r.o) — 1
2048⁵ Charnwood Queen **(45)**(48) (RWArmstrong) 3-7-10 ow1 WCarson(9) (a.p: led wl over 1f out tl ins fnl f) 1¼ 2
Charlie Sillett **(70)**(72) (BWHills) 3-9-7 BThomson(10) (lw: a.p: sltly hmpd ins fnl f: r.o nr fin) ¾ 3
1975⁸ Sizzling **(63)**(63) (RHannon) 3-8-7 (7) DaneO'Neill(3) (a.p: r.o ins fnl f) ½ 4
2137⁶ Vavona **(56)**(56)(Fav)(LJHolt) 3-8-7 JReid(11) (lw: hdwy fnl 2f: nvr nrr) hd 5
1952⁷ Cork Street Girl (IRE) **(53)**(53) (BJMeehan) 3-8-4b BDoyle(16) (led over 4f: r.o) s.h 6
1982⁸ Almasi (IRE) **(65)**(63) (CFWall) 3-9-2 WWoods(1) (gd hdwy over 1f out: wknd wl ins fnl f) ¾ 7
1962¹⁸ Tara Colleen (IRE) **(42)**(40) (CAHorgan) 3-7-7 NAdams(13) (hrd rdn & no hdwy fnl 2f) hd 8
830⁷ Happy Brave **(43)**(33) (PDCundell) 3-7-8 NCarlisle(12) (nvr nr to chal) 3 9
2017³ Amany (IRE) **(46)**(36) (GLewis) 3-7-11 RStreet(15) (lw: hld up in rr: hdwy over 1f out: nvr nr ldrs) s.h 10
1963⁷ Robo Magic (USA) **(56)**(45) (LMontagueHall) 3-8-7 DHarrison(5) (spd over 4f) nk 11
2137⁴ Cedar Girl **(49)**(37) (RJHodges) 3-7-7 (7) AmandaSanders(8) (gd spd over 4f) nk 12
2048⁴ The Mestral **(42)**(30) (MJRyan) 3-7-7b GBardwell(7) (swtg: outpcd) hd 13
2137⁸ Nordman Lass **(49)**(31) (MissJacquelineDoyle) 3-8-0 AMcGlone(6) (swtg: outpcd) 2 14
2067⁸ Hot Snap **(63)**(16) (CFWall) 3-9-0 GDuffield(2) (outpcd) 11 15
1125¹⁹ La Thuile **(42)** (MDIUsher) 3-7-2 (5) MBaird(14) (b: a bhd) nk 16

LONG HANDICAP The Mestral 7-6 Tara Colleen (IRE) 7-4 La Thuile 7-4

5/1 Vavona, **11/2** BEN GUNN, **13/2** Sizzling, Charnwood Queen, **15/2** Amany (IRE), **8/1** The Mestral, **12/1** Cork Street Girl (IRE), Charlie Sillett (op 8/1), Cedar Girl (tchd 7/1), Almasi (IRE), Robo Magic (USA), Hot Snap, **20/1** Nordman Lass, Happy Brave, **25/1** Tara Colleen (IRE), La Thuile, CSF £45.29 CT £403.82 TOTE £5.20: £1.50 £1.70 £3.80 £1.50 (£10.90) Trio £163.30 OWNER Mr Michael White (LAMBOURN) BRED Michael White and Peter Walwyn 16 Rn

1m 12.7 (2.20) SF: 34/8/32/23/16/13/23/-/-/-/5/-/-/-/-/-

OFFICIAL EXPLANATION **Amany: the jockey reported that his instructions were to switch the filly off and push her out with hands and heels.**

2319

CAMELIA BOTNAR MAIDEN STKS (3-Y.O) (Class D) £5,930.00 (£1,790.00: £870.00: £410.00)
1m 67y Stalls: High GOING minus 0.44 sec per fur (F) 9-10 (9-11)

715⁵ **Cap Juluca (IRE)** (81)(Fav)(RCharlton) 3-9-0 PatEddery(2) (lw: 5th st: led over 2f out: r.o wl) — 1
1979² Raise the Stakes **(78)**(76)(Fav)(IABalding) 3-9-0 RCochrane(1) (lw: led over 1f: 4th st: ev ch 2f out: r.o one pce) 2½ 2
1874³ Sejaal (IRE) (75+) (JLDunlop) 3-9-0 WCarson(15) (plld hrd: hmpd over 5f out: 8th st: stdy hdwy fnl 2f: r.o) ¾ 3
637⁷ Victory Team (IRE) (72) (JRFanshawe) 3-9-0 DHarrison(10) (led over 6f out: 6th st: ev ch over 2f out: wknd fnl f) 1¼ 4
675² Prize Pupil (IRE) (69) (CFWall) 3-9-0 GDuffield(16) (hmpd 6f out: 6th st: ev ch over 2f out: wknd fnl f) 1¾ 5
1796⁹ Yeath (IRE) (57) (RAkehurst) 3-9-0 TQuinn(3) (lw: 7th st: no hdwy fnl 2f) 6 6
1979¹² My Brave Girl (50) (HRACecil) 3-8-9 AMcGlone(13) (nvr nr to chal) 1½ 7
1701⁵ Brown Eyed Girl **(70)**(49) (RHannon) 3-8-9 LDettori(12) (lw: 3rd st: hrd rdn 3f out: sn wknd) ½ 8
1796⁷ Zaaleff (USA) (53) (MRStoute) 3-9-0 WRSwinburn(7) (lw: nvr nr ldrs) ½ 9
1312⁵ White Heat (47) (MJHeaton-Ellis) 3-8-9 MRoberts(4) (chsd ldrs tl wknd 2f out) ½ 10
1979¹¹ Dazzler (52) (MarkCampion) 3-8-7 (7) JDoe(11) (lw: a bhd) s.h 11
Istiwa (48) (CJBenstead) 3-9-0 MWigham(6) (str: scope: lw: s.s: a bhd) 2 12
1736⁵ Tap On Tootsie (41) (ICampbell) 3-8-9 MTebbutt(9) (s.s: a bhd) ¾ 13
1796¹⁰ Fern's Governor (35) (WJMusson) 3-8-9 EGuest(14) (swtg: s.s: a bhd) 3½ 14

3/1 CAP JULUCA (IRE), Raise the Stakes (op 5/1), **7/1** Brown Eyed Girl, **8/1** Sejaal (IRE) (6/1-10/1), Zaaleff (USA) (5/1-9/1), **10/1** Victory Team (IRE) (6/1-12/1), Prize Pupil (IRE), **14/1** My Brave Girl, White Heat, **16/1** Yeath (IRE), **20/1** Istiwa, **33/1** Dazzler, Tap On Tootsie, Fern's Governor, CSF £13.42 TOTE £4.40: £1.90 £2.00 £2.80 (£5.80) Trio £32.40 OWNER Mr Martin Myers (BECKHAMPTON) BRED Mrs N. Myers 14 Rn 1m 44.8 (3.20) SF: 32/27/26/23/20/8/1/-/4/-/3/-/-/-

T/Jkpt: £33,268.60 (0.1 Tckts); £42,171.53 to Newmarket 11/7/95. T/Plpt: £48.00 (505.11 Tckts). T/Qdpt: £74.50 (1.5 Tckts). Hn

2102-NEWMARKET (R-H)
Tuesday July 11th (Good to firm)
WEATHER: hot, stormy WIND: almost nil

2320 STRUTT & PARKER MAIDEN STKS (2-Y.O) (Class D) £5,526.50 (£1,652.00: £791.00: £360.50) 7f (July) Stalls: High GOING minus 0.38 sec (F) 2-05 (2-06)

Alhaarth (IRE) *(90+)*(Fav)*(MajorWRHern)* 2-9-0 WCarson(6) (gd sort: scope: trckd ldrs: led over 2f out: hdd wl over 1f out: r.o wl to ld ins fnl f)........— 1
Mark of Esteem (IRE) *(89)* *(HRACecil)* 2-9-0 MJKinane(11) (cmpt: scope: lw: trckd ldrs: led wl over 1f out tl ins fnl f: r.o towards fin)........nk 2
Silver Prey (USA) *(80)* *(EALDunlop)* 2-9-0 PaulEddery(16) (cmpt: bkwd: s.s: hdwy 2f out: r.o)........4 3
Ironheart *(77)* *(JHMGosden)* 2-9-0 LDettori(8) (gd sort: in tch: hdwy 3f out: edgd rt & one pce appr fnl f)........1¼ 4
Polar Prince (IRE) *(74)* *(MAJarvis)* 2-9-0 PRobinson(2) (w'like: bhd: gd hdwy 2f out: nt qckn ins fnl f)........1½ 5
Amber Fort *(74)* *(PFICole)* 2-9-0 TQuinn(10) (leggy: scope: bkwd: cl up: ev ch 3f out: wknd over 1f out)........s.h 6
D'naan (IRE) *(74)* *(WJHaggas)* 2-9-0 RCochrane(13) (str: cmpt: bkwd: bhd tl hdwy 2f out: r.o)........s.h 7
Latin Reign (USA) *(70)* *(PWChapple-Hyam)* 2-9-0 JReid(9) (gd sort: lw: outpcd 3f out: hmpd over 1f out: styd on towards fin)........1¾ 8
St Mawes (FR) *(68)* *(JLDunlop)* 2-9-0 BThomson(1) (w'like: dwlt: hdwy over 2f out: hmpd over 1f out: no imp)........¾ 9
2070² Villeggiatura *(68)* *(BWHills)* 2-9-0 WRSwinburn(12) (lw: chsd ldrs tl wknd over 1f out)........hd 10
Stoop To Conquer *(63)* *(RCharlton)* 2-9-0 PatEddery(5) (leggy: scope: bit bkwd: sn drvn along: a rr div)........2 11
Gumair (USA) *(63)* *(RHannon)* 2-9-0 RHughes(3) (w'like: scope: outpcd & bhd: sme hdwy 2f out: n.d)........nk 12
2083² Maid For Baileys (IRE) *(53)* *(MJohnston)* 2-8-9 DHolland(14) (chsd ldrs tl wknd fnl 2f)........2 13
Village Native (FR) *(55)* *(KOCunningham-Brown)* 2-9-0 JWeaver(4) (w'like: scope: disp ld over 4f: sn lost pl)........1½ 14
2005ᴾ Red Raja *(54)* *(PMitchell)* 2-9-0 TIves(15) (lw: s.s: a bhd)........nk 15
1752⁷ Minsterbeach *(42)* *(CEBrittain)* 2-9-0 MRoberts(7) (disp ld over 4f: sn wknd)........5 16

7/2 ALHAARTH (IRE) (5/2-4/1), **4/1** Mark of Esteem (IRE), **6/1** Latin Reign (USA) (4/1-13/2), Villeggiatura, **10/1** Ironheart, **14/1** Amber Fort (8/1-16/1), Minsterbeach (10/1-16/1), Maid For Baileys (IRE) (10/1-16/1), Stoop To Conquer, **25/1** St Mawes (FR), Silver Prey (USA), **33/1** Gumair (USA), Polar Prince (IRE), D'naan (IRE), **50/1** Village Native (FR), **66/1** Red Raja, CSF £17.37 TOTE £4.20: £1.90 £2.00 £8.00 (£7.90) Trio £112.40 OWNER Mr Hamdan Al Maktoum (LAMBOURN) BRED Shadwell Estate Company Limited 16 Rn
1m 26.32 (1.92) SF: 44/43/34/31/28/28/28/24/22/22/17/17/7/9/8/-

2321 H & K COMMISSIONS H'CAP (0-80) (3-Y.O+) (Class D) £7,895.00 (£2,360.00: £1,130.00: £515.00) 1m (July) Stalls: High GOING minus 0.38 sec per fur (F) 2-35 (2-37)

1808¹² **Samah (62)***(74)*(Fav)*(DNicholls)* 5-8-12 NConnorton(14) (lw: trckd ldrs gng wl: swtchd rt over 3f out: chal & hung lft 1f out: r.o to ld cl home)........— 1
2031⁶ Deevee **(71)***(83)* *(CJBenstead)* 6-9-7 PRobinson(1) (in tch: hdwy over 2f out: led over 1f out: hdd & no ex nr fin)........s.h 2
1778* Western Fame (USA) **(79)***(88)* *(JLDunlop)* 3-9-6 WCarson(6) (a chsng ldrs: hdwy 2f out: kpt on ins fnl f)........1½ 3
1988³ Mo-Addab (IRE) **(71)***(77)* *(ACStewart)* 5-9-7 MRoberts(3) (cl up: effrt over 2f out: no ex fnl f)1¼ 4
1261⁷ Caleman **(78)***(79)* *(RBoss)* 6-10-0 AMcGlone(4) (lw: led tl hdd over 1f out: kpt on same pce)2½ 5
2181* Saifan **(70)***(70)* *(DMorris)* 6-9-6b 5x LDettori(7) (hdwy 3f out: styd on: nt pce to chal)........¾ 6
1926¹² Secret Aly (CAN) **(75)***(74)* *(CEBrittain)* 5-9-11 BDoyle(2) (chsd ldrs: rdn 2f out: one pce)........nk 7

1967* Crown of Sheba (USA) **(77)***(66) (EALDunlop)* 3-9-4 WRSwinburn(8) (prom tl rdn & wknd fnl 2½f) 5 8
2130³ Be Warned **(78)***(67) (NACallaghan)* 4-10-0 PatEddery(5) (bhd: hdwy 2f out: btn appr fnl f) ....hd 9
1244⁴ Thatchmaster (IRE) **(52)***(39) (CAHorgan)* 4-8-2 TWilliams(12) (hld up & bhd: effrt over 2f out: no imp) 1 10
1808¹³ Battle Colours (IRE) **(56)***(42) (DonEnricoIncisa)* 6-8-6 KimTinkler(10) (a outpcd & bhd) ....¾ 11
2032² I'm Outa Here (IRE) **(65)***(49) (RHannon)* 3-8-6 ow1 JReid(9) (lw: cl up tl wknd fnl 2½f) ....½ 12
701⁸ Rapier Point (IRE) **(68)***(50) (PCHaslam)* 4-9-4 JWeaver(11) (cl up 6f: wknd) 1½ 13
2108² Rise Up Singing **(60)***(41) (WJMusson)* 7-8-7b(3) PMcCabe(15) (racd stands' side: cl up tl wknd appr fnl f) ....½ 14
1988⁴ Wellsian (USA) **(73)***(38) (LMCumani)* 3-9-0 MJKinane(13) (outpcd & bhd fnl 3f) 8 15

7/2 SAMAH (op 8/1), **4/1** Western Fame (USA), **7/1** Wellsian (USA), **8/1** Rise Up Singing, Saifan, Crown of Sheba (USA), **10/1** Deevee, Mo-Addab (IRE), **20/1** Caleman, Thatchmaster (IRE), Secret Aly (CAN), Be Warned, I'm Outa Here (IRE), **50/1** Rapier Point (IRE), **66/1** Battle Colours (IRE), CSF £39.34 CT £142.03 TOTE £9.70: £3.30 £2.40 £2.20 (£86.30) Trio £142.03 OWNER Mrs Norma Robinson (THIRSK) BRED Shadwell Estate Company Limited 15 Rn
1m 39.66 (1.96) SF: 45/54/50/48/50/41/45/28/38/10/13/11/21/12/-
WEIGHT FOR AGE 3yo-9lb

2322 HILLSDOWN CHERRY HINTON STKS (Gp 3) (2-Y.O F) (Class A)
£18,360.00 (£5,080.00: £5,080.00: £1,400.00: £600.00: £280.00)
6f (July) Stalls: High GOING minus 0.38 sec per fur (F) 3-05 (3-06)

1893² **Applaud (USA)** *(100) (DRLoder)* 2-8-9 PatEddery(4) (cl up: led 2f out & qcknd: r.o wl fnl f)..— 1
2025* Darling Flame (USA) *(99) (JHMGosden)* 2-8-9 LDettori(2) (trckd ldrs: hdwy to chal over 1f out: r.o) ....½ 2
1849² Dance Sequence (USA) *(99)*(Fav)*(MRStoute)* 2-8-9 WRSwinburn(8) (lw: trckd ldrs: n.m.r & swtchd over 1f out: r.o wl) ....d.h 2
1259* Flying Squaw *(95) (MRChannon)* 2-8-9 RHughes(3) (hld up & bhd: hdwy 2f out: nt qckn ins fnl f) 1½ 4
1769* Amazing Bay *(93) (IABalding)* 2-8-9 RCochrane(5) (lw: hld up: hdwy 2f out: nt qckn fnl f) ....½ 5
Phantom Creek *(89) (SbinSuroor)* 2-8-9 MJKinane(7) (nice filly: lw: plld hrd: trckd ldrs: rdn & rn green: hmpd over 1f out: kpt on towards fin) 1½ 6
1833³ Beautiful Ballad (IRE) **(94)***(84) (BWHills)* 2-8-9 DHolland(1) (b.hind: slt ld 4f: sn rdn & wknd)...2 7
1871² Paloma Bay (IRE) *(MBell)* 2-8-9 MFenton(6) (s.s: p.u sn after s) .... P

9/4 Dance Sequence (USA) (7/4-11/4), **3/1** Phantom Creek, **5/1** Darling Flame (USA), **11/2** APPLAUD (USA), **7/1** Flying Squaw, **14/1** Paloma Bay (IRE), **20/1** Amazing Bay, **40/1** Beautiful Ballad (IRE), CSF A & DS £8.64 A & DF £15.07 TOTE £6.20: £1.60 DS £1.40 DF £1.50 (A & DS £3.40 A & DF £8.20) OWNER Mr Faisal Salman (NEWMARKET) BRED Claiborne Farm and The Gamely Corporation 8 Rn 1m 13.72 (2.22) SF: 31/30/30/26/24/20/15/-

2323 PRINCESS OF WALES'S STKS (Gp 2) (3-Y.O+) (Class A) £35,576.00
(£13,184.00: £6,342.00: £2,610.00: £1,055.00: £433.00)
1m 4f (July) Stalls: High GOING minus 0.38 sec per fur (F) 3-40 (3-41)

1894* **Beauchamp Hero (105)***(121) (JLDunlop)* 5-9-5 JReid(6) (hld up & bhd: outpcd 3f out: gd hdwy 2f out: qcknd to ld wl ins fnl f) ....— 1
1897⁵ Istidaad (USA) **(106)***(117) (ACStewart)* 3-8-3 WCarson(8) (swtg: hld up: hdwy 3f out: disp ld appr fnl f: r.o) 1 2
1611³ Presenting **(119)***(116)*(Fav)*(JHMGosden)* 3-8-3 LDettori(2) (lw: trckd ldrs: led & qcknd over 2f out: hrd rdn fnl f: no ex towards fin) ....½ 3
1894³ Bal Harbour **(104)***(113) (HRACecil)* 4-9-2 PatEddery(4) (hld up: outpcd over 3f out: gd hdwy to chal 1f out: edgd lft & nt qckn) 2½ 4
1897⁶ In Camera (IRE) **(109)***(110) (MRStoute)* 3-8-3 MRoberts(7) (lw: swtg: trckd ldrs: pushed along 4f out: hdwy & ev ch 1f out: sn btn) 1¾ 5
1836³ Needle Gun (IRE) **(112)***(108) (CEBrittain)* 5-9-2 MJKinane(9) (trckd ldrs: nt clr run & swtchd 2f out: r.o one pce) 2 6
898a⁸ Right Win (IRE) **(118)***(97) (RHannon)* 5-9-5 RHughes(5) (lw: hld up: outpcd 3f out: no imp) ..10 7
1894⁶ Time Star (USA) **(120)***(98) (PFICole)* 4-9-7 TQuinn(1) (mde most tl hdd & wknd over 2f out)...1 8
1894² Midnight Legend **(109)***(82) (LMCumani)* 4-9-2 JWeaver(3) (cl up tl wknd 2f out) 8 9

15/8 Presenting, **5/1** In Camera (IRE), **8/1** BEAUCHAMP HERO (op 9/2), Bal Harbour, Needle Gun (IRE), Midnight Legend (op 5/1), **12/1** Istidaad (USA), **14/1** Time Star (USA), **33/1** Right Win (IRE), CSF £82.20 TOTE £7.60: £2.00 £2.70 £1.60 (£29.40) Trio £27.10 OWNER Mr E. Penser (ARUNDEL) BRED E. Penser 9 Rn 2m 28.83 (0.13) SF: 72/55/54/64/48/59/48/49/33
WEIGHT FOR AGE 3yo-13lb

2324
TYPHOO TEA RATED STKS H'CAP (0-100) (3-Y.O) (Class B)
£8,541.00 (£3,159.00: £1,514.50: £617.50: £243.75: £94.25)
6f (July) Stalls: High GOING minus 0.38 sec per fur (F) 4-10 (4-11)

1806[9] **Perryston View (86)***(92) (PCalver)* 3-8-10v MBirch(6) (trckd ldrs: led wl over 1f out: hrd rdn fnl f: r.o)........— 1
1316[2] Actual Fact (USA) **(83)***(88)*(Fav)*(GHarwood)* 3-8-7 PatEddery(4) (outpcd ½-wy: gd hdwy to chal 1f out: kpt on under str pressure)........½ 2
812[7] Gallows Corner (IRE) **(83)***(87) (RHannon)* 3-8-7 JReid(5) (outpcd & bhd tl styd wl u.p fnl f: nrst fin)........nk 3
633[9] Rockville Pike (IRE) **(83)***(85) (SDow)* 3-8-7 MRoberts(2) (lw: in tch: outpcd ½-wy: hdwy & ch over 1f out: nt qckn ins fnl f)........¾ 4
2067* Fairy Wind (IRE) **(85)***(82) (NACallaghan)* 3-8-9 LDettori(8) (b.hind: cl up: chal 2f out: wknd ins fnl f)........2 5
1806[4] French Grit (IRE) **(88)***(84) (MDods)* 3-8-12 JWeaver(3) (lw: hld up: outpcd ½-wy: hdwy 2f out: rdn & btn 1f out)........nk 6
1795[5] Hinton Rock (IRE) **(92)***(74) (MBell)* 3-9-2b MFenton(1) (swtg: led over 4f: sn wknd)........5 7
LONG HANDICAP Gallows Corner (IRE) 8-6 Rockville Pike (IRE) 8-6

2/1 Actual Fact (USA) (6/4-9/4), **3/1** Fairy Wind (IRE), **5/1** French Grit (IRE), **6/1** PERRYSTON VIEW, **12/1** Hinton Rock (IRE), Gallows Corner (IRE), **25/1** Rockville Pike (IRE), CSF £16.72 CT £108.87 TOTE £6.90: £3.00 £1.70 (£6.50) OWNER Mrs Janis MacPherson (RIPON) BRED Mrs V. E. Hughes 7 Rn 1m 13.85 (2.35) SF: 30/26/25/23/20/22/12
STEWARDS' ENQUIRY Birch suspended 20-21/7/95 (improper use of whip)

2325
HARTLEYS JAM RATED STKS H'CAP (0-100) (3-Y.O F) (Class B)
£8,314.80 (£3,073.20: £1,471.60: £598.00: £234.00: £88.40)
7f (July) Stalls: High GOING minus 0.38 sec per fur (F) 4-45 (4-46)

1915* **Bouche Bee (USA) (87)***(95+)*(Fav)*(LMCumani)* 3-8-3 ow1 LDettori(3) (b.hind: hld up far side: qcknd to ld over 1f out: r.o wl)........— 1
1806[6] Doctor's Glory (USA) **(84)***(88) (RHannon)* 3-8-0 BDoyle(7) (hld up stands' side: hdwy to chal over 1f out: kpt on one pce)........2 2
1362* Forest Cat (IRE) **(92)***(96) (MrsJCecil)* 3-8-8 JReid(5) (b.nr fore: cl up stands' side: led ½-wy: nt pce of wnr fnl f)........s.h 3
2066[5] Signs **(92)***(96) (RHannon)* 3-8-8 MRoberts(1) (led far side to ½-wy: led 2f out: sn hdd: hrd rdn & one pce)........hd 4
1787* Courageous Dancer (IRE) **(84)***(85) (BHanbury)* 3-7-11 (3) SSanders(4) (lw: racd stands' side: chal ½-wy: rdn & btn appr fnl f)........1½ 5
1588[5] Hiwaya **(98)***(98) (HThomsonJones)* 3-9-0 WCarson(6) (lw: swtg: led stands' side to ½-wy: wknd wl over 1f out)........½ 6
1370[3] Dashing Water **(92)***(46) (IABalding)* 3-8-8 RCochrane(2) (b.nr hind: trckd ldrs far side: led ½-wy: hdd & wknd qckly 2f out)........20 7
LONG HANDICAP Courageous Dancer (IRE) 7-13

13/8 BOUCHE BEE (USA), **3/1** Forest Cat (IRE), **4/1** Courageous Dancer (IRE) (5/2-9/2), **9/1** Hiwaya, **12/1** Dashing Water, Doctor's Glory (USA) (8/1-14/1), **25/1** Signs, CSF £18.12 TOTE £2.70: £1.60 £4.00 (£25.60) OWNER Miss Gatto Roissard (NEWMARKET) BRED Jones Kamur Partnership 7 Rn 1m 27.06 (2.66) SF: 26/19/27/27/16/29/-

2326
NGK SPARK PLUGS SOHAM H'CAP (0-80) (3-Y.O+) (Class D)
£5,900.00 (£1,760.00: £840.00: £380.00)
5f (July) Stalls: High GOING minus 0.38 sec per fur (F) 5-15 (5-15)

1193* **Broadstairs Beauty (IRE) (75)***(81) (SRBowring)* 5-9-7v(5) CTeague(1) (b: b.hind: led centre: rdn over 2f out: hdd ins fnl f: rallied to ld last stride)........— 1
2013[3] Aragrove **(77)***(83) (JWPayne)* 5-10-0b MTebbutt(2) (lw: b: swtg: a.p centre: rdn to ld ins fnl f: no ex nr fin)........s.h 2
1689[9] Pageboy **(65)***(71)*(Fav)*(PCHaslam)* 6-9-2b JWeaver(5) (lw: racd centre: bhd tl hdwy 2f out: ev ch ins fnl f: kpt on)........s.h 3
1822[5] Lloc **(54)***(60) (JohnBerry)* 3-7-8 (5) NVarley(10) (led stands' side: hung lft 2f out: ev ch tl no ex cl home)........s.h 4
1832[2] Gone Savage **(66)***(71) (WJMusson)* 7-9-3 MJKinane(11) (b.hind: chsd ldr stands' side: hdwy & ev ch 1f out: nt qckn towards fin)........s.h 5
2252* Ned's Bonanza **(71)***(68)*(Fav)*(MDods)* 6-9-8 7x WCarson(7) (drvn along stands' side: styd on fnl 2f: nrst fin)........2½ 6
2079[2] Purple Fling **(71)***(63) (SirMarkPrescott)* 4-9-8 WWoods(3) (s.i.s: hdwy u.p ½-wy: nvr able chal)........1¾ 7

2252[10] Metal Boys **(67)***(55) (MissLCSiddall)* 8-9-4 WNewnes(9) (bhd stands' side: sme hdwy over 1f out: n.d) 1¼ **8**
1700[7] Moujeeb (USA) **(62)***(42) (PatMitchell)* 5-8-13 WRSwinburn(8) (a outpcd & bhd) 2½ **9**
2203[6] Fairy Fay (IRE) **(50)***(14) (BJMcMath)* 3-7-4 (5) MBaird(4) (b.hind: swtg: racd stands' side: a outpcd & bhd) 5 **10**
1942[3] High Priest **(69)***(32) (LMCumani)* 3-9-0 LDettori(6) (lw: racd centre: chsd wnr to ½-wy: sn btn) ....nk **11**

5/1 Ned's Bonanza, Pageboy, **11/2** BROADSTAIRS BEAUTY (IRE), **6/1** Gone Savage, **13/2** Purple Fling, High Priest, **15/2** Aragrove, **14/1** Moujeeb (USA), **16/1** Lloc, **20/1** Metal Boys, **50/1** Fairy Fay (IRE), CSF £43.40 CT £201.60 TOTE £6.80: £1.90 £3.10 £2.10 (£26.60) Trio £105.10 OWNER Mrs Judy Hunt (EDWINSTOWE) BRED Patrick Murnaghan 11 Rn

59.85 secs (0.85) SF: 63/65/53/36/53/50/45/37/24/-/8

WEIGHT FOR AGE 3yo-6lb

STEWARDS' ENQUIRY Tebbutt suspended 20-22/7/95 (improper use of whip)

T/Jkpt: Not Won; £64,209.39 to Newmarket 12/7/95. T/Plpt: £18.60 (2,113.48 Tckts). T/Qdpt: £5.10 (42.25 Tckts). AA

2128-PONTEFRACT (L-H)
Tuesday July 11th (Good to firm)

WEATHER: overcast, hot WIND: almost nil

2327

HYDE SPORTING PROMOTIONS LADIES AMATEUR H'CAP (0-60) (3-Y.O+) (Class F) £3,288.00 (£984.00: £472.00: £216.00)
1m 2f 6y Stalls: Low GOING minus 0.31 sec per fur (GF) 2-20 (2-30)

1881[3] **Harry Browne (IRE) (55)***(63) (MrsJRRamsden)* 3-10-6 (3) MissERamsden(9) (hld up: hdwy over 2f out: r.o wl to ld cl home) ....— **1**
1956[2] Cashmirie **(44)***(51)*(Fav)*(JLEyre)* 3-9-12 MissDianaJones(1) (trckd ldrs: hrd rdn over 1f out: r.o u.p fnl f) ....½ **2**
2254[3] Lord Vivienne (IRE) **(41)***(47) (BSRothwell)* 6-10-3 (3) MissAlexMcCabe(12) (led after 1f: hrd rdn over 1f out: ct nr fin) 1 **3**
1543[4] Larn Fort **(56)***(54) (CWFairhurst)* 5-11-7v MrsSBosley(7) (chsd ldrs: effrt over 2f out: rdn over 1f out: kpt on one pce) 5 **4**
2165* Thaleros **(55)***(45) (GMMoore)* 5-11-6 5x MrsLPearce(3) (hld up: prog 3f out: kpt on fnl 2f: nt pce to chal) 5 **5**
2126[2] Rasayel (USA) **(48)***(37) (PDEvans)* 5-10-13 MissCBurgess(8) (trckd ldr: wknd over 2f out: sn one pce) ....½ **6**
2289[7] Thrower **(46)***(34) (WMBrisbourne)* 4-10-8 (3) MrsSJOwen(4) (prom: rdn over 4f out: sn wknd) .½ **7**
875[2] Boundary Express **(51)***(33) (EJAlston)* 3-10-5 MissRClark(11) (hld up: n.d) 4 **8**
1985* Queens Contractor **(40)***(11) (SMellor)* 5-10-5b MissEJoyce(2) (in tch: sme hdwy 4f out: sn rdn & wknd) 7 **9**
1873[6] Intrepid Fort **(23)** *(BWMurray)* 6-9-2v MissAElsey(14) (a in rr) 2½ **10**
1921[3] Ijab (CAN) **(37)** *(JParkes)* 5-10-2b MrsAFarrell(6) (prom early: rdn & wknd 2f out) 5 **11**
1944[8] Kralingen **(41)** *(NChamberlain)* 3-9-9 ow9 MissCMetcalfe(10) (mid div tl rdn & lost pl over 3f out: sn bhd) ....nk **12**
Crystal Heart (IRE) **(36)** *(FJYardley)* 4-9-12 (3) MissSYardley(13) (n.d) 4 **13**
1883[11] Plum Dennis **(26)** *(NBycroft)* 4-9-2b(3) MissABycroft(5) (unruly s: a bhd) 3½ **14**

LONG HANDICAP Kralingen 8-12

5/1 Cashmirie, **6/1** Thaleros, **13/2** Larn Fort, **7/1** Queens Contractor, **8/1** HARRY BROWNE (IRE), **10/1** Lord Vivienne (IRE), Thrower, Rasayel (USA), **11/1** Ijab (CAN), **16/1** Intrepid Fort, Boundary Express, **25/1** Plum Dennis, **33/1** Crystal Heart (IRE), **50/1** Kralingen, CSF £45.44 CT £377.00 TOTE £7.30: £2.20 £1.60 £6.10 (£36.90) Trio £331.40 OWNER Mrs J. R. Ramsden (THIRSK) BRED Patrick Whelan in Ireland 14 Rn 2m 15.1 (6.80) SF: 43/31/38/45/36/28/25/13/2/-/-/-/-/-

WEIGHT FOR AGE 3yo-11lb

2328

DIANNE NURSERY H'CAP (2-Y.O) (Class E) £4,142.50 (£1,240.00: £595.00: £272.50) **6f** Stalls: Low GOING minus 0.31 sec per fur (GF) 2-50 (2-51)

2085[5] **Benny Glow (82)***(82) (MrsJRRamsden)* 2-9-7 KFallon(4) (mid div: rdn 2f out: edgd rt 1f out: rdn to ld cl home) ....— **1**
2153[3] Bold Times **(69)***(68) (PDEvans)* 2-8-8 JFortune(1) (led tl hdd over 2f out: rdn to ld over 1f out: r.o: ct cl home) ....½ **2**
1266* Russian Rascal (IRE) **(59)***(53) (MHEasterby)* 2-7-12 SMaloney(9) (chsd ldrs: rdn along over 1f out: kpt on one pce fnl f) 1¾ **3**
2131[4] Ramsey Hope **(73)***(66) (CWFairhurst)* 2-8-12 NKennedy(2) (disp ld: rdn to ld over 2f out: hdd over 1f out: wknd fnl f) ....nk **4**

1197[4] Polly Golightly **(80)***(68) (BSmart)* 2-8-12 (7) ADaly(11) (chsd ldrs: rdn 2f out: one pce)..............2 **5**
1159* Thorntoun Jewel (IRE) **(61)***(36) (JBalding)* 2-8-0 ClaireBalding(3) (chsd ldrs: rdn & wknd over 2f out)..........5 **6**
2153[2] Moi Canard **(66)***(40) (JBerry)* 2-8-5 JCarroll(5) (chsd ldrs: rdn & wknd over 2f out).................nk **7**
1678* Doug's Folly **(63)***(34) (MWEasterby)* 2-7-9 (7) RuthCoulter(6) (a in rr)..1 **8**
2116* Shontaine **(80)***(50)*(Fav)*(MJohnston)* 2-9-5 WRyan(10) (prom tl wknd over 2f out)..................½ **9**
2161[11] Lucky Bea **(60)***(26) (MWEasterby)* 2-7-13 LCharnock(7) (unruly s: s.i.s: a bhd).....................1¼ **10**
1413[7] Copper Bright **(57)***(19) (PCHaslam)* 2-7-10 DaleGibson(8) (sn pushed along in rr: n.d).........1½ **11**

11/4 Shontaine, **9/2** BENNY GLOW, **6/1** Doug's Folly, Ramsey Hope, **13/2** Moi Canard, Russian Rascal (IRE), **14/1** Polly Golightly, **20/1** Bold Times, Thorntoun Jewel (IRE), Lucky Bea, **25/1** Copper Bright, CSF £80.31 CT £542.29 TOTE £5.00: £1.90 £3.40 £2.00 (£28.80) Trio £164.90 OWNER Mr Ronald Thorburn (THIRSK) BRED D. H. Jones 11 Rn

1m 18.4 (4.10) SF: 26/12/-/10/12/-/-/-/-/-/-

2329 BRADLEY MAIDEN STKS (3-Y.O+) (Class D) £3,777.50 (£1,145.00: £560.00: £267.50) **1m 2f 6y** Stalls: Low GOING minus 0.31 sec per fur (GF) 3-20 (3-21)

1983[2] **Temora (IRE)** *(86) (HRACecil)* 3-8-5 WRyan(5) (mde all: qcknd clr 2f out: rdn over 1f out: easily)..........— **1**
1946[2] Sherqy (IRE) **(83)***(83)*(Fav)*(JLDunlop)* 3-8-10 GCarter(7) (trckd ldr: hdwy 2f out: sn hrd rdn: no imp)..........5 **2**
1097[17] Debutante Days *(59) (ACStewart)* 3-8-0 (5) MHumphries(4) (hld up: rdn over 3f out: kpt on one pce)..........12 **3**
1417[W] Discorsi *(61) (GWragg)* 3-8-10 FNorton(1) (ss: hdwy ½-wy: rdn 3f out: no imp).......................2 **4**
1916[5] Reaganesque (USA) *(59) (EALDunlop)* 3-8-10 KDarley(3) (chsd wnr: rdn over 2f out: sn wknd)..........1 **5**
Larentia *(14) (JParkes)* 3-8-5 LCharnock(6) (hld up: rdn ½-wy: sn wknd & t.o).......................25 **6**
Bold Joker **(33)** *(GROldroyd)* 4-9-2 (5) GParkin(2) (hld up in rr: wknd ½-wy: t.o)....................30 **7**

11/8 Sherqy (IRE), **6/4** TEMORA (IRE), **11/2** Reaganesque (USA), **10/1** Discorsi, **20/1** Debutante Days, **50/1** Larentia, **500/1** Bold Joker, CSF £3.80 TOTE £2.00: £1.10 £1.50 (£1.30) OWNER Sheikh Mohammed (NEWMARKET) BRED Sheikh Mohammed bin Rashid al Maktoum 7 Rn

2m 11.1 (2.80) SF: 44/41/17/19/17/-/-
WEIGHT FOR AGE 3yo-11lb

2330 NYQUIST H'CAP (0-80) (3-Y.O+) (Class D) £6,264.00 (£1,872.00: £654.00: £654.00) **6f** Stalls: Low GOING minus 0.31 sec per fur (GF) 3-55 (3-55)

1994[4] **Souperficial (57)***(68) (JAGlover)* 4-8-8v GDuffield(10) (hld up: hdwy on outside 2f out: led over 1f out: drvn out)..........— **1**
2096[7] Captain Carat **(64)***(68) (MrsJRRamsden)* 4-9-1 KFallon(7) (hld up: hdwy 2f out: styd on u.p fnl f)..........2½ **2**
2112* Rocketeer (IRE) **(69)***(73) (WRMuir)* 4-9-6b JCarroll(9) (chsd ldrs: hdwy to ld 2f out: hdd over 1f out: unable qckn fnl f)..........s.h **3**
2074[6] Blue Grit **(51)***(55) (MDods)* 9-8-2 DaleGibson(11) (stdd s: hdwy over 2f out: rdn over 1f out: styd on u.p fnl f)..........d.h **3**
2229[7] Birchwood Sun **(59)***(55) (MDods)* 5-8-10b DeanMcKeown(4) (in rr tl sme late hdwy fnl 2f)........3 **5**
2010[11] Tatika **(69)***(61) (GWragg)* 5-9-6b FNorton(8) (trckd ldrs: hrd rdn over 2f out: wknd over 1f out)..........1½ **6**
2229[3] Densben **(49)***(37) (DenysSmith)* 11-8-0 LCharnock(3) (led to 2f out: hrd rdn & wknd)...........1½ **7**
2130[2] Cavers Yangous **(72)***(60)*(Fav)*(MJohnston)* 4-9-9 WRyan(5) (chsd ldrs: rdn 2f out: wknd over 1f out)..........s.h **8**
1827[6] Followmegirls **(54)***(42) (MrsALMKing)* 6-8-2 (3) AGarth(6) (chsd ldrs: rdn 2f out: nt pce to chal)..........hd **9**
2001[6] I'm Your Lady **(73)***(60) (BAMcMahon)* 4-9-10 GCarter(1) (cl up: rdn over 2f out: wknd appr fnl f)..........nk **10**
2163[5] High Domain (IRE) **(67)***(53) (TDBarron)* 4-9-4 JFortune(12) (ss: a in rr)..............................nk **11**
2006[7] Skip to Somerfield **(76)***(9) (KMcAuliffe)* 3-9-6 KDarley(2) (hld up in tch: rdn ½-wy: sn wknd)..........20 **12**

9/2 Cavers Yangous, **11/2** Captain Carat, Rocketeer (IRE), **15/2** Tatika, **9/1** SOUPERFICIAL, **11/1** Densben, **14/1** Blue Grit, Birchwood Sun, Skip to Somerfield, I'm Your Lady, **16/1** High Domain (IRE), Followmegirls, CSF £52.78 CT S, CC & R £136.20 S, CC & BG £313.73 TOTE £9.00: £2.70 £2.30 R £1.10 BG £1.50 (£25.70) Trio S, CC & R £40.50 S, CC & BG £56.90 OWNER Mr M. G. Ridley (WORKSOP) BRED C. L. Loyd 12 Rn

1m 17.1 (2.80) SF: 30/30/35/17/17/23/-/22/4/22/15/-
WEIGHT FOR AGE 3yo-7lb

2331 TANSHELF MAIDEN STKS (3-Y.O+) (Class D) £3,745.00 (£1,135.00: £555.00: £265.00) **1m 4f 8y** Stalls: Low GOING minus 0.31 sec per fur (GF) 4-25 (4-27)

657[12] **Shawahin** *(84) (JLDunlop)* 3-8-8 GCarter(2) (hld up: hmpd & drppd rr 4f out: gd hdwy over 2f out: styd on to ld ins fnl f: pushed clr) — 1
1878[2] Festive Lassie *(71) (TDBarron)* 4-9-2 JFortune(1) (a.p: led over 2f out: drvn clr appr fnl f: hdd ins fnl f: no ex) 6 2
1814[2] Courtown Boy *(72) (OO'Neill)* 5-9-7 VSlattery(8) (mid div: prog 3f out: kpt on one pce fnl f) 3 3
1383[4] Eurolink Shadow *(68) (LMCumani)* 3-8-8 KDarley(6) (led: pushed along over 2f out: sn hdd & grad wknd) 3 4
Winters Cottage (IRE) *(61) (PDEvans)* 7-9-7 GHind(7) (s.i.s: hdwy on outside over 4f out: sn rdn & btn) 5 5
1204[2] Master Charter *(56) (MrsJRRamsden)* 3-8-8 KFallon(5) (trckd ldrs: effrt 3f out: rdn & btn over 1f out) 4 6
Catch the Pigeon *(44) (REBarr)* 6-8-9 (7) PFessey(9) (s.i.s: sn rcvrd: outpcd over 3f out: wknd) 5 7
Sherrington *(25) (ACStewart)* 3-7-12 (5) MHumphries(4) (mid div: rdn over 5f out: sn bhd) 15 8
Calcando *(EWeymes)* 3-8-3 JMarshall(3) (hld up: bdly hmpd over 3f out: eased & virtually p.u after) 20 9
1916[3] Officer (Fav)*(HRACecil)* 3-8-8 WRyan(10) (trckd ldrs tl lost pl over 4f out: sn p.u: broke leg: dead) P

6/4 Officer, **2/1** Eurolink Shadow, **9/1** Festive Lassie, **10/1** Courtown Boy, **11/1** Master Charter, **16/1** SHAWAHIN, **20/1** Sherrington, **33/1** Calcando, **50/1** Winters Cottage (IRE), **100/1** Catch the Pigeon, CSF £134.52 TOTE £17.90: £2.90 £1.90 £2.40 (132.80) Trio £139.10 OWNER Mr Hamdan Al Maktoum (ARUNDEL) BRED Lord Halifax 10 Rn 2m 41.0 (6.70) SF: 26/26/27/10/16/-/-/-/-/-
WEIGHT FOR AGE 3yo-13lb

OFFICIAL EXPLANATION **Master Charter: his jockey explained that he stopped riding in the final stages because both he and the horse were exhausted, had nothing more to give and it was unlikely that they would have finished much closer had he been able to continue riding.**

2332 KING RICHARD III H'CAP (0-70) (3-Y.O+ F & M) (Class E) £3,980.00 (£1,190.00: £570.00: £260.00) **1m 4y** Stalls: Low GOING minus 0.31 sec per fur (GF) 5-00 (5-00)

1945[2] **Prudent Pet (58)***(67) (CWFairhurst)* 3-8-12 (3) JTate(12) (hld up & bhd: gd hdwy over 2f out: styd on to ld ent fnl f: hung lft: r.o wl) — 1
2149* Just Fizzy **(60)***(66) (JHetherton)* 3-9-3 6x NKennedy(10) (led tl ent fnl f: kpt on same pce) 1¾ 2
*2292** Asmarina **(45)***(50) (SRBowring)* 5-8-11b 6x StephenDavies(5) (in rr tl hdwy over 2f out: r.o u.p ins fnl f) ½ 3
1880[8] Simand **(45)***(49) (EWeymes)* 3-8-2 GHind(7) (prom: hrd rdn over 2f out: unable qckn ins fnl f) s.h 4
1675[4] Almizaj **(69)***(71) (HThomsonJones)* 3-9-12 NCarlisle(8) (hld up in tch: rdn over 2f out: kpt on one pce ins fnl f) 1 5
1939[2] Kellaire Girl (IRE) **(46)***(48)*(Fav)*(GLewis)* 3-7-12 (5) AWhelan(3) (a chsng ldrs: rdn over 2f out: sn one pce) nk 6
1811[11] Harvest Rose **(48)***(43) (OO'Neill)* 6-9-0 VSlattery(11) (in tch tl drvn appr st: wknd over 1f out) 3½ 7
2133[2] Hunza Story **(37)***(29) (NPLittmoden)* 3-7-1 (7)ow1 CAdamson(1) (a mid div: rdn 3f out: n.d) ¾ 8
2190[4] Benten **(36)** *(DWChapman)* 3-7-7 JMarshall(9) (plld hrd: cl up tl rdn & wknd over 3f out: sn bhd) 25 9
1649* Chantry Bellini **(46)** (Fav)*(MrsSMAustin)* 6-8-9b(3) DarrenMoffatt(4) (reard s: a bhd: t.o) 8 10
LONG HANDICAP Hunza Story 7-6 Benten 7-5

4/1 Kellaire Girl (IRE), Chantry Bellini, **5/1** Almizaj, **11/2** PRUDENT PET, **13/2** Asmarina, **10/1** Just Fizzy, **16/1** Simand, **20/1** Hunza Story, Harvest Rose, **33/1** Benten, CSF £50.90 CT £325.95 TOTE £6.10: £1.90 £2.40 £2.60 (£17.00) Trio £65.10 OWNER The McLain & Rodda Partnership (MIDDLEHAM) BRED John A. Jones Morgan 10 Rn 1m 46.8 (4.80) SF: 29/28/21/11/33/10/14/-/-/-
WEIGHT FOR AGE 3yo-9lb

OFFICIAL EXPLANATION **Chantry Bellini: appeared to have strained her back muscles when she reared on leaving the stalls.**

2333 MONKHILL LIMITED STKS (0-70) (3-Y.O+) (Class E) £3,191.00 (£968.00: £474.00: £227.00) **1m 2f 6y** Stalls: Low GOING minus 0.31 sec per fur (GF) 5-30 (5-30)

1102[9] **Access Adventurer (IRE) (65)***(83) (RBoss)* 4-9-7 WRyan(1) (led tl hdd over 2f out: rallied to ld nr fin) — 1

2279² Carol's Dream (USA) **(70)***(83) (JWHills)* 3-8-10 JCarroll(4) (chsd ldr: led over 2f out: hrd rdn & ct nr fin)....nk **2**
2139² Finlaggan **(69)***(75) (SirMarkPrescott)* 3-8-7 GDuffield(3) (trckd ldrs: rdn over 2f out: unable qckn)....3 **3**
1966* First Bite (IRE) **(70)***(78) (JLDunlop)* 3-8-12 GCarter(7) (hld up: pushed along on outside over 2f out: nvr nr ldrs)....1¼ **4**
1825³ Carlito Brigante **(70)***(63)*(Fav)*(MrsJRRamsden)* 3-8-10 KFallon(5) (dwlt: sn prom: rdn over 2f out: sn btn)....8 **5**
2088¹¹ Ballard Ring (IRE) **(48)***(42) (JSWainwright)* 4-9-2b ACulhane(2) (ss: a bhd)....10 **6**
2020³ Heathyards Magic (IRE) **(69)***(30) (RHollinshead)* 3-8-12 KDarley(6) (hld up & bhd: rdn over 3f out: sn wknd: eased whn btn)....12 **7**

11/4 Carlito Brigante, **3/1** Finlaggan, **7/2** First Bite (IRE), **9/2** Carol's Dream (USA), **7/1** ACCESS ADVENTURER (IRE), **10/1** Heathyards Magic (IRE), **66/1** Ballard Ring (IRE), CSF £35.32 TOTE £8.60: £2.20 £2.70 (£25.60) OWNER Miss Elaine Williams (NEWMARKET) BRED Barronstown Bloodstock Ltd 7 Rn
2m 12.9 (4.60) SF: 45/34/26/29/14/4/-
WEIGHT FOR AGE 3yo-11lb
T/Plpt: £1371.80 (10.95 Tckts). T/Qdpt: Not Won; £134.60 to Newmarket 12/7/95. DG

2173-FOLKESTONE (R-H)
Wednesday July 12th (Good to firm)
WEATHER: hot WIND: mod half bhd

2334 BRIDGE (S) H'CAP (0-60) (3-Y.O+) (Class G) £2,646.20 (£733.20: £350.60)
1m 1f 149y Stalls: Low GOING minus 0.55 sec per fur (F) 2-20 (2-21)

2246⁵ **Yo Kiri-B (48)***(61) (JFfitch-Heyes)* 4-9-13 GDuffield(5) (lw: 5th st: hrd rdn over 1f out: led nr fin)....— **1**
2174⁹ Mim-Lou-and **(45)***(56) (BRMillman)* 3-8-13 JWilliams(10) (2nd st: rdn over 2f out: ev ch ins fnl f: unable qckn)....1 **2**
2174⁴ Zahid (USA) **(43)***(54)*(Fav)*(KRBurke)* 4-9-8 RCochrane(4) (lw: 3rd st: hrd rdn over 1f out: ev ch ins fnl f: unable qckn)....nk **3**
2050⁹ Head For Heaven **(40)***(51) (RPCHoad)* 5-9-5 PRobinson(1) (led over 7f out: hrd rdn over 1f out: hdd nr fin)....hd **4**
2052⁹ Sharp Gazelle **(38)***(45) (BSmart)* 5-8-10 (7) MarkDenaro(7) (lw: rdn over 2f out: hdwy over 1f out: r.o)....2 **5**
1548⁹ Tocco Jewel **(18)***(24) (MJRyan)* 5-7-6 (5) MBaird(9) (nvr nr to chal)....1 **6**
2037⁵ Malingerer **(33)***(33) (DAWilson)* 4-8-12 AMackay(12) (6th st: wknd over 1f out)....3½ **7**
2089* Bronze Runner **(40)***(36) (SMellor)* 11-8-12b(7) ADaly(2) (a bhd)....2½ **8**
2090⁹ Tout de Val **(31)***(12) (KBishop)* 6-8-10 RPerham(11) (led 2f: 4th st: wknd over 2f out)....9 **9**
1911¹⁰ Pop to Stans **(47)***(27) (JPearce)* 6-9-12 GBardwell(6) (lw: a bhd)....½ **10**
De la Billiere (IRE) **(35)** *(HGRowsell)* 7-8-11 (3) SDrowne(8) (b: prom over 5f)....25 **11**
Billyback **(43)** *(MJRyan)* 5-9-8 AClark(3) (s.s: a bhd)....3 **12**

100/30 Zahid (USA) (9/4-7/2), **4/1** Pop to Stans (op 6/1), **9/2** Bronze Runner (5/2-5/1), **8/1** YO KIRI-B (6/1-9/1), Malingerer (6/1-9/1), **11/1** Head For Heaven (7/1-12/1), **12/1** Tout de Val (8/1-14/1), **14/1** Tocco Jewel (10/1-16/1), Sharp Gazelle (10/1-16/1), **16/1** Mim-Lou-and, **33/1** De la Billiere (IRE), Billyback, CSF £116.13 CT £465.49 TOTE £13.80: £3.40 £2.80 £1.20 (£74.90) Trio £80.90 OWNER Miss L. A. Elliott (LEWES) BRED Crescent (UK) Ltd 12 Rn
2m 2.9 (5.20) SF: 23/7/16/13/7/-/-/-/-/-/-/-
WEIGHT FOR AGE 3yo-11lb
Bt in 3,600gns

2335 DAILY STAR NURSERY H'CAP (2-Y.O) (Class E) £3,187.80 (£950.40: £453.20: £204.60) **5f** Stalls: Centre GOING minus 0.55 sec per fur (F) 2-50 (2-50)

1247³ **Welsh Mountain** *(75) (MJHeaton-Ellis)* 2-9-4 DHolland(5) (chsd ldr: rdn over 3f out: led ins fnl f: r.o wl)....— **1**
1810* Arlington Lady *(66)*(Fav)*(NACallaghan)* 2-8-4 (7) MHenry(2) (b.hind: hld up: hrd rdn over 1f out: ev ch ins fnl f: unable qckn)....¾ **2**
2176* Wingnut (IRE) *(66) (GLewis)* 2-8-12 7x PaulEddery(1) (lw: led: hrd rdn over 1f out: hdd ins fnl f: one pce)....nk **3**
1722* Just Ice *(59) (SirMarkPrescott)* 2-9-7 GDuffield(4) (hld up: rdn 2f out: wknd over 1f out)....5 **4**
2170² Mister Sean (IRE) *(45) (JWPayne)* 2-9-6 RCochrane(7) (lw: hld up: rdn 2f out: wknd over 1f out)....4 **5**
1424ᵁ Mrs McBadger *(26) (BSmart)* 2-8-2 (3) SSanders(6) (lw: prom over 2f)....1¼ **6**
1810⁴ Solva Mist *(18) (LJHolt)* 2-8-1 CAvery(3) (lw: a bhd)....1¼ **7**

5/2 Arlington Lady, **3/1** WELSH MOUNTAIN, **100/30** Just Ice, **5/1** Mister Sean (IRE), **8/1** Mrs McBadger (6/1-9/1), **11/1** Wingnut (IRE) (6/1-12/1), **25/1** Solva Mist, CSF £10.73 TOTE £4.10: £2.00 £2.60 (£8.00) OWNER Canary Thoroughbreds (NEWMARKET) BRED Prof Klaus E. Rohde 7 Rn 59.8 secs (1.20) SF: 19/5/35/26/26/-/-

2336

ST LAWRENCE MAIDEN AUCTION STKS (2-Y.O) (Class F) £2,519.00 (£694.00: £329.00) **6f** Stalls: Centre GOING minus 0.55 sec per fur (F) 3-25 (3-27)

*1089*6 **Times of Times (IRE)** *(54) (DJSCosgrove)* 2-7-11 FNorton(2) (mde virtually all: hrd rdn over 1f out: r.o wl)........— 1
1938 2 Where's Margaret *(49)*(Fav)*(GLewis)* 2-8-1 ow1 PaulEddery(5) (lw: hld up: rdn over 1f out: unable qckn)........3 2
Western Venture (IRE) *(46) (JWPayne)* 2-8-6 ow1 RCochrane(3) (w'like: lw: w wnr: rdn & ev ch over 2f out: 3rd & btn whn hmpd ins fnl f)........3 3
Cherry Garden (IRE) *(9) (TJNaughton)* 2-8-2 (3) SSanders(1) (w'like: swvd lft s: a wl bhd).....14 4
Tartan Express (IRE) *(BAPearce)* 2-8-5 StephenDavies(4) (unf: bit bkwd: bhd fnl 3f)........4 5

2/5 Where's Margaret, **3/1** Western Venture (IRE), **12/1** TIMES OF TIMES (IRE) (op 7/1), **20/1** Cherry Garden (IRE), **50/1** Tartan Express (IRE), CSF £17.27 TOTE £14.20: £1.40 £1.10 (£2.90) OWNER Mrs M. Schneider (NEWMARKET) BRED E. Moloney 5 Rn 1m 13.1 (1.40) SF: 18/13/10/-/-

2337

GODFREY EVANS MEDIAN AUCTION MAIDEN STKS (3 & 4-Y.O) (Class E) £3,102.00 (£924.00: £440.00: £198.00)
6f Stalls: Centre GOING minus 0.55 sec per fur (F) 3-55 (3-55)

2066 7 **Red Rita (IRE) (75)***(67) (WRMuir)* 4-8-13 DHolland(6) (lw: mde all: rdn out)........— 1
2164 2 Agoer *(60)*(Fav)*(CEBrittain)* 3-8-6 WWoods(2) (chsd wnr: rdn over 2f out: ev ch over 1f out: unable qckn)........2½ 2
Mason (IRE) *(56) (SMellor)* 3-8-4 (7) ADaly(1) (hld up: rdn over 2f out: wknd fnl f)........3½ 3
Anjomajasa *(42) (MissGayKelleway)* 3-8-6 RCochrane(3) (unf: s.s: nvr nrr)........3½ 4
2164 5 Don't Look Now **(65)***(35) (DrJDScargill)* 3-8-3 (3) SSanders(5) (lw: bhd fnl 2f)........2½ 5
Wendals Touch *(RMFlower)* 4-8-13 AMorris(4) (bhd fnl 4f)........14 6

Evens Agoer, **7/4** RED RITA (IRE), **6/1** Don't Look Now (4/1-8/1), **7/1** Anjomajasa (op 9/2), **20/1** Mason (IRE), **50/1** Wendals Touch, CSF £4.09 TOTE £2.40: £1.30 £1.30 (£2.10) OWNER Mr T. Brady (LAMBOURN) BRED J. B. Clarke 6 Rn 1m 12.0 (0.30) SF: 47/33/29/15/8/-
WEIGHT FOR AGE 3yo-7lb

2338

LESLIE AMES MEMORIAL H'CAP (0-70) (3-Y.O+) (Class E) £3,044.80 (£906.40: £431.20: £193.60)
5f Stalls: Centre GOING minus 0.55 sec per fur (F) 4-30 (4-30)

2179 2 **Super Rocky (62)***(67)*(Fav)*(RBastiman)* 6-9-5 (5) HBastiman(1) (a.p: nt clr run over 2f out & over 1f out: squeezed thro ins fnl f: led last strides)........— 1
2048 2 Miami Banker **(42)***(47) (WRMuir)* 9-8-4b GBardwell(2) (swtg: led: rdn over 2f out: hdd last strides)........hd 2
1429 7 Tyrian Purple (IRE) **(54)***(54) (TJNaughton)* 7-8-11b(5) JDSmith(3) (hrd rdn over 2f out: hdwy over 1f out: r.o)........1½ 3
2054 8 Splash of Salt (IRE) **(41)***(36) (TJNaughton)* 5-8-0b(3) SSanders(5) (swtg: hrd rdn & hdwy over 1f out: r.o one pce)........1½ 4
2163 3 Halbert **(55)***(46) (MRChannon)* 6-9-3v 7x PaulEddery(4) (lw: a.p: rdn over 2f out: wknd ins fnl f)........1¼ 5

11/8 SUPER ROCKY, **9/4** Miami Banker, **11/4** Halbert (7/4-100/30), **10/1** Tyrian Purple (IRE) (6/1-11/1), **33/1** Splash of Salt (IRE), CSF £4.71 TOTE £2.40: £1.20 £1.60 (£2.90) OWNER Mr I. B. Barker (WETHERBY) BRED J. Berry 5 Rn 59.3 secs (0.70) SF: 49/29/36/18/28

2339

KNOTT H'CAP (0-70) (3-Y.O+ F & M) (Class E) £3,330.80 (£994.40: £475.20: £215.60) **1m 4f** Stalls: Low GOING minus 0.55 sec per fur (F) 5-00 (5-01)

1986 4 **Labibeh (USA) (66)***(76) (JLDunlop)* 3-9-5 WNewnes(2) (swtg: mde all: unchal)........— 1
Unchanged **(60)***(65) (CEBrittain)* 3-8-13 WWoods(6) (6th st: r.o one pce fnl 2f)........3½ 2
2037* Pip's Dream **(41)***(45) (MJRyan)* 4-8-7 AClark(5) (lw: 4th st: one pce fnl 2f)........1 3
Exhibit Air (IRE) **(62)***(65) (RAkehurst)* 5-9-11 (3) SSanders(4) (2nd st: hrd rdn over 1f out: one pce)........¾ 4
1776 3 Hi-Aud **(70)***(70)*(Fav)*(JAkehurst)* 3-9-9 GCarter(1) (5th st: no hdwy fnl 2f)........2½ 5
2028 6 Triple Tie (USA) **(55)***(52) (MBlanshard)* 4-9-7 RCochrane(7) (a bhd)........1¾ 6
1983 3 Hatta Breeze **(70)***(67) (MAJarvis)* 3-9-9 PRobinson(3) (3rd st: wknd over 1f out)........½ 7

11/4 Hi-Aud, **7/2** Exhibit Air (IRE), Pip's Dream, **4/1** Hatta Breeze, **6/1** LABIBEH (USA), **12/1** Unchanged (16/1-10/1), **14/1** Triple Tie (USA), CSF £62.06 TOTE £5.00: £3.50 £6.60 (£67.40) OWNER Mr Hamdan Al Maktoum (ARUNDEL) BRED Shadwell Farm Estate Co Ltd and Shadwell Farm Inc 7 Rn 2m 35.9 (4.70) SF: 29/18/11/31/23/18/20
WEIGHT FOR AGE 3yo-13lb

T/Plpt: £68.90 (128.48 Tckts). T/Qdpt: £19.20 (1.65 Tckts). AK

2005-**KEMPTON (R-H)**
Wednesday July 12th (Good to firm, Firm patches)
WEATHER: very warm WIND: almost nil

2340 E.B.F. BULL AND BEAR MEDIAN AUCTION MAIDEN STKS (2-Y.O) (Class E) £3,420.00 (£1,035.00: £505.00: £240.00)
6f Stalls: Low GOING minus 0.37 sec per fur (F) 6-40 (6-41)

Believe Me *(78) (RHannon)* 2-9-0 RPerham(5) (gd sort: lw: hmpd s: led 1f out: pushed out) — 1
1842[3] White Ensign (IRE) *(76)*(Fav)*(RHannon)* 2-9-0 RHughes(8) (lw: led 5f: r.o) ....¾ 2
2091[5] Grey Legend *(71) (RMFlower)* 2-9-0 MRoberts(7) (hld up: hrd rdn over 2f out: r.o one pce)....2 3
1977[17] Half An Inch (IRE) *(70) (BJMeehan)* 2-9-0 BDoyle(9) (a.p: ev ch over 2f out: one pce)..........nk 4
Xenophon of Cunaxa (IRE) *(62) (MJFetherston-Godley)* 2-9-0 DHarrison(4) (w'like: scope: hmpd s: hdwy over 3f out: ev ch over 2f out: wknd over 1f out) 3 5
Craven Cottage *(61) (CJames)* 2-9-0 AMcGlone(3) (unf: bit bkwd: hmpd s: nvr nr to chal).....½ 6
Sunrise Special (IRE) *(50) (GLewis)* 2-9-0 PaulEddery(6) (w'like: scope: bit bkwd: swvd lft s: bhd fnl 3f)........4 7
Cold Shoulder (IRE) *(49) (JLDunlop)* 2-9-0 TQuinn(2) (neat: bit bkwd: hmpd s: a wl bhd) ......½ 8
1938[9] Efficacious (IRE) *(43) (CJBenstead)* 2-8-9 MWigham(1) (bhd fnl 4f) ....hd 9

5/4 White Ensign (IRE), **9/2** Cold Shoulder (IRE) (3/1-5/1), **9/1** BELIEVE ME (5/1-10/1), Sunrise Special (IRE) (5/1-10/1), **12/1** Grey Legend, **14/1** Half An Inch (IRE) (op 8/1), **20/1** Efficacious (IRE), Xenophon of Cunaxa (IRE), **25/1** Craven Cottage, CSF £18.79 TOTE £7.80: £1.90 £1.10 £2.10 (£4.40) Trio £20.10 OWNER Mr Bruce Adams (MARLBOROUGH) BRED Derek R. Price 9 Rn
1m 13.98 (2.68) SF: 30/28/23/22/14/13/2/1/-

2341 DERIVATIVES MAIDEN STKS (3-Y.O) (Class D) £3,647.50 (£1,105.00: £540.00: £257.50) **1m 4f** Stalls: High GOING minus 0.37 sec per fur (F) 7-05 (7-06)

1473[2] **Hagwah (USA)** **(79)***(77+)*(Fav)*(BHanbury)* 3-8-9 MRimmer(6) (swtg: mde all: qcknd over 1f out: easily) ....— 1
1691[11] Nickitoto *(72) (JLDunlop)* 3-8-9 GDuffield(3) (lw: rdn over 3f out: 3rd st: chsd wnr fnl f: no imp)........4 2
1691[7] Blue And Royal (IRE) *(74) (RHannon)* 3-9-0 RPerham(4) (lw: rdn 6f out: chsd wnr to 1f out: one pce) 1¾ 3
Racing Wings (FR) *(53) (KOCunningham-Brown)* 3-8-9 BDoyle(5) (unf: scope: lw: 4th st: wknd over 2f out) 12 4

8/15 HAGWAH (USA), **4/1** Blue And Royal (IRE), **9/2** Nickitoto, **20/1** Racing Wings (FR), CSF £3.11 TOTE £1.60: (£2.20) OWNER Mr Abdullah Ali (NEWMARKET) BRED Gainsborough Farm Inc 4 Rn 2m 36.98 (6.78) SF: 20/15/17/-

2342 GUARDIAN PROPERTIES H'CAP (0-70) (3-Y.O+) (Class E) £3,842.50 (£1,165.00: £570.00: £272.50)
7f (Jubilee) Stalls: High GOING minus 0.37 sec per fur (F) 7-35 (7-38)

2081[5] **Mr Cube (IRE)** **(53)***(64) (JMBradley)* 5-8-4v(7) RWaterfield(5) (lw: hdwy over 1f out: str run fnl f: led nr fin)........— 1
2113* Soaking **(62)***(71) (PBurgoyne)* 5-9-3 (3) DRMcCabe(6) (6th st: rdn over 2f out: r.o wl ins fnl f)........¾ 2
1676[3] Whatever's Right (IRE) **(70)***(79) (MDIUsher)* 6-10-0 TQuinn(3) (lw: 3rd st: hrd rdn over 1f out: led ins fnl f: hdd nr fin) ....hd 3
2169[4] Dancing Lawyer **(69)***(78) (BJMeehan)* 4-9-13 BDoyle(9) (4th st: led over 2f out tl wl ins fnl f: unable qckn) ....hd 4
2108* Broughtons Turmoil **(60)***(62)*(Fav)*(WJMusson)* 6-9-1 (3) PMcCabe(13) (swtg: 7th st: rdn over 2f out: 3rd whn nt clr run & snatched up ins fnl f: nt rcvr)........3 5
1676[12] Sharp Imp **(35)***(37) (RMFlower)* 5-7-7b NAdams(8) (5th st: hrd rdn over 1f out: one pce)........hd 6
1516[5] Walnut Burl (IRE) **(56)***(52) (LJHolt)* 5-9-0 RHughes(4) (nvr nr to chal) 2½ 7
1664[3] Rising Spray **(55)***(45) (CAHorgan)* 4-8-13 PaulEddery(7) (lw: s.s: nvr nrr) 2½ 8
1502[8] Access Carnival (IRE) **(52)***(40) (RBoss)* 4-8-10 GDuffield(11) (lw: nvr nrr) 1 9

2017[4] Panchellita (USA) **(49)***(34) (GLMoore)* 6-8-7 SWhitworth(2) (2nd st: ev ch wl over 1f out: sn wknd) 1½ **10**
Thunder River (IRE) **(65)***(46) (MJHeaton-Ellis)* 5-9-9 MRoberts(1) (lw: led over 4f: 5th & wkng whn squeezed out over 1f out) 1½ **11**
1541[9] Almapa **(57)***(34) (RJHodges)* 3-8-4 (3) SDrowne(12) (lw: bhd fnl 2f) 1¾ **12**
2084* Blushing Grenadier (IRE) **(54)***(18) (MJFetherston-Godley)* 3-8-4b DHarrison(14) (hdwy on ins over 2f out: wkng whn hmpd over 1f out) 6 **13**
1940[13] Michaelmas Park (IRE) **(47)** *(TMJones)* 4-8-5bow1 RPerham(10) (s.s: a bhd) 8 **14**

LONG HANDICAP Sharp Imp 7-6

4/1 Broughtons Turmoil, **11/2** Dancing Lawyer, Whatever's Right (IRE), **13/2** Blushing Grenadier (IRE), **10/1** Walnut Burl (IRE), Panchellita (USA), **12/1** Rising Spray, MR CUBE (IRE), **14/1** Access Carnival (IRE) (16/1-25/1), Thunder River (IRE), **16/1** Soaking, Almapa, **33/1** Sharp Imp, Michaelmas Park (IRE), CSF £175.68 CT £1,076.41 TOTE £15.40: £4.90 £5.80 £2.80 (£236.90) Trio £338.30 OWNER Mr R. Miles (CHEPSTOW) BRED Lyonstown Stud 14 Rn

1m 25.76 (1.56) SF: 46/53/61/60/44/19/34/27/22/16/28/8/-/-

WEIGHT FOR AGE 3yo-8lb

2343

GLOBE H'CAP (0-90) (3-Y.O+) (Class C) £5,550.00 (£1,680.00: £820.00: £390.00)
1m 2f (Jubilee) Stalls: High GOING minus 0.37 sec per fur (F) 8-05 (8-07)

1926[3] **Sadler's Walk (75)***(86)*(Fav)*(GWragg)* 4-9-5 PaulEddery(3) (lw: 4th st: rdn over 2f out: led ins fnl f: r.o wl) ....— **1**
1814* State Law **(86)***(96) (GHarwood)* 3-9-5 AClark(1) (lw: 3rd st: led over 1f out: edgd rt: hdd ins fnl f: r.o) ....½ **2**
1926[10] Laxford Bridge **(79)***(83) (PWHarris)* 4-9-9 GDuffield(4) (lw: led over 8f: 4th & btn whn n.m.r on ins 1f out) 4 **3**
2056* Second Chance (IRE) **(84)***(87) (PMitchell)* 5-9-7 (7) MHenry(2) (lw: plld hrd: chsd ldr: ev ch over 1f out: sn wknd) ....nk **4**

10/11 SADLER'S WALK, **5/2** State Law, **9/2** Laxford Bridge (op 3/1), **8/1** Second Chance (IRE), CSF £3.42 TOTE £1.80: (£1.70) OWNER Sir Philip Oppenheimer (NEWMARKET) BRED Hascombe and Valiant Studs 4 Rn

2m 12.43 (9.93) SF: -/-/-/1

WEIGHT FOR AGE 3yo-11lb

2344

CHANNEL ONE CLAIMING STKS (3-Y.O+) (Class E) £3,550.00 (£1,075.00: £525.00: £250.00)
6f Stalls: Low GOING minus 0.37 sec per fur (F) 8-35 (8-36)

1614[13] **Coffee 'n Cream (80)***(87) (RHannon)* 3-8-8 MRoberts(1) (swtg: a.p: led over 2f out: comf) ..— **1**
1316[4] Easy Dollar **(78)***(81) (BGubby)* 3-8-8v(5) AWhelan(6) (a.p: hrd rdn over 1f out: unable qckn) 4 **2**
1975[5] Taffeta Silk (USA) **(62)***(67) (WJarvis)* 4-8-6 TQuinn(3) (led over 3f: one pce) ....s.h **3**
1766[6] How's Yer Father **(84)***(69)*(Fav)*(RJHodges)* 9-8-10 RHughes(7) (hld up: hrd rdn over 2f out: one pce) ....¾ **4**
2203[4] Just Like Me **(67)***(57) (RGuest)* 3-7-12 (3)ow1 SSanders(5) (a.p: hrd rdn over 2f out: wknd over 1f out) 3½ **5**
2031[3] Law Commission **(78)***(61) (DRCElsworth)* 5-9-6 BDoyle(4) (lw: hld up: rdn over 2f out: wknd wl over 1f out) 3½ **6**
2093[7] Lore *(RIngram)* 3-8-2 AMcGlone(2) (lw: a bhd: t.o) 20 **7**

5/4 How's Yer Father (Evens-6/4), **5/1** Law Commission (7/2-11/2), **11/2** Taffeta Silk (USA), **6/1** COFFEE 'N CREAM, **13/2** Easy Dollar, **10/1** Just Like Me, **50/1** Lore, CSF £39.48 TOTE £6.50: £3.80 £2.30 (£22.40) OWNER Mr A. Reeves (MARLBOROUGH) BRED R. T. and Mrs Watson 7 Rn

1m 11.51 (0.21) SF: 59/53/46/48/29/40/-

WEIGHT FOR AGE 3yo-7lb

2345

CITY EVENING H'CAP (0-80) (3-Y.O+) (Class D) £4,338.00 (£1,314.00: £642.00: £306.00) **1m (round)** Stalls: High GOING minus 0.37 sec per fur (F) 9-05 (9-06)

1995[5] **Admirals Flame (IRE) (66)***(78+) (CFWall)* 4-9-0 GDuffield(1) (b: 3rd st: led over 1f out: comf) ....— **1**
2222[5] Just Harry **(70)***(74) (MJRyan)* 4-8-11 (7) DGibbs(7) (lw: rdn over 2f out: hdwy over 1f out: r.o one pce) 4 **2**
1173[7] Artful Dane (IRE) **(75)***(78) (MJHeaton-Ellis)* 3-9-0 MRoberts(4) (lw: led over 6f: one pce) ....¾ **3**
2010[5] Court Minstrel **(53)***(53)*(Fav)*(LJHolt)* 6-8-1 AMcGlone(5) (rdn over 2f out: hdwy over 1f out: one pce) 1¼ **4**
Fort Knox (IRE) **(60)***(57) (RMFlower)* 4-8-8 AMorris(6) (4th st: rdn over 2f out: one pce) 1¾ **5**
1542[11] Lady Williams (IRE) **(59)***(44) (LordHuntingdon)* 4-8-7 DHarrison(3) (lw: 6th st: wknd over 2f out) 6 **6**

2222[6] Kingchip Boy **(75)***(59) (MJRyan)* 6-9-9b AClark(8) (5th st: wknd over 1f out) ....s.h 7
2010* Cameron Highland (IRE) **(80)***(34) (PFICole)* 4-10-0 TQuinn(2) (chsd ldr over 5f: eased whn btn over 1f out: fin lame) 15 8

11/4 Court Minstrel, **100/30** Cameron Highland (IRE), **5/1** Artful Dane (IRE), ADMIRALS FLAME (IRE) (3/1-11/2), **7/1** Just Harry, **10/1** Kingchip Boy, **12/1** Lady Williams (IRE) (op 8/1), **33/1** Fort Knox (IRE), CSF £35.65 CT £165.54 TOTE £6.00: £1.70 £1.60 £2.20 (£15.90) OWNER Mr Walter Grubmuller (NEWMARKET) BRED A. Tarry 8 Rn 1m 38.31 (1.11) SF: 57/53/48/32/36/23/38/13
WEIGHT FOR AGE 3yo-9lb
T/Plpt: £113.20 (93.55 Tckts). T/Qdpt: £44.30 (3.9 Tckts). AK

2320-NEWMARKET (R-H)
Wednesday July 12th (Good to firm)
WEATHER: sunny WIND: almost nil

2346
NGK SPARK PLUGS (S) STKS (2-Y.O) (Class E) £4,542.00 (£1,356.00: £648.00: £294.00) **7f (July)** Stalls: High GOING minus 0.51 sec per fur (F) 2-05 (2-06)

1841* **Society Girl** *(74+) (CWThornton)* 2-8-8 DeanMcKeown(5) (a.p: led over 2f out: pushed clr: unchal) ....— 1
2107[8] Again Together *(63)*(Fav)*(NACallaghan)* 2-8-8 LDettori(1) (hld up in tch: hdwy over 2f out: sn hrd rdn & no imp) 5 2
1634[7] General Rose *(73) (RHannon)* 2-9-0 (7) DaneO'Neill(10) (hld up: hdwy over 2f out: rdn & kpt on ins fnl f) 1¼ 3
2011[7] Willie Rushton *(55) (GLMoore)* 2-8-12 SWhitworth(6) (b.hind: plld hrd: a.p: chal over 2f out: grad wknd) 4 4
1540[9] Rothley Imp (IRE) *(47) (JWharton)* 2-8-8 KDarley(8) (r.o fnl 2f: nrst fin) 1½ 5
615[9] Richard House Lad *(55) (CASmith)* 2-9-3 MWigham(7) (hdwy bel dist: r.o fnl f: nvr nrr) ....½ 6
2128[10] In Paradisum (USA) *(49) (MrsJRRamsden)* 2-8-13v KFallon(12) (lw: hld up & bhd: effrt 3f out: nvr able to chal) 1 7
1671[10] Just Another High (IRE) *(39) (DrJDScargill)* 2-8-8 BThomson(4) (led tl hdd & wknd over 2f out) 2 8
2143[10] The Kastarbids (IRE) *(40) (DMorris)* 2-8-13 TIves(9) (a in rr) 2 9
Distant Storm *(21) (MBell)* 2-8-13 JReid(11) (w'like: s.s: a wl bhd & outpcd: t.o) 8 10
Fast Food *(4) (BJMcMath)* 2-9-7 MTebbutt(3) (cmpt: bkwd: bhd fr ½-wy: t.o) 11 11

9/4 Again Together, **100/30** SOCIETY GIRL (9/4-7/2), **5/1** General Rose, **11/2** In Paradisum (USA) (3/1-6/1), **10/1** Distant Storm (op 6/1), **20/1** Rothley Imp (IRE), **25/1** Fast Food, **33/1** Just Another High (IRE), **40/1** The Kastarbids (IRE), Willie Rushton, **50/1** Richard House Lad, CSF £10.17 TOTE £2.80: £1.30 £1.10 £1.90 (£3.20) Trio £6.90 OWNER Mr Guy Reed (MIDDLEHAM) BRED G. Reed 11 Rn 1m 27.38 (2.98) SF: 16/5/15/-/-/-/-/-/-/-/-
Bt in 20,000 gns

2347
SBJ GROUP JULY STKS (Gp 3) (2-Y.O C & G) (Class A) £18,476.00 (£6,884.00: £3,342.00: £1,410.00: £605.00: £283.00)
6f (July) Stalls: High GOING minus 0.51 sec per fur (F) 2-35 (2-36)

1838[4] **Tagula (IRE)** *(100) (IABalding)* 2-8-10 WRSwinburn(6) (a.p: led 2f out: qcknd clr: r.o wl) ....— 1
1838[7] Take A Left *(99) (MrsJRRamsden)* 2-8-10 KFallon(1) (hld up & bhd: swtchd lft over 2f out: str run fnl f: fin fast) ....nk 2
1871* World Premier *(100) (CEBrittain)* 2-8-13 BDoyle(4) (lw: a.p: rdn over 1f out: kpt on towards fin) ....¾ 3
2029* Rio Duvida *(96)*(Fav)*(DRLoder)* 2-8-10 PatEddery(2) (hld up in tch: effrt & swtchd over 2f out: styd on u.p fnl f: nt pce to chal) ....½ 4
2070* Zuhair *(94) (MajorWRHern)* 2-8-10 WCarson(7) (bit bkwd: sn chsng ldr: outpcd bel dist: sn btn) ....¾ 5
1868* Lucky Lionel (USA) *(88) (RHannon)* 2-9-1 LDettori(5) (lw: prom: effrt & outpcd 2f out: eased whn btn fnl f) 4 6
1772* High Priority (IRE) *(78) (MRChannon)* 2-8-10 MJKinane(9) (chsd ldrs on outside: rdn & wknd over 2f out) 2 7
1868[4] First Fiddler *(76) (WJarvis)* 2-8-10b BThomson(3) (hld up: effrt & rdn 2f out: sn outpcd) ....¾ 8
1868[7] Night Parade (USA) *(74) (PWChapple-Hyam)* 2-8-10 JReid(8) (led to 2f out: sn lost tch) ....¾ 9

15/8 Rio Duvida, **7/2** TAGULA (IRE), **9/2** Lucky Lionel (USA), **9/1** Zuhair, **11/1** First Fiddler (8/1-12/1), **14/1** World Premier, **16/1** High Priority (IRE), Night Parade (USA), **25/1** Take A Left, CSF £66.48 TOTE £5.50: £1.70 £8.90 £3.40 (£124.60) Trio £452.50 OWNER Robert & Elizabeth Hitchins (KINGSCLERE) BRED Sean and Patrick Twomey 9 Rn
1m 11.83 (0.33) SF: 47/46/47/43/41/35/25/23/21

2348 H.E. LIMITED DUKE OF CAMBRIDGE H'CAP (0-105) (3-Y.O) (Class B) £19,412.50 (£5,800.00: £2,775.00: £1,262.50)

1m 2f (July) Stalls: Low GOING minus 0.51 sec per fur (F) 3-10 (3-11)

1872 17 **Pilsudski (IRE) (82)***(92) (MRStoute)* 3-8-3 KDarley(3) (b.nr hind: hld up: hdwy over 3f out: qcknd to ld ins fnl f: r.o wl)....— 1
1839 12 Krystallos **(90)***(97) (RHannon)* 3-8-11 MJKinane(6) (drppd rr after 2f: hdwy over 2f out: rdn & ev ch ent fnl f: unable qckn)....2 2
1793 2 Jalfrezi **(82)***(88)*(Fav)*(JARToller)* 3-8-3 JWeaver(4) (stdd s: hdwy over 2f out: ev ch appr fnl f: unable qckn)....½ 3
1839 8 Myrtle Quest **(80)***(84) (RCharlton)* 3-8-1 TSprake(2) (hld up: hdwy & ev ch fr 3f out: rdn & no ex wl ins fnl f)....1 4
2068 2 Rahy Zoman (USA) **(83)***(87) (JRFanshawe)* 3-8-4 DHarrison(5) (lw: hld up: hdwy 3f out: kpt on wl towards fin)....s.h 5
1897 7 Inquisitor (USA) **(99)***(103) (JHMGosden)* 3-9-6 PatEddery(7) (led: hrd rdn & hdd ins fnl f: sn btn)....hd 6
678* Indonesian (IRE) **(84)***(85) (MBell)* 3-8-5 LDettori(1) (chsd ldrs: effrt & outpcd over 1f out: eased whn btn)....1¾ 7
1684* Jandeel (IRE) **(88)***(87)*(Fav)*(ACStewart)* 3-8-9 MRoberts(10) (b.hind: prom tl wknd wl over 1f out)....1½ 8
Craigmill **(86)***(84) (HRACecil)* 3-8-7 WRyan(8) (prom tl wknd over 1f out)....¾ 9
1619* Romios (IRE) **(86)***(77) (PFICole)* 3-8-7 TQuinn(12) (b.nr fore: plld hrd: prom tl wknd over 2f out)....4 10
1269* Nigel's Lad (IRE) **(86)***(53) (PCHaslam)* 3-8-7 MTebbutt(9) (lost tch fnl 4f: t.o)....15 11
1729 8 Yarn (IRE) **(100)***(48) (MRChannon)* 3-9-7 JReid(11) (hld up & bhd: pushed along over 3f out: sn t.o)....12 12

5/1 Jandeel (IRE), Jalfrezi, **11/2** Indonesian (IRE), Inquisitor (USA), **15/2** PILSUDSKI (IRE) (5/1-8/1), **11/1** Myrtle Quest, **12/1** Rahy Zoman (USA), **14/1** Krystallos, **16/1** Craigmill, Romios (IRE), **25/1** Nigel's Lad (IRE), **33/1** Yarn (IRE), CSF £93.10 CT £520.62 TOTE £10.00: £2.90 £5.60 £2.00 (£107.20) Trio £272.30 OWNER Lord Weinstock & The Hon Simon Weinstock (NEWMARKET) BRED Ballymacoll Stud Co 12 Rn 2m 3.9 (1.50) SF: 34/39/30/26/29/45/27/29/26/19/-/-

2349 FALMOUTH STKS (Gp 2) (3-Y.O+ F & M) (Class A) £34,099.25 (£12,293.00: £5,896.50: £2,407.50: £953.75)

1m (July) Stalls: High GOING minus 0.51 sec per fur (F) 3-40 (3-40)

1712a 7 **Caramba** *(112) (RHannon)* 3-8-6 MRoberts(3) (chsd ldr: led 2f out: hrd rdn fnl f: jst hld on)..— 1
1850 5 Gay Gallanta (USA) **(116)***(112) (MRStoute)* 3-8-6 PatEddery(1) (lw: prom: outpcd & rdn over 2f out: rallied fnl f: r.o wl)....s.h 2
1850 3 Harayir (USA) **(120)***(117)*(Fav)*(MajorWRHern)* 3-8-12 WCarson(5) (lw: hld up & bhd: gd hdwy over 1f out: hrd rdn & r.o wl)....nk 3
1927* Arabride *(110) (JARToller)* 3-8-6 JWeaver(4) (led to 2f out: ev ch tl no ex nr fin)....¾ 4
1850 4 Warning Shadows (IRE) *(106) (CEBrittain)* 3-8-6 MJKinane(2) (hld up: rdn 2f out: one pce) 1¾ 5

15/8 Harayir (USA), **9/4** Warning Shadows (IRE), **5/2** CARAMBA, **8/1** Gay Gallanta (USA), **33/1** Arabride, CSF £17.28 TOTE £3.60: £1.70 £1.80 (£10.60) OWNER Lord Carnarvon (MARLBOROUGH) BRED Highclere Stud Ltd 5 Rn 1m 40.17 (2.47) SF: 25/25/30/23/19

2350 MORE O'FERRALL PLC MAIDEN STKS (3-Y.O) (Class D) £4,980.50 (£1,484.00: £707.00: £318.50)

1m 2f (July) Stalls: Low GOING minus 0.51 sec (F) 4-15 (4-17)

691 2 **Royal Circle** *(88)*(Fav)*(RCharlton)* 3-8-9 KDarley(4) (a.p: led bel dist: rn green & hdd ins fnl f: rallied gamely to ld fnl strides)....— 1
1755 3 Bequeath *(93) (HRACecil)* 3-9-0 PatEddery(6) (lw: a.p: hrd drvn over 2f out: swtchd & qcknd to ld ins fnl f: ct cl home)....hd 2
Anne D'Autriche (IRE) *(78) (JHMGosden)* 3-8-9 LDettori(5) (leggy: led after 2f to bel dist: eased whn btn ins fnl f)....6 3
Bay of Islands *(80) (CEBrittain)* 3-9-0 BDoyle(2) (cmpt: led 2f: outpcd 2f out: sn btn)....2 4
1258 3 Early Peace (IRE) *(56) (RHannon)* 3-9-0 WRSwinburn(9) (a bhd: outpcd fnl 4f: t.o)....15 5
Praglia (IRE) *(51) (JLDunlop)* 3-8-9 WCarson(3) (hld up & bhd: lost tch 3f out: t.o)....nk 6
539 14 Anastina *(47) (JHMGosden)* 3-8-9 GHind(1) (a bhd: t.o)....2½ 7

5/4 ROYAL CIRCLE (11/8-10/11), **13/8** Bequeath (op 5/2), **10/1** Anne D'Autriche (IRE) (7/1-12/1), **14/1** Praglia (IRE) (10/1-20/1), **16/1** Early Peace (IRE), **33/1** Bay of Islands, Anastina, CSF £3.38 TOTE £2.00: £1.40 £1.60 (£1.70) Trio £2.00 OWNER Cliveden Stud (BECKHAMPTON) BRED Cliveden Stud 7 Rn 2m 5.86 (3.46) SF: 25/30/15/17/-/-/-

2351

PRINCESS MAIDEN STKS (2-Y.O F) (Class D) £5,526.50 (£1,652.00: £791.00: £360.50) **6f (July)** Stalls: High GOING minus 0.51 sec per fur (F) 4-45 (4-54)

Rouge Rancon (USA) *(101+)*(Fav)*(PFICole)* 2-8-11 TQuinn(14) (w'like: b.nr hind: racd centre: a.p: led wl over 1f out: r.o wl nr fin)......— 1
Dimakya (USA) *(94) (DRLoder)* 2-8-11 MJKinane(6) (leggy: scope: a.p: ev ch over 1f out: nt qckn)......2½ 2
Najiya *(93) (JLDunlop)* 2-8-11 WCarson(11) (neat: in tch: hdwy 2f out: one pce fnl f)......½ 3
Comic Fantasy (AUS) *(85) (PWChapple-Hyam)* 2-8-11 JReid(1) (leggy: scope: led tl hdd wl over 1f out: rdn & no ex fnl f)......3 4
Salty Girl (IRE) *(77) (BWHills)* 2-8-11 WRSwinburn(9) (w'like: s.s: stdy hdwy ½-wy: nvr plcd to chal)......3 5
Carmosa (USA) *(76) (WJarvis)* 2-8-11 BThomson(15) (w'like: scope: in tch 4f: one pce)......nk 6
Fervent Fan (IRE) *(75) (MBell)* 2-8-11 JWeaver(13) (neat: outpcd & bhd tl styd on ins fnl f)......½ 7
1928[5] Al Shadeedah (USA) *(74) (LMCumani)* 2-8-11 LDettori(2) (chsd ldrs 4f)......½ 8
Wandering Star (USA) *(72) (JRFanshawe)* 2-8-11 DHarrison(10) (cmpt: bkwd: nvr nr ldrs)....½ 9
Primrose Path *(71) (CEBrittain)* 2-8-11 MRoberts(3) (w'like: scope: chsd ldrs 4f: sn outpcd) .nk 10
Jezyah (USA) *(65) (RWArmstrong)* 2-8-11 RPrice(8) (w'like: bit bkwd: chsd ldrs: rdn & wknd over 2f out)......2½ 11
2114[2] Moving Up (IRE) *(64) (GLMoore)* 2-8-11 SWhitworth(7) (b.hind: a bhd)......nk 12
Put Off *(57) (BWHills)* 2-8-11 WRyan(4) (cmpt: bkwd: chsd ldrs to ½-wy: sn lost tch)......2½ 13
Sweet Amoret *(44) (RCSpicer)* 2-8-11 DeanMcKeown(5) (w'like: s.s: a bhd: t.o)......5 14
Trafalgar Lady (USA) *(RCharlton)* 2-8-11 PatEddery(12) (w'like: withdrawn not under Starter's orders: ref to ent stalls)...... W

, **100/30** ROUGE RANCON (USA), **4/1** Najiya (9/4-9/2), Dimakya (USA) (3/1-9/2), **11/2** Comic Fantasy (AUS) (3/1-13/2), **8/1** Al Shadeedah (USA) (6/1-12/1), **16/1** Carmosa (USA), **25/1** Fervent Fan (IRE), **33/1** Salty Girl (IRE), Primrose Path, Jezyah (USA), Wandering Star (USA), Put Off, Moving Up (IRE), **66/1** Sweet Amoret, CSF £15.11 TOTE £4.60: £1.50 £1.90 £2.10 (£7.20) Trio £9.10 OWNER Mr Christopher Wright (WHATCOMBE) BRED Cesar Gauterio 14 Rn
1m 12.92 (1.42) SF: 33/26/25/17/9/8/7/6/4/3/-/-/-/-/-

2352

REG DAY MEMORIAL H'CAP (0-90) (3-Y.O+) (Class C) £5,952.00 (£1,776.00: £848.00: £384.00)
2m 24y (July) Stalls: Low GOING minus 0.51 sec per fur (F) 5-20 (5-24)

1300[2] **New Reputation (85)***(101)*(Fav)*(BWHills)* 4-9-10 PatEddery(5) (lw: hld up: rdn over 4f out: styd on to ld bel dist: sn clr)......— 1
2098[4] Noufari (FR) **(74)***(82) (RHollinshead)* 4-8-13 TIves(3) (lw: hld up & bhd: hdwy to chse wnr over 1f out: hung lft & no imp)......8 2
2087[6] Thunderheart **(70)***(77) (LMCumani)* 4-8-9 LDettori(2) (hld up in rr: nvr plcd to chal)......1 3
2026[8] Wurlitzer (USA) **(72)***(79) (JHMGosden)* 3-7-8 NCarlisle(1) (led: clr 3f out: wknd & hdd bel dist)......nk 4
2184[5] Tukano (CAN) **(68)***(65) (JRJenkins)* 4-8-7 MJKinane(4) (chsd ldr: rdn over 4f out: grad wknd: t.o)......10 5

7/4 NEW REPUTATION, **2/1** Noufari (FR) (op 3/1), **3/1** Thunderheart, **8/1** Wurlitzer (USA) (6/1-9/1), **25/1** Tukano (CAN), CSF £5.33 TOTE £2.10: £1.50 £2.10 (£3.10) OWNER Mr R. E. Sangster (LAMBOURN) BRED Seahorse Investments 5 Rn 3m 26.92 (3.92) SF: 48/29/24/9/12
WEIGHT FOR AGE 3yo-17lb

T/Jkpt: £8,814.90 (8.55 Tckts). T/Plpt: £122.90 (305.21 Tckts). T/Qdpt: £19.20 (28.95 Tckts). IM

1943-REDCAR (L-H)
Wednesday July 12th (Firm)

WEATHER: fine, misty WIND: mod half against

2353

TYNE & WEAR (S) APPRENTICE H'CAP (0-60) (3-Y.O) (Class F) £2,703.00 (£758.00: £369.00)
1m 3f Stalls: Low GOING minus 0.51 sec per fur (F) 6-50 (6-51)

2166[7] **Lindisfarne Lady (41)***(53) (MrsMReveley)* 3-8-13 SCopp(6) (trckd ldrs: effrt over 3f out: hung lft: styd on to ld towards fin)......— 1
2089[6] Gulf Bay **(32)***(43)*(Fav)*(MBell)* 3-7-11 (7) RMullen(4) (a chsng ldrs: ev ch fnl f: nt qckn cl home)......¾ 2

1962[3] Perfect Bertie (IRE) **(49)***(60) (GROldroyd)* 3-9-7 GParkin(1) (led: hrd rdn fnl 2f: hdd nr fin) ...s.h **3**
2306[3] Jackmanii **(51)***(59) (WTKemp)* 3-9-9b 5x PRoberts(3) (s.i.s: sn prom: effrt over 3f out: hung lft over 1f out: kpt on)...1¾ **4**
2280[6] Longcroft **(42)***(49) (KWHogg)* 3-8-7 (7) DLockhart(2) (sn bhd: hung bdly lft over 2f out: styd on towards fin) ...1¼ **5**
2129[2] High Flown (USA) **(44)***(49) (RonaldThompson)* 3-9-2 CAdamson(5) (dwlt: sn prom: hmpd 5f out: outpcd 3f out: n.d after) ...1 **6**
Absolute Millions **(39)***(15) (MartynWane)* 3-8-11 CTeague(7) (outpcd & bhd 5f out) ...20 **7**

11/4 Gulf Bay, **3/1** Jackmanii, **7/2** High Flown (USA), **11/2** LINDISFARNE LADY, Perfect Bertie (IRE), **10/1** Longcroft, **25/1** Absolute Millions, CSF £20.47 TOTE £6.40: £3.40 £1.20 (£10.60) OWNER Ken Matthews Racing (SALTBURN) BRED Viscount Leverhulme 7 Rn
2m 22.6 (6.90) SF: 7/-/14/13/3/3/-
No bid

2354 BRITISH STEEL PLATE MAIDEN AUCTION STKS (2-Y.O) (Class F)
£2,735.00 (£760.00: £365.00)
5f Stalls: Centre GOING minus 0.51 sec per fur (F) 7-15 (7-20)

Middle East *(64+)*(Fav)*(TDBarron)* 2-8-2 ow1 KDarley(1) (rangy: chsd ldrs: led 2f out: drvn out) ...— **1**
1977[5] Napoleon's Return *(58) (AGFoster)* 2-8-1 TSprake(2) (a chsng ldrs: effrt ½-wy: ev ch & edgd lft 1f out: nt qckn)...2 **2**
Happy Partner (IRE) *(52) (PCHaslam)* 2-8-1 JQuinn(4) (neat: lw: a chsng ldrs: rdn & edgd rt over 1f out: kpt on same pce)...1¾ **3**
Valise *(46) (MrsMReveley)* 2-8-0 LCharnock(5) (cmpt: bit bkwd: dwlt: outpcd & pushed along: styd on appr fnl f)...1½ **4**
2128[9] Society Sue (IRE) *(33) (RonaldThompson)* 2-7-3 (7) CAdamson(6) (unruly: chsd ldrs tl wknd over 1f out)...3 **5**
Eileen's Girl (IRE) *(7) (MrsMReveley)* 2-7-10 DaleGibson(3) (lt-f: unf: s.i.s: a wl outpcd & sn drvn along) ...8 **6**
1646[6] Quinta Boy *(12) (JBerry)* 2-8-5 JCarroll(7) (lw: led: hung lft & hdd 2f out: wknd qckly) ...1¼ **7**

11/8 MIDDLE EAST, **9/4** Napoleon's Return, **9/2** Quinta Boy, **11/2** Happy Partner (IRE), **25/1** Eileen's Girl (IRE), Valise, **33/1** Society Sue (IRE), CSF £4.94 TOTE £2.80: £1.70 £2.10 (£3.60) OWNER Mr T. Hazell (THIRSK) BRED Miss M. Grantmyre 7 Rn 58.6 secs (1.90) SF: 12/6/-/-/-/-/-

2355 RED CROSS H'CAP (0-65) (3-Y.O+) (Class F) £3,050.00 (£850.00: £410.00)
1m 6f 19y Stalls: Low GOING minus 0.51 sec per fur (F) 7-40 (7-47)

2177* **Nanton Point (USA) (57)***(67+)*(Fav)*(LadyHerries)* 3-8-10 5x JQuinn(11) (trckd ldrs: hdwy to ld over 2f out: drvn out) ...— **1**
Jalcanto **(54)***(62) (MrsMReveley)* 5-9-1 (7) SCopp(2) (bhd: effrt & hmpd over 3f out: hdwy & ev ch ins fnl f: nt qckn)...1½ **2**
2166[3] Instantaneous **(44)***(52) (MHEasterby)* 3-7-11 SMaloney(10) (lw: hld up & plld hrd: hdwy & nt clr run 3f out: styd on same pce appr fnl f) ...s.h **3**
1858[3] Arc Bright (IRE) **(44)***(51) (RHollinshead)* 5-8-9 (3) AGarth(8) (lw: a chsng ldrs: ev ch over 1f out: one pce) ...1¼ **4**
1965[2] Scalp 'em (IRE) **(40)***(41) (PDEvans)* 7-8-8 JFortune(7) (chsd ldrs: led 3f out: sn hdd: wknd over 1f out)...5 **5**
1970[2] Masuri Kabisa (USA) **(33)***(30) (HJCollingridge)* 4-8-1 DaleGibson(1) (rr div: effrt over 3f out: kpt on: nvr nr ldrs) ...3½ **6**
2280[2] Leap in the Dark (IRE) **(33)***(27) (MissLCSiddall)* 6-8-1 GHind(6) (led to 3f out: wknd over 1f out) ...2½ **7**
2306[4] Petal's Jarred **(25)***(19) (WStorey)* 5-7-0v(7) PFessey(3) (s.i.s: bhd: sme hdwy 7f out: nvr nr ldrs) ...hd **8**
2157[2] Brodessa **(59)***(50) (MrsMReveley)* 9-9-13 KDarley(5) (lw: trckd ldrs: wknd over 2f out: eased towards fin)...2½ **9**
2127[4] Nouvelle Cuisine **(52)***(26) (GMMoore)* 7-9-3 (3) JStack(9) (mid div: effrt & hung lft over 3f out: sn lost pl)...15 **10**
2086[7] Readyspex **(42)** *(RDEWoodhouse)* 5-8-10 NConnorton(4) (hld up & racd wd: t.o 6f out) .....dist **11**

4/5 NANTON POINT (USA), **5/1** Instantaneous, **8/1** Brodessa, **10/1** Leap in the Dark (IRE), **12/1** Masuri Kabisa (USA), **16/1** Arc Bright (IRE), **20/1** Scalp 'em (IRE), Jalcanto, **33/1** Nouvelle Cuisine, **50/1** Petal's Jarred, **100/1** Readyspex, CSF £17.85 CT £55.71 TOTE £1.90: £1.10 £2.40 £2.80 (£15.70) Trio £35.20 OWNER Mr L. G. Lazarus (LITTLEHAMPTON) BRED Newgate Stud Farm Inc 11 Rn 3m 2.1 (4.10) SF: 33/43/18/32/22/11/8/-/31/7/-
WEIGHT FOR AGE 3yo-15lb

2356
TEESSIDE CHEMICALS INITIATIVE H'CAP (0-70) (3-Y.O) (Class E) £3,280.00 (£985.00: £475.00: £220.00) **1m 2f** Stalls: Low GOING minus 0.51 sec(F)8-10 (8-14)

2139 11 **Grooms Gold (IRE) (63)***(73)*(Fav)*(PWHarris)* 3-9-0 GHind(3) (lw: prom: outpcd & drvn along 4f out: styd on u.p fnl 2f: led cl home)........— 1
1984 6 Gloriana **(70)***(80) (LadyHerries)* 3-9-7 JQuinn(6) (tongue tied down: led: shkn up & qcknd 3f out: hdd nr fin)........nk 2
1966 11 Highfield Fizz **(60)***(68) (CWFairhurst)* 3-8-8 (3) JTate(7) (hld up: effrt on outside over 3f out: hdwy 2f out: styd on ins fnl f)........1 3
1961 2 Tinklers Folly **(43)***(47) (DenysSmith)* 3-7-8 LCharnock(2) (chsd ldrs: ev ch over 1f out: sn wknd)........2½ 4
2020 6 Eden Dancer **(57)***(58) (MrsMReveley)* 3-8-8 KDarley(1) (hld up bhd: effrt 3f out: nvr nr ldrs).1¾ 5
1666 8 Cumbrian Minstrel **(55)***(55) (MHEasterby)* 3-8-6 MBirch(5) (trckd ldrs: effrt over 3f out: hrd rdn, edgd lft & wknd 2f out)........½ 6
1930 2 Thatcher's Era (IRE) **(65)***(64) (TDBarron)* 3-9-2 JFortune(4) (chsd ldrs: effrt over 3f out: wknd over 2f out)........1 7

3/1 GROOMS GOLD (IRE), **7/2** Gloriana, **4/1** Tinklers Folly, **6/1** Eden Dancer, Thatcher's Era (IRE), **7/1** Cumbrian Minstrel, **14/1** Highfield Fizz, CSF £13.25 TOTE £4.60: £2.00 £2.30 (£12.00) OWNER The French Connection (BERKHAMSTED) BRED Petra Bloodstock Agency Ltd 7 Rn
2m 7.6 (5.10) SF: 17/24/12/-/2/-/8

2357
SOUTH SHIELDS CLAIMING STKS (3-Y.O) (Class F) £2,882.00 (£802.00: £386.00) **7f** Stalls: Centre GOING minus 0.51 sec per fur (F) 8-40 (8-42)

2018 2 **Special-K (60)***(67)*(Fav)*(EWeymes)* 3-8-6 GHind(4) (plld hrd: trckd ldrs: rdn over 2f out: styd on to ld ins fnl f)........— 1
1947 3 Northern Trove (USA) **(72)***(78) (GMMoore)* 3-9-4 (3) JStack(5) (hld up: hdwy to ld 3f out: rdn & edgd lft u.p appr fnl f: hdd ins fnl f)........1¾ 2
2191 8 Full Gloss **(56)***(49) (MrsMReveley)* 3-8-3 KDarley(6) (chsd ldrs: effrt & hung rt over 2f out: styd on one pce)........5 3
2102* Care And Comfort **(62)***(54) (KMcAuliffe)* 3-8-9 (3) JTate(7) (lw: hld up: effrt ½-wy: hung lft u.p: no imp)........1½ 4
1846 6 Self Styled (IRE) *(53) (TDBarron)* 3-8-11 JFortune(3) (trckd ldrs: outpcd 3f out: grad wknd) .hd 5
645 10 L'Eglise Belle **(45)***(38) (MrsALMKing)* 3-7-13 (3) AGarth(8) (mde most to ½-wy: sn wknd)......2½ 6
2018 8 Rambo's Rumtime *(37) (FWatson)* 3-8-2 SMaloney(2) (disp ld 2f: wknd ½-wy)........½ 7
2086 5 Ruby Rock *(16) (BWMurray)* 3-8-4 ACulhane(1) (swtg: chsd ldrs: rdn & lost pl ½-wy: sn bhd)10 8

2/1 SPECIAL-K, **5/2** Northern Trove (USA) (op 6/4), Care And Comfort, **11/1** Ruby Rock, **16/1** Self Styled (IRE), Full Gloss, **33/1** L'Eglise Belle, **50/1** Rambo's Rumtime, CSF £7.19 TOTE £2.90: £1.30 £1.10 £2.40 (£3.10) OWNER Mr G. Falshaw (MIDDLEHAM) BRED Patrick Diamond 8 Rn
1m 25.5 (3.50) SF: 7/18/-/-/-/-/-/-

2358
BEDALE H'CAP (0-80) (3-Y.O+) (Class D) £3,762.50 (£1,130.00: £545.00: £252.50) **7f** Stalls: Centre GOING minus 0.51 sec per fur (F) 9-10 (9-11)

1666 12 **King Chestnut (52)***(62) (MDods)* 4-8-8 JCarroll(5) (in tch tl outpcd ½-wy: rdn & hung lft 2f out: styd on to ld wl ins fnl f)........— 1
1828 4 Kid Ory **(59)***(67) (PCalver)* 4-9-1 MBirch(2) (led to ½-wy: led jst ins fnl f tl towards fin)........¾ 2
1994* Pine Ridge Lad (IRE) **(54)***(61) (JLEyre)* 5-8-10 JFortune(1) (chsd ldrs: kpt on same pce appr fnl f)........¾ 3
1918 5 Willshe Gan **(50)***(50) (DenysSmith)* 5-8-6 KFallon(6) (chsd ldrs: swtchd rt & led over 1f out: sn hdd & wknd)........3 4
1995 11 Gymcrak Flyer **(62)***(58) (GHolmes)* 4-9-1 (3) JStack(7) (b.hind: trckd ldrs: led ½-wy tl over 2f out: grad wknd)........1½ 5
1902* Parliament Piece **(70)***(55)*(Fav)*(MrsMReveley)* 9-9-12v KDarley(9) (trckd ldrs: led over 2f out tl over 1f out: sn wknd)........5 6
2191* Cafe Solo **(41)***(21) (NBycroft)* 4-7-11b NKennedy(8) (sn outpcd & bhd: sme hdwy 2f out: n.d)..2 7
1864 8 Knayton Lass **(59)***(30) (MWEasterby)* 4-8-8 (7) RuthCoulter(4) (plld hrd: trckd ldrs tl lost pl 3f out)........4 8
2021* Green's Bid **(53)** *(DWChapman)* 5-8-9 ACulhane(3) (dwlt: sn w ldrs: lost pl 3f out: eased)....15 9

9/4 Parliament Piece, **5/1** Kid Ory, **11/2** Cafe Solo, **6/1** Green's Bid, **13/2** Pine Ridge Lad (IRE), **7/1** Willshe Gan, **20/1** Gymcrak Flyer, **25/1** KING CHESTNUT, **33/1** Knayton Lass, CSF £130.49 CT £832.18 TOTE £12.50: £2.90 £1.70 £2.40 (£69.80) Trio £137.80 OWNER Mr C. Graham (DARLINGTON) BRED G. E. C. Graham and Partners 9 Rn 1m 24.7 (2.70) SF: 20/25/19/8/16/13/-/-/-
T/Plpt: £156.70 (65.52 Tckts). T/Qdpt: £37.20 (1.75 Tckts). WG

2264-CHEPSTOW (L-H)
Thursday July 13th (Good to firm)
WEATHER: sunny WIND: almost nil

2359 EVENING APPRENTICE H'CAP (0-70) (3-Y.O+) (Class G) £2,437.00 (£682.00: £331.00) **1m 4f 23y** Stalls: Centre GOING minus 0.35 sec per fur (F) 6-45 (6-46)

2007 4 **Wottashambles (37)***(48) (LMontagueHall)* 4-7-11 (3) GMitchell(4) (lw: chsd ldr 6f: 3rd st: rdn over 2f out: led ins fnl f: r.o) — 1
2065 4 Bushehr (IRE) **(65)***(75)*(Fav)*(JWHills)* 3-9-1 MHenry(10) (lw: chsd ldr 6f out: 2nd st: led over 3f out: hdd ins fnl f) 1 2
2175 2 Ismeno **(54)***(58) (SDow)* 4-9-0 (3) ADaly(9) (led over 8f: one pce fnl 2f) 4 3
1926 9 Shabanaz **(65)***(68) (WRMuir)* 10-9-7 (7) RPooles(3) (hld up & bhd: 8th st: styd on fnl 2f: n.d) ¾ 4
2007 13 Shepherds Rest (IRE) **(44)***(39) (SMellor)* 3-7-3 (5)ow1 CarolineHovington(5) (lw: 4th st: rdn over 3f out: wknd over 2f out) 6 5
2122* Duggan **(35)***(30)*(Fav)*(PDEvans)* 8-7-12 5x AmandaSanders(6) (hld up: hdwy over 5f out: 5th & c wd st: wknd 2f out) nk 6
2139 9 Bell Contractors (IRE) **(60)***(51) (CDBroad)* 3-8-10 RHavlin(7) (hld up: 6th st: hrd rdn over 3f out: hung lft 2f out: sn bhd) 3 7
1755 12 Knave of Diamonds **(59)***(30) (RJHodges)* 3-8-9 DGriffiths(1) (lw: plld hrd: lost pl & 7th st: eased whn btn fnl 2f) 15 8
1799 12 Caromandoo (IRE) **(37)** *(ABarrow)* 7-7-11v(3) SLanigan(2) (v.reluctant to race: a wl t.o) dist 9

7/2 Duggan, Bushehr (IRE), **4/1** Ismeno, **5/1** WOTTASHAMBLES, **15/2** Shabanaz, **16/1** Shepherds Rest (IRE), Bell Contractors (IRE), **33/1** Knave of Diamonds, **50/1** Caromandoo (IRE), CSF £20.19 CT £62.15 TOTE £7.00: £1.70 £1.50 £1.90 (£10.70) Trio £11.10 OWNER Dream On Racing Partnership (EPSOM) BRED Arthur Sims 9 Rn 2m 35.5 (4.20) SF: 30/44/40/50/8/12/20/-/-
WEIGHT FOR AGE 3yo-13lb

2360 WELSH RIBAND CONDITIONS STKS (3-Y.O+) (Class B) £10,803.20 (£2,996.80) **1m 4f 23y** Stalls: Centre GOING minus 0.35 sec per fur (F) 7-15 (7-16)

Edbaysaan (IRE) *(109) (RAkehurst)* 5-9-7 LDettori(2) (lw: led: rdn & qcknd 4f out: hdd over 2f out: led 1f out: r.o wl) — 1
2104 3 Waiting **(104)***(112)*(Fav)*(PFICole)* 4-9-11 TQuinn(3) (lw: hld up: 2nd st: slt ld on bit over 2f out: rdn & hdd 1f out: nt qckn) 1 2

4/11 Waiting (1/4-2/5), **2/1** EDBAYSAAN (IRE) (6/4-5/2), TOTE £2.10 OWNER Sheikh Essa Bin Mubarak (EPSOM) BRED Newgate Stud Co 2 Rn 2m 38.0 (6.70) SF: 33/36

2361 ALLBRIGHT BITTER H'CAP (0-80) (3-Y.O) (Class D) £3,787.00 (£1,141.00: £553.00: £259.00) **1m 14y** Stalls: Centre GOING minus 0.35 sec (F) 7-45 (7-46)

1804 3 **Shifting Moon (72)***(81)*(Fav)*(IABalding)* 3-9-6b LDettori(5) (lw: mde all: clr over 4f out: unchal) — 1
1811 7 Maybe Today **(54)***(56) (BRMillman)* 3-7-11 (5) AWhelan(7) (chsd ldr stands' side: r.o ins fnl f: nt trble wnr) 3½ 2
2199 6 African-Pard (IRE) **(73)***(73) (DHaydnJones)* 3-9-7 TQuinn(8) (led stands' side: edgd rt over 1f out: nt qckn ins fnl f) 1¼ 3
2103 6 The Stager (IRE) **(72)***(66) (JRJenkins)* 3-9-6 MRoberts(2) (lw: stdd s: hdwy 4f out: rdn 3f out: one pce: hung rt ins fnl f) 3 4
2054 2 Cedar Dancer **(49)***(38) (RJHodges)* 3-7-6 (5)ow4 NVarley(1) (chsd wnr: rdn over 3f out: no imp: btn whn carried rt ins fnl f) hd 5
1761 2 Nessun Doro **(70)***(52) (SMellor)* 3-9-4 MWigham(3) (rdn 3f out: sn bhd) 6 6
2125 2 Triple Tricks (IRE) **(69)***(50) (WJHaggas)* 3-9-3 RCochrane(6) (hld up: rdn over 3f out: sn bhd) s.h 7

LONG HANDICAP Cedar Dancer 7-6

11/4 SHIFTING MOON, **7/2** Nessun Doro, **4/1** The Stager (IRE), Triple Tricks (IRE), **7/1** African-Pard (IRE), **12/1** Cedar Dancer, **14/1** Maybe Today (10/1-16/1), CSF £32.96 CT £221.74 TOTE £3.60: £1.90 £4.90 (£29.50) OWNER Mr J. C. Smith (KINGSCLERE) BRED Pinfold Stud and Farms Ltd 7 Rn 1m 34.8 (2.30) SF: 49/24/41/34/6/20/18

2362 MAPLE CONDITIONS STKS (3 & 4-Y.O) (Class D) £3,787.00 (£1,141.00: £553.00: £259.00) **7f 16y** Stalls: Centre GOING minus 0.35 sec per fur (F) 8-15 (8-18)

1787 3 **Anam (77)***(86+) (PTWalwyn)* 3-8-3 GHind(2) (chsd ldr 5f out: led over 2f out: sn clr: easily) — 1

1186² Easy Jet (POL) **(82)***(77)*(Fav)*(LordHuntingdon)* 3-8-8 DHarrison(4) (rdn & hdwy over 3f out: chsd wnr over 1f out: no imp) 6 **2**
*322** Hand Craft (IRE) *(80) (WJHaggas)* 3-9-0 RCochrane(5) (lw: hld up: hdwy over 2f out: one pce fnl f) 1½ **3**
2053⁵ Future Options **(65)***(51) (MSSaunders)* 4-8-8 (3) SDrowne(3) (chsd ldrs 2f: rdn over 3f out: wknd over 2f out) 8 **4**
1941⁴ Shen Yang (USA) **(80)***(44) (GLMoore)* 3-8-12 SWhitworth(1) (led: sn clr: edgd rt & hdd over 2f out: sn wknd) 7 **5**
Miss Spent Youth *(8) (RJHodges)* 4-8-4 (7) AmandaSanders(6) (bit bkwd: a bhd: t.o fnl 2f)....12 **6**

10/11 Easy Jet (POL), **7/2** ANAM, **4/1** Hand Craft (IRE), **13/2** Shen Yang (USA) (4/1-7/1), **20/1** Future Options, **66/1** Miss Spent Youth, CSF £7.02 TOTE £4.10: £2.00 £1.50 (£2.70) OWNER Mr Hamdan Al Maktoum (LAMBOURN) BRED Shadwell Estate Company Limited 6 Rn
1m 22.2 (2.20) SF: 30/21/24/3/-/-
WEIGHT FOR AGE 3yo-8lb

2363 ALVESTON MAIDEN H'CAP (0-70) (3-Y.O+) (Class E) £3,337.00 (£1,006.00: £488.00: £229.00) **7f 16y** Stalls: Centre GOING minus 0.35 sec (F) 8-45 (8-46)

555⁹ **Yaa Wale (60)***(70+) (JHMGosden)* 3-9-6 LDettori(4) (lw: hld up: hdwy over 2f out: led 1f out: qckned clr: comf) ....— **1**
2188² Takeshi (IRE) **(61)***(67)*(Fav)*(EALDunlop)* 3-9-4 (3) JTate(6) (a.p: led over 2f out to 1f out: nt qckn) 2 **2**
2018⁷ Trina **(36)***(39) (DLWilliams)* 4-7-11 (7) MHenry(5) (w ldrs: ev ch 2f out: nt qckn) 1¼ **3**
1939⁴ Saltis (IRE) **(58)***(60) (DWPArbuthnot)* 3-9-4 TQuinn(3) (b.hind: chsd ldrs: rdn over 3f out: r.o one pce fnl 2f) ....hd **4**
1546⁸ Indian Lament **(44)***(40) (RJHodges)* 4-8-9 (3) SDrowne(2) (no hdwy fnl 2f) 3 **5**
2032⁸ Miss Laughter **(46)***(41) (JWHills)* 3-8-6 MRoberts(7) (led over 3f: wknd 2f out) ....½ **6**
2202⁵ Lorins Gold **(33)***(25) (AndrewTurnell)* 5-8-1b NAdams(1) (b.nr hind: lw: a.p: led over 3f out tl over 2f out: eased whn btn fnl f) 1 **7**
Swinging Sixties (IRE) **(56)***(47) (GLMoore)* 4-9-10 SWhitworth(12) (b.nr fore: lw: hld up & bhd: sme hdwy over 1f out: nvr plcd to chal) ....½ **8**
334⁶ Main Brace **(46)***(35) (KRBurke)* 4-9-0 ATucker(11) (s.i.s: nvr plcd to chal) ....¾ **9**
2054⁴ Nuthatch (IRE) **(38)***(20) (MDIUsher)* 3-7-5v(7)ow4 AmandaSanders(9) (lw: spd over 5f) 1½ **10**
2032³ Anegre (IRE) **(59)***(27) (LJHolt)* 3-9-5 DHarrison(8) (plld hrd: prom over 4f) 8 **11**
1679¹³ Garlande D'Or **(45)***(6) (JLSpearing)* 3-8-5 GHind(10) (lw: bhd fnl 3f) 3 **12**

11/4 Takeshi (IRE), **4/1** YAA WALE, **13/2** Anegre (IRE), **8/1** Saltis (IRE), **9/1** Trina (op 16/1), Miss Laughter, **14/1** Swinging Sixties (IRE), **16/1** Lorins Gold, Nuthatch (IRE), **25/1** Main Brace, **40/1** Garlande D'Or, **50/1** Indian Lament, CSF £14.36 CT £85.57 TOTE £4.50: £2.20 £2.00 £2.10 (£6.00) Trio £31.70 OWNER Sheikh Ahmed Al Maktoum (NEWMARKET) BRED The Duke of Roxburghe's Stud 12 Rn 1m 22.6 (2.60) SF: 41/38/18/31/19/12/4/26/14/-/-/-
WEIGHT FOR AGE 3yo-8lb

2364 FLEUR DE LYS H'CAP (0-70) (3-Y.O+) (Class E) £2,005.75 (£2,005.75: £449.00: £209.50) **5f 16y** Stalls: Centre GOING minus 0.35 sec per fur (F) 9-15 (9-17)

2092⁶ **Bold Gem (52)***(57) (BJMeehan)* 4-8-10b DHarrison(3) (hld up & bhd: hdwy wl over 1f out: r.o wl ins fnl f) ....— **1**
366⁵ **Delrob (49)***(54) (DHaydnJones)* 4-8-7 TQuinn(2) (lw: chsd ldrs: rdn 3f out: led over 1f out: r.o wl) ....— **1**
2260³ Giggleswick Girl **(63)***(68)*(Fav)*(MRChannon)* 4-9-7 RHughes(1) (lw: hld up: hdwy over 1f out: r.o wl ins fnl f) ....s.h **3**
1972⁹ Ashkernazy (IRE) **(43)***(42) (NEBerry)* 4-8-1 NAdams(5) (chsd ldr over 3f: r.o one pce fnl f) 2 **4**
1451³ Rhythmic Dancer **(67)***(65) (JLSpearing)* 7-9-8 (3) SDrowne(7) (plld hrd: led over 3f: nt qckn ins fnl f) ....hd **5**
2074⁴ Grey Toppa **(46)***(40) (NPLittmoden)* 4-7-11 (7) MHenry(6) (rdn 2f out: nvr nr to chal) 1½ **6**
2096¹⁰ Bayin (USA) **(68)***(49) (MDIUsher)* 6-9-12 RStreet(4) (b.nr fore: lw: hld up & bhd: nvr trbld ldrs) 4 **7**

5/2 Giggleswick Girl, **3/1** Bayin (USA), **5/1** DELROB, Rhythmic Dancer, **15/2** BOLD GEM, **9/1** Ashkernazy (IRE), **14/1** Grey Toppa, CSF BG & D £20.33; D & BG £18.41 TOTE BG £4.80: £3.50; D £3.10: £2.40 (£23.20) OWNER Mr F. C. T. Wilson (UPPER LAMBOURN)/Mrs E. M. Haydn-Jones (PONTYPRIDD) BRED F. C. T. Wilson 7 Rn
59.5 secs (2.50) SF: 21/18/32/6/29/4/13

T/Plpt: £229.00 (47.8 Tckts). T/Qdpt: £21.40 (4 Tckts). KH

2346-NEWMARKET (R-H)
Thursday July 13th (Good to firm, Good fnl 3f)
WEATHER: overcast, rain WIND: almost nil

2365
CHILD & CO. SUPERLATIVE STKS (Listed) (2-Y.O) (Class A) £9,756.75 (£3,513.00: £1,681.50: £682.50: £266.25)
7f (July) Stalls: Low GOING minus 0.19 sec per fur (GF) 2-05 (2-05)

1838[8] **Allied Forces (USA)** *(96+)*(Fav)*(HRACecil)* 2-9-0 PatEddery(2) (lw: a gng wl: led 3f out: shkn up appr fnl f: r.o wl)........— 1
1913* Mons *(93) (LMCumani)* 2-9-0 JReid(5) (bhd: hdwy ½-wy: ch 1f out: r.o: nt pce of wnr)........1¼ 2
1838[5] Dovebrace *(89) (ABailey)* 2-9-2 MWigham(1) (chsd ldrs: hdwy ½-wy: sn rdn: one pce fnl 2f)........2½ 3
1298[3] Galapino *(62) (CEBrittain)* 2-8-11 BDoyle(4) (trckd ldrs: ev ch over 2f out: rdn & btn over 1f out)........10 4
2005* Canons Park *(19) (IABalding)* 2-9-0 WRSwinburn(3) (unruly in stalls: led & sn clr: hdd 3f out: wknd rapidly)........20 5

2/1 ALLIED FORCES (USA) (6/4-9/4), **4/1** Canons Park (op 5/2), Dovebrace, **9/2** Mons, **11/2** Galapino, CSF £9.70 TOTE £2.70: £1.50 £1.80 (£3.80) OWNER Mr A. Altayer (NEWMARKET) BRED Buckram Oak Farm 5 Rn 1m 27.84 (3.44) SF: 42/39/35/8/-

2366
BAHRAIN TROPHY STKS (Listed) (3-Y.O) (Class A) £11,386.80 (£4,096.80: £1,958.40: £792.00: £306.00)
1m 6f 175y (July) Stalls: High GOING minus 0.19 sec per fur (GF) 2-35 (2-36)

1852[6] **Grey Shot (97)***(102) (IABalding)* 3-8-10 LDettori(2) (mde all: qcknd 6f out: styd on fnl 2f)........— 1
1925* Juyush (USA) **(107)***(99)*(Fav)*(BWHills)* 3-8-10 WCarson(4) (lw: trckd ldrs: effrt 4f out: hrd rdn fnl 2f: nt pce to chal)........2½ 2
1852[5] Great Crusader **(99)***(97) (CACyzer)* 3-8-10 JWeaver(5) (trckd ldrs: effrt over 4f out: hung rt fnl 3f: nt qckn appr fnl f)........2½ 3
1987* Eelious (USA) **(86)***(80) (CEBrittain)* 3-8-10 MRoberts(1) (hld up: hdwy 7f out: rdn & wknd fnl 3f)........15 4
2119[3] Cypress Avenue (IRE) **(95)***(69) (RHannon)* 3-8-10 JReid(3) (hld up: outpcd 5f out: sn btn)....11 5

10/11 Juyush (USA) (4/5-Evens), **9/2** GREY SHOT, **6/1** Great Crusader, **13/2** Cypress Avenue (IRE), **8/1** Eelious (USA), CSF £8.65 TOTE £5.10: £1.70 £1.30 (£2.80) OWNER Mr J. C. Smith (KINGSCLERE) BRED Littleton Stud 5 Rn 3m 8.23 (2.23) SF: 68/65/63/46/35

2367
TNT AVIATION H'CAP (0-95) (3-Y.O) (Class C) £9,787.50 (£2,925.00: £1,400.00: £637.50) **1m (July)** Stalls: Low GOING: 0.04 sec per fur (G) 3-05 (3-07)

2103[3] **Nordinex (IRE) (75)***(84) (RWArmstrong)* 3-8-6 RPrice(3) (lw: cl up: led 2f out: hrd rdn & hung lft fnl f: styd on)........— 1
2103* Twilight Patrol **(90)***(97) (RHannon)* 3-9-0 (7) DaneO'Neill(6) (b. nr fore: hld up: hdwy over 2f out: ev ch 1f out: carried lft: btn whn hmpd cl home)........1¼ 2
1554* Blisland **(90)***(96)*(Fav)*(RCharlton)* 3-9-7 PatEddery(5) (hld up: effrt 3f out: hrd rdn to chal appr fnl f: kpt on)........s.h 3
1988[2] Elpidos **(70)***(76) (CEBrittain)* 3-8-1 MRoberts(7) (chsd ldrs: outpcd & n.m.r over 2f out: r.o wl towards fin)........s.h 4
2100* Touch a Million (USA) **(81)***(79) (EALDunlop)* 3-8-12 WRSwinburn(1) (lw: in tch tl wl outpcd 3f out: styd on fnl f)........4 5
1793[9] Tranquillity **(78)***(76) (LordHuntingdon)* 3-8-9 LDettori(4) (led tl hdd 2f out: grad wknd)........hd 6
1269[2] Atlaal (USA) **(80)***(73) (HThomsonJones)* 3-8-11 WCarson(2) (hld up: rdn 3f out: sn btn)........2½ 7

2/1 Blisland, **9/2** NORDINEX (IRE), **5/1** Twilight Patrol (7/2-11/2), **11/2** Touch a Million (USA), **7/1** Elpidos, **9/1** Atlaal (USA), **12/1** Tranquillity, CSF £24.67 TOTE £5.40: £2.50 £2.70 (£8.40) OWNER Mr R. J. Arculli (NEWMARKET) BRED Howard Kaskel in Ireland 7 Rn
1m 42.03 (4.33) SF: 50/63/62/42/45/42/39
STEWARDS' ENQUIRY Price suspended 22 & 24-29/7/95 (careless riding).

2368
JULY CUP STKS (Gp 1) (3-Y.O+) (Class A) £85,774.00 (£31,666.00: £15,133.00: £6,115.00: £2,357.50: £854.50)
6f (July) Stalls: Low GOING: 0.04 sec per fur (G) 3-40 (3-41)

1870[2] **Lake Coniston (IRE) (120)***(134)*(Fav)*(GLewis)* 4-9-6 PatEddery(9) (lw: mde all: qcknd over 1f out: r.o wl)........— 1

1896* Piccolo **(113)***(123) (MRChannon)* 4-9-6 RHughes(6) (lw: hld up: hdwy over 2f out: r.o wl: no ch w wnr)....4 2
1896 8 Hoh Magic **(117)***(114) (MBell)* 3-8-10 WRSwinburn(4) (chsd ldrs: outpcd over 2f out: kpt on wl fnl f)....2½ 3
1364 3 Owington **(120)***(116) (GWragg)* 4-9-6 PaulEddery(2) (hld up: stdy hdwy 2f out: rdn & nt qckn appr fnl f)....nk 4
1896 5 Fard (IRE) **(117)***(114) (DMorley)* 3-8-13 WCarson(5) (lw: chsd ldrs: sn drvn: one pce fnl 2f)...¾ 5
1896 4 Millstream (USA) **(110)***(109) (MJohnston)* 3-8-10 DHolland(3) (swtg: chsd wnr tl rdn & btn wl over 1f out)....¾ 6
1870* So Factual (USA) **(114)***(107) (SbinSuroor)* 5-9-6 RCochrane(8) (effrt ½-wy: hdwy 2f out: sn rdn & btn)....2 7
1848* Sergeyev (IRE) *(103) (RHannon)* 3-8-13 TQuinn(1) (sn pushed along: nvr trbld ldrs)....1¼ 8
1120a* Heart Lake *(77) (SbinSuroor)* 4-9-6 LDettori(7) (trckd ldrs: rdn over 2f out: sn btn & eased)..10 9

13/8 LAKE CONISTON (IRE), **4/1** Owington, **5/1** Sergeyev (IRE), **7/1** Piccolo, **15/2** Heart Lake, **10/1** So Factual (USA) (7/1-12/1), **12/1** Fard (IRE), **20/1** Hoh Magic, **33/1** Millstream (USA), CSF £13.86 TOTE £3.10: £1.50 £2.60 (£10.70) Trio £123.70 OWNER Highclere Thoroughbred Racing Ltd (EPSOM) BRED J. P. McManus 9 Rn 1m 12.42 (0.92) SF: 96/85/69/78/69/64/69/58/39
WEIGHT FOR AGE 3yo-7lb

2369 LADBROKE BUNBURY CUP H'CAP (0-105) (3-Y.O+) (Class B)

£24,270.00 (£7,260.00: £3,480.00: £1,590.00)
7f (July) Stalls: Low GOING: 0.04 sec per fur (G) 4-10 (4-15)

2205 2 **Cadeaux Tryst (97)***(108) (EALDunlop)* 3-9-1 WRSwinburn(17) (b: hld up & bhd stands' side: gd hdwy over 1f out: r.o to ld wl ins fnl f)....— 1
2096 5 Sky Music **(77)***(88) (MissSEHall)* 4-7-10 (7) MHenry(19) (b: trckd ldrs stands' side: led wl over 1f out: edgd lft: hdd & no ex towards fin)....hd 2
1839 14 Anniversarypresent **(95)***(105) (GLewis)* 3-8-13b PaulEddery(12) (bhd stands' side: gd hdwy over 1f out: r.o wl u.p)....nk 3
1851 25 Madly Sharp **(93)***(100) (JWWatts)* 4-9-5 PatEddery(18) (lw: hld up & bhd stands' side: gd hdwy over 2f out: ev ch 1f out: nt qckn)....1¼ 4
2099* Tawafij (USA) **(84)***(88) (TDyer)* 6-8-10 JFortune(14) (hld up stands' side: gd hdwy & ev ch over 1f out: nt qckn)....1½ 5
1915 8 Veloce (IRE) **(72)***(74) (ABailey)* 7-7-12 FNorton(15) (b: a.p stands' side: ev ch over 1f out: sn btn)....1 6
1728* Celestial Key (USA) **(102)***(101) (MJohnston)* 5-10-0 DHolland(1) (hld up & bhd far side: hdwy 2f out: styd on)....1 7
1851 9 Night City **(99)***(95) (LadyHerries)* 4-9-11 RHughes(3) (lw: chsd ldrs far side over 5f)....1½ 8
1299* Elfland (IRE) **(85)***(81)*(Fav)*(LadyHerries)* 4-8-11 RCochrane(2) (b: hld up far side: hdwy & ev ch over 1f out: rdn & sn btn)....s.h 9
1618 6 Jafeica (IRE) **(95)***(90) (RHannon)* 4-9-7 JReid(16) (chsd ldrs stands' side: ev ch 2f out: btn 1f out)....nk 10
1487 5 Montserrat **(79)***(71) (LGCottrell)* 3-7-11 GBardwell(8) (cl up: led far side 3f out tl wknd over 1f out)....1¼ 11
1895 12 Saseedo (USA) **(88)***(77) (WAO'Gorman)* 5-9-0 EmmaO'Gorman(10) (swtg: hld up far side: hdwy ½-wy: btn over 1f out)....1¼ 12
1851 19 Czarna (IRE) **(88)***(76) (CEBrittain)* 4-9-0 MRoberts(5) (b.hind: chsd ldrs far side over 5f)....½ 13
2169 5 Helios **(76)***(62) (NJHWalker)* 7-8-2 BDoyle(7) (led far side 4f: wknd)....¾ 14
2099 8 En Attendant (FR) **(96)***(82) (BHanbury)* 7-9-8v TIves(4) (b.hind: hld up & bhd far side: effrt 3f out: n.d)....nk 15
1070* Moon Strike (FR) **(75)***(61) (WJarvis)* 5-8-1b WCarson(6) (b.off hind: chsd ldrs far side 5f: sn rdn & btn)....s.h 16
1638 3 Shepherd Market (IRE) **(67)***(51) (DAWilson)* 4-7-7 JQuinn(13) (lw: led stands' side tl hung lft & hdd wl over 1f out: sn wknd)....¾ 17
1895 20 Darren Boy (IRE) **(85)***(63) (PFICole)* 4-8-11 TQuinn(11) (swtg: prom stands' side: hung lft u.p fnl 2f & wknd)....2½ 18
2015 2 Done Well (USA) **(98)***(71) (EALDunlop)* 3-9-2 LDettori(9) (swtchd stands' side after s: cl up 5f: wknd qckly)....2½ 19

LONG HANDICAP Shepherd Market (IRE) 7-6

6/1 Elfland (IRE), **15/2** Celestial Key (USA), Madly Sharp, **9/1** Done Well (USA), En Attendant (FR), **10/1** Anniversarypresent, **11/1** Tawafij (USA), **12/1** Sky Music, **14/1** Moon Strike (FR), **16/1** Czarna (IRE), Night City, **20/1** Saseedo (USA), CADEAUX TRYST, Shepherd Market (IRE), Montserrat, **25/1** Darren Boy (IRE), Jafeica (IRE), **33/1** Veloce (IRE), Helios, CSF £231.08 CT £2,323.65 TOTE £21.20: £4.90 £3.00 £2.80 £2.20 (£183.40) Trio £1,461.00 OWNER Maktoum Al Maktoum (NEWMARKET) BRED Gainsborough Stud Management Ltd 19 Rn
1m 26.96 (2.56) SF: 73/61/70/73/61/47/74/68/54/63/36/50/49/35/55/34/24/36/36
WEIGHT FOR AGE 3yo-8lb

2370 E.B.F. NGK SPARK PLUGS MAIDEN STKS (2-Y.O) (Class D) £4,980.50 (£1,484.00: £707.00: £318.50)
6f (July) Stalls: Low GOING: 0.04 sec per fur (G) 4-45 (4-47)

Danehill Dancer (IRE) *(84)*(Fav)*(NACallaghan)* 2-9-0 PatEddery(5) (str: scope: bit bkwd: a cl up: led 1½f out: pushed along & r.o wl fnl f).....— 1
Raheen (USA) *(81+) (MRStoute)* 2-9-0 WRSwinburn(6) (gd sort: trckd ldrs: rdn 2f out: w wnr appr fnl f: r.o wl).....1 2
Albaha (USA) *(71+) (RWArmstrong)* 2-9-0 WCarson(4) (w'like: scope: led tl hdd 1½f out: sn outpcd).....4 3
Mancini *(68+) (MBell)* 2-9-0 RHughes(7) (neat: bhd: drvn along ½-wy: styd on: no imp).....1 4
Papering (IRE) *(56) (LMCumani)* 2-8-9 LDettori(2) (leggy: scope: chsd ldrs tl outpcd fnl 2½f).....2½ 5
Prize Giving *(61) (GWragg)* 2-9-0 PaulEddery(3) (gd sort: scope: s.i.s: bhd: rdn ½-wy: no real hdwy).....s.h 6
Decision Maker (IRE) *(61) (RHannon)* 2-9-0 JReid(1) (w'like: scope: cl up tl outpcd fnl f).....hd 7

7/4 DANEHILL DANCER (IRE), **3/1** Prize Giving, **9/2** Raheen (USA) (5/2-13/2), **5/1** Albaha (USA), **9/1** Papering (IRE) (6/1-10/1), **25/1** Mancini, Decision Maker (IRE), CSF £9.55 TOTE £2.60: £1.70 £2.50 (£4.90) OWNER Mr M. Tabor (NEWMARKET) BRED L. K. and K. McCreery 7 Rn
1m 15.9 (4.40) SF: 40/37/27/24/12/17/17

T/Jkpt; Not won £11,064.88 to Newbury 14/07/95. T/Plpt: £72.70 (471.7 Tckts). T/Qdpt: £29.90 (9.9 Tckts). AA

2353-REDCAR (L-H)
Thursday July 13th (Firm)
WEATHER: fine, thundery last race WIND: slt half bhd

2371 E.B.F. MERMAID MAIDEN STKS (2-Y.O) (Class D) £3,678.00 (£1,104.00: £532.00: £246.00) **5f** Stalls: Centre GOING minus 0.51 sec per fur (F) 6-30 (6-31)

1620³ **Evening Chime (USA)** *(69+)*(Fav)*(MrsJRRamsden)* 2-9-0 KFallon(4) (lw: mde virtually all: pushed clr over 1f out: eased towards fin).....— 1
1919³ Katy-Q (IRE) *(59) (PCalver)* 2-8-9 MBirch(5) (w wnr: rdn & hung lft over 1f out: no ch w wnr).....1½ 2
2221⁷ Superfrills *(46) (MissLCSiddall)* 2-8-9 DeanMcKeown(7) (trckd ldrs: kpt on same pce fnl 2f)...4 3
2116⁴ Relatively Clever (USA) *(47) (MrsJRRamsden)* 2-9-0 MDeering(6) (s.i.s: outpcd tl hdwy ½-wy: nvr nr ldrs).....1¼ 4
1678⁸ Darerock *(38) (MDods)* 2-9-0 JFortune(2) (chsd ldrs: drvn along: outpcd ½-wy: sn wknd).....3 5
1620⁶ Ron's Gem *(38) (WWHaigh)* 2-9-0 DaleGibson(3) (dwlt: a outpcd & drvn along).....hd 6
1935⁵ Ginger Hodgers *(29) (RMWhitaker)* 2-8-9 ACulhane(1) (chsd ldrs tl wknd ½-wy).....1¼ 7

1/3 EVENING CHIME (USA), **5/1** Katy-Q (IRE), **12/1** Relatively Clever (USA) (op 6/1), **20/1** Ginger Hodgers, **25/1** Ron's Gem, **33/1** Darerock, Superfrills, CSF £2.66 TOTE £1.40: £1.20 £1.30 (£1.30) OWNER Mr P. A. Leonard (THIRSK) BRED Bob Berger 7 Rn 58.7 secs (2.00) SF: 19/9/-/-/-/-/-

2372 JOLLY SAILOR (S) H'CAP (0-60) (3-Y.O) (Class G) £2,623.00 (£728.00: £349.00)
5f Stalls: Centre GOING minus 0.51 sec per fur (F) 7-00 (7-02)

2220² **Freckles Kelly (37)***(47) (MHEasterby)* 3-8-0 SMaloney(5) (mde virtually all: drvn out).....— 1
2084¹³ Royal Dome (IRE) **(50)***(56) (MartynWane)* 3-8-13 KFallon(3) (w ldrs: ev ch over 1f out: edgd lft u.p: nt qckn towards fin).....1¼ 2
2124³ Baileys Sunset (IRE) **(58)***(54)*(Fav)*(MJohnston)* 3-9-7b DHolland(6) (swvd rt s: chsd ldrs: nt qckn appr fnl f).....3 3
1523¹⁴ Daily Challenger (USA) **(47)***(38) (RonaldThompson)* 3-8-5 (5) LNewton(7) (bmpd s: hdwy ½-wy: kpt on fnl f).....1¾ 4
2018⁴ Jessica's Secret (IRE) **(34)***(24) (ABailey)* 3-7-11 WHawksley(2) (chsd ldrs: hrd rdn 2f out: edgd lft & kpt on one pce).....nk 5
1847⁷ Double Glow **(45)***(34) (NBycroft)* 3-8-8b JQuinn(9) (chsd ldrs tl wknd wl over 1f out).....nk 6
2124⁸ Oneineverycolour **(43)***(21) (PDEvans)* 3-8-6 JFortune(4) (chsd ldrs: rdn ½-wy: sn wknd).....3½ 7
2162⁹ Malsisio **(30)***(4) (SGNorton)* 3-7-7 NKennedy(8) (dwlt: bhd & drvn along: sme late hdwy).....1¼ 8
Oubeck Princess **(45)***(18) (EWeymes)* 3-8-8 DeanMcKeown(10) (bit bkwd: hdwy ½-wy: sn rdn & wknd).....nk 9
2084¹⁰ Pemley **(33)***(3) (RMWhitaker)* 3-7-10v DaleGibson(1) (sn outpcd & pushed along).....1 10
LONG HANDICAP Malsisio 7-4

7/4 Baileys Sunset (IRE), **7/2** FRECKLES KELLY, **5/1** Pemley, **8/1** Royal Dome (IRE), **9/1** Double Glow, **11/1** Oneineverycolour, **14/1** Daily Challenger (USA), Jessica's Secret (IRE), **20/1** Oubeck Princess, **33/1** Malsisio, CSF £31.24 CT £60.63 TOTE £4.00: £1.70 £5.00 £1.60 (£30.10) Trio £9.20 OWNER Mr T. H. Bennett (MALTON) BRED Bjorn Neilson 10 Rn 58.4 secs (1.70) SF: 12/21/19/3/-/- Bt in 5,800 gns

2373

CROFT AND BLACKBURN COMMERCIAL VEHICLE H'CAP (0-80) (3-Y.O+) (Class D) £3,814.50 (£1,146.00: £553.00: £256.50)
1m 2f Stalls: Low GOING minus 0.51 sec per fur (F) 7-30 (7-30)

2132[5] **Durano (62)***(73) (MHEasterby)* 4-9-5 SMaloney(1) (hld up & plld hrd: hdwy 3f out: squeezed thro & styd on to ld ins fnl f: drvn out) .....— **1**
1944[2] Sycamore Lodge (IRE) **(69)***(78)*(Fav)*(PCalver)* 4-9-12 MBirch(2) (trckd ldrs: led over 2f out: rdn & edgd lft over 1f out: hdd & nt qckn ins fnl f) 1¼ **2**
2122[4] Exclusion **(40)***(48) (JHetherton)* 6-7-11 LCharnock(6) (chsd ldrs: led over 3f out tl over 2f out: hmpd over 1f out: kpt on one pce) .....¾ **3**
1946[4] Once More for Luck (IRE) **(59)***(67)*(Fav)*(MrsMReveley)* 4-9-2 KDarley(4) (lw: hld up: smooth hdwy & ev ch 2f out: sn rdn: styd on one pce) .....s.h **4**
1844[7] First Bid **(66)***(73) (RMWhitaker)* 8-9-9 ACulhane(3) (trckd ldrs: ev ch over 1f out: one pce)....nk **5**
1946[5] Doctor's Remedy **(36)***(38) (MrsJJordan)* 9-7-7b NKennedy(5) (led tl over 3f out: wknd over 2f out) 3½ **6**

LONG HANDICAP Doctor's Remedy 7-1

7/4 Once More for Luck (IRE), Sycamore Lodge (IRE), **8/1** Exclusion, **10/1** DURANO (8/1-12/1), **12/1** First Bid (op 8/1), **14/1** Doctor's Remedy, CSF £25.41 TOTE £15.30: £4.10 £1.50 (£19.40) OWNER Mr A. M. Wragg (MALTON) BRED A. M. Wragg 6 Rn 2m 5.5 (3.00) SF: 37/42/12/31/37/2

2374

SEA PIGEON H'CAP (0-75) (3-Y.O+) (Class D) £3,736.50 (£1,122.00: £541.00: £250.50) **2m 4y** Stalls: Low GOING minus 0.51 sec per fur (F) 8-00 (8-01)

2355* **Nanton Point (USA) (57)***(68)*(Fav)*(LadyHerries)* 3-7-7 4x JQuinn(5) (led to 9f out: led 4f out tl over 1f out: styd on wl to ld ins fnl f: drvn out) .....— **1**
2184* Tu Opes **(70)***(81) (JLHarris)* 4-9-9 4x DHolland(6) (lw: trckd ldrs: chal 3f out: led over 1f out tl ins fnl f: hrd rdn & nt qckn towards fin) .....nk **2**
2098[10] Mondragon **(72)***(82) (MrsMReveley)* 5-9-6 (5) GParkin(2) (bhd: pushed along ½-wy: gd hdwy over 1f out: styd on wl towards fin) 1¼ **3**
2087[2] Good Hand (USA) **(75)***(83) (JWWatts)* 9-10-0 NConnorton(4) (sn trckng ldrs: outpcd & drvn along 7f out: kpt on fnl 3f: nvr nr to chal) 1½ **4**
495[2] Cutthroat Kid (IRE) **(66)***(74) (MrsMReveley)* 5-9-5v KDarley(3) (lw: hld up: effrt & pushed along 5f out: kpt on same pce fnl 3f) .....½ **5**
2186[2] Izza **(40)***(40) (WStorey)* 4-7-0v(7) PFessey(1) (plld hrd: trckd ldr: led 9f out to 4f out: sn wknd) 8 **6**

LONG HANDICAP Nanton Point (USA) 7-2 Izza 7-2

11/8 NANTON POINT (USA), **4/1** Tu Opes, Mondragon, **5/1** Good Hand (USA), **17/2** Cutthroat Kid (IRE), **25/1** Izza, CSF £7.01 TOTE £2.80: £1.70 £2.50 (£6.40) OWNER Mr L. G. Lazarus (LITTLEHAMPTON) BRED Newgate Stud Farm Inc 6 Rn 3m 25.7 (0.70) SF: 35/65/66/67/58/24
WEIGHT FOR AGE 3yo-17lb

2375

LANGBAURGH H'CAP (0-70) (3-Y.O+) (Class E) £3,280.00 (£985.00: £475.00: £220.00) **1m 1f** Stalls: Low GOING minus 0.51 sec per fur (F) 8-30 (8-32)

1669[2] **Bulsara (55)***(67)*(Fav)*(CWFairhurst)* 3-8-9 DeanMcKeown(11) (trckd ldr: led over 1f out: hrd rdn: jst hld on) .....— **1**
2276[7] Habeta (USA) **(36)***(48) (JWWatts)* 9-8-0 LCharnock(5) (prom: chal over 1f out: hrd rdn: jst failed) .....s.h **2**
2276[6] Nobby Barnes **(41)***(51) (DonEnricoIncisa)* 6-8-5 KimTinkler(2) (bhd: hdwy on ins & nt clr run 2f out: styd on ins fnl f) 1¼ **3**
1995[4] Avishayes (USA) **(48)***(56) (MrsMReveley)* 8-8-12 JFanning(4) (lw: hld up & bhd: hdwy on outside 3f out: styd on appr fnl f: nt rch ldrs) 1 **4**
1452[9] Durham Drapes **(55)***(60) (MHEasterby)* 4-9-5 MBirch(8) (trckd ldrs: effrt & hung lft over 1f out: no imp) 1¾ **5**
2126[3] Essayeffsee **(49)***(52) (MrsMReveley)* 6-8-13 KDarley(10) (lw: hld up: nt clr run & swtchd over 1f out: styd on: nvr rchd ldrs) 1 **6**
2073[2] Calder King **(58)***(61) (JLEyre)* 4-9-8v JFortune(6) (mid div: effrt 4f out: nt clr run over 2f out: styd on: nvr nr ldrs) .....hd **7**
2254[4] Fort Vally **(36)***(36) (BWMurray)* 5-7-7 (7) MartinDwyer(9) (unruly in stalls: dwlt: bhd: sme hdwy on outside 3f out: n.d) 1½ **8**

Northwise (IRE) **(45)***(45) (WWHaigh)* 4-8-9 DaleGibson(7) (trckd ldrs: drvn along & outpcd over 3f out: grad wknd)....hd **9**
2061[7] Pleasure Trick (USA) **(60)***(56) (NTinkler)* 4-9-10 GDuffield(1) (swtg: led & sn clr: hdd over 1f out: wknd)....2 **10**

4/1 BULSARA (3/1-9/2), **5/1** Calder King, Essayeffsee, **6/1** Avishayes (USA), **7/1** Durham Drapes, **8/1** Fort Vally, **10/1** Habeta (USA), Nobby Barnes, **16/1** Northwise (IRE), **33/1** Pleasure Trick (USA), CSF £39.53 CT £340.57 TOTE £4.30: £1.60 £2.70 £2.20 (£20.90) Trio £82.90 OWNER Twinacre Nurseries Ltd (MIDDLEHAM) BRED P. and Mrs Blacker 10 Rn

1m 52.8 (3.80) SF: 18/9/12/17/21/13/22/-/6/17

WEIGHT FOR AGE 3yo-10lb

STEWARDS' ENQUIRY McKeown susp. 24-25/7/95 (excessive use of whip).

2376

FARNDALE LIMITED STKS (0-70) (3-Y.O) (Class E) £3,075.25 (£922.00: £443.50: £204.25) **1m** Stalls: Centre GOING minus 0.51 sec per fur (F) 9-00 (9-03)

300[2] **First Crush (68)***(73) (SirMarkPrescott)* 3-8-9 GDuffield(3) (lw: w ldrs: hrd rdn fnl 2f: styd on to ld nr fin)....— **1**
1504[4] Break the Rules **(70)***(78) (MrsMReveley)* 3-9-0 KDarley(5) (lw: chsd ldrs: outpcd ½-wy: swtchd rt: styd on wl ins fnl f: jst failed)....s.h **2**
2103[10] Nordic Doll (IRE) **(70)***(75) (BWHills)* 3-8-6 (5) JDSmith(6) (trckd ldr: led 2f out tl last strides) ..s.h **3**
962[9] Bobanlyn (IRE) **(68)***(68)*(Fav)*(DMorris)* 3-8-9 KFallon(1) (drvn along & outpcd ½-wy: hdwy u.p 2f out: nvr nr to chal)....2½ **4**
2115[4] Sheama (USA) **(69)***(68) (WJarvis)* 3-8-11b JCarroll(2) (trckd ldrs: effrt over 2f out: wknd over 1f out)....¾ **5**
2125* Aoife Alainn (IRE) **(70)** *(JWHills)* 3-8-11 DHolland(4) (led to 2f out: 3rd & wkng whn broke leg over 1f out: dead).... **P**

3/1 Bobanlyn (IRE), **4/1** Break the Rules, **9/2** FIRST CRUSH, **5/1** Nordic Doll (IRE), Sheama (USA), **6/1** Aoife Alainn (IRE), CSF £20.33 TOTE £3.40: £1.60 £2.60 (£5.70) OWNER Mrs L. Burnet (NEWMARKET) BRED Cheveley Park Stud Ltd 6 Rn 1m 37.4 (2.40) SF: 26/31/28/21/21/-

STEWARDS' ENQUIRY Duffield suspended 22 & 24-29/7/95 (excessive use & using whip above shoulder height).

T/Plpt: £54.50 (200.63 Tckts). T/Qdpt: £26.60 (1.3 Tckts). WG

1879-SOUTHWELL (L-H)
Thursday July 13th (Standard)

WEATHER: thundery WIND: almost nil

2377

CHELSEA H'CAP (0-60) (3-Y.O+) (Class F) £2,519.00 (£694.00: £329.00) **1m (Fibresand)** Stalls: Low 2-20 (2-23)

2076[3] **Moneghetti (38)***(50) (RHollinshead)* 4-8-6 NCarlisle(8) (a.p: 6th st: rdn to ld ins fnl f: r.o wl)....— **1**
2073[6] First Gold **(58)***(64) (JWharton)* 6-9-12 KDarley(12) (mid div: hdwy 5th st: led over 1f out: hdd & unable qckn ins fnl f)....3 **2**
1785[2] Legend Dulac (IRE) **(39)***(41) (JAHarris)* 6-8-7 SDWilliams(13) (chsd ldrs: 2nd st: led over 1f out: sn hdd & unable qckn)....2 **3**
1884[5] Puffy **(46)***(47) (MDods)* 8-9-0v DaleGibson(15) (b: s.i.s: hdwy over 2f out: nt rch ldrs)....nk **4**
1568[4] Friar Street (IRE) **(40)***(41) (EJAlston)* 5-8-8 JCarroll(3) (led: hdd over 1f out: styd on same pce)....nk **5**
1940[8] Prenonamoss **(55)***(55) (DWPArbuthnot)* 7-9-9v JWilliams(10) (b.hind: nvr nrr)....½ **6**
2246[17] Genesis Four **(43)***(33) (SRBowring)* 5-8-6b(5) CTeague(11) (lw: mid div: drvn along over 4f out: n.d after)....5 **7**
306[5] Jalmaid **(50)***(37) (BAMcMahon)* 3-8-6 (3) SSanders(9) (nvr trbld ldrs)....1½ **8**
1878[5] Bali Tender **(43)***(22) (MWEasterby)* 4-8-11 LCharnock(14) (prom: 3rd & rdn st: sn wknd)....4 **9**
1880[11] Legally Delicious **(56)***(25) (DWChapman)* 3-9-1 DeanMcKeown(16) (lw: s.s: a in rr)....5 **10**
2073[8] Jairzinho (USA) **(47)***(13) (PHayward)* 6-8-8 (7) AmandaSanders(2) (bhd fr ½-wy)....1¼ **11**
Key Pitch (USA) **(60)***(26) (LordHuntingdon)* 3-9-5 DHarrison(4) (bit bkwd: prom tl 7th & wkng st)....hd **12**
2246[6] Swinging Tich **(44)***(4) (ALForbes)* 6-8-7 (5)ow1 LNewton(7) (s.s: a in rr)....2½ **13**
1714[12] Racing Telegraph **(42)** *(JPearce)* 5-8-10 GBardwell(5) (a in rr)....5 **14**
2156[3] Corona Gold **(42)** (Fav)*(JGFitzGerald)* 5-8-10 KFallon(1) (sn outpcd & bhd)....hd **15**
1843[8] Prim Lass **(47)** *(JHetherton)* 4-9-1 WNewnes(6) (chsd ldrs: 4th & rdn st: sn wknd)....12 **16**

11/2 Corona Gold, **6/1** MONEGHETTI, **7/1** Legend Dulac (IRE), **8/1** Genesis Four, Key Pitch (USA), **11/1** Puffy, **12/1** Legally Delicious, First Gold, **14/1** Jalmaid, Swinging Tich, **16/1** Racing Telegraph, Friar Street (IRE), Prenonamoss, **25/1** Prim Lass, **33/1** Bali Tender, Jairzinho (USA), CSF £72.58 CT £478.26 TOTE £8.20: £2.20 £2.10 £2.50 £3.80 (£41.60) Trio £210.70 OWNER Mr Philip Harvey (UPPER LONGDON) BRED P.G.Harvey 16 Rn 1m 45.8 (6.50) SF: 18/32/9/15/9/23/1/-/-/-/-/-/-/-/-/-
WEIGHT FOR AGE 3yo-9lb

OFFICIAL EXPLANATION **Corona Gold: the trainer's representative stated that the gelding was outpaced early on and resented the kickback. A routine test was ordered.**

2378 HAMPSTEAD CLAIMING STKS (3-Y.O) (Class F) £2,519.00 (£694.00: £329.00) **1m 4f (Fibresand)** Stalls: High 2-50 (2-56)

1986[6] **Last Corner (67)***(64)*(Fav)*(RHollinshead)* 3-9-1 KDarley(13) (trckd ldrs: 2nd st: led wl over 2f out: hdd over 1f out: rallied to ld ins fnl f: drvn out) — **1**
1881[4] Shared Risk **(55)***(66) (SGNorton)* 3-8-12 (5) HKYim(11) (prom: outpcd over 4f out: rallied & 3rd st: led over 1f out: hdd ins fnl f: nt r.o) nk **2**
2142[4] Red Phantom (IRE) *(50) (SMellor)* 3-8-8 (7) ADaly(8) (prom: 4th st: outpcd fnl 2f) 10 **3**
2093[5] Endless Fantasy *(34) (CACyzer)* 3-9-2 DHarrison(7) (hld up: hdwy & 5th st: wknd 2f out) 13 **4**
1881[10] Scale the Summit **(42)***(16) (SirMarkPrescott)* 3-8-3 GDuffield(3) (prom: drvn along over 4f out: 6th & btn st) 3½ **5**
1881[11] Lady Kuynder **(25)***(6) (DrJDScargill)* 3-7-12 NCarlisle(2) (hld up: nvr trbld ldrs) 4 **6**
Ski Chalet *(15) (AHide)* 3-8-10 JWilliams(10) (unf: hld up: plld hrd: effrt 4f out: sn lost tch) 2 **7**
1628[5] Royal Rabbit **(50)***(10) (GLMoore)* 3-8-7 SWhitworth(6) (hld up: outpcd over 5f out: n.d after) 1¾ **8**
2134[8] Northern Spruce (IRE) **(40)** *(MissJacquelineDoyle)* 3-8-9 KFallon(5) (led: hdd wl over 2f out: wknd qckly) dist **9**
2133[3] Panama Hat (IRE) *(PCHaslam)* 3-8-12 (3) JStack(12) (chsd ldr: rdn over 4f out: sn wknd) 5 **10**
1059[8] Anchor Crown *(JRJenkins)* 3-8-8 WNewnes(9) (Withdrawn not under Starter's orders: bolted bef s) **W**
1880[3] Be My Choice *(MrsJCecil)* 3-8-4 GHind(4) (Withdrawn not under Starter's orders: ref to ent stalls) **W**

7/4 LAST CORNER, **4/1** Be My Choice, **6/1** Endless Fantasy, **7/1** Royal Rabbit (op 4/1), **8/1** Scale the Summit, **12/1** Red Phantom (IRE) (op 8/1), Ski Chalet (op 7/1), **14/1** Shared Risk (10/1-16/1), **25/1** Lady Kuynder, Panama Hat (IRE), Anchor Crown, **50/1** Northern Spruce (IRE), CSF £18.37 TOTE £2.10: £1.20 £3.00 £3.00 (£8.10) Trio £43.80 OWNER Mr P. D. Savill (UPPER LONGDON) BRED Aston Park Stud 10 Rn 2m 43.4 (9.20) SF: 32/34/18/2/-/-/-/-/-/-/-
STEWARDS' ENQUIRY Yim suspended 24-25/7/95 (excessive use of whip).

2379 DERRY BUILDING SERVICES H'CAP (0-70) (3-Y.O+) (Class E) £3,559.60 (£1,064.80: £510.40: £233.20) **1m 4f (Fibresand)** Stalls: High 3-25 (3-27)

2138[6] **Carpathian (55)***(66)*(Fav)*(LordHuntingdon)* 4-9-1 DHarrison(11) (hld up in tch: 3rd st: led 2f out: drvn out) — **1**
1683[2] Daleria **(55)***(63) (AHarrison)* 4-8-12 (3) JStack(9) (hld up: hdwy 5f out: 4th st: kpt on ins fnl f) 2½ **2**
*1880** Sudden Spin **(55)***(62) (SGNorton)* 5-9-1 KFallon(7) (chsd ldrs: led 3f out: hdd 2f out: no ex fnl f) nk **3**
2145[2] Locorotondo (IRE) **(65)***(62)*(Fav)*(MBell)* 4-9-4 (7) GFaulkner(13) (chsd ldrs: 3rd st: sn ev ch: wknd fnl f) 8 **4**
2175[3] Progression **(56)***(43) (PCHaslam)* 4-9-2 MTebbutt(12) (prom: rdn over 4f out: 6th & btn st) 7 **5**
2145[3] Sommersby (IRE) **(66)***(51) (MrsNMacauley)* 4-9-12 DeanMcKeown(2) (hld up: hrd rdn over 2f out: no imp) 2 **6**
Sloe Brandy **(39)***(16) (APJarvis)* 5-7-6 (7) CAdamson(6) (hld up: hdwy 5f out: wknd over 2f out) 6 **7**
1694[6] Nothing Doing (IRE) **(40)***(9) (WJMusson)* 6-8-0 TWilliams(5) (hld up in tch: effrt over 3f out: sn btn) 6 **8**
2132[4] Zanzara (IRE) **(49)***(16) (MrsVAAconley)* 4-8-9 JCarroll(3) (prom 4f: grad lost pl) 1½ **9**
*2293** Palacegate Jo (IRE) **(55)***(15) (DWChapman)* 4-9-1 5x ACulhane(4) (lw: led to 3f out: 5th & wkng st) 5 **10**
2293[5] All on **(50)***(10) (JHetherton)* 4-8-10 WNewnes(10) (swtg: w ldr: drvn along 8f out: wknd 5f out) nk **11**
771[10] Hasta la Vista **(45)***(1) (MWEasterby)* 5-8-5b LCharnock(8) (chsd ldrs over 6f) 2½ **12**

5/1 CARPATHIAN, Locorotondo (IRE), **6/1** Sudden Spin, Palacegate Jo (IRE), **7/1** Sommersby (IRE), **10/1** Hasta la Vista (op 16/1), **12/1** Nothing Doing (IRE), All on, Progression, **14/1** Daleria, **20/1** Zanzara (IRE), **25/1** Sloe Brandy, CSF £66.09 CT £394.99 TOTE £4.80: £2.20 £2.60 £2.90 (£76.00) Trio £97.10 OWNER The Queen (WEST ILSLEY) BRED Sheikh Mohammed bin Rashid al Maktoum 12 Rn 2m 43.2 (9.00) SF: 34/31/30/30/11/19/-/-/-/-/-/-

2380 E.B.F. PUTNEY MAIDEN STKS (I) (2-Y.O) (Class D) £3,720.00 (£1,110.00: £530.00: £240.00) 7f (Fibresand) Stalls: Low 3-55 (3-56)

1190[5] **Kingfisher Brave** *(66)*(Fav)*(SGNorton)* 2-9-0 KDarley(10) (chsd ldrs: 3rd st: styd on u.p to ld ins fnl f) ....— 1
1758[2] Ebony Boy *(64) (JWharton)* 2-9-0 JWilliams(6) (lw: chsd ldrs: 2nd st: rdn to ld over 1f out: hdd & unable qckn ins fnl f) 1 2
1597[10] Serif (USA) *(52) (JHMGosden)* 2-9-0 GHind(3) (led over 4f out: hdd & wknd over 1f out) 5 3
1597[13] Oisin An Oir (IRE) *(34) (JBerry)* 2-9-0 JCarroll(7) (lw: prom: 5th st: wknd 2f out) 8 4
810[11] Dorspring (IRE) *(28) (CEBrittain)* 2-9-0 WNewnes(9) (outpcd: effrt & 6th st: nvr trbld ldrs) 2½ 5
2143[4] Sphinx Levelv (IRE) *(APJarvis)* 2-8-7 (7) CAdamson(1) (prom: outpcd after 2f: n.d after) 13 6
2161[6] Colour Counsellor *(KMcAuliffe)* 2-9-0v DHarrison(8) (mid div: drvn along ½-wy: 4th & wkng st) 5 7
African Sun (IRE) *(BHanbury)* 2-8-11 (3) JStack(4) (w'like: sn outpcd & bhd) ....s.h 8
533[16] Hobbs Choice *(MissJFCraze)* 2-8-9 SWebster(5) (led over 2f: wknd over 3f out) 8 9
Kudos Blue *(JDBethell)* 2-8-9 MRimmer(2) (lt-f: unf: s.i.s: sn prom: wknd ½-wy) 25 10

13/8 KINGFISHER BRAVE, **7/2** Serif (USA) (op 6/4), **5/1** Ebony Boy, **8/1** African Sun (IRE) (op 5/1), **10/1** Colour Counsellor, **14/1** Oisin An Oir (IRE), Kudos Blue (op 8/1), **16/1** Dorspring (IRE), **20/1** Sphinx Levelv (IRE), **40/1** Hobbs Choice, CSF £10.60 TOTE £3.10: £1.70 £1.50 £1.60 (£7.60) Trio £7.10 OWNER Mr C. E. Whiteley (BARNSLEY) BRED P. T. Tellwright 10 Rn
1m 32.8 (6.00) SF: 22/20/8/-/-/-/-/-/-/-

2381 E.B.F. PUTNEY MAIDEN STKS (II) (2-Y.O) (Class D) £3,687.50 (£1,100.00: £525.00: £237.50) 7f (Fibresand) Stalls: Low 4-30 (4-32)

1697[3] **Carmentalia** *(73) (SirMarkPrescott)* 2-8-9 GDuffield(8) (chsd ldrs: 3rd st: led over 2f out: hdd over 1f out: rallied to ld ins fnl f: all out) ....— 1
Jack Jennings *(77) (BAMcMahon)* 2-8-11 (3) SSanders(10) (str: bit bkwd: s.v.s: hdwy 4f out: 4th st: ev ch 2f out: unable qckn nr fin) ....½ 2
1190[8] Oversman *(75) (JGFitzGerald)* 2-9-0 KFallon(9) (bit bkwd: hld up in tch: 5th st: led over 1f out: hdd & unable qckn ins fnl f) 1 3
1287[3] Disallowed (IRE) *(62)*(Fav)*(MBell)* 2-8-2 (7) GFaulkner(3) (lw: bhd: outpcd ½-wy: styd on appr fnl f: nvr nrr) 3½ 4
One Life To Live (IRE) *(55) (AHarrison)* 2-8-11 (3) JStack(5) (cmpt: chsd ldr: 2nd st: wknd wl over 1f out) 5 5
2063[7] Scathebury *(41) (SPCWoods)* 2-9-0b WWoods(1) (lw: chsd ldrs: 6th & rdn st: sn btn) 6 6
2107[7] Balpare *(35) (NACallaghan)* 2-8-9 GCarter(4) (led over 4f: grad wknd) ....¾ 7
Makaskamina *(15) (BHanbury)* 2-9-0 NCarlisle(6) (small: hld up: plld hrd: 7th & btn st) 11 8
1954[7] Timson *(JPLeigh)* 2-9-0 SWhitworth(2) (chsd ldrs to ½-wy) 25 9

9/4 Disallowed (IRE), **3/1** CARMENTALIA (op 6/5), **100/30** Scathebury, **6/1** Jack Jennings (op 14/1), Balpare (9/2-7/1), **10/1** Makaskamina (op 6/1), **12/1** Oversman, **33/1** One Life To Live (IRE), **50/1** Timson, CSF £22.33 TOTE £4.10: £1.60 £1.20 £4.00 (£22.33) Trio £74.90 OWNER Hesmonds Stud (NEWMARKET) BRED Hesmonds Stud Ltd 9 Rn 1m 32.0 (5.20) SF: 26/30/28/15/8/-/-/-/-
OFFICIAL EXPLANATION Scathebury: the trainer reported that the colt was not suited by the blinkers and resented the kickback.
Disallowed (IRE): the trainer's representative stated that the filly resented the kickback, lost her place and ran on when switched to the outside in the home straight.

2382 MAYFAIR (S) STKS (2-Y.O F) (Class G) £2,243.00 (£618.00: £293.00) 5f (Fibresand) Stalls: High 5-00 (5-00)

2146[10] **Morning Surprise** *(68) (APJarvis)* 2-7-13 (7) CAdamson(9) (chsd ldrs: led over 1f out: rdn clr) ....— 1
2047[6] Trible Pet *(55) (BGubby)* 2-8-6 GDuffield(5) (b: hmpd s: prom: outpcd ½-wy: r.o ins fnl f) 4 2
2146[4] Touch of Fantasy *(54) (JohnBerry)* 2-8-3 (3) SDrowne(1) (led: hdd over 1f out: sn outpcd) ....½ 3
2185[4] April's Joy *(51) (JNorton)* 2-7-13 (7) AmyGosden(11) (prom: rdn over 1f out: r.o one pce) ....¾ 4
Jessica's Song *(51) (WGMTurner)* 2-8-6 TSprake(10) (b. hind: neat: outpcd ½-wy: r.o ins fnl f) ....hd 5
1977[9] Lunar Gris *(46) (JEBanks)* 2-8-6 AClark(3) (b: outpcd: hdwy 2f out: kpt on) 1½ 6
2128[6] Chamber Music *(41)*(Fav)*(JBerry)* 2-8-6 JCarroll(12) (spd 3f) 1½ 7
1503[3] Miss Impulse *(32) (JWharton)* 2-8-6 AMackay(6) (lw: prom over 3f) 3 8
2185[10] Grimstone Girl *(27) (MWEasterby)* 2-7-13b(7) RuthCoulter(7) (swtg: chsd ldrs over 3f) 1½ 9
2176[4] No Sympathy *(16) (GLMoore)* 2-8-6 SWhitworth(4) (wnt rt s: prom: drvn along ½-wy: sn lost pl) 3½ 10

Sleep Standing (IRE) *(3) (AHarrison)* 2-8-3 (3) JStack(2) (unf: spd over 3f) 4 11
1841 10 Sea of Blue *(MWEasterby)* 2-8-6 GCarter(8) (a outpcd) 1½ 12

3/1 Chamber Music, **9/2** Trible Pet, Lunar Gris (5/2-5/1), **5/1** Miss Impulse, **13/2** No Sympathy, **8/1** Jessica's Song (6/1-10/1), **10/1** April's Joy (op 6/1), Touch of Fantasy, **12/1** Sleep Standing (IRE) (op 8/1), **14/1** Sea of Blue (op 8/1), **16/1** MORNING SURPRISE, **25/1** Grimstone Girl, CSF £96.33 TOTE £45.80: £4.70 £2.80 £2.20 (£106.90) Trio £195.80 OWNER Mrs D. B. Brazier (ASTON UPTHORPE) BRED Miss S. E. Jarvis 12 Rn 62.3 secs (4.30) SF: 10/-/-/-/-/-/-/-/-/-/-/-
No bid.

2383 FULHAM H'CAP (0-60) (3-Y.O+) (Class F) £2,519.00 (£694.00: £329.00)
6f (Fibresand) Stalls: Low 5-30 (5-32)

*1883*4 **Bold Aristocrat (IRE) (45)***(53) (RHollinshead)* 4-8-6 (7) FLynch(14) (hld up: gd hdwy over 1f out: r.o to ld wl ins fnl f) ....— 1
1963 10 Ring the Chief **(54)***(60) (RAkehurst)* 3-8-12 (3) SSanders(13) (chsd ldrs: led over 1f out: hdd wl ins fnl f) ....¾ 2
*2074*3 Old Comrades **(47)***(50) (TDBarron)* 8-8-8 (7) KimberleyHart(16) (prom: rdn over 1f out: r.o) 1 3
1832 14 Grey Charmer (IRE) **(50)***(51) (CJames)* 6-9-4 WNewnes(5) (mid div: hdwy over 1f out: r.o) 1 4
*2074*2 Efficacy **(54)***(51)*(Fav)*(APJarvis)* 4-9-1 (7) CAdamson(8) (lw: chsd ldrs: led over 2f out: hdd & no ex over 1f out) 1¼ 5
1991 7 Titanium Honda (IRE) **(47)***(42) (CEBrittain)* 4-9-1 MRimmer(6) (lw: chsd ldrs: rdn 2f out: no imp fnl f) ....¾ 6
*1883*2 Abigails Boy (HOL) **(40)***(35) (DrJDScargill)* 6-8-1b(7) CDomergue(11) (prom: rdn over 2f out: sn btn) ....nk 7
*1571*4 Jamaica Bridge **(60)***(44) (SGNorton)* 5-9-9 (5) HKYim(3) (chsd ldrs: rdn over 2f out: wknd fnl f) 4 8
*1882*6 Cheerful Groom (IRE) **(39)***(21) (JMackie)* 4-8-7 GCarter(9) (lw: n.d) ....¾ 9
*2074*5 Arc Lamp **(47)***(26) (JAGlover)* 9-9-1 SDWilliams(4) (lw: led over 1f: wknd over 2f out) 1 10
2188 6 Mac's Taxi **(58)***(35) (PCHaslam)* 3-8-12 (7) JulieLemin(1) (chsd ldrs to ½-wy) 1 11
*2074*8 Disco Boy **(53)***(26) (BAMcMahon)* 5-9-7b GDuffield(10) (led over 4f out: hdd over 2f out: sn wknd) 1¼ 12
Chloella **(48)***(19) (CBBBooth)* 3-8-9 SMorris(15) (swtg: bit bkwd: s.s: a in rr) 1 13
1493 6 Mu-Arrik **(47)***(7) (GROldroyd)* 7-8-12v(3) AGarth(12) (lw: prom: hmpd ent st: sn wknd) 4 14
Olifantsfontein **(50)***(7) (DNicholls)* 7-9-4 AlexGreaves(2) (bit bkwd: prom 3f) 1 15

9/2 Efficacy, **6/1** Ring the Chief, **7/1** Old Comrades, **15/2** Jamaica Bridge, **10/1** Arc Lamp (8/1-12/1), Titanium Honda (IRE), Olifantsfontein (12/1-8/1), **12/1** Abigails Boy (HOL), **14/1** Disco Boy, Grey Charmer (IRE), Mac's Taxi, BOLD ARISTOCRAT (IRE), **16/1** Cheerful Groom (IRE), **20/1** Chloella, Mu-Arrik, CSF £96.26 CT £598.59 TOTE £16.20: £4.10 £3.60 £2.70 (£43.90) Trio £91.20 OWNER Mrs J. Hughes (UPPER LONGDON) BRED Scarteen Stud 15 Rn
1m 18.3 (4.80) SF: 24/24/21/22/22/13/6/15/-/-/-/-/-/-/-
WEIGHT FOR AGE 3yo-7lb
T/Plpt: £201.00 (57.93 Tckts). T/Qdpt: £48.30 (1 Tckts). KH

2038a-LES LANDES (Jersey) (L-H)
Thursday June 29th

2384a BARING INTERNATIONAL H'CAP (3-Y.O+) £720.00
7f 7-30 (7-35)

Superensis *(JLeBrocq,Jersey)* 5-10-12 PHolley ....— 1
2038a2 Screech *(ZJones,Guernsey)* 5-8-12 SWhitelam 2 2
Misinterrex *(MissAVibert,Jersey)* 4-8-12 RMcGhin ....½ 3
798a4 Reality Park *(PDJones)* 4-10-12 SNicoll (btn approx 11½l) 5

Tote £4.60: £2.60 £3.00 (£1.50) OWNER Miss J. V. May BRED Woodditton Stud Ltd 6 Rn 1m 30.0

2385a H.S.B.C. H'CAP (3-Y.O+) £900.00
1m 4f 8-00 (8-11)

798a2 **Brown Fairy (USA)** *(JSOArthur,Jersey)* 7-10-5 VSmith ....— 1
798a* Granache (IRE) *(MissAVibert,Jersey)* 6-10-1 PHolley 1 2
799aP Northreel *(HVautier,Jersey)* 4-9-6 MrJCulloty ....½ 3
*1455*3 Love of the North (IRE) *(RTJuckes)* 4-9-7 AMcCabe 7

Tote £3.40: £3.20 £3.20 (£2.30) OWNER Messrs B Winfield and J Potter 7 Rn 2m 46.0 SF: -/-/-/-

2044a-LONGCHAMP (Paris, France) (R-H)
Saturday July 8th (Good)

2386a
PRIX HUBERT DE CHAUDENAY (Gp 2) (3-Y.O) £35,928.00 (£14,371.00: £7,186.00: £3,593.00) **1m 7f** 3-15 (3-21)

1574a[7] **Affidavit (USA)** *(106) (AFabre,France)* 3-8-11 TJarnet (hld up early: 3rd st: r.o wl fnl f: led cl hme) — 1
1885a[3] Peckinpah's Soul (FR) *(106) (DSmaga,France)* 3-8-11 FHead (led 12f out tl hdd 1f out: led again ins fnl f: ct cl hme) nk 2
1852[7] Anchor Clever *(106) (PAKelleway)* 3-8-11 CAsmussen (hld up: rdn 2f out: r.o wl fnl f) s.h 3
1852[4] Wot-If-We (IRE) *(99) (TGMills)* 3-8-11 WNewnes (led 3f: 2nd st: rdn & wknd 2f out) 6 4
Shamardar (IRE) *(91) (AdeRoyerDupre,France)* 3-8-11 GMosse (4th st: rdn to ld 1f out: wnt lame ins fnl f) 8 5
2119[2] Lord Jim (IRE) *(75) (MissGayKelleway)* 3-8-11 DBoeuf (3rd tl rdn and btn st) 15 6

P-M 1.60F: 1.10f 1.60F (SF 5.30F) OWNER Sheikh Mohammed (FRANCE) BRED H.H. Aga Khan Stud S.C. 6 Rn 3m 11.2 SF: -/-/-/-/-/-

2043a-SAN SIRO (Milan, Italy) (R-H)
Sunday July 9th (Firm)

2387a
PREMIO GIUSEPPE DE MONTEL (Listed) (2-Y.O C & G) £17,730.00 (£7,801.00: £4,255.00) **7f 110y** 3-45 (4-01)

2059[2] **Cabcharge Striker** *(MRChannon)* 2-8-13 RHughes — 1
Attimo Fuggente (IRE) *(APeraino,Italy)* 2-8-13 DHolland 5¾ 2
Pierrot Solaire (FR) *(SSaggiamo,Italy)* 2-8-13 GBietolini 2¼ 3

Tote 27L: 16L 27L 30L (151L) OWNER Scuderia Gianni Daniele (UPPER LAMBOURN) BRED J. K. Keegan 9 Rn 1m 33.7 SF: -/-/-

AGNANO (Naples, Italy) (R-H)
Sunday July 9th (Good to firm)

2388a
GRAN PREMIO CITTA DI NAPOLI (Gp 3) (3-Y.O+) £25,248.00 (£11,607.00: £6,477.00) **1m 2f** 9-55 (9-55)

1890a[7] **Guado d'Annibale (IRE)** *(114) (ARenzoni,Italy)* 6-8-13 JacquelineFreda — 1
1118a[10] Sugarland Express (IRE) *(109) (OPessi,Italy)* 4-8-13 GBietolini 3 2
Red Paper (IRE) *(109) (FManganelli,Italy)* 3-8-4 BJovine 1½ 3

Tote 22L: 11L 11L 14L (243L) OWNER Aterno Stud BRED Scuderia Aterno 8 Rn 2m 2.8 SF: -/-/-

HOPPEGARTEN (Berlin, Germany) (R-H)
Sunday July 9th (Good to firm)

2389a
BERLIN BRANDENBURG TROPHY DER LANDESBANK BERLIN (Gp 2) (3-Y.O+) £90,534.00 (£39,095.00: £18,519.00: £10,288.00) **1m** 4-00 (4-10)

1009a[5] **Kill the Crab (IRE)** *(110) (WNeuroth,Norway)* 3-8-1 MLarsen (a.p. 3rd st: chal 2f out: led cl hme) — 1
Royal Abjar (USA) *(120) (AWohler,Germany)* 4-9-7 WRSwinburn (trckd ldr tl led 2f out: rdn & wknd ins fnl f: hdd clhme) nk 2
1586[3] Chato (USA) *(110) (HSteinmetz,Germany)* 3-8-5 AStarke (alwys in tch: r.o wl fnl 2f) 1½ 3
1121a[8] Tristano *(108) (ALowe,Germany)* 3-8-5 AHelfenbein (mid-div: r.o st: nrst fin) 1 4
1892a[3] Devil River Peek (USA) *(108) (BSchutz,Germany)* 3-8-5 ASuborics (mid-div: prog st: r.o) nk 5
1892a* Ladoni *(107) (HRemmert,Germany)* 3-8-5 KWoodburn (4th st: rdn to chal over 1f out: no ex) ½ 6
Fiello (GER) *(114) (Germany)* 5-9-7 MRimmer (hld up in rr: r.o fnl 2f: nt rch ldrs) s.h 7
1121a[9] Siberian Grey *(107) (Germany)* 3-8-5 MO'Reilly (alwys mid-div) hd 8
Star Carnival (USA) *(109) (Germany)* 4-9-7 WRyan (led tl hdd 2f out: wknd) 2½ 9

Tote 143DM: 26DM 14DM 20DM (492DM) OWNER Stall Tricolor BRED Deerpark Stud in Ireland 16 Rn 1m 33.6 SF: -/-/-/-/-/-/-/-/-

1999-CHESTER (L-H)
Friday July 14th (Good to firm, Good patches)
WEATHER: thundery showers WIND: almost nil

2390 H. S. ADMIN. SERVICES APPRENTICE H'CAP (0-70) (3-Y.O+) (Class F) £2,770.25 (£842.00: £413.50: £199.25)
7f 122y Stalls: Low GOING minus 0.09 sec per fur (G) 6-30 (6-31)

*2073** **What a Nightmare (IRE) (53)***(64)*(Fav)*(JAGlover)* 3-8-7b AWhelan(1) (mde all: reminders over 2f out: hld on gamely towards fin)— **1**
2291[6] David James' Girl **(60)***(70) (ABailey)* 3-8-7 (7) AngelaGallimore(3) (swtg: chsd ldrs: 4th st: effrt & ev ch ins fnl f: r.o)nk **2**
1873[10] Resolute Bay **(40)***(49) (RMWhitaker)* 9-8-3v LNewton(7) (lw: hld up: hdwy & 5th st: plld outside appr fnl f: rdn & r.o wl)½ **3**
1843[3] Royal Comedian **(46)***(49) (BWMurray)* 6-8-4 (5) MartinDwyer(2) (chsd ldrs: 3rd st: rdn & one pce fnl f)3 **4**
2061[4] Cee-Jay-Ay **(64)***(66) (JBerry)* 8-9-10 (3) PRoberts(4) (lw: dwlt: hdwy over 2f out: 6th & rdn st: no imp)nk **5**
2191[2] Four of Spades **(58)***(52) (PDEvans)* 4-9-4b(3) AmandaSanders(5) (chsd wnr: 2nd st: wknd wl over 1f out)4 **6**
1855[3] Shuttlecock **(43)***(31) (MrsNMacauley)* 4-8-6 AGarth(8) (lw: bhd & outpcd tl sme late hdwy)3 **7**
2191[6] Delmour **(34)***(14) (WMBrisbourne)* 4-7-6 (5)ow4 SLanigan(6) (swtg: a in rr)1½ **8**
2307[2] At the Savoy (IRE) **(41)***(21) (TDBarron)* 4-7-13b(5) KimberleyHart(10) (in tch: rdn along ½-wy: grad wknd)2 **9**
2191[7] Brigadore Gold **(31)***(6) (FHLee)* 5-7-8 ow1 DarrenMoffatt(9) (rdn & lost pl 3f out: sn bhd)1¾ **10**
LONG HANDICAP Delmour 6-8 Brigadore Gold 7-2

7/2 WHAT A NIGHTMARE (IRE), **4/1** Four of Spades, **9/2** Royal Comedian, **5/1** At the Savoy (IRE), **6/1** Cee-Jay-Ay, **10/1** David James' Girl, Shuttlecock, **20/1** Resolute Bay, **33/1** Delmour, Brigadore Gold, CSF £35.52 CT £554.33 TOTE £3.30: £1.30 £3.20 £4.10 (£37.30) Trio £406.30 OWNER Bassetlaw Bloodstock Agency Ltd (WORKSOP) BRED Carrigbeg Stud Co Ltd 10 Rn
1m 36.45 (4.75) SF: 33/39/27/27/44/30/9/-/-/-
WEIGHT FOR AGE 3yo-9lb

2391 TRANSMERE DISTRIBUTION CLAIMING STKS (3-Y.O+) (Class D) £3,650.50 (£1,099.00: £532.00: £248.50)
1m 4f 66y Stalls: Low GOING minus 0.09 sec per fur (G) 7-00 (7-01)

1198[4] **Sure Care** *(71) (CREgerton)* 4-8-12 GBardwell(2) (set slow pce: mde all: hrd rdn over 2f out: styd on wl)— **1**
2201[5] Pride of May (IRE) **(60)***(72) (RHannon)* 4-8-11v(5) AWhelan(3) (chsd wnr: 2nd st: hrd rdn over 1f out: kpt on same pce)2 **2**
1477[5] Teen Jay **(72)***(67)*(Fav)*(SESherwood)* 5-9-2v GCarter(6) (stdd s: hdwy & 3rd st: nt trble ldrs) ..4 **3**
Malihabad (IRE) *(67) (RHollinshead)* 6-9-2 ACulhane(1) (bkwd: hld up: effrt 3f out: rdn & outpcd over 2f out: 5th & btn st)½ **4**
Viardot (IRE) *(70) (MrsMReveley)* 6-9-12 JFortune(4) (bkwd: hld up: effrt 3f out: 4th st: sn rdn & outpcd)5 **5**
*2076** Backstabber **(29)***(42) (MissSJWilton)* 5-8-12 RPrice(5) (hld up & bhd: effrt & rdn 5f out: 6th & btn st: t.o)11 **6**
Ghedi (POL) *(32) (MissGayKelleway)* 4-9-6 JFanning(7) (lw: plld hrd: prom tl wknd over 3f out: 7th & t.o st)14 **7**

2/1 Teen Jay, **7/2** Viardot (IRE), **9/2** SURE CARE, Pride of May (IRE), **7/1** Backstabber (op 20/1), **12/1** Ghedi (POL), **16/1** Malihabad (IRE), CSF £23.76 TOTE £6.00: £2.80 £2.60 (£13.50) OWNER Mr Charles Egerton (CHADDLEWORTH) BRED Normanby Stud Ltd and C. Shaw 7 Rn
2m 49.88 (13.28) SF: 7/8/3/3/6/-/-
Sure Care clmd Miss S Weatherhouse £11,000. Pride of May (IRE) clmd W Dobson £10,000. Teen Jay clmd K Clark £10,000.

2392 BREITLING WATCHES AND WALTONS OF CHESTER H'CAP (0-90) (3-Y.O+) (Class C) £5,608.00 (£1,684.00: £812.00: £376.00)
1m 4f 66y Stalls: Low GOING minus 0.09 sec per fur (G) 7-30 (7-31)

2305* **Soba Up (62)***(76+) (TJEtherington)* 5-9-0 5x ACulhane(1) (lw: a.p: 2nd st: qcknd to ld wl over 1f out: sn clr: unchal)— **1**
2196[3] Killick **(60)***(68)*(Fav)*(ABailey)* 7-8-12 MWigham(5) (led tl hdd wl over 1f out: sn outpcd)5 **2**

Twice the Groom (IRE) **(66)***(66) (RLee)* 5-9-4 GCarter(3) (b: chsd ldrs: 5th st: kpt on u.p fnl f) 6 3
2014³ Mentor (GR) **(88)***(88) (RCharlton)* 3-9-13 DHarrison(2) (hld up: hmpd 7f out: hdwy 3f out: 3rd st: one pce appr fnl f) ....s.h 4
2139⁴ Myfontaine **(64)***(57) (KTIvory)* 8-9-2 GBardwell(4) (lw: pushed along in rr ½-wy: 6th st: nvr nr to chal) 5 5
1747⁵ Hujjab (USA) **(84)***(75) (JLDunlop)* 3-9-9 WCarson(7) (chsd ldr: rdn & 4th st: sn lost tch) 2 6
2101⁴ Sunderland Echo **(70)***(49) (MrsMReveley)* 6-9-8 JFortune(8) (lw: hld up & bhd: hdwy 4f out: sn rdn & no imp: t.o) 9 7
*894*⁹ In the Money (IRE) **(57)** *(RHollinshead)* 6-8-6 (3) AGarth(6) (chsd ldrs 8f: sn lost tch: t.o) ....dist 8

9/4 Killick, **3/1** SOBA UP, **7/1** Mentor (GR), Sunderland Echo, **8/1** Hujjab (USA), Myfontaine, **10/1** In the Money (IRE), **20/1** Twice the Groom (IRE), CSF £9.93 CT £100.92 TOTE £3.40: £1.50 £1.30 £3.30 (£2.60) OWNER Mrs M. Hills (MALTON) BRED Mrs M. J. Hills 8 Rn
2m 40.59 (3.99) SF: 66/58/56/65/47/52/39/-
WEIGHT FOR AGE 3yo-13lb

2393

SAFFERY CHAMPNESS MAIDEN STKS (3-Y.O F) (Class D) £4,276.00 (£1,288.00: £624.00: £292.00)
7f 122y Stalls: Low GOING minus 0.09 sec per fur (G) 8-00 (8-06)

Hadeel *(90) (HThomsonJones)* 3-8-11 RCochrane(5) (bit bkwd: hld up: hdwy over 3f out: 3rd st: str run to ld nr fin) ....— 1
1675⁹ Azdihaar (USA) **(79)***(89) (JLDunlop)* 3-8-11 WCarson(2) (led 6f out tl ent fnl f: rallied to ld 100 yards out: ct cl home) ....nk 2
613⁴ Splintercat (USA) *(88) (JHMGosden)* 3-8-11 LDettori(4) (a.p: 2nd st: rdn to ld 1f out: sn hdd: unable qckn) ....½ 3
1615⁸ Coryana Dancer (IRE) **(60)***(80) (RHollinshead)* 3-8-11 ACulhane(3) (wl bhd tl hdwy & 6th st: kpt on appr fnl f: nvr nrr) 4 4
1533² Masaafaat (USA) *(78)*(Fav)*(MRStoute)* 3-8-11 WWoods(1) (hld up: effrt & 4th st: sn rdn: no imp) 1 5
2236⁴ Brave Fighter (USA) *(54) (BHanbury)* 3-8-11 DHarrison(6) (lw: led over 1f: 5th st: sn rdn & wknd: eased whn btn: t.o) 11 6
Cent Nouvelles (USA) *(51) (JHMGosden)* 3-8-11 GHind(8) (s.s: chsd ldrs tl wknd 2f out: t.o) 1¾ 7
1905⁹ Last Ambition (IRE) *(50) (CREgerton)* 3-8-11 JFortune(7) (lw: prom over 5f: sn wknd: t.o) ....½ 8

9/4 Masaafaat (USA), **3/1** Azdihaar (USA), **7/2** Splintercat (USA), **6/1** Brave Fighter (USA), **10/1** HADEEL, **16/1** Cent Nouvelles (USA), **20/1** Coryana Dancer (IRE), **25/1** Last Ambition (IRE), CSF £37.93 TOTE £17.70: £2.70 £1.50 £1.50 (£16.40) OWNER Mr Hamdan Al Maktoum (NEWMARKET) BRED Shadwell Estate Company Limited 8 Rn 1m 36.03 (4.33) SF: 41/40/39/31/29/5/2/1

2394

WAYMAN HALES H'CAP (0-95) (3-Y.O) (Class C) £5,569.00 (£1,672.00: £806.00: £373.00) **5f 16y** Stalls: Low GOING minus 0.09 sec per fur (G) 8-30 (8-30)

2311² **Crystal Loop (64)***(76) (ABailey)* 3-7-7 GBardwell(1) (mde all: clr over 1f out: unchal) ....— 1
Quiz Time **(85)***(92) (SirMarkPrescott)* 3-9-0 WWoods(2) (a.p: rdn over 1f out: r.o) 1¾ 2
1806¹⁰ Go Hever Golf **(92)***(95)*(Fav)*(TJNaughton)* 3-9-7 GCarter(3) (b.nr hind: hdwy ent st: swtchd outside bel dist: kpt on: nt pce to chal) 1 3
1489⁸ Total Stranger **(78)***(77) (MrsLPiggott)* 3-8-7 RCochrane(5) (chsd wnr: rdn over 1f out: one pce) 1¼ 4
2252² Stolen Kiss (IRE) **(69)***(56) (MWEasterby)* 3-7-12b WCarson(4) (bhd: effrt & nt clr run 3f out & 2f out: nvr nrr) 4 5
2247⁵ The Happy Fox (IRE) **(72)***(53) (BAMcMahon)* 3-8-1 GHind(7) (lw: sn drvn along: a outpcd) 2 6
1949* Just Dissident (IRE) **(68)***(41) (RMWhitaker)* 3-7-11 JFanning(6) (lw: chsd ldrs: rdn 2f out: sn btn) 2½ 7
2024³ C-Yer-Simmie (IRE) **(64)***(33) (RHollinshead)* 3-7-7 NCarlisle(8) (a bhd & outpcd) 1 8
LONG HANDICAP Crystal Loop 7-4 C-Yer-Simmie (IRE) 7-3

2/1 Go Hever Golf (op 3/1), **11/4** Stolen Kiss (IRE), **6/1** Just Dissident (IRE) (op 4/1), **8/1** The Happy Fox (IRE), Total Stranger, **9/1** CRYSTAL LOOP, Quiz Time, **16/1** C-Yer-Simmie (IRE), CSF £78.73 CT £207.26 TOTE £9.30: £1.90 £2.60 £1.60 (£29.00) OWNER Mr Roy Matthews (TARPORLEY) BRED B. Long 8 Rn 61.43 secs (1.43) SF: 47/63/66/48/27/24/12/4

2395

DHD ENGINEERING CONDITIONS STKS (3-Y.O+) (Class C) £5,812.50 (£1,875.00: £912.50) **1m 2f 75y** Stalls: High GOING minus 0.09 sec (G) 9-00 (9-00)

2118³ **Maeterlinck (IRE) (87)***(88)*(Fav)*(BWHills)* 3-8-7 LDettori(3) (lw: mde all: qcknd 3f out: r.o strly fnl f) ....— 1

1908⁴ Red Valerian **(71)**(93) *(KMcAuliffe)* 4-9-12b RCochrane(2) (lw: hld up: 3rd st: rdn & r.o ins fnl f: nt pce of wnr) 1¾ **2**
1619⁷ Heathyards Rock **(92)**(83) *(RHollinshead)* 3-8-7 DHarrison(4) (chsd wnr fnl 6f: 2nd st: rdn & one pce fnl f) 1½ **3**

1/2 MAETERLINCK (IRE), **11/4** Heathyards Rock, **6/1** Red Valerian (op 4/1), CSF £3.10 TOTE £1.40 (£2.00) OWNER Sheikh Mohammed (LAMBOURN) BRED Sean Collins 3 Rn
2m 16.83 (8.13) SF: 22/38/17
WEIGHT FOR AGE 3yo-11lb
T/Plpt: £118.40 (125.49 Tckts). T/Qdpt: £6.20 (47.35 Tckts). IM

2226-HAMILTON (R-H)
Friday July 14th (Firm)

WEATHER: overcast, showers WIND: almost nil

2396

SUNDAY MAIL AMATEUR H'CAP (0-65) (3-Y.O+) (Class F) £3,566.25 (£1,080.00: £527.50: £251.25)
1m 1f 36y Stalls: High GOING minus 0.61 sec per fur (F) 6-50 (6-50)

2276⁵ **Twin Creeks (47)**(58) *(MDHammond)* 4-12-0 MrCBonner(1) (lw: chsd ldrs: led 4f out: hld on wl fnl f) .... — **1**
2122³ Red Spectacle (IRE) **(47)**(58) *(PCHaslam)* 3-11-1 (3) MrsDKettlewell(4) (a.p: effrt 3f out: styd on u.p fnl f) .... nk **2**
2226* Gold Blade **(47)**(52)(Fav) *(JPearce)* 6-12-0 5x MrsLPearce(11) (lw: hld up & bhd: hdwy ½-wy: chsd ldrs 2f out: one pce appr fnl f) 3 **3**
1824⁹ Rubislaw **(31)**(36) *(CWFairhurst)* 3-9-13v(3) MrsSBosley(10) (effrt ½-wy: styd on u.p: nrst fin) .... hd **4**
2327² Cashmirie **(44)**(45) *(JLEyre)* 3-11-1 MissDianaJones(5) (cl up tl outpcd over 3f out: styd on fnl f) 2½ **5**
2148* Asterix **(49)**(45) *(JMBradley)* 7-12-2v 5x MrJLLlewellyn(2) (lw: hld up: hdwy 6f out: effrt over 3f out: nt pce to chal) 2½ **6**
2122² Thisonesforalice **(39)**(35) *(JSGoldie)* 7-11-6 MissPRobson(6) (chsd ldrs: outpcd over 2f out: n.d after) .... ½ **7**
2232⁶ Runrig (IRE) **(40)**(33) *(MissLAPerratt)* 5-11-7 MrRHale(9) (lw: bhd: effrt 4f out: no imp) 1½ **8**
1161⁶ Sylvan Celebration **(20)** *(MissLAPerratt)* 4-9-10 (5) MrSRutherford(7) (led tl hdd & wknd 4f out) 13 **9**
Drumdonna (IRE) **(47)**(12) *(PBeaumont)* 5-12-0 MrsAFarrell(8) (b: bhd: hrd rdn 3f out: n.d) 3 **10**
*63*¹¹ Princess Shera (IRE) **(45)** *(EJAlston)* 4-11-7 (5) MrPBlane(3) (a bhd: t.o) 20 **11**

2/1 Gold Blade, **9/2** Cashmirie, **5/1** Asterix, **13/2** Thisonesforalice, **8/1** Red Spectacle (IRE), TWIN CREEKS, **16/1** Runrig (IRE), **20/1** Sylvan Celebration, **33/1** Rubislaw, Drumdonna (IRE), **50/1** Princess Shera (IRE), CSF £66.04 CT £162.55 TOTE £12.00: £3.60 £1.80 £1.60 (£24.50) Trio £49.60 OWNER The Armchair Jockeys-Four Seasons Racing (MIDDLEHAM) BRED Crest Stud Ltd
11 Rn 1m 59.1 (4.80) SF: 48/38/42/16/25/35/25/23/-/2/-
WEIGHT FOR AGE 3yo-10lb

2397

SCOTTISHPOWER TROPHY H'CAP (0-80) (3-Y.O+) (Class D) £5,150.65 (£1,559.20: £761.10: £362.05)
1m 65y Stalls: High GOING minus 0.61 sec per fur (F) 7-20 (7-20)

2266⁴ **Sooty Tern (67)**(78) *(JMBradley)* 8-9-8 (3) SDrowne(7) (mde all: kpt on gamely fnl f) .... — **1**
2068⁷ Talented Ting (IRE) **(68)**(75) *(PCHaslam)* 6-9-9 (3) JStack(5) (chsd ldrs: ev ch 3f out: rdn & btn ent fnl f) 2 **2**
1687² Sarmatian (USA) **(64)**(70) *(MDHammond)* 4-9-8 DaleGibson(1) (in tch: hdwy 4f out: kpt on u.p fnl f: nvr able chal) .... ½ **3**
*2292*¹¹ King Curan (USA) **(66)**(61) *(ABailey)* 4-9-10b AMackay(6) (trckd ldrs: rdn 3f out: sn outpcd) 6 **4**
2307³ Spanish Verdict **(68)**(55) *(DenysSmith)* 8-9-7 (5) CTeague(2) (hdwy ½-wy: sn rdn: outpcd fnl 2½f) 4 **5**
2156¹³ Ragazzo (IRE) **(37)**(7) *(JSWainwright)* 5-7-9b LCharnock(3) (chsd ldr tl wknd fnl 3f) 9 **6**
2062² Boldina Bay **(77)** (Fav) *(MJohnston)* 3-9-12b DHolland(4) (bhd: effrt 4f out: broke leg & p.u 3f out: dead) .... **P**

11/4 Boldina Bay, **7/2** Talented Ting (IRE), **9/2** Sarmatian (USA), King Curan (USA), **6/1** Spanish Verdict (op 4/1), SOOTY TERN, **33/1** Ragazzo (IRE), CSF £25.96 TOTE £5.90: £2.40 £2.60 (£9.80) OWNER Mr J. M. Bradley (CHEPSTOW) BRED Sheikh Mohammed bin Rashid al Maktoum
7 Rn 1m 45.0 (1.70) SF: 44/41/36/27/21/-/-
WEIGHT FOR AGE 3yo-9lb

2398 FIELD & LAWN (MARQUEES) LTD (S) STKS (3-Y.O+) (Class G)
£2,507.00 (£702.00: £170.50: £170.50)
6f 5y Stalls: Low GOING minus 0.61 sec per fur (F) 7-50 (7-54)

2156[5] **Blow Dry (IRE) (52)***(60) (MartynWane)* 5-9-7 AMackay(1) (in tch: hdwy over 1f out: r.o to ld wl ins fnl f)..........— 1
2304* Diet **(47)***(57) (MissLAPerratt)* 9-9-0v(7) PFessey(2) (lw: chsd ldrs: ch ins fnl f: kpt on wl)........1¼ 2
2018[6] Brookhead Lady **(57)***(51) (PDEvans)* 4-9-2 DHolland(9) (b.nr fore: led tl hdd & no ex wl ins fnl f)..........nk 3
1996[3] Brisas **(39)***(56) (CWFairhurst)* 8-9-4 (3) JStack(3) (a chsng ldrs: kpt on fnl f)..........d.h 3
1993[3] Best Kept Secret **(65)***(53)*(Fav)*(JBerry)* 4-9-7 JCarroll(5) (in tch: hdwy u.p 2f out: nt run on fnl f)..........1¼ 5
2229[5] Sunday Mail Too (IRE) **(37)***(44) (MissLAPerratt)* 3-8-4b(5) CTeague(4) (lw: s.i.s: hung rt & racd alone far side: jnd ldrs ½-wy: wknd fnl f)..........1¼ 6
887[11] Waverley Star **(40)***(25) (JSWainwright)* 10-9-7 LCharnock(6) (lw: chsd ldrs 4f: sn wknd)..........9 7
Nuclear Express **(47)***(22) (JMBradley)* 8-9-4 (3) SDrowne(8) (b: gd spd 4f)..........1¼ 8

9/4 Best Kept Secret, **7/2** Brookhead Lady, Diet, **5/1** BLOW DRY (IRE), **14/1** Sunday Mail Too (IRE), **20/1** Brisas, Waverley Star, **50/1** Nuclear Express, CSF £20.45 TOTE £8.80: £2.40 £1.20 B £1.10 BL 90p (£9.50) Trio £29.00 B; £9.20 BL OWNER Mr Gerard Moran (RICHMOND) BRED Miss Janet Mehigan 8 Rn 1m 11.9 (1.90) SF: 26/23/17/22/19/3/-/-
WEIGHT FOR AGE 3yo-7lb
No bid.

2399 SCOTTISHPOWER CLASSIC NURSERY H'CAP (2-Y.O) (Class E)
£3,828.80 (£1,159.40: £566.20: £269.60)
5f 4y Stalls: Low GOING minus 0.61 sec per fur (F) 8-20 (8-26)

2223[2] **Desert Tiger** *(79)*(Fav)*(MJohnston)* 2-9-7 DHolland(4) (uns rdr & bolted bef s: mde most: hrd rdn & styd on fnl f)..........— 1
2153* Natural Key *(74) (DHaydnJones)* 2-9-10 7x AMackay(2) (lw: a cl up: nt qckn fnl f)..........2½ 2
2146[2] Boffy (IRE) *(59) (BPJBaugh)* 2-8-10 (5) VHalliday(1) (trckd ldrs: effrt & ev ch over 1f out: nt qckn)..........2 3
1466* Lila Pedigo (IRE) *(45) (JBerry)* 2-8-12 JCarroll(3) (chsd ldrs: pushed along after 2f: sn btn).3½ 4

1/2 DESERT TIGER, **3/1** Natural Key, **9/2** Lila Pedigo (IRE), **12/1** Boffy (IRE), CSF £2.70 TOTE £1.40 (£1.80) OWNER Mrs M. O'Donnell (PONTYPRIDD)/Maktoum Al Maktoum (MIDDLEHAM) BRED Cheveley Park Stud Ltd 4 Rn 60.2 secs (1.90) SF: 16/21/1/-

2400 'JUDGE' CLAIMING STKS (3-Y.O+) (Class F) £2,661.00 (£746.00: £363.00)
1m 3f 16y Stalls: High GOING minus 0.61 sec per fur (F) 8-50 (8-50)

2280[7] **Goodbye Millie (47)***(56) (JLEyre)* 5-8-12v RLappin(2) (led after 1f: mde rest: styd on gamely fnl f)..........— 1
Keep Your Distance **(60)***(65)*(Fav)*(MrsMReveley)* 5-9-9 JCarroll(6) (bhd: pushed along appr st: hdwy 4f out: ev ch ovcer 1f out: hrd rdn: nt qckn)..........1¼ 2
2165[2] Anorak (USA) **(46)***(51) (GMMoore)* 5-9-0v(3) JStack(4) (chsd wnr tl rdn & btn wl over 1f out)....6 3
2353[5] Longcroft **(42)***(41) (KWHogg)* 3-8-0 AMackay(5) (bhd: rdn over 3f out: styd on u.p)..........3½ 4
2245[10] Rubadub **(41)***(33) (JMBradley)* 4-8-7 (3) SDrowne(3) (b: lw: plld hrd & led 1f: trckd ldrs: rdn 3f out: wknd wl over 1f out)..........3½ 5
1960[3] Glenrock Dancer (IRE) *(1) (WTKemp)* 3-7-1b(7) PFessey(1) (chsd ldrs to st: sn rdn, wknd & t.o)..........20 6

13/8 Keep Your Distance, **11/4** GOODBYE MILLIE, **4/1** Anorak (USA), **9/2** Longcroft, **9/1** Rubadub (6/1-10/1), **33/1** Glenrock Dancer (IRE), CSF £7.63 TOTE £3.30: £1.40 £1.50 (£2.30) OWNER Mr K. Meynell (HAMBLETON) BRED G. Corbett 6 Rn 2m 24.2 (5.20) SF: 12/21/7/-/-/-
WEIGHT FOR AGE 3yo-12lb

2401 JOE PUNTER MAIDEN H'CAP (0-60) (3-Y.O+) (Class F) £3,420.00
(£1,035.00: £505.00: £240.00)
1m 4f 17y Stalls: High GOING minus 0.61 sec per fur (F) 9-20 (9-20)

2232[3] **Bark'n'bite (43)***(61) (MrsMReveley)* 3-8-6 LCharnock(3) (lw: chsd ldrs: chal 4f out: r.o u.p to ld ins fnl f)..........— 1
1875[5] Muzrak (CAN) **(52)***(65)*(Fav)*(MDHammond)* 4-10-0 DaleGibson(5) (sn pushed along: hdwy 6f out: led over 4f out tl ins fnl f: no ex)..........3½ 2
2232[4] Never so True **(40)***(41) (MartynWane)* 4-9-2v JCarroll(1) (lw: bhd: hdwy 6f out: ev ch over 4f out: wl outpcd fnl 3f)..........9 3

2224⁷ Parish Walk (IRE) **(40)**_(24)_ _(KWHogg)_ 4-9-2 AMackay(4) (chsd ldrs: one pce fnl 4f)...............13 **4**
2306⁸ Halls Burn **(36)** _(JSGoldie)_ 7-8-5v(7)ow6 NKinnon(6) (led & sn wl clr: hdd over 4f out: wknd qckly).........14 **5**
2082⁸ Frank the Swank **(47)** _(PDEvans)_ 4-9-9 DHolland(2) (lw: chsd clr ldr to st: wknd 4f out)........20 **6**

5/4 Muzrak (CAN), **9/4** BARK'N'BITE (6/4-5/2), **9/2** Never so True, **7/1** Frank the Swank, **16/1** Parish Walk (IRE), **33/1** Halls Burn, CSF £5.42 TOTE £2.50: £1.50 £1.60 (£1.80) OWNER Mr P. D. Savill (SALTBURN) BRED Ian Flockton Developments Ltd 6 Rn 2m 36.7 (4.70) SF: 13/30/6/-/-/-
WEIGHT FOR AGE 3yo-13lb

T/Plpt: £28.30 (351.81 Tckts). T/Qdpt: £6.10 (12 Tckts). AA

2089-LINGFIELD (L-H)
Friday July 14th (Turf Good to firm, AWT Standard)

Race 2 hand stopped.
WEATHER: sunny WIND: mod half bhd

2402 BOWLER CLAIMING STKS (3-Y.O+) (Class F) £2,871.80 (£794.80: £379.40)
5f (Equitrack) Stalls: High GOING minus 0.60 sec per fur (FST) 2-15 (2-15)

_2295⁹_ **Tommy Tempest (29)**_(54)_ _(REPeacock)_ 6-8-3v(3) PMcCabe(2) (mde all: sn clr: hrd rdn over 1f out: r.o wl)........— **1**
2009⁶ Anzio (IRE) **(65)**_(50)_ _(BAPearce)_ 4-8-1b(7) JWilkinson(4) (b: lw: s.i.s: rdn over 2f out: gd hdwy fnl f: r.o wl)........2 **2**
1972⁷ Random **(58)**_(46)_ _(CJames)_ 4-8-5 SWhitworth(3) (chsd wnr: rdn over 2f out: unable qckn) ...s.h **3**
_2144⁴_ Abbey House **(58)**_(33)_ _(RGuest)_ 3-7-9b AMackay(1) (hld up: rdn over 3f out: one pce)............3 **4**
_2142⁸_ Little Saboteur **(69)**_(39)_(Fav)_(PJMakin)_ 6-8-9b AClark(5) (b.nr hind: lw: hld up: rdn over 2f out: one pce)........½ **5**

5/4 Little Saboteur, **9/4** Anzio (IRE), **4/1** Abbey House (5/2-9/2), **11/2** Random, **25/1** TOMMY TEMPEST, CSF £75.21 TOTE £14.20: £2.40 £1.40 (£35.60) OWNER Mr Allan White (MALMESBURY) BRED D. J. Wood 5 Rn 58.55 secs (0.35) SF: 34/30/26/7/19
WEIGHT FOR AGE 3yo-6lb

OFFICIAL EXPLANATION **Tommy Tempest: preferred the faster surface which allowed him to dominate from start to finish.**

2403 MERCHANT (S) STKS (2-Y.O) (Class G) £2,556.60 (£707.60: £337.80)
6f Stalls: Centre GOING minus 0.57 sec per fur (F) 2-50 (2-51)

2204* **Fenna** _(71)_(Fav)_(SPCWoods)_ 2-8-11 WWoods(3) (led 4f out: rdn out)........— **1**
_2143⁷_ Bobsworthatcaspers _(63)_ _(GLewis)_ 2-8-11b SWhitworth(6) (lw: a.p: chsd wnr fnl 3f: unable qckn)........3 **2**
2176² Music Mistress (IRE) _(53)_ _(RHannon)_ 2-7-13 (7) DaneO'Neill(1) (b.nr hind: lw: hld up: rdn over 3f out: one pce)........2 **3**
1981¹¹ Latzio _(29)_ _(BAPearce)_ 2-7-13 (7) JWilkinson(2) (spd over 3f)........9 **4**
Rowlandsons Stud (IRE) _(18)_ _(GLMoore)_ 2-8-11 FNorton(5) (w'like: bit bkwd: s.s: a wl bhd) ..6 **5**
1981⁸ The Clan _(2)_ _(AMoore)_ 2-8-6 GDuffield(4) (bit bkwd: led 2f)........4 **6**

4/5 FENNA (op 6/5), **11/4** Music Mistress (IRE), **5/1** Bobsworthatcaspers (3/1-11/2), **14/1** Rowlandsons Stud (IRE) (6/1-16/1), **20/1** The Clan, **50/1** Latzio, CSF £5.12 TOTE £1.70: £1.30 £2.20 (£4.40) OWNER Mr S. P. C. Woods (NEWMARKET) BRED High Point Bloodstock Ltd and Nigel Fenner Fownes 6 Rn 1m 10.32 (1.32) SF: 28/20/10/-/-/-
Bt in 9,000gns.

2404 AL AMEAD H'CAP (0-70) (3-Y.O+ F & M) (Class E) £3,445.20 (£1,029.60: £492.80: £224.40) **6f** Stalls: Centre GOING minus 0.57 sec per fur (F) 3-20 (3-21)

2088⁵ **Poyle Jezebelle (44)**_(52)_ _(MBlanshard)_ 4-8-2 StephenDavies(9) (lw: a.p: led over 1f out: hrd rdn: r.o wl)........— **1**
2180² Rosa Bonheur **(50)**_(54)_ _(MAJarvis)_ 3-7-10 (5) NVarley(10) (b.hind: hld up: rdn over 3f out: ev ch over 1f out: unable qckn)........1½ **2**
2017² Tonys Gift **(62)**_(64)_ _(RHannon)_ 3-8-6 (7) DaneO'Neill(7) (hld up: rdn over 3f out: one pce fnl f)........¾ **3**
1975* Louisville Belle (IRE) **(54)**_(54)_ _(MDIUsher)_ 6-8-5 (7) CAdamson(6) (b: lw: hld up: nt clr run over 1f out & ins fnl f: nt rcvr)........¾ **4**
2010⁷ La Petite Fusee **(70)**_(65)_ _(RJO'Sullivan)_ 4-10-0 AClark(8) (b.hind: lw: led over 4f)........1¾ **5**
1982⁵ Sally Weld **(59)**_(45)_ _(CJBenstead)_ 3-8-10 MWigham(5) (spd over 3f)........3½ **6**
1963* Hello Hobson's (IRE) **(52)**_(31)_(Fav)_(RBastiman)_ 5-8-10 DeanMcKeown(1) (dwlt: a bhd).......2½ **7**

1516⁴ Myjinka **(35)** *(JO'Donoghue)* 5-7-2b(5) MBaird(4) (prom over 2f)....8 **8**
2113³ Julia's Freebee **(40)** *(TMJones)* 4-7-12 FNorton(3) (lw: a bhd)....4 **9**
Sarasonia **(39)** *(JWPayne)* 4-7-11 AMackay(2) (bhd fnl 4f)....12 **10**

LONG HANDICAP Myjinka 6-13

2/1 Hello Hobson's (IRE) (3/1-7/4), **4/1** La Petite Fusee (3/1-9/2), **11/2** Louisville Belle (IRE) (op 7/2), **8/1** Tonys Gift (op 4/1), POYLE JEZEBELLE (4/1-10/1), **10/1** Sally Weld (op 5/1), Rosa Bonheur (op 6/1), **20/1** Myjinka, **33/1** Julia's Freebee, Sarasonia, CSF £76.85 CT £598.45 TOTE £16.00: £2.70 £2.30 £1.80 (£26.30) Trio £79.00 OWNER Mr Cecil Wiggins (UPPER LAMBOURN) BRED C. Wiggins 10 Rn 1m 9.26 (0.26) SF: 34/29/39/36/47/20/13/-/-/-

WEIGHT FOR AGE 3yo-7lb

2405

BANKERS LIMITED STKS (0-75) (3-Y.O) (Class D) £3,867.50 (£1,154.00: £551.00: £249.50) **7f 140y** Stalls: Centre GOING minus 0.57 sec per fur (F) 3-50 (3-51)

1747³ **Donna Viola (72)***(81) (CFWall)* 3-8-6 WWoods(5) (lw: a.p: led over 3f out: r.o wl)....— **1**
1845⁷ Aldaneh **(75)***(74) (RHannon)* 3-8-2 (7) DaneO'Neill(2) (lw: a.p: chsd wnr over 3f out: hrd rdn over 2f out: unable qckn)....5 **2**
1517⁷ Greenwich Again **(69)***(69) (TGMills)* 3-9-3 TIves(6) (lost pl over 4f out: one pce fnl 2f)....6 **3**
1249⁷ Pelleman **(75)***(56)*(Fav)*(RBoss)* 3-9-0 GDuffield(4) (lw: bhd fnl 2f)....5 **4**
2094* Rising Dough (IRE) **(75)***(53) (GLMoore)* 3-9-0 SWhitworth(1) (led 4f: wknd over 2f out)....1¼ **5**
1907⁶ Made in Heaven **(74)***(24) (JWHills)* 3-7-13 (7) MHenry(3) (swtg: bhd fnl 3f)....10 **6**

3/1 Pelleman, **100/30** DONNA VIOLA, **7/2** Aldaneh (5/2-4/1), Rising Dough (IRE), **7/1** Greenwich Again, **16/1** Made in Heaven, CSF £14.01 TOTE £3.50: £2.10 £2.60 (£10.30) OWNER Mr Kieran Scott (NEWMARKET) BRED Lady Juliet de Chair 6 Rn 1m 27.47 (-0.53) SF: 47/40/35/22/19/-

2406

INNTREPRENEUR ESTATES H'CAP (0-80) (3-Y.O) (Class D) £3,630.90 (£1,081.20: £514.60: £231.30) **1m 3f 106y** Stalls: High GOING minus 0.57 sec per fur (F) 4-20 (4-20)

2199⁵ **No Pattern (73)***(81) (GLMoore)* 3-9-7 SWhitworth(1) (lw: hdwy 4f out: 3rd st: hrd rdn over 1f out: led ins fnl f: all out)....— **1**
1985² Birthday Boy (IRE) **(63)***(71) (RHannon)* 3-8-4v(7) DaneO'Neill(4) (led: clr 9f out: hdd ins fnl f: r.o)....nk **2**
2166² Dance So Suite **(71)***(78)*(Fav)*(PFICole)* 3-9-5 TIves(2) (lw: chsd ldr over 5f out: hrd rdn over 2f out: ev ch ins fnl f: r.o)....hd **3**
1654³ Emphatic Candidate (IRE) **(65)***(60) (RAkehurst)* 3-8-13 AClark(5) (lw: rdn over 6f out: 6th st: nvr nr to chal)....9 **4**
2314⁴ Hotspur Street **(67)***(49) (MJohnston)* 3-9-1 TWilliams(3) (5th st: wknd over 3f out)....9 **5**
2314¹¹ Ewar Imperial **(67)***(42) (CEBrittain)* 3-9-1 WWoods(6) (chsd ldr 6f: 4th st: wknd over 3f out)....5 **6**

6/4 Dance So Suite, **11/4** NO PATTERN, **4/1** Birthday Boy (IRE), **15/2** Hotspur Street (3/1-8/1), **9/1** Emphatic Candidate (IRE) (op 4/1), **14/1** Ewar Imperial, CSF £13.35 TOTE £4.80: £1.80 £2.10 (£16.80) OWNER Mr K. Higson (EPSOM) BRED Mrs N. F. M. Sampson 6 Rn 2m 27.58 (5.58) SF: 21/11/18/-/-/-

2407

KELLY SERVICES H'CAP (0-70) (3-Y.O+) (Class E) £3,330.80 (£994.40: £475.20: £215.60) **1m 2f (Equitrack)** Stalls: Low GOING minus 0.60 sec (FST) 4-50 (4-50)

*1980** **North Reef (IRE) (67)***(79+)*(Fav)*(SirMarkPrescott)* 4-9-11 GDuffield(4) (lw: mde all: clr 3f out: eased fnl f)....— **1**
1789⁵ Water Hazard (IRE) **(56)***(62) (SDow)* 3-7-10 (7) ADaly(7) (in rr 7f: hdwy on ins over 2f out: chsd wnr fnl f: no imp)....4 **2**
*2147** Rolling Waters **(61)***(63) (JARToller)* 5-9-5 6x AClark(6) (a.p: rdn over 4f out: one pce)....2½ **3**
1314⁸ I Recall (IRE) **(60)***(60) (PHayward)* 4-8-11 (7) DaneO'Neill(1) (a.p: rdn over 4f out: wknd fnl f)....1¼ **4**
*1939** El Bailador (IRE) **(63)***(62) (JDBethell)* 4-9-7 TIves(8) (lw: chsd wnr over 4f out to over 1f out: sn wknd)....nk **5**
*347** Carte Blanche **(50)***(48) (CACyzer)* 4-8-8 DeanMcKeown(3) (bhd fnl 5f)....¾ **6**
2089⁵ Tadellal (IRE) **(55)***(52) (BAPearce)* 4-8-6 (7) JWilkinson(2) (lw: bhd fnl 4f)....¾ **7**

7/4 NORTH REEF (IRE), **100/30** El Bailador (IRE), **4/1** Carte Blanche (op 6/1), **11/2** Rolling Waters (3/1-6/1), **10/1** Tadellal (IRE), **12/1** Water Hazard (IRE) (op 5/1), **20/1** I Recall (IRE), CSF £20.11 CT £89.33 TOTE £2.50: £1.60 £3.60 (£9.40) OWNER Mr W. E. Sturt (NEWMARKET) BRED Limestone Stud 7 Rn 2m 5.34 (2.34) SF: 41/13/25/22/24/10/14

WEIGHT FOR AGE 3yo-11lb

T/Plpt: £422.80 (15.14 Tckts). T/Qdpt: £94.90 (0.95 Tckts). AK

2025-NEWBURY (L-H)
Friday July 14th (Good)
WEATHER: fair WIND: fresh half against

2408 E.B.F. ECCHINSWELL MAIDEN STKS (2-Y.O) (Class D) £4,597.50 (£1,380.00: £665.00: £307.50) **6f 8y** Stalls: Centre GOING minus 0.21 sec (GF) 2-30 (2-32)

1893[6] **Shaniko (IRE)** *(95)*(Fav)*(PWChapple-Hyam)* 2-9-0 JReid(11) (lw: mde all: hrd rdn ins fnl f: all out)....— **1**
1134[3] Brilliant Red *(95) (PFICole)* 2-9-0 MRoberts(8) (lw: a.p: n.m.r 2f out: ev ch fnl f: hrd rdn: r.o)s.h **2**
Mongol Warrior (USA) *(87) (LordHuntingdon)* 2-9-0 DHarrison(10) (neat: hdwy 2f out: r.o one pce appr fnl f)....3 **3**
Hidden Oasis *(80) (MRStoute)* 2-9-0 WRSwinburn(3) (gd sort: lw: chsd ldrs: one pce appr fnl f)....2½ **4**
Mukhlles (USA) *(78) (MajorWRHern)* 2-9-0 WCarson(7) (unf: scope: pushed along over 3f out: no hdwy fnl 2f)....1 **5**
1726[9] No Cliches *(74) (GLewis)* 2-9-0 JWilliams(4) (stdy hdwy over 1f out: r.o)....1¼ **6**
General Macarthur *(74) (JLDunlop)* 2-9-0 TSprake(9) (cmpt: bhd: rdn over 3f out: stdy hdwy whn hmpd over 1f out: nvr nrr)....hd **7**
2005[5] Roman Gold (IRE) *(67) (RHannon)* 2-9-0 RPerham(5) (nvr nr ldrs)....2½ **8**
Concert Party (IRE) *(58) (JLDunlop)* 2-9-0 AMcGlone(13) (scope: s.i.s: nvr trbld ldrs)....3½ **9**
Cross The Border *(57) (RHannon)* 2-9-0 RHughes(1) (str: scope: w wnr: rdn & ev ch 2f out: sn wknd)....nk **10**
Gelsemine *(52) (HCandy)* 2-8-9 WNewnes(12) (unf: scope: s.s: stdy hdwy whn hmpd over 2f out: n.d)....d.h **10**
Prime Partner *(55) (WRMuir)* 2-8-11 (3) SSanders(6) (str: bit bkwd: prom over 3f)....1 **12**
Sticks Mckenzie *(31) (BWHills)* 2-9-0 WRyan(2) (cmpt: s.i.s: sn pushed along: bhd fnl 3f)....9 **13**

11/8 SHANIKO (IRE), **7/2** Brilliant Red (op 2/1), **9/2** Mukhlles (USA), **11/2** Hidden Oasis (op 7/2), **16/1** Mongol Warrior (USA), **25/1** Sticks Mckenzie, General Macarthur, Concert Party (IRE), Cross The Border, **33/1** Roman Gold (IRE), Gelsemine, Prime Partner, **50/1** No Cliches, CSF £7.23 TOTE £2.40: £1.30 £1.30 £4.20 (£3.20) Trio £55.30 OWNER Sheikh Mohammed (MARLBOROUGH) BRED Sheikh Mohammed bin Rashid al Maktoum 13 Rn
1m 14.91 (3.11) SF: 38/38/30/23/21/17/17/10/1/-/-/-/-

2409 WATERMILL CONDITIONS STKS (3-Y.O+) (Class C) £5,658.80 (£2,109.20: £1,024.60: £433.00: £186.50: £87.90) **7f 64y (round)** Stalls: Centre GOING minus 0.21 sec per fur (GF) 3-00 (3-03)

*394** **Allemande (IRE)** *(109) (JHMGosden)* 3-8-8 GHind(6) (lw: hld up: 5th st: hdwy 2f out: led over 1f out: r.o wl)....— **1**
Indhar *(106) (JEBanks)* 4-9-3 JQuinn(5) (lw: stmbld s: hld up & bhd: rdn & hdwy 2f out: r.o ins fnl f)....1¾ **2**
1850[8] Mamlakah (IRE) **(105)***(102) (HThomsonJones)* 3-8-9 WCarson(7) (hld up: 4th st: rdn & ev ch over 1f out: one pce)....2 **3**
1618[2] Carranita (IRE) **(105)***(98) (BPalling)* 5-9-2 TSprake(3) (lw: 6th st: nt clr run 3f out: swtchd rt over 2f out: rdn over 1f out: one pce)....1½ **4**
2006[4] Queenfisher **(88)***(86) (RHannon)* 3-8-2 MRoberts(8) (2nd st: rdn 2f out: wknd over 1f out)....2½ **5**
1835[7] Peace Envoy **(109)***(93)*(Fav)*(HRACecil)* 3-9-2b PatEddery(10) (lw: led 6f: sn wknd: eased whn btn)....3 **6**
502* General Sir Peter (IRE) *(66) (PFICole)* 3-8-8 DHarrison(4) (lw: 3rd st: rdn 3f out: sn wknd)....9 **7**
1976[4] Grandinare (USA) **(88)***(65) (PWChapple-Hyam)* 3-8-8 JReid(1) (lw: a wl bhd)....nk **8**
1870[9] Shamanic **(98)***(64) (RHannon)* 3-8-11 WRSwinburn(2) (s.s: a wl bhd)....1¾ **9**
Texanne (BEL) *(PaulSmith,Belgium)* 4-8-11 BDoyle(9) (ref to r: t.n.p).... **R**

2/1 Peace Envoy (7/4-11/4), **100/30** Carranita (IRE), **7/2** Mamlakah (IRE) (5/1-3/1), **10/1** Queenfisher (7/1-12/1), **14/1** Grandinare (USA) (10/1-16/1), **16/1** ALLEMANDE (IRE), Shamanic, **20/1** General Sir Peter (IRE), Indhar, **66/1** Texanne (BEL), CSF £238.21 TOTE £15.40: £2.80 £7.50 £1.40 (£172.90) Trio £273.30 OWNER Sheikh Mohammed (NEWMARKET) 10 Rn
1m 29.03 (0.53) SF: 70/75/63/67/47/54/27/26/25/-
WEIGHT FOR AGE 3yo-8lb

2410 GOLF COURSE & DRIVING RANGE H'CAP (0-90) (3-Y.O+) (Class C) £5,507.50 (£1,660.00: £805.00: £377.50) **5f 34y** Stalls: Centre GOING minus 0.21 sec per fur (GF) 3-30 (3-32)

2027* **Top Banana (84)***(94)*(Fav)*(HCandy)* 4-9-10 WNewnes(3) (lw: mde all: rdn out)....— **1**

2288[5] Robellion **(70)***(73) (DWPArbuthnot)* 4-8-10v ow1 RHughes(6) (lw: hld up: hdwy 2f out: chsd wnr over 1f out: no imp)....2 **2**
1832[17] Macfarlane **(70)***(71) (MJFetherston-Godley)* 7-8-10 WRSwinburn(1) (a.p: rdn 2f out: one pce) 1 **3**
1895[8] Sea-Deer **(88)***(83) (LJHolt)* 6-10-0 AMcGlone(7) (lw: rdn & hdwy over 1f out: r.o one pce)....1¾ **4**
2247[6] John O'Dreams **(54)***(48) (MrsALMKing)* 10-7-8 ow1 JQuinn(2) (b: lw: hld up: rdn & outpcd 2f out: r.o ins fnl f)....s.h **5**
2150[5] Domicksky **(62)***(52) (MRChannon)* 7-8-2 BDoyle(5) (prom: chsd wnr over 2f out tl over 1f out: sn wknd)....1½ **6**
1982[6] Royal Carlton (IRE) **(71)***(61) (RAkehurst)* 3-8-2 (3) SSanders(4) (lw: w wnr over 2f: hrd rdn & wknd 2f out)....s.h **7**

LONG HANDICAP John O'Dreams 7-5

5/4 TOP BANANA, **9/2** Sea-Deer (3/1-5/1), **7/1** Robellion, Macfarlane, **8/1** Domicksky, **11/1** Royal Carlton (IRE) (6/1-12/1), **25/1** John O'Dreams, CSF £9.49 TOTE £1.80: £1.30 £3.50 (£6.00) OWNER Major M. G. Wyatt (WANTAGE) BRED Dunchurch Lodge Stud Co 7 Rn
62.94 secs (2.64) SF: 46/25/23/35/-/4/7
WEIGHT FOR AGE 3yo-6lb

2411 WHITE HORSE H'CAP (0-80) (3-Y.O F) (Class D) £4,077.50 (£1,220.00: £585.00: £267.50) **1m 2f 6y** Stalls: Centre GOING minus 0.21 sec per fur (GF) 4-00 (4-03)

2171[2] **Emily-Mou (IRE) (67)***(79) (BJMeehan)* 3-8-8 BDoyle(6) (b: mde all: rdn & qcknd 2f out: r.o wl)....— **1**
1916* Goonda **(74)***(85) (HRACecil)* 3-9-1 WRyan(8) (lw: chsd wnr: 2nd st: rdn 2f out: one pce fnl f).½ **2**
1990[3] Wells Whisper (FR) **(70)***(81) (GWragg)* 3-8-11 WRSwinburn(3) (3rd st: hrd rdn over 2f out: chsd wnr over 1f out: nt qckn)....s.h **3**
2028[4] Vena (IRE) **(80)***(89) (JLDunlop)* 3-9-7 WCarson(1) (lw: hld up: stmbld & 8th st: hdwy on ins 2f out: r.o one pce appr fnl f)....1½ **4**
2152[3] Santa Fan (IRE) **(75)***(82) (PFICole)* 3-9-2 MRoberts(9) (lw: hdwy & 4th st: rdn 3f out: styd on ins fnl f)....1 **5**
2152[2] Stinging Reply **(75)***(81) (IABalding)* 3-9-2 PatEddery(4) (lw: hld up: 7th st: rdn & hdwy 2f out: no imp)....1 **6**
1770* San Pietra (IRE) **(77)***(78)*(Fav)*(PWChapple-Hyam)* 3-9-4 JReid(5) (lw: 6th st: sn rdn & lost pl st: no hdwy fnl 3f)....3 **7**
1675[3] Wild Rita **(69)***(67) (WRMuir)* 3-8-10 DHarrison(7) (hld up: hdwy & 5th st: rdn over 3f out: wknd 2f out)....1¾ **8**
779[9] Marzipan (IRE) **(70)***(51) (JWHills)* 3-8-11 ow1 RHughes(2) (lw: last st: a bhd)....10 **9**

100/30 San Pietra (IRE), **4/1** Goonda, **9/2** Stinging Reply, **13/2** Wells Whisper (FR), **7/1** Santa Fan (IRE) (op 12/1), **11/1** Vena (IRE) (8/1-12/1), **12/1** EMILY-MOU (IRE), **14/1** Wild Rita, **33/1** Marzipan (IRE), CSF £53.71 CT £308.00 TOTE £13.70: £2.50 £1.60 £1.30 (£20.10) Trio £70.00 OWNER Mr A. S. Reid (UPPER LAMBOURN) BRED W. and R. Barnett Ltd 9 Rn
2m 7.63 (4.63) SF: 38/44/40/48/41/40/37/26/10

2412 CHATTIS HILL MAIDEN STKS (2-Y.O F) (Class D) £3,548.00 (£1,064.00: £512.00: £236.00) **5f 34y** Stalls: Centre GOING minus 0.21 sec per fur (GF) 4-30 (4-31)

1928[3] **Marjaana (IRE)** *(80)*(Fav)*(PTWalwyn)* 2-8-11 WCarson(6) (a.p: shkn up over 2f out: r.o to ld last strides)....— **1**
My Branch *(80) (BWHills)* 2-8-11 PatEddery(4) (unf: w ldr: rdn to ld over 1f out: hdd last strides)....s.h **2**
Repatriate (AUS) *(74) (PWChapple-Hyam)* 2-8-11 JReid(5) (w'like: led over 3f: wknd wl ins fnl f)....1¾ **3**
Chelsea Classic (IRE) *(56) (MRChannon)* 2-8-11 RHughes(1) (unf: s.s: hdwy 2f out: nvr nr ldrs)....6 **4**
2011[6] Sunset Harbour (IRE) *(48) (DAWilson)* 2-8-11 NGwilliams(2) (lw: hld up: outpcd fnl 2f)....2½ **5**
Rose Tint (IRE) *(46) (LordHuntingdon)* 2-8-11 WRSwinburn(3) (unf: a bhd)....¾ **6**
Wild Humour (IRE) *(33) (WRMuir)* 2-8-11 MRoberts(7) (w'like: scope: bkwd: bhd fnl 2f)....4 **7**

4/7 MARJAANA (IRE), **4/1** Repatriate (AUS), **8/1** My Branch (op 5/1), **10/1** Chelsea Classic (IRE) (6/1-12/1), **12/1** Rose Tint (IRE), **33/1** Sunset Harbour (IRE), Wild Humour (IRE), CSF £6.11 TOTE £1.50: £1.20 £3.10 (£5.00) OWNER Mr Hamdan Al Maktoum (LAMBOURN) BRED Shadwell Estate Company Limited 7 Rn 63.82 secs (3.52) SF: 20/20/14/-/-/-/-

2413 JULY H'CAP (0-85) (3-Y.O+) (Class D) £4,299.00 (£1,302.00: £636.00: £303.00) **2m** Stalls: Centre GOING minus 0.21 sec per fur (GF) 5-00 (5-00)

2193* **Kristal's Paradise (IRE) (80)***(94+)*(Fav)*(JLDunlop)* 3-8-6 5x WCarson(2) (lw: 3rd st: led wl over 3f out: clr over 2f out: pushed out)....— **1**

1600[4] Tibetan **(70)***(81) (LadyHerries)* 3-7-10 JQuinn(6) (lw: hdwy & 4th st: chsd wnr over 2f out: no imp) 3 **2**
2007[6] Santana Lady (IRE) **(62)***(69) (MJHeaton-Ellis)* 6-8-5 WRyan(5) (led: c wd & hdd wl over 3f out: one pce) 4 **3**
1784[3] Brave Spy **(56)***(55) (CACyzer)* 4-7-13 ow1 DBiggs(7) (6th st: nvr nr to chal) 7 **4**
2154[4] Brumon (IRE) **(60)***(59) (DWPArbuthnot)* 4-8-3b MRoberts(8) (chsd ldr: 2nd st: wknd 4f out) ..1½ **5**
2284[10] Coleridge **(55)***(38) (JJSheehan)* 7-7-5b(7)ow5 JoHunnam(1) (nvr gng wl: a wl bhd) 11 **6**
1621* Purple Splash **(81)***(65) (PJMakin)* 5-9-10b WRSwinburn(3) (b: hld up: 5th st: rdn 4f out: sn bhd) 3½ **7**
Postage Stamp **(50)***(9) (FMurphy)* 8-7-7 NAdams(4) (7th & wkng st: sn t.o) 25 **8**

LONG HANDICAP Coleridge 7-1

5/4 KRISTAL'S PARADISE (IRE), **9/2** Purple Splash, **5/1** Tibetan (9/2-7/1), **7/1** Postage Stamp, **12/1** Brumon (IRE) (8/1-14/1), **16/1** Brave Spy, Santana Lady (IRE), **50/1** Coleridge, CSF £7.55 CT £57.73 TOTE £1.90: £1.20 £2.00 £2.80 (£7.20) OWNER Windflower Overseas Holdings Inc (ARUNDEL) BRED Windflower Overseas 8 Rn 3m 30.63 (4.13) SF: 55/42/47/33/37/16/43/-
WEIGHT FOR AGE 3yo-17lb

2414

LEVY BOARD H'CAP (0-80) (3-Y.O+) (Class D) £3,952.50 (£1,185.00: £570.00: £262.50) **7f (straight)** Stalls: Centre GOING minus 0.21 sec (GF) 5-30 (5-32)

2130[7] **Safey Ana (USA) (70)***(77) (BHanbury)* 4-9-4 WRyan(10) (hld up: hdwy over 2f out: led over 1f out tl ins fnl f: led post) ....— **1**
1676[6] Chili Heights **(55)***(62) (GBBalding)* 5-8-3v TSprake(11) (hld up & bhd: gd hdwy 2f out: led ins fnl f: hdd post) ....s.h **2**
2169* Fairy Story (IRE) **(74)***(75) (RAkehurst)* 5-9-5 (3) 6x SSanders(4) (lw: led: rdn: edgd rt & hdd over 1f out: nt qckn) 2½ **3**
2010[6] Mullitover **(63)***(63) (MJHeaton-Ellis)* 5-8-11 JReid(7) (a.p: ev ch over 1f out: one pce) ....½ **4**
1542* Sharp Rebuff **(76)***(74) (PJMakin)* 4-9-10 WRSwinburn(1) (lw: prom: edgd rt over 2f out: hrd rdn & ev ch over 1f out: one pce) ....¾ **5**
2010[2] Dawalib (USA) **(67)***(54)*(Fav)*(DHaydnJones)* 5-9-1 WCarson(6) (hld up: hdwy 2f out: eased whn btn ins fnl f) 5 **6**
761[12] Jigadee Creek **(60)***(40) (GHarwood)* 3-8-0 MRoberts(2) (lw: hld up mid div: wknd wl over 1f out) 3 **7**
1969[6] Love Legend **(54)***(30) (DWPArbuthnot)* 10-8-2 JQuinn(5) (lost pl & hmpd over 2f out: sn bhd).2 **8**
1629[4] Rocky Waters (USA) **(75)***(49) (PBurgoyne)* 6-9-6 (3) DRMcCabe(8) (lw: bhd fnl 2f) ....¾ **9**
2051[2] Weather Break **(75)***(49) (HCandy)* 4-9-9 WNewnes(9) (chsd ldr 4f: sn wknd) ....s.h **10**
1732[3] Ahjay **(49)***(21) (DAWilson)* 5-7-11 NAdams(3) (lw: prom 4f) ....¾ **11**

9/2 Dawalib (USA), **5/1** Fairy Story (IRE), **11/2** Jigadee Creek (10/1-5/1), **13/2** Ahjay, **7/1** Sharp Rebuff, **8/1** SAFEY ANA (USA) (6/1-9/1), **10/1** Weather Break, **11/1** Mullitover (7/1-12/1), **16/1** Chili Heights, Love Legend, **33/1** Rocky Waters (USA), CSF £110.72 CT £640.58 TOTE £11.70: £3.70 £3.70 £2.20 (£118.30) Trio £334.30 OWNER The Optimists Racing Partnership (NEWMARKET) BRED Robert N. Clay 11 Rn 1m 26.62 (2.12) SF: 60/45/58/46/57/37/15/13/32/32/4
WEIGHT FOR AGE 3yo-8lb

T/Jpt: £16,070.40 (1.00 Tckt). T/Plpt: £28.80 (678.96 Tckts). T/Qdpt: £8.80 (17.45 Tckts). KH

1803-YORK (L-H)

Friday July 14th (Good to firm)

WEATHER: showers WIND: fresh half bhd

2415

FOSS RATED STKS H'CAP (0-100) (3-Y.O) (Class B) £8,212.50 (£3,037.50: £1,456.25: £593.75: £234.38: £90.62)
1m 3f 195y Stalls: Low GOING minus 0.27 sec per fur (GF) 2-05 (2-12)

1852[9] **Tenorio (98)***(104)*(Fav)*(DRLoder)* 3-9-7 LDettori(6) (lw: trckd ldrs: effrt over 3f out: led jst ins fnl f: readily) ....— **1**
1872[8] Time for Action (IRE) **(87)***(90) (MHTompkins)* 3-8-10 MBirch(4) (lw: hdwy over 3f out: styd on u.p appr fnl f: no ch w wnr) 2 **2**
2004* Crystal Blade **(87)***(90)*(Fav)*(IABalding)* 3-8-10 MJKinane(9) (unruly s: led: qcknd over 4f out: hdd jst ins fnl f) ....nk **3**
1782[3] Royal Scimitar (USA) **(96)***(94) (PFICole)* 3-9-5 RCochrane(1) (b.hind: hld up: hmpd after 1f: bhd tl styd on fnl 2f: nt rch ldrs) 3½ **4**
1800[3] Dawlah **(90)***(88) (HThomsonJones)* 3-8-13 KDarley(7) (chsd ldr: rdn over 4f out: one pce) ....nk **5**
2086[3] Tilaal (USA) **(81)***(75) (EALDunlop)* 3-8-4 JWeaver(2) (hld up & plld hrd: hdwy on outside over 3f out: hung lft u.p: no imp) 3 **6**
1872[16] Al Safeer (IRE) **(82)***(56) (JWHills)* 3-8-5 DHolland(8) (in tch: rdn over 3f out: hung lft & sn wknd: eased over 1f out) 15 **7**

1761* Oneoftheoldones **(81)***(28) (SGNorton)* 3-7-13 (5) HKYim(5) (plld hrd: sn trckng ldrs: wknd over 3f out: sn bhd)....20 8

LONG HANDICAP Tilaal (USA) 8-2 Oneoftheoldones 8-1

7/2 TENORIO, Crystal Blade, **9/2** Time for Action (IRE), Royal Scimitar (USA), **15/2** Dawlah, Tilaal (USA) (7/2-8/1), **9/1** Al Safeer (IRE), **16/1** Oneoftheoldones, CSF £19.21 CT £54.24 TOTE £4.10: £1.50 £1.90 £1.20 (£14.20) Trio £13.50 OWNER Cuadra Africa (NEWMARKET) BRED Sir Eric Parker 8 Rn 2m 28.47 (1.47) SF: 73/59/59/63/57/44/25/-

2416 BLACK DUCK STKS (Listed) (3-Y.O+ F & M) (Class A) £14,328.00 (£4,284.00: £2,052.00: £936.00) 6f Stalls: Centre GOING minus 0.27 sec (GF) 2-40 (2-43)

1895[17] **Tajannub (USA) (100)***(103) (RWArmstrong)* 3-8-7 LDettori(1) (mde all: styd on wl fnl f: jst hld on)....— 1

1848[11] Epagris **(108)***(107)*(Fav)*(HRACecil)* 3-8-11 MJKinane(4) (trckd ldrs: effrt ½-wy: ev ch whn rdn over 1f out: edgd rt: jst failed)....s.h 2

2285[7] Welsh Mist **(94)***(107) (RBoss)* 4-9-4 JWeaver(2) (trckd ldrs: effrt over 2f out: ev ch over 1f out: nt qckn nr fin)....hd 3

2097* Branston Abby (IRE) **(105)***(100) (MJohnston)* 6-9-4 DHolland(6) (racd stands' side: hld up in tch: rdn over 2f out: kpt on same pce)....2½ 4

2066[4] Paris Babe **(92)***(94) (DMorris)* 3-8-7 RCochrane(5) (trckd ldrs: drvn along ½-wy: no imp)....¾ 5

*2066** Marha **(94)** *(HThomsonJones)* 3-8-7 KDarley(3) (Withdrawn: unruly s & rdr inj).... W

15/8 Epagris, **2/1** Branston Abby (IRE), **5/1** TAJANNUB (USA), **13/2** Marha, **9/1** Welsh Mist, **14/1** Paris Babe, CSF £11.71 TOTE £5.90: £2.00 £1.40 (£5.10) OWNER Mr Hamdan Al Maktoum (NEWMARKET) BRED G. Watts Humphrey and Pierce and Pierce Inc in USA 5 Rn

1m 9.99 (0.39) SF: 63/67/74/67/54/-

WEIGHT FOR AGE 3yo-7lb

2417 MANCHESTER-SINGAPORE CONDITIONS STKS (3-Y.O+) (Class B) £8,865.00 (£3,065.00: £1,470.00: £600.00) 7f 202y Stalls: Low GOING minus 0.27 sec per fur (GF) 3-10 (3-15)

1837[2] **Charnwood Forest (IRE) (117)***(97)*(Fav)*(HRACecil)* 3-8-8 MJKinane(2) (lw: trckd ldr: led wl over 2f out: drvn along & styd on strly fnl f)....— 1

Shemaq (USA) *(86) (HThomsonJones)* 3-8-3 PaulEddery(1) (hld up & plld hrd: effrt 3f out: styd on u.p ins fnl f)....3 2

2121* Decorated Hero *(95+) (JHMGosden)* 3-8-12 LDettori(3) (hld up: effrt over 3f out: ev ch tl wknd jst ins fnl f)....s.h 3

Above the Cut (USA) *(86) (PWHarris)* 3-8-13 RCochrane(4) (led tl wl over 2f out: sn wknd) ...5 4

30/100 CHARNWOOD FOREST (IRE), **5/1** Decorated Hero, **9/1** Above the Cut (USA), **12/1** Shemaq (USA), CSF £4.20 TOTE £1.30 (£3.80) OWNER Sheikh Mohammed (NEWMARKET) BRED Sheikh Mohammed bin Rashid al Maktoum 4 Rn 1m 36.2 (0.20) SF: 69/58/67/58

2418 ANTHONY FAWCETT MEMORIAL H'CAP (0-100) (3-Y.O+) (Class C) £7,180.00 (£2,140.00: £1,020.00: £460.00) 5f Stalls: Centre GOING minus 0.27 sec per fur (GF) 3-40 (3-40)

2163* **Lady Sheriff (67)***(73+) (MWEasterby)* 4-7-2b(7) 7x PFessey(4) (trckd ldrs: led over 1f out: edgd lft & hld on wl)....— 1

2194[8] Rich Glow **(65)***(69) (NBycroft)* 4-7-7 NKennedy(3) (sn pushed along: hdwy ½-wy: ev ch fnl f: nt qckn nr fin)....½ 2

2120* Join the Clan **(93)***(94) (MrsNMacauley)* 6-9-4 (3) SDrowne(6) (trckd ldrs gng wl: effrt over 1f out: nt qckn ins fnl f)....1 3

1756[2] Gorinsky (IRE) **(80)***(77) (JBerry)* 7-8-8 JCarroll(1) (led tl over 1f out: wknd towards fin)....1¼ 4

1895[21] Master Planner **(100)***(93) (CACyzer)* 6-10-0 RCochrane(5) (hld up: effrt over 2f out: nvr nr to chal)....1¼ 5

2060[11] Benzoe (IRE) **(82)***(70)*(Fav)*(MrsJRRamsden)* 5-8-10v KFallon(7) (s.i.s: effrt ½-wy: sn outpcd: kpt on fnl f: nvr nr to chal)....1½ 6

2150[4] Ashtina **(91)***(67) (RJHodges)* 10-9-5 LDettori(2) (w ldrs: outpcd & rdn along ½-wy: sn lost pl)....4 7

LONG HANDICAP Rich Glow 7-1

11/4 Benzoe (IRE), **3/1** Join the Clan, **9/2** LADY SHERIFF, **5/1** Master Planner, **7/1** Ashtina, **15/2** Gorinsky (IRE) (op 12/1), **11/1** Rich Glow, CSF £44.78 TOTE £4.80: £2.00 £5.30 (£42.10) OWNER Mr E. J. Mangan (SHERIFF HUTTON) BRED Jeremy Green and Sons 7 Rn

57.51 secs (0.51) SF: 48/44/69/52/68/45/42

2419

TERRINGTON H'CAP (0-90) (3-Y.O+) (Class C) £7,050.00 (£2,100.00: £1,000.00: £450.00) **7f 202y** Stalls: Low GOING minus 0.27 sec per fur (GF) 4-10 (4-10)

1947* **Behaviour (85)***(99+)*(Fav)*(MrsJCecil)* 3-9-5 PaulEddery(2) (lw: hld up: smooth hdwy 3f out: shkn up to ld over 1f out: drvn out)....— 1
2222* Murphy's Gold (IRE) **(57)***(70) (RAFahey)* 4-8-0 5x SMaloney(6) (led: hdd over 1f out: kpt on wl towards fin)....¾ 2
1851 18 Sue's Artiste **(80)***(92) (BWHills)* 4-9-9 DHolland(4) (swtg: trckd ldr: kpt on same pce fnl 2f)....nk 3
1851 14 Star Manager (USA) **(81)***(90) (PFICole)* 5-9-10 RCochrane(5) (stdd s: hld up: hdwy to trck ldrs over 3f out: kpt on same pce)....1½ 4
1926 13 Pride of Pendle **(72)***(74) (DNicholls)* 6-9-1 AlexGreaves(3) (lw: hld up: effrt over 2f out: nvr nr to chal: eased towards fin)....3½ 5
1280 10 Tregaron (USA) **(74)***(66) (PCalver)* 4-9-3 MBirch(1) (trckd ldrs: effrt over 2f out: hung lft & sn wknd)....5 6

10/11 BEHAVIOUR (tchd Evens), **7/2** Pride of Pendle, **7/1** Star Manager (USA), Murphy's Gold (IRE), **15/2** Tregaron (USA), **10/1** Sue's Artiste, CSF £8.09 TOTE £1.90: £1.50 £1.80 (£4.70) OWNER Oceanic Ltd (NEWMARKET) BRED Oceanic Development Co Ltd 6 Rn

1m 37.54 (1.54) SF: 65/45/67/65/49/41
WEIGHT FOR AGE 3yo-9lb

2420

PETERGATE MAIDEN STKS (2-Y.O) (Class D) £4,347.00 (£1,296.00: £618.00: £279.00) **6f 214y** Stalls: Low GOING minus 0.27 sec per fur (GF) 4-40 (4-41)

Vilayet *(75+)*(Fav)*(HRACecil)* 2-9-0 MJKinane(3) (w'like: rangy: dwlt s: sn trckng ldrs: shkn up to ld over 1f out: drvn out)....— 1
Moody's Cat (IRE) *(69+) (BWHills)* 2-8-9 DHolland(2) (tall: s.i.s: hdwy & swtchd ins over 2f out: sn hrd drvn: nt qckn ins fnl f: eased nr fin)....½ 2
2005 2 Gentilhomme *(68) (PFICole)* 2-9-0 RCochrane(5) (swtg: trckd ldr: ev ch over 2f out: nt qckn appr fnl f)....2½ 3
2116 5 Welcome Royale (IRE) *(60) (MHTompkins)* 2-9-0 LDettori(1) (led tl over 1f out: wknd fnl f)..3½ 4
Supermister *(39) (MHEasterby)* 2-9-0 MBirch(4) (w'like: lengthy: prom: n.m.r & wknd over 2f out)....9 5
Dancing Cormorant *(37) (JDBethell)* 2-9-0 JWeaver(6) (w'like: bit bkwd: s.i.s: outpcd & hung lft ½-wy: wknd qckly over 2f out)....1¼ 6

8/13 VILAYET, **9/2** Gentilhomme (op 11/4), **13/2** Moody's Cat (IRE), **8/1** Welcome Royale (IRE), **12/1** Dancing Cormorant, **16/1** Supermister, CSF £5.53 TOTE £1.70: £1.40 £1.90 (£3.90) OWNER Sheikh Mohammed (NEWMARKET) BRED Sheikh Mohammed Bin Rashid Al Maktoum 6 Rn

1m 24.37 (2.87) SF: 40/34/33/25/4/2

2421

LEVY BOARD RATED STKS H'CAP (0-95) (4-Y.O+) (Class B) £8,903.25 (£2,839.50:£1,357.25)
1m 3f 195y Stalls: Low GOING minus 0.27 sec (GF) 5-10 (5-11)

2274* **Lombardic (USA) (90)***(98)*(Fav)*(MrsJCecil)* 4-9-2 3x LDettori(1) (lw: mde all: drvn along 3f out: unchal)....— 1
2274 8 Glide Path (USA) **(95)***(102) (JWHills)* 6-9-7 MJKinane(2) (lw: hld up: effrt & rdn over 3f out: edgd lft & n.m.r over 1f out: styd on ins fnl f)....¾ 2
2241 3 Slasher Jack (IRE) **(81)***(88) (SGNorton)* 4-8-2b(5) HKYim(3) (jnd wnr 5f out: edgd lft: kpt on one pce fnl 2f)....nk 3

10/11 LOMBARDIC (USA), **5/2** Glide Path (USA), **11/4** Slasher Jack (IRE), CSF £3.08 TOTE £1.60 (£1.90) OWNER Bonusprint (NEWMARKET) BRED Juddmonte Farms 3 Rn

2m 29.54 (2.54) SF: 61/65/51
T/Plpt: £25.60 (874.61 Tckts). T/Qdpt: £17.30 (6.70 Tckts). WG

1930-AYR (L-H)
Saturday July 15th (Good)
WEATHER: sunny spells WIND: slt against

2422

E.B.F. FIN ME OOT MEDIAN AUCTION MAIDEN STKS (2-Y.O) (Class E) £3,436.25 (£1,040.00: £507.50: £241.25)
5f Stalls: High GOING minus 0.19 sec per fur (GF) 6-50 (6-53)

Purple Memories *(57+)*(Fav)*(MJohnston)* 2-9-0 DHolland(4) (wl grwn: str: sn w ldr: led after 2f: edgd lft: r.o wl)....— 1

2161[7] Domino Flyer *(53) (MrsASwinbank)* 2-9-0 DaleGibson(1) (led: hung lft & hdd after 2f: kpt on one pce)....1¼ 2
Los Alamos *(48) (CWThornton)* 2-8-9 DeanMcKeown(2) (neat: bit bkwd: sn outpcd: hdwy 2f out: styd on wl towards fin)....hd 3
1063[8] Phantom Dancer (IRE) *(40) (JBerry)* 2-8-7b(7) PRoberts(3) (s.i.s: nvr wnt pce)....4 4

4/5 PURPLE MEMORIES, **7/4** Domino Flyer (9/4-6/4), **12/1** Los Alamos (op 5/1), Phantom Dancer (IRE) (op 4/1), CSF £2.40 TOTE £1.60: (£1.20) OWNER The Mathieson Partnership (MIDDLEHAM) BRED The Mathieson Partnership 4 Rn 61.86 secs (4.86) SF: -/-/-/-

2423 GLASGOW FAIR CONDITIONS STKS (2-Y.O) (Class D) £4,045.50 (£1,224.00: £597.00: £283.50) 5f Stalls: High GOING minus 0.19 sec per fur (GF) 7-20 (7-20)

690[5] **Martara (IRE)** *(74) (MRChannon)* 2-8-12 KDarley(5) (lw: w ldr: led over 1f out: hung lft: kpt on wl)....— 1
1860[3] Red River Valley *(77) (DenysSmith)* 2-9-4 LCharnock(1) (lw: chsd ldrs: chal 2f out: nt qckn ins fnl f)....1 2
Soviet Style (AUS) *(69+)*(Fav)*(PWChapple-Hyam)* 2-8-12 JReid(3) (cmpt: lw: led tl hdd over 1f out: sn outpcd: kpt on towrds fin)....½ 3
2230* No Monkey Nuts *(70) (JBerry)* 2-9-4 JCarroll(2) (lw: cl up tl outpcd & n.m.r 2f out: edgd rt & kpt on fnl f)....1¾ 4
2158[3] Distinctly Swingin (IRE) *(55) (MissLAPerratt)* 2-8-7 DeanMcKeown(4) (b: s.i.s: hdwy ½-wy: nvr able chal)....1¼ 5

7/4 Soviet Style (AUS) (op 4/5), **15/8** MARTARA (IRE), **3/1** No Monkey Nuts, **8/1** Red River Valley, **66/1** Distinctly Swingin (IRE), CSF £13.50 TOTE £3.40: £1.80 £5.00 (£15.10) OWNER Chris Scott & Partners (UPPER LAMBOURN) BRED Alan Dargan 5 Rn 61.77 secs (4.77) SF: -/2/-/-/-

2424 HOURSTONS OF AYR NURSERY H'CAP (2-Y.O) (Class D) £4,240.50 (£1,284.00: £627.00: £298.50) 6f Stalls: High GOING minus 0.19 sec per fur (GF) 7-50 (7-51)

2131[3] **Precious Girl** *(75) (DMoffatt)* 2-8-7 (3) DarrenMoffatt(4) (lw: trckd ldrs: rdn to ld ins fnl f: r.o)....— 1
2399[2] Natural Key *(73) (DHaydnJones)* 2-8-13 JCarroll(2) (led tl hdd ins fnl f: no ex)....1¾ 2
1525* Mystic Tempo (USA) *(79)*(Fav)*(PWChapple-Hyam)* 2-9-7 JReid(1) (lw: cl up: rdn 2f out: nt qckn)....¾ 3
2131[6] Silverdale Knight *(57) (KWHogg)* 2-8-8 DeanMcKeown(5) (lw: bhd: hrd rdn & hdwy 2f out: swtchd lft: no imp)....3½ 4
2192[5] Termon *(39) (MissLAPerratt)* 2-8-6 DaleGibson(3) (outpcd ½-wy: n.d after)....6 5

5/4 Mystic Tempo (USA), **5/2** Natural Key, **9/2** PRECIOUS GIRL, **9/1** Silverdale Knight (5/1-10/1), Termon (op 9/2), CSF £14.88 TOTE £4.70: £1.80 £1.50 (£11.60) OWNER Mr R. E. Sangster (MARLBOROUGH) BRED Swetteham Stud and Ben Sangster 5 Rn 1m 13.43 (3.63) SF: 31/25/27/9/-

2425 ROON BEN H'CAP (0-60) (3-Y.O) (Class F) £3,257.50 (£985.00: £480.00: £227.50) 7f Stalls: Low GOING minus 0.19 sec per fur (GF) 8-20 (8-22)

1692[6] **Quillon Rose (41)***(51)*(Fav)*(CFWall)* 3-8-3 JLowe(11) (b.hind: chsd ldrs: rdn 3f out: hdwy 2f out: r.o u.p to ld cl home)....— 1
2019[2] Legal Issue (IRE) **(58)***(68)*(Fav)*(SirMarkPrescott)* 3-9-6 WWoods(2) (lw: trckd ldrs: led over 2f out: hrd rdn & r.o: jst ct)....hd 2
1932[7] Teejay'n'aitch (IRE) **(52)***(54) (JSGoldie)* 3-9-0 DHolland(9) (in tch: effrt 3f out: styd on: nt pce to chal)....3½ 3
1962[4] Caltha **(39)***(40) (PCalver)* 3-7-10b(5) NVarley(5) (sn cl up: led 2½f out: sn hdd: one pce)....nk 4
651[9] Howqua River **(54)***(47) (PWChapple-Hyam)* 3-8-9 (7) RHavlin(10) (in tch: hrd rdn & hung lft over 2f out: no imp)....3½ 5
1463[5] Salduba **(32)***(22) (TDyer)* 3-7-1 (7) BHalligan(3) (stdd s: sn wl bhd: styd on u.p fnl 2f: n.d)....1¼ 6
1598* Ballard Lady (IRE) **(47)***(26) (JSWainwright)* 3-8-9 LCharnock(8) (lw: chsd ldrs tl rdn & btn over 2f out)....5 7
1524[8] Stand Tall **(59)***(38) (CWThornton)* 3-9-7 DeanMcKeown(1) (led tl hdd & wknd over 2½f out) s.h 8
2162[4] Seenthelight **(42)***(19) (DMoffatt)* 3-8-1v(3) DarrenMoffatt(12) (s.i.s: a bhd)....¾ 9
1956[3] Tee Tee Too (IRE) **(56)** *(PCHaslam)* 3-9-4 DaleGibson(7) (Withdrawn not under Starter's orders).... W

7/2 QUILLON ROSE, Legal Issue (IRE), **6/1** Teejay'n'aitch (IRE), **13/2** Ballard Lady (IRE), **7/1** Seenthelight (op 4/1), **9/1** Stand Tall, **10/1** Tee Tee Too (IRE), **16/1** Caltha, Howqua River, **50/1** Salduba, CSF £13.61 CT £53.02 TOTE £2.90: £1.50 £1.40 £1.40 (£2.80) Trio £12.60 OWNER Sir Philip Oppenheimer (NEWMARKET) BRED Hascombe and Valiant Studs 9 Rn
1m 29.58 (5.58) SF: 8/25/11/-/4/-/-/-/-
STEWARDS' ENQUIRY Lowe suspended 24-25/7/95 (excessive use of whip).

2426 TICKLY TAP MAIDEN STKS (3-Y.O+) (Class D) £3,517.50 (£1,065.00: £520.00: £247.50) **1m 2f** Stalls: Low GOING minus 0.19 sec per fur (GF) 8-50 (8-52)

1764[3] **Honfleur (IRE)** *(72+)*(Fav)*(PWChapple-Hyam)* 3-8-6 JReid(1) (lw: mde most: pushed along 2f out: r.o wl) — 1
Twilight Hour (USA) *(68) (BWHills)* 3-8-6 DHolland(4) (lw: trckd wnr: rdn to chal 2f out: btn ins fnl f) 2½ 2
Victor Laszlo *(49) (JDBethell)* 3-8-11 JCarroll(3) (w'like: s.s: sn in tch: hdwy & rn green 3f out: wl outpcd fnl 2f) 15 3
Senso (IRE) *(36) (JSWainwright)* 4-9-8 DeanMcKeown(2) (chsd ldrs tl outpcd fnl 3f) 8 4

1/3 HONFLEUR (IRE), **5/2** Twilight Hour (USA), **16/1** Senso (IRE), **33/1** Victor Laszlo, CSF £1.65 TOTE £1.40: (£1.20) OWNER Mr R. E. Sangster (MARLBOROUGH) BRED Swettenham Stud 4 Rn 2m 13.21 (8.61) SF: 8/4/-/-
WEIGHT FOR AGE 3yo-11lb

2427 DUNURE H'CAP (0-85) (3-Y.O+) (Class D) £3,582.50 (£1,085.00: £530.00: £252.50) **1m 2f 192y** Stalls: Low GOING minus 0.19 sec per fur (GF) 9-20 (9-23)

2166* **Tessajoe (64)***(76) (MJCamacho)* 3-8-9 LCharnock(5) (a.p: led on bit 2½f out: hrd rdn fnl f: r.o wl) — 1
1616[2] Colorful Ambition **(71)***(82) (MrsASwinbank)* 5-10-0 NConnorton(2) (lw: hld up: hdwy 3f out: rdn to chal 1f out: nt qckn) ½ 2
2226[2] Mentalasanythin **(67)***(74) (ABailey)* 6-9-10 AMackay(1) (in tch: effrt 3f out: r.o one pce) 3 3
1933[3] Keep Battling **(43)***(45) (JSGoldie)* 5-8-0 DaleGibson(7) (lw: plld hrd: trckd ldrs: effrt 2f out: nt qckn) 3½ 4
2312[2] Royal Expression **(57)***(56)*(Fav)*(MrsMReveley)* 3-8-2 KDarley(6) (lw: led tl hdd 2½f out: sn btn) 2 5
2186[7] Kinoko **(40)***(30) (KWHogg)* 7-7-4 (7) DLockhart(4) (stdd s: hld up: outpcd over 3f out: n.d after) 6 6
Wild Rose of York **(57)***(34) (PMonteith)* 4-9-0 DHolland(3) (cl up tl wknd 3f out) 9 7

11/4 Royal Expression, **3/1** TESSAJOE, Mentalasanythin, **4/1** Colorful Ambition, **5/1** Keep Battling, **20/1** Kinoko, **40/1** Wild Rose of York, CSF £15.33 TOTE £4.10: £2.20 £2.00 (£11.00) OWNER Riley Partnership (MALTON) BRED A. and Mrs Rhodes 7 Rn 2m 22.04 (5.84) SF: 36/54/46/17/16/2/6
WEIGHT FOR AGE 3yo-12lb

T/Plpt: £64.90 (104.59 Tckts). T/Qdpt: £24.90 (4.1 Tckts). AA

2390-CHESTER (L-H)
Saturday July 15th (Good)
WEATHER: dry & sunny WIND: mod half against

2428 WATERGATE STREET GALLERY CLAIMING STKS (3-Y.O+) (Class D) £4,328.00 (£1,304.00: £632.00: £296.00) **7f 2y** Stalls: Low GOING minus 0.26 sec per fur (GF) 2-20 (2-21)

2053[2] **Chickawicka (IRE) (80)***(92) (MCPipe)* 4-9-5v(5) LNewton(6) (mde all: sn wl clr: unchal) — 1
563[10] Absolute Magic **(83)***(84) (WJHaggas)* 5-9-8 RCochrane(9) (swtg: chsd ldrs: 3rd & rdn st: kpt on fnl f: no ch w wnr) 2½ 2
2194[6] Rossini Blue **(70)***(70) (ABailey)* 4-8-8 MWigham(7) (hld up: hdwy & 5th st: rdn & r.o wl fnl f) s.h 3
2099[6] Sagebrush Roller **(82)***(77) (JWWatts)* 7-9-2 BThomson(1) (mid div: drvn along & 4th st: no ex cl home) ½ 4
2169[2] Shikari's Son **(90)***(73)*(Fav)*(JWhite)* 8-9-4 BDoyle(3) (a.p: 2nd st: sn rdn: wknd appr fnl f) 2½ 5
Rambo's Hall **(96)***(71) (JAGlover)* 10-9-8 SDWilliams(4) (swtg: hld up: effrt & 6th st: nt rch ldrs) 3 6
972[5] Bee Dee Best (IRE) **(39)***(48) (JPSmith)* 4-8-11 JCarroll(2) (swtg: a bhd & outpcd) 5 7
1993* Respectable Jones **(45)***(39) (RHollinshead)* 9-8-3 (7) FLynch(5) (prom tl rdn & wknd qckly 2f out) 3½ 8

5/2 Shikari's Son, **3/1** Sagebrush Roller, **9/2** CHICKAWICKA (IRE) (3/1-5/1), **6/1** Absolute Magic, **7/1** Rossini Blue, **10/1** Rambo's Hall (6/1-11/1), **16/1** Respectable Jones, **50/1** Bee Dee Best (IRE), CSF £28.82 TOTE £5.30: £1.90 £1.90 £2.10 (£22.60) Trio £30.00 OWNER Merthyr Motor Auctions (WELLINGTON) BRED Charlton Down Stud 8 Rn 1m 27.29 (2.09) SF: 62/54/40/47/43/41/18/9
Rossini Blue clmd Mrs L. Ramsden £4,000.

2429 CHESTER SUMMER H'CAP (0-80) (3-Y.O+) (Class D) £8,812.00 (£2,656.00: £1,288.00: £604.00)
2m 2f 147y Stalls: High GOING minus 0.26 sec per fur (GF) 2-50 (2-50)

2256* **Salaman (FR)** **(78)***(91+)*(Fav)*(JLDunlop)* 3-9-1 RCochrane(6) (lw: hld up & bhd: hdwy 6f out: 4th st: styd on u.p to ld wl ins fnl f) — **1**
2256³ Moonlight Quest **(70)***(83) (BHanbury)* 7-9-12 MRimmer(3) (lw: hld up: hdwy 8f out: 2nd st: led over 1f out: hrd rdn & ct nr fin) ½ **2**
1840²⁶ Upper Mount Clair **(58)***(66) (CEBrittain)* 5-9-0 BDoyle(1) (chsd ldrs: 5th & rdn st: styd on one pce) 5 **3**
2392² Killick **(59)***(66) (ABailey)* 7-9-1 JCarroll(4) (led tl hdd & wknd over 1f out) 1¾ **4**
2284² Paradise Navy **(72)***(75) (CREgerton)* 6-10-0 BThomson(5) (lw: plld hrd: hld up: hdwy 4f out: 3rd st: rdn & wknd bel dist) 5 **5**
998¹⁷ Welshman **(66)***(66) (MBlanshard)* 9-9-8 WNewnes(2) (chsd ldr 14f: 6th & wknd st) 3½ **6**
506⁵ Secret Serenade **(68)** *(CWFairhurst)* 4-9-10 MWigham(7) (b: bkwd: prom 12f: sn lost tch: t.o) dist **7**

6/4 SALAMAN (FR), **4/1** Paradise Navy, **6/1** Moonlight Quest, **8/1** Upper Mount Clair, Killick, **14/1** Welshman, **16/1** Secret Serenade, CSF £9.70 TOTE £2.50: £1.90 £2.60 (£6.50) OWNER Lady Cohen (ARUNDEL) BRED Ridgecourt Stud 7 Rn 4m 11.66 SF: 23/34/17/17/26/17/-
WEIGHT FOR AGE 3yo-19lb

2430 CITY WALL CONDITIONS STKS (3-Y.O+) (Class B) £15,535.00 (£5,815.00: £2,845.00: £1,225.00: £550.00: £280.00)
5f 16y Stalls: Low GOING minus 0.26 sec per fur (GF) 3-20 (3-22)

2237⁴ **Ziggy's Dancer (USA)** **(90)***(100) (EJAlston)* 4-9-2 SDWilliams(3) (lw: chsd ldrs: rdn to ld wl ins fnl f) — **1**
1786² Glorious Aragon *(92) (RFJohnsonHoughton)* 3-8-3 ACulhane(5) (lw: bhd & outpcd tl gd hdwy on ins fnl f: fin fast) nk **2**
1795² Lucky Parkes **(100)***(103)*(Fav)*(JBerry)* 5-9-7 JCarroll(2) (w ldrs: lft in ld ent st: hdd & no ex wl ins fnl f) nk **3**
2066³ Katya (IRE) **(92)***(94) (MRChannon)* 3-8-6 BDoyle(4) (hdwy over 1f out: rdn & r.o ins fnl f) s.h **4**
1572a¹¹ Risky **(108)***(95) (RHannon)* 4-9-0 MRimmer(7) (b: bit bkwd: chsd ldrs: pushed along ½-wy: swtchd lft 1f out: r.o wl) nk **5**
2039a² Ya Malak **(106)***(101) (JWPayne)* 4-9-11 BThomson(9) (lw: w ldrs: ev ch whn carried wd ent st: sn lost pl) 1¾ **6**
1370⁵ Kayrawan (USA) **(90)***(79) (HThomsonJones)* 3-8-10 RCochrane(10) (lw: s.i.s: a bhd & outpcd) 4 **7**
1896⁶ Eveningperformance **(107)***(82)*(Fav)*(HCandy)* 4-9-7 WNewnes(6) (led: hung rt & c wd ent st: sn btn) ½ **8**

11/4 Eveningperformance, Lucky Parkes (op 5/1), **7/2** Ya Malak (op 9/4), **7/1** Risky, **8/1** ZIGGY'S DANCER (USA), **9/1** Katya (IRE), **14/1** Kayrawan (USA), **33/1** Glorious Aragon, CSF £156.70 TOTE £9.00: £1.90 £4.00 £1.30 (£111.20) Trio £45.30 OWNER Mr John Patrick Barry (PRESTON) BRED Warren W. Rosenthal 8 Rn 61.86 secs (1.86) SF: 47/33/50/35/42/48/20/29
WEIGHT FOR AGE 3yo-6lb

2431 E.B.F. MAIDEN STKS (2-Y.O) (Class D) £4,198.00 (£1,264.00: £612.00: £286.00)
5f 16y Stalls: Low GOING minus 0.26 sec per fur (GF) 3-50 (3-51)

1685⁶ **Admiral Jones (IRE)** *(79+) (MJohnston)* 2-9-0 TWilliams(1) (led after 1f: qcknd clr ent fnl f: unchal) — **1**
2128² Clan Chief *(60)*(Fav)*(JRArnold)* 2-9-0 RCochrane(5) (b.hind: prom: rdn & effrt ent st: r.o one pce) 6 **2**
2143⁵ Chemcast *(51) (BJMeehan)* 2-9-0 BDoyle(3) (led 1f: prom tl rdn & outpcd over 1f out) 3 **3**
2146⁷ L A Touch *(45) (JohnBerry)* 2-8-9 CDwyer(2) (chsd ldrs over 3f: sn outpcd) nk **4**
1899⁴ Maysimp (IRE) *(39) (BPJBaugh)* 2-8-9 ACulhane(6) (b.nr hind: s.i.s: a bhd) 1¾ **5**
2221⁶ Magic Lake *(38) (WJHaggas)* 2-8-9 BThomson(7) (b.off hind: effrt over 2f out: sn rdn: no imp) nk **6**
1758⁸ Lawnswood Captain (IRE) *(21) (RHollinshead)* 2-9-0 MWigham(4) (s.i.s: a bhd & outpcd: t.o) 7 **7**

Evens Clan Chief, **7/2** Magic Lake, **11/2** ADMIRAL JONES (IRE), **9/1** Chemcast, **20/1** L A Touch, **25/1** Lawnswood Captain (IRE), **33/1** Maysimp (IRE), CSF £10.58 TOTE £5.20: £2.30 £1.40 (£3.40) OWNER E H Jones (Paints) Ltd (MIDDLEHAM) BRED Sheikh Mohammed Bin Rashid Al Maktoum 7 Rn 62.19 secs (2.19) SF: 40/21/12/6/-/-/-

2432

RETAIL ADVERTISING SERVICES CONDITIONS STKS (2-Y.O) (Class C) £4,710.00 (£1,710.00: £830.00: £350.00: £150.00)
6f 18y Stalls: Low GOING minus 0.26 sec per fur (GF) 4-20 (4-21)

1592* **Depreciate** *(82)*(Fav)*(CJames)* 2-9-0 RCochrane(1) (mde all: hrd rdn fnl f: hld on wl)........— 1
2000* Amaniy (USA) *(77+) (HThomsonJones)* 2-8-9 BThomson(2) (lw: hld up: n.m.r over 1f out: swtchd rt & r.o wl fnl f: unlucky)........hd 2
1608³ Double Point (IRE) *(78) (MBell)* 2-9-0 WNewnes(4) (prom: pushed along 2f out: kpt on ins fnl f)........1¼ 3
2223* Myttons Mistake *(74)*(Fav)*(ABailey)* 2-9-6 MWigham(5) (swtg: chsd ldrs: effrt on outside ent st: sn rdn & outpcd)........4 4
Lagan *(25) (CEBrittain)* 2-8-10 BDoyle(3) (cmpt: bkwd: s.s: a bhd & outpcd: t.o)........15 5

11/4 DEPRECIATE, Myttons Mistake, **3/1** Amaniy (USA), Double Point (IRE), **10/1** Lagan, CSF £10.60 TOTE £3.20: £1.40 £1.80 (£5.80) OWNER Mr V. R. Bedley (NEWBURY) BRED V. R. Bedley 5 Rn
1m 15.33 (2.03) SF: 49/44/45/41/-

2433

CHESHIRE YEOMANRY H'CAP (0-80) (3-Y.O+) (Class D) £7,200.00 (£2,160.00: £1,040.00: £480.00)
1m 2f 75y Stalls: High GOING minus 0.26 sec per fur (GF) 4-50 (4-50)

1825* **Jameel Asmar (68)***(86+) (CREgerton)* 3-8-11 BThomson(3) (lw: hld up: hdwy 4f out: 2nd st: rdn to ld ins fnl f: sn clr)........— 1
Boloardo **(67)***(74) (CEBrittain)* 6-9-7 BDoyle(2) (bit bkwd: chsd ldrs: 4th & rdn st: kpt on ins fnl f)........7 2
2395² Red Valerian **(71)***(78) (KMcAuliffe)* 4-9-11b RCochrane(4) (hld up: hdwy over 4f out: 3rd st: one pce)........hd 3
2298³ Plinth **(56)***(60) (NAGraham)* 4-8-10v MRimmer(7) (led: qcknd clr ½-wy: wknd & ct last 200y) 1¾ 4
2002⁷ Kings Cay (IRE) **(64)***(63) (THCaldwell)* 4-9-4 ACulhane(5) (hld up in rr: effrt & 6th st: nvr nr ldrs)........3½ 5
980⁹ Tidal Reach (USA) **(65)***(61) (ABailey)* 3-8-8 MWigham(8) (prom tl 5th & btn ent st)........1¾ 6
*592*¹⁰ Divertimiento **(57)***(45) (JMackie)* 4-8-11 WNewnes(1) (bkwd: chsd ldrs 7f: sn lost tch)........5 7
1995* Master Ofthe House **(62)***(47)*(Fav)*(MDHammond)* 9-9-2 JMarshall(9) (lw: a bhd)........2 8
2123⁴ Jubran (USA) **(67)***(50) (MJohnston)* 9-9-4 (3) AGarth(6) (lw: dwlt: sn prom: chsd ldr over 6f out: sn rdn & wknd: t.o)........1½ 9

5/2 Master Ofthe House, **3/1** JAMEEL ASMAR, **5/1** Plinth, Jubran (USA), **6/1** Red Valerian (op 4/1), **9/1** Tidal Reach (USA), **14/1** Boloardo, **20/1** Kings Cay (IRE), **33/1** Divertimiento, CSF £41.32 CT £226.16 TOTE £3.40: £1.60 £3.00 £2.20 (£31.50) Trio £102.00 OWNER Mr Abdul Rahman Mubarak (CHADDLEWORTH) BRED Kirtlington Stud Ltd 9 Rn
2m 11.9 (3.20) SF: 50/49/53/35/38/25/20/22/25
WEIGHT FOR AGE 3yo-11lb
T/Plpt: £182.90 (91.6 Tckts). T/Qdpt: £28.40 (15.55 Tckts). IM

2402-LINGFIELD (L-H)
Saturday July 15th (Good to firm)

WEATHER: overcast WIND: mod half across

2434

SURREY CONDITIONS STKS (2-Y.O) (Class D) £4,012.50 (£1,200.00: £575.00: £262.50) **7f** Stalls: Centre GOING minus 0.54 sec per fur (F) 2-30 (2-30)

2183⁴ **Opera** *(69)*(Fav)*(WJarvis)* 2-7-13 (7) MHenry(2) (a.p: led over 1f out: r.o)........— 1
2059³ Dankeston (USA) *(76) (MBell)* 2-9-1v DHarrison(3) (lw: led: hdd over 1f out: rdn & one pce fnl f)........¾ 2
2182³ Proper Blue (USA) *(72) (TGMills)* 2-8-4 (7) JCornally(1) (a.p: ev ch over 1f out: rdn & one pce fnl f)........hd 3
1751⁵ Oscar Rose *(56) (LordHuntingdon)* 2-8-11 AMcGlone(4) (bhd fnl 3f)........7 4
2034⁴ Gallante *(56) (PFICole)* 2-8-11 AClark(5) (prom over 4f)........hd 5
1184¹⁵ Master Lynx (USA) *(48) (GLewis)* 2-8-11 SWhitworth(7) (a bhd)........3½ 6
2315¹¹ Midas Gold *(43) (BJMeehan)* 2-8-8 (3) SSanders(6) (a bhd)........2 7

9/4 OPERA, **5/2** Dankeston (USA), **3/1** Proper Blue (USA), **6/1** Gallante, **12/1** Master Lynx (USA), **16/1** Oscar Rose, **33/1** Midas Gold, CSF £8.09 TOTE £3.10: £1.80 £1.40 (£3.20) OWNER Mrs Doris Allen (NEWMARKET) BRED Stowell Hill Ltd 7 Rn
1m 23.43 (2.83) SF: 11/18/14/-/-/-/-
STEWARDS' ENQUIRY Harrison susp 24-29/7/95 (using whip with unreasonable force).

2435

DAILY MAIL CLASSIFIED NURSERY H'CAP (2-Y.O) (Class C)
£5,677.50 (£1,695.00: £810.00: £367.50)
6f Stalls: Centre GOING minus 0.54 sec per fur (F) 3-00 (3-06)

2242⁴ **Bedside Mail** *(75) (JMPEustace)* 2-9-7 MTebbutt(5) (hld up: hdwy 2f out: led wl ins fnl f: r.o) .... — 1
1810⁶ Don't Tell Vicki *(46) (JSMoore)* 2-7-2 (5) MBaird(6) (led: rdn over 1f out: hdd wl ins fnl f: unable qckn) .... nk 2
1715⁸ Castan (IRE) *(65) (JLDunlop)* 2-9-0 GCarter(2) (hld up: hdwy 2f out: ev ch ins fnl f: unable qckn) .... ¾ 3
2192² Eights High (USA) *(60)*(Fav)*(RHannon)* 2-8-8 (7) DaneO'Neill(1) (lw: a.p: ev ch ins fnl f: one pce) 2½ 4
1259⁶ Lussuria (IRE) *(48) (BJMeehan)* 2-9-0 DHarrison(3) (prom to ½-wy) 4 5
1772⁴ Hoh Majestic (IRE) *(MBell)* 2-8-10b(7) GFaulkner(4) (Withdrawn not under Starter's orders: got loose on wy to s) .... W

11/8 Eights High (USA), **2/1** BEDSIDE MAIL, **4/1** Castan (IRE), **11/2** Hoh Majestic (IRE), **15/2** Lussuria (IRE), Don't Tell Vicki, CSF £14.98 TOTE £3.50: £2.00 £1.40 (£7.10) OWNER Mr Gary Coull (NEWMARKET) BRED R. G. Percival and Miss S. M. Rhodes 5 Rn
1m 9.96 (0.96) SF: 44/-/29/17/34/15

2436

SATURDAY SILVER TROPHY RATED STKS H'CAP (0-105) (Listed) (3-Y.O+) (Class A) £11,456.64 (£4,289.76: £2,099.88: £905.40: £407.70: £208.62)
7f 140y Stalls: Centre GOING minus 0.54 sec per fur (F) 3-30 (3-36)

1618⁷ **Moccasin Run (USA) (100)***(107) (IABalding)* 4-9-2 DGriffiths(10) (swtg: hld up: hdwy over 2f out: led ins fnl f: r.o) .... — 1
Wizard King **(105)***(110) (SirMarkPrescott)* 4-9-7 JLowe(8) (lw: a.p: rdn & ev ch wl ins fnl f: unable qckn) 1 2
2235² Croft Valley **(94)***(99) (RAkehurst)* 8-8-10 SSanders(2) (led: hdd ins fnl f: unable qckn) .... s.h 3
1923² Royal Rebuke **(93)***(97) (RCharlton)* 3-8-0 DHarrison(9) (hld up: hdwy 2f out: rdn over 1f out: r.o one pce fnl f) .... ½ 4
2205⁴ Maid for Walking **(100)***(103) (DRLoder)* 3-8-7 MTebbutt(11) (hld up: hdwy 2f out: ev ch ins fnl f: unable qckn) .... ½ 5
1839* Medaille Militaire **(94)***(93)*(Fav)*(JLDunlop)* 3-8-1 GCarter(7) (chsd ldrs: rdn over 2f out: r.o one pce fnl f) 2 6
1895¹⁹ Everglades (IRE) **(105)***(103) (RCharlton)* 7-9-7 SRaymont(6) (nvr nrr) .... nk 7
2369⁷ Celestial Key (USA) **(102)***(96) (MJohnston)* 5-9-4 AMcGlone(3) (chsd ldrs: rdn over 2f out: wknd fnl f) 2 8
1261¹⁴ Zifta (USA) **(91)***(70) (SCWilliams)* 4-8-7 AMackay(4) (prom 5f) 7 9
2235³ Pinkerton's Pal **(94)***(65) (CEBrittain)* 4-8-10 RPrice(1) (b: prom 5f) 4 10
2030⁴ Prussian Flag **(96)***(54) (RHannon)* 3-8-3 AClark(5) (a bhd) 6 11

LONG HANDICAP Zifta (USA) 7-12

3/1 Medaille Militaire (op 2/1), **7/2** Royal Rebuke, **5/1** Wizard King, **6/1** Celestial Key (USA), **13/2** Croft Valley, **14/1** Everglades (IRE), Maid for Walking, Pinkerton's Pal (8/1-16/1), **16/1** Prussian Flag, **25/1** MOCCASIN RUN (USA), **33/1** Zifta (USA), CSF £139.71 CT £848.20 TOTE £36.90: £6.60 £2.40 £2.20 (£90.00) Trio £356.60 OWNER Mr George Strawbridge (KINGSCLERE) BRED Jayeff B Stables 11 Rn
1m 27.15 (-0.85) SF: 63/66/55/44/50/40/59/52/26/21/1
WEIGHT FOR AGE 3yo-9lb

OFFICIAL EXPLANATION **Moccasin Run: had run too freely in blinkers on his previous run and his improvement was due to being held up this time.**

2437

ROTHMANS ROYALS NORTH SOUTH CHALLENGE SERIES H'CAP (0-90) (3-Y.O) (Class C) £7,375.00 (£2,200.00: £1,050.00: £475.00)
7f Stalls: Centre GOING minus 0.54 sec per fur (F) 4-00 (4-03)

1787⁵ **Muchtarak (IRE) (83)***(89) (CJBenstead)* 3-9-3 AMcGlone(7) (hld up: hdwy over 1f out: led wl ins fnl f: all out) .... — 1
2067⁹ Prima Cominna **(79)***(85) (MBell)* 3-8-13 GCarter(8) (hld up: hdwy over 1f out: str run fnl f: fin wl: jst failed) .... s.h 2
*276** Wild Rice **(78)***(83+)*(Fav)*(GWragg)* 3-8-12 FNorton(2) (a.p: led over 1f out: hdd wl ins fnl f: unable qckn) .... ½ 3
2188³ Concer Un **(61)***(64) (SCWilliams)* 3-7-9 AMackay(5) (led: hdd over 3f out: led over 2f out: hdd over 1f out: one pce) .... ¾ 4
2103⁴ Mister Fire Eyes (IRE) **(73)***(72)*(Fav)*(CEBrittain)* 3-8-7 RPrice(6) (a.p: led over 3f out: hdd over 2f out: one pce) 1¾ 5
2361⁴ The Stager (IRE) **(72)***(68) (JRJenkins)* 3-8-6 MTebbutt(1) (racd far side: prom over 5f) 1¼ 6

2258* Fantasy Racing (IRE) **(75)***(62) (MRChannon)* 3-8-9 AClark(9) (chsd ldrs tl wknd over 1f out) ..4 **7**
1941* Maiandros (GR) **(87)***(60)*(Fav)*(RCharlton)* 3-9-7 DHarrison(3) (hld up: rdn over 2f out: no hdwy)....6 **8**

4/1 Mister Fire Eyes (IRE), Wild Rice (3/1-9/2), Maiandros (GR), **5/1** MUCHTARAK (IRE), Concer Un, **13/2** Fantasy Racing (IRE), **11/1** Prima Cominna (8/1-12/1), **12/1** The Stager (IRE), CSF £52.56 CT £222.72 TOTE £7.80: £1.70 £3.70 £1.80 (£44.40) Trio £189.70 OWNER Mr Hamdan Al Maktoum (EPSOM) BRED E. O'Leary 8 Rn 1m 21.25 (0.65) SF: 46/42/40/21/29/25/19/17

2438

CHAMPAGNE JACQUART MAIDEN STKS (3-Y.O+) (Class D) £4,137.90 (£1,237.20: £592.60: £270.30)
1m 1f Stalls: Centre GOING minus 0.54 sec per fur (F) 4-30 (4-34)

1905[2] **Quandary (USA) (75)***(82)*(Fav)*(HRACecil)* 4-9-2 AMcGlone(6) (lw: chsd ldr: 2nd st: led 2f out: comf)....— **1**
2100[2] Balasara (IRE) **(80)***(81) (DRCElsworth)* 5-9-2 (5) AProcter(10) (lw: led: hdd 2f out: one pce)..3½ **2**
Poddington *(80) (RAkehurst)* 4-9-7 DHarrison(2) (unf: dwlt: sn rcvd: 3rd st: ev ch 2f out: one pce)....½ **3**
2151[4] Tappeto *(64) (HCandy)* 3-8-11 NAdams(1) (chsd ldrs: 5th st: sn rdn: no hdwy fnl 2f)....9 **4**
1927[5] Cavil *(62) (CEBrittain)* 3-8-11 AMackay(5) (7th st: rdn 3f out: nvr nrr)....1¼ **5**
Freddie Baloo *(49) (RTPhillips)* 3-8-11 GCarter(9) (bit bkwd: nvr nrr)....7 **6**
1905[6] RaincheckA *(42) (MarkCampion)* 4-9-7 SRaymont(4) (chsd ldrs: 6th st: sn wknd)....4 **7**
Fastini Gold *(41) (MDIUsher)* 3-8-11 RPrice(8) (unf: chsd ldrs: 4th st: edgd lft & wknd over 1f out)....¾ **8**
2134[9] Dirty Dancer *(27) (MMadgwick)* 6-9-7v CAvery(7) (dwlt: a bhd)....8 **9**
Ilium Bourbon *(RJO'Sullivan)* 3-8-6 AClark(3) (leggy: unf: dwlt: a bhd)....20 **10**

13/8 QUANDARY (USA) (7/4-11/4), **7/4** Balasara (IRE) (3/1-2/1), **6/1** Cavil (tchd 10/1), **7/1** Tappeto (4/1-8/1), **16./1** Poddington, **20/1** RaincheckA, Fastini Gold, Ilium Bourbon, **50/1** Freddie Baloo, Dirty Dancer, CSF £5.13 TOTE £2.10: £1.10 £1.20 £2.40 (£2.20) Trio £15.80 OWNER K.Abdullah (NEWMARKET) BRED Juddmonte Farms 10 Rn 1m 52.4 (0.60 under best) (3.10) SF: 28/27/26/-/-/-/-/-
WEIGHT FOR AGE 3yo-10lb

2439

REIGATE H'CAP (0-65) (3-Y.O+) (Class F) £3,451.40 (£960.40: £462.20)
1m 6f Stalls: Centre GOING minus 0.54 sec per fur (F) 5-00 (5-02)

1622[10] **Persian Smoke (35)***(50) (AHide)* 4-7-10 (7) MHenry(3) (chsd ldrs: led over 6f out: rdn 2f out: r.o wl)....— **1**
277[9] Disputed Call (USA) **(35)***(47) (JFfitch-Heyes)* 6-8-3 RPrice(13) (hdwy over 4f out: 3rd st: ev ch 2f out: one pce)....3 **2**
1937[2] Santella Boy (USA) **(57)***(69) (GHarwood)* 3-8-10 AClark(1) (a.p: 4th st: rdn 2f out: one pce).s.h **3**
2052[5] Bowcliffe **(56)***(66) (JTGifford)* 4-9-10 DHarrison(5) (hdwy over 4f out: 6th st: rdn over 2f out: r.o one pce)....1 **4**
2007[5] Rocquaine Bay **(35)***(37) (MJBolton)* 8-8-3 AMcGlone(12) (nvr nrr)....7 **5**
2201[2] Wild Strawberry **(60)***(62)*(Fav)*(MissBSanders)* 6-9-7 (7) DaneO'Neill(15) (prom: 2nd st: rdn over 2f out: grad wknd)....hd **6**
2177[5] Stormaway (ITY) **(54)***(52) (TGMills)* 3-8-7 AMackay(16) (a mid div)....3½ **7**
2050[4] One Off the Rail (USA) **(42)***(38) (AMoore)* 5-8-10 CandyMorris(11) (chsd ldrs: 5th st: wknd over 2f out)....2 **8**
2172[3] Courbaril **(60)***(55) (SDow)* 3-8-6 (7) ADaly(10) (a mid div)....½ **9**
2175[5] Brunswick Blue (IRE) **(25)***(16) (RMFlower)* 7-7-2b(5) MBaird(8) (prom tl wknd 4f out)....3½ **10**
2268[13] Jarzon Dancer **(30)***(11) (DAWilson)* 7-7-5 (7) RachaelMoody(7) (s.i.s: a bhd)....9 **11**
1940[12] Coalisland **(25)***(3) (RIngram)* 5-7-7 NAdams(9) (a bhd)....3 **12**
1694[9] Wildfire (SWI) **(47)***(25) (RAkehurst)* 4-8-12 (3) SSanders(14) (prom: led 7f out: sn hdd: wknd 4f out)....s.h **13**
1166[7] Brandonhurst **(59)***(33) (LadyHerries)* 5-9-13 GCarter(2) (dwlt: a bhd)....3½ **14**
1319[13] Deliffin **(35)** *(RMFlower)* 9-8-3 AMorris(6) (led 7f)....20 **15**
1960* Medway (IRE) **(65)***(8) (MHTompkins)* 3-9-4 SMulvey(4) (bhd fnl 8f)....7 **16**
LONG HANDICAP Brunswick Blue (IRE) 6-13

3/1 Wild Strawberry (tchd 5/1), **4/1** Santella Boy (USA), **11/2** Medway (IRE) (4/1-6/1), Courbaril, **7/1** Rocquaine Bay, **11/1** Wildfire (SWI), **14/1** Bowcliffe, One Off the Rail (USA), Brandonhurst (10/1-16/1), **16/1** Stormaway (ITY), **20/1** Jarzon Dancer, Deliffin, **25/1** Coalisland, PERSIAN SMOKE, **33/1** Disputed Call (USA), **50/1** Brunswick Blue (IRE), CSF £617.56 CT £3,603.40 TOTE £38.10: £7.10 £13.90 £1.80 £4.00 (£1,394.60) Trio not won; £622.92 to Ayr 16/07/95 OWNER Mrs Andrew Normand (NEWMARKET) BRED Brook Stud Ltd 16 Rn
3m 3.2 (0.43 under best) (7.90) SF: 2/-/6/18/-/14/-/-/-/-/-/-/-/-/-/-
WEIGHT FOR AGE 3yo-15lb
T/Plpt: £576.80 (20.18 Tckts). T/Qdpt: £47.20 (3.7 Tckts). SM

2408-**NEWBURY (L-H)**
Saturday July 15th (Good)
WEATHER: overcast WIND: almost nil

2440
DONCASTER BLOODSTOCK SALES ROSE BOWL STKS (Listed) (2-Y.O) (Class A) £11,240.00 (£3,140.00: £1,520.00)
6f 8y Stalls: Centre GOING: 0.24 sec per fur (G) 2-15 (2-16)

1893³ **Polaris Flight (USA)** *(99) (PWChapple-Hyam)* 2-8-11 JReid(2) (lw: b.hind: chsd ldr: led ins fnl f: drvn out)........— **1**
1803* Kahir Almaydan (IRE) *(101)*(Fav)*(JLDunlop)* 2-9-0 WCarson(1) (lw: led tl ins fnl f: r.o)........½ **2**
2058* Kriscliffe *(34) (PTWalwyn)* 2-9-0 JWeaver(3) (cl up tl wknd qckly 2f out)........25 **3**

8/11 Kahir Almaydan (IRE), **6/4** POLARIS FLIGHT (USA), **9/1** Kriscliffe (6/1-10/1), CSF £2.80 TOTE £2.70 (£1.10) OWNER Mr Richard Kaster (MARLBOROUGH) BRED Bill Van Den Dool 3 Rn
1m 15.86 (4.06) SF: 59/61/-

2441
MTOTO DONNINGTON CASTLE CONDITIONS STKS (2-Y.O) (Class B) £8,078.00 (£3,002.00: £1,451.00: £605.00: £252.50: £111.50)
7f (straight) Stalls: Centre GOING: 0.24 sec per fur (G) 2-45 (2-46)

Zelzelah (USA) *(84+) (PAKelleway)* 2-8-4 ow2 JWeaver(7) (lw: lengthy: a gng wl: led 2f out: sn qcknd clr: easily)........— **1**
Axford (USA) *(82+) (PWChapple-Hyam)* 2-8-7 JReid(4) (lw: w'like: scope: hld up: hdwy whn slipped 2f out: r.o wl fnl f)........3 **2**
Tria Kemata *(79+) (JLDunlop)* 2-8-7 WCarson(2) (gd sort: plld hrd: drppd rr 2f out: gd hdwy 5f out: nt qckn fnl f)........1½ **3**
1781* Kilvine *(81)*(Fav)*(LMCumani)* 2-8-13 KDarley(5) (hmpd & drppd rr 2f out: gd hdwy fnl f)........1½ **4**
2183³ Acharne *(78) (CEBrittain)* 2-8-10 MRoberts(8) (a.p: one pce fnl 2f)........hd **5**
1751* Warning Time *(73) (BJMeehan)* 2-8-13 LDettori(1) (spd 5f)........3½ **6**
1903² Warning Reef *(59) (MRChannon)* 2-8-10 PaulEddery(6) (led tl wknd 2f out)........5 **7**

5/2 Kilvine, **3/1** Warning Time (tchd 9/2), **5/1** Axford (USA) (op 5/2), **6/1** ZELZELAH (USA) (7/2-13/2), **7/1** Tria Kemata (op 4/1), **10/1** Warning Reef, **20/1** Acharne, CSF £31.64 TOTE £12.30: £3.40 £3.00 (£34.80) OWNER Mr P. A. Kelleway (NEWMARKET) BRED Polan, Ross and Polan 7 Rn
1m 30.3 (5.80) SF: 40/38/35/37/34/29/15

2442
WEATHERBYS SUPER SPRINT STKS (2-Y.O) (Class B) £71,214.80 (£26,553.20: £12,906.60: £5,463.00: £2,361.50: £1,120.90)
5f 34y Stalls: Centre GOING: 0.24 sec per fur (G) 3-15 (3-18)

1620* **Blue Iris** *(86) (MAJarvis)* 2-8-1 WCarson(16) (a.p: led 2f out: r.o wl)........— **1**
1928⁴ Needham Star (USA) *(76) (PAKelleway)* 2-8-4 ow2 JWeaver(17) (gd hdwy fnl 2f: nt rch wnr) 3½ **2**
940* Ortolan *(81) (RHannon)* 2-8-8 RPerham(11) (hdwy fnl 2f: nrst fin)........nk **3**
1530⁴ Kunucu (IRE) *(71) (TDBarron)* 2-8-3 KDarley(10) (a.p: led over 2f out: sn hdd: nt qckn)........1¾ **4**
1977* Crocodile Shoes *(66) (RHannon)* 2-8-7 JReid(5) (a.p: one pce fnl 2f)........3 **5**
2182⁶ Sylva Paradise (IRE) *(62) (CEBrittain)* 2-8-9 MRoberts(7) (gd hdwy 2f out: nvr nr to chal) ...1¾ **6**
2216a⁵ Amaretto Bay (IRE) *(64) (BJMeehan)* 2-8-12 RHavlin(15) (outpcd: styd on fnl f)........nk **7**
2085* Maggi For Margaret *(42) (MRChannon)* 2-7-13 JFanning(12) (led 3f out: sn hdd: wknd 2f out)........3 **8**
1868⁸ Eastern Prophets *(46) (GLewis)* 2-8-9 PaulEddery(3) (gd spd 4f)........1¾ **9**
1395a⁷ Mystique Smile *(31) (JBerry)* 2-8-1 PFessey(4) (led 2f: wknd 2f out)........2½ **10**
1343⁶ Kustom Kit (IRE) *(37) (BAMcMahon)* 2-8-8 PMcCabe(8) (nvr trbld ldrs)........s.h **11**
1857⁹ Veesey *(30) (JohnBerry)* 2-8-1 NCarlisle(9) (s.s: a bhd)........hd **12**
2029³ Kandavu *(24) (MMcCormack)* 2-7-13 StephenDavies(2) (outpcd)........1½ **13**
2243* Home Shopping *(27) (KMcAuliffe)* 2-8-6 JTate(6) (bhd fnl 2f)........1¼ **14**
1893¹³ Happy Tycoon (IRE) *(14) (MJHeaton-Ellis)* 2-8-6v SDrowne(13) (gd spd over 2f)........4 **15**
1849⁶ Marl *(11)*(Fav)*(RAkehurst)* 2-8-7 LDettori(1) (wl bhd fnl 2f)........1½ **16**
1054¹² Midnight Cookie *(RJHodges)* 2-8-7 AmandaSanders(14) (a wl bhd: t.o)........9 **17**

7/2 Marl, **5/1** Ortolan (op 3/1), Home Shopping, **13/2** BLUE IRIS, **9/1** Crocodile Shoes, **10/1** Maggi For Margaret, **16/1** Kunucu (IRE), Needham Star (USA), Kandavu, Eastern Prophets, **25/1** Amaretto Bay (IRE), **33/1** Mystique Smile, **50/1** Happy Tycoon (IRE), Sylva Paradise (IRE), Kustom Kit (IRE), **100/1** Veesey, Midnight Cookie, CSF £97.28 TOTE £6.40: £2.00 £6.40 £2.20 (£39.00) Trio £185.80 OWNER Mr M. A. Jarvis (NEWMARKET) BRED North Cheshire Trading and Storage Ltd 17 Rn
64.22 secs (3.92) SF: 42/32/37/27/22/18/20/-/2/-/-/-/-/-/-/-/-

OFFICIAL EXPLANATION **Marl: the jockey reported that the filly did not handle the fast ground.**

2443

HACKWOOD STKS (Listed) (3-Y.O+) (Class A) £13,218.00 (£3,984.00: £1,932.00: £906.00) **6f 8y** Stalls: Centre GOING: 0.24 sec per fur (G) 3-50 (3-51)

1100[12] **Hard to Figure (103)***(115) (RJHodges)* 9-9-7 SDrowne(7) (hdwy 2f out: r.o wl fnl f: led last strides) ....— **1**
2097[2] Inzar (USA) **(105)***(111)*(Fav)*(PFICole)* 3-8-10 WCarson(11) (lw: hdwy over 2f out: led wl over 1f out tl fnl strides).......hd **2**
1870[3] Nuriva (USA) **(104)***(102)*(Fav)*(SbinSuroor)* 3-8-5 LDettori(2) (a.p: ev ch 1f out: nt qckn).......1¼ **3**
934[4] Montendre **(106)***(107) (MMcCormack)* 8-9-7 JReid(4) (hdwy & hrd rdn over 1f out: nt rch ldrs) 1½ **4**
1786* Penny Dip *(91) (RFJohnsonHoughton)* 3-8-5 RPerham(3) (a.p: no hdwy fnl 2f).......3 **5**
1488[7] With the Fairies **(96)***(87) (RHannon)* 3-8-5 JWeaver(8) (chsd ldrs tl wknd over 1f out) 1½ **6**
2285[4] Lennox Lewis **(99)***(81) (APJarvis)* 3-8-10 MRoberts(10) (prom 4f) 4 **7**
2285* Bunty Boo **(101)***(77) (RHannon)* 6-9-2 KDarley(1) (led tl wknd wl over 1f out) 1 **8**
Thousla Rock (IRE) **(107)***(81) (PWChapple-Hyam)* 6-9-10 RHavlin(5) (w ldrs tl wknd 2f out) 1¾ **9**
1305* Star Tulip **(99)***(6) (JLDunlop)* 3-8-9 JTate(6) (w ldrs tl wknd qckly 2f out: t.o) 25 **10**

5/2 Inzar (USA), Nuriva (USA), **15/2** Bunty Boo, **8/1** Montendre (6/1-9/1), **10/1** Lennox Lewis, Star Tulip, **12/1** With the Fairies, **16/1** Penny Dip, **25/1** HARD TO FIGURE, Thousla Rock (IRE), CSF £83.36 TOTE £37.30: £6.00 £1.80 £1.40 (£56.00) Trio £96.60 OWNER Mr J. W. Mursell (SOMERTON) BRED J. W. Mursell 10 Rn 1m 14.53 (2.73) SF: 88/77/68/80/57/53/47/50/54/-
WEIGHT FOR AGE 3yo-7lb

2444

STEVENTON STKS (Listed) (3-Y.O+) (Class A) £12,984.00 (£3,912.00: £1,896.00: £888.00) **1m 2f 6y** Stalls: Low GOING: 0.24 sec per fur (G) 4-25 (4-26)

2008[3] **Ihtiram (IRE) (108)***(117)*(Fav)*(JLDunlop)* 3-8-6 WCarson(1) (3rd st: led ins fnl f: drvn out) ...— **1**
2217a[2] Dance Turn **(109)***(116) (RWArmstrong)* 4-9-3 JReid(5) (2nd tl led 4f out: hdd ins fnl f).......½ **2**
1836[6] Ionio (USA) **(110)***(107) (CEBrittain)* 4-9-3 MRoberts(3) (4th st: ev ch over 2f out: sn wknd) 6 **3**
1616[6] Windrush Lady **(70)***(100) (MMcCormack)* 5-8-12 JWeaver(6) (led 6f: wknd 3f out).......1 **4**
1866* King's Crown *(65) (EALDunlop)* 3-8-6 PaulEddery(2) (5th st: wknd 4f out: t.o).......25 **5**

7/4 IHTIRAM (IRE), **11/4** Dance Turn (op 6/4), Ionio (USA), **13/2** King's Crown, **25/1** Windrush Lady, CSF £6.25 TOTE £2.50: £1.70 £1.50 (£2.30) OWNER Mr Hamdan Al Maktoum (ARUNDEL) BRED Kilcarn Stud 5 Rn 2m 8.42 (5.42) SF: 66/76/67/60/14
WEIGHT FOR AGE 3yo-11lb

2445

HANNINGTON H'CAP (0-90) (3-Y.O+) (Class C) £5,832.50 (£1,760.00: £855.00: £402.50) **1m 5f 61y** Stalls: Low GOING: 0.24 sec per fur (G) 4-55 (4-57)

1872[11] **Celeric (83)***(97) (DMorley)* 3-8-8 LDettori(6) (4th st: hrd rdn over 1f out: led last strides) ......— **1**
2197* Shaft of Light **(77)***(91)*(Fav)*(LordHuntingdon)* 3-8-2 MRoberts(7) (2nd st: led over 2f out tl fnl strides).......hd **2**
1691* Ahla **(85)***(95) (RWArmstrong)* 3-8-10 WCarson(1) (led tl over 2f out: r.o one pce).......3 **3**
1410[3] Bit on the Side (IRE) **(72)***(81) (WJMusson)* 6-8-8 (3) PMcCabe(4) (hdwy on ins & 3rd st: rdn over 1f out: nt qckn) ....¾ **4**
1794[6] Pembridge Place **(73)***(78) (JLDunlop)* 4-8-12 JWeaver(2) (7th st: nvr plcd to chal).......4 **5**
2293[2] Tovarich **(60)***(60) (GLewis)* 4-7-13 StephenDavies(3) (6th st: rdn 2f out: no hdwy).......3½ **6**
1716[2] Warm Spell **(76)***(76) (GLMoore)* 5-9-1 SWhitworth(9) (5th st: wknd 2f out) ....hd **7**
2289[10] Tondres (USA) **(67)***(65) (RIngram)* 4-8-3b(3) SDrowne(5) (8th st: sme hdwy over 2f out: sn wknd).......1¾ **8**

3/1 Shaft of Light, **100/30** CELERIC, **5/1** Warm Spell (7/2-11/2), **11/2** Ahla, **7/1** Pembridge Place, Bit on the Side (IRE) (op 9/2), **12/1** Tovarich (op 8/1), **33/1** Tondres (USA), CSF £13.17 CT £47.46 TOTE £4.00: £1.60 £1.40 £1.90 (£5.60) Trio £6.70 OWNER Mr Christopher Spence (NEWMARKET) BRED Chieveley Manor Enterprises 8 Rn 2m 56.59 (11.29) SF: 44/38/42/42/39/21/37/26
WEIGHT FOR AGE 3yo-14lb

2446

LEVY BOARD SEVENTH RACE H'CAP (0-90) (3-Y.O+) (Class C) £5,832.50 (£1,760.00: £855.00: £402.50)
1m (straight) Stalls: Centre GOING: 0.24 sec per fur (G) 5-25 (5-27)

1851[13] **Show Faith (IRE) (81)***(90) (RHannon)* 5-9-8 LDettori(8) (hdwy 2f out: hrd rdn fnl f: led last strides) ....— **1**
2266* Lord Oberon (IRE) **(56)***(65) (JAkehurst)* 7-7-11 JFanning(6) (hdwy 2f out: led cl home tl fnl strides).......hd **2**

2240* Night Dance **(81)***(89)*(Fav)*(GLewis)* 3-8-8 (5) AWhelan(5) (hdwy 3f out: led over 1f out tl nr fin) ....½ **3**
1839[29] Amrak Ajeeb (IRE) **(80)***(85) (BHanbury)* 3-8-12 MRoberts(4) (hdwy over 2f out: ev ch over 1f out: nt qckn) 1¼ **4**
1476[7] Never Explain (IRE) **(83)***(85) (JLDunlop)* 3-9-1 JWeaver(2) (led: hdd & lost pl over 3f out: r.o fnl f) 1½ **5**
1365[4] Thabit (USA) **(85)***(77) (PTWalwyn)* 4-9-12 WCarson(7) (led over 3f out tl wknd over 1f out) 5 **6**
Dowsong **(67)***(56) (RAkehurst)* 4-8-8 RPerham(1) (w ldrs tl wknd over 1f out) 1½ **7**
1626[5] Nashaat (USA) **(68)***(17) (NJHWalker)* 7-8-6 (3) JTate(3) (t.o fnl 2f) 20 **8**

5/2 Night Dance, **9/2** Lord Oberon (IRE), **5/1** SHOW FAITH (IRE), **11/2** Thabit (USA) (3/1-6/1), **15/2** Amrak Ajeeb (IRE), **9/1** Nashaat (USA), **12/1** Never Explain (IRE) (8/1-14/1), **20/1** Dowsong, CSF £25.21 CT £61.29 TOTE £5.30: £1.60 £1.70 £1.50 (£10.70) OWNER Mr I. A. N. Wight (MARLBOROUGH) BRED M. J. Cassidy 8 Rn 1m 42.68 (5.68) SF: 67/42/57/53/53/54/33/-
WEIGHT FOR AGE 3yo-9lb

T/Jkpt: Not won; £10,578.30 to Ayr 16/07/95. T/Plpt: £105.20 (241.29 Tckts). T/Qdpt: £8.00 (45.7 Tckts). Hn

2245-WARWICK (L-H)
Saturday July 15th (Good to firm)

WEATHER: fair WIND: slt half bhd

2447 'WHEREFORE ART THOU' MAIDEN AUCTION STKS (2-Y.O F) (Class F)
£2,796.20 (£773.20: £368.60)
7f Stalls: Low GOING minus 0.21 sec per fur (GF) 6-40 (6-40)

1798[2] **Sound Check** *(62+)*(Fav)*(BJMeehan)* 2-8-2 NCarlisle(5) (mde all: qcknd clr 2f out: eased cl home) ....— **1**
2025[9] Zdenka *(60) (MBlanshard)* 2-8-2 StephenDavies(7) (hld up: wnt 3rd st: chsd wnr over 1f out: rdn & edgd lft ins fnl f: r.o wl) ....¾ **2**
2198[9] Classic Daisy *(49) (MissGayKelleway)* 2-8-2 GBardwell(6) (b.hind: hld up: rdn & 5th st: hdwy over 1f out: one pce fnl f) 5 **3**
1671[6] Brave Maisie (IRE) *(45) (MMcCormack)* 2-7-12 RStreet(2) (s.s: last st: hdwy over 1f out: one pce fnl f) ....s.h **4**
Lavender Della (IRE) *(41) (MJFetherston-Godley)* 2-8-2 FNorton(1) (cmpt: bkwd: chsd wnr 3f out: 2nd st: wknd over 1f out) 3½ **5**
2161[10] Scenic Air *(34) (EWeymes)* 2-8-2 GHind(3) (plld hrd: 4th st: wknd 2f out) 3 **6**
2195[3] Marmy *(30) (MHEasterby)* 2-8-2 SMaloney(4) (6th & rdn st: wknd 2f out) 1¾ **7**

7/4 SOUND CHECK, **2/1** Marmy, **7/1** Zdenka, Classic Daisy, **9/1** Scenic Air, **10/1** Brave Maisie (IRE), **16/1** Lavender Della (IRE), CSF £14.05 TOTE £2.40: £1.60 £3.20 (£12.80) OWNER Theobalds Stud (UPPER LAMBOURN) BRED Theobalds Stud 7 Rn 1m 28.5 (4.30) SF: 19/17/6/2

2448 PAUL SMITH BENEFIT YEAR H'CAP (0-70) (3-Y.O+) (Class E)
£3,318.75 (£990.00: £472.50: £213.75)
6f Stalls: Low GOING minus 0.21 sec per fur (GF) 7-10 (7-11)

2194[4] **Bargash (65)***(77)*(Fav)*(PDEvans)* 3-9-5 JFortune(7) (hld up: hdwy & 5th st: edgd lft 1f out: led ins fnl f: drvn out) ....— **1**
1832[11] Rambold **(62)***(70) (NEBerry)* 4-9-4 (5) RPainter(4) (led over 4f out: qcknd clr 2f out: hrd rdn over 1f out: hdd ins fnl f) 1½ **2**
2148[7] Exclusive Assembly **(47)***(54) (APJames)* 3-8-1 FNorton(2) (3rd st: r.o one pce fnl f) ....nk **3**
2301[4] Pearl Dawn (IRE) **(60)***(66) (NoelChance)* 5-9-7 TSprake(1) (hld up: bmpd & 4th st: r.o one pce fnl f) ....nk **4**
2009[5] Face the Future **(63)***(63) (LJHolt)* 6-9-3 (7) IonaWands(8) (hld up: last st: hdwy on ins 2f out: one pce appr fnl f) 2½ **5**
2137[11] Norling (IRE) **(52)***(30) (KOCunningham-Brown)* 5-8-13 JWeaver(6) (led over 1f: 2nd st: wknd over 1f out) 8 **6**
1882[7] Gallant Spirit (IRE) **(56)***(30) (RJHodges)* 4-8-10 (7) AmandaSanders(5) (7th st: a bhd) 1¾ **7**
2137[5] Petraco (IRE) **(63)***(33) (NASmith)* 7-9-3 (7) JCornally(3) (6th st: bhd fnl 2f) 1¼ **8**

7/4 BARGASH, **7/2** Face the Future, **4/1** Petraco (IRE) (3/1-9/2), **9/1** Pearl Dawn (IRE) (op 6/1), **10/1** Norling (IRE) (op 5/1), **11/1** Rambold (8/1-14/1), **12/1** Gallant Spirit (IRE) (op 7/1), **16/1** Exclusive Assembly, CSF £20.01 CT £219.85 TOTE £3.70: £1.50 £3.00 £2.80 (£14.70) OWNER Mr John Pugh (WELSHPOOL) BRED Trafalgar Bloodstock and R. West 8 Rn
1m 14.5 (2.50) SF: 51/51/28/47/44/11/11/14
WEIGHT FOR AGE 3yo-7lb

2449

DERMOT REEVE MAIDEN STKS (3-Y.O+ F & M) (Class D) £4,104.10 (£1,226.80: £587.40: £267.70)
1m Stalls: Low GOING minus 0.21 sec per fur (GF) 7-40 (7-41)

1195^{4} **Celtic Fringe** *(86+)*(Fav)*(HRACecil)* 3-8-8 WRyan(1) (mde all: clr wl over 1f out: easily) ......— 1
950^{8} Cyphell (IRE) *(78) (MRStoute)* 3-8-8 DHarrison(3) (dwlt: plld hrd: sn prom: wnt 2nd st: no imp)........................4 2
1736^{12} Incha *(70) (HThomsonJones)* 3-8-8 NCarlisle(4) (hld up & plld hrd: hdwy & 4th st: wknd wl over 1f out) 4 3
1053^{6} Great Tern *(58) (NMBabbage)* 3-8-8 BDoyle(2) (chsd wnr tl 3rd st: wknd 2f out) 6 4
Woodlands Energy *(42) (PAPritchard)* 4-9-3 NAdams(6) (lt-f: 5th & rdn st: wknd 2f out)..........8 5
1905^{7} Gabriel's Lady *(30) (MarkCampion)* 4-9-3 JWilliams(5) (prom tl lost pl & 6th st)........................6 6

4/5 CELTIC FRINGE, **11/4** Incha, **3/1** Cyphell (IRE) (2/1-100/30), **33/1** Great Tern, **50/1** Gabriel's Lady, **66/1** Woodlands Energy, CSF £3.63 TOTE £1.60: £1.40 £2.10 (£2.00) OWNER Lord Howard de Walden (NEWMARKET) BRED Lord Howard de Walden 6 Rn 1m 40.8 (3.80) SF: 36/28/20/8/1/-
WEIGHT FOR AGE 3yo-9lb

2450

BOTTOM (S) H'CAP (0-60) (3-Y.O+) (Class G) £2,243.00 (£618.00: £293.00)
1m 2f 169y Stalls: Low GOING minus 0.21 sec per fur (GF) 8-10 (8-13)

2246^{8} **Deceit the Second (38)***(47) (GLewis)* 3-7-8b NAdams(1) (hmpd & dropped rr after s: gd hdwy on ins 4f out: 3rd st: led over 1f out: r.o wl) ....— 1
2110^{3} Suile Mor **(53)***(59) (BRMillman)* 3-8-9 JWilliams(3) (a.p: led over 3f out tl over 1f out: nt qckn) 2 2
1771^{13} Wharfedale Music **(30)***(36) (MCPipe)* 4-7-12 FNorton(7) (hld up: hdwy over 4f out: 6th st: r.o one pce fnl f)........................nk 3
Becky Boo **(25)***(25) (MrsLAMurphy)* 5-7-7 GBardwell(6) (hdwy 2f out: one pce fnl f) 4 4
2314^{7} Sinclair Lad (IRE) **(40)***(40)*(Fav)*(RJHodges)* 7-8-5b(3) SDrowne(18) (hld up & bhd: hdwy 4f out: 5th st: one pce fnl 2f) ....s.h 5
2332^{8} Hunza Story **(43)***(33) (NPLittmoden)* 3-7-6 (7)ow6 MHenry(4) (7th st: no hdwy fnl 2f)...............2½ 6
1759^{7} Ann Hill (IRE) **(35)***(25) (RHollinshead)* 5-7-10 (7)ow1 AEddery(10) (lw: bhd tl hdwy 3f out: nvr nr to chal) 3 7
2140^{11} Alpine Storm (IRE) **(40)***(28) (MDIUsher)* 3-7-3b(7) CAdamson(16) (nvr nrr)........................2½ 8
2377^{13} Swinging Tich **(43)***(16) (ALForbes)* 6-8-6 (5) LNewton(11) (lw: n.d) 10 9
1950^{4} Mr Moriarty (IRE) **(25)** *(SRBowring)* 4-7-7b NCarlisle(8) (6th st: wknd 2f out) ....hd 10
2291^{11} Pats Folly **(25)** *(FJYardley)* 4-7-2 (5) MBaird(5) (led tl hdd over 3f out: 2nd st: wknd qckly 2f out)........................¾ 11
1902^{5} Club Elite **(37)***(3) (MFBarraclough)* 3-7-0 (7) RMullen(17) (prom 6f)........................3½ 12
415^{8} Coven Moon **(35)** *(DMorris)* 5-8-3 DHarrison(12) (bhd fnl 4f)........................2 13
1971^{4} Jehol **(60)***(13) (NMBabbage)* 9-10-0 BDoyle(15) (prom over 6f) 7 14
2248^{6} Belgran (USA) **(36)** *(WMBrisbourne)* 6-8-4 GCarter(14) (a bhd) ....nk 15
1974^{17} Them Times (IRE) **(30)** *(FJordan)* 6-7-5 (7)ow5 SLanigan(9) (lw: prom tl 8th & wkng st)..........3½ 16
1745^{16} Grand Salt (IRE) **(46)** *(MJHaynes)* 4-8-7 (7) DaneO'Neill(13) (prom tl wknd qckly over 4f out: t.o) 30 17

LONG HANDICAP Mr Moriarty (IRE) 7-6 Becky Boo 7-5 Pats Folly 7-4 Hunza Story 7-5 Them Times (IRE) 7-1 Club Elite 7-2

4/1 Sinclair Lad (IRE), **7/1** DECEIT THE SECOND, Suile Mor, **8/1** Belgran (USA) (op 12/1), Ann Hill (IRE), Mr Moriarty (IRE), **9/1** Jehol, **10/1** Coven Moon, **14/1** Swinging Tich, Wharfedale Music, **16/1** Hunza Story, **20/1** Alpine Storm (IRE), Becky Boo, Grand Salt (IRE), **33/1** Pats Folly, Them Times (IRE), Club Elite, CSF £57.77 CT £634.74 TOTE £9.60: £2.00 £2.90 £4.30 £4.00 (343.10) Trio £284.80 OWNER Mr N. Bedack (EPSOM) 17 Rn 2m 19.8 (6.30) SF: 16/28/17/6/21/2/6/-/-/-/-/-/-/-/-/-/-
WEIGHT FOR AGE 3yo-12lb
Bt in 10,200 gns.

2451

'ALAS! POOR YORICK' H'CAP (0-80) (3-Y.O F) (Class D) £4,036.50 (£1,206.00: £577.00: £262.50)
7f Stalls: Low GOING minus 0.21 sec per fur (GF) 8-40 (8-44)

1787^{7} **Linger (65)***(73+) (LordHuntingdon)* 3-8-6 JWeaver(6) (5th st: hdwy over 1f out: led wl ins fnl f: r.o wl) ....— 1
1603^{2} Grey Again **(55)***(60)*(Fav)*(SRBowring)* 3-7-10b TWilliams(7) (4th st: hdwy over 1f out: ev ch ins fnl f: nt qckn)........................1¼ 2
2033^{2} Never so Rite (IRE) **(61)***(66) (DWPArbuthnot)* 3-8-2 FNorton(5) (3rd st: hdwy on ins to ld 1f out: hdd wl ins fnl f)........................nk 3
2067^{3} Tart and a Half **(80)***(83) (BJMeehan)* 3-9-7b BDoyle(2) (led: hrd rdn & hdd 1f out: nt qckn wl ins fnl f)........................½ 4
2266^{6} Sylvandra **(70)***(68) (PGMurphy)* 3-8-11 JWilliams(3) (6th st: nvr nr to chal) 2½ 5

1831⁹ Nosirrah **(52)**_(38) (CAHorgan)_ 3-7-7 NAdams(4) (w ldr: rdn & 2nd st: wknd over 1f out)...........5 **6**
2088W Anytime Baby **(52)**_(4) (PTDalton)_ 3-7-7 NCarlisle(1) (stdd s: last st: a bhd: t.o)......................15 **7**
LONG HANDICAP Nosirrah 7-0 Anytime Baby 7-1

5/2 Grey Again, **11/4** Never so Rite (IRE), **7/2** Sylvandra, **9/2** Tart and a Half, **8/1** LINGER (6/1-9/1), **14/1** Nosirrah (op 8/1), **25/1** Anytime Baby, CSF £27.53 TOTE £9.50: £3.80 £1.50 (£19.30) OWNER Lord Carnarvon (WEST ILSLEY) BRED Highclere Stud Ltd 7 Rn
1m 27.1 (2.90) SF: 39/26/32/49/34/4/-
STEWARDS' ENQUIRY Doyle suspended 25-26/7/95 (excessive use of whip).

2452

CALIBAN H'CAP (0-70) (3-Y.O+) (Class E) £3,435.75 (£1,026.00:£490.50: £222.75)
1m 6f 194y Stalls: Low GOING minus 0.21 sec per fur (GF) 9-10 (9-12)

2201* **Trazl (IRE) (68)**_(87+)_(Fav)_(JLDunlop)_ 3-9-6 GCarter(5) (lw: a.p: led 4f out: clr 2f out: easily)—- **1**
2175* Stately Home (IRE) **(52)**_(66) (BRMillman)_ 4-9-1 (5) AWhelan(6) (s.s: plld hrd: rdn & hdwy over 3f out: 3rd st: chsd wnr fnl 2f: no imp)..........5 **2**
2201⁴ Wannaplantatree **(56)**_(62) (NMBabbage)_ 4-9-10v JWeaver(3) (led after 2f: sn clr: hdd over 5f out: 2nd st: wknd 2f out)..........7 **3**
2244² Old Swinford (IRE) **(55)**_(54) (BJMeehan)_ 3-8-7 BDoyle(4) (led 2f: led over 5f out tl 4f out: 4th & wkng st)..........7 **4**
1292⁸ Achilles Heel **(46)**_(42) (CNAllen)_ 4-9-0 GBardwell(2) (poor 5th st: a wl bhd) 2½ **5**
2280⁴ Star of the Glen **(29)**_(25) (SCoathup)_ 9-7-11 NAdams(1) (s.s: a bhd) ....s.h **6**

8/13 TRAZL (IRE) (op Evens), **5/1** Old Swinford (IRE), **11/2** Wannaplantatree, **8/1** Stately Home (IRE) (op 5/1), **10/1** Achilles Heel (op 6/1), **40/1** Star of the Glen, CSF £6.30 TOTE £1.70: £1.30 £3.20 (£6.30) OWNER Hesmonds Stud (ARUNDEL) BRED Hesmonds Stud Ltd 6 Rn
3m 17.0 (8.00) SF: 45/40/36/12/16/-
WEIGHT FOR AGE 3yo-16lb
T/Plpt: £79.20 (119.72 Tckts). T/Qdpt: £16.40 (6.7 Tckts). KH

2415-YORK (L-H)
Saturday July 15th (Good to firm)

WEATHER: overcast & heavy showers WIND: slt half bhd

2453

JERVAULX MEDIAN AUCTION MAIDEN STKS (2-Y.O) (Class E)
£3,817.50 (£1,140.00: £545.00: £247.50)
6f Stalls: High GOING minus 0.34 sec per fur (GF) 2-00 (2-00)

1856⁹ **Crackernat (IRE)** _(83) (LMCumani)_ 2-9-0 WRyan(1) (lw: led tl over 1f out: styd on wl to ld ins fnl f)..........—- **1**
2058² Al Shafa _(83)_(Fav)_(JLDunlop)_ 2-9-0 TQuinn(5) (swtg: chsd ldrs: slt ld over 1f out: hung lft: hdd & no ex ins fnl f)..........hd **2**
Nose No Bounds (IRE) _(72+) (MJohnston)_ 2-9-0 DHolland(4) (w'like: str: bit bkwd: s.i.s: outpcd & sn drvn along: hdwy 2f out: styd on ins fnl f)..........4 **3**
Gulf of Siam _(65) (MissSEHall)_ 2-9-0 NConnorton(3) (lengthy: unf: scope: dwlt s: sn chsng ldrs: hung lft ½-wy: wknd 1f out)..........2½ **4**
1597⁵ Bellator _(52) (GBBalding)_ 2-9-0 TIves(2) (prom tl outpcd fr ½-wy)..........5 **5**

8/15 Al Shafa, **4/1** CRACKERNAT (IRE), **6/1** Nose No Bounds (IRE), **12/1** Gulf of Siam, Bellator, CSF £6.69 TOTE £6.50: £2.00 £1.20 (£2.60) OWNER Mr Paul Silver (NEWMARKET) BRED Hamwood Stud 5 Rn 1m 12.74 (3.14) SF: 25/25/14/7/-

2454

ANVIL AT SHEFFIELD CONDITIONS STKS (2-Y.O) (Class C)
£4,947.00 (£1,707.00: £816.00: £330.00)
6f 214y Stalls: High GOING minus 0.34 sec per fur (GF) 2-35 (2-35)

2136³ **Fag End (IRE)** _(79) (MHTompkins)_ 2-8-0 (5) HKYim(4) (trckd ldrs: led over 2f out: wnt rt u.p over 1f out: hld on wl)..........—- **1**
2107* Swift Fandango (USA) _(81)_(Fav)_(PFICole)_ 2-8-12 TQuinn(3) (chsd ldr: effrt ½-wy: rdn over 1f out: styng on same pce whn hmpd & swtchd ins & eased cl home)..........2 **2**
1889a* Semper (IRE) _(76) (LMCumani)_ 2-8-12 JFortune(1) (lengthy: scope: b.nr hind: dwlt: sn pushed along: hdwy over 1f out: kpt on nr fin)..........2½ **3**
2200* Champagne Prince _(73) (PWHarris)_ 2-8-12 WRyan(2) (led tl over 2f out: wknd over 1f out: eased nr fin)..........1¼ **4**

4/9 Swift Fandango (USA) (4/6-2/5), **5/1** Champagne Prince, Semper (IRE) (op 5/2), **14/1** FAG END (IRE) (op 8/1), CSF £20.65 TOTE £8.00 (£4.60) OWNER Mr Michael Keogh (NEWMARKET) BRED St Simon Foundation 4 Rn 1m 23.68 (2.18) SF: 34/36/31/28
STEWARDS' ENQUIRY Obj. to Fag End (IRE) by Quinn overruled.

2455 JOHN SMITH'S BITTER H'CAP (0-90) (3-Y.O+) (Class C) £6,212.00(£1,856.00: £888.00: £404.00) **6f 214y** Stalls: High GOING minus 0.34 sec (GF) 3-05 (3-07)

1932[4] **Allinson's Mate (IRE)** **(71)***(79) (TDBarron)* 7-9-0b JFortune(11) (hld up: hdwy over 2f out: styd on wl u.p to ld post)........— **1**
2061[2] Hi Nod **(82)***(90) (MJCamacho)* 5-9-11 LCharnock(3) (trckd ldrs: effrt over 2f out: styd on wl u.p to ld wl ins fnl f: jst ct)........hd **2**
2188* Russian Heroine **(73)***(80) (MJohnston)* 3-8-8 DHolland(9) (trckd ldr: led ½-wy: sn rdn: hdd cl home)........½ **3**
2103[9] Verde Luna **(69)***(71) (MHTompkins)* 3-7-13 (5) HKYim(5) (bhd: hdwy over 2f out: nvr rchd ldrs)2 **4**
2130* Halmanerror **(68)***(68) (MrsJRRamsden)* 5-8-11 KFallon(8) (s.i.s: hld up & bhd: hdwy on outside ½-wy: styd on appr fnl f: nt rch ldrs)........¾ **5**
1932[3] Don Pepe **(69)***(67) (RBoss)* 4-8-12 WRyan(4) (lw: chsd ldrs: rdn over 2f out: grad wknd)........1 **6**
*383** Dune River **(82)***(79)*(Fav)*(DRLoder)* 6-9-8 (3) DRMcCabe(6) (led to ½-wy: wknd 2f out)........nk **7**
2066[8] Queenbird **(83)***(71) (MJRyan)* 4-9-12 TQuinn(1) (in tch: drvn along ½-wy: sn lost pl)........4 **8**
2246[2] Pusey Street Boy **(53)***(38) (JRBosley)* 8-7-10 GBardwell(7) (t: sn outpcd & drvn along: n.d).1½ **9**
985[8] Corio **(77)***(61) (MissSEHall)* 3-8-12 NConnorton(10) (a in rr)........nk **10**
1808[14] Daawe (USA) **(75)***(52) (MrsVAAconley)* 4-9-4v MDeering(2) (lw: chsd ldrs: rdn ½-wy: sn wknd)3 **11**

3/1 Dune River, **5/1** Russian Heroine, Halmanerror, **6/1** Hi Nod, **13/2** Don Pepe, **8/1** ALLINSON'S MATE (IRE), **12/1** Corio, **14/1** Pusey Street Boy, Verde Luna, **25/1** Queenbird, **33/1** Daawe (USA), CSF £53.85 CT £246.62 TOTE £11.70: £2.80 £2.20 £1.60 (£44.70) Trio £55.20 OWNER Mr Peter Jones (THIRSK) BRED Gay O'Callaghan 11 Rn
1m 22.83 (1.33) SF: 53/64/46/37/42/41/53/45/12/27/26
WEIGHT FOR AGE 3yo-8lb

2456 FOSTER'S SILVER CUP RATED STKS H'CAP (0-105) (Listed) (4-Y.O+) (Class A) £11,285.64 (£4,112.64: £1,966.32: £795.60: £307.80) **1m 5f 194y** Stalls: Low GOING minus 0.34 sec per fur (GF) 3-40 (3-40)

2104* **Saxon Maid (100)***(111)*(Fav)*(LMCumani)* 4-9-5 JFortune(1) (lw: hld up: smooth hdwy 4f out: led over 2f out: styd on wl u.p)........— **1**
2272[3] Magical Retreat (USA) **(98)***(106) (CACyzer)* 5-9-3 DBiggs(5) (chsd ldrs: drvn along over 6f out: styd on wl appr fnl f)........2½ **2**
2098[13] The Flying Phantom **(90)***(92) (MHTompkins)* 4-8-9 WWoods(6) (jnd ldr 9f out: led over 4f out tl over 2f out: one pce)........5 **3**
1479[4] English Invader **(95)***(94) (RAkehurst)* 4-9-0 TQuinn(4) (chsd ldrs: pushed along 6f out: outpcd over 2f out)........3 **4**
2098[17] Tethys (USA) **(92)***(91) (JLEyre)* 4-8-11 TIves(2) (led tl over 4f out: wknd over 2f out)........s.h **5**

5/4 SAXON MAID, **4/1** Magical Retreat (USA), English Invader, **13/2** Tethys (USA), **7/1** The Flying Phantom, CSF £6.15 TOTE £2.00: £1.40 £2.20 (£3.30) OWNER Sheikh Mohammed (NEWMARKET) BRED Cleaboy Farms Co 5 Rn 2m 55.7 (2.10) SF: 64/59/45/47/44

2457 36TH JOHN SMITH'S MAGNET CUP H'CAP (0-110) (3-Y.O+) (Class B) £56,730.00 (£17,040.00: £8,220.00: £3,810.00) **1m 2f 85y** Stalls: Low GOING minus 0.34 sec per fur (GF) 4-15 (4-16)

1839[4] **Naked Welcome (90)***(104) (MJFetherston-Godley)* 3-8-4 DHolland(9) (lw: hld up & bhd: smooth hdwy on outside 3f out: r.o u.p to ld nr fin)........— **1**
2241[6] Ringmaster (IRE) **(84)***(98) (MHTompkins)* 4-8-4 (5) HKYim(14) (hld up: gd hdwy on outside over 3f out: led over 2f out: hdd & nt qckn nr fin)........nk **2**
2241* Yoush (IRE) **(95)***(108)*(Fav)*(MAJarvis)* 3-8-9 8x TIves(1) (swtg: trckd ldrs: effrt 3f out: edgd rt & ev ch ins fnl f: no ex)........nk **3**
2118[2] Rokeby Bowl **(87)***(99) (IABalding)* 3-7-8 (7) MartinDwyer(3) (plld hrd: trckd ldrs: n.m.r & lost pl over 3f out: swtchd rt 2f out: edgd lft & styd on strly fnl f)........¾ **4**
1140[2] Gone for a Burton (IRE) **(86)***(96) (PJMakin)* 5-8-11 JFortune(10) (hld up: hdwy on ins over 3f out: sn outpcd: kpt on wl fnl f)........1 **5**
1926[5] Virtual Reality **(79)***(88) (AHide)* 4-8-4v WWoods(5) (swtg: hld up: smooth hdwy on ins over 3f out: grad wknd fnl f)........1¼ **6**
2241[13] Unforgiving Minute **(81)***(88) (PWHarris)* 6-8-3 (3) DRMcCabe(15) (plld hrd: trckd ldrs: lost pl 4f out: styd on wl fnl f)........¾ **7**
1808[9] Country Lover **(80)***(85) (LordHuntingdon)* 4-8-5 DeanMcKeown(4) (led tl over 2f out: wknd appr fnl f)........1¼ **8**
1610[8] Sherman (IRE) **(96)***(101) (HThomsonJones)* 4-9-7b WRyan(16) (trckd ldrs tl grad wknd fnl 2f)½ **9**
2241[10] The French Friar (IRE) **(74)***(77) (GBBalding)* 4-7-8 (5) NVarley(2) (swtg: plld hrd: trckd ldrs tl wknd over 2f out)........¾ **10**

1853[16] Cedez le Passage (FR) **(98)***(98) (CEBrittain)* 4-9-9 MBirch(7) (w ldr: ev ch tl wknd & eased 2f out) 2 **11**
1808[10] Bold Amusement **(82)***(80) (WSCunningham)* 5-8-2 (5) VHalliday(12) (bhd: wnt lft u.p over 2f out: n.d) 1½ **12**
2307* Legal Fiction **(68)***(66) (MJohnston)* 4-7-7 NKennedy(6) (in tch tl lost pl 3f out) ....nk **13**
1807* Quango **(92)***(88) (JGFitzGerald)* 3-8-6 KFallon(11) (lw: rr div: effrt over 3f out: sn rdn: n.d)...1¼ **14**
2241[7] Old Hickory (IRE) **(99)***(93) (LMCumani)* 4-9-10b TQuinn(13) (in tch: wkng whn hmpd over 2f out) 1¼ **15**
2118[4] Mr Confusion (IRE) **(86)***(78) (MissSEHall)* 7-8-8 (3) JStack(8) (dwlt: hdwy on outside 7f out: sn prom: wknd qckly over 2f out)....1¼ **16**

LONG HANDICAP Legal Fiction 7-1

3/1 Yoush (IRE), **6/1** NAKED WELCOME, Quango, **8/1** Rokeby Bowl, **9/1** Virtual Reality, **11/1** Ringmaster (IRE), **14/1** Sherman (IRE), **16/1** Mr Confusion (IRE), Country Lover, The French Friar (IRE), Gone for a Burton (IRE), Old Hickory (IRE), **25/1** Legal Fiction, **33/1** Unforgiving Minute, **40/1** Cedez le Passage (FR), **50/1** Bold Amusement, CSF £68.23 CT £222.27 TOTE £6.30: £1.90 £3.80 £1.10 £1.90 (£98.50) Trio £113.00 OWNER The Most Welcome Partnership (EAST ILSLEY) BRED W. H. Joyce 16 Rn 2m 10.23 (2.73) SF: 41/46/45/36/44/36/36/33/49/25/46/28/14/25/41/26

WEIGHT FOR AGE 3yo-11lb

2458

WEBSTER'S GREEN LABEL BEST H'CAP (0-90) (3-Y.O+) (Class C) £6,524.00 (£1,952.00: £936.00: £428.00)
6f Stalls: High GOING minus 0.34 sec per fur (GF) 4-45 (4-46)

2194* **Jawlaat (USA) (84)***(94)*(Fav)*(JLDunlop)* 3-9-3 TQuinn(9) (mde all: qcknd clr 2f out: pushed out: readily) ....— **1**
2120[8] Musical Season **(88)***(96) (TDBarron)* 3-9-7 JFortune(6) (a chsng wnr: styd on wl ins fnl f: nvr able chal) ....¾ **2**
2344[4] How's Yer Father **(84)***(89) (RJHodges)* 9-9-7 (3) DRMcCabe(2) (in tch: rdn over 2f out: kpt on wl fnl f) 1¼ **3**
2194[2] Barato **(73)***(77) (MrsJRRamsden)* 4-8-13 KFallon(1) (b.nr hind: swtchd rt s: bhd: hdwy over 2f out: kpt on) ....nk **4**
2001[7] Highborn (IRE) **(82)***(86) (PSFelgate)* 6-9-8 WRyan(5) (chsd ldrs: drvn along ½-wy: kpt on one pce) ....s.h **5**
2096[3] Plum First **(61)***(61) (LRLloyd-James)* 5-7-8v(7) MartinDwyer(3) (b.hind: bhd: swvd lft ½-wy: kpt on fnl f) 1¼ **6**
2096[11] Croft Pool **(81)***(81) (JAGlover)* 4-9-7 TIves(8) (mid div: effrt ½-wy: nvr nr to chal) ....nk **7**
2194[7] Maid O'Cannie **(62)***(62) (MWEasterby)* 4-7-9 (7) RuthCoulter(12) (s.i.s: hdwy on ins ½-wy: n.m.r & n.d) ....s.h **8**
2096[13] Here Comes a Star **(71)***(69) (JMCarr)* 7-8-11 MBirch(11) (in tch: outpcd ½-wy: n.d) ....½ **9**
1151[14] Invigilate **(55)***(40) (MartynWane)* 6-7-9 NKennedy(7) (chsd ldrs tl lost pl wl over 1f out) 5 **10**

15/8 JAWLAAT (USA), **5/1** Barato, **7/1** Musical Season, **15/2** Plum First, Highborn (IRE), **9/1** Here Comes a Star, Croft Pool, **10/1** How's Yer Father, **14/1** Maid O'Cannie, **20/1** Invigilate, CSF £16.38 CT £104.53 TOTE £2.60: £1.70 £2.50 £2.00 (£15.20) Trio £50.00 OWNER Mr Hamdan Al Maktoum (ARUNDEL) BRED Shadwell Farm Inc. in USA 10 Rn
1m 11.64 (2.04) SF: 43/45/45/33/42/17/37/18/25/-

WEIGHT FOR AGE 3yo-7lb

2459

FISHERGATE NURSERY H'CAP (2-Y.O) (Class C) £5,385.00 (£1,605.00: £765.00: £345.00) **5f** Stalls: High GOING minus 0.34 sec per fur (GF) 5-15 (5-16)

1860[4] **Rambo Delight** *(67) (JLEyre)* 2-9-0 RLappin(6) (trckd ldrs: disp ld over 1f out: hrd rdn & kpt on wl nr fin) ....— **1**
1356* White Emir *(64)*(Fav)*(MrsJRRamsden)* 2-8-13 KFallon(3) (unruly in stalls: trckd ldrs: disp ld over 1f out: no ex cl home) ....½ **2**
1177[6] Patrington Park *(37) (MWEasterby)* 2-7-4 (7) MartinDwyer(5) (w ldrs: disp ld ½-wy: nt qckn over 1f out) 3½ **3**
2259* Oriel Lad *(59) (PDEvans)* 2-9-2v(3) DRMcCabe(1) (s.i.s: wl outpcd: styd on over 1f out: nvr nr to chal) ....hd **4**
1893[11] Limerick Princess (IRE) *(58) (JBerry)* 2-9-7 TQuinn(4) (led: hung lft: hdd wl over 1f out) 1 **5**
2077[4] Erupt *(45) (GBBalding)* 2-8-12 TIves(7) (trckd ldrs: effrt 2f out: sn wknd) 1¼ **6**
1899* Pathaze *(NBycroft)* 2-8-6 MBirch(2) (in tch over 1f: sn lost pl: eased: virtually p.u) 12 **7**

9/4 White Emir, **5/1** RAMBO DELIGHT, Pathaze, **11/2** Erupt, Limerick Princess (IRE), **6/1** Oriel Lad, **9/1** Patrington Park, CSF £16.65 TOTE £5.40: £2.50 £1.90 (£4.90) OWNER Mr Thomas Doherty (COCKERHAM) BRED Thomas Doherty 7 Rn 59.79 secs (2.79) SF: 12/13/21/18/-/-/-

T/Plpt: £336.10 (98.78 Tckts). T/Qdpt: £8.90 (46.7 Tckts). WG

2422-AYR (L-H)
Sunday July 16th (Good)
WEATHER: overcast WIND: almost nil

2460 SCOTLAND'S FIRST SUNDAY MAIDEN STKS (3-Y.O+) (Class D)
£4,065.00 (£1,230.00: £600.00: £285.00)
1m Stalls: Low GOING minus 0.08 sec per fur (G) 2-15 (2-17)

Code of Law (USA) *(88+)*(Fav)*(PWChapple-Hyam)* 3-8-12 BThomson(4) (mde all: shkn up & r.o fnl 2f) — 1
2255³ Far Ahead *(81) (MrsVAAconley)* 3-8-12 MDeering(5) (bhd tl styd on u.p fnl 2f: no ch w wnr) 3½ 2
2313³ Ihtimaam (FR) *(79) (MrsASwinbank)* 3-8-12 NConnorton(6) (chsd wnr: shkn up & one pce fnl 2f) 1 3
Melmoth (USA) *(78) (JHMGosden)* 3-8-12 JCarroll(2) (w'like: lengthy: bit bkwd: hld up: effrt 3f out: rdn & no imp fnl 2f) ½ 4
1846³ Dr Caligari (IRE) **(72)***(78) (JBerry)* 3-8-12 KDarley(3) (a.p: hdwy 3f out: btn appr fnl f) s.h 5
Harlech (IRE) *(77) (JHMGosden)* 3-8-12 DaleGibson(1) (gd sort: cmpt: bit bkwd: s.i.s: hdwy u.p 2f out: n.m.r towards fin) ½ 6
1947⁵ Top Skipper (IRE) **(69)***(65) (BHanbury)* 3-8-9 (3) JStack(7) (chsd ldrs tl wknd fnl 2½f) 6 7

4/6 CODE OF LAW (USA) (op Evens), **7/2** Melmoth (USA) (op 2/1), **8/1** Top Skipper (IRE), **14/1** Far Ahead (op 8/1), Dr Caligari (IRE) (op 8/1), **20/1** Harlech (IRE), **66/1** Ihtimaam (FR), CSF £9.86 TOTE £1.90: £1.50 £2.50 (£11.30) OWNER Mr R. E. Sangster (MARLBOROUGH) BRED Seahorse Investments 7 Rn 1m 44.63 (7.83) SF: 11/4/2/1/1/-/-

2461 SUNDAY MAIL H'CAP (0-85) (3-Y.O+) (Class D) £5,800.00 (£1,750.00: £850.00: £400.00) 6f Stalls: High GOING minus 0.08 sec per fur (G) 2-45 (2-53)

2231* **Flashy's Son (64)***(73) (GMMoore)* 7-8-13 (3) JTate(13) (b: trckd ldrs: nt clr run 3f out: hdwy over 1f out: r.o to ld wl ins fnl f) — 1
2096* Al Wujud (IRE) **(57)***(65)*(Fav)*(TDyer)* 4-8-9 JFanning(3) (lw: a.p: led wl over 1f out tl hdd wl ins fnl f) ½ 2
2156⁶ The Happy Loon (IRE) **(51)***(53) (DenysSmith)* 4-8-3 JCarroll(4) (chsd ldrs: chal over 2f out: one pce fnl f) 2 3
*1953*⁸ Desert Invader (IRE) **(59)***(58) (DWChapman)* 4-8-11 ACulhane(10) (hdwy ½-wy: styd on wl fnl f: nrst fin) 1¼ 4
2358⁷ Cafe Solo **(42)***(41) (NBycroft)* 4-7-8b NKennedy(8) (lw: bhd: hdwy 2f out: kpt on towards fin) hd 5
2330⁸ Cavers Yangous **(73)***(70) (MJohnston)* 4-9-11 DHolland(7) (hdwy u.p ½-wy: one pce appr fnl f) ½ 6
2398² Diet **(55)***(48) (MissLAPerratt)* 9-8-7v 7x NConnorton(6) (lw: cl up tl wknd appr fnl f) 1½ 7
2307⁶ Miss Pigalle **(41)***(30) (MissLAPerratt)* 4-7-0b(7) BHalligan(5) (bhd tl sme late hdwy) 1¾ 8
1918³ Lepine (IRE) **(72)***(61) (JWWatts)* 4-9-10 GDuffield(11) (chsd ldrs: effrt ½-wy: hmpd & wknd wl over 1f out) s.h 9
2260* Pharsical **(76)***(61) (MRChannon)* 4-10-0 KDarley(12) (led over 4f: hung lft & sn btn) 1¼ 10
2001⁹ Bold Street (IRE) **(73)***(57) (ABailey)* 5-9-11b MWigham(9) (b: s.i.s: n.d) ½ 11
2397⁶ Ragazzo (IRE) **(44)***(18) (JSWainwright)* 5-7-10bow3 LCharnock(2) (b.hind: a outpcd & bhd) 2½ 12
2229⁴ Suedoro **(41)***(14) (RMMcKellar)* 5-7-0 (7) PFessey(1) (swtg: sn chsng ldrs: wknd 2f out) 1½ 13

LONG HANDICAP Miss Pigalle 7-3 Ragazzo (IRE) 7-3

3/1 Al Wujud (IRE), **5/1** Pharsical, **6/1** Bold Street (IRE), **7/1** Lepine (IRE) (5/1-15/2), **8/1** FLASHY'S SON, Cavers Yangous, **16/1** Cafe Solo, The Happy Loon (IRE), **20/1** Diet, Suedoro, **33/1** Miss Pigalle, Desert Invader (IRE), **50/1** Ragazzo (IRE), CSF £30.10 CT £348.57 TOTE £9.10: £3.00 £1.80 £3.60 (£19.50) Trio £220.80 OWNER Mr K. Lee (MIDDLEHAM) BRED Brian A. Shovelton (North Wales) Ltd 13 Rn 1m 12.43 (2.63) SF: 56/48/36/41/24/53/31/13/44/44/40/1/-

2462 TENNENT TROPHY RATED STKS H'CAP (0-95) (3-Y.O+) (Class B)
£8,120.28 (£2,842.68: £1,391.34: £599.70)
1m 7f Stalls: Low GOING minus 0.08 sec per fur (G) 3-15 (3-15)

2098⁶ **Highflying (77)***(89) (GMMoore)* 9-9-2 (3) JTate(2) (lw: mde all: styd on gamely fnl 2f) — 1
1682* Torch Vert (IRE) **(80)***(88) (BWHills)* 3-8-7 DHolland(1) (trckd wnr: effrt u.p over 2f out: btn appr fnl f) 3½ 2
2238* Blue Blazer **(78)***(76) (BHanbury)* 5-9-3 (3) JStack(4) (hld up: effrt appr st: one pce fnl 2f) 10 3
2022* Batabanoo **(79)***(55)*(Fav)*(MrsMReveley)* 6-9-7 KDarley(3) (chsd ldrs: rdn 7f out: wknd fnl 3½f) 20 4

2/1 Batabanoo, **9/4** HIGHFLYING, **7/2** Blue Blazer, **4/1** Torch Vert (IRE), CSF £9.36 TOTE £3.50: (£10.10) OWNER Mr B. Batey (MIDDLEHAM) BRED Juddmonte Farms 4 Rn
3m 18.99 (8.89) SF: 50/34/37/16
WEIGHT FOR AGE 3yo-15lb

OFFICIAL EXPLANATION **Batabanoo: the jockey reported that the gelding ran flat and had sweated up before the race which had contributed to his poor run.**

2463 JOE PUNTER (S) H'CAP (0-60) (3-Y.O+) (Class F) £2,905.00 (£880.00: £430.00: £205.00) **5f** Stalls: High GOING minus 0.08 sec (G) 3-45 (3-48)

2372[3] **Baileys Sunset (IRE) (59)***(66) (MJohnston)* 3-9-11 DHolland(7) (bhd: hdwy 2f out: r.o to ld nr fin)........— 1
2295[6] Cheeky Chappy **(34)***(39) (DWChapman)* 4-8-5b ACulhane(3) (lw: prom: hdwy to ld wl ins fnl f: nt qckn towards fin)........½ 2
2303[3] Ramborette **(47)***(51)*(Fav)*(DenysSmith)* 3-8-13 KFallon(11) (chsd ldrs: led wl over 1f out tl hdd wl ins fnl f)........nk 3
2124[4] Glow of Hope **(30)***(30) (RMMcKellar)* 5-7-8 (7) PFessey(9) (in tch: rdn 2f out: styd on fnl f: nrst fin)........1¼ 4
2398[7] Waverley Star **(40)***(31) (JSWainwright)* 10-8-11b LCharnock(10) (lw: in tch: rdn ½-wy: no imp)3 5
1739[8] Uppance **(26)***(11) (DANolan)* 7-7-11 ow1 AMackay(1) (bhd tl sme late hdwy)........1½ 6
2398[6] Sunday Mail Too (IRE) **(41)***(27) (MissLAPerratt)* 3-8-7b GDuffield(8) (lw: s.i.s: nvr nrr)........s.h 7
2303[7] Leading Princess (IRE) **(44)***(30) (MissLAPerratt)* 4-9-1b MBirch(5) (led 1½f: cl up tl wknd fnl 2f)........s.h 8
2338[5] Halbert **(55)***(41) (MRChannon)* 6-9-12v KDarley(4) (lw: led after 1½f tl wl over 1f out: grad wknd)........s.h 9
2162[5] Dauntless Fort **(40)***(3) (MrsVAAconley)* 4-8-11b MDeering(6) (nvr wnt pce)........7 10

11/4 Ramborette, **4/1** BAILEYS SUNSET (IRE), Halbert, **8/1** Glow of Hope, **10/1** Sunday Mail Too (IRE) (8/1-12/1), **14/1** Waverley Star, Cheeky Chappy, Leading Princess (IRE), **25/1** Dauntless Fort, **50/1** Uppance, CSF £49.02 CT £158.84 TOTE £4.10: £1.70 £1.80 £2.00 (£21.60) Trio £26.90 OWNER G R Bailey Ltd (Baileys Horse Feeds) (MIDDLEHAM) BRED Vincent and Joseph Fitzpatrick in Ireland 10 Rn 60.55 secs (3.55) SF: 40/18/25/9/10/-/1/9/20/-
WEIGHT FOR AGE 3yo-5lb
No bid

2464 E.B.F. SUNDAY MAIL RACING AHEAD MAIDEN STKS (2-Y.O) (Class D) £4,318.50 (£1,308.00: £639.00: £304.50) **7f** Stalls: Low GOING minus 0.08 sec per fur (G) 4-15 (4-17)

2116[3] **Royal Mark (IRE)** *(84) (JWWatts)* 2-9-0 GDuffield(5) (lw: a.p: led 1½f out: qcknd clr: jst hld on)........— 1
Freedom Flame *(78+) (MJohnston)* 2-8-9 DHolland(6) (w'like: str: rn green & bhd: hdwy over 2f out: str run fnl f: jst failed)........nk 2
2034[2] Detachment (USA) *(74)*(Fav)*(PWChapple-Hyam)* 2-9-0 BThomson(3) (lw: led tl hdd 1½f out: sn btn)........4 3
2192[4] Ciserano (IRE) *(62) (MRChannon)* 2-8-9 KDarley(7) (cl up: effrt over 2f out: r.o one pce)........3 4
2083[4] Grey Galava *(44) (BWHills)* 2-8-9 KFallon(2) (chsd ldrs tl wknd 2f out)........8 5
1935[3] Craignairn *(35) (JBerry)* 2-9-0 JCarroll(4) (chsd ldrs tl outpcd fnl 2f)........6 6
Limyski *(33) (MrsASwinbank)* 2-9-0 NConnorton(1) (w'like: bit bkwd: s.s: hdwy appr st: sn outpcd)........1 7

4/7 Detachment (USA), **11/4** Freedom Flame, **7/1** ROYAL MARK (IRE), **14/1** Grey Galava (10/1-16/1), **20/1** Ciserano (IRE), **50/1** Craignairn, **100/1** Limyski, CSF £25.72 TOTE £5.80: £2.40 £2.00 (£17.90) OWNER Lord Swaythling (RICHMOND) BRED Barronstown Stud And Ron Con Ltd 7 Rn
1m 29.55 (5.55) SF: 27/21/17/5/-/-/-

2465 SCOTTISH RACING CLUB SCOTS WHA'HAE AMATEUR H'CAP (0-70) (3-Y.O+) (Class E) £3,598.75 (£1,090.00: £532.50: £253.75) **1m 5f 13y** Stalls: Low GOING minus 0.08 sec per fur (G) 4-45 (4-46)

2401[4] **Parish Walk (IRE) (43)***(49) (KWHogg)* 4-10-0 (5)ow8 MrKDrewry(2) (mde all: sn clr: jst lasted)........— 1
2293[6] Dusty Point (IRE) **(56)***(70)*(Fav)*(JPearce)* 5-11-4 MrsLPearce(4) (lw: b: bhd: effrt 7f out: r.o wl fnl f: jst failed)........nk 2
2186[9] Yaakum **(35)***(41) (SEKettlewell)* 6-9-11v MrsDKettlewell(1) (lw: chsd clr ldr: shkn up over 1f out: nt qckn)........6 3
1998[5] Balzino (USA) **(42)***(46) (NTinkler)* 6-9-13 (5) MrLSpink(3) (bhd: effrt ent st: n.d)........1¾ 4
2374[5] Cutthroat Kid (IRE) **(66)***(66) (MrsMReveley)* 5-12-0 MrMHNaughton(5) (prom chsng group: effrt over 3f out: n.d)........3½ 5

4/6 Dusty Point (IRE) (op Evens), **9/4** Cutthroat Kid (IRE), **13/2** Balzino (USA) (4/1-7/1), **12/1** Yaakum, **25/1** PARISH WALK (IRE), CSF £43.30 TOTE £18.60: £3.20 £1.20 (£8.70) OWNER Exors of the late Mr P J White (ISLE OF MAN) BRED Mrs A. R. Martin 5 Rn

2m 59.66 (14.86) SF: 22/43/14/19/39

T/Jkpt: Not won; £20,510.18 to Windsor 17/7/95. T/Plpt: £890.80 (16.24 Tckts). T/Qdpt: £32.30 (5 Tckts). AA

2203-YARMOUTH (L-H)
Sunday July 16th (Good to firm)

WEATHER: overcast WIND: mod across

2466

UPTON (S) STKS (3-Y.O) (Class G) £2,444.60 (£675.60: £321.80)
1m 2f 21y Stalls: Low GOING minus 0.34 sec per fur (GF) 2-00 (2-01)

2246⁹ **Today Tonite (43)***(57) (JPearce)* 3-8-6 GBardwell(2) (hld up: 4th st: rdn to ld wl over 1f out: hld on wl) ....— **1**
1854⁵ Kindred Greeting **(37)***(61) (DMorris)* 3-8-11b RCochrane(1) (chsd ldr tl 3rd st: ev ch over 1f out: rdn & r.o) ....½ **2**
1990⁷ The Flying Fiddle *(45) (MHTompkins)* 3-8-6v SMulvey(5) (led tl hdd & n.m.r wl over 1f out: wknd fnl f) 7 **3**
1097⁹ Shooter **(70)***(39)*(Fav)*(PFICole)* 3-8-11 TQuinn(3) (chsd ldrs tl 2nd & slipped ent st: rdn over 3f out: sn btn: lame) 7 **4**
1914⁷ Fair Attraction **(42)***(30) (AHide)* 3-8-11 MTebbutt(4) (stdd s: plld hrd: last st: a bhd) 6 **5**

1/2 Shooter, **11/2** TODAY TONITE (4/1-6/1), **7/1** The Flying Fiddle, **9/1** Kindred Greeting, **12/1** Fair Attraction, CSF £38.82 TOTE £6.50: £2.20 £3.30 (£28.80) OWNER Mrs J. Furlong (NEWMARKET) BRED J. R. Furlong 5 Rn 2m 9.9 (5.50) SF: 20/24/8/2/-

Bt in 4,000 gns

2467

E.B.F. ACLE MAIDEN STKS (2-Y.O) (Class D) £4,425.00 (£1,320.00: £630.00: £285.00) **6f 3y** Stalls: Centre GOING minus 0.34 sec per fur (GF) 2-30 (2-31)

Dublin River (USA) *(74+) (HThomsonJones)* 2-9-0 WCarson(3) (unf: scope: w ldr: led ins fnl f: drvn out) ....— **1**
Kalao Tua (IRE) *(69+) (JRFanshawe)* 2-8-9 DHarrison(5) (lengthy: bkwd: hld up: hdwy & ev ch over 1f out: r.o) ....s.h **2**
2183⁷ Red Nose (IRE) *(74) (MHTompkins)* 2-9-0 WWoods(2) (led tl ins fnl f: r.o) ....hd **3**
2200³ Brecon *(50)*(Fav)*(PFICole)* 2-9-0 TQuinn(1) (in tch: rdn over 2f out: sn btn) 9 **4**
Nosey Native *(42) (JPearce)* 2-9-0 RCochrane(4) (w'like: leggy: dwlt: sn pushed along: hdwy over 3f out: wknd 2f out) 3 **5**

6/4 Brecon, **2/1** DUBLIN RIVER (USA) (6/4-9/4), **9/2** Kalao Tua (IRE) (3/1-11/2), **6/1** Red Nose (IRE), **12/1** Nosey Native (6/1-14/1), CSF £10.37 TOTE £2.70: £1.30 £2.80 (£7.00) OWNER Mr Khalil Alsayegh (NEWMARKET) BRED C. L. Kidder and N. L. Robenalt 5 Rn

1m 12.8 (2.20) SF: 39/34/39/15/7

2468

MAIL ON SUNDAY MILE (QUALIFIER) H'CAP (0-85) (3-Y.O+) (Class D) £7,570.00 (£2,260.00: £1,080.00: £490.00)
1m 3y Stalls: Centre GOING minus 0.34 sec per fur (GF) 3-00 (3-01)

1225¹⁰ **Toujours Riviera (84)***(95) (JPearce)* 5-10-0 GBardwell(7) (chsd ldr tl led 3f out: hld on wl u.p fnl f) ....— **1**
2321⁶ Saifan **(70)***(80) (DMorris)* 6-9-0b RCochrane(8) (dwlt: sn pushed along: gd hdwy over 1f out: ev ch ins fnl f: no ex cl home) ....nk **2**
2253* Hakika (USA) **(86)***(91)*(Fav)*(DMorley)* 3-9-8 WCarson(3) (trckd ldrs: plld out 2f out: sn rdn & no ex) 2½ **3**
2207* Blockade (USA) **(73)***(76) (MBell)* 6-9-3 TQuinn(2) (t: led 5f: wknd fnl f) 1¼ **4**
2031² Samba Sharply **(79)***(79) (AHide)* 4-9-9 WWoods(4) (chsd ldrs over 5f) 1½ **5**
1845² Green Seed (IRE) **(80)***(80) (JRFanshawe)* 3-8-11 (5) NVarley(5) (lw: chsd ldrs tl rdn & btn 2f out) ....s.h **6**
1999² Lunar Mission (IRE) **(72)***(58) (JMPEustace)* 4-8-9 (7) WinChung(6) (swtg: wl bhd fnl 4f) 7 **7**

100/30 Hakika (USA), **7/2** Saifan, Samba Sharply, **9/2** Green Seed (IRE), **5/1** Blockade (USA), **12/1** TOUJOURS RIVIERA, **20/1** Lunar Mission (IRE), CSF £49.89 CT £157.32 TOTE £10.40: £3.00 £2.70 (£35.30) OWNER Mr James Furlong (NEWMARKET) BRED J. L. C. Pearce 7 Rn

1m 36.6 (1.30) SF: 69/54/57/50/53/46/32

WEIGHT FOR AGE 3yo-8lb

STEWARDS' ENQUIRY Bardwell suspended 25-26/7/95 (excessive use of whip).

2469
PLEASURE BEACH MAIDEN STKS (3-Y.O) (Class D) £4,581.00 (£1,368.00: £654.00: £297.00) **7f 3y** Stalls: Centre GOING minus 0.34 sec per fur (GF) 3-30 (3-32)

	Sveltana *(71++) (JRFanshawe)* 3-8-9 DHarrison(6) (leggy: bit bkwd: trckd ldrs: qcknd to ld 1f out: edgd lft: comf)	—	1
	Miswaki Belle (USA) *(70+)*(Fav)*(JHMGosden)* 3-8-9 GHind(7) (unf: scope: chsd ldrs: n.m.r over 1f out: r.o ins fnl f)	½	2
1796[4]	Millazure (USA) *(68)*(Fav)*(RCharlton)* 3-8-9 PaulEddery(1) (w ldr tl led over 3f out: hdd 1f out: one pce)	¾	3
	Prudent Princess *(60) (AHide)* 3-8-9 WWoods(3) (unf: scope: dwlt: sn chsng ldrs: rdn & ev ch over 1f out: no ex)	3½	4
	Melody Wheel *(57) (AHide)* 3-8-9 RCochrane(4) (lengthy: unf: plld hrd: chsd ldrs 5f)	1¼	5
	Sujud (IRE) *(56) (HThomsonJones)* 3-8-9 NCarlisle(8) (unf: chsd ldrs 5f)	¾	6
	To the Roof (IRE) *(15) (PWHarris)* 3-9-0 WRyan(5) (bit bkwd: led over 4f: wknd over 3f out)	20	7
	Mawsam *(11) (EALDunlop)* 3-9-0 WCarson(2) (neat: bwkd: a bhd)	1¾	8

2/1 Miswaki Belle (USA), Millazure (USA), **9/2** Mawsam, **11/2** SVELTANA, **12/1** Sujud (IRE) (op 7/1), **33/1** Prudent Princess, To the Roof (IRE), Melody Wheel, CSF £16.42 TOTE £7.30: £1.50 £1.20 £1.20 (£6.50) OWNER Bottisham Heath Stud and Mr D W Dennis (NEWMARKET) BRED R. H. Cowell 8 Rn 1m 27.8 (5.00) SF: 7/6/4/-/-/-/-/-

STEWARDS' ENQUIRY Obj. to Svetlana by Hind overruled.

2470
TUNSTALL CONDITIONS STKS (3-Y.O F) (Class C) £5,209.60 (£1,926.40: £923.20: £376.00: £148.00: £56.80) **7f 3y** Stalls: Centre GOING minus 0.34 sec per fur (GF) 4-00 (4-02)

1979*	**Felitza (IRE)** *(104+) (HRACecil)* 3-8-13 WRyan(6) (led after 2f: qcknd clr over 1f out: comf)	—	1
1923[4]	Mandarina (USA) **(94)***(97)*(Fav)*(LMCumani)* 3-8-13 TQuinn(5) (chsd ldrs: ev ch over 2f out: sn rdn & outpcd: styd on again fnl f)	3	2
1870[6]	Tanami **(106)***(102) (DRLoder)* 3-9-1 (3) DRMcCabe(4) (lw: s.i.s: hdwy over 2f out: chsd wnr appr fnl f: no imp)	hd	3
2325[5]	Courageous Dancer (IRE) **(83)***(89) (BHanbury)* 3-8-13 TIves(1) (kpt on fnl 2f: nvr nrr)	3½	4
1923[8]	Karayb (IRE) **(96)***(75) (DMorley)* 3-9-3 WCarson(2) (lw: led 2f: wknd over 2f out)	8	5
	Haddeyah (USA) *(25) (HThomsonJones)* 3-8-13 NCarlisle(3) (stumbled s: a bhd)	20	6

2/1 Mandarina (USA), **3/1** FELITZA (IRE), **7/2** Tanami (op 9/4), **11/2** Karayb (IRE), **7/1** Courageous Dancer (IRE), **12/1** Haddeyah (USA) (op 7/1), CSF £9.36 TOTE £3.60: £1.90 £1.90 (£3.90) OWNER Sheikh Mohammed (NEWMARKET) BRED Sheikh Mohammed bin Rashid al Maktoum 6 Rn 1m 24.9 (2.10) SF: 43/36/41/28/14/-

2471
BROADLAND 102 RATED STKS H'CAP (0-100) (3-Y.O C & G) (Class B) £7,962.25 (£2,881.00: £1,390.50: £577.50: £238.75) **7f 3y** Stalls: Centre GOING minus 0.34 sec per fur (GF) 4-30 (4-30)

2030[W]	**Romanzof (99)***(110+) (HRACecil)* 3-9-7 WRyan(1) (mde all: rdn & qcknd clr fnl f)	—	1
2240[10]	Midwich Cuckoo **(86)***(89) (PTWalwyn)* 3-8-8 RCochrane(5) (chsd ldrs: ev ch over 1f out: r.o: nt pce of wnr)	3½	2
1839[18]	Dance Band (USA) **(92)***(92) (BHanbury)* 3-9-0 TIves(2) (lw: prom tl lost pl 2f out: r.o again ins fnl f)	1½	3
2099[4]	Kabil **(87)***(86)*(Fav)*(HThomsonJones)* 3-8-9 WCarson(3) (lw: hld up: hdwy & ev ch over 2f out: btn fnl f)	nk	4
1370[6]	Iblis (IRE) **(94)***(82) (GWragg)* 3-9-2 PaulEddery(4) (lw: hld up: hdwy & ev ch over 2f out: sn rdn: wknd appr fnl f)	5	5

7/4 Kabil, **100/30** ROMANZOF, **7/2** Iblis (IRE), **4/1** Midwich Cuckoo, **7/1** Dance Band (USA), CSF £15.34 TOTE £3.00: £1.40 £1.90 (£8.10) OWNER Sheikh Mohammed (NEWMARKET) BRED Sheikh Mohammed bin Rashid al Maktoum 5 Rn 1m 26.0 (3.20) SF: 38/17/20/14/10

2472
REPPS H'CAP (0-80) (3-Y.O+) (Class D) £4,269.00 (£1,272.00: £606.00: £273.00) **1m 3f 101y** Stalls: Low GOING minus 0.34 sec per fur (GF) 5-00 (5-02)

2069[2]	**Miss Pin Up (77)***(87)*(Fav)*(WJHaggas)* 6-10-0 RMcGhin(2) (hld up: 4th st: qcknd to ld wl over 1f out: sn rdn clr: eased cl home)	—	1
2069[6]	Un Parfum de Femme (IRE) **(63)***(70) (JPearce)* 4-9-0 GBardwell(5) (hld up: hdwy over 2f out: r.o u.p ins fnl f)	2½	2

1730[3] Barford Sovereign **(69)***(75) (JRFanshawe)* 3-8-9 DHarrison(4) (swtg: prom: 3rd st: sn rdn: led over 2f out tl wl over 1f out: one pce) ....nk **3**
2138[4] Eden's Close **(57)***(60) (MHTompkins)* 6-8-8 SMulvey(3) (lw: prom: 2nd st: ev ch over 3f out: sn rdn & no ex) 2 **4**
Top Royal **(72)***(54) (JPearce)* 6-9-9 RCochrane(1) (bit bkwd: led tl hdd over 2f out: sn wknd & eased) 15 **5**

7/4 MISS PIN UP, **11/4** Un Parfum de Femme (IRE), **3/1** Barford Sovereign, **9/2** Eden's Close (op 3/1), **10/1** Top Royal, CSF £6.88 TOTE £2.60: £1.70 £1.60 (£4.30) OWNER Mr E. Baldwin (NEWMARKET) BRED Brook Bloodstock P L C 5 Rn 2m 27.6 (4.60) SF: 52/35/29/25/19
WEIGHT FOR AGE 3yo-11lb

T/Plpt: £358.10 (30.65 Tckts). T/Qdpt: £34.60 (3.8 Tckts). Dk

2460-AYR (L-H)
Monday July 17th (Good)

WEATHER: sunny spells & showers WIND: mod against

2473 RECORD MERIDIAN MAIDEN STKS (2-Y.O) (Class D) £3,501.25 (£1,060.00: £517.50: £246.25) **6f** Stalls: High GOING minus 0.04 sec per fur (G) 2-15 (2-15)

Dismissed (USA) *(79+)*(Fav)*(PFICole)* 2-9-0 TQuinn(4) (w'like: scope: lw: cl up: led over 2f out: rn green & hdd ins fnl f: sn led again: hrd rdn & r.o) ....— **1**
1247[5] Creative Account (USA) *(78) (MrsJRRamsden)* 2-9-0 KFallon(5) (hld up: hdwy over 2f out: slt ld ins fnl f: sn hdd: r.o) ....nk **2**
2161[8] Aztec Flyer (USA) *(62) (MrsMReveley)* 2-9-0 KDarley(2) (bhd tl styd on fnl 2f: nvr nr to chal) 6 **3**
1597[12] Give Me A Ring (IRE) *(58) (CWThornton)* 2-9-0 JFortune(3) (cl up tl wknd fnl 2f) 1½ **4**
2116[2] Lucky Rabbit *(56) (BWHills)* 2-9-0 MHills(1) (led tl hdd over 2f out: wknd over 1f out) ....¾ **5**

4/7 DISMISSED (USA), **5/2** Lucky Rabbit, **13/2** Creative Account (USA), **40/1** Give Me A Ring (IRE), **50/1** Aztec Flyer (USA), CSF £4.49 TOTE £1.60: £1.10 £2.80 (£4.10) OWNER Prince Fahd Salman (WHATCOMBE) BRED David's Farm 5 Rn 1m 13.18 (3.38) SF: 47/46/30/26/24

2474 GARRY OWEN CUP (A NURSERY) H'CAP (2-Y.O) (Class D) £4,359.00 (£1,224.00: £597.00) **5f** Stalls: High GOING minus 0.04 sec per fur (G) 2-45 (2-46)

2023[2] **Imp Express (IRE)** *(63+)*(Fav)*(GMMoore)* 2-8-12 JFortune(3) (lw: a gng wl: led on bit ins fnl f: easily) ....— **1**
2221[4] Alfayza *(51) (JDBethell)* 2-8-6 JWeaver(1) (lw: w ldr: rdn to ld 1f out: sn hdd: no ch w wnr) 1¾ **2**
1584[5] Gwespyr *(58)*(Fav)*(JBerry)* 2-9-7 KDarley(2) (led: rdn 2f out: hdd 1f out: sn btn) 2½ **3**

11/8 Gwespyr, IMP EXPRESS (IRE), **7/2** Alfayza, CSF £4.93 TOTE £2.20: (£2.20) OWNER Lord Mostyn (COCKERHAM)/Ms Sigrid Walter (MIDDLEHAM) BRED R. and Mrs Heathcote 3 Rn
60.85 secs (3.85) SF: 21/26/14

2475 DAILY RECORD H'CAP (0-75) (3-Y.O+) (Class D) £3,745.00 (£1,135.00: £555.00: £265.00) **5f** Stalls: High GOING minus 0.04 sec per fur (G) 3-15 (3-17)

2234* **Shadow Jury (68)***(78) (DWChapman)* 5-9-12b LCharnock(9) (trckd ldrs: led wl over 1f out: r.o strly ins fnl f) ....— **1**
2418[2] Rich Glow **(59)***(61)*(Fav)*(NBycroft)* 4-9-3 SMaloney(7) (lw: in tch: hdwy to chal over 1f out: no ex ins fnl f) 2½ **2**
2160[3] Mister Westsound **(46)***(45) (MissLAPerratt)* 3-7-13b DaleGibson(3) (lw: s.i.s: hdwy 2f out: styd on fnl f) 1 **3**
2160[5] Oriental Air (IRE) **(52)***(50) (EWeymes)* 4-8-10 KDarley(11) (lw: early spd: sn bhd: styd on wl fnl f) ....nk **4**
2096[12] Petite-D-Argent **(62)***(58) (TDyer)* 6-9-6 JFortune(8) (lw: cl up: led over 2f out tl wl over 1f out: one pce) ....½ **5**
2124[5] Murray's Mazda (IRE) **(44)***(37) (JLEyre)* 6-8-2 ow2 RLappin(10) (outpcd & bhd ½-wy: styd on towards fin) ....nk **6**
1900[6] Kenesha (IRE) **(48)***(42) (DANolan)* 5-8-1 (5) VHalliday(1) (bhd: hdwy ½-wy: btn appr fnl f) ....nk **7**
2303* Flashing Sabre **(56)***(47) (JBerry)* 3-8-2 (7) 7x PRoberts(6) (trckd ldrs tl rdn & btn over 1f out) 1 **8**
2303[9] Serious Hurry **(43)***(34) (RMMcKellar)* 7-7-8 (7) PFessey(4) (rdn after 2f: nvr trbld ldrs) ....s.h **9**

2463[8] Leading Princess (IRE) **(44)***(35) (MissLAPerratt)* 4-7-13b(3) JStack(2) (led tl hdd & wknd over 2f out)....hd 10

5/2 Rich Glow, **9/2** SHADOW JURY, **6/1** Oriental Air (IRE), **7/1** Petite-D-Argent, **8/1** Mister Westsound, **10/1** Flashing Sabre, **14/1** Murray's Mazda (IRE), Serious Hurry, **25/1** Kenesha (IRE), **33/1** Leading Princess (IRE), CSF £14.84 CT £77.21 TOTE £4.20: £1.40 £1.70 £1.60 (£4.90) Trio £8.10 OWNER Mrs Jeanne Chapman (YORK) BRED J. S. Bell 10 Rn

59.77 secs (2.77) SF: 58/41/20/30/38/17/22/22/14/15

WEIGHT FOR AGE 3yo-5lb

2476

TENNENTS SCOTTISH CLASSIC STKS (Gp 3) (3-Y.O+) (Class A) £19,984.00 (£7,456.00: £3,628.00: £1,540.00: £670.00: £322.00)
1m 2f Stalls: Low GOING minus 0.04 sec per fur (G) 3-45 (3-45)

2041a[2] **Baron Ferdinand (114)***(121)*(Fav)*(RCharlton)* 5-9-2 KDarley(2) (lw: b: trckd ldrs gng wl: led over 1f out: rdn & edgd rt: styd on)....— 1

1392a[2] Captain Horatius (IRE) **(113)***(124) (JLDunlop)* 6-9-7 WRyan(4) (lw: bhd: gd hdwy over 2f out: kpt on fnl f: nt pce to chal)....1 2

2008* Revere (IRE) **(116)***(118) (PFICole)* 5-9-5 TQuinn(3) (lw: b: led 2½f: cl up: led 3f out tl wl over 1f out: one pce)....2½ 3

2008[2] Young Buster (IRE) **(112)***(106) (GWragg)* 7-9-2 MHills(5) (lw: led after 2½f to 3f out: one pce)....6 4

Fill the Bill (IRE) *(103) (JohnMcLoughlin,Ireland)* 3-8-6 NGMcCullagh(6) (bhd: effrt 3f out: rdn & no imp)....1½ 5

2123[5] Gospel Song **(66)***(101) (WTKemp)* 3-8-6 KFallon(1) (lw: prom early: outpcd appr st: n.d after)....1½ 6

827[5] Desert Shot **(111)***(96) (MRStoute)* 5-9-5 WRSwinburn(7) (chsd ldrs: rdn over 2f out: no rspnse: eased ins fnl f)....5 7

100/30 BARON FERDINAND, **7/2** Revere (IRE), Young Buster (IRE), **4/1** Captain Horatius (IRE), **8/1** Desert Shot, **10/1** Fill the Bill (IRE), **250/1** Gospel Song, CSF £15.00 TOTE £4.00: £2.10 £3.10 (£9.90) OWNER Lady Rothschild (BECKHAMPTON) BRED Exors of the late Mrs D. M. de Rothschild 7 Rn 2m 8.28 (3.68) SF: 68/71/65/53/40/38/43

WEIGHT FOR AGE 3yo-10lb

2477

HOLIDAY H'CAP (0-95) (3-Y.O+) (Class C) £5,602.00 (£1,696.00: £828.00: £394.00) **7f** Stalls: Low GOING minus 0.04 sec per fur (G) 4-15 (4-15)

1603[6] **Somerton Boy (IRE) (71)***(79) (PCalver)* 5-9-2 MBirch(6) (lw: chsd ldrs: led over 1f out: r.o wl)....— 1

2123[3] Persian Fayre **(66)***(71) (JBerry)* 3-8-4 ow1 KFallon(9) (lw: chsd ldrs: outpcd over 2f out: styd on wl towards fin)....1 2

2457[13] Legal Fiction **(67)***(70) (MJohnston)* 4-8-12 5x DHolland(3) (lw: cl up: disp ld 3f out: no ex fnl f)....1 3

2222[8] Celestial Choir **(73)***(75) (JLEyre)* 5-9-4 JFortune(5) (mid div: rdn over 2f out: r.o wl towards fin)....½ 4

1409[10] Tom Morgan **(82)***(83) (PTWalwyn)* 4-9-13 JWeaver(7) (led tl hdd over 1f out: sn hrd rdn & btn)....½ 5

2121[4] Iktasab **(89)***(88) (EALDunlop)* 3-9-13 WRSwinburn(1) (in tch: rdn 3f out: styng on whn hmpd appr fnl f: sn btn)....¾ 6

2461[5] Cafe Solo **(48)***(42) (NBycroft)* 4-7-7b NKennedy(2) (lw: s.i.s: effrt 3f out: nvr trbld ldrs)....2½ 7

1932[9] General Chaos (IRE) **(82)***(71) (JJO'Neill)* 5-9-8 (5)ow5 ARoche(8) (lw: effrt on outside ent st: no imp)....hd 8

2369[6] Veloce (IRE) **(72)***(40)*(Fav)*(ABailey)* 7-9-3b KDarley(4) (b: lw: bhd: rdn 3f out: sn btn)....11 9

LONG HANDICAP Cafe Solo 7-1

7/2 Veloce (IRE), **5/1** Iktasab, **11/2** Legal Fiction, SOMERTON BOY (IRE), **6/1** Persian Fayre, Tom Morgan, **7/1** Celestial Choir, **20/1** Cafe Solo, **40/1** General Chaos (IRE), CSF £35.72 CT £173.10 TOTE £8.00: £1.80 £2.50 £1.80 (£67.20) Trio £39.00 OWNER Mrs Janis MacPherson (RIPON) BRED Mrs A. Whitehead 9 Rn 1m 28.53 (4.53) SF: 43/28/34/39/47/45/6/35/4

WEIGHT FOR AGE 3yo-7lb

2478

WEST SOUND RADIO CLAIMING STKS (3-Y.O+) (Class E) £3,009.00 (£912.00: £446.00: £213.00)
1m 2f 192y Stalls: Low GOING minus 0.04 sec per fur (G) 4-45 (4-47)

2400[2] **Keep Your Distance (60)***(64)*(Fav)*(MrsMReveley)* 5-9-7 KDarley(4) (lw: a.p: led wl over 1f out: shkn up & qcknd: comf)....— 1

2400[3] Anorak (USA) **(47)***(53) (GMMoore)* 5-8-10v(3) JStack(9) (lw: trckd ldrs: chal 2f out: styd on: nt pce of wnr)....2 2

2306* Funny Rose **(23)***(37) (PMonteith)* 5-8-4 DHolland(1) (trckd ldrs: led 3f out tl wl over 1f out: sn outpcd)....5 **3**
Flash of Realm (FR) *(55) (PMonteith)* 9-9-9 (5)ow5 ARoche(7) (hdwy appr st: prom & rdn 2f out: one pce)....½ **4**
1944[9] Brother Barnabas **(45)***(38) (CWThornton)* 4-8-9 KFallon(3) (led tl hdd 3f out: grad wknd)....2 **5**
1818[5] Hutchies Lady **(44)***(29) (RMMcKellar)* 3-7-6 (7) PFessey(2) (effrt appr st: nvr trbld ldrs)....7 **6**
1688[6] Cymbalo *(JSGoldie)* 4-8-11 LCharnock(8) (outpcd appr st: t.o)....20 **7**
2220[3] High Typha **(47)** *(MRChannon)* 4-8-8 JFortune(6) (prom tl rdn & wknd appr st: p.u appr fnl f).... **P**

11/10 KEEP YOUR DISTANCE (Evens-5/4), **3/1** High Typha, **8/1** Anorak (USA) (6/1-10/1), Funny Rose, **14/1** Brother Barnabas, **16/1** Flash of Realm (FR), **20/1** Hutchies Lady, **33/1** Cymbalo, CSF £9.99 TOTE £1.90: £1.30 £1.70 £1.10 (£5.70) Trio £6.50 OWNER Mr P. D. Savill (SALTBURN) BRED Cedric Ford 8 Rn 2m 25.98 (9.78) SF: 31/20/4/22/5/-/-/-
WEIGHT FOR AGE 3yo-11lb

2479 WESTERN HOUSE RESTAURANT H'CAP (0-75) (3-Y.O+) (Class D)
£5,083.75 (£1,540.00: £752.50: £358.75)
1m Stalls: Low GOING minus 0.04 sec per fur (G) 5-15 (5-16)

2117[4] **Kemo Sabo (72)***(87) (MrsJRRamsden)* 3-9-3 (7) TFinn(4) (lw: led after 1f: qcknd clr 3f out: unchal)....— **1**
2227* Second Colours (USA) **(61)***(68)*(Fav)*(MrsMReveley)* 5-9-7 KDarley(9) (lw: hld up: effrt 3f out: styd on: no ch w wnr)....4 **2**
1904[3] Celebration Cake (IRE) **(63)***(67) (MissLAPerratt)* 3-9-1 MBirch(8) (cl up: rdn 3f out: one pce)....1¾ **3**
2276[14] Matisse **(43)***(43) (JDBethell)* 4-8-3 ow2 KFallon(6) (lw: hld up: hdwy 3f out: hrd rdn & no imp fnl f)....¾ **4**
2425[7] Ballard Lady (IRE) **(50)***(39) (JSWainwright)* 3-7-13 (3)ow3 JStack(7) (sme hdwy 3f out: nvr trbld ldrs)....5 **5**
2156[10] Langtonian **(37)***(22) (JLEyre)* 6-7-11v DaleGibson(5) (lw: s.i.s: sn rcvrd & chsd ldrs: rdn & hung lft over 2f out: sn wknd)....3½ **6**
1195[9] Swandale Flyer **(56)***(38) (NBycroft)* 3-8-8 NKennedy(1) (hmpd after s: hld up & bhd: n.d)....1½ **7**
1615[6] Mithraic (IRE) **(65)***(35) (JWWatts)* 3-9-3 NConnorton(2) (pushed along appr st: sn bhd)....6 **8**
2156[4] Seconds Away **(38)***(7) (JSGoldie)* 4-7-12 LCharnock(3) (plld hrd: led 1f: outpcd over 3f out: sn wknd)....½ **9**

5/2 Second Colours (USA), **5/1** KEMO SABO, Matisse, **6/1** Mithraic (IRE), Seconds Away, **7/1** Celebration Cake (IRE), **12/1** Ballard Lady (IRE), **14/1** Langtonian, **16/1** Swandale Flyer, CSF £18.14 CT £82.72 TOTE £4.80: £1.90 £1.60 £1.70 (£5.70) Trio £6.20 OWNER Mr Colin Webster (THIRSK) BRED Stud-On-The-Chart 9 Rn 1m 42.18 (5.38) SF: 49/38/29/13/1/-/-/-/-
WEIGHT FOR AGE 3yo-8lb

T/Plpt: £46.40 (295.8 Tckts). T/Qdpt: £10.10 (20 Tckts). AA

2251-BEVERLEY (R-H)
Monday July 17th (Good, Good to firm patches)
WEATHER: overcast & cloudy WIND: slt half against

2480 POCKLINGTON (S) STKS (3-Y.O) (Class G) £2,390.00 (£665.00: £320.00)
1m 3f 216y Stalls: High GOING minus 0.40 sec per fur (F) 6-45 (6-46)

2129* **Bunker (IRE) (48)***(58)*(Fav)*(JPearce)* 3-9-1 GBardwell(5) (sn bhd & drvn along: hdwy 4f out: hrd rdn & styd on to ld post)....— **1**
2280[8] Remontant (IRE) **(38)***(49) (RHollinshead)* 3-8-3 (3) AGarth(6) (wnt 2nd 6f out: hung rt u.p over 1f out: styd on towards fin)....s.h **2**
2353[6] High Flown (USA) **(46)***(58) (RonaldThompson)* 3-8-10v(5) LNewton(2) (led & sn clr: hrd rdn fnl f: jst ct)....s.h **3**
2400[4] Longcroft **(39)***(41) (KWHogg)* 3-8-10 JFanning(1) (bhd & pushed along 7f out: sme hdwy 4f out: sn rdn & no imp)....9 **4**
2309[4] Samana Cay **(48)***(21) (DNicholls)* 3-8-10 AlexGreaves(3) (hld up: lost tch 5f out: eased)....15 **5**
1065[11] Midnight Mass *(MissJFCraze)* 3-8-6 SWebster(4) (bit bkwd: chsd ldr tl wknd 4f out: sn bhd)20 **6**

5/4 BUNKER (IRE), **7/2** Samana Cay, **9/2** High Flown (USA), **6/1** Longcroft, **8/1** Remontant (IRE), **20/1** Midnight Mass, CSF £10.79 TOTE £2.20: £1.20 £4.90 (£12.50) OWNER Mr Jeff Pearce (NEWMARKET) BRED Bernard Cooke 6 Rn 2m 40.3 (8.80) SF: 12/3/12/-/-/-
No bid.
STEWARDS' ENQUIRY Newton suspended 26-29/7/95 (excessive use of whip).

2481

NORWOOD RATING RELATED MAIDEN LIMITED STKS (0-65) (3-Y.O) (Class F)
£2,672.00 (£742.00: £356.00)
2m 35y Stalls: Centre GOING minus 0.40 sec per fur (F) 7-10 (7-10)

2300[2] **Zuiena (USA) (62)***(69) (PFICole)* 3-8-9 TQuinn(7) (trckd ldrs: led over 3f out: styd on u.p fnl f: jst hld on) — **1**
2082[2] Torreglia (IRE) **(65)***(69)*(Fav)*(JLDunlop)* 3-8-9 JWeaver(3) (hld up: hdwy ½-wy: shkn up to ld over 6f out: hdd 3f out: rallied fnl f: jst failed) hd **2**
2193[7] Blue Smoke (IRE) **(53)***(68) (BAMcMahon)* 3-9-0b JFortune(2) (s.i.s: hld up: effrt over 3f out: sn rdn: one pce) 6 **3**
2244[3] Hong Kong Designer **(46)***(65) (SGNorton)* 3-9-0 GHind(1) (hld up: hmpd 6f out: hdwy over 3f out: nvr nr to chal) 3 **4**
1587[9] Last Spin **(65)***(48) (JRJenkins)* 3-8-9 MTebbutt(4) (hld up: drvn along & hung rt 7f out: hdwy over 3f out: wknd 2f out) 12 **5**
2166[5] Fools of Pride (IRE) **(33)***(46) (RHollinshead)* 3-8-9 TIves(5) (chsd ldr tl lost pl 6f out) 1¾ **6**
2189[4] Brownlows **(43)** *(MPBielby)* 3-9-0 ACulhane(6) (swtg: led: hung lft ½-wy: hdd over 6f out: rn v.wd ent st: sn t.o) dist **7**

5/4 Torreglia (IRE), **7/4** ZUIENA (USA) (9/4-6/4), **5/1** Last Spin, **8/1** Hong Kong Designer, **12/1** Blue Smoke (IRE), **20/1** Fools of Pride (IRE), **33/1** Brownlows, CSF £4.69 TOTE £2.60: £1.60 £1.70 (£2.00) OWNER Prince Fahd Salman (WHATCOMBE) BRED Michael Baum and Reiko Baum 7 Rn
3m 44.5 (14.00) SF: -/-/-/-/-/-/-
STEWARDS' ENQUIRY Tebbutt suspended 26-29/7/95 (careless riding).

2482

I. J. BLAKEY HAULAGE H'CAP (0-80) (3-Y.O+ F & M) (Class D)
£4,352.25 (£1,308.00: £631.50: £293.25)
1m 1f 207y Stalls: High GOING minus 0.40 sec per fur (F) 7-40 (7-41)

1568[6] **Moneefa (62)***(79) (HRACecil)* 4-9-9 WRyan(1) (trckd ldr: led over 1f out: r.o strly) — **1**
1651[4] Phylian **(48)***(61) (SCWilliams)* 4-8-9 JFortune(9) (led 1f: led over 2f out tl over 1f out: kpt on same pce appr fnl f) 2½ **2**
2152* Inchkeith **(72)***(85)*(Fav)*(GWragg)* 3-9-9 MHills(7) (lw: chsd ldrs: pushed along 4f out: n.m.r over 2f out: styd on one pce appr fnl f) nk **3**
1476[4] Makri **(70)***(79) (MrsJCecil)* 3-9-7 TIves(6) (prom: effrt 3f out: one pce) 2½ **4**
721[5] Sariyaa **(63)***(68) (MBrittain)* 4-9-10 MWigham(3) (led after 1f tl over 2f out: grad wknd) 2 **5**
2278* South Rock **(73)***(78) (JAGlover)* 3-9-10 DeanMcKeown(4) (stdd s: hld up: hdwy on outside 3f out: effrt 2f out: wandered: sn wknd) hd **6**
1961[4] Champagne N Dreams **(57)***(62) (DNicholls)* 3-8-8 AlexGreaves(2) (lw: hld up & bhd: hung bdly lft 6f out: hdwy over 3f out: nvr nr to chal) s.h **7**
1863[10] Sharkashka (IRE) **(57)***(60) (MHEasterby)* 5-9-4 SMaloney(8) (sn in tch: drvn & outpcd 3f out) 1¼ **8**
2196[5] Kanat Lee (IRE) **(38)***(30) (DonEnricoIncisa)* 4-7-13 KimTinkler(5) (a last: drvn along 4f out) 7 **9**

11/4 Inchkeith, **7/2** South Rock, Phylian, **13/2** MONEEFA, **8/1** Makri, Champagne N Dreams, **14/1** Sariyaa, Sharkashka (IRE), **25/1** Kanat Lee (IRE), CSF £29.57 CT £72.44 TOTE £7.30: £2.00 £1.30 £1.40 (£14.60) Trio £14.60 OWNER Prince A. A. Faisal (NEWMARKET) BRED Nawara Stud Co Ltd 9 Rn
2m 6.7 (4.20) SF: 41/23/37/31/30/30/14/22/-
WEIGHT FOR AGE 3yo-10lb

2483

EAST YORKSHIRE GLAZING CLAIMING STKS (2-Y.O) (Class F)
£2,838.00 (£849.00: £407.00: £186.00)
5f Stalls: Centre GOING minus 0.40 sec per fur (F) 8-10 (8-12)

1841[2] **The Butterwick Kid** *(69) (RAFahey)* 2-8-9 ACulhane(4) (chsd ldrs: styd on far side fr ½-wy: led towards fin) — **1**
1772[3] Standown *(68) (JBerry)* 2-8-9 JCarroll(10) (led: edgd lft over 1f out: hdd wl ins fnl f) nk **2**
Power Don *(64+) (WGMTurner)* 2-8-4 (3) PMcCabe(3) (rangy: unf: bit bkwd: s.i.s: hdwy ½-wy: styd on wl fnl f) ¾ **3**
Forest Fantasy *(57+) (JWharton)* 2-8-4 JFanning(5) (leggy: unf: scope: s.i.s: bhd: hdwy ½-wy: styd on wl towards fin) 1¼ **4**
2185[6] Bee Health Boy *(57) (MWEasterby)* 2-8-5 MWigham(2) (trckd ldrs: effrt & hung lft 2f out: swtchd rt: nt qckn) hd **5**
2131[5] Never Think Twice *(65)*(Fav)*(KTIvory)* 2-9-0 MTebbutt(1) (b: swtchd lft s: chsd ldrs tl wknd over 1f out) nk **6**
Krishan Power *(52+) (MWEasterby)* 2-8-8 ow3 TIves(9) (bit bkwd: sn outpcd & pushed along: styd on appr fnl f) 1½ **7**
Yougoa *(42+) (MWEasterby)* 2-7-7 (7) RuthCoulter(6) (unf: scope: bkwd: s.s: bhd & drvn along: sme hdwy over 1f out: n.d) 1½ **8**

2158* Sporting Fantasy *(45) (JBalding)* 2-8-7 SDWilliams(8) (chsd ldrs tl wknd over 1f out)...........1¼ 9
China Castle *(32) (PCHaslam)* 2-8-10 JWeaver(7) (cmpt: bit bkwd: s.i.s: a outpcd)..................5 10
Ann's Music *(JMJefferson)* 2-8-2 GHind(11) (cmpt: bit bkwd: unruly s: s.v.s: a wl bhd).........20 11

7/2 Never Think Twice, **4/1** Standown, **9/2** THE BUTTERWICK KID, **6/1** Sporting Fantasy (op 4/1), **8/1** Power Don, **10/1** China Castle (op 6/1), Forest Fantasy, **12/1** Ann's Music, **16/1** Krishan Power, **20/1** Bee Health Boy, **33/1** Yougoa, CSF £22.87 TOTE £5.40: £1.90 £1.40 £2.10 (£9.60) Trio £63.30 OWNER The Butterwick Race Co (MALTON) BRED Scorrier Stud 11 Rn
66.3 secs (4.80) SF: -/-/-/-/-/-/-/-/-/-/-

2484 JWE MOBILEPHONE GROUP H'CAP (0-70) (3-Y.O+) (Class E)
£3,367.75 (£1,012.00: £488.50: £226.75)
7f 100y Stalls: High GOING minus 0.40 sec per fur (F) 8-40 (8-41)

2276[13] **Kilnamartyra Girl (44)***(58) (JParkes)* 5-8-4 (3) PMcCabe(5) (bhd & pushed along: gd hdwy & nt clr run over 1f out: qcknd to ld ins fnl f: sn clr) ....— 1
2327[3] Lord Vivienne (IRE) **(40)***(48) (BSRothwell)* 6-8-3 ACulhane(12) (led: clr 2f out: hdd ins fnl f)..3 2
1666[13] Northern Spark **(46)***(52) (MartynWane)* 7-8-9 JCarroll(7) (lw: chsd ldrs: outpcd over 2f out: kpt on wl fnl f) ....¾ 3
2258[2] Princess Maxine (IRE) **(56)***(61) (JJO'Neill)* 6-9-0 (5) GParkin(11) (mid div: hmpd over 5f out: swtchd outside & styd on strly ins fnl f)...nk 4
2191[3] Reed My Lips (IRE) **(36)***(40) (BPJBaugh)* 4-7-6 (7) IonaWands(13) (bhd & pushed along: styd on fnl 2f: nt rch ldrs) ....½ 5
2220* Dante's Rubicon (IRE) **(48)***(52) (JDBethell)* 4-8-11 TIves(4) (trckd ldrs: effrt over 2f out: kpt on same pce)..s.h 6
2020[2] Euro Sceptic (IRE) **(51)***(52)*(Fav)*(MHEasterby)* 3-8-7b SMaloney(9) (a chsng ldrs: drvn along 3f out: one pce)..1½ 7
2310[10] Northern Chief **(37)***(33) (MissJFCraze)* 5-8-0 JFanning(10) (mid div: effrt over 2f out: nvr rchd ldrs) 2½ 8
2088[2] Sea-Ayr (IRE) **(49)***(37) (MrsSMAustin)* 5-8-9 (3) DarrenMoffatt(2) (b: bhd: hdwy on outside 3f out: edgd lft: nvr nr ldrs)..3½ 9
1873[16] Henry Will **(30)***(16) (WLBarker)* 11-7-7 GBardwell(6) (bhd: sme hdwy on outside 3f out: n.d) ....¾ 10
2187[4] Golden Chip (IRE) **(65)***(48) (JLEyre)* 7-10-0 JFortune(1) (bit bkwd: in tch: effrt 3f out: sn wknd)..1¾ 11
2309[7] Melody Dancer **(50)***(30) (MissJFCraze)* 4-8-13 SWebster(3) (b.off hind: hld up: sme hdwy over 3f out: sn wknd)..1¼ 12
228[9] Grey Kingdom **(40)***(18) (MBrittain)* 4-8-3 JLowe(8) (w ldr tl wknd qckly over 1f out)..................1 13
Arkindale Amber **(41)***(15) (FJO'Mahony)* 3-7-11 ow2 TWilliams(14) (hld up & plld v.hrd: a bhd) ....¾ 14

9/2 Euro Sceptic (IRE), **5/1** Sea-Ayr (IRE), **6/1** Princess Maxine (IRE), **8/1** Northern Spark, Dante's Rubicon (IRE), KILNAMARTYRA GIRL, Lord Vivienne (IRE), **10/1** Reed My Lips (IRE), **12/1** Golden Chip (IRE), **25/1** Henry Will, Northern Chief, Melody Dancer, Grey Kingdom, **33/1** Arkindale Amber, CSF £68.72 CT £494.64 TOTE £16.50: £4.20 £1.90 £3.90 (£65.00) Trio £306.60 OWNER Mr P.J. Cronin (MALTON) BRED F. R. Colley 14 Rn 1m 34.3 (2.30) SF: 35/25/29/38/17/29/22/10/14/-/25/7
WEIGHT FOR AGE 3yo-7lb

2485 HULL MAIDEN STKS (2-Y.O) (Class D) £3,678.00 (£1,104.00: £532.00: £246.00)
7f 100y Stalls: High GOING minus 0.40 sec per fur (F) 9-10 (9-12)

1856[3] **Inchrory** *(80)*(Fav)*(HRACecil)* 2-9-0 WRyan(5) (b.nr hind: trckd ldrs: led over 1f out: hung rt: drvn out) ....— 1
1134[6] Pleasant Surprise *(75+) (MJohnston)* 2-9-0 DHolland(2) (unruly s: prom: pushed along & outpcd over 3f out: styd on u.p over 1f out: no ch w wnr) 2½ 2
1856[2] Munketh (USA) *(71) (JLDunlop)* 2-9-0 JWeaver(6) (lw: led: clr 3f out: hdd over 1f out: grad wknd)..1½ 3
2083[6] Belana *(65+) (JWWatts)* 2-8-9 TIves(4) (sn outpcd & bhd: hdwy over 1f out: edgd rt & styd on towards fin)..½ 4
1842[6] Eric's Bett *(66) (MrsSMAustin)* 2-8-11 (3) DarrenMoffatt(7) (b: chsd ldrs: hmpd over 5f out: one pce fnl 2f)..2 5
Crystal Falls (IRE) *(60+) (JJO'Neill)* 2-9-0 JCarroll(3) (cmpt: bit bkwd: chsd ldrs tl outpcd fnl 2f)..3 6
1877[9] Westcourt Magic *(49) (MWEasterby)* 2-9-0 SDWilliams(1) (hld up & plld hrd: sn w ldrs: lost pl over 2f out: sn bhd) 5 7
Clued Up *(44) (MHEasterby)* 2-8-9 SMaloney(8) (leggy: bkwd: dwlt: a outpcd & bhd)...........s.h 8

5/4 INCHRORY (Evens-11/8), **11/4** Munketh (USA), **3/1** Pleasant Surprise, **10/1** Belana, **16/1** Crystal Falls (IRE), **25/1** Clued Up, **33/1** Westcourt Magic, Eric's Bett, CSF £5.71 TOTE £2.10: £1.10 £1.30 £1.10 (£3.30) OWNER Sir David Wills (NEWMARKET) BRED Sir David Wills 8 Rn
1m 35.4 (3.40) SF: 30/25/21/15/16/10/-/-

T/Plpt: £47.30 (290.18 Tckts). T/Qdpt: £10.80 (7.15 Tckts). WG

2314-WINDSOR (Fig. 8)
Monday July 17th (Good to firm)

WEATHER: overcast WIND: almost nil

2486 HEADWAY (S) H'CAP (0-60) (3-Y.O+) (Class F) £3,107.50 (£870.00: £422.50)
1m 3f 135y Stalls: High GOING minus 0.50 sec per fur (F) 6-30 (6-35)

2379[8] **Nothing Doing (IRE) (30)***(44)*(Fav)*(WJMusson)* 6-8-12 AMcGlone(16) (4th st: led on bit over 2f out: easily) ....— 1
2078[8] Call Me Albi (IRE) **(42)***(51) (GLMoore)* 4-9-10 AClark(4) (lw: 7th st: hrd rdn 3f out: styd on).....4 2
2334[8] Bronze Runner **(40)***(48) (SMellor)* 11-9-8b TSprake(5) (9th st: hdwy over 2f out: nvr nrr).......s.h 3
1974[10] Brown Carpet **(26)***(34)*(Fav)*(CAHorgan)* 8-8-8b PaulEddery(13) (6th st: rdn 2f out: one pce).......nk 4
2246[7] Whispering Loch (IRE) **(40)***(43)*(Fav)*(JAkehurst)* 4-9-8b SWhitworth(3) (8th st: rdn 3f out: one pce: broke leg ins fnl f: dead) 4 5
2134[7] Excelled (IRE) **(30)***(29) (CJDrewe)* 6-8-12 RCochrane(7) (nrst fin).......2½ 6
2310[6] Swynford Flyer **(30)***(24)*(Fav)*(JAHarris)* 6-8-5 (7) CAdamson(12) (3rd st: ev ch over 2f out: wknd over 1f out).......3½ 7
2334[7] Malingerer **(33)***(27) (DAWilson)* 4-9-1 AMackay(2) (bhd tl r.o fnl 2f) ....½ 8
2174[8] Burnt Sienna (IRE) **(28)***(20) (JSMoore)* 3-7-7v(5) MBaird(15) (2nd st: wknd 2f out) 1½ 9
1622[19] The Oil Baron **(20)***(9) (RPCHoad)* 9-7-11 (5) NVarley(18) (bhd tl sme late hdwy).......1½ 10
Concinnity (USA) **(39)***(27) (MMadgwick)* 6-9-7 CAvery(17) (b: bit bkwd: swtg: bhd tl sme late hdwy) 1 11
1974[5] Premier Blues (FR) **(26)***(13) (RJRWilliams)* 5-8-8b DBiggs(14) (led tl wknd over 2f out).......1 12
2134[5] Ballestro (IRE) **(40)***(20) (JFfitch-Heyes)* 3-8-3 (7) MHenry(8) (nvr nr to chal) 5 13
1834[5] Darius The Great (IRE) **(36)***(12) (DMarks)* 3-8-6 StephenDavies(11) (lw: 5th & wd st: wknd 3f out).......3 14
2209[6] Swan Flyer **(23)** *(JJSheehan)* 4-8-2 (3) SDrowne(10) (swtg: a bhd) 4 15
2439[12] Coalisland **(25)** *(RIngram)* 5-8-7b NAdams(6) (a bhd) 2 16
Tigana **(42)** *(MrsLCJewell)* 3-8-12 CRutter(9) (bhd fnl 4f: t.o).......25 17

6/1 NOTHING DOING (IRE), Swynford Flyer, Brown Carpet, Whispering Loch (IRE), **13/2** Bronze Runner, **8/1** Call Me Albi (IRE), Malingerer (op 5/1), **14/1** Premier Blues (FR), Ballestro (IRE) (10/1-16/1), **16/1** Coalisland, **20/1** Excelled (IRE), **33/1** Burnt Sienna (IRE), The Oil Baron, Darius The Great (IRE), Swan Flyer, Concinnity (USA), Tigana, CSF £51.44 CT £294.57 TOTE £7.10: £1.80 £2.70 £1.90 £1.40 (£41.00) Trio £47.80 OWNER Broughton Bloodstock (NEWMARKET) BRED Cleaboy Stud 17 Rn 2m 29.9 (3.90) SF: 31/38/35/21/30/16/11/14/-/-/14/-/-/-/-/-/-
WEIGHT FOR AGE 3yo-12lb
No bid.

2487 E.B.F. SUNLEY BUILDS MEDIAN AUCTION MAIDEN STKS (2-Y.O) (Class E) £3,647.25 (£1,098.00: £531.50: £248.25)
5f 10y Stalls: High GOING minus 0.50 sec per fur (F) 7-00 (7-02)

2000[3] **Nellie North** *(75) (MrsMMcCourt)* 2-8-2 (7) RStudholme(2) (mde all: pushed out).......— 1
2320[14] Village Native (FR) *(79) (KOCunningham-Brown)* 2-9-0 RCochrane(10) (chsd wnr: ev ch fnl f: r.o) ....nk 2
1123[3] Therhea (IRE) *(78)*(Fav)*(BRMillman)* 2-8-9 (5) AWhelan(11) (lw: a.p: ev ch fnl f: r.o) ....nk 3
Maristax *(62) (PJMakin)* 2-8-9 MRoberts(1) (leggy: unf: s.s: gd hdwy over 1f out: fin wl).......3½ 4
Whalley Abbey *(60) (GLMoore)* 2-8-9 SWhitworth(8) (str: scope: bit bkwd: s.s: gd late hdwy: nvr nrr).......¾ 5
Supreme Power *(63) (WRMuir)* 2-9-0 CRutter(6) (str: a mid div) ....½ 6
2230[2] Red Acuisle (IRE) *(63) (MBell)* 2-9-0 JReid(7) (no hdwy fnl 2f).......hd 7
Antonias Melody *(56) (SRBowring)* 2-8-4 (5) CTeague(5) (unf: bit bkwd: hrd rdn over 2f out: no rspnse) ....½ 8
Careful (IRE) *(45) (BWHills)* 2-8-9 PaulEddery(3) (unf: prom 3f) 3½ 9
Tahya (USA) *(23) (HThomsonJones)* 2-8-9 NCarlisle(4) (lt-f: s.s: a bhd).......7 10
2170[4] Windi Imp (IRE) *(BJMeehan)* 2-8-9 BDoyle(9) (Withdrawn not under Starter's orders: broke out of stalls)....... W

3/1 Therhea (IRE), **4/1** Careful (IRE) (op 7/4), **5/1** Red Acuisle (IRE) (op 9/4), **7/1** Village Native (FR) (5/1-8/1), **9/1** Tahya (USA) (4/1-10/1), Maristax (4/1-10/1), **10/1** NELLIE NORTH (6/1-12/1), Antonias Melody (20/1-33/1), **12/1** Windi Imp (IRE), **14/1** Supreme Power, **33/1** Whalley Abbey, CSF £70.10 TOTE £11.10: £2.40 £2.10 £1.30 (£79.80) Trio £20.70 OWNER Mr Geoffrey Greenwood (WANTAGE) BRED Mrs C. A. Wernham 10 Rn 61.1 secs (2.10) SF: 17/21/20/4/2/5/5/-/-/-/-

2488 WILLIAM HILL ROYAL WINDSOR H'CAP (0-80) (3-Y.O+ F & M) (Class D) £4,484.00 (£1,352.00: £656.00: £308.00)
1m 67y Stalls: High GOING minus 0.50 sec per fur (F) 7-30 (7-31)

1793[7] **Ma Petite Anglaise (79)***(90) (WJarvis)* 3-9-2 (7) MHenry(9) (4th st: swtchd rt over 1f out: swtchd lft ins fnl f: qcknd to ld last stride) — 1
2178* Marrowfat Lady (IRE) **(63)***(74) (BRMillman)* 4-8-10 (5) AWhelan(7) (3rd st: led ins fnl f: hdd post) s.h 2
2317[6] Mo's Star **(62)***(72) (SDow)* 3-8-6 MRoberts(4) (lw: 2nd st: led over 2f out tl ins fnl f) ½ 3
2265* Proud Destiny **(80)***(85)*(Fav)*(MRStoute)* 3-9-7 (3) JTate(1) (6th st: hdwy 3f out: one pce fnl 2f) 2½ 4
2246[14] Emma Grimes (IRE) **(41)***(43) (JSMoore)* 4-7-2 (5) MBaird(2) (lw: 5th st: one pce fnl 3f) 1¾ 5
1692[2] Anna-Jane **(64)***(62) (RHannon)* 3-8-8 JReid(3) (swtg: led: hung bdly lft fnl 5f: hdd over 2f out) 1¾ 6
1617[12] Misty Silks **(71)***(54) (MJRyan)* 5-9-9 AClark(6) (a bhd) 8 7
2265[7] Radiance (IRE) **(60)***(33) (RHannon)* 3-8-4 GCarter(8) (a bhd) 5 8
2056[6] Mnemonic **(62)***(24) (HCandy)* 3-8-6 WNewnes(5) (a bhd) 6 9

LONG HANDICAP Emma Grimes (IRE) 7-6

5/2 Proud Destiny, **7/2** Marrowfat Lady (IRE), **9/2** MA PETITE ANGLAISE, **5/1** Anna-Jane, **8/1** Mo's Star, **10/1** Misty Silks, Mnemonic, **20/1** Radiance (IRE), **50/1** Emma Grimes (IRE), CSF £20.44 CT £113.83 TOTE £6.40: £2.00 £1.50 £2.10 (£12.20) Trio £30.60 OWNER Mr K. P. Seow (NEWMARKET) BRED R. P. Williams 9 Rn 1m 45.3 (3.70) SF: 31/23/13/26/-/3/3/-/-
WEIGHT FOR AGE 3yo-8lb

2489 TAP AND SPILE NIMBLE CONDITIONS STKS (2-Y.O F) (Class C) £6,116.50 (£2,273.50: £1,099.25: £458.75: £191.88: £85.12)
5f 217y Stalls: High GOING minus 0.50 sec per fur (F) 8-00 (8-01)

2136* **Tropical Dance (USA)** *(88)*(Fav)*(MrsJCecil)* 2-9-5 JReid(2) (lw: w ldrs: led 3f out: drvn out) — 1
2077* Rhumba Dancer *(75) (RHannon)* 2-8-11 DaneO'Neill(4) (lw: hld up: hdwy over 1f out: r.o: nt rch wnr) 2 2
2328[5] Polly Golightly *(75) (BSmart)* 2-8-13 RCochrane(5) (chsd ldrs: r.o ins fnl f) ½ 3
1893[12] Capture The Moment *(40) (RJRWilliams)* 2-8-13 DBiggs(3) (led 3f: r.o one pce) 1½ 4
1829[2] My Kind *(59) (KMcAuliffe)* 2-8-9 DHarrison(7) (lw: w ldrs tl wknd over 1f out) 3 5
1259[4] Windswept (IRE) *(58) (DJSffrenchDavis)* 2-8-13 NAdams(6) (bhd fnl 3f) 2 6
Azwah (USA) *(51) (PTWalwyn)* 2-8-9 WCarson(1) (w'like: bit bkwd: s.s: hdwy 4f out: ev ch over 2f out: eased whn btn over 1f out) 1 7

4/6 TROPICAL DANCE (USA), **3/1** Azwah (USA) (2/1-4/1), **15/2** Rhumba Dancer (7/2-8/1), **16/1** Windswept (IRE), Capture The Moment, **20/1** Polly Golightly, **33/1** My Kind, CSF £6.41 TOTE £1.70: £1.30 £2.40 (£3.10) OWNER Mr George Ward (NEWMARKET) BRED Charles T Wilson Jr. 7 Rn 1m 11.7 (1.20) SF: 44/31/31/27/15/14/7

2490 BANKERS INSURANCE H'CAP (0-80) (3-Y.O+) (Class D) £4,354.00 (£1,312.00: £636.00: £298.00) **1m 2f 7y** Stalls: High GOING minus 0.50 sec (F) 8-30 (8-33)

1594[4] **Trade Wind (69)***(79) (DRCElsworth)* 4-9-4b(5) AProcter(9) (8th st: hdwy 3f out: hrd rdn over 1f out: led cl home) — 1
262[6] Conspicuous (IRE) **(57)***(65) (LGCottrell)* 5-8-11 MRoberts(5) (2nd st: led over 3f out tl nr fin) 1¼ 2
2246* Mighty Kingdom (IRE) **(43)***(51) (JohnBerry)* 4-7-6 (5) NVarley(10) (lw: 3rd st: r.o one pce fnl 2f) nk 3
1324[5] Persian Elite (IRE) **(74)***(81) (PFICole)* 4-9-7 (7) ADaly(4) (led tl over 3f out: r.o one pce) hd 4
2138* Haroldon (IRE) **(74)***(79) (BPalling)* 6-10-0 TSprake(11) (b: 6th st: no hdwy fnl 2f) 1¼ 5
2314* Just Flamenco **(50)***(51)*(Fav)*(MJRyan)* 4-8-4 5x AClark(3) (lw: hdwy & rdn 3f out: nvr nr to chal) 2½ 6
2317[8] Duello **(60)***(56) (MBlanshard)* 4-9-0 RCochrane(1) (nvr nr to chal) 3½ 7
2293[10] Grand Applause (IRE) **(53)***(46) (MPMuggeridge)* 5-8-7b SWhitworth(12) (a bhd) 2 8
2081[3] Marchman **(47)***(35) (JSKing)* 10-8-1 PaulEddery(8) (7th st: wknd 3f out) 3 9
1831* Dr Edgar **(65)***(49)*(Fav)*(GWragg)* 3-8-9 FNorton(7) (lw: 4th st: wknd qckly over 2f out) 2½ 10
Double Jeopardy **(72)***(40) (JWhite)* 4-9-9 (3) SDrowne(2) (lw: 5th st: wknd 3f out) 10 11

100/30 Just Flamenco, Dr Edgar, **7/1** Marchman, **15/2** Haroldon (IRE) (6/1-10/1), **8/1** TRADE WIND, Conspicuous (IRE), **10/1** Persian Elite (IRE) (7/1-12/1), Duello (7/1-12/1), **12/1** Mighty Kingdom (IRE) (op 8/1), **20/1** Double Jeopardy, **25/1** Grand Applause (IRE), CSF £68.56 CT £710.94 TOTE £9.30: £2.80 £3.70 £3.10 (£24.70) Trio £303.90 OWNER Mr Ray Richards (WHITCOMBE) BRED Mrs M. H. Hunter 11 Rn
2m 7.0 (2.10) SF: 50/36/22/52/50/22/27/17/6/10/11
WEIGHT FOR AGE 3yo-10lb

2491 MARK DAVIES INJURED RIDERS' FUND H'CAP (0-70) (3-Y.O) (Class E) £4,133.00 (£1,244.00: £602.00: £281.00)

5f 217y Stalls: High GOING minus 0.50 sec per fur (F) 9-00 (9-02)

2318[2] **Charnwood Queen (45)**(54)(Fav)*(RWArmstrong)* 3-7-10 ow1 WCarson(7) (mde all: r.o wl)....— **1**
1963[5] Sweet Mate **(43)***(46) (SRBowring)* 3-7-3b(5) MBaird(11) (chsd wnr: ev ch over 1f out: no imp)....2½ **2**
2318[4] Sizzling **(63)***(62) (RHannon)* 3-9-0 MRoberts(13) (a.p: r.o one pce fnl f)....1½ **3**
2318[6] Cork Street Girl (IRE) **(53)***(51) (BJMeehan)* 3-8-4b BDoyle(15) (a.p: hrd rdn 2f out: r.o one pce)....½ **4**
2318[7] Almasi (IRE) **(65)***(60) (CFWall)* 3-9-2 WWoods(9) (a.p: rdn 2f out: nt qckn)....1 **5**
2067[7] Stoppes Brow **(65)***(59) (GLMoore)* 3-9-2v SWhitworth(12) (dwlt: sn prom: one pce fnl 2f)....½ **6**
2033[8] Prince Pellinore **(45)***(36) (JohnBerry)* 3-7-5 (5)ow2 NVarley(14) (w ldrs tl wknd 2f out)....nk **7**
2318[5] Vavona **(55)***(42) (LJHolt)* 3-8-6 ow2 JReid(6) (nvr nrr)....1½ **8**
2168[6] Kensington Freight **(49)***(30) (JAkehurst)* 3-7-7 (7)ow7 MHenry(10) (nvr nr to chal)....nk **9**
2003[8] Silver Tzar **(69)***(47) (WJHaggas)* 3-9-6 RCochrane(1) (s.s: nvr nr ldrs)....4 **10**
2049* Sharp 'n Smart **(70)***(46) (BSmart)* 3-9-0 (7) DaneO'Neill(5) (prom over 3f)....¾ **11**
It'sthebusiness **(60)***(32) (SDow)* 3-8-11 DHarrison(8) (a bhd)....1¼ **12**
2318[8] Tara Colleen (IRE) **(42)***(10) (CAHorgan)* 3-7-7 NAdams(2) (a bhd)....1¾ **13**
1168[15] Henry Weston **(42)** *(PHowling)* 3-7-7 NCarlisle(4) (bhd fnl 2f)....8 **14**
2318[16] La Thuile **(44)** *(MDIUsher)* 3-7-2b(7)ow2 CAdamson(3) (spd 2f)....6 **15**

LONG HANDICAP Kensington Freight 6-13 Tara Colleen (IRE) 7-4 Henry Weston 7-5 La Thuile 7-4

3/1 CHARNWOOD QUEEN, **9/2** Vavona, **6/1** Sizzling (op 4/1), **13/2** Almasi (IRE), **15/2** Stoppes Brow, **8/1** Sweet Mate (11/2-9/1), **10/1** Sharp 'n Smart (7/1-11/1), **14/1** Cork Street Girl (IRE), **20/1** It'sthebusiness, **25/1** Silver Tzar, Tara Colleen (IRE), **33/1** Kensington Freight, Prince Pellinore, Henry Weston, La Thuile, CSF £27.95 CT £128.84 TOTE £3.30: £1.80 £2.50 £2.20 (£14.20) Trio £22.00 OWNER Mr R. V. Cliff (NEWMARKET) BRED Rockhouse Farms Ltd 15 Rn
1m 11.1 (0.60) SF: 31/23/39/28/37/36/13/19/7/24/23/9/-/-/-

T/Jkpt: Not won; £30,116.80 to Beverley 18/7/95. T/Plpt: £106.60 (187.64 Tckts). T/Qdpt: £72.90 (0.25 Tckts); £73.95 to Beverley 18/7/95. Hn

2290-WOLVERHAMPTON (L-H) Monday July 17th (Standard)

WEATHER: cloudy WIND: slt bhd

2492 THORPE VERNON H'CAP (0-65) (3-Y.O+) (Class F) £2,519.00 (£694.00: £329.00)

5f (Fibresand) Stalls: Low GOING: 0.16 sec per fur (SLW) 2-00 (2-00)

2364[4] **Ashkernazy (IRE) (43)***(50) (NEBerry)* 4-8-7 NAdams(4) (led 1f: rdn to ld ins fnl f: r.o wl)....— **1**
2231[2] Southern Dominion **(50)***(52)*(Fav)*(MJohnston)* 3-8-9 DeanMcKeown(9) (led after 1f tl hdd & no ex ins fnl f)....1½ **2**
2234[1] King Rambo **(61)***(61) (RHollinshead)* 4-9-7 (7) AEddery(10) (chsd ldrs: effrt over 1f out: nt pce to chal)....¾ **3**
2267[3] La Belle Dominique **(60)***(49) (SGKnight)* 3-9-5 VSlattery(3) (lw: chsd ldrs: rdn wl over 1f out: nvr able to chal)....3½ **4**
2144[6] Most Uppitty **(55)***(37) (JBerry)* 3-8-7 (7) JoanneWebster(5) (nvr gng pce of ldrs)....2 **5**
2303[6] Featherstone Lane **(62)***(43) (MissLCSiddall)* 4-9-12v WNewnes(8) (outpcd & bhd tl r.o fnl f)....½ **6**
*2295** Bonny Melody **(40)***(17)*(Fav)*(PDEvans)* 4-7-11 (7) AmandaSanders(6) (sn drvn along: a in rr)....1¼ **7**
532[7] Jon's Choice **(52)***(28) (BPreece)* 7-9-2 JLowe(2) (bit bkwd: chsd ldrs over 3f: sn lost pl)....nk **8**
2295[5] Chance Me **(40)***(12) (MJohnston)* 3-7-13 TWilliams(1) (spd 3f: sn rdn & wknd)....1 **9**
2142[9] Sabella **(58)** *(RHarris)* 4-9-8 AMackay(7) (s.i.s: a bhd & outpcd: t.o)....20 **10**

100/30 Bonny Melody, Southern Dominion, **4/1** King Rambo, **6/1** Featherstone Lane, **8/1** Most Uppitty, **12/1** ASHKERNAZY (IRE), Chance Me, **16/1** La Belle Dominique, **20/1** Jon's Choice, **33/1** Sabella, CSF £49.94 CT £176.61 TOTE £20.32: £9.80 £1.90 £1.90 (£50.30) Trio £45.30 OWNER London Bridge II (UPPER LAMBOURN) BRED G. P. Griffin 10 Rn

62.6 secs (4.60) SF: 27/24/41/21/9/20/-/5/-/-
WEIGHT FOR AGE 3yo-5lb

2493

KELLY SERVICES (UK) CLAIMING STKS (3-Y.O+) (Class F) £2,519.00 (£694.00: £329.00) **6f (Fibresand)** Stalls: Low GOING: 0.16 sec per fur (SLW) 2-30 (2-31)

2162* **Sense of Priority (57)***(67)*(Fav)*(DNicholls)* 6-9-2 AlexGreaves(8) (lw: hld up gng wl: qcknd to ld over 1f out: sn clr: eased nr fin).......— **1**
2398 3 Brookhead Lady **(57)***(44) (PDEvans)* 4-8-9 PaulEddery(6) (b.nr fore: hdwy 2f out: kpt on u.p fnl f: no ch w wnr).......6 **2**
2142 6 Petomi **(70)***(52) (SirMarkPrescott)* 3-8-11 GDuffield(7) (hdwy over 2f out: hrd rdn bel dist: one pce).......s.h **3**
1785 14 Assignment **(52)***(35) (JFfitch-Heyes)* 9-8-8b TWilliams(3) (b.off hind: lw: led tl rdn & hdd over 1f out: sn btn).......3 **4**
2071 11 Vengan **(37)***(15) (DHaydnJones)* 3-8-1 AMackay(1) (chsd ldr over 4f: sn rdn & outpcd).......7 **5**
2071 6 Northern Grey **(47)***(13) (JBerry)* 3-8-8 JCarroll(5) (chsd ldrs 4f: sn rdn & wknd).......3½ **6**
Miss The Beat *(11) (SMellor)* 3-8-7 MWigham(4) (cmpt: bkwd: s.s: a bhd & outpcd).......½ **7**
2141 9 Caherass Court (IRE) **(37)** *(BPreece)* 4-8-4v NAdams(2) (dwlt: a bhd & outpcd).......5 **8**

11/8 SENSE OF PRIORITY, **7/4** Petomi, **9/2** Brookhead Lady, **12/1** Northern Grey (op 7/1), **20/1** Assignment, **33/1** Miss The Beat, **50/1** Vengan, Caherass Court (IRE), CSF £7.86 TOTE £2.40: £1.20 £1.30 £1.30 (£3.50) OWNER Mr S. Schofield (THIRSK) BRED Cheveley Park Stud Ltd 8 Rn

1m 15.8 (4.60) SF: 49/26/28/17/-/-/-/-
WEIGHT FOR AGE 3yo-6lb

2494

MUNSLOW PRECISION ENGINEERING MAIDEN STKS (3-Y.O) (Class D) £3,766.10 (£1,122.80: £535.40: £241.70)
1m 4f (Fibresand) Stalls: Low GOING: 0.16 sec per fur (SLW) 3-00 (3-03)

2193 6 **Backview (64)***(73) (BJLlewellyn)* 3-9-0 TWilliams(5) (chsd ldrs: rdn to ld 4f out: sn pushed clr: unchal).......— **1**
2208 5 Racing Hawk (USA) *(66) (HRACecil)* 3-9-0 AMcGlone(6) (chsd ldrs: effrt & ev ch 4f out: 2nd & rdn st: one pce).......5 **2**
1755 6 Cuba **(74)***(61)*(Fav)*(MRStoute)* 3-9-0 DeanMcKeown(4) (hld up: hdwy 5f out: 3rd st: sn hrd rdn: no imp).......4 **3**
Noble Ballerina (USA) *(49) (APJarvis)* 3-8-9 JCarroll(2) (w'like: leggy: prom: led over 5f out to 4f out: 4th & wkng st).......5 **4**
1983 8 Bold Charlie *(14) (SMellor)* 3-9-0 MWigham(7) (led over 6f: 4th & btn ent st: t.o).......30 **5**
Efosa *(2) (MPMuggeridge)* 3-9-0 SWhitworth(3) (nt grwn: bkwd: prom 8f: sn lost pl: 5th & t.o st).......9 **6**
Cariad Ffol *(BJLlewellyn)* 3-8-9 VSlattery(1) (leggy: lt-f: s.s: a in rr: t.o fr ½-wy: 7th st).......25 **7**

5/4 Cuba (8/11-6/4), **2/1** Racing Hawk (USA), **7/2** BACKVIEW, **12/1** Noble Ballerina (USA) (op 5/1), **66/1** Efosa, Cariad Ffol, **100/1** Bold Charlie, CSF £10.25 TOTE £7.20: £2.70 £1.10 (£4.40) OWNER Mr Eamonn O'Malley (BARGOED) BRED G. D. Dalrymple 7 Rn 2m 41.7 (10.70) SF: 40/33/28/16/-/-/-

2495

WOLVERHAMPTON CHAMBER OF COMMERCE & INDUSTRY H'CAP (0-65) (4-Y.O+) (Class F) £2,560.00 (£760.00: £360.00: £160.00)
1m 6f 166y (Fibresand) Stalls: Centre GOING: 0.16 sec per fur (SLW) 3-30 (3-30)

2413 4 **Brave Spy (54)***(66) (CACyzer)* 4-9-4 DBiggs(12) (lw: a.p: led over 3f out tl ins fnl f: rallied to ld cl home).......— **1**
1686 5 Premier Dance **(57)***(69) (DHaydnJones)* 8-9-7 AMackay(5) (lw: hld up: hdwy 5f out: 4th st: shkn up to ld ins fnl f: hdd & no ex nr fin).......hd **2**
2147 4 Swordking (IRE) **(40)***(47)*(Fav)*(JLHarris)* 6-8-4v PaulEddery(10) (hld up: hdwy 5f out: 3rd st: ev ch over 1f out: sn rdn & btn).......5 **3**
1535 4 La Menorquina (USA) **(48)***(54) (DMarks)* 5-8-12 JCarroll(1) (hld up & bhd: hdwy & 6th st: nt rch ldrs).......s.h **4**
1970 8 Gunmaker **(33)***(36) (BJLlewellyn)* 6-7-11 ow3 TWilliams(4) (prom: led over 6f out tl over 3f out: 2nd & rdn st: sn outpcd).......hd **5**
1160 9 Jarrow **(34)***(31) (MrsAMNaughton)* 4-7-12v JLowe(3) (hld up: hdwy 5f out: wknd 3f out).......9 **6**
2293 4 Kierchem (IRE) **(60)***(56) (RFFisher)* 4-9-10 GDuffield(6) (hld up in tch: rdn over 3f out: 5th & btn st).......nk **7**

2293[8] Winn's Pride (IRE) **(35)***(10) (RHollinshead)* 4-7-13 FNorton(2) (lw: chsd ldrs tl wknd over 2f out: t.o) 20 8
415[14] Soda Popinski (USA) **(29)** *(JLHarris)* 7-7-7 NAdams(7) (led 8f: wknd over 4f out) 7 9
Canary Blue (IRE) **(39)***(5) (JGMO'Shea)* 4-8-3 TSprake(8) (lost pl 5f out: sn bhd) ....¾ 10
1955[11] Lone Risk **(55)***(20) (CNAllen)* 4-9-5 GBardwell(9) (swtg: a in rr: reminders 7f out: no imp: t.o) 1½ 11
2090[4] Perfect Ending **(45)** *(CACyzer)* 4-8-6v(3) DRMcCabe(11) (s.s: hdwy 8f out: wknd over 4f out: t.o) 20 12

7/2 Swordking (IRE) (5/1-3/1), **4/1** La Menorquina (USA), Kierchem (IRE), **11/2** BRAVE SPY (4/1-6/1), **8/1** Premier Dance (op 5/1), **14/1** Gunmaker, Winn's Pride (IRE) (10/1-16/1), Lone Risk (op 8/1), **16/1** Jarrow, Perfect Ending, **33/1** Canary Blue (IRE), **50/1** Soda Popinski (USA), CSF £47.35 CT £163.82 TOTE £7.40: £1.80 £2.50 £1.90 (£30.50) Trio £19.50 OWNER Mr R. M. Cyzer (HORSHAM) BRED Floors Farming & London Thoroughbred Services Ltd 12 Rn

3m 21.5 (14.10) SF: 40/43/21/28/10/5/30/-/-/-/-/-

2496 SALOP DESIGN & ENGINEERING (S) STKS (2-Y.O) (Class G) £2,277.00 (£627.00: £297.00) 7f (Fibresand) Stalls: Centre GOING: 0.16 sec(SLW) 4-00 (4-02)

2242[8] **Victoria Venture** *(59) (SPCWoods)* 2-8-6 WWoods(1) (a.p: led ent st: drvn out) ....— 1
2075[5] Pulga Circo *(57) (BAMcMahon)* 2-8-6 FNorton(9) (lw: chsd ldrs: 4th & rdn st: r.o wl fnl f) 1 2
1981[9] Young Butt *(62) (JFfitch-Heyes)* 2-8-11 RPrice(7) (led tl hdd & 2nd st: kpt on u.p) ....hd 3
2294[2] Euskara *(41) (MDIUsher)* 2-8-6 RStreet(4) (b: lw: hld up: hdwy 3f out: 5th st: nvr nr to chal) ...7 4
*2294** Red Simba *(50)*(Fav)*(JBerry)* 2-9-2 JCarroll(2) (w ldr: rdn & 3rd st: grad wknd) ....nk 5
2294[4] Rowhome *(33) (MRChannon)* 2-8-6 (5) PPMurphy(5) (lost pl after 2f: sn bhd: t.o) 5 6
2035[4] Plausilium *(32) (WGMTurner)* 2-8-8 (3) PMcCabe(8) (chsd ldrs: rdn over 2f out: 6th & btn st: t.o) ....¾ 7
1336[7] Public Acclaim *(27) (MBlanshard)* 2-8-6 StephenDavies(6) (bit bkwd: a in rr: t.o) ....s.h 8
2249[4] Impending Danger *(31) (KSBridgwater)* 2-8-11 VSlattery(10) (bit bkwd: s.i.s: sn pushed along to chse ldrs: wknd 3f out: t.o) ....s.h 9
1665[13] Brogans Brush *(30) (CWFairhurst)* 2-8-11v DeanMcKeown(3) (a in rr: t.o) ....½ 10

2/1 Red Simba (op 5/4), **3/1** VICTORIA VENTURE (op 2/1), **7/1** Plausilium, **8/1** Young Butt (tchd 12/1), **9/1** Pulga Circo, **12/1** Euskara (8/1-14/1), **16/1** Public Acclaim, **20/1** Rowhome, Brogans Brush, **50/1** Impending Danger, CSF £27.51 TOTE £3.70: £1.50 £1.90 £1.50 (£14.90) Trio £44.50 OWNER Dr Frank Chao (NEWMARKET) BRED Dr Frank Chao and High Point Bloodstock Ltd 10 Rn

1m 33.3 (9.30) SF: -/-/-/-/-/-/-/-/-/-

Bt in 6,000 gns

2497 AVALON ASSOCIATES APPRENTICE H'CAP (0-60) (3-Y.O) (Class G) £2,270.00 (£645.00: £320.00) 6f (Fibresand) Stalls: Low GOING: 0.16 sec per fur (SLW) 4-30 (4-31)

1541[14] **Mixed Mood (60)***(66) (BJLlewellyn)* 3-9-2 (5) JWilkinson(7) (bhd & outpcd: hdwy over 2f out: r.o to ld wl ins fnl f) ....— 1
2164* Solianna **(55)***(60) (MRChannon)* 3-8-8 (8) DSweeney(1) (chsd ldrs: rdn to ld ins fnl f: ct cl home) ....nk 2
*2144** Jersey Belle **(49)***(45)*(Fav)*(PJMakin)* 3-8-10 ADaly(6) (hdwy & rdn over 2f out: kpt on ins fnl f: nvr nrr) 3½ 3
2144[8] Runs in the Family **(50)***(44) (PGMurphy)* 3-8-8b(3) RWaterfield(8) (lw: chsd ldr: led bel dist tl ins fnl f) ....¾ 4
1664[10] Speedy Snaps Pride **(41)***(31) (PDCundell)* 3-8-2 SLanigan(4) (dwlt: hdwy bel dist: kpt on fnl f) 1½ 5
855[9] Fortunes Leap **(49)***(38) (MrsLAMurphy)* 3-8-5 (5) BHalligan(5) (s.s: effrt over 2f out: nvr nr to chal) ....½ 6
1880[12] Truly Madly Deeply **(40)***(23) (JAHarris)* 3-8-1 CWebb(2) (outpcd: a bhd) 2 7
2088[13] Miss Tri Colour **(34)***(17) (FHLee)* 3-7-2v(7) RMullen(3) (b: set str pce over 4f: wknd qckly) ....hd 8
1457[12] Bex Hill **(49)***(19) (DHaydnJones)* 3-8-0 (10) AnthonyBond(9) (chsd ldrs 4f: wknd qckly: t.o) 5 9

9/4 Jersey Belle (6/4-5/2), **10/3** Solianna (9/4-7/2), **6/1** Speedy Snaps Pride, **9/1** MIXED MOOD (6/1-10/1), **12/1** Fortunes Leap (op 8/1), **14/1** Runs in the Family, **16/1** Miss Tri Colour, Bex Hill, **33/1** Truly Madly Deeply, CSF £33.85 CT £69.66 TOTE £8.80: £1.10 £2.40 £1.40 (£19.20) Trio £9.90 OWNER Millstream Associates (BARGOED) BRED Edward Gregory 9 Rn

1m 17.3 (6.10) SF: 33/27/12/11/-/5/-/-/-

T/Plpt: £26.70 (380.54 Tckts). T/Qdpt: £6.40 (6 Tckts). IM

2480-BEVERLEY (R-H)
Tuesday July 18th (Good)
WEATHER: sunny periods WIND: fresh half against

2498 SAMSUNG MAIDEN AUCTION STKS (2-Y.O) (Class E) £3,276.75 (£984.00: £474.50: £219.75) 5f Stalls: Centre GOING minus 0.09 sec per fur (G) 2-00 (2-03)

2128[5] **Annaberg (IRE)** *(73+)*(Fav)*(MrsJRRamsden)* 2-8-4 KFallon(10) (a.p: rdn to ld ins fnl f: styd on wl) .... — 1
Wrays (USA) *(68+) (MJohnston)* 2-8-0 TWilliams(4) (neat: str: bit bkwd: led tl hdd ins fnl f: rallied) .... nk 2
2336[3] Western Venture (IRE) *(68) (JWPayne)* 2-8-6 ow1 JWeaver(5) (lw: cl up tl rdn & btn ins fnl f) 1½ 3
2221[5] Harriet's Beau *(64) (MWEasterby)* 2-8-7 LCharnock(9) (bhd: hdwy 2f out: nt pce to chal) 2 4
2128[4] Camionneur (IRE) *(60) (MHEasterby)* 2-8-6b MBirch(6) (lw: hld up & bhd: hdwy 2f out: rdn & btn 1f out) 1 5
Answers-To-Thomas *(60) (JMJefferson)* 2-8-7 GHind(7) (lengthy: unf: lw: chsd ldrs tl wknd ent fnl f) .... nk 6
2259[2] Oriole *(70d) (NTinkler)* 2-8-6 KimTinkler(8) (early spd: sn bhd: hdwy 2f out: wknd ins fnl f) ...hd 7
819[6] Mill End Lady *(45) (MWEasterby)* 2-8-2 SMaloney(1) (nvr trbld ldrs) 3 8
Cocoon (IRE) *(21) (CWThornton)* 2-8-1 JFanning(2) (w'like: leggy: spd 3f: wknd qckly) 7 9
1857[10] Stotfold Boy (IRE) *(17) (RHollinshead)* 2-8-9 TIves(3) (prom 3f: sn wknd) 4 10

5/2 ANNABERG (IRE) (9/4-7/2), **7/2** Harriet's Beau, **9/2** Western Venture (IRE), **5/1** Camionneur (IRE) (7/2-11/2), **7/1** Wrays (USA), **8/1** Oriole, **16/1** Cocoon (IRE), Mill End Lady, **20/1** Answers-To-Thomas, Stotfold Boy (IRE), CSF £21.61 TOTE £3.20: £1.30 £3.80 £1.40 (£16.30) Trio £22.00 OWNER Mr Bernard Hathaway (THIRSK) BRED D. J. and Mrs Deer 10 Rn
67.41 secs (5.91) SF: -/-/-/-/-/-/-/-/-/-

2499 WHIRLPOOL CLAIMING STKS (3-Y.O) (Class E) £3,117.50 (£935.00: £450.00: £207.50) 7f 100y Stalls: High GOING minus 0.09 sec per fur (G) 2-30 (2-31)

2357* **Special-K** **(60)***(74)*(Fav)*(EWeymes)* 3-8-4 GHind(5) (led early: a cl up: led wl over 1f out: r.o) .... — 1
1947[4] Hand of Straw (IRE) **(69)***(64) (JWWatts)* 3-8-5 NConnorton(3) (b: a.p: effrt 3f out: hung rt: one pce fnl f) 5 2
2140[8] Distant Princess **(62)***(60) (BWHills)* 3-8-4 DHolland(2) (lw: hdwy on outside over 2f out: rdn & no ex appr fnl f) 1¾ 3
2225[3] Miss Zanzibar **(60)***(57) (RAFahey)* 3-8-4 ACulhane(4) (trckd ldrs: effrt on ins 2f out: n.m.r: one pce fnl f) 1¼ 4
1498[13] Khan **(55)***(53) (CWThornton)* 3-8-4 DeanMcKeown(6) (sn led: hdd & wknd wl over 1f out) 2 5
616[9] Show Flair (IRE) **(45)** *(JSWainwright)* 3-8-4b KFallon(1) (pushed along thrght: lost tch fnl 3f) 30 6

13/8 SPECIAL-K, **11/4** Hand of Straw (IRE) (2/1-3/1), **9/2** Miss Zanzibar, **11/2** Khan (4/1-6/1), **7/1** Distant Princess, **20/1** Show Flair (IRE), CSF £6.49 TOTE £2.60: £1.30 £1.70 (£3.10) OWNER Mr G. Falshaw (MIDDLEHAM) BRED Patrick Diamond 6 Rn 1m 36.4 (4.40) SF: 34/24/20/17/13/-

2500 COMET H'CAP (0-90) (3-Y.O) (Class C) £5,442.50 (£1,640.00: £795.00: £372.50) 7f 100y Stalls: High GOING minus 0.09 sec per fur (G) 3-00 (3-00)

2188[7] **Mountgate** **(69)***(77) (MPBielby)* 3-8-12 (3) DRMcCabe(2) (bhd: hdwy 2f out: r.o wl fnl f to ld nr fin) .... — 1
2437[4] Concer Un **(61)***(68) (SCWilliams)* 3-8-7 KFallon(4) (lw: a cl up: led 2f out: sn hrd drvn: nt qckn towards fin) .... nk 2
2103[11] Seventeens Lucky **(67)***(73) (BobJones)* 3-8-13 NConnorton(5) (chsd ldr: chal over 1f out: no ex cl home) .... ½ 3
2455[3] Russian Heroine **(73)***(79)*(Fav)*(MJohnston)* 3-9-5 DHolland(3) (a.p: hdwy & ev ch over 1f out: nt qckn towards fin) .... hd 4
1847[4] Quilling **(68)***(71) (MDods)* 3-9-0 JWeaver(7) (lw: effrt over 2f out: nvr trbld ldrs) 1¼ 5
2276* Bollin Frank **(59)***(62) (MHEasterby)* 3-8-5 MBirch(1) (led after 1½f to 2f out: kpt on u.p: no ex ins fnl f) .... s.h 6
1953[10] Barrel of Hope **(75)** *(JLEyre)* 3-9-4 (3) JTate(6) (led 1½f: cl up tl wknd fnl 3f: t.o) .... dist 7

13/8 Russian Heroine, **3/1** Concer Un (op 5/1), **9/2** Bollin Frank (op 3/1), **5/1** Quilling, **8/1** Seventeens Lucky, **12/1** Barrel of Hope, **20/1** MOUNTGATE, CSF £77.88 TOTE £20.80: £7.30 £1.70 (£29.00) OWNER Mr J. F. Coupland (GRIMSBY) BRED Llety Stud 7 Rn
1m 35.7 (3.70) SF: 52/43/48/54/46/37/-

2501
SONY H'CAP (0-70) (3-Y.O+) (Class E) £3,208.50 (£963.00: £464.00: £214.50)
2m 35y Stalls: Centre GOING minus 0.09 sec per fur (G) 3-30 (3-30)

1929[5] **Chakalak (45)***(58)*(Fav)*(SDow)* 7-8-2 (7) ADaly(3) (sn pushed along: hdwy ½-wy: styd on wl fr 3f out to ld wl ins fnl f) ....— 1
2157[3] Arian Spirit (IRE) **(32)***(43) (JLEyre)* 4-7-5 (5)ow2 NVarley(5) (lw: led after 3f: clr over 2f out: sn hrd drvn: hdd & no ex wl ins fnl f) ....½ 2
2197[8] Roxy River **(35)***(35) (JLSpearing)* 6-7-13 JFanning(2) (chsd ldrs: ev ch 3f out: one pce) 13 3
2127* Vain Prince **(52)***(47) (NTinkler)* 8-9-2b LCharnock(4) (lw: hld up: hdwy & prom ½-wy: rdn appr st: no imp) 5 4
2224[4] Lightning Quest (IRE) **(33)***(15) (JSWainwright)* 4-7-11bow1 SMaloney(1) (in tch tl outpcd appr st: n.d after) 12 5
2256[2] Eire Leath-Sceal **(60)***(23) (MBrittain)* 8-9-10 JLowe(6) (lw: prom tl hmpd 6f out: n.d after)......20 6
2256[4] Baroski **(31)** *(JLHarris)* 4-7-6b(3)ow2 DarrenMoffatt(7) (lw: led 3f: wknd qckly ½-wy: sn t.o) ...dist 7

LONG HANDICAP Baroski 7-3

7/4 CHAKALAK, **11/4** Vain Prince, **3/1** Eire Leath-Sceal, **7/1** Arian Spirit (IRE), **16/1** Lightning Quest (IRE), Roxy River, **20/1** Baroski, CSF £13.68 TOTE £2.70: £1.70 £2.10 (£7.20) OWNER Mr P. F. Chakko (EPSOM) BRED Seend Stud 7 Rn 3m 42.8 (12.30) SF: 29/14/6/18/-/-/-

2502
TOSHIBA H'CAP (0-60) (3-Y.O+) (Class F) £3,618.00 (£1,089.00: £527.00: £246.00) **5f** Stalls: Centre GOING minus 0.09 sec per fur (G) 4-00 (4-02)

1721[8] **Miss Siham (IRE) (39)***(50+) (DNicholls)* 6-8-7 AlexGreaves(16) (mde all: clr 2f out: r.o wl)...— 1
2358[8] Knayton Lass **(59)***(62) (MWEasterby)* 4-9-6 (7) RuthCoulter(3) (bhd: swtchd & hdwy 2f out: hung rt fnl f: no ch w wnr).......2½ 2
2301* Paley Prince (USA) **(53)***(55)*(Fav)*(MDIUsher)* 9-9-0 (7) CAdamson(18) (b: prom: rdn ½-wy: r.o one pce) ....nk 3
2179[5] Judgement Call **(45)***(45) (PHowling)* 8-8-13 NCarlisle(15) (b: sn chsng ldrs: nt qckn appr fnl f) ....½ 4
2252[8] Gymcrak Tycoon **(44)***(40) (GHolmes)* 6-8-12 KFallon(2) (b: b.hind: in tch: hdwy 2f out: one pce fnl f).......1½ 5
2071[5] Younger Days (IRE) **(32)***(21) (MartynWane)* 4-8-0 TWilliams(8) (styd on fnl 2f: no imp) 2 6
2261[2] Blue Lugana **(42)***(31) (NBycroft)* 3-8-5b SMaloney(4) (prom: kpt on fnl 2f: no imp).................d.h 6
1214[9] Farndale **(38)***(26) (RonaldThompson)* 8-8-1 (5) LNewton(1) (a chsng ldrs: one pce fnl 2f) ....½ 8
1802[3] Superbit **(54)***(40) (BAMcMahon)* 3-9-3 FNorton(13) (lw: prom tl outpcd fnl 2f) ....½ 9
2239[5] Time Is Money (IRE) **(53)***(37) (MHTompkins)* 3-8-11v(5) HKYim(5) (nvr nr to chal)..................¾ 10
2239[6] Secret Miss **(51)***(34) (APJarvis)* 3-8-11 (3) DWright(9) (n.d) ....hd 11
2252[7] Tutu Sixtysix **(40)***(18) (DonEnricoIncisa)* 4-8-8v KimTinkler(14) (lw: sn drvn along: nvr trbld ldrs) 1¾ 12
2303[5] The Institute Boy **(47)***(19) (MissJFCraze)* 5-9-1v SWebster(6) (spd 3f) 1¾ 13
1843[10] Carol Again **(38)***(8) (NBycroft)* 3-8-1 NKennedy(12) (bhd most of wy).......¾ 14
2231[4] Henry the Hawk **(50)***(12) (MDods)* 4-9-4 JWeaver(7) (gd spd 3f: sn wknd) 2½ 15
Nordoora (IRE) **(57)** *(JLHarris)* 6-9-11 SDWilliams(10) (spd 3f: sn wl bhd).......14 16
1677[14] Northgate Raver **(25)** *(RonaldThompson)* 4-7-0 (7) PFessey(17) (bhd fr ½-wy).......3 17

7/2 Paley Prince (USA), **7/1** Judgement Call, Tutu Sixtysix, **15/2** Time Is Money (IRE), **9/1** MISS SIHAM (IRE), Henry the Hawk, Superbit, **10/1** Secret Miss, **12/1** The Institute Boy, **16/1** Gymcrak Tycoon, Blue Lugana, **20/1** Knayton Lass, Farndale, Nordoora (IRE), **33/1** Carol Again, Younger Days (IRE), **50/1** Northgate Raver, CSF £173.37 CT £703.31 TOTE £12.00: £2.30 £14.60 £1.10 £2.30 (£363.50) Trio £1,101.20 OWNER Ardsley Racing (THIRSK) BRED Derby Bloodstock Services Ltd 17 Rn 65.2 secs (3.70) SF: 25/37/30/20/15/-/1/1/10/7/4/-/-/-/-/-/-

WEIGHT FOR AGE 3yo-5lb

2503
VODAFONE APPRENTICE H'CAP (0-65) (3-Y.O) (Class F) £3,436.00 (£1,033.00: £499.00: £232.00)
1m 100y Stalls: High GOING minus 0.09 sec per fur (G) 4-30 (4-31)

2139[8] **Lorelei Lee (IRE) (60)***(69) (JohnBerry)* 3-9-0 (3) HKYim(12) (a.p: led wl over 1f out: hrd rdn fnl f: jst hld on).......— 1
2253[3] Shining Edge **(54)***(63) (MHEasterby)* 3-8-8 (3) LNewton(8) (lw: in tch: hdwy over 1f out: styd on wl towards fin: jst failed).......s.h 2
1569[2] Samaka Hara (IRE) **(55)***(59) (WSCunningham)* 3-8-12 DRMcCabe(9) (bhd: hdwy over 2f out: nrst fin) 2½ 3
1504[7] Tajar (USA) **(63)***(67) (DMorley)* 3-9-1 (5) GMitchell(3) (a.p: effrt 3f out: one pce appr fnl f).......hd 4
2191[4] Proud Image **(63)***(65) (APJarvis)* 3-9-6 DWright(10) (cl up: disp ld over 2f out tl wl over 1f out: grad wknd).......1 5

2250[3] Nautical Jewel **(50)***(48) (MDIUsher)* 3-8-2 (5) CAdamson(13) (b: in tch: hit rails 6f out & 5f out: kpt on one pce fnl 2f) 2 **6**
2228* Three Arch Bridge **(55)***(51)*(Fav)*(MJohnston)* 3-8-12b JTate(1) (mid div: hdwy 2f out: rdn & nvr able to chal) 1¼ **7**
2225* Westcourt Princess **(48)***(41) (MWEasterby)* 3-8-0 (5) RuthCoulter(11) (lw: mde most tl hdd & wknd wl over 1f out) 1½ **8**
2278[5] Evan 'elp Us **(64)***(56)*(Fav)*(JLEyre)* 3-9-4b(3) NVarley(2) (mid div: rdn 3f out: no hdwy) ....½ **9**
2353[3] Perfect Bertie (IRE) **(52)***(38) (GROldroyd)* 3-8-4 (5)ow3 GParkin(5) (n.d) 1¾ **10**
2081[12] My Handsome Prince **(43)***(25) (PJBevan)* 3-7-9 (5) DDenby(7) (bhd: brought wd & effrt 3f out: n.d) 3½ **11**
1649[4] Intendant **(62)***(40) (JGFitzGerald)* 3-9-0 (5) GFaulkner(4) (chsd ldrs tl grad wknd fnl 3f) 2½ **12**
2033[3] Sporting Risk **(54)***(13) (PWHarris)* 3-8-11 JStack(6) (hld up & bhd: brought wd & effrt 3f out: n.d) 10 **13**

6/1 Three Arch Bridge (op 4/1), Evan 'elp Us, **13/2** Westcourt Princess, **7/1** Shining Edge, **9/1** Samaka Hara (IRE), Sporting Risk, **10/1** Intendant, Tajar (USA), LORELEI LEE (IRE), Nautical Jewel, My Handsome Prince, **12/1** Proud Image, **16/1** Perfect Bertie (IRE), CSF £79.48 CT £616.46 TOTE £12.50: £3.60 £2.80 £4.90 (£59.10) Trio £167.60 OWNER Mr L. C. Wadey (NEWMARKET) BRED Sheikh Mohammed bin Rashid al Maktoum 13 Rn
1m 49.3 (5.30) SF: 43/37/33/41/39/22/25/15/30/12/-/14/-

T/Jpt; not won £51,496.85 to Sandown 19/7/95. T/Plpt: £343.80 (63.69 Tckts). T/Qdpt: £50.90 (3 Tckts). AA

2466-YARMOUTH (L-H)
Tuesday July 18th (Good)
WEATHER: overcast WIND: fresh across

2504 SCRATBY H'CAP (0-75) (3-Y.O+) (Class D) £3,664.70 (£1,091.60: £519.80: £233.90) **7f 3y** Stalls: Low GOING minus 0.01 sec per fur (G) 2-15 (2-15)

1786[8] **Khatim (USA) (61)***(71) (HThomsonJones)* 3-9-2 RHills(5) (pushed along bef ½-wy: led 2f out: hrd rdn appr fnl f: r.o) ....— **1**
2199[7] Mighty Marston **(71)***(73) (LadyHerries)* 3-9-5 (7) JO'Dwyer(4) (lw: trckd ldr: outpcd 3f out: hdwy appr fnl f: r.o) 3½ **2**
2358* King Chestnut **(58)***(59) (MDods)* 4-9-6 6x JFortune(2) (trckd ldrs: ev ch over 1f out: one pce) .nk **3**
2337[2] Agoer **(60)***(60)*(Fav)*(CEBrittain)* 3-9-1 BDoyle(6) (swtg: led over 1f: ev ch 2f out: sn one pce) ½ **4**
2203[3] Our Shadee (USA) **(47)***(44) (KTIvory)* 5-8-2v(7) CScally(3) (bhd: hdwy 3f out: ev ch over 1f out: sn wknd) 1¼ **5**
2178[4] Cloette **(63)***(55) (WAO'Gorman)* 3-9-4b EmmaO'Gorman(1) (lw: led over 5f out to 2f out: wknd qckly) 2½ **6**

9/4 Agoer, **3/1** King Chestnut, **9/2** Our Shadee (USA), **5/1** Cloette, **6/1** Mighty Marston, **12/1** KHATIM (USA) (8/1-14/1), CSF £68.72 TOTE £10.40: £3.00 £3.40 (£35.80) OWNER Mr Hamdan Al Maktoum (NEWMARKET) BRED Shadwell Farm Inc and Shadwell Estate Company 6 Rn
1m 29.0 (6.20) SF: 26/28/21/15/6/10
WEIGHT FOR AGE 3yo-7lb

2505 ELIZABETH SIMPSON (S) STKS (2-Y.O) (Class G) £2,489.40 (£688.40: £328.20) **7f 3y** Stalls: Low GOING minus 0.01 sec per fur (G) 2-45 (2-45)

1798[7] **Crimson And Clover** *(66+)*(Fav)*(MBell)* 2-8-6 MHills(1) (swtg: a.p: led over 2f out: clr over 1f out: pushed out: r.o wl) ....— **1**
2346[9] The Kastarbids (IRE) *(62) (DMorris)* 2-8-11v JFortune(2) (trckd ldrs: styd on one pce fnl 2f)....4 **2**
2403[2] Bobsworthatcaspers *(62) (GLewis)* 2-8-11b PaulEddery(4) (lw: pushed along ½-wy: hrd rdn & hdwy to chse wnr over 1f out: no ex fnl f) ....s.h **3**
2346[11] Fast Food *(50) (BJMcMath)* 2-8-11 MTebbutt(7) (wnt rt s: led over 5f out to over 2f out: sn wknd) 5 **4**
1734[4] Comrade Chinnery (IRE) *(48) (JMPEustace)* 2-8-11 RCochrane(6) (trckd ldrs tl wknd wl over 1f out) 1¼ **5**
2176[3] The Imps (IRE) *(46) (BWHills)* 2-9-2 BThomson(5) (lw: led over 1f: ev ch wl over 1f out: sn wknd) 3 **6**

6/4 CRIMSON AND CLOVER, **9/4** Bobsworthatcaspers, **11/4** The Imps (IRE), **14/1** Comrade Chinnery (IRE) (op 8/1), **25/1** Fast Food, The Kastarbids (IRE), CSF £25.15 TOTE £2.90: £1.50 £4.20 (£34.40) OWNER Mr Christopher Wright (NEWMARKET) BRED Mascalls Stud 6 Rn
1m 30.8 (8.00) SF: -/-/-/-/-/-
Wnr sld Mr J.Bates 10,000gs

2506 MEDLER MAIDEN STKS (3-Y.O+) (Class D) £3,698.50 (£1,102.00: £525.00: £236.50) **1m 3f 101y** Stalls: Low GOING minus 0.30 sec per fur (GF) 3-15 (3-15)

1717 10 **Ack's Again** *(79) (BWHills)* 3-8-7 MHills(5) (lw: mde virtually all: rdn over 1f out: r.o wl) ....— 1
1600 2 Anna of Brunswick *(77)*(Fav)*(HRACecil)* 3-8-7 WRyan(2) (trckd wnr: disp ld over 3f out: ev ch ins fnl f: rdn & fnd nil) 1½ 2
1948 2 Lucayan Sunshine (USA) *(70) (LadyHerries)* 3-8-0 (7) JO'Dwyer(1) (swtg: 4th st: effrt over 2f out: one pce fr over 1f out) 5 3
1656 4 Baddi Quest **(66)***(67) (BHanbury)* 3-8-5 (7) MHenry(3) (3rd st: btn 3f out) 6 4
1971 10 Waterloo Belle *(MrsNMacauley)* 4-9-4 JFortune(4) (s.s: a bhd: t.o fnl 3f) ....dist 5

8/15 Anna of Brunswick, **5/2** Lucayan Sunshine (USA), **10/1** Baddi Quest (6/1-12/1), **14/1** ACK'S AGAIN, **100/1** Waterloo Belle, CSF £21.77 TOTE £11.30: £6.50 £1.10 (£4.80) OWNER Mr K. Abdullah (LAMBOURN) BRED Juddmonte Farms 5 Rn 2m 26.0 (3.00) SF: 47/45/38/35/-
WEIGHT FOR AGE 3yo-11lb

2507 NORTH WALSHAM H'CAP (0-95) (3-Y.O) (Class C) £5,744.00 (£1,712.00: £816.00: £368.00) **6f 3y** Stalls: Centre GOING minus 0.01 sec (G) 3-45 (3-45)

2202* **Bowden Rose (70)***(76) (MBlanshard)* 3-8-5b StephenDavies(4) (mde all: qcknd 1f out: rdn out) ....— 1
2239 4 Brockton Flame **(67)***(71) (JMPEustace)* 3-8-2 GCarter(5) (swtg: a.p: rdn & r.o fnl f) ....¾ 2
1487 13 Hakiki (IRE) **(86)***(77) (PTWalwyn)* 3-9-7 RHills(3) (lw: trckd wnr tl rdn & wknd wl over 1f out) ..5 3
2067 2 Mousehole **(71)***(48) (RGuest)* 3-8-6 JFortune(6) (in tch 4f) 5 4
2168* Tafahhus **(86)***(55)*(Fav)*(RWArmstrong)* 3-9-7 WCarson(1) (lw: outpcd fr ½-wy) 3 5
2236 3 Crown of Love (USA) **(68)***(36) (MRStoute)* 3-8-3 PaulEddery(2) (b.hind: a last: lost tch over 2f out) ....½ 6

9/4 Tafahhus, **3/1** Mousehole, **4/1** BOWDEN ROSE, **6/1** Crown of Love (USA), **15/2** Brockton Flame, **8/1** Hakiki (IRE) (6/1-9/1), CSF £28.27 TOTE £4.90: £1.70 £3.50 (£16.00) OWNER The Lower Bowden Syndicate (UPPER LAMBOURN) BRED E. A. Badger 6 Rn
1m 14.4 (3.80) SF: 35/30/36/7/14/-
OFFICIAL EXPLANATION **Tafahhus: was unsuited by the rain-softened ground.**

2508 E.B.F. SCROBY SANDS MAIDEN STKS (2-Y.O) (Class D) £4,230.00 (£1,260.00: £600.00: £270.00)
5f 43y Stalls: Centre GOING minus 0.01 sec per fur (G) 4-15 (4-15)

1579 5 **Stop Play (IRE)** *(74)*(Fav)*(MHTompkins)* 2-8-9 PRobinson(1) (prom: led over 1f out: rdn 1f out: r.o) ....— 1
Sweet Nature (IRE) *(68+) (WJarvis)* 2-8-9 BThomson(4) (unf: bit bkwd: a.p: led 2f out tl over 1f out: unable qckn fnl f) 2 2
Madam Zando *(49+) (JMPEustace)* 2-8-9 MTebbutt(6) (cmpt: str: wnt rt s: bhd tl sme hdwy fr over 1f out) 6 3
Fyors Gift (IRE) *(43) (BHanbury)* 2-8-9 MRimmer(5) (lengthy: unf: bit bkwd: led 3f out to 2f out: sn wknd) 2 4
2170 3 Ichor *(36) (HThomsonJones)* 2-8-9 RHills(3) (led 2f: wknd 2f out) 2½ 5
Buff *(26) (DMorley)* 2-8-9 RCochrane(2) (lt-f: w ldrs 2f: wl bhd fnl 2f) 3 6

7/4 STOP PLAY (IRE), **11/4** Sweet Nature (IRE) (2/1-3/1), **6/1** Ichor (9/2-7/1), **13/2** Buff (9/2-7/1), **8/1** Fyors Gift (IRE) (op 5/1), **20/1** Madam Zando, CSF £6.22 TOTE £2.00: £1.10 £1.60 (£3.30) OWNER Mark Tompkins Racing (NEWMARKET) BRED Michael Doyle 6 Rn
65.0 secs (4.70) SF: 16/10/-/-/-/-

2509 BELTON MAIDEN H'CAP (0-75) (3-Y.O+) (Class D) £3,732.30 (£1,112.40: £530.20: £239.10)
1m 6f 17y Stalls: Low GOING minus 0.30 sec per fur (GF) 4-45 (4-45)

2026 4 **Invest Wisely (68)***(78) (JMPEustace)* 3-9-13 RCochrane(7) (swtg: pressed ldr: 2nd st: led wl over 3f out: drvn out) ....— 1
1093 5 Leading Spirit (IRE) **(57)***(64) (CFWall)* 3-9-2 WWoods(1) (lw: 4th st: chsd wnr fr wl over 1f out: r.o one pce) 2½ 2
2196 2 Innocence **(66)***(68)*(Fav)*(GWragg)* 3-9-11 MHills(5) (led tl wl over 3f out: wknd 2f out) 5 3
1987 5 Kriva **(69)***(66) (RJRWilliams)* 3-10-0 DBiggs(3) (3rd & pushed along st: wknd wl over 2f out) 4 4
2189 5 Coggle **(60)***(34) (NAGraham)* 3-9-5 PaulEddery(4) (6th st: wl bhd fnl 3f) 20 5

2037[15] Dolly Dolittle **(20)** *(HJCollingridge)* 4-7-7 GBardwell(2) (swtg: last st: wl bhd fnl 3f)..................8 **6**
2082[7] Bella Vitessa (IRE) **(56)***(10) (JWHills)* 3-9-1 RHills(6) (5th st: wl bhd fnl 3f)..............................10 **7**
LONG HANDICAP Dolly Dolittle 7-5

6/4 Innocence, **5/2** INVEST WISELY (7/4-11/4), **5/1** Leading Spirit (IRE), **6/1** Coggle, **14/1** Kriva (7/1-16/1), **16/1** Bella Vitessa (IRE), **40/1** Dolly Dolittle, CSF £14.35 TOTE £3.60: £2.10 £2.60 (£7.40) OWNER Mr J. C. Smith (NEWMARKET) BRED Littleton Stud 7 Rn
3m 5.4 (7.40) SF: 46/32/36/34/2/-/-
WEIGHT FOR AGE 3yo-14lb

T/Plpt: £1,036.50 (12.34 Tckts). T/Qdpt: £23.70 (4.65 Tckts). RC

2296-BATH (L-H)
Wednesday July 19th (Firm, Hard patches)
WEATHER: mainly cloudy, humid WIND: almost nil

2510
JAMES & COWPER H'CAP (0-80) (3-Y.O+) (Class D) £3,741.50 (£1,127.00: £546.00: £255.50) **1m 5y** Stalls: Low GOING minus 0.50 sec per fur (F) 2-15 (2-17)

2123[7] **Piquant (62)***(73) (LordHuntingdon)* 8-9-4 DHarrison(3) (lw: chsd ldr over 4f out: 2nd st: led 2f out: edgd rt over 1f out: drvn out)..................— **1**
2187[2] Greatest **(67)***(78)*(Fav)*(RAkehurst)* 4-9-9 TQuinn(5) (led 6f: r.o wl fnl f)..................hd **2**
2317[12] Morocco (IRE) **(55)***(58) (MRChannon)* 6-8-11 AClark(4) (hld up: 6th st: hdwy 2f out: one pce fnl f)..................4 **3**
2037[6] Cracking Prospect **(46)***(43) (BRMillman)* 4-7-11 (5)ow4 AWhelan(1) (lw: s.s: hld up: 7th st: r.o one pce fnl 2f)..................¾ **4**
2291[4] Robsera (IRE) **(72)***(66) (GLewis)* 4-10-0b PaulEddery(7) (3rd st: rdn & wknd over 2f out)......3½ **5**
2246[12] Darakah **(41)***(35) (CJHill)* 8-7-11 GBardwell(2) (s.s: last st: nvr trbld ldrs)..................nk **6**
Tatjana **(55)***(49) (MajorDNChappell)* 4-8-11 BThomson(6) (hld up: 5th st: wknd over 2f out)..hd **7**
1930* Lucky Soph (USA) **(73)***(57) (BWHills)* 3-9-7 JWeaver(8) (swtg: chsd ldr tl rn wd over 4f out: 4th st: wknd over 2f out)..................5 **8**

7/4 Greatest, **4/1** Lucky Soph (USA) (3/1-9/2), **6/1** PIQUANT, **9/1** Darakah, **11/1** Tatjana (8/1-12/1), **12/1** Robsera (IRE) (op 8/1), Morocco (IRE) (op 8/1), **16/1** Cracking Prospect, CSF £15.48 CT £101.06 TOTE £5.50: £1.50 £1.20 £1.90 (£5.40) OWNER The Queen (WEST ILSLEY) BRED The Queen 8 Rn
1m 39.9 (1.40) SF: 47/52/32/17/40/9/23/23
WEIGHT FOR AGE 3yo-8lb

2511
HILDA HOGSTON FIFTY YEARS AT BATH RACECOURSE (S) H'CAP (0-60) (3-Y.O+) (Class G) £2,521.00 (£706.00: £343.00)
1m 5f 22y Stalls: Low GOING minus 0.50 sec per fur (F) 2-45 (2-45)

2197[7] **Bresil (USA) (26)***(37) (KRBurke)* 6-7-8 (7) MHenry(7) (lw: a gng wl: 3rd st: led on bit over 1f out: sn clr)..................— **1**
2450[4] Becky Boo **(23)***(26) (MrsLAMurphy)* 5-7-12 AMackay(2) (chsd ldr: 2nd st: led over 2f out: hrd rdn & hdd over 1f out: one pce)..................7 **2**
2148[5] Formaestre (IRE) **(31)***(32) (RLee)* 5-8-6 GCarter(9) (b: lw: 4th st: r.o one pce fnl 2f)..................1½ **3**
2291[7] Patrice **(44)***(44) (MrsLAMurphy)* 4-9-5 JWilliams(8) (hld up: 5th st: r.o one pce fnl 2f)..................nk **4**
2300[3] Wizzy Lizzy (IRE) **(40)***(37) (DRCElsworth)* 4-9-1 TQuinn(4) (7th st: nvr nr to chal)..................3 **5**
2280[3] Opera Buff (IRE) **(53)***(46) (MCPipe)* 4-9-7b(7) DaneO'Neill(6) (led: clr after 2f: rdn over 3f out: hdd over 2f out: wknd qckly)..................3 **6**
2129[5] Risky Rose **(43)***(36)*(Fav)*(RHollinshead)* 3-8-2 (3) AGarth(3) (hld up & bhd: sme hdwy & 6th st: wknd over 2f out)..................nk **7**
1771[12] Tapping Feet **(31)***(14) (DMHyde)* 3-7-7 NAdams(5) (last st: a bhd)..................8 **8**
1254[14] La Belle Shyanne **(33)***(7) (CJHill)* 4-8-8 GBardwell(1) (8th st: a bhd)..................7 **9**
LONG HANDICAP Tapping Feet 7-6

2/1 Risky Rose, **3/1** Opera Buff (IRE) (2/1-7/2), **7/2** Wizzy Lizzy (IRE), **6/1** Becky Boo, **9/1** La Belle Shyanne (6/1-10/1), **20/1** Formaestre (IRE), **33/1** BRESIL (USA), Patrice, **40/1** Tapping Feet, CSF £198.62 CT £3,671.99 TOTE £43.90: £6.20 £1.90 £4.80 (£91.60) Trio £315.20 OWNER Mr P. Sweeting (WANTAGE) BRED Alec Head 9 Rn
2m 50.6 (4.90) SF: 18/7/13/25/18/27/4/-/-
WEIGHT FOR AGE 3yo-13lb
No bid.

2512
TOTE BOOKMAKERS H'CAP (0-90) (3-Y.O) (Class C) £5,609.75 (£1,688.00: £816.50: £380.75) **5f 11y** Stalls: Low GOING minus 0.50 sec per fur (F) 3-15 (3-16)

2288* **That Man Again (90)***(98)*(Fav)*(GLewis)* 3-9-7b PaulEddery(2) (chsd ldr: hrd rdn to ld wl ins fnl f: r.o)..................— **1**

2250* Colston-C **(62)***(69) (CJHill)* 3-7-7 GBardwell(3) (led: rdn 2f out: hdd wl ins fnl f: r.o wl)...........nk 2
Princess Sadie **(79)***(81) (MRChannon)* 3-8-10 DHarrison(4) (hld up: hdwy on ins over 1f out: nt qckn ins fnl f)...........1½ 3
1832[12] Astral Invader (IRE) **(64)***(54) (MSSaunders)* 3-7-9 NAdams(6) (rdn & hdwy over 2f out: wknd over 1f out)...........4 4
1786[5] Supreme Thought **(70)***(50) (LGCottrell)* 3-8-1 GCarter(5) (swtg: prom over 3f)...........3 5
2194[10] In Love Again (IRE) **(75)***(42) (MRChannon)* 3-8-6 TQuinn(1) (swtg: rdn over 2f out: sn bhd)....4 6

8/11 THAT MAN AGAIN, **6/1** Supreme Thought, **7/1** Colston-C, **8/1** In Love Again (IRE), **11/1** Princess Sadie (6/1-12/1), **16/1** Astral Invader (IRE), CSF £5.86 TOTE £1.60: £1.30 £2.00 (£2.90) OWNER Mr M. Jameson (EPSOM) BRED T. P. Milne and M. Jameson 6 Rn
61.7 secs (1.20) SF: 44/15/27/-/-/-

2513 MANSELL GOLDEN ANNIVERSARY CONDITIONS STKS (3-Y.O) (Class D)
£3,559.50 (£1,071.00: £518.00: £241.50)
5f 11y Stalls: Low GOING minus 0.50 sec per fur (F) 3-45 (3-45)

2267* **Millesime (IRE) (68)***(70)*(Fav)*(BHanbury)* 3-8-7 (7) MHenry(3) (mde virtually all: rdn over 1f out: r.o wl)...........— 1
2267[2] Grand Chapeau (IRE) **(58)***(61) (RHannon)* 3-8-3 (7) DaneO'Neill(4) (w wnr: rdn 2f out: ev ch over 1f out: nt qckn)...........1¾ 2
2497[2] Solianna **(60)***(58) (MRChannon)* 3-8-2 (7) DSweeney(1) (a.p: r.o one pce fnl f)...........½ 3
2502[9] Superbit **(54)***(22) (BAMcMahon)* 3-9-0 FNorton(2) (lw: prom: sn pushed along: wknd 2f out)...........13 4

8/13 MILLESIME (IRE), **4/1** Solianna (3/1-9/2), **11/2** Grand Chapeau (IRE) (3/1-6/1), **8/1** Superbit (5/1-9/1), CSF £3.96 TOTE £1.60: (£2.60) OWNER Boxall Asset Management Ltd (NEWMARKET) BRED Killarkin Stud 4 Rn
63.2 secs (2.70) SF: 14/5/2/-

2514 COMBE GROVE MANOR HOTEL AND COUNTRY CLUB H'CAP (0-70)
(3-Y.O+) (Class E) £3,168.00 (£954.00: £462.00: £216.00)
2m 1f 34y Stalls: Low GOING minus 0.50 sec per fur (F) 4-15 (4-15)

2154[6] **Bardolph (USA) (62)***(74)*(Fav)*(PFICole)* 8-10-0b TQuinn(6) (lw: hld up: 3rd st: hrd rdn to ld wl over 1f out: all out)...........— 1
2355[4] Arc Bright (IRE) **(44)***(56) (RHollinshead)* 5-8-7 (3) AGarth(4) (a.p: led 7f out: hdd wl over 1f out: hrd rdn: r.o wl)...........nk 2
Mr Geneaology (USA) **(55)***(64) (FMurphy)* 5-9-7b RCochrane(2) (6th st: hdwy over 2f out: styd on fnl f)...........3½ 3
1929[8] Sarazar (USA) **(39)***(47) (RAkehurst)* 6-8-5b CRutter(1) (hld up & plld hrd: hdwy 7f out: 4th st: ev ch over 1f out: wknd fnl f)...........¾ 4
2268[3] Phil's Time **(59)***(65) (TGMills)* 4-9-11 JWeaver(8) (lw: led tl hdd 7f out: 2nd & rdn st: wknd over 1f out)...........1½ 5
2078* Rose of Glenn **(51)***(43) (BPalling)* 4-9-3 TSprake(5) (hld up: hdwy 6f out: 5th st: wknd over 2f out)...........15 6
2201[7] Chucklestone **(53)***(34) (JSKing)* 12-9-5 AClark(7) (bit bkwd: chsd ldr tl rdn 8f out: wknd 5f out: t.o)...........12 7
Hacketts Cross (IRE) **(61)***(40) (NoelChance)* 7-9-6 (7) LHagen(3) (7th st: hdwy 6f out: wknd 4f out: t.o)...........2½ 8

5/2 BARDOLPH (USA), **9/2** Arc Bright (IRE), **5/1** Sarazar (USA) (op 3/1), Phil's Time (7/2-11/2), **8/1** Rose of Glenn (op 5/1), Chucklestone (op 7/2), **11/1** Mr Geneaology (USA) (8/1-12/1), **20/1** Hacketts Cross (IRE), CSF £13.41 CT £93.03 TOTE £ 3.50: £1.70 £1.30 £2.20 (£9.10) OWNER Sir George Meyrick (WHATCOMBE) BRED McMillin Bros 8 Rn
3m 47.3 (6.30) SF: 45/27/35/18/36/14/5/11

2515 E.B.F. MELKSHAM MAIDEN STKS (2-Y.O) (Class D) £4,302.00
(£1,296.00: £628.00: £294.00)
5f 11y Stalls: Low GOING minus 0.50 sec per fur (F) 4-45 (4-46)

Splinter (IRE) *(80+)*(Fav)*(RCharlton)* 2-9-0 TQuinn(3) (gd sort: lw: a.p: led on bit over 1f out: jinked rt ins fnl f: r.o wl)...........— 1
2299[2] Dramatic Entry (IRE) *(70) (JARToller)* 2-8-9b WNewnes(5) (swtg: w ldr: led over 2f out: hdd over 1f out: nt qckn)...........1½ 2
2135[6] Dande Flyer *(66) (DWPArbuthnot)* 2-9-0 RPrice(4) (a.p: r.o one pce fnl f)...........3 3
1536[3] Green Bentley (IRE) *(59) (RHannon)* 2-8-9 RPerham(7) (lw: hdwy over 1f out: nvr nrr)...........½ 4
1511[11] Fairy Prince (IRE) *(55) (MrsALMKing)* 2-8-11 (3) AGarth(2) (no hdwy fnl 2f)...........3 5
2025[11] Red Misty (IRE) *(48) (MRChannon)* 2-8-9 CRutter(9) (hrd rdn over 2f out: no hdwy)...........½ 6

1590[11] Bath Knight *(52) (DJSffrenchDavis)* 2-9-0 NAdams(1) (lw: led over 2f: wknd wl over 1f out) ....½ **7**
Water Music Melody *(40) (MartynMeade)* 2-8-9 VSlattery(8) (str: scope: bit bkwd: a bhd) 2 **8**
Mobile King *(40) (APJarvis)* 2-9-0 BThomson(6) (w'like: s.s: a bhd) 1½ **9**

4/6 SPLINTER (IRE), **100/30** Dramatic Entry (IRE), **6/1** Green Bentley (IRE), **14/1** Red Misty (IRE), **20/1** Dande Flyer, Mobile King, **50/1** Fairy Prince (IRE), Bath Knight, Water Music Melody, CSF £3.54 TOTE £1.70: £1.20 £1.10 £3.20 (£2.50) Trio £15.60 OWNER Mr K. Abdullah (BECKHAMPTON) BRED Juddmonte Farms 9 Rn 62.7 secs (2.20) SF: 21/11/7/-/-/-/-/-/-

T/Plpt: £86.60 (147.12 Tckts). T/Qdpt: £3.20 (35.55 Tckts). KH

2185-CATTERICK (L-H)
Wednesday July 19th (Good to firm)
WEATHER: fine & sunny WIND: fresh half against

2516
HUDDERSFIELD (S) STKS (2-Y.O) (Class G) £2,602.00 (£722.00: £346.00)
7f Stalls: Low GOING minus 0.19 sec per fur (GF) 2-30 (2-32)

1943[2] **Catwalk Girl** *(52) (SGNorton)* 2-8-6v KDarley(8) (chsd ldrs: led wl over 1f out: wandered: drvn out) ....— **1**
2195[5] Ginger Glint *(54) (MJHeaton-Ellis)* 2-8-11 DHolland(1) (mid div: styd on fnl 2f: nt qckn ins fnl f) 1½ **2**
2155[2] Veshca Lady (IRE) *(53) (EWeymes)* 2-8-11 JFanning(11) (hdwy 4f out: ev ch 1f out: edgd rt & nt qckn towards fin) ....hd **3**
2251[8] Euro Express *(53) (MHEasterby)* 2-8-11 TWilliams(10) (led: edgd rt 2f out: sn hdd: one pce)nk **4**
2251[7] Ned's Contessa (IRE) *(47) (MDods)* 2-8-6 JCarroll(12) (swtg: s.i.s: hdwy on ins & n.m.r 2f out: styng on same pce whn hmpd towards fin) ....nk **5**
2346[7] In Paradisum (USA) *(44)*(Fav)*(MrsJRRamsden)* 2-8-11 NConnorton(7) (lw: chsd ldrs: drvn & outpcd 3f out: kpt on fnl 2f) 3½ **6**
1841[6] Harsh Times *(36) (MHEasterby)* 2-8-6 SMaloney(14) (b.hind: sn bhd & pushed along: sme hdwy over 1f out: n.d) 1½ **7**
2155[3] Ceilidh (IRE) *(40) (PCHaslam)* 2-8-11 JFortune(3) (chsd ldrs: drvn along & outpcd ½-wy: kpt on appr fnl f) ....nk **8**
2251[4] Frances Mary *(34) (CWFairhurst)* 2-8-6 PRobinson(13) (chsd ldrs: outpcd over 2f out: sn lost pl) ....½ **9**
2251[2] Pat's Choice (IRE) *(25) (MHEasterby)* 2-8-6b MBirch(5) (in tch 3f: sn outpcd & bhd) 4 **10**
1959[5] Borana Lodge (USA) *(11) (MrsJRRamsden)* 2-8-11b LCharnock(9) (b.off hind: in tch tl lost pl ½-wy: eased) 8 **11**
Tilly Tupgill *(MDHammond)* 2-8-6 DaleGibson(4) (small: unf: s.i.s: sn drvn along) 8 **12**
2195[9] Mill House Boy (IRE) *(BSRothwell)* 2-8-11 ACulhane(6) (hmpd & lost pl after 1f) 2½ **13**
2185[W] Royal Romance *(GMMoore)* 2-8-3 (3) JStack(2) (cmpt: unf: s.s: rn green & a wl bhd) ....s.h **14**

3/1 In Paradisum (USA), **100/30** CATWALK GIRL, **5/1** Frances Mary, **11/2** Pat's Choice (IRE), **7/1** Veshca Lady (IRE), **10/1** Borana Lodge (USA) (op 6/1), **11/1** Ginger Glint, **16/1** Ceilidh (IRE), **20/1** Tilly Tupgill, **25/1** Harsh Times, Euro Express, Ned's Contessa (IRE), **33/1** Royal Romance, **50/1** Mill House Boy (IRE), CSF £42.15 TOTE £3.70: £1.30 £3.50 £2.70 (£25.50) Trio £36.50 OWNER Mrs Rosie Richer (BARNSLEY) BRED P. Teasdale and J. Richer 14 Rn
1m 28.8 (5.60) SF: 9/11/10/10/4/1/-/-/-/-/-/-/-/-
No bid.

2517
C.S.S. SDN BHD H'CAP (0-80) (3-Y.O+) (Class D) £3,687.50 (£1,100.00: £525.00: £237.50) **7f** Stalls: Low GOING minus 0.19 sec per fur (GF) 3-00 (3-00)

2187* **Pyramus (USA) (72)***(81+)*(Fav)*(MrsLPiggott)* 4-9-7 (7) GMilligan(5) (b: hld up: smooth hdwy on ins over 2f out: led over 1f out: shkn up & styd on wl) ....— **1**
2390[9] At the Savoy (IRE) **(43)***(50) (TDBarron)* 4-7-13b LCharnock(1) (led: rdn over 2f out: hdd over 1f out: styd on same pce) 1 **2**
2099[5] Bold Angel **(69)***(76) (MHEasterby)* 8-9-11 MBirch(4) (hld up: hdwy to trck ldrs ½-wy: rdn 2f out: kpt on one pce) ....s.h **3**
2390[6] Four of Spades **(59)***(60) (PDEvans)* 4-8-8 (7) AmandaSanders(3) (chsd ldrs: drvn along ½-wy: outpcd fnl 2f) 2½ **4**
2358[3] Pine Ridge Lad (IRE) **(54)***(52) (JLEyre)* 5-8-10 SDWilliams(2) (chsd ldrs: sn drvn along: wl outpcd fnl 2f) 1½ **5**

6/4 PYRAMUS (USA), **100/30** Bold Angel, **4/1** Pine Ridge Lad (IRE), **5/1** At the Savoy (IRE), **8/1** Four of Spades (op 5/1), CSF £8.40 TOTE £2.00: £1.30 £2.30 (£4.60) OWNER Mr Henryk De Kwiatkowski (NEWMARKET) BRED Kennelot Stables Ltd 5 Rn 1m 26.9 (3.70) SF: 51/20/46/30/22

2518 LEYBURN CLAIMING STKS (3-Y.O+) (Class F) £2,966.00 (£826.00: £398.00)
7f Stalls: Low GOING minus 0.19 sec per fur (GF) 3-30 (3-31)

*211*3 **Super Benz (57)***(59) (FJO'Mahony)* 9-8-9 SDWilliams(5) (b: trckd ldrs: qcknd to ld ½-wy: sn clr: drvn out) — **1**
2357² Northern Trove (USA) **(72)***(62)*(Fav)*(GMMoore)* 3-8-5 (3) JStack(4) (swtg: hld up: hdwy on outside: rdn & hung lft over 1f out: no imp) 1½ **2**
2304⁵ Thwaab **(45)***(56) (FWatson)* 3-8-5 SMaloney(2) (hdwy ½-wy: kpt on fnl 2f: nvr nr to chal) 1¼ **3**
*2383*11 Mac's Taxi **(66)***(56) (PCHaslam)* 3-8-10 JFortune(3) (trckd ldr: drvn along over 3f out: wknd over 1f out) 2 **4**
2306⁷ Lordan Velvet (IRE) **(48)***(42) (LLungo)* 3-8-2 DaleGibson(6) (led: edgd rt & hdd ½-wy: sn outpcd) 2½ **5**
*1076*8 Make the Break **(55)***(8) (SCoathup)* 4-8-7 TWilliams(1) (hld up: effrt 3f out: wknd & eased over 1f out) 14 **6**

1/2 Northern Trove (USA), **3/1** Mac's Taxi (op 2/1), **6/1** SUPER BENZ, **33/1** Lordan Velvet (IRE), **50/1** Thwaab, **66/1** Make the Break, CSF £9.25 TOTE £5.50: £2.10 £1.10 (£3.50) OWNER Whitestonecliffe Racing Partnership (HAMBLETON) BRED Scarteen Stud 6 Rn
1m 28.2 (5.00) SF: 19/15/9/9/-/-
WEIGHT FOR AGE 3yo-7lb

2519 HALIFAX H'CAP (0-80) (3-Y.O+ F & M) (Class D) £3,622.50 (£1,080.00: £515.00: £232.50)
5f 212y Stalls: High GOING minus 0.19 sec per fur (GF) 4-00 (4-00)

2130⁴ **Formidable Liz (55)***(66)*(Fav)*(MDHammond)* 5-9-2 KDarley(1) (lw: led 2f: led over 2f out: drvn clr over 1f out) — **1**
1701⁶ Banner (USA) **(73)***(76) (BWHills)* 3-10-0 DHolland(5) (trckd ldrs: effrt over 2f out: edgd lft & styd on fnl f: no ch w wnr) 3 **2**
2261* Dominelle **(51)***(46) (MHEasterby)* 3-8-6 SMaloney(3) (chsd ldrs: ev ch & rdn 2f out: edgd lft & wknd fnl f) 3 **3**
2260² Chiming In **(72)***(60) (MrsJRRamsden)* 3-9-13 JCarroll(2) (swtg: dwlt: outpcd & drvn along ½-wy: nvr nr to chal) 2½ **4**
2394* Crystal Loop **(68)***(55) (ABailey)* 3-9-2 (7) 7x AngelaGallimore(6) (led on outside 4f out: hdd over 2f out: wknd & eased over 1f out) nk **5**
2358⁴ Willshe Gan **(50)** *(DenysSmith)* 5-8-11 JFortune(4) (chsd ldrs tl p.u lame ½-wy: dead) **P**

3/1 FORMIDABLE LIZ, **7/2** Crystal Loop, **9/2** Banner (USA), **5/1** Dominelle, **6/1** Chiming In, Willshe Gan, CSF £15.01 TOTE £4.00: £2.00 £3.10 (£9.00) OWNER Mr J. Johnson (MIDDLEHAM) BRED S. M. Saud 6 Rn
1m 13.4 (2.90) SF: 43/47/17/31/26/-
WEIGHT FOR AGE 3yo-6lb

2520 DEWSBURY MAIDEN STKS (3-Y.O+) (Class D) £3,687.50 (£1,100.00: £525.00: £237.50)
1m 5f 175y Stalls: Low GOING minus 0.19 sec per fur (GF) 4-30 (4-31)

2167³ **Duchess of Alba** *(80+) (RCharlton)* 3-8-1 DaleGibson(2) (pushed along 8f out: hdwy over 5f out: led 2f out: drvn clr: eased nr fin) — **1**
2244⁴ Northern Law **(61)***(75) (BWHills)* 3-8-6 DHolland(5) (chsd ldrs: effrt 4f out: led over 2f out: sn hdd & btn) 9 **2**
1987² Mansur (IRE) **(84)***(64)*(Fav)*(DRLoder)* 3-8-6 KDarley(4) (lw: trckd ldr: led over 7f out tl over 2f out: nt r.o) 9 **3**
2331⁷ Catch the Pigeon *(56) (REBarr)* 6-8-8 (7) PFessey(3) (in tch tl pushed along & outpcd 5f out: sn lost tch) 3 **4**
1473⁶ Shining Dancer *(MRStoute)* 3-7-12 (3) DRMcCabe(1) (bolted gng to s: led: plld hrd & sn clr: rn wd bnd 8f out: sn hdd: rdn & wknd qckly over 5f out: sn wl bhd: t.o 3f out) dist **5**

5/4 Mansur (IRE), **13/8** DUCHESS OF ALBA, **6/1** Northern Law, **7/1** Shining Dancer (op 4/1), **150/1** Catch the Pigeon, CSF £10.05 TOTE £2.10: £1.30 £2.20 (£7.10) OWNER Mr A. J. Morrison (BECKHAMPTON) BRED Fonthill Stud 5 Rn
3m 4.0 (8.80) SF: 22/17/6/12/-
WEIGHT FOR AGE 3yo-14lb

2521 LEEDS H'CAP (0-70) (3-Y.O+) (Class E) £3,314.00 (£992.00: £476.00: £218.00)
5f Stalls: Low GOING minus 0.19 sec per fur (GF) 5-00 (5-02)

2252⁴ **Croft Imperial (61)***(66) (MJohnston)* 8-9-8v TWilliams(1) (chsd ldrs: led 2f out: drvn out) — **1**
2163⁷ Kalar **(41)***(42) (DWChapman)* 6-8-2b DaleGibson(16) (w ldrs stands' side: kpt on wl fnl f) 1¼ **2**

2330[11] High Domain (IRE) **(65)***(65) (TDBarron)* 4-9-12b JFortune(3) (lw: bmpd s: hdwy to chse ldrs ½-wy: kpt on wl u.p fnl f) ....nk 3
2252[6] King Rat (IRE) **(63)***(63) (TJEtherington)* 4-9-10v KDarley(4) (in tch: outpcd ½-wy: styd on fnl f) ....hd 4
2160[7] Kabcast **(50)***(47) (DWChapman)* 10-8-4b(7) PFessey(15) (chsd ldrs stands' side: nt qckn fnl 2f) ....¾ 5
746[3] Prince Belfort **(67)***(63) (JLEyre)* 7-10-0b JCarroll(7) (lw: bhd: hdwy over 1f out: styd on towards fin) ....½ 6
2124[7] Sigama (USA) **(56)***(51) (DNicholls)* 9-9-3 AlexGreaves(9) (led 3f: grad wknd) ....nk 7
1689[13] Lochon **(59)***(49) (JLEyre)* 4-9-6 RLappin(2) (swvd rt s: chsd ldrs tl outpcd fnl 2f) 1½ 8
2364[5] Rhythmic Dancer **(67)***(57) (JLSpearing)* 7-10-0 DeanMcKeown(11) (unruly in stalls: in tch tl wknd over 1f out) ....s.h 9
1582[8] Able Sheriff **(48)***(38) (MWEasterby)* 3-8-4b MBirch(17) (swvd rt s: chsd ldrs stands' side tl wknd over 1f out) ....s.h 10
2163[10] Pete Afrique (IRE) **(65)***(52) (MWEasterby)* 4-9-12 LCharnock(14) (chsd ldrs tl lost pl ½-wy: edgd rt over 1f out) ....¾ 11
2303[8] Pallium (IRE) **(55)***(42) (MrsAMNaughton)* 7-9-2 SDWilliams(8) (sn bhd: rdn ½-wy: n.d) ....s.h 12
2383[15] Olifantsfontein **(50)***(34) (DNicholls)* 7-8-11v NConnorton(5) (a in rr) 1 13
2092[7] Tee-Emm **(42)***(23) (PHowling)* 5-8-3 ow2 ACulhane(10) (b.off hind: chsd ldrs to ½-wy: sn lost pl) ....nk 14
2163[4] Miss Movie World **(61)***(40)*(Fav)*(MDHammond)* 6-9-5 (3) JStack(13) (in tch tl lost pl ½-wy: sddle slipped) 1¼ 15
2303[11] Sandmoor Velvet **(50)***(27) (MHEasterby)* 3-8-6 SMaloney(12) (b.off fore: prom to ½-wy: sn wknd) ....½ 16
1822[8] Breakfast Creek **(62)***(27) (JBerry)* 3-8-11 (7) CLowther(6) (b.nr hind: a outpcd) 4 17

4/1 Miss Movie World, **5/1** CROFT IMPERIAL, **7/1** Pallium (IRE), **8/1** King Rat (IRE), **9/1** High Domain (IRE), **12/1** Able Sheriff, Prince Belfort, Rhythmic Dancer, **16/1** Lochon, Pete Afrique (IRE), Sandmoor Velvet, Sigama (USA), Breakfast Creek, Tee-Emm, **25/1** Olifantsfontein, Kalar, Kabcast, CSF £122.24 CT £1,031.30 TOTE £6.50: £2.20 £12.70 £2.60 £1.30 (£139.90) Trio £835.00; £117.71 to Catterick 20/7/95. OWNER Mrs B. A. Matthews (MIDDLEHAM) BRED Eric Henshaw 17 Rn 59.9 secs (2.40) SF: 48/24/47/45/29/45/33/31/39/15/34/24/16/5/22/4/4
WEIGHT FOR AGE 3yo-5lb
T/Plpt: £83.50 (143.13 Tckts). T/Qdpt: £26.00 (1.4 Tckts). WG

1778-LEICESTER (R-H)
Wednesday July 19th (Good, Good to firm patches)
WEATHER: fine & sunny WIND: slt bhd

2522 BOLLINGER CHAMPAGNE CHALLENGE SERIES AMATEUR H'CAP (0-70) (3-Y.O) (Class E) £3,102.00 (£924.00: £440.00: £198.00)
7f 9y Stalls: High GOING minus 0.50 sec per fur (F) 6-35 (6-36)

1718[7] **Owdbetts (IRE) (51)***(64) (GLMoore)* 3-11-3 (4) MrKGoble(2) (hld up: gd hdwy to ld wl over 1f out: sn clr) ....— 1
2425[2] Legal Issue (IRE) **(58)***(60)*(Fav)*(SirMarkPrescott)* 3-12-0 MrPPritchard-Gordon(3) (lw: hld up: hdwy to ld over 2f out: hdd wl over 1f out: one pce) 5 2
2497[5] Speedy Snaps Pride **(47)***(37) (PDCundell)* 3-11-3 MrRJohnson(6) (chsd ldrs: rdn 2f out: sn lost tch) 5 3
2318[9] Happy Brave **(43)***(22) (PDCundell)* 3-10-13 MrTMcCarthy(4) (led over 3f out tl over 2f out: wknd qckly) 5 4
1952[6] Sound Trick (USA) **(54)***(33) (GCBravery)* 3-11-10 MrJDurkan(1) (bhd: hdwy over 2f out: sn rdn & outpcd) ....s.h 5
1939[7] Pharly Reef **(57)***(31) (IABalding)* 3-11-13 MrABalding(7) (led over 3f: rdn & wknd over 2f out) .2 6
1378[9] Enchanted Cottage **(42)***(13) (MDHammond)* 3-10-12 MrCBonner(5) (w ldrs to ½-wy: sn lost tch) 1¼ 7
2407[2] Water Hazard (IRE) **(42)***(7) (SDow)* 3-10-12 MrTCuff(8) (swtg: effrt & swtchd rt over 2f out: sn rdn & wknd) 3 8

7/4 Legal Issue (IRE), **5/1** Water Hazard (IRE), **13/2** Pharly Reef, **15/2** Speedy Snaps Pride (5/1-8/1), **8/1** OWDBETTS (IRE), **12/1** Enchanted Cottage, Sound Trick (USA), **14/1** Happy Brave, CSF £20.73 CT £95.86 TOTE £8.60: £1.80 £1.10 £2.20 (£10.20) OWNER Mr K. Higson (EPSOM) BRED Maria Goglio 8 Rn 1m 26.1 (3.60) SF: 46/42/19/4/15/13/-/-

2523 RADIO LEICESTER NURSERY H'CAP (2-Y.O) (Class E) £3,502.40 (£1,047.20: £501.60: £228.80) **5f 2y** Stalls: High GOING minus 0.50 sec per fur (F) 7-05 (7-06)

2281* **Gagajulu** *(66) (PDEvans)* 2-8-9 TIves(1) (swtg: hld up: hdwy to ld appr fnl f: rdn out) ....— 1

2328[4] Ramsey Hope *(73) (CWFairhurst)* 2-9-4 NKennedy(6) (led tl appr fnl f: rallied u.p cl home)....½ 2
2315[4] Midnight Escape *(76) (CFWall)* 2-9-7 NCarlisle(7) (chsd ldrs: rdn & edgd lft 1f out: kpt on)....hd 3
2085[2] Born A Lady *(64) (NPLittmoden)* 2-9-0 TGMcLaughlin(9) (prom: rdn over 1f out: one pce)....1¾ 4
2135[3] Magic Imp (IRE) *(50) (WJMusson)* 2-8-5 (3) PMcCabe(3) (lw: dwlt: hdwy 3f out: swtchd lft ent fnl f: no imp)....2½ 5
2459[2] White Emir *(52)*(Fav)*(MrsJRRamsden)* 2-9-0 MHills(8) (hld up in tch: effrt & rdn wl over 1f out: no imp)....1¼ 6
2335[3] Wingnut (IRE) *(30) (GLewis)* 2-8-5 SWhitworth(5) (chsd ldrs: rdn along over 2f out: sn btn)....4 7
2153[6] Members Welcome (IRE) *(19) (PGMurphy)* 2-8-2 JLowe(4) (a bhd: rdn & wandered fnl 2f: no imp)....2½ 8
2223[3] Incapol *(33) (MJRyan)* 2-9-3 AClark(2) (prom to ½-wy: sn rdn & wknd)....nk 9

9/4 White Emir, **7/1** Magic Imp (IRE), Wingnut (IRE), GAGAJULU, **8/1** Born A Lady, **9/1** Incapol, **10/1** Midnight Escape, **20/1** Ramsey Hope, Members Welcome (IRE), CSF £101.34 CT £1,102.21 TOTE £5.70: £1.70 £3.00 £1.60 (£60.50) Trio £74.40 OWNER Mr Mervyn Ayers (NEWMARKET) BRED M. L. Ayers 9 Rn
60.6 secs (2.10) SF: 26/23/-/2/14/16/-/-/-

2524 BLABY (S) STKS (3-Y.O) (Class G) £2,556.60 (£707.60: £337.80)

1m 8y Stalls: High GOING minus 0.50 sec per fur (F) 7-35 (7-36)

1209[11] **Bakers Daughter (45)***(59) (JRArnold)* 3-8-11 JWeaver(7) (led 1f: lost pl ½-wy: hdwy 2f out: led ent fnl f: r.o wl)....— 1
2276[11] Master M-E-N (IRE) **(50)***(62) (NMBabbage)* 3-9-2v WRyan(8) (hld up: hdwy 3f out: led over 1f out: sn hdd: kpt on u.p fnl f)....1 2
1824[3] Mill Dancer (IRE) *(50) (EJAlston)* 3-8-6 AMackay(2) (led after 1f tl over 2f out: kpt on u.p fnl f)....1¼ 3
2149[2] Irie Mon (IRE) **(58)***(55)*(Fav)*(JWHills)* 3-8-9 (7) MHenry(1) (a.p: led over 2f out tl over 1f out: r.o one pce)....2½ 4
2180[3] Corrievarkie **(46)***(44) (MissGayKelleway)* 3-8-7 ow1 WNewnes(9) (hld up: hdwy 2f out: rdn & r.o ins fnl f)....nk 5
2037[7] Tragic Hero **(59)***(41) (IABalding)* 3-8-11b TIves(5) (hld up: hdwy 3f out: wknd fnl 2f)....4 6
2359[7] Bell Contractors (IRE) **(55)***(17) (CDBroad)* 3-8-11v MFenton(6) (chsd ldrs tl rdn & outpcd ½-wy: t.o)....12 7
Dalysnicelitlerner *(3) (JRJenkins)* 3-8-11 CRutter(3) (w'like: bkwd: s.s: a bhd & outpcd: t.o) ...7 8

9/4 Irie Mon (IRE), **11/4** Tragic Hero (7/4-3/1), **13/2** Master M-E-N (IRE), **7/1** Mill Dancer (IRE), **15/2** Bell Contractors (IRE) (5/1-8/1), **8/1** Corrievarkie, **14/1** BAKERS DAUGHTER, **33/1** Dalysnicelitlerner, CSF £90.60 CT £74.40 TOTE £10.90: £2.10 £2.60 £1.90 (£53.10) Trio £44.20 OWNER Mr J. R. Arnold (UPPER LAMBOURN) BRED C. C. Bromley and Son and A. O. Nerses 8 Rn
1m 37.5 (2.50) SF: 28/31/19/24/13/10/-/-
Bt in 3,700 gns

2525 THOMAS GRANT & COMPANY STOCKBROKERS H'CAP (0-90) (3-Y.O+) (Class C) £6,056.00 (£1,808.00: £864.00: £392.00)

1m 3f 183y Stalls: High GOING minus 0.50 sec per fur (F) 8-05 (8-06)

2263* **Vindaloo (78)***(87) (JLHarris)* 3-8-13 DHolland(5) (lw: hld up: 6th st: hdwy to ld 2f out: hrd rdn & ct cl home: fin 2nd, s.h: awrdd r)....— 1
1878* Artic Courier **(77)***(86) (DJSCosgrove)* 4-9-3 (7) DGibbs(2) (hdwy ½-wy: 3rd st: rdn to chal over 1f out: qcknd to ld cl home: fin 1st: disq: plcd 2nd).... 2
1983* Flame War (USA) **(79)***(85)*(Fav)*(HRACecil)* 3-9-0 WRyan(7) (led after 2f to 2f out: rdn & one pce fnl f)....2½ 3
2068[4] Snowy Petrel (IRE) **(77)***(83) (JLDunlop)* 3-8-12 JWeaver(4) (hld up in rr: hdwy over 3f out: styd on appr fnl f: nt rch ldrs)....s.h 4
1853[17] Riparius (USA) **(78)***(79) (HCandy)* 4-9-11b WNewnes(9) (lw: s.i.s: hld up: hdwy 2f out: nvr nr to chal)....4 5
2101[6] Jadwal (USA) **(82)***(72) (DMorley)* 3-9-3 MHills(3) (hld up: effrt & rdn over 2f out: nt trble ldrs)....9 6
2055[3] General Mouktar **(70)***(59) (MCPipe)* 5-9-3v TIves(6) (hld up: effrt & n.m.r over 2f out: nvr able to chal)....1 7
15[4] Meant to Be **(75)***(55) (LadyHerries)* 5-9-1 (7) JO'Dwyer(1) (bit bkwd: prom: 2nd st: wknd over 2f out)....7 8
935[18] Eben Al Habeeb (IRE) **(78)***(58) (MajorWRHern)* 4-9-11 RHills(10) (bkwd: led 2f: 4th st: rdn & wknd over 2f out)....s.h 9

1825[6] Sayyed Alraqs (USA) **(69)***(24) (MAJarvis)* 3-8-4 PRobinson(8) (lw: chsd ldrs: 5th st: wknd wl over 2f out: t.o) 20 **10**

2/1 Flame War (USA), **11/2** Snowy Petrel (IRE), **7/1** Sayyed Alraqs (USA), VINDALOO, **8/1** Artic Courier, **10/1** Riparius (USA), **12/1** General Mouktar, **20/1** Jadwal (USA), Meant to Be, Eben Al Habeeb (IRE), CSF £55.22 CT £136.24 TOTE £5.80: £1.70 £3.20 £1.40 (£22.60) Trio £9.60 OWNER Mr J. D. Abell (MELTON MOWBRAY) BRED Green Park Investments Ltd 10 Rn
2m 30.8 (2.00) SF: 55/66/53/51/58/38/37/32/35/-
WEIGHT FOR AGE 3yo-12lb

2526 TATTERSALLS MAIDEN AUCTION STKS (2-Y.O) (Class E) £3,502.40 (£1,047.20: £501.60: £228.80) **7f 9y** Stalls: High GOING minus 0.50 sec per fur (F) 8-35 (8-39)

Letluce *(83) (JRArnold)* 2-8-2 CRutter(2) (w'like: hld up: hdwy & nt clr run over 2f out: rdn to ld over 1f out: r.o wl) ....— **1**
White Sea (IRE) *(83+) (PFICole)* 2-8-5 AClark(4) (unf: hld up: gd hdwy over 1f out: fin wl) ..1½ **2**
Rostaq *(79) (DJGMurraySmith)* 2-8-6 JWeaver(1) (leggy: lt-f: hld up in tch: effrt over 1f out: r.o) 2 **3**
1715[4] Silver Harrow *(79)*(Fav)*(SirMarkPrescott)* 2-8-8 GDuffield(15) (hld up: led over 2f out tl over 1f out: no ex fnl f) 1 **4**
1798[5] Infantry Dancer *(66) (GCBravery)* 2-7-6 (5) NVarley(3) (a.p: ev ch over 1f out: unable qckn) ....¾ **5**
Bianca Stella (USA) *(69) (MBell)* 2-8-7 MFenton(12) (lengthy: unf: b.nr fore: b.hind: prom: rdn over 1f out: grad wknd) 3 **6**
2063[3] Laurel Crown (IRE) *(69) (JBerry)* 2-8-1 (7) PRoberts(5) (chsd ldrs: rdn appr fnl f: one pce) ....½ **7**
2198[7] Daunting Destiny (BEL) *(57) (RHannon)* 2-8-4 ow1 RPerham(10) (mid div: effrt 2f out: nt pce to chal) 3 **8**
2198[4] The Legions Pride *(58) (JWHills)* 2-8-4 MHills(7) (dwlt: nvr nrr) ....nk **9**
Six Clerks (IRE) *(57) (JGFitzGerald)* 2-8-8 DHolland(8) (w'like: n.m.r 2f out: nvr nr to chal) 2 **10**
2116[6] Winston *(47) (JDBethell)* 2-8-5 ow1 RHills(9) (hld up: swtchd lft 2f out: no imp) 2½ **11**
1024[4] Aussie *(44) (MHTompkins)* 2-8-5 PRobinson(17) (unruly s: nvr nr ldrs) 2 **12**
1798[3] Atlantic Mist *(41) (BRMillman)* 2-8-4 SWhitworth(6) (w ldrs tl wknd 2f out) 1 **13**
2173[5] Be My Bird *(33) (BJMeehan)* 2-8-1 NCarlisle(14) (a in rr) 2 **14**
2135[8] Nottonitejosephine *(30) (RBoss)* 2-7-13 (3)ow3 PMcCabe(13) (led over 4f: wknd fnl 2f) ....nk **15**
High Desire (IRE) *(30) (JRArnold)* 2-8-1 NAdams(11) (w'like: bkwd: a bhd) 1¼ **16**
Onefourseven *(30) (SRBowring)* 2-8-2 StephenDavies(16) (leggy: unf: s.s: a bhd) ....nk **17**

15/8 Silver Harrow (11/4-7/4), **7/2** Bianca Stella (USA), **9/1** Aussie (op 6/1), **10/1** The Legions Pride, **12/1** White Sea (IRE) (8/1-14/1), **14/1** Daunting Destiny (BEL), Laurel Crown (IRE), **16/1** Rostaq, Atlantic Mist, **20/1** Be My Bird, Six Clerks (IRE), **25/1** Winston, LETLUCE, Infantry Dancer, **33/1** Nottonitejosephine, High Desire (IRE), Onefourseven, CSF £294.31 TOTE £42.50: £9.00 £5.30 £4.70 (£599.80) Trio £194.30 OWNER Mr A. H. Robinson (UPPER LAMBOURN) BRED Woodcote Stud Ltd 17 Rn
1m 25.2 (2.70) SF: 13/13/9/9/-/-/-/-/-/-/-/-/-/-/-/-/-

2527 GLEBE MEDIAN AUCTION MAIDEN STKS (3-Y.O F) (Class F) £2,695.40 (£744.40: £354.20) **5f 2y** Stalls: High GOING minus 0.50 sec per fur (F) 9-05 (9-06)

Non Dimenticar Me (IRE) *(71) (SirMarkPrescott)* 3-8-11 GDuffield(2) (swvd lft s: hdwy 2f out: led ins fnl f: readily) ....— **1**
1450[2] Ninety-Five **(67)***(63)*(Fav)*(JGFitzGerald)* 3-8-11 DHolland(5) (led tl hdd & outpcd ins fnl f)....2½ **2**
Flirty Gertie *(60) (RBoss)* 3-8-11 JWeaver(6) (rangy: s.s: hdwy ½-wy: rdn & kpt on ins fnl f) 1 **3**
2071[13] Fiery Footsteps **(48)***(56) (PHowling)* 3-8-11b WNewnes(4) (prom: rdn over 1f out: one pce)..1¼ **4**
2239[8] Sharp Holly (IRE) **(56)***(43) (JABennett)* 3-8-11 RHills(3) (prom: rdn 2f out: sn btn) 4 **5**
2236[12] Four Lane Flyer *(34) (EJAlston)* 3-8-11 AMackay(7) (b: s.s: a bhd & outpcd) 3 **6**
Last World *(30) (JAPickering)* 3-8-11 NCarlisle(1) (hmpd s: hdwy 3f out: wknd wl over 1f out) 1 **7**

4/6 Ninety-Five (op Evens), **5/1** Sharp Holly (IRE), **7/1** Flirty Gertie, **8/1** NON DIMENTICAR ME (IRE), **16/1** Fiery Footsteps, **33/1** Four Lane Flyer, **50/1** Last World, CSF £13.10 TOTE £7.40: £2.70 £1.30 (£5.60) OWNER Mr G. D. Waters (NEWMARKET) BRED G. D. Waters 7 Rn
60.5 secs (2.00) SF: 20/12/9/5/-/-/-

T/Plpt: £1,202.90 (11.67 Tckts). T/Qdpt: Not won; £74.40 to Chepstow 20/7/95. IM

2283-**SANDOWN (R-H)**

Wednesday July 19th (St course Good to firm, Rnd course Good, Good to firm patches)

WEATHER: hot WIND: nil

2528

HARPERS & QUEEN (S) H'CAP (0-60) (3-Y.O+) (Class E) £3,793.75 (£1,150.00: £562.50: £268.75)
1m 14y Stalls: High GOING minus 0.07 sec per fur (G) 6-20 (6-25)

2134[3] **Roi de la Mer (IRE) (55)***(71) (JAkehurst)* 4-9-11 GCarter(13) (3rd st: led wl over 1f out: sn clr: r.o wl) — 1
2166[4] Alltime Dancer (IRE) **(51)***(59)*(Fav)*(MrsJRRamsden)* 3-8-13b KFallon(5) (lw: s.s: rdn over 3f out: hdwy over 1f out: r.o) 4 2
2334[10] Pop to Stans **(47)***(51) (JPearce)* 6-8-10 (7) MNutter(17) (swtg: rdn over 2f out: gd hdwy over 1f out: r.o wl ins fnl f) 2 3
1484[10] Queens Stroller (IRE) **(55)***(56) (CCElsey)* 4-9-11 DHarrison(16) (n.m.r & swtchd lft 2f out: hdwy over 1f out: r.o one pce) 1½ 4
2246[16] Lucknam Style **(43)***(44) (MrsBarbaraWaring)* 7-8-13v JWilliams(7) (b.hind: swtg: 2nd st: ev ch over 2f out: wknd fnl f) hd 5
2134[2] Flair Lady **(47)***(47) (WGMTurner)* 4-8-10 (7) ADaly(14) (led over 6f) ½ 6
1785[4] Finjan **(51)***(50) (AGFoster)* 8-9-2 (5) RPainter(18) (nvr nr to chal) nk 7
2377[14] Racing Telegraph **(42)***(38) (JPearce)* 5-8-12 GBardwell(12) (plld hrd: 5th st: rdn over 2f out: wknd over 1f out) 1¾ 8
2246[3] Zahran (IRE) **(44)***(40) (JMBradley)* 4-8-11 (3) SDrowne(15) (b: lw: hrd rdn over 3f out: hdwy on ins over 2f out: wknd 1f out) s.h 9
2021[4] Rad **(53)***(44) (SPCWoods)* 5-9-9 WWoods(4) (a mid div) 2½ 10
2332[7] Harvest Rose **(48)***(33) (OO'Neill)* 6-9-4 BDoyle(10) (swtg: nvr nrr) 3 11
1027[11] Lawnswood Junior **(53)***(38) (JLSpearing)* 8-9-9 GHind(11) (swtg: dwlt: nvr nrr) s.h 12
2310[9] Ballyhays (IRE) **(46)***(29) (JAHarris)* 6-9-2 PaulEddery(9) (swtg: bhd fnl 3f) 1 13
2363[9] Main Brace **(46)***(23) (KRBurke)* 4-8-13 (3) JTate(2) (swtg: mid div & wkng whn hmpd 2f out) 3 14
2134[4] White Flash **(50)***(23) (DRCElsworth)* 4-9-6 MRoberts(6) (a bhd) 1¾ 15
Arnie (IRE) **(53)***(19) (GLMoore)* 3-9-1 AMcGlone(1) (bhd fnl 2f) 3½ 16
2033[5] South Sound (IRE) **(55)***(20) (RHannon)* 3-9-3 JReid(8) (6th st: wknd over 2f out) ¾ 17
1771[6] Sharp Spring **(46)***(1) (JWhite)* 4-8-13 (3) DWright(3) (4th st: wknd over 2f out) 5 18

5/1 Alltime Dancer (IRE), **11/2** Zahran (IRE), South Sound (IRE), **8/1** Flair Lady, **9/1** White Flash (6/1-10/1), Rad, **10/1** ROI DE LA MER (IRE), Queens Stroller (IRE), **14/1** Finjan, **16/1** Pop to Stans, Main Brace, **20/1** Lucknam Style, **25/1** Sharp Spring, Racing Telegraph, Lawnswood Junior, **33/1** Harvest Rose, Ballyhays (IRE), **50/1** Arnie (IRE), CSF £61.27 CT £765.85 TOTE £12.70: £2.80 £2.10 £3.30 £2.60 (£72.80) Trio £293.90 OWNER Foundation Developments Ltd (LAMBOURN) BRED Yeomanstown Lodge Stud 18 Rn

1m 44.23 (5.03) SF: 52/32/32/37/25/28/31/19/21/25/14/19/10/4/4/-/-/-
WEIGHT FOR AGE 3yo-8lb
No bid.

2529

E.B.F. 'BEST DRESSED RACEGOER' MAIDEN STKS (2-Y.O) (Class D) £4,104.00 (£1,242.00: £606.00: £288.00)
7f 16y Stalls: High GOING minus 0.07 sec per fur (G) 6-50 (6-55)

2283[11] **Oblomov** *(77) (GLewis)* 2-9-0 PaulEddery(6) (mde all: rdn out) — 1
2283[6] Labeed (USA) *(76) (MajorWRHern)* 2-9-0 TQuinn(5) (3rd st: rdn over 3f out: r.o wl ins fnl f) .nk 2
Faateq *(72)*(Fav)*(JLDunlop)* 2-9-0 WCarson(4) (str: scope: mod 4th st: hdwy over 2f out: chsd wnr over 1f out tl ins fnl f: r.o one pce: bttr for r) 1¾ 3
1246[6] Seven Crowns (USA) *(63) (RHannon)* 2-9-0 RCochrane(3) (mod 6th st: rdn over 3f out: hdwy over 1f out: r.o one pce) 4 4
1752[6] Star of Ring (IRE) *(52) (MJHeaton-Ellis)* 2-9-0 MRoberts(2) (2nd st: rdn over 3f out: wknd over 1f out) 5 5
Rayner (IRE) *(51) (PWChapple-Hyam)* 2-9-0 JReid(7) (w'like: scope: lw: s.s: wl bhd over 5f: nvr nrr) nk 6
2005[7] Shamand (USA) *(45) (BJMeehan)* 2-9-0 BDoyle(1) (bit bkwd: a bhd) 3 7
2200[8] Louisiana Purchase *(39) (MrsBarbaraWaring)* 2-9-0 JWilliams(8) (s.s: mod 5th st: wknd over 2f out) 2½ 8

9/4 Faateq (6/4-3/1), **5/2** Star of Ring (IRE), **5/1** Rayner (IRE) (5/2-6/1), **7/1** Labeed (USA) (5/1-8/1), **10/1** Seven Crowns (USA) (op 5/1), Shamand (USA) (8/1-12/1), **33/1** OBLOMOV, Louisiana Purchase, CSF £210.82 TOTE £26.20: £3.00 £1.70 £1.40 (£148.00) OWNER Mr John Manley (EPSOM) BRED Mrs M. Upsdell 8 Rn 1m 33.49 (6.89) SF: 15/14/10/1/-/-/-/-

2530 JENNIFER'S DIARY H'CAP (0-80) (4-Y.O+) (Class D) £4,690.50 (£1,419.00: £692.00: £328.50)
1m 6f Stalls: High GOING minus 0.07 sec per fur (G) 7-20 (7-25)

2238[2] **Midyan Blue (IRE) (72)***(85)*(Fav)*(JMPEustace)* 5-9-9 RCochrane(11) (3rd st: rdn over 3f out: squeezed thro ins fnl f: led last stride) — 1
2284[3] Tudor Island **(75)***(88)*(Fav)*(CEBrittain)* 6-9-12 BDoyle(8) (4th st: rdn over 3f out: led ins fnl f: hdd last stride) s.h 2
2374[2] Tu Opes **(70)***(79)*(Fav)*(JLHarris)* 4-9-7 PaulEddery(9) (2nd st: rdn over 2f out: ev ch ins fnl f: one pce) 3½ 3
2184[3] Ela Man Howa **(56)***(65)*(Fav)*(RAkehurst)* 4-8-7 TQuinn(10) (lw: led: hrd rdn over 1f out: hdd ins fnl f: one pce) nk 4
2280* Romalito **(45)***(51)* *(MBlanshard)* 5-7-5 (5) MBaird(3) (rdn over 3f out: hdwy over 1f out: one pce fnl f) 2 5
2109[2] Dormy Three **(70)***(76)* *(RJHodges)* 5-9-7 JWilliams(4) (hdwy 2f out: one pce fnl f) s.h 6
2289[4] Broughtons Formula **(48)***(52)*(Fav)*(WJMusson)* 5-7-13 AMcGlone(12) (lw: rdn over 3f out: hdwy over 1f out: wknd ins fnl f) 2 7
1749* Flight Lieutenant (USA) **(74)***(77)* *(RHannon)* 6-9-11 JReid(1) (swtg: nvr nr to chal) 1 8
2036[4] King Ubad (USA) **(50)***(49)* *(KOCunningham-Brown)* 6-8-1 MRoberts(13) (swtg: 5th st: wknd over 2f out) 3 9
2289[5] Uncharted Waters **(55)***(54)* *(CACyzer)* 4-8-6 DBiggs(5) (hld up: rdn over 4f out: wknd over 1f out) ½ 10
1109[7] Well Arranged (IRE) **(77)***(75)* *(RAkehurst)* 4-10-0 FNorton(2) (a bhd) 1 11
1840[22] High Five (IRE) **(43)***(40)* *(DAWilson)* 5-7-8 GBardwell(6) (lw: s.s: a bhd) 1 12
1794[7] Fast Forward Fred **(56)***(40)* *(LMontagueHall)* 4-8-7 DHarrison(7) (swtg: 6th st: wknd over 3f out) 11 13

6/1 MIDYAN BLUE (IRE), Tudor Island, Tu Opes, Ela Man Howa, Broughtons Formula, **9/1** Flight Lieutenant (USA), Dormy Three, **10/1** Uncharted Waters, **14/1** High Five (IRE), **20/1** Romalito, Well Arranged (IRE), **25/1** King Ubad (USA), Fast Forward Fred, CSF £40.26 CT £207.44 TOTE £6.20: £2.00 £2.60 £2.90 (£12.30) Trio £31.10 OWNER Mr Keith Palmer (NEWMARKET) BRED Ballykisteen Stud Ltd 13 Rn 3m 3.4 (8.70) SF: 52/55/46/32/18/43/19/44/16/21/42/7/7

2531 PANMURE GORDON H'CAP (0-85) (3-Y.O) (Class D) £4,901.75 (£1,484.00: £724.50: £344.75) **7f 16y** Stalls: High GOING minus 0.07 sec (G) 7-50 (7-55)

2117[2] **Fame Again (76)***(85)*(Fav)*(MrsJRRamsden)* 3-9-1 KFallon(2) (lw: rdn over 2f out: hdwy over 1f out: led ins fnl f: drvn out) — 1
1487[15] Elite Hope (USA) **(80)***(88)* *(CREgerton)* 3-8-12 (7) ADaly(5) (led: rdn over 2f out: hdd ins fnl f: r.o) ½ 2
2003[2] Nordic Breeze (IRE) **(70)***(76)* *(ABailey)* 3-8-9 RCochrane(6) (swtg: 2nd st: rdn over 2f out: unable qckn) 1 3
2068[9] Risky Romeo **(63)***(60)* *(GCBravery)* 3-8-2 FNorton(3) (swtg: hdwy 4f out: 4th st: hrd rdn over 1f out: sn wknd) 4 4
2168[5] Balance of Power **(74)***(65)* *(RAkehurst)* 3-8-13 TQuinn(4) (b: 3rd st: rdn over 2f out: wknd over 1f out) 2½ 5
2324[3] Gallows Corner (IRE) **(82)***(72)* *(RHannon)* 3-9-7 JReid(1) (lw: 5th st: rdn over 2f out: wknd over 1f out) ½ 6
1907[2] Crested Knight (IRE) **(67)***(53)* *(CAHorgan)* 3-8-6 PaulEddery(7) (swtg: 6th st: wknd wl over 1f out) 1¾ 7

13/8 FAME AGAIN, **7/2** Gallows Corner (IRE), **4/1** Nordic Breeze (IRE), **7/1** Crested Knight (IRE), **9/1** Balance of Power, **10/1** Elite Hope (USA), **16/1** Risky Romeo, CSF £16.79 TOTE £3.00: £1.60 £5.70 (£17.80) OWNER Mr M. R. Charlton (THIRSK) BRED R. Barbes 7 Rn
1m 32.6 (6.00) SF: 25/28/16/-/5/12/-

2532 '25TH BIRTHDAY' CLAIMING STKS (3-Y.O) (Class E) £3,598.75 (£1,090.00: £532.50: £253.75) **1m 2f 7y** Stalls: High GOING minus 0.07 sec (G) 8-20 (8-25)

2245[5] **Woodrising (54)***(66)* *(LadyHerries)* 3-7-12 GBardwell(7) (mde all: hrd rdn 2f out: r.o wl) — 1
2028[9] Victoria's Secret (IRE) **(70)***(71)* *(DRCElsworth)* 3-8-9b MRoberts(10) (2nd st: rdn over 2f out: unable qckn) 4 2
2314[8] Night Time **(70)***(70)* *(RHannon)* 3-8-9 JReid(3) (lw: hdwy over 2f out: r.o one pce) ½ 3
2411[5] Santa Fan (IRE) **(73)***(69)*(Fav)*(PFICole)* 3-8-9 TQuinn(2) (5th st: rdn 2f out: no rspnse) nk 4
2065[3] Gentle Irony **(51)***(59)* *(BJMeehan)* 3-8-0b BDoyle(12) (3rd st: rdn over 2f out: one pce) ¾ 5
Devon Peasant *(54)* *(LGCottrell)* 3-8-4 GCarter(13) (str: scope: bit bkwd: s.s: wl bhd over 8f: nvr nrr) 6 6

2309* Prince of Spades **(60)***(60) (CACyzer)* 3-9-0 DBiggs(11) (4th st: rdn over 3f out: wknd over 2f out) 2 **7**
*316** Cannizaro (IRE) *(43) (RJRWilliams)* 3-8-6 RCochrane(5) (lw: 6th st: wknd over 2f out) 6 **8**
*2378*4 Endless Fantasy *(35) (CACyzer)* 3-8-2 ow2 DHarrison(6) (lw: a bhd) 1¼ **9**
1675 10 Dr Frances (IRE) **(47)***(18) (CCElsey)* 3-7-11 FNorton(9) (a bhd) 9 **10**
2280 15 Adjacent Too **(26)***(10) (CCElsey)* 3-7-6 (5) MBaird(8) (lw: s.i.s: a wl bhd) 5 **11**
1691 13 Celestial Fire *(19) (JWhite)* 3-8-6 (3) SDrowne(4) (lw: bhd fnl 7f) 1¾ **12**

5/4 Santa Fan (IRE), **8/1** Victoria's Secret (IRE) (9/2-9/1), Night Time (6/1-9/1), Cannizaro (IRE) (5/1-9/1), Gentle Irony, Prince of Spades, **9/1** WOODRISING (6/1-10/1), **25/1** Dr Frances (IRE), **33/1** Devon Peasant, Endless Fantasy, Adjacent Too, Celestial Fire, CSF £74.39 TOTE £11.80: £2.10 £2.20 £2.10 (£51.90) Trio £50.80 OWNER Seymour Bloodstock (UK) Ltd (LITTLEHAMPTON) BRED Kirtlington Stud Ltd 12 Rn 2m 11.21 (6.91) SF: 23/28/27/26/16/11/17/-/-/-/-/-
Woodrising clmd BGee £4,000; Santa Fan (IRE) clmd EWardBlanchJr £15,000

2533 CHANNEL ONE H'CAP (0-80) (4-Y.O+) (Class D) £4,645.00 (£1,405.00: £685.00: £325.00) **5f 6y** Stalls: High GOING minus 0.23 sec per fur (GF) 8-50 (8-55)

Mr Bergerac (IRE) (70)*(79) (BPalling)* 4-9-6 TSprake(12) (swtg: rdn over 2f out: hdwy over 1f out: led wl ins fnl f: r.o wl) ....— **1**
2288 3 Agwa **(74)***(81)*(Fav)*(RJO'Sullivan)* 6-9-10 RCochrane(10) (chsd ldr: led 1f out tl wl ins fnl f: unable qckn) ....¾ **2**
2079 7 So Intrepid (IRE) **(70)***(73) (JMBradley)* 5-9-3 (3) SDrowne(8) (swtg: a.p: hrd rdn over 1f out: one pce) 1¼ **3**
2364 3 Giggleswick Girl **(63)***(63) (MRChannon)* 4-8-13 TQuinn(9) (a.p: rdn over 2f out: eased & lost pl over 1f out: r.o ins fnl f) 1 **4**
2326 5 Gone Savage **(66)***(65) (WJMusson)* 7-9-2 AMcGlone(3) (b.hind: hdwy over 1f out: r.o) ....nk **5**
2288 4 Magic Orb **(78)***(75) (JLHarris)* 5-10-0 PaulEddery(6) (b: a.p: hrd rdn over 1f out: one pce) ....½ **6**
2137* Great Hall **(59)***(54) (PDCundell)* 6-8-9b DHarrison(11) (s.s: wl bhd 4f: nvr nrr) ....¾ **7**
2326 8 Metal Boys **(65)***(59) (MissLCSiddall)* 8-9-1 GHind(7) (nvr nr to chal) ....nk **8**
2326 6 Ned's Bonanza **(68)***(61) (MDods)* 6-9-4 WCarson(1) (outpcd) ....nk **9**
1900 3 Yet More Roses **(69)***(54) (LadyHerries)* 4-9-5v JReid(5) (b: b.hind: led: clr over 3f out: hdd 1f out: sn wknd) 2½ **10**
2288 12 Green Golightly (USA) **(61)***(39) (DAWilson)* 4-8-11 NGwilliams(4) (outpcd) 2 **11**

100/30 Agwa, **6/1** Giggleswick Girl, **13/2** Magic Orb, Yet More Roses, **8/1** So Intrepid (IRE), Ned's Bonanza, Great Hall (5/1-9/1), Gone Savage (6/1-9/1), **20/1** MR BERGERAC (IRE), **25/1** Metal Boys, **33/1** Green Golightly (USA), CSF £81.26 CT £524.34 TOTE £30.50: £6.70 £2.00 £3.40 (£46.50) Trio £109.80 OWNER Mr P. R. John (COWBRIDGE) BRED Red House Stud 11 Rn
61.19 secs (1.39) SF: 61/63/55/45/47/57/36/41/43/36/21

T/Jckpt: Not won; £85,748.97 to Chepstow 20/07/95. T/Plpt: £282.70 (93.9 Tckts). T/Qdpt: £49.20 (5.9 Tckts). AK

1810-BRIGHTON (L-H)
Thursday July 20th (Firm)
WEATHER: sunny WIND: almost nil

2534 E.B.F. WOODINGDEAN MEDIAN AUCTION MAIDEN STKS (2-Y.O) (Class E) £3,187.80 (£950.40: £453.20: £80.30: £80.30) **6f 209y** Stalls: Low GOING minus 0.62 sec per fur (F) 2-00 (2-01)

Arabian Story *(72+) (LordHuntingdon)* 2-9-0 JWilliams(9) (unf: scope: bit bkwd: rr: hdwy over 1f out: str run to ld wl ins fnl f) ....— **1**
2370 4 Mancini *(71)*(Fav)*(MBell)* 2-9-0 MFenton(4) (led 5f out: rdn over 1f out: hdd wl ins fnl f: unable qckn) ....½ **2**
Lilli Claire *(62) (AGFoster)* 2-8-9 MRimmer(6) (leggy: 5th st: hdwy over 1f out: ev ch ins fnl f: one pce) 1¾ **3**
2408 8 Roman Gold (IRE) *(66) (RHannon)* 2-8-7 (7) DaneO'Neill(1) (s.i.s: sn rcvrd: 7th st: hdwy 2f out: rdn over 1f out: one pce) ....nk **4**
Vasetto *(66) (SirMarkPrescott)* 2-9-0 CNutter(3) (cmpt: bit bkwd: s.i.s: sn rcvrd: rdn 5f out: 6th st: hdwy 2f out: rdn over 1f out: one pce) ....d.h **4**
1977 12 Honestly *(45) (BSmart)* 2-8-6 (3) SSanders(10) (a bhd) 7 **6**
1184 14 North Star (IRE) *(50) (RHannon)* 2-9-0 RPerham(5) (nvr nrr) ....s.h **7**
1424 3 Laughing Buccaneer *(36) (BJMeehan)* 2-9-0 TQuinn(2) (prom: 2nd st: wknd over 1f out) 6 **8**
*2380*5 Dorspring (IRE) *(22) (CEBrittain)* 2-9-0 BDoyle(7) (led 2f: 3rd st: wknd wl over 1f out) 6 **9**
Phoenix House *(GLMoore)* 2-9-0 SWhitworth(8) (w'like: bit bkwd: 4th st: wknd 2f out) 15 **10**

8/11 Mancini (op 5/4), **11/2** Laughing Buccaneer (4/1-6/1), **13/2** North Star (IRE), **10/1** ARABIAN STORY (6/1-12/1), Roman Gold (IRE) (op 5/1), **14/1** Vasetto (8/1-16/1), **33/1** Honestly, Lilli Claire, Dorspring (IRE), Phoenix House, CSF £17.74 TOTE £12.60: £3.10 £1.10 £5.70 (£5.40) Trio £94.30 OWNER The Queen (WEST ILSLEY) BRED The Queen 10 Rn 1m 22.4 (2.40) SF: 16/15/6/10/10/-

2535 KINGSTON (S) H'CAP (0-60) (3-Y.O+) (Class G) £2,489.40 (£688.40: £328.20)
1m 3f 196y Stalls: High GOING minus 0.62 sec per fur (F) 2-35 (2-37)

2090[2] **Valiant Toski (44)***(63)*(Fav)*(MCPipe)* 4-9-5b BDoyle(3) (mde all: qcknd 2f out: pushed out)..— 1
2174[6] Riva Rock **(28)***(43) (TPMcGovern)* 5-8-3 AMcGlone(2) (a.p: 2nd st: rdn 2f out: edgd lft ins fnl f: one pce)..........3 2
2175[6] Total Joy (IRE) **(53)***(66) (PFICole)* 4-10-0b TQuinn(1) (plld hrd: a.p: 3rd st: rdn over 2f out: 3rd & btn whn n.m.r ins fnl f: one pce)..........1½ 3
1937[11] Remember This (IRE) **(28)***(21) (CACyzer)* 5-8-3 DBiggs(6) (mod 4th st: no hdwy)..........15 4
1974[14] Green Green Ruby **(37)***(16) (GLMoore)* 3-8-0v CRutter(5) (rdn 6f out: poor 6th st: a bhd).......10 5
Flatford Princess **(45)***(14) (GLMoore)* 3-8-8 SWhitworth(4) (poor 5th st: bhd fnl 5f)..........8 6

6/5 VALIANT TOSKI, **7/2** Total Joy (IRE) (5/2-4/1), **11/2** Riva Rock, **10/1** Green Green Ruby (6/1-12/1), Flatford Princess (5/1-12/1), **20/1** Remember This (IRE), CSF £7.10 TOTE £2.00: £1.40 £2.20 (£5.10) OWNER Sir John Swaine (WELLINGTON) BRED Corvette Paddocks Ltd 6 Rn
2m 29.7 (0.70) SF: 49/29/52/7/-/-
WEIGHT FOR AGE 3yo-12lb
No bid

2536 PEVENSEY H'CAP (0-70) (3-Y.O) (Class E) £3,330.80 (£994.40: £475.20: £215.60)
1m 1f 209y Stalls: High GOING minus 0.62 sec per fur (F) 3-10 (3-11)

1124[5] **Soviet Bride (IRE) (52)***(61) (SDow)* 3-7-12 (7) ADaly(3) (led 2f: 4th st: led wl over 1f out: sn clr: r.o wl)..........— 1
1985[3] Elite Justice **(63)***(66) (PFICole)* 3-9-2 TQuinn(2) (a.p: 3rd st: led over 2f out: hdd wl over 1f out: one pce)..........4 2
1939[5] Guest Alliance (IRE) **(54)***(53) (AMoore)* 3-8-7 CandyMorris(1) (rdn 5f out: 6th st: hrd rdn fnl 2f: one pce)..........2 3
2033[6] Alerting **(64)***(61) (IABalding)* 3-8-12 (5) DGriffiths(8) (lw: 5th st: rdn over 2f out: one pce).......1½ 4
2406[2] Birthday Boy (IRE) **(63)***(59)*(Fav)*(RHannon)* 3-8-9v(7) DaneO'Neill(4) (led 8f out: hdd over 2f out: wknd over 1f out)..........¾ 5
444[10] Emerald Dream (IRE) **(47)***(23) (CCElsey)* 3-8-0 AMcGlone(9) (a bhd)..........12 6
2167[6] Pedaltothemetal (IRE) **(48)***(22) (PMitchell)* 3-7-10 (5)ow2 AWhelan(6) (b.nr hind: 7th st: rdn 3f out: grad wknd)..........½ 7
2270[3] Indian Jockey **(68)***(40) (MCPipe)* 3-9-7 BThomson(7) (a.p: 2nd st: ev ch over 2f out: wknd over 1f out)..........2½ 8

3/1 Birthday Boy (IRE) (2/1-100/30), **100/30** Elite Justice, **4/1** SOVIET BRIDE (IRE), Indian Jockey, **9/1** Alerting (9/2-10/1), **16/1** Pedaltothemetal (IRE), **25/1** Emerald Dream (IRE), Guest Alliance (IRE), CSF £16.19 CT £253.00 TOTE £4.40: £1.70 £1.20 £6.90 (£9.50) Trio £147.00 OWNER Mr J. E. Mills (EPSOM) BRED Gainsborough Stud Management Ltd 8 Rn
1m 59.9 (1.90) SF: 29/34/21/29/27/-/-/8

2537 JOE BLANKS MEMORIAL CHALLENGE CUP H'CAP (0-80) (3-Y.O) (Class D) £3,799.90 (£1,133.20: £540.60: £244.30)
7f 214y Stalls: Low GOING minus 0.62 sec per fur (F) 3-45 (3-45)

1787[2] **Apollono (67)***(80) (RAkehurst)* 3-8-13 (3) SSanders(2) (3rd st: led 2f out: hrd rdn & edgd lft fnl f: all out)..........— 1
2361* Shifting Moon **(77)***(90)*(Fav)*(IABalding)* 3-9-7b(5) 5x DGriffiths(6) (lw: sn led: hdd 2f out: rallied & hrd rdn ins fnl f: r.o)..........s.h 2
2171* Elite Racing **(68)***(73) (PFICole)* 3-9-3 TQuinn(4) (4th st: rdn over 2f out: one pce)..........4 3
2278[3] Star of Gold **(64)***(63) (CREgerton)* 3-8-13 BThomson(3) (2nd st: rdn over 2f out: grad wknd)..........3 4
2199[2] Kevasingo **(63)***(62) (SDow)* 3-8-7 (5) AWhelan(1) (sn rdn along: 5th st: no hdwy fnl 2f)..........s.h 5
2405[3] Greenwich Again **(69)***(58) (TGMills)* 3-9-4 SWhitworth(7) (6th st: bhd fnl 2f)..........5 6
1979[16] Sovereigns Parade **(64)***(35) (LJHolt)* 3-8-13 AMcGlone(5) (a bhd)..........9 7

3/1 Shifting Moon, **7/2** Elite Racing, Kevasingo, **6/1** APOLLONO (7/2-13/2), **7/1** Star of Gold (5/1-8/1), **8/1** Greenwich Again (5/1-9/1), **16/1** Sovereigns Parade, CSF £22.68 TOTE £5.90: £2.30 £1.50 (£19.10) OWNER Mr J K Ruggles & Mrs A R Ruggles (EPSOM) BRED Miss P. Ambler 7 Rn
1m 33.0 (0.80) SF: 38/48/31/21/20/16/-

2538 ROCK GARDENS CLAIMING STKS (3-Y.O+) (Class F) £2,519.00 (£694.00: £329.00) **6f 209y** Stalls: Low GOING minus 0.62 sec per fur (F) 4-20 (4-21)

2178[2] **Crystal Heights (FR) (63)***(66)*(Fav)*(RJO'Sullivan)* 7-8-9 (3) SSanders(1) (dwlt: sn rcvrd: 5th st: led 2f out: rdn fnl f: r.o)...— 1
1974[11] Thames Side **(47)***(65) (MMadgwick)* 4-8-12 MFenton(6) (bhd: sn rdn along: 8th st: swtchd lft & hdwy over 1f out: str run fnl f: fin wl)...nk 2
2093[2] Dusk in Daytona **(62)***(62) (CJames)* 3-8-6 AMcGlone(3) (led 4f out: hdd 2f out: rdn over 1f out: one pce)...1¾ 3
1546[10] Kencol **(49)***(56) (AGFoster)* 3-7-11 (5)ow1 AWhelan(2) (6th st: rdn 2f out: r.o one pce fnl f)...½ 4
2053[6] The Little Ferret **(63)***(63) (AMoore)* 5-8-11 (5) CChoi(4) (led 3f: 2nd st: ev ch 2f out: one pce)..½ 5
1593[5] Blue Bomber **(74)***(64) (CWeedon)* 4-9-8 MPerrett(7) (3rd st: rdn over 2f out: wknd over 1f out)...2 6
2054[9] Mutinique **(44)***(39) (BAPearce)* 4-8-5b StephenDavies(5) (4th st: wknd over 2f out)...3½ 7
1714[5] Kissavos **(41)***(37) (CCElsey)* 9-8-10v BDoyle(8) (a bhd)...3 8

6/4 CRYSTAL HEIGHTS (FR), **4/1** Dusk in Daytona, **9/2** Blue Bomber (op 3/1), **6/1** The Little Ferret (op 4/1), **20/1** Thames Side, **25/1** Kencol, Kissavos, **33/1** Mutinique, CSF £24.18 TOTE £1.90: £1.30 £1.50 £1.40 (£15.30) OWNER Mr Jack Joseph (BOGNOR REGIS) BRED Ahmad Fustok 8 Rn
1m 21.7 (1.70) SF: 22/21/11/5/19/20/-/-
WEIGHT FOR AGE 3yo-7lb

2539 PRESTON PARK LIMITED STKS (0-60) (3-Y.O+) (Class F) £2,519.00 (£694.00: £329.00) **5f 213y** Stalls: Low GOING minus 0.62 sec per fur (F) 4-55 (4-56)

2054* **Pride of Hayling (IRE) (49)***(67) (PRHedger)* 4-9-1 StephenDavies(4) (4th st: hdwy over 1f out: led wl ins fnl f: r.o)...— 1
2448[4] Pearl Dawn (IRE) **(60)***(63)*(Fav)*(NoelChance)* 5-8-12 BThomson(7) (3rd st: led 1f out: hdd wl ins fnl f: unable qckn)...nk 2
2203[5] Red Admiral **(58)***(63) (PCHaslam)* 5-8-13 (7) NicolaHowarth(2) (led: hdd 1f out: one pce)...3 3
2342[7] Walnut Burl (IRE) **(56)***(55) (LJHolt)* 5-9-3 MFenton(6) (dwlt: 8th st: rdn 2f out: nvr nrr)...2 4
1815[4] Pirates Gold (IRE) **(46)***(54) (JWhite)* 5-9-3 BDoyle(5) (6th st: rdn over 2f out: one pce)...nk 5
2178[6] Singing Rock (IRE) **(60)***(41) (RHannon)* 3-8-6b RPerham(1) (7th st: rdn over 2f out: no hdwy).3 6
1785[15] It's so Easy **(34)***(25) (APJames)* 4-8-12 MRimmer(3) (wnt rt s: 2nd st: wknd 2f out)...6 7
2290[2] Frisky Miss (IRE) **(58)***(23) (KOCunningham-Brown)* 4-8-12 AMcGlone(8) (5th st: wknd 2f out)...¾ 8

9/4 Pearl Dawn (IRE), **7/2** Singing Rock (IRE), **5/1** Frisky Miss (IRE) (3/1-11/2), Walnut Burl (IRE) (4/1-13/2), **6/1** PRIDE OF HAYLING (IRE) (4/1-13/2), **9/1** Red Admiral (op 4/1), **16/1** Pirates Gold (IRE), **33/1** It's so Easy, CSF £19.70 TOTE £9.00: £2.60 £1.90 £2.90 (£14.60) OWNER Mr Bill Broomfield (CHICHESTER) BRED Ewar Stud Farm International 8 Rn
1m 8.4 (equals standard) SF: 45/41/41/33/32/13/3/1
WEIGHT FOR AGE 3yo-6lb

T/Plpt: £75.40 (139.23 Tckts). T/Qdpt: £14.30 (4.5 Tckts). SM

2516-CATTERICK (L-H)
Thursday July 20th (Good to firm)
WEATHER: sunny periods, very warm WIND: slight across

2540 NORA BATTY (S) APPRENTICE H'CAP (0-60) (3-Y.O) (Class G) £2,377.00 (£672.00: £331.00) **7f** Stalls: Low GOING minus 0.34 sec per fur (GF) 6-45 (6-46)

2425[4] **Caltha (39)***(48)*(Fav)*(PCalver)* 3-8-4b NVarley(4) (lw: mde all: clr appr st: drvn out)...— 1
847[6] Dowdency **(54)***(60) (JAPickering)* 3-9-2 (3) SCopp(5) (in tch: hdwy 2f out: hrd rdn & one pce ins fnl f)...1½ 2
2239[7] Prince Rudolf (IRE) **(42)***(44) (MrsNMacauley)* 3-8-4v(3) AmandaSanders(2) (in tch: styd on fnl 2f: nvr able to chal)...1½ 3
1647[7] The Cape Doctor (IRE) **(43)***(42) (AGFoster)* 3-8-8b JDSmith(7) (s.i.s: styd on fnl 3f: nrst fin)...1¼ 4
701[12] Boost **(45)***(43) (CWThornton)* 3-8-3 (7) GMills(6) (bhd tl styd on fnl 2f: nrst fin)...½ 5
2425[W] Tee Tee Too (IRE) **(56)***(54) (PCHaslam)* 3-9-2 (5) CarolDavison(10) (lw: chsd wnr tl wknd fnl 2f)...hd 6
2278[7] Asking **(32)***(29) (JABennett)* 3-7-8v(3) MHenry(8) (chsd ldrs tl wknd fnl 2½f)...nk 7
2220[7] Irchester Lass **(39)***(33) (SRBowring)* 3-8-4 CTeague(12) (lw: racd wd: nvr trbld ldrs)...1¼ 8
2357[6] L'Eglise Belle **(45)***(34) (MrsALMKing)* 3-8-7 (3) RHavlin(3) (lw: s.i.s: n.d)...2½ 9

2246[18] Pash **(34)***(22) (CWFairhurst)* 3-7-10v(3) PFessey(11) (lw: n.d) ....hd **10**
2156[9] Benjarong **(32)***(16) (RMMcKellar)* 3-7-11 MBaird(13) (in tch 4f: sn wknd) 1¾ **11**
1993[6] Saint Amigo **(52)***(11) (JLEyre)* 3-9-3 HKYim(9) (s.i.s: a wl bhd) 11 **12**
1358[14] Shazanni (IRE) **(46)***(1) (JGFitzGerald)* 3-8-6 (5) GFaulkner(1) (b: chsd ldrs to st: sn wknd) 1¾ **13**

7/2 CALTHA (5/1-3/1), **6/1** Prince Rudolf (IRE), Tee Tee Too (IRE), **8/1** Irchester Lass, **12/1** The Cape Doctor (IRE), L'Eglise Belle, Shazanni (IRE), Saint Amigo, **14/1** Dowdency, Asking, Benjarong, **20/1** Pash, **25/1** Boost, CSF £47.33 CT £264.30 TOTE £3.80: £1.80 £3.40 £1.50 (£52.00) Trio £65.00 OWNER Mr D. B. Stanley (RIPON) BRED Mrs G. C. Stanley 13 Rn
1m 26.9 (3.70) SF: 17/29/13/11/12/23/-/2/3/-/-/-/-
No bid

2541 OLIVE OYL NURSERY H'CAP (2-Y.O) (Class E) £3,444.00 (£1,032.00: £496.00: £228.00)
7f Stalls: Low GOING minus 0.34 sec per fur (GF) 7-15 (7-16)

2424[4] **Silverdale Knight** *(75) (KWHogg)* 2-7-13 (5) MBaird(5) (mde most: styd on strly fnl f) ....— **1**
2346* Society Girl *(78)*(Fav)*(CWThornton)* 2-8-12 6x DeanMcKeown(8) (a.p: effrt & ev ch over 2f out: hung lft & nt qckn appr fnl f) 2 **2**
2328[6] Thorntoun Jewel (IRE) *(61) (JBalding)* 2-7-9 ClaireBalding(6) (hdwy on outside 2f out: styd on wl towards fin) ....nk **3**
1943* Sizzling Symphony *(71) (RAFahey)* 2-8-7 ACulhane(7) (lw: s.i.s: sn pushed along: hdwy appr st: hrd rdn & one pce fnl 2f) ....¾ **4**
2354[2] Napoleon's Return *(66) (AGFoster)* 2-8-4 JFortune(1) (bhd tl styd on fnl 2f) ....¾ **5**
2277[4] Don't Forget Mikie (IRE) *(64) (MJHeaton-Ellis)* 2-8-2 JLowe(3) (chsd ldrs tl wknd fnl 2f) ....hd **6**
2059[4] Traceability *(70) (JBerry)* 2-8-12 JCarroll(2) (lw: prom 5f) 2 **7**
2251* Sovitaka (IRE) *(47) (MHEasterby)* 2-7-12 ow1 SMaloney(4) (a outpcd & bhd) 3½ **8**
1650[2] The Frisky Farmer *(57) (WGMTurner)* 2-9-0 (7) AEddery(9) (cl up tl wknd over 2f out) 6 **9**

2/1 Society Girl, **4/1** Sizzling Symphony, **11/2** Don't Forget Mikie (IRE), **8/1** Napoleon's Return, **10/1** Traceability, SILVERDALE KNIGHT, The Frisky Farmer, **12/1** Sovitaka (IRE), **25/1** Thorntoun Jewel (IRE), CSF £29.50 CT £457.22 TOTE £20.00: £4.10 £1.30 £4.80 (£30.00) Trio £84.30 OWNER Mr G. J. Bush (SHERBORNE) BRED Miss Claire Farrow, Dame Elizabeth and Alexander C 9 Rn
1m 27.7 (4.50) SF: -/11/3/4/-/8/-/-/-

2542 PENELOPE PITSTOP MAIDEN STKS (2-Y.O) (Class D) £3,720.00 (£1,110.00: £530.00: £240.00) **5f 212y** Stalls: High GOING minus 0.34 sec (GF) 7-45 (7-46)

1842[4] **Gladys Althorpe (IRE)** *(71) (JLEyre)* 2-8-9 RLappin(3) (chsd clr ldrs: hdwy over 1f out: r.o wl fnl f to ld nr fin) ....— **1**
2095[4] Pharmacy *(71+)*(Fav)*(JWWatts)* 2-8-9 TIves(4) (lw: mde most tl eased ins fnl f: ct nr fin) ....hd **2**
1992[2] Nilgiri Hills (IRE) *(65) (JLDunlop)* 2-9-0 JWeaver(2) (w ldr to st: sn rdn & grad wknd) 4 **3**
Spirito Libro (USA) *(59) (SirMarkPrescott)* 2-8-9 DeanMcKeown(9) (small: neat: a chsng ldrs: no imp fnl 2½f) ....nk **4**
1579[7] Mystic Times *(38) (MissSEHall)* 2-8-9 NConnorton(8) (hld up: stdy hdwy 2f out: nvr plcd to chal: lame) 8 **5**
1877[5] Arc of The Diver (IRE) *(39) (JBerry)* 2-9-0 JCarroll(11) (a same pl) 1¼ **6**
2371[4] Relatively Clever (USA) *(39) (MrsJRRamsden)* 2-8-7 (7) SBuckley(1) (lw: nvr nr to chal) ....hd **7**
2185[8] Spring Silhouette *(34) (MrsVAAconley)* 2-8-9 MDeering(7) (nvr trbld ldrs) ....s.h **8**
1781[5] Four Weddings (USA) *(36) (MBell)* 2-9-0 JFanning(10) (lw: dwlt: a bhd) 1 **9**
Kernof (IRE) *(36) (MDHammond)* 2-9-0 DaleGibson(5) (scope: s.i.s: nvr wnt pce) ....hd **10**
Recall To Mind *(34) (MHEasterby)* 2-9-0 SMaloney(6) (unf: s.i.s: sme hdwy 2f out: sn wknd) ¾ **11**

13/8 Pharmacy, **9/4** Nilgiri Hills (IRE) (3/1-2/1), **6/1** GLADYS ALTHORPE (IRE), **14/1** Spirito Libro (USA), Arc of The Diver (IRE), Relatively Clever (USA), **20/1** Mystic Times, **25/1** Four Weddings (USA), **33/1** Recall To Mind, **66/1** Kernof (IRE), **100/1** Spring Silhouette, CSF £15.16 TOTE £9.50: £1.90 £1.10 £1.10 (18.10) Trio £5.10 OWNER Mr T. S. Ely (HAMBLETON) BRED Mrs R. Kitchin 11 Rn
1m 13.5 (3.00) SF: 23/23/17/11/-/-/-/-/-/-/-

STEWARDS' ENQUIRY Ives susp. 29/7-2/8/95 (failing to ensure best possible placing).

OFFICIAL EXPLANATION **Mystic Times: had stumbled and lost her action six furlongs out and finished lame.**

2543 EHL'S BIRTHDAY H'CAP (0-70) (3-Y.O+) (Class E) £3,348.00 (£999.00: £477.00: £216.00) **1m 3f 214y** Stalls: Low GOING minus 0.34 sec per fur (GF) 8-15 (8-16)

2339* **Labibeh (USA)** **(71)***(82)*(Fav)*(JLDunlop)* 3-10-1 5x JWeaver(10) (cl up: led 5f out tl hdd over 2f out: rallied to ld ins fnl f: r.o) ....— **1**
2355[3] Instantaneous **(47)***(55) (MHEasterby)* 3-8-5 SMaloney(1) (lw: a.p: led over 2f out: sn rdn: hdd & no ex ins fnl f) 2½ **2**

23736 Doctor's Remedy **(31)***(31) (MrsJJordan)* 9-7-8b(7)ow1 MHenry(3) (bhd tl styd on fnl 2f: nrst fin) .5 **3**
672 15 Tancred Mischief **(32)***(32) (WLBarker)* 4-7-13 (3) DarrenMoffatt(6) (swtg: outpcd & bhd tl styd on strly fnl 2f) 1 **4**
2245* Course Fishing **(39)***(39) (BAMcMahon)* 4-8-9 JFortune(4) (lw: chsd ldrs: drvn along & ev ch appr st: btn over 2f out) ....hd **5**
23733 Exclusion **(38)***(23) (JHetherton)* 6-8-8 DeanMcKeown(2) (lw: led tl hdd 5f out: sn outpcd) 11 **6**
23557 Leap in the Dark (IRE) **(35)***(17) (MissLCSiddall)* 6-8-5 TWilliams(9) (chsd ldrs tl outpcd over 4f out) 2 **7**
23075 My Handy Man **(54)***(36) (RAllan)* 4-9-10 JCarroll(7) (in tch: effrt & chsng ldrs appr st: btn over 2f out) ....½ **8**
23323 Asmarina **(39)***(12) (SRBowring)* 5-8-4b(5) CTeague(8) (lw: chsd ldrs tl rdn & wknd 4f out) 6 **9**

7/4 LABIBEH (USA), **5/2** Instantaneous, **11/2** Course Fishing, **7/1** Asmarina, **10/1** Exclusion, **12/1** My Handy Man, **16/1** Leap in the Dark (IRE), **25/1** Doctor's Remedy, **66/1** Tancred Mischief, CSF £6.67 CT £72.81 TOTE £2.70: £1.50 £1.10 £5.80 (£3.10) Trio £60.50 OWNER Mr Hamdan Al Maktoum (ARUNDEL) BRED Shadwell Farm Estate Co Ltd and Shadwell Farm Inc 9 Rn
2m 36.1 (5.10) SF: 52/25/13/14/21/5/-/18/-
WEIGHT FOR AGE 3yo-12lb

2544 EDINA AND PATSY CLAIMING STKS (3-Y.O+) (Class F) £2,798.00 (£778.00: £374.00) **1m 3f 214y** Stalls: Low GOING minus 0.34 sec per fur (GF) 8-45 (8-46)

16866 **Latvian (68)***(76+)*(Fav)*(RAllan)* 8-9-5 JWeaver(1) (hld up: hdwy 6f out: qcknd to ld 1½f out: sn clr) ....— **1**
23312 Festive Lassie *(64)*(Fav)*(TDBarron)* 4-9-1 JFortune(4) (lw: cl up: effrt over 2f out: nt pce of wnr fnl f) 6 **2**
23275 Thaleros **(56)***(66) (GMMoore)* 5-9-1 (3) JTate(3) (lw: mde most tl hdd 1½f out: one pce) ....¾ **3**
24782 Anorak (USA) **(47)***(55) (GMMoore)* 5-8-9v(3) JStack(9) (bhd: effrt appr st: nvr able to chal).......4 **4**
21238 Nonios (IRE) **(75)***(62) (GMMoore)* 4-9-10 JCarroll(7) (pushed along 5f out: nvr trbld ldrs).....3½ **5**
22939 Fearless Wonder **(56)***(56) (MrsMReveley)* 4-8-12b(7) SCopp(5) (outpcd & bhd 6f out: n.d after) ....½ **6**
1596 14 Castletown Count **(45)***(50) (KWHogg)* 3-8-2 SMaloney(2) (lw: cl up: slt ld after 4f to 6½f out: wknd 5f out) ....¾ **7**
21654 Skiddaw Samba *(45) (MrsMReveley)* 6-8-5 (7) DDenby(6) (swtg: chsd ldrs tl wknd over 2f out) 2½ **8**
23558 Petal's Jarred **(32)***(31) (WStorey)* 5-8-0v(7) PFessey(8) (prom tl wknd 4f out) 7 **9**

7/4 LATVIAN, Festive Lassie, **8/1** Thaleros, **12/1** Anorak (USA), Fearless Wonder, **14/1** Skiddaw Samba, **25/1** Castletown Count, Nonios (IRE), **66/1** Petal's Jarred, CSF £4.95 TOTE £2.80: £1.10 £1.20 £2.10 (£1.70) Trio £5.50 OWNER Mr I. Bell (CORNHILL-ON-TWEED) BRED Fittocks Stud Ltd 9 Rn
2m 37.2 (6.20) SF: 36/24/26/15/22/16/-/5/-
WEIGHT FOR AGE 3yo-12lb

2545 LILO LILL H'CAP (0-70) (3-Y.O+) (Class E) £3,210.00 (£960.00: £460.00: £210.00) **1m 7f 177y** Stalls: Low GOING minus 0.34 sec per fur (GF) 9-15 (9-16)

23746 **Izza (34)***(44) (WStorey)* 4-7-5 (7) PFessey(1) (hld up: hdwy 6f out: styd on u.p fnl 2f to ld cl home) ....— **1**
2186* Kilernan **(44)***(54)*(Fav)*(TDBarron)* 4-8-8 JFortune(2) (trckd ldrs: led 5½f out & qcknd: rdn over 1f out: jst ct) ....hd **2**
14356 Great Oration (IRE) **(36)***(44) (FWatson)* 6-8-0 SMaloney(5) (hdwy 7f out: chsng ldrs appr st: kpt on fnl f) 1¾ **3**
16014 Arctic Charmer (USA) **(69)***(75) (JLDunlop)* 3-9-3 JWeaver(4) (lw: chsd ldrs: drvn along 5f out: one pce fnl 2½f) 2 **4**
22632 Opus One **(60)***(62) (MissSEHall)* 4-9-3 (7) MHenry(6) (swtg: hld up: sddle slipped ½-wy: rdn appr st: no imp) 4 **5**
2310 15 Sallyoreally (IRE) **(43)***(43) (WStorey)* 4-8-7 JFanning(3) (bhd: sme hdwy ent st: n.d) 2½ **6**
21864 Don't Cry **(29)***(28) (DonEnricoIncisa)* 7-7-7 KimTinkler(7) (lw: led tl hdd 5½f out: sn outpcd) ....nk **7**
24276 Kinoko **(40)***(38) (KWHogg)* 7-7-11 (7) DLockhart(8) (cl up tl wknd 4f out) 1¼ **8**
LONG HANDICAP Don't Cry 6-13

2/1 Kilernan (6/4-9/4), **5/2** Opus One, **4/1** Great Oration (IRE) (op 6/1), **7/1** Arctic Charmer (USA), **12/1** IZZA (op 7/1), **20/1** Don't Cry, **25/1** Kinoko, **50/1** Sallyoreally (IRE), CSF £33.89 CT £103.94 TOTE £13.50: £2.40 £1.10 £1.50 (£18.80) OWNER Mr D. C. Batey (CONSETT) 8 Rn
3m 31.8 (10.80) SF: 5/15/5/20/23/4/-/-
WEIGHT FOR AGE 3yo-16lb

T/Plpt: £9.00 (1,399.14 Tckts). T/Qdpt: £1.90 (27.60 Tckts). AA

2359-CHEPSTOW (L-H)
Thursday July 20th (Good to firm)
Race 5 - flip start
WEATHER: sunny & hot WIND: nil

2546 LYSAGHT AMATEUR H'CAP (0-70) (3-Y.O+) (Class G) £2,633.00 (£738.00: £359.00) **1m 4f 23y** Stalls: High GOING minus 0.52 sec per fur (F) 6-30 (6-34)

1937⁴ **Strat's Legacy (43)***(56) (DWPArbuthnot)* 8-11-2 MrsDArbuthnot(9) (b.hind: mde virtually all: qcknd clr 2f out: r.o wl).....— 1
2197² Our Bessie **(46)***(51) (DMarks)* 4-11-5 MissKMarks(5) (w wnr: 2nd st: outpcd 3f out: styd on fnl f).....6 2
2233² Outstayed Welcome **(49)***(54) (MJHaynes)* 3-10-10 MissYHaynes(13) (lw: 3rd st: chsd wnr over 3f out: edgd lft 2f out: wknd ins fnl f).....hd 3
2226⁵ Ice Magic **(26)***(28) (FJYardley)* 8-9-8v(5) MissSYardley(15) (hdwy & 5th st: one pce fnl 3f).....2 4
1674⁷ Last Laugh (IRE) **(58)***(59)*(Fav)*(MCPipe)* 3-11-5 MrRJohnson(7) (hld up & bhd: hdwy & hung lft 3f out: nt r.o).....¾ 5
2007¹² Lunar Risk **(38)***(39) (MissBSanders)* 5-10-11 MissDianaJones(8) (nvr nr to chal).....nk 6
2356* Grooms Gold (IRE) **(65)***(64) (PWHarris)* 3-11-12 5x MissAElsey(1) (7th st: no hdwy fnl 3f).....1¼ 7
*514*⁷ How's it Goin (IRE) **(55)***(53) (WRMuir)* 4-12-0 MrJDurkan(6) (8th st: no hdwy fnl 3f).....1¼ 8
2138³ Scenic Dancer **(46)***(42) (AHide)* 7-11-5 MrsLPearce(2) (s.s: a bhd).....1½ 9
2129⁷ Gigfy **(38)***(20) (BJLlewellyn)* 3-9-13b MrJLLlewellyn(14) (plld hrd: prom: 4th st: wknd over 3f out).....10 10
*1762*¹⁴ Reigning Royal **(35)***(14) (DBurchell)* 4-10-3 (5) MissEJJones(10) (plld hrd: 6th st: wknd 4f out).....2½ 11
2154⁷ Lajadhal (FR) **(20)** *(KBishop)* 6-9-2 (5) MissAPurdy(4) (prom tl wknd rapidly over 5f out).....1 12
1996¹⁰ Dance and Sing (IRE) **(29)** *(DLWilliams)* 5-9-11 (5) MrsCWilliams(3) (s.s: a bhd).....7 13
2151⁵ Handson **(47)***(12) (BRMillman)* 3-10-3 (5) MrLJefford(12) (a bhd).....2½ 14
LONG HANDICAP Lajadhal (FR) 9-4

11/4 Last Laugh (IRE), **6/1** Grooms Gold (IRE) (op 7/2), Scenic Dancer, **7/1** Our Bessie, STRAT'S LEGACY, **15/2** Outstayed Welcome, **10/1** How's it Goin (IRE), **12/1** Lunar Risk, **25/1** Ice Magic, Gigfy, **33/1** Reigning Royal, Handson, **50/1** Lajadhal (FR), Dance and Sing (IRE), CSF £53.27 CT £351.22 TOTE £6.70: £2.60 £2.20 £2.50 (£24.70) Trio £54.80 OWNER Mr Jack Blumenow (COMPTON) BRED Exors of the late T. Stratton Smith 14 Rn
2m 38.4 (7.10) SF: 39/34/25/11/30/22/35/36/25/-/-/-/-/-
WEIGHT FOR AGE 3yo-12lb

2547 GOLDEN DAFFODIL STKS (Listed) (3-Y.O+ F & M) (Class A) £11,185.20 (£4,186.80: £2,048.40: £882.00: £396.00: £201.60) **1m 2f 36y** Stalls: High GOING minus 0.52 sec per fur (F) 7-00 (7-03)

2008⁶ **Frustration (104)***(105) (LadyHerries)* 4-9-1 DHarrison(4) (4th st: hrd rdn & hdwy over 3f out: led 1f out: r.o wl).....— 1
997³ Najmat Alshemaal (IRE) *(102) (MajorWRHern)* 3-8-6 ow1 RCochrane(5) (lw: led: rdn 2f out: hdd 1f out: nt qckn).....2 2
2241¹² Pearl Venture **(93)***(98) (SPCWoods)* 3-8-5 WWoods(3) (hld up & bhd: hdwy on ins 3f out: ev ch over 1f out: one pce fnl f).....2½ 3
1976* Red Azalea **(104)***(92)*(Fav)*(SirMarkPrescott)* 3-8-5 GDuffield(7) (lw: plld hrd: chsd ldr 2f: 3rd st: rdn & wknd over 2f out).....3½ 4
2316⁵ Roufontaine *(90) (WRMuir)* 4-9-1 DHolland(1) (lw: 6th st: nvr nr to chal).....1¾ 5
2151* Razana (IRE) *(83) (JHMGosden)* 3-8-5 LDettori(2) (lw: chsd ldr 8f out: 2nd st: rdn 3f out: wknd 2f out).....4 6
*2292*⁸ Dynamis (IRE) **(55)***(74) (KOCunningham-Brown)* 4-9-1 NAdams(6) (hld up: a in rr).....6 7

5/6 Red Azalea (op 5/4), **9/2** Najmat Alshemaal (IRE), **11/2** Razana (IRE), **13/2** FRUSTRATION, **10/1** Pearl Venture, **40/1** Roufontaine, **100/1** Dynamis (IRE), CSF £32.57 TOTE £6.20: £2.60 £2.00 (£11.80) OWNER Lavinia Duchess of Norfolk (LITTLEHAMPTON) BRED Lavinia Duchess of Norfolk 7 Rn
2m 6.7 (2.40) SF: 38/25/21/15/23/6/7
WEIGHT FOR AGE 3yo-10lb

2548 WORTHINGTON BEST BITTER MAIDEN AUCTION STKS (2-Y.O) (Class E) £3,317.50 (£1,000.00: £485.00: £227.50) **6f 16y** Stalls: High GOING minus 0.52 sec per fur (F) 7-30 (7-34)

2308³ **Jubilee Place (IRE)** *(66?) (TThomsonJones)* 2-7-13 StephenDavies(13) (mde all: clr over 1f out: r.o wl).....— 1

2077[5] Seaford Star (IRE) *(61) (MRChannon)* 2-8-7 AClark(4) (a.p: chsd wnr fnl 3f: no imp) 5 2
2277[8] Rock Sharp *(61) (RHannon)* 2-8-1 (7) DaneO'Neill(1) (lw: s.s: hdwy over 2f out: r.o wl ins fnl f)½ 3
2143[2] Weetman's Weigh (IRE) *(57)*(Fav)*(RHollinshead)* 2-8-6 LDettori(3) (hdwy 3f out: one pce fnl 2f)..........¾ 4
1981[4] Time Clash (IRE) *(47) (BPalling)* 2-7-11 TSprake(10) (lw: a.p: one pce fnl 2f) ....hd 5
2277[9] Soviet Sakti (IRE) *(44) (PMitchell)* 2-8-7 RPerham(6) (prom 4f) 5 6
Blue Adelaide *(40) (PFICole)* 2-8-3 TQuinn(7) (w'like: b.hind: no hdwy fnl 2f) ....s.h 7
1977[8] Bailiwick *(41) (NAGraham)* 2-8-9 JReid(8) (prom: lost pl 3f out: sme hdwy whn nt clr run over 1f out) 2 8
Day Tripper *(34) (GBBalding)* 2-8-4 ow1 JWilliams(2) (w'like: dwlt: a bhd) ....hd 9
2075[10] Lucky Revenge *(27) (MartynMeade)* 2-7-11 ow1 AMackay(11) (s.s: a bhd)..............................nk 10
Winged Prince *(34) (BJMeehan)* 2-8-4 BDoyle(5) (w'like: bhd fnl 2f) ....nk 11
2198[6] Little Kenny *(29) (MJFetherston-Godley)* 2-8-1 FNorton(14) (s.s: a bhd)..................................¾ 12
1327[2] Duralock Fencer *(18) (PGMurphy)* 2-7-11 (7)ow3 RWaterfield(12) (a bhd)..................................4 13
One Shot (IRE) *(WRMuir)* 2-8-10 DHolland(9) (w'like: scope: a bhd: t.o) 30 14

3/1 Weetman's Weigh (IRE), **5/1** JUBILEE PLACE (IRE), **6/1** Blue Adelaide, **10/1** Bailiwick, **11/1** One Shot (IRE) (8/1-12/1), **12/1** Rock Sharp, Duralock Fencer (op 8/1), Seaford Star (IRE), Little Kenny, Time Clash (IRE), **20/1** Lucky Revenge, Winged Prince, **25/1** Day Tripper, **50/1** Soviet Sakti (IRE), CSF £60.82 TOTE £5.70: £1.80 £3.70 £4.00 (£43.00) Trio £286.00 OWNER Mr Timothy Chick (LAMBOURN) BRED Labelon Co Ltd 14 Rn 1m 10.1 (1.10) SF: 23/18/18/14/4/1/-/-/-/-/-/-/-/-

2549 UNIVERSITY AND LITERARY CLUB H'CAP (0-70) (3-Y.O+) (Class E) £3,493.00 (£1,054.00: £512.00: £241.00)
7f 16y Stalls: High GOING minus 0.52 sec per fur (F) 8-00 (8-03)

2363* **Yaa Wale (66)***(76++)*(Fav)*(JHMGosden)* 3-9-3 6x LDettori(8) (lw: mde all: v.easily)..............— 1
2396[6] Asterix **(50)***(56) (JMBradley)* 7-8-5v(3) SDrowne(9) (a.p: chsd wnr over 1f out: no imp) 2 2
1950[5] Mislemani (IRE) **(51)***(56) (AGNewcombe)* 5-8-4 (5) DGriffiths(5) (chsd wnr over 5f: one pce)..hd 3
2088* Belleminette (IRE) **(56)***(61) (DHaydnJones)* 4-9-0 AMackay(10) (s.s: plld hrd: rdn & hdwy 2f out: r.o one pce fnl f)..........hd 4
2276[4] Vanborough Lad **(55)***(57) (MJBolton)* 6-8-13 WCarson(14) (hld up: nt clr run over 1f out: hdwy & n.m.r fnl f: nvr nrr)..........1¼ 5
2016* Blasted **(63)***(65) (RHannon)* 3-9-0 JReid(13) (hld up: r.o one pce fnl 2f) ....hd 6
2414[8] Love Legend **(54)***(53) (DWPArbuthnot)* 10-8-12 TQuinn(12) (a.p: no hdwy fnl 2f)..................1¼ 7
1995[10] Bogart **(56)***(55) (CWFairhurst)* 4-9-0 RCochrane(7) (lw: hld up: plld hrd: hmpd over 2f out: hdwy over 1f out: one pce fnl f)..........hd 8
2317[3] Super Serenade **(54)***(51) (GBBalding)* 6-8-12 JWilliams(6) (hld up: nvr nr to chal) ....¾ 9
2137[3] Bold Cyrano (IRE) **(52)***(46) (BPalling)* 4-8-10 TSprake(11) (prom 5f) 1¼ 10
2229[8] Persian Affair (IRE) **(67)***(60) (DHaydnJones)* 4-9-11 DHolland(3) (lw: hld up: hmpd over 2f out: n.d after)..........½ 11
2246[10] Safe Secret **(35)***(15) (RBrotherton)* 4-7-7 GBardwell(2) (prom 4f) 6 12
2003[6] Cool Tactician **(55)***(27) (RHollinshead)* 3-8-6 DHarrison(1) (bhd fnl 2f) 3½ 13
2400[5] Rubadub **(39)***(8) (JMBradley)* 4-7-8 (3)ow3 DWright(4) (plld hrd: stmbld over 3f out: a bhd)......hd 14
LONG HANDICAP Safe Secret 7-4

5/4 YAA WALE, **7/1** Super Serenade, **9/1** Blasted, **11/1** Belleminette (IRE) (8/1-12/1), Vanborough Lad, **12/1** Asterix, **14/1** Bogart, Bold Cyrano (IRE), **16/1** Love Legend, Persian Affair (IRE), **20/1** Mislemani (IRE), **25/1** Safe Secret, **33/1** Cool Tactician, Rubadub, CSF £18.36 CT £213.60 TOTE £1.90: £1.50 £2.60 £9.10 (£11.30) Trio £326.90 OWNER Sheikh Ahmed Al Maktoum(NEWMARKET) BRED The Duke of Roxburghe's Stud 14 Rn 1m 21.3 (1.30) SF: 39/26/26/31/27/28/23/25/21/16/30
WEIGHT FOR AGE 3yo-7lb

2550 SIR GORDON RICHARDS H'CAP (0-80) (3-Y.O) (Class D) £3,559.50 (£1,071.00: £518.00: £241.50)
2m 49y Stalls: High GOING minus 0.52 sec per fur (F) 8-30 (8-30)

2296[2] **Carnbrea Belle (IRE) (60)***(72) (MBell)* 3-8-5 MFenton(1) (5th st: hdwy over 3f out: edgd lft over 1f out: led ins fnl f: all out)..........— 1
2244* John Lee Hooker **(62)***(74) (DWPArbuthnot)* 3-8-7 TQuinn(2) (b.hind: led after 2f tl 10f out: led 7f out tl ins fnl f: r.o wl)..........s.h 2
1379[8] Greycoat Boy **(60)***(63) (BJMeehan)* 3-8-5 BDoyle(3) (led after 1f to after 2f: 3rd st: one pce fnl 2f)..........9 3
1600* Tonnerre **(76)***(75)*(Fav)*(CWFairhurst)* 3-9-7 RCochrane(4) (led 1f: 4th st: hrd rdn 3f out: wknd 2f out)..........4 4
2300* Toraja **(76)***(73)*(Fav)*(JLDunlop)* 3-9-7 5x WCarson(6) (hld up: hdwy to ld 10f out: hdd 7f out: 2nd st: wknd 2f out)..........2½ 5
1731[7] Vaporize **(48)** *(DMHyde)* 3-7-7 NAdams(5) (last st: a bhd: t.o fnl 3f) ....dist 6
LONG HANDICAP Vaporize 7-1

5/2 Tonnerre, Toraja, **7/2** CARNBREA BELLE (IRE), **4/1** John Lee Hooker, **7/1** Greycoat Boy (op 4/1), **66/1** Vaporize, CSF £16.42 TOTE £4.10: £1.40 £1.90 (£5.10) OWNER Mrs S. M. Crompton (NEWMARKET) BRED Limestone Stud 6 Rn 3m 34.7 (6.70) SF: 18/20/9/21/19/-

2551 LUNDY ISLAND H'CAP (0-70) (3-Y.O+) (Class E) £3,220.00 (£970.00: £470.00: £220.00) **5f 16y** Stalls: High GOING minus 0.52 sec per fur (F) 9-00 (9-02)

2410² **Robellion (68)***(75)*(Fav)*(DWPArbuthnot)* 4-9-12v TQuinn(6) (lw: chsd ldr: led ins fnl f: drvn out)......— **1**
2338² Miami Banker **(44)***(48) (WRMuir)* 9-8-2b GBardwell(8) (led tl ins fnl f: r.o)......1 **2**
2247² Windrush Boy **(62)***(65) (JRBosley)* 5-8-13 (7) AimeeCook(9) (a.p: swtchd lft 1f out: nt qckn ins fnl f)......nk **3**
2017⁶ Tinker Osmaston **(66)***(59) (MSSaunders)* 4-9-7 (3) SDrowne(7) (lw: hld up: hdwy 2f out: one pce fnl f)......3 **4**
2410⁶ Domicksky **(62)***(50) (MRChannon)* 7-9-1 (5) PPMurphy(3) (nvr nr to chal)......1¾ **5**
2410⁵ John O'Dreams **(49)***(31) (MrsALMKing)* 10-8-4 (3) AGarth(4) (lw: prom: hrd rdn wl over 1f out: sn wknd)......2 **6**
2301² The Noble Oak (IRE) **(47)***(25) (MJBolton)* 7-7-12 (7) GMitchell(1) (prom: rdn 2f out: sn wknd) 1¼ **7**
2288¹¹ Bryan Robson (USA) **(62)***(14) (GBBalding)* 4-9-6 JReid(2) (bhd fnl 2f)......8 **8**

9/4 ROBELLION, **100/30** Miami Banker, **6/1** Windrush Boy, **8/1** Domicksky (6/1-9/1), **10/1** Tinker Osmaston (op 5/1), John O'Dreams, The Noble Oak (IRE), Bryan Robson (USA), CSF £9.80 CT £34.78 TOTE £2.90: £1.60 £1.10 £2.80 (£3.60) Trio £4.30 OWNER Mr George Thompson (COMPTON) BRED Pitts Farm Stud 8 Rn 58.3 secs (1.30) SF: 41/14/31/25/16/-/-/-

T/Jkpt: £23,440.60 (3.98 Tckts). T/Plpt: £174.00 (124.74 Tckts). T/Qdpt £42.90 (3.0 Tckts). KH

2528-SANDOWN (R-H)
Thursday July 20th (St course Good to firm, Rnd Good, Good to firm patches)

WEATHER: very hot WIND: nil

2552 TATTERSALLS MAIDEN AUCTION STKS (2-Y.O) (Class E) £3,598.75 (£1,090.00: £532.50: £253.75) **5f 6y** Stalls: High GOING minus 0.31 sec per fur (GF)2-15 (2-16)

2135⁴ **Dil Dil** *(57) (RHannon)* 2-8-2 MRoberts(5) (swtg: a.p: chsd ldr 2f out: hrd rdn over 1f out: led last stride)......— **1**
2336² Where's Margaret *(54)*(Fav)*(GLewis)* 2-7-13 WCarson(4) (swtg: led: rdn fnl f: hdd last stride)......s.h **2**
2264⁴ Kiss Me Again (IRE) *(53) (RHannon)* 2-8-4 KDarley(7) (a.p: nt clr run on ins over 2f out: swtchd lft: r.o ins fnl f)......2 **3**
Second Time Lucky (IRE) *(53)*(Fav)*(LordHuntingdon)* 2-8-5 LDettori(6) (w'like: rdn over 2f out: hdwy over 1f out: r.o one pce)......nk **4**
2412⁵ Sunset Harbour (IRE) *(46) (DAWilson)* 2-7-13 NGwilliams(11) (chsd ldr 3f: hrd rdn over 1f out: one pce)......nk **5**
2408¹² Prime Partner *(49) (WRMuir)* 2-8-9 MHills(10) (nvr nr to chal)......2 **6**
2114³ Fayre Holly (IRE) *(35) (MJHeaton-Ellis)* 2-8-3 GCarter(8) (swtg: squeezed out s: nvr nrr) 2½ **7**
Quakers Field *(38) (GLMoore)* 2-8-9 AClark(2) (w'like: hdwy over 2f out: sn wknd)......1 **8**
1938⁵ Step On Degas *(26)*(Fav)*(SDow)* 2-7-11 FNorton(9) (lw: a bhd)......hd **9**
2135² Polish Bear (IRE) *(22) (BJMeehan)* 2-8-3 DHarrison(3) (swtg: prom over 3f)......3 **10**
1849¹⁰ Mimosa *(18) (LJHolt)* 2-8-6 ow2 JReid(1) (swtg: a bhd)......1½ **11**

4/1 Second Time Lucky (IRE) (op 8/1), Where's Margaret (5/2-9/2), Step On Degas (3/1-9/2), **6/1** Polish Bear (IRE), **15/2** Mimosa, **9/1** DIL DIL, **10/1** Fayre Holly (IRE) (8/1-12/1), **12/1** Kiss Me Again (IRE) (op 8/1), **25/1** Quakers Field, Prime Partner, **33/1** Sunset Harbour (IRE), CSF £43.80 TOTE £12.00: £2.40 £1.70 £3.50 (£20.90) Trio £58.10 OWNER Khanmaher (MARLBOROUGH) BRED Barouche Stud Ltd 11 Rn 61.66 secs (1.86) SF: 30/27/26/26/19/22/8/11/-/-/-

2553 HEATHROW MAIDEN STKS (3-Y.O+) (Class D) £3,810.00 (£1,155.00: £565.00: £270.00) **1m 14y** Stalls: High GOING minus 0.07 sec per fur (G) 2-50 (2-53)

1927² **Grand du Lac (USA)** *(93)*(Fav)*(DRLoder)* 3-8-12 LDettori(6) (lw: chsd ldr over 6f out: led 2f out: rdn out)......— **1**
1990² Goalwah *(88) (HThomsonJones)* 3-8-7 RHills(10) (led 6f: hrd rdn: ev ch fnl f: r.o wl)......hd **2**
Keen To The Last (FR) *(85) (GHarwood)* 3-8-12 AClark(15) (leggy: scope: rdn & hdwy over 2f out: r.o one pce)......4 **3**

715[W] Night Flare (FR) *(81) (RHannon)* 3-8-12 SRaymont(11) (str: scope: bit bkwd: 6th st: rdn over 3f out: one pce) 1¾ 4
Ranosh (USA) *(67) (EALDunlop)* 3-8-7 PaulEddery(1) (b: b.hind: w'like: scope: s.s: stdy hdwy fnl 2f: nvr plcd to chal) 5 5
Regal Portrait (IRE) *(66) (HRACecil)* 3-8-7 WRyan(13) (unf: scope: 3rd st: rdn over 2f out: wknd over 1f out) ....s.h 6
Roseberry Ray (IRE) *(66) (GWragg)* 3-8-12 MHills(5) (bit bkwd: nvr nr to chal) 2½ 7
Darcey Bussell *(58) (BWHills)* 3-8-7 KDarley(16) (b: w'like: scope: dwlt: nvr nrr) 1¾ 8
1979[4] Florismart *(62) (JARToller)* 3-8-12 WNewnes(14) (a mid div) ....nk 9
Golden Pound (USA) *(60) (EALDunlop)* 3-8-12 WRSwinburn(7) (w'like: scope: bit bkwd: 5th st: shkn up 2f out: eased whn btn fnl f: bttr for r) 1¼ 10
Fasih *(59) (ACStewart)* 3-8-12 WCarson(4) (nt clr run over 2f out & over 1f out: nvr plcd to chal) ....½ 11
2319[4] Victory Team (IRE) *(55) (JRFanshawe)* 3-8-12 DHarrison(2) (swtg: hdwy over 2f out: wknd over 1f out) 2 12
1615[4] Monument *(47) (RCharlton)* 3-8-12 TSprake(3) (a bhd) 4 13
2082[5] Celestial Dollar *(27) (OO'Neill)* 4-9-6 VSlattery(12) (swtg: 4th st: wknd 3f out) 10 14
Paddys Cherub *(2) (JRArnold)* 3-8-4 (3) DRMcCabe(8) (str: scope: bkwd: bhd fnl 6f) 10 15

6/4 GRAND DU LAC (USA), **4/1** Goalwah (3/1-9/2), **8/1** Regal Portrait (IRE) (op 4/1), **10/1** Golden Pound (USA) (6/1-12/1), **12/1** Monument, Victory Team (IRE) (op 6/1), **14/1** Fasih (8/1-16/1), Darcey Bussell, **20/1** Florismart, Roseberry Ray (IRE), Keen To The Last (FR), **25/1** Ranosh (USA), **33/1** Night Flare (FR), **50/1** Paddys Cherub, **66/1** Celestial Dollar, CSF £8.74 TOTE £2.10: £1.40 £1.80 £9.40 (£3.20) Trio £82.60 OWNER Mrs Virginia KraftPayson (NEWMARKET) BRED Virginia Kraft Payson 15 Rn 1m 43.07 (3.87) SF: 52/47/44/40/26/25/25/17/21/19/18/14/6/-/-
WEIGHT FOR AGE 3yo-8lb

OFFICIAL EXPLANATION Ranosh (USA): the jockey reported that the filly was slowly away and then short of room in the straight.The trainer reported that she suffered with navicular as a two year old and is afflicted by splints.

2554 MILCARS STAR STKS (Listed) (2-Y.O F) (Class A) £10,260.00 (£3,105.00: £1,515.00: £720.00) **7f 16y** Stalls: High GOING minus 0.07 sec (G) 3-25 (3-27)

2275* **Tamnia** *(79) (JLDunlop)* 2-8-12 JReid(5) (4th st: led over 1f out: rdn out) ....— 1
2106[4] Solar Crystal (IRE) *(76) (HRACecil)* 2-8-12 WRyan(4) (led over 5f: hrd rdn: unable qckn ins fnl f) 1¼ 2
2257* Lac Dessert (USA) *(73) (DRLoder)* 2-8-12 DRMcCabe(2) (3rd st: rdn 3f out: one pce fnl f)..1¼ 3
2106[2] Persian Secret (FR) *(72)*(Fav)*(JWWatts)* 2-8-12 LDettori(1) (lw: 5th st: rdn 2f out: wandered over 1f out: one pce) ....¾ 4
1968* Key To A Million (IRE) *(65) (RHannon)* 2-8-9 MRoberts(3) (2nd st: wknd over 1f out) 1¾ 5

5/4 Persian Secret (FR) (Evens-10/11), **5/2** TAMNIA, **6/1** Lac Dessert (USA) (3/1-13/2), **13/2** Solar Crystal (IRE) (op 7/2), **12/1** Key To A Million (IRE), CSF £15.22 TOTE £3.40 £1.80 £2.80 (£10.60) OWNER Prince A. A. Faisal (ARUNDEL) BRED Nawara Stud Co Ltd 5 Rn
1m 31.06 (4.46) SF: 40/37/34/33/26

OFFICIAL EXPLANATION Persian Secret (FR): the jockey reported that the filly had hung badly in the straight and appeared to be inconvenienced by the ground, despite having won on the firm previously this season.

2555 PYCRAFT & ARNOLD H'CAP (0-90) (3-Y.O) (Class C) £5,602.00 (£1,696.00: £828.00: £394.00) **1m 6f** Stalls: High GOING minus 0.07 sec per fur (G)4-00 (4-00)

2172[4] **Thaljanah (IRE) (82)***(91) (ACStewart)* 3-9-4 RHills(3) (b.hind: swtg: mde virtually all: drvn out) ....— 1
1872[10] Dangerous Guest (IRE) **(84)***(91) (SirMarkPrescott)* 3-9-6 GDuffield(2) (lw: 3rd st: hrd rdn over 1f out: r.o one pce) 1½ 2
2014[2] Haniya (IRE) **(85)***(91)*(Fav)*(JLDunlop)* 3-9-7 WCarson(4) (2nd st: ev ch over 1f out: one pce) 1¼ 3
2193[2] Executive Design **(79)***(85) (MrsMReveley)* 3-9-1 KDarley(5) (rdn & hdwy 2f out: one pce) .....hd 4
2406[3] Dance So Suite **(72)***(76) (PFICole)* 3-8-8 JReid(1) (6th st: rdn over 2f out: wknd 1f out)........1¼ 5
2452[4] Old Swinford (IRE) **(57)***(57) (BJMeehan)* 3-7-7 GBardwell(7) (5th st: wknd over 2f out) 4 6
2266[7] Sea Victor **(78)***(49) (JLHarris)* 3-9-0 LDettori(6) (4th st: wknd 3f out: t.o) 25 7
LONG HANDICAP Old Swinford (IRE) 7-5

3/1 Haniya (IRE) (2/1-10/3), **100/30** Dangerous Guest (IRE), **5/1** Executive Design, **11/2** THALJANAH (IRE) (4/1-6/1), **6/1** Dance So Suite (4/1-13/2), **9/1** Sea Victor, **14/1** Old Swinford (IRE), CSF £21.97 TOTE £7.40: £3.50 £2.30 (£26.30) OWNER Mr Hamdan Al Maktoum (NEWMARKET) BRED Abbeville Stud 7 Rn 3m 5.01 (10.31) SF: 38/38/38/32/23/4/-

2556 RAILWAY H'CAP (0-80) (3-Y.O) (Class D) £4,201.50 (£1,272.00: £621.00: £295.50)
5f 6y Stalls: High GOING minus 0.31 sec per fur (GF) 4-35 (4-35)

2239* **Tedburrow (72)***(81+) (MrsAMNaughton)* 3-9-1 LDettori(1) (swtg: hld up: plld out wl over 1f out: sn led: comf) — 1
2239³ The Kings Ransom **(68)***(71)*(Fav)*(MrsJRRamsden)* 3-8-11v KFallon(2) (hld up: rdn over 2f out: ev ch over 1f out: unable qckn) 2 2
2168² Jo Maximus **(73)***(71) (SDow)* 3-9-2 MRoberts(5) (led over 3f: one pce) 1½ 3
2271³ The Scythian **(74)***(71) (BobJones)* 3-9-3 GDuffield(4) (lw: a.p: ev ch over 1f out: one pce) nk 4
2009² Youdontsay **(78)***(72) (RCurtis)* 3-9-7 JReid(3) (swtg: a.p: ev ch over 1f out: one pce) 1 5

2/1 The Kings Ransom, **3/1** TEDBURROW (op 7/4), **4/1** Youdontsay, **5/1** Jo Maximus, The Scythian, CSF £8.96 TOTE £2.80: £1.70 £1.80 (£3.20) OWNER Mr Philip Davies (RICHMOND) BRED Lady Matthews 5 Rn 60.71 secs (0.91) SF: 58/48/48/48/49

2557 WELLINGTON APPRENTICE H'CAP (0-70) (3-Y.O+) (Class E)
£3,316.50 (£1,017.00: £506.00: £250.50)
1m 2f 7y Stalls: High GOING minus 0.07 sec per fur (G) 5-10 (5-10)

2139³ **Zacaroon (65)***(75+) (LordHuntingdon)* 4-9-8 (6) AimeeCook(4) (4th st: rdn over 1f out: led ins fnl f: r.o wl) — 1
1978⁴ Wet Patch (IRE) **(60)***(68) (RHannon)* 3-8-3 (10) EGreehy(3) (swtg: hdwy 2f out: hrd rdn over 1f out: unable qckn wl ins fnl f) 1 2
1747⁷ Edan Heights **(67)***(71) (SDow)* 3-9-3 (3) ADaly(8) (swtg: 5th st: hmpd & lost pl on ins over 2f out: swtchd lft wl over 1f out: n.m.r & swtchd lft 1f out: r.o one pce) 2½ 3
2189² Domitia (USA) **(62)***(64) (MBell)* 3-8-5 (10) RMullen(7) (lw: led 6f: 3rd st: hrd rdn over 2f out: one pce) 1¼ 4
1940⁴ Hatta Sunshine (USA) **(39)***(37) (AMoore)* 5-7-11 (5) JWilkinson(2) (hld up: led 4f out: rn wd st: hdd ins fnl f: sn wknd) 2½ 5
2246¹³ Nita's Choice **(30)***(24) (AGNewcombe)* 5-7-7 SLanigan(1) (s.s: nvr nr to chal) 3 6
2174³ Dia Georgy **(47)***(39) (RGuest)* 4-8-10 CWebb(5) (swtg: 6th st: rdn over 2f out: wknd fnl f) 1¼ 7
687⁶ Contrafire (IRE) **(66)***(56) (WJarvis)* 3-9-0 (5) RStudholme(6) (swtg: 2nd st: wknd wl over 1f out) 1¼ 8
2314² Anlace **(53)***(40)*(Fav)*(SMellor)* 6-8-11 (5) CarolineHovington(9) (bhd fnl 6f) 2 9

LONG HANDICAP Nita's Choice 7-4

9/2 Anlace, **5/1** Wet Patch (IRE), Domitia (USA) (op 3/1), **11/2** Contrafire (IRE) (7/2-6/1), **6/1** Dia Georgy, **13/2** ZACAROON, **10/1** Hatta Sunshine (USA), Edan Heights (12/1-8/1), Nita's Choice, CSF £37.72 CT £298.59 TOTE £9.30: £2.20 £1.40 £2.90 (£18.60) Trio £89.00 OWNER Mr P.A. Leonard (WEST ILSLEY) BRED Juddmonte Farms 9 Rn 2m 12.33 (8.03) SF: 42/25/28/21/4/-/6/13/7
WEIGHT FOR AGE 3yo-10lb

T/Plpt: £312.40 (54.77 Tckts). T/Qdpt: £207.40 (0.25 Tckts); £210.30 to Ascot 21/07/95. AK

MAISONS-LAFFITTE (France)
Tuesday July 11th (Holding)

2558a PRIX MESSIDOR (Gp 3) (3-Y.O+) £26,347.00 (£9,581.00: £4,790.00) **1m** 2-45 (2-43)

Nec Plus Ultra (FR) *(114) (AdeRoyerDupre,France)* 4-9-2 TGillet — 1
713⁸ Bishop of Cashel *(114) (JRFanshawe)* 3-8-7 DHarrison hd 2
Tellurium (USA) *(106) (JCunnington,France)* 4-9-2 FSanchez 4 3
1586⁴ Sonic Boy *(98) (RFJohnsonHoughton)* 3-8-7 JQuinn (btn approx 8l) 6

P-M 8.30F: 2.80F 4.20F 5.40F (DF 55.70F) OWNER Marquesa de Moratalla BRED Mrs G Forien & Marquise de Moratalla in France 10 Rn 1m 36.5 SF: -/-/-/-
DS

DOWN ROYAL (Lisburn, Ireland) (R-H)
Thursday July 13th (Good)

2559a ULSTER HARP DERBY H'CAP (0-110) (3-Y.O+) £32,500.00 (£9,500.00: £4,500.00: £1,500.00) **1m 4f 68y** 3-45 (3-53)

Munif (IRE) *(DKWeld,Ireland)* 3-8-10 MJKinane — 1
Danaa Minni (IRE) *(JSBolger,Ireland)* 3-7-13 JAHeffernan hd 2

Tarajan (USA) (Fav)*(JOxx,Ireland)* 3-8-13 JPMurtagh 2 3
1661* Northern Union (CAN) *(MAJarvis)* 4-8-13 PRobinson (b.d 3f out).... B
1524[7] Greenspan (IRE) *(WRMuir)* 3-7-13b CRutter (s.u 3f out).... S

4/1 Tarajan (USA), **9/2** MUNIF (IRE), **5/1** Northern Union (CAN), **12/1** Danaa Minni (IRE), Greenspan (IRE), OWNER Mr Hamdan Al Maktoum BRED Shadwell Estate Company Ltd 10 Rn
2m 33.5 SF: -/-/-/-/-
NR

2213a-SAINT-CLOUD (France) (L-H) Friday July 14th (Good)

2560a PRIX EUGENE ADAM (Gp 2) (3-Y.O) £35,928.00 (£14,371.00: £7,186.00: £3,593.00) 1m 2f
3-20 (3-18)

978* **Royal Solo (IRE)** *(104) (PWChapple-Hyam)* 3-8-11 BThomson (a.p: rdn over 1f out: styd on to ld cl home)....— 1
2111* Montjoy (USA) *(104) (PFICole)* 3-8-11 TQuinn (hld up: swtchd & hdwy over 3f out: led over 1f out: hdd cl home)....nk 2
1230a[4] Vaguely Gay *(103) (MmeCHead,France)* 3-8-11 ODoleuze (trckd ldrs: rdn 2f out: r.o fnl f: nrst fin)....hd 3
1007a[3] East of Heaven(IRE) *(103) (AFabre,France)* 3-8-11 TJarnet (a.p: rdn & outpcd 2f out: r.o fnl f)....s.nk 4
Silent Warrior (IRE) *(103) (JEHammond,France)* 3-8-11 CAsmussen (lw: hld up in rr: n.m.r & rdn over 2f out: kpt on fnl f)....s.nk 5
Senneville (USA) *(102) (AFabre,France)* 3-8-11 OPeslier (led tl hdd over 1f out: one pce)....¾ 6
1230a* Tzar Rodney (FR) *(95) (GDoleuze,France)* 3-8-11 ESaint-Martin (plld hrd in rr: nvr able to chal)....4 7

P-M 12.60F: 7.40F 3.50F (SF 76.10) OWNER Mr R. E. Sangster (MARLBOROUGH) BRED Littleton Stud and Camas Park Stud 7 Rn
2m 8.3 (4.80) SF: -/-/-/-/-/-/-
DS

2041a-EVRY (France) (R-H) Saturday July 15th (Good)

2561a PRIX CHLOE (Gp 3) (3-Y.O F) £26,347.00 (£9,581.00: £4,790.00) 1m 1f
2-25 (2-34)

1712a[8] **Garden Rose (IRE)** *(114) (PBary,France)* 3-8-9 DBoeuf ....— 1
1116a[15] Take Liberties *(114) (AFabre,France)* 3-8-9 TJarnet ....hd 2
1712a[4] Balanka (IRE) *(113) (AdeRoyerDupre,France)* 3-8-9 GMosse ....¾ 3
1923* Cask *(109) (JHMGosden)* 3-8-9 WRSwinburn (btn approx 4½l).... 6

P-M 4.20F: 2.70F 2.90F (SF 27.40F) OWNER Mrs A. O'Reilly BRED Petra Bloodstock Agency 7 Rn
1m 54.75 (4.75) SF: -/-/-/-

2562a PRIX DE RIS-ORANGIS (Gp 3) (3-Y.O+) £26,347.00 (£9,581.00: £4,790.00: £2,395.00) 6f
3-20 (3-26)

1572a[2] **Diffident (FR)** *(117) (AFabre,France)* 3-8-8 TJarnet ....— 1
2039a* Linoise (FR) *(113) (ELeGuen,France)* 3-8-5 OPeslier ....½ 2
1870[4] Wessam Prince *(115) (CLaffon-Parias,France)* 4-9-4 WRSwinburn 1½ 3
1572a[9] Key of Luck (USA) *(107) (MmeCHead,France)* 4-9-0 FHead 1½ 4

P-M 1.50F: 1.10F 1.20F (SF 2.70F) OWNER Sheikh Mohammed (FRANCE) BRED Haras d'Etreham & R Ades in France 4 Rn
1m 13.79 (3.79) SF: -/-/-/-
DS

2216a-CURRAGH (Newbridge, Ireland) (R-H) Sunday July 16th (Soft)

2563a KILDANGAN STUD IRISH OAKS (Gp 1) (3-Y.O F) £112,700.00 (£38,700.00: £18,700.00: £6,700.00) 1m 4f
3-45 (3-53)

1587[3] **Pure Grain** *(118) (MRStoute)* 3-9-0 JReid (a.p: 3rd st: led over 2f out: rdn clr over 1f out: r.o strly)....— 1

2211a[2] Russian Snows (IRE) *(110) (JOxx,Ireland)* 3-9-0 MJKinane (hld up: 5th st: rdn over 2f out: no ch w wnr) 6 2
1237a* Valley of Gold (FR) *(105) (AFabre,France)* 3-9-0 LDettori (trckd ldrs: pushed along 4f out: 4th st: rdn over 2f out: styd on fnl f) 4 3
1867[3] Musetta (IRE) *(104) (CEBrittain)* 3-9-0 MRoberts (led tl hdd over 2f out: kpt on) ....nk 4
1729* Larrocha (IRE) *(104) (LMCumani)* 3-9-0 WRSwinburn (2nd st: ev ch over 2f out: unable qckn) ....s.h 5
1587[5] Asterita *(103) (RHannon)* 3-9-0 JWeaver (mid div: 6th st: rdn 2f out: one pce) 1 6
Bluffing (USA) *(70) (JSBolger,Ireland)* 3-9-0 KJManning (hld up: prog 5f out: sn wknd: t.o)...25 7
Riyama (IRE) *(69) (JOxx,Ireland)* 3-9-0 JPMurtagh (nvr nr to chal) ....½ 8
Crystal Bird (IRE) *(66) (MJGrassick,Ireland)* 3-9-0 PVGilson (a bhd) 2 9
2211a[5] Alisidora (IRE) *(66) (CO'Brien,Ireland)* 3-9-0 CRoche (in tch tl lost pl ½-wy: rdn over 4f out: sn wknd) ....s.h 10

CSF £29.99 TOTE £4.50: £1.80 £1.70 £1.70 (£20.10) OWNER Mr R. Barnett (NEWMARKET) BRED W. and R. Barnett Ltd 10 Rn
2m 33.6 (4.90) SF: -/-/-/-/-/-/-/-/-/-

2564a CURRAGH STKS (Gp 3) (2-Y.O) £16,250.00 (£4,750.00: £2,250.00) **5f**
4-20 (4-24)

Almaty (IRE) *(100) (CCollins,Ireland)* 2-8-10 PVGilson ....— 1
2216a[2] Sweet Robin (IRE) *(94) (MJohnston)* 2-8-7 LDettori 1 2
Sunset Reigns (IRE) *(90) (APO'Brien,Ireland)* 2-8-11 CRoche 2½ 3

CSF £10.59 TOTE £4.20: £2.70 £1.30 (£4.60) OWNER Mr P. D. Savill BRED P. E. Banahan 6 Rn
61.8 secs (3.30) SF: -/-/-

2565a RAGUSA STUD MINSTREL STKS (Listed) (3-Y.O+) £9,675.00 (£2,775.00: £1,275.00) **1m**
4-50 (4-50)

Hushang (IRE) *(110) (JOxx,Ireland)* 5-9-3 JPMurtagh ....— 1
2217a[6] Ivory Frontier (IRE) *(110) (JSBolger,Ireland)* 5-9-3 KJManning ....hd 2
1573a[4] Two O'Clock Jump (IRE) *(110) (RHannon)* 3-8-12 LDettori 1½ 3

CSF £26.24 TOTE £3.60: £1.20 £4.30 £1.70 (£20.90) OWNER Aga Khan BRED H H Aga Khan Stud S C 8 Rn
1m 39.5 (3.50) SF: -/-/-

2387a-SAN SIRO (Milan, Italy) (R-H)
Sunday July 16th (Good to firm)

2566a PREMIO LEGNANO (Gp 3) (3-Y.O+ F & M) £25,768.00 (£6,738.00: £3,369.00) **1m**
4-10 (4-29)

1237a[2] **Olimpia Dukakis (ITY)** *(99) (GBotti,Italy)* 3-8-5 GForte ....— 1
1237a[5] Rosi Zambotti (IRE) *(98) (BGrizzetti,Italy)* 3-8-5 ACarboni ....½ 2
Senebrova *(97) (VValliani)* 4-9-0 EBotti 1¼ 3

TOTE 13L: 12L 19L 25L (42L) OWNER Scuderia Siba (ITALY) BRED Scuderia Siba in Italy 11 Rn
1m 37.0 SF: -/-/-

FRANKFURT (Germany) (L-H)
Sunday July 16th (Good)

2567a AMMERSCHLAGER FRANKFURT-POKAL (Gp 3) (3-Y.O+) £24,691.00 (£9,877.00: £4,938.00) **1m 2f**
3-50 (3-58)

Solon (GER) *(110) (HJentzsch,Germany)* 3-8-0 PSchiergen ....— 1
2046a[7] Silent Lake (GER) *(111) (HRemmert,Germany)* 4-9-0 DBoeuf 2 2
No Dancer (GER) *(111) (MHofer,Germany)* 4-9-0b NGrant ....hd 3

TOTE 35DM: 17DM 32DM 46DM (SF 597DM) OWNER Gestut Schlenderhan BRED Gestut Schlenderhan 13 Rn
2m 6.32 SF: -/-/-

1923-**ASCOT (R-H)**

Friday July 21st (Good to firm)

WEATHER: very hot WIND: almost nil

2568 STANLEY CAYZER MAIDEN STKS (3-Y.O) (Class D) £6,872.50 (£2,080.00: £1,015.00: £482.50)
1m 2f Stalls: High GOING minus 0.13 sec per fur (G) 2-30 (2-30)

2319⁵ **Prize Pupil (IRE)** *(79) (CFWall)* 3-9-0 MRoberts(5) (chsd ldr: led over 2f out: clr over 1f out: r.o wl) — 1
Maftun (USA) *(73) (MajorWRHern)* 3-9-0 WCarson(3) (w'like: scope: lw: rdn over 5f out: mod 5th st: hdwy over 1f out: r.o) 3½ 2
1691⁹ Spread The Word *(66) (LGCottrell)* 3-8-9 BThomson(4) (lw: rdn over 4f out: 3rd st: chsd wnr over 1f out to ins fnl f: unable qckn) 1¼ 3
1587⁷ Bint Zamayem (IRE) **(97)***(52)*(Fav)*(BWHills)* 3-8-9 MHills(6) (led: rdn over 3f out: hdd over 2f out: wknd over 1f out) 9 4
Toskano *(33) (IABalding)* 3-9-0 WRyan(1) (lw: mod 5th st: a wl bhd) 15 5

8/11 Bint Zamayem (IRE) (1/2-4/5), **5/2** Maftun (USA), **13/2** PRIZE PUPIL (IRE) (3/1-7/1), **14/1** Toskano (op 5/1), **50/1** Spread The Word, CSF £20.64 TOTE £6.60: £1.90 £1.20 (£7.20) OWNER Mr Shunya Seki (NEWMARKET) BRED Shunya Seki 5 Rn 2m 12.56 (8.26) SF: 23/17/10/-/-

2569 CLIPSAL BROWN JACK H'CAP (0-80) (3-Y.O+) (Class D) £10,845.00 (£3,285.00: £1,605.00: £765.00)
2m 45y Stalls: High GOING minus 0.13 sec per fur (G) 3-00 (3-00)

2462* **Highflying** **(80)***(95)*(Fav)*(GMMoore)* 9-9-11 (3) 3x JTate(7) (mde all: clr over 2f out: hrd rdn: r.o wl) — 1
2154³ Art Form (USA) **(66)***(76) (CACyzer)* 8-9-0 DBiggs(10) (lw: rdn over 7f out: hdwy over 3f out: 5th st: hrd rdn over 2f out: r.o one pce) 5 2
2098¹⁴ Blaze Away (USA) **(77)***(87) (IABalding)* 4-9-11 LDettori(5) (swtg: chsd wnr: hrd rdn over 2f out: one pce) ½ 3
2268* Gentleman Sid **(45)***(53) (PGMurphy)* 5-7-7 NAdams(9) (lw: 3rd st: hrd rdn over 2f out: one pce) 1½ 4
2270* Hillzah (USA) **(76)***(82) (RBastiman)* 7-9-5 (5) HBastiman(11) (swtg: hdwy over 2f out: r.o one pce) 1¾ 5
2201⁸ Head Turner **(46)***(42) (CPWildman)* 7-7-8 GBardwell(12) (lost pl over 14f out: r.o one pce fnl 2f) 11 6
2452² Stately Home (IRE) **(52)***(46) (BRMillman)* 4-8-0 MRoberts(4) (rdn over 6f out: 4th st: wknd over 2f out) 2 7
1973⁴ Ibsen **(67)***(60) (RAkehurst)* 7-9-1 TQuinn(6) (b: lw: nvr nr to chal) 1 8
2490⁸ Grand Applause (IRE) **(53)***(39) (MPMuggeridge)* 5-8-1b CRutter(3) (swtg: a bhd) 7 9
2186³ Chez Catalan **(48)***(27)*(Fav)*(RAkehurst)* 4-7-7b(3)ow3 DWright(8) (lw: hdwy over 3f out: 6th st: wknd over 2f out) 4 10
2248³ Pomorie (IRE) **(60)***(38) (JWPayne)* 4-8-8 RCochrane(1) (prom 9f) 3½ 11
2248² Tarthooth (IRE) **(66)***(39)*(Fav)*(CJBenstead)* 4-9-0 WCarson(2) (swtg: bhd fnl 6f) 5 12

LONG HANDICAP Gentleman Sid 7-4

11/2 HIGHFLYING, Tarthooth (IRE), Chez Catalan (op 7/2), **13/2** Stately Home (IRE), **15/2** Art Form (USA), **9/1** Blaze Away (USA), **10/1** Ibsen, **14/1** Hillzah (USA), **16/1** Gentleman Sid, **20/1** Head Turner, **25/1** Pomorie (IRE), **66/1** Grand Applause (IRE), CSF £40.38 CT £325.89 TOTE £5.50: £2.00 £3.30 £2.90 (£18.90) Trio £56.30 OWNER Mr B. Batey (MIDDLEHAM) BRED Juddmonte Farms 12 Rn 3m 34.78 (8.28) SF: 61/42/53/19/48/8/12/26/5/-/4/5

2570 BERNARD MATTHEWS RATED STKS H'CAP (0-100) (3-Y.O+) (Class B) £15,433.50 (£5,776.50: £2,825.75: £1,216.25: £545.63: £277.37)
5f Stalls: Centre GOING minus 0.13 sec per fur (G) 3-30 (3-30)

2120³ **Name the Tune** **(83)***(91) (PHowling)* 4-8-9 PaulEddery(8) (b.hind: swtg: hld up: rdn over 1f out: led wl ins fnl f: all out) — 1
*1953** Sailormaite **(81)***(89) (SRBowring)* 4-8-7 SWebster(5) (a.p: rdn over 1f out: ev ch ins fnl f: r.o wl) s.h 2
1766⁵ Jayannpee **(95)***(102) (IABalding)* 4-9-7 WRyan(7) (lw: w ldr: led over 3f out tl wl ins fnl f: r.o) nk 3
1895⁷ Royale Figurine (IRE) **(95)***(100) (MJFetherston-Godley)* 4-9-7 WRSwinburn(1) (lw: hld up: nt clr run 2f out, over 1f out & ins fnl f: nt rcvr) ½ 4
1895²³ Mister Jolson **(85)***(85) (RJHodges)* 6-8-8 (3) SDrowne(4) (b.nr fore: lw: rdn over 2f out: hdwy & nt clr run over 1f out: one pce) 1¾ 5

2430* Ziggy's Dancer (USA) **(94)***(91) (EJAlston)* 4-9-6 3x KFallon(6) (rdn over 2f out: hdwy over 1f out: one pce) ....¾ 6
2418[3] Join the Clan **(93)***(89)*(Fav)*(MrsNMacauley)* 6-9-5 LDettori(2) (lw: stumbled s: hdwy over 1f out: one pce) ....½ 7
2418[7] Ashtina **(89)***(62) (RJHodges)* 10-9-1 RCochrane(3) (led over 1f: wknd over 1f out) 7 8
LONG HANDICAP Sailormaite 8-4

4/1 Join the Clan, **5/1** Ziggy's Dancer (USA), Jayannpee, Royale Figurine (IRE), **6/1** NAME THE TUNE, Sailormaite, **12/1** Mister Jolson, **14/1** Ashtina, CSF £37.06 CT £172.54 TOTE £7.20: £2.10 £1.70 £1.90 (£15.30) OWNER Mr C. Hammond (NEWMARKET) BRED Derek R. Price 8 Rn
62.18 secs (2.68) SF: 38/36/49/47/32/38/36/9

2571 IVECO FORD BALMORAL H'CAP (0-90) (3-Y.O) (Class C) £8,715.00 (£2,640.00: £1,290.00: £615.00)
1m 2f Stalls: High GOING minus 0.13 sec per fur (G) 4-05 (4-08)

1793[6] **River Keen (IRE) (73)***(85) (RWArmstrong)* 3-8-6b WCarson(4) (lw: mde all: rdn out) ....— 1
1589[9] Polydamas **(80)***(92) (MRStoute)* 3-8-13 WRSwinburn(11) (lw: a.p: chsd wnr over 4f out: hrd rdn over 2f out: r.o wl ins fnl f) ....nk 2
1793[4] Major Change **(86)***(91) (RHannon)* 3-9-5 JReid(7) (4th st: hrd rdn over 2f out: unable qckn)....4 3
*2145** Persian Conquest (IRE) **(64)***(66) (RIngram)* 3-7-11b NAdams(8) (lw: chsd wnr over 5f: 3rd st: hrd rdn over 2f out: one pce) 2 4
2433* Jameel Asmar **(73)***(73)*(Fav)*(CREgerton)* 3-8-6 5x BThomson(10) (rdn over 5f out: 5th st: one pce fnl 2f) 1 5
1834* Painted Hall (USA) **(77)***(73) (JARToller)* 3-8-10 WNewnes(5) (nvr nr to chal) 2½ 6
2086* Star of Persia (IRE) **(83)***(77) (PWHarris)* 3-9-2 MFenton(6) (swtg: nvr nrr) 1½ 7
2199* Rockforce **(82)***(74) (MRChannon)* 3-9-1 RHughes(1) (hdwy 2f out: wknd over 1f out) 1¼ 8
2314[3] Braydon Forest **(67)***(58) (CJDrewe)* 3-8-0 AMcGlone(3) (lw: bhd fnl 3f) ....¾ 9
2030[3] Peutetre **(88)***(79) (CEBrittain)* 3-9-7 MRoberts(2) (lw: bhd fnl 2f) ....hd 10
1831[10] Kilcoran Bay **(78)***(66) (IABalding)* 3-8-11 LDettori(9) (rdn over 5f out: hdwy on ins 3f out: 6th st: wknd over 2f out) 1½ 11

2/1 Jameel Asmar, **11/2** Rockforce, **7/1** Star of Persia (IRE), **8/1** Major Change, **10/1** Polydamas, **14/1** RIVER KEEN (IRE), Kilcoran Bay, **16/1** Braydon Forest, Painted Hall (USA), **20/1** Persian Conquest (IRE), **25/1** Peutetre, CSF £126.87 CT £1,081.01 TOTE £15.40: £3.20 £2.40 £2.00 (£40.10) Trio £123.10 OWNER Dr Meou Tsen Geoffrey Yeh (NEWMARKET) BRED Ballylinch Stud Ltd 11 Rn
2m 9.24 (4.94) SF: 41/48/47/22/29/29/33/30/14/35/22

2572 DUKE OF EDINBURGH'S AWARD MAIDEN STKS (2-Y.O F) (Class D) £6,710.00 (£2,030.00: £990.00: £470.00)
6f Stalls: Centre GOING minus 0.13 sec per fur (G) 4-35 (4-35)

Bint Shadayid (USA) *(90t+)*(Fav)*(JLDunlop)* 2-8-11 WCarson(3) (leggy: scope: hld up: shkn up 2f out: led 1f out: qcknd: comf) ....— 1
Alessandra *(81t) (BWHills)* 2-8-11 MHills(2) (b: str: scope: bit bkwd: led: rdn 2f out: hdd 1f out: unable qckn) 3½ 2
Celandine *(81t) (RCharlton)* 2-8-11 TQuinn(1) (unf: scope: hld up: rdn over 2f out: wandered, bmpd & ev ch over 1f out: one pce) ....s.h 3
Sistar Act *(59t) (MRChannon)* 2-8-11 JReid(4) (w'like: scope: bit bkwd: hld up: rdn over 2f out: wknd wl over 1f out) 8 4

1/3 BINT SHADAYID (USA), **9/2** Celandine (op 3/1), **12/1** Alessandra (op 5/1), **16/1** Sistar Act, CSF £4.09 TOTE £1.30 (£3.40) OWNER Mr Hamdan Al Maktoum (ARUNDEL) BRED Shadwell Estate Company Limited 4 Rn
1m 19.26 (5.66) SF: 10/1/1/-

2573 E.B.F. SANDWICH MAIDEN STKS (2-Y.O) (Class D) £6,872.50 (£2,080.00: £1,015.00: £482.50)
7f Stalls: Centre GOING minus 0.13 sec per fur (G) 5-05 (5-08)

Jarah (USA) *(78) (BHanbury)* 2-9-0 WCarson(2) (b.off hind: str: scope: bit bkwd: s.s: swtchd lft & hdwy over 1f out: str run fnl f: led last strides) ....— 1
Skillington (USA) *(78+)*(Fav)*(IABalding)* 2-9-0 MHills(5) (gd sort: hld up: rdn over 3f out: led ins fnl f: hdd last strides: bttr for r) ....hd 2
2283[2] Kings Witness (USA) *(76) (WJHaggas)* 2-9-0 RCochrane(3) (w ldr: led over 2f out tl ins fnl f: one pce) ....¾ 3
Hammerstein *(72+) (MRStoute)* 2-9-0 JReid(7) (str: scope: bit bkwd: rdn over 3f out: hdwy over 2f out: ev ch 1f out: one pce: bttr for r) 2 4
Wilawander *(71+)*(Fav)*(BWHills)* 2-9-0 WRSwinburn(6) (w'like: scope: lw: rdn over 3f out: hdwy over 2f out: r.o one pce) ....nk 5

Lord of Men *(71) (JHMGosden)* 2-9-0 LDettori(8) (w'like: scope: hld up: rdn over 2f out: wknd over 1f out)....7 6
Alzanti *(55) (PFICole)* 2-9-0 TQuinn(4) (str: scope: 3rd whn stumbled bdly over 3f out: nt rcvr)....d.h 6
2107[4] Henry The Fifth *(39) (CEBrittain)* 2-9-0 BDoyle(1) (led over 4f)....7 8

3/1 Skillington (USA) (5/2-9/2), Wilawander (op 2/1), **4/1** Kings Witness (USA) (5/2-11/2), **8/1** JARAH (USA) (12/1-7/1), Lord of Men (op 5/1), **9/1** Hammerstein (op 7/2), **20/1** Alzanti, **25/1** Henry The Fifth, CSF £29.20 TOTE £7.70: £1.90 £1.70 £1.40 (£23.60) OWNER Mr Hamdan Al Maktoum (NEWMARKET) BRED Shadwell Farm Inc 8 Rn 1m 29.77 (3.27) SF: 50/50/48/44/43/27/27/11

T/Jkpt: Not won; £9,983.84 to Newmarket 22/7/95. T/Plpt: £187.20 (49.27 Tckts). T/Qdpt: £28.30 (15.85 Tckts). AK

2365-NEWMARKET (R-H)
Friday July 21st (Good to firm, Good last 8f)
WEATHER: cloudy, warm WIND: almost nil

2574 YELLOW LABEL CLAIMING STKS (3-Y.O) (Class D) £4,347.00 (£1,296.00: £618.00: £279.00) 1m (July) Stalls: High GOING minus 0.32 sec (GF) 6-30 (6-30)

1962[12] **La Fille de Cirque (42)***(57) (RJRWilliams)* 3-8-3 DBiggs(2) (hld up: hdwy over 2f out: led ins fnl f: sn pushed clr)....— 1
2282[6] Kama Simba **(59)***(63) (NACallaghan)* 3-9-0 PaulEddery(3) (w ldrs: led 4f out: clr over 2f out: hdd & no ex ins fnl f)....2½ 2
2166[6] Coneygree **(32)***(47) (JWharton)* 3-8-5 JWilliams(5) (plld hrd: prom: ev ch 4f out: sn outpcd)....3½ 3
2093[9] Nyali Beach (IRE) **(51)***(36) (DrJDScargill)* 3-7-8 (5) NVarley(1) (hld up & plld hrd: rdn 4f out: no imp)....2½ 4
1625[6] Sastrugi (IRE) *(37) (SPCWoods)* 3-8-4b WWoods(6) (swvd rt s: led 7f out: hdd 4f out: sn wknd)....2 5
2102[6] Empower (IRE) **(75)** (Fav)*(RHannon)* 3-8-12 GCarter(4) (led 1f: rdn over 3f out: sn wknd: virtually p.u appr fnl f: lame)....dist 6

11/8 Empower (IRE), **9/4** Kama Simba, **15/2** Nyali Beach (IRE), **10/1** Sastrugi (IRE), **14/1** LA FILLE DE CIRQUE, **16/1** Coneygree, CSF £40.59 TOTE £12.60: £3.20 £1.50 (£15.00) OWNER Mr Richard Morris Jr (NEWMARKET) BRED James Wigan 6 Rn 1m 41.49 (3.79) SF: 24/30/14/3/4/-

2575 ST PETERSBURG CONDITIONS STKS (3-Y.O+) (Class C) £5,425.60 (£1,873.60: £896.80: £364.00) 1m 4f (July) Stalls: High GOING minus 0.32 sec per fur (GF) 7-00 (7-01)

1926[2] **Burooj (102)***(113)*(Fav)*(DMorley)* 5-9-12 WCarson(1) (lw: hld up: hdwy 3f out: rdn to ld wl ins fnl f)....— 1
1894[5] Wind in Her Hair (IRE) **(110)***(104) (JWHills)* 4-9-3 RHills(4) (lw: led: clr over 2f out: hdd & no ex wl ins fnl f)....hd 2
2366[3] Great Crusader **(99)***(92) (CACyzer)* 3-8-6 DBiggs(3) (chsd ldr: rdn over 3f out: sn btn)....10 3
2119[5] Djais (FR) *(RTPhillips)* 6-9-2 TQuinn(2) (chsd ldrs: shkn up 4f out: hung lft & fnd nil)....dist 4

6/5 BUROOJ, **7/4** Wind in Her Hair (IRE), **4/1** Great Crusader, **14/1** Djais (FR) (10/1-16/1), CSF £3.47 TOTE £1.90 (£1.50) OWNER Mr Hamdan Al Maktoum (NEWMARKET) BRED Shadwell Estate Company Limited 4 Rn 2m 30.79 (2.09) SF: 70/61/37/-
WEIGHT FOR AGE 3yo-12lb

2576 NICOLE PONSARDIN MAIDEN STKS (3-Y.O+) (Class D) £4,659.00 (£1,392.00: £666.00: £151.50: £151.50) 6f (July) Stalls: High GOING minus 0.32 sec per fur (GF) 7-25 (7-27)

2344[2] **Easy Dollar (78)***(89) (BGubby)* 3-9-0b JWeaver(12) (lw: led 5f: rdn & r.o to ld again nr fin)....— 1
My Cadeaux *(83) (RGuest)* 3-8-9 MRoberts(1) (leggy: unf: w ldrs: led 1f out: rdn & edgd left: hdd & eased nr fin)....nk 2
1544[2] Sea Thunder *(83) (IABalding)* 3-8-9 MHills(9) (chsd ldrs: rdn & r.o wl fnl f)....hd 3
Dictation (USA) *(88)*(Fav)*(RCharlton)* 3-9-0 TQuinn(2) (cmpt: trckd ldrs: ev ch over 1f out: sn rdn: wknd ins fnl f)....hd 4
1168[7] Double Matt (IRE) **(77)***(88) (RHannon)* 3-9-0 RHughes(4) (bhd: hdwy over 1f out: fin wl)....d.h 4
Zahwa *(76) (RWArmstrong)* 3-8-9 WCarson(11) (hld up: hdwy wl over 1f out: nvr plcd to chal)....2½ 6

1846[4] Mystic Lure **(72)***(76) (EALDunlop)* 3-8-9 WRSwinburn(3) (b.hind: in tch: hmpd over 2f out: sn rdn & no imp) ....s.h 7
Golden Envoy (USA) *(68) (JHMGosden)* 3-8-9 LDettori(5) (h.d.w: dwlt: hdwy over 2f out: nvr rchd ldrs) 3 8
1486[4] Hugwity *(73) (BHanbury)* 3-9-0 WRyan(6) (s.s: wl bhd tl r.o appr fnl f) ....hd 9
Utr (USA) *(52) (HThomsonJones)* 3-8-9 RHills(8) (chsd ldrs over 4f) 6 10
2303[10] Fiveaday **(57)***(51) (BHanbury)* 3-8-11 (3) JStack(10) (lw: w wnr over 3f) 2 11
2049[2] Bold Revival *(30) (MrsPSly)* 3-8-9 WWoods(7) (prom tl wknd over 2f out) 6 12

11/4 Dictation (USA) (7/4-3/1), **4/1** Sea Thunder (3/1-9/2), **7/1** Mystic Lure, **15/2** EASY DOLLAR, **10/1** Hugwity (op 6/1), Golden Envoy (USA), Zahwa, Utr (USA) (op 6/1), **16/1** My Cadeaux, **20/1** Double Matt (IRE), **33/1** Fiveaday, Bold Revival, CSF £108.76 TOTE £7.70: £2.40 £5.00 £1.70 (£112.10) Trio £190.50 OWNER Brian Gubby Ltd (BAGSHOT) BRED Brian Gubby Ltd 12 Rn
1m 12.22 (0.72) SF: 61/55/55/60/60/48/48/40/45/24/23/2

2577

PRIX DE LA GRANDE DAME H'CAP (0-95) (4-Y.O+) (Class C) £6,920.00 (£2,060.00: £980.00: £440.00)
1m 2f (July) Stalls: High GOING minus 0.32 sec per fur (GF) 7-55 (7-56)

1753* **Special Dawn (IRE) (89)***(102)*(Fav)*(JLDunlop)* 5-10-0 PaulEddery(1) (lw: hld up: hdwy over 1f out: led ins fnl f: sn hdd & no ex: fin 2nd, 1¼l: awrdd r) ....— 1
1908* My Learned Friend **(79)***(91)*(Fav)*(AHide)* 4-9-4 JWilliams(2) (lw: a.p: led over 1f out tl bmpd & hdd ins fnl f: kpt on: fin 3rd, 3/4l: plcd 2nd) 2
2333* Access Adventurer (IRE) **(70)***(78)*(Fav)*(RBoss)* 4-8-9 5x WRyan(6) (led over 8f: no ex whn hmpd ins fnl f: fin 4th, 2½l: plcd 3rd) 3
2174[2] Ruby Heights **(54)***(57) (RHannon)* 4-7-7 GBardwell(3) (plld hrd: rdn 3f out: nvr trbld ldrs: fin 5th, 3½l: plcd 4th) 4
2028[7] Dancing Heights (IRE) **(75)***(72) (IABalding)* 4-9-0 LDettori(7) (chsd ldrs 8f: fin 6th, 3l: plcd 5th) 5
2080[4] Aeroking (USA) **(81)***(70) (GHarwood)* 4-9-6 AClark(5) (chsd ldr: ev ch over 2f out: wkng whn hmpd over 1f out) 1 7
1912[3] Ball Gown **(72)***(87) (DTThom)* 5-8-8 (3) DRMcCabe(4) (lw: b.hind: hld up: hdwy & n.m.r over 1f out: squeezed thro to ld wl ins fnl f: fin 1st: disq: plcd last) .... D

LONG HANDICAP Ruby Heights 7-3

4/1 SPECIAL DAWN (IRE), My Learned Friend, Access Adventurer (IRE), **5/1** Ball Gown, **6/1** Dancing Heights (IRE), **8/1** Aeroking (USA), Ruby Heights, CSF £18.74 TOTE £4.20: £2.20 £2.00 (£5.00) OWNER Windflower Overseas Holdings Inc (ARUNDEL) BRED Windflower Overseas 7 Rn
2m 5.76 (3.36) SF: 57/46/33/12/27/32/42
STEWARDS' ENQUIRY McCabe susp. 30/7-3/8/95 (irresponsible riding).

2578

CLICQUOT ROSE H'CAP (0-80) (3-Y.O+) (Class D) £4,854.00 (£1,452.00: £696.00: £318.00) **6f (July)** Stalls: High GOING minus 0.32 sec (GF) 8-25 (8-25)

2194[3] **Miss Aragon (45)***(55) (MissLCSiddall)* 7-7-13 NCarlisle(4) (dwlt: hdwy over 1f out: qcknd to ld ins fnl f) ....— 1
2206[4] Macs Maharanee **(70)***(77) (PSFelgate)* 8-9-7 (3) JStack(1) (w ldrs: led over 1f out tl ins fnl f: no ex) 1 2
2404[4] Louisville Belle (IRE) **(54)***(61) (MDIUsher)* 6-8-1 (7) CAdamson(7) (b: led over 4f: r.o) ....s.h 3
2326[3] Pageboy **(65)***(69)*(Fav)*(PCHaslam)* 6-9-5b JWeaver(2) (racd alone far side: gd spd over 4f) .1¼ 4
2414[2] Chili Heights **(55)***(57) (GBBalding)* 5-8-9v TSprake(5) (b.hind: sn bhd & pushed along: r.o appr fnl f: nvr nrr) ....¾ 5
2330* Souperficial **(63)***(62) (JAGlover)* 4-9-3v 6x GDuffield(3) (dwlt: hdwy over 2f out: no ex ins fnl f) 1¼ 6
2203[2] Samsolom **(67)***(65) (PHowling)* 7-9-7 PaulEddery(8) (lw: rdn 2f out: nvr nr to chal) ....nk 7
2009[3] Dashing Dancer (IRE) **(58)***(54) (RAkehurst)* 4-8-12 TQuinn(11) (prom: one pce appr fnl f: eased nr fin) ....¾ 8
*2290** My Gallery (IRE) **(53)***(48) (ABailey)* 4-8-4 (3) SSanders(12) (chsd ldrs: rdn over 2f out: no imp)nk 9
2203* Tharwa (IRE) **(64)***(50)*(Fav)*(NACallaghan)* 3-8-12 LDettori(6) (b: b.hind: prom tl wknd appr fnl f) 3½ 10
2317[7] Spectacle Jim **(50)***(29) (JO'Donoghue)* 6-8-4b FNorton(9) (a bhd) 2½ 11
2168[7] Southern Ridge **(67)***(35) (CAHorgan)* 4-9-7 DHarrison(10) (b.hind: prom 4f) 4 12

9/2 Pageboy, Tharwa (IRE), **6/1** Dashing Dancer (IRE), **7/1** Chili Heights, Souperficial, Samsolom, **8/1** My Gallery (IRE), **10/1** MISS ARAGON, **12/1** Macs Maharanee (op 8/1), **14/1** Louisville Belle (IRE), **25/1** Spectacle Jim, Southern Ridge, CSF £119.13 CT £1,540.49 TOTE £13.00: £3.30 £4.80 £5.70 (£61.80) Trio £449.40 OWNER Miss L. C. Siddall (TADCASTER) BRED J. A. Griffiths 12 Rn
1m 12.94 (1.44) SF: 37/59/43/51/39/44/47/36/30/26/11/17
WEIGHT FOR AGE 3yo-6lb

2579 WIDOW MAIDEN STKS (2-Y.O F) (Class D) £4,503.00 (£1,344.00: £642.00: £291.00) **7f (July)** Stalls: High GOING minus 0.32 sec per fur (GF) 8-55 (8-56)

Matiya (IRE) *(78)*(Fav)*(BHanbury)* 2-8-11 RHills(4) (gd sort: hld up: qcknd to ld 1f out: pushed out)....— **1**
17812 Sibbertoft (IRE) *(76) (PFICole)* 2-8-11 TQuinn(2) (prom: led over 1f out: sn hdd & no ex)....1 **2**
Parrot Jungle (IRE) *(72+) (JLDunlop)* 2-8-11 PaulEddery(3) (neat: lw: hld up & bhd: hdwy over 1f out: r.o)....1¾ **3**
Just Nuisance *(66) (CEBrittain)* 2-8-11 MRoberts(5) (cmpt: bit bkwd: led over 5f: one pce)..2½ **4**
Silver Wing (USA) *(63) (MBell)* 2-8-11 MFenton(1) (w'like: b.off hind: in tch: effrt 2f out: wknd fnl f)....1½ **5**
20703 Fikra (USA) *(61) (DMorley)* 2-8-11 WCarson(6) (hld up: nvr trbld ldrs)....½ **6**
20256 Hawanafa *(56) (RHannon)* 2-8-11 LDettori(7) (prom: ev ch over 1f out: eased whn btn ins fnl f)....2½ **7**

2/1 MATIYA (IRE), **3/1** Fikra (USA), **100/30** Sibbertoft (IRE) (9/4-7/2), **8/1** Hawanafa (6/1-10/1), **10/1** Silver Wing (USA), Parrot Jungle (IRE) (op 4/1), **12/1** Just Nuisance, CSF £9.14 TOTE £4.50: £2.10 £2.40 (£6.80) OWNER Mr Hamdan Al Maktoum (NEWMARKET) BRED Barronstown Stud 7 Rn 1m 28.05 (3.65) SF: 27/25/21/15/12/10/5

T/Plpt: £482.10 (34.45 Tckts). T/Qdpt: £161.10 (1.6 Tckts). Dk

1841-THIRSK (L-H)
Friday July 21st (Good)
WEATHER: sunny WIND: mod bhd

2580 E.B.F. JONATHAN COWAP MAIDEN STKS (2-Y.O F) (Class D) £4,110.00 (£1,230.00: £590.00: £270.00) **6f** Stalls: Centre GOING minus 0.44 sec (F) 2-10 (2-10)

22752 **Thrilling Day** *(70+)*(Fav)*(NAGraham)* 2-8-11 DHolland(4) (lw: trckd ldr: led ins fnl f: shkn up & r.o)....— **1**
19772 Auriga *(66) (IABalding)* 2-8-11 JWeaver(5) (lw: led tl hdd ins fnl f: kpt on)....1½ **2**
12985 Swing Mania (IRE) *(39) (SGNorton)* 2-8-11 KDarley(1) (chsd ldrs tl outpcd fr ½-wy)....10 **3**
She's Simply Great (IRE) *(33) (JJO'Neill)* 2-8-11 GDuffield(3) (leggy: unf: sn pushed along: nvr trbld ldrs)....2½ **4**
24838 Yougoa *(14) (MWEasterby)* 2-8-11 LCharnock(2) (dwlt: a outpcd & bhd)....7 **5**

2/5 THRILLING DAY, **5/2** Auriga (op 6/4), **16/1** Swing Mania (IRE), **25/1** She's Simply Great (IRE), **50/1** Yougoa, CSF £1.82 TOTE £1.50: £1.10 £1.10 (£1.30) OWNER Bloomsbury Stud (NEWMARKET) BRED Bloomsbury Stud 5 Rn 1m 11.8 (2.10) SF: 28/24/-/-/-

2581 BBC RADIO YORK CONDITIONS STKS (2-Y.O) (Class D) £3,940.00 (£1,090.00: £520.00) **7f** Stalls: Low GOING minus 0.17 sec per fur (GF) 2-40 (2-42)

Exalted (IRE) *(67+) (SirMarkPrescott)* 2-8-10 GDuffield(2) (w'like: bit bkwd: a.p: shkn up to ld 1f out: r.o)....— **1**
20255 Rumpipumpy *(56)*(Fav)*(LordHuntingdon)* 2-8-5 JWeaver(3) (lw: sn trckng ldr: rdn over 2f out: r.o one pce)....2½ **2**
15623 Arajaan (USA) *(61) (BHanbury)* 2-8-10 RHills(1) (led: hung rt 2f out: hdd 1f out: no ex)....s.h **3**

4/5 Rumpipumpy, **11/4** EXALTED (IRE), Arajaan (USA), CSF £5.01 TOTE £3.40 (£1.80) OWNER Mrs F. R. Watts (NEWMARKET) BRED Rowanstown Stud 3 Rn 1m 28.4 (5.70) SF: 13/2/7

2582 JULIA BOOTH (S) H'CAP (0-60) (3-Y.O) (Class G) £2,780.60 (£771.60: £369.80) **1m** Stalls: Low GOING minus 0.17 sec per fur (GF) 3-10 (3-12)

23324 **Simand (45)***(59)*(Fav)*(EWeymes)* 3-9-4 KDarley(5) (lw: sn pushed along: hdwy 2f out: r.o to ld wl ins fnl f)....— **1**
18738 Summer Villa **(42)***(55)*(Fav)*(PCHaslam)* 3-9-1 JWeaver(2) (a cl up: slt ld 2f out: nt qckn ins fnl f)....½ **2**
215611 Malzoom **(33)***(45) (SEKettlewell)* 3-8-6 JFortune(1) (lw: chsd ldrs: led 3f out to 2f out: ev ch tl hrd rdn & one pce ins fnl f)....½ **3**
196210 Trumble **(48)***(53) (CWThornton)* 3-9-7 AMackay(7) (lw: a.p: hdwy u.p over 2f out: nt pce to chal)....3½ **4**
22583 Bitch **(39)***(43) (DNicholls)* 3-8-12b AlexGreaves(3) (a chsng ldrs: effrt 3f out: no imp)....nk **5**

1873[7] Milltown Classic (IRE) **(35)***(31) (JParkes)* 3-8-8 LCharnock(10) (lw: in tch: no hdwy fnl 3f).......4 6
141[8] Lass of Kinloch **(33)***(27) (MBrittain)* 3-8-6 JLowe(11) (s.i.s: nrst fin) 1¼ 7
2149[3] Miltak **(41)***(27) (PJMakin)* 3-9-0 DHarrison(12) (effrt ent st: no imp) 4 8
1962[2] Magical Bid (IRE) **(46)***(30) (JMBradley)* 3-9-0 (5) HKYim(9) (b: rdn ½-wy: a rr div) 1 9
2239[11] Jet Classic **(36)***(15) (MissJFCraze)* 3-8-9 JFanning(6) (b.hind: s.i.s: n.d)..............................2½ 10
2037[17] Rozalina Lady **(43)***(21) (NAGraham)* 3-9-2 DHolland(14) (nvr bttr than mid div) ....½ 11
1583[8] Magnums Secret **(48)***(23) (JLEyre)* 3-9-7 RLappin(13) (swtg: bhd & rdn appr st: n.d)............1¼ 12
1569[12] Nebrangus (IRE) **(40)***(10) (NBycroft)* 3-8-13b SMaloney(4) (plld hrd: a bhd)..........................2½ 13
1993[11] West Farm Boy **(39)***(3) (JJO'Neill)* 3-8-12b GDuffield(8) (led tl hdd 3f out: wknd qckly) 3 14

9/2 SIMAND, Summer Villa, **6/1** Malzoom, **13/2** Bitch, Magical Bid (IRE), **7/1** Miltak, **9/1** Magnums Secret (op 6/1), **10/1** Trumble, Milltown Classic (IRE), **16/1** Rozalina Lady, **20/1** West Farm Boy, **33/1** Jet Classic, Lass of Kinloch, **50/1** Nebrangus (IRE), CSF £26.71 CT £121.11 TOTE £4.70: £1.80 £1.50 £2.50 (£8.70) Trio £29.90 OWNER Mr W. G. Martin (MIDDLEHAM) BRED R. V. Young 14 Rn 1m 42.0 (6.40) SF: 22/18/8/16/6/-/-/-/-/-/-/-/-/-
No bid.

2583 STANNINGLEY ENGINEERING MAIDEN STKS (3-Y.O) (Class D)
£3,915.00 (£1,170.00: £560.00: £255.00)
7f Stalls: Low GOING minus 0.17 sec per fur (GF) 3-40 (3-41)

547[4] **Russian Maid** *(77+)*(Fav)*(JRFanshawe)* 3-8-9 DHarrison(1) (b.hind: trckd ldrs: qcknd to ld over 1f out: shkn up & r.o wl) ....— 1
2236[6] Iktamal (USA) **(78)***(79) (EALDunlop)* 3-9-0 JWeaver(2) (lw: hld up: smooth hdwy whn bmpd wl over 1f out: sn disp ld: nt qckn ins fnl f)..1¼ 2
2236[2] Young Benson **(76)***(76) (BAMcMahon)* 3-9-0 JFortune(3) (lw: led tl hdd over 1f out: r.o one pce) 1½ 3
Unfuwaanah *(64) (HThomsonJones)* 3-8-9 RHills(5) (w'like: s.s: sn rcvrd: kpt on fnl 2f: nvr able to chal)..3 4
2255[2] Reefa's Mill (IRE) **(76)***(60) (JWHills)* 3-9-0 KDarley(4) (lw: cl up tl edgd rt & wknd wl over 1f out)..4 5

10/11 RUSSIAN MAID, **7/2** Iktamal (USA), **11/2** Unfuwaanah, **6/1** Young Benson, **7/1** Reefa's Mill (IRE), CSF £4.69 TOTE £2.10: £1.50 £1.80 (£2.60) OWNER Sheikh Mohammed (NEWMARKET) BRED Sheikh Mohammed bin Rashid al Maktoum 5 Rn 1m 27.5 (4.80) SF: 22/24/21/9/5

2584 ROYAL ARTILLERY HERITAGE H'CAP (0-80) (3-Y.O+) (Class D)
£4,092.00 (£1,221.00: £583.00: £264.00)
1m 4f Stalls: Low GOING minus 0.17 sec per fur (GF) 4-10 (4-12)

2224[5] **Ashover (53)***(69) (TDBarron)* 5-9-3 JFortune(4) (lw: trckd ldr: led & qcknd 4f out: r.o wl)......— 1
2392* Soba Up **(63)***(77)*(Fav)*(TJEtherington)* 5-9-13 5x ACulhane(1) (lw: hld up: chsd ldr appr st: r.o u.p: nvr able to chal)..1¼ 2
2238[7] Chimanimani **(60)***(61) (NTinkler)* 4-9-10 GDuffield(2) (hld up: sme hdwy 2½f out: no imp) 10 3
2233[4] Persian Soldier **(45)***(37) (EJAlston)* 8-8-9 DHolland(3) (lw: set slow pce tl hdd 4f out: sn outpcd)..7 4

4/5 Soba Up, **3/1** ASHOVER, **11/2** Persian Soldier, **15/2** Chimanimani, CSF £5.54 TOTE £3.40 (£2.00) OWNER Mr Timothy Cox (THIRSK) BRED Bridge End Bloodstock 4 Rn
2m 39.4 (9.40) SF: 26/34/18/-

2585 'BACK A WINNER BY TRAIN-TOTE' H'CAP (0-80) (3-Y.O+) (Class D)
£4,378.00 (£1,309.00: £627.00: £286.00)
6f Stalls: Centre GOING minus 0.44 sec per fur (F) 4-45 (4-46)

2330[3] **Rocketeer (IRE) (69)***(78)*(Fav)*(WRMuir)* 4-9-8b JWeaver(9) (lw: dwlt: outpcd & bhd tl hdwy 2f out: led ins fnl f: sn clr) ....— 1
2521[3] High Domain (IRE) **(65)***(69) (TDBarron)* 4-9-4b JFortune(6) (lw: cl up: led 2½f out tl ins fnl f: no ex)..1¾ 2
1441[6] Boursin (IRE) **(69)***(67) (PCalver)* 6-9-8 DaleGibson(3) (lw: led 3½f: ev ch ins fnl f: nt qckn) ..2½ 3
2458[9] Here Comes a Star **(71)***(64) (JMCarr)* 7-9-10 ACulhane(4) (lw: hld up: hdwy ½-wy: rdn & nt qckn fnl f) 1¾ 4
20[10] Mustn't Grumble (IRE) **(64)***(54) (WSCunningham)* 5-9-3 GDuffield(7) (in tch: effrt 2f out: nt qckn)..1 5
2458[6] Plum First **(61)***(49) (LRLloyd-James)* 5-9-0 JFanning(8) (lw: b.hind: chsd ldrs: outpcd fnl 2f) ..¾ 6
1996[2] Heart Broken **(57)***(19) (JGFitzGerald)* 5-8-10 DHolland(2) (lw: outpcd fr ½-wy) 10 7
2163[6] My Abbey **(57)***(15) (EJAlston)* 6-8-10 AMackay(1) (racd alone centre: spd 4f)........................1¼ 8
2475[4] Oriental Air (IRE) **(52)** *(EWeymes)* 4-8-5 KDarley(5) (lw: prom over 3f: eased & virually p.u) ....dist 9

2/1 ROCKETEER (IRE), **11/2** Heart Broken, **6/1** Oriental Air (IRE), **13/2** Plum First, **15/2** High Domain (IRE), **8/1** Here Comes a Star, **10/1** Boursin (IRE), **14/1** Mustn't Grumble (IRE) (op 8/1), My Abbey, CSF £17.22 CT £115.20 TOTE £2.70: £1.30 £2.30 £4.10 (£20.10) Trio £73.00 OWNER Mrs J. M. Muir (LAMBOURN) BRED Mrs T. Bracken in Ireland 9 Rn

1m 10.2 (0.50) SF: 61/52/50/47/37/32/2/-/-

2586

LEVY BOARD APPRENTICE H'CAP (0-70) (3-Y.O+) (Class E) £2,923.25 (£896.00: £445.50: £220.25)
1m Stalls: Low GOING minus 0.17 sec per fur (GF) 5-15 (5-15)

2390[3] **Resolute Bay (40)***(49) (RMWhitaker)* 9-8-0v FLynch(5) (lw: sn outpcd & bhd: hdwy & rn wd st: styd on to ld wl ins fnl f: hung lft)........— 1
2332[2] Just Fizzy **(59)***(67) (JHetherton)* 3-8-11 JWilkinson(2) (mde most: clr over 2f out: hdd wl ins fnl f)........½ 2
2220[5] Bex Boy (IRE) **(33)***(36) (MWEasterby)* 4-7-2b(5) RMullen(4) (chsd ldrs: outpcd appr st: kpt on fnl f)........2½ 3
1945[6] Rambo Waltzer **(52)***(43) (SGNorton)* 3-8-4v CLowther(1) (cl up tl outpcd appr st: no imp after)........6 4
2397* Sooty Tern **(73)***(50)*(Fav)*(JMBradley)* 8-10-5 6x GFaulkner(3) (lw: w ldr tl wknd fnl 2f)........7 5

LONG HANDICAP Bex Boy (IRE) 7-3

7/4 Sooty Tern, **3/1** Just Fizzy, **4/1** Rambo Waltzer, **9/2** RESOLUTE BAY, **10/1** Bex Boy (IRE), CSF £16.22 TOTE £3.90: £1.30 £2.10 (£5.00) OWNER Mr R. M. Whitaker (LEEDS) BRED R. T. and Mrs Watson 5 Rn

1m 41.9 (6.30) SF: 7/17/-/-/8
WEIGHT FOR AGE 3yo-8lb

T/Plpt: £103.20 (59.34 Tckts). T/Qdpt: £33.90 (1.65 Tckts). AA

2492-WOLVERHAMPTON (L-H)
Friday July 21st (Standard)

WEATHER: cloudy WIND: slt half against

2587

ABOYEUR MAIDEN H'CAP (0-60) (3-Y.O+) (Class F) £2,519.00 (£694.00: £329.00) **7f** **(Fibresand)** Stalls: High GOING minus 0.01 sec (STD) 2-20 (2-23)

2137[7] **Caddy's First (52)***(64) (SMellor)* 3-9-8 MWigham(9) (led over 4f out: clr ent st: unchal)........— 1
2250[4] Diamond Market **(46)***(52) (RHollinshead)* 3-9-2 TIves(12) (hdwy 3f out: 2nd st: kpt on nr fin: no ch w wnr)........2½ 2
2164[3] Md Thompson **(56)***(49) (SCWilliams)* 3-9-12 MRimmer(1) (a.p: 4th & rdn st: kpt on one pce)..6 3
2140[4] Fyne Song **(36)***(29) (WJMusson)* 3-8-3 (3) PMcCabe(6) (lw: lost pl after 2f: rdn & styd on ins fnl f)........s.h 4
2076[6] Mezzoramio **(46)***(31) (KAMorgan)* 3-8-11v(5) DGriffiths(3) (led over 2f: 3rd st: rdn & wknd appr fnl f)........3½ 5
2084[7] Backhander (IRE) **(58)***(42)*(Fav)*(JARToller)* 3-9-11 (3) SSanders(8) (bhd: rdn 3f out: kpt on appr fnl f: nvr nrr)........hd 6
1701[11] Vezelay (USA) **(55)***(34) (JHMGosden)* 3-9-11 GHind(7) (bhd: effrt & rdn ½-wy: no imp)........2½ 7
2088[14] Arctic Poppy (USA) **(42)***(16) (IABalding)* 3-8-12 AClark(4) (lw: prom: rdn over 3f out: 5th & wknd st)........2 8
2528[14] Main Brace **(36)***(8) (KRBurke)* 4-8-6b(7) MHenry(10) (chsd ldrs: 6th & btn ent st)........¾ 9
2088[10] Just Whistle **(47)***(11) (CWThornton)* 3-9-3 DeanMcKeown(2) (sn pushed along: a in rr)........3½ 10
1873[11] Rosina's Folly **(40)***(4) (JLHarris)* 4-9-3 NCarlisle(11) (racd wd: a bhd)........s.h 11
2202[7] Pacific Girl (IRE) **(57)***(17) (BPalling)* 3-9-13 TSprake(5) (chsd ldrs 4f: sn rdn & wknd)........2 12

5/1 Backhander (IRE), **11/2** Fyne Song, **6/1** Md Thompson, **8/1** Diamond Market, **10/1** Main Brace, **12/1** CADDY'S FIRST, Vezelay (USA) (op 5/1), **14/1** Mezzoramio, Arctic Poppy (USA), **20/1** Just Whistle, Rosina's Folly, Pacific Girl (IRE), CSF £87.71 CT £529.95 TOTE £19.70: £2.70 £2.30 £2.70 (£96.50) Trio £52.90 OWNER Mr Stan Mellor (SWINDON) BRED Mrs Rosemary Tennant 12 Rn

1m 30.2 (6.20) SF: 32/20/17/-/-/10/2/-/-/-/-/-
WEIGHT FOR AGE 3yo-7lb

2588

GEORGE MARTIN CLAIMING STKS (3-Y.O+) (Class F) £2,519.00 (£694.00: £329.00)
1m 100y (Fibresand) Stalls: Centre GOING minus 0.01 sec(STD) 2-50 (2-52)

2291[5] **Wentbridge Lad (IRE) (82)***(82) (PDEvans)* 5-9-7v(3) SSanders(6) (chsd ldrs: led 2f out: rdn & swvd lft ins fnl f: sn clr)........— 1
2291[3] Northern Celadon (IRE) **(65)***(74) (MJHeaton-Ellis)* 4-9-6 AClark(7) (w ldrs: led over 5f out tl hdd & 2nd st: rdn & one pce fnl f)........2 2

2291[2] Bentico **(73)***(76) (MrsNMacauley)* 6-9-3b(5) CTeague(2) (lw: a.p: 3rd st: sn rdn: unable qckn)........s.h **3**
1761[5] Rock Scene (IRE) *(68) (RHollinshead)* 3-8-12 TIves(9) (hld up: hdwy ½-wy: 4th st: one pce fnl 2f)........3 **4**
*2291** No Submission (USA) **(72)***(59)*(Fav)*(DWChapman)* 9-9-4 DeanMcKeown(3) (lw: sn drvn along: slt ld over 3f: 5th & outpcd st)........4 **5**
Loki (IRE) *(53) (GLewis)* 7-8-9 (7) ALakeman(5) (b: bkwd: s.i.s: bhd tl sme late hdwy)........2 **6**
1542[6] Private Fixture (IRE) **(70)***(51) (DMarks)* 4-9-3 (3) AGarth(12) (a in rr)........3 **7**
646[14] Educated Pet **(46)***(45) (BPreece)* 6-9-0 GHind(8) (b: bkwd: chsd ldrs tl 6th & rdn st)........s.h **8**
1971[5] Lady Valensina (IRE) **(42)***(31) (BJLlewellyn)* 4-8-5 RPrice(10) (lw: sn rdn along: a bhd)........3 **9**
2292[5] Brackenthwaite **(59)***(35) (LRLloyd-James)* 5-9-2b TWilliams(1) (a bhd)........3½ **10**
2391[7] Ghedi (POL) *(35) (MissGayKelleway)* 4-8-9 (7) DaneO'Neill(4) (prom tl rdn & wknd over 3f out)........hd **11**
Bowcliffe Grange (IRE) *(16) (DWChapman)* 3-7-13 (7) PFessey(11) (bkwd: a bhd: t.o)........9 **12**
2357[4] Care And Comfort **(62)** *(KMcAuliffe)* 3-8-7 SWhitworth(13) (sn drvn along: a bhd: t.o)........9 **13**

9/4 No Submission (USA), **6/1** WENTBRIDGE LAD (IRE), Bentico, **7/1** Loki (IRE) (op 7/2), **10/1** Northern Celadon (IRE), **12/1** Care And Comfort (op 8/1), **20/1** Ghedi (POL), Brackenthwaite, **25/1** Rock Scene (IRE), **33/1** Lady Valensina (IRE), Educated Pet, Bowcliffe Grange (IRE), Private Fixture (IRE), CSF £55.27 TOTE £9.20: £2.40 £1.70 £1.80 (£25.20) Trio £17.70 OWNER Mr John Pugh (WELSHPOOL) BRED Peter Doyle 13 Rn 1m 50.9 (6.90) SF: 41/33/35/19/18/12/10/4/-/-/-/-/-
WEIGHT FOR AGE 3yo-8lb

2589 DAILY STAR TOP TIPSTER H'CAP (0-90) (3-Y.O) (Class C)

£5,588.00 (£1,664.00: £792.00: £356.00)
1m 1f 79y (Fibresand) Stalls: Centre GOING minus 0.01 sec per fur (STD) 3-20 (3-20)

2525* **Vindaloo (65)***(71) (JLHarris)* 3-7-10 5x NCarlisle(5) (led over 2f: led 3f out: sn hdd: 3rd st: rallied to ld ins fnl f: r.o wl)........— **1**
2503[7] Three Arch Bridge **(64)***(68) (MJohnston)* 3-7-9b TWilliams(6) (chsd ldrs: led over 2f out tl ins fnl f: hrd rdn: nt qckn)........1 **2**
1589[8] Bardon Hill Boy (IRE) **(84)***(85)*(Fav)*(BHanbury)* 3-8-12 (3) JStack(4) (hld up & bhd: hdwy ½-wy: 2nd st: ev ch over 1f out: sn rdn: no ex)........2 **3**
2433[6] Tidal Reach (USA) **(66)***(62) (ABailey)* 3-7-11 FNorton(1) (a.p: led 7f out to 3f out: 4th & rdn st: one pce)........3 **4**
2395[3] Heathyards Rock **(90)***(85) (RHollinshead)* 3-9-7 TIves(3) (lost tch over 4f out: 6th & btn st)....½ **5**
1953[9] Montanelli (FR) **(81)***(54) (KMcAuliffe)* 3-8-12 SWhitworth(2) (lw: in rr & drvn along ½-wy: 5th & lost tch st: t.o)........13 **6**

7/4 Bardon Hill Boy (IRE) (op 3/1), **9/4** VINDALOO, **11/2** Tidal Reach (USA), **6/1** Three Arch Bridge, **10/1** Montanelli (FR), **11/1** Heathyards Rock, CSF £14.57 TOTE £2.30: £2.10 £3.50 (£6.40) OWNER Mr J. D. Abell (MELTON MOWBRAY) BRED Green Park Investments Ltd 6 Rn
2m 3.1 (7.10) SF: 20/17/34/11/34/3

2590 LEX TRANSFLEET H'CAP (0-65) (3-Y.O) (Class F) £2,519.00 (£694.00: £329.00)

5f (Fibresand) Stalls: Centre GOING: minus 0.01 sec per fur (STD) 3-50 (3-50)

2295[3] **Malibu Man (62)***(77+)*(Fav)*(SMellor)* 3-9-6 TSprake(4) (mde all: wl clr ent fnl f: eased nr fin)........— **1**
1201[7] Magical Manoeuvers **(56)***(58) (BAMcMahon)* 3-9-0 SDWilliams(5) (chsd wnr fr ½-wy: no imp)........4 **2**
2383[2] Ring the Chief **(57)***(58) (RAkehurst)* 3-8-12 (3) SSanders(1) (swtg: sn drvn along & outpcd: rdn wl over 1f out: nvr nr to chal)........nk **3**
2024[5] Frans Lad **(63)***(35) (JBerry)* 3-9-0v(7) PRoberts(3) (a outpcd & bhd: t.o)........9 **4**
I'm Playing **(50)***(14) (MJohnston)* 3-8-8 TWilliams(2) (bit bkwd: spd over 2f: sn lost tch: t.o)........2½ **5**

11/10 MALIBU MAN (op 7/4), **5/2** Ring the Chief, **11/2** Magical Manoeuvers, **7/1** Frans Lad (op 4/1), **9/1** I'm Playing (op 6/1), CSF £7.15 TOTE £1.90: £1.10 £2.50 (£4.90) OWNER Church Racing Partnership (SWINDON) BRED Mrs M. Chubb 5 Rn 62.8 secs (4.80) SF: 22/3/3/-/-

2591 MYSTERIOUS (S) STKS (2-Y.O F) (Class G) £2,243.00 (£618.00: £293.00)

6f (Fibresand) Stalls: Centre GOING minus 0.01 sec per fur (STD) 4-20 (4-20)

1287[7] **Welsh Melody** *(53) (KRBurke)* 2-8-6 TWilliams(6) (s.i.s: bhd: hdwy over 2f out: led ins fnl f: r.o wl)........— **1**
2249[3] Saint Rosalina *(50) (CJHill)* 2-7-13c(7) MHenry(7) (eyecover: s.i.s: bhd & outpcd: hdwy 2f out: r.o wl fnl f)........1 **2**

2336* Times of Times (IRE) *(53)*(Fav)*(DJSCosgrove)* 2-8-7 (5) LNewton(3) (b: led 3f out tl hdd & no ex ins fnl f)....1¼ 3
*2496*4 Euskara *(42) (MDIUsher)* 2-8-6 RStreet(4) (b: dwlt: sn chsng ldrs: rdn over 2f out: outpcd)....1¼ 4
*2382*5 Jessica's Song *(38) (WGMTurner)* 2-8-6 TSprake(5) (b.hind: prom tl rdn & wknd 2f out)......1½ 5
*2294*3 February *(28) (MRChannon)* 2-7-13 (7) DSweeney(1) (lw: gd spd over 3f)....4 6
23357 Solva Mist *(9) (LJHolt)* 2-8-6 CAvery(2) (led to ½-wy: wknd qckly: t.o)....7 7

11/8 Times of Times (IRE), **2/1** Jessica's Song (op 4/1), **4/1** Saint Rosalina (op 2/1), **8/1** Solva Mist, **10/1** February, **14/1** WELSH MELODY, Euskara, CSF £70.23 TOTE £16.50: £2.00 £3.70 (£42.40) OWNER Mr M. Deren (WANTAGE) BRED Llety Stud 7 Rn 1m 17.7 (6.50) SF: 1/-/1/-/-/-/-
No bid.

2592 PERSIMMON AMATEUR H'CAP (0-60) (3-Y.O+) (Class G) £2,243.00 (£618.00: £293.00)

2m 46y (Fibresand) Stalls: High GOING minus 0.01 sec per fur (STD) 4-55 (4-55)

2232* **Claireswan (IRE) (49)***(66) (SCWilliams)* 3-9-13 (7) MissKWright(7) (a.p: disp ld fr ½-wy: 2nd st: led over 1f out: r.o wl)....— 1
21542 Flashman **(35)***(51)*(Fav)*(BJLlewellyn)* 5-10-8 MrJLLlewellyn(3) (hld up: hdwy 6f out: sn rdn: 4th st: r.o wl ins fnl f)....1¼ 2
23555 Scalp 'em (IRE) **(47)***(62) (PDEvans)* 7-11-2 (4) MrWMcLaughlin(6) (hld up gng wl: hdwy to ld 3f out: hdd over 1f out: sn rdn & no ex)....1 3
21973 Stalled (IRE) **(48)***(62)*(Fav)*(PTWalwyn)* 5-11-3 (4) MarchionessBlandford(2) (led after 5f to 3f out: 3rd st: kpt on one pce)....¾ 4
*2147*5 Child Star (FR) **(40)***(39) (DMarks)* 6-10-13e MissKMarks(12) (eyecover: hdwy 7f out: poor 5th st: n.d)....15 5
196511 Drimard (IRE) **(38)***(22) (KMcAuliffe)* 4-10-11 MrTMcCarthy(8) (chsd ldrs: sn rdn along: lost tch 4f out: poor 6th st: t.o)....15 6
24136 Coleridge **(44)***(20) (JJSheehan)* 7-10-13b(4) MrPClose(4) (sn bhd & drvn along: no imp: t.o)....9 7
2465* Parish Walk (IRE) **(39)***(5) (KWHogg)* 4-10-8 (4) 4x MrKDrewry(11) (hdwy 7f out: poor 5th st: n.d)....10 8
228013 Verro (USA) **(19)** *(KBishop)* 8-9-2e(4)ow4 MissAPurdy(1) (eyecover: led after 2f to 11f out: wknd 7f out: t.o)....3 9
21976 Sadler's Pearl **(38)***(1) (BJMeehan)* 3-9-9b MissJAllison(9) (lw: s.s: a bhd: t.o)....d.h 9
*45*13 Crab 'n Lobster (IRE) **(26)** *(BPreece)* 5-9-6 (7) MissLBoswell(10) (bit bkwd: s.s: a wl bhd: t.o)10 11
Snickersnee **(21)** *(PaddyFarrell)* 7-9-4 (4) MissJSouthcombe(5) (bkwd: led 2f: lost pl ½-wy: t.o)....25 12

7/2 Stalled (IRE), Flashman, **5/1** Child Star (FR), **11/2** CLAIRESWAN (IRE) (4/1-6/1), **8/1** Parish Walk (IRE) (20/1-7/1), **10/1** Scalp 'em (IRE), **16/1** Drimard (IRE), **20/1** Coleridge, Sadler's Pearl, **40/1** Verro (USA), **50/1** Snickersnee, **66/1** Crab 'n Lobster (IRE), CSF £23.28 CT £171.45 TOTE £9.00: £2.20 £1.80 £1.60 (£15.50) Trio £21.70 OWNER Mr J. Wright (NEWMARKET) BRED Thomas Bean 12 Rn 3m 44.8 SF: 32/33/44/44/21/4/2/-/-/-/-/-
WEIGHT FOR AGE 3yo-16lb

T/Plpt: £177.70 (40.77 Tckts). T/Qdpt: £9.30 (2 Tckts). IM

2568-ASCOT (R-H)
Saturday July 22nd (Good to firm)

WEATHER: sunny WIND: slt across

2593 HORTENSIA DIAMOND CONDITIONS (LADIES) AMATEUR STKS (3-Y.O+) (Class C) £7,100.00 (£2,150.00: £1,050.00: £500.00)

1m (round) Stalls: High GOING minus 0.12 sec per fur (G) 2-00 (2-02)

2319* **Cap Juluca (IRE)** *(102) (RCharlton)* 3-9-11 MissEJohnsonHoughton(6) (led 6f out: r.o wl)...— 1
24713 Dance Band (USA) **(92)***(97) (BHanbury)* 3-9-11 MrsLPearce(8) (lw: 2nd st: rdn over 1f out: unable qckn)....2½ 2
21112 Green Green Desert (FR) **(100)***(86)*(Fav)*(MRStoute)* 4-9-13 (3) MrsJHills(4) (swtg: stdy hdwy fnl 2f: r.o: too much to do)....4 3
21672 Dorothea Brooke (IRE) **(77)***(77) (PWHarris)* 3-9-0 MissAElsey(12) (3rd st: rdn 2f out: one pce)....¾ 4
16267 Rory **(79)***(74) (MrsJCecil)* 4-10-5 MrsJCrossley(14) (hdwy over 1f out: nvr nrr)....7 5
21153 Polly Peculiar **(56)***(61) (BSmart)* 4-9-8 MissVMarshall(13) (b.hind: hdwy on ins over 3f out: 4th st: wknd over 1f out)....1 6
Padre Mio (IRE) *(65) (CPEBrooks)* 7-9-10 (3) MrsMiriamFrancome(1) (nvr nr to chal)....nk 7
22694 Sweet Trentino (IRE) **(54)***(64) (MTate)* 4-10-0 (3) MrsHNeedham(9) (nvr nrr)....2½ 8
2110* Desert Power **(65)***(61) (DBurchell)* 6-10-8 MissEJJones(3) (6th st: wknd over 2f out)....4 9

2076[5] Flashfeet **(54)***(40) (KBishop)* 5-9-13 MissAPurdy(11) (lw: dwlt: a bhd) 6 **10**
2236[5] Highspeed (IRE) *(34) (SEKettlewell)* 3-9-5 MrsDKettlewell(10) (bhd fnl 2f) 3 **11**
2451[4] Tart and a Half **(80)***(32) (BJMeehan)* 3-9-6b MrsJBoggis(7) (5th st: wkng whn sddle slipped over 2f out) 1½ **12**
2317[15] Real Madrid **(37)***(28) (GPEnright)* 4-9-10 (3) MrsMEnright(5) (lw: bhd fnl 3f) 1½ **13**
2171[6] Fosters Top **(32)***(20) (JFfitch-Heyes)* 3-9-2 (3) MissJEwer(2) (lw: led 2f: wknd over 3f out) 4 **14**

11/4 Green Green Desert (FR) (op 6/4), **3/1** CAP JULUCA (IRE), Dance Band (USA), **9/1** Dorothea Brooke (IRE), **11/1** Rory (8/1-12/1), **20/1** Tart and a Half, **33/1** Desert Power, **50/1** Highspeed (IRE), Polly Peculiar, **100/1** Padre Mio (IRE), Flashfeet, Sweet Trentino (IRE), Real Madrid, Fosters Top, CSF £10.68 TOTE £4.00: £1.50 £1.60 £1.60 (£6.40) Trio £4.50 OWNER Mr Martin Myers (BECKHAMPTON) BRED Mrs N. Myers 14 Rn 1m 41.88 (2.28) SF: 76/71/68/51/56/43/47/46/43/22/8/6/10/-
WEIGHT FOR AGE 3yo-8lb

OFFICIAL EXPLANATION **Tart and a Half: the saddle slipped causing her to interfere with Highspeed.**

2594

PRINCESS MARGARET STKS (Gp 3) (2-Y.O F) (Class A) £21,770.00 (£8,237.25: £4,031.13: £1,836.62)
6f Stalls: Centre GOING minus 0.12 sec per fur (G) 2-35 (2-35)

1849* **Blue Duster (USA)** *(104+)*(Fav)*(DRLoder)* 2-9-0 MJKinane(1) (lw: hld up: led over 1f out: qcknd: easily) ....— **1**
2216a[3] Ribot's Secret (IRE) *(90) (APO'Brien,Ireland)* 2-8-9v JReid(2) (neat: bdly hmpd 3f out: hdwy over 1f out: r.o one pce) 3½ **2**
2173[2] Myrtle *(83) (RHannon)* 2-8-9 LDettori(7) (lw: hld up: carried rt & led over 2f out: hdd over 1f out: one pce) 2½ **3**
2242[5] White Whispers *(83) (BJMeehan)* 2-8-9 BDoyle(4) (swtg: bmpd & lost pl 3f out: r.o one pce fnl f) ....s.h **4**
2025[3] Lyzia (IRE) *(81) (CEBrittain)* 2-8-9 TJarnet(5) (a.p: ev ch over 2f out: wknd over 1f out) ....¾ **5**
2315[2] Roses In The Snow (IRE) *(80) (JWHills)* 2-8-9 RHills(6) (hld up: ev ch over 1f out: sn wknd) nk **6**
2264* Kossolian *(27) (BPalling)* 2-8-9 TSprake(3) (lw: led tl swvd rt & hdd over 2f out: sn wknd) 20 **7**

30/100 BLUE DUSTER (USA), **8/1** Ribot's Secret (IRE) (op 5/1), **9/1** Lyzia (IRE), **14/1** Myrtle (10/1-16/1), **20/1** Roses In The Snow (IRE), **50/1** White Whispers, Kossolian, CSF £3.56 TOTE £1.40: £1.10 £2.00 (£2.00) OWNER Sheikh Mohammed (NEWMARKET) BRED Darley Stud Management Inc 7 Rn 1m 16.2 (2.60) SF: 53/39/32/32/30/29/-

2595

KING GEORGE VI & QUEEN ELIZABETH DIAMOND STKS (Gp 1) (3-Y.O+) (Class A) £278,760.00 (£103,713.00: £49,306.50: £20,920.50)
1m 4f Stalls: High GOING minus 0.12 sec per fur (G) 3-20 (3-21)

1611* **Lammtarra (USA)** *(127+)*(Fav)*(SbinSuroor)* 3-8-9 LDettori(3) (lw: rdn & hdwy over 3f out: 4th st: led ins fnl f: r.o wl) ....— **1**
1897* Pentire **(120)***(127+) (GWragg)* 3-8-9 MHills(1) (lw: hdwy over 3f out: 5th st: led over 2f out tl ins fnl f: r.o) ....nk **2**
1890a[3] Strategic Choice (USA) **(115)***(125) (PFICole)* 4-9-7 TQuinn(7) (lw: 2nd st: hrd rdn & ev ch over 1f out: 3rd & btn whn n.m.r on ins wl ins fnl f) 1½ **3**
2218a* Winged Love (IRE) *(125) (AFabre,France)* 3-8-9 OPeslier(5) (6th st: rdn over 2f out: r.o one pce fnl f) ....hd **4**
1890a[2] Broadway Flyer (USA) **(116)***(124) (JWHills)* 4-9-7 RHills(2) (lw: led over 9f: hrd rdn: one pce) ....hd **5**
2213a* Carnegie (IRE) *(123) (AFabre,France)* 4-9-7 TJarnet(6) (lw: 7th st: rdn over 2f out: r.o one pce fnl f) 1¼ **6**
2286[4] Environment Friend **(112)***(117) (CEBrittain)* 7-9-7 BDoyle(4) (lw: 3rd st: wknd over 2f out) 4 **7**

9/4 LAMMTARRA (USA) (3/1-7/4), **11/4** Carnegie (IRE), **3/1** Pentire (op 7/4), **9/2** Winged Love (IRE), **12/1** Broadway Flyer (USA), **25/1** Strategic Choice (USA), **50/1** Environment Friend, CSF £9.04 TOTE £2.90: £1.90 £2.10 (£4.10) OWNER Mr Saeed Maktoum Al Maktoum (NEWMARKET) BRED Gainsborough Farm Inc. in USA 7 Rn 2m 31.01 (1.51) SF: 74/74/84/72/83/82/76
WEIGHT FOR AGE 3yo-12lb

2596

VENETIA DIAMOND RATED STKS H'CAP (0-105) (3-Y.O+) (Class B) £11,975.60 (£4,480.40: £2,190.20: £941.00: £420.50: £212.30)
1m 2f Stalls: High GOING minus 0.12 sec per fur (G) 4-00 (4-00)

2241[17] **Aljazzaf (96)***(109) (RAkehurst)* 5-9-5 JWeaver(5) (mde all: hrd rdn over 1f out: r.o wl) ....— **1**
1853[8] Taufan's Melody **(98)***(107) (LadyHerries)* 4-9-7 JReid(6) (3rd st: chsd wnr over 2f out: hrd rdn over 1f out: no imp) 2½ **2**

1388a* El Supremo (USA) **(99)***(107) (DRLoder)* 3-8-12 LDettori(3) (5th st: rdn over 2f out: swtchd lft wl over 1f out: one pce) ....½ **3**
2274[5] Marsoom (CAN) **(98)***(105)*(Fav)*(BHanbury)* 4-9-7 TIves(1) (b: b.hind: 4th st: rdn over 2f out: one pce) ....½ **4**
2104[4] Garden of Heaven (USA) **(95)***(94) (CEBrittain)* 6-9-4 BDoyle(2) (dwlt: 6th st: a bhd) 5 **5**
Fragrant Belle (USA) **(96)***(93) (LGCottrell)* 4-9-5 TQuinn(4) (bit bkwd: 2nd st: wkng whn hmpd wl over 1f out) 1½ **6**

5/2 Marsoom (CAN), **11/4** El Supremo (USA) (6/4-3/1), **7/2** Taufan's Melody, **9/2** ALJAZZAF, **10/1** Garden of Heaven (USA), **20/1** Fragrant Belle (USA), CSF £18.38 TOTE £4.50: £2.00 £2.70 (£11.70) OWNER Y. M. Y. Partnership (EPSOM) BRED Gainsborough Stud Management Ltd 6 Rn
2m 7.74 (3.44) SF: 66/64/54/62/51/50
WEIGHT FOR AGE 3yo-10lb

2597 E.B.F. GRANVILLE MAIDEN STKS (2-Y.O C & G) (Class D) £8,169.00 (£2,472.00: £1,206.00: £573.00)
6f Stalls: Centre GOING minus 0.12 sec per fur (G) 4-30 (4-32)

Tamhid (USA) *(87) (HThomsonJones)* 2-8-11 RHills(2) (str: scope: bit bkwd: s.s: hld up: led over 1f out: rdn out) ....— **1**
Elshabiba (USA) *(85+)*(Fav)*(JLDunlop)* 2-8-11 WCarson(1) (w'like: scope: hld up: rdn over 3f out: swtchd rt over 1f out: r.o wl ins fnl f) ....¾ **2**
Dancing Image *(78) (IABalding)* 2-8-11 LDettori(5) (leggy: scope: led over 4f: unable qckn) 2½ **3**
Straight Thinking (USA) *(62) (PFICole)* 2-8-11 TQuinn(3) (w'like: scope: hld up: swtchd rt over 2f out: wknd over 1f out) 6 **4**

4/5 Elshabiba (USA) (8/11-5/4), **9/4** TAMHID (USA) (6/4-5/2), **4/1** Dancing Image (5/1-8/1), **10/1** Straight Thinking (USA) (op 6/1), CSF £4.59 TOTE £3.50 (£2.10) OWNER Mr Hamdan Al Maktoum (NEWMARKET) BRED Shadwell Farm 4 Rn 1m 17.19 (3.59) SF: 37/35/28/12

2598 CROCKER BULTEEL H'CAP (0-105) (3-Y.O+) (Class B) £13,810.00 (£4,180.00: £2,040.00: £970.00)
1m (straight) Stalls: Centre GOING minus 0.12 sec per fur (G) 5-00 (5-00)

2031[4] **Kayvee (98)***(108) (GHarwood)* 6-9-7 AClark(1) (lw: stdy hdwy over 2f out: led 1f out: rdn out) ....— **1**
2117* Bettergeton **(91)***(100) (PJBevan)* 3-8-6 NCarlisle(7) (lw: hld up: rdn over 1f out: r.o ins fnl f) ....½ **2**
2436[2] Wizard King **(106)***(114)*(Fav)*(SirMarkPrescott)* 4-10-1 MJKinane(10) (a.p: led over 2f out to 1f out: unable qckn) ....¾ **3**
1728[2] Roving Minstrel **(88)***(93) (BAMcMahon)* 4-8-11 TQuinn(6) (lw: rdn & hdwy over 1f out: r.o ins fnl f) 1½ **4**
2367* Nordinex (IRE) **(79)***(78) (RWArmstrong)* 3-7-8 ow1 SLanigan(8) (lw: led over 5f: wknd over 1f out) 2½ **5**
1851[20] Ham N'Eggs **(86)***(84) (RHannon)* 4-8-9 JReid(5) (nvr nr to chal) 1 **6**
1895[10] Belfry Green (IRE) **(93)***(86) (CAHorgan)* 5-9-2 WWoods(2) (lw: rdn & hdwy 2f out: wknd fnl f) 2½ **7**
2457[11] Cedez le Passage (FR) **(94)***(82) (CEBrittain)* 4-9-3b BDoyle(4) (lw: prom over 5f) 2½ **8**
2266[2] Fionn de Cool (IRE) **(73)***(57) (RAkehurst)* 4-7-10 ow1 WCarson(3) (lw: prom 6f) 1¼ **9**
1851[6] Moving Arrow **(89)***(69) (MissSEHall)* 4-8-12v NConnorton(9) (lw: bhd fnl 2f) 2½ **10**

100/30 Wizard King, **4/1** Bettergeton, **6/1** Fionn de Cool (IRE), **13/2** KAYVEE, **8/1** Nordinex (IRE), Belfry Green (IRE) (11/2-9/1), Moving Arrow, **10/1** Roving Minstrel (7/1-12/1), **12/1** Ham N'Eggs, **25/1** Cedez le Passage (FR), CSF £32.57 CT £95.65 TOTE £7.70: £2 20 £1.60 £1.70 (£17.70) Trio £13.20 OWNER Mr J. H. Richmond-Watson (PULBOROUGH) BRED Normanby Stud Ltd 10 Rn
1m 41.72 (2.52) SF: 70/54/76/55/32/46/48/44/19/31
WEIGHT FOR AGE 3yo-8lb

2599 BLACKNEST H'CAP (0-90) (3-Y.O+) (Class C) £6,937.50 (£2,100.00: £1,025.00: £487.50)
1m 4f Stalls: High GOING minus 0.12 sec per fur (G) 5-35 (5-35)

2289[3] **Dancing Sensation (USA) (65)***(78) (RAkehurst)* 8-8-7 JReid(4) (4th st: led over 1f out: rdn out) ....— **1**
2241[14] Benfleet **(78)***(90)*(Fav)*(RWArmstrong)* 4-9-6 WCarson(6) (lw: 5th st: nt clr run over 2f out: nt clr run & swtchd lft over 1f out: r.o wl ins fnl f) ....½ **2**
2012[3] Swallows Dream (IRE) **(82)***(90) (JLDunlop)* 4-9-10 MJKinane(8) (lw: 2nd st: led over 2f out tl over 1f out: unable qckn) 3½ **3**

2289* Bookcase **(65)***(73) (DRCElsworth)* 8-8-7 BDoyle(2) (lw: hdwy & nt clr run on ins over 1f out: one pce) ....hd 4
2472* Miss Pin Up **(81)***(88) (WJHaggas)* 6-9-9 RMcGhin(5) (3rd st: nt clr run wl over 1f out & over 1f out: swtchd lft: nt rcvr) ....hd 5
2055² Global Dancer **(72)***(77) (SDow)* 4-9-0 JWeaver(7) (led over 9f: wknd over 1f out) 1¾ 6
2082* Woodcrest **(81)***(79) (HCandy)* 3-8-11 WNewnes(1) (lw: a bhd) 5 7
1717⁵ En Vacances (IRE) **(66)***(55) (AGFoster)* 3-7-10 NCarlisle(3) (lw: 6th st: wknd over 2f out) 7 8

3/1 Benfleet, **4/1** Woodcrest, **6/1** Swallows Dream (IRE), Global Dancer, Miss Pin Up, **15/2** Bookcase, **9/1** DANCING SENSATION (USA), **25/1** En Vacances (IRE), CSF £33.54 CT £158.82 TOTE £8.20: £1.90 £1.30 £2.10 (£13.20) OWNER Chelgate Public Relations Ltd (EPSOM) BRED Martin W. Bach and Chris Vonderlohe 8 Rn 2m 33.1 (3.60) SF: 58/70/70/53/68/57/47/23
WEIGHT FOR AGE 3yo-12lb

T/Plpt: £38.60 (1,118.07 Tckts). T/Qdpt: £66.00 (10.8 Tckts). AK

2434-LINGFIELD (L-H)
Saturday July 22nd (Turf Good to firm, AWT Standard)
WEATHER: sunny WIND: almost nil

2600 SPORTSMAN CASINO MAIDEN APPRENTICE H'CAP (0-70) (3-Y.O+) (Class F) £2,595.50 (£738.00: £366.50)
1m 2f (Equitrack) Stalls: Centre GOING minus 0.65 sec per fur (FST) 6-20 (6-20)

2140² **She Said No (54)***(62)*(Fav)*(LordHuntingdon)* 3-8-11 (6) AimeeCook(4) (a.p: led ins fnl f: r.o) .— 1
2167⁴ Mighty Squaw **(57)***(64) (MissGayKelleway)* 3-8-13 (7) KSked(6) (hld up: hdwy over 1f out: r.o) ....½ 2
2439¹¹ Jarzon Dancer **(27)***(31) (DAWilson)* 7-7-4 (10) RachaelMoody(2) (hld up: hdwy over 3f out: r.o one pce fnl 2f) 2 3
2032⁶ Memory's Music **(54)***(57) (IABalding)* 3-8-9 (8) JBramhill(7) (lw: chsd ldr tl led over 7f out: chal 3f out: hdd ins fnl f: no ex) ....¾ 4
1016⁸ Woolverstone Hall (IRE) **(50)***(38) (DJGMurraySmith)* 3-8-8 (5) DSweeney(1) (chsd ldrs: rdn over 2f out: grad wknd) 9 5
290³ Come on Dancer (IRE) **(54)***(41) (JWhite)* 7-9-3 (10) CCarver(3) (bhd fnl 3f) ....¾ 6
Think of England **(39)** *(SDow)* 3-7-13 (3) ADaly(5) (led over 2f: wknd 5f out) 20 7

6/4 SHE SAID NO, **5/2** Mighty Squaw, **5/1** Memory's Music, **10/1** Come on Dancer (IRE) (8/1-12/1), Woolverstone Hall (IRE), **12/1** Jarzon Dancer (op 7/1), Think of England (op 7/1), CSF £5.84 CT £28.71 TOTE £2.20: £1.50 £1.70 (£3.00) OWNER Mr J. R. Bailey (WEST ILSLEY) BRED K. V. and Mrs Stenborg 7 Rn 2m 7.97 (4.97) SF: 10/12/-/5/-/-/-
WEIGHT FOR AGE 3yo-10lb

2601 SOUTHGATE MANAGEMENT (S) STKS (2-Y.O) (Class G) £2,534.20 (£701.20: £334.60) **5f** Stalls: Centre GOING minus 0.65 sec per fur (HD) 6-50 (6-51)

2403³ **Music Mistress (IRE)** *(53) (RHannon)* 2-8-0 (7)ow1 DaneO'Neill(6) (a.p: led over 2f out: rdn ins fnl f: r.o) ....— 1
1977¹³ Velvet Jones *(56)*(Fav)*(PFICole)* 2-8-11 TQuinn(3) (chsd ldrs: rdn 2f out: r.o one pce fnl f)....¾ 2
2403⁴ Latzio *(49) (BAPearce)* 2-7-13 (7) JWilkinson(4) (chsd ldrs: rdn 2f out: r.o one pce fnl f) ....½ 3
1035⁶ Ghostly Apparition *(52) (JohnUpson)* 2-8-11 DHarrison(5) (a.p: outpcd 2f out: rdn & edgd lft over 1f out: r.o one pce fnl f) ....¾ 4
2382² Trible Pet *(42) (BGubby)* 2-8-1 (5) AWhelan(2) (chsd ldrs: rdn over 1f out: one pce) 1½ 5
2176⁵ Fortuitious (IRE) *(35) (JRJenkins)* 2-8-6 BThomson(1) (led over 2f: wkng whn n.m.r over 1f out) 2 6

7/4 Velvet Jones, **2/1** MUSIC MISTRESS (IRE), **5/2** Trible Pet, **9/1** Fortuitious (IRE), **20/1** Ghostly Apparition, **33/1** Latzio, CSF £5.94 TOTE £3.00: £1.30 £2.20 (£3.90) OWNER Mrs Derek Strauss (MARLBOROUGH) BRED Baronrath Stud 6 Rn 60.48 secs (3.48) SF: 6/9/2/5/-/-
No bid

2602 A. R. DENNIS BOOKMAKERS H'CAP (0-80) (3-Y.O+) (Class D) £4,137.90 (£1,237.20: £592.60: £270.30)
7f 140y Stalls: Centre GOING minus 0.65 sec per fur (HD) 7-20 (7-23)

2178⁵ **Norsong (52)***(60) (RAkehurst)* 3-7-11 FNorton(9) (a.p: led appr fnl f: rdn ins fnl f: r.o) ....— 1
2051³ Mr Nevermind (IRE) **(65)***(70) (GLMoore)* 5-9-4 SWhitworth(8) (chsd ldrs: rdn & swtchd lft over 1f out: r.o one pce fnl f) 1½ 2
1859⁴ Mutabassim (IRE) **(69)***(74) (ACStewart)* 3-9-0 RHills(6) (hld up: led gng wl over 1f out: sn hdd: rdn ins fnl f: one pce) ....s.h 3

2317* Kindergarten Boy (IRE) **(62)***(62)*(Fav)*(RBoss)* 4-9-1 JWeaver(7) (led 6f: one pce) 2½ **4**
2414* Safey Ana (USA) **(75)***(70) (BHanbury)* 4-10-0 WRyan(4) (a.p: ev ch over 1f out: one pce)....2 **5**
*2407*6 Carte Blanche **(46)***(31) (CACyzer)* 4-7-13 ow3 DBiggs(3) (chsd ldrs: rdn 2f out: one pce) 3½ **6**
1381 4 Serious Option (IRE) **(69)***(36) (PFICole)* 4-9-8 TQuinn(2) (chsd ldrs tl wknd over 2f out)....10 **7**
1673 11 Green City **(72)***(36) (RHannon)* 3-9-3 BThomson(5) (rdn 4f out: a bhd) 1½ **8**
2345 5 Fort Knox (IRE) **(58)***(18) (RMFlower)* 4-8-11 AMorris(1) (chsd ldrs tl wknd over 2f out)....2 **9**

5/2 Kindergarten Boy (IRE) (op 4/1), **7/2** Mutabassim (IRE), **5/1** Mr Nevermind (IRE), Safey Ana (USA) (op 3/1), **7/1** NORSONG, **8/1** Serious Option (IRE), **14/1** Carte Blanche (op 8/1), **16/1** Green City, Fort Knox (IRE), CSF £41.91 CT £134.58 TOTE £11.60: £3.90 £1.40 £1.10 (£26.80) Trio £25.30 OWNER The Fairy Story Partnership (EPSOM) BRED Deepwood Farm Stud 9 Rn
1m 30.23 (2.23) SF: 30/48/44/40/48/9/14/6/-
WEIGHT FOR AGE 3yo-8lb

2603

DAILY STAR H'CAP (0-70) (3-Y.O) (Class E) £3,130.60 (£932.80: £444.40: £200.20) **2m** Stalls: Centre GOING minus 0.65 sec per fur (HD) 7-50 (7-51)

2550* **Carnbrea Belle (IRE) (65)***(78)*(Fav)*(MBell)* 3-9-12 5x MFenton(2) (a.p: 2nd st: led over 1f out: r.o) ....— **1**
2248 5 Euro Forum **(54)***(67) (GLMoore)* 3-9-1 PaulEddery(4) (hld up: 3rd st: hdwy over 1f out: one pce) ....½ **2**
2439 3 Santella Boy (USA) **(58)***(69) (GHarwood)* 3-9-5 AClark(1) (led tl over 1f out: one pce) 2 **3**
1379 11 Tommyknocker (IRE) **(35)***(19) (JRJenkins)* 3-7-10 ow2 FNorton(3) (chsd ldr 12f out tl over 4f out: 4th st: sn wknd) 25 **4**

11/10 CARNBREA BELLE (IRE) (4/5-5/4), **2/1** Santella Boy (USA), **100/30** Euro Forum, **10/1** Tommyknocker (IRE), CSF £4.91 TOTE £2.00 (£3.40) OWNER Mrs S. M. Crompton (NEWMARKET) BRED Limestone Stud 4 Rn 3m 36.67 (12.67) SF: 24/13/15/-

2604

EDMUNDSON ELECTRICAL H'CAP (0-70) (3-Y.O) (Class E) £3,044.80 (£906.40: £431.20: £193.60)
1m 4f (Equitrack) Stalls: Centre GOING minus 0.65 sec per fur (FST) 8-20 (8-20)

*2589** **Vindaloo (65)***(70)*(Fav)*(JLHarris)* 3-9-2 5x JWeaver(1) (hld up in tch: hdwy to ld over 1f out: r.o) ....— **1**
2026 6 Rocky Forum **(47)***(48) (GLMoore)* 3-7-12 FNorton(2) (led: rdn over 2f out: hdd over 1f out: one pce) 3 **2**
1986 8 Quillwork (USA) **(60)***(53) (MrsJCecil)* 3-8-11 PaulEddery(3) (plld hrd: chsd ldr: ev ch over 1f out: sn wknd) 6 **3**
2262* Harry Welsh (IRE) **(70)***(23) (KMcAuliffe)* 3-9-7 DHarrison(4) (bhd fnl 4f) 30 **4**

10/11 VINDALOO (8/11-11/10), **100/30** Rocky Forum, **7/2** Harry Welsh (IRE), **6/1** Quillwork (USA) (tchd 9/1), CSF £4.15 TOTE £1.70 (£2.40) OWNER Mr J. D. Abell (MELTON MOWBRAY) BRED Green Park Investments Ltd 4 Rn 2m 29.28 (0.02 under best) (-0.12) SF: 49/27/32/2

2605

MANDY PACKHAM BIRTHDAY LIMITED STKS (0-65) (3-Y.O+) (Class F) £2,947.40 (£816.40: £390.20)
1m 2f (Equitrack) Stalls: Centre GOING minus 0.65 sec per fur (FST) 8-50 (8-50)

*2379*4 **Locorotondo (IRE) (60)***(66) (MBell)* 4-9-0 MFenton(1) (hld up in tch: led over 1f out: r.o wl) ....— **1**
*2407*3 Rolling Waters **(61)***(69) (JARToller)* 5-9-9 WNewnes(6) (outpcd & bhd tl styd on fnl f: r.o) 4 **2**
1095 3 Ultimate Warrior **(64)***(66) (CACyzer)* 5-9-7 DBiggs(3) (chsd ldr: led 2f out: sn hdd: rdn over 1f out: one pce) ....nk **3**
2538 5 The Little Ferret **(60)***(63) (AMoore)* 5-9-0 (5) CChoi(5) (led to 2f out: ev ch over 1f out: one pce) ....¾ **4**
2376* First Crush **(63)***(58)*(Fav)*(SirMarkPrescott)* 3-8-6b CNutter(2) (prom: ev ch 2f out: sn rdn & one pce) 1½ **5**
2202 8 Words of Wisdom (IRE) **(59)***(57) (CACyzer)* 5-8-12 (7) ADaly(4) (chsd ldrs: rdn over 2f out: no hdwy) 2 **6**

11/10 First Crush (5/4-2/1), **9/4** LOCOROTONDO (IRE) (3/1-2/1), **9/2** Ultimate Warrior (4/1-7/1), **8/1** Rolling Waters (5/1-9/1), **12/1** The Little Ferret (8/1-14/1), Words of Wisdom (IRE), CSF £19.13 TOTE £3.90: £1.90 £2.20 (£10.40) OWNER The P 1 Partnership (NEWMARKET) BRED Irish National Stud Co Ltd 6 Rn 2m 5.15 (2.15) SF: 29/32/29/26/11/20
WEIGHT FOR AGE 3yo-10lb

T/Plpt: £30.10 (221.45 Tckts). T/Qdpt: £28.90 (3.6 Tckts). SM

2095-**NEWCASTLE (L-H)**
Saturday July 22nd (Good to firm)
WEATHER: fine, overcast WIND: fresh half against

2606 SEAHOUSES (S) STKS (2-Y.O) (Class F) £2,675.60 (£751.60: £366.80)
5f Stalls: Centre GOING: 0.18 sec per fur (G) 2-10 (2-11)

2485 7 **Westcourt Magic** *(63+) (MWEasterby)* 2-8-12 JFanning(2) (lw: mde all: clr over 1f out: eased nr fin)...— 1
2483 5 Bee Health Boy *(57) (MWEasterby)* 2-8-5 (7) RuthCoulter(7) (chsd ldr: kpt on fnl 2f: no ch w wnr)...2 2
2192 8 Europex *(37) (MHEasterby)* 2-8-12 MBirch(3) (chsd wnr tl wknd over 1f out)...6 3
2185 11 Julgarant (IRE) *(33) (MDods)* 2-8-12 TWilliams(6) (effrt ½-wy: wandered u.p: nvr nr to chal)...1½ 4
2399 3 Boffy (IRE) *(28)*(Fav)*(BPJBaugh)* 2-8-12 ACulhane(4) (lw: hld up: effrt 2f out: sn wknd)...1½ 5
2371 5 Darerock *(12) (MDods)* 2-8-12 JLowe(5) (s.s: sn drvn along & chsng ldrs: lost pl over 2f out)...5 6
2158 2 Chilibang Bang *(7) (JBerry)* 2-8-11v SDWilliams(1) (hld up: effrt over 2f out: sn wknd)...1¼ 7

11/4 Boffy (IRE), **10/3** Chilibang Bang, Europex, **9/2** Bee Health Boy, **10/1** WESTCOURT MAGIC, **12/1** Darerock (op 8/1), **14/1** Julgarant (IRE), CSF £49.49 TOTE £23.00: £6.60 £2.70 (£37.80) OWNER Mr K. Hodgson (SHERIFF HUTTON) BRED C. R. and V. M. Withers 7 Rn
63.78 secs (5.38) SF: 21/15/-/-/-/-/-
No bid

2607 WIDE OPEN H'CAP (0-80) (3-Y.O+) (Class D) £3,775.20
(£1,143.60: £558.80: £266.40)
1m (round) Stalls: Low GOING minus 0.17 sec per fur (GF) 2-40 (2-41)

2181 2 **Ninia (USA)** **(55)***(67)*(Fav)*(MJohnston)* 3-8-0 TWilliams(7) (lw: trckd ldrs: effrt over 2f out: rdn to ld over 1f out: drvn out)...— 1
2397 5 Spanish Verdict **(66)***(76) (DenysSmith)* 8-9-0 (5) CTeague(2) (lw: chsd wnr: effrt u.p over 2f out: nt qckn fnl f)...1 2
2375 4 Avishayes (USA) **(47)***(56) (MrsMReveley)* 8-8-0 JFanning(4) (lw: s.i.s: sn pushed along: hdwy 3f out: outpcd over 1f out: kpt on nr fin)...½ 3
2375 5 Durham Drapes **(54)***(62) (MHEasterby)* 4-8-7 MBirch(3) (chsd ldrs: effrt u.p over 2f out: kpt on one pce)...nk 4
2586 5 Sooty Tern **(71)***(78) (JMBradley)* 8-9-7 (3) SDrowne(5) (dwlt: sn trckng ldrs: effrt over 2f out: n.m.r: kpt on one pce)...¾ 5
2123 2 Lancashire Life (IRE) **(53)***(59) (EJAlston)* 4-8-6 SDWilliams(1) (lw: led tl over 1f out: eased nr fin)...½ 6
2461 4 Desert Invader (IRE) **(57)***(51) (DWChapman)* 4-8-10 ACulhane(6) (lw: hld up & bhd: n.d)...6 7

6/4 NINIA (USA), **5/1** Desert Invader (IRE) (6/1-4/1), **13/2** Avishayes (USA), Lancashire Life (IRE), **8/1** Sooty Tern (5/1-9/1), **9/1** Spanish Verdict, **10/1** Durham Drapes, CSF £13.87 TOTE £2.10: £1.70 £3.10 (£8.00) OWNER Mrs D. R. Schreiber (MIDDLEHAM) BRED Newgate Stud Farm Inc 7 Rn
1m 43.66 (4.66) SF: 25/42/22/28/44/25/17
WEIGHT FOR AGE 3yo-8lb

2608 TATTERSALLS MAIDEN AUCTION STKS (2-Y.O) (Class E) £3,166.90 (£959.20: £468.60: £223.30) **6f** Stalls: Centre GOING: 0.18 sec per fur (G) 3-10 (3-11)

1871 6 **Missile Toe (IRE)** *(65) (JEBanks)* 2-8-1 (3) SDrowne(6) (lw: mde all: qcknd clr over 1f out: pushed out nr fin)...— 1
Rocky's Meteor *(57+) (RAFahey)* 2-8-4 ACulhane(4) (lengthy: unf: s.i.s: bhd tl hdwy over 2f out: hrd rdn & styd on fnl f: no ch w wnr)...3 2
2161 3 Tabriz *(32) (JDBethell)* 2-7-12 TWilliams(3) (chsd ldrs: drvn along 3f out: one pce)...7 3
2192 3 Cumbrian Maestro *(44)*(Fav)*(MHEasterby)* 2-8-10 MBirch(1) (chsd ldrs: rdn over 2f out: one pce)...nk 4
Principal Boy (IRE) *(34+) (TJEtherington)* 2-8-6 JLowe(2) (w'like: scope: bit bkwd: in tch: effrt over 2f out: grad wknd)...2 5
Cerise (IRE) *(15) (CWCElsey)* 2-7-12 ow1 JFanning(7) (leggy: unf: s.s: a outpcd & bhd)...4 6
2302 2 Monkey Zanty (IRE) *(9) (JBerry)* 2-7-5 (7) PFessey(5) (chsd ldr tl wknd over 2f out: sn bhd) .2½ 7

2/1 Cumbrian Maestro, **3/1** MISSILE TOE (IRE), **9/2** Tabriz, **11/2** Monkey Zanty (IRE), **11/1** Rocky's Meteor (8/1-12/1), **14/1** Principal Boy (IRE) (op 8/1), Cerise (IRE) (10/1-16/1), CSF £29.66 TOTE £3.70: £2.30 £3.10 (£20.80) OWNER Stag and Huntsman (NEWMARKET) BRED Dr E. Grant and Miss Susan McKeon 7 Rn
1m 17.94 (6.44) SF: 15/7/-/-/-/-/-

2609

RAMBLING RIVER H'CAP (0-95) (3-Y.O+) (Class C) £5,647.00 (£1,696.00: £818.00: £379.00)
5f Stalls: Centre GOING: 0.18 sec per fur (G) 3-40 (3-44)

2533[3] **So Intrepid (IRE) (70)***(79) (JMBradley)* 5-8-10 (3) SDrowne(7) (lw: hdwy ½-wy: styd on wl u.p fnl f to ld nr fin)....— **1**
2418[*] Lady Sheriff **(71)***(78)*(Fav)*(MWEasterby)* 4-8-7b(7) RuthCoulter(6) (lw: w ldrs: led ½-wy: hdd & nt qckn nr fin)....½ **2**
2252[3] Shashi (IRE) **(77)***(80) (DMorley)* 3-9-1b JLowe(2) (rr div: swtchd rt ½-wy: kpt on wl u.p fnl f) .1½ **3**
2475[2] Rich Glow **(67)***(68) (NBycroft)* 4-8-3 (7) PFessey(3) (chsd ldrs: ev ch over 1f out: unable qckn)....½ **4**
2324[7] Hinton Rock (IRE) **(90)***(88) (MBell)* 3-9-7b(7) GFaulkner(8) (s.i.s: sn chsng ldrs: nt qckn fnl f) ...1 **5**
2271[2] Bollin Harry **(70)***(61) (MHEasterby)* 3-8-8 MBirch(1) (chsd ldrs tl outpcd appr fnl f)....2 **6**
2060[8] Tuscan Dawn **(80)***(59) (JBerry)* 5-9-2 (7) PRoberts(10) (reard s: bhd: sme hdwy ½-wy: sn wknd)....4 **7**
2252[5] Twice in Bundoran (IRE) **(54)***(27) (PSFelgate)* 4-7-8 (3) DWright(5) (led to ½-wy: wknd over 1f out)....1¾ **8**
2247[3] Allwight Then (IRE) **(74)** *(FHLee)* 4-9-3 TWilliams(9) (w ldrs tl wknd qckly over 1f out: virtually p.u)....15 **9**
2252[W] Magic Pearl **(74)** *(EJAlston)* 5-9-3 SDWilliams(4) (bolted gng to s: s.i.s: sn wl bhd: t.o 2f out)....dist **10**

11/2 Lady Sheriff, **6/1** SO INTREPID (IRE), Shashi (IRE), Rich Glow, Bollin Harry, **8/1** Magic Pearl, Allwight Then (IRE), **9/1** Hinton Rock (IRE), **10/1** Twice in Bundoran (IRE), **16/1** Tuscan Dawn, CSF £36.81 CT £189.73 TOTE £7.80: £3.10 £1.60 £1.90 (£20.00) Trio £39.50 OWNER Mr E. A. Hayward (CHEPSTOW) BRED Crest Stud Ltd 10 Rn 61.98 secs (3.58) SF: 52/51/48/41/56/29/32/-
WEIGHT FOR AGE 3yo-5lb

2610

COUPLAND H'CAP (0-85) (3-Y.O+) (Class D) £3,707.60 (£1,122.80: £548.40: £261.20) **1m 2f 32y** Stalls: Low GOING minus 0.17 sec per fur (GF) 4-10 (4-10)

2226[4] **Imperial Bid (FR) (52)***(62) (DenysSmith)* 7-8-6 TWilliams(1) (lw: dwlt: sn chsng ldrs: shkn up over 4f out: styd on u.p fnl 2f: led ins fnl f: drvn clr)....— **1**
2254[*] Ooh Ah Cantona **(64)***(70)*(Fav)*(JLEyre)* 4-9-4 RLappin(3) (trckd ldrs: led 3f out: sn rdn: hdd & nt qckn ins fnl f)....2½ **2**
1598[2] Frontiersman **(54)***(56) (JWWatts)* 3-7-12 JLowe(6) (drvn along 5f out: outpcd & rdn over 3f out: styd on fnl f)....2½ **3**
2373[2] Sycamore Lodge (IRE) **(70)***(70) (PCalver)* 4-9-10b MBirch(5) (hld up & bhd: effrt over 2f out: kpt on: nvr nr to chal)....1¼ **4**
2427[4] Keep Battling **(42)***(42) (JSGoldie)* 5-7-3 (7) PFessey(4) (plld hrd: trckd ldrs: ev ch 3f out: wknd 1f out)....hd **5**
2356[6] Cumbrian Minstrel **(52)***(41) (MHEasterby)* 3-7-7 (3) DWright(2) (led to 3f out: wknd over 1f out)....7 **6**

13/8 Ooh Ah Cantona, **4/1** Frontiersman, **9/2** Sycamore Lodge (IRE), **6/1** Keep Battling, **8/1** IMPERIAL BID (FR), Cumbrian Minstrel, CSF £20.58 TOTE £15.30: £4.10 £1.40 (£8.50) OWNER Lord Durham (BISHOP AUCKLAND) BRED David Grenfell 6 Rn 2m 10.9 (4.20) SF: 44/52/28/52/24/13
WEIGHT FOR AGE 3yo-10lb

2611

JACKIE MILBURN MEMORIAL APPRENTICE H'CAP (0-80) (3-Y.O+) (Class F) £2,729.00 (£769.00: £377.00)
7f Stalls: Low GOING: 0.18 sec per fur (G) 4-40 (4-40)

2342[*] **Mr Cube (IRE) (55)***(67) (JMBradley)* 5-8-12v(3) RWaterfield(5) (lw: trckd ldrs: shkn up to ld jst ins fnl f: pushed out)....— **1**
2330[5] Birchwood Sun **(58)***(64) (MDods)* 5-9-4b VHalliday(1) (chsd ldrs: sn drvn along: kpt on fnl f: no ch w wnr)....2½ **2**
2484[*] Kilnamartyra Girl **(49)***(55)*(Fav)*(JParkes)* 5-8-4 (5) 5x GFaulkner(3) (w ldrs: led over 3f out: hrd rdn & hdd jst ins fnl f: kpt on same pce)....nk **3**
2290[7] Star Performer (IRE) **(53)***(55) (MrsMReveley)* 4-8-10 (3) DDenby(4) (hld up: styd on fnl 2f: nt rch ldrs)....1¾ **4**
1355[3] Winter Scout (USA) **(64)***(59) (MrsMReveley)* 7-9-10 SCopp(9) (hld up: effrt over 2f out: nvr nr ldrs)....3 **5**
1873[4] Tolls Choice (IRE) **(55)***(50) (MWEasterby)* 6-8-12 (3) RuthCoulter(7) (s.i.s: hld up: hdwy ½-wy: edgd lft & wknd appr fnl f)....hd **6**
2425[3] Teejay'n'aitch (IRE) **(52)***(35) (JSGoldie)* 3-8-5 PFessey(6) (w ldrs: disp ld ½-wy to 2f out: sn wknd)....5 **7**

2276[2] Move Smartly (IRE) **(51)***(32) (FHLee)* 5-8-11v DGriffiths(8) (w ldrs: rdn & hung lft 2f out: sn lost pl)....¾ 8
Kummel King **(59)***(29) (EJAlston)* 7-9-5 PRoberts(2) (b: led tl over 3f out: edgd lft & sn lost pl)....5 9

9/4 Kilnamartyra Girl, **5/1** MR CUBE (IRE), **13/2** Winter Scout (USA), Move Smartly (IRE), **7/1** Teejay'n'aitch (IRE), **10/1** Birchwood Sun, Tolls Choice (IRE), **12/1** Star Performer (IRE), Kummel King (op 8/1), CSF £49.06 CT £130.57 TOTE £4.80: £2.00 £2.50 £1.30 (£36.70) Trio £26.10 OWNER Mr R. Miles (CHEPSTOW) BRED Lyonstown Stud 9 Rn

1m 30.88 (6.58) SF: 37/34/25/25/29/20/-/2/-

WEIGHT FOR AGE 3yo-7lb

STEWARDS' ENQUIRY Faulkner susp. 31/7-1/8/95 (excessive use of whip).

T/Plpt: £315.30 (26.72 Tckts). T/Qdpt: £10.20 (14.5 Tckts). WG

2574-NEWMARKET (R-H)
Saturday July 22nd (Good to firm, Good last 8f)
WEATHER: sunny WIND: almost nil

2612
FOOD BROKERS-GLOYSTARNE H'CAP (0-85) (4-Y.O+) (Class D) £4,935.00 (£1,470.00: £700.00: £315.00)
1m 6f 175y (July) Stalls: High GOING minus 0.48 sec per fur (F) 2-10 (2-11)

2119[4] **College Don (60)***(78) (MPBielby)* 4-8-9 (3) DRMcCabe(8) (hld up: rdn & chsd ldr over 2f out: styd on wl to ld ins fnl f)....— 1
2472[4] Eden's Close **(54)***(69) (MHTompkins)* 6-8-6v PRobinson(2) (led: clr 5f out: rdn over 1f out: hdd & unable qckn ins fnl f)....2½ 2
2069* Pharamineux **(66)***(69)*(Fav)*(RAkehurst)* 9-9-4 WRSwinburn(3) (lw: hld up: effrt 6f out: kpt on fnl 2f)....11 3
2238[3] Cuango (IRE) **(70)***(72)*(Fav)*(RHollinshead)* 4-9-8 WRyan(7) (lw: bhd: pushed along 6f out: styd on fnl 3f)....1¼ 4
2530* Midyan Blue (IRE) **(76)***(78) (JMPEustace)* 5-9-11 (3) 4x JStack(1) (chsd ldrs: rdn & outpcd 5f out: wknd 2f out)....nk 5
1623[5] Sharazi (USA) **(66)***(46) (DJSCosgrove)* 4-9-4 MRimmer(6) (rdn over 5f out: a bhd)....20 6
2450[15] Belgran (USA) **(48)** *(WMBrisbourne)* 6-8-0 ow7 AMcGlone(5) (chsd ldr 10f: sn wknd)....25 7
1840[27] Maradonna (USA) **(62)** *(JWhite)* 6-9-0 MFenton(4) (prom: shkn up whn broke leg & p.u 4f out: dead).... P

LONG HANDICAP Belgran (USA) 6-6

7/2 Cuango (IRE), Pharamineux, **4/1** Midyan Blue (IRE), **11/2** COLLEGE DON, **7/1** Maradonna (USA), **10/1** Eden's Close, **14/1** Sharazi (USA), **66/1** Belgran (USA), CSF £48.38 CT £180.94 TOTE £6.70: £1.50 £2.10 £1.50 (£28.60) OWNER Mr J. F. Coupland (GRIMSBY) BRED Chippenham Lodge Stud 8 Rn 3m 8.28 (2.28) SF: 46/37/37/40/46/14/-/-

2613
INVESCO H'CAP (0-80) (3-Y.O+) (Class D) £5,526.50 (£1,652.00: £791.00: £360.50) **1m (July)** Stalls: Low GOING minus 0.48 sec per fur (F) 2-45 (2-47)

2240[13] **Sheer Danzig (IRE) (71)***(82) (RWArmstrong)* 3-8-12 WRSwinburn(6) (chsd ldrs: pushed along 4f out: qcknd to ld ins fnl f)....— 1
2321[4] Mo-Addab (IRE) **(70)***(79) (ACStewart)* 5-9-5 MRoberts(7) (trckd ldrs: ev ch over 1f out tl unable qckn ins fnl f)....1¼ 2
1809[16] Reverand Thickness **(73)***(81) (SCWilliams)* 4-9-8 RHughes(5) (in tch: plld out over 1f out: r.o wl fnl f)....½ 3
2266[3] Zermatt (IRE) **(70)***(77) (MDIUsher)* 5-9-5 BThomson(8) (lw: prom: led 2f out tl hdd & no ex ins fnl f)....½ 4
2266[5] Dontforget Insight (IRE) **(72)***(78) (PFICole)* 4-9-7 GCarter(1) (b.hind: in tch: hdwy over 1f out: no ex ins fnl f)....½ 5
2103[12] Sarasota Storm **(66)***(66) (MBell)* 3-8-7 MFenton(13) (led 6f: wknd fnl f)....3 6
2206* Cutpurse Moll **(75)***(70) (JRFanshawe)* 3-9-2 DHarrison(2) (chsd ldrs: rdn over 2f out: wknd fnl f)....2½ 7
2345* Admirals Flame (IRE) **(75)***(64)*(Fav)*(CFWall)* 4-9-5 (5) LNewton(9) (b: chsd ldrs: ev ch wl over 1f out: wknd fnl f)....3 8
2269[6] Zingibar **(66)***(53) (BWHills)* 3-8-7b DHolland(4) (lw: b.off hind: hld up: effrt over 2f out: rdn & edgd lft over 1f out: sn wknd)....¾ 9
1967[4] Saltando (IRE) **(60)***(47) (PatMitchell)* 4-8-9 SO'Gorman(12) (chsd ldrs tl rdn & btn 3f out)....s.h 10
2321[9] Be Warned **(75)***(61) (NACallaghan)* 4-9-10b PaulEddery(3) (bhd: rdn over 2f out: nvr nr ldrs)....½ 11

1786[12] Try-Haitai (IRE) **(62)***(40) (RAkehurst)* 4-8-8 (3) SSanders(11) (prom: rdn over 2f out: sn wknd).4 **12**
Ruby Estate (IRE) **(60)***(30) (APJames)* 4-8-9 FNorton(10) (pushed along 4f out: sn bhd).........4 **13**

3/1 Admirals Flame (IRE), **4/1** Mo-Addab (IRE), **7/1** Zermatt (IRE), SHEER DANZIG (IRE), Cutpurse Moll, **10/1** Dontforget Insight (IRE), **20/1** Zingibar, Try-Haitai (IRE), Be Warned, **25/1** Reverand Thickness, Sarasota Storm, **33/1** Saltando (IRE), Ruby Estate (IRE), CSF £32.61 CT £600.89 TOTE £6.50: £1.90 £2.10 £7.20 (£14.40) Trio £124.40 OWNER Mr R. J. Arculli (NEWMARKET) BRED Mrs Max Morris 13 Rn 1m 37.94 (0.24) SF: 55/60/62/58/59/39/43/45/26/28/42/21/11
WEIGHT FOR AGE 3yo-8lb

2614 FOOD BROKERS APHRODITE STKS (Listed) (3-Y.O+ F & M) (Class A) £13,041.00 (£3,888.00: £1,854.00: £837.00)
1m 4f (July) Stalls: High GOING minus 0.48 sec per fur (F) 3-15 (3-15)

2341* **Hagwah (USA) (79)***(102) (BHanbury)* 3-8-4 MRoberts(2) (plld hrd: mde all: rdn & styd on wl appr fnl f)....................— **1**
2208* Tinashaan (IRE) **(90)***(99) (JRFanshawe)* 3-8-4 DHarrison(4) (lw: hld up: plld out 3f out: kpt on wl appr fnl f)....................2½ **2**
1867[2] Tillandsia (IRE) **(110)***(97)*(Fav)*(DRLoder)* 3-8-4 WRyan(5) (lw: chsd ldrs: rdn & no ex appr fnl f)....................1½ **3**
1800[2] Ellie Ardensky **(92)***(95) (JRFanshawe)* 3-8-4 BThomson(3) (hld up: rdn 3f out: no imp appr fnl f)....................1½ **4**
1704a[5] Llia **(100)***(81) (JLDunlop)* 3-8-4 GCarter(1) (plld hrd: prom tl rdn & wknd 3f out)....................10 **5**

10/11 Tillandsia (IRE) (4/6-Evens), **4/1** Tinashaan (IRE), **5/1** Llia, **15/2** HAGWAH (USA), **10/1** Ellie Ardensky (tchd 5/1), CSF £31.74 TOTE £5.50: £1.60 £2.30 (£13.50) OWNER Mr Abdullah Ali (NEWMARKET) BRED Gainsborough Farm Inc 5 Rn 2m 29.11 (0.41) SF: 47/44/42/40/26

2615 PRIMULA MAIDEN STKS (2-Y.O) (Class D) £4,620.00 (£1,380.00: £660.00: £300.00) **6f (July)** Stalls: Low GOING minus 0.48 sec per fur (F) 3-45 (3-47)

2182[5] **Akalim** *(77) (DMorley)* 2-9-0 WRyan(9) (mde all: rdn & hld on wl fnl f)....................— **1**
Do Not Disturb (USA) *(76+) (JLDunlop)* 2-9-0 GCarter(6) (neat: s.i.s: hdwy fnl 2f: fin wl).......nk **2**
Red Nymph *(69+) (WJarvis)* 2-8-9 BThomson(1) (leggy: scope: hld up: qcknd to chal wl over 1f out: wknd ins fnl f)....................1 **3**
2058[4] Shock-A-Lot (IRE) *(63) (GLewis)* 2-9-0 PaulEddery(5) (chsd ldrs: outpcd fnl 2f)....................4 **4**
2408[13] Sticks Mckenzie *(63) (BWHills)* 2-9-0 SWhitworth(4) (in tch: sn pushed along: no imp fnl 2f) hd **5**
Wee Hope (USA) *(61)*(Fav)*(MRStoute)* 2-9-0 WRSwinburn(3) (gd sort: bit bkwd: prom tl wknd 2f out: eased whn btn)....................¾ **6**
1443[6] Film Buff *(50) (BWHills)* 2-8-2 (7) GBrace(10) (lw: racd centre: dwlt: effrt over 2f out: n.d) 2 **7**
Stoney End (USA) *(52) (MRChannon)* 2-9-0 RHughes(11) (wl grwn: bkwd: s.i.s: nvr trbld ldrs)....................1¼ **8**
Samuel Scott *(48) (MBell)* 2-9-0 MFenton(12) (gd sort: s.i.s: sn chsng ldrs: wknd 2f out).....1½ **9**
Generous Present *(21) (JWPayne)* 2-9-0 AMcGlone(7) (w'like: chsd ldrs 3f)....................10 **10**
Munakeb (FR) *(RWArmstrong)* 2-9-0 MRimmer(8) (Withdrawn not under Starter's orders)..... **W**

9/4 Wee Hope (USA), **3/1** Stoney End (USA), **5/1** Red Nymph, **7/1** Do Not Disturb (USA), **8/1** AKALIM, Munakeb (FR), **10/1** Shock-A-Lot (IRE), **14/1** Film Buff, Samuel Scott, **16/1** Sticks Mckenzie, **25/1** Generous Present, CSF £62.29 TOTE £14.30: £2.80 £2.20 £1.90 (£36.60) Trio £182.10 OWNER Mr Hamdan Al Maktoum (NEWMARKET) BRED R. Powell-Tuck and Partners 10 Rn 1m 12.66 (1.16) SF: 42/41/34/28/28/26/15/17/13/-/-

2616 FOOD BROKERS ANIMAL HEALTH TRUST TROPHY H'CAP (0-100) (3-Y.O) (Class B) £17,150.00 (£6,350.00: £3,050.00: £1,250.00: £500.00: £200.00)
1m (July) Stalls: Low GOING minus 0.48 sec per fur (F) 4-15 (4-15)

1839[7] **Restructure (IRE) (92)***(102)*(Fav)*(MrsJCecil)* 3-9-1 PaulEddery(11) (a.p: led 2f out tl over 1f out: led ins fnl f: drvn out)....................— **1**
1839[5] Bin Rosie **(93)***(103) (DRLoder)* 3-8-13v(3) DRMcCabe(2) (trckd ldrs: led over 1f out tl ins fnl f: r.o wl)....................s.h **2**
1851[26] Hoh Express **(96)***(101) (IABalding)* 3-9-5 MRoberts(6) (plld hrd in tch: hdwy 2f out: r.o)........2½ **3**
2006[3] Blue Zulu (IRE) **(91)***(94) (JRFanshawe)* 3-9-0 DHarrison(5) (hld up & bhd: hdwy 2f out: r.o wl ins fnl f)....................1 **4**
2240[7] Stone Ridge (IRE) **(87)***(86)*(Fav)*(RHannon)* 3-8-10 RHughes(3) (stdd s: hdwy over 2f out: no imp fnl f)....................2 **5**
1941[2] Te Amo (IRE) **(84)***(83) (RAkehurst)* 3-8-4 (3) SSanders(4) (w ldr 6f)....................s.h **6**
2325[2] Doctor's Glory (USA) **(84)***(77) (RHannon)* 3-8-7 BThomson(1) (hld up: effrt 3f out: nvr rchd ldrs)....................3 **7**

2348[11] Nigel's Lad (IRE) **(84)***(71) (PCHaslam)* 3-8-7 GCarter(7) (prom tl wknd over 2f out)..................3 8
2121[3] Sotoboy (IRE) **(93)***(80) (PWHarris)* 3-9-2 MFenton(9) (in tch over 5f)..................s.h 9
1754[9] Jibereen **(86)***(67) (GLewis)* 3-8-9 SWhitworth(8) (led 6f: sn wknd)..................3 10
2369[19] Done Well (USA) **(98)***(77) (EALDunlop)* 3-9-7 WRSwinburn(10) (hld up: gd hdwy over 3f out: wknd 2f out)..................1 11

LONG HANDICAP Nigel's Lad (IRE) 8-6 Te Amo (IRE) 8-5

9/2 RESTRUCTURE (IRE), Stone Ridge (IRE), **6/1** Hoh Express, Bin Rosie, **7/1** Blue Zulu (IRE), **15/2** Done Well (USA) (op 14/1), **8/1** Doctor's Glory (USA), **9/1** Te Amo (IRE), **10/1** Sotoboy (IRE), **20/1** Jibereen, Nigel's Lad (IRE), CSF £32.23 CT £152.80 TOTE £4.60: £2.20 £2.80 £2.90 (£9.70) Trio £37.80 OWNER Mr Martin Myers (NEWMARKET) BRED J. H. Stone 11 Rn

1m 37.43 (-0.27) SF: 63/64/62/55/47/44/38/32/41/28/38

2617 CHEMIST BROKERS - SALON SELECTIVES H'CAP (0-100) (3-Y.O+) (Class C) £5,692.00 (£1,696.00: £808.00: £364.00)

5f (July) Stalls: Low GOING minus 0.48 sec per fur (F) 4-45 (4-45)

2060[2] **Sweet Magic (81)***(87)*(Fav)*(LJHolt)* 4-8-11 AMcGlone(5) (led over 1f: led over 1f out: rdn fnl f: all out)..................— 1
2060[6] Princess Oberon (IRE) **(85)***(91) (MBell)* 5-9-1 MFenton(6) (hld up: hdwy wl over 1f out: r.o wl ins fnl f: jst failed)..................s.h 2
2150[2] Ansellman **(73)***(72) (JBerry)* 5-8-3 GCarter(2) (chsd ldrs: no hdwy fnl 2f)..................2 3
2418[5] Master Planner **(98)***(95) (CACyzer)* 6-10-0 DBiggs(4) (lw: outpcd after 2f: r.o wl appr fnl f).....¾ 4
2324[5] Fairy Wind (IRE) **(85)***(71) (NACallaghan)* 3-8-5 (5) MHenry(1) (b.hind: dwlt: led over 3f out tl over 1f out: sn wknd)..................3½ 5
Inherent Magic (IRE) **(92)***(65) (WRMuir)* 6-9-8 WRSwinburn(3) (b: spd 3f)..................4 6

9/4 SWEET MAGIC, **5/2** Fairy Wind (IRE) (op 6/4), **4/1** Princess Oberon (IRE), **13/2** Ansellman, **9/1** Master Planner (op 6/1), **10/1** Inherent Magic (IRE), CSF £10.74 TOTE £2.80 £1.90 £2.30 (£7.40) OWNER Mrs John Crawford (BASINGSTOKE) BRED Miss K. S. Waddington 6 Rn

58.12 secs (0.40 under best) (-0.88) SF: 70/74/55/78/49/48

WEIGHT FOR AGE 3yo-5lb

2618 CHEMIST BROKERS CONDITIONS STKS (2-Y.O) (Class C) £5,276.80 (£1,820.80: £870.40: £352.00)

5f (July) Stalls: Low GOING minus 0.48 sec per fur (F) 5-20 (5-20)

2442[8] **Maggi For Margaret** *(85) (MRChannon)* 2-8-9 RHughes(1) (w ldr: led over 2f out: rdn over 1f out: eased nr fin)..................— 1
2095* Atraf *(85)*(Fav)*(DMorley)* 2-9-0 WRyan(2) (lw: hld up: rdn & r.o fnl f)..................1½ 2
2242[6] Arctic Romancer (IRE) *(79) (GLewis)* 2-8-10 PaulEddery(4) (hld up: hdwy over 1f out: no ex fnl f)..................¾ 3
2435[W] Hoh Majestic (IRE) *(76) (MBell)* 2-8-10b MFenton(3) (led over 2f: wknd fnl f)..................¾ 4

11/10 Atraf (Evens-5/4), **9/4** MAGGI FOR MARGARET, **7/2** Arctic Romancer (IRE) (op 9/4), **7/1** Hoh Majestic (IRE) (4/1-8/1), CSF £5.11 TOTE £3.30 (£2.10) OWNER Mr Michael Foy (UPPER LAMBOURN) BRED Brook Stud Ltd 4 Rn

59.22 secs (0.22) SF: -/-/-/-

T/Jkpt: Not won; £22,978.43 to 24/7/95. T/Plpt: £813.2 Tckts). T/Qdpt: £46.70 (6.05 Tckts). Dk

2308-RIPON (R-H)

Saturday July 22nd (Good to firm)

WEATHER: sunny WIND: fresh across

2619 E.B.F. KILBURN WHITE HORSE APPEAL MAIDEN STKS (2-Y.O) (Class D) £4,182.00 (£1,266.00: £618.00: £294.00)

5f Stalls: Centre GOING minus 0.21 sec per fur (GF) 2-35 (2-37)

2412[2] **My Branch** *(72+)*(Fav)*(BWHills)* 2-8-4 (5) JDSmith(3) (lw: chsd ldrs: led 2f out: sn qcknd clr)..................— 1
1620[7] Sepoy (IRE) *(61) (CWThornton)* 2-9-0 DeanMcKeown(4) (b: plld hrd: hdwy ½-wy: styd on wl: no ch w wnr)..................5 2
2143[8] Katie Komaite *(46) (CaptJWilson)* 2-8-9 JFortune(5) (led 3f: r.o one pce)..................3 3
2259[3] Silver Welcome *(50) (MHEasterby)* 2-9-0 SMaloney(1) (bhd tl hdwy over 1f out: put hd in air: r.o)..................nk 4
1685[5] Power Game *(47) (JBerry)* 2-9-0 JCarroll(6) (chsd ldrs tl rdn & btn 2f out)..................1 5
Privileged *(46+) (MrsJRRamsden)* 2-9-0 KFallon(9) (cmpt: scope: dwlt: wl bhd tl r.o strly fnl f)..................nk 6

5337 Goretski (IRE) *(42) (NTinkler)* 2-9-0 KDarley(10) (prom: nt qckn fnl 2f) 1½ **7**
18574 Soul of Honour (FR) *(34) (MrsJRRamsden)* 2-9-0 MDeering(11) (lw: prom 3f: wknd) 2½ **8**
Golden Tyke (IRE) *(27) (MDHammond)* 2-9-0 DaleGibson(8) (leggy: scope: lw: drvn along thrght: nvr able to chal) 2 **9**
78811 Kiwud *(11) (GMMoore)* 2-8-6 (3) JTate(7) (spd 3f: sn lost pl) 3½ **10**
23023 Fancy Clancy *(5) (MissLCSiddall)* 2-8-9 GHind(2) (prom to ½-wy: sn bhd) 2 **11**

4/6 MY BRANCH (4/7-8/1), **4/1** Power Game, **11/1** Sepoy (IRE) (20/1-33/1), **12/1** Privileged (op 6/1), Golden Tyke (IRE), **14/1** Soul of Honour (FR) (op 8/1), **20/1** Goretski (IRE), Fancy Clancy, Silver Welcome, **33/1** Kiwud, Katie Komaite, CSF £10.64 TOTE £1.70: £1.10 £6.00 £4.20 (£15.10) Trio £191.30; £13.47 to 24/7/95. OWNER Mr Wafic Said (LAMBOURN) BRED Addison Racing Ltd Inc 11 Rn
60.0 secs (2.00) SF: 42/31/16/20/17/16/12/4/-/-/-

2620 CENTAUR CENTENARY (S) STKS (3-Y.O+) (Class F) £2,570.00 (£770.00: £370.00: £170.00) **1m** Stalls: High GOING minus 0.21 sec per fur (GF) 3-05 (3-05)

25035 **Proud Image (63)***(69)*(Fav)*(APJarvis)* 3-8-8v KDarley(10) (lw: chsd ldr: led wl over 2f out: r.o) ....— **1**
232111 Battle Colours (IRE) **(50)***(68) (DonEnricoIncisa)* 6-9-7 KimTinkler(11) (lw: led over 5f: kpt on u.p) 3 **2**
24995 Khan **(55)***(60) (CWThornton)* 3-8-8 DeanMcKeown(6) (a chsng ldrs: no imp whn sltly hmpd 1f out) 1¾ **3**
23078 Moofaji **(55)***(58) (FWatson)* 4-9-2 SMaloney(9) (a chsng ldrs: one pce fnl 3f) 1 **4**
18088 Roseate Lodge **(60)***(60) (NBycroft)* 9-9-4 (3) JTate(3) (lw: hld up & bhd: hdwy 3f out: nvr rchd ldrs) 1½ **5**
*1880*7 Wordsmith (IRE) **(41)***(48) (JLHarris)* 5-9-7 KFallon(8) (lw: bhd tl styd on fnl 2f) 6 **6**
22549 Canny Lad **(25)***(37) (MPBielby)* 5-9-2v JCarroll(2) (bhd: shkn up 4f out: no imp) 3 **7**
*363*6 Komlucky **(47)***(32) (FJO'Mahony)* 3-8-8 AMackay(7) (b: prom tl wknd fnl 3f) 2½ **8**
19986 Musical March **(30)***(26) (EWeymes)* 4-8-11 GHind(5) (nvr nr ldrs) ....hd **9**
164710 Gamzatti **(23)***(16) (CBBBooth)* 4-8-11v JFortune(4) (nvr bttr than mid div) 5 **10**
23096 Brandon Lane *(19) (RMWhitaker)* 4-9-2 DaleGibson(1) (bhd: effrt ½-wy: n.d) 1 **11**

6/4 PROUD IMAGE, **5/2** Roseate Lodge, **4/1** Khan, **12/1** Moofaji, **14/1** Battle Colours (IRE), Komlucky, **16/1** Wordsmith (IRE), **20/1** Brandon Lane, **25/1** Gamzatti, Musical March, **33/1** Canny Lad, CSF £24.40 TOTE £2.40: £1.30 £2.80 £1.70 (£16.90) Trio £37.30 OWNER Mr L. Fust (ASTON UPTHORPE) BRED Miss S. E. Jarvis 11 Rn 1m 41.2 (3.50) SF: 40/47/31/37/39/27/16/3/5/-/-
WEIGHT FOR AGE 3yo-8lb
No bid

2621 LEEDS HOSPITAL FUND H'CAP (0-80) (3-Y.O+) (Class D) £4,175.00 (£1,250.00: £600.00: £275.00) **1m 2f** Stalls: High GOING minus 0.21 sec per fur (GF) 3-35 (3-36)

2167* **Future Act (USA) (80)***(96++)*(Fav)*(HRACecil)* 3-9-12 GHind(4) (lw: trckd ldr: led over 3f out: sn clr: easily) ....— **1**
110210 Gallardini (IRE) **(52)***(57) (BSRothwell)* 6-8-8 LCharnock(1) (a chsng ldrs: outpcd 3f out: styd on wl nr fin: no ch w wnr) 7 **2**
2373* Durano **(66)***(71) (MHEasterby)* 4-9-8 SMaloney(3) (hld up: effrt 4f out: rdn & one pce fnl 2f)..hd **3**
22092 Blaze of Oak (USA) **(69)***(71) (WJHaggas)* 4-9-11 KDarley(2) (lw: led tl over 3f out: sn rdn & btn) 1½ **4**
16519 Braille (IRE) **(61)***(62) (MGMeagher)* 4-9-3 JFortune(5) (in tch tl outpcd over 3f out: kpt on nr fin) ....½ **5**
25557 Sea Victor **(78)***(68) (JLHarris)* 3-9-10 KFallon(7) (a bhd) 7 **6**
16667 Mca Below the Line **(60)***(46) (JLEyre)* 7-8-13 (3) JTate(6) (a wl bhd) 2½ **7**

8/11 FUTURE ACT (USA) (op Evens), **7/2** Blaze of Oak (USA), **4/1** Durano, **12/1** Braille (IRE) (tchd 8/1), **14/1** Sea Victor, **16/1** Mca Below the Line, **25/1** Gallardini (IRE), CSF £18.24 TOTE £1.80: £1.20 £5.40 (£26.10) OWNER Buckram Oak Holdings (NEWMARKET) BRED Cabin Creek Farm 7 Rn
2m 6.9 (3.40) SF: 65/36/50/50/41/37/25
WEIGHT FOR AGE 3yo-10lb

2622 LEEDS AND HOLBECK BUILDING SOCIETY BELL-RINGER H'CAP (0-95) (3-Y.O+) (Class C) £7,010.00 (£2,105.00: £1,015.00: £470.00) **1m 4f 60y** Stalls: High GOING minus 0.21 sec per fur (GF) 4-05 (4-05)

2427* **Tessajoe (69)***(78) (MJCamacho)* 3-9-6 LCharnock(1) (lw: hld up: smooth hdwy over 2f out: led appr fnl f: hrd rdn & r.o) ....— **1**
11942 Top Lady (IRE) **(69)***(78)*(Fav)*(MRStoute)* 3-9-3 (3) JTate(3) (lw: trckd ldr: led over 3f out: sn rdn: hdd over 1f out: rallied) ....s.h **2**

1681³ Eau de Cologne **(70)***(76) (CWThornton)* 3-9-7 AMackay(4) (bhd: hdwy 3f out: kpt on wl fnl f: nvr able to chal)........2 3
2391² Pride of May (IRE) **(61)***(62) (CWFairhurst)* 4-9-10b DeanMcKeown(2) (led tl over 3f out: outpcd appr fnl f)........4 4

4/6 Top Lady (IRE), **9/4** TESSAJOE, **8/1** Eau de Cologne (op 9/2), Pride of May (IRE), CSF £4.10 TOTE £3.60: (£1.60) OWNER Riley Partnership (MALTON) BRED A. and Mrs Rhodes 4 Rn
2m 41.0 (7.00) SF: 42/42/40/38
WEIGHT FOR AGE 3yo-12lb

2623

CONTINUUM-RA MEDIAN AUCTION MAIDEN STKS (3-Y.O) (Class E) £3,210.00 (£960.00: £460.00: £210.00)
1m 1f Stalls: High GOING minus 0.21 sec per fur (GF) 4-35 (4-36)

362² **Hand Woven** *(79) (WJHaggas)* 3-9-0 KDarley(1) (lw: hld up: hdwy 3f out: led wl over 1f out: r.o)........— 1
2583⁵ Reefa's Mill (IRE) **(76)***(78) (JWHills)* 3-8-9 (5) HKYim(4) (lw: trckd ldrs: outpcd over 3f out: hdwy over 1f out: r.o)........½ 2
1615³ Karaar *(69)*(Fav)*(JHMGosden)* 3-9-0 GHind(2) (lw: trckd ldr: led 3f out: hdd wl over 1f out: rdn & fnd nil)........5 3
2208⁷ Chalky Dancer *(55) (HJCollingridge)* 3-9-0 KFallon(3) (led to 3f out: ev ch tl wknd wl over 1f out)........8 4

8/15 Karaar, **3/1** HAND WOVEN, **5/1** Reefa's Mill (IRE), **25/1** Chalky Dancer, CSF £14.14 TOTE £4.00: (£6.60) OWNER Mrs M. M. Haggas (NEWMARKET) BRED Waverton Farm (Stow) 4 Rn
1m 55.2 (5.00) SF: 25/24/15/1

OFFICIAL EXPLANATION **Karaar: the jockey reported that the colt had not let himself down on the ground.**

2624

HARTWELL MOTOR CONTRACTS MAIDEN H'CAP (0-70) (3-Y.O+) (Class E) £3,210.00 (£960.00: £460.00: £210.00)
6f Stalls: Centre GOING minus 0.21 sec per fur (GF) 5-05 (5-06)

2428³ **Rossini Blue (68)***(73) (MrsJRRamsden)* 4-10-0 KFallon(2) (racd stands' side: hdwy 3f out: r.o u.p to ld wl ins fnl f)........— 1
2500⁵ Quilling **(68)***(71) (MDods)* 3-9-3v(5) CTeague(11) (lw: prom: led far side 1f out: hdd & nt qckn nr fin)........¾ 2
789⁴ Michellisa **(51)***(50) (JDBethell)* 4-8-6 (5) JDSmith(8) (lw: cl up far side: led 3f out to 1f out: nt qckn)........1½ 3
2377⁹ Bali Tender **(39)***(34) (MWEasterby)* 4-7-6 (7) MartinDwyer(9) (cl up far side: wandered u.p ½-wy: kpt on one pce)........1½ 4
1882⁵ Cemaes Bay **(70)***(64) (JBerry)* 3-9-3 (7) CLowther(1) (led stands' side over 4f: sn wknd)........½ 5
2502¹¹ Secret Miss **(51)***(45) (APJarvis)* 3-8-2 (3) JTate(3) (racd stands' side: spd 4f: sn wknd)........s.h 6
2191⁵ Saltz (IRE) **(54)***(47) (PTDalton)* 3-8-3 (5) HKYim(7) (sme hdwy 2f out: no imp)........nk 7
2363³ Trina **(36)***(22) (DLWilliams)* 4-7-10 ow1 AMackay(12) (lw: chsd ldrs far side over 4f)........2 8
1371⁴ Best of Bold **(67)***(54)*(Fav)*(NAGraham)* 3-9-7 JFortune(10) (nvr trbld ldrs)........hd 9
2220⁴ Monkey Face **(39)***(25) (JHetherton)* 4-7-13 NKennedy(5) (cl up far side tl wknd wl over 1f out)........nk 10
2310¹² Coney Hills **(36)***(19) (NBycroft)* 4-7-7 (3)ow3 DarrenMoffatt(13) (spd far side to ½-wy: sn wknd)........s.h 11
2071⁹ Samsung Lovelylady (IRE) **(50)***(33) (EWeymes)* 3-8-4 JMarshall(4) (lw: swtchd rt after s & racd far side: n.d)........1¼ 12
2084² Skiptamaloo **(33)***(15) (DonEnricoIncisa)* 4-7-7b KimTinkler(6) (lw: outpcd far side fr ½-wy)........½ 13
2502⁶ Younger Days (IRE) **(41)***(13) (MartynWane)* 4-7-8 (7)ow8 FLynch(14) (led far side to ½-wy: sn wknd)........½ 14

LONG HANDICAP Coney Hills 6-12 Skiptamaloo 7-4 Younger Days (IRE) 7-6

5/2 Best of Bold, **11/2** Trina, **6/1** ROSSINI BLUE, **7/1** Michellisa, **9/1** Secret Miss, Cemaes Bay, Quilling, **11/1** Saltz (IRE), **14/1** Monkey Face, Skiptamaloo, Samsung Lovelylady (IRE), **20/1** Younger Days (IRE), **25/1** Bali Tender, **33/1** Coney Hills, CSF £62.91 CT £373.79 TOTE £6.20: £2.60 £3.50 £1.90 (£37.00) Trio £57.50 OWNER Richard Flood Bloodstock Ltd (THIRSK) BRED Castle Farm Stud 14 Rn 1m 12.9 (2.70) SF: 55/47/32/16/40/21/23/4/30/7/1/9/-/-
WEIGHT FOR AGE 3yo-6lb

T/Plpt: £184.70 (45.47 Tckts). T/Qdpt: £96.30 (0.8 Tckts). AA

2377-SOUTHWELL (L-H)
Saturday July 22nd (Standard)

WEATHER: cloudy WIND: slt bhd

2625

DUBONNET MEDIAN AUCTION MAIDEN STKS (2-Y.O) (Class F) £2,519.00 (£694.00: £329.00)
7f (Fibresand) Stalls: Low GOING minus 0.05 sec per fur (STD) 6-10 (6-13)

2380^{2} **Ebony Boy** *(64)*(Fav)*(JWharton)* 2-9-0 JWilliams(6) (lw: mde all: rdn over 1f out: all out) .....— **1**
2192^{11} Sedbergh (USA) *(59) (MrsMReveley)* 2-9-0 MWigham(2) (lw: prom: chsd wnr over 4f out: 2nd st: rdn over 1f out: no imp) 2 **2**
Blenheim Terrace *(48) (CBBBooth)* 2-9-0 ACulhane(4) (lt-f: chsd ldrs: 3rd st: hrd rdn over 1f out: wknd fnl f) 5 **3**
2485^{8} Clued Up *(32) (MHEasterby)* 2-8-9 SMaloney(1) (prom: 4th & rdn st: sn wknd) 5 **4**
Let's Hang On (IRE) *(WWHaigh)* 2-8-9 DaleGibson(5) (neat: bkwd: s.i.s: sn outpcd & bhd: 6th & t.o st) 25 **5**
2336^{5} Tartan Express (IRE) *(BAPearce)* 2-9-0 StephenDavies(7) (prom tl 5th & wkng st) 2 **6**

4/7 EBONY BOY, **11/2** Sedbergh (USA) (7/2-6/1), **9/1** Clued Up (op 6/1), **10/1** Blenheim Terrace, Let's Hang On (IRE) (op 5/1), **14/1** Tartan Express (IRE), CSF £4.31 TOTE £1.50 £1.10 £2.30 (£2.70) OWNER Mr P. W. Lambert (MELTON MOWBRAY) BRED D. R. Botterill 6 Rn

1m 34.0 (7.20) SF: 13/8/-/-/-/-

2626

B & K BUILDING SERVICES CLAIMING MAIDEN STKS (3-Y.O+) (Class F) £2,519.00 (£694.00: £329.00)
1m 4f (Fibresand) Stalls: High GOING minus 0.05 sec per fur (STD) 6-40 (6-42)

2378^{3} **Red Phantom (IRE)** *(71) (SMellor)* 3-8-12 MWigham(5) (hld up: hdwy over 6f out: 2nd st: led over 2f out: styd on u.p) ....— **1**
2279^{9} Oleron **(52)***(56) (JNorton)* 3-8-1 DaleGibson(1) (mid div: 3rd st: ev ch fr 2f out tl no ex fnl f).....3 **2**
2378^{W} Be My Choice *(55)*(Fav)*(MrsJCecil)* 3-8-5 GHind(3) (lw: chsd ldrs: outpcd 8f out: hdwy over 4f out: 4th st: styd on same pce fnl 2f) 4 **3**
355^{4} Aviator's Dream **(43)***(49) (JPearce)* 5-8-12 JWilliams(2) (s.i.s: outpcd & bhd: hdwy 7f out: 5th st: rdn 2f out: styd on same pce) ....nk **4**
2378^{6} Lady Kuynder **(25)***(28) (DrJDScargill)* 3-7-2 (5) MBaird(6) (chsd ldrs: led over 5f out: hdd over 2f out: sn hrd rdn & wknd) 11 **5**
1718^{14} Ace Chapel (IRE) **(36)***(6) (CCElsey)* 3-7-12 JFanning(7) (prom: drvn along 4f out: 6th & btn st) 20 **6**
2495^{10} Canary Blue (IRE) **(39)** *(JGMO'Shea)* 4-8-7 DeanMcKeown(4) (chsd ldrs tl wknd over 4f out) 2½ **7**
2378^{W} Anchor Crown *(JRJenkins)* 3-7-4 (7) CAdamson(8) (led over 6f: grad wknd) 20 **8**

11/8 Be My Choice, **85/40** RED PHANTOM (IRE), **13/2** Aviator's Dream, **12/1** Oleron, **14/1** Ace Chapel (IRE), Canary Blue (IRE), **20/1** Lady Kuynder, Anchor Crown, CSF £24.90 TOTE £2.70: £1.10 £2.10 (£21.10) OWNER Mr Stan Mellor (SWINDON) BRED K. and Mrs CULLEN 8 Rn

2m 45.2 (11.00) SF: 22/7/6/12/-/-/-/-
WEIGHT FOR AGE 3yo-12lb

2627

FIBRESAND H'CAP (0-60) (3-Y.O+) (Class F) £3,199.40 (£888.40: £426.20)
5f (Fibresand) Stalls: High GOING minus 0.05 sec per fur (STD) 7-10 (7-11)

2475^{*} **Shadow Jury (65)***(75) (DWChapman)* 5-10-5b 7x LCharnock(6) (chsd ldrs: led ins fnl f: r.o wl) ....— **1**
2372^{*} Freckles Kelly **(44)***(53) (MHEasterby)* 3-8-7 SMaloney(11) (a.p: ev ch over 1f out: r.o)....nk **2**
1565^{5} The Real Whizzbang (IRE) **(47)***(50) (PSFelgate)* 4-8-12b(3) PMcCabe(2) (led tl hdd & unable qckn ins fnl f) 2 **3**
2492^{2} Southern Dominion **(50)***(53)*(Fav)*(MJohnston)* 3-8-13 DHolland(12) (lw: w ldrs: rdn over 1f out: styd on same pce) ....s.h **4**
2463^{2} Cheeky Chappy **(37)***(35) (DWChapman)* 4-8-5b ACulhane(7) (lw: chsd ldrs: rdn over 1f out: no imp) 1½ **5**
2402^{*} Tommy Tempest **(43)***(39) (REPeacock)* 6-8-4v(7) GMitchell(1) (chsd ldrs tl outpcd fnl f)....½ **6**
1445^{6} Name That Tune **(43)***(31) (CJHill)* 3-8-6 DeanMcKeown(5) (nvr rchd ldrs) 2½ **7**
583^{9} Superlativemaximus (IRE) **(60)***(45) (JABennett)* 7-10-0 TSprake(4) (b: bit bkwd: chsd ldrs over 3f) 1 **8**
2364^{6} Grey Toppa **(38)***(22) (NPLittmoden)* 4-7-13 (7) CAdamson(8) (outpcd fr ½-wy) ....nk **9**
2497^{7} Truly Madly Deeply **(40)***(24) (JAHarris)* 3-8-3 JFanning(13) (s.i.s: sn outpcd & bhd)....hd **10**
Pretty Average **(30)***(10) (BRichmond)* 5-7-12 ClaireBalding(3) (bkwd: spd to ½-wy) 1¼ **11**

*1789*7 Pat Poindestres **(30)** *(BAPearce)* 5-7-12 StephenDavies(9) (b: prom to ½-wy) 10 **12**
1975 14 Rotherfield Park (IRE) **(46)** *(CSmith)* 3-8-9 GHind(10) (s.i.s: a outpcd) 3½ **13**

5/2 Southern Dominion (op 5/1), **4/1** SHADOW JURY, Name That Tune, **7/1** Freckles Kelly, **8/1** The Real Whizzbang (IRE), **9/1** Cheeky Chappy (8/1-12/1), **10/1** Tommy Tempest, **12/1** Rotherfield Park (IRE) (tchd 8/1), **16/1** Grey Toppa, **20/1** Superlativemaximus (IRE), **25/1** Pretty Average, **33/1** Pat Poindestres, Truly Madly Deeply, CSF £35.07 CT £210.38 TOTE £5.30: £1.90 £2.50 £2.80 (£28.10) Trio £30.10 OWNER Mrs Jeanne Chapman (YORK) BRED J. S. Bell 13 Rn
59.3 secs (1.30) SF: 58/31/33/31/18/22/9/28/5/2/-/-/-
WEIGHT FOR AGE 3yo-5lb

2628

MAUN MOTORS H'CAP (0-70) (3-Y.O+) (Class E) £3,388.00 (£1,012.00: £484.00: £220.00) **7f (Fibresand)** Stalls: Low GOING minus 0.05 sec (STD) 7-40 (7-42)

*2073*9 **Ism (63)***(71) (MajorWRHern)* 3-9-4 TSprake(4) (chsd ldrs: led over 3f out: rdn out) ......— **1**
*2383*9 Cheerful Groom (IRE) **(39)***(42) (JMackie)* 4-8-1 GHind(5) (hld up in tch: 4th st: chsd wnr 2f out: styd on u.p) 2 **2**
2282 7 Top Fella (USA) **(58)***(57) (WAO'Gorman)* 3-8-13v EmmaO'Gorman(6) (trckd ldrs: chal & 5th st: sn outpcd: rdn over 1f out: no imp) 1¾ **3**
*2377*2 First Gold **(59)***(57)*(Fav)*(JWharton)* 6-9-7 JWilliams(2) (lw: hld up in tch: 6th st: nvr able to chal) ......¾ **4**
2390 7 Shuttlecock **(62)***(44) (MrsNMacauley)* 4-9-10 DeanMcKeown(1) (lw: led over 3f: 3rd st: sn rdn & wknd) 7 **5**
*2383*7 Abigails Boy (HOL) **(40)***(18) (DrJDScargill)* 6-8-2b JFanning(7) (chsd ldrs: 2nd st: rdn & wknd 2f out) 1½ **6**
1599 11 Bells of Longwick **(61)***(26) (WWHaigh)* 6-9-9 DaleGibson(3) (a in rr) 6 **7**

85/40 First Gold, **7/2** Top Fella (USA), **5/1** ISM, **6/1** Shuttlecock, **13/2** Abigails Boy (HOL), **8/1** Bells of Longwick, **12/1** Cheerful Groom (IRE) (8/1-14/1), CSF £51.61 TOTE £5.80: £2.50 £4.70 (£47.10) OWNER Mrs W. R. Hern (LAMBOURN) BRED Mrs R. D. Peacock 7 Rn
1m 31.9 (5.10) SF: 40/18/26/33/20/-/2
WEIGHT FOR AGE 3yo-7lb

2629

EAST MIDLANDS ELECTRICITY-LINCOLN (S) STKS (2-Y.O) (Class G) £2,489.40 (£688.40: £328.20)
6f (Fibresand) Stalls: Low GOING minus 0.05 sec per fur (STD) 8-10 (8-11)

2195 6 **Ticka Ticka Timing** *(69?) (BWMurray)* 2-8-8 (3) PMcCabe(10) (hld up: hdwy over 2f out: led ins fnl f: rdn out) ......— **1**
*2382** Morning Surprise *(68)*(Fav)*(APJarvis)* 2-8-4 (7) CAdamson(9) (hld up: hdwy over 2f out: r.o ins fnl f) ......nk **2**
2431 6 Magic Lake *(47) (WJHaggas)* 2-8-6 DHolland(4) (b.off hind: led over 1f: led over 2f out: hdd & wknd ins fnl f) 6 **3**
2302 4 Efipetite *(47) (NBycroft)* 2-8-6 SMaloney(7) (trckd ldrs: rdn over 1f out: r.o one pce) ......s.h **4**
2155 4 Don't Tell Anyone *(31) (JBerry)* 2-8-11 GHind(1) (chsd ldr: led over 4f out tl over 2f out: wknd fnl f) 8 **5**
Craigmore Magic (USA) *(30) (MissMKMilligan)* 2-8-11 JFanning(8) (w'like: nvr trbld ldrs) ......nk **6**
2447 7 Marmy *(22) (MHEasterby)* 2-8-6b DeanMcKeown(6) (chsd ldrs over 3f) 1 **7**
2023 6 Cawdor Lady *(4) (TJEtherington)* 2-8-6 LCharnock(5) (chsd ldrs 4f) 7 **8**
Farida Seconda *(JBalding)* 2-8-6 ClaireBalding(2) (leggy: bkwd: outpcd fr ½-wy: t.o) 30 **9**
*2381*9 Timson *(JPLeigh)* 2-8-11 ACulhane(3) (outpcd: t.o) ......dist **10**

2/1 Morning Surprise, **7/2** Magic Lake, **6/1** Marmy, Cawdor Lady, **8/1** Don't Tell Anyone, **12/1** Efipetite, **14/1** Craigmore Magic (USA) (20/1-33/1), **16/1** Timson, **25/1** Farida Seconda, **33/1** TICKA TICKA TIMING, CSF £96.98 TOTE £24.70: £7.10 £1.40 £2.00 (£109.30) Trio £111.50; £117.80 to 24/7/95. OWNER Mrs M. Lingwood (MALTON) BRED Mrs M. Lingwood 10 Rn
1m 19.7 (6.20) SF: 9/8/-/-/-/-/-/-/-/-
No bid; Magic Lake clmd PEbdon £6,000

2630

WHISKY H'CAP (0-60) (3-Y.O+ F & M) (Class F) £2,519.00 (£694.00: £329.00)
1m 4f (Fibresand) Stalls: High GOING minus 0.05 sec per fur (STD) 8-40 (8-41)

1957 8 **Philmist (48)***(55) (CWCElsey)* 3-8-12 NKennedy(14) (bhd: hdwy over 4f out: 4th st: r.o u.p to ld last strides) ......— **1**
*2292*2 Fen Terrier **(55)***(62)*(Fav)*(WJHaggas)* 3-9-0 (5) MHenry(12) (hld up: hdwy over 4f out: 2nd st: led 2f out: hdd post) ......s.h **2**
2282 3 Silver Rondo (USA) **(51)***(55) (LordHuntingdon)* 3-9-1 JWilliams(16) (hld up: hdwy 6f out: 5th st: rdn & hung lft over 1f out: nt r.o) 2 **3**

1252[2] Stoproveritate **(50)***(50) (MrsMReveley)* 6-9-5 (7) SCopp(8) (lw: mid div: drvn along 4f out: styd on u.p appr fnl f: n.d)....3½ **4**
2379[10] Palacegate Jo (IRE) **(52)***(32) (DWChapman)* 4-10-0 ACulhane(5) (lw: prom: 6th & rdn st: sn wknd)....15 **5**
1881[7] Lucidity **(48)***(24) (CWThornton)* 3-8-12 DeanMcKeown(9) (led 10f out: rdn & hdd 2f out: sn wknd)....3 **6**
Brooks Masquerade **(32)***(4) (NJHWalker)* 4-8-8 SMaloney(17) (bkwd: prom 8f)....2½ **7**
1990[10] Mystoski **(49)***(18) (MHTompkins)* 3-8-8 (5) HKYim(6) (in tch: rdn over 4f out: grad wknd)....2½ **8**
2225[4] Skedaddle **(57)***(22) (JGFitzGerald)* 3-9-7 DHolland(4) (led 2f: rdn 8f out: 7th & wkng st)....3 **9**
512[5] Tilly Owl **(46)***(11) (JAHarris)* 4-9-8 JO'Reilly(11) (chsd ldrs: plld hrd: 5th & wkng st)....s.h **10**
1718[13] Pink Petal **(32)** *(CJHill)* 3-7-3 (7) CAdamson(3) (hld up: nvr rchd ldrs)....1¼ **11**
2450[6] Hunza Story **(37)** *(NPLittmoden)* 3-8-1 ow1 TGMcLaughlin(7) (b.hind: hld up: hdwy 7f out: rdn & wknd over 3f out)....nk **12**
2072[8] Lady Tjonger **(30)** *(DrJDScargill)* 4-8-6 JFanning(2) (hld up: a in rr)....6 **13**
2327[12] Kralingen **(30)** *(NChamberlain)* 3-7-8 JMarshall(15) (prom: rdn over 4f out: grad wknd)....¾ **14**
2166[9] Prime Property (IRE) **(38)** *(MWEasterby)* 3-8-2b LCharnock(13) (chsd ldr over 7f: sn wknd: t.o)....20 **15**

7/2 Fen Terrier, **5/1** Stoproveritate, **13/2** Silver Rondo (USA), **7/1** Skedaddle, **8/1** Palacegate Jo (IRE), **9/1** Lucidity, **11/1** Tilly Owl, **12/1** Mystoski, Lady Tjonger, **16/1** Prime Property (IRE), **20/1** Pink Petal, PHILMIST, **25/1** Hunza Story, **50/1** Brooks Masquerade, Kralingen, CSF £89.57 CT £486.62 TOTE £46.30: £14.50 £1.90 £2.20 (£109.80) Trio £219.50; £278.34 to 24/7/95. OWNER Mr C. D. Barber-Lomax (MALTON) BRED Mrs M. Morley 15 Rn

2m 44.9 (10.70) SF: 24/31/24/31/13/-/-/-/-/-/-/-/-/-/-

WEIGHT FOR AGE 3yo-12lb

T/Plpt: £77.30 (96.53 Tckts). T/Qdpt: Not won; £46.20 to 24/7/95. CR

2587-WOLVERHAMPTON (L-H)
Saturday July 22nd (Standard)

WEATHER: sunny intervals WIND: mod across

2631 PROVISION (BUSINESS MANAGEMENT) LIMITED STKS (0-55) (3-Y.O+) (Class F) £2,381.00 (£656.00: £311.00)
5f (Fibresand) Stalls: Low GOING: 0.11 sec per fur (SLW) 7-00 (7-01)

2288[10] **Evening Falls (55)***(53) (CJames)* 4-8-11 CRutter(7) (hld up: hdwy wl over 1f out: r.o to ld wl ins fnl f)....— **1**
2326[4] Lloc **(53)***(51)(Fav)(JohnBerry)* 3-8-1 (5) NVarley(2) (b: led 2f: rdn to ld ins fnl f: sn hdd: nt qckn)....¾ **2**
2383[12] Disco Boy **(51)***(55) (BAMcMahon)* 5-8-13b(3) SSanders(8) (led 3f out tl hdd & no ex ins fnl f)....hd **3**
2492[8] Jon's Choice **(52)***(51) (BPreece)* 7-8-9 (7) AEddery(10) (hdwy ½-wy: rdn over 1f out: nt pce to chal)....1½ **4**
2295[12] Pats Delight **(37)***(33) (SCoathup)* 3-7-13 (7) AmandaSanders(9) (bhd & outpcd tl r.o ins fnl f)....4 **5**
2239[12] Tomal **(47)***(37) (RIngram)* 3-8-11 NAdams(4) (prom tl wknd bel dist)....hd **6**
1963[15] Lady-Bo-K **(54)***(28) (CaptJWilson)* 4-8-8 (3) JStack(11) (b.hind: chsd ldrs over 3f: sn wknd)....1½ **7**
2502[13] The Institute Boy **(50)***(28) (MissJFCraze)* 5-9-2v SWebster(1) (rdn along fr ½-wy: nvr nr ldrs)....1½ **8**
2229[10] Indian Crystal **(49)***(20) (MrsMReveley)* 4-8-11b JCarroll(5) (s.i.s: a bhd)....¾ **9**
1377[13] Tarn Lane (IRE) **(42)***(14) (JPearce)* 3-8-6 GBardwell(6) (outpcd: a bhd)....2 **10**
2316[10] Carnegie Blue **(32)** *(AJChamberlain)* 4-8-8b(5)ow2 RPainter(3) (b: b.hind: outpcd: a bhd: t.o) .20 **11**

5/2 Lloc, **9/2** Disco Boy, **5/1** EVENING FALLS, The Institute Boy, **8/1** Indian Crystal, **10/1** Jon's Choice, **16/1** Lady-Bo-K, Tarn Lane (IRE), Tomal, **25/1** Carnegie Blue, **33/1** Pats Delight, CSF £17.94 TOTE £10.60: £3.40 £2.10 £1.10 (£17.70) Trio £24.50 OWNER Mrs Carol Welch (NEWBURY) BRED M. V. S. and Mrs Aram 11 Rn 62.9 secs (4.90) SF: 22/15/24/20/-/1/-/-/-/-/-

WEIGHT FOR AGE 3yo-5lb

2632 BLACKBERRY CLAIMING STKS (3 & 4-Y.O) (Class F) £2,381.00 (£656.00: £311.00) 1m 6f 166y (Fibresand) Stalls: High GOING: 0.11 sec (SLW) 7-30 (7-30)

2481[6] **Fools of Pride (IRE) (33)***(55)(Fav)(RHollinshead)* 3-8-0 ow1 GCarter(4) (lw: a.p: led 4f out: clr ent fnl f: eased cl home)....— **1**
2450[12] Club Elite **(35)***(47) (MFBarraclough)* 3-7-6 (5)ow4 NVarley(5) (s.i.s: rdn along 7f out: 2nd st: rdn & btn appr fnl f)....2 **2**
2004[5] The Cottonwool Kid **(37)***(50) (THCaldwell)* 3-8-1 (3) JStack(3) (led 8f: ev ch 3f out: 3rd & outpcd ent st)....7 **3**

1749[5] Yo-Mate *(48) (JFfitch-Heyes)* 4-9-7 WWoods(1) (bit bkwd: hld up: hdwy to jn ldrs 7f out: rdn & 4th st: sn btn) 4 **4**
2385a[7] Love of the North (IRE) **(30)***(43) (RTJuckes)* 4-8-13 (3) AGarth(2) (hld up: led over 6f out to 4f out: wknd qckly & 5th st) ....hd **5**

7/4 FOOLS OF PRIDE (IRE), **2/1** Yo-Mate, **9/2** Love of the North (IRE), **8/1** Club Elite, **9/1** The Cottonwool Kid, CSF £12.75 TOTE £3.20: £1.80 £3.30 (£7.30) OWNER Mr L. A. Morgan (UPPER LONGDON) BRED Barronstown Stud and Ron Con Ltd 5 Rn 3m 29.7 (22.30) SF: -/-/-/-/-
WEIGHT FOR AGE 3yo-15lb

2633 E.B.F. TAYBERRY MAIDEN STKS (2-Y.O) (Class D) £3,882.50 (£1,160.00: £555.00: £252.50)
6f (Fibresand) Stalls: Low GOING: 0.11 sec per fur (SLW) 8-00 (8-03)

2381[6] **Scathebury** *(71) (SPCWoods)* 2-9-0v WWoods(6) (chsd ldr: led over 3f out: rdn fnl f: hld on gamely) ....— **1**
2143[3] Charterhouse Xpres *(71) (MMcCormack)* 2-9-0 PRobinson(5) (led over 2f: rallied fnl f: jst failed) ....hd **2**
Music Theatre *(49) (SirMarkPrescott)* 2-9-0 KFallon(1) (gd sort: bkwd: dwlt: outpcd & bhd tl r.o fnl 2f) 8 **3**
1652[5] Nkapen Rocks (SPA) *(49) (CaptJWilson)* 2-9-0 JFortune(9) (bit bkwd: s.i.s: sn chsng ldng pair: rdn over 2f out: nvr on terms) ....hd **4**
2198[3] Kinnescash (IRE) *(36)*(Fav)*(RIngram)* 2-9-0 AMcGlone(4) (outpcd: a bhd) 5 **5**
Rhythmic Ball *(28) (TRWatson)* 2-8-9 GCarter(3) (lt-f: outpcd: a bhd) 1¼ **6**
1670[18] Noble Colours *(25) (JBerry)* 2-9-0 JCarroll(2) (lw: outpcd fr ½-wy) 3 **7**
Potenza *(6) (RHollinshead)* 2-8-11 (3) AGarth(7) (leggy: lt-f: outpcd: a bhd: t.o) 7 **8**
1690[8] Dyanko *(MSSaunders)* 2-8-11 (3) SDrowne(8) (Withdrawn not under Starter's orders: ref to ent stalls) .... **W**

11/4 Kinnescash (IRE), **3/1** SCATHEBURY, **4/1** Music Theatre (op 5/2), Charterhouse Xpres, **9/1** Nkapen Rocks (SPA), **14/1** Noble Colours, **16/1** Dyanko, **20/1** Potenza, Rhythmic Ball, CSF £14.93 TOTE £4.00: £1.70 £1.20 £1.70 (£7.40) Trio £6.90 OWNER Mr Mark Johnson (NEWMARKET) BRED The Duke Of Marlborough 8 Rn 1m 16.6 (5.40) SF: 32/32/10/10/-/-/-/-

2634 ROTHMANS ROYALS NORTH SOUTH CHALLENGE SERIES H'CAP (0-75) (3-Y.O+) (Class D) £4,698.00 (£1,404.00: £672.00: £306.00)
1m 100y (Fibresand) Stalls: Low GOING: 0.11 sec per fur (SLW) 8-30 (8-31)

2222[4] **Equerry (58)***(68) (MJohnston)* 4-8-11 PRobinson(9) (hld up: hdwy 3f out: 3rd st: hrd rdn to ld nr fin) ....— **1**
1830[5] Daytona Beach (IRE) **(62)***(72) (PBurgoyne)* 5-8-10 (5) NVarley(12) (lw: led 6f out tl hdd last stride) ....hd **2**
Segala (IRE) **(75)***(80) (SirMarkPrescott)* 4-10-0 WWoods(8) (bit bkwd: hld up: hdwy over 2f out: 5th st: kpt on u.p fnl f) 2½ **3**
2051[5] Shanghai Venture (USA) **(69)***(72) (SPCWoods)* 4-9-1 (7) CWebb(2) (hld up gng wl: 2nd st: rdn over 1f out: one pce) 1 **4**
2390[5] Cee-Jay-Ay **(60)***(62) (JBerry)* 8-8-13 JCarroll(7) (dwlt: bhd tl hdwy over 2f out: 7th st: kpt on fnl f) ....½ **5**
2276[8] Marowins **(68)***(61)*(Fav)*(EJAlston)* 6-9-7 KFallon(10) (sn wl bhd & rdn along: r.o fnl 2f: nvr nrr) 5 **6**
2342[5] Broughtons Turmoil **(58)***(49) (WJMusson)* 6-8-8 (3) DRMcCabe(6) (led over 2f: 4th & rdn st: grad wknd) 1 **7**
1459[7] Ayunli **(60)***(49) (SCWilliams)* 4-8-10 (3) SSanders(3) (lw: prom tl rdn & outpcd over 2f out: 6th & btn st) 1¼ **8**
1980[2] Kinnegad Kid **(69)***(57) (RIngram)* 6-9-8 AMcGlone(11) (chsd ldrs: rdn along over 3f out: sn lost tch) ....½ **9**
2362[4] Future Options **(60)***(34) (MSSaunders)* 4-8-10 (3) SDrowne(13) (hld up: hdwy 4f out: rdn & wknd ent st) 7 **10**
1280[5] Gadge **(72)***(35)*(Fav)*(DMorris)* 4-9-11 JFortune(1) (prom tl drvn along & lost pl ½-wy: sn bhd) 6 **11**
2292[3] Mam'zelle Angot **(63)***(20) (AHarrison)* 5-8-13 (3) JStack(5) (lw: chsd ldrs 5f: sn wknd) 3 **12**
2290[3] Indiahra **(52)** *(RHollinshead)* 4-8-5 GCarter(4) (dwlt: a bhd: t.o) 20 **13**

9/2 Gadge, Marowins, **5/1** Broughtons Turmoil, **7/1** Daytona Beach (IRE), Segala (IRE), Kinnegad Kid, **8/1** EQUERRY, **12/1** Cee-Jay-Ay, Ayunli, **16/1** Shanghai Venture (USA), Mam'zelle Angot, **25/1** Future Options, Indiahra, CSF £65.69 CT £389.61 TOTE £7.30: £1.80 £2.60 £3.00 (£16.10) Trio £246.80; £128.66 to 24/7/95 OWNER Mr J. R. Good (MIDDLEHAM) BRED J. R. and Mrs P. Good 13 Rn 1m 50.0 (6.00) SF: 47/51/59/51/41/40/28/28/36/13/14/-/-

OFFICIAL EXPLANATION **Gadge: resented the kick-back and was never travelling.**

2635

GOOSEBERRY (S) STKS (2-Y.O) (Class G) £2,070.00 (£570.00: £270.00)
7f (Fibresand) Stalls: High GOING: 0.11 sec per fur (SLW) 9-00 (9-01)

2035² **Arch Angel (IRE)** *(59) (DJSffrenchDavis)* 2-8-11 NAdams(4) (mde virtually all: hrd rdn fnl f: all out) — 1
La Haye Sainte *(53) (DJSCosgrove)* 2-8-0 (5) LNewton(1) (lenthy: s.s: hdwy & 6th st: hrd rdn & r.o wl ins fnl f) hd 2
*2496** Victoria Venture *(58)*(Fav)*(SPCWoods)* 2-8-11 WWoods(8) (a.p: 2nd st: ev ch ins fnl f: unable qckn) nk 3
1829⁸ Two Socks *(55) (MMcCormack)* 2-8-10 PRobinson(2) (prom tl lost pl 3f out: effrt u.p appr fnl f: fin wl) 1 4
2380⁷ Colour Counsellor *(53) (KMcAuliffe)* 2-8-10b JFortune(9) (hld up: hdwy 3f out: 3rd st: rdn & wknd fnl f) 1 5
2346⁶ Richard House Lad *(46) (CASmith)* 2-8-10 MWigham(3) (hdwy ½-wy: 4th st: rdn & wknd over 1f out) 3 6
2035⁷ Welsh Owl *(37) (KRBurke)* 2-8-5 KFallon(5) (lw: chsd ldrs: 5th & rdn st: wknd over 1f out) 1¾ 7
Tamarind Cove *(7) (BJMeehan)* 2-8-7 (3) SSanders(6) (cmpt: bkwd: s.s: a bhd: t.o) 15 8

11/10 Victoria Venture, **7/2** ARCH ANGEL (IRE) (3/1-9/2), **4/1** Richard House Lad (8/1-7/2), **10/1** Colour Counsellor (op 6/1), Tamarind Cove, **14/1** La Haye Sainte (op 8/1), **16/1** Two Socks, **25/1** Welsh Owl, CSF £45.63 TOTE £3.60: £2.30 £3.50 £1.10 (£49.10) Trio £18.10 OWNER Mr R.J. Lorenz (UPPER LAMBOURN) BRED Mrs P. Grubb 8 Rn

1m 32.6 (0.60 under 2y best) (8.60) SF: 5/-/4/1/-/-/-/-

No bid

2636

STRAWBERRY MAIDEN H'CAP (0-65) (3-Y.O) (Class F) £2,381.00 (£656.00: £311.00)
1m 4f (Fibresand) Stalls: Low GOING: 0.11 sec per fur (SLW) 9-30 (9-31)

1691¹⁵ **Canton Venture (59)***(71+) (SPCWoods)* 3-9-7 WWoods(3) (hld up: hdwy 4f out: 5th st: rdn to ld ins fnl f: sn clr) — 1
1628⁴ My Boy Josh **(56)***(66) (RGuest)* 3-9-4 JCarroll(5) (lw: led 1f: rdn to ld 3f out: hdd & no ex ins fnl f) 1¾ 2
2353² Gulf Bay **(33)***(29)*(Fav)*(MBell)* 3-7-2 (7) RMullen(6) (chsd ldrs: 3rd & rdn st: sn wknd) 10 3
1674⁸ Grandes Oreilles (IRE) **(58)***(53) (NJHWalker)* 3-9-6v PRobinson(7) (led after 1f to 5f out: 4th & rdn st: sn btn) 1 4
2359⁵ Shepherds Rest (IRE) **(38)***(26) (SMellor)* 3-8-0 NAdams(1) (lw: hmpd s: sn rcvrd to chse ldrs: slt ld 5f out to 3f out: 2nd st: wknd over 1f out) 5 5
Evaporate **(43)***(26) (APJones)* 3-7-12 (7) AmandaSanders(8) (bit bkwd: bhd & outpcd tl sme late hdwy) 4 6
2293¹¹ Kristal Breeze **(41)***(19) (WRMuir)* 3-8-3v CRutter(2) (lw: hld up: effrt u.p 4f out: 6th & no imp st) 3½ 7
144⁸ Cuban Reef **(37)***(1) (WJMusson)* 3-7-13 AMackay(4) (bit bkwd: bhd & outpcd tl sme late hdwy) 11 8
1950⁹ Beecham **(42)***(5) (PCHaslam)* 3-8-4 GBardwell(9) (chsd ldrs 9f: sn wknd: t.o) ½ 9

9/4 Gulf Bay (op 5/4), **11/4** My Boy Josh, Shepherds Rest (IRE) (op 12/1), **7/1** Grandes Oreilles (IRE) (op 4/1), **8/1** Beecham, **10/1** Cuban Reef, **14/1** CANTON VENTURE (op 8/1), Kristal Breeze, **16/1** Evaporate, CSF £57.48 CT £118.07 TOTE £17.20: £3.70 £1.60 £1.10 (£47.90) £13.20 OWNER Dr Frank Chao (NEWMARKET) BRED High Point B/stock Ltd & Chao Racing & B/stock Ltd 9 Rn

2m 44.2 (13.20) SF: 27/22/-/9/-/-/-/-/-

T/Plpt: £17.50. T/Qdpt: £11.10. IM

2534-BRIGHTON (L-H)
Monday July 24th (Firm)
WEATHER: hot WIND: almost nil

2637

RAGGETTS (S) STKS (2-Y.O) (Class G) £2,243.00 (£618.00: £293.00)
6f 209y Stalls: Low GOING minus 0.59 sec per fur (F) 2-30 (2-32)

2346¹⁰ **Distant Storm** *(66) (MBell)* 2-8-11b MHills(3) (lw: s.s: outpcd: mod 6th st: hdwy over 1f out: led ins fnl f: r.o wl) — 1
2435⁵ Lussuria (IRE) *(60)*(Fav)*(BJMeehan)* 2-8-11 GBardwell(2) (3rd st: led over 1f out tl ins fnl f: unable qckn) 3 2
2346⁴ Willie Rushton *(54) (GLMoore)* 2-8-6 SWhitworth(5) (lw: 2nd st: led over 2f out tl over 1f out: one pce) hd 3
2381⁸ Makaskamina *(51) (BHanbury)* 2-8-11 MRimmer(4) (4th st: rdn over 2f out: one pce) 3½ 4

2505[3] Bobsworthatcaspers *(39) (GLewis)* 2-8-11b PaulEddery(7) (lw: led over 4f: wknd over 1f out) .5 **5**
2505[4] Fast Food *(12) (BJMcMath)* 2-8-11 MTebbutt(6) (lw: bhd fnl 5f: mod 5th st) 12 **6**
2249* Spanish Luck *(JWHills)* 2-8-11 KDarley(1) (s.s: a wl bhd) 7 **7**

2/1 Lussuria (IRE), **3/1** Willie Rushton, **5/1** Spanish Luck (3/1-11/2), **11/2** Bobsworthatcaspers (3/1-6/1), **10/1** DISTANT STORM (7/1-11/1), **20/1** Makaskamina, **33/1** Fast Food, CSF £27.24 TOTE £10.80: £3.30 £1.10 (£15.30) OWNER Mr B. R. H. Burrough (NEWMARKET) BRED Stratford Place Stud 7 Rn 1m 23.5 (3.50) SF: 3/-/-/-/-/-/-
Bt in 4,400 gns

2638

CHIPPENDALE MAIDEN STKS (3-Y.O+ F & M) (Class D) £3,630.90 (£1,081.20: £514.60: £231.30) **7f 214y** Stalls: Low GOING minus 0.59 sec (F) 3-00 (3-03)

2297[2] **Avignon (IRE) (82)***(88)*(Fav)*(PWChapple-Hyam)* 3-8-10 JReid(3) (lw: 3rd st: led wl over 1f out: comf) ....— **1**
2279[5] Shady Deed (USA) **(62)***(68) (JWHills)* 3-8-10b MHills(2) (lw: led over 6f: unable qckn) 10 **2**
2393[6] Brave Fighter (USA) *(67) (BHanbury)* 3-8-10 MRimmer(4) (4th st: rdn over 3f out: one pce) .nk **3**
Tafia (IRE) *(59) (JPearce)* 4-9-4 GBardwell(6) (lw: rdn over 4f out: 2nd st: wknd over 2f out) ..4 **4**
2337[4] Anjomajasa *(47) (MissGayKelleway)* 3-8-7 (3) SDrowne(5) (5th st: wknd over 3f out) 6 **5**
Estrela Castanha *(44) (RMFlower)* 3-8-10b AMorris(1) (6th st: a bhd) 1½ **6**

4/7 AVIGNON (IRE), **6/1** Brave Fighter (USA) (9/2-7/1), Tafia (IRE), **8/1** Shady Deed (USA) (5/1-9/1), **25/1** Anjomajasa, **100/1** Estrela Castanha, CSF £5.15 TOTE £1.40: £1.10 £1.80 (£4.20) OWNER Lord Weinstock & The Hon Simon Weinstock (MARLBOROUGH) BRED Ballymacoll Stud Farm Ltd 6 Rn 1m 33.2 (1.00) SF: 33/13/12/12/-/-
WEIGHT FOR AGE 3yo-8lb

2639

BRIGHTON SUMMER CHALLENGE CUP H'CAP (0-80) (3-Y.O+) (Class D) £3,833.70 (£1,143.60: £545.80: £246.90)
1m 3f 196y Stalls: High GOING minus 0.59 sec per fur (F) 3-30 (3-33)

1773[4] **Prince Danzig (IRE) (54)***(66) (DJGMurraySmith)* 4-8-2 PaulEddery(4) (lw: chsd ldr: rdn over 2f out: edgd lft & led ins fnl f: r.o wl) ....— **1**
2339[4] Exhibit Air (IRE) **(62)***(74)*(Fav)*(RAkehurst)* 5-8-7b(3) SSanders(2) (led: hrd rdn over 1f out: hdd ins fnl f: r.o) ....nk **2**
2525[2] Artic Courier **(77)***(85) (DJSCosgrove)* 4-9-4 (7) DGibbs(3) (swtg: 4th st: rdn over 2f out: edgd lft ins fnl f: unable qckn) 3 **3**
2069[3] Lookingforarainbow (IRE) **(78)***(80) (BobJones)* 7-9-12 MWigham(1) (lw: 3rd st: rdn over 2f out: wknd over 1f out) 4 **4**
2298* Silently **(81)***(70) (IABalding)* 3-9-3 KDarley(5) (lw: 5th st: wknd over 2f out) 10 **5**

2/1 Exhibit Air (IRE), **5/2** Silently, **4/1** Artic Courier, **11/2** Lookingforarainbow (IRE) (4/1-6/1), **13/2** PRINCE DANZIG (IRE), CSF £18.50 TOTE £7.50: £3.30 £1.40 (£11.20) OWNER Mr A. H. Ulrick (LAMBOURN) BRED J. N. McCaffrey in Ireland 5 Rn 2m 31.6 (2.60) SF: 23/31/42/37/15
WEIGHT FOR AGE 3yo-12lb

2640

BEAU BRUMMEL CLAIMING STKS (3-Y.O+) (Class F) £2,519.00 (£694.00: £329.00) **1m 1f 209y** Stalls: High GOING minus 0.59 sec per fur (F) 4-00 (4-03)

445[9] **Zuno Noelyn (54)***(63)*(Fav)*(RAkehurst)* 4-8-12 (3) SSanders(5) (lw: hdwy over 5f out: 4th st: led over 1f out: rdn out: dead) ....— **1**
2538[2] Thames Side **(47)***(63) (MMadgwick)* 4-9-2 CAvery(3) (hrd rdn & hdwy over 1f out: edgd lft ins fnl f: r.o) ....½ **2**
2174[5] Kirov Protege (IRE) **(44)***(52) (HJCollingridge)* 3-8-8 MRimmer(1) (hdwy over 4f out: 6th st: rdn over 2f out: wknd over 1f out) 8 **3**
2309[2] Malindi Bay **(30)***(44) (BJMcMath)* 7-8-10 MTebbutt(7) (hld up: led over 3f out tl over 1f out: sn wknd) ....hd **4**
1498[15] Dance of Joy **(52)***(35) (JLDunlop)* 3-8-5 PaulEddery(2) (led 2f: 5th st: wknd over 2f out) 9 **5**
2033[9] Chase the Melody **(26)***(31) (MJHeaton-Ellis)* 3-7-9v(7) AmandaSanders(4) (led 8f out tl over 4f out: 3rd st: wknd over 2f out) ....½ **6**
2549[14] Rubadub **(36)***(9) (JMBradley)* 4-8-2v(3) SDrowne(6) (b: led over 4f out tl over 3f out: 2nd st: wknd over 2f out) 9 **7**

2/1 ZUNO NOELYN, **3/1** Thames Side, **6/1** Dance of Joy (op 7/2), **13/2** Kirov Protege (IRE), **8/1** Malindi Bay (op 9/2), Rubadub, **40/1** Chase the Melody, CSF £7.79 TOTE £2.70: £1.90 £2.80 (£3.60) OWNER Planflow (Leasing) Ltd (EPSOM) BRED R. B. Warren 7 Rn
2m 1.0 (3.00) SF: 25/25/4/6/-/-/-
WEIGHT FOR AGE 3yo-10lb

2641

A. R. DENNIS BOOKMAKERS JULY H'CAP (0-70) (3-Y.O+) (Class E)
£3,044.80 (£906.40: £431.20: £193.60)
5f 213y Stalls: Low GOING minus 0.59 sec per fur (F) 4-30 (4-32)

2342[6] **Sharp Imp (33)***(44) (RMFlower)* 5-7-12b DBiggs(2) (chsd ldr: led over 1f out: rdn out) ....— 1
2539[3] Red Admiral **(58)***(60)*(Fav)*(PCHaslam)* 5-9-9 MTebbutt(8) (lw: led over 4f: unable qckn) 3½ 2
2539[5] Pirates Gold (IRE) **(46)***(43) (JWhite)* 5-8-8 (3) SDrowne(1) (lw: 5th st: rdn 3f out: one pce).....1¾ 3
2491[6] Stoppes Brow **(65)***(61) (GLMoore)* 3-9-5v(5) CChoi(7) (6th st: rdn over 2f out: one pce) ....nk 4
2491[4] Cork Street Girl (IRE) **(52)***(41) (BJMeehan)* 3-8-11b PaulEddery(5) (3rd st: wknd wl over 1f out) 2½ 5
2491[10] Silver Tzar **(69)***(58) (WJHaggas)* 3-10-0 RMcGhin(3) (a bhd)..........d.h 5
2021[7] Ain'tlifelikethat **(38)***(23) (TJNaughton)* 8-8-3b AMcGlone(4) (b: s.s: sme hdwy over 1f out: sn wknd)..........1½ 7
2363[7] Lorins Gold **(31)***(12) (AndrewTurnell)* 5-7-10b NAdams(6) (b.nr hind: 4th st: wknd 2f out)......1¾ 8

3/1 Red Admiral, **100/30** Silver Tzar (12/1-20/1), Cork Street Girl (IRE), **4/1** Stoppes Brow, **5/1** Pirates Gold (IRE), **7/1** SHARP IMP, **12/1** Ain'tlifelikethat, **16/1** Lorins Gold, CSF £27.02 CT £104.67 TOTE £7.10: £1.80 £1.40 £2.20 (£16.90) OWNER Mrs G. M. Temmerman (JEVINGTON) BRED James Wigan 8 Rn 1m 8.6 (0.20) SF: 29/45/28/40/20/37/8/-
WEIGHT FOR AGE 3yo-6lb

2642

FITZHERBERT H'CAP (0-60) (3-Y.O+) (Class F) £2,846.60 (£787.60: £375.80)
5f 59y Stalls: Low GOING minus 0.59 sec per fur (F) 5-00 (5-02)

2338[3] **Tyrian Purple (IRE) (54)***(62) (TJNaughton)* 7-9-5b(5) JDSmith(1) (mde virtually all: hrd rdn over 1f out: r.o wl) ....— 1
2492[4] La Belle Dominique **(56)***(59) (SGKnight)* 3-9-7 VSlattery(5) (4th st: hrd rdn over 1f out: unable qckn)..........1¾ 2
2054[6] Tachycardia **(52)***(53)*(Fav)*(RJO'Sullivan)* 3-9-0 (3) SSanders(7) (lw: 2nd st: ev ch 2f out: one pce) ....½ 3
2144[2] Hong Kong Dollar **(53)***(50) (BJMeehan)* 3-8-11b(7) RHavlin(8) (5th st: rdn over 2f out: r.o one pce) 1¼ 4
2301[W] Another Batchworth **(54)***(50) (SMellor)* 3-8-12 (7) ADaly(3) (s.s: 6th st: rdn over 1f out: one pce) ....½ 5
2398[8] Nuclear Express **(43)***(33) (JMBradley)* 8-8-10 (3) SDrowne(6) (b: lw: a bhd) 2 6
2049[6] Can't Say (IRE) **(33)***(19) (JMBradley)* 3-7-12v DBiggs(4) (a bhd)..........1¼ 7
2402[4] Abbey House **(47)***(27) (RGuest)* 3-8-5v(7) CWebb(2) (3rd st: wknd over 2f out)..........2 8

11/4 Tachycardia, **3/1** TYRIAN PURPLE (IRE), **7/2** Hong Kong Dollar, **10/1** La Belle Dominique (5/1-12/1), **12/1** Another Batchworth (7/1-14/1), **14/1** Can't Say (IRE) (op 8/1), Abbey House (8/1-16/1), **16/1** Nuclear Express, CSF £27.48 CT £74.72 TOTE £4.00: £1.70 £2.00 £1.20 (£23.50) OWNER Mr T. O'Flaherty (EPSOM) BRED Niels Schibbye 8 Rn 62.6 secs (2.60) SF: 15/7/1/-/-/-/-/-
WEIGHT FOR AGE 3yo-5lb
T/Plpt: £22.80 (500.48 Tckts). T/Qdpt: £4.00 (23.5 Tckts). AK

2606-NEWCASTLE (L-H)
Monday July 24th (Good to firm)

WEATHER: sunny periods WIND: slt bhd

2643

SQUIRE ORDE MAIDEN STKS (3-Y.O+) (Class D) £3,849.20 (£1,081.20: £527.60)
1m 2f 32y Stalls: Low GOING minus 0.21 sec per fur (GF) 2-15 (2-16)

2329[2] **Sherqy (IRE) (83)***(75)*(Fav)*(JLDunlop)* 3-8-11 WCarson(3) (lw: mde all: qcknd over 2f out: r.o: comf) ....— 1
1967[2] Chevalier (USA) *(73) (HRACecil)* 3-8-11 WRyan(1) (lw: trckd wnr: rdn over 2f out: r.o: nt pce to chal)..........1½ 2
Take A Right *(NChamberlain)* 3-8-11 SWebster(2) (w'like: bkwd: sn outpcd & bhd)..........dist 3

4/6 SHERQY (IRE), **5/4** Chevalier (USA) (op 4/6), **66/1** Take A Right, CSF £1.69 TOTE £1.40 (£1.10) OWNER Mr Hamdan Al Maktoum (ARUNDEL) BRED Shadwell Estate Company Limited 3 Rn 2m 11.6 (4.90) SF: 44/42/-

2644

JOHN CARTWRIGHT NURSERY H'CAP STKS (2-Y.O) (Class E)
£3,009.60 (£910.80: £444.40: £211.20)
6f Stalls: Centre GOING minus 0.21 sec per fur (GF) 2-45 (2-45)

2328[9] **Shontaine** *(78)*(Fav)*(MJohnston)* 2-9-7 DHolland(2) (lw: mde all: rdn along & r.o wl fnl f) .....— 1

2459[4] Oriel Lad *(73) (PDEvans)* 2-9-3v(3) DRMcCabe(4) (hld up: hdwy & ev ch appr fnl f: hrd rdn & nt qckn)....1½ 2
2328[3] Russian Rascal (IRE) *(45)*(Fav)*(MHEasterby)* 2-8-5 MBirch(1) (w ldr tl rdn & wknd 2f out)......5 3
2328[11] Copper Bright *(26) (PCHaslam)* 2-7-7 NKennedy(3) (sn pushed along: nvr able to chal)......2½ 4

7/4 SHONTAINE, Russian Rascal (IRE), **9/4** Oriel Lad, **11/1** Copper Bright, CSF £5.74 TOTE £2.20 (£2.90) OWNER Mr Paul Dean (MIDDLEHAM) BRED Mark Johnston Racing Ltd 4 Rn
1m 14.94 (3.44) SF: 40/35/7/-

2645 EURO-AMERICAN CHALLENGE AMATEUR H'CAP (0-70) (3-Y.O+) (Class E) £3,403.75 (£1,030.00: £502.50: £238.75)
6f Stalls: Centre GOING minus 0.21 sec per fur (GF) 3-15 (3-17)

2194[5] **Chinour (IRE) (61)***(75) (EJAlston)* 7-11-1 MrTSchmeer(6) (mde most: rdn clr fnl f)....— 1
2475[6] Murray's Mazda (IRE) **(42)***(43) (JLEyre)* 6-9-10 MissCGVonKageneck(7) (b: disp ld to ½-wy: one pce after)....5 2
2578[4] Pageboy **(65)***(56)*(Fav)*(PCHaslam)* 6-11-5b MrsDKettlewell(5) (lw: chsd ldrs: hrd rdn over 1f out: r.o one pce)....3½ 3
2330[3] Blue Grit **(52)***(38) (MDods)* 9-10-6 MissCClagett(1) (chsd ldrs tl rdn over 2f out: no imp after)....2 4
1044[7] Miss Whittingham (IRE) **(52)***(9) (JBerry)* 5-10-6 MrSFileccia(3) (lw: spd 3f)....11 5
2461* Flashy's Son **(70)***(17) (GMMoore)* 7-11-10 MissARushton(2) (lw: b: spd to ½-wy: sn wknd)..3½ 6
2337[3] Mason (IRE) **(60)** *(SMellor)* 3-10-8 MrTMaher(4) (lw: a outpcd & bhd: t.o)....dist 7

7/4 Pageboy, **5/1** CHINOUR (IRE), Blue Grit, Flashy's Son, **8/1** Murray's Mazda (IRE), Mason (IRE), **10/1** Miss Whittingham (IRE), CSF £39.25 TOTE £4.30: £2.70 £4.20 (£41.90) OWNER Mr Frank McKevitt (PRESTON) BRED His Highness The Aga Khans Studs S.C. 7 Rn
1m 15.13 (3.63) SF: 57/25/38/20/-/-/-
WEIGHT FOR AGE 3yo-6lb

OFFICIAL EXPLANATION **Mason (IRE): was found to be in a distressed state after the race.**

2646 BEESWING STKS (Gp 3) (3-Y.O+) (Class A) £21,450.00 (£7,950.00: £3,825.00: £1,575.00: £637.50: £262.50)
7f Stalls: Centre GOING minus 0.21 sec per fur (GF) 3-45 (3-45)

1848[2] **Shahid (106)***(118) (JLDunlop)* 3-8-7 WCarson(5) (lw: trckd ldrs: hdwy to ld ins fnl f: r.o)....— 1
2105[4] Mistle Cat (USA) **(111)***(116) (SPCWoods)* 5-9-0 WWoods(7) (led: qcknd 4f out: hdd ins fnl f: kpt on wl)....1 2
2409[6] Peace Envoy **(109)***(113) (HRACecil)* 3-8-7 WRyan(4) (lw: cl up: rdn 2f out: r.o one pce)....1 3
2105* Pipe Major (IRE) **(120)***(112)*(Fav)*(PCHaslam)* 3-8-11 JWeaver(2) (lw: chsd ldrs: rdn over 2f out: r.o one pce)....2½ 4
1835[2] Nijo **(109)***(108) (DRLoder)* 4-9-0 LDettori(1) (lw: trckd ldrs: effrt over 2f out: edgd lft & nt qckn)....hd 5
1613[2] Green Perfume (USA) **(107)***(105) (PFICole)* 3-8-7 TQuinn(3) (hld up: effrt over 2f out: rdn & btn appr fnl f)....1 6
2368[8] Sergeyev (IRE) **(112)***(106) (RHannon)* 3-8-11 RHughes(6) (hld up & bhd: effrt over 2f out: sn rdn & btn: eased ins fnl f)....1¼ 7

11/4 Pipe Major (IRE), **3/1** SHAHID, **7/2** Nijo, **9/2** Sergeyev (IRE), **10/1** Green Perfume (USA), **11/1** Mistle Cat (USA), **16/1** Peace Envoy, CSF £30.11 TOTE £3.70: £1.80 £3.80 (£19.80) OWNER Mr Hamdan Al Maktoum (ARUNDEL) BRED Somerhall Bloodstock Ltd and Lord Chelsea 7 Rn
1m 25.21 (0.91) SF: 64/69/59/58/61/51/52
WEIGHT FOR AGE 3yo-7lb

OFFICIAL EXPLANATION **Sergeyev (IRE): lost his action and ran flat.**

2647 HARRY PEACOCK MEMORIAL CHALLENGE CUP RATED H'CAP (0-95) (3-Y.O+) (Class B) £7,909.80 (£2,938.20: £1,419.10: £590.50: £245.25: £107.15)
7f Stalls: Centre GOING minus 0.21 sec per fur (GF) 4-15 (4-15)

2455[2] **Hi Nod (85)***(94) (MJCamacho)* 5-9-7 LCharnock(8) (lw: trckd ldrs: stdy hdwy to ld 1½f out: shkn up & sn qcknd clr)....— 1
2455* Allinson's Mate (IRE) **(75)***(79) (TDBarron)* 7-8-11b JFortune(2) (lw: hld up: effrt over 2f out: styd on fnl f: nt pce to chal)....2 2
2235[4] Gymcrak Premiere **(82)***(86) (GHolmes)* 7-9-4 KFallon(7) (lw: sn pushed along: styd on wl fnl 2f: nvr able to chal)....s.h 3
2369[2] Sky Music **(81)***(82) (MissSEHall)* 4-8-10 (7) PFessey(4) (b: mde most tl hdd 1½f out: one pce)1½ 4
2369[5] Tawafij (USA) **(84)***(84) (TDyer)* 6-9-6 JWeaver(6) (hld up & bhd: hdwy 2f out: sn rdn & no imp)....½ 5

24372 Prima Cominna **(81)**_(79) (MBell)_ 3-8-10 MFenton(1) (trckd ldrs: effrt over 2f out: wknd over 1f out)....¾ 6
22402 Khamseh **(84)**_(79)_(Fav)_(JWWatts)_ 3-8-13 LDettori(5) (chsd ldrs: effrt 3f out: wknd over 1f out)....1½ 7
24369 Zifta (USA) **(82)**_(71) (SCWilliams)_ 4-9-4 AMackay(3) (disp ld 4f: sn rdn & wknd)....2½ 8

3/1 Khamseh, **4/1** Sky Music, **11/2** HI NOD, Tawafij (USA), **6/1** Prima Cominna, **13/2** Allinson's Mate (IRE), **14/1** Gymcrak Premiere, **16/1** Zifta (USA), CSF £37.14 CT £428.58 TOTE £6.20: £2.10 £2.30 £2.30 (£11.00) OWNER Mr Brian Nordan (MALTON) BRED B. Nordan 8 Rn
1m 26.99 (2.69) SF: 56/41/48/44/46/34/34/33
WEIGHT FOR AGE 3yo-7lb

2648

DOCTOR SYNTAX H'CAP (0-80) (3-Y.O+) (Class D) £3,555.50 (£1,076.00: £525.00: £249.50) **1m 4f 93y** Stalls: Low GOING minus 0.21 sec (GF) 4-45 (4-45)

20873 **Lord Hastie (USA) (44)**_(55) (CWThornton)_ 7-8-0 AMackay(2) (lw: a.p: rdn to ld ins fnl f: r.o)— 1
9685 Turnpole (IRE) **(63)**_(71) (MrsMReveley)_ 4-9-5 LDettori(3) (trckd ldrs: led 1½f out: hdd & one pce ins fnl f)....2½ 2
2544* Latvian **(73)**_(79) (RAllan)_ 8-10-1 5x JWeaver(4) (lw: hld up: effrt 3f out: styd on nr fin: n.d) 1½ 3
15582 Wonderful Day **(68)**_(74)_(Fav)_(SCWilliams)_ 4-9-10 JFortune(5) (lw: led tl hdd 1½f out: wknd) s.h 4
21893 Dawn Mission **(54)**_(50) (MHEasterby)_ 3-7-12 ow2 SMaloney(1) (hld up: shkn up 3f out: n.d)......6 5

6/4 Wonderful Day, **7/2** Turnpole (IRE), Latvian, LORD HASTIE (USA), **12/1** Dawn Mission (op 8/1), CSF £14.81 TOTE £5.20: £3.10 £1.50 (£8.20) OWNER Mrs Joy Bendall (MIDDLEHAM) BRED Upland Park Stud 5 Rn
2m 43.85 (5.35) SF: 35/51/59/54/18
WEIGHT FOR AGE 3yo-12lb

2649

NEWMINSTER MAIDEN STKS (3-Y.O+) (Class D) £3,538.60 (£1,070.80: £522.40: £248.20) **5f** Stalls: Low GOING minus 0.21 sec per fur (GF) 5-15 (5-16)

Pentre Ffynnon (IRE) _(84) (JBerry)_ 3-8-9 JCarroll(4) (mde all: rdn & r.o strly fnl 2f)....— 1
24757 Kenesha (IRE) **(48)**_(53) (DANolan)_ 5-8-4 (5) VHalliday(1) (chsd wnr tl wl outpcd fnl 2f)....8 2
232611 High Priest **(68)**_(47)_(Fav)_(LMCumani)_ 3-8-9 LDettori(2) (lw: hld up: effrt ½-wy: sn rdn & fnd nil)....3½ 3
223610 Respect A Secret _(33) (SEKettlewell)_ 3-8-4 NRodgers(3) (outpcd & bhd fr ½-wy) 3 4

4/11 High Priest, **4/1** PENTRE FFYNNON (IRE), **6/1** Kenesha (IRE), **16/1** Respect A Secret, CSF £20.41 TOTE £3.70 (£14.10) OWNER Lord Mostyn (COCKERHAM) BRED Green Ireland Properties Ltd 4 Rn
60.03 secs (1.63) SF: 48/22/11/-
WEIGHT FOR AGE 3yo-5lb
OFFICIAL EXPLANATION High Priest: no explanation offered.

T/Plpt: £1,676.40 (5.55 Tckts). T/Qdpt: £92.60 (0.2 Tckts); £100.16 to Goodwood 25/7/95. AA

2277-NOTTINGHAM (L-H)
Monday July 24th (Good to firm, firm patches)
WEATHER: fine & sunny WIND: almost nil

2650

KPMG PASAS (S) H'CAP (0-60) (3-Y.O) (Class G) £2,511.80 (£694.80: £331.40) **1m 6f 15y** Stalls: Low GOING minus 0.38 sec per fur (F) 6-30 (6-33)

25556 **Old Swinford (IRE) (53)**_(70) (BJMeehan)_ 3-9-7 AClark(1) (chsd ldrs: 3rd st: shkn up to chal 2f out: led over 1f out: r.o wl) ....— 1
23052 Can She Can Can **(45)**_(61)_(Fav)_(MJohnston)_ 3-8-13 DHolland(2) (chsd ldr: 2nd st: led over 3f out tl over 1f out: kpt on u.p nr fin)....½ 2
24508 Alpine Storm (IRE) **(33)**_(27) (MDIUsher)_ 3-7-8b(7) CAdamson(5) (lw: led: clr ½-wy: wknd & hdd over 3f out: sn btn) 20 3
22965 Nellyssia (FR) **(45)**_(27) (GLMoore)_ 3-8-13v CandyMorris(4) (unruly stalls: prom tl stumbled & lost pl paddock bnd: 5th & rdn st: no imp: t.o)....10 4
2353* Lindisfarne Lady **(44)**_(22) (MrsMReveley)_ 3-8-5 (7) SCopp(6) (lw: hld up: outpcd & 4th ent st: sn bhd: t.o)....4 5

11/8 Can She Can Can, **2/1** OLD SWINFORD (IRE) (op 5/4), **3/1** Lindisfarne Lady, **16/1** Alpine Storm (IRE), **20/1** Nellyssia (FR), CSF £4.98 TOTE £2.40: £1.40 £1.30 (£2.10) OWNER Old Swinford Betting Partnership (UPPER LAMBOURN) BRED Owen Bourke 5 Rn
3m 3.8 (5.30) SF: 46/37/3/3/-
Bt in 4,400 gns

2651 SHEFFIELD STAR MAIDEN AUCTION STKS (2-Y.O F) (Class F) £3,199.40 (£888.40: £426.20) **6f 15y** Stalls: Centre GOING minus 0.38 sec (F) 7-00 (7-02)

2277³ **Pharaoh's Joy** *(67) (JWPayne)* 2-8-0 PRobinson(8) (swtg: hld up: swtchd lft over 1f out: shkn up to ld ins fnl f: r.o) ....— 1
1823⁶ Yuppy Girl (IRE) *(60) (CaptJWilson)* 2-7-10 JMarshall(2) (b.off hind: a.p: led wl over 1f out tl ins fnl f: unable qckn) 1 2
Real Gem *(64) (PJMakin)* 2-8-0 GCarter(9) (lt-f: unf: s.s: bhd tl gd hdwy appr fnl f: fin wl) ....s.h 3
2308⁵ Rebel County (IRE) *(55)*(Fav)*(DJSCosgrove)* 2-7-10 FNorton(11) (swtg: chsd ldrs: outpcd 2f out: rallied fnl f: r.o) 2 4
2198⁵ Pearls of Thought (IRE) *(58) (PTWalwyn)* 2-8-0 TSprake(12) (bhd: rdn 2f out: kpt on wl ins fnl f) ....nk 5
2308² Lia Fail (IRE) *(58)*(Fav)*(RHollinshead)* 2-8-0 NCarlisle(3) (w ldr: ev ch & rdn bel dist: one pce) ....s.h 6
Fairly Sure (IRE) *(48) (NEBerry)* 2-8-0 JFanning(6) (lt-f: bit bkwd: chsd ldrs 4f: sn lost tch) 4 7
Total Aloof *(46) (MrsLPiggott)* 2-7-8 (7)ow1 VictoriaAppleby(7) (lt-f: unf: b: b.hind: s.i.s: sn led: hdd & wknd over 1f out) ....¾ 8
Dulford Dolly *(43) (BRMillman)* 2-8-0 CRutter(5) (w'like: scope: b.hind: b.nr fore: s.i.s: outpcd: a in rr) 1 9
2487⁵ Whalley Abbey *(41) (GLMoore)* 2-8-0 CandyMorris(4) (b: bhd: rdn along over 2f out: no rspnse) ....¾ 10
Sassetta (IRE) *(38) (NTinkler)* 2-8-3 ow3 KimTinkler(1) (lt-f: s.s: a bhd & outpcd) 1 11

3/1 Lia Fail (IRE), Rebel County (IRE), **100/30** PHARAOH'S JOY, **7/1** Pearls of Thought (IRE), **10/1** Whalley Abbey, **12/1** Real Gem (op 7/1), **16/1** Fairly Sure (IRE), **20/1** Total Aloof, Yuppy Girl (IRE), **25/1** Dulford Dolly, Sassetta (IRE), CSF £61.56 TOTE £4.10: £1.30 £3.20 £4.10 (£186.40) Trio Not won; £145.91 to 25/7/95 OWNER Pyramid Racing Club (NEWMARKET) BRED Mrs L. Popely 11 Rn
1m 14.1 (3.10) SF: 10/3/7/-/1/1/-/-/-/-/-

2652 TOTE NOTTINGHAM STEWARDS CUP H'CAP (0-85) (3-Y.O+) (Class D) £7,197.50 (£2,180.00: £1,065.00: £507.50) **6f 15y** Stalls: Centre GOING minus 0.38 sec per fur (F) 7-30 (7-31)

Double Bounce (65)*(72) (PJMakin)* 5-8-12 DHolland(6) (b: swtg: hld up: hdwy over 1f out: str run to ld nr fin) ....— 1
2458⁷ Croft Pool **(80)***(86) (JAGlover)* 4-9-13 WRyan(9) (hld up: gd hdwy to ld over 1f out: hrd rdn & ct cl home) ....nk 2
2578² Macs Maharanee **(70)***(76) (PSFelgate)* 8-9-0 (3) JStack(10) (lw: hld up: hdwy wl over 1f out: ev ch ins fnl f: unable qckn) ....s.h 3
2458⁴ Barato **(72)***(75)*(Fav)*(MrsJRRamsden)* 4-9-5 KFallon(8) (b.nr hind: lw: stdd s: hdwy bel dist: r.o fnl f: nt pce to chal) 1¼ 4
*2627** Shadow Jury **(75)***(75)*(Fav)*(DWChapman)* 5-9-8b 7x LCharnock(3) (a.p: ev ch over 1f out: wknd ins fnl f) 1¼ 5
2330² Captain Carat **(65)***(64) (MrsJRRamsden)* 4-8-12 PRobinson(5) (chsd ldrs: effrt bel dist: one pce ins fnl f) ....nk 6
2448⁸ Petraco (IRE) **(61)***(57) (NASmith)* 7-8-8 SDWilliams(4) (led tl hdd over 1f out: sn outpcd) 1 7
2455⁸ Queenbird **(78)***(71) (MJRyan)* 4-9-11 AClark(7) (chsd ldrs 4f: sn lost pl) 1¼ 8
2533⁷ Great Hall **(59)***(52) (PDCundell)* 6-8-6b GCarter(1) (spd over 4f) ....hd 9
2448* Bargash **(70)***(60) (PDEvans)* 3-8-11 JFortune(2) (prom: rdn along 2f out: outpcd appr fnl f).....1 10

9/2 Barato, Shadow Jury, **5/1** Macs Maharanee, **11/2** Captain Carat, **13/2** Bargash, **9/1** Great Hall, **11/1** Croft Pool, **14/1** DOUBLE BOUNCE, Petraco (IRE), **25/1** Queenbird, CSF £137.68 CT £796.44 TOTE £16.00: £4.10 £1.70 £1.70 (£59.30) Trio £209.60 OWNER Mrs P. Scott-Dunn (MARLBOROUGH) BRED Mrs P. Scott-Dunn 10 Rn
1m 13.3 (2.30) SF: 32/46/36/35/35/24/17/31/12/14
WEIGHT FOR AGE 3yo-6lb

2653 ALLIED DUNBAR MEDIAN AUCTION MAIDEN STKS (3-Y.O F) (Class E) £3,130.60 (£932.80: £444.40: £200.20) **1m 1f 213y** Stalls: Low GOING minus 0.38 sec per fur (F) 8-00 (8-01)

1128⁵ **Prague Spring (68)***(69)*(Fav)*(BWHills)* 3-8-11 RHills(6) (led after 2f: qcknd ent st: rdn over 2f out: r.o wl) ....— 1
2329³ Debutante Days *(67) (ACStewart)* 3-8-6 (5) MHumphries(5) (hld up & bhd: 6th st: hdwy 4f out: ev ch over 1f out: unable qckn) 1¼ 2
2094⁴ Forest Mill *(63) (DWPArbuthnot)* 3-8-11 AClark(3) (b.hind: bit bkwd: led 2f: 3rd st: rdn over 2f out: r.o one pce) 2½ 3

2167[5] Special Beat *(63) (PFICole)* 3-8-11 CRutter(4) (plld hrd: hld up & bhd: 5th st: effrt & drvn along 3f out: nvr nr to chal) ....hd **4**
1967[3] Doonyasha *(53) (JLDunlop)* 3-8-11 GCarter(1) (plld hrd: hld up: 4th st: hdwy 4f out: rdn & wknd over 2f out) 6 **5**
Dillyetta *(RonaldThompson)* 3-8-11 SDWilliams(7) (unf: bkwd: prom: 2nd st: rdn & wknd 4f out: sn t.o) ....dist **6**

13/8 PRAGUE SPRING, **2/1** Doonyasha, **4/1** Special Beat, **15/2** Debutante Days (5/1-8/1), **20/1** Forest Mill, **50/1** Dillyetta, CSF £12.20 TOTE £2.70: £1.40 £4.00 (£9.80) OWNER Mr W. J. Gredley (LAMBOURN) BRED Stetchworth Park Stud Ltd 6 Rn 2m 11.0 (8.50) SF: -/-/-/-/-/-

2654

ALLIED DUNBAR H'CAP (0-80) (3-Y.O) (Class D) £4,002.70 (£1,195.60: £571.80: £259.90) **1m 54y** Stalls: Low GOING minus 0.38 sec per fur (F) 8-30 (8-33)

2362[3] **Hand Craft (IRE) (74)***(79)*(Fav)*(WJHaggas)* 3-9-3 RHills(3) (lw: hld up: 4th st: hdwy 3f out: rdn to ld appr fnl f: r.o wl) ....— **1**
2313* Pennycairn **(78)***(81) (HRACecil)* 3-9-7 WRyan(1) (a.p: 2nd st: led over 2f out tl over 1f out: rdn & no ex nr fin) 1¼ **2**
2455[4] Verde Luna **(69)***(71) (MHTompkins)* 3-8-12 PRobinson(5) (hld up in rr: 6th st: hdwy wl over 1f out: fin wl) ....½ **3**
2613[9] Zingibar **(66)***(67) (BWHills)* 3-8-9b DHolland(6) (pushed along in ld: hdd over 2f out: rallied ent fnl f: kpt on) ....nk **4**
1165[14] El Don **(60)***(47) (MJRyan)* 3-8-3 AClark(2) (bit bkwd: hld up: 5th st: rdn 3f out: sn outpcd) 7 **5**
2278[2] Spumante **(64)***(42) (RChampion)* 3-8-7 GCarter(4) (lw: chsd ldrs: 3rd st: rdn over 2f out: wknd wl over 1f out) 5 **6**

7/4 HAND CRAFT (IRE), **2/1** Pennycairn, **7/2** Verde Luna, **5/1** Spumante, **12/1** Zingibar, **20/1** El Don, CSF £6.02 TOTE £2.90: £1.80 £1.90 (£1.30) OWNER Mrs M. M. Haggas (NEWMARKET) BRED D. and N. Wallace 6 Rn 1m 43.6 (4.00) SF: 30/32/22/18/-/-

2655

AMERICAN ADVENTURE THEME PARK LIMITED STKS (0-60) (3-Y.O+) (Class F) £2,519.00 (£694.00: £329.00) **1m 1f 213y** Stalls: Low GOING minus 0.38 sec per fur (F) 9-00 (9-01)

2145[7] **Music Maker (60)***(69)*(Fav)*(SirMarkPrescott)* 3-8-7 WWoods(8) (hld up: 5th st: hdwy to ld 2f out: hld on gamely fnl f) ....— **1**
1966[2] Lady Highfield **(55)***(70) (MJRyan)* 4-9-5 AClark(2) (hld up: 7th st: jnd wnr over 1f out: hrd rdn fnl f: nt qckn) ....½ **2**
2292[7] Aljawab (USA) **(57)***(68) (JLDunlop)* 4-9-8 GCarter(4) (hld up & bhd: hdwy over 2f out: r.o u.p fnl f: nt rch ldrs) 3½ **3**
2450[2] Suile Mor **(59)***(60) (BRMillman)* 3-8-5 DHolland(6) (a.p: 2nd st: led over 2f out: sn hdd: rdn & one pce fnl f) ....nk **4**
2377[8] Jalmaid **(50)***(60) (BAMcMahon)* 3-8-5 JFortune(1) (a.p: 3rd st: effrt on ins & hmpd 2f out: swtchd rt & nt clr run over 1f out: nt rcvr) ....nk **5**
1598[5] Rushen Raider **(56)***(65) (KWHogg)* 3-8-5 (7) ADaly(5) (led tl over 2f out: wknd over 1f out) ....¾ **6**
2148[4] Salska **(58)***(55) (ALForbes)* 4-9-1 SDWilliams(3) (prom: 6th st: rdn 2f out: sn btn) 2 **7**
1093[12] Slapy Dam **(50)***(57) (JMackie)* 3-8-12 PRobinson(7) (bit bkwd: hld up in rr: rdn 3f out: no imp) 3½ **8**
2396[4] Rubislaw **(31)***(54) (CWFairhurst)* 3-8-10v LCharnock(9) (chsd ldrs: 4th st: rdn & hung lft 2f out: sn btn) ....hd **9**

3/1 MUSIC MAKER, **7/2** Lady Highfield (5/1-10/3), Aljawab (USA), **5/1** Suile Mor, **9/1** Slapy Dam, Rushen Raider (6/1-10/1), **12/1** Salska, **16/1** Jalmaid, **25/1** Rubislaw, CSF £14.21 TOTE £3.50: £1.70 £1.30 £2.30 (£7.80) Trio £4.90 OWNER Cheveley Park Stud (NEWMARKET) BRED Cheveley Park Stud Ltd 9 Rn 2m 8.1 (5.60) SF: 16/27/25/7/7/12/12/4/1

WEIGHT FOR AGE 3yo-10lb

STEWARDS' ENQUIRY Woods susp. 2-4/8/95 (careless riding).

T/Plpt: £83.40 (150.89 Tckts). T/Qdpt: £19.20 (0.5 Tckts); £13.00 to Goodwood 25/7/95. IM

2486-WINDSOR (Fig. 8)
Monday July 24th (Good to firm)

WEATHER: fine WIND: nil

2656

JOHN DISHAW RETIREMENT (S) STKS (2-Y.O) (Class G) £2,507.00 (£702.00: £341.00) **5f 217y** Stalls: High GOING minus 0.54 sec per fur (F) 6-15 (6-16)

Lindas Delight *(54) (JSMoore)* 2-8-6 TWilliams(7) (w'like: bit bkwd: hdwy over 2f out: led wl over 1f out: all out) ....— **1**

2204[5] Ivory's Grab Hire *(59) (KTIvory)* 2-8-4 (7) CScally(4) (b: gd hdwy over 1f out: fin wl) ....s.h **2**
2047[7] Pinocchio Boy (IRE) *(46) (BJMeehan)* 2-8-11 MTebbutt(8) (w ldrs: one pce fnl 2f) 5 **3**
2299[6] Beeny *(44) (APJarvis)* 2-8-8 (3) JTate(9) (w ldrs: outpcd 2f out: styd on ins fnl f)......................¾ **4**
2195[2] Domettes (IRE) *(42)*(Fav)*(RHannon)* 2-8-11 JReid(6) (w ldrs: hrd rdn over 2f out: no rspnse: fin lame)..½ **5**
1031[7] Cupla Focail *(19) (WRMuir)* 2-8-6 MHills(1) (hdwy over 2f out: wknd over 1f out) 7 **6**
Baker *(19) (HCandy)* 2-8-11 WNewnes(2) (unf: bit bkwd: bhd fnl 2f)......................................1½ **7**
2403[5] Rowlandsons Stud (IRE) *(GLMoore)* 2-8-11 SWhitworth(5) (led tl wknd qckly wl over 1f out) 14 **8**
Back In The Black *(MrsJCecil)* 2-8-11 KDarley(3) (leggy: lw: a wl bhd) 7 **9**

4/5 Domettes (IRE) (tchd 5/4), **3/1** Back In The Black (op 6/4), **15/2** Ivory's Grab Hire (7/2-8/1), **10/1** Beeny, **14/1** Baker (op 6/1), **20/1** LINDAS DELIGHT, **25/1** Pinocchio Boy (IRE), Rowlandsons Stud (IRE), Cupla Focail, CSF £151.58 TOTE £20.20: £2.70 £2.00 £3.70 (£94.50) Trio Not won; £188.07 to 25/7/95 OWNER Mr Liam Doherty (EAST GARSTON) BRED M. Yiapatos 9 Rn
1m 14.3 (3.80) SF: -/-/-/-/-/-/-/-/-
Bt in 4,400 gns

2657

COAXIS H'CAP (0-70) (3-Y.O+) (Class E) £4,588.00 (£1,384.00: £672.00: £316.00)
1m 2f 7y Stalls: High GOING minus 0.54 sec per fur (F) 6-45 (6-47)

2490[6] **Just Flamenco (51)***(61)*(Fav)*(MJRyan)* 4-8-13 WCarson(8) (hdwy 3f out: led wl over 1f out: drvn out) ....— **1**
2488[5] Emma Grimes (IRE) **(40)***(48) (JSMoore)* 4-7-9 (7) MartinDwyer(12) (gd hdwy 2f out: r.o ins fnl f)..1½ **2**
2314[6] Lady Lacey **(46)***(53) (GBBalding)* 8-8-8v JWilliams(11) (wl bhd tl gd late hdwy) ....½ **3**
2175[4] Ikhtiraa (USA) **(37)***(43) (RJO'Sullivan)* 5-7-8 (5) MHenry(7) (3rd st: hrd rdn over 2f out: one pce) ....½ **4**
2296[3] Hadabet **(60)***(64) (MissJacquelineDoyle)* 3-8-12 JReid(13) (hdwy on ins 3f out: ev ch over 1f out: wknd fnl f)..1¼ **5**
403[7] Bandita **(47)***(46) (DJSffrenchDavis)* 4-8-9 WWewnes(14) (led tl wknd wl over 1f out)...............3 **6**
2321[10] Thatchmaster (IRE) **(49)***(48) (CAHorgan)* 4-8-11 TWilliams(2) (lw: hdwy 3f out: wknd over 1f out) ....nk **7**
2445[8] Tondres (USA) **(62)***(60) (RIngram)* 4-9-10b AMcGlone(5) (s.s: nvr nrr).................................½ **8**
2490[3] Mighty Kingdom (IRE) **(43)***(22) (JohnBerry)* 4-8-0 (5) NVarley(1) (7th st: wknd over 2f out) 12 **9**
1940* Mister O'Grady (IRE) **(45)***(18) (RAkehurst)* 4-8-7 TQuinn(10) (lw: 4th st: wknd over 2f out)...3½ **10**
2317[4] Secret Ballad (IRE) **(63)***(35) (JAkehurst)* 3-9-1 SWhitworth(9) (5th st: wknd over 2f out) ....¾ **11**
2319[10] White Heat **(63)***(33) (MJHeaton-Ellis)* 3-9-1 MRoberts(3) (b: 6th st: wknd 3f out)...................1¼ **12**
1628[10] Shy Paddy (IRE) **(47)***(8) (KOCunningham-Brown)* 3-7-13 GBardwell(4) (2nd st: wknd over 3f out) 6 **13**
Manila Bay (USA) **(55)***(15) (JSKing)* 5-9-3 StephenDavies(6) (bit bkwd: a bhd).......................½ **14**

7/2 JUST FLAMENCO, **9/2** Mister O'Grady (IRE), **11/2** Hadabet, Secret Ballad (IRE), **6/1** Mighty Kingdom (IRE), **10/1** Lady Lacey (8/1-12/1), Ikhtiraa (USA) (8/1-12/1), **12/1** Emma Grimes (IRE) (20/1-10/1), White Heat (op 8/1), Thatchmaster (IRE), **14/1** Tondres (USA), **16/1** Bandita, **20/1** Shy Paddy (IRE), **25/1** Manila Bay (USA), CSF £51.22 CT £391.63 TOTE £3.80: £1.80 £3.80 £2.80 (£99.90) Trio £346.60 OWNER Mrs S. M. Martin (NEWMARKET) BRED Mrs L. Martin 14 Rn
2m 6.9 (2.00) SF: 38/25/30/20/31/23/25/37/-/-/2/-/-/-
WEIGHT FOR AGE 3yo-10lb

2658

SMS H'CAP (0-70) (3-Y.O+) (Class E) £4,276.00 (£1,288.00: £624.00: £292.00)
1m 3f 135y Stalls: High GOING minus 0.54 sec per fur (F) 7-15 (7-18)

2050[5] **Paradise Waters (57)***(67)*(Fav)*(RFJohnsonHoughton)* 3-8-6 JReid(1) (led tl over 2f out: rallied to ld ins fnl f: all out)..— **1**
2138[5] Admirals Secret (USA) **(67)***(76) (CFWall)* 6-9-9 (5) LNewton(4) (lw: 6th st: rdn & outpcd over 2f out: str run fnl f: r.o) ....½ **2**
2224[2] Jean de Florette (USA) **(33)***(41) (JohnBerry)* 4-7-3 (5)ow1 NVarley(6) (5th st: led over 1f out tl ins fnl f: r.o)...nk **3**
1970[6] Faustino **(50)***(59) (PFICole)* 3-7-13 StephenDavies(5) (2nd st: led over 2f out tl over 1f out: r.o)..s.h **4**
2557[9] Anlace **(54)***(57) (SMellor)* 6-9-1 MWigham(3) (nvr nrr)..4 **5**
2392[5] Myfontaine **(64)***(65) (KTIvory)* 8-9-11 GBardwell(8) (lw: hdwy 4f out: ev ch 2f out: wknd fnl f)..1¾ **6**
2314[9] Make a Stand **(52)***(43) (HCandy)* 4-8-13b WNewnes(2) (3rd st: wknd 3f out) 7 **7**
1844[4] Stevie's Wonder (IRE) **(58)***(40) (MJRyan)* 5-9-5 WCarson(9) (hmpd & snatched up over 5f out: nt rcvr)...7 **8**
*2494** Backview **(69)***(49) (BJLlewellyn)* 3-9-4 5x TWilliams(7) (4th st: wknd over 3f out)......................1 **9**

3/1 PARADISE WATERS, **7/2** Stevie's Wonder (IRE), **11/2** Backview, **7/1** Anlace (5/1-8/1), **9/1** Admirals Secret (USA) (op 5/1), Myfontaine, Jean de Florette (USA), Faustino, **16/1** Make a Stand, CSF £28.43 CT £202.82 TOTE £3.70: £1.60 £4.10 £2.60 (£20.30) Trio £45.60 OWNER Mr R. Crutchley (DIDCOT) BRED R. E. Crutchley 9 Rn 2m 27.6 (1.60) SF: 37/58/23/29/39/47/25/22/19

WEIGHT FOR AGE 3yo-12lb

2659 BOWMAN BOOKMAKERS H'CAP (0-80) (3-Y.O+ F & M) (Class D) £5,540.00 (£1,670.00: £810.00: £380.00)

5f 217y Stalls: High GOING minus 0.54 sec per fur (F) 7-45 (7-51)

2491*	**Charnwood Queen (54)***(60) (RWArmstrong)* 3-8-1 7x WCarson(8) (lw: mde virtually all: rdn out)	—	1
2202⁴	Winsome Wooster **(64)***(70) (PGMurphy)* 4-9-0 (3) SDrowne(13) (a.p: r.o wl ins fnl f)	hd	2
2344³	Taffeta Silk (USA) **(64)***(70) (WJarvis)* 4-8-12 (5) MHenry(10) (a.p: ev ch over 1f out: r.o)	hd	3
2507²	Brockton Flame **(67)***(67) (JMPEustace)* 3-9-0 MHills(6) (a.p: one pce fnl 2f)	2	4
2079⁷	Midnight Break **(65)***(65) (PTWalwyn)* 3-8-12 JReid(11) (w wnr: ev ch 2f out: one pce)	hd	5
2364*	Bold Gem **(53)***(50) (BJMeehan)* 4-8-6b TQuinn(12) (nrst fin)	1¼	6
2491⁹	Kensington Freight **(46)***(42) (JAkehurst)* 3-7-7 NAdams(9) (nvr nrr)	s.h	7
2096²	Patsy Grimes **(66)***(54) (LJHolt)* 5-9-5 AMcGlone(2) (nvr nr to chal)	3	8
2330¹⁰	I'm Your Lady **(71)***(57) (BAMcMahon)* 4-9-7 (3) SSanders(4) (spd over 4f)	1	9
1660²	Lough Erne **(71)***(50)*(Fav)*(CFWall)* 3-9-4 TIves(14) (lw: prom 4f)	2½	10
2393⁸	Last Ambition (IRE) **(47)***(18) (CREgerton)* 3-7-3 (5)ow1 NVarley(1) (spd 4f)	2½	11
2404*	Poyle Jezebelle **(51)***(15) (MBlanshard)* 4-8-4 StephenDavies(3) (spd 4f)	3	12
2301³	Raisa Point **(47)** *(WRMuir)* 4-8-0 GBardwell(5) (swtg: a wl bhd)	10	13

LONG HANDICAP Last Ambition (IRE) 7-1 Kensington Freight 6-9

7/2 Lough Erne (9/2-3/1), **4/1** CHARNWOOD QUEEN, Brockton Flame, **11/2** Patsy Grimes, **10/1** Poyle Jezebelle, Bold Gem (8/1-12/1), **12/1** Taffeta Silk (USA), Midnight Break, **16/1** Winsome Wooster, **20/1** Raisa Point, I'm Your Lady, **50/1** Last Ambition (IRE), Kensington Freight, CSF £64.34 CT £668.31 TOTE £4.10: £1.80 £4.30 £2.80 (£53.20) Trio £163.70 OWNER Mr R. V. Cliff (NEWMARKET) BRED Rockhouse Farms Ltd 13 Rn

1m 11.0 (0.50) SF: 33/49/49/40/38/29/15/33/36/23/-/-/-

WEIGHT FOR AGE 3yo-6lb

2660 SANGRIA DESIGNS 25TH ANNIVERSARY MAIDEN STKS (2-Y.O) (Class D) £5,572.50 (£1,680.00: £815.00: £382.50)

5f 10y Stalls: High GOING minus 0.54 sec per fur (F) 8-15 (8-17)

1406²	**Rambling Bear** *(91) (MBlanshard)* 2-9-0 StephenDavies(13) (lw: a.p: led 2f out: r.o wl)	—	1
2408¹⁰	Cross The Border *(82) (RHannon)* 2-9-0 KDarley(10) (a.p: ev ch over 1f out: r.o)	3	2
	Fond Embrace *(76) (HCandy)* 2-8-9 WNewnes(2) (unf: bit bkwd: hdwy over 1f out: r.o ins fnl f)	hd	3
1751³	Forest Robin *(78) (RFJohnsonHoughton)* 2-9-0 BThomson(8) (lw: mid div tl r.o fnl f)	1	4
690⁴	Friendly Forester (USA) *(74) (RCharlton)* 2-9-0 TQuinn(11) (bit bkwd: chsd ldrs: one pce fnl 2f)	1¼	5
2351⁴	Comic Fantasy (AUS) *(69)*(Fav)*(PWChapple-Hyam)* 2-8-9 JReid(7) (wnt lft s: led to 2f out: wknd 1f out)	s.h	6
	Hurtleberry (IRE) *(67) (LordHuntingdon)* 2-8-9 JWilliams(5) (leggy: nvr nr to chal)	½	7
2487⁶	Supreme Power *(66) (WRMuir)* 2-9-0 TIves(1) (lw: spd over 2f)	2	8
	Ma Bulsie *(56) (BAMcMahon)* 2-8-6 (3) SSanders(6) (leggy: hmpd s: nvr nrr)	1½	9
	Maraschino *(51) (MJHeaton-Ellis)* 2-8-9 MRoberts(12) (leggy: bit bkwd: dwlt: a bhd)	1½	10
	Golina (IRE) *(32) (BWHills)* 2-8-9 MHills(3) (unf: bit bkwd: spd over 2f)	6	11
	Longhill Boy *(26) (BJMeehan)* 2-9-0 RHughes(9) (w'like: bit bkwd: a bhd)	3½	12
1481⁷	Ben'a'vachei Boy *(25) (JDBethell)* 2-9-0 WCarson(4) (plld hrd: w ldrs 2f: wknd qckly)	nk	13

6/5 Comic Fantasy (AUS), **5/1** Cross The Border, **7/1** RAMBLING BEAR (4/1-8/1), Golina (IRE) (8/1-12/1), Fond Embrace (op 3/1), **8/1** Friendly Forester (USA) (op 4/1), Forest Robin (5/1-10/1), **9/1** Hurtleberry (IRE) (10/1-16/1), **16/1** Ben'a'vachei Boy, Supreme Power, **20/1** Longhill Boy, **25/1** Maraschino, **33/1** Ma Bulsie, CSF £50.44 TOTE £8.10: £2.50 £2.30 £3.90 (£36.70) Trio £223.30 OWNER Mrs Michael Hill (UPPER LAMBOURN) BRED E. A. Badger 13 Rn

60.2 secs (1.20) SF: 32/23/17/19/15/10/8/7/-/-/-/-/-

2661 CHAMPAGNE LANSON CLAIMING STKS (3-Y.O+) (Class F) £3,077.00 (£926.00: £448.00: £209.00)

1m 67y Stalls: High GOING minus 0.54 sec per fur (F) 8-45 (8-45)

2057³	**Reprehend (86)***(84)*(Fav)*(RHannon)* 4-9-2 JReid(3) (4th st: rdn to ld over 2f out: all out)	—	1

*2292*6 Waldo **(65)***(78) (LordHuntingdon)* 4-8-5v(7) AimeeCook(8) (lw: 7th st: hdwy 3f out: ev ch fnl 2f: no ex)....1 **2**
2433 3 Red Valerian **(71)***(82) (KMcAuliffe)* 4-9-10b MPerrett(6) (5th st: r.o one pce fnl 2f)....4 **3**
2602 7 Serious Option (IRE) **(69)***(73) (PFICole)* 4-9-4b TQuinn(2) (6th st: ev ch over 2f out: one pce)....2 **4**
2037 12 Code of Silence **(41)***(56) (GFHCharles-Jones)* 3-8-0 (3)ow2 PMcCabe(4) (nvr nrr)....4 **5**
2486 9 Burnt Sienna (IRE) **(28)***(48) (JSMoore)* 3-7-3v(5) NVarley(5) (2nd st: wknd over 2f out)....½ **6**
1371 9 Sorisky **(39)***(45) (BGubby)* 3-7-10 (5) MHenry(1) (led tl wknd over 2f out)....5 **7**
1754 10 Daswaki (CAN) **(65)***(47) (GLMoore)* 7-8-11 SWhitworth(7) (b: swtg: 3rd st: wknd over 3f out)....nk **8**
2016 10 Scboo *(6) (REPeacock)* 6-8-9 JWilliams(9) (a bhd: t.o)....20 **9**

11/8 REPREHEND (Evens-6/4), **11/4** Red Valerian, **9/2** Serious Option (IRE), **7/1** Waldo, **16/1** Burnt Sienna (IRE), **20/1** Daswaki (CAN), **50/1** Sorisky, Code of Silence, Scboo, CSF £11.01 TOTE £2.20: £1.20 £1.70 £1.30 (£5.80) Trio £6.20 OWNER Mrs C. J. Powell (MARLBOROUGH) BRED Shanbally House Stud 9 Rn 1m 44.0 (2.40) SF: 33/27/31/22/-/-/-/-/-
WEIGHT FOR AGE 3yo-8lb

T/Jkpt: Not won; £34,380.51 to Goodwood 25/7/95. T/Plpt: £2,223.40 (9.1 Tckts). T/Qdpt: £122.50 (1.6 Tckts). Hn

2498-**BEVERLEY (R-H)**
Tuesday July 25th (Good to firm)
WEATHER: sunny & hot WIND: slt bhd

2662
LADYGATE (S) H'CAP (0-60) (3-Y.O) (Class F) £2,798.00 (£778.00: £374.00)
1m 3f 216y Stalls: High GOING minus 0.58 sec per fur (F) 2-20 (2-21)

2232 5 **Coast Along (IRE) (31)***(45) (CWThornton)* 3-7-12 SMaloney(3) (a chsng ldrs: effrt ent st: led 1f out: all out)....— **1**
2480 3 High Flown (USA) **(44)***(56)*(Fav)*(RonaldThompson)* 3-8-6 (5) LNewton(2) (w ldrs: led 6½f out to 1f out: kpt on)....1¾ **2**
2480 2 Remontant (IRE) **(38)***(48)*(Fav)*(RHollinshead)* 3-8-2 (3) AGarth(1) (chsd ldrs: hdwy 4f out: one pce fnl 2f)....1½ **3**
2480* Bunker (IRE) **(54)***(64) (JPearce)* 3-9-7 6x AMackay(4) (lw: hdwy appr st: chsng ldrs 2f out: r.o one pce)....hd **4**
2129 4 Our Rainbow **(36)***(28) (MrsSMAustin)* 3-8-0 (3) DarrenMoffatt(5) (b: bhd: hdwy over 3f out: sn in tch: wknd fnl 2f)....13 **5**
2282 9 Drumochter **(54)***(41) (DMorley)* 3-9-7 WRyan(6) (hdwy 5f out: sn prom: wl outpcd fnl 2f)....4 **6**
2544 7 Castletown Count **(45)***(25) (KWHogg)* 3-8-5 (7) ADaly(8) (led tl hdd 6½f out: wknd 3f out)....5 **7**
1801 9 Our Bairn **(52)** *(RThompson)* 3-9-5 NAdams(7) (wl bhd fnl 6f: t.o)....dist **8**

7/2 High Flown (USA), Remontant (IRE), **4/1** Drumochter, **9/2** Bunker (IRE), **11/2** COAST ALONG (IRE), **8/1** Our Rainbow, **20/1** Castletown Count, Our Bairn, CSF £24.25 CT £68.61 TOTE £7.10: £1.40 £1.60 £1.60 (£13.20) OWNER The Challengers (MIDDLEHAM) BRED John Poynton 8 Rn
2m 39.8 (8.30) SF: -/-/-/5/-/-/-/-
No bid.

2663
MAX JAFFA MEMORIAL H'CAP (0-70) (3-Y.O+) (Class E) £3,163.00 (£949.00: £457.00: £211.00)
1m 3f 216y Stalls: High GOING minus 0.58 sec per fur (F) 2-50 (2-51)

2545 8 **Kinoko (35)***(48) (KWHogg)* 7-7-6 (5) MBaird(1) (unruly in stalls: stdd s: hdwy 4f out: led wl over 1f out: r.o)....— **1**
2159* North Ardar **(57)***(69)*(Fav)*(MrsMReveley)* 5-8-12 (7) SCopp(4) (trckd ldrs: smooth hdwy to ld over 2f out: sn rdn: hdd & one pce)....¾ **2**
2355 6 Masuri Kabisa (USA) **(31)***(34) (HJCollingridge)* 4-7-7 NAdams(2) (lw: led 2f: chsd ldrs: rdn appr st: one pce)....7 **3**
2373 5 First Bid **(66)***(68) (RMWhitaker)* 8-10-0 ACulhane(5) (pushed along 5f out: hdwy 3f out: one pce fnl 2f)....nk **4**
2400* Goodbye Millie **(49)***(38) (JLEyre)* 5-8-11v RLappin(3) (lw: led after 2f: sn pushed along: hdd over 2f out: sn btn)....10 **5**
LONG HANDICAP Masuri Kabisa (USA) 7-5

Evens North Ardar, **5/2** First Bid, **11/2** Goodbye Millie, **6/1** Masuri Kabisa (USA), **12/1** KINOKO, CSF £24.78 TOTE £12.30: £3.40 £1.20 (£9.40) OWNER Mr Anthony White (ISLE OF MAN) BRED Auldyn Stud Ltd 5 Rn 2m 37.9 (6.40) SF: -/18/-/17/-

2664 TIMEFORM LADIES RACE FOR THE DOROTHY LAIRD TROPHY H'CAP (0-80) (3-Y.O+) (Class E) £3,185.75 (£956.00: £460.50: £212.75)
1m 1f 207y Stalls: High GOING minus 0.58 sec per fur (F) 3-25 (3-25)

2327* **Harry Browne (IRE) (60)***(70) (MrsJRRamsden)* 3-8-10 (5)ow2 MissERamsden(1) (hld up: hdwy on outside appr st: led appr fnl f: r.o) ....— 1
2396³ Gold Blade **(47)***(57)*(Fav)*(JPearce)* 6-8-12 MrsLPearce(9) (lw: disp ld: led & qcknd 3f out: hdd appr fnl f: no ex) 1¼ 2
2449² Cyphell (IRE) **(70)***(80) (MRStoute)* 3-9-6 (5) MrsSEddery(8) (trckd ldrs: nt clr run 2f out: kpt on fnl f) ....nk 3
2621² Gallardini (IRE) **(52)***(61) (BSRothwell)* 6-8-12 (5) MissAlexMcCabe(3) (lw: hld up: effrt & swtchd 2f out: styd on towards fin) ....hd 4
2343³ Laxford Bridge **(77)***(86) (PWHarris)* 4-11-0 MissAElsey(7) (lw: disp ld tl hdd 3f out: rdn & one pce) ....s.h 5
2254² Self Expression **(55)***(62) (MrsJRRamsden)* 7-9-1 (5) MissFHaynes(6) (lw: s.s: hld up & bhd: effrt on ins over 2f out: n.m.r & n.d) 1¼ 6
2375⁸ Fort Vally **(42)***(46) (BWMurray)* 5-8-7v AmandaSanders(2) (dwlt: hld up & bhd: rdn over 2f out: n.d) 2 7
1845⁵ Shift Again (IRE) **(77)***(73) (WJarvis)* 3-9-13 (5) MissIFoustok(5) (lw: plld hrd: trckd ldrs tl outpcd fnl 2f) 5 8

LONG HANDICAP Fort Vally 7-13

5/2 Gold Blade, **9/2** HARRY BROWNE (IRE), Laxford Bridge, **5/1** Self Expression, **6/1** Cyphell (IRE), **10/1** Gallardini (IRE), Shift Again (IRE), **20/1** Fort Vally, CSF £15.93 CT £62.29 TOTE £6.50: £1.80 £1.20 £1.50 (£5.80) Trio £7.40 OWNER Mrs J. R. Ramsden (THIRSK) BRED Patrick Whelan in Ireland 8 Rn 2m 13.0 (10.50) SF: -/-/-/-/-/-/-/-
WEIGHT FOR AGE 3yo-10lb

2665 'GO RACING IN YORKSHIRE' CLAIMING STKS (3-Y.O+) (Class F) £2,924.00 (£814.00: £392.00)
5f Stalls: Centre GOING minus 0.58 sec per fur (F) 4-00 (4-01)

2585⁴ **Here Comes a Star (69)***(71) (JMCarr)* 7-9-0 ACulhane(4) (a.p: led appr fnl f: hrd rdn & r.o) .— 1
2521⁹ Rhythmic Dancer **(65)***(62) (JLSpearing)* 7-8-5 (3) SDrowne(1) (a chsng ldrs: effrt over 1f out: styd on) 1 2
2418⁴ Gorinsky (IRE) **(79)***(69)*(Fav)*(JBerry)* 7-9-2 GCarter(2) (dwlt: hdwy ½-wy: kpt on fnl f) ....nk 3
2492³ King Rambo **(63)***(69) (RHollinshead)* 4-9-2 WRyan(7) (hld up: hdwy 2f out: one pce ins fnl f) ....hd 4
2521¹³ Olifantsfontein **(50)***(56) (DNicholls)* 7-8-6 NConnorton(5) (lw: hld up: hdwy over 1f out: nvr plcd to chal) ....¾ 5
2295⁸ Super Sonata **(59)***(52) (PDEvans)* 3-7-12v SMaloney(8) (led tl hdd appr fnl f: no ex) ....nk 6
2533⁸ Metal Boys **(64)***(54) (MissLCSiddall)* 8-8-10 GHind(6) (lw: sn drvn along: nvr trbld ldrs) 1¾ 7
2502⁸ Farndale **(38)***(42) (RonaldThompson)* 8-8-3 (5) LNewton(3) (outpcd fr ½-wy) 3 8
1909⁴ Cradle Days **(62)***(27) (RCSpicer)* 6-8-12b RPerham(9) (bolted gng to s: cl up to ½-wy: wknd qckly) 6 9

2/1 Gorinsky (IRE), **3/1** HERE COMES A STAR, **6/1** King Rambo, **7/1** Rhythmic Dancer, Metal Boys, **8/1** Super Sonata, **10/1** Cradle Days, **16/1** Olifantsfontein, **33/1** Farndale, CSF £24.60 TOTE £3.70: £1.60 £2.40 £1.40 (£20.10) Trio £18.60 OWNER Mrs June Goodridge (MALTON) BRED A. and M. Scarfe 9 Rn 63.5 secs (2.00) SF: 20/11/18/18/5/-/3/-/-
WEIGHT FOR AGE 3yo-5lb

2666 FAMILY DAY MAIDEN AUCTION STKS (2-Y.O F) (Class F) £2,910.00 (£810.00: £390.00) 5f
Stalls: Centre GOING minus 0.58 sec per fur (F) 4-30 (4-34)

Little Noggins (IRE) *(65) (JohnBerry)* 2-7-7 (5) NVarley(6) (leggy: unf: mde all: rdn & r.o wl fnl f) ....— 1
2221³ Arrhythmic (IRE) *(62)*(Fav)*(MBrittain)* 2-8-4 ow6 KFallon(2) (lw: chsd ldrs: smooth hdwy 2f out: chal appr fnl f: rdn & nt qckn) 1 2
1278¹¹ Scenicris (IRE) *(54) (RHollinshead)* 2-7-9 (3) AGarth(8) (hdwy 2f out: styd on: nrst fin) 2½ 3
2498² Wrays (USA) *(49) (MJohnston)* 2-8-1 TWilliams(5) (spd 3f: sn rdn & btn) 2½ 4
Needwood Fantasy *(35) (BAMcMahon)* 2-7-12 FNorton(1) (unf: drvn along thrght: nvr trbld ldrs) 3½ 5
Salilian Twilight *(JPearce)* 2-7-12 AMackay(4) (lt-f: unf: s.s: a bhd) 11 6
Babsy Babe *(JJQuinn)* 2-8-1 DaleGibson(3) (Withdrawn not under Starter's orders: ref to ent stalls) .... W
Northern Falcon *(MWEasterby)* 2-8-1 SMaloney(7) (Withdrawn not under Starter's orders: unruly in stalls: jockey inj) .... W

11/10 Arrhythmic (IRE), **9/4** Wrays (USA), **9/2** Babsy Babe, **10/1** Salilian Twilight, LITTLE NOGGINS (IRE), **14/1** Scenicris (IRE), **20/1** Needwood Fantasy, Northern Falcon, CSF £17.67 TOTE £12.40: £1.70 £1.40 (£8.10) OWNER Mr M. E. Hall (NEWMARKET) BRED A. M. F. Persse 6 Rn
62.9 secs (1.40) SF: 14/11/3/-/-/-/-/-

2667 E.B.F. MINSTER MOORGATE MAIDEN STKS (2-Y.O) (Class D)
£3,977.00 (£1,196.00: £578.00: £269.00)
7f 100y Stalls: High GOING minus 0.58 sec per fur (F) 5-00 (5-03)

1485[3] **Modern Day (USA)** *(86)*(Fav)*(HRACecil)* 2-9-0 WRyan(7) (lw: unruly stalls: in tch: rdn over 2f out: r.o u.p to ld wl ins fnl f) ....— 1
2485[2] Pleasant Surprise *(85) (MJohnston)* 2-9-0 TWilliams(2) (led: clr 3f out: hdd wl ins fnl f: kpt on).......½ 2
1964[3] Lionel Edwards (IRE) *(77) (PFICole)* 2-9-0 GCarter(9) (lw: chsd ldrs: rdn 3f out: one pce) ...3½ 3
2005[6] Nabhaan (IRE) *(77) (DMorley)* 2-9-0 MTebbutt(1) (shkn up & hdwy 3f out: styd on wl towards fin) ....s.h 4
Serious Trust *(60) (SirMarkPrescott)* 2-9-0 WWoods(4) (unf: outpcd tl hdwy u.p over 2f out: nvr rchd ldrs) 8 5
2380[9] Hobbs Choice *(44) (MissJFCraze)* 2-8-9v SWebster(8) (chsd ldr tl rdn & btn over 2f out).........5 6
1856[8] Lahik (IRE) *(39) (TThomsonJones)* 2-9-0 StephenDavies(5) (sn outpcd & bhd: n.d).......5 7
Noir Esprit *(37) (JMCarr)* 2-9-0 SMorris(6) (leggy: bit bkwd: a outpcd & bhd).......1 8
2420[5] Supermister *(15) (MHEasterby)* 2-9-0 MBirch(3) (chsd ldrs 4f: wknd qckly) 10 9

4/9 MODERN DAY (USA), **9/2** Lionel Edwards (IRE), **7/1** Pleasant Surprise, **8/1** Serious Trust (op 5/1), **14/1** Lahik (IRE), **20/1** Supermister, Nabhaan (IRE), **50/1** Noir Esprit, **100/1** Hobbs Choice, CSF £5.61 TOTE £1.40: £1.10 £1.60 (£3.60) Trio £3.40 OWNER Mr K. Abdullah (NEWMARKET) BRED Juddmonte Farms 9 Rn 1m 33.6 (1.60) SF: 34/33/25/25/8/-/-/-/-

2668 MALTON H'CAP (0-80) (3-Y.O+) (Class D) £4,323.00 (£1,299.00: £627.00: £291.00) **1m 100y** Stalls: High GOING minus 0.58 sec per fur (F) 5-30 (5-31)

2457[12] **Bold Amusement (78)***(90) (WSCunningham)* 5-9-11 (3) DRMcCabe(1) (lw: dwlt: hdwy appr st: led over 1f out: r.o wl) ....— 1
2375[3] Nobby Barnes **(43)***(52) (DonEnricoIncisa)* 6-7-7 KimTinkler(5) (lw: bhd tl hdwy 2f out: r.o towards fin).......1½ 2
2503* Lorelei Lee (IRE) **(62)***(69) (JohnBerry)* 3-8-4 ow2 KFallon(2) (in tch: hdwy over 2f out: ev ch over 1f out: nt qckn) ....nk 3
2484[2] Lord Vivienne (IRE) **(43)***(47) (BSRothwell)* 6-7-7 JMarshall(4) (disp ld tl led ½-wy: hdd over 1f out: grad wknd).......2½ 4
2332[10] Chantry Bellini **(46)***(39) (MrsSMAustin)* 6-7-7b(3) DarrenMoffatt(3) (b: b.hind: outpcd ent st: n.d after) 6 5
2123[6] Prizefighter **(63)***(55) (JLEyre)* 4-8-13 StephenDavies(7) (disp ld 4f: wknd fnl 2f) ....hd 6
2419[2] Murphy's Gold (IRE) **(58)***(46)*(Fav)*(RAFahey)* 4-8-8 ACulhane(6) (chsd ldrs: rdn & n.m.r over 2f out: sn wknd).......2½ 7

LONG HANDICAP Nobby Barnes 7-5 Lord Vivienne (IRE) 7-6

2/1 Murphy's Gold (IRE), **7/2** Lorelei Lee (IRE), **5/1** BOLD AMUSEMENT, **11/2** Lord Vivienne (IRE), **6/1** Prizefighter (op 10/1), **13/2** Chantry Bellini, **10/1** Nobby Barnes, CSF £47.98 TOTE £7.70: £3.80 £3.70 (£20.20) OWNER Mr David Bell (YARM) BRED Cheveley Park Stud Ltd 7 Rn
1m 47.0 (3.00) SF: 36/-/7/-/-/1/-
WEIGHT FOR AGE 3yo-8lb

T/Plpt: £6.50 (2,022.72 Tckts). T/Qdpt: £3.00 (40.7 Tckts). AA

2053-GOODWOOD (R-H)
Tuesday July 25th (Good to firm st, Firm Rnd)
WEATHER: very hot WIND: fresh behind

2669 CITROEN XANTIA H'CAP (0-85) (3-Y.O+) (Class D) £8,025.00 (£2,400.00: £1,150.00: £525.00) **1m** Stalls: High GOING minus 0.33 sec (GF) 2-30 (2-32)

2321[7] **Secret Aly (CAN) (73)***(90+) (CEBrittain)* 5-9-2 MRoberts(8) (lw: 2nd st: led over 3f out: clr over 1f out: r.o wl) ....— 1
1638[13] Pay Homage **(84)***(89) (IABalding)* 7-9-13 LDettori(11) (4th st: rdn over 3f out: r.o one pce)......6 2
2321[5] Caleman **(75)***(80)*(Fav)*(RBoss)* 6-9-4 JWeaver(3) (3rd st: rdn over 3f out: one pce).......hd 3
2139[10] Fairelaine **(58)***(62) (APJarvis)* 3-7-0 (7) CAdamson(1) (lw: rdn over 3f out: hdwy over 1f out: r.o one pce) ....nk 4
2240[3] Captain's Day **(82)***(85) (TGMills)* 3-9-3 KDarley(9) (5th st: rdn over 3f out: r.o ins fnl f) ....½ 5

2056[5] Another Fiddle (IRE) **(66)***(66) (RAkehurst)* 5-8-9 TQuinn(6) (lw: 6th st: nt clr run over 2f out: one pce)............1½ 6
2345[7] Kingchip Boy **(73)***(70) (MJRyan)* 6-9-2v AClark(5) (rdn over 4f out: hdwy on ins 2f out: wknd over 1f out)............1½ 7
1131[7] Tiler (IRE) **(81)***(77) (MJohnston)* 3-9-2 PRobinson(2) (lw: led over 4f: wknd fnl f)............¾ 8
2446[3] Night Dance **(82)***(58) (GLewis)* 3-9-3 PaulEddery(4) (a bhd)............10 9

LONG HANDICAP Fairelaine 7-6

4/1 Caleman, **5/1** Night Dance, **6/1** Captain's Day, Another Fiddle (IRE) (4/1-13/2), **7/1** Pay Homage, **15/2** Kingchip Boy, **11/1** SECRET ALY (CAN) (8/1-12/1), Tiler (IRE), **25/1** Fairelaine, CSF £73.07 CT £306.41 TOTE £14.20: £4.10 £2.20 £1.40 (£45.10) Trio £56.60 OWNER Mr B. H. Voak (NEWMARKET) BRED Northern Equine Thoroughbred Productions 9 Rn

1m 37.45 (-0.15) SF: 75/74/65/39/62/51/55/54/35

WEIGHT FOR AGE 3yo-8lb

2670 WESTMINSTER TAXI INSURANCE GORDON STKS (Gp 3) (3-Y.O) (Class A) £22,183.00 (£8,197.00: £3,923.50: £1,592.50: £621.25: £232.75) **1m 4f** Stalls: Low GOING minus 0.33 sec per fur (GF) 3-10 (3-11)

2323[3] **Presenting (119)***(119)*(Fav)*(JHMGosden)* 3-8-10 LDettori(4) (2nd st: led 3f out: hrd rdn over 1f out: r.o wl)............— 1
2273* Don Corleone **(113)***(117) (RCharlton)* 3-8-10 KDarley(1) (4th st: hrd rdn over 2f out: ev ch wl over 1f out: unable qckn)............1½ 2
2323[2] Istidaad (USA) **(113)***(116) (ACStewart)* 3-8-10 WCarson(6) (lw: 5th st: rdn 1f out: one pce)....½ 3
2323[5] In Camera (IRE) **(109)***(112) (MRStoute)* 3-8-10 WRSwinburn(5) (lw: 6th st: rdn over 3f out: one pce)............3 4
1897[3] Kalabo (USA) **(113)***(109) (HRACecil)* 3-8-10 MJKinane(2) (chsd ldr: led over 8f out tl over 6f out: led over 4f out to 3f out: wknd over 1f out)............2½ 5
2273[2] Indian Light **(104)***(108) (JLDunlop)* 3-8-10 TQuinn(3) (7th st: a bhd)............½ 6
2044a[8] Painter's Row (IRE) **(111)** *(PWChapple-Hyam)* 3-8-13 JReid(7) (lw: led over 3f: led over 6f out tl over 4f out: 3rd st: wknd over 3f out: t.o whn p.u ins fnl f: lame)............ P

7/4 PRESENTING, **11/4** Kalabo (USA), **11/2** Don Corleone, **6/1** Istidaad (USA), **12/1** Painter's Row (IRE), **14/1** In Camera (IRE), **20/1** Indian Light, CSF £10.81 TOTE £2.70: £1.40 £2.70 (£6.60) OWNER Mr George Strawbridge (NEWMARKET) BRED George Strawbridge 7 Rn

2m 31.57 (0.27 under best) (-0.43) SF: 72/70/69/65/62/61/-

2671 KING GEORGE STKS (Gp 3) (3-Y.O+) (Class A) £27,920.00 (£10,456.00: £5,028.00: £2,196.00) **5f** Stalls: Low GOING minus 0.65 sec (HD) 3-45 (3-47)

2212a* **Hever Golf Rose (107)***(118) (TJNaughton)* 4-9-5 JWeaver(2) (lw: n.m.r 3f out: swtchd lft over 1f out: rapid hdwy fnl f: led last strides)............— 1
2430[8] Eveningperformance **(105)***(108) (HCandy)* 4-8-11 WNewnes(9) (chsd ldr: led over 1f out: rdn & hdd last strides)............½ 2
2285[2] Saint Express **(104)***(111) (MrsMReveley)* 5-9-0 KDarley(10) (lw: a.p: rdn 2f out: r.o ins fnl f) .hd 3
2368[6] Millstream (USA) **(110)***(113) (MJohnston)* 3-8-11 MJKinane(7) (hld up: rdn 3f out: r.o ins fnl f)............hd 4
2416[3] Welsh Mist **(102)***(104) (RBoss)* 4-8-11 LDettori(4) (rdn over 2f out: hdwy over 1f out: r.o).....1¼ 5
2039a[3] Palacegate Episode (IRE) **(107)***(107) (JBerry)* 5-9-2 JCarroll(6) (lw: led over 3f)............½ 6
2285[W] Mistertopogigo (IRE) **(106)***(105) (WSCunningham)* 5-9-0 MRoberts(1) (b. off hind: nvr nr to chal)............hd 7
2285[8] Loch Patrick **(106)***(105) (LJHolt)* 5-9-0 AMcGlone(3) (lw: outpcd: rdn & hdwy over 1f out: one pce ins fnl f)............hd 8
1637[2] Don't Worry Me (IRE) **(100)***(96) (FHLee)* 3-8-6 PaulEddery(8) (prom over 3f)............1¾ 9
1896[2] Struggler *(98)*(Fav)*(CLaffon-Parias,France)* 3-9-0 WRSwinburn(5) (bhd fnl 3f)............2 10
1364[4] Raah Algharb (USA) **(109)***(92) (MRStoute)* 3-8-9 MHills(11) (s.s: outpcd)............nk 11

11/4 Struggler, **7/1** Millstream (USA), Saint Express, Loch Patrick, **8/1** Eveningperformance, **10/1** HEVER GOLF ROSE, **12/1** Mistertopogigo (IRE), Welsh Mist, **14/1** Raah Algharb (USA), **20/1** Don't Worry Me (IRE), Palacegate Episode (IRE), CSF £77.78 TOTE £9.50: £2.40 £3.50 £3.10 (£66.00) Trio £162.40 OWNER Mr M. P. Hanson (EPSOM) BRED Ronald Popely 11 Rn

56.25 secs (0.06 under best) (-0.45) SF: 54/44/47/44/40/43/41/41/27/29/23

WEIGHT FOR AGE 3yo-5lb

2672 WILLIAM HILL CUP H'CAP (4-Y.O+) (Class B) £35,337.50 (£10,700.00: £5,225.00: £1,243.75: £1,243.75) **1m 2f** Stalls: High GOING minus 0.33 sec (GF) 4-15 (4-20)

2241[9] **Silver Groom (IRE) (65)***(79+) (RAkehurst)* 5-7-6 (5) MHenry(12) (3rd st: led 2f out: clr 1f out: comf)............— 1

1851[7] Hunters of Brora (IRE) **(87)***(97) (JDBethell)* 5-9-5 TIves(7) (13th st: nt clr run over 3f out tl over 1f out: swtchd lft: gd hdwy fnl f: fin wl) 2½ **2**
2118* Knave's Ash (USA) **(92)***(101) (MRStoute)* 4-9-7 (3) JTate(8) (7th st: ev ch wl over 1f out: unable qckn) ....½ **3**
2343* Sadler's Walk **(79)***(84) (GWragg)* 4-8-11 MHills(9) (8th st: hdwy over 2f out: hrd rdn over 1f out: one pce) 2½ **4**
2433[9] Jubran (USA) **(64)***(73) (MJohnston)* 9-7-3 (7) BHalligan(14) (4th st: hrd rdn & ev ch 2f out: one pce) ....d.h **4**
2028* Legendary Leap **(75)***(80) (LordHuntingdon)* 5-8-7 JReid(4) (9th st: nvr nr to chal) ....s.h **6**
2419[4] Star Manager (USA) **(80)***(80) (PFICole)* 5-8-12 TQuinn(2) (lw: lost pl over 5f out: 12th st: hrd rdn 2f out: r.o one pce) 3 **7**
2457[8] Country Lover **(78)***(78) (LordHuntingdon)* 4-8-10 MRoberts(11) (lw: 5th st: wknd over 1f out) ....hd **8**
*2407** North Reef (IRE) **(72)***(69)*(Fav)*(SirMarkPrescott)* 4-8-4 WCarson(1) (lw: chsd ldr: led over 5f out to 2f out: wknd over 1f out) 2 **9**
2419[3] Sue's Artiste **(80)***(76) (BWHills)* 4-8-12 RHills(13) (hdwy over 4f out: 6th st: n.m.r & swtchd lft over 1f out: sn wknd) ....½ **10**
2457[2] Ringmaster (IRE) **(88)***(78) (MHTompkins)* 4-9-6 PRobinson(10) (11th st: a bhd) 4 **11**
2446* Show Faith (IRE) **(84)***(70) (RHannon)* 5-9-2 LDettori(6) (10th st: nt clr run 3f out & 2f out: hdwy & n.m.r over 1f out: sn wknd) 2½ **12**
2117[3] Up in Flames (IRE) **(79)***(64) (MDHammond)* 4-8-11 KDarley(5) (bhd fnl 6f: 14th st) ....nk **13**
2391* Sure Care **(64)***(43) (BJMeehan)* 4-7-10 NCarlisle(3) (led over 4f: 2nd st: wknd wl over 1f out) .4 **14**

5/1 North Reef (IRE), **11/2** Sadler's Walk, **6/1** SILVER GROOM (IRE), **8/1** Knave's Ash (USA), **10/1** Country Lover, Legendary Leap, Ringmaster (IRE) (7/1-11/1), Hunters of Brora (IRE), **12/1** Up in Flames (IRE), **16/1** Sue's Artiste, Show Faith (IRE), **25/1** Jubran (USA), Star Manager (USA), **33/1** Sure Care, CSF £60.48 CT £446.69 TOTE £8.00: £2.80 £2.80 £3.30 (£41.10) Trio £163.60
OWNER The Silver Darling Partnership (EPSOM) BRED Holborn Trust Co 14 Rn
2m 5.64 (0.64) SF: 51/69/73/56/45/52/52/50/41/48/50/42/36/15

2673 OAK TREE STKS (Listed) (3-Y.O+ F & M) (Class A) £20,817.50 (£6,215.00: £2,970.00: £1,347.50)
7f Stalls: High GOING minus 0.33 sec per fur (GF) 4-45 (4-48)

1850[9] **Brief Glimpse (IRE) (94)***(109) (MajorDNChappell)* 3-8-7 MHills(10) (hdwy over 4f out: 5th st: n.m.r 2f out: led ins fnl f: rdn out) ....— **1**
2271* Cheyenne Spirit **(102)***(104) (BHanbury)* 3-8-7 WCarson(3) (led tl ins fnl f: unable qckn) 2 **2**
2416[2] Epagris **(105)***(107)*(Fav)*(HRACecil)* 3-8-10 MJKinane(2) (lw: 4th st: rdn over 3f out: ev ch 1f out: one pce) ....nk **3**
1850[6] A la Carte (IRE) **(100)***(103) (JLDunlop)* 3-8-7 JReid(1) (9th st: rdn over 2f out: hdwy over 1f out: r.o) ....½ **4**
2409[3] Mamlakah (IRE) **(102)***(98) (HThomsonJones)* 3-8-7 RHills(8) (lw: 3rd st: rdn over 2f out: one pce) 2 **5**
2212a[11] Daring Destiny **(102)***(95) (KRBurke)* 4-9-3 JTate(6) (7th st: hdwy over 2f out: hrd rdn: one pce) 2½ **6**
2349[2] Gay Gallanta (USA) **(112)***(87) (MRStoute)* 3-8-7 LDettori(9) (lw: 2nd st: hrd rdn over 2f out: wknd over 1f out) 2½ **7**
2287* Lap of Luxury **(103)***(81) (WJarvis)* 6-9-0 BThomson(5) (6th st: wknd over 2f out) 2½ **8**
1101[5] Germane **(105)***(79) (MBell)* 3-8-7 MFenton(7) (8th st: bhd fnl 3f) ....¾ **9**
2409[5] Queenfisher **(88)***(75) (RHannon)* 3-8-7b MRoberts(4) (10th st: a bhd) 2 **10**

11/4 Epagris, **3/1** Gay Gallanta (USA) (op 2/1), **8/1** Lap of Luxury, **9/1** A la Carte (IRE), Cheyenne Spirit, **10/1** Daring Destiny (8/1-12/1), Mamlakah (IRE), **14/1** BRIEF GLIMPSE (IRE), **20/1** Germane, **25/1** Queenfisher, CSF £117.55 TOTE £33.10: £5.10 £1.50 £1.50 (£83.60) Trio £154.60
OWNER Whiteways Racing (WHITSBURY) BRED J. C. Condon in Ireland 10 Rn
1m 23.88 (0.84 under best) (-0.52) SF: 71/66/69/65/60/64/49/50/41/37
WEIGHT FOR AGE 3yo-7lb

2674 EVENING STANDARD NURSERY H'CAP (2-Y.O) (Class C) £7,505.00 (£2,240.00: £1,070.00: £485.00)
6f Stalls: Low GOING minus 0.65 sec per fur (HD) 5-20 (5-22)

2221* **April The Eighth** *(95)*(Fav)*(BWHills)* 2-9-7 MHills(5) (a.p: led over 2f out: r.o wl) ....— **1**
2183[5] Prince of Florence (IRE) *(83) (LMCumani)* 2-9-0 WRSwinburn(6) (hrd rdn & hdwy over 1f out: edgd rt ins fnl f: r.o) 2 **2**
2173[6] Vera's First (IRE) *(71) (GLewis)* 2-8-6 PaulEddery(10) (lw: hld up: rdn over 2f out: ev ch over 1f out: unable qckn) 1¼ **3**

2192* King of Peru (77) (APJarvis) 2-8-11 (3) JTate(9) (hrd rdn & hdwy over 1f out: 4th & btn whn n.m.r ins fnl f) ....¾ 4
2299³ Proud Monk (65) (GLMoore) 2-8-10 SWhitworth(1) (s.s: nvr nr to chal) 3 5
2335² Arlington Lady (60) (NACallaghan) 2-8-5 MRoberts(4) (a.p: rdn 2f out: wknd over 1f out) ....s.h 6
2170* Centurion (64) (RHannon) 2-8-9 LDettori(8) (plld hrd: a.p: ev ch over 1f out: wknd fnl f) ....hd 7
2618⁴ Hoh Majestic (IRE) (52) (MBell) 2-8-10b MFenton(3) (led over 3f) 5 8
2424³ Mystic Tempo (USA) (53) (PWChapple-Hyam) 2-9-2 JReid(7) (prom over 4f) 1¾ 9
2601⁶ Fortuitious (IRE) (20) (JRJenkins) 2-7-8 NCarlisle(2) (lw: bhd fnl 5f) 4 10

100/30 APRIL THE EIGHTH, **7/2** King of Peru, **9/2** Centurion, **8/1** Arlington Lady, Mystic Tempo (USA), **9/1** Prince of Florence (IRE), **14/1** Hoh Majestic (IRE) (10/1-16/1), **20/1** Proud Monk, Vera's First (IRE), **50/1** Fortuitious (IRE), CSF £29.45 CT £462.39 TOTE £4.40: £1.70 £2.50 £3.80 (£22.90) Trio £117.20 OWNER Mr Michael Siu (LAMBOURN) BRED Miss E. Aldous 10 Rn

1m 10.08 (-0.12) SF: 51/9/39/33/21/8/20/27/16/-

2675

FINDON MAIDEN STKS (2-Y.O F) (Class D) £6,970.00 (£2,110.00: £1,030.00: £490.00) **6f** Stalls: Low GOING minus 0.65 sec per fur (HD) 5-50 (5-52)

Silk Masque (USA) (83+)(Fav)(PWChapple-Hyam) 2-8-11 JReid(3) (leggy: unf: a.p: rdn over 1f out: led ins fnl f: r.o wl) ....— 1
2106⁶ Naissant (82) (CEBrittain) 2-8-11 MJKinane(4) (chsd ldr: led over 2f out: rdn over 1f out: hdd ins fnl f: r.o) ....nk 2
Astuti (IRE) (73) (APJarvis) 2-8-11 JTate(7) (leggy: dwlt: hdwy 3f out: rdn over 1f out: unable qckn) 3½ 3
1833⁶ Invigorating (66) (RHannon) 2-8-11 LDettori(1) (led over 3f: wknd over 1f out) 2½ 4
Iberian Dancer (CAN) (61) (JWHills) 2-8-11 RHills(6) (unf: dwlt: hld up: rdn over 2f out: wknd over 1f out) 2 5
Thracian (58) (JLDunlop) 2-8-11 WCarson(2) (scope: bit bkwd: bhd fnl 3f) 1¼ 6
Bold Enough (51) (BWHills) 2-8-11 MHills(5) (leggy: unf: hld up: rdn over 2f out: wknd over 1f out) 2½ 7

Evens SILK MASQUE (USA), **5/1** Thracian (4/1-6/1), **11/2** Naissant (3/1-6/1), **15/2** Astuti (IRE) (10/1-16/1), **12/1** Iberian Dancer (CAN), **14/1** Invigorating (op 7/1), **20/1** Bold Enough, CSF £6.69 TOTE £1.90: £1.40 £2.90 (£6.00) OWNER Mr R. E. Sangster (MARLBOROUGH) BRED Swettenham Stud 7 Rn

1m 10.71 (0.51) SF: 33/32/23/16/11/8/1

T/Jkpt; not won £64,303.08 to Epsom 26/07/95. T/Plpt: £702.00 (82.99 Tckts). T/Qdpt: £89.80 (6 Tckts). AK

2116-DONCASTER (L-H)
Wednesday July 26th (Good to firm, Firm patches)

WEATHER: sunny, v.hot WIND: fresh bhd

2676

SUNSHINE (S) STKS (3, 4 & 5-Y.O) (Class E) £3,172.50 (£945.00: £450.00: £202.50) **1m 4f** Stalls: Low GOING minus 0.64 sec per fur (F) 2-45 (2-46)

2544⁶ **Fearless Wonder** (**56**)(67) (MrsMReveley) 4-9-7b KDarley(4) (trckd ldrs: rdn to ld ins fnl f: styd on u.p) ....— 1
2486² Call Me Albi (IRE) (**42**)(65) (GLMoore) 4-9-7 AClark(7) (lw: cl up: led over 4f out tl ins fnl f: kpt on) 1½ 2
2165⁶ Pillow Talk (IRE) (**44**)(55) (SWCampion) 4-9-2 GCarter(2) (hld up: hdwy over 4f out: one pce fnl 2f) 4 3
2396⁵ Cashmirie (**46**)(52)(Fav)(JLEyre) 3-7-13 (5) HKYim(1) (sddle slipped after s: a in tch: swtchd 2f out: no imp) 1¾ 4
2478⁵ Brother Barnabas (**45**)(49) (CWThornton) 4-9-7 DeanMcKeown(6) (lw: led tl over 4f out: sn outpcd) 6 5
2449⁴ Great Tern (35) (NMBabbage) 3-8-4 KFallon(5) (hld up: effrt 4f out: sn rdn & btn) 7 6
Whitegatesprincess (IRE) (BEllison) 4-9-2 TIves(3) (sn outpcd & bhd: wl t.o) ....dist 7

2/1 Cashmirie, **7/2** Call Me Albi (IRE), Great Tern, **4/1** FEARLESS WONDER, **8/1** Pillow Talk (IRE), **16/1** Brother Barnabas, **33/1** Whitegatesprincess (IRE), CSF £17.81 TOTE £6.60: £2.50 £1.60 (£8.50) OWNER Mr William Davies (SALTBURN) BRED W. L. Caley 7 Rn

2m 34.1 (3.50) SF: 32/30/20/5/14/-/-

WEIGHT FOR AGE 3yo-12lb

No bid

2677 VAUX SAMSON CONDITIONS STKS (3-Y.O+) (Class C) £5,376.00 (£1,856.00: £888.00: £360.00) 6f Stalls: High GOING minus 0.64 sec per fur (F) 3-20 (3-21)

2066² **Iltimas (USA) (89)***(92)*(Fav)*(PTWalwyn)* 3-8-9 KDarley(4) (cl up: led over 2f out tl disp ld ins fnl f: rallied to ld nr fin) — 1
571⁸ Averti (IRE) **(100)***(97) (WRMuir)* 4-9-6 JCarroll(1) (lw: trckd ldrs: rdn to ld ins fnl f: hdd nr fin: r.o) s.h 2
2237² Bahith (USA) **(96)***(92) (HThomsonJones)* 3-9-0b PRobinson(3) (led over 3f: hrd rdn & one pce) 2 3
2324⁴ Rockville Pike (IRE) **(82)***(34) (SDow)* 3-8-10 GHind(2) (lw: outpcd after 2f: lost action ½-wy: n.d after) 20 4

11/8 ILTIMAS (USA), **2/1** Bahith (USA), **100/30** Averti (IRE), **8/1** Rockville Pike (IRE), CSF £5.68 TOTE £2.00 (£4.20) OWNER Mr Hamdan Al Maktoum (LAMBOURN) BRED Shadwell Farm in USA 4 Rn
1m 9.74 (0.46 under best) (-1.26) SF: 57/68/57/-
WEIGHT FOR AGE 3yo-6lb

2678 WARDS BEST BITTER H'CAP (0-85) (3-Y.O+) (Class D) £4,425.00 (£1,320.00: £630.00: £285.00) 1m 2f 60y Stalls: Low GOING minus 0.64 sec (F) 3-55 (3-56)

2333⁵ **Carlito Brigante (68)***(79) (MrsJRRamsden)* 3-8-8 KFallon(6) (lw: trckd ldrs: disp ld 2f out: r.o u.p fnl f) — 1
2373⁴ Once More for Luck (IRE) **(59)***(69) (MrsMReveley)* 4-8-9 KDarley(2) (lw: a in tch: outpcd 2f out: swtchd over 1f out: r.o wl) ½ 2
2391³ Teen Jay **(68)***(76) (MJRyan)* 5-9-4b AClark(4) (trckd ldrs: hdwy to disp ld 2f out: no ex ins fnl f) 1¼ 3
2321¹⁵ Wellsian (USA) **(71)***(78) (LMCumani)* 3-8-11 OUrbina(5) (lw: w ldr: led over 3f out to 2f out: kpt on one pce) 1 4
1940⁵ Rival Bid (USA) **(58)***(51) (MAJarvis)* 7-8-8 PRobinson(3) (hld up: effrt over 2f out: sn btn) 9 5
2427² Colorful Ambition **(74)***(56)*(Fav)*(MrsASwinbank)* 5-9-10 NConnorton(7) (b.off hind: lw: dwlt: sn rcvrd: effrt 3f out: sn btn) 7 6
2253⁴ Lancer (USA) **(79)***(55) (MBell)* 3-9-5 JCarroll(1) (mde most tl hdd & wknd over 3f out) 4 7

3/1 Colorful Ambition, **5/1** Wellsian (USA), Teen Jay, **11/2** Rival Bid (USA), CARLITO BRIGANTE, **7/1** Lancer (USA), **8/1** Once More for Luck (IRE), CSF £41.27 TOTE £7.00: £2.90 £2.10 (£16.00) OWNER Mr Bernard Hathaway (THIRSK) BRED Whitsbury Manor Stud 7 Rn
2m 5.48 (0.92 under best) (-1.52) SF: 53/53/60/52/35/40/29
WEIGHT FOR AGE 3yo-10lb
STEWARDS' ENQUIRY Urbina susp. 4-7/8/95 (incorrect use of whip).

2679 STALLITE BATTERIES H'CAP (0-85) (3-Y.O F) (Class D) £4,698.00 (£1,404.00: £672.00: £306.00) 1m (round) Stalls: High GOING minus 0.64 sec (F) 4-30 (4-31)

1990* **Bonne Etoile (79)***(87+)*(Fav)*(DRLoder)* 3-9-3 (3) DRMcCabe(7) (a.p: led 2f out: r.o: eased ins fnl f) — 1
2152⁴ Cap And Gown (IRE) **(80)***(83) (PFICole)* 3-9-7 JFortune(3) (in tch: drvn along over 3f out: styd on fnl f: no imp) 2½ 2
1701* Nawaasi **(75)***(78) (HThomsonJones)* 3-9-2 KDarley(2) (lw: cl up: led 3f out to 2f out: r.o one pce) hd 3
2006⁸ Varvarka **(78)***(81) (JWWatts)* 3-9-5 JCarroll(6) (lw: bhd: effrt on outside 3f out: styd on nr fin) s.h 4
2451² Grey Again **(56)***(54) (SRBowring)* 3-7-11b TWilliams(4) (hld up: effrt on ins over 2f out: n.m.r & sn btn) 2½ 5
2499* Special-K **(66)***(64) (EWeymes)* 3-8-4 (3) 6x SSanders(5) (led 2f: chsd ldrs tl outpcd fnl 2½f) hd 6
2362* Anam **(79)***(69) (PTWalwyn)* 3-9-6 GHind(1) (lw: led after 2f to 3f out: wknd 2f out) 4 7

6/4 BONNE ETOILE, **9/2** Nawaasi, **5/1** Anam, **6/1** Special-K, **10/1** Cap And Gown (IRE), **14/1** Grey Again, Varvarka, CSF £14.67 TOTE £2.20: £1.60 £3.20 (£10.60) OWNER Miss D. F. Fleming (NEWMARKET) BRED Kirtlington Stud Ltd 7 Rn 1m 36.93 (0.63) SF: 45/41/36/39/12/22/27

2680 HEINEKEN H'CAP (0-70) (3-Y.O) (Class E) £3,552.75 (£1,062.00: £508.50: £231.75) 5f Stalls: High GOING minus 0.64 sec per fur (F) 5-05 (5-06)

2409⁷ **General Sir Peter (IRE) (68)***(73) (PFICole)* 3-9-6 KDarley(2) (a.p: rdn to ld ins fnl f: styd on wl) — 1

2394[6] The Happy Fox (IRE) **(69)***(72)*(Fav)*(BAMcMahon)* 3-9-7b GCarter(4) (lw: chsd ldrs: outpcd 2f out: hdwy 1f out: fin wl) .... ½ 2
2519[3] Dominelle **(51)***(54) (MHEasterby)* 3-8-3 SMaloney(1) (lw: cl up: led over 1f out tl ins fnl f: no ex) .... hd 3
2372[2] Royal Dome (IRE) **(54)***(56) (MartynWane)* 3-8-6v KFallon(5) (cl up: hung rt ins fnl f: styd on nr fin) .... nk 4
2394[8] C-Yer-Simmie (IRE) **(61)***(62) (RHollinshead)* 3-8-13 TIves(10) (led tl over 1f out: grad wknd) . ½ 5
2463* Baileys Sunset (IRE) **(63)***(61) (MJohnston)* 3-9-1 PRobinson(9) (bhd tl styd on fnl f) .... ¾ 6
2491[2] Sweet Mate **(43)***(41) (SRBowring)* 3-7-9b NKennedy(6) (chsd ldrs: nt clr run & eased ins fnl f) .... hd 7
2295[4] Pursuance (IRE) **(54)***(45) (JBalding)* 3-8-6v GHind(3) (lw: s.i.s: sn rcvrd & cl up: wknd fnl 2f) 2 8

9/2 The Happy Fox (IRE), **5/1** GENERAL SIR PETER (IRE), Dominelle, Sweet Mate, **11/2** Baileys Sunset (IRE), **15/2** Royal Dome (IRE), **8/1** Pursuance (IRE), **10/1** C-Yer-Simmie (IRE), CSF £25.79 CT £106.46 TOTE £5.90: £2.20 £1.50 £1.90 (£24.00) Trio £34.30 OWNER Mr Yahya Nasib (WHATCOMBE) BRED Hamilton Bloodstock (UK) Ltd 8 Rn 58.55 secs (0.15) SF: 47/46/28/30/36/35/15/19

2681 SILVERDALE MAIDEN STKS (2-Y.O) (Class D) £3,987.55 (£1,194.40: £573.70: £263.35) **7f** Stalls: High GOING minus 0.64 sec per fur (F) 5-35 (5-37)

2381[2] **Jack Jennings** *(83) (BAMcMahon)* 2-9-0 GCarter(12) (cl up: led over 1f out: r.o wl) .... — 1
2464[2] Freedom Flame *(75+)*(Fav)*(MJohnston)* 2-8-9 PRobinson(10) (trckd ldrs: nt clr run & outpcd 2f out: squeezed thro ent fnl f: r.o) 1¼ 2
2242[3] Taufan Boy *(80) (PWHarris)* 2-9-0 GHind(5) (cl up: effrt 2f out: nt qckn fnl f) .... hd 3
2183[6] Khabar *(77) (DMorley)* 2-9-0 DeanMcKeown(3) (led tl over 1f out: one pce) 1¼ 4
Weet-A-Minute (IRE) *(77) (RHollinshead)* 2-9-0 TIves(2) (w'like: dwlt: rn green & bhd tl r.o fnl 2f) .... hd 5
2107[3] Snow Falcon *(74) (MBell)* 2-9-0 JCarroll(6) (in tch: rdn over 2f out: one pce) 1¼ 6
2070[5] Cool Fire *(60) (SPCWoods)* 2-9-0 WWoods(7) (prom 5f: sn wknd) 6 7
2381[3] Oversman *(53) (JGFitzGerald)* 2-9-0 KFallon(1) (outpcd fnl 3f) 3 8
Poetic Dance (USA) *(40) (JLDunlop)* 2-9-0 KDarley(9) (w'like: scope: s.s: rn green thrght: n.d) 6 9
Bandit Boy *(31) (JMPEustace)* 2-9-0 NKennedy(8) (w'like: leggy: s.s: a bhd) 4 10

11/8 Freedom Flame (op 4/5), **3/1** Taufan Boy, **11/2** JACK JENNINGS, **8/1** Poetic Dance (USA) (op 5/1), Snow Falcon, **14/1** Khabar, **20/1** Oversman, Cool Fire, **25/1** Bandit Boy, **33/1** Weet-A-Minute (IRE), CSF £14.09 TOTE £6.20: £1.70 £1.30 £1.50 (£3.10) Trio £6.60 OWNER Mr G. Whitaker (TAMWORTH) BRED Southcourt Stud 10 Rn 1m 25.53 (2.13) SF: 20/12/17/14/14/11/-/-/-/-

T/Plpt: £101.70 (111.08 Tckts). T/Qdpt: £51.20 (2.4 Tckts). AA

2167-EPSOM (L-H)
Wednesday July 26th (Good)

Race 6 hand-timed
WEATHER: sunny WIND: almost nil

2682 WARREN APPRENTICE H'CAP (0-75) (3-Y.O+) (Class E) £4,201.50 (£1,272.00: £621.00: £295.50) **1m 2f 18y** Stalls: Centre GOING minus 0.45 sec per fur (F) 6-05 (6-07)

2536* **Soviet Bride (IRE) (58)***(66)*(Fav)*(SDow)* 3-8-1 (5) 6x ADaly(4) (a gng wl: 3rd st: rdn to ld over 1f out: pushed clr) .... — 1
2026[7] Negative Equity **(47)***(49) (KRBurke)* 3-7-9v NVarley(2) (led: rdn & hdd over 1f out: one pce) .3½ 2
2450* Deceit the Second **(47)***(49) (GLewis)* 3-7-9b MBaird(6) (4th st: rdn over 2f out: r.o one pce fnl f) .... s.h 3
2064[9] Maurangi **(52)***(49) (BWMurray)* 4-8-5 (5) MartinDwyer(7) (6th st: rdn over 2f out: kpt on one pce fnl f) 3½ 4
2115* Roman Reel (USA) **(66)***(60) (GLMoore)* 4-9-5 (5) CarolineHovington(5) (2nd st: rdn 2f out: wknd over 1f out) 1½ 5
2269[3] Newport Knight **(63)***(53) (RAkehurst)* 4-9-2 (5) RMoogan(1) (5th st: hrd rdn 2f out: no hdwy) 3 6
2076[4] Captain Marmalade **(47)***(31) (DTThom)* 6-8-2 (3)ow4 DGriffiths(3) (a bhd) 1 7

10/11 SOVIET BRIDE (IRE) (op 6/4), **7/1** Newport Knight (4/1-8/1), Maurangi, **8/1** Deceit the Second (5/1-9/1), **10/1** Negative Equity, Roman Reel (USA) (op 5/1), Captain Marmalade, CSF £10.14 TOTE £1.80: £1.40 £1.90 (£8.40) OWNER Mr J. E. Mills (EPSOM) BRED Gainsborough Stud Management Ltd 7 Rn 2m 7.5 (3.50) SF: 27/10/10/20/31/24/2

WEIGHT FOR AGE 3yo-10lb

2683

E.B.F. WALTON MEDIAN AUCTION MAIDEN STKS (2-Y.O F) (Class D) £3,403.75 (£1,030.00: £502.50: £238.75)
6f Stalls: Centre GOING minus 0.45 sec per fur (F) 6-35 (6-38)

2381[7] **Balpare** *(59) (NACallaghan)* 2-8-11 BDoyle(2) (3rd st: rdn over 1f out: led ins fnl f: r.o) ....— 1
Charming Bride *(54) (SCWilliams)* 2-8-8 (3) JStack(8) (unf: dwlt: 7th st: hdwy 2f out: led over 1f out tl ins fnl f: unable qckn) 1¾ 2
Janies Girl (IRE) *(50) (KRBurke)* 2-8-11 JQuinn(3) (w'like: bit bkwd: 9th st: rdn over 1f out: r.o one pce) 1¾ 3
2552[5] Sunset Harbour (IRE) *(48) (DAWilson)* 2-8-11 MWigham(7) (chsd ldr: 2nd st: ev ch 1f out: one pce) ....½ 4
Anna Settic *(47) (DrJDScargill)* 2-8-11 MFenton(1) (unf: bit bkwd: dwlt: 10th st: hdwy fnl f: styd on wl) ....½ 5
Bellacardia *(47)*(Fav)*(GLewis)* 2-8-11 PaulEddery(6) (w'like: 6th st: rdn 2f out: one pce) ....hd 6
2091[4] Heaven Sent (IRE) *(40) (PMitchell)* 2-8-11 RPerham(4) (led tl over 1f out: sn wknd) 2½ 7
Fair To Middling (IRE) *(40) (GLMoore)* 2-8-11 SWhitworth(9) (neat: 4th st: wknd 2f out) ....hd 8
1977[14] Tarry *(33) (LordHuntingdon)* 2-8-11 JWilliams(5) (sn outpcd: 8th st: a bhd) 2½ 9
2198[8] Move Darling *(25) (CACyzer)* 2-8-11 DBiggs(10) (5th st: wknd over 2f out) 3 10

2/1 Bellacardia, **4/1** Sunset Harbour (IRE) (op 5/2), **6/1** BALPARE (5/2-13/2), **13/2** Tarry, **15/2** Janies Girl (IRE), **10/1** Charming Bride (8/1-14/1), **12/1** Move Darling, **14/1** Heaven Sent (IRE) (10/1-16/1), Fair To Middling (IRE), **20/1** Anna Settic, CSF £62.17 TOTE £11.50: £4.00 £4.60 £2.30 (£31.40) Trio £231.30 OWNER Mr Michael Hill (NEWMARKET) BRED G. R. Smith (Thriplow) Ltd 10 Rn
1m 11.22 (3.22) SF: 10/5/1/-/-/-/-/-/-/-

2684

CHANNEL ONE CLAIMING STKS (3-Y.O) (Class E) £3,403.75 (£1,030.00: £502.50: £238.75) **1m 114y** Stalls: Centre GOING minus 0.45 sec (F) 7-05 (7-05)

2532[5] **Gentle Irony (51)***(61) (BJMeehan)* 3-8-0b BDoyle(5) (2nd st: rdn 2f out: led 1f out: r.o) ....— 1
2537[3] Elite Racing **(68)***(68)*(Fav)*(PFICole)* 3-8-8b TQuinn(7) (led to 1f out: rallied ins fnl f: r.o) ....½ 2
2282[8] Chastleton **(38)***(49) (MRChannon)* 3-7-7 (5)ow2 PPMurphy(6) (4th st: rdn over 2f out: one pce) 4 3
2332[6] Kellaire Girl (IRE) **(45)***(46) (GLewis)* 3-7-10 JQuinn(4) (5th st: rdn over 2f out: one pce) 1½ 4
*2093** Mediate (IRE) **(55)***(51) (RHannon)* 3-7-13 (7)ow1 DaneO'Neill(1) (4th st: rdn 2f out: wknd over 1f out) 1¾ 5
263[9] Rowlandsons Silver (FR) *(38) (DJGMurraySmith)* 3-8-1 CRutter(3) (6th st: a bhd) 5 6
1675[13] Barbrallen **(39)***(34) (DJSffrenchDavis)* 3-8-4 NAdams(2) (s.s: a bhd) 4 7

8/11 Elite Racing, **11/2** GENTLE IRONY (4/1-13/2), Mediate (IRE) (op 3/1), **6/1** Kellaire Girl (IRE), **16/1** Chastleton, **33/1** Rowlandsons Silver (FR), **50/1** Barbrallen, CSF £9.63 TOTE £4.90: £1.90 £1.20 (£2.90) OWNER Mr A. S. Reid (UPPER LAMBOURN) BRED Red House Stud 7 Rn
1m 45.01 (3.01) SF: 19/26/7/4/9/-/-

2685

RING & BRYMER H'CAP (0-70) (3-Y.O+) (Class E) £4,702.00 (£1,426.00: £698.00: £334.00)
7f Stalls: Centre GOING minus 0.45 sec per fur (F) 7-35 (7-37)

2549[3] **Mislemani (IRE) (51)***(65) (AGNewcombe)* 5-8-5 (5) DGriffiths(2) (3rd st: led wl over 1f out: r.o wl) ....— 1
2342[2] Soaking **(62)***(67)*(Fav)*(PBurgoyne)* 5-9-7 PaulEddery(3) (10th st: hdwy 2f out: rdn over 1f out: r.o fnl f) 4 2
2528[8] Racing Telegraph **(42)***(46) (JPearce)* 5-8-1 GBardwell(10) (13th st: hdwy over 1f out: styd on strly fnl f) ....nk 3
2539* Pride of Hayling (IRE) **(55)***(59) (PRHedger)* 4-9-0 6x StephenDavies(4) (6th st: rdn over 1f out: r.o one pce) ....nk 4
2641* Sharp Imp **(39)***(42) (RMFlower)* 5-7-12b 6x DBiggs(9) (chsd ldr: 2nd st: ev ch wl over 1f out: wknd ins fnl f) ....hd 5
2342[4] Dancing Lawyer **(69)***(68) (BJMeehan)* 4-9-7 (7) RHavlin(7) (7th st: rdn over 2f out: one pce) 2 6
2073[10] Nakita **(47)***(43) (CNAllen)* 4-8-6 JQuinn(6) (11th st: nvr nrr) 1 7
2202[3] Paddy's Rice **(56)***(52) (LJHolt)* 4-9-1 AMcGlone(14) (9th st: a mid div) ....nk 8
2342[10] Panchellita (USA) **(47)***(39) (GLMoore)* 6-8-6v SWhitworth(5) (led tl wl over 1f out: sn wknd) 1 9
2446[7] Dowsong **(64)***(49) (RAkehurst)* 4-9-9 TQuinn(15) (5th st: wknd over 2f out) 3 10
2369[17] Shepherd Market (IRE) **(66)***(47) (DAWilson)* 4-9-11 JWilliams(12) (a bhd) 2 11

22026 Media Express **(66)***(47) (RHannon)* 3-8-11 (7) DaneO'Neill(1) (8th st: wknd over 2f out) .... s.h **12**
24882 Marrowfat Lady (IRE) **(63)***(36) (BRMillman)* 4-9-3 (5) AProcter(13) (12th st: a bhd) 3½ **13**
76219 Tuigamala **(37)***(10) (RIngram)* 4-7-10 NAdams(8) (dwlt: a bhd) .... s.h **14**
25103 Morocco (IRE) **(53)***(21) (MRChannon)* 6-8-12 RHughes(16) (dwlt: a bhd) 2 **15**
23904 Royal Comedian **(46)** *(BWMurray)* 6-8-2 (3) PMcCabe(17) (4th st: wknd qckly over 2f out) 11 **16**

3/1 Soaking (op 8/1), **9/2** Dowsong, **7/1** Marrowfat Lady (IRE), Sharp Imp, **8/1** Pride of Hayling (IRE), **9/1** Paddy's Rice, **10/1** Shepherd Market (IRE), **11/1** Dancing Lawyer, **12/1** Morocco (IRE), **14/1** Royal Comedian, Media Express, **20/1** Panchellita (USA), MISLEMANI (IRE), **25/1** Racing Telegraph, Nakita, **33/1** Tuigamala, CSF £88.10 CT £1,504.99 TOTE £39.70: £4.50 £1.50 £6.90 £2.70 (£61.30) Trio £1,152.80; £649.50 to 27/7/95 OWNER Mrs Pamela Cann (BARNSTAPLE) BRED Gainsborough Stud Management Ltd 16 Rn

1m 22.22 (1.92) SF: 32/34/13/26/9/35/10/19/6/16/14/7/3/-/-/-

WEIGHT FOR AGE 3yo-7lb

2686

OLYMPIC H'CAP (0-80) (3-Y.O+) (Class D) £5,158.50 (£1,563.00: £764.00: £364.50) **5f** Stalls: Centre GOING minus 0.45 sec per fur (F) 8-05 (8-06)

25512 **Miami Banker (45)***(51)*(Fav)*(WRMuir)* 9-7-7b GBardwell(6) (led 4f out: j.path over 3f out: rdn ins fnl f: r.o) .... — **1**
2247* Bashful Brave **(71)***(75) (JWPayne)* 4-9-5 MRimmer(3) (chsd ldrs: rdn over 1f out: r.o) .... ½ **2**
*2631*2 Lloc **(54)***(52) (JohnBerry)* 3-7-6 (5) NVarley(4) (prom: rdn over 1f out: one pce) 2 **3**
25515 Domicksky **(61)***(55) (MRChannon)* 7-8-4 (5) PPMurphy(7) (in rr whn rdn 2f out: one pce) 1¼ **4**
22474 Halliard **(57)***(48) (TMJones)* 4-8-5 ow1 RPerham(8) (in rr: rdn 2f out: one pce) .... ½ **5**
26097 Tuscan Dawn **(80)***(70) (JBerry)* 5-9-7 (7) PRoberts(1) (led 1f: ev ch 2f out: wknd ins fnl f) .... ¾ **6**
252115 Miss Movie World **(61)***(47) (MDHammond)* 6-8-6 (3) JStack(2) (chsd ldrs tl wknd 1f out) 1¼ **7**
24107 Royal Carlton (IRE) **(69)***(53) (RAkehurst)* 3-8-12 TQuinn(5) (a bhd) .... ½ **8**

3/1 MIAMI BANKER, **4/1** Bashful Brave, Miss Movie World, **9/2** Lloc, **13/2** Halliard, **9/1** Tuscan Dawn, **11/1** Royal Carlton (IRE) (8/1-12/1), **12/1** Domicksky (8/1-14/1), CSF £15.61 CT £49.86 TOTE £4.70: £1.30 £1.80 £1.70 (£7.20) OWNER Mr J. J. Amass (LAMBOURN) BRED J. D. Wheeler 8 Rn

54.92 secs (0.42) SF: 30/54/26/34/27/49/26/27

WEIGHT FOR AGE 3yo-5lb

2687

LONSDALE H'CAP (0-65) (3-Y.O+) (Class F) £3,533.75 (£1,070.00: £522.50: £248.75) **1m 4f 10y** Stalls: Centre GOING minus 0.45 sec per fur (F) 8-40 (8-41)

24395 **Rocquaine Bay (30)***(48) (MJBolton)* 8-7-10 JQuinn(11) (hld up: hdwy 6f out: led wl over 3f out: clr over 1f out: r.o wl) .... — **1**
*2379** Carpathian **(55)***(64) (LordHuntingdon)* 4-9-7 JWilliams(13) (hld up: hdwy 5f out: 4th st: rdn over 2f out: wnt 2nd ent fnl f: no imp) 7 **2**
26583 Jean de Florette (USA) **(32)***(39) (JohnBerry)* 4-7-7v(5) NVarley(10) (hdwy 6f out: 3rd st: chsd wnr over 3f out tl ins fnl f: one pce) 1¼ **3**
*2600*3 Jarzon Dancer **(30)***(26) (DAWilson)* 7-7-3 (7)ow3 RachaelMoody(3) (bhd: hdwy 2f out: nvr nrr) .. 6 **4**
24525 Achilles Heel **(44)***(41) (CNAllen)* 4-8-10 GBardwell(7) (s.s: bhd: hdwy 2f out: nvr nrr) 1¾ **5**
20892 Harding Brown (USA) **(50)***(43) (GHarwood)* 3-7-11v(7) GayeHarwood(5) (led over 10f out tl wl over 3f out: 2nd st: wknd over 2f out) 3 **6**
253010 Uncharted Waters **(55)***(46) (CACyzer)* 4-9-7 DBiggs(6) (7th st: sn rdn: wknd 3f out) 1½ **7**
20502 Bag of Tricks (IRE) **(54)***(45) (SDow)* 5-8-13 (7) ADaly(8) (prom 7f: 8th st: wknd 3f out) .... s.h **8**
23413 Blue And Royal (IRE) **(65)***(48) (RHannon)* 3-8-12 (7) DaneO'Neill(2) (5th st: wknd 3f out) 6 **9**
2174* Araboybill **(62)***(41) (MPMuggeridge)* 4-10-0b SWhitworth(4) (bhd fr ½-wy) 3 **10**
25466 Lunar Risk **(38)***(8) (MissBSanders)* 5-8-1 (3) SSanders(1) (prom 7f) 7 **11**
2532* Woodrising **(59)***(22)*(Fav)*(GLewis)* 3-8-13 5x PaulEddery(9) (led over 1f: wknd 6f out) 5 **12**
2359* Wottashambles **(43)***(5) (LMontagueHall)* 4-8-9 StephenDavies(14) (chsd ldrs: 6th st: sn wknd) .... nk **13**

9/4 Woodrising (op 4/1), **3/1** Carpathian, **6/1** ROCQUAINE BAY (op 10/1), **8/1** Wottashambles (op 12/1), **10/1** Lunar Risk (7/1-11/1), Harding Brown (USA) (7/1-11/1), **12/1** Blue And Royal (IRE) (op 8/1), Bag of Tricks (IRE) (op 8/1), **14/1** Uncharted Waters, **16/1** Jean de Florette (USA), Araboybill, **20/1** Achilles Heel, **33/1** Jarzon Dancer, CSF £27.00 CT £277.19 TOTE £7.60: £2.10 £2.10 £3.40 (£13.10) Trio £78.80 OWNER Mr D. C. Woollard (SHREWTON) BRED Anne L. Woollard 13 Rn

2m 37.7 (2.70) SF: 29/45/20/7/22/12/27/26/17/22/-/-/-

WEIGHT FOR AGE 3yo-12lb

T/Jkpt: Not won; £101,270.87 to Goodwood 27/7/95. T/Plpt: £73.30 (223.05 Tckts). T/Qdpt: £15.50 (8.7 Tckts). SM

2669-GOODWOOD (R-H)
Wednesday July 26th (St course Good to firm, Rnd Firm)
WEATHER: very warm WIND: moderate half against

2688 COUNTRY CLUB HOTELS GOODWOOD H'CAP (0-90) (3-Y.O+) (Class C)
£12,427.00 (£3,706.00: £1,768.00: £799.00)
2m 4f GOING: minus 0.23 sec per fur (GF) 2-30 (2-30)

1840⁸ **Imad (USA) (60)***(77) (JWhite)* 5-7-12 DaleGibson(7) (4th st: rdn 3f out: led ins fnl f: r.o wl)...— 1
2429³ Upper Mount Clair **(56)***(73) (CEBrittain)* 5-7-8 JQuinn(6) (swtg: chsd ldr: led 7f out to ins fnl f: unable qckn)...½ 2
2429* Salaman (FR) **(83)***(97) (JLDunlop)* 3-8-2 MRoberts(5) (lw: lost pl over 5f out: 6th st: rallied over 1f out: r.o)...3½ 3
1840* Harlestone Brook **(89)***(103)*(Fav)*(JLDunlop)* 5-9-13 WCarson(2) (5th st: nt clr run on ins over 2f out: swtchd lft: r.o one pce)...hd 4
2284⁸ Nawar (FR) **(71)***(85) (JRJenkins)* 5-8-2 (7) DaneO'Neill(4) (swtg: hdwy 6f out: 3rd st: hrd rdn over 3f out: one pce)...nk 5
2154* Tamarpour (USA) **(60)***(73) (MCPipe)* 8-7-12v AMcGlone(3) (b.nr fore: lw: a bhd)...1¼ 6
2514* Bardolph (USA) **(62)***(74) (PFICole)* 8-8-0 CRutter(1) (hdwy 7f out: 2nd st: wknd over 3f out)..½ 7
2193³ Astrolabe **(80)***(80) (BWHills)* 3-7-13b BDoyle(8) (led 13f: wknd over 5f out)...15 8

7/4 Harlestone Brook, **4/1** Salaman (FR), **15/2** Bardolph (USA), **8/1** Tamarpour (USA), **9/1** Astrolabe, **12/1** Upper Mount Clair, **16/1** IMAD (USA), **25/1** Nawar (FR), CSF £148.15 CT £706.24 TOTE £18.30: £3.50 £2.10 £1.30 (£64.90) OWNER Mr Alan Brackley (WENDOVER) BRED Geoffrey C. Hughes 8 Rn 4m 27.4 (10.40) SF: 25/21/26/51/33/21/22/9
WEIGHT FOR AGE 3yo-19lb

2689 SUSSEX STKS (Gp 1) (3-Y.O+) (Class A) £111,220.00 (£41,863.50: £20,306.75: £9,059.75) **1m** Stalls: High GOING minus 0.23 sec per fur (GF) 3-10 (3-12)

1835⁵ **Sayyedati (120)***(125) (CEBrittain)* 5-9-4 BDoyle(4) (lw: 6th st: stdy hdwy over 2f out: led over 1f out: rdn out)...— 1
1837* Bahri (USA) **(120)***(127)*(Fav)*(JLDunlop)* 3-8-13 WCarson(5) (lw: 3rd st: led 2f out to over 1f out: ev ch ins fnl f: r.o)...nk 2
2217a* Darnay *(120) (SbinSuroor)* 4-9-7 LDettori(6) (lw: chsd ldr: led over 2f out: sn hdd: unable qckn)...3½ 3
1835* Nicolotte **(113)***(113) (GWragg)* 4-9-7 MHills(2) (lw: 5th st: rdn over 2f out: carried bdly lft over 1f out: nt rcvr: fin 5th, s.h: plcd 4th)... 4
1835³ Soviet Line (IRE) **(120)***(113) (MRStoute)* 5-9-7 WRSwinburn(3) (lw: 4th st: rdn 2f out: hung bdly lft over 1f out: nt rcvr: fin 4th, 3½l: disq: plcd 5th)... 5
2030* Sulb (USA) *(101) (ACStewart)* 3-8-13 RHills(1) (b.hind: lw: led over 5f)...6 6

Evens Bahri (USA), **5/1** Soviet Line (IRE), **11/2** SAYYEDATI, **7/1** Nicolotte, **9/1** Darnay, **50/1** Sulb (USA), CSF £10.50 TOTE £6.60: £2.50 £1.40 (£4.90) OWNER Mr Mohamed Obaida (NEWMARKET) 6 Rn 1m 36.17 (-1.43) SF: 100/94/95/88/88/68
WEIGHT FOR AGE 3yo-8lb

2690 LANSON CHAMPAGNE VINTAGE STKS (Gp 3) (2-Y.O) (Class A)
£22,540.00 (£8,424.50: £4,037.25: £1,748.25)
7f Stalls: High GOING minus 0.23 sec per fur (GF) 3-45 (3-45)

2320* **Alhaarth (IRE)** *(99+)*(Fav)*(MajorWRHern)* 2-8-11 WCarson(5) (lw: 3rd st: hmpd on ins over 2f out: swtchd lft over 1f out: led ins fnl f: pushed out)...— 1
2365* Allied Forces (USA) *(100) (HRACecil)* 2-9-0 WRyan(1) (lw: 4th st: edgd rt & led over 2f out: hdd ins fnl f: unable qckn)...1 2
2034* More Royal (USA) *(96) (IABalding)* 2-8-11 LDettori(2) (lw: 6th st: rdn over 2f out: r.o ins fnl f)½ 3
2059* Mushahid (USA) *(91) (JLDunlop)* 2-8-11 RHills(6) (led 6f out to over 2f out: ev ch over 1f out: one pce)...2 4
2340* Believe Me *(82) (RHannon)* 2-8-11 RPerham(4) (5th st: rdn over 3f out: nt clr run over 2f out: swtchd lft: sn wknd)...4 5
2058³ Oberons Boy (IRE) *(77) (BJMeehan)* 2-8-11 WRSwinburn(3) (lw: led 1f: 2nd st: hmpd over 2f out: sn wknd)...2 6

5/6 ALHAARTH (IRE) (5/4-4/5), **4/1** Allied Forces (USA) (op 2/1), **11/2** More Royal (USA) (4/1-6/1), **15/2** Mushahid (USA), **25/1** Believe Me, **33/1** Oberons Boy (IRE), CSF £4.24 TOTE £2.00: £1.40 £1.90 (£2.50) OWNER Mr Hamdan Al Maktoum (LAMBOURN) BRED Shadwell Estate Company Limited 6 Rn 1m 26.21 (1.81) SF: 55/56/52/47/38/33

2691

TOTE GOLD TROPHY H'CAP (0-105) (3-Y.O) (Class B) £37,270.00 (£11,260.00: £5,480.00: £2,590.00)
1m 4f Stalls: Low GOING minus 0.23 sec per fur (GF) 4-15 (4-20)

2348* **Pilsudski (IRE) (89)***(100) (MRStoute)* 3-8-12 WRSwinburn(14) (hdwy over 4f out: 6th st: plld out over 3f out: led over 1f out: rdn out)......— **1**
2457^{4} Rokeby Bowl **(90)***(101)*(Fav)*(IABalding)* 3-8-13 LDettori(6) (lw: swtchd rt & hdwy over 3f out: rdn over 2f out: r.o wl ins fnl f)......nk **2**
2062* Grand Selection (IRE) **(79)***(86) (MBell)* 3-8-2 MFenton(3) (led over 5f out to over 3f out: led over 2f out to over 1f out: unable qckn)......3 **3**
1872^{6} Burning (USA) **(98)***(105) (GHarwood)* 3-9-7 RHills(8) (lw: rdn over 3f out: swtchd rt & hdwy over 2f out: swtchd lft over 1f out: r.o ins fnl f)......hd **4**
1308* Sanmartino (IRE) **(91)***(97) (BWHills)* 3-9-0 MHills(12) (lw: rdn over 3f out: nvr nr to chal)......¾ **5**
2172^{2} Vaugrenier (IRE) **(81)***(81) (RHannon)* 3-8-4 MRoberts(10) (led over 6f: 2nd st: led over 3f out to over 2f out: 4th & btn whn n.m.r on ins over 1f out)......4 **6**
2289^{6} Lovely Lyca **(78)***(78) (JWHills)* 3-7-10 (5) MHenry(4) (lw: rdn over 3f out: hdwy over 1f out: nvr nrr)......½ **7**
1872^{4} At Liberty (IRE) **(91)***(90) (RHannon)* 3-9-0 JReid(2) (lw: rdn over 3f out: nvr nr to chal)......nk **8**
1872^{2} Bob's Ploy **(89)***(88) (RAkehurst)* 3-8-12 BThomson(9) (4th st: rdn over 3f out: wknd over 1f out)......s.h **9**
1672^{5} Danjing (IRE) **(93)***(81) (PFICole)* 3-9-2 WCarson(15) (bhd whn hmpd on ins over 2f out)......8 **10**
2437^{6} The Stager (IRE) **(70)***(57) (JRJenkins)* 3-7-7 GBardwell(11) (5th st: wknd over 2f out)......¾ **11**
1527* Dont Shoot Fairies **(71)***(50) (CEBrittain)* 3-7-8 JQuinn(5) (3rd st: wknd over 3f out)......6 **12**
2411^{7} San Pietra (IRE) **(75)***(49) (PWChapple-Hyam)* 3-7-12 FNorton(13) (a bhd)......4 **13**
2348^{9} Craigmill **(84)***(56) (HRACecil)* 3-8-7 WRyan(1) (prom tl wknd & hmpd 4f out)......1½ **14**
2348^{5} Rahy Zoman (USA) **(83)***(52) (JRFanshawe)* 3-8-6 JWeaver(7) (bhd fnl 3f)......2½ **15**

5/1 Rokeby Bowl, **11/2** PILSUDSKI (IRE) (4/1-6/1), Bob's Ploy, **8/1** Burning (USA), At Liberty (IRE), **10/1** Grand Selection (IRE), **11/1** Craigmill, **12/1** Sanmartino (IRE), **14/1** Rahy Zoman (USA), **20/1** Dont Shoot Fairies, **25/1** Danjing (IRE), Lovely Lyca, San Pietra (IRE), Vaugrenier (IRE), **66/1** The Stager (IRE), CSF £31.15 CT £249.58 TOTE £5.70: £2.40 £2.00 £2.60 (£15.00) Trio £46.40 OWNER Lord Weinstock & The Hon Simon Weinstock (NEWMARKET) BRED Ballymacoll Stud Co
15 Rn 2m 34.32 (2.32) SF: 63/64/49/68/60/44/41/53/51/44/20/13/12/19/15

2692

CHARLTON H'CAP (0-80) (3-Y.O+) (Class D) £7,440.00 (£2,220.00: £1,060.00: £480.00)
5f Stalls: Low GOING minus 0.47 sec per fur (F) 4-45 (4-52)

2326^{2} **Aragrove (77)***(86)*(Fav)*(JWPayne)* 5-10-0 LDettori(6) (hld up: led over 1f out: rdn out)......— **1**
2120^{4} Beau Venture (USA) **(76)***(84) (FHLee)* 7-9-13 RLappin(3) (hld up: hrd rdn over 1f out: r.o wl ins fnl f)......nk **2**
2533^{4} Giggleswick Girl **(64)***(67) (MRChannon)* 4-9-1 RHughes(2) (hrd rdn & hdwy over 1f out: r.o ins fnl f)......1½ **3**
2330^{9} Followmegirls **(51)***(54) (MrsALMKing)* 6-7-13 (3) AGarth(11) (hdwy 2f out: ev ch ins fnl f: unable qckn)......hd **4**
2627^{4} Southern Dominion **(65)***(62) (MJohnston)* 3-8-11 MRoberts(5) (led over 3f)......2 **5**
2288^{13} Another Jade **(67)***(62) (APJarvis)* 5-9-1 (3) JTate(10) (lw: hld up: ev ch over 1f out: sn wknd)..½ **6**
2027^{4} Barossa Valley (IRE) **(74)***(68) (PWChapple-Hyam)* 4-9-4b(7) RHavlin(8) (lw: rdn 2f out: nt clr run wl over 1f out: swtchd rt & hdwy over 1f out: hung rt fnl f: nvr nrr)......nk **7**
2067^{6} Taylord **(66)***(60) (RHannon)* 3-8-12 JReid(7) (hld up: ev ch over 1f out: sn wknd)......s.h **8**
2394^{4} Total Stranger **(77)***(67) (MrsLPiggott)* 3-9-9 WRyan(4) (w ldr over 3f)......1¼ **9**
1910^{4} Mazzarello (IRE) **(43)***(22) (RCurtis)* 5-7-8v GBardwell(9) (hld up: ev ch over 1f out: sn wknd)3½ **10**

7/2 ARAGROVE, **6/1** Mazzarello (IRE), Total Stranger, **13/2** Giggleswick Girl, **15/2** Beau Venture (USA), **8/1** Barossa Valley (IRE) (6/1-9/1), **12/1** Southern Dominion, **14/1** Another Jade, Taylord (10/1-16/1), **16/1** Followmegirls, CSF £26.67 CT £145.73 TOTE £3.60: £1.60 £3.50 £1.50 (£15.50) Trio £32.40 OWNER Mr Dennis Purkiss (NEWMARKET) BRED Mrs J. R. Hine and Miss J. Bunting
10 Rn 58.02 secs (1.32) SF: 47/45/28/15/18/23/29/16/23/-
WEIGHT FOR AGE 3yo-5lb

2693

E.B.F. SELSEY MAIDEN STKS (2-Y.O C & G) (Class D) £6,872.50 (£2,080.00: £1,015.00: £482.50)
6f Stalls: Low GOING minus 0.47 sec per fur (F) 5-20 (5-21)

690^{8} **Woodborough (USA)** *(83)*(Fav)*(PWChapple-Hyam)* 2-8-11 JReid(4) (lw: a.p: rdn over 1f out: led wl ins fnl f: r.o wl)......— **1**
2063^{2} Bijou d'Inde *(82) (MJohnston)* 2-8-11 MRoberts(3) (a.p: rdn 2f out: r.o ins fnl f)......nk **2**

2370² Raheen (USA) *(81) (MRStoute)* 2-8-11 WRSwinburn(5) (led: rdn 2f out: wandered fnl f: hdd wl ins fnl f: unable qckn) .... ½ **3**
Love Bird (IRE) *(62) (MJohnston)* 2-8-11 JWeaver(7) (neat: nvr nr to chal) 7 **4**
Statoyork *(60) (BWHills)* 2-8-11 MHills(8) (wl grwn: spd over 4f) 1 **5**
1715⁷ La Tansani (IRE) *(50) (RHannon)* 2-8-11 LDettori(1) (a bhd) 3½ **6**
2340⁷ Sunrise Special (IRE) *(10) (GLewis)* 2-8-11 WRyan(2) (a bhd) 15 **7**

2/1 WOODBOROUGH (USA) (6/4-9/4), **9/4** Raheen (USA), **5/2** Bijou d'Inde, **16/1** Statoyork, **20/1** Love Bird (IRE), **25/1** La Tansani (IRE), **33/1** Sunrise Special (IRE), CSF £6.84 TOTE £3.00: £1.80 £1.90 (£5.00) OWNER Mr R. E. Sangster (MARLBOROUGH) BRED Swettenham Stud 7 Rn
1m 11.15 (0.95) SF: 42/41/40/21/19/9/-

2694

DRAYTON H'CAP (0-90) (3-Y.O+ F & M) (Class C) £7,830.00 (£2,340.00: £1,120.00: £510.00) **1m 1f** Stalls: High GOING minus 0.23 sec (GF) 5-50 (5-51)

2199⁴ **Ron's Secret (71)***(86) (JWPayne)* 3-8-9 LDettori(6) (4th st: nt clr run over 3f out & over 2f out: bmpd, squeezed thro & led over 1f out: hrd rdn: r.o wl) .... — **1**
2287⁵ Sue's Return **(88)***(102) (APJarvis)* 3-9-9 (3) JTate(1) (6th st: led wl over 1f out: sn hdd & edgd rt: r.o) .... ½ **2**
2139* Quivira **(68)***(82) (TTClement)* 4-9-1 MRimmer(7) (rdn over 3f out: hdwy on ins over 2f out: nt clr run over 1f out: r.o ins fnl f) .... nk **3**
2607* Ninia (USA) **(55)***(66)*(Fav)*(MJohnston)* 3-7-7 GBardwell(5) (3rd st: rdn over 3f out: ev ch whn bmpd over 1f out: unable qckn) 1¾ **4**
2287⁹ Shot At Love (IRE) **(80)***(89) (CACyzer)* 4-9-13 JReid(4) (5th st: nt clr run over 3f out: rdn over 2f out: one pce) 1 **5**
2411* Emily-Mou (IRE) **(70)***(73) (BJMeehan)* 3-8-8 JWeaver(8) (led over 7f) 3½ **6**
1923⁵ Menas Gold **(89)***(91) (SDow)* 3-9-13 MRoberts(3) (a bhd) .... hd **7**
2241⁸ Lesley's Fashion **(64)***(65) (DJSffrenchDavis)* 4-8-6 (5) MHenry(9) (a bhd) .... ½ **8**
2449* Celtic Fringe **(82)***(83)*(Fav)*(HRACecil)* 3-9-6 WRyan(2) (lw: 2nd st: rdn over 2f out: btn whn hmpd over 1f out) .... nk **9**

4/1 Ninia (USA), Celtic Fringe (5/2-9/2), **5/1** RON'S SECRET, **11/2** Emily-Mou (IRE), **13/2** Menas Gold, **10/1** Sue's Return, Lesley's Fashion, **12/1** Quivira (op 8/1), **25/1** Shot At Love (IRE), CSF £47.07 CT £511.42 TOTE £5.30: £1.60 £2.70 £3.50 (£24.20) Trio £134.90 OWNER Mrs Linda Popely (NEWMARKET) BRED Mrs L. Popely 9 Rn 1m 55.32 (4.62) SF: 34/50/39/14/46/21/39/22/31
WEIGHT FOR AGE 3yo-9lb

T/Plpt: £48.50 (1,115.52 Tckts). T/Qdpt: £13.70 (56.35 Tckts). AK

2676-DONCASTER (L-H)
Thursday July 27th (Firm, Good to firm patches)

WEATHER: fine & sunny WIND: almost nil

2695

DONCASTER RACECOURSE SUNDAY MARKET AMATEUR H'CAP (0-80) (3-Y.O+) (Class F) £3,028.00 (£904.00: £432.00: £196.00)
2m 110y Stalls: Low GOING minus 0.36 sec per fur (F) 6-30 (6-31)

2603* **Carnbrea Belle (IRE) (63)***(77+) (MBell)* 3-9-12 (5) 3x MrRWakley(7) (hld up gng wl: stdy hdwy 9f out: swtchd 4f out: led 2f out: sn wl clr: eased towards fin) .... — **1**
2545² Kilernan **(44)***(55) (TDBarron)* 4-10-0 MrsAFarrell(6) (swtg: plld hrd: led after 3f: clr 5f out: hdd 2f out: no ch w wnr) 3½ **2**
2501* Chakalak **(48)***(50) (SDow)* 7-10-4 3x MrTCuff(1) (lw: led 3f: rdn & lost pl 8f out: bhd tl styd on fnl 2f) 9 **3**
2465² Dusty Point (IRE) **(56)***(58)*(Fav)*(JPearce)* 5-10-12 MrsLPearce(8) (hdwy 8f out: effrt & hmpd 4f out: kpt on one pce fnl 2f) .... s.h **4**
2127² Hit the Canvas (USA) **(65)***(67) (MrsMReveley)* 4-11-7b MrMHNaughton(2) (trckd ldrs: pushed along 5f out: rdn over 2f out: sn wknd) .... nk **5**
2546⁴ Ice Magic **(30)***(23) (FJYardley)* 8-8-9v(5) MissSYardley(5) (s.i.s: drvn along 10f out: sme hdwy 5f out: edgd rt & lost pl over 3f out) 9 **6**
1643⁸ Al Jinn **(36)***(20) (RCurtis)* 4-9-1 (5) MrMAllen(3) (drvn along & hdwy 6f out: edgd lft 4f out: hrd rdn & hung lft: sn wknd) 9 **7**
1359⁷ Bajan Affair **(46)** *(JRBostock)* 5-9-11 (5)ow16 MrKLoads(4) (prom early: lost pl 9f out: sn t.o) ..20 **8**

LONG HANDICAP Ice Magic 8-10 Bajan Affair 8-6

5/2 Dusty Point (IRE) (op 4/1), **11/4** CARNBREA BELLE (IRE), **100/30** Chakalak, **4/1** Kilernan, **6/1** Hit the Canvas (USA), **16/1** Ice Magic, **33/1** Al Jinn, Bajan Affair, CSF £14.66 CT £35.13 TOTE £3.10: £1.20 £1.80 £1.30 (£8.00) OWNER Mrs S. M. Crompton (NEWMARKET) BRED Limestone Stud 8 Rn 3m 38.99 (9.99) SF: 39/33/28/36/45/1/-/-
WEIGHT FOR AGE 3yo-16lb

2696 DONCASTER STALLHOLDERS CONDITIONS STKS (2-Y.O) (Class C)
£5,040.00 (£1,740.00: £832.50: £337.50)
6f Stalls: High GOING minus 0.36 sec per fur (F) 7-00 (7-00)

2328* **Benny Glow** *(63+)*(Fav)*(MrsJRRamsden)* 2-8-10 KFallon(3) (swtg: trckd ldr: shkn up to ld over 1f out: drvn out).........— 1
*1879** Jimjareer (IRE) *(60) (CaptJWilson)* 2-8-10 SDWilliams(4) (led: hung lft & hdd ½-wy: sn wl outpcd: styd on ins fnl f).........1 2
2422* Purple Memories *(58) (MJohnston)* 2-8-10 JCarroll(1) (lw: trckd ldrs: effrt & hmpd over 2f out: carried lft: styd on same pce u.p fnl f).........1 3
1670[17] Petrefuz (IRE) *(57?) (EWeymes)* 2-8-10 NRodgers(2) (sn w ldr: hung lft & led ½-wy: edgd lft: hdd over 1f out: one pce).........nk 4

10/11 BENNY GLOW, **7/4** Purple Memories (4/1-6/4), **5/1** Jimjareer (IRE) (op 8/1), **25/1** Petrefuz (IRE), CSF £5.12 TOTE £1.90 (£3.10) OWNER Mr Ronald Thorburn (THIRSK) BRED D. H. Jones 4 Rn
1m 13.71 (2.71) SF: 27/24/22/21

2697 'DAZZLING DONCASTER MARKETS' H'CAP (0-85) (3-Y.O) (Class D)
£4,737.00 (£1,416.00: £678.00: £309.00)
6f Stalls: High GOING minus 0.36 sec per fur (F) 7-30 (7-30)

2556* **Tedburrow (79)***(88)*(Fav)*(MrsAMNaughton)* 3-9-4 7x JCarroll(2) (trckd ldr: led wl over 1f out: pushed clr ins fnl f: readily).........— 1
2271[5] Prolific Lady (IRE) **(74)***(78) (MBrittain)* 3-8-13b KFallon(3) (reard s: hld up: effrt & swtchd over 1f out: kpt on same pce).........2 2
2179* Arasong **(63)***(66) (EWeymes)* 3-8-2 DaleGibson(4) (led: drvn along ½-wy: hdd wl over 1f out: one pce).........hd 3
Super Park **(82)***(75) (MHEasterby)* 3-9-7 MBirch(1) (h.d.w: trckd ldrs tl rdn & wknd over 1f out: eased nr fin).........4 4

6/4 TEDBURROW (op Evens), **15/8** Arasong, **4/1** Prolific Lady (IRE), **11/2** Super Park (4/1-6/1), CSF £6.83 TOTE £1.90 (£2.50) OWNER Mr Philip Davies (RICHMOND) BRED Lady Matthews 4 Rn
1m 15.15 (4.15) SF: 15/5/-/2

2698 WARD'S THORNE BEST BITTER H'CAP (0-70) (3-Y.O+) (Class E)
£3,816.00 (£1,143.00: £549.00: £252.00)
7f Stalls: High GOING minus 0.36 sec per fur (F) 8-00 (8-02)

2279[4] **Anonym (IRE) (63)***(71) (JLDunlop)* 3-9-3 NConnorton(5) (trckd ldrs: led 2f out: hung rt: drvn out).........— 1
2358[2] Kid Ory **(60)***(65) (PCalver)* 4-9-7 MBirch(6) (trckd ldrs: swtchd lft ½-wy: n.m.r over 1f out: kpt on wl ins fnl f).........1½ 2
1847[8] It's Academic **(58)***(62) (MrsJRRamsden)* 3-8-12 KFallon(17) (hld up: hdwy over 2f out: n.m.r over 1f out: styd on wl ins fnl f).........nk 3
2477[7] Cafe Solo **(41)***(44) (NBycroft)* 4-8-2b SMaloney(2) (trckd ldrs: ev ch & wandered over 1f out: one pce).........½ 4
2383[10] Arc Lamp **(38)***(40) (JAGlover)* 9-7-13 DaleGibson(7) (hld up & plld hrd: hdwy ½-wy: kpt on wl fnl f).........nk 5
2377[3] Legend Dulac (IRE) **(46)***(44) (JAHarris)* 6-8-7 SDWilliams(3) (lw: w ldrs tl wknd over 1f out)....2 6
2342[11] Thunder River (IRE) **(63)***(60) (MJHeaton-Ellis)* 5-9-10 TIves(10) (w ldrs: effrt over 2f out: kpt on same pce u.p fnl f: n.m.r towards fin).........hd 7
2330[7] Densben **(48)***(42) (DenysSmith)* 11-8-9 ACulhane(4) (hdwy over 2f out: n.m.r over 1f out: nvr nr to chal).........1½ 8
2484[5] Reed My Lips (IRE) **(35)***(23) (BPJBaugh)* 4-7-3 (7) IonaWands(18) (swtg: in tch: drvn along ½-wy: sn outpcd).........2½ 9
2634[13] Indiahra **(51)***(36) (RHollinshead)*4-8-9(3) AGarth(15) (chsd ldrs: led over 2f out: sn hdd: wknd)1¼ 10
2549[2] Asterix **(49)***(30)*(Fav)*(JMBradley)* 7-8-7v(3) SDrowne(8) (mid div: drvn along ½-wy: swtchd lft & styd on appr fnl f: n.d).........2 11
2448[3] Exclusive Assembly **(46)***(20) (APJames)* 3-8-0 JQuinn(14) (in tch tl wknd over 2f out).........3 12
2484[3] Northern Spark **(46)***(16) (MartynWane)* 7-8-7 JCarroll(12) (lw: mid div: effrt & hung lft ½-wy: swtchd rt: nvr nr ldrs).........1½ 13
2549[4] Belleminette (IRE) **(56)***(25) (DHaydnJones)* 4-9-3 NRodgers(16) (s.s: a wl bhd).........½ 14
2491[12] It'sthebusiness **(60)***(28) (SDow)* 3-8-11 (3) DRMcCabe(11) (s.s: a wl bhd).........½ 15
2162[7] Kajostar **(35)** *(SWCampion)* 5-7-10 JMarshall(9) (swtg: sn bhd).........5 16
2451[7] Anytime Baby **(42)** *(PTDalton)* 3-7-7 (3) DWright(13) (led & sn clr: hdd over 2f out: wknd)......12 17
2355[11] Readyspex **(32)** *(RDEWoodhouse)* 5-7-7 NKennedy(1) (racd far side: sn wl bhd).........4 18
LONG HANDICAP Readyspex 7-0

6/1 Asterix, **8/1** Legend Dulac (IRE), It's Academic, Belleminette (IRE), Kid Ory, **17/2** ANONYM (IRE), **10/1** Northern Spark, It'sthebusiness, **11/1** Exclusive Assembly, **12/1** Reed My Lips (IRE), Thunder River (IRE), **14/1** Cafe Solo, **16/1** Densben, **20/1** Arc Lamp, Indiahra, **50/1** Kajostar, Anytime Baby, **100/1** Readyspex, CSF £76.17 CT £537.87 TOTE £9.90: £2.10 £1.90 £3.00 £5.60 (£27.60) Trio £78.00 OWNER Mr J. L. Dunlop (ARUNDEL) BRED T. G. Mooney 18 Rn
1m 25.5 (2.10) SF: 46/47/37/26/22/26/42/24/5/18/12/-/-/7/3/-/-/-
WEIGHT FOR AGE 3yo-7lb

2699 'COME TO DONCASTER MARKETS' CONDITIONS STKS (3-Y.O+) (Class C) £5,536.80 (£1,996.80: £958.40: £392.00: £156.00)
7f Stalls: High GOING minus 0.36 sec per fur (F) 8-30 (8-30)

2409[2] **Indhar (102)***(106)*(Fav)*(JEBanks)* 4-9-6 JQuinn(6) (lw: trckd ldrs: effrt 2f out: styd on u.p to ld ins fnl f: jst hld on)........— 1
1100[7] Monaassib (IRE) **(94)***(105) (EALDunlop)* 4-9-5 TIves(1) (w ldr: led 3f out tl jst ins fnl f: styd on wl)........s.h 2
2097[6] Storiths (IRE) **(106)***(93) (JWWatts)* 5-9-0 NConnorton(4) (lw: b: trckd ldrs: pushed along ½-wy: effrt over 2f out: rdn & hung lft over 1f out: n.m.r ins fnl f: eased towards fin)........3 3
2436[5] Maid for Walking **(99)***(77) (DRLoder)* 3-8-11 (3) DRMcCabe(5) (hld up: effrt over 2f out: wknd over 1f out)........10 4
Tabook (IRE) **(102)***(68) (EALDunlop)* 4-9-6 JCarroll(2) (plld hrd: led to 3f out: wknd over 1f out)........3½ 5

13/8 INDHAR, **3/1** Maid for Walking, **7/2** Storiths (IRE), **4/1** Monaassib (IRE), **6/1** Tabook (IRE), CSF £8.53 TOTE £2.60: £1.30 £2.10 (£4.90) OWNER Miss P. Rovera (NEWMARKET) BRED Patrick Eddery Ltd 5 Rn
1m 24.5 (1.10) SF: 61/60/48/25/23
WEIGHT FOR AGE 3yo-7lb

2700 DONCASTER GOOSEHILL MARKET LIMITED STKS (0-70) (3-Y.O+) (Class E) £3,273.60 (£976.80: £466.40: £211.20)
6f GOING minus 0.36 sec per fur (F) 9-00 (9-01)

2326[7] **Purple Fling (70)***(77)*(Fav)*(SirMarkPrescott)* 4-9-6 JCarroll(6) (trckd ldr: led over 1f out: drvn out)........— 1
2652[10] Bargash **(70)***(74) (PDEvans)* 3-9-0 TIves(4) (effrt over 2f out: kpt on same pce fnl f: nvr able to chal)........1¼ 2
2240[16] Bedouin Invader **(70)***(70) (MRStoute)* 3-8-8v(3) DRMcCabe(3) (chsd ldrs: effrt over 2f out: kpt on same pce fnl f)........hd 3
2609* So Intrepid (IRE) **(70)***(78) (JMBradley)* 5-9-9 (3) SDrowne(7) (trckd ldrs: effrt over 2f out: n.m.r: nt qckn fnl f: wknd towards fin)........½ 4
2585[3] Boursin (IRE) **(69)***(53) (PCalver)* 6-9-3 DaleGibson(5) (led tl over 1f out: wknd & eased ins fnl f)........6 5

5/2 PURPLE FLING, **3/1** Boursin (IRE), **7/2** So Intrepid (IRE), **4/1** Bedouin Invader, Bargash, CSF £11.99 TOTE £2.90: £1.60 £2.50 (£6.60) OWNER Cheveley Park Stud (NEWMARKET) BRED Mrs P. Lewis 5 Rn
1m 12.64 (1.64) SF: 51/42/38/52/27
WEIGHT FOR AGE 3yo-6lb
T/Plpt: £36.10 (246.73 Tckts). T/Qdpt: £21.20 (4.75 Tckts). WG

2688-GOODWOOD (R-H)
Thursday July 27th (St Good, Rnd Firm, both Good to firm patches)

7th race, flag start
WEATHER: fair WIND: almost nil

2701 CROWTHER HOMES RATED STKS H'CAP (0-95) (3-Y.O) (Class B) £9,802.80 (£3,625.20: £1,737.60: £708.00: £279.00: £107.40)
1m 6f Stalls: High GOING minus 0.28 sec per fur (GF) 2-30 (2-34)

1872[5] **Cherrington (81)***(94)*(Fav)*(GWragg)* 3-9-4 MHills(1) (4th st: led wl over 1f out: rdn & r.o wl)........— 1
2445[2] Shaft of Light **(79)***(92)*(Fav)*(LordHuntingdon)* 3-9-2 LDettori(4) (led over 12f: ev ch ins fnl f: r.o)........nk 2
2284[4] Red Bustaan **(83)***(89) (ACStewart)* 3-9-6b MRoberts(5) (2nd st: rdn over 3f out: wknd over 1f out)........6 3

2604* Vindaloo **(81)***(85) (JLHarris)* 3-9-4 3x JWeaver(2) (lw: 6th st: rdn over 3f out: nvr nr to chal) 1¼ 4
2462[2] Torch Vert (IRE) **(79)***(75) (BWHills)* 3-9-2 RHills(7) (lw: 3rd st: rdn over 3f out: 4th & wkng whn hit in face by whip & stumbled over 1f out) 7 5
2172* High Flying Adored (IRE) **(84)***(75)*(Fav)*(JLDunlop)* 3-9-7 WCarson(3) (lw: 5th st: a bhd)....5 6

7/2 CHERRINGTON, Shaft of Light, High Flying Adored (IRE), **5/1** Torch Vert (IRE) (5/2-11/2), **11/2** Red Bustaan, **8/1** Vindaloo, CSF £14.52 TOTE £4.30: £2.40 £1.90 (£5.40) OWNER Sheikh Mohammed (NEWMARKET) BRED Sheikh Mohammed bin Rashid al Maktoum 6 Rn

3m 2.26 (3.26) SF: 62/60/57/53/43/43

2702 TIFFANY GOODWOOD CUP STKS (Gp 2) (3-Y.O+) (Class A) £36,080.00 (£13,491.50: £6,470.75: £2,807.75)

2m Stalls: High GOING minus 0.28 sec per fur (GF) 3-10 (3-11)

1869* **Double Trigger (IRE) (117)***(127)*(Fav)*(MJohnston)* 4-9-5 JWeaver(7) (swtg: mde virtually all: drvn out)....— 1
2218a[10] Double Eclipse (IRE) **(105)***(122) (MJohnston)* 3-7-12 TWilliams(6) (swtg: 3rd st: hrd rdn over 2f out: ev ch ins fnl f: r.o wl)....nk 2
2219a[5] Khamaseen **(109)***(118) (JLDunlop)* 4-9-0 JReid(8) (5th st: nt clr run over 2f out: swtchd lft over 1f out: r.o one pce) 4 3
2098* Bold Gait **(110)***(115) (JRFanshawe)* 4-9-0 WRSwinburn(1) (lw: 4th st: rdn over 2f out: hung rt ins fnl f: one pce)....2½ 4
1869[3] Admiral's Well (IRE) **(108)***(115) (RAkehurst)* 5-9-0 TQuinn(3) (lw: 2nd st: rdn over 3f out: wknd over 1f out)....s.h 5
2456* Saxon Maid **(106)***(110) (LMCumani)* 4-8-11 LDettori(2) (lost pl 7f out: 7th st: no hdwy fnl 3f)...2 6
1898* Cuff Link (IRE) **(108)***(112) (MajorWRHern)* 5-9-0 PaulEddery(5) (lw: 6th st: rdn over 3f out: wknd fnl f) 1 7
2366[2] Juyush (USA) **(107)***(110) (BWHills)* 3-7-12 WCarson(9) (9th st: a bhd)....2½ 8
2119* Further Flight **(107)***(107) (BWHills)* 9-9-0 MHills(4) (b.hind: 8th st: a bhd) 3 9

2/1 DOUBLE TRIGGER (IRE), **100/30** Bold Gait (9/4-7/2), **6/1** Saxon Maid, **15/2** Double Eclipse (IRE), **12/1** Admiral's Well (IRE), **14/1** Juyush (USA), **20/1** Cuff Link (IRE), Further Flight, **25/1** Khamaseen, CSF £15.23 TOTE £3.30: £1.40 £2.60 £3.80 (£7.90) Trio £126.90 OWNER Mr R. W. Huggins (MIDDLEHAM) BRED Dene Investments N V 9 Rn

3m 25.86 (1.36) SF: 75/54/66/63/63/58/60/42/55

WEIGHT FOR AGE 3yo-16lb

2703 SCHWEPPES GOLDEN MILE H'CAP (3-Y.O+) (Class B) £48,250.00 (£14,500.00: £7,000.00: £3,250.00)

1m Stalls: High GOING minus 0.28 sec per fur (GF) 3-45 (3-50)

2287[2] **Khayrapour (IRE) (83)***(94) (BJMeehan)* 5-7-13b BDoyle(1) (20th st: plld out over 3f out: gd hdwy over 1f out: str run fnl f: led nr fin) ....— 1
2241[4] Realities (USA) **(105)***(116) (GHarwood)* 5-9-7 LDettori(6) (16th st: swtchd lft over 2f out: hdwy wl over 1f out: led ins fnl f: hrd rdn: hdd nr fin)....s.h 2
2080[3] Desert Green (FR) **(94)***(102) (RHannon)* 6-8-10 RPerham(10) (13th st: hdwy 2f out: nt clr run wl over 1f out: r.o wl ins fnl f)....1½ 3
2217a[4] Fraam **(108)***(114) (EALDunlop)* 6-9-10v WRSwinburn(5) (b: swtg: 15th st: hdwy over 2f out: led over 1f out tl ins fnl f: one pce) ....¾ 4
2436[4] Royal Rebuke **(93)***(98) (RCharlton)* 3-7-12 (3) SSanders(20) (3rd st: led 2f out tl over 1f out: one pce ins fnl f)....½ 5
1851[3] Indian Fly **(94)***(96) (RHannon)* 4-8-10 JReid(21) (9th st: hdwy over 2f out: rdn over 1f out: one pce ins fnl f)....1½ 6
1839[19] Classicy **(94)***(88) (MRStoute)* 3-7-13 (3)ow2 JTate(12) (5th st: rdn over 2f out: hung rt over 1f out: sn wknd)....3 7
2287[7] Embankment (IRE) **(85)***(80) (RHannon)* 5-8-1 GCarter(8) (17th st: rdn over 3f out: hdwy over 1f out: nvr nrr) ....¾ 8
2222[2] Queens Consul (IRE) **(80)***(73) (BSRothwell)* 5-7-10 FNorton(13) (4th st: rdn over 3f out: nt clr run over 2f out: btn whn bdly hmpd over 1f out)....1 9
2369[8] Night City **(99)***(90) (LadyHerries)* 4-9-1 PaulEddery(18) (swtg: 10th st: hdwy & n.m.r over 1f out: wknd fnl f)....¾ 10
2419* Behaviour **(88)***(78)*(Fav)*(MrsJCecil)* 3-7-10 3x WCarson(7) (lw: 4t st: hdwy 2f out: hmpd on ins over 1f out: nt rcvr)....½ 11
2287[8] Classic Sky (IRE) **(99)***(89) (BHanbury)* 4-9-1 WRyan(9) (12th st: a mid div)....nk 12
2436[10] Pinkerton's Pal **(95)***(84) (CEBrittain)* 4-8-11 JWeaver(15) (b: lw: 11th st: mid div whn nt clr run 2f out)....nk 13

2436[8] Celestial Key (USA) **(102)***(91) (MJohnston)* 5-9-4 PRobinson(22) (6th st: nt clr run over 2f out: btn whn hmpd over 1f out)...nk **14**
1851[23] Allez Cyrano (IRE) **(89)***(76) (MBell)* 4-8-5 MFenton(19) (19th st: hung rt over 2f out: nvr nrr)..¾ **15**
1915[3] Cyrano's Lad (IRE) **(90)***(72) (JohnBerry)* 6-8-3 (3) DRMcCabe(14) (led over 3f: 2nd st: ev ch 2f out: wknd over 1f out)...2½ **16**
1409[4] Bagshot **(80)***(61) (RHannon)* 4-7-10 NCarlisle(4) (18th st: a bhd)...½ **17**
2031* Weaver Bird **(85)***(61) (HCandy)* 5-8-1 NAdams(16) (7th st: wknd over 3f out)...2½ **18**
2468* Toujours Riviera **(87)***(62) (JPearce)* 5-8-0 (3) 3x JStack(2) (lw: chsd ldr: led over 4f out to 2f out: wkng whn hmpd over 1f out)...½ **19**
2287[4] Beauchamp Jazz **(100)***(57) (JLDunlop)* 3-8-8 TQuinn(11) (lw: 8th st: wknd over 2f out)...9 **20**
1839[3] Bedivere (USA) **(95)***(45) (PWChapple-Hyam)* 3-7-12 (5) MHenry(3) (21st st: a bhd)...3½ **21**

7/1 Behaviour, **15/2** KHAYRAPOUR (IRE), **9/1** Indian Fly, **11/1** Fraam, Realities (USA) (8/1-14/1), Beauchamp Jazz, Classicy (8/1-12/1), Royal Rebuke, **14/1** Bedivere (USA), **16/1** Desert Green (FR), Toujours Riviera, **20/1** Night City, Celestial Key (USA), **25/1** Bagshot, Allez Cyrano (IRE), Weaver Bird, Cyrano's Lad (IRE), **33/1** Classic Sky (IRE), Embankment (IRE), Queens Consul (IRE), **40/1** Pinkerton's Pal, CSF £82.15 CT £1,193.00 TOTE £10.30: £2.60 £3.10 £3.60 £2.80 (£55.70) Trio £351.70 OWNER Miss J. Semple (UPPER LAMBOURN) BRED His Highness The Aga Khans Stud S.C. 21 Rn
1m 36.88 (-0.72) SF: 69/91/77/89/65/71/55/55/48/65/45/64/59/66/51/47/36/36/37/24/12
WEIGHT FOR AGE 3yo-8lb

2704 RICHMOND STKS (Gp 2) (2-Y.O C & G) (Class A) £31,325.00 (£11,761.25: £5,680.63: £2,508.12) 6f Stalls: Low GOING minus 0.28 sec (GF) 4-15 (4-20)

2440* **Polaris Flight (USA)** *(99) (PWChapple-Hyam)* 2-8-11 JReid(2) (lw: hdwy over 1f out: hrd rdn fnl f: led nr fin)...— **1**
2243[3] Mubhij (IRE) *(98) (BWHills)* 2-8-11 RHills(5) (led: hrd rdn over 1f out: hdd nr fin)...nk **2**
2440[2] Kahir Almaydan (IRE) *(93) (JLDunlop)* 2-8-11 WCarson(6) (lw: hld up: rdn over 2f out: one pce fnl f)...2 **3**
1838[13] Wisam *(91) (RHannon)* 2-8-11 WRSwinburn(3) (rdn & hdwy over 2f out: one pce fnl f)...¾ **4**
2243[5] Norwegian Blue (IRE) *(82) (APJarvis)* 2-8-11 BThomson(1) (prom 4f)...3½ **5**
1893* Kuantan (USA) *(72d)*(Fav)*(PFICole)* 2-8-11 TQuinn(4) (spd over 3f)...3½ **6**

13/8 Kuantan (USA) (11/10-7/4), **9/4** POLARIS FLIGHT (USA), **7/2** Kahir Almaydan (IRE), **8/1** Wisam, **14/1** Mubhij (IRE) (8/1-16/1), **50/1** Norwegian Blue (IRE), CSF £24.84 TOTE £3.70: £1.60 £3.40 (£27.50) OWNER Mr R. E. Sangster (MARLBOROUGH) BRED Bill Van Den Dool 6 Rn
1m 11.27 (1.07) SF: 56/55/50/48/39/29

2705 E.B.F. NEW HAM MAIDEN STKS (2-Y.O F) (Class D) £7,035.00 (£2,130.00: £1,040.00: £495.00) 7f Stalls: High GOING minus 0.28 sec per fur (GF) 4-45 (4-48)

2370[5] **Papering (IRE)** *(88) (LMCumani)* 2-8-11 LDettori(3) (lw: 4th st: led over 1f out: r.o wl)...— **1**
2025[4] Ailesbury Hill (USA) *(80)*(Fav)*(PWChapple-Hyam)* 2-8-11 JReid(5) (lw: led over 5f: unable qckn)...3½ **2**
2351[5] Salty Girl (IRE) *(75)*(Fav)*(BWHills)* 2-8-11 MHills(1) (2nd st: ev ch over 1f out: one pce)...2 **3**
2173[3] Streete Dancer (IRE) *(73) (PFICole)* 2-8-11 TQuinn(6) (3rd st: swtchd lft over 1f out: one pce)...1¼ **4**
2025[8] Eccola *(69) (IABalding)* 2-8-11 WRyan(4) (lw: 6th st: a bhd)...1½ **5**
Shernadeed (FR) *(63) (MJohnston)* 2-8-11 MRoberts(2) (w'like: scope: s.s: 5th st: a bhd)...2½ **6**

2/1 Ailesbury Hill (USA), Salty Girl (IRE), **11/2** Shernadeed (FR) (7/2-6/1), **6/1** PAPERING (IRE), **10/1** Streete Dancer (IRE) (6/1-12/1), **16/1** Eccola, CSF £17.30 TOTE £4.30: £1.90 £1.70 (£6.30) OWNER Sheikh Mohammed (NEWMARKET) BRED Sheikh Mohammed bin Rashid al Maktoum 6 Rn
1m 28.21 (3.81) SF: 28/20/15/13/9/3

2706 LAVANT NURSERY H'CAP (2-Y.O) (Class C) £7,700.00 (£2,300.00: £1,100.00: £500.00) 5f Stalls: Low GOING minus 0.28 sec per fur (GF) 5-20 (5-21)

2431* **Admiral Jones (IRE)** *(92+)*(Fav)*(MJohnston)* 2-9-7 MRoberts(2) (mde all: rdn out)...— **1**
2335[4] Just Ice *(75) (SirMarkPrescott)* 2-9-0 WWoods(6) (hld up: rdn over 2f out: unable qckn)...3 **2**
2223[4] Krystal Max (IRE) *(77) (TDBarron)* 2-9-3 JFortune(7) (hld up: rdn over 2f out: r.o one pce)...nk **3**
2459* Rambo Delight *(81) (JLEyre)* 2-9-7 RLappin(10) (a.p: rdn 2f out: one pce)...nk **4**
2085[9] Pleasure Time *(65) (CSmith)* 2-8-6b NCarlisle(1) (lw: a.p: hrd rdn over 1f out: one pce)...s.h **5**
2474* Imp Express (IRE) *(72) (GMMoore)* 2-9-2 (3) 6x JTate(13) (outpcd: hdwy 2f out: hrd rdn over 1f out: one pce fnl f)...2 **6**
1590* Bozeman (IRE) *(51) (RHannon)* 2-8-9 MHills(12) (hdwy 2f out: sn wknd)...3½ **7**

2552[2] Where's Margaret *(46) (GLewis)* 2-8-7 PaulEddery(8) (a bhd)....¾ 8
2483[2] Standown *(50) (JBerry)* 2-8-12 WCarson(11) (lw: prom over 2f)....½ 9
2302* Branston Danni *(50) (MrsJRRamsden)* 2-9-0 TQuinn(3) (a bhd)....½ 10
2431[3] Chemcast *(44) (BJMeehan)* 2-8-8 PRobinson(4) (bhd fnl 2f)....s.h 11
2382[3] Touch of Fantasy *(13) (JohnBerry)* 2-7-0 (7) RMullen(9) (prom over 2f)....5 12

4/1 ADMIRAL JONES (IRE), **11/2** Branston Danni (4/1-13/2), **13/2** Where's Margaret, **8/1** Bozeman (IRE), Standown (tchd 12/1), **9/1** Imp Express (IRE), **10/1** Rambo Delight (8/1-12/1), Pleasure Time, **14/1** Just Ice, Krystal Max (IRE), **33/1** Chemcast, Touch of Fantasy, CSF £52.15 CT £641.71 TOTE £3.90: £1.70 £4.70 £5.10 (£58.10) Trio £247.90 OWNER E H Jones (Paints) Ltd (MIDDLEHAM) BRED Sheikh Mohammed Bin Rashid Al Maktoum 12 Rn

58.72 secs (2.02) SF: 45/34/25/30/28/3/3/4/-/-/18/-

2707 DRAWING ROOM H'CAP (0-80) (3-Y.O+) (Class D) £8,025.00 (£2,400.00: £1,150.00: £525.00)

1m 1f Stalls: High GOING minus 0.28 sec per fur (GF) 5-50 (5-59)

2411[4] **Vena (IRE) (80)***(90) (JLDunlop)* 3-9-6 GCarter(6) (rdn over 3f out: nt clr run 2f out: swtchd lft & hdwy over 1f out: led wl ins fnl f: r.o wl)....— 1
2490[2] Conspicuous (IRE) **(57)***(65) (LGCottrell)* 5-8-6 TQuinn(12) (lw: 4th st: led over 2f out tl wl ins fnl f: unable qckn)....1 2
2319[2] Raise the Stakes **(78)***(84) (IABalding)* 3-9-4 MHills(3) (lw: led 2f: 2nd st: rdn over 2f out: one pce)....1½ 3
2557[5] Hatta Sunshine (USA) **(44)***(50) (AMoore)* 5-7-7 NAdams(1) (hdwy over 1f out: r.o)....s.h 4
2479[2] Second Colours (USA) **(61)***(64) (MrsMReveley)* 5-8-10 WRyan(9) (6th st: rdn over 2f out: one pce)....1¼ 5
1344[10] Gypsy Love (USA) **(68)***(70) (PWChapple-Hyam)* 3-8-8 JReid(2) (nvr nr to chal)....¾ 6
2028[2] Douce Maison (IRE) **(54)***(54) (APJarvis)* 4-8-0 (3) JTate(8) (3rd st: rdn over 3f out: wknd over 1f out)....1 7
2477[4] Celestial Choir **(73)***(71) (JLEyre)* 5-9-8 JFortune(7) (7th st: rdn 2f out: wknd over 1f out)....1¼ 8
2602[6] Carte Blanche **(44)***(39) (CACyzer)* 4-7-7 NCarlisle(11) (hmpd on ins over 1f out: a bhd)....1½ 9
2367[4] Elpidos **(70)***(51)*(Fav)*(CEBrittain)* 3-8-10 MRoberts(10) (5th st: wknd over 3f out)....8 10
2571* River Keen (IRE) **(79)***(57) (RWArmstrong)* 3-9-5b 6x RHills(5) (led 7f out tl over 2f out: sn wknd)....1¾ 11

LONG HANDICAP Carte Blanche 7-6 Hatta Sunshine (USA) 7-2

9/2 Elpidos, **5/1** VENA (IRE), **6/1** Raise the Stakes, River Keen (IRE), **7/1** Second Colours (USA), Douce Maison (IRE), **12/1** Conspicuous (IRE), Gypsy Love (USA), **14/1** Celestial Choir, **16/1** Carte Blanche, **33/1** Hatta Sunshine (USA), CSF £57.01 CT £335.92 TOTE £5.80: £2.00 £3.20 £2.30 (£70.00) Trio £255.10 OWNER Skyline Racing Ltd (ARUNDEL) BRED J. Throsby 11 Rn

1m 52.81 (1.43 under best) (2.11) SF: 62/46/56/31/45/42/35/52/20/23/29

WEIGHT FOR AGE 3yo-9lb

T/Jkpt: £50,739.90 (2.69 Tckts). T/Plpt: £268.00 (274.52 Tckts). T/Qdpt: £98.00 (8.1 Tckts). AK

2197-SALISBURY (R-H)
Thursday July 27th (Good)

Race 6: flip start (hand-timed).
WEATHER: warm & sunny WIND: almost nil

2708 NEWNHAM MAIDEN STKS (3-Y.O+) (Class D) £3,850.00 (£1,150.00: £550.00: £250.00) 6f Stalls: High GOING minus 0.05 sec per fur (G) 6-20 (6-22)

2576[3] **Sea Thunder** *(85)*(Fav)*(IABalding)* 3-8-7 LDettori(4) (hld up: swtchd lft & hdwy over 2f out: edgd rt & led ins fnl f: r.o wl)....— 1
1172[11] La Gran Senorita (USA) **(75)***(78) (PFICole)* 3-8-7 MFenton(9) (led tl ins fnl f)....2½ 2
1786[6] Safety Factor (USA) *(83) (GHarwood)* 4-9-4 AClark(10) (a.p: rdn over 1f out: r.o one pce)....nk 3
2576[4] Double Matt (IRE) **(77)***(72) (RHannon)* 3-8-12 RHughes(3) (hld up & bhd: rdn & hdwy over 1f out: r.o one pce fnl f)....4 4
2469[3] Millazure (USA) *(63) (RCharlton)* 3-8-7 JWeaver(8) (swtg: chsd ldr: rdn over 2f out: wknd over 1f out)....1½ 5
522[3] Nottash (IRE) *(62) (JRFanshawe)* 3-8-2 (5) NVarley(1) (prom tl wknd over 1f out)....½ 6
1982[7] Dark Menace **(64)***(63) (SMellor)* 3-8-5 (7) ADaly(11) (nvr trbld ldrs)....1½ 7
Arecibo (FR) *(56) (GLMoore)* 3-8-12 SWhitworth(5) (w'like: bit bkwd: chsd ldrs over 3f)....2½ 8
2049[4] Marwell Indigo *(45) (JARToller)* 3-8-12 WNewnes(7) (b.nr hind: s.s: plld hrd: a bhd)....4 9
2449[6] Gabriel's Lady *(35) (MarkCampion)* 4-8-13 JWilliams(2) (a bhd)....2 10

6/4 SEA THUNDER, **9/2** Nottash (IRE), Double Matt (IRE), **5/1** Millazure (USA) (op 3/1), **9/1** La Gran Senorita (USA), **20/1** Safety Factor (USA), **33/1** Dark Menace, Marwell Indigo, **40/1** Arecibo (FR), **66/1** Gabriel's Lady, CSF £14.79 TOTE £2.10: £1.10 £3.50 £3.00 (£19.60) Trio £56.90 OWNER Greenfield Stud (KINGSCLERE) 10 Rn 1m 15.92 (3.62) SF: 38/31/42/25/16/15/16/9/-/-
WEIGHT FOR AGE 3yo-6lb

2709

MAGDALENE H'CAP (0-80) (3-Y.O+ F & M) (Class D) £4,045.00 (£1,210.00: £580.00: £265.00) **6f 212y** Stalls: High GOING minus 0.05 sec (G) 6-50 (6-52)

2236* **Alarming (76)***(88+)*(Fav)*(JHMGosden)* 3-9-10 LDettori(4) (hld up: hdwy over 2f out: led wl over 1f out: edgd rt 1f out: r.o) — 1
2451 5 Sylvandra **(68)***(79) (PGMurphy)* 3-9-2 JWilliams(7) (hld up: ev ch whn hmpd 1f out: swtchd lft ins fnl f: r.o wl) ½ 2
2451* Linger **(68)***(67) (LordHuntingdon)* 3-9-2 JWeaver(6) (led over 5f: wknd fnl f) 5 3
2405 2 Aldaneh **(71)***(69) (RHannon)* 3-8-12 (7) DaneO'Neill(3) (lw: w ldr tl wknd over 1f out) ¾ 4
2363 5 Indian Lament **(41)***(4) (RJHodges)* 4-7-5 (5) NVarley(1) (b.nr hind: swvd bdly lft s: bhd fnl 2f: t.o) 15 5
2003 5 Itab (USA) **(75)***(32) (EALDunlop)* 3-9-9 WCarson(2) (b.nr hind: lw: prom over 4f: t.o) 2½ 6

Evens ALARMING, **4/1** Linger, Aldaneh, **5/1** Itab (USA) (4/1-6/1), **11/1** Sylvandra (op 7/1), **50/1** Indian Lament, CSF £11.51 TOTE £2.20: £1.40 £3.80 (£14.10) OWNER Mr K. Abdullah (NEWMARKET) BRED Juddmonte Farms 6 Rn 1m 30.73 (5.03) SF: 45/36/24/26/-/-
WEIGHT FOR AGE 3yo-7lb

2710

TRINITY CONDITIONS STKS (2-Y.O) (Class C) £5,017.00 (£1,892.00: £896.00: £380.00: £165.00) **6f** Stalls: High GOING minus 0.05 sec per fur (G) 7-20 (7-21)

2441 6 **Warning Time** *(87+) (BJMeehan)* 2-9-0 BDoyle(2) (lw: hld up & bhd: gd hdwy to ld over 1f out: r.o wl) — 1
2198* Last Token *(72) (JSMoore)* 2-8-5 (5) NVarley(7) (chsd ldr: ev ch over 1f out: one pce fnl f) 4 2
2315* Lacryma Cristi (IRE) *(76)*(Fav)*(MrsJCecil)* 2-9-0 PaulEddery(3) (hld up: hdwy 2f out: ev ch over 1f out: one pce) s.h 3
2299* Vola Via (USA) *(71) (IABalding)* 2-9-0 LDettori(6) (lw: a.p: led over 1f out: sn hdd: wknd ins fnl f) 2 4
2315 12 Muhandam (IRE) *(51) (MRStoute)* 2-8-10 JWeaver(5) (lw: led over 4f: sn wknd) 6 5

2/7 Lacryma Cristi (IRE), **11/2** Vola Via (USA) (4/1-6/1), **6/1** WARNING TIME (7/2-7/1), **12/1** Last Token (10/1-16/1), **25/1** Muhandam (IRE), CSF £50.70 TOTE £6.80: £2.10 £2.10 (£26.40) OWNER Mr F. C. T. Wilson (UPPER LAMBOURN) BRED F. C. T. Wilson 5 Rn 1m 15.66 (3.36) SF: -/-/-/-/-

2711

SPIRE FM H'CAP (0-70) (3-Y.O) (Class E) £3,392.00 (£1,016.00: £488.00: £224.00) **1m** Stalls: High GOING minus 0.05 sec per fur (G) 7-50 (7-52)

2199 3 **Almond Rock (67)***(82) (JRFanshawe)* 3-9-2 (5) NVarley(8) (hld up: led 2f out: r.o wl) — 1
1788 6 Anistop **(45)***(50) (RAkehurst)* 3-7-10 (3) SSanders(9) (a.p: led 3f out to 2f out: one pce) 5 2
2342 13 Blushing Grenadier (IRE) **(54)***(58) (MJFetherston-Godley)* 3-8-8b LDettori(2) (hld up: hung bdly lft over 2f out: one pce) ¾ 3
2536 2 Elite Justice **(63)***(57)*(Fav)*(PFICole)* 3-9-3 TQuinn(5) (w ldrs: ev ch 2f out: wknd over 1f out) 5 4
2245 4 Jewel Trader **(48)***(38) (CJBenstead)* 3-8-2b JLowe(1) (lw: prom over 6f) 1¾ 5
2488 6 Anna-Jane **(64)***(53) (RHannon)* 3-8-11 (7) DaneO'Neill(4) (hld up & plld hrd: rdn & hung lft 2f out: sn wknd) nk 6
2318 10 Amany (IRE) **(47)***(19)*(Fav)*(GLewis)* 3-8-1 ow1 PaulEddery(6) (hld up: a bhd) 8 7
1939 10 Claudia Habibi (IRE) **(45)***(12) (CCElsey)* 3-7-8 (5) MHenry(10) (lw: led 5f) 3 8
2049 5 With Intent **(61)***(21) (CJames)* 3-9-1 WNewnes(7) (plld hrd: a bhd) 3½ 9
1755 7 Red Morning **(65)***(13) (DRCElsworth)* 3-9-0 (5) AProcter(3) (a bhd) 6 10

7/2 Elite Justice, Amany (IRE), **9/2** ALMOND ROCK, **13/2** Anna-Jane, **7/1** Red Morning, Blushing Grenadier (IRE) (op 53/1), **8/1** Jewel Trader (4/1-9/1), **14/1** Anistop (op 8/1), **20/1** With Intent, **33/1** Claudia Habibi (IRE), CSF £61.08 CT £407.81 TOTE £5.20: £2.40 £3.40 £1.30 (£47.20) Trio £150.70 OWNER C I T Racing Ltd (NEWMARKET) BRED Lord Halifax 10 Rn
1m 44.11 (4.81) SF: 53/21/29/28/9/24/-/-/-/-

2712

DOWNING CLAIMING STKS (3-Y.O) (Class F) £2,861.00 (£796.00: £383.00) **6f** Stalls: High GOING minus 0.05 sec per fur (G) 8-20 (8-21)

2404 2 **Rosa Bonheur (52)***(64) (MAJarvis)* 3-7-8 (5) NVarley(7) (lw: a.p: led over 1f out: hrd rdn ins fnl f: r.o wl) — 1

1718[10] Astrojoy (IRE) **(47)***(60) (LordHuntingdon)* 3-7-5 (5) MHenry(10) (hld up & bhd: plld out over 3f out: hdwy 2f out: ev ch ins fnl f: r.o)....nk 2
2404[3] Tonys Gift **(62)***(63)*(Fav)*(RHannon)* 3-8-0 (7) DaneO'Neill(1) (hld up: hdwy 2f out: rdn over 1f out: one pce)....3 3
2437[7] Fantasy Racing (IRE) **(73)***(65) (MRChannon)* 3-8-10 ow1 RHughes(2) (hld up: hdwy 2f out: rdn over 1f out: one pce)....hd 4
2513[3] Solianna **(60)***(52) (MRChannon)* 3-7-8 (5) PPMurphy(5) (w ldr: led 4f out tl over 1f out: one pce)....1 5
2361[5] Cedar Dancer **(44)***(49) (RJHodges)* 3-7-8 (7) AmandaSanders(8) (no hdwy fnl 2f)....2 6
2661[5] Code of Silence **(41)***(41) (GFHCharles-Jones)* 3-7-11 (7) ADaly(6) (lw: hrd rdn 3f out: sn bhd)..4 7
1731[6] Thehillsarealive (IRE) *(51) (DRCElsworth)* 3-9-5 (5) AProcter(4) (lw: prom: hrd rdn & wknd over 2f out)....4 8
2337[5] Don't Look Now **(54)***(8) (DrJDScargill)* 3-7-9b NAdams(3) (led 2f: wknd qckly over 2f out)....5 9
2576[11] Fiveaday **(53)***(1) (BHanbury)* 3-7-13 (5) AWhelan(9) (s.s: a bhd)....6 10

2/1 Tonys Gift, **5/2** Fantasy Racing (IRE) (op 6/4), **5/1** ROSA BONHEUR, **11/2** Solianna, **11/1** Don't Look Now (8/1-12/1), **20/1** Astrojoy (IRE), Thehillsarealive (IRE), Cedar Dancer, **33/1** Code of Silence, Fiveaday, CSF £85.07 TOTE £5.80: £1.70 £4.90 £1.50 (£32.30) Trio £73.40 OWNER Mrs Mary Taylor (NEWMARKET) BRED Mrs Mary Taylor 10 Rn

1m 15.71 (3.41) SF: 33/29/32/34/21/18/10/20/-/-

2713 PEMBROKE H'CAP (0-70) (4-Y.O+) (Class E) £3,236.00 (£968.00: £464.00: £212.00) **1m 6f** Stalls: High GOING minus 0.05 sec per fur (G) 8-50 (8-50)

2007[3] **Supreme Star (USA) (50)***(61) (PRHedger)* 4-8-9 (5) NVarley(8) (hld up: hrd rdn & hdwy over 2f out: led over 1f out: r.o wl)....— 1
2472[2] Un Parfum de Femme (IRE) **(63)***(72)*(Fav)*(JPearce)* 4-9-13 JWeaver(5) (lw: hld up: hdwy over 2f out: ev ch over 1f out: r.o ins fnl f)....1½ 2
2439* Persian Smoke **(43)***(47) (AHide)* 4-8-0 (7)ow2 DaneO'Neill(10) (led 4f: ev ch over 1f out: one pce)....2½ 3
2511* Bresil (USA) **(31)***(37) (KRBurke)* 6-7-4 (5) 5x MHenry(7) (plld hrd: chsd ldr: led 10f out: hdd over 1f out: one pce)....½ 4
2530[5] Romalito **(42)***(45) (MBlanshard)* 5-8-6 WNewnes(4) (lw: hld up & bhd: hdwy over 1f out: nvr nrr)....2½ 5
2439[4] Bowcliffe **(56)***(58) (JTGifford)* 4-9-6 MFenton(1) (hld up: rdn & hdwy over 3f out: wknd 1f out)....1¼ 6
2721a* Bee Beat **(42)***(43) (AJChamberlain)* 7-8-6 JWilliams(2) (b: prom tl wknd over 2f out)....½ 7
2232[2] Amiarge **(31)***(21) (MBrittain)* 5-7-9 JLowe(3) (a bhd)....10 8
Gushy **(29)***(15) (RJBaker)* 9-7-7 NAdams(9) (prom tl wknd over 3f out)....3 9

LONG HANDICAP Gushy 7-5

4/1 Un Parfum de Femme (IRE), **9/2** Romalito, **5/1** SUPREME STAR (USA), Persian Smoke, Bresil (USA) (3/1-11/2), Amiarge, **10/1** Bowcliffe, **16/1** Bee Beat, **33/1** Gushy, CSF £25.12 CT £98.15 TOTE £7.80: £2.10 £1.60 £2.20 (£12.40) Trio £26.60 OWNER Mr J. J. Whelan (CHICHESTER) BRED Peter M. Brant 9 Rn

3m 17.74 (19.54) SF: -/-/-/-/-/-/-/-/-

T/Plpt: £650.40 (17.41 Tckts). T/Qdpt: £35.50 (3.4 Tckts). KH

2504-YARMOUTH (L-H)
Thursday July 27th (Good to firm)

WEATHER: overcast WIND: fresh half against

2714 THURNE H'CAP (0-75) (3-Y.O+) (Class D) £3,766.10 (£1,122.80: £535.40: £241.70) **6f 3y** Stalls: Low GOING minus 0.34 sec per fur (GF) 2-15 (2-18)

2578[7] **Samsolom (67)***(75)*(Fav)*(PHowling)* 7-9-9 KDarley(2) (lw: hld up: hdwy over 2f out: rdn to ld ins fnl f)....— 1
2652[5] Shadow Jury **(75)***(78) (DWChapman)* 5-10-3b 7x ACulhane(5) (trckd ldr: led 2f out: hdd & no ex ins fnl f)....1¾ 2
2203[7] Awesome Venture **(52)***(47) (MCChapman)* 5-8-5 (3) PMcCabe(3) (lw: led tl rdn & hdd 2f out: wknd ins fnl f)....3 3
2585[6] Plum First **(61)***(48) (LRLloyd-James)* 5-9-3b MPerrett(1) (prom over 3f: sn rdn & btn)....3 4
2504[5] Our Shadee (USA) **(52)***(24) (KTIvory)* 5-8-1v(7)ow5 CScally(6) (effrt 2f out: nvr trbld ldrs)....4 5

11/8 SAMSOLOM, **5/2** Shadow Jury, **9/2** Our Shadee (USA), **5/1** Plum First, **7/1** Awesome Venture, CSF £5.42 TOTE £2.20: £1.40 £1.60 (£3.20) OWNER Mr C. Hammond (NEWMARKET) BRED C. R. Mason 5 Rn

1m 13.9 (3.30) SF: 49/52/21/22/-

2715

BASTWICK (S) STKS (2-Y.O) (Class G) £2,422.20 (£669.20: £318.60)
6f 3y Stalls: Low GOING minus 0.34 sec per fur (GF) 2-45 (2-47)

2204[9] **Down The Yard** *(56) (MCChapman)* 2-8-3 (3) PMcCabe(1) (hdwy over 2f out: led over 1f out: pushed out)........— 1
2508[3] Madam Zando *(55)*(Fav)*(JMPEustace)* 2-8-6 AMcGlone(2) (mde most tl over 1f out: one pce)........½ 2
2153[4] Our Tom's Boy *(46) (KTIvory)* 2-8-4b(7) CScally(3) (w ldr: rdn over 2f out: sn btn)........5 3
2526[12] Aussie *(40d) (MHTompkins)* 2-8-6 (5) HKYim(5) (prom 4f)........2½ 4
2251[6] Nonconformist (IRE) *(35) (MRChannon)* 2-8-11 MRimmer(4) (plld hrd: trckd ldrs over 3f)....1¾ 5
1652[6] Princess Renata (IRE) *(25) (RHarris)* 2-8-6 AMackay(7) (chsd ldrs over 3f)........2 6
2508[6] Buff *(14) (DMorley)* 2-8-6 KDarley(6) (nvr trbld ldrs)........4 7

4/5 Madam Zando (op 5/4), **3/1** Nonconformist (IRE), **100/30** Aussie, **13/2** Buff, **8/1** Our Tom's Boy, DOWN THE YARD, **14/1** Princess Renata (IRE), CSF £18.62 TOTE £10.10: £3.00 £1.20 (£12.20) OWNER Mr Geoff Whiting (MARKET RASEN) BRED Fonthill Stud 7 Rn 1m 16.8 (6.20) SF: -/-/-/-/-/-/-
No bid

2716

COTMAN CONDITIONS STKS (2-Y.O F) (Class C) £5,251.50 (£1,674.00: £799.50)
5f 43y Stalls: Low GOING minus 0.34 sec per fur (GF) 3-20 (3-21)

2442[4] **Kunucu (IRE)** *(83+)*(Fav)*(TDBarron)* 2-8-12 KDarley(3) (chsd ldr: led over 1f out: pushed out)— 1
2114* Defined Feature (IRE) *(75) (MRStoute)* 2-8-9 GHind(1) (outpcd tl styd on appr fnl f)........1¾ 2
2515[2] Dramatic Entry (IRE) *(71) (JARToller)* 2-8-9b AMcGlone(2) (led over 3f: no ex)........1¼ 3

8/11 KUNUCU (IRE), **7/4** Defined Feature (IRE), **4/1** Dramatic Entry (IRE), CSF £2.39 TOTE £1.70 (£1.40) OWNER Mr P. D. Savill (THIRSK) BRED Mrs Rita Fitzgerald 3 Rn
63.5 secs (3.20) SF: 33/25/21

2717

TATTERSALLS MAIDEN AUCTION STKS (2-Y.O F) (Class E) £3,315.45 (£987.60: £470.30: £211.65)
7f 3y Stalls: Low GOING minus 0.34 sec per fur (GF) 3-55 (3-56)

2277[2] **Hurricane Dancer (IRE)** *(63) (SPCWoods)* 2-7-13 AMcGlone(3) (chsd ldr tl led over 2f out: drvn out)........— 1
2447[2] Zdenka *(63) (MBlanshard)* 2-7-13 StephenDavies(5) (led: hdd & rdn over 2f out: rallied & ev ch ins fnl f: r.o: fin 3rd, hd: plcd 2nd)........ 2
1823[5] Posen Gold (IRE) *(61) (PAKelleway)* 2-8-3 ow4 KDarley(2) (hld up: ev ch over 1f out: no ex ins fnl f: fin 4th, ½l: plcd 3rd)........ 3
2526[2] White Sea (IRE) *(69?)*(Fav)*(PFICole)* 2-8-5 CRutter(1) (hld up: n.m.r over 2f out: squeezed thro ins fnl f: jst failed: fin 2nd, hd: disq plcd 4th)........ 4
2346[2] Again Together *(NACallaghan)* 2-8-2 AMackay(4) (reard s: t.n.p)........ R

4/7 White Sea (IRE), **4/1** Zdenka, **5/1** Posen Gold (IRE) (op 3/1), **6/1** Again Together, **9/1** HURRICANE DANCER (IRE) (op 5/1), CSF £41.79 TOTE £9.70: £2.90 £2.60 (£17.90) OWNER Mr Andrew Rutter (NEWMARKET) BRED H and Y Bloodstock Co 5 Rn 1m 30.5 (7.70) SF: -/-/-/-/-

2718

WROXHAM H'CAP (0-70) (3-Y.O+) (Class E) £3,388.00 (£1,012.00: £484.00: £220.00) **7f 3y** Stalls: Low GOING minus 0.34 sec per fur (GF) 4-30 (4-31)

1966[4] **Midnight Jazz (IRE) (69)***(83) (WAO'Gorman)* 5-9-13 EmmaO'Gorman(1) (hld up: hdwy over 3f out: led 2f out: pushed clr fnl f)........— 1
2504* Khatim (USA) **(67)***(75)*(Fav)*(HThomsonJones)* 3-9-4 6x KDarley(3) (chsd ldrs: outpcd 2f out: styd on fnl f)........2½ 2
2108[10] Spanish Stripper (USA) **(66)***(69) (MCChapman)* 4-9-7 (3) PMcCabe(5) (led 1f: led over 2f out: sn hdd: one pce fnl f)........2½ 3
2318[13] The Mestral **(42)***(41) (MJRyan)* 3-7-2v(5) MBaird(6) (chsd ldrs 4f)........1¾ 4
1906[6] Delight of Dawn **(67)***(63) (KTIvory)* 3-8-11 (7) CScally(4) (drppd rr & rdn over 3f out: n.d after)1¼ 5
2108[7] As Such (IRE) **(43)** *(NACallaghan)* 4-8-1b AMackay(7) (led 6f out tl over 2f out: sn wknd & eased)........25 6

LONG HANDICAP The Mestral 7-6

Evens Khatim (USA), **4/1** MIDNIGHT JAZZ (IRE) (5/2-9/2), Spanish Stripper (USA), **5/1** Delight of Dawn, **8/1** The Mestral (5/1-10/1), **12/1** As Such (IRE) (8/1-14/1), CSF £9.24 TOTE £6.50: £2.00 £1.30 (£4.10) OWNER Mr S. Fustok (NEWMARKET) BRED S. Fustok in Ireland 6 Rn
1m 27.0 (4.20) SF: 49/34/35/-/22/-
WEIGHT FOR AGE 3yo-7lb
STEWARDS' ENQUIRY McCabe susp. 5 & 7-10/8/95 (excessive use of whip).

2719 DAMGATE H'CAP (0-70) (3-Y.O+ F & M) (Class E) £3,330.80 (£994.40: £475.20: £215.60)
1m 2f 21y Stalls: Low GOING minus 0.34 sec per fur (GF) 5-00 (5-01)

1539⁷ **Aqua Rigia (IRE)** **(44)***(58+)*(Fav)*(HCandy)* 3-8-0 AMcGlone(4) (swtg: prom: 4th st: led wl over 2f out: r.o wl) ....— **1**
2209⁴ Hard Love **(62)***(68) (SPCWoods)* 3-8-11 (7) CWebb(2) (lw: led after 2f: clr 5f out: hdd wl over 2f out: sn rdn & no ex)....5 **2**
2279* Bellateena **(54)***(57)*(Fav)*(HJCollingridge)* 3-8-10 MRimmer(3) (prom: 3rd st: one pce fnl 3f)....2 **3**
2152⁵ Cephista **(60)***(62) (PTWalwyn)* 3-9-2 GHind(10) (rdn & hdwy 3f out: no ex fnl 2f)....¾ **4**
*263*¹² Maronetta **(37)***(39) (MJRyan)* 3-7-2 (5) MBaird(8) (bhd tl rdn & r.o fnl 3f)....hd **5**
*2140*¹⁰ Loving Legacy **(58)***(59) (WJHaggas)* 4-9-10 RMcGhin(9) (chsd ldrs: 6th st: no imp fnl 3f)....½ **6**
2376⁴ Bobanlyn (IRE) **(66)***(65) (DMorris)* 3-9-8 CNutter(6) (bhd tl sme hdwy 3f out)....1 **7**
2307⁷ Mary Macblain **(37)***(27) (JLHarris)* 6-8-3 AMackay(7) (sn bhd)....6 **8**
2280¹⁴ Britannia Mills **(28)***(17) (MCChapman)* 4-7-8 SLanigan(1) (led 2f: 2nd st: wknd 2f out)....½ **9**
1535¹⁵ Yengema **(36)** *(RCSpicer)* 4-7-9b(7)ow9 TThomas(5) (dwlt: sn rcvrd: 6th & stumbled st: sn rdn & bhd)....25 **10**

LONG HANDICAP Maronetta 7-5 Yengema 7-5

3/1 AQUA RIGIA (IRE) (op 5/1), Bellateena, **4/1** Cephista, **9/2** Hard Love, **5/1** Bobanlyn (IRE) (op 3/1), **10/1** Mary Macblain (op 6/1), Loving Legacy (op 6/1), **12/1** Britannia Mills (op 8/1), **25/1** Maronetta, **33/1** Yengema, CSF £19.18 CT £44.44 TOTE £3.80: £1.20 £1.80 £2.10 (£13.60) Trio £16.70 OWNER Mrs C. M. Poland (WANTAGE) BRED Newgate Stud Co 10 Rn

2m 7.9 (3.50) SF: 30/40/29/34/11/41/37/9/-/-
WEIGHT FOR AGE 3yo-10lb
T/Plpt: £37.30 (211.59 Tckts). T/Qdpt: £18.40 (2.55 Tckts). Dk

0099a-LES LANDES (Jersey) (L-H)
Saturday July 15th (Good)

2720a CORAL HALKETT STREET SPRINT H'CAP (3-Y.O+) £750.00
5f 100y 3-05 (3-06)

2384a³ **Misinterrex** *(MissAVibert,Jersey)* 4-8-9 RMcGhin ....— **1**
2384a² Screech *(ZJones,Guernsey)* 5-9-3 BPowell 1 **2**
2384a* Superensis *(JLeBrocq,Jersey)* 5-10-12 PHolley 3 **3**
2384a⁵ Reality Park *(PDJones)* 4-10-4 SNicoll 4 **4**

Tote £14.60: (£4.60) OWNER La Closerie Syndicate 4 Rn 1m 8.0 SF: -/-/-/-

2721a CORAL CHANNEL ISLANDS H'CAP (3-Y.O+) £750.00
1m 7f 4-15 (4-15)

2109R **Bee Beat** *(AJChamberlain)* 7-9-4 BPowell ....— **1**
799a³ Fortensky (USA) *(CMcCready,Jersey)* 5-10-12 RMcGhin 6 **2**
Our Topsie *(JSOArthur,Jersey)* 8-8-5 SNicoll 3 **3**
2038a⁶ Muscat (IRE) *(PDJones)* 8-8-12 MrPClose (btn approx 19l) **5**

Tote £4.00: (£3.70) OWNER Mr D. P. Travers-Clark (SWINDON) BRED E. A. Badger 5 Rn 3m 24.0

2558a-MAISONS-LAFFITTE (France)
Monday July 17th (Holding)

2722a PRIX NIMBUS (Listed) (3-Y.O C & G) £16,766.00 (£5,748.00: £3,593.00) **1m 4f** 3-15 (3-15)

1339* **Song of Tara (IRE)** *(84++) (PWChapple-Hyam)* 3-9-2 JReid ....— **1**
Another Felix (USA) *(82) (JEHammond,France)* 3-9-2 CAsmussen 1½ **2**
El Angelo (USA) *(82) (PBary,France)* 3-9-2 DBoeuf ....nk **3**

P-M 2.00F: 1.50F 2.20F (SF 15.90F) OWNER Mr A. J. F. O'Reilly (MARLBOROUGH) BRED Kilcarn Stud 7 Rn
2m 38.8 (10.50) SF: -/-/-

2561a-EVRY (France) (R-H)
Tuesday July 18th (Good)

2723a PRIX MINERVE (Gp 3) (3-Y.O F) £26,347.00 (£9,581.00: £4,790.00) **1m 4f** 3-30 (0-33)

Danefair *(99) (MZilber,France)* 3-8-9 GGuignard ...— 1
Angel In My Heart (FR) *(99) (JEHammond,France)* 3-8-9 CAsmussen ...s.nk 2
Daraydala (IRE) *(98) (AdeRoyerDupre,France)* 3-8-9 GMosse ...½ 3

P-M 1.60F: 1.30F 2.30F (SF 11.80F) OWNER Mr K. Abdullah BRED Juddmonte Farms 6 Rn
2m 40.73 (11.23) SF: -/-/-

2566a-SAN SIRO (Milan, Italy) (R-H)
Wednesday July 19th (Good)

2724a PREMIO QUASSO (3-Y.O) £5,910.00 **1m** 2-00 (2-02)

2030[2] **Albinor (IRE)** *(78+) (JLDunlop)* 3-8-8 ow1 FJovine ...— 1
Digarah (IRE) *(83) (Italy)* 3-9-3 MLatorre ...2½ 2
Peco's Bill (IRE) *(79) (Italy)* 3-9-0 EBotti ...½ 3

Tote 12L: 11L 14L (36L) OWNER Diamond Thoroughbreds Inc (ARUNDEL) BRED Allevamento Annarosa di V. Schirone 5 Rn 1m 42.3 SF: -/-/-

2725a PREMIO SALASCO MAIDEN (2-Y.O) £4,925.00 **6f** 2-50 (2-55)

Camp Follower *(61) (JLDunlop)* 2-8-11 FJovine ...— 1
1889a[3] Selenia (IRE) *(61) (Italy)* 2-8-11 GForte ...hd 2
Gun Ballad (IRE) *(47) (Italy)* 2-8-7 ADiNardo ...3½ 3

Tote 17L: 11L 11L 17L (23L) OWNER J.L.Dunlop (ARUNDEL) BRED T.Whitaker 10 Rn 1m 11.9

2722a-MAISONS-LAFFITTE (France)
Sunday July 23rd (Good)

2726a PRIX ROBERT PAPIN (Gp 2) (2-Y.O C & F) £41,916.00 (£16,766.00: £8,383.00: £4,192.00) **5f 110y** 3-15 (3-15)

2347[6] **Lucky Lionel (USA)** *(99) (RHannon)* 2-9-2 JReid (hld up: hdwy to ld over 1f out: hdd cl hme: rallied to ld post)...— 1
2210a[2] Shining Molly (FR) *(96) (PBary,France)* 2-8-13 OPeslier (hld up: prog 2f out: chal to ld cl hme: hdd post) ...nse 2
Barricade (USA) *(98) (AFabre,France)* 2-9-2 SGuillot (racd in 3rd: rdn 2f out: r.o) ...nk 3
Blushing Gleam *(88) (MmeCHead,France)* 2-8-13 ODoleuze (mid-div: effrt 2f out: ne pce)..2½ 4
2210a* Media Nox *(83) (AFabre,France)* 2-8-13 TJarnet (rr early: hrd rdn 2f out: nvr plcd to chal)...1½ 5
Miss Ebene (FR) *(81) (DSmaga,France)* 2-8-13 FHead (led 2f: rdn 2f out: fdd) ...¾ 6
2347[7] High Priority (IRE) *(70) (MRChannon)* 2-9-2 RHughes (rcd wide: led after 2f tl hdd over 1f out: wknd)...5 7
Sacramento (IRE) *(69) (BTevels,France)* 2-9-2 RVindevogel (mid-div: chal 2f out: wknd 1½f out) ...nk 8

P-M 6.50F: 2.20F 1.60F 1.70F (17.30F) OWNER Mr A. Balzarini (MARLBOROUGH) BRED Richard & Mrs Kaster 8 Rn 66.1 secs (2.60) SF: -/-/-/-/-/-/-/-

2727a PRIX CERES (Listed) (3-Y.O F) £16,766.00 (£5,748.00: £3,593.00) **7f** 3-45 (3-44)

Miss Satamixa (IRE) *(103) (AFabre,France)* 3-8-11 TJarnet ...— 1
Yavari (USA) *(96) (JEHammond,France)* 3-8-11 CAsmussen ...3 2
1572a[10] Doree (USA) *(93) (MmeCHead,France)* 3-8-11 FHead ...1½ 3
2443[6] With the Fairies *(89) (RHannon)* 3-8-11 JReid (btn over 6½l) ... 7

P-M 3.10F: 2.00F 3.00F (SF 18.80F) OWNER Mr J-L. Lagardere (FRANCE) BRED J-L. Lagardere 7 Rn 1m 28.0 SF: -/-/-/-

1009a-DUSSELDORF (Germany) (R-H)
Sunday July 23rd (Good)

2728a
PREIS DER DUSSELDORFER IMMOBILIENWIRTSCHAFT (Listed) (3-Y.O+) £12,346.00 (£4,938.00: £2,469.00) **7f** 2-30 (2-35)

Henessy (GER) *(103) (ALowe,Germany)* 3-8-5 PSchiergen (fin 2nd btn 1½l: awrdd r) ....— 1
2212a3 Matula (USA) *(106) (BSchutz,Germany)* 3-8-9 ASuborics (fin 3rd btn nk: plcd 2nd).................. 2
24164 Branston Abby (IRE) *(103+) (MJohnston)* 6-8-9 MRoberts (fin 1st: disq: plcd last: carried wrong weight)........ D

Tote 24DM: 18DM 21DM (SF 215DM) OWNER Stall Nicoletta BRED W.Jackson & Gestut Quenhorn 5 Rn
1m 25.4 SF: -/-/-

2729a
PREIS DER PRIVATBANKIERS MERCK FINCK & CO (Gp 1) (3-Y.O+) £98,765.00 (£39,095.00: £18,519.00: £8,230.00) **1m 4f** 3-35 (3-41)

1890a* **Lando (GER)** *(123+) (HJentzsch,Germany)* 5-9-7 PSchiergen (trckd ldrs: 3rd st: led & qcknd 1½f out: cmftbly)........— 1
2046a3 Laroche (GER) *(120) (HJentzsch,Germany)* 4-9-7 ATylicki (led tl hdd by wnr: r.o)...............2½ 2
2046a4 Kornado *(116) (ALowe,Germany)* 5-9-7 GBocskai (a.p: 2nd st: chal over 1f out: one pce)......3 3
2215a2 Manzoni (GER) *(112) (AWohler,Germany)* 3-8-6 ABoschert (hld up: hdwy & 4th st: no ex)....½ 4
2046a5 Protektor (GER) *(112) (ALowe,Germany)* 6-9-7 MLarsen (rr tl hdwy ent st: no imp) 2 5
1231a3 Flying Dream *(108) (BSchutz,Germany)* 5-9-3 ASuborics (6th st: no ex)...............................nk 6
2046a9 Aratikos (GER) *(93) (HBlume,Germany)* 4-9-7 OSchick (prom tl wknd 4f out).......................14 7
2046a6 Bad Bertrich (IRE) *(85) (ALowe,Germany)* 4-9-7 AHelfenbein (alwys rr) 6 8

Tote 16DM: 11DM 15DM 15DM (SF 64DM) OWNER Gestut Haus Ittlingen BRED Gestut Hof Ittlingen 8 Rn
2m 26.6 SF: -/-/-/-/-/-/-/-

ARLINGTON PARK (Chicago, USA) (L-H)
Sunday July 23rd (Yielding)

2730a
AMERICAN DERBY (Gp 2) (3-Y.O) £115,385.00 (£38,462.00: £21,154.00: £11,538.00) **1m 1f 110y** 10-47 (10-47)

2044a6 **Gold and Steel (FR)** *(114) (J-CRouget,France)* 3-8-2 AGryder ....— 1
2044a4 Torrential (USA) *(118) (JHMGosden)* 3-8-8 LDettori 1¼ 2
Unanimous Vote (IRE) *(118) (TAmoss,USA)* 3-8-8 CBorel ....hd 3
Mecke (USA) *(114) (ETortora,USA)* 3-8-5 HCastillojnr ....½ 4
Dixie Dynasty (USA) *(110) (USA)* 3-8-5 THerbert 2½ 5
Synergetic (FR) *(103) (USA)* 3-8-2 JSantos 2½ 6
Arctic Explosion (USA) *(93) (USA)* 3-8-2 RRomero 5½ 7

P-M £11.20: £4.60 £3.60 Show £3.20 £2.80 £3.80 (SF £27.60 DF £134.00) OWNER Mr Gary Tanaka BRED G.Rollain 7 Rn
1m 44.0 SF: -/-/-/-/-/-/-

2302-EDINBURGH (R-H)
Friday July 28th (Firm)
WEATHER: humid & overcast WIND: nil

2731
OLD COURSE LIMITED STKS (0-55) (3-Y.O+) (Class F) £2,274.00 (£639.00: £312.00) **1m 3f 32y** Stalls: Low GOING minus 0.58 sec per fur (F) 6-50 (6-54)

22248 **Our Main Man** **(55)***(64) (RMWhitaker)* 5-9-6 ACulhane(7) (mde all: rdn 2f out: kpt on gamely fnl f)..........— 1
25033 Samaka Hara (IRE) **(55)***(64) (WSCunningham)* 3-8-11 TIves(1) (hld up & bhd: stdy hdwy 3f out: rdn to chal 2f out: no ex ins fnl f)..........1½ 2
26203 Khan **(55)***(59) (CWThornton)* 3-8-9 DeanMcKeown(4) (prom: rdn & ev ch over 2f out: styd on same pce)..........1¾ 3
2610* Imperial Bid (FR) **(52)***(63) (DenysSmith)* 7-9-10 2x TWilliams(5) (hld up: hdwy ent st: sn outpcd: rallied u.p & kpt on fnl 2f)..........nk 4
26302 Fen Terrier **(55)***(57)*(Fav)*(WJHaggas)* 3-8-5 (3) JStack(6) (rn wd ent st: hdwy wl over 2f out: sn rdn: one pce)..........½ 5

17574 Father Dan (IRE) **(50)***(59) (MissGayKelleway)* 6-9-5 (3) SDrowne(3) (hld up: rdn 3f out: no imp fnl 2f)....¾ **6**
2484 12 Melody Dancer **(48)***(46) (MissJFCraze)* 4-9-6 SWebster(8) (chsd ldrs: rdn over 3f out: sn bhd)....8 **7**
24277 Wild Rose of York **(54)** *(PMonteith)* 4-9-1 JFortune(2) (Withdrawn not under Starter's orders: lame).... **W**

7/4 Fen Terrier, **3/1** Father Dan (IRE), **9/2** Imperial Bid (FR), **6/1** Samaka Hara (IRE), **16/1** Khan, OUR MAIN MAN, **33/1** Wild Rose of York, **40/1** Melody Dancer, CSF £90.33 TOTE £15.30: £4.10 £2.00 (£89.20) OWNER Mr Christopher Cooke (LEEDS) BRED Pinfold Stud and Farms Ltd 7 Rn
2m 27.2 (7.50) SF: 7/-/-/6/-/2/-/-
WEIGHT FOR AGE 3yo-11lb

2732 NEW COURSE (S) STKS (2-Y.O) (Class G) £2,232.00 (£627.00: £306.00)
7f 15y Stalls: Low GOING minus 0.58 sec per fur (F) 7-20 (7-21)

25417 **Traceability** *(63)*(Fav)*(JBerry)* 2-8-9 (7) PRoberts(3) (cl up: rdn 2f out: led ent fnl f: r.o u.p) ...— **1**
25165 Ned's Contessa (IRE) *(52) (MDods)* 2-8-6 JFortune(4) (trckd ldrs: hdwy to chal appr fnl f: sn rdn: r.o one pce u.p)....½ **2**
24473 Classic Daisy *(49)*(Fav)*(MissGayKelleway)* 2-8-3b(3) SDrowne(5) (set stdy pce: qcknd appr st: hdd ent fnl f: nt qckn)....1¼ **3**
18995 Silent Soprano *(40) (DenysSmith)* 2-8-6 TWilliams(1) (hld up: hdwy over 2f out: sn rdn: btn ent fnl f)....4 **4**
21853 Fergal (USA) *(37) (GMMoore)* 2-8-8 (3) JStack(2) (hld up & bhd: hdwy & rdn 2f out: sn wknd)....3½ **5**

7/4 TRACEABILITY (op 4/5), Classic Daisy, **4/1** Fergal (USA), **8/1** Ned's Contessa (IRE), **10/1** Silent Soprano, CSF £13.23 TOTE £2.00: £1.70 £2.40 (£7.10) OWNER Mr J. Clayton (COCKERHAM) BRED J. S. A. and Mrs Shorthouse 5 Rn 1m 33.0 (7.00) SF: -/-/-/-/-
No bid

2733 LATE NIGHT H'CAP (0-60) (3-Y.O+) (Class F) £2,431.50 (£684.00: £334.50)
1m 16y Stalls: Low GOING minus 0.58 sec per fur (F) 7-50 (7-51)

23564 **Tinklers Folly (43)***(58) (DenysSmith)* 3-8-4 TWilliams(9) (trckd ldrs: led over 2f out: sn drvn clr: styd on wl)....— **1**
24844 Princess Maxine (IRE) **(60)***(68) (JJO'Neill)* 6-9-10 (5)ow2 ARoche(11) (in tch: hdwy 3f out: sn rdn: styd on same pce ins fnl f)....2½ **2**
25822 Summer Villa **(44)***(53) (PCHaslam)* 3-8-2 (3) JStack(10) (led: rdn over 4f out: hdd over 2f out: one pce)....¾ **3**
24848 Northern Chief **(35)***(42) (MissJFCraze)* 5-8-4 SWebster(7) (a.p: rdn over 2f out: styd on one pce)....¾ **4**
24794 Matisse **(43)***(45)*(Fav)*(JDBethell)* 4-8-12 TIves(5) (in tch: hdwy over 3f out: sn rdn & no imp)....2½ **5**
2586* Resolute Bay **(43)***(44) (RMWhitaker)* 9-8-12v ACulhane(6) (mid div: rdn along ½-wy: nvr trbld ldrs)....¾ **6**
2528 12 Lawnswood Junior **(55)***(46) (JLSpearing)* 8-9-10 DeanMcKeown(1) (bhd: rdn 3f out: nvr trbld ldrs)....5 **7**
13107 Nornax Lad (USA) **(55)***(45) (MartynMeade)* 7-9-10b VSlattery(2) (a rr: nvr nr to chal) ....nk **8**
2540* Caltha **(40)***(24)*(Fav)*(PCalver)* 3-7-12b(3) DWright(8) (cl up: rdn & ev ch 3f out: sn lost pl)....3 **9**
24796 Langtonian **(39)***(23) (JLEyre)* 6-8-8v RLappin(4) (s.s: hdwy ½-wy: rdn & in tch 2f out: sn btn).nk **10**
24015 Halls Burn **(30)** *(JSGoldie)* 7-7-13v JFanning(3) (s.i.s: a bhd: t.o fnl 3f)....25 **11**

4/1 Caltha, Matisse, **5/1** Summer Villa, **11/2** TINKLERS FOLLY, **9/1** Princess Maxine (IRE) (6/1-10/1), Resolute Bay (op 6/1), **12/1** Lawnswood Junior, **16/1** Langtonian, **25/1** Northern Chief, **33/1** Nornax Lad (USA), **66/1** Halls Burn, CSF £47.33 CT £235.71 TOTE £6.00: £1.60 £2.00 £1.90 (£16.60) Trio £29.60 OWNER Mr R. O. Manners (BISHOP AUCKLAND) BRED Qualitair Stud Ltd 11 Rn 1m 41.2 (2.60) SF: 16/34/11/8/11/10/12/11/-/-/-
WEIGHT FOR AGE 3yo-8lb

2734 EVENING H'CAP (0-60) (3-Y.O+) (Class F) £2,305.50 (£648.00: £316.50)
1m 7f 16y Stalls: Low GOING minus 0.58 sec per fur (F) 8-20 (8-20)

25012 **Arian Spirit (IRE) (30)***(44) (JLEyre)* 4-8-13 RLappin(6) (trckd ldrs: hdwy on outside over 3f out: chal u.p over 2f out: styd on to ld nr fin) ....— **1**
25453 Great Oration (IRE) **(36)***(50)*(Fav)*(FWatson)* 6-9-5 NConnorton(3) (hld up: hdwy ent st: led 2½f out: hdd wl ins fnl f: kpt on) ....nk **2**

2359[6] Duggan **(31)***(42) (PDEvans)* 8-9-0 JFortune(2) (hld up & bhd: hdwy over 2f out: sn rdn & styd on: nvr able to chal) 2½ 3
1957[3] Sharp Sensation **(41)***(46) (WLBarker)* 5-9-10 AlexGreaves(5) (mid div: hdwy appr st: rdn over 2f out: btn appr fnl f) 6 4
2226[6] Lord Advocate **(36)***(31) (DANolan)* 7-9-0b(5) VHalliday(1) (chsd ldrs: rdn & lost pl ent st: n.d after) 9 5
2127[3] Milngavie (IRE) **(34)***(25) (MJohnston)* 5-9-3 TWilliams(7) (s.i.s: sn cl up: rdn ½-wy: wknd over 3f out) 3½ 6
2501[3] Roxy River **(35)***(25) (JLSpearing)* 6-9-4 DeanMcKeown(4) (led: rdn & hdd 2½f out: wknd over 3f out) 1 7
2157[4] Daleside **(26)***(5) (AHarrison)* 7-8-6 (3) JStack(8) (prom: rdn ent st: sn wknd) 11 8

5/2 Great Oration (IRE), **4/1** Milngavie (IRE), **5/1** ARIAN SPIRIT (IRE), **6/1** Lord Advocate, **9/1** Duggan (op 6/1), **10/1** Sharp Sensation (op 6/1), **14/1** Daleside, **20/1** Roxy River, CSF £16.22 CT £89.56 TOTE £4.30: £1.40 £1.90 £1.80 (£7.00) OWNER Mr Martin West (HAMBLETON) BRED M. Ervine in Ireland 8 Rn
3m 17.2 (6.70) SF: 18/24/16/20/5/-/-/-

2735 MORNING AFTER CLAIMING STKS (2-Y.O) (Class F) £2,253.00 (£633.00: £309.00) 5f Stalls: Low GOING minus 0.58 sec per fur (F) 8-50 (8-54)

1833[5] **Miss Bigwig** *(63)*(Fav)*(JBerry)* 2-8-5 (7) PFessey(6) (mde all: qcknd clr appr fnl f: unchal) — 1
2308[6] Hickleton Miss *(38) (MrsMReveley)* 2-8-9 JFortune(2) (prom: chsd wnr fnl 2f: no imp) 7 2
2382[9] Grimstone Girl *(13) (MWEasterby)* 2-8-0 JFanning(5) (outpcd & rdn ½-wy: styd on u.p fnl f: nvr nr to chal) 5 3
2483[9] Sporting Fantasy *(28) (JBalding)* 2-8-10 (7) JEdmunds(1) (cl up tl rdn & wknd over 2f out) ½ 4
Time For A Glass *(WTKemp)* 2-7-12 TWilliams(4) (neat: bkwd: s.i.s: a wl bhd & outpcd) 3 5
2185[12] Miss Hotshot *(RBastiman)* 2-8-4 ACulhane(3) (gd spd to ½-wy: sn wknd) 8 6

4/5 MISS BIGWIG (Evens-11/10), **7/4** Hickleton Miss (5/4-9/4), **8/1** Sporting Fantasy (5/1-9/1), **20/1** Grimstone Girl, **33/1** Time For A Glass, **100/1** Miss Hotshot, CSF £2.49 TOTE £1.70: £1.50 £1.30 (£2.20) OWNER Bigwigs Entertainments (COCKERHAM) BRED Ravenstonedale Fold and Bloodstock 6 Rn
59.6 secs (1.90) SF: 15/-/-/-/-/-

2736 FINAL DRAM H'CAP (0-70) (3-Y.O+) (Class E) £2,718.50 (£766.00: £375.50) 5f Stalls: Low GOING minus 0.58 sec per fur (F) 9-20 (9-23)

2338* **Super Rocky** **(66)***(73)*(Fav)*(RBastiman)* 6-9-9 (5) HBastiman(8) (chsd ldrs: led appr fnl f: r.o wl) — 1
2649[2] Kenesha (IRE) **(48)***(53) (DANolan)* 5-8-5b(5) VHalliday(5) (a w ldrs: rdn 2f out: sn led: hdd appr fnl f: no ex) ½ 2
2073[7] Walk the Beat **(62)***(63) (MartynMeade)* 5-9-10 VSlattery(11) (chsd ldrs: rdn 2f out: kpt on ins fnl f) 1½ 3
2163[8] The Fed **(52)***(51) (RMWhitaker)* 5-9-0v ACulhane(1) (spd stands' side 3f: rdn wl over 1f out: styd on) ½ 4
2475[10] Leading Princess (IRE) **(40)***(38) (MissLAPerratt)* 4-8-2b JFanning(7) (led: rdn 2f out: sn hdd: one pce) nk 5
2463[6] Uppance **(32)***(28) (DANolan)* 7-7-8bow1 WHawksley(3) (in tch: hdwy 2f out: kpt on u.p appr fnl f) nk 6
2475[9] Serious Hurry **(43)***(35) (RMMcKellar)* 7-8-5 ClaireBalding(6) (chsd ldrs: rdn ½-wy: sn outpcd) 1¾ 7
2475[3] Mister Westsound **(46)***(37) (MissLAPerratt)* 3-8-3b NConnorton(4) (s.i.s: rdn & prom ½-wy: sn btn) hd 8
2463[4] Glow of Hope **(31)***(17) (RMMcKellar)* 5-7-0 (7) PFessey(2) (spd stands' side over 3f: sn btn) 1½ 9
2521[5] Kabcast **(50)***(32) (DWChapman)* 10-8-12b DaleGibson(10) (cl up: rdn ½-wy: grad lost pl) 1½ 10
2463[3] Ramborette **(49)***(25) (DenysSmith)* 3-8-6 TWilliams(9) (w ldrs: rdn ½-wy: sn wknd) 1¾ 11
LONG HANDICAP Glow of Hope 7-6 Uppance 7-1

5/2 SUPER ROCKY, **3/1** Ramborette, **9/2** Mister Westsound, **9/1** Kabcast, The Fed (op 6/1), **10/1** Glow of Hope, **14/1** Kenesha (IRE) (10/1-16/1), **16/1** Walk the Beat, **25/1** Serious Hurry, Leading Princess (IRE), **66/1** Uppance, CSF £35.11 CT £438.06 TOTE £4.00: £1.90 £2.90 £3.10 (£24.50) Trio £93.20 OWNER Mr I. B. Barker (WETHERBY) BRED J. Berry 11 Rn
58.8 secs (1.10) SF: 43/23/33/21/8/-/5/2/-/2/-
WEIGHT FOR AGE 3yo-5lb

T/Plpt: £230.00 (36.69 Tckts). T/Qdpt: £9.80 (4.2 Tckts). GB

2701-**GOODWOOD (R-H)**

Friday July 28th (St Good, Rnd Firm, both Good to firm patches)

WEATHER: humid WIND: almost nil

2737

SEEBOARD H'CAP (0-100) (3-Y.O) (Class C) £19,820.00 (£5,960.00: £2,880.00: £1,340.00) **7f** Stalls: High GOING minus 0.20 sec per fur (GF) 2-30 (2-32)

2576* **Easy Dollar (84)***(95) (BGubby)* 3-8-12b 6x RHughes(14) (2nd st: led 3f out: r.o wl) ....— 1
1487[7] Three Stops (USA) **(78)***(88) (MRStoute)* 3-8-6 KDarley(7) (rdn & hdwy over 2f out: ev ch ins fnl f: r.o) ....½ 2
2318* Ben Gunn **(72)***(78) (PTWalwyn)* 3-7-9 (5) MHenry(10) (lw: 7th st: rdn over 3f out: one pce)....1½ 3
2367[2] Twilight Patrol **(90)***(95) (RHannon)* 3-9-4 JReid(6) (hdwy over 2f out: n.m.r over 1f out: r.o ins fnl f) ....¾ 4
2325* Bouche Bee (USA) **(93)***(98) (LMCumani)* 3-9-7 LDettori(4) (lw: rdn over 2f out: hdwy over 1f out: r.o) ....hd 5
2240[4] Hawa Al Nasamaat (USA) **(83)***(84) (EALDunlop)* 3-8-11 RHills(15) (lw: 4th st: ev ch over 1f out: wknd ins fnl f) 1¾ 6
2500[4] Russian Heroine **(75)***(74) (MJohnston)* 3-8-3 MRoberts(9) (5th st: rdn over 3f out: wknd over 1f out) ....¾ 7
2003[4] Self Reliance **(73)***(70) (MBell)* 3-8-1 MFenton(3) (nvr nrr) 1 8
2099[2] Emerging Market **(90)***(86) (JLDunlop)* 3-9-4 WCarson(13) (lw: bhd whn nt clr run over 2f out: hdwy over 1f out: r.o) ....s.h 9
2325[7] Dashing Water **(90)***(86) (IABalding)* 3-9-4 MHills(16) (lw: hdwy over 1f out: wknd fnl f) ....hd 10
2549* Yaa Wale **(72)***(68)*(Fav)*(JHMGosden)* 3-8-0 6x NCarlisle(8) (hdwy & nt clr run over 1f out: one pce) ....nk 11
2325[4] Signs **(92)***(86) (RHannon)* 3-9-6 PaulEddery(2) (a bhd) ....½ 12
2479* Kemo Sabo **(78)***(71) (MrsJRRamsden)* 3-8-6 6x TQuinn(12) (lw: 3rd st: hrd rdn over 2f out: wknd over 1f out) ....½ 13
2369[11] Montserrat **(79)***(71) (LGCottrell)* 3-8-7 GBardwell(11) (6th st: wknd over 2f out) ....½ 14
2240[5] Roderick Hudson **(86)***(76) (JARToller)* 3-8-11 (3) SSanders(1) (8th st: wknd over 2f out)..........¾ 15
1754[7] Warning Shot **(80)***(57) (MartynMeade)* 3-8-8 BThomson(17) (swtg: led 4f: wknd over 1f out)...6 16

9/4 Yaa Wale, **13/2** Bouche Bee (USA), **8/1** Kemo Sabo (6/1-9/1), **11/1** Roderick Hudson, **12/1** Emerging Market, Hawa Al Nasamaat (USA) (op 8/1), **14/1** Ben Gunn, **16/1** Twilight Patrol, Three Stops (USA), Russian Heroine, **33/1** EASY DOLLAR, Dashing Water, **40/1** Warning Shot, Montserrat, Signs, **50/1** Self Reliance, CSF £414.27 CT £6,769.57 TOTE £27.70: £4.80 £5.00 £2.90 £2.90 (£460.40) Trio £1,217.20 OWNER Brian Gubby Ltd (BAGSHOT) BRED Brian Gubby Ltd
16 Rn 1m 25.44 (1.04) SF: 68/61/51/68/71/57/47/43/59/59/41/59/44/44/49/30

2738

VOLVO TRUCK FINANCE SPITFIRE H'CAP (0-110) (3-Y.O) (Class B) £33,630.00 (£10,140.00: £4,920.00: £2,310.00) **1m 2f** Stalls: High GOING minus 0.20 sec per fur (GF) 3-10 (3-11)

2348[3] **Jalfrezi (84)***(94) (JARToller)* 3-7-10 (3) SSanders(6) (14th st: rdn over 2f out: hdwy over 1f out: led wl ins fnl f: r.o wl) ....— 1
2367[3] Blisland **(90)***(99) (RCharlton)* 3-8-5 KDarley(13) (10th st: rdn over 3f out: hdwy wl over 1f out: led ins fnl f: sn hdd: r.o) ....½ 2
2571[3] Major Change **(86)***(91) (RHannon)* 3-8-1 GCarter(8) (6th st: rdn 3f out: unable qckn fnl f).....2½ 3
2343[2] State Law **(88)***(92) (GHarwood)* 3-8-3 AClark(5) (13th st: rdn over 3f out: nt clr run over 2f out: swtchd lft: hdwy over 1f out: r.o ins fnl f) ....¾ 4
2395* Maeterlinck (IRE) **(87)***(90) (BWHills)* 3-8-2 MHills(9) (swtg: 3rd st: rdn over 1f out: ev ch ins fnl f: one pce) ....¾ 5
1872[7] Kimbridge Knight (IRE) **(82)***(84) (PTWalwyn)* 3-7-11v NCarlisle(2) (lw: 2nd st: rdn over 2f out: ev ch over 1f out: one pce) ....nk 6
2348[7] Indonesian (IRE) **(84)***(85) (MBell)* 3-7-13 BDoyle(10) (lw: 5th st: rdn over 3f out: one pce)......¾ 7
1636[5] Dahik **(106)***(107) (MajorWRHern)* 3-9-7 WCarson(7) (lw: 4th st: rdn over 2f out: wknd fnl f)...hd 8
2062[4] Danegold (IRE) **(80)***(81) (MRChannon)* 3-7-9v GBardwell(14) (s.s: 11th st: rdn over 3f out: nvr nrr) ....nk 9
2316* Warning Order **(98)***(97) (JLDunlop)* 3-8-13 MRoberts(1) (lw: led: rdn over 2f out: hdd ins fnl f: sn wknd) 1 10
2457* Naked Welcome **(96)***(92)*(Fav)*(MJFetherston-Godley)* 3-8-11 JReid(4) (lw: 12th st: a bhd)...1¾ 11
1782[2] Triquetti (IRE) **(96)***(91) (LMCumani)* 3-8-11 LDettori(12) (lw: 8th st: rdn & hdwy over 3f out: eased whn btn ins fnl f) ....½ 12
2297* Sparrowhawk (IRE) **(84)***(79) (BWHills)* 3-7-8 (5) MHenry(11) (7th st: rdn over 3f out: sn wknd)hd 13
2110[F] Stage Struck (IRE) **(80)***(62) (MRStoute)* 3-7-9 JQuinn(3) (b.nr hind: swtg: 9th st: bhd fnl 3f) 8 14

4/1 Naked Welcome, **6/1** JALFREZI, **7/1** Triquetti (IRE) (5/1-15/2), **9/1** Maeterlinck (IRE), **10/1** Indonesian (IRE), **11/1** Blisland (8/1-12/1), **12/1** Stage Struck (IRE) (op 8/1), **14/1** State Law, **16/1** Kimbridge Knight (IRE), Sparrowhawk (IRE), **20/1** Major Change, Danegold (IRE), Dahik, **25/1** Warning Order, CSF £62.56 CT £1,123.16 TOTE £6.30: £2.30 £4.60 £5.60 (£62.00) Trio £362.80 OWNER Hamthor Ltd (The Rannerdale Trust) (WHITSBURY) BRED Rannerdale Trust 14 Rn
2m 6.43 (1.43) SF: 57/62/54/55/53/47/48/70/44/60/55/54/42/25

2739 SCHRODERS GLORIOUS RATED STKS H'CAP (0-110) (Listed) (4-Y.O+) (Class A) £27,470.40 (£10,233.60: £4,966.80: £2,094.00: £897.00: £418.20)
1m 4f Stalls: Low GOING minus 0.20 sec per fur (GF) 3-45 (3-47)

2323⁹ **Midnight Legend (109)***(120) (LMCumani)* 4-9-7 LDettori(7) (led 11f out: rdn over 2f out: r.o wl) ....— 1
2444³ Ionio (USA) **(107)***(116) (CEBrittain)* 4-9-5 MRoberts(3) (b: lw: 3rd st: rdn over 2f out: chsd wnr over 1f out: unable qckn) 1½ 2
2274⁷ Source of Light **(101)***(108) (RCharlton)* 6-8-13 KDarley(5) (5th st: rdn over 2f out: one pce) .1¾ 3
1853* Son of Sharp Shot (IRE) **(98)***(104)*(Fav)*(JLDunlop)* 5-8-10 PaulEddery(4) (lw: 6th st: rdn over 2f out: n.m.r on ins over 1f out: swtchd lft: r.o one pce) ....¾ 4
1768* Wishing (USA) **(96)***(100) (RAkehurst)* 4-8-8 TQuinn(2) (lw: 4th st: rdn over 3f out: wknd over 2f out) 1 5
2008⁴ Florid (USA) **(107)***(111) (HRACecil)* 4-9-5 WRyan(6) (swtg: led 1f: 2nd st: rdn over 2f out: wknd fnl f) ....nk 6
2421² Glide Path (USA) **(95)***(94) (JWHills)* 6-8-7 MHills(1) (lw: 7th st: rdn over 2f out: wknd over 1f out) 4 7

11/4 Son of Sharp Shot (IRE) (7/4-3/1), **7/2** MIDNIGHT LEGEND (op 7/1), **5/1** Source of Light, **11/2** Wishing (USA) (7/2-6/1), **7/1** Glide Path (USA), **10/1** Florid (USA), **14/1** Ionio (USA) (10/1-16/1), CSF £38.81 TOTE £4.90: £2.30 £3.50 (£29.80) OWNER Umm Qarn Racing (NEWMARKET) BRED Limestone Stud 7 Rn
2m 33.81 (1.81) SF: 78/74/66/62/58/69/52
OFFICIAL EXPLANATION **Midnight Legend: the trainer explained the colt had reared up and boiled over in the stalls last time, and thus ran a poor race.**

2740 MOLECOMB STKS (Gp 3) (2-Y.O) (Class A) £19,500.00 (£7,290.00: £3,495.00: £1,515.00) **5f** Stalls: Low GOING minus 0.20 sec per fur (GF) 4-15 (4-23)

2564a* **Almaty (IRE)** *(104) (CCollins,Ireland)* 2-9-3 KDarley(8) (leggy: unf: lw: mde all: edgd lft over 1f out: hrd rdn: r.o wl) ....— 1
2243⁴ Cayman Kai (IRE) *(94) (RHannon)* 2-8-12 RHughes(4) (lw: a.p: rdn 2f out: r.o one pce) 1½ 2
1833* Baize *(89)*(Fav)*(RFJohnsonHoughton)* 2-8-7 TQuinn(6) (outpcd: hdwy 2f out: one pce fnl f) s.h 3
2322⁵ Amazing Bay *(83) (IABalding)* 2-8-7 LDettori(9) (lw: a.p: ev ch over 1f out: one pce) 1¾ 4
2408* Shaniko (IRE) *(82) (PWChapple-Hyam)* 2-8-12 JReid(1) (swtg: lost pl over 2f out: rallied over 1f out: edgd rt: one pce) 2 5
2487* Nellie North *(64) (MrsMMcCourt)* 2-8-7 WCarson(5) (prom over 2f) 4 6
2347⁹ Night Parade (USA) *(68) (PWChapple-Hyam)* 2-8-12 BThomson(7) (prom over 3f) ....½ 7
1868⁹ Prince Aslia *(MJohnston)* 2-8-12 MRoberts(2) (Withdrawn not under Starter's orders: kicked in stalls) .... W
2487² Village Native (FR) *(KOCunningham-Brown)* 2-8-12 JWeaver(3) (Withdrawn not under Starter's orders: unruly in stalls) .... W

3/1 Baize, **9/2** ALMATY (IRE), Amazing Bay, **5/1** Cayman Kai (IRE), **11/2** Shaniko (IRE) (7/2-6/1), **7/1** Prince Aslia, **16/1** Night Parade (USA), **20/1** Nellie North, **25/1** Village Native (FR), CSF £20.65 TOTE £4.80: £2.60 £2.80 (£15.10) Trio £18.40 OWNER Mr P. D. Savill BRED P. E. Banahan 7 Rn
58.17 secs (1.47) SF: 58/48/43/37/36/18/22/-/-
STEWARDS' ENQUIRY Darley susp. 7-8/8/95 (careless riding).

2741 E.B.F. FOXHALL MAIDEN STKS (2-Y.O C & G) (Class D) £7,035.00 (£2,130.00: £1,040.00: £495.00)
7f Stalls: High GOING minus 0.20 sec per fur (GF) 4-45 (4-50)

2320² **Mark of Esteem (IRE)** *(84+)*(Fav)*(HRACecil)* 2-8-11 WRyan(3) (lw: 3rd st: led 2f out: comf) ....— 1
Tawkil (USA) *(77+) (BWHills)* 2-8-11 WCarson(1) (unf: scope: 5th st: rdn over 2f out: unable qckn fnl f) 3 2
Reinhardt (IRE) *(77+) (PWChapple-Hyam)* 2-8-11 JReid(5) (w'like: scope: 6th st: rdn over 3f out: r.o one pce fnl 2f: rn green) ....nk 3
2283⁴ Night Watch (USA) *(74) (IABalding)* 2-8-11 LDettori(7) (lw: led 5f: one pce) 1 4

Serendipity (FR) *(74) (JLDunlop)* 2-8-11 TQuinn(6) (str: scope: 4th st: rdn over 2f out: wknd over 1f out) .... nk 5
Civil Liberty *(70) (GLewis)* 2-8-11 PaulEddery(4) (wl grwn: 2nd st: rdn over 2f out: wknd over 1f out) 1½ 6
910[7] Current Leader *(66) (RHannon)* 2-8-11 KDarley(2) (a bhd) 2 7
Minnisam *(43) (JLDunlop)* 2-8-11 RHughes(8) (unf: s.s: a bhd) 10 8

8/15 MARK OF ESTEEM (IRE), **11/2** Night Watch (USA), **7/1** Tawkil (USA) (op 9/2), **8/1** Reinhardt (IRE) (op 9/2), **12/1** Serendipity (FR), **25/1** Civil Liberty, **33/1** Minnisam, **40/1** Current Leader, CSF £5.54 TOTE £1.60: £1.10 £1.80 £1.50 (£4.80) OWNER Sheikh Mohammed (NEWMARKET) BRED Sheikh Mohammed Bin Rashid Al Maktoum 8 Rn 1m 27.22 (2.82) SF: 45/38/38/35/35/31/27/4

2742

CHICHESTER CITY H'CAP (0-90) (3-Y.O) (Class C) £7,180.00 (£2,140.00: £1,020.00: £460.00)
5f Stalls: Low GOING minus 0.20 sec per fur (GF) 5-20 (5-21)

2239[2] **Crowded Avenue (67)***(81)*(Fav)*(PJMakin)* 3-8-2 PaulEddery(5) (swtg: hld up: a gng wl: led ins fnl f: easily) .... — 1
2344* Coffee 'n Cream **(83)***(92)*(Fav)*(RHannon)* 3-9-4 JReid(2) (swtg: led 4f out tl ins fnl f: unable qckn) 1½ 2
2394[2] Quiz Time **(86)***(82) (SirMarkPrescott)* 3-9-7 WWoods(4) (a.p: rdn over 2f out: ev ch over 1f out: wknd fnl f) 4 3
2692[5] Southern Dominion **(65)***(57) (MJohnston)* 3-8-0 MRoberts(1) (lw: led 1f: wknd 3f out) 1½ 4
2512[3] Princess Sadie **(79)***(64) (MRChannon)* 3-9-0 RHughes(3) (s.s: hdwy over 2f out: hrd rdn over 1f out: sn wknd) 2 5
1802[4] Endless Wave **(62)***(44) (MBell)* 3-7-11 NCarlisle(6) (bhd fnl 2f) 1 6

3/1 CROWDED AVENUE, Coffee 'n Cream, **100/30** Quiz Time (2/1-7/2), **5/1** Princess Sadie, **8/1** Southern Dominion (op 12/1), **12/1** Endless Wave, CSF £11.19 TOTE £4.00: £1.70 £1.70 (£4.90) OWNER Mr T. W. Wellard (MARLBOROUGH) BRED The Duke of Marlborough 6 Rn
58.19 secs (1.49) SF: 43/54/44/19/26/6

2743

KINRARA APPRENTICE LIMITED STKS (0-80) (4-Y.O+) (Class D) £6,840.00 (£2,070.00: £1,010.00: £480.00)
6f Stalls: Low GOING minus 0.20 sec per fur (GF) 5-50 (5-50)

2206[3] **First Veil (80)***(70) (JRFanshawe)* 5-8-7 NVarley(5) (rdn over 2f out: hdwy over 1f out: led wl ins fnl f: r.o wl) .... — 1
2402[3] Random **(51)***(69) (CJames)* 4-8-4 (3) CAdamson(7) (dwlt: rdn & hdwy over 1f out: led ins fnl f: sn hdd: r.o) .... ½ 2
2692* Aragrove **(77)***(83) (JWPayne)* 5-9-13 3x SSanders(3) (b: swtg: a.p: led over 1f out to ins fnl f: unable qckn) 2 3
2402[2] Anzio (IRE) **(67)***(71) (BAPearce)* 4-8-10b(5) JWilkinson(2) (b: a.p: rdn over 2f out: one pce) .... nk 4
2288[9] Thatcherella **(79)***(65)*(Fav)*(MajorDNChappell)* 4-8-8 (5) AimeeCook(6) (swtg: hld up: rdn over 1f out: one pce fnl f) 1¼ 5
1915[7] Jolto **(73)***(64) (KOCunningham-Brown)* 6-9-1 CTeague(4) (led over 4f) 1¼ 6
2414[9] Rocky Waters (USA) **(71)***(54) (PBurgoyne)* 6-8-9 (3) MHenry(1) (a bhd) 2½ 7

7/4 Thatcherella, **11/4** Aragrove, **4/1** FIRST VEIL (5/2-9/2), **7/1** Jolto (5/1-8/1), **11/1** Rocky Waters (USA), **14/1** Anzio (IRE), **25/1** Random, CSF £64.94 TOTE £5.00: £2.50 £4.10 (£52.60) OWNER Mr Raymond Tooth (NEWMARKET) BRED Mrs P. D. Rossdale and Mrs D. H. Clifton 7 Rn
1m 11.73 (1.53) SF: 53/52/66/54/48/47/37

T/Jkpt: Not won; £16,938.52 to Goodwood 29/7/95. T/Plpt: £962.50 (£57.15 Tckts). T/Qdpt: £67.30 (11.1 Tckts). AK

2612-NEWMARKET (R-H)
Friday July 28th (Good to firm, Good fnl 8f)
WEATHER: hot WIND: almost nil

2744

SIDE HILL (S) STKS (3-Y.O+) (Class E) £3,850.00 (£1,150.00: £550.00: £250.00)
1m (July) Stalls: High GOING minus 0.45 sec per fur (F) 6-15 (6-16)

2280[11] **Lincoln Treasure (IRE) (42)***(55) (MCChapman)* 4-9-1 (3) DRMcCabe(4) (swtg: hld up: hdwy over 1f out: led ins fnl f: rdn out) .... — 1

2477[9] Veloce (IRE) **(72)***(58)*(Fav)*(ABailey)* 7-9-9 GCarter(3) (lw: hld up: smooth hdwy 2f out: led 1f out: sn rdn & hdd: unable qckn)....1¼ 2
1945[8] Miss Felixstowe (USA) **(49)***(47) (MrsMReveley)* 3-8-5 RHills(5) (swtg: in tch: rdn over 3f out: kpt on fnl f: nrst fin)....hd 3
1873* Guesstimation (USA) **(62)***(57) (JPearce)* 6-9-9 GBardwell(9) (swtg: hld up: hdwy 2f out: rdn & ev ch over 1f out: no ex fnl f)....hd 4
2246[19] Keys Seminar **(40)***(49) (JohnBerry)* 3-8-10 CDwyer(10) (chsd ldrs: led over 1f out: sn hdd & no ex)....1½ 5
2065[9] Watch My Lips *(47) (MHTompkins)* 3-8-10 SMulvey(6) (lw: stdd s: hld up: hdwy & ev ch over 1f out: sn btn)....1¼ 6
2528[3] Pop to Stans **(47)***(48) (JPearce)* 6-9-2 (7) MNutter(11) (lw: hld up: n.m.r over 1f out: nvr plcd to chal)....1¾ 7
Chancey Fella **(60)***(27) (KTIvory)* 4-9-4v MWigham(7) (b: led after 2f to over 1f out: sn wknd)..8 8
2491[15] La Thuile **(35)***(21) (MDIUsher)* 3-8-5 DBiggs(2) (led 2f: ev ch over 2f out: sn wknd)....½ 9
1951[W] Sweetlittlemystery **(27)***(5) (EJAlston)* 4-8-13 SDWilliams(1) (prom: sn pushed along: wknd 3f out)....8 10
2466[3] The Flying Fiddle **(39)** *(MHTompkins)* 3-8-5v PRobinson(8) (chsd ldrs: rdn over 2f out: sn wknd)....7 11

6/4 Veloce (IRE), **2/1** Guesstimation (USA), **8/1** Miss Felixstowe (USA), **12/1** Pop to Stans, **16/1** Chancey Fella, **20/1** The Flying Fiddle, LINCOLN TREASURE (IRE), **25/1** Watch My Lips, **40/1** Sweetlittlemystery, Keys Seminar, **50/1** La Thuile, CSF £47.77 TOTE £23.80: £4.20 £1.20 £2.00 (£32.30) Trio £100.10 OWNER Mr Mattie O'Toole (MARKET RASEN) BRED Thomas and Mrs Marie Ryan 11 Rn 1m 41.75 (4.05) SF: 25/28/9/27/11/9/18/-/-/-/-

WEIGHT FOR AGE 3yo-8lb
No bid

2745 LUCINDA STOPFORD SACKVILLE LADIES H'CAP (0-80) (4-Y.O+) (Class E) £3,687.50 (£1,100.00: £525.00: £237.50)

1m 4f (July) Stalls: High GOING minus 0.45 sec per fur (F) 6-45 (6-46)

1607[2] **Fruitful Affair (IRE) (43)***(56) (TThomsonJones)* 6-8-9 (5) MissKEllis(4) (hdwy 8f out: led over 1f out: rdn clr ins fnl f)....— 1
2238[4] Minnesota Viking **(58)***(68)*(Fav)*(LadyHerries)* 4-10-1 MrsMCowdrey(3) (in tch: hdwy 5f out: ev ch over 1f out: sn rdn & no ex)....2½ 2
2664[2] Gold Blade **(47)***(56) (JPearce)* 6-9-4 MrsLPearce(9) (b: trckd ldrs tl lost pl 6f out: n.m.r fr 2f out tl r.o ins fnl f: gng on fin)....¾ 3
2228[3] Song of Years (IRE) **(57)***(65) (JWHills)* 4-9-9 (5) MrsGBell(2) (swtg: hld up: hdwy to ld 2f out: hdd over 1f out: nt qckn)....¾ 4
2639[4] Lookingforarainbow (IRE) **(78)***(81) (BobJones)* 7-11-2 (5) MissGJones(8) (hld up: hdwy over 1f out: no ex appr fnl f)....3½ 5
2546* Strat's Legacy **(47)***(49) (DWPArbuthnot)* 8-9-4 4x MrsDArbuthnot(1) (b.hind: led after 3f to 7f out: wknd 3f out)....½ 6
2546[9] Scenic Dancer **(46)***(43) (AHide)* 7-9-3 MissLHide(7) (in tch: no imp fnl 3f)....4 7
2022[4] Credit Squeeze **(71)***(67) (RFJohnsonHoughton)* 5-11-0 MissEJohnsonHoughton(6) (prom: led 7f out to 2f out: sn wknd)....¾ 8
2546[2] Our Bessie **(46)***(40) (DMarks)* 4-9-3 MissKMarks(5) (led 3f: wknd 3f out)....1¼ 9

LONG HANDICAP Fruitful Affair (IRE) 8-10

11/4 Minnesota Viking, **4/1** Gold Blade, **9/2** Strat's Legacy, **6/1** Credit Squeeze, **10/1** Song of Years (IRE), Lookingforarainbow (IRE), **11/1** Our Bessie, **14/1** Scenic Dancer, **33/1** FRUITFUL AFFAIR (IRE), CSF £113.52 CT £414.85 TOTE £16.10: £3.20 £1.60 £1.40 (£46.60) Trio £177.80 OWNER Mr E. S. G. Faber (LAMBOURN) BRED Rathbarry Stud 9 Rn

2m 32.41 (3.71) SF: 37/49/37/46/62/30/24/48/21

2746 VARDY CONTINENTAL H'CAP (0-90) (3-Y.O+) (Class C) £7,830.00 (£2,340.00: £1,120.00: £510.00)

6f (July) Stalls: High GOING minus 0.45 sec per fur (F) 7-15 (7-19)

2578* **Miss Aragon (52)***(60) (MissLCSiddall)* 7-7-7 7x NCarlisle(8) (lw: in tch: hdwy over 1f out: rdn & r.o wl to ld nr fin)....— 1
2364[7] Bayin (USA) **(67)***(23) (MDIUsher)* 6-8-8 RStreet(2) (b: lw: dwlt: hld up: hdwy over 2f out: led over 1f out: ct nr fin)....hd 2
1738[2] Cool Edge (IRE) **(72)***(28) (MHTompkins)* 4-8-13 PRobinson(5) (lw: prom: pushed along & led wl over 1f out: sn hdd & no ex)....2 3
2617[2] Princess Oberon (IRE) **(85)***(34)*(Fav)*(MBell)* 5-9-12 MFenton(10) (w ldrs tl led over 2f out: hdd wl over 1f out: no ex)....nk 4
2009* Dry Point **(72)***(34) (JARToller)* 9-8-13 WNewnes(1) (chsd ldrs: one pce fnl 2f)....1¼ 5

2369 12 Saseedo (USA) **(87)***(37) (WAO'Gorman)* 5-10-0 EmmaO'Gorman(9) (swtg: dwlt: bhd tl r.o appr fnl f) ....nk 6
1599 4 Cumbrian Waltzer **(75)***(36) (MHEasterby)* 10-9-2 LDettori(6) (in tch: rdn 3f out: styd on fnl f)....nk 7
2410 4 Sea-Deer **(86)***(37) (LJHolt)* 6-9-13 JReid(4) (swtg: chsd ldrs: no imp appr fnl f) 1¾ 8
2369 13 Czarna (IRE) **(87)***(23) (CEBrittain)* 4-10-0 MRoberts(12) (swtg: w ldrs over 3f)....5 9
Bello Gallico (IRE) **(76)***(81) (LadyHerries)* 4-9-3v PaulEddery(7) (led over 3f) ....½ 10
1862 4 Pengamon **(85)***(50) (HJCollingridge)* 3-9-6 MRimmer(3) (a bhd)....15 11
Ikaab (USA) **(88)***(95) (MajorWRHern)* 3-9-9 WCarson(11) (bit bkwd: spd 3f: sn wknd & eased) ....½ 12

5/1 Princess Oberon (IRE), **6/1** Cool Edge (IRE), **13/2** Dry Point, Sea-Deer, Ikaab (USA), **7/1** Cumbrian Waltzer, **9/1** MISS ARAGON, **12/1** Pengamon, **14/1** Bayin (USA), **16/1** Czarna (IRE), **20/1** Bello Gallico (IRE), Saseedo (USA), CSF £115.71 CT £740.81 TOTE £9.30: £2.70 £4.90 £2.00 (£85.60) Trio £162.50 OWNER Miss L. C. Siddall (TADCASTER) BRED J. A. Griffiths 12 Rn
1m 12.67 (1.17) SF: 25/40/39/52/35/50/37/43/31/18/-/-
WEIGHT FOR AGE 3yo-6lb

2747

WEATHERBYS 'NEWCOMERS' SERIES H'CAP (0-70) (3-Y.O+) (Class E)
£4,893.00 (£1,464.00: £702.00: £321.00)
1m 2f (July) Stalls: High GOING minus 0.45 sec per fur (F) 7-45 (7-48)

1681 5 **Floating Line (58)***(69) (EJAlston)* 7-9-8 SDWilliams(11) (swtg: trckd ldrs: led wl over 2f out: rdn out) ....— 1
1945 10 Pass Mark **(60)***(69) (JRFanshawe)* 3-9-0 WRyan(3) (swtg: plld hrd: in tch: hdwy 4f out: chsd wnr fnl 2f: r.o)....1½ 2
2657 5 Hadabet **(60)***(66)*(Fav)*(MissJacquelineDoyle)* 3-9-0 JReid(13) (lw: in tch: n.m.r 3f out: hdwy over 1f out: r.o)....1½ 3
2499 4 Miss Zanzibar **(60)***(64) (RAFahey)* 3-9-0 JQuinn(4) (chsd ldrs: kpt on same pce fnl 3f)....1½ 4
2531 4 Risky Romeo **(63)***(61) (GCBravery)* 3-9-3 MHills(7) (s.i.s: hdwy 2f out: nrst fin)....3½ 5
2246 11 Aldwick Colonnade **(41)***(31) (MDIUsher)* 8-8-5 DBiggs(5) (hdwy 3f out: nvr able to chal) 5 6
2407 7 Tadellal (IRE) **(55)***(42) (BAPearce)* 4-9-5 StephenDavies(10) (led tl wl over 2f out: no ex)....1¾ 7
2181 4 World Traveller **(51)***(38) (WAO'Gorman)* 4-9-1b EmmaO'Gorman(14) (bhd tl sme late hdwy)....s.h 8
1473 10 Rockusa **(54)***(32) (LadyHerries)* 3-8-8 PaulEddery(9) (lw: dwlt: nvr trbld ldrs)....6 9
Chilly Lad **(54)***(31) (MJRyan)* 4-9-4 AClark(12) (swtg: bhd: pushed along 5f out: n.m.r over 1f out: nvr trbld ldrs) ....½ 10
1830 7 Nunnery Grove (IRE) **(43)***(10) (TThomsonJones)* 3-7-11 NAdams(1) (lw: plld hrd: prom 7f)....6 11
2613 13 Ruby Estate (IRE) **(60)***(27) (APJames)* 4-9-10 FNorton(2) (bhd: rdn & hdwy 5f out: wknd 2f out)....s.h 12
1596 16 Dahlenburg (IRE) **(66)***(33) (JHMGosden)* 3-9-6v LDettori(8) (lw: chsd ldrs tl rdn & btn over 3f out: eased appr fnl f)....s.h 13
Supermick **(42)***(5) (PJMcBride)* 4-8-6 MFenton(6) (swtg: prom 6f: wknd qckly)....2½ 14

5/1 Hadabet, **6/1** Dahlenburg (IRE), **8/1** FLOATING LINE (6/1-9/1), Miss Zanzibar, Chilly Lad, **9/1** Risky Romeo, World Traveller, **10/1** Pass Mark, Rockusa, **20/1** Nunnery Grove (IRE), Ruby Estate (IRE), **25/1** Tadellal (IRE), Aldwick Colonnade, **33/1** Supermick, CSF £78.68 CT £405.28 TOTE £12.70: £3.50 £3.80 £1.80 (£83.80) Trio £247.10 OWNER Mr G. Lowe (PRESTON) BRED R. Kalman 14 Rn 2m 4.74 (2.34) SF: 50/40/37/35/32/12/23/19/3/12/-/8/4/-
WEIGHT FOR AGE 3yo-10lb

2748

NGK SPARK PLUGS CONDITIONS STKS (3-Y.O+ F & M) (Class C)
£5,163.20 (£1,908.80: £914.40: £372.00: £146.00: £55.60)
6f (July) Stalls: High GOING minus 0.45 sec per fur (F) 8-15 (8-16)

2416 5 **Paris Babe (92)***(96) (DMorris)* 3-9-4 LDettori(6) (trckd ldrs: led over 1f out: rdn & r.o strly) ...— 1
She's Dynamite (IRE) **(85)***(84) (WJarvis)* 3-9-0 BThomson(3) (bit bkwd: outpcd over 3f out: styd on wl appr fnl f) 3 2
2443 5 Penny Dip **(85)***(81) (RFJohnsonHoughton)* 3-8-12 JReid(1) (chsd ldrs: rdn & ev ch over 1f out: sn btn)....nk 3
2181 3 Karinska **(64)***(79) (MCChapman)* 5-9-7 (3) DRMcCabe(4) (t.o tl r.o wl fnl 2f) 3 4
2458* Jawlaat (USA) **(90)***(61)*(Fav)*(JLDunlop)* 3-9-4 WCarson(5) (lw: led over 4f: sn rdn & wknd) 7 5
2609 10 Magic Pearl **(74)***(32) (EJAlston)* 5-9-5 SDWilliams(2) (prom over 3f: rdn, hung lft & sn wknd) ..9 6

Evens Jawlaat (USA), **3/1** Penny Dip, **9/2** PARIS BABE, **8/1** She's Dynamite (IRE) (6/1-9/1), **16/1** Karinska, **20/1** Magic Pearl, CSF £33.40 TOTE £4.40: £2.00 £2.10 (£16.70) OWNER Mrs Susan Parry (NEWMARKET) BRED I. W. Parry 6 Rn 1m 13.55 (2.05) SF: 36/24/21/25/1/-
WEIGHT FOR AGE 3yo-6lb

2749 E.B.F. DEXA'TEX MAIDEN STKS (2-Y.O) (Class D) £4,542.00 (£1,356.00: £648.00: £294.00) **7f (July)** Stalls: High GOING minus 0.45 sec (F) 8-45 (8-46)

Subterfuge *(78t+)*(Fav)*(HRACecil)* 2-8-9 WRyan(3) (leggy: unf: hld up: qcknd to ld ins fnl f: rdn out) — 1
Rash Gift *(78+) (LordHuntingdon)* 2-8-9 LDettori(1) (w'like: unf: trckd ldr: led 1f out: sn hdd: rallied nr fin) hd 2
2107[6] Samim (USA) *(75) (JLDunlop)* 2-9-0 WCarson(4) (set stdy pce: qcknd 2f out: hdd 1f out: sn btn) 3½ 3
Midtime (IRE) *(75) (MRStoute)* 2-9-0 RHills(2) (scope: bkwd: hld up: qcknd & ev ch over 1f out: sn rdn & no ex) s.h 4

4/5 SUBTERFUGE, **3/1** Rash Gift, **9/2** Samim (USA), **8/1** Midtime (IRE) (op 4/1), CSF £3.41 TOTE £1.80 (£2.40) OWNER Lord Howard de Walden (NEWMARKET) 4 Rn 1m 31.95 (7.55) SF: -/-/-/-

T/Plpt: £511.80 (27.84 Tckts). T/Qdpt: £183.20 (0.4 Tckts); £148.62 to Newmarket 29/7/95. Dk

2327-PONTEFRACT (L-H)
Friday July 28th (Good to firm)
WEATHER: fine & sultry WIND: almost nil

2750 JACK BERRY APPEAL CLAIMING STKS (2-Y.O) (Class F) £3,083.50 (£856.00: £410.50) **6f** Stalls: Low GOING minus 0.33 sec per fur (GF) 6-40 (6-41)

2498* **Annaberg (IRE)** *(74+)*(Fav)*(MrsJRRamsden)* 2-8-9 KFallon(1) (hld up: qcknd to ld wl over 1f out: shkn up & sn clr) — 1
2328[7] Moi Canard *(64) (JBerry)* 2-8-7 JCarroll(2) (trckd ldrs: effrt over 2f out: chal over 1f out: kpt on same pce) 3 2
2431[7] Lawnswood Captain (IRE) *(58) (RHollinshead)* 2-8-1 (3) AGarth(5) (w ldr: hung lft ½-wy: outpcd 2f out: kpt on u.p fnl f) 1 3
The Black Dubh (IRE) *(58) (JJQuinn)* 2-8-7 MBirch(3) (leggy: bit bkwd: led: drvn along ½-wy: hdd wl over 1f out: one pce) 1¼ 4
1964[4] Victoria Sioux *(54) (JWharton)* 2-8-6 JWilliams(4) (b: trckd ldrs: effrt over 2f out: sn wl outpcd: n.d after) 1¼ 5

8/13 ANNABERG (IRE), **4/1** Victoria Sioux, **5/1** Moi Canard, **10/1** The Black Dubh (IRE), **33/1** Lawnswood Captain (IRE), CSF £4.00 TOTE £1.60: £1.10 £2.00 (£1.90) OWNER Mr Bernard Hathaway (THIRSK) BRED D. J. and Mrs Deer 5 Rn 1m 19.3 (5.00) SF: 2/-/-/-/-

2751 YORKSHIRE-TYNE TEES TELEVISION H'CAP (0-70) (3-Y.O) (Class E) £3,275.00 (£980.00: £470.00: £215.00) **1m 4f 8y** Stalls: Low GOING minus 0.33 sec per fur (GF) 7-05 (7-07)

2401* **Bark'n'bite (50)***(61) (MrsMReveley)* 3-9-5 JCarroll(3) (led: qcknd 4f out: drvn clr over 1f out: unchal) — 1
1957[7] Kildrummy Castle **(52)***(61)*(Fav)*(MrsJRRamsden)* 3-9-7 KFallon(4) (hld up: effrt 5f out: rdn over 3f out: chsd wnr over 1f out: nvr able to chal) 1¼ 2
2511[7] Risky Rose **(43)***(40) (RHollinshead)* 3-8-9 (3) AGarth(1) (trckd ldrs: effrt 3f out: wknd 1f out) 9 3
2225[9] Gifted **(28)** *(DonEnricoIncisa)* 3-7-11 KimTinkler(2) (trckd ldr: pushed along 4f out: wknd 2f out: eased) 25 4

6/4 Kildrummy Castle, **13/8** BARK'N'BITE, **5/2** Risky Rose, **20/1** Gifted, CSF £4.33 TOTE £2.50 (£1.50) OWNER Mr P. D. Savill (SALTBURN) BRED Ian Flockton Developments Ltd 4 Rn 2m 44.1 (9.80) SF: 16/16/-/-

2752 CORAL INJURED JOCKEYS FUND HOLIDAY H'CAP (0-80) (3-Y.O+) (Class D) £4,503.00 (£1,344.00: £642.00: £291.00) **1m 2f 6y** Stalls: Low GOING minus 0.33 sec per fur (GF) 7-30 (7-32)

1661[9] **Wathbat Mtoto (80)***(94+) (LMCumani)* 3-9-0 (7) JoHunnam(4) (lw: led to 4f out: led 3f out: shkn up & clr wl over 1f out: unchal) — 1
2557* Zacaroon **(65)***(75)*(Fav)*(LordHuntingdon)* 4-9-2 JWilliams(3) (hld up: outpcd & drvn along over 3f out: styd on appr fnl f: nt rch wnr) 2½ 2
2241[5] Hazard a Guess (IRE) **(77)***(82) (MrsJRRamsden)* 5-10-0 KFallon(2) (hld up: outpcd & drvn along over 3f out: styd on appr fnl f: nvr nr to chal) 3 3

24827 Champagne N Dreams **(57)***(40) (DNicholls)* 3-7-12 JLowe(1) (unruly: trckd ldr: qcknd to ld 4f out: hdd 3f out: wknd qckly over 1f out)....14 **4**

11/8 Zacaroon, **2/1** Hazard a Guess (IRE), **7/2** WATHBAT MTOTO, **13/2** Champagne N Dreams, CSF £8.32 TOTE £4.30 (£4.70) OWNER Sheikh Ahmed Al Maktoum (NEWMARKET) BRED Sheikh Ahmed bin Rashid al Maktoum 4 Rn 2m 19.8 (11.50) SF: -/-/-/-
WEIGHT FOR AGE 3yo-10lb

2753

ANTONIA DEUTERS H'CAP (0-80) (3-Y.O+) (Class D) £4,207.50 (£1,260.00: £605.00: £277.50) **5f** Stalls: Low GOING minus 0.33 sec per fur (GF) 8-00 (8-03)

25562 **The Kings Ransom (68)***(86)*(Fav)*(MrsJRRamsden)* 3-9-5v KFallon(8) (lw: bhd: gd hdwy ½-wy: qcknd to ld wl over 1f out: drvn clr)....— **1**
27142 Shadow Jury **(75)***(77) (DWChapman)* 5-10-3b 7x JWilliams(7) (chsd ldrs: styd on appr fnl f: no ch w wnr)....5 **2**
26657 Metal Boys **(64)***(64) (MissLCSiddall)* 8-8-13 (7) TSiddall(5) (rr div: hdwy & swtchd ins over 1f out: styd on)....¾ **3**
26654 King Rambo **(63)***(61) (RHollinshead)* 4-8-12 (7) AEddery(3) (a in tch: effrt 2f out: kpt on same pce appr fnl f)....½ **4**
25214 King Rat (IRE) **(63)***(60) (TJEtherington)* 4-9-5 JLowe(9) (chsd ldrs: outpcd 2f out: kpt on fnl f)....nk **5**
24927 Bonny Melody **(48)***(43) (PDEvans)* 4-7-11 (7) AmandaSanders(4) (w ldrs: chal 2f out: one pce)....½ **6**
23032 Sir Tasker **(53)***(46) (JLHarris)* 7-8-9v AMackay(1) (lw: sn drvn along w ldrs: wknd over 1f out)....¾ **7**
23108 General Gubbins **(58)***(43) (JHetherton)* 4-9-0 NKennedy(2) (unruly in stalls: s.s: a in rr)....2½ **8**
22347 Call to the Bar (IRE) **(63)***(45) (MDods)* 6-9-5 JCarroll(10) (s.i.s: a bhd)....1 **9**
24758 Flashing Sabre **(53)***(32) (JBerry)* 3-7-11 (7) CLowther(6) (mde most tl wl over 1f out: sn lost pl)....1 **10**

5/2 THE KINGS RANSOM, **7/2** Sir Tasker, **6/1** Shadow Jury (op 4/1), King Rat (IRE), **7/1** King Rambo, **12/1** General Gubbins, Flashing Sabre, **14/1** Metal Boys, **20/1** Bonny Melody, Call to the Bar (IRE), CSF £17.94 CT £160.34 TOTE £3.40: £1.60 £2.40 £2.40 (£9.40) Trio £82.10 OWNER Mr M. J. Simmonds (THIRSK) BRED M. J. Simmonds 10 Rn
62.6 secs (1.10) SF: 58/54/41/38/37/20/23/20/22/4
WEIGHT FOR AGE 3yo-5lb

2754

ST JOHN AMBULANCE MAIDEN STKS (3-Y.O) (Class D) £3,842.50 (£1,080.00: £527.50) **1m 4f 8y** Stalls: Low GOING minus 0.33 sec per fur (GF) 8-30 (8-30)

10382 **Saleel (IRE) (81)***(75) (ACStewart)* 3-9-0 SWhitworth(2) (lw: chsd ldr: pushed along 8f out: hdwy over 3f out: styd on to ld over 1f out: drvn out)....— **1**
22083 Iridal **(85)***(66)*(Fav)*(HRACecil)* 3-9-0 AMcGlone(3) (lw: led: drvn along over 4f out: hdd over 1f out: eased towards fin)....7 **2**
21334 Roscommon Lad (IRE) **(32)***(33) (RHollinshead)* 3-8-11v(3) AGarth(1) (sn pushed along: lost tch 4f out)....25 **3**

2/5 Iridal, **9/4** SALEEL (IRE), **25/1** Roscommon Lad (IRE), CSF £3.35 TOTE £2.60 (£1.10) OWNER Sheikh Ahmed Al Maktoum (NEWMARKET) BRED Doverlodge Stud 3 Rn
2m 36.6 (2.30) SF: 58/49/16

2755

RED SHIRT NIGHT CLAIMING STKS (3-Y.O+) (Class F) £2,936.50 (£814.00: £389.50) **1m 4y** Stalls: Low GOING minus 0.33 sec per fur (GF) 9-00 (9-01)

237510 **Pleasure Trick (USA) (56)***(70) (NTinkler)* 4-9-0 KimTinkler(2) (swtg: chsd ldrs: pushed along 5f out: sn outpcd: hdwy over 2f out: styd on to ld ins fnl f: drvn out)....— **1**
25862 Just Fizzy **(61)***(61)*(Fav)*(JHetherton)* 3-8-1 NKennedy(5) (trckd ldr: led over 1f out tl hdd & no ex ins fnl f)....2 **2**
24605 Dr Caligari (IRE) **(70)***(66) (JBerry)* 3-8-8 JCarroll(1) (prom: drvn along 3f out: sn outpcd: kpt on appr fnl f)....1¼ **3**
26207 Canny Lad **(25)***(55) (MPBielby)* 5-8-12v KFallon(4) (led tl over 1f out: sn wknd)....3½ **4**
23586 Parliament Piece **(67)***(52)*(Fav)*(MrsMReveley)* 9-8-12v(5) GParkin(7) (prom: ev ch & rdn over 2f out: wknd over 1f out)....4 **5**
185418 Juice Plus **(21)***(25) (JParkes)* 4-8-11 (3) PMcCabe(6) (in tch: outpcd & drvn along over 2f out: sn bhd)....12 **6**
258813 Care And Comfort **(62)** *(KMcAuliffe)* 3-8-1v JLowe(3) (plld hrd: trckd ldrs: sddle slipped & lost pl 3f out: eased)....10 **7**

2/1 Just Fizzy, Parliament Piece, **5/1** Dr Caligari (IRE), **6/1** Care And Comfort, **10/1** PLEASURE TRICK (USA), **33/1** Canny Lad, **40/1** Juice Plus, CSF £28.47 TOTE £17.10: £3.30 £1.40 (£21.70) OWNER Mr J.D.Gordon (MALTON) BRED W.S.Farish 7 Rn 1m 44.1 (2.10) SF: 52/35/40/37/34/7/-

WEIGHT FOR AGE 3yo-8lb

T/Plpt: £207.60 (32.66 Tckts). T/Qdpt: Not won; £48.20 to Goodwood 29/7/95. WG

2580-THIRSK (L-H)
Friday July 28th (Good to firm)

WEATHER: very hot WIND: slt against

2756

GOLDEN FLEECE CLAIMING STKS (2-Y.O) (Class F) £3,293.50 (£916.00: £440.50) **7f** Stalls: Low GOING minus 0.29 sec per fur (GF) 2-15 (2-18)

1511[9] **Hotlips Houlihan** *(73) (RJRWilliams)* 2-8-3 DBiggs(6) (lw: mde most: rdn & styd on wl fnl f) — 1
1977[4] Pacific Grove *(73) (PFICole)* 2-8-9 CRutter(2) (cl up: rn sltly wd st: sn rdn: nt qckn appr fnl f) 2½ 2
2526[4] Silver Harrow *(78)*(Fav)*(SirMarkPrescott)* 2-9-0 JLowe(4) (chsd wnr: rdn over 2f out: nt qckn fnl f) hd 3
1503[4] How Could-I (IRE) *(53) (MHEasterby)* 2-8-0 SMaloney(5) (styd on fnl 3f: nvr rchd ldrs) 5 4
2629[6] Craigmore Magic (USA) *(54) (MissMKMilligan)* 2-8-3 JFanning(7) (chsd ldrs: rdn ent st: no imp) ¾ 5
2483[10] China Castle *(58) (PCHaslam)* 2-8-7 JFortune(10) (bdly hmpd s: nt rcvr) s.h 6
La Fandango (IRE) *(46) (MWEasterby)* 2-7-9 (7) RuthCoulter(3) (w'like: nvr nr ldrs) 3 7
2251[9] The Wad *(21) (MWEasterby)* 2-8-11 MBirch(9) (bdly hmpd s: nt rcvr) 15 8
2516[14] Royal Romance *(GMMoore)* 2-7-13 TWilliams(8) (swvd bdly rt leaving stalls & uns rdr) U
2526[7] Laurel Crown (IRE) *(JBerry)* 2-8-11 JCarroll(1) (Withdrawn not under starters' orders: vet's advice) W

6/5 Silver Harrow, **5/2** Pacific Grove, **5/1** HOTLIPS HOULIHAN, **8/1** Laurel Crown (IRE), **12/1** China Castle, **16/1** How Could-I (IRE), La Fandango (IRE), **25/1** The Wad, **33/1** Royal Romance, Craigmore Magic (USA), CSF £17.60 TOTE £5.10: £1.10 £1.20 £1.20 (£7.60) Trio £2.20 OWNER Mr Harry Ormesher (NEWMARKET) BRED P. Young 9 Rn 1m 27.1 (4.40) SF: 12/12/17/-/-/-/-/-/-

2757

LEWIS GEIPEL MEMORIAL CHALLENGE CUP NURSERY H'CAP (2-Y.O) (Class D) £3,850.00 (£1,150.00: £550.00: £250.00) **6f** Stalls: Centre GOING minus 0.39 sec per fur (F) 2-50 (2-50)

2498[7] **Oriole** *(62) (NTinkler)* 2-8-9 KimTinkler(2) (cl up: rdn to ld ins fnl f: hung rt: styd on) — 1
2489[5] My Kind *(65) (KMcAuliffe)* 2-8-13 JCarroll(1) (b.nr hind: mde most tl hdd over 1f out: rallied ins fnl f) ½ 2
2644[2] Oriel Lad *(72)*(Fav)*(PDEvans)* 2-9-7b JFortune(3) (swtg: a w ldrs: kpt on one pce ins fnl f) hd 3
2459[3] Patrington Park *(47) (MWEasterby)* 2-7-6 (7) PFessey(5) (swtg: hld up: hdwy to ld over 1f out: hdd ins fnl f: btn whn hmpd towards fin) 1¼ 4
2629[4] Efipetite *(47) (NBycroft)* 2-8-2 SMaloney(4) (disp ld tl wknd ent fnl f) 1 5

2/1 Oriel Lad, **5/2** My Kind, **3/1** Patrington Park (2/1-100/30), **5/1** ORIOLE, **10/1** Efipetite, CSF £16.65 TOTE £8.10: £3.40 £1.50 (£15.10) OWNER Kendall White & Co Ltd (WELSHPOOL) BRED D. J. Watkins 5 Rn 1m 12.7 (3.00) SF: 28/21/18/3/3

2758

GO RACING IN YORKSHIRE H'CAP (0-80) (3-Y.O+) (Class D) £4,235.00 (£1,265.00: £605.00: £275.00) **6f** Stalls: Centre GOING minus 0.39 sec per fur (F) 3-25 (3-26)

2533[9] **Ned's Bonanza (68)***(77) (MDods)* 6-9-2 SWhitworth(6) (hdwy 2f out: led ins fnl f: jst hld on) — 1
2418[6] Benzoe (IRE) **(80)***(89) (MrsJRRamsden)* 5-10-0 KFallon(9) (lw: in tch: hdwy 2f out: led ins fnl f: sn hdd: wknd towards fin) s.h 2
2461[9] Lepine (IRE) **(70)***(72) (JWWatts)* 4-9-4v JCarroll(2) (swtg: led & sn wl clr: hdd & no ex ins fnl f) 2½ 3
2519* Formidable Liz **(62)***(61) (MDHammond)* 5-8-10 7x DaleGibson(4) (in tch: rdn ½-wy: styd on: no imp) 1¼ 4
*2493** Sense of Priority **(64)***(59)*(Fav)*(DNicholls)* 6-8-12 7x AlexGreaves(7) (outpcd & hung lft ½-wy: no imp after) 1½ 5
2458[8] Maid O'Cannie **(59)***(51) (MWEasterby)* 4-8-0 (7) RuthCoulter(3) (nvr nr to chal) 1¼ 6
2585[2] High Domain (IRE) **(64)***(55) (TDBarron)* 4-8-12b JFortune(1) (racd alone far side: chsd ldrs: rdn & nt qckn fnl 2f) nk 7

2652[9] Great Hall **(59)***(45) (PDCundell)* 6-8-2b(5) DGriffiths(5) (s.i.s: n.d) 1¾ **8**
2060[9] High Ranking **(65)***(49) (MHEasterby)* 3-8-7 MBirch(10) (n.d) ....¾ **9**
2521[6] Prince Belfort **(67)** *(JLEyre)* 7-8-10b(5) HKYim(8) (b: in tch: effrt over 2f: p.u lame 2f out: dead). **P**

9/2 Sense of Priority, **5/1** High Domain (IRE), Benzoe (IRE), **6/1** NED'S BONANZA, **13/2** Formidable Liz, **8/1** Lepine (IRE), Prince Belfort, **9/1** Maid O'Cannie, **10/1** Great Hall, **16/1** High Ranking, CSF £36.14 CT £227.56 TOTE £7.20: £2.40 £2.00 £2.80 (£19.00) Trio £68.20 OWNER Mr Ned Jones (DARLINGTON) BRED D. W. McHarg 10 Rn
1m 10.2 (0.50) SF: 60/72/55/44/42/34/38/28/26/-
WEIGHT FOR AGE 3yo-6lb

2759 PETER BELL MEMORIAL H'CAP (0-70) (3-Y.O+ F & M) (Class E)
£3,637.25 (£1,088.00: £521.50: £238.25)
1m 4f Stalls: Low GOING minus 0.29 sec per fur (GF) 3-55 (4-00)

2543[2] **Instantaneous (47)***(56)*(Fav)*(MHEasterby)* 3-7-9 JLowe(5) (trckd ldr: led 3f out: comf) ....— **1**
2479[5] Ballard Lady (IRE) **(50)***(51) (JSWainwright)* 3-7-12 ow5 SMaloney(4) (chsd ldrs: kpt on fnl 2f: nt pce to chal) 2 **2**
2482[5] Sariyaa **(63)***(67) (MBrittain)* 4-9-9 MWigham(3) (led tl hdd 3f out: one pce) 1½ **3**
2543[4] Tancred Mischief **(35)***(35) (WLBarker)* 4-7-6 (3)ow2 DarrenMoffatt(6) (swtg: outpcd & bhd: styd on fnl 3f) 2 **4**
2547[5] Roufontaine **(68)***(69) (WRMuir)* 4-10-0 JCarroll(1) (unruly in stalls: hld up: effrt appr st: no imp) ....½ **5**
2305[3] Missus Murhill (IRE) **(36)***(17) (NTinkler)* 4-7-10 KimTinkler(2) (lw: s.s: a bhd) 15 **6**
LONG HANDICAP Tancred Mischief 7-6

5/4 INSTANTANEOUS, **11/4** Roufontaine, **9/2** Missus Murhill (IRE) (5/2-5/1), **8/1** Ballard Lady (IRE) (op 5/1), Sariyaa, **12/1** Tancred Mischief, CSF £11.30 TOTE £1.80: £1.10 £5.60 (£11.00) OWNER Mr Reg Griffin (MALTON) BRED Mrs Anne Sutton 6 Rn 2m 35.1 (5.10) SF: 24/19/47/15/49/-
WEIGHT FOR AGE 3yo-12lb

2760 STOKESLEY MAIDEN STKS (3-Y.O+) (Class D) £4,230.00 (£1,260.00: £600.00: £270.00) 1m Stalls: Low GOING minus 0.29 sec per fur (GF) 4-25 (4-25)

1436[3] **Dance King (66)***(58)*(Fav)*(DNicholls)* 3-8-11 AlexGreaves(2) (mde all: r.o fnl 2f: comf) ....— **1**
2587[6] Backhander (IRE) **(58)***(52) (JARToller)* 3-8-11 SWhitworth(3) (lw: chsd wnr: effrt over 2f out: hung lft & nt r.o) 3 **2**
Woodlands Lad Too *(12) (PAPritchard)* 3-8-11 CRutter(4) (leggy: s.i.s: sn in tch: rn wd st: sn rdn & btn) 20 **3**
Ghalayan *(4) (HThomsonJones)* 3-8-11 AMcGlone(1) (w'like: scope: s.i.s: sn rcvrd: rdn & wknd 3f out) 4 **4**

8/11 DANCE KING (11/10-4/6), **9/4** Ghalayan (op Evens), **4/1** Backhander (IRE), **20/1** Woodlands Lad Too, CSF £3.97 TOTE £2.00 (£5.30) OWNER Mr Terry Connors (THIRSK) BRED A. Aikin 4 Rn
1m 40.0 (4.40) SF: 26/20/-/-

2761 COWESBY MAIDEN APPRENTICE H'CAP (0-70) (3-Y.O+) (Class F)
£2,595.50 (£738.00: £366.50)
7f Stalls: Low GOING minus 0.29 sec per fur (GF) 4-55 (4-56)

2122[6] **Upex le Gold Too (33)***(43+) (LRLloyd-James)* 3-7-6 (5) KSked(3) (lw: chsd ldr: led wl over 1f out: r.o u.p) ....— **1**
2522[3] Speedy Snaps Pride **(47)***(51) (PDCundell)* 3-8-11 GFaulkner(2) (chsd ldrs: hdwy 2f out: nt qckn fnl f) 2½ **2**
2624[11] Coney Hills **(24)***(25) (NBycroft)* 4-7-9 BHalligan(1) (swtg: led tl hdd wl over 1f out: sn rdn & btn) 1½ **3**
2540[5] Boost **(45)***(39) (CWThornton)* 3-8-4 (5) GMills(4) (lw: in tch: rdn over 2f out: no imp) 3 **4**
1533[7] Bella Sedona **(64)***(56)*(Fav)*(LadyHerries)* 3-10-0 PDoe(7) (racd wd: sme hdwy 3f out: wknd 2f out) 1 **5**
65[13] Woodlands Electric **(22)***(13) (PAPritchard)* 5-7-7 JoHunnam(6) (outpcd appr st: n.d) ....nk **6**
LONG HANDICAP Woodlands Electric 7-3

5/2 Bella Sedona, **3/1** Boost, Speedy Snaps Pride, **7/2** UPEX LE GOLD TOO, **14/1** Coney Hills, **33/1** Woodlands Electric, CSF £13.19 TOTE £4.30: £2.10 £1.50 (£5.30) OWNER Mr J. B. Slatcher (MALTON) BRED Shaunlara Stud 6 Rn 1m 27.1 (4.40) SF: 6/14/-/2/19/-
WEIGHT FOR AGE 3yo-7lb

T/Plpt: £75.60 (106.44 Tckts). T/Qdpt: £29.50 (2.35 Tckts). AA

2737-**GOODWOOD (R-H)**

Saturday July 29th (St Good to firm, Rnd Firm, Good to firm patches)

WEATHER: hot WIND: almost nil

2762 VODAPAGE CONDITIONS STKS (3-Y.O) (Class B) £13,366.00 (£4,816.00: £2,308.00: £940.00: £370.00)

1m Stalls: High GOING minus 0.22 sec per fur (GF) 2-00 (2-01)

Tamayaz (CAN) *(113+) (SbinSuroor)* 3-8-11 LDettori(3) (h.d.w: mde all: clr over 1f out: easily) ....— **1**

1848³ First Island (IRE) **(105)***(110)*(Fav)*(GWragg)* 3-9-2 MHills(1) (lw: 4th st: chsd wnr over 2f out: no imp) 4 **2**

2008⁵ Be Mindful **(101)***(103) (JRFanshawe)* 3-9-1 TQuinn(2) (3rd st: rdn over 2f out: one pce).......3 **3**

713⁷ Knight Commander (USA) **(95)***(98) (RHannon)* 3-8-11 MRoberts(5) (5th st: nvr nr to chal) ....nk **4**

2205* Solar Flight **(100)***(83) (BWHills)* 3-9-2 KDarley(6) (lw: plld hrd: chsd wnr over 5f) 10 **5**

5/4 First Island (IRE), **5/2** TAMAYAZ (CAN) (op 6/4), **5/1** Solar Flight, **9/1** Be Mindful (6/1-10/1), **16/1** Knight Commander (USA), CSF £5.49 TOTE £2.70: £1.40 £1.40 (£1.90) OWNER Maktoum Al Maktoum (NEWMARKET) BRED Windfields Farm 5 Rn 1m 38.58 (0.98) SF: 68/65/58/53/38

2763 VODAFONE NASSAU STKS (Gp 2) (3-Y.O+ F & M) (Class A) £46,300.00 (£17,347.50: £8,348.75: £3,653.75)

1m 2f Stalls: High GOING minus 0.22 sec per fur (GF) 2-40 (2-41)

2349* **Caramba** *(117+)*(Fav)*(RHannon)* 3-8-9 MRoberts(3) (lw: 4th st: rdn over 2f out: led ins fnl f: r.o wl) ....— **1**

2349⁵ Warning Shadows (IRE) **(111)***(113) (CEBrittain)* 3-8-6 BDoyle(6) (led tl ins fnl f: r.o).......½ **2**

1120a⁸ Erin Bird (FR) *(110) (PWChapple-Hyam)* 4-9-2 RHughes(4) (2nd st: rdn 3f out: ev ch wl over 1f out: unable qckn) 1¾ **3**

1923³ Western Reel (USA) **(91)***(110) (PFICole)* 3-8-6 TQuinn(1) (6th st: rdn over 2f out: one pce) ..hd **4**

1729² Poppy Carew (IRE) **(106)***(110) (PWHarris)* 3-8-6 LDettori(5) (lw: 3rd st: rdn 3f out: one pce).hd **5**

2211a⁷ Subya **(107)***(101) (JLDunlop)* 3-8-6 WCarson(2) (5th st: rdn 3f out: wknd over 1f out).......6 **6**

5/2 CARAMBA (7/4-3/1), **4/1** Erin Bird (FR), Subya (3/1-9/2), **9/2** Warning Shadows (IRE), **6/1** Poppy Carew (IRE) (10/1-11/2), **12/1** Western Reel (USA), CSF £12.43 TOTE £3.10: £1.60 £2.60 (£5.40) OWNER Lord Carnarvon (MARLBOROUGH) BRED Highclere Stud Ltd 6 Rn 2m 8.65 (3.65) SF: 47/43/50/40/40/31

WEIGHT FOR AGE 3yo-10lb

2764 VODAC STEWARDS' CUP H'CAP (3-Y.O+) (Class B) £50,525.00 (£15,200.00: £7,350.00: £3,425.00)

6f Stalls: Low GOING minus 0.22 sec per fur (GF) 3-15 (3-24)

2428⁵ **Shikari's Son (92)***(103) (JWhite)* 8-8-13 ow4 RHughes(30) (s.s: swtchd lft 2f out: gd hdwy over 1f out: hrd rdn & led ins fnl f: r.o wl) ....— **1**

2410* Top Banana **(79)***(92)*(Fav)*(HCandy)* 4-8-0 MRoberts(26) (rdn over 2f out: hdwy over 1f out: ev ch ins fnl f: unable qckn).......¾ **2**

2570³ Jayannpee **(95)***(108) (IABalding)* 4-9-2 WCarson(10) (lw: hld up: rdn over 2f out: n.m.r over 1f out: r.o wl ins fnl f) ....s.h **3**

1924* Espartero (IRE) **(99)***(112) (SirMarkPrescott)* 3-9-0 LDettori(4) (hld up: rdn over 1f out: ev ch ins fnl f: r.o) ....s.h **4**

2150* Sir Joey (USA) **(84)***(97) (PGMurphy)* 6-8-5 JWilliams(15) (hld up: rdn fnl f: r.o) ....s.h **5**

2288¹⁴ No Extras (IRE) **(89)***(100) (GLMoore)* 5-8-10 SWhitworth(24) (hdwy over 2f out: hrd rdn & ev ch ins fnl f: one pce).......¾ **6**

1895²⁷ My Best Valentine **(82)***(93) (JWhite)* 5-7-12 (5) AWhelan(23) (lw: outpcd: hdwy over 1f out: r.o) ....s.h **7**

2443² Inzar (USA) **(105)***(115) (PFICole)* 3-9-6b TQuinn(22) (hdwy 3f out: hrd rdn over 1f out: ev ch ins fnl f: one pce) ....hd **8**

2533² Agwa **(74)***(83) (RJO'Sullivan)* 6-7-6 (3) DarrenMoffatt(8) (lw: a.p: hrd rdn over 2f out: ev ch over 1f out: one pce).......nk **9**

2001³ Silent Expression **(79)***(88) (BJMeehan)* 5-8-0 BDoyle(17) (rdn & lost pl 3f out: r.o one pce fnl f).......nk **10**

2092* Jade Pet **(80)***(87) (RHannon)* 4-8-1 MFenton(9) (nvr nrr) ....½ **11**

2617³ Ansellman **(72)***(79) (JBerry)* 5-7-2 (5) MBaird(19) (lw: a.p: rdn over 2f out: ev ch over 1f out: wknd ins fnl f) ....hd **12**

2443* Hard to Figure **(110)**_(117) (RJHodges)_ 9-10-0 (3) 7x SDrowne(2) (nvr nrr) ....hd **13**
1895* Astrac (IRE) **(94)**_(101) (RAkehurst)_ 4-8-12 (3) SSanders(21) (lw: hdwy 4f out: led wl over 1f out tl ins fnl f: sn wknd) ....s.h **14**
1895[3] Brave Edge **(100)**_(107) (RHannon)_ 4-9-7 WNewnes(27) (rdn over 2f out: hdwy 1f out: one pce) ....d.h **14**
2288[2] Master of Passion **(81)**_(86) (JMPEustace)_ 6-7-13 (3) JTate(29) (a.p: hrd rdn over 2f out: ev ch ins fnl f: sn wknd) ....½ **16**
2458[3] How's Yer Father **(84)**_(89) (RJHodges)_ 9-8-5 RPerham(20) (lw: rdn over 3f out: hdwy over 1f out: eased whn btn ins fnl f) ....nk **17**
2673[6] Daring Destiny **(102)**_(105) (KRBurke)_ 4-9-4b(5) MHenry(25) (s.s: hdwy over 2f out: wknd fnl f) ....½ **18**
2533[11] Green Golightly (USA) **(72)**_(74) (DAWilson)_ 4-7-7 NAdams(7) (outpcd) ....½ **19**
2404[5] La Petite Fusee **(74)**_(72) (RJO'Sullivan)_ 4-7-6 (3)ow2 DWright(11) (prom 3f) ....¾ **20**
2326* Broadstairs Beauty (IRE) **(75)**_(75) (SRBowring)_ 5-7-10v NKennedy(16) (lw: led over 4f) ....hd **21**
1806* Bold Effort (FR) **(97)**_(96) (KOCunningham-Brown)_ 3-8-12 JWeaver(6) (spd over 4f) ....hd **22**
2617[4] Master Planner **(100)**_(97) (CACyzer)_ 6-9-7 DBiggs(28) (lw: prom over 3f) ....¾ **23**
2079[5] Napoleon Star (IRE) **(72)**_(63) (MSSaunders)_ 4-7-7 SLanigan(3) (lw: a bhd) 2½ **24**
1614* Saddlehome (USA) **(82)**_(65) (TDBarron)_ 6-8-3 KDarley(18) (hdwy over 2f out: wkng whn nt clr run over 1f out) 3 **25**
2001[4] Palacegate Touch **(90)**_(72) (JBerry)_ 5-8-11v JCarroll(1) (lw: bhd fnl 3f) ....hd **26**
2271[6] Prime Match (IRE) **(82)**_(64) (PWHarris)_ 3-7-11b StephenDavies(5) (lw: s.s: a bhd) ....nk **27**
_2743[5]_ Thatcherella **(79)** _(MajorDNChappell)_ 4-8-0 TSprake(14) (Withdrawn not under Starter's orders: Veterinary advice) .... **W**
_2096[9]_ Castlerea Lad **(88)** _(RHollinshead)_ 6-8-4 (5) DGriffiths(12) (Withdrawn not under Starter's orders: Veterinary advice) .... **W**
_2533[6]_ Magic Orb **(78)** _(JLHarris)_ 5-7-13 JQuinn(13) (Withdrawn not under Starter's orders: v.unruly & broke out of stalls) .... **W**

LONG HANDICAP La Petite Fusee 7-5 Napoleon Star (IRE) 7-5 Green Golightly (USA) 7-5 Ansellman 7-5

9/2 Top Banana, **7/1** Espartero (IRE), **10/1** Astrac (IRE), **11/1** Brave Edge, **14/1** Agwa, Bold Effort (FR), **16/1** Saddlehome (USA), Master of Passion, Broadstairs Beauty (IRE), Inzar (USA), **20/1** Jayannpee, Jade Pet, **25/1** Castlerea Lad, Daring Destiny, Silent Expression, **33/1** Sir Joey (USA), How's Yer Father, Thatcherella, Hard to Figure, Master Planner, **40/1** SHIKARI'S SON, **50/1** Magic Orb, No Extras (IRE), **66/1** La Petite Fusee, Ansellman, My Best Valentine, Napoleon Star (IRE), Palacegate Touch, Prime Match (IRE), **200/1** Green Golightly (USA), CSF £190.82 CT £3,347.50 TOTE £77.60: £11.40 £1.40 £3.50 £2.80 (£194.10) Trio £1,483.80 OWNER Mr Alan Spargo (WENDOVER) BRED W. H. Joyce 27 Rn 1m 10.86 (0.66)
SF:69/58/74/72/63/66/59/75/49/54/53/45/83/67/73/52/55/71/40/38/41/56/63/29/31/38/24/-/-/-
WEIGHT FOR AGE 3yo-6lb

2765 VODATA NURSERY H'CAP (2-Y.O) (Class C) £7,245.00 (£2,160.00: £1,030.00: £465.00) 7f Stalls: High GOING minus 0.22 sec per fur (GF) 3-50 (3-55)

2135[10] **Vanishing Point** _(70) (GLewis)_ 2-7-10 WCarson(4) (mde all: rdn over 2f out: r.o wl) ....— **1**
2283[9] Urgent Swift _(66) (APJarvis)_ 2-7-2 (7) CAdamson(7) (lw: hdwy over 2f out: ev ch over 1f out: wandered: unable qckn) 1¼ **2**
2434* Opera _(74) (WJarvis)_ 2-8-1 (5) MHenry(9) (4th st: rdn over 3f out: one pce) 1½ **3**
2441[4] Kilvine _(89)_(Fav)_(LMCumani)_ 2-9-7 LDettori(1) (6th st: rdn over 2f out: r.o one pce) ....hd **4**
2489[3] Polly Golightly _(74) (BSmart)_ 2-8-3 (5) DGriffiths(2) (3rd st: rdn over 2f out: one pce) ....¾ **5**
1774* Jaleel _(70) (RHannon)_ 2-8-6 MRoberts(6) (plld hrd: 2nd st: ev ch 2f out: wknd fnl f) ....¾ **6**
2442[7] Amaretto Bay (IRE) _(78) (BJMeehan)_ 2-8-13 (7) RHavlin(8) (5th st: nt clr run over 2f out: wknd over 1f out) 2½ **7**
1734* Miss Offset _(35) (MJohnston)_ 2-7-7b JQuinn(5) (a bhd) 7 **8**
2435[2] Don't Tell Vicki _(31) (JSMoore)_ 2-7-2 (5) MBaird(3) (hdwy over 2f out: wknd over 1f out) 2 **9**

11/4 Kilvine, **4/1** Jaleel, **5/1** VANISHING POINT, Opera, **7/1** Miss Offset (op 7/2), **9/1** Amaretto Bay (IRE), **16/1** Polly Golightly, **25/1** Don't Tell Vicki, **33/1** Urgent Swift, CSF £108.68 CT £779.11 TOTE £6.40: £1.80 £5.80 £1.80 (£89.50) Trio £133.40 OWNER Sheikh Mohammed (NEWMARKET) BRED Sheikh Mohammed bin Rashid al Maktoum 9 Rn 1m 28.14 (3.74) SF: 38/27/23/23/19/19/15/-/-

2766 TURF CLUB CLAIMING STKS (3-Y.O+) (Class D) £7,700.00 (£2,300.00: £1,100.00: £500.00) 1m Stalls: High GOING minus 0.22 sec per fur (GF) 4-25 (4-26)

2117[5] **Mellottie (87)**_(98) (MrsMReveley)_ 10-9-2 RHughes(3) (stdy hdwy 3f out: led 2f out: hung rt over 1f out: r.o wl) ....— **1**
2537[2] Shifting Moon **(82)**_(93)_(Fav)_(IABalding)_ 3-8-6b LDettori(7) (led 6f: 2nd & btn whn squeezed out on ins over 1f out) 1¾ **2**

2310* Chairmans Choice **(46)***(88) (APJarvis)* 5-8-12 JTate(10) (3rd st: rdn over 1f out: one pce)....1¼ **3**
2468[4] Blockade (USA) **(71)***(76) (MBell)* 6-8-12 MFenton(4) (lw: 2nd st: rdn over 2f out: wknd over 1f out)....6 **4**
2613[5] Dontforget Insight (IRE) **(72)***(77) (PFICole)* 4-9-2b TQuinn(9) (b.hind: plld hrd: nvr nr to chal)....1½ **5**
2343[4] Second Chance (IRE) **(82)***(81) (PMitchell)* 5-9-7 MHenry(8) (lw: 6th st: rdn over 3f out: wknd over 1f out)....nk **6**
Wave Hill *(64) (PRHedger)* 6-8-9 MPerrett(6) (lw: hld up: nt clr run on ins 3f out to 2f out: wknd over 1f out)....2½ **7**
1613[5] Great Bear **(94)***(63) (RFJohnsonHoughton)* 3-8-8 TSprake(2) (bhd fnl 5f)....4 **8**
2103[2] Eurolink the Rebel (USA) **(80)***(66) (RAkehurst)* 3-9-1 SSanders(1) (4th st: wknd over 2f out)..2 **9**
2661* Reprehend **(86)***(57) (RHannon)* 4-9-2 4x RPerham(5) (5th st: wknd over 2f out)....1¼ **10**

7/2 Shifting Moon, **9/2** MELLOTTIE (3/1-5/1), **5/1** Eurolink the Rebel (USA), **13/2** Great Bear, **7/1** Reprehend (op 9/2), Blockade (USA), **12/1** Second Chance (IRE), **20/1** Dontforget Insight (IRE), **33/1** Chairmans Choice, Wave Hill, CSF £18.81 TOTE £6.20: £2.40 £1.40 £2.40 (£8.70) Trio £41.00 OWNER Mrs J. G. Fulton (SALTBURN) BRED Mrs G. R. Reveley and Partners 10 Rn
1m 37.84 (0.24) SF: 80/67/70/58/59/63/46/37/40/39
WEIGHT FOR AGE 3yo-8lb
Shifting Moon clmd TRobertHindle £12000

2767 RICHARD BAERLEIN MAIDEN STKS (2-Y.O) (Class D) £7,067.50 (£2,140.00: £1,045.00: £497.50) 6f Stalls: Low GOING minus 0.22 sec per fur (GF) 4-55 (4-58)

Charwelton *(76t) (PFICole)* 2-8-9 TQuinn(7) (unf: a.p: hrd rdn & carried rt over 1f out: led ins fnl f: r.o wl)....— **1**
Raed *(80+)*(Fav)*(PTWalwyn)* 2-9-0 WCarson(3) (w'like: scope: rdn & lost pl over 2f out: rallied & hung rt over 1f out: rn green)....½ **2**
Brandon Magic *(79) (IABalding)* 2-9-0 LDettori(2) (w'like: scope: w ldr: led 4f out: hrd rdn & edgd rt over 1f out: hdd ins fnl f: unable qckn)....nk **3**
Parsis (USA) *(68) (LadyHerries)* 2-9-0 JO'Dwyer(6) (w'like: scope: s.s: hdwy over 2f out: wknd over 1f out)....4 **4**
Abundant *(65) (BGubby)* 2-9-0 BDoyle(1) (leggy: lw: led 2f: rdn over 2f out: wknd over 1f out)....1¼ **5**
Nakhal *(65) (DJGMurraySmith)* 2-9-0 JWeaver(9) (leggy: scope: lw: s.s: a bhd)....s.h **6**
Singing Patriarch (IRE) *(65) (JLDunlop)* 2-9-0 SWhitworth(8) (unf: hld up: rdn over 1f out: sn wknd)....hd **7**

5/2 Raed (op 6/4), **3/1** Parsis (USA), **9/2** Brandon Magic, **7/1** CHARWELTON, Singing Patriarch (IRE) (op 4/1), **12/1** Abundant, **14/1** Nakhal, CSF £22.92 TOTE £8.50: £3.30 £1.70 (£13.20) Trio £8.90 OWNER Mr Bernard Gover (WHATCOMBE) 7 Rn 1m 12.99 (2.79) SF: 35/39/38/27/24/24/24

2768 TRUNDLE H'CAP (0-90) (3-Y.O+) (Class C) £7,570.00 (£2,260.00: £1,080.00: £490.00) 1m 4f Stalls: Low GOING minus 0.22 sec per fur (GF) 5-25 (5-26)

2379[5] **Progression (54)***(74) (PCHaslam)* 4-7-2b(5) MBaird(4) (hdwy over 4f out: 6th st: led over 1f out: r.o wl)....— **1**
1853[7] Proton **(73)***(84) (RAkehurst)* 5-8-12 JWeaver(9) (3rd st: rdn over 2f out: unable qckn)....7 **2**
1853[12] Mystic Hill **(89)***(97) (RCharlton)* 4-9-11 (3) SSanders(2) (4th st: led 3f out tl over 1f out: one pce)....2 **3**
1514[16] Niknaks Nephew **(70)***(78) (DJSffrenchDavis)* 3-7-6 (5) MHenry(5) (5th st: hrd rdn & lost pl over 3f out: r.o one pce fnl 2f)....hd **4**
2599[6] Global Dancer **(70)***(76) (SDow)* 4-8-2 (7) ADaly(3) (led over 8f: wknd over 1f out)....1¾ **5**
2433[2] Boloardo **(67)***(67) (CEBrittain)* 6-8-6 BDoyle(6) (2nd st: led over 3f out: sn hdd: wknd over 1f out)....4 **6**
2530[11] Well Arranged (IRE) **(70)***(70) (RAkehurst)* 4-8-9 TQuinn(1) (a bhd)....nk **7**
2289[2] Fairy Knight **(75)***(73) (RHannon)* 3-8-2 MFenton(8) (lw: hdwy over 6f out: wknd over 3f out).1¼ **8**
2599[2] Benfleet **(82)***(79)*(Fav)*(RWArmstrong)* 4-9-7 WCarson(7) (a bhd)....1¼ **9**
LONG HANDICAP Progression 7-4

11/4 Benfleet, **9/2** Mystic Hill, **5/1** Fairy Knight (7/2-11/2), **13/2** Boloardo, **7/1** Proton, Global Dancer, **14/1** Well Arranged (IRE), **16/1** Niknaks Nephew, **33/1** PROGRESSION, CSF £217.45 CT £1,130.58 TOTE £28.70: £4.50 £2.20 £1.90 (£71.40) Trio £134.60 OWNER Mr Alex Gorrie (MIDDLEHAM) 9 Rn 2m 34.69 (2.69) SF: 43/53/66/35/45/36/39/30/48
WEIGHT FOR AGE 3yo-12lb

T/Jkpt: Not won; £38,178.26 to Lingfield 30/7/95. T/Plpt: £70.10 (695.08 Tckts). T/Qdpt: £18.40 (31.25 Tckts). AK

2396-**HAMILTON (R-H)**
Saturday July 29th (Firm)
WEATHER: sunny WIND: almost nil

2769 BURNBANK (S) STKS (3-Y.O+) (Class G) £2,423.00 (£678.00: £329.00)
1m 65y Stalls: High GOING minus 0.61 sec per fur (F) 6-35 (6-37)

2102[7] **Rock Foundation (62)***(61) (PCHaslam)* 3-8-12 TWilliams(2) (lw: swtg: hld up: led over 2f out: shkn up & sn qcknd clr: easily)......— 1
2587[10] Just Whistle **(47)***(50) (CWThornton)* 3-8-7 NConnorton(1) (outpcd & bhd tl hdwy & swtchd over 2f out: styd on wl towards fin)......3 2
2620[2] Battle Colours (IRE) **(50)***(54)*(Fav)*(DonEnricoIncisa)* 6-9-6 KimTinkler(3) (lw: chsd ldrs: effrt 3f out: one pce)......¾ 3
2304[3] Ricana **(39)***(39) (WTKemp)* 3-8-4 (3) PMcCabe(6) (cl up: rdn over 3f out: outpcd fnl 2f)......5 4
2396[9] Sylvan Celebration **(15)***(34) (MissLAPerratt)* 4-9-1 JFanning(7) (cl up: rdn over 3f out: wknd over 2f out)......2½ 5
2304[6] Valley of Time (FR) **(23)***(34) (DANolan)* 7-8-10 (5) VHalliday(9) (led tl hdd over 2f out: sn btn) nk 6
2165[8] Venture Fourth **(21)***(35) (EJAlston)* 6-9-6 AMackay(5) (hld up: hdwy ½-wy: rdn & no ex fnl 2½f)......1¾ 7
2396[10] Drumdonna (IRE) **(44)***(24) (PBeaumont)* 5-8-8 (7) MCotton(8) (b: chsd ldrs 5f: wknd)......3½ 8
Hod-Mod (IRE) *(21) (MissZAGreen)* 5-9-6 JLowe(4) (wl outpcd fnl 3f)......4 9

6/4 Battle Colours (IRE), **2/1** ROCK FOUNDATION, **7/1** Ricana, **9/1** Just Whistle (op 6/1), **20/1** Drumdonna (IRE), **33/1** Venture Fourth, **66/1** Valley of Time (FR), Sylvan Celebration, **100/1** Hod-Mod (IRE), CSF £17.07 TOTE £3.40: £1.30 £2.30 £1.10 (£10.80) Trio £9.00 OWNER Patrick Haslam Racing Club (MIDDLEHAM) BRED R. P. Williams 9 Rn 1m 46.3 (3.00) SF: 20/9/21/-/1/1/2/-/-
WEIGHT FOR AGE 3yo-8lb
Bt in 5,200 gns

2770 ROTHMANS ROYALS NORTH SOUTH CHALLENGE SERIES H'CAP (0-80) (3-Y.O) (Class D) £4,810.75 (£1,456.00: £710.50: £337.75)
1m 1f 36y Stalls: High GOING minus 0.61 sec per fur (F) 7-05 (7-06)

2589[2] **Three Arch Bridge (55)***(67) (MJohnston)* 3-8-3b TWilliams(6) (lw: chsd ldr: led over 2f out: all out)......— 1
2623* Hand Woven **(72)***(84)*(Fav)*(WJHaggas)* 3-9-3 (3) JStack(9) (a.p: effrt 3f out: styd on strly towards fin)......hd 2
2376[2] Break the Rules **(73)***(78) (MrsMReveley)* 3-9-7 KDarley(8) (lw: effrt ½-wy: styd on u.p: nt pce to chal)......4 3
2250[2] Opera Fan (IRE) **(58)***(59) (SirMarkPrescott)* 3-8-6 JLowe(2) (lw: bhd: effrt 5f out: hdwy 3f out: one pce fnl 3f)......2½ 4
2327[8] Boundary Express **(50)***(40) (EJAlston)* 3-7-12v AMackay(4) (led & sn clr: hdd over 2f out: sn btn)......6 5
2611[7] Teejay'n'aitch (IRE) **(51)***(37) (JSGoldie)* 3-7-13 JFanning(3) (bhd: effrt on outside 4f out: nvr able to chal)......2½ 6
2477[2] Persian Fayre **(68)***(36) (JBerry)* 3-9-2 JCarroll(5) (prom tl wknd fnl 3f)......10 7
2460[3] Ihtimaam (FR) **(70)***(36) (MrsASwinbank)* 3-9-4 NConnorton(1) (b: outpcd & bhd fnl 4f)......1½ 8
2476[6] Gospel Song **(67)***(26) (WTKemp)* 3-8-12b(3) PMcCabe(7) (in tch: rdn ½-wy: sn wknd)......3½ 9

4/1 Hand Woven, **9/2** Break the Rules, **5/1** Ihtimaam (FR), **11/2** Gospel Song, **6/1** THREE ARCH BRIDGE (op 4/1), Persian Fayre, **10/1** Opera Fan (IRE) (op 6/1), **20/1** Teejay'n'aitch (IRE), **33/1** Boundary Express, CSF £28.10 CT £106.77 TOTE £5.90: £1.70 £1.90 £1.80 (£14.50) Trio £16.90 OWNER Mr R. N. Pennell (MIDDLEHAM) BRED R. Taylor 9 Rn
1m 54.2 (-0.10) SF: 40/57/51/32/13/10/9/9/-

2771 WESTWOOD MAIDEN STKS (2-Y.O) (Class D) £3,846.35 (£1,164.80: £568.90: £270.95) **6f 5y** Stalls: Low GOING minus 0.61 sec per fur (F) 7-35 (7-35)

2283[10] **Classic Victory** *(85?) (SCWilliams)* 2-9-0 AMackay(1) (lw: mde all: rdn & styd on wl fnl f)....— 1
1620[8] Larghetto (IRE) *(78)*(Fav)*(JBerry)* 2-9-0 JCarroll(3) (lw: trckd ldrs: hdwy 2f out: chsng wnr appr fnl f: nt qckn)......2½ 2
1919[2] Meeting Point *(65) (MrsMReveley)* 2-8-9 KDarley(4) (trckd wnr: chal 2f out: sn rdn & fnd nil)..3 3
2542[4] Spirito Libro (USA) *(65) (SirMarkPrescott)* 2-8-9 JLowe(2) (lw: chsd ldrs tl outpcd ½-wy: n.d after)......hd 4

9/4 Larghetto (IRE), **5/2** CLASSIC VICTORY (3/1-2/1), **3/1** Spirito Libro (USA), **4/1** Meeting Point, CSF £7.33 TOTE £5.10 (£6.80) OWNER Classic Bloodstock Plc (NEWMARKET) BRED G. King and Genesis Green Stud Ltd 4 Rn 1m 11.5 (1.50) SF: 25/18/5/5

2772 HORSELL ANITEC H'CAP (0-70) (3-Y.O+ F & M) (Class E) £3,793.70 (£1,148.60: £560.80: £266.90) **6f 5y** Stalls: Low GOING minus 0.61 sec per fur (F) 8-05 (8-07)

2461 13 **Suedoro (40)***(48) (RMMcKellar)* 5-7-12 JFanning(1) (mde most: styd on wl fnl f)...— 1
2502 12 Tutu Sixtysix **(38)***(41) (DonEnricoIncisa)* 4-7-10v KimTinkler(6) (lw: a.p: hdwy & ev ch over 1f out: nt qckn)...1¾ 2
2461 8 Miss Pigalle **(37)***(38) (MissLAPerratt)* 4-7-9b AMackay(4) (b: dwlt: hdwy 2f out: styd on wl towards fin)...¾ 3
2736 9 Glow of Hope **(35)***(32)(RMMcKellar)* 5-7-7 ClaireBalding(2) (in tch: hdwy 2f out: nt qckn fnl f)1¾ 4
2736 2 Kenesha (IRE) **(47)***(29) (DANolan)* 5-8-0b(5)ow1 VHalliday(5) (sn drvn along: nvr trbld ldrs)...5 5
2463 7 Sunday Mail Too (IRE) **(41)***(22) (MissLAPerratt)* 3-7-7b JLowe(7) (lw: disp ld: hung rt & hdd ½-wy: grad wknd)...¾ 6
2645 5 Miss Whittingham (IRE) **(52)***(26)*(Fav)*(JBerry)* 5-8-10 JCarroll(3) (outpcd after 2f: n.d after)...3 7
2163 9 Marjorie's Memory (IRE) **(70)***(37) (MrsASwinbank)* 4-10-0 NConnorton(8) (prom 4f)...2½ 8
2478 6 Hutchies Lady **(44)***(3) (RMMcKellar)* 3-7-10bow3 TWilliams(9) (outpcd & bhd fr ½-wy)...1¾ 9
LONG HANDICAP Sunday Mail Too (IRE) 7-6 Glow of Hope 7-2 Hutchies Lady 7-6

4/1 Miss Whittingham (IRE), **9/2** Tutu Sixtysix (3/1-5/1), Kenesha (IRE), **13/2** SUEDORO (4/1-7/1), **9/1** Miss Pigalle, Sunday Mail Too (IRE), **10/1** Glow of Hope (op 6/1), **14/1** Marjorie's Memory (IRE), **33/1** Hutchies Lady, CSF £31.00 CT £209.18 TOTE £7.20: £2.00 £1.40 £2.20 (£15.80) Trio £23.50 OWNER Mr Ray Vardy (LESMAHAGOW) BRED R. Vardy 9 Rn
1m 10.6 (0.60) SF: 23/16/13/7/4/-/1/12/-
WEIGHT FOR AGE 3yo-6lb

2773 RUTHERGLEN MAIDEN AUCTION STKS (2-Y.O) (Class F) £2,745.00 (£770.00: £375.00) **5f 4y** Stalls: Low GOING minus 0.61 sec per fur (F) 8-35 (8-36)

1798 9 **Wilfull Lad (IRE)** *(72) (MartynMeade)* 2-8-10 VSlattery(1) (lw: chsd ldrs: led ins fnl f: r.o)...— 1
2483 3 Power Don *(62)*(Fav)*(WGMTurner)* 2-8-3 (3) PMcCabe(2) (disp ld tl led 2f out: edgd rt: hdd ins fnl f: kpt on)...1¾ 2
2354 4 Valise *(42) (MrsMReveley)* 2-8-5 KDarley(3) (outpcd: hdwy u.p 2f out: no imp)...6 3
2608 7 Monkey Zanty (IRE) *(35) (JBerry)* 2-8-3 ow2 JCarroll(7) (lw: disp ld 3f: sn rdn & btn)...1 4
Ready Teddy (IRE) *(33) (MissLAPerratt)* 2-8-5 JLowe(6) (w'like: bkwd: drvn along thrght: nvr trbld ldrs)...2 5
2371 3 Superfrills *(MissLCSiddall)* 2-7-11 TWilliams(4) (disp ld to ½-wy: eased whn btn fnl f)...20 6

5/4 Power Don, **7/2** Superfrills, **9/2** Valise, **8/1** Monkey Zanty (IRE), **10/1** WILFULL LAD (IRE), **33/1** Ready Teddy (IRE), CSF £21.34 TOTE £17.50: £7.80 £1.10 (£15.10) OWNER Mr R G Hardie & Mr P H Ling (MALMESBURY) BRED John I. O'Byrne 6 Rn 59.0 secs (0.70) SF: 31/21/1/-/-/-

2774 PENROSE HILL H'CAP (0-70) (3-Y.O+) (Class E) £3,811.25 (£1,154.00: £563.50: £268.25) **1m 3f 16y** Stalls: High GOING minus 0.61 sec per fur (F) 9-05 (9-07)

2356 5 **Eden Dancer (54)***(65) (MrsMReveley)* 3-9-1 KDarley(5) (mde all: rdn along & r.o wl fnl 3f)..— 1
2396 2 Red Spectacle (IRE) **(51)***(61)*(Fav)*(PCHaslam)* 3-8-9 (3) JStack(2) (lw: dwlt: sn trckng ldrs: chal over 2f out: r.o wl)...½ 2
2353 4 Jackmanii **(49)***(48) (WTKemp)* 3-8-10b NConnorton(4) (trckd ldr: effrt over 3f out: sn outpcd)..8 3
2356 3 Highfield Fizz **(60)***(47) (CWFairhurst)* 3-9-7 JLowe(6) (in tch tl outpcd fnl 3f)...8 4
1824 13 Elite Number (USA) **(40)** *(RMMcKellar)* 3-8-1 TWilliams(3) (b: plld hrd: rdn & wknd 5f out: t.o)...dist 5

7/4 Red Spectacle (IRE), **3/1** Highfield Fizz, Jackmanii, **5/1** EDEN DANCER, **16/1** Elite Number (USA), CSF £13.15 TOTE £6.10: £2.40 £1.80 (£4.70) OWNER Mr Ashley Graham (SALTBURN) BRED B. D. Cantle 5 Rn 2m 25.2 (6.20) SF: 8/4/-/-/-
T/Plpt: £104.10 (69.56 Tckts). T/Qdpt: £37.20 (0.1 Tckts); £45.36 to Lingfield 30/7/95 AA

2744-NEWMARKET (R-H)
Saturday July 29th (Good to firm)
WEATHER: sunny WIND: almost nil

2775 COLMAN'S SAUCES CONDITIONS STKS (2-Y.O) (Class C) £5,298.80 (£1,908.80: £914.40: £372.00: £146.00)
7f (July) Stalls: Low GOING minus 0.37 sec per fur (F) 2-10 (2-11)

2283* **Mawwal (USA)** *(85+)*(Fav)*(RWArmstrong)* 2-9-1 BThomson(5) (lw: mde all: shkn up & hld on fnl f)...— 1

2454* Fag End (IRE) *(79) (MHTompkins)* 2-8-12 PRobinson(3) (chsd wnr: rdn over 2f out: no ex ins fnl f) 1¼ 2
2581* Exalted (IRE) *(80) (SirMarkPrescott)* 2-9-1 WWoods(2) (outpcd: hdwy wl over 1f out: r.o) .....¾ 3
2454[3] Semper (IRE) *(60) (LMCumani)* 2-9-1 WRyan(1) (lw: wl bhd tl r.o appr fnl f) 9 4
2183* Classic Flyer (IRE) *(37) (SCWilliams)* 2-8-10 AMackay(4) (lw: prom over 3f: sn rdn & wknd) ..8 5

Evens MAWWAL (USA), **7/2** Classic Flyer (IRE), **6/1** Exalted (IRE) (op 4/1), Fag End (IRE), **12/1** Semper (IRE) (8/1-14/1), CSF £6.53 TOTE £1.80 £1.30 £1.40 (£4.00) OWNER Mr Hamdan Al Maktoum (NEWMARKET) BRED Shadwell Estate Co., Ltd. and Shadwell Farm Inc. 5 Rn
1m 26.64 (2.24) SF: 42/36/37/17/-

2776 FLORA CLAIMING STKS (3-Y.O) (Class D) £4,581.00 (£1,368.00: £654.00: £297.00) **7f (July)** Stalls: Low GOING minus 0.37 sec per fur (F) 2-40 (2-42)

2718[5] **Delight of Dawn (67)***(76) (KTIvory)* 3-8-1 (7) CScally(8) (b: bhd: hdwy 2f out: led over 1f out: rdn out) ....— 1
2493[3] Petomi **(70)***(66) (SirMarkPrescott)* 3-8-2 CNutter(3) (swtg: dwlt: sn trckng ldrs: rdn & ev ch over 1f out: edgd rt & r.o) 1¾ 2
1549[3] By The Bay **(66)***(69) (BWHills)* 3-8-6 WRyan(4) (swtg: in tch: hdwy over 1f out: nrst fin) ....nk 3
1956* Okay Baby (IRE) **(48)***(63) (MHTompkins)* 3-8-0 PRobinson(7) (led over 5f: one pce) ....nk 4
2108[9] Cats Bottom **(67)***(68)*(Fav)*(DJSCosgrove)* 3-8-8 MRimmer(9) (swtg: bhd: hdwy wl over 1f out: no imp fnl f) 1¼ 5
2102[8] Contract Venture (IRE) **(62)***(61) (WJarvis)* 3-8-3b AMcGlone(6) (trckd ldrs: ev ch over 1f out: nt qckn fnl f) ....¾ 6
2532[8] Cannizaro (IRE) **(50)***(37) (RJRWilliams)* 3-8-6 WWoods(1) (lw: prom 4f) 12 7
1544[7] Jalwa (USA) **(70)***(11) (KTIvory)* 3-8-8 MWigham(2) (swtg: prom over 3f) 12 8
1654[6] Sapphire Son (IRE) **(60)***(6) (CNWilliams)* 3-8-2v(3) DRMcCabe(5) (lw: chsd ldr over 4f)............1 9

7/2 Cats Bottom, **9/2** By The Bay, **11/2** Petomi, **13/2** Sapphire Son (IRE), **7/1** Okay Baby (IRE), **8/1** DELIGHT OF DAWN, **12/1** Contract Venture (IRE) (op 8/1), **14/1** Cannizaro (IRE), **20/1** Jalwa (USA), CSF £45.49 TOTE £12.80: £3.20 £1.90 £1.90 (£54.20) Trio £27.90 OWNER Mr K. T. Ivory (RADLETT) BRED John Hayter 9 Rn 1m 26.04 (1.64) SF: 43/33/36/30/35/28/4/-/-

2777 E.B.F. COLMAN'S MUSTARD MAIDEN STKS (2-Y.O) (Class D) £4,425.00 (£1,320.00: £630.00: £285.00) **6f (July)** Stalls: Low GOING minus 0.37 sec per fur (F) 3-10 (3-11)

Witch of Fife (USA) *(71+) (BWHills)* 2-8-9 BThomson(3) (lengthy: unf: plld hrd: trckd ldrs: rdn to ld ins fnl f) ....— 1
1726[6] Surtees *(73)*(Fav)*(RCharlton)* 2-9-0 WRyan(5) (led after 1f tl ins fnl f: rdn & r.o) 1¼ 2
Sava River (IRE) *(69+) (MRStoute)* 2-9-0 PaulEddery(4) (scope: prom: ev ch over 1f out: no ex fnl f) 1½ 3
Quality (IRE) *(67+) (WAO'Gorman)* 2-9-0 EmmaO'Gorman(2) (str: bit bkwd: trckd ldrs: kpt on ins fnl f) ....¾ 4
Cowboy Dreams (IRE) *(32) (MHTompkins)* 2-9-0 PRobinson(1) (unf: scope: led 1f: wknd over 2f out) 13 5

4/6 Surtees, **7/2** Sava River (IRE) (5/2-4/1), **6/1** WITCH OF FIFE (USA) (op 4/1), **14/1** Cowboy Dreams (IRE) (10/1-16/1), **16/1** Quality (IRE), CSF £10.09 TOTE £5.70: £1.80 £1.10 (£2.70) OWNER Sheikh Mohammed (LAMBOURN) BRED Darley Stud Management Inc 5 Rn
1m 14.71 (3.21) SF: 19/21/17/15/-

2778 P.G. TIPS H'CAP (0-80) (3-Y.O) (Class D) £4,659.00 (£1,392.00: £666.00: £303.00) **1m (July)** Stalls: Low GOING minus 0.37 sec per fur (F) 3-45 (3-47)

1512[5] **Noble Neptune (55)***(68) (WJMusson)* 3-7-13 GCarter(5) (hld up: hdwy to ld over 1f out: rdn out) ....— 1
2531[3] Nordic Breeze (IRE) **(71)***(83) (ABailey)* 3-9-1 MWigham(10) (hld up: hdwy over 2f out: ev ch over 1f out: unable qckn) ....nk 2
1550[4] Make Time **(67)***(69) (JPearce)* 3-8-11 GBardwell(9) (bhd: gd hdwy over 1f out: nrst fin)...........5 3
2405* Donna Viola **(77)***(77)*(Fav)*(CFWall)* 3-9-7 WWoods(6) (chsd ldr tl led over 3f out: hdd over 1f out: no ex) 1 4
1859* Princess Danielle **(57)***(50) (CCElsey)* 3-8-1 CRutter(4) (chsd ldrs: swtchd over 3f out: wandered 2f out: sn btn)....3½ 5
1825[11] Mr Christie **(59)***(51) (MissLCSiddall)* 3-8-3 DeanMcKeown(7) (swtg: prom over 5f) ....½ 6
2613[6] Sarasota Storm **(63)***(52) (MBell)* 3-8-7 KFallon(1) (lw: led: sn pushed along: hdd over 3f out: sn btn) 1¾ 7
2376[5] Sheama (USA) **(67)***(51) (WJarvis)* 3-8-11b PaulEddery(3) (plld hrd: trckd ldrs 5f) 2½ 8

1549[6] Merrie le Bow **(52)***(26) (PatMitchell)* 3-7-5 (5) NVarley(8) (bhd fnl 3f)....................5 9
2500* Mountgate **(71)** *(MPBielby)* 3-8-12 (3) DRMcCabe(2) (lw: dwlt & stmbld s: hld up: clipped heels & uns rdr 2f out)........................ U

9/4 Donna Viola, **11/2** Nordic Breeze (IRE), **13/2** Mountgate, **8/1** Princess Danielle, **9/1** Make Time, Sarasota Storm, **14/1** Sheama (USA), NOBLE NEPTUNE, **20/1** Mr Christie, **33/1** Merrie le Bow, CSF £77.98 CT £653.76 TOTE £20.00: £3.60 £2.00 £2.70 (£67.80) Trio £45.10 OWNER Mrs Rita Brown (NEWMARKET) BRED E. A. Badger 10 Rn 1m 40.48 (2.78) SF: 26/41/27/35/8/9/10/9/-/-

2779 COLMAN'S OF NORWICH NURSERY H'CAP (2-Y.O) (Class C)
£18,600.00 (£5,550.00: £2,650.00: £1,200.00)
6f (July) Stalls: Low GOING minus 0.37 sec per fur (F) 4-15 (4-17)

1838[11] **Rabican (IRE)** *(87) (GCBravery)* 2-8-8 (3) DRMcCabe(1) (sn pushed along & bhd: gd hdwy 2f out: led ins fnl f: rdn out).................— 1
2136[2] Forentia *(92) (JRFanshawe)* 2-9-7 WRyan(4) (hld up: hdwy to ld 2f out: hdd & nt qckn ins fnl f: sddle slipped)..................1¾ 2
1992* Flying North (IRE) *(79) (MrsMReveley)* 2-8-8 DeanMcKeown(10) (lw: hld up: hdwy over 2f out: r.o ins fnl f)..................s.h 3
2489[2] Rhumba Dancer *(77) (RHannon)* 2-8-5 (7) DaneO'Neill(6) (in tch: bmpd after 1f: plld out over 1f out: r.o)..................2½ 4
2182* Ned Al Sheeba *(82) (WJHaggas)* 2-9-5 MHills(8) (lw: chsd ldrs: wnt lft over 1f out: no imp) ...¾ 5
2085[7] Foreman *(57) (WAO'Gorman)* 2-7-12b FNorton(11) (swtg: w ldrs: ev ch 2f out: nt qckn) 1¼ 6
2508* Stop Play (IRE) *(63)*(Fav)*(MHTompkins)* 2-8-5 PRobinson(3) (plld hrd: chsd ldrs: btn whn hmpd wl over 1f out)..................½ 7
2435* Bedside Mail *(69) (JMPEustace)* 2-9-5 AMcGlone(2) (swtg: chsd ldrs 4f: sn btn & eased) 3 8
2335* Welsh Mountain *(55) (MJHeaton-Ellis)* 2-8-10 WWoods(9) (led 2f: ev ch 2f out: sn wknd).......2 9
2403* Fenna *(40) (SPCWoods)* 2-7-9 (5) NVarley(5) (chsd ldrs: bmpd after 1f: btn whn hmpd wl over 1f out)..................1¾ 10
2371* Evening Chime (USA) *(45) (MrsJRRamsden)* 2-8-13 KFallon(7) (lw: led after 2f tl 2f out: sn hmpd & bhd)..................3 11

3/1 Stop Play (IRE), **9/2** Ned Al Sheeba, **11/2** Evening Chime (USA), **8/1** Flying North (IRE), RABICAN (IRE), **9/1** Fenna, **10/1** Foreman, **12/1** Forentia, **14/1** Welsh Mountain, Rhumba Dancer, Bedside Mail, CSF £94.29 CT £734.70 TOTE £12.30: £3.10 £3.00 £2.50 (£67.60) Trio £165.30 OWNER Mrs Nicolas Kairis (NEWMARKET) BRED Clarents Racing Ltd 11 Rn
1m 13.3 (1.80) SF: 45/22/35/-/30/40/8/32/16/-/10
STEWARDS' ENQUIRY Hills susp. 7-9/8/95 (careless riding).

2780 NGK SPARK PLUGS H'CAP (0-90) (3-Y.O+) (Class C) £6,160.00 (£1,840.00: £880.00: £400.00) **1m 2f (July)** Stalls: High GOING minus 0.37 sec (F) 4-45 (4-47)

2008[7] **Pursuit of Glory (75)***(89) (CACyzer)* 4-9-7 KFallon(3) (swtg: chsd ldr: rdn to ld 1f out: hld on wl)..................— 1
2240[9] Out on a Promise (IRE) **(77)***(89) (GWragg)* 3-8-13 MHills(1) (lw: chsd ldrs: rdn 4f out: ev ch 1f out: unable qckn ins fnl f)..................1¼ 2
2525[6] Jadwal (USA) **(78)***(88) (DMorley)* 3-9-0 BThomson(9) (hld up: hdwy 2f out: r.o) 1½ 3
2577[D] Ball Gown **(76)***(84)*(Fav)*(DTThom)* 5-9-5 (3) DRMcCabe(8) (hld up & wl bhd: hdwy over 2f out: btn fnl f)..................1¼ 4
2616[8] Nigel's Lad (IRE) **(81)***(85) (PCHaslam)* 3-9-3 GCarter(2) (led & sn clr: rdn over 2f out: wknd & hdd 1f out)..................2½ 5
2207[2] Action Jackson **(68)***(69) (BJMcMath)* 3-8-4 EJohnson(4) (swtg: chsd ldrs: rdn 4f out: sn btn)..................1½ 6
2457[6] Virtual Reality **(78)***(79) (AHide)* 4-9-10 WWoods(6) (swtg: hld up & wl bhd: effrt over 2f out: nvr plcd to chal)..................nk 7
813[17] Divina Mia **(70)***(65) (JWHills)* 3-8-6 PaulEddery(5) (a bhd)..................3½ 8

2/1 Ball Gown, **3/1** Virtual Reality, **9/2** Out on a Promise (IRE), **8/1** Action Jackson, **12/1** PURSUIT OF GLORY, Nigel's Lad (IRE), **14/1** Jadwal (USA), **25/1** Divina Mia, CSF £58.95 CT £692.59 TOTE £17.60: £3.50 £1.50 £2.20 (£25.10) Trio £76.90 OWNER Mr R. M. Cyzer (HORSHAM) BRED Gerald W. Leigh 8 Rn 2m 8.05 (5.65) SF: 30/20/19/25/16/-/20/-
WEIGHT FOR AGE 3yo-10lb

2781 JIF LEMON H'CAP (0-70) (3-Y.O) (Class E) £4,425.00 (£1,320.00: £630.00: £285.00) **1m 4f (July)** Stalls: Low GOING minus 0.37 sec per fur (F) 5-20 (5-21)

2282[2] **Silktail (IRE) (50)***(61+)*(Fav)*(JohnBerry)* 3-8-3 GCarter(2) (swtg: trckd ldrs: chal on bit over 2f out: led over 1f out: easily)..................— 1

978[8] Istabraq (IRE) **(68)**_(77) (JHMGosden)_ 3-9-7 AMcGlone(4) (chsd ldr tl led 4f out: rdn & hdd over 1f out: no ch w wnr)....1½ **2**
1372[12] Rock Group **(53)**_(62) (JPearce)_ 3-8-6 GBardwell(6) (lw: hld up: hdwy over 3f out: rdn & ev ch over 1f out: one pce)....nk **3**
2532[3] Night Time **(65)**_(56) (RHannon)_ 3-8-11 (7) DaneO'Neill(1) (lw: chsd ldrs tl rdn & wknd over 3f out)....13 **4**
1978[9] Admiral's Guest (IRE) **(57)**_(48) (GHarwood)_ 3-8-10 AClark(7) (lw: prom: rdn 4f out: sn wknd).½ **5**
1922[3] Mill Thyme **(59)**_(34) (MrsMReveley)_ 3-8-12 DeanMcKeown(3) (led 8f: sn bhd)....12 **6**
1663[8] Lord Palmerston (USA) **(62)**_(31) (PFICole)_ 3-9-1 KFallon(5) (b: swtg: s.i.s: a bhd)....4 **7**

15/8 SILKTAIL (IRE), **4/1** Istabraq (IRE) (3/1-9/2), **9/2** Night Time, **6/1** Admiral's Guest (IRE), **8/1** Mill Thyme, **12/1** Lord Palmerston (USA), **16/1** Rock Group, CSF £9.13 TOTE £2.80: £1.60 £2.40 (£4.50) OWNER Mrs Monica Caine (NEWMARKET) BRED Sheikh Mohammed bin Rashid al Maktoum 7 Rn 2m 33.64 (4.94) SF: 26/42/27/21/13/-/-

T/Plpt: £285.50 (77.08 Tckts). T/Qdpt: £317.90 (0.65 Tckts); £150.40 to Lingfield 30/7/95 Dk

2756-THIRSK (L-H)
Saturday July 29th (Firm)
WEATHER: fine & sunny WIND: slt half bhd

2782
E.B.F. SUTTON MAIDEN STKS (2-Y.O) (Class D) £4,509.50 (£1,346.00: £643.00: £291.50) **5f** Stalls: Centre GOING minus 0.40 sec per fur (F) 2-20 (2-21)

1137[4] **Hear The Music (IRE)** _(73)_(Fav)_(BWHills)_ 2-8-4 (5) JDSmith(8) (swtg: a.p: led 2f out: sn rdn clr: r.o)....— **1**
2666[2] Arrhythmic (IRE) _(67) (MBrittain)_ 2-8-6 (3) PMcCabe(9) (hld up: hdwy bel dist: rdn & r.o wl fnl f)....1¾ **2**
2275[5] Crissem (IRE) _(64) (RHollinshead)_ 2-8-9 RHills(4) (slt ld 3f: rdn over 1f out: kpt on nr fin)....1 **3**
Oh Whataknight _(51+) (RMWhitaker)_ 2-8-9 ACulhane(6) (w'like: scope: bkwd: s.s: rn green: hdwy over 1f out: nt rch ldrs)....4 **4**
Szloto _(51) (TDBarron)_ 2-9-0 JFortune(2) (w'like: swtg: bhd & pushed along: hdwy over 1f out: nvr nrr)....1¾ **5**
2483[7] Krishan Power _(41) (MWEasterby)_ 2-9-0 SMaloney(11) (in tch stands' side tl wknd wl over 1f out)....3 **6**
1652[8] Good To Talk _(37) (MHEasterby)_ 2-9-0 MBirch(1) (bit bkwd: chsd ldrs over 3f)....1¼ **7**
_1879[3]_ Chillam _(33) (JPLeigh)_ 2-9-0 GHind(7) (led 3f: sn rdn & wknd)....1¼ **8**
2619[9] Golden Tyke (IRE) _(33) (MDHammond)_ 2-9-0 DaleGibson(5) (racd keenly: w ldrs 3f: sn rdn & outpcd)....s.h **9**
Redbrook Lady _(28) (SGNorton)_ 2-8-9 TWilliams(3) (scope: bit bkwd: dwlt: effrt & rdn 2f out: wknd appr fnl f)....s.h **10**
Prince Mike (IRE) _(14) (JBerry)_ 2-9-0 SDWilliams(10) (w'like: leggy: bit bkwd: outpcd & bhd: t.o)....6 **11**

Evens HEAR THE MUSIC (IRE), **100/30** Arrhythmic (IRE), **9/1** Prince Mike (IRE), **11/1** Chillam, Crissem (IRE), **12/1** Golden Tyke (IRE), **14/1** Good To Talk, **16/1** Oh Whataknight, **20/1** Szloto, Krishan Power, **33/1** Redbrook Lady, CSF £5.65 TOTE £2.10: £1.40 £1.60 £2.40 (£3.10) Trio £7.80 OWNER Lady Harrison (LAMBOURN) BRED Gay O'Callaghan 11 Rn
58.4 secs (1.20) SF: 29/23/20/7/7/-/-/-/-/-/-

2783
COOPERS & LYBRAND CONDITIONS STKS (2-Y.O F) (Class C) £5,452.50 (£1,740.00: £832.50) **6f** Stalls: Centre GOING minus 0.40 sec (F) 2-50 (2-50)

2432[2] **Amaniy (USA)** _(83) (HThomsonJones)_ 2-9-0 RHills(3) (lw: hld up: led over 1f out: r.o: comf)— **1**
2412* Marjaana (IRE) _(80)_(Fav)_(PTWalwyn)_ 2-9-0 MBirch(2) (swtg: led tl hdd over 1f out: rdn & hung lft fnl f: no ex)....1¼ **2**
2523[4] Born A Lady _(74?) (NPLittmoden)_ 2-8-9 TGMcLaughlin(1) (hld up & bhd: shkn up to chal bel dist: unable qckn)....nk **3**

8/13 Marjaana (IRE), **13/8** AMANIY (USA), **11/1** Born A Lady, CSF £2.87 TOTE £2.30 (£1.10) OWNER Mr Hamdan Al Maktoum (NEWMARKET) BRED Shadwell Farm Inc 3 Rn 1m 15.4 (5.70)

2784
ROCOM LADIES (S) H'CAP (0-60) (3-Y.O+) (Class E) £3,959.00 (£1,187.00: £571.00: £111.00: £111.00) **6f** Stalls: Centre GOING minus 0.40 sec (F) 3-25 (3-27)

_2627[11]_ **Pretty Average (30)**_(38) (BRichmond)_ 5-9-4 (4) MrsMMorris(5) (bit bkwd: mde all: clr 2f out: hld on wl)....— **1**

24846 Dante's Rubicon (IRE) **(47)***(52) (JDBethell)* 4-10-11 MissEJohnsonHoughton(10) (a.p: rdn & kpt on towards fin) 1¼ 2
18287 Panther (IRE) **(57)***(58) (JHetherton)* 5-11-3 (4) MissAElsey(8) (hdwy 2f out: rdn & r.o wl ins fnl f) 1½ 3
26452 Murray's Mazda (IRE) **(42)***(43) (JLEyre)* 6-10-6 MissDianaJones(3) (swtg: hdwy 3f out: rdn over 1f out: one pce) ....¾ 4
24932 Brookhead Lady **(52)***(51) (PDEvans)* 4-10-12 (4) MrsSEddery(7) (b.nr fore: chsd ldrs: rdn over 1f out: nt pce to chal)....d.h 4
21623 Pakol (IRE) **(45)***(43) (MrsASwinbank)* 6-10-9 MrsAFarrell(18) (swtg: hdwy u.p over 1f out: nrst fin)....nk 6
26684 Lord Vivienne (IRE) **(42)***(37) (BSRothwell)* 6-9-13 (7) MissAlexMcCabe(1) (swtg: racd alone: sme hdwy fnl f: nvr nrr) 1 7
26279 Grey Toppa **(43)***(38) (NPLittmoden)* 4-10-3 (4) MrsDMcHale(11) (prom over 4f: rdn & outpcd)s.h 8
22285 Passion Sunday **(45)***(33) (LRLloyd-James)* 4-10-5 (4) MissADeniel(13) (b.hind: nvr nrr)....2½ 9
238314 Mu-Arrik **(52)***(40) (GROldroyd)* 7-10-9v(7) MissABycroft(16) (lw: nvr nr to chal)....nk 10
21417 Campaspe **(42)***(28) (JGFitzGerald)* 3-9-10 (4) MissERamsden(17) (swtg: a bhd)....½ 11
18436 Bill Moon **(31)***(17) (DTThom)* 9-9-9 MissJFeilden(4) (dwlt: a in rr) ....nk 12
245810 Invigilate **(53)***(37) (MartynWane)* 6-11-3 MrsLPearce(6) (dwlt: hdwy ½-wy: rdn & wknd appr fnl f) ....½ 13
23728 Malsisio **(28)***(11) (SGNorton)* 3-8-10 (4) MissKWright(14) (mid div: hmpd over 2f out: nvr nr to chal)....nk 14
25186 Make the Break **(48)***(31) (SCoathup)* 4-10-5b(7) MrsCWilliams(2) (in rr most of wy)....nk 15
207613 Christian Warrior **(32)***(5) (REPeacock)* 6-9-3v(7)ow9 MrsCPeacock(15) (b: spd over 3f) ....nk 16
25406 Tee Tee Too (IRE) **(53)***(13)*(Fav)*(PCHaslam)* 3-10-7 (4) MrsDKettlewell(9) (lw: outpcd & bhd: effrt u.p 2f out: eased whn btn appr fnl f: t.o)....8 17
22604 Oscar the Second (IRE) **(30)** *(CWFairhurst)* 5-9-4 (4) MrsSBosley(12) (spd to ½-wy: sn wknd: t.o)....2 18

LONG HANDICAP Malsisio 8-10

7/1 Tee Tee Too (IRE), **8/1** Murray's Mazda (IRE), Dante's Rubicon (IRE), Invigilate, **17/2** Pakol (IRE), Panther (IRE), **9/1** Lord Vivienne (IRE), **10/1** Brookhead Lady, **12/1** Campaspe, **14/1** Mu-Arrik, **16/1** Oscar the Second (IRE), Bill Moon, **20/1** PRETTY AVERAGE, Grey Toppa, **25/1** Christian Warrior, **33/1** Make the Break, Malsisio, Passion Sunday, CSF £168.00 CT £1,353.23 TOTE £90.00: £11.10 £2.20 £3.30 BL £1.00, MM £0.70 (£691.60) Trio Not won; £684.74 to Chester 30/7/95 OWNER Miss P. Hamilton (WELLINGORE) 18 Rn

1m 12.3 (2.60) SF: 26/40/46/31/39/31/25/26/21/28/10/5/25/-/19/-/-/-
WEIGHT FOR AGE 3yo-6lb
No bid

2785 BARCLAYS BANK H'CAP (0-80) (3-Y.O+) (Class D) £5,336.25 (£1;590.00: £757.50: £341.25)

1m 4f Stalls: High GOING minus 0.40 sec per fur (F) 4-00 (4-01)

2543* **Labibeh (USA) (80)***(95)*(Fav)*(JLDunlop)* 3-9-11 RHills(6) (led tl over 2f out: rdn to ld bel dist: styd on strly)....— 1
22386 Solomon's Dancer (USA) **(60)***(72) (WWHaigh)* 5-9-3 DaleGibson(2) (lw: hld up: effrt & 4th st: rdn & r.o ins fnl f) 2½ 2
2584* Ashover **(58)***(68) (TDBarron)* 5-9-1 JFortune(5) (a.p: 2nd st: led over 2f out to bel dist: hrd rdn: r.o) 1 3
24822 Phylian **(51)***(53) (SCWilliams)* 4-8-8 GHind(3) (chsd wnr 6f: 3rd st: rdn & wknd 2f out: eased whn btn)....6 4
25433 Doctor's Remedy **(37)***(18) (MrsJJordan)* 9-7-8bow1 JMarshall(4) (swtg: a bhd: 6th st: t.o fnl 3f)15 5
26634 First Bid **(66)** *(RMWhitaker)* 8-9-9 ACulhane(1) (lw: hld up: 5th st: broke down & p.u over 2f out) .... P

LONG HANDICAP Doctor's Remedy 7-1

5/4 LABIBEH (USA), **3/1** Ashover, **6/1** Solomon's Dancer (USA), Phylian, **7/1** First Bid (5/1-8/1), **20/1** Doctor's Remedy, CSF £8.83 TOTE £2.00: £1.40 £3.70 (£7.80) OWNER Mr Hamdan Al Maktoum (ARUNDEL) BRED Shadwell Farm Estate Co Ltd and Shadwell Farm Inc 6 Rn

2m 32.9 (2.90) SF: 57/46/42/27/-/-
WEIGHT FOR AGE 3yo-12lb

2786 SUN ALLIANCE MAIDEN H'CAP (0-70) (3-Y.O+) (Class E) £4,045.00 (£1,210.00: £580.00: £265.00) 6f Stalls: Centre GOING minus 0.40 sec per fur (F) 4-30 (4-35)

13806 **Statius (69)***(76)*(Fav)*(TDBarron)* 3-9-11 JFortune(3) (lw: a w ldrs: led over 2f out: rdn out)...— 1
24697 To the Roof (IRE) **(60)***(65) (PWHarris)* 3-9-2 MBirch(5) (bit bkwd: hld up: hdwy 2f out: ev ch whn faltered ins fnl f: nt rcvr)....¾ 2
26243 Michellisa **(51)***(51) (JDBethell)* 4-8-8 (5) JDSmith(1) (lw: a.p: hrd rdn bel dist: kpt on one pce) ..2 3
26242 Quilling **(70)***(69) (MDods)* 3-9-12v GHind(4) (lw: hld up: hdwy 2f out: hrd rdn & unable qckn fnl f)....hd 4

2624[4] Bali Tender **(37)***(30) (MWEasterby)* 4-7-6 (7) PFessey(8) (prom: led ½-wy: sn hdd: wknd appr fnl f) 2½ 5
2318[15] Hot Snap **(59)***(50) (CFWall)* 3-9-1 NCarlisle(6) (effrt u.p wl over 1f out: unable chal) ....½ 6
748[9] Anotherone to Note **(54)***(29) (NPLittmoden)* 4-9-2 TGMcLaughlin(2) (swtg: b: chsd ldrs tl rdn & wknd wl over 1f out) 6 7
2239[9] Sooty (IRE) **(55)***(21) (HThomsonJones)* 3-8-11 RHills(7) (lw: chsd ldrs over 4f: rdn & wknd) 3½ 8
Hoswinoname **(37)** *(DNicholls)* 3-7-7b JMarshall(9) (swtg: bkwd: plld hrd: led 3f: wknd wl over 1f out: t.o) 14 9

LONG HANDICAP Hoswinoname 7-5

5/2 STATIUS, **7/2** Quilling, **4/1** Michellisa, **13/2** Bali Tender, **10/1** To the Roof (IRE), Hot Snap (op 20/1), Sooty (IRE), **20/1** Anotherone to Note, **33/1** Hoswinoname, CSF £25.70 CT £90.02 TOTE £2.90: £1.50 £3.10 £1.30 (£30.60) Trio £38.50 OWNER Mr Alex Gorrie (THIRSK) BRED Will Edmeades Bloodstock 9 Rn 1m 10.6 (0.90) SF: 52/41/33/45/12/26/11/-/-
WEIGHT FOR AGE 3yo-6lb

2787 LORDS TAVERNERS MAIDEN STKS (3-Y.O F) (Class D) £3,752.50 (£1,120.00: £535.00: £242.50) 7f Stalls: Low GOING minus 0.40 sec per fur (F) 5-00 (5-03)

2519[2] **Banner (USA) (73)***(81) (BWHills)* 3-8-6 (5) JDSmith(2) (swtg: mde all: rdn bel dist: kpt on gamely nr fin) ....— 1
2393[2] Azdihaar (USA) **(74)***(80)*(Fav)*(JLDunlop)* 3-8-11 RHills(3) (hld up: 3rd st: rdn over 2f out: ev ch ins fnl f: r.o) ....½ 2
2393[7] Cent Nouvelles (USA) *(79) (JHMGosden)* 3-8-11 GHind(4) (lw: plld hrd: sn chsng wnr: 2nd st: disp ld over 2f out: rdn & put hd in air bel dist: kpt on ins fnl f) ....½ 3
2576[7] Mystic Lure **(72)***(75) (EALDunlop)* 3-8-11 JFortune(1) (b.hind: hld up & bhd: effrt & rdn 2f out: nt pce to chal) 1¾ 4

4/5 Azdihaar (USA) (10/11-Evens), **100/30** BANNER (USA) (9/4-7/2), Mystic Lure, **10/1** Cent Nouvelles (USA) (8/1-12/1), CSF £6.31 TOTE £3.70 (£1.60) OWNER Mr K. Abdullah (LAMBOURN) BRED Juddmonte Farms 4 Rn 1m 25.5 (2.80) SF: 29/28/27/23

2788 LORDS TAVERNERS H'CAP (0-80) (3-Y.O+) (Class D) £5,433.75 (£1,620.00: £772.50: £348.75) 1m Stalls: Low GOING minus 0.40 sec per fur (F) 5-35 (5-38)

*2634** **Equerry (67)***(81) (MJohnston)* 4-9-9 RHills(5) (swtg: mde virtually all: qcknd clr over 2f out: unchal) ....— 1
2419[5] Pride of Pendle **(71)***(77)*(Fav)*(DNicholls)* 6-9-13 AlexGreaves(6) (hld up: 6th st: hdwy 2f out: kpt on u.p fnl f: no ch w wnr) 4 2
2062[5] Striffolino **(74)***(79) (TDBarron)* 3-9-8 JFortune(7) (a.p: 2nd st: rdn 2f out: r.o one pce) ....¾ 3
2310[4] Thatched (IRE) **(50)***(54) (REBarr)* 5-7-13 (7) PFessey(3) (lw: hld up in rr: 7th st: r.o ins fnl f: nvr nrr) ....hd 4
2051[4] Polonez Prima **(61)***(64) (JLSpearing)* 8-9-3 ACulhane(8) (chsd ldrs: 5th st: hrd rdn wl over 1f out: no imp) ....½ 5
2484[7] Euro Sceptic (IRE) **(51)***(51) (MHEasterby)* 3-7-13 SMaloney(4) (chsd ldrs: 4th st: rdn bel dist: sn wknd) 1½ 6
2376[3] Nordic Doll (IRE) **(70)***(67) (BWHills)* 3-8-13 (5) JDSmith(1) (unruly s: prom: 3rd st: hrd rdn & n.m.r over 1f out: sn btn) 1¾ 7

5/2 Pride of Pendle, **11/2** Thatched (IRE), **6/1** Striffolino, EQUERRY, Euro Sceptic (IRE), Nordic Doll (IRE), **10/1** Polonez Prima (8/1-12/1), CSF £19.56 CT £78.16 TOTE £4.70: ££2.30 £2.00 (£5.00) OWNER Mr J. R. Good (MIDDLEHAM) BRED J. R. and Mrs P. Good 7 Rn
1m 39.1 (3.50) SF: 37/33/27/10/20/-/15
WEIGHT FOR AGE 3yo-8lb

T/Plpt: £57.70 (140.39 Tckts). T/Qdpt: £20.30 (5.2 Tckts). IM

2656-WINDSOR (Fig. 8)
Saturday July 29th (Good to firm)

WEATHER: sunny WIND: almost nil

2789 DAVY (S) APPRENTICE H'CAP (0-60) (3-Y.O+) (Class G) £2,553.50 (£726.00: £360.50) 1m 67y Stalls: Centre GOING minus 0.49 sec per fur (F) 6-15 (6-22)

2661[6] **Burnt Sienna (IRE) (27)***(38) (JSMoore)* 3-7-2 (5) RMullen(13) (mde all: clr over 2f out: r.o wl) ....— 1
2524[6] Tragic Hero **(52)***(60) (IABalding)* 3-9-1 (3) CScudder(4) (6th st: hdwy over 2f out: rdn over 1f out: one pce) 1¾ 2
2624[8] Trina **(35)***(40) (DLWilliams)* 4-8-9 RStudholme(2) (2nd st: rdn over 1f out: one pce) 1½ 3

2549⁷ Love Legend **(52)***(54) (DWPArbuthnot)* 10-9-4 (8) CSangster(9) (hld up: hdwy 3f out: rdn over 1f out: r.o) 1½ **4**
2428⁷ Bee Dee Best (IRE) **(39)***(41) (JPSmith)* 4-8-13 DSweeney(16) (4th st: rdn over 2f out: r.o one pce) ....hd **5**
2246⁴ Jobber's Fiddle **(48)***(44)*(Fav)*(DJSffrenchDavis)* 3-9-0v JBramhill(14) (8th st: rdn over 2f out: r.o one pce) 3 **6**
2549⁹ Super Serenade **(54)***(48)*(Fav)*(GBBalding)* 6-10-0 ALakeman(3) (dwlt: hdwy over 2f out: nvr nrr) ....¾ **7**
2317⁹ Chieftain's Crown (USA) **(38)***(30) (JWhite)* 4-8-4 (8) CCarver(7) (3rd st: rdn 3f out: wknd over 2f out) 1¼ **8**
2081⁶ Mai Pen Rai **(32)***(19) (RJHodges)* 7-8-6 JoHunnam(10) (a mid div) 2½ **9**
1016¹² Arrasas Lady **(24)***(6) (JCPoulton)* 5-7-7 (5) TField(17) (5th st: wknd over 2f out) 2½ **10**
2246¹⁵ Shanghai Lil **(33)***(14) (MJFetherston-Godley)* 3-7-13 GFaulkner(11) (bhd fnl 4f) ....½ **11**
2486⁷ Swynford Flyer **(25)** *(JAHarris)* 6-7-13 CLowther(5) (bhd fnl 4f) 4 **12**
2687⁴ Jarzon Dancer **(25)** *(DAWilson)* 7-7-5 (8) RachaelMoody(18) (a bhd) ....nk **13**
2450¹⁷ Grand Salt (IRE) **(38)***(6) (MJHaynes)* 4-8-7 (5) JCornally(6) (bhd fnl 3f) 2½ **14**
2052¹² Il Furetto **(29)** *(JSKing)* 3-7-4 (5) RhonaGent(12) (a bhd) 11 **15**
2056¹⁰ Amber Nectar **(29)** *(BAPearce)* 9-8-3 JWilkinson(15) (a bhd) 2 **16**
2148² Courting Newmarket **(44)** *(MrsAKnight)* 7-9-4 FLynch(1) (a bhd) **17**
2574⁴ Nyali Beach (IRE) **(42)** *(DrJDScargill)* 3-8-0 (8) CDomergue(8) (Withdrawn not under Starter's orders) .... **W**

LONG HANDICAP Burnt Sienna (IRE) 7-1

13/2 Jobber's Fiddle, Super Serenade, **8/1** Love Legend, **10/1** Trina, Chieftain's Crown (USA), Swynford Flyer, Tragic Hero (8/1-12/1), **12/1** Courting Newmarket, Mai Pen Rai, **14/1** Nyali Beach (IRE), Bee Dee Best (IRE), **16/1** Jarzon Dancer, **20/1** Amber Nectar, Shanghai Lil, BURNT SIENNA (IRE), **33/1** Arrasas Lady, Grand Salt (IRE), Il Furetto, CSF £180.67 CT £1,667.98 TOTE £20.80: £3.90 £3.00 £3.00 £2.10 (£197.00) Trio £313.50; £401.88 to 31/7/95 OWNER Mr Alex Gorrie (EAST GARSTON) BRED Mrs Margaret Tully and R. Cutler 17 Rn

1m 46.6 (5.00) SF: -/-/-/-/-/-/-/-/-/-/-/-/-/-/-/-/-/-
WEIGHT FOR AGE 3yo-8lb
No bid

2790

INDEFATIGABLE MAIDEN STKS (3-Y.O+) (Class D) £4,474.50 (£1,356.00: £663.00: £316.50)
1m 2f 7y Stalls: Centre GOING minus 0.49 sec per fur (F) 6-45 (6-50)

2241¹¹ **Country Star (IRE) (72)***(82) (HCandy)* 4-9-7 WNewnes(15) (lw: 3rd st: led over 1f out: r.o)..— **1**
2316² Persian Saint (IRE) **(79)***(78)*(Fav)*(DRCElsworth)* 4-9-2 (5) AProcter(13) (lw: 2nd st: led 3f out: hdd over 1f out: one pce) 2½ **2**
2438⁴ Tappeto *(72) (HCandy)* 3-8-11 NAdams(5) (lw: 7th st: hdwy 2f out: rdn over 1f out: one pce) .4 **3**
2426² Twilight Hour (USA) *(65) (BWHills)* 3-8-6 MHills(10) (4th st: rdn over 2f out: one pce) ....¾ **4**
2316³ Frozen Sea (USA) *(70) (GPEnright)* 4-9-7 MPerrett(4) (10th st: hdwy over 2f out: rdn over 1f out: one pce) ....s.h **5**
2568² Maftun (USA) *(66) (MajorWRHern)* 3-8-11 WCarson(14) (led: hdd 3f out: wknd 2f out) 2½ **6**
As You Like it (USA) *(66) (JHMGosden)* 3-8-11 LDettori(2) (hdwy 5f out: 5th st: rdn 2f out: one pce) ....½ **7**
2316⁴ Nobby North *(66) (LordHuntingdon)* 3-8-4 (7) AimeeCook(3) (6th st: rdn 2f out: sn wknd) ....s.h **8**
2329⁴ Discorsi *(64) (GWragg)* 3-8-11 FNorton(6) (9th st: a mid div) 1¼ **9**
Dtoto *(63) (MRStoute)* 3-8-8 (3) JTate(1) (w'like: bit bkwd: nvr nrr) ....s.h **10**
1736¹⁰ Hala Halina *(50) (JEBanks)* 3-8-6 JQuinn(11) (a bhd) 5 **11**
2553¹⁴ Celestial Dollar *(46) (OO'Neill)* 4-9-7 JWilliams(8) (a bhd) 6 **12**
Minneola *(36) (RTPhillips)* 3-8-6 WRyan(9) (unf: bit bkwd: dwlt: a bhd) 3 **13**
2331⁸ Sherrington *(4) (ACStewart)* 3-8-6 MRoberts(12) (8th st: sn wknd) 20 **14**

5/2 Persian Saint (IRE), **3/1** Maftun (USA), **11/2** COUNTRY STAR (IRE) (7/1-4/1), **6/1** Twilight Hour (USA) (op 4/1), **8/1** As You Like it (USA), **10/1** Dtoto, **12/1** Sherrington (op 8/1), **16/1** Frozen Sea (USA), Discorsi, **20/1** Nobby North, **25/1** Tappeto, Minneola, Hala Halina, **50/1** Celestial Dollar, CSF £21.68 TOTE £7.20: £2.20 £2.00 £6.70 (£10.40) Trio £263.70 OWNER Prince Fahd Salman (WANTAGE) BRED M. L. Page 14 Rn 2m 7.5 (2.60) SF: 45/41/25/18/33/19/19/19/17/16/3/9/-/-
WEIGHT FOR AGE 3yo-10lb

2791

E.B.F. APOLLO MEDIAN AUCTION MAIDEN STKS (2-Y.O) (Class E) £4,037.50 (£1,225.00: £600.00: £287.50)
5f 217y Stalls: Centre GOING minus 0.49 sec per fur (F) 7-15 (7-19)

2552³ **Kiss Me Again (IRE)** *(70) (RHannon)* 2-8-9 RPerham(3) (a.p: led over 2f out: hrd rdn ins fnl f: r.o wl) ....— **1**
2552⁴ Second Time Lucky (IRE) *(74)*(Fav)*(LordHuntingdon)* 2-9-0 LDettori(17) (lw: a.p: rdn & ev ch wl ins fnl f: r.o) ....nk **2**

Sondos (68) (JWHills) 2-8-9 WCarson(6) (w'like: a.p: ev ch & rdn wl ins fnl f: r.o wl) ....nk 3
2552[7] Fayre Holly (IRE) (63) (MJHeaton-Ellis) 2-8-9 WWoods(5) (chsd ldrs: rdn 2f out: ev ch ins fnl f: one pce) 2 4
2548[14] One Shot (IRE) (61) (WRMuir) 2-8-11 (3) JTate(14) (chsd ldrs: rdn 2f out: one pce) 2½ 5
Swift Maiden (53) (MrsLAMurphy) 2-8-9 JWilliams(9) (w'like: bit bkwd: hdwy fnl 2f: nvr nrr) .1¼ 6
849[2] Princely Sound (56) (MBell) 2-9-0 MFenton(11) (led: hdd over 2f out: wknd over 1f out) ....¾ 7
2487[9] Careful (IRE) (50) (BWHills) 2-8-9 MHills(2) (hld up: swtchd rt 3f out: styd on fnl 2f: nvr nrr) ..½ 8
2340[8] Cold Shoulder (IRE) (44) (JLDunlop) 2-9-0 SWhitworth(8) (nvr nrr).............4 9
2264[5] Coastguards Hero (39) (MDIUsher) 2-9-0 DBiggs(16) (prom over 3f).............1¾ 10
2336[4] Cherry Garden (IRE) (39) (TJNaughton) 2-9-0 PaulEddery(15) (a bhd).............s.h 11
Quiet Moments (IRE) (36) (PGMurphy) 2-8-7 (7) RWaterfield(12) (leggy: bit bkwd: dwlt: a bhd).............1¼ 12
Hartfields Boy (35) (BJMeehan) 2-9-0 BDoyle(7) (neat: a bhd).............½ 13
Boston Tea Party (22) (IABalding) 2-8-9 WRyan(10) (neat: a bhd).............3 14
Tablets of Stone (IRE) (13) (JRBosley) 2-9-0 CRutter(1) (w'like: bit bkwd: a bhd).............5 15
Match The Colour (MRChannon) 2-9-0 RHughes(18) (w'like: dwlt: sn rcvrd: wknd 3f out)...20 16

9/4 Second Time Lucky (IRE), **9/2** KISS ME AGAIN (IRE) (op 8/1), **5/1** Princely Sound, **10/1** Sondos, Match The Colour (op 6/1), **14/1** Boston Tea Party, Hartfields Boy (op 6/1), Careful (IRE) (op 8/1), Cold Shoulder (IRE), **16/1** Fayre Holly (IRE), **20/1** One Shot (IRE), **25/1** Tablets of Stone (IRE), **33/1** Swift Maiden, Cherry Garden (IRE), **40/1** Quiet Moments (IRE), **50/1** Coastguards Hero, CSF £15.59 TOTE £5.70: £1.90 £1.20 £2.00 (£5.80) Trio £8.90 OWNER Mr Bob Lalemant (MARLBOROUGH) BRED Alain Storme 16 Rn 1m 13.6 (3.10) SF: 10/14/8/3/1/-/-/-/-/-/-/-/-/-/-/-

2792

AMERADA HESS GAS H'CAP (0-75) (3-Y.O+) (Class D) £5,272.25 (£1,598.00: £781.50: £373.25) **1m 3f 135y** Stalls: Centre GOING minus 0.49 sec (F) 7-45 (7-47)

1813[2] **Quest Again (61)**(73) (DWPArbuthnot) 4-9-3 TQuinn(1) (4th st: led over 2f out: r.o).............— 1
2530[7] Broughtons Formula **(47)**(54) (WJMusson) 5-8-3b JQuinn(2) (5th st: hdwy 3f out: ev ch over 1f out: one pce).............3½ 2
2317[10] Witney-de-Bergerac (IRE) **(57)**(64) (JSMoore) 3-7-10 (5) NVarley(3) (7th st: hdwy 3f out: ev ch over 1f out: one pce).............½ 3
2298[6] Endowment **(73)**(77) (MajorWRHern) 3-9-3b WCarson(4) (s.i.s: 8th st: hdwy 3f out: ch over 1f out: one pce).............1¾ 4
2490* Trade Wind **(72)**(69) (DRCElsworth) 4-9-9b(5) AProcter(7) (6th st: hdwy over 2f out: wknd over 1f out).............5 5
2413[3] Santana Lady (IRE) **(60)**(50)(Fav)(MJHeaton-Ellis) 6-9-2 MRoberts(6) (led: hdd 6f out: 2nd st: led 4f out: hdd over 2f out: sn wknd).............5 6
2050* Mr Browning (USA) **(70)**(26) (RAkehurst) 4-9-9b(3) SSanders(8) (chsd ldr: led 6f out: hdd 4f out: sn wknd).............25 7
2571[4] Persian Conquest (IRE) **(62)**(16) (RIngram) 3-8-6b AMcGlone(5) (3rd st: wknd over 2f out) ..1½ 8

7/2 Santana Lady (IRE), **4/1** Mr Browning (USA), **9/2** QUEST AGAIN, **5/1** Broughtons Formula, **11/2** Trade Wind (op 3/1), **6/1** Persian Conquest (IRE), Endowment, **20/1** Witney-de-Bergerac (IRE), CSF £27.50 CT £385.02 TOTE £5.60: £2.00 £1.70 £3.70 (£20.10) OWNER Miss P. E. Decker (COMPTON) BRED Miss P. E. Decker 8 Rn 2m 27.1 (1.10) SF: 55/36/34/47/51/32/8/-
WEIGHT FOR AGE 3yo-12lb

2793

AMETHYST H'CAP (0-70) (3-Y.O+) (Class E) £3,956.25 (£1,200.00: £587.50: £281.25) **5f 10y** Stalls: Centre GOING minus 0.49 sec per fur (F) 8-15 (8-15)

2513[2] **Grand Chapeau (IRE) (59)**(64) (RHannon) 3-8-12 LDettori(3) (chsd ldrs: rdn over 1f out: r.o to ld last stride).............— 1
2512[2] Colston-C **(65)**(70)(Fav)(CJHill) 3-9-4 JWeaver(6) (led: rdn & edgd lft over 1f out: ct last stride).............s.h 2
2137[9] Rocky Two **(52)**(56) (PHowling) 4-8-10b JQuinn(5) (a.p: ev ch wl ins fnl f: r.o).............nk 3
2551[7] The Noble Oak (IRE) **(47)**(51) (MJBolton) 7-7-12 (7) GMitchell(2) (a.p: ev ch wl ins fnl f: r.o) ...hd 4
2551[3] Windrush Boy **(62)**(55) (JRBosley) 5-8-13 (7) AimeeCook(1) (prom: rdn over 1f out: one pce)3½ 5
542[8] Speedy Classic (USA) **(60)**(49) (MJHeaton-Ellis) 6-9-4 MRoberts(7) (chsd ldrs: rdn over 2f out: no hdwy).............1 6
1545[5] Mister Raider **(50)**(38) (SMellor) 3-7-10 (7) ADaly(8) (a bhd).............nk 7
191[3] Milos **(67)**(46) (TJNaughton) 4-9-11 PaulEddery(4) (a bhd).............3 8

5/2 Colston-C, **7/2** Windrush Boy, **4/1** GRAND CHAPEAU (IRE), **6/1** Speedy Classic (USA), **8/1** Mister Raider, **9/1** Milos (op 6/1), **10/1** The Noble Oak (IRE), **14/1** Rocky Two, CSF £14.65 CT £118.79 TOTE £3.10: £1.30 £1.50 £3.70 (£3.50) OWNER Mr Robert Whitworth (MARLBOROUGH) BRED Norelands Bloodstock 8 Rn 60.9 secs (1.90) SF: 23/29/20/15/19/13/-/10
WEIGHT FOR AGE 3yo-5lb

2794 BERYL MAIDEN STKS (3-Y.O) (Class D) £4,377.00 (£1,326.00: £648.00: £309.00)
1m 67y Stalls: Centre GOING minus 0.49 sec per fur (F) 8-45 (8-46)

2345³ **Artful Dane (IRE) (74)***(80) (MJHeaton-Ellis)* 3-9-0 MRoberts(5) (mde all: hrd rdn & edgd lft fnl f: r.o)........— **1**
916* Catercap (IRE) *(80)*(Fav)*(JHMGosden)* 3-9-0 LDettori(12) (lw: 2nd st: ev ch fnl 2f: r.o)........hd **2**
2265² Western Sal *(75) (WJarvis)* 3-8-9 PRobinson(11) (3rd st: rdn 2f out: r.o fnl f)........hd **3**
Almuhimm (USA) *(73) (EALDunlop)* 3-8-11 (3) JTate(3) (w'like: scope: s.i.s: 12th st: hdwy 2f out: r.o)........3½ **4**
677⁷ Viyapari (IRE) **(83)***(72) (LMCumani)* 3-9-0 RHughes(2) (bit bkwd: 5th st: rdn over 2f out: one pce)........½ **5**
Troubadour Song *(71) (IABalding)* 3-9-0 SO'Gorman(4) (unf: bit bkwd: 9th st: hdwy 2f out: sn rdn: one pce)........nk **6**
2438⁸ Fastini Gold *(62) (MDIUsher)* 3-9-0 DBiggs(10) (plld hrd: 4th st: wknd 3f out)........5 **7**
2319⁶ Yeath (IRE) *(58) (RAkehurst)* 3-9-0 TQuinn(7) (6th st: sn wknd)........2 **8**
Sheraz (IRE) **(65)***(58) (GWragg)* 3-9-0 FNorton(6) (8th st: rdn 3f out: no hdwy)........hd **9**
Fataana (USA) *(52) (BWHills)* 3-8-9 MHills(9) (w'like: bit bkwd: dwlt: sn rcvrd: 7th st: wknd over 2f out)........½ **10**
1979¹³ Indescent Blue **(59)***(47) (DWPArbuthnot)* 3-8-9 AClark(8) (10th st: a bhd)........2½ **11**
2319¹² Istiwa *(23) (CJBenstead)* 3-9-0 WCarson(1) (11th st: a bhd)........15 **12**

7/2 Catercap (IRE), **4/1** Viyapari (IRE), **9/2** Western Sal, **5/1** Almuhimm (USA), **15/2** ARTFUL DANE (IRE), **8/1** Fataana (USA), **14/1** Sheraz (IRE), **16/1** Yeath (IRE), Istiwa, **20/1** Indescent Blue, Troubadour Song, **33/1** Fastini Gold, CSF £34.98 TOTE £8.50: £1.90 £1.80 £1.30 (£12.50) Trio £9.40 OWNER Mr S. P. Lansdown (WROUGHTON) BRED R. A. Keogh 12 Rn
1m 46.9 (5.30) SF: 10/10/5/3/2/1/-/-/-/-/-/-

T/Plpt: £174.10 (71.57 Tckts). T/Qdpt: £18.90 (5.5 Tckts). SM

2428-CHESTER (L-H)
Sunday July 30th (Good to firm)
WEATHER: sunny, very hot WIND: slt half against

2795 CHESTER CATHEDRAL APPEAL CONDITIONS STKS (3-Y.O+) (Class B) £9,000.60 (£3,148.60: £1,539.30: £661.50)
7f 122y Stalls: Low GOING minus 0.44 sec per fur (F) 2-30 (2-30)

1839²¹ **Lipizzaner (IRE) (90)***(95)*(Fav)*(BWHills)* 3-8-13 MHills(1) (lw: s.i.s: hdwy 3f out: 3rd st: led ins fnl f: all out)........— **1**
2205³ Hedera (USA) **(90)***(90) (MRStoute)* 3-8-8 WRyan(2) (swtg: chsd ldr: 2nd st: led over 1f out tl ins fnl f: rallied u.p cl home)........hd **2**
2169³ Emirates Express **(86)***(84) (JWHills)* 3-8-13 TQuinn(3) (swtg: led tl hdd over 1f out: sn rdn & outpcd)........5 **3**
2003⁷ Hey Up Dolly (IRE) **(67)***(67) (JBerry)* 3-8-6 JCarroll(4) (chsd ldrs tl rdn & outpcd over 2f out: 4th & btn st)........5 **4**

6/4 LIPIZZANER (IRE), **13/8** Hedera (USA), **7/2** Emirates Express, **12/1** Hey Up Dolly (IRE), CSF £4.04 TOTE £2.70 (£1.50) OWNER Sheikh Mohammed (LAMBOURN) BRED Colin G. R. Booth 4 Rn
1m 33.49 (1.79) SF: 42/37/31/14

2796 E.B.F. SALTNEY MAIDEN STKS (2-Y.O) (Class D) £4,302.00 (£1,296.00: £628.00: £294.00) **7f 2y** Stalls: Low GOING minus 0.44 sec per fur (F) 3-00 (3-01)

2183² **Bonarelli (IRE)** *(81+)*(Fav)*(MRStoute)* 2-9-0 WRyan(6) (lw: hdwy 3f out: 2nd st: rdn to ld 100y out: r.o)........— **1**
2264² Ramooz (USA) *(75) (BHanbury)* 2-9-0b PRobinson(5) (b: lw: led after 1f: sn clr: rdn & hdd ins fnl f: no ex)........2½ **2**
2315⁹ Alamein (USA) *(72) (MrsLPiggott)* 2-8-7 (7) GMilligan(1) (bit bkwd: led 1f: rdn & 3rd st: r.o one pce)........1¼ **3**
2173⁴ Martha Quest *(58) (BWHills)* 2-8-9 MHills(3) (prom tl lost pl & 4th st)........4 **4**
2320¹¹ Stoop To Conquer *(50) (RCharlton)* 2-9-0b TQuinn(2) (swtg: dwlt: a in rr: 5th & rdn st: no imp)........6 **5**
2146⁸ Just Rory *(25) (EJAlston)* 2-9-0 JCarroll(4) (chsd ldrs 4f: sn rdn & wknd: 6th st: t.o)........11 **6**

Evens BONARELLI (IRE), **9/2** Ramooz (USA), Stoop To Conquer, **5/1** Martha Quest, **20/1** Alamein (USA), **50/1** Just Rory, CSF £5.52 TOTE £2.10: £1.70 £1.60 (£2.90) OWNER Sheikh Mohammed (NEWMARKET) BRED Robert Griffin 6 Rn 1m 27.16 (1.96) SF: 39/33/30/16/8/-

2797 MAIL ON SUNDAY MILE (QUALIFIER) H'CAP (0-85) (3-Y.O+) (Class D) £8,910.00 (£2,700.00: £1,320.00: £630.00)

7f 122y Stalls: Low GOING minus 0.44 sec per fur (F) 3-30 (3-33)

*2588** **Wentbridge Lad (IRE) (56)***(73) (PDEvans)* 5-8-5v GHind(1) (a.p: 3rd st: rdn to ld wl ins fnl f: r.o)..........— 1
2607⁵ Sooty Tern **(71)***(87) (JMBradley)* 8-9-3 (3) SDrowne(2) (led tl hdd wl ins fnl f: rallied gamely)...½ 2
2611* Mr Cube (IRE) **(62)***(70) (JMBradley)* 5-8-4v(7) RWaterfield(3) (hld up: hdwy & 5th st: nt rch ldrs)..........4 3
2634⁵ Cee-Jay-Ay **(63)***(65) (JBerry)* 8-8-12 JCarroll(10) (s.s: hdwy on ins ent st: fin wl)..........2½ 4
2607⁶ Lancashire Life (IRE) **(52)***(54) (EJAlston)* 4-7-12 (3) DWright(8) (w ldr: 2nd st: rdn & wknd appr fnl f)..........hd 5
2345² Just Harry **(70)***(71) (MJRyan)* 4-9-0 (5) MBaird(11) (hld up & bhd: hdwy over 2f out: nvr plcd to chal)..........nk 6
*2142** Sweet Supposin (IRE) **(64)***(61) (JohnBerry)* 4-8-13 TQuinn(12) (lw: in rr: effrt u.p ent st: no imp)..........2 7
2578⁹ My Gallery (IRE) **(54)***(50) (ABailey)* 4-7-10 (7)ow1 AngelaGallimore(5) (chsd ldrs: 4th st: wknd qckly bel dist)..........s.h 8
2397⁴ King Curan (USA) **(65)***(62) (ABailey)* 4-9-0 AMackay(6) (lw: prom early: sn lost pl)..........hd 9
2517* Pyramus (USA) **(75)***(67)*(Fav)*(MrsLPiggott)* 4-9-3 (7) GMilligan(7) (b: chsd ldrs: 6th & rdn st: sn lost tch)..........2½ 10
2461⁶ Cavers Yangous **(72)***(61) (MJohnston)* 4-9-7 PRobinson(4) (prom tl lost pl & 7th st: sn bhd)...1 11

4/1 Pyramus (USA), **5/1** Mr Cube (IRE), **13/2** Sweet Supposin (IRE), **15/2** Just Harry, **8/1** WENTBRIDGE LAD (IRE), **9/1** Sooty Tern, Cavers Yangous, **11/1** Cee-Jay-Ay, Lancashire Life (IRE), **12/1** King Curan (USA), My Gallery (IRE), CSF £73.95 CT £367.30 TOTE £12.60: £2.90 £2.80 £2.70 (£48.80) Trio £94.90 OWNER Mr John Pugh (WELSHPOOL) BRED Peter Doyle 11 Rn
1m 32.97 (1.27) SF: 40/54/37/32/21/38/28/17/29/34/28

2798 'BARBARA HIGGINS HAPPY BIRTHDAY' H'CAP (0-85) (3-Y.O+ F & M) (Class D) £4,120.00 (£1,240.00: £600.00: £280.00)

1m 4f 66y Stalls: Low GOING minus 0.44 sec per fur (F) 4-00 (4-00)

1808¹¹ **No Comebacks (55)***(67+) (EJAlston)* 7-8-7 KFallon(2) (stdd s: hld up & bhd: effrt & 4th st: c wd & led ins fnl f: sn clr)..........— 1
2584² Soba Up **(72)***(81)*(Fav)*(TJEtherington)* 5-9-10 ACulhane(3) (lw: a.p: 3rd st: led on ins bel dist: hdd & no ex ins fnl f)..........2½ 2
2327⁶ Rasayel (USA) **(45)***(49) (PDEvans)* 5-7-11 GBardwell(1) (lw: dwlt: gd hdwy 5f out: jnd ldr 3f out: 2nd & rdn st: one pce)..........3½ 3
2411³ Wells Whisper (FR) **(71)***(70) (GWragg)* 3-8-11 MHills(4) (swtg: chsd ldrs: led 4f out tl bel dist: outpcd appr fnl f)..........4 4
2429⁴ Killick **(62)***(49) (ABailey)* 7-9-0 JCarroll(5) (led 8f: sn rdn & wknd: 5th & btn st: t.o)..........9 5

2/1 Soba Up, **9/4** Wells Whisper (FR), **11/4** Killick, **7/1** Rasayel (USA), **8/1** NO COMEBACKS, CSF £23.32 TOTE £8.50: £2.80 £1.20 (£7.90) OWNER Mr Lionel Snowden (PRESTON) BRED Newmarket Thoroughbred Breeders P L C 5 Rn 2m 38.02 (1.42) SF: 48/62/30/39/30
WEIGHT FOR AGE 3yo-12lb

2799 CORBETT BOOKMAKERS RATED STKS H'CAP (0-95) (4-Y.O+) (Class B) £9,265.30 (£3,362.80: £1,631.40: £687.00: £293.50)

1m 7f 195y Stalls: Low GOING minus 0.44 sec per fur (F) 4-30 (4-31)

2429² **Moonlight Quest (73)***(86) (BHanbury)* 7-7-11 NCarlisle(4) (chsd ldrs: gd hdwy to ld ent st: sn clr)..........— 1
2098⁷ Latahaab (USA) **(86)***(93) (RAkehurst)* 4-8-10 TQuinn(1) (chsd ldr: led 2f out: hdd & 2nd st: sn outpcd)..........6 2
2352² Noufari (FR) **(74)***(80) (RHollinshead)* 4-7-12 AMackay(3) (in rr: outpcd 4f out: sn rdn: 5th st: styd on ins fnl f: nvr nrr)..........1 3
2352* New Reputation **(90)***(93)*(Fav)*(BWHills)* 4-9-0 MHills(5) (hld up: chsd ldrs: outpcd 4f out: rdn & 4th st: no imp)..........2½ 4
2530³ Tu Opes **(73)***(68) (JLHarris)* 4-7-11 GBardwell(2) (b: led: hrd rdn & hdd 2f out: 3rd & wkng st)..........8 5
LONG HANDICAP Moonlight Quest 7-10 Tu Opes 7-8

15/8 New Reputation, **5/2** Latahaab (USA), **9/2** MOONLIGHT QUEST, **11/2** Noufari (FR), **6/1** Tu Opes, CSF £14.88 TOTE £4.30: £1.90 £1.80 (£10.10) OWNER Mr B. Hanbury (NEWMARKET) BRED Raintree Stud 5 Rn 3m 24.53 (0.47 under best) (1.63) SF: 40/47/34/47/22

2800 DIES DOMINICA DEVAE NURSERY H'CAP (2-Y.O) (Class D) £4,146.00 (£1,248.00: £604.00: £282.00)
6f 18y Stalls: Low GOING minus 0.44 sec per fur (F) 5-00 (5-01)

2328[2] **Bold Times** *(77) (PDEvans)* 2-9-7 JFortune(1) (chsd ldrs: drvn ½-wy: hrd rdn to ld ins fnl f).— **1**
2185* U-No-Harry (IRE) *(65)*(Fav)*(RHollinshead)* 2-8-7 (3) AGarth(3) (led after 2f tl ins fnl f: rallied)..½ **2**
1849[12] Whittle Rock *(72) (EJAlston)* 2-9-6 KFallon(4) (hld up & bhd: hdwy over 2f out: ev ch ent fnl f: rdn & unable qckn)....1 **3**
2085[3] Amy Leigh (IRE) *(48) (CaptJWilson)* 2-9-0 JCarroll(2) (chsd ldrs: effrt & hrd rdn 2f out: outpcd appr fnl f)....7 **4**
2204[4] Dancing Lottie (IRE) *(18) (PAKelleway)* 2-7-8 JLowe(5) (led 2f: wknd ent st)....3½ **5**
2431[4] L A Touch *(2) (JohnBerry)* 2-8-1 GBardwell(6) (chsd ldrs 4f: sn rdn & outpcd: t.o)....9 **6**

3/1 U-No-Harry (IRE), **7/2** Whittle Rock, BOLD TIMES, **4/1** Amy Leigh (IRE), **11/2** Dancing Lottie (IRE), **12/1** L A Touch, CSF £13.46 TOTE £3.80: £2.00 £1.60 (£4.50) OWNER Mr J. Hardman (WELSHPOOL) BRED Mrs P. E. Bell 6 Rn 1m 16.0 (2.70) SF: 32/27/3/20/-/-

T/Plpt: £85.10 (212.18 Tckts). T/Qdpt: £18.70 (17.8 Tckts). IM

2600-LINGFIELD (L-H)
Sunday July 30th (Good to firm becoming Good to soft)
WEATHER: humid, thunder & fresh after WIND: nil

2801 DOM RUINART CHAMPAGNE SUNDAY MAIDEN STKS (2-Y.O) (Class D) £4,455.00 (£1,350.00: £660.00: £315.00)
6f Stalls: High GOING minus 0.47 sec per fur (F) 2-15 (2-17)

Yarob (IRE) *(82+) (HThomsonJones)* 2-9-0 RHills(2) (neat: lw: mde all: easily)....— **1**
2552[6] Prime Partner *(71) (WRMuir)* 2-8-11 (3) SSanders(3) (chsd wnr: rdn over 2f out: unable qckn) 4 **2**
2340[3] Grey Legend *(68) (RMFlower)* 2-9-0 DBiggs(4) (swtg: a.p: rdn 3f out: one pce)....1¼ **3**
Hever Golf Hero *(60)*(Fav)*(TJNaughton)* 2-9-0 JQuinn(8) (w'like: scope: bit bkwd: rdn over 2f out: hdwy over 1f out: one pce)....3 **4**
Budding Annie *(42) (JRBosley)* 2-8-9 RPerham(6) (unf: hld up: wkng whn nt clr run over 2f out & bmpd over 1f out)....5 **5**
Stand Your Ground *(45) (GLMoore)* 2-9-0 SWhitworth(5) (neat: hld up: rdn over 2f out: wknd wl over 1f out)....½ **6**
2434[4] Oscar Rose *(27) (LordHuntingdon)* 2-9-0 AMcGlone(7) (a bhd)....7 **7**
2408[9] Concert Party (IRE) *(19) (JLDunlop)* 2-9-0 GCarter(1) (lw: a bhd)....3 **8**
Mogin *(JFfitch-Heyes)* 2-8-9 RPrice(10) (leggy: bit bkwd: s.s: a wl bhd)....10 **9**

9/4 Hever Golf Hero, **5/2** YAROB (IRE) (op 6/4), **13/2** Prime Partner, Grey Legend, **12/1** Oscar Rose (op 8/1), **14/1** Concert Party (IRE) (op 8/1), **25/1** Stand Your Ground, **33/1** Budding Annie, Mogin, CSF £16.73 TOTE £3.50: £1.60 £1.40 £2.00 (£13.40) Trio £13.10 OWNER Mr Hamdan Al Maktoum (NEWMARKET) 9 Rn 1m 11.59 (2.59) SF: 21/10/7/-/-/-/-/-/-

2802 WILLIAM HILL H'CAP (0-90) (3-Y.O) (Class C) £5,602.00 (£1,696.00: £828.00: £394.00) **6f** Stalls: High GOING minus 0.47 sec per fur (F) 2-45 (2-48)

2311* **Rasas (IRE) (85)***(92) (HThomsonJones)* 3-9-6 RHills(3) (lw: a.p: led over 1f out: rdn out)....— **1**
2507* Bowden Rose **(77)***(76)*(Fav)*(MBlanshard)* 3-8-12b JQuinn(4) (led over 4f: unable qckn)....3 **2**
2405[4] Pelleman **(72)***(67) (RBoss)* 3-8-4 (3) SSanders(5) (hld up: rdn over 3f out: one pce fnl 2f)....1½ **3**
2362[5] Shen Yang (USA) **(80)***(64) (GLMoore)* 3-9-1 SWhitworth(6) (swtg: rdn over 3f out: hdwy over 2f out: wknd over 1f out)....4 **4**
2556[3] Jo Maximus **(73)***(57) (SDow)* 3-8-1 (7) ADaly(7) (swtg: w ldr over 3f)....nk **5**
2271[8] Try to Please (IRE) **(80)***(50) (EALDunlop)* 3-8-12 (3) JTate(2) (bhd fnl 2f)....5 **6**
2507[5] Tafahhus **(86)***(32) (RWArmstrong)* 3-9-7 WCarson(1) (bhd fnl 4f)....9 **7**

9/4 Bowden Rose, **7/2** RASAS (IRE), **5/1** Tafahhus, Jo Maximus, **7/1** Pelleman (5/1-8/1), **14/1** Try to Please (IRE), **20/1** Shen Yang (USA), CSF £10.87 TOTE £4.10: £2.60 £2.00 (£4.90) OWNER Mr Hamdan Al Maktoum (NEWMARKET) BRED Shadwell Estate Company Limited 7 Rn
1m 8.61 (-0.39) SF: 69/53/44/41/34/27/9

2803 BONUSPRINT H'CAP (0-100) (3-Y.O+) (Class C) £5,837.50 (£5,837.50: £1,320.00: £625.00) **7f** Stalls: Centre GOING minus 0.47 sec per fur (F) 3-15 (3-15)

2414[3] **Fairy Story (IRE) (74)***(81)*(Fav)*(RAkehurst)* 5-8-3 (3) SSanders(6) (lw: a.p: led over 1f out: all out: jnd post)....— **1**

2593² **Dance Band (USA) (91)***(98)*(Fav)*(BHanbury)* 3-8-13 (3) JStack(8) (swtg: a.p: led over 2f out tl over 1f out: hrd rdn: jnd ldr post)........— 1
2337* Red Rita (IRE) **(75)***(81) (WRMuir)* 4-8-7 CRutter(9) (lw: led over 4f: rdn & r.o ins fnl f)........½ 3
2477³ Legal Fiction **(68)***(68) (MJohnston)* 4-8-0 TWilliams(2) (lw: hrd rdn over 3f out: hdwy over 2f out: eased whn btn ins fnl f)........2½ 4
2100³ Takhlid (USA) **(79)***(76) (HThomsonJones)* 4-8-11 RHills(3) (swtg: lost pl 4f out: rallied over 1f out: one pce)........1¼ 5
2477⁶ Iktasab **(89)***(83) (EALDunlop)* 3-8-11 (3) JTate(1) (rdn over 3f out: nvr nr to chal)........1¼ 6
2443⁷ Lennox Lewis **(99)***(91) (APJarvis)* 3-9-10 GCarter(10) (lw: a bhd)........1¼ 7
1728¹² Waikiki Beach (USA) **(85)***(67) (GLMoore)* 4-9-3 SWhitworth(7) (lw: dwlt: hld up: rdn over 3f out: wknd 2f out)........4 8
*2437** Muchtarak (IRE) **(86)** *(CJBenstead)* 3-8-11 WCarson(5) (Withdrawn not under Starter's orders: Veterinary advice)........W

7/2 FAIRY STORY (IRE), DANCE BAND (USA), **5/1** Muchtarak (IRE), **11/2** Legal Fiction (op 53/1), **6/1** Lennox Lewis, **7/1** Iktasab, **15/2** Takhlid (USA), **10/1** Red Rita (IRE), **14/1** Waikiki Beach (USA) (12/1-20/1), CSF DB & FS £7.56, FS & DB £7.56 CT DB, FS & RR £49.27, FS, DB & RR £49.27 TOTE DB £2.00, FS £1.70: DB £1.30, FS £1.70 £1.90 (£5.20) Trio £15.20 OWNER The Fairy Story Partnership (EPSOM)/Mr Abdullah Ali (NEWMARKET) BRED Deepwood Farm Stud 8 Rn
1m 21.61 (1.01) SF: 36/46/36/23/31/31/39/22/-
WEIGHT FOR AGE 3yo-7lb

2804 SUNDAY EXPRESS BEST FOR SPORT (QUALIFIER) H'CAP (0-80) (3-Y.O+) (Class D) £5,147.00 (£1,556.00: £758.00: £359.00) **1m 2f** Stalls: Low GOING: 0.06 sec per fur (G) 3-45 (3-52)

1747⁰ **Better Offer (IRE) (77)***(89) (GHarwood)* 3-9-11 MPerrett(1) (chsd ldr 2f: 3rd st: led over 1f out: r.o wl)........— 1
2490¹⁰ Dr Edgar **(64)***(68) (GWragg)* 3-8-12 FNorton(3) (led over 8f: unable qckn)........5 2
2197⁵ Top Pet (IRE) **(55)***(56) (RAkehurst)* 5-8-13 JQuinn(2) (lost pl over 5f out: 4th st: r.o one pce fnl 2f)........2 3
2557² Wet Patch (IRE) **(59)***(59)*(Fav)*(RHannon)* 3-8-0 (7) DaneO'Neill(4) (dwlt: chsd ldr 8f out: ev ch 2f out: one pce)........½ 4

6/4 Wet Patch (IRE), **11/4** BETTER OFFER (IRE), **7/2** Dr Edgar, **4/1** Top Pet (IRE), CSF £10.63 TOTE £4.70 (£7.60) OWNER Mrs Wendy Sainer (PULBOROUGH) BRED John McLoughlin 4 Rn
2m 9.5 (6.50) SF: 61/40/38/31
WEIGHT FOR AGE 3yo-10lb

2805 KPMG MAIDEN STKS (3-Y.O+) (Class D) £3,712.50 (£1,125.00: £550.00: £262.50) **1m 1f** Stalls: Low GOING: 0.06 sec per fur (G) 4-15 (4-20)

2356² **Gloriana (72)***(78) (LadyHerries)* 3-8-7 JQuinn(1) (mde all: clr over 2f out: r.o wl)........— 1
2438² Balasara (IRE) **(78)***(71)*(Fav)*(DRCElsworth)* 5-9-2b(5) AProcter(2) (chsd wnr: hrd rdn over 2f out: no imp)........7 2
Mr Medley *(63) (RHannon)* 3-8-5 (7) DaneO'Neill(3) (unf: 4th st: one pce fnl 3f)........4 3
2568⁵ Toskano *(55) (IABalding)* 3-8-12 AClark(5) (3rd st: one pce fnl 3f)........5 4
2438⁷ RaincheckA *(39) (MarkCampion)* 4-9-7 CAvery(4) (b: 5th st: a bhd)........9 5

Evens Balasara (IRE), **13/8** GLORIANA, **6/1** Mr Medley (4/1-7/1), **9/1** Toskano (12/1-8/1), **33/1** RaincheckA, CSF £3.71 TOTE £2.80: £1.70 £1.00 (£1.10) OWNER Mr David Blacker (LITTLEHAMPTON) BRED D. Blacker 5 Rn
2m 1.76 (12.46) SF: -/-/-/-/-
WEIGHT FOR AGE 3yo-9lb

2806 'BIG APPLE' (S) STKS (3-Y.O+) (Class E) £3,745.00 (£1,135.00: £555.00: £265.00) **1m 6f** Stalls: High GOING: 0.06 sec per fur (G) 4-45 (4-45)

2157* **Faugeron (70)***(71)*(Fav)*(NTinkler)* 6-9-12 GCarter(6) (b: mde all: clr over 1f out: rdn out)........— 1
Born To Be Wild *(50) (WGMTurner)* 3-7-13 (3) PMcCabe(2) (w'like: 2nd st: rdn over 2f out: eased whn btn ins fnl f)........10 2
*2378*⁸ Royal Rabbit **(52)***(47) (GLMoore)* 3-8-7 (5) AWhelan(5) (prom 8f: mod 3rd st)........11 3
2486¹⁰ The Oil Baron **(15)***(19) (RPCHoad)* 9-9-7 RPerham(4) (poor 4th st: nvr nr to chal)........20 4
*2632*² Club Elite **(27)***(10) (MFBarraclough)* 3-7-11 (5) NVarley(7) (a bhd)........3½ 5
1513¹² Captain Starlight (IRE) **(33)***(11) (RAkehurst)* 4-9-4b(3) SSanders(8) (bhd fnl 8f)........4 6
*2632*⁴ Yo-Mate *(JFfitch-Heyes)* 4-9-7 RPrice(9) (bhd fnl 7f: t.o)........dist 7

8/11 FAUGERON, **7/2** Captain Starlight (IRE), **9/2** Royal Rabbit, **10/1** Club Elite, **14/1** Born To Be Wild, **16/1** Yo-Mate, **33/1** The Oil Baron, CSF £12.03 TOTE £1.30: £3.80 £2.50 (£10.80) Trio £28.90 OWNER Elite Racing Club (MALTON) BRED J. L. C. Pearce 7 Rn

3m 18.57 (23.27) SF: -/-/-/-/-/-/-
WEIGHT FOR AGE 3yo-14lb
No bid

2807

LEVY BOARD SUNDAY H'CAP (0-70) (3-Y.O+) (Class E) £3,225.00 (£975.00: £475.00: £225.00)
7f 140y Stalls: Centre GOING: 0.06 sec per fur (G) 5-15 (5-17)

2620* **Proud Image (63)***(78) (APJarvis)* 3-8-10v(3) JTate(2) (mde all: rdn out) — 1
2321 12 I'm Outa Here (IRE) **(61)***(74)*(Fav)*(RHannon)* 3-8-4 (7) DaneO'Neill(10) (hld up: chsd wnr over 2f out: r.o ins fnl f) 1 2
2276 12 Runic Symbol **(40)***(30) (MBlanshard)* 4-7-12 CRutter(3) (lw: hdwy over 1f out: r.o one pce) 11 3
2528 5 Lucknam Style **(42)***(27) (MrsBarbaraWaring)* 7-8-0v AMcGlone(8) (b.hind: a.p: rdn over 2f out: sn wknd) 2½ 4
1649 13 Just Lucky (IRE) **(52)***(30) (RWArmstrong)* 3-8-2 RPrice(11) (nvr nr to chal) 3 5
2488 3 Mo's Star **(64)***(34) (SDow)* 3-8-7 (7) ADaly(9) (prom over 4f) 4 6
2522* Owdbetts (IRE) **(63)***(28) (GLMoore)* 3-8-13 SWhitworth(1) (bhd fnl 4f: sddle slipped) 2½ 7
Tower Green **(70)***(28) (LadyHerries)* 4-10-0 JQuinn(6) (t: b.hind: bit bkwd: swtg: a bhd) 3 8
Mister Fox **(41)** *(RJHodges)* 4-7-8 (5)ow1 NVarley(7) (b.off fore: a bhd) 9 9

7/2 I'm Outa Here (IRE), **4/1** Mo's Star, **9/2** Owdbetts (IRE), **5/1** PROUD IMAGE, **6/1** Tower Green, **10/1** Runic Symbol, **14/1** Lucknam Style, **16/1** Just Lucky (IRE), **33/1** Mister Fox, CSF £21.46 CT £152.02 TOTE £4.40: £2.40 £1.10 £2.70 (£14.50) Trio £87.80 OWNER Mr L. Fust (ASTON UPTHORPE) BRED Miss S. E. Jarvis 9 Rn 1m 33.15 (5.15) SF: 44/40/4/1/-/-/-/2/-

WEIGHT FOR AGE 3yo-8lb
T/Jkpt: £671.90 (76.41 Tckts). T/Plpt: £19.40 (693.53 Tckts). T/Qdpt: £47.30 (3.4 Tckts). AK

2637-BRIGHTON (L-H)
Monday July 31st (Firm)
WEATHER: hot WIND: almost nil

2808

DAILY STAR APPRENTICE H'CAP (0-70) (3-Y.O+) (Class F) £2,745.80 (£758.80: £361.40) **7f 214y** Stalls: Low GOING minus 0.69 sec per fur (HD) 6-05 (6-07)

1013 8 **Inderaputeri (54)***(66) (MissGayKelleway)* 5-8-13 (3) DaneO'Neill(4) (2nd st: hrd rdn over 2f out: led ins fnl f: r.o wl) — 1
2682 5 Roman Reel (USA) **(66)***(75) (GLMoore)* 4-9-9 (5) LSuthern(3) (lw: led: rdn over 1f out: hdd ins fnl f: unable qckn) 1½ 2
2661 2 Waldo **(65)***(73) (LordHuntingdon)* 4-9-8v(5) AimeeCook(5) (lw: mod 6th st: rdn over 2f out: hdwy over 1f out: r.o) ¾ 3
2093 6 Equilibrium **(50)***(53) (JWHills)* 3-8-1 (3) MHenry(6) (3rd st: hrd rdn over 2f out: sn wknd) 2½ 4
2528 10 Rad **(51)***(50) (SPCWoods)* 5-8-8 (5) CWebb(7) (mod 4th st: rdn over 2f out: hdwy & n.m.r on ins over 1f out: r.o one pce) 1¾ 5
2537 5 Kevasingo **(63)***(62)*(Fav)*(SDow)* 3-9-0 (3) ADaly(2) (lw: mod 5th st: nvr nr to chal) s.h 6
2668 3 Lorelei Lee (IRE) **(65)***(24) (JohnBerry)* 3-9-5 HKYim(1) (bhd fnl 4f) 20 7

11/4 Kevasingo, **4/1** Lorelei Lee (IRE) (op 5/2), Waldo (3/1-9/2), **11/2** Roman Reel (USA), **6/1** INDERAPUTERI, **10/1** Equilibrium, **16/1** Rad, CSF £33.98 TOTE £10.90: £3.40 £2.60 (£27.00) OWNER H.R.H. Sultan Ahmad Shah (WHITCOMBE) BRED G. Haywood 7 Rn

1m 33.5 (1.30) SF: 27/36/34/6/11/15/-
WEIGHT FOR AGE 3yo-8lb

2809

E.B.F. ALFRISTON MAIDEN STKS (2-Y.O) (Class D) £4,141.80 (£1,144.80: £545.40) **5f 213y** Stalls: Low GOING minus 0.69 sec per fur (HD) 6-35 (6-39)

2453 2 **Al Shafa** *(63+)*(Fav)*(JLDunlop)* 2-9-0 TQuinn(3) (swtg: mde all: shkn up over 1f out: eased ins fnl f) — 1
2135 7 Miss Carottene *(31) (MJRyan)* 2-8-9 AClark(2) (chsd wnr: rdn over 2f out: wknd over 1f out) 10 2
Suparoy *(TGMills)* 2-9-0 PaulEddery(1) (Withdrawn not under Starter's orders: unruly in stalls) W

1/12 AL SHAFA, **12/1** Suparoy, **20/1** Miss Carottene, TOTE £1.10 OWNER Prince A. A. Faisal (ARUNDEL) BRED Fonthill Stud 2 Rn 1m 9.9 (1.50) SF: 18/-/-

2810 DOWNS (S) STKS (3-Y.O+) (Class G) £2,243.00 (£618.00: £293.00)
5f 213y Stalls: Low GOING minus 0.69 sec per fur (HD) 7-05 (7-05)

2680⁶ **Baileys Sunset (IRE) (63)**_(67)_(Fav)_(MJohnston)_ 3-9-4 WWoods(1) (lw: 3rd st: rdn over 2f out: led 1f out: edgd lft ins fnl f: r.o wl)........— **1**
2641³ Pirates Gold (IRE) **(46)**_(56) (JWhite)_ 5-9-4 TQuinn(3) (lw: 5th st: n.m.r & swtchd rt over 2f out: r.o wl ins fnl f)........2 **2**
2642* Tyrian Purple (IRE) **(54)**_(60) (TJNaughton)_ 7-9-5b(5) JDSmith(2) (b: lw: led 5f: 2nd & btn whn hmpd & stumbled ins fnl f)........½ **3**
2642⁴ Hong Kong Dollar **(53)**_(48) (BJMeehan)_ 3-8-12b PaulEddery(5) (4th st: hrd rdn over 2f out: one pce)........2½ **4**
2593¹⁴ Fosters Top **(32)**_(29) (JFfitch-Heyes)_ 3-8-12 RPrice(4) (lw: 2nd st: wknd over 2f out)........7 **5**

2/1 BAILEYS SUNSET (IRE), **9/4** Tyrian Purple (IRE), **5/2** Hong Kong Dollar, **5/1** Pirates Gold (IRE) (4/1-6/1), **25/1** Fosters Top, CSF £11.06 TOTE £2.20: £1.50 £2.60 (£9.30) OWNER G R Bailey Ltd (Baileys Horse Feeds) (MIDDLEHAM) BRED Vincent and Joseph Fitzpatrick in Ireland 5 Rn
1m 9.2 (0.80) SF: 31/26/30/12/-
WEIGHT FOR AGE 3yo-6lb
No bid
STEWARDS' ENQUIRY Woods susp. 9-10/8/95 (careless riding).

2811 A R DENNIS BOOKMAKERS EVENING H'CAP (0-75) (3-Y.O) (Class D)
£4,180.00 (£1,155.00: £550.00)
1m 1f 209y Stalls: High GOING minus 0.69 sec per fur (HD) 7-35 (7-36)

2532⁷ **Prince of Spades (59)**_(70) (CACyzer)_ 3-9-2 DBiggs(2) (3rd st: led over 1f out: rdn out)........— **1**
2682* Soviet Bride (IRE) **(58)**_(69)_(Fav)_(SDow)_ 3-8-8 (7) ADaly(1) (led 8f out tl over 1f out: r.o)........nk **2**
1382⁵ Paper Cloud **(64)**_(65) (CEBrittain)_ 3-9-7 WWoods(3) (lw: led 2f: 2nd st: wknd over 2f out)........6 **3**

1/3 Soviet Bride (IRE) (2/9-4/9), **5/1** Paper Cloud (7/2-11/2), **11/2** PRINCE OF SPADES (4/1-6/1), CSF £7.52 TOTE £5.70 (£1.80) OWNER Mr Stephen Crown (HORSHAM) BRED S. Crown 3 Rn
2m 0.8 (2.80) SF: 20/19/15

2812 DUKE OF NORFOLK MEMORIAL H'CAP (0-75) (3-Y.O) (Class D)
£4,152.00 (£1,236.00: £588.00: £264.00)
1m 3f 196y Stalls: High GOING minus 0.69 sec per fur (HD) 8-05 (8-05)

2439⁹ **Courbaril (56)**_(68) (SDow)_ 3-8-8 (7) ADaly(2) (lw: 3rd st: hrd rdn over 3f out: led ins fnl f: r.o wl)........— **1**
2687⁶ Harding Brown (USA) **(50)**_(60) (GHarwood)_ 3-8-2v(7) GayeHarwood(3) (lw: led: hrd rdn over 2f out: hdd ins fnl f: unable qckn)........1¾ **2**
2658⁴ Faustino **(50)**_(58) (PFICole)_ 3-8-9 TQuinn(1) (lw: chsd ldr: hrd rdn & wandered over 1f out: one pce)........1½ **3**
2339² Unchanged **(62)**_(52)_(Fav)_(CEBrittain)_ 3-9-7 WWoods(5) (bhd fnl 5f)........13 **4**
2282⁴ Ruddigore **(48)**_(31) (RHannon)_ 3-8-7 SRaymont(4) (lw: 4th st: wknd 3f out)........5 **5**

7/4 Unchanged, **11/4** Faustino, COURBARIL (2/1-3/1), **8/1** Harding Brown (USA) (op 4/1), **11/1** Ruddigore (5/1-12/1), CSF £18.96 TOTE £4.20: £2.20 £3.10 (£18.00) OWNER Mr G. Steinberg (EPSOM) BRED George & Mrs Steinberg 5 Rn 2m 29.9 (0.90) SF: 44/36/34/28/7

2813 SOUTHERN FM LIMITED STKS (0-50) (3-Y.O) (Class F) £2,872.00 (£856.00: £408.00: £184.00) 7f 214y Stalls: Low GOING minus 0.69 sec (HD) 8-35 (8-38)

2363⁶ **Miss Laughter (43)**_(62) (JWHills)_ 3-8-2 (5) MHenry(3) (swtg: mde all: qcknd 2f out: r.o wl)........— **1**
2574* La Fille de Cirque **(48)**_(54)_(Fav)_(RJRWilliams)_ 3-8-9 DBiggs(2) (lw: 6th st: rdn over 3f out: r.o one pce)........5 **2**
2149⁴ Tirollac (IRE) **(45)**_(51) (LGCottrell)_ 3-8-7 MFenton(5) (2nd st: rdn over 2f out: one pce)........nk **3**
2540³ Prince Rudolf (IRE) **(41)**_(49) (MrsNMacauley)_ 3-8-5v(7) AmandaSanders(7) (4th st: rdn over 2f out: wknd over 1f out)........3½ **4**
2225⁶ Indian Rhapsody **(47)**_(48) (MRChannon)_ 3-8-11 TQuinn(8) (rdn over 2f out: nvr nr to chal)........nk **5**
1401⁵ Fair Ella (IRE) **(35)**_(43) (JFfitch-Heyes)_ 3-8-7 RPrice(1) (lw: a bhd)........½ **6**
I Remember it Well (IRE) **(45)**_(39) (SirMarkPrescott)_ 3-8-7 CNutter(6) (bit bkwd: 3rd st: wknd over 2f out)........2 **7**
2538⁴ Kencol **(49)**_(40) (AGFoster)_ 3-8-7 (5) AWhelan(4) (b.hind: swtg: hmpd on ins over 4f out: 5th st: wknd over 2f out)........2 **8**

5/2 La Fille de Cirque, **11/4** Indian Rhapsody, **13/2** Prince Rudolf (IRE) (7/2-7/1), **7/1** MISS LAUGHTER (7/2-8/1), **8/1** Tirollac (IRE), I Remember it Well (IRE), Kencol, **33/1** Fair Ella (IRE), CSF £24.05 TOTE £10.00: £2.00 £1.30 £2.30 (£30.70) OWNER Miss J. Wilkinson (LAMBOURN) BRED Miss J. Wilkinson 8 Rn
1m 34.2 (2.00) SF: 12/4/1/-/-/-/-/-

T/Plpt: £1,002.70 (8.01 Tckts). T/Qdpt: £46.60 (0.1 Tckts). AK

2258-CARLISLE (R-H)
Monday July 31st (Firm, Hard patches)
WEATHER: sunny WIND: slt across

2814 CARLISLE CHAMPION APPRENTICE H'CAP (0-70) (3-Y.O+) (Class E) £3,109.70 (£941.60: £459.80: £218.90)
7f 214y Stalls: High GOING minus 0.69 sec per fur (HD) 6-20 (6-20)

2607² **Spanish Verdict (67)***(80)*(Fav)*(DenysSmith)* 8-9-13 CTeague(7) (mde all: kpt on wl fnl f) ....— 1
2607³ Avishayes (USA) **(47)***(57) (MrsMReveley)* 8-8-2 (5) DDenby(5) (hld up: stdy hdwy over 2f out: chal ins fnl f: kpt on) 1½ 2
2611³ Kilnamartyra Girl **(51)***(58) (JParkes)* 5-8-11 LNewton(6) (hld up: effrt over 2f out: styd on towards fin) 1½ 3
2733² Princess Maxine (IRE) **(56)***(61) (JJO'Neill)* 6-8-13 (3) PRoberts(4) (lw: cl up: rdn 3f out: btn appr fnl f) 1¼ 4
2621⁷ Mca Below the Line **(58)***(61) (JLEyre)* 7-9-4v NVarley(1) (drvn along ½-wy: no imp) ....¾ 5
1523⁷ Level Edge **(44)***(40) (MDHammond)* 4-8-4 DWright(3) (chsd ldrs tl rdn & wknd over 2f out)..3½ 6
2620⁹ Musical March **(33)** *(EWeymes)* 4-7-7 DarrenMoffatt(2) (cl up tl rdn & wknd over 3f out).......20 7
LONG HANDICAP Musical March 7-4

5/2 SPANISH VERDICT, **3/1** Kilnamartyra Girl, Princess Maxine (IRE), **4/1** Avishayes (USA), **12/1** Mca Below the Line, **20/1** Level Edge, **50/1** Musical March, CSF £12.04 TOTE £3.10: £2.20 £1.80 (£4.20) OWNER Cox & Allen (Kendal) Ltd (BISHOP AUCKLAND) BRED Hyde Stud 7 Rn
1m 39.9 (0.90) SF: 46/23/24/27/27/6/-

2815 KIRKSTONE CLAIMING STKS (3-Y.O) (Class F) £2,773.00 (£778.00: £379.00)
6f 206y Stalls: High GOING minus 0.69 sec per fur (HD) 6-50 (6-53)

2582* **Simand (47)***(61) (EWeymes)* 3-8-2 KDarley(6) (lw: hdwy over 2f out: swtchd over 1f out: led jst ins fnl f: smoothly) ....— 1
2390² David James' Girl **(62)***(56)*(Fav)*(ABailey)* 3-8-0 SMaloney(7) (trckd ldrs: pushed along over 2f out: swtchd & r.o wl fnl f: too much to do)....1¼ 2
2755³ Dr Caligari (IRE) **(70)***(66) (JBerry)* 3-8-10 JCarroll(5) (lw: led tl hdd 3f out: led wl over 1f out tl jst ins fnl f: one pce) ....hd 3
2549¹³ Cool Tactician **(52)***(53) (RHollinshead)* 3-8-9 GCarter(3) (chsd ldrs: rdn & one pce fnl 2f)........5 4
2480⁵ Samana Cay **(43)***(42) (DNicholls)* 3-7-13 DaleGibson(2) (cl up: outpcd 3f out: sn btn) ....¾ 5
*350*¹⁰ Evan Can Wait (IRE) *(17) (JLEyre)* 3-8-2 RLappin(1) (a bhd)....12 6
*2588*¹² Bowcliffe Grange (IRE) *(7) (DWChapman)* 3-8-4 DeanMcKeown(4) (bhd: rapid hdwy to ld 3f out: hdd & wknd wl over 1f out)....5 7

6/4 David James' Girl, **3/1** Dr Caligari (IRE), **4/1** SIMAND, **11/2** Cool Tactician, **9/1** Samana Cay (5/1-10/1), **50/1** Bowcliffe Grange (IRE), **100/1** Evan Can Wait (IRE), CSF £10.00 TOTE £4.00: £1.80 £1.20 (£3.20) OWNER Mr W. G. Martin (MIDDLEHAM) BRED R. V. Young 7 Rn
1m 27.5 (1.80) SF: 12/7/17/4/-/-/-

2816 CUMBERLAND NEWS H'CAP (0-80) (3-Y.O+) (Class D) £3,538.60 (£1,070.80: £522.40: £248.20)
1m 4f Stalls: Low GOING minus 0.69 sec per fur (HD) 7-20 (7-20)

Master Hyde (USA) (55)*(68) (WStorey)* 6-7-11 (7) PFessey(4) (hld up: pushed thro over 3f out: led over 2f out: styd on)....— 1
2462⁴ Batabanoo **(79)***(87) (MrsMReveley)* 6-10-0 KDarley(1) (lw: hld up: hdwy to jn ldr ½-wy: led over 3f out tl over 2f out: nt qckn) 3½ 2
2785³ Ashover **(58)***(62)*(Fav)*(TDBarron)* 5-8-7 JFortune(3) (lw: plld hrd: chsd ldrs: effrt & bmpd over 3f out: one pce after)....3 3
2734⁵ Lord Advocate **(46)***(34) (DANolan)* 7-7-4b(5)ow2 NVarley(2) (led tl hdd over 3f out: sn btn) 11 4
LONG HANDICAP Lord Advocate 6-13

11/10 Ashover, **5/4** Batabanoo (op 4/5), **8/1** MASTER HYDE (USA), **14/1** Lord Advocate, CSF £17.33 TOTE £9.00 (£6.00) OWNER Mr D. Callaghan (CONSETT) BRED Saddle Home Farm 4 Rn
2m 29.4 (0.90 under best) (-1.60) SF: 45/64/39/11
STEWARDS' ENQUIRY Fessey susp. 9-16/8/95 (careless riding).

2817 WRYNOSE MAIDEN AUCTION STKS (2-Y.O) (Class E) £3,023.90 (£915.20: £446.60: £212.30) **5f** Stalls: High GOING minus 0.69 sec per fur (HD) 7-50 (7-50)

2548⁴ **Weetman's Weigh (IRE)** *(66)*(Fav)*(RHollinshead)* 2-8-3 KDarley(2) (chsd ldrs: rdn to ld 1f out: r.o) ....— **1**
2498⁶ Answers-To-Thomas *(67) (JMJefferson)* 2-8-6 GHind(3) (w ldr: disp ld 2f out to 1f out: kpt on wl) ....½ **2**
977⁶ Secret Voucher *(57) (BAMcMahon)* 2-8-0 GCarter(4) (led tl hdd 1f out: no ex) 1½ **3**
2308⁴ Paper Maze *(39) (JAHarris)* 2-7-9 DaleGibson(5) (a chsng ldrs: drvn along ½-wy: no imp) 4 **4**
Palacegate Chief *(25) (JBerry)* 2-8-10 JCarroll(1) (w'like: scope: lw: sn outpcd & wl bhd) 9 **5**

9/4 WEETMAN'S WEIGH (IRE), **3/1** Palacegate Chief, **4/1** Secret Voucher, Answers-To-Thomas, **5/1** Paper Maze, CSF £10.58 TOTE £2.70: £1.60 £2.00 (£4.90) OWNER Ed Weetman (Haulage & Storage) Ltd (UPPER LONGDON) BRED David Commins 5 Rn 60.7 secs (0.50) SF: 23/24/14/-/-

2818 HARD KNOTT (S) H'CAP (0-60) (3-Y.O) (Class G) £2,549.00 (£714.00: £347.00) **5f 207y** Stalls: High GOING minus 0.69 sec per fur (HD) 8-20 (8-21)

2016⁶ **Commander Glen (IRE) (44)***(59) (MartynMeade)* 3-9-0b VSlattery(7) (lw: outpcd & bhd: hdwy ½-wy: led 1f out: r.o wl) ....— **1**
2372⁴ Daily Challenger (USA) **(43)***(42)*(Fav)*(RonaldThompson)* 3-8-8 (5) LNewton(9) (w ldrs: kpt on fnl f: no ch w wnr) 6 **2**
*2493*⁶ Northern Grey **(51)***(47) (JBerry)* 3-9-0 (7) PRoberts(8) (mde most tl hdd 1f out: one pce) 1 **3**
2620⁸ Komlucky **(44)***(40) (FJO'Mahony)* 3-8-11b(3) PMcCabe(6) (b: chsd ldrs: effrt 2f out: kpt on one pce fnl f) ....hd **4**
2772⁶ Sunday Mail Too (IRE) **(40)***(31) (MissLAPerratt)* 3-8-10b JCarroll(2) (plld hrd: hmpd after 2f: hung rt fnl 2f: nvr able to chal) 1¾ **5**
2518⁵ Lordan Velvet (IRE) **(43)***(33) (LLungo)* 3-8-13 DaleGibson(10) (chsd ldrs: nt qckn fnl 2f: nvr trbld ldrs) ....½ **6**
2372⁹ Oubeck Princess **(40)***(23) (EWeymes)* 3-8-10 GHind(3) (s.i.s: nvr trbld ldrs) 2½ **7**
2425⁹ Seenthelight **(42)***(25) (DMoffatt)* 3-8-9 (3) DarrenMoffatt(4) (cl up tl wknd wl over 1f out) ....s.h **8**
2332⁹ Benten **(33)***(11) (DWChapman)* 3-8-3b NCarlisle(11) (dwlt: n.d) 1¾ **9**
*2144*⁷ Lawnswood Lady **(43)***(2) (RHollinshead)* 3-8-13 KDarley(1) (nvr trbld ldrs) 7 **10**
2582¹⁴ West Farm Boy **(33)** *(JJO'Neill)* 3-8-3b GDuffield(5) (cl up 4f: sn wknd) 6 **11**

7/2 Daily Challenger (USA), **9/2** COMMANDER GLEN (IRE), **5/1** Seenthelight, **13/2** Komlucky, **7/1** Lordan Velvet (IRE), Benten, **12/1** Lawnswood Lady, Northern Grey, **14/1** Sunday Mail Too (IRE), **20/1** Oubeck Princess, **33/1** West Farm Boy, CSF £20.69 CT £167.49 TOTE £6.20: £2.00 £2.30 £3.70 (£16.50) Trio £28.80 OWNER Ladyswood Racing Club (MALMESBURY) BRED Des Vere Hunt Farming Co 11 Rn 1m 12.8 (0.50) SF: 35/18/23/16/7/9/-/1/-/-/-
Bt in 3,100 gns

2819 WHINLATTER LIMITED STKS (0-70) (3-Y.O+) (Class E) £3,656.40 (£897.60) **6f 206y** Stalls: High GOING minus 0.69 sec per fur (HD) 8-50 (8-51)

2700* **Purple Fling (70)***(82)*(Fav)*(SirMarkPrescott)* 4-9-10 3x GDuffield(2) (lw: mde all: pushed along 2f out: r.o wl) ....— **1**
2507⁶ Crown of Love (USA) **(65)***(63) (MRStoute)* 3-8-6 GHind(1) (trckd wnr: effrt 2f out: hung rt & nt r.o) 3½ **2**

4/7 PURPLE FLING, **6/4** Crown of Love (USA), TOTE £1.80 OWNER Cheveley Park Stud (NEWMARKET) BRED Mrs P. Lewis 2 Rn 1m 28.2 (2.50) SF: 24/-
WEIGHT FOR AGE 3yo-7lb

T/Plpt: £194.10 (48.28 Tckts). T/Qdpt: £31.90 (0.25 Tckts). AA

2619-RIPON (R-H)
Monday July 31st (Good to firm, Firm patches)
WEATHER: sunny & v.hot WIND: nil

2820 E.B.F. ROUNDABOUT MAIDEN STKS (2-Y.O) (Class D) £4,260.00 (£1,290.00: £630.00: £300.00) **6f** Stalls: Low GOING minus 0.44 sec per fur (F) 2-30 (2-31)

2619⁶ **Privileged** *(72+)*(Fav)*(MrsJRRamsden)* 2-9-0 KFallon(8) (lw: s.i.s: hld up: hdwy ½-wy: led over 1f out: drvn out) ....— **1**
2534⁴ Vasetto *(69)*(Fav)*(SirMarkPrescott)* 2-9-0 GDuffield(3) (led tl over 1f out: kpt on u.p) 1 **2**

24735 Lucky Rabbit *(69) (BWHills)* 2-9-0 RHughes(7) (swtg: trckd ldrs: effrt 2f out: hung lft u.p: nt qckn fnl f) ....s.h 3
Jo Mell *(66+) (MHEasterby)* 2-9-0 MBirch(2) (unf: dwlt: hld up & plld hrd: hdwy 2f out: sn outpcd)....1¼ 4
Ancestral Jane *(56+) (MrsJRRamsden)* 2-8-9 RCochrane(4) (lengthy: scope: bit bkwd: dwlt: hld up & plld hrd: stdy hdwy ½-wy: kpt on wl fnl f) 1¾ 5
Phantom Haze *(53) (MissSEHall)* 2-9-0 NConnorton(5) (small: bit bkwd: dwlt: sn w ldrs: hung lft & wknd over 1f out)....3 6
*1212*11 Miletrian City *(40) (JBerry)* 2-9-0 JCarroll(1) (bit bkwd: chsd ldrs: rdn ½-wy: sn lost pl)....5 7
22574 Sonya Marie *(31) (JGFitzGerald)* 2-8-9 JFortune(9) (sn outpcd & pushed along: wnt rt 2f out: sn wknd)....1½ 8
Dino's Mistral *(7) (FHLee)* 2-9-0 LDettori(6) (tall: bit bkwd: chsd ldrs: edgd rt & wknd 2f out: eased & sn bhd)....11 9

11/4 PRIVILEGED, Vasetto, **3/1** Lucky Rabbit, **9/1** Dino's Mistral, Ancestral Jane, **12/1** Jo Mell, Miletrian City, **20/1** Phantom Haze, **25/1** Sonya Marie, CSF £10.93 TOTE £3.50: £1.40 £1.30 £1.60 (£4.70) Trio £3.10 OWNER L C and A E Sigsworth (THIRSK) BRED L. C. and Mrs A. E. Sigsworth 9 Rn 1m 13.1 (2.90) SF: 21/18/18/15/5/2/-/-/-

2821 BOUNCING CASTLE (S) H'CAP (0-60) (3-Y.O+) (Class F) £2,944.00 (£892.00: £436.00: £208.00)

5f Stalls: Low GOING minus 0.44 sec per fur (F) 3-00 (3-01)

2521 12 **Pallium (IRE) (55)***(62)*(Fav)*(MrsAMNaughton)* 7-10-0 JWeaver(2) (hld up: effrt & swtchd rt over 2f out: led ins fnl f: hld on wl)....— 1
26985 Arc Lamp **(38)***(43) (JAGlover)* 9-8-11 SDWilliams(1) (lw: w ldr: led ½-wy tl ins fnl f: kpt on wl) ....¾ 2
2784* Pretty Average **(35)***(38) (BRichmond)* 5-8-8 5x ClaireBalding(3) (led to ½-wy: ev ch 1f out: unable qckn)....½ 3
23983 Brisas **(41)***(40) (CWFairhurst)* 8-9-0 RCochrane(7) (s.s: bhd: hdwy over 1f out: styd on u.p towards fin)....1¼ 4
26658 Farndale **(35)***(28) (RonaldThompson)* 8-8-3 (5) LNewton(5) (sn outpcd & pushed along: styd on fnl 2f)....1¾ 5
17395 China Hand (IRE) **(51)***(41) (MartynWane)* 3-9-5 KFallon(4) (chsd ldrs tl wknd over 1f out)....1 6
*2627*5 Cheeky Chappy **(36)***(26) (DWChapman)* 4-8-9b ACulhane(8) (sn outpcd: effrt & wandered ½-wy: kpt on: nvr nr ldrs)....s.h 7
2390 10 Brigadore Gold **(25)***(7) (FHLee)* 5-7-12b NCarlisle(9) (outpcd fr ½-wy) 2½ 8
2484 14 Arkindale Amber **(39)***(8) (FJO'Mahony)* 3-8-7 JFortune(11) (swtg: sn chsng ldrs: wknd & hung bdly 2f out) 4 9
*2590*5 I'm Playing **(46)***(7) (MJohnston)* 3-9-0 TWilliams(6) (prom early: bhd fr ½-wy)....2½ 10

7/2 PALLIUM (IRE), **4/1** Pretty Average, **5/1** Arc Lamp, **11/2** Brisas, Cheeky Chappy, **14/1** I'm Playing, China Hand (IRE), **16/1** Farndale, **25/1** Brigadore Gold, **33/1** Arkindale Amber, CSF £19.73 CT £65.14 TOTE £4.10: £1.60 £1.90 £1.70 (£12.20) Trio £22.80 OWNER Mr W. J. Kelly (RICHMOND) BRED North Ridge Farm Inc 10 Rn 59.7 secs (1.70) SF: 45/26/21/23/11/19/9/-/-/-
WEIGHT FOR AGE 3yo-5lb
No bid

2822 TOMMY SHEDDEN CHALLENGE TROPHY H'CAP (0-90) (3-Y.O) (Class C) £5,569.00 (£1,672.00: £806.00: £373.00)

1m 1f Stalls: High GOING minus 0.44 sec per fur (F) 3-30 (3-31)

25718 **Rockforce (82)***(93) (MRChannon)* 3-9-7 RHughes(4) (trckd ldrs: effrt over 2f out: styd on u.p to ld wl ins fnl f) ....— 1
24375 Mister Fire Eyes (IRE) **(71)***(82) (CEBrittain)* 3-8-10 BDoyle(5) (led: edgd lft u.p ins fnl f: hdd nr fin)....nk 2
27702 Hand Woven **(72)***(78)*(Fav)*(WJHaggas)* 3-8-11 RCochrane(3) (lw: trckd ldrs: pushed along 4f out: outpcd fnl 2f)....2½ 3
17355 Juweilla **(63)***(66) (JWPayne)* 3-8-2 GBardwell(1) (hld up: rn wd ent st: sn chsng ldrs: wknd wl over 1f out)....2 4
2375* Bulsara **(58)***(55) (CWFairhurst)* 3-7-11 JLowe(6) (hld up: effrt over 3f out: rdn & wknd wl over 1f out) 3 5
25032 Shining Edge **(58)***(53) (MHEasterby)* 3-7-11 NCarlisle(2) (hld up & plld hrd: rn wd ent st: effrt on outside over 2f out: wnt rt & sn wknd) 1¼ 6

9/4 Hand Woven, **5/2** ROCKFORCE, **5/1** Mister Fire Eyes (IRE), **11/2** Bulsara, **6/1** Shining Edge, **10/1** Juweilla, CSF £14.20 TOTE £3.10: £1.90 £3.40 (£8.30) OWNER Mr G. Z. Mizel (UPPER LAMBOURN) BRED Guest Leasing and Bloodstock Co 6 Rn 1m 52.8 (2.60) SF: 46/35/31/19/8/6

2823 ARMSTRONG MEMORIAL CHALLENGE CUP RATED STKS H'CAP (0-95) (3-Y.O+) (Class B) £8,223.00 (£3,057.00: £1,478.50: £617.50: £258.75: £115.25)
6f Stalls: Low GOING minus 0.44 sec per fur (F) 4-00 (4-01)

2096[6] **Rock Symphony (87)***(95)*(Fav)*(WJHaggas)* 5-9-2 RCochrane(4) (lw: hld up: stdy hdwy 2f out: n.m.r, swtchd & ev ch ins fnl f: hrd rdn & led post) — 1
2652[2] Croft Pool **(80)***(88) (JAGlover)* 4-8-9 LDettori(5) (chsd ldrs: drvn along ½-wy: styd on to ld ins fnl f: jst ct) s.h 2
2324* Perryston View **(90)***(93) (PCalver)* 3-8-13v MBirch(3) (lw: trckd ldrs: led 2f out tl ins fnl f: nt qckn) 1¾ 3
1100[11] Lord Olivier (IRE) **(92)***(92) (WJarvis)* 5-9-7 MTebbutt(2) (w ldrs: pushed along ½-wy: edgd rt & kpt on same pce) 1¼ 4
2764[26] Palacegate Touch **(87)***(86) (JBerry)* 5-9-2v JCarroll(1) (led to 2f out: hung lft u.p & grad wknd fnl f) ½ 5
2288[8] Takadou (IRE) **(83)***(58) (MissLCSiddall)* 4-8-12 DHarrison(6) (sn outpcd: drvn along ½-wy: sn lost tch) 9 6

5/2 ROCK SYMPHONY, **11/4** Perryston View, **7/2** Croft Pool, **7/1** Palacegate Touch, Takadou (IRE), **10/1** Lord Olivier (IRE), CSF £10.78 TOTE £3.20: £1.40 £2.00 (£4.10) OWNER Mrs C. E. Feather (NEWMARKET) BRED J. R. and Mrs Haggas 6 Rn 1m 10.7 (0.50) SF: 56/49/48/53/47/19
WEIGHT FOR AGE 3yo-6lb

2824 'GO RACING IN YORKSHIRE' H'CAP (0-70) (3-Y.O+) (Class E) £3,217.60 (£974.80: £476.40: £227.20)
1m 4f 60y Stalls: High GOING minus 0.44 sec per fur (F) 4-30 (4-31)

2648* **Lord Hastie (USA) (49)***(61) (CWThornton)* 7-9-1 5x AMackay(6) (trckd ldrs: edgd lft ins fnl f: led nr fin: hld on wl) — 1
2663[2] North Ardar **(57)***(69)*(Fav)*(MrsMReveley)* 5-9-2 (7) SCopp(1) (hld up: trckd ldrs: wnt lft & led over 2f out: hung rt: hrd rdn, hdd & nt qckn towards fin) nk 2
2546[3] Outstayed Welcome **(51)***(55) (MJHaynes)* 3-8-0 (5) MBaird(4) (b.off hind: trckd ldrs: led over 3f out: hdd & n.m.r over 2f out: one pce) 6 3
1205[7] Gold Desire **(33)***(26) (MBrittain)* 5-7-13 JLowe(3) (hdwy ½-wy: sn wl outpcd) 8 4
91[7] Non Vintage (IRE) **(58)***(41) (MCChapman)* 4-9-7 (3) PMcCabe(5) (swtg: s.i.s: bhd: sme hdwy 2f out: n.d) 8 5
2586[3] Bex Boy (IRE) **(29)***(7) (MWEasterby)* 4-7-2b(7) PFessey(2) (racd wd: sn w ldrs: rdn & wknd over 2f out) 4 6
Le Temeraire **(27)***(4) (DonEnricoIncisa)* 9-7-7 KimTinkler(7) (led tl over 3f out: wknd over 2f out) ½ 7

LONG HANDICAP Le Temeraire 7-5

7/4 North Ardar, **3/1** LORD HASTIE (USA), **4/1** Outstayed Welcome, **7/1** Bex Boy (IRE), **12/1** Gold Desire, **14/1** Le Temeraire, **16/1** Non Vintage (IRE), CSF £8.37 TOTE £4.00: £2.00 £1.60 (£3.40) OWNER Mrs Joy Bendall (MIDDLEHAM) BRED Upland Park Stud 7 Rn
2m 38.3 (4.30) SF: 37/45/19/2/17/-/-
WEIGHT FOR AGE 3yo-12lb

2825 SEE-SAW MAIDEN STKS (3-Y.O+) (Class D) £3,969.20 (£1,202.60: £587.80: £280.40) **1m 2f** Stalls: High GOING minus 0.44 sec per fur (F) 5-00 (5-00)

Ninette (USA) *(67++)*(Fav)*(JHMGosden)* 3-8-6 LDettori(1) (str: cmpt: swvd lft s: sn trckng ldr: led on bit over 2f out: readily) — 1
2506[4] Baddi Quest **(65)***(68) (BHanbury)* 3-8-11 JWeaver(4) (led: sn drvn along: hdd over 2f out: no ch w wnr) 2½ 2
Dream Sweet Dreams (USA) *(23) (FHLee)* 6-9-2 MWigham(3) (lost tch fnl 4f) 25 3
2520[4] Catch the Pigeon *(REBarr)* 6-8-9 (7) PFessey(2) (reluctant to r: swvd lft s: uns rdr: rmntd) dist 4

4/5 NINETTE (USA) (4/7-10/11), **5/4** Baddi Quest (4/7-10/11), **14/1** Catch the Pigeon (op 25/1), **33/1** Dream Sweet Dreams (USA), CSF £2.09 TOTE £1.60 (£1.10) OWNER Mr K. Abdullah (NEWMARKET) BRED Juddmonte Farms 4 Rn
2m 6.7 (3.20) SF: 30/31/-/-
WEIGHT FOR AGE 3yo-10lb

T/Jkpt: £793.20 (8.95 Tckts). T/Plpt: £12.50 (1,288.08 Tckts). T/Qdpt: £13.20 (6.75 Tckts). WG

2808-**BRIGHTON (L-H)**
Tuesday August 1st (Firm)
WEATHER: v.hot WIND: almost nil

2826
JIMMY HEAL MEMORIAL TROPHY NURSERY H'CAP (2-Y.O) (Class D)
£4,191.00 (£1,248.00: £594.00: £267.00)
5f 59y Stalls: Low GOING minus 0.52 sec per fur (F) 2-00 (2-02)

2523* **Gagajulu** *(72) (PDEvans)* 2-9-6 GHind(2) (lw: 4th st: hrd rdn over 1f out: led nr fin) ....— 1
2515³ Dande Flyer *(66) (DWPArbuthnot)* 2-9-1 RPrice(3) (b.nr hind: 5th st: led over 1f out: hrd rdn ins fnl f: hdd nr fin) ....nk 2
2674⁷ Centurion *(68)*(Fav)*(RHannon)* 2-9-7 RHughes(4) (led over 3f: one pce) 1¼ 3
2683* Balpare *(62) (NACallaghan)* 2-9-4 7x BDoyle(5) (lw: outpcd: 6th st: hdwy fnl f: r.o) 1¼ 4
2281³ Nameless *(24) (DJSCosgrove)* 2-8-2 (3) PMcCabe(6) (lw: 3rd st: hrd rdn over 1f out: sn wknd)8 5
2515⁷ Bath Knight *(3) (DJSffrenchDavis)* 2-8-5 TQuinn(1) (w ldr over 2f) 7 6

13/8 Centurion, **7/2** Nameless, **4/1** GAGAJULU (3/1-9/2), **9/2** Balpare, **14/1** Dande Flyer (8/1-16/1), **20/1** Bath Knight, CSF £41.04 TOTE £5.60: £2.60 £5.50 (£21.90) OWNER Mr George Teo (MARLBOROUGH)/Mr R. F. F. Mason (WELSHPOOL) BRED Roger C. Denton 6 Rn
62.2 secs (2.20) SF: 19/23/13/17/-/-

2827
BLACK ROCK CONDITIONS STKS (3-Y.O+) (Class D) £4,439.20 (£1,070.80)
7f 214y Stalls: Low GOING minus 0.52 sec per fur (F) 2-30 (2-30)

2405⁵ **Rising Dough (IRE) (72)***(85) (GLMoore)* 3-9-0 SWhitworth(1) (lw: mde all: qcknd 2f out: hrd rdn over 2f out: r.o wl) ....— 1
1373⁶ Veuve Hoornaert (IRE) **(87)***(72)*(Fav)*(RHannon)* 3-8-8 RPerham(2) (lw: chsd wnr: ev ch over 2f out: hrd rdn over 1f out: unable qckn) 3½ 2

1/2 Veuve Hoornaert (IRE), **7/4** RISING DOUGH (IRE), TOTE £2.00 OWNER Mr Bryan Pennick (EPSOM) BRED David John Brown 2 Rn
1m 33.9 (1.70) SF: 45/32

2828
STANMER CLAIMING STKS (3-Y.O) (Class F) £2,519.00 (£694.00: £329.00)
7f 214y Stalls: Low GOING minus 0.52 sec per fur (F) 3-00 (3-00)

*2605*⁵ **First Crush (69)***(70)*(Fav)*(SirMarkPrescott)* 3-8-10b TQuinn(5) (mde all: clr 1f out: rdn out) ..— 1
2549⁶ Blasted **(62)***(74) (RHannon)* 3-9-5 RHughes(3) (lw: 3rd st: chsd wnr over 1f out: unable qckn) 2½ 2
2522⁸ Water Hazard (IRE) **(37)***(62) (SDow)* 3-8-0 (7) ADaly(2) (swtg: in rr 6f: hdwy over 1f out: r.o one pce) ....hd 3
2574² Kama Simba **(58)***(65) (NACallaghan)* 3-8-13 RCochrane(4) (lw: 4th st: rdn over 2f out: one pce) 1¼ 4
2684* Gentle Irony **(51)***(55) (BJMeehan)* 3-8-5b BDoyle(1) (chsd wnr over 6f) 1¼ 5

5/4 FIRST CRUSH, **3/1** Gentle Irony (op 2/1), **9/2** Kama Simba, Blasted, **20/1** Water Hazard (IRE), CSF £6.68 TOTE £2.30: £1.70 £1.90 (£5.00) OWNER Mrs L. Burnet (NEWMARKET) BRED Cheveley Park Stud Ltd 5 Rn
1m 34.3 (2.10) SF: 28/32/20/23/13

2829
BRIGHTON CHALLENGE CUP H'CAP (0-80) (4-Y.O+) (Class D)
£3,841.75 (£1,144.00: £544.50: £244.75)
1m 3f 196y Stalls: High GOING minus 0.52 sec per fur (F) 3-30 (3-31)

2687² **Carpathian (55)***(70) (LordHuntingdon)* 4-8-3 DHarrison(1) (lw: 3rd st: led wl over 1f out: edgd lft: r.o wl) ....— 1
2639* Prince Danzig (IRE) **(59)***(69) (DJGMurraySmith)* 4-8-7 5x PaulEddery(4) (lw: led over 9f: ev ch wl over 1f out: unable qckn) 3½ 2
2639² Exhibit Air (IRE) **(62)***(63)*(Fav)*(RAkehurst)* 5-8-10b TQuinn(3) (lw: 2nd st: led over 2f out tl wl over 1f out: wknd fnl f) 7 3
2657² Emma Grimes (IRE) **(46)***(45) (JSMoore)* 4-7-3 (5)ow1 NVarley(2) (4th st: wknd over 2f out) ....½ 4
2599⁵ Miss Pin Up **(80)***(78) (WJHaggas)* 6-10-0 RMcGhin(7) (5th st: wknd over 3f out) 1½ 5
LONG HANDICAP Emma Grimes (IRE) 7-0

15/8 Exhibit Air (IRE), **5/2** CARPATHIAN, **3/1** Miss Pin Up, **5/1** Prince Danzig (IRE), **14/1** Emma Grimes (IRE) (10/1-16/1), CSF £13.30 TOTE £3.50: £1.70 £2.50 (£7.70) OWNER The Queen (WEST ILSLEY) BRED Sheikh Mohammed bin Rashid al Maktoum 5 Rn
2m 29.7 (0.70) SF: 42/41/35/17/50

2830 GORING (S) H'CAP (0-60) (3-Y.O+) (Class G) £2,243.00 (£618.00: £293.00)
1m 3f 196y Stalls: High GOING minus 0.52 sec per fur (F) 4-00 (4-01)

*2090** **Glow Forum (29)***(40) (GLMoore)* 4-9-1 TQuinn(2) (qcknd & led 8f out: hrd rdn over 1f out: r.o wl)........— **1**
2536[3] Guest Alliance (IRE) **(51)***(55) (AMoore)* 3-9-12 CandyMorris(1) (lw: led 4f: 3rd st: chsd wnr fnl 3f: unable qckn)........5 **2**
2129[6] Presto Boy **(45)***(45)*(Fav)*(MBell)* 3-9-6 DHarrison(4) (rdn over 4f out: 2nd st: wknd over 1f out)........3½ **3**
2486[16] Coalisland **(18)** *(RIngram)* 5-8-4b NAdams(3) (t.o fnl 7f)........dist **4**

6/4 Presto Boy, **9/4** GLOW FORUM, **5/2** Guest Alliance (IRE), **12/1** Coalisland (8/1-14/1), CSF £7.25 TOTE £3.00 (£3.50) OWNER The Forum Ltd (EPSOM) BRED Forum Bloodstock Ltd 4 Rn
2m 44.4 (15.40) SF: -/-/-/-
WEIGHT FOR AGE 3yo-11lb
No bid

2831 HASSOCKS H'CAP (0-70) (3-Y.O) (Class E) £3,557.50 (£1,060.00: £505.00: £227.50) **6f 209y** Stalls: Low GOING minus 0.52 sec per fur (F) 4-30 (4-30)

2404[6] **Sally Weld (56)***(62) (CJBenstead)* 3-8-10 MWigham(3) (2nd st: rdn over 2f out: led wl ins fnl f: r.o wl)........— **1**
2500[3] Seventeens Lucky **(67)***(71) (BobJones)* 3-9-7v RCochrane(2) (led: rdn over 2f out: hdd wl ins fnl f: unable qckn)........¾ **2**
2451[3] Never so Rite (IRE) **(61)***(65)*(Fav)*(DWPArbuthnot)* 3-9-1 TQuinn(5) (4th st: rdn over 2f out: r.o ins fnl f)........nk **3**
2641[4] Stoppes Brow **(63)***(65) (GLMoore)* 3-9-3v SWhitworth(4) (swtg: 5th st: rdn over 1f out: one pce)........½ **4**
2631[6] Tomal **(47)***(44) (RIngram)* 3-8-1 NAdams(6) (6th st: a bhd)........2½ **5**
1983[5] See You Again **(63)***(46) (RHannon)* 3-9-3 RHughes(1) (3rd st: wknd 2f out)........6 **6**

13/8 Never so Rite (IRE), **2/1** Seventeens Lucky (6/4-9/4), **5/1** Stoppes Brow, **10/1** SALLY WELD (6/1-12/1), **11/1** See You Again (5/1-12/1), **16/1** Tomal, CSF £28.45 TOTE £12.80: £1.50 £1.10 (£11.60) OWNER Mr R. Lamb (EPSOM) BRED R. P. Williams 6 Rn
1m 22.5 (2.50) SF: 19/28/22/22/1/3

T/Plpt: £308.20 (29.09 Tckts). T/Qdpt: £23.10 (8.55 Tckts). AK

2540-CATTERICK (L-H)
Tuesday August 1st (Good to firm)
WEATHER: sunny WIND: mod half against

2832 5TH REGIMENT ROYAL ARTILLERY CHAMPAGNE POL ROGER H'CAP (0-60) (3-Y.O+) (Class F) £3,206.00 (£891.00: £428.00)
7f Stalls: Low GOING minus 0.18 sec per fur (GF) 2-15 (2-17)

2390* **What a Nightmare (IRE) (56)***(67) (JAGlover)* 3-8-13b(5) AWhelan(17) (mde all: eased towards fin)........— **1**
2698[3] It's Academic **(58)***(66)*(Fav)*(MrsJRRamsden)* 3-9-6 KFallon(1) (lw: hld up & bhd: effrt appr st: swtchd outside: r.o: nrst fin)........1¼ **2**
2549[8] Bogart **(55)***(61) (CWFairhurst)* 4-9-6 (3) JTate(9) (in tch: hdwy 2f out: styd on one pce fnl f).....¾ **3**
766[6] Bedazzle **(35)***(37) (MBrittain)* 4-8-3 GBardwell(8) (b: chsd ldrs: kpt on same pce fnl f)........1¾ **4**
2758[5] Sense of Priority **(57)***(59) (DNicholls)* 6-9-11 AlexGreaves(13) (lw: chsd ldrs: edgd lft & nt qckn fnl f)........s.h **5**
2179[6] Mitsis **(41)***(40) (GCBravery)* 4-8-9b MFenton(15) (a in tch: hdwy 2f out: one pce fnl f)........1½ **6**
2517[2] At the Savoy (IRE) **(43)***(37) (TDBarron)* 4-8-11b JFortune(3) (a chsng ldrs: one pce fnl 2f).......2 **7**
St Louis Lady **(60)***(53) (WJarvis)* 4-9-9 (5) MBaird(4) (nvr bttr than mid div)........¾ **8**
2631[7] Lady-Bo-K **(54)***(46) (CaptJWilson)* 4-9-8b JWeaver(14) (b.hind: s.i.s: hdwy & swtchd over 2f out: no imp)........hd **9**
2630[15] Prime Property (IRE) **(31)***(23) (MWEasterby)* 3-7-0b(7) PFessey(12) (sn chsng ldrs: hdwy ent st: wknd 2f out)........nk **10**
2390[8] Delmour **(27)***(14) (WMBrisbourne)* 4-7-2 (7)ow2 MartinDwyer(5) (nvr trbld ldrs)........1¼ **11**
2290[4] Tyrone Flyer **(50)***(39) (RHarris)* 6-9-4 AMackay(16) (chsd wnr to st: sn wknd)........hd **12**
2772[3] Miss Pigalle **(37)***(25) (MissLAPerratt)* 4-8-5b GDuffield(6) (b: dwlt: hdwy appr st: sn btn).........½ **13**
2484[10] Henry Will **(27)***(13) (WLBarker)* 11-7-6 (3) DarrenMoffatt(11) (a rr div)........¾ **14**
2698[13] Northern Spark **(46)***(31) (MartynWane)* 7-9-0 SMaloney(2) (broke wl: sn lost pl & bhd: n.d)....½ **15**
Wacky (IRE) **(26)** *(DNicholls)* 4-7-8 JLowe(18) (bmpd over 2f out: n.d)........10 **16**

1074[12] T'Niel **(25)** *(GFierro)* 4-7-7 NKennedy(7) (bhd fr ½-wy) ½ **17**
Steady Risk **(35)** *(MrsAMNaughton)* 4-8-3 JFanning(10) (in tch to st: sn lost pl) 6 **18**
LONG HANDICAP Delmour 6-13 T'Niel 7-6 Prime Property (IRE) 7-4

9/4 It's Academic, **5/1** At the Savoy (IRE), **6/1** WHAT A NIGHTMARE (IRE), Sense of Priority, **10/1** Bogart, **12/1** Miss Pigalle, St Louis Lady, **14/1** Northern Spark, **16/1** Lady-Bo-K, Mitsis, **20/1** Bedazzle, **25/1** Tyrone Flyer, **33/1** Henry Will, Prime Property (IRE), **50/1** Delmour, **66/1** Wacky (IRE), T'Niel, **100/1** Steady Risk, CSF £20.74 CT £136.69 TOTE £7.10: £1.10 £1.40 £2.30 £7.50 (£15.30) Trio £101.20 OWNER Bassetlaw Bloodstock Agency Ltd (WORKSOP) BRED Carrigbeg Stud Co Ltd 18 Rn 1m 27.6 (4.40) SF: 35/34/35/11/33/14/11/27/20/-/-/13/-/-/5/-/-/-
WEIGHT FOR AGE 3yo-6lb

2833 FRAGGLES CONDITIONS STKS (2-Y.O) (Class D) £3,687.50 (£1,100.00: £525.00: £237.50) 7f Stalls: Low GOING minus 0.18 sec per fur (GF) 2-45 (2-45)

2434[2] **Dankeston (USA)** *(84) (MBell)* 2-9-1v MFenton(2) (lw: trckd ldrs: led 1½f out: r.o) — **1**
2453* Crackernat (IRE) *(82)*(Fav)*(LMCumani)* 2-9-3 LDettori(1) (lw: led tl put hd in air & hdd 1½f out: swtchd ent fnl f: nt qckn) 1¾ **2**
2523[2] Ramsey Hope *(64) (CWFairhurst)* 2-9-3 NKennedy(3) (a chsng ldrs: no imp fnl 2f) 8 **3**
2354* Middle East *(60) (TDBarron)* 2-9-1 JFortune(4) (hld up & bhd: rn wd appr st: nvr plcd to chal) ¾ **4**

4/6 Crackernat (IRE) (10/11-Evens), **3/1** Middle East, **4/1** DANKESTON (USA) (op 5/2), **10/1** Ramsey Hope (op 6/1), CSF £7.24 TOTE £4.00 (£1.90) OWNER Mr Luciano Gaucci (NEWMARKET) BRED Donald MacRae 4 Rn 1m 28.6 (5.40) SF: 21/19/1/-

2834 HONDEGHEM (S) STKS (3 & & 5-Y.O) (Class G) £2,602.00 (£722.00: £346.00) 1m 5f 175y Stalls: Low GOING minus 0.18 sec per fur (GF) 3-15 (3-15)

2379[9] **Zanzara (IRE) (37)***(62) (MrsVAAconley)* 4-9-4 MDeering(1) (hdwy 5f out: rdn appr st: styd on to ld ins fnl f) — **1**
2676* Fearless Wonder **(50)***(65)*(Fav)*(MrsMReveley)* 4-9-9b KDarley(4) (lw: hdwy 7f out: sn cl up: rdn to ld over 1f out: sn hdd & no ex) 2 **2**
2481[4] Hong Kong Designer **(51)***(64) (SGNorton)* 3-8-5 (5) HKYim(3) (led after 3f tl over 1f out: sn btn) nk **3**
Dawn Palace *(TWDonnelly)* 4-9-9 SDWilliams(5) (prom tl outpcd 6f out: sn t.o) dist **4**
1430[6] Ladys Promise **(34)** *(GROldroyd)* 3-8-5 MMcAndrew(2) (led 3f: outpcd 8f out: sn t.o) 14 **5**

4/5 Fearless Wonder (10/11-Evens), **11/8** Hong Kong Designer, **12/1** ZANZARA (IRE) (op 8/1), **100/1** Dawn Palace, Ladys Promise, CSF £21.00 TOTE £9.00: £2.80 £1.10 (£4.80) OWNER Mr J. Chan (WESTOW) BRED Miss Ruth Lonergan 5 Rn 3m 6.1 (10.90) SF: 27/30/16/-/-
WEIGHT FOR AGE 3yo-13lb
No bid

2835 DRAGON TROOP H'CAP (0-75) (3-Y.O+) (Class D) £3,622.50 (£1,080.00: £515.00: £232.50) 1m 5f 175y Stalls: Low GOING minus 0.18 sec per fur (GF) 3-45 (3-50)

2658[2] **Admirals Secret (USA) (67)***(78)*(Fav)*(CFWall)* 6-9-9 (5) LNewton(2) (lw: trckd ldrs: hdwy gng wl appr st: led over 2f out: sn clr) — **1**
2734[6] Milngavie (IRE) **(34)***(43) (MJohnston)* 5-7-9b TWilliams(1) (swtg: led: qcknd over 4f out: hdd over 2f out: no ch w wnr) 2 **2**
2359[2] Bushehr (IRE) **(69)***(67) (JWHills)* 3-8-12 (5) MHenry(4) (lw: hld up: effrt ent st: hung lft & hit rails wl over 1f out: sn btn & eased) 9 **3**
2312[5] Manful **(69)***(50) (JHetherton)* 3-9-3 NKennedy(3) (b: unruly & led to s: chsd ldr tl outpcd appr st: sn btn) 15 **4**

11/8 ADMIRALS SECRET (USA), **6/4** Bushehr (IRE), **9/2** Milngavie (IRE), **8/1** Manful (5/1-10/1), CSF £6.88 TOTE £2.10 (£3.60) OWNER B. R. A. T. S (NEWMARKET) BRED Haras Santa Maria de Araras & Peter M. Brant 4 Rn 3m 6.4 (11.20) SF: 34/-/10/-
WEIGHT FOR AGE 3yo-13lb

2836 SANNA'S POST CLAIMING STKS (3-Y.O+) (Class F) £2,985.50 (£828.00: £396.50) 7f Stalls: Low GOING minus 0.18 sec per fur (GF) 4-15 (4-17)

2517[3] **Bold Angel (69)***(76)*(Fav)*(MHEasterby)* 8-8-10 MBirch(1) (a.p: rdn to ld ins fnl f) — **1**
2518* Super Benz **(60)***(73) (FJO'Mahony)* 9-8-10 SDWilliams(2) (lw: b: cl up: led over 2f out tl ins fnl f: kpt on) 1½ **2**
2518[2] Northern Trove (USA) **(68)***(56) (GMMoore)* 3-8-8 KDarley(5) (led tl hdd over 2f out: sn outpcd) 9 **3**

2527* Non Dimenticar Me (IRE) **(72)** *(SirMarkPrescott)* 3-8-5 GDuffield(3) (lw: sddle slipped after s: eased & lost tch after 3f) 25 **4**
Axed Again *(NBycroft)* 3-8-5 SMaloney(4) (sn outpcd & t.o) ....nk **5**

5/4 BOLD ANGEL, **2/1** Non Dimenticar Me (IRE), **4/1** Northern Trove (USA), **6/1** Super Benz, **66/1** Axed Again, CSF £8.36 TOTE £2.50: £1.20 £2.20 (£5.40) OWNER Mr A. M. Wragg (MALTON) BRED A. M. Wragg 5 Rn 1m 27.2 (4.00) SF: 32/29/6/-/-
WEIGHT FOR AGE 3yo-6lb

2837 LILLIBULERO H'CAP (0-65) (3-Y.O+) (Class F) £2,887.50 (£800.00: £382.50)
5f Stalls: Low GOING minus 0.18 sec per fur (GF) 4-45 (4-46)

2521² **Kalar (49)***(49)*(Fav)*(DWChapman)* 6-8-11b KDarley(2) (mde most: kpt on wl fnl f) ....— **1**
2521¹⁰ Able Sheriff **(53)***(50) (MWEasterby)* 3-8-11b MBirch(4) (hmpd s: smooth hdwy ½-wy: ev ch ins fnl f: nt qckn) 1 **2**
2753¹⁰ Flashing Sabre **(60)***(52) (JBerry)* 3-8-11 (7) PRoberts(5) (hmpd s: bhd tl hdwy 2f out: styd on wl) 1½ **3**
2736¹¹ Ramborette **(56)***(40) (DenysSmith)* 3-9-0 JWeaver(7) (a chsng ldrs: nt qckn fnl 2f) 2½ **4**
2736⁵ Leading Princess (IRE) **(46)***(28) (MissLAPerratt)* 4-8-8b GDuffield(6) (wnt lft s: in tch: no imp fr ½-wy) ....½ **5**
2821* Pallium (IRE) **(62)***(40) (MrsAMNaughton)* 7-9-10 7x ACulhane(8) (sn bhd & drvn: no imp) 1½ **6**
2680³ Dominelle **(57)***(32) (MHEasterby)* 3-9-1 SMaloney(1) (lw: disp ld to ½-wy: sn rdn & btn) ....¾ **7**
2582¹⁰ Jet Classic **(38)** *(MissJFCraze)* 3-7-7v(3) DWright(3) (b.hind: wnt rt s: spd to ½-wy: sn btn) 7 **8**
LONG HANDICAP Jet Classic 7-3

9/4 KALAR, **11/4** Dominelle, **6/1** Able Sheriff, **7/1** Flashing Sabre, **8/1** Ramborette, **9/1** Pallium (IRE) (op 6/1), **16/1** Leading Princess (IRE), **25/1** Jet Classic, CSF £15.05 CT £72.99 TOTE £3.00: £1.10 £2.10 £2.50 (£9.50) OWNER Mr E. Stockdale (YORK) BRED C. C. and Mrs Pryor 8 Rn
60.3 secs (2.80) SF: 32/29/31/19/11/23/11/-
WEIGHT FOR AGE 3yo-4lb

T/Jkpt: Not won; £6,725 to Nottingham 2/8/95. T/Plpt: £119.50 (109.69 Tckts). T/Qdpt: £39.60 (2.3 Tckts). AA

2826-BRIGHTON (L-H)
Wednesday August 2nd (Firm)
WEATHER: sunny WIND: fresh half bhd

2838 RINGMER (S) STKS (2-Y.O) (Class G) £2,243.00 (£618.00: £293.00)
5f 213y Stalls: Low GOING minus 0.71 sec per fur (HD) 2-15 (2-16)

2637² **Lussuria (IRE) (75)***(74+)*(Fav)*(BJMeehan)* 2-8-11 BDoyle(1) (mde all: hung rt over 3f out: rdn out) ....— **1**
*2382*¹⁰ No Sympathy **(56)***(61) (GLMoore)* 2-8-6 SWhitworth(4) (3rd st: chsd wnr over 2f out: rdn over 1f out: one pce) 3 **2**
*2591*⁵ Jessica's Song *(48) (WGMTurner)* 2-8-6 TSprake(2) (2nd st: rdn over 2f out: wknd over 1f out) 5 **3**
*1073*⁵ Fiddles Delight *(46) (MRChannon)* 2-8-6 PaulEddery(5) (4th st: rdn over 2f out: no hdwy) ....½ **4**
2666⁶ Salilian Twilight *(46) (JPearce)* 2-8-3 (3) JTate(3) (6th st: a bhd) ....s.h **5**
*1213*⁵ Iron And Steel *(AMoore)* 2-8-11 CandyMorris(6) (5th st: a bhd) 20 **6**

8/13 LUSSURIA (IRE) (Evens-4/7), **11/2** Fiddles Delight (4/1-6/1), **13/2** No Sympathy (7/2-7/1), **10/1** Jessica's Song (5/1-11/1), **16/1** Salilian Twilight, **20/1** Iron And Steel, CSF £4.87 TOTE £1.60: £1.20 £3.10 (£4.40) OWNER Mr Mario Lanfranchi (UPPER LAMBOURN) BRED Blandford Bloodstock 6 Rn 1m 8.8 (0.40) SF: 28/15/2/-/-/-
No bid.

2839 MARINA MAIDEN AUCTION STKS (2-Y.O) (Class E) £3,245.00 (£968.00: £462.00: £209.00)
6f 209y Stalls: Low GOING minus 0.71 sec per fur (HD) 2-45 (2-45)

2534² **Mancini** *(84)*(Fav)*(MBell)* 2-8-10 MFenton(5) (3rd st: led wl over 1f out: r.o wl) ....— **1**
2340⁴ Half An Inch (IRE) *(68) (BJMeehan)* 2-8-1 PaulEddery(4) (lw: led: rdn & hdd wl over 1f out: one pce) 3 **2**
2077³ Essentialselection **(76)***(72) (WJHaggas)* 2-8-2 (7) ElizabethTurner(6) (chsd ldr: 2nd st: rdn over 1f out: one pce) 2½ **3**
*2146*⁵ Dhulikhel *(56) (DMarks)* 2-7-9 NAdams(1) (6th st: rdn & sme hdwy fnl f: nvr nrr) ....nk **4**
2526⁵ Infantry Dancer *(55) (GCBravery)* 2-7-4 (5) NVarley(2) (4th st: rdn 3f out: one pce) ....nk **5**
Diego *(62) (CEBrittain)* 2-8-9 BDoyle(3) (5th st: a bhd) 3 **6**

6/4 MANCINI, **3/1** Half An Inch (IRE), **4/1** Infantry Dancer, **7/1** Essentialselection (op 9/2), **8/1** Diego (op 4/1), **33/1** Dhulikhel, CSF £6.10 TOTE £2.30: £1.60 £1.30 (£2.60) OWNER Mrs Anne Yearley (NEWMARKET) BRED Mrs J. Shipway-Pratt 6 Rn 1m 20.5 (0.50) SF: 27/11/13/-/-/5

2840 TOTE SPRINT H'CAP (0-80) (3-Y.O+) (Class D) £4,889.50 (£1,456.00: £693.00: £311.50) **5f 213y** Stalls: Low GOING minus 0.71 sec per fur (HD) 3-15 (3-15)

2539[4] **Walnut Burl (IRE) (54)***(59) (LJHolt)* 5-8-7 MFenton(4) (dwlt: 5th st: hdwy to ld 2f out: r.o) ....— 1
2714* Samsolom **(74)***(76)*(Fav)*(PHowling)* 7-9-13 7x PaulEddery(3) (hld up: 4th st: hdwy over 1f out: r.o) 1¼ 2
1963[9] Lugana Vision **(52)***(34) (RHarris)* 3-8-0b JQuinn(2) (2nd st: ev ch 2f out: rdn over 1f out: sn wknd: fin 4th, 5l: plcd 3rd) 3
2491[11] Sharp 'n Smart **(68)***(36) (BSmart)* 3-9-2 TQuinn(5) (led to 2f out: wkng whn hmpd over 1f out: fin 5th, 5l: plcd 4th) 4
1827* Prima Silk **(74)***(69)*(Fav)*(MJRyan)* 4-9-8 (5) MBaird(1) (3rd st: squeezed thro & edgd lft over 1f out: one pce: fin 3rd, 2½l: disq: plcd last) 0

5/2 Samsolom, Prima Silk, **3/1** WALNUT BURL (IRE), **6/1** Lugana Vision, **7/1** Sharp 'n Smart, CSF £9.94 TOTE £4.00: £1.80 £1.10 (£4.80) OWNER Mr G. Steinberg (BASINGSTOKE) BRED Limestone Stud 5 Rn 1m 7.9 (-0.50) SF: 37/54/7/9/47

WEIGHT FOR AGE 3yo-5lb

STEWARDS' ENQUIRY Baird susp. 11-15/8/95 (irresponsible riding).

2841 CLIFTONVILLE MEDIAN AUCTION MAIDEN STKS (3-Y.O F) (Class F) £2,519.00 (£694.00: £329.00) **1m 3f 196y** Stalls: High GOING minus 0.71 sec per fur (HD) 3-45 (3-46)

2509[5] **Coggle (55)***(63+)*(Fav)*(NAGraham)* 3-8-11b PaulEddery(2) (mde all: clr over 1f out: easily)..— 1
1136[17] Equasion (IRE) *(59) (GLMoore)* 3-8-11 CandyMorris(1) (reluctant to r: sn rdn to r in tch: chsd wnr 5f out: 2nd st: hrd rdn 2f out: no imp) 3 2
2262[2] Hanifa **(55)** (Fav)*(MissGayKelleway)* 3-8-11 TQuinn(3) (chsd wnr over 6f: 3rd st: sn wl bhd: t.o) ....dist 3

6/4 COGGLE, Hanifa, **11/4** Equasion (IRE) (6/4-3/1), CSF £4.75 TOTE £2.40 (£2.40) OWNER Mr R. D. Hollingsworth (NEWMARKET) BRED R. D. Hollingsworth 3 Rn 2m 35.2 (6.20) SF: -/-/-

OFFICIAL EXPLANATION **Hanifa: the trainer reported that the filly was weak and unable to handle the firm ground.**

2842 BRIGHTON SUMMER H'CAP (0-60) (3-Y.O+) (Class F) £3,149.00 (£874.00: £419.00) **1m 1f 209y** Stalls: High GOING minus 0.71 sec per fur (HD) 4-15 (4-16)

2657[10] **Mister O'Grady (IRE) (45)***(57) (RAkehurst)* 4-9-3 TQuinn(4) (3rd st: chsd ldr over 2f out: led ins fnl f: r.o) ....— 1
2433[4] Plinth **(56)***(66)*(Fav)*(NAGraham)* 4-10-0v AMcGlone(9) (led 7f out: clr 2f out: hdd ins fnl f: unable qckn) 1½ 2
2657[4] Ikhtiraa (USA) **(37)***(44) (RJO'Sullivan)* 5-8-9v WNewnes(10) (a.p: 2nd st: rdn over 2f out: r.o one pce fnl f) 1½ 3
2334[9] Tout de Val **(33)***(29) (KBishop)* 6-8-5 ow5 RPerham(6) (8th st: styd on fnl 2f: nvr nrr) 4 4
2305[4] Western Horizon (USA) **(40)***(41) (CEBrittain)* 3-8-3 BDoyle(5) (9th st: styd on fnl 2f: nvr nrr) ....hd 5
Salvatore Giuliano **(42)***(36) (AGFoster)* 5-9-0 TSprake(12) (11th st: nvr nrr) 4 6
2254[7] Dots Dee **(28)***(8) (JMBradley)* 6-8-0 JQuinn(7) (5th st: wknd over 2f out) 9 7
2528[7] Finjan **(50)***(30) (AGFoster)* 8-9-3 (5) JDSmith(11) (10th st: a bhd) ....s.h 8
2282[5] Maziere **(47)***(20) (MJHeaton-Ellis)* 3-8-10 RHughes(8) (led 3f: 4th st: sn wknd) 4 9
2682[3] Deceit the Second **(47)***(16) (GLewis)* 3-8-10b PaulEddery(1) (6th st: sn wknd) 2½ 10
2334[5] Sharp Gazelle **(36)** *(BSmart)* 5-8-1 (7) DaneO'Neill(2) (7th st: sn wknd) 8 11

100/30 Plinth, **5/1** MISTER O'GRADY (IRE) (4/1-6/1), **11/2** Deceit the Second, **6/1** Sharp Gazelle, **8/1** Dots Dee (op 5/1), Western Horizon (USA), **9/1** Ikhtiraa (USA) (op 6/1), **12/1** Maziere (op 8/1), **25/1** Finjan, **33/1** Tout de Val, Salvatore Giuliano, CSF £20.91 CT £131.75 TOTE £5.10: £2.50 £1.20 £2.40 (£8.30) Trio £43.50 OWNER City Industrial Supplies Ltd (EPSOM) BRED A. Ross 11 Rn 1m 59.5 (1.50) SF: 29/38/16/1/4/8/-/2/-/-/-

WEIGHT FOR AGE 3yo-9lb

2843 LEVY BOARD MAIDEN H'CAP (0-60) (3-Y.O+) (Class F) £3,123.80 (£866.80: £415.40) **6f 209y** Stalls: Low GOING minus 0.71 sec per fur (HD) 4-45 (4-46)

2685[14] **Tuigamala (37)***(43) (RIngram)* 4-9-5 NAdams(2) (3rd st: led over 1f out: r.o) ....— 1

2137 10 Green Apache **(28)***(25) (TJNaughton)* 3-7-13 (5) JDSmith(5) (6th st: hdwy 2f out: rdn & edgd lft over 1f out: r.o one pce fnl f)....4 2
2711 7 Amany (IRE) **(46)***(39)*(Fav)*(GLewis)* 3-9-8 PaulEddery(11) (led tl over 1f out: one pce)....1½ 3
2528 18 Sharp Spring **(42)***(33) (JWhite)* 4-9-5 (5) AWhelan(6) (4th st: rdn 2f out: one pce)....1 4
2659 7 Kensington Freight **(41)***(29) (JAkehurst)* 3-9-3 WNewnes(8) (9th st: nvr nrr)....1½ 5
2587 8 Arctic Poppy (USA) **(42)***(23) (IABalding)* 3-9-4 SO'Gorman(7) (8th st: rdn 2f out: one pce)....3 6
2404 10 Sarasonia **(30)***(8) (JWPayne)* 4-8-7 (5) NVarley(13) (2nd st: ev ch over 2f out: grad wknd)....1¼ 7
2404 9 Julia's Freebee **(36)***(13) (TMJones)* 4-9-4 RPerham(10) (7th st: wknd 2f out)....½ 8
251 6 Zeliba **(36)***(13) (CEBrittain)* 3-8-12 BDoyle(4) (5th st: rdn over 2f out: sn wknd)....s.h 9
2149 7 Amber Lily **(31)***(4) (JMBradley)* 3-8-2 (5)ow1 DGriffiths(9) (11th st: a bhd)....1¼ 10
2451 6 Nosirrah **(45)***(16) (CAHorgan)* 3-9-7 MPerrett(3) (12th st: a bhd)....1 11
1545 9 False Pretences (IRE) **(35)** *(BAPearce)* 3-8-4 (7) DaneO'Neill(12) (10th st: a bhd)....7 12
2789 10 Arrasas Lady **(24)** *(JCPoulton)* 5-8-6 RPrice(1) (ref to r: t.n.p).... R

2/1 Amany (IRE), **4/1** Kensington Freight, **6/1** Arctic Poppy (USA), **8/1** Sharp Spring (op 5/1), **12/1** TUIGAMALA (op 8/1), Zeliba (op 8/1), Nosirrah (op 6/1), **14/1** Sarasonia, **20/1** Julia's Freebee, **25/1** Green Apache, Amber Lily, False Pretences (IRE), Arrasas Lady, CSF £244.84 CT £766.25 TOTE £32.20: £7.60 £13.70 £1.20 (£267.50) Trio £344.90 OWNER Mr C. G. Adams (EPSOM) BRED Mrs S. Ingram 13 Rn 1m 20.6 (0.60) SF: 35/11/25/25/15/9/-/5/-/-/2/-/-
WEIGHT FOR AGE 3yo-6lb

2844

EDBURTON MAIDEN H'CAP (0-70) (3-Y.O+) (Class E) £3,557.50 (£1,060.00: £505.00: £227.50)
5f 59y Stalls: Low GOING minus 0.71 sec per fur (HD) 5-15 (5-15)

1258 10 **Hever Golf Star (58)***(70+)*(Fav)*(TJNaughton)* 3-8-13 (5) JDSmith(5) (mde virtually all: clr 2f out: r.o wl)....— 1
2642 5 Another Batchworth **(54)***(54) (SMellor)* 3-9-0 CAvery(1) (reard stalls: 5th st: rdn 2f out: chsd wnr over 1f out: one pce)....4 2
2708 7 Dark Menace **(64)***(59) (SMellor)* 3-9-10 RPerham(6) (2nd st: rdn 2f out: one pce)....1½ 3
2491 7 Prince Pellinore **(41)***(26) (JohnBerry)* 3-7-10 (5) NVarley(4) (w ldr 1f: 4th st: rdn over 2f out: sn wknd)....3½ 4
1972 6 Chief's Lady **(52)***(33) (RHarris)* 3-8-5 (7) GFaulkner(3) (dwlt: sn rcvrd: 3rd st: wknd 2f out)....1¼ 5
2527 4 Fiery Footsteps **(52)***(31) (PHowling)* 3-8-5 (7) TThomas(2) (6th st: a bhd)....½ 6

2/1 HEVER GOLF STAR, **7/2** Chief's Lady, **4/1** Another Batchworth, **9/2** Prince Pellinore, **11/2** Fiery Footsteps, **8/1** Dark Menace (5/1-9/1), CSF £10.52 TOTE £2.30: £1.90 £3.00 (£9.90) OWNER Mr M. P. Hanson (EPSOM) BRED Mrs L. Popely 6 Rn 59.5 secs (-0.50) SF: 48/32/37/4/11/9

T/Plpt: £26.00 (439.82 Tckts). T/Qdpt: £60.30 (0.25 Tckts) £61.20 to Pontefract 3/8/95. SM

2340-KEMPTON (R-H)
Wednesday August 2nd (Good to firm, Firm patches)

WEATHER: hot WIND: almost nil

2845

CHANNEL ONE APPRENTICE H'CAP (0-70) (3-Y.O+) (Class E) £3,582.50 (£1,085.00: £530.00: £252.50)
1m 4f Stalls: High GOING minus 0.65 sec per fur (HD) 6-00 (6-00)

2792 2 **Broughtons Formula (47)***(60)*(Fav)*(WJMusson)* 5-8-5b PMcCabe(5) (lw: wl bhd 9f out tl over 2f out: rapid hdwy over 1f out: led ins fnl f: r.o wl)....— 1
961 3 Roisin Clover **(67)***(77) (SDow)* 4-9-8 (3) ADaly(6) (lw: 3rd st: rdn over 2f out: n.m.r over 1f out: r.o one pce)....2 2
2289 9 Rock The Barney (IRE) **(56)***(65)*(Fav)*(PBurgoyne)* 6-9-0 JTate(1) (lw: 2nd st: led over 1f out tl ins fnl f: one pce)....¾ 3
2785 4 Phylian **(51)***(58) (SCWilliams)* 4-8-9b JStack(2) (led 7f out: clr over 4f out: hdd over 1f out: sn wknd)....2 4
2525 7 General Mouktar **(67)***(63) (MCPipe)* 5-9-11v LNewton(3) (lw: bhd fnl 4f)....8 5
1987 8 Vanola **(56)***(36) (PHowling)* 3-7-12 (5) DebbieBiggs(4) (led 5f: wknd over 3f out: 4th st)....12 6

11/4 BROUGHTONS FORMULA, Rock The Barney (IRE), **100/30** Roisin Clover (9/4-7/2), **11/2** Phylian, **7/1** General Mouktar, **33/1** Vanola, CSF £10.90 TOTE £3.20: £1.90 £1.70 (£4.80) OWNER Crawford Gray & Aylett (NEWMARKET) BRED The Lavington Stud 6 Rn
2m 35.06 (4.86) SF: 8/25/13/6/11/-
WEIGHT FOR AGE 3yo-11lb

2846 E.B.F. RIVERMEAD MAIDEN STKS (2-Y.O) (Class D) £3,680.00 (£1,115.00: £545.00: £260.00) 7f (Jubilee) GOING minus 0.65 sec per fur (HD) 6-30 (6-32)

2315³ **Winter Quarters (USA)** *(81) (IABalding)* 2-9-0 MHills(6) (lw: led over 4f out: clr 2f out: r.o wl) — 1
2200⁴ Flying Green (FR) *(76)*(Fav)*(RCharlton)* 2-9-0 PaulEddery(3) (lw: 2nd st: rdn over 2f out: unable qckn) 2 2
1964⁶ Golden Pond (IRE) *(66) (RFJohnsonHoughton)* 2-8-9 JQuinn(13) (hdwy over 2f out: hrd rdn over 1f out: r.o one pce) 2½ 3
825⁷ Nikita's Star (IRE) *(69) (DJGMurraySmith)* 2-9-0 TQuinn(2) (hdwy 4f out: 5th st: rdn over 2f out: one pce) ¾ 4
Storm Trooper (USA) *(66+)*(Fav)*(HRACecil)* 2-9-0 WRyan(17) (leggy: scope: 6th st: hmpd over 2f out: one pce) 1¼ 5
Mystic Knight *(66+) (RCharlton)* 2-9-0 TSprake(4) (leggy: unf: s.s: hdwy & nt clr run over 1f out: r.o) s.h 6
2408⁷ General Macarthur *(65) (JLDunlop)* 2-9-0 MRoberts(14) (lw: prom 3f) ½ 7
Paint It Black *(63) (RHannon)* 2-9-0 RHughes(5) (s.s: nvr nrr) ¾ 8
2548¹¹ Winged Prince *(55) (BJMeehan)* 2-9-0 BDoyle(16) (nvr nrr) 3½ 9
2529² Labeed (USA) *(55)*(Fav)*(MajorWRHern)* 2-9-0 WCarson(10) (nvr nr to chal) nk 10
2447⁴ Brave Maisie (IRE) *(46) (MMcCormack)* 2-8-6 (3) JTate(9) (4th st: wknd over 2f out) 1½ 11
2200⁷ Island Victory *(47) (IABalding)* 2-9-0 SO'Gorman(8) (hld up: j.path 5f out: rdn over 3f out: nt clr run on ins over 2f out: sn wknd) 2 12
Petite Heritiere *(39) (MJRyan)* 2-8-4 (5) MBaird(11) (leggy: unf: led over 2f: 3rd st: wknd over 2f out) 1¼ 13
Fit To Ski *(34) (MHTompkins)* 2-8-9 PRobinson(12) (leggy: unf: a bhd) 2 14
John-T *(35) (JLDunlop)* 2-9-0 SWhitworth(15) (scope: bit bkwd: bhd fnl 2f) 2 15

4/1 Flying Green (FR) (7/2-11/2), Labeed (USA) (3/1-5/1), Storm Trooper (USA) (3/1-9/2), **11/2** WINTER QUARTERS (USA) (4/1-7/1), **7/1** General Macarthur, **10/1** Paint It Black (8/1-14/1), **12/1** Nikita's Star (IRE) (8/1-14/1), **14/1** Golden Pond (IRE) (8/1-16/1), **16/1** Mystic Knight, **20/1** Fit To Ski, **25/1** Island Victory, John-T, **33/1** Petite Heritiere, Brave Maisie (IRE), Winged Prince, CSF £29.64 TOTE £7.80: £2.10 £1.90 £6.50 (£18.10) Trio £200.50 OWNER Maverick Productions Ltd (KINGSCLERE) BRED Maverick Productions Ltd 15 Rn
1m 24.87 (0.67) SF: 37/32/22/25/22/22/21/19/11/11/2/3/-/-/-

2847 LYDE GREEN NURSERY H'CAP (2-Y.O) (Class D) £3,501.25 (£1,060.00: £517.50: £246.25) 6f Stalls: High GOING minus 0.65 sec per fur (HD) 7-00 (7-01)

2706² **Just Ice (73)***(80) (SirMarkPrescott)* 2-9-2 MRoberts(7) (lw: led 1f: led over 2f out: drvn out) — 1
2467³ Red Nose (IRE) **(71)***(75) (MHTompkins)* 2-9-0 PRobinson(4) (hld up: rdn over 2f out: chsd wnr over 1f out: unable qckn ins fnl f) 1¼ 2
2674³ Vera's First (IRE) **(72)***(69) (GLewis)* 2-9-1 PaulEddery(5) (rdn over 2f out: hdwy over 1f out: r.o one pce) 2½ 3
2423* Martara (IRE) **(70)***(64)*(Fav)*(MRChannon)* 2-8-13 RHughes(2) (lw: rdn over 2f out: hdwy over 1f out: one pce) 1¼ 4
2315⁶ Croeso Cynnes **(72)***(59) (BPalling)* 2-9-1 TSprake(3) (b: hld up: rdn over 2f out: sn wknd) 2½ 5
1608⁶ Jolis Present **(78)***(60) (MJRyan)* 2-9-7 WCarson(1) (led 5f out tl j.path & hdd 4f out: wknd over 1f out) 2 6
2346³ General Rose **(71)***(42) (RHannon)* 2-9-0 TQuinn(8) (lw: hdwy 3f out: wkng whn hmpd on ins 1f out) 4 7
2487ᵂ Windi Imp (IRE) **(64)***(30) (BJMeehan)* 2-8-7 BDoyle(6) (led 4f out tl over 2f out: wkng whn squeezed out over 1f out) 2 8

7/2 Martara (IRE), **4/1** JUST ICE, **9/2** Red Nose (IRE), **11/2** Vera's First (IRE), **7/1** Jolis Present, **10/1** Croeso Cynnes, **12/1** General Rose, **14/1** Windi Imp (IRE), CSF £20.12 CT £86.32 TOTE £3.20: £1.70 £1.70 £2.00 (£8.00) OWNER Canary Thoroughbreds (NEWMARKET) BRED Prof Klaus E. Rohde 8 Rn
1m 11.15 (-0.15) SF: 48/43/37/32/27/28/10/-

2848 WIDGEON H'CAP (0-90) (3-Y.O) (Class C) £5,602.00 (£1,696.00: £828.00: £394.00) 7f (round) Stalls: High GOING minus 0.65 sec per fur (HD) 7-30 (7-31)

2437³ **Wild Rice (79)***(91+)*(Fav)*(GWragg)* 3-9-2 MHills(7) (b: lw: hld up: led on bit over 1f out: qcknd: comf) — 1
2616⁷ Doctor's Glory (USA) **(84)***(89) (RHannon)* 3-9-0 (7) DaneO'Neill(3) (lw: 5th st: rdn over 2f out: r.o one pce) 3 2
2488⁴ Proud Destiny **(79)***(84) (MRStoute)* 3-8-13 (3) JTate(4) (3rd st: ev ch over 1f out: one pce) s.h 3

1222⁸ Dancing Heart **(72)***(69) (BJMeehan)* 3-8-9 BDoyle(6) (led over 5f)....3½ **4**
2367⁶ Tranquillity **(73)***(69) (LordHuntingdon)* 3-8-10 TQuinn(2) (lw: 6th st: nvr nr to chal)....½ **5**
2015⁴ Marocco (USA) **(82)***(73) (HRACecil)* 3-9-5 WRyan(1) (a bhd)....2 **6**
2009⁴ Q Factor **(72)***(59) (DHaydnJones)* 3-8-9 WCarson(5) (lw: 2nd st: wknd wl over 1f out)....2 **7**

5/2 WILD RICE, **5/1** Q Factor, **6/1** Tranquillity, Proud Destiny, **13/2** Marocco (USA), **7/1** Dancing Heart, **8/1** Doctor's Glory (USA), CSF £19.49 TOTE £2.40: £1.60 £3.00 (£12.70) OWNER Sir Philip Oppenheimer (NEWMARKET) BRED Hascombe and Valiant Studs 7 Rn
1m 23.59 (1.23 under best) (-0.91) SF: 57/55/50/35/35/39/25

2849

CORAL BRIGHTON & HOVE GREYHOUND STADIUM CLAIMING STKS (3-Y.O) (Class F) £2,736.00 (£828.00: £404.00: £192.00)
1m 2f (Jubilee) Stalls: High GOING minus 0.65 sec per fur (HD) 8-00 (8-02)

2694⁶ **Emily-Mou (IRE) (70)***(81)*(Fav)*(BJMeehan)* 3-8-12 BDoyle(4) (b: led 7f out: clr over 2f out: r.o wl)....— **1**
2037¹³ Oakbury (IRE) **(58)***(75) (RHannon)* 3-9-0 MRoberts(5) (b.nr fore: lw: led 3f: 3rd st: chsd wnr over 2f out: no imp)....5 **2**
691¹⁰ Streaky Hawk (USA) *(71) (PFICole)* 3-9-4 TQuinn(1) (lw: rdn over 4f out: 2nd st: wknd over 2f out)....5 **3**
2684³ Chastleton **(38)***(56) (MRChannon)* 3-7-13 ⁽⁵⁾ PPMurphy(3) (lw: bhd fnl 4f)....½ **4**
2297³ Isshereal (IRE) *(21) (BPalling)* 3-8-1 TSprake(2) (bhd fnl 3f)....20 **5**

8/11 EMILY-MOU (IRE), **7/2** Streaky Hawk (USA) (7/4-4/1), **7/1** Oakbury (IRE) (op 4/1), Chastleton, **14/1** Isshereal (IRE) (10/1-16/1), CSF £5.87 TOTE £1.60: £1.10 £2.20 (£5.10) OWNER Mr A. S. Reid (UPPER LAMBOURN) BRED W. and R. Barnett Ltd 5 Rn 2m 1.64 (-0.86) SF: 50/44/40/25/-

2850

LALEHAM H'CAP (0-70) (3-Y.O+) (Class E) £3,501.25 (£1,060.00: £517.50: £246.25) **5f** Stalls: High GOING minus 0.65 sec per fur (HD) 8-30 (8-31)

2686* **Miami Banker (51)***(55) (WRMuir)* 9-8-11b ⁶ˣ GBardwell(1) (led: rdn over 2f out: hdd ins fnl f: led last strides)....— **1**
2301⁵ Miriam **(50)***(54) (MJFetherston-Godley)* 4-8-3 ⁽⁷⁾ DaneO'Neill(7) (a.p: hrd rdn over 1f out: led ins fnl f: hdd last strides)....hd **2**
2364* Delrob **(50)***(47) (DHaydnJones)* 4-8-10 WCarson(6) (rdn thrght: hdwy 2f out: one pce fnl f)....2 **3**
2686⁴ Domicksky **(60)***(56) (MRChannon)* 7-9-6 RHughes(4) (lw: hld up: rdn over 1f out: one pce)....½ **4**
2793³ Rocky Two **(52)***(47) (PHowling)* 4-8-12b JQuinn(5) (hld up: rdn over 2f out: one pce)....hd **5**
2513* Millesime (IRE) **(68)***(59)*(Fav)*(BHanbury)* 3-9-3 ⁽⁷⁾ PBowe(3) (lw: a.p: rdn & ev ch 2f out: wknd fnl f)....1¼ **6**
2692⁴ Followmegirls **(51)***(34) (MrsALMKing)* 6-8-11 MRoberts(2) (hld up: rdn over 2f out: sn wknd)2½ **7**

7/2 Millesime (IRE), **9/2** MIAMI BANKER, Delrob, **5/1** Followmegirls, **13/2** Rocky Two, **8/1** Miriam, Domicksky, CSF £33.63 TOTE £4.90: £2.20 £5.00 (£35.80) OWNER Mr J. J. Amass (LAMBOURN) BRED J. D. Wheeler 7 Rn 59.1 secs (1.30) SF: 18/17/10/19/10/18/-
WEIGHT FOR AGE 3yo-4lb

T/Plpt: £35.00 (339.94 Tckts). T/Qdpt; not declared. AK

2643-NEWCASTLE (L-H)
Wednesday August 2nd (Firm, Hard patches)

WEATHER: sunny, v.hot WIND: slt bhd

2851

LOBLEY HILL (S) STKS (3-Y.O) (Class F) £2,625.20 (£737.20: £359.60)
1m 4f 93y Stalls: Low GOING minus 0.58 sec per fur (F) 2-30 (2-30)

2731³ **Khan (54)***(60)*(Fav)*(CWThornton)* 3-9-0 DeanMcKeown(2) (lw: trckd ldrs: rdn to chal 1f out: styd on to ld wl ins fnl f)....— **1**
2650⁵ Lindisfarne Lady **(44)***(53) (MrsMReveley)* 3-8-9 KDarley(4) (lw: cl up: led over 2f out tl wl ins fnl f: kpt on same pce)....1¼ **2**
2662² High Flown (USA) **(44)***(60) (RonaldThompson)* 3-9-0 ⁽⁵⁾ LNewton(1) (lw: led tl over 2f out: one pce)....2½ **3**
2662⁴ Bunker (IRE) **(48)***(59)*(Fav)*(JPearce)* 3-9-5 GBardwell(3) (lw: last & pushed along 6f out: sme hdwy over 2f out: sn btn)....¾ **4**

9/4 KHAN, Bunker (IRE) (op 6/4), **3/1** Lindisfarne Lady, **4/1** High Flown (USA), CSF £7.98 TOTE £2.70 (£4.50) OWNER Mr Simon Brown (MIDDLEHAM) BRED Wheelersland Stud 4 Rn
2m 42.16 (3.66) SF: 30/23/30/29
No bid.

2852 SWALWELL MEDIAN AUCTION MAIDEN STKS (2-Y.O) (Class F) £2,738.60 (£769.60: £375.80)

6f Stalls: Centre GOING minus 0.58 sec per fur (F) 3-00 (3-01)

Nostoi *(55+)*(Fav)*(SirMarkPrescott)* 2-8-9 GDuffield(4) (w'like: lw: dwlt: sn chsng ldrs: nt clr run over 1f out: qcknd to ld wl ins fnl f: rn green) — 1
2619⁴ Silver Welcome *(57) (MHEasterby)* 2-9-0 MBirch(7) (cl up: led 2f out tl wl ins fnl f: kpt on) 1 2
1877⁷ Time To Fly *(53) (BWMurray)* 2-9-0 JFortune(5) (lw: led 4f: styd on u.p: no ex ins fnl f) 1¾ 3
2354⁵ Society Sue (IRE) *(44) (RonaldThompson)* 2-8-9 SDWilliams(2) (plld hrd: cl up: effrt 2f out: one pce appr fnl f) 1¼ 4
2498⁴ Harriet's Beau **(68)***(33) (MWEasterby)* 2-9-0 KDarley(1) (lw: cl up 4f: sn rdn & btn) 6 5
2464⁶ Craignairn **(60)***(28) (JBerry)* 2-8-7 (7) PFessey(6) (spd over 3f: sn lost tch) 2 6
2483¹¹ Ann's Music *(JMJefferson)* 2-8-9 KFallon(3) (plld hrd early: lost action ½-wy: sn t.o) dist 7

2/1 NOSTOI (op 11/10), **9/4** Harriet's Beau, **3/1** Silver Welcome (2/1-100/30), **8/1** Craignairn (op 5/1), **14/1** Time To Fly (op 8/1), **20/1** Ann's Music, **33/1** Society Sue (IRE), CSF £8.15 TOTE £1.90: £1.50 £1.80 (£3.40) OWNER Hesmonds Stud (NEWMARKET) BRED Hesmonds Stud Ltd 7 Rn
1m 13.9 (2.40) SF: 13/15/11/2/-/-/-

2853 WHICKHAM H'CAP (0-85) (3-Y.O+) (Class D) £3,538.60 (£1,070.80: £522.40: £248.20) 7f

Stalls: Centre GOING minus 0.58 sec per fur (F) 3-30 (3-33)

2358⁵ **Gymcrak Flyer (59)***(72) (GHolmes)* 4-8-11 KFallon(1) (lw: mde all: qcknd clr 2f out: r.o wl u.p) — 1
2836² Super Benz **(60)***(72) (FJO'Mahony)* 9-8-12 SDWilliams(4) (lw: trckd ldr: rdn to chal ins fnl f: r.o) nk 2
2647² Allinson's Mate (IRE) **(75)***(76)*(Fav)*(TDBarron)* 7-9-13b JFortune(3) (lw: hld up: effrt over 2f out: sn rdn & btn) 5 3
2698⁴ Cafe Solo **(41)***(35) (NBycroft)* 4-7-0b(7) PFessey(2) (hld up: hdwy over 2f out: sn rdn & btn) 3 4

11/10 Allinson's Mate (IRE), **7/2** GYMCRAK FLYER (5/2-4/1), **4/1** Cafe Solo, **5/1** Super Benz (op 3/1), CSF £15.73 TOTE £4.70 (£9.10) OWNER The Gymcrak Thoroughbred Racing Club (PICKERING) BRED D. G. Mason 4 Rn
1m 25.77 (1.47) SF: 31/31/35/-

2854 WEATHERBYS 'NEWCOMERS' SERIES H'CAP (0-70) (3-Y.O+) (Class E) £3,052.50 (£924.00: £451.00: £214.50)

2m 19y Stalls: Centre GOING minus 0.58 sec per fur (F) 4-00 (4-02)

2238⁵ **Star Rage (IRE) (70)***(85) (MJohnston)* 5-10-0 JWeaver(1) (hld up: hdwy appr st: rdn to ld over 1f out: styd on wl) — 1
2177² Hever Golf Lady **(54)***(66) (TJNaughton)* 3-7-11 ow1 JFanning(2) (b.off hind: cl up: led 3f out tl over 1f out: no ex) 2½ 2
2695⁵ Hit the Canvas (USA) **(65)***(73) (MrsMReveley)* 4-9-9 KDarley(3) (cl up tl lost pl ½-wy: styd on fnl 3f: nvr nr to chal) 5 3
2695² Kilernan **(46)***(53) (TDBarron)* 4-8-4 JFortune(6) (led to 3f out: sn outpcd) ½ 4
2622⁴ Pride of May (IRE) **(57)***(62) (CWFairhurst)* 4-9-1 DeanMcKeown(9) (lw: hld up: effrt 5f out: outpcd fnl 3f) 1¾ 5
2545* Izza **(37)***(40) (WStorey)* 4-7-2 (7) PFessey(8) (hld up: hdwy ½-wy: chsng ldrs ent st: sn rdn & btn) 2½ 6
2280¹⁰ Green's Seago (USA) **(37)***(34) (JAHarris)* 7-7-6 (3)ow2 DarrenMoffatt(7) (chsd ldrs: pushed along 6f out: wknd appr st) 4 7
2785² Solomon's Dancer (USA) **(60)** (Fav)*(WWHaigh)* 5-9-4 DaleGibson(5) (Withdrawn not under Starter's orders: ref to ent stalls) W

LONG HANDICAP Green's Seago (USA) 6-13

11/4 Solomon's Dancer (USA), **100/30** STAR RAGE (IRE), **11/2** Kilernan, **6/1** Hever Golf Lady, Izza, **8/1** Hit the Canvas (USA), **10/1** Pride of May (IRE), **50/1** Green's Seago (USA), CSF £13.11 CT £53.16 TOTE £3.30: £1.90 £1.50 (£4.30) Trio £7.30 OWNER Mr J. D. Abell (MIDDLEHAM) BRED Killarkin Stud 7 Rn
3m 31.56 (6.06) SF: 37/3/25/5/14/-/-/-
WEIGHT FOR AGE 3yo-15lb

2855 TYNE BRIDGE NURSERY H'CAP (2-Y.O) (Class E) £3,209.80 (£972.40: £475.20: £226.60) 7f

Stalls: Centre GOING minus 0.58 sec per fur (F) 4-30 (4-32)

2474² **Alfayza (64)***(63)*(Fav)*(JDBethell)* 2-8-5 JWeaver(2) (racd alone far side: mde all: jst hld on) — 1
2195⁴ Homeland **(56)***(55) (CWThornton)* 2-7-11 AMackay(11) (swtg: a in tch: hdwy 2f out: hung lft: r.o wl nr fin) s.h 2

2516³ Veshca Lady (IRE) **(57)***(54) (EWeymes)* 2-7-12 JFanning(3) (lw: a chsng ldrs: kpt on u.p fnl f: nvr able to chal) 1 3
2606³ Europex **(57)***(44) (MHEasterby)* 2-7-12 ow1 SMaloney(7) (led main group 3f out tl outpcd fnl 2f) 4 4
2541³ Thorntoun Jewel (IRE) **(60)***(38) (JBalding)* 2-8-1 ClaireBalding(5) (in tch: effrt over 2f out: sn rdn & btn) 4 5
2606² Bee Health Boy **(63)***(28) (MWEasterby)* 2-8-4 KDarley(4) (lw: in tch: rdn & no imp fnl 2f) 6 6
2541* Silverdale Knight **(74)***(9)*(Fav)*(KWHogg)* 2-8-12 (3) AGarth(10) (led main group: hung lft thrght: hdd 3f out: sn wknd: bit slipped) 13 7
1798⁴ Anshan's Deity **(65)** *(CWFairhurst)* 2-8-6 TWilliams(8) (lw: prom over 4f) ....½ 8

9/2 ALFAYZA (op 3/1), Silverdale Knight, **11/2** Bee Health Boy, Homeland, **6/1** Anshan's Deity, **7/1** Europex (op 9/2), **15/2** Thorntoun Jewel (IRE) (5/1-8/1), **10/1** Veshca Lady (IRE), CSF £26.85 CT £210.57 TOTE £3.80: £2.20 £1.20 £2.90 (£11.80) Trio £57.80 OWNER Sheikh Amin Dahlawi (MIDDLEHAM) BRED Al Dahlawi Stud Co Ltd 8 Rn 1m 26.71 (2.41) SF: 15/7/6/-/-/-/-/-

OFFICIAL EXPLANATION Silverdale Knight: had hung left and his bit had slipped through his mouth.

2856

DERWENT LIMITED STKS (0-70) (3-Y.O) (Class E) £2,981.00 (£902.00: £440.00: £209.00)
1m 1f 9y Stalls: Low GOING minus 0.58 sec per fur (F) 5-00 (5-00)

2678* **Carlito Brigante (68)***(88)*(Fav)*(MrsJRRamsden)* 3-8-13 KFallon(2) (lw: trckd ldrs: led 2f out: rdn clr) ....— 1
2332⁵ Almizaj **(68)***(75) (HThomsonJones)* 3-8-6 RHills(3) (hld up: swtchd over 2f out: styd on: no ch w wnr) 3½ 2
2770⁹ Gospel Song **(67)***(81) (WTKemp)* 3-9-1 GDuffield(1) (led after 1½f to 2f out: one pce) 1¾ 3
2510⁸ Lucky Soph (USA) **(70)***(72) (BWHills)* 3-8-8 JWeaver(4) (b.off hind: led 1½f: cl up: chal over 2f out: wknd over 1f out) 1 4

11/10 CARLITO BRIGANTE, **2/1** Almizaj, **4/1** Lucky Soph (USA), **10/1** Gospel Song (8/1-12/1), CSF £3.53 TOTE £1.90 (£1.70) OWNER Mr Bernard Hathaway (THIRSK) BRED Whitsbury Manor Stud 4 Rn 1m 54.33 (2.03) SF: 33/20/26/17

T/Plpt: £367.60 (23.66 Tckts). T/Qdpt: £44.50 (1.2 Tckts). AA

2650-NOTTINGHAM (L-H)
Wednesday August 2nd (Good to firm, Firm patches)
WEATHER: fine & sunny WIND: fresh half bhd

2857

GREASLEY MINERS' WELFARE 'JAMAICA' (S) STKS (2-Y.O) (Class G) £2,243.00 (£618.00: £293.00)
6f 15y Stalls: High GOING minus 0.56 sec per fur (F) 6-15 (6-19)

*2591*³ **Times of Times (IRE) (68)***(57)*(Fav)*(DJSCosgrove)* 2-8-11 MRimmer(3) (b: a.p: led 2f out: rdn & r.o wl) ....— 1
*2591*² Saint Rosalina *(49) (CJHill)* 2-8-1c(5) MHenry(4) (eyecover: led: c stands' side: hdd 2f out: kpt on u.p nr fin) 1 2
*2380*⁶ Sphinx Levelv (IRE) *(52) (APJarvis)* 2-8-11 BThomson(5) (lw: effrt & rdn bel dist: kpt on ins fnl f: nrst fin) ....¾ 3
2601⁴ Ghostly Apparition **(52)***(46) (JohnUpson)* 2-8-11 DHarrison(8) (bhd: rdn along ½-wy: kpt on fnl f: nvr nrr) 2½ 4
1943⁸ Miletrian Refurb (IRE) **(55)***(45) (MRChannon)* 2-8-11 DHolland(7) (spd over 4f: sn outpcd) ....½ 5
*2382*⁸ Miss Impulse *(38) (JWharton)* 2-8-6 JWilliams(1) (nvr gng pce of ldrs) ....½ 6
*2496*⁵ Red Simba *(47) (JBerry)* 2-8-9 (7) PRoberts(2) (lw: racd centre: chsd ldrs 4f: sn rdn & wknd) .nk 7
Jenaxa *(MRLeach)* 2-8-6 JLowe(6) (w'like: bkwd: s.s: a bhd: t.o) 25 8

9/4 TIMES OF TIMES (IRE), **7/2** Saint Rosalina, Miletrian Refurb (IRE), **15/2** Sphinx Levelv (IRE) (8/1-12/1), **9/1** Red Simba (op 6/1), **12/1** Miss Impulse (op 8/1), Ghostly Apparition, **33/1** Jenaxa, CSF £10.12 TOTE £3.90: £1.40 £1.60 £2.10 (£4.20) OWNER Mrs M. Schneider (NEWMARKET) BRED E. Moloney 8 Rn 1m 13.4 (2.40) SF: 15/7/10/4/3/-/5/-
Bt in 7,200gns.

2858

RAINWORTH MINERS' WELFARE 'BARBADOS' H'CAP (0-60) (3-Y.O+) (Class F) £2,519.00 (£694.00: £329.00)
5f 13y Stalls: High GOING minus 0.56 sec per fur (F) 6-45 (6-45)

2680⁴ **Royal Dome (IRE) (54)***(66+) (MartynWane)* 3-9-4 DHolland(4) (chsd ldr: led appr fnl f: r.o wl) ....— 1

*2492** Ashkernazy (IRE) **(41)***(48) (NEBerry)* 4-8-4 (5) RPainter(1) (led tl hdd ent fnl f: r.o one pce)...1½ **2**
2736⁴ The Fed **(52)***(53) (RMWhitaker)* 5-9-6v ACulhane(5) (chsd ldrs: hrd rdn fnl 2f: nt pce to chal)...2 **3**
2502² Knayton Lass **(60)***(60)*(Fav)*(MWEasterby)* 4-10-0 DHarrison(3) (reard s: hdwy 2f out: rdn & r.o fnl f: nvr nrr) ....nk **4**
2627⁷ Name That Tune **(43)***(41) (CJHill)* 3-8-2 (5) MHenry(6) (lw: chsd ldrs: rdn 2f out: one pce) ....½ **5**
2513⁴ Superbit **(53)***(51) (BAMcMahon)* 3-9-3 FNorton(8) (lw: sn chsng ldrs: rdn 2f out: nt pce to chal) ....nk **6**
2753⁶ Bonny Melody **(48)***(36) (PDEvans)* 4-8-9 (7) AmandaSanders(2) (a bhd & outpcd) 3 **7**
2624⁶ Secret Miss **(49)***(31) (APJarvis)* 3-8-13b BThomson(9) (lw: bhd: rdn along ½-wy: no imp) 2 **8**

7/2 Knayton Lass, **4/1** Ashkernazy (IRE) (op 6/1), The Fed, **11/2** ROYAL DOME (IRE), **15/2** Name That Tune, **9/1** Secret Miss, **10/1** Superbit, **14/1** Bonny Melody, CSF £25.85 CT £87.74 TOTE £6.90: £2.00 £1.70 £1.10 (£13.90) Trio £20.70 OWNER Mr G. W. Jones (RICHMOND) BRED Michael F. Fogarty 8 Rn 59.0 secs (0.30) SF: 49/35/40/47/24/34/23/14

WEIGHT FOR AGE 3yo-4lb

2859 LEABROOKS CLUB 'TRINIDAD & TOBAGO' CLAIMING STKS (2-Y.O) (Class F) £2,519.00 (£694.00: £329.00)

5f 13y Stalls: High GOING minus 0.56 sec per fur (F) 7-15 (7-18)

2047* **Tymeera (63)***(68) (BPalling)* 2-8-1 (3) SSanders(5) (b: mde virtually all: rdn & drifted lft fnl f: r.o) ....— **1**
2674⁸ Hoh Majestic (IRE) **(78)***(74)*(Fav)*(MBell)* 2-9-0v MFenton(4) (lw: a.p: rdn over 1f out: r.o one pce) 1¼ **2**
2382⁴ April's Joy **(49)***(54) (JNorton)* 2-7-12 DaleGibson(7) (prom: rdn over 1f out: unable qckn).....1¼ **3**
2656⁴ Beeny **(62)***(69) (APJarvis)* 2-8-13 BThomson(8) (lw: w ldrs: rdn over 1f out: hung lft fnl f: unable qckn) ....hd **4**
Swynford Dream *(67) (JFBottomley)* 2-9-3 JLowe(1) (w'like: bkwd: swvd lft s: effrt 2f out: kpt on appr fnl f) 1¾ **5**
2782⁶ Krishan Power *(63) (MWEasterby)* 2-8-13 SDWilliams(6) (w ldrs over 3f: sn rdn & outpcd) ..s.h **6**
2195⁷ Doubleyoubeay **(51)***(52) (JBerry)* 2-8-8 (7) PRoberts(3) (lw: bhd: effrt & rdn 2f out: no imp).......4 **7**
1779⁶ Tin Man *(44) (BAMcMahon)* 2-8-7 GCarter(2) (lw: in tch: effrt 2f out: nt rch ldrs) ....hd **8**
2757⁴ Patrington Park **(55)***(54) (MWEasterby)* 2-8-12 (5) MHenry(9) (chsd ldrs: swtchd lft after 2f: sn rdn: nvr able to chal) ....s.h **9**
Jenopis *(16) (MRLeach)* 2-8-4 NKennedy(10) (cmpt: bkwd: s.s: a bhd: t.o) 8 **10**

11/10 Hoh Majestic (IRE), **7/2** TYMEERA, **8/1** Patrington Park, Doubleyoubeay (11/2-9/1), **12/1** April's Joy, Swynford Dream, **16/1** Krishan Power, Beeny, **20/1** Tin Man, **33/1** Jenopis, CSF £8.09 TOTE £3.70: £1.70 £1.10 £3.60 (£2.30) Trio £5.30 OWNER Glenbrook Associates (COWBRIDGE) BRED R. T. Lingwood 10 Rn 60.9 secs (2.20) SF: 5/11/-/6/4/-/-/-/-/-

2860 RJB MINING H'CAP (0-65) (3-Y.O+) (Class F) £3,502.40 (£1,047.20: £501.60: £228.80)

2m 9y Stalls: Low GOING minus 0.56 sec per fur (F) 7-45 (7-46)

2713⁸ **Amiarge (32)***(43) (MBrittain)* 5-7-7 (3)ow1 DWright(1) (hld up: effrt & nt clr run 3f out: swtchd rt over 1f out: str run to ld post) ....— **1**
2268² Tommy Cooper **(43)***(55) (MrsBarbaraWaring)* 4-8-4 (3) SDrowne(7) (b.hind: chsd ldrs: 4th st: styd on wl ins fnl f) ....nk **2**
2413⁵ Brumon (IRE) **(57)***(69) (DWPArbuthnot)* 4-9-7v JWilliams(5) (b: hld up: hdwy over 2f out: rdn & styd on wl fnl f) ....hd **3**
2481² Torreglia (IRE) **(65)***(76)*(Fav)*(JLDunlop)* 3-9-0 JWeaver(9) (chsd ldr: 2nd st: hrd rdn & kpt on fnl f) ....nk **4**
2514² Arc Bright (IRE) **(46)***(57) (RHollinshead)* 5-8-5 (5) MHenry(12) (sn led: hrd rdn 2f out: hdd wl ins fnl f) ....hd **5**
2713⁵ Romalito **(42)***(51) (MBlanshard)* 5-8-6 RCochrane(3) (lw: hld up: rdn 2f out: kpt on ins fnl f) 2 **6**
2147ᵂ Danus Rex (IRE) **(58)***(66) (CASmith)* 3-8-7 ow1 MWigham(4) (chsd ldrs: 5th st: rdn over 2f out: sn btn) ....½ **7**
2688⁶ Tamarpour (USA) **(60)***(65) (MCPipe)* 8-9-10v AMcGlone(2) (b.nr fore: hld up: effrt & rdn over 3f out: no imp) 4 **8**
2650² Can She Can Can **(45)***(49) (MJohnston)* 3-7-8 JLowe(8) (hld up in tch: 6th st: rdn & wknd fnl 2f) ....½ **9**
2514⁶ Rose of Glenn **(49)***(38) (BPalling)* 4-8-10 (3) SSanders(11) (in rr most of wy: t.o)....15 **10**
2481³ Blue Smoke (IRE) **(58)***(45) (BAMcMahon)* 3-8-7b JFortune(10) (lw: prom: 3rd st: rdn & wknd qckly 2f out: t.o)....2½ **11**
2543⁷ Leap in the Dark (IRE) **(29)***(9) (MissLCSiddall)* 6-7-7 NCarlisle(6) (lw: a in rr: t.o fnl 3f)...........7 **12**

LONG HANDICAP Leap in the Dark (IRE) 7-6

7/2 Torreglia (IRE), **5/1** Can She Can Can, **6/1** Tamarpour (USA) (op 4/1), Arc Bright (IRE), **10/1** Brumon (IRE) (op 6/1), Romalito, Danus Rex (IRE), Tommy Cooper, **12/1** Blue Smoke (IRE) (op 8/1), **20/1** Rose of Glenn, **25/1** AMIARGE, Leap in the Dark (IRE), CSF £233.98 CT £2,413.41 TOTE £55.80: £10.80 £2.60 £4.90 (£184.90) Trio £371.80 OWNER Miss D. J. Woods (WARTHILL) 12 Rn 3m 28.1 (3.70) SF: 20/32/46/38/34/28/28/42/11/15/7/-

WEIGHT FOR AGE 3yo-15lb

2861 CLIPSTONE MINERS' SOCIAL CLUB 'CARIBBEAN' H'CAP (0-70) (3-Y.O+) (Class E) £3,759.80 (£1,126.40: £541.20: £248.60)

1m 1f 213y Stalls: Low GOING minus 0.56 sec per fur (F) 8-15 (8-17)

2407[5] **El Bailador (IRE) (58)***(71) (JDBethell)* 4-9-6 JWeaver(13) (mde all: clr ent st: styd on strly)......— 1
2678[2] Once More for Luck (IRE) **(59)***(69)*(Fav)*(MrsMReveley)* 4-9-7 DHolland(10) (lw: hld up: hdwy over 2f out: styd on fnl f: nt rch wnr)......1¾ 2
2655[8] Slapy Dam **(50)***(57) (JMackie)* 3-8-0 (3) SSanders(1) (lw: hld up & bhd: hdwy over 2f out: styd on ins fnl f)......2 3
2655[2] Lady Highfield **(55)***(61) (MJRyan)* 4-9-3 AClark(5) (hld up: 6th st: effrt over 2f out: rdn & btn fnl f)......¾ 4
2543[5] Course Fishing **(36)***(40) (BAMcMahon)* 4-7-12 FNorton(6) (hld up: hdwy 3f out: rdn & one pce appr fnl f)......1¼ 5
2687[10] Araboybill **(62)***(60) (MPMuggeridge)* 4-9-10b RCochrane(3) (chsd wnr to ½-wy: 3rd st: rdn 2f out: sn btn)......3½ 6
2511[9] La Belle Shyanne **(31)***(25) (CJHill)* 4-7-0 (7) RMullen(14) (s.s: rapid hdwy ½-wy: 4th st: wknd over 2f out)......2½ 7
2307[4] Demurrer **(36)***(30) (MrsAMNaughton)* 5-7-12 JLowe(7) (nvr trbld ldrs)......hd 8
1029[4] Modest Hope (USA) **(48)***(39) (BRichmond)* 8-8-10 AlexGreaves(11) (bkwd: a in rr)......2 9
2333[4] First Bite (IRE) **(70)***(59) (JLDunlop)* 3-9-9 GCarter(9) (chsd ldrs: 5th st: rdn & wknd over 2f out)......1¼ 10
Pat's Splendour **(50)***(33) (HJCollingridge)* 4-8-12 MRimmer(4) (bkwd: prom: 2nd st: wknd wl over 2f out)......3½ 11
2528[4] Queens Stroller (IRE) **(54)** *(CCElsey)* 4-9-2 DHarrison(8) (withdrawn not under starters' orders: spread plate s)...... W

LONG HANDICAP La Belle Shyanne 7-4

5/2 Once More for Luck (IRE), **3/1** Lady Highfield, **11/2** First Bite (IRE), **7/1** EL BAILADOR (IRE), **10/1** Course Fishing, Araboybill, Queens Stroller (IRE), **12/1** Slapy Dam, **14/1** Demurrer, Modest Hope (USA), **20/1** La Belle Shyanne, **25/1** Pat's Splendour, CSF £25.74 CT £201.72 TOTE £11.30: £4.20 £1.50 £1.90 (£29.10) Trio £171.10 OWNER Mrs John Lee (MIDDLEHAM) BRED Miss Anne Reid 11 Rn 2m 5.9 (3.40) SF: 31/29/8/21/-/20/-/-/-/10/-/-

WEIGHT FOR AGE 3yo-9lb

2862 OLLERTON/BEVERCOTES MINERS' WELFARE 'MONSERRAT' H'CAP (0-70) (3-Y.O+ F & M) (Class E) £3,359.40 (£1,003.20: £479.60: £217.80)

1m 54y Stalls: Low GOING minus 0.56 sec per fur (F) 8-45 (8-46)

2088[6] **Racing Brenda (51)***(63) (BAMcMahon)* 4-9-4 GCarter(8) (hld up & bhd: 6th st: hdwy to chse ldr bel dist: rdn to ld wl ins fnl f)......— 1
2770* Three Arch Bridge **(60)***(69)*(Fav)*(MJohnston)* 3-9-6b 5x DHolland(3) (a.p: 2nd st: led over 3f out: hrd rdn & ct nr fin)......1½ 2
2669[4] Fairelaine **(57)***(58) (APJarvis)* 3-9-3 BThomson(2) (lw: chsd ldrs: 4th st: rdn & one pce fnl 2f)......4 3
2718[4] The Mestral **(42)***(38) (MJRyan)* 3-8-2v ow1 AClark(1) (chsd ldrs: 5th st: hrd rdn & outpcd 3f out: kpt on appr fnl f)......2 4
2755[2] Just Fizzy **(61)***(54) (JHetherton)* 3-9-7 NKennedy(6) (lw: led tl hdd over 3f out: sn rdn: grad wknd)......2½ 5
1645[12] Fiaba **(42)***(33) (MrsNMacauley)* 7-8-2 (7) AmandaSanders(4) (lw: plld hrd: prom: 3rd st: wknd over 2f out)......¾ 6
2794[11] Indescent Blue **(59)***(49) (DWPArbuthnot)* 3-9-5 RPrice(5) (b.hind: hld up & bhd: 7th st: effrt on outside 3f out: no imp)......½ 7

2/1 Three Arch Bridge (7/1-85/40), **4/1** Fairelaine (3/1-9/2), **9/2** Just Fizzy, **5/1** RACING BRENDA, **10/1** The Mestral (7/1-11/1), Indescent Blue (7/1-11/1), **16/1** Fiaba, CSF £14.52 CT £38.25 TOTE £5.80: £2.00 £1.80 (£6.40) OWNER Mr G. Whitaker (TAMWORTH) BRED D. J. and Mrs Deer 7 Rn 1m 42.0 (2.40) SF: 32/31/20/-/16/2/11

WEIGHT FOR AGE 3yo-7lb

T/Jkpt; not won £12,468.70 to Pontefract 03/08/95. T/Plpt: £169.70 (101.46 Tckts). T/Qdpt: £48.20 (0.3 Tckts) £45.64 to Pontefract 03/08/95. IM

2510-BATH (L-H)
Thursday August 3rd (Hard)
WEATHER: sunny, hot WIND: slt across

2863 SILKWOOD MAIDEN H'CAP (0-80) (3-Y.O+) (Class D) £3,809.75 (£1,148.00: £556.50: £260.75)
1m 2f 46y Stalls: Low GOING minus 0.57 sec per fur (F) 2-30 (2-32)

1984[2] **Sweet Pavlova (USA) (65)***(76)*(Fav)*(PFICole)* 3-9-2 TQuinn(1) (mde all: hrd rdn over 1f out: r.o wl)........— 1
Zeetaro **(68)***(75) (MajorWRHern)* 4-10-0 TSprake(3) (lw: hld up: 5th st: hdwy over 7f out: ev ch over 1f out: sn rdn: no imp)........2½ 2
2411[9] Marzipan (IRE) **(64)***(67) (JWHills)* 3-9-1 RHughes(7) (lw: chsd wnr over 5f: 3rd st: wknd over 1f out)........2½ 3
2510[4] Cracking Prospect **(42)***(44) (BRMillman)* 4-7-11 (5) AWhelan(5) (s.i.s: hld up: hdwy 7f out: 4th st: one pce fnl 2f)........1 4
1526[4] Alaraby (IRE) **(70)***(71) (IABalding)* 3-9-7 WNewnes(6) (prom: chsd wnr over 4f out: 2nd st: rdn over 2f out: wknd over 1f out)........nk 5
2600[2] Mighty Squaw **(58)***(48) (MissGayKelleway)* 3-8-9 MWigham(2) (lw: 6th st: rdn over 2f out: sn bhd)........7 6
Jacks to Open (USA) **(49)** *(MJHeaton-Ellis)* 4-8-9 RPerham(4) (bit bkwd: a bhd: lost tch fnl 4f: t.o)........dist 7

2/1 SWEET PAVLOVA (USA), **4/1** Alaraby (IRE) (op 5/2), **11/2** Mighty Squaw, Cracking Prospect, **7/1** Zeetaro, **9/1** Marzipan (IRE) (op 6/1), **50/1** Jacks to Open (USA), CSF £14.07 TOTE £2.40: £1.10 £2.30 (£7.60) OWNER Mr M. Arbib (WHATCOMBE) BRED W. S. & Bayard farish & Sharp 7 Rn
2m 8.5 (0.80) SF: 49/57/40/26/44/21/-
WEIGHT FOR AGE 3yo-9lb

2864 BE HOPEFUL MEMORIAL H'CAP (0-75) (3-Y.O) (Class D) £4,068.00 (£1,224.00: £592.00: £276.00)
1m 5y Stalls: Low GOING minus 0.57 sec per fur (F) 3-00 (3-01)

2500[2] **Concer Un (61)***(71) (SCWilliams)* 3-8-9 RHughes(2) (led over 5f out: clr over 1f out: eased ins fnl f)........— 1
2522[2] Legal Issue (IRE) **(62)***(69)*(Fav)*(SirMarkPrescott)* 3-8-10 GDuffield(5) (3rd st: hrd rdn & chsd wnr over 2f out: no imp)........1½ 2
2411[6] Stinging Reply **(73)***(66)*(Fav)*(IABalding)* 3-9-7 TQuinn(4) (lw: led 7f out tl over 5f out: 2nd st: wknd 2f out)........7 3
2504[2] Mighty Marston **(71)***(57) (LadyHerries)* 3-9-5 JWeaver(3) (lw: led 1f: stdd & drppd rr: 5th & rdn st: no hdwy fnl 2f)........3½ 4
2342[12] Almapa **(55)***(20) (RJHodges)* 3-8-0 (3)ow1 SDrowne(1) (4th & rdn st: a bhd)........10 5

9/4 Legal Issue (IRE), Stinging Reply, **5/2** CONCER UN, **9/2** Mighty Marston, **20/1** Almapa, CSF £8.21 TOTE £3.50: £1.10 £1.50 (£3.00) OWNER Miss L. J. Ward (NEWMARKET) BRED Lloyd Bros 5 Rn
1m 40.0 (1.50) SF: 32/30/27/18/-

2865 AUGUST CLAIMING STKS (3-Y.O+) (Class E) £3,122.50 (£940.00: £455.00: £212.50) **5f 161y** Stalls: Low GOING minus 0.57 sec per fur (F) 3-30 (3-32)

2539[2] **Pearl Dawn (IRE) (59)***(68) (NoelChance)* 5-8-7 BThomson(1) (mde all: rdn over 2f out: edgd rt over 1f out: sn clr)........— 1
2712[4] Fantasy Racing (IRE) **(73)***(59)*(Fav)*(MRChannon)* 3-8-7 TQuinn(3) (a.p: rdn over 2f out: r.o one pce fnl f)........5 2
2587[12] Pacific Girl (IRE) **(53)***(54) (BPalling)* 3-8-6 TSprake(2) (a.p: rdn over 2f out: one pce)........1½ 3
2665[2] Rhythmic Dancer **(64)***(50) (JLSpearing)* 7-8-8 (3) SDrowne(5) (swtg: plld hrd: a.p: rdn over 2f out: wknd fnl f)........1¼ 4
2631[11] Carnegie Blue **(27)** *(AJChamberlain)* 4-8-5 (5)ow4 RPainter(4) (b: b.hind: sn outpcd: t.o)........20 5

7/4 Fantasy Racing (IRE), **2/1** PEARL DAWN (IRE), **9/4** Rhythmic Dancer, **25/1** Pacific Girl (IRE), **100/1** Carnegie Blue, CSF £5.30 TOTE £2.50: £1.40 £1.30 (£2.00) OWNER Mrs M. Chance (LAMBOURN) BRED Niall Creighton 5 Rn
1m 10.4 (1.10) SF: 29/15/10/11/-
WEIGHT FOR AGE 3yo-5lb

2866

FRANCASAL (S) STKS (2-Y.O) (Class G) £2,563.00 (£718.00: £349.00)
5f 161y Stalls: Low GOING minus 0.57 sec per fur (F) 4-00 (4-01)

*2633*5 **Kinnescash (IRE) (68)***(64?)*(Fav)*(RIngram)* 2-8-11 AMcGlone(5) (lw: chsd ldr: hrd rdn to ld over 1f out: r.o wl) ....— 1
2706 11 Chemcast **(67)***(36) (BJMeehan)* 2-8-11 RHughes(4) (led tl hrd rdn & hdd over 1f out: eased whn btn ins fnl f) 10 2
2515 8 Water Music Melody *(31) (MartynMeade)* 2-8-6 AClark(1) (chsd ldrs: rdn over 2f out: one pce) ....s.h 3
2791 16 Match The Colour *(25) (MRChannon)* 2-8-11 JeanPierreLopez(2) (a bhd: eased whn no ch ins fnl f) 4 4
Dells Dream (IRE) *(6) (MRChannon)* 2-8-6 TQuinn(3) (neat: bit bkwd: s.i.s: outpcd) 5 5

5/4 KINNESCASH (IRE), **9/4** Chemcast, **4/1** Dells Dream (IRE) (3/1-9/2), **10/1** Match The Colour, **16/1** Water Music Melody, CSF £4.25 TOTE £1.90: £1.30 (£1.90) OWNER Mr J. B. Wilcox (EPSOM) BRED Frank Barry 5 Rn 1m 11.4 (2.10) SF: 19/-/-/-/-
Sold MSaunders 6,000gns

2867

WHIRLWIND SPRINT H'CAP (0-85) (3-Y.O+) (Class D) £4,120.00 (£1,240.00: £600.00: £280.00) **5f 11y** Stalls: Low GOING minus 0.57 sec per fur (F) 4-30 (4-30)

1106 12 **Spender (71)***(78) (PWHarris)* 6-9-12 WNewnes(1) (chsd ldr: rdn 2f out: led ins fnl f: r.o wl) ..— 1
*2627*6 Tommy Tempest **(38)***(42) (REPeacock)* 6-7-7v SLanigan(3) (led tl ins fnl f: r.o) 1 2
2502 3 Paley Prince (USA) **(60)***(63) (MDIUsher)* 9-9-1 RPrice(5) (a.p: ev ch 1f out: nt qckn) ....nk 3
2659 6 Bold Gem **(53)***(56) (BJMeehan)* 4-8-8b RPerham(7) (swtchd rt & hdwy over 2f out: hung lft over 1f out: nt clr run ins fnl f: r.o) ....hd 4
2692 3 Giggleswick Girl **(64)***(61)*(Fav)*(MRChannon)* 4-9-5 CRutter(2) (hdwy on ins 2f out: one pce fnl f) 1¾ 5
2533 10 Yet More Roses **(68)***(63) (LadyHerries)* 4-9-9 AClark(8) (b: b.hind: rdn & no hdwy fnl 2f) ....½ 6
2609 3 Shashi (IRE) **(76)***(69)*(Fav)*(DMorley)* 3-9-13 AMcGlone(6) (rdn 3f out: no hdwy fnl 2f) ....¾ 7

LONG HANDICAP Tommy Tempest 7-2

7/2 Shashi (IRE), Giggleswick Girl, **9/2** Paley Prince (USA), **5/1** SPENDER, **11/2** Yet More Roses, **6/1** Bold Gem, **16/1** Tommy Tempest, CSF £61.07 CT £346.39 TOTE £6.50: £2.80 £5.10 (£90.20) OWNER The Entrepreneurs (BERKHAMSTED) BRED The Mount Coote Partnership 7 Rn
61.5 secs (1.00) SF: 46/10/31/24/29/31/33
WEIGHT FOR AGE 3yo-4lb

2868

COLERNE APPRENTICE H'CAP (0-80) (3-Y.O) (Class E) £3,218.00 (£898.00: £434.00) **2m 1f 34y** Stalls: Low GOING minus 0.57 sec per fur (F) 5-00 (5-00)

2509 4 **Kriva (63)***(71) (RJRWilliams)* 3-8-9 SSanders(3) (mde all: qcknd over 6f out: rdn over 3f out: drvn out) ....— 1
2520* Duchess of Alba **(75)***(80)*(Fav)*(RCharlton)* 3-9-0 (7) RBrisland(2) (hld up: chsd wnr 10f out: 2nd st: rdn 3f out: no imp) 3 2
2650* Old Swinford (IRE) **(60)** *(BJMeehan)* 3-8-6 ow2 5x RPainter(1) (chsd ldr over 7f: rdn over 4f out: 3rd & wkng st: t.o) ....dist 3

Evens Duchess of Alba, **7/4** Old Swinford (IRE), **4/1** KRIVA, CSF £7.45 TOTE £5.40 (£2.20) OWNER Mr Hamad Al Ghowais (NEWMARKET) BRED Sheikh Mohammed bin Rashid al Maktoum 3 Rn 3m 51.0 (10.00) SF: 6/15/-
T/Plpt: £384.90 (25.74 Tckts). T/Qdpt: £48.70 (1 Tckt). KH

2769-HAMILTON (R-H)
Thursday August 3rd (Firm)

WEATHER: sunny, warm WIND: almost nil

2869

LEE (S) STKS (2-Y.O) (Class F) £2,689.00 (£754.00: £367.00)
5f 4y Stalls: Low GOING minus 0.54 sec per fur (F) 6-15 (6-16)

2735 2 **Hickleton Miss** *(57)*(Fav)*(MrsMReveley)* 2-8-1 (5) NVarley(4) (cl up: rdn to ld ins fnl f: r.o) ....— 1
2606 7 Chilibang Bang **(55)***(49) (JBerry)* 2-8-11 JCarroll(3) (cl up: led after 1½f tl ins fnl f: kpt on) 1¼ 2
Rattle *(52) (JJO'Neill)* 2-8-11 JFanning(5) (unf: scope: s.i.s: sn chsng ldrs: nt qckn fnl f) 1¾ 3
*2629*8 Cawdor Lady *(28) (TJEtherington)* 2-8-6 AMackay(2) (led 1½f out: hung rt: rdn & btn 2f out) 6 4
Hardenfast *(DNicholls)* 2-8-6 JLowe(1) (leggy: scope: dwlt: hung bdly rt thrght: sn t.o) ....dist 5

11/10 HICKLETON MISS, **7/2** Chilibang Bang, **5/1** Rattle (op 9/4), **7/1** Cawdor Lady (op 4/1), **15/2** Hardenfast (5/1-8/1), CSF £5.08 TOTE £2.10: £1.40 £1.30 (£1.70) OWNER Mrs Linda Leech (SALTBURN) BRED Derek Leech 5 Rn 60.6 secs (2.30) SF: 7/8/2/-/-
No bid

2870 ARTHUR BALDING H'CAP (0-70) (3-Y.O+) (Class E) £3,916.55 (£1,186.40: £579.70: £276.35)
6f 5y Stalls: Low GOING minus 0.54 sec per fur (F) 6-45 (6-46)

2461[7] **Diet (51)***(57)*(Fav)*(MissLAPerratt)* 9-9-0v JCarroll(2) (w ldr: led 2f out: styd on wl) — 1
2736[3] Walk the Beat **(62)***(67)*(Fav)*(MartynMeade)* 5-9-11 VSlattery(6) (trckd ldrs: hdwy 2f out: ev ch ins fnl f: kpt on) ½ 2
2611[2] Birchwood Sun **(60)***(64)*(Fav)*(MDods)* 5-9-9b JLowe(3) (sn bhd: hdwy over 1f out: nt clr run & swtchd ins fnl f: nrst fin) nk 3
2772* Suedoro **(47)***(43)* *(RMMcKellar)* 5-8-10 7x JFanning(5) (led 4f: rdn & btn appr fnl f) 3 4
2304[4] Annie Fay (IRE) **(57)***(46)* *(JLHarris)* 3-8-10 (5) NVarley(4) (cl up tl outpcd fnl 2f) 2½ 5
2590[4] Frans Lad **(59)***(47)* *(JBerry)* 3-8-10 (7) PRoberts(1) (in tch: hung rt most of wy: btn wl over 1f out) ½ 6

7/2 DIET, Walk the Beat, Birchwood Sun, **9/2** Suedoro, **6/1** Annie Fay (IRE), **12/1** Frans Lad (op 8/1), CSF £14.09 TOTE £2.90: £1.90 £2.50 (£9.20) OWNER Mrs M. S. J. Clydesdale (AYR) BRED Rowcliffe Stud 6 Rn 1m 11.5 (1.50) SF: 31/41/38/17/15/16
WEIGHT FOR AGE 3yo-5lb

2871 LANGS SUPREME SCOTCH WHISKY H'CAP (0-80) (3-Y.O+) (Class D) £4,463.40 (£1,351.20: £659.60: £313.80)
1m 5f 9y Stalls: High GOING minus 0.54 sec per fur (F) 7-15 (7-17)

2733[8] **Nornax Lad (USA) (53)***(67)* *(MartynMeade)* 7-9-3b VSlattery(6) (lw: cl up: led 7f out: rdn & hld on wl fnl 2f) — 1
2824* Lord Hastie (USA) **(48)***(62)*(Fav)*(CWThornton)* 7-8-12 4x AMackay(2) (hld up & bhd: stdy hdwy 4f out: chal 2f out: kpt on: nt qckn towards fin) nk 2
2816[4] Lord Advocate **(36)***(39)* *(DANolan)* 7-7-9b(5) NVarley(4) (chsd ldrs: drvn along 6f out: n.m.r over 3f out: styd on one pce) 9 3
2751* Bark'n'bite **(54)***(56)* *(MrsMReveley)* 3-8-6 4x KDarley(5) (lw: hld up: effrt 5f out: rdn & n.m.r over 3f out: one pce after) nk 4
2759[3] Sariyaa **(60)***(62)* *(MBrittain)* 4-9-5 (5) VHalliday(1) (led 6f: cl up: edgd lft fnl 4f: grad wknd fnl 2½f) hd 5
2224* Abalene **(38)***(35)* *(TWDonnelly)* 6-8-2 JLowe(3) (prom: c wd st: sn rdn & btn) 4 6

5/4 Lord Hastie (USA), **3/1** Bark'n'bite, **6/1** Abalene (op 4/1), **8/1** NORNAX LAD (USA), **9/1** Sariyaa (op 6/1), **20/1** Lord Advocate, CSF £17.40 TOTE £9.00: £4.20 £1.40 (£10.80) OWNER Mrs B. Taylor (MALMESBURY) BRED Hillfields Farm 6 Rn 2m 48.9 (3.20) SF: 40/35/12/17/35/8
WEIGHT FOR AGE 3yo-12lb

2872 HAMILTON HEAVY PLANT EXHIBITION MAIDEN H'CAP (0-65) (3-Y.O+) (Class F) £3,231.90 (£979.20: £478.60: £228.30)
1m 65y Stalls: High GOING minus 0.54 sec per fur (F) 7-45 (7-46)

779[13] **Pleasant Memories (53)***(60+)* *(LordHuntingdon)* 3-9-9 DHarrison(4) (lw: mde most: qcknd 3f out: sn clr) — 1
2228[4] Flyaway Blues **(54)***(55)*(Fav)*(MrsMReveley)* 3-9-10v KDarley(3) (trckd wnr: wnt lft over 3f out: rdn & no ch after) 3 2
2832[4] Bedazzle **(35)***(34)*(Fav)*(MBrittain)* 4-8-12 JLowe(1) (lw: hld up: stdy hdwy ½-wy: bmpd over 3f out: rdn & fnd nil) 1 3
2479[9] Seconds Away **(35)***(5)* *(JSGoldie)* 4-8-5 (7) PFessey(2) (plld hrd: bhd: wl outpcd fnl 3f) 15 4

2/1 Flyaway Blues, Bedazzle, **7/2** PLEASANT MEMORIES, **9/2** Seconds Away, CSF £9.67 TOTE £2.50 (£3.00) OWNER Team Valor (WEST ILSLEY) BRED Mrs S. Smart and Mrs J. J. Hindley 4 Rn
1m 46.5 (3.20) SF: 33/28/14/-
WEIGHT FOR AGE 3yo-7lb

2873 COREHOUSE CLAIMING STKS (3-Y.O) (Class F) £2,661.00 (£746.00: £363.00)
1m 65y Stalls: High GOING minus 0.54 sec per fur (F) 8-15 (8-15)

2769* **Rock Foundation (62)***(63++)*(Fav)*(PCHaslam)* 3-8-10 TWilliams(4) (hld up: smooth hdwy to ld 2½f out: sn clr: v.easily) — 1
2815[3] Dr Caligari (IRE) **(70)***(66)* *(JBerry)* 3-9-4 JCarroll(2) (lw: hld up: led 3f out: sn hdd: no ch w wnr) 2½ 2

2815[5] Samana Cay **(43)***(44) (DNicholls)* 3-8-3b JLowe(1) (led tl hdd 3f out: sn outpcd)........................4 **3**
2425[6] Salduba **(29)***(30) (TDyer)* 3-8-1 JFanning(3) (cl up tl wl outpcd fnl 3f) 6 **4**

1/2 ROCK FOUNDATION, **5/2** Dr Caligari (IRE), **12/1** Samana Cay (op 6/1), **33/1** Salduba, CSF £1.94 TOTE £1.50 (£1.10) OWNER Patrick Haslam Racing Club (MIDDLEHAM) BRED R. P. Williams 4 Rn 1m 46.9 (3.60) SF: 18/21/-/-
Rock Foundation clmd ADinsmore £6,000

2874 GAETAN BILLIARD CHAMPAGNE MAIDEN H'CAP (0-60) (3-Y.O+) (Class F) £3,131.80 (£948.40: £463.20: £220.60)

1m 3f 16y Stalls: High GOING minus 0.54 sec per fur (F) 8-45 (8-45)

2401[3] **Never so True (37)***(50) (MartynWane)* 4-9-6 JCarroll(2) (lw: mde most: all out).....................— **1**
2306[2] Portite Sophie **(37)***(50) (MBrittain)* 4-9-1 (5) VHalliday(4) (lw: hld up: hdwy on ins 4f out: ev ch ins fnl f: nt qckn cl home) ....nk **2**
2630[3] Silver Rondo (USA) **(48)***(56)*(Fav)*(LordHuntingdon)* 3-9-7 DHarrison(1) (chsd ldrs: ev ch 3f out: wknd ins fnl f)..3 **3**
1669[4] Highbank **(51)***(51) (MrsMReveley)* 3-9-10 KDarley(5) (chsd ldrs tl outpcd over 4f out: no imp after) 6 **4**
2769[5] Sylvan Celebration **(15)***(9) (MissLAPerratt)* 4-7-12 JFanning(3) (cl up tl wknd 3f out)................4 **5**
Bdoore (IRE) **(37)***(24) (DANolan)* 7-9-1 (5) NVarley(6) (a bhd: wl outpcd fnl 4f)............................5 **6**

13/8 Silver Rondo (USA), **7/4** Highbank (5/4-15/8), **5/1** Portite Sophie (4/1-6/1), **11/1** NEVER SO TRUE (7/1-12/1), **12/1** Sylvan Celebration, **66/1** Bdoore (IRE), CSF £54.52 TOTE £13.80: £3.50 £1.90 (£16.50) OWNER James S Kennerley and Miss Jenny Hall (RICHMOND) BRED Cheveley Park Stud Ltd 6 Rn 2m 23.2 (4.20) SF: 32/32/28/23/-/6
WEIGHT FOR AGE 3yo-10lb
T/Plpt: £136.50 (57.23 Tckts). T/Qdpt: Not won £80.60 to Southwell 4/8/95. AA

2750-PONTEFRACT (L-H)
Thursday August 3rd (Good to firm)

WEATHER: sunny, hot WIND: mod half against

2875 BOLLINGER CHAMPAGNE CHALLENGE SERIES (FOR GENTLEMAN RIDERS) AMATEUR H'CAP (0-70) (3-Y.O+) (Class F) £3,002.00 (£896.00: £428.00: £194.00)

1m 2f 6y Stalls: Low GOING minus 0.49 sec per fur (F) 2-45 (2-46)

2375[6] **Essayeffsee (48)***(62) (MrsMReveley)* 6-11-0 MrMHNaughton(10) (lw: chsd ldrs: styd on appr fnl f: led last strides) ....— **1**
2225[2] Bold Top **(39)***(53) (BSRothwell)* 3-9-10b MrRJohnson(9) (trckd ldr: led over 2f out tl nr fin).....hd **2**
2797* Wentbridge Lad (IRE) **(61)***(70) (PDEvans)* 5-11-9v(4) 5x MrWMcLaughlin(5) (bhd: hdwy on outside over 2f out: hung lft u.p: kpt on wl: nvr nr to chal)...3 **3**
2433[8] Master Ofthe House **(61)***(70)*(Fav)*(MDHammond)* 9-11-13 MrCBonner(6) (hld up & bhd: hdwy over 2f out: kpt on same pce: nvr nr to chal)...hd **4**
2544[3] Thaleros **(56)***(62) (GMMoore)* 5-11-8 MrRHale(3) (led tl over 2f out: wknd fnl f) 2 **5**
2184[7] Record Lover (IRE) **(36)***(35) (MCChapman)* 5-9-12 (4) MrMMackley(2) (prom tl wknd over 2f out) 4 **6**
2751[2] Kildrummy Castle **(52)***(43) (MrsJRRamsden)* 3-10-9v MrSSwiers(4) (lw: chsd ldrs: effrt u.p 3f out: lost pl over 2f out)...5 **7**
2655[7] Salska **(58)***(48) (ALForbes)* 4-11-6 (4) MrPClinton(7) (chsd ldrs: rdn 4f out: sn wknd) 1 **8**
2536[4] Alerting **(63)***(45) (IABalding)* 3-11-6v MrABalding(11) (lw: hld up: effrt over 3f out: sn rdn: nt r.o fnl 2f) 5 **9**
2695[8] Bajan Affair **(35)***(6) (JRBostock)* 5-9-11 (4)ow8 MrKLoads(8) (bhd & rdn 4f out: sn t.o) 1¾ **10**
LONG HANDICAP Bajan Affair 9-2

7/2 Master Ofthe House, **4/1** Wentbridge Lad (IRE), **5/1** Kildrummy Castle, Alerting, **6/1** ESSAYEFFSEE, **8/1** Bold Top, **11/1** Thaleros, **33/1** Salska, Record Lover (IRE), **50/1** Bajan Affair, CSF £48.16 CT £194.80 TOTE £5.20: £1.70 £1.80 £2.00 (£20.50) Trio £54.90 OWNER Mrs S. D. Murray (SALTBURN) BRED Mrs L. F. Rathbone 10 Rn 2m 13.9 (5.60) SF: 43/25/51/51/43/16/15/29/17/-
WEIGHT FOR AGE 3yo-9lb

2876 CORNMILL HOTEL (HULL) MAIDEN STKS (2-Y.O) (Class D) £3,598.75 (£1,090.00: £532.50: £253.75)

6f Stalls: Low GOING minus 0.49 sec per fur (F) 3-15 (3-17)

2182[2] **Laafee** *(81)*(Fav)*(HThomsonJones)* 2-9-0 RHills(4) (mde all: qcknd clr over 1f out: easily) ...— **1**
2485[6] Crystal Falls (IRE) *(65) (JJO'Neill)* 2-9-0 JFortune(3) (a chsng wnr: kpt on u.p fnl 2f) 6 **2**
2572[3] Celandine *(56) (RCharlton)* 2-8-9 KDarley(8) (sn trckng ldrs: effrt 2f out: kpt on same pce)..1½ **3**

2526[10] Six Clerks (IRE) *(56) (JGFitzGerald)* 2-9-0 KFallon(10) (mid div: kpt on wl appr fnl f) 2 4
2693[4] Love Bird (IRE) *(55) (MJohnston)* 2-9-0 DHolland(1) (in tch: effrt u.p over 2f out: kpt on: nvr rchd ldrs) ....hd 5
Keepers Dawn (IRE) *(32) (RFJohnsonHoughton)* 2-8-9 PaulEddery(5) (leggy: scope: unruly s: s.s: bhd tl sme hdwy fnl 2f) 7 6
Hever Golf Queen *(21) (TJNaughton)* 2-8-4 (5) JDSmith(11) (cmpt: bit bkwd: s.i.s: bhd tl sme late hdwy) 4 7
Warming Trends *(21) (SirMarkPrescott)* 2-9-0 CNutter(12) (unf: nvr wnt pce) 2 8
523[5] Uncle George *(18) (MHTompkins)* 2-9-0 PRobinson(9) (in tch: effrt over 2f out: sn wknd) 1 9
2351[14] Sweet Amoret *(12) (RCSpicer)* 2-8-9 DeanMcKeown(7) (swvd lft s: chsd ldrs over 3f: sn wknd) ....½ 10
Larry Lambrusco *(13) (MAJarvis)* 2-9-0 TIves(6) (leggy: unf: a outpcd & sn drvn along) 1¼ 11
2299[7] Bluetong *(11) (PTWalwyn)* 2-9-0b MHills(2) (s.i.s: bhd: rdn ½-wy: nt r.o) 1 12

6/4 LAAFEE, **2/1** Celandine, **7/1** Love Bird (IRE), **8/1** Keepers Dawn (IRE), **14/1** Larry Lambrusco, Hever Golf Queen, **16/1** Uncle George, Bluetong, **20/1** Warming Trends, Crystal Falls (IRE), **50/1** Sweet Amoret, Six Clerks (IRE), CSF £34.16 TOTE £2.70: £1.30 £4.80 £1.40 (£40.40) Trio £31.70 OWNER Mr Hamdan Al Maktoum (NEWMARKET) BRED Shadwell Estate Company Limited 12 Rn
1m 16.2 (1.90) SF: 34/18/9/9/8/-/-/-/-/-/-/-

2877 AUGUST CLAIMING STKS (3-Y.O) (Class F) £2,789.50 (£772.00: £368.50)
5f Stalls: Low GOING minus 0.49 sec per fur (F) 3-45 (3-46)

2680[2] **The Happy Fox (IRE) (69)***(84) (BAMcMahon)* 3-9-0b JFortune(5) (trckd ldrs gng wl: effrt 2f out: led on bit ins fnl f: pushed clr: eased nr fin) ....— 1
2680[5] C-Yer-Simmie (IRE) **(61)***(64) (RHollinshead)* 3-7-9 (3) AGarth(2) (led tl ins fnl f: no ch w wnr) 1¼ 2
2665[6] Super Sonata **(59)***(51) (PDEvans)* 3-7-10v FNorton(3) (trckd ldr: effrt 2f out: kpt on one pce) 3½ 3
2521[17] Breakfast Creek **(59)***(53) (JBerry)* 3-7-7 (7) PFessey(4) (b.off fore: sn outpcd & drvn along: hdwy on outside over 2f out: wknd over 1f out) ....½ 4
2697[3] Arasong **(63)***(52)*(Fav)*(EWeymes)* 3-8-3 KDarley(1) (chsd ldrs: effrt & drvn along ½-wy: outpcd & hrd rdn over 1f out: sn wknd) 1¼ 5

6/4 Arasong, **3/1** THE HAPPY FOX (IRE), C-Yer-Simmie (IRE), **13/2** Super Sonata, **10/1** Breakfast Creek, CSF £11.48 TOTE £3.40: £1.50 £1.60 (£4.70) OWNER Mr G. Whitaker (TAMWORTH) BRED Abbey Lodge Stud 5 Rn
63.0 secs (1.50) SF: 35/15/2/4/3

2878 ROGERTHORPE MANOR HOTEL H'CAP (0-90) (3-Y.O+) (Class C) £7,505.00 (£2,240.00: £1,070.00: £485.00)
1m 4f 8y Stalls: Low GOING minus 0.49 sec per fur (F) 4-15 (4-21)

2648[3] **Latvian (68)***(81) (RAllan)* 8-9-1 JFortune(4) (led tl over 1f out: kpt on wl u.p to ld ins fnl f) ....— 1
2087[7] Hullbank **(60)***(73) (WWHaigh)* 5-8-7 DaleGibson(5) (lw: b: sn trckng ldr: pushed along over 3f out: slt ld over 1f out: hdd & nt qckn nr fin) ....nk 2
2270[2] Augustan **(62)***(68) (SGollings)* 4-8-9 DHolland(3) (drvn along & outpcd over 4f out: kpt on fnl 2f: nvr able to chal) 5 3
2639[5] Silently **(81)***(82)*(Fav)*(IABalding)* 3-9-3 MHills(1) (lw: trckd ldrs: effrt over 3f out: sn outpcd: wknd over 1f out) 4 4
2415[5] Dawlah **(88)** *(HThomsonJones)* 3-9-10 RHills(2) (Withdrawn not under Starters' orders: lame at s) .... W

7/4 Silently, **5/2** Hullbank, **11/4** Dawlah, **3/1** Augustan, LATVIAN (op 9/2), CSF £10.09 TOTE £4.00: £3.30 (£5.00) OWNER Mr I. Bell (CORNHILL-ON-TWEE) BRED Fittocks Stud Ltd 4 Rn
2m 40.7 (6.40) SF: 21/13/8/11/-
WEIGHT FOR AGE 3yo-11lb

2879 CHAPLINS CLUB H'CAP (0-70) (3-Y.O+) (Class E) £3,655.00 (£1,090.00: £520.00: £235.00)
5f Stalls: Low GOING minus 0.49 sec per fur (F) 4-45 (4-50)

2521[8] **Lochon (55)***(59) (JLEyre)* 4-9-5 RLappin(5) (chsd ldrs: outpcd ½-wy: hrd rdn over 1f out: styd on u.p to ld nr fin) ....— 1
1559[2] Nite-Owl Dancer **(57)***(59) (JAHarris)* 3-9-3 RHills(4) (hld up & bhd: gd hdwy 2f out: led ins fnl f tl nr fin) ....½ 2
2736[10] Kabcast **(48)***(48) (DWChapman)* 10-8-12b ACulhane(7) (led: clr 2f out: hdd & no ex ins fnl f)..¾ 3
2821[7] Cheeky Chappy **(36)***(33) (DWChapman)* 4-8-0b DaleGibson(1) (unruly in stalls: sn drvn along: hdwy ½-wy: kpt on same pce appr fnl f) 1 4
2680[7] Sweet Mate **(45)***(31)*(Fav)*(SRBowring)* 3-8-0b(5) CTeague(9) (swvd rt s: sn chsng ldrs: rdn 2f out: sn wknd) 3½ 5

2665[9] Cradle Days **(62)***(40) (RCSpicer)* 6-9-12 DeanMcKeown(6) (chsd ldrs tl hrd rdn & wknd 2f out)........2½ 6
2772[2] Tutu Sixtysix **(38)***(11) (DonEnricoIncisa)* 4-8-2v KimTinkler(10) (chsd ldrs: outpcd ½-wy: wnt lft & lost pl over 1f out)........1½ 7
2502[16] Nordoora (IRE) **(54)** *(JLHarris)* 6-9-4 KFallon(2) (Withdrawn not under Starters' orders: lame at s)........W

5/2 Sweet Mate, **3/1** Nite-Owl Dancer, **4/1** LOCHON, Tutu Sixtysix (3/1-9/2), **8/1** Kabcast, Cheeky Chappy, **10/1** Nordoora (IRE), **12/1** Cradle Days, CSF £16.87 CT £86.26 TOTE £5.90: £2.80 £1.80 (£14.40) Trio £49.40 OWNER Mrs A. Harker (HAMBLETON) BRED M. and Mrs Young 7 Rn
63.7 secs (2.20) SF: 28/24/17/2/-/9/-/-
WEIGHT FOR AGE 3yo-4lb
STEWARDS' ENQUIRY Lappin susp. 12-15/8/95 (excessive use of whip).

2880 MATTY BOWN MEMORIAL MAIDEN STKS (3-Y.O+) (Class D) £3,761.25 (£1,140.00: £557.50: £266.25)
1m 4y Stalls: Low GOING minus 0.49 sec per fur (F) 5-15 (5-15)

1296[7] **Pumice (82)***(79) (LMCumani)* 3-8-9 KFallon(6) (lw: prom: drvn along 4f out: r.o strly fnl f: led towards fin: readily)........— 1
2707[3] Raise the Stakes **(78)***(83) (IABalding)* 3-9-0 PaulEddery(5) (led 2f: led 4f out: rdn clr over 1f out: hdd & no ex wl ins fnl f)........¾ 2
2553[7] Roseberry Ray (IRE) *(77) (GWragg)* 3-9-0 MHills(2) (lw: dwlt: bhd: swtchd ins & hdwy over 1f out: kpt on wl)........3 3
2583[3] Young Benson **(76)***(76) (BAMcMahon)* 3-9-0 JFortune(4) (swtg: chsd ldrs: effrt over 2f out: kpt on same pce over 1f out)........½ 4
2553[11] Fasih *(70)*(Fav)*(ACStewart)* 3-9-0 WCarson(1) (lw: sn bhd & pushed along: sme hdwy 2f out: nvr nr ldrs)........3 5
Duke Valentino *(67) (RHollinshead)* 3-9-0 TIves(8) (trckd ldrs: effrt over 2f out: wknd over 1f out)........1½ 6
2469[6] Sujud (IRE) *(50) (HThomsonJones)* 3-8-9 RHills(7) (s.i.s: bhd & drvn along: eased over 1f out)........6 7
2313[4] Galafron *(53) (JHMGosden)* 3-9-0b GHind(3) (hung rt thrght: led after 2f: hdd 4f out: wknd wl over 1f out: sn bhd)........1 8

7/4 Fasih, **9/4** Raise the Stakes, **5/1** PUMICE, **6/1** Roseberry Ray (IRE), **10/1** Young Benson, **12/1** Sujud (IRE), **16/1** Duke Valentino, Galafron, CSF £17.60 TOTE £5.70: £1.90 £1.30 £2.20 (£10.20) OWNER Lord Halifax (NEWMARKET) BRED Lord Halifax 8 Rn
1m 44.6 (2.60) SF: 30/34/28/27/21/18/1/4

2881 TALLY HO H'CAP (0-65) (3-Y.O) (Class F) £3,132.50 (£870.00: £417.50)
1m 4y Stalls: Low GOING minus 0.49 sec per fur (F) 5-45 (5-47)

2528[2] **Alltime Dancer (IRE) (54)***(64)*(Fav)*(MrsJRRamsden)* 3-9-0b KFallon(3) (lw: hld up: hdwy 3f out: styd on appr fnl f: led ins fnl f: eased nr fin)........— 1
2624[7] Saltz (IRE) **(51)***(59) (PTDalton)* 3-8-8 (3) PMcCabe(6) (trckd ldrs: led 2f out: hdd & no ex ins fnl f)........1 2
2628[3] Top Fella (USA) **(49)***(55) (WAO'Gorman)* 3-8-9 EmmaO'Gorman(7) (hld up: effrt 3f out: styd on appr fnl f: nvr nr to chal)........1 3
2503[13] Sporting Risk **(52)***(52) (PWHarris)* 3-8-12 GHind(1) (chsd ldrs tl rdn & outpcd fnl 2f)........3 4
Hee's a Dancer **(44)***(43) (MJCamacho)* 3-8-4 DaleGibson(5) (swtg: chsd ldrs tl wknd over 1f out)........¾ 5
2317[17] Embezzler **(47)***(40) (SGollings)* 3-8-7 DMcKeown(4) (s.i.s: hld up & plld hrd: hung lft & lost pl ½-wy: n.d after)........3 6
907[3] Eden's Star (IRE) **(61)***(53) (MHTompkins)* 3-9-7 PRobinson(2) (plld hrd: led to 2f out: sn wknd)........½ 7
2500[6] Bollin Frank **(59)***(35) (MHEasterby)* 3-9-5 MBirch(8) (swtg: chsd ldrs tl wknd 2f out: hung lft & virtually p.u towards fin)........8 8

2/1 ALLTIME DANCER (IRE), **5/2** Bollin Frank, **11/2** Top Fella (USA), **8/1** Eden's Star (IRE), **9/1** Sporting Risk, **20/1** Embezzler, Saltz (IRE), Hee's a Dancer, CSF £32.56 CT £170.72 TOTE £2.40: £1.40 £3.30 £1.50 (£11.40) Trio £37.00 OWNER Mr Colin Webster (THIRSK) BRED K. and Mrs Prendergast 8 Rn 1m 45.0 (3.00) SF: 31/26/22/19/10/7/20/2
OFFICIAL EXPLANATION **Bollin Frank: No explanation offered.**

T/Jkpt: £16,812.10 (0.3 Tckts) £16,575.41 to Southwell 4/8/95. T/Plpt: £170.00 (118.15 Tckts). T/Qdpt: £94.50 (2.40 Tckts). WG

2714-YARMOUTH (L-H)
Thursday August 3rd (Good to firm)
WEATHER: warm, sunny WIND: mod half bhd

2882 FOSTERS LAGER H'CAP (0-80) (3-Y.O+) (Class D) £3,732.30 (£1,112.40: £530.20: £239.10) **1m 6f 17y** Stalls: High GOING minus 0.42 sec (F) 6-00 (6-00)

2509* **Invest Wisely (74)***(86) (JMPEustace)* 3-8-9 RCochrane(2) (lw: led 7f: 2nd st: led 4f out: rdn clr appr fnl f) ....— 1
2184⁴ Toy Princess (USA) **(69)***(74) (CEBrittain)* 3-8-4 MRoberts(3) (b: chsd ldrs: pushed along & 3rd st: rdn & ev ch over 3f out: kpt on: nt trble wnr) 6 2
2622² Top Lady (IRE) **(72)***(74)*(Fav)*(MRStoute)* 3-8-4v(3) JTate(1) (led 7f out tl rdn & hdd 4f out: one pce) 2½ 3
2462³ Blue Blazer **(77)***(75) (BHanbury)* 5-9-8 (3) JStack(4) (lw: hld up: last st: rdn & btn over 3f out)...4 4

6/4 Top Lady (IRE), **9/4** INVEST WISELY, **9/2** Blue Blazer (3/1-5/1), **6/1** Toy Princess (USA) (7/2-13/2), CSF £11.40 TOTE £2.50 (£11.40) OWNER Mr J. C. Smith (NEWMARKET) BRED Littleton Stud 4 Rn 3m 1.4 (3.40) SF: 41/29/29/43
WEIGHT FOR AGE 3yo-13lb

2883 SIDEGATE MOTORS MAIDEN STKS (3-Y.O+) (Class D) £4,526.50 (£1,254.00: £599.50) **1m 3f 101y** Stalls: Low GOING minus 0.42 sec per fur (F) 6-30 (6-33)

2350³ **Anne D'Autriche (IRE)** *(81+)*(Fav)*(JHMGosden)* 3-8-6 LDettori(4) (hld up: 3rd st: led 3f out: comf) ....— 1
2333² Carol's Dream (USA) **(74)***(82) (JWHills)* 3-8-11 RCochrane(1) (lw: trckd ldrs: 2nd st: led over 3f out: sn hdd: ev ch ins fnl f: no ex) 3 2
2438⁵ Cavil *(61) (CEBrittain)* 3-8-11 MRoberts(3) (led tl over 3f out: sn btn & eased) 15 3
2094³ Adonisis *(TTClement)* 3-8-11 StephenDavies(2) (Withdrawn not under Starter's orders)......... W

4/11 ANNE D'AUTRICHE (IRE), **7/2** Carol's Dream (USA), **8/1** Cavil (op 4/1), **33/1** Adonisis, CSF £1.84 TOTE £1.30 (£1.30) OWNER Sheikh Mohammed (NEWMARKET) BRED Sheikh Mohammed bin Rashid al Maktoum 3 Rn 2m 25.2 (2.20) SF: 41/42/21/-

2884 WARWICK SHUBROOK CLAIMING STKS (3-Y.O) (Class F) £2,821.40 (£780.40: £372.20) **1m 2f 21y** Stalls: Low GOING minus 0.42 sec per fur (F) 7-00 (7-01)

2687¹² **Woodrising (62)***(66)*(Fav)*(GLewis)* 3-7-5 (5) MHenry(2) (mde all: rdn clr fnl f) ....— 1
2314⁵ Darling Clover **(56)***(64)*(Fav)*(DMorley)* 3-8-1 ow1 MFenton(3) (chsd wnr: 2nd st: ev ch 3f out tl no ex fnl f) 4 2
2245⁸ Fresh Look (IRE) **(55)***(62) (RFJohnsonHoughton)* 3-8-6 LDettori(4) (lw: chsd ldrs: 3rd st: one pce fnl 3f) 5 3
2466² Kindred Greeting **(39)***(39) (DMorris)* 3-7-13b GBardwell(1) (sn pushed along: 4th st: nvr trbld ldrs) 10 4
Greenway Lady *(34) (CNAllen)* 3-8-1 ow1 GCarter(6) (unf: bit bkwd: last st: a bhd) 3½ 5
Nushka Babushka *(BobJones)* 3-7-9 ow1 JQuinn(5) (hld up & plld hrd: 4th & rdn st: wknd qckly) 20 6

7/4 WOODRISING (5/4-15/8), Darling Clover, **5/1** Fresh Look (IRE), **7/1** Kindred Greeting, **25/1** Greenway Lady, **33/1** Nushka Babushka, CSF £4.82 TOTE £2.30: £1.90 £1.10 (£2.60) OWNER Mr C. F. Sparrowhawk (EPSOM) BRED Kirtlington Stud Ltd 6 Rn 2m 5.4 (1.00) SF: 39/37/35/12/7/-

2885 ROTARY INTERNATIONAL (S) H'CAP (0-60) (3 & 4-Y.O) (Class G) £2,467.00 (£682.00: £325.00) **1m 3y** Stalls: Low GOING minus 0.42 sec per fur (F) 7-30 (7-31)

2587⁴ **Fyne Song (36)***(47) (WJMusson)* 3-8-8 LDettori(3) (led after 2f: rdn & hld on wl fnl f) ....— 1
2279¹¹ Colosse **(51)***(60) (MAJarvis)* 3-9-9 WRyan(8) (lw: chsd ldrs: ev ch over 1f out: unable qckn fnl f) 1¼ 2
2813⁴ Prince Rudolf (IRE) **(41)***(47) (MrsNMacauley)* 3-8-6v(7) AmandaSanders(6) (stdd s: hdwy 2f out: nrst fin) 1¼ 3
2528⁹ Zahran (IRE) **(44)***(48)*(Fav)*(JMBradley)* 4-9-9 JQuinn(7) (b: lw: in tch: rdn & hdwy 4f out: no ex appr fnl f) 1¼ 4
2528⁶ Flair Lady **(46)***(43) (WGMTurner)* 4-9-4 (7) ADaly(5) (w ldrs over 5f) 3½ 5
Bayou (IRE) **(47)***(42) (JAHarris)* 4-9-12 SDWilliams(4) (lw: led 2f: wknd over 2f out) ....¾ 6
2718⁶ As Such (IRE) **(43)***(20) (NACallaghan)* 4-9-8 MRoberts(1) (bhd fnl 3f) 9 7
2712¹⁰ Fiveaday **(53)***(12) (BHanbury)* 3-9-8 (3) JStack(2) (stdd s: plld hrd: shkn up 4f out: a bhd).........9 8

7/2 Zahran (IRE) (5/2-4/1), **4/1** Flair Lady, **9/2** Colosse (op 3/1), **5/1** FYNE SONG (3/1-6/1), **15/2** Prince Rudolf (IRE) (6/1-10/1), **10/1** As Such (IRE) (op 5/1), **16/1** Bayou (IRE), Fiveaday, CSF £24.43 CT £137.16 TOTE £3.70: £1.70 £1.70 £2.30 (£12.00) OWNER Mrs P. A. Linton (NEWMARKET) BRED Stud-On-The-Chart 8 Rn 1m 39.6 (4.30) SF: 14/27/14/22/17/16/-/-
WEIGHT FOR AGE 3yo-7lb
No bid

2886 ANGLIAN WATER CONDITIONS STKS (2-Y.O F) (Class C) £4,900.50 (£1,690.50: £807.75: £326.25)
7f 3y Stalls: Low GOING minus 0.42 sec per fur (F) 8-00 (8-00)

2554[5] **Key To A Million (IRE) (92)***(73) (RHannon)* 2-8-11 MRoberts(3) (set stdy pce: qcknd 4f out: rdn over 2f out: unchal)........— 1
2173* Gryada *(72) (WJarvis)* 2-8-13 WRyan(2) (trckd ldrs: rdn over 1f out: kpt on: nt trble wnr).....1½ 2
2277* She's My Love *(66)*(Fav)*(JEBanks)* 2-8-11 JQuinn(1) (trckd wnr over 5f: sn rdn & no rspnse)........1½ 3
Flame Valley (USA) *(60+) (MRStoute)* 2-8-9 LDettori(4) (leggy: scope: dwlt: hld up: rdn 3f out: no imp)........1¾ 4

2/1 She's My Love, **9/4** Flame Valley (USA) (6/4-5/2), **3/1** Gryada, **7/2** KEY TO A MILLION (IRE), CSF £12.42 TOTE £4.20 (£6.60) OWNER Million In Mind Part(4) (MARLBOROUGH) BRED Leo Collins 4 Rn 1m 23.7 (0.90) SF: 49/48/42/36

2887 COURAGE H'CAP (0-70) (3-Y.O+) (Class E) £3,016.20 (£897.60: £426.80: £191.40) **5f 43y** Stalls: Low GOING minus 0.42 sec per fur (F) 8-30 (8-30)

2502[4] **Judgement Call (45)***(51) (PHowling)* 8-8-9 NCarlisle(2) (b: lw: outpcd: hdwy 2f out: rdn & r.o wl to ld ins fnl f)........— 1
2850[6] Millesime (IRE) **(68)***(72) (BHanbury)* 3-9-11 (3) JStack(1) (led over 3f out: clr over 1f out: hdd & no ex nr fin)........¾ 2
2502[10] Time Is Money (IRE) **(52)***(50) (MHTompkins)* 3-8-7 (5) HKYim(3) (lw: kpt on fnl 2f: nrst fin)....1¾ 3
2521[14] Tee-Emm **(40)***(23) (PHowling)* 5-8-4 JQuinn(5) (led over 1f: wknd appr fnl f)........5 4
2641[2] Red Admiral **(59)***(41)*(Fav)*(PCHaslam)* 5-9-9 MTebbutt(6) (prom: rdn after 2f: sn bhd)........nk 5
2071[12] Sizzling Romp **(56)***(33) (DTThom)* 3-8-13 (3) JTate(4) (a bhd)........1½ 6

2/1 Red Admiral, **3/1** JUDGEMENT CALL, **4/1** Time Is Money (IRE) (3/1-9/2), Millesime (IRE) (op 5/2), **9/1** Tee-Emm (5/1-10/1), **16/1** Sizzling Romp, CSF £14.34 TOTE £3.20: £2.20 £2.40 (£7.50) OWNER Mr K. Weston (NEWMARKET) BRED T. P. Kelly 6 Rn 62.1 secs (1.80) SF: 28/45/23/-/18/6
WEIGHT FOR AGE 3yo-4lb
T/Plpt: £141.60 (50.23 Tckts). T/Qdpt: £18.40 (4 Tckts). Dk

TIPPERARY (Ireland) (L-H)
Sunday July 23rd (Good)

2888a TIPPERARY SPRINT RACE (Listed) (3-Y.O+) £9,675.00 (£2,775.00: £1,275.00: £375.00) **5f** 4-00 (4-02)

707a[3] **Sharp Point (IRE)** *(103) (DKWeld,Ireland)* 3-8-7 MJKinane........— 1
1572a[6] Dairine's Delight (IRE) *(106) (MCunningham,Ireland)* 5-9-3 JPMurtagh........½ 2
Tourandot (IRE) *(100) (TStack,Ireland)* 4-9-1 SCraine........1½ 3
2285[5] Double Quick (IRE) *(96) (MJohnston)* 3-8-7 JWeaver........nk 4

CSF £30.13 TOTE £5.40: £1.90 £1.40 £1.80 (£11.70) OWNER Moyglare Stud Farm Ltd 9 Rn
56.2 secs SF: -/-/-/-
NR

2723a-EVRY (France) (R-H)
Thursday July 27th (Good)

2889a PRIX DAPHNIS (Gp 3) (3-Y.O C & G) £26,347.00 (£9,581.00: £4,790.00) **1m 1f** 2-55 (2-59)

2560a[5] **Silent Warrior (IRE)** *(120) (JEHammond,France)* 3-8-9 CAsmussen........— 1
291a[2] Sharpest Image (IRE) *(117) (RCollet,France)* 3-8-9 GGuignard........1½ 2
Shannjar *(117) (AdeRoyerDupre,France)* 3-8-9 GMosse........nse 3
2105[2] Prince of India *(108) (LordHuntingdon)* 3-8-9 OPeslier (btn approx 6l)........ 6

P-M 1.90F: 1.60F 5.10F (SF 32.00F) OWNER Mr S. S. Niarchos 7 Rn 1m 50.57 (0.57) SF: -/-/-/-

3035a-MAISONS-LAFFITTE (France)
Saturday July 29th (Good)

2890a PRIX MAURICE DE NIEUIL (Gp 2) (3-Y.O+) £35,928.00 (£14,371.00: £7,186.00) **1m 4f 110y** 3-20 (3-27)

1709a7 **Partipral (USA)** *(117) (ELellouche,France)* 6-9-8 DBoeuf (racd prom: rdn 2f out: led 1f out: kpt on wl u.p) ....— 1
2560a7 Tzar Rodney (FR) *(112) (GDoleuze,France)* 3-8-5 OPeslier (hld up in rr: hrd rdn wl over 1f out: r.o wl) ....s.nk 2
2323* Beauchamp Hero *(119) (JLDunlop)* 5-9-11 CAsmussen (hld up gng wl: rdn over 1f out: unable qckn) ....¾ 3
896a3 L'ile Tudy (IRE) *(109) (MmeMBollack-Badel,France)* 5-9-1 ABadel (led: rdn & hdd over 1f out: kpt on u.p ins fnl f) ....s.h 4
1239a2 Nononito (FR) *(112) (JLesbordes,France)* 4-9-4 GMosse (trckd ldrs: rdn over 1f out: one pce ins fnl f) ....s.nk 5

P-M: 7.60F: 4.60F 3.70F (SF 49.60F) OWNER E. Sarasola BRED Thorpe Investments in USA 5 Rn
2m 48.6 (14.10) SF: -/-/-/-/-

2563a-CURRAGH (Newbridge, Ireland) (R-H)
Saturday July 29th (Good)

2891a MELD STKS (Gp 3) (3-Y.O+) £16,250.00 (£4,750.00: £2,250.00) **1m 2f** 4-30 (4-34)

2323[6] **Needle Gun (IRE)** *(119) (CEBrittain)* 5-9-3 MJKinane ....— 1
2565a* Hushang (IRE) *(119) (JOxx,Ireland)* 5-9-3 JPMurtagh ....nk 2
Kayaara (IRE) *(104) (NoelFurlong,Ireland)* 3-8-7 PShanahan 9 3
2211a3 Ballykett Nancy (IRE) *(99) (JSBolger,Ireland)* 4-9-0 JAHeffernan 1½ 4
2476[5] Fill the Bill (IRE) *(102) (JohnMcLoughlin,Ireland)* 3-8-7 NGMcCullagh ....s.h 5
2218a7 I'm Supposin (IRE) *(KPrendergast,Ireland)* 3-8-7 WJSupple 6

CSF £8.10 TOTE £2.00: £1.80 £1.30 (£3.10) OWNER Mr Saeed Manana (NEWMARKET) BRED Saeed Manana 6 Rn
2m 1.6 (-0.70) SF: -/-/-/-/-/-
NR

1713a-COLOGNE (Germany) (R-H)
Sunday July 30th (Good to firm)

2892a OPPENHEIM-RENNEN (Listed) (2-Y.O) £12,346.00 (£4,938.00: £2,469.00) **6f** 2-30 (2-33)

Happy Boy *(99) (HJentzsch,Germany)* 2-9-2 ATylicki ....— 1
2322[4] Flying Squaw *(95) (MRChannon)* 2-8-12 RHughes ....hd 2
La Blue *(89) (BSchutz,Germany)* 2-8-12 ASuborics 2 3

TOTE 59DM: 16DM 12DM 16DM (SF 175DM) OWNER Gestut Fahrhof BRED Gestut Fahrhof 8 Rn
1m 10.9 SF: -/-/-

2893a OSTERMANN-POKAL (Gp 3) (3-Y.O+) £24,691.00 (£9,876.00: £4,938.00) **1m** 4-10 (4-17)

2215a9 **A Magicman (FR)** *(103) (HSteguweit,Germany)* 3-8-5 NGrant ....— 1
1848[14] Silca Blanka (IRE) *(102) (MRChannon)* 3-8-5 KDarley ....nk 2
2105[7] Mr Martini (IRE) *(107) (CEBrittain)* 5-9-5 JWeaver ....¾ 3

TOTE 66DM: 25DM 42DM 27DM (SF 668DM) OWNER Stall Dagobert BRED H. Voegele & Maria Koenig 10 Rn
1m 33.7 SF: -/-/-

1122a-MUNICH (Germany) (L-H)
Sunday July 30th (Good to firm)

2894a DR POTH-BAYERISCHES ZUCHTRENNEN (Gp 1) (3-Y.O+) £90,535.00 (£39,094.00: £18,518.00: £10,288.00) **1m 2f** 3-20 (3-21)

2046a2 **Germany (USA)** *(121) (BSchutz,Germany)* 4-9-6 LDettori (mde all: pushed out: easily) ....— 1

1711a* Kaldounevees(FR) *(119) (JEHammond,France)* 4-9-6 FSanchez (mid div: effrt over 2f out: r.o: nvr nrr)....1½ 2
2286[8] Tryphosa (IRE) *(110) (AWohler,Germany)* 3-8-3 ABoschert (hld up in rr: str run fnl f: nrst fin).1 3
2218a[2] Definite Article *(113) (DKWeld,Ireland)* 3-8-7 MJKinane (a.p: shkn up 1½f out: no rspnse) ....½ 4
Hondero (GER) *(115) (Germany)* 5-9-6 DRegnard (racd 2nd: one pce fnl f) ....½ 5
2215a[12] Centaine *(104) (HRemmert,Germany)* 3-8-3 MRoberts (racd in rr: hdwy 3f out: unable qckn fnl 1½f)....2½ 6
Flying Anshan *(107) (Germany)* 4-9-6 PHeugl (a in rr: nvr able to chal) 3 7
2215a[7] Speedster *(81) (BSchutz,Germany)* 3-8-7 GHuber (hld up mid div: rdn over 2f out: sn btn)...14 8
1394a[4] Thames (FR) *(76) (LAudon,France)* 4-9-6 WMongil (racd in 4th: grad wknd) 5 9

TOTE 51DM: 19DM 33DM 30DM (SF 637DM) OWNER Mr Jaber Abdullah BRED Curative Ltd 9 Rn
2m 5.2 SF: -/-/-/-/-/-/-/-/-

2895a GROSSER SPRINT PREIS (Listed) (3-Y.O+) £9,876.00 (£3,951.00: £2,016.00) **6f 110y** 4-35 (4-36)

Macanal (USA) *(117) (HJentzsch,Germany)* 3-9-3 SEccles ....— 1
2728a[D] Branston Abby (IRE) *(113) (MJohnston)* 6-9-8 MRoberts 1¼ 2
Grappolo *(97) (RSuerland,Germany)* 3-8-6 FSanchez 2½ 3
2430[4] Katya (IRE) *(MRChannon)* 3-8-8 DHarrison (btn approx 4l).... 5

TOTE 29DM: 12DM 13DM 17DM (SF 76DM) OWNER Gestut Fahrhof BRED Bruce Hundley in USA 10 Rn
1m 18.0 SF: -/-/-/-

DEAUVILLE (France) (R-H)
Sunday July 30th (Good to soft)

2896a PRIX YACOWLEF (Listed) (2-Y.O) £16,766.00 (£5,748.00: £3,593.00) **6f (straight)** 2-00 (1-52)

Sangria (USA) *(AFabre,France)* 2-8-13 GGuignard ....— 1
West Memphis (USA) *(AFabre,France)* 2-9-2 TJarnet ....s.nk 2
Titus Livius (FR) *(JEPease,France)* 2-9-2 CAsmussen 1 3
Magic Galop (USA) *(DRCElsworth)* 2-9-2 PaulEddery 15 4

P-M 4.90F: 1.70F 1.10F (9.90F) OWNER Sheikh Mohammed (FRANCE) BRED Keswick Stables 4 Rn
1m 14.4 (5.90) SF: -/-/-/-

2897a PRIX D'ASTARTE (Gp 2) (3-Y.O+ F & M) £35,928.00 (£14,371.00: £7,186.00: £3,593.00) **1m (straight)** 2-30 (2-23)

1850[2] **Smolensk (USA)** *(115) (AFabre,France)* 3-8-7 TJarnet (trckd ldrs: hdwy on outside over 2f out: led 1f out: r.o wl)....— 1
1712a[6] Shaanxi (USA) *(114) (ELellouche,France)* 3-8-7 DBoeuf (mid div: rdn over 1f out: bmpd ins fnl f: kpt on)....½ 2
1711a[3] Agathe (USA) *(110) (AFabre,France)* 4-9-0 OPeslier (led tl rdn & hdd 1f out: one pce) 1½ 3
1390a[4] Ghostly (IRE) *(110) (PBary,France)* 3-8-7 CAsmussen (in rr: hdwy 2f out: unable qckn ins fnl f)....¾ 4
2214a* Fairy Path (USA) *(109) (DSmaga,France)* 3-8-7 FHead (hld up in rr: rdn over 2f out: sme hdwy ins fnl f)....hd 5
2214a[2] Nagnagnag (IRE) *(104) (SDow)* 3-8-7 GMosse (prom: rdn 2f out: wknd over 1f out) 2½ 6
1850[10] Macoumba (USA) *(100) (MmeCHead,France)* 3-8-7 ODoleuze (trckd ldr: rdn & wknd over 2f out)....2 7

P-M 2.10F: 1.20F 1.50F (5.80F) OWNER Mme P. de Moussac (FRANCE) 7 Rn 1m 35.6 (1.30)

2898a PRIX BERTEUX (Gp 3) (3-Y.O) £26,347.00 (£9,581.00: £4,790.00) **1m 7f** 3-30 (3-23)

2386a* **Affidavit (USA)** *(115) (AFabre,France)* 3-9-4 TJarnet ....— 1
2386a[2] Peckinpah's Soul (FR) *(106) (DSmaga,France)* 3-8-11 FHead 2 2
2045a[5] Enquiry (FR) *(101) (MmePBarbe,France)* 3-8-8 TThulliez 1½ 3
2386a[4] Wot-If-We (IRE) *(96) (TGMills)* 3-8-8 PaulEddery 5 4

P-M 2.30F: 1.10F 1.10F (3.40F) OWNER Sheikh Mohammed (FRANCE) BRED H.H. Aga Khan Stud S.C. 4 Rn
3m 15.8 SF: -/-/-/-

2899a PRIX DU CERCLE (Listed) (3-Y.O+) £16,766.00 (£5,748.00: £3,593.00: £1,898.00) 5f **(straight)** 4-00 (3-54)

Kerulen *(107) (JEPease,France)* 4-8-10 CAsmussen ......— 1
Super Vite (USA) *(108) (CLaffon-Parias,France)* 3-8-6 OPeslier ......nse 2
Baba Thong (USA) *(111) (MmeCHead,France)* 3-8-9 ODoleuze ......s.h 3
2430[6] Ya Malak *(114) (JWPayne)* 4-9-4 BThomson ......s.nk 4

P-M 22.30F: 4.30F 2.80F 2.00F (83.10F) OWNER Mr George Strawbridge BRED London Thoroughbred Services Ltd 9 Rn 58.7 secs SF: -/-/-/-

2388a-AGNANO (Naples, Italy) (R-H) Sunday July 30th (Soft)

2900a CRITERIUM PARTENOPEO (Listed) (2-Y.O) £17,730.00 (£7,801.00: £3,617.00) 7f 110y 9-55 (10-03)

2387a[3] **Pierrot Solaire (FR)** *(SSaggiamo,Italy)* 2-8-9 FJovine ......— 1
Marintisse (ITY) *(SSantella,Italy)* 2-8-9 GLigas 1 2
Boccadirosa (IRE) *(PGuarsegnati,Italy)* 2-8-6 OFancera 1 3
2432[3] Double Point (IRE) *(MBell)* 2-8-9 MFenton (btn approx 12l)...... 8

TOTE 97L: 54L 70L 46L (2829L) OWNER Scuderia Tamara BRED Haras D'Ommeel 13 Rn 1m 32.3

2270-HAYDOCK (L-H) Friday August 4th (Good to firm)

WEATHER: fine, sunny WIND: fresh bhd

2901 HAYDOCK PARK PONY CLUB CLAIMING STKS (3-Y.O+) (Class F) £2,689.00 (£754.00: £367.00) 1m 2f 120y Stalls: High GOING minus 0.39 sec (F) 6-15 (6-16)

2676[4] **Cashmirie (46)***(60)*(Fav)*(JLEyre)* 3-7-4 (5)ow1 NVarley(5) (lw: chsd ldr: 2nd st: led wl over 1f out: hld on gamely)......— 1
Smart Family (USA) **(75)***(72)*(Fav)*(MCPipe)* 4-9-2 DHolland(1) (bit bkwd: hld up & bhd: 5th st: hdwy 3f out: hrd rdn & r.o wl towards fin)......s.h 2
1854[11] Torrey Pines (IRE) **(38)***(61) (DHaydnJones)* 3-7-9 (3) AMackay(4) (set slow pce: rdn & hdd wl over 1f out: sn btn)......2 3
2391[4] Malihabad (IRE) *(65) (RHollinshead)* 6-8-13 WRyan(2) (bit bkwd: chsd ldrs: 3rd st: rdn over 2f out: wknd appr fnl f)......½ 4
2147[3] Awestruck **(41)***(42) (BPreece)* 5-8-5 (3) JStack(3) (hld up: 4th st: rdn & wknd 3f out: t.o)......12 5

7/4 CASHMIRIE, Smart Family (USA), **4/1** Malihabad (IRE), **9/1** Awestruck, **20/1** Torrey Pines (IRE), CSF £4.81 TOTE £2.90: £1.20 £1.60 (£2.20) OWNER Mr Ernest Spencer (HAMBLETON) BRED G. E. Peace 5 Rn 2m 17.84 (6.34) SF: 3/25/4/18/-
WEIGHT FOR AGE 3yo-10lb

2902 DON DARIAS H'CAP (0-85) (3-Y.O) (Class D) £3,764.25 (£1,134.00: £549.50: £257.25) 1m 3f 200y Stalls: High GOING minus 0.39 sec per fur (F) 6-45 (6-46)

2781* **Silktail (IRE) (55)***(70+)*(Fav)*(CADwyer)* 3-7-5 (5) 5x NVarley(3) (s.i.s: 4th st: rdn over 3f out: led wl over 1f out: sn clr)......— 1
2752* Wathbat Mtoto **(85)***(91) (LMCumani)* 3-9-5 (7) 5x JoHunnam(1) (chsd ldr: 2nd st: led over 2f out tl over 1f out: sn outpcd)......7 2
2506[3] Lucayan Sunshine (USA) **(75)***(77) (LadyHerries)* 3-9-2b GCarter(2) (lw: chsd ldrs: 4th st: drppd rr 3f out: styd on u.p appr fnl f)......3 3
2571[6] Painted Hall (USA) **(74)***(73) (JARToller)* 3-9-1 WNewnes(6) (led tl over 2f out: sn rdn & btn) 1¾ 4
2589[3] Bardon Hill Boy (IRE) **(78)***(74) (BHanbury)* 3-9-2 (3) JStack(4) (s.i.s: hld up in rr: 5th st: rdn over 2f out: nvr nr to chal)......2½ 5
2555[4] Executive Design **(79)***(72) (MrsMReveley)* 3-9-6 KDarley(5) (hld up: 6th st: effrt 3f out: rdn & wknd 2f out)......2½ 6

11/10 SILKTAIL (IRE) (6/4-Evens), **5/1** Wathbat Mtoto (7/2-11/2), **6/1** Executive Design, **7/1** Painted Hall (USA), Bardon Hill Boy (IRE), **8/1** Lucayan Sunshine (USA), CSF £6.91 TOTE £2.20: £1.40 £2.40 (£3.20) OWNER Mrs Monica Caine (NEWMARKET) BRED Sheikh Mohammed bin Rashid al Maktoum 6 Rn 2m 30.37 (2.37) SF: 34/55/41/37/38/36

2903

HALEWOOD INTERNATIONAL MISSISSIPPI STEAMER H'CAP (0-85) (3-Y.O+) (Class D) £3,787.00 (£1,141.00: £553.00: £259.00)
1m 2f 120y Stalls: High GOING minus 0.39 sec per fur (F) 7-15 (7-15)

2446[4] **Amrak Ajeeb (IRE) (79)***(91) (BHanbury)* 3-9-5 MRimmer(5) (lw: stdd s: 4th st: hdwy 2f out: led ent fnl f: r.o wl) — 1
2269* Senorita Dinero (USA) **(83)***(95)*(Fav)*(MRStoute)* 3-9-9 DHolland(1) (hld up: 3rd st: effrt & rdn 3f out: led 2f out tl appr fnl f: rallied u.p cl home) nk 2
2490[4] Persian Elite (IRE) **(74)***(78) (PFICole)* 4-9-10 KDarley(2) (led 7f out to 2f out: rdn & n.m.r bel dist: sn outpcd) 5 3
2525[3] Flame War (USA) **(79)***(75) (HRACecil)* 3-9-5 WRyan(3) (led over 3f: 2nd st: rdn & btn whn hmpd bel dist) 5 4

11/8 Senorita Dinero (USA) (Evens-6/4), **2/1** Flame War (USA), **100/30** Persian Elite (IRE), **6/1** AMRAK AJEEB (IRE), CSF £14.06 TOTE £6.40 (£4.60) OWNER Mr A. Merza (NEWMARKET) BRED Ovidstown Investments Ltd 4 Rn 2m 12.65 (1.15) SF: 63/67/60/47
WEIGHT FOR AGE 3yo-10lb
STEWARDS' ENQUIRY Obj. to Amrak Ajeeb (IRE) by Holland overruled. Holland fined £55 (no reasonable grounds for obj.).

2904

COUNTRYWIDE FREIGHT CONDITIONS STKS (2-Y.O) (Class C) £4,829.00 (£1,754.00: £852.00: £360.00: £155.00)
6f Stalls: High GOING minus 0.39 sec per fur (F) 7-45 (7-45)

2063* **Mazeed (IRE)** *(84+)*(Fav)*(HThomsonJones)* 2-9-2 RHills(3) (mde all: clr ½-wy: canter) — 1
2541[9] The Frisky Farmer **(80)***(70) (WGMTurner)* 2-8-4 (7) ADaly(2) (a.p: rdn to go 2nd wl ins fnl f: no ch w wnr) 3½ 2
2619[5] Power Game **(71)***(70) (JBerry)* 2-8-11 JCarroll(4) (lw: chsd wnr: rdn & no ex fnl f) 1¾ 3
2696[2] Jimjareer (IRE) **(77)***(46) (CaptJWilson)* 2-8-11 KFallon(5) (lw: a bhd: rdn over 2f out: no imp) .7 4
Distant King *(SCoathup)* 2-8-11b TWilliams(1) (bkwd: s.i.s: a bhd: t.o fnl 2f) 30 5

4/9 MAZEED (IRE), **11/2** The Frisky Farmer, Jimjareer (IRE), **10/1** Power Game (op 6/1), **25/1** Distant King, CSF £3.49 TOTE £1.50: £1.20 £1.70 (£2.70) OWNER Mr Hamdan Al Maktoum (NEWMARKET) BRED Shadwell Estate Company Limited 5 Rn 1m 13.54 (1.84) SF: 42/28/23/4/-
OFFICIAL EXPLANATION Jimjareer: the jockey stated that the colt had lost his action two furlongs out.

2905

NATIONAL GROCERS BENEVOLENT FUND CLAIMING STKS (3-Y.O+) (Class F) £2,787.00 (£782.00: £381.00)
6f Stalls: High GOING minus 0.39 sec per fur (F) 8-15 (8-17)

2753[4] **King Rambo (63)***(70) (RHollinshead)* 4-8-7 WRyan(3) (lw: stdd s: plld hrd: swtchd outside over 1f out: qcknd to ld ins fnl f: hld on wl) — 1
2611[9] Kummel King **(59)***(66) (EJAlston)* 7-8-4 ow1 KFallon(2) (led: rdn over 1f out: hdd ins fnl f: rallied cl home) hd 2
2665* Here Comes a Star **(69)***(69) (JMCarr)* 7-8-11 ACulhane(1) (hld up: hdwy 2f out: ev ch ent fnl f: unable qckn) 1¾ 3
2611[5] Winter Scout (USA) **(64)***(60) (MrsMReveley)* 7-8-9 KDarley(5) (lw: prom: ev ch ent fnl f: rdn & one pce) 2½ 4
2712* Rosa Bonheur **(52)***(49)*(Fav)*(MAJarvis)* 3-7-8 (5) NVarley(7) (b.hind: chsd ldrs: rdn over 1f out: sn btn) 2½ 5
2784[15] Make the Break **(48)***(48) (SCoathup)* 4-8-3b TWilliams(6) (hld up in rr: effrt & rdn over 1f out: no imp) hd 6
2493[5] Vengan **(47)** *(DHaydnJones)* 3-7-11 ow4 AMackay(4) (withdrawn not under starters' orders: ref to ent stalls) W

9/4 Rosa Bonheur, **11/4** Here Comes a Star, **4/1** KING RAMBO, **9/2** Winter Scout (USA), **9/1** Kummel King, **25/1** Vengan, **33/1** Make the Break, CSF £30.77 TOTE £4.80: £2.30 £3.10 (£17.40) OWNER Mr J. D. Graham (UPPER LONGDON) BRED G. Johnson 6 Rn
1m 13.38 (1.68) SF: 36/32/35/26/10/14/-
WEIGHT FOR AGE 3yo-5lb

2906

GATE HOUSE H'CAP (0-70) (3-Y.O+) (Class E) £3,176.25 (£960.00: £467.50: £221.25) **1m 30y** Stalls: Low GOING minus 0.39 sec per fur (F) 8-45 (8-45)

2446[2] **Lord Oberon (IRE) (58)***(70)*(Fav)*(JAkehurst)* 7-9-5 GCarter(3) (lw: mde all: qcknd 3f out: rdn & r.o wl) — 1

2227[2] Sir Arthur Hobbs **(57)***(67) (JLEyre)* 8-9-4 RLappin(1) (hld up: 4th st: hdwy over 2f out: str chal fnl f: r.o)..........1 2
2668[2] Nobby Barnes **(41)***(48) (DonEnricoIncisa)* 6-8-2 KimTinkler(5) (a.p: 3rd st: rdn ent fnl f: unable qckn)..........1½ 3
2814[4] Princess Maxine (IRE) **(56)***(58) (JJO'Neill)* 6-9-3 JCarroll(4) (lw: a.p: 2nd st: rdn 2f out: one pce)..........2½ 4
2549[11] Persian Affair (IRE) **(65)***(67) (DHaydnJones)* 4-9-12 AMackay(2) (lw: hld up & bhd: 5th st: effrt & rdn 2f out: nt pce to chal)..........s.h 5

13/8 LORD OBERON (IRE), **7/2** Sir Arthur Hobbs, **4/1** Nobby Barnes, **11/2** Princess Maxine (IRE), Persian Affair (IRE), CSF £7.16 TOTE £2.40: £1.60 £2.20 (£3.40) OWNER Mrs John Akehurst (LAMBOURN) BRED H. Ward 5 Rn
1m 45.85 (5.45) SF: 19/16/-/7/16
STEWARDS' ENQUIRY Lappin susp. 18-19/8/95 (incorrect use of whip).

T/Plpt: £231.10 (53.5 Tckts). T/Qdpt: £147.50 (0.4 Tckts); £119.64 to Haydock 5/8/95. IM

2775-NEWMARKET (R-H)
Friday August 4th (Good to firm)
WEATHER: warm, sunny WIND: mod bhd

2907
HEADLAND INTERNATIONAL PROPERTIES H'CAP (0-90) (3-Y.O+) (Class C) £5,744.00 (£1,712.00: £816.00: £368.00)
2m 24y (July) Stalls: High GOING minus 0.31 sec per fur (GF) 6-00 (6-01)

2612* **College Don (65)***(78) (MPBielby)* 4-8-3 (3) DRMcCabe(1) (trckd ldrs: styd on wl u.p to ld ins fnl f)..........— 1
2284* Shining High **(83)***(96)*(Fav)*(JLDunlop)* 3-8-9 WCarson(5) (lw: trckd ldr: plld out over 2f out: rdn to ld over 1f out: hdd & unable qckn ins fnl f)..........nk 2
2569* Highflying **(87)***(97) (GMMoore)* 9-9-11 (3) JTate(2) (led: hdd over 1f out: rdn & no ex ins fnl f)..........2½ 3
2374[3] Mondragon **(72)***(72) (MrsMReveley)* 5-8-13 DeanMcKeown(6) (hld up: effrt 4f out: sn rdn & btn)..........10 4
2695* Carnbrea Belle (IRE) **(73)***(61) (MBell)* 3-7-6 (7) 4x RMullen(4) (in tch: rdn over 3f out: sn wknd)12 5

2/1 Shining High, **100/30** COLLEGE DON, **9/2** Highflying (op 3/1), Carnbrea Belle (IRE) (op 3/1), **5/1** Mondragon, CSF £9.68 TOTE £3.90: £1.40 £1.70 (£3.80) OWNER Mr J. F. Coupland (GRIMSBY) BRED Chippenham Lodge Stud 5 Rn
3m 30.04 (7.04) SF: 32/35/51/26/-
WEIGHT FOR AGE 3yo-15lb

2908
TEAM ENGLAND TOILETRY RANGE (S) STKS (2-Y.O) (Class E) £3,622.50 (£1,080.00: £515.00: £232.50)
7f (July) Stalls: High GOING minus 0.31 sec per fur (GF) 6-30 (6-31)

2683[9] **Tarry** *(60) (LordHuntingdon)* 2-8-6 JWeaver(4) (rdn & hdwy 3f out: styd on wl to ld wl ins fnl f)..........— 1
2715[4] Aussie **(58)***(63) (MHTompkins)* 2-8-11 PRobinson(5) (lw: hld up: hdwy 2f out: led over 1f out tl wl ins fnl f: unable qckn)..........¾ 2
2717[R] Again Together **(68)***(57)*(Fav)*(NACallaghan)* 2-8-6 PatEddery(3) (b: led 2f: ev ch over 1f out tl no ex nr fin)..........½ 3
2542[10] Kernof (IRE) *(54) (MDHammond)* 2-8-11 DaleGibson(2) (chsd ldrs: ev ch over 1f out: one pce)..........3½ 4
2635[3] Victoria Venture **(55)***(52) (SPCWoods)* 2-8-11 BDoyle(1) (prom: led after 2f: hdd over 1f out: sn wknd)..........¾ 5
2346[5] Rothley Imp (IRE) *(36) (JWharton)* 2-8-6 JQuinn(6) (lw: trckd ldrs: nt clr run 2f out: nvr trbld ldrs)..........5 6
2035[5] Compensate (IRE) *(22) (MJHaynes)* 2-8-1 (5) MBaird(7) (dwlt: plld hrd & sn prom: wknd qckly over 1f out)..........6 7
2505[2] The Kastarbids (IRE) **(60)***(22) (DMorris)* 2-8-11v LDettori(8) (plld hrd: prom: ev ch over 2f out: sn rdn & btn)..........2½ 8
1989[6] Imprimis (IRE) **(53)***(13) (CNAllen)* 2-8-1 (5) MHenry(9) (chsd ldrs 4f: sn rdn & wknd)..........1¾ 9

6/4 Again Together, **9/2** Victoria Venture (3/1-5/1), **5/1** The Kastarbids (IRE), **8/1** TARRY (6/1-9/1), **10/1** Aussie (6/1-12/1), **12/1** Imprimis (IRE) (8/1-16/1), **16/1** Rothley Imp (IRE), **33/1** Compensate (IRE), Kernof (IRE), CSF £73.05 TOTE £11.90: £2.40 £2.00 £1.40 (£44.60) Trio £75.10 OWNER Lord Carnarvon (WEST ILSLEY) BRED Highclere Stud Ltd 9 Rn
1m 28.62 (4.22) SF: 16/19/13/10/8/-/-/-/-
sold Mr C Williams 6,500gns.

2909 BERNARD LLOYD/PAUL STANBROOK H'CAP (0-90) (3-Y.O+) (Class C)

£6,524.00 (£1,952.00: £936.00: £428.00)
6f (July) Stalls: High GOING minus 0.31 sec per fur (GF) 7-00 (7-01)

2461^{2} **Al Wujud (IRE) (61)***(75) (TDyer)* 4-8-6 JQuinn(4) (swtg; hld up centre: hdwy to ld over 1f out: sn clr: easily) — 1
2271^{7} Bajan Rose **(79)***(80) (MBlanshard)* 3-9-5 StephenDavies(2) (chsd ldr centre: ev ch over 1f out: sn outpcd) 5 2
2585* Rocketeer (IRE) **(75)***(74)*(Fav)*(WRMuir)* 4-9-6b JWeaver(9) (plld out & hdwy over 2f out: no ex fnl f) ½ 3
1414^{3} Showery **(72)***(70) (JWWatts)* 3-8-12 LDettori(11) (chsd clr ldr stands' side: kpt on fnl f) s.h 4
2746^{12} Ikaab (USA) **(88)***(79) (MajorWRHern)* 3-10-0b WCarson(6) (led centre over 4f) 2½ 5
2745^{5} Lookingforarainbow (IRE) **(78)***(60) (BobJones)* 7-9-9 MWigham(3) (dwlt: racd centre: styd on fnl 2f) 3½ 6
2001^{10} Moonlight Saunter (USA) **(88)***(66) (EALDunlop)* 3-9-11 (3) JTate(1) (racd centre: chsd ldrs 4f) 1½ 7
2764^{19} Green Golightly (USA) **(58)***(34) (DAWilson)* 4-8-3 NAdams(10) (stdd s: nvr plcd to chal) ¾ 8
2533^{5} Gone Savage **(66)***(39) (WJMusson)* 7-8-11 AMcGlone(12) (b: a bhd) 1¼ 9
1637^{5} Insider Trader **(77)***(45) (RGuest)* 4-9-8v GDuffield(8) (b: lw: led & sn clr stands' side: wknd & hdd over 1f out) 1¾ 10
2326^{9} Moujeeb (USA) **(60)***(21) (PatMitchell)* 5-8-5 BDoyle(7) (chsd ldrs over 3f) 2½ 11
2659^{2} Winsome Wooster **(64)***(22) (PGMurphy)* 4-8-6 (3) SDrowne(13) (chsd ldrs: rdn 3f out: sn btn) 1¼ 12

4/1 Rocketeer (IRE), **5/1** AL WUJUD (IRE), Showery, **6/1** Winsome Wooster, **9/1** Gone Savage, **11/1** Ikaab (USA), **12/1** Insider Trader, Green Golightly (USA), **20/1** Moonlight Saunter (USA), Moujeeb (USA), **33/1** Lookingforarainbow (IRE), Bajan Rose, CSF £122.71 CT £646.82 TOTE £4.40: £2.10 £6.20 £2.10 (£125.20) Trio £112.10 OWNER Mr Mike Flynn (INVERGOWRIE) BRED Shadwell Estate Company Limited 12 Rn 1m 12.03 (0.53) SF: 57/57/56/47/56/42/43/16/21/27/3/4
WEIGHT FOR AGE 3yo-5lb

2910 TUDOR GATE HOTEL & RESTAURANT CONDITIONS STKS (3-Y.O+) (Class C)

£5,060.80 (£1,820.80: £870.40: £352.00: £136.00)
1m 2f (July) Stalls: High GOING minus 0.31 sec per fur (GF) 7-30 (7-30)

1574a^{11} **Commoner (USA) (101)***(107)*(Fav)*(RHannon)* 3-8-11 PatEddery(2) (lw: trckd ldrs: led over 1f out: pushed clr nr fin) — 1
2593^{3} Green Green Desert (FR) **(100)***(104) (MRStoute)* 4-9-4 WCarson(1) (lw: hld up: hdwy 2f out: ev ch ins fnl f: rdn & no ex) ¾ 2
2012^{2} Godwin (USA) **(81)***(94) (HRACecil)* 4-9-1 AMcGlone(3) (trckd ldr: led over 2f out tl over 1f out: sn outpcd) 4 3
*468** Bencher Q C (USA) *(93) (JHMGosden)* 3-8-11 LDettori(5) (led over 7f: wknd appr fnl f) 4 4
2596^{6} Fragrant Belle (USA) **(94)***(75) (LGCottrell)* 4-8-13 MRoberts(4) (lw: plld hrd: in tch 6f: sn rdn & btn) 7 5

9/4 COMMONER (USA), **3/1** Green Green Desert (FR), **7/2** Godwin (USA), **9/2** Bencher Q C (USA), **7/1** Fragrant Belle (USA), CSF £8.49 TOTE £2.90: £1.60 £1.60 (£3.00) OWNER Mr B. E. Nielsen (MARLBOROUGH) BRED Pamela H. Firman, G. W. and Louise Humphrey in USA 5 Rn
2m 8.26 (5.86) SF: 23/29/19/9/-
WEIGHT FOR AGE 3yo-9lb

2911 EMPLAS TRADE WINDOWS NURSERY H'CAP (2-Y.O) (Class D)

£4,503.00 (£1,344.00: £642.00: £291.00)
7f (July) Stalls: High GOING minus 0.31 sec per fur (GF) 8-00 (8-00)

2464* **Royal Mark (IRE) (78)***(85+)*(Fav)*(JWWatts)* 2-9-7 PatEddery(2) (lw: hld up: hdwy over 1f out: led ins fnl f: pushed out) — 1
2515^{4} Green Bentley (IRE) **(64)***(70) (RHannon)* 2-8-7 RPerham(4) (hld up: nt clr run fr 2f out tl squeezed thro ins fnl f: r.o wl: nt rch wnr) ½ 2
2541^{2} Society Girl **(78)***(77) (CWThornton)* 2-9-7 DeanMcKeown(1) (b.hind: lw: trckd ldrs: led over 1f out tl ins fnl f: one pce) 3 3
2505* Crimson And Clover **(62)***(51) (RAkehurst)* 2-8-5 ow1 LDettori(5) (trckd ldr: ev ch over 1f out: one pce whn hmpd ins fnl f) 4 4
2467^{4} Brecon **(75)***(42) (PFICole)* 2-9-4 TQuinn(3) (led: qcknd over 2f out: hdd & wknd over 1f out) 10 5

Evens ROYAL MARK (IRE), **4/1** Green Bentley (IRE), Crimson And Clover, **6/1** Society Girl (op 7/2), **14/1** Brecon (op 6/1), CSF £5.13 TOTE £2.00: £1.20 £2.20 (£3.30) OWNER Lord Swaythling (RICHMOND) BRED Barronstown Stud And Ron Con Ltd 5 Rn 1m 28.63 (4.23) SF: 30/15/22/-/-

2912 CARWIN MAIDEN STKS (2-Y.O) (Class D) £4,815.00 (£1,440.00: £690.00: £315.00) **7f (July)** Stalls: High GOING minus 0.31 sec per fur (GF) 8-30 (8-30)

2573[6] **Lord of Men** *(84+) (JHMGosden)* 2-9-0 LDettori(3) (sn trckng ldrs: led over 1f out: rdn clr)...— **1**
2573[5] Wilawander *(76)*(Fav)*(BWHills)* 2-9-0 BThomson(5) (led over 5f: kpt on same pce) 3½ **2**
Threesome (USA) *(69+) (LMCumani)* 2-8-9 JWeaver(7) (unf: stdd s: hdwy 2f out: r.o wl fnl f)......¾ **3**
Kass Alhawa *(69+) (MRStoute)* 2-9-0 PaulEddery(11) (w'like: scope: hld up: hdwy over 2f out: kpt on fnl f)......2½ **4**
Majdak Jereeb (IRE) *(68+) (MajorWRHern)* 2-9-0 TSprake(6) (str: bkwd: bhd: rdn over 1f out: hdwy fnl f: nrst fin) ......nk **5**
Diminutive (USA) *(63) (JWHills)* 2-9-0 MHills(2) (neat: scope: lw: chsd ldrs: one pce fnl 2f) 2 **6**
2200[5] Tapintime (USA) *(63) (PFICole)* 2-9-0 TQuinn(10) (plld hrd: prom: ev ch 2f out: sn wknd).....nk **7**
Magic Ron *(59) (MBell)* 2-9-0 MFenton(4) (unf: scope: lw: s.i.s: sn pushed along: nvr nrr) ...1½ **8**
Consordino *(53) (LMCumani)* 2-8-2 (7) GMitchell(12) (scope: bkwd: chsd ldrs over 5f) ....¾ **9**
Murheb *(56) (RWArmstrong)* 2-9-0 RPrice(8) (lt-f: unf: trckd ldrs 5f)......s.h **10**
Muhtadi (IRE) *(40) (JLDunlop)* 2-9-0 WCarson(13) (rangy: unf: s.i.s: a bhd)......7 **11**
2161[9] Vague Spirit *(40) (CEBrittain)* 2-9-0 MRoberts(1) (w ldrs: rdn 3f out: sn btn)......hd **12**

5/4 Wilawander (tchd Evens), **7/2** LORD OF MEN (5/2-4/1), **8/1** Muhtadi (IRE) (6/1-10/1), **9/1** Threesome (USA) (8/1-12/1), **10/1** Magic Ron, **12/1** Murheb (10/1-16/1), **20/1** Kass Alhawa, Tapintime (USA), **33/1** Diminutive (USA), Consordino, Majdak Jereeb (IRE), Vague Spirit, CSF £8.22 TOTE £4.90: £1.80 £1.40 £2.10 (£4.20) Trio £11.80 OWNER Sheikh Mohammed (NEWMARKET) BRED Sheikh Mohammed bin Rashid al Maktoum 12 Rn
1m 26.21 (1.81) SF: 51/43/36/36/35/30/30/26/20/23/7/7

T/Plpt: £10.10 (1,762.28 Tckts). T/Qdpt: £7.60 (31.75 Tckts). Dk

2371-REDCAR (L-H)
Friday August 4th (Firm, Good to firm patches)
WEATHER: overcast, cool WIND: mod half against

2913 STAINTONDALE (S) STKS (3-Y.O+) (Class F) £2,882.00 (£802.00: £386.00) **7f** Stalls: Centre GOING minus 0.16 sec per fur (GF) 2-40 (2-43)

2611[8] **Move Smartly (IRE) (51)***(61+) (FHLee)* 5-9-4v RCochrane(6) (lw: trckd ldrs gng wl: led over 2f out: edgd lft & r.o)......— **1**
2698[6] Legend Dulac (IRE) **(46)***(53) (JAHarris)* 6-9-4 LDettori(2) (a cl up: kpt on one pce fnl 2f) 3½ **2**
2398[5] Best Kept Secret **(62)***(42) (JBerry)* 4-8-11 (7) PFessey(9) (trckd ldrs: effrt over 2f out: put hd in air & styd on one pce)......5 **3**
2461[12] Ragazzo (IRE) **(35)***(44) (JSWainwright)* 5-9-9b BThomson(10) (b.hind: a chsng ldrs: nt qckn fnl 2f)......1 **4**
2832[5] Sense of Priority **(57)***(44) (DNicholls)* 6-9-9 AlexGreaves(3) (s.i.s: effrt ½-wy: no imp) ....s.h **5**
2396[11] Princess Shera (IRE) **(35)***(34) (EJAlston)* 4-8-13 KFallon(7) (hld up: effrt ½-wy: rdn & no rspnse)......s.h **6**
Palace River (IRE) *(31) (DMoffatt)* 7-8-10 (3) DarrenMoffatt(4) (dwlt: outpcd & bhd tl sme late hdwy)......1½ **7**
1297[14] Broctune Gold **(68)***(34)*(Fav)*(MrsMReveley)* 4-9-4 (5) GParkin(8) (lw: led after 1f tl over 2f out: sn wknd)......3 **8**
Easby Jester *(20) (SEKettlewell)* 4-9-4 JFortune(5) (prom over 4f) 4 **9**
2698[16] Kajostar **(35)***(12) (SWCampion)* 5-8-13 JLowe(1) (swtg: led 1f: wknd ½-wy) 1 **10**
2676[7] Whitegatesprincess (IRE) *(BEllison)* 4-8-13v NConnorton(11) (a outpcd & bhd)......20 **11**

15/8 Broctune Gold (5/4-2/1), **5/2** Sense of Priority, **5/1** Best Kept Secret, **6/1** MOVE SMARTLY (IRE), Legend Dulac (IRE), **40/1** Princess Shera (IRE), **50/1** Ragazzo (IRE), Easby Jester, **100/1** Kajostar, **150/1** Palace River (IRE), Whitegatesprincess (IRE), CSF £38.37 TOTE £8.10: £2.20 £1.50 £1.40 (£8.90) Trio £12.50 OWNER Mr F. H. Lee (WILMSLOW) BRED Ballysheehan Stud in Ireland 11 Rn 1m 26.7 (4.70) SF: 32/24/13/15/15/5/2/5/-/-/-
No bid

2914 TATTERSALLS NURSERY AUCTION H'CAP (2-Y.O) (Class E) £3,670.00 (£1,105.00: £535.00: £250.00) **6f** Stalls: Centre GOING minus 0.16 sec per fur (GF) 3-10 (3-12)

2423[2] **Red River Valley (74)***(82) (DenysSmith)* 2-9-6 KFallon(2) (lw: ld up: qcknd to ld 1½f out: sn clr)......— **1**
1823[P] Diminuet **(75)***(76) (JWWatts)* 2-9-7 NConnorton(5) (lw: hld up: effrt 2f out: styd on: no imp)..2½ **2**

2371[2] Katy-Q (IRE) **(62)***(57)*(Fav)*(PCalver)* 2-8-8 MBirch(1) (lw: w ldrs: led ½-wy tl 1½f out: one pce) 2½ **3**
2498[5] Camionneur (IRE) **(65)***(57) (MHEasterby)* 2-8-11 LDettori(7) (w ldrs: rdn & nt qckn appr fnl f) .1 **4**
1842[10] Northern Clan **(57)***(49) (MWEasterby)* 2-8-3 JFanning(3) (cl up: disp ld ½-wy: wknd fnl 2f)....hd **5**
2257[3] Contradictory **(52)***(43) (MWEasterby)* 2-7-5 (7) PFessey(6) (sn pushed along: chsd ldrs tl wknd 2f out) ....nk **6**
2757[5] Efipetite **(60)***(38) (NBycroft)* 2-8-6 ow2 JWeaver(4) (led to ½-wy: sn wknd)....4 **7**

7/4 Katy-Q (IRE), **4/1** RED RIVER VALLEY, **9/2** Camionneur (IRE), **5/1** Diminuet, **8/1** Contradictory, **12/1** Northern Clan (op 8/1), **14/1** Efipetite, CSF £22.66 TOTE £5.20: £2.00 £3.40 (£23.20) OWNER Mr J. A. Bianchi (BISHOP AUCKLAND) BRED R. J. Vines 7 Rn 1m 14.0 (4.70) SF: 24/18/-/-/-/-/-

2915 CLEVELAND MAIDEN STKS (3-Y.O+) (Class D) £3,736.50 (£1,122.00: £541.00: £250.50) **7f** Stalls: Centre GOING minus 0.16 sec per fur (GF) 3-40 (3-42)

2583[2] **Iktamal (USA)** **(79)***(83)*(Fav)*(EALDunlop)* 3-8-12 JWeaver(3) (lw: plld hrd: bhd tl hdwy 3f out: chal 1f out: rdn to ld post) ....— **1**
2576[8] Golden Envoy (USA) *(78) (JHMGosden)* 3-8-7 LDettori(1) (led: qcknd 3f out: r.o: jst ct) ....s.h **2**
2527[6] Four Lane Flyer *(44) (EJAlston)* 3-8-7 KFallon(4) (b: cl up 4f: sn outpcd)....15 **3**
2255[4] Gymcrak Jareer (IRE) *(46) (GHolmes)* 3-8-12 NConnorton(2) (chsd ldrs 4f: sn rdn & btn)....1 **4**

5/6 IKTAMAL (USA) (10/11-Evens), **11/10** Golden Envoy (USA), **20/1** Gymcrak Jareer (IRE), **50/1** Four Lane Flyer, CSF £2.01 TOTE £1.90 (£1.10) OWNER Maktoum Al Maktoum (NEWMARKET) BRED Green Ireland Properties Ltd 4 Rn 1m 26.1 (4.10) SF: 32/27/-/-

2916 YUILL HOMES H'CAP (0-80) (3-Y.O+ F & M) (Class D) £3,658.50 (£1,098.00: £529.00: £244.50) **5f** Stalls: Centre GOING minus 0.16 sec per fur (GF) 4-10 (4-13)

2879[2] **Nite-Owl Dancer** **(57)***(62) (JAHarris)* 3-8-7 LDettori(4) (lw: trckd ldr stands' side: led ins fnl f: r.o) ....— **1**
2609[2] Lady Sheriff **(74)***(78)*(Fav)*(MWEasterby)* 4-9-7b(7) PFessey(3) (racd stands' side: led tl hdd ins fnl f: rallied)....nk **2**
2631[9] Indian Crystal **(40)***(33) (MrsMReveley)* 4-7-5v(3)ow1 DarrenMoffatt(1) (trckd ldr centre: effrt ½-wy: nt qckn)....3 **3**
2194[9] Encore M'Lady (IRE) **(73)***(48) (FHLee)* 4-9-13v RCochrane(2) (swtg: racd centre: cl up: rdn ½-wy: grad wknd)....6 **4**

LONG HANDICAP Indian Crystal 7-6

4/5 Lady Sheriff, **11/4** Encore M'Lady (IRE), **3/1** NITE-OWL DANCER, **25/1** Indian Crystal, CSF £5.73 TOTE £2.60 (£2.00) OWNER Burntwood Sports Ltd (SOUTHWELL) BRED Irwin Kramer 4 Rn 59.3 secs (2.60) SF: 31/51/6/21

WEIGHT FOR AGE 3yo-4lb

2917 PAT PHONENIX H'CAP (0-70) (3-Y.O+) (Class E) £3,579.00 (£1,077.00: £521.00: £243.00) **1m 3f** Stalls: Low GOING minus 0.16 sec per fur (GF) 4-40 (4-41)

2648[2] **Turnpole (IRE)** **(63)***(72)*(Fav)*(MrsMReveley)* 4-9-9 JFortune(5) (cl up: rdn over 4f out: styd on to ld ins fnl f)....— **1**
2132[3] Bardia **(33)***(42) (DonEnricoIncisa)* 5-7-7 KimTinkler(1) (lw: trckd ldrs: styd on to chal 1f out: kpt on) ....nk **2**
2621[3] Durano **(66)***(72) (MHEasterby)* 4-9-12 MBirch(4) (dwlt: hld up: styd on fnl 2f: nvr plcd to chal)....1¾ **3**
2774[4] Highfield Fizz **(60)***(64) (CWFairhurst)* 3-8-10 RCochrane(2) (led: qcknd over 4f out: hdd & wknd ins fnl f) 1¾ **4**
569[5] Antartictern (USA) **(53)***(48) (GROldroyd)* 5-8-13 JFanning(3) (s.i.s: sn prom: outpcd fnl 4f) 6 **5**

LONG HANDICAP Bardia 7-5

10/11 TURNPOLE (IRE) (Evens-5/6), **9/4** Durano, **6/1** Bardia, **7/1** Highfield Fizz, **33/1** Antartictern (USA), CSF £6.40 TOTE £1.80: £1.50 £2.30 (£3.90) OWNER Mr W. J. Williams (SALTBURN) BRED Old Meadow Stud 5 Rn 2m 27.0 (11.30) SF: 13/-/13/-/-

WEIGHT FOR AGE 3yo-10lb

2918 MIDDLETON MEDIAN AUCTION MAIDEN STKS (2-Y.O F) (Class F) £3,890.00 **5f** GOING minus 0.16 sec per fur (GF) 5-10 (-)

2782[2] **Arrhythmic (IRE)** *(MBrittain)* 2-8-11 RCochrane(3) (walked over) ....— **1**

OWNER Consultco Ltd (WARTHILL) BRED Patrick J. Farrington

T/Plpt: £51.70 (169.31 Tckts). T/Qdpt: Not won; £43.00 to Redcar 5/8/95. AA

2625-SOUTHWELL (L-H)
Friday August 4th (Standard)

WEATHER: sunny, hot WIND: slt half against

2919 TURNER H'CAP (0-60) (3-Y.O+) (Class F) £2,519.00 (£694.00: £329.00)
1m 6f (Fibresand) Stalls: Low GOING minus 0.01 sec per fur (STD) 2-20 (2-21)

2327[11] **Ijab (CAN) (37)***(49) (JParkes)* 5-8-6b GBardwell(10) (trckd ldrs: styd on u.p fnl 2f: led ins fnl f) — 1
*2630** Philmist **(51)***(63) (CWCElsey)* 3-8-7 NKennedy(5) (bhd: gd hdwy 6f out: sn w ldrs: led over 1f out tl ins fnl f: nt qckn nr fin) nk 2
2147[7] Who's the Best (IRE) **(43)***(52) (APJarvis)* 5-8-9 (3) DWright(15) (lw: chsd ldrs: led 7f out tl over 1f out: wknd ins fnl f) 2½ 3
2293[3] Barti-Ddu **(57)***(63) (SCWilliams)* 4-9-9 (3) JTate(16) (prom: effrt & outpcd over 3f out: kpt on fnl 2f) 2½ 4
2452[3] Wannaplantatree **(56)***(61) (NMBabbage)* 4-9-4 (7) SallySandes(3) (hdwy 5f out: one pce fnl 2f) ¾ 5
2687[3] Jean de Florette (USA) **(32)***(34) (CADwyer)* 4-7-10v(5) NVarley(2) (bhd: hdwy on outside over 2f out: nvr rchd ldrs) 3 6
2509[2] Leading Spirit (IRE) **(60)***(56)*(Fav)*(CFWall)* 3-9-2 GDuffield(11) (lw: trckd ldrs tl lost pl over 3f out) 5 7
1036[4] Murphys Way **(40)***(32) (JLEyre)* 6-8-9v CRutter(13) (chsd ldrs tl wknd 2f out) 3½ 8
2592[6] Drimard (IRE) **(34)***(20) (KMcAuliffe)* 4-8-3vow1 DHarrison(17) (chsd ldrs tl grad wknd fnl 3f) 4 9
Turner Prize (IRE) **(57)***(42) (MJRyan)* 5-9-12 AClark(12) (prom tl wknd over 3f out) 2 10
3[6] Top Prize **(35)***(14) (MBrittain)* 7-8-4 KDarley(4) (sn bhd) 5 11
1643[2] Inn At the Top **(60)***(37) (JNorton)* 3-9-2v DaleGibson(1) (sn bhd & drvn along) 2½ 12
1086[9] Desert Force (IRE) **(38)***(11) (RHarris)* 6-8-7 AMackay(9) (sn drvn along: chsd ldrs 7f out tl wknd 3f out) 3 13
1477[10] Risky Tu **(52)***(25) (PAKelleway)* 4-9-7 MWigham(7) (hdwy to chse ldrs 4f out: sn wknd) nk 14
1332[6] Absalom's Pillar **(59)***(30) (JMackie)* 5-10-0 GCarter(14) (led 4f: chsd ldrs tl lost pl 5f out) 1½ 15
2263[4] Mhemeanles **(43)***(7) (CaptJWilson)* 5-8-12 SMaloney(8) (b.hind: bhd: gd hdwy ½-wy: chsd ldrs tl wknd 3f out) 6 16
2495[3] Swordking (IRE) **(38)***(2) (JLHarris)* 6-8-7 PaulEddery(6) (led after 4f to 7f out: sn lost pl) nk 17

5/1 Leading Spirit (IRE), **7/1** Philmist, Inn At the Top, Swordking (IRE), **10/1** Jean de Florette (USA), **11/1** Barti-Ddu (8/1-12/1), **12/1** Top Prize, Risky Tu, Who's the Best (IRE), Absalom's Pillar, **14/1** IJAB (CAN), **16/1** Wannaplantatree, Murphys Way, **20/1** Mhemeanles, Turner Prize (IRE), Drimard (IRE), **25/1** Desert Force (IRE), CSF £111.34 CT £1,144.01 TOTE £20.70: £4.70 £2.20 £3.90 £3.00 (£221.70) Trio £135.60 OWNER Mrs Lynn Parkes (MALTON) BRED R. M. Anderson 17 Rn
3m 11.7 (12.00) SF: 25/26/28/39/37/10/19/8/-/18/-/-/-/1/6/-/-
WEIGHT FOR AGE 3yo-13lb

2920 KANDINSKY CLAIMING STKS (I) (3-Y.O+) (Class F) £2,519.00 (£694.00: £329.00)
1m 3f (Fibresand) Stalls: Low GOING minus 0.01 sec per fur (STD) 2-50 (2-55)

2658[8] **Stevie's Wonder (IRE) (70)***(69)*(Fav)*(MJRyan)* 5-8-13 (7) DGibbs(3) (mde all: styd on u.p fnl 2f: all out) — 1
*2378** Last Corner **(62)***(68)*(Fav)*(RHollinshead)* 3-8-10 KDarley(6) (trckd ldrs: rdn over 2f out: hung lft: swtchd outside over 1f out: styd on wl towards fin) ¾ 2
2445[6] Tovarich **(56)***(66) (GLewis)* 4-9-4 SWhitworth(2) (trckd ldrs: effrt over 2f out: kpt on same pce fnl f: eased nr fin) s.h 3
2626[2] Oleron **(49)***(48) (JNorton)* 3-8-3 DaleGibson(7) (b: trckd ldrs: hdwy & ev ch 3f out: wknd over 1f out) 9 4
Annyban *(32) (JParkes)* 5-8-9 GBardwell(4) (trckd ldrs: pushed along 6f out: sn lost pl) 8 5
Greenacres Lady *(22) (BAMcMahon)* 5-8-9 SDWilliams(5) (unruly s: s.s: bhd & drvn along: sme hdwy over 4f out: sn wknd) 7 6
Phils Fortune *(KSBridgwater)* 3-7-13 NCarlisle(1) (bit bkwd: v.unruly s: s.s: bhd & drvn along: t.o 4f out) 30 7
Fearless Dove *(JHetherton)* 3-7-4 (7) CAdamson(9) (unruly: chsd ldrs: drvn along 6f out: sn lost pl: t.o 4f out) 30 8

2/1 STEVIE'S WONDER (IRE), Last Corner, **11/4** Tovarich, **12/1** Oleron (op 7/1), **20/1** Greenacres Lady, **25/1** Fearless Dove, **33/1** Phils Fortune, Annyban, CSF £6.22 TOTE £2.70: £1.10 £1.20 £1.20 (£3.10) Trio £2.40 OWNER Newmarket Consortium (NEWMARKET) BRED Ovidstown Investments Ltd in Ireland 8 Rn
2m 31.6 (10.10) SF: 33/22/30/2/-/-/-/-
WEIGHT FOR AGE 3yo-10lb

2921

KANDINSKY CLAIMING STKS (II) (3-Y.O+) (Class F) £2,519.00 (£694.00: £329.00)
1m 3f (Fibresand) Stalls: Low GOING minus 0.01 sec per fur (STD) 3-20 (3-22)

1022[5] **Mad Militant (IRE) (68)***(79)*(Fav)*(ALForbes)* 6-9-1 (7) DDenby(2) (lw: in tch: hdwy to ld 3f out: sn clr: drvn out)........— **1**
2378[2] Shared Risk **(55)***(63)*(Fav)*(SGNorton)* 3-8-7 (5) HKYim(7) (chsd ldrs: drvn along 4f out: hrd rdn & styd on one pce fnl f)........11 **2**
2626[4] Aviator's Dream **(43)***(49) (JPearce)* 5-8-8v GBardwell(6) (sn prom: chsd wnr over 2f out: one pce)........nk **3**
2588[5] No Submission (USA) **(72)***(52)*(Fav)*(DWChapman)* 9-9-0 ACulhane(3) (lw: prom early: sn bhd & drvn along: sme hdwy on outside over 2f out: n.d)........1½ **4**
2494[4] Noble Ballerina (USA) *(35) (APJarvis)* 3-8-0 (3) DWright(8) (jnd ldrs 7f out: wknd over 2f out) 11 **5**
2663[5] Goodbye Millie **(33)***(28) (JLEyre)* 5-8-4v(5) NVarley(1) (lw: s.i.s: bhd & sn drvn along: nvr nr ldrs)........2½ **6**
Ameeri (USA) *(21) (NPLittmoden)* 3-8-4 TGMcLaughlin(4) (hld up: effrt on outside over 3f out: sn wknd)........8 **7**
2587[5] Mezzoramio **(43)***(15) (KAMorgan)* 3-7-12b TWilliams(5) (b: led tl 3f out: sn lost pl)........nk **8**

3/1 MAD MILITANT (IRE), Shared Risk, No Submission (USA) (2/1-7/2), **7/1** Goodbye Millie, **11/1** Noble Ballerina (USA) (8/1-12/1), **12/1** Aviator's Dream, Ameeri (USA), **25/1** Mezzoramio, CSF £11.84 TOTE £4.40: £1.90 £1.70 £2.10 (£6.00) OWNER Mr K. Nicholls (UTTOXETER) BRED Cloghran Stud Farm Co in Ireland 8 Rn 2m 31.4 (52.10) SF: 36/10/6/9/-/-/-/-
WEIGHT FOR AGE 3yo-10lb

2922

LUXFER GAS CYLINDERS LIMITED STKS (0-65) (3-Y.O+) (Class F)
£2,947.40 (£816.40: £390.20)
1m (Fibresand) Stalls: Low GOING minus 0.01 sec per fur (STD) 3-50 (3-53)

2707[9] **Carte Blanche (47)***(69) (CACyzer)* 4-9-1 DBiggs(7) (trckd ldr: led over 2f out: styd on wl ins fnl f)........— **1**
749[8] Sandmoor Denim **(65)***(71) (SRBowring)* 8-9-1 (5) CTeague(9) (b: s.i.s: hdwy to chse ldrs ½-wy: chal over 1f out: nt qckn ins fnl f)........1¼ **2**
2588[2] Northern Celadon (IRE) **(65)***(51) (MJHeaton-Ellis)* 4-9-6 AClark(3) (chsd ldrs: effrt over 2f out: sn wl outpcd)........10 **3**
1792[2] Yoxall Lodge **(60)***(44) (HJCollingridge)* 5-9-3 JQuinn(5) (chsd ldrs: effrt 3f out: sn rdn & wl outpcd)........2 **4**
2503[9] Evan 'elp Us **(62)***(43) (JLEyre)* 3-8-10b RLappin(6) (sn drvn along: in tch tl lost pl over 4f out: n.d after)........½ **5**
Erlking (IRE) **(62)***(42) (SMellor)* 5-9-3 MWigham(8) (trckd ldrs: effrt 2f out: grad wknd)........½ **6**
2225[8] Persistent (IRE) **(65)***(40) (MHEasterby)* 3-8-10 SMaloney(10) (a in rr)........1 **7**
2655* Music Maker **(60)***(36)*(Fav)*(SirMarkPrescott)* 3-8-11 GDuffield(4) (led tl over 2f out: wknd over 1f out)........2½ **8**
2636[7] Kristal Breeze **(35)***(16) (WRMuir)* 3-8-5v CRutter(2) (sn bhd: sme hdwy ½-wy: sn wknd)........7 **9**
Family Rose **(33)** *(RHarris)* 6-9-3 AMackay(11) (racd wde: sn outpcd & drvn along: t.o)........30 **10**
1884* Major Mouse **(65)** *(WWHaigh)* 7-9-9 DaleGibson(1) (withdrawn not under Starter's orders: v.unruly & broke out of front of stalls)........ **W**

11/4 Music Maker, **4/1** Yoxall Lodge, **6/1** Evan 'elp Us, **15/2** Northern Celadon (IRE), **8/1** Major Mouse, Sandmoor Denim, **10/1** CARTE BLANCHE, **12/1** Persistent (IRE) (op 8/1), **20/1** Erlking (IRE), **25/1** Kristal Breeze, Family Rose, CSF £68.73 TOTE £10.50: £2.30 £2.20 £1.70 (£40.50) Trio £93.40 OWNER Mr R. M. Cyzer (HORSHAM) BRED Cotswold Stud 10 Rn
1m 46.3 (19.50) SF: 29/31/11/4/-/2/-/-/-/-
WEIGHT FOR AGE 3yo-7lb

2923

QUALITY BUILDING SERVICES H'CAP (0-70) (3-Y.O+) (Class E)
£3,645.40 (£1,091.20: £523.60: £239.80)
7f (Fibresand) Stalls: Low GOING minus 0.01 sec per fur (STD) 4-20 (4-29)

2585[7] **Heart Broken (70)***(73) (JGFitzGerald)* 5-10-0be MWigham(12) (a chsng ldrs: hrd rdn & styd on fnl 2f: led nr fin)........— **1**
2698[12] Exclusive Assembly **(54)***(57) (APJames)* 3-8-6 FNorton(14) (chsd ldr: led 2f out: hrd rdn: jst ct)........hd **2**
Penmar **(55)***(54) (TJEtherington)* 3-8-7 LCharnock(15) (chsd ldrs: edgd lft u.p appr fnl f: kpt on wl)........1¾ **3**
2504[6] Cloette **(69)***(66) (WAO'Gorman)* 3-9-7 EmmaO'Gorman(1) (lw: in tch: styd on fnl 2f: nvr nr to chal)........¾ **4**
2832[12] Tyrone Flyer **(54)***(50) (RHarris)* 6-8-12 AMackay(16) (chsd ldrs: styd on one pce appr fnl f)...nk **5**

27848 Grey Toppa (36)(19) (NPLittmoden) 4-7-1 (7) CAdamson(6) (mid div: rdn over 2f out: no imp)..6 6
25174 Four of Spades (70)(53) (PDEvans) 4-9-7v(7) AmandaSanders(9) (led to 2f out: sn wknd).....d.h 6
2377* Moneghetti (45)(19)(Fav)(RHollinshead) 4-8-3 NCarlisle(2) (sn drvn along & outpcd: n.d) 4 8
20767 Arrogant Boy (35)(8) (DWChapman) 6-7-7 NKennedy(8) (bhd: sme hdwy fnl 2f: n.d) ....hd 9
19616 Miss Iron Heart (USA) (47)(17) (DJSCosgrove) 3-7-13 CRutter(7) (a rr div)...........................1¼ 10
114810 On Y Va (USA) (46)(15) (RJRWilliams) 8-8-4 DBiggs(10) (lw: a rr div).......................................½ 11
2497* Mixed Mood (66)(26) (BJLlewellyn) 3-9-4 RPrice(5) (in tch tl rdn & lost pl ½-wy) 4 12
103415 Lady Silk (68)(28) (JHetherton) 4-9-12 SWebster(13) (unruly s: racd wd: a bhd) ....s.h 13
19829 Dancing Sioux (70)(29) (RGuest) 3-9-8 GDuffield(4) (sn chsng ldrs: wknd over 2f out)...........nk 14
26857 Nakita (50) (CNAllen) 4-8-8 JQuinn(3) (b: s.i.s: a wl bhd) 9 15
19568 Orthorhombus (57) (DJSCosgrove) 6-8-10b(5) LNewton(11) (s.i.s: a bhd & rn wd ent st)........12 16

LONG HANDICAP Arrogant Boy 6-11

7/2 Moneghetti, **7/1** On Y Va (USA), **15/2** Cloette (5/1-8/1), **8/1** Mixed Mood, **9/1** HEART BROKEN (6/1-10/1), **11/1** Four of Spades (8/1-12/1), **12/1** Exclusive Assembly, Dancing Sioux, Penmar, **14/1** Orthorhombus, **16/1** Nakita, Tyrone Flyer, **20/1** Lady Silk, **25/1** Grey Toppa, **33/1** Miss Iron Heart (USA), **50/1** Arrogant Boy, CSF £108.03 CT £1,206.45 TOTE £9.00: £2.30 £4.70 £3.50 £1.70 (£96.30) Trio £466.00; £406.99 to Newmarket 5/8/95 OWNER Mr J. G. FitzGerald (MALTON) BRED J. H. Burbidge 16 Rn 1m 31.8 (5.00) SF: 53/31/28/40/30/-/33/-/-/-/-/-/8/3/-/-

WEIGHT FOR AGE 3yo-6lb

STEWARDS' ENQUIRY Wigham susp. 21-23/8/95 (excessive use of whip).

2924

EAST MIDLANDS ELECTRICITY (S) STKS (2-Y.O) (Class G) £2,780.60 (£771.60: £369.80) **7f (Fibresand)** Stalls: Low GOING minus 0.01 sec (STD) 4-50 (4-57)

27566 **China Castle** (64+) (PCHaslam) 2-8-11 MTebbutt(4) (trckd ldrs: led 4f out: drvn clr 1f out: eased nr fin)..— 1
25167 Harsh Times (51) (MHEasterby) 2-8-6 SMaloney(6) (chsd ldrs: kpt on u.p fnl 2f: no ch w wnr)..3½ 2
26354 Two Socks (56)(54) (MMcCormack) 2-8-11 AClark(8) (sltly hmpd s: hdwy over 2f out: styd on one pce fnl f)..1 3
22513 Kratz (IRE) (61)(45) (BSRothwell) 2-8-11v MFenton(13) (in rr tl hdwy on outside over 2f out: nvr nr ldrs)..4 4
24969 Impending Danger (37) (KSBridgwater) 2-8-8 (3) SDrowne(7) (sltly hmpd s: sn chsng ldrs: rdn 3f out: grad wknd)..3½ 5
26352 La Haye Sainte (28) (DJSCosgrove) 2-8-1 (5) LNewton(10) (sn bhd: sme hdwy ½-wy: nvr nr to chal)..1½ 6
Irish Oasis (IRE) (32) (BSRothwell) 2-8-11 DHarrison(2) (leggy: s.s: bhd: sme hdwy 2f out: n.d)..½ 7
251612 Tilly Tupgill (MDHammond) 2-8-6 JMarshall(9) (sltly hmpd s: sn in tch: lost pl ½-wy) 13 8
21469 Waitingforwalnuts (IRE) (CASmith) 2-8-3 (3) AGarth(5) (in tch tl rdn & wknd 3f out) 5 9
11909 Topaglow (IRE) (PTDalton) 2-8-11 LCharnock(1) (prom tl lost pl ½-wy)..............................10 10
2516* Catwalk Girl (56) (Fav)(SGNorton) 2-8-11v TWilliams(3) (led to 4f out: wknd qckly & eased over 2f out: t.o)..11 11
26569 Back In The Black (MrsJCecil) 2-8-11b GDuffield(12) (sn bhd & drvn along: t.o ½-wy)..........¾ 12
Jereed's Tut (IRE) (JWharton) 2-8-6 JWilliams(11) (small: unf: bit bkwd: sn wl bhd: t.o)........7 13

5/2 Catwalk Girl (2/1-3/1), **3/1** La Haye Sainte, **4/1** CHINA CASTLE (7/1-3/1), **15/2** Kratz (IRE) (4/1-8/1), **9/1** Back In The Black (6/1-10/1), **10/1** Two Socks, **14/1** Irish Oasis (IRE) (8/1-16/1), **20/1** Harsh Times, Topaglow (IRE), **25/1** Impending Danger, Jereed's Tut (IRE), **33/1** Tilly Tupgill, Waitingforwalnuts (IRE), CSF £79.03 TOTE £6.10: £1.50 £11.50 £2.40 (£107.20) Trio £295.50 OWNER Mr J. M. Davis (MIDDLEHAM) BRED Mrs Frances Cronin 13 Rn

1m 33.6 (20.10) SF: 18/5/8/-/-/-/-/-/-/-/-/-/-

Bt in 9,200 gns

2925

PICASSO H'CAP (0-60) (3-Y.O+) (Class F) £2,519.00 (£694.00: £329.00) **6f (Fibresand)** Stalls: Low GOING minus 0.01 sec per fur (STD) 5-20 (5-27)

22957 **Matthew David** (38)(45) (SRBowring) 5-8-9b SWebster(10) (chsd ldrs: effrt & hung lft 2f out: led 1f out: jst hld on)..— 1
23834 Grey Charmer (IRE) (49)(56) (CJames) 6-9-6 CRutter(5) (in tch: effrt on outside 2f out: r.o wl ins fnl f)..hd 2
2383* Bold Aristocrat (IRE) (49)(53)(Fav)(RHollinshead) 4-8-13 (7) FLynch(13) (lw: hld up & bhd: hdwy on outside 2f out: r.o wl fnl f)..1 3
7694 Beveled Edge (55)(48) (BPalling) 6-9-12 TSprake(2) (a chsng ldrs: kpt on one pce appr fnl f)..4 4
238313 Chloella (45)(36) (CBBBooth) 3-8-11 SMorris(3) (in tch: effrt over 2f out: nvr nr to chal)...........1 5
27867 Anotherone to Note (49)(32) (NPLittmoden) 4-9-6b TGMcLaughlin(6) (prom tl wknd over 1f out)..3 6

1523[17] Dundeelin **(42)***(22) (JLEyre)* 4-8-13v AClark(8) (hld up & bhd: sme hdwy 2f out: n.d) 1 **7**
2840[3] Lugana Vision **(43)***(22) (RHarris)* 3-8-9b JWilliams(9) (bhd: sme hdwy 2f out: n.d) ....nk **8**
1377[4] Gate of Heaven **(26)** *(CADwyer)* 5-7-11 GBardwell(12) (b.hind: nvr bttr than mid div) 2 **9**
2295[10] Pretty Chic **(26)** *(DWChapman)* 6-7-11 NKennedy(14) (sn outpcd & bhd) 1½ **10**
2627[3] The Real Whizzbang (IRE) **(47)***(9) (PSFelgate)* 4-9-1b(3) PMcCabe(1) (led: hdd 1f out: wknd & eased) 3 **11**
2220[10] Petova (IRE) **(36)** *(MJCamacho)* 3-8-2 LCharnock(15) (swtg: a in rr) 3½ **12**
1516[11] Distant Dynasty **(55)** *(BAPearce)* 5-9-12 SWhitworth(7) (dwlt s: bhd: hdwy over 3f out: sn wknd) 3 **13**
2627[8] Superlativemaximus (IRE) **(57)** *(JABennett)* 7-10-0 MFenton(4) (chsd ldrs tl wknd over 2f out: p.u lame 1f out) .... **P**

4/1 Bold Aristocrat (IRE), **11/2** Grey Charmer (IRE), **6/1** The Real Whizzbang (IRE), **7/1** Lugana Vision, **15/2** MATTHEW DAVID, **10/1** Beveled Edge, **12/1** Distant Dynasty (op 8/1), **16/1** Dundeelin, Gate of Heaven, Pretty Chic, Chloella, Anotherone to Note, **20/1** Petova (IRE), Superlativemaximus (IRE), CSF £48.15 CT £176.12 TOTE £9.80: £2.40 £2.50 £1.60 (£20.50) Trio £24.10 OWNER Mrs Katherine Fogg (EDWINSTOWE) BRED MDM Racing (Thoroughbreds) Ltd 14 Rn
1m 18.4 (4.90) SF: 27/38/35/30/13/14/4/-/-/-/-/-/-/-
WEIGHT FOR AGE 3yo-5lb

T/Jkpt: Not won; £23, 064.71 to Newmarket 5/8/95. T/Plpt: £534.50 (32.28 Tckts). T/Qdpt: £102.70 (0.1 Tckts); £124.92 to Newmarket 5/8/95. WG

2473-AYR (L-H)
Saturday August 5th (Good to firm)

WEATHER: sunny & hot WIND: almost nil

2926 BARASSIE MEDIAN AUCTION MAIDEN STKS (2-Y.O) (Class E)
£3,044.50 (£916.00: £443.00: £206.50)
7f Stalls: Low GOING minus 0.09 sec per fur (G) 2-05 (2-06)

2005[3] **Beauchamp King** *(79+)*(Fav)*(JLDunlop)* 2-9-0 GCarter(1) (lw: hld up: stdy hdwy over 2f out: led 1½f out: shkn up & r.o) ....— **1**
2264[3] Emperegrine (USA) **(76)***(70) (CFWall)* 2-9-0 GDuffield(4) (cl up: led 3f out to 1½f out: one pce ins fnl f) 4 **2**
2485[5] Eric's Bett *(65) (MrsSMAustin)* 2-9-0 JCarroll(3) (b: led tl hdd 3f out: one pce) 2 **3**
1356[11] Rapid Liner *(62) (AHarrison)* 2-8-11 (3) JStack(5) (bhd: effrt on outside ent st: chsng ldrs 2f out: wknd appr fnl f) 1½ **4**
2615[5] Sticks Mckenzie *(62) (BWHills)* 2-8-9 (5) JDSmith(2) (lw: chsd ldrs tl rdn & btn over 2f out) ....hd **5**

8/13 BEAUCHAMP KING (4/5-Evens), **11/4** Emperegrine (USA), **11/2** Sticks Mckenzie (7/2-6/1), **16/1** Eric's Bett, **20/1** Rapid Liner, CSF £2.85 TOTE £1.50: £1.10 £1.10 (£1.60) OWNER Mr E. Penser (ARUNDEL) BRED E. Penser 5 Rn 1m 31.04 (7.04) SF: 9/-/-/-/-

2927 OLD PRESTWICK (S) H'CAP (0-60) (3-Y.O) (Class F) £2,833.00 (£788.00: £379.00) 7f Stalls: Low GOING minus 0.09 sec per fur (G) 2-35 (2-36)

2733[9] **Caltha (42)***(53) (PCalver)* 3-9-2b(3) DarrenMoffatt(5) (b.hind: mde most: edgd lft & hld on wl fnl f) ....— **1**
2761[4] Boost **(42)***(52) (CWThornton)* 3-9-5 JCarroll(7) (chsd ldrs: chal over 1f out: kpt on)................nk **2**
2818* Commander Glen (IRE) **(49)***(58)*(Fav)*(MartynMeade)* 3-9-12b 5x MWigham(3) (lw: in tch: effrt over 2f out: nt clr run & swtchd fnl f: r.o towards fin) ....¾ **3**
2733[3] Summer Villa **(42)***(39) (PCHaslam)* 3-9-2 (3) JStack(6) (a chsng ldrs: one pce fnl 3f)..................5 **4**
492[6] Achill Princess **(42)***(34) (WTKemp)* 3-9-5 GDuffield(1) (hld up: effrt 3f out: no imp) 2½ **5**
2582[13] Nebrangus (IRE) **(35)***(24) (NBycroft)* 3-8-12b SMaloney(4) (s.i.s: a bhd) 1¼ **6**
2627[10] Truly Madly Deeply **(35)***(8) (JAHarris)* 3-8-12 GCarter(2) (lw: chsd wnr tl outpcd appr st: sn bhd) 7 **7**

6/4 Commander Glen (IRE), **7/4** Summer Villa, **6/1** CALTHA (9/2-7/1), **8/1** Boost, **25/1** Achill Princess, Truly Madly Deeply, **100/1** Nebrangus (IRE), CSF £43.98 TOTE £9.80: £2.40 £2.70 (£17.70) OWNER Mr D. B. Stanley (RIPON) BRED Mrs G. C. Stanley 7 Rn
1m 30.51 (6.51) SF: 20/19/25/6/1/-/-
No bid

2928 DAILY STAR H'CAP (0-80) (3-Y.O+) (Class D) £4,302.00 (£1,296.00: £628.00: £294.00) 1m Stalls: Low GOING minus 0.09 sec per fur (G) 3-05 (3-05)

2504[3] **King Chestnut (57)***(64) (MDods)* 4-8-7 JCarroll(5) (bhd: hdwy 2f out: led ins fnl f: r.o) ....— **1**

2778[2] Nordic Breeze (IRE) **(74)**_(80)_(Fav)_(ABailey)_ 3-9-3v MWigham(6) (pushed along appr st: hdwy & edgd lft 2f out: r.o towards fin) ....nk 2
2613[8] Admirals Flame (IRE) **(74)**_(78)_ _(CFWall)_ 4-9-10 GDuffield(1) (lw: b: hld up: smooth hdwy on ins to ld appr fnl f: sn hdd & no ex) 1¼ 3
_2634_[2] Daytona Beach (IRE) **(62)**_(65)_ _(DJSffrenchDavis)_ 5-8-7 (5) JDSmith(2) (lw: mde most tl edgd rt & hdd appr fnl f: sn btn) ....½ 4
2803[4] Legal Fiction **(67)**_(69)_ _(MJohnston)_ 4-9-0 (3) JStack(3) (chsd ldrs: effrt 3f out: btn whn sltly hmpd over 1f out) ....½ 5
2479[3] Celebration Cake (IRE) **(62)**_(61)_ _(MissLAPerratt)_ 3-8-5 GCarter(4) (b: disp ld to st: ev ch tl wknd appr fnl f) 1¼ 6

11/4 Nordic Breeze (IRE), **100/30** Daytona Beach (IRE), **4/1** Admirals Flame (IRE), Legal Fiction, **8/1** Celebration Cake (IRE), **9/1** KING CHESTNUT, CSF £31.03 TOTE £9.60: £2.90 £2.00 (£12.40) OWNER Mr C. Graham (DARLINGTON) BRED G. E. C. Graham and Partners 6 Rn

1m 42.0 (5.20) SF: 31/40/45/32/36/21
WEIGHT FOR AGE 3yo-7lb

2929 SEAFIELD MAIDEN STKS (3-Y.O+) (Class D) £3,934.00 (£1,099.00: £532.00) **1m 2f** Stalls: Low GOING minus 0.09 sec per fur (G) 3-35 (3-36)

2446[5] **Never Explain (IRE) (80)**_(83+)_(Fav)_(JLDunlop)_ 3-8-6 GCarter(3) (lw: a gng wl: led over 2f out: v.easily) ....— 1
2100[4] Venice Beach **(75)**_(86)_ _(BWHills)_ 3-8-6 (5) JDSmith(1) (lw: led tl hdd over 2f out: no ch w wnr) 1¼ 2
Your Most Welcome _(65?)_ _(DJSffrenchDavis)_ 4-9-1 GDuffield(2) (b.hind: a last: wl outpcd fnl 3f) 10 3

8/13 NEVER EXPLAIN (IRE), **7/4** Venice Beach, **8/1** Your Most Welcome, CSF £1.97 TOTE £1.60 (£1.10) OWNER Sir Andrew LloydWebber (ARUNDEL) BRED Barronstown Stud 3 Rn

2m 12.29 (7.69) SF: 23/26/14
WEIGHT FOR AGE 3yo-9lb

2930 STAR FORM H'CAP (0-75) (3-Y.O+) (Class D) £3,809.75 (£1,148.00: £556.50: £260.75) **6f** Stalls: High GOING minus 0.09 sec per fur (G) 4-05 (4-08)

2736[8] **Mister Westsound (45)**_(57)_ _(MissLAPerratt)_ 3-7-2b(7) JBramhill(2) (bhd: hdwy over 2f out: hung bdly lft: led over 1f out: hung lft: r.o) ....— 1
2870[2] Walk the Beat **(62)**_(67)_ _(MartynMeade)_ 5-9-3 GCarter(1) (hld up: hdwy 2f out: nt qckn fnl f)..2½ 2
2060[12] White Sorrel **(66)**_(66)_ _(AHarrison)_ 4-9-2b(5) JDSmith(8) (w ldrs: nt qckn fnl f) 2 3
2645[3] Pageboy **(64)**_(61)_(Fav)_(PCHaslam)_ 6-9-2 (3) JStack(5) (lw: chsd ldrs: rdn 2f out: hmpd over 1f out: r.o one pce) 1 4
2870* Diet **(58)**_(55)_ _(MissLAPerratt)_ 9-8-6v(7) 7x PFessey(7) (slt ld tl hung lft, hdd & hmpd over 1f out: sn btn) ....s.h 5
2758* Ned's Bonanza **(73)**_(66)_ _(MDods)_ 6-10-0 JCarroll(3) (lw: bhd: hdwy 2f out: hmpd over 1f out: nt rcvr) 1½ 6
2610[5] Keep Battling **(40)**_(30)_ _(JSGoldie)_ 5-7-6 (3) DarrenMoffatt(9) (nvr wnt pce) 1¼ 7
2837[5] Leading Princess (IRE) **(38)**_(15)_ _(MissLAPerratt)_ 4-7-7b ClaireBalding(10) (w ldrs over 3f: sn rdn & btn) 5 8
1614[6] Craigie Boy **(59)**_(35)_ _(NBycroft)_ 5-9-0 SMaloney(6) (drvn along ½-wy: nvr trbld ldrs) ....hd 9
2736[6] Uppance **(41)** _(DANolan)_ 7-7-10bow3 WHawksley(4) (a bhd) 10 10

LONG HANDICAP Uppance 6-8

7/2 Pageboy, **4/1** Walk the Beat, Ned's Bonanza, **7/1** Craigie Boy, **9/1** Diet (op 6/1), White Sorrel (op 6/1), **11/1** Keep Battling, **14/1** MISTER WESTSOUND, **25/1** Leading Princess (IRE), **100/1** Uppance, CSF £63.04 CT £486.71 TOTE £17.80: £2.20 £1.50 £4.40 (£31.00) Trio £43.50 OWNER Mr R. McLean (AYR) BRED Red House Stud 10 Rn

1m 12.52 (2.72) SF: 34/49/48/43/37/48/12/-/17/-
WEIGHT FOR AGE 3yo-5lb

STEWARDS' ENQUIRY Bramhill susp. 14-17/8/95 (careless riding) & 18-19 & 20-21/8/95 (excessive use of whip).

2931 PORTLAND AMATEUR H'CAP (0-70) (3-Y.O+) (Class E) £3,168.00 (£954.00: £462.00: £216.00) **1m 7f** Stalls: Low GOING minus 0.09 sec per fur (G) 4-35 (4-35)

_2592*_ **Claireswan (IRE) (55)**_(69)_(Fav)_(SCWilliams)_ 3-10-11 (4) MissKWright(1) (lw: mde all: kpt on wl fnl 2f) ....— 1
2545[4] Arctic Charmer (USA) **(68)**_(76)_ _(JLDunlop)_ 3-12-0 MrTCuff(3) (chsd wnr: rdn 3f out: one pce) .6 2
2871[6] Abalene **(38)**_(45)_ _(TWDonnelly)_ 6-10-12b MrMHNaughton(7) (lw: a chsng ldrs: one pce fnl 3f) ½ 3
879[17] Dawn Rock **(28)**_(22)_ _(RMMcKellar)_ 4-9-9b(7) MrsCWilliams(5) (wl bhd tl sme late hdwy) 12 4
568[16] Kalko **(35)**_(8)_ _(JSGoldie)_ 6-10-5 (4) MrKSantana(2) (outpcd & lost tch 7f out) 20 5

763[11] Pilib (IRE) **(48)** *(JPearce)* 4-11-8 MrsLPearce(4) (b: chsd ldrs tl rdn & wknd appr st: t.o) .....dist 6
477[7] Carondra **(33)** *(RMMcKellar)* 3-9-3b(4) MrSRutherford(6) (outpcd & wl bhd fnl 7f: t.o)..............15 7

LONG HANDICAP Carondra 9-1

4/5 CLAIRESWAN (IRE) (op Evens), **100/30** Arctic Charmer (USA), **9/2** Pilib (IRE), **6/1** Abalene, **10/1** Kalko, **16/1** Dawn Rock, **100/1** Carondra, CSF £4.68 CT £10.54 TOTE £2.20: £1.40 £2.00 (£2.50) OWNER Mr J. Wright (NEWMARKET) BRED Thomas Bean 7 Rn

3m 26.63 (16.53) SF: 33/40/23/-/-/-/-
WEIGHT FOR AGE 3yo-14lb

T/Plpt: £131.60 (47.32 Tckts). T/Qdpt: £18.00 (5.45 Tckts). AA

2901-HAYDOCK (L-H)
Saturday August 5th (Good to firm)
WEATHER: hot, sunny WIND: slt bhd

2932
TATTERSALLS MAIDEN AUCTION STKS (2-Y.O) (Class E) £3,208.75 (£970.00: £472.50: £223.75)
5f Stalls: High GOING minus 0.43 sec per fur (F) 2-00 (2-00)

2782[3] **Crissem (IRE)** *(69)*(Fav)*(RHollinshead)* 2-8-4 ow1 LDettori(2) (a.p: led ins fnl f: hrd rdn: all out)..........— 1
2651[8] Total Aloof *(64) (MrsLPiggott)* 2-7-12 JQuinn(10) (b.hind: a.p: jnd wnr ins fnl f: r.o) ....s.h 2
1448[8] Contract Bridge (IRE) *(60) (CWThornton)* 2-7-13 AMackay(9) (several positions: rdn & r.o wl fnl f: nvr nrr)..........1½ 3
2548[2] Seaford Star (IRE) *(66) (MRChannon)* 2-8-5 TQuinn(8) (led after 1f to 2f out: kpt on u.p cl home)..........s.h 4
1935[4] Globe Runner *(63) (JJO'Neill)* 2-8-2 FNorton(1) (hdwy appr fnl f: r.o ins fnl f: nvr nrr) ....s.h 5
Angus McCoatup (IRE) *(63) (BAMcMahon)* 2-8-5 JFortune(4) (cmpt: bkwd: prom: led 2f out tl ins fnl f: sn rdn & wknd)..........1 6
Lawn Order *(53) (MrsJRRamsden)* 2-8-0 MDeering(7) (neat: bit bkwd: s.s: bhd tl sme late hdwy)..........1½ 7
2619[3] Katie Komaite **(58)***(46) (CaptJWilson)* 2-7-12 JMarshall(3) (led 1f: wknd bel dist)..................1½ 8
2431[5] Maysimp (IRE) **(56)***(39) (BPJBaugh)* 2-7-6 (7) IonaWands(5) (b.hind: nvr trbld ldrs) 2½ 9
Whothehellisharry *(34) (JBerry)* 2-8-7 TIves(6) (lt-f: bkwd: dwlt: a bhd & outpcd).....................4 10

13/8 CRISSEM (IRE), **3/1** Seaford Star (IRE), **8/1** Total Aloof, **12/1** Katie Komaite, Whothehellisharry, **14/1** Angus McCoatup (IRE), Lawn Order, Globe Runner, **33/1** Contract Bridge (IRE), Maysimp (IRE), CSF £14.08 TOTE £2.30: £1.50 £1.80 £7.20 (£9.30) Trio £119.30 OWNER Mrs Christine Johnson (UPPER LONGDON) BRED Islanmore Stud 10 Rn

60.46 secs (1.46) SF: 28/23/19/25/22/22/12/5/-/-

2933
HARVEY JONES RATED STKS H'CAP (0-95) (3-Y.O+) (Class B) £7,964.60 (£2,971.40: £1,445.70: £613.50: £266.75: £128.05)
1m 30y Stalls: Low GOING minus 0.43 sec per fur (F) 2-30 (2-30)

2598[10] **Moving Arrow (87)***(95) (MissSEHall)* 4-8-10 JWeaver(6) (plld hrd: mde all: rdn out) ....— 1
1839[27] Hardy Dancer **(87)***(92) (GLMoore)* 3-8-3 PaulEddery(2) (prom: 3rd st: rdn appr fnl f: kpt on ins fnl f: no ch w wnr)..........1¾ 2
2703[17] Bagshot **(77)***(82) (RHannon)* 4-8-0 JQuinn(3) (hld up: 5th st: hdwy over 2f out: rdn & one pce appr fnl f)..........s.h 3
1839[15] Chattaroy (IRE) **(89)***(87)*(Fav)*(JHMGosden)* 3-8-5 LDettori(1) (lw: hld up & bhd: 6th st: effrt u.p 2f out: no imp)..........3½ 4
2235* Band on the Run **(91)***(85) (BAMcMahon)* 8-9-0 JFortune(4) (lw: sn chsng wnr: 2nd st: rdn wl over 1f out: wknd)..........1¾ 5
2694[5] Shot At Love (IRE) **(80)***(64) (CACyzer)* 4-8-3 DBiggs(5) (chsd ldrs: 4th st: rdn along 3f out: sn lost tch)..........5 6

3/1 Chattaroy (IRE), **100/30** Band on the Run, **7/2** Hardy Dancer, **9/2** MOVING ARROW, **11/2** Bagshot, **10/1** Shot At Love (IRE), CSF £18.96 TOTE £5.40: £2.70 £2.20 (£9.30) OWNER Mr G. W. Westgarth (MIDDLEHAM) BRED W. G. Barker 6 Rn

1m 40.2 (0.15 under best) (-0.20) SF: 62/52/49/47/52/31
WEIGHT FOR AGE 3yo-7lb

2934
E.B.F. HERMITAGE GREEN MAIDEN STKS (2-Y.O F) (Class D) £4,458.00 (£1,344.00: £652.00: £306.00)
6f Stalls: High GOING minus 0.43 sec per fur (F) 3-00 (3-00)

2351[3] **Najiya** *(98+)*(Fav)*(JLDunlop)* 2-8-11 RHills(1) (a.p: led over 2f out: readily)..........— 1

2351² Dimakya (USA) *(93)*(Fav)*(DRLoder)* 2-8-11 LDettori(4) (lw: chsd ldrs: effrt & rdn over 1f out: unable qckn) 2 2
Royal Jade *(91+)* *(BWHills)* 2-8-11 BThomson(2) (b.hind: w'like: hld up: hdwy 2f out: nt pce to chal: improve) ....¾ 3
2275³ Willisa *(72)* *(JDBethell)* 2-8-11 TIves(3) (led over 3f: wknd appr fnl f) 7 4
Needwood Epic *(70)* *(BAMcMahon)* 2-8-11 JFortune(5) (tall: bkwd: sn outpcd: a bhd) ....¾ 5

11/8 NAJIYA, Dimakya (USA), **5/1** Royal Jade, **14/1** Willisa, **25/1** Needwood Epic, CSF £3.55 TOTE £2.60: £1.30 £1.30 (£1.50) OWNER Mr Hamdan Al Maktoum (ARUNDEL) BRED Shadwell Estate Company Limited 5 Rn 1m 12.86 (1.16) SF: 44/39/37/18/16

2935 CORAL H'CAP (0-100) (3-Y.O+) (Class C) £10,755.00 (£3,240.00: £1,570.00: £735.00) **5f** Stalls: High GOING minus 0.43 sec per fur (F) 3-30 (3-31)

2512* **That Man Again (94)***(102)* *(GLewis)* 3-9-7b(5) AWhelan(8) (a.p: led wl over 1f out: rdn & hld on gamely nr fin) ....— 1
2758³ Lepine (IRE) **(70)***(77)*(Fav)*(JWWatts)* 4-8-6v JWeaver(12) (swtg: led tl hdd wl over 1f out: rallied u.p nr fin) ....nk 2
2692² Beau Venture (USA) **(79)***(80)* *(FHLee)* 7-9-1 RLappin(9) (lw: chsd ldrs: kpt on u.p ins fnl f: nt pce to chal) 1¾ 3
2742² Coffee 'n Cream **(85)***(86)* *(RHannon)* 3-9-3 TQuinn(7) (lw: chsd ldrs: rdn over 1f out: unable qckn) ....s.h 4
2609⁴ Rich Glow **(65)***(65)* *(NBycroft)* 4-8-1 JQuinn(14) (hdwy over 1f out: fin wl) ....½ 5
2764W Castlerea Lad **(87)***(79)* *(RHollinshead)* 6-9-9 LDettori(3) (racd alone centre: edgd rt & r.o ins fnl f) 2½ 6
2652³ Macs Maharanee **(72)***(59)* *(PSFelgate)* 8-8-8 JFortune(13) (chsd ldrs: no hdwy fnl 2f) 1½ 7
2234⁸ Gondo **(57)***(42)* *(EJAlston)* 8-7-7v SLanigan(10) (nvr trbld ldrs) ....½ 8
2519⁵ Crystal Loop **(68)***(53)* *(ABailey)* 3-7-11 (3) DWright(11) (lw: spd stands' side 3f) ....s.h 9
2867⁵ Giggleswick Girl **(63)***(47)* *(MRChannon)* 4-7-8 (5) PPMurphy(5) (s.s: nvr nrr) ....½ 10
2570* Name the Tune **(86)***(66)* *(PHowling)* 4-9-8 PaulEddery(1) (b.hind: lw: chsd ldr far side: nvr on terms) 1¼ 11
2753² Shadow Jury **(76)***(51)* *(DWChapman)* 5-8-12b BDoyle(6) (lw: nvr nr to chal) 1½ 12
2665³ Gorinsky (IRE) **(77)***(45)* *(JBerry)* 7-8-13 TIves(2) (lw: spd far side 3f) 2 13
2609⁹ Allwight Then (IRE) **(74)***(30)* *(FHLee)* 4-8-10b RHills(4) (led & clr far side: lost tch fnl 2f) 4 14

LONG HANDICAP Gondo 6-10

5/1 Lepine (IRE), **13/2** Coffee 'n Cream, **15/2** Name the Tune, **8/1** Beau Venture (USA), Macs Maharanee, **9/1** THAT MAN AGAIN, Shadow Jury, **10/1** Gorinsky (IRE), **11/1** Rich Glow, **12/1** Castlerea Lad, **14/1** Allwight Then (IRE), Crystal Loop, **20/1** Giggleswick Girl, **33/1** Gondo, CSF £53.43 CT £356.07 TOTE £10.30: £2.20 £2.50 £3.20 (£40.50) Trio £75.90 OWNER Mr M. Jameson (EPSOM) BRED T. P. Milne and M. Jameson 14 Rn
58.6 secs (0.30 under best) (-0.40) SF: 80/59/62/64/47/61/41/24/31/29/48/33/27/12
WEIGHT FOR AGE 3yo-4lb

2936 ROSE OF LANCASTER STKS (Gp 3) (3-Y.O+) (Class A) £21,760.00 (£8,218.00: £4,009.00: £1,813.00) **1m 2f 120y** Stalls: High GOING minus 0.43 sec(F) 4-00 (4-03)

2273³ **Fahal (USA) (117)***(120)* *(DMorley)* 3-8-7 RHills(4) (lw: hld up: 5th st: led 2f out: rdn & styd on strly) ....— 1
2476⁴ Young Buster (IRE) **(112)***(116)* *(GWragg)* 7-9-3 PaulEddery(1) (lw: s.i.s: bhd: hdwy 3f out: rdn & styd on ins fnl f: nvr nrr) 2½ 2
2558a⁶ Sonic Boy **(114)***(114)* *(RFJohnsonHoughton)* 3-8-7 JQuinn(6) (led to 2f out: kpt on u.p fnl f) 1¼ 3
2476* Baron Ferdinand **(113)***(109)*(Fav)*(RCharlton)* 5-9-7 TSprake(8) (b: swtg: bhd: hdwy 3f out: nt rch ldrs) 6 4
2273⁴ Stiffelio (IRE) **(100)***(104)* *(RHannon)* 3-8-7 RPerham(2) (lw: prom: 3rd st: rdn & outpcd over 2f out) ....¾ 5
2476³ Revere (IRE) **(116)***(102)* *(PFICole)* 5-9-7 TQuinn(7) (b: lw: chsd ldr: 2nd st: wknd over 2f out) 4 6
2563a⁴ Musetta (IRE) **(110)***(72)* *(CEBrittain)* 3-8-4 BDoyle(3) (chsd ldrs: 4th st: wknd wl over 2f out: t.o) 15 7
2241² Salt Lake **(102)***(71)* *(PWChapple-Hyam)* 4-9-3 BThomson(9) (lw: a bhd: t.o) 2½ 8
2118⁷ Wainwright (USA) **(103)** *(JHMGosden)* 6-9-3 LDettori(5) (bit bkwd: bhd: effrt & 6th st: n.m.r & fell 3f out: broke leg: dead) .... F

9/4 Baron Ferdinand, **3/1** FAHAL (USA) (op 2/1), **7/1** Revere (IRE), **15/2** Young Buster (IRE), **8/1** Musetta (IRE), **9/1** Salt Lake, **12/1** Sonic Boy, Wainwright (USA), **25/1** Stiffelio (IRE), CSF £24.55 TOTE £3.20: £1.60 £1.70 £3.80 (£10.30) Trio £43.00 OWNER Mr Hamdan Al Maktoum (NEWMARKET) BRED Jones/Jayeff B PTNR in USA 9 Rn
2m 8.53 (1.06 under best) (-2.97) SF: 81/87/75/80/65/73/33/42/-
WEIGHT FOR AGE 3yo-10lb

2937 NORTH LANCASHIRE H'CAP (0-85) (3-Y.O+) (Class D) £3,951.00 (£1,188.00: £574.00: £267.00) **1m 6f** Stalls: Low GOING minus 0.43 sec per fur (F) 4-30 (4-32)

2274[6] **Foundry Lane (78)***(88)*(Fav)*(MrsMReveley)* 4-9-12 JFortune(2) (lw: plld hrd: a.p: 3rd st: led appr fnl f: styd on strly)........— **1**
2312* Royal York **(71)***(79) (MissSEHall)* 3-8-6 NConnorton(4) (lw: led tl hdd over 7f out: 2nd st: led 2f out: sn hdd: rdn & kpt on nr fin)........1¾ **2**
2366[4] Eelious (USA) **(80)***(88) (CEBrittain)* 3-9-1 BDoyle(5) (lw: chsd ldrs: effrt over 2f out: kpt on u.p fnl f)........nk **3**
1863[7] Chantry Beath **(52)***(59) (CWThornton)* 4-8-0 AMackay(9) (hld up: 6th st: hdwy 3f out: styd on one pce fnl f)........¾ **4**
2374[4] Good Hand (USA) **(74)***(80) (JWWatts)* 9-9-8 BThomson(3) (lw: hld up: 5th st: styd on u.p fnl 2f: nvr able to chal)........1 **5**
2612[4] Cuango (IRE) **(68)***(58) (RHollinshead)* 4-9-2 TQuinn(8) (hld up: hdwy over 3f out: nt trble ldrs)........14 **6**
2745[8] Credit Squeeze **(70)***(58) (RFJohnsonHoughton)* 5-9-4 JQuinn(1) (hdwy to ld over 7f out: hdd 2f out: eased whn btn fnl f)........1¾ **7**
2621[5] Braille (IRE) **(59)***(44) (MGMeagher)* 4-8-7 JWeaver(7) (a bhd: t.o)........2½ **8**
2331* Shawahin **(84)***(57) (JLDunlop)* 3-9-5 RHills(6) (prom: 4th st: wknd 3f out: eased whn btn: t.o)10 **9**

100/30 FOUNDRY LANE, **7/2** Shawahin, **9/2** Royal York, **11/2** Cuango (IRE), **8/1** Eelious (USA), **9/1** Good Hand (USA), **10/1** Credit Squeeze, **12/1** Chantry Beath, **20/1** Braille (IRE), CSF £18.51 CT £103.25 TOTE £4.40: £1.60 £2.00 £2.10 (£8.30) Trio £29.30 OWNER Mr A. Sharratt (SALTBURN) 9 Rn 3m 0.88 (2.68) SF: 61/39/48/32/53/31/31/17/17
WEIGHT FOR AGE 3yo-13lb
T/Plpt: £72.00 (356.31 Tckts). T/Qdpt: £15.10 (24.75 Tckts). IM

2801-LINGFIELD (L-H)
Saturday August 5th (Turf Good to firm, AWT Standard)
WEATHER: hot WIND: almost nil

2938 COURIER NEWSPAPERS (S) H'CAP (0-60) (3-Y.O+) (Class G) £2,780.60 (£771.60: £369.80) **1m 2f (Equitrack)** Stalls: Low GOING minus 0.67 sec per fur (FST) 5-50 (5-52)

2747[7] **Tadellal (IRE) (51)***(60) (BAPearce)* 4-9-0 (7) JWilkinson(6) (lw: led over 6f out: r.o wl)........— **1**
1971[3] Tropical Jungle (USA) **(50)***(56) (PJMakin)* 5-9-6b WNewnes(4) (hdwy over 2f out: rdn over 1f out: r.o one pce)........2 **2**
2524* Bakers Daughter **(43)***(49)*(Fav)*(JRArnold)* 3-8-8 (5) MHenry(8) (a.p: rdn over 4f out: chsd wnr over 3f out: one pce)........s.h **3**
2744[4] Guesstimation (USA) **(48)***(52)*(Fav)*(JPearce)* 6-9-4 GBardwell(11) (s.s: hdwy over 3f out: rdn over 2f out: one pce)........1¼ **4**
2450[3] Wharfedale Music **(36)***(32) (MCPipe)* 4-8-6 RPrice(3) (no hdwy fnl 3f)........5 **5**
2862[6] Fiaba **(42)***(33) (MrsNMacauley)* 7-8-5 (7) AmandaSanders(10) (nvr nr to chal)........3 **6**
2640[4] Malindi Bay **(32)***(18) (BJMcMath)* 7-7-13 (3)ow2 SSanders(7) (nvr nrr)........1¾ **7**
War Requiem (IRE) **(41)***(28) (MissGayKelleway)* 5-8-11 RCochrane(9) (bit bkwd: a mid div)..½ **8**
2605[4] The Little Ferret **(58)***(41) (AMoore)* 5-9-7 (7) LSuthern(1) (b.hind: lw: nvr nrr)........3 **9**
240[3] Rockstine (IRE) **(55)***(34) (PMitchell)* 4-9-4 (7) DaneO'Neill(5) (b.hind: a bhd)........2 **10**
2292[4] Shansi (IRE) **(41)***(16) (MDIUsher)* 4-8-11v RStreet(2) (b: led over 3f: wknd over 2f out)........2½ **11**
2377[11] Jairzinho (USA) **(42)** *(PHayward)* 6-8-9 (3) SDrowne(12) (prom over 5f)........12 **12**
2744[9] La Thuile **(25)** *(MDIUsher)* 3-7-2be(7)ow1 CAdamson(13) (b: bhd fnl 4f)........½ **13**

4/1 Guesstimation (USA), Bakers Daughter, **5/1** Tropical Jungle (USA), **8/1** War Requiem (IRE), Wharfedale Music (5/1-10/1), **11/1** Shansi (IRE), **12/1** The Little Ferret, Malindi Bay (8/1-14/1), Rockstine (IRE), **20/1** Fiaba, **25/1** TADELLAL (IRE), **33/1** Jairzinho (USA), **50/1** La Thuile, CSF £137.93 CT £566.01 TOTE £98.90: £15.20 £1.30 £2.20 (£168.00) Trio £262.00 OWNER Mr Brian Arthur Pearce (LIMPSFIELD) 13 Rn 2m 5.12 (2.12) SF: 34/30/23/26/6/7/-/2/15/8/-/-/-
Sold OJStokes 5,100 gns

2939 E.B.F. LADY MARGARET MEDIAN AUCTION MAIDEN STKS (2-Y.O F) (Class F) £2,897.00 (£802.00: £383.00) **6f** Stalls: High GOING minus 0.37 sec per fur (F) 6-20 (6-22)

2351[7] **Fervent Fan (IRE)** *(68+)*(Fav)*(MBell)* 2-8-11 MFenton(6) (lw: mde all: shkn up over 1f out: comf)........— **1**
2651[10] Whalley Abbey *(60) (GLMoore)* 2-8-11v SWhitworth(2) (b: lw: rdn over 3f out: hdwy over 1f out: r.o one pce)........3 **2**

Shaw House *(52) (DWPArbuthnot)* 2-8-11 RPrice(7) (unf: hld up: chsd wnr over 2f out to ins fnl f: sn wknd)....3 **3**
2683[2] Charming Bride *(33) (SCWilliams)* 2-8-8 (3) JTate(1) (a.p: rdn over 2f out: eased whn btn fnl f)....7 **4**
Image Maker (IRE) *(29) (DWPArbuthnot)* 2-8-11 GBardwell(3) (unf: bit bkwd: a bhd)....1½ **5**
1481[10] Reclaimed *(29) (JSMoore)* 2-8-4 (7) DaneO'Neill(4) (lw: chsd wnr over 3f)....s.h **6**
2651[7] Fairly Sure (IRE) *(NEBerry)* 2-8-11 WNewnes(5) (Withdrawn not under Starters' orders: very unruly in stalls).... **W**

8/15 FERVENT FAN (IRE) (op 5/4), **5/2** Charming Bride (op 5/4), **12/1** Shaw House, **20/1** Whalley Abbey, Fairly Sure (IRE), **33/1** Image Maker (IRE), Reclaimed, CSF £10.26 TOTE £1.70: £1.30 £2.70 (£10.30) OWNER Major W. R. Paton-Smith (NEWMARKET) BRED EDMOND AND RICHARD KENT 6 Rn 1m 11.74 (2.74) SF: 25/17/9/-/-/-/-

OFFICIAL EXPLANATION **Charming Bride: the jockey stated that the filly had struck into herself about a furlong out, and that he had not persevered.**

2940 COOLSCREEN BLINDS CONDITIONS STKS (2-Y.O) (Class D) £3,901.30 (£1,164.40: £556.20: £252.10)

5f Stalls: High GOING minus 0.37 sec per fur (F) 6-50 (6-51)

2423[3] **Soviet Style (AUS)** *(97?) (PWChapple-Hyam)* 2-8-3 (7) RHavlin(1) (lw: chsd ldr: led over 1f out: rdn & r.o wl)....— **1**
1298[4] Caricature (IRE) **(83)***(84)*(Fav)*(GLewis)* 2-8-10 SWhitworth(2) (hld up: rdn 2f out: chsd wnr over 1f out: no imp)....4 **2**
2508[4] Fyors Gift (IRE) *(68) (BHanbury)* 2-8-0 (5) MHenry(4) (hld up: rdn 3f out: one pce)....3½ **3**
1833[2] Just Lady *(64) (WGMTurner)* 2-8-6 (3) SSanders(8) (led over 3f)....2½ **4**
2608* Missile Toe (IRE) **(85)***(63) (JEBanks)* 2-8-13 (3) SDrowne(6) (lw: bhd fnl 3f)....2½ **5**
1608[5] Hever Golf Express **(77)***(63) (TJNaughton)* 2-9-2 MHills(7) (b.off hind: a.p: rdn over 2f out: sn wknd)....hd **6**
2683[7] Heaven Sent (IRE) **(60)***(29) (PMitchell)* 2-7-13 (7)ow1 DaneO'Neill(5) (bhd fnl 3f)....7 **7**
Burj *(NAGraham)* 2-8-10 WCarson(3) (w'like: s.i.s: a wl bhd)....11 **8**

5/2 Caricature (IRE), **7/2** Hever Golf Express, **9/2** Missile Toe (IRE), **11/2** SOVIET STYLE (AUS), **6/1** Just Lady (9/2-7/1), **7/1** Burj (6/1-10/1), **14/1** Fyors Gift (IRE) (op 8/1), **50/1** Heaven Sent (IRE), CSF £19.46 TOTE £6.20: £1.90 £1.40 £4.10 (£6.10) OWNER Mr R. E. Sangster (MARLBOROUGH) BRED Swettenham Stud 8 Rn 57.64 secs (0.64) SF: 51/38/22/18/17/17/-/-

2941 HORSELL ANITEC LIMITED STKS (0-80) (3-Y.O+) (Class D) £3,935.10 (£1,174.80: £561.40: £254.70)

7f Stalls: High GOING minus 0.37 sec per fur (F) 7-20 (7-21)

2679[7] **Anam** **(77)***(84+)*(Fav)*(PTWalwyn)* 3-8-10 WCarson(3) (lw: mde all: comf)....— **1**
1923[10] Regal Fanfare (IRE) **(80)***(75) (JWHills)* 3-8-7b MHills(1) (hld up: rdn 2f out: unable qckn)....2½ **2**
2598[5] Nordinex (IRE) **(78)***(86) (RWArmstrong)* 3-9-4 RPrice(4) (lw: hld up: swtchd lft & rdn 2f out: one pce)....nk **3**
2802[4] Shen Yang (USA) **(77)***(80) (GLMoore)* 3-9-1 SWhitworth(2) (lw: a.p: rdn over 2f out: one pce)....1 **4**

5/4 ANAM, **15/8** Nordinex (IRE) (5/4-2/1), **9/2** Regal Fanfare (IRE) (4/1-6/1), **9/1** Shen Yang (USA) (4/1-10/1), CSF £6.09 TOTE £2.20 (£3.80) OWNER Mr Hamdan Al Maktoum (LAMBOURN) BRED Shadwell Estate Company Limited 4 Rn 1m 23.89 (3.29) SF: 23/14/25/19

2942 NORMAN HILL GROUP H'CAP (0-70) (3-Y.O+) (Class E) £3,302.20 (£985.60: £470.80: £213.40)

2m (Equitrack) Stalls: Low GOING minus 0.67 sec per fur (FST) 7-50 (7-51)

2604[2] **Rocky Forum** **(52)***(70+)*(Fav)*(GLMoore)* 3-7-2 (7)ow2 CAdamson(5) (hld up: led 3f out: clr 2f out: comf)....— **1**
2688[7] Bardolph (USA) **(63)***(74) (PFICole)* 8-9-7b RCochrane(2) (led over 12f: chsd wnr fnl f: no imp)....9 **2**
*2495** Brave Spy **(58)***(65) (CACyzer)* 4-9-2 DBiggs(4) (chsd ldr: led over 3f out: sn hdd: one pce)....4 **3**
2605[2] Rolling Waters **(63)***(69)*(Fav)*(JARToller)* 5-9-7 WNewnes(3) (hld up: rdn over 4f out: one pce)....1½ **4**
1794[10] Jaraab **(66)***(67) (GLewis)* 4-9-10v SWhitworth(1) (lw: hld up: rdn over 4f out: wknd over 2f out)....5 **5**
2514[4] Sarazar (USA) **(36)***(36) (RAkehurst)* 6-7-8b GBardwell(6) (lw: bhd fnl 4f)....½ **6**

LONG HANDICAP Rocky Forum 7-6

3/1 ROCKY FORUM, Rolling Waters, **100/30** Bardolph (USA), **5/1** Sarazar (USA), **7/1** Jaraab (5/1-8/1), **8/1** Brave Spy (6/1-9/1), CSF £12.59 TOTE £3.70: £1.70 £2.00 (£5.70) OWNER The Forum Ltd (EPSOM) BRED Forum Bloodstock Ltd 6 Rn 3m 21.74 (-1.76) SF: 36/55/46/50/48/17
WEIGHT FOR AGE 3yo-15lb

2943

ROADWAYS & CAR PARKS H'CAP (0-70) (3-Y.O+) (Class E) £3,359.40 (£1,003.20: £479.60: £217.80)
6f Stalls: High GOING minus 0.37 sec per fur (FST) 8-20 (8-22)

2318[11] **Robo Magic (USA)** **(54)***(60) (LMontagueHall)* 3-8-10 RCochrane(2) (rdn over 2f out: hdwy over 1f out: led last strides)......— 1
2578[8] Dashing Dancer (IRE) **(57)***(63) (RAkehurst)* 4-9-1 (3) SSanders(10) (lw: hld up: rdn over 2f out: led nr fin: hdd last strides)......hd 2
2685[5] Sharp Imp **(41)***(45) (RMFlower)* 5-8-2b DBiggs(6) (rdn over 3f out: hdwy over 1f out: led ins fnl f: hdd nr fin)......½ 3
2887[5] Red Admiral **(59)***(58) (PCHaslam)* 5-9-6 MTebbutt(12) (lw: a.p: rdn over 2f out: one pce fnl f) .2 4
1400[2] Texas Cowgirl (IRE) **(45)***(39) (HVanderdussen,Belgium)* 5-8-6 MO'Callaghan(5) (lw: hld up: led over 2f out tl ins fnl f: sn wknd)......2 5
1429[6] Dahiyah (USA) **(61)***(48) (GLMoore)* 4-9-1 (7) LSuthern(1) (swtg: rdn over 2f out: nvr nr to chal)......2½ 6
2448[2] Rambold **(62)***(49) (NEBerry)* 4-9-4 (5) RPainter(8) (prom over 4f)......s.h 7
2578[3] Louisville Belle (IRE) **(55)***(42) (MDIUsher)* 6-8-9 (7) CAdamson(9) (b: b.hind: lw: prom 4f)......s.h 8
2010[12] Lucky Lucaya (USA) **(69)***(48) (LadyHerries)* 3-9-11 MHills(7) (bhd fnl 2f)......3 9
2659* Charnwood Queen **(58)***(32)*(Fav)*(RWArmstrong)* 3-9-0 WCarson(4) (lw: bhd fnl 2f)......1¾ 10
2642[3] Tachycardia **(51)***(24) (RJO'Sullivan)* 3-8-7 StephenDavies(11) (lw: led over 3f)......nk 11
2538[6] Blue Bomber **(67)** *(CWeedon)* 4-10-0 MPerrett(3) (lw: a bhd)......20 12

7/4 Charnwood Queen, **7/1** Louisville Belle (IRE), **15/2** Rambold (4/1-8/1), **8/1** Dashing Dancer (IRE), **9/1** Texas Cowgirl (IRE), Sharp Imp (8/1-12/1), **10/1** Red Admiral (7/1-11/1), **14/1** Dahiyah (USA) (10/1-20/1), Lucky Lucaya (USA), **16/1** Tachycardia, **20/1** ROBO MAGIC (USA), Blue Bomber, CSF £166.51 CT £1,416.90 TOTE £26.70: £5.70 £2.70 £3.50 (£131.70) Trio £239.20 OWNER Mr A D Green and Partners (EPSOM) BRED Curtis C. Green 12 Rn
1m 10.82 (1.82) SF: 36/44/26/39/20/29/30/23/24/8/-/-
WEIGHT FOR AGE 3yo-5lb

T/Plpt: £229.40 (40.8 Tckts). T/Qdpt: £149.70 (1.1 Tckts). AK

2907-NEWMARKET (R-H)
Saturday August 5th (Good to firm)

WEATHER: warm, sunny WIND: almost nil

2944

MONTANA WINES MAIDEN STKS (3-Y.O+) (Class D) £4,581.00 (£1,368.00: £654.00: £297.00) **1m 4f (July)** Stalls: High GOING minus 0.36 sec (F) 2-10 (2-10)

1147[4] **Jellaby Askhir** *(96) (RAkehurst)* 3-8-10 DHarrison(6) (dwlt: sn prom: rdn & outpcd 3f out: styd on wl to ld ins fnl f)......— 1
764[14] Pampas Breeze (IRE) *(89) (WJarvis)* 3-8-0 (5) MHenry(3) (hld up: plld hrd: hdwy over 2f out: ev ch ins fnl f: kpt on)......1¼ 2
2547[2] Najmat Alshemaal (IRE) **(97)***(89)*(Fav)*(MajorWRHern)* 3-8-5 RCochrane(2) (tckd ldrs: led over 1f out tl wknd & hdd ins fnl f)......½ 3
1346[4] Jambia *(83) (HRACecil)* 3-8-5 WRyan(1) (led tl hdd & wknd over 1f out)......4 4
Reem Dubai (IRE) *(83) (JHMGosden)* 3-8-5 PRobinson(7) (lengthy: unf: bkwd: chsd ldrs 8f: sn rdn & wknd)......hd 5
1587[8] Kshessinskaya **(95)***(77) (CEBrittain)* 3-8-5 MRoberts(5) (lw: chsd ldrs tl rdn & wknd 2f out)......5 6
Mutammaddin *(48) (JHMGosden)* 3-8-10 WCarson(4) (unf: bit bkwd: b.hind: s.i.s: a bhd)......25 7

11/8 Najmat Alshemaal (IRE), **9/2** Kshessinskaya, **11/2** Mutammaddin (op 3/1), **13/2** JELLABY ASKHIR (5/1-8/1), **8/1** Jambia (5/1-9/1), **16/1** Reem Dubai (IRE), **50/1** Pampas Breeze (IRE), CSF £133.85 TOTE £9.30: £3.20 £6.90 (£98.90) OWNER Sheikh Essa Bin Mubarak (EPSOM) BRED Side Hill Stud and Floors Farming 7 Rn 2m 32.8 (4.10) SF: 38/31/31/25/25/19/-

2945

BROOKS OF NORWICH CLAIMING STKS (3-Y.O+) (Class D) £4,737.00 (£1,416.00: £678.00: £309.00)
7f (July) Stalls: Low GOING minus 0.36 sec per fur (F) 2-40 (2-40)

2755[5] **Parliament Piece** **(67)***(84) (MrsMReveley)* 9-9-1 RCochrane(3) (lw: trckd ldrs: rdn to ld wl ins fnl f)......— 1

2766[4] Blockade (USA) **(71)***(80)*(Fav)*(MBell)* 6-8-12 MFenton(5) (t: swtg: led tl hdd & unable qckn wl ins fnl f)....½ 2
2807* Proud Image **(63)***(69) (APJarvis)* 3-8-6 (3) JTate(8) (chsd ldr over 5f: one pce)....6 3
2321[13] Rapier Point (IRE) **(66)***(60) (PCHaslam)* 4-9-0 MTebbutt(1) (prom tl rdn & btn over 1f out) ...3½ 4
Scorpius *(66) (CNWilliams)* 5-9-6 PRobinson(4) (b.off hind: lw: bhd: sn rdn: kpt on fnl 2f)....s.h 5
2744* Lincoln Treasure (IRE) **(42)***(59) (MCChapman)* 4-8-10 (3) DRMcCabe(2) (hld up: nvr trbld ldrs)....s.h 6
1991[9] Magication **(34)** *(CNAllen)* 5-7-12 (5) MBaird(7) (stdd s: a bhd)....dist 7
Circle of Friends (IRE) **(56)** *(RAkehurst)* 4-8-0 (3) SSanders(6) (prom tl broke down & p.u over 3f out: dead).... P

13/8 Blockade (USA), **7/2** Proud Image, **5/1** PARLIAMENT PIECE, **8/1** Circle of Friends (IRE), **16/1** Rapier Point (IRE), Lincoln Treasure (IRE), Scorpius, **33/1** Magication, CSF £12.21 TOTE £4.50: £1.50 £1.10 £1.60 (£4.60) OWNER Mr G. A. Farndon (SALTBURN) BRED Patrick Headon 8 Rn
1m 25.38 (0.98) SF: 58/54/37/34/40/33/-/-
WEIGHT FOR AGE 3yo-6lb

2946 DANDELION INVITATION LADIES' H'CAP (0-65) (3-Y.O+) (Class F)

£4,179.00 (£1,272.00: £626.00: £303.00)
1m (July) Stalls: Low GOING minus 0.36 sec per fur (F) 3-15 (3-15)

2602[9] **Fort Knox (IRE) (49)***(61) (RMFlower)* 4-10-5 MrsGabriellaMartin(12) (swtg: bhd: hdwy over 1f out: led nr fin)....— 1
2052[4] Don't Drop Bombs (USA) **(30)***(40) (DTThom)* 6-9-0v MissAElsey(3) (led 2f: led 4f out: clr over 1f out: wknd & ct nr fin)....1¼ 2
2814[2] Avishayes (USA) **(47)***(56)*(Fav)*(MrsMReveley)* 8-10-3 MissCCashman(2) (lw: hdwy 2f out: r.o fnl f)....½ 3
2363[4] Saltis (IRE) **(57)***(65) (DWPArbuthnot)* 3-10-6 MrsDArbuthnot(10) (b.hind: hdwy 4f out: ev ch over 2f out: wknd over 1f out)....½ 4
2682[7] Captain Marmalade **(42)***(49) (DTThom)* 6-9-12 MissJWinter(9) (b: hdwy over 1f out: nrst fin)s.h 5
2685* Mislemani (IRE) **(59)***(59) (AGNewcombe)* 5-11-1 MissKSchlick(6) (chsd ldrs: outpcd over 2f out: kpt on fnl f)....3½ 6
2657[9] Mighty Kingdom (IRE) **(43)***(43) (CADwyer)* 4-9-13 MissReneeKierans(5) (b.off fore: prom: rdn 2f out: wknd over 1f out)....s.h 7
2396* Twin Creeks **(52)***(47) (MDHammond)* 4-10-8 MrsAPerrett(7) (lw: prom: rdn 3f out: sn btn) ...2½ 8
2789[3] Trina **(35)***(30) (DLWilliams)* 4-9-5 MissLJarven(4) (plld hrd: led after 2f to 4f out: sn wknd) ....nk 9
2276[9] Daring Ryde **(48)***(35) (JPSmith)* 4-10-4 MissLGrizzetti(11) (nvr nr to chal)....4 10
2538[8] Kissavos **(41)***(16) (CCElsey)* 9-9-11 MissAMHojfeldt(8) (s.i.s: a bhd)....6 11
2748[4] Karinska **(69)***(43) (MCChapman)* 5-11-11 MissKMarks(1) (s.i.s: a bhd) ....nk 12
LONG HANDICAP Don't Drop Bombs (USA) 8-11

3/1 Avishayes (USA), **5/1** Twin Creeks, **6/1** Mislemani (IRE), **10/1** Karinska, FORT KNOX (IRE), **11/1** Mighty Kingdom (IRE), **14/1** Saltis (IRE), Captain Marmalade (op 8/1), **16/1** Don't Drop Bombs (USA), Trina, **20/1** Daring Ryde, **33/1** Kissavos, CSF £133.59 CT £538.34 TOTE £16.20: £4.20 £3.10 £1.80 (£134.30) Trio £138.20 OWNER Miss C. Markowiak (JEVINGTON) BRED Leo Collins 12 Rn
1m 41.55 (3.85) SF: 48/27/43/45/36/46/30/34/17/22/3/30
WEIGHT FOR AGE 3yo-7lb

2947 ENZA NEW ZEALAND SWEET SOLERA STKS (Listed) (2-Y.O F) (Class A) £12,560.00 (£4,640.00: £2,220.00: £900.00: £350.00: £130.00)

7f (July) Stalls: Low GOING minus 0.36 sec per fur (F) 3-45 (3-47)

1928* **Bint Salsabil (USA)** *(91+)*(Fav)*(JLDunlop)* 2-8-8 WCarson(3) (trckd ldrs: led over 1f out: rdn & hld on wl fnl f)....— 1
2083* Staffin *(90) (JRFanshawe)* 2-8-8 DHarrison(5) (lw: hld up: hdwy over 2f out: ev ch over 1f out: unable qckn ins fnf f) ....nk 2
2777* Witch of Fife (USA) *(89) (BWHills)* 2-8-8 DHolland(4) (hld up: hdwy over 1f out: r.o wl fnl f: nrst fin)....¾ 3
2242* Honest Guest (IRE) *(87) (MHTompkins)* 2-8-11 PRobinson(2) (lw: led 1f: wknd 2f out)....2 4
2489* Tropical Dance (USA) **(98)***(81) (MrsJCecil)* 2-8-11 RHughes(7) (led after 1f tl over 1f out: sn wknd)....2½ 5
2594[4] White Whispers **(93)***(77) (BJMeehan)* 2-8-8 AClark(6) (prom over 4f)....¾ 6
2675[3] Astuti (IRE) *(APJarvis)* 2-8-8 JTate(1) (Withdrawn not under Starter's orders: veterinary advice).... W

Evens BINT SALSABIL (USA), **5/1** Staffin, **6/1** Honest Guest (IRE), **8/1** Witch of Fife (USA) (op 14/1), Tropical Dance (USA) (5/1-9/1), **20/1** Astuti (IRE), **40/1** White Whispers, CSF £5.59 TOTE £1.50: £1.30 £2.70 (£3.90) OWNER Mr Hamdan Al Maktoum (ARUNDEL) BRED Shadwell Estate Company Limited 6 Rn
1m 25.68 (1.28) SF: 48/47/46/44/38/34/-

2948

NEW ZEALAND H'CAP (0-105) (3-Y.O+) (Class B) £18,600.00 (£5,550.00: £2,650.00: £1,200.00) **7f (July)** Stalls: Low GOING minus 0.36 sec (F) 4-20 (4-21)

1839[10] **Verzen (IRE) (94)***(102)*(Fav)*(DRLoder)* 3-8-10 (3) DRMcCabe(11) (hld up: effrt 3f out: r.o wl appr fnl f to ld nr fin)........— 1
2647* Hi Nod **(92)***(99) (MJCamacho)* 5-9-3 LCharnock(3) (swtg: trckd ldrs: rdn to ld ins fnl f: ct nr fin)........nk 2
2703[14] Celestial Key (USA) **(100)***(107) (MJohnston)* 5-9-11 DHolland(13) (lw: hdwy over 1f out: fin wl)........s.h 3
2531[2] Elite Hope (USA) **(83)***(87) (CREgerton)* 3-8-2 MRoberts(8) (led tl hdd & no ex ins fnl f)........1¼ 4
2647[5] Tawafij (USA) **(83)***(87) (TDyer)* 6-8-8v StephenDavies(9) (hdwy 2f out: no ex ins fnl f)........nk 5
2647[3] Gymcrak Premiere **(84)***(86) (GHolmes)* 7-8-9 KFallon(6) (lw: hdwy 2f out: nvr able to chal)....¾ 6
2703[16] Cyrano's Lad (IRE) **(89)***(89) (CADwyer)* 6-9-0 RHughes(1) (chsd ldrs: no imp fnl 2f)........¾ 7
2598* Kayvee **(103)***(102) (GHarwood)* 6-10-0 AClark(2) (hdwy over 2f out: no imp fnl f)........¾ 8
2764[7] My Best Valentine **(82)***(77) (JWhite)* 5-8-7 DHarrison(12) (lw: hld up: effrt over 1f out: no imp)........1¾ 9
2743* First Veil **(78)***(70) (JRFanshawe)* 5-7-12 (5) NVarley(7) (chsd ldr over 5f)........1¼ 10
2428[2] Absolute Magic **(83)***(67) (WJHaggas)* 5-8-8 MHills(10) (b.off hind: rdn 3f out: no imp)........3½ 11
2369* Cadeaux Tryst **(102)***(82) (EALDunlop)* 3-9-7 WCarson(4) (b: lw: a bhd)........1¾ 12
2428[6] Rambo's Hall **(90)***(61) (JAGlover)* 10-9-1 DeanMcKeown(5) (lw: a bhd)........4 13

11/2 VERZEN (IRE), **7/1** My Best Valentine, Cadeaux Tryst, **8/1** Celestial Key (USA), Hi Nod, Tawafij (USA), **11/1** First Veil, Kayvee, Gymcrak Premiere, **14/1** Elite Hope (USA), Cyrano's Lad (IRE), Absolute Magic, **40/1** Rambo's Hall, CSF £45.51 CT £322.73 TOTE £6.20: £1.80 £2.70 £3.50 (£33.90) Trio £123.20 OWNER Mr Saeed Manana (NEWMARKET) BRED Sheikh Mohammed bin Rashid al Maktoum 13 Rn 1m 23.98 (-0.42) SF: 73/76/84/58/64/63/66/79/54/47/44/53/38

WEIGHT FOR AGE 3yo-6lb

OFFICIAL EXPLANATION **Cadeaux Tryst: the trainer stated the colt did not act on the ground.**

2949

ANZ. BANKING GROUP MAIDEN STKS (3-Y.O) (Class D) £4,503.00 (£1,344.00: £642.00: £291.00) **6f (July)** Stalls: Low GOING minus 0.36 sec (F) 4-50 (4-52)

2576[2] **My Cadeaux** *(83) (RGuest)* 3-8-9 MRoberts(6) (a.p: rdn to ld nr fin)........— 1
2576[4] Dictation (USA) *(87)*(Fav)*(RCharlton)* 3-9-0 DHarrison(2) (lw: led after 2f: hrd rdn fnl f: ct nr fin)........nk 2
1473[4] Latching (IRE) **(75)***(79) (RFJohnsonHoughton)* 3-8-9 MHills(5) (in tch: rdn & r.o appr fnl f)...1¼ 3
442[7] Daysman (USA) *(83) (BWHills)* 3-9-0 DHolland(4) (chsd ldrs: effrt 2f out: no ex ins fnl f)........½ 4
2469[4] Prudent Princess *(71) (AHide)* 3-8-9 MTebbutt(9) (lw: s.s: sn chsng ldrs: no imp fnl 2f)........2½ 5
752[10] Merlin's Fancy *(70) (WJarvis)* 3-8-9 WRyan(7) (trckd ldrs tl wknd 2f out)........nk 6
2576[10] Utr (USA) *(49) (HThomsonJones)* 3-8-9 PRobinson(8) (swtg: led 2f: sn bhd)........8 7
2236[9] Akola Angel *(42) (CREgerton)* 3-8-9 RHughes(1) (sn bhd)........2½ 8
1979[14] Arabian Flight *(46) (TTClement)* 3-9-0 EGuest(3) (b: s.i.s: a bhd)........nk 9

11/8 Dictation (USA), **2/1** MY CADEAUX, **13/2** Latching (IRE) (9/2-7/1), **9/1** Daysman (USA), **12/1** Prudent Princess (op 8/1), **25/1** Utr (USA), **33/1** Merlin's Fancy, **50/1** Akola Angel, Arabian Flight, CSF £4.98 TOTE £2.90: £1.20 £1.20 £1.10 (£1.90) Trio £2.20 OWNER Mr C. J. Mills (NEWMARKET) BRED Jim and Mrs Strange 9 Rn 1m 13.0 (1.50) SF: 43/47/39/43/31/30/9/2/6

2950

LANSON CHAMPAGNE H'CAP (0-95) (3-Y.O+) (Class C) £5,952.00 (£1,776.00: £848.00: £384.00)
1m 2f (July) Stalls: High GOING minus 0.36 sec per fur (F) 5-20 (5-20)

2571[7] **Star of Persia (IRE) (81)***(85) (PWHarris)* 3-8-11 DHolland(1) (hld up: hdwy to ld over 1f out: jst hld on)........— 1
2804* Better Offer (IRE) **(83)***(87) (GHarwood)* 3-8-13 MPerrett(3) (lw: set slow pce 3f: ev ch 1f out: jst failed)........s.h 2
2780[4] Ball Gown **(75)***(73)*(Fav)*(DTThom)* 5-8-11 (3) DRMcCabe(4) (plld hrd: led after 3f: clr 4f out: hdd over 1f out: sn btn)........4 3
2746[9] Czarna (IRE) **(85)***(78) (CEBrittain)* 4-9-10 MRoberts(2) (lw: hld up & plld hrd: effrt 3f out: btn appr fnl f)........3 4

7/4 Ball Gown, **9/4** Better Offer (IRE), **100/30** Czarna (IRE), **11/2** STAR OF PERSIA (IRE) (3/1-6/1), CSF £15.53 TOTE £5.70 (£7.40) OWNER The Saturday Club (BERKHAMSTED) BRED Mrs Kiki Ward Platt 4 Rn 2m 14.94 (12.54) SF: -/-/-/-

WEIGHT FOR AGE 3yo-9lb

T/Jkpt: £32,651.50 (0.2 Tckts); £36,790.51 to Windsor 7/8/95. T/Plpt: £218.40 (154.29 Tckts). T/Qdpt: £9.00 (65.95 Tckts). Dk

2913-REDCAR (L-H)
Saturday August 5th (Firm, Good to firm patches)
WEATHER: fine WIND: slt half against

2951
BEDALE (S) STKS (2-Y.O) (Class F) £2,798.00 (£778.00: £374.00)
6f Stalls: Centre GOING minus 0.28 sec per fur (GF) 2-15 (2-16)

2619[7] **Goretski (IRE)** *(66+)*(Fav)*(NTinkler)* 2-8-11 KDarley(8) (w ldrs gng wl: led ½-wy: pushed clr over 1f out: eased nr fin) — 1
2580[5] Yougoa *(53) (MWEasterby)* 2-8-6 JFanning(6) (swtg: hld up & plld hrd: sn trckng ldrs: outpcd ½-wy: kpt on appr fnl f: no ch w wnr) 3 2
2629[5] Don't Tell Anyone **(52)***(55) (JBerry)* 2-8-11 AMcGlone(3) (led to ½-wy: kpt on same pce) 1¼ 3
Bumblefoot (IRE) *(49) (MJohnston)* 2-8-6 TWilliams(10) (unf: dwlt: sn chsng ldrs: rdn & edgd lft 2f out: kpt on) nk 4
1356[10] Taurean Fire *(52) (MrsMReveley)* 2-8-4 (7) DDenby(2) (hdwy ½-wy: kpt on fnl 2f: nvr nr to chal) ¾ 5
*2629** Ticka Ticka Timing *(44) (BWMurray)* 2-8-11 (5) GParkin(7) (w ldrs: rdn along ½-wy: sn wknd) .5 6
Baroness Gold *(32) (MHEasterby)* 2-8-6 MBirch(4) (b.hind: unf: s.s: a outpcd & bhd) ½ 7
2542[8] Spring Silhouette *(30) (MrsVAAconley)* 2-8-1 (5) CTeague(1) (swtg: trckd ldrs tl wknd over 2f out) ¾ 8
2328[10] Lucky Bea **(58)***(34) (MWEasterby)* 2-8-11 SDWilliams(5) (chsd ldrs: drvn ½-wy: sn wl outpcd)nk 9
Nuclear Jewel *(13) (RMWhitaker)* 2-8-6 ACulhane(9) (leggy: unf: unruly in stalls: s.i.s: a wl outpcd) 6 10

4/5 GORETSKI (IRE), **6/1** Don't Tell Anyone, **7/1** Ticka Ticka Timing, **8/1** Taurean Fire, **9/1** Bumblefoot (IRE) (op 6/1), **11/1** Lucky Bea, **12/1** Baroness Gold (op 6/1), **20/1** Yougoa, Nuclear Jewel, **50/1** Spring Silhouette, CSF £19.83 TOTE £2.00: £1.10 £2.40 £1.80 (£26.80) Trio £47.20 OWNER Mr P.D.Savill (MALTON) BRED Pierre Brichart 10 Rn 1m 13.2 (3.90) SF: 16/3/5/-/2/-/-/-/-/-
Bt in 5,400 gns.

2952
ROTHMANS ROYALS NORTH SOUTH CHALLENGE SERIES H'CAP (0-85) (3-Y.O+) (Class D) £4,206.00 (£1,263.00: £609.00: £282.00)
1m Stalls: Centre GOING minus 0.28 sec per fur (GF) 2-45 (2-52)

2694[4] **Ninia (USA) (58)***(67) (MJohnston)* 3-7-10 TWilliams(6) (led: shkn up & clr over 2f out: hdd ins fnl f: styd on u.p to ld last stride) — 1
2788[2] Pride of Pendle **(72)***(81) (DNicholls)* 6-9-3 AlexGreaves(1) (trckd ldrs: effrt 2f out: rdn to ld ins fnl f: jst ct) hd 2
2797[4] Cee-Jay-Ay **(63)***(68) (JBerry)* 8-8-1 (7) PRoberts(4) (dwlt: pushed along ½-wy: styd on fnl f: nvr nr to chal) 1¾ 3
2468[2] Saifan **(72)***(77)*(Fav)*(DMorris)* 6-9-3b KDarley(7) (lw: s.i.s: sn trckng ldrs: effrt over 2f out: styd on same pce u.p appr fnl f) hd 4
2668* Bold Amusement **(83)***(87) (WSCunningham)* 5-9-7 (7) SCopp(3) (lw: dwlt: sn trckng ldrs: effrt over 2f out: kpt on one pce fr over 1f out) ¾ 5
2645* Chinour (IRE) **(69)***(59) (EJAlston)* 7-9-0 SDWilliams(5) (swtg: chsd ldrs: rdn over 2f out: wknd over 1f out: eased) 7 6
1566[11] Gorodenka Boy **(49)***(14) (MrsJJordan)* 5-7-8 ow1 JLowe(2) (swtg: plld hrd: w ldrs tl rdn & wknd qckly over 2f out: sn bhd & eased) 12 7

LONG HANDICAP Gorodenka Boy 6-8

11/4 Saifan, **7/2** Pride of Pendle, NINIA (USA), **4/1** Bold Amusement, **7/1** Chinour (IRE), **10/1** Cee-Jay-Ay, **66/1** Gorodenka Boy, CSF £15.20 TOTE £3.60: £1.70 £1.70 (£5.20) OWNER Mrs D.R. Schreiber (MIDDLEHAM) BRED Newgate Stud Farm Inc 7 Rn
1m 37.3 (2.30) SF: 34/55/42/51/61/33/-
WEIGHT FOR AGE 3yo-7lb

2953
MARY REVELEY RACING CLUB CLAIMING STKS (3-Y.O) (Class F) £2,843.00 (£854.00: £412.00: £191.00)
1m 2f Stalls: Low GOING minus 0.28 sec per fur (GF) 3-20 (3-20)

2655[6] **Rushen Raider (56)***(71) (KWHogg)* 3-8-12 (7) ADaly(4) (trckd ldrs: led & hung lft over 1f out: drvn out) — 1
Barton Heights *(67) (MrsMReveley)* 3-8-10 (7) SCopp(3) (s.s: bhd: hdwy 2f out: styd on strly ins fnl f) 1½ 2
2479[8] Mithraic (IRE) **(60)***(66) (JWWatts)* 3-9-3 MBirch(5) (mde most: reminders 5f out: hdd over 1f out: one pce) nk 3
Soupreme *(65) (MrsMReveley)* 3-8-11 (5) GParkin(6) (small: lengthy: bit bkwd: s.i.s: bhd: pushed along & rn green: hdwy over 1f out: styd on nr fin) s.h 4

2233* Durgams First (IRE) **(60)***(69)*(Fav)*(MrsMReveley)* 3-9-7 KDarley(2) (trckd ldrs: effrt 3f out: rdn & wknd appr fnl f) ....½ 5
2582[7] Lass of Kinloch **(30)***(34) (MBrittain)* 3-8-2 JLowe(1) (w ldr: drvn along over 3f out: wknd over 2f out: eased) 10 6

4/6 Durgams First (IRE), **7/2** Mithraic (IRE), **9/2** RUSHEN RAIDER, **20/1** Soupreme, **25/1** Barton Heights, Lass of Kinloch, CSF £63.29 TOTE £6.80: £2.00 £5.40 (£36.30) OWNER Exors of the late Mr P J White (ISLE OF MAN) BRED M. H. D. Madden and Partners 6 Rn
2m 8.2 (5.70) SF: 34/30/29/28/32/-
Mithraic (IRE) clmd WSCunningham £8,000

2954

BONUSPRINT H'CAP (0-75) (3-Y.O+) (Class D) £4,440.00 (£1,335.00: £645.00: £300.00) **1m 2f** Stalls: Low GOING minus 0.28 sec per fur (GF) 3-50 (3-51)

2610[2] **Ooh Ah Cantona (65)***(75) (JLEyre)* 4-9-8 (5) DGriffiths(6) (trckd ldrs: qcknd to ld over 1f out: edgd lft: drvn out) ....— 1
1966[10] Bold Look **(56)***(65) (PWHarris)* 4-9-4 MBirch(5) (chsd ldrs: rdn & outpcd over 3f out: swtchd outside over 1f out: styd on wl nr fin) ....¾ 2
2731* Our Main Man **(56)***(65) (RMWhitaker)* 5-9-4 ACulhane(7) (trckd ldrs: led over 3f out: hdd over 1f out: styd on same pce) ....hd 3
2805* Gloriana **(75)***(83)*(Fav)*(LadyHerries)* 3-9-7 (7) JO'Dwyer(3) (led tl over 3f out: edgd rt & kpt on same pce appr fnl f) ....½ 4
2731[4] Imperial Bid (FR) **(56)***(63) (DenysSmith)* 7-9-4 TWilliams(1) (lw: chsd ldrs: effrt over 4f out: hung rt: kpt on fnl 2f: nvr nr to chal) ....nk 5
2482[9] Kanat Lee (IRE) **(34)***(39) (DonEnricoIncisa)* 4-7-10 KimTinkler(2) (s.i.s: bhd: sme hdwy & sltly hmpd over 1f out: nvr nr ldrs) 1½ 6
2503[10] Perfect Bertie (IRE) **(49)***(51) (GROldroyd)* 3-8-2 JFanning(4) (hld up: effrt 4f out: nvr nr ldrs) ..2 7
1917* Pine Essence (USA) **(59)***(58) (MrsMReveley)* 4-9-7 KDarley(8) (hld up: effrt, drvn along & outpcd 4f out: n.d after) 1½ 8

11/4 Gloriana, **100/30** OOH AH CANTONA, **5/1** Pine Essence (USA), **6/1** Our Main Man, **7/1** Bold Look (5/1-3/1), Imperial Bid (FR), **14/1** Perfect Bertie (IRE), **20/1** Kanat Lee (IRE), CSF £24.78 CT £122.04 TOTE £3.40: £1.60 £1.50 £2.30 (£37.50) OWNER Mrs Eve Sweetman (HAMBLETON) BRED R. M. Whitaker and E. Wilkinson 8 Rn 2m 6.3 (3.80) SF: 57/47/47/56/45/21/24/40
WEIGHT FOR AGE 3yo-9lb

2955

BET WITH THE TOTE MAIDEN APPRENTICE H'CAP (0-65) (3-Y.O+) (Class F) £2,656.75 (£814.00: £404.50: £199.75)
1m 1f Stalls: Low GOING minus 0.28 sec per fur (GF) 4-15 (4-16)

2607[4] **Durham Drapes (54)***(63)*(Fav)*(MHEasterby)* 4-9-12 GFaulkner(5) (hld up in tch: led over 2f out: drvn out) ....— 1
2279[6] Master Fiddler **(27)***(35) (EWeymes)* 5-7-13 KSked(7) (bhd: hit rail over 5f out: hdwy on ins over 2f out: styd on wl nr fin) ....¾ 2
2375[9] Northwise (IRE) **(42)***(49) (WWHaigh)* 4-9-0 JoHunnam(2) (chsd ldr: ev ch over 3f out: kpt on one pce appr fnl f) ....½ 3
2744[3] Miss Felixstowe (USA) **(49)***(51) (MrsMReveley)* 3-8-5 (8) SamanthaRooks(4) (chsd ldrs: edgd rt 3f out: edgd lft over 1f out: kpt on same pce) 2½ 4
2587[3] Md Thompson **(56)***(57) (SCWilliams)* 3-9-6 RMullen(6) (s.s: sn chsng ldrs: led over 3f out: hdd over 2f out: wknd appr fnl f) ....¾ 5
2611[4] Star Performer (IRE) **(54)***(53) (MrsMReveley)* 4-9-4 (8)ow1 KPrendergast(3) (hld up: effrt, hung rt & hmpd over 2f out: swtchd ins: n.m.r over 1f out: nvr nr ldrs) ....½ 6
2620[10] Gamzatti **(24)***(19) (CBBBooth)* 4-7-10 ow1 FLynch(8) (sn bhd: sme hdwy on outside over 3f out: n.d) 2½ 7
2761[3] Coney Hills **(22)** *(NBycroft)* 4-7-8 BHalligan(1) (swtg: led & plld hrd: hdd over 3f out: lost pl).13 8

7/4 DURHAM DRAPES (op 11/4), **4/1** Star Performer (IRE), **5/1** Md Thompson (op 3/1), **6/1** Miss Felixstowe (USA), **8/1** Northwise (IRE), **12/1** Master Fiddler, Coney Hills, **33/1** Gamzatti, CSF £20.77 CT £124.10 TOTE £3.10: £1.50 £1.60 £1.70 (£17.30) OWNER Durham Drapes Ltd (MALTON) BRED Mrs M. Upsdell 8 Rn 1m 53.9 (4.90) SF: 42/14/28/22/28/32/-/-
WEIGHT FOR AGE 3yo-8lb

2956

GO RACING IN YORKSHIRE CLAIMING H'CAP (0-60) (3-Y.O+) (Class F) £2,861.00 (£796.00: £383.00)
6f Stalls: Centre GOING minus 0.28 sec per fur (GF) 4-45 (4-46)

2821[2] **Arc Lamp (38)***(45)*(Fav)*(JAGlover)* 9-8-10 SDWilliams(8) (lw: trckd ldrs: effrt over 1f out: led jst ins fnl f: drvn out) ....— 1

2753[7] Sir Tasker **(52)***(58)*(Fav)*(JLHarris)* 7-9-10v KDarley(2) (led tl over 1f out: kpt on wl nr fin).......nk 2
2540[8] Irchester Lass **(38)***(40)* *(SRBowring)* 3-8-0 (5)ow2 CTeague(5) (s.i.s: sn in tch: edgd lft & kpt on wl fnl f)......¾ 3
2450[10] Mr Moriarty (IRE) **(21)***(25)* *(SRBowring)* 4-7-7b NKennedy(6) (chsd ldrs: drvn along & wl outpcd ½-wy: kpt on wl fnl f)......hd 4
2784[13] Invigilate **(52)***(55)* *(MartynWane)* 6-9-10 TWilliams(3) (lw: chsd ldrs: led over 1f out tl jst ins fnl f: wknd nr fin)......½ 5
2665[5] Olifantsfontein **(50)***(47)* *(DNicholls)* 7-9-8 MBirch(4) (lw: hld up: effrt & outpcd over 2f out: kpt on: nvr nr to chal)......2 6
2463[5] Waverley Star **(37)***(32)* *(JSWainwright)* 10-8-9b JFanning(7) (chsd ldrs: rdn along & lost pl ½-wy)......¾ 7
2624[13] Skiptamaloo **(30)***(23)* *(DonEnricoIncisa)* 4-8-2b KimTinkler(1) (s.s: a in rr)......1 8
2772[7] Miss Whittingham (IRE) **(50)***(38)* *(JBerry)* 5-9-1 (7) PRoberts(9) (in tch: rdn ½-wy: sn lost pl) .1¾ 9

LONG HANDICAP Mr Moriarty (IRE) 7-4

3/1 ARC LAMP, Sir Tasker (op 9/2), **9/2** Olifantsfontein, **7/1** Invigilate, **9/1** Irchester Lass, **10/1** Miss Whittingham (IRE), **12/1** Waverley Star, **16/1** Skiptamaloo, Mr Moriarty (IRE), CSF £12.21 CT £66.07 TOTE £3.20: £1.80 £1.50 £3.70 (£5.70) Trio £46.10 OWNER Mr B. Bruce (WORKSOP) BRED H. J. Joel 9 Rn 1m 12.4 (3.10) SF: 26/39/16/6/36/28/13/4/19

WEIGHT FOR AGE 3yo-5lb

2957

E.B.F. SINNINGTON MAIDEN STKS (2-Y.O F) (Class D) £4,055.00 (£1,220.00: £590.00: £275.00)
7f Stalls: Low GOING minus 0.28 sec per fur (GF) 5-15 (5-16)

2579[3] **Parrot Jungle (IRE)** *(72+)*(Fav)*(JLDunlop)* 2-8-11 KDarley(5) (lw: hld up: smooth hdwy to jn ldr 2f out: shkn up & led jst ins fnl f: pushed out)......— 1
2320[13] Maid For Baileys (IRE) **(74)***(72)* *(MJohnston)* 2-8-11 TWilliams(1) (lw: led tl jst ins fnl f: kpt on u.p nr fin)......hd 2
Flaming June (USA) *(60+)* *(HRACecil)* 2-8-11 AMcGlone(3) (leggy: unf: scope: chsd ldr: rdn 2f out: sn outpcd)......5 3
2608[6] Cerise (IRE) *(52)* *(CWCElsey)* 2-8-11 JFanning(2) (chsd ldrs: drvn along ½-wy: wknd 2f out)......3½ 4
2651[11] Sassetta (IRE) *(23)* *(NTinkler)* 2-8-11 KimTinkler(6) (bit bkwd: chsd ldrs: drvn along ½-wy: sn wknd)......13 5

10/11 PARROT JUNGLE (IRE), **13/8** Flaming June (USA), **11/2** Maid For Baileys (IRE) (7/2-6/1), **25/1** Cerise (IRE), **50/1** Sassetta (IRE), CSF £5.94 TOTE £1.70: £1.20 £1.60 (£2.80) OWNER Sultan Al Kabeer (ARUNDEL) BRED Lyonstown Stud, Swettenham Stud and Ron Con Ltd 5 Rn

1m 24.9 (2.90) SF: 37/37/25/17/-

T/Plpt: £432.40 (20.61 Tckts). T/Qdpt: £42.10 (3.15 Tckts). WG

2631-WOLVERHAMPTON (L-H)
Saturday August 5th (Standard)

WEATHER: sunny WIND: nil

2958

E.B.F. STARFISH MAIDEN STKS (2-Y.O) (Class D) £4,110.00 (£1,230.00: £590.00: £270.00)
7f (Fibresand) Stalls: Low GOING minus 0.25 sec per fur (FST) 7-00 (7-02)

1856[10] **Double Diamond (IRE) (76)***(73)* *(MJohnston)* 2-9-0 JWeaver(6) (swtg: mde all: r.o wl)......— 1
2633[3] Music Theatre *(64)*(Fav)*(SirMarkPrescott)* 2-9-0 GDuffield(2) (chsd ldrs: 4th st: rdn appr fnl f: one pce)......4 2
2380[3] Serif (USA) *(57)* *(JHMGosden)* 2-9-0 NCarlisle(9) (swtg: plld hrd: a.p: 2nd st: sn wknd)......3 3
1454[6] Capilano Princess **(68)***(49)* *(DHaydnJones)* 2-8-9 AMackay(11) (dwlt: racd wd: hdwy 4f out: 6th & rdn st: no hdwy fr over 1f out)......1¼ 4
1746[5] Pendley Rose *(45)* *(PWHarris)* 2-8-9 PaulEddery(3) (bit bkwd: chsd wnr tl 3rd & wknd ent st)......2 5
Threesocks *(35)* *(BSmart)* 2-8-9 RPerham(7) (w'like: bit bkwd: s.i.s: wl bhd tl kpt on fnl 2f: n.d)......4 6
1856[11] Classic Call (IRE) *(39)* *(MRStoute)* 2-9-0 KFallon(5) (swtg: mid div: pushed along over 2f out: 6th & btn st)......¾ 7
825[11] Mr Speaker (IRE) *(37)* *(CFWall)* 2-8-9 (5) LNewton(4) (in tch: drvn ½-wy: sn wknd)......¾ 8
1670[12] Stately *(31)* *(SirMarkPrescott)* 2-8-9 CNutter(12) (a rr)......nk 9
2625[3] Blenheim Terrace *(36)* *(CBBBooth)* 2-9-0 ACulhane(1) (prom: sn drvn along: wknd ½-wy)...hd 10
John's Law (IRE) *(MJHeaton-Ellis)* 2-9-0 DaleGibson(10) (w'like: str: lost tch 3f out: t.o)......20 11

2/1 Music Theatre, **4/1** Pendley Rose (7/1-9/2), **6/1** DOUBLE DIAMOND (IRE), **13/2** Serif (USA), **12/1** Stately, Classic Call (IRE) (op 8/1), **14/1** Capilano Princess, **16/1** Mr Speaker (IRE), **25/1** John's Law (IRE), **33/1** Blenheim Terrace, Threesocks, CSF £17.47 TOTE £4.90: £1.20 £1.70 £2.20 (£6.50) Trio £4.90 OWNER The 2nd Middleham Partnership (MIDDLEHAM) BRED Dene Investments N V 11 Rn 1m 31.4 (1.80 under 2y best) (7.40) SF: 32/23/16/8/4/-/-/-/-/-/-

2959 SEA BREEZE CLAIMING STKS (3-Y.O) (Class F) £2,519.00 (£694.00: £329.00)
1m 1f 79y (Fibresand) Stalls: Low GOING minus 0.25 sec per fur (FST) 7-30 (7-34)

*2626** **Red Phantom (IRE) (63)***(75) (SMellor)* 3-8-13 MWigham(4) (bhd: hdwy over 2f out: 6th st: styd on to ld wl ins fnl f) — 1
2406[4] Emphatic Candidate (IRE) **(63)***(69) (RAkehurst)* 3-8-11 TQuinn(2) (chsd ldr: led over 3f out: rdn & hdd appr fnl f: rallied to ld ins fnl f: hdd & no ex nr fin) 2½ 2
2747[4] Miss Zanzibar **(61)***(62) (RAFahey)* 3-8-6 ACulhane(9) (lw: chsd ldr fr ½-wy: 2nd st: rdn to ld bel dist: hdd & unable to qckn ins fnl f) ¾ 3
*2140** Equity's Darling (IRE) **(64)***(56)*(Fav)*(MBell)* 3-8-8 GDuffield(6) (chsd ldrs: 3rd st: grad wknd) 5 4
2588[4] Rock Scene (IRE) *(56) (RHollinshead)* 3-8-11 TIves(10) (prom: 4th st: kpt on one pce) 1¾ 5
2574[5] Sastrugi (IRE) *(44) (SPCWoods)* 3-8-1b NAdams(8) (sn outpcd: styd on fr 3f out: n.d) 1 6
2582[8] Miltak **(38)***(18) (PJMakin)* 3-8-0 NCarlisle(7) (prom tl drvn & wknd ½-wy: t.o) 15 7
591[14] All Honour *(15) (DWChapman)* 3-8-3 LCharnock(5) (bhd fr ½-wy: t.o) 3 8
2438[6] Freddie Baloo **(42)***(16) (RTPhillips)* 3-8-7 RPerham(11) (a bhd: t.o) 1¾ 9
2540[4] The Cape Doctor (IRE) **(60)***(6) (AGFoster)* 3-8-5b TSprake(1) (led 6f: 5th & btn st) 5 10
2493[7] Miss The Beat *(SMellor)* 3-7-11 (7) ADaly(3) (drvn & lost tch 5f out: t.o) 10 11

5/2 Equity's Darling (IRE), **7/2** Rock Scene (IRE) (op 6/1), **5/1** Emphatic Candidate (IRE), **6/1** Miss Zanzibar, **9/1** RED PHANTOM (IRE), **16/1** Sastrugi (IRE), Miltak, **25/1** The Cape Doctor (IRE), **33/1** Miss The Beat, Freddie Baloo, **50/1** All Honour, CSF £48.40 TOTE £7.60: £2.50 £2.20 £1.30 (£15.90) Trio £27.80 OWNER Mr Stan Mellor (SWINDON) BRED K. and Mrs CULLEN 11 Rn
2m 5.0 (9.00) SF: 40/34/27/21/21/9/-/-/-/-/-

2960 CHEMIQUE ADHESIVES MAIDEN H'CAP (0-70) (3-Y.O+) (Class E) £3,502.40 (£1,047.20: £501.60: £228.80)
1m 4f (Fibresand) Stalls: Low GOING minus 0.25 sec per fur (FST) 8-00 (8-02)

1784[4] **Chahaya Timor (IRE) (66)***(73) (PFICole)* 3-10-0 TQuinn(10) (lw: trckd ldrs gng wl: 2nd st: led on bit wl over 1f out: r.o) — 1
2503[6] Nautical Jewel **(55)***(58) (MDIUsher)* 3-9-3 MWigham(7) (b: hld up: hdwy 3f out: 4th st: chsd wnr appr fnl f: rdn & r.o one pce) 3 2
2760[2] Backhander (IRE) **(55)***(45)*(Fav)*(JARToller)* 3-9-3 JWeaver(3) (led tl rdn & hdd wl over 1f out: sn wknd) 10 3
2587[2] Diamond Market **(48)***(37)*(Fav)*(RHollinshead)* 3-8-10 TIves(4) (towards rr: drvn along 4f out: styd on appr fnl f: nvr nrr) nk 4
2630[7] Brooks Masquerade **(25)***(14) (NJHWalker)* 4-7-12 FNorton(2) (chsd ldrs: 3rd & rdn st: wknd appr fnl f) nk 5
1657[5] Joys First **(35)***(24) (HJCollingridge)* 4-8-8 JQuinn(6) (bit bkwd: hld up: effrt over 4f out: 6th & btn st) nk 6
1881[8] Hard Try **(54)***(40) (MJCamacho)* 3-9-2 LCharnock(8) (in tch: rdn 3f out: 5th & btn st) 2 7
2592[11] Crab 'n Lobster (IRE) **(30)** *(BPreece)* 5-7-10 (7)ow10 AEddery(9) (a in rr: t.o) 13 8
2494[5] Bold Charlie **(40)***(8) (SMellor)* 3-8-2 NAdams(1) (lw: bhd fr ½-wy: t.o) ½ 9
1509[13] Broughtons Bird (IRE) **(36)** *(WJMusson)* 4-8-9 KFallon(5) (swtg: bkwd: prom tl drppd rr 5f out: sn t.o) dist 10

4/1 Diamond Market, Backhander (IRE), **9/2** Hard Try, CHAHAYA TIMOR (IRE), **8/1** Joys First, Nautical Jewel, **16/1** Broughtons Bird (IRE), **20/1** Bold Charlie, **33/1** Crab 'n Lobster (IRE), Brooks Masquerade, CSF £36.01 CT £137.84 TOTE £5.20: £2.00 £2.00 £2.10 (£27.40) Trio £29.30 OWNER H.R.H. Sultan Ahmad Shah (WHATCOMBE) BRED J. R. Mitchell 10 Rn
2m 46.3 (15.30) SF: 31/16/3/-/-/-/-/-/-/-
WEIGHT FOR AGE 3yo-11lb

2961 SUN PUNTERS CLUB H'CAP (0-60) (3-Y.O+) (Class F) £2,519.00 (£694.00: £329.00)
1m 1f 79y (Fibresand) Stalls: Low GOING minus 0.25 sec per fur (FST) 8-30 (8-31)

2634[8] **Ayunli (58)***(65) (SCWilliams)* 4-9-12 GHind(8) (b.off hind: in tch: hdwy to ld over 3f out: clr over 1f out: pushed out) — 1
1830[9] Sparkling Roberta **(35)***(40) (MDIUsher)* 4-8-3 DHarrison(13) (a.p: 3rd st: rdn & r.o one pce) 1¼ 2
2814[6] Level Edge **(49)***(52) (MDHammond)* 4-9-3 GDuffield(1) (lw: a.p: 2nd & ev ch st: rdn & unable qckn) 1¼ 3

2557[7] Dia Georgy **(52)***(39) (RGuest)* 4-8-13 (7) CWebb(5) (hdwy over 2f out: 6th st: nrst fin)..............9 4
1630[5] Delgarth Lady **(27)***(14) (JLSpearing)* 4-7-9 NAdams(10) (in tch: rdn over 2f out: 5th st: r.o same pce)..............½ 5
2292[U] Studio Thirty **(48)***(34) (RHollinshead)* 3-8-1 (7) AEddery(11) (dwlt: bhd tl styd on fr over 2f out: n.d)..............s.h 6
1884[6] Ivan the Terrible (IRE) **(47)***(30)*(Fav)*(BEllison)* 7-9-1 TQuinn(2) (b: led over 3f: styd prom tl 4th & btn st)..............2 7
2770[5] Boundary Express **(47)***(16) (EJAlston)* 3-8-7v KFallon(4) (prom tl rdn & wknd over 2f out)........8 8
2391[6] Backstabber **(37)***(6) (MissSJWilton)* 5-8-5 JQuinn(9) (hld up: effrt 5f out: eased whn btn wl over 1f out)..............nk 9
2450[13] Coven Moon **(30)** *(DMorris)* 5-7-12 DaleGibson(7) (dwlt: a bhd)..............nk 10
2821[8] Brigadore Gold **(25)** *(FHLee)* 5-7-7b NCarlisle(12) (led 6f out: hdd over 3f out: sn wknd).........4 11
329[7] Knightrider **(46)** *(CDBroad)* 4-9-0 JWeaver(6) (bit bkwd: a bhd: t.o)..............dist 12
Master Showman (IRE) **(60)** *(HOliver)* 4-9-7 (7) FLynch(3) (bkwd: lost tch ½-wy: t.o)..............12 13

LONG HANDICAP Brigadore Gold 7-6

3/1 Ivan the Terrible (IRE), **6/1** Dia Georgy, **7/1** Backstabber, AYUNLI, **8/1** Sparkling Roberta, **10/1** Studio Thirty, **12/1** Boundary Express, **14/1** Level Edge, Coven Moon, **16/1** Delgarth Lady, Knightrider, **20/1** Master Showman (IRE), **33/1** Brigadore Gold, CSF £59.09 CT £706.88 TOTE £21.30: £3.80 £2.60 £4.60 (£58.70) Trio not won; £253.20 to Windsor 7/8/95 OWNER Mr I. A. Southcott (NEWMARKET) BRED I. A. Southcott 13 Rn 2m 5.7 (9.70) SF: 47/22/34/21/-/8/12/-/-/-
WEIGHT FOR AGE 3yo-8lb

2962 CANDY-FLOSS (S) STKS (2-Y.O) (Class G) £2,243.00 (£618.00: £293.00)
6f (Fibresand) Stalls: Low GOING minus 0.25 sec per fur (FST) 9-00 (9-04)

1352[5] **Ultra Barley** *(68) (PCHaslam)* 2-8-11 JWeaver(8) (mde all: pushed along 2f out: clr appr fnl f: comf)..............— 1
2601[2] Velvet Jones *(52)*(Fav)*(PFICole)* 2-8-11 TQuinn(13) (a.p: chsd wnr fr ½-wy: 2nd & ev ch st: outpcd)..............6 2
2839[4] Dhulikhel *(40) (DMarks)* 2-8-6 GDuffield(9) (a.p: 3rd & rdn st: sn wknd)..............2½ 3
2637[5] Bobsworthatcaspers **(48)***(36) (GLewis)* 2-8-11b PaulEddery(10) (chsd ldrs: rdn 2f out: 4th & btn st)..............3½ 4
Vital Evidence *(30) (DCO'Brien)* 2-8-3 (3) DRMcCabe(5) (b.hind: lt-f: s.i.s: sn outpcd & wl bhd: styd on fnl 2f: nrst fin)..............½ 5
2715[3] Our Tom's Boy **(59)***(35) (KTIvory)* 2-8-4b(7) CScally(2) (b: nrst fin)..............s.h 6
2075[7] Cottesloe Beach *(34) (KTIvory)* 2-8-11 MWigham(6) (b: nvr on terms)..............hd 7
1740[6] Monsieur Culsyth **(62)***(37) (JBerry)* 2-9-2 KFallon(11) (mid div: pushed along 4f out: 6th & btn st)..............1 8
Still Here (IRE) *(31) (MJHeaton-Ellis)* 2-8-11 DaleGibson(1) (w'like: bit bkwd: nvr trbld ldrs) .hd 9
*2591** Welsh Melody **(68)***(13) (KRBurke)* 2-8-11 TWilliams(4) (chsd ldrs: 5th & drvn st: sn btn: eased)..............7 10
2635[5] Colour Counsellor **(54)***(9) (KMcAuliffe)* 2-8-11b DHarrison(7) (outpcd)..............1½ 11
2198[11] Dish The Dosh *(PGMurphy)* 2-7-13 (7) RWaterfield(3) (a bhd: t.o)..............11 12

5/2 Velvet Jones, **9/2** Welsh Melody, **7/1** Bobsworthatcaspers, Colour Counsellor, **8/1** ULTRA BARLEY, **10/1** Monsieur Culsyth, **14/1** Our Tom's Boy, Dhulikhel, Still Here (IRE), **25/1** Cottesloe Beach, Vital Evidence, **33/1** Dish The Dosh, CSF £27.42 TOTE £9.30: £3.20 £2.10 £2.40 (£15.30) Trio £34.50 OWNER Pet Express Ltd T/A Nutrimix (MIDDLEHAM) BRED Benham Stud 12 Rn
1m 17.7 (6.50) SF: 26/10/-/-/-/-/-/-/-/-/-/-
No bid

2963 SAND CASTLE H'CAP (0-65) (3-Y.O+) (Class F) £2,519.00 (£694.00: £329.00)
7f (Fibresand) Stalls: Low GOING minus 0.25 sec per fur (FST) 9-30 (9-31)

2141[2] **Legatee (58)***(65)*(Fav)*(BJMeehan)* 4-9-8 BDoyle(8) (lw: mde all: clr over 1f out: edgd lft drvn out)..............— 1
*2587** Caddy's First **(59)***(63) (SMellor)* 3-9-3 MWigham(11) (chsd wnr: drvn & outpcd 2f out: 2nd st: rdn & edgd rt appr fnl f: r.o)..............1½ 2
521[13] Lilac Rain **(41)***(42) (JRArnold)* 3-7-13 JQuinn(6) (lw: wl bhd tl styd on fr over 2f out: r.o wl fnl f)..............1¼ 3
2497[3] Jersey Belle **(49)***(44) (PJMakin)* 3-8-7 GDuffield(12) (in tch: hdwy over 2f out: 3rd st: rdn & wknd fnl f)..............2½ 4
2797[8] My Gallery (IRE) **(64)***(50) (ABailey)* 4-9-11 (3) DWright(5) (lw: hld up in tch: 5th & drvn st: one pce)..............4 5
2112[5] Calling (USA) **(35)***(19) (WMBrisbourne)* 4-7-10 (3) AGarth(1) (dwlt: bhd: kpt on fr over 1f out: n.d)..............¾ 6
2631[4] Jon's Choice **(52)***(36) (BPreece)* 7-8-9 (7) AEddery(4) (in tch: drvn along ½-wy: 6th st: no imp)..............s.h 7

2539⁷ It's so Easy **(38)***(19)* *(APJames)* 4-8-2 FNorton(9) (nvr trbld ldrs) 1½ 8
1421¹¹ Peacefull Reply (USA) **(45)***(20)* *(FHLee)* 5-8-9b DaleGibson(10) (chsd ldrs: rdn over 2f out: 4th & btn st) 2½ 9
2497⁶ Fortunes Leap **(47)***(13)* *(MrsLAMurphy)* 3-8-5 ow1 JWilliams(7) (dwlt: a bhd) 3½ 10
2497⁴ Runs in the Family **(49)***(10)* *(PGMurphy)* 3-8-0b(7) RWaterfield(2) (prom to ½-wy: btn 2f out) 2½ 11
2491¹³ Tara Colleen (IRE) **(56)** *(CAHorgan)* 3-9-0 TWilliams(3) (b: sn t.o: p.u ins fnl f: dismntd).... P

2/1 LEGATEE (op 4/1), **4/1** Caddy's First, **7/1** Jersey Belle, My Gallery (IRE), **8/1** Jon's Choice, **12/1** Runs in the Family, **14/1** Peacefull Reply (USA), **16/1** Fortunes Leap, **20/1** Tara Colleen (IRE), **25/1** Lilac Rain, It's so Easy, Calling (USA), CSF £10.77 CT £138.37 TOTE £3.60: £1.40 £1.80 £4.50 (£8.40) Trio £313.10 OWNER Mr Alan Cunliffe (UPPER LAMBOURN) BRED Mrs J. E. Young 12 Rn
1m 32.4 (8.40) SF: 28/20/-/1/13/-/-/-/-/-/-/-
WEIGHT FOR AGE 3yo-6lb

T/Plpt: £100.50 (121.06 Tckts). T/Qdpt: £63.90 (1.4 Tckts). J

2522-LEICESTER (R-H)
Monday August 7th (Good to firm)

WEATHER: cloudy WIND: slt half across

2964 E.B.F. MENPHYS MEDIAN AUCTION MAIDEN STKS (2-Y.O F) (Class E) £3,502.40 (£1,047.20: £501.60: £228.80)

7f 9y Stalls: Low GOING minus 0.16 sec per fur (GF) 6-00 (6-00)

Baltic Dream (USA) *(77)* *(KRBurke)* 2-8-11 MFenton(4) (scope: bit bkwd: hld up: hdwy 2f out: hrd rdn to ld cl home) ....— 1
1968⁴ Mountain Valley **(79)***(77)* *(PFICole)* 2-8-11 TQuinn(2) (a.p: led over 1f out: hrd rdn & ct post) ....s.h 2
2705⁶ Shernadeed (FR) *(66)* *(MJohnston)* 2-8-11 WRSwinburn(6) (bit bkwd: led tl hdd over 1f out: sn btn) 5 3
2083³ Frezeliere *(61)*(Fav)*(JLDunlop)* 2-8-11 WCarson(8) (lw: prom: drvn & effrt 2f out: one pce) 2 4
2666³ Scenicris (IRE) *(60)* *(RHollinshead)* 2-8-11 TIves(7) (chsd ldrs: rdn over 2f out: sn outpcd) ...½ 5
Miss Swing King (IRE) *(55)* *(RHannon)* 2-8-12 ow1 RHughes(9) (w'like: leggy: s.s: hdwy ½-wy: wknd over 1f out) 2 6
2351¹³ Put Off *(52)* *(BWHills)* 2-8-11 AMcGlone(1) (a in rr) 1½ 7
2791⁸ Careful (IRE) *(50)* *(BWHills)* 2-8-11 RStreet(5) (outpcd: a bhd) 1 8
Somer Solo *(18)* *(PMitchell)* 2-8-11 GDuffield(3) (lt-f: unf: bkwd: s.s: a bhd: t.o) 14 9

8/11 Frezeliere, **9/2** Shernadeed (FR) (3/1-5/1), **8/1** Mountain Valley (op 5/1), **10/1** BALTIC DREAM (USA) (25/1-8/1), **12/1** Careful (IRE) (op 6/1), **14/1** Miss Swing King (IRE), **20/1** Scenicris (IRE), **25/1** Put Off, **33/1** Somer Solo, CSF £81.04 TOTE £17.10: £2.70 £2.60 £1.80 (£45.50) Trio £58.60 OWNER Mr W. J. P. Jackson (WANTAGE) BRED Margaux Stud, L. Collins, M. M. Della-Penna, et. a
9 Rn 1m 27.3 (4.80) SF: 25/25/14/9/8/3/-/-/-

2965 LANGHAM NURSERY (S) H'CAP (2-Y.O) (Class G) £2,534.20 (£701.20: £334.60)

5f 218y Stalls: Low GOING minus 0.16 sec per fur (GF) 6-30 (6-31)

2548⁵ **Time Clash (IRE) (58)***(58)* *(BPalling)* 2-9-2 TSprake(4) (a.p: led over 1f out: sn clr: easily)...— 1
2800⁶ L A Touch **(50)***(42)* *(CADwyer)* 2-8-5 (3) SDrowne(9) (hld up: swtchd rt & effrt over 1f out: nt pce of wnr) 3 2
2656³ Pinocchio Boy (IRE) **(56)***(41)* *(BJMeehan)* 2-9-0 MTebbutt(10) (chsd ldrs: rdn over 1f out: r.o one pce) 2½ 3
2656² Ivory's Grab Hire **(63)***(43)* *(KTIvory)* 2-9-0 (7) CScally(2) (b: dwlt: bhd tl styd on appr fnl f) 2 4
2644⁴ Copper Bright **(43)***(22)*(Fav)*(PCHaslam)* 2-8-1v DaleGibson(3) (lw: led tl hdd over 1f out: sn rdn & outpcd) ....nk 5
2591⁴ Euskara **(45)***(22)* *(MDIUsher)* 2-8-3b RStreet(7) (b: prom: rdn & wknd over 2f out) ....¾ 6
2800⁵ Dancing Lottie (IRE) **(46)***(10)* *(PAKelleway)* 2-8-1 (3) JTate(5) (plld hrd: hld up in rr: rdn 2f out: sn lost tch) 5 7
2869⁴ Cawdor Lady **(47)** *(TJEtherington)* 2-8-5b GDuffield(8) (lw: spd over 3f: sn wknd: t.o) 7 8
2765⁹ Don't Tell Vicki **(56)** *(JSMoore)* 2-8-9 (5) DGriffiths(6) (Withdrawn not under Starters' orders: broke out of stalls) .... W

4/1 Copper Bright (7/1-9/2), **9/2** Don't Tell Vicki, **11/2** Ivory's Grab Hire, Dancing Lottie (IRE), **6/1** TIME CLASH (IRE), **10/1** Cawdor Lady (7/1-11/1), **11/1** Pinocchio Boy (IRE), Euskara, **16/1** L A Touch, CSF £56.98 CT £543.94 TOTE £6.20: £1.60 £3.70 £2.50 (£31.00) Trio £28.40 OWNER Mrs R. M. Williams (COWBRIDGE) BRED Terry Minahan 8 Rn 1m 15.3 (5.30) SF: 13/-/-/-/-/-/-/-
No bid

2966

INSTITUTE OF INSURANCE BROKERS H'CAP (0-70) (3-Y.O) (Class E) £3,652.00 (£1,012.00: £484.00)
1m 8y Stalls: Low GOING minus 0.16 sec per fur (GF) 7-00 (7-00)

2698* **Anonym (IRE) (68)**_(76)_(Fav)_(JLDunlop)_ 3-9-6 WCarson(2) (plld hrd: hld up: effrt & rdn 2f out: led ins fnl f: sn clr) — 1
2623[4] Chalky Dancer **(42)**_(48) (HJCollingridge)_ 3-7-8 JQuinn(3) (led tl rdn & hdd ins fnl f: sn outpcd) 1¼ 2
2574[3] Coneygree **(43)**_(37) (JWharton)_ 3-7-2 (7)ow2 CAdamson(4) (swtg: lw: s.i.s: chsd wnr 5f out tl over 2f out: wknd appr fnl f) 5 3

LONG HANDICAP Coneygree 7-2

2/5 ANONYM (IRE), **5/2** Chalky Dancer, **9/1** Coneygree, CSF £1.75 TOTE £1.30 (£1.30) OWNER Mr J. L. Dunlop (ARUNDEL) BRED T. G. Mooney 3 Rn 1m 41.7 (6.70) SF: 21/-/-

2967

LUMBERS GRANDE CLASSIQUE H'CAP (0-80) (3-Y.O+) (Class D) £3,833.70 (£1,143.60: £545.80: £246.90)
1m 1f 218y Stalls: Low GOING minus 0.43 sec per fur (F) 7-30 (7-30)

2903[3] **Persian Elite (IRE) (74)**_(86) (PFICole)_ 4-9-10b TQuinn(1) (mde all: sn wl clr: rdn over 2f out: hld on wl) — 1
2274[9] Adolescence (IRE) **(78)**_(86) (KMcAuliffe)_ 5-9-11 (3) DRMcCabe(3) (s.i.s: hld up & bhd: 5th st: gd hdwy bel dist: nt rch wnr) 2½ 2
2525[9] Eben Al Habeeb (IRE) **(72)**_(78) (MajorWRHern)_ 4-9-8 WCarson(4) (chsd wnr: 2nd st: hrd drvn 2f out: kpt on) 1¼ 3
2490[5] Haroldon (IRE) **(73)**_(79) (BPalling)_ 6-9-9 TSprake(5) (b: swtg: hld up: 4th st: hdwy to chse wnr over 3f out: rdn & no ex appr fnl f) s.h 4
2752[2] Zacaroon **(67)**_(71)_(Fav)_(LordHuntingdon)_ 4-8-10 (7) AimeeCook(2) (lw: chsd ldrs: 3rd st: effrt 2f out: nvr able to chal) 1¼ 5

11/4 Zacaroon, **3/1** PERSIAN ELITE (IRE), **4/1** Haroldon (IRE), Adolescence (IRE), **5/1** Eben Al Habeeb (IRE), CSF £13.22 TOTE £3.10: £1.40 £2.30 (£9.80) OWNER Elite Racing Club (WHATCOMBE) BRED Mrs M. E. Farrell 5 Rn 2m 7.7 (5.00) SF: 33/33/25/26/18

2968

TRAVELSPHERE CLAIMING STKS (3-Y.O) (Class F) £3,174.20 (£881.20: £422.60) **7f 9y** Stalls: Low GOING minus 0.16 sec per fur (GF) 8-00 (8-01)

2776* **Delight of Dawn (72)**_(76) (KTIvory)_ 3-8-12 (7) CScally(1) (b: hld up: hdwy to ld bel dist: rdn & hld on wl) — 1
2684[5] Mediate (IRE) **(52)**_(72) (RHannon)_ 3-9-1 RHughes(9) (bhd: swtchd rt & hdwy wl over 1f out: str run fnl f: jst failed) hd 2
2776[3] By The Bay **(66)**_(66) (BWHills)_ 3-8-13 DHolland(4) (a.p: ev ch over 1f out: kpt on u.p fnl f) 1½ 3
2836[4] Non Dimenticar Me (IRE) **(72)**_(66)_(Fav)_(SirMarkPrescott)_ 3-9-5 GDuffield(8) (lw: chsd ldrs: rdn along over 2f out: sn ev ch: one pce appr fnl f) 3 4
2540[9] L'Eglise Belle **(41)**_(44) (MrsALMKing)_ 3-8-1 (3) AGarth(5) (hld up: hdwy over 2f out: wknd appr fnl f) 3 5
2518[3] Thwaab **(46)**_(57) (FWatson)_ 3-9-4 SMaloney(2) (led after 1f tl bel dist: rdn & drifted rt fnl f: sn btn) ½ 6
2776[4] Okay Baby (IRE) **(51)**_(37) (MHTompkins)_ 3-8-10 PRobinson(7) (lw: racd far side: prom tl rdn & wknd 2f out) 5 7
2776[9] Sapphire Son (IRE) **(57)**_(13) (CNWilliams)_ 3-8-12v(3) DRMcCabe(6) (led 1f: wknd over 2f out: eased whn btn: t.o) 13 8
2357[3] Full Gloss **(48)** _(MrsMReveley)_ 3-8-6 JQuinn(10) (a in rr) 1¾ 9
Ballysheila _(GFHCharles-Jones)_ 3-8-0 (7) RStudholme(3) (neat: unf: bkwd: s.s: rdn & wl bhd ½-wy: t.o) 20 10

5/2 Non Dimenticar Me (IRE), **4/1** DELIGHT OF DAWN, **5/1** By The Bay (op 3/1), **8/1** Okay Baby (IRE), Thwaab, **10/1** Mediate (IRE), **12/1** Full Gloss, **14/1** Sapphire Son (IRE), **50/1** L'Eglise Belle, Ballysheila, CSF £38.35 TOTE £7.50: £2.20 £3.50 £1.90 (£19.00) Trio £41.60 OWNER Mr K. T. Ivory (RADLETT) BRED John Hayter 10 Rn 1m 27.8 (5.30) SF: 26/22/16/16/-/7/-/-/-/-
By The Bay clmd C.Elsey £8,000

2969

EVANS OF LEICESTER MERCEDES-BENZ LIMITED STKS (0-65) (3-Y.O) (Class F) £2,796.20 (£773.20: £368.60)
1m 3f 183y Stalls: Low GOING minus 0.43 sec per fur (F) 8-30 (8-31)

2341[2] **Nickitoto (63)**_(68)_(Fav)_(JLDunlop)_ 3-8-9 WCarson(1) (s.i.s: hld up & bhd: 5th st: effrt 3f out: sn rdn: styd on strly to ld wl ins fnl f) — 1

2658* Paradise Waters **(60)***(69)*(Fav)*(RFJohnsonHoughton)* 3-8-11 TQuinn(4) (chsd ldr: 2nd st: led over 3f out tl wl ins fnl f) ..... ¾ **2**
*2604*4 Harry Welsh (IRE) **(65)***(70) (KMcAuliffe)* 3-9-2 DHarrison(6) (chsd ldrs: 3rd st: rdn over 2f out: kpt on one pce) 3 **3**
23397 Hatta Breeze **(65)***(44) (MAJarvis)* 3-8-9b PRobinson(5) (lw: led tl hdd over 3f out: rdn & wknd fnl 2f: eased: t.o) 14 **4**
*2636** Canton Venture **(59)***(40) (SPCWoods)* 3-9-2 WWoods(3) (hld up: 4th st: c wd to r alone 3f out: sn rdn & wl bhd: t.o) 8 **5**
*2520*2 Northern Law **(65)** *(BWHills)* 3-9-0 DHolland(2) (Withdrawn not under Starters' orders: jockey unwell) ..... **W**

9/4 NICKITOTO, Paradise Waters, **4/1** Hatta Breeze, **6/1** Harry Welsh (IRE), **13/2** Canton Venture, **9/1** Northern Law, CSF £7.16 TOTE £2.80: £1.50 £1.40 (£2.60) OWNER Hesmonds Stud (ARUNDEL) BRED Hesmonds Stud Ltd 5 Rn 2m 32.0 (3.20) SF: 38/39/40/14/10/-

T/Plpt: £99.40 (109.2 Tckts). T/Qdpt: £4.80 (14.9 Tckts). IM

2782-THIRSK (L-H)
Monday August 7th (Good to firm)
WEATHER: overcast WIND: mod half against

2970 E.B.F. BOWNCROFT MEDIAN AUCTION MAIDEN STKS (2-Y.O) (Class E) £3,454.50 (£1,029.00: £490.00: £220.50)
5f Stalls: High GOING minus 0.40 sec per fur (F) 6-15 (6-16)

26602 **Cross The Border** *(80+)*(Fav)*(RHannon)* 2-9-0 JCarroll(3) (lw: trckd ldrs: led 2f out: shkn up & r.o fnl f) ..... — **1**
Baroness Blixen *(69) (DJGMurraySmith)* 2-8-9 JWeaver(1) (unf: lw: outpcd early: hdwy ½-wy: chsd wnr fnl f: r.o) 2 **2**
20634 La Finale *(57) (MHEasterby)* 2-8-9 KFallon(2) (dwlt: bhd tl r.o fnl f) 3½ **3**
27827 Good To Talk *(58?) (MHEasterby)* 2-9-0 MBirch(5) (cl up 3f: sn wknd) 1¼ **4**
278210 Redbrook Lady *(50?) (SGNorton)* 2-8-9 JFortune(4) (led 3f: sn rdn & btn) 1 **5**

1/3 CROSS THE BORDER, **4/1** Baroness Blixen (3/1-6/1), **10/1** La Finale, **33/1** Good To Talk, **50/1** Redbrook Lady, CSF £2.05 TOTE £1.30: £1.30 £1.60 (£2.00) OWNER Mr P. D. Savill (MARLBOROUGH) BRED Brook Stud Ltd 5 Rn 59.4 secs (2.20) SF: 26/15/3/4/-

2971 TATTERSALLS MAIDEN AUCTION STKS (2-Y.O) (Class E) £3,388.00 (£1,012.00: £484.00: £220.00)
7f Stalls: Low GOING minus 0.32 sec per fur (GF) 6-45 (6-47)

25483 **Rock Sharp** *(78)*(Fav)*(RHannon)* 2-8-5 PaulEddery(7) (lw: unruly s: cl up: rdn to ld cl home) ..... — **1**
25263 Rostaq *(78)*(Fav)*(DJGMurraySmith)* 2-8-6 JWeaver(4) (lw: led tl ct cl home) ..... nk **2**
27567 La Fandango (IRE) *(66) (MWEasterby)* 2-7-13 LCharnock(1) (chsd ldrs: swtchd rt ent fnl f: nt qckn) 2½ **3**
26085 Principal Boy (IRE) *(71) (TJEtherington)* 2-8-6 JLowe(5) (swtchd rt & effrt wl over 1f out: styd on: nt pce to chal) ..... ¾ **4**
26512 Yuppy Girl (IRE) *(59) (CaptJWilson)* 2-7-11 JMarshall(8) (b.off hind: bhd: hit rails appr st: styd on fnl 2f) 1½ **5**
21614 Danico *(63) (SCWilliams)* 2-8-2 JCarroll(3) (in tch: drvn along appr st: one pce after) ..... nk **6**
28206 Phantom Haze *(62) (MissSEHall)* 2-8-3 NConnorton(9) (bhd: effrt ent st: bmpd wl over 1f out: sn wknd) ..... ¾ **7**
252617 Onefourseven *(59) (SRBowring)* 2-8-0b(5)ow3 CTeague(2) (lw: in tch tl rdn ent st: no imp) ..... ¾ **8**
10414 Domoor *(66) (MJohnston)* 2-8-10 TWilliams(6) (chsd ldrs: rdn over 2f out: wknd over 1f out) ..... ¾ **9**
Goldmart (IRE) *(2) (TJEtherington)* 2-8-3 JFanning(10) (w'like: bkwd: dwlt: hung lft fnl 3f: eased) 25 **10**

5/2 ROCK SHARP, Rostaq (7/4-11/4), **7/2** Danico, **7/1** Yuppy Girl (IRE) (6/1-9/1), **14/1** Principal Boy (IRE), Phantom Haze, **16/1** Domoor, **33/1** La Fandango (IRE), Goldmart (IRE), **40/1** Onefourseven, CSF £8.98 TOTE £3.50: £1.30 £1.40 £9.10 (£3.10) Trio £105.20 OWNER Noodles Racing (MARLBOROUGH) BRED R. M. Whitaker 10 Rn 1m 28.0 (5.30) SF: 1/1/-/-/-/-/-/-/-/-

2972 WEST YORKSHIRE (S) H'CAP (0-60) (3-Y.O+) (Class F) £3,304.10 (£917.60: £440.30) 1m Stalls: Low GOING minus 0.32 sec per fur (GF) 7-15 (7-18)

26647 **Fort Vally (34)***(45) (BWMurray)* 5-8-6v(5) GParkin(14) (bhd: hdwy u.p over 2f out: styd on to ld cl home: edgd lft) ..... — **1**

2220 12 Golden Fish **(48)***(59) (JLEyre)* 3-9-4 RLappin(9) (b.off fore: a.p: styd on to ld wl ins fnl f: no ex & hdd towards fin)....hd **2**
2377 7 Genesis Four **(33)***(44) (SRBowring)* 5-8-10b SWebster(15) (lw: hdwy over 2f out: styd on wl towards fin)....hd **3**
2755 4 Canny Lad **(32)***(42) (MPBielby)* 5-8-9v KFallon(2) (led tl ct wl ins fnl f)....hd **4**
2630 12 Hunza Story **(35)***(45) (NPLittmoden)* 3-8-0 (5) CTeague(3) (in tch: hdwy 3f out: ev ch over 1f out: nt qckn)....hd **5**
2832 7 At the Savoy (IRE) **(43)***(53) (TDBarron)* 4-9-6b JFortune(8) (lw: hdwy u.p over 2f out: nrst fin)....s.h **6**
2733 6 Resolute Bay **(42)***(50) (RMWhitaker)* 9-9-5v ACulhane(18) (lw: bhd: hdwy ent st: nvr able to chal)....1¼ **7**
2784 7 Lord Vivienne (IRE) **(42)***(46) (BSRothwell)* 6-9-5 JMarshall(13) (prom: hung lft fnl 3f: no imp)....1¾ **8**
2873 3 Samana Cay **(43)***(46) (DNicholls)* 3-8-13b AlexGreaves(12) (nvr btr than mid div)....½ **9**
1843 11 My Godson **(40)***(41) (FJO'Mahony)* 5-9-3b SDWilliams(4) (b.hind: chsd ldrs tl wknd over 2f out)....1¼ **10**
2824 6 Bex Boy (IRE) **(29)***(30) (MWEasterby)* 4-8-6b LCharnock(1) (s.i.s: n.d)....s.h **11**
2927 4 Summer Villa **(42)***(39)*(Fav)*(PCHaslam)* 3-8-12 JWeaver(17) (hmpd appr st: sn bhd)....1¾ **12**
1966 9 Leave it to Lib **(49)***(41) (PCalver)* 8-9-12 MBirch(7) (lw: chsd ldrs 6f)....2½ **13**
2784 6 Pakol (IRE) **(43)***(29) (MrsASwinbank)* 6-9-6 NConnorton(5) (lw: chsd ldrs tl wknd fnl 2f)....3 **14**
2832 14 Henry Will **(27)***(12) (WLBarker)* 11-8-1 (3) DarrenMoffatt(10) (lw: a rr div)....¾ **15**
2624 10 Monkey Face **(37)***(21) (JHetherton)* 4-9-0 PaulEddery(11) (prom 5f: sn wknd)....s.h **16**
2927 3 Commander Glen (IRE) **(49)***(32)*(Fav)*(MartynMeade)* 3-9-5b 5x VSlattery(16) (lw: a bhd)....½ **17**
2784 9 Passion Sunday **(41)***(17) (LRLloyd-James)* 4-8-13 (5) LNewton(6) (b.hind: lost pl appr st: n.d after)....3½ **18**

5/1 Commander Glen (IRE), Summer Villa, **8/1** Leave it to Lib (6/1-10/1), **9/1** Resolute Bay, **10/1** At the Savoy (IRE), **11/1** Lord Vivienne (IRE), **12/1** Canny Lad, **14/1** FORT VALLY, Pakol (IRE), Bex Boy (IRE), **16/1** Golden Fish, Samana Cay, Monkey Face, **20/1** Genesis Four, My Godson, **33/1** Passion Sunday, Hunza Story, **50/1** Henry Will, CSF £210.45 CT £4,044.16 TOTE £21.00: £4.60 £4.30 £6.70 £2.70 (£138.20) Trio £570.50 OWNER Mrs M. Lingwood (MALTON) BRED Norton Grove Stud Ltd 18 Rn 1m 39.7 (4.10) SF: 27/34/26/24/20/35/32/28/21/23/12/14/23/11/-/3/7/-

WEIGHT FOR AGE 3yo-7lb

No bid

STEWARDS' ENQUIRY Parkin susp. 18/8/95 (careless riding).

2973 ASENBY H'CAP (0-80) (3-Y.O) (Class D) £3,877.50 (£1,155.00: £550.00: £247.50)

5f Stalls: High GOING minus 0.40 sec per fur (F) 7-45 (7-46)

2311 3 **Brecongill Lad (74)***(84) (MissSEHall)* 3-9-7b NConnorton(2) (chsd ldrs: hung rt: led 2f out: styd on u.p)....— **1**
2659 5 Midnight Break **(64)***(68) (PTWalwyn)* 3-8-11 PaulEddery(6) (lw: chsd ldrs: swtchd 2f out: kpt on wl fnl f)....1¾ **2**
1876 6 Hannah's Usher **(68)***(64) (PCHaslam)* 3-9-1 JWeaver(3) (dwlt: hdwy ½-wy: hmpd wl over 1f out: r.o one pce)....2½ **3**
2758 9 High Ranking **(61)***(45) (MHEasterby)* 3-8-8 MBirch(1) (disp ld 3f: sn rdn & one pce)....4 **4**
2837 2 Able Sheriff **(46)***(24)*(Fav)*(MWEasterby)* 3-7-0b(7) PFessey(4) (lw: disp ld 3f: hung lft: sn btn)1¾ **5**
Question Ali **(65)***(33) (JBerry)* 3-8-12 JCarroll(5) (cl up 3f: hmpd, swtchd & sn btn)....3 **6**

9/4 Able Sheriff, **5/2** Midnight Break, **7/2** BRECONGILL LAD, **9/2** Hannah's Usher, **10/1** Question Ali, **20/1** High Ranking, CSF £12.10 TOTE £4.60: £2.20 £1.80 (£5.20) OWNER Three Horse Shoes Partnership (MIDDLEHAM) BRED Miss S. E. Hall 6 Rn 58.8 secs (1.60) SF: 42/26/22/3/-/-

STEWARDS' ENQUIRY Connorton susp. 18-19/8/95 (careless riding).

2974 CHEQUE BOOK H'CAP (0-80) (3-Y.O) (Class D) £4,425.00 (£1,320.00: £630.00: £285.00)

1m Stalls: Low GOING minus 0.32 sec per fur (GF) 8-15 (8-16)

2864* **Concer Un (66)***(76)*(Fav)*(SCWilliams)* 3-8-13 5x KFallon(1) (lw: cl up: led 2½f out: pushed clr: comf)....— **1**
2760* Dance King **(68)***(75) (DNicholls)* 3-9-1 AlexGreaves(7) (led tl hdd 2½f out: one pce)....1¾ **2**
2733* Tinklers Folly **(47)***(53) (DenysSmith)* 3-7-8 LCharnock(2) (in tch: rdn 3f out: styd on: nt pce to chal)....½ **3**
2188 4 So Amazing **(60)***(65) (MissSEHall)* 3-8-7 JWeaver(4) (b: dwlt: hdwy 3f out: hung lft fnl 2f: one pce fnl f)....hd **4**
2788 3 Striffolino **(74)***(73) (TDBarron)* 3-9-7 JFortune(5) (lw: chsd ldrs tl rdn & wknd fnl 2f)....3 **5**
*72** Biya (IRE) **(63)***(48) (MJohnston)* 3-8-10 TWilliams(3) (s.i.s: sn rcvrd: rdn ent st: sn outpcd)....7 **6**
2679 5 Grey Again **(58)***(28) (SRBowring)* 3-8-0b(5)ow3 CTeague(6) (rn wd ent st: n.d)....6 **7**

6/4 CONCER UN (op 3/1), **4/1** Striffolino (7/2-9/1), **9/2** Biya (IRE), **6/1** So Amazing, **7/1** Dance King, Tinklers Folly, **10/1** Grey Again, CSF £13.19 TOTE £3.20: £1.80 £3.20 (£12.60) OWNER Miss L. J. Ward (NEWMARKET) BRED Lloyd Bros 7 Rn 1m 38.8 (3.20) SF: 38/37/15/27/35/10/-

2975 YORKSHIRE PUDDING CONDITIONS STKS (3-Y.O) (Class D) £6,420.00
1m 4f 8-30 (8-30)

2525[4] **Snowy Petrel (IRE) (77)** *(JLDunlop)* 3-9-0 JWeaver(1) (walked over) ....— 1

OWNER Sir Thomas Pilkington (ARUNDEL) BRED Sir Thomas Pilkington

T/Plpt: £107.20 (98.08 Tckts). T/Qdpt: Not won; £50.40 to Bath 8/8/95 AA

2789-WINDSOR (Fig. 8)
Monday August 7th (Good to firm)
WEATHER: overcast WIND: slt half against

2976 STRATFIELDSAYE (S) STKS (3-Y.O+) (Class G) £2,451.00 (£686.00: £333.00)
1m 3f 135y Stalls: Low GOING minus 0.69 sec per fur (HD) 2-00 (2-01)

2359[4] **Shabanaz (65)***(53+)*(Fav)*(WRMuir)* 10-9-13 CRutter(7) (6th st: hdwy 4f out: led over 2f out: rdn out) ....— 1
2486[6] Excelled (IRE) *(43) (CJDrewe)* 6-9-5 RCochrane(3) (lw: 4th st: chsd wnr fnl 2f: r.o) 1¾ 2
2466* Today Tonite **(40)***(44) (JPearce)* 3-8-11 GBardwell(1) (9th st: hdwy 3f out: one pce fnl 2f)....1½ 3
2486[3] Bronze Runner **(40)***(48) (SMellor)* 11-9-6b(7) ADaly(9) (7th st: rdn & hdwy 3f out: one pce fnl 2f)................¾ 4
2532[9] Endless Fantasy **(45)***(39) (CACyzer)* 3-8-8 DBiggs(6) (lw: 5th st: rdn & lost pl 3f out: rallied & r.o fnl f) ....hd 5
2946[9] Trina **(35)***(38) (DLWilliams)* 4-9-0 (5) DGriffiths(10) (2nd st: ev ch over 2f out: wknd over 1f out) 1¼ 6
2450[14] Jehol **(50)***(38) (NMBabbage)* 9-9-3 (7) LSuthern(2) (b: led tl wknd over 2f out)................3½ 7
2806[4] The Oil Baron **(15)***(38) (RPCHoad)* 9-9-10 PRobinson(11) (wl bhd tl rdn & hdwy 2f out: nvr nr to chal) ....hd 8
2806[3] Royal Rabbit **(52)***(39) (GLMoore)* 3-9-2 SWhitworth(5) (3rd st: wknd over 2f out)................1¼ 9
2334[6] Tocco Jewel **(15)***(23) (MJRyan)* 5-9-0 (5) DGibbs(8) (8th st: a bhd)................6 10
2478[P] High Typha **(47)** *(MRChannon)* 4-9-5 RHughes(4) (hmpd bnd 6f out: bhd fnl 3f: eased 2f out: t.o) 30 11

1/2 SHABANAZ, **6/1** Today Tonite, **10/1** Bronze Runner (6/1-11/1), High Typha (6/1-12/1), **14/1** Trina, Royal Rabbit (op 8/1), **20/1** Excelled (IRE), Endless Fantasy, **25/1** Jehol, **50/1** Tocco Jewel, The Oil Baron, CSF £14.32 TOTE £1.70: £1.20 £4.10 £1.80 (£17.30) Trio £43.20 OWNER Fayzad Thoroughbred Ltd (LAMBOURN) BRED The Overbury Stud 11 Rn
2m 29.2 (3.20) SF: 35/25/15/30/10/20/20/20/10/5/-
WEIGHT FOR AGE 3yo-11lb
No bid

2977 SEDGWICK NOBLE LOWNDES MAIDEN STKS (3-Y.O+) (Class D)
£4,396.50 (£1,332.00: £651.00: £310.50)
1m 67y Stalls: Low GOING minus 0.69 sec per fur (HD) 2-30 (2-32)

1927[2] **Mackook (USA) (87)***(86)*(Fav)*(MRStoute)* 3-9-0 WRSwinburn(5) (mde all: rdn 2f out: r.o wl) ....— 1
Clan Ben (IRE) *(85) (HRACecil)* 3-9-0 WRyan(3) (str: scope: 6th st: hdwy 4f out: rdn over 2f out: r.o)................½ 2
2553[10] Golden Pound (USA) *(78) (EALDunlop)* 3-8-11 (3) JTate(1) (lw: 4th st: rdn 2f out: one pce fnl f)................3½ 3
Wild Palm *(74) (WAO'Gorman)* 3-9-0 EmmaO'Gorman(2) (w'like: scope: lw: 7th st: hdwy 3f out: one pce fnl 2f)................2½ 4
2653[4] Special Beat *(63) (PFICole)* 3-8-9 TQuinn(10) (lw: 3rd st: wknd 2f out) 3 5
Our Little Lady *(61) (JEBanks)* 3-8-9 JQuinn(4) (leggy: unf: bit bkwd: rdn over 2f out: nvr nr to chal) 1 6
Sweet Allegiance *(55) (JCPoulton)* 5-9-2 AMorris(12) (s.i.s: 5th st: wknd 2f out)................3 7
2708[8] Arecibo (FR) *(45) (GLMoore)* 3-9-0 SWhitworth(7) (swtg: a bhd)................8 8
Dunloe (IRE) *(39) (GWragg)* 3-8-9 FNorton(9) (leggy: bit bkwd: dwlt: 8th st: bhd fnl 2f)..........½ 9
2449[5] Woodlands Energy *(35) (PAPritchard)* 4-9-2 NAdams(8) (s.s: a bhd)................1¾ 10
2949[9] Arabian Flight *(37) (TTClement)* 3-9-0 AMackay(11) (b: 2nd st: wknd over 2f out: eased whn btn fnl f) 1½ 11

4/9 MACKOOK (USA) (op 4/6), **7/2** Clan Ben (IRE) (5/2-4/1), **12/1** Golden Pound (USA), **14/1** Special Beat (10/1-16/1), **16/1** Dunloe (IRE), **33/1** Wild Palm, **50/1** Our Little Lady, **66/1** Sweet Allegiance, Arecibo (FR), **100/1** Woodlands Energy, Arabian Flight, CSF £2.73 TOTE £1.50: £1.10 £1.30 £2.30 (£1.60) Trio £5.20 OWNER Maktoum Al Maktoum (NEWMARKET) BRED Cormal Investments Inc. 11 Rn 1m 44.3 (2.70) SF: 17/16/9/5/-/-/-/-/-/-/-
WEIGHT FOR AGE 3yo-7lb

2978 SMS CONDITIONS STKS (2-Y.O) (Class C) £6,334.00 (£2,356.00: £1,140.50: £477.50: £201.25: £90.75)
5f 217y Stalls: Low GOING minus 0.49 sec per fur (F) 3-00 (3-02)

2615³ **Red Nymph** *(83+) (WJarvis)* 2-8-5 BThomson(1) (lw: chsd ldr: led 3f out: edgd lft fnl f: rdn out) — **1**
2726a⁷ High Priority (IRE) **(98)***(73) (MRChannon)* 2-9-0 RHughes(2) (swtg: reard s: hdd 3f out: rdn 2f out: unable qckn) 7 **2**
2135* Rushcutter Bay *(71) (TTClement)* 2-8-12 DGibbs(9) (lw: a.p: rdn 3f out: edgd rt wl over 1f out: one pce) nk **3**
2432* Depreciate **(88)***(75)*(Fav)*(CJames)* 2-9-6 RCochrane(7) (lw: led 3f: one pce fnl 2f) 1½ **4**
2779⁸ Bedside Mail **(85)***(68) (JMPEustace)* 2-9-2 MTebbutt(6) (rdn & no hdwy fnl 2f) 1 **5**
2615⁴ Shock-A-Lot (IRE) *(43) (GLewis)* 2-8-10 PaulEddery(4) (lw: wl bhd tl styd on fnl 2f) 7 **6**
2765⁶ Jaleel **(80)***(34) (RHannon)* 2-8-12 MRoberts(5) (prom 4f) 4 **7**
Prime Secret *(BJMeehan)* 2-8-10 BDoyle(8) (unf: s.s: a wl bhd: t.o) 30 **8**

5/2 Depreciate, **10/3** RED NYMPH (9/2-3/1), **5/1** High Priority (IRE) (op 11/4), **7/1** Bedside Mail (op 4/1), **8/1** Jaleel, **9/1** Rushcutter Bay, **14/1** Prime Secret (6/1-16/1), **25/1** Shock-A-Lot (IRE), CSF £18.42 TOTE £3.40: £1.40 £1.70 £1.90 (£5.70) Trio £63.50 OWNER The Who Needs Partners?, Partnership (NEWMARKET) BRED P. V. Jackson 8 Rn 1m 12.3 (1.80) SF: 24/14/12/16/9/-/-/-

2979 TOTE BOOKMAKERS H'CAP (0-70) (3-Y.O+) (Class E) £6,417.50 (£1,940.00: £945.00: £447.50) 1m 67y Stalls: Low GOING minus 0.69 sec (HD) 3-30 (3-30)

2414⁴ **Mullitover (62)***(77) (MJHeaton-Ellis)* 5-9-6 MRoberts(9) (lw: 2nd st: led over 1f out: comf) — **1**
1663⁷ Mr Rough **(62)***(71) (DMorris)* 4-9-6 DHarrison(16) (4th st: rdn 4f out: ev ch wl over 1f out: unable qckn) 3 **2**
2537⁴ Star of Gold **(64)***(64) (CREgerton)* 3-9-1 BThomson(7) (lw: led 7f: wknd fnl f) 5 **3**
2549⁵ Vanborough Lad **(55)***(51) (MJBolton)* 6-8-13 WRSwinburn(13) (10th st: rdn & hdwy over 1f out: one pce) 2 **4**
2789⁷ Super Serenade **(52)***(47) (GBBalding)* 6-8-10 JWilliams(20) (lw: rdn & hdwy fnl 3f: nvr nrr) ½ **5**
2766⁷ Wave Hill **(62)***(54) (PRHedger)* 6-9-6 MPerrett(21) (lw: 5th st: one pce fnl 3f) 1¼ **6**
2718* Midnight Jazz (IRE) **(75)***(65) (WAO'Gorman)* 5-10-5 EmmaO'Gorman(15) (lw: dwlt: rdn & hdwy 3f out: wknd fnl f) 1¼ **7**
1693⁸ Astral Weeks (IRE) **(70)***(59) (RHannon)* 4-9-7 (7) DaneO'Neill(8) (lw: 6th st: wknd over 1f out) nk **8**
2510⁵ Robsera (IRE) **(70)***(59) (GLewis)* 4-10-0 PaulEddery(17) (lw: 9th st: rdn & no hdwy fnl 4f) nk **9**
2797⁶ Just Harry **(69)***(57) (MJRyan)* 4-9-8 (5) DGibbs(6) (lw: 11th st: n.m.r over 2f out: r.o one pce) nk **10**
2685² Soaking **(63)***(50)*(Fav)*(PBurgoyne)* 5-9-4 (3) DRMcCabe(19) (hld up: shkn up 3f out: nt clr run wl over 1f out: nvr nr to chal) ½ **11**
Romansh **(48)***(34) (BJMeehan)* 6-8-6 SWhitworth(10) (s.i.s: wl bhd tl r.o fnl f) ¾ **12**
*472*³ Digpast (IRE) **(59)***(44) (RJO'Sullivan)* 5-9-3b DBiggs(12) (lw: hmpd 6f out: 12th st: a mid div) nk **13**
1788⁴ South Eastern Fred **(56)***(40) (HJCollingridge)* 4-9-0 MRimmer(4) (3rd st: wknd 2f out) ¾ **14**
2747⁵ Risky Romeo **(61)***(42) (GCBravery)* 3-8-12 RCochrane(5) (dwlt: hdwy 3f out: wknd wl over 1f out) 1½ **15**
2788⁵ Polonez Prima **(60)***(41) (JLSpearing)* 8-9-4b AMcGlone(1) (lw: 8th st: wknd 2f out) hd **16**
2744⁸ Chancey Fella **(58)***(36) (KTIvory)* 4-9-2v MWigham(18) (b: lw: s.s: rdn 3f out: sme hdwy 2f out: sn wknd) 1½ **17**
2468⁷ Lunar Mission (IRE) **(66)***(37) (JMPEustace)* 4-9-10 MTebbutt(3) (a bhd) 3½ **18**
2672¹⁴ Sure Care **(61)***(31) (BJMeehan)* 4-9-5 BDoyle(14) (lw: a bhd) ½ **19**
2719⁷ Bobanlyn (IRE) **(62)***(28) (DMorris)* 3-8-13 CNutter(11) (wl bhd fnl 3f) 2 **20**
2578¹² Southern Ridge **(60)***(20) (CAHorgan)* 4-9-4 JQuinn(2) (b.hind: 7th st: wknd wl over 1f out) 3½ **21**

9/2 Soaking (op 7/1), **13/2** Risky Romeo, **9/1** Just Harry, **10/1** MULLITOVER, Digpast (IRE), Vanborough Lad, **12/1** Midnight Jazz (IRE), **14/1** Star of Gold (12/1-20/1), Mr Rough, South Eastern Fred, Super Serenade, **16/1** Wave Hill, Sure Care, Robsera (IRE), Lunar Mission (IRE), Polonez Prima, Bobanlyn (IRE), **25/1** Southern Ridge, **33/1** Astral Weeks (IRE), Chancey Fella, Romansh, CSF £151.54 CT £1,838.16 TOTE £7.70: £1.90 £4.10 £4.80 £2.20 (£67.00) Trio £875.60 OWNER Mrs D. B. Mulley (WROUGHTON) BRED Mrs D. B. Mulley 21 Rn
1m 43.2 (1.60) SF: 33/27/13/7/3/10/21/15/15/13/6/-/-/-/-/-/-/-/-/-/-
WEIGHT FOR AGE 3yo-7lb

2980 SHADWELL STUD SERIES APPRENTICE H'CAP (0-80) (3-Y.O+) (Class E) £3,465.25 (£1,042.00: £503.50: £234.25)
1m 2f 7y Stalls: Low GOING minus 0.69 sec per fur (HD) 4-00 (4-00)

2747[3] **Hadabet (60)***(74+) (MissJacquelineDoyle)* 3-8-1 AWhelan(5) (lw: mde all: hrd rdn wl over 1f out: eased ins fnl f) — 1
2780[2] Out on a Promise (IRE) **(80)***(88) (GWragg)* 3-9-4 (3) GMilligan(4) (lw: 2nd st: rdn & ev ch 2f out: unable qckn) 4 2
2657[3] Lady Lacey **(46)***(54) (GBBalding)* 8-7-5v(5) IonaWands(3) (rdn 4f out: hdwy & n.m.r ins fnl f: r.o wl nr fin) s.h 3
2201[6] Acquittal (IRE) **(60)***(65) (JRFanshawe)* 3-8-1v NVarley(8) (3rd st: hrd rdn 2f out: one pce) 1¾ 4
2269[2] Uncle Oswald **(78)***(82)*(Fav)*(RHannon)* 4-10-0 DaneO'Neill(2) (lw: 5th st: one pce fnl 2f) nk 5
2298[5] Tonka **(64)***(62) (PJMakin)* 3-8-5 SSanders(7) (4th st: wknd 3f out) 4 6
2745[4] Song of Years (IRE) **(56)***(49) (JWHills)* 4-8-6 MHenry(1) (swtg: rdn 6f out: hmpd & stumbled bnd 5f out: nt rcvr) 3 7
2657* Just Flamenco **(55)***(42) (MJRyan)* 4-8-5 DGibbs(6) (lw: 6th st: hdwy 4f out: hrd rdn over 2f out: sn wknd) 4 8

5/2 Uncle Oswald (tchd 1/4), **100/30** Out on a Promise (IRE), **7/2** Just Flamenco, **7/1** Song of Years (IRE), **8/1** HADABET (6/1-9/1), **9/1** Lady Lacey (8/1-12/1), **12/1** Acquittal (IRE), **20/1** Tonka, CSF £33.97 CT £227.48 TOTE £10.50: £2.10 £1.70 £1.80 (£24.80) OWNER The Basics (LAMBOURN) BRED Stetchworth Park Stud Ltd 8 Rn 2m 7.3 (2.40) SF: 13/27/2/4/30/1/-/-
WEIGHT FOR AGE 3yo-9lb

2981 BOLLINGER CHAMPAGNE CHALLENGE SERIES GENTLEMENS' H'CAP (0-70) (3-Y.O+) (Class E) £3,207.00 (£966.00: £468.00: £219.00)
1m 3f 135y Stalls: Low GOING minus 0.69 sec per fur (HD) 4-30 (4-30)

2731[6] **Father Dan (IRE) (50)***(64) (MissGayKelleway)* 6-11-2 MrMArmytage(11) (lw: 5th st: rdn & led wl over 1f out: r.o wl) — 1
2829* Carpathian **(62)***(69)*(Fav)*(LordHuntingdon)* 4-12-0 5x MrJDurkan(2) (lw: 6th st: ev ch 2f out: unable qckn) 5 2
2222[7] Montone (IRE) **(55)***(57) (KRBurke)* 5-11-3 (4) MrMMannish(4) (4th st: one pce fnl 3f) 3½ 3
2824[5] Non Vintage (IRE) **(58)***(60) (MCChapman)* 4-11-6 (4) MrMMackley(10) (3rd st: hrd rdn 2f out: one pce) s.h 4
2065[8] Try Omnipotent **(43)***(44) (CNAllen)* 3-9-8 (4) MrVLukaniuk(8) (2nd st: led 3f out tl wl over 1f out: wknd fnl f) ¾ 5
2658[5] Anlace **(51)***(47) (SMellor)* 6-11-3 MrTCuff(7) (rdn & hdwy 3f out: one pce fnl 2f) 4 6
2789[13] Jarzon Dancer **(27)***(18) (DAWilson)* 7-9-7 MrTMcCarthy(9) (b: hrd rdn 4f out: nvr nr to chal) 3½ 7
1622[21] The Chairman (IRE) **(50)***(6) (FJordan)* 4-10-12 (4) MrGShenkin(1) (led over 8f: wknd 2f out: eased whn btn 1f out: t.o) 25 8
Ler Cru (IRE) **(30)** *(JFfitch-Heyes)* 6-9-6 (4) MrSFindlay(6) (lw: s.s: a bhd: t.o) 5 9
1644[8] Mr Butch **(62)** *(RCurtis)* 5-11-10 (4) MrMAllen(5) (rdn 5f out: wl bhd fnl 4f: t.o) 20 10
Mr Poppleton **(34)** *(RBrotherton)* 6-9-10 (4)ow6 MrJBarton(3) (b: lw: a wl bhd: t.o fnl 5f) 2½ 11
LONG HANDICAP Jarzon Dancer 9-3

4/5 Carpathian, **100/30** FATHER DAN (IRE), **5/1** Anlace, **10/1** Montone (IRE) (8/1-12/1), **16/1** Jarzon Dancer, **20/1** Non Vintage (IRE), **33/1** Try Omnipotent, **50/1** The Chairman (IRE), Mr Butch, Mr Poppleton, **100/1** Ler Cru (IRE), CSF £6.41 CT £23.30 TOTE £5.10: £1.40 £1.30 £2.60 (£2.70) Trio £6.60 OWNER Wessex Fm (Whitcombe) Racing Club Ltd (WHITCOMBE) BRED John Michael 11 Rn 2m 31.1 (5.10) SF: 38/43/31/34/7/21/-/-/-/-/-
WEIGHT FOR AGE 3yo-11lb

2982 SWAN NURSERY H'CAP (2-Y.O F) (Class D) £4,354.00 (£1,312.00: £636.00: £298.00) **5f 217y** Stalls: Low GOING minus 0.49 sec per fur (F) 5-00 (5-01)

2548* **Jubilee Place (IRE) (70)***(73)*(Fav)*(TThomsonJones)* 2-9-3 StephenDavies(1) (mde all: rdn out) — 1
2674[6] Arlington Lady **(66)***(65) (NACallaghan)* 2-8-8 (5) MHenry(5) (b.hind: a.p: rdn 3f out: one pce) 1½ 2
2198[2] Bearnaise (IRE) **(63)***(62) (RHannon)* 2-8-3 (7) DaneO'Neill(2) (lw: s.i.s: sn prom: one pce fnl 2f) hd 3
2779[10] Fenna **(66)***(51) (SPCWoods)* 2-8-13 WWoods(4) (chsd wnr over 4f: wknd fnl f) 5 4
1650[3] Deerly **(74)***(59) (DMorris)* 2-9-7 RCochrane(7) (lw: rdn & lost pl 3f out: rallied & r.o fnl f) nk 5
2847[8] Windi Imp (IRE) **(66)***(45) (BJMeehan)* 2-8-13 BDoyle(8) (lw: hdwy 3f out: wknd over 1f out) 2 6
2591[6] February **(51)***(25) (MRChannon)* 2-7-12 CRutter(6) (bhd fnl 3f) 2 7
2523[5] Magic Imp (IRE) **(65)***(37) (WJMusson)* 2-8-12 GCarter(3) (hld up: hrd rdn over 2f out: wknd over 1f out: eased whn btn ins fnl f) ¾ 8

7/4 JUBILEE PLACE (IRE) (9/4-6/4), **9/2** Arlington Lady (4/1-6/1), Bearnaise (IRE) (7/1-4/1), **11/2** Fenna, **7/1** Magic Imp (IRE), **10/1** Deerly (7/1-12/1), **20/1** Windi Imp (IRE), **25/1** February, CSF £10.00 CT £27.95 TOTE £2.80: £1.30 £1.80 £1.80 (£8.30) OWNER Mr Timothy Chick (LAMBOURN) BRED Labelon Co Ltd 8 Rn
1m 13.4 (2.90) SF: 19/11/8/-/5/-/-/-

T/Jkpt: £20,172.10 (2.07 Tckts). T/Plpt: £34.70 (574.79 Tckts). T/Qdpt: £63.80 (1.1 Tckts). AK

2863-BATH (L-H)
Tuesday August 8th (Hard)
WEATHER: sunny WIND: mod across

2983
AUGUST (S) STKS (3-Y.O+) (Class G) £2,479.00 (£694.00: £337.00)
1m 5y Stalls: Low GOING minus 0.53 sec per fur (F) 2-00 (2-02)

2789[2] **Tragic Hero (54)***(60)*(Fav)*(IABalding)* 3-8-5 RCochrane(9) (lw: led 1f: 2nd st: led over 2f out: r.o wl).......— **1**
2685[15] Morocco (IRE) **(52)***(58) (MRChannon)* 6-9-1 RHughes(5) (hld up: 5th st: ev ch whn swtchd lft over 1f out: hrd rdn: no imp).......2½ **2**
2808[5] Rad **(51)***(58) (SPCWoods)* 5-9-1 WWoods(7) (8th st: hdwy over 2f out: r.o ins fnl f).......s.h **3**
2528[15] White Flash **(46)***(46) (DRCElsworth)* 4-8-5b TQuinn(11) (hld up & bhd: hdwy fnl 2f: r.o).......1 **4**
2744[7] Pop to Stans **(47)***(55) (JPearce)* 6-8-8 (7) MNutter(2) (lw: hld up: 7th st: nvr nr to chal).......½ **5**
2528[17] South Sound (IRE) **(53)***(52) (RHannon)* 3-8-0b(7)ow2 DaneO'Neill(10) (lw: 3rd st: one pce fnl 2f).......hd **6**
2549[12] Safe Secret **(32)***(29) (RBrotherton)* 4-8-5 RPrice(8) (a bhd).......8 **7**
1791[8] Margaret Modes **(38)***(27) (CACyzer)* 3-8-0v DBiggs(1) (lw: pushed along: sn prom: 4th st: wknd qckly 3f out).......1¾ **8**
2450[11] Pats Folly **(17)***(21) (FJYardley)* 4-8-0 (5) MHenry(3) (led after 1f: hdd over 2f out: wknd qckly)..2 **9**
2784[16] Christian Warrior **(23)***(24) (REPeacock)* 6-8-10v JWilliams(6) (6th st: wknd over 2f out).......1¼ **10**

15/8 TRAGIC HERO, **7/2** Morocco (IRE), **6/1** South Sound (IRE), **7/1** Pop to Stans, **15/2** White Flash (5/1-8/1), **10/1** Rad, **14/1** Margaret Modes (10/1-16/1), **33/1** Safe Secret, **66/1** Pats Folly, **100/1** Christian Warrior, CSF £8.50 TOTE £3.00: £1.70 £1.70 £2.00 (£4.70) Trio £12.50 OWNER The Cromhall Stud Partnership (KINGSCLERE) BRED Derek R. Price 10 Rn
1m 40.6 (2.10) SF: 26/31/31/19/28/18/2/-/-/-
WEIGHT FOR AGE 3yo-7lb
Sold DPipe 9,100 gns

2984
MILE MAIDEN H'CAP (0-65) (3-Y.O+) (Class F) £2,950.00 (£825.00: £400.00)
1m 5y Stalls: Low GOING minus 0.53 sec per fur (F) 2-30 (2-31)

2638[2] **Shady Deed (USA) (62)***(72) (JWHills)* 3-9-8b(5) MHenry(2) (mde all: sn clr: hrd rdn 2f out: r.o wl).......— **1**
2861[7] La Belle Shyanne **(28)***(35) (CJHill)* 4-7-7 (7) CAdamson(3) (s.s: hdwy & 6th st: nt clr run over 2f out: chsd wnr over 1f out: r.o).......1¾ **2**
2657[6] Bandita **(44)***(46) (DJSffrenchDavis)* 4-9-2 DHarrison(6) (hld up: nt clr run on ins over 4f out: 4th st: hdwy 3f out: one pce fnl 2f).......2½ **3**
2278[4] Just-Mana-Mou (IRE) **(48)***(36)*(Fav)*(GLewis)* 3-8-13 PaulEddery(8) (rdn thrght: 3rd st: wknd 2f out).......7 **4**
2831[6] See You Again **(63)***(49) (RHannon)* 3-10-0 JReid(4) (prom: rdn over 4f out: 2nd st: wknd 2f out).......¾ **5**
2781[7] Lord Palmerston (USA) **(56)***(34) (PFICole)* 3-9-7 TQuinn(5) (b: swtg: a bhd).......4 **6**
Irish Dominion **(40)***(18) (ABarrow)* 5-8-12 JWilliams(7) (a bhd).......nk **7**
2843[4] Sharp Spring **(42)***(10) (JWhite)* 4-8-11 (3) SDrowne(9) (5th st: wknd over 2f out).......5 **8**

13/8 Just-Mana-Mou (IRE), **4/1** SHADY DEED (USA) (3/1-9/2), **8/1** La Belle Shyanne, **9/1** Sharp Spring (op 6/1), See You Again, Lord Palmerston (USA), **10/1** Bandita, **66/1** Irish Dominion, CSF £30.38 CT £245.71 TOTE £4.00: £1.60 £1.80 £2.10 (£16.90) Trio £27.30 OWNER Wyck Hall Stud (LAMBOURN) BRED Lincoln Collins and J. and Della-Penna 8 Rn
1m 41.9 (3.40) SF: 34/4/15/-/11/-/-/-
WEIGHT FOR AGE 3yo-7lb

2985
TRIPLEPRINT MAIDEN STKS (2-Y.O F) (Class D) £3,556.25 (£1,070.00: £517.50: £241.25)
5f 11y Stalls: Low GOING minus 0.53 sec per fur (F) 3-00 (3-01)

2660[6] **Comic Fantasy (AUS)** *(85?)*(Fav)*(PWChapple-Hyam)* 2-8-11b JReid(7) (mde all: clr over 2f out: easily).......— **1**

Kirov Lady (IRE) *(66) (RHannon)* 2-8-11 RHughes(3) (unf: a.p: r.o fnl f: no ch w wnr).............6 2
2716[3] Dramatic Entry (IRE) **(70)***(55) (JARToller)* 2-8-11 TQuinn(2) (lw: sn chsng wnr: rdn over 2f out: wknd ins fnl f) 3½ 3
1653[9] Zuno Princess (IRE) *(36) (GLewis)* 2-8-11 PaulEddery(1) (a bhd)..6 4
852[8] Gracious Gretclo *(26) (CJHill)* 2-8-6 (5) AWhelan(6) (chsd ldrs: edgd rt wl over 1f out: wknd)...3 5
Martins Folly *(14) (JWhite)* 2-8-8 (3) SDrowne(4) (lt-f: s.s: outpcd)..4 6
2660[11] Golina (IRE) *(12) (BWHills)* 2-8-11 BThomson(5) (spd 2f) ....½ 7

6/4 COMIC FANTASY (AUS), **2/1** Dramatic Entry (IRE), **5/1** Kirov Lady (IRE) (7/2-11/2), **7/1** Golina (IRE), **10/1** Gracious Gretclo, **33/1** Zuno Princess (IRE), **50/1** Martins Folly, CSF £9.26 TOTE £2.10: £1.40 £2.60 (£6.70) OWNER Mr R. E. Sangster (MARLBOROUGH) BRED Swettenham Stud 7 Rn 61.5 secs (1.00) SF: 35/16/5/-/-/-/-

2986 BBC RADIO BRISTOL H'CAP (0-80) (3-Y.O+) (Class D) £3,673.25 (£1,106.00: £535.50: £250.25) 2m 1f 34y Stalls: Low GOING minus 0.53 sec (F) 3-30 (3-30)

2860[5] **Arc Bright (IRE) (44)***(56) (RHollinshead)* 5-7-13 (5) MHenry(5) (lw: chsd ldr: led 8f out to 2f out: led over 1f out: r.o wl)...— 1
2514[3] Mr Geneaology (USA) **(54)***(64) (FMurphy)* 5-9-0b RCochrane(4) (hld up: hdwy 5f out: 3rd st: ev ch whn swtchd rt 2f out: r.o one pce)...2½ 2
2452* Trazl (IRE) **(79)***(87)*(Fav)*(JLDunlop)* 3-9-10 GCarter(6) (lw: hld up: chsd wnr 6f out: 2nd st: led 2f out: sn hdd: wknd fnl f)..1¾ 3
2514[7] Chucklestone **(48)***(50) (JSKing)* 12-8-8 PaulEddery(1) (led tl rdn & hdd 8f out: 5th & wkng st).6 4
2546[12] Lajadhal (FR) **(33)***(35) (KBishop)* 6-7-4 (3) NVarley(3) (4th st: wknd 2f out)..............................nk 5
2713[9] Gushy **(33)** *(RJBaker)* 9-7-7 NAdams(2) (lost tch 7f out: last & t.o st).................................dist 6
LONG HANDICAP Lajadhal (FR) 6-3 Gushy 6-10

4/5 Trazl (IRE), **3/1** ARC BRIGHT (IRE), **9/2** Mr Geneaology (USA), **8/1** Chucklestone, **100/1** Lajadhal (FR), Gushy, CSF £15.19 TOTE £3.30: £1.30 £2.20 (£4.20) OWNER Mr J. E. Bigg (UPPER LONGDON) BRED Tsarina Stud 6 Rn 3m 45.8 (4.80) SF: 27/35/43/21/6/-
WEIGHT FOR AGE 3yo-15lb

2987 LUCKINGTON LIMITED STKS (0-70) (3-Y.O+) (Class E) £2,947.00 (£886.00: £428.00: £199.00) 5f 11y Stalls: Low GOING minus 0.53 sec per fur (F) 4-00 (4-00)

2865[2] **Fantasy Racing (IRE) (70)***(73) (MRChannon)* 3-8-12 (7) JDennis(1) (a.p: rdn to ld cl home) .— 1
Bangles **(70)***(64) (LordHuntingdon)* 5-9-0 DHarrison(4) (led: hrd rdn over 1f out: hdd cl home)...hd 2
2935[10] Giggleswick Girl **(63)***(69) (MRChannon)* 4-9-2 (7) DSweeney(5) (s.s: hdwy & plld out 2f out: edgd rt wl over 1f out: r.o one pce)...1¼ 3
1778[3] Master Millfield (IRE) **(65)***(67) (CJHill)* 3-9-4 StephenDavies(2) (lw: prom: rdn over 2f out: r.o one pce) ....hd 4
636[11] Dark Eyed Lady (IRE) **(68)***(48) (DWPArbuthnot)* 5-9-0 TQuinn(6) (w ldr: ev ch over 1f out: wknd ins fnl f) 3½ 5
2867[3] Paley Prince (USA) **(60)***(52)*(Fav)*(MDIUsher)* 9-8-12 (7) CAdamson(3) (lw: hld up: hdwy & ev ch 2f out: wknd over 1f out) ....½ 6

3/1 Paley Prince (USA), **7/2** Bangles (op 2/1), Dark Eyed Lady (IRE), **6/1** Giggleswick Girl, **7/1** FANTASY RACING (IRE), **8/1** Master Millfield (IRE), CSF £27.55 TOTE £5.50: £2.40 £2.10 (£14.70) OWNER Aldridge Racing Ltd (UPPER LAMBOURN) BRED Barronstown Stud and Ron Con Ltd 6 Rn 61.0 secs (0.50) SF: 51/46/51/45/30/34
WEIGHT FOR AGE 3yo-4lb

2988 NUNNEY NURSERY H'CAP (2-Y.O) (Class E) £3,142.00 (£946.00: £458.00: £214.00) 5f 161y Stalls: Low GOING minus 0.53 sec per fur (F) 4-30 (4-30)

2023* **Albert The Bear (61)***(65) (JBerry)* 2-8-7 JCarroll(2) (lw: w ldr: rdn over 2f out: led over 1f out: drvn out)...— 1
2601* Music Mistress (IRE) **(51)***(54) (RHannon)* 2-7-6 (5) MHenry(3) (a.p: ev ch fnl f: r.o) ....½ 2
2660[5] Friendly Forester (USA) **(75)***(75)*(Fav)*(RCharlton)* 2-9-7 TQuinn(1) (lw: rdn over 3f out: hdwy over 2f out: r.o one pce fnl f)..1 3
2800[2] U-No-Harry (IRE) **(68)***(65) (RHollinshead)* 2-8-11 (3) AGarth(4) (lw: led tl over 1f out: no ex ins fnl f)...1 4
2962[6] Our Tom's Boy **(59)***(45) (KTIvory)* 2-8-5b GBardwell(5) (rdn over 3f out: a bhd) 4 5

7/4 Friendly Forester (USA), **9/4** ALBERT THE BEAR, **100/30** Music Mistress (IRE), **5/1** U-No-Harry (IRE), **33/1** Our Tom's Boy, CSF £9.18 TOTE £3.00: £1.80 £1.40 (£4.20) OWNER Mr Chris Deuters (COCKERHAM) BRED Rockhouse Farms Ltd 5 Rn 1m 11.4 (2.10) SF: 19/8/29/19/-

2989 ROYAL CRESCENT H'CAP (0-80) (3-Y.O+) (Class D) £3,536.75 (£1,064.00: £514.50: £239.75)
1m 3f 144y Stalls: Low GOING minus 0.53 sec per fur (F) 5-00 (5-00)

2792[4] **Endowment (71)***(80) (MajorWRHern)* 3-9-10b WCarson(2) (3rd st: swtchd rt & rdn over 1f out: r.o to ld last stride) — **1**
2829[2] Prince Danzig (IRE) **(58)***(67) (DJGMurraySmith)* 4-9-8 PaulEddery(3) (chsd ldr: 2nd st: rdn to ld over 2f out: hdd last stride) s.h **2**
2653* Prague Spring **(68)***(72)*(Fav)*(BWHills)* 3-9-7 BThomson(1) (led tl over 2f out: wknd over 1f out) 3½ **3**
2657[14] Manila Bay (USA) **(50)***(52) (JSKing)* 5-9-0 JWilliams(4) (last st: a bhd) 1¾ **4**

7/4 Prague Spring (op 11/10), **15/8** ENDOWMENT, **2/1** Prince Danzig (IRE), **20/1** Manila Bay (USA), CSF £5.57 TOTE £2.50 (£2.80) OWNER Mr Hamdan Al Maktoum (LAMBOURN) BRED Bloomsbury Stud 4 Rn
2m 31.7 (5.00) SF: 32/30/24/15
WEIGHT FOR AGE 3yo-11lb
T/Jkpt: £7,100.00 (0.76 Tckts) £1,545.55 to Sandown 09/08/95. T/Plpt: £118.40 (149.09 Tckts).
T/Qdpt: £33.60 (4.50 Tckts). KH

2662-BEVERLEY (R-H)
Wednesday August 9th (Good to firm)
WEATHER: sunny, hot WIND: slt half bhd

2990 GRAPE LANE (S) STKS (3-Y.O+) (Class F) £2,693.00 (£748.00: £359.00)
1m 3f 216y Stalls: High GOING minus 0.51 sec per fur (F) 2-00 (2-01)

2126[6] **Diamond Crown (IRE) (44)***(62) (MartynWane)* 4-9-4 KFallon(2) (s.s: hld up: effrt over 3f out: hdwy on ins to ld ins fnl f: hld on nr fin) — **1**
2806* Faugeron **(70)***(67)*(Fav)*(NTinkler)* 6-9-10 KimTinkler(1) (b: dwlt: led after 1f: hrd rdn & edgd lft over 1f out: hdd wl ins fnl f: styd on nr fin) ½ **2**
2662[3] Remontant (IRE) **(38)***(53) (RHollinshead)* 3-7-13 (3) AGarth(6) (led 1f: chsd ldrs: chal 2f out: nt qckn fnl f) 2½ **3**
2834[2] Fearless Wonder **(50)***(63) (MrsMReveley)* 4-9-10b JFortune(4) (lw: trckd ldrs: effrt over 3f out: rdn & hung rt over 1f out: nt r.o) ½ **4**
Charmed Life **(40)***(31) (MrsALMKing)* 6-8-11 (7) MSemple(3) (hld up: effrt over 5f out: sn outpcd: wknd 2f out) 20 **5**
Billytobinslad *(17) (MrsVAAconley)* 4-9-4 MDeering(5) (leggy: plld hrd: sn trckng ldrs: wknd qckly over 2f out) 10 **6**

8/13 Faugeron, **4/1** Fearless Wonder, **11/2** Remontant (IRE), **9/1** DIAMOND CROWN (IRE) (op 6/1), **16/1** Charmed Life, **33/1** Billytobinslad, CSF £15.25 TOTE £11.50: £2.90 £1.20 (£7.70) OWNER Mr J. M. Pickup (RICHMOND) BRED Dene Investments N V 6 Rn
2m 41.3 (9.80) SF: 1/6/-/2/-/-
WEIGHT FOR AGE 3yo-11lb
No bid.

2991 CONTRAC COMPUTER SUPPLIES NURSERY H'CAP (2-Y.O) (Class D) £4,352.25 (£1,308.00: £631.50: £293.25)
5f Stalls: Centre GOING minus 0.51 sec per fur (F) 2-30 (2-33)

2606* **Westcourt Magic (66)***(68) (MWEasterby)* 2-7-11 TWilliams(6) (mde all: drvn over 1f out: unchal) — **1**
2442[9] Eastern Prophets **(90)***(86) (GLewis)* 2-9-7 PaulEddery(2) (swtg: a chsng wnr: effrt & hung rt over 1f out: no imp) 2 **2**
2779[7] Stop Play (IRE) **(74)***(54)*(Fav)*(MHTompkins)* 2-8-5 PRobinson(8) (sn outpcd & drvn along: hdwy over 1f out: styd on nr fin) 5 **3**
2085[8] Dancing Rainbow **(65)***(71d) (MJCamacho)* 2-7-10 LCharnock(10) (swtg: a chsng ldrs: sn drvn along: one pce fr ½-wy) 1¼ **4**
2918* Arrhythmic (IRE) **(86)***(59) (MBrittain)* 2-9-3 7x RCochrane(7) (chsd ldrs: kpt on one pce fnl 2f) ¾ **5**
2706[10] Branston Danni **(70)***(39) (MrsJRRamsden)* 2-8-1 GCarter(3) (b.nr hind: swvd rt s: sn chsng ldrs: wknd wl over 1f out) 1¼ **6**
1454[7] Briganoone **(62)***(26) (SRBowring)* 2-7-7b NKennedy(9) (in tch tl lost pl ½-wy) 1½ **7**
*2625** Ebony Boy **(65)***(18) (JWharton)* 2-7-10 AMackay(5) (s.i.s: a outpcd) 3½ **8**
2508[5] Ichor **(62)***(15) (HThomsonJones)* 2-7-7 NCarlisle(4) (unruly s: a outpcd & sn drvn along) s.h **9**
2771[3] Meeting Point **(67)***(12) (MrsMReveley)* 2-7-12 SMaloney(1) (sn wl outpcd & wl bhd) 2½ **10**
LONG HANDICAP Ichor 7-5 Briganoone 7-1

2/1 Stop Play (IRE) (op 4/1), **5/1** Eastern Prophets, **11/2** WESTCOURT MAGIC, **7/1** Branston Danni, **8/1** Dancing Rainbow, **9/1** Ebony Boy, **11/1** Arrhythmic (IRE), **12/1** Meeting Point (op 8/1), Ichor, **25/1** Briganoone, CSF £33.34 CT £69.06 TOTE £7.50: £2.20 £1.70 £1.50 (£15.30) Trio £30.50 OWNER Mr K. Hodgson (SHERIFF HUTTON) BRED C. R. and V. M. Withers 10 Rn
62.4 secs (0.90) SF: 27/45/13/-/18/-/-/-/-/-

2992 STRUTHERS AND CARTER H'CAP (0-80) (3-Y.O+) (Class D) £4,557.00 (£1,371.00: £663.00: £309.00)
5f Stalls: Centre GOING minus 0.51 sec per fur (F) 3-00 (3-03)

2736* **Super Rocky (71)***(80) (RBastiman)* 6-9-7 (5) HBastiman(6) (chsd ldrs: drvn along ½-wy: styd on u.p to ld ins fnl f: hld on wl) ....— **1**
2714[4] Plum First **(59)***(66) (LRLloyd-James)* 5-9-0 RCochrane(11) (led: edgd lft & hdd ins fnl f)....¾ **2**
2652[4] Barato **(72)***(72) (MrsJRRamsden)* 4-9-6 (7) SBuckley(7) (b.nr hind: hld up & bhd: hdwy ½-wy: n.m.r & swtchd lft 1f out: kpt on same pce)....2 **3**
2837[6] Pallium (IRE) **(62)***(61) (MrsAMNaughton)* 7-9-3 7x KFallon(8) (sn outpcd & drvn along: hdwy ½-wy: kpt on same pce appr fnl f)....½ **4**
2628[4] First Gold **(60)***(53) (JWharton)* 6-9-1 PRobinson(9) (lw: sn outpcd & bhd: styd on appr fnl f).1¾ **5**
2858[4] Knayton Lass **(60)***(51) (MWEasterby)* 4-8-10 (5) LNewton(3) (s.i.s: hung lft thrght: outpcd: sme hdwy ½-wy: nvr nr to chal)....½ **6**
2551* Robellion **(71)***(51)*(Fav)*(DWPArbuthnot)* 4-9-12v JWeaver(10) (b: trckd ldr: effrt over 1f out: sn rdn & wknd qckly)....3½ **7**
2551[6] John O'Dreams **(47)***(24) (MrsALMKing)* 10-7-13 (3) AGarth(4) (s.s: bhd tl sme late hdwy)....1 **8**
2858[3] The Fed **(51)***(28) (RMWhitaker)* 5-8-6 ACulhane(5) (b.hind: chsd ldrs tl rdn & wknd wl over 1f out)....s.h **9**
2521* Croft Imperial **(66)***(43) (MJohnston)* 8-9-7 TWilliams(1) (chsd ldrs: sn drvn along: hrd rdn & outpcd 2f out: sn wknd)....hd **10**

7/4 Robellion, **6/1** SUPER ROCKY, **15/2** Knayton Lass, Croft Imperial, **9/1** Barato, **10/1** The Fed, Plum First, First Gold, **12/1** Pallium (IRE), **20/1** John O'Dreams, CSF £60.48 CT £496.19 TOTE £6.10: £2.10 £2.70 £3.00 (£32.30) Trio £74.50 OWNER Mr I. B. Barker (WETHERBY) BRED J. Berry 10 Rn
62.9 secs (1.40) SF: 46/32/38/27/19/17/17/-/-/9

2993 HULL DAILY MAIL H'CAP (0-70) (3-Y.O) (Class E) £4,352.25 (£1,308.00: £631.50: £293.25) **1m 1f 207y** Stalls: High GOING minus 0.51 sec per fur (F) 3-30 (3-32)

2664* **Harry Browne (IRE) (63)***(71)*(Fav)*(MrsJRRamsden)* 3-9-6 KFallon(9) (lw: hld up & bhd: effrt over 2f out: gd hdwy over 1f out: qcknd to ld wl ins fnl f: readily)....— **1**
2503[8] Westcourt Princess **(45)***(52) (MWEasterby)* 3-8-2 GCarter(10) (sn led: drvn clr over 2f out: hdd & no ex wl ins fnl f)....½ **2**
2503[4] Tajar (USA) **(63)***(66) (DMorley)* 3-9-6 RCochrane(2) (hld up & bhd: effrt over 2f out: hung rt & styd on one pce fr over 1f out)....2½ **3**
1970[10] Court Joker (IRE) **(53)***(53) (MHTompkins)* 3-8-10 PRobinson(5) (in tch: effrt over 2f out: kpt on one pce)....1¾ **4**
2953* Rushen Raider **(61)***(57) (KWHogg)* 3-8-11 (7) 5x FLynch(7) (in tch: effrt & edgd lft over 2f out: nvr nr to chal)....2½ **5**
2881[6] Embezzler **(49)***(43) (SGollings)* 3-8-6 ow2 ACulhane(3) (hld up & bhd: sme hdwy over 2f out: nvr nr ldrs)....s.h **6**
1922[2] Dancing Destiny **(64)***(51) (RBastiman)* 3-9-2 (5) HBastiman(4) (s.i.s: a in rr)....6 **7**
2406[6] Ewar Imperial **(60)***(44) (CEBrittain)* 3-9-3 JWeaver(8) (led early: chsd ldrs: drvn along over 4f out: wknd over 2f out)....1¾ **8**
2774* Eden Dancer **(59)***(43) (MrsMReveley)* 3-9-2 KDarley(6) (trckd ldrs: effrt & 2nd over 3f out: wknd qckly over 1f out)....hd **9**
2822[4] Juweilla **(63)** *(JWPayne)* 3-9-6 GBardwell(1) (ref to r: virtually t.n.p).... **R**

6/4 HARRY BROWNE (IRE) (op 5/2), **6/1** Eden Dancer, **13/2** Court Joker (IRE), **7/1** Tajar (USA), **8/1** Westcourt Princess, **9/1** Juweilla, Dancing Destiny, **11/1** Rushen Raider, **14/1** Ewar Imperial, **25/1** Embezzler, CSF £15.37 CT £68.09 TOTE £2.90: £1.30 £2.40 £2.30 (£11.20) Trio £35.50 OWNER Mrs J. R. Ramsden (THIRSK) BRED Patrick Whelan in Ireland 10 Rn
2m 6.3 (3.80) SF: 32/13/27/14/18/4/12/5/4/-

2994 ALLDERS OF HULL CLAIMING STKS (3-Y.O+) (Class E) £3,254.00 (£977.00: £471.00: £218.00) **1m 100y** Stalls: High GOING minus 0.51 sec (F) 4-00 (4-03)

2707[5] **Second Colours (USA) (61)***(72) (MrsMReveley)* 5-9-8 KDarley(4) (lw: trckd ldrs: effrt over 3f out: nt clr run & swtchd lft 2f out: styd on u.p to ld ins fnl f: drvn out)....— **1**
2885[6] Bayou (IRE) **(47)***(57) (JAHarris)* 4-8-8 SDWilliams(7) (sn drvn along: led tl hdd & nt qckn ins fnl f)....½ **2**

2117[8] Forever Diamonds **(79)***(66)*(Fav)*(MHEasterby)* 8-9-6 MBirch(3) (lw: hld up: smooth hdwy & swtchd ins over 2f out: nt clr run: nt qckn appr fnl f) 1½ 3
1736[7] Hello Peter (IRE) *(59) (MHTompkins)* 3-8-4 (5) HKYim(1) (a chsng ldrs: pushed along 4f out: one pce fnl 2f) 1¾ 4
2755* Pleasure Trick (USA) **(65)***(53) (NTinkler)* 4-9-4 KimTinkler(2) (chsd ldrs: drvn along 3f out: one pce) 4 5
2329[6] Larentia **(48)***(39) (JParkes)* 3-8-6 KFallon(5) (dwlt s: a bhd: drvn along 5f out: n.d) 5 6
2620[4] Moofaji **(53)***(42) (FWatson)* 4-9-2 SMaloney(8) (trckd ldrs: plld hrd: lost pl over 4f out: n.d after) ....hd 7
2446[8] Nashaat (USA) **(66)***(40) (NJHWalker)* 7-9-4 RCochrane(6) (trckd ldrs: ev ch over 2f out: sn lost pl: eased) 2 8

11/8 Forever Diamonds, **11/4** SECOND COLOURS (USA), **4/1** Nashaat (USA) (op 5/2), **7/1** Pleasure Trick (USA), **12/1** Hello Peter (IRE) (op 25/1), **14/1** Moofaji, **25/1** Bayou (IRE), **33/1** Larentia, CSF £53.53 TOTE £3.90: £1.10 £3.70 £1.30 (£78.90) OWNER Mr P. D. Savill (SALTBURN) BRED Dinnaken Farm in USA 8 Rn 1m 47.5 (3.50) SF: 32/17/26/12/13/-/2/-
WEIGHT FOR AGE 3yo-7lb

2995 JOURNAL MAIDEN STKS (2-Y.O) (Class D) £4,159.00 (£1,252.00: £606.00: £283.00) 7f 100y Stalls: High GOING minus 0.51 sec per fur (F) 4-30 (4-34)

2667[2] **Pleasant Surprise (91)***(85)*(Fav)*(MJohnston)* 2-9-0 DHolland(11) (trckd ldrs: styd on wl to ld ins fnl f: drvn out) ....— 1
2485[4] Belana *(77) (JWWatts)* 2-8-9 TIves(12) (lw: trckd ldrs: led over 3f out: hdd & nt qckn ins fnl f) 1¼ 2
2529[3] Faateq *(72) (JLDunlop)* 2-9-0 GCarter(6) (trckd ldrs: effrt 2f out: kpt on same pce over 1f out) 5 3
2749[4] Midtime (IRE) *(70) (MRStoute)* 2-9-0 KDarley(3) (chsd ldrs: drvn along & n.m.r over 2f out: kpt on one pce) ....¾ 4
2667[8] Noir Esprit *(57) (JMCarr)* 2-9-0 SMorris(1) (bhd: hdwy 2f out: hung rt: n.d) 6 5
Shu Gaa (IRE) *(57+) (MrsLPiggott)* 2-9-0 RCochrane(4) (rangy: bit bkwd: s.i.s: bhd: pushed along: rn green: swtchd outside & styd on over 1f out) ....s.h 6
2542[11] Recall To Mind *(55) (MHEasterby)* 2-9-0 MBirch(10) (led tl over 3f out: wknd over 1f out) 1 7
Mon Pere *(54) (KMcAuliffe)* 2-9-0 JWeaver(9) (unf: chsd ldr: drvn along ½-wy: wknd 2f out) ....nk 8
2667[5] Serious Trust *(52) (SirMarkPrescott)* 2-9-0 CNutter(8) (bhd: sme hdwy fnl 2f: nvr nr ldrs) 1 9
No More Hassle (IRE) *(50) (MrsMReveley)* 2-9-0 ACulhane(7) (leggy: unf: bit bkwd: sn bhd & pushed along) ....¾ 10
2420[4] Welcome Royale (IRE) *(47) (MHTompkins)* 2-9-0 PRobinson(5) (unruly in stalls: s.i.s: bhd: hdwy on outside over 4f out: sn chsng ldrs: rdn & wnt rt over 1fout: sn wknd) 1½ 11
Oxgang (IRE) *(26) (JGFitzGerald)* 2-9-0 KFallon(2) (w'like: cmpt: bit bkwd: in tch: hung rt & lost pl 3f out: sn bhd & eased) 10 12
2107[9] Double Vintage (IRE) *(MCChapman)* 2-8-7 (7) CMunday(13) (mid div: sn drvn along: outpcd ½-wy: sn bhd) 20 13

6/5 PLEASANT SURPRISE (7/4-Evens), **7/4** Faateq (6/4-5/2), **6/1** Midtime (IRE), **10/1** Belana, **12/1** Welcome Royale (IRE) (8/1-14/1), **14/1** Shu Gaa (IRE), Serious Trust, **20/1** Oxgang (IRE), **25/1** No More Hassle (IRE), **33/1** Recall To Mind, Mon Pere, **50/1** Noir Esprit, **66/1** Double Vintage (IRE), CSF £17.44 TOTE £2.40: £1.20 £3.00 £1.40 (£9.30) Trio £10.50 OWNER Mr Abdullah Ali (MIDDLEHAM) BRED Highclere Stud Ltd 13 Rn 1m 33.7 (1.70) SF: 39/31/26/24/11/11/9/8/6/4/1/-/-

2996 CHARLES ELSEY MEMORIAL CHALLENGE TROPHY H'CAP (0-80) (3-Y.O+) (Class D) £4,147.50 (£1,245.00: £600.00: £277.50) 2m 35y Stalls: High GOING minus 0.51 sec per fur (F) 5-00 (5-01)

2854* **Star Rage (IRE) (75)***(86)*(Fav)*(MJohnston)* 5-9-12 5x JWeaver(6) (lw: hld up: nt clr run over 3f out: effrt & chsd ldr 2f out: styd on wl u.p to ld jst ins fnl f) ....— 1
2701[3] Red Bustaan **(80)***(91) (ACStewart)* 3-9-2 RCochrane(4) (stmbld s: sn led: hdd jst ins fnl f: kpt on u.p) ....nk 2
2355[2] Jalcanto **(58)***(68) (MrsMReveley)* 5-8-9 KDarley(3) (hld up: effrt on outside 3f out: hung rt u.p over 1f out: kpt on same pce) ....½ 3
2799* Moonlight Quest **(77)***(81) (BHanbury)* 7-10-0 NCarlisle(5) (lw: led early: trckd ldrs: pushed along over 5f out: outpcd 3f out: n.d after) 6 4
2429[5] Paradise Navy **(70)***(74) (CREgerton)* 6-9-7 TIves(2) (trckd ldrs: pushed along 4f out: outpcd fnl 2f) ....½ 5
2550[5] Toraja **(75)***(66) (JLDunlop)* 3-8-11 GCarter(1) (effrt over 4f out: rdn over 2f out: nvr able chal: btn whn hung rt & eased 1f out) 13 6

6/4 STAR RAGE (IRE) (op 3/1), **7/2** Moonlight Quest, **9/2** Paradise Navy, Jalcanto (op 3/1), **11/2** Red Bustaan, **15/2** Toraja, CSF £10.79 TOTE £2.90: £1.50 £2.80 (£7.80) OWNER Mr J. D. Abell (MIDDLEHAM) BRED Killarkin Stud 6 Rn 3m 36.4 (5.90) SF: 43/33/25/38/31/8
WEIGHT FOR AGE 3yo-15lb

T/Plpt: £23.60 (581.8 Tckts). T/Qdpt: £5.70 (16.4 Tckts). WG

2869-HAMILTON (R-H)
Wednesday August 9th (Firm)
WEATHER: sunny WIND: alm nil

2997
SCOTTISH RIFLES APPRENTICE H'CAP (0-70) (3-Y.O+) (Class E)
£3,323.00 (£1,019.00: £507.00: £251.00)
5f 4y Stalls: Low GOING minus 0.51 sec per fur (F) 6-15 (6-23)

2736[7] **Serious Hurry (40)***(51) (RMMcKellar)* 7-7-10b(5) KSked(6) (mde all: sn clr: r.o wl) ....— 1
1827[5] Just Bob **(67)***(67) (SEKettlewell)* 6-9-11 (3) GFaulkner(7) (s.s: r.o fnl 2f: nrst fin).....................3½ 2
2818[3] Northern Grey **(51)***(50) (JBerry)* 3-8-3b(5) CLowther(8) (a.p: hdwy 2f out: one pce fnl f)...........nk 3
2930[2] Walk the Beat **(62)***(61) (MartynMeade)* 5-9-9 PBowe(3) (s.i.s: hdwy 2f out: nvr rchd ldrs) ......hd 4
2879[4] Cheeky Chappy **(36)***(29) (DWChapman)* 4-7-8b(3) JoHunnam(5) (unruly s: chsd wnr 3f: sn rdn & btn).....................................1¾ 5
2818[5] Sunday Mail Too (IRE) **(39)***(31) (MissLAPerratt)* 3-7-5b(5) JBramhill(2) (in tch: rdn ½-wy: no hdwy) ....nk 6
2930[8] Leading Princess (IRE) **(38)***(30) (MissLAPerratt)* 4-7-8b(5) RMullen(9) (in tch: effrt ½-wy: no imp).....................................hd 7
2935[9] Crystal Loop **(68)***(56)*(Fav)*(ABailey)* 3-9-4 (7) AngelaGallimore(11) (prom: hung lft after 1f: wknd fnl 2f).....................................1¼ 8
2772[4] Glow of Hope **(32)***(12) (RMMcKellar)* 5-7-2 (5) BHalligan(10) (unruly s: hmpd & lost pl after 1½f: n.d after).....................................2½ 9
2930[10] Uppance **(42)***(11) (DANolan)* 7-7-12b(5)ow10 CarolDavison(4) (s.i.s: hdwy ½-wy: sn wknd)......nk 10
2772[5] Kenesha (IRE) **(51)***(11) (DANolan)* 5-8-12b DDenby(1) (s.s: a bhd)..6 11
LONG HANDICAP Glow of Hope 7-4 Uppance 7-0

9/2 Crystal Loop, **5/1** Walk the Beat, Just Bob, **7/1** Cheeky Chappy, **10/1** Kenesha (IRE), **11/1** Northern Grey (8/1-12/1), **12/1** Glow of Hope, **14/1** SERIOUS HURRY, **16/1** Leading Princess (IRE), Sunday Mail Too (IRE), **66/1** Uppance, CSF £70.60 CT £660.35 TOTE £14.70: £2.20 £1.80 £2.00 (£49.70) Trio £202.00 OWNER Miss S. A. Corcoran (LESMAHAGOW) BRED The Duke of Marlborough 11 Rn 59.2 secs (0.90) SF: 29/45/24/39/7/5/8/30/-/-/-
WEIGHT FOR AGE 3yo-4lb

2998
HYNDFORD CLAIMING STKS (2-Y.O) (Class F) £2,717.00 (£762.00: £371.00)
6f 5y Stalls: Low GOING minus 0.51 sec per fur (F) 6-45 (6-52)

2750[2] **Moi Canard (64)***(66) (JBerry)* 2-8-11 JFortune(2) (trckd ldrs: led & hung lft wl over 1f out: r.o) ....— 1
2542[5] Mystic Times **(65)***(58) (MissSEHall)* 2-8-8 NConnorton(1) (b.hind: cl up: hmpd after 2f & 2f out: chal 1f out: n.m.r & nt qckn).....................................2 2
2756[3] Silver Harrow **(83)***(78d)*(Fav)*(SirMarkPrescott)* 2-9-7b GDuffield(3) (lw: reminders after s: cl up: led ½-wy tl wl over 1f out: edgd lft).....................................4 3
2838[4] Fiddles Delight **(48)***(20) (MRChannon)* 2-7-13 (3) NVarley(5) (led tl hdd 3f out: wknd wl over 1f out).....................................8 4
1670[9] Larrylukeathugh *(4) (JJO'Neill)* 2-8-13b DMcKeown(4) (lw: w ldrs 4f: sn wknd) 10 5

13/8 Silver Harrow, **5/2** Mystic Times (op 6/4), **11/4** MOI CANARD, **13/2** Fiddles Delight, **7/1** Larrylukeathugh, CSF £10.10 TOTE £3.90: £2.30 £2.90 (£8.20) OWNER Bloy & Hughes (COCKERHAM) BRED Llety Stud 5 Rn 1m 12.8 (2.80) SF: 13/5/7/-/-
STEWARDS' ENQUIRY Obj. to Moi Canard by Connorton overruled.

2999
WILLIAM HILL SCOTTISH TROPHY H'CAP (0-70) (3-Y.O+) (Class E)
£7,230.00 (£2,190.00: £1,070.00: £510.00)
1m 65y Stalls: High GOING minus 0.51 sec per fur (F) 7-15 (7-24)

2397[3] **Sarmatian (USA) (63)***(74) (MDHammond)* 4-9-4 (5) DGriffiths(5) (chsd ldrs: slt ld wl over 1f out: all out).....................................— 1
2375[2] Habeta (USA) **(38)***(49) (JWWatts)* 9-7-12 LCharnock(11) (in tch: hdwy ½-wy: chal over 1f out: hrd drvn & r.o) ....hd 2

2397² Talented Ting (IRE) **(68)***(78) (PCHaslam)* 6-10-0 JFortune(1) (cl up: led ½-wy tl wl over 1f out: rallied fnl f)....nk 3
2788⁴ Thatched (IRE) **(50)***(60) (REBarr)* 5-8-10 NConnorton(12) (bhd: drvn along over 4f out: styd on wl fnl 2f: gng on fin)....nk 4
2906² Sir Arthur Hobbs **(57)***(55)*(Fav)*(JLEyre)* 8-9-3 RLappin(2) (b: led to ½-wy: r.o one pce)....6 5
2862² Three Arch Bridge **(60)***(53) (MJohnston)* 3-8-13b TWilliams(4) (hmpd after s: chsd ldrs tl outpcd fnl 3f)....2½ 6
2928⁵ Legal Fiction **(67)***(59) (MJohnston)* 4-9-13 DeanMcKeown(3) (lw: hmpd after s: chsd ldrs: outpcd ½-wy: no imp after)....½ 7
2927⁵ Achill Princess **(43)***(33) (WTKemp)* 3-7-10 ow1 DaleGibson(6) (hmpd after s: in tch tl outpcd fnl 3f)....½ 8
2906⁴ Princess Maxine (IRE) **(59)***(47) (JJO'Neill)* 6-9-5 GDuffield(8) (lw: rdn ½-wy: a rr div)....1¾ 9
2797⁹ King Curan (USA) **(63)***(48) (ABailey)* 4-9-9b AMackay(7) (a bhd)....1¾ 10
2668⁵ Chantry Bellini **(43)***(8) (MrsSMAustin)* 6-8-3b JLowe(10) (b: b.hind: s.i.s: a bhd)....10 11

9/2 Sir Arthur Hobbs, **5/1** Three Arch Bridge, **6/1** Talented Ting (IRE), SARMATIAN (USA), **8/1** Habeta (USA), **17/2** Thatched (IRE), **11/1** King Curan (USA) (8/1-12/1), **12/1** Legal Fiction (op 8/1), **20/1** Chantry Bellini, Princess Maxine (IRE), **66/1** Achill Princess, CSF £46.06 CT £267.57 TOTE £8.10: £3.00 £3.60 £2.60 (£31.80) Trio £37.10 OWNER Mr Stuart Thomas Brankin (MIDDLEHAM) BRED David Allan 11 Rn 1m 44.4 (1.10) SF: 55/30/59/41/36/27/40/7/28/29/-

WEIGHT FOR AGE 3yo-7lb

3000 CAMERONIANS H'CAP (0-70) (3-Y.O) (Class E) £3,758.60 (£1,137.80: £555.40: £264.20)

6f 5y Stalls: Low GOING minus 0.51 sec per fur (F) 7-45 (7-50)

2930* **Mister Westsound (52)***(62)*(Fav)*(MissLAPerratt)* 3-8-5b 7x GDuffield(1) (s.s: gd hdwy 2f out: led ins fnl f: r.o)....— 1
2972¹⁷ Commander Glen (IRE) **(51)***(57) (MartynMeade)* 3-8-4 7x TWilliams(7) (prom: hdwy ½-wy: ev ch ins fnl f: kpt on)....1½ 2
2784¹⁷ Tee Tee Too (IRE) **(52)***(53) (PCHaslam)* 3-8-5 JFortune(8) (lw: cl up: led 2f out: hdd ins fnl f: no ex)....1¾ 3
2624⁵ Cemaes Bay **(68)***(69) (JBerry)* 3-9-0 (7) PRoberts(3) (led 4f: rdn & r.o one pce)....hd 4
2770⁶ Teejay'n'aitch (IRE) **(48)***(46) (JSGoldie)* 3-7-12v(3) NVarley(4) (chsd ldrs tl rdn & btn appr fnl f)....1 5
2712⁵ Solianna **(59)***(56) (MRChannon)* 3-8-12 AMackay(2) (chsd ldrs: rdn 2f out: r.o one pce)....¾ 6
2818⁷ Oubeck Princess **(40)***(15) (EWeymes)* 3-7-7 JMarshall(6) (unruly leaving paddock: dwlt: n.d)....8 7
2502⁶ Blue Lugana **(43)***(17) (NBycroft)* 3-7-10b ow1 DaleGibson(5) (b: prom tl rdn & wknd fr ½-wy)....hd 8

11/4 MISTER WESTSOUND (2/1-3/1), **9/2** Solianna, Cemaes Bay, **6/1** Commander Glen (IRE), **13/2** Teejay'n'aitch (IRE), **7/1** Blue Lugana, **10/1** Tee Tee Too (IRE), **33/1** Oubeck Princess, CSF £18.13 CT £128.64 TOTE £3.80: £1.70 £2.30 £1.90 (£11.00) OWNER Mr R. McLean (AYR) BRED Red House Stud 8 Rn 1m 11.1 (1.10) SF: 31/26/22/38/15/25/-/-

3001 ORBISTON LIMITED STKS (0-55) (3-Y.O+) (Class F) £2,689.00 (£754.00: £367.00)

1m 3f 16y Stalls: High GOING minus 0.51 sec per fur (F) 8-15 (8-16)

2871* **Nornax Lad (USA) (48)***(66)*(Fav)*(MartynMeade)* 7-9-1b(7) RHavlin(3) (lw: sn trckng ldrs: led over 2f out: r.o u.p)....— 1
2851* Khan **(53)***(65) (CWThornton)* 3-8-12 DeanMcKeown(5) (hld up: hdwy 3f out: chsd wnr fnl 2f: r.o)....1 2
2731W Wild Rose of York **(54)***(50) (PMonteith)* 4-8-12 (3) NVarley(2) (led tl hdd over 2f out: rdn & one pce)....5 3
2774² Red Spectacle (IRE) **(54)***(55) (PCHaslam)* 3-8-10 TWilliams(4) (lw: hld up: effrt over 3f out: rdn & no rspnse)....hd 4
2584³ Chimanimani **(55)***(44) (NTinkler)* 4-9-6 GDuffield(1) (chsd ldrs tl wknd fnl 3f)....8 5

2/1 NORNAX LAD (USA), **9/4** Red Spectacle (IRE), **7/2** Khan (op 9/4), **6/1** Chimanimani, **14/1** Wild Rose of York, CSF £8.28 TOTE £3.10: £1.30 £2.00 (£6.00) OWNER Mrs B. Taylor (MALMESBURY) BRED Hillfields Farm 5 Rn 2m 21.4 (2.40) SF: 48/37/32/27/26

WEIGHT FOR AGE 3yo-10lb

3002

EARNOCK H'CAP (0-70) (3-Y.O+) (Class E) £3,828.80 (£1,159.40: £566.20: £269.60)
1m 5f 9y Stalls: High GOING minus 0.51 sec per fur (F) 8-45 (8-45)

2501[4] **Vain Prince (51)**_(62) (NTinkler)_ 8-9-5b LCharnock(2) (lw: trckd ldrs: shkn up over 3f out: led ins fnl f: styd on u.p)...— **1**
2835[2] Milngavie (IRE) **(30)**_(40) (MJohnston)_ 5-7-12b TWilliams(3) (lw: led 3f: led 4f out tl ins fnl f: kpt on wl)...½ **2**
2545[5] Opus One **(58)**_(67)_(Fav)_(MissSEHall)_ 4-9-12 NConnorton(7) (swtg: hld up: effrt 3f out: chal 1f out: no ex towards fin)...1 **3**
2871[3] Lord Advocate **(33)**_(36) (DANolan)_ 7-7-12b(3) NVarley(5) (trckd ldrs tl lost pl 8f out: rdn & hdwy 4f out: one pce fnl 2f)...5 **4**
2856[3] Gospel Song **(64)**_(65) (WTKemp)_ 3-9-6b GDuffield(6) (plld hrd: led after 3f to 4f out: grad wknd fnl 2½f)...1¾ **5**
1093[14] Elation **(58)**_(55) (GRichards)_ 3-9-0 DMcKeown(1) (hld up: hdwy over 4f out: wknd fnl 2f)......3½ **6**

11/10 Opus One, **9/2** Milngavie (IRE), **5/1** VAIN PRINCE (7/2-6/1), **9/1** Gospel Song, **10/1** Lord Advocate (7/1-11/1), **16/1** Elation, CSF £23.60 TOTE £5.20: £2.00 £1.20 (£8.10) OWNER Mr A. C. Findlay (MALTON) BRED Lodge Park Stud 6 Rn 2m 49.9 (4.20) SF: 38/16/43/12/29/19
WEIGHT FOR AGE 3yo-12lb
T/Plpt: £243.80 (51.89 Tckts). T/Qdpt: £89.90 (1.2 Tckts). AA

2708-SALISBURY (R-H)
Wednesday August 9th (Firm)

WEATHER: sunny, cloudy later WIND: almost nil

3003

E.B.F. SANDOWN MAIDEN STKS (2-Y.O) (Class D) £4,263.00 (£1,284.00: £622.00: £291.00)
6f Stalls: High GOING minus 0.50 sec per fur (F) 2-15 (2-16)

1017[4] **Bewitching (USA)** _(75) (JARToller)_ 2-8-6 (3) SSanders(3) (lw: a.p: led wl over 1f out: drvn out)...— **1**
Tina's Ridge _(79) (RHannon)_ 2-9-0 JReid(5) (unf: hld up: hdwy over 2f out: r.o ins fnl f).........½ **2**
2777[2] Surtees _(72)_(Fav)_(RCharlton)_ 2-9-0 WRyan(4) (lw: a.p: rdn over 1f out: one pce)...2½ **3**
2487[3] Therhea (IRE) _(72) (BRMillman)_ 2-9-0 BThomson(9) (led over 4f: r.o one pce)...s.h **4**
2801[2] Prime Partner **(80)**_(56) (WRMuir)_ 2-9-0 DHarrison(7) (prom over 3f)...6 **5**
2534[4] Roman Gold (IRE) **(84)**_(53) (RHannon)_ 2-9-0 MRoberts(2) (lw: nvr trbld ldrs)...1¼ **6**
The Man _(52) (MRChannon)_ 2-9-0 RHughes(8) (cmpt: prom 4f)...nk **7**
2876[8] Warming Trends _(52) (SirMarkPrescott)_ 2-9-0 JCarroll(1) (dwlt: a bhd)...hd **8**
2791[15] Tablets of Stone (IRE) _(30) (JRBosley)_ 2-9-0 VSlattery(6) (prom 3f)...8 **9**

8/11 Surtees, **6/1** Therhea (IRE), **13/2** BEWITCHING (USA), **12/1** Tina's Ridge (op 8/1), The Man (6/1-14/1), **14/1** Prime Partner (10/1-16/1), Roman Gold (IRE) (10/1-16/1), **33/1** Warming Trends, **66/1** Tablets of Stone (IRE), CSF £71.01 TOTE £8.40: £1.60 £2.90 £1.20 (£39.40) Trio £29.60 OWNER Mr P. C. J. Dalby (WHITSBURY) BRED B. Ned Jones and Dr James R. Cook 9 Rn
1m 14.06 (1.76) SF: 28/32/25/25/9/6/5/5/-

3004

H.S. LESTER MEMORIAL CHALLENGE CUP H'CAP (0-70) (3-Y.O+) (Class E) £3,626.00 (£1,088.00: £524.00: £242.00)
1m 1f 209y Stalls: High GOING minus 0.50 sec per fur (F) 2-45 (2-45)

2599[4] **Bookcase (65)**_(73)_(Fav)_(DRCElsworth)_ 8-9-11 MRoberts(5) (lw: hld up: stdy hdwy 2f out: r.o to ld wl ins fnl f)...— **1**
2861[W] Queens Stroller (IRE) **(54)**_(62) (CCElsey)_ 4-9-0 BDoyle(1) (led: rdn 2f out: hdd wl ins fnl f)....nk **2**
1732[8] Posing (IRE) **(67)**_(71) (JRFanshawe)_ 3-9-4 DHarrison(6) (chsd ldr: ev ch 2f out: nt qckn ins fnl f)...2 **3**
2698[15] It'sthebusiness **(56)**_(57) (SDow)_ 3-8-7 ow1 BThomson(4) (hld up: rdn over 3f out: hdwy over 2f out: one pce fnl f)...1¾ **4**
2316[7] Chocolate Charlie **(68)**_(57) (RCharlton)_ 4-10-0 TSprake(3) (prom: rdn over 3f out: wknd over 2f out)...8 **5**

5/4 BOOKCASE, **5/1** Queens Stroller (IRE), It'sthebusiness, **11/2** Posing (IRE), Chocolate Charlie, CSF £6.99 TOTE £2.00: £1.40 £1.90 (£2.80) OWNER Adept (80) Ltd (WHITCOMBE) BRED The Sussex Stud 5 Rn 2m 7.72 (3.02) SF: 45/34/34/20/29
WEIGHT FOR AGE 3yo-9lb

3005

AMESBURY CONDITIONS STKS (3-Y.O+ F & M) (Class C) £4,909.00
(£1,831.00: £890.50: £377.50: £163.75: £78.25)
5f Stalls: High GOING minus 0.50 sec per fur (F) 3-15 (3-18)

2677* **Iltimas (USA)** **(95)***(96)*(Fav)*(PTWalwyn)* 3-9-4 WCarson(5) (a.p: rdn over 2f out: ev ch whn hmpd ins fnl f: r.o wl: fin 2nd, s.h: awrdd r) ....— 1
2430[3] Lucky Parkes **(100)***(100)*(Fav)*(JBerry)* 5-9-12 JCarroll(2) (w ldr: led over 2f out: edgd lft ins fnl f: all out: fin 1st: disq: plcd 2nd)........ 2
2895a[5] Katya (IRE) **(92)***(95) (MRChannon)* 3-9-4 RHughes(1) (hld up: rdn & hdwy over 1f out: r.o wl ins fnl f) ....nk 3
1795[3] Overbrook **(96)***(97) (IABalding)* 3-9-6 WRSwinburn(3) (lw: hld up: nt clr run over 1f out: hdwy fnl f: r.o) ....s.h 4
1795[6] Painted Desert **(90)***(85) (RCharlton)* 3-8-12 JReid(6) (led over 2f: one pce fnl f)........1¼ 5
2570[7] Join the Clan **(93)***(85) (MrsNMacauley)* 6-9-9 (3) SDrowne(4) (hld up: n.m.r on ins over 2f out & over 1f out: nt rcvr)........3½ 6

9/4 ILTIMAS (USA), Lucky Parkes, **5/1** Katya (IRE) (3/1-11/2), **6/1** Overbrook, **7/1** Join the Clan, **10/1** Painted Desert, CSF £7.45 TOTE £3.40: £1.70 £1.60 (£3.80) OWNER Mr Hamdan Al Maktoum (LAMBOURN) BRED Shadwell Farm in USA 6 Rn

59.68 secs (-0.32) SF: 66/74/65/67/56/50
WEIGHT FOR AGE 3yo-4lb

3006

HEINEKEN H'CAP (0-70) (3-Y.O+ F & M) (Class E) £3,366.00
(£1,008.00: £484.00: £222.00)
1m 4f Stalls: High GOING minus 0.50 sec per fur (F) 3-45 (3-46)

2687* **Rocquaine Bay** **(40)***(48)*(Fav)*(MJBolton)* 8-8-1 JQuinn(4) (hld up: hdwy 5f out: slt ld 3f out: hrd rdn over 1f out: all out) ....— 1
2811[2] Soviet Bride (IRE) **(63)***(71) (SDow)* 3-8-6 (7) ADaly(6) (b.nr hind: plld hrd: led after 1f to 3f out: ev ch tl nt qckn ins fnl f) ....nk 2
2532[2] Victoria's Secret (IRE) **(66)***(70) (DRCElsworth)* 3-9-2b MRoberts(3) (led 1f: rdn over 2f out: r.o one pce fnl f) 3 3
2759[5] Roufontaine **(67)***(70) (WRMuir)* 4-9-11b(3) JTate(5) (hld up: hdwy 3f out: one pce fnl 2f)........¾ 4
Delicious **(60)***(57) (MajorDNChappell)* 3-8-10 BThomson(2) (rdn 4f out: sn bhd)........4 5
1824[7] Huish Cross **(58)***(43) (SGKnight)* 3-8-8 VSlattery(1) (plld hrd: prom tl wknd over 3f out)........9 6

15/8 ROCQUAINE BAY, **9/4** Soviet Bride (IRE), **7/2** Victoria's Secret (IRE), **8/1** Delicious, **10/1** Roufontaine (op 6/1), **12/1** Huish Cross (op 8/1), CSF £6.49 TOTE £2.60: £2.10 £1.40 (£2.90) OWNER Mr D. C. Woollard (SHREWTON) BRED Anne L. Woollard 6 Rn

2m 37.33 (4.73) SF: 17/29/28/39/15/1
WEIGHT FOR AGE 3yo-11lb

3007

UPAVON STKS (Listed) (3-Y.O+ F & M) (Class A) £11,268.00
(£4,212.00: £2,056.00: £880.00: £390.00: £194.00)
1m 1f 209y Stalls: High GOING minus 0.50 sec per fur (F) 4-15 (4-16)

2614[4] **Ellie Ardensky** **(90)***(102) (JRFanshawe)* 3-8-5 DHarrison(3) (lw: hdwy over 2f out: edgd lft over 1f out: led ins fnl f: drvn out) ....— 1
2561a[6] Cask **(97)***(105) (JHMGosden)* 3-8-9 JReid(8) (lw: chsd ldr: led over 2f out tl ins fnl f) ....¾ 2
2707* Vena (IRE) **(85)***(99) (JLDunlop)* 3-8-5 WCarson(7) (a.p: ev ch 1f out: nt qckn) 1¼ 3
Alusha *(95) (GWragg)* 3-8-5 RHills(2) (hdwy over 2f out: hrd rdn over 1f out: one pce) 2½ 4
2738* Jalfrezi **(90)***(94) (JARToller)* 3-8-5 SSanders(6) (hdwy on ins 3f out: hrd rdn 2f out: one pce)........nk 5
2621* Future Act (USA) **(94)***(92)*(Fav)*(HRACecil)* 3-8-5 WRyan(1) (prom tl rdn & wknd over 2f out) 1½ 6
2694[3] Quivira **(72)***(83) (TTClement)* 4-9-0 MRimmer(5) (prom tl wknd 3f out) 3 7
2780* Pursuit of Glory **(80)***(88) (CACyzer)* 4-9-0 DBiggs(9) (swtg: led tl wknd over 2f out) 2½ 8
Persian Bailiwick (IRE) *(35) (FJordan)* 3-8-5 JWilliams(4) (plld hrd: wknd 6f out: t.o fnl 3f)....30 9

13/8 Future Act (USA), **3/1** Jalfrezi, **9/2** Cask, **8/1** Alusha (6/1-9/1), **9/1** Vena (IRE), **12/1** ELLIE ARDENSKY (op 8/1), **20/1** Pursuit of Glory, **33/1** Quivira, **100/1** Persian Bailiwick (IRE), CSF £61.48 TOTE £11.90: £2.50 £1.60 £1.50 (£28.60) Trio £82.80 OWNER The Snailwell Stud Company Ltd (NEWMARKET) BRED Snailwell Stud Co Ltd 9 Rn

2m 6.13 (1.43) SF: 39/42/36/32/31/29/29/34/-
WEIGHT FOR AGE 3yo-9lb

3008 BEMBRIDGE CLAIMING STKS (2-Y.O) (Class F) £3,008.00 (£838.00: £404.00)
6f 212y Stalls: High GOING minus 0.50 sec per fur (F) 4-45 (4-46)

2732* **Traceability (70)**(70)(Fav)*(JBerry)* 2-9-1 JCarroll(1) (lw: hld up: led over 2f out: r.o wl).........— 1
2526[8] Daunting Destiny (BEL) *(71) (RHannon)* 2-9-5 JReid(6) (lw: hdwy 2f out: r.o one pce fnl f) ..1½ 2
2771[4] Spirito Libro (USA) *(63) (SirMarkPrescott)* 2-9-0 DHarrison(9) (led tl over 2f out: r.o one pce)1¼ 3
*2635** Arch Angel (IRE) **(58)***(43) (DJSffrenchDavis)* 2-8-6 NAdams(8) (w ldr: rdn 3f out: wknd 2f out)..........5 4
2846[12] Island Victory *(40) (IABalding)* 2-8-7 MRoberts(5) (nvr nrr)..........1¾ 5
1690[5] Back By Dawn **(56)***(52) (DRCElsworth)* 2-9-0 (5) AProcter(7) (b.hind: lw: prom tl wknd over 2f out)..........nk 6
1288[4] Chik's Secret *(40) (BPalling)* 2-8-10 TSprake(2) (rdn over 3f out: nvr nr to chal)..........1 7
2637[7] Spanish Luck **(62)***(27) (JWHills)* 2-8-6 BThomson(3) (prom tl wknd over 2f out)..........4 8
2656* Lindas Delight *(31) (JSMoore)* 2-9-0 AClark(4) (a bhd)..........1¾ 9

7/2 TRACEABILITY, **9/2** Arch Angel (IRE), **5/1** Spirito Libro (USA), Lindas Delight, **7/1** Island Victory, Back By Dawn, **8/1** Daunting Destiny (BEL), **20/1** Chik's Secret, Spanish Luck, CSF £29.48 TOTE £3.60: £1.70 £1.80 £1.60 (£20.90) Trio £58.50 OWNER Mr J. Clayton (COCKERHAM) BRED J. S. A. and Mrs Shorthouse 9 Rn 1m 27.39 (1.69) SF: 39/40/32/12/9/21/9/-/-
Traceability clmd MKirby £8,000

3009 ISLE OF WIGHT MAIDEN STKS (I) (2-Y.O) (Class D) £3,808.00 (£1,144.00: £552.00: £256.00)
6f 212y Stalls: High GOING minus 0.50 sec per fur (F) 5-15 (5-17)

2320[9] **St Mawes (FR)** *(75+)*(Fav)*(JLDunlop)* 2-9-0 WCarson(7) (hdwy 2f out: led ins fnl f: r.o wl)....— 1
2434[3] Proper Blue (USA) **(86)***(72) (TGMills)* 2-9-0 JCarroll(4) (a.p: led wl over 1f out tl ins fnl f: r.o)1¼ 2
2580[2] Auriga *(66) (IABalding)* 2-8-9 WRSwinburn(3) (chsd ldr: led over 2f out tl wl over 1f out: r.o one pce)..........½ 3
2370[7] Decision Maker (IRE) *(67) (RHannon)* 2-9-0 RPerham(5) (a.p: one pce fnl 2f)..........1¾ 4
Waterland (USA) *(60) (RCharlton)* 2-8-9 DHarrison(9) (a.p: ev ch 2f out: one pce)..........1 5
Take Note (IRE) *(37) (NAGraham)* 2-9-0 AMcGlone(8) (unf: dwlt: bhd fnl 3f)..........12 6
Macmorris (USA) *(36) (PFICole)* 2-9-0 JReid(10) (w'like: led tl wknd over 2f out)..........½ 7
2526[16] High Desire (IRE) *(25) (JRArnold)* 2-8-9 NAdams(1) (a bhd)..........2½ 8
Ben Bowden *(30) (MBlanshard)* 2-9-0 StephenDavies(2) (unf: a bhd)..........s.h 9

7/4 ST MAWES (FR), **15/8** Auriga, **11/2** Proper Blue (USA), **7/1** Waterland (USA), **9/1** Macmorris (USA) (op 6/1), **14/1** Ben Bowden, **20/1** Decision Maker (IRE), **33/1** Take Note (IRE), **50/1** High Desire (IRE), CSF £12.49 TOTE £3.30: £1.30 £1.70 £1.10 (£9.20) Trio £3.70 OWNER Lord Swaythling (ARUNDEL) BRED Societe Aland 9 Rn 1m 27.95 (2.25) SF: 32/29/23/24/17/-/-/-/-

3010 ISLE OF WIGHT MAIDEN STKS (II) (2-Y.O) (Class D) £3,808.00 (£1,144.00: £552.00: £256.00)
6f 212y Stalls: High GOING minus 0.50 sec per fur (F) 5-45 (5-52)

2320[10] **Villeggiatura** *(76) (BWHills)* 2-9-0 WRSwinburn(9) (a.p: led over 2f out: r.o)..........— 1
2370[6] Prize Giving *(74) (GWragg)* 2-9-0 FNorton(1) (gd hdwy over 1f out: r.o: nt rch wnr)..........¾ 2
2408[10] Gelsemine *(68) (HCandy)* 2-8-9 WNewnes(8) (led: jinked lft 4f out: hdd over 2f out: r.o) ....¾ 3
Wood Magic *(71+)*(Fav)*(DRLoder)* 2-8-11 (3) DRMcCabe(2) (gd sort: bhd & plld hrd: hdwy 2f out: r.o ins fnl f)..........½ 4
Utmost Zeal (USA) *(67) (PWHarris)* 2-9-0 BThomson(4) (unf: a.p: ev ch 2f out: one pce) 2 5
Financial Star (IRE) *(57) (JLDunlop)* 2-8-9 SWhitworth(10) (leggy: unf: hdwy 2f out: nvr nr to chal)..........2 6
East India (IRE) *(59) (RCharlton)* 2-9-0 DHarrison(5) (w'like: scope: bit bkwd: chsd ldr: hmpd 4f out: wknd 2f out)..........1½ 7
Dramatic Moment *(48) (IABalding)* 2-8-9 SO'Gorman(6) (unf: scope: bit bkwd: prom tl wknd over 2f out)..........2½ 8
Veiled Dancer (IRE) *(42) (JLDunlop)* 2-8-9 MRoberts(3) (w'like: scope: bit bkwd: a bhd) 2½ 9
2526[13] Atlantic Mist *(44) (BRMillman)* 2-9-0 JWilliams(7) (bhd fnl 2f)..........1¼ 10

9/4 Wood Magic, **11/4** VILLEGGIATURA, **3/1** Prize Giving (9/2-11/4), **10/1** Gelsemine, Veiled Dancer (IRE), **14/1** East India (IRE) (op 8/1), **20/1** Utmost Zeal (USA), Dramatic Moment, **33/1** Financial Star (IRE), Atlantic Mist, CSF £11.52 TOTE £3.60: £1.30 £1.90 £3.10 (£7.70) Trio £22.60 OWNER Maktoum Al Maktoum (LAMBOURN) BRED GAINSBOROUGH STUD MANAGEMENT LTD 10 Rn 1m 28.18 (2.48) SF: 30/28/22/25/21/11/13/2/-/-

T/Plpt: £25.60 (599.51 Tckts). T/Qdpt: £11.70 (6.7 Tckts). KH

2552-SANDOWN (R-H)
Wednesday August 9th (Good to firm)
WEATHER: very warm WIND: almost nil

3011
PACEMAKER & THOROUGHBRED BREEDER RACING SCHOOLS APPRENTICE H'CAP (0-80) (3-Y.O+) (Class E) £4,123.50 (£1,248.00: £609.00: £289.50)
1m 14y Stalls: High GOING minus 0.17 sec per fur (GF) 5-55 (5-55)

2668[6] **Prizefighter (60)**_(70)_(Fav)_(JLEyre)_ 4-8-11 JTate(6) (mde all: r.o wl) — 1
2537* Apollono **(73)**_(80) (RAkehurst)_ 3-9-3 SSanders(8) (6th st: chsd wnr over 2f out: unable qckn) 1¾ 2
2031[5] Desert Time **(77)**_(83) (MRChannon)_ 5-9-11 (3) DSweeney(5) (nt clr run on ins over 2f out: swtchd lft: hdwy over 1f out: r.o one pce) ½ 3
2808* Inderaputeri **(59)**_(58) (MissGayKelleway)_ 5-8-10 5x SDrowne(7) (3rd st: rdn over 2f out: wknd over 1f out) 3½ 4
2369[14] Helios **(74)**_(66) (NJHWalker)_ 7-9-11 RPainter(2) (lw: nvr nr to chal) 3½ 5
2669[7] Kingchip Boy **(72)**_(61) (MJRyan)_ 6-9-9v MBaird(3) (5th st: wknd over 3f out) 1¼ 6
2946* Fort Knox (IRE) **(54)**_(43) (RMFlower)_ 4-8-5b 5x CTeague(1) (a bhd) s.h 7
2602[2] Mr Nevermind (IRE) **(67)**_(55) (GLMoore)_ 5-9-4 LSuthern(9) (2nd st: wknd over 1f out) ½ 8
2843* Tuigamala **(42)**_(29) (RIngram)_ 4-7-1 (6) 5x JFowle(4) (lw: 4th st: wknd over 3f out) ¾ 9
LONG HANDICAP Tuigamala 6-12

7/2 PRIZEFIGHTER, **9/2** Apollono (op 3/1), Fort Knox (IRE), **6/1** Desert Time, **7/1** Kingchip Boy, **9/1** Inderaputeri, **10/1** Mr Nevermind (IRE), **16/1** Helios, Tuigamala, CSF £18.43 CT £82.25 TOTE £4.20: £1.50 £2.20 £2.20 (£8.20) Trio £25.80 OWNER Diamond Racing Ltd (HAMBLETON) BRED J. K. Bloodstock Ltd 9 Rn 1m 42.7 (3.50) SF: 47/50/60/35/43/38/20/32/6
WEIGHT FOR AGE 3yo-7lb

3012
SQUASH & FITNESS CENTRE MEDIAN AUCTION MAIDEN STKS (2-Y.O) (Class F) £3,371.25 (£1,020.00: £497.50: £236.25)
5f 6y Stalls: High GOING minus 0.54 sec per fur (F) 6-25 (6-26)

2660[8] **Supreme Power** _(70) (WRMuir)_ 2-9-0b CRutter(3) (lw: mde all: clr over 3f out: unchal) — 1
2651[4] Rebel County (IRE) _(54) (DJSCosgrove)_ 2-8-9 MRimmer(5) (lw: a.p: rdn over 2f out: unable qckn) 3½ 2
1977[15] It's A Ripper _(53) (GLewis)_ 2-9-0 PaulEddery(6) (lw: lost pl over 2f out: rallied fnl f: r.o) 2 3
Lady Caroline Lamb (IRE) _(47) (MRChannon)_ 2-8-9 RHughes(4) (unf: a.p: rdn 2f out: one pce) nk 4
2791[13] Hartfields Boy _(40) (BJMeehan)_ 2-9-0 BDoyle(7) (lw: outpcd) 3½ 5
Toe Tappin Music (USA) _(40) (MartynMeade)_ 2-9-0 VSlattery(2) (w'like: bit bkwd: hld up: rdn over 2f out: sn wknd) s.h 6
1935[6] Saturiba (USA) _(24) (MJohnston)_ 2-8-11 (3) JStack(1) (lw: prom over 2f) 5 7
2801[3] Grey Legend **(80)**_(68d)_(Fav)_(RMFlower)_ 2-9-0b DBiggs(8) (swtg: a wl bhd: t.o) dist 8

3/1 Grey Legend, **7/2** Lady Caroline Lamb (IRE), **4/1** Rebel County (IRE), **13/2** SUPREME POWER, **7/1** Saturiba (USA) (5/1-15/2), **10/1** It's A Ripper (6/1-12/1), **12/1** Hartfields Boy (op 7/1), **25/1** Toe Tappin Music (USA), CSF £29.97 TOTE £8.80: £2.10 £1.40 £2.70 (£16.00) OWNER Mr A. J. de V Patrick (LAMBOURN) BRED Richard M. Whitaker 8 Rn 61.38 secs (1.58) SF: 27/11/10/4/-/-/-/-

3013
SANDOWN EXHIBITION CENTRE CONDITIONS STKS (3-Y.O+) (Class C) £5,292.00 (£1,852.00: £906.00: £390.00)
1m 14y Stalls: High GOING minus 0.17 sec per fur (GF) 6-55 (6-55)

2417[2] **Shemaq (USA) (90)**_(98) (HThomsonJones)_ 3-8-6 RHills(1) (lw: mde all: rdn over 2f out: r.o wl) — 1
2471* Romanzof **(106)**_(108)_(Fav)_(HRACecil)_ 3-9-5 WRyan(4) (lw: chsd wnr: rdn over 2f out: ev ch 1f out: unable qckn) 1¾ 2
Jumilla (USA) **(85)**_(83) (GWragg)_ 3-8-4 PaulEddery(5) (s.s: 4th st: nvr nr to chal) 5 3
Scenic Heights (IRE) _(66) (RWArmstrong)_ 3-8-11 RPrice(2) (3rd st: rdn over 2f out: wknd over 1f out) 12 4

Evens Romanzof, **5/4** SHEMAQ (USA), **12/1** Jumilla (USA) (op 6/1), Scenic Heights (IRE) (6/1-14/1), CSF £2.79 TOTE £2.50: (£1.30) OWNER Mr Hamdan Al Maktoum (NEWMARKET) BRED Thomas P. Whitney in USA 4 Rn 1m 42.42 (3.22) SF: 45/55/30/13

3014
GOLF CLUB H'CAP (0-70) (3-Y.O+) (Class E) £3,501.25
(£1,060.00: £517.50: £246.25)
5f 6y Stalls: High GOING minus 0.54 sec per fur (F) 7-25 (7-27)

2753[5] **King Rat (IRE) (62)***(68) (TJEtherington)* 4-9-10b WCarson(5) (lw: chsd ldr: led over 1f out: pushed out)......— 1
Correspondence (CAN) **(40)***(43) (MartynMeade)* 5-7-11 (5) MHenry(4) (swtg: a.p: ev ch ins fnl f: unable qckn)......1 2
2887* Judgement Call **(52)***(51) (PHowling)* 8-9-0 7x PaulEddery(8) (b: led over 3f: one pce)......1¼ 3
2491[3] Sizzling **(62)***(59) (RHannon)* 3-9-6 JReid(7) (hld up: rdn over 3f out: r.o one pce)......¾ 4
2909[11] Moujeeb (USA) **(60)***(56) (PatMitchell)* 5-9-5v(3) JTate(9) (lw: rdn over 2f out: hdwy over 1f out: r.o one pce)......s.h 5
2850[4] Domicksky **(59)***(49) (MRChannon)* 7-9-7 RHughes(2) (lw: nvr nr to chal)......2 6
2867[4] Bold Gem **(53)***(43)*(Fav)*(BJMeehan)* 4-9-1b BDoyle(6) (a bhd)......hd 7
2850[2] Miriam **(50)***(36) (MJFetherston-Godley)* 4-8-5 (7) DaneO'Neill(3) (hld up: rdn wl over 1f out: sn wknd)......1¼ 8
2190[2] Diebiedale **(55)***(31) (RBoss)* 3-8-13 WRyan(1) (lw: bhd fnl 2f)......3 9

4/1 Bold Gem, **5/1** Sizzling, **11/2** Miriam, **13/2** KING RAT (IRE), **7/1** Judgement Call, **8/1** Moujeeb (USA), **10/1** Diebiedale (8/1-12/1), **11/1** Domicksky, **16/1** Correspondence (CAN), CSF £83.46 CT £668.57 TOTE £6.00: £2.00 £3.30 £2.20 (£75.40) Trio £310.80 OWNER Mr Paul Daniels (MALTON) BRED Airlie Stud 9 Rn
60.54 secs (0.74) SF: 50/25/33/37/38/31/25/18/9
WEIGHT FOR AGE 3yo-4lb

3015
SURREY RACING H'CAP (0-90) (3-Y.O+) (Class C) £5,446.00
(£1,648.00: £804.00: £382.00)
1m 6f Stalls: High GOING minus 0.17 sec per fur (GF) 7-55 (7-57)

2845* **Broughtons Formula (48)***(59) (WJMusson)* 5-7-10b JQuinn(4) (lw: 5th st: led wl over 1f out: rdn: r.o wl)......— 1
2555* Thaljanah (IRE) **(87)***(96)*(Fav)*(ACStewart)* 3-9-8 WCarson(3) (b.hind: lw: plld hrd: chsd ldr: rdn over 2f out: ev ch wl over 1f out: unable qckn)......1¾ 2
2530[4] Ela Man Howa **(55)***(61) (RAkehurst)* 4-8-0 (3) SSanders(5) (b.nr fore: led over 12f: one pce) .2½ 3
1872[14] Nine Barrow Down (IRE) **(75)***(80) (HRACecil)* 3-8-10 WRyan(2) (lw: plld hrd: 4th st: rdn over 2f out: one pce)......¾ 4
2829[5] Miss Pin Up **(80)***(76) (WJHaggas)* 6-10-0 RMcGhin(1) (3rd st: wknd over 2f out)......8 5

5/2 Thaljanah (IRE) (7/4-11/4), **100/30** BROUGHTONS FORMULA, **7/2** Ela Man Howa (tchd 9/4), **9/2** Nine Barrow Down (IRE), **11/2** Miss Pin Up, CSF £10.81 TOTE £3.60: £1.40 £1.50 (£3.00) OWNER Crawford Gray & Aylett (NEWMARKET) BRED The Lavington Stud 5 Rn
3m 4.37 (9.67) SF: 13/37/15/21/30
WEIGHT FOR AGE 3yo-13lb

3016
CHANNEL ONE MAIDEN STKS (3-Y.O+) (Class D) £3,842.50
(£1,165.00: £570.00: £272.50)
1m 2f 7y Stalls: High GOING minus 0.17 sec per fur (GF) 8-25 (8-33)

2571[2] **Polydamas (84)***(87)*(Fav)*(MRStoute)* 3-8-12 WRSwinburn(14) (4th st: led over 2f out: r.o wl)— 1
1339[4] Step Aloft *(81) (LordHuntingdon)* 3-8-7 DHarrison(10) (lw: 6th st: rdn over 2f out: r.o ins fnl f)¾ 2
2553[5] Ranosh (USA) *(78) (EALDunlop)* 3-8-7 PaulEddery(15) (b: b.hind: lw: 7th st: nt clr run over 3f out & wl over 1f out: r.o one pce)......1¾ 3
Lost Lagoon (USA) *(83) (HRACecil)* 3-8-12 WRyan(7) (b: w'like: scope: lw: 5th st: ev ch wl over 1f out: one pce)......nk 4
2790[2] Persian Saint (IRE) **(76)***(80) (DRCElsworth)* 4-9-2 (5) AProcter(8) (3rd st: rdn over 2f out: one pce)......1¾ 5
Chief Bee *(74) (JLDunlop)* 4-9-2 WCarson(19) (bit bkwd: stdy hdwy fnl 2f: r.o: bttr for r)......¾ 6
2553[3] Keen To The Last (FR) *(78) (GHarwood)* 3-8-12 AClark(12) (swtg: nvr nr to chal)......½ 7
2790[7] As You Like it (USA) *(77) (JHMGosden)* 3-8-12 GHind(6) (nvr plcd to chal)......¾ 8
1675[6] Knotally Wood (USA) *(70) (JWHills)* 3-8-2 (5) MHenry(3) (a mid div)......1¼ 9
888[3] Suvalu (USA) **(78)***(55) (PFICole)* 3-8-12 CRutter(4) (nvr nrr)......1 10
Election Day (IRE) *(49) (MRStoute)* 3-8-12 JReid(18) (leggy: scope: nvr nrr)......4 11
1983[6] Dixiemelody *(47) (RHannon)* 3-8-12 RPerham(13) (nvr nrr)......1 12
2553[4] Night Flare (FR) *(44) (RHannon)* 3-8-12 SRaymont(11) (lw: led over 7f)......2½ 13
2711[10] Red Morning **(60)***(38) (DRCElsworth)* 3-8-7 BDoyle(2) (bhd fnl 3f)......½ 14
673[6] Tabdeel *(39) (ACStewart)* 3-8-7 (5) MHumphries(1) (a bhd)......2½ 15
2684[7] Barbrallen **(35)***(29) (DJSffrenchDavis)* 3-8-7 RPrice(9) (lw: bhd fnl 2f)......3 16
2532[6] Devon Peasant *(28) (LGCottrell)* 3-8-7 BThomson(5) (2nd st: wknd 3f out)......½ 17

Flora's Temple (USA) *(4) (JARToller)* 4-9-2 WNewnes(17) (w'like: bit bkwd: a bhd) 15 **18**

2/1 POLYDAMAS, **7/2** Keen To The Last (FR), **5/1** Ranosh (USA) (7/2-11/2), **9/1** Lost Lagoon (USA) (5/1-10/1), **12/1** As You Like it (USA), Chief Bee (8/1-14/1), **14/1** Election Day (IRE) (op 8/1), Persian Saint (IRE) (10/1-16/1), Night Flare (FR) (12/1-20/1), **16/1** Knotally Wood (USA), **20/1** Suvalu (USA), **25/1** Step Aloft, Flora's Temple (USA), **33/1** Devon Peasant, **40/1** Dixiemelody, **50/1** Red Morning, Tabdeel, **100/1** Barbrallen, CSF £57.55 TOTE £3.30: £1.60 £5.60 £2.40 (£36.40) Trio £88.60 OWNER Mr Athos Christodoulou (NEWMARKET) 18 Rn

2m 8.44 (4.14) SF: 50/44/41/46/52/46/41/40/33/18/12/10/7/1/2/-/-/-

WEIGHT FOR AGE 3yo-9lb

T/Jkpt: Not won; £6,962.66 to Salisbury 10/8/95. T/Plpt: £135.30 (124.78 Tckts). T/Qdpt: £63.50 (6.5 Tckts). AK

2990-BEVERLEY (R-H)
Thursday August 10th (Good to firm)
WEATHER: sunny, v.hot WIND: slt half bhd

3017
TOLL GAVEL (S) H'CAP (0-60) (3-Y.O+) (Class E) £3,189.00 (£957.00: £461.00: £213.00)
2m 35y Stalls: Centre GOING minus 0.65 sec per fur (HD) 2-15 (2-16)

2355⁹ **Brodessa (57)***(67)*(Fav)*(MrsMReveley)* 9-10-0 KDarley(5) (hld up: hdwy on outside 6f out: led over 2f out: drvn out).................................— **1**

*2632** Fools of Pride (IRE) **(37)***(45) (RHollinshead)* 3-7-7 JQuinn(8) (trckd ldrs: styd on fnl 2f: no imp).................................2½ **2**

2860⁹ Can She Can Can **(48)***(51) (MJohnston)* 3-8-4 DHolland(7) (led tl over 2f out: one pce) 5 **3**

2919¹¹ Top Prize **(30)***(25) (MBrittain)* 7-8-1 JLowe(1) (chsd ldrs: pushed along after 4f: outpcd fnl 2f).8 **4**

2785⁵ Doctor's Remedy **(27)***(13) (MrsJJordan)* 9-7-5b(7) JoHunnam(2) (bhd & pushed along 10f out: kpt on fnl 3f: n.d).................................9 **5**

Little Conker **(25)***(4) (ASmith)* 7-7-10 LCharnock(6) (b: in tch: rdn along ½-wy: lost pl over 3f out).................................7 **6**

2509⁶ Dolly Dolittle **(25)** *(HJCollingridge)* 4-7-10 ow3 AMackay(4) (chsd ldrs: pushed along 6f out: lost pl 4f out).................................25 **7**

Aston Court **(29)** *(BEllison)* 10-8-0 NKennedy(3) (hld up & bhd: pushed along ½-wy: t.o 4f out).................................dist **8**

LONG HANDICAP Dolly Dolittle 7-0 Fools of Pride (IRE) 7-3

11/8 BRODESSA, **3/1** Can She Can Can, **5/1** Fools of Pride (IRE), **11/2** Top Prize, **9/1** Doctor's Remedy, **20/1** Little Conker, Dolly Dolittle, **33/1** Aston Court, CSF £9.10 CT £17.33 TOTE £2.30: £1.20 £1.20 £1.60 (£3.60) OWNER Mr R. W. S. Jevon (SALTBURN) BRED B. Fairs 8 Rn

3m 34.6 (4.10) SF: 43/6/12/1/-/-/-/-

WEIGHT FOR AGE 3yo-15lb

No bid

3018
HOLDERNESS PONY CLUB CLAIMING STKS (2-Y.O) (Class E) £3,345.00 (£1,005.00: £485.00: £225.00)
5f Stalls: Centre GOING minus 0.65 sec per fur (HD) 2-45 (2-48)

2423⁴ **No Monkey Nuts (70)***(81)*(Fav)*(JBerry)* 2-8-10 JCarroll(8) (mde all: drvn clr over 1f out: unchal).................................— **1**

2859² Hoh Majestic (IRE) **(76)***(68) (MBell)* 2-8-8v MFenton(2) (a chsng wnr: rdn 2f out: no imp)......3½ **2**

2859³ April's Joy **(49)***(47) (JNorton)* 2-7-11 DaleGibson(13) (a chsng ldrs: kpt on same pce u.p fr ½-wy) 3 **3**

Colway Bridge *(55+) (MrsMReveley)* 2-9-0 KDarley(4) (w'like: cmpt: bit bkwd: sn outpcd & drvn along: hdwy ½-wy: styd on fnl f).................................3 **4**

1213⁶ Melos *(45) (RonaldThompson)* 2-8-9 SDWilliams(12) (chsd ldrs tl wknd over 1f out)............1½ **5**

2750³ Lawnswood Captain (IRE) **(56)***(35) (RHollinshead)* 2-8-1 (3) AGarth(10) (mid div: rdn & hung lft ½-wy: styng on whn n.m.r ins fnl f).................................1½ **6**

Candy Dancer *(36) (CWThornton)* 2-8-6 DeanMcKeown(5) (cmpt: unf: outpcd & bhd: sme hdwy 2f out: n.d).................................nk **7**

2666ᵂ Northern Falcon *(35) (MWEasterby)* 2-8-9 LCharnock(11) (unf: s.s: wl bhd tl sme hdwy fnl 2f).................................1¼ **8**

Jenny's Charmer *(28) (SEKettlewell)* 2-8-8 JWeaver(1) (cmpt: bit bkwd: s.i.s: a bhd)...........1¾ **9**

2496¹⁰ Brogans Brush **(45)***(12) (CWFairhurst)* 2-8-0 JLowe(3) (sn bhd & pushed along: wandered ½-wy).................................2½ **10**

Mulhollande Lad (IRE) *(10) (MCChapman)* 2-8-11 (3) DRMcCabe(9) (str: cmpt: bkwd: s.s: a wl bhd).................................5 **11**

Macs Clan *(NPLittmoden)* 2-8-1 ow2 TGMcLaughlin(7) (unf: b.hind: outpcd fr ½-wy)..............5 **12**

Lugana Boy *(ASmith)* 2-9-0b MBirch(6) (leggy: swvd bdly lft s: virtually t.n.p) 13

11/8 NO MONKEY NUTS, **15/8** Hoh Majestic (IRE), **7/1** April's Joy, **9/1** Lawnswood Captain (IRE), **12/1** Colway Bridge, **16/1** Candy Dancer, **20/1** Northern Falcon, Jenny's Charmer, **25/1** Macs Clan, Brogans Brush, Lugana Boy, **33/1** Mulhollande Lad (IRE), **50/1** Melos, CSF £5.13 TOTE £2.40: £1.30 £1.40 £1.60 (£2.70) Trio £3.00 OWNER The Monkey Racing Club Ltd (COCKERHAM) BRED Miss C. Tagart 13 Rn 62.6 secs (1.10) SF: 25/12/-/-/-/-/-/-/-/-/-/-/-

3019

KINGSWOOD NURSERY H'CAP (2-Y.O) (Class D) £3,574.00
(£1,072.00: £516.00: £238.00)
7f 100y Stalls: High GOING minus 0.65 sec per fur (HD) 3-15 (3-17)

2454[4] **Champagne Prince (81)***(89) (PWHarris)* 2-9-7 JWeaver(4) (lw: trckd ldrs: led over 2f out: drvn clr over 1f out: styd on strly) .... — 1
2644[3] Russian Rascal (IRE) **(66)***(65) (MHEasterby)* 2-8-6 MBirch(3) (trckd ldrs: effrt over 2f out: hung rt: kpt on: no imp) 4 2
2855[2] Homeland **(56)***(55) (CWThornton)* 2-7-10 AMackay(5) (sn bhd: hdwy on outside over 2f out: styd on ins fnl f) .... nk 3
2765* Vanishing Point **(76)***(73)*(Fav)*(GLewis)* 2-9-2 PaulEddery(10) (sn drvn along & chsng ldrs: kpt on one pce appr fnl f) 1 4
1226* Takapuna (IRE) **(60)***(53) (TJNaughton)* 2-8-0 JQuinn(2) (s.i.s: sn drvn along: hdwy on outside 3f out: sn outpcd) 1½ 5
2855[7] Silverdale Knight **(74)***(62) (KWHogg)* 2-8-7 (7) ADaly(1) (led tl over 2f out: wknd over 1f out) .2½ 6
2914[6] Contradictory **(53)***(41) (MWEasterby)* 2-7-7 JLowe(6) (hld up: effrt over 2f out: sn rdn: n.d) ...hd 7
2715* Down The Yard **(61)***(41) (MCChapman)* 2-7-8 (7)ow1 CMunday(7) (hmpd after 1f: a in rr) 3 8
2516[10] Pat's Choice (IRE) **(57)***(38) (MHEasterby)* 2-7-11 SMaloney(8) (chsd ldrs: effrt & n.m.r over 1f out: sn wknd) .... s.h 9
2914[5] Northern Clan **(57)***(25) (MWEasterby)* 2-7-11 LCharnock(9) (hmpd after 1f: a bhd) 6 10

LONG HANDICAP Contradictory 7-6

5/2 Vanishing Point, **7/2** Takapuna (IRE), Homeland, **5/1** CHAMPAGNE PRINCE, **12/1** Russian Rascal (IRE), Silverdale Knight, **14/1** Pat's Choice (IRE), **16/1** Contradictory, Northern Clan, **20/1** Down The Yard, CSF £60.65 CT £222.43 TOTE £6.40: £2.20 £2.60 £1.70 (£40.70) Trio £44.90 OWNER Magnum Force (BERKHAMSTED) BRED Cheveley Park Stud Ltd 10 Rn
1m 33.3 (1.30) SF: 39/15/5/23/3/12/-/-/-/-

3020

EAST RIDING YEOMANRY CHALLENGE TROPHY AMATEUR H'CAP (0-80) (3-Y.O+) (Class E) £3,231.25 (£970.00: £467.50: £216.25)
7f 100y Stalls: High GOING minus 0.65 sec per fur (HD) 3-45 (3-46)

2814[3] **Kilnamartyra Girl (51)***(59) (JParkes)* 5-10-5 MrsDKettlewell(3) (effrt on ins over 2f out: styd on u.p to ld ins fnl f) .... — 1
2737[13] Kemo Sabo **(80)***(85)*(Fav)*(MrsJRRamsden)* 3-11-10 (4) MissERamsden(6) (lw: led 1f: trckd ldrs: led over 2f out: edgd lft: hdd & nt qckn ins fnl f) 1¼ 2
1323[5] Breezed Well **(43)***(46) (BRCambidge)* 9-9-7 (4) MrsHNoonan(1) (w ldrs: chal 3f out: nt qckn appr fnl f) 1¼ 3
2789[4] Love Legend **(52)***(48) (DWPArbuthnot)* 10-10-6 MrsDArbuthnot(2) (mde most after 1f tl over 2f out: wknd over 1f out) 3 4
2718[3] Spanish Stripper (USA) **(65)***(59) (MCChapman)* 4-11-1 (4) MrMMackley(4) (swtg: s.i.s: hdwy ½-wy: no imp fnl 2f) 1¼ 5
2664[8] Shift Again (IRE) **(72)***(60) (WJarvis)* 3-11-2 (4) MissIFoustok(5) (s.s: bhd: hdwy on outside 3f out: wknd over 1f out) 2½ 6

7/4 Kemo Sabo, **11/4** KILNAMARTYRA GIRL, **9/2** Love Legend, **13/2** Shift Again (IRE), Spanish Stripper (USA), **10/1** Breezed Well, CSF £8.04 TOTE £3.90: £1.60 £1.30 (£3.10) OWNER Mr P. J. Cronin (MALTON) BRED F. R. Colley 6 Rn 1m 34.2 (2.20) SF: 40/60/27/29/40/35
WEIGHT FOR AGE 3yo-6lb

3021

RAPID LAD H'CAP (0-90) (3-Y.O+) (Class C) £5,637.50
(£1,700.00: £825.00: £387.50)
1m 1f 207y Stalls: High GOING minus 0.65 sec per fur (HD) 4-15 (4-16)

2766* **Mellottie (87)***(99) (MrsMReveley)* 10-9-11 KDarley(6) (lw: hld up: effrt over 2f out: r.o wl to ld wl ins fnl f) .... — 1
2327[4] Larn Fort **(55)***(67) (CWFairhurst)* 5-7-7v LCharnock(4) (hld up: effrt & hmpd over 2f out: led jst ins fnl f: hung rt: hdd & nt qckn towards fin) .... s.h 2

2593[9] Desert Power **(65)***(73) (DBurchell)* 6-8-3 RPrice(9) (trckd ldrs: hdwy on ins to ld wl over 1f out: hdd jst ins fnl f: nt qckn)....2½ **3**
2903[2] Senorita Dinero (USA) **(83)***(87)*(Fav)*(MRStoute)* 3-8-12 DHolland(5) (w ldrs: led over 2f out: sn hdd: kpt on same pce)....2½ **4**
2672[4] Jubran (USA) **(64)***(68) (MJohnston)* 9-8-2 TWilliams(7) (plld hrd: trckd ldrs: effrt & n.m.r 2f out: kpt on one pce)....hd **5**
2752[3] Hazard a Guess (IRE) **(77)***(78) (MrsJRRamsden)* 5-9-1 KFallon(3) (hld up: effrt on outside over 2f out: wknd over 1f out)....2 **6**
2701[4] Vindaloo **(82)***(79) (JLHarris)* 3-8-11 JWeaver(2) (racd wd: hdwy to trck ldrs after 2f: effrt & hmpd over 2f out: sn wknd)....2½ **7**
Who's Tef (IRE) **(55)***(49) (MHEasterby)* 7-7-7 JQuinn(8) (led tl over 7f out: n.m.r & wknd 2f out)....1¾ **8**
2643* Sherqy (IRE) **(83)***(73) (JLDunlop)* 3-8-12 PaulEddery(1) (racd wd: led over 7f out tl over 2f out: sn wknd)....2½ **9**

LONG HANDICAP Who's Tef (IRE) 7-1

5/2 Senorita Dinero (USA), **9/2** Vindaloo, Sherqy (IRE), MELLOTTIE, **13/2** Hazard a Guess (IRE), **7/1** Jubran (USA), **12/1** Desert Power, **16/1** Larn Fort, **33/1** Who's Tef (IRE), CSF £65.48 CT £753.05 TOTE £6.80: £1.90 £3.20 £2.70 (£91.60) Trio £168.00 OWNER Mrs J. G. Fulton (SALTBURN) BRED Mrs G. R. Reveley and Partners 9 Rn 2m 4.3 (1.80) SF: 42/10/16/21/11/21/13/-/7

WEIGHT FOR AGE 3yo-9lb

STEWARDS' ENQUIRY Quinn fined £250 (leaving course before weighed-in signal).

3022 E.B.F. WESTWOOD MAIDEN STKS (2-Y.O F) (Class D) £3,548.00 (£1,064.00: £512.00: £236.00)

5f Stalls: Centre GOING minus 0.65 sec per fur (HD) 4-45 (4-47)

1928[2] **Prancing** *(65+)*(Fav)*(DRLoder)* 2-8-11 KDarley(1) (lw: mde all: pushed clr over 1f out: easily)....— **1**
2487[8] Antonias Melody *(54) (SRBowring)* 2-8-11 SWebster(4) (chsd ldrs: sn drvn along: styd on u.p fnl f: no ch w wnr)....3½ **2**
671[10] Rustic Song (IRE) *(49) (JWharton)* 2-8-11 KFallon(2) (chsd wnr tl wknd over 1f out)....1½ **3**
2483[4] Forest Fantasy *(30) (JWharton)* 2-8-11 JFanning(5) (sn outpcd & pushed along)....6 **4**
Holloway Melody *(20) (BAMcMahon)* 2-8-11 SDWilliams(3) (cmpt: bit bkwd: dwlt: sn reminders: a wl outpcd)....3 **5**

1/12 PRANCING, **14/1** Forest Fantasy, **16/1** Antonias Melody, **50/1** Rustic Song (IRE), Holloway Melody, CSF £2.59 TOTE £1.10: £1.10 £1.50 (£3.10) OWNER Cheveley Park Stud (NEWMARKET) BRED Mrs P. D. Rossdale and Mrs D. H. Clifton 5 Rn

61.5 secs (0.50 under 2y best) (0.00) SF: 43/32/27/8/-

T/Plpt: £33.50 (366.16 Tckts). T/Qdpt: £11.40 (6.5 Tckts). WG

3003-SALISBURY (R-H)
Thursday August 10th (Firm)

WEATHER: sunny & hot WIND: slt half bhd

3023 BROAD CHALKE MAIDEN STKS (3-Y.O F) (Class D) £3,970.50 (£1,194.00: £577.00: £268.50)

6f 212y Stalls: High GOING minus 0.52 sec per fur (F) 2-00 (2-03)

Polar Queen *(85) (JHMGosden)* 3-8-11 GHind(8) (unf: scope: lw: hld up: swtchd lft 2f out: gd hdwy over 1f out: str run to ld last strides)....— **1**
1242[9] Fresh Fruit Daily **(80)***(85) (PAKelleway)* 3-8-11 MWigham(2) (w ldr: led over 2f out: hdd last strides)....hd **2**
2787[2] Azdihaar (USA) **(72)***(83)*(Fav)*(JLDunlop)* 3-8-11 WCarson(7) (lw: a.p: rdn 2f out: r.o one pce fnl f)....1 **3**
1128[6] Academy Life *(81) (PFICole)* 3-8-11 TQuinn(11) (lw: a.p: rdn 2f out: one pce fnl f)....¾ **4**
Swiss Bank *(76) (LordHuntingdon)* 3-8-11 DHarrison(13) (a.p: one pce fnl 2f)....2 **5**
1240[6] Hasaid Lady (IRE) **(69)***(67) (RHannon)* 3-8-11 JReid(5) (plld hrd early & hld up: no hdwy fnl 3f)....4 **6**
2553[8] Darcey Bussell *(58) (BWHills)* 3-8-11 BThomson(9) (bit bkwd: no hdwy fnl 3f)....4 **7**
Jilly Beveled *(52) (RHannon)* 3-8-11 RPerham(6) (lt-f: rdn over 3f out: nvr trbld ldrs)....2½ **8**
Spandrel *(47) (HCandy)* 3-8-11 WNewnes(10) (unf: scope: bit bkwd: dwlt: a bhd)....2 **9**
1979[17] River May *(47) (AndrewTurnell)* 3-8-11 NAdams(4) (s.s: a bhd)....nk **10**
Midnight Walker *(43) (MrsSDWilliams)* 3-8-11 JWilliams(12) (w'like: bit bkwd: a bhd)....1½ **11**
2583[4] Unfuwaanah *(39) (HThomsonJones)* 3-8-11 NCarlisle(3) (plld hrd: led over 4f: wknd qckly)....2 **12**
2438[10] Ilium Bourbon *(RJO'Sullivan)* 3-8-11 DBiggs(1) (lw: s.s: a bhd: t.o)....20 **13**

2/1 Azdihaar (USA), **5/1** POLAR QUEEN (op 3/1), Fresh Fruit Daily (op 5/2), **6/1** Academy Life (op 4/1), **8/1** Unfuwaanah (6/1-9/1), **10/1** Swiss Bank, **12/1** Darcey Bussell, Spandrel (op 6/1), **20/1** Hasaid Lady (IRE), **33/1** Midnight Walker, River May, **40/1** Jilly Beveled, Ilium Bourbon, CSF £31.19 TOTE £6.20: £1.90 £1.80 £1.20 (£25.70) Trio £12.90 OWNER Mr George Strawbridge (NEWMARKET) BRED George Strawbridge 13 Rn
1m 26.25 (0.55) SF: 47/47/45/43/38/29/20/14/9/9/5/1/-

3024 VIOLET APPLIN CHALLENGE CUP H'CAP (0-70) (3-Y.O+) (Class E)

£3,262.00 (£976.00: £468.00: £214.00)
1m 6f Stalls: High GOING minus 0.52 sec per fur (F) 2-30 (2-32)

2439² **Disputed Call (USA) (36)***(48) (JFfitch-Heyes)* 6-7-8 (5) MHenry(7) (sn chsng ldr: led over 4f out: clr whn edgd lft wl over 1f out: r.o wl) — 1
2713* Supreme Star (USA) **(55)***(58)*(Fav)*(PRHedger)* 4-9-1 (3) NVarley(5) (chsd wnr over 4f out: hrd rdn over 2f out: no imp) 8 2
2687¹³ Wottashambles **(47)***(39) (LMontagueHall)* 4-8-3 (7)ow7 GMitchell(8) (rdn & outpcd over 3f out: styd on one pce fnl 2f) 3½ 3
2514⁸ Hacketts Cross (IRE) **(53)***(51) (NoelChance)* 7-9-2 BThomson(2) (hmpd s: hld up in rr: hdwy 3f out: one pce fnl 2f) ¾ 4
2713² Un Parfum de Femme (IRE) **(65)***(56) (JPearce)* 4-9-11 (3) SSanders(6) (hld up & plld hrd: rdn 5f out: wknd over 3f out) 6 5
2829⁴ Emma Grimes (IRE) **(41)***(32) (JSMoore)* 4-8-4 AMcGlone(1) (prom: rdn 6f out: wknd 3f out) .nk 6
1513⁷ Saafi (IRE) **(50)** *(RJBaker)* 4-8-13 JWilliams(3) (plld hrd: led & sn clr: hdd over 4f out: wknd qckly: t.o fnl 3f) dist 7
2713⁷ Bee Beat **(37)** *(AJChamberlain)* 7-8-0 NCarlisle(4) (w.r.s: ref to r: t.n.p) R

7/4 Supreme Star (USA), **100/30** Un Parfum de Femme (IRE), **5/1** Wottashambles, **6/1** DISPUTED CALL (USA), **10/1** Emma Grimes (IRE) (op 6/1), **14/1** Bee Beat, **20/1** Hacketts Cross (IRE), Saafi (IRE), CSF £16.30 CT £49.67 TOTE £6.50: £1.40 £1.30 £1.90 (£8.10) OWNER Mr A. S. Champion (LEWES) BRED Ralph Wilson Jnr 8 Rn 3m 4.18 (5.98) SF: 11/21/2/14/19/-/-/-

3025 TATTERSALLS MAIDEN AUCTION STKS (2-Y.O) (Class E) £3,678.00

(£1,104.00: £532.00: £246.00)
6f Stalls: High GOING minus 0.52 sec per fur (F) 3-00 (3-01)

2660⁷ **Hurtleberry (IRE)** *(77) (LordHuntingdon)* 2-7-8 (5) MHenry(2) (a.p: led over 2f out tl wl over 1f out: led ins fnl f: r.o wl) — 1
2548¹⁰ Lucky Revenge **(50)***(75) (MartynMeade)* 2-7-8 (3) NVarley(3) (hld up: led wl over 1f out tl ins fnl f: r.o) hd 2
2660³ Fond Embrace *(67)*(Fav)*(HCandy)* 2-7-13 WCarson(4) (lw: plld hrd: a.p: rdn over 2f out: one pce fnl f) 3½ 3
2548⁹ Day Tripper *(64) (GBBalding)* 2-8-3 ow1 JWilliams(7) (lw: hld up & bhd: hdwy fnl 2f: nvr nrr) .2½ 4
1662³ Stronz (IRE) *(69) (RAkehurst)* 2-8-7 TQuinn(6) (rdn over 3f out: hdwy 2f out: one pce fnl f) ..hd 5
2932⁴ Seaford Star (IRE) *(56) (MRChannon)* 2-8-5 AClark(5) (led over 4f out tl over 2f out: one pce)4 6
2846⁴ Nikita's Star (IRE) *(56) (DJGMurraySmith)* 2-8-8 RCochrane(9) (bhd fnl 3f) 1 7
2340⁹ Efficacious (IRE) *(48) (CJBenstead)* 2-8-2 CRutter(8) (a bhd) ¾ 8
1123⁴ Delaunay (IRE) *(33) (RHannon)* 2-8-5 MRoberts(10) (prom over 3f) 7 9
2660¹² Longhill Boy *(27) (BJMeehan)* 2-8-6 BDoyle(1) (led over 1f: wknd 2f out) 2½ 10

4/6 Fond Embrace (op 5/4), **7/2** HURTLEBERRY (IRE) (5/2-4/1), **7/1** Stronz (IRE) (op 4/1), **9/1** Seaford Star (IRE), **10/1** Nikita's Star (IRE) (8/1-14/1), **11/1** Delaunay (IRE) (op 5/1), **50/1** Lucky Revenge, Longhill Boy, **66/1** Efficacious (IRE), Day Tripper, CSF £117.11 TOTE £6.40: £1.60 £5.60 £1.20 (£194.40) Trio £77.90 OWNER Mrs Ian Pilkington (WEST ILSLEY) BRED D. Maher 10 Rn 1m 13.25 (0.95) SF: 28/26/18/15/20/7/7/-/-/-

3026 TOTE BOOKMAKERS H'CAP (0-90) (3-Y.O+) (Class C) £5,832.50

(£1,760.00: £855.00: £402.50)
1m Stalls: High GOING minus 0.52 sec per fur (F) 3-30 (3-31)

2598⁹ **Fionn de Cool (IRE) (70)***(81) (RAkehurst)* 4-8-12 TQuinn(4) (mde all: r.o wl) — 1
2711* Almond Rock **(76)***(86)*(Fav)*(JRFanshawe)* 3-8-11 DHarrison(8) (hld up: nt clr run on ins over 1f out: hdwy fnl f: r.o) ¾ 2
2703¹⁸ Weaver Bird **(82)***(91) (HCandy)* 5-9-10 WNewnes(5) (lw: plld hrd in rr: nt clr run & plld out 2f out: hdwy fnl f: r.o) ½ 3
2685⁶ Dancing Lawyer **(68)***(76) (BJMeehan)* 4-8-10 BDoyle(1) (plld hrd: hdwy 2f out: edgd rt over 1f out: one pce fnl f) s.h 4
2367⁷ Atlaal (USA) **(75)***(80) (HThomsonJones)* 3-8-10 WCarson(6) (hld up: hdwy over 2f out: one pce fnl f) 1¾ 5

2906* Lord Oberon (IRE) **(64)**(66) (JAkehurst) 7-8-1 (5) 6x MHenry(2) (hld up mid div: nt clr run over 2f out: hmpd over 1f out: one pce) 1¼ 6
2811* Prince of Spades **(65)**(55) (CACyzer) 3-8-0 6x DBiggs(7) (chsd wnr tl wknd 2f out) 6 7
2436[11] Prussian Flag **(89)**(67) (RHannon) 3-9-10 JReid(3) (lw: prom: rdn & wkng whn hmpd 1f out) ...6 8

7/2 Almond Rock, **4/1** Weaver Bird, **9/2** FIONN DE COOL (IRE) (3/1-5/1), Lord Oberon (IRE), **9/1** Dancing Lawyer, **10/1** Atlaal (USA), **12/1** Prince of Spades (op 7/1), **14/1** Prussian Flag, CSF £18.83 CT £59.64 TOTE £5.90: £1.30 £1.80 £1.60 (£15.30) OWNER Mr R. F. Kilby (EPSOM) BRED Ciaran Quigley 8 Rn 1m 41.92 (2.62) SF: 29/27/39/24/21/14/-/8
WEIGHT FOR AGE 3yo-7lb

3027 WHITCHURCH CONDITIONS STKS (3-Y.O+) (Class C) £4,967.00 (£1,853.00: £901.50: £382.50: £166.25: £79.75)
6f 212y Stalls: High GOING minus 0.52 sec per fur (F) 4-00 (4-02)

2762[4] **Knight Commander (USA) (95)**(98) (RHannon) 3-8-12 MRoberts(1) (lw: hld up: led & edgd rt ins fnl f: r.o wl) ....— 1
Muktabas (IRE) (95)(Fav)(JHMGosden) 3-8-12 WCarson(6) (lw: chsd ldr: led over 1f out tl ins fnl f) 1¼ 2
2237[3] Hindaawee (USA) **(90)**(91) (EALDunlop) 3-8-9 (3) JTate(5) (hmpd s: hld up: hrd rdn 2f out: r.o one pce fnl f) 1¾ 3
2436[7] Everglades (IRE) **(103)**(101) (RCharlton) 7-10-0 TQuinn(3) (lw: swvd rt s: hld up: hrd rdn over 1f out: one pce) ....hd 4
Scotsky (IRE) (96) (JLDunlop) 3-9-4 WNewnes(4) (hmpd s: rdn 3f out: nvr nr to chal) ....½ 5
2409[9] Shamanic **(95)**(100) (RHannon) 3-9-8 JReid(2) (lw: led over 5f: sn btn) ....hd 6

15/8 Muktabas (IRE) (3/1-7/4), **2/1** Everglades (IRE) (op 5/4), **100/30** KNIGHT COMMANDER (USA), **15/2** Hindaawee (USA) (op 7/2), **14/1** Shamanic (8/1-16/1), **16/1** Scotsky (IRE), CSF £9.88 TOTE £3.20: £2.10 £1.60 (£4.70) OWNER Highclere Thoroughbred Racing Ltd (MARLBOROUGH) BRED Mrs J. G. Jones Snr and Ronald Judy 6 Rn 1m 26.67 (0.97) SF: 43/40/36/52/41/45
WEIGHT FOR AGE 3yo-6lb

3028 FRESHWATER H'CAP (0-80) (3-Y.O+) (Class D) £3,944.50(£1,186.00: £573.00: £266.50) 6f Stalls: High GOING minus 0.52 sec per fur (F) 4-30 (4-32)

2344[6] **Law Commission (77)**(85) (DRCElsworth) 5-9-11 MRoberts(9) (led early: stdd & sn bhd: plld out 2f out: nt clr run & swtchd lft over 1f out: rapid hdwy to ld nr fin) ....— 1
2652* Double Bounce **(69)**(76)(Fav)(PJMakin) 5-9-3 RCochrane(12) (hld up: n.m.r 2f out: hdwy over 1f out: r.o wl ins fnl f) ....nk 2
2448[6] Norling (IRE) **(47)**(53) (KOCunningham-Brown) 5-7-9 NCarlisle(1) (chsd ldr: led over 2f out: hdd nr fin) ....nk 3
2746[5] Dry Point **(71)**(77) (JARToller) 9-9-5 WNewnes(11) (lw: a.p: ev ch ins fnl f: nt qckn) ....nk 4
2531[5] Balance of Power **(73)**(69) (RAkehurst) 3-8-13 (3) SSanders(5) (nvr nr to chal) 3½ 5
2764[9] Agwa **(76)**(72) (RJO'Sullivan) 6-9-10 RHughes(3) (rdn over 2f out: no hdwy) ....s.h 6
2743[4] Anzio (IRE) **(67)**(59) (BAPearce) 4-9-1 SWhitworth(10) (b: chsd ldrs 4f) 1½ 7
1832[16] Slivovitz **(55)**(39) (MJHeaton-Ellis) 5-8-3b AClark(4) (sn led: hdd over 2f out: sn wknd) 3 8
Oare Sparrow **(73)**(56) (PTWalwyn) 5-9-7 DHarrison(2) (bit bkwd: prom over 4f) ....nk 9
2659[12] Poyle Jezebelle **(51)**(30) (MBlanshard) 4-7-13 StephenDavies(6) (n.d) 1½ 10
2737[16] Warning Shot **(75)**(38) (MartynMeade) 3-9-4 VSlattery(7) (rdn 4f out: sn bhd) 6 11
2470[6] Haddeyah (USA) **(80)**(33) (HThomsonJones) 3-9-9 WCarson(8) (lw: a bhd: t.o fnl 3f) 4 12

7/4 Double Bounce (op 3/1), **100/30** Agwa, **7/1** Dry Point, **10/1** Balance of Power (op 6/1), **11/1** Slivovitz (op 7/1), Haddeyah (USA) (10/1-20/1), **14/1** LAW COMMISSION (op 8/1), Poyle Jezebelle, **16/1** Anzio (IRE), Norling (IRE), Warning Shot, **20/1** Oare Sparrow, CSF £40.98 CT £405.47 TOTE £13.70: £3.50 £1.70 £3.50 (£12.10) Trio £44.60 OWNER Mr Raymond Tooth (WHITCOMBE) BRED Airlie Stud 12 Rn 1m 13.23 (0.93) SF: 53/44/21/45/32/40/27/7/24/-/1/-
WEIGHT FOR AGE 3yo-5lb

T/Jkpt: Not won; £14,079.77 to Newbury 11/8/95. T/Plpt: £16.80 (1,076.75 Tckts). T/Qdpt: £8.60 (9.5 Tckts). KH

2882-YARMOUTH (L-H)
Thursday August 10th (Good to firm)

WEATHER: sunny becoming cool WIND: fresh across

3029 BOTTON BROTHERS LADIES' H'CAP (0-70) (3-Y.O+) (Class G) £2,556.60 (£707.60: £337.80)
1m 6f 17y Stalls: High GOING minus 0.34 sec per fur (GF) 5-45 (5-46)

2824[3] **Outstayed Welcome (47)**(61) (MJHaynes) 3-9-10 MissYHaynes(10) (b.off hind: prom: led 6f out: clr 2f out: comf) ....— 1

2931* Claireswan (IRE) **(59)***(69)*(Fav)*(SCWilliams)* 3-10-8 4x MissKWright(6) (lw: led 8f: 2nd st: rdn over 2f out: kpt on: no ch w wnr) 3½ 2
2695 4 Dusty Point (IRE) **(55)***(64)* *(JPearce)* 5-11-3v MrsLPearce(8) (b: prom: 4th st: rdn over 3f out: one pce) ....¾ 3
2861 9 Modest Hope (USA) **(48)***(56)* *(BRichmond)* 8-10-10 MissDianaJones(3) (bhd tl r.o fnl 3f: nvr able to chal) ....¾ 4
2695 6 Ice Magic **(24)***(29)* *(FJYardley)* 8-8-11v(3) MissSYardley(4) (prom: 3rd st: sn chsng wnr: btn 2f out) 3 5
2745* Fruitful Affair (IRE) **(47)***(49)* *(TThomsonJones)* 6-10-9 MissKEllis(9) (plld hrd: prom: 5th & rdn st: no imp) 3 6
2745 2 Minnesota Viking **(59)***(43)*(Fav)*(LadyHerries)* 4-11-7 MrsMCowdrey(2) (swtg: hld up & bhd: hdwy 9f out: 7th st: eased whn btn over 1f out) 15 7
2713 4 Bresil (USA) **(40)** *(KRBurke)* 6-9-13 (3)ow9 MrsHSweeting(1) (lw: s.i.s: racd wd: bhd fnl 7f) 15 8
1696 10 Amercius **(45)** *(JEBanks)* 3-9-8 MissKMarks(7) (in tch: 6th st: sn btn) 25 9
2713 3 Persian Smoke **(43)** *(AHide)* 4-10-5 MissLHide(5) (s.i.s: a bhd) 25 10

LONG HANDICAP Ice Magic 8-12

7/2 Minnesota Viking, Claireswan (IRE), **4/1** Dusty Point (IRE), **11/2** Fruitful Affair (IRE), **15/2** Persian Smoke, **9/1** OUTSTAYED WELCOME, **10/1** Modest Hope (USA), **16/1** Amercius, **25/1** Bresil (USA), **33/1** Ice Magic, CSF £40.01 CT £137.40 TOTE £6.60: £1.80 £2.10 £2.00 (£32.10) Trio £18.20 OWNER Mrs B. Bell (EPSOM) BRED Hesmonds Stud Ltd 10 Rn

3m 5.6 (7.60) SF: 39/47/55/47/20/40/34/-/-/-
WEIGHT FOR AGE 3yo-13lb

3030 DAMGATE CONDITIONS STKS (3 & 4-Y.O) (Class D) £3,935.10 (£1,174.80: £561.40: £254.70)

1m 2f 21y Stalls: Low GOING minus 0.34 sec per fur (GF) 6-15 (6-19)

1807 3 **Sayeh (IRE) (92)***(95)* *(HThomsonJones)* 3-9-0 RHills(3) (lw: mde all: rdn & hld on wl appr fnl f) ....— 1
2703 10 Night City **(96)***(88)*(Fav)*(LadyHerries)* 4-8-10 (7) JO'Dwyer(5) (lw: hld up: hdwy & 3rd st: shkn up 3f out: r.o ins fnl f: nt rch wnr) ....¾ 2
Karttikeya (FR) *(84)* *(MrsNMacauley)* 4-9-3 PRobinson(2) (b: trckd ldrs: 5th st: plld out & rdn 2f out: one pce) 2½ 3
1846 2 Al Baha **(69)***(76)* *(HRACecil)* 3-8-3 WRyan(1) (chsd wnr: 2nd st: ev ch over 1f out: wknd ins fnl f) 1¾ 4
2638 4 Tafia (IRE) **(78)***(56)* *(JPearce)* 4-8-12 GBardwell(6) (stdd s: 6th st: nvr nr ldrs) 13 5
Persian Flower *(55)* *(GCBravery)* 3-8-5 ow2 MHills(4) (unf: bkwd: last st: rdn 3fout: a bhd) ....nk 6
Legaitak *(55)* *(BHanbury)* 3-8-5 (3) JStack(7) (leggy: unf: bit bkwd: bhd: effrt & 4th st: sn rdn & wknd) 3 7

11/10 Night City, **100/30** SAYEH (IRE), **4/1** Al Baha, **12/1** Karttikeya (FR) (op 8/1), **14/1** Tafia (IRE) (op 8/1), **16/1** Legaitak, **33/1** Persian Flower, CSF £7.16 TOTE £3.20: £2.10 £1.30 (£2.80) OWNER Mr Hamdan Al Maktoum (NEWMARKET) BRED Lord Harrington in Ireland 7 Rn

2m 7.2 (2.80) SF: 48/50/46/29/18/8/8
WEIGHT FOR AGE 3yo-9lb

3031 COBHOLM H'CAP (0-80) (3-Y.O F) (Class D) £3,968.90 (£1,185.20: £566.60: £257.30)

1m 2f 21y Stalls: Low GOING minus 0.34 sec per fur (GF) 6-45 (6-46)

2393* **Hadeel (75)***(88+)* *(HThomsonJones)* 3-9-2 RHills(1) (hld up: plld hrd: last st: hdwy 3f out: led over 1f out: rdn out) ....— 1
2557 4 Domitia (USA) **(60)***(70)* *(MBell)* 3-8-1 MFenton(5) (prom: led after 2f: hdd 3f out: ev ch ins fnl f: unable qckn) 1¾ 2
2798 4 Wells Whisper (FR) **(70)***(78)*(Fav)*(GWragg)* 3-8-11 MHills(2) (lw: sn prom: 2nd & c wd st: sn outpcd: r.o fnl f) 1¼ 3
2679 2 Cap And Gown (IRE) **(80)***(86)* *(PFICole)* 3-9-7 TQuinn(4) (prom: 3rd st: led 3f out tl over 1f out: sn btn) 1¾ 4
935 P College Night (IRE) **(74)***(68)* *(CADwyer)* 3-8-10 (5) LNewton(3) (led 2f: 4th st: btn over 3f out) 7 5

13/8 Wells Whisper (FR), **7/4** HADEEL, **9/2** Cap And Gown (IRE), **6/1** Domitia (USA) (op 4/1), **20/1** College Night (IRE), CSF £10.90 TOTE £2.30: £1.40 £3.00 (£10.70) OWNER Mr Hamdan Al Maktoum (NEWMARKET) BRED Shadwell Estate Company Limited 5 Rn

2m 6.5 (2.10) SF: 56/38/46/54/36

3032 PEDDARS CROSS NURSERY H'CAP (2-Y.O) (Class E) £3,559.85 (£1,062.80: £507.90: £230.45)
6f 3y Stalls: Centre GOING minus 0.34 sec per fur (GF) 7-15 (7-15)

27162 **Defined Feature (IRE) (84)***(87) (MRStoute)* 2-9-7 MHills(2) (mde all: hld on wl fnl f)...........— 1
16527 Badger Bay (IRE) **(60)***(63) (CADwyer)* 2-7-8 (3) NVarley(5) (chsd ldrs: ev ch 2f out: r.o wl ins fnl f)...........s.h 2
2619* My Branch **(73)***(72)*(Fav)*(BWHills)* 2-8-5 (5) JDSmith(4) (hld up: hdwy over 1f out: ev ch ins fnl f: no ex nr fin)...........1½ 3
28472 Red Nose (IRE) **(71)***(62) (MHTompkins)* 2-8-8 PRobinson(3) (hld up: effrt over 2f out:sn btn) .3 4
24877 Red Acuisle (IRE) **(61)***(45) (MBell)* 2-7-5 (7) RMullen(1) (lw: w wnr 4f)...........2½ 5

4/5 My Branch, **9/4** Red Nose (IRE), **11/2** DEFINED FEATURE (IRE), **10/1** Red Acuisle (IRE), **20/1** Badger Bay (IRE), CSF £57.98 TOTE £6.30: £1.70 £2.70 (£29.00) OWNER Mr Saeed Suhail (NEWMARKET) BRED Gainsborough Stud Management Ltd 5 Rn
1m 13.1 (2.50) SF: 41/17/26/16/-

3033 STOKESLEY CONDITIONS STKS (3-Y.O+) (Class C) £5,376.00 (£1,856.00: £888.00: £360.00)
6f 3y Stalls: Centre GOING minus 0.34 sec per fur (GF) 7-45 (7-45)

26732 **Cheyenne Spirit (102)***(110)*(Fav)*(BHanbury)* 3-9-2 WRyan(2) (lw: mde all: rdn over 2f out: hld on wl ins fnl f)...........— 1
27648 Inzar (USA) **(105)***(115) (PFICole)* 3-9-7 TQuinn(1) (lw: trckd wnr: qcknd to chal ins fnl f: no ex cl home)...........s.h 2
26995 Tabook (IRE) **(100)***(98) (EALDunlop)* 4-9-6 MHills(4) (prom: rdn over 1f out: sn btn)...........4 3
2416W Marha **(94)***(95) (HThomsonJones)* 3-9-2 RHills(3) (stdd s: hld up & plld hrd: rdn over 1f out: no imp)...........1½ 4

6/4 CHEYENNE SPIRIT, **7/4** Inzar (USA), **100/30** Marha, **8/1** Tabook (IRE) (6/1-10/1), CSF £4.32 TOTE £2.40 (£2.40) OWNER Mr C. Mauritzon (NEWMARKET) BRED J. McGarry 4 Rn
1m 10.6 (0.00) SF: 72/77/65/57
WEIGHT FOR AGE 3yo-5lb

3034 LOWESTOFT H'CAP (0-70) (3-Y.O+ F & M) (Class E) £3,302.20 (£985.60: £470.80: £213.40)
7f 3y Stalls: Centre GOING minus 0.34 sec per fur (GF) 8-15 (8-16)

24993 **Distant Princess (60)***(70+) (BWHills)* 3-9-7 MHills(6) (lw: racd stands' side: chsd ldrs: led over 1f out: sn pushed clr: easily)...........— 1
27783 Make Time **(66)***(69) (JPearce)* 3-9-13 GBardwell(7) (lw: plld hrd: hdwy over 2f out: r.o fnl f) 3 2
27789 Merrie le Bow **(44)***(47) (PatMitchell)* 3-8-2 (3) NVarley(5) (prom: led 3f out tl over 1f out: wknd fnl f)...........nk 3
29457 Magication **(34)***(21) (CNAllen)* 5-8-1 JQuinn(3) (chsd ldrs: lost pl 3f out: n.d after)...........7 4
Hylters Girl **(42)***(28) (MJRyan)* 3-7-12 (5) MBaird(2) (bit bkwd: led 4f: sn wknd)...........nk 5
26383 Brave Fighter (USA) **(62)***(41)*(Fav)*(BHanbury)* 3-9-6 (3) JStack(4) (lw: hld up & plld hrd: hdwy 4f out: wknd wl over 1f out)...........3 6
22073 Jurassic Sue **(59)***(15) (PHowling)* 3-9-6b PRobinson(1) (lw: chsd ldrs 4f: sn rdn & btn)...........10 7

9/4 Brave Fighter (USA), **11/4** Make Time (6/4-3/1), **7/2** Jurassic Sue, **5/1** DISTANT PRINCESS, **11/2** Magication (op 14/1), **20/1** Hylters Girl, **25/1** Merrie le Bow, CSF £19.14 TOTE £5.30: £2.30 £2.10 (£9.00) OWNER Mr Wafic Said (LAMBOURN) BRED Addison Racing Ltd Inc 7 Rn
1m 25.3 (2.50) SF: 46/45/23/3/4/17/-
WEIGHT FOR AGE 3yo-6lb
T/Plpt: £189.10 (51.47 Tckts). T/Qdpt: £46.40 (1.45 Tckts). Dk

2726a-MAISONS-LAFFITTE (France)
Tuesday July 25th (Good)

3035a PRIX MADAME JEAN COUTURIE (Listed) (3-Y.O F) £16,766.00 (£5,748.00: £3,593.00) **1m 2f** 3-00 (2-59)

Redwood Falls (IRE) *(AFabre,France)* 3-9-2 OPeslier...........— 1
2045a4 Powder Bowl (USA) *(JEPease,France)* 3-9-2 CAsmussen...........½ 2
Saderlina (IRE) *(RCollet,France)* 3-9-2 ESaint-Martin...........1 3
18677 Fleet Hill (IRE) *(MRChannon)* 3-9-2 RHughes (btn approx 5½l)........... 5

P-M 8.70F: 2.30F 1.20F (28.10F) OWNER Mr D. Wildenstein (FRANCE) BRED Dayton Ltd 6 Rn
2m 8.0 SF: -/-/-/-

VICHY (France) (R-H)
Monday July 31st (Good)

3036a GRAND PRIX DE VICHY (Gp 3) (3-Y.O+) £26,347.00 (£9,581.00: £4,790.00) **1m 2f** 9-05 (9-26)

2041a* **Marildo (FR)** *(124) (DSmaga,France)* 8-9-6 GGuignard .....— **1**
2041a3 Solidoun (FR) *(115) (ELellouche,France)* 4-9-2 DBoeuf 3 **2**
Captain Haddock (FR) *(115) (FRossi,France)* 4-9-2 OBenoist .....nk **3**

P-M 2.70F: 1.30F 1.80F 1.90F (8.40F)
OWNER Mr D. Smaga BRED Warnerton Farm 8 Rn 2m 5.5 SF: -/-/-

2896a-DEAUVILLE (France) (R-H)
Tuesday August 1st (Good)

3037a PRIX DE CABOURG (Gp 3) (2-Y.O) £26,347.00 (£9,581.00: £4,790.00: £2,395.00) **6f** 3-05 (3-05)

With Fascination (USA) *(JEPease,France)* 2-8-8 CAsmussen .....— **1**
2210a3 Kistena (FR) *(MmeCHead,France)* 2-8-8 ODoleuze 3 **2**
Anziyan (USA) *(AFabre,France)* 2-8-11 TJarnet .....½ **3**
2442 14 Home Shopping *(KMcAuliffe)* 2-8-8 GMosse .....hd **4**

P-M 3.30F: 1.90F 2.70F (SF 14.20F) OWNER Mr George Strawbridge BRED G.Strawbridge jnr et al
5 Rn 1m 12.6 (4.10) SF: -/-/-/-

3037a-DEAUVILLE (France) (R-H)
Thursday August 3rd (Good)

3038a PRIX DE TOURGEVILLE (Listed) (3-Y.O C & G) £16,766.00 (£5,748.00: £3,593.00) **1m** 3-35 (3-34)

Philanthrop (FR) *(108) (JEPease,France)* 3-8-12 CAsmussen .....— **1**
2889a2 Sharpest Image (IRE) *(111) (RCollet,France)* 3-9-2 GGuignard .....nk **2**
Super Gascon *(107) (TLallie,France)* 3-8-12 DRegnard .....hd **3**
2596 3 El Supremo (USA) *(108) (DRLoder)* 3-9-2 LDettori (btn approx 2l) **5**

P-M 7.50F: 2.40F 2.10F 2.60F (24.90F) OWNER Mr S. S. Niarchos 8 Rn 1m 41.3 SF: -/-/-/-

GROSSETO (Italy) (R-H)
Saturday August 5th (Good)

3039a PREMIO CITTA DI GROSSETO (Listed) (3-Y.O) £17,730.00 (£7,801.00: £4,255.00) **1m 165y** 10-20 (10-35)

Naga (ITY) *(100+) (LAgosta,Italy)* 3-8-7 AHerrera .....— **1**
2724a* Albinor (IRE) *(89) (JLDunlop)* 3-8-7 FJovine 6 **2**
Toaff (IRE) *(87) (MTellini,Italy)* 3-8-7 SLandi 1¼ **3**

Tote 293L: 58L 17L 28L (476L) OWNER . Scuderia Dual BRED Allevamento Annarosa di Schirone
12 Rn 1m 38.7 SF: -/-/-

3038a-DEAUVILLE (France) (R-H)
Saturday August 5th (Good)

3040a PRIX DE PSYCHE (Gp 3) (3-Y.O F) £26,347.00 (£9,581.00: £4,790.00: £599.00) **1m 2f** 2-40 (2-45)

2723a2 **Angel In My Heart (FR)** *(107) (JEHammond,France)* 3-8-12 CAsmussen .....— **1**

2561a[2] Take Liberties *(101) (AFabre,France)* 3-8-12 TJarnet 4 2
1238a[3] Secret Quest *(102) (PBary,France)* 3-9-2 DBoeuf 1½ 3
1238a[2] Marble Falls (IRE) *(95) (ELellouche,France)* 3-8-12 OPeslier 2 4
2547[3] Pearl Venture *(95) (SPCWoods)* 3-8-12 WWoods ....d.h 4

P-M 3.70F: 1.70F 1.40F (SF 7.90F) OWNER Mr S. S. Niarchos BRED S.Niarchos 5 Rn
2m 7.2 (5.60) SF: -/-/-/-/-

3040a-DEAUVILLE (France) (R-H)
Sunday August 6th (Good)

3041a PRIX DE POMONE (Gp 2) (3-Y.O+ F & M) £35,928.00 (£14,371.00: £7,186.00: £3,593.00) **1m 5f 110y** 3-10 (3-08)

1709a[4] **Sunrise Song (FR)** *(114) (FDoumen,France)* 4-9-4 GMosse (3rd st: effrt to ld ins fnl f: r.o) ..— 1
2272* Fanjica (IRE) *(113) (JLDunlop)* 3-8-6 MJKinane (2nd tl led over 5f out: hdd & no ex ins fnl f) ....¾ 2
2890a[4] L'ile Tudy (IRE) *(112) (MmeMBollack-Badel,France)* 3-8-6 ABadel (hld up: last st: r.o u.p fnl 2f) 1 3
2045a[3] Genovefa (USA) *(112) (AFabre,France)* 3-8-6 TJarnet (4th st: rdn over 2f out: one pce)....hd 4
1709a[8] Truly a Dream (IRE) *(108) (RCollet,France)* 4-9-4 OPeslier (5th & rdn st: no imp) 3 5
2272[2] Totality *(106) (HRACecil)* 4-9-4 PatEddery (led tl over 5f out: 2nd & rdn st: sn wknd) 2 6
Lafille de General *(100) (PLenogue,France)* 4-9-4 FSanchez (a bhd) 5 7

P-M 15.30F: 4.50F 2.70F (39.10F) OWNER J. Percepied BRED C.Schmidt 7 Rn
2m 59.4 (10.40) SF: -/-/-/-/-/-/-

3042a PRIX MAURICE DE GHEEST (Gp 1) (3-Y.O+) £59,880.00 (£23,952.00: £11,976.00: £5,988.00) **6f 110y** 3-40 (3-39)

2040a* **Cherokee Rose (IRE)** *(122) (JEHammond,France)* 4-8-12 CAsmussen (hld up: hdwy 2f out: led ins fnl f: jst hld on) ....— 1
1835[4] Young Ern *(125) (SDow)* 5-9-1 TQuinn (4th early: rdn to ld over 1f out: hdd ins fnl f: rallied wl cl hme) ....s.h 2
2562a[3] Wessam Prince *(118) (CLaffon-Parias,France)* 4-9-1 WRSwinburn (mid div: hdwy 2f out: r.o)3 3
2562a* Diffident (FR) *(117) (AFabre,France)* 3-8-11 TJarnet (rr early: hdwy 2f out: ev ch 1f out: no ex) ....¾ 4
2368[3] Hoh Magic *(113) (MBell)* 3-8-8 MHills (mid div: rdn 2f out: unable qckn) ....hd 5
1577a[2] Lavinia Fontana (IRE) *(109) (JLDunlop)* 6-8-12 MJKinane (led tl rdn & hdd over 1f out: wknd) 1½ 6
1837[4] Atticus (USA) *(112) (MmeCHead,France)* 3-8-11 ODoleuze (prom tl rdn & wknd 2f out).....s.nk 7
2368[5] Fard (IRE) *(110) (DMorley)* 3-8-11b WCarson (m.n.s) 1 8
2558a* Nec Plus Ultra (FR) *(96) (AdeRoyerDupre,France)* 4-9-1 GMosse (prom 3f) 5 9
1117a[6] General Monash (USA) *(96) (PWChapple-Hyam)* 3-8-11 BThomson (2nd early: rdn & wknd over 2f out) ....½ 10

P-M 1.80F: 1.80F 3.20F 2.90F (30.00F) OWNER Sheikh Mohammed BRED Sheikh Mohammed 10 Rn
1m 16.5 SF: -/-/-/-/-/-/-/-/-/-

JAGERSRO (Malmo, Sweden) (L-H)
Sunday August 6th (Good)

3043a ITT SHERATON SCANDINAVIA CUP (3-Y.O+ F & M) £6,449.00 (£3,224.00: £1,548.00) **1m** 1-25 (1-25)

Next Going (IRE) *(84) (MKahn,Sweden)* 3-8-7 FJohansson ....— 1
Clearwater Lady (IRE) *(64) (JBjordal,Norway)* 3-8-7 WWilliams 10 2
Mrs. Yazzo (SWE) *(62) (JTorok,Sweden)* 4-9-3 SMcCann 2½ 3
23105 Comanche Companion *(TJNaughton)* 5-9-3 JWeaver (btn approx 15½l) 7

Tote 24.60KR: 14KR 20KR 40KR (152.50KR) OWNER Stall Lambada AB BRED Mrs A. Whitehead 11 Rn
1m 39.8 SF: -/-/-/-

3044a VERDEXA CUP (Listed) (3-Y.O+) £8,230.00 (£5,417.00: £2,580.00) **6f** 2-40 (2-40)

Sharp Matt *(110) (MKahn,Sweden)* 4-9-2 FDiaz ....— 1
Melmac (SWE) *(102) (HMeisel,Sweden)* 4-9-2 MadeleineSmith 3 2

Mr. Ibrahim (DEN) *(101) (SChristiansen,Denmark)* 8-9-2 LVillarroel ....½ 3
2394³ Go Hever Golf *(TJNaughton)* 3-8-10 JWeaver (btn approx 5 3/4l) 7

Tote 286.50KR: 69KR 34KR 90KR (1991.50KR) OWNER Stall Kebo BRED Juddmonte Farms 15 Rn
1m 12.1 SF: -/-/-/-

GELSENKIRCHEN-HORST (Gelsenkirchen, Germany) (R-H) Sunday August 6th (Good)

3045a

SILBERNE PEITSCHE (Listed) (3-Y.O+) £8,230.00 (£3,292.00: £1,646.00) **7f** 2-30 (2-31)

2895a² **Branston Abby (IRE)** *(115) (MJohnston)* 6-9-2 MRoberts ....— 1
Platin Lady (IRE) *(112) (ALowe,Germany)* 3-8-8 AHelfenbein ....½ 2
2389a⁷ Fiello (GER) *(108) (NSauer,Germany)* 5-9-2 ABest 2½ 3

Tote 21DM: 22DM 39DM 23DM (SF 401DM)
OWNER Mr J. D. Abell (MIDDLEHAM) BRED John David Abell 8 Rn 1m 27.0 SF: -/-/-

3046a

ARAL POKAL (Gp 1) (3-Y.O+) £86,420.00 (£37,037.00: £20,576.00: £10,288.00) **1m 4f** 3-40 (3-40)

2575² **Wind in Her Hair (IRE)** *(115) (JWHills)* 4-9-2 RHills (mid div: hdwy to ld 2f out: easily) ....— 1
2215a⁸ Lecroix (GER) *(114) (MHofer,Germany)* 3-8-7 ManfredHofer (hld up: last st: r.o fnl 2f: nt rch wnr) 2 2
2046a⁸ Concepcion (GER) *(112) (AWohler,Germany)* 5-9-6 ABoschert (5th st: r.o fnl 2f) 3 3
2729a³ Kornado *(111) (ALowe,Germany)* 5-9-6 GBocskai (led 2f: 2nd tl rdn & r.o one pce fnl 2f) ....¾ 4
2046a* Monsun (GER) *(111) (HJentzsch,Germany)* 5-9-6 PSchiergen (led after 2f tl rdn & hdd 2f out: sn wknd) ....½ 5
2729a⁵ Protektor (GER) *(111) (ALowe,Germany)* 6-9-6 AHelfenbein (4th st: no ex fnl 2f) ....hd 6
2739² Ionio (USA) *(107) (CEBrittain)* 4-9-6 MRoberts (a in rr) 2½ 7

Tote 138DM: 26DM 18DM 44DM (SF 858DM) OWNER Mrs David Nagle (LAMBOURN) BRED Swettenham Stud and Barronstown Stud in Ireland 7 Rn 2m 36.0 SF: -/-/-/-/-/-/-

2832-CATTERICK (L-H) Friday August 11th (Good to firm)

WEATHER: sunny WIND: almost nil

3047

INTERNATIONAL RACECOURSE MANAGEMENT AMATEUR H'CAP (0-70) (3-Y.O+) (Class E) £3,158.00 (£944.00: £452.00: £206.00)
1m 3f 214y Stalls: Low GOING minus 0.18 sec per fur (GF) 6-00 (6-02)

866⁶ **Salinger (28)***(46) (JParkes)* 7-10-6 MrMHNaughton(1) (trckd ldrs: smooth hdwy ½-wy: led 2f out: shkn up & qcknd clr) ....— 1
Smocking **(32)***(43) (JPearce)* 5-10-10 MrsLPearce(8) (chsd ldr: hdwy 6f out: led ent st: hdd 2f out: one pce) 5 2
2946² Don't Drop Bombs (USA) **(27)***(38) (DTThom)* 6-10-5v MissJFeilden(2) (lw: led: rdn 4f out: hdd ent st: kpt on same pce) ....hd 3
2379³ Sudden Spin **(40)***(49)*(Fav)*(SGNorton)* 5-11-4 MrRHale(5) (chsd ldrs: hdwy 6f out: outpcd over 2f out: kpt on fnl f) 1¾ 4
2842⁷ Dots Dee **(28)***(34) (JMBradley)* 6-10-6 MissEJJones(4) (stumbled bdly after 4f: hdwy ½-wy: rdn & no imp fnl 2½f) 2 5
2734³ Duggan **(30)***(33) (PDEvans)* 8-10-8 MrWMcLaughlin(9) (lw: bhd: effrt ½-wy: no imp) 2½ 6
2875⁶ Record Lover (IRE) **(36)***(39) (MCChapman)* 5-11-0 MrMMackley(6) (nvr trbld ldrs) ....hd 7
3001⁴ Red Spectacle (IRE) **(54)***(53) (PCHaslam)* 3-11-7 MrsDKettlewell(3) (lw: chsd ldrs: rdn over 4f out: wknd ent st) 3 8
2824⁷ Le Temeraire **(25)***(12) (DonEnricoIncisa)* 9-9-12 (5) MrLSpink(7) (a bhd) 9 9

11/4 Sudden Spin, **100/30** Don't Drop Bombs (USA) (9/2-3/1), **9/2** Duggan, **6/1** SALINGER, **10/1** Red Spectacle (IRE), **11/1** Dots Dee (op 6/1), **12/1** Smocking (op 7/1), **33/1** Record Lover (IRE), Le Temeraire, CSF £63.13 CT £248.64 TOTE £12.60: £2.20 £3.20 £1.50 (£63.70) Trio £57.70 OWNER Mr Vince Dolan (MALTON) BRED D. J. and Mrs Deer 9 Rn
2m 41.4 (10.40) SF: 35/32/27/38/23/22/28/31/1
WEIGHT FOR AGE 3yo-11lb

3048 NORTHERN AGGREGATES (S) STKS (2-Y.O) (Class G) £2,518.00 (£698.00: £334.00) 7f Stalls: Low GOING minus 0.18 sec per fur (GF) 6-30 (6-31)

2855[3] **Veshca Lady (IRE) (57)***(50)*(Fav)*(EWeymes)* 2-8-6 JFanning(1) (bhd: hdwy on ins over 2f out: led ins fnl f: styd on) — **1**
2516[4] Euro Express **(56)***(53) (MHEasterby)* 2-8-11 TWilliams(2) (lw: cl up tl outpcd ½-wy: hdwy to disp ld 1f out: kpt on one pce) ¾ **2**
2422[4] Phantom Dancer (IRE) *(45) (JBerry)* 2-8-11 GCarter(4) (lw: s.i.s: hdwy on outside appr st: led over 2f out tl jst ins fnl f: wknd) 3½ **3**
2516[2] Ginger Glint **(58)***(38) (MJHeaton-Ellis)* 2-8-11 MFenton(3) (s.i.s: sn chsng ldrs: rdn & hung rt ent st: one pce after) 3 **4**
2637[4] Makaskamina *(30) (BHanbury)* 2-8-8 (3) JStack(5) (cl up tl outpcd fnl 2f) 3½ **5**
2541[8] Sovitaka (IRE) **(60)***(9) (MHEasterby)* 2-8-6 KFallon(6) (led tl hdd & wknd over 2f out) 7 **6**
2750[4] The Black Dubh (IRE) *(3) (JJQuinn)* 2-8-8 (3) SDrowne(7) (cl up to st: sn rdn & btn) 5 **7**

6/4 VESHCA LADY (IRE), **9/2** Ginger Glint, **5/1** Sovitaka (IRE), **6/1** Phantom Dancer (IRE), The Black Dubh (IRE), **7/1** Euro Express, **12/1** Makaskamina, CSF £12.81 TOTE £2.30: £1.50 £3.80 (£13.60) OWNER Mr J. O'Malley (MIDDLEHAM) BRED A. F. O'Callaghan 7 Rn

1m 29.6 (6.40) SF: 1/4/-/-/-/-/-
No bid

3049 OKAY FRANZEN NURSERY H'CAP (2-Y.O) (Class E) £3,106.00(£928.00:£444.00: £202.00) 5f 212y Stalls: High GOING minus 0.18 sec per fur (GF) 7-00 (7-02)

2988* **Albert The Bear (68)***(65)*(Fav)*(JBerry)* 2-8-9 7x GCarter(1) (lw: cl up early: hdwy 2f out: led wl ins fnl f: r.o: eased nr fin) — **1**
2619[8] Soul of Honour (FR) **(67)***(63) (MrsJRRamsden)* 2-8-8 KFallon(4) (lw: bhd: hdwy to ld ins fnl f: hrd rdn & hdd wl ins fnl f: kpt on wl) nk **2**
2489[4] Capture The Moment **(79)***(37d) (RJRWilliams)* 2-9-1 (5) AWhelan(6) (s.i.s: sn rcvrd & chsd ldrs: led over 1f out tl ins fnl f: sn btn) 4 **3**
2771* Classic Victory **(80)***(57) (SCWilliams)* 2-9-7 AMackay(3) (lw: led tl hdd over 1f out: no ex) 3 **4**
1959* Everyone Can Dream **(63)***(22)*(Fav)*(DenysSmith)* 2-8-4 LCharnock(2) (lw: chsd ldrs: hrd drvn ent st: sn outpcd) 7 **5**
2800* Bold Times **(80)** *(PDEvans)* 2-9-7 JFortune(5) (cl up tl p.u ent st: dead) **P**

3/1 ALBERT THE BEAR, Everyone Can Dream, **100/30** Classic Victory, **11/2** Bold Times, Soul of Honour (FR), **6/1** Capture The Moment, CSF £18.43 TOTE £3.90: £2.00 £2.60 (£17.00) OWNER Mr Chris Deuters (COCKERHAM) BRED Rockhouse Farms Ltd 6 Rn

1m 15.2 (4.70) SF: 13/11/13/5/-/-

3050 CHARLES CLINKARD FINE FOOTWEAR H'CAP (0-70) (3-Y.O+) (Class E) £3,366.00 (£1,008.00: £484.00: £222.00) 7f Stalls: Low GOING minus 0.18 sec per fur (GF) 7-30 (7-35)

2786[3] **Michellisa (50)***(61) (JDBethell)* 4-8-10 KFallon(7) (lw: effrt ½-wy: r.o u.p fr 2f out to ld ins fnl f) — **1**
2698[2] Kid Ory **(62)***(72) (PCalver)* 4-9-8 GCarter(6) (b.hind: chsd ldr: chal 2f out: disp ld ins fnl f: kpt on) nk **2**
2832* What a Nightmare (IRE) **(62)***(69)*(Fav)*(JAGlover)* 3-8-11b(5) 6x AWhelan(4) (led tl hdd ins fnl f: no ex) 1½ **3**
2797[3] Mr Cube (IRE) **(62)***(62) (JMBradley)* 5-9-1v(7) RWaterfield(1) (a chsng ldrs: one pce fnl 2f) 3 **4**
2461[3] The Happy Loon (IRE) **(51)***(47) (DenysSmith)* 4-8-11 AMackay(2) (a chsng ldrs: swtchd over 1f out: one pce) 1¾ **5**
2679[6] Special-K **(64)***(56) (EWeymes)* 3-9-1 (3) SDrowne(3) (outpcd & bhd tl styd on fnl 2f) 2 **6**
2832[13] Miss Pigalle **(36)***(25) (MissLAPerratt)* 4-7-10b JLowe(8) (chsd ldr tl outpcd fnl 2f) 1¼ **7**
2786[5] Bali Tender **(35)***(23) (MWEasterby)* 4-7-9 LCharnock(9) (nvr wnt pce) hd **8**
2450[16] Them Times (IRE) **(33)***(15) (FJordan)* 6-7-7 SLanigan(5) (s.i.s: n.d) 3 **9**
2700[2] Bargash **(70)***(51) (PDEvans)* 3-9-10 JFortune(10) (chsd ldrs: racd wd appr st: wknd over 2f out) hd **10**

LONG HANDICAP Them Times (IRE) 6-7

7/4 What a Nightmare (IRE), **5/1** Kid Ory, **6/1** Mr Cube (IRE), **8/1** MICHELLISA, **10/1** The Happy Loon (IRE), Special-K, Bargash, **20/1** Bali Tender, Miss Pigalle, **100/1** Them Times (IRE), CSF £43.81 CT £91.96 TOTE £10.60: £2.00 £1.50 £1.60 (£14.40) Trio £19.80 OWNER Mrs S. M. Burley (MIDDLEHAM) BRED W. and R. Barnett Ltd 10 Rn

1m 27.7 (4.50) SF: 26/37/28/27/12/15/-/-/-/10
WEIGHT FOR AGE 3yo-6lb

3051
TATTERSALLS BOOKMAKERS CLAIMING STKS (3-Y.O+) (Class F)
£2,863.00 (£793.00: £379.00)
5f Stalls: Low GOING minus 0.18 sec per fur (GF) 8-00 (8-01)

2764 12 **Ansellman (72)***(80) (JBerry)* 5-8-11 GCarter(6) (outpcd tl hdwy ½-wy: r.o wl to ld post) ....— 1
2060 10 Elle Shaped (IRE) **(72)***(78) (ABailey)* 5-8-9 AMackay(2) (s.i.s: sn trckng ldrs: led over 1f out: r.o: jst ct) ....s.h 2
2743 3 Aragrove **(81)***(77)*(Fav)*(JWPayne)* 5-8-13 MTebbutt(4) (swtg: b: hld up: swtchd rt & hdwy over 1f out: nrst fin) 1½ 3
2905 3 Here Comes a Star **(70)***(71) (JMCarr)* 7-8-8 ACulhane(3) (in tch: effrt over 1f out: nt qckn ins fnl f) ....nk 4
2686 7 Miss Movie World **(58)***(63) (MDHammond)* 6-7-12 (3) JStack(7) (lw: chsd ldrs: ev ch over 1f out: edgd lft & nt qckn) ....½ 5
2758 7 High Domain (IRE) **(65)***(64) (TDBarron)* 4-8-6b JFortune(1) (led tl hdd over 1f out: sn btn) 1¼ 6
2609 5 Hinton Rock (IRE) **(87)***(70) (MBell)* 3-8-12 MFenton(5) (chsd ldrs over 3f: btn whn hmpd towards fin) 1 7
2956 6 Olifantsfontein **(50)***(57) (DNicholls)* 7-8-5 KFallon(8) (lw: nvr wnt pce) ....¾ 8
2877 3 Super Sonata **(57)***(32) (PDEvans)* 3-7-9v LCharnock(9) (spd to ½-wy: sn wknd) 6 9

85/40 Aragrove, **5/2** Hinton Rock (IRE), **5/1** ANSELLMAN, **8/1** Here Comes a Star, Elle Shaped (IRE), **10/1** Miss Movie World, **12/1** High Domain (IRE) (op 7/1), **33/1** Super Sonata, **50/1** Olifantsfontein, CSF £41.74 TOTE £5.80: £1.90 £2.60 £1.60 (£58.90) Trio £38.70 OWNER Ansells of Watford (COCKERHAM) BRED W. L. Caley 9 Rn

59.2 secs (1.70) SF: 50/48/47/41/33/34/36/27/-
WEIGHT FOR AGE 3yo-4lb
STEWARDS' ENQUIRY Mackay susp. 21-24/8/95 (excessive use of whip).

3052
PLANTATION STUD MAIDEN H'CAP (0-70) (3-Y.O+) (Class E)
£3,184.00 (£952.00: £456.00: £208.00)
1m 7f 177y GOING minus 0.18 sec per fur (GF) 8-30 (8-31)

2969 W **Northern Law (65)***(81)*(Fav)*(BWHills)* 3-9-10 MFenton(6) (lw: set slow pce: qcknd 6f out: qcknd again over 2f out: drvn out) ....— 1
1682 3 Gymcrak Diamond (IRE) **(30)***(46) (GHolmes)* 5-8-4 KFallon(1) (lw: hld up: hdwy 5f out: r.o u.p fnl 2f: too much to do) ....½ 2
2759 4 Tancred Mischief **(29)***(39) (WLBarker)* 4-8-0 (3) DarrenMoffatt(7) (swtg: hld up: hdwy 6f out: chsd wnr ent st: one pce) 5 3
2545 7 Don't Cry **(21)***(29) (DonEnricoIncisa)* 7-7-9 KimTinkler(3) (chsd ldrs tl outpcd 5f out: styd on again fnl 2f) 2½ 4
1194 10 Silverdale Count **(43)***(48) (KWHogg)* 3-7-9 (7)ow1 ADaly(5) (chsd wnr tl rdn & wknd fnl 3f) 2 5
Sakura (IRE) **(39)***(32) (MDHammond)* 4-8-8 (5) DGriffiths(2) (trckd ldrs: effrt appr st:sn btn) ...13 6
1506 14 Heavens Above **(38)***(25) (MrsJRRamsden)* 3-7-11 LCharnock(4) (lw: hld up & bhd: n.d) 6 7

7/4 NORTHERN LAW, **7/2** Gymcrak Diamond (IRE), **4/1** Heavens Above, **9/2** Tancred Mischief, **10/1** Don't Cry, **25/1** Silverdale Count, Sakura (IRE), CSF £7.94 TOTE £2.50: £1.50 £2.50 (£5.10) OWNER Mr John Bradley (LAMBOURN) BRED Charlton Down Stud 7 Rn

3m 45.7 (24.70) SF: -/-/-/-/-/-/-
WEIGHT FOR AGE 3yo-15lb
T/Plpt: £39.80 (301.75 Tckts). T/Qdpt: £11.10 (7.6 Tckts). AA

2334-FOLKESTONE (R-H)
Friday August 11th (Firm)
WEATHER: sunny WIND: almost nil

3053
E.B.F. BURWASH MAIDEN STKS (2-Y.O) (Class D) £4,127.75
(£1,232.00: £588.50: £266.75)
5f Stalls: Low GOING minus 0.55 sec per fur (F) 2-30 (2-31)

2498 3 **Western Venture (IRE)** *(68) (JWPayne)* 2-9-0 MRimmer(5) (chsd ldr: rdn over 1f out: led nr fin) ....— 1
1772 2 Tarf (USA) **(90)***(63+)*(Fav)*(PTWalwyn)* 2-8-9 PRobinson(4) (led: sn clr: several l in front whn sddle slipped appr fnl f: ct nr fin: unlucky) ....hd 2
716 8 Little Lucky *(52) (GLewis)* 2-8-9 PaulEddery(1) (chsd ldrs: rdn 3f out: one pce fnl 2f) 3½ 3
Beldray Park (IRE) *(54) (MrsALMKing)* 2-9-0 JQuinn(2) (unf: swvd rt s: sme hdwy over 2f out: rdn over 1f out: one pce) ....¾ 4
2660 10 Maraschino *(49) (MJHeaton-Ellis)* 2-8-9 WNewnes(3) (chsd ldrs: rdn & one pce fnl 2f) ....s.h 5

2615W Munakeb (FR) *(22) (RWArmstrong)* 2-9-0 RPrice(6) (neat: bit bkwd: s.v.s: sn wl bhd)...........10 6

2/7 Tarf (USA), **11/2** WESTERN VENTURE (IRE), **15/2** Munakeb (FR) (op 4/1), **16/1** Maraschino, Little Lucky, **20/1** Beldray Park (IRE), CSF £8.00 TOTE £12.00: £2.20 £1.10 (£3.30) OWNER Mr J. P. Power (NEWMARKET) BRED S. Morrin and B. Powell 6 Rn

60.0 secs (1.40) SF: 28/23/12/14/9/-

3054 SMARDEN (S) STKS (2-Y.O F) (Class G) £2,243.00 (£618.00: £293.00)
6f Stalls: Low GOING minus 0.55 sec per fur (F) 3-00 (3-02)

2857* **Times of Times (IRE) (68)***(69)*(Fav)*(DJSCosgrove)* 2-9-0 MRimmer(1) (chsd ldrs gng wl: hdwy to ld appr fnl f: r.o)...........— 1
2523⁷ Wingnut (IRE) **(66)***(65) (GLewis)* 2-9-0 PaulEddery(5) (led: hdd appr fnl f: sn rdn: one pce)..1½ 2
1253⁷ Mrs Nevermind *(45) (GLMoore)* 2-8-10 SWhitworth(3) (chsd ldrs: rdn 2f out: wknd 1f out)......6 3
Sally State *(5) (MrsMMcCourt)* 2-8-3 (7) RStudholme(6) (a bhd)...........15 4
Touch of Snow *(JABennett)* 2-8-10 TSprake(4) (bhd fnl 3f)...........8 5
2635⁷ Welsh Owl *(KRBurke)* 2-8-7 (3) NVarley(2) (bhd fnl 3f)...........2 6

4/6 TIMES OF TIMES (IRE), **9/4** Wingnut (IRE), **7/1** Mrs Nevermind (op 4/1), **33/1** Sally State, **40/1** Touch of Snow, **50/1** Welsh Owl, CSF £2.45 TOTE £1.70: £1.20 £1.40 (£1.50) OWNER Mrs M. Schneider (NEWMARKET) BRED E. Moloney 6 Rn 1m 13.8 (2.10) SF: 24/20/-/-/-/-

Bt in 5,200 gns

3055 GRAFTY GREEN H'CAP (0-60) (3-Y.O+) (Class F) £3,123.80 (£866.80: £415.40)
6f Stalls: Low GOING minus 0.55 sec per fur (F) 3-30 (3-32)

2943⁴ **Red Admiral (59)***(67) (PCHaslam)* 5-9-7 (7) NicolaHowarth(3) (chsd ldr: led ins fnl f: r.o) ......— 1
2652⁷ Petraco (IRE) **(59)***(67) (NASmith)* 7-10-0 MRimmer(4) (chsd ldrs: ev ch ins fnl f: r.o) ....hd 2
1785¹² Waders Dream (IRE) **(43)***(51) (PatMitchell)* 6-8-12v PRobinson(10) (mid div: rdn & hdwy over 1f out: ev ch wl ins fnl f: r.o)...........hd 3
2793⁷ Mister Raider **(49)***(53) (SMellor)* 3-8-13b TSprake(5) (mid div: hdwy over 1f out: r.o one pce fnl f)...........1¼ 4
2844* Hever Golf Star **(65)***(66)*(Fav)*(TJNaughton)* 3-9-10 (5) 7x JDSmith(11) (led tl hdd & wknd ins fnl f) 1¼ 5
2844⁵ Chief's Lady **(52)***(52) (RHarris)* 3-8-11 (5) DGibbs(7) (dwlt: nvr nrr) ....nk 6
2789¹⁵ Il Furetto **(30)***(16) (JSKing)* 3-7-8 ow1 JQuinn(2) (swtg: hdwy over 2f out: sn rdn & wknd)..........5 7
1692¹⁴ Mrs Tigger **(38)***(23) (RWArmstrong)* 3-8-2 RPrice(8) (a bhd)...........½ 8
2925⁹ Gate of Heaven **(24)***(3) (CADwyer)* 5-7-4 (3) NVarley(9) (a bhd)...........2½ 9
2708¹⁰ Gabriel's Lady **(40)***(13) (MarkCampion)* 4-8-9 CAvery(6) (prom over 3f)...........2 10
2448⁷ Gallant Spirit (IRE) **(53)***(18) (RJHodges)* 4-9-1 (7) AmandaSanders(12) (prom to ½-wy)............3 11
1750⁵ Half Tone **(47)***(11) (RMFlower)* 3-8-11 AMorris(1) (a bhd)...........½ 12

LONG HANDICAP Il Furetto 7-2 Gate of Heaven 7-3

11/8 Hever Golf Star, **6/1** RED ADMIRAL (op 4/1), Half Tone (op 4/1), **13/2** Petraco (IRE) (op 4/1), **7/1** Mister Raider, **12/1** Chief's Lady (op 8/1), **16/1** Gallant Spirit (IRE), Waders Dream (IRE), Gate of Heaven, **20/1** Mrs Tigger, **33/1** Il Furetto, Gabriel's Lady, CSF £46.04 CT £560.63 TOTE £4.20: £2.00 £1.50 £7.60 (£14.10) Trio £67.40 OWNER Sackville House Racing (MIDDLEHAM) BRED Hesmonds Stud Ltd 12 Rn 1m 13.1 (1.40) SF: 46/46/30/27/40/26/-/-/-/-/-/-

WEIGHT FOR AGE 3yo-5lb

3056 PAUL COOK MAIDEN H'CAP (0-60) (3-Y.O+) (Class F) £2,519.00 (£694.00: £329.00)
1m 4f Stalls: Low GOING minus 0.55 sec per fur (F) 4-00 (4-01)

2663³ **Masuri Kabisa (USA) (27)***(41) (HJCollingridge)* 4-8-4v JQuinn(8) (chsd ldrs: 4th st: led over 1f out: r.o wl)...........— 1
2603³ Santella Boy (USA) **(58)***(68)*(Fav)*(GHarwood)* 3-9-10 MPerrett(5) (led after 1f: hdd over 1f out: one pce) 3 2
2919⁶ Jean de Florette (USA) **(33)***(43) (CADwyer)* 4-8-10 MRimmer(6) (hdwy 4f out: 5th st: rdn over 1f out: r.o one pce fnl f) ....nk 3
2812³ Faustino **(50)***(58) (PFICole)* 3-9-2b PaulEddery(3) (led 1f: chsd ldr: 2nd st: ev ch over 1f out: one pce) 1¼ 4
2037³ Euro Singer **(55)***(59)*(Fav)*(RAkehurst)* 3-9-7 AMcGlone(7) (a.p: 3rd st: rdn 2f out: wknd over 1f out)...........3 5
2244⁵ Born to Please (IRE) **(45)***(45) (PWHarris)* 3-8-11 WNewnes(4) (nvr nrr) 3 6
2279³ Lady Sabina **(38)***(37) (WJMusson)* 5-8-12 (3) PMcCabe(1) (a mid div) 1 7
Annabel's Baby (IRE) **(25)***(10) (MrsMMcCourt)* 6-7-9 (7) RStudholme(2) (a bhd) 10 8

2486⁸ Malingerer **(27)***(11) (DAWilson)* 4-8-4 GBardwell(11) (mid div: 6th st: sn wknd)......¾ 9
2245² Jubilee Line **(33)***(16) (NEBerry)* 5-8-10 RPerham(9) (bhd fnl 3f)......1¼ 10
2805⁵ RaincheckA **(40)***(20) (MarkCampion)* 4-9-3 CAvery(10) (bhd fnl 5f)......1¾ 11

9/2 Santella Boy (USA), Euro Singer, **5/1** Faustino, **11/2** MASURI KABISA (USA) (op 10/1), **6/1** Lady Sabina, **7/1** Jean de Florette (USA), **8/1** Jubilee Line, **14/1** Born to Please (IRE), Malingerer, **33/1** RaincheckA, **50/1** Annabel's Baby (IRE), CSF £30.07 CT £164.68 TOTE £7.60: £2.30 £2.00 £2.50 (£24.40) Trio £59.70 OWNER Mr N. P. Etches (NEWMARKET) BRED Stonereath Farms 11 Rn
2m 34.7 (3.50) SF: 23/39/25/29/30/16/19/-/-/-/2
WEIGHT FOR AGE 3yo-11lb

3057 HIGH HALDEN H'CAP (0-65) (3-Y.O+) (Class F) £3,174.20 (£881.20: £422.60)
6f 189y Stalls: Low GOING minus 0.55 sec per fur (F) 4-30 (4-35)

2685¹⁰ **Dowsong (62)***(73) (RAkehurst)* 4-10-0 RPerham(3) (chsd ldrs: 2nd st: led over 1f out: r.o) ..— 1
2831⁵ Tomal **(47)***(54) (RIngram)* 3-8-7 AMcGlone(7) (hld up: rdn over 2f out: hdwy over 1f out: r.o)1¾ 2
2807⁴ Lucknam Style **(40)***(42) (MrsBarbaraWaring)* 7-8-6v WNewnes(8) (led: hdd over 1f out: one pce)......2 3
*2943*³ Sharp Imp **(41)***(43)*(Fav)*(RMFlower)* 5-8-2b⁽⁵⁾ JDSmith(5) (stmbld s: rr: rdn over 2f out: hdwy over 1f out: r.o fnl f)......nk 4
2363² Takeshi (IRE) **(62)***(54)*(Fav)*(EALDunlop)* 3-9-8 PaulEddery(9) (4th st: rdn 2f out: wknd over 1f out)......4 5
2843⁷ Sarasonia **(30)***(21) (JWPayne)* 4-7-7 ⁽³⁾ NVarley(10) (3rd st: wknd 2f out)......½ 6
2178³ Zinbaq **(30)***(21) (CJBenstead)* 9-7-10 JQuinn(1) (6th st: rdn 2f out: no hdwy)......s.h 7
2807⁵ Just Lucky (IRE) **(47)***(37) (RWArmstrong)* 3-8-7 RPrice(6) (nvr nrr)......nk 8
2808⁷ Lorelei Lee (IRE) **(64)***(52) (JohnBerry)* 3-9-5 ⁽⁵⁾ HKYim(4) (5th st: wknd over 1f out)......1 9
*2634*¹⁰ Future Options **(53)***(37) (MSSaunders)* 4-9-5 MRimmer(2) (bhd fnl 3f)......1¾ 10

9/4 Sharp Imp, Takeshi (IRE), **7/1** Zinbaq, **8/1** DOWSONG (op 5/1), **10/1** Lorelei Lee (IRE) (op 6/1), **14/1** Lucknam Style, **20/1** Tomal, Just Lucky (IRE), **33/1** Sarasonia, **50/1** Future Options, CSF £124.56 CT £1.968.19 TOTE £11.80: £3.30 £2.40 £2.80 (£57.60) Trio £396.00 OWNER The Fairy Story Partnership (EPSOM) BRED Deepwood Farm Stud 10 Rn
1m 23.6 (2.00) SF: 41/16/10/11/16/-/-/-/14/5
WEIGHT FOR AGE 3yo-6lb

3058 JOHN MCCARTHY MAIDEN H'CAP (0-70) (3-Y.O+) (Class E) £3,674.00 (£1,100.00: £528.00: £242.00)
1m 1f 149y Stalls: Low GOING minus 0.55 sec per fur (F) 5-00 (5-01)

2863² **Zeetaro (68)***(79)*(Fav)*(MajorWRHern)* 4-10-0 TSprake(3) (hld up gng wl: 5th st: led over 1f out: sn clr: easily)......— 1
2109³ Harvey White (IRE) **(54)***(59) (JPearce)* 3-8-5 GBardwell(1) (chsd ldr: 2nd st: led wl over 1f out: sn hdd: one pce)......3½ 2
2334² Mim-Lou-and **(46)***(49) (BRMillman)* 3-7-11 JQuinn(4) (chsd ldrs: 3rd st: ev ch over 1f out: one pce)......1¼ 3
2780⁶ Action Jackson **(66)***(67) (BJMcMath)* 3-9-3 MRimmer(6) (led: hdd wl over 1f out: one pce)...1¼ 4
2711⁵ Jewel Trader **(49)***(42) (CJBenstead)* 3-8-0b^ow4 PRobinson(5) (rr whn sltly hmpd 5f out: 7th st: styd on wl fnl f: nvr nrr)......2½ 5
1991⁸ Prince's Feather (IRE) **(69)***(59) (KRBurke)* 3-9-3 ⁽³⁾ NVarley(7) (plld hrd: chsd ldrs: wknd 2f out)4 6
2638⁶ Estrela Castanha **(42)***(24) (RMFlower)* 3-7-0b⁽⁷⁾ RMullen(2) (a bhd)......5 7
LONG HANDICAP Estrela Castanha 7-4

7/4 ZEETARO, **11/4** Mim-Lou-and, **4/1** Action Jackson, **7/1** Harvey White (IRE), **8/1** Prince's Feather (IRE) (op 5/1), **9/1** Jewel Trader (op 6/1), **50/1** Estrela Castanha, CSF £13.90 TOTE £2.80: £1.60 £2.70 (£9.80) OWNER The Dayspring Company Ltd (LAMBOURN) BRED D. Aykroyd 7 Rn
2m 1.9 (4.20) SF: 32/3/-/11/-/3/-
WEIGHT FOR AGE 3yo-9lb
T/Plpt: £279.60 (29.02 Tckts). T/Qdpt: £245.70 (0.8 Tckts); £66.42 to Newbury 12/8/95. SM

2932-HAYDOCK (L-H)
Friday August 11th (Good to firm)
WEATHER: fine, v.warm WIND: slt half bhd becoming almost nil

3059 WIGAN RUGBY LEAGUE APPRENTICE H'CAP (0-80) (3-Y.O+) (Class F) £2,801.00 (£786.00: £383.00)
1m 3f 200y Stalls: High GOING minus 0.46 sec per fur (F) 5-45 (5-46)

2937⁸ **Braille (IRE) (59)***(75) (MGMeagher)* 4-9-5 AGarth(1) (led after 3f: qckd clr 3f out: unchal)..— 1

2427[3] Mentalasanythin **(66)***(73)*(Fav)*(ABailey)* 6-9-12 DWright(4) (sn chsng wnr: 2nd st: rdn & outpcd 3f out: no imp) 7 2
2022[6] Hill Farm Dancer **(48)***(53) (WMBrisbourne)* 4-8-5 (3) VHalliday(3) (s.i.s: hld up: 3rd st: rdn over 2f out: one pce) 1½ 3
2520[3] Mansur (IRE) **(77)***(61) (DRLoder)* 3-9-12 DRMcCabe(2) (lw: set v.slow pce 3f: drppd rr & 4th st: sn t.o) 15 4

4/5 Mentalasanythin, **3/1** Mansur (IRE) (op 7/4), **5/1** Hill Farm Dancer, **11/2** BRAILLE (IRE) (op 7/2), CSF £10.31 TOTE £6.40 (£4.50) OWNER The Winning Feature Partnership (ORMSKIRK) BRED John McLoughlin 4 Rn

2m 44.51 (16.51) SF: -/-/-/-
WEIGHT FOR AGE 3yo-11lb

3060 ORRELL R.U.F.C. (S) STKS (3-Y.O) (Class F) £2,829.00 (£794.00: £387.00)

1m 30y Stalls: Low GOING minus 0.46 sec per fur (F) 6-15 (6-16)

2524[3] **Mill Dancer (IRE) (40)***(52)*(Fav)*(EJAlston)* 3-8-9 SDWilliams(3) (mde all: clr 3f out: eased fnl f: canter) ....— 1
Katy Koo *(23) (PJBevan)* 3-8-9 NCarlisle(1) (lw: wl grwn: bkwd: s.s: 3rd st: chsd wnr fnl 4f: no imp) 15 2
824[10] Mr Personality **(54)***(6) (MrsMReveley)* 3-9-0 DeanMcKeown(2) (swvd rt s: plld hrd: hld up: 4th st: rdn over 2f out: no imp) 11 3
Merger Mania *(MissJFCraze)* 3-9-0 SWebster(4) (w'like: str: bkwd: b: chsd wnr: 2nd st: wknd over 3f out: t.o) 14 4

8/11 MILL DANCER (IRE), **9/4** Mr Personality (op 6/4), **13/2** Katy Koo, **14/1** Merger Mania (op 8/1), CSF £5.01 TOTE £1.70 (£3.00) OWNER Mrs Dot Jones (PRESTON) BRED William Flood 4 Rn

1m 44.24 (3.84) SF: 19/-/-/-
No bid

3061 BELLCHARM MOTOR COMPANY H'CAP (0-70) (3-Y.O+) (Class E) £3,176.25 (£960.00: £467.50: £221.25)

1m 2f 120y Stalls: High GOING minus 0.46 sec per fur (F) 6-45 (6-46)

2226[3] **Askern (66)***(81) (DHaydnJones)* 4-9-11 (3) DRMcCabe(8) (mde all: drvn clr 2f out: r.o wl) ....— 1
2861[2] Once More for Luck (IRE) **(61)***(75)*(Fav)*(MrsMReveley)* 4-9-9 KDarley(6) (lw: stdd s: hdwy over 2f out: chsd wnr appr fnl f: r.o) 1 2
2557[8] Contrafire (IRE) **(64)***(68) (WJarvis)* 3-8-11 (5) MHenry(9) (a.p: 3rd st: rdn 2f out: kpt on same pce) 6 3
2861[3] Slapy Dam **(49)***(53) (JMackie)* 3-8-1 NCarlisle(7) (hld up & bhd: effrt over 2f out: nt pce to chal) ....nk 4
1596[7] Beauman **(65)***(67) (PDEvans)* 5-9-13 GHind(2) (lw: chsd ldrs: 4th st: rdn over 2f out: one pce) 1¼ 5
2747* Floating Line **(63)***(54) (EJAlston)* 7-9-11 SDWilliams(1) (chsd ldrs: 5th st: rdn along 3f out: sn btn) 7 6
2327[7] Thrower **(43)***(34) (WMBrisbourne)* 4-8-2 (3) AGarth(4) (w wnr: 2nd st: outpcd 3f out: sn bhd) ...½ 7
2759[2] Ballard Lady (IRE) **(48)***(38) (JSWainwright)* 3-8-0 SMaloney(5) (lw: hld up: a bhd) ....nk 8
2733[7] Lawnswood Junior **(48)***(37) (JLSpearing)* 8-8-10 DeanMcKeown(3) (hld up: 6th st: effrt over 3f out: sn wknd) ....½ 9

9/4 Once More for Luck (IRE), **4/1** Floating Line, **5/1** Slapy Dam, **13/2** Contrafire (IRE), **9/1** Ballard Lady (IRE), ASKERN, **12/1** Beauman, **16/1** Thrower, **20/1** Lawnswood Junior, CSF £28.80 CT £132.11 TOTE £11.20: £2.60 £1.40 £2.10 (£8.80) Trio £26.80 OWNER Mrs M. O'Donnell (PONTYPRIDD) BRED Highclere Stud Ltd 9 Rn 2m 13.01 (1.51) SF: 63/57/40/25/49/36/16/10/19

WEIGHT FOR AGE 3yo-10lb

3062 BOLTON GREYHOUND STADIUM CONDITIONS STKS (3-Y.O+ F & M) (Class C) £6,541.00 (£1,809.00)

7f 30y Stalls: Low GOING minus 0.46 sec per fur (F) 7-15 (7-16)

Didina (103)*(97++)*(Fav)*(RCharlton)* 3-8-10 KDarley(1) (lw: hld up: 2nd st: jnd ldr 2f out: led on bit appr fnl f: hrd hld) ....— 1
1754[3] Shefoog **(90)***(94) (RWArmstrong)* 3-8-10 RPrice(2) (lw: set str pce: rdn 2f out: hdd appr fnl f: sn btn) 1¼ 2

2/5 DIDINA, **2/1** Shefoog, TOTE £1.30 OWNER Mr K. Abdullah (BECKHAMPTON) BRED Juddmonte Farms 2 Rn

1m 28.46 (1.16) SF: 44/41

3063 CLAUDE HARRISON MEMORIAL CHALLENGE TROPHY H'CAP (0-70) (3-Y.O+) (Class E) £3,322.50 (£1,005.00: £490.00: £232.50)
1m 30y Stalls: Low GOING minus 0.46 sec per fur (F) 7-45 (7-48)

1649[14] **Rood Music (54)***(63) (MGMeagher)* 4-8-12 JCarroll(4) (mde all: hrd rdn & edgd lft nr fin).....— 1
2913* Move Smartly (IRE) **(56)***(62) (FHLee)* 5-9-0v 5x PaulEddery(5) (lw: a.p: 3rd st: rdn to chal ins fnl f: btn whn n.m.r nr fin)....1½ 2
2875[3] Wentbridge Lad (IRE) **(61)***(64)*(Fav)*(PDEvans)* 5-9-5v GHind(7) (chsd ldrs: 5th st: rdn 2f out: kpt on ins fnl f)....1½ 3
Snake Plissken (IRE) **(47)***(50) (DHaydnJones)* 4-8-2 (3) DRMcCabe(10) (bit bkwd: prom: 4th st: rdn over 2f out: kpt on)....nk 4
2479[7] Swandale Flyer **(51)***(44) (NBycroft)* 3-8-2 SMaloney(2) (bhd: styd on fnl 2f: nvr nrr)....5 5
2807[3] Runic Symbol **(40)***(32) (MBlanshard)* 4-7-12 StephenDavies(11) (chsd ldrs: 6th st: rdn over 2f out: sn btn)....½ 6
2744[2] Veloce (IRE) **(70)***(55) (ABailey)* 7-9-11 (3) DWright(3) (b: hld up: effrt on ins over 2f out: sn rdn: nvr able to chal)....3½ 7
Edgar Kirby **(60)***(40) (PWHarris)* 4-9-4 KDarley(8) (bkwd: prom: 2nd st: wknd over 2f out)....2½ 8
2634[6] Marowins **(47)***(26) (EJAlston)* 6-8-5 SDWilliams(1) (a in rr)....nk 9
2961[11] Brigadore Gold **(36)***(11) (FHLee)* 5-7-8 ow1 NCarlisle(6) (hld up: effrt 3f out: no imp)....1¾ 10
2832[11] Delmour **(39)** *(WMBrisbourne)* 4-7-8 (3)ow4 AGarth(9) (a bhd: t.o)....20 11

LONG HANDICAP Brigadore Gold 6-11 Delmour 6-3

7/2 Wentbridge Lad (IRE), **4/1** Veloce (IRE), **9/2** Move Smartly (IRE), **15/2** Snake Plissken (IRE), Marowins (op 5/1), **10/1** Edgar Kirby, Runic Symbol, **12/1** ROOD MUSIC, **20/1** Swandale Flyer, **33/1** Brigadore Gold, **66/1** Delmour, CSF £61.00 CT £211.79 TOTE £14.10: £2.60 £1.50 £1.60 (£25.90) Trio £77.90 OWNER Mr M. R. Johnson (ORMSKIRK) BRED T. R. G. Vestey 11 Rn
1m 42.72 (2.32) SF: 36/35/37/23/10/5/28/13/-/-/-
WEIGHT FOR AGE 3yo-7lb

3064 JOHN PARROTT SNOOKER NURSERY H'CAP (2-Y.O) (Class E)£3,241.25 (£980.00: £477.50: £226.25)
5f Stalls: High GOING minus 0.46 sec per fur (F) 8-15 (8-16)

2706[5] **Pleasure Time (65)***(67) (CSmith)* 2-8-7b NCarlisle(9) (a.p: rdn to ld ent fnl f: all out)....— 1
2779[9] Welsh Mountain **(74)***(75) (MJHeaton-Ellis)* 2-9-2 DHolland(6) (hdwy 2f out: ev ch ins fnl f: unable qckn)....nk 2
2826[3] Centurion **(72)***(71) (RHannon)* 2-9-0 BDoyle(4) (w ldrs 3f: rallied u.p towards fin)....¾ 3
2706[3] Krystal Max (IRE) **(77)***(76) (TDBarron)* 2-9-5 DeanMcKeown(3) (chsd ldrs: led bel dist tl rdn & hdd ent fnl f: one pce)....s.h 4
2459[7] Pathaze **(64)***(61) (NBycroft)* 2-8-6 SMaloney(7) (dwlt: hdwy fnl 2f: fin wl)....½ 5
2735* Miss Bigwig **(75)***(67) (JBerry)* 2-9-3 JCarroll(5) (led over 3f: sn rdn: one pce)....1½ 6
2988[4] U-No-Harry (IRE) **(68)***(55) (RHollinshead)* 2-8-7 (3) AGarth(11) (disp ld over 3f)....1¾ 7
1678[3] Montrestar **(67)***(53) (PDEvans)* 2-8-9 GHind(1) (prom: rdn & wknd wl over 1f out)....nk 8
2618[3] Arctic Romancer (IRE) **(79)***(61)*(Fav)*(GLewis)* 2-9-7b PaulEddery(8) (rdn along ½-wy: nvr nr to chal)....1¼ 9
2424[2] Natural Key **(76)***(57) (DHaydnJones)* 2-9-4 KDarley(12) (prom: hrd rdn & ev ch 2f out: sn wknd)....hd 10
2706[6] Imp Express (IRE) **(76)***(55) (GMMoore)* 2-9-4 StephenDavies(2) (spd over 3f)....¾ 11
2773* Wilfull Lad (IRE) **(79)***(58) (MartynMeade)* 2-9-7 VSlattery(10) (sn drvn along: a bhd)....s.h 12

4/1 Arctic Romancer (IRE) (op 6/1), **11/2** Miss Bigwig, **6/1** Centurion, **7/1** Natural Key, **15/2** Krystal Max (IRE) (op 5/1), **9/1** Wilfull Lad (IRE), Welsh Mountain, **10/1** PLEASURE TIME, U-No-Harry (IRE), **11/1** Imp Express (IRE), **14/1** Montrestar, **25/1** Pathaze, CSF £95.50 CT £549.25 TOTE £20.80: £4.40 £2.00 £2.60 (£47.90) Trio £77.00 OWNER The Temple Bruers (WELLINGORE) BRED John David Abell 12 Rn
60.61 secs (1.61) SF: 26/34/30/35/20/26/14/12/20/16/14/17
T/Plpt: £322.80 (23.87 Tckts). T/Qdpt: £19.50 (7.5 Tckts). IM

2440-NEWBURY (L-H)
Friday August 11th (Good to firm)
WEATHER: very hot WIND: almost nil

3065 JACK COLLING POLAR JEST APPRENTICE H'CAP (0-90) (3-Y.O+) (Class E) £3,782.00 (£1,136.00: £548.00: £254.00)
6f 8y Stalls: Centre GOING minus 0.23 sec per fur (GF) 2-10 (2-12)

2758[8] **Great Hall (57)***(65) (PDCundell)* 6-7-5b(5) MartinDwyer(1) (lw: rdn thrght: gd hdwy fnl f: led nr fin)....— 1

2764 17 How's Yer Father **(83)***(88) (RJHodges)* 9-9-8 DGriffiths(5) (swtchd lft over 2f out: hdwy wl over 1f out: led ins fnl f: hdd nr fin) 1 **2**
2448 5 Face the Future **(62)***(67) (LJHolt)* 6-7-10 (5) IonaWands(11) (s.s: hdwy over 1f out: ev ch ins fnl f: one pce) ....nk **3**
2935 4 Coffee 'n Cream **(85)***(88)*(Fav)*(RHannon)* 3-9-2 (3) MarkDenaro(8) (lw: a.p: rdn over 2f out: one pce) ....¾ **4**
2428* Chickawicka (IRE) **(88)***(90) (MCPipe)* 4-9-13v LNewton(6) (lw: hld up: rdn over 3f out: r.o one pce) ....s.h **5**
2802 2 Bowden Rose **(78)***(78) (MBlanshard)* 3-8-9b(3) ADaly(9) (led: clr over 3f out: hdd ins fnl f: sn wknd) ....¾ **6**
2764 11 Jade Pet **(82)***(82) (RHannon)* 4-9-4 (3) DaneO'Neill(3) (a.p: rdn over 2f out: one pce) ....s.h **7**
2743 7 Rocky Waters (USA) **(68)***(64) (PBurgoyne)* 6-8-7 RPainter(7) (b.hind: a bhd) 1½ **8**
1468 10 Knobbleeneeze **(74)***(65) (MRChannon)* 5-8-8v(5) DSweeney(2) (lw: bhd fnl 2f) 2 **9**
2909 8 Green Golightly (USA) **(61)***(50) (DAWilson)* 4-8-0 PPMurphy(4) (prom 4f) ....¾ **10**
2692 7 Barossa Valley (IRE) **(72)***(54) (PWChapple-Hyam)* 4-8-4 (7) RCody-Boutcher(10) (lw: bhd fnl 2f) 2½ **11**

4/1 Coffee 'n Cream, **9/2** Bowden Rose, **5/1** Jade Pet, **10/1** Barossa Valley (IRE) (op 5/1), Chickawicka (IRE), How's Yer Father, **11/1** Face the Future, **12/1** GREAT HALL, **14/1** Knobbleeneeze, **16/1** Green Golightly (USA), **20/1** Rocky Waters (USA), CSF £109.82 CT £1,224.39 TOTE £17.20: £3.70 £2.40 £2.80 (£44.30) Trio £205.90 OWNER Miss M. C. Fraser (NEWBURY) BRED Dorothea Viscountess Kelburn 11 Rn
1m 13.61 (1.81) SF: 37/60/39/55/62/45/54/36/37/22/26
WEIGHT FOR AGE 3yo-5lb

3066 BONUSPRINT H'CAP (0-100) (3-Y.O) (Class C) £9,878.00 (£2,984.00: £1,452.00: £686.00)
1m 2f 6y Stalls: Low GOING minus 0.23 sec per fur (GF) 2-40 (2-44)

2593* **Cap Juluca (IRE) (96)***(108)*(Fav)*(RCharlton)* 3-9-7 JWeaver(4) (mde all: rdn out) ....— **1**
2691 3 Grand Selection (IRE) **(79)***(89) (MBell)* 3-8-4 MFenton(3) (a.p: chsd wnr 5f out: rdn over 2f out: unable qckn) 1½ **2**
2568* Prize Pupil (IRE) **(75)***(81) (CFWall)* 3-8-0 MRoberts(1) (swtg: 5th st: lost pl 3f out: rallied fnl f: r.o) 2 **3**
2822 2 Mister Fire Eyes (IRE) **(71)***(76) (CEBrittain)* 3-7-10v FNorton(7) (swtg: 4th st: rdn over 2f out: one pce) 1 **4**
2822* Rockforce **(87)***(89) (MRChannon)* 3-8-12 5x RHughes(5) (hdwy on ins over 4f out: hrd rdn over 1f out: one pce) 1½ **5**
2803* Dance Band (USA) **(93)***(91) (BHanbury)* 3-9-4 WRSwinburn(2) (chsd wnr 5f: 3rd st: wknd over 3f out) 3 **6**
2738 4 State Law **(88)***(85) (GHarwood)* 3-8-13 AClark(6) (nvr nr to chal) ....½ **7**
2348 2 Krystallos **(93)***(90) (RHannon)* 3-9-4 JReid(12) (lw: nvr nrr) ....s.h **8**
2691 10 Danjing (IRE) **(90)***(83) (PFICole)* 3-9-1 TQuinn(8) (b.hind: hdwy on ins over 3f out: wknd over 2f out) 2½ **9**
2795 2 Hedera (USA) **(89)***(81) (MRStoute)* 3-9-0 MJKinane(13) (6th st: wknd over 2f out) ....¾ **10**
2571 11 Kilcoran Bay **(75)***(66) (IABalding)* 3-8-0 WCarson(11) (a bhd) ....½ **11**
2738 5 Maeterlinck (IRE) **(86)***(74) (BWHills)* 3-8-11 MHills(10) (lw: a bhd) 1½ **12**
2409 8 Grandinare (USA) **(88)***(37) (PWChapple-Hyam)* 3-8-13 BThomson(9) (a bhd) 25 **13**

4/1 CAP JULUCA (IRE), **13/2** Hedera (USA), **7/1** Grand Selection (IRE), Krystallos, **8/1** State Law, **9/1** Prize Pupil (IRE), **11/1** Maeterlinck (IRE), **12/1** Mister Fire Eyes (IRE), **14/1** Dance Band (USA), **16/1** Rockforce, **25/1** Danjing (IRE), **33/1** Kilcoran Bay, Grandinare (USA), CSF £29.23 CT £212.95 TOTE £4.90: £1.70 £2.30 £2.90 (£10.00) Trio £31.90 OWNER Mr Martin Myers (BECKHAMPTON) BRED Mrs N. Myers 13 Rn 2m 5.67 (2.67) SF: 65/46/38/33/46/48/42/47/40/38/23/31/-

3067 HUNGERFORD STKS (Gp 3) (3-Y.O+) (Class A) £23,100.00 (£8,670.00: £4,185.00: £1,845.00)
7f 64y (round) Stalls: Centre GOING minus 0.23 sec per fur (GF) 3-10 (3-12)

2349 3 **Harayir (USA) (118)***(121)*(Fav)*(MajorWRHern)* 3-8-13 WCarson(5) (lw: 5th st: led over 1f out: rdn: r.o wl) ....— **1**
2646 5 Nijo **(109)***(114) (DRLoder)* 4-9-0 JReid(1) (lw: 3rd st: nt clr run over 1f out: r.o ins fnl f) ....¾ **2**
2689 3 Darnay **(115)***(119) (SbinSuroor)* 4-9-5 MJKinane(8) (2nd st: led over 2f out tl over 1f out: unable qckn) ....hd **3**
2703 4 Fraam **(109)***(111) (EALDunlop)* 6-9-0v WRSwinburn(7) (b: swtg: 4th st: rdn over 1f out: one pce) 1¼ **4**
2737* Easy Dollar **(90)***(111) (BGubby)* 3-8-8b JWeaver(2) (lw: led 5f: rdn: one pce) ....s.h **5**
2646 6 Green Perfume (USA) **(102)***(106) (PFICole)* 3-8-8 TQuinn(6) (plld hrd: nvr nr to chal) 2½ **6**

2671[11] Raah Algharb (USA) **(109)***(105) (MRStoute)* 3-8-8 RHills(4) (plld hrd: 6th st: one pce fnl 3f) ..nk **7**
2673* Brief Glimpse (IRE) **(106)***(101) (MajorDNChappell)* 3-8-5 MHills(9) (hdwy over 2f out: wknd over 1f out) ....½ **8**
2369[10] Jafeica (IRE) **(93)***(93) (RHannon)* 4-9-0 MRoberts(3) (lw: bhd fnl 5f) 5 **9**

9/4 HARAYIR (USA), **5/2** Darnay, **4/1** Brief Glimpse (IRE), **15/2** Fraam (op 5/1), **8/1** Nijo (op 5/1), **20/1** Green Perfume (USA), **33/1** Raah Algharb (USA), **50/1** Easy Dollar, **66/1** Jafeica (IRE), CSF £18.51 TOTE £3.30: £1.20 £2.30 £1.50 (£15.80) Trio £9.30 OWNER Mr Hamdan Al Maktoum (LAMBOURN) BRED Shadwell Farm Inc in USA 9 Rn 1m 28.3 (-0.20) SF: 81/80/85/77/71/66/65/61/59
WEIGHT FOR AGE 3yo-6lb

3068 WASHINGTON SINGER STKS (Listed) (2-Y.O) (Class A) £10,294.00 (£3,112.00: £1,516.00: £718.00)
7f (straight) Stalls: Centre GOING minus 0.23 sec per fur (GF) 3-40 (3-41)

2365[2] **Mons** *(95)*(Fav)*(LMCumani)* 2-9-0 JWeaver(4) (lw: led: rdn over 2f out: hdd wl over 1f out: led ins fnl f: r.o wl) ....— **1**
2801* Yarob (IRE) *(91) (HThomsonJones)* 2-9-0 RHills(7) (a.p: rdn over 2f out: led wl over 1f out tl ins fnl f: unable qckn) 1¾ **2**
2131[2] Line Dancer *(90) (WJarvis)* 2-9-0 TQuinn(5) (b.off fore: lw: hld up: rdn over 2f out: one pce fnl f) ....nk **3**
2320[8] Latin Reign (USA) *(78) (PWChapple-Hyam)* 2-8-11 JReid(2) (lw: a.p: ev ch 2f out: wknd over 1f out) 4 **4**
2572[2] Alessandra *(72) (BWHills)* 2-8-6 MHills(3) (b: b.nr hind: a.p: ev ch 2f out: wknd over 1f out) ..¾ **5**
2681* Jack Jennings *(78) (BAMcMahon)* 2-9-0 GCarter(1) (lw: swvd lft s: a bhd) ....½ **6**
Light Reflections *(45) (BWHills)* 2-8-8 WRSwinburn(8) (leggy: unf: scope: s.s: a bhd) 12 **7**
Regal Eagle *(11) (IABalding)* 2-8-8 WRyan(6) (str: scope: bit bkwd: a bhd) 15 **8**

13/8 MONS, **4/1** Yarob (IRE) (op 5/2), **6/1** Latin Reign (USA), **10/1** Jack Jennings (op 6/1), **12/1** Alessandra, Regal Eagle, **14/1** Line Dancer (op 7/1), **16/1** Light Reflections, CSF £7.70 TOTE £2.30: £1.20 £1.60 £2.90 (£2.80) OWNER Mrs E. H. Vestey (NEWMARKET) BRED Sir Eric Parker 8 Rn 1m 26.87 (2.37) SF: 51/47/46/34/28/34/1/-

3069 SPARSHOLT MAIDEN STKS (2-Y.O F) (Class D) £4,016.00 (£1,208.00: £584.00: £272.00)
6f 8y Stalls: Centre GOING minus 0.23 sec per fur (GF) 4-10 (4-15)

Bosra Sham (USA) *(105+)*(Fav)*(HRACecil)* 2-8-11 MJKinane(20) (w'like: scope: lw: a.p: led over 2f out: qcknd: r.o wl) ....— **1**
Faraway Waters *(96) (DWPArbuthnot)* 2-8-11 TQuinn(19) (b.hind: unf: hld up: rdn over 2f out: unable qckn) 3½ **2**
Dark Deed (USA) *(95) (BWHills)* 2-8-11 MHills(5) (w'like: scope: hdwy over 2f out: rdn over 1f out: one pce) ....nk **3**
Tsarnista *(87) (JLDunlop)* 2-8-11 JReid(22) (leggy: hld up: rdn over 2f out: one pce) 3 **4**
Possessive Artiste *(85+) (MRStoute)* 2-8-11 WRSwinburn(7) (b.hind: unf: scope: bit bkwd: rdn over 2f out: hdwy over 1f out: r.o one pce) ....¾ **5**
Min Elreeh (USA) *(82+) (MajorWRHern)* 2-8-11 RHills(9) (unf: nvr plcd to chal) 1¼ **6**
Ruznama (USA) *(80+) (BWHills)* 2-8-11 WCarson(11) (w'like: scope: lw: s.s: nvr plcd to chal) ....½ **7**
2876[6] Keepers Dawn (IRE) *(80) (RFJohnsonHoughton)* 2-8-11 AClark(18) (led over 3f) ....nk **8**
Victoria Regia (IRE) *(79) (RCharlton)* 2-8-11 SRaymont(23) (w'like: scope: bit bkwd: nvr nr to chal: rn green) ....nk **9**
1497[4] Watch Me (IRE) *(77) (RHannon)* 2-8-4 (7) DaneO'Neill(14) (a.p: rdn over 2f out: wknd fnl f) ....½ **10**
Sabaah Elfull *(73) (ACStewart)* 2-8-11 MRoberts(2) (leggy: lw: s.s: shkn up & hdwy 1f out: no ch whn bdly hmpd ins fnl f) 1¾ **11**
2675[7] Bold Enough *(71) (BWHills)* 2-8-11 RStreet(16) (a mid div) ....¾ **12**
Arcady *(66) (PTWalwyn)* 2-8-11 JWeaver(6) (leggy: unf: a mid div) 1¾ **13**
Lady Thiang *(65) (CFWall)* 2-8-6 (5) LNewton(21) (w'like: bit bkwd: nvr nrr) ....nk **14**
Classic Look (IRE) *(55) (MajorDNChappell)* 2-8-11 BThomson(1) (leggy: lt-f: s.s: nvr nrr) 4 **15**
Fiddes (IRE) *(55) (JLDunlop)* 2-8-11 RCochrane(17) (str: bkwd: s.s: nvr nrr) ....s.h **16**
1348[8] Flash In The Pan (IRE) *(50) (MBell)* 2-8-11 MFenton(3) (a bhd) 1¾ **17**
2135[12] Cotytto *(47) (MJFetherston-Godley)* 2-8-11 FNorton(10) (bhd fnl 2f) 1¼ **18**
2572[4] Sistar Act *(45) (MRChannon)* 2-8-4 (7) DSweeney(8) (bhd fnl 2f) ....½ **19**
Eskimo Kiss (IRE) *(32) (MJFetherston-Godley)* 2-8-8 (3) JTate(4) (w'like: bit bkwd: a bhd) 5 **20**
Friday Night (USA) *(30) (IABalding)* 2-8-11 WRyan(12) (unf: bhd fnl 2f) 1 **21**
Poly By Staufan (IRE) *(MRChannon)* 2-8-11 RHughes(13) (leggy: spd 4f) 11 **22**

4/5 BOSRA SHAM (USA), **11/1** Watch Me (IRE), **12/1** Classic Look (IRE), **14/1** Ruznama (USA), **16/1** Possessive Artiste, **25/1** Dark Deed (USA), Min Elreeh (USA), Keepers Dawn (IRE), **33/1** Tsarnista, Poly By Staufan (IRE), Sabaah Elfull, Friday Night (USA), **40/1** Victoria Regia (IRE), Fiddes (IRE), **50/1** Sistar Act, Flash In The Pan (IRE), Bold Enough, Arcady, **66/1** Faraway Waters, Eskimo Kiss (IRE), Lady Thiang, **100/1** Cotytto, CSF £52.97 TOTE £1.60: £1.20 £10.50 £6.30 (£106.00) Trio £735.30 OWNER Mr Wafic Said (NEWMARKET) BRED Gerald W. Leigh 22 Rn
1m 13.87 (2.07) SF: 47/38/37/29/27/24/22/22/21/19/15/13/8/7/-/-/-/-/-/-/-/-

3070 NEWTOWN CONDITIONS STKS (3-Y.O+) (Class C) £5,037.25 (£1,831.00: £890.50: £377.50: £163.75)
1m 4f 5y Stalls: Low GOING minus 0.23 sec per fur (GF) 4-40 (4-44)

1780[6] **Wayne County (IRE) (105)**_(114) (RAkehurst)_ 5-9-7 JWeaver(1) (led 11f out: rdn over 2f out: r.o wl)......— 1
2910* Commoner (USA) **(101)**_(113) (RHannon)_ 3-8-11 MJKinane(4) (led 1f: 2nd st: rdn over 2f out: unable qckn)......1¾ 2
1780[3] Blush Rambler (USA) **(109)**_(108) (MRStoute)_ 5-9-4 WRSwinburn(5) (4th st: rdn over 2f out: r.o one pce)......nk 3
2323[4] Bal Harbour **(108)**_(106)_(Fav)_(HRACecil)_ 4-9-4 WRyan(2) (3rd st: rdn over 2f out: one pce) ..1¾ 4
1122a[4] Dreamer (USA) **(103)**_(82) (PFICole)_ 3-8-10 TQuinn(3) (plld hrd: 5th st: a bhd)......20 5

5/4 Bal Harbour, **11/4** Blush Rambler (USA), **5/1** Commoner (USA), **6/1** Dreamer (USA) (op 4/1), **14/1** WAYNE COUNTY (IRE), CSF £65.37 TOTE £13.20: £3.90 £1.80 (£28.00) OWNER Mrs A. Naughton (EPSOM) BRED Swettenham Stud 5 Rn 2m 33.22 (3.92) SF: 60/48/54/52/17
WEIGHT FOR AGE 3yo-11lb

3071 LEVY BOARD H'CAP (0-95) (3-Y.O+) (Class C) £5,670.00 (£1,710.00: £830.00: £390.00)
2m Stalls: Low GOING minus 0.23 sec per fur (GF) 5-10 (5-10)

2569[3] **Blaze Away (USA) (79)**_(92) (IABalding)_ 4-10-0 WRyan(3) (swtg: mde all: rdn over 2f out: r.o wl)......— 1
2445* Celeric **(86)**_(99)_(Fav)_(DMorley)_ 3-9-6 RHills(6) (5th st: swtchd rt over 2f out: rdn over 1f out: unable qckn)......½ 2
2550[2] John Lee Hooker **(67)**_(79) (DWPArbuthnot)_ 3-8-1 MRoberts(5) (2nd st: ev ch wl over 1f out: one pce)......¾ 3
1929* French Ivy (USA) **(62)**_(73) (FMurphy)_ 8-8-11 RCochrane(4) (b: lw: hdwy over 10f out: 3rd st: rdn over 3f out: one pce)......½ 4
2996* Star Rage (IRE) **(75)**_(81) (MJohnston)_ 5-9-10 5x JWeaver(2) (lw: 4th st: wknd over 1f out)......5 5
Atours (USA) **(79)**_(76) (DRCElsworth)_ 7-9-9 (5) AProcter(1) (b: 6th st: a bhd)......9 6

2/1 Celeric, **11/4** Star Rage (IRE), **4/1** French Ivy (USA), **13/2** John Lee Hooker, BLAZE AWAY (USA), **12/1** Atours (USA) (op 8/1), CSF £19.21 TOTE £8.10: £3.30 £2.00 (£14.10) OWNER Mr Paul Mellon (KINGSCLERE) BRED Paul Mellon 6 Rn 3m 35.43 (8.93) SF: 51/43/23/32/40/35
WEIGHT FOR AGE 3yo-15lb
T/Jkpt: £17,704.50 (0.1 Tckts); £22,442.41 to Newbury 12/8/95. T/Plpt: £513.10 (54.99 Tckts). T/Qdpt: £63.00 (5.5 Tckts). AK

2958-WOLVERHAMPTON (L-H)
Friday August 11th (Standard)
WEATHER: sunny, hot WIND: nil

3072 JAPONICA H'CAP (0-65) (3-Y.O+) (Class F) £2,560.00 (£760.00: £360.00: £160.00)
6f (Fibresand) Stalls: Low GOING: 0.12 sec per fur (SLW) 2-20 (2-24)

_2631*_ **Evening Falls (55)**_(61) (CJames)_ 4-9-5 CRutter(13) (hdwy 3f out: wnt 2nd st: led wl ins fnl f: r.o)......— 1
_1763[5]_ Chadwell Hall **(61)**_(66) (SRBowring)_ 4-9-6b(5) CTeague(8) (led: rdn over 1f out: hdd wl ins fnl f)......nk 2
2786[2] To the Roof (IRE) **(64)**_(65) (PWHarris)_ 3-9-9 MBirch(6) (a.p: 3rd st: ev ch over 1f out: nt qckn)......1¾ 3
2776[2] Petomi **(65)**_(65) (SirMarkPrescott)_ 3-9-10 GDuffield(11) (swtg: hdwy 3f out: 5th st: r.o one pce fnl f)......hd 4
_2925[3]_ Bold Aristocrat (IRE) **(49)**_(49) (RHollinshead)_ 4-8-6 (7) FLynch(12) (lw: hdwy & 7th st: r.o one pce fnl f)......hd 5
_2963[7]_ Jon's Choice **(52)**_(44) (BPreece)_ 7-9-2 GHind(10) (prom: rdn over 2f out: 6th st: no hdwy) 3 6

2590[3] Ring the Chief **(56)***(45) (RAkehurst)* 3-8-12 (3) SSanders(1) (lw: nvr nr to chal) 1¼ 7
831[7] Primula Bairn **(60)***(43) (DNicholls)* 5-9-10 AlexGreaves(9) (chsd ldrs 4f)....................2 8
2692[6] Another Jade **(64)***(47)*(Fav)*(APJarvis)* 5-10-0 KDarley(5) (prom: 4th st: wknd over 1f out) .....nk 9
2631[3] Disco Boy **(55)***(34) (BAMcMahon)* 5-9-5b SDWilliams(3) (prom 3f) 1½ 10
2229[6] Tael of Silver **(57)***(34) (KRBurke)* 3-9-2 DHolland(2) (a bhd) ....½ 11
2963[5] My Gallery (IRE) **(64)***(37) (ABailey)* 4-10-0 WHawksley(4) (lw: rdn 4f out: a bhd) 1½ 12
2742[6] Endless Wave **(57)** *(MBell)* 3-9-2 DHarrison(7) (chsd ldrs 3f: eased whn btn over 1f out)......12 13

6/1 Another Jade, **7/1** Petomi, **15/2** Bold Aristocrat (IRE) (op 5/1), **8/1** To the Roof (IRE), EVENING FALLS, Ring the Chief (op 5/1), Tael of Silver, **9/1** Primula Bairn, **10/1** Chadwell Hall, Disco Boy, **12/1** Jon's Choice, **14/1** My Gallery (IRE), Endless Wave, CSF £84.77 CT £620.10 TOTE £7.30: £1.90 £3.40 £4.10 (£82.30) Trio Not won; £248.62 to Newbury 12/8/95 OWNER Mrs Carol Welch (NEWBURY) BRED M. V. S. and Mrs Aram 13 Rn
1m 16.2 (5.00) SF: 43/48/42/42/31/26/22/25/29/16/11/19/-
WEIGHT FOR AGE 3yo-5lb

3073

CLEMATIS CLAIMING STKS (I) (3-Y.O+) (Class F) £2,519.00 (£694.00: £329.00)
7f (Fibresand) Stalls: Low GOING: 0.12 sec per fur (SLW) 2-50 (2-54)

2797[7] **Sweet Supposin (IRE) (87)***(87)*(Fav)*(CADwyer)* 4-9-10b DHarrison(12) (s.i.s: hdwy over 3f out: led wl over 1f out: pushed out) ....— 1
2588[3] Bentico **(73)***(71) (MrsNMacauley)* 6-9-2b DeanMcKeown(9) (a.p: jnd ldr over 4f out: 3rd st: ev ch over 1f out: nt qckn) 3½ 2
*2963** Legatee **(58)***(52) (BJMeehan)* 4-8-3 BDoyle(3) (led over 5f: one pce) 2½ 3
2784[4] Brookhead Lady **(57)***(46) (PDEvans)* 4-8-5 GHind(10) (b.nr fore: hdwy 3f out: 4th st:one pce)3½ 4
2276[15] Maple Bay (IRE) **(52)***(50) (ABailey)* 6-8-5 (5) VHalliday(5) (nvr nrr) ....¾ 5
Cape Colony *(58) (CFWall)* 3-9-0 WWoods(7) (neat: s.s: hdwy 3f out: 7th st: one pce) ....¾ 6
2815[4] Cool Tactician **(67)***(38) (RHollinshead)* 3-8-10 TIves(4) (chsd ldrs: 6th & wkng st) 7 7
2383[8] Jamaica Bridge **(60)***(34) (SGNorton)* 5-8-12 KDarley(11) (prom: 5th & wkng st) ....s.h 8
2921[5] Noble Ballerina (USA) *(19) (APJarvis)* 3-8-2 (3) DWright(8) (n.d) 6 9
1951[10] Princethorpe *(14) (BRCambidge)* 8-8-8 GDuffield(6) (a bhd) 1 10
1906* Brass Tacks **(64)***(10) (RTPhillips)* 3-8-0 (5) MHenry(2) (spd 2f: sn bhd) 3 11
2309[5] Indian Colours *(JNorton)* 4-8-5 DaleGibson(1) (bhd fnl 3f) 3 12

15/8 SWEET SUPPOSIN (IRE) (3/1-13/8), **3/1** Legatee, **8/1** Maple Bay (IRE) (op 12/1), **9/1** Brass Tacks, **10/1** Cool Tactician, **11/1** Bentico (op 6/1), **14/1** Jamaica Bridge, Brookhead Lady, **33/1** Cape Colony, Noble Ballerina (USA), Princethorpe, Indian Colours, CSF £21.93 TOTE £2.50: £1.90 £1.70 £1.60 (£13.60) Trio £7.90 OWNER Mr James Robertson (NEWMARKET) BRED Ballylinch Stud Ltd 12 Rn
1m 29.8 (5.80) SF: 49/33/14/8/12/14/-/-/-/-/-/-
WEIGHT FOR AGE 3yo-6lb
Legatee clmd DPawlitta £4,000

3074

CLEMATIS CLAIMING STKS (II) (3-Y.O+) (Class F) £2,519.00 (£694.00: £329.00)
7f (Fibresand) Stalls: Low GOING: 0.12 sec per fur (SLW) 3-20 (3-21)

Ashgore (85)*(80)*(Fav)*(MJohnston)* 5-9-4 DHolland(12) (a.p: 3rd st: led over 1f out: r.o wl)..— 1
2972[6] At the Savoy (IRE) **(62)***(73) (TDBarron)* 4-8-12b KDarley(6) (chsd ldrs: rdn 4f out: 5th st: ev ch ins fnl f: r.o) ....nk 2
2517[5] Pine Ridge Lad (IRE) **(70)***(72) (JLEyre)* 5-9-2 SDWilliams(3) (a.p: ev ch over 1f out: nt qckn)2½ 3
2538* Crystal Heights (FR) **(65)***(67) (RJO'Sullivan)* 7-8-9 (3) SSanders(8) (b: dwlt: hdwy 1f out: nvr nrr) ....nk 4
2836* Bold Angel **(69)***(66) (MHEasterby)* 8-9-0 MBirch(7) (rdn & hdwy over 3f out: r.o ins fnl f) 1¼ 5
2538[3] Dusk in Daytona **(60)***(63) (CJames)* 3-8-5 CRutter(2) (led over 5f: wknd fnl f) ....hd 6
2586[4] Rambo Waltzer **(80)***(68) (SGNorton)* 3-9-0 MTebbutt(4) (hdwy over 3f out: 6th st: ev ch over 1f out: wknd fnl f) 1½ 7
2605[6] Words of Wisdom (IRE) **(57)***(66) (CACyzer)* 5-9-6 DBiggs(1) (prom: 2nd st: ev ch over 1f out: wknd fnl f) 1 8
2913[5] Sense of Priority **(71)***(46) (DNicholls)* 6-9-0 AlexGreaves(11) (n.d) 6 9
2493[8] Caherass Court (IRE) **(32)***(7) (BPreece)* 4-8-1 ow1 GHind(5) (s.s: a bhd: t.o) 11 10
Chili Lass *(2) (JWharton)* 3-7-11 DaleGibson(9) (a in rr: t.o) ....nk 11
2540[11] Benjarong **(46)***(2) (RMMcKellar)* 3-7-6 (5) MHenry(10) (bhd fnl 2f: t.o) 3½ 12

15/8 ASHGORE, **9/2** Bold Angel, **7/1** Crystal Heights (FR), **8/1** Sense of Priority, At the Savoy (IRE), Rambo Waltzer, **9/1** Pine Ridge Lad (IRE), **12/1** Words of Wisdom (IRE), **16/1** Dusk in Daytona, **50/1** Caherass Court (IRE), Chili Lass, Benjarong, CSF £18.12 TOTE £2.70: £1.70 £2.70 £2.30 (£11.50) Trio £186.90 OWNER Mr Harvey Ashworth (MIDDLEHAM) BRED D. A. and Mrs Hicks 12 Rn
1m 30.5 (6.50) SF: 35/28/27/22/21/12/17/21/1/-/-/-
WEIGHT FOR AGE 3yo-6lb

3075

H & V NEWS H'CAP (0-70) (3-Y.O+) (Class E) £3,502.40 (£1,047.20: £501.60: £228.80)
1m 100y (Fibresand) Stalls: Low GOING: 0.12 sec per fur (SLW) 3-50 (3-53)

*2634*9 **Kinnegad Kid (67)***(78) (RIngram)* 6-9-11v BDoyle(7) (hdwy over 3f out: led wl over 1f out: r.o wl) — 1
2707 7 Douce Maison (IRE) **(59)***(68) (APJarvis)* 4-9-3 DHarrison(10) (hdwy 3f out: 5th st: r.o ins fnl f) 1¼ 2
*2634*4 Shanghai Venture (USA) **(68)***(70) (SPCWoods)* 4-9-12 WWoods(5) (hld up: stdy hdwy & 6th st: btn whn hmpd ins fnl f) 3½ 3
2737 8 Self Reliance **(60)***(62) (MBell)* 3-8-4 (7) GFaulkner(12) (hdwy over 4f out: 3rd st: btn whn hung rt ins fnl f) hd 4
2881 4 Sporting Risk **(52)***(46) (PWHarris)* 3-7-12 (5) MHenry(3) (led over 6f out: hdd & 2nd st: sn wknd) 4 5
*2634*12 Mam'zelle Angot **(62)***(54) (AHarrison)* 5-9-6 TIves(13) (no hdwy fnl 3f) 1 6
*2922*2 Sandmoor Denim **(65)***(54)*(Fav)*(SRBowring)* 8-9-4 (5) CTeague(6) (b: b.hind: rdn 4f out: nvr nrr) 2 7
*2922** Carte Blanche **(52)***(40) (CACyzer)* 4-8-10 5x DBiggs(2) (prom: 4th & wkng st) hd 8
2815 2 David James' Girl **(65)***(48) (ABailey)* 3-8-13 (3) SSanders(9) (chsd ldrs tl wknd 2f out) 3 9
2776 8 Jalwa (USA) **(60)***(26) (KTIvory)* 3-8-11 GDuffield(8) (led 2f: wknd 3f out) 9 10
1933 5 Dosses Dan (IRE) **(69)***(28) (BPreece)* 3-9-6 GHind(4) (a bhd) 3½ 11
*2377*6 Prenonamoss **(53)** *(DWPArbuthnot)* 7-8-11v JWilliams(11) (lw: a bhd: t.o) 8 12
1512 11 Lees Please (IRE) **(58)** *(KOCunningham-Brown)* 3-8-9 DHolland(1) (prom 4f: t.o) 14 13

3/1 Sandmoor Denim, **5/1** Carte Blanche, **11/2** David James' Girl, **6/1** Douce Maison (IRE), Self Reliance, **10/1** Prenonamoss, **12/1** Shanghai Venture (USA), KINNEGAD KID, **14/1** Mam'zelle Angot, **25/1** Jalwa (USA), Sporting Risk, Lees Please (IRE), **33/1** Dosses Dan (IRE), CSF £82.52 CT £830.54 TOTE £19.10: £3.90 £2.80 £3.60 (£34.70) Trio £173.90 OWNER Mr J. B. Wilcox (EPSOM) BRED Airlie Stud and Miss K. Rausing 13 Rn

1m 51.9 (7.90) SF: 43/33/35/20/4/19/19/5/6/-/-/-/-
WEIGHT FOR AGE 3yo-7lb

3076

WILD ROSE H'CAP (0-70) (3-Y.O+ F & M) (Class E) £3,159.20 (£941.60: £448.80: £202.40)
1m 4f (Fibresand) Stalls: Low GOING: 0.12 sec per fur (SLW) 4-20 (4-21)

2759* **Instantaneous (47)***(60)*(Fav)*(MHEasterby)* 3-8-7 MBirch(7) (a gng wl: led over 2f out: clr over 1f out: r.o wl) — 1
*2379*2 Daleria **(57)***(61)*(Fav)*(AHarrison)* 4-10-0 TIves(3) (hld up: hdwy over 4f out: 3rd st: r.o fnl f: no ch w wnr) 7 2
2719 2 Hard Love **(64)***(68) (SPCWoods)* 3-9-10 WWoods(6) (a.p: led over 4f out tl over 2f out: 2nd st: one pce) hd 3
*2140*3 Rosevear (IRE) **(49)***(43) (SMellor)* 3-8-9 MWigham(8) (hld up: hdwy 5f out: 4th st: wknd over 1f out) 7 4
*2961*2 Sparkling Roberta **(35)***(19) (MDIUsher)* 4-7-13 (7) CAdamson(1) (hld up: hdwy 6f out: wknd 3f out: 5th & no ch st) 8 5
*2920*4 Oleron **(49)***(29) (JNorton)* 3-8-9 DaleGibson(5) (rdn over 5f out: sn bhd) 2½ 6
*2919*14 Risky Tu **(52)** *(PAKelleway)* 4-9-2 (7) AdelleGibbons(4) (led 9f out tl over 4f out: sn wknd: poor 6th st: t.o) 25 7
2731 5 Fen Terrier **(57)** *(WJHaggas)* 3-8-12 (5) MHenry(2) (bhd fnl 4f: t.o) 3 8
2719 4 Cephista **(59)***(1) (PTWalwyn)* 3-9-5v DHolland(9) (led 3f: wknd qckly over 4f out: t.o) 1 9

4/1 INSTANTANEOUS, Daleria, **5/1** Fen Terrier, Rosevear (IRE), **6/1** Sparkling Roberta, **13/2** Cephista, Hard Love, **11/1** Risky Tu, **16/1** Oleron, CSF £21.37 CT £98.09 TOTE £4.90: £1.50 £2.40 £3.10 (£16.40) Trio £29.70 OWNER Mr Reg Griffin (MALTON) BRED Mrs Anne Sutton 9 Rn

2m 43.2 (12.20) SF: 21/33/29/4/-/-/-/-/-
WEIGHT FOR AGE 3yo-11lb

3077

PLUMBAGO (S) STKS (2-Y.O) (Class G) £2,374.00 (£654.00: £310.00)
5f (Fibresand) Stalls: Low GOING: 0.12 sec per fur (SLW) 4-50 (4-52)

2869 2 **Chilibang Bang (55)***(60) (JBerry)* 2-8-11 JCarroll(7) (a.p: 3rd st: edgd lft ins fnl f: r.o to ld last strides) — 1
2866 2 Chemcast **(64)***(60) (BJMeehan)* 2-8-11 BDoyle(1) (led tl hdd last strides) hd 2
2580 3 Swing Mania (IRE) *(45)*(Fav)*(SGNorton)* 2-8-6 KDarley(9) (chsd ldrs: outpcd 2f out: r.o fnl f) 3 3
2505 6 The Imps (IRE) **(68)***(54) (BWHills)* 2-9-2 DHolland(2) (a.p: 5th st: r.o one pce fnl f) ½ 4
2185 9 Peters Folly *(40) (JLEyre)* 2-8-6 RLappin(8) (nvr nr to chal) 1¼ 5

Mullagh Hill Lad (IRE) *(44) (BAMcMahon)* 2-8-8 (3) SSanders(6) (leggy: unf: w ldrs: 2nd st: ev ch wl over 1f out: hung lft: sn wknd)....s.h 6
1670[16] Brockville Bairn *(40) (MrsASwinbank)* 2-8-11 NConnorton(11) (nvr trbld ldrs)....1½ 7
Golden Wedding *(36) (DCO'Brien)* 2-8-11 TIves(3) (unf: prom: 6th st: wknd over 1f out)....1 8
Forecast *(32) (JWharton)* 2-8-11 JWilliams(12) (unf: s.s: a bhd)....1¼ 9
2221[9] General Equation *(28) (JBalding)* 2-8-4 (7) JEdmunds(10) (prom: 4th st: wknd over 1f out)...1¼ 10
2633[8] Potenza *(20) (RHollinshead)* 2-8-4 (7) AEddery(4) (a bhd)....2½ 11
1829[12] Mandy's Risk *(17) (TMJones)* 2-8-11v DaleGibson(13) (bhd fnl 3f)....1 12
2515[9] Mobile King *(11) (APJarvis)* 2-8-11 DHarrison(5) (s.s: a bhd)....2 13

4/1 Swing Mania (IRE), **9/2** CHILIBANG BANG, **5/1** The Imps (IRE) (op 3/1), Mullagh Hill Lad (IRE) (5/2-11/2), **11/2** Chemcast, **11/1** Mobile King, **16/1** General Equation, **20/1** Peters Folly, Golden Wedding, Mandy's Risk, Potenza, Brockville Bairn, **25/1** Forecast, CSF £29.64 TOTE £3.90: £1.20 £1.80 £1.60 (£7.60) Trio £12.70 OWNER Mr Ian Crawford (COCKERHAM) BRED G. W. Hampson
13 Rn 65.2 secs (7.20) SF: -/-/-/-/-/-/-/-/-/-/-/-/-
Bt in 6,400 gns

3078

HONEYSUCKLE MAIDEN AMATEUR H'CAP (0-65) (3-Y.O+) (Class G)
£2,243.00 (£618.00: £293.00)
1m 6f 166y (Fibresand) Stalls: Low GOING: 0.12 sec per fur (SLW) 5-20 (5-20)

1596[6] **Nordic Mine (IRE) (44)***(53) (PJHobbs)* 5-10-13 (5) MrsSHobbs(10) (hld up: stdy hdwy over 3f out: 3rd st: led ins fnl f: r.o wl)....— 1
2599[8] En Vacances (IRE) **(61)***(67) (AGFoster)* 3-11-7 MissJAllison(7) (hld up: lost pl 7f out: hdwy & 5th st: r.o fnl f: nt trble wnr)....2½ 2
2745[9] Our Bessie **(29)***(34)*(Fav)*(DMarks)* 4-10-3e MissKMarks(9) (hdwy over 6f out: led over 4f out tl ins fnl f)....1 3
2648[5] Dawn Mission **(48)***(51) (MHEasterby)* 3-10-8 MrCBonner(6) (a.p: led 5f out: sn hdd: 2nd st: ev ch over 1f out: wknd fnl f)....2½ 4
2981[7] Jarzon Dancer **(23)***(22) (DAWilson)* 7-9-11 MrsSBosley(5) (s.s: hdwy 6f out: 6th st: nvr nr ldrs)....3 5
2090[8] Rejects Reply **(27)***(25) (WJMusson)* 5-10-1 MrTMcCarthy(3) (prom: 3rd st: wknd over 1f out)....1¼ 6
2535[4] Remember This (IRE) **(28)***(4) (CACyzer)* 5-9-11 (5) MissAWilcox(1) (led to 5f out: wknd over 2f out: t.o)....20 7
1957[9] Goldenberry **(32)** *(KGWingrove)* 4-10-1 (5)ow9 MrKLoads(4) (plld hrd: sn chsng ldr: wknd 6f out: t.o)....6 8
122[4] The Frog Lady (IRE) **(46)***(11) (DWPArbuthnot)* 4-11-6 MrsDArbuthnot(8) (b: dropped rr 7f out: t.o)....4 9

9/4 Our Bessie (3/1-2/1), **9/2** Dawn Mission, **5/1** NORDIC MINE (IRE), Rejects Reply, The Frog Lady (IRE), **11/2** En Vacances (IRE), **14/1** Jarzon Dancer, **16/1** Remember This (IRE), **33/1** Goldenberry, CSF £33.68 CT £74.86 TOTE £9.80: £4.00 £1.90 £1.10 (£32.20) Trio £64.90 OWNER Mr N. C. Savery (MINEHEAD) BRED D. H. W. Dobson 9 Rn
3m 28.4 (21.00) SF: 28/28/9/12/-/-/-/-/-
WEIGHT FOR AGE 3yo-14lb
T/Plpt: £216.00 (44.52 Tckts). T/Qdpt: £10.00 (2.2 Tckts). KH

2938-LINGFIELD (L-H)
Saturday August 12th (Turf Good to firm, AWT Standard)
WEATHER: sunny WIND: slt bhd

3079

BLACKBERRY LANE APPRENTICE H'CAP (0-60) (3-Y.O+) (Class G)
£2,357.50 (£670.00: £332.50)
7f 140y Stalls: Centre GOING minus 0.49 sec per fur (F) 5-45 (5-49)

2425* **Quillon Rose (46)***(67)*(Fav)*(CFWall)* 3-8-1 (10) PClarke(14) (swtg: hld up gng wl: hdwy over 3f out: led over 2f out: r.o)....— 1
2685[8] Paddy's Rice **(56)***(74) (LJHolt)* 4-9-8 (6) IonaWands(1) (racd far side: a.p: ev ch fnl 2f: unable qckn)....1¼ 2
2789* Burnt Sienna (IRE) **(35)***(30) (JSMoore)* 3-7-9 (5) RMullen(11) (chsd ldrs: rdn over 2f out: one pce)....11 3
2404[8] Myjinka **(27)***(22) (JO'Donoghue)* 5-7-8b(5) PDoe(3) (chsd ldrs: rdn over 2f out: one pce)....hd 4
2593[13] Real Madrid **(37)***(26) (GPEnright)* 4-8-4b(5) FLynch(12) (chsd ldrs: rdn over 2f out: one pce)....3 5
2761[6] Woodlands Electric **(21)***(8) (PAPritchard)* 5-7-4 (3) JoHunnam(16) (led: hdd over 2f out: sn rdn: one pce)....¾ 6
315[8] Paronomasia **(40)***(22) (MBell)* 3-7-13 (6) GFaulkner(8) (nvr nrr)....2½ 7

30117 Fort Knox (IRE) **(53)**_(31) (RMFlower)_ 4-9-11b AEddery(2) (prom 5f) 1¾ **8**
23638 Swinging Sixties (IRE) **(56)**_(34) (GLMoore)_ 4-9-11 (3) LSuthern(9) (b: in rr: rdn 3f out: no hdwy) ....hd **9**
1855 12 Dragonflight **(33)**_(8) (DHaydnJones)_ 4-7-9 (10)ow1 AnthonyBond(6) (swtg: mid div: edgd lft 4f out: wknd 3f out) 1¼ **10**
2843R Arrasas Lady **(27)** _(JCPoulton)_ 5-7-6 (7)ow6 TField(7) (a bhd) ....hd **11**
25367 Pedaltothemetal (IRE) **(41)**_(13) (PMitchell)_ 3-8-1b(5) RStudholme(4) (b.hind: mid div tl wknd 3f out) 1¾ **12**
_2925_13 Distant Dynasty **(46)**_(17) (BAPearce)_ 5-9-1 (3) JWilkinson(5) (swtg: mid div: edgd lft over 3f out: sn rdn & wknd) ....nk **13**
28326 Mitsis **(39)**_(4) (GCBravery)_ 4-8-11b RWaterfield(13) (lw: prom 5f) 3 **14**
LONG HANDICAP Woodlands Electric 7-1

7/2 QUILLON ROSE, **11/2** Fort Knox (IRE) (4/1-6/1), Burnt Sienna (IRE) (4/1-6/1), **7/1** Paddy's Rice (5/1-9/1), **8/1** Swinging Sixties (IRE), Pedaltothemetal (IRE) (op 16/1), **12/1** Myjinka, **14/1** Mitsis, Distant Dynasty (8/1-16/1), **20/1** Real Madrid, **25/1** Paronomasia, **33/1** Dragonflight, **50/1** Woodlands Electric, Arrasas Lady, CSF £27.16 CT £123.31 TOTE £5.30: £2.60 £2.00 £2.00 (£38.80) Trio £32.70 OWNER Sir Philip Oppenheimer (NEWMARKET) BRED Hascombe and Valiant Studs 14 Rn
1m 28.92 (0.92) SF: 43/57/6/5/9/-/-/14/17/-/-/-/-/-
WEIGHT FOR AGE 3yo-7lb

3080 LAMBERT & FOSTER (S) STKS (2-Y.O) (Class G) £2,646.20 (£733.20: £350.60)

6f Stalls: High GOING minus 0.49 sec per fur (F) 6-15 (6-16)

2534 10 **Phoenix House** _(66) (GLMoore)_ 2-8-11v RPerham(8) (led after 1f: clr 3f out: rdn & hung lft over 1f out: all out) ....— **1**
28473 Vera's First (IRE) **(73)**_(61d)_(Fav)_(GLewis)_ 2-8-6 PaulEddery(4) (lw: hld up: rdn 3f out: chsd wnr over 2f out: hrd rdn fnl f: jst failed) ....hd **2**
27915 One Shot (IRE) _(64) (WRMuir)_ 2-8-8 (3) JTate(3) (hdwy over 2f out: rdn over 1f out: r.o one pce) ....¾ **3**
_2962_5 Vital Evidence _(59) (DCO'Brien)_ 2-8-3 (3) DRMcCabe(5) (hdwy 2f out: rdn over 1f out: r.o one pce fnl f) ....s.h **4**
_2962_7 Cottesloe Beach _(50) (KTIvory)_ 2-8-4 (7) CScally(6) (b: b.hind: chsd ldrs tl wknd over 1f out) 5 **5**
_2939_6 Reclaimed _(35) (JSMoore)_ 2-7-13 (7) DaneO'Neill(7) (led 1f: chsd wnr tl wknd over 2f out) 4 **6**
_2625_6 Tartan Express (IRE) _(30) (BAPearce)_ 2-8-4b(7) JWilkinson(2) (edgd lft s: a bhd) 3½ **7**
Bellapais (IRE) _(1) (WRMuir)_ 2-8-6 DHarrison(1) (w'like: sltly hmpd s: a bhd) 9 **8**

4/11 Vera's First (IRE), **9/2** One Shot (IRE) (3/1-5/1), **11/2** Vital Evidence, **10/1** Bellapais (IRE) (5/1-12/1), **25/1** Reclaimed, **40/1** PHOENIX HOUSE, Tartan Express (IRE), Cottesloe Beach, CSF £59.69 TOTE £19.40: £3.30 £1.10 £1.20 (£22.70) OWNER Pennine Partners (EPSOM) BRED K. Higson 8 Rn
1m 11.68 (2.68) SF: 16/11/14/9/-/-/-/-
Bt in 4,000 gns

3081 FELCOURT MEDIAN AUCTION MAIDEN STKS (3-Y.O+) (Class F) £2,846.60 (£787.60: £375.80)

7f 140y Stalls: Centre GOING minus 0.49 sec per fur (F) 6-45 (6-45)

28076 **Mo's Star (62)**_(72)_(Fav)_(SDow)_ 3-8-2 (7) ADaly(1) (chsd ldr: led 3f out: hrd rdn fnl f: r.o) ....— **1**
26535 Doonyasha _(72) (JLDunlop)_ 3-8-9 PaulEddery(2) (lw: led: hdd 3f out: hrd rdn & ev ch fnl f: r.o) ....s.h **2**
26533 Forest Mill _(61) (DWPArbuthnot)_ 3-8-9 TQuinn(5) (b.hind: outpcd & bhd: sme hdwy over 1f out: kpt on one pce fnl f) 5 **3**
21495 Sobeloved **(49)**_(63) (NEBerry)_ 3-9-0 RPerham(3) (chsd ldrs: rdn 3f out: wknd 2f out) 1½ **4**
2486 17 Tigana **(30)**_(52) (MrsLCJewell)_ 3-8-9 NGwilliams(4) (bhd fnl 3f) 3 **5**

7/4 MO'S STAR, **2/1** Forest Mill, **9/4** Doonyasha, **8/1** Sobeloved (op 12/1), **33/1** Tigana, CSF £6.04 TOTE £2.60: £1.50 £2.00 (£2.90) OWNER Mrs A. M. Upsdell (EPSOM) BRED Mrs John Trotter 5 Rn
1m 30.88 (2.88) SF: 20/20/9/11/-

3082 SAXBY H'CAP (0-65) (3-Y.O+) (Class F) £2,997.80 (£830.80:£397.40)

1m 2f (Equitrack) Stalls: Low GOING minus 0.55 sec per fur (FST) 7-15 (7-17)

27477 **Tadellal (IRE) (56)**_(66) (WGMTurner)_ 4-8-12 (7) JWilkinson(4) (lw: s.s: sn rcvrd to chse ldrs: led 1f out: hrd rdn fnl f: r.o) ....— **1**
_2961_4 Dia Georgy **(51)**_(60) (RGuest)_ 4-9-0 PaulEddery(2) (chsd ldrs: led over 1f out: sn hdd: hrd rdn fnl f: r.o) ....½ **2**

2808³ Waldo **(60)***(68)*(Fav)*(LordHuntingdon)* 4-9-9v DHarrison(11) (chsd ldrs: rdn over 1f out: r.o) ...¾ **3**
2828³ Water Hazard (IRE) **(56)***(60) (SDow)* 3-8-3 (7) ADaly(13) (chsd ldrs: rdn 2f out: r.o one pce fnl f)....................2½ **4**
*2605*³ Ultimate Warrior **(61)***(64) (CACyzer)* 5-9-10 DBiggs(12) (chsd ldr: led 3f out: hdd over 1f out: one pce) ....¾ **5**
2942⁴ Rolling Waters **(62)***(52) (JARToller)* 5-9-11 RHughes(14) (lw: a mid div) 8 **6**
Pennine Lad (IRE) **(55)***(45) (BGubby)* 5-8-13 (5) AWhelan(7) (nvr nrr) ....hd **7**
*2588*⁶ Loki (IRE) **(65)***(54) (GLewis)* 7-9-7 (7) ALakeman(6) (b: a mid div) ....¾ **8**
2881³ Top Fella (USA) **(58)***(47) (WAO'Gorman)* 3-8-12 EmmaO'Gorman(1) (nvr nrr)....................hd **9**
2946⁵ Captain Marmalade **(51)***(39) (DTThom)* 6-8-11 (3) DRMcCabe(5) (a bhd) ....½ **10**
2808² Roman Reel (USA) **(60)***(48) (GLMoore)* 4-9-9 SWhitworth(10) (lw: led: hdd 3f out: sn wknd).hd **11**
2707⁴ Hatta Sunshine (USA) **(51)***(36) (AMoore)* 5-8-7 (7) DaneO'Neill(8) (bhd fnl 4f) 1¾ **12**
*240*³ Rockstine (IRE) **(53)***(36) (PMitchell)* 4-9-2 GDuffield(3) (a bhd)....................1 **13**
Jo N Jack (IRE) **(47)** *(RIngram)* 7-8-10 AMcGlone(9) (swtg: a bhd: t.o)....................25 **14**

4/1 Waldo (op 6/1), **6/1** Roman Reel (USA), **7/1** Hatta Sunshine (USA), Rolling Waters, **8/1** Captain Marmalade, **10/1** Loki (IRE), **11/1** Top Fella (USA) (8/1-12/1), **12/1** TADELLAL (IRE), Dia Georgy, Rockstine (IRE), Ultimate Warrior, **14/1** Water Hazard (IRE) (10/1-16/1), **33/1** Pennine Lad (IRE), Jo N Jack (IRE), CSF £142.42 CT £627.04 TOTE £16.80: £5.30 £2.90 £2.40 (£154.00) Trio £208.60 OWNER Mr O. J. Stokes (SHERBORNE) 14 Rn
2m 5.74 (2.74) SF: 37/31/39/22/35/23/16/25/9/10/19/7/7/-
WEIGHT FOR AGE 3yo-9lb

3083

EDMUNDSON ELECTRICAL H'CAP (0-70) (3-Y.O+) (Class E) £3,159.20 (£941.60: £448.80: £202.40)
1m 3f 106y Stalls: Low GOING minus 0.49 sec per fur (F) 7-45 (7-45)

2682⁶ **Newport Knight (60)***(73) (RAkehurst)* 4-9-8 AMcGlone(1) (hld up: rdn 8f out: hdwy 4f out: 3rd st: led over 1f out: edgd lft ins fnl f: r.o) ....— **1**
668¹¹ Lear Dancer (USA) **(64)***(76) (PMitchell)* 4-9-12b GDuffield(6) (chsd ldr: 2nd st: led over 2f out: hdd over 1f out: rdn & rallied ins fnl f: r.o) ....½ **2**
2661⁴ Serious Option (IRE) **(63)***(68) (PFICole)* 4-9-11 TQuinn(4) (chsd ldrs: 4th st: rdn 2f out: one pce) 5 **3**
2745⁷ Scenic Dancer **(42)***(39) (AHide)* 7-8-4 ow1 JWilliams(5) (s.s: 5th st: rdn 2f out: nvr nrr)....................5 **4**
2989² Prince Danzig (IRE) **(60)***(54)*(Fav)*(DJGMurraySmith)* 4-9-8 PaulEddery(2) (led: hdd over 2f out: sn wknd)....................3 **5**
Karon Beach **(50)***(9) (JRBostock)* 4-8-12 SWhitworth(3) (6th st: a bhd) 25 **6**

10/11 Prince Danzig (IRE) (op 11/8), **4/1** NEWPORT KNIGHT, **7/1** Serious Option (IRE) (5/1-15/2), Scenic Dancer, Lear Dancer (USA) (5/1-15/2), **25/1** Karon Beach, CSF £27.18 TOTE £4.80: £2.30 £2.30 (£22.60) OWNER Muirmax Alper Partnership (EPSOM) BRED Pendley Farm 6 Rn
2m 27.33 (5.33) SF: 30/33/25/-/11/-

3084

TOY'S HILL LIMITED STKS (0-70) (3-Y.O) (Class E) £3,044.80(£906.40: £431.20: £193.60) **2m(Equitrack)** Stalls: Low GOING minus 0.55 sec (FST) 8-15 (8-15)

2333³ **Finlaggan (65)***(76)*(Fav)*(SirMarkPrescott)* 3-8-9 GDuffield(4) (hld up in tch gng wl: led 1f out: r.o) ....— **1**
*2960** Chahaya Timor (IRE) **(73)***(80) (PFICole)* 3-9-0 TQuinn(2) (chsd ldr: led 2f out: hdd 1f out: one pce) ....¾ **2**
2868* Kriva **(66)***(66) (RJRWilliams)* 3-8-7 DBiggs(1) (led: rdn 3f out: hdd 2f out: wknd over 1f out)....7 **3**
2825² Baddi Quest **(65)***(64) (BHanbury)* 3-8-9 (3) JStack(3) (bhd fnl 3f)....................7 **4**

7/4 FINLAGGAN, **15/8** Chahaya Timor (IRE), **11/4** Kriva, **7/1** Baddi Quest (op 4/1), CSF £5.12 TOTE £2.30 (£2.40) OWNER Mrs C. R. Philipson (NEWMARKET) BRED Mrs C. R. Philipson 4 Rn
3m 28.53 (5.03) SF: 26/30/16/14
T/Plpt: £193.30 (51.49 Tckts). T/Qdpt: £80.50 (1 Tckt). SM

3065-NEWBURY (L-H)
Saturday August 12th (Good to firm)

WEATHER: very hot WIND: almost nil

3085

ANDOVER RATED STKS H'CAP (0-100) (3-Y.O+) (Class B) £9,736.80 (£3,631.20: £1,765.60: £748.00: £324.00: £154.40)
7f 64y (round) Stalls: High GOING minus 0.26 sec per fur (GF) 2-00 (2-02)

2948⁶ **Gymcrak Premiere (83)***(94) (GHolmes)* 7-8-7v KFallon(13) (b.hind: lw: hdwy over 2f out: nt clr run & snatched up ins fnl f: swtchd rt: led last stride) ....— **1**

2417[3] Decorated Hero **(98)***(109) (JHMGosden)* 3-9-2 PRobinson(7) (7th st: led wl over 1f out tl ins fnl f: led wl ins fnl f: hdd last stride) .... s.h **2**
2616[2] Bin Rosie **(99)***(110)*(Fav)*(DRLoder)* 3-9-3v WRSwinburn(4) (lw: 6th st: swtchd rt over 2f out: led ins fnl f: sn hdd: r.o) .... s.h **3**
2703[12] Classic Sky (IRE) **(97)***(103) (EALDunlop)* 4-9-7 WRyan(11) (nt clr run & swtchd lft over 2f out: nt clr run wl over 1f out: hdwy fnl f: r.o wl) 2 **4**
2764[6] No Extras (IRE) **(89)***(94) (GLMoore)* 5-8-13 SWhitworth(14) (swtg: hdwy over 3f out: rdn over 2f out: r.o one pce) .... ½ **5**
2737[9] Emerging Market **(89)***(93) (JLDunlop)* 3-8-7 RHills(6) (hdwy over 3f out: rdn over 2f out: one pce) .... ¾ **6**
2795* Lipizzaner (IRE) **(95)***(95) (BWHills)* 3-8-13 MHills(2) (lw: 3rd st: rdn over 2f out: eased whn btn wl ins fnl f) 1½ **7**
2255* Akil (IRE) **(83)***(83) (RWArmstrong)* 3-8-1 WCarson(9) (5th st: lost pl over 3f out: r.o one pce fnl f) .... nk **8**
2598[6] Ham N'Eggs **(84)***(83) (RHannon)* 4-8-8 JReid(12) (lw: nvr nrr) .... nk **9**
2703[15] Allez Cyrano (IRE) **(86)***(81) (MBell)* 4-8-10 MFenton(8) (s.s: nvr nrr) 2 **10**
2764* Shikari's Son **(96)***(84) (JWhite)* 8-9-6 RHughes(5) (hdwy on ins over 1f out: eased whn btn ins fnl f) 3 **11**
2737[10] Dashing Water **(88)***(71) (IABalding)* 3-8-6 KDarley(1) (lw: led 6f) 2½ **12**
2436[3] Croft Valley **(95)***(51) (RAkehurst)* 8-9-5 TQuinn(10) (lw: 2nd st: wknd over 2f out) 12 **13**
1728[9] Bide Our Time (USA) **(93)***(36) (JARToller)* 3-8-11 JWeaver(3) (lw: 4th st: wknd over 4f out) 6 **14**

LONG HANDICAP Akil (IRE) 7-13

9/2 Bin Rosie (5/2-11/2), **13/2** Decorated Hero, **7/1** Akil (IRE) (op 3/1), **8/1** Croft Valley, **10/1** Lipizzaner (IRE), GYMCRAK PREMIERE, **12/1** Emerging Market (op 8/1), Ham N'Eggs (10/1-16/1), **14/1** Classic Sky (IRE), **16/1** Allez Cyrano (IRE), **20/1** No Extras (IRE), Shikari's Son, **25/1** Dashing Water, Bide Our Time (USA), CSF £66.40 CT £302.04 TOTE £10.10: £2.70 £2.90 £2.40 (£55.30) Trio £56.20 OWNER The Gymcrak Thoroughbred Racing Club (PICKERING) BRED Cheveley Park Stud Ltd 14 Rn 1m 29.41 (0.91) SF: 60/69/70/69/60/53/55/43/49/47/50/31/17/-

WEIGHT FOR AGE 3yo-6lb

3086 MANTON ST HUGH'S STKS (Listed) (2-Y.O F) (Class A) £10,566.00 (£3,168.00: £1,524.00: £702.00)

5f 34y Stalls: Centre GOING minus 0.26 sec per fur (GF) 2-30 (2-31)

2740[4] **Amazing Bay (100)***(96)*(Fav)*(IABalding)* 2-8-11 WRyan(4) (lw: hld up: led over 1f out: shkn up: comf) .... — **1**
2618* Maggi For Margaret **(84)***(87) (MRChannon)* 2-8-11 RHughes(3) (lw: led over 3f: unable qckn) 3 **2**
2782* Hear The Music (IRE) **(90)***(71) (BWHills)* 2-8-8 MHills(6) (lw: a.p: rdn wl over 1f out: sn wknd) 4 **3**
2716* Kunucu (IRE) **(90)***(73) (TDBarron)* 2-8-11 KDarley(2) (lw: a.p: rdn over 2f out: wknd over 1f out) .... nk **4**
2412[3] Repatriate (AUS) *(63) (PWChapple-Hyam)* 2-8-8b JReid(1) (lw: a.p: rdn over 2f out: wknd over 1f out) 2½ **5**
1849[9] Top Cat (FR) **(95)***(43) (EWeymes)* 2-8-13 DeanMcKeown(5) (lw: a.p: rdn over 2f out: sn wknd) 8 **6**

11/4 AMAZING BAY, **9/2** Top Cat (FR), **5/1** Repatriate (AUS), **11/2** Hear The Music (IRE), **6/1** Kunucu (IRE) (op 7/2), Maggi For Margaret, CSF £16.04 TOTE £3.10: £1.70 £2.30 (£9.70) OWNER Mr J. C. Smith (KINGSCLERE) BRED R. G. Percival 6 Rn 62.76 secs (2.46) SF: 33/24/8/10/-/-

3087 STRATTON H'CAP (0-95) (3-Y.O+) (Class C) £5,605.00 (£1,690.00: £820.00: £385.00)

5f 34y Stalls: Centre GOING minus 0.26 sec per fur (GF) 3-00 (3-00)

2764[16] **Master of Passion (82)***(94) (JMPEustace)* 6-9-3 (3) JTate(8) (hld up: rdn over 2f out: led nr fin) .... — **1**
2748[3] Penny Dip **(82)***(92) (RFJohnsonHoughton)* 3-9-2 JReid(7) (a.p: led over 1f out: hrd rdn ins fnl f: hdd nr fin) .... ½ **2**
2533* Mr Bergerac (IRE) **(76)***(83) (BPalling)* 4-9-0 TSprake(9) (hld up: rdn over 2f out: n.m.r 1f out: one pce) 1¼ **3**
2992[7] Robellion **(71)***(77) (DWPArbuthnot)* 4-8-9v TQuinn(1) (hld up: rdn over 1f out: one pce ins fnl f) .... hd **4**
2909[2] Bajan Rose **(80)***(77) (MBlanshard)* 3-9-0 StephenDavies(4) (hld up: rdn over 1f out: one pce) 3 **5**
2617* Sweet Magic **(85)***(77)*(Fav)*(LJHolt)* 4-9-9 AMcGlone(6) (led over 3f) 1¾ **6**
2867* Spender **(75)***(65) (PWHarris)* 6-8-13 GDuffield(5) (s.s: a bhd) .... ½ **7**
2686[2] Bashful Brave **(75)***(60) (JWPayne)* 4-8-13 MRimmer(3) (lw: w ldr over 3f: wknd fnl f) 1¾ **8**
2458[2] Musical Season **(90)***(56) (TDBarron)* 3-9-10 KDarley(2) (lw: prom over 2f) 6 **9**

7/2 Sweet Magic, **5/1** MASTER OF PASSION, **6/1** Penny Dip (4/1-13/2), **7/1** Bajan Rose, **8/1** Musical Season (6/1-9/1), Spender (6/1-9/1), **11/1** Mr Bergerac (IRE), Bashful Brave (7/1-12/1), **12/1** Robellion, CSF £31.01 CT £279.43 TOTE £5.90: £1.90 £2.00 £3.30 (£13.50) Trio £65.90 OWNER Mr & Mrs Michael Kwee (NEWMARKET) BRED Stratford Place Stud 9 Rn

62.41 secs (2.11) SF: 47/41/36/30/26/30/18/13/5

WEIGHT FOR AGE 3yo-4lb

3088 TRIPLEPRINT GEOFFREY FREER STKS (Gp 2) (3-Y.O+) (Class A) £43,970.00 (£16,469.75: £7,922.38: £3,462.87)

1m 5f 61y Stalls: High GOING minus 0.26 sec per fur (GF) 3-30 (3-32)

2670* **Presenting (119)***(120+)*(Fav)*(JHMGosden)* 3-8-5 JReid(5) (chsd ldr: led over 2f out: pushed out)........— **1**
2739* Midnight Legend **(109)***(116) (LMCumani)* 4-9-3 JWeaver(4) (lw: led 11f: unable qckn)........3 **2**
2670² Don Corleone **(113)***(116) (RCharlton)* 3-8-5 DHarrison(6) (4th st: rdn over 3f out: ev ch over 2f out: one pce)........s.h **3**
2575* Burooj **(107)***(113) (DMorley)* 5-9-3 WCarson(2) (5th st: rdn over 2f out: one pce)........3 **4**
2323⁷ Right Win (IRE) **(113)***(115) (RHannon)* 5-9-6b TQuinn(3) (3rd st: rdn over 2f out: sn wknd).....¾ **5**
2350* Royal Circle *(99) (RCharlton)* 3-8-2 KDarley(1) (lw: 6th st: a bhd)........8 **6**

10/11 PRESENTING (4/5-Evens), **9/2** Don Corleone, **5/1** Midnight Legend (7/2-11/2), **11/2** Burooj, **10/1** Royal Circle, **40/1** Right Win (IRE), CSF £5.85 TOTE £1.80: £1.30 £2.20 (£3.50) OWNER Mr George Strawbridge (NEWMARKET) BRED George Strawbridge 6 Rn

2m 47.43 (2.13) SF: 56/64/52/61/63/35

WEIGHT FOR AGE 3yo-12lb

3089 E.B.F YATTENDON MAIDEN STKS (2-Y.O) (Class D) £4,952.00 (£1,496.00: £728.00: £344.00)

7f (straight) Stalls: Centre GOING minus 0.26 sec per fur (GF) 4-05 (4-06)

2320³ **Silver Prey (USA)** *(80) (EALDunlop)* 2-9-0 WRSwinburn(17) (a.p: rdn wl over 1f out: led last stride)........— **1**
2741³ Reinhardt (IRE) *(80) (PWChapple-Hyam)* 2-9-0 JReid(6) (lw: a.p: led over 1f out: hrd rdn ins fnl f: hdd last stride)........s.h **2**
Coldstream *(77+) (LMCumani)* 2-9-0 JWeaver(20) (leggy: scope: led over 5f: one pce)........1½ **3**
Double Bluff (IRE) *(73) (IABalding)* 2-9-0 SO'Gorman(21) (unf: scope: a.p: rdn over 2f out: one pce)........1¾ **4**
2320⁵ Polar Prince (IRE) *(69) (MAJarvis)* 2-9-0 PRobinson(5) (hld up: rdn over 2f out: one pce)....1½ **5**
2573² Skillington (USA) *(69)*(Fav)*(IABalding)* 2-9-0 KDarley(7) (lw: stumbled s: hld up: rdn over 2f out: one pce)........s.h **6**
Oliver Rock *(68+) (MajorDNChappell)* 2-9-0 RHills(13) (w'like: bit bkwd: s.s: nt clr run over 1f out: hdwy fnl f: r.o)........nk **7**
1726¹¹ Prince of My Heart *(64) (BWHills)* 2-9-0 AMcGlone(1) (rdn & hdwy over 1f out: eased whn btn ins fnl f)........2 **8**
Prince Kinsky *(63) (LordHuntingdon)* 2-9-0 DHarrison(11) (leggy: hdwy over 1f out: nvr nrr) .nk **9**
Hal Hoo Yaroom *(61) (MajorWRHern)* 2-9-0 TSprake(2) (leggy: unf: nt clr run over 1f out: nvr plcd to chal)........¾ **10**
Nereus *(57) (BWHills)* 2-9-0 MHills(10) (cmpt: bit bkwd: a mid div)........1¾ **11**
2320⁶ Amber Fort *(54) (PFICole)* 2-9-0 TQuinn(14) (prom over 4f)........1¼ **12**
Mischief Star *(49) (DRCElsworth)* 2-8-9 GDuffield(8) (leggy: s.s: rdn thrght: nvr nrr)........s.h **13**
2846⁹ Winged Prince *(54) (BJMeehan)* 2-9-0 BDoyle(12) (nt clr run wl over 1f out: a mid div)........hd **14**
One Pound *(52) (BWHills)* 2-9-0 RStreet(4) (w'like: bit bkwd: a bhd)........¾ **15**
Dark Waters (IRE) *(50) (MRStoute)* 2-9-0 PaulEddery(9) (str: scope: bit bkwd: nvr nrr)........1¼ **16**
Time Allowed *(44) (MRStoute)* 2-8-9 WRyan(18) (leggy: unf: bhd fnl 2f)........hd **17**
2846³ Golden Pond (IRE) *(44) (RFJohnsonHoughton)* 2-8-9 JQuinn(16) (prom 5f)........hd **18**
Verulam (IRE) *(46) (JARToller)* 2-9-0 RHughes(3) (leggy: lt-f: a bhd)........1½ **19**
High Note *(40) (RCharlton)* 2-8-9 SRaymont(19) (leggy: unf: s.s: mid div & wkng whn nt clr run on ins over 1f out)........nk **20**
2529⁷ Shamand (USA) *(36) (BJMeehan)* 2-9-0 WNewnes(22) (a bhd)........4 **21**
Even Handed *(31) (PFICole)* 2-9-0 MFenton(15) (leggy: prom over 4f)........2 **22**

9/4 Skillington (USA), **4/1** SILVER PREY (USA), **9/2** Coldstream (4/1-6/1), **9/1** Reinhardt (IRE), **12/1** Nereus (8/1-14/1), **16/1** Polar Prince (IRE), **20/1** Amber Fort, Dark Waters (IRE), Time Allowed, **25/1** Hal Hoo Yaroom, Golden Pond (IRE), **33/1** High Note, Double Bluff (IRE), Verulam (IRE), **40/1** Prince Kinsky, Oliver Rock, **50/1** Winged Prince, Prince of My Heart, One Pound, Even Handed, **66/1** Mischief Star, Shamand (USA), CSF £40.56 TOTE £5.30: £2.00 £2.50 £2.60 (£12.30) Trio £25.00 OWNER Maktoum Al Maktoum (NEWMARKET) BRED Henrietta K. Alexander 22 Rn

1m 28.0 (3.50) SF: 36/36/33/29/25/25/24/20/19/17/13/10/5/10/8/6/-/-/2/-/-/-

3090 LEVY BOARD NURSERY H'CAP (2-Y.O) (Class C) £5,507.50 (£1,660.00: £805.00: £377.50)
7f 64y (round) Stalls: High GOING minus 0.26 sec per fur (GF) 4-35 (4-37)

2756[2] **Pacific Grove (68)***(78) (PFICole)* 2-8-2 DBiggs(8) (led 2f: 3rd st: rdn over 2f out: led ins fnl f: r.o wl)........— 1
2911[2] Green Bentley (IRE) **(64)***(71)*(Fav)*(RHannon)* 2-7-12 JQuinn(10) (5th st: led over 2f out tl ins fnl f: unable qckn)........1¼ 2
2710[4] Vola Via (USA) **(77)***(82) (IABalding)* 2-8-11 KDarley(11) (rdn over 2f out: hdwy over 1f out: r.o)........1¼ 3
2441[7] Warning Reef **(78)***(82) (MRChannon)* 2-8-12 RHughes(6) (swtg: rdn & hdwy over 2f out: r.o ins fnl f)........hd 4
2526[9] The Legions Pride **(64)***(65) (JWHills)* 2-7-7 (5) MHenry(3) (led over 5f out tl over 2f out: one pce)........1½ 5
2485[3] Munketh (USA) **(87)***(87) (JLDunlop)* 2-9-7 WCarson(2) (s.s: nvr plcd to chal)........nk 6
1536* Agnella (IRE) **(77)***(76)*(Fav)*(GLMoore)* 2-8-11 SWhitworth(5) (lw: hdwy 5f out: 6th st: rdn over 1f out: wknd ins fnl f)........½ 7
2826[4] Balpare **(66)***(62) (NACallaghan)* 2-8-0 StephenDavies(1) (4th st: wknd over 1f out)........1½ 8
2534[8] Laughing Buccaneer **(75)***(69) (BJMeehan)* 2-8-9 BDoyle(4) (bhd fnl 4f)........¾ 9
1460[3] Elmswood (USA) **(78)***(72) (PWChapple-Hyam)* 2-8-12 JReid(12) (hdwy over 2f out: wknd fnl f)........nk 10
2637* Distant Storm **(67)***(39) (MBell)* 2-8-1b MFenton(7) (2nd st: ev ch over 2f out: sn wknd)........10 11
2801[7] Oscar Rose **(65)** *(LordHuntingdon)* 2-7-13v AMcGlone(9) (b: a bhd: t.o)........25 12

11/4 Agnella (IRE) (7/2-9/4), Green Bentley (IRE), **9/1** Munketh (USA) (6/1-10/1), **11/1** Balpare, Elmswood (USA) (6/1-12/1), **12/1** Distant Storm (op 8/1), **14/1** The Legions Pride (12/1-20/1), PACIFIC GROVE (op 8/1), Vola Via (USA), **16/1** Warning Reef, **33/1** Laughing Buccaneer, Oscar Rose, CSF £49.35 CT £510.00 TOTE £18.40: £2.80 £1.50 £3.90 (£21.20) Trio £77.70 OWNER Elite Racing Club (WHATCOMBE) BRED Tarworth Bloodstock Investments Ltd 12 Rn
1m 31.24 (2.74) SF: 35/28/39/39/22/44/33/19/26/29/-/-

3091 AUGUST H'CAP (0-100) (3-Y.O+) (Class C) £5,803.00 (£1,744.00:£842.00: £391.00) **1m 4f 5y** Stalls: High GOING minus 0.26 sec per fur (GF) 5-05 (5-06)

2577[2] **My Learned Friend (79)***(92) (AHide)* 4-9-2 JWilliams(3) (hdwy over 1f out: led ins fnl f: r.o wl)— 1
2768[2] Proton **(74)***(83)*(Fav)*(RAkehurst)* 5-8-11 JWeaver(7) (lw: 2nd st: led over 1f out tl ins fnl f: unable qckn)........3 2
2525[5] Riparius (USA) **(78)***(85) (HCandy)* 4-9-1b WNewnes(8) (lw: s.s: 6th st: rdn over 2f out: one pce)........1¼ 3
2738[7] Indonesian (IRE) **(82)***(89) (MBell)* 3-8-8 MFenton(4) (lw: 5th st: nt clr run & swtchd rt over 1f out: one pce)........s.h 4
2878[W] Dawlah **(88)***(93) (HThomsonJones)* 3-9-0 RHills(2) (led over 10f)........1½ 5
2274[4] Seasonal Splendour (IRE) **(87)***(92) (MCPipe)* 5-9-10 DBiggs(5) (hdwy over 5f out: 3rd st: rdn over 2f out: wknd fnl f)........nk 6
2790[8] Nobby North **(71)***(67) (LordHuntingdon)* 3-7-6 (5)ow4 MHenry(1) (4th st: wknd 2f out)........3½ 7
Judge Advocate (IRE) **(80)***(67) (MajorDNChappell)* 3-8-6 StephenDavies(6) (s.s: a bhd)........10 8
LONG HANDICAP Nobby North 7-6

11/4 Proton, **7/2** Seasonal Splendour (IRE), **9/2** MY LEARNED FRIEND (3/1-5/1), Indonesian (IRE), **15/2** Judge Advocate (IRE), **10/1** Dawlah, **14/1** Riparius (USA), **16/1** Nobby North, CSF £16.95 CT £146.58 TOTE £5.10: £1.30 £1.40 £3.30 (£6.00) OWNER Mrs J. Roberts (NEWMARKET) BRED A. D. G. Oldrey 8 Rn
2m 32.63 (3.33) SF: 57/48/50/43/47/57/21/21
WEIGHT FOR AGE 3yo-11lb
T/Jkpt: Not won; £40,326.91 to Kempton 13/8/95. T/Plpt: £101.60 (437.65 Tckts). T/Qdpt: £18.20 (16.55 Tckts). AK

2857-NOTTINGHAM (L-H)
Saturday August 12th (Good to firm)
WEATHER: bright WIND: almost nil

3092 'LADIES NIGHT' (S) H'CAP (0-60) (3-Y.O+) (Class G) £2,243.00 (£618.00: £293.00)
1m 6f 15y Stalls: Low GOING minus 0.37 sec per fur (F) 6-00 (6-01)

3017[4] **Top Prize (30)***(42) (MBrittain)* 7-8-11v JLowe(3) (a.p: 3rd st: rdn to ld bel dist: all out)........— 1
2860[12] Leap in the Dark (IRE) **(25)***(37) (MissLCSiddall)* 6-8-6 GHind(4) (chsd ldrs: 4th st: led over 2f out: hdd over 1f out: ev ch ins fnl f: r.o)........s.h 2

3029[8] Bresil (USA) **(31)**_(43) (KRBurke)_ 6-8-12 KFallon(8) (lw: hld up: hdwy over 2f out: ev ch fnl f: r.o) ....hd **3**
2806[5] Club Elite **(27)**_(34) (MFBarraclough)_ 3-7-6 (3) NVarley(5) (s.i.s: bhd: styd on appr fnl f: nrst fin)....4 **4**
2052[7] Persian Bud (IRE) **(39)**_(43) (JRBosley)_ 7-8-13 (7) AimeeCook(7) (lw: hld up: styd on fnl 2f)....2½ **5**
_2630_[8] Mystoski **(41)**_(44) (MHTompkins)_ 3-8-9 PRobinson(11) (led 10f: wknd over 1f out) 1 **6**
3017[3] Can She Can Can **(44)**_(46)_(Fav)_(MJohnston)_ 3-8-12 TWilliams(2) (chsd ldr: 2nd st: led 4f out: hdd over 2f out: wknd over 1f out)....1 **7**
2942[6] Sarazar (USA) **(36)**_(34) (RAkehurst)_ 6-9-0 (3) SSanders(9) (lw: chsd ldrs: 5th st: wknd 3f out) ..4 **8**
2450[7] Ann Hill (IRE) **(29)**_(24) (RHollinshead)_ 5-8-7 (3) AGarth(10) (hld up: hdwy & 6th st: wknd over 2f out)....2 **9**
2233[5] Little Blackfoot **(34)**_(25) (JLHarris)_ 7-9-1 AMackay(6) (s.i.s: n.d) 4 **10**
1344[8] Buster **(43)** _(MrsBarbaraWaring)_ 7-9-7 (3) SDrowne(1) (a outpcd: t.o fnl 6f)....dist **11**

5/2 Can She Can Can, **3/1** Sarazar (USA), **13/2** Bresil (USA), **10/1** Leap in the Dark (IRE), **11/1** TOP PRIZE, Persian Bud (IRE), **12/1** Ann Hill (IRE), **14/1** Club Elite, **20/1** Mystoski, Little Blackfoot, Buster, CSF £105.69 CT £694.22 TOTE £10.10: £2.30 £1.80 £2.40 (£43.40) Trio £114.40 OWNER Northgate Lodge Racing Ltd (WARTHILL) BRED The Overbury Stud 11 Rn
3m 4.5 (6.00) SF: 33/28/34/12/34/22/24/25/15/16/-
WEIGHT FOR AGE 3yo-13lb
No bid

3093

'SILK STOCKINGS' MAIDEN STKS (2-Y.O) (Class D) £4,175.00 (£1,250.00: £600.00: £275.00)
6f 15y Stalls: High GOING minus 0.37 sec per fur (F) 6-30 (6-30)

2777[3] **Sava River (IRE)** _(65+)_(Fav)_(MRStoute)_ 2-9-0 WRyan(5) (chsd ldrs: led over 1f out: rdn out)— **1**
1842[5] Rose of Siberia (USA) _(57) (MBell)_ 2-8-9 PRobinson(2) (hld up: hdwy 2f out: r.o ins fnl f) 1 **2**
2315[10] Sheilana (IRE) _(57+) (TGMills)_ 2-8-9 JQuinn(6) (hld up in tch: nt clr run fnl 2f: r.o)....nk **3**
Gold Kicker _(60) (MJRyan)_ 2-9-0 AClark(10) (cmpt: prom: rdn & ev ch fnl f: eased whn btn nr fin)....¾ **4**
2173[7] Oare Budgie _(49) (PTWalwyn)_ 2-8-9 NCarlisle(9) (led over 4f: no ex fnl f) 2 **5**
Penny Ghent _(20) (PSFelgate)_ 2-8-9 GHind(8) (small: bkwd: hld up: rdn ½-wy: grad wknd)..11 **6**
2221[8] Gresham Flyer _(12) (BRichmond)_ 2-9-0 SDWilliams(4) (bit bkwd: w ldr over 4f) 5 **7**
Tallulah Belle _(6) (NPLittmoden)_ 2-8-9 TGMcLaughlin(1) (unf: bkwd: s.s: a outpcd) ....nk **8**

2/5 SAVA RIVER (IRE), **6/1** Rose of Siberia (USA), **11/1** Oare Budgie (8/1-12/1), **14/1** Penny Ghent (10/1-16/1), Gold Kicker, **16/1** Sheilana (IRE), **33/1** Tallulah Belle, **40/1** Gresham Flyer, CSF £3.82 TOTE £1.50: £1.40 £1.20 £2.80 (£1.90) Trio £4.00 OWNER Sheikh Mohammed (NEWMARKET) BRED Sheikh Mohammed 8 Rn
1m 17.0 (6.00) SF: -/-/-/-/-/-/-/-

3094

SUNDAY EXPRESS 'BEST FOR SPORT' SERIES H'CAP (0-75) (3-Y.O+) (Class D) £4,435.00 (£1,330.00: £640.00: £295.00)
1m 1f 213y Stalls: Low GOING minus 0.37 sec per fur (F) 7-00 (7-00)

2790[3] **Tappeto (70)**_(81) (HCandy)_ 3-9-2 WNewnes(6) (chsd ldrs: 5th st: led over 2f out: rdn out) ...— **1**
2875[8] Salska **(45)**_(54) (AStreeter)_ 4-8-0 NCarlisle(5) (chsd ldr: 2nd st: led wl over 2f out: sn hdd: styd on u.p fnl f)....1 **2**
2298[2] Fieldridge **(73)**_(81) (MPMuggeridge)_ 6-10-0 GCarter(1) (lw: dwlt: hld up: hdwy over 3f out: rdn over 1f out: no imp)....¾ **3**
2804[3] Top Pet (IRE) **(53)**_(55) (RAkehurst)_ 5-8-8 JQuinn(4) (led over 7f: no ex fnl f)....4 **4**
2310[3] No Speeches (IRE) **(55)**_(56)_(Fav)_(CACyzer)_ 4-8-10 KFallon(7) (hld up: 7th & rdn st: styd on appr fnl f: nt pce to chal) ....¾ **5**
2861[6] Araboybill **(60)**_(53) (MPMuggeridge)_ 4-9-1b PRobinson(2) (chsd ldrs: 4th st: wknd over 2f out)....5 **6**
2917[2] Bardia **(38)**_(29) (DonEnricoIncisa)_ 5-7-7 KimTinkler(3) (s.i.s: bhd: 8th st: rdn over 4f out: wknd 3f out)....1¼ **7**
2861[4] Lady Highfield **(55)**_(45) (MJRyan)_ 4-8-10 AClark(8) (b.hind: hld up: 6th st: rdn & wknd 2f out) ½ **8**
2878[3] Augustan **(61)**_(43) (SGollings)_ 4-8-11v(5) VHalliday(9) (s.i.s: sn prom: 3rd st: rdn & wknd 3f out)....5 **9**

LONG HANDICAP Bardia 7-2

7/2 No Speeches (IRE), **9/2** Lady Highfield, **11/2** TAPPETO, **6/1** Top Pet (IRE), **7/1** Fieldridge, Augustan, **9/1** Bardia, **20/1** Araboybill, **25/1** Salska, CSF £98.35 CT £870.68 TOTE £8.50: £2.80 £3.60 £1.60 (£276.40) Trio £167.30 OWNER Mrs David Blackburn (WANTAGE) BRED Mrs D. Blackburn 9 Rn
2m 6.5 (4.00) SF: 38/20/47/21/22/19/-/11/9
WEIGHT FOR AGE 3yo-9lb

3095

'LADIES IN HALF PRICE' H'CAP (0-80) (3-Y.O) (Class D)£4,272.50 (£1,280.00: £615.00: £282.50) **1m 54y** Stalls: Low GOING minus 0.37 sec per fur (F)7-30 (7-31)

2778[4] **Donna Viola (75)***(86) (CFWall)* 3-8-12 (5) LNewton(5) (lw: hld up: 5th st: hdwy to ld 2f out: sn clr: eased nr fin) ....— 1
1547* Mukhatab **(79)***(83)*(Fav)*(HThomsonJones)* 3-9-7 RHills(1) (trckd ldrs: plld hrd: 4th st: hmpd 2f out: sn ev ch: chsd wnr over 1f out: no imp) 3½ 2
2778[5] Princess Danielle **(55)***(55) (CCElsey)* 3-7-11 FNorton(2) (led 2f: 2nd st: rdn & edgd lft over 2f out: styd on same pce) 2 3
2602* Norsong **(57)***(52) (RAkehurst)* 3-7-13 JQuinn(3) (a.p: 3rd & rdn st: styd on same pce fnl 2f)....3 4
2880[4] Young Benson **(72)***(64) (BAMcMahon)* 3-9-0 GCarter(4) (lw: led 6f out: hdd 2f out: sn btn) ..1¼ 5

6/5 Mukhatab, **7/2** Norsong, **4/1** DONNA VIOLA, **7/1** Young Benson (5/1-15/2), **11/1** Princess Danielle, CSF £8.70 TOTE £4.10: £1.60 £1.60 (£4.30) OWNER Mr Kieran Scott (NEWMARKET) BRED Lady Juliet de Chair 5 Rn 1m 44.8 (5.20) SF: 20/17/-/-/-

3096

'BEST DRESSED LADY' CLAIMING STKS (3-Y.O) (Class F) £2,519.00 (£694.00: £329.00) **1m 54y** Stalls: Low GOING minus 0.37 sec per fur (F) 8-00 (8-01)

2828[5] **Gentle Irony (55)***(69) (BJMeehan)* 3-8-8b BDoyle(1) (chsd ldr: 2nd st: rdn to ld over 1f out: edgd rt & lft ins fnl f: r.o) ....— 1
2828* First Crush **(68)***(72)*(Fav)*(SirMarkPrescott)* 3-9-2b KDarley(6) (led: hdd over 1f out: styd on same pce) 2½ 2
2885[2] Colosse **(53)***(53) (MAJarvis)* 3-8-2 PRobinson(8) (lw: chsd ldrs: ev ch 2f out: nt qckn fnl f) ...2½ 3
2776[6] Contract Venture (IRE) **(60)***(58) (WJarvis)* 3-8-6b(5) MHenry(4) (prom: 6th st: rdn 2f out: styd on same pce) 2 4
2540[7] Asking **(30)***(49) (JABennett)* 3-8-9 JQuinn(2) (chsd ldrs: 3rd st: wknd over 2f out).......4 5
2884[6] Nushka Babushka *(39) (BobJones)* 3-8-0 FNorton(9) (nvr rchd ldrs).......nk 6
1412[8] Red River Rose (IRE) **(42)***(38) (NPLittmoden)* 3-8-1b(5) CTeague(3) (s.i.s: a in rr) 3½ 7
2983[8] Margaret Modes **(38)***(27) (CACyzer)* 3-8-12 KFallon(7) (chsd ldrs: 5th st: wknd over 2f out)....9 8
2921[7] Ameeri (USA) *(27) (NPLittmoden)* 3-8-13 TGMcLaughlin(5) (lw: hld up: hdwy, rn wd & 7th st: wknd over 2f out) ....nk 9

11/10 First Crush (Evens-6/5), **7/2** Colosse, **5/1** Contract Venture (IRE), **13/2** GENTLE IRONY (4/1-7/1), **20/1** Margaret Modes, Red River Rose (IRE), **33/1** Nushka Babushka, Asking, **40/1** Ameeri (USA), CSF £13.68 TOTE £4.70: £1.90 £1.30 £1.40 (£6.10) Trio £3.90 OWNER Mr A. S. Reid (UPPER LAMBOURN) BRED Red House Stud 9 Rn 1m 43.9 (4.30) SF: 20/23/4/9/-/-/-/-/-
Colosse clmd SGoodwin £3,600

3097

'LADIES FIRST' RATING RELATED MAIDEN LIMITED STKS (0-65) (3-Y.O) (Class F) £2,519.00 (£694.00: £329.00)
1m 1f 213y Stalls: Low GOING minus 0.37 sec per fur (F) 8-30 (8-30)

2653[2] **Debutante Days (65)***(68)*(Fav)*(ACStewart)* 3-8-9 RHills(3) (chsd ldr: 2nd st: led 2f out: rdn out) ....— 1
2863[3] Marzipan (IRE) **(61)***(65) (JWHills)* 3-8-4 (5) MHenry(1) (chsd ldrs: 3rd st: outpcd over 2f out: r.o ins fnl f).......1¾ 2
2805[4] Toskano **(57)***(68) (IABalding)* 3-9-0 KDarley(4) (trckd ldrs: plld hrd: 4th st: ev ch over 1f out: nt qckn).......1¼ 3
2881[7] Eden's Star (IRE) **(59)***(63) (MHTompkins)* 3-9-0 PRobinson(2) (led: rdn & hdd 2f out: wknd fnl f) 3½ 4
2655[5] Jalmaid **(54)***(48) (BAMcMahon)* 3-8-9 GCarter(6) (hld up: 5th st: rdn 3f out: no imp) 6 5
2393[4] Coryana Dancer (IRE) **(65)***(46) (RHollinshead)* 3-8-9 WRyan(5) (hld up & bhd: 6th st: no imp) 1 6

2/1 DEBUTANTE DAYS, **11/4** Marzipan (IRE), **7/2** Coryana Dancer (IRE), **8/1** Jalmaid, **11/1** Toskano (7/1-12/1), **12/1** Eden's Star (IRE) (op 7/1), CSF £7.29 TOTE £2.60: £1.70 £1.90 (£3.30) OWNER Lady McAlpine (NEWMARKET) BRED Lady McAlpine 6 Rn
2m 6.6 (4.10) SF: 31/28/31/26/11/9
T/Plpt: £85.40 (130.6 Tckts). T/Qdpt: £30.70 (2.65 Tckts). CR

2820-RIPON (R-H)

Saturday August 12th (Good to firm, Firm patches)

WEATHER: cloudy WIND: fresh across

3098

STABLE LADS WELFARE TRUST APPRENTICE H'CAP (0-70) (3-Y.O+) (Class E) £3,207.00 (£966.00: £468.00: £219.00)
6f Stalls: Low GOING minus 0.50 sec per fur (F) 2-15 (2-16)

2956* **Arc Lamp (40)***(50)*(Fav)*(JAGlover)* 9-8-4 (5) VictoriaAppleby(2) (lw: prom: led over 2f out: hung rt: r.o) ....— 1

2832[10] Prime Property (IRE) **(29)***(32) (MWEasterby)* 3-7-4b(3) MartinDwyer(9) (wnt rt s: bhd tl hdwy ½-wy: nt qckn u.p fnl f)....2½ 2
2502[15] Henry the Hawk **(48)***(48) (MDods)* 4-9-0 (3) CWebb(1) (a in tch: kpt on wl fnl f)....1¼ 3
2784[4] Murray's Mazda (IRE) **(42)***(41) (JLEyre)* 6-8-11 DGibbs(10) (prom: effrt ½-wy: kpt on fnl f)....½ 4
2784[3] Panther (IRE) **(57)***(54) (JHetherton)* 5-9-5 (7) TSiddall(6) (lw: bhd: hdwy over 2f out: nvr able to chal)....½ 5
2923[6] Four of Spades **(58)***(53) (PDEvans)* 4-9-13 AmandaSanders(5) (a chsng ldrs: kpt on one pce fnl 2f)....1 6
2992[2] Plum First **(59)***(47) (LRLloyd-James)* 5-9-9 (5) KSked(3) (b.hind: lw: prom tl outpcd ½-wy: n.d after)....2½ 7
2714[3] Awesome Venture **(50)***(35) (MCChapman)* 5-9-5 CMunday(11) (w ldrs 4f: wknd)....1 8
2853[4] Cafe Solo **(41)***(26) (NBycroft)* 4-8-10b GMitchell(8) (lw: nvr trbld ldrs)....nk 9
2832[18] Steady Risk **(30)***(11) (MrsAMNaughton)* 4-7-8 (5) BHalligan(4) (spd 4f)....1¼ 10
3000[3] Tee Tee Too (IRE) **(52)***(17) (PCHaslam)* 3-8-11 (5) CarolDavison(7) (lw: led over 3f: wknd qckly)....6 11

LONG HANDICAP Prime Property (IRE) 7-5

7/2 ARC LAMP, **4/1** Plum First, **7/1** Tee Tee Too (IRE), Panther (IRE), **8/1** Murray's Mazda (IRE), **9/1** Cafe Solo, **10/1** Four of Spades, Awesome Venture, **14/1** Prime Property (IRE), Henry the Hawk, **50/1** Steady Risk, CSF £47.29 CT £566.77 TOTE £4.30: £2.00 £3.90 £4.00 (£64.10) Trio £217.20 OWNER Mr B. Bruce (WORKSOP) BRED H. J. Joel 11 Rn

1m 11.7 (1.50) SF: 30/7/28/21/34/33/27/15/6/-/-

WEIGHT FOR AGE 3yo-5lb

3099 WHARFEDALE (S) H'CAP (0-60) (3-Y.O) (Class F) £2,853.00 (£864.00: £422.00: £201.00)

1m 2f Stalls: High GOING minus 0.50 sec per fur (F) 2-45 (2-47)

2972[5] **Hunza Story (35)***(46) (NPLittmoden)* 3-7-11 (7) CAdamson(1) (b.hind: hld up: smooth hdwy 4f out: led over 1f out: all out)....— 1
2955[4] Miss Felixstowe (USA) **(47)***(58)*(Fav)*(MrsMReveley)* 3-9-2 GCarter(13) (hdwy 4f out: r.o wl fnl f: jst failed)....s.h 2
2610[6] Cumbrian Minstrel **(47)***(57) (MHEasterby)* 3-9-2 MBirch(5) (lw: hld up: hdwy 4f out: ev ch appr fnl f: styd on u.p)....½ 3
2640[3] Kirov Protege (IRE) **(44)***(52) (HJCollingridge)* 3-8-13 GHind(11) (chsd ldrs: ch 2f out: one pce fnl f)....1¼ 4
2851[3] High Flown (USA) **(49)***(56) (RonaldThompson)* 3-8-13v(5) LNewton(8) (led: clr ent st: hdd over 1f out: no ex)....½ 5
2582[12] Magnums Secret **(45)***(48) (JLEyre)* 3-8-9 (5) DGriffiths(9) (a.p: one pce fnl 4f)....3 6
2881[5] Hee's a Dancer **(42)***(41) (MJCamacho)* 3-8-11 LCharnock(7) (a chsng ldrs: effrt 4f out: outpcd fnl 2f)....2½ 7
2954[7] Perfect Bertie (IRE) **(47)***(42) (GROldroyd)* 3-8-11 (5) GParkin(12) (bhd: effrt & hmpd appr st: hdwy 3f out: no imp)....2 8
2636[3] Gulf Bay **(35)***(24)*(Fav)*(MBell)* 3-8-1 (3)ow2 SSanders(14) (bhd: hdwy on ins 4f out: no imp)...2½ 9
2140[6] Qualitair Pride **(52)***(41) (JFBottomley)* 3-9-7b JLowe(3) (lw: nvr trbld ldrs)....1¾ 10
1436[4] Island Cascade **(45)***(18) (DonEnricoIncisa)* 3-9-0 KimTinkler(15) (lw: stdd s: n.d)....10 11
2662[5] Our Rainbow **(31)***(1) (MrsSMAustin)* 3-8-0 DaleGibson(10) (b: a rr div)....1½ 12
2953[6] Lass of Kinloch **(30)** *(MBrittain)* 3-7-10 (3) DWright(2) (chsd ldrs 6f: sn wknd)....5 13
2129[9] Beyaateh **(32)** *(MCChapman)* 3-7-8 (7)ow8 CMunday(4) (prom to st)....2 14
Mr Eglantine **(40)** *(ASmith)* 3-8-9 JFanning(16) (hmpd & lost pl appr st: n.d after)....1¾ 15
2927[6] Nebrangus (IRE) **(30)** *(NBycroft)* 3-7-13 SMaloney(6) (chsd ldr to st: sn lost pl: t.o)....11 16

LONG HANDICAP Beyaateh 7-1

4/1 Gulf Bay, Miss Felixstowe (USA) (op 6/1), **7/1** HUNZA STORY, Hee's a Dancer, **8/1** Cumbrian Minstrel, Kirov Protege (IRE), **9/1** High Flown (USA), **10/1** Perfect Bertie (IRE), Magnums Secret, **16/1** Qualitair Pride, Island Cascade, Our Rainbow, **33/1** Lass of Kinloch, Mr Eglantine, Nebrangus (IRE), **50/1** Beyaateh, CSF £38.41 CT £228.70 TOTE £18.20: £3.40 £2.00 £2.00 £1.60 (£44.20) Trio £145.20 OWNER Mr M. S. Moule (NEWARK) BRED V. O'Donoghue 16 Rn

2m 7.3 (3.80) SF: 19/31/30/25/29/21/14/15/-/14/-/-/-/-/-/-

No bid

3100 RIPON HORN BLOWER CONDITIONS STKS (2-Y.O) (Class C) £6,822.50 (£2,372.50: £1,148.75: £481.25)

5f Stalls: Low GOING minus 0.50 sec per fur (F) 3-15 (3-16)

2940* **Soviet Style (AUS)** *(95) (PWChapple-Hyam)* 2-8-12 RHavlin(2) (lw: led to 1f out: r.o u.p to ld wl ins fnl f)....— 1
2740[W] Prince Aslia **(98)***(98)*(Fav)*(MJohnston)* 2-9-2 DHolland(4) (lw: w wnr: slt ld 1f out tl wl ins fnl f: nt qckn nr fin)....nk 2

2833[3] Ramsey Hope **(82)***(84) (CWFairhurst)* 2-8-10 NKennedy(1) (a chsng ldrs: kpt on fnl 2f: nvr able to chal)....2½ **3**
2826* Gagajulu **(76)***(75) (PDEvans)* 2-8-7 GHind(3) (pushed along ½-wy: chsd ldrs tl wknd appr fnl f)....2 **4**

10/11 Prince Aslia, **15/8** SOVIET STYLE (AUS), **9/2** Gagajulu, **14/1** Ramsey Hope, CSF £3.95 TOTE £2.30 (£1.70) OWNER Mr R. E. Sangster (MARLBOROUGH) BRED Swettenham Stud 4 Rn
58.8 secs (0.80) SF: 40/43/29/20

3101

ROTHMANS ROYALS NORTH SOUTH CHALLENGE SERIES H'CAP (0-80) (3-Y.O+) (Class D) £7,205.00 (£2,165.00: £1,045.00: £485.00)
1m 1f Stalls: High GOING minus 0.50 sec per fur (F) 3-45 (3-46)

2654* **Hand Craft (IRE) (78)***(89)*(Fav)*(WJHaggas)* 3-9-10 GHind(9) (lw: hld up: hdwy 3f out: led over 1f out: r.o)....— **1**
2875[5] Thaleros **(54)***(64) (GMMoore)* 5-8-8 JFortune(3) (lw: chsd ldrs: chal over 4f out: led over 2f out tl over 1f out: r.o u.p)....¾ **2**
2917[5] Antartictern (USA) **(43)***(50) (GROldroyd)* 5-7-11 LCharnock(10) (bhd: hdwy on ins 3f out: n.m.r appr fnl f: r.o nr fin)....1¼ **3**
2780[5] Nigel's Lad (IRE) **(79)***(86) (PCHaslam)* 3-9-11 MTebbutt(7) (hld up: effrt over 3f out: sn rdn & chsng ldrs: one pce fnl f)....s.h **4**
2814* Spanish Verdict **(70)***(75) (DenysSmith)* 8-9-5 (5) CTeague(6) (a chsng ldrs: one pce fnl3f)....1¼ **5**
2906[3] Nobby Barnes **(43)***(47) (DonEnricoIncisa)* 6-7-11 KimTinkler(1) (dwlt: bhd tl r.o fnl 2f)....½ **6**
2602[4] Kindergarten Boy (IRE) **(62)***(64) (RBoss)* 4-9-2 JCarroll(5) (led tl hdd over 2f out: sn btn)....1¼ **7**
2862* Racing Brenda **(58)***(48) (BAMcMahon)* 4-8-12 GCarter(8) (bhd: effrt on outside ½-wy: n.d)....7 **8**
2822[6] Shining Edge **(55)***(40) (MHEasterby)* 3-8-1 SMaloney(4) (trckd ldrs: effrt 3f out: sn btn)....2½ **9**
2719[9] Britannia Mills **(47)***(14) (MCChapman)* 4-7-8 (7)ow8 CMunday(2) (chsd ldrs to ½-wy: sn lost pl)....6 **10**

LONG HANDICAP Britannia Mills 6-5

7/4 HAND CRAFT (IRE), **11/2** Nigel's Lad (IRE), **6/1** Spanish Verdict, Racing Brenda, **7/1** Kindergarten Boy (IRE), **8/1** Shining Edge, **10/1** Nobby Barnes, **12/1** Thaleros, **33/1** Antartictern (USA), **50/1** Britannia Mills, CSF £23.22 CT £503.56 TOTE £2.90: £1.30 £2.80 £8.00 (£29.90) Trio £189.20 OWNER Mrs M. M. Haggas (NEWMARKET) BRED D. and N. Wallace 10 Rn
1m 51.5 (1.30) SF: 55/38/24/52/49/21/38/22/6/-
WEIGHT FOR AGE 3yo-8lb

3102

CROWTHER HOMES H'CAP (0-80) (3-Y.O+) (Class D) £4,165.00 (£1,240.00: £590.00: £265.00)
1m 4f 60y Stalls: High GOING minus 0.50 sec per fur (F) 4-15 (4-15)

2678[4] **Wellsian (USA) (69)***(79) (LMCumani)* 3-9-0 OUrbina(5) (hld up: hdwy 3f out: rdn to ld ins fnl f: r.o)....— **1**
717[3] Deano's Beeno **(79)***(89)*(Fav)*(MJohnston)* 3-9-10 DHolland(1) (lw: mde most tl hdd ins fnl f: kpt on)....nk **2**
2379[12] Hasta la Vista **(41)***(48) (MWEasterby)* 5-7-4b(7)ow1 MartinDwyer(4) (lw: cl up: disp ld over 3f out: rdn & btn ins fnl f)....1 **3**
2917[3] Durano **(66)***(63) (MHEasterby)* 4-9-8 MBirch(3) (trckd ldrs tl outpcd fnl 2½f)....9 **4**
2954[3] Our Main Man **(57)***(53) (RMWhitaker)* 5-8-13 ACulhane(2) (lw: trckd ldrs: rdn over 3f out: wknd over 2f out)....nk **5**

6/5 Deano's Beeno, **11/4** WELLSIAN (USA), **4/1** Our Main Man, **5/1** Durano, **12/1** Hasta la Vista, CSF £6.61 TOTE £3.70: £1.80 £1.40 (£2.90) OWNER Sheikh Mohammed (NEWMARKET) BRED Darley Stud Management Co. Inc. 5 Rn
2m 37.4 (3.40) SF: 37/47/17/32/22
WEIGHT FOR AGE 3yo-11lb

3103

WENSLEYDALE MAIDEN STKS (3-Y.O+) (Class D) £3,776.15(£1,143.20: £558.10: £265.55) **5f** Stalls: Low GOING minus 0.50 sec per fur (F) 4-50 (4-51)

Mr Oscar *(88+) (MJohnston)* 3-9-0 DHolland(7) (mde all: clr ½-wy: r.o strly)....— **1**
2527[3] Flirty Gertie *(64) (RBoss)* 3-8-9 MTebbutt(2) (lw: in tch: effrt 2f out: styd on wl: no ch w wnr)....6 **2**
2949[4] Daysman (USA) *(59)*(Fav)*(BWHills)* 3-9-0 JCarroll(1) (lw: a.p: effrt ½-wy: one pce appr fnl f) .3 **3**
2923[14] Dancing Sioux **(70)***(59) (RGuest)* 3-9-0 LCharnock(3) (chsd ldrs: rdn ½-wy: no imp)....s.h **4**
2357[5] Self Styled (IRE) *(11) (TDBarron)* 3-9-0 JFortune(5) (t: swtg: nvr trbld ldrs)....15 **5**
Jacques Point *(3) (ASmith)* 3-8-9 MBirch(6) (chsd ldrs over 3f: sn wknd)....1 **6**
Woolaw Girl *(JSHaldane)* 7-8-13 DaleGibson(4) (nvr wnt pce)....10 **7**

4/5 Daysman (USA) (op 1/2), **7/2** MR OSCAR, **5/1** Flirty Gertie, **9/1** Dancing Sioux, **20/1** Self Styled (IRE), **50/1** Jacques Point, **100/1** Woolaw Girl, CSF £19.18 TOTE £5.20: £2.00 £1.90 (£9.80) OWNER Mr W. McKeown (MIDDLEHAM) BRED Zetland Stud 7 Rn

58.5 secs (0.50) SF: 47/23/18/18/-/-/-

WEIGHT FOR AGE 3yo-4lb

T/Plpt: £172.00 (75.62 Tckts). T/Qdpt: £39.20 (3.45 Tckts). AA

2845-KEMPTON (R-H)
Sunday August 13th (Good to firm)

WEATHER: hot WIND: almost nil

3104 HERMIT MAIDEN STKS (2-Y.O) (Class D) £4,338.00 (£1,314.00: £642.00: £306.00)
6f Stalls: High GOING minus 0.29 sec per fur (GF) 2-00 (2-02)

2552[8] **Quakers Field** *(80) (GLMoore)* 2-9-0 SWhitworth(6) (a.p: led over 2f out: clr over 1f out: r.o wl) — 1
2615[2] Do Not Disturb (USA) *(71)*(Fav)*(JLDunlop)* 2-9-0 GCarter(3) (dwlt: hld up: rdn over 2f out: chsd wnr fnl f: r.o one pce) 3½ 2
2107[5] White Settler *(55) (RHannon)* 2-9-0 MRoberts(1) (led over 3f) 6 3
Jean-Pierre *(44) (JPearce)* 2-9-0 RCochrane(4) (neat: hld up: rdn over 2f out: sn wknd) 4 4
2809[W] Suparoy *(28) (TGMills)* 2-9-0 TQuinn(2) (neat: spd over 2f) 6 5
424[9] Clint *(25) (JFfitch-Heyes)* 2-9-0 GDuffield(5) (a bhd) 1 6

2/7 Do Not Disturb (USA), **11/2** White Settler, **14/1** Suparoy (8/1-16/1), **25/1** Jean-Pierre, **33/1** QUAKERS FIELD, **50/1** Clint, CSF £41.70 TOTE £30.50: £6.50 £1.10 (£13.90) OWNER Pennine Partners (EPSOM) BRED Summertree Stud 6 Rn

1m 13.08 (1.78) SF: 49/40/24/13/-/-

3105 KNOWLE GREEN MAIDEN STKS (3-Y.O) (Class D) £4,279.50 (£1,296.00: £633.00: £301.50)
1m (Jubilee) Stalls: High GOING minus 0.29 sec per fur (GF) 2-30 (2-31)

2553[13] **Monument** *(85) (RCharlton)* 3-9-0 TSprake(3) (3rd st: hrd rdn over 1f out: led nr fin) — 1
2880[2] Raise the Stakes **(77)***(85)*(Fav)*(IABalding)* 3-9-0 RCochrane(2) (lw: led over 4f: 2nd st: led over 1f out: hrd rdn: hdd nr fin) hd 2
2593[4] Dorothea Brooke (IRE) **(77)***(76) (PWHarris)* 3-8-9 GDuffield(1) (chsd ldr: led over 3f out tl over 1f out: one pce) 2 3
2805[3] Mr Medley *(79) (RHannon)* 3-8-7 (7) DaneO'Neill(5) (4th st: hrd rdn over 2f out: one pce) ¾ 4
Our Kris *(61) (GHarwood)* 3-9-0 AClark(4) (b.off hind: leggy: scope: s.s: 5th st: wknd 3f out) 9 5

11/10 Raise the Stakes, **5/2** Dorothea Brooke (IRE), **11/2** Our Kris (4/1-6/1), **10/1** MONUMENT (7/1-12/1), **16/1** Mr Medley, CSF £19.98 TOTE £13.30: £3.70 £1.30 (£10.70) OWNER Lady Rothschild (BECKHAMPTON) BRED Exors of the late Mrs D. M. de Rothschild 5 Rn

1m 41.55 (4.55) SF: 28/28/19/22/4

OFFICIAL EXPLANATION **Monument: the trainer explained that the gelding pulled very hard to post and refused to settle last time, but had settled in this small field.**

3106 SUNDAY EXPRESS 'BEST FOR SPORT' SERIES (QUALIFIER) H'CAP (0-85) (3-Y.O+) (Class D) £5,681.75 (£1,724.00: £844.50: £404.75)
1m 2f (Jubilee) Stalls: High GOING minus 0.29 sec per fur (GF) 3-00 (3-01)

2707[2] **Conspicuous (IRE)** **(59)***(71) (LGCottrell)* 5-8-3 JQuinn(4) (lw: 7th st: led wl over 1f out: rdn out) — 1
2790* Country Star (IRE) **(80)***(89) (HCandy)* 4-9-10 MRoberts(6) (rdn over 2f out: hdwy over 1f out: r.o) 2 2
2694* Ron's Secret **(76)***(83) (JWPayne)* 3-8-11 RCochrane(5) (4th st: rdn over 2f out: one pce) 1¼ 3
2768[8] Fairy Knight **(75)***(81) (RHannon)* 3-8-10 TQuinn(3) (lw: rdn over 2f out: hdwy over 1f out: r.o one pce) nk 4
1619[3] Francfurter **(77)***(83) (RCharlton)* 3-8-12 TSprake(7) (lw: nt clr run over 2f out: hdwy over 1f out: r.o one pce) s.h 5
2457[10] The French Friar (IRE) **(72)***(72) (GBBalding)* 4-9-2 AClark(9) (lw: hdwy & n.m.r over 2f out: rdn over 1f out: one pce) 4 6
2672* Silver Groom (IRE) **(75)***(74)*(Fav)*(RAkehurst)* 5-9-0 (5) MHenry(13) (lw: 6th st: bdly hmpd over 2f out: one pce) ¾ 7

2909[6] Lookingforarainbow (IRE) **(77)***(75) (BobJones)* 7-9-7 MWigham(8) (lw: led 5f out tl wl over 1f out: sn wknd)....nk **8**
2694[8] Lesley's Fashion **(62)***(58) (DJSffrenchDavis)* 4-8-6 MTebbutt(12) (lw: a bhd)....1½ **9**
2664[5] Laxford Bridge **(77)***(71) (PWHarris)* 4-9-7 GDuffield(11) (lw: 5th st: n.m.r on ins over 2f out: sn wknd)....1 **10**
Slaney Project (IRE) **(76)***(70) (WRMuir)* 3-8-11 DHarrison(1) (b: lw: led 5f: 2nd st: wknd 2f out)....hd **11**
2115[6] Chief of Staff **(65)***(59) (JPearce)* 6-8-9 JWilliams(2) (s.s: a bhd)....s.h **12**
2528* Roi de la Mer (IRE) **(65)***(35) (JAkehurst)* 4-8-9 GCarter(14) (3rd st: wknd over 2f out)....15 **13**

2/1 Silver Groom (IRE), **9/1** Ron's Secret, CONSPICUOUS (IRE), **10/1** Country Star (IRE), **11/1** Francfurter (8/1-12/1), **12/1** The French Friar (IRE), **14/1** Slaney Project (IRE), Roi de la Mer (IRE), **16/1** Lookingforarainbow (IRE), Lesley's Fashion, Fairy Knight, Laxford Bridge, **20/1** Chief of Staff, CSF £86.54 CT £760.32 TOTE £10.20: £2.00 £3.50 £2.00 (£45.00) Trio £93.40 OWNER Mrs Jenny Hopkins (CULLOMPTON) BRED Gerry Canavan 13 Rn

2m 6.36 (3.86) SF: 33/51/36/34/36/34/36/37/20/33/23/21/-

WEIGHT FOR AGE 3yo-9lb

3107 NIMBUS RATED STKS H'CAP (0-100) (3-Y.O+) (Class B) £12,359.30 (£4,506.80: £2,203.40: £947.00: £423.50)

1m 4f Stalls: High GOING minus 0.29 sec per fur (GF) 3-30 (3-30)

2768[3] **Mystic Hill (87)***(93)*(Fav)*(RCharlton)* 4-9-7 TQuinn(4) (2nd st: led over 2f out: wandered over 1f out: hdd ins fnl f: hrd rdn: led last strides)....— **1**
2639[3] Artic Courier **(80)***(86) (DJSCosgrove)* 4-8-9 (5) DGibbs(2) (lw: 3rd st: rdn over 2f out: r.o wl ins fnl f)....s.h **2**
2738[3] Major Change **(86)***(92) (RHannon)* 3-8-2 (7) DaneO'Neill(1) (led over 9f: hrd rdn: led ins fnl f: hdd last strides)....hd **3**
2738[10] Warning Order **(96)***(100) (JLDunlop)* 3-9-5 MRoberts(6) (5th st: rdn over 2f out: one pce)....1¾ **4**
3004* Bookcase **(73)***(75) (DRCElsworth)* 8-8-2 (5) 3x MHenry(5) (4th st: rdn over 2f out: one pce)....1½ **5**

LONG HANDICAP Bookcase 7-13

9/4 MYSTIC HILL, **5/2** Major Change, **7/2** Bookcase, **5/1** Artic Courier, **7/1** Warning Order, CSF £11.99 TOTE £2.50: £1.80 £2.10 (£8.70) OWNER Sir Philip Oppenheimer (BECKHAMPTON) BRED Hascombe and Valiant Studs 5 Rn

2m 36.26 (6.06) SF: 42/35/30/38/24

WEIGHT FOR AGE 3yo-11lb

3108 HENDON (S) STKS (3-Y.O+) (Class E) £3,647.50 (£1,105.00: £540.00: £257.50)

1m 1f (round) Stalls: Low GOING minus 0.29 sec per fur (GF) 4-00 (4-01)

2744[4] **Guesstimation (USA) (62)***(70) (JPearce)* 6-9-10 RCochrane(2) (hdwy over 2f out: hrd rdn ins fnl f: led last strides)....— **1**
2678[5] Rival Bid (USA) **(56)***(66)*(Fav)*(MAJarvis)* 7-9-6 MTebbutt(11) (6th st: led over 1f out: hrd rdn: hdd last strides)....hd **2**
2976* Shabanaz **(65)***(69) (WRMuir)* 10-9-10 DHarrison(1) (5th st: hrd rdn over 2f out: r.o)....½ **3**
2334[3] Zahid (USA) **(43)***(58) (KRBurke)* 4-9-1b(5) MHenry(9) (lw: 2nd st: led over 2f out tl over 1f out: wknd fnl f)....4 **4**
2334* Yo Kiri-B **(51)***(56) (JFfitch-Heyes)* 4-9-5 GDuffield(6) (lw: hdwy over 1f out: one pce)....nk **5**
2843[5] Kensington Freight **(41)***(48) (JAkehurst)* 3-8-7 GCarter(5) (nvr nr to chal)....2½ **6**
2976[11] High Typha **(47)***(45) (MRChannon)* 4-9-1v AClark(10) (nvr nrr)....1¾ **7**
2661[8] Daswaki (CAN) **(58)***(44) (GLMoore)* 7-9-6 SWhitworth(7) (b: swtg: led over 6f)....3 **8**
Khalyani (IRE) *(40) (RRowe)* 5-9-6 MPerrett(3) (4th st: wknd over 2f out)....2½ **9**
526[8] Total Rach (IRE) **(69)***(33) (RIngram)* 3-8-7 AMcGlone(4) (a bhd)....1 **10**
2334[4] Head For Heaven **(40)***(20) (RPCHoad)* 5-9-6 RPerham(8) (3rd st: wknd over 2f out)....10 **11**

3/1 Rival Bid (USA), **7/2** Shabanaz (5/2-4/1), **5/1** GUESSTIMATION (USA), **8/1** Total Rach (IRE) (5/1-10/1), Yo Kiri-B, **9/1** Zahid (USA) (14/1-8/1), **12/1** Khalyani (IRE), **20/1** Kensington Freight, **25/1** Daswaki (CAN), High Typha, Head For Heaven, CSF £19.56 TOTE £5.80: £1.80 £ 2.10 £2.00 (£6.40) Trio £7.60 OWNER Quintet Partnership (NEWMARKET) BRED Oak Crest Farm 11 Rn

1m 53.97 (3.97) SF: 48/44/47/36/34/18/23/22/18/3/-

WEIGHT FOR AGE 3yo-8lb

No bid

3109 AIRBORNE H'CAP (0-90) (3-Y.O+) (Class C) £5,732.00 (£1,736.00: £848.00: £404.00)

7f (round) Stalls: High GOING minus 0.29 sec per fur (GF) 4-30 (4-30)

2414[6] **Dawalib (USA) (66)***(75) (DHaydnJones)* 5-8-8 RCochrane(3) (swtg: hdwy over 3f out: 4th st: led over 1f out: all out)....— **1**

2669[9] Night Dance **(80)***(89) (GLewis)* 3-8-11 (5) AWhelan(8) (hdwy over 1f out: r.o ins fnl f)..............hd 2
2906[5] Persian Affair (IRE) **(63)***(72) (DHaydnJones)* 4-8-5 AMackay(2) (lw: carried wd bnd over 4f out: hdwy over 1f out: r.o ins fnl f)..............s.h 3
2831[2] Seventeens Lucky **(67)***(73) (BobJones)* 3-8-3 GDuffield(5) (lw: 3rd st: nt clr run 2f out tl over 1f out: r.o one pce)..............1¼ 4
2803[3] Red Rita (IRE) **(76)***(76) (WRMuir)* 4-9-4 TQuinn(1) (2nd st: led over 2f out tl over 1f out: sn wknd)..............2½ 5
2602[5] Safey Ana (USA) **(74)***(63) (BHanbury)* 4-8-11 (5) MHenry(6) (lw: 5th st: rdn over 2f out: sn wknd)..............5 6
2787* Banner (USA) **(73)***(60)*(Fav)*(BWHills)* 3-8-4 (5) JDSmith(7) (rn wd bnd over 4f out: 6th st: wknd over 2f out)..............¾ 7
2199[9] Landlord **(70)***(56) (JARToller)* 3-8-6b MRoberts(4) (4th whn carried wd bnd over 4f out: sn wknd)..............½ 8
2803[8] Waikiki Beach (USA) **(82)***(59) (GLMoore)* 4-9-10v SWhitworth(9) (lw: led over 4f)..............4 9

9/2 Banner (USA), **5/1** DAWALIB (USA), Safey Ana (USA), **11/2** Night Dance, Red Rita (IRE), **13/2** Seventeens Lucky, **9/1** Persian Affair (IRE), **10/1** Landlord, **20/1** Waikiki Beach (USA), CSF £30.96 CT £220.80 TOTE £6.80: £2.00 £3.60 £3.10 (£31.80) Trio £76.40 OWNER Jack Brown (Bookmaker) Ltd (PONTYPRIDD) BRED Hilary J. Boone Jnr 9 Rn
1m 26.59 (2.09) SF: 44/52/41/36/45/32/23/19/28
WEIGHT FOR AGE 3yo-6lb
T/Jkpt: Not won; £68,811.22 to Windsor 14/8/95. T/Plpt: £36.20 (508.18 Tckts). T/Qdpt: £18.00 (23.95 Tckts). AK

2875-PONTEFRACT (L-H)
Sunday August 13th (Good to firm)
WEATHER: sunny periods WIND: mod bhd

3110
E.B.F SUNDAY PLATE MAIDEN STKS (2-Y.O) (Class D) £4,240.50 (£1,284.00: £627.00: £298.50)
5f Stalls: Low GOING minus 0.39 sec per fur (F) 2-15 (2-17)

1938[8] **Clincher Club** *(73) (MJohnston)* 2-8-9 DHolland(9) (trckd ldrs: effrt 2f out: r.o told wl ins fnl f)— 1
617[2] Johayro *(76)*(Fav)*(WGMTurner)* 2-8-11 (3) SSanders(6) (led tl hdd wl ins fnl f: r.o)..............¾ 2
Juicy *(70+) (WJHaggas)* 2-9-0 KDarley(7) (cmpt: scope: bit bkwd: dwlt: outpcd & bhd tl hdwy 2f out: r.o)..............1¾ 3
My Millie *(60+) (RBoss)* 2-8-9 JWeaver(3) (leggy: lt-f: trckd ldrs: effrt & hung lft 2f out: styd on fnl f)..............1½ 4
2852[3] Time To Fly **(68)***(64?) (BWMurray)* 2-9-0 KFallon(8) (chsd ldrs: rdn & nt qckn fnl 2f)..............½ 5
Finisterre (IRE) *(54) (JJO'Neill)* 2-9-0 DeanMcKeown(1) (unf: lw: w ldr tl rdn & wknd 1f out)...3 6
Jive Baby *(9) (NBycroft)* 2-9-0 SMaloney(4) (unf: sn outpcd & wl bhd)..............14 7
Dispol Conqueror (IRE) *(4) (GROldroyd)* 2-9-0 JFanning(2) (cmpt: bit bkwd: dwlt: a outpcd & wl bhd)..............1½ 8

11/8 Johayro, **9/4** Juicy, **7/1** My Millie, **15/2** Finisterre (IRE) (op 12/1), **12/1** Time To Fly, **14/1** CLINCHER CLUB, **25/1** Jive Baby, Dispol Conqueror (IRE), CSF £33.53 TOTE £22.90: £3.90 £1.40 £1.50 (£11.70) Trio £33.50 OWNER Brian Yeardley Continental Ltd (MIDDLEHAM) BRED Jeremy Green and Sons 8 Rn 63.6 secs (2.10) SF: 28/31/25/15/19/9/-/-

3111
MAGIC 828 (S) STKS (3-Y.O) (Class F) £2,745.00 (£770.00:£375.00)
1m 4f 8y Stalls: Low GOING minus 0.39 sec per fur (F) 2-45 (2-53)

2961[8] **Boundary Express (45)***(58) (EJAlston)* 3-9-0 KFallon(1) (mde all: qcknd 3f out: r.o wl)........— 1
2582[4] Trumble **(47)***(56) (CWThornton)* 3-9-0 DeanMcKeown(3) (trckd wnr: ev ch & rdn over 1f out: nt qckn towards fin)..............1¼ 2
1824[8] Never Time (IRE) **(37)***(55) (MrsVAAconley)* 3-9-0 MDeering(2) (hld up: hdwy 4f out: sn chsng ldrs: nt qckn ins fnl f)..............1¼ 3
2851[2] Lindisfarne Lady **(43)***(49)*(Fav)*(MrsMReveley)* 3-8-9 KDarley(5) (hld up: hdwy 6f out: hrd rdn over 1f out: no rspnse)..............¾ 4
2806[2] Born To Be Wild *(35) (WGMTurner)* 3-8-6 (3) SSanders(4) (cl up tl rdn & wknd over 2f out) ...10 5

11/8 Lindisfarne Lady, **7/2** Born To Be Wild, **4/1** Trumble, **9/2** BOUNDARY EXPRESS, **14/1** Never Time (IRE) (op 8/1), CSF £19.44 TOTE £8.60: £2.30 £2.10 (£22.00) OWNER Mrs Stella Barclay (PRESTON) BRED W. Gott and Mrs I. Bird 5 Rn 2m 41.1 (6.80) SF: 25/23/22/16/2
Bt in 3,700 gns
STEWARDS' ENQUIRY Darley susp. 22-24/8/95 (excessive use of whip).

3112 STANLEY LEISURE H'CAP (0-85) (3-Y.O+) (Class D) £5,758.00 (£1,744.00: £852.00: £406.00)

6f Stalls: Low GOING minus 0.39 sec per fur (F) 3-15 (3-21)

2455[5] **Halmanerror (67)***(72)*(Fav)*(MrsJRRamsden)* 5-8-13 KFallon(11) (lw: bhd: hdwy over 2f out: r.o wl to ld cl home: edgd lft)....— 1
2786* Statius **(75)***(79) (TDBarron)* 3-9-2 JFortune(3) (chsd ldrs: rdn to ld wl ins fnl f: hdd nr fin)....nk 2
2987[4] Master Millfield (IRE) **(65)***(65) (CJHill)* 3-8-6 StephenDavies(4) (cl up: led wl over 1f out tl hdd & no ex wl ins fnl f)....1½ 3
2915* Iktamal (USA) **(79)***(76) (EALDunlop)* 3-9-3 (3) JTate(1) (unruly gng to s: trckd ldrs: nt clr run fnl 2f: nt rcvr)....1¼ 4
2470[4] Courageous Dancer (IRE) **(83)***(77) (BHanbury)* 3-9-7 (3) JStack(7) (bhd: effrt 2f out: nt clr run over 1f out: nrst fin)....1 5
2698[8] Densben **(47)***(37) (DenysSmith)* 11-7-4 (3) NVarley(13) (lw: bhd: hdwy & c wd st: nrst fin)....1½ 6
2455[6] Don Pepe **(69)***(56) (RBoss)* 4-9-1 JWeaver(2) (lw: led over 4f: r.o one pce)....1¼ 7
2764[W] Magic Orb **(77)***(56) (JLHarris)* 5-9-6 (3) SSanders(12) (lw: b: in tch: c wd st: no imp after)....3 8
2758[4] Formidable Liz **(63)***(37) (MDHammond)* 5-8-4 (5)ow1 DGriffiths(5) (hld up: effrt over 2f out: sn rdn & no imp)....1½ 9
2840[0] Prima Silk **(74)***(33) (MJRyan)* 4-9-6 KDarley(6) (chsd ldrs 4f: sn wknd)....6 10
681[7] Here Comes Risky **(82)***(39) (MJohnston)* 3-9-9 DHolland(8) (lw: outpcd fr ½-wy)....¾ 11
2578[6] Souperficial **(64)***(18) (JAGlover)* 4-8-10v PRobinson(10) (lw: effrt ½-wy: wknd wl over 1f out)1¼ 12
3050[10] Bargash **(70)** *(PDEvans)* 3-8-11 GHind(9) (bhd fr ½-wy)....10 13

4/1 HALMANERROR, **7/1** Souperficial, Don Pepe, **8/1** Prima Silk, Iktamal (USA), **9/1** Master Millfield (IRE), **10/1** Statius, **11/1** Formidable Liz, Courageous Dancer (IRE), **12/1** Magic Orb, **14/1** Bargash, **16/1** Densben, **20/1** Here Comes Risky, CSF £42.91 CT £322.20 TOTE £5.90: £2.20 £4.70 £3.00 (£41.00) Trio £138.60 OWNER Mrs Joan Smith(Lincoln) (THIRSK) BRED Ulceby Vale Stud Ltd 13 Rn 1m 15.9 (1.60) SF: 45/47/33/44/45/10/29/29/10/6/7/-/-

WEIGHT FOR AGE 3yo-5lb

STEWARDS' ENQUIRY Tate susp. 22-23/8/95 (careless riding).

3113 ROTHMANS ROYALS NORTH SOUTH CHALLENGE SERIES H'CAP (0-90) (3-Y.O+) (Class C) £7,327.50 (£2,220.00: £1,085.00: £517.50)

1m 4y Stalls: Low GOING minus 0.39 sec per fur (F) 3-45 (3-48)

2613[2] **Mo-Addab (IRE) (72)***(78)*(Fav)*(ACStewart)* 5-8-13 JCarroll(2) (swtg: prom: led 1½f out tl ins fnl f: nt qckn: fin 2nd, 4l: awrdd r)....— 1
2952[2] Pride of Pendle **(74)***(79) (DNicholls)* 6-9-1 AlexGreaves(10) (hld up: hdwy over 2f out: bmpd over 1f out: hung lft & styd on: fin 3rd, ½l: plcd 2nd).... 2
2707[8] Celestial Choir **(70)***(84) (JLEyre)* 5-8-6 (5) DGriffiths(1) (trckd ldrs: hdwy & swtchd over 1f out: led ins fnl f: r.o wl: fin 1st: disq: plcd 3rd).... 3
2703[19] Toujours Riviera **(87)***(90) (JPearce)* 5-10-0 GBardwell(5) (cl up: led 3f out to 1½f out: kpt on one pce)....1¼ 4
3063[3] Wentbridge Lad (IRE) **(61)***(62) (PDEvans)* 5-8-2v GHind(7) (trckd ldrs: effrt over 2f out: one pce appr fnl f)....¾ 5
2362[2] Easy Jet (POL) **(78)***(78) (LordHuntingdon)* 3-8-12 KFallon(9) (lw: bhd tl styd on fnl 3f: nrst fin)....½ 6
2672[8] Country Lover **(76)***(73) (LordHuntingdon)* 4-9-3 DHolland(11) (bhd tl styd on fnl 2f)....1½ 7
2482[6] South Rock **(73)***(68) (JAGlover)* 3-8-7 DeanMcKeown(3) (hdwy 3f out: n.m.r: one pce fnl 2f)1¼ 8
2797[5] Lancashire Life (IRE) **(55)** *(EJAlston)* 4-7-7 (3)ow3 DWright(4) (led 5f: grad wknd)....11 9
2613[4] Zermatt (IRE) **(70)** *(MDIUsher)* 5-8-11 RPrice(12) (chsd ldrs tl rdn & wknd fnl 2f)....8 10
2669[2] Pay Homage **(84)** *(IABalding)* 7-9-11 KDarley(8) (lw: bhd: effrt ½-wy: sn btn)....15 11
2669[3] Caleman **(75)** *(RBoss)* 6-9-2 JWeaver(6) (lw: cl up tl wknd qckly 3f out: p.u over 1f out: swallowed tongue).... P

LONG HANDICAP Lancashire Life (IRE) 7-6

5/1 MO-ADDAB (IRE), **11/2** Pride of Pendle, **15/2** Pay Homage, **8/1** Celestial Choir, Caleman, Easy Jet (POL), Zermatt (IRE), Toujours Riviera, **9/1** Country Lover, **11/1** Wentbridge Lad (IRE), **14/1** South Rock, **20/1** Lancashire Life (IRE), CSF £33.09 CT £206.64 TOTE £6.10: £1.90 £2.100 £2.60 (£11.20) Trio £26.50 OWNER Mr S. J. Hammond (NEWMARKET) BRED Mrs M. Upsdell 12 Rn

1m 43.2 (1.20) SF: 47/48/53/59/31/40/42/30/28/30/14/-

WEIGHT FOR AGE 3yo-7lb

STEWARDS' ENQUIRY Griffiths susp. 22-25/8/95 (irresponsible riding).

OFFICIAL EXPLANATION Caleman: was pulled up when he swallowed his tongue.

3114 'GO RACING IN YORKSHIRE' H'CAP (0-65) (3-Y.O+) (Class F) £2,829.00 (£794.00: £387.00)
2m 1f 22y Stalls: Low GOING minus 0.39 sec per fur (F) 4-15 (4-15)

2734[2] **Great Oration (IRE) (38)***(52)*(Fav)*(FWatson)* 6-9-1 JWeaver(2) (lw: trckd ldrs: hdwy gng wl 3f out: led wl over 1f out: r.o u.p)........— 1
2834* Zanzara (IRE) **(47)***(60) (MrsVAAconley)* 4-9-10 MDeering(1) (prom tl outpcd 4f out: hdwy u.p 2f out: ch ins fnl f: kpt on)........1¼ 2
2860* Amiarge **(34)***(45) (MBrittain)* 5-8-8 (3) DWright(3) (hld up: hdwy 6f out: ev ch 2f out: sn rdn & one pce)........1¾ 3
2734* Arian Spirit (IRE) **(33)***(42) (JLEyre)* 4-8-7 (3) NVarley(5) (led tl hdd 7f out: hdwy u.p 3f out: one pce appr fnl f)........2½ 4
3002[2] Milngavie (IRE) **(34)***(38) (MJohnston)* 5-8-11b TWilliams(4) (cl up: led & qcknd 7f out: hdd wl over 1f out: wknd)........5 5

7/4 GREAT ORATION (IRE), **9/4** Arian Spirit (IRE), **4/1** Amiarge, **9/2** Milngavie (IRE), **8/1** Zanzara (IRE) (6/1-10/1), CSF £13.64 TOTE £2.40: £1.40 £2.60 (£12.30) OWNER M D Hetherington (Packaging) Ltd (SEDGEFIELD) BRED P. F. I. Cole 5 Rn 3m 57.4 (17.40) SF: -/8/-/-/-

3115 KIDS COME FREE MAIDEN STKS (3-Y.O+) (Class D) £3,566.25 (£1,080.00: £527.50: £251.25)
1m 4y Stalls: Low GOING minus 0.39 sec per fur (F) 4-45 (4-46)

2794[2] **Catercap (IRE)** *(79)*(Fav)*(JHMGosden)* 3-8-12 JCarroll(2) (mde all: jst hld on)........— 1
2794[6] Troubadour Song *(79) (IABalding)* 3-8-12 KDarley(4) (lw: trckd ldrs: effrt over 1f out: rdn ins fnl f: fin fast)........s.h 2
2415[6] Tilaal (USA) **(78)***(74) (EALDunlop)* 3-8-12 JWeaver(1) (hld up: hdwy over 3f out: rdn & nt qckn fnl 2f)........2½ 3
Graceful Lady *(9) (EJAlston)* 5-9-0 KFallon(5) (str: bkwd: hld up: effrt over 3f out: wknd over 2f out)........30 4
Stray Rein *(JJQuinn)* 3-8-7 MBirch(3) (w'like: str: bit bkwd: prom 5f: eased whn btn)........dist 5

11/8 CATERCAP (IRE) (4/5-6/4), **5/2** Troubadour Song, Tilaal (USA), **16/1** Graceful Lady, **25/1** Stray Rein, CSF £4.86 TOTE £2.00: £1.40 £1.90 (£2.40) OWNER Sheikh Mohammed (NEWMARKET) BRED Upstream Ltd 5 Rn 1m 46.4 (4.40) SF: 24/24/19/-/-
WEIGHT FOR AGE 3yo-7lb

3116 FAMILY DAY H'CAP (0-65) (3-Y.O+) (Class F) £3,053.00 (£858.00: £419.00)
5f Stalls: Low GOING minus 0.39 sec per fur (F) 5-15 (5-19)

3055[2] **Petraco (IRE) (59)***(69) (NASmith)* 7-9-10 SDWilliams(11) (a.p: rdn to ld ins fnl f: r.o)........— 1
2956[5] Invigilate **(51)***(55) (MartynWane)* 6-9-2 KFallon(15) (mid div: c wd st: r.o ins fnl f)........1¾ 2
2837[4] Ramborette **(47)***(50) (DenysSmith)* 3-8-3 (5) CTeague(14) (hdwy over 1f out: r.o wl towards fin)........½ 3
2821[4] Brisas **(41)***(44) (CWFairhurst)* 8-8-6 DeanMcKeown(1) (a chsng ldrs: ev ch 1f out: nt qckn)..hd 4
2879* Lochon **(58)***(57)*(Fav)*(JLEyre)* 4-9-4 (5) DGriffiths(4) (lw: chsd ldrs: effrt 2f out: r.o one pce)......1 5
Trioming **(46)***(44) (APJones)* 9-8-6 (5) RPainter(10) (mid div: styd on fnl f: nvr able to chal)......nk 6
2879[3] Kabcast **(47)***(44) (DWChapman)* 10-8-12b KDarley(6) (led tl hdd & wknd ins fnl f)........½ 7
2916[3] Indian Crystal **(36)***(26) (MrsMReveley)* 4-8-1 PRobinson(8) (dwlt: bhd tl r.o ins fnl f)........2 8
2585[8] My Abbey **(56)***(42) (EJAlston)* 6-9-7 JFortune(13) (cl up over 3f: wknd)........1¼ 9
2492[6] Featherstone Lane **(54)***(38) (MissLCSiddall)* 4-9-5v JWeaver(2) (dwlt: sme hdwy u.p over 1f out: n.d)........¾ 10
1566[8] Grand Time **(33)***(12) (CJHill)* 6-7-12b GBardwell(5) (nvr trbld ldrs)........1½ 11
2879[W] Nordoora (IRE) **(54)***(31) (JLHarris)* 6-9-2 (3) SSanders(9) (lw: w ldrs 3f: wknd)........¾ 12
2521[16] Sandmoor Velvet **(47)***(8) (MHEasterby)* 3-8-8 MBirch(3) (s.i.s: a bhd)........5 13
2502* Miss Siham (IRE) **(47)** *(DNicholls)* 6-8-12 AlexGreaves(12) (b.hind: unruly stalls: outpcd & bhd fr ½-wy)........4 14

4/1 Lochon, **7/1** Kabcast, Miss Siham (IRE), **15/2** PETRACO (IRE), Invigilate, **8/1** Featherstone Lane, **9/1** Indian Crystal, **12/1** My Abbey, Brisas, Grand Time (op 8/1), **14/1** Ramborette, **16/1** Sandmoor Velvet, **20/1** Nordoora (IRE), **25/1** Trioming, CSF £63.76 CT £730.21 TOTE £18.40: £4.40 £3.10 £5.80 (£60.00) Trio £445.40
OWNER Mr Bernard Gover (UPTON SNODSBURY) BRED Mrs M. Beaumont 14 Rn
63.5 secs (2.00) SF: 44/30/21/19/32/19/19/1/17/13/-/6/-/-
WEIGHT FOR AGE 3yo-4lb
T/Plpt: £96.80 (155.20 Tckts). T/Qdpt: £14.50 (15.20 Tckts). AA

2997-HAMILTON (R-H)
Monday August 14th (Firm)
WEATHER: overcast WIND: almost nil

3117
E.B.F SILVERWELL HOUSE MAIDEN STKS (2-Y.O) (Class D)
£4,143.00 (£1,254.00: £612.00: £291.00)
6f 5y Stalls: Low GOING minus 0.40 sec per fur (F) 2-15 (2-18)

2771[2] **Larghetto (IRE) (75)***(78) (JBerry)* 2-9-0 JCarroll(5) (mde all: qcknd 2f out: hld on gamely) ...— 1
2473[2] Creative Account (USA) *(70)*(Fav)*(MrsJRRamsden)* 2-9-0 KFallon(2) (lw: trckd ldr: effrt 2f out: disp ld wl ins fnl f: r.o)....hd 2
2453[3] Nose No Bounds (IRE) *(63) (MJohnston)* 2-9-0 DHolland(4) (a.p: no hdwy fnl 2f)....2½ 3
2908[4] Kernof (IRE) *(62?) (MDHammond)* 2-9-0 DaleGibson(1) (lw: chsd ldrs: nt qckn appr fnl f).....nk 4
Distinctlyfoster's (IRE) *(52) (MJohnston)* 2-8-9 TWilliams(3) (lt-f: unruly s: dwlt: swtchd & sme hdwy ½-wy: nvr able to chal)....2 5

8/13 Creative Account (USA), **5/2** Nose No Bounds (IRE), **5/1** LARGHETTO (IRE), **25/1** Distinctlyfoster's (IRE), **40/1** Kernof (IRE), CSF £8.57 TOTE £5.70: £1.80 £1.10 (£2.10) OWNER Godolphin (COCKERHAM) BRED Sheikh Mohammed bin Rashid al Maktoum 5 Rn
1m 12.3 (2.30) SF: 32/32/25/24/14

3118
HAZELBANK (S) H'CAP (0-60) (3-Y.O+) (Class G) £2,409.00
(£674.00: £327.00)
1m 1f 36y Stalls: High GOING minus 0.60 sec per fur (F) 2-45 (2-45)

2885[4] **Zahran (IRE) (43)***(56) (JMBradley)* 4-10-0 KFallon(4) (b: hdwy 4f out: led 2f out: r.o: comf)..— 1
2874* Never so True **(41)***(51) (MartynWane)* 4-9-12 JCarroll(3) (led tl hdd 2f out: kpt on wl)....1¾ 2
2972[7] Resolute Bay **(42)***(51) (RMWhitaker)* 9-9-13 ACulhane(9) (lw: hdwy 3f out: chsng ldrs ent fnl f: nt qckn nr fin)....½ 3
2874[2] Portite Sophie **(40)***(46) (MBrittain)* 4-9-6 (5) VHalliday(8) (chsd ldrs: effrt over 3f out: one pce)1¾ 4
2972[8] Lord Vivienne (IRE) **(42)***(42) (BSRothwell)* 6-9-13 JFortune(5) (cl up: effrt over 3f out: sn rdn & no rspnse)....3½ 5
2913[4] Ragazzo (IRE) **(35)***(33) (JSWainwright)* 5-9-6 LCharnock(2) (bhd: styd on u.p fnl 3f: n.d).....1¼ 6
2861[8] Demurrer **(34)***(27) (MrsAMNaughton)* 5-9-5 TWilliams(6) (cl up tl wknd 3f out)....2½ 7
2972[2] Golden Fish **(48)***(6)*(Fav)*(JLEyre)* 3-9-11 SDWilliams(1) (prom tl rdn & wknd over 3f out)......20 8
2769[9] Hod-Mod (IRE) **(30)** *(MissZAGreen)* 5-9-1 JLowe(7) (t: a bhd)....8 9

7/2 Golden Fish, **9/2** ZAHRAN (IRE), **5/1** Never so True, **6/1** Portite Sophie, Lord Vivienne (IRE), **9/1** Demurrer, **10/1** Resolute Bay, **16/1** Ragazzo (IRE), **100/1** Hod-Mod (IRE), CSF £24.25 CT £185.97 TOTE £5.50: £1.70 £1.50 £1.60 (£15.50) Trio £22.60 OWNER Mr D. Smith(Saul) (CHEPSTOW) BRED S. Niarchos 9 Rn
1m 56.7 (2.40) SF: 41/36/36/31/27/18/12/-/-
WEIGHT FOR AGE 3yo-8lb
No bid
OFFICIAL EXPLANATION **Golden Fish: no explanation offered.**

3119
CAPTAIN J. C. STEWART MEMORIAL H'CAP (0-75) (3-Y.O+) (Class D) £4,546.60 (£1,376.80: £672.40: £320.20)
1m 65y Stalls: High GOING minus 0.60 sec per fur (F) 3-15 (3-15)

2880[3] **Roseberry Ray (IRE) (73)***(86)*(Fav)*(GWragg)* 3-9-8 PRobinson(2) (hld up: effrt 3f out: led jst ins fnl f: r.o wl)....— 1
2999[3] Talented Ting (IRE) **(68)***(78) (PCHaslam)* 6-9-10 JFortune(3) (w ldr: rdn to ld 2f out: sn hdd: kpt on fnl f)....1½ 2
2875[4] Master Ofthe House **(61)***(70) (MDHammond)* 9-8-12 (5) DGriffiths(5) (lw: hld up: hdwy 3f out: led 1½f out tl hdd & wknd ins fnl f)....½ 3
2974[3] Tinklers Folly **(47)***(47) (DenysSmith)* 3-7-10 LCharnock(4) (led tl hdd 2f out: sn btn)....5 4
2733[10] Langtonian **(39)***(15) (JLEyre)* 6-7-6v(3)ow2 NVarley(1) (lw: hdwy to jn ldrs appr st: rdn 3f out: sn btn)....11 5
LONG HANDICAP Langtonian 7-3

11/8 ROSEBERRY RAY (IRE) (op Evens), **2/1** Talented Ting (IRE), **6/1** Master Ofthe House, **13/2** Tinklers Folly, **33/1** Langtonian, CSF £4.08 TOTE £1.90: £1.10 £1.50 (£2.40) OWNER Mrs Nicola Bscher (NEWMARKET) BRED Kilcarn Stud 5 Rn
1m 46.4 (3.10) SF: 29/28/20/-/-
WEIGHT FOR AGE 3yo-7lb

3120
ROSEBANK CLAIMING STKS (2-Y.O) (Class F) £2,647.00 (£742.00: £361.00)
6f 5y Stalls: Low GOING minus 0.40 sec per fur (F) 3-45 (3-45)

*2962** **Ultra Barley** *(74+) (PCHaslam)* 2-8-13 JFortune(2) (mde all: pushed along 2f out: sn clr) ....— 1
2998* Moi Canard **(64)***(64)*(Fav)*(JBerry)* 2-8-11 JCarroll(4) (lw: trckd wnr: effrt 2f out: rdn & no imp)........3 2
2606[4] Julgarant (IRE) **(53)***(39) (MDods)* 2-8-7v DeanMcKeown(3) (plld hrd: effrt over 2f out: sn btn)..8 3
Autofyr *(18) (JSWainwright)* 2-8-2 LCharnock(1) (unf: bkwd: prom 4f: sn lost pl) 6 4

8/11 Moi Canard, **5/4** ULTRA BARLEY, **20/1** Julgarant (IRE), **33/1** Autofyr, CSF £2.46 TOTE £2.10 (£1.10) OWNER Pet Express Ltd T/A Nutrimix (MIDDLEHAM) BRED Benham Stud 4 Rn
1m 12.5 (2.50) SF: 28/18/-/-

3121
TEAM MANAGEMENT H'CAP (0-70) (3-Y.O+) (Class E) £3,811.25 (£1,154.00: £563.50: £268.25)
6f 5y Stalls: Low GOING minus 0.40 sec per fur (F) 4-15 (4-17)

2870[4] **Suedoro (45)***(52) (RMMcKellar)* 5-8-2 (7) CAdamson(4) (disp ld tl led 2f out: r.o) ....— 1
2930[5] Diet **(54)***(59) (MissLAPerratt)* 9-9-4v JCarroll(3) (disp ld 4f: kpt on wl u.p)........¾ 2
2652[6] Captain Carat **(64)***(68)*(Fav)*(MrsJRRamsden)* 4-9-7 (7) TFinn(5) (lw: hdwy ½-wy: sn rdn & chsng ldrs: styd on fnl f)........nk 3
2742[4] Southern Dominion **(62)***(65) (MJohnston)* 3-9-7 TWilliams(2) (lw: in tch: styd on wl fnl f: nrst fin)........nk 4
2870[3] Birchwood Sun **(61)***(64) (MDods)* 5-9-11b DeanMcKeown(6) (lw: cl up: rdn over 2f out: r.o one pce)........hd 5
2810* Baileys Sunset (IRE) **(63)***(63) (MJohnston)* 3-9-8 DHolland(8) (lw: hld up: nt clr run fnl 2f: nt rcvr)........1¼ 6
2930[4] Pageboy **(63)***(56)*(Fav)*(PCHaslam)* 6-9-13b JFortune(7) (lw: bhd: hdwy ½-wy: rdn & btn over 1f out)........2½ 7
2956[7] Waverley Star **(34)***(9) (JSWainwright)* 10-7-12b LCharnock(1) (lw: a bhd)........7 8

7/2 Pageboy, Captain Carat, **9/2** Baileys Sunset (IRE), **6/1** Diet, **13/2** Birchwood Sun, **8/1** SUEDORO, **11/1** Southern Dominion (8/1-12/1), **16/1** Waverley Star, CSF £49.91 CT £179.82 TOTE £14.00: £2.50 £1.90 £1.60 (£24.70) OWNER Mr Ray Vardy (LESMAHAGOW) BRED R. Vardy 8 Rn
1m 12.2 (2.20) SF: 28/35/44/36/40/34/32/-
WEIGHT FOR AGE 3yo-5lb

3122
CARSTAIRS APPRENTICE H'CAP (0-70) (3-Y.O+) (Class F) £2,906.00 (£816.00: £398.00)
1m 4f 17y Stalls: High GOING minus 0.60 sec per fur (F) 4-45 (4-45)

2543[6] **Exclusion (38)***(48) (JHetherton)* 6-8-0 (3) CAdamson(2) (lw: mde all: styd on strly fnl2f)........— 1
3001* Nornax Lad (USA) **(64)***(70)*(Fav)*(MartynMeade)* 7-9-12b(3) 5x RHavlin(3) (lw: trckd wnr: effrt 2f out: one pce fnl f)........3 2
3002[4] Lord Advocate **(33)***(36) (DANolan)* 7-7-12b NVarley(1) (prom: outpcd 5f out: sme hdwy u.p 3f out: no imp)........2½ 3

4/7 Nornax Lad (USA), **7/2** EXCLUSION, Lord Advocate, CSF £5.61 TOTE £4.10 (£1.90) OWNER Mr James Byrne (MALTON) BRED Roan Rocket Partners 3 Rn 2m 34.5 (2.50) SF: 25/47/13
T/Plpt: £222.90 (35.98 Tckts). T/Qdpt: £10.70 (0.5 Tckts); £7.25 to York 15/8/95 AA

2964-LEICESTER (R-H)
Monday August 14th (Good to firm)
WEATHER: cloudy & dry WIND: slt across

3123
LEICESTERSHIRE COUNTY CRICKET CLUB H'CAP (0-70) (3-Y.O+) (Class E) £3,245.00 (£968.00: £462.00: £209.00)
5f 2y Stalls: Low GOING minus 0.44 sec per fur (F) 6-00 (6-01)

2793[5] **Windrush Boy (62)***(60) (JRBosley)* 5-9-7 (7) AimeeCook(4) (swtg: chsd ldrs: led ent fnl f: pushed out)........— 1
2925[8] Lugana Vision **(51)***(48) (RHarris)* 3-8-13b MFenton(1) (s.i.s: hdwy 2f out: ev ch ins fnl f: r.o) ..nk 2
646* Double Splendour (IRE) **(50)***(45) (PSFelgate)* 5-8-13 (3) DWright(11) (b: dwlt: hdwy ½-wy: ev ch 1f out: kpt on u.p)........¾ 3

2887[4] Tee-Emm **(39)***(29) (PHowling)* 5-8-5 JQuinn(2) (b.hind: lw: a.p centre: led bel dist: sn hdd & no ex) 1½ **4**
3055* Red Admiral **(64)***(49) (PCHaslam)* 5-9-9 (7) 6x NicolaHowarth(6) (chsd ldrs centre: rdn wl over 1f out: btn whn edgd rt fnl f) 1½ **5**
2631[8] The Institute Boy **(45)***(30) (MissJFCraze)* 5-8-11v SWebster(10) (chsd ldr far side: shkn up wl over 1f out: sn btn) ....hd **6**
2502[5] Gymcrak Tycoon **(42)***(24)*(Fav)*(GHolmes)* 6-8-8 KFallon(5) (b: chsd ldrs over 3f: sn rdn & outpcd) ....¾ **7**
2850[7] Followmegirls **(49)***(29) (MrsALMKing)* 6-9-1 MWigham(7) (dwlt: effrt & rdn 2f out: nt rch ldrs).¾ **8**
2837* Kalar **(47)***(27) (DWChapman)* 6-8-13b WRyan(8) (led tl hdd bel dist: eased whn btn) ....hd **9**
2865[3] Pacific Girl (IRE) **(53)***(29) (BPalling)* 3-9-1b TSprake(3) (a bhd: hrd rdn 2f out: nt rch ldrs).....1¼ **10**
2858[6] Superbit **(51)***(27) (BAMcMahon)* 3-8-13 TQuinn(9) (lw: outpcd & bhd: rdn 2f out: no imp) .....s.h **11**

7/2 Gymcrak Tycoon, **5/1** Kalar, **11/2** Double Splendour (IRE), **7/1** Red Admiral, **8/1** Followmegirls, **10/1** WINDRUSH BOY (8/1-12/1), **12/1** Tee-Emm, **14/1** Lugana Vision, The Institute Boy, Superbit, **16/1** Pacific Girl (IRE), CSF £124.37 CT £772.82 TOTE £12.70: £2.50 £5.20 £1.80 (£159.70) Trio £62.90 OWNER Mr J. Westley (WANTAGE) BRED M. A. Wilkins 11 Rn

60.4 secs (1.90) SF: 42/26/27/11/31/12/6/11/9/7/5

WEIGHT FOR AGE 3yo-4lb

3124 HANSIE CRONJE (S) STKS (2-Y.O) (Class G) £2,646.20 (£733.20:£350.60)
5f 218y Stalls: Low GOING minus 0.44 sec per fur (F) 6-25 (6-26)

2965[2] **L A Touch (50)***(61)*(Fav)*(CADwyer)* 2-8-3 (3) JStack(4) (lw: hld up: hdwy to ld 1f out: rdn & drifted rt fnl f: hld on) ....— **1**
2908[6] Rothley Imp (IRE) *(60) (JWharton)* 2-8-6 JQuinn(3) (hld up: led over 2f out to 1f out: rallied u.p fnl f) ....½ **2**
2939[5] Image Maker (IRE) *(52) (DWPArbuthnot)* 2-8-6 TQuinn(6) (prom: rdn over 2f out: kpt on one pce ins fnl f) 3 **3**
2951[3] Don't Tell Anyone **(52)***(53) (JBerry)* 2-8-11 AMcGlone(2) (a.p: rdn over 1f out: one pce).......1¼ **4**
2023[5] Poppy My Love *(32) (RHarris)* 2-8-6 AMackay(1) (led over 3f: wknd bel dist) 6 **5**
2859[8] Tin Man *(BAMcMahon)* 2-8-11 GCarter(7) (lw: chsd ldrs over 3f: sn rdn & wknd: t.o) 14 **6**
2951[5] Taurean Fire *(MrsMReveley)* 2-8-11 KDarley(5) (plld hrd: spd to ½-wy: sn lost tch: t.o) 9 **7**

11/4 L A TOUCH, **100/30** Taurean Fire, **7/2** Don't Tell Anyone, **5/1** Rothley Imp (IRE), **12/1** Image Maker (IRE), Tin Man, **20/1** Poppy My Love, CSF £14.78 TOTE £3.00: £1.60 £2.70 (£14.90) OWNER Mr C. A. Rosen (NEWMARKET) BRED J. K. S. Cresswell 7 Rn

1m 14.8 (4.80) SF: -/-/-/-/-/-/-

No bid

3125 NIGEL BRIERS H'CAP (0-70) (3-Y.O) (Class E) £3,616.80 (£1,082.40: £519.20: £237.60)
1m 8y Stalls: Low GOING minus 0.44 sec per fur (F) 6-55 (6-57)

2707[10] **Elpidos (69)***(83) (CEBrittain)* 3-9-7 MRoberts(6) (led 2f: rdn 2f out: led ins fnl f: r.o wl) ....— **1**
2974* Concer Un **(70)***(80)*(Fav)*(SCWilliams)* 3-9-8 5x KFallon(4) (a.p stands' side: led 2f out: hrd rdn & hdd ins fnl f: no ex) 2 **2**
2253[5] Primo Lara **(66)***(74) (PWHarris)* 3-9-4 MFenton(1) (chsd ldrs stands' side: rdn wl over 1f out: kpt on towards fin) 1 **3**
2864[2] Legal Issue (IRE) **(62)***(68) (SirMarkPrescott)* 3-9-0 GDuffield(2) (lw: led stands' side after 2f: hdd 2f out: rdn & n.m.r ent fnl f: nt rcvr) 1 **4**
2968[5] L'Eglise Belle **(41)***(41) (MrsALMKing)* 3-7-7 NCarlisle(5) (chsd ldrs stands' side: rdn over 2f out: one pce) 3 **5**
1180[5] Another Time **(53)***(50+) (SPCWoods)* 3-8-5 WWoods(9) (bit bkwd: chsd ldrs: edgd lft u.p 2f out: kpt on) 1¾ **6**
2711[2] Anistop **(45)***(34) (RAkehurst)* 3-7-11 JQuinn(8) (rdn over 2f out: nvr nrr) 4 **7**
2747[13] Dahlenburg (IRE) **(61)***(49) (JHMGosden)* 3-8-13v GHind(3) (lw: swtg: prom stands' side 5f: sn rdn & btn) ....nk **8**
2813[2] La Fille de Cirque **(48)***(18) (RJRWilliams)* 3-8-0 DBiggs(7) (b: w ldrs far side over 5f: wknd qckly) 9 **9**
*1952** Super High **(60)***(22) (PHowling)* 3-8-12 RCochrane(10) (lw: prom far side 5f) 4 **10**
2966[3] Coneygree **(41)** *(JWharton)* 3-7-7 GBardwell(12) (swtg: w ldrs far side over 4f) 3 **11**
2815[7] Bowcliffe Grange (IRE) **(41)** *(DWChapman)* 3-7-7 NKennedy(11) (t.o) 10 **12**
Asian Elegance **(53)** *(HThomsonJones)* 3-8-5 KDarley(13) (still unf: swtg: racd far side: bhd fr ½-wy: t.o) 30 **13**

LONG HANDICAP Coneygree 7-2 Bowcliffe Grange (IRE) 6-10

100/30 Concer Un, **5/1** Super High (7/2-11/2), **6/1** ELPIDOS, **13/2** Legal Issue (IRE), **10/1** Another Time, Anistop, La Fille de Cirque, **11/1** Dahlenburg (IRE), **14/1** Primo Lara, **20/1** Asian Elegance, **25/1** Coneygree, **33/1** L'Eglise Belle, **50/1** Bowcliffe Grange (IRE), CSF £25.30 CT £251.89 TOTE £7.20: £2.00 £1.80 £6.40 (£10.20) Trio £27.80 OWNER The Dayspring Company Ltd (NEWMARKET) BRED Ewar Stud Farms 13 Rn 1m 37.2 (2.20) SF: 45/42/36/30/3/12/-/11/-/-/-/-/-

3126 TIM BOON BENEFIT CLAIMING STKS (3-Y.O) (Class F) £2,735.00 (£760.00: £365.00) 1m 1f 218y Stalls: Low GOING minus 0.23 sec per fur (GF) 7-25 (7-27)

2884* **Woodrising (59)***(70)*(Fav)*(GLewis)* 3-8-3 (5) AWhelan(2) (lw: mde all: qcknd clr over 3f out: styd on strly) — 1
2849² Oakbury (IRE) **(58)***(75) (RHannon)* 3-9-5 MRoberts(1) (b.nr fore: chsd wnr: 2nd st: c wd 4f out: sn rdn: kpt on one pce) 3½ 2
2884² Darling Clover **(56)***(60) (DMorley)* 3-8-10 MFenton(3) (prom: 3rd st: effrt 3f out: sn rdn & wknd appr fnl f) 4 3
2776⁵ Cats Bottom **(67)***(44) (DJSCosgrove)* 3-8-12 MRimmer(5) (lw: chsd ldrs: 4th st: rdn along over 2f out: sn btn) 11 4
*2631*⁵ Pats Delight **(37)***(16) (SCoathup)* 3-7-13 (7) AmandaSanders(4) (hld up in rr: 6th st: t.o fnl 3f) 14 5
2849⁵ Isshereal (IRE) **(33)***(9) (BPalling)* 3-8-0 TSprake(6) (t: prom early: lost pl & 5th st: t.o fnl 3f) ¾ 6

13/8 WOODRISING, **3/1** Darling Clover, Cats Bottom, **9/2** Oakbury (IRE), **16/1** Isshereal (IRE), **40/1** Pats Delight, CSF £8.97 TOTE £2.40: £1.30 £3.30 (£4.70) OWNER Mr Geoff Lewis (EPSOM) BRED Kirtlington Stud Ltd 6 Rn 2m 7.2 (4.50) SF: 38/43/28/12/-/-
Woodrising clmd Elite Racing Club £6,000
STEWARDS' ENQUIRY Whelan susp. 23-24/8/95 (excessive use of whip).

3127 WEATHERBYS 'NEWCOMERS' SERIES H'CAP (0-80) (3-Y.O+) (Class D) £4,036.50 (£1,206.00: £577.00: £262.50) 1m 3f 183y Stalls: Low GOING minus 0.23 sec per fur (GF) 7-55 (7-58)

*1955*³ **Charlie Bigtime (46)***(57) (RHarris)* 5-8-4 AMackay(4) (b.hind: chsd ldrs: 4th st: hdwy 4f out: sn rdn: styd on ins fnl f to ld cl home) — 1
2780³ Jadwal (USA) **(78)***(89) (DMorley)* 3-9-11 GDuffield(6) (s.i.s: hld up: 5th st: hdwy 3f out: rdn to ld ins fnl f: ct cl home) nk 2
2854² Hever Golf Lady **(57)***(66) (TJNaughton)* 3-8-4 PaulEddery(1) (led: rdn 2f out: hdd ins fnl f: kpt on) 1 3
2612³ Pharamineux **(65)***(73)*(Fav)*(RAkehurst)* 9-9-9 TQuinn(5) (lw: dwlt: hld up & bhd: 6th st: c wd: rdn & outpcd over 3f out: styd on ins fnl f) 1¼ 4
2339⁶ Triple Tie (USA) **(50)***(56) (MBlanshard)* 4-8-8 RCochrane(3) (swtg: hld up: 3rd st: hdwy over 2f out: ev ch dist: wknd towards fin) 1¼ 5
Hatta River (USA) **(59)***(45) (JAHarris)* 5-9-3 KFallon(7) (bit bkwd: chsd ldr: 2nd st: c wd: wknd over 2f out: t.o) 15 6

11/4 Pharamineux, **100/30** Jadwal (USA), **7/2** Hever Golf Lady, **4/1** CHARLIE BIGTIME, **12/1** Triple Tie (USA), **16/1** Hatta River (USA), CSF £15.30 TOTE £5.20: £2.70 £2.10 (£9.80) OWNER Mr T. J. Dawson (NEWMARKET) BRED Sir Stanley Grinstead 6 Rn 2m 35.7 (6.90) SF: 25/46/23/41/24/13
WEIGHT FOR AGE 3yo-11lb

3128 PAUL NIXON LIMITED STKS (0-65) (3-Y.O+) (Class F) £3,174.20 (£881.20: £422.60) 7f 9y Stalls: Low GOING minus 0.44 sec per fur (F) 8-25 (8-26)

2979³ **Star of Gold (64)***(74) (CREgerton)* 3-8-10 TQuinn(1) (led 2f: rdn to ld over 1f out: hld on gamely) — 1
2853* Gymcrak Flyer **(62)***(71)*(Fav)*(GHolmes)* 4-9-0 KFallon(4) (b.hind: lw: hld up & bhd: hdwy & rdn over 2f out: chal fnl f: jst failed) nk 2
2984* Shady Deed (USA) **(62)***(66) (JWHills)* 3-8-3b(5) MHenry(3) (lw: led after 2f: rdn, wnt rt & hdd over 1f out: sn btn) 2½ 3
2549¹⁰ Bold Cyrano (IRE) **(50)***(63) (BPalling)* 4-9-2 TSprake(2) (hld up: hdwy u.p over 2f out: nt pce to chal) 2 4
2819² Crown of Love (USA) **(62)***(42) (MRStoute)* 3-8-5 KDarley(5) (b.nr fore: b.hind: prom: rdn along 3f out: sn lost tch: eased whn btn) 7 5
*256*⁸ Lovely Me (IRE) **(65)***(34) (RFJohnsonHoughton)* 4-8-11 RCochrane(7) (bit bkwd: hld up: hdwy 3f out: wknd fnl 2f) 3½ 6
2491⁵ Almasi (IRE) **(62)***(27) (CFWall)* 3-8-0 (5) LNewton(6) (hld up: effrt over 2f out: sn rdn & wknd) 3 7

3/1 Gymcrak Flyer, **7/2** Shady Deed (USA), **4/1** Almasi (IRE), Crown of Love (USA), **5/1** STAR OF GOLD, **16/1** Lovely Me (IRE), **20/1** Bold Cyrano (IRE), CSF £19.26 TOTE £6.00: £2.80 £1.60 (£8.00) OWNER Normanby Stud Ltd (CHADDLEWORTH) BRED Normanby Stud Ltd and C. Shaw 7 Rn
1m 25.1 (2.60) SF: 26/29/18/21/-/-/-
WEIGHT FOR AGE 3yo-6lb
T/Plpt: £316.90 (43.12 Tckts). T/Qdpt: £43.80 (1.9 Tckts). IM

2976-WINDSOR (Fig. 8)
Monday August 14th (Good to firm)
WEATHER: hot WIND: almost nil

3129
BELMEAD (S) STKS (3-Y.O+) (Class G) £2,810.00 (£785.00: £380.00)
1m 2f 7y Stalls: High GOING minus 0.31 sec per fur (GF) 2-30 (2-32)

Latin Leader *(70) (CREgerton)* 5-9-4 MRoberts(1) (hdwy over 3f out: led over 2f out: r.o wl)— 1
2640² Thames Side **(55)***(65) (MMadgwick)* 4-9-4 MFenton(8) (hdwy 3f out: chsd wnr over 2f out: unable qckn)....3 2
2979¹⁸ Lunar Mission (IRE) **(66)***(65)*(Fav)*(JMPEustace)* 4-9-4 RCochrane(3) (lw: hdwy over 3f out: rdn over 2f out: one pce)....hd 3
2983⁴ White Flash **(46)***(44) (DRCElsworth)* 4-8-13b TQuinn(2) (6th st: wknd over 2f out)....10 4
2486¹² Premier Blues (FR) **(22)***(44) (RJRWilliams)* 5-8-13b DBiggs(4) (3rd st: ev ch 2f out: sn wknd) nk 5
Take Two *(42) (JWhite)* 7-8-13 (5) AWhelan(10) (bit bkwd: 4th st: led over 3f out tl over 2f out: sn wknd)....4 6
2849⁴ Chastleton **(40)***(31) (MRChannon)* 3-8-10 CandyMorris(9) (w ldr: led 6f out tl over 3f out: sn wknd)....8 7
2640⁴ Malindi Bay **(30)***(28) (BJMcMath)* 7-9-4 MTebbutt(7) (nvr nrr)....¾ 8
Antiguan Flyer **(57)***(20) (RHarris)* 6-9-4 AMackay(11) (b: swtg: 5th st: wknd over 3f out)....5 9
2807⁹ Mister Fox **(35)***(8) (RJHodges)* 4-9-1 (3) SDrowne(13) (b: lw: led 4f: 2nd st: wknd 4f out)....8 10
2863⁷ Jacks to Open (USA) **(41)***(2) (MJHeaton-Ellis)* 4-9-4 RPerham(12) (b: lw: bhd fnl 4f)....3½ 11
Swaynes Lad *(CPWildman)* 3-8-6 (3) SSanders(6) (unf: a bhd)....3½ 12
Lobkov *(RCurtis)* 3-8-4 GBardwell(5) (swtg: bhd fnl 4f)....5 13

9/4 Lunar Mission (IRE), **11/4** Thames Side, **5/1** White Flash, **15/2** LATIN LEADER, **8/1** Take Two (op 4/1), **12/1** Chastleton (8/1-14/1), Antiguan Flyer, **33/1** Premier Blues (FR), Malindi Bay, Mister Fox, Jacks to Open (USA), Swaynes Lad, Lobkov, CSF £28.04 TOTE £8.70: £2.60 £1.50 £1.50 (£23.30) Trio £13.70 OWNER Elite Racing Club (CHADDLEWORTH) BRED Cheveley Park Stud Ltd 13 Rn
2m 8.6 (3.70) SF: 48/43/43/22/22/20/-/6/-/-/-/-/-
WEIGHT FOR AGE 3yo-9lb
No bid

3130
QUORTINA CHALLENGE CUP H'CAP (0-80) (3-Y.O) (Class D) £4,276.00 (£1,288.00: £624.00: £292.00)
1m 3f 135y Stalls: High GOING minus 0.31 sec per fur (GF) 3-00 (3-00)

2599⁷ **Woodcrest (76)***(88) (HCandy)* 3-9-5 WNewnes(5) (lw: 3rd st: rdn over 2f out: led ins fnl f: all out)....— 1
2849* Emily-Mou (IRE) **(69)***(81)*(Fav)*(BJMeehan)* 3-8-12 BDoyle(2) (led: rdn over 2f out: hdd ins fnl f: r.o wl)....s.h 2
2812* Courbaril **(60)***(72) (SDow)* 3-7-10 (7) ADaly(1) (lw: 2nd st: rdn over 2f out: r.o wl)....nk 3
2406* No Pattern **(76)***(84) (GLMoore)* 3-9-5 SWhitworth(4) (hdwy over 3f out: rdn over 2f out: unable qckn)....2½ 4
1948⁴ Junior Ben (IRE) **(63)***(71) (PHowling)* 3-8-6 PaulEddery(3) (4th st: rdn over 2f out: one pce) s.h 5
1194⁶ Snow Valley **(78)***(84) (LMCumani)* 3-9-7 KDarley(6) (bit bkwd: 5th st: rdn over 2f out: one pce)....1½ 6
2536⁵ Birthday Boy (IRE) **(63)***(61)*(Fav)*(RHannon)* 3-8-6 PatEddery(7) (6th st: wknd 3f out)....6 7

3/1 Birthday Boy (IRE), Emily-Mou (IRE), **4/1** WOODCREST, **13/2** Courbaril, **7/1** Snow Valley, No Pattern, **12/1** Junior Ben (IRE), CSF £15.79 TOTE £5.90: £2.60 £1.70 (£11.30) OWNER Major M. G. Wyatt (WANTAGE) BRED Dunchurch Lodge Stud Co 7 Rn
2m 32.0 (6.00) SF: 38/31/22/34/21/34/11

3131
THEALE CONDITIONS STKS (3-Y.O+) (Class C) £5,126.50 (£1,864.00: £907.00: £385.00: £167.50)
1m 2f 7y Stalls: High GOING minus 0.31 sec per fur (GF) 3-30 (3-31)

2936⁵ **Stiffelio (IRE) (100)***(105) (RHannon)* 3-8-11 MRoberts(1) (lw: chsd ldr: rdn over 4f out: led wl over 1f out: r.o wl)....— 1

1479[3] Golden Ball (IRE) **(105)***(100)*(Fav)*(MRStoute)* 4-9-2 PatEddery(5) (lw: led over 8f: edgd lft: ev ch fnl f: r.o)....½ 2
2738[8] Dahik **(104)***(106) (MajorWRHern)* 3-9-1 WCarson(2) (lw: 3rd st: rdn over 2f out: r.o)....1¼ 3
1839[22] Bernard Seven (IRE) **(90)***(95) (SPCWoods)* 3-8-13v WWoods(4) (lw: 4th st: wknd over 2f out)....6 4
Palatial Style **(92)***(79) (PJMakin)* 8-9-0 GDuffield(3) (b: bit bkwd: 5th st: a bhd)....5 5

Evens Golden Ball (IRE), **2/1** Dahik, **7/2** STIFFELIO (IRE) (5/2-4/1), **20/1** Bernard Seven (IRE), **25/1** Palatial Style, CSF £7.44 TOTE £4.50: £1.80 £1.30 (£2.60) OWNER Mr B. E. Nielsen (MARLBOROUGH) BRED D. J. and Mrs Deer 5 Rn

2m 6.6 (1.70) SF: 57/61/58/47/40
WEIGHT FOR AGE 3yo-9lb

3132 ROYAL BANK OF SCOTLAND NURSERY H'CAP (2-Y.O) (Class D)

£4,380.00 (£1,320.00: £640.00: £300.00)
5f 217y Stalls: High GOING minus 0.31 sec per fur (GF) 4-00 (4-01)

2791* **Kiss Me Again (IRE) (72)***(71) (RHannon)* 2-8-10 PatEddery(6) (a.p: led over 1f out: hrd rdn: r.o wl)....— 1
2847* Just Ice **(82)***(80) (SirMarkPrescott)* 2-9-6 GDuffield(1) (lw: led over 4f: rdn: r.o)....nk 2
2978[5] Bedside Mail **(83)***(75) (JMPEustace)* 2-9-7 RCochrane(9) (s.s: swtchd lft over 3f out: hdwy over 2f out: rdn over 1f out: unable qckn)....2½ 3
2951* Goretski (IRE) **(64)***(44) (NTinkler)* 2-8-2 ow2 KDarley(2) (a.p: rdn over 1f out: wknd fnl f)....3½ 4
2552[10] Polish Bear (IRE) **(72)***(49) (BJMeehan)* 2-8-10 BDoyle(5) (hld up: rdn over 2f out: wknd over 1f out)....2 5
2962[2] Velvet Jones **(55)***(31) (PFICole)* 2-7-7 NCarlisle(4) (prom over 3f)....nk 6
2809[2] Miss Carottene **(65)***(38) (MJRyan)* 2-8-3 AClark(7) (nvr nrr)....1¼ 7
2847[4] Martara (IRE) **(68)***(40)*(Fav)*(MRChannon)* 2-8-1 (5) PPMurphy(3) (lw: spd over 4f)....hd 8
2904[2] The Frisky Farmer **(75)***(29) (WGMTurner)* 2-8-6 (7) SO'Shea(8) (rdr lost iron s: prom 3f)....7 9
2308* All She Surveys **(71)***(20) (JAkehurst)* 2-8-9 GCarter(10) (a bhd)....1¾ 10

5/2 Martara (IRE), **9/2** KISS ME AGAIN (IRE), **5/1** Just Ice, Goretski (IRE), **11/1** Velvet Jones (8/1-12/1), The Frisky Farmer (8/1-12/1), **12/1** Bedside Mail (8/1-14/1), **16/1** All She Surveys, **25/1** Polish Bear (IRE), **33/1** Miss Carottene, CSF £25.40 CT £228.89 TOTE £4.90: £1.70 £1.90 £3.30 (£6.30) Trio £28.70 OWNER Mr Bob Lalemant (MARLBOROUGH) BRED Alain Storme 10 Rn

1m 12.8 (2.30) SF: 36/45/40/9/14/-/3/5/-/-

3133 E.B.F. BRACKNELL MAIDEN STKS (2-Y.O) (Class D) £4,406.00

(£1,328.00: £644.00: £302.00)
5f 10y Stalls: High GOING minus 0.31 sec per fur (GF) 4-30 (4-32)

Branston Jewel (IRE) *(75+)*(Fav)*(MJohnston)* 2-8-9 MRoberts(6) (w'like: scope: lw: mde all: drvn out)....— 1
2594[6] Roses In The Snow (IRE) **(92)***(75) (JWHills)* 2-8-9 RHills(2) (chsd wnr: ev ch fnl 2f: r.o wl)....hd 2
Star And Garter *(62) (GWragg)* 2-8-9 MHills(10) (s.s: hdwy over 2f out: rdn over 1f out: unable qckn)....4 3
Prima Volta *(54) (RHannon)* 2-8-9 PatEddery(3) (w'like: hld up: rdn over 2f out: one pce)....2½ 4
2412[7] Wild Humour (IRE) *(53) (WRMuir)* 2-8-9 TIves(4) (a.p: rdn over 2f out: one pce)....½ 5
2846[13] Petite Heritiere *(37) (MJRyan)* 2-8-9 AClark(5) (outpcd)....5 6
849[5] Northern Saga (IRE) *(37) (AndrewTurnell)* 2-9-0 NAdams(1) (nvr nr to chal)....1½ 7
2693[7] Sunrise Special (IRE) *(37) (GLewis)* 2-9-0 PaulEddery(7) (bhd fnl 3f)....hd 8
2483[6] Never Think Twice **(70)***(36) (KTIvory)* 2-8-7 (7) CScally(9) (b: bhd fnl 3f)....s.h 9
2982[6] Windi Imp (IRE) **(61)***(19) (BJMeehan)* 2-8-9b BDoyle(8) (prom over 3f)....4 10

4/5 BRANSTON JEWEL (IRE) (6/4-9/4), **9/4** Roses In The Snow (IRE), **11/2** Star And Garter (op 7/2), **10/1** Prima Volta (op 7/2), **25/1** Never Think Twice, **33/1** Wild Humour (IRE), **50/1** Northern Saga (IRE), Sunrise Special (IRE), Petite Heritiere, Windi Imp (IRE), CSF £3.31 TOTE £2.00: £1.20 £1.30 £2.10 (£2.30) Trio £6.10 OWNER Mr J. D. Abell (MIDDLEHAM) BRED John David Abell 10 Rn

61.3 secs (2.30) SF: 29/29/16/8/7/-/-/-/-/-

3134 ADDITIONAL APPRENTICE H'CAP (0-70) (3-Y.O+) (Class F)

£2,660.00 (£815.00: £405.00: £200.00)
5f 10y Stalls: High GOING minus 0.31 sec per fur (GF) 5-00 (5-00)

3028[7] **Anzio (IRE) (67)***(76) (BAPearce)* 4-9-11b JWilkinson(3) (b: lw: rdn & hdwy over 2f out: led ins fnl f: r.o wl)....— 1
2659[8] Patsy Grimes **(66)***(75) (LJHolt)* 5-9-2 (8) NicholaHyde(6) (hdwy over 1f out: r.o wl ins fnl f)....s.h 2

2641[5] Cork Street Girl (IRE) **(51)***(52) (BJMeehan)* 3-8-5b CScudder(2) (lw: led tl ins fnl f: unable qckn) 2½ 3
3014[2] Correspondence (CAN) **(40)***(33) (MartynMeade)* 5-7-12 BHalligan(1) (a.p: hrd rdn over 1f out: sn wknd) 2½ 4
2858[2] Ashkernazy (IRE) **(43)***(32)*(Fav)*(NEBerry)* 4-8-1 JoHunnam(10) (lw: hld up: rdn over 2f out: one pce) 1¼ 5
2850[5] Rocky Two **(52)***(39) (PHowling)* 4-8-7b(3) DebbieBiggs(4) (hld up: one pce fnl 2f) ....½ 6
3014[8] Miriam **(53)***(40) (MJFetherston-Godley)* 4-8-11 GFaulkner(5) (bhd fnl 2f) ....nk 7
3014[6] Domicksky **(58)***(44) (MRChannon)* 7-8-13 (3) JDennis(9) (lw: a bhd) ....hd 8
2793[4] The Noble Oak (IRE) **(47)***(21) (MJBolton)* 7-8-5 IonaWands(7) (lw: bhd fnl 2f) 4 9
2202[9] Riskie Things **(43)***(12) (JSMoore)* 4-8-1 RMullen(8) (a bhd) 1½ 10

5/2 Ashkernazy (IRE), **3/1** Correspondence (CAN), **9/1** Domicksky, **10/1** Miriam, Patsy Grimes (op 6/1), The Noble Oak (IRE) (7/1-11/1), **12/1** Cork Street Girl (IRE) (op 7/1), **14/1** ANZIO (IRE), Rocky Two, **25/1** Riskie Things, CSF £126.76 CT £1,558.98 TOTE £18.10: £2.60 £1.70 £2.90 (£52.30) Trio £208.00 OWNER Mr Richard Gray (LIMPSFIELD) BRED Rathduff Stud 10 Rn

61.2 secs (2.20) SF: 45/44/17/2/1/8/9/13/-/-

WEIGHT FOR AGE 3yo-4lb

T/Jkpt: £82,257.70 (0.3 Tckts); £81,099.23 to York 15/8/95. T/Plpt: £52.90 (396.42 Tckts). T/Qdpt: £11.20 (5.5 Tckts). AK

3053-FOLKESTONE (R-H)
Tuesday August 15th (Firm)

WEATHER: very hot WIND: slight half against

3135

PAT MARSH LAUGHTERNOON (S) STKS (2-Y.O) (Class G) £2,243.00 (£618.00: £293.00)
6f 189y Stalls: Low GOING minus 0.41 sec per fur (F) 2-20 (2-21)

2965[3] **Pinocchio Boy (IRE) (56)** *(BJMeehan)* 2-8-11 MTebbutt(2) (2nd st: led over 2f out: drvn out) ....— 1
2683[5] Anna Settic (Fav)*(DrJDScargill)* 2-8-6 MRimmer(4) (4th st: hrd rdn & chsd wnr over 1f out: r.o) ....½ 2
2965[4] Ivory's Grab Hire **(63)** *(KTIvory)* 2-8-4 (7) CScally(5) (b: mod 5th st: hdwy over 1f out: r.o one pce) 2 3
Deedeejay *(JMBradley)* 2-8-5 (5)ow4 RHavlin(8) (neat: bit bkwd: led over 4f: wknd over 1f out) 5 4
2908[8] The Kastarbids (IRE) **(53)** *(DMorris)* 2-8-11v DHarrison(1) (3rd st: wknd over 1f out) 1 5
2962[4] Bobsworthatcaspers **(53)** *(GLewis)* 2-8-6 (5) AWhelan(7) (lw: a bhd) 4 6
2496[7] Plausilium **(50)** *(WGMTurner)* 2-8-4b(7) ADaly(3) (stumbled over 5f out: mod 6th st: a bhd) 4 7

11/10 Anna Settic, **7/2** Ivory's Grab Hire (op 2/1), **6/1** PINOCCHIO BOY (IRE) (op 3/1), **13/2** Bobsworthatcaspers (op 4/1), **9/1** The Kastarbids (IRE) (5/1-10/1), **20/1** Plausilium, **25/1** Deedeejay, CSF £12.89 TOTE £6.10: £3.10 £1.30 (£7.10) OWNER Mr K. C. Gomm (UPPER LAMBOURN) BRED Owen Bourke 7 Rn

1m 26.4 (4.80) SF: 5/-/-/-/-/-/-

No bid.

3136

LE SHUTTLE MAIDEN STKS (2-Y.O F) (Class D) £3,915.00 (£1,170.00: £560.00: £255.00)
6f 189y Stalls: Low GOING minus 0.41 sec per fur (F) 2-50 (2-51)

Expensive Taste *(76+)*(Fav)*(MRStoute)* 2-8-11 DHarrison(7) (leggy: unf: 4th st: rdn over 2f out: led ins fnl f: r.o wl) ....— 1
Smile Forever (USA) *(75) (PFICole)* 2-8-11 GCarter(1) (w'like: bit bkwd: chsd ldr: rdn over 1f out: ev ch ins fnl f: r.o) ....½ 2
2351[10] Primrose Path *(71) (CEBrittain)* 2-8-11 WWoods(6) (led: rdn over 1f out: hdd ins fnl f: unable qckn) 1¾ 3
2534[3] Lilli Claire *(64) (AGFoster)* 2-8-11 MRimmer(5) (3rd st: rdn over 2f out: wknd over 1f out) 3 4
Mignonnette (FR) *(52) (IABalding)* 2-8-11 WRyan(4) (neat: bit bkwd: dwlt: nvr nr to chal) 5 5
2964[9] Somer Solo *(40) (PMitchell)* 2-8-11 RPerham(3) (5th st: bhd fnl 4f) 5 6
1746[6] Queen's Music (USA) *(37) (PFICole)* 2-8-11 DBiggs(2) (b.nr hind: 6th st: a bhd) 1½ 7

8/11 EXPENSIVE TASTE (op 5/4), **7/2** Mignonnette (FR) (9/4-4/1), **8/1** Primrose Path (op 7/2), **10/1** Lilli Claire (4/1-12/1), Smile Forever (USA) (op 4/1), **16/1** Queen's Music (USA), **50/1** Somer Solo, CSF £8.69 TOTE £1.60: £1.20 £4.10 (£10.80) OWNER Maktoum Al Maktoum (NEWMARKET) BRED Gainsborough Stud Management Ltd 7 Rn

1m 25.4 (3.80) SF: 16/15/11/4/-/-/-

3137

HOTEL BURSTIN H'CAP (0-70) (3-Y.O+) (Class E) £3,302.20 (£985.60: £470.80: £213.40)
1m 4f Stalls: Low GOING minus 0.41 sec per fur (F) 3-25 (3-26)

2089[7] **Pearly River (58)***(68) (DrJDScargill)* 4-9-11 MRimmer(8) (4th st: rdn over 1f out: led ins fnl f: r.o wl) — **1**
1539[12] All the Joys **(36)***(44) (CACyzer)* 4-8-3 DBiggs(5) (lw: a.p: led over 3f out tl ins fnl f: unable qckn) 1¼ **2**
2687[8] Bag of Tricks (IRE) **(51)***(59)*(Fav)*(SDow)* 5-9-4 DHarrison(4) (hdwy over 4f out: rdn over 2f out: 3rd st: one pce fnl 2f) ½ **3**
2842[5] Western Horizon (USA) **(37)***(44)*(Fav)*(CEBrittain)* 3-7-7 GBardwell(7) (lw: rdn 7f out: lost pl over 3f out: rallied over 1f out: r.o one pce) ¾ **4**
3056[9] Malingerer **(27)***(33) (DAWilson)* 4-7-8 AMackay(1) (hdwy over 2f out: 5th st: hrd rdn over 1f out: one pce) nk **5**
2781[5] Admiral's Guest (IRE) **(52)***(57) (GHarwood)* 3-8-8 AClark(3) (lw: led over 8f: 2nd st: wknd fnl f) ¾ **6**
2979[19] Sure Care **(61)***(57) (BJMeehan)* 4-9-7 (7) DaneO'Neill(6) (lw: a bhd) 7 **7**
2863[4] Cracking Prospect **(38)***(26) (BRMillman)* 4-8-5 JWilliams(2) (chsd wnr 8f out to 4f out: sn wknd: 6th st) 6 **8**

7/2 Western Horizon (USA) (5/2-4/1), Bag of Tricks (IRE), **4/1** Cracking Prospect, **5/1** Sure Care, **7/1** Admiral's Guest (IRE) (op 9/2), **8/1** All the Joys (op 5/1), **14/1** Malingerer, **16/1** PEARLY RIVER, CSF £120.56 CT £502.18 TOTE £33.90: £3.90 £2.20 £1.40 (£90.60) OWNER Manor Farm Packers Ltd (NEWMARKET) BRED Newgate Stud Co 8 Rn 2m 38.1 (6.90) SF: 31/7/22/-/-/9/20/-
WEIGHT FOR AGE 3yo-11lb

3138

KENT TODAY MEDIAN AUCTION MAIDEN STKS (3 & 4-Y.O) (Class F) £2,720.60 (£751.60: £357.80)
6f Stalls: Low GOING minus 0.61 sec per fur (F) 4-00 (4-01)

232[2] **Always Grace (57)***(80) (MissGayKelleway)* 3-8-7 (7)ow5 DaneO'Neill(6) (mde virtually all: rdn out) — **1**
3103[4] Dancing Sioux **(68)***(80) (RGuest)* 3-9-0 LCharnock(5) (hld up: ev ch over 1f out: unable qckn ins fnl f) 1¾ **2**
2949[5] Prudent Princess *(70)*(Fav)*(AHide)* 3-8-9 MTebbutt(2) (hld up: ev ch 2f out: one pce) 2 **3**
2844[6] Fiery Footsteps **(48)***(59) (PHowling)* 3-8-9b WNewnes(1) (a.p: ev ch 2f out: sn wknd) 4 **4**
Jeux Interdits *(61) (PaulSmith)* 3-9-0v GCarter(4) (w'like: swtg: bhd fnl 3f) 1¼ **5**
2844[2] Another Batchworth **(54)** *(SMellor)* 3-8-2 (7) ADaly(3) (Withdrawn not under Starter's orders: injured in saddling box) **W**

, **8/13** Prudent Princess, **7/2** ALWAYS GRACE (5/2-4/1), **5/1** Dancing Sioux (op 3/1), **12/1** Fiery Footsteps (op 5/1), Jeux Interdits (6/1-14/1), CSF £18.71 TOTE £3.80: £1.70 £2.60 (£7.30) OWNER Easy Going Partnership (WHITCOMBE) BRED Zetland Stud 5 Rn
1m 13.1 (1.40) SF: 29/29/19/8/10/-

3139

KENTISH EXPRESS LIMITED STKS (0-50) (3-Y.O+) (Class F) £2,519.00 (£694.00: £329.00)
6f Stalls: Low GOING minus 0.61 sec per fur (F) 4-30 (4-32)

3057[4] **Sharp Imp (42)***(56) (RMFlower)* 5-9-3b DBiggs(2) (a.p: led over 3f out: all out) — **1**
2578[11] Spectacle Jim **(50)***(53) (JO'Donoghue)* 6-8-11b(3) DRMcCabe(4) (rdn over 2f out: hdwy over 1f out: r.o wl ins fnl f) s.h **2**
3055[3] Waders Dream (IRE) **(43)***(53) (PatMitchell)* 6-9-0v AClark(1) (rdn 4f out: hdwy over 1f out: r.o wl ins fnl f) s.h **3**
3055[4] Mister Raider **(49)***(47) (SMellor)* 3-8-2b(7) ADaly(3) (lw: a.p: ev ch over 1f out: one pce) 2 **4**
3055[12] Half Tone **(47)***(42) (RMFlower)* 3-8-9b MRimmer(8) (lw: hld up: rdn over 2f out: one pce) 2 **5**
3028[3] Norling (IRE) **(47)***(42)*(Fav)*(KOCunningham-Brown)* 5-9-0 LCharnock(10) (lw: a.p: rdn over 2f out: wknd fnl f) s.h **6**
2714[5] Our Shadee (USA) **(45)***(43) (KTIvory)* 5-8-10v(7) CScally(5) (lw: nvr nrr) ¾ **7**
2698[11] Asterix **(50)***(42) (JMBradley)* 7-8-10v(7) RWaterfield(11) (nvr nrr) ½ **8**
2641[7] Ain'tlifelikethat **(36)***(37) (TJNaughton)* 8-8-9b(5) JDSmith(7) (b: s.s: nvr nrr) ½ **9**
3079[13] Distant Dynasty **(46)***(33) (BAPearce)* 5-8-7 (7) JWilkinson(6) (bhd fnl 2f) 1¾ **10**
3134[9] The Noble Oak (IRE) **(47)***(31) (MJBolton)* 7-8-7 (7) GMitchell(12) (lw: a.p: rdn 3f out: wknd fnl f) ¾ **11**
2659[13] Raisa Point **(45)***(18) (WRMuir)* 4-8-9 RPerham(9) (bhd fnl 2f) 3 **12**
2318[12] Cedar Girl **(45)** *(RJHodges)* 3-7-11 (7) AmandaSanders(13) (lw: led over 2f: wknd over 2f out) 12 **13**

11/4 Norling (IRE), **5/1** SHARP IMP, **11/2** Mister Raider (4/1-6/1), **13/2** Waders Dream (IRE) (3/1-7/1), **9/1** Spectacle Jim, **10/1** Half Tone, **12/1** Asterix (op 8/1), **14/1** Our Shadee (USA) (10/1-16/1), Cedar Girl, **16/1** Ain'tlifelikethat, The Noble Oak (IRE), Raisa Point, Distant Dynasty, CSF £51.43 TOTE £5.60: £2.30 £3.20 £2.70 (£28.80) Trio £78.40 OWNER Mrs G. M. Temmerman (JEVINGTON) BRED James Wigan 13 Rn 1m 12.6 (0.90) SF: 38/35/35/24/19/24/25/24/19/15/13/-/-

WEIGHT FOR AGE 3yo-5lb

3140 BBC RADIO KENT UNBRIDLED AND UNRIVALLED APPRENTICE H'CAP (0-70) (3-Y.O) (Class F) £2,581.50 (£734.00: £364.50)

2m 93y Stalls: Low GOING minus 0.41 sec per fur (F) 5-00 (5-00)

2812² **Harding Brown (USA) (51)***(61) (GHarwood)* 3-8-0v(3) GayeHarwood(5) (mde all: qcknd over 1f out: r.o wl)......— 1
2481* Zuiena (USA) **(66)***(74) (PFICole)* 3-8-10b(8) DavidO'Neill(1) (lw: 4th st: hrd drvn over 1f out: r.o one pce)......2½ 2
2969³ Harry Welsh (IRE) **(65)***(70) (KMcAuliffe)* 3-9-0v(3) SMcCarthy(4) (lw: chsd wnr: rdn over 1f out: one pce)......3 3
2907⁵ Carnbrea Belle (IRE) **(69)***(72)*(Fav)*(MBell)* 3-9-4 (3) GFaulkner(3) (lw: hdwy 5f out: 3rd st: rdn over 1f out: sn wknd)......1½ 4
2976⁵ Endless Fantasy **(45)***(41) (CACyzer)* 3-7-11 RMullen(6) (a bhd)......7 5
2845⁶ Vanola **(46)***(37) (PHowling)* 3-7-9 (3) DebbieBiggs(2) (bhd fnl 4f)......6 6

11/8 Carnbrea Belle (IRE), **11/4** Zuiena (USA) (2/1-3/1), **4/1** HARDING BROWN (USA), **9/2** Harry Welsh (IRE) (op 3/1), **12/1** Endless Fantasy (op 7/1), **33/1** Vanola, CSF £15.12 TOTE £5.80: £2.20 £2.30 (£5.60) OWNER Mr Seymour Cohn (PULBOROUGH) BRED Patricia Elia and Christopher Elia 6 Rn 3m 37.1 (6.10) SF: 28/41/37/39/8/4

STEWARDS' ENQUIRY O'Neil susp. 24-27/8/95 (improper riding).
T/Plpt: £198.00 (61.56 Tckts). T/Qdpt: £14.10 (8.8 Tckts). AK

2453-YORK (L-H)
Tuesday August 15th (Good to firm)

WEATHER: sunny & hot WIND: fresh half against

3141 DEPLOY ACOMB CONDITIONS STKS (2-Y.O) (Class B) £13,140.00 (£4,860.00: £2,330.00: £950.00: £375.00: £145.00)

6f 214y Stalls: High GOING minus 0.31 sec per fur (GF) 2-05 (2-06)

2693² **Bijou d'Inde** *(98+) (MJohnston)* 2-8-10 DHolland(4) (mde all: styd on strly fnl 2f)......— 1
2573⁴ Hammerstein *(89) (MRStoute)* 2-8-10 MJKinane(6) (lw: a chsng wnr: drvn along over 2f out: kpt on: no imp)......3½ 2
2573* Jarah (USA) *(91)*(Fav)*(BHanbury)* 2-9-0 WCarson(3) (lw: b.off hind: chsd ldrs: drvn along & outpcd ½-wy: styd on u.p fnl 2f: nvr nr to chal)......½ 3
2690⁵ Believe Me *(63) (RHannon)* 2-8-10 PatEddery(2) (chsd ldrs: drvn along ½-wy: wknd over 2f out: eased towards fin)......9 4
2320¹² Gumair (USA) *(58) (RHannon)* 2-8-10 JReid(1) (lw: s.i.s: a outpcd & bhd)......2 5
Chelsea My Love (USA) *(29) (PAKelleway)* 2-8-5 JWeaver(5) (w'like: leggy: s.s: sn trckng ldrs: rdn & wknd 3f out: eased ins fnl f)......9 6

13/8 Jarah (USA), **11/4** BIJOU D'INDE, **4/1** Hammerstein, **8/1** Believe Me (op 5/1), **10/1** Chelsea My Love (USA), **33/1** Gumair (USA), CSF £12.42 TOTE £3.40: £2.00 £1.90 (£5.70) OWNER Mr J. S. Morrison (MIDDLEHAM) BRED Whitsbury Manor Stud 6 Rn

1m 23.53 (13.93) SF: 43/35/38/13/9/-

3142 STAKIS CASINOS MELROSE RATED STKS H'CAP (0-100) (3-Y.O) (Class B) £16,142.25 (£5,811.00: £2,780.50: £1,127.50:£438.75)

1m 5f 194y Stalls: Low GOING minus 0.31 sec per fur (GF) 2-35 (2-36)

2754* **Saleel (IRE) (88)***(96) (ACStewart)* 3-8-12 MRoberts(4) (lw: pushed along 11f out: hdwy 3f out: chal 1f out: styd on u.p to ld post)......— 1
2366* Grey Shot **(97)***(105) (IABalding)* 3-9-7 PatEddery(2) (trckd ldrs: effrt over 3f out: led over 1f out: jst ct)......s.h 2
2701² Shaft of Light **(83)***(89)*(Fav)*(LordHuntingdon)* 3-8-7 JWeaver(5) (lw: trckd ldr: effrt 4f out: led 3f out tl over 1f out: kpt on same pce ins fnl f)......1¾ 3
2575³ Great Crusader **(93)***(98) (CACyzer)* 3-9-3b KFallon(1) (dwlt: hld up: effrt over 4f out: sn outpcd: styd on appr fnl f: nvr nr to chal)......1¼ 4
2415³ Crystal Blade **(88)***(79) (IABalding)* 3-8-12 MJKinane(3) (led to 3f out: wknd 2f out: eased)......12 5

LONG HANDICAP Shaft of Light 8-6

2/1 Shaft of Light, **5/2** Grey Shot, **4/1** SALEEL (IRE), **5/1** Crystal Blade, **10/1** Great Crusader, CSF £12.88 TOTE £5.30: £2.00 £1.50 (£8.80) OWNER Sheikh Ahmed Al Maktoum (NEWMARKET) BRED Doverlodge Stud 5 Rn 2m 54.73 (1.13) SF: 65/74/58/67/48

3143

JUDDMONTE INTERNATIONAL STKS (Gp 1) (3-Y.O+) (Class A)
£161,720.00 (£59,480.00: £28,240.00: £11,200.00: £4,100.00:£1,260.00)
1m 2f 85y Stalls: Low GOING minus 0.31 sec per fur (GF) 3-10 (3-10)

2286* **Halling (USA) (120)***(130+)*(Fav)*(SbinSuroor)* 4-9-6 WRSwinburn(2) (lw: trckd ldrs: shkn up to ld over 2f out: qckmd & edgd rt: r.o v.wl) ....— 1
2689² Bahri (USA) **(120)***(125) (JLDunlop)* 3-8-11 WCarson(4) (lw: hld up: hdwy over 3f out: chsd wnr fnl 2f: kpt on wl: no imp) 3½ 2
2218a³ Annus Mirabilis (FR) **(119)***(122) (MRStoute)* 3-8-11 MJKinane(3) (lw: chsd ldrs: effrt u.p over 3f out: hung rt & sn outpcd: kpt on fnl f) 1¾ 3
2891a* Needle Gun (IRE) **(114)***(121) (CEBrittain)* 5-9-6 RCochrane(1) (lw: led early: led over 3f out tl over 2f out: kpt on same pce) ....½ 4
2286⁵ Eltish (USA) **(120)***(116) (HRACecil)* 3-8-11 PatEddery(6) (swtg: sn led: hdd over 3f out: wknd wl over 1f out) 3½ 5
1807² Ela-Aristokrati (IRE) **(105)***(115) (MRStoute)* 3-8-11 MHills(5) (hld up: effrt over 3f out: rdn & wknd over 2f out) ....nk 6

9/4 HALLING (USA), **11/4** Bahri (USA) (7/4-3/1), **100/30** Annus Mirabilis (FR), **7/2** Eltish (USA), **16/1** Needle Gun (IRE), **33/1** Ela-Aristokrati (IRE), CSF £8.34 TOTE £3.00: £1.80 £2.20 (£4.40) OWNER Godolphin (NEWMARKET) BRED Cyril Humphries 6 Rn 2m 6.42 (-1.08) SF: 88/74/71/79/65/64
WEIGHT FOR AGE 3yo-9lb

3144

GREAT VOLTIGEUR STKS (Gp 2) (3-Y.O C & G) (Class A)
£49,736.60 (£17,164.60: £8,207.30: £3,321.50)
1m 3f 195y Stalls: Low GOING minus 0.31 sec per fur (GF) 3-45 (3-46)

2595² **Pentire (120)***(129)*(Fav)*(GWragg)* 3-8-12 MHills(1) (lw: hld up: effrt over 2f out: slt ld 1f out: jst hld on) ....— 1
2286² Singspiel (IRE) **(120)***(126) (MRStoute)* 3-8-9 MJKinane(3) (trckd ldrs: led over 2f out: hrd rdn & styd on wl fnl f) ....s.h 2
2213a² Luso **(120)***(126) (CEBrittain)* 3-9-0 RCochrane(4) (led: shkn up & qcknd over 3f out: hdd over 2f out: kpt on same pce appr fnl f) 3½ 3
2444* Ihtiram (IRE) **(109)***(116) (JLDunlop)* 3-8-9 WCarson(2) (lw: dwlt: hld up: effrt on outside over 3f out: hung rt & wknd over 1f out) 4 4

4/5 PENTIRE, **5/2** Singspiel (IRE) (7/4-11/4), **5/1** Luso, **11/1** Ihtiram (IRE), CSF £3.03 TOTE £1.70 (£1.70) OWNER Mollers Racing (NEWMARKET) BRED Lord Halifax 4 Rn
2m 29.86 (2.86) SF: 52/49/49/39

3145

EAGLE LANE H'CAP (0-100) (3-Y.O+) (Class C) £14,953.75(£4,480.00: £2,152.50: £988.75) **6f** Stalls: High GOING minus 0.31 sec per fur (GF) 4-15 (4-18)

2669⁸ **Tiler (IRE) (78)***(90) (MJohnston)* 3-8-5 DHolland(16) (mde most: styd on wl fnl f) ....— 1
2823⁴ Lord Olivier (IRE) **(90)***(100) (WJarvis)* 5-9-8 JReid(7) (a chsng ldrs: nt qckn ins fnl f) ....¾ 2
2746² Bayin (USA) **(72)***(81) (MDIUsher)* 6-8-4 RStreet(11) (b: hld up & bhd: gd hdwy & swtchd rt 2f out: r.o) ....½ 3
2758² Benzoe (IRE) **(84)***(86) (MrsJRRamsden)* 5-9-2 KFallon(12) (lw: sn w ldrs: edgd rt & kpt on same pce appr fnl f) 2½ 4
2764¹⁰ Silent Expression **(80)***(81) (BJMeehan)* 5-8-12 MJKinane(20) (prom: rdn & outpcd over 2f out: swtchd lft: styd on fnl f) ....½ 5
2803⁷ Lennox Lewis **(97)***(96) (APJarvis)* 3-9-7 (3) JTate(13) (w ldrs tl wknd over 1f out: sltly hmpd ins fnl f) ....¾ 6
3065² How's Yer Father **(83)***(81) (RJHodges)* 9-8-10 (5) DGriffiths(3) (swtchd lft & hdwy over 1f out: r.o towards fin) ....hd 7
1639⁷ Loveyoumillions (IRE) **(94)***(91) (MJohnston)* 3-9-7b JWeaver(19) (lw: chsd ldrs: wnt rt & outpcd over 2f out: styd on fnl f) ....½ 8
2823* Rock Symphony **(91)***(86) (WJHaggas)* 5-9-9 MHills(1) (lw: s.i.s: bhd tl sme hdwy fnl 2f) ....¾ 9
2369⁴ Madly Sharp **(94)***(88) (JWWatts)* 4-9-12 PatEddery(8) (lw: hld up: effrt over 2f out: nvr nr ldrs) ....nk 10
2935⁶ Castlerea Lad **(85)***(79) (RHollinshead)* 6-9-3 WRSwinburn(4) (trckd ldrs: effrt over 2f out: wknd over 1f out) ....nk 11
2764⁵ Sir Joey (USA) **(87)***(79) (PGMurphy)* 6-9-2 (3) SDrowne(6) (hld up: sme hdwy over 1f out: styd on towards fin) ....½ 12
2935⁵ Rich Glow **(64)***(55) (NBycroft)* 4-7-10 WCarson(2) (in tch far side over 3f) ....nk 13

2877* The Happy Fox (IRE) **(79)***(69) (BAMcMahon)* 3-8-6b JFortune(17) (lw: chsd ldrs: rdn ½-wy: sn wknd) .... ½ **14**
2764[23] Master Planner **(96)***(85) (CACyzer)* 6-9-9 (5) CTeague(18) (lw: in tch: wkng whn hmpd on ins over 2f out) .... ½ **15**
2930[9] Craigie Boy **(61)***(47) (NBycroft)* 5-7-7b JLowe(9) (s.i.s: a in rr) 1 **16**
2624* Rossini Blue **(72)***(56) (MrsJRRamsden)* 4-8-4 MRoberts(15) (sn chsng ldrs: wknd over 2f out) .... ¾ **17**
2613[11] Be Warned **(74)***(56) (NACallaghan)* 4-8-6b PaulEddery(14) (sn bhd) .... ¾ **18**
2823[2] Croft Pool **(83)***(64) (JAGlover)* 4-9-1 PRobinson(5) (stumbled s: bhd: wnt lft 2f out:n.d) .... ½ **19**
2909* Al Wujud (IRE) **(72)** (Fav)*(TDyer)* 4-8-4 JQuinn(10) (swtg: s.i.s: sn prom: p.u lame over 1f out). **P**

LONG HANDICAP Craigie Boy 7-3

11/2 Al Wujud (IRE), **10/1** Lord Olivier (IRE), Rossini Blue, Madly Sharp, **11/1** Sir Joey (USA), Castlerea Lad, **12/1** Rock Symphony, Silent Expression, **14/1** Croft Pool, How's Yer Father, Rich Glow, Benzoe (IRE), Be Warned, **16/1** Master Planner, The Happy Fox (IRE), **20/1** Loveyoumillions (IRE), Bayin (USA), TILER (IRE), **25/1** Lennox Lewis, **50/1** Craigie Boy, CSF £206.36 CT £3,704.84 TOTE £22.10: £4.20 £2.80 £8.10 £3.10 (£163.70) Trio £4,676.20 OWNER Mrs C. Robinson (MIDDLEHAM) BRED J. Mamakos 20 Rn

1m 11.17 (1.57) SF: 41/56/37/42/37/47/37/42/42/44/35/35/11/20/41/3/12/12/20/-

WEIGHT FOR AGE 3yo-5lb

3146 LONSDALE STKS (Listed) (3-Y.O+) (Class A) £12,444.00

(£4,596.00: £2,198.00: £890.00: £345.00: £127.00)
1m 7f 195y Stalls: Low GOING minus 0.31 sec per fur (GF) 4-45 (4-45)

2702[2] **Double Eclipse (IRE) (115)***(115)*(Fav)*(MJohnston)* 3-8-0 TWilliams(5) (trckd ldr: led over 6f out: styd on strly u.p fnl 3f) .... — **1**
2702[7] Cuff Link (IRE) **(107)***(112) (MajorWRHern)* 5-9-0 PaulEddery(1) (chsd ldrs: rdn & outpcd over 3f out: hung rt: hdwy to chse wnr fnl f: no imp) 2 **2**
2098[5] Always Aloof (USA) **(88)***(111) (MRStoute)* 4-9-0 WRSwinburn(6) (hld up: effrt over 3f out: sn outpcd: swtchd ins & styd on appr fnl f) 1 **3**
2702[3] Khamaseen **(111)***(115) (JLDunlop)* 4-9-5 JReid(2) (trckd ldrs: plld hrd: chsd wnr 4f out: one pce appr fnl f) .... ¾ **4**
1869[5] Old Rouvel (USA) **(98)***(95) (DJGMurraySmith)* 4-9-0 JWeaver(3) (hld up: effrt & rn wd ent st: sn lost pl: eased towards fin) 15 **5**
2360* Edbaysaan (IRE) **(107)***(80) (RAkehurst)* 5-9-0 PatEddery(4) (led tl over 6f out: sn drvn along: lost pl over 3f out: eased fnl 2f) 15 **6**

10/11 DOUBLE ECLIPSE (IRE) (4/5-Evens), **4/1** Edbaysaan (IRE), **11/2** Khamaseen, **15/2** Cuff Link (IRE), **12/1** Old Rouvel (USA), Always Aloof (USA), CSF £7.93 TOTE £1.90: £1.40 £1.90 (£5.70) OWNER The Middleham Partnership (MIDDLEHAM) BRED Dene Investments N V in Ireland 6 Rn

3m 22.78 (2.78) SF: 47/59/58/62/42/27

WEIGHT FOR AGE 3yo-15lb

3147 EGLINTON NURSERY H'CAP (2-Y.O) (Class C) £12,135.00

(£3,630.00: £1,740.00: £795.00)
6f 214y Stalls: High GOING minus 0.31 sec per fur (GF) 5-15 (5-16)

2779[11] **Evening Chime (USA) (77)***(79) (MrsJRRamsden)* 2-8-3 KFallon(10) (lw: mde most: clr over 1f out: edgd rt: kpt on wl) .... — **1**
2608[3] Tabriz **(70)***(68) (JDBethell)* 2-7-10 ow1 WCarson(13) (a chsng ldrs: kpt on u.p fnl f) 1¼ **2**
2833* Dankeston (USA) **(89)***(85) (MBell)* 2-9-1v MFenton(6) (trckd ldrs: nt qckn appr fnl f) 1¼ **3**
3003[6] Roman Gold (IRE) **(73)***(69)*(Fav)*(RHannon)* 2-7-13 MRoberts(11) (lw: in tch: sn drvn along: outpcd ½-wy: hdwy over 1f out: styd on towards fin) .... hd **4**
2765[4] Kilvine **(95)***(88) (LMCumani)* 2-9-7 MJKinane(9) (lw: chsd ldrs: rdn over 2f out: edgd lft: nvr able chal) 1½ **5**
3049[2] Soul of Honour (FR) **(67)***(56) (MrsJRRamsden)* 2-7-7 JLowe(7) (bmpd s: bhd: hdwy on ins ½-wy: styd on fnl f) 1½ **6**
2765[2] Urgent Swift **(72)***(59) (APJarvis)* 2-7-5 (7) CAdamson(4) (lw: in tch: outpcd ½-wy: kpt on fnl f) ..1 **7**
2765[7] Amaretto Bay (IRE) **(88)***(75) (BJMeehan)* 2-9-0 WRSwinburn(14) (hld up: effrt over 2f out: nvr rchd ldrs) .... hd **8**
*2380** Kingfisher Brave **(72)***(58) (SGNorton)* 2-7-12 TWilliams(12) (sn drvn along: outpcd: hrd rdn & lost pl ½-wy: hmpd over 2f out: kpt on appr fnl f) .... ½ **9**
2161* Too Hasty **(85)***(68) (MHEasterby)* 2-8-11 MBirch(15) (lw: hdwy on outside ½-wy: edgd lft: n.d)1 **10**
2757[3] Oriel Lad **(77)***(59) (PDEvans)* 2-8-3 GHind(16) (effrt on outside ½-wy: n.d) .... ¾ **11**
2644* Shontaine **(82)***(62) (MJohnston)* 2-8-8 DHolland(1) (w wnr tl wknd wl over 1f out: eased) .... ½ **12**
2765[3] Opera **(80)***(56) (WJarvis)* 2-8-1 (5) MHenry(5) (swvd rt s: drvn along ½-wy: n.d) 2 **13**
2542* Gladys Althorpe (IRE) **(82)***(35) (JLEyre)* 2-8-8 PatEddery(3) (bmpd s: bhd fr ½-wy: eased)...10 **14**

1375* Amanita **(78)**_(28) (JWWatts)_ 2-8-4 JWeaver(2) (hld up & bhd: hdwy over 2f out: wandered & sn wknd)....1¼ **15**

7/1 Roman Gold (IRE), **15/2** Kilvine, Soul of Honour (FR), Amanita, **9/1** Shontaine, Opera, **10/1** Dankeston (USA), **11/1** Urgent Swift, **12/1** Tabriz, EVENING CHIME (USA), Gladys Althorpe (IRE), Too Hasty, **14/1** Kingfisher Brave, **16/1** Oriel Lad, Amaretto Bay (IRE), CSF £145.51 CT £1,385.01 TOTE £17.40: £5.20 £3.20 £3.80 (£123.90) Trio £1,137.80 OWNER Mr P. A. Leonard (THIRSK) BRED Bob Berger 15 Rn 1m 24.97 (3.47) SF: 20/9/26/10/29/-/-/16/-/9/-/3/-/-/-
T/Jkpt £10,920.60 (10.65 Tckts). T/Plpt: £131.10 (363.36 Tckts). T/Qdpt: £26.60 (27.15 Tckts). WG

2814-CARLISLE (R-H)
Wednesday August 16th (Hard)
WEATHER: sunny WIND: slight half against

3148
MILLER GENUINE DRAFT (S) STKS (3-Y.O+) (Class G) £2,367.00 (£662.00: £321.00) **1m 4f** Stalls: Low GOING minus 0.68 sec per fur (HD) 2-20 (2-20)

3017[5] **Doctor's Remedy (27)**_(57) (MrsJJordan)_ 9-8-12 (7) JoHunnam(1) (led tl hdd 5½f out: sn pushed along: kpt on wl fnl 2f to ld nr fin)....— **1**
2990* Diamond Crown (IRE) **(44)**_(62)_(Fav)_(MartynWane)_ 4-9-10 JFortune(3) (lw: hld up: hdwy on bit 2f out: shkn up to ld ins fnl f: r.o: jst ct)....hd **2**
Persiansky (IRE) **(66)**_(55) (WTKemp)_ 5-9-5 GCarter(4) (w ldr: led 5½f out tl ins fnl f: nt qckn)1½ **3**
2751[3] Risky Rose **(38)**_(22) (RHollinshead)_ 3-8-2 (7) FLynch(2) (lw: trckd ldrs: rdn over 3f out: sn btn)25 **4**

8/13 Diamond Crown (IRE), **2/1** Risky Rose, **9/1** Persiansky (IRE) (6/1-10/1), **25/1** DOCTOR'S REMEDY, CSF £40.06 TOTE £13.20 (£7.00) OWNER Mr J. O. Addison (YARM) BRED Miss R. Jeffreys 4 Rn 2m 33.1 (2.10) SF: 36/41/34/-
WEIGHT FOR AGE 3yo-10lb
No bid

3149
E.B.F. BULMERS STRONGBOW MEDIAN AUCTION MAIDEN STKS (2-Y.O) (Class F) £2,684.00 (£812.00: £396.00: £188.00)
5f Stalls: High GOING minus 0.68 sec per fur (HD) 2-50 (2-51)

3012[4] **Lady Caroline Lamb (IRE)** _(57) (MRChannon)_ 2-8-6 (3) JStack(1) (lw: trckd ldrs: led ½-wy: qcknd wl over 1f out: r.o)....— **1**
2852[2] Silver Welcome **(71)**_(56)_(Fav)_(MHEasterby)_ 2-9-0 MBirch(2) (chsd ldrs: outpcd ½-wy: styd on fnl f: nvr able chal)....1¾ **2**
3110[5] Time To Fly **(68)**_(53) (BWMurray)_ 2-9-0 JFortune(4) (led to ½-wy: rdn & one pce)....1¾ **3**
Two Timer _(28) (MJohnston)_ 2-9-0 MMcAndrew(3) (w'like: s.s: rn green & a bhd)....7 **4**

11/8 Silver Welcome (Evens-7/4), **9/4** Two Timer, **5/2** LADY CAROLINE LAMB (IRE), **5/1** Time To Fly, CSF £6.52 TOTE £2.90 (£2.50) OWNER Mr W. H. Ponsonby (UPPER LAMBOURN) BRED Tally-Ho Stud 4 Rn 61.0 secs (0.80) SF: 22/21/16/-

3150
BODDINGTONS BITTER H'CAP (0-80) (3-Y.O+) (Class D) £3,707.60 (£1,122.80: £548.40: £261.20)
5f Stalls: High GOING minus 0.68 sec per fur (HD) 3-25 (3-28)

3051[4] **Here Comes a Star (69)**_(79) (JMCarr)_ 7-9-8 ACulhane(3) (in tch: qcknd to ld ins fnl f: r.o)....— **1**
2858* Royal Dome (IRE) **(61)**_(70) (MartynWane)_ 3-8-11 JFortune(2) (lw: chsd ldrs: led appr fnl f: sn hdd: r.o)....nk **2**
2837[7] Dominelle **(51)**_(54) (MHEasterby)_ 3-8-1 SMaloney(5) (lw: a chsng ldrs: kpt on fnl f)....2 **3**
2997* Serious Hurry **(40)**_(43) (RMMcKellar)_ 7-7-0b(7) CAdamson(1) (led tl hdd appr fnl f: kpt on one pce)....s.h **4**
2992[4] Pallium (IRE) **(59)**_(54) (MrsAMNaughton)_ 7-8-12 GDuffield(4) (lw: outpcd & drvn along ½-wy: nvr trbld ldrs)....2½ **5**
2935[12] Shadow Jury **(75)**_(63) (DWChapman)_ 5-10-0b LCharnock(8) (chsd ldrs tl wknd appr fnl f)....2 **6**
2992[6] Knayton Lass **(60)**_(47) (MWEasterby)_ 4-8-6b(7) RuthCoulter(7) (a outpcd & bhd)....½ **7**
_2649*_ Pentre Ffynnon (IRE) **(75)** (Fav)_(JBerry)_ 3-9-11 GCarter(6) (withdrawn not under Starters' orders: ref to ent stalls).... **W**

3/1 Pentre Ffynnon (IRE), **100/30** Serious Hurry, **6/1** Royal Dome (IRE), HERE COMES A STAR, Pallium (IRE), **8/1** Dominelle (6/1-9/1), **10/1** Shadow Jury, **14/1** Knayton Lass, CSF £23.73 CT £111.40 TOTE £5.90: £2.90 £2.20 (£30.50) OWNER Mrs June Goodridge (MALTON) BRED A. and M. Scarfe 7 Rn 59.6 secs (0.20 under best) (-0.60) SF: 58/46/30/22/33/42/26/-
WEIGHT FOR AGE 3yo-3lb

3151
BRITVIC SOFT DRINKS H'CAP (0-70) (3-Y.O+ F & M) (Class E)
£3,066.80 (£928.40: £453.20: £215.60)
7f 214y Stalls: High GOING minus 0.68 sec per fur (HD) 4-00 (4-01)

2955* **Durham Drapes (56)***(68)*(Fav)*(MHEasterby)* 4-9-10 MBirch(4) (lw: mde all: pushed along & r.o wl fnl f)........— 1
2831³ Never so Rite (IRE) **(60)***(66)*(Fav)*(DWPArbuthnot)* 3-9-5 (3) JStack(3) (a chsng wnr: rdn & nt qckn fnl 2f)........3 2
2959³ Miss Zanzibar **(58)***(60) (RAFahey)* 3-9-6 ACulhane(2) (chsd ldrs: rdn over 3f out: r.o one pce)2 3
2815* Simand **(59)***(61) (EWeymes)* 3-9-7 JFortune(1) (lw: hld up: effrt u.p over 2f out: sn btn)........hd 4

5/2 DURHAM DRAPES, Never so Rite (IRE), **11/4** Simand, **3/1** Miss Zanzibar, CSF £8.11 TOTE £2.70 (£3.60) OWNER Durham Drapes Ltd (MALTON) BRED Mrs M. Upsdell 4 Rn
1m 39.8 (0.80) SF: 46/38/32/33
WEIGHT FOR AGE 3yo-6lb

3152
HOEGAARDEN WHEAT BEER LIMITED STKS (0-60) (3-Y.O+) (Class F)
£2,773.00 (£778.00: £379.00)
6f 206y Stalls: High GOING minus 0.68 sec per fur (HD) 4-30 (4-31)

2983² **Morocco (IRE) (52)***(71) (MRChannon)* 6-9-3 (3) JStack(2) (lw: trckd ldrs: stdy hdwy to ld appr fnl f: rdn & r.o)........— 1
2769³ Battle Colours (IRE) **(60)***(67) (DonEnricoIncisa)* 6-9-3 KimTinkler(1) (lw: a.p: rdn 2f out: r.o) ..½ 2
2813* Miss Laughter **(55)***(58) (JWHills)* 3-8-10 JFortune(5) (swtg: w ldr: rdn over 2f out: r.o one pce)3 3
2870⁶ Frans Lad **(57)***(63) (JBerry)* 3-9-1b GCarter(3) (mde most tl hdd appr fnl f: sn btn)........s.h 4
2770⁴ Opera Fan (IRE) **(54)***(59)*(Fav)*(SirMarkPrescott)* 3-8-12 GDuffield(4) (lw: bhd & outpcd over 3f out: no imp)........½ 5

13/8 Opera Fan (IRE), **7/4** Miss Laughter, **5/1** MOROCCO (IRE), **7/1** Frans Lad, **8/1** Battle Colours (IRE) (6/1-9/1), CSF £33.85 TOTE £4.90: £2.00 £3.30 (£14.70) OWNER Mr Martin Myers (UPPER LAMBOURN) BRED Nikita Investments 5 Rn 1m 26.5 (0.80) SF: 41/37/23/28/24
WEIGHT FOR AGE 3yo-5lb

3153
HEINEKEN LAGER MAIDEN H'CAP (0-60) (3-Y.O+) (Class F)
£2,689.00 (£754.00: £367.00)
1m 6f 32y Stalls: Low GOING minus 0.68 sec per fur (HD) 5-00 (5-00)

2312⁴ **Punch (51)***(62) (NTinkler)* 3-9-10b GCarter(6) (lw: trckd ldrs: led 2f out: drvn out)........— 1
3052⁴ Don't Cry **(21)***(30) (DonEnricoIncisa)* 7-8-6 KimTinkler(1) (lw: hld up & bhd: hdwy 4f out: ev ch over 1f out: kpt on one pce)........2 2
2813⁷ I Remember it Well (IRE) **(42)***(50) (SirMarkPrescott)* 3-9-1 GDuffield(3) (chsd ldrs: led over 3f out tl hdd 2f out: kpt on one pce)........½ 3
2990³ Remontant (IRE) **(38)***(43)*(Fav)*(RHollinshead)* 3-8-8 (3) AGarth(2) (hdwy 6f out: disp ld over 3f out: outpcd fnl 1½f)........2½ 4
1647⁸ Leedons Park **(38)***(26) (MWEasterby)* 3-8-11 LCharnock(4) (hdwy 5f out: wknd 3f out) 15 5
1607⁹ Black Ice Boy (IRE) **(35)***(23) (RBastiman)* 4-9-1b(5) HBastiman(5) (led tl hdd over 3f out: sn btn)........½ 6

7/4 Remontant (IRE), **11/4** I Remember it Well (IRE), **4/1** PUNCH, **9/2** Don't Cry, **10/1** Black Ice Boy (IRE), **11/1** Leedons Park, CSF £21.06 TOTE £4.50: £2.00 £3.30 (£5.80) OWNER Mrs D. Wright (MALTON) BRED Hillwood Stud 6 Rn 3m 6.7 (6.70) SF: 19/-/7/-/-/-
WEIGHT FOR AGE 3yo-12lb

T/Plpt: £6,510.70 (0.35 Tckts); £8,798.30 to York 17/8/95. T/Qdpt: £83.40 (0.1 Tckts); £101.52 to York 17/8/95. AA

3104-KEMPTON (R-H)
Wednesday August 16th (Good to firm)
WEATHER: very hot WIND: almost nil

3154
FORESTER APPRENTICE H'CAP (0-70) (3-Y.O) (Class E) £3,452.50 (£1,045.00: £510.00: £242.50)
1m 2f (Jubilee) Stalls: High GOING minus 0.37 sec per fur (F) 5-35 (5-35)

2804⁴ **Wet Patch (IRE) (57)***(72) (RHannon)* 3-9-2 MarkDenaro(4) (lw: hdwy 2f out: led 1f out: r.o wl)........— 1
2922⁸ Music Maker **(56)***(68) (SirMarkPrescott)* 3-9-1 VHalliday(9) (3rd st: ev ch over 1f out: unable qckn)........2 2

*1952*5 Mega Tid **(41)***(48) (BAPearce)* 3-7-9 (5)ow4 JWilkinson(5) (4th st: rdn over 2f out: r.o ins fnl f)..½ 3
3006 2 Soviet Bride (IRE) **(62)***(71)*(Fav)*(SDow)* 3-9-7 ADaly(2) (b.nr hind: chsd ldr: led over 1f out: sn hdd: one pce)....1½ 4
2682 2 Negative Equity **(47)***(52) (KRBurke)* 3-8-6v DGibbs(3) (lw: led over 8f)....2 5
*2600*4 Memory's Music **(51)***(52) (IABalding)* 3-8-5 (5) CScudder(6) (lw: hdwy over 3f out: 5th st: wknd 2f out)....3 6
2980* Hadabet **(65)***(62) (MissJacquelineDoyle)* 3-9-10 5x DaneO'Neill(7) (lw: bhd fnl 2f)....2½ 7
2319 11 Dazzler **(58)***(37) (MarkCampion)* 3-9-3 PRoberts(8) (a bhd)....11 8
*2963*3 Lilac Rain **(44)***(14) (JRArnold)* 3-8-3 ow3 RHavlin(1) (hdwy over 3f out: 6th st: wknd 2f out)....4 9

5/2 Soviet Bride (IRE), **7/2** Hadabet, **5/1** Negative Equity, **13/2** WET PATCH (IRE), **10/1** Music Maker (8/1-12/1), **12/1** Mega Tid (op 8/1), Memory's Music (8/1-14/1), **16/1** Lilac Rain, **25/1** Dazzler, CSF £60.23 CT £684.72 TOTE £5.40: £1.60 £2.00 £3.40 (£17.30) Trio £93.50 OWNER Mr Peter Hammond (MARLBOROUGH) BRED S. Niarchos 9 Rn
2m 5.56 (3.06) SF: 45/41/21/44/25/25/35/10/-

3155

E.B.F. CONFEDERACY MAIDEN STKS (2-Y.O) (Class D) £3,826.25 (£1,160.00: £567.50: £271.25)
7f (Jubilee) Stalls: High GOING minus 0.37 sec per fur (F) 6-05 (6-09)

2408 2 **Brilliant Red** *(90+)*(Fav)*(PFICole)* 2-9-0 TQuinn(10) (chsd ldr: led 3f out: clr over 1f out: pushed out)....— 1
2467 5 Nosey Native *(82) (JPearce)* 2-9-0 PRobinson(2) (4th st: hrd rdn over 2f out: r.o one pce) ..3½ 2
2675 5 Iberian Dancer (CAN) *(77) (JWHills)* 2-8-9 MHills(3) (3rd st: rdn over 2f out: one pce)....s.h 3
Major Dundee (IRE) *(81) (RHannon)* 2-8-7 (7) DaneO'Neill(4) (unf: scope: hdwy over 1f out: r.o)....½ 4
Time of Night (USA) *(72) (RGuest)* 2-8-9 MFenton(9) (w'like: bit bkwd: nvr nr to chal) 1½ 5
2597 3 Dancing Image *(77) (IABalding)* 2-9-0 PatEddery(8) (swtg: led 4f: 2nd st: rdn over 2f out: eased whn btn ins fnl f)....nk 6
Benatom (USA) *(65) (HRACecil)* 2-9-0 WRyan(6) (str: scope: bkwd: nvr nrr)....5 7
3025 9 Delaunay (IRE) *(58) (RHannon)* 2-9-0 RPerham(11) (a bhd)....3 8
Angel Face (USA) *(53) (EALDunlop)* 2-8-6 (3) JTate(7) (w'like: scope: s.s: hdwy over 3f out: 5th st: wknd wl over 1f out)....hd 9
2801 8 Concert Party (IRE) *(42) (JLDunlop)* 2-9-0 AMcGlone(5) (lw: 6th st: wknd over 2f out)....7 10
Easy To Remember (IRE) *(JRFanshawe)* 2-9-0 DHarrison(1) (scope: a bhd)....25 11

11/8 BRILLIANT RED, **11/4** Dancing Image (2/1-7/2), **6/1** Benatom (USA) (op 5/2), **16/1** Easy To Remember (IRE), Iberian Dancer (CAN), **20/1** Angel Face (USA), **25/1** Time of Night (USA), Major Dundee (IRE), **33/1** Concert Party (IRE), Delaunay (IRE), **50/1** Nosey Native, CSF £51.87 TOTE £2.30: £1.10 £7.70 £2.40 (£46.70) Trio £178.50 OWNER Prince Fahd Salman (WHATCOMBE) BRED Newgate Stud Co 11 Rn 1m 26.6 (2.40) SF: 39/31/26/30/21/26/14/7/2/-/-

3156

CHANNEL ONE H'CAP (0-90) (3-Y.O+) (Class C) £5,550.00(£1,680.00: £820.00: £390.00) **1m 4f** Stalls: High GOING minus 0.37 sec per fur (F) 6-35 (6-36)

2950 2 **Better Offer (IRE) (85)***(97) (GHarwood)* 3-9-10 MPerrett(1) (lw: 5th st: shkn up over 1f out: led ins fnl f: r.o wl)....— 1
2738 14 Stage Struck (IRE) **(77)***(87) (MRStoute)* 3-9-2 PatEddery(5) (3rd st: led over 1f out tl ins fnl f: unable qckn)....1½ 2
3066 2 Grand Selection (IRE) **(79)***(86)*(Fav)*(MBell)* 3-9-4 MFenton(4) (led over 10f: one pce)....2 3
2792* Quest Again **(67)***(73) (DWPArbuthnot)* 4-9-2 TQuinn(2) (lw: chsd ldr over 9f: one pce)....1¼ 4
2967 4 Haroldon (IRE) **(73)***(76) (BPalling)* 6-9-8 TSprake(8) (b: 4th st: rdn over 2f out: wknd wl over 1f out) 2 5
3030 3 Karttikeya (FR) **(75)***(77) (MrsNMacauley)* 4-9-10 PRobinson(3) (b: nvr nr to chal)....¾ 6
2845 2 Roisin Clover **(68)***(69) (SDow)* 4-9-3 WRyan(6) (6th st: wknd over 1f out) 1 7
2981 2 Carpathian **(61)***(44) (LordHuntingdon)* 4-8-10 DHarrison(7) (lw: a bhd)....13 8

2/1 Grand Selection (IRE), **7/2** Quest Again, **13/2** Roisin Clover, **7/1** Carpathian (5/1-8/1), **15/2** BETTER OFFER (IRE), Stage Struck (IRE), **10/1** Karttikeya (FR) (12/1-8/1), **16/1** Haroldon (IRE), CSF £57.11 CT £141.33 TOTE £8.50: £3.10 £2.70 £1.00 (£51.00) OWNER Mrs Wendy Sainer (PULBOROUGH) BRED John McLoughlin 8 Rn 2m 33.47 (3.27) SF: 57/47/46/43/46/47/39/14
WEIGHT FOR AGE 3yo-10lb

3157

E.B.F. WIGAN MEDIAN AUCTION MAIDEN STKS (2-Y.O) (Class F) £2,918.00 (£884.00: £432.00: £206.00)
6f Stalls: Low GOING minus 0.37 sec per fur (F) 7-05 (7-08)

2985 2 **Kirov Lady (IRE)** *(66)*(Fav)*(RHannon)* 2-8-9 PatEddery(3) (a.p: rdn over 2f out: led ins fnl f: r.o wl) ....— 1

2308[7] Time For Tea (IRE) *(61) (CACyzer)* 2-8-9 DBiggs(4) (lw: a.p: led 3f out tl ins fnl f: unable qckn) 1¾ **2**
Dragon's Back (IRE) *(56) (MrsJCecil)* 2-9-0 PaulEddery(10) (str: scope: lw: hld up: rdn over 3f out: r.o ins fnl f) 4 **3**
Lancashire Legend *(54) (SDow)* 2-9-0 WRyan(7) (w'like: bit bkwd: s.s: rdn & hdwy over 2f out: r.o) ....½ **4**
2939[3] Shaw House *(48) (DWPArbuthnot)* 2-8-9 TQuinn(11) (led 3f: wknd fnl f) ....½ **5**
2408[6] No Cliches *(50) (GLewis)* 2-9-0 SWhitworth(2) (lw: s.s: nvr nr to chal) 1 **6**
2340[6] Craven Cottage *(48) (CJames)* 2-9-0 AMcGlone(6) (prom 4f) ....¾ **7**
1913[5] Classic Artiste (USA) *(35) (SCWilliams)* 2-8-9 AMackay(12) (dwlt: nvr nrr) 3 **8**
2777[5] Cowboy Dreams (IRE) *(36) (MHTompkins)* 2-9-0 PRobinson(8) (lw: a bhd) 1½ **9**
3012[5] Hartfields Boy *(33) (BJMeehan)* 2-9-0 MTebbutt(5) (bhd fnl 2f) 1¼ **10**
Signs R Us (IRE) *(26) (DrJDScargill)* 2-9-0 MRimmer(14) (neat: spd over 4f) 2½ **11**
1774[6] Double Or Bust *(19) (RJBaker)* 2-8-9 JWilliams(13) (swtg: bhd fnl 2f) 1 **12**
Spiral Flyer (IRE) *(18) (MDIUsher)* 2-8-9 RPrice(1) (str: bhd fnl 2f) ....nk **13**

11/8 KIROV LADY (IRE), **13/2** Classic Artiste (USA), **7/1** Dragon's Back (IRE) (3/1-15/2), No Cliches (op 9/2), **10/1** Shaw House (8/1-12/1), **14/1** Lancashire Legend (8/1-16/1), Craven Cottage (8/1-16/1), **16/1** Hartfields Boy, **20/1** Cowboy Dreams (IRE), Signs R Us (IRE), **33/1** Time For Tea (IRE), Double Or Bust, Spiral Flyer (IRE), CSF £44.47 TOTE £2.40: £1.10 £7.10 £2.90 (£46.50) Trio £334.20 OWNER Mr David Seale (MARLBOROUGH) BRED David Seale 13 Rn
1m 14.38 (3.08) SF: 20/15/10/8/2/4/2/-/-/-/-/-/-

3158 PUREFOY CONDITIONS STKS (2-Y.O) (Class C) £5,249.60

(£1,966.40: £963.20: £416.00: £188.00: £96.80)
7f Stalls: High GOING minus 0.37 sec per fur (F) 7-35 (7-35)

2467* **Dublin River (USA)** *(91) (HThomsonJones)* 2-9-3 RHills(3) (lw: 2nd st: led over 1f out: rdn out) ....— **1**
2741[6] Civil Liberty *(84) (GLewis)* 2-8-11 PaulEddery(1) (rdn & hdwy over 1f out: r.o wl ins fnl f) ....nk **2**
2594[3] Myrtle **(94)***(74)*(Fav)*(RHannon)* 2-8-6 PatEddery(8) (5th st: rdn over 2f out: nt clr run over 1f out: swtchd lft: r.o ins fnl f) 2½ **3**
1871[4] La Modiste **(92)***(73) (SDow)* 2-8-6 TQuinn(7) (4th st: rdn over 2f out: unable qckn) ....½ **4**
2485* Inchrory **(85)***(83) (HRACecil)* 2-9-3 WRyan(5) (plld hrd: a.p: led over 3f out tl over 1f out: one pce) ....hd **5**
2526* Letluce *(68) (JRArnold)* 2-8-6 (3) DRMcCabe(4) (lw: nt clr run over 2f out: hdwy wl over 1f out: sn wknd) 3 **6**
*2939** Fervent Fan (IRE) *(57) (MBell)* 2-8-6 MFenton(2) (lw: 6th st: wknd over 2f out) 3½ **7**
2548[6] Soviet Sakti (IRE) *(44) (PMitchell)* 2-8-11v RPerham(6) (led over 3f: 2nd st: wknd over 2f out) 8 **8**

9/4 Myrtle, **4/1** Inchrory (op 9/4), **5/1** Letluce, **11/2** DUBLIN RIVER (USA) (op 7/2), **6/1** Civil Liberty, **7/1** La Modiste, **9/1** Fervent Fan (IRE), **50/1** Soviet Sakti (IRE), CSF £36.66 TOTE £5.70: £2.00 £3.20 £1.50 (£32.60) OWNER Mr Khalil Alsayegh (NEWMARKET) BRED C. L. Kidder and N. L. Robenalt 8 Rn
1m 27.58 (3.08) SF: 31/24/14/13/23/8/-/-

3159 CUNLIFFE H'CAP (0-70) (3-Y.O+) (Class E) £3,615.00

(£1,095.00: £535.00: £255.00)
7f (round) Stalls: High GOING minus 0.37 sec per fur (F) 8-05 (8-05)

2979* **Mullitover (67)***(83) (MJHeaton-Ellis)* 5-9-11 5x WWoods(12) (led over 1f: 2nd st: led 2f out: clr over 1f out: r.o wl) ....— **1**
2342[3] Whatever's Right (IRE) **(70)***(77) (MDIUsher)* 6-10-0 TQuinn(11) (b: 4th st: rdn over 2f out: unable qckn) 4 **2**
2051[6] Double Rush (IRE) **(51)***(55) (TGMills)* 3-8-4 RHills(3) (hdwy over 1f out: r.o ins fnl f) 1¼ **3**
3079* Quillon Rose **(46)***(49)*(Fav)*(CFWall)* 3-7-13 JLowe(10) (swtg: 7th st: rdn over 2f out: bmpd ins fnl f: one pce) ....nk **4**
2698[14] Belleminette (IRE) **(56)***(58) (DHaydnJones)* 4-9-0 AMackay(9) (s.s: hdwy over 1f out: r.o wl ins fnl f) ....½ **5**
2700[3] Bedouin Invader **(67)***(66) (MRStoute)* 3-9-6v PatEddery(6) (lw: led over 5f out to 2f out: wknd fnl f) 1½ **6**
2979[11] Soaking **(63)***(60) (PBurgoyne)* 5-9-4 (3) DRMcCabe(2) (lw: 6th st: wknd wl over 1f out) ....¾ **7**
2181[5] Keston Pond (IRE) **(67)***(63) (DAWilson)* 5-9-11 WNewnes(1) (nvr nr to chal) ....½ **8**
1967[5] Valetta **(47)***(39) (BJMeehan)* 4-8-5 DHarrison(4) (3rd st: wknd over 1f out) 1¾ **9**
2946[4] Saltis (IRE) **(57)***(42) (DWPArbuthnot)* 3-8-10 RPrice(7) (b.hind: 5th st: wknd wl over 1f out) 3 **10**
2711[9] With Intent **(56)***(32) (CJames)* 3-8-9 AMcGlone(5) (s.s: a bhd) 4 **11**
2945[5] Scorpius **(70)***(43) (CNWilliams)* 5-10-0 PRobinson(8) (b.nr fore: a bhd) 1½ **12**

5/2 Quillon Rose, **11/2** MULLITOVER, **6/1** Whatever's Right (IRE), **13/2** Soaking, **15/2** Bedouin Invader, **8/1** Keston Pond (IRE) (tchd 12/1), **16/1** Saltis (IRE), Belleminette (IRE), **33/1** Valetta, Double Rush (IRE), With Intent, Scorpius, CSF £34.71 CT £879.45 TOTE £6.40: £2.00 £2.40 £6.10 (£19.30) Trio £242.50 OWNER Mrs D. B. Mulley (WROUGHTON) BRED Mrs D. B. Mulley 12 Rn
1m 25.6 (1.10) SF: 65/59/32/26/40/43/42/45/21/19/9/25
WEIGHT FOR AGE 3yo-5lb

T/Plpt: £139.70 (99.39 Tckts). T/Qdpt: £24.30 (8.5 Tckts). AK

3141-YORK (L-H)
Wednesday August 16th (Good to firm)
WEATHER: hot & sunny WIND: fresh half bhd

3160 EAST COAST ROUS (S) STKS (2-Y.O) (Class E) £14,655.00 (£4,440.00: £2,170.00: £1,035.00)
6f Stalls: High GOING minus 0.15 sec per fur (GF) 2-05 (2-06)

3018* **No Monkey Nuts (67)***(81)*(Fav)*(JBerry)* 2-8-11 JCarroll(6) (lw: a.p: shkn up 2f out: r.o to ld wl ins fnl f)...— 1
2523⁶ White Emir **(78)***(78) (MrsJRRamsden)* 2-8-11 KFallon(11) (led: hrd rdn ent fnl f: ct nr fin)...1 2
2820³ Lucky Rabbit **(80)***(72+) (BWHills)* 2-8-11 MHills(8) (s.s: hdwy & nt clr run over 2f out: styd on wl ins fnl f)...2½ 3
2839³ Essentialselection **(76)***(62) (WJHaggas)* 2-8-11v RHills(7) (b.nr hind: hdwy u.p fnl 2f: nrst fin)...3½ 4
2838* Lussuria (IRE) **(66)***(56) (BJMeehan)* 2-8-6 BDoyle(2) (chsd ldrs: rdn along over 2f out: kpt on one pce)...½ 5
Dunmebrains (IRE) *(54) (JSMoore)* 2-8-6 JFEgan(12) (leggy: unf: chsd ldrs: rdn & outpcd over 2f out: drvn lft ins fnl f)...¾ 6
*2958*¹⁰ Blenheim Terrace *(56) (CBBBooth)* 2-8-11 DaleGibson(5) (s.i.s: rdn ½-wy: nvr nr to chal)...1¼ 7
2422² Domino Flyer **(62)***(55) (MrsASwinbank)* 2-8-11 JReid(3) (chsd ldrs: rdn along over 2f out: sn btn)...nk 8
2982² Arlington Lady **(66)***(48) (NACallaghan)* 2-8-6 MJKinane(4) (b.hind: in tch: drvn along ½-wy: sn lost pl)...¾ 9
2998² Mystic Times **(65)***(43) (MissSEHall)* 2-8-6 NConnorton(1) (b.hind: chsd ldrs: hrd rdn over 2f out: sn wknd)...1¾ 10
2706⁷ Bozeman (IRE) **(66)***(35) (RHannon)* 2-8-11 PatEddery(10) (chsd ldrs over 3f: sn lost tch: t.o)...5 11
2914⁷ Efipetite **(53)***(19) (NBycroft)* 2-8-1b(5) MHenry(9) (swtg: s.i.s: a wl bhd: t.o)...4 12

5/2 NO MONKEY NUTS, **7/2** White Emir, **13/2** Lucky Rabbit, Arlington Lady (9/2-7/1), **8/1** Lussuria (IRE), **9/1** Bozeman (IRE), **10/1** Essentialselection, **14/1** Mystic Times, **20/1** Domino Flyer, **25/1** Dunmebrains (IRE), Efipetite, **40/1** Blenheim Terrace, CSF £12.29 TOTE £2.90: £1.40 £2.00 £1.80 (£5.20) Trio £9.30 OWNER The Monkey Racing Club Ltd (COCKERHAM) BRED Miss C. Tagart 12 Rn
1m 12.62 (3.02) SF: 39/36/30/20/14/12/14/13/6/1/-/-
Bt in 18,200gns
White Emir clmd MrsBMeehan £10,000

3161 ASTON UPTHORPE YORKSHIRE OAKS STKS (Gp 1) (3-Y.O+ F & M) (Class A) £82,730.50 (£30,449.50: £14,474.75: £5,761.25: £2,130.63: £678.37)
1m 3f 195y Stalls: Low GOING minus 0.15 sec per fur (GF) 2-35 (2-40)

2563a* **Pure Grain (118)***(118)*(Fav)*(MRStoute)* 3-8-8 JReid(2) (hld up in tch: 3rd st: led over 2f out: hrd rdn & hld on wl towards fin)...— 1
2456² Magical Retreat (USA) **(100)***(118) (CACyzer)* 5-9-4 DBiggs(6) (led tl hdd over 2f out: rallied gamely u.p fnl f: no ex cl home)...hd 2
3046a* Wind in Her Hair (IRE) **(100)***(115) (JWHills)* 4-9-4 RHills(4) (lw: chsd ldrs: 5th st: hdwy over 2f out: styd on strly towards fin)...2 3
2211a⁴ Royal Ballerina (IRE) *(114) (MKauntze,Ireland)* 5-9-4 WJO'Connor(1) (swtg: hld up: 6th st: hdwy on ins 2f out: kpt on fnl f)...1¼ 4
1385⁵ La Confederation **(116)***(113) (DRLoder)* 4-9-4 MJKinane(3) (lw: hld up & bhd: 8th st: hdwy over 2f out: sn hrd rdn: nvr able chal)...hd 5

1867^{4} Dance a Dream **(116)***(113) (MRStoute)* 3-8-8 WRSwinburn(7) (sn chsng ldr: 2nd st: rdn 3f out: wknd bel dist) ....½ **6**
2272^{4} Noble Rose (IRE) **(107)***(110) (LMCumani)* 4-9-4 JWeaver(8) (hld up & bhd: 7th st: effrt on outside 3f out: nvr nr ldrs) 2 **7**
1867^{*} Phantom Gold **(109)***(101) (LordHuntingdon)* 3-8-8 PatEddery(5) (prom: 4th st: sn rdn & drppd rr: t.o) 7 **8**

11/10 PURE GRAIN (5/4-Evens), **7/1** La Confederation, Wind in Her Hair (IRE), Phantom Gold, Dance a Dream, **9/1** Noble Rose (IRE), **14/1** Royal Ballerina (IRE), **33/1** Magical Retreat (USA), CSF £29.25 TOTE £2.00: £1.10 £5.70 £1.50 (£41.50) OWNER Mr R. Barnett (NEWMARKET) BRED W. and R. Barnett Ltd 8 Rn 2m 28.68 (1.68) SF: 69/79/76/75/74/64/71/52
WEIGHT FOR AGE 3yo-10lb

3162 TOTE EBOR H'CAP (3-Y.O+) (Class B) £98,255.00 (£29,540.00: £14,270.00: £6,635.00)
1m 5f 194y Stalls: Low GOING minus 0.15 sec per fur (GF) 3-10 (3-18)

2691^{5} **Sanmartino (IRE) (91)***(104) (BWHills)* 3-7-11 WCarson(21) (hld up mid div: hdwy u.p over 3f out: hrd rdn & edgd lft: led cl home) ....— **1**
2612^{5} Midyan Blue (IRE) **(76)***(89) (JMPEustace)* 5-7-8 4x NKennedy(1) (chsd ldrs: wnt 3rd st: led 3f out tl ct nr fin) ....s.h **2**
2937^{*} Foundry Lane **(78)***(89)*(Fav)*(MrsMReveley)* 4-7-5 (5) MHenry(6) (lw: hld up: hdwy on ins over 3f out: hung rt: unable qckn fnl f) 2 **3**
2739^{4} Son of Sharp Shot (IRE) **(98)***(109) (JLDunlop)* 5-9-2 PatEddery(3) (hld up & bhd: gd hdwy 3f out: rdn & hmpd over 1f out: styd on nr fin) ....s.h **4**
2274^{2} Diaghilef (IRE) **(107)***(118) (MJohnston)* 3-8-13 DHolland(11) (lw: hld up mid div: hdwy on ins 3f out: nt clr run bel dist: swtchd ins fnl f: styd on strly) ....s.h **5**
2274^{3} Shadow Leader **(81)***(88) (DJSffrenchDavis)* 4-7-13 BDoyle(16) (chsd ldrs: chal 3f out: one pce appr fnl f) 3 **6**
2272^{5} Misbelief **(97)***(102) (JRFanshawe)* 5-9-1 DHarrison(15) (hld up & bhd: gd hdwy 3f out: n.m.r & swtchd over 1f out: r.o) 1½ **7**
2055^{*} Embracing **(89)***(92)*(Fav)*(MRStoute)* 3-7-9 JQuinn(4) (lw: chsd ldrs tl rdn & outpcd over 3f out: styd on fnl f) 1¾ **8**
3061^{*} Askern **(75)***(71) (DHaydnJones)* 4-7-7 AMackay(12) (led after 4f to 3f out: sn rdn & outpcd)....6 **9**
2907^{*} College Don **(77)***(70) (MPBielby)* 4-7-2 (7)ow2 7x MartinDwyer(8) (s.i.s: bhd tl sme late hdwy)....1 **10**
3071^{5} Star Rage (IRE) **(77)***(72) (MJohnston)* 5-7-9 7x TWilliams(13) (bhd: drvn along 6f out: n.d) ....nk **11**
2530^{8} Flight Lieutenant (USA) **(75)***(68) (RHannon)* 6-7-7 NCarlisle(7) (a in rr) 1½ **12**
1853^{14} Whitechapel (USA) **(86)***(76) (LordHuntingdon)* 7-8-4 MHills(9) (led 4f: 4th st: wknd 3f out) 3 **13**
2530^{2} Tudor Island **(75)***(65) (CEBrittain)* 6-7-7 GBardwell(14) (swtg: prom tl wknd over 3f out)........hd **14**
1853^{11} Blushing Flame (USA) **(90)***(77) (MRStoute)* 4-8-8 WRSwinburn(5) (in rr: rdn along ent st: no imp) 2½ **15**
2456^{5} Tethys (USA) **(91)***(77) (JLEyre)* 4-8-9 TIves(2) (prom: 2nd st: wknd 3f out) 1 **16**
2702^{6} Saxon Maid **(106)***(91) (LMCumani)* 4-9-10 MJKinane(20) (lw: racd wd: effrt 3f out: sn rdn: no imp) ....nk **17**
2739^{5} Wishing (USA) **(96)***(69) (RAkehurst)* 4-9-0 TQuinn(19) (lw: racd wd: chsd ldrs tl wknd over 3f out: eased: t.o) 11 **18**
2981^{4} Non Vintage (IRE) **(75)***(46) (MCChapman)* 4-7-2 (5) MBaird(17) (swtg: a bhd: t.o)....1¼ **19**
2691^{4} Burning (USA) **(98)***(69) (GHarwood)* 3-8-4 RHills(10) (chsd ldrs: 6th st: sn lost pl: eased whn btn: t.o) ....hd **20**
2421^{*} Lombardic (USA) **(93)***(61) (MrsJCecil)* 4-8-11 JReid(18) (lw: chsd ldrs: 5th st: wknd qckly over 2f out: t.o) 2½ **21**
LONG HANDICAP Flight Lieutenant (USA) 7-6 Non Vintage (IRE) 6-4 Askern 6-13 College Don 6-6

7/1 Embracing, Foundry Lane, **15/2** Burning (USA), **8/1** SANMARTINO (IRE), Son of Sharp Shot (IRE), **9/1** Wishing (USA), **10/1** Diaghilef (IRE), **12/1** Lombardic (USA), Blushing Flame (USA), **14/1** Saxon Maid, **16/1** Tudor Island, **25/1** Shadow Leader, **28/1** Star Rage (IRE), Midyan Blue (IRE), **33/1** Whitechapel (USA), College Don, Flight Lieutenant (USA), Misbelief, **50/1** Askern, Tethys (USA), **150/1** Non Vintage (IRE), CSF £195.66 CT £1,520.19 TOTE £10.30: £2.30 £7.20 £2.00 £2.20 (£363.90) Trio £1,248.90 OWNER Mr K. Abdullah (LAMBOURN) BRED Juddmonte Farms 21 Rn 2m 53.62 (0.02) SF: 71/68/68/88/85/67/81/59/50/49/51/47/55/44/56/56/70/48/25/36/40
WEIGHT FOR AGE 3yo-12lb

3163 SCOTTISH EQUITABLE GIMCRACK STKS (Gp 2) (2-Y.O C & G) (Class A) £70,143.70 (£25,346.20: £12,205.60: £5,038.00: £2,051.50)
6f Stalls: High GOING minus 0.15 sec per fur (GF) 3-45 (3-47)

1838^{*} **Royal Applause** *(104)*(Fav)*(BWHills)* 2-9-0 WRSwinburn(1) (led after 2f: hrd rdn fnl f: jst hld on) ....— **1**

2091* Tumbleweed Ridge **(95)***(101) (BJMeehan)* 2-8-11 BDoyle(2) (lw: hld up in tch: chal 1f out: rdn & r.o wl cl home) ....hd **2**
2347² Take A Left **(100)***(96) (MrsJRRamsden)* 2-8-11 KFallon(4) (hld up: hdwy & n.m.r over 1f out: kpt on same pce) 1¾ **3**
1838¹⁰ Gothenberg (IRE) **(98)***(89) (MJohnston)* 2-8-11 DHolland(3) (swtg: chsd ldrs 3f: sn rdn & outpcd: kpt on u.p fnl f) 2½ **4**
2597* Tamhid (USA) *(83) (HThomsonJones)* 2-8-11 RHills(5) (led 2f: wknd wl over 1f out) 2½ **5**

4/6 ROYAL APPLAUSE, **4/1** Take A Left, **5/1** Tamhid (USA), **8/1** Tumbleweed Ridge, **11/1** Gothenberg (IRE), CSF £6.40 TOTE £1.40: £1.20 £3.30 (£6.40) OWNER Maktoum Al Maktoum (LAMBOURN) BRED Gainsborough Stud Management Ltd 5 Rn
1m 11.42 (1.82) SF: 59/56/51/44/38

3164 MOTABILITY RATED STKS H'CAP (0-105) (3-Y.O+) (Class B)

£9,942.00 (£3,678.00: £1,764.00: £720.00: £285.00: £111.00)
1m 2f 85y Stalls: Low GOING minus 0.15 sec per fur (GF) 4-15 (4-17)

2436⁶ **Medaille Militaire (93)***(105+)*(Fav)*(JLDunlop)* 3-8-4 MJKinane(5) (chsd ldrs: 4th st: qcknd to ld ins fnl f: sn clr) ....— **1**
2596² Taufan's Melody **(99)***(107) (LadyHerries)* 4-9-4 JReid(10) (chsd ldr: 2nd st: led 2f out tl ins fnl f) 2½ **2**
2616* Restructure (IRE) **(99)***(107) (MrsJCecil)* 3-8-10 PaulEddery(4) (prom: 3rd st: effrt 2f out: kpt on same pce fnl f) ....nk **3**
2616³ Hoh Express **(97)***(105) (IABalding)* 3-8-8 WRSwinburn(1) (hld up & bhd: gd hdwy on ins over 2f out: one pce fnl f) ....s.h **4**
1306⁴ Mezaan (IRE) **(88)***(96) (MRStoute)* 3-7-13 WCarson(7) (chsd ldrs: 5th st: rdn & outpcd 3f out: styd on u.p fnl f) ....hd **5**
2596* Aljazzaf **(102)***(102) (RAkehurst)* 5-9-7 JWeaver(9) (lw: led 8f: sn rdn & wknd) 5 **6**
2672² Hunters of Brora (IRE) **(92)***(88) (JDBethell)* 5-8-11 TIves(8) (hld up & bhd: effrt on outside 3f out: n.d) 2½ **7**
2457⁹ Sherman (IRE) **(94)***(86) (HThomsonJones)* 4-8-13b RHills(2) (lw: hld up: effrt 3f out: wknd fnl 2f) 2½ **8**
1585⁶ Penny a Day (IRE) **(98)***(85) (MrsMReveley)* 5-9-3 RCochrane(6) (chsd ldrs: 6th st: sn rdn & lost pl) 3 **9**
LONG HANDICAP Mezaan (IRE) 7-12

7/2 MEDAILLE MILITAIRE, **4/1** Hunters of Brora (IRE), **6/1** Restructure (IRE), **13/2** Sherman (IRE) (10/1-6/1), **7/1** Penny a Day (IRE), **15/2** Aljazzaf, **9/1** Taufan's Melody, Mezaan (IRE), **10/1** Hoh Express (7/1-11/1), CSF £33.36 CT £171.46 TOTE £4.00: £1.80 £3.80 £2.30 (£37.90) Trio £69.30 OWNER Mr James Hartnett (ARUNDEL) BRED Fares Stables Ltd 9 Rn
2m 7.43 (-0.07) SF: 78/88/80/78/69/83/69/67/66
WEIGHT FOR AGE 3yo-8lb

3165 ROSES STKS (Listed) (2-Y.O C & G) (Class A) £10,282.50

(£3,060.00: £1,455.00: £652.50)
5f Stalls: Low GOING minus 0.15 sec per fur (GF) 4-45 (4-46)

2704² **Mubhij (IRE) (100)***(98)*(Fav)*(BWHills)* 2-8-11 WCarson(4) (mde all: hung lft fr ½-wy: drvn out)— **1**
2660* Rambling Bear *(97) (MBlanshard)* 2-8-11 StephenDavies(3) (lw: chsd wnr: rdn & outpcd appr fnl f: rallied nr fin) ....nk **2**
2978² High Priority (IRE) **(98)***(96?) (MRChannon)* 2-8-11 JReid(1) (swvd rt s: rdn along 2f out: gd hdwy fnl f: fin wl) ....nk **3**
2706* Admiral Jones (IRE) **(89)***(91) (MJohnston)* 2-9-0 TWilliams(2) (bmpd s: chsd ldrs: rdn & outpcd ½-wy: styd on fnl f) 2½ **4**

11/10 MUBHIJ (IRE), **9/4** Admiral Jones (IRE), **9/2** Rambling Bear, **10/1** High Priority (IRE), CSF £5.36 TOTE £1.70 (£3.80) OWNER Mr Hamdan Al Maktoum (LAMBOURN) BRED Shadwell Estate Company Limited 4 Rn
59.01 secs (2.01) SF: 47/46/45/40

3166 FALMOUTH H'CAP (0-100) (3-Y.O) (Class C) £11,160.00

(£3,330.00: £1,590.00: £720.00)
5f Stalls: High GOING minus 0.15 sec per fur (GF) 5-15 (5-16)

2617⁵ **Fairy Wind (IRE) (84)***(94) (NACallaghan)* 3-8-5 MJKinane(12) (b.hind: lw: chsd ldrs stands' side: led over 1f out: r.o wl) ....— **1**
2742* Crowded Avenue **(79)***(83)*(Fav)*(PJMakin)* 3-7-11 (3)ow1 SSanders(3) (a.p: rdn over 1f out: kpt on: nt rch wnr) 1½ **2**
2916* Nite-Owl Dancer **(76)***(69) (JAHarris)* 3-7-6 (5)ow4 MHenry(6) (in tch: styd on fnl 2f) 2½ **3**

2593[12] Tart and a Half **(80)***(77) (BJMeehan)* 3-8-1b BDoyle(11) (s.i.s: bhd tl hdwy over 1f out: nvr nrr)s.h **4**
2394[5] Stolen Kiss (IRE) **(72)***(67) (MWEasterby)* 3-7-7b GBardwell(4) (lw: chsd ldr: chal over 1f out: wknd ins fnl f) .... ¾ **5**
2697* Tedburrow **(85)***(78) (MrsAMNaughton)* 3-8-6 JWeaver(9) (chsd ldrs: effrt 2f out: kpt on: nt pce to chal) .... ½ **6**
2237[5] Lago Di Varano **(100)***(91) (JBerry)* 3-9-7b JCarroll(2) (dwlt: sn chsng ldrs: rdn & wknd over 1f out) .... ¾ **7**
2120[7] Karina Heights (USA) **(79)***(68) (JWWatts)* 3-8-0v WCarson(1) (swvd lft s: racd alone: led over 3f) .... ½ **8**
Silk Cottage **(72)***(57) (RMWhitaker)* 3-7-4 (3) NVarley(10) (bit bkwd: chsd ldrs: rdn & hung lft ½-wy: sn wknd) 1¼ **9**
3027[6] Shamanic **(95)***(76) (RHannon)* 3-9-2 JReid(5) (sn bhd & pushed along: no imp) 1¼ **10**
2697[4] Super Park **(82)***(58) (MHEasterby)* 3-8-3 JQuinn(8) (hld up: a bhd) 1½ **11**
1602* Premium Gift **(74)***(39) (CBBBooth)* 3-7-9 ow2 DaleGibson(7) (lw: s.i.s: a bhd) 3 **12**
LONG HANDICAP Silk Cottage 7-1 Nite-Owl Dancer 6-8 Premium Gift 6-13

3/1 Crowded Avenue, **100/30** Tedburrow, **13/2** FAIRY WIND (IRE), **10/1** Lago Di Varano, Karina Heights (USA), Shamanic, **11/1** Stolen Kiss (IRE), **12/1** Super Park, Premium Gift (op 20/1), **14/1** Tart and a Half, **20/1** Nite-Owl Dancer, **33/1** Silk Cottage, CSF £26.38 CT £353.36 TOTE £7.50: £2.20 £1.90 £3.90 (£16.30) Trio £145.30 OWNER Mr N. A. Callaghan (NEWMARKET) BRED Ron Con Ltd 12 Rn 57.73 secs (0.73) SF: 64/53/39/47/37/48/61/38/27/46/28/9
T/Jkpt: £405.30 (35.03 Tckts). T/Plpt: £18.90 (3,028.35 Tckts). T/Qdpt: £16.30 (67.7 Tckts). IM

2926-AYR (L-H)
Thursday August 17th (Firm)

5th race: hand start
WEATHER: sunny & warm WIND: almost nil

3167 BURNS MEDIAN AUCTION MAIDEN STKS (3-Y.O) (Class E) £2,944.00 (£892.00: £436.00: £208.00)
7f Stalls: Low GOING minus 0.22 sec per fur (GF) 6-00 (6-02)

2593[11] **Highspeed (IRE)** *(57) (SEKettlewell)* 3-8-11 (3) JStack(1) (hld up: hdwy ent st: led 1½f out: hung lft: r.o) .... — **1**
2999[8] Achill Princess **(39)***(50) (WTKemp)* 3-8-9 KFallon(2) (lw: hld up: smooth hdwy ent st: effrt 2f out: swtchd lft over 1f out: r.o u.p) .... ¾ **2**
2927[2] Boost **(44)***(53)*(Fav)*(CWThornton)* 3-9-0 JFortune(3) (lw: trckd ldrs: led 3f out: sn rdn: hdd 1½f out: hung rt & nt qckn) 1 **3**
2164[4] Ballindalloch *(27) (TJEtherington)* 3-8-9 JLowe(6) (unruly s: effrt ent st: rdn & btn 2f out) 9 **4**
2357[7] Rambo's Rumtime *(24) (FWatson)* 3-8-9 TWilliams(5) (led tl hdd 3f out: sn outpcd) 1½ **5**
Alex *(RAllan)* 3-8-9 SMaloney(4) (w'like: bit bkwd: prom to st: rn green: sn t.o) .... dist **6**

7/4 Boost, **9/4** HIGHSPEED (IRE), **6/1** Achill Princess, Ballindalloch (op 4/1), **33/1** Rambo's Rumtime, **50/1** Alex, CSF £12.60 TOTE £3.80: £1.60 £3.50 (£12.20) OWNER Mr David Wright (MIDDLEHAM) BRED R.McQuillan 6 Rn 1m 30.85 (6.85) SF: 2/-/-/-/-/-

3168 DICK PEACOCK NURSERY H'CAP (2-Y.O) (Class E) £3,062.50 (£925.00: £450.00: £212.50)
1m Stalls: Low GOING minus 0.22 sec per fur (GF) 6-30 (6-31)

*2381** **Carmentalia (79)***(89) (SirMarkPrescott)* 2-9-7 WWoods(5) (lw: chsd ldrs: led over 2f out: rdn & r.o) .... — **1**
2732[4] Silent Soprano **(51)***(54) (DenysSmith)* 2-7-7 JLowe(3) (lw: hld up: hdwy over 3f out: chsng wnr appr fnl f: kpt on) 3½ **2**
2750* Annaberg (IRE) **(75)***(73)*(Fav)*(MrsJRRamsden)* 2-9-3 KFallon(2) (lw: hld up: hdwy 3f out: rdn & nt qckn fnl 2f) 2½ **3**
3019[6] Silverdale Knight **(74)***(69) (KWHogg)* 2-8-13 (3) DWright(1) (lw: led tl hdd over 2f out: hrd rdn & sn btn) 1½ **4**
2765[8] Miss Offset **(64)***(39) (MJohnston)* 2-8-6b TWilliams(4) (chsd ldrs tl rdn & btn 2½f out: eased fnl f) 10 **5**
LONG HANDICAP Silent Soprano 7-4

10/11 Annaberg (IRE) (op Evens), **9/4** CARMENTALIA, **7/1** Miss Offset, **8/1** Silverdale Knight, **33/1** Silent Soprano, CSF £32.27 TOTE £2.90: £2.20 £3.10 (£23.30) OWNER Hesmonds Stud (NEWMARKET) BRED Hesmonds Stud Ltd 5 Rn 1m 42.69 (5.89) SF: 27/-/11/7/-

3169 GAYMER OLDE ENGLISH H'CAP (0-80) (3-Y.O+) (Class D) £3,675.00 (£1,110.00: £540.00: £255.00)
1m 2f Stalls: Low GOING minus 0.22 sec per fur (GF) 7-00 (7-01)

3059* **Braille (IRE) (52)***(69+)*(Fav)*(MGMeagher)* 4-7-13 (3) AGarth(5) (a.p: led 2f out: r.o wl)........— 1
2967[2] Adolescence (IRE) **(78)***(90) (KMcAuliffe)* 5-9-11 (3) JStack(6) (lw: c wd st: hdwy 3f out: nt pce of wnr fnl f)........3 2
3020[2] Kemo Sabo **(80)***(86) (MrsJRRamsden)* 3-9-8 KFallon(8) (lw: led: qcknd over 3f out: hdd 2f out: no ex)........4 3
3021[2] Larn Fort **(55)***(59) (CWFairhurst)* 5-8-5v WWoods(2) (lw: chsd ldrs: outpcd 3f out: kpt on u.p)........1¼ 4
2993[5] Rushen Raider **(60)***(63) (KWHogg)* 3-7-9 (7) FLynch(7) (cl up tl outpcd & hmpd over 2f out: styd on towards fin)........¾ 5
2930[7] Keep Battling **(43)***(45) (JSGoldie)* 5-7-7 JLowe(3) (hld up & bhd: stdy hdwy 3f out: effrt 2f out: no rspnse)........½ 6
2836[3] Northern Trove (USA) **(65)***(64) (GMMoore)* 3-8-7 JFortune(1) (swtg: hld up: effrt over 3f out: no rspnse)........1½ 7
2954[5] Imperial Bid (FR) **(56)***(49) (DenysSmith)* 7-8-6 TWilliams(4) (lw: hld up & bhd: hdwy on ins 3f out: rdn & btn 2f out)........4 8

LONG HANDICAP Keep Battling 7-4

5/2 BRAILLE (IRE), **4/1** Larn Fort, **5/1** Kemo Sabo, **6/1** Adolescence (IRE), **9/1** Imperial Bid (FR), **14/1** Keep Battling, Rushen Raider, **25/1** Northern Trove (USA), CSF £15.16 CT £50.12 TOTE £4.00: £1.30 £1.70 £1.30 (£28.80) OWNER The Winning Feature Partnership (ORMSKIRK) BRED John McLoughlin 8 Rn
2m 11.44 (6.84) SF: 16/37/25/6/2/-/3/-
WEIGHT FOR AGE 3yo-8lb

3170 E.B.F. KIRKOSWALD MAIDEN STKS (2-Y.O F) (Class D) £3,436.25 (£1,040.00: £507.50: £241.25)
6f Stalls: High GOING minus 0.22 sec per fur (GF) 7-30 (7-33)

2542[2] **Pharmacy (85)***(68+)*(Fav)*(JWWatts)* 2-8-11 NConnorton(6) (lw: led after 2f: sn clr: easily)...— 1
2820[5] Ancestral Jane *(52) (MrsJRRamsden)* 2-8-11 KFallon(2) (bit bkwd: bhd: hdwy 2f out: r.o: nvr plcd to chal)........6 2
Baileys First (IRE) *(51) (MJohnston)* 2-8-11 TWilliams(4) (neat: bit bkwd: chsd ldrs: drvn along ½-wy: r.o one pce)........½ 3
2580[4] She's Simply Great (IRE) *(32) (JJO'Neill)* 2-8-11 JFortune(3) (led 2f: wknd over 2f out)........7 4
Polish Saga *(29) (MDods)* 2-8-11 WWoods(5) (neat: unf: bit bkwd: chsd ldrs tl wknd over 2f out)........1¼ 5

1/2 PHARMACY, **11/4** Ancestral Jane (6/4-3/1), **6/1** Baileys First (IRE) (4/1-7/1), **25/1** Polish Saga, **40/1** She's Simply Great (IRE), CSF £2.40 TOTE £1.60: £1.20 £1.40 (£1.90) OWNER Lady Jane Kaplan (RICHMOND) BRED Stanley Estate and Stud Co 5 Rn
1m 11.57 (1.77) SF: 51/35/34/15/12

3171 DUMFRIES (S) STKS (3-Y.O+) (Class F) £2,675.00 (£750.00: £365.00)
1m 5f 13y Stalls: Low GOING minus 0.22 sec per fur (GF) 8-00 (8-00)

3052[5] **Silverdale Count (42)***(57) (KWHogg)* 3-8-1 (7) FLynch(1) (hld up: hdwy to ld 3f out: rdn & hung lft: r.o)........— 1
3001[3] Wild Rose of York **(54)***(50) (PMonteith)* 4-8-11 (3) DWright(3) (trckd ldrs: hdwy gng wl ent st: rdn over 2f out: btn whn sltly hmpd ins fnl f)........2 2
2990[2] Faugeron **(70)***(35)*(Fav)*(NTinkler)* 6-9-10b KimTinkler(2) (lw: b: s.s: sn rcvrd: led ent st: hdd 3f out: sn rdn & no rspnse)........20 3
2874[5] Sylvan Celebration **(11)***(19) (MissLAPerratt)* 4-9-0v NConnorton(4) (led tl hdd ent st:sn btn) 5 4

4/5 Faugeron, **6/4** Wild Rose of York, **6/1** SILVERDALE COUNT, **33/1** Sylvan Celebration, CSF £14.63 TOTE £13.50 (£7.90) OWNER Mr Anthony White (ISLE OF MAN) BRED Auldyn Stud Ltd 4 Rn
2m 57.01 (12.21) SF: 4/8/-/-
WEIGHT FOR AGE 3yo-11lb
No bid

3172 SUMMER EVENING H'CAP (0-70) (3-Y.O+) (Class E) £3,225.00 (£975.00: £475.00: £225.00)
7f Stalls: Low GOING minus 0.22 sec per fur (GF) 8-30 (8-32)

2832[2] **It's Academic (59)***(68)*(Fav)*(MrsJRRamsden)* 3-9-3 KFallon(8) (in tch: hdwy to ld over 1f out: hung lft: r.o u.p)........— 1

3000* Mister Westsound **(58)***(66) (MissLAPerratt)* 3-8-13b(3) 6x JStack(1) (lw: bhd: hdwy whn nt clr rn appr fnl f: swtchd & r.o strly) ....½ 2
2832 3 Bogart **(55)***(62) (CWFairhurst)* 4-9-4 WWoods(5) (bhd: hdwy on outside over 2f out: hung lft: kpt on fnl f) ....nk 3
2220 6 Ashdren **(54)***(57) (AHarrison)* 8-9-3 JFanning(4) (trckd ldrs: outpcd whn hmpd appr fnl f: nt rcvr) 2 4
3050 7 Miss Pigalle **(36)***(35) (MissLAPerratt)* 4-7-13b TWilliams(6) (lw: hld up: effrt on ins 2f out: nt pce to chal) 1¾ 5
2770 7 Persian Fayre **(66)***(62) (JBerry)* 3-9-10 JFortune(2) (lw: cl up: led 3f out tl over 1f out: sn btn) 1 6
2304 2 King of Show (IRE) **(50)***(35) (RAllan)* 4-8-13 SMaloney(7) (b: cl up tl wknd 2f out) 5 7
2872 4 Seconds Away **(30)***(4) (JSGoldie)* 4-7-7v JLowe(3) (led tl hdd 3f out: sn btn) 5 8

13/8 IT'S ACADEMIC, **9/2** Mister Westsound, Persian Fayre, **5/1** Bogart, **12/1** Ashdren, King of Show (IRE), **25/1** Miss Pigalle, Seconds Away, CSF £8.93 CT £25.59 TOTE £2.30: £1.30 £1.20 £1.70 (£5.90) OWNER Mr J. R. Chester (THIRSK) BRED W. H. F. Carson 8 Rn

1m 29.75 (5.75) SF: 16/14/15/10/-/10/-/-
WEIGHT FOR AGE 3yo-5lb
T/Plpt: £412.30 (19.42 Tckts). T/Qdpt: Not won; £74.20 to Sandown 18/8/95. AA

3023-SALISBURY (R-H)
Thursday August 17th (Good to firm, Firm patches)
6th race: hand start
WEATHER: sunny, warm WIND: almost nil

3173 WOODFORD APPRENTICE H'CAP (0-70) (3-Y.O+) (Class F) £2,613.00 (£743.00: £369.00) **1m** Stalls: Low GOING minus 0.43 sec per fur (F) 5-45 (5-50)

1940 10 **Oozlem (IRE) (39)***(49) (JCPoulton)* 6-8-0b(3)ow5 GFaulkner(1) (s.s: sn rcvrd: led over 4f out: edgd lft over 1f out: r.o wl) ....— 1
2979 5 Super Serenade **(52)***(64) (GBBalding)* 6-8-11 (5) ALakeman(7) (s.s: sn rcvrd: r.o one pce fnl f) 1½ 2
2747 6 Aldwick Colonnade **(37)***(49) (MDIUsher)* 8-8-1 AimeeCook(11) (hld up: hdwy over 2f out: r.o one pce fnl f) ....hd 3
2979 17 Chancey Fella **(58)***(67) (KTIvory)* 4-9-5v(3) CScally(6) (b: s.s: hrd rdn over 4f out: hdwy over 1f out: nvr nrr) 1½ 4
3057 10 Future Options **(53)***(62) (MSSaunders)* 4-9-0 (3) JDennis(2) (hdwy over 2f out: one pce) ....hd 5
2789 9 Mai Pen Rai **(33)***(24) (RJHodges)* 7-7-11 ow4 RWaterfield(10) (nvr trbld ldrs) 7 6
2864 4 Mighty Marston **(70)***(62) (LadyHerries)* 3-9-11 (3) JO'Dwyer(3) (prom: rdn & wknd over 2f out) 1½ 7
2807 2 I'm Outa Here (IRE) **(65)***(55)*(Fav)*(RHannon)* 3-8-13 (10) EGreehy(8) (prom tl wknd over 2f out) ....¾ 8
2981 8 The Chairman (IRE) **(50)***(12) (FJordan)* 4-9-0 AEddery(4) (w ldr over 3f: wknd over 2f out: t.o) 14 9
2976 6 Trina **(37)** *(DLWilliams)* 4-7-10 (5)ow2 RStudholme(5) (led over 3f: wknd 3f out: t.o) 3 10
2961 12 Knightrider **(48)** *(CDBroad)* 4-8-2 (10) DHarnett(9) (prom over 4f: t.o) 7 11

5/2 I'm Outa Here (IRE), **5/1** Super Serenade, **6/1** Mighty Marston, **8/1** Mai Pen Rai, Trina, **9/1** OOZLEM (IRE), **14/1** Aldwick Colonnade (op 8/1), **16/1** The Chairman (IRE), **25/1** Chancey Fella, Future Options, **33/1** Knightrider, CSF £48.29 CT £566.47 TOTE £12.20: £3.10 £1.80 £4.20 (£34.90) Trio £26.30 OWNER Brooknight Guarding Ltd (LEWES) BRED J. R. Jameson 11 Rn

1m 42.59 (3.29) SF: 21/36/21/39/34/-/28/21/-/-/-
WEIGHT FOR AGE 3yo-6lb

3174 NETHERAVON MAIDEN STKS (2-Y.O) (Class D) £4,146.00 (£1,248.00: £604.00: £282.00) **6f 212y** Stalls: Low GOING minus 0.43 sec per fur (F) 6-15 (6-18)

2573 6 **Alzanti** *(66) (PFICole)* 2-9-0 TQuinn(15) (mde all: all out) ....— 1
2912 6 Diminutive (USA) *(66) (JWHills)* 2-9-0 RCochrane(14) (a.p: ev ch ins fnl f: hrd rdn: r.o) ....s.h 2
2846 8 Paint It Black *(62) (RHannon)* 2-9-0 RHughes(3) (lw: prom: rdn over 2f out: ev ch over 1f out: nt qckn ins fnl f) 1¾ 3
Danesman (IRE) *(56) (JHMGosden)* 2-9-0 KDarley(5) (wl grwn: bit bkwd: hld up: hdwy 3f out: one pce fnl 2f) 2½ 4
Masquerade *(54) (LMCumani)* 2-9-0 RPerham(12) (str: w'like: no hdwy fnl 2f) 1 5
2441 3 Tria Kemata *(42)*(Fav)*(JLDunlop)* 2-9-0 WCarson(1) (swtg: plld hrd: chsd ldr over 5f) 5 6
Sandabar *(42+) (MRStoute)* 2-9-0 PaulEddery(6) (gd sort: nvr nr to chal) ....nk 7

Wire Act (USA) *(41) (MartynMeade)* 2-9-0 VSlattery(2) (scope: nvr nrr)....½ **8**
2453[5] Bellator *(40) (GBBalding)* 2-9-0 JWilliams(7) (n.d)....hd **9**
Idle Fancy *(33) (LordHuntingdon)* 2-8-9 DHarrison(10) (leggy: scope: a bhd)....1 **10**
3009[4] Decision Maker (IRE) *(33) (RHannon)* 2-8-7 (7) DaneO'Neill(9) (a bhd)....2 **11**
Autumn (FR) *(26) (PFICole)* 2-8-9 DBiggs(4) (leggy: prom 5f)....1¼ **12**
1343[5] Etterby Park (USA) *(24) (MDIUsher)* 2-9-0 MWigham(13) (prom over 4f)....3 **13**
1829[7] Emei Shan *(PGMurphy)* 2-8-2 (7) RWaterfield(8) (bhd fnl 3f)....8 **14**
Peggy Ess *(APJames)* 2-8-9 NAdams(11) (neat: lt-f: dwlt: a bhd: t.o)....15 **15**

13/8 Tria Kemata (5/4-2/1), **3/1** Sandabar, **5/1** Danesman (IRE), **13/2** ALZANTI, **14/1** Diminutive (USA), Masquerade, Paint It Black (op 8/1), Decision Maker (IRE), **25/1** Autumn (FR), Idle Fancy, **33/1** Bellator, Etterby Park (USA), **66/1** Wire Act (USA), Emei Shan, Peggy Ess, CSF £95.15 TOTE £7.60: £1.80 £3.30 £4.80 (£44.20) Trio £228.50 OWNER Elite Racing Club (WHATCOMBE) BRED J. Weinfeld 15 Rn 1m 27.75 (2.05) SF: 40/40/36/30/28/16/16/15/14/7/7/-/-/-/-

3175

BBC WILTSHIRE SOUND H'CAP (0-85) (3-Y.O+) (Class D) £3,944.50 (£1,186.00: £573.00: £266.50)
6f 212y Stalls: Low GOING minus 0.43 sec per fur (F) 6-45 (6-45)

2743[6] **Jolto (72)***(82) (KOCunningham-Brown)* 6-9-1 (3) DRMcCabe(4) (mde all: rdn 2f out: all out)..— **1**
3065* Great Hall **(57)***(66) (PDCundell)* 6-8-3b DHarrison(3) (bhd: rdn 3f out: gd hdwy fnl f: fin wl) ....nk **2**
2053[3] Blurred Image (IRE) **(72)***(80)*(Fav)*(MissGayKelleway)* 4-9-4 RCochrane(10) (hld up: hdwy over 2f out: nt qckn ins fnl f)....¾ **3**
2941* Anam **(78)***(86) (PTWalwyn)* 3-9-5 WCarson(1) (dwlt: hdwy 2f out: r.o ins fnl f)....s.h **4**
3011[3] Desert Time **(77)***(84) (MRChannon)* 5-9-9 RHughes(9) (hld up: hdwy & n.m.r over 1f out: r.o ins fnl f)....hd **5**
2709[2] Sylvandra **(71)***(75) (PGMurphy)* 3-8-12 JWilliams(8) (prom tl wknd over 1f out)....1½ **6**
2271[4] Masruf (IRE) **(74)***(74) (TThomsonJones)* 3-9-1 StephenDavies(2) (sn chsng wnr: rdn over 2f out: wknd over 1f out)....1½ **7**
1907[3] Scharnhorst **(73)***(73) (SDow)* 3-8-7 (7) ADaly(6) (prom: hung rt & wknd over 2f out) ....nk **8**
2909[7] Moonlight Saunter (USA) **(83)***(77) (EALDunlop)* 3-9-10 PaulEddery(5) (prom: rdn over 2f out: wknd over 1f out: eased whn btn ins fnl f)....2½ **9**
Jaazim **(70)***(61) (MMadgwick)* 5-9-2 KDarley(7) (plld hrd: bhd fnl 5f)....1½ **10**

4/1 Blurred Image (IRE), **5/1** Anam, Desert Time, **6/1** Sylvandra, **7/1** Scharnhorst, **8/1** JOLTO, Great Hall (6/1-10/1), **9/1** Jaazim, **16/1** Moonlight Saunter (USA), Masruf (IRE), CSF £66.92 CT £272.11 TOTE £9.50: £2.60 £2.90 £1.70 (£17.80) Trio £82.70
OWNER Mrs G. M. Gooderham (STOCKBRIDGE) BRED Mrs G. Gooderham 10 Rn
1m 27.57 (1.87) SF: 46/30/44/45/48/34/33/32/36/25
WEIGHT FOR AGE 3yo-5lb

3176

NIGHTFALL CONDITIONS STKS (2-Y.O) (Class C) £4,611.60 (£1,724.40: £842.20: £361.00: £160.50: £80.30)
5f Stalls: Low GOING minus 0.43 sec per fur (F) 7-15 (7-19)

3053[2] **Tarf (USA) (90)***(95)*(Fav)*(PTWalwyn)* 2-8-5 WCarson(1) (plld hrd: mde virtually all: shkn up ins fnl f: r.o wl)....— **1**
2970* Cross The Border **(80)***(89) (RHannon)* 2-8-10 KDarley(7) (w wnr: rdn over 1f out: one pce)..3½ **2**
2985* Comic Fantasy (AUS) **(90)***(74) (PWChapple-Hyam)* 2-8-3b(5) RHavlin(2) (w ldrs: rdn over 2f out: one pce)....4 **3**
1511[3] Sonic Mail **(95)***(70) (KMcAuliffe)* 2-8-10 RCochrane(4) (a.p: one pce fnl 2f)....1¾ **4**
2489[6] Windswept (IRE) **(70)***(68) (DJSffrenchDavis)* 2-8-8 WNewnes(6) (outpcd: nvr nrr) ....s.h **5**
Almushtarak (IRE) *(41) (MissGayKelleway)* 2-8-10 MWigham(3) (leggy: scope: bkwd: s.s: a in rr)....9 **6**

15/8 TARF (USA) (5/4-2/1), **2/1** Comic Fantasy (AUS), **3/1** Cross The Border, **11/2** Sonic Mail, **20/1** Windswept (IRE), **40/1** Almushtarak (IRE), CSF £7.82 TOTE £2.50: £1.60 £1.80 (£4.20) OWNER Mr Hamdan Al Maktoum (LAMBOURN) BRED Shadwell Farm Inc 6 Rn
59.8 secs (0.09 under 2y best) (-0.20) SF: 57/51/36/32/30/3

3177

ELITE RACING CLUB CLAIMING H'CAP (0-60) (3-Y.O+) (Class F) £3,092.00 (£862.00: £416.00)
6f Stalls: Low GOING minus 0.43 sec per fur (F) 7-45 (7-47)

3139[6] **Norling (IRE) (47)***(57) (KOCunningham-Brown)* 5-9-1 RCochrane(16) (mde all: rdn 2f out: drvn out)....— **1**
2943[6] Dahiyah (USA) **(59)***(65) (GLMoore)* 4-9-6v(7) LSuthern(7) (sn chsng wnr: ev ch 2f out: nt qckn)....1½ **2**

3139[7] Our Shadee (USA) **(45)***(49) (KTIvory)* 5-8-6v(7) CScally(5) (hld up: hdwy 2f out: r.o one pce fnl f)..........¾ **3**
2743[2] Random **(54)***(57) (CJames)* 4-9-1 (7) CAdamson(8) (hld up & bhd: hdwy 2f out: r.o ins fnl f)..........½ **4**
3139[8] Asterix **(50)***(53) (JMBradley)* 7-9-1v(3) DRMcCabe(10) (bhd: hdwy 2f out: r.o ins fnl f)..........s.h **5**
2968[2] Mediate (IRE) **(52)***(48)*(Fav)*(RHannon)* 3-9-2 KDarley(13) (lw: plld out over 1f out: late hdwy: nrst fin)..........2½ **6**
3134[4] Correspondence (CAN) **(40)***(36) (MartynMeade)* 5-8-8 VSlattery(15) (prom: rdn over 2f out: eased whn btn ins fnl f)..........hd **7**
2180[5] La Bossette (IRE) **(44)***(35) (JRArnold)* 3-8-8v WCarson(4) (lw: nvr nr to chal)..........1¾ **8**
2712[6] Cedar Dancer **(44)***(30) (RJHodges)* 3-8-1 (7) AmandaSanders(2) (lw: prom over 3f)..........2 **9**
1012[7] Ilustre (IRE) **(50)***(34) (LJHolt)* 3-9-0 MPerrett(9) (n.d)..........½ **10**
2522[4] Happy Brave **(38)***(20) (PDCundell)* 3-8-2 DHarrison(6) (bhd: hdwy & edgd rt over 1f out: sn wknd)..........¾ **11**
2685[4] Pride of Hayling (IRE) **(55)***(33) (PRHedger)* 4-9-9 StephenDavies(12) (lw: prom over 3f: eased whn btn fnl f)..........1½ **12**
2301[6] Harry's Coming **(55)***(33) (RJHodges)* 11-9-6 (3) SDrowne(14) (chsd ldrs: hrd rdn & wknd 2f out)..........hd **13**
1963[16] Classic Pet (IRE) **(47)***(24) (CAHorgan)* 3-8-11 PaulEddery(3) (b: plld hrd: prom over 3f)..........nk **14**
2984[7] Irish Dominion **(40)***(15) (ABarrow)* 5-8-8 JWilliams(11) (a bhd)..........1 **15**
3007[9] Persian Bailiwick (IRE) **(40)***(9) (FJordan)* 3-8-4 DBiggs(1) (s.i.s: sn rcvrd: wknd 3f out)..........2 **16**

3/1 Mediate (IRE) (tchd 9/2), **4/1** Pride of Hayling (IRE), **11/2** NORLING (IRE), **8/1** Random, **11/1** Correspondence (CAN) (7/1-12/1), **12/1** Asterix, **14/1** Dahiyah (USA), Harry's Coming, **16/1** La Bossette (IRE), **20/1** Cedar Dancer, Happy Brave, Our Shadee (USA), Classic Pet (IRE), **25/1** Ilustre (IRE), **66/1** Irish Dominion, Persian Bailiwick (IRE), CSF £78.36 CT £1,342.48 TOTE £5.70: £1.40 £5.80 £5.00 £1.90 (£72.10) Trio £248.30 OWNER Mr S. Pedersen (STOCKBRIDGE) BRED Mrs A. Whitehead 16 Rn 1m 14.67 (2.37) SF: 32/40/24/32/28/19/11/6/1/5/-/8/8/-/-/-
WEIGHT FOR AGE 3yo-4lb

3178 ODSTOCK MAIDEN STKS (3-Y.O+) (Class D) £3,866.50 (£1,162.00: £561.00: £260.50)

1m 6f Stalls: Low GOING minus 0.43 sec per fur (F) 8-15 (8-17)

2781[2] **Istabraq (IRE) (71)***(79)*(Fav)*(JHMGosden)* 3-8-5 WCarson(6) (b: plld hrd: lost pl 7f out: hrd rdn 3f out: rallied 2f out: styd on to ld ins fnl f)..........— **1**
3016[12] Dixiemelody *(76) (RHannon)* 3-8-5 KDarley(3) (lw: chsd ldr: led 6f out tl ins fnl f)..........2½ **2**
2284[6] Sea Freedom **(69)***(76) (GBBalding)* 4-9-3 JWilliams(1) (a.p: jnd ldr 5f out: ev ch 1f out: one pce)..........hd **3**
2931[2] Arctic Charmer (USA) **(68)***(62) (JLDunlop)* 3-8-5 RCochrane(5) (led 8f: wknd over 3f out)..........12 **4**
3024[7] Saafi (IRE) **(50)***(57) (RJBaker)* 4-9-3 BPowell(4) (hld up & bhd: hdwy 5f out: wknd over 3f out)..........5 **5**
2842[6] Salvatore Giuliano **(40)***(54) (AGFoster)* 5-9-3 TSprake(7) (hld up: hdwy 5f out: wknd 3f out) 2½ **6**
Fortunes Rose (IRE) *(35) (JSKing)* 3-8-2 ow2 DBiggs(9) (unf: wl bhd fnl 6f: t.o)..........12 **7**
513[7] Shared (IRE) *(38) (MMadgwick)* 3-8-5 CAvery(2) (plld hrd: prom 12f: t.o)..........2 **8**
Andre's Affair *(26) (DJSffrenchDavis)* 4-9-3 WNewnes(8) (lengthy: bkwd: wl bhd fnl 7f: t.o)..10 **9**
Ceilidh Dancer *(4) (PRHedger)* 4-8-12 StephenDavies(10) (lt-f: a bhd: t.o)..........15 **10**

5/6 ISTABRAQ (IRE) (4/6-Evens), **5/2** Sea Freedom, **7/2** Arctic Charmer (USA), **12/1** Dixiemelody, **50/1** Fortunes Rose (IRE), **66/1** Saafi (IRE), Salvatore Giuliano, Shared (IRE), Andre's Affair, Ceilidh Dancer, CSF £11.67 TOTE £2.10: £1.30 £1.60 £1.40 (£9.10) Trio £11.70 OWNER Mr Hamdan Al Maktoum (NEWMARKET) BRED Shadwell Estate Company Limited 10 Rn
3m 7.98 (9.78) SF: 4/1/13/-/-/-/-/-/-/-
WEIGHT FOR AGE 3yo-12lb
T/Plpt: £352.20 (33.54 Tckts). T/Qdpt: £12.60 (7.4 Tckts). KH

3029-YARMOUTH (L-H)
Thursday August 17th (Good to firm)

WEATHER: warm & sunny WIND: fresh half bhd

3179 MARSTONS PEDIGREE H'CAP (0-70) (3-Y.O+ F & M) (Class E) £3,260.25 (£972.00: £463.50: £209.25)

6f 3y Stalls: Centre GOING minus 0.53 sec per fur (F) 2-20 (2-21)

2265[6] **Awayil (USA) (70)***(84) (HThomsonJones)* 3-10-0 RHills(6) (dwlt: sn prom: qcknd to ld ins fnl f: sn clr)..........— **1**
2943[10] Charnwood Queen **(58)***(63) (RWArmstrong)* 3-9-2 RPrice(7) (led tl ins fnl f: unable qckn)....3½ **2**

2956[3] Irchester Lass **(37)***(37) (SRBowring)* 3-7-9 JQuinn(1) (chsd ldrs centre: kpt on appr fnl f) 1¾ 3
3034[3] Merrie le Bow **(44)***(41) (PatMitchell)* 3-7-13 (3) NVarley(2) (lw: chsd ldr centre: edgd lft & ev ch 2f out: wknd appr fnl f) 1 4
2404[7] Hello Hobson's (IRE) **(52)***(36)*(Fav)*(RBastiman)* 5-9-0 DeanMcKeown(5) (chsd ldrs 3f: wknd).5 5
3072[4] Petomi **(64)***(47) (SirMarkPrescott)* 3-9-8 CNutter(3) (swtg: in tch over 3f) ....½ 6
2171[3] Medieval Miss **(63)***(46) (MrsNMacauley)* 3-9-7v PRobinson(4) (lw: led centre over 2f: sn bhd)s.h 7

9/4 Hello Hobson's (IRE), **9/2** Charnwood Queen, **11/2** Petomi (4/1-6/1), **6/1** AWAYIL (USA) (op 4/1), Irchester Lass, **8/1** Medieval Miss, **16/1** Merrie le Bow, CSF £29.12 TOTE £6.70: £3.00 £1.80 (£24.90) OWNER Mr Hamdan Al Maktoum (NEWMARKET) BRED Shadwell Farm 7 Rn
1m 11.9 (1.30) SF: 48/27/1/5/4/11/10
WEIGHT FOR AGE 3yo-4lb

3180 E.B.F. FOSTERS ICE MAIDEN STKS (2-Y.O) (Class D) £4,620.00 (£1,380.00: £660.00: £300.00)
6f 3y Stalls: Centre GOING minus 0.53 sec per fur (F) 2-50 (2-52)

2876[9] **Uncle George** *(73) (MHTompkins)* 2-9-0 PRobinson(8) (in tch: rdn over 2f out: r.o wl fnl f to ld nr fin) ....— 1
Sasuru *(73) (GWragg)* 2-9-0 MHills(5) (lengthy: bkwd: chsd ldrs: r.o appr fnl f: jst failed) ......hd 2
2796[3] Alamein (USA) *(73) (MrsLPiggott)* 2-8-7 (7) GMilligan(7) (w ldrs: led wl over 1f out: edgd lft & ct nr fin) ....hd 3
1551[2] Unsold *(70)*(Fav)*(JRFanshawe)* 2-8-11 (3) NVarley(6) (bit bkwd: chsd ldrs: rdn 2f out: kpt on fnl f) 1 4
2912[9] Consordino *(65) (LMCumani)* 2-8-2 (7) GMitchell(9) (hld up: stdy hdwy appr fnl f: nrst fin) ......hd 5
1485[10] Dubai College (IRE) *(54) (CEBrittain)* 2-9-0 WRyan(4) (bit bkwd: in tch over 3f) 6 6
3003[8] Warming Trends *(52) (SirMarkPrescott)* 2-9-0 CNutter(3) (nvr nr to chal) ....½ 7
A-Aasem *(48) (HThomsonJones)* 2-9-0 RHills(1) (tall: scope: plld hrd: led centre: hdd & hung lft wl over 1f out: sn wknd & eased) 1¾ 8
A Million At Last (IRE) *(34) (MBell)* 2-9-0 MFenton(2) (w'like: scope: a bhd) 5 9

5/4 Unsold, **5/2** A-Aasem, **6/1** Sasuru (7/2-13/2), **8/1** Consordino, **12/1** Alamein (USA) (8/1-14/1), **14/1** A Million At Last (IRE), **33/1** UNCLE GEORGE, Warming Trends, Dubai College (IRE), CSF £203.74 TOTE £26.70: £3.00 £2.40 £2.40 (£96.50) Trio £209.10 OWNER Mr J. A. Fuller (NEWMARKET) BRED R. W. and Mrs J. R. Fidler 9 Rn 1m 14.1 (3.50) SF: 6/6/6/3/-/-/-/-/-

3181 COCA-COLA AND SCHWEPPES H'CAP (0-80) (3-Y.O+) (Class D) £4,137.90 (£1,237.20: £592.60: £270.30)
7f 3y Stalls: Centre GOING minus 0.53 sec per fur (F) 3-25 (3-28)

2602[3] **Mutabassim (IRE) (71)***(82) (ACStewart)* 3-9-3 SWhitworth(8) (swtg: a.p: led over 2f out: clr appr fnl f: pushed out) ....— 1
2718[2] Khatim (USA) **(68)***(73)*(Fav)*(HThomsonJones)* 3-9-0 RHills(4) (lw: chsd ldrs: shkn up over 3f out: no imp fnl f) 2½ 2
2832[8] St Louis Lady **(60)***(61) (WJarvis)* 4-8-11b JQuinn(2) (b.off hind: led over 4f: unable qckn) 1¾ 3
1778[8] Wandering Minstrel (IRE) **(64)***(64) (JMPEustace)* 3-8-10 PRobinson(3) (chsd ldrs: rdn over 2f out: kpt on fnl f) ....½ 4
2504[4] Agoer **(60)***(55) (CEBrittain)* 3-8-6 WRyan(7) (nvr nrr) 2½ 5
2979[7] Midnight Jazz (IRE) **(75)***(67) (WAO'Gorman)* 5-9-12 EmmaO'Gorman(5) (lw: hld up: hdwy & rdn 3f out: wknd over 1f out) 1 6
3159[8] Keston Pond (IRE) **(67)***(55) (DAWilson)* 5-9-4 DeanMcKeown(6) (hld up: effrt 3f out: n.d) 1¾ 7
1676[9] Fleet Cadet **(49)***(34) (NAGraham)* 4-8-0b AMcGlone(9) (swtg: chsd ldrs: rdn over 3f out: sn btn) 1½ 8
2787[3] Cent Nouvelles (USA) **(71)** *(JHMGosden)* 3-9-3 GHind(1) (Withdrawn not under Starters' orders: ref to ent stalls) .... W

11/4 Khatim (USA), **11/2** Midnight Jazz (IRE), Cent Nouvelles (USA), **7/1** MUTABASSIM (IRE), **8/1** Agoer, Wandering Minstrel (IRE) (5/1-9/1), Keston Pond (IRE), **14/1** St Louis Lady, **20/1** Fleet Cadet, CSF £19.03 CT £143.44 TOTE £6.40: £1.90 £1.40 £1.50 £1.90 (£7.90) Trio £45.30 OWNER Mr Hamdan Al Maktoum (NEWMARKET) BRED Shadwell Estate Company Limited 8 Rn
1m 22.9 (0.10) SF: 55/46/39/37/28/45/33/12/-
WEIGHT FOR AGE 3yo-5lb

3182 STRONGBOW ICE LIMITED STKS (0-60) (3-Y.O+) (Class F) £3,502.40 (£1,047.20: £501.60: £228.80)
1m 3y Stalls: Centre GOING minus 0.53 sec per fur (F) 4-00 (4-01)

3034* **Distant Princess (60)***(75)*(Fav)*(BWHills)* 3-8-10 MHills(4) (lw: prom: c stands side 4f out: led over 1f out: rdn out) ....— 1

2883[3] Cavil **(58)***(75) (CEBrittain)* 3-8-13 WRyan(7) (bhd: c stands side 4f out: rdn & hdwy over 1f out: r.o) 1¾ 2
3031[2] Domitia (USA) **(60)***(68) (MBell)* 3-8-8 MFenton(8) (w ldr: led 2f out: sn hdd & one pce) 1 3
2537[7] Sovereigns Parade **(60)***(66) (JEBanks)* 3-8-13 JQuinn(5) (b.hind: lw: chsd ldrs: rdn 2f out: no imp) 3½ 4
1911[9] Able Choice (IRE) **(48)***(54) (RWArmstrong)* 5-9-5h RPrice(6) (prom tl wknd over 2f out) 6 5
2979[14] South Eastern Fred **(56)***(46) (HJCollingridge)* 4-9-5 MRimmer(2) (nvr trbld ldrs) 4 6
1696[6] Star Fighter **(46)***(45) (WAO'Gorman)* 3-8-13 EmmaO'Gorman(1) (racd far side: rdn over 3f out: a bhd) ....½ 7
3011* Prizefighter **(60)***(44) (JLEyre)* 4-9-5 GHind(3) (lw: led 6f: sn wknd & eased) ....hd 8

6/4 DISTANT PRINCESS, **2/1** Prizefighter, **5/1** Domitia (USA), **8/1** South Eastern Fred (5/1-9/1), **12/1** Cavil, **16/1** Sovereigns Parade, **25/1** Star Fighter, **33/1** Able Choice (IRE), CSF £19.10 TOTE £2.20: £1.20 £2.00 £1.20 (£7.70) OWNER Mr Wafic Said (LAMBOURN) BRED Addison Racing Ltd Inc 8 Rn
1m 36.1 (0.80) SF: 42/42/35/33/27/19/12/17
WEIGHT FOR AGE 3yo-6lb

OFFICIAL EXPLANATION **Prizefighter: the trainer reported that the gelding may prefer running on an uphill course.**

3183

DIAMOND WHITE MAIDEN STKS (3-Y.O+) (Class D) £4,002.70 (£1,195.60: £571.80: £259.90)
1m 2f 21y Stalls: Low GOING minus 0.53 sec per fur (F) 4-30 (4-31)

544[3] **Jumairah Sun (IRE) (84)***(81) (LMCumani)* 3-8-7 OUrbina(2) (prom: 4th st: qcknd to ld over 1f out: rdn out) ....— 1
2794[9] Sheraz (IRE) **(65)***(84) (GWragg)* 3-8-12 MHills(3) (lw: led tl over 1f out: kpt on) 1½ 2
2350[4] Bay of Islands *(80) (CEBrittain)* 3-8-12 WRyan(1) (bit bkwd: chsd ldr: 2nd st: ev ch 2f out: one pce) 2½ 3
664[7] Merry Festival (USA) *(69) (JHMGosden)* 3-8-7 GHind(4) (prom: 3rd st: plld out over 3f out: sn rdn & hng lft: no imp) 3½ 4
2794[4] Almuhimm (USA) *(63)*(Fav)*(EALDunlop)* 3-8-12 RHills(5) (plld hrd: trckd ldrs: 5th st: plld out over 3f out: btn appr fnl f) 7 5
2977[6] Our Little Lady *(34) (JEBanks)* 3-8-7 JQuinn(6) (6th st: a bhd) 15 6
1720[4] Never So Fit **(40)***(23) (RBastiman)* 4-9-1 (5) HBastiman(7) (b: bit bkwd: wl bhd fnl 6f) 10 7

13/8 Almuhimm (USA), **5/2** Merry Festival (USA), **4/1** JUMAIRAH SUN (IRE) (3/1-9/2), **6/1** Bay of Islands, **10/1** Sheraz (IRE) (6/1-11/1), **16/1** Our Little Lady, **33/1** Never So Fit, CSF £37.62 TOTE £3.30: £2.40 £3.80 (£14.60) OWNER Sheikh Ahmed Al Maktoum (NEWMARKET) BRED Michael Doyle 7 Rn
2m 7.6 (3.20) SF: 24/27/23/12/6/-/-
WEIGHT FOR AGE 3yo-8lb

3184

JOHN SMITHS MAIDEN H'CAP (0-65) (3-Y.O+) (Class F) £3,023.00 (£838.00: £401.00)
1m 3f 101y Stalls: Low GOING minus 0.53 sec per fur (F) 5-00 (5-00)

2245[7] **Marchant Ming (IRE) (55)***(75) (MAJarvis)* 3-9-5b WRyan(6) (lw: led after 2f: clr over 2f out: rdn out) ....— 1
2509[3] Innocence **(64)***(74)*(Fav)*(GWragg)* 3-10-0 MHills(3) (in tch: 5th st: effrt over 3f out: chsd wnr appr fnl f: no imp) 7 2
2830[3] Presto Boy **(41)***(47) (MBell)* 3-8-5v MFenton(7) (hld up: last st: hdwy over 2f out: r.o fnl f) 3 3
2884[3] Fresh Look (IRE) **(53)***(58) (RFJohnsonHoughton)* 3-9-3 RHills(5) (led 2f: 2nd st: rdn & no ex fnl 2f) 1 4
2532[10] Dr Frances (IRE) **(38)***(42) (CCElsey)* 3-8-2 FNorton(1) (sn chsg ldrs: 3rd st: rdn 3f out: sn btn) ....¾ 5
2981[5] Try Omnipotent **(43)***(40) (CNAllen)* 3-8-7 JQuinn(4) (6th st: rdn 4f out: nvr nr ldrs) 5 6
2960[6] Joys First **(34)***(3) (HJCollingridge)* 4-8-7 MRimmer(2) (chsd ldrs: 4th st: rdn & wknd over 3f out) 20 7

7/4 Innocence, **7/2** MARCHANT MING (IRE) (2/1-4/1), **4/1** Presto Boy, **9/2** Fresh Look (IRE), **14/1** Try Omnipotent (8/1-16/1), Joys First (8/1-16/1), **33/1** Dr Frances (IRE), CSF £9.59 TOTE £5.30: £2.20 £1.50 (£4.70) OWNER S Marchant & Son (NEWMARKET) BRED Etablissement Equine Investments 7 Rn
2m 24.8 (1.80) SF: 48/47/20/31/15/13/-
WEIGHT FOR AGE 3yo-9lb

T/Plpt: £70.00 (181.14 Tckts). T/Qdpt: £6.70 (15.85 Tckts). Dk

3160-**YORK (L-H)**
Thursday August 17th (Good to firm)
WEATHER: sunny & v.hot WIND: slt half bhd

3185 MOORESTYLE CONVIVIAL MAIDEN STKS (2-Y.O) (Class D) £9,381.25 (£2,800.00: £1,337.50: £606.25)
6f Stalls: High GOING minus 0.18 sec per fur (GF) 2-05 (2-05)

Desert Boy (IRE) *(87+) (PWChapple-Hyam)* 2-9-0 JReid(5) (w'like: leggy: mde virtually all: styd on wl u.p fnl f: jst hld on)........— 1
Leonine (IRE) *(87+) (PFICole)* 2-9-0 TQuinn(2) (rangy: sn chsng ldrs: hrd rdn & sltly hmpd over 1f out: styd on strly towards fin)........s.h 2
Russian Music *(84+) (PCHaslam)* 2-9-0 MTebbutt(7) (w'like: scope: bit bkwd: s.i.s: sn chsng ldrs: n.m.r over 2f out: styd on wl cl home)........1¼ 3
2693³ Raheen (USA) *(83)*(Fav)*(MRStoute)* 2-9-0 WRSwinburn(1) (trckd ldrs: rdn & edgd rt over 1f out: sltly hmpd: eased nr fin)........s.h 4
2675² Naissant **(94)***(69) (CEBrittain)* 2-8-9 MJKinane(6) (w ldrs tl wknd over 1f out)........3½ 5
Sabot *(70) (BWHills)* 2-9-0 BThomson(4) (w'like: leggy: bit bkwd: dwlt: sn chsng ldrs: outpcd ½-wy: n.d after)........1½ 6
Mukabir (USA) *(62)*(Fav)*(MajorWRHern)* 2-9-0 WCarson(8) (gd sort: lw: sn trckng ldrs: rdn over 2f out: wknd over 1f out: eased)........3 7
Jerry Cutrona (IRE) *(9) (NACallaghan)* 2-9-0 PatEddery(3) (w'like: scope: bkwd: s.s: a wl bhd)........20 8

9/4 Raheen (USA) (5/1-2/1), Mukabir (USA), **100/30** DESERT BOY (IRE), **6/1** Leonine (IRE), **9/1** Naissant, **20/1** Sabot, **25/1** Russian Music, Jerry Cutrona (IRE), CSF £22.93 TOTE £5.10: £1.40 £1.90 £5.10 (£21.70) OWNER Lord Weinstock & The Hon Simon Weinstock (MARLBOROUGH) BRED Ballymacoll Stud Farm Ltd 8 Rn 1m 12.22 (2.62) SF: 45/45/42/41/27/28/20/-

3186 LOWTHER STKS (Gp 2) (2-Y.O F) (Class A) £40,521.40 (£15,022.60: £7,231.30: £2,981.50: £1,210.75: £502.45)
6f Stalls: High GOING minus 0.18 sec per fur (GF) 2-35 (2-37)

2322² **Dance Sequence (USA) (100)***(101)*(Fav)*(MRStoute)* 2-8-11 WRSwinburn(8) (trckd ldrs: styd on wl to ld ins fnl f)........— 1
1849³ My Melody Parkes **(100)***(99) (JBerry)* 2-8-11 JCarroll(4) (lw: led tl ins fnl f)........¾ 2
2564a² Sweet Robin (IRE) *(95) (MJohnston)* 2-8-11 MJKinane(7) (lw: chsd ldrs: drvn along & outpcd ½-wy: hdwy over 1f out: styng on sme pce whn swtchd lft nr fin)........1½ 3
2580* Thrilling Day **(100)***(88) (NAGraham)* 2-8-11 DHolland(5) (sn chsng ldrs: kpt on same pce appr fnl f)........2½ 4
2740³ Baize *(88) (RFJohnsonHoughton)* 2-8-11 JReid(2) (unruly in stalls: chsd ldrs: kpt on same pce u.p fnl 2f)........nk 5
2779² Forentia **(90)***(85) (JRFanshawe)* 2-8-11 DHarrison(9) (swtg: in tch: effrt over 2f out: nvr nr to chal)........1 6
2947W Astuti (IRE) *(80) (APJarvis)* 2-8-11 PatEddery(3) (lw: unruly s: s.i.s: bhd: hdwy 2f out: n.m.r: n.d)........1¾ 7
2322² Darling Flame (USA) **(100)***(56) (JHMGosden)* 2-8-11 LDettori(6) (s.i.s: sn drvn along & outpcd: wknd qckly 2f out: virtually p.u nr fin)........9 8
3037a⁴ Home Shopping **(100)***(47) (KMcAuliffe)* 2-8-11 TQuinn(1) (swtg: effrt on outside ½-wy: sn lost pl: eased)........3½ 9

5/4 DANCE SEQUENCE (USA), **4/1** Darling Flame (USA), **8/1** My Melody Parkes, Sweet Robin (IRE), **9/1** Baize, **10/1** Forentia, **14/1** Thrilling Day, **16/1** Home Shopping, **20/1** Astuti (IRE), CSF £12.27 TOTE £2.10: £1.30 £2.10 £1.50 (£9.20) Trio £14.00 OWNER Cheveley Park Stud (NEWMARKET) BRED John C Mabee and Mrs Mabee 9 Rn
1m 11.59 (1.99) SF: 51/49/45/38/38/35/30/6/-
OFFICIAL EXPLANATION Darling Flame: was found to be in season.

3187 NUNTHORPE STKS (Gp 1) (Class A) £72,029.50 (£26,390.50: £12,445.25: £4,838.75: £1,669.38: £401.62)
5f Stalls: High GOING minus 0.18 sec per fur (GF) 3-10 (3-12)

2368⁷ **So Factual (USA) (115)***(127) (SbinSuroor)* 5-9-6 LDettori(5) (lw: hld up gng wl: smooth hdwy & swtchd lft 2f out: led over 1f out: edgd rt: drvn out)........— 1
2899a⁴ Ya Malak **(106)***(122) (JWPayne)* 4-9-6 BThomson(8) (racd stands' side: trckd ldrs: r.o wl ins fnl f)........1½ 2

2671* Hever Golf Rose **(107)***(114) (TJNaughton)* 4-9-3 JWeaver(1) (b.hind: led to ½-wy: hung rt & kpt on same pce appr fnl f) 1½ 3
2888a* Sharp Point (IRE) *(111) (DKWeld,Ireland)* 3-9-0b MJKinane(6) (hld up: effrt ½-wy: sn outpcd: styd on fnl f) 1 4
1896⁷ Millyant **(113)***(111) (RGuest)* 5-9-3 CAsmussen(4) (chsd ldrs: outpcd ½-wy: kpt on fnl f) ....s.h 5
1896³ Mind Games **(120)***(113)*(Fav)*(JBerry)* 3-9-3 JCarroll(3) (lw: dwlt: sn trckng ldrs: led ½-wy: hdd over 1f out: edgd rt: wknd towards fin) ....nk 6
2671⁴ Millstream (USA) **(110)***(101) (MJohnston)* 3-9-0 DHolland(2) (swtg: chsd ldrs: drvn along & outpcd ½-wy: wknd over 1f out) 3 7
2671⁷ Mistertopogigo (IRE) **(106)***(99) (WSCunningham)* 5-9-6 MRoberts(7) (lw: b.off hind: hld up: effrt on outside 2f out: sn wknd) 1½ 8

10/11 Mind Games, **4/1** Hever Golf Rose (op 9/4), **9/2** SO FACTUAL (USA), **11/1** Millstream (USA), **12/1** Millyant, **16/1** Sharp Point (IRE), **20/1** Ya Malak, **25/1** Mistertopogigo (IRE), CSF £70.91 TOTE £5.00: £1.70 £4.10 £1.70 (£95.40) OWNER Godolphin (NEWMARKET) BRED Juddmonte Farms Inc 8 Rn
57.47 secs (0.47) SF: 80/75/67/61/64/63/51/52
WEIGHT FOR AGE 3yo-3lb

3188

BRADFORD & BINGLEY RATED STKS H'CAP (0-105) (3-Y.O+) (Class B) £23,604.00 (£8,736.00: £4,193.00: £1,715.00: £682.50: £269.50)
7f 202y Stalls: Low GOING minus 0.18 sec per fur (GF) 3-45 (3-46)

3066* **Cap Juluca (IRE) (99)***(113+)*(Fav)*(RCharlton)* 3-8-11 3x JWeaver(1) (mde all: styd on strly fnl 3f: readily) ....— 1
2703⁶ Indian Fly **(94)***(106) (RHannon)* 4-8-12 JReid(2) (hld up: effrt & nt clr run over 1f out: swtchd: r.o wl) 1¼ 2
2703¹¹ Behaviour **(89)***(99) (MrsJCecil)* 3-8-1 PaulEddery(6) (in tch: effrt & chsd wnr over 1f out: kpt on same pce) ....¾ 3
2672³ Knave's Ash (USA) **(95)***(102) (MRStoute)* 4-8-10 (3) JTate(4) (a chsng ldrs: kpt on same pce u.p fnl 2f) 1½ 4
2737⁵ Bouche Bee (USA) **(93)***(97) (LMCumani)* 3-8-5 PatEddery(5) (b.hind: chsd ldrs: drvn along over 3f out: one pce) 1¼ 5
2933* Moving Arrow **(91)***(92) (MissSEHall)* 4-8-9 MJKinane(9) (lw: trckd ldrs: rdn over 2f out: grad wknd over 1f out) 1½ 6
2948³ Celestial Key (USA) **(102)***(103) (MJohnston)* 5-9-6 DHolland(7) (lw: mid div: effrt over 2f out: n.m.r: nvr nr ldrs) ....nk 7
2598² Bettergeton **(95)***(93) (PJBevan)* 3-8-4 (3) SSanders(3) (lw: hld up & bhd: hdwy u.p over 2f out: nvr nr to chal) 1½ 8
2241¹⁵ Billy Bushwacker **(89)***(85) (MrsMReveley)* 4-8-7 RCochrane(8) (s.i.s: bhd tl hdwy on outside over 2f out: hung lft & eased ins fnl f) ....¾ 9
2694² Sue's Return **(92)***(81) (APJarvis)* 3-8-4 DHarrison(13) (lw: hld up & bhd: sme hdwy 2f out: n.d) 3½ 10
2673⁸ Lap of Luxury **(103)***(88) (WJarvis)* 6-9-2 (5) MHenry(14) (hld up & bhd: effrt 3f out: n.d) 2 11
2948² Hi Nod **(94)***(67) (MJCamacho)* 5-8-12 LCharnock(12) (lw: hld up: plld hrd: effrt 3f out: sn wknd: eased) 6 12
2948⁵ Tawafij (USA) **(89)***(60) (TDyer)* 6-8-2v(5) AWhelan(11) (lw: mid div: hrd rdn 3f out: sn wknd) 1 13
2689⁶ Sulb (USA) **(94)***(60) (ACStewart)* 3-8-6 WCarson(10) (chsd ldrs tl rdn & wknd 3f out) 2½ 14
2436* Moccasin Run (USA) **(103)***(69) (IABalding)* 4-9-2 (5) DGriffiths(15) (swtg: hld up & bhd: effrt on outside 3f out: sn wknd) ....s.h 15
LONG HANDICAP Billy Bushwacker 8-5 Tawafij (USA) 8-1 Behaviour 8-0

7/2 CAP JULUCA (IRE), **4/1** Behaviour, **7/1** Bouche Bee (USA), **11/1** Sulb (USA), Billy Bushwacker, **12/1** Moving Arrow, Bettergeton, Indian Fly, **14/1** Knave's Ash (USA), Celestial Key (USA), Hi Nod, **16/1** Lap of Luxury, **20/1** Moccasin Run (USA), **25/1** Sue's Return, **33/1** Tawafij (USA), CSF £45.28 CT £169.12 TOTE £4.40: £2.50 £3.70 £2.60 (£31.50) Trio £58.20 OWNER Mr Martin Myers (BECKHAMPTON) BRED Mrs N. Myers 15 Rn
1m 35.76 (-0.24) SF: 84/83/70/79/68/69/80/64/62/52/65/44/37/31/46
WEIGHT FOR AGE 3yo-6lb

3189

LADBROKE KNAVESMIRE H'CAP (0-95) (3-Y.O+) (Class C) £15,660.00 (£4,680.00: £2,240.00: £1,020.00)
1m 3f 195y Stalls: Low GOING minus 0.18 sec per fur (GF) 4-15 (4-17)

2768* **Progression (65)***(81+) (PCHaslam)* 4-8-1b(5) MBaird(9) (swtg: s.i.s: hld up & bhd: gd hdwy on ins over 2f out: nt clr run & swtchd outside over 1f out: qcknd to ld ins fnl f: wnt rt) ....— 1

2571[5] Jameel Asmar **(77)**(90) *(CREgerton)* 3-8-8 BThomson(12) (hdwy over 3f out: led over 1f out: hdd & nt qckn ins fnl f)....2½ **2**
3021[7] Vindaloo **(82)**(94) *(JLHarris)* 3-8-13 JWeaver(11) (lw: mid div: hdwy & ev ch over 2f out: kpt on same pce ins fnl f)....½ **3**
2871[2] Lord Hastie (USA) **(53)**(64) *(CWThornton)* 7-7-8 AMackay(13) (trckd ldrs: led over 2f out: hdd over 1f out: one pce)....1 **4**
2907[3] Highflying **(87)**(92) *(GMMoore)* 9-9-11 (3) JTate(1) (hld up: gd hdwy on ins 4f out: kpt on same pce)....4 **5**
2880* Pumice **(76)**(78)(Fav)*(LMCumani)* 3-8-7 PatEddery(14) (prom: pushed along 5f out: outpcd & n.m.r 2f out: nvr able to chal)....2½ **6**
3094[9] Augustan **(61)**(63) *(SGollings)* 4-8-2 WCarson(2) (hld up & bhd: styd on fnl 3f: nvr nr ldrs)....nk **7**
2768[6] Boloardo **(67)**(68) *(CEBrittain)* 6-8-8 BDoyle(15) (in tch tl outpcd fnl 3f)....nk **8**
3102[2] Deano's Beeno **(79)**(78) *(MJohnston)* 3-8-10 DHolland(5) (lw: led tl over 2f out: sn wknd)....1¼ **9**
2816* Master Hyde (USA) **(60)**(57) *(WStorey)* 6-7-8 (7) PFessey(7) (racd wd: nvr nr ldrs)....1¾ **10**
2902* Silktail (IRE) **(67)**(62) *(CADwyer)* 3-7-12 GCarter(6) (swtg: hld up: plld hrd & bhd: sme hdwy over 3f out: sn wknd)....1¾ **11**
2937[2] Royal York **(72)**(62) *(MissSEHall)* 3-7-12 (5) MHenry(16) (lw: chsd ldrs tl wknd over 2f out)...3½ **12**
2856* Carlito Brigante **(72)**(61) *(MrsJRRamsden)* 3-8-3 MRoberts(3) (chsd ldrs: n.m.r 3f out: hmpd over 2f out: sn wknd)....¾ **13**
2824[2] North Ardar **(60)**(47) *(MrsMReveley)* 5-7-10 (5) AWhelan(8) (bhd & pushed along 6f out: sme hdwy 3f out: eased over 1f out)....1½ **14**
3102[5] Our Main Man **(57)**(37) *(RMWhitaker)* 5-7-12v DaleGibson(4) (b.nr hind: chsd ldrs tl lost pl over 3f out: sn bhd)....5 **15**

4/1 Pumice, **5/1** Deano's Beeno, **6/1** Carlito Brigante, **7/1** Silktail (IRE), Royal York, **12/1** PROGRESSION, **14/1** Jameel Asmar, Highflying, **16/1** Lord Hastie (USA), North Ardar, Vindaloo, Master Hyde (USA), **25/1** Boloardo, Augustan, **33/1** Our Main Man, CSF £160.92 CT £2,463.04 TOTE £19.80: £5.00 £5.00 £3.90 (£113.10) Trio £1,653.60 OWNER Mr Alex Gorrie (MIDDLEHAM) 15 Rn
2m 28.04 (1.04) SF: 69/68/72/52/80/56/51/56/56/45/40/40/39/35/25
WEIGHT FOR AGE 3yo-10lb

3190 GALTRES STKS (Listed) (3-Y.O+ F & M) (Class A) £14,620.00 (£4,360.00: £2,080.00: £940.00)

1m 3f 195y Stalls: Low GOING minus 0.18 sec per fur (GF) 4-45 (4-47)

2563a[5] **Larrocha (IRE)** (111+)(Fav)*(LMCumani)* 3-9-0 MJKinane(3) (lw: hld up: effrt & outpcd over 2f out: led wl over 1f out: wnt clr fnl f: easily)....— **1**
1867[5] Segovia (93) *(HRACecil)* 3-8-8 PatEddery(2) (led 2f: led over 3f out: no ch w wnr: eased towards fin)....9 **2**
Majestic Role (FR) (92) *(MKauntze,Ireland)* 4-9-4 WJO'Connor(1) (dwlt: led after 2f tl over 3f out: sn btn)....½ **3**
2944[6] Kshessinskaya **(95)**(91) *(CEBrittain)* 3-8-8 BDoyle(4) (pushed along ½-wy: rdn over 4f out: nvr nr to chal)....1¼ **4**

4/11 LARROCHA (IRE), **100/30** Segovia, **11/1** Majestic Role (FR) (8/1-12/1), **20/1** Kshessinskaya, CSF £1.97 TOTE £1.30 (£1.40) OWNER Sheikh Mohammed (NEWMARKET) BRED K. and Mrs Prendergast 4 Rn
2m 28.54 (1.54) SF: 74/56/65/54
WEIGHT FOR AGE 3yo-10lb

3191 CITY OF YORK STKS (Listed) (3-Y.O+) (Class A) £14,211.00 (£4,248.00: £2,034.00: £927.00)

6f 214y Stalls: High GOING minus 0.18 sec per fur (GF) 5-15 (5-16)

3062* **Didina (103)**(110++) *(RCharlton)* 3-8-4 PatEddery(1) (lw: trckd ldrs: n.m.r 2f out: qcknd to ld 1f out: sn clr: impressive)....— **1**
Foxhound (USA) (109)(Fav)*(SbinSuroor)* 4-9-0 JCarroll(4) (lw: chsd ldrs: effrt over 2f out: edgd lft & chal over 1f out: nt pce of wnr)....2½ **2**
2646[3] Peace Envoy **(109)**(114) *(HRACecil)* 3-9-0 WJO'Connor(10) (hld up: hdwy 2f out: styd on u.p ins fnl f)....nk **3**
2699[3] Storiths (IRE) **(102)**(107) *(JWWatts)* 5-9-0 BThomson(7) (lw: b: dwlt: bhd: hdwy on outside over 2f out: hung lft: no imp ins fnl f)....¾ **4**
2671[5] Welsh Mist **(102)**(102) *(RBoss)* 4-9-0 JReid(8) (trckd ldrs: effrt over 2f out: nvr able to chal)....2 **5**
2097[4] Venture Capitalist **(106)**(99) *(DNicholls)* 6-9-0 AlexGreaves(3) (lw: trckd ldrs: styng on same pce whn hmpd over 1f out)....1¼ **6**
2677[2] Averti (IRE) **(100)**(98) *(WRMuir)* 4-9-0 JWeaver(11) (rr div: sme hdwy u.p over 2f out: nvr nr to chal)....½ **7**
2237* Cool Jazz **(102)**(95) *(CEBrittain)* 4-9-0 MJKinane(9) (lw: trckd ldrs: led & wnt lft 2f out: sn hdd & wknd)....1¼ **8**

2699[2] Monaassib (IRE) **(100)***(95) (EALDunlop)* 4-9-0 TIves(6) (b.hind: trckd ldrs: led over 2f out: sn hdd, hmpd & wknd)....hd 9
2105[6] Star of Zilzal (USA) **(102)***(95) (MRStoute)* 3-8-9 WRSwinburn(5) (lw: hld up: stdy hdwy on ins over 2f out: hmpd over 1f out: eased)....nk 10
3193a* Wizard King **(108)***(97) (SirMarkPrescott)* 4-9-5 GDuffield(2) (led tl over 2f out: wkng whn hmpd over 1f out: eased ins fnl f)....1 11

7/4 Foxhound (USA), **100/30** DIDINA, **9/2** Wizard King, **11/1** Star of Zilzal (USA), **12/1** Peace Envoy, Venture Capitalist, **20/1** Storiths (IRE), Welsh Mist, Monaassib (IRE), Cool Jazz, **25/1** Averti (IRE), CSF £9.64 TOTE £3.80: £1.80 £1.50 £3.20 (£4.20) Trio £28.20 OWNER Mr K. Abdullah (BECKHAMPTON) BRED Juddmonte Farms 11 Rn

1m 22.2 (0.70) SF: 65/69/69/67/62/59/58/55/55/50/57

WEIGHT FOR AGE 3yo-5lb

T/Jkpt: £8,658.50 (1.64 Tckts). T/Plpt: £797.40 (69.4 Tckts). T/Qdpt: £136.00 (6.05 Tckts). WG

3041a-DEAUVILLE (France) (R-H)
Tuesday August 8th (Good)

3192a PRIX DE LA CALONNE (Listed) (3-Y.O F) £16,766.00 (£5,748.00: £3,593.00) 1m

3-15 (3-20)

2349[4] **Arabride** *(88) (JARToller)* 3-8-11 JWeaver ....— 1
Marie de Ken (FR) *(87) (AdeRoyerDupre,France)* 3-8-11 GMosse ....nk 2
Beyrouth (USA) *(86) (JEHammond,France)* 3-8-11 CAsmussen ....½ 3

P-M 5.20F: 1.90F 1.60F 1.50F (13.00F) OWNER Blandford (WHITSBURY) BRED W. H. F. Carson 9 Rn

1m 43.2 SF: -/-/-

FAIRYHOUSE (Dublin, Ireland) (R-H)
Wednesday August 9th (Firm)

3193a PLATINUM STKS (Listed) (3-Y.O+) £9,675.00 (£2,775.00: £1,275.00) 1m

6-00 (6-00)

2598[3] **Wizard King** *(111)*(Fav)*(SirMarkPrescott)* 4-9-3 MJKinane ....— 1
Idris (IRE) *(109) (JSBolger,Ireland)* 5-9-3 KJManning 1 2
1390a[8] Park Charger *(102) (APO'Brien,Ireland)* 3-8-7 WJSupple 2 3

Evens WIZARD KING, **6/4** Idris (IRE), **8/1** Park Charger, Tote £1.50: £1.20 £1.70 (£1.10) OWNER Sheikh Ahmed bin Saeed Al Maktoum (NEWMARKET) BRED Sheikh Mohammed bin Rashid al Maktoum 5 Rn

1m 35.4 SF: -/-/-

3192a-DEAUVILLE (France) (R-H)
Thursday August 10th (Good)

3194a PRIX DE REUX (Listed) (3-Y.O+) £16,766.00 (£5,748.00: £3,593.00) 1m 4f 110y

3-30 (3-28)

1885a* **Swain (IRE)** *(110) (AFabre,France)* 3-8-13 TJarnet ....— 1
Lord of Appeal *(103) (AFabre,France)* 3-8-6 SGuillot ....nk 2
898a[3] Richard of York *(100) (JHMGosden)* 5-9-4 CAsmussen 2½ 3

P-M 1.10F: 1.90F 2.40F (£5.40) OWNER Sheikh Mohammed (FRANCE) BRED Sheikh Mohammed 6 Rn

2m 43.3 (8.00) SF: -/-/-

2389a-HOPPEGARTEN (Berlin, Germany) (R-H)
Saturday August 12th (Good)

3195a GROSSER PREIS VON BERLIN (Gp 3) (3-Y.O+) £35,391.00 (£14,815.00: £7,407.00) 6f 110y

3-45 (4-03)

2212a[2] **Desidera (IRE)** *(108) (HBlume,Germany)* 3-8-6 AStarke ....— 1
2389a[8] Siberian Grey *(111) (CSprengel,Germany)* 3-8-10 MO'Reilly ....½ 2

1393a2 Glenlivet (SWE) *(111) (LKelp,Sweden)* 7-9-6 JohnFortune 2 3
3045a* Branston Abby (IRE) *(109) (MJohnston)* 6-9-2 MRoberts (btn approx 3¼l) 5
1145 7 Fire Dome (IRE) *(103) (RHannon)* 3-8-10 RCochrane (btn approx 4l) 8
2646 2 Mistle Cat (USA) *(SPCWoods)* 5-9-6 WWoods (btn over 7½l) 10

Tote 43DM: 20DM 22DM 46DM (SF 367DM) OWNER Gestut Rottgen BRED Gestut Rottgen 11 Rn
1m 16.1 SF: -/-/-/-/-/-

3194a-DEAUVILLE (France) (R-H) Saturday August 12th (Good)

3196a PRIX DE THIBERVILLE (Listed) (3-Y.O F) £16,766.00 (£5,748.00: £3,593.00) **1m 4f 110y** 3-05 (3-02)

Pont Audemer (USA) *(99) (ELellouche,France)* 3-8-9 OPeslier ....— 1
2723a3 Daraydala (IRE) *(99) (AdeRoyerDupre,France)* 3-8-9 GMosse ....hd 2
2045a2 Ultra Finesse *(99) (MmeCHead,France)* 3-8-9 ODoleuze ....s.nk 3
2426* Honfleur (IRE) *(PWChapple-Hyam)* 3-8-9 BThomson (btn over 4½l) 6

P-M 8.50F: 3.10F 1.60F (13.70F) OWNER Mr D. Wildenstein BRED Allez France Stables 7 Rn
2m 49.5 (14.20) SF: -/-/-/-

1706a-LEOPARDSTOWN (Dublin, Ireland) (L-H) Sunday August 13th (Good to firm)

3197a HEINZ 57 PHOENIX STKS (Gp 1) (2-Y.O C & F) £98,000.00 (£29,000.00: £14,000.00: £5,000.00) **6f** 3-20 (3-23)

2370* **Danehill Dancer (IRE)** *(104)*(Fav)*(NACallaghan)* 2-9-0 PatEddery (trckd ldr: rdn to ld 1½f out: r.o wl u.p) ....— 1
2693* Woodborough (USA) *(103) (PWChapple-Hyam)* 2-9-0 JReid (trckd ldrs: rdn to chal 1f out: r.o) ....nk 2
Catch A Glimpse (USA) *(96) (DKWeld,Ireland)* 2-8-11 MJKinane (rr early: gd hdwy over 1f out: fin wl) 1½ 3
2892a2 Flying Squaw *(94) (MRChannon)* 2-8-11 RHughes (a.p: rdn & no ex fnl 1½f) ....¾ 4
2564a3 Sunset Reigns (IRE) *(85) (APO'Brien,Ireland)* 2-8-11 CRoche (led tl hdd by wnr: rdn & wknd) 3½ 5
2674* April The Eighth *(88) (BWHills)* 2-9-0 WCarson (a.p: rdn over 2f out: wknd fnl f) ....s.h 6
Rockcorry Rose (IRE) *(KPrendergast,Ireland)* 2-8-11 WJSupple (prom tl rdn & wknd over 2f out) 7
2594 2 Ribot's Secret (IRE) *(APO'Brien,Ireland)* 2-8-11b PVGilson (prom tl rdn over 2f out: wknd) 8
Deed of Love (USA) *(JSBolger,Ireland)* 2-9-0b KJManning (prom: rdn 2f out: wknd qckly fnl f) 9
Nymph In The Ski (IRE) *(WJFitzpatrick,Ireland)* 2-8-11 PShanahan (a bhd: t.o) 10

2/1 DANEHILL DANCER (IRE), **5/1** Sunset Reigns (IRE), **11/2** Woodborough (USA), **6/1** April The Eighth, **7/1** Deed of Love (USA), **8/1** Ribot's Secret (IRE), Flying Squaw, **25/1** Catch A Glimpse (USA), **40/1** Rockcorry Rose (IRE), **500/1** Nymph In The Ski (IRE), Tote £3.30: £1.80 £1.20 £7.10 (£5.40) OWNER Mr M. Tabor (NEWMARKET) BRED L. K. and K. McCreery 10 Rn
1m 14.6 (3.40) SF: -/-/-/-/-/-/-/-/-/-

3198a PHOENIX SPRINT STKS (Gp 3) (3-Y.O+) £16,250.00 (£4,750.00: £2,250.00) **6f** 3-55 (3-55)

1706a* **Desert Style (IRE)** *(124)*(Fav)*(JSBolger,Ireland)* 3-9-3 KJManning ....— 1
1703a3 Petite Fantasy *(107) (APO'Brien,Ireland)* 3-8-7 JFEgan 2½ 2
3033* Cheyenne Spirit *(103) (BHanbury)* 3-8-7 WRyan 1½ 3
2443 8 Bunty Boo *(RHannon)* 6-8-12 JReid (btn over 5l) 6
2097 7 Roger the Butler (IRE) *(MBell)* 5-9-1 MFenton 9

4/1 DESERT STYLE (IRE), **5/1** Petite Fantasy, Cheyenne Spirit, **9/1** Bunty Boo, **10/1** Roger the Butler (IRE), Tote £4.10: £2.00 £2.30 £2.40 (£18.40) OWNER Maktoum Al Maktoum (IRELAND) BRED Ovidstown Investments Ltd 9 Rn
1m 14.0 (2.80) SF: -/-/-/-/-

3196a-DEAUVILLE (France) (R-H)
Sunday August 13th (Good)

3199a
PRIX DU HARAS DE FRESNAY-LE-BUFFARD JACQUES LE MAROIS (Gp 1) (3-Y.O+ C & F) £119,760.00 (£47,904.00: £23,952.00: £11,976.00) **1m** 2-45 (2-48)

2727a* **Miss Satamixa (IRE)** *(124) (AFabre,France)* 3-8-8 SGuillot (mid div: rdn 1½f out: qcknd to ld ins fnl f: r.o wl) — 1
2689* Sayyedati *(122) (CEBrittain)* 5-9-1 BDoyle (hld up: smooth hdwy to ld over 1f out: rdn & hdd ins fnl f) 1 2
2897a2 Shaanxi (USA) *(119) (ELellouche,France)* 3-8-8 DBoeuf (hld up: trckd 2nd fr ½-way: r.o fnl f) 1½ 3
2762* Tamayaz (CAN) *(119) (SbinSuroor)* 3-8-11 CAsmussen (led after 1f tl rdn & hdd over 1f out: rallied fnl f) 1½ 4
1394a* Green Tune (USA) *(119) (MmeCHead,France)* 4-9-4 ODoleuze (trckd ldr: hrd rdn over 2f out: one pce fnl f) hd 5
1234a5 Prince Arthur (IRE) *(116) (PWChapple-Hyam)* 3-8-11 BThomson (led 1f: racd in 2nd: rdn & outpcd 2f out) 1½ 6
26894 Nicolotte *(114) (GWragg)* 4-9-4 MHills (hld up: rdn over 2f out: nvr plcd to chal) 1 7
2897a* Smolensk (USA) *(109) (AFabre,France)* 3-8-8 TJarnet (mid div: rdn over 2f out: outpcd) 1 8
1712a* Carling (FR) *(97) (MmePBarbe,France)* 3-8-8 TThulliez (plld: rcd in 4th: outpcd & bhd fnl 2f) .6 9

P-M 22.70F: 4.60F 1.80F 3.30F (72.60F) OWNER Mr J-L. Lagardere (FRANCE) BRED J-L. Lagardere 9 Rn
1m 35.7 SF: -/-/-/-/-/-/-/-/-

3195a-HOPPEGARTEN (Berlin, Germany) (R-H)
Sunday August 13th (Good to firm)

3200a
BMW EUROCHAMPIONAT (Gp 2) (3-Y.O) £164,609.00 (£61,728.00: £32,922.00: £16,461.00) **1m 4f** 3-30 (3-36)

2215a* **All My Dreams (IRE)** *(108) (HRemmert,Germany)* 3-9-2 KWoodburn (racd in 3rd: chal to ld over 1f out: hung rt: r.o strly) — 1
2215a6 Oxalagu (GER) *(103) (BSchutz,Germany)* 3-9-2 ASuborics (4th st: r.o fnl 2f: no imp) 4 2
2215a16 Kalimnos (GER) *(91) (HBlume,Germany)* 3-9-2 OSchick (trckd ldr: hmpd over 1f out: r.o) 9 3
161112 Korambi *(90) (CEBrittain)* 3-9-2 WWoods (led tl hdd by wnr: wknd) ½ 4
Coronar (GER) *(83) (Germany)* 3-9-2 WMongil (a rr) 5 5
Moltaire (GER) *(79) (Germany)* 3-9-2 THellier (a rr) 3 6

Tote 13DM: 12DM 23DM (SF71DM) OWNER Stall Rheinwiese BRED J.C.Condon 6 Rn
2m 26.2 SF: -/-/-/-/-/-

2983-BATH (L-H)
Friday August 18th (Hard)
WEATHER: sunny WIND: nil

3201
BOWOOD MAIDEN STKS (3-Y.O) (Class D) £3,860.50 (£1,078.00: £521.50) **1m 5y** Stalls: Low GOING minus 0.56 sec per fur (F) 5-45 (5-47)

23193 **Sejaal (IRE) (80)***(65++)*(Fav)*(JLDunlop)* 3-9-0 WCarson(3) (lw: dwlt: sn chsng ldr: 2nd st: nt clr run over 2f out: led on bit over 1f out: v.easily) — 1
27947 Fastini Gold *(63) (MDIUsher)* 3-9-0 MWigham(2) (dwlt: 3rd st: hdwy to ld over 2f out: hdd over 1f out: no ch w wnr) 1¼ 2
254013 Shazanni (IRE) **(40)** *(MRChannon)* 3-8-9 RHughes(4) (led: sn clr: rdn over 3f out: hdd over 2f out: sn btn & eased) dist 3

1/6 SEJAAL (IRE), **6/1** Fastini Gold (op 4/1), **14/1** Shazanni (IRE), CSF £1.55 TOTE £1.20 (£1.30) OWNER Mr Mirza Al Sayegh (ARUNDEL) BRED Norton Brookes 3 Rn 1m 43.4 (4.90) SF: 6/4/-

3202
WHITE HORSE (S) STKS (4-Y.O+) (Class G) £2,409.00 (£674.00: £327.00)
1m 3f 144y Stalls: Low GOING minus 0.56 sec per fur (F) 6-15 (6-15)

29762 **Excelled (IRE) (25)***(55)*(Fav)*(CJDrewe)* 6-9-0 RHughes(4) (3rd st: hrd rdn over 2f out: r.o to ld cl home) — 1

2860[10] Rose of Glenn **(47)***(59)*(Fav)*(BPalling)* 4-9-2 (3) SSanders(5) (led: rdn over 2f out: hdd cl home)....½ 2
2983[5] Pop to Stans **(47)***(48) (JPearce)* 6-9-3 (7) MNutter(3) (hld up: 4th st: rdn & hdwy 3f out: wknd wl over 1f out)....12 3
1771[11] Old Master (IRE) *(25) (RJBaker)* 4-9-5 MPerrett(2) (w ldr: 2nd st: wknd over 2f out: t.o)....13 4
3024[R] Bee Beat **(37)** *(AJChamberlain)* 7-9-10b 5x BPowell(1) (b: ref to r: t.n.p).... R

2/1 EXCELLED (IRE), Rose of Glenn, **9/4** Pop to Stans, **14/1** Bee Beat, **33/1** Old Master (IRE), CSF £5.84 TOTE £2.40: £1.40 £1.40 (£2.30) OWNER Mrs J. Strange (DIDCOT) BRED Leo Collins 5 Rn 2m 31.6 (4.90) SF: 22/26/15/-/-
Bt in 5,200 gns

3203

AVEBURY MEDIAN AUCTION MAIDEN STKS (2-Y.O) (Class D) £3,044.50 (£916.00: £443.00: £206.50)
5f 161y Stalls: Low GOING minus 0.56 sec per fur (F) 6-45 (6-45)

2340[5] **Xenophon of Cunaxa (IRE)** *(80) (MJFetherston-Godley)* 2-9-0 WNewnes(4) (mde virtually all: rdn clr 1f out: comf)....— 1
Meg's Memory (IRE) *(64) (JohnBerry)* 2-8-9 MFenton(1) (cmpt: bit bkwd: chsd wnr: rdn over 2f out: r.o one pce fnl f)....4 2
1823[2] Corniche Quest (IRE) **(69)***(64)*(Fav)*(MRChannon)* 2-8-9 RHughes(3) (hld up: chsd wnr 2f out: hung rt over 1f out: no imp)....hd 3
3069[12] Bold Enough *(59) (BWHills)* 2-8-9 WCarson(2) (hld up: a bhd)....1¾ 4

6/4 Corniche Quest (IRE), **9/4** Bold Enough, **5/2** XENOPHON OF CUNAXA (IRE), **8/1** Meg's Memory (IRE) (5/1-10/1), CSF £15.30 TOTE £3.90 (£9.20) OWNER Abigail Ltd (EAST ILSLEY) BRED Newtownbarry House Stud and Miss S. Von Schilcher 4 Rn 1m 11.6 (2.30) SF: 20/4/4/-

3204

STEVE VICK INTERNATIONAL SPRINT H'CAP (0-80) (3-Y.O+) (Class D) £3,673.25 (£1,106.00: £535.50: £250.25)
5f 161y Stalls: Low GOING minus 0.56 sec per fur (F) 7-15 (7-16)

2793[2] **Colston-C (66)***(71)*(Fav)*(CJHill)* 3-9-0 StephenDavies(1) (mde all: r.o wl)....— 1
2987* Fantasy Racing (IRE) **(75)***(77) (MRChannon)* 3-9-9 7x RHughes(7) (hld up: hdwy on ins 2f out: r.o ins fnl f)....1¼ 2
2512[4] Astral Invader (IRE) **(62)***(63) (MSSaunders)* 3-8-10 NAdams(8) (a.p: ev ch wl over 1f out: r.o one pce)....hd 3
2909[12] Winsome Wooster **(65)***(65) (PGMurphy)* 4-9-0 (3) SDrowne(6) (a.p: ev ch wl over 1f out: one pce)....nk 4
2708[2] La Gran Senorita (USA) **(75)***(71) (PFICole)* 3-9-2 (7) CRafter(4) (hdwy over 3f out: ev ch over 2f out: one pce fnl f)....1¾ 5
3028[4] Dry Point **(71)***(53)*(Fav)*(JARToller)* 9-9-9 WNewnes(3) (prom: rdn over 2f out: wknd over 1f out)....5 6
3116[6] Trioming **(46)***(16) (APJones)* 9-7-5 (7) CAdamson(5) (chsd ldrs: rdn over 2f out: wknd over 1f out)....4 7
1335[4] Maydaan (IRE) **(80)***(47) (BHanbury)* 3-9-11 (3) SSanders(2) (prom 3f)....1¼ 8

7/2 COLSTON-C, Dry Point, **9/2** Fantasy Racing (IRE), **7/1** Winsome Wooster, Maydaan (IRE), **8/1** La Gran Senorita (USA) (op 5/1), **12/1** Trioming, **16/1** Astral Invader (IRE), CSF £17.82 CT £194.34 TOTE £3.90: £1.60 £1.40 £2.90 (£6.90) Trio £62.10 OWNER Mr John Hill (BARNSTAPLE) BRED R. M. Eggo 8 Rn 1m 10.6 (1.30) SF: 34/40/26/32/34/20/-/10
WEIGHT FOR AGE 3yo-4lb

3205

LONGLEAT CLAIMING STKS (3-Y.O+) (Class F) £2,845.00 (£795.00: £385.00)
5f 11y Stalls: Low GOING minus 0.56 sec per fur (F) 7-45 (7-45)

2865* **Pearl Dawn (IRE) (64)***(72)*(Fav)*(NoelChance)* 5-8-11 JFEgan(6) (mde all: hrd rdn over 1f out: edgd rt ins fnl f: r.o wl)....— 1
3051* Ansellman **(72)***(77) (JBerry)* 5-9-10 GCarter(2) (outpcd: hdwy over 1f out: r.o ins fnl f)....2½ 2
2987[6] Paley Prince (USA) **(60)***(63) (MDIUsher)* 9-8-3 (7) CAdamson(5) (lw: a.p: chsd wnr wl over 1f out: one pce)....hd 3
2987[3] Giggleswick Girl **(63)***(52) (MRChannon)* 4-9-1 RHughes(4) (dwlt: hdwy 3f out: wknd over 1f out)....5 4
3123[10] Pacific Girl (IRE) **(53)***(48) (BPalling)* 3-8-9 (3) SSanders(7) (chsd wnr: rdn over 2f out: wknd over 1f out)....1¼ 5
2054[5] Nomadic Dancer (IRE) **(45)***(23) (MSSaunders)* 3-8-12 NAdams(1) (dwlt: a bhd)....8 6
2968[10] Ballysheila *(GFHCharles-Jones)* 3-7-8b(7)ow1 RStudholme(3) (b: s.s: a in rr: t.o)....8 7

15/8 PEARL DAWN (IRE), **2/1** Ansellman, **7/2** Giggleswick Girl, **6/1** Paley Prince (USA), **25/1** Pacific Girl (IRE), Nomadic Dancer (IRE), **100/1** Ballysheila, CSF £5.80 TOTE £2.30: £1.50 £1.60 (£2.50) OWNER Mrs M. Chance (LAMBOURN) BRED Niall Creighton 7 Rn

61.1 secs (0.60) SF: 39/44/30/19/12/-/-
WEIGHT FOR AGE 3yo-3lb

3206

WESTONBIRT H'CAP (0-70) (3-Y.O+ F & M) (Class E) £3,103.00 (£934.00: £452.00: £211.00)
1m 2f 46y Stalls: Low GOING minus 0.56 sec per fur (F) 8-15 (8-15)

2719* **Aqua Rigia (IRE) (52)***(61+)*(Fav)*(HCandy)* 3-9-8 WNewnes(4) (lw: 3rd st: rdn to ld over 1f out: r.o wl) — 1
2842⁴ Tout de Val **(28)***(32) (KBishop)* 6-8-6 RPerham(1) (sn chsng ldr: led 4f out tl over 1f out: one pce) 3 2
2655⁴ Suile Mor **(54)***(53) (BRMillman)* 3-9-10 JWilliams(2) (hld up & plld hrd: 4th st: one pce fnl 2f) 3½ 3
3034⁴ Magication **(34)***(31) (CNAllen)* 5-8-12 JQuinn(5) (hld up: last st: nvr nr to chal) 1 4
3129⁷ Chastleton **(40)***(37) (MRChannon)* 3-8-10 CandyMorris(6) (hld up: 5th st: hdwy over 2f out: wknd over 1f out) s.h 5
2984³ Bandita **(44)***(29) (DJSffrenchDavis)* 4-9-5 (3) SSanders(3) (led: hdd 4f out: 2nd st: hrd rdn over 2f out: sn wknd) 8 6

Evens AQUA RIGIA (IRE), **9/2** Suile Mor, **7/1** Bandita, **8/1** Tout de Val (6/1-10/1), **10/1** Magication, **11/1** Chastleton (op 6/1), CSF £8.33 TOTE £1.90: £1.30 £2.50 (£7.00) OWNER Mrs C. M. Poland (WANTAGE) BRED Newgate Stud Co 6 Rn 2m 11.2 (3.50) SF: 34/13/26/12/10/10

WEIGHT FOR AGE 3yo-8lb
T/Plpt: £37.00 (192.52 Tckts). T/Qdpt: £31.90 (1.6 Tckts). KH

2795-CHESTER (L-H)
Friday August 18th (Good to firm)

WEATHER: cloudy, v.warm WIND: almost nil

3207

WIRRAL APPRENTICE H'CAP (0-70) (3-Y.O+) (Class F) £2,656.75 (£814.00: £404.50: £199.75)
1m 2f 75y Stalls: High GOING minus 0.31 sec per fur (GF) 2-30 (2-31)

3169* **Braille (IRE) (58)***(76)*(Fav)*(MGMeagher)* 4-9-2 6x GFaulkner(1) (chsd ldrs: wnt 2nd ½-wy: rdn 2f out: styd on to ld ins fnl f) — 1
2928⁴ Daytona Beach (IRE) **(61)***(75) (DJSffrenchDavis)* 5-9-5 JDennis(2) (led: drvn clr over 2f out: hdd & no ex ins fnl f) 2½ 2
2798³ Rasayel (USA) **(44)***(49) (PDEvans)* 5-8-2 JoHunnam(9) (a.p: 3rd & outpcd ent st: sn btn) 6 3
*2919*¹⁶ Mhemeanles **(45)***(48) (CaptJWilson)* 5-8-3 VictoriaAppleby(6) (b.hind: hld up: effrt, stumbled & almost uns rdr 3f out: 5th & rdn st: nt rch ldrs) 1½ 4
3063⁷ Veloce (IRE) **(70)***(68) (ABailey)* 7-9-6 (8) AngelaGallimore(5) (b: plld hrd: hld up: hdwy 3f out: 4th st: wknd appr fnl f) 3 5
*2961*⁶ Studio Thirty **(45)***(33) (RHollinshead)* 3-7-6 (3)ow2 FLynch(3) (swtg: dwlt: a in rr) 5 6
*1211*⁷ Komreyev Dancer **(70)***(51) (ABailey)* 3-9-6 KSked(4) (bkwd: lost pl ½-wy: sn bhd: t.o) 6 7
Fair Flyer (IRE) **(55)***(35) (PJBevan)* 6-8-13 RMullen(8) (bkwd: a bhd: t.o fnl 3f) ¾ 8
*2292*⁴ Shansi (IRE) **(38)***(13) (MDIUsher)* 4-7-10b BHalligan(7) (b: prom: 7f: sn wknd: 6th & btn st: t.o) 3 9

LONG HANDICAP Studio Thirty 7-4

11/8 BRAILLE (IRE), **5/1** Daytona Beach (IRE), Rasayel (USA), **11/1** Veloce (IRE) (8/1-12/1), **12/1** Komreyev Dancer (op 8/1), **14/1** Mhemeanles, **16/1** Studio Thirty, **20/1** Shansi (IRE), **25/1** Fair Flyer (IRE), CSF £8.09 CT £23.04 TOTE £2.40: £1.30 £1.40 £1.50 (£3.80) Trio £5.50 OWNER The Winning Feature Partnership (ORMSKIRK) BRED John McLoughlin 9 Rn

2m 11.04 (2.34) SF: 57/56/30/29/49/6/24/16/-
WEIGHT FOR AGE 3yo-8lb

3208

E.B.F. GREY FRIARS MAIDEN STKS (2-Y.O) (Class D) £4,276.00 (£1,288.00: £624.00: £292.00)
7f 2y Stalls: Low GOING minus 0.31 sec per fur (GF) 3-00 (3-00)

2741² **Tawkil (USA)** *(92+)*(Fav)*(BWHills)* 2-9-0 RHills(4) (mde all: qcknd clr ent st: drvn out fnl f) — 1
2408⁴ Hidden Oasis *(89) (MRStoute)* 2-9-0 WRSwinburn(2) (hld up: 2nd st: effrt bel dist: r.o wl fnl f) 1¼ 2
2681⁵ Weet-A-Minute (IRE) *(76) (RHollinshead)* 2-9-0 TIves(3) (a.p: 3rd & rdn st: kpt on one pce) 6 3
2441⁵ Acharne *(66) (CEBrittain)* 2-9-0 BDoyle(5) (lw: s.s: hdwy ½-wy: rdn & 4th st: sn outpcd) 4 4
2995⁹ Serious Trust *(53) (SirMarkPrescott)* 2-9-0 GDuffield(1) (sn wl bhd & outpcd: 5th st: t.o) 6 5

4/6 TAWKIL (USA) (10/11-Evens), **5/2** Hidden Oasis, **6/1** Acharne, **9/1** Weet-A-Minute (IRE), **20/1** Serious Trust, CSF £2.99 TOTE £1.60: £1.10 £1.50 (£1.60) OWNER Mr Hamdan Al Maktoum (LAMBOURN) BRED Braeburn Farm Corp 5 Rn 1m 27.13 (1.93) SF: 50/47/34/24/11

3209 EASTGATE RATED H'CAP (0-95) (3-Y.O) (Class B) £8,168.76
(£3,048.84: £1,484.42: £631.10: £275.55: £133.33)
7f 2y Stalls: Low GOING minus 0.31 sec per fur (GF) 3-30 (3-30)

2848* **Wild Rice (87)***(93)*(Fav)*(GWragg)* 3-9-3 MHills(3) (b: b.off hind: a.p: effrt & 3rd st: led ins fnl f: all out)......— 1
3145* Tiler (IRE) **(81)***(87) (MJohnston)* 3-8-11 3x DHolland(4) (led tl ins fnl f: rallied gamely nr fin)...hd 2
2471[4] Kabil **(86)***(92) (HThomsonJones)* 3-9-2 RHills(1) (lw: hld up & bhd: gd hdwy & 4th st: str chal fnl f: jst failed)......hd 3
2647[7] Khamseh **(83)***(86) (JWWatts)* 3-8-13 JWeaver(6) (hld up: hdwy over 2f out: 5th st: kpt on fnl f: nt pce to chal)......1¼ 4
2616[9] Sotoboy (IRE) **(91)***(80) (PWHarris)* 3-9-7 GDuffield(5) (swtg: sn chsng ldr: 2nd st: rdn & wknd bel dist)......6 5
2748[2] She's Dynamite (IRE) **(85)***(68) (WJarvis)* 3-9-1 BThomson(7) (prom: rdn along ½-wy: wknd fnl 2f)......2½ 6
1605[7] Last Roundup **(82)***(64) (CWThornton)* 3-8-12 DeanMcKeown(2) (lw: prom tl 6th & btn st)........½ 7

6/4 WILD RICE, **7/2** Tiler (IRE), **11/2** Kabil, **6/1** She's Dynamite (IRE), **9/1** Khamseh, **16/1** Sotoboy (IRE), **25/1** Last Roundup, CSF £6.74 TOTE £2.20: £1.50 £2.10 (£2.50) OWNER Sir Philip Oppenheimer (NEWMARKET) BRED Hascombe and Valiant Studs 7 Rn
1m 25.67 (0.47) SF: 70/64/69/63/57/45/41

3210 COMBERMERE CONDITIONS STKS (2-Y.O F) (Class C) £4,755.70
(£1,733.20: £846.60: £363.00: £161.50)
6f 18y Stalls: Low GOING minus 0.31 sec per fur (GF) 4-00 (4-03)

2947[5] **Tropical Dance (USA) (99)***(88)*(Fav)*(MrsJCecil)* 2-9-6 JReid(1) (mde all: rdn out: comf)......— 1
1530[5] Red Stream (USA) *(74) (MRStoute)* 2-8-11 WRSwinburn(4) (hld up & bhd: effrt & rdn over 2f out: kpt on fnl f: no ch w wnr)......2 2
2800[3] Whittle Rock **(76)***(69) (EJAlston)* 2-8-11 KFallon(2) (swtg: chsd wnr tl rdn & wknd ins fnl f)...1¾ 3
2459[5] Limerick Princess (IRE) **(76)***(64) (JBerry)* 2-8-11 JCarroll(3) (lw: chsd ldrs: rdn 2f out: r.o one pce)......2 4
2143[W] Steal 'Em *(32) (ABailey)* 2-8-8 KDarley(5) (bit bkwd: s.s: sn rcvrd: rdn over 2f out: sn btn: t.o)11 5

11/8 TROPICAL DANCE (USA), **15/8** Red Stream (USA), **11/2** Limerick Princess (IRE), **7/1** Whittle Rock, **14/1** Steal 'Em (op 8/1), CSF £4.22 TOTE £2.00: £1.50 £1.60 (£1.80) OWNER Mr George Ward (NEWMARKET) BRED Charles T Wilson Jr. 5 Rn 1m 15.22 (1.92) SF: 52/38/33/28/-

3211 BLACK FRIARS H'CAP (0-80) (3-Y.O+) (Class D) £4,802.00
(£1,436.00: £688.00: £314.00)
1m 7f 195y Stalls: Low GOING minus 0.31 sec per fur (GF) 4-35 (4-35)

2284[9] **Fujiyama Crest (IRE) (64)***(78) (MRStoute)* 3-8-1 PRobinson(6) (b.nr hind: mde all: clr ent st: unchal)......— 1
2429[6] Welshman **(58)***(65) (MBlanshard)* 9-8-9 KDarley(3) (chsd wnr fr 7f out: sn rdn: 2nd st: no imp)7 2
2986* Arc Bright (IRE) **(50)***(56) (RHollinshead)* 5-8-1 4x BDoyle(1) (chsd wnr 9f: rdn & outpcd over 3f out: 4th & btn st)......¾ 3
2798* No Comebacks **(61)***(67) (EJAlston)* 7-8-12 KFallon(5) (hld up & bhd: hdwy 3f out: 5th st: sn rdn: nt rch ldrs)......hd 4
2996[4] Moonlight Quest **(77)***(73)*(Fav)*(BHanbury)* 7-9-11 (3) JStack(2) (drppd rr ½-wy: effrt & rdn over 3f out: no imp: 6th st: eased)......10 5
2835* Admirals Secret (USA) **(70)***(64) (CFWall)* 6-9-2 (5) LNewton(4) (hld up: hdwy 4f out: 5th st: wknd wl over 1f out)......2½ 6

2/1 Moonlight Quest, **4/1** Admirals Secret (USA), **5/1** No Comebacks, Arc Bright (IRE), **8/1** FUJIYAMA CREST (IRE), Welshman, CSF £54.73 TOTE £8.50: £2.40 £2.80 (£27.70) OWNER Mr Seisuke Hata (NEWMARKET) BRED B. Kennedy 6 Rn 3m 27.24 (4.34) SF: 40/41/32/43/49/40
WEIGHT FOR AGE 3yo-14lb

3212 RED DEER H'CAP (0-100) (3-Y.O+) (Class C) £5,881.00
(£1,768.00: £854.00: £397.00)
7f 2y Stalls: Low GOING minus 0.31 sec per fur (GF) 5-10 (5-11)

2369[15] **En Attendant (FR) (94)***(106) (BHanbury)* 7-10-0 JReid(4) (b: b.hind: hld up: hdwy 3f out: 4th st: r.o to ld wl ins fnl f)......— 1

3051² Elle Shaped (IRE) **(72)***(83) (ABailey)* 5-8-3 (3) DWright(7) (swtg: led tl hdd wl ins fnl f)............½ 2
2952⁶ Chinour (IRE) **(69)***(72) (EJAlston)* 7-8-3 BDoyle(13) (s.s: bhd tl hdwy ent st: fin wl)...............3½ 3
2737⁷ Russian Heroine **(75)***(78) (MJohnston)* 3-8-4 DHolland(3) (chsd ldr: rdn & 3rd st: kpt on same pce).......................hd 4
3109³ Persian Affair (IRE) **(63)***(62) (DHaydnJones)* 4-7-11 AMackay(1) (bhd tl gd hdwy appr fnl f: nrst fin).......................1¼ 5
2948⁴ Elite Hope (USA) **(83)***(80) (CREgerton)* 3-8-12 BThomson(5) (lw: chsd ldrs: effrt & 5th st: nvr trbld ldrs).......................1 6
2909³ Rocketeer (IRE) **(75)***(71)*(Fav)*(WRMuir)* 4-8-9b JWeaver(2) (lw: swtg: bhd tl r.o appr fnl f: nvr nrr).......................½ 7
3112¹³ Bargash **(70)***(57) (PDEvans)* 3-7-6 (7) AmandaSanders(6) (prom: 6th st: wknd ent fnl f)............4 8
2099⁷ Selhurstpark Flyer (IRE) **(82)***(69) (JBerry)* 4-9-2 JCarroll(11) (lw: prom: 2nd st: wknd qckly over 1f out).......................s.h 9
2458⁵ Highborn (IRE) **(81)***(54) (PSFelgate)* 6-9-1 KDarley(9) (lw: nvr nr to chal)...............................6 10
2001⁸ Champagne Grandy **(77)***(46) (MRChannon)* 5-8-8 (3) JStack(8) (a in rr) 1½ 11
3065⁵ Chickawicka (IRE) **(88)***(55) (MCPipe)* 4-9-3v(5) LNewton(12) (chsd ldrs over 4f: sn wknd) 1¼ 12
2948¹¹ Absolute Magic **(80)***(43) (WJHaggas)* 5-9-0 MHills(10) (b.off hind: a bhd)............................1½ 13

11/2 Rocketeer (IRE), **13/2** Persian Affair (IRE), **7/1** Elite Hope (USA), Russian Heroine, **9/1** Elle Shaped (IRE), Highborn (IRE), **10/1** Champagne Grandy, **12/1** Chickawicka (IRE), **14/1** EN ATTENDANT (FR), Absolute Magic, Selhurstpark Flyer (IRE), **20/1** Chinour (IRE), **33/1** Bargash, CSF £119.57 CT £2,269.88 TOTE £18.20: £5.20 £2.20 £7.60 (£50.70) Trio £312.70 OWNER Mrs B. Newton (NEWMARKET) BRED Marystead Farm 13 Rn

1m 25.63 (0.43) SF: 81/58/47/48/37/50/46/27/44/29/21/30/18
WEIGHT FOR AGE 3yo-5lb
T/Plpt: £102.20 (146.09 Tckts). T/Qdpt: £57.20 (2.1 Tckts). IM

3011-SANDOWN (R-H)
Friday August 18th (Good to firm)
WEATHER: very hot WIND: almost nil

3213 ORLEANS NURSERY H'CAP (2-Y.O) (Class D) £4,221.00 (£1,278.00: £624.00: £297.00)
5f 6y Stalls: Low GOING minus 0.30 sec per fur (GF) 2-00 (2-02)

2991* **Westcourt Magic (71)***(88+)*(Fav)*(MWEasterby)* 2-8-8 5x GCarter(8) (mde all: clr over 1f out: r.o wl).......................— 1
3064* Pleasure Time **(70)***(68) (CSmith)* 2-8-7b 5x NCarlisle(1) (lw: chsd wnr: hrd rdn over 1f out: unable qckn).......................6 2
2618² Atraf **(84)***(78) (DMorley)* 2-9-7 WCarson(3) (rdn over 2f out: hdwy over 1f out: r.o one pce)..1¼ 3
3064³ Centurion **(72)***(65) (RHannon)* 2-8-9 PatEddery(2) (swtg: rdn over 3f out: hdwy over 1f out: one pce).......................nk 4
2459⁶ Erupt **(67)***(58) (GBBalding)* 2-8-1 (3) NVarley(9) (rdn & hdwy over 2f out: one pce)..................¾ 5
2940² Caricature (IRE) **(83)***(73) (GLewis)* 2-9-6 PaulEddery(7) (a.p: rdn over 2f out: one pce).........hd 6
1938¹⁰ Rowlandsons Charm (IRE) **(64)***(53) (GLMoore)* 2-8-1 FNorton(5) (bit bkwd: a bhd) ....½ 7
1938⁴ Meranti **(73)***(59) (LJHolt)* 2-8-10 MFenton(4) (lw: a bhd).......................¾ 8
3100⁴ Gagajulu **(75)***(60) (PDEvans)* 2-8-12 GHind(6) (prom over 3f).......................nk 9

15/8 WESTCOURT MAGIC, **4/1** Atraf, **5/1** Centurion, **8/1** Caricature (IRE) (op 5/1), **10/1** Pleasure Time, Gagajulu, **20/1** Erupt, Meranti, **33/1** Rowlandsons Charm (IRE), CSF £18.68 CT £60.37 TOTE £2.70: £1.20 £3.00 £1.50 (£15.70) Trio £31.50 OWNER Mr K. Hodgson (SHERIFF HUTTON) BRED C. R. and V. M. Withers 9 Rn 60.91 secs (1.11) SF: 49/29/39/26/19/34/14/20/21

3214 ALBERT H'CAP (0-90) (3-Y.O) (Class C) £5,810.00 (£1,760.00: £860.00: £410.00)
1m 14y Stalls: High GOING minus 0.08 sec per fur (G) 2-35 (2-39)

2111³ **Alkateb (87)***(93) (MissGayKelleway)* 3-9-7 RCochrane(6) (lw: rdn over 2f out: hdwy over 1f out: led last strides).......................— 1
2583* Russian Maid **(80)***(85)*(Fav)*(JRFanshawe)* 3-9-0 DHarrison(3) (b.hind: 5th st: led over 1f out: hrd rdn: hdd last strides).......................nk 2
2654² Pennycairn **(79)***(84) (HRACecil)* 3-8-13 WRyan(5) (4th st: led over 2f out tl over 1f out: hrd rdn: ev ch ins fnl f: r.o wl).......................s.h 3
2933² Hardy Dancer **(87)***(91) (GLMoore)* 3-9-7 SWhitworth(8) (swtg: 3rd st: rdn over 2f out: r.o ins fnl f).......................¾ 4
2616⁵ Stone Ridge (IRE) **(86)***(85) (RHannon)* 3-9-6 RHughes(11) (rdn over 2f out: hdwy over 1f out: r.o one pce).......................2½ 5

Red Light **(75)***(72) (LordHuntingdon)* 3-8-9 TQuinn(9) (nvr nr to chal).....................................1 6
2669[5] Captain's Day **(81)***(77) (TGMills)* 3-8-8 (7) DToole(10) (lw: 6th st: rdn over 2f out: one pce).....nk 7
2803[W] Muchtarak (IRE) **(86)***(81) (CJBenstead)* 3-9-6 WCarson(4) (swtg: nvr plcd to chal)................¾ 8
2794[8] Yeath (IRE) **(65)***(59) (RAkehurst)* 3-7-13 JQuinn(7) (lw: nvr nrr)..½ 9
2738[6] Kimbridge Knight (IRE) **(81)***(73) (PTWalwyn)* 3-9-1v PatEddery(1) (swtg: 2nd st: ev ch over 2f out: wknd over 1f out)...¾ 10
3125* Elpidos **(75)***(64) (CEBrittain)* 3-8-9 6x MRoberts(12) (7th st: rdn over 2f out: wknd over 1f out)1¾ 11
2616[10] Jibereen **(80)***(61) (GLewis)* 3-9-0 PaulEddery(2) (led over 5f) 4 12
2803[6] Iktasab **(86)***(63) (EALDunlop)* 3-9-3 (3) JTate(13) (rdn over 2f out: hdwy over 1f out: nt clr run on ins & eased ins fnl f) 2 13

7/2 Russian Maid, **6/1** Kimbridge Knight (IRE), **13/2** Hardy Dancer, Pennycairn, **7/1** Elpidos, **9/1** Stone Ridge (IRE), **10/1** Muchtarak (IRE), **14/1** Yeath (IRE) (10/1-16/1), Captain's Day, **16/1** Red Light, ALKATEB, Iktasab, **33/1** Jibereen, CSF £71.13 CT £384.43 TOTE £11.40: £4.40 £1.90 £2.00 (£78.60) Trio £130.40 OWNER Mr Steve May (WHITCOMBE) BRED Greenland Park Stud 13 Rn
1m 43.99 (4.79) SF: 50/42/41/48/42/29/34/38/16/30/21/18/20

3215 CHARTERHOUSE CONDITIONS STKS (2-Y.O) (Class C) £4,779.50 (£1,742.00: £851.00: £365.00: £162.50)

1m 14y Stalls: High GOING minus 0.08 sec per fur (G) 3-10 (3-12)

2796* **Bonarelli (IRE)** *(89) (MRStoute)* 2-8-13 PatEddery(1) (swtg: 3rd st: led over 2f out: r.o wl)...— 1
2690[4] Mushahid (USA) **(100)***(92)*(Fav)*(JLDunlop)* 2-9-3 WCarson(2) (swtg: 2nd st: ev ch fnl 2f: r.o).½ 2
2529* Oblomov **(84)***(78) (GLewis)* 2-8-13 PaulEddery(3) (lw: led over 5f: hrd rdn over 1f out: unable qckn)...5 3
2420* Vilayet *(78) (HRACecil)* 2-8-13 WRyan(5) (lw: 5th st: rdn over 2f out: one pce)......................nk 4
2320[16] Minsterbeach *(46) (CEBrittain)* 2-8-11 MRoberts(4) (4th st: wknd over 3f out) 15 5

Evens Mushahid (USA), **5/2** Vilayet, **100/30** BONARELLI (IRE), **25/1** Oblomov, **50/1** Minsterbeach, CSF £6.63 TOTE £4.10: £2.10 £1.10 (£3.10) OWNER Sheikh Mohammed (NEWMARKET) BRED Robert Griffin 5 Rn 1m 45.11 (5.91) SF: 32/35/21/21/-

3216 SOLARIO STKS (Gp 3) (2-Y.O) (Class A) £21,480.00 (£8,049.00: £3,874.50: £1,696.50)

7f 16y Stalls: High GOING minus 0.08 sec per fur (G) 3-45 (3-45)

2690* **Alhaarth (IRE)** *(104+)*(Fav)*(MajorWRHern)* 2-9-2 WCarson(4) (lw: chsd ldr: led 2f out: easily) ....— 1
2947[2] Staffin **(100)***(87) (JRFanshawe)* 2-8-6 DHarrison(2) (4th st: rdn 3f out: r.o one pce).................3 2
2473* Dismissed (USA) *(88) (PFICole)* 2-8-11 TQuinn(1) (b.nr hind: lw: 3rd st: hrd rdn & ev ch over 1f out: one pce)...2 3
2947[6] White Whispers **(93)***(65) (BJMeehan)* 2-8-6 AClark(3) (swtg: led 5f)..8 4

30/100 ALHAARTH (IRE), **4/1** Staffin (op 5/2), **12/1** Dismissed (USA) (op 7/1), **100/1** White Whispers, CSF £1.74 TOTE £1.20 (£1.10) OWNER Mr Hamdan Al Maktoum (LAMBOURN) BRED Shadwell Estate Company Limited 4 Rn 1m 31.0 (4.40) SF: 43/26/27/4

3217 CLAYGATE STAYERS H'CAP (0-70) (3-Y.O+) (Class E) £3,793.75 (£1,150.00: £562.50: £268.75)

2m 78y Stalls: High GOING minus 0.08 sec per fur (G) 4-15 (4-16)

2569[4] **Gentleman Sid (45)***(57) (PGMurphy)* 5-8-3 NAdams(10) (3rd st: led over 3f out: clr 2f out: hrd rdn over 1f out: r.o wl) ....— 1
2184[2] Swivel **(68)***(78)*(Fav)*(JRFanshawe)* 3-8-12 DHarrison(6) (nt clr run & swtchd lft 3f out: hdwy over 2f out: chsd wnr over 1f out: r.o) 2 2
549[9] Southampton **(35)***(44) (GBBalding)* 5-7-4 (3) NVarley(11) (rdn & hdwy over 2f out: r.o ins fnl f) ¾ 3
2860[3] Brumon (IRE) **(57)***(64) (DWPArbuthnot)* 4-9-1 JWilliams(9) (b: lw: hdwy over 1f out: r.o) 2½ 4
3029[10] Persian Smoke **(43)***(50) (AHide)* 4-7-10 (5) MHenry(8) (4th st: rdn over 3f out: one pce) ....hd 5
2860[2] Tommy Cooper **(45)***(50) (MrsBarbaraWaring)* 4-8-0 (3)ow1 SDrowne(3) (b.hind: 6th st: nt clr run over 3f out & over 2f out: one pce)..¾ 6
2688* Imad (USA) **(65)***(69) (JWhite)* 5-9-9 DaleGibson(4) (5th st: rdn over 3f out: one pce) 2 7
2986[4] Chucklestone **(48)***(52) (JSKing)* 12-8-6 PaulEddery(14) (led over 14f out tl over 8f out: 2nd st: wknd over 2f out) ....½ 8
2695[3] Chakalak **(47)***(42) (SDow)* 7-8-5 MRoberts(2) (lw: a bhd)...9 9
2657[8] Tondres (USA) **(59)***(39) (RIngram)* 4-9-3b AMcGlone(13) (swtg: a bhd) 15 10
2514[5] Phil's Time **(55)***(16) (TGMills)* 4-8-6 (7) JCornally(1) (prom 12f)...20 11
2942[2] Bardolph (USA) **(63)***(12) (PFICole)* 8-9-7b TQuinn(5) (b.off hind: swtg: led 2f: led over 8f out tl over 3f out: sn wknd) 12 12

2569[2] Art Form (USA) **(68)** *(CACyzer)* 8-9-12 DBiggs(7) (rdn 7f out: 9th whn stumbled & fell bnd over 3f out)........ F

LONG HANDICAP Southampton 7-5

9/2 Swivel, **5/1** Art Form (USA), **6/1** Chakalak, **13/2** Imad (USA) (9/2-7/1), **7/1** GENTLEMAN SID, **9/1** Bardolph (USA), **10/1** Brumon (IRE), Tommy Cooper, **14/1** Phil's Time, **16/1** Tondres (USA), **20/1** Persian Smoke, **25/1** Chucklestone, **33/1** Southampton, CSF £38.10 CT £916.99 TOTE £10.70: £2.90 £1.90 £11.20 (£25.50) Trio £919.70 OWNER Miss J. Collison (BRISTOL) BRED D. I. Heathcote 13 Rn 3m 39.15 (9.15) SF: 38/45/25/45/31/31/50/33/23/20/-/-/-

WEIGHT FOR AGE 3yo-14lb

STEWARDS' ENQUIRY Harrison susp. 2-15/9/95 (irresponsible riding).

3218

HOGS BACK CLAIMING STKS (3-Y.O) (Class D) £3,582.50 (£1,085.00: £530.00: £252.50) **1m 1f** Stalls: High GOING minus 0.08 sec per fur (G) 4-50 (4-52)

2103[13] **Sharpical (67)***(75) (JRFanshawe)* 3-8-4 DHarrison(8) (4th st: rdn over 1f out: led ins fnl f: r.o wl)........— 1
2319[8] Brown Eyed Girl **(68)***(69) (RHannon)* 3-8-1 GCarter(3) (lw: 5th st: rdn over 3f out: ev ch over 1f out: unable qckn)........1½ 2
3057[9] Lorelei Lee (IRE) **(64)***(73) (JohnBerry)* 3-8-5 MRoberts(4) (lw: 2nd st: led over 2f out tl ins fnl f: one pce)........s.h 3
3016[14] Red Morning **(60)***(60) (DRCElsworth)* 3-8-6 PatEddery(7) (6th st: hrd rdn over 2f out: one pce)8 4
2684[2] Elite Racing **(67)***(53)*(Fav)*(PFICole)* 3-8-4b TQuinn(2) (b. hind: led over 6f: wknd over 1f out)..3 5
3096* Gentle Irony **(55)***(47) (BJMeehan)* 3-7-13b JQuinn(6) (3rd st: wknd over 1f out)........nk 6
715[23] Sunoma Valley *(45) (JMPEustace)* 3-8-11 MTebbutt(5) (lw: s.s: a bhd)........8 7
2181[8] Red Dragon **(59)***(44) (GWragg)* 3-8-11 PaulEddery(1) (a bhd)........¾ 8

15/8 Elite Racing, **100/30** Brown Eyed Girl, **7/2** Gentle Irony, **7/1** SHARPICAL, **10/1** Red Morning, Lorelei Lee (IRE), **16/1** Red Dragon, **33/1** Sunoma Valley, CSF £29.78 TOTE £8.70: £1.90 £1.80 £2.20 (£17.80) OWNER Mrs Mary Watt (NEWMARKET) BRED E. R. W. Stanley and New England Stud Farm Ltd 8 Rn 1m 57.15 (5.75) SF: 31/25/29/16/9/3/1/-

Sharpical clmd A.S.Reid £8,000

3219

SURREY RACING H'CAP (0-80) (3-Y.O+) (Class D) £3,777.50(£1,145.00: £560.00: £267.50) **5f 6y** Stalls: Low GOING minus 0.30 sec per fur (GF) 5-20 (5-23)

3087[3] **Mr Bergerac (IRE) (76)***(85) (BPalling)* 4-9-13 TSprake(3) (hld up: rdn over 3f out: led over 1f out: r.o wl)........— 1
3014* King Rat (IRE) **(69)***(72) (TJEtherington)* 4-9-6b 7x PatEddery(4) (lw: a.p: stumbled over 2f out: unable qckn fnl f)........1¾ 2
3014[3] Judgement Call **(49)***(48) (PHowling)* 8-8-0 NCarlisle(1) (b: lost pl over 3f out: rallied fnl f: r.o)1½ 3
3028[2] Double Bounce **(69)***(64)*(Fav)*(PJMakin)* 5-9-6 RCochrane(9) (rdn over 2f out: hdwy over 1f out: one pce)........1¼ 4
2850* Miami Banker **(55)***(45) (WRMuir)* 9-8-6b GBardwell(7) (lw: led over 2f: wknd over 1f out)........1½ 5
2680* General Sir Peter (IRE) **(72)***(62) (PFICole)* 3-9-6 TQuinn(2) (lw: nvr nr to chal)........s.h 6
3116[10] Featherstone Lane **(54)***(42) (MissLCSiddall)* 4-8-5v DHarrison(8) (a.p: led over 2f out tl over 1f out: sn wknd)........½ 7
3087[4] Robellion **(71)***(58) (DWPArbuthnot)* 4-9-8v WWoods(5) (prom over 3f)........nk 8
3014[5] Moujeeb (USA) **(58)***(43) (PatMitchell)* 5-8-9v AClark(6) (lw: rdn over 3f out: hdwy 2f out: eased whn btn ins fnl f)........¾ 9

15/8 Double Bounce, **5/1** King Rat (IRE), General Sir Peter (IRE) (7/2-11/2), **6/1** MR BERGERAC (IRE), **8/1** Judgement Call, **10/1** Miami Banker (8/1-12/1), Robellion (7/1-12/1), **20/1** Featherstone Lane, Moujeeb (USA), CSF £34.78 CT £218.94 TOTE £8.40: £2.30 £1.20 £2.60 (£15.70) Trio £47.20 OWNER Mr P. R. John (COWBRIDGE) BRED Red House Stud 9 Rn

60.86 secs (1.06) SF: 68/55/31/47/28/42/25/41/26

WEIGHT FOR AGE 3yo-3lb

T/Jkpt: Not won; £7,091.84 to Sandown 19/8/95. T/Plpt: £84.20 (318.80 Tckts). T/Qdpt: £31.80 (5.90 Tckts). AK

3207-CHESTER (L-H)

Saturday August 19th (Good to firm)

WEATHER: sunny & hot WIND: slt half bhd

3220

LINENHALL CONDITIONS STKS (2-Y.O C & G) (Class C) £6,677.00 (£2,337.00: £1,143.50: £492.50)
6f 18y Stalls: Low GOING minus 0.32 sec per fur (GF) 1-55 (1-56)

2365[3] **Dovebrace (100)***(106) (ABailey)* 2-9-6 DHolland(2) (chsd ldrs: rdn to disp ld ins fnl f: led last stride)........— 1

2904* Mazeed (IRE) **(87)**(*104*)(Fav)*(HThomsonJones)* 2-9-4 NCarlisle(3) (s.i.s: shkn up & hdwy 2f out: swtchd lft & r.o strly fnl f: jst failed)........s.h **2**
2243[6] Tadeo **(96)**(*99*) *(MJohnston)* 2-8-13 MRoberts(1) (led tl hrd rdn & ct post)........s.h **3**
3049* Albert The Bear **(76)**(*91?*) *(JBerry)* 2-8-10 JCarroll(4) (chsd ldrs: rdn over 1f out: r.o one pce)........1¾ **4**

6/5 Mazeed (IRE) (Evens-5/4), **5/2** Tadeo, **3/1** DOVEBRACE, **9/1** Albert The Bear (6/1-10/1), CSF £6.65 TOTE £3.90 (£2.50) OWNER Mr David Jones (TARPORLEY) BRED Mrs M. Christian 4 Rn
1m 15.93 (2.63) SF: 42/40/35/27

3221

ROWTON MOOR H'CAP (0-85) (3-Y.O+) (Class D) £8,318.00 (£2,504.00: £1,212.00: £566.00)
5f 16y Stalls: Low GOING minus 0.32 sec per fur (GF) 2-30 (2-32)

3212[2] **Elle Shaped (IRE) (72)**(*86*)(Fav)*(ABailey)* 5-9-1 (3) DWright(3) (swtg: chsd ldrs: led 1f out: qcknd clr: easily)........— **1**
1777[10] Ann's Pearl (IRE) **(77)**(*78*) *(JWHills)* 4-9-4 (5) MHenry(2) (hld up: hdwy 2f out: r.o ins fnl f: nvr nrr)........4 **2**
3116[9] My Abbey **(55)**(*53*) *(EJAlston)* 6-8-1 GHind(12) (swtg: hdwy on outside wl over 1f out: fin wl)..1 **3**
2992[10] Croft Imperial **(66)**(*62*) *(MJohnston)* 8-8-12v TWilliams(9) (a.p: rdn along ½-wy: kpt on fnl f)....¾ **4**
2916[2] Lady Sheriff **(75)**(*69*) *(MWEasterby)* 4-9-0b(7) PFessey(11) (w ldrs: led bel dist: sn hdd: unable qckn)........½ **5**
2764[25] Saddlehome (USA) **(81)**(*74*) *(TDBarron)* 6-9-13 JFortune(1) (lw: hld up in tch: hdwy ent st: sn rdn: nt pce to chal)........nk **6**
2905* King Rambo **(64)**(*57*) *(RHollinshead)* 4-8-10 DHarrison(4) (in tch: no hdwy fnl 2f)........s.h **7**
2909[10] Insider Trader **(75)**(*67*) *(RGuest)* 4-9-7b MRoberts(8) (b: lw: hdwy & swtchd rt appr fnl f: r.o) ..½ **8**
2700[4] So Intrepid (IRE) **(74)**(*65*) *(JMBradley)* 5-9-3 (3) SDrowne(6) (mid div tl wknd appr fnl f)........nk **9**
2935[8] Gondo **(47)**(*32*) *(EJAlston)* 8-7-2v(5) MBaird(14) (s.s: a bhd)........1¾ **10**
2686[6] Tuscan Dawn **(76)**(*60*) *(JBerry)* 5-9-8 JCarroll(10) (lw: s.s: a bhd & outpcd)........½ **11**
2867[2] Tommy Tempest **(47)**(*25*) *(REPeacock)* 6-7-7v JLowe(5) (swtg: led to bel dist: sn wknd)........1¾ **12**
2935[14] Allwight Then (IRE) **(72)**(*42*) *(FHLee)* 4-9-4b NCarlisle(7) (gd spd 3f)........2½ **13**
2692[9] Total Stranger **(76)**(*42*) *(MrsLPiggott)* 3-8-12 (7) GMilligan(13) (chsd ldrs over 3f: sn outpcd) .1¼ **14**

LONG HANDICAP Tommy Tempest 6-13 Gondo 7-6

3/1 ELLE SHAPED (IRE), **7/1** Lady Sheriff, Insider Trader, **8/1** Saddlehome (USA) (6/1-9/1), **9/1** King Rambo, **10/1** So Intrepid (IRE), **14/1** Croft Imperial, Tuscan Dawn (op 8/1), Total Stranger (10/1-16/1), **16/1** Gondo, Ann's Pearl (IRE), **20/1** My Abbey, Allwight Then (IRE), **33/1** Tommy Tempest, CSF £47.19 CT £769.17 TOTE £3.50: £2.00 £5.10 £6.30 (£24.00) Trio £1,179.10 OWNER Simple Technology UK Ltd (TARPORLEY) BRED Dan Daly 14 Rn
60.64 secs (0.64) SF: 64/56/31/40/47/52/35/45/43/10/38/3/20/17
WEIGHT FOR AGE 3yo-3lb

3222

ROTHMANS ROYALS NORTH SOUTH CHALLENGE SERIES H'CAP (0-90) (3-Y.O+) (Class C) £7,749.50 (£2,336.00: £1,133.00: £531.50)
7f 122y Stalls: Low GOING minus 0.32 sec per fur (GF) 3-00 (3-04)

3113[2] **Pride of Pendle (74)**(*85*) *(DNicholls)* 6-9-0 AlexGreaves(13) (hld up: hdwy over 2f out: led wl ins fnl f: r.o wl)........— **1**
3074[5] Bold Angel **(68)**(*78*) *(MHEasterby)* 8-8-8 TWilliams(1) (swtg: hld up: hdwy ½-wy: 4th st: led ins fnl f: sn hdd & kpt on)........½ **2**
2853[3] Allinson's Mate (IRE) **(77)**(*84*) *(TDBarron)* 7-9-3b JFortune(9) (lw: hld up: hdwy 2f out: rdn & edgd lft & r.o strly ins fnl f)........1½ **3**
3113[5] Wentbridge Lad (IRE) **(61)**(*67*) *(PDEvans)* 5-8-1 ow1 GHind(11) (lw: hld up: hdwy 2f out: swtchd lft appr fnl f: fin wl)........s.h **4**
2803* Fairy Story (IRE) **(75)**(*79*)(Fav)*(RAkehurst)* 5-8-12 (3) SSanders(2) (chsd ldrs: 3rd st: ev ch 1f out: btn whn n.m.r nr fin)........1¼ **5**
2979[2] Mr Rough **(64)**(*67*) *(DMorris)* 4-8-4 DHarrison(7) (chsd ldrs: 5th st: kpt on u.p ins fnl f)........nk **6**
3207[2] Daytona Beach (IRE) **(61)**(*64*) *(DJSffrenchDavis)* 5-7-12 (3) DWright(15) (lw: led after 2f: sn clr: hdd & wknd ins fnl f)........nk **7**
481[4] Bassmaat (USA) **(75)**(*75*) *(WJHaggas)* 4-8-8 (7) GMilligan(16) (bit bkwd: chsd ldrs: rdn over 1f out: one pce)........1¼ **8**
3207[5] Veloce (IRE) **(68)**(*68*) *(ABailey)* 7-8-8 GBardwell(3) (b: nvr trbld ldrs)........nk **9**
2794* Artful Dane (IRE) **(75)**(*73*) *(MJHeaton-Ellis)* 3-8-9 DHolland(5) (led 2f: 2nd st: rdn & wknd whn n.m.r appr fnl f)........½ **10**
2488* Ma Petite Anglaise **(83)**(*81*) *(WJarvis)* 3-8-12 (5) MHenry(17) (a in rr)........nk **11**
2598[4] Roving Minstrel **(88)**(*83*) *(BAMcMahon)* 4-10-0 SDWilliams(8) (lw: mid div: effrt & 6th st: wknd over 1f out)........1¼ **12**
2952[3] Cee-Jay-Ay **(63)**(*56*) *(JBerry)* 8-8-3 JCarroll(18) (s.v.s: nvr nrr)........1¼ **13**

2669* Secret Aly (CAN) **(83)***(73) (CEBrittain)* 5-9-9 MRoberts(14) (lw: effrt 3f out: rdn & no imp ent st: sn eased)....1¼ **14**
2797[2] Sooty Tern **(75)***(46) (JMBradley)* 8-8-12 (3) SDrowne(10) (prom 4f: sn lost tch: t.o)....9 **15**
2905[2] Kummel King **(60)***(24) (EJAlston)* 7-7-9 (5) MBaird(12) (prom to ½-wy: sn lost tch: t.o)....3 **16**
Monis (IRE) **(72)***(11) (JBalding)* 4-8-12 NCarlisle(6) (bkwd: prom over 4f: wknd qckly: t.o)....12 **17**

4/1 Fairy Story (IRE), **9/1** PRIDE OF PENDLE, Bold Angel, **10/1** Secret Aly (CAN), Cee-Jay-Ay, Artful Dane (IRE), **11/1** Mr Rough, **12/1** Ma Petite Anglaise, Roving Minstrel, Daytona Beach (IRE), **14/1** Sooty Tern, **16/1** Wentbridge Lad (IRE), Veloce (IRE), Allinson's Mate (IRE), **20/1** Bassmaat (USA), Kummel King, Monis (IRE), CSF £88.66 CT £1,181.52 TOTE £7.00: £1.70 £2.30 £3.50 £4.70 (£54.40) Trio £134.70 OWNER Mrs Linda Miller (THIRSK) BRED James Simpson 17 Rn
1m 32.71 (1.01) SF: 61/54/60/43/55/43/40/51/44/43/51/59/32/49/22/-/-
WEIGHT FOR AGE 3yo-6lb

3223 CHESTER RATED STKS H'CAP (0-110) (Listed) (3-Y.O+) (Class A)
£15,982.40 (£5,574.40: £2,712.20: £1,151.00)
1m 5f 89y Stalls: Low GOING minus 0.32 sec per fur (GF) 3-30 (3-34)

2739[3] **Source of Light (100)***(99+)*(Fav)*(RCharlton)* 6-9-7 DHarrison(4) (lw: s.i.s: hld up: hdwy to ld over 2f out: comf)....— **1**
2785* Labibeh (USA) **(87)***(85)*(Fav)*(JLDunlop)* 3-7-11 JLowe(3) (s.i.s: led after 1f tl hdd & 2nd st: kpt on u.p fnl f)....1¼ **2**
2798[2] Soba Up **(86)***(79) (TJEtherington)* 5-8-7 ACulhane(2) (lw: swtg: led 1f: chsd ldr tl 3rd & rdn st: sn outpcd)....3½ **3**
868[10] Opera Lover (IRE) **(101)***(90) (MRStoute)* 3-8-11 DHolland(1) (bit bkwd: hld up & bhd: rdn & hdwy 4f out: 4th st: eased whn btn)....4 **4**
LONG HANDICAP Soba Up 7-8

6/4 SOURCE OF LIGHT, Labibeh (USA), **11/2** Soba Up, Opera Lover (IRE), CSF £4.01 TOTE £2.60 (£1.80) OWNER Mr K. Abdullah (BECKHAMPTON) BRED Juddmonte Farms 4 Rn
2m 54.04 (4.04) SF: 56/31/36/36
WEIGHT FOR AGE 3yo-11lb

3224 ROUGE ROSE MAIDEN STKS (3-Y.O F) (Class D) £4,172.00
(£1,256.00: £608.00: £284.00)
1m 4f 66y Stalls: Low GOING minus 0.32 sec per fur (GF) 4-00 (4-00)

2208[4] **Danesrath (IRE) (76)***(85) (ACStewart)* 3-8-11 MRoberts(4) (mde all: hrd rdn & edgd rt ins fnl f: r.o)....— **1**
2882[3] Top Lady (IRE) **(70)***(85) (MRStoute)* 3-8-11 DHolland(2) (chsd wnr: rdn over 2f out: 2nd st: rallied gamely towards fin)....nk **2**
2944[5] Reem Dubai (IRE) *(72)*(Fav)*(JHMGosden)* 3-8-11 JCarroll(3) (bit bkwd: hld up & bhd: effrt over 3f out: 4th st: nvr trbld ldrs)....10 **3**
2944[2] Pampas Breeze (IRE) *(69)*(Fav)*(WJarvis)* 3-8-6 (5) MHenry(5) (hdwy ½-wy: 3rd & rdn ent st: sn outpcd)....1¾ **4**
2004[4] Victoria Day *(54) (JWWatts)* 3-8-11 GHind(1) (lw: drppd rr 7f out: outpcd 4f out: 5th & btn st)....12 **5**

9/4 Pampas Breeze (IRE), Reem Dubai (IRE), **5/2** DANESRATH (IRE), **9/2** Top Lady (IRE), **20/1** Victoria Day, CSF £12.60 TOTE £3.90: £1.90 £1.40 (£4.40) OWNER Mr M. Hawkes (NEWMARKET) BRED Major V. McCalmont 5 Rn 2m 39.54 (2.94) SF: 52/52/39/36/21

3225 LEVY BOARD NURSERY H'CAP (2-Y.O) (Class C) £5,442.50
(£1,640.00: £795.00: £372.50)
7f 2y Stalls: Low GOING minus 0.32 sec per fur (GF) 4-30 (4-33)

3019* **Champagne Prince (89)***(90)*(Fav)*(PWHarris)* 2-9-2 (5) MHenry(6) (lw: a.p: led ent st: hrd rdn fnl f: jst hld on)....— **1**
2964[5] Scenicris (IRE) **(68)***(69) (RHollinshead)* 2-8-0 NCarlisle(1) (s.i.s: hdwy ent st: ev ch fnl f: r.o)....s.h **2**
2629[3] Magic Lake **(61)***(62) (EJAlston)* 2-7-2 (5) MBaird(8) (hld up gng wl: 5th st: ev ch fnl f: r.o)....hd **3**
3147[11] Oriel Lad **(77)***(74) (PDEvans)* 2-8-9v GHind(2) (swtg: a.p: 3rd st: ev ch 1f out: unable qckn) .1¾ **4**
3003[4] Therhea (IRE) **(88)***(80) (BRMillman)* 2-9-6 DHolland(9) (hld up: hdwy 3f out: 6th st: one pce appr fnl f)....2 **5**
2926[2] Emperegrine (USA) **(76)***(65) (CFWall)* 2-8-8 MRoberts(4) (chsd ldr tl led over 2f out: hdd & 2nd st: wknd fnl f)....1¼ **6**
2756* Hotlips Houlihan **(77)***(59) (RJRWilliams)* 2-8-6 (3) SSanders(3) (led over 4f: 4th & rdn st: sn btn)....3 **7**
3048[2] Euro Express **(61)***(34) (MHEasterby)* 2-7-7 JLowe(5) (sn pushed along: a bhd)....4 **8**

2195* Flood's Fancy **(63)***(34) (ABailey)* 2-7-6 (3)ow2 DWright(7) (prom tl wknd wl over 1f out)...........s.h **9**
2328[8] Doug's Folly **(63)***(27) (MWEasterby)* 2-7-9 GBardwell(10) (bhd) 4 **10**

LONG HANDICAP Magic Lake 6-7 Flood's Fancy 7-6

6/4 CHAMPAGNE PRINCE, **7/1** Doug's Folly, Emperegrine (USA), **8/1** Flood's Fancy, Hotlips Houlihan, **10/1** Euro Express, Oriel Lad, **14/1** Scenicris (IRE), Therhea (IRE), **33/1** Magic Lake, CSF £22.15 CT £473.96 TOTE £2.50: £1.50 £5.00 £6.40 (£34.40) Trio £572.00 OWNER Magnum Force (BERKHAMSTED) BRED Cheveley Park Stud Ltd 10 Rn

1m 27.76 (2.56) SF: 49/28/21/33/39/24/18/-/-/-

3226

PARADISE MAIDEN STKS (3-Y.O+) (Class D) £4,224.00 (£1,272.00: £616.00: £288.00)
7f 2y Stalls: Low GOING minus 0.32 sec per fur (GF) 5-05 (5-06)

2393[3] **Splintercat (USA)** *(80+) (JHMGosden)* 3-8-8 JCarroll(3) (chsd ldr: led on bit 2f out: sn clr: eased cl home) ....— **1**
355[9] Miss Charlie **(40)***(69) (ABailey)* 5-8-13 GBardwell(4) (set str pce: hdd 2f out: 2nd st: one pce)...........5 **2**
2949[2] Dictation (USA) *(67)*(Fav)*(RCharlton)* 3-8-13 DHarrison(2) (swtg: chsd ldrs: drvn along ½-wy: 3rd & rdn st: nvr able to chal)...........3 **3**
3030[7] Legaitak *(51) (BHanbury)* 3-8-10 (3) JStack(1) (bit bkwd: s.s: sn drvn along: a bhd: 4th st).......7 **4**

4/5 Dictation (USA), **5/4** SPLINTERCAT (USA) (op Evens), **14/1** Legaitak (12/1-20/1), **20/1** Miss Charlie, CSF £13.33 TOTE £2.10 (£14.30) OWNER Sheikh Mohammed (NEWMARKET) BRED Overbrook Farm 4 Rn 1m 26.45 (1.25) SF: 52/46/39/23

WEIGHT FOR AGE 3yo-5lb

T/Plpt: £372.40 (36.49 Tckts). T/Qdpt: £72.00 (3.3 Tckts) IM

3098-RIPON (R-H)
Saturday August 19th (Good to firm)

WEATHER: sunny, v.hot WIND: almost nil

3227

BOROUGHBRIDGE MAIDEN STKS (3-Y.O+) (Class D) £3,793.70 (£1,148.60: £560.80: £266.90)
1m Stalls: High GOING minus 0.39 sec per fur (F) 2-10 (2-10)

Strumming (IRE) *(82) (JHMGosden)* 3-8-7 WRyan(4) (b.hind: trckd ldrs: effrt 3f out: led over 1f out: jst hld on) ....— **1**
2977[3] Golden Pound (USA) *(87)*(Fav)*(EALDunlop)* 3-8-12 WRSwinburn(3) (trckd ldr: effrt over 2f out: ev ch fnl f: styd on u.p) ....hd **2**
Afsaat *(83) (MRStoute)* 3-8-12 KFallon(1) (w'like: bit bkwd: dwlt: bhd & pushed along 6f out: hdwy over 2f out: r.o strly ins fnl f: eased nr fin)...........1¾ **3**
2883[2] Carol's Dream (USA) **(73)***(80) (JWHills)* 3-8-12 RCochrane(5) (lw: led: sn clr: hdd over 1f out: one pce) 1½ **4**
2503[11] My Handsome Prince **(40)** *(PJBevan)* 3-8-12 GDuffield(2) (reluctant to go to s: sn bhd: lost tch 6f out: t.o) ....dist **5**

6/5 Golden Pound (USA) (4/5-5/4), **2/1** Carol's Dream (USA) (op 9/2), **9/2** Afsaat, STRUMMING (IRE), **33/1** My Handsome Prince, CSF £10.65 TOTE £6.50: £2.10 £1.20 (£3.40) OWNER Sheikh Mohammed (NEWMARKET) BRED Harry McCalmont and Major V. McCalmont 5 Rn

1m 38.8 (1.10) SF: 49/54/50/47/-

3228

YORKSHIRE RACING CLUB CONDITIONS STKS (2-Y.O) (Class D) £3,550.00 (£1,075.00: £525.00: £250.00)
6f Stalls: Low GOING minus 0.39 sec per fur (F) 2-40 (2-41)

3100[3] **Ramsey Hope (82)***(84) (CWFairhurst)* 2-9-3 NKennedy(7) (mde all: styd on u.p fnl f: all out)...........— **1**
2876[2] Crystal Falls (IRE) *(78) (JJO'Neill)* 2-8-11 KFallon(4) (chsd ldrs: styd on wl u.p appr fnl f: jst failed)...........hd **2**
2011[4] Splicing *(73) (JRFanshawe)* 2-8-3 (3) NVarley(5) (lw: chsd ldrs: ev ch & hung rt u.p fnl f: nt qckn towards fin) ....hd **3**
2852* Nostoi *(73)*(Fav)*(SirMarkPrescott)* 2-8-10 GDuffield(3) (lw: s.i.s: sn chsng ldrs: drvn along & outpcd ½-wy: hdwy & swtchd outside 2f out: no imp ins fnl f)...........1½ **4**
2833[2] Crackernat (IRE) **(87)***(66) (LMCumani)* 2-9-3 WRyan(1) (lw: w ldr: hung bdly lft over 2f out: lost pl over 1f out)...........5 **5**

2970[3] La Finale *(51) (MHEasterby)* 2-8-6 SMaloney(2) (dwlt: outpcd & bhd: kpt on fnl f)................1½ 6
1597[6] West Austria (IRE) *(38) (JBerry)* 2-8-11 GCarter(6) (dwlt: a outpcd: bhd fr ½-wy)....................7 7

9/4 Nostoi, **5/2** Crackernat (IRE), **7/2** Splicing, **7/1** West Austria (IRE), **8/1** Crystal Falls (IRE), La Finale (op 12/1), **9/1** RAMSEY HOPE, CSF £72.26 TOTE £14.40: £3.40 £3.00 (£83.80) OWNER Mr C. D. Barber-Lomax (MIDDLEHAM) BRED Norton Grove Stud Ltd 7 Rn
1m 12.2 (2.00) SF: 40/34/29/29/22/7/-

3229

BILLY NEVETT MEMORIAL CHALLENGE CUP H'CAP (0-80) (3-Y.O+) (Class D) £4,250.00 (£1,280.00: £620.00: £290.00)
1m 4f 60y Stalls: High GOING minus 0.39 sec per fur (F) 3-15 (3-16)

3102[3] **Hasta la Vista (43)***(54) (MWEasterby)* 5-7-4b(3) NVarley(10) (chsd ldrs: drvn along over 3f out: styd on to ld ins fnl f: all out).......................................— 1
3007[7] Quivira **(74)***(85) (TTClement)* 4-9-10 RCochrane(8) (swtg: a.p: hdwy to ld over 2f out: hdd ins fnl f: styd on).......................................hd 2
2792[6] Santana Lady (IRE) **(58)***(66) (MJHeaton-Ellis)* 6-8-8 GCarter(9) (led to 9f out: a.p: effrt over 2f out: styd on same pce appr fnl f).......................................2½ 3
2975* Snowy Petrel (IRE) **(77)***(83)*(Fav)*(JLDunlop)* 3-9-3 JWeaver(7) (lw: trckd ldr: led 9f out tl hdd over 2f out: one pce).......................................1¼ 4
3001[2] Khan **(54)***(59) (CWThornton)* 3-7-8 ow1 AMackay(6) (lw: hdwy & prom over 3f out: one pce fnl 2f).......................................nk 5
2663* Kinoko **(43)***(36) (KWHogg)* 7-7-7 NKennedy(1) (hld up & bhd: sme hdwy on outside over 3f out: nvr nr ldrs).......................................10 6
2186[5] New Inn **(56)***(48) (EWeymes)* 4-8-6 DaleGibson(5) (in tch: drvn along & outpcd 5f out: n.d after).......................................½ 7
2816[3] Ashover **(57)***(48) (TDBarron)* 5-8-7 WRyan(3) (bhd: sme hdwy over 3f out: n.d)......................¾ 8
3015[5] Miss Pin Up **(78)***(61) (WJHaggas)* 6-10-0 RMcGhin(2) (sn trckng ldrs: wknd 3f out: eased).....6 9
2790[9] Discorsi **(63)** *(GWragg)* 3-8-3 FNorton(4) (lw: in tch: drvn along & lost pl 6f out: bhd whn eased 2f out: t.o).......................................dist 10
LONG HANDICAP Hasta la Vista 7-5 Kinoko 7-6

7/2 Snowy Petrel (IRE), **9/2** HASTA LA VISTA, **5/1** Ashover, **8/1** Quivira, Khan, **9/1** Kinoko, New Inn, **10/1** Santana Lady (IRE), Miss Pin Up, Discorsi, CSF £39.69 CT £322.02 TOTE £36.40: £1.70 £2.50 £3.90 (£31.70) Trio £164.80 OWNER Mr K. Hodgson (SHERIFF HUTTON) BRED Clanville Lodge Stud 10 Rn
2m 35.8 (1.80) SF: 36/67/48/55/31/18/30/30/43/-
WEIGHT FOR AGE 3yo-10lb
OFFICIAL EXPLANATION **Discorsi: appeared to have pulled a muscle in his quarters and was heard to gurgle when pulled up.**

3230

WILLIAM HILL GREAT ST WILFRID H'CAP (0-105) (3-Y.O+) (Class B) £19,430.00 (£5,840.00: £2,820.00: £1,310.00)
6f Stalls: Low GOING minus 0.39 sec per fur (F) 3-50 (3-52)

934[8] **Double Blue (101)***(112) (MJohnston)* 6-9-13 JWeaver(7) (lw: mde all: r.o strly fnl f) ....— 1
3145[6] Lennox Lewis **(97)***(101) (APJarvis)* 3-9-2 (3) JTate(5) (chsd wnr: styd on ins fnl f: no imp)......2½ 2
2764[2] Top Banana **(89)***(92)*(Fav)*(HCandy)* 4-9-1 WNewnes(2) (lw: b.off hind: drvn along & wandered over 2f out: styd on wl u.p fnl f: nt rch ldrs).......................................½ 3
3112[2] Statius **(78)***(78) (TDBarron)* 3-7-11 (3) NVarley(3) (lw: a chsng ldrs: kpt on same pce fnl 2f)...1¼ 4
3145[3] Bayin (USA) **(72)***(70) (MDIUsher)* 6-7-12 RStreet(8) (b: hld up: swtchd outside ½-wy: kpt on fnl 2f: nvr nr to chal).......................................½ 5
2823[3] Perryston View **(90)***(80) (PCalver)* 3-8-12v MBirch(6) (chsd ldrs tl grad wknd over 1f out).........3 6
3145[9] Rock Symphony **(91)***(81) (WJHaggas)* 5-9-3 RCochrane(11) (s.i.s: bhd: hdwy 2f out: nt rch ldrs).......................................hd 7
2853[2] Super Benz **(68)***(56) (FJO'Mahony)* 9-7-8 ow1 AMackay(12) (b: mid div: drvn along & outpcd ½-wy: kpt on fnl f).......................................nk 8
2930[6] Ned's Bonanza **(73)***(58) (MDods)* 6-7-13 AMcGlone(1) (sn bhd: sme hdwy 2f out: n.d).........1¾ 9
3145[17] Rossini Blue **(73)***(56) (MrsJRRamsden)* 4-7-13 ow1 GCarter(4) (nvr wnt pce)..........................nk 10
3112[9] Formidable Liz **(70)***(49) (MDHammond)* 5-7-10bow3 DaleGibson(10) (swtchd lft s: chsd ldrs tl wknd 2f out).......................................¾ 11
3098[7] Plum First **(67)***(47) (LRLloyd-James)* 5-7-7b NKennedy(9) (b.hind: sn bhd & drvn along).........¾ 12
2645[6] Flashy's Son **(71)***(49) (GMMoore)* 7-7-11 ow1 SMaloney(14) (b: b.hind: chsd ldrs on outside tl wknd over 1f out).......................................nk 13
2840[2] Samsolom **(74)***(49) (PHowling)* 7-8-0 FNorton(13) (sn outpcd: rdn ½-wy: n.d).......................1½ 14
LONG HANDICAP Super Benz 7-2 Plum First 7-1 Formidable Liz 7-1

7/4 Top Banana, **7/1** Statius, **15/2** DOUBLE BLUE, **8/1** Bayin (USA), **9/1** Perryston View, Rock Symphony, **12/1** Lennox Lewis, Rossini Blue, **14/1** Samsolom, Ned's Bonanza, Flashy's Son, **33/1** Super Benz, Plum First, Formidable Liz, CSF £94.76 CT £211.35 TOTE £8.40: £2.40 £4.30 £1.40 (£32.60) Trio £66.10 OWNER Mr R. W. Huggins (MIDDLEHAM) BRED The Queen 14 Rn

1m 10.1 (-0.10) SF: 79/64/59/41/37/43/48/23/25/23/16/14/16/16

WEIGHT FOR AGE 3yo-4lb

STEWARDS' ENQUIRY Newnes fined £55 for making frivolous obj.

3231 TATTERSALLS MAIDEN AUCTION STKS (2-Y.O) (Class E) £3,360.60 (£1,018.80: £498.40: £238.20)
6f Stalls: Low GOING minus 0.39 sec per fur (F) 4-20 (4-25)

1111a3 **Greek Icon** *(72+)*(Fav)*(JLDunlop)* 2-8-4 ow1 JWeaver(6) (w ldr: led over 2f out: r.o strly fnl f) — **1**
29323 Contract Bridge (IRE) *(59) (CWThornton)* 2-7-13 AMackay(2) (sn drvn along: hdwy & nt clr run over 2f out: swtchd outside & styd on wl appr fnl f)......3½ **2**
28764 Six Clerks (IRE) *(63) (JGFitzGerald)* 2-8-8 KFallon(3) (hdwy ½-wy: styd on u.p appr fnl f)...1¾ **3**
Ocean Stream (IRE) *(60+) (JLEyre)* 2-8-7 RCochrane(16) (sn chsng ldrs: effrt 2f out: kpt on same pce appr fnl f)......¾ **4**
26679 Supermister *(53) (MHEasterby)* 2-8-4b MBirch(10) (chsd ldrs tl wknd over 1f out)......1½ **5**
29704 Good To Talk **(66)***(44) (MHEasterby)* 2-8-2 SMaloney(4) (led to ½-wy: wknd wl over 3f out).2½ **6**
295110 Nuclear Jewel *(31) (RMWhitaker)* 2-7-8 (3) NVarley(11) (chsd ldrst tl edgd lft & wknd 1f out) ...3 **7**
Gymcrak Gem (IRE) *(32) (GHolmes)* 2-7-8 (7)ow1 RuthCoulter(5) (s.i.s: hld up: sme hdwy whn hmpd over 1f out: nvr plcd to chal)......¾ **8**
*770*5 Mysterious Times **(46)***(28) (BWMurray)* 2-7-4 (7) MartinDwyer(1) (chsd ldrs: outpcd ½-wy: rdn & hung rt over 1f out: sn wknd)......½ **9**
29574 Cerise (IRE) *(20) (CWCElsey)* 2-7-11 JFanning(17) (unruly: chsd ldrs on outside tl wknd over 2f out)......3 **10**
Forgie (IRE) *(31) (PCalver)* 2-8-8 WNewnes(9) (lengthy: unf: bit bkwd: s.i.s: a outpcd)......hd **11**
29717 Phantom Haze *(25) (MissSEHall)* 2-8-3 JMarshall(14) (mid div: drvn along ½-wy: n.d)......nk **12**
29327 Lawn Order *(20) (MrsJRRamsden)* 2-8-0 MDeering(13) (in tch tl grad wknd fnl 2f)......¾ **13**
25155 Fairy Prince (IRE) *(27) (MrsALMKing)* 2-8-11 ow1 MWigham(7) (s.i.s: a outpcd & bhd: rn green)......1¼ **14**
Bold Future (IRE) *(12) (JWWatts)* 2-8-3 GDuffield(8) (s.i.s: a bhd)......3 **15**
Power Princess *(RMWhitaker)* 2-7-11 DaleGibson(12) (s.i.s: a outpcd & sn drvn along) 5 **16**
Danamich (IRE) *(JBerry)* 2-8-10 GCarter(15) (lengthy: bit bkwd: s.i.s: a outpcd & bhd)......6 **17**

9/4 GREEK ICON, **9/2** Six Clerks (IRE) (op 10/1), **5/1** Ocean Stream (IRE) (6/1-4/1), **11/2** Contract Bridge (IRE), **10/1** Danamich (IRE), Lawn Order, **12/1** Supermister, **14/1** Bold Future (IRE), **16/1** Good To Talk, Cerise (IRE), Forgie (IRE), **25/1** Fairy Prince (IRE), Power Princess, Gymcrak Gem (IRE), Phantom Haze, **33/1** Nuclear Jewel, Mysterious Times, CSF £18.48 TOTE £2.70: £1.40 £2.00 £2.30 (£5.90) Trio £10.80 OWNER Mr A. M. Cati (ARUNDEL) BRED Kirtlington Stud 17 Rn

1m 12.5 (2.30) SF: 24/11/15/12/5/-/-/-/-/-/-/-/-/-/-/-/-

3232 HARROGATE H'CAP (0-80) (3-Y.O+) (Class D) £4,458.00 (£1,344.00: £652.00: £306.00)
1m 2f Stalls: High GOING minus 0.39 sec per fur (F) 4-50 (4-54)

31012 **Thaleros (57)***(65) (GMMoore)* 5-8-6 JWeaver(4) (mde all: styd on u.p fnl 2f: hld on wl) ......— **1**
31013 Antartictern (USA) **(46)***(52) (GROldroyd)* 5-7-9 ow2 AMackay(7) (bhd: pushed along over 4f out: hdwy 2f out: styd on wl u.p ins fnl f: nt rch wnr)......nk **2**
22545 Touch Above **(45)***(52) (TDBarron)* 9-7-5 (3) NVarley(5) (sn pushed along: prom: chal over 3f out: hung rt & kpt on wl fnl f)......s.h **3**
3058* Zeetaro **(75)***(82)*(Fav)*(MajorWRHern)* 4-9-10 TSprake(2) (lw: trckd ldrs: chal 2f out: sn rdn: kpt on one pce ins fnl f)......½ **4**
26104 Sycamore Lodge (IRE) **(69)***(72) (PCalver)* 4-9-4 MBirch(3) (hld up: hdwy over 2f out: nvr nr to chal)......2½ **5**
30218 Who's Tef (IRE) **(49)***(37) (MHEasterby)* 7-7-12 SMaloney(1) (chsd ldrs: rdn & wknd over 2f out)......9 **6**
*927*10 Seckar Vale (USA) **(80)** *(JHanson)* 3-9-7 GCarter(6) (Withdrawn not under Starter's orders: v.unruly s: ref to ent stalls)...... **W**

LONG HANDICAP Antartictern (USA) 7-6

Evens Zeetaro, **4/1** THALEROS, **5/1** Sycamore Lodge (IRE), **7/1** Antartictern (USA), Seckar Vale (USA), **8/1** Touch Above, **12/1** Who's Tef (IRE), CSF £25.46 TOTE £4.10: £2.20 £2.60 (£13.50) OWNER Mr M. Gleason (MIDDLEHAM) BRED A. Christodoulou 6 Rn

2m 5.8 (2.30) SF: 41/28/28/58/48/13/-

WEIGHT FOR AGE 3yo-8lb

T/Plpt: £1,006.30 (13.21 Tckts). T/Qdpt: £32.50 (5.1 Tckts). WG

3213-SANDOWN (R-H)
Saturday August 19th (Good to firm)
WEATHER: very hot WIND: almost nil

3233 EMBASSY LEISURE BREAKS NURSERY (S) H'CAP (2-Y.O) (Class E)
£2,900.00 (£875.00: £425.00: £200.00)
7f 16y Stalls: High GOING minus 0.03 sec per fur (G) 2-00 (2-04)

3019³ **Homeland (58)***(62)*(Fav)*(CWThornton)* 2-9-0 WCarson(1) (swtg: 4th st: hrd rdn over 2f out: led ins fnl f: r.o wl)....— 1
2637³ Willie Rushton **(56)***(58) (GLMoore)* 2-8-12 SWhitworth(7) (7th st: rdn over 2f out: r.o fnl f)....¾ 2
2505⁵ Comrade Chinnery (IRE) **(46)***(45) (JMPEustace)* 2-8-2b JQuinn(10) (lw: hdwy over 1f out: r.o wl ins fnl f)....1½ 3
2988² Music Mistress (IRE) **(55)***(53) (RHannon)* 2-8-4 (7) DaneO'Neill(2) (swtg: 5th st: rdn over 2f out: unable qckn fnl f)....nk 4
*2962*¹¹ Colour Counsellor **(54)***(51) (KMcAuliffe)* 2-8-10 RHills(3) (lw: w ldr: ev ch 2f out: one pce fnl f)¾ 5
3008⁸ Spanish Luck **(53)***(49) (JWHills)* 2-8-9b TQuinn(6) (led tl hdd ins fnl f: one pce)....s.h 6
3135* Pinocchio Boy (IRE) **(60)***(52) (BJMeehan)* 2-9-2 4x MTebbutt(4) (3rd st: rdn over 2f out: n.m.r 1f out: sn wknd)....2 7
2826⁶ Bath Knight **(48)***(37) (DJSffrenchDavis)* 2-8-4 NAdams(9) (b.hind: swtg: a bhd)....1¼ 8
2857³ Sphinx Levelv (IRE) **(65)***(51) (APJarvis)* 2-9-7 KDarley(8) (lw: rdn & hdwy on ins over 2f out: hmpd & eased ins fnl f)....1½ 9
3008⁹ Lindas Delight **(58)***(38) (JSMoore)* 2-9-0 JFEgan(5) (swtg: 6th st: wknd over 2f out)....2½ 10

9/4 HOMELAND, **4/1** Pinocchio Boy (IRE), **5/1** Music Mistress (IRE), **9/1** Willie Rushton, **12/1** Sphinx Levelv (IRE), **14/1** Lindas Delight, **20/1** Comrade Chinnery (IRE), Bath Knight, Spanish Luck, **25/1** Colour Counsellor, CSF £19.58 CT £262.86 TOTE £2.80: £1.50 £2.50 £6.70 (£12.00) Trio £147.50 OWNER Mr Guy Reed (MIDDLEHAM) BRED P. D. and Mrs Player 10 Rn

1m 33.48 (6.88) SF: 18/14/1/9/7/5/8/-/7/-
Homeland sold R. Barber 6,800 gns

3234 RIVERDANCE AMATEUR LIMITED STKS (0-70) (3-Y.O+) (Class E)
£3,545.00 (£1,070.00: £520.00: £245.00)
1m 2f 7y Stalls: High GOING minus 0.03 sec per fur (G) 2-35 (2-36)

2577³ **Access Adventurer (IRE) (70)***(76)*(Fav)*(RBoss)* 4-11-10 MrsMCowdrey(4) (swtg: led 7f out: clr over 4f out: hung lft 2f out: r.o wl)....— 1
2010¹⁰ Wayfarers Way (USA) **(67)***(73) (RHannon)* 4-11-8 MrCVigors(1) (lw: 5th st: chsd wnr over 2f out: ev ch over 1f out: unable qckn)....¾ 2
2780⁸ Divina Mia **(67)***(65) (JWHills)* 3-10-9 MissEJohnsonHoughton(9) (led over 1f: 2nd st: one pce fnl 2f)....1¾ 3
2664³ Cyphell (IRE) **(70)***(65) (MRStoute)* 3-10-9 MrsSEddery(8) (hdwy 3f out: rdn 1f out: one pce).hd 4
2954² Bold Look **(57)***(70) (PWHarris)* 4-11-10 MissAElsey(2) (hdwy over 1f out: r.o one pce)....1½ 5
3108⁴ Zahid (USA) **(43)***(65) (KRBurke)* 4-11-9 ow1 MrSAstaire(3) (lw: hdwy 2f out: r.o one pce)....1½ 6
2981³ Montone (IRE) **(52)***(65) (KRBurke)* 5-11-8 MrMMannish(12) (hdwy 3f out: one pce fnl 2f)....nk 7
3029⁶ Fruitful Affair (IRE) **(44)***(57) (TThomsonJones)* 6-11-1 (4) MrsSFaber(7) (led over 8f out tl over 7f out: 4th st: wknd over 2f out)....3 8
2979¹² Romansh **(48)***(59) (BJMeehan)* 6-11-8 MissJAllison(5) (lw: 3rd st: wknd over 1f out)....½ 9
*1759*⁶ Maraady (USA) **(21)***(45) (GPEnright)* 6-11-4 (4) MrsMEnright(6) (b: a bhd)....9 10
*1078*⁴ Starlight Flyer **(25)***(43) (JELong)* 8-11-4b(4) MrTWaters(11) (b: b.hind: prom 5f)....1¼ 11
Don't Give Up **(31)***(30) (PBurgoyne)* 7-11-4b(4) MissMO'Sullivan(13) (lw: a wl bhd)....8 12

7/4 ACCESS ADVENTURER (IRE), **9/4** Cyphell (IRE) (6/4-5/2), **7/1** Bold Look (6/1-9/1), **8/1** Divina Mia (6/1-10/1), **12/1** Wayfarers Way (USA) (op 7/1), **14/1** Montone (IRE) (10/1-16/1), **20/1** Fruitful Affair (IRE), **33/1** Romansh, **40/1** Zahid (USA), **66/1** Maraady (USA), Starlight Flyer, Don't Give Up, CSF £21.91 TOTE £3.00: £1.30 £2.80 £2.60 (£13.50) Trio £34.50 OWNER Miss Elaine Williams (NEWMARKET) BRED Barronstown Bloodstock Ltd 12 Rn

2m 13.46 (9.16) SF: 58/55/39/39/52/47/47/39/41/27/25/12
WEIGHT FOR AGE 3yo-8lb
STEWARDS' ENQUIRY Enright susp. 28-29/8/95 (excessive use of whip).

3235 BANK OF SCOTLAND TERCENTENARY 'ATALANTA' MILE STKS (Listed)
(3-Y.O+ F & M) (Class A) £12,487.50 (£3,780.00: £1,845.00:£877.50)
1m 14y Stalls: High GOING minus 0.03 sec per fur (G) 3-10 (3-11)

2006* **Private Line (USA) (99)***(106)*(Fav)*(HRACecil)* 3-8-8 PatEddery(5) (lw: chsd ldr: led over 1f out: hrd rdn: r.o wl)....— 1

Louis' Queen (IRE) *(103) (JLDunlop)* 3-8-8 KDarley(2) (6th st: rdn over 2f out: r.o ins fnl f)..1½ 2
2673⁴ A la Carte (IRE) **(101)***(102) (JLDunlop)* 3-8-8 TQuinn(3) (swtg: 4th st: hrd rdn over 1f out: r.o one pce) ....nk 3
2006² Amanah (USA) **(98)***(101) (JHMGosden)* 3-8-8 WCarson(7) (swtg: 3rd st: hrd rdn over 1f out: one pce) ....½ 4
2673⁵ Mamlakah (IRE) **(100)***(101) (HThomsonJones)* 3-8-8b RHills(6) (swtg: led: sn clr: hdd over 1f out: one pce) ....hd 5
2737⁴ Twilight Patrol **(90)***(89) (RHannon)* 3-8-8 RHughes(1) (b.nr fore: 5th st: wknd over 1f out) 6 6

9/4 PRIVATE LINE (USA), **5/2** Amanah (USA), **3/1** A la Carte (IRE), **7/1** Mamlakah (IRE), **10/1** Twilight Patrol, **12/1** Louis' Queen (IRE), CSF £23.07 TOTE £2.60 £1.70 £2.90 (£17.80) OWNER Mr K. Abdullah (NEWMARKET) BRED Juddmonte Farms in USA 6 Rn
1m 43.81 (4.61) SF: 44/41/40/39/39/27

3236

SUNLEY RATED STKS H'CAP (0-100) (3-Y.O+) (Class B) £7,335.00 (£2,745.00: £1,342.50: £577.50: £258.75: £131.25)
5f 6y Stalls: Low GOING minus 0.23 sec per fur (GF) 3-40 (3-42)

2935¹¹ **Name the Tune (86)***(94) (PHowling)* 4-8-7 PaulEddery(1) (b.hind: hld up: led over 1f out: rdn out) ....— 1
2742³ Quiz Time **(86)***(91) (SirMarkPrescott)* 3-8-4 WWoods(4) (hld up: hrd rdn over 1f out: unable qckn ins fnl f) 1 2
3005⁵ Painted Desert **(86)***(90) (RCharlton)* 3-8-4 KDarley(5) (swtg: led over 3f: one pce)....nk 3
2285⁹ Hello Mister **(94)***(95) (JO'Donoghue)* 4-8-12 (3) DRMcCabe(3) (swtg: dwlt: rdn over 2f out: hdwy fnl f: r.o wl) 1 4
3051³ Aragrove **(86)***(79) (JWPayne)* 5-8-2 (5) DGriffiths(6) (b: swtg: a.p: rdn over 1f out: one pce)...2½ 5
2764³ Jayannpee **(97)***(90)*(Fav)*(IABalding)* 4-9-4 LDettori(2) (lw: rdn over 2f out: hdwy over 1f out: one pce)....s.h 6
2746⁴ Princess Oberon (IRE) **(88)***(77) (MBell)* 5-8-9 MFenton(7) (prom over 3f)....1¼ 7
3005⁶ Join the Clan **(92)***(76) (MrsNMacauley)* 6-8-13 DeanMcKeown(8) (spd over 3f) 1½ 8
2764¹⁴ Brave Edge **(100)***(68) (RHannon)* 4-9-7 PatEddery(9) (hdwy 2f out: wknd over 1f out)....5 9
LONG HANDICAP Aragrove 8-2 Quiz Time 8-3

15/8 Jayannpee, **100/30** Brave Edge, **7/1** Princess Oberon (IRE), NAME THE TUNE, **9/1** Quiz Time, **10/1** Join the Clan, **14/1** Painted Desert, **16/1** Aragrove, Hello Mister, CSF £62.26 CT £783.83 TOTE £7.70: £2.00 £2.40 £3.60 (£31.60) Trio £171.60 OWNER Mr C. Hammond (NEWMARKET) BRED Derek R. Price 9 Rn 60.81 secs (1.01) SF: 56/50/49/57/41/52/39/38/30
WEIGHT FOR AGE 3yo-3lb

3237

WILLIAM HILL H'CAP (0-90) (3-Y.O+) (Class C) £5,160.00 (£1,560.00: £760.00: £360.00)
1m 2f 7y Stalls: High GOING minus 0.03 sec per fur (G) 4-15 (4-19)

3106⁵ **Francfurter (77)***(89)*(Fav)*(RCharlton)* 3-8-9b PatEddery(5) (4th st: led over 2f out: pushed out)....— 1
2903* Amrak Ajeeb (IRE) **(84)***(93) (BHanbury)* 3-9-2 WCarson(1) (b: swtg: s.s: hdwy 4f out: 6th st: hrd rdn over 1f out: r.o one pce)....2 2
2910⁴ Bencher Q C (USA) **(85)***(91) (JHMGosden)* 3-9-3 LDettori(2) (lw: 5th st: rdn over 2f out: one pce) 2 3
815⁷ High Patriarch (IRE) **(77)***(78) (JLDunlop)* 3-8-9 SWhitworth(8) (rdn over 2f out: hdwy over 1f out: one pce) 3 4
3113¹⁰ Zermatt (IRE) **(69)***(70) (MDIUsher)* 5-8-9 PaulEddery(6) (swtg: led over 1f: 3rd st: rdn over 2f out: one pce)....hd 5
2766⁵ Dontforget Insight (IRE) **(71)***(67) (PFICole)* 4-8-11 TQuinn(3) (led over 8f out tl over 2f out: wknd over 1f out)....3 6
2546⁷ Grooms Gold (IRE) **(66)***(61) (PWHarris)* 3-7-12 JQuinn(4) (swtg: 2nd st: wknd over 2f out) ...nk 7
2240⁸ Bring on the Choir **(82)***(77) (RBoss)* 3-9-0 WWoods(9) (nvr nr to chal)....nk 8
3091⁸ Judge Advocate (IRE) **(78)***(70) (MajorDNChappell)* 3-8-10 RHills(11) (lw: a bhd) 2 9
3007⁸ Pursuit of Glory **(80)***(71) (CACyzer)* 4-9-6 DBiggs(7) (swtg: a bhd) ....½ 10
3085¹⁰ Allez Cyrano (IRE) **(84)***(73) (MBell)* 4-9-10 MFenton(10) (lw: s.s: a bhd) 1½ 11

9/4 FRANCFURTER, **100/30** Amrak Ajeeb (IRE), **7/1** Bencher Q C (USA) (5/1-8/1), **10/1** Judge Advocate (IRE) (8/1-14/1), Zermatt (IRE), **14/1** High Patriarch (IRE) (8/1-16/1), Pursuit of Glory (op 8/1), **16/1** Grooms Gold (IRE), **20/1** Dontforget Insight (IRE), **25/1** Bring on the Choir, Allez Cyrano (IRE), CSF £9.53 CT £38.34 TOTE £2.70: £1.50 £1.50 £2.40 (£4.20) Trio £7.70 OWNER Cliveden Stud (BECKHAMPTON) BRED Cliveden Stud Ltd 11 Rn
2m 10.87 (6.57) SF: 39/43/41/28/28/25/11/27/20/29/31
WEIGHT FOR AGE 3yo-8lb

3238 BUTLIN'S HOLIDAYS H'CAP (0-80) (3-Y.O+) (Class D) £4,190.00 (£1,265.00: £615.00: £290.00)
1m 6f Stalls: High GOING minus 0.03 sec per fur (G) 4-45 (4-49)

3024² **Supreme Star (USA) (58)***(66) (PRHedger)* 4-8-11 (7) DaneO'Neill(6) (4th st: rdn over 2f out: led ins fnl f: r.o wl) — 1
2248* Casual Water (IRE) **(64)***(72) (AGNewcombe)* 4-9-7 (3) DRMcCabe(3) (hdwy 4f out: 6th st: ev ch fnl 2f: r.o) nk 2
3024* Disputed Call (USA) **(46)***(52) (JFfitch-Heyes)* 6-8-6 RPrice(4) (swtg: hdwy 7f out: led over 4f out tl ins fnl f: unable qckn) 1¼ 3
3015* Broughtons Formula **(54)***(60)*(Fav)*(WJMusson)* 5-9-0b JQuinn(2) (lw: 5th st: rdn over 2f out: r.o one pce) nk 4
2937⁴ Chantry Beath **(52)***(56) (CWThornton)* 4-8-12 DeanMcKeown(5) (swtg: 3rd st: hrd rdn 2f out: one pce) 2 5
3094⁵ No Speeches (IRE) **(53)***(48) (CACyzer)* 4-8-13 DBiggs(8) (bhd fnl 3f) 8 6
2569⁸ Ibsen **(62)***(44) (RAkehurst)* 7-9-1 (7) RMoogan(7) (b: lw: 2nd st: wknd over 2f out) 11 7
Recluse **(60)** *(LadyHerries)* 4-9-6 WCarson(1) (swtg: led over 9f: t.o) dist 8

5/2 Broughtons Formula (7/2-9/4), **100/30** Casual Water (IRE), **5/1** Chantry Beath, **6/1** Disputed Call (USA) (5/1-13/), **10/1** SUPREME STAR (USA) (7/1-11/1), Recluse, **12/1** No Speeches (IRE), **20/1** Ibsen, CSF £39.87 CT £197.59 TOTE £12.40: £2.40 £1.70 £2.30 (£25.70) OWNER Mr J. J. Whelan (CHICHESTER) BRED Peter M. Brant 8 Rn 3m 12.97 (18.27) SF: -/5/-/-/-/-/-/-

3239 TONY HUNT MEMORIAL MAIDEN STKS (3-Y.O F) (Class D) £3,545.00 (£1,070.00: £520.00: £245.00)
1m 14y Stalls: High GOING minus 0.03 sec per fur (G) 5-20 (5-22)

2553² **Goalwah** *(83+)*(Fav)*(HThomsonJones)* 3-8-11 RHills(3) (2nd st: led 3f out: clr over 1f out: easily) — 1
868⁷ Miss Haversham **(85)***(73) (CACyzer)* 3-8-11 DBiggs(9) (bit bkwd: 4th st: rdn over 2f out: unable qckn) 5 2
Belmez Melody *(71) (IABalding)* 3-8-11 PatEddery(6) (led 5f: one pce fnl 2f) 1¼ 3
1675⁸ Fragaria *(70) (IABalding)* 3-8-6 (5) DGriffiths(5) (6th st: rdn over 3f out: one pce) nk 4
2790¹⁴ Sherrington *(60) (ACStewart)* 3-8-11 SWhitworth(7) (nvr nr to chal) 5 5
Fire of London *(53) (JHMGosden)* 3-8-11 LDettori(8) (b.hind: w'like: scope: bit bkwd: 5th st: wknd over 2f out) 3½ 6
Urania *(52) (MAJarvis)* 3-8-8 (3) DRMcCabe(2) (w'like: scope: bit bkwd: hdwy & nt clr run over 1f out: sn wknd) ½ 7
3023⁸ Jilly Beveled *(48) (RHannon)* 3-8-11 RPerham(1) (swtg: 3rd st: wknd over 1f out) 2 8
Dance Treat (USA) *(45) (MRStoute)* 3-8-11 PaulEddery(10) (lw: bhd fnl 2f) 1¾ 9
Ozubeck (USA) *(41) (BHanbury)* 3-8-11 RHughes(4) (str: scope: bkwd: s.s: a bhd) 2 10

8/11 GOALWAH (1/2-4/5), **3/1** Fire of London (5/2-9/2), **7/1** Miss Haversham (5/1-8/1), **16/1** Dance Treat (USA), Belmez Melody, **20/1** Ozubeck (USA), **40/1** Jilly Beveled, Fragaria, **50/1** Urania, Sherrington, CSF £6.84 TOTE £1.70: £1.10 £1.70 £2.60 (£4.60) Trio £15.10 OWNER Mr Hamdan Al Maktoum (NEWMARKET) BRED Shadwell Estate Company Limited 10 Rn
1m 45.18 (5.98) SF: 33/23/21/20/10/3/2/-/-/-
T/Jckpt: £14,128.40 (0.7 Tckts); £5,969.78 to Nottingham 21/8/95. T/Plpt: £158.70 (275.72 Tckts). T/Qdpt: £67.80 (5.5 Tckts) AK

3072-WOLVERHAMPTON (L-H)
Saturday August 19th (Standard)
WEATHER: warm, sunny WIND: almost nil

3240 BEATTIES FASHION AMATEUR H'CAP (0-70) (3-Y.O+) (Class G) £2,243.00 (£618.00: £293.00)
1m 1f 79y (Fibresand) Stalls: Low GOING: 0.13 sec per fur (SLW) 7-00 (7-00)

*266*⁵ **Can Can Charlie (58)***(67) (JPearce)* 5-11-9 MrsLPearce(13) (rn wd after 2f: hdwy 5f out: 2nd st: sn led: rdn out) — 1
*2961** Ayunli **(63)***(70) (SCWilliams)* 4-11-9 (5) MissKWright(10) (lw: b.off hind: prom: led 5f out to 4f out: led 2f out: sn hdd & one pce) 1¼ 2
*3075*² Douce Maison (IRE) **(63)***(67) (APJarvis)* 4-11-7 (7) MrsEBurke(6) (chsd ldrs: 6th st: kpt on fnl f) 1¾ 3
2375⁷ Calder King **(63)***(64) (JLEyre)* 4-12-0v MissDianaJones(7) (hdwy 6f out: 5th st: wknd fnl f) 1¾ 4

*2630*5 Palacegate Jo (IRE) **(51)***(48) (DWChapman)* 4-10-11 (5) MrJCulloty(1) (lw: r.o u.p fnl 2f: nrst fin) 2½ 5
*3075*8 Carte Blanche **(62)***(48) (CACyzer)* 4-11-6 (7) MissAWilcox(9) (lw: prom: led 4f out tl hdd & 3rd st: sn wknd) 6 6
28627 Indescent Blue **(55)***(41) (DWPArbuthnot)* 3-10-13 MrsDArbuthnot(4) (lw: b.off hind: chsd ldrs tl 7th & btn st) ....½ 7
73816 Royal Acclaim **(45)***(30) (JMBradley)* 10-10-5v(5) MrsDMcHale(5) (wl bhd tl r.o fnl 3f) ....nk 8
31192 Talented Ting (IRE) **(62)***(47)*(Fav)*(PCHaslam)* 6-11-13v MrCBonner(12) (racd wd: hdwy 6f out: wknd over 2f out) ....hd 9
25938 Sweet Trentino (IRE) **(54)***(36) (MTate)* 4-10-12 (7) MrsHNeedham(3) (chsd ldrs over 5f) 1½ 10
29742 Dance King **(64)***(12) (DNicholls)* 3-11-3 (5) MissRClark(2) (lw: prom 5f: wkng whn rn v. wd over 2f out) 20 11
*2922*6 Erlking (IRE) **(60)***(4) (SMellor)* 5-11-4 (7) MrSHearn(8) (led over 4f: sn wknd) 2½ 12

7/2 Talented Ting (IRE), **4/1** Ayunli, **6/1** Dance King, **13/2** Calder King, **7/1** CAN CAN CHARLIE, **8/1** Douce Maison (IRE) (op 5/1), **12/1** Palacegate Jo (IRE), Carte Blanche, **25/1** Indescent Blue, Sweet Trentino (IRE), Royal Acclaim, Erlking (IRE), CSF £33.57 CT £204.82 TOTE £6.10: £1.50 £2.20 £3.30 (£37.30) Trio £66.10 OWNER Mr G. H. Tufts (NEWMARKET) BRED J. L. Woolford 12 Rn
2m 7.1 (11.10) SF: 49/52/49/46/30/30/16/12/29/18/-/-
WEIGHT FOR AGE 3yo-7lb

3241 CABLE MIDLANDS CLAIMING STKS (3-Y.O+) (Class F) £2,519.00 (£694.00: £329.00)
1m 100y (Fibresand) Stalls: Low GOING: 0.13 sec per fur (SLW) 7-30 (7-33)

2994* **Second Colours (USA) (70)***(76)*(Fav)*(MrsMReveley)* 5-9-5 KDarley(9) (swtg: hld up: hdwy over 3f out: 4th st: rdn to ld ins fnl f) ....— 1
*3073*2 Bentico **(72)***(73) (MrsNMacauley)* 6-9-3b DeanMcKeown(3) (chsd ldrs: 5th st: kpt on wl fnl f) ....½ 2
*3074*7 Rambo Waltzer **(76)***(77) (SGNorton)* 3-9-1 MTebbutt(6) (lw: led 3f: led 3f out tl ins fnl f: one pce) ....hd 3
*3074*3 Pine Ridge Lad (IRE) **(70)***(72) (JLEyre)* 5-9-3 SDWilliams(7) (hdwy & 6th st: no ex ins fnl f) ..nk 4
*3073*5 Maple Bay (IRE) **(52)***(59) (ABailey)* 6-8-4 (3) DWright(4) (led after 3f to 3f out: 2nd st: rdn & btn appr fnl f) 1¾ 5
*2959*2 Emphatic Candidate (IRE) **(65)***(63) (RAkehurst)* 3-8-8 (3) SSanders(13) (b: lw: sn prom: 3rd st: wknd over 1f out) 3 6
*2921*4 No Submission (USA) **(70)***(54) (DWChapman)* 9-8-13v ACulhane(12) (lw: sn rdn along: hdwy 5f out: wknd over 2f out) 3 7
*3073*3 Legatee **(63)***(44) (AStreeter)* 4-8-1 (5) LNewton(1) (in tch 6f) 1½ 8
*1629*W Chadleigh Lane (USA) **(67)***(52) (RHollinshead)* 3-8-11 GCarter(11) (lw: nvr nrr) 1½ 9
*2959*4 Equity's Darling (IRE) **(64)***(46) (MBell)* 3-8-6 GDuffield(2) (in tch: rdn 4f out: sn btn) ....½ 10
*2922*3 Northern Celadon (IRE) **(65)***(42) (MJHeaton-Ellis)* 4-9-3 AClark(5) (prom over 4f) 5 11
30836 Karon Beach **(50)***(32) (JRBostock)* 4-8-1 (7) MDavies(10) (a bhd) ....nk 12

15/8 SECOND COLOURS (USA) (op 3/1), **6/1** Bentico, No Submission (USA), **13/2** Emphatic Candidate (IRE), Northern Celadon (IRE), **8/1** Maple Bay (IRE) (6/1-10/1), **10/1** Legatee (8/1-12/1), **12/1** Equity's Darling (IRE) (op 8/1), **14/1** Chadleigh Lane (USA), **16/1** Pine Ridge Lad (IRE), **33/1** Rambo Waltzer, **50/1** Karon Beach, CSF £15.33 TOTE £2.70: £1.50 £2.10 £5.70 (£5.60) Trio £139.70 OWNER Mr P. D. Savill (SALTBURN) BRED Dinnaken Farm in USA 12 Rn
1m 51.7 (7.70) SF: 40/37/35/36/23/21/18/8/10/4/6/-
WEIGHT FOR AGE 3yo-6lb

3242 BEATTIES 'A BETTER PLACE TO SHOP' H'CAP (0-80) (3-Y.O+) (Class D) £3,968.90 (£1,185.20: £566.60: £257.30)
6f (Fibresand) Stalls: Low GOING: 0.13 sec per fur (SLW) 8-00 (8-01)

30986 **Four of Spades (68)***(73) (PDEvans)* 4-8-9 (7) AmandaSanders(13) (lw: chsd ldrs: 4th st: rdn over 1f out: led nr fin) ....— 1
311212 Souperficial **(66)***(70) (JAGlover)* 4-9-0v JFortune(11) (s.i.s: hdwy & 7th st: no ex ins fnl f) ....nk 2
22345 Sing With the Band **(69)***(73) (BAMcMahon)* 4-9-3 GCarter(1) (led: clr over 1f out: ct nr fin) ...s.h 3
28676 Yet More Roses **(66)***(63) (LadyHerries)* 4-9-0 AClark(12) (bhd: hdwy over 3f out: 5th st: no ex fnl f) 2½ 4
*2590** Malibu Man **(72)***(69)*(Fav)*(SMellor)* 3-9-2 TSprake(8) (prom: 2nd st: no imp appr fnl f) ....nk 5
31506 Shadow Jury **(70)***(62) (DWChapman)* 5-9-4b KDarley(10) (chsd ldrs: 3rd st: sn btn) 1¾ 6
29303 White Sorrel **(80)***(71) (AHarrison)* 4-9-9b(5) JDSmith(5) (nvr nrr) ....nk 7
2819* Purple Fling **(73)***(48) (SirMarkPrescott)* 4-9-7 GDuffield(4) (chsd ldrs tl 6th & btn st) 6 8
276427 Prime Match (IRE) **(75)***(46) (PWHarris)* 3-9-5 MFenton(9) (nvr nr to chal) 1½ 9
302811 Warning Shot **(70)***(25) (MartynMeade)* 3-9-0 VSlattery(2) (spd 3f) 6 10

Pharaoh's Dancer **(70)**(21) (PBurgoyne) 8-8-13 (5) DGibbs(3) (lw: s.s: a bhd) 1¾ 11
1599 13 Leigh Crofter **(78)**(25) (PDCundell) 6-9-7 (5) DGriffiths(6) (prom over 2f) 1¼ 12
2802 6 Try to Please (IRE) **(76)**(19) (EALDunlop) 3-9-6 WWoods(7) (sn rdn: in tch 3f) 1¾ 13

2/1 Malibu Man (op 9/2), **3/1** Purple Fling, **11/2** White Sorrel, **8/1** Sing With the Band, Shadow Jury, **9/1** Souperficial, **12/1** Pharaoh's Dancer, Prime Match (IRE), **14/1** Yet More Roses, **20/1** FOUR OF SPADES, **25/1** Try to Please (IRE), Leigh Crofter, **33/1** Warning Shot, CSF £198.63 CT £1,461.13 TOTE £20.80: £6.80 £3.50 £2.30 (£53.60) Trio £156.50 OWNER Mrs Anna Sanders (WELSHPOOL) BRED Hesmonds Stud Ltd 13 Rn 1m 15.6 (4.40) SF: 50/47/50/40/42/39/48/25/19/-/-/2/-
WEIGHT FOR AGE 3yo-4lb

3243 BEATTIES PERFUMERY MAIDEN AUCTION STKS (2-Y.O) (Class F) £2,519.00 (£694.00: £329.00)
7f (Fibresand) Stalls: High GOING: 0.13 sec per fur (SLW) 8-30 (8-34)

2951 4 **Bumblefoot (IRE)** (61+)(Fav)(MJohnston) 2-7-10 TWilliams(1) (led over 4f: 2nd st: led 1f out: rdn clr) .... — 1
1024 5 Rozel Bay (53) (JLSpearing) 2-7-10 NAdams(10) (a.p: 3rd st: no ex appr fnl f) 3½ 2
2791 11 Cherry Garden (IRE) (60) (TJNaughton) 2-8-1 (5)ow1 JDSmith(4) (hld up: 6th st: hdwy over 1f out: fin wl) .... ¾ 3
2962 9 Still Here (IRE) (60) (MJHeaton-Ellis) 2-8-5 AClark(7) (lw: chsd ldrs: led over 2f out tl wknd & hdd 1f out) .... nk 4
2773 2 Power Don (56)(Fav)(WGMTurner) 2-7-12 (7) JWilkinson(8) (prom: 4th st: sn rdn & wknd) ... 1½ 5
2924 6 La Haye Sainte (46) (DJSCosgrove) 2-7-12 (3)ow1 SSanders(12) (swtg: chsd ldrs tl rdn & lost pl over 3f out: n.d after) 2½ 6
Shermood (39) (MBell) 2-7-10 DaleGibson(9) (leggy: lt-f: chsd ldrs tl poor 5th & btn st) 1¼ 7
1798 6 Cry Baby (44) (KTIvory) 2-8-5 WWoods(11) (lw: reard s: wl bhd tl hdwy after 3f: nt rch ldrs) 1½ 8
2971 8 Onefourseven (40) (SRBowring) 2-8-0b(5)ow4 CTeague(6) (sn outpcd) .... nk 9
What Jim Wants (IRE) (JJO'Neill) 2-8-5 JCarroll(5) (w'like: bit bkwd: bhd fnl 4f) 20 10
Ricochet (IRE) (SGNorton) 2-8-1 DBiggs(2) (lt-f: unf: b.hind: sn bhd: t.o) .... dist 11
Eurobox Boy (APJarvis) 2-8-2 (3) JTate(3) (Withdrawn not under Starter's orders: ref to ent stalls) .... W

5/2 BUMBLEFOOT (IRE) (3/1-2/1), Power Don, **4/1** La Haye Sainte, **6/1** Cry Baby, **10/1** What Jim Wants (IRE) (8/1-12/1), **12/1** Ricochet (IRE) (op 8/1), Shermood (op 8/1), Eurobox Boy, **16/1** Cherry Garden (IRE), **25/1** Onefourseven, **33/1** Still Here (IRE), Rozel Bay, CSF £69.43 TOTE £3.10: £1.40 £7.90 £4.70 (£60.40) Trio £97.00 OWNER G & P Partners (MIDDLEHAM) BRED Rathbarry Stud 11 Rn 1m 33.3 (9.30) SF: -/-/-/-/-/-/-/-/-/-/-

3244 BEATTIES MENSWEAR (S) STKS (2-Y.O F) (Class G) £2,547.00(£702.00: £333.00) **6f (Fibresand)** Stalls: Low GOING: 0.13 sec per fur (SLW) 9-00 (9-03)

*3077** **Chilibang Bang (59)**(62+)(Fav)(JBerry) 2-9-0 JCarroll(10) (lw: w ldrs tl led 2f out: sn clr: pushed out) .... — 1
3093 8 Tallulah Belle (52) (NPLittmoden) 2-8-9 TGMcLaughlin(9) (lw: hdwy & 6th st: stayed on wl fnl f: nt rch wnr) 1¾ 2
2516 9 Frances Mary (48) (CWFairhurst) 2-8-9 WWoods(1) (lw: chsd ldrs: 3rd st: r.o one pce) 1¾ 3
3077 3 Swing Mania (IRE) **(49)**(47) (SGNorton) 2-8-9 KDarley(3) (lw: chsd ldrs: 5th st: no imp appr fnl f) .... hd 4
3124 5 Poppy My Love (31) (RHarris) 2-8-9 AMackay(5) (lw: led 4f: 2nd st: wknd over 1f out) 6 5
Moniques Venture (5) (DJSCosgrove) 2-8-9 MRimmer(7) (s.i.s: nvr nr to chal) 10 6
2924 13 Jereed's Tut (IRE) (JWharton) 2-8-9 AClark(8) (chsd ldrs 3f) 7 7
1981 5 Laser Life Star (CNWilliams) 2-8-9 MFenton(6) (w ldr tl 4th st: eased whn btn appr fnl f) .... hd 8
1213 4 Braes'O'Shieldhill **(42)** (ABailey) 2-8-6 (3) DWright(2) (lw: dwlt: a bhd) 12 9

10/11 CHILIBANG BANG (5/4-4/5), **3/1** Swing Mania (IRE), **7/1** Laser Life Star (op 4/1), Moniques Venture (op 4/1), **9/1** Frances Mary (6/1-10/1), **14/1** Braes'O'Shieldhill, **25/1** Poppy My Love, **33/1** Tallulah Belle, **40/1** Jereed's Tut (IRE), CSF £29.78 TOTE £2.10: £1.20 £4.00 £2.10 (£19.00) Trio £38.20 OWNER Mr Ian Crawford (COCKERHAM) BRED G. W. Hampson 9 Rn
1m 19.3 (8.10) SF: -/-/-/-/-/-/-/-/-
Bt in 6,400 gns

3245 BEATTIES ARAMIS H'CAP (0-65) (3-Y.O+) (Class F) £2,519.00 (£694.00: £329.00)
1m 6f 166y (Fibresand) Stalls: High GOING: 0.13 sec per fur (SLW) 9-30 (9-31)

2919 4 **Barti-Ddu (55)**(65) (SCWilliams) 4-9-1 (3) JTate(9) (chsd ldrs: led 3f out tl over 1f out: led ins fnl f: rdn out) .... — 1

*2495*2 Premier Dance **(60)***(70) (DHaydnJones)* 8-9-9 JCarroll(5) (dwlt: hdwy 5f out: 3rd & rdn st: led over 1f out tl ins fnl f: no ex)....nk **2**
*3078*2 En Vacances (IRE) **(64)***(72) (AGFoster)* 3-9-0 TSprake(8) (lw: a.p: 2nd st: kpt on wl fnl f).....1½ **3**
*2920** Stevie's Wonder (IRE) **(65)***(70) (MJRyan)* 5-9-9 (5) DGibbs(1) (led over 11f: 4th st: snbtn).....2½ **4**
*3082*6 Rolling Waters **(60)***(51) (JARToller)* 5-9-9 WNewnes(3) (hld up: hdwy 5f out: 6th st: no imp).13 **5**
866 2 Environmentalist (IRE) **(55)***(45)*(Fav)*(RHarris)* 4-9-4 AMackay(12) (b.hind: hld up: hdwy over 5f out: 5th & btn st)....1 **6**
2849 3 Streaky Hawk (USA) **(62)***(42) (PFICole)* 3-8-12 KDarley(2) (lw: chsd ldr tl 6th & wkng st) 9 **7**
*2919*15 Absalom's Pillar **(55)***(35) (JMackie)* 5-9-4 NCarlisle(6) (chsd ldrs 8f)....nk **8**
2969 5 Canton Venture **(65)***(42) (SPCWoods)* 3-9-1b WWoods(10) (hld up: hdwy 7f out: rdn over 4f out: sn wknd)....2½ **9**
2942 3 Brave Spy **(58)***(32) (CACyzer)* 4-9-7 DBiggs(7) (lw: lost pl after 6f: n.d after)....3 **10**
2942 5 Jaraab **(62)***(32) (GLewis)* 4-9-6v(5) AWhelan(11) (lw: a bhd)....4 **11**
1858 7 Handmaiden **(54)***(24) (AHarrison)* 5-8-12 (5) JDSmith(4) (lw: prom: rdn over 6f out: wknd 4f out)....s.h **12**

5/2 Environmentalist (IRE), **5/1** Jaraab, **6/1** Streaky Hawk (USA), **7/1** Premier Dance, Rolling Waters, Brave Spy, BARTI-DDU, **8/1** Stevie's Wonder (IRE) (6/1-10/1), **12/1** Handmaiden (op 6/1), **14/1** En Vacances (IRE) (op 8/1), Canton Venture, **33/1** Absalom's Pillar, CSF £61.50 CT £650.19 TOTE £13.00: £3.10 £2.10 £6.60 (£24.10) Trio £53.60 OWNER Miss L. J. Ward (NEWMARKET) BRED Lloyd Bros 12 Rn 3m 22.7 (15.30) SF: 31/36/25/36/17/11/-/1/-/-/-/-
WEIGHT FOR AGE 3yo-13lb
T/Plpt: £841.30 (19.68 Tckts). T/Qdpt: £33.60 (2 Tckts). Dk

2838-**BRIGHTON (L-H)**
Monday August 21st (Firm)
WEATHER: very hot WIND: almost nil

3246 HENFIELD MAIDEN AUCTION STKS (2-Y.O) (Class E) £3,130.60 (£932.80: £444.40: £200.20)
6f 209y Stalls: Low GOING minus 0.45 sec per fur (F) 5-30 (5-31)

2964 2 **Mountain Valley (79)***(77)*(Fav)*(PFICole)* 2-8-0 DBiggs(4) (3rd st: led over 1f out: rdn out) ...— **1**
2741 7 Current Leader *(76) (RHannon)* 2-8-2 AMcGlone(3) (led 6f out tl over 1f out: unable qckn ins fnl f)....1½ **2**
2791 9 Cold Shoulder (IRE) *(66) (JLDunlop)* 2-8-6 SWhitworth(1) (led 1f: 2nd st: hrd rdn over 1f out: sn wknd)....6 **3**
Madonna da Rossi *(61) (SirMarkPrescott)* 2-8-2 CNutter(2) (w'like: bit bkwd: plld hrd: 4th st: swtchd rt over 1f out: sn wknd)....nk **4**
May King Mayhem *(48) (WRMuir)* 2-8-5 DHarrison(5) (cmpt: bhd fnl 4f) 7 **5**

4/5 MOUNTAIN VALLEY, **11/4** Current Leader, **7/1** Madonna da Rossi, **8/1** Cold Shoulder (IRE) (5/1-10/1), **16/1** May King Mayhem, CSF £3.36 TOTE £2.10: £1.10 £1.10 (£1.40) OWNER Mr Christopher Wright (WHATCOMBE) BRED P. J. McCalmont 5 Rn 1m 22.3 (2.30) SF: 18/17/7/2/-

3247 DITCHLING CLAIMING STKS (3-Y.O+ F & M) (Class F) £2,771.00 (£766.00: £365.00)
1m 1f 209y Stalls: High GOING minus 0.45 sec per fur (F) 6-00 (6-00)

2807 7 **Owdbetts (IRE) (63)***(65) (GLMoore)* 3-8-6 SWhitworth(1) (3rd st: swtchd rt 2f out: led over 1f out: rdn & r.o wl) ....— **1**
3125 9 La Fille de Cirque **(48)***(61) (RJRWilliams)* 3-8-8 DBiggs(2) (lw: 2nd st: ev ch over 1f out: unable qckn)....4 **2**
3218 3 Lorelei Lee (IRE) **(62)***(60)*(Fav)*(JohnBerry)* 3-8-12 TQuinn(4) (led over 8f)....3 **3**
2993R Juweilla **(63)** *(JWPayne)* 3-8-8 GBardwell(3) (hung bdly lft s & virtually ref to r: a t.o) ....dist **4**

2/1 Lorelei Lee (IRE) (6/4-9/4), **9/4** OWDBETTS (IRE), **100/30** Juweilla, **9/2** La Fille de Cirque, CSF £9.91 TOTE £3.30 (£7.80) OWNER Mr K. Higson (EPSOM) BRED Maria Goglio 4 Rn
2m 0.9 (2.90) SF: 29/25/24/-

3248 MADEIRA H'CAP (0-70) (3-Y.O+) (Class E) £3,187.80 (£950.40: £453.20: £204.60)
7f 214y Stalls: Low GOING minus 0.45 sec per fur (F) 6-30 (6-30)

3011 4 **Inderaputeri (58)***(74)*(Fav)*(MissGayKelleway)* 5-8-9 (7) DaneO'Neill(7) (2nd st: led over 1f out: r.o wl)....— **1**

2169[7] Confronter **(70)***(80) (SDow)* 6-10-0 RHughes(1) (lw: rdn over 2f out: hdwy over 1f out: r.o one pce) 3 **2**
3026[4] Dancing Lawyer **(68)***(73)*(Fav)*(BJMeehan)* 4-9-12 DHarrison(2) (6th st: n.m.r on ins over 2f out & ins fnl f: one pce) 2½ **3**
2862[3] Fairelaine **(57)***(60) (APJarvis)* 3-8-9 TQuinn(4) (5th st: hung lft over 1f out: one pce) 1 **4**
3082[12] Hatta Sunshine (USA) **(42)***(44) (AMoore)* 5-8-0 NAdams(5) (s.s: hdwy 4f out: hrd rdn over 1f out: wknd fnl f) ....¾ **5**
3057[3] Lucknam Style **(44)***(39) (MrsBarbaraWaring)* 7-7-13b(3)ow4 SDrowne(3) (b.hind: led: clr 6f out: hdd over 1f out: sn wknd) 1¼ **6**
3011[9] Tuigamala **(43)***(38) (RIngram)* 4-8-1 AMcGlone(6) (lw: 3rd st: wknd over 2f out) 1¾ **7**

11/4 INDERAPUTERI, Dancing Lawyer, **4/1** Confronter, **7/1** Hatta Sunshine (USA) (8/1-12/1), **8/1** Fairelaine, Lucknam Style, **20/1** Tuigamala, CSF £13.13 CT £28.33 TOTE £1.10: £1.00 £10.90 (£7.90) OWNER H.R.H. Sultan Ahmad Shah (WHITCOMBE) BRED G. Haywood 7 Rn

1m 33.2 (1.00) SF: 51/57/50/31/21/16/15
WEIGHT FOR AGE 3yo-6lb

3249 GORING MEDIAN AUCTION MAIDEN STKS (3-Y.O) (Class F) £2,519.00 (£694.00: £329.00)

6f 209y Stalls: Low GOING minus 0.45 sec per fur (F) 7-00 (7-01)

3074[6] **Dusk in Daytona (60)***(66+)*(Fav)*(CJames)* 3-8-9 AMcGlone(3) (lw: mde all: clr over 1f out: r.o wl) ....— **1**
2984[5] See You Again **(58)***(63) (RHannon)* 3-9-0 JReid(1) (lost pl & 5th st: rallied fnl f: r.o) 3½ **2**
2844[3] Dark Menace **(63)***(61) (SMellor)* 3-9-0 TSprake(4) (2nd st: rdn over 2f out: unable qckn) 1 **3**
3081[4] Sobeloved **(49)***(42) (NEBerry)* 3-9-0 TQuinn(2) (4th st: hung lft over 1f out: sn wknd) 8 **4**
2843[12] False Pretences (IRE) **(30)***(35) (BAPearce)* 3-9-0b StephenDavies(5) (swtg: 3rd st: rdn over 3f out: wknd over 1f out) 3 **5**

13/8 DUSK IN DAYTONA, **15/8** Dark Menace, **3/1** See You Again, **10/1** Sobeloved (7/1-12/1), **33/1** False Pretences (IRE), CSF £6.40 TOTE £3.10: £1.70 £1.80 (£4.10) OWNER Mr Barry Ross (NEWBURY) BRED B. Minty 5 Rn

1m 22.2 (2.20) SF: 28/25/23/4/-

3250 BRIGHTON HOLIDAY H'CAP (0-80) (3-Y.O+) (Class D) £3,766.10 (£1,122.80: £535.40: £241.70)

5f 59y Stalls: Low GOING minus 0.45 sec per fur (F) 7-30 (7-30)

2463[9] **Halbert (54)***(68) (MRChannon)* 6-8-0v(7) DSweeney(4) (mde all: clr over 3f out: r.o wl) ....— **1**
3087[8] Bashful Brave **(75)***(74)*(Fav)*(JWPayne)* 4-10-0 MRimmer(5) (lw: 3rd st: chsd wnr over 2f out: no imp) 5 **2**
2697[2] Prolific Lady (IRE) **(74)***(65) (MBrittain)* 3-9-10b JWilliams(1) (lw: 4th st: one pce fnl 2f) 2½ **3**
Granmas Delight **(50)***(31) (MMcCormack)* 4-8-3 StephenDavies(2) (lw: 5th st: a bhd) 3½ **4**
2987[5] Dark Eyed Lady (IRE) **(62)***(27) (DWPArbuthnot)* 5-9-1 TQuinn(3) (chsd wnr over 2f: wknd over 1f out) 5 **5**

9/4 Bashful Brave (6/4-5/2), **5/2** Prolific Lady (IRE), **4/1** HALBERT, Dark Eyed Lady (IRE), **9/1** Granmas Delight, CSF £12.30 TOTE £6.10: £2.60 £2.00 (£6.00) OWNER Miss Bridget Coyle (UPPER LAMBOURN) BRED Mr and Mrs J. K. S. Cresswell 5 Rn

60.4 secs (0.40) SF: 46/52/40/9/5
WEIGHT FOR AGE 3yo-3lb

3251 ALDRINGTON H'CAP (0-70) (3-Y.O) (Class E) £3,492.50 (£1,040.00: £495.00: £222.50)

5f 213y Stalls: Low GOING minus 0.45 sec per fur (F) 8-00 (8-00)

3204[2] **Fantasy Racing (IRE) (70)***(79) (MRChannon)* 3-9-7 RHughes(4) (mde all: hrd rdn over 1f out: r.o wl) ....— **1**
1739[6] Portelet **(55)***(61) (RGuest)* 3-8-6 GDuffield(2) (chsd wnr: rdn over 1f out: ev ch ins fnl f: unable qckn) 1 **2**
3121[6] Baileys Sunset (IRE) **(63)***(61)*(Fav)*(MJohnston)* 3-9-0 JReid(1) (lw: 4th st: rdn over 2f out: one pce) 3 **3**
2649[3] High Priest **(65)***(59) (LMCumani)* 3-9-2 OUrbina(3) (5th st: rdn over 2f out: one pce) 1½ **4**
3139[5] Half Tone **(47)***(31) (RMFlower)* 3-7-12bow1 DBiggs(5) (lw: 3rd st: wknd over 1f out) 3½ **5**

15/8 Baileys Sunset (IRE), **9/4** FANTASY RACING (IRE), **5/1** Portelet, **13/2** High Priest (3/1-7/1), Half Tone (3/1-7/1), CSF £11.78 TOTE £2.90: £1.60 £1.90 (£4.20) OWNER Aldridge Racing Ltd (UPPER LAMBOURN) BRED Barronstown Stud and Ron Con Ltd 5 Rn
1m 9.3 (0.90) SF: 53/35/35/33/5
T/Plpt: £35.00 (208.83 Tckts). T/Qdpt: £32.00 (1.7 Tckts). AK

3148-CARLISLE (R-H)
Monday August 21st (Hard)
WEATHER: sunny & hot WIND: slt across

3252 CRUMMOCK WATER APPRENTICE H'CAP (0-65) (4-Y.O+) (Class F) £2,801.00 (£786.00: £383.00)
5f Stalls: High GOING minus 0.77 sec per fur (HD) 5-45 (5-46)

3150^4 **Serious Hurry (47)***(55) (RMMcKellar)* 7-8-8b$^{(5)}$ KSked(1) (mde all: kpt on wl fnl f)........— **1**
2997^5 Cheeky Chappy **(34)***(36) (DWChapman)* 4-7-9b$^{(5)}$ JoHunnam(9) (a chsng ldrs: kpt on same pce fnl f)........1¾ **2**
3116^4 Brisas **(41)***(43) (CWFairhurst)* 8-8-7 JStack(8) (in tch: styd on fnl f: nrst fin)........hd **3**
3116^7 Kabcast **(47)***(45) (DWChapman)* 10-8-10b$^{(3)}$ DGibbs(7) (lw: a chsng ldrs: rdn & btn appr fnl f)........1¼ **4**
2913^3 Best Kept Secret **(58)***(54) (JBerry)* 4-9-7 $^{(3)}$ PFessey(3) (lw: racd wd in tch: kpt on fnl f)........¾ **5**
3116^8 Indian Crystal **(34)***(28) (MrsMReveley)* 4-7-9v$^{(5)}$ DDenby(4) (s.s: racd wd: nvr trbld ldrs)........½ **6**
3123^6 The Institute Boy **(45)***(39) (MissJFCraze)* 5-8-11v DWright(2) (s.s: swtchd rt & gd hdwy ½-wy: rdn & btn over 1f out)........hd **7**
3116^2 Invigilate **(52)***(38)*(Fav)*(MartynWane)* 6-9-4 LNewton(5) (lw: racd wd: drvn along ½-wy: no imp)........2½ **8**
3098^3 Henry the Hawk **(47)***(23) (MDods)* 4-8-8 $^{(5)}$ CWebb(6) (lw: racd wd: outpcd fr ½-wy)........3 **9**

9/4 Invigilate, **9/2** Brisas, **6/1** Best Kept Secret, **15/2** SERIOUS HURRY, **10/1** Henry the Hawk, **11/1** Indian Crystal, **12/1** The Institute Boy, Kabcast, **16/1** Cheeky Chappy, CSF £96.37 CT £540.46 TOTE £5.90: £2.70 £5.40 1.70 (£98.70) Trio £80.50 OWNER Miss S. A. Corcoran (LESMAHAGOW) BRED The Duke of Marlborough 9 Rn
59.4 secs (0.40 under best) (-0.80) SF: 47/28/35/37/46/20/31/30/15

3253 WASTWATER (S) STKS (2-Y.O) (Class G) £2,465.00 (£690.00: £335.00)
5f Stalls: High GOING minus 0.77 sec per fur (HD) 6-15 (6-17)

3018^3 **April's Joy (46)***(47)*(Fav)*(JNorton)* 2-8-6 DaleGibson(6) (mde all: styd on wl fnl f)........— **1**
2852^4 Society Sue (IRE) **(60)***(44) (RonaldThompson)* 2-8-1 $^{(5)}$ LNewton(4) (trckd ldrs gng wl: effrt appr fnl f: nt qckn)........1 **2**
2859^7 Doubleyoubeay **(51)***(43) (JBerry)* 2-9-2 JCarroll(1) (lw: cl up tl rdn & btn appr fnl f)........3½ **3**
3048^7 The Black Dubh (IRE) *(31) (JJQuinn)* 2-8-11 ACulhane(8) (chsd ldrs: hrd drvn ½-wy: r.o one pce)........2 **4**
3018^7 Candy Dancer *(29) (CWThornton)* 2-8-11 DeanMcKeown(7) (chsd ldrs: rdn ½-wy: no imp after)........¾ **5**
3120^3 Julgarant (IRE) **(50)***(16) (MDods)* 2-8-11v JFortune(5) (spd over 3f)........4 **6**
2796^6 Just Rory **(65)** *(MissZAGreen)* 2-8-8 $^{(3)}$ JStack(2) (s.s: hdwy on outside ½-wy: wknd wl over 1f out)........10 **7**
Princess Briana *(DMoffatt)* 2-8-3 $^{(3)}$ DarrenMoffatt(3) (neat: scope: bkwd: sn outpcd & bhd) 12 **8**

5/2 APRIL'S JOY, **7/2** Society Sue (IRE), **5/1** Doubleyoubeay, Candy Dancer, **11/1** The Black Dubh (IRE), **12/1** Julgarant (IRE) (op 20/1), **14/1** Princess Briana (op 8/1), **33/1** Just Rory, CSF £10.50 TOTE £3.20: £1.20 £1.50 £2.00 (£4.50) OWNER Mrs Sylvia Blakeley (BARNSLEY) BRED Red House Stud 8 Rn
61.8 secs (1.60) SF: 3/-/-/-/-/-/-/-
No bid

3254 SUNDAY NEWS & STAR H'CAP (0-70) (3-Y.O) (Class E) £2,966.70 (£897.60: £437.80: £207.90)
1m 4f Stalls: Low GOING minus 0.77 sec per fur (HD) 6-45 (6-46)

3047^8 **Red Spectacle (IRE) (49)***(64) (PCHaslam)* 3-8-3 $^{(3)}$ JStack(3) (mde all: styd on wl fnl 2f)........— **1**
3111^2 Trumble **(46)***(56) (CWThornton)* 3-8-3 DeanMcKeown(4) (plld hrd: sn trckng wnr: effrt 3f out: nvr able to chal)........4 **2**
2920^2 Last Corner **(52)***(57)*(Fav)*(RHollinshead)* 3-8-9 KDarley(2) (lw: hld up: outpcd over 3f out: no imp after)........3½ **3**

3076[3] Hard Love **(64)***(69) (SPCWoods)* 3-9-0 (7) CWebb(1) (lw: hld up: effrt 4f out: hung lft: no imp)....nk 4

5/4 Last Corner, **2/1** Hard Love, **9/2** Trumble, **7/1** RED SPECTACLE (IRE) (4/1-8/1), CSF £28.62 TOTE £6.70 (£7.50) OWNER Mr David Morgan (MIDDLEHAM) BRED J. Beckett 4 Rn
2m 33.2 (2.20) SF: 16/8/9/21

3255 BONNIE PRINCE CHARLIE H'CAP (0-80) (3-Y.O+) (Class D) £3,606.20 (£1,091.60: £532.80: £253.40)
7f 214y Stalls: High GOING minus 0.77 sec per fur (HD) 7-15 (7-18)

2999[4] **Thatched (IRE) (50)***(70+) (REBarr)* 5-7-12 (7) PFessey(4) (lw: prom: qcknd to ld 2f out: r.o wl: sn clr)....— 1
3101[5] Spanish Verdict **(69)***(73)*(Fav)*(DenysSmith)* 8-9-5 (5) CTeague(6) (lw: led tl hdd 2f out: one pce)....8 2
2999[6] Three Arch Bridge **(61)***(62) (MJohnston)* 3-8-10b TWilliams(5) (cl up: effrt over 3f out: r.o one pce)....1½ 3
3240[9] Talented Ting (IRE) **(68)***(62) (PCHaslam)* 6-9-9 JFortune(3) (drvn along appr st: nvr trbld ldrs)....3½ 4
2814[5] Mca Below the Line **(56)***(50) (JLEyre)* 7-8-11v SDWilliams(2) (outpcd & bhd fr ½-wy: n.d)......hd 5
3151* Durham Drapes **(61)***(55)*(Fav)*(MHEasterby)* 4-9-2 5x SMaloney(1) (lw: cl up: rdn 3f out: sn wknd)....hd 6

3/1 Spanish Verdict, Durham Drapes (op 2/1), **9/2** THATCHED (IRE), Talented Ting (IRE), **11/2** Three Arch Bridge, **8/1** Mca Below the Line, CSF £17.13 TOTE £5.50: £2.20 £1.70 (£7.10) OWNER Mr J. C. Garbutt (MIDDLESBROUGH) BRED D. P. O'Brien 6 Rn
1m 37.3 (0.80 under best) (-1.70) SF: 45/48/31/37/25/30
WEIGHT FOR AGE 3yo-6lb

3256 BUTTERMERE CLAIMING STKS (3-Y.O+) (Class F) £2,871.00 (£806.00: £393.00)
5f 207y Stalls: High GOING minus 0.77 sec per fur (HD) 7-45 (7-49)

3073[4] **Brookhead Lady (49)***(62)*(Fav)*(PDEvans)* 4-8-4 GHind(5) (mde most: rdn & styd on wl appr fnl f)....— 1
3116[3] Ramborette **(47)***(51) (DenysSmith)* 3-7-12 TWilliams(7) (a chsng ldrs: hdwy over 2f out: nt qckn appr fnl f)....3½ 2
2913[8] Broctune Gold **(65)***(52) (MrsMReveley)* 4-8-11 KDarley(4) (lw: w wnr: rdn 2f out: grad wknd)....3 3
2821[5] Farndale **(35)***(35) (RonaldThompson)* 8-8-0 (5) LNewton(2) (outpcd ½-wy: styd on: no imp) 4 4
3063[10] Brigadore Gold **(22)***(28) (FHLee)* 5-8-0b RLappin(1) (chsd ldrs to ½-wy: sn wknd)....¾ 5
1778[10] Delightful Dancer (IRE) **(57)***(26) (JNorton)* 3-7-12b(7) AmyGosden(6) (lw: nvr wnt pce)....4 6
2913[7] Palace River (IRE) *(19) (DMoffatt)* 7-7-13 (3) DarrenMoffatt(3) (dwlt: a outpcd & bhd)....s.h 7

2/1 BROOKHEAD LADY, **9/4** Ramborette, Broctune Gold, **12/1** Farndale, **14/1** Delightful Dancer (IRE) (tchd 33/1), **40/1** Brigadore Gold, Palace River (IRE), CSF £6.69 TOTE £2.60: £1.50 £1.60 (£3.20) OWNER Mr J. E. Abbey (WELSHPOOL) BRED Theakston Stud 7 Rn
1m 11.9 (-0.40) SF: 32/17/22/5/-/-/-
WEIGHT FOR AGE 3yo-4lb

3257 RYDAL WATER RATING RELATED MAIDEN LIMITED STKS (0-60) (3-Y.O) (Class F) £2,675.00 (£750.00: £365.00)
5f 207y Stalls: High GOING minus 0.77 sec per fur (HD) 8-15 (8-16)

3167[2] **Achill Princess (38)***(49) (WTKemp)* 3-8-9 KDarley(6) (lw: sn chsng ldrs: swtchd 2f out: r.o u.p to ld cl home)....— 1
2997[3] Northern Grey **(50)***(54) (JBerry)* 3-9-0 JCarroll(4) (lw: cl up: led 1½f out: hrd rdn: jst ct) ....s.h 2
2974[4] So Amazing **(60)***(44)*(Fav)*(MissSEHall)* 3-8-9 NConnorton(3) (b: chsd ldrs: led 2½f out to 1½f out: btn whn hmpd wl ins fnl f)....2 3
3000[7] Oubeck Princess **(32)***(30) (EWeymes)* 3-8-9 GHind(5) (outpcd ½-wy: n.d after)....5 4
2818[2] Daily Challenger (USA) **(44)***(34) (RonaldThompson)* 3-8-9 (5) LNewton(2) (led 3½f: sn btn)....nk 5

4/5 So Amazing, **3/1** Northern Grey, **9/2** Daily Challenger (USA), **9/1** ACHILL PRINCESS, **33/1** Oubeck Princess, CSF £32.27 TOTE £7.80: £3.60 £1.90 (£8.30) OWNER Drakemyre Racing (DUNS) BRED Barrettstown Stud Farms Ltd 5 Rn 1m 13.3 (1.00) SF: 18/23/13/-/3

T/Plpt: £365.70 (26.26 Tckts). T/Qdpt: £20.10 (2.4 Tckts). AA

3092-NOTTINGHAM (L-H)
Monday August 21st (Good to firm, firm patches)
WEATHER: hot & sunny WIND: almost nil

3258 'ENCOURAGE THE YOUNG' (S) H'CAP (0-60) (I) (3-Y.O+) (Class G) £2,243.00 (£618.00: £293.00)
1m 1f 213y Stalls: High GOING minus 0.49 sec per fur (F) 2-15 (2-16)

2317[11] **Threshfield (USA) (44)**(57) (BJCurley) 9-9-5 WRyan(9) (b: mde all: rdn & hld on gamely nr fin)........— **1**
3056[7] Lady Sabina **(35)**(48) (WJMusson) 5-8-7 (3) PMcCabe(10) (hld up: 4th st: ev ch fr bel dist: rdn & r.o wl)........s.h **2**
3099[8] Perfect Bertie (IRE) **(43)**(50) (GROldroyd) 3-8-10v KFallon(5) (bhd: hdwy on ins 3f out: hrd rdn appr fnl f: nt rch ldrs)........3½ **3**
2789[12] Swynford Flyer **(23)**(29) (JAHarris) 6-7-7 (5) MHenry(2) (lw: hdwy & 5th st: styd on u.p ins fnl f)¾ **4**
3129[5] Premier Blues (FR) **(22)**(24) (RJRWilliams) 5-7-11b NCarlisle(7) (chsd wnr: 2nd st: hrd rdn & wknd wl over 1f out)........2½ **5**
3118* Zahran (IRE) **(49)**(50)(Fav)(JMBradley) 4-9-7 (3) 6x SDrowne(6) (b: chsd ldrs: wnt 3rd st: hrd rdn 2f out: sn btn)........¾ **6**
3099* Hunza Story **(38)**(35) (NPLittmoden) 3-7-12 (7) CAdamson(3) (b.hind: a in rr)........2½ **7**
2064[2] Straw Thatch **(49)**(38) (RBastiman) 6-9-5 (5) HBastiman(4) (hld up: 6th st: rdn 3f out: no imp)..5 **8**
2884[4] Kindred Greeting **(38)**(8) (DMorris) 3-8-5b JFanning(8) (a in rr: t.o fnl 2f)........12 **9**
2832[17] T'Niel **(18)** (GFierro) 4-7-0 (7) BHalligan(1) (s.i.s: sn rcvrd to chse ldrs: racd wd: wknd over 4f out: t.o)........dist **10**

LONG HANDICAP T'Niel 7-6

4/1 Zahran (IRE), **9/2** THRESHFIELD (USA), **11/2** Straw Thatch, **7/1** Hunza Story (op 4/1), Perfect Bertie (IRE), **15/2** Lady Sabina, **9/1** Kindred Greeting, **10/1** Swynford Flyer, **16/1** Premier Blues (FR), **50/1** T'Niel, CSF £34.89 CT £211.59 TOTE £5.20: £2.30 £2.40 £1.30 (£24.30) Trio £36.90
OWNER Mrs B. J. Curley (NEWMARKET) BRED Aisco Farms 10 Rn

2m 7.1 (4.60) SF: 27/18/12/-/-/20/-/8/-/-
WEIGHT FOR AGE 3yo-8lb
No bid

3259 'ENCOURAGE THE YOUNG' (S) H'CAP (0-60) (II) (3-Y.O+) (Class G) £2,243.00 (£618.00: £293.00)
1m 1f 213y Stalls: High GOING minus 0.49 sec per fur (F) 2-45 (2-48)

2961[10] **Coven Moon (26)**(41) (DMorris) 5-7-8v ow1 JQuinn(5) (a.p: 2nd st: led 4f out: sn clr: rdn & hld on ins fnl f)........— **1**
2861[5] Course Fishing **(35)**(49) (BAMcMahon) 4-8-3 FNorton(6) (a.p: 4th st: chsd wnr fnl 3f: hrd rdn: one pce)........1¼ **2**
2813[5] Indian Rhapsody **(46)**(60) (MJohnston) 3-8-6 DHolland(2) (hld up: nt clr run 3f out: gd hdwy over 2f out: fin wl)........hd **3**
2901* Cashmirie **(45)**(48) (JLEyre) 3-8-2 (3) NVarley(3) (b: hld up: hdwy & 5th st: rdn over 2f out: nvr nr to chal)........7 **4**
3099[2] Miss Felixstowe (USA) **(49)**(36)(Fav)(MrsMReveley) 3-8-9 GCarter(10) (swtg: mid div: 6th st: effrt u.p over 2f out: nvr nr to chal)........10 **5**
3118[4] Portite Sophie **(40)**(19) (MBrittain) 4-8-8 JLowe(9) (swtg: led after 1f to 4f out: wknd over 2f out)........5 **6**
2961[9] Backstabber **(30)** (MissSJWilton) 5-7-12 ow1 JFanning(7) (hdwy ½-wy: 3rd st: rdn & wknd over 3f out: t.o)........12 **7**
2582[11] Rozalina Lady **(40)** (NAGraham) 3-8-0b ow2 BDoyle(8) (s.s: hdwy ½-wy: wknd ent st: t.o)........10 **8**
232[8] Captain Sinbad **(34)** (KSBridgwater) 3-7-8 ow1 NCarlisle(4) (bit bkwd: led 1f: 5th st: wknd 3f out: t.o)........15 **9**
2961[13] Master Showman (IRE) **(60)** (HOliver) 4-10-0 KFallon(1) (swtg: a bhd: t.o fnl 3f)........13 **10**

LONG HANDICAP Captain Sinbad 7-4

11/4 Miss Felixstowe (USA), **4/1** Cashmirie, **5/1** Indian Rhapsody, Course Fishing, **10/1** Portite Sophie, **12/1** Backstabber, **14/1** COVEN MOON, Rozalina Lady, **25/1** Master Showman (IRE), **50/1** Captain Sinbad, CSF £75.20 CT £365.29 TOTE £13.60: £2.00 £1.60 £2.00 (£28.20) Trio £124.70
OWNER Mrs Sara Pepper (NEWMARKET) BRED Mrs S. Pepper 10 Rn

2m 5.6 (3.10) SF: 15/23/26/14/2/-/-/-/-/-
WEIGHT FOR AGE 3yo-8lb
No bid

3260 'PUNCH AND JUDY' MAIDEN AUCTION STKS (2-Y.O) (Class E) £3,559.60 (£1,064.80: £510.40: £233.20)
6f 15y Stalls: Low GOING minus 0.49 sec per fur (F) 3-15 (3-17)

3069² **Faraway Waters** *(90+)*(Fav)*(DWPArbuthnot)* 2-8-5 TQuinn(11) (b.hind: lw: mde virtually all: qcknd clr fnl f: easily) — 1
3025² Lucky Revenge **(75)***(76) (MartynMeade)* 2-7-9 (3) NVarley(6) (dwlt: hdwy 3f out: effrt & nt clr run ent fnl f: no ch w wnr) 2½ 2
2281⁴ Impington (IRE) *(68) (MAJarvis)* 2-8-3 PRobinson(3) (b.hind: hdwy 2f out: wknd appr fnl f) 5 3
Iceni (IRE) *(61) (ACStewart)* 2-8-2 MRoberts(2) (lt-f: hld up: swtchd stands' side: r.o fnl f: improve) 2½ 4
1781⁹ Our Albert (IRE) *(64) (JAGlover)* 2-8-6 SDWilliams(5) (bit bkwd: settled mid div: hdwy wl over 1f out: nvr nrr) hd 5
3089²² Even Handed *(64) (PFICole)* 2-8-7 AClark(10) (disp ld 4f: sn rdn & outpcd) ½ 6
*2958*⁸ Mr Speaker (IRE) *(61) (CFWall)* 2-8-9 NCarlisle(4) (lw: hld up: hdwy bel dist: styng on whn n.m.r fnl f) 1¾ 7
3053⁵ Maraschino *(47) (MJHeaton-Ellis)* 2-8-5 WWoods(9) (lw: chsd ldrs 4f: sn lost tch) 4 8
2161² Sharp Monty **(77)***(36) (RHollinshead)* 2-8-5 WRyan(8) (gd spd over 3f: grad wknd) 4 9
Impeccable *(11) (JLDunlop)* 2-8-3 WCarson(7) (neat: scope: bit bkwd: swvd rt s: sn rdn & bhd: t.o) 9 10
2978⁸ Prime Secret *(11) (BJMeehan)* 2-8-5 BDoyle(1) (nvr gng pce of ldrs: lost tch fnl 2f: t.o) ¾ 11

10/11 FARAWAY WATERS, **6/1** Lucky Revenge (op 10/1), Impeccable, **7/1** Iceni (IRE) (op 4/1), **10/1** Impington (IRE), **11/1** Sharp Monty, **16/1** Prime Secret, **25/1** Even Handed, **33/1** Maraschino, **40/1** Mr Speaker (IRE), Our Albert (IRE), CSF £7.90 TOTE £2.00: £1.40 £1.80 £1.90 (£7.30) Trio £23.80 OWNER Mr R. Crutchley (COMPTON) BRED R. E. Crutchley 11 Rn
1m 13.9 (2.90) SF: 9/-/-/-/-/-/-/-/-/-/-

OFFICIAL EXPLANATION **Mr Speaker: reportedly got outpaced early on, was not striding out on the fast ground and then got slightly hampered in the later stages.**

3261 'CHILDRENS DAY' CONDITIONS STKS (3-Y.O) (Class C) £5,227.20 (£1,803.20: £861.60: £348.00)
1m 54y Stalls: High GOING minus 0.49 sec per fur (F) 3-45 (3-47)

3027² **Muktabas (IRE)** *(96)*(Fav)*(JHMGosden)* 3-8-12 WCarson(1) (lw: chsd ldr: 2nd st: led wl over 1f out: drvn out) — 1
1729⁷ Miasma (USA) **(99)***(90) (JARToller)* 3-8-7 JWeaver(3) (swtg: led: rdn 2f out: sn hdd: rallied gamely fnl f) ¾ 2
3066¹⁰ Hedera (USA) **(89)***(90) (MRStoute)* 3-8-9 WRyan(4) (lw: hld up: 3rd st: rdn 2f out: kpt on wl towards fin) ¾ 3
3027³ Hindaawee (USA) **(90)***(83) (EALDunlop)* 3-8-9 (3) JTate(2) (lw: s.v.s: 4th st: outpcd fnl 2f) 5 4

Evens MUKTABAS (IRE), **11/4.** Hedera (USA), **5/1** Hindaawee (USA), **7/1** Miasma (USA) (op 7/2), CSF £6.46 TOTE £1.80 (£3.20) OWNER Mr Hamdan Al Maktoum (NEWMARKET) BRED Ardenode Stud Ltd. in Ireland 4 Rn
1m 42.0 (2.40) SF: 32/26/26/19

3262 'CHILDREN FREE TODAY' H'CAP (0-80) (3-Y.O+) (Class D) £3,799.90 (£1,133.20: £540.60: £244.30)
1m 6f 15y Stalls: High GOING minus 0.49 sec per fur (F) 4-15 (4-16)

*2919*⁵ **Wannaplantatree (54)***(64) (NMBabbage)* 4-8-4 AClark(4) (hld up: 3rd st: shkn up to chal ins fnl f: r.o to ld nr fin) — 1
3162¹¹ Star Rage (IRE) **(78)***(86) (MJohnston)* 5-10-0 JWeaver(2) (led: rdn & qcknd over 1f out: hdd & no ex wl ins fnl f) 1¾ 2
2986³ Trazl (IRE) **(79)***(86)*(Fav)*(JLDunlop)* 3-9-3 GCarter(1) (lw: chsd ldr: 2nd st: ev ch fnl 2f: rdn & unable qckn fnl f) ½ 3
2954⁶ Kanat Lee (IRE) **(43)***(33) (DonEnricoIncisa)* 4-7-7 KimTinkler(3) (lw: hld up & bhd: 4th & outpcd ent st: sn lost tch: t.o) 15 4
LONG HANDICAP Kanat Lee (IRE) 6-10

Evens Trazl (IRE), **7/4** Star Rage (IRE), **7/2** WANNAPLANTATREE, **33/1** Kanat Lee (IRE), CSF £9.40 TOTE £4.10 (£3.20) OWNER Royal Oak, Kinnersley, Racing (CHELTENHAM) BRED Stetchworth Park Stud Ltd 4 Rn
3m 2.3 (3.80) SF: 29/51/39/-
WEIGHT FOR AGE 3yo-12lb

3263 'PLAYGROUND' LIMITED STKS (0-55) (3-Y.O+) (Class F) £2,519.00 (£694.00: £329.00)
1m 6f 15y Stalls: High GOING minus 0.49 sec per fur (F) 4-45 (4-46)

7214 **Bellara (47)***(63) (NMBabbage)* 3-8-5 JQuinn(6) (bit bkwd: swtg: a chsng ldrs: 4th st: rdn to ld ins fnl f: all out) — 1
29862 Mr Geneaology (USA) **(55)***(68) (FMurphy)* 5-9-8b JWeaver(4) (hld up & bhd: drvn along 4f out: hdwy 3f out: str chal fnl f: jst failed) s.h 2
*3076** Instantaneous **(55)***(61)*(Fav)*(MHEasterby)* 3-8-9 MBirch(7) (hld up: hdwy 6f out: 5th st: rdn 3f out: led bel dist tl hdd ins fnl f: all out) 5 3
3029* Outstayed Welcome **(51)***(62) (MJHaynes)* 3-8-9 (5) MBaird(9) (lw: chsd ldr: 2nd st: led over 3f out to bel dist) 4 4
22299 Phase One (IRE) **(51)***(46) (JLEyre)* 5-9-3 MRoberts(2) (b: hld up & bhd: rdn 4f out: styd on fnl 2f: nvr nrr) 6 5
3140* Harding Brown (USA) **(51)***(50) (GHarwood)* 3-8-3v(7) GayeHarwood(3) (lw: led: clr 10f out: hdd over 3f out: sn rdn: wknd bel dist) 1¼ 6
15358 Limosa **(37)***(42) (RFJohnsonHoughton)* 4-9-3 AClark(10) (hld up: 7th st: rdn over 4f out: no imp) 2 7
286011 Blue Smoke (IRE) **(53)***(42) (BAMcMahon)* 3-8-10b FNorton(5) (hld up: effrt & rdn 4f out: no imp: t.o) 5 8
25097 Bella Vitessa (IRE) **(50)***(14) (JWHills)* 3-8-0b(5) MHenry(1) (plld hrd: prom: 3rd st: wknd 3f out: t.o) 20 9

13/8 Instantaneous, **4/1** Harding Brown (USA), Outstayed Welcome, **5/1** Mr Geneaology (USA), **10/1** Limosa, **12/1** Phase One (IRE), **14/1** Blue Smoke (IRE), **20/1** Bella Vitessa (IRE), **33/1** BELLARA, CSF £184.66 TOTE £32.50: £3.70 £1.80 £1.60 (£96.00) Trio £72.20 OWNER Mr B. Babbage (CHELTENHAM) BRED John White 9 Rn 3m 0.6 (81.00) SF: 40/57/38/39/35/27/31/19/-
WEIGHT FOR AGE 3yo-12lb

3264 'FUN FOR ALL AGES' H'CAP (0-70) (3-Y.O+) (Class E) £3,473.80 (£1,038.40: £497.20: £226.60)
1m 54y Stalls: High GOING minus 0.49 sec per fur (F) 5-15 (5-18)

28812 **Saltz (IRE) (52)***(65) (PTDalton)* 3-8-4 (3) PMcCabe(8) (lw: chsd ldrs: 3rd st: led over 2f out: sn clr) — 1
3050* Michellisa **(54)***(67) (JDBethell)* 4-9-1 KFallon(3) (hld up & bhd: 6th st: hdwy & rdn along 2f out: str chal fnl f: jst failed) hd 2
31016 Nobby Barnes **(41)***(49) (DonEnricoIncisa)* 6-8-2 KimTinkler(6) (hld up: 5th st: styd on appr fnl f: nvr nrr) 2½ 3
30266 Lord Oberon (IRE) **(61)***(64)*(Fav)*(JAkehurst)* 7-9-8 GCarter(4) (hld up: 4th st: rdn over 2f out: nvr nr to chal) 2½ 4
28723 Bedazzle **(34)***(33) (MBrittain)* 4-7-9 JLowe(2) (chsd ldr: 2nd st: wknd over 2f out) 2 5
11915 Slytly Beveled **(54)***(50) (NPLittmoden)* 3-8-9b TGMcLaughlin(1) (swtg: a bhd: 7th st: rdn 3f out: no imp) 1½ 6
2885* Fyne Song **(41)***(20) (WJMusson)* 3-7-10 JQuinn(5) (led tl hdd & wknd over 2f out: t.o) 9 7
310612 Chief of Staff **(63)** *(JPearce)* 6-9-10 WNewnes(7) (Withdrawn not under Starter's orders: bolted 2 circuits bef s) W

2/1 Lord Oberon (IRE), **3/1** Michellisa, **5/1** Nobby Barnes, **11/2** SALTZ (IRE), Fyne Song, **10/1** Chief of Staff, **14/1** Bedazzle, **16/1** Slytly Beveled, CSF £21.82 CT £80.43 TOTE £7.10: £1.90 £2.90 (£15.70) OWNER Mrs Julie Martin (BURTON-ON-TRENT) BRED John B. Hughes 7 Rn
1m 42.9 (3.30) SF: 19/27/9/24/-/4/-/-
WEIGHT FOR AGE 3yo-6lb

T/Jkpt: Not won; £11,688.12 to Pontefract 22/8/95. T/Plpt: £369.40 (48.62 Tckts). T/Qdpt: £35.90 (4.55 Tckts). IM

3246-BRIGHTON (L-H)
Tuesday August 22nd (Firm)
WEATHER: hot WIND: almost nil

3265 FRIENDS OF QUEEN'S PARK (S) APPRENTICE H'CAP (0-60) (3-Y.O) (Class G) £2,243.00 (£618.00: £293.00)
1m 3f 196y Stalls: High GOING minus 0.66 sec per fur (HD) 2-30 (2-31)

30824 **Water Hazard (IRE) (42)***(59)*(Fav)*(SDow)* **3-9-6** ADaly(5) (swtg: led over 5f out: hrd rdn over 2f out: r.o wl) — 1

2976[9] Royal Rabbit **(43)**(55) (GLMoore) 3-9-2 (5) ALakeman(1) (led 11f out tl over 5f out: 3rd st: rdn over 2f out: r.o one pce fnl f) 4 2
2976[3] Today Tonite **(37)**(49)(Fav)(JPearce) 3-9-1 DGibbs(6) (2nd st: ev ch over 2f out: edgd rt ins fnl f: one pce) ....s.h 3
2959[7] Miltak **(38)**(47) (PJMakin) 3-9-2 RHavlin(4) (4th st: ev ch over 2f out: one pce) 1¾ 4
3184[3] Presto Boy **(41)**(48) (MBell) 3-9-2v(3) GFaulkner(3) (5th st: hrd rdn over 2f out: wknd over 1f out) 2 5
1939[6] Most Welcome News **(42)**(22) (JRJenkins) 3-9-3b(3) RWaterfield(2) (led 1f: wknd over 5f out) 20 6
3096[8] Margaret Modes **(35)**(9) (CACyzer) 3-8-13b CAdamson(7) (a bhd) 4 7
2626[8] Anchor Crown **(28)** (JRJenkins) 3-7-13 (7) SallyWall(8) (bhd fnl 6f) 11 8

2/1 WATER HAZARD (IRE), Today Tonite, **11/2** Presto Boy (7/2-6/1), **10/1** Royal Rabbit (op 6/1), **14/1** Margaret Modes, **20/1** Most Welcome News, Miltak, **50/1** Anchor Crown, CSF £18.81 CT £35.20 TOTE £3.00: £1.20 £2.20 £1.20 (£16.20) OWNER Mr Ken Butler (EPSOM) BRED Mrs A. C. Belcher and P. B. Hayden in Ireland 8 Rn

2m 33.4 (4.40) SF: 23/19/13/11/12/-/-/-
Bt in 6,000gns

3266 E.B.F. GARDEN AWARD MAIDEN STKS (2-Y.O) (Class D) £3,557.50 (£1,060.00: £505.00: £227.50)

7f 214y Stalls: Low GOING minus 0.66 sec per fur (HD) 3-00 (3-01)

3090[6] **Munketh (USA) (87)**(72+)(Fav)(JLDunlop) 2-9-0 WCarson(6) (4th st: led ins fnl f: pushed out) ....— 1
2820[2] Vasetto (69) (SirMarkPrescott) 2-9-0 WWoods(1) (lw: 3rd st: led over 2f out tl ins fnl f: unable qckn) 1½ 2
3104[5] Suparoy (61) (TGMills) 2-9-0 PaulEddery(3) (hdwy over 4f out: 5th st: swtchd rt 2f out: one pce) 4 3
3174[12] Autumn (FR) (54) (PFICole) 2-8-9 CRutter(7) (s.s: rdn 3f out: hdwy over 1f out: nvr nrr) 1¼ 4
2529[4] Seven Crowns (USA) (58) (RHannon) 2-9-0 JReid(4) (lw: 6th st: nvr nr to chal) ....s.h 5
Happy Taipan (IRE) (58) (MJHeaton-Ellis) 2-9-0 WNewnes(2) (w'like: bit bkwd: led over 5f: wknd over 1f out) ....hd 6
2434[5] Gallante (50) (PFICole) 2-9-0 TQuinn(5) (2nd st: wknd 2f out) 4 7

1/2 MUNKETH (USA), **7/2** Vasetto, **8/1** Seven Crowns (USA) (5/1-10/1), **14/1** Gallante (10/1-16/1), **25/1** Happy Taipan (IRE), **33/1** Suparoy, **50/1** Autumn (FR), CSF £2.83 TOTE £1.40: £1.10 £1.50 (£2.00) OWNER Mr Hamdan Al Maktoum (ARUNDEL) BRED Dr. Thomas D. Brokken and Wilma J. Miller 7 Rn

1m 35.2 (3.00) SF: 11/8/-/-/-/-/-

3267 ARTHUR BURROW KING MEMORIAL NURSERY H'CAP (2-Y.O) (Class E) £3,159.20 (£941.60: £448.80: £202.40)

6f 209y Stalls: Low GOING minus 0.66 sec per fur (HD) 3-30 (3-31)

3009[2] **Proper Blue (USA) (84)**(92) (TGMills) 2-9-7 JReid(4) (3rd st: hrd rdn fnl f: led last stride) ....— 1
2847[7] General Rose **(66)**(74) (RHannon) 2-8-3 WCarson(3) (2nd st: led over 1f out: rdn: hdd last stride) ....s.h 2
3019[4] Vanishing Point **(76)**(75)(Fav)(GLewis) 2-8-13 PaulEddery(7) (led 1f: 4th st: lost pl over 3f out: r.o one pce fnl f) 4 3
3090* Pacific Grove **(78)**(76) (PFICole) 2-8-8 (7) ADaly(5) (5th st: rdn over 3f out: one pce fnl f) ....hd 4
3019[5] Takapuna (IRE) **(60)**(49) (TJNaughton) 2-7-11 FNorton(6) (6th st: nvr nr to chal) 4 5
3090[11] Distant Storm **(67)**(52) (MBell) 2-8-4b MFenton(2) (lw: a bhd) 2 6
2732[3] Classic Daisy **(61)**(35) (MissGayKelleway) 2-7-7v(5)ow5 MHenry(1) (b. hind: led 6f out tl over 1f out: sn wknd) 2½ 7

11/4 Vanishing Point, **3/1** Pacific Grove, **5/1** Takapuna (IRE) (4/1-6/1), **11/2** PROPER BLUE (USA), **13/2** General Rose, **8/1** Classic Daisy, **16/1** Distant Storm, CSF £36.03 TOTE £5.20: £2.20 £2.20 (£11.50) OWNER Mr M. J. Legg (EPSOM) BRED Claibome Farm and The Gamely Corporation 7 Rn

1m 22.2 (2.20) SF: 22/4/5/6/-/-/-

3268 QUEEN'S PARK CENTENARY CHALLENGE CUP H'CAP (0-80) (4-Y.O+) (Class D) £3,698.50 (£1,102.00: £525.00: £236.50)

6f 209y Stalls: Low GOING minus 0.66 sec per fur (HD) 4-00 (4-00)

2803[5] **Takhlid (USA) (77)**(85) (HThomsonJones) 4-10-0 WCarson(1) (lw: led over 4f: led wl ins fnl f: r.o wl) ....— 1
3139* Sharp Imp **(48)**(55) (RMFlower) 5-7-13b 6x DBiggs(7) (6th st: rdn over 1f out: led ins fnl f: sn hdd: r.o) ....nk 2

3057* Dowsong **(68)**(*75*) (*RAkehurst*) 4-9-5 TQuinn(4) (2nd st: hrd rdn over 1f out: ev ch ins fnl f: r.o)....s.h 3
2840* Walnut Burl (IRE) **(58)**(*65*)(Fav)(*LJHolt*) 5-8-9 MFenton(2) (lw: 4th st: rdn over 2f out: r.o ins fnl f)....nk 4
3175[3] Blurred Image (IRE) **(72)**(*77*) (*MissGayKelleway*) 4-9-2 (7) DaneO'Neill(3) (lw: 3rd st: led over 2f out tl ins fnl f: unable qckn)....¾ 5
2605[4] The Little Ferret **(60)**(*30*) (*AMoore*) 5-8-11 CandyMorris(6) (lw: 5th st: wknd over 2f out)....15 6
2979[13] Digpast (IRE) **(57)** (*RJO'Sullivan*) 5-8-3b(5) MHenry(5) (lw: a bhd: t.o fnl 4f)....dist 7

3/1 Walnut Burl (IRE), **9/2** Blurred Image (IRE), Dowsong, **5/1** Sharp Imp, **11/2** Digpast (IRE), **7/1** TAKHLID (USA), **14/1** The Little Ferret, CSF £37.22 TOTE £5.20: £3.00 £3.10 (£15.60) OWNER Mr Hamdan Al Maktoum (NEWMARKET) BRED Cheveley Park Stud Ltd 7 Rn
1m 21.0 (1.00) SF: 42/12/32/22/34/-/-

3269

SADDLESCOMBE CLAIMING STKS (3-Y.O+) (Class F) £2,519.00 (£694.00: £329.00)
7f 214y Stalls: Low GOING minus 0.66 sec per fur (HD) 4-30 (4-30)

2945[2] **Blockade (USA) (71)**(*80*)(Fav)(*MBell*) 6-9-3 MFenton(4) (t: swtg: mde all: rdn out)....— 1
2669[6] Another Fiddle (IRE) **(65)**(*65*)(Fav)(*RAkehurst*) 5-8-11 TQuinn(2) (3rd st: rdn over 2f out: n.m.r 1f out: swtchd rt: r.o one pce: fin 3rd, nk: plcd 2nd).... 2
3011[6] Kingchip Boy **(70)**(*76*) (*MJRyan*) 6-9-7v AClark(3) (4th st: rdn over 2f out: hung lft over 1f out: unable qckn fnl f: fin 2nd, 4l: plcd 3rd).... 3
*317** Masnun (USA) **(69)**(*58*) (*RJO'Sullivan*) 10-8-6 (5) MHenry(1) (bit bkwd: 5th st: rdn over 2f out: wknd fnl f)....3½ 4
3073[11] Brass Tacks **(64)**(*57*) (*RTPhillips*) 3-7-13 (7) ADaly(6) (6th st: hrd rdn over 2f out: swtchd lft: wknd over 1f out)....1 5
3096[2] First Crush **(68)**(*60*) (*SirMarkPrescott*) 3-8-10b WWoods(5) (2nd st: wknd over 1f out)....nk 6

11/4 BLOCKADE (USA) (2/1-3/1), Another Fiddle (IRE), **7/2** First Crush, **9/2** Masnun (USA), **10/1** Brass Tacks (6/1-11/1), Kingchip Boy (op 6/1), CSF £10.09 TOTE £3.00: £1.70 £2.30 (£6.20) OWNER Mr A. M. Warrender (NEWMARKET) BRED Patricia C. Warrender 6 Rn
1m 33.1 (0.90) SF: 35/20/31/13/6/9
WEIGHT FOR AGE 3yo-6lb

3270

RACE HILL MEDIAN AUCTION MAIDEN STKS (3-Y.O F) (Class F) £2,519.00 (£694.00: £329.00)
1m 1f 209y Stalls: High GOING minus 0.66 sec per fur (HD) 5-00 (5-01)

3081[2] **Doonyasha (62)**(*52*)(Fav)(*JLDunlop*) 3-8-11 WCarson(1) (mde virtually all: pushed out)....— 1
3201[3] Shazanni (IRE) **(40)**(*48*) (*MRChannon*) 3-8-4 (7) DSweeney(3) (3rd st: ev ch ins fnl f: unable qckn)....2½ 2
1175[10] Easter Coul (IRE) (*34*) (*MJFetherston-Godley*) 3-8-11 JReid(2) (chsd wnr: rdn over 2f out: sn wknd)....9 3

1/18 DOONYASHA (1/4-1/20), **20/1** Easter Coul (IRE), **25/1** Shazanni (IRE), CSF £1.87 TOTE £1.10 (£1.87) OWNER Mr J. L. Dunlop (ARUNDEL) BRED Mrs R. C. Langmead 3 Rn
2m 5.9 (7.90) SF: -/-/-
T/Plpt: £28.60 (438.22 Tckts). T/Qdpt £11.00 (4.25 Tckts). AK

3110-PONTEFRACT (L-H)
Tuesday August 22nd (Good to firm)
WEATHER: sunny & very hot WIND: almost nil

3271

COMPUTER TIMEFORM NURSERY H'CAP (2-Y.O) (Class D) £3,850.00 (£1,150.00: £550.00: £250.00)
6f Stalls: Low GOING minus 0.29 sec per fur (GF) 2-45 (2-46)

2399* **Desert Tiger (81)**(*88*)(Fav)(*MJohnston*) 2-9-6 MRoberts(2) (reard s: sn rcvrd & chsd ldrs: led ins fnl f: r.o)....— 1
3220[4] Albert The Bear **(76)**(*80*) (*JBerry*) 2-9-1 JCarroll(11) (lw: cl up: led appr fnl f: sn hdd & nt qckn)....1¼ 2
2964[4] Frezeliere **(82)**(*85*) (*JLDunlop*) 2-9-7 WRSwinburn(6) (lw: stdd s: c wd st: hrd rdn appr fnl f: r.o)....hd 3
3120* Ultra Barley **(74)**(*72*) (*PCHaslam*) 2-8-13 7x JFortune(10) (trckd ldrs: effrt 2f out: styd on: nt pce to chal)....2 4
2940[5] Missile Toe (IRE) **(75)**(*72*) (*JEBanks*) 2-8-11 (3) SDrowne(8) (led tl hdd appr fnl f: one pce)....nk 5

2817* Weetman's Weigh (IRE) **(68)***(55) (RHollinshead)* 2-8-7 WRyan(5) (drvn along ½-wy: styd on: nvr trbld ldrs) 4 6
2951² Yougoa **(54)***(34) (MWEasterby)* 2-7-4 (3) NVarley(12) (cl up over 4f: wknd) 2½ 7
3064¹² Wilfull Lad (IRE) **(75)***(54) (MartynMeade)* 2-9-0 VSlattery(7) (outpcd ½-wy: no imp after) ....nk 8
2991¹⁰ Meeting Point **(62)***(28) (MrsMReveley)* 2-8-1 SMaloney(4) (a outpcd & bhd) 5 9
2855⁶ Bee Health Boy **(60)***(26) (MWEasterby)* 2-7-13 RuthCoulter(1) (hmpd after s: a bhd)....s.h 10
*2633** Scathebury **(62)***(25) (SPCWoods)* 2-8-1v AMcGlone(9) (prom over 3f)....1 11

LONG HANDICAP Yougoa 7-4

11/4 DESERT TIGER, **3/1** Ultra Barley, **5/1** Albert The Bear, **7/1** Scathebury, **9/1** Frezeliere, **11/1** Missile Toe (IRE), **12/1** Weetman's Weigh (IRE), **16/1** Meeting Point, **25/1** Bee Health Boy, **33/1** Yougoa, Wilfull Lad (IRE), CSF £16.69 CT £100.25 TOTE £3.50: £1.30 £1.90 £2.40 (£8.80) Trio £29.50 OWNER Maktoum Al Maktoum (MIDDLEHAM) BRED Gainsborough Stud Management Ltd 11 Rn
1m 18.3 (4.00) SF: 28/20/25/12/12/-/-/-/-/-/-

3272 TIMEFORM RACE CARD (S) STKS (3-Y.O+) (Class G) £2,560.00 (£710.00: £340.00)

1m 2f 6y Stalls: Low GOING minus 0.29 sec per fur (GF) 3-15 (3-19)

2954⁸ **Pine Essence (USA) (57)***(62)*(Fav)*(MrsMReveley)* 4-9-2 JFortune(8) (swtg: s.s: hdwy 4f out: led wl over 1f out: hung lft: r.o u.p) ....— 1
2620⁶ Wordsmith (IRE) **(41)***(55) (JLHarris)* 5-9-0 KFallon(5) (in tch: hdwy 3f out: chsd wnr fnl f: kpt on)....3 2
3094⁷ Bardia **(33)***(47) (DonEnricoIncisa)* 5-8-9 KimTinkler(6) (hld up & bhd: hdwy 4f out: styd on u.p fnl f)....1¾ 3
2983³ Rad **(48)***(50) (SPCWoods)* 5-9-0 WRyan(3) (trckd ldrs: chal 2f out: hmpd & swtchd appr fnl f: nt qckn)....1½ 4
3118⁸ Golden Fish **(49)***(44) (JLEyre)* 3-8-6 RLappin(4) (chsd ldrs: qcknd to ld 3f out: hdd wl over 1f out)....4 5
Monica Maguire *(7) (GMMoore)* 3-8-1 NKennedy(9) (unf: bit bkwd: sn drvn along: t.o 6f out)20 6
2913⁶ Princess Shera (IRE) **(30)***(1) (EJAlston)* 4-8-9 SDWilliams(2) (unruly to post: cl up tl wknd over 2f out: eased considerably fnl f: t.o) 3½ 7
2990⁶ Billytobinslad *(3) (MrsVAAconley)* 4-9-0 MDeering(1) (led tl hdd & wknd qckly 3f out: t.o)....1¾ 8

11/10 PINE ESSENCE (USA) (4/5-6/5), **3/1** Rad, **11/2** Golden Fish, **9/1** Wordsmith (IRE), **10/1** Bardia, **20/1** Monica Maguire, **25/1** Princess Shera (IRE), **40/1** Billytobinslad, CSF £11.39 TOTE £2.10: £1.20 £2.00 £2.10 (£7.90) Trio £13.00 OWNER Dab Hand Racing (SALTBURN) BRED David E. Hager II 8 Rn
2m 16.3 (8.00) SF: 17/10/2/5/-/-/-/-
WEIGHT FOR AGE 3yo-8lb
Sold KMeynall 6200gns

3273 TIMEFORM FUTURITY STKS (2-Y.O) (Class C) £6,584.00 (£2,304.00: £1,127.00: £485.00)

6f Stalls: Low GOING minus 0.29 sec per fur (GF) 3-45 (3-45)

3032* **Defined Feature (IRE) (96)***(87) (MRStoute)* 2-8-10 WRSwinburn(3) (mde most: r.o gamely fnl f) ....— 1
2876* Laafee *(89)*(Fav)*(HThomsonJones)* 2-9-1 RHills(4) (lw: w ldr: slt ld wl over 1f out: sn rdn & hdd: no ex fnl f) 1 2
2579* Matiya (IRE) *(79) (BHanbury)* 2-8-10 WRyan(2) (lw: b.nr hind: hld up: effrt over 2f out: nt pce to chal)....2 3
1727³ Double Oscar (IRE) *(65) (MJohnston)* 2-9-1 JWeaver(1) (lw: sn chsng ldrs: rdn over 2f out: wknd wl over 1f out) 7 4

11/10 Laafee, **9/4** Matiya (IRE), **9/2** Double Oscar (IRE), **5/1** DEFINED FEATURE (IRE), CSF £10.75 TOTE £4.40 (£2.90) OWNER Mr Saeed Suhail (NEWMARKET) BRED Gainsborough Stud Management Ltd 4 Rn
1m 16.8 (2.50) SF: 38/40/30/16

3274 PHIL BULL TROPHY STKS (3-Y.O+) (Class C) £5,267.20 (£1,843.20: £901.60: £388.00)

2m 1f 216y Stalls: Centre GOING minus 0.29 sec per fur (GF) 4-15 (4-16)

2688³ **Salaman (FR) (83)***(62+)*(Fav)*(JLDunlop)* 3-8-5 RCochrane(2) (lw: trckd ldr: lft in ld ½-wy: qcknd over 4f out: comf) ....— 1
3162¹⁹ Non Vintage (IRE) **(55)***(58) (MCChapman)* 4-9-6 JWeaver(3) (hld up: chsd wnr fnl 4f: put hd in air & nt qckn fnl 2f)....3½ 2

3148² Diamond Crown (IRE) **(49)***(53) (MartynWane)* 4-9-3 KFallon(1) (led tl swvd rt & hdd ½-wy: outpcd 4f out: hdwy 2f out: nt qckn fnl f)....2½ **3**
3047⁷ Record Lover (IRE) **(33)***(49) (MCChapman)* 5-8-10 (7) CMunday(4) (hld up: effrt 4f out: rdn & no imp)....4 **4**

1/9 SALAMAN (FR), **10/1** Non Vintage (IRE), **16/1** Diamond Crown (IRE), **33/1** Record Lover (IRE), CSF £1.95 TOTE £1.20 (£1.60) OWNER Lady Cohen (ARUNDEL) BRED Ridgecourt Stud 4 Rn
4m 38.7 (46.70) SF: -/-/-/-
WEIGHT FOR AGE 3yo-16lb

3275 PHIL BULL BIOGRAPHY H'CAP (0-70) (3-Y.O+) (Class E) £3,288.00 (£984.00: £472.00: £216.00)
6f Stalls: Low GOING minus 0.29 sec per fur (GF) 4-45 (4-47)

3098² **Prime Property (IRE) (36)***(41) (MWEasterby)* 3-7-2b(7)ow2 MartinDwyer(13) (swtg: hdwy on outside 2f out: r.o to ld nr fin)....— **1**
3121³ Captain Carat **(64)***(70)*(Fav)*(MrsJRRamsden)* 4-9-13 KFallon(10) (stdd s: hld up & bhd: hdwy 2f out: chal wl ins fnl f: r.o)....nk **2**
3121⁵ Birchwood Sun **(61)***(67) (MDods)* 5-9-10b JWeaver(12) (s.i.s: hdwy 2f out: r.o to disp ld wl ins fnl f: r.o)....hd **3**
3112⁶ Densben **(45)***(50) (DenysSmith)* 11-8-3 (5) CTeague(3) (lw: hdwy 2f out: r.o to chal wl ins fnl f: no ex nr fin)....nk **4**
3116⁵ Lochon **(58)***(63) (JLEyre)* 4-9-7 RLappin(5) (trckd ldrs: led 1½f out tl ct cl home)....hd **5**
3098⁸ Awesome Venture **(48)***(50) (MCChapman)* 5-8-4 (7) CMunday(11) (led tl hdd 1½f out: kpt on one pce)....1¼ **6**
2877⁵ Arasong **(62)***(60) (EWeymes)* 3-9-7 DHarrison(1) (sn drvn along: hdwy ½-wy: one pce fnl f) 1¼ **7**
3116* Petraco (IRE) **(65)***(57) (NASmith)* 7-10-0 SDWilliams(6) (in tch: hdwy 2f out: wknd fnl f)....2½ **8**
2879⁷ Tutu Sixtysix **(38)***(27) (DonEnricoIncisa)* 4-8-1v KimTinkler(15) (s.i.s: nvr nr to chal)....1 **9**
3121² Diet **(54)***(42) (MissLAPerratt)* 9-9-3v JCarroll(2) (lw: chsd ldrs tl outpcd fnl 2f)....nk **10**
2698¹⁰ Indiahra **(48)***(35) (RHollinshead)* 4-8-11 WRSwinburn(8) (bhd: effrt 2f out: no imp)....½ **11**
3125¹² Bowcliffe Grange (IRE) **(34)***(19) (DWChapman)* 3-7-7 NKennedy(4) (s.s: effrt over 1f out: wknd ins fnl f)....¾ **12**
2972³ Genesis Four **(33)***(4) (SRBowring)* 5-7-10b TWilliams(7) (outpcd fr ½-wy)....5 **13**
2913¹⁰ Kajostar **(30)***(1) (SWCampion)* 5-7-7 JLowe(9) (b.nr hind: sn bhd)....nk **14**
LONG HANDICAP Prime Property (IRE) 7-3 Bowcliffe Grange (IRE) 7-3

7/2 Captain Carat, **4/1** Diet (op 7/1), **15/2** Lochon, **8/1** Petraco (IRE), Densben, **11/1** Birchwood Sun (8/1-12/1), **12/1** PRIME PROPERTY (IRE), Indiahra, **16/1** Genesis Four, Arasong, **20/1** Awesome Venture, **25/1** Tutu Sixtysix, **100/1** Bowcliffe Grange (IRE), Kajostar, CSF £50.63 CT £444.87 TOTE £12.20: £2.70 £2.20 £2.70 (£32.20) Trio £143.20 OWNER Alan Black & Co (SHERIFF HUTTON) BRED Gestut Romerhof 14 Rn 1m 17.2 (2.90) SF: 19/52/49/32/45/32/38/39/9/24/17/-/-/-
WEIGHT FOR AGE 3yo-4lb

3276 TIMEFORM PERSPECTIVE AND RACE RATINGS H'CAP (0-80) (3-Y.O+) (Class D) £3,817.50 (£1,140.00: £545.00: £247.50)
1m 4y Stalls: Low GOING minus 0.29 sec per fur (GF) 5-15 (5-16)

3113³ **Celestial Choir (78)***(90)*(Fav)*(JLEyre)* 5-10-0 SDWilliams(3) (trckd ldrs: swtchd & qcknd to ld ins fnl f: r.o wl)....— **1**
3101⁴ Nigel's Lad (IRE) **(79)***(85) (PCHaslam)* 3-9-9 JFortune(6) (lw: cl up: led over 1f out tl ins fnl f: kpt on same pce)....3 **2**
2406⁵ Hotspur Street **(67)***(70) (MJohnston)* 3-8-11 DHolland(1) (bhd tl styd on wl fnl 2f: nrst fin) 1¾ **3**
3115³ Tilaal (USA) **(75)***(77) (EALDunlop)* 3-9-5 WRSwinburn(5) (lw: led tl hdd over 1f out: hrd rdn & no ex)....½ **4**
2946³ Avishayes (USA) **(47)***(42) (MrsMReveley)* 8-7-11 JFanning(7) (hld up: hdwy 3f out: rdn 2f out: nt qckn)....3½ **5**
2510* Piquant **(67)***(59) (LordHuntingdon)* 8-9-3 DHarrison(4) (chsd ldrs: drvn along over 3f out: sn outpcd)....1½ **6**
2999¹¹ Chantry Bellini **(43)***(33) (MrsSMAustin)* 6-7-7 JLowe(2) (b: b.hind: outpcd 3f out: n.d after)....¾ **7**

2/1 CELESTIAL CHOIR, **3/1** Nigel's Lad (IRE), **4/1** Avishayes (USA), **7/1** Piquant, **8/1** Tilaal (USA), **11/1** Hotspur Street, **40/1** Chantry Bellini, CSF £7.98 TOTE £2.80: £1.70 £2.00 (£6.90) OWNER Lowlands Racing Ltd (HAMBLETON) BRED J. L. Eyre 7 Rn 1m44.5 (2.50) SF: 64/53/38/45/16/33/7
WEIGHT FOR AGE 3yo-6lb

T/Jkpt: £1,151.80 (14.80 Tckts). T/Plpt: £59.10 (332.99 Tckts). T/Qdpt: £13.20 (10.30 Tckts). AA

2593-ASCOT (R-H)
Wednesday August 23rd (Good to firm becoming Good)
WEATHER: raining becoming fresh WIND: almost nil

3277
BUCKINGHAM PALACE APPRENTICE H'CAP (0-80) (3-Y.O+) (Class E) £4,104.00 (£1,242.00: £606.00: £288.00)
1m 4f Stalls: High GOING: 0.06 sec per fur (G) 5-20 (5-21)

1984[5] **Tirolette (IRE) (57)***(66) (RJRWilliams)* 3-7-13b(3)ow3 AimeeCook(2) (lw: hdwy 2f out: led over 1f out: r.o wl) — 1
2557[3] Edan Heights **(67)***(77) (SDow)* 3-8-12 ADaly(8) (lw: hdwy on ins over 2f out: 4th st: ev ch over 1f out: unable qckn) 1¼ 2
2790[5] Frozen Sea (USA) **(69)***(74) (GPEnright)* 4-9-10 DGibbs(5) (lw: hdwy over 2f out: 5th st: hrd rdn over 1f out: one pce) 4 3
2193[4] Daily Starlight (USA) **(78)***(76)*(Fav)*(MissGayKelleway)* 3-9-9 DaneO'Neill(9) (2nd st: ev ch over 2f out: wknd over 1f out) 5 4
Big Pat **(73)***(70) (KMcAuliffe)* 6-9-9 (5) SMcCarthy(1) (hld up: led over 3f out tl over 1f out: sn wknd) ¾ 5
1401* Krayyan Dawn **(59)***(52) (RAkehurst)* 5-8-9 (5) TAshley(6) (lw: prom 9f) 3½ 6
3122* Exclusion **(42)***(25) (JHetherton)* 6-7-11 4x CAdamson(7) (lw: led over 7f: 3rd st: wknd over 2f out) 7 7
Moultazim (USA) **(47)** *(RJPrice)* 5-7-11 (5) FLynch(4) (lw: a.p: led over 4f out tl over 3f out: 6th st: wknd over 2f out) 30 8

11/4 Daily Starlight (USA), **100/30** Edan Heights, **4/1** Krayyan Dawn (3/1-9/2), **6/1** Exclusion, **10/1** Big Pat (8/1-12/1), **12/1** Frozen Sea (USA), **14/1** TIROLETTE (IRE), **25/1** Moultazim (USA), CSF £54.48 CT £513.44 TOTE £14.50: £2.50 £1.70 £2.90 (£22.50) Trio £77.20 OWNER Mr Richard Morris Jr (NEWMARKET) BRED W. J. O'Regan 8 Rn 2m 37.59 (8.09) SF: 38/49/56/48/52/34/7/-
WEIGHT FOR AGE 3yo-10lb

3278
STARFORM CONDITIONS STKS (3-Y.O F) (Class B) £9,690.00 (£3,390.00: £1,657.50: £712.50)
1m 2f Stalls: High GOING: 0.06 sec per fur (G) 5-50 (5-51)

2763[5] **Poppy Carew (IRE) (106)***(93+)*(Fav)*(PWHarris)* 3-8-10 PatEddery(1) (2nd st: led 2f out: rdn out) — 1
2825* Ninette (USA) *(89) (JHMGosden)* 3-8-11 LDettori(4) (chsd ldr: led over 3f out to 2f out: unable qckn fnl f) 3 2
3013[3] Jumilla (USA) **(85)***(83) (GWragg)* 3-8-10 MHills(3) (rdn over 3f out: 3rd st: one pce fnl 2f) 3½ 3
3130[2] Emily-Mou (IRE) **(69)***(38) (BJMeehan)* 3-8-13 MTebbutt(2) (b: led over 6f: sn wknd: 4th st) 30 4

8/13 POPPY CAREW (IRE), **11/4** Ninette (USA), **7/1** Jumilla (USA), **20/1** Emily-Mou (IRE), CSF £2.44 TOTE £1.70 (£1.50 OWNER Mrs P. W. Harris (BERKHAMSTED) BRED Pendley Farm 4 Rn
2m 11.89 (7.59) SF: 39/35/29/-

3279
INVOSHIRE GROUP H'CAP (0-90) (3-Y.O+) (Class C) £7,067.50 (£2,140.00: £1,045.00: £497.50)
5f Stalls: Centre GOING: 0.06 sec per fur (G) 6-20 (6-21)

3065[4] **Coffee 'n Cream (85)***(100) (RHannon)* 3-9-6 MRoberts(1) (w ldr: led over 2f out: comf) — 1
3134* Anzio (IRE) **(67)***(74) (BAPearce)* 4-8-2b(3) DRMcCabe(9) (b: lw: rdn over 2f out: hdwy over 1f out: r.o) 2½ 2
2935[2] Lepine (IRE) **(74)***(73)*(Fav)*(JWWatts)* 4-8-12v PatEddery(12) (racd alone: a.p: ev ch over 1f out: unable qckn) 2½ 3
1766[10] Croeso-I-Cymru **(88)***(84) (RAkehurst)* 4-9-9 (3) SSanders(6) (a.p: rdn over 2f out: one pce) 1 4
3145[12] Sir Joey (USA) **(87)***(79) (PGMurphy)* 6-9-8 (3) SDrowne(8) (hld up: rdn over 1f out: sn wknd) 1¼ 5
3065[6] Bowden Rose **(77)***(68) (MBlanshard)* 3-8-12b StephenDavies(2) (led over 2f: wknd over 1f out) nk 6
2823[6] Takadou (IRE) **(82)***(66) (MissLCSiddall)* 4-9-6 JReid(4) (nvr nr to chal) 2 7
2992[3] Barato **(71)***(47) (MrsJRRamsden)* 4-8-9v JWeaver(11) (rdn over 2f out: hdwy over 1f out: sn wknd) 2½ 8
2935[3] Beau Venture (USA) **(79)***(55) (FHLee)* 7-9-3 RLappin(5) (lw: bhd fnl 2f) s.h 9
2992* Super Rocky **(77)***(48) (RBastiman)* 6-8-10 (5) HBastiman(10) (bhd fnl 2f) 1¾ 10
2909[5] Ikaab (USA) **(85)***(48) (MajorWRHern)* 3-9-6v WCarson(3) (prom over 3f) 2½ 11

100/30 Lepine (IRE), **8/1** COFFEE 'N CREAM, Barato, **9/1** Croeso-I-Cymru, Beau Venture (USA), **11/1** Super Rocky, **12/1** Takadou (IRE), Anzio (IRE), Ikaab (USA), Sir Joey (USA), **14/1** Bowden Rose, CSF £83.06 CT £332.26 TOTE £7.00: £2.10 £4.00 £1.90 (£67.10) Trio £49.30 OWNER Mr A. Reeves (MARLBOROUGH) BRED R. T. and Mrs Watson 11 Rn
62.25 secs (2.75) SF: 63/40/39/50/45/31/32/13/21/14/11
WEIGHT FOR AGE 3yo-3lb

3280 JAMES WETENHALL MAIDEN STKS (2-Y.O) (Class D) £6,840.00 (£2,070.00: £1,010.00: £480.00)
1m (round) Stalls: High GOING: 0.06 sec per fur (G) 6-50 (6-51)

2420[2] **Moody's Cat (IRE)** *(78) (BWHills)* 2-8-9 MHills(6) (mde all: rdn out) — **1**
Bright Heritage (IRE) *(81+)*(Fav)*(DRLoder)* 2-9-0 PatEddery(5) (gd sort: lw: chsd wnr over 3f out: ev ch fnl 2f: unable qckn wl ins fnl f) 1¼ **2**
3089[6] Skillington (USA) *(79) (IABalding)* 2-9-0 LDettori(3) (lw: 3rd st: rdn over 2f out: swtchd rt ins fnl f: one pce) 1 **3**
2912[11] Muhtadi (IRE) *(72) (JLDunlop)* 2-9-0 WCarson(1) (rdn & hdwy 2f out: one pce) 3½ **4**
3141[5] Gumair (USA) *(71) (RHannon)* 2-9-0 JReid(9) (lw: 4th st: wknd over 2f out) s.h **5**
Flyfisher (IRE) *(51) (GLewis)* 2-9-0 PaulEddery(2) (w'like: scope: bit bkwd: s.s: a bhd) 10 **6**
3089[7] Oliver Rock *(33) (MajorDNChappell)* 2-9-0 BThomson(4) (5th st: wknd over 2f out) 9 **7**
2801[4] Hever Golf Hero *(7) (TJNaughton)* 2-9-0 JWeaver(8) (6th st: wknd over 2f out) 13 **8**

5/4 Bright Heritage (IRE), **11/4** Skillington (USA), **5/1** MOODY'S CAT (IRE) (7/2-11/2), **8/1** Oliver Rock (5/1-9/1), **11/1** Muhtadi (IRE) (12/1-20/1), **16/1** Hever Golf Hero, **40/1** Flyfisher (IRE), Gumair (USA), CSF £11.55 TOTE £5.80: £1.50 £1.30 £1.30 (£5.40) Trio £2.80 OWNER K. Al-Said (LAMBOURN) BRED Charlton Down Stud 8 Rn 1m 46.2 (6.60) SF: 33/36/34/27/26/6/-/-

3281 GLOBE NURSERY H'CAP (2-Y.O) (Class C) £6,905.00 (£1,555.00:£1,555.00: £485.00) 7f Stalls: Centre GOING: 0.06 sec per fur (G) 7-20 (7-21)

2971* **Rock Sharp (75)***(78) (RHannon)* 2-8-11 JReid(6) (chsd ldr: led 1f out: rdn out) — **1**
2674[2] Prince of Florence (IRE) **(84)***(86) (LMCumani)* 2-9-6 LDettori(4) (lw: hld up: ev ch over 1f out: one pce) 1¼ **2**
2911* Royal Mark (IRE) **(85)***(84+)*(Fav)*(JWWatts)* 2-9-7 PatEddery(3) (lw: hld up: nt clr run over 1f out & ins fnl f: r.o one pce) d.h **2**
2978[6] Shock-A-Lot (IRE) **(66)***(65) (GLewis)* 2-8-2 PaulEddery(2) (lw: led 6f: one pce) s.h **4**
3090[5] The Legions Pride **(64)***(60) (JWHills)* 2-7-9 (5) MHenry(5) (a.p: ev ch wl over 1f out: one pce) 1¼ **5**
3049[3] Capture The Moment **(79)***(25) (RJRWilliams)* 2-9-1 DBiggs(1) (bhd fnl 2f) 9 **6**

13/8 Royal Mark (IRE), **7/2** Prince of Florence (IRE), **9/2** ROCK SHARP, **5/1** Shock-A-Lot (IRE), **14/1** The Legions Pride (10/1-16/1), **20/1** Capture The Moment, CSF R,RM £5.55 RS,PF £8.94 TOTE £4.30: £1.90 RM £0.70 PF £1.10 (RS,RM £1.30 RS,PF £3.70) OWNER Noodles Racing (MARLBOROUGH) BRED R. M. Whitaker 6 Rn 1m 32.09 (5.59) SF: 36/42/43/24/19/14

3282 CRANBOURNE CHASE MAIDEN STKS (3-Y.O) (Class D) £5,368.00 (£1,624.00: £792.00: £376.00)
7f Stalls: Centre GOING: 0.06 sec per fur (G) 7-50 (7-50)

Starry Eyed *(90+)*(Fav)*(JHMGosden)* 3-8-9 LDettori(5) (w'like: hld up: led over 1f out: rdn out) — **1**
3023[2] Fresh Fruit Daily **(74)***(87) (PAKelleway)* 3-8-9 PatEddery(4) (w ldr: ev ch over 1f out: unable qckn) 1¼ **2**
2708[4] Double Matt (IRE) **(77)***(88) (RHannon)* 3-9-0 JReid(3) (led over 5f) 2 **3**
Sky Girl *(64) (CBBBooth)* 3-8-9 MBirch(1) (w'like: hld up: rdn over 2f out: sn wknd) 8 **4**
Awasha (IRE) *(48)*(Fav)*(MissGayKelleway)* 3-8-9 JWeaver(2) (w'like: bhd fnl 3f) 7 **5**

15/8 STARRY EYED, Awasha (IRE), **100/30** Fresh Fruit Daily, **7/1** Double Matt (IRE), **12/1** Sky Girl, CSF £8.04 TOTE £2.70: £1.70 £1.30 (£2.70) OWNER Mr K. Abdullah (NEWMARKET) BRED Juddmonte Farms 5 Rn 1m 30.33 (3.83) SF: 54/51/52/28/12

T/Jkpt: Not won; £6,313.17 to Lingfield 24/8/95. T/Plpt: £26.50 (766.74 Tckts). T/Qdpt: £3.40 (98.1 Tckts). AK

3265-BRIGHTON (L-H)
Wednesday August 23rd (Firm)
WEATHER: overcast WIND: slt across

3283 E.B.F MEDIAN AUCTION MAIDEN STKS (2-Y.O F) (Class F) £2,796.20 (£773.20: £368.60)
5f 213y Stalls: Low GOING minus 0.47 sec per fur (F) 2-30 (2-30)

3158[4] **La Modiste (92)***(66+)*(Fav)*(SDow)* 2-8-11 TQuinn(2) (5th st: hdwy over 2f out: led over 1f out: comf)......— 1
2515[6] Red Misty (IRE) *(62) (MRChannon)* 2-8-11 RHughes(3) (led: hdd over 1f out: one pce)........1½ 2
2982[7] February **(45)***(49) (MRChannon)* 2-8-4 (7) DSweeney(1) (4th st: rdn over 2f out: one pce) 5 3
3157[2] Time For Tea (IRE) *(38) (CACyzer)* 2-8-11 DBiggs(4) (2nd st: rdn 2f out: wknd over 1f out) ...4 4
2683[3] Janies Girl (IRE) *(14) (KRBurke)* 2-8-11 JQuinn(5) (3rd st: rdn over 2f out: sn wknd) 9 5

4/6 LA MODISTE, **5/2** Time For Tea (IRE), **13/2** Janies Girl (IRE) (4/1-7/1), **14/1** Red Misty (IRE) (12/1-20/1), **50/1** February, CSF £8.57 TOTE £1.60: £1.10 £2.50 (£6.60) OWNER Mrs G. R. Smith (EPSOM) BRED G. R. Smith (Thriplow) Ltd 5 Rn 1m 10.0 (1.60) SF: 32/28/15/4/-

3284 NEWHAVEN NURSERY H'CAP (2-Y.O) (Class E) £3,130.60 (£932.80: £444.40: £200.20)
5f 59y Stalls: Low GOING minus 0.47 sec per fur (F) 3-00 (3-00)

2838[2] **No Sympathy (55)***(64) (GLMoore)* 2-8-7 SWhitworth(2) (6th st: hdwy on ins over 2f out: led over 1f out: r.o) ......— 1
3018[2] Hoh Majestic (IRE) **(63)***(64)*(Fav)*(MBell)* 2-9-1v MFenton(3) (2nd st: ev ch 2f out: rdn over 1f out: one pce) 2½ 2
3064[8] Montrestar **(67)***(65) (PDEvans)* 2-9-5b GHind(6) (5th st: ev ch 2f out: rdn over 1f out: one pce) 1¼ 3
2826[2] Dande Flyer **(69)***(64) (DWPArbuthnot)* 2-9-7 RPrice(5) (dwlt: sn in tch: 3rd st: ev ch over 1f out: wknd ins fnl f) ......¾ 4
3054[2] Wingnut (IRE) **(65)***(55) (GLewis)* 2-9-3 PaulEddery(4) (4th st: rdn over 2f out: no hdwy)........1¾ 5
3133[10] Windi Imp (IRE) **(60)***(48) (BJMeehan)* 2-8-12b TQuinn(1) (led: hdd over 1f out: wknd fnl f)......¾ 6

6/4 Hoh Majestic (IRE), **4/1** Dande Flyer, **5/1** Wingnut (IRE), **6/1** Montrestar, **8/1** NO SYMPATHY, **14/1** Windi Imp (IRE), CSF £18.99 TOTE £11.50: £2.70 £1.10 (£6.40) OWNER Pennine Partners (EPSOM) BRED Mrs Sara Hood 6 Rn 62.9 secs (2.90) SF: 5/5/6/5/-/-

3285 SEAGULLS (S) STKS (2-Y.O) (Class G) £2,243.00 (£618.00: £293.00)
6f 209y Stalls: Low GOING minus 0.47 sec per fur (F) 3-30 (3-32)

2962[3] **Dhulikhel (61)***(56) (DMarks)* 2-8-6 GDuffield(5) (led: hdd wl over 1f out: rallied to ld ins fnl f: r.o) ......— 1
3160[5] Lussuria (IRE) **(64)***(59d)*(Fav)*(BJMeehan)* 2-8-11 BDoyle(2) (5th st: hdwy over 2f out: led wl over 1f out: hdd ins fnl f: one pce) ......¾ 2
3135[2] Anna Settic *(51) (DrJDScargill)* 2-8-6 MRimmer(6) (3rd st: rdn 2f out: r.o one pce fnl f).........1½ 3
3124[3] Image Maker (IRE) *(47) (DWPArbuthnot)* 2-8-6 TQuinn(1) (chsd ldr: 2nd st: rdn 2f out: one pce) 1½ 4
2683[8] Fair To Middling (IRE) *(47) (GLMoore)* 2-8-6 SWhitworth(3) (4th st: rdn 2f out: one pce)......s.h 5

10/11 Lussuria (IRE) (8/11-Evens), **9/4** Anna Settic, **11/2** Image Maker (IRE), **11/1** Fair To Middling (IRE) (5/1-12/1), **14/1** DHULIKHEL (8/1-20/1), CSF £27.14 TOTE £17.10: £4.50 £1.20 (£5.90) OWNER Mr G. J. King (UPPER LAMBOURN) BRED M. H. D. Madden and Partners 5 Rn
1m 24.2 (4.20) SF: -/3/-/-/-
Bt in 4,000gns

3286 ROTTINGDEAN LIMITED STKS (0-70) (3-Y.O) (Class E) £3,159.20 (£941.60: £448.80: £202.40)
6f 209y Stalls: Low GOING minus 0.47 sec per fur (F) 4-00 (4-01)

3159[6] **Bedouin Invader (67)***(80) (MRStoute)* 3-9-0b JReid(5) (4th st: hdwy 2f out: led ins fnl f: r.o wl) ......— 1
2848[4] Dancing Heart **(70)***(77) (BJMeehan)* 3-9-3 BDoyle(3) (chsd ldr: led 4f out: hdd ins fnl f: one pce) 2½ 2
3112[3] Master Millfield (IRE) **(65)***(70) (CJHill)* 3-9-3 StephenDavies(4) (5th st: rdn 2f out: one pce) 3 3

2691[11] The Stager (IRE) **(67)***(70) (JRJenkins)* 3-9-3b TQuinn(1) (led: hdd 4f out: 2nd st: rdn over 1f out: one pce) ....hd **4**
2941[2] Regal Fanfare (IRE) **(70)***(58)*(Fav)*(JWHills)* 3-8-9b MHills(2) (3rd st: rdn over 2f out: wknd over 1f out) 2 **5**
3109[4] Seventeens Lucky **(67)***(56) (BobJones)* 3-9-0 GDuffield(7) (sn outpcd: 6th st: rdn over 2f out: no hdwy) 3 **6**
3081* Mo's Star **(62)***(49) (SDow)* 3-8-12 MRoberts(6) (a bhd) 2 **7**

100/30 Regal Fanfare (IRE), **7/2** Dancing Heart, **5/1** Mo's Star, Seventeens Lucky, **13/2** The Stager (IRE) (9/2-7/1), **8/1** BEDOUIN INVADER, **9/1** Master Millfield (IRE) (9/2-10/1), CSF £33.20 TOTE £7.10: £3.30 £2.20 (£55.00) OWNER Mr Salem Suhail (NEWMARKET) BRED Mrs R. B. Kennard 7 Rn 1m 21.2 (1.20) SF: 43/40/33/33/21/19/12

3287

GEARGE ROBEY CHALLENGE TROPHY H'CAP (0-70) (3-Y.O+ F & M) (Class E) £3,388.00 (£1,012.00: £484.00: £220.00)
1m 3f 196y Stalls: High GOING minus 0.47 sec per fur (F) 4-30 (4-31)

3056* **Masuri Kabisa (USA) (33)***(45) (HJCollingridge)* 4-8-7v MRimmer(1) (a.p: 2nd st: led over 3f out: r.o strly fnl f) ....— **1**
3137[2] All the Joys **(36)***(43) (CACyzer)* 4-8-10 DBiggs(6) (3rd st: ev ch over 1f out: one pce) 3½ **2**
3006* Rocquaine Bay **(43)***(45)*(Fav)*(MJBolton)* 8-9-3 JQuinn(3) (4th st: rdn & ev ch over 2f out: one pce) 4 **3**
Chanson D'Avril **(42)***(42) (DAWilson)* 4-9-2 GDuffield(2) (chsd ldr 7f: 5th st: hrd rdn over 2f out: no hdwy) 1¾ **4**
2841* Coggle **(59)***(40) (NAGraham)* 3-9-9b PaulEddery(4) (led over 8f) 14 **5**

11/8 Rocquaine Bay, **3/1** MASURI KABISA (USA) (op 2/1), **5/1** All the Joys, **7/1** Coggle (5/1-9/1), **8/1** Chanson D'Avril, CSF £15.09 TOTE £3.40: £1.70 £3.00 (£9.30) OWNER Mr N. P. Etches (NEWMARKET) BRED Stonereath Farms 5 Rn 2m 33.2 (4.20) SF: 27/25/27/24/12
WEIGHT FOR AGE 3yo-10lb

3288

BRIGHTON AMATEUR H'CAP (0-70) (3-Y.O+) (Class G) £2,579.00 (£714.00: £341.00 **1m 1f 209y** Stalls: Low GOING minus 0.47 sec per fur (F) 5-00 (5-02)

3047[3] **Don't Drop Bombs (USA) (31)***(45) (DTThom)* 6-9-8v MissJFeilden(5) (mde all: clr over 2f out: unchal) ....— **1**
3094[6] Araboybill **(58)***(62) (MPMuggeridge)* 4-11-7b MrEWilliams(3) (chsd wnr: rdn over 2f out: no imp) 6 **2**
3265* Water Hazard (IRE) **(42)***(46)*(Fav)*(SDow)* 3-9-11 MrsMCowdrey(6) (hdwy 5f out: 6th st: rdn over 2f out: r.o one pce) ....½ **3**
2655[3] Aljawab (USA) **(57)***(53) (JLDunlop)* 4-11-6 MissEJohnsonHoughton(1) (3rd st: rdn over 2f out: one pce) 5 **4**
3047[2] Smocking **(36)***(28) (JPearce)* 5-9-13 MrsLPearce(4) (4th st: rdn over 2f out: one pce) 2½ **5**
3234[7] Montone (IRE) **(52)***(42) (KRBurke)* 5-11-1 MrMMannish(8) (7th st: rdn over 2f out: no hdwy) .¾ **6**
2830[2] Guest Alliance (IRE) **(50)***(40) (AMoore)* 3-10-5 MrsJMoore(2) (10th st: nvr nrr) ....nk **7**
3108[10] Total Rach (IRE) **(58)***(41) (RIngram)* 3-10-8 (5) MrsSIngram(7) (5th st: rdn over 2f out: wknd over 1f out) 4 **8**
3234[9] Romansh **(48)***(28) (BJMeehan)* 6-10-11 MissJAllison(9) (8th st: a bhd) 2 **9**
3020[3] Breezed Well **(42)***(9) (BRCambidge)* 9-10-5 MrsHNoonan(10) (9th st: a bhd) 8 **10**
3078[8] Goldenberry **(43)** *(KGWingrove)* 4-10-1 (5)ow20 MrKLoads(11) (11th st: a bhd) 5 **11**
LONG HANDICAP Goldenberry 8-9

5/2 Water Hazard (IRE), **4/1** Smocking, **9/2** Aljawab (USA), **7/1** Montone (IRE), **8/1** DON'T DROP BOMBS (USA), **10/1** Araboybill, **12/1** Guest Alliance (IRE), **16/1** Breezed Well, **20/1** Romansh, **25/1** Total Rach (IRE), **66/1** Goldenberry, CSF £79.23 CT £236.93 TOTE £6.30: £2.00 £2.30 £1.80 (£40.20) Trio £91.00 OWNER Miss J. Feilden (NEWMARKET) BRED Hurstland Farm Incorporated 11 Rn 2m 2.9 (4.90) SF: 26/43/19/34/9/23/13/14/9/-/-
WEIGHT FOR AGE 3yo-8lb

T/Plpt: £105.50 (103.56 Tckts). T/Qdpt: £81.60 (0.35 Tckts); £71.76 to Lingfield 24/8/95. SM

3123-LEICESTER (R-H)
Wednesday August 23rd (Good)

WEATHER: fine & sunny WIND: almost nil

3289

LOROS GERARD GAMBLE NURSERY H'CAP (2-Y.O) (Class E) £3,702.60 (£1,108.80: £532.40: £244.20)
5f 218y Stalls: Low GOING minus 0.22 sec per fur (GF) 5-35 (5-36)

2581[3] **Arajaan (USA) (81)***(85) (BHanbury)* 2-9-0 (3) JStack(1) (lw: mde all: clr 1f out: pushed out)..— **1**

2991[6] Branston Danni **(66)***(65) (MrsJRRamsden)* 2-8-2 JFEgan(5) (swtg: chsd ldrs: rdn & r.o ins fnl f: no ch w wnr) 1¾ **2**
3110* Clincher Club **(71)***(64)*(Fav)*(MJohnston)* 2-8-7 DHolland(4) (hdwy 2f out: sn rdn: kpt on one pce) 2½ **3**
2982[5] Deerly **(68)***(53) (DMorris)* 2-8-4 RCochrane(6) (a.p: rdn wl over 1f out: one pce) 3 **4**
2200[6] Goodwood Rocket **(73)***(52) (JLDunlop)* 2-8-9 WNewnes(7) (lw: s.s: hdwy & swtchd rt bel dist: styd on) 2 **5**
2629[2] Morning Surprise **(61)***(39) (APJarvis)* 2-7-8 (3) DWright(3) (s.s: hdwy ½-wy: wknd over 1f out) ½ **6**
2740[6] Nellie North **(85)***(50) (MrsMMcCourt)* 2-9-0 (7) RStudholme(2) (lw: chsd ldrs stands' side: swtchd rt 2f out: sn btn) 5 **7**
3124* L A Touch **(59)***(16) (CADwyer)* 2-7-6 (3)ow1 5x NVarley(8) (hdwy ½-wy: rdn 2f out: sn lost tch)2½ **8**
3049[4] Classic Victory **(76)***(29) (SCWilliams)* 2-8-12 DBatteate(10) (w ldrs 4f: sn rdn & outpcd) 2 **9**
2552* Dil Dil **(72)***(17) (RHannon)* 2-8-8 RPerham(9) (spd over 3f: sn wknd) 3 **10**
2991[8] Ebony Boy **(62)***(3) (JWharton)* 2-7-12 GBardwell(11) (lw: prom to ½-wy: sn lost pl) 1¼ **11**

5/1 Clincher Club (op 3/1), **11/2** Goodwood Rocket, **6/1** Dil Dil, L A Touch, **7/1** ARAJAAN (USA), **8/1** Branston Danni, **10/1** Morning Surprise, **11/1** Classic Victory, **12/1** Deerly, **20/1** Nellie North, Ebony Boy, CSF £56.60 CT £274.27 TOTE £8.30: £3.30 £3.00 £2.60 (£32.90) Trio £43.20 OWNER Mr Hamdan Al Maktoum (NEWMARKET) BRED Mrs Gail Beitz 11 Rn
1m 13.8 (3.80) SF: 29/9/8/-/-/-/-/-/-/-/-

3290 SUTTON (S) STKS (2-Y.O) (Class G) £2,780.60 (£771.60: £369.80)
5f 2y Stalls: Low GOING minus 0.22 sec per fur (GF) 6-05 (6-07)

2606[5] **Boffy (IRE) (65)***(70) (BPJBaugh)* 2-8-4 (7) IonaWands(10) (hld up: hdwy 2f out: r.o to ld ins fnl f: r.o wl) ....— **1**
3124[2] Rothley Imp (IRE) **(54)***(59) (JWharton)* 2-8-6 PRobinson(12) (lw: a.p: rdn & ev ch 1f out: unable qckn) 1¾ **2**
3064[7] U-No-Harry (IRE) **(68)***(69)*(Fav)*(RHollinshead)* 2-9-2 TIves(6) (lw: a.p: ev ch ins fnl f: rdn & unable qckn) ....nk **3**
2185[5] Apartments Abroad *(55) (KMcAuliffe)* 2-8-6b DHarrison(4) (s.i.s: hdwy over 1f out: rdn & r.o wl fnl f) 1¼ **4**
2817[3] Secret Voucher *(58) (BAMcMahon)* 2-8-11 GCarter(8) (led after 2f tl hdd & wknd ins fnl f) ....½ **5**
3032[5] Red Acuisle (IRE) **(61)***(57) (MBell)* 2-8-11 DHolland(14) (lw: chsd ldrs: rdn wl over 1f out: one pce) ....nk **6**
2601[5] Trible Pet **(44)***(50) (BGubby)* 2-8-6b JFEgan(1) (chsd ldrs: rdn wl over 1f out: nvr able to chal)½ **7**
3048[5] Makaskamina **(56)***(51) (BHanbury)* 2-8-8 (3) JStack(7) (chsd ldrs over 3f: sn outpcd) 1½ **8**
2998[4] Fiddles Delight **(48)***(26) (MRChannon)* 2-8-1 (5) PPMurphy(2) (leggy: bit bkwd: dwlt: a bhd & outpcd) 6 **9**
2924[9] Waitingforwalnuts (IRE) *(17) (CASmith)* 2-8-7 ow1 VSlattery(11) (led 2f: wknd fnl 2f) 3 **10**
So Select *(14) (APJarvis)* 2-8-3 (3) DWright(5) (cmpt: bkwd: s.s: a bhd & outpcd) 1 **11**
Fantasy Fair *(4) (RBoss)* 2-8-6 WWoods(9) (s.s: a bhd) 3 **12**
2985[4] Zuno Princess (IRE) **(62)** *(GLewis)* 2-8-6 RCochrane(13) (spd to ½-wy: sn lost tch) 2 **13**

3/1 U-No-Harry (IRE), **9/2** Secret Voucher, **6/1** Red Acuisle (IRE), **7/1** Rothley Imp (IRE), **8/1** Zuno Princess (IRE), **14/1** BOFFY (IRE) (10/1-16/1), Fantasy Fair, **16/1** Apartments Abroad, Makaskamina, Trible Pet, So Select, **20/1** Fiddles Delight, **33/1** Waitingforwalnuts (IRE), CSF £103.67 TOTE £19.30: £3.60 £1.80 £2.30 (£35.40) Trio £44.70 OWNER Mr Stan Baugh (LITTLE HAYWOOD) BRED J. Hayden 13 Rn 62.0 secs (3.50) SF: 18/7/17/3/6/5/-/-/-/-/-/-/-
No bid

3291 DICKINSON & MORRIS H'CAP (0-80) (3-Y.O+) (Class D) £4,070.30 (£1,216.40: £582.20: £265.10)
7f 9y Stalls: Low GOING minus 0.22 sec per fur (GF) 6-35 (6-37)

2952[4] **Saifan (72)***(84)*(Fav)*(DMorris)* 6-9-12b RCochrane(2) (hld up: hdwy 2f out: rdn to ld ins fnl f: readily) ....— **1**
3020[4] Love Legend **(50)***(58) (DWPArbuthnot)* 10-8-4 AClark(5) (chsd ldrs: rdn over 1f out: r.o wl towards fin) 1¾ **2**
2966* Anonym (IRE) **(71)***(77) (JLDunlop)* 3-9-6 NConnorton(1) (hld up: hdwy over 2f out: rdn bel dist: nt pce to chal) 1 **3**
3152* Morocco (IRE) **(57)***(61) (MRChannon)* 6-8-11 5x RHughes(9) (prom: rdn & outpcd bel dist: rallied nr fin) 1 **4**
2490[7] Duello **(57)***(58) (MBlanshard)* 4-8-11 DeanMcKeown(3) (a.p: ev ch 1f out: no ex fnl f) 1¼ **5**
2992[5] First Gold **(58)***(57) (JWharton)* 6-8-12 PRobinson(10) (hdwy 2d out: sn hrd rdn: kpt on) ....¾ **6**
3212[4] Russian Heroine **(75)***(72) (MJohnston)* 3-9-10 DHolland(7) (mde most tl hrd rdn & hdd ins fnl f) ....¾ **7**
3050[4] Mr Cube (IRE) **(62)***(59) (JMBradley)* 5-8-9v(7) RWaterfield(8) (chsd ldrs: effrt 2f out: wknd appr fnl f) ....hd **8**

3031[5] College Night (IRE) **(68)***(45) (CADwyer)* 3-9-3 DHarrison(6) (w ldrs tl hrd rdn & wknd wl over 1f out: t.o)....9 9
2588[8] Educated Pet **(50)***(26) (BPreece)* 6-8-4v NAdams(4) (outpcd: a bhd: t.o)....hd 10

11/4 SAIFAN, **7/2** Anonym (IRE), **6/1** Russian Heroine, **7/1** Morocco (IRE), First Gold, **12/1** Duello, Mr Cube (IRE), **14/1** Love Legend, **33/1** College Night (IRE), Educated Pet, CSF £35.79 CT £122.79 TOTE £4.00: £1.60 £2.60 £1.90 (£23.60) Trio £19.80 OWNER Ms L. Hawes (NEWMARKET) BRED M. M. Nashar 10 Rn 1m 25.3 (2.80) SF: 57/31/45/34/31/30/40/32/13/-
WEIGHT FOR AGE 3yo-5lb

3292 SOTHEBY'S CLAIMING STKS (3-Y.O+) (Class F) £2,922.20 (£809.20: £386.60)
1m 3f 183y Stalls: Low GOING minus 0.22 sec per fur (GF) 7-05 (7-09)

2658[7] **Make a Stand (45)***(76+) (HCandy)* 4-9-2 WNewnes(4) (hld up: hdwy & 6th st: led over 2f out: sn clr: eased nr fin)....— 1
2835[3] Bushehr (IRE) **(65)***(75) (JWHills)* 3-8-8 DHolland(9) (hld up: hdwy ent st: rdn to chal 2f out: nt pce of wnr)....2½ 2
3126[2] Oakbury (IRE) **(58)***(71) (RHannon)* 3-8-10 RHughes(2) (b.nr fore: chsd ldrs: 3rd st: ev ch & rdn 2f out: one pce)....4 3
2868[3] Old Swinford (IRE) **(53)***(55) (BJMeehan)* 3-8-1 GBardwell(3) (chsd ldr: 2nd st: rdn & wknd wl over 1f out)....5 4
3015[3] Ela Man Howa **(53)***(58)*(Fav)*(RAkehurst)* 4-9-0 TQuinn(5) (lw: led: sn clr: rdn & hdd over 2f out: sn btn)....hd 5
3082[7] Pennine Lad (IRE) **(51)***(48) (BGubby)* 5-8-7 (3) JStack(1) (chsd ldrs: 5th & c wd st: wknd 3f out)....5 6
815[9] Alzoomo (IRE) *(52) (JAGlover)* 3-9-0 SDWilliams(8) (bkwd: chsd ldrs: 7th st: wknd 3f out)....7 7
2901[5] Awestruck **(36)***(33) (BPreece)* 5-8-10b PRobinson(11) (a in rr)....4 8
2959[6] Sastrugi (IRE) **(46)***(22) (SPCWoods)* 3-8-0b NAdams(6) (b.nr fore: chsd ldrs: 4th st: wknd 3f out: t.o)....8 9
2920[7] Phils Fortune *(18) (KSBridgwater)* 3-7-11 NCarlisle(7) (bkwd: lost pl ½-wy: t.o)....½ 10
Sonny Place *(JLHarris)* 4-8-12 RCochrane(10) (w'like: str: bkwd: s.s: a wl bhd & t.o)....20 11

3/1 Ela Man Howa, **7/2** Bushehr (IRE), **4/1** Oakbury (IRE), **6/1** Old Swinford (IRE), **14/1** Pennine Lad (IRE), Alzoomo (IRE), **16/1** MAKE A STAND, **20/1** Awestruck, Sonny Place, **33/1** Sastrugi (IRE), **50/1** Phils Fortune, CSF £65.02 TOTE £14.30: £3.40 £1.60 £1.90 (£31.40) Trio £112.80 OWNER Kingstone Warren Partners (WANTAGE) BRED R. M. West 11 Rn
2m 34.8 (6.00) SF: 43/32/28/12/25/15/9/-/-/-/-
WEIGHT FOR AGE 3yo-10lb
Make a Stand clmd MPipe £8,000, Bushehr(IRE) clmd SCoathup £9,000.

3293 PEDIGREE PET FOODS H'CAP (0-70) (3-Y.O+) (Class E) £3,645.40 (£1,091.20: £523.60: £239.80)
5f 218y Stalls: Low GOING minus 0.22 sec per fur (GF) 7-35 (7-37)

3179[3] **Irchester Lass (37)***(42) (SRBowring)* 3-7-10 NCarlisle(1) (hdwy bel dist: led ins fnl f: jst hld on)....— 1
3123[7] Gymcrak Tycoon **(42)***(47) (GHolmes)* 6-8-5v WNewnes(5) (b: b.off hind: lw: hld up & bhd: hdwy wl over 1f out: fin wl)....s.h 2
3072[3] To the Roof (IRE) **(64)***(67) (PWHarris)* 3-9-9 PRobinson(7) (chsd ldrs: effrt over 1f out: ev ch fnl f: unable qckn)....¾ 3
3098* Arc Lamp **(46)***(49) (JAGlover)* 9-8-2 (7) VictoriaAppleby(3) (lw: a.p: led over 2f out tl hdd & no ex ins fnl f)....hd 4
2943[2] Dashing Dancer (IRE) **(59)***(58) (RAkehurst)* 4-9-8 TQuinn(8) (hld up: hdwy 2f out: rdn & ev ch appr fnl f: nt qckn)....1¼ 5
3139[3] Waders Dream (IRE) **(44)***(42) (PatMitchell)* 6-8-7v DHolland(9) (hdwy bel dist: r.o wl fnl f)....½ 6
*2943** Robo Magic (USA) **(58)***(52) (LMontagueHall)* 3-9-3 RCochrane(16) (chsd ldrs: rdn over 1f out: one pce)....1½ 7
3123[3] Double Splendour (IRE) **(50)***(41)*(Fav)*(PSFelgate)* 5-8-10 (3) DWright(17) (b: hdwy 2f out: sn rdn & ev ch: no ex fnl f)....1 8
2925[4] Beveled Edge **(51)***(42) (BPalling)* 6-9-0 TSprake(14) (swtg: w ldrs tl rdn & outpcd ins fnl f)....s.h 9
3079[6] Woodlands Electric **(34)***(20) (PAPritchard)* 5-7-4 (7)ow4 JoHunnam(10) (w ldrs tl outpcd appr fnl f)....½ 10
769[9] Cretan Gift **(54)***(42) (NPLittmoden)* 4-9-3 TGMcLaughlin(12) (bkwd: nvr nr to chal)....½ 11
3072[6] Jon's Choice **(57)***(41) (BPreece)* 7-9-6 NAdams(11) (lw: hdwy over 2f out: sn ev ch: rdn & wknd appr fnl f)....1½ 12
2093[3] Montague Dawson (IRE) **(63)***(47) (MrsNMacauley)* 3-9-1 (7) AmandaSanders(6) (b.hind: lw: chsd ldrs 4f: sn wknd)....nk 13
3175[2] Great Hall **(61)***(43) (PDCundell)* 6-9-10b DHarrison(2) (dwlt: a bhd)....¾ 14

2956⁴ Mr Moriarty (IRE) **(30)***(11) (SRBowring)* 4-7-7b NKennedy(15) (outpcd) ....nk **15**
3050⁹ Them Times (IRE) **(31)***(6) (FJordan)* 6-7-5 (3)ow1 NVarley(4) (sn rdn along: a outpcd) 2 **16**
3028⁸ Slivovitz **(50)***(2) (MJHeaton-Ellis)* 5-8-13b AClark(18) (lw: racd alone far side: led over 3f: sn wknd: t.o) 9 **17**

LONG HANDICAP Woodlands Electric 6-6 Mr Moriarty (IRE) 6-11 Them Times (IRE) 6-10
9/2 Double Splendour (IRE), **6/1** Arc Lamp, **7/1** Dashing Dancer (IRE), Great Hall, **15/2** Robo Magic (USA), **10/1** To the Roof (IRE), **11/1** Waders Dream (IRE), **12/1** Gymcrak Tycoon, Slivovitz, **14/1** Beveled Edge, **16/1** Montague Dawson (IRE), IRCHESTER LASS, **25/1** Mr Moriarty (IRE), Cretan Gift, Jon's Choice, **50/1** Woodlands Electric, Them Times (IRE), CSF £191.28 CT £1,858.28 TOTE £23.10: £4.00 £3.20 £4.20 £1.90 (£100.80) Trio £510.50 OWNER Mr D. M. Hacker (EDWINSTOWE) BRED R. Hacker 17 Rn 1m 13.0 (3.00) SF: 20/29/45/31/40/24/30/23/24/2/24/23/25/25/-/-/-
WEIGHT FOR AGE 3yo-4lb

3294 MOUNTSORREL MEDIAN AUCTION MAIDEN STKS (3 & 4-Y.O) (Class F)
£3,199.40 (£888.40: £426.20)
1m 1f 218y Stalls: Low GOING minus 0.22 sec per fur (GF) 8-05 (8-07)

2794³ **Western Sal (70)***(77) (WJarvis)* 3-8-8 PRobinson(11) (hld up: hdwy over 3f out: led appr fnl f: drvn out) ....— **1**
2790¹⁰ Dtoto *(78) (MRStoute)* 3-8-13 DHolland(6) (bit bkwd: chsd ldrs: 3rd st: led bel dist: sn hdd: outpcd fnl f) 2½ **2**
3016⁷ Keen To The Last (FR) *(76) (GHarwood)* 3-8-13 AClark(3) (lw: chsd ldrs: 5th st: rdn wl over 2f out: kpt on fnl f) 1¼ **3**
3115² Troubadour Song *(75)*(Fav)*(IABalding)* 3-8-13 TQuinn(7) (chsd ldrs: 4th st: led 2f out tl bel dist: unable qckn) ....½ **4**
2621⁴ Blaze of Oak (USA) **(67)***(75) (WJHaggas)* 4-9-7 RCochrane(8) (lw: hld up in tch: 6th st: hdwy & ev ch bel dist: one pce) ....nk **5**
2612⁶ Sharazi (USA) **(60)***(75) (DJSCosgrove)* 4-9-7b DHarrison(1) (chsd ldr: rdn & ev ch 2f out: kpt on one pce) ....s.h **6**
Fighting Times *(68) (CASmith)* 3-8-13 ACulhane(5) (wl grwn: bkwd: s.s: wl bhd tl sme late hdwy) 4 **7**
2553⁹ Florismart **(68)***(62) (JARToller)* 3-8-13 WNewnes(12) (led to 2f out: eased whn btn fnl f) 4 **8**
2977¹⁰ Woodlands Energy *(56) (PAPritchard)* 4-9-2 NAdams(9) (a in rr) ....nk **9**
Sungai Mas (USA) *(61) (SPCWoods)* 3-8-13 WWoods(10) (w'like: bkwd: a in rr) ....s.h **10**
2319¹³ Tap On Tootsie *(54) (ICampbell)* 3-8-8 GBardwell(2) (bit bkwd: chsd ldrs to ½-wy: sn lost tch) 1¼ **11**
2790¹³ Minneola *(14) (RTPhillips)* 3-8-8 RPerham(4) (b.hind: bkwd: a bhd: t.o) 25 **12**

2/1 Troubadour Song (op 3/1), **9/4** Keen To The Last (FR), **9/2** WESTERN SAL, **8/1** Dtoto, **10/1** Blaze of Oak (USA), **16/1** Florismart, **20/1** Sungai Mas (USA), **25/1** Sharazi (USA), **33/1** Tap On Tootsie, **50/1** Minneola, Fighting Times, **66/1** Woodlands Energy, CSF £39.18 TOTE £4.50: £1.40 £2.10 £1.70 (£11.40) Trio £26.20 OWNER Mrs James McAllister (NEWMARKET) BRED Fluorocarbon Bloodstock 12 Rn 2m 10.7 (8.00) SF: 11/12/10/9/17/17/2/-/-/-/-/-
WEIGHT FOR AGE 3yo-8lb
T/Plpt: £96.80 (134.02 Tckts). T/Qdpt: £48.50 (1.5 Tckts). IM

2951-REDCAR (L-H)
Wednesday August 23rd (Good to firm)
WEATHER: sunny WIND: slt across

3295 FURNITURE FACTORS RACING SCHOOLS APPRENTICE H'CAP (0-70)
(3-Y.O+) (Class E) £3,046.25 (£920.00: £447.50: £211.25)
1m Stalls: High GOING minus 0.31 sec per fur (GF) 2-15 (2-15)

Dana Point (IRE) (60)*(70) (TDBarron)* 3-8-13 (4) KimberleyHart(7) (a.p: led wl over 1f out: hld on wl) ....— **1**
2156⁷ Mary's Case (IRE) **(53)***(62) (MJohnston)* 5-9-2b RHavlin(1) (lw: hld up: hdwy 3f out: chal ins fnl f: nt r.o cl home) ....½ **2**
3119³ Master Ofthe House **(61)***(70)*(Fav)*(MDHammond)* 9-9-10 SCopp(5) (hld up: hdwy over 2f out: ev ch ins fnl f: nt qckn towards fin) ....s.h **3**
3234⁶ Zahid (USA) **(43)***(48) (KRBurke)* 4-8-6v RPainter(6) (hdwy 3f out: rdn & one pce fnl 2f) 2 **4**
2761* Upex le Gold Too **(40)***(37) (LRLloyd-James)* 3-7-7 (4)ow2 KSked(4) (lw: led over 6f: sn wknd) ...3 **5**
3118³ Resolute Bay **(41)***(39) (RMWhitaker)* 9-8-4b GMitchell(2) (lw: in tch: effrt u.p 3f out: sn btn) ....½ **6**
2968⁹ Full Gloss **(44)***(38) (MrsMReveley)* 3-7-11 (4) DDenby(8) (effrt over 3f out: rdn & no rspnse) .1¾ **7**
2755⁶ Juice Plus **(30)***(16) (JParkes)* 4-7-7 MBaird(3) (spd to ½-wy: sn bhd) 4 **8**
LONG HANDICAP Juice Plus 6-12

11/4 Master Ofthe House, **4/1** Zahid (USA), **5/1** Mary's Case (IRE), Resolute Bay, Upex le Gold Too, **10/1** Full Gloss, **12/1** DANA POINT (IRE), **33/1** Juice Plus, CSF £65.04 CT £194.26 TOTE £26.80: £6.10 £1.40 £1.50 (£63.20) OWNER Mr J. Baggott (THIRSK) BRED T. N. Leonard 8 Rn
1m 37.8 (2.80) SF: 46/44/52/30/13/21/14/-
WEIGHT FOR AGE 3yo-6lb

3296 RUNSWICK BAY (S) STKS (3-Y.O+) (Class F) £2,672.00 (£742.00: £356.00)

1m 6f 19y Stalls: Low GOING minus 0.31 sec per fur (GF) 2-45 (2-45)

3017* **Brodessa (61)**_(59+)_(Fav)_(MrsMReveley)_ 9-9-3 (7) SCopp(3) (lw: hdwy appr st: led over 3f out: sn pushed clr) — 1
3153[2] Don't Cry **(18)**_(38) (DonEnricoIncisa)_ 7-9-0 KimTinkler(4) (hld up: effrt 4f out: styd on: no ch w wnr) 10 2
3148* Doctor's Remedy **(25)**_(33) (MrsJJordan)_ 9-9-3 (7) JoHunnam(1) (led 6f: outpcd ent st: c wd: n.d after) 13 3
3118[2] Never so True **(41)**_(23) (MartynWane)_ 4-9-5 JCarroll(2) (lw: cl up: led 8f out tl over 3f out: wknd) 4 4

1/8 BRODESSA, **9/1** Never so True, **20/1** Don't Cry, Doctor's Remedy, CSF £3.43 TOTE £1.20 (£3.10) OWNER Mr R. W. S. Jevon (SALTBURN) BRED B. Fairs 4 Rn 3m 6.9 (8.90) SF: 34/13/8/-
No bid

3297 BOLLINGER CHAMPAGNE CHALLENGE SERIES GENTLEMENS' AMATEUR H'CAP (0-70) (3-Y.O+) (Class F) £2,735.00 (£760.00: £365.00)

1m 3f Stalls: Low GOING minus 0.31 sec per fur (GF) 3-15 (3-15)

3047* **Salinger (37)**_(52)_(Fav)_(JParkes)_ 7-10-5 MrCBonner(8) (mde most: kpt on wl fnl f) — 1
2875* Essayeffsee **(52)**_(63) (MrsMReveley)_ 6-11-6 MrMHNaughton(1) (lw: trckd ldrs: hmpd 5½f out: ev ch over 2f out: one pce fnl f) 2½ 2
3094[2] Salska **(46)**_(55) (AStreeter)_ 4-10-10 (4) MrPClinton(2) (racd wd: a.p: hung lft over 1f out: r.o one pce) 2 3
3127[6] Hatta River (USA) **(59)**_(67) (JAHarris)_ 5-11-9 (4) MrGaryWoodward(6) (in tch: effrt & wnt lft 2f out: nt pce to chal) ½ 4
2759[6] Missus Murhill (IRE) **(31)**_(33) (NTinkler)_ 4-9-9 (4) MrLSpink(7) (lw: s.s: styd on fnl 3f: n.d) 4 5
2825[4] Catch the Pigeon **(47)**_(49) (REBarr)_ 6-11-1 MrSSwiers(5) (nvr trbld ldrs) nk 6
2544[2] Festive Lassie **(60)**_(60) (TDBarron)_ 4-12-0 MrRJohnson(4) (chsd ldrs: effrt over 3f out: sddle slipped: sn rdn & btn) ¾ 7
1921[5] Fret (USA) **(50)**_(33) (JSWainwright)_ 5-11-0 (4) MrKGreen(3) (prom to st: sn rdn & bhd) 12 8

5/2 SALINGER, **11/4** Essayeffsee, **4/1** Festive Lassie, **5/1** Salska, **10/1** Missus Murhill (IRE), **14/1** Fret (USA), **33/1** Catch the Pigeon, Hatta River (USA), CSF £9.24 CT £26.74 TOTE £3.10: £1.70 £1.50 £1.90 (£3.50) OWNER Mr Vince Dolan (MALTON) BRED D. J. and Mrs Deer 8 Rn
2m 24.2 (8.50) SF: 30/41/33/45/11/27/38/11
STEWARDS' ENQUIRY Spink susp. 1-4/9/95 (careless riding).

3298 ANDERSONS H'CAP (0-85) (3-Y.O) (Class D) £4,381.50 (£1,317.00: £636.00: £295.50)

6f Stalls: High GOING minus 0.31 sec per fur (GF) 3-45 (3-48)

3112[4] **Iktamal (USA) (80)**_(91)_(Fav)_(EALDunlop)_ 3-9-7 WRyan(1) (lw: hld up: smooth hdwy to ld wl over 1f out: rdn & r.o fnl f) — 1
2909[4] Showery **(72)**_(79) (JWWatts)_ 3-8-13 NConnorton(7) (lw: hld up: effrt ½-wy: outpcd 2f out: styd on fnl f) 1½ 2
2679[3] Nawaasi **(75)**_(78) (HThomsonJones)_ 3-9-2 RHills(4) (hld up: swtchd & effrt 2f out: hrd rdn & nt qckn fnl f) 1½ 3
2949[3] Latching (IRE) **(75)**_(69) (RFJohnsonHoughton)_ 3-9-2b ACulhane(3) (a chsng ldrs: one pce fnl 2f) 3½ 4
2742[5] Princess Sadie **(78)**_(61) (MJohnston)_ 3-9-5 TWilliams(6) (in tch: effrt ½-wy: sn btn) 4 5
2973[6] Question Ali **(62)**_(45) (JBerry)_ 3-8-3 JCarroll(2) (lw: led over 4f: sn btn) hd 6
2973[4] High Ranking **(57)**_(33) (MHEasterby)_ 3-7-12 SMaloney(5) (plld hrd: prom over 3f) 2½ 7

2/1 IKTAMAL (USA), **3/1** Nawaasi, **7/2** Showery, **7/1** Latching (IRE) (9/2-8/1), **8/1** Princess Sadie (5/1-9/1), **12/1** High Ranking, **14/1** Question Ali, CSF £9.47 TOTE £3.60: £2.00 £1.90 (£6.10) OWNER Maktoum Al Maktoum (NEWMARKET) BRED Green Ireland Properties Ltd 7 Rn
1m 10.4 (1.10) SF: 62/50/49/40/32/16/4

3299 YORKSHIRE-TYNE TEES TELEVISION H'CAP (0-70) (3-Y.O) (Class E) £3,185.75 (£956.00: £460.50: £212.75)
1m 6f 19y Stalls: Low GOING minus 0.31 sec per fur (GF) 4-15 (4-17)

3254* **Red Spectacle (IRE) (53)***(65) (PCHaslam)* 3-8-6 (5) 4x MBaird(2) (mde all: qcknd 4f out: r.o wl)......— 1
2969* Nickitoto **(63)***(72)*(Fav)*(JLDunlop)* 3-9-7 GCarter(4) (lw: hld up: outpcd 4f out: styd on u.p fnl 2f: nrst fin)......2½ 2
3111* Boundary Express **(47)***(56) (EJAlston)* 3-8-5 DeanMcKeown(7) (chsd wnr: effrt over 3f out: one pce)......s.h 3
3153* Punch **(55)***(60) (NTinkler)* 3-8-13b 4x WRyan(6) (lw: trckd ldrs: effrt 3f out: rdn & btn 2f out)......4 4
*3078*4 Dawn Mission **(48)***(52) (MHEasterby)* 3-8-6 SMaloney(5) (a chsng ldrs: rdn 4f out: no imp after)......hd 5
3099 11 Island Cascade **(42)***(45) (DonEnricoIncisa)* 3-8-0 KimTinkler(3) (hld up & bhd: rdn 4f out: n.d) 1 6
2871 4 Bark'n'bite **(51)***(53) (MrsMReveley)* 3-8-9 JCarroll(1) (in tch: one pce fnl 4f)......1¼ 7

1/2 Nickitoto, **7/1** Punch, **8/1** Bark'n'bite, **10/1** Boundary Express, RED SPECTACLE (IRE), **14/1** Dawn Mission, **50/1** Island Cascade, CSF £15.59 TOTE £8.30: £2.20 £1.20 (£5.50) OWNER Mr David Morgan (MIDDLEHAM) BRED J. Beckett 7 Rn 3m 4.6 (6.60) SF: 34/41/25/29/21/14/22

3300 WESTERDALE MAIDEN AUCTION STKS (2-Y.O) (Class E) £3,029.75 (£908.00: £436.50: £200.75)
5f Stalls: High GOING minus 0.31 sec per fur (GF) 4-45 (4-47)

2666W **Babsy Babe** *(51+)*(Fav)*(JJQuinn)* 2-8-0 DaleGibson(2) (neat: scope: trckd ldrs: led 1f out: pushed along & r.o wl)......— 1
2354 3 Happy Partner (IRE) *(52)*(Fav)*(PCHaslam)* 2-7-12 (5) MBaird(3) (lw: w ldr: led ½-wy: hdd 1f out: r.o)......¾ 2
2128 7 Niteowl Raider (IRE) *(27) (JAHarris)* 2-8-7 RHills(1) (slt ld to ½-wy: wknd)......9 3
1857 5 Stealth Attack (IRE) **(61)***(2) (JBerry)* 2-8-8 JCarroll(4) (lw: a outpcd & bhd)......8 4

7/4 BABSY BABE, Happy Partner (IRE), **9/4** Stealth Attack (IRE), **12/1** Niteowl Raider (IRE), CSF £4.99 TOTE £3.10 (£2.20) OWNER Mrs Carol Bloom (MALTON) BRED John Gaines 4 Rn
58.5 secs (1.80) SF: 27/28/3/-

3301 WHITBY CONDITIONS STKS (2-Y.O) (Class C) £5,343.50 (£1,721.00: £835.50)
7f Stalls: High GOING minus 0.31 sec per fur (GF) 5-15 (5-16)

3147 3 **Dankeston (USA) (89)***(86) (MBell)* 2-8-8v(7) GFaulkner(2) (lw: trckd ldrs: disp ld over 2f out: r.o wl)......— 1
2667* Modern Day (USA) *(86)*(Fav)*(HRACecil)* 2-9-1 WRyan(1) (lw: hld up: hdwy, wnt lft & qcknd to disp ld over 2f out: r.o wl)......hd 2
2257 2 Leith Academy (USA) **(90)***(53) (BWHills)* 2-8-5 RHills(3) (lw: led over 4f: sn outpcd)......10 3

8/15 Modern Day (USA), **5/2** DANKESTON (USA), **13/2** Leith Academy (USA), CSF £4.01 TOTE £3.20 (£1.30) OWNER Mr Luciano Gaucci (NEWMARKET) BRED Donald MacRae 3 Rn
1m 24.3 (2.30) SF: 45/45/12
T/Plpt: £83.00 (117.24 Tckts). T/Qdpt: Not won; £39.00 to Lingfield 24/8/95 AA

3017-BEVERLEY (R-H)
Thursday August 24th (Good to firm)
WEATHER: overcast & cool WIND: fresh half against

3302 WOODMANSEY MAIDEN APPRENTICE H'CAP (0-60) (3-Y.O+) (Class F) £2,620.00 (£745.00: £370.00)
1m 1f 207y Stalls: High GOING minus 0.25 sec per fur (GF) 5-15 (5-21)

2577 4 **Ruby Heights (50)***(65)*(Fav)*(RHannon)* 4-9-9 (5) EGreehy(8) (chsd ldr: led 3f out: hld on towards fin)......— 1
1368 10 Broughton's Pride (IRE) **(48)***(62) (JAGlover)* 4-9-12 VictoriaAppleby(7) (in tch: hdwy to chse ldrs over 2f out: chal ins fnl f: nt qckn nr fin)......½ 2
2972 11 Bex Boy (IRE) **(27)***(27) (MWEasterby)* 4-8-5b TFinn(9) (chsd ldr: led 5f out to 3f out: wknd over 1f out)......9 3
2955 2 Master Fiddler **(28)***(10) (EWeymes)* 5-8-6 KSked(6) (bhd: hdwy on outside over 2f out: sn rdn & wknd)......11 4

*2960*4 Diamond Market **(46)***(26)*(Fav)*(RHollinshead)* 3-9-2 FLynch(3) (bhd: sme hdwy on outside over 2f out: hung rt & sn wknd)....1¼ **5**
2582 6 Milltown Classic (IRE) **(32)***(6) (JParkes)* 3-8-2 JGotobed(2) (stdd s: bhd: sme hdwy over 2f out: n.d)....4 **6**
2994 6 Larentia **(43)***(10) (JParkes)* 3-8-13 SBuckley(1) (pushed along 7f out: hmpd over 3f out: wnt rt & sn wknd)....4 **7**
2955 3 Northwise (IRE) **(42)***(4) (WWHaigh)* 4-9-6 JoHunnam(4) (uns rdr gng to s: chsd ldrs tl outpcd over 3f out: sn rdn & wknd)....3½ **8**
3099 10 Qualitair Pride **(47)***(2) (JFBottomley)* 3-9-3b DSweeney(5) (plld hrd: led: racd wd: hdd over 5f out: sn lost pl)....4 **9**

7/2 RUBY HEIGHTS (op 9/4), Diamond Market, **9/2** Master Fiddler, **5/1** Northwise (IRE), **8/1** Broughton's Pride (IRE), Larentia, Bex Boy (IRE), **12/1** Milltown Classic (IRE), Qualitair Pride, CSF £31.71 CT £200.32 TOTE £3.30 £1.50 £2.80 £1.60 (£19.00) Trio £28.00 OWNER Mr G. S. Shropshire (MARLBOROUGH) BRED Mrs M. Burrell 9 Rn 2m 8.1 (5.60) SF: 46/43/8/-/-/-/-/-/-
WEIGHT FOR AGE 3yo-8lb

3303 DRIFFIELD (S) H'CAP (0-60) (3-Y.O+) (Class G) £2,539.00 (£704.00: £337.00)
2m 35y Stalls: Centre GOING minus 0.25 sec per fur (GF) 5-45 (5-46)

3092* **Top Prize (34)***(52) (MBrittain)* 7-9-7v JLowe(6) (chsd ldrs: rdn over 3f out: styd on to ld over 1f out: sn wnt clr)....— **1**
3114 4 Arian Spirit (IRE) **(32)***(42)*(Fav)*(JLEyre)* 4-9-5 RLappin(9) (hdwy ½-wy: led over 2f out tl over 1f out: one pce)....8 **2**
3092 7 Can She Can Can **(42)***(51) (MJohnston)* 3-9-1 DHolland(3) (mde most to 7f out: outpcd 3f out: styd on appr fnl f)....¾ **3**
2676 3 Pillow Talk (IRE) **(41)***(46) (SWCampion)* 4-10-0 GCarter(7) (jnd ldrs 7f out: led over 3f out tl over 2f out: wknd over 1f out)....4 **4**
3092 4 Club Elite **(25)***(29) (MFBarraclough)* 3-7-7 (5) MBaird(10) (sn bhd: drvn along ½-wy: sme hdwy over 2f out: nvr nr ldrs)....1¼ **5**
3017 2 Fools of Pride (IRE) **(38)***(39) (RHollinshead)* 3-8-11 TIves(5) (chsd ldrs: drvn along 7f out: wknd 3f out)....3 **6**
3083 4 Scenic Dancer **(37)***(38) (AHide)* 7-9-10 JWilliams(4) (bhd: sme hdwy over 3f out: hung rt: nvr nr ldrs)....nk **7**
1036 7 Brusque (USA) **(20)***(17) (DonEnricoIncisa)* 11-8-7 KimTinkler(1) (sn chsng ldrs: lost pl 10f out: sn wl bhd: sme hdwy 2f out: n.d)....4 **8**
3056 8 Annabel's Baby (IRE) **(20)***(13) (MrsMMcCourt)* 6-8-0 (7) RStudholme(2) (w ldr: led 7f out tl over 3f out: sn wknd)....4 **9**
3029 5 Ice Magic **(20)** *(FJYardley)* 8-8-7v DHarrison(8) (rr div: hdwy u.p over 4f out: sn wknd & bhd)20 **10**

3/1 Arian Spirit (IRE), **5/1** TOP PRIZE, Can She Can Can, **11/2** Scenic Dancer (4/1-6/1), **6/1** Fools of Pride (IRE) (op 4/1), Annabel's Baby (IRE) (op 14/1), **8/1** Ice Magic, **9/1** Club Elite, **10/1** Pillow Talk (IRE), **20/1** Brusque (USA), CSF £22.80 CT £79.27 TOTE £6.00: £2.00 £2.10 £1.70 (£12.40) Trio £16.80 OWNER Northgate Lodge Racing Ltd (WARTHILL) BRED The Overbury Stud 10 Rn
3m 43.5 (13.00) SF: 25/15/10/19/-/-/11/-/-/-
WEIGHT FOR AGE 3yo-14lb
No bid

3304 SNOWY GRAY MEMORIAL MAIDEN STKS (3-Y.O+) (Class D) £3,743.00 (£1,124.00: £542.00: £251.00)
2m 35y Stalls: Centre GOING minus 0.25 sec per fur (GF) 6-15 (6-15)

3016 15 **Tabdeel** *(81) (ACStewart)* 3-8-7 MRoberts(4) (led 1f: drvn along & outpcd 5f out: styd on to ld ins fnl f: edgd lft: drvn out)....— **1**
2860 4 Torreglia (IRE) **(65)***(75)*(Fav)*(JLDunlop)* 3-8-2 WCarson(2) (pushed along 6f out: n.m.r over 2f out: hrd rdn over 1f out: kpt on same pce)....1½ **2**
Yougo *(78) (MJohnston)* 3-8-7 DHolland(3) (wl grwn: trckd ldrs: led over 3f out tl ins fnl f: edgd lft & kpt on same pace)....1¼ **3**
Batty's Island *(49) (BPreece)* 6-9-7 GHind(1) (led after 1f: pushed along ½-wy: hdd over 3f out: sn wknd: eased)....30 **4**

4/7 Torreglia (IRE) (1/2-4/5), **11/4** TABDEEL (4/1-5/2), **8/1** Yougo, Batty's Island (op 5/1), CSF £4.77 TOTE £4.30: (£1.70) OWNER Sheikh Ahmed Al Maktoum (NEWMARKET) BRED Hamilton Bloodstock (UK) Ltd 4 Rn
3m 44.7 (14.20) SF: 7/1/4/-
WEIGHT FOR AGE 3yo-14lb

3305 ST JOHN AMBULANCE H'CAP (0-70) (3-Y.O+) (Class E) £3,678.00 (£1,104.00: £532.00: £246.00)
7f 100y Stalls: High GOING minus 0.25 sec per fur (GF) 6-45 (6-46)

2952* **Ninia (USA) (61)***(72)*(Fav)*(MJohnston)* 3-9-9 MRoberts(8) (trckd ldrs on ins: effrt & swtchd lft over 1f out: styd on to ld ins fnl f: drvn out) — **1**
2966² Chalky Dancer **(42)***(51) (HJCollingridge)* 3-8-4 MHills(7) (led tl ins fnl f: kpt on u.p) 1 **2**
3050⁶ Special-K **(62)***(69) (EWeymes)* 3-9-10 GHind(5) (chsd ldrs: rdn 3f out: styd on same pce appr fnl f) ¾ **3**
3113⁹ Lancashire Life (IRE) **(51)***(57) (EJAlston)* 4-9-4 KFallon(4) (trckd ldrs: effrt u.p & hung rt over 1f out: kpt on: nvr rchd ldrs) ½ **4**
2611⁶ Tolls Choice (IRE) **(54)***(60) (MWEasterby)* 6-9-7b TIves(9) (hld up: hdwy on ins over 2f out: n.m.r: styd on same pce ins fnl f) nk **5**
Watch Me Go (IRE) **(37)***(36) (BobJones)* 6-8-4 ow1 NConnorton(1) (b: bhd: hdwy on outside 2f out: hung rt: nvr nr ldrs) 2½ **6**
3096⁷ Red River Rose (IRE) **(42)***(23) (NPLittmoden)* 3-7-11b(7) CAdamson(10) (dwlt: a bhd) 9 **7**
2972⁴ Canny Lad **(32)***(4) (MPBielby)* 5-7-13v JFEgan(6) (chsd ldr: drvn along ½-wy: chal 3f out: sn wknd & eased) 4 **8**
2993⁶ Embezzler **(43)***(10) (SGollings)* 3-8-5 ACulhane(3) (chsd ldrs: ev ch 3f out: sn wknd: eased) 2½ **9**
3098¹⁰ Steady Risk **(26)** *(MrsAMNaughton)* 4-7-0 (7) BHalligan(2) (hld up: effrt on outside over 2f out: sn rdn & wknd) 6 **10**

LONG HANDICAP Steady Risk 7-4

5/4 NINIA (USA), **5/1** Chalky Dancer (4/1-6/1), **6/1** Lancashire Life (IRE), **8/1** Special-K, Canny Lad (6/1-9/1), **10/1** Tolls Choice (IRE), **12/1** Embezzler, **14/1** Watch Me Go (IRE), **16/1** Red River Rose (IRE), **33/1** Steady Risk, CSF £9.62 CT £38.09 TOTE £2.40: £1.50 £1.80 £2.10 (£5.50) Trio £8.60 OWNER Mrs D. R. Schreiber (MIDDLEHAM) BRED Newgate Stud Farm Inc 10 Rn
1m 35.5 (3.50) SF: 49/28/46/39/42/18/-/-/-/-
WEIGHT FOR AGE 3yo-5lb

3306 E.B.F. WILLERBY MAIDEN STKS (2-Y.O F) (Class D) £4,081.00 (£1,228.00: £594.00: £277.00)
7f 100y Stalls: High GOING minus 0.25 sec per fur (GF) 7-15 (7-18)

3158³ **Myrtle (94)***(83)*(Fav)*(RHannon)* 2-8-11 MRoberts(6) (lw: chsd ldrs: hmpd ½-wy: styd on u.p to ld ins fnl f: drvn out) — **1**
1697⁵ Toffee *(80?) (JRFanshawe)* 2-8-11 DHarrison(7) (swtg: bhd whn hmpd ½-wy: hdwy over 1f out: styd on wl towards fin) 1½ **2**
Fijon (IRE) *(80?) (BWHills)* 2-8-11 MHills(4) (cmpt: chsd ldrs: led over 2f out tl ins fnl f: no ex) hd **3**
3018⁸ Northern Falcon *(62) (MWEasterby)* 2-8-11 MBirch(8) (stdd s: bhd tl sme hdwy fnl f: n.d) 8 **4**
2971³ La Fandango (IRE) *(60) (MWEasterby)* 2-8-4 (7) RuthCoulter(1) (in tch: effrt over 2f out: sn wknd) 1 **5**
Candy's Delight *(55) (JLEyre)* 2-8-11 RLappin(9) (lt-f: unf: b: chsd ldrs tl wknd over 2f out) 2½ **6**
2852⁷ Ann's Music *(36) (JMJefferson)* 2-8-11 KFallon(5) (plld hrd: led tl over 2f out: wknd over 1f out) 9 **7**
Alis Princess *(MPBielby)* 2-8-11 ACulhane(3) (rangy: bit bkwd: sn trckng ldrs: lost pl 3f out: eased) 20 **8**
3010⁶ Financial Star (IRE) *(JLDunlop)* 2-8-11 WCarson(2) (sn drvn along & bhd: hdwy to chse ldrs whn broke leg ½-wy: p.u: dead) **P**

8/13 MYRTLE, **3/1** Financial Star (IRE), **6/1** Fijon (IRE) (op 7/2), **12/1** Toffee, **16/1** Northern Falcon, **20/1** La Fandango (IRE), **40/1** Ann's Music, Alis Princess, Candy's Delight, CSF £10.31 TOTE £1.70: £1.20 £1.60 £1.50 (£7.30) Trio £7.70 OWNER Lord Carnarvon (MARLBOROUGH) BRED Highclere Stud Ltd 9 Rn
1m 37.8 (5.80) SF: 14/11/11/-/-/-/-/-/-

3307 MANOR ROAD MAIDEN STKS (2-Y.O) (Class D) £3,600.00 (£1,080.00: £520.00: £240.00)
1m 100y Stalls: High GOING minus 0.25 sec per fur (GF) 7-45 (7-47)

2995² **Belana (83)***(76) (JWWatts)* 2-8-9 TIves(6) (lw: hld up: effrt & n.m.r over 2f out: styd on wl to ld ins fnl f: drvn out) — **1**
2957² Maid For Baileys (IRE) **(85)***(72)*(Fav)*(MJohnston)* 2-8-9 MRoberts(1) (lw: trckd ldrs: led over 1f out: sn hdd & unable qckn) 2 **2**
2749³ Samim (USA) *(66) (JLDunlop)* 2-9-0 WCarson(3) (lw: unruly s: sn drvn along & chsng ldrs: chal 2f out: outpcd appr fnl f) 6 **3**
2995⁷ Recall To Mind *(64) (MHEasterby)* 2-9-0 MBirch(5) (led 1f: led 2f out: sn hdd: one pce) 1 **4**

2932[10] Whothehellisharry *(55) (JBerry)* 2-9-0 GCarter(4) (bit bkwd: sn bhd: sme hdwy 2f out: nvr nr ldrs) 5 **5**
3110[8] Dispol Conqueror (IRE) *(36) (GROldroyd)* 2-9-0 KFallon(2) (bhd: hrd drvn & sme hdwy ½-wy: lost pl over 2f out) 10 **6**
1597[15] Swish *(22) (NTinkler)* 2-9-0 ACulhane(7) (plld hrd: led after 1f to 2f out: sn lost pl & eased)....7 **7**

13/8 Maid For Baileys (IRE), **7/4** BELANA, **11/4** Samim (USA), **16/1** Whothehellisharry, **25/1** Recall To Mind, **33/1** Swish, **66/1** Dispol Conqueror (IRE), CSF £4.92 TOTE £2.80: £1.40 £1.80 (£2.40) OWNER Sheikh Mohammed (RICHMOND) BRED Lilliemore Stud and Darley Stud Management Co Ltd 7 Rn 1m 50.7 (6.70) SF: 11/7/1/-/-/-/-
T/Plpt: £68.50 (147.36 Tckts). T/Qdpt: £24.80 (3.3 Tckts). WG

2731-EDINBURGH (R-H)
Thursday August 24th (Good to firm)
WEATHER: overcast
WIND: mod half against

3308

TANGIER 1680 CLAIMING STKS (3-Y.O+) (Class F) £2,759.00 (£774.00: £377.00)
1m 7f 16y Stalls: High GOING minus 0.31 sec per fur (GF) 2-15 (2-15)

2478* **Keep Your Distance (60)***(63+)*(Fav)*(MrsMReveley)* 5-9-10 JFortune(1) (a gng wl: led on bit 1f out: v.easily)....— **1**
3171[2] Wild Rose of York **(47)***(58) (PMonteith)* 4-9-2 (3) DWright(3) (plld hrd: trckd ldr: led 3f out: hdd 1f out: no ch w wnr)....½ **2**
938[7] Iron Gent (USA) **(73)***(59) (SEKettlewell)* 4-9-3 (7) GFaulkner(2) (led tl hdd 3f out: one pce)....3½ **3**

4/5 KEEP YOUR DISTANCE (8/11-Evens), **5/4** Iron Gent (USA), **10/1** Wild Rose of York, CSF £5.30 TOTE £2.10: (£2.00) OWNER Mr P. D. Savill (SALTBURN) BRED Cedric Ford 3 Rn
3m 27.5 (17.00) SF: -/-/-

3309

STEVE WOOD MEMORIAL NURSERY H'CAP (2-Y.O) (Class E) £2,820.00 (£840.00: £400.00: £180.00)
7f 15y Stalls: High GOING minus 0.31 sec per fur (GF) 2-45 (2-46)

3168[2] **Silent Soprano (48)***(54) (DenysSmith)* 2-8-3 TWilliams(2) (lw: chsd ldrs: led appr st: styd on strly fnl f)....— **1**
3225[3] Magic Lake **(47)***(52)*(Fav)*(EJAlston)* 2-7-13 (3) NVarley(3) (lw: cl up: lft in ld appr st: sn hdd: rdn to disp ld over 1f out: no ex wl ins fnl f)....nk **2**
3048* Veshca Lady (IRE) **(57)***(61) (EWeymes)* 2-8-12 JFanning(1) (chsd ldrs: rdn over 2f out: kpt on: nt pce to chal)....¾ **3**
2855* Alfayza **(66)***(65) (JDBethell)* 2-9-7 JFortune(4) (a.p: effrt 3f out: r.o one pce)....2 **4**
2852[6] Craignairn **(56)***(52) (JBerry)* 2-8-4 (7) PFessey(5) (cl up tl carried wd & lost pl appr st: hdwy 3f out: wknd fnl f)....1¼ **5**
*2924** China Castle **(64)***(56) (PCHaslam)* 2-9-5 MTebbutt(6) (lw: led tl rn wd & lost pl appr st: n.d after)....2 **6**

11/8 Magic Lake (Evens-6/4), **9/2** Alfayza, China Castle, **6/1** Veshca Lady (IRE), **9/1** SILENT SOPRANO, **16/1** Craignairn, CSF £20.33 TOTE £12.70: £4.50 £1.70 (£12.60) OWNER Mr Jim Blair (BISHOP AUCKLAND) BRED Mrs Evelyn Cunningham 6 Rn 1m 31.6 (5.60) SF: -/-/7/11/-/2

3310

EDMONDS H'CAP (0-70) (3-Y.O) (Class E) £3,126.00 (£948.00: £464.00: £222.00)
7f 15y Stalls: High GOING minus 0.31 sec per fur (GF) 3-15 (3-17)

3125[4] **Legal Issue (IRE) (62)***(75) (SirMarkPrescott)* 3-9-3 WWoods(5) (lw: in tch: hdwy u.p 2f out: qcknd to ld wl ins fnl f)....— **1**
2927* Caltha **(45)***(51) (PCalver)* 3-7-11b(3) NVarley(3) (b.hind: led: wl clr ent st: hdd & no ex wl ins fnl f)....3 **2**
3119[4] Tinklers Folly **(47)***(52) (DenysSmith)* 3-8-2 JFanning(4) (chsd ldrs tl rdn & btn over 2f out: n.d)....½ **3**
3121[4] Southern Dominion **(62)***(64) (MJohnston)* 3-9-3 TWilliams(2) (a chsng ldrs: rdn 3f out: one pce)....1¼ **4**
3172[6] Persian Fayre **(66)***(68) (JBerry)* 3-9-0 (7) PFessey(7) (in tch: rdn 3f out: no imp)....s.h **5**
3172[2] Mister Westsound **(60)***(54)*(Fav)*(MissLAPerratt)* 3-9-1b DeanMcKeown(6) (lw: s.s: hrd rdn over 2f out: n.d)....3½ **6**

3257* Achill Princess **(43)***(32) (WTKemp)* 3-7-9 (3) 5x DWright(1) (lw: nvr wnt pce) 2½ 7

2/1 Mister Westsound, **3/1** LEGAL ISSUE (IRE), **11/2** Southern Dominion, **8/1** Tinklers Folly (6/1-9/1), Achill Princess, **9/1** Caltha, **10/1** Persian Fayre, CSF £26.07 TOTE £2.70: £2.20 £3.30 (£14.00) OWNER Cheveley Park Stud (NEWMARKET) BRED Naver Enterprises Ltd 7 Rn

1m 29.1 (3.10) SF: 40/16/17/29/33/19/-

3311 ROYAL SCOTS H'CAP (0-70) (3-Y.O+) (Class E) £3,139.00 (£952.00: £466.00: £223.00)

1m 4f 31y Stalls: High GOING minus 0.31 sec per fur (GF) 3-45 (3-45)

3122[3] **Lord Advocate (30)***(41) (DANolan)* 7-8-4b VHalliday(3) (mde most: drvn along 3f out: eased towards fin) .... — 1
2396[7] Thisonesforalice **(36)***(45) (JSGoldie)* 7-8-3 (7) PFessey(1) (chsd ldrs: hdwy 3f out: ev ch over 1f out: edgd rt & nt qckn) 1¼ 2
2980[4] Acquittal (IRE) **(59)***(68)*(Fav)*(JRFanshawe)* 3-9-6v(3) NVarley(4) (lw: chsd ldrs: rdn appr st: styd on towards fin) ....½ 3
3114[5] Milngavie (IRE) **(31)***(32) (MJohnston)* 5-8-5b TWilliams(2) (lw: w wnr tl wknd 3f out)....6 4
573[6] Spirituelle **(60)***(49) (JJO'Neill)* 3-9-10 JFortune(5) (b.off hind: a outpcd & last)....9 5

15/8 Acquittal (IRE), **5/2** Thisonesforalice, **3/1** Milngavie (IRE), **5/1** LORD ADVOCATE, **20/1** Spirituelle, CSF £16.24 TOTE £5.70: £2.10 £2.10 (£6.90) OWNER Mrs J. McFadyen-Murray (WISHAW) BRED London Thoroughbred Services Ltd 5 Rn

2m 39.2 (6.70) SF: 21/25/38/12/19
WEIGHT FOR AGE 3yo-10lb

3312 SALAMANCA (S) STKS (2-Y.O) (Class F) £2,703.00 (£758.00: £369.00)

5f Stalls: High GOING minus 0.31 sec per fur (GF) 4-15 (4-21)

3008[3] **Spirito Libro (USA) (64)***(58+)*(Fav)*(SirMarkPrescott)* 2-8-6 WWoods(1) (sn outpcd: hdwy ½-wy: led ins fnl f: sn clr).... — 1
3124[4] Don't Tell Anyone **(52)***(50) (JBerry)* 2-8-4b(7) PFessey(4) (lw: led to ½-wy: hung lft: kpt on same pce)....4 2
3018[9] Jenny's Charmer *(49) (SEKettlewell)* 2-8-11 JFortune(3) (cl up: slt ld ½-wy: hdd & wknd ins fnl f) ....½ 4
3253[2] Society Sue (IRE) **(60)** *(RonaldThompson)* 2-8-6 SDWilliams(2) (Withdrawn not under Starter's orders: ref to ent stalls) .... **W**

8/11 SPIRITO LIBRO (USA) (Evens-11/10), **4/1** Society Sue (IRE), **9/2** Don't Tell Anyone (3/1-5/1), **6/1** Jenny's Charmer (7/2-7/1), CSF £2.42 TOTE £1.10 (£1.10) OWNER Mrs Timothy Rooney (NEWMARKET) BRED T. J. Rooney 3 Rn

61.4 secs (3.70) SF: 2/-/-/-
Bt in 6,400 gns

3313 PERGODA APPRENTICE H'CAP (0-70) (3-Y.O+) (Class F) £2,913.00 (£818.00: £399.00)

5f Stalls: High GOING minus 0.31 sec per fur (GF) 4-45 (4-46)

3252[2] **Cheeky Chappy (34)***(49) (DWChapman)* 4-7-9b DarrenMoffatt(1) (lw: racd alone stands' side: w ldrs: led 2f out: clr fnl f: r.o wl) .... — 1
3252* Serious Hurry **(54)***(50) (RMMcKellar)* 7-8-8b(7) 7x NKinnon(8) (disp ld 3f: edgd lft & kpt on one pce)....6 2
3221[10] Gondo **(46)***(41) (EJAlston)* 8-8-2 (5) JEdmunds(7) (lw: chsd ldrs: hdwy u.p over 1f out: nt qckn ins fnl f) ....nk 3
2997[11] Kenesha (IRE) **(50)***(42) (DANolan)* 5-8-11b NVarley(3) (chsd ldrs: rdn ½-wy: styd on)....1 4
2997[2] Just Bob **(67)***(59)*(Fav)*(SEKettlewell)* 6-9-9 (5) GFaulkner(4) (lw: s.s: hdwy 2f out: nt rch ldrs)s.h 5
3256[2] Ramborette **(47)***(38) (DenysSmith)* 3-8-5 CTeague(10) (disp ld 3f: grad wknd)....nk 6
2997[6] Sunday Mail Too (IRE) **(36)***(19) (MissLAPerratt)* 3-7-3v(5) JBramhill(2) (prom over 3f) 2½ 7
1972[10] Daily Starshine (IRE) **(54)***(27) (JBerry)* 3-8-7b(5) CLowther(9) (s.i.s: rdn & no imp fr ½-wy) 3 8
Bruz **(36)***(8) (WTKemp)* 4-7-8 (3) PFessey(5) (sn outpcd & bhd)....nk 9
2997[10] Uppance **(32)** *(DANolan)* 7-7-7 DWright(6) (in tch: rdn ½-wy: sn wknd) 2½ 10

LONG HANDICAP Uppance 7-0

2/1 Just Bob, **7/2** Serious Hurry, **9/2** Ramborette, **13/2** CHEEKY CHAPPY (9/2-7/1), **10/1** Daily Starshine (IRE), **12/1** Kenesha (IRE), Gondo, **16/1** Sunday Mail Too (IRE), **50/1** Bruz, **66/1** Uppance, CSF £28.62 CT £247.72 TOTE £8.30: £1.90 £1.30 £2.20 (£10.80) Trio £91.00 OWNER Mrs Jeanne Chapman (YORK) BRED Ian W. Glenton 10 Rn

59.0 secs (1.30) SF: 31/32/23/24/41/17/-/6/-/-
WEIGHT FOR AGE 3yo-3lb
T/Plpt: £139.70 (56.39 Tckts). T/Qdpt: £11.30 (4.4 Tckts). AA

3079-LINGFIELD (L-H)
Thursday August 24th (Turf Good to firm, AWT Standard)
WEATHER: warm WIND: almost nil

3314
BRITVIC SOFT DRINKS CLAIMING STKS (2-Y.O) (Class F) £3,149.00 (£874.00: £419.00)
6f Stalls: High GOING minus 0.34 sec per fur (GF) 2-00 (2-02)

2666* **Little Noggins (IRE)** *(72)*(Fav)*(CADwyer)* 2-8-6 (3) JStack(12) (w ldr: led 4f out: rdn out) ......— 1
3064[9] Arctic Romancer (IRE) **(78)***(79) (GLewis)* 2-9-3 PaulEddery(4) (lw: led 2f: ev ch fnl 2f: r.o) .....½ 2
3054* Times of Times (IRE) **(68)***(68) (DJSCosgrove)* 2-8-8 MRimmer(7) (a.p: hrd rdn over 1f out: r.o ins fnl f)........½ 3
3054[3] Mrs Nevermind *(49) (GLMoore)* 2-7-13 JFEgan(11) (hld up: rdn over 3f out: unable qckn)......4 4
3120[2] Moi Canard **(72)***(57) (JBerry)* 2-8-9 JCarroll(6) (hld up: rdn over 2f out: one pce) ....½ 5
2998[3] Silver Harrow **(72)***(45) (SirMarkPrescott)* 2-8-7 GDuffield(1) (prom 4f).........4 6
1282* Lunar Mist *(44) (MartynMeade)* 2-8-9 VSlattery(10) (outpcd)..........1 7
1047[7] Hurricane Horn (IRE) *(41) (WRMuir)* 2-8-11 JWeaver(2) (bit bkwd: prom over 3f) 2 8
1327[W] Mindrace *(34) (KTIvory)* 2-8-4 (7) CScally(9) (leggy: a bhd) 2½ 9
3077[8] Golden Wedding *(20) (DCO'Brien)* 2-8-1 (3) DRMcCabe(5) (s.s: a bhd) 2½ 10
2382[6] Lunar Gris *(24) (JEBanks)* 2-8-8 AClark(8) (b: a bhd) ....hd 11

5/2 LITTLE NOGGINS (IRE), **11/2** Times of Times (IRE) (op 3/1), Silver Harrow, **13/2** Moi Canard, **7/1** Lunar Mist (5/1-8/1), Arctic Romancer (IRE) (4/1-15/2), **12/1** Hurricane Horn (IRE) (op 5/1), **20/1** Lunar Gris, **25/1** Mrs Nevermind, **33/1** Golden Wedding, **50/1** Mindrace, CSF £19.29 TOTE £3.30 £1.50 £2.10 £2.00 (£14.50) Trio £22.90 OWNER Mr M. E. Hall (NEWMARKET) BRED A. M. F. Persse 11 Rn 1m 11.2 (2.20) SF: 33/40/29/10/18/6/5/2/-/-/-

3315
CORONA CONDITIONS STKS (2-Y.O) (Class C) £5,703.75 (£1,822.50: £873.75)
7f 140y Stalls: Centre GOING minus 0.34 sec per fur (GF) 2-30 (2-32)

2912* **Lord of Men** *(95+)*(Fav)*(JHMGosden)* 2-9-0 LDettori(3) (mde all: shkn up 2f out: easily) ......— 1
3093* Sava River (IRE) *(78) (MRStoute)* 2-9-0 WRSwinburn(2) (lw: hld up: rdn over 2f out: no imp).8 2
2964* Baltic Dream (USA) *(65) (KRBurke)* 2-8-7 MFenton(1) (hld up: rdn over 2f out: sn wknd)........3 3

1/3 LORD OF MEN, **9/2** Sava River (IRE), **6/1** Baltic Dream (USA) (op 3/1), CSF £2.04 TOTE £1.30 (£1.50) OWNER Sheikh Mohammed (NEWMARKET) BRED Sheikh Mohammed bin Rashid al Maktoum 3 Rn 1m 31.24 (3.24) SF: 33/16/3

3316
WHITBREAD CONDITIONS STKS (3-Y.O+) (Class C) £5,302.40 (£1,961.60: £940.80: £384.00: £152.00: £59.20)
5f Stalls: High GOING minus 0.34 sec per fur (GF) 3-00 (3-01)

2671[9] **Don't Worry Me (IRE) (100)***(101) (FHLee)* 3-8-9 PaulEddery(5) (swtg: mde all: pushed out)— 1
2097[5] Wavian **(101)***(102) (RCharlton)* 3-9-2b PatEddery(6) (a.p: rdn over 2f out: unable qckn)...........2 2
3005[2] Lucky Parkes **(99)***(105) (JBerry)* 5-9-9 JCarroll(2) (lw: a.p: rdn over 2f out: one pce)..............nk 3
3191[7] Averti (IRE) **(100)***(95)*(Fav)*(WRMuir)* 4-9-0 JWeaver(4) (hld up: rdn 2f out: r.o ins fnl f)..........hd 4
3085[12] Dashing Water **(85)***(67) (IABalding)* 3-8-8 LDettori(3) (b.nr fore: b.hind: bhd fnl 3f)..........8 5
2802[7] Tafahhus **(84)***(48) (RWArmstrong)* 3-9-1 RPrice(1) (outpcd) 8 6

11/4 Averti (IRE), **3/1** DON'T WORRY ME (IRE), **100/30** Wavian, **7/2** Lucky Parkes, **14/1** Dashing Water (7/1-16/1), **33/1** Tafahhus, CSF £11.75 TOTE £3.80: £1.80 £2.20 (£8.00) OWNER Mr Michael Caveney (WILMSLOW) BRED Irish National Stud Co Ltd 6 Rn
56.3 secs (-0.70) SF: 77/78/84/74/43/24
WEIGHT FOR AGE 3yo-3lb

3317
LEVY BOARD MAIDEN STKS (3-Y.O+) (Class D) £3,732.30 (£1,112.40: £530.20: £239.10)
1m 6f Stalls: High GOING minus 0.34 sec per fur (GF) 3-30 (3-30)

2863[5] **Alaraby (IRE) (66)***(80) (IABalding)* 3-7-13 (7) MartinDwyer(4) (b.nr hind: chsd ldr 11f out: led over 1f out: rdn out) ....— 1
3130[6] Snow Valley **(78)***(84)*(Fav)*(LMCumani)* 3-8-11 LDettori(3) (led: rdn over 2f out: hdd over 1f out: unable qckn ins fnl f) ....½ 2
Mr Darcy *(CACyzer)* 3-8-11 DBiggs(2) (bhd fnl 6f: t.o) ....dist 3

30587 Estrela Castanha **(30)** *(RMFlower)* 3-8-6b AMorris(1) (bhd fnl 7f: t.o)....25 4

30/100 Snow Valley, **3/1** ALARABY (IRE) (2/1-100/30), **25/1** Mr Darcy, **66/1** Estrela Castanha, CSF £4.15 TOTE £3.60 (£1.20) OWNER Mr George Strawbridge (KINGSCLERE) BRED George Strawbridge 4 Rn
3m 4.4 (9.10) SF: 13/17/-/-

3318 STRONGBOW CIDER H'CAP (0-60) (3-Y.O) (Class F) £2,897.00 (£802.00: £383.00)

2m (Equitrack) Stalls: Low GOING minus 0.55 sec per fur (FST) 4-00 (4-02)

30292 **Claireswan (IRE) (54)***(70)*(Fav)*(SCWilliams)* 3-9-2 (3) JTate(6) (lw: chsd ldr: led over 8f out: clr over 3f out: r.o wl)....— 1
31405 Endless Fantasy **(50)***(57) (CACyzer)* 3-9-1 DBiggs(2) (lw: a.p: chsd wnr fnl 3f: no imp)....9 2
284210 Deceit the Second **(43)***(48) (GLewis)* 3-8-3b(5) MHenry(8) (lw: rdn & hdwy over 4f out: r.o one pce)....2 3
26032 Euro Forum **(56)***(58) (GLMoore)* 3-9-7 PaulEddery(7) (hld up: hrd rdn 4f out: one pce)....3 4
29192 Philmist **(53)***(53) (CWCElsey)* 3-9-4 NKennedy(9) (hdwy over 4f out: sn wknd)....2½ 5
31273 Hever Golf Lady **(55)***(52) (TJNaughton)* 3-9-6 JWeaver(1) (b: led over 7f: wknd over 3f out) 2½ 6
26366 Evaporate **(38)***(35) (APJones)* 3-7-10 (7) AmandaSanders(3) (bhd fnl 2f)....nk 7
20506 Premazing **(33)***(22) (JPearce)* 3-7-12 GBardwell(10) (lw: a bhd)....8 8
31543 Mega Tid **(53)***(27) (BAPearce)* 3-8-13 (5) DaneO'Neill(5) (bhd fnl 5f)....15 9
31533 I Remember it Well (IRE) **(42)***(6) (SirMarkPrescott)* 3-8-7 GDuffield(4) (lw: prom 10f)....10 10

5/2 CLAIRESWAN (IRE), **3/1** Hever Golf Lady, **5/1** Euro Forum, **13/2** Philmist (9/2-7/1), **10/1** I Remember it Well (IRE) (op 6/1), **14/1** Deceit the Second, Mega Tid (op 8/1), **20/1** Endless Fantasy, Premazing, **33/1** Evaporate, CSF £44.24 CT £539.79 TOTE £3.90: £1.40 £7.40 £2.60 (£96.10) Trio £562.20) OWNER Mr J. Wright (NEWMARKET) BRED Thomas Bean 10 Rn
3m 28.79 (5.29) SF: 34/21/12/22/17/16/-/-/-/-
OFFICIAL EXPLANATION **Hever Golf Lady: finished distressed.**

3319 LANSON CHAMPAGNE H'CAP (0-80) (3-Y.O+) (Class D) £4,340.70 (£1,299.60: £623.80: £285.90)

7f (Equitrack) Stalls: Low GOING minus 0.55 sec per fur (FST) 4-30 (4-33)

31825 **Able Choice (IRE) (70)***(79) (RWArmstrong)* 5-9-6 LDettori(6) (hdwy over 3f out: rdn over 2f out: led wl ins fnl f: r.o wl)....— 1
322215 Sooty Tern **(47)***(55) (JMBradley)* 8-7-11 GBardwell(3) (led 1f: led over 3f out tl wl ins fnl f: r.o)....½ 2
31893 Vindaloo **(74)***(74)*(Fav)*(JLHarris)* 3-9-5 JWeaver(13) (lw: led 6f out to 5f out: rdn 3f out: unable qckn)....3½ 3
31723 Bogart **(57)***(51) (CWFairhurst)* 4-8-7 PaulEddery(8) (lw: a.p: rdn over 3f out: one pce)....2½ 4
236311 Anegre (IRE) **(57)***(48) (SDow)* 3-7-9 (7) ADaly(12) (lw: led 5f out tl over 3f out: wknd over 1f out)....1¼ 5
30727 Ring the Chief **(56)***(47) (RAkehurst)* 3-8-1 JQuinn(5) (lw: hld up: rdn over 2f out: one pce)....hd 6
9114 Mr Frosty **(66)***(56) (WJarvis)* 3-8-6 (5) MHenry(1) (bit bkwd: hld up: rdn over 2f out: one pce)..nk 7
311211 Here Comes Risky **(78)***(66) (MJohnston)* 3-9-9 JCarroll(10) (lw: hdwy over 3f out: wknd over 2f out)....1¼ 8
31773 Our Shadee (USA) **(59)***(46) (KTIvory)* 5-8-2v(7) CScally(7) (lw: bhd fnl 3f)....nk 9
5464 Kintwyn **(74)***(57) (CCElsey)* 5-9-10 WNewnes(9) (b: b.hind: a bhd)....1¾ 10
25855 Mustn't Grumble (IRE) **(77)***(53) (WSCunningham)* 5-9-13 GDuffield(11) (a bhd)....3 11
43310 Flowing Ocean **(78)***(51) (MissGayKelleway)* 5-10-0 RCochrane(4) (bit bkwd: a bhd)....1¼ 12

4/1 Vindaloo, **11/2** Sooty Tern, **13/2** Flowing Ocean (4/1-7/1), **7/1** Bogart, **15/2** Here Comes Risky, **8/1** Mr Frosty, **9/1** Ring the Chief, **10/1** Mustn't Grumble (IRE) (7/1-12/1), Our Shadee (USA), Kintwyn, **16/1** ABLE CHOICE (IRE), **20/1** Anegre (IRE), CSF £102.84 CT £397.76 TOTE £26.30: £6.70 £2.70 £1.30 (£64.30) Trio £56.30 OWNER Dr Cornel Li (NEWMARKET) BRED Rathasker Stud in Ireland 12 Rn
1m 25.57 (2.57) SF: 28/4/18/-/-/-/-/10/-/6/2/-
WEIGHT FOR AGE 3yo-5lb

3320 HEINEKEN LAGER H'CAP (0-80) (3-Y.O+) (Class D) £3,799.90 (£1,133.20: £540.60: £244.30)

1m 3f 106y Stalls: High GOING minus 0.34 sec per fur (GF) 5-00 (5-01)

30613 **Contrafire (IRE) (63)***(75) (WJarvis)* 3-8-13 (3) SSanders(4) (lw: 3rd st: led 3f out: rdn out)....— 1
2196* Lucky Coin **(68)***(77) (CEBrittain)* 3-9-7 BDoyle(5) (2nd st: ev ch over 1f out: unable qckn)....2 2
29544 Gloriana **(75)***(82) (LadyHerries)* 3-10-0 JQuinn(2) (lw: 5th st: rdn over 2f out: one pce)....1¾ 3
2842* Mister O'Grady (IRE) **(49)***(53)*(Fav)*(RAkehurst)* 4-8-11 JWeaver(6) (4th st: rdn over 2f out: one pce)....1¾ 4

3184* Marchant Ming (IRE) **(60)***(62)*(Fav)*(MAJarvis)* 3-8-13b 5x PRobinson(7) (led over 8f) 2 5
3169[4] Larn Fort **(59)***(52) (CWFairhurst)* 5-9-7v RCochrane(3) (lw: 6th st: a bhd) 6 6
3081[3] Forest Mill **(60)***(53) (DWPArbuthnot)* 3-8-13 AClark(1) (b.hind: lw: a bhd) ....s.h 7

100/30 Mister O'Grady (IRE), Marchant Ming (IRE), **7/2** Lucky Coin, **11/2** Gloriana (4/1-6/1), **6/1** CONTRAFIRE (IRE), **12/1** Larn Fort (8/1-14/1), **16/1** Forest Mill, CSF £24.82 TOTE £8.90: £4.80 £2.40 (£14.60) OWNER Miss V. R. Jarvis (NEWMARKET) BRED Thoroughbred Trust in Ireland 7 Rn 2m 27.22 (5.22) SF: 36/38/43/23/23/22/14
WEIGHT FOR AGE 3yo-9lb
T/Jkpt: 9,476.30 (0.28 Tckts); £9,609.79 to Newmarket 25/8/95. T/Plpt: £152.60 (91.56 Tckts). T/Qdpt: £63.70 (2.9 Tckts). AK

0137a-LES LANDES (Jersey) (L-H)
Sunday August 13th (Good)

3321a ST. HELIER GARAGES H'CAP (3-Y.O+) £900.00 **1m 6f** 4-40 (4-44)

2721a[2] **Fortensky (USA)** *(CMcCready,Jersey)* 5-10-12 RMcGhin ....— 1
361[5] Wollboll *(JSOArthur,Jersey)* 5-9-5 VSmith 1 2
Time to Move (IRE) *(PDJones)* 5-9-4 MrJCulloty 6 3

Tote £7.00 (£1.40) OWNER F Goody & J G P Wheeler (JERSEY) 3 Rn 3m 20.0 SF: -/-/-

3322a KENSINGTON SPORTING PAINTINGS H'CAP (3-Y.O+) £720.00 **1m 4f** 5-50 (5-55)

2721a[3] **Our Topsie** *(JSOArthur,Jersey)* 8-9-7 VSmith ....— 1
800a[2] Time Lapse *(JSOArthur,Jersey)* 6-10-10 RMcGhin 1 2
Avanti Xiquet *(RLePennec,Jersey)* 4-9-11 MrDCuthbert 20 3
2720a[4] Reality Park *(PDJones)* 4-10-12 MrJCulloty 10 4

Tote £4.20 (£2.00) OWNER Mr K. Aston 4 Rn 2m 48.0 SF: -/-/-/-

3199a-DEAUVILLE (France) (R-H)
Tuesday August 15th (Good)

3323a PRIX GUILLAUME D'ORNANO (Gp 2) (3-Y.O) £35,928.00 (£14,371.00: £7,186.00: £3,593.00) **1m 2f** 3-00 (3-00)

2560a[2] **Montjoy (USA)** *(117) (PFICole)* 3-8-11 TQuinn (rcd in 3rd: rdn to ld 1f out: r.o wl u.p) ....— 1
2763[2] Warning Shadows (IRE) *(114) (CEBrittain)* 3-8-8 BDoyle (plld early: mid div: rdn to chal ins fnl f: r.o) ....nk 2
2889a* Silent Warrior (IRE) *(115) (JEHammond,France)* 3-8-11 CAsmussen (hld up: rdn 2f out: styd on fnl f) 1 3
2560a* Royal Solo (IRE) *(120) (PWChapple-Hyam)* 3-9-2 BThomson (trckd ldr: led 2f out: hdd 1f out: one pce) ....s.nk 4
3038a[2] Sharpest Image (IRE) *(114) (RCollet,France)* 3-8-11 OPeslier (rr early: r.o u.p 2f out: nrst fin) ½ 5
2560a[3] Vaguely Gay *(113) (MmeCHead,France)* 3-8-11 ODoleuze (led tl hdd 2f out: wknd) ....½ 6
1115a[3] Angel Falls (FR) *(111) (AFabre,France)* 3-8-11 TJarnet (hld up: nvr plcd to chal) 1 7

P-M 8.00F: 3.40F 3.80F (SF 38.80F) OWNER Sir George Meyrick (WHATCOMBE) BRED Anthony M. Warrender 7 Rn 2m 11.1 (9.50) SF: -/-/-/-/-/-/-

3323a-DEAUVILLE (France) (R-H)
Wednesday August 16th (Good)

3324a PRIX DE LA VALLEE D'AUGE (Listed) (2-Y.O) £16,766.00 (£5,748.00: £3,593.00) **5f** 1-50 (1-51)

3086[2] **Maggi For Margaret** *(96) (MRChannon)* 2-8-8 RHughes ....— 1
3100[2] Prince Aslia *(97) (MJohnston)* 2-8-11 MRoberts ....¾ 2
3037a[2] Kistena (FR) *(89) (MmeCHead,France)* 2-8-8 ODoleuze 1½ 3

P-M 5.90F: 2.60F 2.00F (SF 11.70F) OWNER Mr Michael Foy (UPPER LAMBOURN) BRED Brook Stud Ltd 7 Rn 59.1 secs (3.30) SF: -/-/-

2891a-CURRAGH (Newbridge, Ireland) (R-H)
Saturday August 19th (Good to firm)

3325a DESMOND STKS (Gp 3) (3-Y.O+) £16,250.00 (£4,750.00: £2,250.00: £750.00) **1m** 3-00 (3-01)

2893a3 **Mr Martini (IRE)** *(114) (CEBrittain)* 5-9-4 BDoyle (fin 3rd, btn hd & sh. hd: plcd 1st) ....— 1
2565a2 Ivory Frontier (IRE) *(111) (JSBolger,Ireland)* 5-9-0 KJManning (fin 1st by hd: plcd 2nd) 2
Timarida (IRE) *(107)*(Fav)*(JOxx,Ireland)* 3-8-5 CRoche (fin 2nd btn hd: plcd 3rd)...................... 3
24442 Dance Turn *(108) (RWArmstrong)* 4-9-0 JReid (btn approx 1l)..¾ 4

5/4 Timarida (IRE), **6/4** Dance Turn, **6/1** Ivory Frontier (IRE), MR MARTINI (IRE), Tote £11.90: £3.70 £3.00 (£22.90) OWNER Parrot Racing (NEWMARKET) BRED Mrs W. Hanson 5 Rn
1m 37.1 (1.10) SF: -/-/-/-

3326a ROYAL WHIP STKS (Gp 3) (3-Y.O+) £16,250.00 (£4,750.00: £2,250.00) **1m 2f** 4-30 (4-44)

2217a7 **Shemaran (IRE)** *(121) (JOxx,Ireland)* 3-8-13 JPMurtagh ....— 1
2563a2 Russian Snows (IRE) *(111)*(Fav)*(JOxx,Ireland)* 3-8-5 ow1 CRoche ....½ 2
Al Mohaajir (USA) *(113) (JSBolger,Ireland)* 4-9-1 KJManning ....½ 3

11/10 Russian Snows (IRE), **5/1** SHEMARAN (IRE), Al Mohaajir (USA), Tote £6.70: £3.20 £1.10 (£4.50) OWNER Aga Khan BRED H.H. Aga Khan Studs S.C. 5 Rn 2m 2.9 (0.60) SF: -/-/-

3324a-DEAUVILLE (France) (R-H)
Saturday August 19th (Good)

3327a PRIX GONTAUT-BIRON (Gp 3) (4-Y.O+) £26,347.00 (£9,581.00: £4,790.00) **1m 2f** 2-10 (2-11)

898a5 **Hernando (FR)** *(122) (JEHammond,France)* 5-8-9 CAsmussen ....— 1
1398a* Freedom Cry *(129) (AFabre,France)* 4-9-4 OPeslier 1½ 2
898a10 Millkom *(118) (J-CRouget,France)* 4-8-9 J-RDubosc 1 3
27633 Erin Bird (FR) *(116) (PWChapple-Hyam)* 4-8-8 BThomson (btn approx 3¼l) 5

P-M 2.30F: 1.40F 1.60F 1.80F (6.40F) OWNER Mr S. S. Niarchos BRED S. Niarchos in France 9 Rn
2m 7.3 (5.70) SF: -/-/-/-

3328a CRITERIUM DU FONDS EUROPEEN DE L'ELEVAGE (Listed) (2-Y.O) £59,880.00 (£29,940.00: £17,964.00) **6f 110y** 3-10 (0-31)

2779* **Rabican (IRE)** *(87+) (GCBravery)* 2-8-11 MHills ....— 1
Mayoumbe *(86) (JEPease,France)* 2-8-11 CAsmussen ....nk 2
Princess Bilbao *(80) (NClement,France)* 2-8-8 ESaint-Martin 1½ 3
Woodbury Lad (USA) *(60) (WRMuir)* 2-8-11 TIves (btn approx 9l) 7

P-M 6.00F: 2.70F 2.10F 3.80F (20.30F) OWNER Mr Michael Hwang (NEWMARKET) BRED Charles O'Connor 9 Rn 1m 20.0 SF: -/-/-/-

3327a-DEAUVILLE (France) (R-H)
Sunday August 20th (Good)

3329a PRIX KERGORLAY (Gp 2) (3-Y.O+) £35,928.00 (£14,371.00: £7,186.00: £3,593.00) **1m 7f** 2-00 (1-59)

2898a2 **Peckinpah's Soul (FR)** *(118) (DSmaga,France)* 3-8-5bow1 FHead (2nd early: led after 7f: qcknd cl over 1f out: unchal)...— 1
2890a5 Nononito (FR) *(116) (JLesbordes,France)* 4-9-4 GMosse (trckd ldr thrght: hrd rdn 2f out: nt rch wnr) 2½ 2
1239a3 Epaphos (GER) *(115) (PBary,France)* 5-9-4 DBoeuf (last st: styd on fnl f)...........................1½ 3
Lac Ladoga *(114) (H-APantall,France)* 4-9-4 JBoisnard (4th st: nvr plcd to chal) ....nk 4

Lafille du General (FR) *(101) (PLenogue,France)* 4-9-1 FSanchez (led 7f: 3rd & rdn st: btn 2f out) 10 **5**

P-M 3.40F: 1.50F 1.20F (7.60F) OWNER Ecurie Leader BRED Manita Investment Corporation 5 Rn
3m 18.7 SF: -/-/-/-/-

3330a PRIX MORNY PIAGET (Gp 1) (2-Y.O C & F) £95,808.00 (£38,323.00: £19,162.00: £9,581.00) **6f** 3-00 (0-30)

2347* **Tagula (IRE)** *(106) (IABalding)* 2-9-0 WRSwinburn (rcd in 5th: prog to ld over 1f out: r.o wl fnl f) ....— **1**
3037a* With Fascination (USA) *(100) (JEPease,France)* 2-8-11 CAsmussen (trckd ldr: rdn over 1f out: r.o fnl f) 1 **2**
2726a³ Barricade (USA) *(101) (AFabre,France)* 2-9-0 TJarnet (hld up; rdn over 2f out: r.o)....¾ **3**
1838² Russian Revival (USA) *(99) (PWChapple-Hyam)* 2-9-0 BThomson (led tl hdd by wnr: no ex) .1 **4**
2726a² Shining Molly (FR) *(88) (PBary,France)* 2-8-11 OPeslier (swtg: 4th early: rdn 2f out: no imp)..3 **5**
2347³ World Premier *(91) (CEBrittain)* 2-9-0 BDoyle (2nd early: rdn 2f out: wknd) ....s.h **6**
2726a* Lucky Lionel (USA) *(85) (RHannon)* 2-9-0 JReid (m.n.s) 2 **7**
2896a* Sangria (USA) *(66) (JFellows,France)* 2-8-11 GGuignard (a bhd) 6 **8**

P-M 9.70F: 2.10F 1.40F 1.50F (17.40F) OWNER Mr Robert Hitchins (KINGSCLERE) BRED Sean and Patrick Twomey 8 Rn
1m 11.6 (3.10) SF: -/-/-/-/-/-/-/-

3331a COUPE DU FONDS EUROPEEN DE L'ELEVAGE (Listed) (3-Y.O F) £59,880.00 (£29,940.00: £17,964.00) **1m 2f** 3-30 (3-33)

2561a³ **Balanka (IRE)** *(115) (AdeRoyerDupre,France)* 3-8-12 GMosse ....— **1**
2614³ Tillandsia (IRE) *(115) (DRLoder)* 3-8-12 LDettori ....hd **2**
3040a² Take Liberties *(112) (AFabre,France)* 3-8-12 TJarnet 2 **3**
2763⁴ Western Reel (USA) *(98) (PFICole)* 3-8-12 TQuinn (btn approx 11¼l) **11**

P-M 3.90F: 1.60F 1.70F 1.40F (7.60F) OWNER Aga Khan BRED H.H. Aga Khan Studs S.C. 12 Rn
2m 11.9 (10.30) SF: -/-/-/-

OVREVOLL (Oslo, Norway) (L-H)
Sunday August 20th (Good)

3332a MARIT SVEAAS MINNELOP (Listed) (3-Y.O+) £23,629.00 (£11,815.00: £5,671.00) **1m 1f** 2-40 (2-40)

Philidor *(98) (ALund,Norway)* 6-9-6 FDiaz ....— **1**
Regal Parade *(93) (OStenstrom,Sweden)* 11-9-2 FJohansson ....½ **2**
Dulford Lad *(97) (JFretheim,Norway)* 4-9-6 MSantos ....hd **3**
793⁹ Our Rita *(70) (DrJDScargill)* 6-8-7 DHolland (btn over 14l) **9**

Tote 22.30Kr: (82.60Kr) OWNER Stall Bonne Nuit BRED John A. Jones Morgan 10 Rn
1m 48.8 SF: -/-/-/-

2762-GOODWOOD (R-H)
Friday August 25th (Good to firm)
WEATHER: sunny WIND: mod half against

3333 ROOKWOOD APPRENTICE H'CAP (0-70) (3-Y.O+) (Class E) £3,720.00 (£1,110.00: £530.00: £240.00) **5f** Stalls: Low GOING minus 0.13 sec per fur (G) 5-20 (5-22)

3205³ **Paley Prince (USA) (59)***(65) (MDIUsher)* 9-9-4 (3) CAdamson(5) (hld up: hdwy over 1f out: led wl ins fnl f: r.o)....— **1**
3055⁵ Hever Golf Star **(67)***(70)*(Fav)*(TJNaughton)* 3-9-12 JDSmith(2) (lw: b.off hind: sn led: hdd wl ins fnl f: one pce)....1 **2**
3134⁸ Domicksky **(57)***(60) (MRChannon)* 7-9-0 (5) DSweeney(6) (a.p: ev ch 1f out: one pce)....hd **3**
3123² Lugana Vision **(51)***(50) (RHarris)* 3-8-7b(3) ADaly(7) (chsd ldrs: rdn over 1f out: one pce)....1 **4**
3065¹⁰ Green Golightly (USA) **(57)***(52) (DAWilson)* 4-9-5 LNewton(4) (bhd: gd hdwy fnl f: nvr nrr) ...1½ **5**
3139¹¹ The Noble Oak (IRE) **(47)***(38) (MJBolton)* 7-8-6 (3) GMitchell(3) (spd over 3f)....1¼ **6**
2987² Bangles **(64)***(54) (LordHuntingdon)* 5-9-7 (5) AimeeCook(10) (chsd ldrs: rdn over 1f out: wknd ins fnl f)....nk **7**
3123⁴ Tee-Emm **(39)***(25) (PHowling)* 5-7-10 (5) DebbieBiggs(8) (prom: ev ch 2f out: wknd ent fnl f).1¼ **8**
·2837³ Flashing Sabre **(52)***(31) (JBerry)* 3-8-8 (3) PRoberts(9) (prom: ev ch 2f out: wknd over 1f out) ..2 **9**

27449 La Thuile **(34)***(5) (MDIUsher)* 3-7-7b MBaird(1) (b: a bhd) 2½ **10**
LONG HANDICAP La Thuile 7-3

9/4 Hever Golf Star, **7/2** Bangles, **11/2** Lugana Vision (4/1-6/1), **7/1** Flashing Sabre, **8/1** PALEY PRINCE (USA) (op 5/1), **11/1** Domicksky (7/1-12/1), **12/1** Green Golightly (USA), Tee-Emm, **20/1** The Noble Oak (IRE), **66/1** La Thuile, CSF £26.01 CT £188.38 TOTE £10.30: £2.60 £1.70 £1.60 (£17.00) Trio £42.50 OWNER . Shirval Partners (SWINDON) BRED Larry Deaton 10 Rn
60.09 secs (3.39) SF: 34/36/29/16/21/7/23/-/-/-
WEIGHT FOR AGE 3yo-3lb

3334 GOODWOOD GOLF CLUB CONDITIONS STKS (3-Y.O+) (Class C)
£5,326.40 (£1,838.40: £879.20: £356.00)
7f Stalls: Low GOING minus 0.13 sec per fur (G) 5-50 (5-51)

30332 **Inzar (USA) (106)***(115)*(Fav)*(PFICole)* 3-9-7 TQuinn(2) (lw: chsd ldr gng wl: 2nd st: led 1f out: rdn ins fnl f: r.o) ....— **1**
31882 Indian Fly **(94)***(107) (RHannon)* 4-9-7 MTebbutt(3) (hld up in tch: 3rd st: hrd rdn 1f out: one pce) 1¼ **2**
Delta One (IRE) *(101) (IABalding)* 4-9-2 PaulEddery(1) (led: hdd 1f out: one pce) ....½ **3**
30274 Everglades (IRE) **(100)***(82) (RCharlton)* 7-9-8 PatEddery(4) (hld up: 4th st: rdn over 2f out: wknd over 1f out) 11 **4**

2/1 INZAR (USA), **5/2** Indian Fly, **3/1** Everglades (IRE), **9/2** Delta One (IRE) (9/4-5/1), CSF £6.38 TOTE £2.60 (£2.30) OWNER Prince Fahd Salman (WHATCOMBE) BRED Newgate Stud Farm Inc in USA 4 Rn
1m 27.41 (3.01) SF: 59/56/50/31
WEIGHT FOR AGE 3yo-5lb

3335 HORSE RACING ABROAD NURSERY CLAIMING H'CAP (2-Y.O) (Class E)
£3,460.00 (£1,030.00: £490.00: £220.00)
5f Stalls: Low GOING minus 0.13 sec per fur (G) 6-20 (6-22)

30772 **Chemcast (63)***(61) (BJMeehan)* 2-8-6 TQuinn(1) (mde all: rdn ins fnl f: r.o) ....— **1**
30646 Miss Bigwig **(78)***(72)*(Fav)*(JBerry)* 2-9-0 (7) PRoberts(3) (a.p: ev ch ins fnl f: one pce) 1¼ **2**
306411 Imp Express (IRE) **(76)***(70) (GMMoore)* 2-9-5 MTebbutt(5) (outpcd early: hdwy 2f out: n.m.r over 1f out: swtchd lft: r.o fnl f) ....s.h **3**
27068 Where's Margaret **(69)***(50) (GLewis)* 2-8-12 PaulEddery(7) (spd over 3f) 4 **4**
29828 Magic Imp (IRE) **(63)***(44) (WJMusson)* 2-8-6v JReid(6) (spd over 3f) ....s.h **5**
32909 Fiddles Delight **(50)***(20) (MRChannon)* 2-7-7v NAdams(4) (dwlt: a bhd) 3½ **6**
LONG HANDICAP Fiddles Delight 7-5

9/4 Miss Bigwig, **7/2** Where's Margaret, **9/2** Imp Express (IRE) (op 3/1), **5/1** CHEMCAST, **6/1** Magic Imp (IRE), **14/1** Fiddles Delight, CSF £15.22 TOTE £4.60: £1.80 £1.90 (£5.90) OWNER Mrs Kim Parker (UPPER LAMBOURN) BRED C. R. and V. M. Withers 6 Rn 61.49 secs (4.79) SF: -/9/7/-/-

3336 HUDSON DENTAL EQUIPMENT H'CAP (0-95) (3-Y.O+) (Class C)
£6,807.50 (£2,060.00: £1,005.00: £477.50)
1m 4f Stalls: Low GOING minus 0.13 sec per fur (G) 6-50 (6-50)

23488 **Jandeel (IRE) (86)***(100) (ACStewart)* 3-9-10 MRoberts(5) (lw: b: b.hind: chsd ldr: 2nd st: led 3f out: rdn over 1f out: r.o wl) ....— **1**
3189* Progression **(70)***(81)*(Fav)*(PCHaslam)* 4-8-13b(5) 5x MBaird(2) (s.i.s: hld up: 4th st: hrd rdn over 1f out: r.o one pce) 2 **2**
25258 Meant to Be **(73)***(83) (LadyHerries)* 5-9-7 PatEddery(1) (led: hdd 3f out: rdn over 1f out: one pce) 1¼ **3**
30669 Danjing (IRE) **(86)***(95) (PFICole)* 3-9-10 TQuinn(4) (5th st: rdn over 3f out: r.o one pce fnl f) ..½ **4**
2599* Dancing Sensation (USA) **(70)***(78) (RAkehurst)* 8-9-4 JReid(3) (chsd ldrs: 3rd st: rdn over 1f out: wknd ins fnl f) ....¾ **5**

6/5 Progression (Evens-5/4), **100/30** JANDEEL (IRE), **9/2** Dancing Sensation (USA), **9/1** Danjing (IRE) (op 6/1), **10/1** Meant to Be, CSF £7.10 TOTE £4.50: £2.20 £1.60 (£3.50) OWNER Sheikh Ahmed Al Maktoum (NEWMARKET) BRED Biddestone Stud 5 Rn
2m 37.48 (5.48) SF: 62/53/55/57/50
WEIGHT FOR AGE 3yo-10lb

3337 HALL AND COMPANY BUILDING MATERIALS SUPPLIER MEDIAN AUCTION MAIDEN STKS (2-Y.O) (Class E) £3,980.00 (£1,190.00: £570.00:£260.00)
6f Stalls: Low GOING minus 0.13 sec per fur (G) 7-20 (7-21)

31867 **Astuti (IRE)** *(69)*(Fav)*(APJarvis)* 2-8-9 PatEddery(5) (lw: a.p: led over 1f out: hrd rdn u.p fnl f: r.o wl) ....— **1**

690[7] Extra Hour (IRE) *(71) (WRMuir)* 2-9-0 CRutter(6) (hld up: plld hrd: hdwy 2f out: rdn over 1f out: r.o) 1 **2**
3157[3] Dragon's Back (IRE) *(70) (MrsJCecil)* 2-9-0 PaulEddery(4) (lw: prom: rdn & outpcd 3f out: rdn over 1f out: r.o fnl f: fin 4th, hd: plcd 3rd) **3**
South Pagoda (IRE) *(70) (PWChapple-Hyam)* 2-9-0 JReid(10) (unf: scope: bit bkwd: hdwy whn sltly hmpd 3f out: rdn over 1f out: r.o one pce fnl f: fin 5th, nk: plcd 4th) **4**
Philistar *(69) (JMPEustace)* 2-9-0 RCochrane(3) (w'like: bit bkwd: s.s: rr: rdn 3f out: styd on fnl f: fin 6th, hd: plcd 5th) **5**
2940[8] Burj *(67) (NAGraham)* 2-9-0 AMcGlone(7) (prom: sltly outpcd over 2f out: r.o one pce fnl f)...¾ **7**
Sihafi (USA) *(63) (EALDunlop)* 2-9-0 RHills(9) (unf: scope: plld hrd: prom: led over 3f out: hdd over 1f out: eased whn btn ins fnl f) 1¾ **8**
3053[4] Beldray Park (IRE) *(23) (MrsALMKing)* 2-9-0 JQuinn(2) (led over 3f: sn wknd)....15 **9**
3025[5] Stronz (IRE) *(71) (RAkehurst)* 2-9-0 AClark(1) (hdwy & swtchd rt 3f out: hrd rdn fnl f: r.o: fin 3rd, nk: disp: plcd last).... **0**

11/10 ASTUTI (IRE), **9/2** Dragon's Back (IRE), **7/1** Sihafi (USA), **8/1** South Pagoda (IRE) (op 4/1), **12/1** Stronz (IRE) (op 8/1), **14/1** Extra Hour (IRE), **16/1** Philistar, **33/1** Beldray Park (IRE), Burj, CSF £15.77 TOTE £2.30: £1.50 £3.40 £1.40 (£25.80) Trio £25.00 OWNER Mrs D. B. Brazier (ASTON UPTHORPE) BRED Patrick J. Power 9 Rn 1m 14.46 (4.26) SF: 23/25/24/24/23/21/17/-/25
STEWARDS' ENQUIRY Clark susp. 4-9 &11/9/95 (irresponsible riding).

3338

WEST DEAN MAIDEN STKS (3-Y.O) (Class D) £4,142.50 (£1,240.00: £595.00: £272.50)
1m 2f Stalls: Low GOING minus 0.13 sec per fur (G) 7-50 (7-53)

2944[3] **Najmat Alshemaal (IRE)** **(97)***(86+)*(Fav)*(MajorWRHern)* 3-8-9 RCochrane(3) (hld up in tch gng wl: 3rd st: qcknd to ld 1f out: sn clr: easily)....— **1**
Mayreau *(82) (GHarwood)* 3-8-9 AClark(1) (chsd ldr: 2nd st: rdn 2f out: ev ch 1f out: one pce)2½ **2**
1852[11] United Force (IRE) **(86)***(87) (PWChapple-Hyam)* 3-9-0 JReid(4) (led: rdn over 1f out: hdd 1f out: one pce)....hd **3**
1097[13] Prophets Honour *(83) (CACyzer)* 3-9-0 DBiggs(5) (5th st: rdn over 2f out: one pce)....2½ **4**
3016[10] Suvalu (USA) **(73)***(79) (PFICole)* 3-9-0 TQuinn(6) (plld hrd: hld up: 4th st: rdn over 2f out: wknd over 1f out: eased whn btn fnl f)....2½ **5**
King of Babylon (IRE) *(76) (LadyHerries)* 3-9-0 PaulEddery(2) (leggy: bit bkwd: 6th st: rdn 3f out: no hdwy)....2 **6**

13/8 NAJMAT ALSHEMAAL (IRE) (4/5-7/4), **3/1** United Force (IRE), **5/1** Prophets Honour, **13/2** Suvalu (USA), **7/1** Mayreau, **10/1** King of Babylon (IRE), CSF £12.23 TOTE £2.00: £1.40 £2.50 (£6.10) OWNER Sheikh Ahmed Al Maktoum (LAMBOURN) BRED Darley Stud Management Co Ltd 6 Rn 2m 10.5 (5.50) SF: 39/35/40/36/32/29
T/Plpt: £18.50 (595.86 Tckts). T/Qdpt: £3.90 (40.90 Tckts). SM

2944-NEWMARKET (R-H)
Friday August 25th (Good to firm, Good fnl 8f)

WEATHER: bright & sunny WIND: fresh half bhd

3339

BLUE PETER MAIDEN STKS (2-Y.O F) (Class D) £4,971.00 (£1,488.00: £714.00: £327.00)
7f (July) Stalls: High GOING minus 0.68 sec per fur (HD) 2-00 (2-01)

3069[7] **Ruznama (USA)** *(97) (BWHills)* 2-8-11 WCarson(9) (chsd ldrs: led bel dist: rdn & r.o wl)....— **1**
Ta Rib (USA) *(95+) (EALDunlop)* 2-8-11 RHills(11) (w'like: scope: hld up: hdwy 2f out: r.o ins fnl f)....1 **2**
3069[9] Victoria Regia (IRE) *(95) (RCharlton)* 2-8-11 RHughes(16) (hld up: hdwy over 2f out: r.o wl fnl f)....hd **3**
Mezzogiorno *(94) (GWragg)* 2-8-11 MHills(2) (wl grwn: a.p: led 2f out to bel dist: rallied fnl f)nk **4**
2912[3] Threesome (USA) *(91) (LMCumani)* 2-8-11 JWeaver(10) (led over 4f: rdn & no ex ins fnl f).1¼ **5**
Inchyre *(88+) (RCharlton)* 2-8-11 SRaymont(13) (neat: dwlt: hdwy ½-wy: styd on ins fnl f) ..1¼ **6**
3069[4] Tsarnista *(84) (JLDunlop)* 2-8-11 JReid(15) (lw: prom over 5f)....1¾ **7**
3069[5] Possessive Artiste *(78) (MRStoute)* 2-8-11 WRSwinburn(18) (b.hind: in tch: no hdwy fnl 2f)2½ **8**
Lovely Prospect *(76) (RGuest)* 2-8-11 BThomson(3) (cmpt: chsd ldrs 5f)....1¼ **9**
Overruled (IRE) *(75+)*(Fav)*(DRLoder)* 2-8-11 PatEddery(14) (w'like: prom: ev ch 2f out: eased whn btn fnl f)....s.h **10**
Ship's Dancer *(75) (JLDunlop)* 2-8-11 KDarley(1) (neat: lt-f: a bhd)....s.h **11**
Ceilidh Star (IRE) *(75) (BWHills)* 2-8-11 MFenton(6) (w'like: leggy: lw: chsd ldrs 5f)....nk **12**
1525[6] Satin Secret (IRE) *(74) (JMPEustace)* 2-8-11 RCochrane(8) (prom: led over 2f out: sn hdd & wknd)....nk **13**

Angel Chimes *(74) (JEBanks)* 2-8-8 (3) JStack(4) (scope: effrt ½-wy: wknd wl over 1f out).....hd 14
32105 Steal 'Em *(70) (ABailey)* 2-8-8 (3) DWright(5) (nvr trbld ldrs)....1½ 15
Diamond Heart *(47) (HRACecil)* 2-8-11 AMcGlone(17) (cmpt: bkwd: a bhd: t.o)....10 16
2846 14 Fit To Ski *(46) (MHTompkins)* 2-8-11 PRobinson(12) (prom 4f: sn lost tch: t.o)....½ 17
17464 Conquistajade (USA) *(12) (SPCWoods)* 2-8-11 WWoods(7) (lw: rdn ½-wy: sn wl bhd: t.o) ...15 18

3/1 Overruled (IRE), **7/2** RUZNAMA (USA) (op 6/1), **4/1** Threesome (USA), **9/1** Possessive Artiste, Tsarnista (6/1-10/1), **12/1** Ta Rib (USA) (op 6/1), **16/1** Diamond Heart, Victoria Regia (IRE), **20/1** Mezzogiorno, Inchyre, Ship's Dancer, **33/1** Lovely Prospect, Satin Secret (IRE), **50/1** Ceilidh Star (IRE), Angel Chimes, Steal 'Em, Fit To Ski, Conquistajade (USA), CSF £45.70 TOTE £5.30: £1.90 £3.50 £5.30 (£12.00) Trio £131.10 OWNER Mr Hamdan Al Maktoum (LAMBOURN) BRED Shadwell Estate Co., Ltd. and Shadwell Farm Inc. 18 Rn

1m 24.46 (0.47 under 2y best) (0.06) SF: 39/37/37/36/33/30/26/20/18/17/17/17/16/16/12/-/-/-

3340 PORT OF TILBURY MAIDEN STKS (2-Y.O C & G) (Class D)

£5,049.00 (£1,512.00: £726.00: £333.00)
7f (July) Stalls: High GOING minus 0.68 sec per fur (HD) 2-35 (2-37)

15516 **Even Top (IRE)** *(78) (MHTompkins)* 2-8-11 PRobinson(8) (chsd ldr: rdn to ld ent fnl f: rdn out)....— 1
2912 10 Murheb *(75) (RWArmstrong)* 2-8-11 RHills(10) (mde most tl hdd ent fnl f: unable qckn fnl f) 1¼ 2
30102 Prize Giving *(71) (GWragg)* 2-8-11 MHills(15) (s.i.s: sn rcvrd to chse ldrs: rdn & one pce appr fnl f)....1¾ 3
Hal's Pal *(68+)(Fav)(DRLoder)* 2-8-11 PatEddery(16) (gd sort: hld up: hdwy over 2f out: rdn & kpt on one pce fnl f)....1½ 4
Dabka Dancer *(68+) (ACStewart)* 2-8-11 RCochrane(4) (str: scope: hld up: hdwy wl over 1f out: fin wl)....hd 5
26935 Statoyork *(62) (BWHills)* 2-8-11 KDarley(6) (chsd ldrs: no hdwy fnl 2f)....2½ 6
Hamlet (IRE) *(62) (MBell)* 2-8-11 MFenton(5) (w'like: leggy: chsd ldrs over 4f)....hd 7
Tirols Tyrant (IRE) *(58) (MrsASwinbank)* 2-8-11 NConnorton(7) (cmpt: scope: prom tl wknd wl over 1f out)....1½ 8
27674 Parsis (USA) *(55) (LadyHerries)* 2-8-11 WRSwinburn(12) (chsd ldrs 5f: eased whn btn appr fnl f)....1¼ 9
Well Drawn *(52) (HCandy)* 2-8-11 WNewnes(18) (w'like: leggy: in tch tl wknd fnl 3f)....1½ 10
Select Few *(52) (LMCumani)* 2-8-11 OUrbina(3) (wl grwn: prom 5f: wknd qckly)....1¼ 11
Fursan (USA) *(49) (NAGraham)* 2-8-11 WCarson(9) (w'like: bkwd: s.s: nvr trbld ldrs)....d.h 11
Humourless *(48) (LMCumani)* 2-8-11 RPerham(17) (cmpt: bkwd: sn bhd & pushed along: no imp)....nk 13
3089 15 One Pound *(47) (BWHills)* 2-8-11 BThomson(2) (a bhd)....¾ 14
Hever Golf Eagle *(46) (TJNaughton)* 2-8-11 JWeaver(11) (w'like: scope: bkwd: bhd & rdn after 2f: nvr nr ldrs)....hd 15
Spanking Roger *(43) (BWHills)* 2-8-11 JReid(14) (str: wl grwn: lw: nvr bttr than mid div)......1½ 16
No Hiding Place *(43) (BHanbury)* 2-8-8 (3) JStack(1) (neat: prom: hung lft 2f out: wknd over 1f out)....s.h 17
Umberston (IRE) *(35) (LMCumani)* 2-8-4 (7) JoHunnam(19) (w'like: scope: s.s: a bhd)....3½ 18
Polar Champ *(21) (SPCWoods)* 2-8-11 WWoods(13) (w'like: a bhd & outpcd: t.o)....6 19

3/1 Hal's Pal (op 2/1), **4/1** Prize Giving, **6/1** Hamlet (IRE) (op 4/1), **7/1** Dabka Dancer, **8/1** Parsis (USA), **11/1** Statoyork, **12/1** EVEN TOP (IRE) (6/1-16/1), **14/1** Murheb (10/1-16/1), **16/1** Spanking Roger, Fursan (USA), **20/1** Hever Golf Eagle, Humourless, **25/1** No Hiding Place, Polar Champ, Well Drawn, **33/1** Select Few, One Pound, **50/1** Tirols Tyrant (IRE), Umberston (IRE), CSF £177.73 TOTE £26.70: £5.30 £7.70 £1.90 (£148.10) Trio £211.00 OWNER Mr B. Schmidt-Bodner (NEWMARKET) BRED M. Dwan 19 Rn 1m 25.4 (1.00) SF: 28/25/21/18/18/12/12/8/5/2/2/-/-/-/-/-/-/-/-

3341 NGK SPARK PLUGS APPRENTICE H'CAP (0-80) (3-Y.O+) (Class E)

£4,279.50 (£1,296.00: £633.00: £301.50)
6f (July) Stalls: High GOING minus 0.68 sec per fur (HD) 3-05 (3-06)

29562 **Sir Tasker (54)***(62)*(Fav)*(JLHarris)* 7-8-10 SSanders(7) (mde all: clr ½-wy: unchal)....— 1
2199 10 Squire Corrie **(60)***(64) (JEBanks)* 3-8-12 JStack(1) (chsd ldrs: rdn over 1f out: kpt on fnl f: no ch w wnr)....1½ 2
2321 14 Rise Up Singing **(58)***(61) (WJMusson)* 7-9-0b PMcCabe(2) (hld up & bhd: hdwy over 1f out: fin wl)....nk 3
27113 Blushing Grenadier (IRE) **(54)***(55) (MJFetherston-Godley)* 3-8-3b(3) DGibbs(5) (prom tl rdn & outpcd over 1f out)....1 4
21413 Forzair **(72)***(69) (SRBowring)* 3-9-10b CTeague(3) (lw: hdwy over 2f out: sn hrd rdn & no imp)1¼ 5
32199 Moujeeb (USA) **(56)***(44) (PatMitchell)* 5-8-12v NVarley(6) (dwlt: sn chsng ldrs: rdn & btn 2f out)....3½ 6

2712[2] Astrojoy (IRE) **(52)***(32) (SGKnight)* 3-8-4 DRMcCabe(8) (a wl bhd)....3 7
Green Dollar **(56)***(25) (PHowling)* 12-8-12 SDrowne(4) (lw: prom to ½-wy: sn lost tch)....4 8

3/1 SIR TASKER, **5/1** Astrojoy (IRE), Rise Up Singing, **11/2** Blushing Grenadier (IRE), **13/2** Squire Corrie, **8/1** Moujeeb (USA), **9/1** Forzair, **20/1** Green Dollar, CSF £20.42 CT £83.29 TOTE £3.70: £1.40 £3.40 £1.30 (£26.80) OWNER Mr J. F. Coupland (MELTON MOWBRAY) BRED W. H. Joyce 8 Rn
1m 12.6 (1.10) SF: 23/21/22/12/26/5/-/-
WEIGHT FOR AGE 3yo-4lb

3342

ALEX SCOTT HOPEFUL STKS (Listed) (3-Y.O+) (Class A)
£12,974.40 (£4,809.60: £2,314.80: £954.00: £387.00: £160.20)
6f (July) Stalls: High GOING minus 0.68 sec per fur (HD) 3-35 (3-36)

3198a[3] **Cheyenne Spirit (102)***(107)*(Fav)*(BHanbury)* 3-8-5 JStack(8) (lw: mde all: drvn out fnl f: jst hld on)....— 1
2570[4] Royale Figurine (IRE) **(95)***(107) (MJFetherston-Godley)* 4-8-9 WRSwinburn(5) (chsd ldrs: rdn over 1f out: r.o wl towards fin: jst failed)....s.h 2
3067[5] Easy Dollar **(107)***(111)*(Fav)*(BGubby)* 3-8-10b JWeaver(11) (lw: w wnr: rdn & kpt on wl ins fnl f)....½ 3
2671[3] Saint Express **(107)***(107) (MrsMReveley)* 5-9-0 KDarley(1) (chsd ldrs: rdn appr fnl f: r.o)....1¼ 4
2764[13] Hard to Figure **(110)***(111) (RJHodges)* 9-9-4 SDrowne(2) (hdwy 2f out: hrd rdn ent fnl f: nvr able to chal)....s.h 5
3005* Iltimas (USA) **(95)***(95) (PTWalwyn)* 3-8-5 WCarson(9) (chsd ldrs: rdn over 1f out: eased whn btn fnl f)....2½ 6
2748* Paris Babe **(95)***(95) (DMorris)* 3-8-5 RCochrane(6) (lw: hld up: effrt 2f out: nt pce to chal)....s.h 7
3033[4] Marha **(94)***(82) (HThomsonJones)* 3-8-5 RHills(3) (spd over 4f)....5 8
953[8] Miss Sacha (IRE) **(105)***(79) (DRLoder)* 4-8-9 PatEddery(4) (s.i.s: nvr nr to chal)....1 9
3195a[8] Fire Dome (IRE) **(101)***(79) (RHannon)* 3-8-10 JReid(10) (rdn along after 2f: a bhd)....2 10
3145[11] Castlerea Lad **(85)***(68) (RHollinshead)* 6-9-0 MHills(7) (lw: sn pushed along: a bhd)....4 11

5/1 CHEYENNE SPIRIT, Easy Dollar, **6/1** Hard to Figure, Saint Express, **13/2** Royale Figurine (IRE), **9/1** Iltimas (USA), **10/1** Miss Sacha (IRE), **12/1** Paris Babe, **16/1** Marha, Fire Dome (IRE), **40/1** Castlerea Lad, CSF £34.01 TOTE £5.80: £2.00 £1.70 £2.10 (£14.30) Trio £17.10 OWNER Mr C. Mauritzon (NEWMARKET) BRED J. McGarry 11 Rn
1m 10.35 (-1.15) SF: 49/53/53/53/57/37/37/24/25/21/14
WEIGHT FOR AGE 3yo-4lb

3343

BREHENY H'CAP (0-95) (3-Y.O+) (Class C) £5,900.00 (£1,760.00: £840.00: £380.00)
1m 6f 175y (July) Stalls: High GOING minus 0.68 sec per fur (HD) 4-10 (4-12)

2799[2] **Latahaab (USA) (84)***(98)*(Fav)*(RAkehurst)* 4-9-9 JWeaver(1) (a.p: led 3f out: rdn & hld on wl)— 1
Shonara's Way **(89)***(102) (RCharlton)* 4-10-0 KDarley(3) (chsd ldrs: wnt 2nd 3f out: hrd rdn fnl f: kpt on)....¾ 2
3015[2] Thaljanah (IRE) **(88)***(93) (ACStewart)* 3-9-0 WCarson(4) (b.hind: a.p: drvn along & outpcd fnl 2f)....8 3
3129[9] Antiguan Flyer **(57)***(58) (RHarris)* 6-7-10 AMackay(6) (b: lw: led: qcknd 5f out: hdd 3f out: edgd lft: sn btn)....3½ 4
3015[4] Nine Barrow Down (IRE) **(73)***(70) (HRACecil)* 3-7-13 ow1 AMcGlone(2) (lw: prom tl wknd 3f out)....2½ 5
3106[8] Lookingforarainbow (IRE) **(75)***(73) (BobJones)* 7-9-0 MWigham(5) (nvr nr ldrs)....½ 6
Sun of Spring **(85)***(70) (JWhite)* 5-9-10 RHughes(10) (bit bkwd: hld up: effrt 4f out: sn wknd: t.o)....12 7
2882[4] Blue Blazer **(76)***(57) (BHanbury)* 5-8-12 (3) JStack(7) (hld up: pushed along 4f out: no rspnse: t.o)....3 8
947[12] Warluskee **(74)***(39) (MJohnston)* 3-8-0 TWilliams(8) (chsd ldrs 9f: sn wknd: t.o)....15 9
2284[7] Robingo (IRE) **(75)** *(MrsLAMurphy)* 6-9-0b BThomson(9) (Withdrawn not under Starter's orders: Veterinary advice).... W

100/30 LATAHAAB (USA), **7/2** Thaljanah (IRE), **9/2** Nine Barrow Down (IRE), **13/2** Sun of Spring, **8/1** Blue Blazer, **9/1** Lookingforarainbow (IRE), **11/1** Shonara's Way, **14/1** Warluskee, **33/1** Robingo (IRE), **50/1** Antiguan Flyer, CSF £34.62 CT £122.23 TOTE £4.10: £1.60 £3.30 £1.20 (£23.50) Trio £28.80 OWNER Ascot Racing Partnership (EPSOM) BRED Gainsborough Farm Inc 9 Rn
3m 6.1 (0.10) SF: 53/57/35/13/12/28/25/12/-/-
WEIGHT FOR AGE 3yo-13lb

3344 BEAUFORT (S) H'CAP (0-60) (3 & 4-Y.O) (Class E) £4,402.50 (£1,320.00: £635.00: £292.50)
7f (July) Stalls: High GOING minus 0.68 sec per fur (HD) 4-40 (4-45)

3259[3] **Indian Rhapsody (46)**(57) (MJohnston) 3-9-0 JWeaver(15) (lw: hdwy 3f out: led bel dist: rdn out)........— **1**
3055[6] Chief's Lady **(49)**(57) (RHarris) 3-9-0 (3) SSanders(20) (led stands' side over 3f: kpt on u.p towards fin)........1½ **2**
2636[8] Cuban Reef **(40)**(47) (WJMusson) 3-8-5 (3) PMcCabe(14) (a.p stands' side: rdn over 1f out: r.o)........nk **3**
2808[4] Equilibrium **(47)**(52) (JWHills) 3-9-1 RHills(17) (a chsng ldrs stands' side: rdn & no ex ins fnl f)........1 **4**
3173[4] Chancey Fella **(55)**(58) (KTIvory) 4-10-0 RCochrane(1) (b: chsd ldrs far side: r.o wl ins fnl f)..¾ **5**
2524[2] Master M-E-N (IRE) **(51)**(53) (NMBabbage) 3-9-5v JFEgan(12) (chsd ldrs: rdn & no imp ins fnl f)........nk **6**
2744[5] Keys Seminar **(43)**(37) (JohnBerry) 3-8-8b(3) JStack(11) (chsd ldrs: rdn over 1f out: one pce)3½ **7**
2747[14] Supermick **(37)**(23)(Fav)(PJMcBride) 4-8-10 JLowe(4) (led far side 4f: eased whn btn appr fnl f)........3½ **8**
3074[2] At the Savoy (IRE) **(42)**(28) (TDBarron) 4-9-1v KDarley(13) (effrt wl over 1f out: nvr nrr).........nk **9**
2994[2] Bayou (IRE) **(45)**(30) (JAHarris) 4-9-4 SDWilliams(9) (mid div: rdn along 3f out: no imp).......s.h **10**
63[8] Buckley Boys **(46)**(30) (ABailey) 4-9-2b(3) DWright(19) (prom tl rdn & wknd 2f out)........½ **11**
2843[8] Julia's Freebee **(32)**(11) (TMJones) 4-8-2v(3) DRMcCabe(16) (lw: nvr nr ldrs)........2½ **12**
2923[6] Grey Toppa **(40)**(14) (NPLittmoden) 4-8-13 MFenton(7) (nvr nr to chal)........2 **13**
3264[7] Fyne Song **(41)**(15) (WJMusson) 3-8-9 AMackay(2) (lw: s.s: swtchd centre 3f out: nvr trbld ldrs)........hd **14**
2744[6] Watch My Lips **(43)**(17) (MHTompkins) 3-8-11 PRobinson(18) (a in rr)........s.h **15**
3305[7] Red River Rose (IRE) **(42)**(11) (NPLittmoden) 3-8-10b TGMcLaughlin(10) (a in rr)........2 **16**
2488[8] Radiance (IRE) **(52)**(15) (RHannon) 3-9-6b RHughes(5) (a in rr)........2½ **17**
3000[2] Commander Glen (IRE) **(54)**(13) (MartynMeade) 3-9-8 VSlattery(8) (m.n.s)........1¾ **18**
3072[5] Bold Aristocrat (IRE) **(42)** (RHollinshead) 4-8-8 (7) FLynch(6) (chsd ldr far side 5f: sn wknd)....3 **19**
3129[11] Jacks to Open (USA) **(41)** (MJHeaton-Ellis) 4-9-0 RPerham(3) (reluctant to r: a t.o)........8 **20**

9/2 Supermick (op 33/1), **6/1** At the Savoy (IRE), **13/2** INDIAN RHAPSODY, **9/1** Bayou (IRE), Master M-E-N (IRE), **10/1** Commander Glen (IRE), **11/1** Fyne Song (7/1-12/1), **12/1** Equilibrium, **14/1** Radiance (IRE), Chancey Fella, Watch My Lips, **16/1** Keys Seminar, **20/1** Buckley Boys, Cuban Reef, Chief's Lady, **33/1** Red River Rose (IRE), Grey Toppa, Bold Aristocrat (IRE), **50/1** Julia's Freebee, Jacks to Open (USA), CSF £131.71 CT £2,316.94 TOTE £5.10: £1.40 £4.90 £14.30 £3.00 (£68.60) Trio £1,434.20 OWNER Mr J. R. Good (MIDDLEHAM) BRED Mrs P. Good 20 Rn 1m 24.95 (0.55) SF: 36/36/26/31/42/32/16/7/12/14/14/-/-/-/-/-/-/-/-/-

WEIGHT FOR AGE 3yo-5lb
Sold to N Hall 6,500 gns.

3345 SAXHAM NURSERY H'CAP (2-Y.O) (Class C) £6,004.00 (£1,792.00: £856.00: £388.00)
1m (July) Stalls: High GOING minus 0.68 sec per fur (HD) 5-10 (5-10)

3008* **Traceability (71)**(70) (SCWilliams) 2-8-11 KDarley(2) (hld up: hdwy 2f out: led appr fnl f: rdn out)........— **1**
2381[4] Disallowed (IRE) **(69)**(66) (MBell) 2-8-9 MFenton(5) (led 4f: ev ch & n.m.r ent fnl f: swtchd & rallied nr fin)........1¼ **2**
3147[4] Roman Gold (IRE) **(73)**(69)(Fav)(RHannon) 2-8-13 RHughes(1) (lw: chsd ldrs gng wl: effrt over 1f out: r.o wl cl home)........hd **3**
2886[3] She's My Love **(81)**(76) (JEBanks) 2-9-7 JWeaver(6) (plld hrd: hld up: hdwy to ld ½-wy: rdn & hdd ent fnl f: no ex)........¾ **4**
3168* Carmentalia **(84)**(77) (SirMarkPrescott) 2-9-10 5x WWoods(3) (lw: prom: ev ch 2f out: hrd rdn & outpcd fnl f)........1 **5**
2908* Tarry **(58)**(51) (CNWilliams) 2-7-9 (3) NVarley(7) (chsd ldrs stands' side: swtchd lft: fin wl)......hd **6**
2447* Sound Check **(67)**(20) (BJMeehan) 2-8-7 NCarlisle(4) (lw: prom tl rdn & wknd over 3f out: t.o)........20 **7**

3/1 Roman Gold (IRE), **7/2** Carmentalia, **9/2** Tarry, **5/1** TRACEABILITY, **13/2** Disallowed (IRE), **7/1** She's My Love, **9/1** Sound Check, CSF £33.98 TOTE £5.40: £2.60 £3.00 (£31.00) OWNER Mr J. W. Lovitt (NEWMARKET) BRED J. S. A. and Mrs Shorthouse 7 Rn

1m 39.01 (0.57 under 2y best) (1.31) SF: 27/23/26/33/34/8/-

T/Jkpt; Not won £15,657.08 to Newmarket 26/8/95. T/Plpt: £496.90 (54.96 Tckts). T/Qdpt: £17.20 (15.25 Tckts). Dk

3233-SANDOWN (R-H)
Friday August 25th (Good to firm)
WEATHER: warm WIND: mod half against

3346
DEPOSITORS MAIDEN STKS (2-Y.O F) (Class D) £4,143.00 (£1,254.00: £612.00: £291.00)
1m 14y Stalls: Low GOING: 0.08 sec per fur (G) 2-15 (2-16)

Pricket (USA) *(62+)*(Fav)*(HRACecil)* 2-8-11 WRyan(1) (w'like: scope: lw: 3rd st: rdn & led over 1f out: edgd rt: rn green)........— 1
Introducing *(58+) (JHMGosden)* 2-8-11 LDettori(4) (neat: chsd ldr: rdn over 2f out: ev ch over 1f out: r.o ins fnl f)........2 2
2964 6 Miss Swing King (IRE) *(57) (RHannon)* 2-8-11 MRoberts(3) (4th st: rdn over 3f out: r.o ins fnl f)........nk 3
2581 2 Rumpipumpy *(56) (LordHuntingdon)* 2-8-11 TQuinn(5) (led over 6f: unable qckn)........¾ 4
Celestial Sister *(CDBroad)* 2-8-11 JWilliams(2) (w'like: s.s: a bhd: t.o)........dist 5

4/9 PRICKET (USA), **11/4** Introducing (13/8-3/1), **11/1** Rumpipumpy (7/2-12/1), **33/1** Miss Swing King (IRE), **100/1** Celestial Sister, CSF £1.94 TOTE £1.40: £1.10 £1.50 (£1.50) OWNER Sheikh Mohammed (NEWMARKET) BRED Mrs.Dillman 5 Rn 1m 47.06 (7.86) SF: 24/20/19/18/-

3347
BASING VIEW MAIDEN STKS (3-Y.O+ F) (Class D) £3,837.50 (£1,160.00: £565.00: £267.50)
7f 16y Stalls: Low GOING: 0.08 sec per fur (G) 2-45 (2-46)

2708 6 **Nottash (IRE) (67)***(78) (JRFanshawe)* 3-8-9 DHarrison(4) (5th st: rdn over 2f out: led 1f out: r.o wl)........— 1
1240 3 Summer Retreat (USA) *(76)*(Fav)*(JHMGosden)* 3-8-9 LDettori(7) (2nd st: led 3f out 1f out: bmpd on ins ins fnl f: unable qckn)........1 2
2576 6 Zahwa *(76) (RWArmstrong)* 3-8-9 RPrice(3) (3rd st: ev ch 1f out: one pce)........hd 3
2977 7 Sweet Allegiance *(62) (JCPoulton)* 5-9-0 AMorris(2) (swtg: 4th st: rdn over 2f out: one pce)...6 4
2265 3 Jareer Do (IRE) *(51) (BPalling)* 3-8-9 TSprake(5) (swtg: nvr nr to chal)........5 5
Mad About The Girl (IRE) *(50) (DJSCosgrove)* 3-8-9 MRimmer(1) (w'like: scope: 6th st: rdn over 2f out: sn wknd)........nk 6
3239 3 Belmez Melody *(36) (IABalding)* 3-8-9 WRyan(6) (led 4f)........6 7

11/8 Summer Retreat (USA), **11/4** Zahwa (2/1-3/1), **7/2** Belmez Melody (op 2/1), **8/1** NOTTASH (IRE) (6/1-10/1), **12/1** Jareer Do (IRE) (8/1-14/1), **33/1** Mad About The Girl (IRE), **66/1** Sweet Allegiance, CSF £18.82 TOTE £9.30: £3.00 £1.40 (£7.40) OWNER Lord Vestey (NEWMARKET) BRED J. P. McManus 7 Rn 1m 31.43 (4.83) SF: 44/42/42/33/17/16/2
WEIGHT FOR AGE 3yo-5lb

3348
SUN LIFE OF CANADA H'CAP (0-85) (3-Y.O+) (Class D) £4,377.00 (£1,326.00: £648.00: £309.00)
1m 14y Stalls: Low GOING: 0.08 sec per fur (G) 3-20 (3-23)

3085 8 **Akil (IRE) (81)***(94) (RWArmstrong)* 3-9-5 RPrice(6) (hdwy over 2f out: led wl over 1f out: rdn out)........— 1
3026* Fionn de Cool (IRE) **(74)***(84) (RAkehurst)* 4-9-4 TQuinn(3) (swtg: 5th st: rdn over 2f out: ev ch wl over 1f out: unable qckn)........1½ 2
3113P Caleman **(75)***(83) (RBoss)* 6-9-5 WRyan(10) (led over 6f: one pce)........1 3
3159* Mullitover **(76)***(77)*(Fav)*(MJHeaton-Ellis)* 5-9-6 6x MRoberts(2) (4th st: rdn over 2f out: eased whn btn ins fnl f)........3½ 4
1130 3 Quintus Decimus **(79)***(79) (LordHuntingdon)* 3-9-3 DHarrison(4) (lw: hdwy over 2f out: one pce)........½ 5
3085 9 Ham N'Eggs **(82)***(82) (RHannon)* 4-9-5 (7) MarkDenaro(7) (lw: hdwy over 1f out: nvr nrr)........s.h 6
2737 11 Yaa Wale **(76)***(71) (JHMGosden)* 3-9-0 LDettori(9) (2nd st: wknd over 1f out)........2½ 7
3269 3 Kingchip Boy **(70)***(62) (MJRyan)* 6-9-0v AClark(5) (6th st: wknd over 2f out)........1¾ 8
2321 2 Deevee **(75)***(62) (CJBenstead)* 6-9-5 MRimmer(8) (swtg: dwlt: a bhd)........2½ 9
3105* Monument **(78)***(64) (RCharlton)* 3-9-2 TSprake(1) (3rd st: wknd wl over 1f out)........½ 10

7/2 Mullitover, **5/1** Yaa Wale, **11/2** Deevee, **7/1** Monument, **8/1** Fionn de Cool (IRE), Quintus Decimus, **10/1** Ham N'Eggs, **11/1** Caleman, **14/1** AKIL (IRE), **20/1** Kingchip Boy, CSF £108.85 CT £1,161.11 TOTE £16.50: £2.80 £2.50 £2.60 (£60.70) Trio £276.90 OWNER Mr Hamdan Al Maktoum (NEWMARKET) BRED Denis Noonan 10 Rn 1m 43.59 (4.39) SF: 65/61/60/54/50/59/42/39/39/35
WEIGHT FOR AGE 3yo-6lb

3349 INVESTORS LIMITED STKS (0-80) (3-Y.O+) (Class D) £4,045.50 (£1,224.00: £597.00: £283.50)
1m 3f 91y Stalls: Low GOING: 0.08 sec per fur (G) 3-50 (3-50)

*3082*8 **Loki (IRE) (80)***(80) (GLewis)* 7-8-13 (5) AWhelan(2) (lw: s.s: 5th st: rdn over 3f out: swtchd lft 2f out: led ins fnl f: r.o wl) — 1
3102* Wellsian (USA) **(73)***(81)*(Fav)*(LMCumani)* 3-8-11 LDettori(4) (lw: 3rd st: rdn over 1f out: ev ch ins fnl f: r.o) ½ 2
26917 Lovely Lyca **(77)***(75) (JWHills)* 3-8-1 (5) MHenry(1) (lw: 2nd st: led over 3f out to ins fnl f: unable qckn) ¾ 3
20029 Chatham Island **(69)***(77) (CEBrittain)* 7-9-6 BDoyle(6) (lw: led 8f: one pce) 2½ 4
11986 Typhoon Eight (IRE) **(80)***(75) (BWHills)* 3-8-9 MRoberts(3) (swtg: 4th st: rdn over 2f out: one pce) hd 5

11/10 Wellsian (USA) (4/6-6/5), **6/4** Lovely Lyca, **7/1** Typhoon Eight (IRE) (6/1-10/1), **11/1** Chatham Island (9/2-12/1), **20/1** LOKI (IRE), CSF £41.73 TOTE £12.20: £2.30 £1.40 (£19.20) OWNER Mr Michael Watt (EPSOM) BRED Abbey Lodge Stud 5 Rn

2m 30.96 (9.26) SF: 43/35/29/40/29
WEIGHT FOR AGE 3yo-9lb

3350 POLICYHOLDERS NURSERY (S) H'CAP (2-Y.O) (Class E) £3,436.25 (£1,040.00: £507.50: £241.25)
1m 14y Stalls: Low GOING: 0.08 sec per fur (G) 4-20 (4-22)

29082 **Aussie (60)***(63)*(Fav)*(MHTompkins)* 2-9-4 LDettori(6) (5th st: led over 1f out: r.o wl) — 1
31326 Velvet Jones **(58)***(53) (PFICole)* 2-8-11 (5) DaneO'Neill(2) (lw: 4th st: ev ch wl over 1f out: unable qckn) 4 2
32335 Colour Counsellor **(54)***(45) (KMcAuliffe)* 2-8-12 DHarrison(7) (lw: rdn over 6f out: 3rd st: one pce fnl 2f) 2 3
267410 Fortuitious (IRE) **(44)***(35) (JRJenkins)* 2-7-11 (5) AWhelan(3) (6th st: led wl over 1f out: sn hdd: wknd fnl f) nk 4
32333 Comrade Chinnery (IRE) **(46)***(35)*(Fav)*(JMPEustace)* 2-8-4b JQuinn(1) (lw: led over 6f) 1 5
31353 Ivory's Grab Hire **(63)***(42) (KTIvory)* 2-9-0 (7) CScally(4) (b: a bhd) 5 6
31355 The Kastarbids (IRE) **(53)***(16) (DMorris)* 2-8-11v BDoyle(5) (lw: 2nd st: wknd over 2f out) 8 7

5/2 AUSSIE, Comrade Chinnery (IRE), **6/1** Ivory's Grab Hire (op 10/1), Velvet Jones (op 4/1), **8/1** Colour Counsellor, **12/1** The Kastarbids (IRE), **14/1** Fortuitious (IRE), CSF £15.85 TOTE £2.10: £1.80 £3.00 (£6.10) OWNER Mr T. N. Claydon (NEWMARKET) BRED Floors Farming 7 Rn

1m 47.11 (7.91) SF: 30/20/12/2/2/9/-
Bt in 8,200 gns

3351 SURREY RACING H'CAP (0-80) (3-Y.O) (Class D) £3,954.50 (£1,196.00: £583.00: £276.50)
1m 6f Stalls: Low GOING: 0.08 sec per fur (G) 4-50 (4-52)

3211* **Fujiyama Crest (IRE) (68)***(87)*(Fav)*(MRStoute)* 3-8-9 4x LDettori(7) (b.nr hind: mde all: rdn over 2f out: r.o wl) — 1
2374* Nanton Point (USA) **(64)***(81) (LadyHerries)* 3-8-5 JQuinn(5) (3rd st: chsd wnr 3f out: ev ch over 2f out: hrd rdn: unable qckn) 1¾ 2
31782 Dixiemelody **(59)***(65) (RHannon)* 3-8-0 MRoberts(2) (5th st: wknd over 2f out) 10 3
29373 Eelious (USA) **(80)***(84) (CEBrittain)* 3-9-7 BDoyle(3) (lw: 4th st: wknd over 2f out) 1 4
30713 John Lee Hooker **(67)***(71) (DWPArbuthnot)* 3-8-8 JWilliams(4) (b.hind: chsd wnr over 11f out to 3f out: sn wknd) ½ 5
28682 Duchess of Alba **(75)***(71) (RCharlton)* 3-9-2 DHarrison(1) (lw: 6th st: a bhd) 7 6
23395 Hi-Aud **(69)** *(JAkehurst)* 3-8-10 AClark(6) (p.u 11f out: lame) P

11/4 FUJIYAMA CREST (IRE), **100/30** Dixiemelody, **7/2** Nanton Point (USA) (3/1-9/2), **6/1** Eelious (USA), **7/1** John Lee Hooker, **8/1** Duchess of Alba, **16/1** Hi-Aud, CSF £12.31 TOTE £3.50: £1.90 £2.40 (£6.10) OWNER Mr Seisuke Hata (NEWMARKET) BRED B. Kennedy 7 Rn

3m 3.89 (9.19) SF: 47/41/25/44/31/31/-
T/Plpt: £55.70 (211.64 Tckts). T/Qdpt: £98.60 (0.8 Tckts); £26.66 to Newmarket 26/8/95. AK

2970-THIRSK (L-H)
Friday August 25th (St course Good to firm, Rnd Firm)
WEATHER: overcast WIND: fresh bhd

3352 E.B.F. JAMES HETHERTON MAIDEN STKS (2-Y.O) (Class D)
£4,532.65 (£1,355.20: £649.10: £296.05)
6f Stalls: High GOING minus 0.69 sec per fur (HD) 2-25 (2-25)

30536 **Munakeb (FR)** *(73) (RWArmstrong)* 2-9-0 KFallon(6) (mde all: hung bdly lft fnl f: r.o) ....— 1
31103 Juicy *(69)*(Fav)*(WJHaggas)* 2-9-0 TIves(1) (lw: chsd ldr: ev ch over 1f out: btn whn hmpd ins fnl f)............1½ 2
Basood (USA) *(57) (EALDunlop)* 2-8-6 (3) JTate(3) (leggy: unf: prom: ev ch over 1f out: nt qckn)............2½ 3
Hilaala (USA) *(56) (PTWalwyn)* 2-8-9 DHolland(4) (leggy: unf: in tch: swtchd lft & rn green ½-wy: kpt on fnl f)............½ 4
27825 Szloto *(56) (TDBarron)* 2-9-0 JFortune(2) (in tch: kpt on fnl 2f)............1¾ 5
Calypso Run *(45) (MBell)* 2-8-2 (7) GFaulkner(8) (unf: scope: sn rdn: outpcd ½-wy: n.d after)2½ 6
30776 Mullagh Hill Lad (IRE) *(36) (BAMcMahon)* 2-9-0 FNorton(7) (hung lft most of wy: a outpcd & bhd)............5 7
Stereo Dancer *(26) (EALDunlop)* 2-9-0 GCarter(5) (w'like: unf: scope: s.i.s: n.d)............4 8

11/8 Juicy, **2/1** Hilaala (USA) (11/8-9/4), **11/2** Calypso Run, **10/1** Stereo Dancer, **12/1** MUNAKEB (FR), **14/1** Szloto (op 8/1), Basood (USA) (op 8/1), **33/1** Mullagh Hill Lad (IRE), CSF £29.94 TOTE £14.30: £2.00 £1.20 £2.80 (£15.30) OWNER Mr Hamdan Al Maktoum (NEWMARKET) BRED Pierre Talvard and Jean-Claude Seroul 8 Rn 1m 12.7 (3.00) SF: -/-/-/-/-/-/-/-

3353 MALCOLM JEFFERSON (S) STKS (2-Y.O) (Class F) £3,122.80
(£865.80: £414.40)
7f Stalls: High GOING minus 0.27 sec per fur (GF) 2-55 (2-56)

30484 **Ginger Glint (58)***(61) (MJHeaton-Ellis)* 2-8-11 DHolland(5) (b: trckd ldrs: led ins fnl f: all out)............— 1
32258 Euro Express **(61)***(60) (MHEasterby)* 2-8-11 MBirch(1) (led tl hdd ins fnl f: rallied towards fin)nk 2
27322 Ned's Contessa (IRE) **(59)***(53)*(Fav)*(MDods)* 2-8-6 JFortune(8) (lw: stdy hdwy 3f out: effrt over 1f out: no ex u.p)............1¼ 3
30483 Phantom Dancer (IRE) **(56)***(46) (JBerry)* 2-8-11 JCarroll(7) (s.i.s: hdwy ent st: effrt 2f out: one pce appr fnl f)............5 4
29517 Baroness Gold *(37) (MHEasterby)* 2-8-6 SMaloney(3) (b.hind: chsd ldrs tl rdn & btn over 1f out)............2 5
20758 Magic Bird (IRE) *(35) (JNorton)* 2-8-6 DaleGibson(2) (lw: disp ld tl wknd fnl 2f)............¾ 6
Mister Joel *(40) (MWEasterby)* 2-8-11 KFallon(6) (w'like: bit bkwd: s.i.s: outpcd & bhd tl sme late hdwy)............hd 7
11596 Sikosarki (USA) *(23) (GMMoore)* 2-8-3 (3) JTate(9) (lw: chsd ldrs: rn wd st: wknd 2f out)............5 8
32535 Candy Dancer *(25) (CWThornton)* 2-8-11 DeanMcKeown(10) (lw: s.i.s: a bhd)............1¼ 9
42412 Go-Go-Power-Ranger *(9) (BEllison)* 2-8-11 NKennedy(4) (in tch to st)............7 10
26376 Fast Food **(49)** *(BJMcMath)* 2-8-11 GCarter(11) (sn bhd: t.o)............dist 11

11/4 Ned's Contessa (IRE), **7/2** Phantom Dancer (IRE), Euro Express, **6/1** GINGER GLINT (op 4/1), **11/1** Sikosarki (USA), **12/1** Candy Dancer (op 8/1), **20/1** Baroness Gold, **25/1** Fast Food, **33/1** Mister Joel, Go-Go-Power-Ranger, Magic Bird (IRE), CSF £25.78 TOTE £5.20: £1.70 £1.80 £1.70 (£10.40) Trio £8.10 OWNER Mr F. J. Sainsbury (WROUGHTON) BRED Stetchworth Park Stud Ltd 11 Rn 1m 27.6 (4.90) SF: 15/14/7/-/-/-/-/-/-/-/-
Bt in 4,800 gns
STEWARDS' ENQUIRY Birch susp. 4-6/9/95 (excessive use of whip).

3354 JOHN QUINN NURSERY H'CAP (2-Y.O) (Class D) £4,017.60
(£1,198.80: £572.40: £259.20)
6f Stalls: High GOING minus 0.69 sec per fur (HD) 3-25 (3-27)

3213* **Westcourt Magic (84)***(88+)*(Fav)*(MWEasterby)* 2-9-6 7x GCarter(3) (lw: mde all: pushed along 2f out: r.o wl fnl f)............— 1
2914* Red River Valley **(85)***(80) (DenysSmith)* 2-9-7 KFallon(6) (lw: chsd ldrs: hdwy over 1f out: nt pce of wnr)............3½ 2
32714 Ultra Barley **(74)***(55) (PCHaslam)* 2-8-10 7x JFortune(2) (chsd wnr: rdn over 2f out: nt qckn) ...5 3
2757* Oriole **(67)***(35) (NTinkler)* 2-8-3 KimTinkler(4) (a outpcd & bhd)............5 4
19924 Mooncusser **(58)***(18) (JGFitzGerald)* 2-7-8 NKennedy(5) (outpcd & bhd after 2f)............3 5

8/11 WESTCOURT MAGIC, **7/2** Red River Valley, **4/1** Ultra Barley (3/1-9/2), **11/1** Mooncusser (8/1-12/1), **14/1** Oriole, CSF £3.84 TOTE £1.70: £1.10 £2.30 (£2.80) OWNER Mr K. Hodgson (SHERIFF HUTTON) BRED C. R. and V. M. Withers 5 Rn 1m 9.2 (0.40 under best) (-0.50) SF: 52/44/19/-/-

3355

BOB WOODHOUSE H'CAP (0-75) (3-Y.O+) (Class D) £4,269.00 (£1,272.00: £606.00: £273.00)
2m Stalls: High GOING minus 0.27 sec per fur (GF) 3-55 (3-56)

3052* **Northern Law (69)***(80) (BWHills)* 3-9-10 DHolland(4) (mde all: r.o strly fnl 3f: eased fnl f) ....— 1
*3084** Finlaggan **(67)***(77)*(Fav)*(SirMarkPrescott)* 3-9-8 GDuffield(3) (lw: hdwy to chse wnr 6f out: rdn 3f out: one pce) ....¾ 2
3002* Vain Prince **(53)***(58) (NTinkler)* 8-9-8b GCarter(1) (lw: chsd ldrs: outpcd over 3f out: no imp after) 5 3
2825[3] Dream Sweet Dreams (USA) **(33)** *(FHLee)* 6-8-2 ow3 RLappin(2) (in tch tl rdn & btn appr st)dist 4

8/11 Finlaggan, **3/1** NORTHERN LAW, Vain Prince, **50/1** Dream Sweet Dreams (USA), CSF £5.47 TOTE £3.30 (£1.80) OWNER Mr John Bradley (LAMBOURN) BRED Charlton Down Stud 4 Rn
3m 32.3 (9.30) SF: 41/38/33/-
WEIGHT FOR AGE 3yo-14lb

3356

JOHN CARR CONDITIONS STKS (3 & 4-Y.O) (Class D) £3,841.75 (£1,144.00: £544.50: £244.75)
1m Stalls: High GOING minus 0.27 sec per fur (GF) 4-25 (4-25)

3097[4] **Eden's Star (IRE) (56)***(87) (MHTompkins)* 3-8-12 TIves(3) (mde all: r.o wl fnl 3f) ....— 1
3023[3] Azdihaar (USA) **(72)***(79)*(Fav)*(JLDunlop)* 3-8-7 GCarter(1) (lw: hld up: effrt 2f out: styd on: nt pce to chal) 1¾ 2
3095[5] Young Benson **(69)***(79) (BAMcMahon)* 3-8-12 JFortune(4) (trckd wnr: effrt & ch 2f out: nt qckn) 2½ 3
2649[4] Respect A Secret *(50) (SEKettlewell)* 3-8-7 NRodgers(2) (s.i.s: rdn ent st: sn lost tch) 12 4

8/15 Azdihaar (USA), **11/4** Young Benson (2/1-3/1), **9/2** EDEN'S STAR (IRE), **50/1** Respect A Secret, CSF £7.40 TOTE £3.80 (£2.50) OWNER Mrs M. Barwell (NEWMARKET) BRED Mount Coote Stud 4 Rn 1m 39.4 (3.80) SF: 35/27/27/-

3357

TIM ETHERINGTON H'CAP (0-70) (3-Y.O+) (Class E) £3,932.25 (£1,176.00: £563.50: £257.25)
5f Stalls: High GOING minus 0.69 sec per fur (HD) 4-55 (4-57)

3123[9] **Kalar (47)***(51)*(Fav)*(DWChapman)* 6-8-10b DHolland(16) (led tl hdd over 1f out: rallied to ld post) ....— 1
3252[8] Invigilate **(52)***(56)*(Fav)*(MartynWane)* 6-9-1 KFallon(14) (cl up: led over 1f out tl ct last stride)s.h 2
3128[6] Lovely Me (IRE) **(65)***(61) (RFJohnsonHoughton)* 4-10-0 ACulhane(13) (a in tch: kpt on wl fnl f) 2½ 3
3252[7] The Institute Boy **(45)***(39) (MissJFCraze)* 5-8-8 SWebster(12) (lw: in tch: styd on fnl 2f: nvr able chal) ....½ 4
3051[5] Miss Movie World **(58)***(49)*(Fav)*(MDHammond)* 6-9-7b TIves(6) (lw: w ldrs tl wknd fnl f) 1 5
3150[3] Dominelle **(51)***(37) (MHEasterby)* 3-8-11 SMaloney(8) (chsd ldrs tl rdn & btn over 1f out) 1½ 6
3252[6] Indian Crystal **(34)***(16) (MrsMReveley)* 4-7-11v FNorton(15) (s.i.s: nrst fin) 1¼ 7
2492[5] Most Uppitty **(56)***(33) (JBerry)* 3-8-9 (7) JoanneWebster(11) (in tch: rdn ½-wy: no imp) 1¾ 8
3252[4] Kabcast **(47)***(24) (DWChapman)* 10-8-10b DeanMcKeown(4) (lw: racd far side: gd spd 4f)....s.h 9
2973[5] Able Sheriff **(48)***(20) (MWEasterby)* 3-8-8b MBirch(10) (nvr nr to chal) 1½ 10
2955[8] Coney Hills **(30)** *(NBycroft)* 4-7-7 ClaireBalding(3) (lw: racd far side: outpcd fr ½-wy)....4 11
3098[4] Murray's Mazda (IRE) **(40)** *(JLEyre)* 6-8-3 RLappin(7) (b.hind: outpcd fr ½-wy)....1½ 12
3103[5] Self Styled (IRE) **(49)** *(TDBarron)* 3-8-9 JFortune(9) (t: n.d) 1¼ 13
3166[9] Silk Cottage **(66)***(16) (RMWhitaker)* 3-9-5 (7) GFaulkner(2) (swtchd rt after s: chsd ldrs: hung bdly lft fnl 2f: wknd) ....s.h 14
2834[5] Ladys Promise **(35)** *(GROldroyd)* 3-7-6 (3)ow2 DarrenMoffatt(5) (n.d)....½ 15
6[8] Chardonnay Girl **(38)** *(JMCarr)* 4-8-1 NKennedy(1) (racd centre: outpcd fr ½-wy) 1¼ 16

LONG HANDICAP Ladys Promise 6-13 Coney Hills 6-6

5/1 KALAR, Invigilate, Miss Movie World, **15/2** Dominelle, **10/1** Indian Crystal, Murray's Mazda (IRE), Able Sheriff, **12/1** Silk Cottage, Kabcast, **16/1** Most Uppitty, The Institute Boy, Lovely Me (IRE), **20/1** Self Styled (IRE), **100/1** Coney Hills, Ladys Promise, Chardonnay Girl, CSF £29.84 CT £353.46 TOTE £4.60: £1.70 £2.10 £4.60 £2.90 (£10.90) Trio £26.20 OWNER Mr E. Stockdale (YORK) BRED C. C. and Mrs Pryor 16 Rn 57.3 secs (0.10) SF: 33/38/43/21/31/16/-/12/6/-/-/-/-/-/-/-
WEIGHT FOR AGE 3yo-3lb

T/Plpt: £191.10 (40.12 Tckts). T/Qdpt: £73.50 (0.95 Tckts) £4.97 to Newmarket 26/8/95. AA

3333-GOODWOOD (R-H)
Saturday August 26th (Good to firm, Firm patches)
WEATHER: hot WIND: mod against

3358
SPORT ON 5 RATED STKS H'CAP (0-105) (3-Y.O+) (Class B)
£9,400.40 (£3,503.60: £1,701.80: £719.00: £309.50: £145.70)
7f Stalls: High GOING minus 0.16 sec per fur (GF) 2-00 (2-01)

2416* **Tajannub (USA) (100)***(109) (RWArmstrong)* 3-9-0 WCarson(6) (lw: chsd ldr: rdn 2f out: led wl ins fnl f: r.o wl) — 1
3188 15 Moccasin Run (USA) **(102)***(111) (IABalding)* 4-9-7 LDettori(5) (swtg: 3rd st: rdn 2f out: ev ch ins fnl f: r.o wl) hd 2
3188 3 Behaviour **(92)***(101)*(Fav)*(MrsJCecil)* 3-8-6 PaulEddery(2) (lw: 4th st: rdn over 2f out: ev ch fnl f: r.o) s.h 3
3085 13 Croft Valley **(95)***(103) (RAkehurst)* 8-8-11 (3) SSanders(1) (lw: led: rdn over 2f out: hdd wl ins fnl f: r.o) nk 4
2703 3 Desert Green (FR) **(97)***(100) (RHannon)* 6-9-2 RPerham(3) (swtg: 6th st: rdn over 2f out: one pce) 2 5
3188 7 Celestial Key (USA) **(101)***(96) (MJohnston)* 5-9-6 PRobinson(7) (stmbld bdly s: nt rcvr) 3½ 6
3085 11 Shikari's Son **(96)***(91) (JWhite)* 8-9-1 RHughes(4) (hdwy on ins over 2f out: wknd over 1f out) nk 7
3212* En Attendant (FR) **(101)***(90) (BHanbury)* 7-9-6 JReid(8) (b: b.hind: 5th st: wknd 2f out) 2½ 8

11/4 Behaviour, **4/1** Desert Green (FR), **6/1** TAJANNUB (USA), **13/2** En Attendant (FR), Celestial Key (USA), **10/1** Moccasin Run (USA), **12/1** Croft Valley (op 8/1), Shikari's Son, CSF £53.64 CT £179.36 TOTE £5.10: £1.80 £2.20 £1.60 (£22.40) OWNER Mr Hamdan Al Maktoum (NEWMARKET) BRED G. Watts Humphrey and Pierce and Pierce Inc in USA 8 Rn

1m 26.57 (2.17) SF: 59/66/51/58/55/51/46/45
WEIGHT FOR AGE 3yo-5lb

3359
LADBROKE RACING SPRINT H'CAP (0-95) (3-Y.O+) (Class C)
£14,915.00 (£4,520.00: £2,210.00: £1,055.00)
6f Stalls: Low GOING minus 0.16 sec per fur (GF) 2-30 (2-33)

3085 5 **No Extras (IRE) (89)***(101) (GLMoore)* 5-9-10 SWhitworth(13) (s.s: hdwy over 1f out: led ins fnl f: rdn out) — 1
3145 13 Rich Glow **(64)***(75) (NBycroft)* 4-7-6 (7) MartinDwyer(22) (hld up: led over 1f out: edgd lft: hdd ins fnl f: unable qckn) ½ 2
2948 9 My Best Valentine **(82)***(89) (JWhite)* 5-9-3 RHughes(8) (lw: hdwy over 1f out: r.o) 1¼ 3
3230 14 Samsolom **(74)***(75) (PHowling)* 7-8-9 PaulEddery(17) (b.hind: hld up: rdn & n.m.r 2f out: r.o ins fnl f) 2½ 4
2708* Sea Thunder **(82)***(83) (IABalding)* 3-8-13 LDettori(19) (lw: hdwy over 1f out: one pce) s.h 5
3275 8 Petraco (IRE) **(65)***(65) (NASmith)* 7-7-7 (7) NicolaHowarth(18) (hld up: hrd rdn over 2f out: nt clr run over 1f out: r.o one pce) s.h 6
3028 6 Agwa **(75)***(75) (RJO'Sullivan)* 6-8-10 DBiggs(16) (a.p: led over 2f out to over 1f out: wknd ins fnl f) nk 7
2570 5 Mister Jolson **(83)***(81) (RJHodges)* 6-9-1 (3) SDrowne(20) (b.nr fore: hdwy over 1f out: one pce) ½ 8
2802 5 Jo Maximus **(72)***(70) (SDow)* 3-7-10 (7) ADaly(23) (lw: led over 3f: wknd 1f out) hd 9
3145 2 Lord Olivier (IRE) **(92)***(87)*(Fav)*(WJarvis)* 5-9-13 JReid(2) (lw: hld up: rdn over 1f out: eased whn btn ins fnl f) 1¼ 10
3134 2 Patsy Grimes **(69)***(59) (LJHolt)* 5-8-4 AMcGlone(3) (hld up: rdn over 2f out: one pce) 1¾ 11
3236 4 Hello Mister **(93)***(80) (JO'Donoghue)* 4-9-11 (3) PMcCabe(4) (hmpd over 5f out: rdn & hdwy over 1f out: one pce) 1 12
3221 9 So Intrepid (IRE) **(74)***(58) (JMBradley)* 5-8-4 (5) DGriffiths(6) (swtg: nvr nrr) 1¼ 13
3028 5 Balance of Power **(72)***(50) (RAkehurst)* 3-8-0 (3)ow1 SSanders(1) (b: nvr nrr) 1¾ 14
3221* Elle Shaped (IRE) **(82)***(59) (ABailey)* 5-9-0 (3) DWright(24) (spd 4f) ¾ 15
3112 10 Prima Silk **(72)***(48) (MJRyan)* 4-8-7 WCarson(10) (hdwy over 2f out: wknd over 1f out) ½ 16
2943 7 Rambold **(62)***(38) (NEBerry)* 4-7-11 NAdams(7) (bhd fnl 2f) s.h 17
3028 9 Oare Sparrow **(71)***(42) (PTWalwyn)* 5-8-6 GCarter(14) (bhd fnl 3f) 2 18
3209 2 Tiler (IRE) **(84)***(51) (MJohnston)* 3-9-1 PRobinson(9) (prom 3f) 1¼ 19
3175 10 Jaazim **(67)***(33) (MMadgwick)* 5-8-2 CAvery(11) (swtg: prom 3f) nk 20
Wardara **(73)***(38) (MissGayKelleway)* 3-7-13 (5) MBaird(15) (swtg: a bhd) ½ 21
2764 W Thatcherella **(78)***(43) (MajorDNChappell)* 4-8-13 RHills(12) (prom over 4f) hd 22

8/1 Lord Olivier (IRE), **9/1** Hello Mister, Sea Thunder (12/1-8/1), **10/1** Tiler (IRE), **12/1** Agwa, **14/1** Patsy Grimes, Elle Shaped (IRE), Wardara, **16/1** NO EXTRAS (IRE), Balance of Power, **20/1** My Best Valentine, Rich Glow, Oare Sparrow, Mister Jolson, Prima Silk, Thatcherella, **25/1** Samsolom, So Intrepid (IRE), Jo Maximus, **33/1** Petraco (IRE), Rambold, **50/1** Jaazim, CSF £269.78 CT £5,690.17 TOTE £17.80: £3.60 £4.60 £4.80 £5.40 (£88.30) Trio £2,292.90 OWNER Mr K. Higson (EPSOM) BRED R. J. Cullen 22 Rn

1m 11.74 (1.54) SF: 72/46/60/46/50/36/46/52/37/58/30/51/29/17/30/19/9/13/18/4/5/14

WEIGHT FOR AGE 3yo-4lb

3360 TRIPLEPRINT CELEBRATION MILE STKS (Gp 2) (3-Y.O+) (Class A)

£35,387.50 (£13,112.50: £6,306.25: £2,593.75: £1,046.88: £428.12)

1m Stalls: High GOING minus 0.16 sec per fur (GF) 3-10 (3-10)

3067* **Harayir (USA) (118)***(122)*(Fav)*(MajorWRHern)* 3-8-12 WCarson(3) (4th st: led over 2f out: rdn fnl f: r.o wl) — 1

3067³ Darnay **(115)***(121) (SbinSuroor)* 4-9-4 JReid(4) (3rd st: nt clr run over 2f out tl barged thro 1f out: r.o ins fnl f) ½ 2

2703² Realities (USA) **(111)***(116) (GHarwood)* 5-9-1 PaulEddery(2) (lw: 6th st: rdn 2f out: bmpd over 1f out & 1f out: r.o one pce) 1¼ 3

805a⁴ Emperor Jones (USA) **(118)***(115) (SbinSuroor)* 5-9-4 LDettori(6) (chsd ldr: led over 3f out to over 2f out: ev ch 1f out: 2nd & btn whn squeezed out ins fnl f) 1¾ 4

2646* Shahid **(113)***(102) (JLDunlop)* 3-8-9 RHills(5) (lw: 5th st: swtchd lft over 2f out: wknd wl over 1f out) 5 5

3325a⁴ Dance Turn **(108)***(88) (RWArmstrong)* 4-9-1v MRoberts(1) (led over 4f) 7 6

5/4 HARAYIR (USA), **7/2** Emperor Jones (USA), **4/1** Shahid (9/4-9/2), **9/1** Realities (USA), Darnay (5/1-10/1), **16/1** Dance Turn, CSF £11.41 TOTE £2.30: £1.60 £3.00 (£9.40) OWNER Mr Hamdan Al Maktoum (LAMBOURN) BRED Shadwell Farm Inc in USA 6 Rn

1m 36.73 (-0.87) SF: 94/99/94/93/74/66

WEIGHT FOR AGE 3yo-6lb

3361 CHICHESTER OBSERVER STKS (4-Y.O+) (Class C) £6,817.50(£2,205.00: £1,077.50) 2m Stalls: High GOING minus 0.16 sec per fur (GF) 3-40 (3-43)

2702⁵ **Admiral's Well (IRE) (108)***(81+)*(Fav)*(RAkehurst)* 5-9-1 LDettori(1) (chsd ldr: led over 3f out: rdn over 2f out: r.o wl) — 1

2456³ The Flying Phantom **(88)***(75) (MHTompkins)* 4-9-2 PRobinson(3) (led over 12f: rdn over 2f out: eased whn btn ins fnl f) 7 2

1535⁶ By Arrangement (IRE) **(30)***(53) (SWoodman)* 6-8-5 PaulEddery(2) (bhd fnl 5f) 11 3

1/3 ADMIRAL'S WELL (IRE), **5/2** The Flying Phantom, **20/1** By Arrangement (IRE), CSF £1.49 TOTE £1.40 (£1.20) OWNER Mr A. D. Spence (EPSOM) BRED Barronstown Bloodstock Ltd 3 Rn

3m 31.55 (7.05) SF: 52/46/24

3362 RICHMOND-BRISSAC TROPHY GENTLEMENS' H'CAP (0-85) (3-Y.O+)

(Class E) £3,720.00 (£1,110.00: £530.00: £240.00)

1m 1f Stalls: High GOING minus 0.16 sec per fur (GF) 4-15 (4-15)

3169² **Adolescence (IRE) (80)***(90) (KMcAuliffe)* 5-11-6 MrLAUrbano(2) (2nd st: led over 3f out: rdn out) — 1

962⁸ Tribal Peace (IRE) **(66)***(76) (BGubby)* 3-9-13 MrCMosse(1) (3rd st: ev ch fnl 3f: r.o) nk 2

2805² Balasara (IRE) **(75)***(83)*(Fav)*(DRCElsworth)* 5-11-1b MrMArmytage(5) (led tl brought wd st: edgd lft & hdd over 3f out: rdn over 1f out: r.o ins fnl f) 1 3

3129² Thames Side **(57)***(62) (MMadgwick)* 4-9-11 MrTMcCarthy(4) (5th st: hrd rdn over 2f out: ev ch over 1f out: unable qckn) 1¾ 4

3113¹¹ Pay Homage **(84)***(89) (IABalding)* 7-11-10 MrABalding(3) (6th st: no hdwy fnl 2f) s.h 5

3234² Wayfarers Way (USA) **(69)***(54) (RHannon)* 4-10-9 MrCVigors(6) (lw: 4th st: wknd over 2f out) 11 6

3/1 Balasara (IRE), **100/30** ADOLESCENCE (IRE), **7/2** Pay Homage, **9/2** Wayfarers Way (USA), **11/2** Tribal Peace (IRE), **10/1** Thames Side (8/1-12/1), CSF £19.40 TOTE £4.30: £2.30 £3.40 (£22.10) OWNER Mrs F. D. McAuley (LAMBOURN) BRED F.D. McAuley 6 Rn

1m 58.13 (7.43) SF: 51/30/44/23/50/15

WEIGHT FOR AGE 3yo-7lb

3363 PILLEY GREEN CLAIMING H'CAP (0-70) (3-Y.O+) (Class E)
£3,817.50 (£1,140.00: £545.00: £247.50)
1m 2f Stalls: High GOING minus 0.16 sec per fur (GF) 4-45 (4-45)

2983* **Tragic Hero** **(54)***(64)*(Fav)*(MCPipe)* 3-8-6 RHills(5) (2nd st: led over 2f out: rdn out) ....— 1
3218* Sharpical **(67)***(75)*(Fav)*(BJMeehan)* 3-9-5 SWhitworth(4) (6th st: rdn 2f out: ev ch ins fnl f: unable qckn) 1 2
2875⁹ Alerting **(61)***(65) (IABalding)* 3-8-13 LDettori(1) (5th st: rdn over 2f out: swtchd rt over 1f out: one pce) 2½ 3
2781⁴ Night Time **(62)***(66) (RHannon)* 3-9-0 GCarter(9) (rdn over 2f out: hdwy over 1f out: r.o) ....nk 4
2980⁶ Tonka **(62)***(63) (PJMakin)* 3-8-11 (3) SSanders(3) (swtg: plld hrd: hdwy 5f out: 3rd st: rdn over 2f out: one pce) 1¾ 5
3129³ Lunar Mission (IRE) **(57)***(58) (JMPEustace)* 4-9-3v MTebbutt(7) (lw: 4th st: rdn over 2f out: one pce)..nk 6
2345⁶ Lady Williams (IRE) **(53)***(44) (LordHuntingdon)* 4-8-13v PRobinson(6) (lw: a bhd) 6 7
Western Valley **(34)***(21) (CPWildman)* 5-7-8 ow1 NCarlisle(8) (b: led over 7f: wknd over 1f out) 2 8

LONG HANDICAP Western Valley 7-4

3/1 TRAGIC HERO, Sharpical, **5/1** Alerting, **6/1** Night Time, **15/2** Lady Williams (IRE), **10/1** Lunar Mission (IRE), **12/1** Tonka, **50/1** Western Valley, CSF £11.40 CT £36.42 TOTE £3.90: £1.20 £1.50 £1.80 (£4.60) Trio £7.20 OWNER 0336 405200 Racing (WELLINGTON) BRED Derek R. Price 8 Rn
2m 11.39 (6.39) SF: 27/38/28/29/26/29/15/-
WEIGHT FOR AGE 3yo-8lb

3364 E.B.F. SOLENT MAIDEN STKS (2-Y.O F) (Class D) £4,659.00(£1,392.00: £666.00: £303.00) **7f** Stalls: High GOING minus 0.16 sec per fur (GF) 5-20 (5-20)

2025² **Min Alhawa (USA)** *(74)*(Fav)*(MajorWRHern)* 2-8-11 RHills(3) (chsd ldr: hrd rdn over 1f out: led ins fnl f: r.o wl)..— 1
Aerleon Jane *(74+) (JHMGosden)* 2-8-11 LDettori(2) (w'like: bit bkwd: 4th st: nt clr run over 1f out: swtchd lft 1f out: fin wl) ....hd 2
1746² Scarlet Plume *(73) (JLDunlop)* 2-8-11 GCarter(5) (led tl ins fnl f: unable qckn) ....½ 3
1169⁶ Ocean Grove (IRE) *(71) (PWChapple-Hyam)* 2-8-6 (5) RHavlin(4) (3rd st: rdn over 1f out: r.o) ....¾ 4
Miss Prism *(14) (JLDunlop)* 2-8-11 SWhitworth(1) (leggy: bit bkwd: s.s: 5th st: a bhd) 25 5

8/15 MIN ALHAWA (USA), **7/2** Scarlet Plume, **6/1** Aerleon Jane, **12/1** Ocean Grove (IRE) (10/1-20/1), **33/1** Miss Prism, CSF £4.20 TOTE £1.60: £1.20 £1.80 (£3.20) OWNER Mr Hamdan Al Maktoum (LAMBOURN) BRED Shadwell Farm Inc 5 Rn 1m 27.98 (3.58) SF: 40/40/39/37/-
T/Plpt: £279.90 (100.27 Tckts). T/Qdpt: £39.80 (18.65 Tckts). AK

2851-NEWCASTLE (L-H)
Saturday August 26th (Good, Good to firm back st)
Races 3 & 6 hand-timed WIND: almost nil

3365 GALLOWGATE CLAIMING APPRENTICE STKS (3-Y.O+) (Class F)£2,750.00 (£775.00: £380.00)
6f Stalls: High GOING: 0.16 sec per fur (G) 2-15 (2-20)

2905⁴ **Winter Scout (USA)** **(62)***(63) (MrsMReveley)* 7-8-11 SCopp(10) (racd stands' side: hdwy to ld appr fnl f: all out)..— 1
2968⁴ Non Dimenticar Me (IRE) **(70)***(59)*(Fav)*(SirMarkPrescott)* 3-8-4 GParkin(8) (prom: rdn over 2f out: led over 1f out: sn hdd: one pce)..nk 2
3252⁵ Best Kept Secret **(58)***(58) (JBerry)* 4-9-1 PFessey(1) (lw: cl up: chal 2f out: rdn & r.o one pce)3 3
2972¹⁸ Passion Sunday **(37)***(47) (LRLloyd-James)* 4-8-2 (3) KimberleyHart(9) (b.hind: led 1½f: cl up: led 2f out: sn hdd: one pce) ....½ 4
3251³ Baileys Sunset (IRE) **(63)***(52) (MJohnston)* 3-8-6 (5) KSked(7) (chsd ldrs: outpcd 2½f out: no imp after) 2 5
2945⁴ Rapier Point (IRE) **(63)***(44) (PCHaslam)* 4-8-6 (5) CarolDavison(4) (b: s.i.s: led after 1½f tl 2f out: sn rdn & btn) 1½ 6
2972¹⁴ Pakol (IRE) **(41)***(19) (MrsASwinbank)* 6-8-3 (5)ow8 CLowther(5) (nvr rchd ldrs) 5 7
2753⁹ Call to the Bar (IRE) **(60)***(18) (MDods)* 6-8-9 (3) CWebb(2) (bhd fr ½-wy)..................................5 8
2398* Blow Dry (IRE) **(54)***(1) (MartynWane)* 5-8-8 (3) AEddery(3) (lw: uns rdr & bolted bef s: bhd fr ½-wy) 6 9

9/4 Non Dimenticar Me (IRE), **5/2** WINTER SCOUT (USA), **5/1** Baileys Sunset (IRE), **10/1** Best Kept Secret, Blow Dry (IRE), Rapier Point (IRE) (op 6/1), **14/1** Call to the Bar (IRE), **20/1** Pakol (IRE), **33/1** Passion Sunday, CSF £8.33 TOTE £3.90: £1.40 £1.30 £1.80 (£4.80) Trio £17.80 OWNER Mr John Hughes (SALTBURN) BRED Virginia Kraft Payson 9 Rn

1m 18.13 (6.63) SF: 18/10/13/2/3/-/-/-/-

WEIGHT FOR AGE 3yo-4lb

3366 E.B.F. NEWGATE MAIDEN STKS (2-Y.O F) (Class D) £3,452.50 (£1,045.00: £510.00: £242.50)

7f Stalls: High GOING: 0.16 sec per fur (G) 2-50 (2-50)

Longing (USA) *(72+) (DRLoder)* 2-8-8 (3) DRMcCabe(3) (lt-f: in tch: led appr fnl f: r.o wl) .....— 1
2579⁶ Fikra (USA) *(63) (DMorley)* 2-8-11 RCochrane(2) (lw: w ldrs: rdn over 2f out: kpt on fnl f: no ch w wnr) 4 2
2083⁵ Islay Brown (IRE) *(63) (CWCElsey)* 2-8-4 (7) PFessey(5) (led tl hdd appr fnl f: no ex).............hd 3
2735⁵ Time For A Glass *(17) (WTKemp)* 2-8-11 TWilliams(1) (cl up 3f: sn rdn & wknd qckly)..........20 4
2964³ Shernadeed (FR) (Fav)*(MJohnston)* 2-8-11 DHolland(4) (in tch tl wl outpcd fr ½-wy: eased fnl 2f)....9 5

13/8 Shernadeed (FR), **2/1** Fikra (USA) (op 3/1), **9/4** LONGING (USA) (op Evens), **20/1** Islay Brown (IRE), **50/1** Time For A Glass, CSF £6.66 TOTE £2.80: £1.40 £1.80 (£3.40) OWNER Mrs Virginia KraftPayson (NEWMARKET) BRED Questroyal Stable 5 Rn 1m 30.66 (6.36) SF: 34/25/25/-/-

3367 THOMAS LONSDALE GALLAGHER H'CAP (0-75) (3-Y.O+) (Class D) £3,673.80 (£1,112.40: £543.20: £258.60)

1m 2f 32y Stalls: Low GOING minus 0.19 sec per fur (GF) 3-25 (3-27)

2824⁴ **Gold Desire (28)***(38) (MBrittain)* 5-7-7 JLowe(4) (bhd: effrt 4f out: styd on u.p to ld wl ins fnl f)....— 1
2993* Harry Browne (IRE) **(67)***(77)*(Fav)*(MrsJRRamsden)* 3-9-10 KFallon(9) (hld up: hdwy over 2f out: disp ld wl ins fnl f: no ex nr fin) ....nk 2
3169⁸ Imperial Bid (FR) **(55)***(63) (DenysSmith)* 7-9-6 TWilliams(1) (lw: a cl up: led 1f out tl wl ins fnl f: kpt on same pce) ....¾ 3
2064⁸ Kalou **(56)***(64) (CWCElsey)* 4-9-0v(7) PFessey(5) (trckd ldrs: led over 2f out tl hdd 1f out: kpt on one pce)....s.h 4
3232³ Touch Above **(45)***(51) (TDBarron)* 9-8-7 (3) NVarley(8) (prom: outpcd over 3f out: styd on appr fnl f) 1¼ 5
3232² Antartictern (USA) **(46)***(47) (GROldroyd)* 5-8-11 AMackay(3) (lw: hld up & bhd: effrt 3f out: nvr rchd ldrs) 3½ 6
2263³ Microlite (USA) **(57)***(39) (MDHammond)* 4-9-5v(3) JStack(2) (prom: rdn over 4f out: sn wknd) 12 7
3232* Thaleros **(58)***(39) (GMMoore)* 5-9-9 DHolland(7) (disp ld tl hdd over 2f out: wknd over 1f out: eased) ....½ 8
3063* Rood Music **(59)***(39) (MGMeagher)* 4-9-10 RCochrane(6) (disp ld tl hdd & wknd over 2f out) .½ 9

LONG HANDICAP Gold Desire 7-5

7/4 Harry Browne (IRE), **6/1** Antartictern (USA), **13/2** Rood Music, **7/1** Thaleros, **9/1** GOLD DESIRE (op 16/1), **10/1** Kalou, **11/1** Touch Above (op 7/1), **12/1** Microlite (USA), Imperial Bid (FR), CSF £24.65 CT £180.09 TOTE £9.30: £1.70 £1.70 £4.10 (£11.50) Trio £68.80 OWNER Mr Mel Brittain (WARTHILL) BRED Northgate Lodge Stud Ltd 9 Rn

2m 12.33 (5.63) SF: 20/51/45/46/33/29/21/21/21

WEIGHT FOR AGE 3yo-8lb

3368 ROTHMANS ROYALS NORTH SOUTH CHALLENGE SERIES H'CAP (0-85) (3-Y.O+) (Class D) £7,643.75 (£2,300.00: £1,112.50: £518.75)

1m (round) Stalls: Low GOING minus 0.19 sec per fur (GF) 4-00 (4-02)

2061* **Scaraben (62)***(75+) (SEKettlewell)* 7-8-8 (3) JStack(5) (trckd ldrs gng wl: led appr fnl f: r.o wl)....— 1
3255* Thatched (IRE) **(55)***(65) (REBarr)* 5-7-11 (7) 5x PFessey(4) (a.p: ev ch over 1f out: r.o) 1½ 2
3026² Almond Rock **(78)***(87)*(Fav)*(JRFanshawe)* 3-9-4 (3) NVarley(13) (lw: prom: hdwy u.p 2f out: kpt on towards fin)....¾ 3
3169³ Kemo Sabo **(80)***(88) (MrsJRRamsden)* 3-9-2 (7) TFinn(3) (led tl hdd appr fnl f: kpt on same pce)....½ 4
1619⁵ Clifton Fox **(83)***(89) (JAGlover)* 3-9-12 SDWilliams(1) (chsd ldrs: outpcd 2f out: kpt on fnl f) 1 5
2994³ Forever Diamonds **(70)***(75) (MHEasterby)* 8-9-5 MBirch(7) (trckd ldrs: effrt 2f out: r.o one pce) ....½ 6
3295² Mary's Case (IRE) **(53)***(56) (MJohnston)* 5-8-2b TWilliams(2) (effrt 3f out: styd on u.p: n.d) .....¾ 7
1306³ Crumpton Hill (IRE) **(85)***(87) (NAGraham)* 3-10-0 DHolland(12) (lw: in tch: effrt 3f out: one pce) ....½ 8

3063⁹ Marowins **(47)***(47) (EJAlston)* 6-7-10 ow2 AMackay(6) (hld up & bhd: effrt 3f out: sme late hdwy) ....s.h 9
785⁹ Current Speech (IRE) **(72)***(73) (MHEasterby)* 4-9-7 SMaloney(8) (nvr trbld ldrs) ....½ 10
3175⁵ Desert Time **(77)***(77) (MRChannon)* 5-9-5 (7) DSweeney(9) (effrt ent st: no imp) ....nk 11
1687⁴ Shinerolla **(76)***(75) (MrsJRRamsden)* 3-9-5 KFallon(11) (hld up & bhd: nvr plcd to chal) ....½ 12
2468³ Hakika (USA) **(85)** *(DMorley)* 3-10-0 RCochrane(10) (lw: in tch: rdn over 2f out: sn btn: sddle slipped & eased appr fnl f: virtually p.u) ....dist 13

9/2 Almond Rock, **11/2** Thatched (IRE), **7/1** Crumpton Hill (IRE), Forever Diamonds, **15/2** SCARABEN, **8/1** Shinerolla (op 9/2), **10/1** Desert Time, Hakika (USA), **12/1** Mary's Case (IRE), **16/1** Clifton Fox, Kemo Sabo, **20/1** Marowins, **33/1** Current Speech (IRE), CSF £47.43 CT £194.81 TOTE £8.60: £2.50 £2.00 £3.00 (£21.90) Trio £51.20 OWNER Mr J. Tennant (MIDDLEHAM) BRED Burton Agnes Stud Co Ltd 13 Rn 1m 44.15 (5.15) SF: 29/19/35/36/37/29/10/35/1/27/31/23/-
WEIGHT FOR AGE 3yo-6lb

3369

JAMES FLETCHER MARQUEES NURSERY H'CAP (2-Y.O) (Class D) £3,640.00 (£1,102.00: £538.00: £256.00)
5f Stalls: High GOING: 0.16 sec per fur (G) 4-30 (4-32)

3284² **Hoh Majestic (IRE) (66)***(71) (MBell)* 2-7-5v(3)ow1 NVarley(7) (chsd ldrs: styd on to ld wl ins fnl f) ....— 1
3220³ Tadeo **(96)***(97)*(Fav)*(MJohnston)* 2-9-10 TWilliams(4) (led: rdn over 1f out: hdd wl ins fnl f)..1½ 2
3064² Welsh Mountain **(81)***(66) (MJHeaton-Ellis)* 2-8-9 DHolland(6) (a.p: hrd drvn 2f out: kpt on same pce) 5 3
2442¹⁰ Mystique Smile **(68)***(44) (JBerry)* 2-7-3 (7) PFessey(3) (cl up tl rdn & btn appr fnl f) 3 4
3049⁵ Everyone Can Dream **(65)***(60d) (DenysSmith)* 2-7-7 JLowe(2) (dwlt: sn drvn along: nvr trbld ldrs) 1 5
2991⁴ Dancing Rainbow **(65)***(66) (MJCamacho)* 2-7-7v NKennedy(5) (s.i.s: sn in tch: rdn & btn 2f out) 3 6
3064⁵ Pathaze **(69)***(12) (NBycroft)* 2-7-11 ow1 SMaloney(1) (chsd ldrs: hrd rdn ½-wy: sn btn) 6 7

LONG HANDICAP Everyone Can Dream 6-13 Dancing Rainbow 7-5 Hoh Majestic (IRE) 7-5

11/4 Tadeo, **100/30** Mystique Smile, **4/1** Welsh Mountain, HOH MAJESTIC (IRE), **8/1** Pathaze, **11/1** Dancing Rainbow, **14/1** Everyone Can Dream, CSF £14.87 TOTE £3.40: £2.20 £2.30 (£4.80) OWNER Mr D. F. Allport (NEWMARKET) BRED Ballinacurra Stud 7 Rn
62.63 secs (4.23) SF: 21/47/16/-/-/-/-

3370

WESTGATE MAIDEN H'CAP (0-65) (3-Y.O+) (Class F) £2,940.20(£827.20: £404.60) **1m (round)** Stalls: Low GOING minus 0.19 sec per fur (GF) 5-05 (5-09)

3263⁵ **Phase One (IRE) (51)***(62) (JLEyre)* 5-9-8 RLappin(3) (swtg: cl up: led 1½f out: styd on u.p).— 1
2733⁵ Matisse **(39)***(49) (JDBethell)* 4-8-10 KFallon(6) (lw: mid div: hdwy over 2f out: ev ch ins fnl f: nt qckn) ....½ 2
2923⁹ Arrogant Boy **(22)***(24) (DWChapman)* 6-7-7 NKennedy(5) (a.p: kpt on u.p fnl 2f: nvr able to chal) 4 3
2955⁵ Md Thompson **(53)***(54) (SCWilliams)* 3-9-1 (3) DRMcCabe(2) (cl up: effrt over 2f out: r.o) ....¾ 4
2396⁸ Runrig (IRE) **(37)***(36) (MissLAPerratt)* 5-8-1 (7) PFessey(4) (hdwy over 2f out: nvr trbld ldrs) 1 5
3079⁷ Paronomasia **(38)***(28) (MBell)* 3-8-0v(3)ow2 JStack(7) (led tl hdd 1½f out: sn outpcd) 3½ 6
3099⁷ Hee's a Dancer **(38)***(26) (MJCamacho)* 3-8-3 DaleGibson(15) (prom: rdn over 3f out: one pce)2 7
3000⁵ Teejay'n'aitch (IRE) **(46)***(27) (JSGoldie)* 3-8-11 DHolland(1) (effrt 3f out: nvr rchd ldrs) 3½ 8
3302³ Bex Boy (IRE) **(27)***(6) (MWEasterby)* 4-7-12b JLowe(13) (prom to st) 1 9
3167³ Boost **(44)***(16) (CWThornton)* 3-8-9 AMackay(16) (in tch tl outpcd fnl 3f) 3½ 10
1797⁵ Rinus Manor (IRE) **(40)** *(EJAlston)* 4-8-11 SDWilliams(10) (n.d) 7 11
2915⁴ Gymcrak Jareer (IRE) **(53)** *(GHolmes)* 3-8-11 (7) RuthCoulter(12) (n.d) 7 12
3103⁷ Woolaw Girl **(26)** *(JSHaldane)* 7-7-11 ow1 SMaloney(9) (a bhd) 15 13
1944⁷ Bollin Sophie **(42)** *(MHEasterby)* 3-8-7 MBirch(11) (cl up tl wknd 3f out) 8 14
2856² Almizaj **(63)** (Fav)*(HThomsonJones)* 3-10-0b RCochrane(18) (lw: bhd ent st: p.u 2f out: dead) .. P
2582³ Malzoom **(33)** *(SEKettlewell)* 3-7-9 (3) NVarley(8) (lw: reard leaving stalls & uns rdr) .... U

5/2 Almizaj (4/1-7/4), **4/1** Md Thompson (op 8/1), **8/1** Matisse, **10/1** PHASE ONE (IRE), Boost, Malzoom, **11/1** Hee's a Dancer, **12/1** Bex Boy (IRE) (op 8/1), Paronomasia, **14/1** Teejay'n'aitch (IRE), **20/1** Runrig (IRE), Rinus Manor (IRE), **25/1** Gymcrak Jareer (IRE), Bollin Sophie, **50/1** Arrogant Boy, Woolaw Girl, CSF £90.22 CT £3,532.73 TOTE £17.30: £3.50 £2.10 £8.90 £2.70 (£71.20) Trio Not won; £572.75 to Goodwood 27/8/95 OWNER Blackfield Racing (HAMBLETON) BRED St Simon Foundation 16 Rn 1m 44.9 (5.90) SF: 32/19/-/18/6/-/-/-/-/-/-/-/-/-/-/-
WEIGHT FOR AGE 3yo-6lb

T/Plpt: £84.00 (124.35 Tckts). T/Qdpt: £305.80 (1.8 Tckts). AA

3339-NEWMARKET (R-H)
Saturday August 26th (Good to firm)
WEATHER: fine WIND: mod bhd

3371
E.B.F. PARK LODGE MAIDEN STKS (2-Y.O) (Class D) £4,932.00 (£1,476.00: £708.00: £324.00)
6f (July) Stalls: Low GOING minus 0.52 sec per fur (F) 2-10 (2-11)

My Mariam *(75) (CREgerton)* 2-8-9 BThomson(14) (neat: lw: sn chsng ldrs: led 1f out: rdn & hld on wl)......— **1**
Promptly (IRE) *(74+) (MRStoute)* 2-8-9 WRSwinburn(4) (neat: scope: hld up: hdwy 2f out: nt clr run & swtchd lft ins fnl f: fin wl)......nk **2**
3003[7] The Man *(71) (MRChannon)* 2-9-0 BDoyle(8) (lw: a.p: rdn wl over 1f out: one pce)......3 **3**
690[6] Man of Wit (IRE) *(70) (APJarvis)* 2-8-11 (3) JTate(13) (led tl hdd 1f out: edgd rt & no ex ins fnl f)......nk **4**
690[10] Hoh Returns (IRE) *(70) (MBell)* 2-9-0 MFenton(1) (chsd ldrs: rdn over 1f out: one pce)......nk **5**
Keiko *(61+) (JHMGosden)* 2-8-9 PatEddery(12) (neat: chsd ldrs: bmpd over 1f out: sn btn).1½ **6**
3185[7] Mukabir (USA) *(65)*(Fav)*(MajorWRHern)* 2-9-0 TSprake(2) (lw: hld up: hdwy over 1f out: nrst fin)......nk **7**
Sharp Pearl *(61) (RCharlton)* 2-9-0 WRyan(6) (w'like: scope: hld up: hdwy wl over 1f out: nrst fin)......1½ **8**
Ecstatic Madam (IRE) *(51) (BWHills)* 2-8-9 MHills(5) (leggy: scope: nvr nr to chal)......2 **9**
Diamond Beach *(51) (BWHills)* 2-9-0 KDarley(10) (w'like: scope: lw: dwlt: hdwy 3f out: rdn 2f out: sn wknd)......1¾ **10**
Prince Zizim *(50) (CADwyer)* 2-9-0 MWigham(7) (neat: str: in tch 3f: sn wknd)......½ **11**
Old School House *(48) (CNAllen)* 2-9-0 StephenDavies(9) (w'like: bkwd: chsd ldrs over 3f)...½ **12**
17817[7] Night of Glass *(48) (DMorris)* 2-9-0 DeanMcKeown(3) (dwlt: a bhd)......s.h **13**
Blueberry Fields *(42) (CFWall)* 2-8-9 WWoods(11) (cmpt: bkwd: s.s: a bhd)......nk **14**

100/30 Mukabir (USA), **5/1** Man of Wit (IRE), **7/1** Promptly (IRE), Keiko, Sharp Pearl, **12/1** Ecstatic Madam (IRE), **20/1** Hoh Returns (IRE), Old School House, **25/1** Diamond Beach, **33/1** MY MARIAM, The Man, Prince Zizim, Night of Glass, Blueberry Fields, CSF £209.00 TOTE £43.30: £7.20 £2.00 £4.80 (£182.80) Trio £405.00; £370.83 to Goodwood 27/8/95 OWNER Mr Abdul Rahman Mubarak (CHADDLEWORTH) BRED Miss S. McCreery and Stowell Hill Ltd 14 Rn
1m 12.7 SF: 34/33/30/29/29/20/24/20/10/10/9/7/7/1

3372
NGK SPARK PLUGS CLAIMING STKS (3-Y.O) (Class D) £4,815.00 (£1,440.00: £690.00: £315.00)
7f (July) Stalls: Low GOING minus 0.52 sec per fur (F) 2-45 (2-45)

2968* **Delight of Dawn** **(72)***(78)*(Fav)*(KTIvory)* 3-8-3 (7) CScally(6) (b: dwlt: hdwy 3f out: led over 1f out: edgd lft: rdn out)......— **1**
2872[2] Flyaway Blues **(54)***(72) (MrsMReveley)* 3-8-6b KDarley(8) (hld up in rr: hdwy over 2f out: styd on u.p fnl f)......1 **2**
2905[5] Rosa Bonheur **(56)***(54) (MAJarvis)* 3-7-9 JQuinn(2) (b.hind: chsd ldrs: rdn over 1f out: kpt on one pce)......3 **3**
3096[4] Contract Venture (IRE) **(57)***(57) (WJarvis)* 3-7-12 (5) MHenry(1) (lw: hld up: effrt over 2f out: nt pce to chal)......2 **4**
3344[18] Commander Glen (IRE) **(54)***(63) (MartynMeade)* 3-8-9 VSlattery(4) (sn rdn along: chsd ldrs: outpcd 3f out: kpt on fnl f)......s.h **5**
3126[4] Cats Bottom **(65)***(60) (DJSCosgrove)* 3-8-2b(5) AWhelan(7) (lw: chsd ldr: led 3f out tl over 1f out: wknd fnl f)......½ **6**
2945[3] Proud Image **(70)***(34) (APJarvis)* 3-8-12v(3) JTate(5) (led 4f: wknd wl over 1f out: eased whn btn)......15 **7**

2/1 DELIGHT OF DAWN, **4/1** Rosa Bonheur, **6/1** Proud Image (op 4/1), **13/2** Cats Bottom, **7/1** Flyaway Blues, **12/1** Contract Venture (IRE) (op 8/1), **20/1** Commander Glen (IRE), CSF £13.64 TOTE £2.70: £1.90 £1.90 (£6.90) OWNER Mr K. T. Ivory (RADLETT) BRED John Hayter 7 Rn
1m 25.22 SF: 42/36/18/21/27/24/-

3373
VIXEN HILL GAZEBOS H'CAP (0-90) (3-Y.O) (Class C) £7,505.00 (£2,240.00: £1,070.00: £485.00)
7f (July) Stalls: Low GOING minus 0.52 sec per fur (F) 3-20 (3-23)

3235[6] **Twilight Patrol** **(90)***(101) (RHannon)* 3-9-2 (5) DaneO'Neill(5) (b.nr fore: hdwy 4f out: led over 1f out: rdn out)......— **1**

2848[3] Proud Destiny **(79)***(88) (MRStoute)* 3-8-10 WRSwinburn(11) (lw: chsd ldrs: outpcd 2f out: rdn & r.o wl ins fnl f)....1 2
3085[6] Emerging Market **(88)***(96) (JLDunlop)* 3-9-5 KDarley(6) (hld up: hdwy over 2f out: rdn & r.o ins fnl f)....½ 3
3182[3] Domitia (USA) **(63)***(67) (MBell)* 3-7-1 (7)ow1 RMullen(9) (swtg: mde most tl hdd & no ex over 1f out)....1¼ 4
2324[6] French Grit (IRE) **(88)***(92) (MDods)* 3-9-5 WWoods(8) (lw: s.s: hdwy over 2f out: nt rch ldrs)..½ 5
1474[10] Desert Harvest **(77)***(77) (RCharlton)* 3-8-8 PatEddery(7) (bhd: rdn & hdwy over 2f out: styd on fnl f)....1½ 6
2709* Alarming **(82)***(81)*(Fav)*(JHMGosden)* 3-8-13 JCarroll(3) (disp ld 5f: rdn over 1f out: sn btn)....½ 7
3182* Distant Princess **(69)***(66) (BWHills)* 3-8-0 BDoyle(1) (chsd ldrs over 5f: sn lost tch)....1 8
3209[7] Last Roundup **(76)***(71) (CWThornton)* 3-8-7 DeanMcKeown(10) (lw: bhd: rdn over 2f out: no imp)....¾ 9
2578[10] Tharwa (IRE) **(64)***(58) (NACallaghan)* 3-7-9 JQuinn(4) (b. b.hind: plld hrd: chsd ldrs 5f)....½ 10

5/1 Alarming, **11/2** Distant Princess, **6/1** Proud Destiny, **13/2** Desert Harvest, **7/1** French Grit (IRE), TWILIGHT PATROL, Emerging Market, **16/1** Domitia (USA), Tharwa (IRE), **20/1** Last Roundup, CSF £43.33 CT £274.01 TOTE £7.80: £2.40 £1.60 £2.50 (£15.80) Trio £78.60 OWNER Cheveley Park Stud (MARLBOROUGH) BRED Cheveley Park Stud Ltd 10 Rn
1m 24.96 SF: 55/42/50/21/46/31/35/20/25/12

3374 DANEPAK CLASSIC RATED STKS H'CAP (0-100) (3-Y.O+) (Class B) £10,046.40 (£3,717.60: £1,256.40: £1,256.40: £289.50: £113.70)
1m 2f (July) Stalls: High GOING minus 0.52 sec per fur (F) 3-50 (3-53)

2950* **Star of Persia (IRE) (84)***(96+) (PWHarris)* 3-8-5 GHind(2) (s.i.s: sn chsng ldrs: led wl over 1f out: clr fnl f)....— 1
3237[2] Amrak Ajeeb (IRE) **(87)***(94)*(Fav)*(BHanbury)* 3-8-8 MRimmer(1) (b: plld hrd: sn chsng ldr: ev ch over 1f out: one pce fnl f)....3 2
3107[4] Warning Order **(94)***(101) (JLDunlop)* 3-9-1b KDarley(10) (lw: hdwy 6f out: rdn over 1f out: nt qckn fnl f)....½ 3
2672[11] Ringmaster (IRE) **(88)***(94) (MHTompkins)* 4-9-3 WRyan(3) (hld up: rdn & hdwy 3f out: styd on ins fnl f)....d.h 3
2967* Persian Elite (IRE) **(78)***(84) (PFICole)* 4-8-7 TQuinn(7) (led tl hdd wl over 1f out: rdn & kpt on fnl f)....s.h 5
2589[5] Heathyards Rock **(86)***(83) (RHollinshead)* 3-8-7b TIves(8) (lw: dwlt: in rr & pushed along 5f out: nvr rchd ldrs)....6 6
2672[12] Show Faith (IRE) **(84)***(81) (RHannon)* 5-8-8 (5) DaneO'Neill(5) (lw: nvr nr to chal)....hd 7
3188[10] Sue's Return **(88)***(78) (APJarvis)* 3-8-9 PatEddery(9) (chsd ldrs over 7f: sn rdn & wknd)....4 8
2598[8] Cedez le Passage (FR) **(92)***(80) (CEBrittain)* 4-9-7 BDoyle(4) (chsd ldrs 6f: grad wknd)....1½ 9
3131[5] Palatial Style **(88)***(63) (PJMakin)* 8-9-3 BThomson(6) (b: bhd: rdn & effrt 3f out: no imp)....8 10

11/4 Amrak Ajeeb (IRE), **5/1** Ringmaster (IRE), **6/1** STAR OF PERSIA (IRE), **7/1** Persian Elite (IRE), **15/2** Sue's Return, **10/1** Warning Order, **12/1** Show Faith (IRE), **14/1** Cedez le Passage (FR), **16/1** Heathyards Rock, **20/1** Palatial Style, CSF £21.37 CT SOP, AA & R £40.19, SOP, AA & WO £73.66 TOTE £6.50: £2.10 £1.20 R £1.20 WO £1.80 (£10.50) Trio SOP-AA-R £9.70, SOP-AA-WO £15.80 OWNER The Saturday Club (BERKHAMSTED) BRED Mrs Kiki Ward Platt 10 Rn
2m 4.04 SF: 34/32/39/40/30/21/27/16/26/9
WEIGHT FOR AGE 3yo-8lb

3375 TOTE MULTIBET NURSERY H'CAP (2-Y.O) (Class C) £25,930.00 (£7,840.00: £3,820.00: £1,810.00)
6f (July) Stalls: Low GOING minus 0.52 sec per fur (F) 4-20 (4-21)

3117[2] **Creative Account (USA) (74)***(83+) (MrsJRRamsden)* 2-8-7 JFEgan(5) (lw: hld up & bhd: hdwy over 1f out: str run to ld wl ins fnl f)....— 1
3032[3] My Branch **(80)***(85) (BWHills)* 2-8-13 MHills(6) (lw: a.p: led over 2f out: hrd rdn & hdd wl ins fnl f)....1½ 2
3213[3] Atraf **(84)***(84) (DMorley)* 2-9-3 BThomson(7) (lw: chsd ldrs til outpcd 2f out: styd on fnl f)....1¾ 3
3328a* Rabican (IRE) **(88)***(84)*(Fav)*(GCBravery)* 2-9-7 WRSwinburn(10) (hld up in tch: effrt & rdn over 1f out: no imp ins fnl f)....1¾ 4
3147[8] Amaretto Bay (IRE) **(84)***(74) (BJMeehan)* 2-9-3b BDoyle(1) (hdwy over 2f out: one pce fnl f)....2 5
2978[3] Rushcutter Bay **(82)***(69) (TTClement)* 2-8-10v(5) DGibbs(12) (hung lft: mde most over 3f: wknd fnl f)....1¼ 6
2779[3] Flying North (IRE) **(82)***(66) (MrsMReveley)* 2-9-1 KDarley(8) (hld up: hdwy 2f out: styd on ins fnl f)....1¼ 7

3090[8] Balpare **(63)**_(47) (NACallaghan)_ 2-7-10 GBardwell(9) (bhd tl rdn & styd on fnl f)....................s.h **8**
3160* No Monkey Nuts **(82)**_(64) (JBerry)_ 2-9-1 JCarroll(13) (spd 4f)....................½ **9**
2223[5] Safio **(87)**_(63d) (CSmith)_ 2-9-3 (3) JTate(4) (b.nr hind: dwlt: a bhd)....................2½ **10**
2432[4] Myttons Mistake **(85)**_(59) (ABailey)_ 2-9-4 WRyan(11) (a bhd)....................¾ **11**
2674[4] King of Peru **(81)**_(54) (APJarvis)_ 2-9-0 PatEddery(2) (chsd ldrs far side: rdn & btn 2f out: eased)....................nk **12**
2900a[8] Double Point (IRE) **(85)**_(53) (MBell)_ 2-9-4 MFenton(3) (prom over 3f)....................1¾ **13**
1492* Satellite Star (IRE) **(80)**_(43) (MRChannon)_ 2-8-13 WNewnes(15) (s.s: a bhd)....................1¾ **14**
2435[4] Eights High (USA) **(72)**_(30) (RHannon)_ 2-8-5 MRoberts(14) (b.off hind: in tch tl rdn & btn 2f out)....................2 **15**

2/1 Rabican (IRE), **8/1** My Branch, **9/1** No Monkey Nuts, CREATIVE ACCOUNT (USA), **10/1** Flying North (IRE), **12/1** Amaretto Bay (IRE), Atraf, Myttons Mistake, King of Peru, **16/1** Balpare, Eights High (USA), **20/1** Rushcutter Bay, **25/1** Double Point (IRE), Satellite Star (IRE), **50/1** Safio, CSF £77.52 CT £811.26 TOTE £10.30: £2.10 £3.00 £3.80 (£57.80) Trio £155.30 OWNER Mr P. A. Leonard (THIRSK) BRED Rankin, Sanderlin and Lenihan 15 Rn

1m 12.3 SF: 37/39/38/38/28/23/20/1/18/17/13/8/7/-/-

3376 TOTE LADIES IN RED LADIES AMATEUR H'CAP (0-85) (3-Y.O+) (Class E) £5,572.00 (£1,666.00: £798.00: £364.00)

5f (July) Stalls: Low GOING minus 0.52 sec per fur (F) 4-50 (4-51)

2997[8] **Crystal Loop (66)**_(72) (ABailey)_ 3-9-8 (5) MissBridgetGatehouse(8) (mde virtually all: hld on wl fnl f)....................— **1**
3219[8] Robellion **(70)**_(76) (DWPArbuthnot)_ 4-10-6 MrsDArbuthnot(12) (lw: hld up: hdwy over 1f out: r.o wl ins fnl f)....................s.h **2**
3205[2] Ansellman **(74)**_(80) (JBerry)_ 5-10-10 MrsDKettlewell(3) (w ldrs: shkn up over 2f out: ev ch over 1f out: r.o fnl f)....................s.h **3**
3341[6] Moujeeb (USA) **(55)**_(58) (PatMitchell)_ 5-9-5v MrsAPerrett(6) (bhd: rdn 2f out: gd hdwy fnl f: fin wl)....................¾ **4**
3236[2] Quiz Time **(88)**_(90)_(Fav)_(SirMarkPrescott)_ 3-11-7 MissDianaJones(7) (in tch: effrt over 1f out: r.o wl nr fin)....................nk **5**
3087[7] Spender **(74)**_(74) (PWHarris)_ 6-10-10 MissAElsey(5) (s.s: hdwy over 2f out: nvr able to chal) ¾ **6**
3123* Windrush Boy **(66)**_(66) (JRBosley)_ 5-10-2 MrsSBosley(9) (chsd ldrs: effrt appr fnl f: nt qckn) hd **7**
3112[8] Magic Orb **(75)**_(74) (JLHarris)_ 5-10-6 (5) MrsSEddery(1) (b: spd far side over 3f)....................s.h **8**
_3242_[6] Shadow Jury **(73)**_(70) (DWChapman)_ 5-10-4b(5) MissRClark(11) (lw: racd centre: spd over 3f)¾ **9**
3014[7] Bold Gem **(53)**_(48) (BJMeehan)_ 4-9-3b MissJAllison(2) (s.s: effrt 2f out: nt trble ldrs)....................¾ **10**
2887[2] Millesime (IRE) **(71)**_(60) (BHanbury)_ 3-10-4 MissEJohnsonHoughton(10) (spd over 3f)........1¾ **11**
_3072_* Evening Falls **(55)**_(28) (CJames)_ 4-9-0 (5) MissCCorbett(4) (unruly stalls: a bhd)....................5 **12**

7/2 Quiz Time, **6/1** Millesime (IRE), Ansellman, **7/1** Evening Falls, **10/1** Windrush Boy, **12/1** Moujeeb (USA), Spender (op 8/1), **14/1** Magic Orb, Robellion (op 8/1), Bold Gem (8/1-16/1), Shadow Jury (10/1-16/1), **16/1** CRYSTAL LOOP, CSF £194.09 CT £1,358.94 TOTE £45.10: £8.50 £4.60 £1.90 (£191.70) Trio £890.70; £632.24 to Goodwood 27/8/95 OWNER Mr Roy Matthews (TARPORLEY) BRED B. Long 12 Rn 59.91 secs SF: 51/58/62/40/69/56/48/56/52/30/39/10

WEIGHT FOR AGE 3yo-3lb

3377 STANLEY HOUSE MAIDEN STKS (3-Y.O+) (Class D) £4,425.00 (£1,320.00: £630.00: £285.00)

1m (July) Stalls: Low GOING minus 0.52 sec per fur (F) 5-25 (5-26)

2977[2] **Clan Ben (IRE)** _(84)_(Fav)_(HRACecil)_ 3-8-11 WRyan(6) (trckd ldrs: led over 2f out: pushed out)—**1**
695[10] Prickwillow (USA) _(77) (JHMGosden)_ 3-8-6 GHind(2) (a.p: ev ch over 2f out tl no ex ins fnl f).1 **2**
2553[12] Victory Team (IRE) **(72)**_(72) (JRFanshawe)_ 3-8-11 JCarroll(9) (led over 5f: one pce appr fnl f)5 **3**
3023[7] Darcey Bussell _(59) (BWHills)_ 3-8-6 MHills(3) (b: in tch: kpt on fnl 2f: nt pce tochal)....................4 **4**
Kalamata _(54) (ACStewart)_ 3-8-11 MRoberts(8) (w'like: bkwd: dwlt: wl bhd tl styd on fnl f)......5 **5**
1314[5] Arzani (USA) **(68)**_(53) (DJSCosgrove)_ 4-9-3 MRimmer(5) (lw: chsd ldrs: eased whn btn appr fnl f)....................¾ **6**
1507[3] Houghton Venture (USA) **(72)**_(41) (SPCWoods)_ 3-8-11 WWoods(10) (hdwy 4f out: wknd & eased over 1f out)....................6 **7**

4/11 CLAN BEN (IRE), **7/1** Kalamata (op 7/2), **10/1** Prickwillow (USA) (op 5/1), **12/1** Houghton Venture (USA), **28/1** Arzani (USA), **33/1** Victory Team (IRE), **50/1** Darcey Bussell, CSF £4.62 TOTE £1.50: £1.10 £2.50 (£3.30) Trio £17.20 OWNER Angus Dundee Ltd (NEWMARKET) BRED T. Hillman 7 Rn 1m 38.35 SF: 46/39/34/21/16/21/3

WEIGHT FOR AGE 3yo-6lb

T/Jkpt: Not won; £25,373.65 to Goodwood 27/8/95. T/Plpt: £516.80 (64.66 Tckts). T/Qdpt: £655.20 (1.25 Tckts). Dk

3129-WINDSOR (Fig. 8)
Saturday August 26th (Good to firm, St Good)
WEATHER: overcast WIND: mod half bhd

3378 GREAT CHARTER (S) STKS (2-Y.O) (Class F) £2,810.00 (£785.00 £380.00)
5f 217y Stalls: High GOING minus 0.25 sec per fur (GF) 5-15 (5-18)

3136[4] **Lilli Claire** *(64) (AGFoster)* 2-8-6 TSprake(3) (lw: a.p: rdn to ld ins fnl f: r.o)........— 1
3133[9] Never Think Twice **(70)***(64) (KTIvory)* 2-8-11 NAdams(9) (b: a.p: led over 1f out: hdd ins fnl f: one pce)........2 2
3233[4] Music Mistress (IRE) **(55)***(56)*(Fav)*(RHannon)* 2-8-11 RHughes(10) (lw: chsd ldrs: rdn over 1f out: eased whn btn ins fnl f)........3 3
Killatty Lark (IRE) *(46) (WJMusson)* 2-8-3 (3) PMcCabe(8) (w'like: bit bkwd: hdwy over 1f out: nvr nrr)........1¾ 4
3290[4] Apartments Abroad *(43) (KMcAuliffe)* 2-8-1b(5) MHenry(14) (b.hind: led: hdd over 1f out: wknd fnl f)........1¼ 5
3244[6] Moniques Venture *(37) (DJSCosgrove)* 2-8-6 DBiggs(13) (dwlt: hdwy over 2f out: rdn & wknd over 1f out)........2 6
3080[8] Bellapais (IRE) *(29) (WRMuir)* 2-8-6b RPerham(11) (dwlt: nvr nrr)........3 7
2656[6] Cupla Focail *(21) (WRMuir)* 2-8-6 CRutter(6) (bhd fnl 3f)........3 8
2176[8] Peterrex *(20) (MRChannon)* 2-8-11 AClark(12) (chsd ldrs tl rdn & wknd 3f out)........2½ 9
2962[12] Dish The Dosh *(11) (PGMurphy)* 2-7-13b(7) RWaterfield(7) (bhd fnl 3f)........1¼ 10
3135[4] Deedeejay *(JMBradley)* 2-8-3 (3) SDrowne(1) (bhd fnl 3f)........5 11
3077[13] Mobile King *(APJarvis)* 2-8-11 GDuffield(4) (bhd fnl 3f)........7 12
3180[9] A Million At Last (IRE) *(MBell)* 2-8-4 (7) GFaulkner(5) (bhd fnl 3f)........5 13

5/2 Music Mistress (IRE), **7/2** LILLI CLAIRE, **6/1** Never Think Twice, Apartments Abroad (7/2-13/2), **8/1** A Million At Last (IRE), **12/1** Peterrex, **14/1** Deedeejay, **16/1** Cupla Focail, **20/1** Moniques Venture, Killatty Lark (IRE), **25/1** Mobile King, **33/1** Bellapais (IRE), Dish The Dosh, CSF £25.39 TOTE £4.30: £1.80 £2.00 £1.40 (£10.80) Trio £12.20 OWNER Miss Juliet Reed (LAMBOURN) BRED Roger C. Denton 13 Rn 1m 13.7 (3.20) SF: 25/25/17/7/4/-/-/-/-/-/-/-/-
Bt in 6,400gns

3379 KING JOHN MAIDEN AUCTION STKS (2-Y.O) (Class E) £3,616.50 (£1,092.00: £531.00: £250.50)
5f 217y Stalls: High GOING minus 0.25 sec per fur (GF) 5-45 (5-49)

3069[14] **Lady Thiang** *(82) (CFWall)* 2-8-2 GDuffield(13) (chsd ldrs: rdn to ld ins fnl f: r.o)........— 1
2277[6] Manderella *(77) (JAkehurst)* 2-7-12 DBiggs(10) (b.off hind: chsd ldrs: rdn over 1f out: ev ch wl ins fnl f: r.o)........nk 2
2552[9] Step On Degas *(67) (SDow)* 2-7-8 (7)ow3 ADaly(1) (a.p: led over 2f out: sn clr: wknd & hdd ins fnl f)........4 3
2791[3] Sondos *(64)*(Fav)*(JWHills)* 2-8-2 WCarson(21) (chsd ldrs: hrd rdn over 1f out: one pce)......2½ 4
2541[5] Napoleon's Return **(67)***(62) (AGFoster)* 2-8-3 TSprake(9) (chsd ldrs: rdn over 1f out: one pce)........1¼ 5
Mam'selle Bergerac (IRE) *(56) (PMitchell)* 2-7-9 (3) DWright(6) (unf: chsd ldrs: rdn 2f out: one pce)........s.h 6
Fran Godfrey *(60) (PTWalwyn)* 2-7-11 (5) MHenry(23) (leggy: nvr nrr)........s.h 7
2548[13] Duralock Fencer *(61) (PGMurphy)* 2-7-10 (7) RWaterfield(7) (b.hind: hld up: hdwy 2f out: rdn over 1f out: one pce)........s.h 8
Daffodil Express (IRE) *(53) (MJRyan)* 2-7-7 (5) MBaird(25) (unf: bit bkwd: led: hdd over 2f out: wknd over 1f out)........1¼ 9
3069[22] Poly By Staufan (IRE) *(51) (MRChannon)* 2-7-11 (5) PPMurphy(19) (prom 4f)........2 10
2198[10] Dragonjoy *(52) (LJHolt)* 2-8-3 AMcGlone(18) (prom 4f)........s.h 11
2299[5] Indira *(50) (HCandy)* 2-8-2 CRutter(14) (chsd ldrs tl wknd 2f out)........½ 12
3025[4] Day Tripper *(50) (GBBalding)* 2-8-4 ow1 JWilliams(3) (a mid div)........½ 13
2548[12] Little Kenny *(49) (MJFetherston-Godley)* 2-7-11 (5) AWhelan(20) (nvr nrr)........s.h 14
3069[20] Eskimo Kiss (IRE) *(48) (MJFetherston-Godley)* 2-8-2 JQuinn(16) (a mid div)........nk 15
Absolutelystunning *(42) (MrsBarbaraWaring)* 2-8-4 (5)ow7 DGriffiths(11) (unf: s.s: hdwy 2f out: rdn & swtchd lft over 1f out: no ex)........2 16
2548[8] Bailiwick *(47) (NAGraham)* 2-8-7 PaulEddery(8) (a bhd)........nk 17
725[5] Sharp Shuffle (IRE) *(37) (RHannon)* 2-8-4 ow1 RPerham(5) (a bhd)........2 18
Soldier Mak *(34) (AHide)* 2-8-3 CNutter(12) (w'like: bit bkwd: a bhd)........1¼ 19
2939[W] Fairly Sure (IRE) *(28) (NEBerry)* 2-7-12 NAdams(4) (a bhd)........nk 20
2791[12] Quiet Moments (IRE) *(31) (PGMurphy)* 2-8-0 (3) SDrowne(17) (a bhd)........¾ 21
3069[18] Cotytto *(29) (MJFetherston-Godley)* 2-8-2 FNorton(15) (a bhd)........½ 22

2135[9] Soul Risk *(24) (JARToller)* 2-8-7 AClark(24) (prom 4f) 3½ **23**
Forliando *(7) (MSSaunders)* 2-8-3 RPrice(2) (unf: bit bkwd: dwlt: a bhd) 5 **24**

5/4 Sondos, **5/1** LADY THIANG (9/2-7/1), **9/1** Napoleon's Return, **10/1** Day Tripper (8/1-14/1), Manderella, **14/1** Step On Degas, Fran Godfrey, **16/1** Indira, Poly By Staufan (IRE), **20/1** Sharp Shuffle (IRE), **25/1** Duralock Fencer, **33/1** Daffodil Express (IRE), Soldier Mak, Little Kenny, Eskimo Kiss (IRE), Soul Risk, Bailiwick, Dragonjoy, Cotytto, Fairly Sure (IRE), Forliando, **50/1** Mam'selle Bergerac (IRE), Absolutelystunning, Quiet Moments (IRE), CSF £61.57 TOTE £9.70: £3.40 £3.40 £7.10 (£71.80) Trio £329.00; £231.72 to 29/8/95 OWNER Mr W. Wallick (NEWMARKET) BRED Dodford Stud 24 Rn 1m 13.4 (2.90) SF: 25/20/10/7/5/-/3/4/-/-/-/-/-/-/-/-/-/-/-/-/-/-/-/-

3380 SHEET & ROLL CONVERTORS POLY CONDITIONS STKS (3-Y.O+) (Class C) £5,678.50 (£1,831.00: £890.50)

1m 3f 135y Stalls: High GOING minus 0.25 sec per fur (GF) 6-15 (6-15)

2670[3] **Istidaad (USA) (113)***(117)*(Fav)*(ACStewart)* 3-8-7 WCarson(1) (mde all: pushed out) ....— **1**
3070[4] Bal Harbour **(108)***(112) (HRACecil)* 4-9-1 PatEddery(2) (chsd wnr: 2nd st: rdn 3f out: one pce fnl f) 2½ **2**
2910[2] Green Green Desert (FR) **(98)***(103) (MRStoute)* 4-9-2 WRSwinburn(3) (hld up: 3rd st: rdn over 2f out: wknd over 1f out: eased ins fnl f) 7 **3**

8/13 ISTIDAAD (USA), **5/2** Bal Harbour, **4/1** Green Green Desert (FR), CSF £2.38 TOTE £1.60 (£1.50) OWNER Mr Hamdan Al Maktoum (NEWMARKET) BRED Shadwell Farm Inc and Shadwell Estate Co Ltd 3 Rn 2m 29.7 (3.70) SF: 47/52/43
WEIGHT FOR AGE 3yo-10lb

3381 WINTER HILL STKS (Gp 3) (3-Y.O+) (Class A) £23,460.00 (£8,808.00: £4,254.00: £1,878.00)

1m 2f 7y Stalls: High GOING minus 0.25 sec per fur (GF) 6-45 (6-47)

2476[7] **Desert Shot (110)***(119) (MRStoute)* 5-9-4 WRSwinburn(6) (hld up: 9th st: gd hdwy over 1f out: led ins fnl f: r.o) ....— **1**
2476[2] Captain Horatius (IRE) **(113)***(113)*(Fav)*(JLDunlop)* 6-9-0 PatEddery(2) (7th st: sn rdn: hdwy 2f out: ev ch ins fnl f: unable qckn) 1½ **2**
1385* Alriffa **(113)***(116) (RHannon)* 4-9-4 RHughes(3) (5th st: hdwy over 2f out: rdn & ev ch ins fnl f: one pce) ....½ **3**
2936[8] Salt Lake **(102)***(110) (PWChapple-Hyam)* 4-9-0 JReid(5) (2nd st: led over 2f out: hdd over 1f out: ev ch ins fnl f: one pce) 1 **4**
3143[6] Ela-Aristokrati (IRE) **(105)***(109) (MRStoute)* 3-8-6 LDettori(1) (6th st: hdwy to ld over 1f out: hdd ins fnl f: one pce) ....½ **5**
2936[2] Young Buster (IRE) **(115)***(105) (GWragg)* 7-9-0 PaulEddery(4) (s.i.s: 8th st: hdwy 2f out: rdn over 1f out: one pce) 2½ **6**
2218a[12] Munwar **(116)***(105) (PTWalwyn)* 3-8-10 WCarson(8) (4th st: rdn over 2f out: wknd over 1f out) 3 **7**
2699* Indhar **(102)***(86) (JEBanks)* 4-9-0 BThomson(9) (3rd st: rdn over 2f out: wkng whn bmpd over 1f out) 9 **8**
2936[3] Sonic Boy **(114)***(75) (RFJohnsonHoughton)* 3-8-6 JQuinn(7) (led: hdd over 2f out: sn wknd)...7 **9**

7/4 Captain Horatius (IRE), **100/30** Young Buster (IRE) (9/2-3/1), **5/1** Munwar, **15/2** Ela-Aristokrati (IRE) (5/1-8/1), **8/1** Sonic Boy, **12/1** Alriffa (7/1-14/1), DESERT SHOT (7/1-14/1), **20/1** Indhar, Salt Lake, CSF £33.93 TOTE £15.30: £2.90 £1.50 £3.60 (£22.60) Trio £51.60 OWNER Maktoum Al Maktoum (NEWMARKET) BRED The Lavington Stud 9 Rn
2m 6.4 (1.50) SF: 70/64/67/61/52/56/48/37/18
WEIGHT FOR AGE 3yo-8lb

3382 FOUR SEASONS RACING RATED STKS H'CAP (0-100) (4-Y.O+) (Class B) £8,047.68 (£3,009.12: £1,469.56: £629.80: £279.90: £139.94)

1m 67y Stalls: High GOING minus 0.25 sec per fur (GF) 7-15 (7-17)

3026[3] **Weaver Bird (83)***(93) (HCandy)* 5-8-7 WNewnes(3) (hld up: 12th st: hdwy 2f out: led over 1f out: r.o wl) ....— **1**
2068[5] Wakeel (USA) **(87)***(95) (SDow)* 3-7-12 (7) ADaly(9) (6th st: hdwy 2f out: rdn & ev ch over 1f out: one pce) 1¼ **2**
2616[4] Blue Zulu (IRE) **(91)***(96) (JRFanshawe)* 3-8-9 DHarrison(12) (3rd st: rdn & ev ch over 1f out: one pce) 1½ **3**
2977* Mackook (USA) **(87)***(84)*(Fav)*(MRStoute)* 3-8-5 JReid(11) (led 6f out: hdd over 2f out: rdn & ev ch over 1f out: wknd fnl f) 4 **4**

2766[6] Second Chance (IRE) **(83)***(80) (PMitchell)* 5-8-2 (5) MHenry(5) (5th st: hdwy to ld over 2f out: hdd over 1f out: wknd ins fnl f)....s.h **5**
3113[4] Toujours Riviera **(86)***(83) (JPearce)* 5-8-10 GBardwell(8) (led over 2f: 2nd st: ev ch over 1f out: sn wknd)....s.h **6**
3085[4] Classic Sky (IRE) **(97)***(90) (EALDunlop)* 4-9-7 LDettori(7) (7th st: hdwy 2f out: wknd over 1f out)....2 **7**
2446[6] Thabit (USA) **(83)***(66) (PTWalwyn)* 4-8-7 WCarson(4) (10th st: a bhd)....5 **8**
3237[5] Zermatt (IRE) **(83)***(64) (MDIUsher)* 5-8-7 BThomson(2) (9th st: a bhd)....1¼ **9**
2470[2] Mandarina (USA) **(94)***(70) (LMCumani)* 3-8-12 PatEddery(10) (8th st: hdwy over 2f out: wknd over 1f out)....2½ **10**
2737[12] Signs **(90)***(61) (RHannon)* 3-8-8 PaulEddery(1) (11th st: a bhd)....2½ **11**
3085[14] Bide Our Time (USA) **(90)***(54) (JARToller)* 3-8-5b(3) SSanders(6) (4th st: sn wknd)....4 **12**
LONG HANDICAP Zermatt (IRE) 7-6 Thabit (USA) 8-5 Second Chance (IRE) 8-5

7/2 Mackook (USA), **4/1** Blue Zulu (IRE), **5/1** Mandarina (USA), **11/2** Classic Sky (IRE), **6/1** Toujours Riviera, WEAVER BIRD, **15/2** Thabit (USA), **16/1** Second Chance (IRE), Signs, **20/1** Wakeel (USA), **33/1** Zermatt (IRE), Bide Our Time (USA), CSF £114.81 CT £505.70 TOTE £7.80: £2.20 £6.80 £2.00 (£74.00) Trio £561.70 OWNER Mrs Henry Candy (WANTAGE) BRED W. and R. Barnett Ltd 12 Rn 1m 44.1 (2.50) SF: 47/43/44/32/34/37/44/20/18/18/9/2
WEIGHT FOR AGE 3yo-6lb

3383

RUNNYMEDE H'CAP (0-75) (3-Y.O+ F & M) (Class D) £4,536.00 (£1,368.00: £664.00: £312.00)
1m 67y Stalls: High GOING minus 0.25 sec per fur (GF) 7-45 (7-45)

2709[4] **Aldaneh (69)***(80) (RHannon)* 3-9-11 JReid(10) (7th st: hdwy 2f out: led ins fnl f: r.o)....— **1**
2862[4] The Mestral **(40)***(49) (MJRyan)* 3-7-10 ow1 WCarson(8) (led over 2f: 2nd st: led over 2f out: hdd ins fnl f: r.o)....½ **2**
3151[2] Never so Rite (IRE) **(60)***(66) (DWPArbuthnot)* 3-9-2v RHughes(11) (4th st: hdwy gng wl 2f out: ev ch over 1f out: one pce)....2 **3**
2861[11] Pat's Splendour **(46)***(52) (HJCollingridge)* 4-8-8 JQuinn(9) (11th st: hdwy over 1f out: r.o fnl f)....hd **4**
3286[7] Mo's Star **(62)***(66) (SDow)* 3-8-11 (7) ADaly(3) (3rd st: ev ch 2f out: one pce)....1¼ **5**
3218[5] Elite Racing **(62)***(65) (PFICole)* 3-9-4 TQuinn(7) (6th st: rdn 2f out: one pce)....nk **6**
3248[4] Fairelaine **(57)***(52) (APJarvis)* 3-8-13v GDuffield(6) (10th st: rdn & sme hdwy over 2f out: wknd over 1f out)....4 **7**
2747[11] Nunnery Grove (IRE) **(38)***(31) (TThomsonJones)* 3-7-8 NAdams(5) (led 6f out: hdd over 2f out: sn wknd)....1¼ **8**
2361[2] Maybe Today **(54)***(28) (BRMillman)* 3-8-5 (5) AWhelan(2) (8th st: a bhd)....10 **9**
1990[4] Bibliotheque (USA) **(67)***(23)*(Fav)*(JHMGosden)* 3-9-9 LDettori(4) (5th st: sn wknd)....9 **10**
3206[5] Chastleton **(39)** *(MRChannon)* 3-7-4 (5)ow2 MBaird(1) (9th st: a bhd)....7 **11**
LONG HANDICAP Chastleton 7-6

13/8 Bibliotheque (USA), **5/1** Elite Racing, **11/2** Never so Rite (IRE), **13/2** ALDANEH, **8/1** Maybe Today, **10/1** The Mestral, **12/1** Mo's Star (8/1-14/1), **14/1** Chastleton, **16/1** Fairelaine, Nunnery Grove (IRE), **25/1** Pat's Splendour, CSF £70.38 CT £360.89 TOTE £10.50: £3.30 £3.00 £1.70 (£39.00) Trio £60.80 OWNER Sheikh Essa Bin Mubarak (MARLBOROUGH) BRED M. B. Small 11 Rn 1m 47.5 (5.90) SF: 31/-/17/9/17/16/3/-/-/-/-
WEIGHT FOR AGE 3yo-6lb
T/Plpt: £240.40 (37.73 Tckts). T/Qdpt: £27.80 (6.3 Tckts). SM

3358-GOODWOOD (R-H)
Sunday August 27th (Good to firm, Firm patches)
WEATHER: sunny WIND: mod across

3384

UCELLO II TROPHY (FOR NATIONAL HUNT JOCKEYS) H'CAP (0-70) (4-Y.O+) (Class E) £3,615.00 (£1,095.00: £535.00: £255.00)
1m 4f Stalls: Low GOING minus 0.62 sec per fur (F) 1-45 (1-46)

2792[7] **Mr Browning (USA) (68)***(79) (RAkehurst)* 4-11-10b DBridgwater(15) (mde all: clr over 3f out: hrd rdn over 1f out: r.o wl)....— **1**
3238* Supreme Star (USA) **(62)***(68) (PRHedger)* 4-11-4 MRichards(14) (lw: hdwy over 4f out: rdn over 3f out: chsd wnr fnl f: r.o one pce)....4 **2**
Kandyan **(63)***(69)*(Fav)*(MHTompkins)* 4-11-5 DGallagher(13) (lw: rdn over 3f out: hdwy over 2f out: r.o one pce)....hd **3**
2981* Father Dan (IRE) **(58)***(61) (MissGayKelleway)* 6-11-0 AMaguire(2) (lw: 3rd st: chsd wnr 3f out to 1f out: one pce)....2 **4**

Curtelace **(57)***(48) (LadyHerries)* 5-10-13 EMurphy(8) (hdwy & hung rt over 2f out: sn wknd)..9 **5**
3107[5] Bookcase **(68)***(59) (DRCElsworth)* 8-11-10 AMcCabe(11) (lw: rdn 3f out: hdwy over 1f out: nvr nrr)....hd **6**
3056[3] Jean de Florette (USA) **(44)***(31) (CADwyer)* 4-10-0 NWilliamson(16) (6th st: wknd over 3f out)....2½ **7**
3234[5] Bold Look **(58)***(45) (PWHarris)* 4-11-0 DSkyrme(6) (nvr nr to chal)....s.h **8**
Scotoni **(44)***(29) (RJO'Sullivan)* 9-10-0 CLlewellyn(12) (lw: 4th st: wknd over 3f out)....2 **9**
2201[3] Ginger Jim **(60)***(44) (PRHedger)* 4-11-2 MPerrett(5) (lw: 5th st: wknd over 2f out)....¾ **10**
2327[9] Queens Contractor **(44)***(21) (SMellor)* 5-10-0b AKondrat(10) (2nd st: wknd over 2f out)....5 **11**
3304 Little Miss Ribot **(47)***(13) (RJO'Sullivan)* 5-10-3 ow3 DO'Sullivan(1) (7th st: wknd over 3f out)...6 **12**
2486* Nothing Doing (IRE) **(44)***(10) (WJMusson)* 6-10-0 JOsborne(7) (lw: bhd fnl 4f)....2 **13**
3234[12] Don't Give Up **(44)** *(PBurgoyne)* 7-10-0b ILawrence(9) (lw: a bhd)....8 **14**
1383[13] Monrush (IRE) **(45)** *(SDow)* 4-10-1 ADicken(4) (lw: a bhd)....15 **15**
Good Fetch **(47)** *(JABennett)* 4-10-3 BPowell(3) (prom over 6f)....2 **16**

LONG HANDICAP Queens Contractor 9-9 Scotoni 9-13 Nothing Doing (IRE) 9-8 Don't Give Up 8-12 Little Miss Ribot 9-13 Jean de Florette (USA) 9-4

5/1 Kandyan, **6/1** Bookcase, Supreme Star (USA), Father Dan (IRE), **9/1** MR BROWNING (USA), **10/1** Ginger Jim, Nothing Doing (IRE), **12/1** Curtelace (8/1-14/1), Bold Look, **16/1** Queens Contractor, **25/1** Little Miss Ribot, Jean de Florette (USA), **66/1** Scotoni, Don't Give Up, Monrush (IRE), Good Fetch, CSF £57.31 CT £274.57 TOTE £11.20: £2.70 £1.70 £2.40 £1.30 (£31.60) Trio £195.90 OWNER Mrs M. E. O'Shea (EPSOM) BRED Lord Carnarvon 16 Rn

2m 37.2 (5.20) SF: 51/40/41/33/20/31/3/17/1/16/-/-/-/-/-/-

OFFICIAL EXPLANATION Mr Browning: was unable to dictate the pace on his previous run and did not like being taken on, whilst today he was able to make all.

3385 BOLLINGER CHAMPAGNE CHALLENGE SERIES GENTLEMENS' H'CAP (0-70) (3-Y.O+) (Class F) £2,872.00 (£856.00: £408.00: £184.00)

1m Stalls: High GOING minus 0.62 sec per fur (F) 2-20 (2-26)

Southern Memories (IRE) (50)*(60) (WJMusson)* 5-12-0 MrTMcCarthy(4) (mde all: r.o wl)...— **1**
3082[13] Rockstine (IRE) **(39)***(47)*(Fav)*(PMitchell)* 4-11-3v MrLAUrbano(2) (b.hind: 6th st: chsd wnr over 1f out: r.o)....1 **2**
2641[8] Lorins Gold **(28)***(31) (AndrewTurnell)* 5-10-6 MrJRees(5) (b.nr hind: lw: hdwy wl over 1f out: r.o one pce)....2½ **3**
2813[3] Tirollac (IRE) **(44)***(40) (LGCottrell)* 3-10-12 (4) MrLJefford(1) (5th st: rdn over 2f out: one pce)....3½ **4**
3234[11] Starlight Flyer **(21)***(17) (JELong)* 8-9-9b(4) MrTWaters(6) (b.hind: 3rd st: rdn over 2f out: one pce)....hd **5**
2946[7] Mighty Kingdom (IRE) **(43)***(29)*(Fav)*(CADwyer)* 4-11-3 (4) MrVLukaniuk(9) (lw: nvr nr to chal)..5 **6**
3055[9] Gate of Heaven **(18)** *(CADwyer)* 5-9-10 MrRJohnson(10) (b.hind: a bhd)....2 **7**
1513[19] Formidable Lass **(32)***(12) (LGCottrell)* 4-10-10 MrJCulloty(8) (lw: 4th st: hrd rdn over 2f out: wknd over 1f out)....¾ **8**
3206[4] Magication **(30)***(6) (CNAllen)* 5-10-4 (4) MrKSantana(3) (b: 2nd st: hrd rdn over 2f out: sn wknd)....2 **9**
3264[6] Slytly Beveled **(54)***(8) (NPLittmoden)* 3-11-12b MrJDurkan(7) (lw: a bhd)....11 **10**

4/1 Mighty Kingdom (IRE) (op 5/2), Rockstine (IRE), **9/2** Slytly Beveled, **11/2** Magication (4/1-6/1), **6/1** Tirollac (IRE), **16/1** Lorins Gold, SOUTHERN MEMORIES (IRE), **25/1** Gate of Heaven, Starlight Flyer, **50/1** Formidable Lass, CSF £68.67 CT £868.76 TOTE £22.00: £4.90 £1.80 £2.50 (£38.40) Trio £131.60 OWNER Broughton Thermal Insulation (NEWMARKET) BRED Jim Horgan 10 Rn

1m 41.09 (3.49) SF: 52/39/23/26/9/21/-/4/-/-

WEIGHT FOR AGE 3yo-6lb

STEWARDS' ENQUIRY Urbano suspended 5-6/9/95.(Improper riding)

3386 PAYNE & GUNTER (S) STKS (2-Y.O) (Class E) £7,115.00 (£2,120.00: £1,010.00: £455.00)

6f Stalls: Low GOING minus 0.62 sec per fur (F) 2-50 (2-51)

2982[4] **Fenna (65)***(71) (SPCWoods)* 2-8-11 WWoods(7) (lw: hld up: led 2f out: clr over 1f out: r.o wl)— **1**
3260[2] Lucky Revenge **(75)***(61)*(Fav)*(MartynMeade)* 2-8-6 RCochrane(4) (lost pl over 3f out: nt clr run over 2f out: swtchd rt: chsd wnr over 1f out: r.o one pce)....2 **2**
3160[9] Arlington Lady **(67)***(56) (NACallaghan)* 2-8-1b(5) DaneO'Neill(6) (b.off hind: hld up: nt clr run over 2f out: r.o one pce)....1¾ **3**
3314[5] Moi Canard **(70)***(53) (JBerry)* 2-9-2 JCarroll(2) (lw: a.p: rdn over 2f out: wknd 1f out)....5 **4**
3133[7] Northern Saga (IRE) *(37) (AndrewTurnell)* 2-8-11 PatEddery(1) (lw: led 4f)....4 **5**
3283[2] Red Misty (IRE) *(29) (MRChannon)* 2-8-6 BDoyle(5) (spd over 4f)....1 **6**

6/4 Lucky Revenge, **100/30** Arlington Lady, **9/2** Red Misty (IRE), **7/1** Moi Canard (5/1-8/1), **8/1** FENNA (6/1-9/1), **10/1** Northern Saga (IRE), CSF £19.90 TOTE £11.60: £3.70 £1.80 (£12.50) OWNER Mr S. P. C. Woods (NEWMARKET) BRED High Point Bloodstock Ltd and Nigel Fenner Fownes 6 Rn
1m 13.19 (2.99) SF: 3/-/-/-/-/-
Bt in 7,500 gns

3387 CROWSON PRESTIGE STKS (Gp 3) (2-Y.O F) (Class A) £18,700.00 (£6,998.75: £3,361.88: £1,464.37)
7f Stalls: High GOING minus 0.62 sec per fur (F) 3-20 (3-21)

2572* **Bint Shadayid (USA)** *(92+)*(Fav)*(JLDunlop)* 2-8-9 WCarson(1) (4th st: swtchd rt over 2f out: swtchd lft over 1f out: str run ins fnl f: led last strides) — 1
2705* Papering (IRE) *(92) (LMCumani)* 2-8-9 PatEddery(3) (2nd st: led 2f out: hrd rdn ins fnl f: hdd last strides) hd 2
2775² Fag End (IRE) **(90)***(87) (MHTompkins)* 2-8-9 PRobinson(6) (led 5f: ev ch ins fnl f: unable qckn) 2 3
3003* Bewitching (USA) **(90)***(86) (JARToller)* 2-8-9 SSanders(5) (lw: 5th st: rdn over 2f out: one pce) ¾ 4
2106³ React **(100)***(81) (WJarvis)* 2-8-9 TQuinn(4) (3rd st: rdn over 2f out: one pce) 2 5
Fancy Design (IRE) *(35) (PMitchell)* 2-8-9 GDuffield(2) (w'like: bit bkwd: 6th st: a bhd) 20 6

Evens BINT SHADAYID (USA), **100/30** Papering (IRE), **11/2** Fag End (IRE), **7/1** React, **25/1** Bewitching (USA), **66/1** Fancy Design (IRE), CSF £4.22 TOTE £1.80: £1.50 £1.60 (£2.10) OWNER Mr Hamdan Al Maktoum (ARUNDEL) BRED Shadwell Estate Company Limited 6 Rn
1m 26.27 (1.87) SF: 21/21/16/15/10/-

3388 SUNDAY EXPRESS BEST FOR SPORT SERIES FINAL H'CAP (3-Y.O+) (Class B) £27,880.00 (£8,440.00: £4,120.00: £1,960.00)
1m 2f Stalls: High GOING minus 0.62 sec per fur (F) 3-50 (3-52)

3094³ **Fieldridge (73)***(85) (MPMuggeridge)* 6-9-5 (5) DaneO'Neill(13) (lw: 2nd st: rdn over 2f out: led ins fnl f: r.o wl) — 1
3106* Conspicuous (IRE) **(66)***(76) (LGCottrell)* 5-9-3 JQuinn(1) (stdy hdwy 3f out: led over 1f out tl ins fnl f: unable qckn) 1¼ 2
3106⁷ Silver Groom (IRE) **(75)***(85)*(Fav)*(RAkehurst)* 5-9-7 (5) MHenry(6) (lw: 3rd st: led 3f out tl over 1f out: one pce) nk 3
2068* Herr Trigger **(71)***(80) (DrJDScargill)* 4-9-8b RCochrane(14) (hdwy over 1f out: r.o wl ins fnl f) ½ 4
3189¹¹ Silktail (IRE) **(67)***(74) (CADwyer)* 3-8-7 (3) JStack(9) (hrd rdn over 2f out: hdwy over 1f out: one pce) 1¼ 5
3297³ Salska **(46)***(51) (AStreeter)* 4-7-11 NCarlisle(11) (led over 1f: 4th st: rdn over 2f out: one pce) 1 6
3106⁴ Fairy Knight **(75)***(79) (RHannon)* 3-9-4 TQuinn(10) (b.hind: lw: 5th st: rdn over 2f out: one pce) ¾ 7
2861* El Bailador (IRE) **(62)***(55) (JDBethell)* 4-8-13 GDuffield(8) (led over 8f out tl over 7f out: wknd over 3f out) 7 8
3106³ Ron's Secret **(76)***(61) (JWPayne)* 3-9-5 PRobinson(4) (hdwy 5f out: 6th st: wknd 3f out) 5 9
2110² Exemption **(71)***(55) (HCandy)* 4-9-8 WNewnes(15) (lw: led over 7f out to 3f out: sn wknd) nk 10
3156² Stage Struck (IRE) **(80)***(62) (MRStoute)* 3-9-9 WCarson(3) (lw: bhd fnl 6f) 1½ 11
3237* Francfurter **(85)***(67) (RCharlton)* 3-10-0b PatEddery(2) (lw: rdn & hdwy over 2f out: sn wknd) s.h 12
3106¹¹ Slaney Project (IRE) **(74)***(54) (WRMuir)* 3-9-3 TIves(5) (lw: bhd fnl 5f) 1 13
3288² Araboybill **(58)***(37) (MPMuggeridge)* 4-8-9b GBardwell(12) (a bhd) ¾ 14

7/2 Silver Groom (IRE) (9/2-3/1), **4/1** Francfurter (3/1-9/2), **6/1** Herr Trigger, **7/1** Conspicuous (IRE), **9/1** Stage Struck (IRE), **12/1** Exemption, Ron's Secret, **16/1** Fairy Knight, **20/1** FIELDRIDGE, El Bailador (IRE), **25/1** Silktail (IRE), **33/1** Salska, Slaney Project (IRE), Araboybill, CSF £141.95 CT £554.66 TOTE £22.40: £5.40 £3.00 £2.00 (£169.00) Trio £329.10 OWNER The Charleston Partnership (NEWBURY) BRED Mrs John Trotter 14 Rn
2m 6.44 (1.44) SF: 47/38/47/42/28/13/33/17/15/17/16/21/8/-
WEIGHT FOR AGE 3yo-8lb

OFFICIAL EXPLANATION **Francfurter: was unable to handle the firm ground coming down the hill.**

3389 EUROLINK MARCH STKS (Listed) (3-Y.O) (Class A) £16,492.00 (£4,508.00)
1m 6f Stalls: High GOING minus 0.62 sec per fur (F) 4-20 (4-24)

2944* **Jellaby Askhir** *(101)*(Fav)*(RAkehurst)* 3-8-11 RCochrane(3) (mde all: rdn over 2f out: r.o wl) — 1

2898a4 Wot-If-We (IRE) **(100)***(99) (TGMills)* 3-8-11 WNewnes(1) (chsd wnr: ev ch wl over 1f out: unable qckn)....2 **2**

4/6 JELLABY ASKHIR, **5/4** Wot-If-We (IRE) (Evens-11/8), TOTE £1.40 OWNER Sheikh Essa Bin Mubarak (EPSOM) BRED Side Hill Stud and Floors Farming 2 Rn 3m 3.04 (4.04) SF: 25/23

3390

SINGLETON H'CAP (0-75) (3-Y.O) (Class D) £4,020.50 (£1,199.00: £572.00: £258.50)
7f Stalls: High GOING minus 0.62 sec per fur (F) 4-50 (4-53)

2831[4] **Stoppes Brow (62)***(72) (GLMoore)* 3-8-8 AClark(1) (lw: 3rd st: led over 2f out: hrd rdn over 1f out: r.o wl)....— **1**
3286[4] The Stager (IRE) **(67)***(72) (JRJenkins)* 3-8-13b RCochrane(9) (lw: led over 4f: rdn: unable qckn)....2 **2**
3109[8] Landlord **(67)***(67) (JARToller)* 3-8-13b WNewnes(4) (hrd rdn & hdwy 2f out: r.o ins fnl f)....2½ **3**
2963[2] Caddy's First **(48)***(47) (SMellor)* 3-7-8 NAdams(6) (4th st: rdn over 3f out: one pce)....nk **4**
3251* Fantasy Racing (IRE) **(82)***(79) (MRChannon)* 3-10-0 7x RHughes(3) (w ldr: ev ch 2f out: wknd ins fnl f)....¾ **5**
3319[5] Anegre (IRE) **(57)***(53) (SDow)* 3-7-10 (7) ADaly(10) (lw: nvr nr to chal)....¾ **6**
1660[4] Bella Coola **(51)***(42) (CAHorgan)* 3-7-11 ow1 CRutter(5) (lw: nvr nrr)....1¾ **7**
3075[9] David James' Girl **(62)***(51) (ABailey)* 3-8-5 (3) DWright(11) (lw: rdn over 3f out: sme hdwy over 1f out: sn wknd)....1¼ **8**
1949[3] Crystal Gift **(66)***(53) (PFICole)* 3-8-12 TQuinn(2) (lw: 5th st: rdn over 3f out: wknd over 1f out)¾ **9**
2831* Sally Weld **(58)***(41) (CJBenstead)* 3-8-4 PRobinson(8) (lw: bhd fnl 2f)....2 **10**
2915[2] Golden Envoy (USA) **(74)***(34)*(Fav)*(JHMGosden)* 3-9-6 PatEddery(7) (6th st: wknd over 3f out)....10 **11**

15/8 Golden Envoy (USA), **13/2** Fantasy Racing (IRE), **7/1** Sally Weld, **9/1** Caddy's First, **10/1** STOPPES BROW (8/1-12/1), **12/1** Bella Coola (8/1-14/1), David James' Girl, Crystal Gift, **14/1** Landlord, **16/1** The Stager (IRE), Anegre (IRE), CSF £138.16 CT £2,023.80 TOTE £18.40: £4.30 £3.50 £3.60 (£104.30) Trio £193.70 OWNER Mr C. J. Pennick (EPSOM) BRED Dodford Stud 11 Rn 1m 26.08 (1.68) SF: 22/22/17/-/29/3/-/1/3/-/-

OFFICIAL EXPLANATION Golden Envoy (USA): got upset before the race and was never travelling well.

T/Jkpt: Not won; £41,859.67 to Epsom 28/8/95. T/Plpt: £56.30 (443.99 Tckts). T/Qdpt: £15.20 (66.1 Tckts). AK

3295-REDCAR (L-H)
Sunday August 27th (Good to firm, Firm patches)
WEATHER: overcast, showers WIND: mod against

3391

D.F.S H'CAP (0-80) (3-Y.O+) (Class D) £6,450.00 (£1,950.00: £950.00: £450.00)
1m 6f 19y Stalls: Low GOING minus 0.21 sec per fur (GF) 2-10 (2-10)

2882* **Invest Wisely (80)***(91)*(Fav)*(JMPEustace)* 3-9-0 (3) JTate(4) (cl up: led 4f out: edgd lft: hld on wl fnl f)....— **1**
2816[2] Batabanoo **(79)***(90) (MrsMReveley)* 6-10-0 KDarley(3) (trckd ldrs: effrt 3f out: styd on u.p fnl f: nrst fin)....nk **2**
2506* Ack's Again **(80)***(87) (BWHills)* 3-9-3 RHills(2) (lw: led tl hdd 4f out: outpcd fnl 2f)....3½ **3**
1686[4] Persuasive **(46)***(53) (MrsMReveley)* 8-7-9 DaleGibson(1) (hld up: effrt over 3f out: rdn & no imp fnl 2f)....s.h **4**

7/4 INVEST WISELY, **2/1** Ack's Again, **5/2** Batabanoo, **5/1** Persuasive, CSF £6.27 TOTE £2.70: (£3.60) OWNER Mr J. C. Smith (NEWMARKET) BRED Littleton Stud 4 Rn
3m 3.0 (5.00) SF: 57/68/53/31
WEIGHT FOR AGE 3yo-12lb

3392

PAUL DANIELS MAIDEN STKS (3-Y.O+) (Class D) £6,450.00 (£1,950.00: £950.00: £450.00)
1m 1f Stalls: Low GOING minus 0.21 sec per fur (GF) 2-40 (2-45)

3016[6] **Chief Bee** *(78)*(Fav)*(JLDunlop)* 4-9-0 KDarley(2) (trckd ldrs: chal 2f out: n.m.r fnl 1½f: r.o: fin 2nd, s.h: awrdd r)....— **1**
3227[3] Afsaat *(83) (MRStoute)* 3-8-12 KFallon(5) (lw: hld up: hdwy to chal over 1f out: sn led: edgd lft: r.o: fin 1st: disq: plcd 2nd).... **2**
3016[3] Ranosh (USA) *(78) (EALDunlop)* 3-8-7 PaulEddery(6) (b: b.hind: lw: trckd ldr: led & qcknd over 2f out: hdd 1f out: kpt on wl)....s.h **3**

1524⁹ Night Wink (USA) **(69)***(69) (DNicholls)* 3-8-12 AlexGreaves(1) (hld up: effrt over 3f out: sn outpcd)....8 4
957¹¹ Supreme (USA) *(57) (MDHammond)* 3-8-7 DaleGibson(3) (in tch tl outpcd fnl 3f)....4 5
Caribbean Surfer (USA) *(51) (JSGoldie)* 6-9-5 AMcGlone(4) (b: led tl hdd over 2f out: sn wknd)....6 6

7/4 CHIEF BEE, **15/8** Afsaat, **3/1** Ranosh (USA), **12/1** Night Wink (USA), **20/1** Caribbean Surfer (USA), **33/1** Supreme (USA), CSF £5.20 TOTE £2.60: £1.30 £1.70 (£2.70) OWNER Mrs Mark Burrell (ARUNDEL) BRED Mrs M. Burrell 6 Rn
1m 54.4 (5.40) SF: 32/30/25/16/4/5
WEIGHT FOR AGE 3yo-7lb

3393 MAIL ON SUNDAY MILE (QUALIFIER) H'CAP (0-85) (3-Y.O+) (Class D) £7,457.50 (£2,260.00: £1,105.00: £527.50)
1m Stalls: Centre GOING minus 0.21 sec per fur (GF) 3-10 (3-20)

2770³ **Break the Rules (71)***(81) (MrsMReveley)* 3-8-8 KDarley(6) (lw: hld up: hdwy to ld over 1f out: r.o)....— 1
3095² Mukhatab **(79)***(87)*(Fav)*(HThomsonJones)* 3-9-2 RHills(2) (lw: led tl hdd over 1f out: kpt on) 1¼ 2
3295³ Master Ofthe House **(67)***(65) (MDHammond)* 9-8-5 (5)ow6 DGriffiths(1) (trckd ldrs: hdwy to disp ld 2f out: wknd ins fnl f)....2 3
3128² Gymcrak Flyer **(62)***(65) (GHolmes)* 4-8-5 KFallon(4) (b.hind: chsd ldrs: ev ch 2f out: r.o one pce)....nk 4
3222⁴ Wentbridge Lad (IRE) **(61)***(54) (PDEvans)* 5-8-4 PaulEddery(10) (a bhd: effrt 3f out: no imp)..5 5
3255³ Three Arch Bridge **(61)***(47) (MJohnston)* 3-7-12b TWilliams(5) (cl up over 5f: grad wknd)......3½ 6
2118⁶ Colway Rock (USA) **(71)***(52) (JWWatts)* 5-9-0 NConnorton(3) (lw: outpcd over 3f out: n.d)...2½ 7
Flag Fen (USA) **(85)***(63) (MartynMeade)* 4-10-0 VSlattery(9) (bhd: hung rt fnl 3f: n.d)..........1½ 8
1280⁶ Top Guide (USA) **(80)** *(EALDunlop)* 4-9-6 (3) JTate(8) (unruly in stalls: bhd: swtchd stands' side after 3f: n.d: p.u fnl f)....dist 9

100/30 Mukhatab, **4/1** Gymcrak Flyer, **11/2** BREAK THE RULES, Wentbridge Lad (IRE), **13/2** Master Ofthe House, **8/1** Three Arch Bridge, **9/1** Top Guide (USA), **10/1** Flag Fen (USA), **20/1** Colway Rock (USA), CSF £23.99 CT £113.80 TOTE £6.20: £1.40 £1.70 £2.00 (£7.90) Trio £28.20 OWNER Mr P. D. Savill (SALTBURN) BRED Cleaboy Farms Co 9 Rn
1m 37.7 (2.70) SF: 47/53/37/37/26/13/24/35/-
WEIGHT FOR AGE 3yo-6lb

OFFICIAL EXPLANATION **Top Guide (USA): got upset in the stalls and his jockey had eased him down in the closing stages.**

3394 TRAFALGAR HOUSE NURSERY H'CAP (2-Y.O) (Class C) £6,450.00 (£1,950.00: £950.00: £450.00)
6f Stalls: Centre GOING minus 0.21 sec per fur (GF) 3-40 (3-44)

1646* **Mybotye (64)***(65+) (GROldroyd)* 2-8-0 AMackay(4) (hld up & bhd: smooth hdwy 2f out: led ins fnl f: r.o wl)....— 1
3147¹² Shontaine **(78)***(78) (MJohnston)* 2-9-0 DHolland(5) (prom: led over 1f out: hdd ins fnl f: r.o) ...½ 2
2833⁴ Middle East **(77)***(63) (TDBarron)* 2-8-13 KDarley(1) (swtg: trckd ldrs: disp ld over 2f out: hdd over 1f out: no ex)....5 3
2608⁴ Cumbrian Maestro **(72)***(53) (MHEasterby)* 2-8-8 MBirch(6) (chsd ldrs: outpcd 2f out: no imp after)....2 4
3117* Larghetto (IRE) **(75)***(55)*(Fav)*(JBerry)* 2-8-11 GCarter(8) (prom: hdwy & ev ch 2f out: sn rdn & btn)....nk 5
2914³ Katy-Q (IRE) **(62)***(32) (PCalver)* 2-7-9 (3) NVarley(7) (rdn ½-wy: nvr trbld ldrs)....4 6
3170* Pharmacy **(85)***(54) (JWWatts)* 2-9-7 NConnorton(3) (lw: w ldrs tl rdn & wknd fnl 2f)....nk 7
3225⁴ Oriel Lad **(77)***(24) (PDEvans)* 2-8-13 PaulEddery(2) (led over 3f out: sn wknd)....8 8

11/4 Larghetto (IRE), **3/1** Pharmacy, **5/1** Shontaine, **11/2** Middle East, **6/1** MYBOTYE, **9/1** Katy-Q (IRE), Oriel Lad, **10/1** Cumbrian Maestro, CSF £36.39 CT £164.85 TOTE £7.90: £1.40 £2.20 £2.70 (£23.00) OWNER Mr Anthony Moroney (YORK) BRED R. S. A. Urquhart 8 Rn
1m 13.7 (4.40) SF: 11/24/9/-/1/-/-/-

3395 MARSHALL AMPLIFICATION LIMITED STKS (0-70) (3-Y.O+) (Class E) £6,450.00 (£1,950.00: £950.00: £450.00)
1m 3f Stalls: Low GOING minus 0.21 sec per fur (GF) 4-10 (4-11)

*2605** **Locorotondo (IRE) (65)***(73)*(Fav)*(MBell)* 4-9-3 MFenton(2) (trckd ldr: slt ld wl over 1f out: all out)....— 1

3234[3] Divina Mia **(62)***(71) (JWHills)* 3-8-6 RHills(7) (lw: led tl hdd wl over 1f out: rallied u.p)....nk 2
2861[10] First Bite (IRE) **(68)***(75) (JLDunlop)* 3-8-13 KDarley(4) (hld up: effrt 4f out: edgd rt: styd on fnl f: nvr rchd ldrs)....1½ 3
3004[3] Posing (IRE) **(66)***(60) (JRFanshawe)* 3-8-6 DHarrison(6) (lw: in tch: effrt 4f out: one pce fnl 2f)....6 4
3297[4] Hatta River (USA) **(54)***(60) (JAHarris)* 5-9-6 KFallon(5) (chsd ldrs tl outpcd fnl 3f)....3½ 5
2544[5] Nonios (IRE) **(70)***(59) (GMMoore)* 4-9-6 JTate(3) (in tch tl outpcd fnl 3f)....½ 6

7/4 LOCOROTONDO (IRE), **3/1** Posing (IRE), **4/1** Divina Mia, First Bite (IRE), **10/1** Nonios (IRE), **14/1** Hatta River (USA), CSF £9.07 TOTE £2.50: £1.50 £2.80 (£6.90) OWNER The P 1 Partnership (NEWMARKET) BRED Irish National Stud Co Ltd 6 Rn 2m 22.2 (6.50) SF: 37/26/30/15/24/23

WEIGHT FOR AGE 3yo-9lb

3396 WEATHERBYS 'NEWCOMERS' SERIES H'CAP (0-80) (3-Y.O+) (Class D) £4,474.50 (£1,356.00: £663.00: £316.50)
7f Stalls: Centre GOING minus 0.21 sec per fur (GF) 4-40 (4-44)

3219[2] **King Rat (IRE) (72)***(83) (TJEtherington)* 4-9-10b GCarter(4) (lw: trckd ldrs: led over 1f out: r.o wl)....— 1
3050[2] Kid Ory **(65)***(69) (PCalver)* 4-9-3 MBirch(1) (b.hind: cl up: led ½-wy tl over 1f out: no ex)....3 2
2928* King Chestnut **(60)***(64)*(Fav)*(MDods)* 4-8-12 KFallon(5) (bhd: hdwy 3f out: styd on fnl f: nvr able to chal)....nk 3
2913[2] Legend Dulac (IRE) **(45)***(43) (JAHarris)* 6-7-11 DaleGibson(3) (led to ½-wy: r.o one pce)....2½ 4
2955[6] Star Performer (IRE) **(51)***(45) (MrsMReveley)* 4-8-3 KDarley(7) (effrt 3f out: nvr rchd ldrs)....1½ 5
3057[5] Takeshi (IRE) **(61)***(53) (EALDunlop)* 3-8-5 (3) JTate(6) (w ldrs tl wknd fnl 2f)....1 6
2668[7] Murphy's Gold (IRE) **(58)***(48) (RAFahey)* 4-8-10 ACulhane(15) (lw: b: chsd ldrs centre: hdwy 3f out: no imp)....1 7
3212[8] Bargash **(67)***(55) (PDEvans)* 3-9-0 NConnorton(14) (effrt centre ½-wy: no imp)....1 8
3275[4] Densben **(45)***(30) (DenysSmith)* 11-7-8 (3) NVarley(11) (lw: effrt centre 3f out: n.d)....1 9
3258[4] Swynford Flyer **(43)***(25) (JAHarris)* 6-7-2 (7)ow2 CAdamson(12) (n.d)....½ 10
2974[5] Striffolino **(72)***(54) (TDBarron)* 3-9-5 DeanMcKeown(10) (spd centre over 4f)....¾ 11
3151[3] Miss Zanzibar **(57)***(38) (RAFahey)* 3-8-4 SMaloney(9) (prom centre over 4f)....½ 12
3063[2] Move Smartly (IRE) **(59)***(39) (FHLee)* 5-8-11v PaulEddery(13) (led centre group over 4f: edgd rt & wknd)....½ 13
3139[9] Ain'tlifelikethat **(41)***(19) (TJNaughton)* 8-7-7b JLowe(8) (b: dwlt: hdwy ½-wy: sn wknd)....¾ 14
3344[10] Bayou (IRE) **(45)***(19) (JAHarris)* 4-7-11 AMackay(2) (outpcd fr ½-wy)....1¾ 15
2528[13] Ballyhays (IRE) **(44)** *(JAHarris)* 6-7-5 (5) MBaird(16) (n.d)....10 16

LONG HANDICAP Ain'tlifelikethat 7-2 Swynford Flyer 6-3

4/1 King Chestnut (op 6/1), **7/1** KING RAT (IRE), **8/1** Kid Ory, Move Smartly (IRE), Star Performer (IRE), Murphy's Gold (IRE), **10/1** Takeshi (IRE), Legend Dulac (IRE), **12/1** Densben, Bayou (IRE), Striffolino, **16/1** Miss Zanzibar, **25/1** Bargash, **50/1** Ain'tlifelikethat, Swynford Flyer, Ballyhays (IRE), CSF £62.18 CT £239.32 TOTE £8.60: £2.20 £1.90 £1.90 £3.20 (£23.80) Trio £16.00 OWNER Mr Paul Daniels (MALTON) BRED Airlie Stud 16 Rn

1m 24.0 (2.00) SF: 66/52/47/26/28/31/31/33/13/8/32/16/22/2/2/-

WEIGHT FOR AGE 3yo-5lb

T/Plpt: £107.70 (140.79 Tckts). T/Qdpt: £56.90 (4.4 Tckts). AA

2546-CHEPSTOW (L-H)
Monday August 28th (Good to firm, Firm patches)
WEATHER: fair WIND: slt bhd

3397 E.B.F. JULIET MAIDEN STKS (2-Y.O F) (Class D) £4,328.00 (£1,304.00: £632.00: £296.00)
1m 14y Stalls: High GOING minus 0.57 sec per fur (F) 1-50 (1-53)

3009[5] **Waterland (USA)** *(81) (RCharlton)* 2-8-11 TSprake(1) (lw: w ldr: led over 2f out: shkn up & edgd rt over 1f out: pushed out)....— 1
2705[2] Ailesbury Hill (USA) *(78)*(Fav)*(PWChapple-Hyam)* 2-8-11 JReid(6) (hld up: hdwy 2f out: swtchd lft ins fnl f: no imp)....1¾ 2
2791[6] Swift Maiden *(75) (MrsLAMurphy)* 2-8-4 (7) RWaterfield(9) (a.p: r.o one pce fnl f)....1½ 3
3155[5] Time of Night (USA) *(73) (RGuest)* 2-8-11 AClark(5) (hld up & plld hrd: rdn & hdwy 2f out: one pce fnl f)....¾ 4
2958[6] Threesocks *(72) (BSmart)* 2-8-11 RPerham(2) (prom: rdn 3f out: no ex fnl f)....¾ 5
3010[8] Dramatic Moment *(65) (IABalding)* 2-8-11 GHind(4) (lw: hld up: nvr trbld ldrs)....3½ 6

2934[5] Needwood Epic *(62) (BAMcMahon)* 2-8-6 (5) JDSmith(3) (lw: plld hrd: prom tl wknd over 1f out)........1¼ 7
3009[8] High Desire (IRE) *(59) (JRArnold)* 2-8-11 NAdams(8) (led over 5f: wknd over 1f out)........1¾ 8
2083[8] Perfect Gift *(47) (PFICole)* 2-8-8 (3) DWright(7) (lw: plld hrd: a bhd)........6 9

8/11 Ailesbury Hill (USA), **9/2** Time of Night (USA) (3/1-11/2), **11/2** WATERLAND (USA), **12/1** Perfect Gift, **14/1** Dramatic Moment (op 8/1), **20/1** Needwood Epic, Swift Maiden, **33/1** Threesocks, **50/1** High Desire (IRE), CSF £9.86 TOTE £6.70: £1.30 £1.10 £5.80 (£3.00) Trio £58.40 OWNER Mr K. Abdullah (BECKHAMPTON) BRED Juddmonte Farms 9 Rn
1m 35.3 (2.80) SF: 16/13/10/8/7/-/-/-/-

3398

E.B.F. ROMEO MAIDEN STKS (2-Y.O C & G) (Class D) £4,406.00 (£1,328.00: £644.00: £302.00)
1m 14y Stalls: High GOING minus 0.57 sec per fur (F) 2-20 (2-22)

Ski Academy (IRE) *(68+)*(Fav)*(PWChapple-Hyam)* 2-8-11 JReid(1) (w'like: a.p: led ins fnl f: pushed out)........— 1
3010[7] East India (IRE) *(67) (RCharlton)* 2-8-11 TSprake(4) (chsd ldr: led 2f out tl ins fnl f: r.o)........½ 2
3089[8] Prince of My Heart *(64) (BWHills)* 2-8-6 (5) JDSmith(7) (hld up: hdwy over 2f out: r.o ins fnl f)........1½ 3
3089[19] Verulam (IRE) *(63) (JARToller)* 2-8-11 GHind(6) (led 6f: one pce fnl f)........nk 4
Montecristo *(62) (RGuest)* 2-8-11 EGuest(3) (neat: hld up: rdn & hdwy 3f out: one pce fnl 2f)¾ 5
1485[6] Shaha *(52) (RHannon)* 2-8-11 RPerham(8) (prom: rdn 4f out: wknd over 2f out)........5 6
Genereux *(22) (PFICole)* 2-8-11 AClark(5) (w'like: bhd: rdn over 4f out: t.o fnl 2f)........15 7
2315[8] Samara Song *(22) (RJBaker)* 2-8-11 NAdams(2) (plld hrd: drppd rr over 3f out: t.o)........hd 8

5/4 SKI ACADEMY (IRE), **9/2** Shaha, **5/1** Prince of My Heart, **15/2** Genereux (op 3/1), **10/1** East India (IRE), Montecristo, **25/1** Verulam (IRE), **33/1** Samara Song, CSF £13.42 TOTE £2.10: £1.30 £2.20 £1.10 (£9.70) OWNER Mr R. E. Sangster (MARLBOROUGH) BRED Swettenham Stud 8 Rn
1m 33.1 (1.50 under 2y best) (0.60) SF: 40/39/36/35/34/24/-/-

3399

FRANKIE DETTORI TON-UP CONDITIONS STKS (3-Y.O+ F & M) (Class C) £5,747.20 (£1,850.20: £897.60)
7f 16y Stalls: High GOING minus 0.57 sec per fur (F) 2-50 (2-51)

2673[10] **Queenfisher (88)***(90+) (RHannon)* 3-8-11 RPerham(1) (trckd ldr: led wl over 1f out: comf)..— 1
3261[2] Miasma (USA) **(99)***(82)*(Fav)*(JARToller)* 3-8-11 JReid(2) (led: rdn over 2f out: hdd wl over 1f out: one pce)........3½ 2
2943[8] Louisville Belle (IRE) **(55)***(69) (MDIUsher)* 6-9-0 TSprake(3) (b: hld up: rdn & ev ch 2f out: wknd over 1f out)........5 3

4/6 Miasma (USA), **7/4** QUEENFISHER, **9/1** Louisville Belle (IRE), CSF £3.07 TOTE £2.80 (£1.20) OWNER Mr K. Higson (MARLBOROUGH) BRED Glazeley Stud 3 Rn 1m 20.6 (0.60) SF: 38/30/22
WEIGHT FOR AGE 3yo-5lb

3400

BANK HOLIDAY NURSERY H'CAP (2-Y.O) (Class D) £3,692.75 (£1,112.00: £538.50: £251.75)
5f 16y Stalls: High GOING minus 0.57 sec per fur (F) 3-20 (3-22)

3213[9] **Gagajulu (75)***(75) (PDEvans)* 2-8-10 GHind(2) (lw: rdn over 2f out: hdwy over 1f out: led ins fnl f: all out)........— 1
3176[3] Comic Fantasy (AUS) **(86)***(86)*(Fav)*(PWChapple-Hyam)* 2-9-7b JReid(4) (led over 3f: rallied ins fnl f: r.o wl)........s.h 2
2800[4] Amy Leigh (IRE) **(70)***(68) (CaptJWilson)* 2-8-5 AClark(3) (a.p: led over 1f out: edgd lft: hdd ins fnl f: r.o)........½ 3
2431[2] Clan Chief **(67)***(53)*(Fav)*(JRArnold)* 2-7-11 (5) AWhelan(1) (prom over 3f)........4 4
2866* Kinnescash (IRE) **(73)***(58) (MSSaunders)* 2-8-8 NAdams(5) (rdn over 2f out: a bhd)........hd 5

9/4 Clan Chief, Comic Fantasy (AUS), **5/1** Amy Leigh (IRE), Kinnescash (IRE), **7/1** GAGAJULU (op 9/2), CSF £20.66 TOTE £6.90: £2.30 £1.70 (£10.20) OWNER Mr R. F. F. Mason (WELSHPOOL) BRED Mrs P. E. Bell 5 Rn 58.3 secs (1.30) SF: 20/31/13/-/3

3401

JOHN HYLTON WATTS CLAIMING STKS (3-Y.O+) (Class F) £2,862.50 (£860.00: £415.00: £192.50)
1m 4f 23y Stalls: High GOING minus 0.57 sec per fur (F) 3-50 (3-52)

2546[5] **Last Laugh (IRE) (56)***(69) (MCPipe)* 3-8-4 (5) JDSmith(6) (hld up: hdwy 8f out: led 4f out: clr over 1f out: r.o wl)........— 1

3056[6] Born to Please (IRE) **(40)***(61) (PWHarris)* 3-8-6 GHind(3) (3rd st: chsd wnr fnl 2f: no imp).......4 **2**
3006[5] Delicious **(55)***(59) (MajorDNChappell)* 3-8-5 AClark(2) (4th st: r.o one pce fnl 2f)....................¾ **3**
2901[3] Torrey Pines (IRE) **(38)***(60) (DHaydnJones)* 3-8-5 (3) DWright(1) (rdn & 7th st: hdwy 2f out: hung lft over 1f out: nt rch ldrs)..1¼ **4**
2745[6] Strat's Legacy **(46)***(51)*(Fav)*(DWPArbuthnot)* 8-8-12 JReid(9) (b.hind: led over 8f: wknd fnl f)2½ **5**
2989[4] Manila Bay (USA) **(45)***(48) (JSKing)* 5-9-0 TSprake(4) (hld up & plld hrd: 6th st: hdwy 4f out: wknd 3f out)..3½ **6**
654* Peter Monamy **(63)***(54) (MCPipe)* 3-8-9 (5) AWhelan(8) (5th st: rdn over 4f out: wknd 3f out)....3 **7**
1012[8] Fly the Eagle **(40)***(19) (MPMuggeridge)* 3-8-5 RStreet(10) (a bhd: t.o)..................................20 **8**
Lady Woodstock *(8) (PGMurphy)* 3-7-12 (7) RWaterfield(5) (bkwd: plld hrd: prom 6f: t.o) 8 **9**
Most Becoming *(JRArnold)* 3-8-5 RPerham(7) (cmpt: bkwd: a bhd: t.o) 8 **10**

2/1 Strat's Legacy, **4/1** LAST LAUGH (IRE), Peter Monamy (op 2/1), **9/1** Delicious, Born to Please (IRE), **12/1** Manila Bay (USA) (op 8/1), Torrey Pines (IRE) (op 8/1), **20/1** Lady Woodstock, **33/1** Fly the Eagle, Most Becoming, CSF £36.73 TOTE £4.40: £1.60 £1.90 £2.80 (£26.40) Trio £83.30 OWNER Charles Eden Ltd (WELLINGTON) BRED Brigitte Wolff in Ireland 10 Rn
2m 35.6 (4.30) SF: 21/13/11/12/13/10/6/-/-/-
WEIGHT FOR AGE 3yo-10lb

3402 SEVERN BRIDGE H'CAP (0-65) (3-Y.O+) (Class F) £3,135.50 (£944.00: £457.00: £213.50)
1m 2f 36y Stalls: High GOING minus 0.57 sec per fur (F) 4-20 (4-26)

3259[2] **Course Fishing (35)***(54)*(Fav)*(BAMcMahon)* 4-7-13 (7) MartinDwyer(2) (hld up: hdwy over 3f out: led over 1f out: rdn out)..— **1**
3004[4] It'sthebusiness **(53)***(67) (SDow)* 3-9-2 JReid(12) (hdwy 4f out: led over 2f out tl over 1f out: one pce)..3 **2**
*3082** Tadellal (IRE) **(53)***(58) (WGMTurner)* 4-9-5 (5) JDSmith(9) (s.s: gd hdwy after 2f: 2nd st: led 4f out tl over 2f out: one pce)..6 **3**
3058[3] Mim-Lou-and **(45)***(48) (BRMillman)* 3-8-3 (5) AWhelan(4) (prom: lost pl 6f out: rallied 3f out: rdn & one pce fnl f)..1½ **4**
3097[2] Marzipan (IRE) **(61)***(57) (JWHills)* 3-9-10 AClark(11) (lw: 3rd st: wknd over 2f out)...................4 **5**
3063[6] Runic Symbol **(37)***(32) (MBlanshard)* 4-8-8 TSprake(10) (hdwy over 2f out: nvr nr to chal) .....½ **6**
3004[2] Queens Stroller (IRE) **(56)***(51) (CCElsey)* 4-9-13 GHind(14) (hdwy & 6th st: wknd over 1f out: eased whn btn fnl f)..nk **7**
2790[12] Celestial Dollar **(51)***(45) (OO'Neill)* 4-9-1 (7) LSuthern(6) (5th st: wknd 3f out)...........................½ **8**
3206[2] Tout de Val **(29)***(23) (KBishop)* 6-7-9 (5) PPMurphy(7) (n.d)..nk **9**
3207[4] Mhemeanles **(44)***(38) (CaptJWilson)* 5-8-8 (7) VictoriaAppleby(1) (prom: lost pl 6f out: n.d after)..hd **10**
Sylvan Starlight **(49)***(37) (JMBradley)* 5-8-13 (7) RWaterfield(5) (swtg: a bhd)........................3½ **11**
3092[11] Buster **(37)***(23) (MrsBarbaraWaring)* 7-8-8 RStreet(13) (a bhd)..1 **12**
2081[8] Pacific Overture **(49)***(20) (CRBarwell)* 3-8-9 (3) DWright(8) (lw: led over 6f) 10 **13**
1979[8] Park Ridge **(59)** *(TGMills)* 3-9-1 (7) DToole(16) (prom: 7th st: wknd 4f out: t.o) 25 **14**
3056[10] Jubilee Line **(30)** *(NEBerry)* 5-8-1 NAdams(15) (prom: 4th & rdn st: wknd over 3f out: bhd whn stumbled & uns rdr over 1f out) .... **U**

9/2 COURSE FISHING, **6/1** It'sthebusiness, Tadellal (IRE), Marzipan (IRE), **8/1** Mim-Lou-and, Queens Stroller (IRE), **12/1** Tout de Val, Mhemeanles, **16/1** Park Ridge, Runic Symbol, **20/1** Jubilee Line, **25/1** Celestial Dollar, **33/1** Pacific Overture, Sylvan Starlight, Buster, CSF £31.04 CT £151.35 TOTE £4.60: £2.40 £2.10 £2.80 (£15.10) Trio £16.80 OWNER Mr G. D. Bull (TAMWORTH) BRED Hyde Stud 15 Rn
2m 6.9 (2.60) SF: 23/28/27/9/18/1/20/14/-/7/6/-/-/-/-
WEIGHT FOR AGE 3yo-8lb
T/Plpt: £96.40 (58.64 Tckts). T/Qdpt: £50.30 (1.4 Tckts). KH

2682-EPSOM (L-H)
Monday August 28th (Good to firm, Good fnl 4f)
WEATHER: sunny WIND: mod across

3403 CICERO CLAIMING STKS (3-Y.O) (Class E) £3,485.00 (£1,055.00: £515.00: £245.00)
1m 2f 18y Stalls: Low GOING minus 0.32 sec per fur (GF) 2-05 (2-05)

3058[2] **Harvey White (IRE) (54)***(70) (JPearce)* 3-8-9 GBardwell(4) (mde all: all out) ....— **1**
3218[6] Gentle Irony **(62)***(63) (BJMeehan)* 3-8-2b PaulEddery(3) (4th st: nt clr run on ins over 2f out: hrd rdn over 1f out: r.o wl ins fnl f)..s.h **2**
1984[3] Charm Dancer **(52)***(75) (MCPipe)* 3-9-2 RCochrane(1) (nt clr run over 2f out: hdwy over 1f out: r.o one pce)..1½ **3**

3338[5] Suvalu (USA) **(73)***(78) (PFICole)* 3-9-7 TQuinn(5) (6th st: rdn over 2f out: one pce) ......¾ 4
3130[7] Birthday Boy (IRE) **(60)***(65) (RHannon)* 3-8-4 (5) DaneO'Neill(7) (3rd st: wknd wl over 1f out) ..¾ 5
3247* Owdbetts (IRE) **(63)***(58)*(Fav)*(GLMoore)* 3-8-2 JFEgan(2) (5th st: no hdwy fnl 3f) ......hd 6
3241[6] Emphatic Candidate (IRE) **(63)***(60) (RAkehurst)* 3-8-2 (3) SSanders(6) (b: lw: 2nd st: hrd rdn 2f out: wknd fnl f) ......¾ 7

2/1 Owdbetts (IRE), **4/1** Gentle Irony, **5/1** Emphatic Candidate (IRE), **6/1** Birthday Boy (IRE), **10/1** Suvalu (USA) (8/1-12/1), **12/1** HARVEY WHITE (IRE) (op 6/1), **14/1** Charm Dancer (op 8/1), CSF £51.53 TOTE £9.80: £2.90 £2.30 (£32.90) OWNER The Harvey White Partnership (NEWMARKET) BRED Mrs C. L. Weld 7 Rn 2m 10.81 (6.81) SF: 14/7/19/22/9/2/4

3404 LADAS MAIDEN STKS (2-Y.O) (Class D) £4,201.50 (£1,272.00: £621.00: £295.50)

6f Stalls: High GOING minus 0.32 sec per fur (GF) 2-35 (2-37)

3003[2] **Tina's Ridge** *(82) (RHannon)* 2-8-9 (5) DaneO'Neill(4) (lw: 4th st: hrd rdn over 2f out: swtchd rt over 1f out: str run fnl f: led nr fin) ......— 1
3133[2] Roses In The Snow (IRE) **(90)***(76)*(Fav)*(JWHills)* 2-8-9 MHills(6) (lw: 2nd st: led over 1f out: hrd rdn ins fnl f: hdd nr fin) ......½ 2
3213[6] Caricature (IRE) **(82)***(79) (GLewis)* 2-9-0b PaulEddery(5) (led over 4f: hrd rdn: r.o) ......½ 3
2442[6] Sylva Paradise (IRE) *(66) (CEBrittain)* 2-9-0 MPerrett(7) (3rd st: wknd over 2f out) 5 4
3093[3] Sheilana (IRE) *(58) (TGMills)* 2-8-6 (3) SSanders(2) (5th st: wknd over 2f out) 1 5
2681[6] Snow Falcon *(61) (MBell)* 2-9-0 TQuinn(3) (s.i.s: a bhd) ......¾ 6
3176[6] Almushtarak (IRE) *(61) (MissGayKelleway)* 2-9-0 RCochrane(1) (lw: 6th st: wknd over 2f out) ......s.h 7
1318[9] Rawi *(51) (CJBenstead)* 2-9-0 SWhitworth(9) (lw: a bhd) 4 8

2/1 Roses In The Snow (IRE), **9/4** TINA'S RIDGE, **9/2** Caricature (IRE), **8/1** Snow Falcon, **12/1** Sylva Paradise (IRE) (op 8/1), **16/1** Sheilana (IRE), **33/1** Almushtarak (IRE), Rawi, CSF £6.73 TOTE £3.30: £1.40 £1.10 £1.50 (£3.00) Trio £2.90 OWNER Mrs Chris Harrington (MARLBOROUGH) BRED P. J. AND MRS SANDS 8 Rn 1m 10.66 (2.66) SF: 32/26/29/16/8/11/11/1

3405 TADWORTH NURSERY H'CAP (2-Y.O) (Class D) £4,221.00 (£1,278.00: £624.00: £297.00)

7f Stalls: Low GOING minus 0.32 sec per fur (GF) 3-05 (3-05)

2988[3] **Friendly Forester (USA)** **(77)***(79) (RCharlton)* 2-8-6b(3) SSanders(5) (2nd st: hrd rdn over 1f out: led last strides) ......— 1
3090[3] Vola Via (USA) **(81)***(83) (IABalding)* 2-8-13 MHills(6) (5th st: led over 2f out: hrd rdn ins fnl f: hdd last strides) ......s.h 2
3267[2] General Rose **(66)***(60)*(Fav)*(RHannon)* 2-7-12 JFEgan(3) (lw: 3rd st: hrd rdn over 2f out: one pce) 3½ 3
3012[3] It's A Ripper **(62)***(50) (GLewis)* 2-7-8 GBardwell(4) (lw: led over 4f: wknd over 1f out) 2½ 4
2651* Pharaoh's Joy **(71)***(50) (JWPayne)* 2-8-3 PaulEddery(1) (bhd fnl 5f) 4 5
2365[4] Galapino **(89)***(65) (CEBrittain)* 2-9-7 RCochrane(2) (4th st: wknd 2f out) 1½ 6

5/2 General Rose, **4/1** It's A Ripper, **9/2** Vola Via (USA), **5/1** FRIENDLY FORESTER (USA), Pharaoh's Joy, **8/1** Galapino, CSF £24.39 TOTE £5.90: £2.70 £2.80 (£12.30) OWNER Mrs Shirley Robins (BECKHAMPTON) BRED Robert and Virginia White 6 Rn
1m 23.81 (3.51) SF: 23/27/4/-/-/9

3406 MOET & CHANDON SILVER MAGNUM GENTLEMENS' H'CAP (0-90) (3-Y.O+) (Class C) £10,357.50 (£3,135.00: £1,530.00: £727.50)

1m 4f 10y Stalls: Low GOING minus 0.32 sec per fur (GF) 3-40 (3-41)

3091[2] **Proton** **(76)***(89)*(Fav)*(RAkehurst)* 5-11-4 MrTMcCarthy(8) (3rd st: led over 3f out: hrd rdn over 2f out: bmpd nr fin) ......— 1
3238[2] Casual Water (IRE) **(66)***(78) (AGNewcombe)* 4-10-8 MrGrassoCaprioli(6) (hdwy over 2f out: ev ch whn edgd lft wl ins fnl f: r.o) ......½ 2
3162[12] Flight Lieutenant (USA) **(72)***(82) (RHannon)* 6-11-0 MrCVigors(3) (lw: hdwy over 2f out: rdn over 1f out: 3rd & ev ch whn bdly hmpd nr fin) 1¾ 3
3156[7] Roisin Clover **(67)***(72) (SDow)* 4-10-9 MrCMosse(5) (lw: 6th st: rdn over 2f out: wknd over 1f out) 3½ 4
2878* Latvian **(72)***(76) (RAllan)* 8-11-0 MrVLukaniuk(2) (led over 10f out tl over 3f out: wknd wl over 1f out) ......¾ 5
3083[2] Lear Dancer (USA) **(68)***(72)*(Fav)*(PMitchell)* 4-10-10b MrLAUrbano(10) (led over 1f: 5th st: wknd over 2f out) ......½ 6
3091[6] Seasonal Splendour (IRE) **(86)***(82) (MCPipe)* 5-12-0 MrJDurkan(7) (bhd fnl 3f) 6 7

Golden Arrow (IRE) **(82)**_(77) (IABalding)_ 4-11-10 MrABalding(1) (lw: 2nd st: wknd over 2f out) ...... ¾ **8**
2445[7] Warm Spell **(74)**_(66) (GLMoore)_ 5-11-2 MrMKeller(9) (lw: 4th st: wknd 3f out) 2 **9**
3108[2] Rival Bid (USA) **(57)**_(29) (MrsNMacauley)_ 7-9-13 MrPPritchard-Gordon(4) (bhd fnl 3f) 15 **10**

4/1 PROTON, Lear Dancer (USA), **9/2** Casual Water (IRE), **13/2** Seasonal Splendour (IRE), **9/1** Latvian, **14/1** Flight Lieutenant (USA), Rival Bid (USA), Golden Arrow (IRE), **16/1** Warm Spell, **20/1** Roisin Clover, CSF £19.96 CT £201.05 TOTE £4.30: £1.50 £1.60 £2.60 (£7.50) Trio £61.00 OWNER The Persian War Partnership (EPSOM) BRED Lord Halifax 10 Rn
2m 40.07 (5.07) SF: 71/60/64/54/58/54/64/59/48/11
STEWARDS' ENQUIRY Caprioli susp. 6-7/9/95 (careless riding).

3407 INDIGENOUS H'CAP (0-95) (3-Y.O+) (Class C) £13,875.00 (£4,200.00: £2,050.00: £975.00)
5f Stalls: High GOING minus 0.32 sec per fur (GF) 4-10 (4-11)

3166[2] **Crowded Avenue (82)**_(89)_(Fav)_(PJMakin)_ 3-9-1 PaulEddery(3) (lw: hld up: rdn over 1f out: squeezed thro to ld ins fnl f: r.o wl) ...... — **1**
3221[8] Insider Trader **(73)**_(76) (RGuest)_ 4-8-4b(5) DaneO'Neill(10) (b: a.p: led over 1f out tl ins fnl f: unable qckn) 1¼ **2**
3166[4] Tart and a Half **(79)**_(81) (BJMeehan)_ 3-8-12b MTebbutt(4) (lw: rdn over 2f out: hdwy over 1f out: r.o) ...... nk **3**
3219[5] Miami Banker **(57)**_(59) (WRMuir)_ 9-7-7b GBardwell(8) (a.p: led over 2f out tl over 1f out: one pce ins fnl f) ...... s.h **4**
3250* Halbert **(60)**_(62) (MRChannon)_ 6-7-7v(3) 6x NVarley(11) (lw: hld up: rdn over 2f out: one pce) s.h **5**
3221[2] Ann's Pearl (IRE) **(79)**_(77) (JWHills)_ 4-9-1 MHills(9) (nvr nr to chal) 1¼ **6**
3236[3] Painted Desert **(87)**_(83) (RCharlton)_ 3-9-6 TQuinn(7) (lw: hld up: rdn over 2f out: one pce) ...... ½ **7**
3044a[7] Go Hever Golf **(92)**_(82) (TJNaughton)_ 3-9-8 (3) SSanders(6) (b.nr hind: prom 3f) 2 **8**
2570[8] Ashtina **(87)**_(76) (RJHodges)_ 10-9-9 RCochrane(5) (hld up: rdn over 2f out: wknd over 1f out) ...... hd **9**
2168[4] Allthruthenight (IRE) **(84)**_(72) (LJHolt)_ 6-9-6 MPerrett(1) (lw: hdwy & nt clr run over 1f out: sn wknd) ...... ½ **10**
1637[10] Windmachine (SWE) **(92)**_(48) (RHarris)_ 4-10-0 SWhitworth(2) (b: led over 2f: wknd over 1f out) 10 **11**
LONG HANDICAP Miami Banker 7-3

100/30 CROWDED AVENUE, **5/1** Painted Desert, **11/2** Halbert, **6/1** Insider Trader, **10/1** Go Hever Golf, Ann's Pearl (IRE), Allthruthenight (IRE), **14/1** Tart and a Half, **16/1** Ashtina, Miami Banker, **25/1** Windmachine (SWE), CSF £22.29 CT £226.19 TOTE £3.80: £1.60 £2.10 £3.80 (£15.50) Trio £108.70 OWNER Mr T. W. Wellard (MARLBOROUGH) BRED The Duke of Marlborough 11 Rn
54.92 secs (0.42) SF: 62/52/54/35/38/53/56/55/52/48/24
WEIGHT FOR AGE 3yo-3lb

3408 ROTHMANS ROYALS NORTH SOUTH CHALLENGE SERIES H'CAP (0-90) (3-Y.O) (Class C) £7,035.00 (£2,130.00: £1,040.00: £495.00)
1m 114y Stalls: Low GOING minus 0.32 sec per fur (GF) 4-40 (4-40)

3011[2] **Apollono (74)**_(89) (RAkehurst)_ 3-8-7 (3) SSanders(4) (3rd st: led over 1f out: rdn out) ...... — **1**
3125[2] Concer Un **(72)**_(82) (SCWilliams)_ 3-8-3 (5) DaneO'Neill(6) (lw: a.p: led over 3f out tl over 1f out: unable qckn fnl f) 2½ **2**
3031* Hadeel **(80)**_(84)_(Fav)_(HThomsonJones)_ 3-9-2 MHills(2) (6th st: rdn over 2f out: one pce) 3½ **3**
2827* Rising Dough (IRE) **(72)**_(70) (GLMoore)_ 3-8-8 SWhitworth(1) (led 5f: 2nd st: wknd over 2f out) 3 **4**
2392[6] Hujjab (USA) **(82)**_(75) (JLDunlop)_ 3-9-4 TQuinn(7) (4th st: wknd over 2f out) 2½ **5**
2778* Noble Neptune **(61)**_(51) (WJMusson)_ 3-7-11 ow1 JFEgan(3) (lw: a bhd) 1¼ **6**
3214[8] Muchtarak (IRE) **(85)**_(75) (CJBenstead)_ 3-9-7 RCochrane(8) (lw: dwlt: a bhd) ...... ¾ **7**
2571[10] Peutetre **(85)**_(56) (CEBrittain)_ 3-9-7 PaulEddery(5) (lw: 5th st: wknd over 3f out) 10 **8**

5/2 Hadeel, **5/1** APOLLONO, Concer Un, Rising Dough (IRE), **13/2** Noble Neptune, **9/1** Muchtarak (IRE), **12/1** Hujjab (USA), **25/1** Peutetre, CSF £27.34 CT £68.30 TOTE £4.80: £1.90 £1.90 £1.50 (£14.30) OWNER Mr J K Ruggles & Mrs A R Ruggles (EPSOM) BRED Miss P. Ambler 8 Rn
1m 43.39 (1.39) SF: 54/47/49/35/40/16/40/21

3409 SHERWOOD MAIDEN STKS (3-Y.O+) (Class D) £4,045.50 (£1,224.00: £597.00: £283.50)
7f Stalls: Low GOING minus 0.32 sec per fur (GF) 5-10 (5-10)

2712[3] **Tonys Gift (62)**_(71) (RHannon)_ 3-8-4 (5) DaneO'Neill(6) (chsd ldr: hrd rdn over 1f out: led ins fnl f: r.o wl) ...... — **1**

3105[2] Raise the Stakes **(77)***(75)*(Fav)*(IABalding)* 3-9-0 PaulEddery(4) (lw: led: hrd rdn over 1f out: hdd ins fnl f: r.o)....½ 2
2393[5] Masaafaat (USA) **(73)***(65) (MRStoute)* 3-8-9 RCochrane(1) (4th st: rdn over 1f out: unable qckn)....2 3
2794[12] Istiwa *(61) (CJBenstead)* 3-9-0 TQuinn(3) (s.s: 5th st: wknd over 2f out)....4 4
Star Anise *(38) (MRChannon)* 3-8-9 MHills(2) (unf: s.s: hdwy over 4f out: 3rd st: wknd 2f out) 8 5

4/5 Raise the Stakes, **5/2** Masaafaat (USA), **5/1** TONYS GIFT (op 8/1), **16/1** Star Anise, **40/1** Istiwa, CSF £9.07 TOTE £4.80: £1.60 £1.20 (£2.90) OWNER Mr A. F. Harrington (MARLBOROUGH) BRED Mrs Sean Kelly and West Lodge Stud 5 Rn 1m 24.73 (4.43) SF: 12/16/6/2/-

T/Jkpt: £16,186.40 (3.09 Tckts). T/Plpt: £43.80 (655.05 Tckts). T/Qdpt: £18.80 (20.60 Tckts). AK

3365-NEWCASTLE (L-H)
Monday August 28th (Good, Good to firm patches back st)

1st & 4th race: hand timed
WEATHER: fine WIND: mod half against

3410 QUAYSIDE (S) STKS (3-Y.O+) (Class F) £2,650.40 (£744.40: £363.20)
1m 4f 93y Stalls: Low GOING minus 0.40 sec per fur (F) 2-15 (2-15)

3254[2] **Trumble (46)***(60)*(Fav)*(CWThornton)* 3-8-11 JWeaver(1) (mde all: styd on ins fnl 2f: drvn out)....— 1
2990[4] Fearless Wonder **(50)***(63) (MrsMReveley)* 4-9-5 (7) SCopp(7) (lw: trckd ldrs: effrt over 2f out: kpt on towards fin)....1¼ 2
3111[4] Lindisfarne Lady **(42)***(53) (MrsMReveley)* 3-8-6 KDarley(5) (lw: trckd ldrs: effrt & ev ch over 1f out: nt qckn ins fnl f)....hd 3
3296[4] Never so True **(41)***(51) (MartynWane)* 4-9-7 KFallon(4) (trckd ldrs: rdn over 2f out: wknd over 1f out)....6 4
3296[3] Doctor's Remedy **(30)***(50) (MrsJJordan)* 9-9-5 (7) JoHunnam(6) (prom: pushed along 6f out: outpcd fnl 3f)....4 5
3258[8] Straw Thatch **(49)***(48) (RBastiman)* 6-9-7 (5) HBastiman(3) (s.i.s: sn drvn along: rn in snatches: effrt 3f out: sn lost pl)....1½ 6
3272[6] Monica Maguire *(6) (GMMoore)* 3-8-6 NKennedy(2) (reminders s: sn drvn along: bhd fnl 5f) 25 7

6/4 TRUMBLE, **4/1** Lindisfarne Lady, **5/1** Fearless Wonder, Straw Thatch, **11/2** Never so True, **20/1** Doctor's Remedy, **25/1** Monica Maguire, CSF £9.35 TOTE £2.20: £1.40 £3.30 (£5.30) OWNER Mr Ben Pocock (MIDDLEHAM) BRED C. J. Sexton 7 Rn 2m 45.2 (6.70) SF: 23/36/16/24/23/21/-
WEIGHT FOR AGE 3yo-10lb
No bid

3411 NORTHERN RACING H'CAP (0-90) (3-Y.O+) (Class C) £11,080.00 (£3,340.00: £1,620.00: £760.00)
7f Stalls: High GOING minus 0.40 sec per fur (F) 2-50 (2-52)

2321[3] **Western Fame (USA) (80)***(89)*(Fav)*(JLDunlop)* 3-9-1 PatEddery(13) (chsd ldrs: styd on to ld 1f out: drvn out)....— 1
2477* Somerton Boy (IRE) **(76)***(81) (PCalver)* 5-9-2 MBirch(15) (chsd ldrs: ev ch ins fnl f: nt qckn) 1¾ 2
3112* Halmanerror **(71)***(73) (MrsJRRamsden)* 5-8-11 KFallon(7) (lw: hld up: effrt over 2f out: styd on ins fnl f: nt rch ldrs)....1½ 3
3065[9] Knobbleeneeze **(70)***(70) (MRChannon)* 5-8-10v WWoods(14) (a chsng ldrs: kpt on same pce appr fnl f)....½ 4
3230[13] Flashy's Son **(69)***(69) (GMMoore)* 7-8-6 (3) JTate(11) (b: b.hind: led stands' side to 1f out: kpt on same pce)....nk 5
3166[6] Tedburrow **(85)***(81) (MrsAMNaughton)* 3-9-6 NConnorton(10) (trckd ldrs: effrt over 2f out: sltly hmpd 1f out: grad wknd)....1¾ 6
3085* Gymcrak Premiere **(88)***(83) (GHolmes)* 7-10-0v WRSwinburn(4) (b.hind: racd far side: effrt over 2f out: edgd rt fnl f: nvr nr ldrs)....½ 7
3222[3] Allinson's Mate (IRE) **(77)***(71) (TDBarron)* 7-9-3b KDarley(3) (lw: chsd ldr far side: wknd over 1f out)....hd 8
*3074** Ashgore **(84)***(73) (MJohnston)* 5-9-10 JWeaver(2) (led far side: rdn 3f out: wknd over 1f out) 2½ 9
3188[13] Tawafij (USA) **(83)***(66) (TDyer)* 6-9-9v LDettori(9) (lw: hld up: effrt over 2f out: nvr nr ldrs)....2½ 10
2948[7] Cyrano's Lad (IRE) **(88)***(55) (CADwyer)* 6-9-11 (3) JStack(8) (chsd ldrs tl wknd over 2f out: eased)....7 11
1306[8] Impulsive Air (IRE) **(82)***(44) (EWeymes)* 3-9-3 DHarrison(5) (racd far side: a in rr)....2 12
3230[8] Super Benz **(62)***(24) (FJO'Mahony)* 9-8-2 JFanning(6) (b: sn drvn along & outpcd: n.d)....nk 13

2797[11] Cavers Yangous **(71)***(24) (MJohnston)* 4-8-11 MRoberts(12) (chsd ldrs tl lost pl over 2f out: eased) 4 14

5/2 WESTERN FAME (USA), **13/2** Tawafij (USA), **9/1** Somerton Boy (IRE), Gymcrak Premiere, Halmanerror (op 6/1), **10/1** Allinson's Mate (IRE), **11/1** Ashgore, **14/1** Tedburrow, Cyrano's Lad (IRE), Super Benz, **16/1** Knobbleeneeze, Cavers Yangous, **20/1** Flashy's Son, **33/1** Impulsive Air (IRE), CSF £25.63 CT £171.58 TOTE £3.00: £1.80 £3.50 £3.00 (£21.40) Trio £67.30 OWNER Mr S. Khaled (ARUNDEL) BRED Palides Investments N V 14 Rn

1m 26.34 (2.04) SF: 42/39/31/28/27/34/41/29/31/24/13/-/-/-
WEIGHT FOR AGE 3yo-5lb

3412 ST MODWEN PERKINS MEMORIAL CUP H'CAP (3-Y.O+) (Class B) £13,745.00 (£4,160.00: £2,030.00: £965.00)

2m 19y Stalls: Low GOING minus 0.40 sec per fur (F) 3-20 (3-22)

3262[2] **Star Rage (IRE) (77)***(90) (MJohnston)* 5-9-4 JWeaver(3) (hld up: hdwy & swtchd outside 3f out: led 2f out: hld on wl) ....— 1
2937[5] Good Hand (USA) **(73)***(86) (JWWatts)* 9-9-0 NConnorton(6) (pushed along 6f out: outpcd over 3f out: rallied over 1f out: styd on wl towards fin) ....½ 2
2996[2] Red Bustaan **(80)***(92) (ACStewart)* 3-8-7 MRoberts(7) (w ldr: led over 3f out to 2f out: styd on wl u.p appr fnl f: no ex towards fin) ....nk 3
3162[3] Foundry Lane **(82)***(91)*(Fav)*(MrsMReveley)* 4-9-9 KDarley(2) (trckd ldrs: effrt over 3f out: rdn & kpt on same pce fnl 2f) 3 4
3189[10] Master Hyde (USA) **(60)***(61) (WStorey)* 6-7-8 (7) PFessey(4) (racd wd: hdwy on outside 12f out: sn chsng ldrs: grad wknd fnl 2f) 8 5
3162[10] College Don **(69)***(59) (MPBielby)* 4-8-7 (3) DRMcCabe(8) (hld up & bhd: hdwy on outside 9f out: effrt 3f out: sn wknd) 11 6
3189[5] Highflying **(87)***(73) (GMMoore)* 9-9-11 (3) JTate(1) (led tl over 3f out: wknd 2f out) 4 7
2907[2] Shining High **(86)***(70) (JLDunlop)* 3-8-13 PatEddery(5) (unruly s: chsd ldrs: pushed along 4f out: rdn & wknd over 2f out: eased) 2 8

3/1 Foundry Lane, **7/2** Shining High, **4/1** Red Bustaan, **5/1** College Don, **8/1** Good Hand (USA), Highflying, **10/1** STAR RAGE (IRE), **20/1** Master Hyde (USA), CSF £78.63 CT £341.88 TOTE £8.90: £2.00 £2.30 £1.30 (£32.00) OWNER Mr J. D. Abell (MIDDLEHAM) BRED Killarkin Stud 8 Rn

3m 30.38 (4.88) SF: 47/43/35/48/18/16/30/13
WEIGHT FOR AGE 3yo-14lb

OFFICIAL EXPLANATION **Shining High: was reported to have been unsuited by the ground.**

3413 CITY OF NEWCASTLE UPON TYNE VIRGINIA RATED STKS H'CAP (0-105) (Listed) (3-Y.O+ F & M) (Class A) £11,153.88 (£4,174.92: £2,042.46: £879.30: £394.65: £200.79)

1m 2f 32y Stalls: Low GOING minus 0.40 sec per fur (F) 3-55 (3-58)

2679* **Bonne Etoile (87)***(98)*(Fav)*(DRLoder)* 3-8-8 DRMcCabe(2) (lw: trckd ldrs: effrt & nt clr run over 2f out: styd on u.p fnl f: led last strides) ....— 1
3007[3] Vena (IRE) **(90)***(101) (JLDunlop)* 3-8-11 PatEddery(7) (chsd ldrs: led over 2f out tl hdd nr fin) ....s.h 2
3007* Ellie Ardensky **(94)***(101) (JRFanshawe)* 3-9-1 DHarrison(5) (hld up: effrt u.p over 2f out: styd on fnl f: nt rch ldrs) 2½ 3
2902[2] Wathbat Mtoto **(87)***(94) (LMCumani)* 3-8-8 KDarley(4) (chsd ldrs: n.m.r over 2f out: kpt on same pce) ....nk 4
3013* Shemaq (USA) **(97)***(100) (HThomsonJones)* 3-9-4 RHills(8) (trckd ldrs: chal over 2f out: wknd over 1f out) 2½ 5
3040a[4] Pearl Venture **(91)***(87) (SPCWoods)* 3-8-12 WWoods(1) (bhd: drvn along over 3f out: n.d) 4 6
3164[7] Hunters of Brora (IRE) **(91)***(86) (JDBethell)* 5-9-6 WRSwinburn(3) (sn bhd: effrt over 3f out: n.d) ....¾ 7
2547[4] Red Azalea **(100)***(94) (SirMarkPrescott)* 3-9-7 GDuffield(6) (led tl over 2f out: wkng whn bdly hmpd wl over 1f out) ....½ 8
2679[4] Varvarka **(78)***(68) (JWWatts)* 3-7-13 JFanning(9) (hld up & plld hrd: hdwy on outside 7f out: rn wd & lost pl ent st) 2½ 9

15/8 BONNE ETOILE, **11/2** Vena (IRE), **6/1** Hunters of Brora (IRE), Shemaq (USA), **7/1** Ellie Ardensky, **8/1** Pearl Venture, **11/1** Wathbat Mtoto, **14/1** Varvarka, **16/1** Red Azalea, CSF £12.98 CT £57.25 TOTE £3.20: £1.30 £2.20 £2.50 (£13.60) Trio £22.20 OWNER Miss D. F. Fleming (NEWMARKET) BRED Kirtlington Stud Ltd 9 Rn

2m 11.6 (4.90) SF: 23/26/26/19/25/12/19/19/-
WEIGHT FOR AGE 3yo-8lb

STEWARDS' ENQUIRY McCabe susp. 6-12/9/95 (careless riding).

3414 STANLEY CLARKE LEISURE NURSERY H'CAP (2-Y.O) (Class C)
£7,205.00 (£2,165.00: £1,045.00: £485.00)
7f Stalls: High GOING minus 0.40 sec per fur (F) 4-25 (4-31)

*2958** **Double Diamond (IRE) (74)***(83+)*(Fav)*(MJohnston)* 2-8-7 JWeaver(1) (lw: swtchd rt sn after s: mde all: styd on strly & drew clr ins fnl f) ....— 1
3168³ Annaberg (IRE) **(73)***(76) (MrsJRRamsden)* 2-8-6 KFallon(7) (hld up & bhd: effrt over 2f out: chal 1f out: kpt on same pce) 2½ 2
3228⁴ Nostoi **(73)***(72) (SirMarkPrescott)* 2-8-6 GDuffield(4) (chsd ldrs: drvn along & outpcd over 2f out: kpt on fnl f) 1¾ 3
3010* Villeggiatura **(88)***(87) (BWHills)* 2-9-7 WRSwinburn(2) (trckd ldrs: effrt over 2f out: hung rt: wknd ins fnl f) ....s.h 4
3117⁴ Kernof (IRE) **(66)***(64) (MDHammond)* 2-7-13 DaleGibson(5) (chsd ldrs: outpcd over 2f out: kpt on ins fnl f) ....¾ 5
3147¹⁰ Too Hasty **(80)***(77+) (MHEasterby)* 2-8-13 MBirch(6) (hld up: nt clr run fnl 2f: nt rcvr) ....hd 6
3147¹⁴ Gladys Althorpe (IRE) **(74)***(70) (JLEyre)* 2-8-7 RLappin(3) (chsd ldrs: drvn along ½-wy: outpcd over 1f out) ....¾ 7

11/4 DOUBLE DIAMOND (IRE), **100/30** Villeggiatura, **7/2** Nostoi, **5/1** Annaberg (IRE), **7/1** Kernof (IRE), **8/1** Too Hasty, **14/1** Gladys Althorpe (IRE), CSF £16.34 TOTE £2.80: £1.90 £2.40 (£4.70) OWNER The 2nd Middleham Partnership (MIDDLEHAM) BRED Dene Investments N V 7 Rn
1m 27.75 (3.45) SF: 19/12/8/23/-/13/6

3415 RIVER TYNE CLAIMING STKS (2-Y.O) (Class F) £2,738.60
(£769.60: £375.80)
5f Stalls: High GOING minus 0.40 sec per fur (F) 4-55 (4-59)

1919⁶ **Opening Chorus** *(62+) (MrsJRRamsden)* 2-8-8 KFallon(9) (hld up: hdwy 2f out: styd on wl u.p to ld wl ins fnl f) ....— 1
3253* April's Joy **(46)***(54) (JNorton)* 2-8-2 DaleGibson(4) (trckd ldr: led ins fnl f tl wl ins fnl f: nt qckn towards fin) ....¾ 2
2869* Hickleton Miss **(57)***(48)*(Fav)*(MrsMReveley)* 2-8-4 KDarley(5) (led tl ins fnl f: kpt on) 2½ 3
2869³ Rattle *(48) (JJO'Neill)* 2-8-12 GDuffield(7) (chsd ldrs: outpcd over 2f out: kpt on u.p fnl f) 2½ 4
1959⁴ Ultra Power *(40+) (PCHaslam)* 2-8-5 (7) JulieLemin(8) (trckd ldrs tl grad wknd fnl 2f) 2½ 5
2185⁷ Princess Pamgaddy **(69)***(30) (JBerry)* 2-7-12 (7) PFessey(6) (sn chsng ldrs: drvn along over 2f out: one pce) ....¾ 6
2696⁴ Petrefuz (IRE) *(27) (EWeymes)* 2-8-10 DHarrison(3) (chsd ldrs: hung lft ½-wy: wknd over 1f out) 2½ 7
2971⁹ Domoor *(23) (MJohnston)* 2-9-0 JWeaver(2) (bhd & rdn ½-wy: wnt rt: n.d) 2½ 8
2991⁹ Ichor **(57)** *(HThomsonJones)* 2-8-1 ow2 RHills(1) (unruly s: s.s: sn chsng ldrs: rdn & fnd nil over 1f out: eased) 9 9

7/4 Hickleton Miss (op 3/1), **5/1** Princess Pamgaddy, **13/2** Petrefuz (IRE), **7/1** Ichor, OPENING CHORUS, April's Joy, **11/1** Domoor, **14/1** Rattle, **25/1** Ultra Power, CSF £52.47 TOTE £9.70: £2.80 £1.70 £1.50 (£60.80) Trio £26.30 OWNER Mr J. D. Abell (THIRSK) BRED N. F. and Mrs E. E. Tebbutt 9 Rn
62.07 secs (3.67) SF: -/-/-/-/-/-/-/-/-
Opening Chorus clmd PSavill £7,000

3416 E.B.F. MAIDEN STKS (2-Y.O C & G) (Class D) £3,533.75
(£1,070.00: £522.50: £248.75)
7f Stalls: High GOING minus 0.40 sec per fur (F) 5-25 (5-29)

3089³ **Coldstream** *(86+)*(Fav)*(LMCumani)* 2-8-11 LDettori(7) (lw: chsd ldrs: styd on u.p to ld ins fnl f: drvn out) ....— 1
2846⁵ Storm Trooper (USA) *(83+) (HRACecil)* 2-8-11 PatEddery(3) (trckd ldrs: led over 2f out: hdd ins fnl f: eased nr fin) 1¼ 2
3228² Crystal Falls (IRE) **(76)***(77) (JJO'Neill)* 2-8-11 KFallon(4) (in tch: sn pushed along: kpt on wl ins fnl f) 2½ 3
2820⁴ Jo Mell *(77+) (MHEasterby)* 2-8-11 MBirch(9) (hld up & plld hrd: nt clr run 2f out: kpt on wl ins fnl f) ....hd 4
Desert Cat (IRE) *(73+) (HThomsonJones)* 2-8-11 RHills(5) (rangy: chsd ldrs: outpcd 2f out: wknd towards fin) 2 5
Cheerful Aspect (IRE) *(59) (EALDunlop)* 2-8-11 WRSwinburn(1) (rangy: scope: b.hind: uns rdr & bolted gng to s: sn bhd: swtchd rt & reminders ½-wy: n.d) 6 6
Mister Aspecto (IRE) *(51+) (MJohnston)* 2-8-11 JWeaver(2) (lengthy: scope: sn drvn along & outpcd: sme hdwy over 2f out: n.d) 3½ 7
Mental Pressure *(42) (MRChannon)* 2-8-11 KDarley(6) (leggy: scope: s.i.s: nvr wnt pce) 4 8

2192[9] Sheemore (IRE) *(33) (JDBethell)* 2-8-11 GDuffield(8) (sn pushed along in tch: outpcd ½-wy: sn lost pl)....4 9
2380[4] Oisin An Oir (IRE) *(29) (JBerry)* 2-8-11 WWoods(10) (led: hung lft & hdd over 2f out: sn wknd)....1¾ 10

5/6 COLDSTREAM, **4/1** Storm Trooper (USA), **5/1** Desert Cat (IRE) (7/1-9/2), **6/1** Mister Aspecto (IRE), **12/1** Crystal Falls (IRE), **14/1** Jo Mell, **20/1** Cheerful Aspect (IRE), Mental Pressure, **50/1** Sheemore (IRE), Oisin An Oir (IRE), CSF £5.76 TOTE £1.90: £1.10 £1.50 £2.10 (£2.70) Trio £10.50 OWNER Mr Robert Russell (NEWMARKET) BRED A. L. and J. Chapman 10 Rn
1m 26.29 (1.99) SF: 39/36/30/30/26/12/4/-/-/-
T/Plpt: £44.40 (438.14 Tckts). T/Qdpt: £9.50 (12.15 Tckts). WG

3227-RIPON (R-H)
Monday August 28th (Good, Good to firm patches)
WEATHER: overcast WIND: almost nil

3417 STAINLEY (S) STKS (2-Y.O) (Class F) £2,879.00 (£872.00: £426.00: £203.00)
6f Stalls: Low GOING minus 0.32 sec per fur (GF) 2-10 (2-12)

3160[10] **Mystic Times (64)***(60) (MissSEHall)* 2-8-6 WRyan(3) (in tch: hdwy over 2f out: r.o fnl f to ld cl home)....— 1
2857[5] Miletrian Refurb (IRE) **(60)***(65) (MRChannon)* 2-8-11 RHughes(7) (mde most tl ct nr fin)....hd 2
3243[5] Power Don **(65)***(63)*(Fav)*(WGMTurner)* 2-8-8 (3) PMcCabe(1) (lw: a w ldrs: rdn 2f out: nt qckn towards fin)....½ 3
3160[8] Domino Flyer **(62)***(54) (MrsASwinbank)* 2-8-11 DHolland(9) (a in tch: kpt on fnl 2f: nt pce to chal)....3½ 4
2951[9] Lucky Bea **(50)***(53) (MWEasterby)* 2-8-11b BThomson(11) (cl up: effrt over 2f out: one pce)..nk 5
3271[10] Bee Health Boy **(60)***(50) (MWEasterby)* 2-8-6b(5) LNewton(12) (w ldrs: nt qckn fnl 2f)....1¼ 6
2629[7] Marmy *(32) (MHEasterby)* 2-8-6 TWilliams(10) (s.i.s: n.d)....5 7
3353[7] Mister Joel *(35) (MWEasterby)* 2-8-4 (7) RuthCoulter(8) (dwlt: nrst fin)....¾ 8
2857[7] Red Simba **(63)***(36) (JBerry)* 2-9-2 JCarroll(5) (prom 4f)....1¼ 9
3077[7] Brockville Bairn *(27) (MrsASwinbank)* 2-8-11 JMarshall(6) (s.i.s: n.d)....1½ 10
3353[5] Baroness Gold *(22) (MHEasterby)* 2-8-6 SMaloney(2) (b.hind: chsd ldrs over 4f)....nk 11
3231[9] Mysterious Times **(46)***(21) (BWMurray)* 2-8-6 ACulhane(4) (s.i.s: a bhd)....nk 12
1943[5] Mels Baby (IRE) **(54)***(25) (JLEyre)* 2-8-11v SDWilliams(13) (bhd fr ½-wy)....nk 13

7/4 Power Don (op 3/1), **100/30** MYSTIC TIMES, **11/2** Domino Flyer, **9/1** Miletrian Refurb (IRE) (op 6/1), **10/1** Mels Baby (IRE), Red Simba, **11/1** Lucky Bea, Bee Health Boy, **14/1** Marmy, **16/1** Baroness Gold, **20/1** Mister Joel, Mysterious Times, **25/1** Brockville Bairn, CSF £38.21 TOTE £4.20: £1.30 £2.30 £1.50 (£18.60) Trio £10.00 OWNER Footballers' Racing Club (MIDDLEHAM) BRED Miss S. E. Hall 13 Rn
1m 14.0 (3.80) SF: 11/16/14/5/4/1/-/-/-/-/-/-/-
No bid

3418 BONUSPRINT H'CAP (0-80) (3-Y.O+) (Class D) £4,354.00 (£1,312.00: £636.00: £298.00)
6f Stalls: Low GOING minus 0.32 sec per fur (GF) 2-40 (2-41)

3221[4] **Croft Imperial (65)***(71) (MJohnston)* 8-9-4v TWilliams(10) (a chsng ldrs: disp ld over 1f out: r.o)....— 1
2288[6] Colway Rake **(69)***(75)*(Fav)*(JWWatts)* 4-9-8b WCarson(1) (hdwy ½-wy: disp ld over 1f out: r.o)....s.h 2
2758[6] Maid O'Cannie **(58)***(61) (MWEasterby)* 4-8-11 SMaloney(4) (hld up & bhd: hdwy over 1f out: n.m.r: fin wl)....1 3
3275[2] Captain Carat **(64)***(67) (MrsJRRamsden)* 4-8-10 (7) SBuckley(11) (lw: bhd: hdwy 2f out: nt clr run & swtchd ins fnl f: r.o wl)....s.h 4
2746[7] Cumbrian Waltzer **(73)***(74) (MHEasterby)* 10-9-7 (5) LNewton(2) (in tch: hdwy 2f out: nt clr run fnl f)....¾ 5
3230[9] Ned's Bonanza **(72)***(73) (MDods)* 6-9-11 JCarroll(8) (a chsng ldrs: nt qckn ins fnl f)....hd 6
3150* Here Comes a Star **(73)***(72) (JMCarr)* 7-9-12 ACulhane(7) (hld up: effrt over 2f out: nvr able to chal)....¾ 7
2394[7] Just Dissident (IRE) **(68)***(67) (RMWhitaker)* 3-9-3 DaleGibson(3) (disp ld over 4f: wknd)....hd 8
3359[16] Prima Silk **(72)***(67) (MJRyan)* 4-9-6b(5) DGibbs(6) (disp ld over 4f: hung lft & grad wknd)....1¼ 9
2628[7] Bells of Longwick **(61)***(48) (WWHaigh)* 6-9-0 DeanMcKeown(9) (in tch over 4f)....3 10
3275[5] Lochon **(58)***(40) (JLEyre)* 4-8-11 SDWilliams(5) (lw: chsd ldrs: outpcd over 2f out: bdly hmpd & snatched up ent fnl f)....2 11

7/2 Colway Rake, **9/2** Captain Carat, **13/2** Here Comes a Star, **7/1** Lochon, **8/1** Maid O'Cannie, Cumbrian Waltzer, **10/1** CROFT IMPERIAL, Just Dissident (IRE), **12/1** Prima Silk, Ned's Bonanza, **33/1** Bells of Longwick, CSF £44.51 CT £278.27 TOTE £12.20 £3.60 £1.90 £2.90 (£21.20) Trio £94.50 OWNER Mrs B. A. Matthews (MIDDLEHAM) BRED Eric Henshaw 11 Rn

1m 14.1 (3.90) SF: 21/25/11/17/24/23/22/13/17/-/-

WEIGHT FOR AGE 3yo-4lb

3419 RIPON ROWELS H'CAP (0-100) (3-Y.O+) (Class C) £7,253.75 (£2,180.00: £1,052.50: £488.75)

1m Stalls: High GOING minus 0.32 sec per fur (GF) 3-10 (3-16)

3255[2] **Spanish Verdict (69)***(79) (DenysSmith)* 8-8-2 (5) CTeague(7) (lw: mde all: all out) ....— 1
3276* Celestial Choir **(83)***(93)*(Fav)*(JLEyre)* 5-9-7 5x SDWilliams(8) (lw: trckd ldrs: nt clr run over 1f out: hdwy ins fnl f: fin wl) ....hd 2
2999[7] Legal Fiction **(66)***(76) (MJohnston)* 4-8-4 DeanMcKeown(1) (lw: a.p: effrt 2f out: hrd rdn fnl f: r.o) ....s.h 3
3095* Donna Viola **(83)***(90) (CFWall)* 3-8-10 (5) LNewton(4) (lw: hld up & bhd: hmpd over 3f out: gd hdwy 2f out: nt qckn ins fnl f) 1¼ 4
2952[5] Bold Amusement **(82)***(85) (WSCunningham)* 5-9-6 JCarroll(6) (chsd wnr: rdn over 3f out: one pce appr fnl f) 2 5
3222* Pride of Pendle **(78)***(79) (DNicholls)* 6-9-2 AlexGreaves(5) (hld up: hdwy over 2f out: nvr nr to chal) 1 6
3027[5] Scotsky (IRE) **(95)***(89)*(Fav)*(JLDunlop)* 3-9-13 WCarson(2) (bhd: swtchd wl over 1f out: no imp) 3½ 7
3188[6] Moving Arrow **(90)***(84) (MissSEHall)* 4-10-0 WRyan(3) (hld up: effrt 3f out: no imp) ....nk 8
2417[4] Above the Cut (USA) **(94)***(84) (PWHarris)* 3-9-12 BThomson(9) (unruly bef s: bhd: effrt 4f out: n.d) 2 9

7/2 Scotsky (IRE), Celestial Choir, **4/1** Donna Viola, **11/2** Pride of Pendle, **13/2** Moving Arrow, **8/1** Legal Fiction (op 14/1), **9/1** Above the Cut (USA), **12/1** Bold Amusement, SPANISH VERDICT, CSF £55.81 CT £342.32 TOTE £14.80: £2.70 £1.70 £2.30 (£31.30) Trio £134.80 OWNER Cox & Allen (Kendal) Ltd (BISHOP AUCKLAND) BRED Hyde Stud 9 Rn

1m 39.9 (2.20) SF: 43/57/40/48/49/43/47/48/42

WEIGHT FOR AGE 3yo-6lb

3420 BONUSPRINT CHAMPION TWO YRS OLD TROPHY STKS (Listed) (2-Y.O) (Class A) £13,178.00 (£4,778.00: £2,314.00: £970.00: £410.00)

6f Stalls: Low GOING minus 0.32 sec per fur (GF) 3-45 (3-45)

2704[3] **Kahir Almaydan (IRE) (100)***(109t)*(Fav)*(JLDunlop)* 2-8-11 WCarson(1) (lw: mde all: r.o wl fnl 2f: pushed out) ....— 1
3165[3] High Priority (IRE) **(100)***(85) (MRChannon)* 2-8-11 RHughes(3) (hdwy over 2f out: styd on: no ch w wnr) 9 2
2554[4] Persian Secret (FR) **(100)***(67) (JWWatts)* 2-8-6 WRyan(2) (lw: chsd wnr tl rdn & btn 2f out) 5 3
2978* Red Nymph *(60) (WJarvis)* 2-8-9 BThomson(5) (chsd ldrs: rdn over 2f out: sn btn) 3½ 4
3220* Dovebrace **(100)***(67) (ABailey)* 2-9-2 DHolland(4) (lw: prom to ½-wy: sn rdn & btn) ....s.h 5

6/4 KAHIR ALMAYDAN (IRE), **2/1** Red Nymph (op 3/1), **5/1** Persian Secret (FR), **11/2** Dovebrace, **7/1** High Priority (IRE), CSF £11.20 TOTE £2.20: £1.30 £3.20 (£7.70) OWNER Mr Mirza Al Sayegh (ARUNDEL) BRED B. Ryan 5 Rn

1m 10.9 (0.10 under 2y best) (0.70) SF: 58/34/16/9/16

3421 GRASSINGTON MAIDEN STKS (3-Y.O) (Class D) £3,811.25 (£1,154.00: £563.50: £268.25)

1m 4f 60y Stalls: High GOING minus 0.32 sec per fur (GF) 4-15 (4-16)

2754[2] **Iridal (81)***(74)*(Fav)*(HRACecil)* 3-9-0 WRyan(1) (lw: trckd ldrs: led wl over 2f out: r.o: comf) ....— 1
2790[4] Twilight Hour (USA) **(65)***(66) (BWHills)* 3-8-9 DHolland(4) (led tl hdd wl over 2f out: kpt on u.p) 2 2
Darter (IRE) *(69) (LMCumani)* 3-9-0 OUrbina(5) (w'like: scope: bkwd: hld up: hdwy 4f out: styd on: nt pce to chal) 1¾ 3
New Broom (IRE) *(55) (MHEasterby)* 3-8-9 SMaloney(3) (unf: scope: a.p: ev ch 3f out: wknd wl over 1f out) 7 4
2426[3] Victor Laszlo *(55) (JDBethell)* 3-9-0 WCarson(2) (hld up: effrt 4f out: n.d) 4 5

5/6 IRIDAL, **5/2** Twilight Hour (USA), **9/2** Darter (IRE) (op 5/2), **10/1** Victor Laszlo (12/1-8/1), **20/1** New Broom (IRE), CSF £3.44 TOTE £1.60: £1.20 £1.90 (£2.50) OWNER Lord Howard de Walden (NEWMARKET) BRED Lord Howard de Walden 5 Rn
2m 41.7 (7.70) SF: 24/16/19/5/5

3422 PATELEY H'CAP (0-70) (3-Y.O) (Class E) £3,260.50 (£988.00: £483.00: £230.50)
1m 2f Stalls: High GOING minus 0.32 sec per fur (GF) 4-50 (4-51)

2993[2] **Westcourt Princess (51)***(65+) (MWEasterby)* 3-7-13 (5)ow3 LNewton(11) (lw: mde all: shkn up over 2f out: r.o wl) ....— **1**
2630[6] Lucidity **(52)***(65) (CWThornton)* 3-8-5 DeanMcKeown(3) (chsd wnr: rdn 3f out: kpt on one pce) 2½ **2**
3207[7] Komreyev Dancer **(67)***(76) (ABailey)* 3-9-6 OUrbina(8) (lw: hdwy 3f out: r.o fnl f: nrst fin) 2½ **3**
3247[2] La Fille de Cirque **(46)***(55) (RJRWilliams)* 3-7-10 (3) DarrenMoffatt(6) (b: swtchd lft & hdwy over 2f out: hung rt ins fnl f: kpt on) ....nk **4**
2719[3] Bellateena **(53)***(59) (HJCollingridge)* 3-8-6 DHolland(13) (lw: chsd ldrs: effrt over 3f out: one pce) 1½ **5**
3099[3] Cumbrian Minstrel **(48)***(53) (MHEasterby)* 3-8-1 SMaloney(4) (a.p: hdwy 3f out: wknd fnl f)....¾ **6**
2875[2] Bold Top **(42)***(45) (BSRothwell)* 3-7-9b JMarshall(12) (chsd ldrs tl wknd fnl 3f).......1 **7**
3258[7] Hunza Story **(44)***(41) (NPLittmoden)* 3-7-4 (7)ow4 JoHunnam(9) (hdwy & prom appr st: wknd fnl 2½f) 1½ **8**
Dally Boy **(53)***(53) (MHEasterby)* 3-8-6 TWilliams(10) (nvr trbld ldrs) ....¾ **9**
2630[9] Skedaddle **(56)***(32) (JGFitzGerald)* 3-8-9 ACulhane(1) (pushed along thrght: bhd fnl 3f)........15 **10**
2207[4] Orchidarma **(56)***(28) (JJQuinn)* 3-8-9 JCarroll(14) (bhd fr ½-wy) 2½ **11**
3258[3] Perfect Bertie (IRE) **(43)***(14) (GROldroyd)* 3-7-10v NKennedy(2) (nvr wnt pce) ....nk **12**
3099[15] Mr Eglantine **(40)** *(ASmith)* 3-7-0 (7) BHalligan(7) (a bhd: t.o) 9 **13**
2880[5] Fasih **(68)***(18)*(Fav)*(ACStewart)* 3-9-7 WCarson(5) (lw: a bhd: t.o).......4 **14**
LONG HANDICAP Mr Eglantine 7-2 Hunza Story 7-5

2/1 Fasih (9/4-7/2), **11/4** WESTCOURT PRINCESS (5/1-5/2), **13/2** La Fille de Cirque, **9/1** Bellateena, **10/1** Perfect Bertie (IRE), Bold Top, **12/1** Cumbrian Minstrel (op 8/1), **16/1** Lucidity, Komreyev Dancer, Skedaddle, **20/1** Hunza Story, Dally Boy, Orchidarma, **50/1** Mr Eglantine, CSF £50.75 CT £610.93 TOTE £3.60: £1.70 £3.60 £8.80 (£54.60) Trio £448.10 OWNER Mr K. Hodgson (SHERIFF HUTTON) BRED Britton House Stud 14 Rn
2m 6.5 (3.00) SF: 39/39/50/29/33/27/19/15/27/6/2/-/-/-
OFFICIAL EXPLANATION Fasih: finished lame behind.
T/Plpt: £124.60 (77.4 Tckts). T/Qdpt: £21.80 (9.65 Tckts). AA

2447-WARWICK (L-H)
Monday August 28th (Firm)
WEATHER: fine & sunny WIND: mod across

3423 PINLEY NURSERY H'CAP (2-Y.O) (Class E) £3,611.25 (£1,080.00: £517.50: £236.25) **6f** Stalls: Low GOING minus 0.65 sec per fur (HD) 2-00 (2-01)

3314[3] **Times of Times (IRE) (68)***(69)*(Fav)*(DJSCosgrove)* 2-8-7 GCarter(2) (a.p: 3rd st: led ins fnl f: rdn out) ....— **1**
3132[7] Miss Carottene **(57)***(57) (MJRyan)* 2-7-5b(5) MBaird(9) (led after 1f tl ins fnl f: rallied u.p cl home) ....½ **2**
3289[6] Morning Surprise **(61)***(58) (APJarvis)* 2-7-7 (7) CAdamson(3) (dwlt: bhd & outpcd tl gd hdwy appr fnl f: fin fast) 1 **3**
2765[5] Polly Golightly **(82)***(72) (BSmart)* 2-9-7 WNewnes(5) (lw: led 1f: 2nd st: rdn bel dist: wknd fnl f) 2½ **4**
2757[2] My Kind **(66)***(50) (KMcAuliffe)* 2-8-5 MFenton(6) (chsd ldrs: 5th & rdn st: wknd over 1f out)..2½ **5**
3090[9] Laughing Buccaneer **(72)***(50) (BJMeehan)* 2-8-11b BDoyle(8) (lw: outpcd: a bhd) 2 **6**
3090[10] Elmswood (USA) **(78)***(51) (PWChapple-Hyam)* 2-8-12 (5) RHavlin(4) (chsd ldrs: 5th st: sn rdn & lost pl) 2 **7**
3003[5] Prime Partner **(73)***(41) (WRMuir)* 2-8-12 PRobinson(1) (in rr: drvn along & 6th st: no imp).......2 **8**
2924[5] Impending Danger **(54)** *(KSBridgwater)* 2-7-7 JLowe(7) (sn drvn along & outpcd: t.o) 25 **9**
LONG HANDICAP Impending Danger 6-13

3/1 TIMES OF TIMES (IRE), **4/1** My Kind, **9/2** Elmswood (USA), **5/1** Polly Golightly, **8/1** Prime Partner, **10/1** Laughing Buccaneer (op 6/1), **12/1** Morning Surprise (op 7/1), **14/1** Miss Carottene, **50/1** Impending Danger, CSF £38.29 CT £400.51 TOTE £3.40: £1.50 £3.60 £3.90 (£32.70) Trio £109.70 OWNER Mrs M. Schneider (NEWMARKET) BRED E. Moloney 9 Rn
1m 12.3 (0.30) SF: 34/22/23/37/15/15/16/6/-

3424

WARWICKSHIRE CLAIMING STKS (3-Y.O+) (Class F) £3,174.20 (£881.20: £422.60)
5f Stalls: Low GOING minus 0.65 sec per fur (HD) 2-30 (2-37)

2865[4] **Rhythmic Dancer (61)**(56) (JLSpearing) 7-8-2 (3)ow1 SDrowne(5) (mde virtually all: rdn & r.o wl fnl f)...— 1
3051[7] Hinton Rock (IRE) **(84)**(62) (MBell) 3-8-11b MFenton(4) (w wnr: rdn over 1f out: unable qckn)1¼ 2
3205* Pearl Dawn (IRE) **(68)**(51)(Fav)(NoelChance) 5-8-7 PRobinson(12) (a.p: rdn over 1f out: nt pce to chal)...1¼ 3
3221[3] My Abbey **(55)**(45) (EJAlston) 6-8-7 AMackay(15) (chsd ldrs: rdn & kpt on ins fnl f)...1¾ 4
2992[8] John O'Dreams **(45)**(47) (MrsALMKing) 10-8-10 AGarth(3) (bhd tl r.o u.p appr fnl f: nvr nrr) ..nk 5
2527[7] Last World **(42)**(40) (JAPickering) 3-8-0 JQuinn(13) (chsd ldrs over 3f: sn rdn: wknd fnl f) .....nk 6
1918[6] Sound the Trumpet (IRE) **(74)**(49) (AStreeter) 3-8-2v(7) DSweeney(16) (chsd ldrs: hrd rdn bel dist: kpt on one pce)...d.h 6
3177[13] Harry's Coming **(53)**(40) (RJHodges) 11-8-2 (5)ow3 DGriffiths(11) (hdwy wl over 1f out: nvr nrr)...nk 8
2712[8] Thehillsarealive (IRE) (47) (DRCElsworth) 3-8-13 JWilliams(14) (s.i.s: nvr gng pce of ldrs)..1¾ 9
3134[3] Cork Street Girl (IRE) **(50)**(24) (BJMeehan) 3-8-0bow2 BDoyle(7) (a in rr)...2½ 10
2642[7] Can't Say (IRE) **(30)**(23) (JMBradley) 3-8-3v RPrice(2) (outpcd)...1¾ 11
3259[9] Captain Sinbad **(30)**(14) (KSBridgwater) 3-8-7 VSlattery(1) (outpcd: a bhd)...4 12
3123[11] Superbit **(50)**(13) (BAMcMahon) 3-8-7 GCarter(9) (outpcd)...½ 13
2843[10] Amber Lily **(25)** (JMBradley) 3-7-5 (7) CAdamson(10) (outpcd)...1¼ 14
3205[7] Ballysheila (GFHCharles-Jones) 3-7-10b JLowe(8) (s.s: a bhd & outpcd: t.o)...15 15
1763[U] Come on Winn **(35)** (RHollinshead) 3-7-9 (7) FLynch(6) (swvd bdly rt & uns rdr s)... U

2/1 Pearl Dawn (IRE) (6/4-9/4), **3/1** Hinton Rock (IRE), **15/2** RHYTHMIC DANCER, **8/1** My Abbey, Cork Street Girl (IRE), **12/1** Harry's Coming, **14/1** Sound the Trumpet (IRE) (op 8/1), **20/1** John O'Dreams, Superbit, **40/1** Thehillsarealive (IRE), **50/1** Can't Say (IRE), **66/1** Last World, Captain Sinbad, Amber Lily, Ballysheila, Come on Winn, CSF £29.49 TOTE £7.50: £2.00 £1.80 £1.50 (£20.00) Trio £10.40 OWNER Mrs Robert Heathcote (ALCESTER) BRED Heathavon Stables Ltd 16 Rn 58.8 secs (0.80) SF: 21/24/16/10/12/2/11/5/9/-/-/-/-/-/-/-
WEIGHT FOR AGE 3yo-3lb
Hinton Rock (IRE) clmd PFreeman £7,000

3425

WARWICK CESAREWITCH H'CAP (0-80) (3-Y.O+) (Class D) £3,935.10 (£1,174.80: £561.40: £254.70)
2m 20y Stalls: Low GOING minus 0.65 sec per fur (HD) 3-00 (3-02)

3217[4] **Brumon (IRE) (56)**(72) (DWPArbuthnot) 4-9-8v JWilliams(6) (lw: hld up & bhd: hdwy over 3f out: 4th st: rdn to ld ins fnl f)...— 1
2569[10] Chez Catalan **(45)**(61) (RAkehurst) 4-8-11b JQuinn(2) (hld up: hdwy 4f out: led over 2f out tl ins fnl f: r.o)...nk 2
3084[3] Kriva **(66)**(78) (RJRWilliams) 3-9-4 DBiggs(8) (b.off hind: lost pl & rdn along ½-wy: hdwy 4f out: 3rd st: styd on one pce u.p)...4 3
2688[2] Upper Mount Clair **(58)**(64) (CEBrittain) 5-9-10 BDoyle(5) (hld up & bhd: effrt u.p over 3f out: 6th st: nvr rchd ldrs)...6 4
3140[3] Harry Welsh (IRE) **(63)**(64) (KMcAuliffe) 3-8-10v(5) MHenry(7) (chsd ldrs: led 4f out tl over 2f out: wknd)...5 5
3217[8] Chucklestone **(42)**(40) (JSKing) 12-8-8 NCarlisle(1) (led after 3f to 5f out: 7th & wkng ent st)2½ 6
3211[2] Welshman **(58)**(48) (MBlanshard) 9-9-10 StephenDavies(3) (jnd ldr 9f out: led 5f out: sn hdd: 5th & btn st)...8 7
3355* Northern Law **(74)** (Fav)(BWHills) 3-9-12 5x MFenton(4) (led 3f: led over 4f out: sn hdd & wknd: 8th st: t.o)...dist 8

9/4 Northern Law, **9/2** Upper Mount Clair, **11/2** Chez Catalan, **6/1** BRUMON (IRE), **7/1** Harry Welsh (IRE), Kriva (op 12/1), **8/1** Welshman, **16/1** Chucklestone, CSF £37.07 CT £217.55 TOTE £8.10: £2.20 £2.50 £1.80 (£36.20) OWNER Mr Christopher Wright (COMPTON) BRED Warner L. Jones 8 Rn 3m 29.6 (3.60) SF: 38/27/30/30/16/6/14/-
WEIGHT FOR AGE 3yo-14lb

3426

ST NICHOLAS (S) STKS (3-Y.O+) (Class G) £2,243.00 (£618.00: £293.00)
1m 2f 169y Stalls: Low GOING minus 0.65 sec per fur (HD) 3-30 (3-41)

3108[3] **Shabanaz (60)**(57)(Fav)(WRMuir) 10-9-10 CRutter(3) (hld up: hdwy 4f out: 5th st: led 1f out: rdn & r.o wl)...— 1

2976⁴ Bronze Runner **(40)***(56) (SMellor)* 11-9-5b(5) DGriffiths(15) (hld up in tch: effrt & 6th st: chal ent fnl f: r.o)....1 **2**
Irish Groom *(52) (AStreeter)* 8-9-0 (7) DSweeney(6) (mid div: hdwy 2f out: rdn & r.o strly fnl f)....nk **3**
3205⁵ Pacific Girl (IRE) **(51)***(43) (BPalling)* 3-8-7 GCarter(7) (hld up in tch: rapid hdwy to ld ent st: hdd 1f out: sn wknd)....2½ **4**
3206³ Suile Mor **(52)***(43) (BRMillman)* 3-8-7 JWilliams(16) (hld up: outpcd ent st: styd on ins fnl f) ...½ **5**
3202³ Pop to Stans **(47)***(46) (JPearce)* 6-9-3 (7) MNutter(5) (hld up: gd hdwy 4f out: 2nd st: rdn over 1f out: one pce)....3 **6**
3092⁹ Ann Hill (IRE) **(24)***(37) (RHollinshead)* 5-8-9 (7) AEddery(1) (dwlt: hdwy 4f out: nt rch ldrs) ......½ **7**
3249⁵ False Pretences (IRE) **(30)***(31) (BAPearce)* 3-8-12 StephenDavies(10) (a in rr)....8 **8**
3079¹⁴ Mitsis **(37)***(25) (GCBravery)* 4-9-7b MFenton(14) (chsd ldrs: rdn along 3f out: grad wknd)........4 **9**
1683⁷ Moonlight Air *(14) (JLSpearing)* 4-9-2 RPrice(2) (mid div tl wknd 3f out)....3½ **10**
1285²⁰ Portolano (FR) **(34)***(18) (WClay)* 4-9-2v(5) RHavlin(12) (prom over 6f)....¾ **11**
2983⁹ Pats Folly **(17)***(12) (FJYardley)* 4-9-2 JQuinn(8) (chsd ldrs tl 7th & wkng st)....¾ **12**
Causley **(65)***(14) (DMHyde)* 10-9-7 VSlattery(11) (b: bkwd: w ldr: led 6f out tl hdd & 3rd st: sn wknd)....2 **13**
1428⁶ Portland Way **(40)***(9) (APJarvis)* 3-8-5 (7) CAdamson(4) (prom 6f: sn wknd)....3½ **14**
Rightacres Lad *(JMBradley)* 4-9-4 (3) SDrowne(9) (a bhd : t.o)....15 **15**
1407⁷ Dick Christian **(35)** *(BJMeehan)* 3-8-12b BDoyle(13) (swtg: led over 4f: ev ch & 4th st: wknd qckly: t.o)....1¾ **16**

13/8 SHABANAZ, **7/2** Suile Mor, **7/1** Pacific Girl (IRE) (op 20/1), **9/1** Causley, **10/1** Pop to Stans (8/1-12/1), **12/1** Bronze Runner, **16/1** Moonlight Air, **20/1** Dick Christian, Ann Hill (IRE), **25/1** False Pretences (IRE), Portolano (FR), **33/1** Mitsis, Portland Way, **50/1** Pats Folly, Rightacres Lad, Irish Groom, CSF £23.39 TOTE £2.80: £1.40 £3.30 £10.60 (£12.20) Trio £410.50; £202.37 to Ripon 29/8/95 OWNER Fayzad Thoroughbred Ltd (LAMBOURN) BRED The Overbury Stud 16 Rn
2m 16.3 (2.80) SF: 35/34/30/12/12/24/15/-/3/-/-/-/-/-/-/-
WEIGHT FOR AGE 3yo-9lb
No bid

3427 RUGBY MAIDEN AUCTION STKS (2-Y.O) (Class F) £3,199.40 (£888.40: £426.20)
7f Stalls: Low GOING minus 0.65 sec per fur (HD) 4-00 (4-09)

Just Millie (USA) *(74+) (JEBanks)* 2-7-10 JQuinn(8) (tall: a.p: 5th st: led bel dist: sn clr: unchal)....— **1**
3225² Scenicris (IRE) **(71)***(66) (RHollinshead)* 2-7-10 NCarlisle(7) (hld up: hdwy 3f out: r.o wl ins fnl f: no ch w wnr)....3½ **2**
2839² Half An Inch (IRE) **(72)***(69)*(Fav)*(BJMeehan)* 2-8-1 BDoyle(11) (led: rdn & hdd bel dist: kpt on same pce)....1 **3**
3185⁸ Jerry Cutrona (IRE) *(66) (NACallaghan)* 2-8-5 GCarter(3) (bit bkwd: rdn along ½-wy: swtchd rt over 1f out: styd on)....3 **4**
2717² Zdenka **(59)***(57) (MBlanshard)* 2-8-0 StephenDavies(1) (hld up: effrt ent st: nvr nr to chal) ...1¾ **5**
2447⁵ Lavender Della (IRE) *(55) (MJFetherston-Godley)* 2-8-0 FNorton(5) (chsd ldrs: 3rd st: rdn & wknd over 1f out)....¾ **6**
3243⁷ Shermood *(51) (MBell)* 2-7-3 (7) RMullen(9) (s.s: nvr nr ldrs)....nk **7**
2846¹¹ Brave Maisie (IRE) **(58)***(50) (MMcCormack)* 2-7-7 (5)ow2 MHenry(10) (prom: 2nd st: rdn & wknd wl over 1f out)....hd **8**
3243⁸ Cry Baby *(50) (KTIvory)* 2-8-5 CRutter(6) (outpcd: a bhd)....4 **9**
3283³ February **(45)***(38) (MRChannon)* 2-7-7 (7) DSweeney(2) (a bhd: t.o)....3 **10**
3080⁷ Tartan Express (IRE) *(16) (BAPearce)* 2-7-12 (7) JWilkinson(12) (prom tl 6th & wkng st: t.o)..12 **11**
1054¹⁰ Masbro Bird *(BRMillman)* 2-7-10 JLowe(4) (chsd ldrs: 4th & rdn st: sn wknd: t.o)....5 **12**

3/1 Half An Inch (IRE) (op 5/1), **7/2** JUST MILLIE (USA) (9/2-3/1), Scenicris (IRE) (op 9/4), **5/1** Zdenka, **12/1** February, **14/1** Brave Maisie (IRE), **16/1** Cry Baby, Jerry Cutrona (IRE), Masbro Bird, **20/1** Lavender Della (IRE), **33/1** Shermood, **50/1** Tartan Express (IRE), CSF £16.54 TOTE £5.40: £1.90 £1.60 £1.70 (£10.50) Trio £7.50 OWNER Mr E. Carter (NEWMARKET) BRED Golden Gate Stud 12 Rn
1m 24.9 (0.70) SF: 20/12/15/12/3/1/-/-/-/-/-/-

3428 BARFORD MAIDEN STKS (3-Y.O+ F & M) (Class D) £4,070.30 (£1,216.40: £582.20: £265.10)
1m Stalls: Low GOING minus 0.65 sec per fur (HD) 4-30 (4-36)

2977⁹ **Dunloe (IRE)** *(60) (GWragg)* 3-8-11 FNorton(1) (lw: a.p: led ent st: rdn clr appr fnl f: hld on) — **1**
3239⁷ Urania *(58) (MAJarvis)* 3-8-11 PRobinson(3) (hld up & bhd: 6th st: str run fnl f: fin fast)....1 **2**
3239⁴ Fragaria *(56)*(Fav)*(IABalding)* 3-8-6 (5) DGriffiths(4) (led 2f: 3rd st: kpt on u.p ins fnl f)....1¼ **3**

3270[2] Shazanni (IRE) **(40)***(52) (MRChannon)* 3-8-4 (7) DSweeney(5) (s.s: effrt & 5th st: nt pce to chal)....1¾ 4
3125[5] L'Eglise Belle **(39)***(46) (MrsALMKing)* 3-8-11 NCarlisle(2) (chsd ldrs: 4th st: c wd to race alone: no imp)....3 5
3115[4] Graceful Lady *(39) (EJAlston)* 5-9-3 AMackay(6) (bit bkwd: led after 2f tl hdd & 2nd st: wknd wl over 1f out)....3½ 6

5/4 Fragaria, **11/4** Urania, **9/2** Shazanni (IRE), **6/1** DUNLOE (IRE) (op 4/1), **10/1** L'Eglise Belle, **20/1** Graceful Lady, CSF £22.18 TOTE £6.00: £2.10 £2.30 (£15.80) OWNER Ahmed Ali Shaiba (NEWMARKET) BRED Sheikh Mohammed bin Rashid al Maktoum 6 Rn

1m 39.9 (2.90) SF: 14/12/10/6/-/-
WEIGHT FOR AGE 3yo-6lb

3429 TEMPLE HILL H'CAP (0-70) (3-Y.O) (Class E) £3,845.25 (£1,152.00: £553.50: £254.25)

1m Stalls: Low GOING minus 0.65 sec per fur (HD) 5-00 (5-02)

2979[15] **Risky Romeo (59)***(68) (GCBravery)* 3-8-11 MFenton(8) (hld up: 6th st: gd hdwy bel dist: rdn to ld nr fin)....— 1
3356* Eden's Star (IRE) **(62)***(70)*(Fav)*(MHTompkins)* 3-9-0 6x PRobinson(6) (chsd ldr: 2nd st: led wl over 1f out: hrd rdn & hdd ins fnl f)....¾ 2
3057[2] Tomal **(49)***(55) (RIngram)* 3-8-1 AMcGlone(2) (hld up: 5th st: rdn to chal 1f out: unable qckn nr fin)....1 3
2789[6] Jobber's Fiddle **(46)***(50) (DJSffrenchDavis)* 3-7-12v JQuinn(7) (hdwy ½-wy: 3rd st: ev ch over 1f out: one pce)....¾ 4
3201[2] Fastini Gold **(64)***(54) (MDIUsher)* 3-9-2 MWigham(4) (lw: stdd s: wl bhd & outpcd ent st: styd on fnl 2f)....7 5
3128[3] Shady Deed (USA) **(64)***(51) (JWHills)* 3-8-11b(5) MHenry(5) (led & sn wl clr: wknd & hdd wl over 1f out)....1¾ 6
3264* Saltz (IRE) **(58)***(35) (PTDalton)* 3-8-7 (3) 6x PMcCabe(3) (chsd ldrs 5f: sn lost tch)....5 7
3060* Mill Dancer (IRE) **(43)***(17) (EJAlston)* 3-7-4 (5)ow2 MBaird(1) (chsd ldrs: 4th st: wknd 2f out)....nk 8
2333[7] Heathyards Magic (IRE) **(69)***(15) (RHollinshead)* 3-9-7 GCarter(9) (a bhd: t.o)....15 9

LONG HANDICAP Mill Dancer (IRE) 7-6

9/4 Eden's Star (IRE) (op 7/2), **9/2** Mill Dancer (IRE), **11/2** Saltz (IRE), Tomal, **6/1** Shady Deed (USA), **10/1** RISKY ROMEO, **11/1** Jobber's Fiddle, **12/1** Heathyards Magic (IRE), **14/1** Fastini Gold, CSF £33.71 CT £132.47 TOTE £13.90: £3.10 £1.70 £1.90 (£35.50) Trio £115.10 OWNER Miss Sonja Quince (NEWMARKET) BRED Mrs S. Quince 9 Rn

1m 36.8 (-0.20) SF: 44/46/31/26/30/27/11/-/-
T/Plpt: £189.90 (38.36 Tckts). T/Qdpt: £63.20 (1.25 Tckts). IM

3417-RIPON (R-H)
Tuesday August 29th (Good to firm)

WEATHER: overcast WIND: almost nil

3430 CLARO MAIDEN AUCTION STKS (2-Y.O) (Class E) £3,203.30 (£970.40: £474.20: £226.10)

5f Stalls: Low GOING minus 0.26 sec per fur (GF) 2-30 (2-30)

3290[5] **Secret Voucher** *(61) (BAMcMahon)* 2-8-3 GCarter(3) (mde all: drvn out)....— 1
3012[2] Rebel County (IRE) **(61)***(55)*(Fav)*(DJSCosgrove)* 2-7-12 TWilliams(6) (lw: sn cl up: outpcd wl over 1f out: styd on strly towards fin)....nk 2
Air Wing *(56) (MHTompkins)* 2-8-3 PRobinson(9) (leggy: lw: a cl up: rdn 2f out: r.o one pce)....1¼ 3
2498[9] Cocoon (IRE) *(43) (CWThornton)* 2-8-0 AMackay(1) (s.i.s: hdwy u.p ½-wy: nvr able to chal)..3 4
1841[7] Marketeer Magic **(60)***(42) (JBerry)* 2-8-7 JCarroll(7) (outpcd tl styd on wl fnl f)....2½ 5
3231[16] Power Princess *(33) (RMWhitaker)* 2-7-12 DaleGibson(2) (sn drvn along: nvr trbld ldrs)....s.h 6
2756[8] The Wad *(37) (MWEasterby)* 2-8-5 LCharnock(10) (in tch: no imp fr ½-wy)....1 7
2852[5] Harriet's Beau **(68)***(33) (MWEasterby)* 2-8-7 MBirch(4) (gd spd to ½-wy: sn wknd)....2 8
3231[13] Lawn Order *(21) (MrsJRRamsden)* 2-8-2 MDeering(5) (s.i.s: nvr nr to chal)....2 9
3157[11] Signs R Us (IRE) *(DrJDScargill)* 2-8-5 JFanning(8) (outpcd fr ½-wy)....8 10

7/4 Rebel County (IRE), **4/1** SECRET VOUCHER (3/1-9/2), **6/1** Air Wing, Harriet's Beau, **7/1** Cocoon (IRE), **10/1** Lawn Order, **12/1** Marketeer Magic, **16/1** Signs R Us (IRE), Power Princess, **33/1** The Wad, CSF £12.11 TOTE £4.60: £1.80 £1.20 £2.30 (£5.00) Trio £9.10 OWNER Mr Ian Guise (TAMWORTH) BRED R. R. Evans 10 Rn 60.4 secs (2.40) SF: 25/19/20/7/6/-/1/-/-/-

3431

DEVERELL CLAIMING STKS (3-Y.O+) (Class F) £2,944.00 (£892.00: £436.00: £208.00)
1m Stalls: High GOING minus 0.26 sec per fur (GF) 3-00 (3-01)

3305³ **Special-K (62)***(74) (EWeymes)* 3-8-2 GHind(4) (a.p: chal over 1f out: carried rt: r.o wl to ld post) — **1**
3392⁴ Night Wink (USA) **(69)***(73) (DNicholls)* 3-8-1 JQuinn(7) (hld up & bhd: hdwy on bit to ld appr fnl f: edgd rt: r.o) s.h **2**
2945* Parliament Piece **(75)***(69)*(Fav)*(MrsMReveley)* 9-8-11 RCochrane(6) (lw: hld up: hdwy over 3f out: styd on: nt pce to chal) 4 **3**
3073⁶ Cape Colony *(67) (CFWall)* 3-8-6 GDuffield(8) (unruly s: hld up & bhd: hdwy 2f out: nrst fin) 1½ **4**
3152² Battle Colours (IRE) **(56)***(58) (DonEnricoIncisa)* 6-8-5 KimTinkler(1) (chsd ldrs tl rdn & btn appr fnl f) 1 **5**
3256⁶ Delightful Dancer (IRE) **(57)***(52) (JNorton)* 3-7-12 DaleGibson(3) (lw: chsd ldrs tl wknd fnl 2f) 2½ **6**
3305⁸ Canny Lad **(32)***(49) (MPBielby)* 5-8-6v KFallon(2) (lw: led tl hdd & wknd appr fnl f) 2½ **7**
Here Comes Herbie *(WStorey)* 3-7-12 JFanning(5) (hdwy & prom appr st: wknd fnl 3f) 30 **8**

Evens Parliament Piece, **5/2** SPECIAL-K, **5/1** Night Wink (USA), **10/1** Cape Colony, Battle Colours (IRE), **20/1** Delightful Dancer (IRE), **25/1** Canny Lad, **50/1** Here Comes Herbie, CSF £15.77 TOTE £3.30: £1.10 £1.90 £1.20 (£7.40) OWNER Mr G. Falshaw (MIDDLEHAM) BRED Patrick Diamond 8 Rn
1m 40.7 (3.00) SF: 35/34/36/28/25/13/16/-
WEIGHT FOR AGE 3yo-6lb

3432

E.B.F SAPPER MAIDEN STKS (2-Y.O) (Class D) £4,416.00 (£1,338.00: £654.00: £312.00)
6f Stalls: Low GOING minus 0.26 sec per fur (GF) 3-30 (3-30)

2091² **Dashing Blue (80)***(85) (IABalding)* 2-9-0 KDarley(10) (cl up: led ½-wy: r.o) — **1**
3069³ Dark Deed (USA) *(75)*(Fav)*(BWHills)* 2-8-9 MHills(11) (trckd ldrs: effrt over 2f out: hrd rdn & kpt on fnl f) 2 **2**
3170³ Baileys First (IRE) *(73) (MJohnston)* 2-8-9 JWeaver(6) (led to ½-wy: kpt on wl fnl f) ¾ **3**
3180³ Alamein (USA) **(78)***(70) (MrsSPiggott)* 2-9-0 RCochrane(7) (in tch: hdwy 2f out: styd on towards fin) 3 **4**
2473⁴ Give Me A Ring (IRE) *(63) (CWThornton)* 2-9-0 DeanMcKeown(1) (dwlt: hdwy over 2f out: r.o) 2½ **5**
3022² Antonias Melody *(57) (SRBowring)* 2-8-9 SWebster(4) (lw: in tch: kpt on wl fnl f) nk **6**
2660⁹ Ma Bulsie *(52) (BAMcMahon)* 2-8-9 GCarter(3) (effrt ½-wy: nvr nr to chal) 2 **7**
Escobar (IRE) *(54) (PCalver)* 2-9-0 MBirch(2) (cmpt: unf: chsd ldrs over 4f) 1¼ **8**
3170² Ancestral Jane *(41) (MrsJRRamsden)* 2-8-9 KFallon(5) (s.i.s: stdy hdwy 2f out: nvr plcd to chal) 3 **9**
1798¹⁰ Simply Silly (IRE) *(34) (WLBarker)* 2-8-9 LCharnock(14) (nvr trbld ldrs) 2½ **10**
First Maite *(35) (SRBowring)* 2-8-9b(5) CTeague(16) (w'like: s.i.s: n.d) 1½ **11**
1722⁴ Boundary Bird (IRE) *(33) (MJohnston)* 2-9-0 TWilliams(12) (n.d) ¾ **12**
2381⁵ One Life To Live (IRE) *(33) (AHarrison)* 2-8-11 (3) JStack(13) (nvr trbld ldrs) s.h **13**
Forzara *(24) (JBerry)* 2-8-9 JCarroll(8) (b.hind: s.i.s: hdwy ½-wy: wknd wl over 1f out) 1½ **14**
Glorious Sound *(13) (JHanson)* 2-9-0 ACulhane(9) (cmpt: str: bkwd: dwlt: a bhd) 6 **15**
3093⁷ Gresham Flyer *(BRichmond)* 2-9-0 SDWilliams(15) (sn outpcd: t.o) 20 **16**

4/6 Dark Deed (USA), **9/2** DASHING BLUE, **8/1** Alamein (USA), **12/1** Baileys First (IRE), **14/1** Ancestral Jane, **16/1** Forzara, Antonias Melody, **20/1** Glorious Sound, Escobar (IRE), Give Me A Ring (IRE), **25/1** Ma Bulsie, **33/1** Boundary Bird (IRE), First Maite, **50/1** One Life To Live (IRE), Simply Silly (IRE), Gresham Flyer, CSF £8.76 TOTE £6.40: £1.50 £1.20 £1.80 (£4.10) Trio £8.60 OWNER Mrs Duncan Allen (KINGSCLERE) BRED Mrs I. A. Balding 16 Rn
1m 13.3 (3.10) SF: 33/23/21/18/11/5/-/2/-/-/-/-/-/-/-/-

3433

STEVE NESBITT CHALLENGE TROPHY H'CAP (0-90) (3-Y.O+) (Class C) £6,750.00 (£2,025.00: £975.00: £450.00)
1m 2f Stalls: High GOING minus 0.26 sec per fur (GF) 4-00 (4-01)

3021* **Mellottie (90)***(101) (MrsMReveley)* 10-10-0 KDarley(12) (lw: hld up: effrt over 2f out: r.o wl to ld nr fin) — **1**
3319³ Vindaloo **(84)***(95)*(Fav)*(JLHarris)* 3-9-0 JWeaver(5) (lw: hld up: effrt 3f out: led appr fnl f: r.o: jst ct) hd **2**
2186⁶ Mowlaie **(67)***(75) (DWChapman)* 4-8-5 ACulhane(6) (hld up: effrt 3f out: n.m.r over 1f out: styd on wl) 2 **3**

3021[5] Jubran (USA) **(64)***(70) (MJohnston)* 9-8-2 TWilliams(1) (led tl hdd over 3f out: led 2f out tl appr fnl f: no ex) ¾ 4
2948[13] Rambo's Hall **(87)***(87) (JAGlover)* 10-9-11 DeanMcKeown(11) (hld up: swtchd 3f out: styd on fnl f) 4 5
2878[4] Silently **(79)***(78) (IABalding)* 3-8-4 (5) DGriffiths(8) (lw: a.p: rdn 3f out: r.o one pce) ½ 6
3367[8] Thaleros **(58)***(57) (GMMoore)* 5-7-10 JQuinn(7) (chsd ldr: led over 3f out tl hdd 2f out: wknd) nk 7
2253[2] Shayim (USA) **(82)***(79) (RWArmstrong)* 3-8-12 RHills(4) (a.p: effrt 3f out: ev ch 2f out: wknd appr fnl f) 1 8
2004[3] Game Ploy (POL) **(74)***(66) (FMurphy)* 3-8-4 RCochrane(2) (nvr trbld ldrs) 3½ 9
1543[7] Museum (IRE) **(74)***(56) (DNicholls)* 4-8-12 AlexGreaves(10) (nvr nr ldrs) 6 10
676[10] Hunters' Heaven (USA) **(56)***(19) (JMackie)* 4-7-8 NCarlisle(9) (prom tl wknd fnl 3f) 12 11

4/1 Vindaloo, **9/2** MELLOTTIE, Shayim (USA), Jubran (USA), **8/1** Silently, **10/1** Game Ploy (POL), **11/1** Thaleros, **14/1** Rambo's Hall, **20/1** Museum (IRE), **25/1** Mowlaie, Hunters' Heaven (USA), CSF £22.26 CT £368.36 TOTE £5.80: £2.10 £1.60 £9.10 (£7.70) Trio £232.00 OWNER Mrs J. G. Fulton (SALTBURN) BRED Mrs G. R. Reveley and Partners 11 Rn
2m 5.2 (1.70) SF: 77/63/51/46/63/46/33/47/34/32/-
WEIGHT FOR AGE 3yo-8lb

3434 CURFEW NURSERY H'CAP (2-Y.O) (Class D) £4,224.00 (£1,272.00: £616.00: £288.00)
5f Stalls: Low GOING minus 0.26 sec per fur (GF) 4-30 (4-30)

3132[3] **Bedside Mail (83)***(88) (JMPEustace)* 2-8-8 RCochrane(1) (lw: chsd ldrs: r.o u.p to ld wl ins fnl f) — 1
3213[2] Pleasure Time **(74)***(74) (CSmith)* 2-7-13b NCarlisle(2) (led: hung bdly rt fnl f: hdd wl ins fnl f) 1½ 2
3290[3] U-No-Harry (IRE) **(73)***(67) (RHollinshead)* 2-7-7 (5)ow5 MHenry(3) (a.p: kpt on u.p fnl f) ½ 3
3225[10] Doug's Folly **(70)***(66) (MWEasterby)* 2-7-2 (7)ow2 MartinDwyer(5) (outpcd tl styd on wl fnl f: nrst fin) hd 4
3369[2] Tadeo **(96)***(93)*(Fav)*(MJohnston)* 2-9-7 JWeaver(8) (lw: sn chsng ldrs: rdn ½-wy: kpt on one pce) ½ 5
3064[4] Krystal Max (IRE) **(84)***(78) (TDBarron)* 2-8-9b DeanMcKeown(4) (cl up tl rdn & btn over 1f out) ¾ 6
3210[4] Limerick Princess (IRE) **(74)***(60) (JBerry)* 2-7-6 (7) PFessey(6) (s.i.s: nvr wnt pce) 2½ 7
1877[6] Theatre Magic **(68)***(19) (TJEtherington)* 2-7-7b JLowe(7) (lw: s.i.s: wl outpcd & bhd fr ½-wy) 11 8
LONG HANDICAP Doug's Folly 6-13 Theatre Magic 7-3

6/4 Tadeo, **4/1** BEDSIDE MAIL, **5/1** Pleasure Time, **6/1** Krystal Max (IRE), **13/2** Limerick Princess (IRE), U-No-Harry (IRE), **20/1** Doug's Folly, Theatre Magic, CSF £24.91 CT £118.59 TOTE £5.80: £1.60 £1.60 £1.80 (£9.80) OWNER Mr Gary Coull (NEWMARKET) BRED R. G. Percival and Miss S. M. Rhodes 8 Rn 60.2 secs (2.20) SF: 33/19/12/11/38/23/5/-

3435 WAKEMAN STAYERS' H'CAP (0-70) (3-Y.O+) (Class E) £3,260.50 (£988.00: £483.00: £230.50)
2m Stalls: Low GOING minus 0.26 sec per fur (GF) 5-00 (5-01)

3263[2] **Mr Geneaology (USA) (55)***(68) (FMurphy)* 5-9-7b RCochrane(6) (in tch: swtchd over 1f out: r.o u.p to ld wl ins fnl f) — 1
2919[12] Inn At the Top **(56)***(68) (JNorton)* 3-8-8 DaleGibson(7) (cl up: led appr fnl f: hdd & no ex wl ins fnl f) ¾ 2
3303[2] Arian Spirit (IRE) **(32)***(44) (JLEyre)* 4-7-9 (3) NVarley(13) (lw: led 2f: chsd ldrs: n.m.r 2f out: styd on towards fin) s.h 3
2996[3] Jalcanto **(58)***(69) (MrsMReveley)* 5-9-10 KDarley(14) (lw: hld up: effrt 4f out: hdwy over 1f out: nt pce to chal) 1 4
2860[6] Romalito **(40)***(50) (MBlanshard)* 5-8-6 KFallon(5) (lw: bhd: rdn over 3f out: styd on: nvr able to chal) 1½ 5
1696[2] Bobby's Dream **(45)***(54)*(Fav)*(MHTompkins)* 3-7-11 JQuinn(8) (lw: a.p: effrt & ev ch 3f out: one pce appr fnl f) ¾ 6
2854[6] Izza **(35)***(44) (WStorey)* 4-7-8 (7) PFessey(4) (plld hrd: stdy hdwy 4f out: rdn & one pce appr fnl f) s.h 7
3029[4] Modest Hope (USA) **(46)***(55) (BRichmond)* 8-8-12 JWeaver(9) (led after 2f: qcknd 4f out: hdd appr fnl f: one pce) s.h 8
556[9] Nahri (USA) **(47)***(55) (JMackie)* 4-8-13 GCarter(10) (trckd ldrs tl wknd fnl 2f) ½ 9
3114[3] Amiarge **(34)***(42) (MBrittain)* 5-7-11 (3) DWright(1) (hld up: hdwy over 2f out: nt clr run fnl 1½f) ½ 10
3274[4] Record Lover (IRE) **(35)***(40) (MCChapman)* 5-7-8 (7)ow2 CMunday(11) (bhd: outpcd 4f out: styd on towards fin) ½ 11

642[15] King of the Horse (IRE) **(37)***(24) (WStorey)* 4-8-3 JFanning(2) (in tch tl outpcd fnl 3f)............20 **12**

11/4 Bobby's Dream, **7/2** Jalcanto, **9/2** MR GENEAOLOGY (USA), **8/1** Romalito, Arian Spirit (IRE), **10/1** Izza, Amiarge, **14/1** Inn At the Top, Modest Hope (USA), Nahri (USA), **33/1** Record Lover (IRE), King of the Horse (IRE), CSF £65.48 CT £464.38 TOTE £4.50: £1.20 £5.50 £2.50 (£32.20) Trio £136.40 OWNER A-Men Partnership (WELLINGTON) BRED Way-Oak Cliff Stable Ltd in USA 12 Rn
3m 36.5 (11.50) SF: 30/16/6/31/12/2/6/17/17/4/2/-
WEIGHT FOR AGE 3yo-14lb

T/Jkpt: £7,100.00 (0.29 Tckts); £4,417.12 to York 30/8/95. T/Plpt: £11.40 (2,232.69 Tckts). T/Qdpt: £21.40 (6.2 Tckts). AA

3346-SANDOWN (R-H)
Wednesday August 30th (Good to firm, Good patches)
WEATHER: sunny WIND: almost nil

3436 CLAYGATE MEDIAN AUCTION MAIDEN STKS (I) (2-Y.O) (Class E) £3,533.75 (£1,070.00: £522.50: £248.75)
7f 16y Stalls: High GOING minus 0.13 sec per fur (G) 1-50 (1-52)

Al Abraq (IRE) *(84+)*(Fav)*(JWHills)* 2-9-0 RHills(10) (str: scope: 6th st: led 2f out: r.o wl).....— **1**
Glenrazie (IRE) *(80+) (PWChapple-Hyam)* 2-8-9 (5) RHavlin(8) (w'like: 5th st: lost pl over 3f out: rallied over 1f out: r.o)............1¼ **2**
2283[8] Warbrook *(75) (IABalding)* 2-9-0 GDuffield(3) (lw: 3rd st: lost pl over 2f out: rallied over 1f out: r.o one pce)............1½ **3**
Energy Man *(74+) (JRFanshawe)* 2-9-0 DHarrison(2) (str: scope: 4th st: rdn over 3f out: one pce)............½ **4**
Spring Campaign (IRE) *(66) (MCPipe)* 2-9-0 JWilliams(11) (leggy: unf: rdn & hdwy over 2f out: one pce)............2½ **5**
Lay The Blame *(64) (WJarvis)* 2-9-0 BThomson(7) (b.off hind: w'like: scope: led over 5f out: edgd rt over 2f out: sn hdd: wknd fnl f)............½ **6**
Flint And Steel *(63) (RHannon)* 2-8-9 (5) DaneO'Neill(6) (str: bit bkwd: nvr nrr)............½ **7**
Classic Defence (IRE) *(62) (JWHills)* 2-9-0 DHolland(12) (str: scope: bit bkwd: nvr nrr)........s.h **8**
2995[8] Mon Pere *(58) (KMcAuliffe)* 2-9-0 MTebbutt(4) (bhd fnl 2f)............1¼ **9**
Skram *(58) (RDickin)* 2-9-0 PRobinson(9) (unf: led over 1f: 2nd st: wknd over 2f out)...........s.h **10**
Dauphin (IRE) *(26) (WJMusson)* 2-9-0 GHind(13) (str: bkwd: a bhd)............10 **11**
Sylvan Princess *(20) (CNAllen)* 2-8-9 GBardwell(5) (unf: s.s: a bhd)............½ **12**
Not Quite Grey *(KMcAuliffe)* 2-9-0 WWoods(1) (w'like: bit bkwd: swvd lft & uns rdr s)............ **U**

9/4 AL ABRAQ (IRE), **11/2** Lay The Blame (4/1-7/1), **7/1** Not Quite Grey, **8/1** Energy Man (op 4/1), **10/1** Glenrazie (IRE) (op 3/1), Warbrook (op 5/1), **12/1** Flint And Steel (8/1-14/1), **20/1** Classic Defence (IRE), **25/1** Spring Campaign (IRE), **33/1** Dauphin (IRE), **50/1** Mon Pere, Sylvan Princess, Skram, CSF £21.85 TOTE £2.70: £1.50 £1.50 £2.10 (£5.90) Trio £32.30 OWNER Mr Ziad Galadari (LAMBOURN) BRED Lordship and Egerton Studs Ltd 13 Rn
1m 32.32 (32.52) SF: 23/19/14/13/5/3/2/1/-/-/-/-/-

3437 HEATHCOTE MAIDEN STKS (2-Y.O) (Class D) £3,468.75 (£1,050.00: £512.50: £243.75)
1m 1f Stalls: High GOING minus 0.13 sec per fur (G) 2-20 (2-26)

2741[4] **Night Watch (USA)** *(75)*(Fav)*(IABalding)* 2-9-0 BThomson(3) (lw: 4th st: led over 2f out: comf)............— **1**
Canon Can (USA) *(68+) (HRACecil)* 2-9-0 WRyan(1) (w'like: scope: lw: 2nd st: led over 3f out tl over 2f out: unable qckn)............4 **2**
2839[6] Diego *(66) (CEBrittain)* 2-9-0 BDoyle(4) (led 1f: 3rd st: rdn over 2f out: one pce)............1¼ **3**
2796[4] Martha Quest *(57) (BWHills)* 2-8-9 DHolland(6) (b.off hind: 5th st: rdn over 3f out: one pce)...2 **4**
Zaforum *(62) (LMontagueHall)* 2-9-0 RPerham(7) (w'like: bkwd: nvr nr to chal)............nk **5**
3266[5] Seven Crowns (USA) **(72)***(58) (RHannon)* 2-9-0 RHills(5) (lw: 6th st: wknd over 2f out)...........2 **6**
Hencarlam (IRE) *(56) (MRChannon)* 2-9-0 WWoods(8) (w'like: bit bkwd: a bhd)............1¼ **7**
Princely Sword (USA) *(51) (PFICole)* 2-9-0 CRutter(2) (leggy: scope: lw: led 8f out tl over 3f out: wknd 2f out)............3 **8**

6/5 NIGHT WATCH (USA), **3/1** Canon Can (USA) (7/4-100/30), **8/1** Martha Quest (op 12/1), **12/1** Princely Sword (USA) (op 6/1), Seven Crowns (USA) (op 8/1), Hencarlam (IRE) (20/1-33/1), **16/1** Diego, **33/1** Zaforum, CSF £5.01 TOTE £1.90: £1.10 £1.60 £5.40 (£2.40) Trio £21.50 OWNER The Queen (KINGSCLERE) BRED The Queen 8 Rn
1m 57.62 (0.12 under 2y best) (6.22) SF: 33/26/24/15/20/16/14/9

3438

MATTHIAS CONSTRUCTION MATERIALS MAIDEN STKS (3-Y.O+) (Class D) £4,299.00 (£1,302.00: £636.00: £303.00)
1m 3f 91y Stalls: High GOING minus 0.13 sec per fur (G) 2-50 (2-57)

Fire on Ice (IRE) *(89+) (MRStoute)* 3-8-12 DHolland(3) (bit bkwd: 4th st: led over 2f out: r.o wl)........— 1
Anchorena *(81) (RCharlton)* 3-8-7 DHarrison(9) (leggy: unf: 6th st: chsd wnr over 1f out: unable qckn)........2½ 2
1872[20] Dr Zhivago **(75)***(83) (MAJarvis)* 3-8-12 PRobinson(1) (swtg: 5th st: rdn over 2f out: one pce)..2 3
715[17] Queens Theatre *(74) (BWHills)* 3-8-0 (7) GBrace(11) (lw: hdwy over 1f out: r.o)........2½ 4
3224[3] Reem Dubai (IRE) *(70) (JHMGosden)* 3-8-7 GHind(2) (2nd st: wknd 2f out)........3 5
Timeless *(66)*(Fav)*(HRACecil)* 3-8-7 WRyan(10) (w'like: scope: 3rd st: nt clr run on ins over 2f out: sn wknd: bttr for r)........3 6
3105[5] Our Kris *(70) (GHarwood)* 3-8-12 AClark(8) (b.off fore: lw: a mid div)........¾ 7
1526[14] Wassl Street (IRE) *(67) (JHMGosden)* 3-8-12v AMcGlone(7) (nvr nr to chal)........2 8
2884[5] Greenway Lady *(59) (CNAllen)* 3-8-7 GBardwell(4) (b.hind: lw: nvr nrr)........2 9
2929[3] Your Most Welcome *(57) (DJSffrenchDavis)* 4-9-2 GDuffield(5) (b.nr hind: a bhd)........1¾ 10
1283[6] Rainelle **(72)***(53) (CEBrittain)* 3-8-7 BDoyle(13) (bit bkwd: led over 8f)........2½ 11
1696[7] Good (IRE) **(45)***(54) (DTThom)* 3-8-12 MPerrett(12) (swtg: prom 6f)........3 12
3178[10] Ceilidh Dancer *(PRHedger)* 4-9-2 CAvery(6) (bhd fnl 6f: t.o)........dist 13

5/2 Timeless, **100/30** FIRE ON ICE (IRE), **6/1** Dr Zhivago, **7/1** Reem Dubai (IRE) (5/1-8/1), **8/1** Anchorena (6/1-9/1), **12/1** Rainelle, **16/1** Our Kris, **25/1** Wassl Street (IRE), Queens Theatre, **33/1** Good (IRE), Your Most Welcome, **66/1** Greenway Lady, Ceilidh Dancer, CSF £27.98 TOTE £4.00: £1.60 £2.40 £1.60 (£18.10) Trio £55.60 OWNER Mr Mana Al Maktoum (NEWMARKET) BRED Dene Investments N V 13 Rn 2m 27.7 (6.00) SF: 44/36/38/29/25/21/25/22/14/21/8/9/-
WEIGHT FOR AGE 3yo-9lb

3439

DORKING H'CAP (0-70) (3-Y.O+) (Class E) £4,435.50 (£1,344.00: £657.00: £313.50)
7f 16y Stalls: High GOING minus 0.13 sec per fur (G) 3-20 (3-29)

2634[7] **Broughtons Turmoil (60)***(72)*(Fav)*(WJMusson)* 6-9-4 GHind(12) (lw: 4th st: led over 1f out: drvn out)........— 1
3248[3] Dancing Lawyer **(68)***(80) (BJMeehan)* 4-9-12 BDoyle(1) (lw: hdwy over 2f out: hrd rdn over 1f out: r.o wl ins fnl f)........hd 2
3159[2] Whatever's Right (IRE) **(70)***(80)*(Fav)*(MDIUsher)* 6-10-0 DHolland(7) (b: lw: w ldr: led over 2f out tl over 1f out: unable qckn)........¾ 3
3291[5] Duello **(57)***(61) (MBlanshard)* 4-9-1 WRyan(10) (lw: hdwy over 1f out: r.o)........2½ 4
3268[2] Sharp Imp **(51)***(53) (RMFlower)* 5-8-9b DBiggs(6) (hdwy over 1f out: nvr nrr)........1 5
3128* Star of Gold **(64)***(63) (CREgerton)* 3-9-3 BThomson(15) (3rd st: hrd rdn over 1f out: one pce)1¼ 6
3248* Inderaputeri **(64)***(63) (MissGayKelleway)* 5-9-3 (5) 6x DaneO'Neill(3) (no hdwy fnl 3f)........s.h 7
3291[4] Morocco (IRE) **(60)***(59) (MRChannon)* 6-9-4 WWoods(2) (lw: nvr nrr)........nk 8
3159[5] Belleminette (IRE) **(55)***(49) (DHaydnJones)* 4-8-13 AMackay(11) (lw: s.s: nvr nrr)........2 9
3181[3] St Louis Lady **(60)***(48) (WJarvis)* 4-9-4b JQuinn(5) (b.off hind: 5th st: wknd over 2f out)........2½ 10
Rakis (IRE) **(70)***(58) (MBrittain)* 5-10-0 JWilliams(8) (b: nvr nrr)........nk 11
2578[5] Chili Heights **(58)***(38) (GBBalding)* 5-9-2v TSprake(13) (b.hind: a bhd)........3½ 12
3222[7] Daytona Beach (IRE) **(61)***(40) (DJSffrenchDavis)* 5-9-5 JFEgan(9) (led over 4f: wknd 1f out) .½ 13
2793[8] Milos **(65)***(38) (TJNaughton)* 4-9-6 (3) SSanders(14) (b.nr hind: lw: a bhd)........2½ 14
2685[11] Shepherd Market (IRE) **(65)***(32) (DAWilson)* 4-9-9 NGwilliams(16) (lw: 6th st: wknd over 2f out)........2½ 15
3065[8] Rocky Waters (USA) **(65)***(27) (PBurgoyne)* 6-9-6 (3) DRMcCabe(4) (b.hind: bhd fnl 3f)........2½ 16

6/1 BROUGHTONS TURMOIL, Whatever's Right (IRE), **13/2** Star of Gold, **8/1** Inderaputeri (op 5/1), **10/1** Chili Heights, **12/1** Sharp Imp (op 8/1), Daytona Beach (IRE), Dancing Lawyer, **14/1** St Louis Lady (10/1-16/1), Belleminette (IRE), **16/1** Morocco (IRE), Milos, Shepherd Market (IRE), **20/1** Duello, Rocky Waters (USA), **33/1** Rakis (IRE), CSF £72.47 TOTE £7.70: £2.10 £3.00 £1.40 £5.20 (£54.10) Trio £66.00 OWNER Broughton & Westwood (NEWMARKET) BRED Tally Ho Stud Co (U.K.) Ltd and Ninevah Ltd 16 Rn
1m 29.83 (3.23) SF: 54/62/62/43/35/40/45/41/31/30/40/20/22/20/14/9
WEIGHT FOR AGE 3yo-5lb

3440

MATTHIAS CONSTRUCTION MATERIALS H'CAP (0-80) (3-Y.O+) (Class D) £4,879.00 (£1,477.00: £721.00: £343.00)
1m 2f 7y Stalls: High GOING minus 0.13 sec per fur (G) 3-50 (4-01)

1808[3] **Tykeyvor (IRE) (75)***(86)*(Fav)*(LadyHerries)* 5-9-9 GDuffield(6) (b.hind: 4th st: rdn over 3f out: led last strides)........— 1

29025 Bardon Hill Boy (IRE) **(76)***(87) (BHanbury)* 3-9-2 BThomson(11) (5th st: led over 1f out: hrd rdn: hdd last strides)....hd **2**
3362* Adolescence (IRE) **(85)***(95) (KMcAuliffe)* 5-10-0 (5) 5x MHenry(7) (3rd st: led over 3f out tl over 1f out: r.o)....nk **3**
32324 Zeetaro **(74)***(82) (MajorWRHern)* 4-9-8v TSprake(10) (lw: rdn & hdwy 2f out: r.o ins fnl f)......1¼ **4**
30169 Knotally Wood (USA) **(66)***(72) (JWHills)* 3-8-6 RHills(3) (rdn over 3f out: hdwy over 1f out: r.o one pce)....1½ **5**
29803 Lady Lacey **(46)***(51) (GBBalding)* 8-7-5v(3) NVarley(5) (lw: rdn & hdwy on ins over 2f out: one pce)....¾ **6**
26875 Achilles Heel **(45)***(47) (CNAllen)* 4-7-7 GBardwell(2) (led 6f out tl over 3f out: wknd 2f out)...1½ **7**
26577 Thatchmaster (IRE) **(46)***(44) (CAHorgan)* 4-7-8 JQuinn(4) (lw: a bhd)....3 **8**
26544 Zingibar **(65)***(57) (BWHills)* 3-8-5b DHolland(1) (6th st: wknd over 2f out)....3½ **9**
24943 Cuba **(72)***(51) (MRStoute)* 3-8-12 WRyan(8) (lw: a bhd)....8 **10**
Erin's Lad **(59)***(24) (RDickin)* 4-8-7 PRobinson(9) (led 4f: 2nd st: wknd 3f out)....9 **11**

LONG HANDICAP Achilles Heel 7-2

11/4 TYKEYVOR (IRE), **11/2** Zeetaro, **6/1** Knotally Wood (USA), **7/1** Lady Lacey, **8/1** Adolescence (IRE) (6/1-9/1), Zingibar, **9/1** Bardon Hill Boy (IRE), **12/1** Cuba, Thatchmaster (IRE), **16/1** Achilles Heel, **33/1** Erin's Lad, CSF £27.41 CT £168.98 TOTE £3.00: £1.70 £3.70 £2.00 (£23.90) Trio £53.60 OWNER Seymour Bloodstock (UK) Ltd (LITTLEHAMPTON) BRED H. Key 11 Rn

2m 9.12 (4.82) SF: 58/51/67/54/36/23/19/16/21/15/-
WEIGHT FOR AGE 3yo-8lb

3441 CLAYGATE MEDIAN AUCTION MAIDEN STKS (II) (2-Y.O) (Class E) £3,517.50 (£1,065.00: £520.00: £247.50)
7f 16y Stalls: High GOING minus 0.13 sec per fur (G) 4-20 (4-37)

Bullfinch *(93+) (PTWalwyn)* 2-9-0 DHolland(10) (w'like: hdwy over 2f out: led & edgd rt over 1f out: rdn out)....— **1**
30895 Polar Prince (IRE) *(87)*(Fav)*(MAJarvis)* 2-9-0 PRobinson(3) (2nd st: led over 2f out tl over 1f out: unable qckn)....2½ **2**
27174 White Sea (IRE) *(73) (PFICole)* 2-8-9 BThomson(7) (4th st: rdn over 2f out: one pce)....4 **3**
Fog City *(73) (WJarvis)* 2-9-0 EmmaO'Gorman(13) (w'like: scope: s.s: hdwy 6f out: 5th st: nt clr run over 2f out: one pce)....2½ **4**
20343 Ice Pick (IRE) **(86)***(73) (RHannon)* 2-8-9 (5) DaneO'Neill(6) (3rd st: rdn over 2f out: one pce).s.h **5**
Righteous Gent *(57) (KMcAuliffe)* 2-9-0 MPerrett(2) (leggy: bit bkwd: nvr nr to chal)....7 **6**
Safecracker *(52) (JWHills)* 2-9-0 RHills(1) (w'like: scope: bit bkwd: nvr nrr)....2 **7**
30096 Take Note (IRE) *(52) (NAGraham)* 2-9-0 AMcGlone(12) (6th st: wknd over 2f out)....hd **8**
33148 Hurricane Horn (IRE) *(51) (WRMuir)* 2-9-0 CRutter(11) (led over 4f)....½ **9**
279114 Boston Tea Party *(30) (IABalding)* 2-8-9 WRyan(8) (a bhd)....7 **10**
Spa Lane *(33) (CJDrewe)* 2-9-0 AClark(4) (w'like: bit bkwd: dwlt: a bhd)....¾ **11**
193812 Victory Commander *(32) (TJNaughton)* 2-9-0 DHarrison(5) (a bhd)....½ **12**
30099 Ben Bowden *(MBlanshard)* 2-9-0 StephenDavies(9) (Withdrawn not under Starters' orders: ref to ent stalls).... **W**

11/10 Polar Prince (IRE) (Evens-5/4), **7/2** White Sea (IRE) (Evens-4/1), Ice Pick (IRE), **10/1** BULLFINCH (op 4/1), **16/1** Fog City, **33/1** Hurricane Horn (IRE), Safecracker, Boston Tea Party, **50/1** Righteous Gent, Ben Bowden, **66/1** Take Note (IRE), Spa Lane, Victory Commander, CSF £20.78 TOTE £14.50: £2.10 £1.20 £1.40 (£15.70) Trio £9.60 OWNER Mr R. Cooper (LAMBOURN) BRED Exors of the late Mrs D. M. de Rothschild 12 Rn

1m 30.72 (4.12) SF: 40/34/20/20/20/4/-/-/-/-/-/-

3442 SURREY RACING H'CAP (0-70) (3-Y.O+) (Class E) £4,455.00 (£1,350.00: £660.00: £315.00)
5f 6y Stalls: Low GOING minus 0.13 sec per fur (G) 4-50 (5-06)

317714 **Classic Pet (IRE) (43)***(51) (CAHorgan)* 3-7-12 NAdams(17) (racd far side: led over 3f out: rdn out)....— **1**
22887 Jobie **(65)***(71) (BWHills)* 5-9-9 DHolland(16) (racd far side: led over 1f: rdn over 2f out: r.o)....¾ **2**
23445 Just Like Me **(61)***(66) (RGuest)* 3-9-2 DHarrison(18) (racd far side: a.p: rdn over 2f out: r.o)....nk **3**
29099 Gone Savage **(65)***(54) (WJMusson)* 7-9-9 AMcGlone(12) (hdwy over 1f out: r.o one pce)....5 **4**
3333* Paley Prince (USA) **(59)***(46) (MDIUsher)* 9-8-10 (7) CAdamson(4) (nvr nr to chal)....½ **5**
3313* Cheeky Chappy **(35)***(22) (DWChapman)* 4-7-7b JQuinn(10) (lw: a.p: rdn over 2f out: one pce)s.h **6**
31238 Followmegirls **(47)***(28) (MrsALMKing)* 6-8-5 AGarth(14) (no hdwy fnl 2f)....2 **7**
32932 Gymcrak Tycoon **(40)***(20)*(Fav)*(GHolmes)* 6-7-12v JFEgan(6) (b: b.off hind: lw: hld up: rdn over 2f out: one pce)....hd **8**
3138* Always Grace **(67)***(43) (MissGayKelleway)* 3-9-3 (5) DaneO'Neill(15) (nvr nrr)....1¼ **9**

Relentless Pursuit (IRE) **(56)***(30) (PWChapple-Hyam)* 7-8-7 (7) RCody-Boutcher(3) (b: b.off hind: spd over 3f) ¾ 10
3219[3] Judgement Call **(49)***(20) (PHowling)* 8-8-7 NCarlisle(8) (b: lw: prom over 2f) 1 11
2247[7] Jucea **(63)***(34) (JLSpearing)* 6-9-4 (3) SDrowne(1) (lw: outpcd) s.h 12
2850[3] Delrob **(49)***(19) (DHaydnJones)* 4-8-7 AMackay(7) (outpcd) nk 13
2627[13] Rotherfield Park (IRE) **(44)***(13) (CSmith)* 3-7-10 (3) NVarley(2) (prom over 2f) nk 14
3251[5] Half Tone **(45)***(11) (RMFlower)* 3-8-0b DBiggs(9) (lw: prom over 3f) 1 15
2949[6] Merlin's Fancy **(66)***(28) (WJarvis)* 3-9-7 WRyan(13) (lw: a bhd) 1 16
1376[7] Nordico Princess **(70)***(31) (MBrittain)* 4-10-0 JWilliams(5) (lw: bhd fnl 2f) ½ 17
3219[7] Featherstone Lane **(51)***(10) (MissLCSiddall)* 4-8-6v(3) DRMcCabe(11) (bhd fnl 2f) ½ 18

LONG HANDICAP Cheeky Chappy 7-6

6/1 Gymcrak Tycoon, **13/2** Cheeky Chappy, **7/1** Paley Prince (USA), **8/1** Jobie, **10/1** Delrob, Judgement Call, Always Grace, **12/1** Jucea, **14/1** Merlin's Fancy, Gone Savage, Just Like Me, **16/1** Nordico Princess, **20/1** Followmegirls, Relentless Pursuit (IRE), Featherstone Lane, **25/1** Half Tone, Rotherfield Park (IRE), **33/1** CLASSIC PET (IRE), CSF £274.32 CT £3,544.61 TOTE £92.00: £9.20 £2.00 £5.90 £4.60 (£160.10) Trio £62.50 OWNER Friary Bloodstock Company Ltd (BILLINGBEAR) BRED G. J. King 18 Rn 61.13 secs (1.33) SF: 33/56/48/39/31/7/13/5/25/15/5/19/4/-/-/10/16/-

WEIGHT FOR AGE 3yo-3lb

T/Plpt: £22.70 (574.56 Tckts). T/Qdpt: £104.00 (8 Tckts). AK

3185-YORK (L-H)

Wednesday August 30th (Good to firm, Good patches)

WEATHER: overcast WIND: almost nil

3443

LEVY BOARD STRAVINSKY VODKA CLAIMING STKS (3-Y.O+) (Class D) £5,344.50 (£1,596.00: £763.00: £346.50)
1m 205y Stalls: Low GOING minus 0.21 sec per fur (GF) 2-10 (2-11)

*3241** **Second Colours (USA) (61)***(78) (MrsMReveley)* 5-9-2 KDarley(1) (swtg: hdwy 4f out: led ins fnl f: all out) — 1
3294[5] Blaze of Oak (USA) **(67)***(78) (WJHaggas)* 4-9-2 RCochrane(2) (sn prom: slt ld over 2f out: hdd ins fnl f: kpt on u.p) s.h 2
3108* Guesstimation (USA) **(62)***(74) (JPearce)* 6-9-0 LDettori(3) (lw: chsd ldrs: outpcd over 2f out: hdwy & swtchd over 1f out: nt qckn ins fnl f) 1¼ 3
3269* Blockade (USA) **(71)***(72)*(Fav)*(MBell)* 6-9-1 MFenton(5) (t: mde most tl hdd over 2f out: r.o one pce) 1¼ 4
3247[3] Lorelei Lee (IRE) **(63)***(62) (JohnBerry)* 3-8-5 KFallon(9) (effrt 4f out: chsd ldrs over 2f out: sn btn) 4 5
3291[6] First Gold **(58)***(59) (JWharton)* 6-9-1 MRoberts(8) (lw: bhd: pushed along 4f out: hdwy over 2f out: no imp) 3½ 6
2961[7] Ivan the Terrible (IRE) **(62)***(32) (BEllison)* 7-8-11 NKennedy(6) (b: w ldrs tl outpcd 4f out: wknd over 3f out) 13 7

2/1 Blockade (USA), **4/1** SECOND COLOURS (USA), **9/2** Guesstimation (USA), **6/1** Blaze of Oak (USA), **9/1** Lorelei Lee (IRE), First Gold, **14/1** Ivan the Terrible (IRE), CSF £24.86 TOTE £4.10: £2.40 £2.80 (£14.40) Trio £19.00 OWNER Mr P. D. Savill (SALTBURN) BRED Dinnaken Farm in USA 7 Rn 1m 51.5 (2.50) SF: 60/60/56/54/37/41/14

WEIGHT FOR AGE 3yo-7lb

STEWARDS' ENQUIRY Dettori susp. 8-11/9/95 (improper riding). Cochrane susp. 8-11/9/95 (excessive use of whip).

3444

BEST BUY PRODUCTS CONDITIONS STKS (2-Y.O) (Class C) £5,276.80 (£1,820.80: £870.40: £352.00)
5f Stalls: High GOING minus 0.21 sec per fur (GF) 2-40 (2-40)

3133* **Branston Jewel (IRE)** *(88+) (MJohnston)* 2-8-7 MRoberts(4) (lw: led after 2f: hung lft: kpt on wl fnl f) — 1
3354* Westcourt Magic **(87)***(95)*(Fav)*(MWEasterby)* 2-9-2 GCarter(3) (disp ld 2f: hmpd & swtchd rt: r.o towards fin) ¾ 2
3100* Soviet Style (AUS) **(92)***(94) (PWChapple-Hyam)* 2-9-2 JReid(2) (lw: disp ld 2f: carried lft: nt qckn fnl f) s.h 3
2782[4] Oh Whataknight *(83?) (RMWhitaker)* 2-8-5 LDettori(1) (lw: chsd ldrs: hdwy centre ½-wy: sn ev ch: nt qckn fnl f) nk 4

13/8 Westcourt Magic, **7/4** BRANSTON JEWEL (IRE), **5/2** Soviet Style (AUS), **20/1** Oh Whataknight, CSF £4.63 TOTE £2.70 (£2.90) OWNER Mr J. D. Abell (MIDDLEHAM) BRED John David Abell 4 Rn

60.25 secs (3.25) SF: 18/25/24/13

3445

BATLEYS CASH & CARRY H'CAP (0-90) (3-Y.O+) (Class C)
£8,090.00 (£2,420.00: £1,160.00: £530.00)
1m 5f 194y Stalls: Low GOING minus 0.21 sec per fur (GF) 3-10 (3-12)

3071² **Celeric (87)***(99)*(Fav)*(DMorley)* 3-9-7 LDettori(1) (lw: a.p: hdwy 2f out: r.o u.p to ld nr fin)......— 1
3178* Istabraq (IRE) **(74)***(86) (JHMGosden)* 3-8-8 WCarson(8) (b: led after 1f to 2f out: led ins fnl f: hdd & nt qckn nr fin)......hd 2
2701* Cherrington **(85)***(96) (GWragg)* 3-9-5 PaulEddery(11) (lw: a.p: slt ld 2f out tl ins fnl f: no ex)......1 3
3061⁶ Floating Line **(62)***(71) (EJAlston)* 7-8-8 KFallon(10) (swtg: trckd ldrs: n.m.r over 2f out & appr fnl f: nt rcvr)......1½ 4
3162² Midyan Blue (IRE) **(82)***(88) (JMPEustace)* 5-10-0 RCochrane(9) (cl up: rdn over 2f out: one pce)......3 5
3171³ Faugeron **(64)***(69) (NTinkler)* 6-8-10 KimTinkler(4) (s.s: r.o fnl 2f: nrst fin)......½ 6
3412* Star Rage (IRE) **(80)***(84) (MJohnston)* 5-9-12 3x MRoberts(13) (lw: hld up: hdwy over 3f out: ev ch 2f out: nt qckn)......1 7
3238⁵ Chantry Beath **(51)***(54) (CWThornton)* 4-7-11 LCharnock(2) (sme hdwy u.p 3f out: n.d)......¾ 8
2937⁶ Cuango (IRE) **(65)***(67) (RHollinshead)* 4-8-11 PatEddery(3) (in tch: rdn 4f out: no imp)......½ 9
3162⁸ Embracing **(86)***(87) (MRStoute)* 3-9-6 KDarley(7) (lw: in tch: pushed along 4f out: wl outpcd fnl 2f)......1 10
3189⁷ Augustan **(59)***(57) (SGollings)* 4-8-0 (5) LNewton(6) (bhd & rdn 4f out: n.d)......2½ 11
3274² Non Vintage (IRE) **(55)***(53) (MCChapman)* 4-7-8 (7) CMunday(12) (led 1f: cl up tl wknd fnl 2f)......s.h 12
2937⁹ Shawahin **(80)** *(JLDunlop)* 3-9-0 GCarter(5) (stumbled bdly after 2f & lost pl: wl bhd after)......dist 13

3/1 CELERIC, **9/2** Cherrington, **11/2** Embracing, **15/2** Istabraq (IRE), **9/1** Midyan Blue (IRE), Star Rage (IRE), **14/1** Cuango (IRE), Chantry Beath, **16/1** Shawahin, **20/1** Floating Line, Augustan, **33/1** Non Vintage (IRE), Faugeron, CSF £25.27 CT £93.46 TOTE £3.40: £1.20 £2.20 £1.60 (£13.90) Trio £25.50 OWNER Mr Christopher Spence (NEWMARKET) BRED Chieveley Manor Enterprises
13 Rn 2m 59.12 (5.52) SF: 56/43/53/40/57/38/53/23/36/44/26/22/-
WEIGHT FOR AGE 3yo-12lb

3446

LAWRENCE BATLEY RATED STKS H'CAP (0-105) (3-Y.O+) (Class B)
£13,256.00 (£4,904.00: £2,352.00: £960.00: £380.00: £148.00)
6f Stalls: High GOING minus 0.21 sec per fur (GF) 3-40 (3-42)

3195a⁵ **Branston Abby (IRE) (105)***(117)*(Fav)*(MJohnston)* 6-9-7 MRoberts(14) (trckd ldrs: led ins fnl f: r.o wl)......— 1
3191⁶ Venture Capitalist **(105)***(114) (DNicholls)* 6-9-7b AlexGreaves(12) (s.s: hdwy 2f out: r.o wl: nrst fin)......1 2
3359¹² Hello Mister **(93)***(102) (JO'Donoghue)* 4-8-6 (3) PMcCabe(3) (hdwy ½-wy: led over 1f out: sn hdd: r.o)......s.h 3
3236⁶ Jayannpee **(97)***(102) (IABalding)* 4-8-13 LDettori(9) (cl up: led 2f out: sn hdd & wknd)......1¾ 4
3230² Lennox Lewis **(98)***(92) (APJarvis)* 3-8-10 KDarley(8) (hdwy ½-wy: sn chsng ldrs: nt qckn fnl f)4 5
3033³ Tabook (IRE) **(95)***(84) (EALDunlop)* 4-8-11 JTate(2) (lw: w ldrs tl wknd appr fnl f)......2 6
3236⁸ Join the Clan **(91)***(79) (MrsNMacauley)* 6-8-7 DeanMcKeown(7) (in tch tl outpcd 2f out: btn whn hmpd over 1f out)......nk 7
2748⁵ Jawlaat (USA) **(91)***(78) (JLDunlop)* 3-8-3 WCarson(10) (led 4f: wknd appr fnl f)......nk 8
3067⁶ Green Perfume (USA) **(102)***(88) (PFICole)* 3-9-0 TQuinn(11) (hdwy on ins whn hmpd over 3f out: n.d after)......½ 9
3145¹⁵ Master Planner **(94)***(76) (CACyzer)* 6-8-5 (5) CTeague(1) (lw: cl up tl wknd wl over 1f out)......1½ 10
3191⁵ Welsh Mist **(102)***(78) (RBoss)* 4-9-4 PatEddery(4) (cl up tl wknd fnl 2f)......2 11
2570⁶ Ziggy's Dancer (USA) **(95)***(34) (EJAlston)* 4-8-11 KFallon(5) (sn drvn along: n.d)......14 12
LONG HANDICAP Join the Clan 8-6 Jawlaat (USA) 8-2

100/30 BRANSTON ABBY (IRE) (5/1-3/1), **6/1** Jawlaat (USA), **7/1** Green Perfume (USA), Lennox Lewis, **15/2** Jayannpee, **8/1** Hello Mister, Venture Capitalist, Welsh Mist, **12/1** Master Planner, Tabook (IRE), **14/1** Ziggy's Dancer (USA), **16/1** Join the Clan, CSF £32.24 CT £195.69 TOTE £4.10: £1.80 £3.10 £3.60 (£18.20) Trio £105.20 OWNER Mr J. D. Abell (MIDDLEHAM) BRED John David Abell 12 Rn
1m 10.99 (1.39) SF: 67/64/52/52/38/34/29/24/34/26/28/-
WEIGHT FOR AGE 3yo-4lb

3447

MCIVOR SCOTCH WHISKY H'CAP (0-80) (3-Y.O+) (Class D)
£6,264.00 (£1,872.00: £896.00: £408.00)
7f 202y Stalls: Low GOING minus 0.21 sec per fur (GF) 4-10 (4-11)

2766[3] **Chairmans Choice (50)***(62) (APJarvis)* 5-8-0 JTate(8) (a cl up: led 2f out: drvn out) ....— 1
2613* Sheer Danzig (IRE) **(76)***(87)*(Fav)*(RWArmstrong)* 3-9-6 LDettori(10) (lw: a.p: effrt 3f out: outpcd 2f out: r.o towards fin) ....nk 2
2881[8] Bollin Frank **(59)***(67) (MHEasterby)* 3-8-3 JCarroll(6) (led tl hdd 2f out: r.o one pce)..............1¾ 3
3264[3] Nobby Barnes **(43)***(51) (DonEnricoIncisa)* 6-7-7 KimTinkler(1) (sn bhd: hdwy 3f out: r.o towards fin)....s.h 4
2117[9] Master Beveled **(75)***(82) (PDEvans)* 5-9-11 TQuinn(3) (lw: prom: effrt 3f out: kpt on: nt pce to chal) ....nk 5
2613[3] Reverand Thickness **(74)***(79) (SCWilliams)* 4-9-10 KDarley(2) (lw: prom: swtchd ins 2f out: no imp after) 1 6
3020* Kilnamartyra Girl **(53)***(57) (JParkes)* 5-8-3 MRoberts(4) (chsd ldrs: rdn 3f out: eased whn btn appr fnl f)....½ 7
3276[5] Avishayes (USA) **(47)***(51) (MrsMReveley)* 8-7-4 (7) PFessey(7) (lw: bhd: effrt over 3f out: nvr rchd ldrs)....s.h 8
3212[3] Chinour (IRE) **(69)***(66) (EJAlston)* 7-9-5 KFallon(9) (s.i.s: a rr div)..........3½ 9
2778[6] Mr Christie **(54)***(39) (MissLCSiddall)* 3-7-12 TWilliams(11) (s.i.s: a bhd) 6 10
360[4] Sarasi **(65)***(49) (MJCamacho)* 3-8-9 LCharnock(5) (nvr nr ldrs)..........½ 11

LONG HANDICAP Nobby Barnes 7-5

3/1 Sheer Danzig (IRE), **7/2** CHAIRMANS CHOICE, **5/1** Reverand Thickness, **13/2** Kilnamartyra Girl, **8/1** Chinour (IRE), **10/1** Master Beveled, **12/1** Avishayes (USA), **14/1** Bollin Frank, **16/1** Sarasi, **20/1** Nobby Barnes, **25/1** Mr Christie, CSF £14.74 CT £125.29 TOTE £4.40: £1.70 £1.40 £4.90 (£5.40) Trio £42.90 OWNER Mrs D. B. Brazier (ASTON UPTHORPE) BRED D. V. Wakefield 11 Rn
1m 38.92 (2.92) SF: 37/56/36/26/57/54/32/26/41/8/18
WEIGHT FOR AGE 3yo-6lb

3448

MAYFIELD BITTER & LAGER MAIDEN STKS (3-Y.O) (Class D)
£5,071.50 (£1,512.00: £721.00: £325.50)
1m 2f 85y Stalls: Low GOING minus 0.21 sec per fur (GF) 4-40 (4-43)

3183[3] **Bay of Islands** *(80) (CEBrittain)* 3-9-0 WCarson(2) (lw: chsd ldrs: lft in ld appr st: r.o u.p fnl f)........— 1
2460[6] Harlech (IRE) *(76) (JHMGosden)* 3-9-0b PatEddery(8) (hld up: hdwy 3f out: ev ch ins fnl f: nt qckn)........2½ 2
Moon Magic *(65) (LadyHerries)* 3-8-9 KDarley(6) (w'like: bit bkwd: in tch: hdwy & ch 2f out: sn btn)........4 3
3239[6] Fire of London *(63) (JHMGosden)* 3-8-9 LDettori(3) (b.hind: trckd ldrs: carried v.wd appr st: sn rcvrd & ev ch: btn appr fnl f)........1 4
3218[7] Sunoma Valley *(53) (JMPEustace)* 3-9-0 RCochrane(5) (nvr nr to chal) 10 5
Kanika *(BHanbury)* 3-8-6 (3) JStack(7) (neat: unf: rel to r: a t.o) ....dist 6
3338[3] United Force (IRE) **(86)** (Fav)*(PWChapple-Hyam)* 3-9-0 JReid(1) (lw: led tl broke down & p.u appr st: dead)........ P
2313[2] Office Hours **(72)** *(CACyzer)* 3-9-0 KFallon(4) (lw: swvd rt & uns rdr leaving stalls) .... U

11/8 United Force (IRE), **4/1** Fire of London, **6/1** Moon Magic (4/1-13/2), BAY OF ISLANDS, Office Hours, **10/1** Harlech (IRE), **16/1** Kanika, **33/1** Sunoma Valley, CSF £58.22 TOTE £6.70: £1.80 £2.00 £1.60 (£25.90) OWNER Bloomsbury Stud (NEWMARKET) BRED Bloomsbury Stud 8 Rn
2m 12.52 (5.02) SF: 42/38/27/25/15/-/-/-

3449

KNIGHTSBRIDGE GIN MAIDEN STKS (2-Y.O) (Class D) £5,390.00
(£1,610.00: £770.00: £350.00)
6f 214y Stalls: High GOING minus 0.21 sec per fur (GF) 5-10 (5-11)

Red Robbo (CAN) *(85+) (HRACecil)* 2-9-0 PatEddery(8) (w'like: wl grwn: lw: in tch: gd hdwy 2f out: led ins fnl f: all out) ....— 1
3180[2] Sasuru *(85) (GWragg)* 2-9-0 PaulEddery(7) (cl up: led over 2f out tl ins fnl f: rallied)........s.h 2
1803[4] Intidab (USA) *(84+) (JHMGosden)* 2-9-0 LDettori(5) (a.p: effrt over 2f out: hdwy over 1f out: r.o)........½ 3
Astor Place (IRE) *(80+)*(Fav)*(PWChapple-Hyam)* 2-9-0 JReid(1) (w'like: scope: lw: cl up: chal 3f out: rdn & rn green 2f out: kpt on)........1¾ 4
Terdad (USA) *(77+) (MRStoute)* 2-9-0 KDarley(4) (w'like: scope: bhd: rdn ½-wy: hdwy 2f out: nvr nr to chal) 1 5

2370[3] Albaha (USA) *(75) (RWArmstrong)* 2-9-0 WCarson(2) (led tl over 2f out: sn btn)....1¼ 6
Eagle Canyon (IRE) *(59) (BHanbury)* 2-8-11 (3) JStack(3) (w'like: scope: bit bkwd: outpcd ½-wy: n.d after)....7 7
3104[4] Jean-Pierre *(47) (JPearce)* 2-9-0 RCochrane(9) (lw: bhd & rdn ½-wy: n.d after)....5 8
Sis Garden *(21) (MHEasterby)* 2-8-9 MBirch(6) (neat: bit bkwd: dwlt: a outpcd & bhd)....9 9

4/6 Astor Place (IRE), **7/2** Albaha (USA), **6/1** RED ROBBO (CAN) (op 4/1), **8/1** Sasuru, **10/1** Intidab (USA), **14/1** Terdad (USA), **25/1** Eagle Canyon (IRE), **40/1** Jean-Pierre, **50/1** Sis Garden, CSF £53.58 TOTE £5.10: £1.40 £2.10 £2.20 (£18.30) Trio £21.00 OWNER Lucayan Stud (NEWMARKET) BRED Richard D. Maynard 9 Rn 1m 25.55 (4.05) SF: 31/31/30/26/23/21/5/-/-

T/Jkpt: £7,125.70 (1.2 Tckts). T/Plpt: £371.70 (82.53 Tckts). T/Qdpt: £110.70 (10 Tckts). AA

3173-SALISBURY (R-H)
Thursday August 31st (Good to firm, Firm patches)

Race 5 hand-timed
WEATHER: fair WIND: slt against

3450

E.B.F. QUIDHAMPTON MAIDEN STKS (2-Y.O F) (Class D) £4,419.00 (£1,332.00: £646.00: £303.00)
6f 212y Stalls: High GOING minus 0.52 sec per fur (F) 2-20 (2-23)

More Than You Know (IRE) *(75+) (RHannon)* 2-8-11 RPerham(3) (unf: bhd: hdwy over 2f out: led over 1f out: pushed out)....— 1
Generosa *(69) (HCandy)* 2-8-11 WNewnes(7) (w'like: bit bkwd: bhd: rdn over 4f out: hdwy 2f out: r.o ins fnl f)....2½ 2
Cebwob *(65) (PFICole)* 2-8-11 CRutter(11) (small: lt-f: b.hind: a.p: led over 2f out tl over 1f out: one pce)....1¾ 3
3180[5] Consordino *(64) (LMCumani)* 2-8-11 OUrbina(5) (chsd ldrs: r.o one pce fnl f)....¾ 4
3346[3] Miss Swing King (IRE) *(63) (RHannon)* 2-8-6 (5) DaneO'Neill(9) (lw: led: hrd rdn: edgd lft & hdd over 2f out: wknd over 1f out)....s.h 5
3089[20] High Note *(60) (RCharlton)* 2-8-11 DHolland(6) (prom: ev ch whn carried lft over 2f out: wknd over 1f out)....1½ 6
2594[5] Lyzia (IRE) *(58)(Fav)(CEBrittain)* 2-8-11 BDoyle(1) (prom: rdn over 2f out: sn wknd)....¾ 7
Faraway Lass *(47) (LordHuntingdon)* 2-8-11 WWoods(8) (scope: w ldr: carried lft over 2f out: wknd qckly)....5 8
Bianca Cappello (IRE) *(24) (JLDunlop)* 2-8-11 WCarson(2) (lengthy: scope: bkwd: a bhd: t.o fnl 3f)....10 9
Silhouette (IRE) *(DRCElsworth)* 2-8-11 JWilliams(10) (neat: bkwd: s.s: a bhd: t.o fnl 3f)....20 10
Giggleswick Gamble *(MRChannon)* 2-8-11 RHughes(4) (Withdrawn not under Starter's orders: ref to ent stalls).... W

7/4 Lyzia (IRE), **5/1** High Note (op 12/1), Consordino, **13/2** Miss Swing King (IRE) (op 4/1), **9/1** Bianca Cappello (IRE) (5/1-10/1), **12/1** Generosa (op 6/1), **14/1** Cebwob (op 8/1), **25/1** Faraway Lass, Giggleswick Gamble, Silhouette (IRE), **33/1** MORE THAN YOU KNOW (IRE), CSF £326.30 TOTE £49.40: £8.70 £3.50 £3.60 (£306.00) Trio £210.60; £163.14 to Kempton 1/9/95 OWNER Mr Bob Lalemant (MARLBOROUGH) BRED John F. Tuthill and Mrs A. Whitehead 10 Rn 1m 27.07 (1.37) SF: 38/32/28/27/26/23/21/10/-/-/-

3451

'WESSEX STALLIONS' H'CAP (0-85) (3-Y.O+ F & M) (Class D) £3,892.50 (£1,170.00: £565.00: £262.50)
6f 212y Stalls: High GOING minus 0.52 sec per fur (F) 2-50 (2-53)

3145[5] **Silent Expression (79)***(92) (BJMeehan)* 5-10-0 RHughes(5) (lw: hld up: stdy hdwy over 2f out: shkn up to ld ins fnl f: comf)....— 1
3226* Splintercat (USA) **(72)***(83)(Fav)(JHMGosden)* 3-9-2 GHind(1) (lw: led: rdn over 1f out: hdd ins fnl f: nt qckn)....1 2
3204[4] Winsome Wooster **(64)***(69) (PGMurphy)* 4-8-10 (3) SDrowne(7) (lw: hld up: swtchd lft over 1f out: hdwy fnl f)....2½ 3
3372* Delight of Dawn **(77)***(81) (KTIvory)* 3-9-0 (7) 5x CScally(3) (b: prom: hrd rdn 2f out: one pce)....½ 4
3181[5] Agoer **(58)***(56) (CEBrittain)* 3-8-2 BDoyle(2) (b.hind: prom: rdn 4f out: no hdwy fnl 2f)....2½ 5
2531[6] Gallows Corner (IRE) **(84)***(81) (RHannon)* 3-9-9 (5) DaneO'Neill(4) (stdd s: rdn 4f out: no hdwy fnl 2f)....nk 6
2948[10] First Veil **(76)***(69) (JRFanshawe)* 5-9-8 (3) NVarley(8) (plld hrd: prom: rdn over 2f out: sn wknd)....1¾ 7
3175[4] Anam **(78)***(62) (PTWalwyn)* 3-9-8 WCarson(6) (chsd ldr tl wknd 2f out)....4 8

15/8 Splintercat (USA), **3/1** Anam (op 5/1), **4/1** SILENT EXPRESSION, **10/1** Delight of Dawn (8/1-12/1), **11/1** First Veil, **12/1** Gallows Corner (IRE), **14/1** Agoer, **16/1** Winsome Wooster, CSF £11.69 CT £97.34 TOTE £4.60: £1.60 £1.30 £2.50 (£5.70) OWNER Mr A. S. Reid (UPPER LAMBOURN) BRED J. B. H. Stevens 8 Rn 1m 26.31 (0.61) SF: 62/48/39/46/21/46/39/27

WEIGHT FOR AGE 3yo-5lb

3452

DICK POOLE CONDITIONS STKS (2-Y.O F) (Class C) £5,251.50 (£1,674.00: £799.50)
6f Stalls: High GOING minus 0.52 sec per fur (F) 3-20 (3-23)

2934* **Najiya** *(89+)*(Fav)*(JLDunlop)* 2-8-9 WCarson(1) (chsd ldr: led on bit over 2f out: easily) ....— **1**
3216⁴ White Whispers **(93)***(82) (BJMeehan)* 2-8-7 BDoyle(3) (swtg: led over 3f: no ch w wnr) 1¾ **2**
Temptress *(2) (PTWalwyn)* 2-8-7 DHolland(2) (lengthy: bkwd: uns rdr & bolted to s: sn rdn & outpcd) 30 **3**

2/9 NAJIYA, **5/1** White Whispers (4/1-6/1), **8/1** Temptress (op 4/1), CSF £1.78 TOTE £1.20: (£1.20) OWNER Mr Hamdan Al Maktoum (ARUNDEL) BRED Shadwell Estate Company Limited 3 Rn

1m 13.28 (0.98) SF: 37/30/-

3453

BLANDFORD H'CAP (0-80) (3-Y.O+) (Class D) £3,606.50 (£1,082.00: £521.00: £240.50)
5f Stalls: High GOING minus 0.52 sec per fur (F) 3-50 (3-51)

3333⁷ **Bangles (64)***(75) (LordHuntingdon)* 5-9-2 WWoods(3) (mde all: rdn over 1f out: r.o wl) ....— **1**
3333³ Domicksky **(55)***(60) (MRChannon)* 7-8-2 (5) PPMurphy(5) (a.p: rdn over 2f out: r.o one pce fnl f) 2 **2**
3407³ Tart and a Half **(79)***(81)*(Fav)*(BJMeehan)* 3-9-9b(5) DaneO'Neill(2) (lw: s.i.s: sn prom: rdn 2f out: one pce) ....¾ **3**
3205⁴ Giggleswick Girl **(64)***(61) (MRChannon)* 4-9-2 RHughes(4) (lw: hld up: hdwy over 1f out: nt rch ldrs) 1½ **4**
2973² Midnight Break **(65)***(58) (PTWalwyn)* 3-9-0 DHolland(7) (rdn over 2f out: nvr nr to chal) 1½ **5**
3221¹² Tommy Tempest **(42)***(24) (REPeacock)* 6-7-5v(3)ow1 NVarley(1) (prom tl rdn & wknd over 2f out) 3 **6**
3333⁶ The Noble Oak (IRE) **(46)***(28) (MJBolton)* 7-7-12b WCarson(6) (lw: a bhd) ....nk **7**

LONG HANDICAP Tommy Tempest 7-4

5/2 Tart and a Half, **9/2** Domicksky, Midnight Break, **5/1** BANGLES, **7/1** Giggleswick Girl, The Noble Oak (IRE), **16/1** Tommy Tempest, CSF £25.02 TOTE £6.70: £3.00 £2.00 (£12.00) OWNER Mr John Rose (WEST ILSLEY) BRED John Rose 7 Rn 59.87 secs (-0.13) SF: 59/44/62/45/39/8/12

WEIGHT FOR AGE 3yo-3lb

3454

SALISBURY FESTIVAL CONDITIONS STKS (3-Y.O+) (Class C) £5,645.00 (£1,820.00: £885.00)
1m 6f Stalls: High GOING minus 0.52 sec per fur (F) 4-20 (4-20)

3223* **Source of Light (104)***(111+)*(Fav)*(RCharlton)* 6-9-9 (5) MHenry(2) (lw: hld up: led on bit over 2f out: sn clr) ....— **1**
3146⁶ Edbaysaan (IRE) **(102)***(84) (RAkehurst)* 5-9-10 RHughes(4) (lw: led: rdn 5f out: hdd over 2f out: eased whn btn 1f out) 20 **2**
One Voice (USA) **(84)***(66) (KBishop)* 5-9-9 JWilliams(1) (hld up: lost tch 6f out:t.o) 15 **3**

4/9 SOURCE OF LIGHT, **9/4** Edbaysaan (IRE), **10/1** One Voice (USA), CSF £1.75 TOTE £1.30: (£1.20) OWNER Mr K. Abdullah (BECKHAMPTON) BRED Juddmonte Farms 3 Rn

3m 8.5 (10.30) SF: 15/-/-

3455

WINTERBOURNE H'CAP (0-65) (3-Y.O+) (Class F) £3,365.00 (£940.00: £455.00)
1m Stalls: High GOING minus 0.52 sec per fur (F) 4-50 (4-53)

3101⁷ **Kindergarten Boy (IRE) (60)***(73) (RBoss)* 4-9-9 WCarson(5) (a.p: led over 3f out: drvn out)— **1**
2314¹⁰ Saucy Maid (IRE) **(56)***(68) (MajorDNChappell)* 4-9-5 BThomson(8) (a.p: ev ch over 1f out: r.o) ....nk **2**
Kestrel Forboxes (IRE) **(63)***(75) (CMcCready,Jersey)* 7-9-12 RMcGhin(6) (led over 4f: ev ch over 1f out: r.o) ....s.h **3**
3173² Super Serenade **(52)***(64) (GBBalding)* 6-9-1 JWilliams(7) (hdwy over 2f out: hung lft over 1f out: r.o) ....nk **4**
2345⁴ Court Minstrel **(52)***(63) (LJHolt)* 6-9-1 MPerrett(12) (bhd: hdwy 2f out: r.o ins fnl f) ....½ **5**

2037[14] Rock Oyster **(49)***(59) (BJMeehan)* 3-8-6 JFEgan(13) (bit bkwd: dwlt: rdn 3f out: hdwy fnl 2f: nrst fin)....½ 6
North Esk (USA) **(57)***(63) (CADwyer)* 6-9-6 MWigham(2) (prom: rdn over 2f out: wknd ins fnl f)....2 7
2808[6] Kevasingo **(62)***(66) (SDow)* 3-8-12 (7) ADaly(16) (chsd ldrs tl wknd over 1f out)....¾ 8
2524* Bakers Daughter **(49)***(49) (JRArnold)* 3-8-1 (5) MHenry(1) (prom over 6f)....2 9
3177[6] Mediate (IRE) **(58)***(57) (RHannon)* 3-8-10 (5) DaneO'Neill(18) (lw: nvr nrr)....½ 10
3344[5] Chancey Fella **(55)***(54) (KTIvory)* 4-8-11v(7) CScally(3) (b: mid div whn hmpd over 3f out: sn bhd)....nk 11
3159[3] Double Rush (IRE) **(50)***(45)*(Fav)*(TGMills)* 3-8-7 PaulEddery(10) (mid div: rdn 3f out: n.m.r 2f out: n.d)....2 12
2993[8] Ewar Imperial **(55)***(40) (CEBrittain)* 3-8-12 BDoyle(17) (lw: bhd fnl 3f)....5 13
3075[5] Sporting Risk **(50)***(33) (PWHarris)* 3-8-7b GHind(4) (prom over 4f)....1 14
2425[5] Howqua River **(51)***(30) (PWChapple-Hyam)* 3-8-1 (7) RCody-Boutcher(15) (chsd ldrs over 5f)1¾ 15
3079[8] Fort Knox (IRE) **(51)***(27) (RMFlower)* 4-9-0 DBiggs(11) (prom over 4f)....1½ 16
2709[5] Indian Lament **(41)** *(RJHodges)* 4-8-1b(3) SDrowne(14) (drppd rr 4f out: sn t.o)....dist 17

6/1 Double Rush (IRE), **13/2** Kestrel Forboxes (IRE), **8/1** KINDERGARTEN BOY (IRE), Super Serenade, Kevasingo, **9/1** Mediate (IRE), **10/1** Bakers Daughter, Court Minstrel (8/1-14/1), **11/1** Fort Knox (IRE), **16/1** Chancey Fella, Sporting Risk, Saucy Maid (IRE), **20/1** North Esk (USA), **25/1** Ewar Imperial, Rock Oyster, **33/1** Howqua River, **50/1** Indian Lament, CSF £123.66 CT £820.92 TOTE £4.50: £1.50 £4.60 £2.20 £2.10 (£107.30) Trio £113.10 OWNER Mrs Joan Root (NEWMARKET) BRED Bernard Eivers 17 Rn 1m 42.41 (3.11) SF: 34/29/36/25/24/14/24/21/4/12/15/-/-/-/-/-/-
WEIGHT FOR AGE 3yo-6lb
T/Plpt: £907.70 (12.75 Tckts). T/Qdpt: £27.70 (3.8 Tckts). KH

3443-YORK (L-H)
Thursday August 31st (Good to firm, Good patches)
WEATHER: overcast WIND: slt against

3456 HEARTHSTEAD HOMES MAIDEN STKS (2-Y.O) (Class D) £5,162.50 (£1,540.00: £735.00: £332.50)
6f Stalls: High GOING minus 0.22 sec per fur (GF) 2-10 (2-11)

3185[2] **Leonine (IRE)** *(94+)*(Fav)*(PFICole)* 2-9-0 TQuinn(3) (sn trckng ldrs: led on bit appr fnl f: shkn up & r.o: comf)....— 1
Musick House (IRE) *(91+) (PWChapple-Hyam)* 2-9-0 JReid(1) (cmpt: unf: dwlt: sn rcvrd: chal over 1f out: r.o)....1¼ 2
3185[3] Russian Music *(81) (PCHaslam)* 2-9-0 JWeaver(6) (led tl hdd appr fnl f: sn btn)....3½ 3
3231[4] Ocean Stream (IRE) *(57) (JLEyre)* 2-9-0 RLappin(5) (cl up: edgd lft most of wy: btn wl over 1f out)....9 4
2667[6] Hobbs Choice *(26) (MissJFCraze)* 2-8-9v PatEddery(4) (spd 2f: sn outpcd & bhd)....10 5

8/11 LEONINE (IRE) (op Evens), **9/4** Russian Music, **5/1** Musick House (IRE) (3/1-11/2), **16/1** Ocean Stream (IRE), **100/1** Hobbs Choice, CSF £4.69 TOTE £1.80: £1.20 £1.80 (£2.30) OWNER Prince Fahd Salman (WHATCOMBE) BRED Irelandia Holdings Ltd 5 Rn
1m 13.25 (3.65) SF: 28/25/15/-/-

3457 QUINTIN GILBEY SILVER TROPHY H'CAP (0-75) (3-Y.O+) (Class D) £6,524.00 (£1,952.00: £936.00: £428.00)
6f 214y Stalls: High GOING minus 0.22 sec per fur (GF) 2-40 (2-42)

2321* **Samah (67)***(75)*(Fav)*(DNicholls)* 5-9-8 NConnorton(1) (trckd ldrs: led over 1f out: r.o wl)....— 1
2746[3] Cool Edge (IRE) **(72)***(79) (MHTompkins)* 4-9-13 PRobinson(14) (led over 2f out tl over 1f out: r.o)....½ 2
3109[6] Safey Ana (USA) **(73)***(77) (BHanbury)* 4-10-0 WRyan(7) (b: b.hind: bhd: hdwy over 2f out: styd on: nrst fin)....1¼ 3
2764[24] Napoleon Star (IRE) **(69)***(72) (MSSaunders)* 4-9-10 NAdams(10) (plld hrd: bhd tl swtchd & hdwy over 2f out: r.o towards fin)....½ 4
1679[10] Ochos Rios (IRE) **(62)***(65) (BSRothwell)* 4-9-3 MFenton(15) (hdwy to chal 2f out: sn rdn & r.o one pce)....hd 5
3319[11] Mustn't Grumble (IRE) **(63)***(63) (WSCunningham)* 5-9-4 LDettori(13) (in tch: hdwy over 2f out: nt qckn appr fnl f)....1 6
2130[6] Jato **(73)***(70) (SCWilliams)* 6-10-0 KDarley(6) (lw: trckd ldrs: nt clr run & swtchd 2f out: one pce after)....1½ 7
3241[4] Pine Ridge Lad (IRE) **(54)***(47) (JLEyre)* 5-8-9 SDWilliams(4) (bhd tl r.o appr fnl f)....1½ 8
3172[4] Ashdren **(54)***(45) (AHarrison)* 8-8-9 KFallon(16) (outpcd & bhd: hdwy over 2f out: no imp)...1¼ 9

3237[6] Dontforget Insight (IRE) **(70)***(59) (PFICole)* 4-9-11 TQuinn(17) (chsd ldrs 5f: wknd) ....½ **10**
2698[7] Thunder River (IRE) **(62)***(49) (MJHeaton-Ellis)* 5-9-3 MRoberts(8) (lw: hdwy u.p ½-wy: sn wknd) 1¼ **11**
2946[12] Karinska **(69)***(55) (MCChapman)* 5-9-3 (7) CMunday(11) (nvr wnt pce) ....nk **12**
2916[4] Encore M'Lady (IRE) **(70)***(52) (FHLee)* 4-9-11 RCochrane(18) (bhd: hdwy 3f out: ev ch 2f out: sn wknd) 1¾ **13**
3098[9] Cafe Solo **(41)***(21) (NBycroft)* 4-7-3b(7)ow1 MartinDwyer(12) (n.d) ....nk **14**
592[12] Monte Cavo **(53)***(31) (MBrittain)* 4-8-8 JLowe(5) (drvn along thrght: lost tch fr ½-wy) 1¼ **15**
3291[7] Russian Heroine **(75)***(53) (MJohnston)* 3-9-11 JWeaver(9) (lw: cl up: led ½-wy tl over 2f out: wknd) ....nk **16**
3341[3] Rise Up Singing **(58)***(1) (WJMusson)* 7-8-13b PatEddery(3) (dwlt: a outpcd & bhd: t.o) 15 **17**
Barik (IRE) **(63)** *(MrsASwinbank)* 5-9-4 RHills(2) (led to ½-wy: wknd qckly: t.o) 8 **18**

7/2 SAMAH, **9/2** Rise Up Singing, **10/1** Cool Edge (IRE), Jato, Thunder River (IRE), **11/1** Safey Ana (USA), **12/1** Mustn't Grumble (IRE), **14/1** Russian Heroine, Dontforget Insight (IRE), **16/1** Pine Ridge Lad (IRE), Barik (IRE), Ochos Rios (IRE), **20/1** Napoleon Star (IRE), Cafe Solo, Encore M'Lady (IRE), Karinska, **25/1** Ashdren, **33/1** Monte Cavo, CSF £40.83 CT £349.08 TOTE £6.10: £1.70 £2.70 £3.10 £5.50 (£40.30) Trio £107.40 OWNER Mrs Norma Robinson (THIRSK) BRED Shadwell Estate Company Limited 18 Rn

1m 25.01 (3.51) SF: 44/48/46/41/34/32/39/16/14/28/18/24/21/-/-/17/-/-

WEIGHT FOR AGE 3yo-5lb

OFFICIAL EXPLANATION **Rise Up Singing: the jockey reported that the horse's head was turned to one side as the gates opened and he lost many lengths.**

3458 FAMOUS GROUSE STRENSALL STKS (Listed) (3-Y.O+) (Class A)

£12,525.00 (£3,750.00: £1,800.00: £825.00)
1m 205y Stalls: Low GOING minus 0.22 sec per fur (GF) 3-10 (3-11)

Triarius (USA) *(112+)*(Fav)*(SbinSuroor)* 5-9-2 LDettori(1) (lw: trckd ldrs gng wl: led 2f out: shkn up & r.o wl) ....— **1**
3381[9] Sonic Boy **(113)***(110) (RFJohnsonHoughton)* 3-8-9 JQuinn(3) (led tl hdd 2f out: r.o) 1¼ **2**
2738[11] Naked Welcome **(96)***(108) (MJFetherston-Godley)* 3-8-9 PatEddery(4) (lw: bhd: outpcd 4f out: styd on u.p fnl 2f: nvr able chal) 1¼ **3**
2762[3] Be Mindful **(101)***(107) (JRFanshawe)* 3-8-9 DHarrison(2) (chsd ldrs: rdn 3f out: one pce) ....nk **4**

5/6 TRIARIUS (USA), **9/4** Sonic Boy, **5/1** Naked Welcome, **7/1** Be Mindful, CSF £3.18 TOTE £1.60: (£1.60) OWNER Godolphin (NEWMARKET) BRED Tyra Black and Summa Stables 4 Rn

1m 51.36 (2.36) SF: 61/52/50/49

WEIGHT FOR AGE 3yo-7lb

3459 SUN LIFE OF CANADA GARROWBY RATED STKS H'CAP (0-105) (3-Y.O)

(Class B) £12,583.20 (£4,648.80: £2,224.40: £902.00: £351.00: £130.60)
1m 3f 195y Stalls: Low GOING minus 0.22 sec per fur (GF) 3-40 (3-40)

3164[5] **Mezaan (IRE) (88)***(101) (MRStoute)* 3-9-0 JReid(1) (lw: trckd ldrs: hdwy to ld appr fnl f: r.o u.p) ....— **1**
2691[2] Rokeby Bowl **(95)***(103)*(Fav)*(IABalding)* 3-9-7 LDettori(5) (hld up: qcknd to ld 2½f out: hdd appr fnl f: kpt on) 3½ **2**
2026[2] Eurolink Mischief **(78)***(86) (LMCumani)* 3-8-4 PatEddery(7) (lw: b.hind: bhd: outpcd 4f out: hdwy u.p 2f out) ....nk **3**
3433[2] Vindaloo **(84)***(91) (JLHarris)* 3-8-10 RCochrane(2) (in tch: effrt 3f out: hrd rdn & n.m.r 1f out) .½ **4**
3189[9] Deano's Beeno **(81)***(82) (MJohnston)* 3-8-7 JWeaver(3) (led tl hdd 2½f out: one pce) 5 **5**
2445[3] Ahla **(84)***(84) (RWArmstrong)* 3-8-10 RHills(6) (cl up: chal 4f out: wknd fnl 2f) ....nk **6**
3066[3] Prize Pupil (IRE) **(78)***(51) (CFWall)* 3-8-4 MRoberts(4) (chsd ldrs: outpcd whn sltly hmpd wl over 2f out: sn wknd: sddle slipped) 20 **7**

LONG HANDICAP Prize Pupil (IRE) 8-2

5/2 Rokeby Bowl, **4/1** Vindaloo, **9/2** MEZAAN (IRE), **11/2** Prize Pupil (IRE), **6/1** Ahla, **13/2** Eurolink Mischief, **9/1** Deano's Beeno, CSF £16.19 TOTE £6.00: £3.00 £2.00 (£10.60) OWNER Mr Mana Al Maktoum (NEWMARKET) BRED Barronstown Stud and Ron Con Ltd. 7 Rn

2m 29.15 (2.15) SF: 66/68/51/56/47/49/16

3460 T.E.F. FREIGHT NURSERY H'CAP (2-Y.O) (Class C) £7,505.00

(£2,240.00: £1,070.00: £485.00)
7f 202y Stalls: Low GOING minus 0.22 sec per fur (GF) 4-10 (4-11)

2796[2] **Ramooz (USA) (80)***(79) (BHanbury)* 2-9-7 WRyan(10) (lw: hld up & bhd: smooth hdwy over 2f out: led 1½f out: r.o) ....— **1**

3345² Disallowed (IRE) **(69)***(66)*(Fav)*(MBell)* 2-8-10 MFenton(4) (lw: led after 1½f to 1½f out: kpt on) 1¼ **2**
1943⁴ Jackson Park **(52)***(38) (MHEasterby)* 2-7-7 JLowe(6) (lw: chsd ldrs: effrt 2f out: one pce) 5 **3**
1035⁷ Exactly (IRE) **(54)***(30) (JLEyre)* 2-7-9 ow2 TWilliams(1) (led 1½f: cl up tl outpcd fnl 2f) 4 **4**
2473³ Aztec Flyer (USA) **(62)***(39) (MrsMReveley)* 2-8-3 DeanMcKeown(5) (bhd: effrt u.p over 3f out: nvr rchd ldrs) ....½ **5**
3354⁴ Oriole **(63)***(35) (NTinkler)* 2-8-4 KimTinkler(7) (lost pl 4f out: hdwy u.p 3f out: n.d) 2½ **6**
3019⁸ Down The Yard **(54)***(26) (MCChapman)* 2-7-6 (3) DWright(2) (bhd tl sme late hdwy) ....s.h **7**
2914⁴ Camionneur (IRE) **(64)***(33) (MHEasterby)* 2-8-5 MBirch(8) (plld hrd: trckd ldrs tl rdn & fnd nil 2f out) 1½ **8**
3160⁷ Blenheim Terrace **(64)***(31) (CBBBooth)* 2-8-5 NKennedy(9) (swtg: a bhd) 1¼ **9**
1798* Evidence In Chief **(68)***(34) (PFICole)* 2-8-9 TQuinn(11) (s.i.s: hdwy appr st: rdn & wknd 3f out) ....nk **10**
2924⁴ Kratz (IRE) **(61)***(21) (BSRothwell)* 2-8-2 DHarrison(3) (prom tl rdn & wknd 3f out) 3 **11**

LONG HANDICAP Exactly (IRE) 7-3

9/4 Disallowed (IRE), **9/2** Evidence In Chief, **5/1** Aztec Flyer (USA) (op 3/1), **11/2** RAMOOZ (USA),**10/1** Camionneur (IRE), **14/1** Jackson Park, **16/1** Oriole, Blenheim Terrace, Kratz (IRE), **20/1** Exactly (IRE), Down The Yard, CSF £18.19 CT £152.09 TOTE £5.30: £2.00 £1.20 £4.40 (£4.60) Trio £65.60 OWNER Mr Hilal Salem (NEWMARKET) BRED Gainsborough Stud Management Ltd 11 Rn
1m 40.02 (4.02) SF: 45/32/4/-/5/1/-/-/-/-/-

3461 PRINCE OF WALES'S OWN REGIMENT OF YORKSHIRE MAIDEN STKS (3-Y.O+) (Class D) £4,844.00 (£1,442.00: £686.00: £308.00)

7f 202y Stalls: Low GOING minus 0.22 sec per fur (GF) 4-40 (4-41)

Delta Soleil (USA) *(92)*(Fav)*(PWHarris)* 3-8-12 PatEddery(2) (lw: mde all: shkn up over 1f out: sn clr & eased) ....— **1**
2794⁵ Viyapari (IRE) **(74)***(76) (LMCumani)* 3-8-12 LDettori(4) (chsd wnr: c wd & ev ch 2f out: rdn & no rspnse) 8 **2**
908³ Our Robert **(60)***(68) (JGFitzGerald)* 3-8-12 KFallon(1) (bhd tl styd on fnl 3f: no imp) 4 **3**
Fatehalkhair (IRE) *(58) (BEllison)* 3-8-12 NKennedy(5) (leggy: b: s.i.s: sn in tch: wknd 3f out) 5 **4**
384⁴ Docklands Courier *(53) (BJMcMath)* 3-8-12 RCochrane(3) (prom tl wl outpcd fnl 3f) 2½ **5**

5/4 DELTA SOLEIL (USA), **11/8** Viyapari (IRE), **6/1** Our Robert, **14/1** Docklands Courier, **33/1** Fatehalkhair (IRE), CSF £3.22 TOTE £2.30: £1.40 £1.20 (£1.60) OWNER American Connection I (BERKHAMSTED) BRED Robert S. Silver and Gaines-GTL P/S 5 Rn
1m 39.15 (3.15) SF: 46/30/22/12/7

3462 RACING SCHOOLS APPRENTICE H'CAP (0-70) (3-Y.O+) (Class E) £3,850.00 (£1,150.00: £550.00: £250.00)

1m 2f 85y Stalls: Low GOING minus 0.22 sec per fur (GF) 5-10 (5-11)

3207³ **Rasayel (USA) (44)***(61) (PDEvans)* 5-8-2 GMitchell(1) (sn in tch: qcknd to ld 3f out: r.o wl) ..— **1**
3384³ Kandyan **(63)***(75) (MHTompkins)* 4-9-7 JWilkinson(8) (a.p: chal 3f out: one pce appr fnl f) ...3½ **2**
3367* Gold Desire **(35)***(34) (MBrittain)* 5-7-7 5x MBaird(15) (b.nr hind: bhd: hdwy ent st: styd on strly: nrst fin) 8 **3**
3422* Westcourt Princess **(53)***(48)*(Fav)*(MWEasterby)* 3-8-3 5x PFessey(6) (led 8f out to 3f out: one pce) 2½ **4**
430¹¹ Sweet Mignonette **(70)***(63) (MrsMReveley)* 7-10-0 SCopp(9) (hdwy u.p over 3f out: hrd rdn & nvr able chal) 1½ **5**
3061⁸ Ballard Lady (IRE) **(46)***(32) (JSWainwright)* 3-7-7 (3)ow1 FLynch(5) (effrt 4f out: styd on: no imp) 4 **6**
3422⁷ Bold Top **(43)***(30) (BSRothwell)* 3-7-7 DDenby(4) (led tl hdd 8f out: cl up tl wknd fnl 3f) ....nk **7**
2954* Ooh Ah Cantona **(69)***(54) (JLEyre)* 4-9-13 DGriffiths(13) (lw: bhd: styd on fnl 3f: n.d) ....¾ **8**
3255⁶ Durham Drapes **(62)***(46) (MHEasterby)* 4-9-6 SSanders(12) (b.off hind: prom tl outpcd fnl 2½f) 1 **9**
3297* Salinger **(42)***(25) (JParkes)* 7-8-0 5x CTeague(2) (prom tl wknd fnl 3f) ....¾ **10**
2917⁴ Highfield Fizz **(59)***(26) (CWFairhurst)* 3-8-9 JTate(11) (a bhd) 10 **11**
1669⁷ Toshiba Talk (IRE) **(49)***(16) (BEllison)* 3-7-13 RWaterfield(14) (in tch tl outpcd fnl 4f) ....½ **12**
2972¹³ Leave it to Lib **(46)***(7) (PCalver)* 8-8-4 AEddery(3) (lw: chsd ldrs tl wknd over 3f out) 3½ **13**
2731² Samaka Hara (IRE) **(56)***(13) (WSCunningham)* 3-8-6 RHavlin(10) (in tch tl wknd fnl 3f) 3 **14**
3229⁸ Ashover **(55)** *(TDBarron)* 5-8-13 KimberleyHart(7) (lw: mid div whn sddle slipped & uns rdr over 4f out) .... **U**

LONG HANDICAP Gold Desire 6-12 Bold Top 7-6

11/4 Westcourt Princess, **13/2** Salinger, **7/1** Kandyan, Ooh Ah Cantona, **9/1** Gold Desire, **10/1** Sweet Mignonette, **12/1** Durham Drapes, Samaka Hara (IRE), **14/1** Ashover, **16/1** RASAYEL (USA), **20/1** Highfield Fizz, Bold Top, **25/1** Ballard Lady (IRE), Leave it to Lib, Toshiba Talk (IRE), CSF £123.02 CT £990.25 TOTE £34.40: £6.80 £2.90 £2.40 (£115.30) Trio £209.00 OWNER Pentons Haulage and Cold Storage Ltd (WELSHPOOL) BRED Gainsborough Farm 15 Rn
2m 9.91 (2.41) SF: 50/64/23/29/52/13/11/43/35/14/7/-/-/-/-
WEIGHT FOR AGE 3yo-8lb

T/Jkpt: £3,550.00 (2 Tckts). T/Plpt: £11.40 (2,499.52 Tckts). T/Qdpt: £5.90 (51.35 Tckts). AA

3059-HAYDOCK (L-H)
Friday September 1st (Good)
WEATHER: cloudy WIND: slt against

3463 BLACKBURN MEDIAN AUCTION MAIDEN STKS (2-Y.O) (Class E)
£3,257.50 (£985.00: £480.00: £227.50)
1m 30y Stalls: Low GOING minus 0.47 sec per fur (F) 2-15 (2-16)

Mick's Love (IRE) *(85+) (MJohnston)* 2-9-0 JWeaver(9) (w'like: leggy: bit bkwd: prom: 3rd st: shkn up over 1f out: styd on to ld nr fin) ....— **1**
3089[4] Double Bluff (IRE) *(84)*(Fav)*(IABalding)* 2-9-0 LDettori(11) (lw: led: rdn fnl f: hdd cl home)....nk **2**
3208[3] Weet-A-Minute (IRE) *(78) (RHollinshead)* 2-9-0 MRoberts(5) (chsd ldrs: 6th st: effrt over 2f out: kpt on one pce) 3½ **3**
3174[8] Wire Act (USA) *(60) (MartynMeade)* 2-9-0 VSlattery(3) (bit bkwd: bhd: hdwy u.p on ins over 3f out: nvr nrr) 9 **4**
2926[3] Eric's Bett **(74)***(54) (MrsSMAustin)* 2-9-0v JMarshall(6) (b: chsd ldr: 2nd st: hrd rdn 2f out: wknd over 1f out)....3 **5**
2625[2] Sedbergh (USA) *(52) (MrsMReveley)* 2-9-0 KDarley(2) (lw: chsd ldrs: 4th st: drvn along 2f out: sn btn)....1¼ **6**
2912[8] Magic Ron *(51) (MBell)* 2-9-0 MFenton(10) (bit bkwd: chsd ldrs: 5th st: rdn & wknd 3f out) ....½ **7**
3307[5] Whothehellisharry *(50) (JBerry)* 2-9-0 JCarroll(1) (lw: effrt 3f out: wknd fnl 2f)....s.h **8**
2876[11] Larry Lambrusco *(47) (MAJarvis)* 2-9-0 PRobinson(4) (lw: a in rr)....1¾ **9**
2971[4] Principal Boy (IRE) *(42) (TJEtherington)* 2-9-0 GCarter(13) (lw: a in rr)....2½ **10**
2995[5] Noir Esprit *(38) (JMCarr)* 2-9-0 SMorris(14) (mid div tl rdn & wknd 2f out:)....2 **11**
Young Saffy *(24) (MrsMReveley)* 2-8-9 (5) GParkin(7) (w'like: scope: bit bkwd: dwlt: a bhd: t.o)7 **12**
2464[7] Limyski *(15) (MrsASwinbank)* 2-9-0 NConnorton(12) (a in rr: t.o) 5 **13**
Gunner B Special *(14) (SRBowring)* 2-8-9 (5) CTeague(8) (w'like: leggy: bkwd: s.s: a bhd: t.o)hd **14**

4/5 Double Bluff (IRE), **11/2** Magic Ron, **7/1** Weet-A-Minute (IRE), MICK'S LOVE (IRE), **12/1** Sedbergh (USA), **20/1** Principal Boy (IRE), **25/1** Larry Lambrusco, **33/1** Eric's Bett, Whothehellisharry, Young Saffy, **50/1** Wire Act (USA), Noir Esprit, Limyski, Gunner B Special, CSF £12.98 TOTE £5.80: £1.60 £1.30 £1.50 (£4.30) Trio £6.50 OWNER Mr M. Doyle (MIDDLEHAM) BRED Collinstown Stud Farm Ltd 14 Rn 1m 43.6 (3.20) SF: 29/28/22/4/-/-/-/-/-/-/-/-/-/-

3464 BOLLINGER CHAMPAGNE CHALLENGE SERIES GENTLEMENS' H'CAP (0-70)
(3-Y.O) (Class E) £3,013.75 (£910.00: £442.50: £208.75)
1m 3f 200y Stalls: High GOING minus 0.47 sec per fur (F) 2-45 (2-45)

3299[3] **Boundary Express** **(47)***(63) (EJAlston)* 3-10-12 MrRJohnson(8) (led 9f out: qcknd clr 3f out: unchal)....— **1**
3320* Contrafire (IRE) **(67)***(75) (WJarvis)* 3-12-4 4x MrPPritchard-Gordon(4) (lw: chsd ldrs: 6th st: swtchd rt & chsd wnr appr fnl f: no imp) 6 **2**
3002[6] Elation **(53)***(58) (GRichards)* 3-11-4 MrRHale(7) (lw: chsd ldrs: 4th st: rdn & hung rt over 2f out: nt pce to chal)....2 **3**
3111[3] Never Time (IRE) **(40)***(45) (MrsVAAconley)* 3-10-1 (4) MrKGreen(6) (hld up: hdwy 7f out: wnt 2nd st: wknd appr fnl f) ....½ **4**
3299[5] Dawn Mission **(48)***(49) (MHEasterby)* 3-10-13 MrSSwiers(3) (bhd: n.m.r 6f out: 5th st: nvr nr to chal)....3 **5**
1269[6] Grate British (IRE) **(58)***(54) (EWeymes)* 3-11-5 (4) MrJWeymes(2) (lw: hld up in rr: rdn 3f out: nvr rchd ldrs) 3½ **6**
3229[5] Khan **(53)***(49) (CWThornton)* 3-11-4 MrCBonner(5) (lw: a bhd)....hd **7**
3277* Tirolette (IRE) **(54)***(46)*(Fav)*(RJRWilliams)* 3-11-5b MrJDurkan(9) (lw: dwlt: rdn ent st: a bhd) 2½ **8**
1881[9] Ranger Sloane **(41)***(24) (GFierro)* 3-10-6 MrTMcCarthy(1) (led 3f: 3rd st: sn hrd rdn & wknd: t.o) 7 **9**

13/8 Tirolette (IRE), **7/2** Contrafire (IRE), **5/1** Khan, **8/1** BOUNDARY EXPRESS, **12/1** Dawn Mission, Grate British (IRE), **16/1** Never Time (IRE), Elation, **20/1** Ranger Sloane, CSF £34.99 CT £405.36 TOTE £7.80: £2.00 £2.10 £2.00 (£13.90) Trio £195.00 OWNER Mrs Stella Barclay (PRESTON) BRED W. Gott and Mrs I. Bird 9 Rn 2m 34.23 (6.23) SF: 44/56/39/26/30/35/30/27/5
OFFICIAL EXPLANATION Tirolette (IRE): reportedly felt flat and prefers greater cut in the ground

3465 E.B.F. BIRKENHEAD MAIDEN STKS (2-Y.O) (Class D) £4,211.00 (£1,268.00: £614.00: £287.00)
5f Stalls: Low GOING minus 0.29 sec per fur (GF) 3-15 (3-18)

*2143*11 **Some Horse (IRE)** *(84) (MGMeagher)* 2-9-0 KFallon(14) (hdwy 2f out: sn hrd rdn: r.o to ld last stride) — **1**
2704 5 Norwegian Blue (IRE) **(94)***(84) (APJarvis)* 2-9-0 KDarley(11) (led stands' side: sn clr: hung lft ½-wy: rdn to ld wl ins fnl f: ct cl home) s.h **2**
Kazimiera (IRE) *(78+) (MJohnston)* 2-8-9 JWeaver(1) (lt-f: s.i.s: sn chsng ldrs far side: led 1f out: hdd nr fin) nk **3**
2315 5 Sketchbook *(80) (GLewis)* 2-9-0 DHolland(16) (wnt rt s: hdwy 2f out: rdn & r.o wl ins fnl f) 1 **4**
1311 4 King of The East (IRE) *(72)*(Fav)*(MRStoute)* 2-9-0 LDettori(18) (bit bkwd: prom stands' side: rdn over 1f out: one pce) 2½ **5**
3025 3 Fond Embrace *(64) (HCandy)* 2-8-9 WNewnes(2) (lw: led to 1f out: rdn & wknd fnl f) ¾ **6**
3110 2 Johayro **(75)***(68) (WGMTurner)* 2-8-11 (3) PMcCabe(15) (prom stands' side: rdn ½-wy: no imp) nk **7**
3328a 7 Woodbury Lad (USA) *(64) (WRMuir)* 2-9-0 WRyan(5) (prom far side over 3f) 1¼ **8**
2932 6 Angus McCoatup (IRE) *(56) (BAMcMahon)* 2-9-0 GCarter(12) (lw: sn outpcd: hdwy over 1f out: nvr nrr) 2½ **9**
3133 5 Wild Humour (IRE) *(42) (WRMuir)* 2-8-9 CRutter(17) (b: bhd fnl 2f) 3 **10**
Amington Lass *(40) (BAMcMahon)* 2-8-9 SDWilliams(4) (lengthy: unf: s.s: a in rr) ½ **11**
1642 2 Pekay **(78)***(40) (JBerry)* 2-9-0 JCarroll(7) (lw: racd far side: a bhd) 1¾ **12**
2242 7 Awafeh *(39) (JWPayne)* 2-9-0 MTebbutt(9) (n.d) s.h **13**
2619 10 Kiwud *(33) (GMMoore)* 2-8-9 GHind(10) (prom stands' side 3f) ½ **14**
Mister Woodstick (IRE) *(36) (MAJarvis)* 2-9-0 PRobinson(13) (cmpt: s.s: a bhd) ½ **15**
3110 6 Finisterre (IRE) *(27) (JJO'Neill)* 2-9-0 DeanMcKeown(8) (lw: a bhd) 3 **16**
2715 2 Madam Zando *(12) (JBalding)* 2-8-3b(7)ow1 JEdmunds(6) (spd to ½-wy: sn wknd) 3 **17**
2619 11 Fancy Clancy **(50)***(12) (MissLCSiddall)* 2-8-9 MRoberts(3) (outpcd) s.h **18**

6/4 King of The East (IRE), **9/2** Woodbury Lad (USA) (6/1-4/1), **11/2** Norwegian Blue (IRE) (4/1-6/1), **15/2** Kazimiera (IRE), **10/1** Fond Embrace, Sketchbook, **11/1** Johayro, **14/1** Pekay, **16/1** Mister Woodstick (IRE), **20/1** SOME HORSE (IRE), Angus McCoatup (IRE), Wild Humour (IRE), **33/1** Finisterre (IRE), Awafeh, **50/1** Kiwud, Amington Lass, Madam Zando, Fancy Clancy, CSF £139.87 TOTE £56.40: £7.80 £1.90 £2.80 (£189.70) Trio £435.70 OWNER The Anfield Hombres (ORMSKIRK) BRED Luisa Salini 18 Rn 61.1 secs (2.10) SF: 39/39/33/35/27/19/23/19/11/-/-/-/-/-/-/-/-/-

3466 MELLING LIMITED STKS (0-80) (3-Y.O) (Class D) £3,792.00 (£1,146.00: £558.00: £264.00)
6f Stalls: Low GOING minus 0.29 sec per fur (GF) 3-45 (3-45)

3298* **Iktamal (USA) (80)***(98)*(Fav)*(EALDunlop)* 3-9-3 WRyan(9) (lw: hld up & bhd: smooth hdwy to ld bel dist: sn clr: edgd lft: impressive) — **1**
3087 5 Bajan Rose **(79)***(76) (MBlanshard)* 3-8-6 StephenDavies(4) (led to bel dist: rdn & one pce fnl f) 4 **2**
*1953*7 Midnight Spell **(80)***(76) (MrsJCecil)* 3-8-6 KDarley(2) (w ldr: rdn over 1f out: one pce) nk **3**
3145 14 The Happy Fox (IRE) **(78)***(83) (BAMcMahon)* 3-9-0b GCarter(7) (chsd ldrs: rdn 2f out: kpt on ins fnl f) s.h **4**
2737 14 Montserrat **(77)***(72) (LGCottrell)* 3-8-6 GBardwell(5) (outpcd tl kpt on ins fnl f) 1¼ **5**
3109 7 Banner (USA) **(73)***(74) (BWHills)* 3-8-9 DHolland(6) (prom: rdn over 2f out: eased whn btn fnl f) nk **6**
2949* My Cadeaux **(78)***(72) (RGuest)* 3-8-9 MRoberts(3) (prom 4f) 1 **7**
3166 11 Super Park **(78)***(44) (MHEasterby)* 3-8-11 MBirch(8) (chsd ldrs 4f: sn outpcd t.o) 11 **8**
1151 9 Thick as Thieves **(77)***(31) (RonaldThompson)* 3-8-11 SDWilliams(1) (bit bkwd: rdn over 2f out: a bhd: t.o) 5 **9**

2/1 IKTAMAL (USA), **7/2** My Cadeaux, **5/1** Bajan Rose, **8/1** Midnight Spell, **9/1** Banner (USA), The Happy Fox (IRE), **10/1** Montserrat, **14/1** Super Park, **25/1** Thick as Thieves, CSF £12.74 TOTE £3.00: £1.40 £1.60 £4.20 (£8.60) Trio £59.00 OWNER Maktoum Al Maktoum (NEWMARKET) BRED Green Ireland Properties Ltd 9 Rn 1m 13.68 (1.98) SF: 49/27/27/34/23/25/23/-/-

3467 OUTLAND (S) H'CAP (0-60) (3-Y.O+) (Class G) £2,857.00 (£802.00: £391.00)

6f Stalls: Low GOING minus 0.29 sec per fur (GF) 4-15 (4-21)

3396[9] **Densben (45)***(54) (DenysSmith)* 11-9-1 KFallon(3) (lw: hdwy over 1f out: hrd rdn: str run to ld post)........— 1
3256* Brookhead Lady **(56)***(65) (PDEvans)* 4-9-12 7x GHind(8) (lw: sn led far side: clr ent fnl f: wknd & ct nr fin)........hd 2
3241[5] Maple Bay (IRE) **(49)***(57) (ABailey)* 6-9-2 (3) DWright(22) (lw: hdwy 2f out: hrd rdn & fin strly).nk 3
2832[15] Northern Spark **(44)***(48) (MartynWane)* 7-8-7 (7) GMills(14) (chsd ldrs centre: rdn & one pce fnl f)........1½ 4
3344[19] Bold Aristocrat (IRE) **(42)***(39) (RHollinshead)* 4-8-5 (7) FLynch(17) (lw: hld up: hdwy 2f out: nrst fin)........2½ 5
3252[3] Brisas **(41)***(35) (CWFairhurst)* 8-8-11 DeanMcKeown(2) (chsd ldrs far side: rdn over 1f out: one pce)........1¼ 6
2858[8] Secret Miss **(48)***(41) (APJarvis)* 3-9-1v JTate(11) (hld up: hdwy 2f out: rdn & r.o ins fnl f)........½ 7
2540[12] Saint Amigo **(49)***(42) (JLEyre)* 3-9-2v RLappin(23) (chsd ldrs: rdn 2f out: one pce)........s.h 8
3098[5] Panther (IRE) **(56)***(47) (JHetherton)* 5-9-12 NKennedy(24) (led stands' side: rdn appr fnl f: kpt on one pce)........¾ 9
3357[2] Invigilate **(52)***(42)*(Fav)*(MartynWane)* 6-9-8 KDarley(16) (lw: wnt rt after 1f: prom tl rdn & wknd over 1f out)........s.h 10
2858[7] Bonny Melody **(44)***(32) (PDEvans)* 4-8-7 (7) AmandaSanders(20) (lw: prom stands side over 4f)........¾ 11
2887[3] Time Is Money (IRE) **(51)***(38) (MHTompkins)* 3-9-4 PRobinson(4) (spd far side 4f)........½ 12
2784[10] Mu-Arrik **(50)***(37) (GROldroyd)* 7-9-1v(5) DGriffiths(1) (lw: n.d)........s.h 13
3128[4] Bold Cyrano (IRE) **(50)***(33) (BPalling)* 4-9-6 TSprake(5) (a in rr)........1½ 14
1565[6] Cronk's Courage **(47)***(29) (MGMeagher)* 9-8-10v(7) GFaulkner(18) (early spd: rdn over 2f out: sn bhd)........nk 15
2999[9] Princess Maxine (IRE) **(56)***(37) (JJO'Neill)* 6-9-12 GDuffield(9) (lw: prom over 3f)........½ 16
3250[4] Granmas Delight **(50)***(31) (MMcCormack)* 4-9-6 JWeaver(7) (a bhd)........s.h 17
2870[5] Annie Fay (IRE) **(55)***(34) (JLHarris)* 3-9-8 LDettori(13) (bhd fnl 3f)........¾ 18
3293[4] Arc Lamp **(46)***(21) (JAGlover)* 9-9-2 SDWilliams(6) (chsd ldrs far side 4f)........1¼ 19
3313[3] Gondo **(44)***(19) (EJAlston)* 8-8-7 (7) JEdmunds(12) (prom 4f: sn outpcd)........s.h 20
1738[5] Aquiletta **(44)***(17) (CBBBooth)* 5-9-0 MBirch(15) (early spd: sn lost pl)........1 21
3252[9] Henry the Hawk **(47)***(9) (MDods)* 4-8-10 (7) CWebb(10) (a bhd)........4 22
1433[11] Noosa (IRE) **(60)** *(DMoffatt)* 3-9-10 (3) DarrenMoffatt(19) (prom tl fell after 1f: dead)........F
1721[12] First Option **(55)** *(RBastiman)* 5-9-6 (5) HBastiman(21) (in rr whn b.d after 1f)........U

4/1 Invigilate (7/1-7/2), **9/1** Arc Lamp, **10/1** DENSBEN, Time Is Money (IRE), Gondo, **11/1** Panther (IRE) (16/1-10/1), **12/1** Bold Cyrano (IRE), Brookhead Lady, Annie Fay (IRE), **14/1** Bonny Melody, **16/1** Maple Bay (IRE), Henry the Hawk, Princess Maxine (IRE), Granmas Delight, Brisas, **20/1** Noosa (IRE), Mu-Arrik, **25/1** Saint Amigo, Bold Aristocrat (IRE), Northern Spark, Aquiletta, Cronk's Courage, Secret Miss, First Option, CSF £130.80 CT £1,775.12 TOTE £15.00: £3.20 £4.20 £7.10 £9.20 (£316.10) Trio £1,099.50; £1,115.04 to Haydock 2/9/95) OWNER Mrs Janet Pike (BISHOP AUCKLAND) BRED D. W. Pike 24 Rn

1m 14.54 (2.84) SF: 36/47/39/30/21/17/20/21/29/24/14/17/19/15/11/19/13/13/3/1/-/-/-/-

WEIGHT FOR AGE 3yo-3lb

No bid

3468 BOLD HEATH CLAIMING STKS (2-Y.O) (Class F) £2,997.00 (£842.00: £411.00)

6f Stalls: Low GOING minus 0.29 sec per fur (GF) 4-45 (4-48)

3290* **Boffy (IRE) (65)***(74) (BPJBaugh)* 2-7-9 (7) IonaWands(13) (racd stands' side: shkn up 2f out: led over 1f out: r.o wl)........— 1
3394[8] Oriel Lad **(77)***(73) (PDEvans)* 2-8-4b GHind(14) (led stands' side tl hdd over 1f out: rallied nr fin)........1 2
2911[3] Society Girl **(76)***(74) (CWThornton)* 2-8-9 DeanMcKeown(1) (led far side: sn clr: r.o u.p)........1½ 3
Addie Pray (IRE) *(65) (MAJarvis)* 2-8-1 PRobinson(4) (lengthy: unf: chsd ldrs: rdn & kpt on ins fnl f)........½ 4
3246[4] Madonna da Rossi *(48) (SirMarkPrescott)* 2-8-0 CNutter(8) (chsd ldrs far side: nvr on terms).6 5
Nutcracker *(37) (CBBBooth)* 2-7-10 NKennedy(5) (leggy: lt-f: bit bkwd: sn wl bhd: styd on appr fnl f: nvr nrr)........2½ 6
3354[3] Ultra Barley **(79)***(48) (PCHaslam)* 2-8-7 JWeaver(11) (chsd ldr stands' side: wknd qckly over 1f out)........nk 7
2998[5] Larrylukeathugh **(56)***(44) (JJO'Neill)* 2-8-4 GDuffield(9) (nvr trbld ldrs)........nk 8

2904³ Power Game **(72)***(50) (JBerry)* 2-8-10 JCarroll(7) (lw: chsd ldrs far side: rdn 2f out: no imp)....s.h 9
3012⁷ Saturiba (USA) *(40) (MJohnston)* 2-8-1 TWilliams(6) (effrt u.p 2f out: no rspnse)....hd 10
Hannahs Bay *(34) (MGMeagher)* 2-7-12 ow1 SMaloney(12) (small: s.s: a bhd: t.o)....¾ 11
3080³ One Shot (IRE) **(65)***(41) (WRMuir)* 2-8-4 CRutter(3) (prom far side to ½-wy: sn outpcd)....nk 12
3290¹¹ So Select *(31) (APJarvis)* 2-7-12 (3) DWright(2) (spd far side 3f)....2½ 13
3010³ Gelsemine *(28)*(Fav)*(HCandy)* 2-8-5 WNewnes(10) (prom far side over 3f)....2½ 14

11/4 Gelsemine, **3/1** Society Girl, **4/1** Ultra Barley, **6/1** Oriel Lad, **9/1** Madonna da Rossi, **10/1** Power Game, **12/1** BOFFY (IRE), Addie Pray (IRE), **14/1** One Shot (IRE), **16/1** Saturiba (USA), **25/1** Larrylukeathugh, Nutcracker, So Select, Hannahs Bay, CSF £90.42 TOTE £20.10: £3.30 £1.90 £1.80 (£43.40) Trio £48.20 OWNER Mr Stan Baugh (LITTLE HAYWOOD) BRED J. Hayden 14 Rn
1m 14.89 (3.19) SF: 19/18/19/10/-/-/-/-/-/-/-/-/-/-

OFFICIAL EXPLANATION **Gelsemine: was always hanging left and proved very difficult to ride out in the closing stages.**

3469

KIRKBY H'CAP (0-80) (3-Y.O) (Class D) £3,948.00 (£1,194.00: £582.00: £276.00)
1m 2f 120y Stalls: High GOING minus 0.47 sec per fur (F) 5-15 (5-17)

2691¹² **Dont Shoot Fairies (71)***(81) (CEBrittain)* 3-8-13 BDoyle(10) (mde all: rdn over 1f out: hld on gamely)....— 1
2902³ Lucayan Sunshine (USA) **(74)***(84) (LadyHerries)* 3-9-2 LDettori(7) (swtg: chsd wnr: 2nd st: ev ch fnl 2f: hrd rdn & r.o)....nk 2
3367² Harry Browne (IRE) **(67)***(76)*(Fav)*(MrsJRRamsden)* 3-8-9 KFallon(1) (hld up in rr: hdwy over 2f out: fin wl)....½ 3
2028⁵ Blue Nile (IRE) **(68)***(75) (ACStewart)* 3-8-10 MRoberts(5) (hld up: hdwy 3f out: rdn & edgd lft over 1f out: kpt on)....1 4
1251² Voila Premiere (IRE) **(67)***(73) (MHTompkins)* 3-8-9 PRobinson(6) (bit bkwd: hld up & plld hrd: 6th st: rdn over 2f out: edgd rt: one pce)....¾ 5
3276² Nigel's Lad (IRE) **(79)***(80) (PCHaslam)* 3-9-7 JWeaver(11) (lw: hld up & bhd: effrt over 2f out: nvr nr ldrs)....3½ 6
3094* Tappeto **(74)***(70) (HCandy)* 3-9-2 WNewnes(8) (prom: 3rd st: rdn & wknd wl over 1f out)....3½ 7
1725⁴ On a Pedestal (IRE) **(53)***(46) (MrsJRRamsden)* 3-7-9 LCharnock(3) (chsd ldrs: 7th st: wknd over 2f out)....1¾ 8
2822³ Hand Woven **(75)***(68) (WJHaggas)* 3-9-3 KDarley(4) (lw: chsd ldrs: 5th st: wknd 2f out:)....s.h 9
3063⁵ Swandale Flyer **(53)***(44) (NBycroft)* 3-7-2 (7)ow2 MartinDwyer(2) (a in rr)....hd 10
3422² Lucidity **(52)***(44) (CWThornton)* 3-7-8 NCarlisle(9) (lw: hld up: hdwy & 4th st: wknd over 2f out)....½ 11

LONG HANDICAP Swandale Flyer 7-4

4/1 Harry Browne (IRE), **9/2** Tappeto, **6/1** Hand Woven, **13/2** Voila Premiere (IRE), **7/1** Nigel's Lad (IRE), **8/1** Blue Nile (IRE) (op 5/1), **9/1** DONT SHOOT FAIRIES, **10/1** Lucayan Sunshine (USA), **14/1** On a Pedestal (IRE), Lucidity, **33/1** Swandale Flyer, CSF £89.66 CT £384.96 TOTE £12.40: £3.00 £2.00 £1.70 (£38.90) Trio £69.00 OWNER Mrs Celia Miller (NEWMARKET) BRED Mrs Celia Miller 11 Rn 2m 14.62 (3.12) SF: 36/39/31/30/28/35/25/1/23/-/-

T/Plpt: £316.60 (58.98 Tckts). T/Qdpt: £117.40 (1.1 Tckts). IM

3154-KEMPTON (R-H)

Friday September 1st (Jubilee Good, Rest Good to firm)

WEATHER: overcast WIND: almost nil

3470

WATFORD H'CAP (0-70) (3-Y.O+) (Class E) £3,631.25 (£1,100.00: £537.50: £256.25)
1m 6f 92y Stalls: High GOING: minus 0.31 sec per fur (GF) 2-05 (2-07)

3292⁵ **Ela Man Howa (53)***(65) (RAkehurst)* 4-8-9 (3) SSanders(1) (lw: hdwy 7f out: 3rd st: led over 2f out: rdn out)....— 1
3178³ Sea Freedom **(69)***(80) (GBBalding)* 4-10-0 JWilliams(14) (rdn over 3f out: hdwy over 1f out: r.o)....¾ 2
2550³ Greycoat Boy **(64)***(75) (BJMeehan)* 3-8-12 PatEddery(12) (hdwy 7f out: 4th st: hrd rdn over 2f out: r.o ins fnl f)....hd 3
3024³ Wottashambles **(40)***(51) (LMontagueHall)* 4-7-13 JFEgan(2) (b: 5th st: hrd rdn over 2f out: r.o ins fnl)....½ 4
2069⁷ Silver Hunter (USA) **(59)***(67) (GCBravery)* 4-9-4v MHills(3) (lw: gd hdwy 7f out: 2nd st: ev ch over 2f out: wknd fnl f)....2½ 5

3238⁴ Broughtons Formula **(54)***(60) (WJMusson)* 5-8-13b JQuinn(5) (lw: rdn & hdwy over 1f out: r.o one pce) 1¾ **6**
3156⁴ Quest Again **(67)***(65)*(Fav)*(DWPArbuthnot)* 4-9-12 TQuinn(9) (lw: chsd ldr: led 7f out tl over 2f out: sn wknd) 7 **7**
3211⁶ Admirals Secret (USA) **(67)***(64) (CFWall)* 6-9-7 (5) LNewton(4) (lw: hdwy 4f out: 6th st: eased whn btn over 1f out) 1¼ **8**
2472⁵ Top Royal **(66)***(61) (JPearce)* 6-9-11 MJKinane(10) (lost pl over 6f out: r.o one pce fnl 2f)....1¾ **9**
2530⁹ King Ubad (USA) **(42)***(34) (KOCunningham-Brown)* 6-8-1 AMcGlone(6) (prom over 7f)....2½ **10**
3024⁴ Hacketts Cross (IRE) **(52)***(40) (NoelChance)* 7-8-11 BThomson(7) (s.s: a bhd)....4 **11**
3234⁸ Fruitful Affair (IRE) **(44)***(30) (TThomsonJones)* 6-8-3 PaulEddery(13) (a bhd) 1¼ **12**
3202* Excelled (IRE) **(44)***(29) (CJDrewe)* 6-8-3 ow1 AClark(11) (bhd fnl 5f)....½ **13**
277⁶ Mr Copyforce **(45)***(30) (MissBSanders)* 5-8-4v WCarson(8) (led over 7f) ....nk **14**

5/1 Quest Again, **11/2** Broughtons Formula (op 7/2), **6/1** ELA MAN HOWA, **13/2** Admirals Secret (USA), **12/1** Sea Freedom (8/1-14/1), Top Royal, Fruitful Affair (IRE), **14/1** Wottashambles (10/1-16/1), Silver Hunter (USA) (10/1-16/1), Excelled (IRE), **16/1** Hacketts Cross (IRE), Greycoat Boy, Mr Copyforce, **33/1** King Ubad (USA), CSF £70.00 CT £1,006.27 TOTE £5.90: £2.10 £2.50 £4.50 (£32.50) Trio £171.00 OWNER Arlington Bloodstock (EPSOM) BRED Sheikh Ahmed bin Rashid al Maktoum 14 Rn 3m 11.51 (8.51) SF: 26/41/25/12/28/21/26/25/22/-/1/-/-/-
WEIGHT FOR AGE 3yo-11lb

3471 STANMORE NURSERY H'CAP (2-Y.O) (Class D) £4,435.50 (£1,344.00: £657.00: £313.50)
6f Stalls: High GOING minus 0.31 sec per fur (GF) 2-35 (2-37)

2011* **Willow Dale (IRE) (74)***(78) (DRCElsworth)* 2-9-7 TQuinn(7) (lw: hld up: rdn 2f out: led 1f out: r.o wl) ....— **1**
2660¹³ Ben'a'vachei Boy **(60)***(61) (JDBethell)* 2-8-7b DHarrison(8) (hdwy over 2f out: ev ch ins fnl f: unable qckn) 1 **2**
3213⁷ Rowlandsons Charm (IRE) **(62)***(63) (GLMoore)* 2-8-9 BThomson(6) (lw: led 5f: one pce ins fnl f) ....s.h **3**
3289¹⁰ Dil Dil **(69)***(70) (RHannon)* 2-8-11 (5) DaneO'Neill(5) (lw: a.p: rdn over 2f out: ev ch over 1f out: one pce ins fnl f) ....hd **4**
2847⁶ Jolis Present **(70)***(58) (MJRyan)* 2-9-3 WCarson(4) (nvr nr to chal)....5 **5**
3225⁶ Emperegrine (USA) **(74)***(55) (CFWall)* 2-9-2 (5) LNewton(2) (hld up: rdn over 2f out: sn wknd)....2½ **6**
3008² Daunting Destiny (BEL) **(72)***(52)*(Fav)*(RHannon)* 2-9-5 PatEddery(3) (lw: prom over 4f)....½ **7**
3089¹⁸ Golden Pond (IRE) **(72)***(50) (RFJohnsonHoughton)* 2-9-5 JReid(1) (lw: a bhd) ....¾ **8**

3/1 Daunting Destiny (BEL) (op 2/1), **100/30** Jolis Present, **9/2** WILLOW DALE (IRE), **6/1** Dil Dil, **7/1** Emperegrine (USA), **9/1** Golden Pond (IRE), **14/1** Ben'a'vachei Boy (10/1-16/1), **20/1** Rowlandsons Charm (IRE), CSF £53.20 CT £1,021.64 TOTE £5.20: £1.90 £3.60 £4.60 (£41.60) OWNER Michael Jackson Bloodstock Ltd (WHITCOMBE) BRED Shunya Seki 8 Rn
1m 14.51 (3.21) SF: 35/18/20/27/15/12/9/7

3472 MILCARS CHERTSEY LOCK STKS (2-Y.O C & G) (Class C) £4,658.00 (£1,742.00: £851.00: £365.00: £162.50: £81.50)
7f (Jubilee) Stalls: High GOING minus 0.15 sec per fur (GF) 3-05 (3-06)

Double Leaf *(86+) (MRStoute)* 2-8-10 WCarson(5) (gd sort: lw: hdwy to chse ldr 2f out: led ins fnl f: r.o wl)....— **1**
Ashjar (USA) *(79) (HThomsonJones)* 2-8-10 RHills(7) (w'like: scope: led over 5f out : clr 2f out: hdd ins fnl f: unable qckn)....3 **2**
Callaloo *(68+)*(Fav)*(MrsJCecil)* 2-8-10 PaulEddery(6) (leggy: unf: scope: s.s: hdwy over 5f out: lost pl over 3f out: 6th st: squeezed out & stumbled over 2f out: rallied over 1f out: r.o one pce)....5 **3**
Trojan Risk *(59) (GLewis)* 2-8-10 SWhitworth(1) (str: scope: bkwd: 3rd st: wknd 1f out)....4 **4**
Johnny Jones (USA) *(56) (PWChapple-Hyam)* 2-8-10 JReid(3) (w'like: 5th st: wknd 2f out).1¼ **5**
Apache Len (USA) *(44) (RHannon)* 2-8-10 PatEddery(8) (w'like: bit bkwd: led over 1f: 2nd st: wknd over 2f out)....5 **6**
Flagstaff (USA) *(40) (RHannon)* 2-8-10 RPerham(2) (cmpt: 4th st: wknd over 2f out)....1¾ **7**

9/4 Callaloo (11/10-5/2), **4/1** Apache Len (USA), **9/2** Johnny Jones (USA) (3/1-6/1), **5/1** DOUBLE LEAF (3/1-11/2), **11/2** Ashjar (USA) (4/1-6/1), **16/1** Trojan Risk, Flagstaff (USA), CSF £28.92 TOTE £4.60: £2.40 £2.10 (£9.10) OWNER Mr Mana Al Maktoum (NEWMARKET) BRED Gainsborough Stud Management Ltd 7 Rn 1m 28.0 (3.80) SF: 37/30/19/10/7/-/-

3473

MILCARS TEMPLE FORTUNE STKS (Listed) (3-Y.O+) (Class A)
£12,604.50 (£3,816.00: £1,863.00: £886.50)
1m (Jubilee) Stalls: High GOING minus 0.15 sec per fur (GF) 3-40 (3-40)

1002a2 **Bin Ajwaad (IRE) (112)***(122) (BHanbury)* 5-9-6 JReid(5) (s.s: 6th st: squeezed thro over 1f out: led ins fnl f: comf) ....— 1
33603 Realities (USA) **(111)***(114)*(Fav)*(GHarwood)* 5-9-0 MJKinane(7) (lw: 3rd st: led 1f out tl ins fnl f: unable qckn).......1 2
318811 Lap of Luxury **(102)***(109) (WJarvis)* 6-8-9 BThomson(6) (5th st: led over 1f out: sn hdd: one pce) ....hd 3
319110 Star of Zilzal (USA) **(102)***(110) (MRStoute)* 3-8-9 WCarson(3) (nvr nr to chal).......2 4
33423 Easy Dollar **(107)***(108) (BGubby)* 3-8-9v PaulEddery(1) (2nd st: led wl over 1f out: edgd lft & sn hdd: one pce) ....¾ 5
19762 That Old Feeling (IRE) **(94)***(103) (RHannon)* 3-8-9 TQuinn(2) (lw: led over 6f: wknd fnl f).....2½ 6
31913 Peace Envoy **(109)***(86) (HRACecil)* 3-8-12 PatEddery(4) (4th st: rdn over 2f out: btn whn bdly hmpd over 1f out).......10 7

10/11 Realities (USA), **9/2** Peace Envoy, **7/1** Star of Zilzal (USA), **8/1** BIN AJWAAD (IRE), **10/1** Lap of Luxury, Easy Dollar (7/1-12/1), **40/1** That Old Feeling (IRE), CSF £15.42 TOTE £8.30: £3.00 £1.30 (£6.50) OWNER Mr A. Merza (NEWMARKET) BRED Tullamaine Castle Stud and Partners in Ireland 7 Rn
1m 40.86 (3.86) SF: 52/44/39/35/33/28/11
WEIGHT FOR AGE 3yo-5lb

3474

MILCARS STKS (2-Y.O F) (Class C) £4,660.50 (£1,698.00: £829.00: £355.00: £157.50)
7f (Jubilee) Stalls: High GOING minus 0.15 sec per fur (GF) 4-10 (4-10)

Sea Spray (IRE) *(74+)*(Fav)*(PWChapple-Hyam)* 2-8-8 JReid(4) (unf: scope: 3rd st: led over 1f out: qcknd: comf) ....— 1
3157* Kirov Lady (IRE) **(80)***(65) (RHannon)* 2-8-8 PatEddery(1) (lw: chsd ldr: ev ch over 1f out: unable qckn).......4 2
28864 Flame Valley (USA) *(64) (MRStoute)* 2-8-8 WCarson(2) (lw: led over 5f: one pce) ....nk 3
308913 Mischief Star *(48) (DRCElsworth)* 2-8-8 TQuinn(5) (poor 4th st: a bhd).......7 4
Bursul Lady *(14) (MissBSanders)* 2-8-8 PaulEddery(3) (str: bit bkwd: poor 5th st: a bhd)......15 5

1/2 SEA SPRAY (IRE), **9/2** Kirov Lady (IRE) (3/1-5/1), Flame Valley (USA) (5/2-5/1), **20/1** Mischief Star, **50/1** Bursul Lady, CSF £3.10 TOTE £1.50: £1.10 £1.50 (£1.90) OWNER Lord Weinstock & The Hon Simon Weinstock (MARLBOROUGH) BRED Ballymacoll Stud Farm Ltd 5 Rn
1m 27.58 (3.38) SF: 40/31/30/14/-

3475

RADLETT MAIDEN H'CAP (0-70) (3-Y.O+) (Class E) £3,810.00 (£1,155.00: £565.00: £270.00)
7f (round) Stalls: High GOING minus 0.31 sec per fur (GF) 4-40 (4-41)

33443 **Cuban Reef (40)***(52)*(Fav)*(WJMusson)* 3-7-10 JQuinn(9) (5th st: led 1f out: rdn out) ....— 1
27116 Anna-Jane **(63)***(72) (RHannon)* 3-9-5 JReid(14) (swtg: 4th st: led over 2f out to 1f out: unable qckn).......1½ 2
261310 Saltando (IRE) **(53)***(58) (PatMitchell)* 4-8-8 (5) DaneO'Neill(12) (rdn over 2f out: hdwy over 1f out: r.o).......1½ 3
32645 Bedazzle **(34)***(38) (MBrittain)* 4-7-8 JLowe(6) (lw: swtchd lft 2f out: hdwy over 1f out: r.o ins fnl f).......½ 4
301616 Barbrallen **(43)***(36) (DJSffrenchDavis)* 3-7-6 (7)ow6 CAdamson(3) (nt clr run over 2f out: swtchd rt: hdwy over 1f out: one pce fnl f).......2 5
14768 Twice Purple (IRE) **(62)***(59) (BJMeehan)* 3-9-4 PatEddery(10) (lw: led over 1f: 2nd st: ev ch wl over 1f out: wknd ins fnl f).......1¼ 6
29683 By The Bay **(64)***(58) (CCElsey)* 3-9-6 DHarrison(2) (3rd st: wknd wl over 1f out).......1¼ 7
27612 Speedy Snaps Pride **(46)***(40) (PDCundell)* 3-8-2 JFEgan(5) (hrd rdn over 2f out: hdwy & hmpd over 1f out: r.o one pce).......s.h 8
252816 Arnie (IRE) **(51)***(42) (GLMoore)* 3-8-7 AClark(4) (lost pl over 3f out: r.o one pce fnl 2f).......1¼ 9
317710 Ilustre (IRE) **(48)***(37) (LJHolt)* 3-7-11 (7) ADaly(13) (a mid div).......1 10
17767 Zuno Flyer (USA) **(46)***(31) (GLewis)* 3-7-11 (5) AWhelan(7) (7th st: wknd over 2f out) 1¾ 11
315910 Saltis (IRE) **(55)***(36) (DWPArbuthnot)* 3-8-11 TQuinn(15) (lw: hdwy over 2f out: wkng whn n.m.r on ins over 1f out).......1½ 12
33448 Supermick **(37)***(16) (PJMcBride)* 4-7-11 DaleGibson(1) (lw: bhd fnl 3f) ....¾ 13
315911 With Intent **(51)***(30) (CJames)* 3-8-7 AMcGlone(11) (led over 5f out tl over 2f out: sn wknd) ..hd 14
23598 Knave of Diamonds **(49)***(1) (RJHodges)* 3-8-5 RPerham(8) (prom 3f).......12 15

2269[5] Rasmi (CAN) **(68)***(19) (PHowling)* 4-10-0 PaulEddery(17) (lw: hdwy on ins over 3f out: wknd wl over 1f out) ....½ **16**
Miss Electra **(43)** *(MBlanshard)* 3-7-8 (5) MHenry(16) (6th st: wknd over 1f out) ....hd **17**

LONG HANDICAP Barbrallen 7-5

5/1 CUBAN REEF (7/2-11/2), **7/1** Anna-Jane, **8/1** Saltis (IRE), Speedy Snaps Pride (11/2-9/1), Twice Purple (IRE), **9/1** Supermick (6/1-10/1), Ilustre (IRE), **10/1** By The Bay, Bedazzle, Zuno Flyer (USA), **16/1** Rasmi (CAN), **20/1** Saltando (IRE), With Intent, **25/1** Miss Electra, **33/1** Arnie (IRE), Knave of Diamonds, Barbrallen, CSF £41.48 CT £615.37 TOTE £5.10: £1.90 £1.30 £9.50 £2.10 (£27.00) Trio £352.70 OWNER Mr W. J. Musson (NEWMARKET) BRED Angley Stud Ltd 17 Rn
1m 27.37 (2.87) SF: 22/42/32/12/6/29/28/10/12/7/1/6/-/-/-/-/-
WEIGHT FOR AGE 3yo-4lb

T/Jkpt: Not won; £5,488.20 to Haydock 2/9/95. T/Plpt: £187.00 (126.77 Tckts). T/Qdpt: £10.00 (16.75 Tckts). AK

3329a-DEAUVILLE (France) (R-H)
Tuesday August 22nd (Good to soft)

3476a PRIX DE MEAUTRY (Gp 3) (3-Y.O+) £26,347.00 (£9,581.00: £4,790.00) 6f
3-30 (3-27)

1187[3] **Missed Flight** *(119) (CFWall)* 5-9-5 GDuffield ....— 1
2285[3] Warning Star *(106) (BWHills)* 3-8-6 MHills 1½ 2
1895[2] Alzianah *(103) (JDBethell)* 4-8-9 BThomson ....¾ 3
2764[22] Bold Effort (FR) *(KOCunningham-Brown)* 3-8-9 DBoeuf (btn approx 6l) 9

P-M 3.20F: 1.90F 6.40F 2.90F (50.30F) OWNER Mr Walter Grubmuller (NEWMARKET) BRED Crest Stud Ltd 10 Rn
1m 12.9 (4.40) SF: -/-/-/-
DS

1398a-BADEN-BADEN (Germany) (L-H)
Friday August 25th (Good)

3477a KRONIMUS-RENNEN (Listed) (2-Y.O) £10,288.00 (£4,115.00: £2,551.00) 7f
2-45 (2-48)

2846* **Winter Quarters (USA)** *(IABalding)* 2-8-11 GHind ....— 1
Personal Love (USA) *(HSteinmetz,Germany)* 2-8-7 AStarke ....s.h 2
3090[7] Agnella (IRE) *(GLMoore)* 2-8-7 SWhitworth 2 3

TOTE 27DM: 13DM 14DM 19DM (SF 73DM) OWNER Maverick Productions Ltd (KINGSCLERE) BRED Maverick Productions Ltd 8 Rn
1m 24.47 SF: -/-/-

3476a-DEAUVILLE (France) (R-H)
Saturday August 26th (Good to soft)

3478a PRIX QUINCEY (Gp 3) (3-Y.O+) £26,347.00 (£9,581.00: £4,790.00: £2,395.00) 1m (straight)
2-55 (2-54)

2565a[3] **Two O'Clock Jump (IRE)** *(112) (RHannon)* 3-8-8 GMosse ....— 1
2558a[2] Bishop of Cashel *(119) (JRFanshawe)* 3-9-1 DHarrison ....hd 2
3038a* Philanthrop (FR) *(112) (JEHammond,France)* 3-8-8 CAsmussen ....hd 3
Pollen Count (USA) *(111) (SbinSuroor)* 6-9-0 TJarnet ....½ 4
3192a* Arabride *(JARToller)* 3-8-5 JWeaver (btn approx 4l) 6

P-M 9.50F: 3.50F 2.30F SF (38.60F) OWNER Mr Bob Lalemant (MARLBOROUGH) BRED D Hollyday 7 Rn
1m 40.0 (5.70) SF: -/-/-/-/-

3479a PRIX MICHEL HOUYVET (Listed) (3-Y.O) £16,766.00 (£5,748.00: £3,593.00) 1m 5f 110y
3-30 (3-27)

3196a[6] **Honfleur (IRE)** *(80) (PWChapple-Hyam)* 3-8-13 DHarrison ....— 1
Karaysar *(83) (AdeRoyerDupre,France)* 3-9-2 GMosse ....nk 2
Periple *(82) (AFabre,France)* 3-9-2 TJarnet ....½ 3

P-M 5.70F: 1.90F 1.50F (SF 11.00F) OWNER Mr R. E. Sangster (MARLBOROUGH) BRED Swettenham Stud 6 Rn
3m 15.9 (26.90) SF: -/-
DS

2730a-ARLINGTON PARK (Chicago, USA) (L-H)
Saturday August 26th (Firm)

3480a BEVERLY D STKS (Gp 1) (3-Y.O+ F & M) £192,308.00 (£64,103.00: £35,256.00: £19,231.00) **1m 1f 110y** 21-45 (21-46)

Possibly Perfect (USA) *(120) (RFrankel,USA)* 5-8-11 CNakatani ....— 1
Alice Springs *(119) (JonathanSheppard,USA)* 5-8-11 RDouglas ....¾ 2
Alpride (IRE) *(119) (RMcAnally,USA)* 4-8-11 CMcCarron ....nse 3
31615 La Confederation *(119) (DRLoder)* 4-8-11 RDavis ....hd 4

P-M: WIN 3.40: 2.60 4.40 Show 2.20 3.00 2.60 (DF 13.40) OWNER Blue Vista Inc 7 Rn
1m 54.8 SF: -/-/-/-

3197a-LEOPARDSTOWN (Dublin, Ireland) (L-H)
Saturday August 26th (Good to firm)

3481a BALLYCULLEN STKS (Listed) (3-Y.O+) £10,275.00 (£2,775.00: £1,275.00) **1m 6f** 5-30 (5-31)

2219a* **Vintage Crop** *(124)*(Fav)*(DKWeld,Ireland)* 8-10-4 MJKinane ....— 1
2219a4 Johansson (USA) *(103) (JOxx,Ireland)* 3-8-13b JPMurtagh 12 2
Lake Kariba *(83) (CO'Brien,Ireland)* 4-9-6 CRoche 13 3

2/5 VINTAGE CROP, **4/1** Johansson (USA), **9/2** Lake Kariba, CSF £2.24 TOTE £1.40 (£1.90) OWNER Dr Michael Smurfit BRED Bertram & Mrs R. Firestone 3 Rn 3m 1.4 (5.10) SF: -/-/-

3478a-DEAUVILLE (France) (R-H)
Sunday August 27th (Good)

3482a GRAND PRIX DE DEAUVILLE LANCEL (Gp 2) (3-Y.O+) £59,880.00 (£23,952.00: £11,976.00: £5,988.00) **1m 4f 110y** 2-15 (2-14)

3194a* **Swain (IRE)** *(118) (AFabre,France)* 3-8-7 TJarnet (mid div: pushed along over 3f out: hrd rdn wl over 1f out: chal 1f out: led ins fnl f: r.o) ....— 1
18944 Zilzal Zamaan (USA) *(118) (MRStoute)* 4-9-4 WRSwinburn (trckd ldr: rdn to ld over 2f out: hdd ins fnl f: no ex) ....¾ 2
3041a* Sunrise Song (FR) *(116) (FDoumen,France)* 4-9-4 FSanchez (in rr: rdn over 2f out: r.o ins fnl f) 1½ 3
2729a2 Laroche (GER) *(118) (HJentzsch,Germany)* 4-9-7 JReid (trckd ldrs: pushed along over 3f out: kpt on one pce) ....¾ 4
2890a* Partipral (USA) *(118) (ELellouche,France)* 6-9-7 DBoeuf (hld up in rr: sme hdwy u.p fnl 2f) ..hd 5
3041a3 L'ile Tudy (IRE) *(111) (MmeMBollack-Badel,France)* 5-9-1 ABadel (in rr: hdwy over 2f out: kpt on fnl f: nvr nr to chal) ....½ 6
2890a2 Tzar Rodney (FR) *(113) (GDoleuze,France)* 3-8-7 ODoleuze (hld up in rr: n.d) ....s.nk 7
25955 Broadway Flyer (USA) *(111) (JWHills)* 4-9-4 MHills (led: pushed along ent st: hdd over 2f out: one pce) 2½ 8
3323a4 Royal Solo (IRE) *(113) (PWChapple-Hyam)* 3-8-10 BThomson (mid div: rdn 4f out: sn one pce) ....hd 9

P-M 1.90F: 1.20F 2.20F 2.30F (10.00F) OWNER Sheikh Mohammed (FRANCE) BRED Sheikh Mohammed 9 Rn
2m 46.1 (10.80) SF: -/-/-/-/-/-/-/-/-

3483a PRIX DU HARAS DE LA HUDERIE (Listed) (2-Y.O C & G) £16,766.00 (£5,748.00: £3,593.00) **7f** 3-50 (3-50)

26903 **More Royal (USA)** *(IABalding)* 2-9-2 LDettori ....— 1
Starmaniac (USA) *(France)* 2-9-2 FHead 1½ 2
Restless Carl (IRE) *(AFabre,France)* 2-9-2 SGuillot 1½ 3

P-M 2.50F: 1.70F 1.80F (SF 6.90F) OWNER Mr George Strawbridge (KINGSCLERE) BRED Gatesby W. Clay 5 Rn
1m 29.7 SF: -/-/-
DS

1707a-TABY (Stockholm, Sweden) (L-H)
Sunday August 27th (Good)

3484a
TABY OPEN SPRINT CHAMPIONSHIP (Listed) (3-Y.O+) £30,954.00 (£8,598.00: £6,879.00) **6f** 1-45 (1-50)

3187[3] **Hever Golf Rose** *(100) (TJNaughton)* 4-9-2 JWeaver ....— 1
1707a[2] Cajun Cadet *(100) (WNeuroth,Norway)* 4-9-6 MLarsen 1½ 2
Parios (FR) *(92) (WUppstrom,Sweden)* 7-9-6 FJohansson 3 3

TOTE 17.40SKr: 12.00SKr 29.00SKr 55.00SKr (SF 113.20SKr) OWNER Mr M. P. Hanson (EPSOM) BRED Ronald Popely 12 Rn 1m 9.0 SF: -/-/-

3485a
STOCKHOLM CUP (Gp 3) (3-Y.O+) £51,591.00 (£17,197.00: £8,598.00)
1m 4f 2-15 (2-21)

2739[7] **Glide Path (USA)** *(99) (JWHills)* 6-9-9 JWeaver ....— 1
Theatrician (USA) *(99) (NLindgren,Sweden)* 6-9-9 FJohansson ....s.h 2
In Waiting (IRE) *(91) (MKahn,Sweden)* 3-8-7 FDiaz 1½ 3

TOTE 72.70SKr: 25.00SKr 19.00SKr 21.00SKr (SF 465.00SKr) OWNER Jampot Partnership (LAMBOURN) BRED John T. L. Jones Jnr. & Robert S. Folsom 12 Rn 2m 33.2 SF: -/-/-

BADEN-BADEN (Germany) (L-H)
Sunday August 27th (Good)

3486a
FURSTENBURG-RENNEN (Gp 3) (3-Y.O) £30,864.00 (£12,345.00: £6,173.00) **1m 3f** 3-25 (3-27)

2567a* **Solon (GER)** *(109) (HJentzsch,Germany)* 3-8-11 PSchiergen ....— 1
Jural *(104) (MJohnston)* 3-8-7 MRoberts ....¾ 2
1574a[8] Rifapour (IRE) *(110) (AdeRoyerDupre,France)* 3-8-13 GMosse ....s.h 3
2691[9] Bob's Ploy *(98) (RAkehurst)* 3-8-9 SWhitworth (btn approx 9l) 7

TOTE 31DM: 11DM 13DM 12DM (SF 140DM) OWNER Gestut Schlenderhan BRED Gestut Schlenderhan 8 Rn 2m 18.5 SF: -/-/-/-

3487a
PREIS DES CASINOS BADEN-BADEN (Listed) (3-Y.O) £16,461.00 (£6,584.00: £4,115.00) **1m** 5-35 (5-36)

3164[4] **Hoh Express** *(103) (IABalding)* 3-8-5 GHind ....— 1
2389a[5] Devil River Peek (USA) *(113) (BSchutz,Germany)* 3-9-2 THellier ....nk 2
Assia (IRE) *(98) (HJentzsch,Germany)* 3-8-1 PSchiergen ....s.h 3
3214[4] Hardy Dancer *(90) (GLMoore)* 3-8-5 SWhitworth (btn approx 6½l) 5

TOTE 43: 21DM 22DM 21DM (SF 349DM) OWNER Mr D. F. Allport (KINGSCLERE) BRED Mrs M. Upsdell 8 Rn 1m 38.42 SF: -/-/-/-

3463-HAYDOCK (L-H)
Saturday September 2nd (Good)
WEATHER: cloudy WIND: fresh against

3488
STANLEY LEISURE GROUP H'CAP (0-90) (3-Y.O+) (Class C)
£6,232.00 (£1,876.00: £908.00: £424.00)
7f 30y Stalls: Low GOING: 0.11 sec per fur (G) 2-00 (2-01)

3113[8] **South Rock (71)***(81) (JAGlover)* 3-8-5 PaulEddery(10) (mde all: clr 2f out: rdn & hld on wl) .— 1
3457[2] Cool Edge (IRE) **(72)***(81)*(Fav)*(MHTompkins)* 4-8-10 PRobinson(3) (hld up: 5th st: str chal fnl f: r.o) ....nk 2
2933[5] Band on the Run **(90)***(98) (BAMcMahon)* 8-10-0 GCarter(5) (hld up: hdwy 2f out: hrd rdn & r.o wl fnl f) ....½ 3

3209⁴ Khamseh **(83)**_(85) (JWWatts)_ 3-9-3b CAsmussen(11) (stdd s: hdwy 2f out: nt rch ldrs)............3 4
3419³ Legal Fiction **(66)**_(67) (MJohnston)_ 4-8-4 DeanMcKeown(6) (lw: chsd ldrs: 4th st: rdn wl over 1f out: grad wknd)............nk 5
3373² Proud Destiny **(81)**_(79) (MRStoute)_ 3-9-1 DHolland(12) (chsd ldrs: 2nd st: brought stands' side to r alone: rdn 2f out: one pce)............1¼ 6
3209³ Kabil **(88)**_(83) (HThomsonJones)_ 3-9-8 RHills(4) (lw: dwlt: hdwy on ins 3f out: hrd drvn over 1f out: sn btn)............1¼ 7
3212⁵ Persian Affair (IRE) **(64)**_(46) (DHaydnJones)_ 4-8-2 AMackay(1) (lw: a in rr)............6 8
2471² Midwich Cuckoo **(86)**_(67) (PTWalwyn)_ 3-9-6 PatEddery(8) (lw: hdwy 4f out: rdn 2f out: sn wknd)............nk 9
3222² Bold Angel **(71)**_(47) (MHEasterby)_ 8-8-9 MBirch(7) (nvr nr to chal: t.o)............2½ 10
3396¹³ Move Smartly (IRE) **(58)**_(28) (FHLee)_ 5-7-10v NCarlisle(2) (chsd ldrs: 6th st: rdn & wknd over 2f out: t.o)............2½ 11
3222⁸ Bassmaat (USA) **(74)**_(43) (WJHaggas)_ 4-8-12 LDettori(9) (lw: prom: 3rd st: drvn along & wknd 3f out: t.o)............nk 12

100/30 Cool Edge (IRE), **7/1** Proud Destiny, **15/2** Kabil, **8/1** Legal Fiction, Midwich Cuckoo, Bassmaat (USA), **17/2** Band on the Run, **9/1** Khamseh, **11/1** Bold Angel, **14/1** Persian Affair (IRE), **20/1** SOUTH ROCK, Move Smartly (IRE), CSF £84.21 CT £573.89 TOTE £54.00: £9.60 £1.80 £2.30 (£96.60) Trio £910.40 OWNER Mr B. H. Farr (WORKSOP) BRED Worksop Manor Stud Farm
12 Rn 1m 31.68 (4.38) SF: 49/53/70/53/39/47/51/18/35/19/-/15
WEIGHT FOR AGE 3yo-4lb

3489 CECIL FRAIL RATED STKS H'CAP (0-100) (3-Y.O+) (Class B)
£8,025.80 (£2,982.20: £1,441.10: £600.50: £250.25: £110.15)
1m 3f 200y Stalls: High GOING: 0.11 sec per fur (G) 2-30 (2-31)

2348⁶ **Inquisitor (USA) (99)**_(115+)_(Fav)_(JHMGosden)_ 3-8-11 PatEddery(9) (lw: hld up: 4th st: led wl over 2f out: sn clr: hld on nr fin)............— 1
3156* Better Offer (IRE) **(92)**_(107) (GHarwood)_ 3-8-4 MPerrett(4) (lw: hld up & bhd: 8th st: hdwy over 2f out: rdn & edgd lft fnl f: r.o wl towards fin)............¾ 2
3162⁶ Shadow Leader **(86)**_(86) (DJSffrenchDavis)_ 4-8-4 (3) DRMcCabe(8) (bhd: 9th st: effrt & rdn over 2f out: styd on)............11 3
3162¹⁶ Tethys (USA) **(86)**_(84) (JLEyre)_ 4-8-7 RLappin(2) (lw: led tl hdd over 3f out: rdn & outpcd bel dist)............1½ 4
1794⁵ Johns Act (USA) **(86)**_(74) (DHaydnJones)_ 5-8-7 AMackay(5) (chsd ldrs: 2nd st: rdn 2f out: sn outpcd)............8 5
1768² Arctic Thunder (USA) **(94)**_(80) (LadyHerries)_ 4-9-1 KDarley(6) (b: hld up: 6th st: effrt 3f out: no imp)............1¼ 6
3162¹⁸ Wishing (USA) **(94)**_(74) (RAkehurst)_ 4-9-1 LDettori(7) (lw: sn pushed along: 7th st: nvr nr ldrs)4 7
735² Linpac West **(100)**_(70) (CWCElsey)_ 9-9-7 JCarroll(3) (bit bkwd: hld up in tch: 5th st: rdn & wknd over 2f out)............8 8
2274¹⁰ Mokhtar (IRE) **(88)**_(24) (JLDunlop)_ 4-8-9 RHills(1) (prom: 3rd st: slt ld over 3f out: sn hdd & wknd: eased whn btn: t.o)............25 9
LONG HANDICAP Johns Act (USA) 7-8 Shadow Leader 8-2 Tethys (USA) 8-6

2/1 INQUISITOR (USA), **3/1** Arctic Thunder (USA), **11/2** Wishing (USA), **7/1** Better Offer (IRE), **10/1** Shadow Leader, **14/1** Linpac West, Tethys (USA), Mokhtar (IRE), **50/1** Johns Act (USA), CSF £15.60 CT £103.56 TOTE £2.90: £1.60 £1.80 £2.40 (£9.70) Trio £27.60 OWNER Mr K. Abdullah (NEWMARKET) BRED Juddmonte Farms 9 Rn 2m 32.25 (4.25) SF: 76/68/56/54/44/50/44/40/-
WEIGHT FOR AGE 3yo-9lb
OFFICIAL EXPLANATION Mokhtar (IRE): finished distressed.

3490 ST ANNES CONDITIONS STKS (2-Y.O) (Class B) £6,663.37
(£2,416.50: £1,170.75: £491.25: £208.13)
1m 30y Stalls: Low GOING: 0.11 sec per fur (G) 3-00 (3-01)

2926* **Beauchamp King** _(94+) (JLDunlop)_ 2-8-10 LDettori(5) (sn chsng ldr: 2nd st: led over 2f out: sn clr: styd on strly)............— 1
3273³ Matiya (IRE) **(88)**_(84) (BHanbury)_ 2-8-7 CAsmussen(4) (lw: hld up in rr: 5th st: hdwy over 2f out: kpt on fnl f: no ch w wnr)............3½ 2
3155* Brilliant Red _(88)_(Fav)_(PFICole)_ 2-8-12 PatEddery(2) (lw: led over 5f: hrd rdn wl over 1f out: sn outpcd)............½ 3
3068⁶ Jack Jennings **(95)**_(74) (BAMcMahon)_ 2-8-12 GCarter(3) (lw: dwlt: hld up: 4th st: effrt & rdn over 2f out: no imp)............7 4
3158* Dublin River (USA) _(76) (HThomsonJones)_ 2-9-0 RHills(1) (chsd ldng pair: 3rd st: rdn along over 2f out: sn btn)............s.h 5

9/4 Brilliant Red, **11/4** Matiya (IRE), **3/1** Dublin River (USA), **7/2** BEAUCHAMP KING, **9/1** Jack Jennings, CSF £12.82 TOTE £3.70: £1.70 £2.00 (£9.10) OWNER Mr E. Penser (ARUNDEL) BRED E. Penser 5 Rn
1m 46.24 (5.84) SF: 45/35/39/25/27

3491

HAYDOCK PARK SPRINT CUP STKS (Gp 1) (3-Y.O+) (Class A)
£72,160.00 (£26,440.00: £12,470.00: £4,850.00: £1,675.00:£405.00)
6f Stalls: High GOING minus 0.01 sec per fur (G) 3-30 (3-30)

3042a* **Cherokee Rose (IRE)** *(121+) (JEHammond,France)* 4-8-11 CAsmussen(4) (lw: hld up gng wl: n.m.r bel dist: qcknd to ld wl ins fnl f: impressive) — **1**
3446* Branston Abby (IRE) **(105)***(117) (MJohnston)* 6-8-11 DHolland(3) (outpcd & drvn along early: hdwy ½-wy: led ins fnl f: sn hdd: one pce) 1½ **2**
2368⁴ Owington **(120)***(118) (GWragg)* 4-9-0 PaulEddery(2) (lw: hld up & bhd: gd hdwy 2f out: rdn to ld ins fnl f: sn hdd: unable qckn) ¾ **3**
2368* Lake Coniston (IRE) **(130)***(111)*(Fav)*(GLewis)* 4-9-0 PatEddery(7) (lw: w ldrs: pushed along over 2f out: slt ld over 1f out tl ins fnl f: no ex) 2½ **4**
3187⁶ Mind Games **(121)***(90) (JBerry)* 3-8-11 JCarroll(5) (slt ld whn hdd & outpcd over 1f out) 8 **5**
3582a² Lavinia Fontana (IRE) **(113)***(74) (JLDunlop)* 6-8-11 LDettori(6) (gd spd over 3f: wknd fnl 2f) 5 **6**

1/3 Lake Coniston (IRE), **5/1** CHEROKEE ROSE (IRE), **10/1** Lavinia Fontana (IRE), **11/1** Owington, **14/1** Branston Abby (IRE) (10/1-16/1), **20/1** Mind Games, CSF £53.66 TOTE £6.20: £2.10 £4.20 (£52.80) OWNER Sheikh Mohammed BRED Sheikh Mohammed 6 Rn
1m 13.74 (2.04) SF: 66/62/63/56/32/19
WEIGHT FOR AGE 3yo-3lb

OFFICIAL EXPLANATION Lake Coniston (IRE): the jockey stated that the colt was never going well.

3492

OLLERTON H'CAP (0-80) (3-Y.O+) (Class D) £4,820.25
(£1,452.00: £703.50: £329.25)
6f Stalls: High GOING minus 0.01 sec per fur (G) 4-00 (4-03)

3219⁴ **Double Bounce (70)***(80)*(Fav)*(PJMakin)* 5-9-8 DHolland(18) (b: lw: hld up in tch: shkn up to ld ins fnl f: sn clr) — **1**
1487¹⁶ Sue Me (IRE) **(70)***(75) (WRMuir)* 3-9-5 CAsmussen(11) (hdwy to ld over 1f out: hdd & unable qckn ins fnl f) 2 **2**
3230¹⁰ Rossini Blue **(71)***(69) (MrsJRRamsden)* 4-9-9 KFallon(7) (hdwy over 1f out: nrst fin) 2½ **3**
2067⁴ Intiaash (IRE) **(72)***(70) (PTWalwyn)* 3-9-7 RHills(15) (chsd ldrs: ev ch over 1f out: unable qckn fnl f) s.h **4**
2746* Miss Aragon **(58)***(53) (MissLCSiddall)* 7-8-10 NCarlisle(8) (lw: hld up: hdwy over 1f out: nvr nrr) 1 **5**
2318³ Charlie Sillett **(70)***(62)*(Fav)*(BWHills)* 3-9-5 PatEddery(16) (lw: chsd ldrs: rdn & effrt over 1f out: nt pce to chal) 1¼ **6**
3109* Dawalib (USA) **(68)***(56) (DHaydnJones)* 5-9-6 LDettori(1) (lw: r.o appr fnl f: nvr nrr) 1½ **7**
3418⁵ Cumbrian Waltzer **(73)***(59) (MHEasterby)* 10-9-11 MBirch(13) (nvr trbld ldrs) ¾ **8**
3376⁸ Magic Orb **(73)***(56) (JLHarris)* 5-9-11 PaulEddery(19) (prom: ev ch 2f out: wknd appr fnl f) 1¼ **9**
3242² Souperficial **(62)***(44) (JAGlover)* 4-9-0v KDarley(5) (chsd ldrs: led wl over 1f out: sn hdd: outpcd fnl f) s.h **10**
3145¹⁶ Craigie Boy **(56)***(34) (NBycroft)* 5-8-8b GHind(9) (hld up: effrt 2f out: rdn & outpcd appr fnl f) 1¾ **11**
3179⁶ Petomi **(62)***(39) (SirMarkPrescott)* 3-8-11 CNutter(12) (nvr nr to chal) nk **12**
3467²⁰ Gondo **(44)***(19) (EJAlston)* 8-7-10 AMackay(20) (outpcd) ¾ **13**
3418² Colway Rake **(69)***(42) (JWWatts)* 4-9-7b NConnorton(4) (lw: a outpcd) ¾ **14**
3399³ Louisville Belle (IRE) **(55)***(28) (MDIUsher)* 6-8-7 TSprake(3) (b: lw: spd on outside 4f) s.h **15**
3275¹¹ Indiahra **(45)***(18) (RHollinshead)* 4-7-11 AGarth(2) (chsd ldr: rdn 2f out: sn lost tch) s.h **16**
3319⁸ Here Comes Risky **(73)***(44) (MJohnston)* 3-9-8 JCarroll(6) (outpcd) ¾ **17**
2425⁸ Stand Tall **(56)***(25) (CWThornton)* 3-8-5 DeanMcKeown(10) (lw: led tl hdd & wknd wl over 1f out) ½ **18**
3341* Sir Tasker **(59)***(24) (JLHarris)* 7-8-11 PRobinson(14) (w ldr over 3f: sn lost tch) 1¾ **19**
2700⁵ Boursin (IRE) **(65)***(23) (PCalver)* 6-9-3 DaleGibson(17) (t: spd over 3f: sn wknd) 2½ **20**

11/2 DOUBLE BOUNCE, Charlie Sillett, **7/1** Dawalib (USA), **9/1** Colway Rake, **10/1** Miss Aragon, **11/1** Sir Tasker, **12/1** Here Comes Risky, **14/1** Rossini Blue, Souperficial, **16/1** Intiaash (IRE), Cumbrian Waltzer, Petomi, **20/1** Gondo, Craigie Boy, Boursin (IRE), Magic Orb, Sue Me (IRE), **25/1** Stand Tall, Indiahra, Louisville Belle (IRE), CSF £113.77 CT £1,383.51 TOTE £6.10: £2.10 £5.10 £4.20 £3.50 (£98.50) Trio £2,515.80 OWNER Mrs P. Scott-Dunn (MARLBOROUGH) BRED Mrs P. Scott-Dunn 20 Rn
1m 14.79 (3.09) SF: 62/54/51/49/35/41/38/41/38/26/16/18/1/24/10/-/23/4/6/5
WEIGHT FOR AGE 3yo-3lb

3493 SPEKE LIMITED STKS (0-65) (3-Y.O+) (Class F) £3,272.00 (£986.00: £478.00: £224.00)
1m 30y Stalls: Low GOING: 0.11 sec per fur (G) 4-30 (4-35)

3393[4] **Gymcrak Flyer (62)***(72) (GHolmes)* 4-8-11 KFallon(15) (lw: hld up: hdwy 2f out: led ins fnl f: hrd rdn: jst hld on) — 1
3429[2] Eden's Star (IRE) **(67)***(77) (MHTompkins)* 3-8-11 PRobinson(14) (lw: led after 1f tl ins fnl f: rallied u.p cl home) s.h 2
3264[W] Chief of Staff **(63)***(73) (JPearce)* 6-9-2 GBardwell(5) (stdd s: hdwy 2f out: rdn & kpt on wl fnl f) 2 3
3440[9] Zingibar **(65)***(71) (BWHills)* 3-8-9 DHolland(12) (hdwy over 2f out: rdn & kpt on wl ins fnl f) hd 4
3222[16] Kummel King **(59)***(68) (EJAlston)* 7-8-9 (5) LNewton(4) (led 1f: 3rd st: rdn bel dist: one pce) 1¼ 5
3061[5] Beauman **(62)***(68) (PDEvans)* 5-9-0 GHind(6) (lw: prom: 4th st: rdn 2f out: kpt on one pce) s.h 6
3242[10] Warning Shot **(65)***(61) (MartynMeade)* 3-8-9 VSlattery(13) (rdn & effrt 3f out: nvr rchd ldrs) 3½ 7
3270[*] Doonyasha **(60)***(52)*(Fav)*(JLDunlop)* 3-8-6 PatEddery(10) (hld up: 6th st: rdn over 3f out: eased whn btn appr fnl f) 3½ 8
3291[10] Educated Pet **(43)***(53) (BPreece)* 6-8-11v(3) SDrowne(3) (nvr plcd to chal) ¾ 9
2499[2] Hand of Straw (IRE) **(64)***(49) (JWWatts)* 3-8-9 NConnorton(7) (mid div tl wknd over 2f out) 2 10
2698[9] Reed My Lips (IRE) **(34)***(49) (BPJBaugh)* 4-8-7 (7) IonaWands(8) (a bhd) nk 11
2733[4] Northern Chief **(32)***(48) (MissJFCraze)* 5-9-0 SWebster(2) (a in rr) hd 12
2620[5] Roseate Lodge **(58)***(49) (NBycroft)* 9-8-13 (3) DRMcCabe(11) (b: a in rr) ¾ 13
2484[11] Golden Chip (IRE) **(62)***(44) (JLEyre)* 7-9-0 GCarter(9) (prom: 2nd st: wknd wl over 2f out) 1½ 14
Miss Springtime **(60)***(38) (JJO'Neill)* 4-8-9 JCarroll(1) (bit bkwd: chsd ldrs: 5th st: wknd 3f out) nk 15

3/1 Doonyasha, **5/1** Eden's Star (IRE), **13/2** GYMCRAK FLYER, **8/1** Beauman (op 12/1), **9/1** Zingibar, **11/1** Hand of Straw (IRE) (8/1-12/1), Kummel King, **14/1** Miss Springtime, **16/1** Warning Shot, Golden Chip (IRE), **20/1** Chief of Staff, Roseate Lodge, **25/1** Reed My Lips (IRE), **33/1** Educated Pet, Northern Chief, CSF £38.86 TOTE £6.60: £2.00 £1.90 £6.60 (£13.80) Trio £50.30 OWNER The Gymcrak Thoroughbred Racing Club (PICKERING) BRED D. G. Mason 15 Rn

1m 46.69 (6.29) SF: 42/42/43/36/38/38/26/17/23/14/19/18/19/14/8

WEIGHT FOR AGE 3yo-5lb

3494 E.B.F. ALTRINCHAM MAIDEN STKS (2-Y.O) (Class D) £4,445.00 (£1,340.00: £650.00: £305.00)
7f 30y Stalls: Low GOING: 0.11 sec per fur (G) 5-00 (5-02)

2573[3] **Kings Witness (USA)** *(76) (WJHaggas)* 2-9-0 KDarley(9) (lw: hld up: 6th st: hdwy 2f out: rdn to ld ins fnl f: r.o) — 1
3174[4] Danesman (IRE) *(73)*(Fav)*(JHMGosden)* 2-9-0 LDettori(1) (sn led: rdn & hdd ins fnl f: no ex) 1½ 2
Van Gurp *(68) (BAMcMahon)* 2-9-0 GCarter(8) (lt-f: hld up: hdwy 2f out: rdn & kpt on ins fnl f) 2 3
1726[8] Stellar Line (USA) *(65) (BWHills)* 2-9-0 PatEddery(2) (hld up in tch: 4th st: ev ch wl over 1f out: no ex fnl f) 1¼ 4
Danish Circus (IRE) *(63) (MJHeaton-Ellis)* 2-9-0 DHolland(11) (unf: bit bkwd: prom: 3rd st: ev ch 2f out: wknd fnl f) 1¼ 5
Firle Phantasy *(61) (PCalver)* 2-9-0 DaleGibson(4) (w'like: nvr nr to chal) ¾ 6
2912[5] Majdak Jereeb (IRE) *(58) (MajorWRHern)* 2-9-0 PaulEddery(3) (bit bkwd: chsd ldrs: 5th st: wknd 2f out) 1½ 7
Alfahaal (IRE) *(51) (HThomsonJones)* 2-9-0 RHills(12) (w'like: str: bkwd: dwlt: hdwy over 2f out: sn rdn: eased whn btn ins fnl f) 3 8
Burnt Offering *(37) (CEBrittain)* 2-9-0 GHind(6) (lt-f: hdwy on ins over 3f out: nvr trbld ldrs) 6 9
3157[9] Cowboy Dreams (IRE) *(13) (MHTompkins)* 2-9-0 PRobinson(10) (a bhd: t.o) 11 10
Three Weeks *(11) (WRMuir)* 2-9-0 JCarroll(5) (lt-f: prom: 2nd st: jnd ldr 3f out: wknd wl over 1f out: t.o) ¾ 11

5/4 Danesman (IRE) (op 2/1), **11/4** KINGS WITNESS (USA), **9/2** Majdak Jereeb (IRE) (3/1-5/1), **5/1** Alfahaal (IRE), **7/1** Stellar Line (USA), **12/1** Van Gurp, **16/1** Danish Circus (IRE), **20/1** Burnt Offering, **25/1** Three Weeks, **33/1** Cowboy Dreams (IRE), Firle Phantasy, CSF £8.07 TOTE £4.40: £1.60 £1.20 £4.10 (£3.30) Trio £87.70 OWNER Highclere Thoroughbred Racing Ltd (NEWMARKET) BRED T. Holmes, M. Levy & R. Trontz 11 Rn

1m 33.71 (6.41) SF: 34/31/26/23/21/19/16/9/-/-/-

T/Jkpt: Not won; £14,679.94 to 4/9/95. T/Plpt: £1,245.20 (28.73 Tckts). T/Qdpt: £239.10 (0.8 Tckts). Pool of £64.63 to 4/9/95. IM

3470-KEMPTON (R-H)
Saturday September 2nd (Good)
WEATHER: overcast WIND: almost nil

3495 E.B.F. ARION MAIDEN STKS (2-Y.O F) (Class D) £3,761.25 (£1,140.00: £557.50: £266.25) **6f** Stalls: High GOING minus 0.09 sec per fur (G) 2-10 (2-13)

3133[4] **Prima Volta** *(86) (RHannon)* 2-8-11 RHughes(1) (hdwy over 2f out: hrd rdn over 1f out: led nr fin)........— 1
Obsessive (USA) *(85+) (MRStoute)* 2-8-11 WRSwinburn(3) (unf: a.p: led over 1f out: rdn fnl f: hdd nr fin)........nk 2
3133[3] Star And Garter *(77)*(Fav)*(GWragg)* 2-8-11 MHills(12) (lw: a.p: rdn over 2f out: r.o one pce) ..3 3
Petit Point (IRE) *(77) (RHannon)* 2-8-6 (5) DaneO'Neill(14) (neat: hdwy over 2f out: ev ch over 1f out: one pce)........s.h 4
Mighty Phantom (USA) *(74) (JWHills)* 2-8-11 BThomson(2) (neat: bit bkwd: rdn over 2f out: hdwy over 1f out: r.o: bttr for r)........1 5
Beauchamp Kate *(66) (HCandy)* 2-8-11 WNewnes(9) (b.hind: unf: hdwy over 1f out: nvr nrr) .3 6
3371[9] Ecstatic Madam (IRE) *(62) (BWHills)* 2-8-6 (5) JDSmith(7) (rdn over 2f out: nvr nr to chal) 1½ 7
3379[2] Manderella *(62) (JAkehurst)* 2-8-11 BDoyle(6) (b.off hind: hld up: rdn over 2f out: sn wknd).s.h 8
Wildwood Flower *(62) (RHannon)* 2-8-11 SRaymont(16) (unf: bit bkwd: a.p: led over 2f out tl over 1f out: sn wknd)........hd 9
3069[16] Fiddes (IRE) *(51) (JLDunlop)* 2-8-11 WCarson(11) (hdwy over 2f out: wknd over 1f out).........4 10
3133[6] Petite Heritiere *(50) (MJRyan)* 2-8-11 AClark(15) (a.p: led over 3f out tl over 2f out: wknd wl over 1f out)........½ 11
Astra Martin *(39) (PGMurphy)* 2-8-4 (7) RWaterfield(10) (w'like: bit bkwd: s.s: a bhd) 4 12
669[6] Lillibella *(36) (IABalding)* 2-8-11 WRyan(13) (led tl hung lft & hdd over 3f out: wknd over 2f out)........1¼ 13
Ostia *(25) (MrsJCecil)* 2-8-11 EGuest(8) (b.off hind: leggy: unf: prom 3f)........4 14
On The Home Run *(16) (JRJenkins)* 2-8-11 JWilliams(5) (w'like: bkwd: a bhd)........3½ 15
2876[10] Sweet Amoret *(RCSpicer)* 2-8-11 JQuinn(4) (Withdrawn not under Starter's orders: ref to go to s)........ W

2/1 Star And Garter (6/4-5/2), **11/2** Obsessive (USA) (4/1-6/1), **7/1** PRIMA VOLTA (4/1-8/1), Manderella, **8/1** Lillibella, **10/1** Ostia (12/1-8/1), **12/1** Petit Point (IRE) (8/1-14/1), **16/1** Ecstatic Madam (IRE), Fiddes (IRE), **25/1** Beauchamp Kate, Mighty Phantom (USA), Petite Heritiere, **33/1** Wildwood Flower, **50/1** Astra Martin, On The Home Run, **66/1** Sweet Amoret, CSF £45.46 TOTE £10.60: £2.80 £2.70 £1.40 (£44.40) Trio £34.00 OWNER The Boardroom Syndicate (MARLBOROUGH) BRED Bearstone Stud 15 Rn 1m 15.38 (4.08) SF: 31/30/22/22/19/11/7/7/7/-/-/-/-/-/-

3496 TEDDINGTON CONDITIONS STKS (3-Y.O+ F & M) (Class C) £5,454.00 (£1,764.00: £862.00) **1m 4f** Stalls: High GOING minus 0.09 sec (G) 2-40 (2-40)

2614[2] **Tinashaan (IRE) (93)***(99)*(Fav)*(JRFanshawe)* 3-8-11 TQuinn(2) (lw: chsd ldr: led 3f out: sn clr: unchal)........— 1
3229[2] Quivira **(77)***(76) (TTClement)* 4-9-3 EGuest(1) (lw: hdwy over 4f out: 3rd st: chsd wnr over 2f out: no imp)........15 2
2883* Anne D'Autriche (IRE) *(JHMGosden)* 3-8-11 WRSwinburn(3) (lw: led 9f: eased whn btn over 2f out: t.o)........dist 3

8/15 TINASHAAN (IRE), **5/2** Anne D'Autriche (IRE) (op 13/8), **7/1** Quivira (5/1-8/1), CSF £3.42 TOTE £1.60 (£3.20) OWNER Mrs James McAllister (NEWMARKET) BRED Chippenham Lodge Stud 3 Rn 2m 41.6 (11.40) SF: 14/-/-
WEIGHT FOR AGE 3yo-9lb

OFFICIAL EXPLANATION **Anne D'Autriche (IRE): the trainer's representative reported that the filly had finished slightly distressed.**

3497 GEOFFREY HAMLYN H'CAP (0-80) (3-Y.O) (Class D) £4,416.00 (£1,338.00: £483.00: £483.00) **1m (Jubilee)** Stalls: High GOING: 0.07 sec (G) 3-10 (3-11)

3408[2] **Concer Un (72)***(84)*(Fav)*(SCWilliams)* 3-9-1 TQuinn(10) (lw: 2nd st: led over 2f out: rdn out)........— 1
3363[2] Sharpical **(69)***(76) (BJMeehan)* 3-8-12 RHughes(8) (hdwy over 3f out: 4th st: ev ch over 1f out: unable qckn)........2½ 2
2941[3] Nordinex (IRE) **(78)***(83) (RWArmstrong)* 3-9-7 MHills(14) (lw: 5th st: ev ch over 2f out: hrd rdn over 1f out: one pce)........1 3
3026[5] Atlaal (USA) **(73)***(78) (HThomsonJones)* 3-9-2 WCarson(15) (led over 5f: one pce)..............d.h 3

2103[7] My Gina **(72)***(74) (MRStoute)* 3-9-1 WRSwinburn(3) (lw: hdwy over 2f out: eased whn btn fnl f) 1¾ 5
614[11] Cyrus the Great (IRE) **(73)***(74) (MBell)* 3-9-2 MFenton(5) (lw: nvr nr to chal) ....s.h 6
3429[3] Tomal **(50)***(43) (RIngram)* 3-7-7b NAdams(12) (gd hdwy 4f out: rn wd st: wknd 2f out) 4 7
2654[3] Verde Luna **(69)***(50) (MHTompkins)* 3-8-12 WRyan(11) (lw: hdwy over 2f out: sn wknd)....6 8
3095[4] Norsong **(55)***(36) (RAkehurst)* 3-7-12 FNorton(9) (hdwy over 2f out: sn wknd)....s.h 9
3239[5] Sherrington **(60)***(37) (ACStewart)* 3-8-3 RPrice(2) (hld up: rdn over 3f out: sn wknd)....2 10
3175[6] Sylvandra **(70)***(46) (PGMurphy)* 3-8-13 JWilliams(7) (3rd st: wknd over 2f out)....¾ 11
3214[11] Elpidos **(75)***(48) (CEBrittain)* 3-9-4 BDoyle(13) (prom over 4f)....1¼ 12
3383[5] Mo's Star **(61)***(34) (SDow)* 3-7-11 (7) ADaly(4) (lw: 6th st: wknd over 2f out) ....nk 13
2537[6] Greenwich Again **(67)***(20) (TGMills)* 3-8-10 StephenDavies(6) (prom over 3f) 10 14
3377[3] Victory Team (IRE) **(70)***(11) (JRFanshawe)* 3-8-13 BThomson(1) (prom 5f) 6 15

LONG HANDICAP Tomal 7-6

6/1 CONCER UN, **8/1** Nordinex (IRE), **9/1** Norsong, Atlaal (USA), Elpidos, **10/1** My Gina, **11/1** Sherrington (7/1-12/1), Verde Luna, Sharpical, **14/1** Sylvandra, Victory Team (IRE), **20/1** Tomal, Greenwich Again, Mo's Star, **33/1** Cyrus the Great (IRE), CSF £63.15 CT £242.68 CU, S & N, £269.56 CU, S & A TOTE £5.00: £2.30 £3.40 £1.30 N £1.10 A (£17.70) Trio £19.30 CU,S & N, £39.00 CU, S & A OWNER Miss L. J. Ward (NEWMARKET) BRED Lloyd Bros 15 Rn

1m 43.18 (6.18) SF: 42/34/41/36/32/32/1/8/-/-/4/6/-/-/-

3498

BONUSPRINT SEPTEMBER STKS (Gp 3) (3-Y.O+) (Class A) £22,380.00 (£8,394.00: £4,047.00: £1,779.00)
1m 3f 30y Stalls: High GOING minus 0.09 sec per fur (G) 3-40 (3-42)

3088[4] **Burooj (109)***(116) (DMorley)* 5-9-0 BThomson(7) (lw: 3rd st: led 2f out: edgd rt fnl f: drvn out) ....— 1
3070[2] Commoner (USA) **(105)***(116) (RHannon)* 3-8-8 ow2 RHughes(2) (lw: led 1f: led 8f out tl over 6f out: 4th st: rdn over 2f out: r.o wl ins fnl f) ....s.h 2
3070* Wayne County (IRE) **(108)***(110) (RAkehurst)* 5-9-0 SWhitworth(1) (lw: led over 6f out to 2f out: wknd ins fnl f) 4 3
3323a[2] Warning Shadows (IRE) **(111)***(107) (CEBrittain)* 3-8-3 BDoyle(3) (2nd st: ev ch 2f out: wknd over 1f out)....½ 4
3144[4] Ihtiram (IRE) **(110)***(81) (JLDunlop)* 3-8-6 WCarson(5) (lw: 5th st: wknd over 2f out) 20 5
3381* Desert Shot **(110)***(67) (MRStoute)* 5-9-3 WRSwinburn(6) (poor 6th st: a bhd) 12 6
3088[2] Midnight Legend **(114)** (Fav)*(LMCumani)* 4-9-0 TQuinn(8) (lw: led 10f out to 8f out: wknd over 4f out: t.o whn virtually p.u fnl 3f)....dist 7

9/4 Midnight Legend (6/4-5/2), **7/2** Warning Shadows (IRE), **5/1** Desert Shot, **13/2** Wayne County (IRE), **15/2** Ihtiram (IRE), **8/1** BUROOJ (6/1-9/1), **25/1** Commoner (USA), CSF £117.70 TOTE £9.50: £2.50 £6.80 (£89.90) OWNER Mr Hamdan Al Maktoum (NEWMARKET) BRED Shadwell Estate Company Limited 7 Rn 2m 23.27 (5.67) SF: 50/42/44/33/7/1/-

WEIGHT FOR AGE 3yo-8lb

STEWARDS' ENQUIRY Obj. to Burooj by Hughes overruled.

OFFICIAL EXPLANATION: Midnight Legend & Desert Shot were unsuited by the rain-softened ground.

3499

BONUSPRINT SIRENIA STKS (Listed) (2-Y.O) (Class A) £10,560.00 (£3,180.00: £1,540.00: £720.00)
6f Stalls: High GOING minus 0.09 sec per fur (G) 4-10 (4-17)

3165[2] **Rambling Bear (100)***(97) (MBlanshard)* 2-8-11 StephenDavies(4) (lw: mde virtually all: r.o wl) ....— 1
2991[2] Eastern Prophets **(95)***(97) (GLewis)* 2-8-11 SWhitworth(5) (a.p: j.path over 3f out: hrd rdn over 1f out: r.o wl ins fnl f)....s.h 2
3273* Defined Feature (IRE) **(94)***(89)*(Fav)*(MRStoute)* 2-8-6 MHills(6) (lw: a.p: hrd rdn over 1f out: unable qckn)....1¼ 3
2767[5] Abundant *(88) (BGubby)* 2-8-11v RHughes(3) (lw: dwlt: hdwy 2f out: hrd rdn over 1f out: r.o one pce) 2 4
3210* Tropical Dance (USA) **(99)***(59) (MrsJCecil)* 2-8-6 BThomson(2) (bhd fnl 2f) 9 5
3220[2] Mazeed (IRE) **(100)***(64)*(Fav)*(HThomsonJones)* 2-8-11 WCarson(1) (lw: rdn over 4f out: bhd fnl 2f)....s.h 6

3/1 Defined Feature (IRE), Mazeed (IRE), **7/2** RAMBLING BEAR (5/2-4/1), Tropical Dance (USA), **6/1** Eastern Prophets, **33/1** Abundant, CSF £21.20 TOTE £4.80: £1.80 £3.30 (£21.30) OWNER Mrs Michael Hill (UPPER LAMBOURN) BRED E. A. Badger 6 Rn

1m 13.53 (2.23) SF: 57/57/49/48/19/24

STEWARDS' ENQUIRY Obj. to Rambling Bear by Whitworth overruled.

3500 SPELTHORNE H'CAP (0-90) (3-Y.O+) (Class C) £7,132.50 (£2,160.00: £1,055.00: £502.50) **1m 4f** Stalls: High GOING minus 0.09 sec per fur (G) 4-40 (4-40)

3374[5] **Persian Elite (IRE) (78)***(90) (PFICole)* 4-9-6 TQuinn(1) (lw: mde virtually all: c stands' side st: hrd rdn over 1f out: r.o wl)......— 1
3066[7] State Law **(88)***(97) (GHarwood)* 3-9-7 AClark(3) (lw: c stands' side st: hdwy over 2f out: hrd rdn & swtchd rt over 1f out: unable qckn)......2½ 2
3106[2] Country Star (IRE) **(82)***(88) (HCandy)* 4-9-10 WNewnes(4) (lw: 5th & c stands' side st: hrd rdn over 1f out: one pce)......1¾ 3
3107[2] Artic Courier **(81)***(86) (DJSCosgrove)* 4-9-4 (5) DGibbs(10) (lw: hdwy over 4f out: 5th st: ev ch over 1f out: one pce)......1¼ 4
2768[9] Benfleet **(82)***(86) (RWArmstrong)* 4-9-10 RPrice(2) (lw: rdn & hdwy over 2f out: one pce)......nk 5
3224* Danesrath (IRE) **(76)***(80)*(Fav)*(ACStewart)* 3-8-9 BThomson(5) (nvr nr to chal)......nk 6
3130[3] Courbaril **(62)***(62) (SDow)* 3-7-4 (5)ow2 MBaird(7) (lw: hdwy over 3f out: 6th st: wknd over 1f out)......1¼ 7
3349* Loki (IRE) **(79)***(75) (GLewis)* 7-9-2 (5) MHenry(8) (b: lw: hld up: rdn over 2f out: wknd wl over 1f out)......5 8
2829[3] Exhibit Air (IRE) **(65)***(54) (RAkehurst)* 5-8-4 (3) SSanders(9) (lw: 2nd st: wknd wl over 1f out)...5 9
1813* Yet Again **(62)***(47) (BHanbury)* 3-7-9 JQuinn(6) (lw: hdwy over 3f out: wknd over 2f out)......3 10
3277[5] Big Pat **(71)***(53) (KMcAuliffe)* 6-8-8 (5) DaneO'Neill(11) (4th st: wknd over 2f out)......2½ 11

5/1 Danesrath (IRE), **11/2** Big Pat, **6/1** Country Star (IRE), **7/1** State Law, **8/1** Exhibit Air (IRE), Benfleet, **9/1** Loki (IRE), **10/1** Yet Again, **11/1** Artic Courier (8/1-12/1), **12/1** Courbaril, PERSIAN ELITE (IRE) (op 8/1), CSF £88.81 CT £513.03 TOTE £16.20: £3.60 £2.20 £2.20 (£54.10) Trio £149.30 OWNER Elite Racing Club (WHATCOMBE) BRED Mrs M. E. Farrell 11 Rn
2m 35.56 (5.36) SF: 61/59/59/57/57/42/24/46/25/9/24
WEIGHT FOR AGE 3yo-9lb

3501 GREBE APPRENTICE H'CAP (0-70) (3-Y.O+) (Class E) £3,598.75 (£1,090.00: £532.50: £253.75) **1m 2f** Stalls: High GOING minus 0.09 sec (G) 5-10 (5-10)

3258[2] **Lady Sabina (38)***(50) (WJMusson)* 5-7-9 (3) JWilkinson(3) (lw: hdwy over 4f out: 3rd st: led over 2f out: r.o wl)......— 1
2658[6] Myfontaine **(61)***(70) (KTIvory)* 8-9-4 (3) CScally(4) (hdwy over 1f out: r.o ins fnl f)......1¾ 2
3173[3] Aldwick Colonnade **(37)***(41) (MDIUsher)* 8-7-11 CAdamson(7) (hdwy over 3f out: 4th st: unable qckn fnl 2f)......3½ 3
3455[3] Kestrel Forboxes (IRE) **(63)***(62)*(Fav)*(CMcCready,Jersey)* 7-9-4 (5) DSweeney(2) (led over 7f: wknd fnl f)......3 4
2776[7] Cannizaro (IRE) **(50)***(34) (RJRWilliams)* 3-8-3 DaneO'Neill(9) (nvr nr to chal)......9 5
3154[7] Hadabet **(66)***(50) (MissJacquelineDoyle)* 3-9-5 GMitchell(1) (lw: prom over 6f)......s.h 6
2520[5] Shining Dancer **(65)***(48) (SDow)* 3-9-4 ADaly(8) (hld up: rdn 3f out: sn wknd)......1 7
3079[4] Myjinka **(33)***(13) (JO'Donoghue)* 5-7-2b(5) PDoe(10) (hdwy 3f out: 6th st: wknd over 2f out) ..1¾ 8
1908[6] Caerle Lad (IRE) **(65)***(43) (GHarwood)* 4-9-6 (5) GayeHarwood(5) (2nd st: wknd over 2f out).1½ 9
3402[U] Jubilee Line **(33)***(8) (NEBerry)* 5-7-2 (5) JBramhill(6) (lw: hdwy over 3f out: 5th st: wknd over 2f out)......1¾ 10

LONG HANDICAP Myjinka 7-0 Jubilee Line 7-4

3/1 Kestrel Forboxes (IRE), **4/1** LADY SABINA, **5/1** Myfontaine, **7/1** Hadabet (5/1-8/1), **8/1** Aldwick Colonnade, **10/1** Caerle Lad (IRE), **14/1** Cannizaro (IRE), Shining Dancer, **33/1** Myjinka, Jubilee Line, CSF £21.95 CT £134.20 TOTE £4.00: £1.90 £1.50 £2.70 (£10.70) Trio £59.50 OWNER Mr W.J. Musson (NEWMARKET) BRED E. A. Badger 10 Rn 2m 8.53 (6.03) SF: 27/47/18/39/4/20/18/-/20/-
WEIGHT FOR AGE 3yo-7lb

T/Plpt: £1,069.60 (23.41 Tckts). T/Qdpt: £170.20 (0.25 Tckts). AK

3352-THIRSK (L-H)
Saturday September 2nd (Good to firm)
WEATHER: overcast WIND: slt half bhd

3502 LLOYDS PRIVATE BANKING MAIDEN AUCTION STKS (2-Y.O) (Class F) £3,299.30 (£914.80: £437.90)
7f Stalls: Low GOING minus 0.17 sec per fur (GF) 2-15 (2-19)

3149[2] **Silver Welcome (62)***(66) (MHEasterby)* 2-8-7 SMaloney(15) (mde most: edgd rt & kpt on wl fnl f)......— 1
2971[5] Yuppy Girl (IRE) **(60)***(56) (CaptJWilson)* 2-7-9 (7)ow4 FLynch(14) (in tch: gd hdwy to disp ld 1f out: no ex towards fin)......½ 2
3246[2] Current Leader **(74)***(56)*(Fav)*(RHannon)* 2-8-7 AMcGlone(11) (lw: chsd ldrs: brought wd st: rdn & no imp appr fnl f)......4 3

3231[10] Cerise (IRE) **(58)***(39) (CWCElsey)* 2-7-5 (7) PFessey(10) (s.i.s: hdwy appr st: r.o)....................3½ 4
3117[5] Distinctlyfoster's (IRE) *(39) (MJohnston)* 2-8-2 TWilliams(4) (w wnr tl grad wknd fnl 2f).........1¾ 5
3231[2] Contract Bridge (IRE) **(67)***(38) (CWThornton)* 2-7-13 (3) NVarley(6) (lw: in tch: hmpd appr st: styd on fnl 3f)....................nk 6
3306[4] Northern Falcon *(30) (MWEasterby)* 2-7-9 (7) MartinDwyer(3) (wandered bdly u.p 2f out: nvr trbld ldrs)....................3½ 7
2957[5] Sassetta (IRE) *(27) (NTinkler)* 2-8-2 KimTinkler(5) (stdd after s: bhd tl sme late hdwy) 1½ 8
1035[8] Cottage Prince (IRE) *(20) (JJQuinn)* 2-8-3 JLowe(8) (unruly in stalls: s.i.s: n.d)....................3½ 9
General Glow *(21) (NBycroft)* 2-8-7 RCochrane(13) (leggy: bit bkwd: s.s: wl bhd tl r.o fnl f) 1 10
3307[6] Dispol Conqueror (IRE) *(17) (GROldroyd)* 2-8-7v LCharnock(12) (chsd ldrs tl wknd fnl 2½f)....2 11
3018[11] Mulhollande Lad (IRE) *(13) (MCChapman)* 2-8-0 (7) CMunday(2) (prom 4f)....................1½ 12
2625[4] Clued Up *(6) (MHEasterby)* 2-8-4 ow2 ACulhane(1) (sn outpcd & bhd)....................1 13
3231[15] Bold Future (IRE) *(8) (JWWatts)* 2-8-7 GDuffield(9) (drvn along & sn in tch: outpcd fnl 3f) ...1¼ 14
3231[6] Good To Talk **(64)***(1) (MHEasterby)* 2-8-0 (3) JStack(7) (prom to st: wknd qckly)....................1½ 15

11/8 Current Leader (op 9/4), **11/4** Contract Bridge (IRE), **8/1** SILVER WELCOME, **9/1** Distinctlyfoster's (IRE) (5/1-10/1), **11/1** Northern Falcon (op 7/1), Yuppy Girl (IRE), **20/1** Good To Talk, **25/1** Cerise (IRE), Bold Future (IRE), **33/1** Clued Up, **40/1** General Glow, Dispol Conqueror (IRE), **50/1** Cottage Prince (IRE), **66/1** Mulhollande Lad (IRE), Sassetta (IRE), CSF £90.84 TOTE £6.20: £1.90 £2.90 £1.40 (£32.20) Trio £25.10 OWNER Mr Peter Hurst (MALTON) BRED Ahmed M. Foustok 15 Rn 1m 28.3 (5.60) SF: 11/1/1/-/-/-/-/-/-/-/-/-/-/-/-

3503

E.B.F. UNDERWOOD MAIDEN STKS (2-Y.O) (Class D) £4,092.00 (£1,221.00: £583.00: £264.00) **1m** Stalls: Low GOING minus 0.17 sec per fur (GF) 2-45 (2-47)

2667[4] **Nabhaan (IRE)** *(90+)*(Fav)*(DMorley)* 2-9-0 RCochrane(5) (cl up: led after 3f: shkn up & r.o strly fnl 3f)....................— 1
2542[6] Arc of The Diver (IRE) *(66) (JBerry)* 2-9-0 SDWilliams(4) (prom: hdwy 3f out: styd on: no ch w wnr)....................12 2
Anchor Venture *(64) (SPCWoods)* 2-9-0 WWoods(3) (unf: scope: chsd ldrs: effrt 3f out: one pce)....................1¼ 3
3231[5] Supermister *(44) (MHEasterby)* 2-9-0 SMaloney(2) (led 3f: cl up tl wknd 3f out)....................10 4
3307[7] Swish *(43) (NTinkler)* 2-9-0 LCharnock(1) (plld hrd: outpcd ent st: n.d)....................nk 5

4/7 NABHAAN (IRE), **9/4** Anchor Venture, **8/1** Arc of The Diver (IRE), **14/1** Supermister, **33/1** Swish, CSF £5.65 TOTE £1.60: £1.10 £2.10 (£3.40) OWNER Mr Hamdan Al Maktoum (NEWMARKET) BRED Shadwell Estate Company Limited 5 Rn 1m 41.2 (5.60) SF: 26/2/-/-/-

3504

YORKSHIRE-TYNE TEES TELEVISION (S) STKS (3-Y.O+) (Class G) £3,164.40 (£878.40: £421.20)
1m Stalls: Low GOING minus 0.17 sec per fur (GF) 3-15 (3-21)

3125[6] **Another Time (53)***(64+)*(Fav)*(SPCWoods)* 3-8-9 WWoods(14) (a in tch: qcknd to ld 1½f out: sn clr)....................— 1
2972[10] My Godson **(38)***(54) (FJO'Mahony)* 5-8-11b(3) JStack(4) (trckd ldrs: chal 2f out: sn rdn: one pce)....................5 2
3272[5] Golden Fish **(48)***(52) (JLEyre)* 3-8-6 (3) NVarley(8) (chsd ldrs: rdn & one pce fnl 3f)....................1¼ 3
2994[5] Pleasure Trick (USA) **(60)***(56) (NTinkler)* 4-9-6 KimTinkler(5) (lw: sn pushed along: a in tch: kpt on fnl f)....................¾ 4
2972[16] Monkey Face **(35)***(40) (JHetherton)* 4-8-9b MWigham(10) (mde most tl hdd 1½f out: sn btn).2½ 5
3385[9] Magication **(30)***(35) (CNAllen)* 5-8-9 MTebbutt(13) (bhd: stdy hdwy over 2f out: nvr nr to chal)....................2½ 6
3256[3] Broctune Gold **(65)***(39) (MrsMReveley)* 4-9-1 (5) GParkin(11) (lw: cl up: disp ld over 2f out tl over 1f out: wknd)....................3½ 7
2357[8] Ruby Rock **(42)***(20) (BWMurray)* 3-7-11v(7) MartinDwyer(1) (nvr bttr than mid div)....................4 8
1736[11] Dozen Dirham (USA) *(25) (JNorton)* 3-8-6 (3) PMcCabe(6) (bit bkwd: n.d)....................hd 9
3295[6] Resolute Bay **(41)***(19) (RMWhitaker)* 9-9-0v ACulhane(7) (lw: in tch: outpcd ent st: sn btn) 3 10
3060[2] Katy Koo *(12) (PJBevan)* 3-8-4 JLowe(2) (s.s: a bhd)....................¾ 11
2815[6] Evan Can Wait (IRE) *(11) (JLEyre)* 3-8-4 SDWilliams(3) (chsd ldrs to st: sn lost pl)....................¾ 12
1412[10] Legal Brief **(40)***(13) (JSWainwright)* 3-8-9 SMaloney(12) (sn wl bhd)....................1½ 13

13/8 ANOTHER TIME (3/1-6/4), **5/1** Broctune Gold (7/2-11/2), **11/2** Pleasure Trick (USA) (4/1-6/1), **8/1** Katy Koo, Golden Fish, Resolute Bay (op 5/1), **14/1** Magication, **16/1** My Godson, **20/1** Monkey Face, **25/1** Dozen Dirham (USA), Ruby Rock, **33/1** Evan Can Wait (IRE), Legal Brief, CSF £30.19 TOTE £2.60: £1.30 £5.30 £2.20 (£53.00) Trio £92.80 OWNER Mr D. Sullivan (NEWMARKET) BRED W. G. Barker 13 Rn 1m 41.0 (5.40) SF: 24/19/12/21/5/-/4/-/-/-/-/-/-

WEIGHT FOR AGE 3yo-5lb
Bt in 7,000 gns

3505

TOTE HAMBLETON CUP H'CAP (0-80) (3-Y.O+) (Class D) £5,872.50 (£1,755.00: £840.00: £382.50)
1m 4f Stalls: High GOING minus 0.17 sec per fur (GF) 3-45 (3-46)

3367[4] **Kalou (56)***(70) (CWCElsey)* 4-8-5 (7) PFessey(5) (in tch: qcknd to ld 2f out: r.o wl) ....— 1
3061[2] Once More for Luck (IRE) **(63)***(70) (MrsMReveley)* 4-9-5 ACulhane(4) (lw: trckd ldrs: ev ch over 2f out: kpt on one pce) 5 2
3237[4] High Patriarch (IRE) **(77)***(82)*(Fav)*(JLDunlop)* 3-9-10 RCochrane(3) (lw: a.p: outpcd over 3f out: styd on: nt pce to chal) 1½ 3
3127[2] Jadwal (USA) **(78)***(83) (DMorley)* 3-9-11 GDuffield(10) (hdwy ent st: styd on u.p: nrst fin) .....hd 4
2622* Tessajoe **(74)***(77) (MJCamacho)* 3-9-7 LCharnock(11) (chsd ldrs: ev ch 3f out: one pce) 1½ 5
3263[3] Instantaneous **(51)***(53) (MHEasterby)* 3-7-12 SMaloney(1) (plld hrd: trckd ldrs: swtchd over 2f out: nt clr run & eased fnl f) ....¾ 6
2871[5] Sariyaa **(57)***(59) (MBrittain)* 4-8-13 MWigham(2) (disp ld to st: wknd 2f out) ....½ 7
3229* Hasta la Vista **(47)***(49) (MWEasterby)* 5-8-0b(3) NVarley(7) (b.nr hind: disp ld tl led appr st: hdd 2f out: wknd) ....s.h 8
954[5] Faal Mario (USA) **(72)***(60) (MrsJRRamsden)* 4-10-0 SDWilliams(9) (lost tch fnl 3f) 10 9
3367[6] Antartictern (USA) **(45)***(27) (GROldroyd)* 5-8-1 NKennedy(8) (nvr wnt pce) 5 10
3238[8] Recluse **(53)***(8) (MDHammond)* 4-8-6 (3) JStack(6) (a wl bhd: t.o) 20 11

11/10 High Patriarch (IRE), **6/1** Once More for Luck (IRE), Tessajoe, **7/1** Instantaneous, **15/2** Jadwal (USA), **8/1** Hasta la Vista, **12/1** KALOU, **16/1** Sariyaa, Faal Mario (USA), **20/1** Antartictern (USA), **33/1** Recluse, CSF £87.64 CT £136.64 TOTE £16.70: £3.60 £1.60 £1.30 (£54.30) Trio £116.70 OWNER Mrs M. C. Butler (MALTON) BRED Bridge End Bloodstock 11 Rn
2m 35.1 (5.10) SF: 49/49/52/53/47/23/38/28/39/6/-
WEIGHT FOR AGE 3yo-9lb

3506

MOORLAND POULTRY H'CAP (0-75) (3-Y.O+ F & M) (Class D) £5,089.50 (£1,521.00: £728.00: £331.50)
1m Stalls: Low GOING minus 0.17 sec per fur (GF) 4-15 (4-16)

3305* **Ninia (USA) (65)***(80)*(Fav)*(MJohnston)* 3-9-10 TWilliams(5) (lw: w ldr: led over 2f out: r.o wl)—- 1
3264[2] Michellisa **(58)***(68) (JDBethell)* 4-9-8 RCochrane(7) (lw: in tch: hdwy 2f out: nt pce of wnr)...2½ 2
3230[11] Formidable Liz **(60)***(60) (MDHammond)* 5-9-10 GDuffield(4) (swtg: effrt ent st: sn chsng ldrs: one pce appr fnl f) 5 3
3370* Phase One (IRE) **(55)***(52) (JLEyre)* 5-9-5 SDWilliams(8) (a chsng ldrs: rdn & nt qckn fnl 2f) .1¾ 4
2685[16] Royal Comedian **(46)***(41) (BWMurray)* 6-8-3 (7) MartinDwyer(1) (led tl hdd over 2f out: grad wknd) 1 5
3457[14] Cafe Solo **(40)***(29) (NBycroft)* 4-8-4b SMaloney(3) (a outpcd & bhd) 3 6
Doo Han (IRE) **(48)***(35) (MDHammond)* 3-8-7 JMarshall(6) (nvr trbld ldrs) ....¾ 7
3357[16] Chardonnay Girl **(31)** *(JMCarr)* 4-7-9 NKennedy(2) (chsd ldrs 5f: hung bdly rt & sn btn: eased) 30 8

Evens NINIA (USA), **7/2** Michellisa, **6/1** Phase One (IRE) (op 4/1), **11/1** Formidable Liz, **12/1** Royal Comedian, **14/1** Cafe Solo, **16/1** Doo Han (IRE), **50/1** Chardonnay Girl, CSF £5.02 CT £21.32 TOTE £1.90: £1.20 £1.40 £1.80 (£2.50) OWNER Mrs D. R. Schreiber (MIDDLEHAM) BRED Newgate Stud Farm Inc 8 Rn 1m 40.9 (5.30) SF: 39/32/24/16/5/-/-/-
WEIGHT FOR AGE 3yo-5lb

3507

YORKSHIRE CANCER RESEARCH MAIDEN STKS (3-Y.O+) (Class D) £4,199.25 (£1,254.00: £599.50: £272.25)
6f Stalls: High GOING minus 0.17 sec per fur (GF) 4-45 (4-45)

3282[3] **Double Matt (IRE) (77)***(84) (RHannon)* 3-8-11 AMcGlone(6) (chsd ldrs: rdn to ld ins fnl f: r.o) ....— 1
1786[3] Allyana (IRE) **(73)***(75)*(Fav)*(IABalding)* 3-7-13 (7) MartinDwyer(5) (lw: led tl hdd & no ex ins fnl f) 1½ 2
3103[2] Flirty Gertie *(74) (RBoss)* 3-8-6 MTebbutt(2) (lw: a chsng ldrs: rdn ½-wy: styd on towards fin) ....½ 3
3282[4] Sky Girl *(63) (CBBBooth)* 3-8-6 GDuffield(8) (lw: s.i.s: edgd lft most of wy: sn chsng ldrs: effrt over 2f out: nt qckn) 4 4
Kira *(56) (JLEyre)* 5-8-9 SDWilliams(1) (b.off hind: w ldr tl wknd over 1f out) 2½ 5
Yeast *(57) (WJHaggas)* 3-8-11 RCochrane(4) (wl grwn: bit bkwd: s.s: styd on fnl 2f: nrst fin) 1½ 6
965[14] Sheroot *(25) (DMoffatt)* 3-8-8 (3) DarrenMoffatt(7) (a outpcd & bhd) 12 7
3356[4] Respect A Secret *(18) (SEKettlewell)* 3-8-3 (3) JStack(3) (outpcd after 2f: n.d after) ....¾ 8

7/4 Allyana (IRE), **5/2** DOUBLE MATT (IRE), **5/1** Flirty Gertie, Sky Girl (op 10/1), **15/2** Yeast (4/1-8/1), **33/1** Kira, **50/1** Sheroot, Respect A Secret, CSF £7.15 TOTE £3.50: £1.50 £1.40 £1.20 (£2.60) OWNER Mr A. F. Merritt (MARLBOROUGH) BRED S. Gollogly 8 Rn

1m 13.3 (3.60) SF: 30/21/20/9/5/3/-/-

WEIGHT FOR AGE 3yo-3lb

3508 CRATHORNE MAIDEN H'CAP (0-60) (3-Y.O+) (Class F) £3,370.50 (£1,008.00: £483.00: £220.50) 5f Stalls: High GOING minus 0.17 sec per fur (GF) 5-15 (5-23)

3251 2 **Portelet (58)***(74) (RGuest)* 3-10-0 GDuffield(15) (lw: led after 1f: r.o strly appr fnl f) ....— 1
3257 2 Northern Grey **(50)***(47)*(Fav)*(JBerry)* 3-8-13b(7) PRoberts(16) (outpcd tl styd on wl fnl 2f: nrst fin) 6 2
3275 12 Bowcliffe Grange (IRE) **(27)***(17) (DWChapman)* 3-7-11 NKennedy(18) (chsd ldrs: ev ch 2f out: wknd appr fnl f) 2 3
2821 6 China Hand (IRE) **(48)***(30) (MartynWane)* 3-9-4 MTebbutt(3) (led far side: no imp fnl 2f) 2½ 4
2372 10 Pemley **(30)***(12) (RMWhitaker)* 3-7-11 (3) NVarley(1) (lw: racd far side: styd on fnl 2f: no imp)s.h 5
3050 8 Bali Tender **(32)***(10) (MWEasterby)* 4-7-11b(7) MartinDwyer(5) (racd far side: no imp) 1¼ 6
3424 6 Last World **(42)***(19) (JAPickering)* 3-8-5 (7) SCopp(8) (racd far side: cl up tl rdn & btn over 1f out) ....½ 7
2925 5 Chloella **(45)***(17) (CBBBooth)* 3-9-1 SMorris(6) (racd far side: chsd ldrs over 3f) 1½ 8
3313 4 Kenesha (IRE) **(48)***(20) (DANolan)* 5-9-6 VHalliday(13) (in tch: rdn ½-wy: no imp) ....s.h 9
1846 8 Young Ben (IRE) **(53)***(24) (JSWainwright)* 3-9-2 (7) FLynch(2) (racd far side: nvr trbld ldrs).....nk 10
861 8 Undawaterscubadiva **(35)** *(MPBielby)* 3-8-2 (3) PMcCabe(10) (bit bkwd: effrt centre ½-wy: sn rdn & btn) 3½ 11
3357 11 Coney Hills **(21)** *(NBycroft)* 4-7-7 ClaireBalding(11) (swtg: chsd ldr 3f: sn wknd) ....d.h 11
1847 14 Gilpa Trinkets **(25)** *(DWChapman)* 3-7-9b LCharnock(17) (led 1f: outpcd & lost tch fr ½-wy).s.h 13
Loch Mariner **(45)** *(JLEyre)* 3-9-1b RLappin(12) (bit bkwd: chsd ldr 3f: sn wknd) 1½ 14
2956 8 Skiptamaloo **(28)** *(DonEnricoIncisa)* 4-8-0b KimTinkler(14) (dwlt: a bhd) 1½ 15
3103 6 Jacques Point **(33)** *(ASmith)* 3-8-3 JLowe(9) (in tch tl wknd fr ½-wy) 4 16
2997 9 Glow of Hope **(29)** *(RMMcKellar)* 5-8-1 TWilliams(7) (withdrawn not under starter's orders: ref to ent stalls) .... W

LONG HANDICAP Coney Hills 7-1

5/2 Northern Grey, **7/2** PORTELET, **9/1** Kenesha (IRE) (op 6/1), **10/1** Last World, **12/1** Bowcliffe Grange (IRE), Skiptamaloo, Bali Tender, **14/1** Glow of Hope, China Hand (IRE), **16/1** Loch Mariner, Chloella, **20/1** Coney Hills, **25/1** Gilpa Trinkets, Pemley, Young Ben (IRE), **33/1** Jacques Point, Undawaterscubadiva, CSF £12.64 CT £82.98 TOTE £3.50: £1.40 £1.20 £2.80 £2.20 (£3.60) Trio £10.50 OWNER Lord Matthews (NEWMARKET) BRED Lord Victor Matthews 16 Rn

59.4 secs (2.20) SF: 58/31/1/14/-/-/3/1/6/8/-/-/-/-/-/-

WEIGHT FOR AGE 3yo-2lb

STEWARDS' ENQUIRY Dwyer susp. 11/9/95 (incorrect use of whip).

T/Plpt: £6.20 (1,896.69 Tckts). T/Qdpt: £3.70 (24.75 Tckts). AA

3240-WOLVERHAMPTON (L-H)
Saturday September 2nd (Standard)

WEATHER: fair WIND: almost nil

3509 TATTERSALLS MAIDEN AUCTION STKS (2-Y.O) (Class E) £3,132.00 (£936.00: £448.00: £204.00) 6f (Fibresand) Stalls: Low GOING: 0.19 sec (SLW) 7-00 (7-00)

1327 6 **Vax New Way** *(71) (JLSpearing)* 2-8-2 (3) SDrowne(11) (plld hrd: led over 2f: led over 2f out: rdn out) ....— 1
Forest Boy *(68) (KMcAuliffe)* 2-8-6 ow1 RCochrane(13) (unf: bit bkwd: a.p: 2nd st: ev ch over 1f out: r.o) 1¼ 2
Miss Pickpocket (IRE) *(60) (PAKelleway)* 2-7-13 GBardwell(10) (unf: s.s: hdwy & 6th st: r.o fnl f) ....¾ 3
2633 2 Charterhouse Xpres **(64)***(66) (MMcCormack)* 2-8-6 DeanMcKeown(1) (led over 3f out tl over 2f out: r.o one pce) ....nk 4
3243 4 Still Here (IRE) *(58) (MJHeaton-Ellis)* 2-8-3 ow1 AClark(6) (prom: rdn & 4th st: one pce fnl f).1½ 5
2651 3 Real Gem *(45) (PJMakin)* 2-7-12 NCarlisle(2) (hdwy & 7th st: nvr trbld ldrs) 3½ 6
The Barnsley Belle (IRE) *(38)*(Fav)*(SGNorton)* 2-7-11 FNorton(5) (lengthy: outpcd: nvr nr ldrs) 2 7
3022 3 Rustic Song (IRE) *(37) (JWharton)* 2-8-5 KFallon(3) (chsd ldrs: 5th st: wknd over 1f out).....3½ 8
2608 2 Rocky's Meteor *(36) (RAFahey)* 2-8-4 ACulhane(8) (prom over 3f) ....hd 9
2817 4 Paper Maze **(66)***(25) (JAHarris)* 2-7-11 DaleGibson(4) (a bhd) 1½ 10
Risking *(25) (GLewis)* 2-8-4 PaulEddery(9) (lengthy: unf: prom over 3f) 2½ 11
Castle Governor *(21) (PCHaslam)* 2-8-3 GCarter(7) (lengthy: a bhd) 1¼ 12

3/1 The Barnsley Belle (IRE), **4/1** Charterhouse Xpres, **6/1** Rocky's Meteor, Real Gem, **7/1** Risking (5/1-8/1), **10/1** Miss Pickpocket (IRE), Forest Boy, **11/1** Rustic Song (IRE), **12/1** Still Here (IRE), Paper Maze, Castle Governor (8/1-14/1), **20/1** VAX NEW WAY, CSF £210.92 TOTE £30.40: £6.20 £5.60 £3.90 (£67.00) OWNER Vax Ltd (ALCESTER) BRED Aquamin Limited 12 Rn
1m 17.3 (6.10) SF: 21/18/10/16/8/-/-/-/-/-/-/-

3510 PRIORY STEEL ANNIVERSARY CLAIMING STKS (3-Y.O+) (Class F) £2,381.00 (£656.00: £311.00) 7f (Fibresand) Stalls: Low GOING: 0.19 sec (SLW) 7-30 (7-31)

*3241*2 **Bentico (72)***(78)*(Fav)*(MrsNMacauley)* 6-8-11b(7) AmandaSanders(10) (lw: sn prom: led 3f out: r.o wl)........— 1
3467 3 Maple Bay (IRE) **(52)***(60) (ABailey)* 6-8-3 (3) DWright(1) (a.p: 2nd st: hrd rdn: r.o one pce) 2½ 2
High Premium *(57) (RAFahey)* 7-9-7 ACulhane(9) (b: lw: prom: 5th st: wknd over 1f out) 8 3
3249* Dusk in Daytona **(60)***(44) (CJames)* 3-8-9 AMcGlone(12) (led over 4f out to 3f out: 4th st: wknd over 1f out)........2 4
3439 11 Rakis (IRE) **(70)***(49) (MBrittain)* 5-9-7 JWilliams(6) (b: prom: 3rd st: wknd over 1f out)..........1½ 5
3365 3 Best Kept Secret **(70)***(30) (JBerry)* 4-9-4 JCarroll(2) (nvr nr ldrs)........7 6
3269 4 Masnun (USA) **(67)***(24) (RJO'Sullivan)* 10-8-12 RCochrane(5) (nvr nr ldrs) ....s.h 7
2974 7 Grey Again **(57)***(11) (SRBowring)* 3-8-3b AClark(11) (dwlt: hdwy over 4f out: 6th & wkng st) .3½ 8
2968 8 Sapphire Son (IRE) **(48)***(16) (CNWilliams)* 3-8-11 PaulEddery(7) (lw: led over 2f: wknd qckly over 2f out)........1¼ 9
*2497*9 Bex Hill **(46)***(4) (DHaydnJones)* 3-8-3 AMackay(4) (a bhd)........1¾ 10
*3241*9 Chadleigh Lane (USA) **(65)***(15) (RHollinshead)* 3-9-3 MWigham(8) (a bhd)........1¼ 11
563 13 Aljaz **(58)***(5) (RHarris)* 5-9-1 DBatteate(3) (hld up: sn bhd)........2 12

2/1 BENTICO (op 100/30), **11/2** Masnun (USA), **7/1** Maple Bay (IRE), High Premium, Grey Again, **9/1** Dusk in Daytona, **11/1** Best Kept Secret, **12/1** Chadleigh Lane (USA), **16/1** Sapphire Son (IRE), Aljaz, **25/1** Rakis (IRE), **33/1** Bex Hill, CSF £17.61 TOTE £3.50: £1.80 £2.80 £1.90 (£12.90) Trio £69.10 OWNER Mr G. Wiltshire (MELTON MOWBRAY) BRED Britton House Stud 12 Rn
1m 29.6 (5.60) SF: 51/33/30/13/22/3/-/-/-/-/-/-
WEIGHT FOR AGE 3yo-4lb

3511 VITTORIA H'CAP (0-70) (3-Y.O+) (Class E) £3,080.00 (£920.00: £440.00: £200.00) 1m 1f 79y (Fibresand) Stalls: Low GOING: 0.19 sec per fur (SLW) 8-00 (8-00)

*3075*3 **Shanghai Venture (USA) (68)***(80+)*(Fav)*(SPCWoods)* 4-10-0 WWoods(8) (lw: hld up: stdy hdwy over 4f out: led over 3f out: clr over 1f out: easily) ....— 1
3047 4 Sudden Spin **(57)***(64) (SGNorton)* 5-9-3 KFallon(4) (a.p: 2nd st: no ch w wnr)........3 2
3127* Charlie Bigtime **(48)***(51) (RHarris)* 5-8-8 AMackay(5) (b.hind: outpcd: 8th & c wd st: hdwy over 1f out: nvr nrr) 2½ 3
3293 12 Jon's Choice **(50)***(53) (BPreece)* 7-8-10 NAdams(7) (hdwy 4f out: 3rd st: one pce) ....s.h 4
*3240*4 Calder King **(61)***(63) (JLEyre)* 4-9-7v SDWilliams(11) (hld up: hdwy over 3f out: 6th st: no imp)........s.h 5
*2961*3 Level Edge **(49)***(45) (MDHammond)* 4-8-9 DaleGibson(12) (lw: prom: 5th & wkng st) 4 6
*3240*2 Ayunli **(66)***(62) (SCWilliams)* 4-9-12 GHind(2) (b.off hind: lw: led 6f: 4th & wkng st) ....d.h 6
*3082*2 Dia Georgy **(54)***(39) (MrsNMacauley)* 4-9-0 DeanMcKeown(3) (lw: prom: 7th & wkng st).........6 8
*3240** Can Can Charlie **(64)***(39) (JPearce)* 5-9-10 GBardwell(6) (rdn over 6f out: sn bhd)........6 9
495 5 Golden Torque **(59)***(27) (RBastiman)* 8-9-0 (5) HBastiman(1) (bkwd: a bhd) 4 10
*3240*12 Erlking (IRE) **(50)***(17) (SMellor)* 5-8-10 MWigham(10) (bhd fnl 4f)........1 11
*3240*5 Palacegate Jo (IRE) **(50)***(16) (DWChapman)* 4-8-10 ACulhane(9) (prom tl wknd qckly over 2f out: b.b.v) ....½ 12
3058 4 Action Jackson **(64)***(18) (BJMcMath)* 3-8-11 (7) RMoogan(13) (b: a bhd) 7 13

9/2 SHANGHAI VENTURE (USA), **6/1** Sudden Spin, Charlie Bigtime, Ayunli, Dia Georgy, Can Can Charlie, **8/1** Calder King, Level Edge, **12/1** Palacegate Jo (IRE), **16/1** Action Jackson, **20/1** Jon's Choice, Erlking (IRE), Golden Torque, CSF £34.64 CT £156.51 TOTE £6.10: £2.10 £1.90 £2.50 (£33.70) Trio £124.40 OWNER Dr Frank Chao (NEWMARKET) BRED David Garvin & Michael J. Ryan 13 Rn
2m 3.5 (7.50) SF: 62/46/33/35/45/27/44/21/21/9/-/-/-
WEIGHT FOR AGE 3yo-6lb

3512 OPC 25TH ANNIVERSARY H'CAP (0-70) (3-Y.O+) (Class E) £3,158.00 (£944.00: £452.00: £206.00) 6f (Fibresand) Stalls: Low GOING: 0.19 sec per fur (SLW) 8-30 (8-32)

2607 7 **Desert Invader (IRE) (62)***(67) (DWChapman)* 4-9-6 ACulhane(12) (lw: hdwy over 2f out: 8th & c wd st: edgd lft over 1f out: edgd lft & led wl ins fnl f: r.o) ....— 1
*3242** Four of Spades **(70)***(73)*(Fav)*(PDEvans)* 4-9-7 (7) AmandaSanders(8) (led 1f: 4th st: led over 1f out tl wl ins fnl f)........¾ 2

2628* Ism **(70)**(72)(Fav)*(MajorWRHern)* 3-9-11 TSprake(4) (hdwy on ins & 6th st: ev ch over 1f out: r.o ins fnl f)....nk **3**
1510[10] Oggi **(67)**(67) *(PJMakin)* 4-9-11b PaulEddery(11) (hdwy over 2f out: 7th & c wd st: ev ch whn hmpd over 1f out: swtchd rt: r.o)....¾ **4**
1544[6] Anita's Contessa (IRE) **(68)**(67) *(BPalling)* 3-9-6 (3) SSanders(10) (prom: 3rd st: ev ch over 1f out: n.m.r ins fnl f: nt qckn)....½ **5**
3293[13] Montague Dawson (IRE) **(65)**(62) *(MrsNMacauley)* 3-9-6 DeanMcKeown(9) (led 5f out to 4f out: 2nd st: ev ch over 1f out: wknd fnl f)....¾ **6**
3121[7] Pageboy **(63)**(53) *(PCHaslam)* 6-9-7 MTebbutt(5) (lw: prom 4f)....2½ **7**
3242[11] Pharaoh's Dancer **(67)**(48) *(PBurgoyne)* 8-9-6 (5) DGibbs(1) (prom: 5th st: ev ch wl over 1f out: sn wknd)....3½ **8**
2923[13] Lady Silk **(63)**(44) *(MissJFCraze)* 4-9-7 SWebster(13) (n.d)....s.h **9**
3242[4] Yet More Roses **(64)**(41) *(LadyHerries)* 4-9-8 AClark(3) (led 4f out tl over 1f out: sn wknd)...1¼ **10**
3376[12] Evening Falls **(60)**(34) *(CJames)* 4-9-4 CRutter(7) (bhd fnl 3f)....1¼ **11**
3341[5] Forzair **(70)**(42) *(SRBowring)* 3-9-6b(5) CTeague(6) (bhd fnl 2f)....¾ **12**
2923[12] Mixed Mood **(66)**(37) *(BJLlewellyn)* 3-9-0 (7) JWilkinson(2) (s.i.s: a bhd)....nk **13**

9/2 Four of Spades, Ism, **11/2** Evening Falls, **6/1** Yet More Roses, **9/1** Oggi, Pageboy, **10/1** Forzair (8/1-12/1), **12/1** Mixed Mood, DESERT INVADER (IRE), **14/1** Montague Dawson (IRE) (12/1-20/1), **16/1** Anita's Contessa (IRE), **20/1** Pharaoh's Dancer, **25/1** Lady Silk, CSF £66.30 CT £267.41 TOTE £33.20: £5.30 £2.10 £2.00 (£169.70) Trio £120.20 OWNER Mr Michael Hill (YORK) BRED Gainsborough Stud Management Ltd 13 Rn

1m 16.4 (5.20) SF: 47/53/49/47/44/39/33/28/24/21/14/19/14

WEIGHT FOR AGE 3yo-3lb

3513 VULCAN KIRKLAND (S) H'CAP (0-60) (3, 4 & 5-Y.O) (Class G) £2,174.00 (£599.00: £284.00)

1m 4f (Fibresand) Stalls: Low GOING: 0.19 sec per fur (SLW) 9-00 (9-00)

2920[3] **Tovarich (56)**(62+)(Fav)*(GLewis)* 4-10-0b SWhitworth(4) (a gng wl: hdwy over 4f out: led over 2f out: v.easily)....— **1**
3292[8] Awestruck **(40)**(41) *(BPreece)* 5-8-12b VSlattery(6) (sn wl bhd: gd hdwy over 1f out: r.o fnl f: no ch w wnr)....3½ **2**
2291[8] Greek Night Out (IRE) **(33)**(32) *(JLEyre)* 4-8-5 SDWilliams(10) (led over 8f: 3rd st: one pce) 1¾ **3**
1799[10] Kismetim **(39)**(38) *(BJMeehan)* 5-8-11 AClark(11) (prom: wnt 2nd 6f out: led over 3f out tl over 2f out: 2nd st: wknd over 1f out)....nk **4**
2921[3] Aviator's Dream **(43)**(35) *(JPearce)* 5-9-1 GBardwell(1) (prom: rdn over 5f out: wknd 3f out: poor 5th st)....5 **5**
546[14] Ever Friends **(49)**(37) *(RHarris)* 3-8-12 DBatteate(12) (prom over 7f: poor 6th st)....3 **6**
592[6] Always Greener (IRE) **(49)**(10) *(MrsNMacauley)* 4-9-7 DeanMcKeown(5) (b: prom over 7f: t.o)....20 **7**
3241[12] Karon Beach **(45)**(6) *(JRBostock)* 4-8-12 (5) DaneO'Neill(9) (prom tl wknd over 3f out: t.o)....hd **8**
3259[6] Portite Sophie **(34)** *(MBrittain)* 4-8-6 JLowe(7) (plld hrd: hdwy over 5f out: wknd over 3f out: t.o)....hd **9**
3099[5] High Flown (USA) **(51)** *(RonaldThompson)* 3-8-9 (5) LNewton(8) (rdn over 6f out: a bhd: t.o)...9 **10**
3292[9] Sastrugi (IRE) **(46)** *(SPCWoods)* 3-8-9v NAdams(3) (a bhd: t.o)....12 **11**
Euchan Falls (IRE) **(51)** *(PDEvans)* 3-9-0 GHind(2) (bhd fnl 5f: t.o)....15 **12**

4/5 TOVARICH, **7/1** Aviator's Dream (op 4/1), **8/1** High Flown (USA), Awestruck, **10/1** Portite Sophie, **12/1** Kismetim, Always Greener (IRE) (8/1-14/1), **14/1** Euchan Falls (IRE), **16/1** Karon Beach, Greek Night Out (IRE), **20/1** Sastrugi (IRE), Ever Friends, CSF £10.62 CT £76.47 TOTE £2.10: £1.50 £1.90 £2.50 (£4.60) Trio £64.60 OWNER Mr Geoff Lewis (EPSOM) BRED Sir John Astor 12 Rn

2m 45.3 (14.30) SF: 33/12/3/9/6/-/-/-/-/-/-/-

WEIGHT FOR AGE 3yo-9lb

Sld RThompson 10,200gns

3514 DEAUVILLE MAIDEN H'CAP (0-65) (3-Y.O+) (Class F) £2,381.00 (£656.00: £311.00)

1m 100y (Fibresand) Stalls: Low GOING: 0.19 sec per fur (SLW) 9-30 (9-31)

2969[4] **Hatta Breeze (60)**(67) *(MAJarvis)* 3-9-6b(3) DRMcCabe(2) (led over 6f out tl over 5f out: led over 4f out: rdn clr over 1f out: r.o wl)....— **1**
2923[3] Penmar **(55)**(56) *(TJEtherington)* 3-9-4 LCharnock(12) (hld up: hdwy 4f out: 3rd & rdn st: chsd wnr over 1f out: no imp)....3 **2**
3370[4] Md Thompson **(54)**(52) *(SCWilliams)* 3-9-3 KFallon(7) (a.p: hrd rdn & wnt 2nd st: one pce)....2 **3**
2747[9] Rockusa **(50)**(41) *(LadyHerries)* 3-8-13 PaulEddery(8) (hld up: hdwy over 3f out: 5th st: no imp)....3½ **4**

3063[4] Snake Plissken (IRE) **(50)***(39) (DHaydnJones)* 4-9-4 AMackay(1) (wl bhd 5f out: hdwy over 1f out: nvr nrr)....1¼ **5**
2466[4] Shooter **(65)***(47) (PFICole)* 3-9-9 (5) DaneO'Neill(10) (lw: prom: pushed along over 6f out: 7th & wkng st)....3½ **6**
Hornpipe **(59)***(39) (JWharton)* 3-9-8 SDWilliams(5) (led 2f: 6th st: wknd over 1f out)....1¼ **7**
3154[6] Memory's Music **(51)***(30) (IABalding)* 3-8-9 (5) DGriffiths(13) (lw: led over 5f out tl over 4f out: 8th & wkng st)....½ **8**
1201[9] Saatchmo **(64)***(38) (JLSpearing)* 3-9-10 (3) SDrowne(4) (dwlt: wl bhd fnl 4f)....2½ **9**
3169[7] Northern Trove (USA) **(62)***(31) (GMMoore)* 3-9-11 MTebbutt(3) (swtg: hdwy on ins 4f out: hrd rdn over 3f out: 4th st: wknd qckly over 1f out)....2½ **10**
2645[7] Mason (IRE) **(60)***(18) (SMellor)* 3-9-9 MWigham(9) (lw: wl bhd fnl 4f)....6 **11**
3218[2] Brown Eyed Girl **(60)***(1)*(Fav)*(RHannon)* 3-9-2 (7) MarkDenaro(6) (rdn over 5f out: sn wl bhd: t.o)....9 **12**
Port Hedland **(50)** *(MMcCormack)* 3-8-13 AClark(11) (wl bhd fnl 4f: t.o)....5 **13**

9/4 Brown Eyed Girl, **5/1** Shooter, **11/2** Snake Plissken (IRE) (4/1-6/1), **7/1** Penmar, Md Thompson, **9/1** HATTA BREEZE, **10/1** Memory's Music, **14/1** Northern Trove (USA), Saatchmo, **20/1** Rockusa, Hornpipe, Mason (IRE), **25/1** Port Hedland, CSF £74.44 CT £446.34 TOTE £12.20: £3.30 £2.30 £2.40 (£75.30) Trio £131.20 OWNER Sheikh Ahmed Al Maktoum (NEWMARKET) BRED Grange Stud (UK) 13 Rn 1m 53.9 (9.90) SF: 28/17/13/2/5/8/-/-/-/-/-/-/-
WEIGHT FOR AGE 3yo-5lb

T/Plpt: £748.30 (16.17 Tckts). T/Qdpt: £28.20 (5.5 Tckts). KH

3201-**BATH (L-H)**
Monday September 4th (Hard)
WEATHER: fair WIND: nil

3515
AUTUMN (S) H'CAP (0-60) (3 & 4-Y.O) (Class G) £2,689.00 (£754.00: £367.00)
1m 5y Stalls: Low GOING minus 0.40 sec per fur (F) 1-45 (1-46)

3372[5] **Commander Glen (IRE) (54)***(66) (MartynMeade)* 3-9-12b VSlattery(2) (5th st: led ins fnl f: r.o wl)....— **1**
3385[6] Mighty Kingdom (IRE) **(43)***(53) (CADwyer)* 4-9-3 (3) SSanders(6) (lw: 3rd st: led wl over 1f out tl ins fnl f)....1¼ **2**
3344[6] Master M-E-N (IRE) **(50)***(58) (NMBabbage)* 3-9-8v JQuinn(18) (gd hdwy 2f out: hrd rdn fnl f: r.o)....1 **3**
2844[4] Prince Pellinore **(39)***(46) (CADwyer)* 3-8-11 CDwyer(15) (hdwy over 2f out: ev ch wl over 1f out: r.o ins fnl f)....nk **4**
2789[5] Bee Dee Best (IRE) **(39)***(40) (JPSmith)* 4-9-2 NAdams(11) (swtg: 7th st: rdn to ld over 2f out: hdd wl over 1f out: sn wknd)....3 **5**
3341[7] Astrojoy (IRE) **(50)***(51) (SGKnight)* 3-9-3 (5) DaneO'Neill(9) (hdwy fnl 2f: nvr nrr)....hd **6**
3173[11] Knightrider **(40)***(39) (CDBroad)* 4-9-3 JWilliams(16) (hdwy 2f out: one pce fnl f)....¾ **7**
3428[5] L'Eglise Belle **(39)***(37) (MrsALMKing)* 3-8-11b NCarlisle(3) (s.s: hdwy on ins 2f out: nt rch ldrs)....¾ **8**
2984[2] La Belle Shyanne **(28)***(26) (CJHill)* 4-7-12 (7) CAdamson(17) (no hdwy fnl 3f)....s.h **9**
3383[11] Chastleton **(32)***(27) (MRChannon)* 3-7-13 (5) PPMurphy(10) (n.d)....1¼ **10**
2383[6] Titanium Honda (IRE) **(30)***(10) (CEBrittain)* 4-8-7 BDoyle(4) (6th st: wknd over 2f out)....1¼ **11**
2362[6] Miss Spent Youth **(35)***(29) (RJHodges)* 4-8-7 (5) MHenry(7) (n.d)....½ **12**
2789[14] Grand Salt (IRE) **(34)***(22) (CLPopham)* 4-8-11 RPerham(14) (t: a bhd)....3 **13**
3249[4] Sobeloved **(49)***(34) (NEBerry)* 3-9-7 WNewnes(13) (lw: dwlt: a bhd)....1¾ **14**
3390[6] Anegre (IRE) **(55)***(39) (SDow)* 3-9-13 TQuinn(12) (led after 2f tl over 5f out: wknd over 2f out)....½ **15**
1498[17] Stylish Interval **(56)***(39) (RJHodges)* 3-9-9 (5) DGriffiths(5) (bhd fnl 3f)....½ **16**
Cnocma (IRE) **(40)***(13)*(Fav)*(WGMTurner)* 4-9-0 (3) PMcCabe(8) (2nd st: ev ch over 2f out: sn wknd)....3½ **17**
60[5] Bills Ploughgirl **(38)** *(JSMoore)* 3-8-10 JFEgan(1) (bit bkwd: led 1f: led over 5f out tl over 2f out: wknd qckly: t.o)....dist **18**

9/2 Cnocma (IRE), **5/1** Master M-E-N (IRE), **6/1** La Belle Shyanne, **7/1** Mighty Kingdom (IRE), **10/1** L'Eglise Belle, **12/1** Titanium Honda (IRE), Anegre (IRE) (op 8/1), Sobeloved (8/1-14/1), **14/1** Astrojoy (IRE) (op 8/1), COMMANDER GLEN (IRE), **16/1** Bee Dee Best (IRE), Miss Spent Youth, Chastleton, **20/1** Prince Pellinore, **33/1** Stylish Interval, Knightrider, **50/1** Grand Salt (IRE), Bills Ploughgirl, CSF £110.96 CT £528.96 TOTE £17.10: £4.30 £1.80 £1.60 £8.30 (£78.30) Trio £172.30 OWNER Ladyswood Racing Club (MALMESBURY) BRED Des Vere Hunt Farming Co 18 Rn 1m 41.9 (3.40) SF: 43/35/35/23/22/28/21/14/8/4/-/11/4/11/16/16/-/-
WEIGHT FOR AGE 3yo-5lb
No bid

3516

BATHFORD NURSERY H'CAP (2-Y.O) (Class C) £5,312.50 (£1,600.00: £775.00: £362.50) **1m 5y** Stalls: Low GOING minus 0.40 sec per fur (F) 2-15 (2-16)

3267[4] **Pacific Grove (78)***(80) (PFICole)* 2-8-7 (5) DaneO'Neill(1) (hld up: 4th st: nt clr run over 1f out: swtchd rt ins fnl f: qckned to ld last strides) — 1
3405* Friendly Forester (USA) **(83)***(84) (RCharlton)* 2-9-0b(3) 6x SSanders(3) (3rd st: led over 1f out tl ins fnl f: led cl home: hdd last strides) ½ 2
3375[8] Balpare **(60)***(61) (NACallaghan)* 2-7-8 JQuinn(10) (hdwy & 7th st: rdn over 2f out: led ins fnl f: hdd cl home) hd 3
3414[3] Nostoi **(73)***(68) (SirMarkPrescott)* 2-8-7 GDuffield(9) (sn pushed along: lost pl 5f out: hdwy & nt clr run over 2f out: one pce) 3 4
3271[8] Wilfull Lad (IRE) **(65)***(57) (MartynMeade)* 2-7-8 (5) MBaird(8) (led 4f: 2nd st: led over 2f out tl over 1f out: sn wknd) 1½ 5
3136[7] Queen's Music (USA) **(64)***(48) (PFICole)* 2-7-7b(5)ow4 MHenry(5) (6th st: no hdwy fnl 2f) 1¾ 6
3266* Munketh (USA) **(87)***(75)*(Fav)*(JLDunlop)* 2-9-7 WCarson(4) (hld up & plld hrd: 5th st: wknd 3f out) nk 7
3400[5] Kinnescash (IRE) **(70)***(56) (MSSaunders)* 2-8-4 NAdams(7) (a bhd) 1 8
3345[7] Sound Check **(62)***(48) (BJMeehan)* 2-7-10 NCarlisle(2) (prom: led 4f out tl over 2f out: sn wknd) s.h 9
3174[14] Emei Shan **(61)***(15) (PGMurphy)* 2-7-2 (7)ow2 CAdamson(6) (bhd fnl 3f: t.o) 15 10

LONG HANDICAP Emei Shan 7-2

6/4 Munketh (USA), **4/1** Nostoi, Friendly Forester (USA), **7/1** PACIFIC GROVE, **8/1** Balpare, **12/1** Sound Check, **20/1** Kinnescash (IRE), Queen's Music (USA), **33/1** Wilfull Lad (IRE), **66/1** Emei Shan, CSF £35.14 CT £215.78 TOTE £8.40: £1.90 £1.60 £2.00 (£11.20) Trio £40.40 OWNER Elite Racing Club (WHATCOMBE) BRED Tarworth Bloodstock Investments Ltd 10 Rn

1m 41.6 (3.10) SF: 33/37/14/21/10/1/28/9/1/-

3517

BRISTOL ROVERS MAIDEN STKS (3-Y.O+) (Class D) £3,582.25 (£1,078.00: £382.38: £382.38)
1m 3f 144y Stalls: Low GOING minus 0.40 sec per fur (F) 2-45 (2-45)

3016[5] **Persian Saint (IRE) (76)***(89) (DRCElsworth)* 4-9-7 PatEddery(3) (swtg: mde all: hrd rdn over 1f out: r.o wl) — 1
3338[2] Mayreau **(80)***(82)*(Fav)*(GHarwood)* 3-8-7 JReid(4) (2nd st: hrd rdn & ev ch over 1f out: nt qckn) 1¾ 2
2967[3] Eben Al Habeeb (IRE) **(72)***(74) (MajorWRHern)* 4-9-7 WCarson(2) (hld up: rdn 4f out: wknd 2f out) 10 3
1691[2] Berkeley Bounder (USA) **(78)***(74) (PFICole)* 3-8-12 TQuinn(1) (3rd & rdn st: wknd over 2f out) d.h 3
Just by Chance *(ABarrow)* 3-8-12 NAdams(5) (s.s: a wl bhd) dist 5

4/5 Mayreau (6/4-8/11), **11/4** PERSIAN SAINT (IRE) (7/4-3/1), **11/2** Eben Al Habeeb (IRE) (3/1-6/1), **6/1** Berkeley Bounder (USA) (7/2-13/2), **100/1** Just by Chance, CSF £5.32 TOTE £4.60: £2.00 £1.50 (£2.60) OWNER Whitcombe Manor Racing Stables Ltd (WHITCOMBE) BRED P. Bolton 5 Rn

2m 29.0 (2.30) SF: 58/42/43/34/-
WEIGHT FOR AGE 3yo-9lb

3518

SHERSTON STKS (2-Y.O F) (Class C) £4,848.00 (£1,688.00: £819.00: £345.00)
1m 5y Stalls: Low GOING minus 0.40 sec per fur (F) 3-15 (3-16)

3283* **La Modiste (92)***(77) (SDow)* 2-8-8 TQuinn(1) (chsd ldr: 2nd st: led wl over 1f out: r.o wl) — 1
2957* Parrot Jungle (IRE) *(76) (JLDunlop)* 2-8-12 WCarson(2) (hld up & plld hrd: 3rd st: hdwy over 2f out: ev ch over 1f out: nt qckn) 2½ 2
3397* Waterland (USA) *(60)*(Fav)*(RCharlton)* 2-8-12 PatEddery(3) (led over 6f: eased whn btn ins fnl f) 8 3
3378[7] Bellapais (IRE) *(32) (WRMuir)* 2-8-8b RPerham(4) (hdwy 4f out: last st: wknd over 2f out) 12 4

Evens Waterland (USA), **13/8** Parrot Jungle (IRE), **9/2** LA MODISTE, **100/1** Bellapais (IRE), CSF £11.05 TOTE £4.10 (£4.20) OWNER Mrs G. R. Smith (EPSOM) BRED G. R. Smith (Thriplow) Ltd 4 Rn

1m 41.6 (3.10) SF: 29/28/12/-

3519

SEPTEMBER H'CAP (0-80) (3-Y.O+) (Class D) £3,900.75 (£1,176.00: £570.50: £267.75)
5f 161y Stalls: Low GOING minus 0.40 sec per fur (F) 3-45 (3-54)

3286[3] **Master Millfield (IRE) (65)***(71) (CJHill)* 3-8-6 (5) DaneO'Neill(4) (a.p: led wl over 1f out: r.o wl) — 1

3453[4] Giggleswick Girl **(64)***(68) (MRChannon)* 4-8-6 (7) JDennis(10) (hdwy over 2f out: ev ch over 1f out: nt qckn)....¾ 2
3279[6] Bowden Rose **(77)***(81) (MBlanshard)* 3-9-4b(5) MBaird(6) (bhd: gd hdwy over 1f out: fin wl)...s.h 3
3424[5] John O'Dreams **(46)***(43) (MrsALMKing)* 10-7-9 ow1 AGarth(3) (b: hdwy 2f out: nt qckn fnl f)......2 4
3177[4] Random **(53)***(47) (CJames)* 4-7-9 (7) CAdamson(12) (hdwy & swtchd rt over 1f out: swvd lft ins fnl f: nt clr run on ins: r.o)....1½ 5
3204[3] Astral Invader (IRE) **(62)***(56) (MSSaunders)* 3-8-8 NAdams(7) (hdwy over 2f out: rdn over 1f out: one pce)....s.h 6
3418[9] Prima Silk **(70)***(64) (MJRyan)* 4-9-5 WCarson(14) (prom: ev ch over 1f out: wknd fnl f)....hd 7
3357[3] Lovely Me (IRE) **(63)***(47) (RFJohnsonHoughton)* 4-8-12 DHolland(1) (prom over 3f)....3½ 8
3376[10] Bold Gem **(52)***(32) (BJMeehan)* 4-8-1b BDoyle(13) (n.d)....1¼ 9
3390[5] Fantasy Racing (IRE) **(78)***(49) (MRChannon)* 3-9-10 RHughes(5) (lw: chsd ldrs over 3f)......3½ 10
3250[5] Dark Eyed Lady (IRE) **(56)***(17) (DWPArbuthnot)* 5-8-5b TQuinn(9) (prom over 3f)....3½ 11
3204* Colston-C **(70)***(26)*(Fav)*(RJHodges)* 3-9-2 StephenDavies(11) (uns rdr & bolted bef s: prom 3f)....1¾ 12
3249[3] Dark Menace **(61)***(17) (SMellor)* 3-8-7b TSprake(2) (a bhd)....hd 13
3453[6] Tommy Tempest **(45)** *(REPeacock)* 6-7-8vow1 JQuinn(8) (led: hdd wl over 1f out: wknd qckly) 4 14

LONG HANDICAP Tommy Tempest 7-1

5/1 Colston-C (4/1-7/1), **7/1** MASTER MILLFIELD (IRE), **8/1** Bowden Rose, Astral Invader (IRE), Random, **9/1** Lovely Me (IRE), **10/1** John O'Dreams, Prima Silk (7/1-12/1), Giggleswick Girl, **11/1** Fantasy Racing (IRE) (op 7/1), **12/1** Bold Gem (7/1-14/1), **14/1** Dark Eyed Lady (IRE), **20/1** Dark Menace, Tommy Tempest, CSF £74.45 CT £532.20 TOTE £7.20: £2.50 £3.40 £5.80 (£38.40) Trio £137.80 OWNER Mr John Hill (BARNSTAPLE) BRED A. M. F. Persse 14 Rn

1m 10.8 (1.50) SF: 41/41/51/16/20/26/37/20/5/19/-/-/-/-

WEIGHT FOR AGE 3yo-3lb

3520 TWERTON MAIDEN STKS (2-Y.O F) (Class E) £2,986.00 (£898.00: £434.00: £202.00) 5f 11y Stalls: Low GOING minus 0.40 sec per fur (F) 4-15 (4-22)

2838[3] **Jessica's Song (48)***(66) (WGMTurner)* 2-7-8 (5) MBaird(2) (b.hind: mde all: hrd rdn over 1f out: r.o wl)....— 1
3203[2] Meg's Memory (IRE) *(62) (JohnBerry)* 2-8-1 ow1 MFenton(3) (outpcd: hdwy over 1f out: r.o ins fnl f)....1¾ 2
2683[4] Sunset Harbour (IRE) **(58)***(62) (DAWilson)* 2-8-1 JQuinn(4) (stdd after s: plld hrd: hdwy 2f out: r.o one pce fnl f)....nk 3
Simply Miss Chief (IRE) *(55) (DWPArbuthnot)* 2-8-0 BDoyle(1) (lt-f: unf: a.p: one pce fnl 2f)....1¾ 4
2985[3] Dramatic Entry (IRE) **(70)***(61)*(Fav)*(JARToller)* 2-8-3b(3) SSanders(6) (bmpd after s: plld hrd: prom: ev ch over 1f out: hrd rdn: wknd fnl f)....s.h 5
3379[10] Poly By Staufan (IRE) *(52) (MRChannon)* 2-7-11 (5) PPMurphy(5) (bmpd after s: prom: ev ch 2f out: wknd over 1f out)....1½ 6

Evens Dramatic Entry (IRE), **5/1** Sunset Harbour (IRE), **11/2** Meg's Memory (IRE) (7/2-6/1), **6/1** Poly By Staufan (IRE) (4/1-13/2), **14/1** JESSICA'S SONG (tchd 25/1), Simply Miss Chief (IRE) (op 6/1), CSF £73.74 TOTE £18.80: £4.30 £1.60 (£22.30) OWNER Mr John Woods (SHERBORNE) BRED C. J. Sexton 6 Rn 63.6 secs (3.10) SF: 2/-/-/-/-/-

3521 KENNET MAIDEN H'CAP (0-70) (3-Y.O+) (Class E) £3,181.00 (£958.00: £464.00: £217.00) 1m 5f 22y Stalls: Low GOING minus 0.40 sec per fur (F) 4-45 (4-46)

2037[9] **Missed the Boat (IRE) (37)***(50) (AGNewcombe)* 5-8-5 (5) DGriffiths(7) (hld up & bhd: gd hdwy over 1f out: led ins fnl f: qcknd clr)....— 1
3137[4] Western Horizon (USA) **(36)***(45) (CEBrittain)* 3-7-13 JQuinn(11) (lw: hld up: 5th st: hrd rdn 2f out: r.o one pce fnl f)....3½ 2
3056[2] Santella Boy (USA) **(60)***(68)*(Fav)*(GHarwood)* 3-9-9v WCarson(10) (led: hrd rdn & hdd ins fnl f)....½ 3
2569[9] Grand Applause (IRE) **(45)***(52) (MPMuggeridge)* 5-9-4 SWhitworth(8) (hdwy 6f out: 7th st: styd on fnl f)....¾ 4
2977[5] Special Beat **(60)***(67) (PFICole)* 3-9-9 TQuinn(3) (3rd & rdn st: one pce fnl 2f)....nk 5
3384[7] Jean de Florette (USA) **(34)***(41) (CADwyer)* 4-8-4v(3) SSanders(5) (lw: hdwy over 4f out: hrd rdn & 6th st: styd on ins fnl f)....nk 6
3287[4] Chanson D'Avril **(41)***(45) (DAWilson)* 4-9-0 RHughes(6) (2nd st: hrd rdn & ev ch 2f out: wknd 1f out)....1¾ 7
3184[5] Dr Frances (IRE) **(37)***(36) (CCElsey)* 3-8-0 ow2 BDoyle(12) (prom: 8th st: wknd over 2f out)....2½ 8
3076[9] Cephista **(57)***(58) (PTWalwyn)* 3-9-6 DHolland(1) (5th st: wknd 2f out)....hd 9
3058[5] Jewel Trader **(44)***(44) (CJBenstead)* 3-8-7b GDuffield(9) (a bhd)....1¼ 10
3401[8] Fly the Eagle **(40)***(21) (MPMuggeridge)* 3-8-3 NAdams(2) (a bhd: t.o)....15 11

3006[3] Victoria's Secret (IRE) **(63)***(44) (DRCElsworth)* 3-9-12 PatEddery(4) (lw: hdwy 7f out: wknd over 4f out: t.o)....½ **12**

11/4 Santella Boy (USA), **9/2** Victoria's Secret (IRE), **11/2** Special Beat, **6/1** MISSED THE BOAT (IRE), Western Horizon (USA), **8/1** Jean de Florette (USA), **10/1** Jewel Trader, **12/1** Grand Applause (IRE) (op 20/1), Cephista (op 8/1), **14/1** Chanson D'Avril, **33/1** Dr Frances (IRE), Fly the Eagle, CSF £44.68 CT £116.18 TOTE £19.00: £4.00 £2.20 £1.40 (£63.70) Trio £261.30 OWNER Mr R. Harding (BARNSTAPLE) BRED Eamon O'Mahony 12 Rn

2m 51.3 (5.60) SF: 30/15/38/32/37/21/25/6/28/14/-/14

WEIGHT FOR AGE 3yo-10lb

OFFICIAL EXPLANATION **Victoria's Secret: the jockey stated that the filly was reluctant to race without her usual blinkers.**

T/Plpt: £908.40 (15.72 Tckts). T/Qdpt: £68.60 (0.5 Tckts); £46.40 to Leicester 5/9/95. KH

2919-SOUTHWELL (L-H)
Monday September 4th (Standard)

WEATHER: fine & sunny WIND: almost nil

3522

ALEX LAWRIE FACTORS CLAIMING STKS (I) (3-Y.O+) (Class F) £2,972.60 (£823.60: £393.80)
5f (Fibresand) Stalls: High GOING minus 0.20 sec per fur (FST) 1-30 (1-32)

693[9] **Spaniards Close (90)***(83+)*(Fav)*(PJMakin)* 7-9-5 LDettori(8) (trckd ldrs: led 2f out: pushed out: comf)....— **1**
3221[7] King Rambo **(65)***(66) (RHollinshead)* 4-8-7 WRyan(12) (lw: hld up: hdwy ½-wy: nt qckn appr fnl f)....1½ **2**
3357[8] Most Uppitty **(54)***(44) (JBerry)* 3-7-9 (7) JoanneWebster(1) (in tch: kpt on one pce appr fnl f)....6 **3**
3492[19] Sir Tasker **(85)***(57) (JLHarris)* 7-9-5 KDarley(4) (led 3f: wknd over 1f out)....¾ **4**
1847[10] Nadwaty (IRE) **(52)***(40) (MCChapman)* 3-7-11 (7) CMunday(10) (swvd lft s: sn chsng ldrs: rdn & outpcd 2f out)....1 **5**
994[3] Nineacres **(60)***(41) (CASmith)* 4-8-7v ACulhane(15) (w ldrs: hrd rdn & wknd 2f out)....hd **6**
2925[6] Anotherone to Note **(45)***(37) (NPLittmoden)* 4-8-5b TGMcLaughlin(11) (s.s: bhd tl styd on appr fnl f)....¾ **7**
3424[6] Sound the Trumpet (IRE) **(74)***(42) (AStreeter)* 3-8-2v(7) DSweeney(13) (chsd ldrs: rdn ½-wy: sn btn)....nk **8**
2810[3] Tyrian Purple (IRE) **(62)***(40) (TJNaughton)* 7-8-4b(5) JDSmith(6) (w ldrs: rdn ½-wy: sn wknd) s.h **9**
3051[9] Super Sonata **(52)** *(PDEvans)* 3-7-5 (7)ow2 AmandaSanders(7) (b.nr hind: prom tl lost pl ½-wy)....9 **10**
2372[6] Double Glow **(40)***(6) (NBycroft)* 3-8-8 TWilliams(5) (chsd ldrs: rdn 2f out: sn lost pl)....1¾ **11**
2959[11] Miss The Beat *(SMellor)* 3-8-6b DaleGibson(9) (hmpd s: a wl bhd)....3 **12**
3121[8] Waverley Star **(36)** *(JSWainwright)* 10-8-7v LCharnock(3) (lw: outpcd & sn wl bhd)....2½ **13**
Gilpa Bliss *(DWChapman)* 4-8-0 SLanigan(2) (w'like: bkwd: s.i.s: a wl outpcd & wl bhd)....20 **14**

11/4 SPANIARDS CLOSE (7/4-3/1), **3/1** King Rambo, **5/1** Sir Tasker, **6/1** Tyrian Purple (IRE), **12/1** Super Sonata, **14/1** Nadwaty (IRE), Most Uppitty, Nineacres, **16/1** Sound the Trumpet (IRE), **33/1** Anotherone to Note, Gilpa Bliss, **50/1** Miss The Beat, Waverley Star, Double Glow, CSF £11.56 TOTE £3.30: £1.40 £1.50 £5.10 (£6.50) Trio £46.00 OWNER Avon Industries Ltd (MARLBOROUGH) BRED Avon Industries Bath Ltd 14 Rn 59.2 secs (1.20) SF: 65/48/24/39/20/23/19/22/22/-/-/-/-/-

WEIGHT FOR AGE 3yo-2lb

3523

E.B.F. COLOGNE MAIDEN STKS (I) (2-Y.O) (Class D) £3,785.00 (£1,130.00: £540.00: £245.00)
7f (Fibresand) Stalls: Low GOING: 0.08 sec per fur (STD) 2-00 (2-03)

3010[4] **Wood Magic** *(78+)*(Fav)*(DRLoder)* 2-9-0 LDettori(2) (lw: led after 2f: pushed clr over 1f out: v.easily)....— **1**
Kings Harmony (IRE) *(57+) (PJMakin)* 2-9-0 RCochrane(8) (w'like: scope: lw: unruly s: s.i.s: rn green & swtchd outside after 1f: hdwy to chse ldrs ½-wy: kpt on fnl 2f)....9 **2**
3432[12] Boundary Bird (IRE) *(54) (MJohnston)* 2-9-0 JWeaver(9) (sn outpcd & bhd: styd on fnl 2f) ..1½ **3**
1856[12] Classic Delight (USA) *(43) (SCWilliams)* 2-8-9 AMackay(6) (led 2f: one pce fnl 3f)....2½ **4**
Daira *(43) (JDBethell)* 2-8-9 KFallon(3) (leggy: scope: in tch: sn outpcd & pushed along: styd on same pce fr ½-wy)....s.h **5**
3244[2] Tallulah Belle *(32) (NPLittmoden)* 2-8-9 TGMcLaughlin(4) (chsd ldrs tl wknd over 2f out)....5 **6**
Maiteamia *(31) (SRBowring)* 2-8-9b(5) CTeague(1) (w'like: dwlt s: nvr nr ldrs)....2½ **7**
3314[9] Mindrace *(15) (KTIvory)* 2-8-7 (7) CScally(11) (chsd ldrs tl wknd 2f out)....7 **8**
2924[7] Irish Oasis (IRE) *(10) (BSRothwell)* 2-8-11 (3) JStack(7) (reard s: a wl bhd)....2¼ **9**

2855[8] Anshan's Deity **(56)***(9) (CWFairhurst)* 2-9-0 TWilliams(10) (sn outpcd & bhd)..........................nk 10
Arrogant Heir *(6) (SGNorton)* 2-9-0 KDarley(5) (w'like: str: bkwd: s.s: a wl bhd: t.o ½-wy).....1½ 11

2/5 WOOD MAGIC, **9/1** Boundary Bird (IRE) (5/1-10/1), **10/1** Kings Harmony (IRE) (6/1-12/1), **12/1** Daira (8/1-14/1), **14/1** Tallulah Belle, **16/1** Arrogant Heir, **20/1** Classic Delight (USA), Anshan's Deity, **33/1** Maiteamia, Mindrace, **50/1** Irish Oasis (IRE), CSF £6.73 TOTE £1.40: £1.10 £2.70 £1.50 (£5.00) Trio £6.30 OWNER Sheikh Mohammed (NEWMARKET) BRED Sheikh Mohammed bin Rashid al Maktoum 11 Rn 1m 33.3 (6.50) SF: 31/10/7/-/-/-/-/-/-/-/-

3524 ALEX LAWRIE FACTORS CLAIMING STKS (II) (3-Y.O+) (Class F) £2,972.60 (£823.60: £393.80)
5f (Fibresand) Stalls: High GOING minus 0.20 sec per fur (FST) 2-30 (2-34)

3424* **Rhythmic Dancer (75)***(66) (JLSpearing)* 7-8-2 (3) SDrowne(14) (unruly s: w ldrs: led over 1f out: drvn out) ....— 1
2877[2] C-Yer-Simmie (IRE) **(62)***(57) (RHollinshead)* 3-8-2 GCarter(3) (chsd ldr far side: kpt on fnl f) 2½ 2
2038a* Newbury Coat *(60) (BJMeehan)* 5-8-7b MTebbutt(2) (lw: led far side: nt qckn ins fnl f)..........s.h 3
2527[2] Ninety-Five **(65)***(55)*(Fav)*(JGFitzGerald)* 3-8-3beow1 KFallon(6) (lw: led tl over 1f out: kpt on same pce)....................½ 4
3072[8] Primula Bairn **(58)***(51) (DNicholls)* 5-8-7bow1 AlexGreaves(7) (lw: in tch: effrt 2f out: nvr rchd ldrs) 2 5
498[7] Daaniera (IRE) **(50)***(49) (PHowling)* 5-8-11b PaulEddery(12) (a chsng ldrs: kpt on one pce fnl 2f)....................2 6
2124[9] My Cherrywell **(50)***(40) (LRLloyd-James)* 5-8-7 ow1 RCochrane(9) (b.hind: sn pushed along: kpt on fnl f: n.d)....................1¼ 7
2925[7] Dundeelin **(38)***(34) (JLEyre)* 4-8-0v TWilliams(8) (chsd ldrs: rdn ½-wy: hung lft tl wknd over 1f out)....................s.h 8
3275[7] Arasong **(61)***(44) (EWeymes)* 3-8-8 KDarley(15) (sn outpcd & pushed along: kpt on fnl f: n.d) ....s.h 9
3365[6] Rapier Point (IRE) **(52)***(43) (PCHaslam)* 4-8-10 JWeaver(11) (lw: sltly hmpd s: sme hdwy ½-wy: n.d) ....nk 10
1321[6] Lift Boy (USA) **(62)***(41) (AMoore)* 6-8-9 CandyMorris(10) (b.hind: outpcd fr ½-wy) ....½ 11
890[5] Dark Shot (IRE) **(67)***(34) (JBerry)* 3-8-7 JCarroll(1) (hung rt ½-wy: nvr nr ldrs) 2 12
High Holme *(8) (DTThom)* 4-9-1 JTate(5) (chsd ldrs tl wknd ½-wy: eased & sn bhd).............10 13
Polhymnia *(GCBravery)* 4-7-12v SLanigan(4) (b.nr fore: b.hind: reluctant to go to s: nvr wnt pce)....................1¼ 14
Sundries *(JAHarris)* 5-8-5 SDWilliams(13) (s.i.s: a outpcd & wl bhd)....................hd 15

4/1 Ninety-Five, **11/2** RHYTHMIC DANCER, **13/2** Dark Shot (IRE), **7/1** Primula Bairn (op 4/1), **8/1** C-Yer-Simmie (IRE), **9/1** Newbury Coat (6/1-10/1), My Cherrywell, Arasong, **12/1** Lift Boy (USA), Rapier Point (IRE), **20/1** Dundeelin, **25/1** Daaniera (IRE), Polhymnia, **33/1** High Holme, Sundries, CSF £50.67 TOTE £5.70: £2.70 £1.30 £4.80 (£16.40) Trio £90.40 OWNER Mrs Robert Heathcote (ALCESTER) BRED Heathavon Stables Ltd 15 Rn
59.7 secs (1.70) SF: 43/32/37/30/28/26/17/11/19/20/18/9/-/-/-
WEIGHT FOR AGE 3yo-2lb
Rhythmic Dancer clmd RJohnson £3,000

3525 E.B.F. COLOGNE MAIDEN STKS (II) (2-Y.O) (Class D) £3,752.50 (£1,120.00: £535.00: £242.50)
7f (Fibresand) Stalls: Low GOING: 0.08 sec per fur (STD) 3-00 (3-06)

2681[3] **Taufan Boy** *(80)*(Fav)*(PWHarris)* 2-9-0 GHind(10) (chsd ldrs: led over 1f out: drvn out) ....— 1
3117[3] Nose No Bounds (IRE) *(77+) (MJohnston)* 2-9-0 JWeaver(9) (chsd ldrs: hmpd over 2f out: styd on u.p fnl f: nt rch wnr)....................1¼ 2
2667[3] Lionel Edwards (IRE) **(84)***(74) (PFICole)* 2-9-0 LDettori(2) (lw: led tl over 1f out: wknd nr fin)1¼ 3
2777[4] Quality (IRE) *(66) (WAO'Gorman)* 2-9-0 EmmaO'Gorman(5) (w ldrs: rdn over 2f out: styd on one pce)....................3½ 4
Pleasureland (IRE) *(59) (PJMakin)* 2-9-0 RCochrane(11) (w'like: sn pushed along: kpt on fnl 2f: nvr nr to chal)....................3 5
2995[4] Midtime (IRE) *(59) (MRStoute)* 2-9-0 KDarley(7) (in tch: drvn along ½-wy: nvr able chal)......hd 6
2756[5] Craigmore Magic (USA) *(43) (MissMKMilligan)* 2-9-0 JFanning(6) (sn drvn along: bhd fr ½-wy) 7 7
Jump The Lights *(40) (SPCWoods)* 2-9-0 WWoods(4) (unf: scope: dwlt s: a in rr) 1½ 8
3432[11] First Maite *(39) (SRBowring)* 2-8-9b(5) CTeague(1) (sn chsng ldrs: lost pl over 2f out) ....nk 9
Royal Oddsox *(NPLittmoden)* 2-9-0 TGMcLaughlin(3) (lt-f: b: s.i.s: sn wl bhd: t.o ½-wy)....dist 10
3243[W] Eurobox Boy *(APJarvis)* 2-9-0 JTate(8) (Withdrawn not under Starter's orders: ref to ent stalls)....................W

3/1 TAUFAN BOY, **7/2** Lionel Edwards (IRE), Quality (IRE), **9/2** Midtime (IRE), **5/1** Nose No Bounds (IRE), **14/1** Pleasureland (IRE), Jump The Lights (6/1-16/1), **25/1** First Maite, Eurobox Boy, **33/1** Royal Oddsox, **50/1** Craigmore Magic (USA), CSF £18.89 TOTE £4.20: £1.40 £1.20 £1.80 (£8.90) Trio £6.90 OWNER Supreme Team (BERKHAMSTED) BRED Pendley Farm 10 Rn

1m 32.8 SF: 36/33/30/22/15/15/-/-/-/-

STEWARDS' ENQUIRY Obj. to Taufan Boy by Weaver overruled.

3526

SHOOSMITH & HARRISON MAIDEN H'CAP (0-70) (3-Y.O+) (Class E) £3,445.20 (£1,029.60: £492.80: £224.40)
1m 3f (Fibresand) Stalls: Low GOING: 0.08 sec per fur (STD) 3-30 (3-34)

30762 **Daleria (57)***(63)*(Fav)*(AHarrison)* 4-9-4 (3) JStack(8) (trckd ldrs: chal over 4f out: led over 3f out: styd on wl fnl f)......— 1
15323 Shining Example **(67)***(71) (PJMakin)* 3-9-9 RCochrane(9) (hdwy 5f out: chal 3f out: no ex fnl f)......1½ 2
Northern Highlight **(53)***(51) (TPMcGovern)* 4-9-0 (3) DRMcCabe(4) (b: a chsng ldrs: rdn & one pce fnl 3f)......4 3
32457 Streaky Hawk (USA) **(57)***(54) (PFICole)* 3-8-13 CRutter(10) (in tch: drvn along 5f out: styd on fnl 2f: no imp)......¾ 4
19166 Pretoria Dancer **(65)***(62) (JHMGosden)* 3-9-7 LDettori(5) (s.i.s: pushed along & hdwy after 2f: outpcd 4f out: no imp after)......nk 5
32763 Hotspur Street **(66)***(60) (MJohnston)* 3-9-8 JWeaver(6) (lw: s.i.s: drvn along & hmpd over 5f out: styd on: no imp)......1½ 6
30829 Top Fella (USA) (56)*(50) (WAO'Gorman)* 3-8-12b EmmaO'Gorman(13) (s.i.s: wnt prom after 3f: led over 4f out tl over 3f out: wknd)......nk 7
29602 Nautical Jewel **(59)***(24) (MDIUsher)* 3-9-1 MWigham(12) (s.i.s: nvr rchd ldrs)......20 8
34229 Dally Boy **(68)***(30) (MHEasterby)* 3-9-10 SMaloney(11) (in tch tl outpcd 5f out: n.d after)......1¾ 9
29844 Just-Mana-Mou (IRE) **(62)***(24) (GLewis)* 3-8-11 (7) AEddery(14) (lw: in tch: drvn along 5f out: wknd fnl 2f)......½ 10
24815 Last Spin **(55)***(12) (JRJenkins)* 3-8-11 MRimmer(2) (led tl hdd & wknd over 4f out)......3 11
31305 Junior Ben (IRE) **(61)** *(PHowling)* 3-9-3 PaulEddery(3) (chsd ldrs tl wknd 5f out)......15 12
33207 Forest Mill **(56)** *(DWPArbuthnot)* 3-8-12 KDarley(7) (b.hind: cl up tl wknd 5f out: eased fnl 2f)12 13
22456 Fabillion **(62)** *(CASmith)* 3-9-4 ACulhane(1) (Withdrawn not under Starter's orders: ref to ent stalls)...... W

4/1 DALERIA (op 7/1), **9/2** Hotspur Street (op 5/2), **5/1** Pretoria Dancer (3/1-11/2), **7/1** Junior Ben (IRE), **8/1** Just-Mana-Mou (IRE), **10/1** Streaky Hawk (USA), Shining Example, Top Fella (USA), Nautical Jewel, **12/1** Forest Mill, **14/1** Dally Boy (10/1-16/1), **20/1** Fabillion, **33/1** Northern Highlight, Last Spin, CSF £45.40 CT £1,106.91 TOTE £4.90: £1.50 £3.50 £9.10 (£26.90) Trio £318.10 OWNER Mr R. Fenwick-Gibson (MIDDLEHAM) 13 Rn 2m 31.7 (10.20) SF: 40/40/28/23/31/29/19/-/-/-/-/-/-

WEIGHT FOR AGE 3yo-8lb

3527

PEVERIL HOMES H'CAP (0-65) (3-Y.O+) (Class F) £3,224.60 (£895.60: £429.80)
2m (Fibresand) Stalls: High GOING: 0.08 sec per fur (STD) 4-00 (4-03)

29193 **Who's the Best (IRE) (43)***(57) (APJarvis)* 5-8-8 (3) DWright(9) (a gng wl: led on bit over 4f out: rdn & styd on wl fnl f)......— 1
*2919** Ijab (CAN) **(41)***(52) (JParkes)* 5-8-9b GBardwell(11) (lw: hdwy u.p 5f out: chsng ldrs ent st: styd on fnl f)......3½ 2
31784 Arctic Charmer (USA) **(65)***(74) (JLDunlop)* 3-9-6 KDarley(13) (trckd ldrs gng wl: effrt 3f out: one pce)......2 3
32456 Environmentalist (IRE) **(50)***(49) (RHarris)* 4-9-4 AMackay(16) (effrt ½-wy: sn chsng ldrs & rdn: outpcd fnl 2½f)......10 4
33185 Philmist **(50)***(48) (CWCElsey)* 3-8-5 NKennedy(15) (lw: bhd: hdwy u.p 5f out: no imp)......1 5
24954 La Menorquina (USA) **(46)***(43)*(Fav)*(DMarks)* 5-9-0 KFallon(7) (in tch: outpcd 5f out: no imp after)......hd 6
30739 Noble Ballerina (USA) **(45)***(38) (APJarvis)* 3-8-0 JTate(3) (chsd ldrs tl wknd fnl 3f)......4 7
64910 Ballymac Girl **(51)***(32) (JMBradley)* 7-9-5 JWeaver(4) (b: cl up: led 7f out tl over 4f out: wknd)......12 8
28607 Danus Rex (IRE) **(55)***(35) (CASmith)* 3-8-10 ACulhane(1) (chsd ldrs: drvn along most of wy: wl outpcd fnl 4f)......1¼ 9
32458 Absalom's Pillar **(50)***(30) (JMackie)* 5-9-4 GCarter(12) (led tl hdd 7f out: sn wknd)......nk 10
324511 Jaraab **(60)***(20) (GLewis)* 4-9-9v(5) AWhelan(14) (lw: a bhd: eased fnl 3f: t.o)......20 11
29212 Shared Risk **(58)** *(SGNorton)* 3-8-13 JCarroll(10) (outpcd & lost tch fnl 6f: t.o)......20 12
31142 Zanzara (IRE) **(42)** *(MrsVAAconley)* 4-8-10 MDeering(6) (lw: a outpcd & bhd: t.o)......1¼ 13
28545 Pride of May (IRE) **(60)** *(CWFairhurst)* 4-10-0v DeanMcKeown(8) (chsd ldrs tl wknd over 6f out: eased fnl 3f: t.o)......4 14
85114 Iron N Gold **(48)** *(AMoore)* 3-8-3 CandyMorris(5) (bhd fr ½-wy: t.o)......dist 15

4/1 La Menorquina (USA) (3/1-9/2), **7/1** Environmentalist (IRE) (5/1-8/1), **8/1** Ijab (CAN), Philmist, **9/1** Arctic Charmer (USA), **10/1** WHO'S THE BEST (IRE), Ballymac Girl, Shared Risk, **12/1** Zanzara (IRE), Jaraab, Iron N Gold, **14/1** Pride of May (IRE), Danus Rex (IRE), **20/1** Absalom's Pillar, **33/1** Noble Ballerina (USA), CSF £89.24 CT £705.14 TOTE £13.00: £3.40 £2.00 £3.50 (£30.50) Trio £128.10 OWNER Mrs Ann Jarvis (ASTON UPTHORPE) BRED F. Feeney 15 Rn
3m 48.5 SF: -/-/-/-/-/-/-/-/-/-/-/-/-/-/-
WEIGHT FOR AGE 3yo-13lb

3528

SUNLINE DIRECT MAIL NURSERY (S) H'CAP (0-65) (2-Y.O) (Class F) £3,098.60 (£859.60: £411.80)
6f (Fibresand) Stalls: Low GOING: 0.08 sec per fur (STD) 4-30 (4-32)

*2924*2 **Harsh Times (48)***(52) (MHEasterby)* 2-8-7 SMaloney(3) (cl up: led 3f out: put hd in air: drvn out) — **1**
3285 4 Image Maker (IRE) **(53)***(50) (DWPArbuthnot)* 2-8-9 (3) DRMcCabe(10) (outpcd tl c wd & styd on wl fnl 2½f) 2½ **2**
3160 12 Efipetite **(47)***(42) (NBycroft)* 2-8-6 KFallon(4) (a in tch: drvn along: kpt on: nt pce to chal) 1 **3**
*3244*3 Frances Mary **(49)***(43) (CWFairhurst)* 2-8-8 WWoods(13) (cl up: led 4f out to 3f out: one pce) nk **4**
3386 5 Northern Saga (IRE) **(53)***(36) (AndrewTurnell)* 2-8-12 PaulEddery(5) (chsd ldrs: drvn along ½-wy: no imp) 4 **5**
*2496*3 Young Butt **(58)***(40) (JFfitch-Heyes)* 2-9-3 RPrice(6) (a chsng ldrs: rdn & one pce fr ½-wy) ½ **6**
3417 9 Red Simba **(59)***(39) (JBerry)* 2-8-11 (7) PFessey(7) (s.i.s: hdwy 3f out: nvr rchd ldrs) ¾ **7**
2857 4 Ghostly Apparition **(59)***(38) (JohnUpson)* 2-8-11 (7) DSweeney(16) (b.hind: w ldrs tl grad wknd fnl 2f) nk **8**
3417 10 Brockville Bairn **(48)***(27) (MrsASwinbank)* 2-8-7 RMcGhin(15) (prom: sn drvn along: outpcd fr ½-wy) s.h **9**
3430 5 Marketeer Magic **(60)***(30) (JBerry)* 2-8-12 (7) PRoberts(8) (lw: b: nvr trbld ldrs) 3½ **10**
3155 10 Concert Party (IRE) **(50)***(6) (DWChapman)* 2-8-9 ACulhane(11) (lw: a in rr) 5 **11**
*3244*4 Swing Mania (IRE) **(49)***(2)*(Fav)*(SGNorton)* 2-8-8b KDarley(9) (s.i.s: nvr wnt pce) 1¼ **12**
3378 8 Cupla Focail **(50)** *(WRMuir)* 2-8-9 JWeaver(12) (nvr wnt pce) 4 **13**
2951 6 Ticka Ticka Timing **(62)***(2) (BWMurray)* 2-9-2 (5) GParkin(14) (a outpcd & bhd) ¾ **14**
1810 7 Caveat Emptor (IRE) **(50)** *(SDow)* 2-8-2 (7) ADaly(1) (lw: led 2f: wknd over 3f out) 14 **15**
2000 6 Derek's Bo **(46)** *(NBycroft)* 2-8-5 TWilliams(2) (w ldrs to ½-wy: wknd qckly: virtually p.u) 25 **16**

11/2 Swing Mania (IRE), **6/1** HARSH TIMES (op 4/1), Frances Mary, **13/2** Ticka Ticka Timing, **8/1** Young Butt, Northern Saga (IRE), **9/1** Red Simba, **10/1** Image Maker (IRE), Marketeer Magic, **11/1** Efipetite, **12/1** Ghostly Apparition, **14/1** Concert Party (IRE), Cupla Focail, Caveat Emptor (IRE), **33/1** Brockville Bairn, Derek's Bo, CSF £72.25 CT £628.42 TOTE £5.20: £1.80 £2.90 £2.70 £1.80 (£24.10) Trio £254.80; £17.95 to Leicester 5/9/95. OWNER Mr David Faulkner (MALTON) BRED Robert T. Cartwright 16 Rn
1m 19.7 SF: 15/13/5/6/-/3/2/1/-/-/-/-/-/-/-/-
Bt in 4,000 gns

3529

DON NOBLE BOOKMAKER AMATEUR H'CAP (0-70) (3-Y.O+) (Class G) £2,243.00 (£618.00: £293.00)
1m (Fibresand) Stalls: Low GOING: 0.08 sec per fur (STD) 5-00 (5-02)

2332* **Prudent Pet (57)***(67) (CWFairhurst)* 3-10-12 (3) MrsSBosley(12) (hdwy over 2f out: styd on wl fnl f to ld cl home) — **1**
3368 7 Mary's Case (IRE) **(54)***(63) (MJohnston)* 5-11-0b(3) MrsDKettlewell(1) (lost pl after 2f: hdwy ent st: led jst ins fnl f: hung lft: hdd & no ex cl home) ½ **2**
3385 2 Rockstine (IRE) **(51)***(52)*(Fav)*(PMitchell)* 4-11-0 MrTMcCarthy(9) (lw: dwlt: hdwy 3f out: styd on towards fin) 4 **3**
*2588*10 Brackenthwaite **(59)***(59) (LRLloyd-James)* 5-11-1v(7) MrDSpiteri(13) (b: b.hind: racd wd: sn drvn along: styd on fnl 2f: nrst fin) ½ **4**
3406 10 Rival Bid (USA) **(57)***(55) (MrsNMacauley)* 7-11-6 MrRJohnson(16) (s.i.s: hdwy 3f out: styd on: nvr able chal) 1¼ **5**
1472 15 Ripsnorter (IRE) **(52)***(49) (KBishop)* 6-10-10 (5) MissAPurdy(10) (lw: hdwy over 2f out: c wd: nrst fin) nk **6**
*3073*8 Jamaica Bridge **(58)***(53) (SGNorton)* 5-11-4 (3) MrMHNaughton(8) (chsd ldrs: led over 2f out tl jst ins fnl f: wknd) 1 **7**
3119 5 Langtonian **(48)***(37) (JLEyre)* 6-10-11v MissDianaJones(14) (led tl hdd & wknd over 2f out) 3 **8**
*3240*7 Indescent Blue **(50)***(38) (DWPArbuthnot)* 3-10-8 MrsDArbuthnot(7) (b.hind: drvn along ½-wy: no imp) nk **9**
820 16 Bold Habit **(53)***(36) (JPearce)* 10-11-2 MrsLPearce(5) (outpcd & bhd most of wy) 2½ **10**
*231*4 Certain Way (IRE) **(53)***(35) (NPLittmoden)* 5-10-9 (7) MrMSalaman(3) (chsd ldrs to st) ½ **11**
3277 8 Moultazim (USA) **(42)***(23) (RJPrice)* 5-10-2 (3) MrJCulloty(11) (chsd ldrs 5f: sn wknd) ½ **12**
3288 10 Breezed Well **(42)***(22) (BRCambidge)* 9-10-0 (5) MrsHNoonan(6) (b: outpcd fr ½-wy) ¾ **13**

3641[11] Off the Air (IRE) **(49)***(19) (BJLlewellyn)* 4-10-12b MrJLLlewellyn(2) (spd to ½-wy: wknd qckly)....5 **14**
2358[9] Green's Bid **(57)** *(DWChapman)* 5-11-1 (5) MissRClark(15) (chsd ldrs tl wknd wl over 2f out)....25 **15**
560[2] Bon Secret (IRE) **(70)** *(TJNaughton)* 3-11-9 (5) MrsJNaughton(4) (a bhd: t.o)....12 **16**

3/1 Rockstine (IRE), **11/2** PRUDENT PET, **6/1** Rival Bid (USA), **15/2** Mary's Case (IRE), **8/1** Bold Habit, **11/1** Jamaica Bridge (8/1-12/1), **12/1** Green's Bid, Langtonian, Off the Air (IRE), Certain Way (IRE), Bon Secret (IRE), **14/1** Brackenthwaite (10/1-16/1), **16/1** Moultazim (USA), Indescent Blue, **20/1** Breezed Well, **33/1** Ripsnorter (IRE), CSF £52.89 CT £146.23 TOTE £7.80: £2.30 £1.70 £1.10 £5.10 (£46.50) Trio £96.90 OWNER The McLain & Rodda Partnership (MIDDLEHAM) BRED John A. Jones Morgan 16 Rn 1m 49.1 (9.80) SF: 35/36/25/32/28/22/26/10/6/9/8/-/-/-/-/-

WEIGHT FOR AGE 3yo-5lb

STEWARDS' ENQUIRY Llewellyn susp. 13-15/9/95 (incorrect use of whip).

T/Jkpt: £8,991.00 (1.5 Tckts). T/Plpt: £44.00 (339.21 Tckts). T/Qdpt: £53.10 (5 Tckts). WG/AA

3289-LEICESTER (R-H)
Tuesday September 5th (Firm)

WEATHER: overcast WIND: almost nil

3530 REMPSTONE MAIDEN STKS (I) (2-Y.O) (Class D) £3,947.50 (£1,180.00: £565.00: £257.50) 7f 9y Stalls: High GOING minus 0.46 sec per fur (F) 1-45 (1-46)

Caxton Star *(81+) (HRACecil)* 2-9-0 AMcGlone(6) (b: unf: a.p: r.o to ld wl ins fnl f)....— **1**
2767[7] Singing Patriarch (IRE) *(78) (JLDunlop)* 2-9-0 PatEddery(13) (a.p: led over 2f out tl wl ins fnl f)....1½ **2**
Lasseman *(49) (RBoss)* 2-9-0 DHolland(10) (str: scope: bit bkwd: dwlt: rdn 3f out: hdwy 2f out: r.o)....¾ **3**
Illuminate *(75) (JARToller)* 2-9-0 WNewnes(3) (small: unf: s.s: plld hrd: gd hdwy over 1f out: r.o)....nk **4**
Robamaset (IRE) *(70+) (LMCumani)* 2-9-0 KDarley(9) (unf: scope: rdn over 3f out: hdwy over 2f out: nvr nr to chal)....2½ **5**
3436[U] Not Quite Grey *(67) (KMcAuliffe)* 2-9-0 JTate(4) (prom tl wknd over 1f out)....1¼ **6**
3427[4] Jerry Cutrona (IRE) *(63) (NACallaghan)* 2-9-0 GCarter(2) (nvr trbld ldrs)....1½ **7**
Sheath Kefaah *(63) (WJHaggas)* 2-9-0 BThomson(12) (unf: w ldrs tl wknd over 2f out)....nk **8**
3008[7] Chik's Secret **(50)***(49) (BPalling)* 2-8-9 TSprake(11) (w ldrs tl wknd over 2f out)....4 **9**
Badri (USA) *(50+)*(Fav)*(JHMGosden)* 2-9-0 LDettori(5) (unf: scope: a bhd: rdn 3f out: no rspnse)....1½ **10**
3246[5] May King Mayhem *(27) (WRMuir)* 2-9-0 FNorton(1) (dwlt: a bhd: t.o)....10 **11**
Mushahadah (IRE) *(DMorley)* 2-8-9 JLowe(8) (w'like: scope: bkwd: led tl wknd over 2f out: broke leg & p.u over 1f out: dead).... **P**

11/8 Badri (USA) (Evens-6/4), **7/2** CAXTON STAR (2/1-4/1), **5/1** Singing Patriarch (IRE), **13/2** Robamaset (IRE), **10/1** Not Quite Grey, **11/1** Lasseman, **16/1** Sheath Kefaah, **20/1** Illuminate, Mushahadah (IRE), Jerry Cutrona (IRE), **50/1** May King Mayhem, Chik's Secret, CSF £23.26 TOTE £7.40: £1.70 £2.20 £5.90 (£9.20) Trio £33.50 OWNER Famestar Ltd (NEWMARKET) BRED Mrs E. Longton 12 Rn 1m 26.6 (4.10) SF: 11/8/6/5/-/-/-/-/-/-/-

3531 STAG APPRENTICE H'CAP (0-75) (3-Y.O+) (Class E) £3,347.00 (£1,016.00: £498.00: £239.00) 1m 1f 218y Stalls: High GOING minus 0.46 sec per fur (F) 2-15 (2-19)

1553[3] **Hawkish (USA) (48)***(61) (DMorley)* 6-8-4 (3) GMitchell(1) (lw: dwlt: hdwy on ins 3f out: led over 1f out: r.o)....— **1**
3240[3] Douce Maison (IRE) **(52)***(64) (APJarvis)* 4-8-8 (3) CAdamson(16) (9th st: hdwy & hrd rdn over 2f out: squeezed over 1f out: r.o ins fnl f)....½ **2**
3207* Braille (IRE) **(65)***(75)*(Fav)*(MGMeagher)* 4-9-5 (5) JWilkinson(5) (lw: 3rd st: led over 3f out tl over 1f out: r.o one pce)....1¼ **3**
3384[5] Curtelace **(54)***(63)*(Fav)*(LadyHerries)* 5-8-10 (3) GParkin(19) (bhd tl hdwy 3f out: nt clr run & swtchd lft over 1f out: hrd rdn & r.o ins fnl f)....½ **4**
3154* Wet Patch (IRE) **(61)***(68)*(Fav)*(RHannon)* 3-8-10 (3) MarkDenaro(9) (swtg: wl bhd tl r.o fnl 2f)....1½ **5**
3286[5] Regal Fanfare (IRE) **(67)***(72) (JWHills)* 3-9-5 MHenry(4) (lw: nvr nrr)....1½ **6**
3402* Course Fishing **(44)***(49) (BAMcMahon)* 4-8-0 (3) 5x MartinDwyer(17) (dwlt: wl bhd tl hdwy 2f out: nvr nr to chal)....s.h **7**
3388[6] Salska **(45)***(48) (AStreeter)* 4-7-13 (5) DSweeney(10) (hdwy over 1f out: nrst fin)....¾ **8**

3362² Tribal Peace (IRE) **(68)***(69) (BGubby)* 3-9-6 AWhelan(6) (7th st: wandered fnl 3f: wknd fnl f) 1¼ **9**
3433⁴ Jubran (USA) **(64)***(65)*(Fav)*(MJohnston)* 9-9-4 (5) BHalligan(11) (4th st: wknd over 2f out) ½ **10**
3305⁴ Lancashire Life (IRE) **(51)***(51) (EJAlston)* 4-8-10 LNewton(3) (5th st: wknd 2f out) s.h **11**
2778⁷ Sarasota Storm **(57)***(57) (MBell)* 3-8-4 (5) GFaulkner(8) (lw: 6th st: ev ch 2f out: sn wknd) nk **12**
1626¹² Vin St Koola **(70)***(49) (MCChapman)* 3-9-5 (3) CMunday(2) (a bhd: t.o) 13 **13**
882¹⁷ Shot the Sheriff **(55)***(31) (PFICole)* 3-8-0 (7) DavidO'Neill(13) (dwlt: hdwy & c wd st: wknd 3f out: t.o) 2 **14**
3294³ Keen To The Last (FR) **(71)***(37)*(Fav)*(GHarwood)* 3-9-4 (5) GayeHarwood(18) (led 6f out tl hdd & wknd over 3f out: t.o) 6 **15**
3493⁹ Educated Pet **(43)** *(BPreece)* 6-8-2 DWright(7) (led 4f: 2nd st: wknd 4f out: t.o) 6 **16**
2946¹⁰ Daring Ryde **(46)** *(JPSmith)* 4-8-0 (5) RStudholme(14) (bhd fnl 4f: t.o) 4 **17**

8/1 Jubran (USA), Wet Patch (IRE), Braille (IRE), Curtelace, Keen To The Last (FR), **17/2** Douce Maison (IRE), **10/1** Course Fishing, **12/1** Tribal Peace (IRE), Regal Fanfare (IRE), **14/1** Salska, Sarasota Storm, HAWKISH (USA), **20/1** Lancashire Life (IRE), **25/1** Shot the Sheriff, **33/1** Vin St Koola, Daring Ryde, **50/1** Educated Pet, CSF £119.86 CT £940.74 TOTE £16.00: £2.40 £2.30 £2.90 £3.00 (£58.50) Trio £212.40 OWNER Mrs M. F. D. Morley (NEWMARKET) BRED Joseph Manzi 17 Rn 2m 5.6 (2.90) SF: 31/34/45/33/31/35/19/18/32/35/21/20/12/-/-/-/-
WEIGHT FOR AGE 3yo-7lb

3532 E.B.F. FILBERT MAIDEN STKS (2-Y.O F) (Class D) £3,984.75 (£1,188.00: £566.50: £255.75) 1m 8y Stalls: High GOING minus 0.46 sec per fur (F) 2-45 (2-48)

Caribbean Quest *(87+) (BHanbury)* 2-8-11 WRSwinburn(4) (lt-f: hld up in rr: swtchd lft 2f out: rapid hdwy to ld ins fnl f: sn clr) — **1**
3306³ Fijon (IRE) *(77) (BWHills)* 2-8-11 DHolland(1) (w ldrs: led over 1f out tl ins fnl f) 5 **2**
Catumbella (USA) *(75+)*(Fav)*(JHMGosden)* 2-8-11 LDettori(11) (w'like: a.p: led 2f out: sn hdd: one pce) 1¼ **3**
Pike Creek (USA) *(74) (IABalding)* 2-8-11 KDarley(3) (lengthy: scope: styd on u.p fnl 2f: nvr nrr) ½ **4**
Pine Needle *(71) (DMorley)* 2-8-11 BThomson(10) (hdwy 3f out: rdn 2f out: wknd fnl f) 1¼ **5**
Age of Reality (USA) *(68) (HCandy)* 2-8-11 WNewnes(2) (hld up: effrt 2f out: one pce fnl f) 1½ **6**
2579⁴ Just Nuisance *(67) (CEBrittain)* 2-8-11 MRoberts(7) (w ldrs tl wknd 2f out) ¾ **7**
Flahuil *(67) (RHannon)* 2-8-11 TQuinn(5) (w ldrs tl wknd 2f out) d.h **7**
Galaka *(61) (LMCumani)* 2-8-11 OUrbina(8) (w'like: hdwy over 2f out: wknd over 1f out) 3 **9**
Home Cookin' *(53) (DrJDScargill)* 2-8-11 TIves(9) (w'like: scope: led tl hdd & wknd 2f out) 4 **10**
Charnwood Nell (USA) *(52) (PAKelleway)* 2-8-11 PatEddery(6) (small: dwlt: rdn 3f out: bhd fnl 2f) ½ **11**

6/4 Catumbella (USA) (5/4-2/1), **9/2** Fijon (IRE) (op 3/1), **11/2** Charnwood Nell (USA) (4/1-6/1), **6/1** CARIBBEAN QUEST (op 4/1), **9/1** Just Nuisance, **10/1** Pike Creek (USA), **12/1** Pine Needle, **14/1** Age of Reality (USA), **16/1** Galaka, **20/1** Flahuil, **33/1** Home Cookin', CSF £35.47 TOTE £4.90: £1.90 £1.90 £1.20 (£19.30) Trio £5.30 OWNER Maktoum Al Maktoum (NEWMARKET) BRED GAINSBOROUGH STUD MANAGEMENT LTD 11 Rn 1m 38.4 (3.40) SF: 22/12/10/9/6/3/2/2/-/-/-

3533 RANCLIFFE NURSERY (S) H'CAP (0-65) (2-Y.O) (Class G) £2,892.60 (£803.60: £385.80) 1m 8y Stalls: High GOING minus 0.46 sec per fur (F) 3-15 (3-21)

2516⁶ **In Paradisum (USA) (54)***(57) (MrsJRRamsden)* 2-8-10 KFallon(10) (stdd s: bhd tl hdwy 2f out: led ins fnl f: r.o) — **1**
3233⁸ Bath Knight **(45)***(45) (DJSffrenchDavis)* 2-8-1 NAdams(3) (a.p: led over 2f out tl ins fnl f) 1¾ **2**
3350² Velvet Jones **(57)***(56) (PFICole)* 2-8-13 TQuinn(12) (a.p: ev ch 1f out: nt qckn) nk **3**
3233² Willie Rushton **(58)***(57)*(Fav)*(GLMoore)* 2-9-0 SWhitworth(7) (a.p: hrd rdn over 2f out: r.o one pce) hd **4**
3285³ Anna Settic **(56)***(50) (DrJDScargill)* 2-8-12v LDettori(8) (hdwy 2f out: nvr nrr) 2½ **5**
2756⁴ How Could-I (IRE) **(52)***(40) (MHEasterby)* 2-8-8 SMaloney(13) (prom tl rdn & wknd over 1f out) 3 **6**
3417⁷ Marmy **(45)***(30) (MHEasterby)* 2-8-1 LCharnock(4) (prom tl wknd over 1f out) 1¼ **7**
*2075** Multi Franchise **(66)***(44) (BGubby)* 2-9-1 (7) CScally(6) (hrd rdn 3f out: nvr nr to chal) 3½ **8**
3378¹⁰ Dish The Dosh **(48)***(22) (PGMurphy)* 2-7-11b(7)ow3 RWaterfield(2) (nvr trbld ldrs) ½ **9**
3353³ Ned's Contessa (IRE) **(55)***(30) (MDods)* 2-8-11 JCarroll(15) (nvr nr ldrs) 1 **10**
1336³ Shanoora (IRE) **(56)***(30) (BPalling)* 2-8-12 TSprake(9) (rdn over 1f out: nvr nr ldrs) ½ **11**
2143⁹ Priddy Fair **(56)***(27) (RBoss)* 2-8-12 MRoberts(16) (bit bkwd: hdwy 4f out: wknd over 2f out) 1½ **12**
2908⁵ Victoria Venture **(59)***(29) (SPCWoods)* 2-8-8 (7) CWebb(1) (lw: outpcd) ¾ **13**
3008⁵ Island Victory **(52)***(19) (IABalding)* 2-8-8v KDarley(18) (led tl hdd & wknd over 2f out) 1¼ **14**
2204⁷ Herald Angel (IRE) **(45)***(11) (MHTompkins)* 2-8-1 SMulvey(19) (outpcd) ¾ **15**
3353¹¹ Fast Food **(42)** *(BJMcMath)* 2-7-12b EJohnson(14) (spd 4f) 4 **16**

3233[7] Pinocchio Boy (IRE) **(62)***(17) (BJMeehan)* 2-9-4 MTebbutt(17) (prom tl hrd rdn & wknd over 2f out) 1½ **17**
2995[13] Double Vintage (IRE) **(45)** *(MCChapman)* 2-7-8 (7) CMunday(11) (lw: a outpcd) 1½ **18**
2496[2] Pulga Circo **(57)** *(BAMcMahon)* 2-8-13 FNorton(20) (lw: t.o) 9 **19**

7/2 Willie Rushton, **7/1** Velvet Jones, **8/1** Island Victory, IN PARADISUM (USA), **9/1** Anna Settic, **10/1** Priddy Fair, **14/1** Ned's Contessa (IRE), How Could-I (IRE), **16/1** Victoria Venture, Pulga Circo, **20/1** Shanoora (IRE), Pinocchio Boy (IRE), Multi Franchise, Herald Angel (IRE), **33/1** Bath Knight, Fast Food, Marmy, Double Vintage (IRE), Dish The Dosh, CSF £232.69 CT £1,758.85 TOTE £10.20: £2.70 £5.50 £1.70 £1.80 (£227.80) Trio £399.90 OWNER Mrs J. R. Ramsden (THIRSK) BRED Audley Farm Inc. 19 Rn 1m 38.6 (3.60) SF: 19/7/18/19/12/2/-/6/-/-/-/-/-/-/-/-/-/-/-
Bt in 4,000 gns; Velvet Jones clmd GCharles-Jones

3534 SWAN H'CAP (0-70) (3-Y.O+) (Class E) £3,817.00 (£1,144.00: £550.00: £253.00) **7f 9y** Stalls: High GOING minus 0.46 sec per fur (F) 3-45 (3-49)

3181[7] **Keston Pond (IRE) (65)***(77) (DAWilson)* 5-9-9 GCarter(15) (a.p: led over 1f out: r.o wl) ....— **1**
3172* It's Academic **(61)***(69)*(Fav)*(MrsJRRamsden)* 3-9-1 KFallon(19) (hdwy over 2f out: swtchd rt over 1f out: r.o ins fnl f) 2 **2**
1209[2] Heathyards Lady (USA) **(48)***(55) (RHollinshead)* 4-8-6 KDarley(13) (a.p: r.o one pce fnl f) ....hd **3**
3439[3] Whatever's Right (IRE) **(70)***(72)*(Fav)*(MDIUsher)* 6-10-0 BThomson(11) (led over 5f: one pce) 2½ **4**
2802[3] Pelleman **(70)***(67)*(Fav)*(RBoss)* 3-9-10 DHolland(7) (a.p: hrd rdn & ev ch 2f out: one pce) 2 **5**
3079[2] Paddy's Rice **(60)***(56) (LJHolt)* 4-9-4 MPerrett(20) (a.p: r.o one pce fnl 2f) ....nk **6**
3447[7] Kilnamartyra Girl **(53)***(47) (JParkes)* 5-8-8 (3) PMcCabe(9) (rdn 3f out: no hdwy fnl 2f) 1¼ **7**
3367[9] Rood Music **(59)***(52) (MGMeagher)* 4-9-3 PatEddery(14) (w ldr tl wknd over 1f out) ....s.h **8**
3396[6] Takeshi (IRE) **(60)***(51) (EALDunlop)* 3-9-0 WRSwinburn(4) (hld up: nvr nr to chal) 1¼ **9**
3291[2] Love Legend **(52)***(42) (DWPArbuthnot)* 10-8-10 SWhitworth(16) (b: nvr nrr) ....s.h **10**
2088[15] Cavatina **(65)***(55) (TWDonnelly)* 5-9-9 CRutter(10) (n.d) ....s.h **11**
3439[9] Belleminette (IRE) **(55)***(45) (DHaydnJones)* 4-8-13 AMackay(12) (stumbled s: sn rcvrd: bhd fnl 2f) ....s.h **12**
1979[3] Sharp Consul (IRE) **(69)***(58) (HCandy)* 3-9-9 WNewnes(18) (hld up: a bhd) ....½ **13**
3511[4] Jon's Choice **(52)***(39) (BPreece)* 7-8-10 NAdams(8) (a bhd) 1 **14**
1680[4] Johnnie the Joker **(53)***(40) (JPLeigh)* 4-8-11 DaleGibson(17) (a bhd) ....hd **15**
2832[9] Lady-Bo-K **(51)***(36) (CaptJWilson)* 4-8-2 (7) FLynch(5) (b.hind: prom 5f) ....½ **16**
3396[3] King Chestnut **(61)***(26) (MDods)* 4-9-5 JCarroll(2) (a bhd) 9 **17**
1571[14] Penny's Wishing **(64)***(22) (JPLeigh)* 3-9-4 DeanMcKeown(1) (a bhd) 3 **18**
3293[14] Great Hall **(60)***(16)*(Fav)*(PDCundell)* 6-9-4b LDettori(6) (sn rdn along: a bhd) 1 **19**
3510[8] Grey Again **(54)***(8) (SRBowring)* 3-8-3b(5) CTeague(3) (b: rdn over 3f out: hung rt: sn bhd) 1 **20**

8/1 Whatever's Right (IRE), It's Academic, Great Hall, Pelleman, **9/1** King Chestnut, **10/1** Rood Music, Kilnamartyra Girl, **12/1** Takeshi (IRE), KESTON POND (IRE), **14/1** Love Legend, Heathyards Lady (USA), Paddy's Rice, **16/1** Sharp Consul (IRE), Belleminette (IRE), **20/1** Grey Again, **25/1** Penny's Wishing, **33/1** Lady-Bo-K, Cavatina, Jon's Choice, Johnnie the Joker, CSF £104.88 CT £1,264.60 TOTE £14.10: £3.50 £2.70 £3.20 £2.00 (£62.50) Trio £376.80 OWNER Mr T. S. M. S. Riley-Smith (EPSOM) BRED John Harrington in Ireland 20 Rn
1m 23.1 (0.60) SF: 60/48/38/55/46/39/30/35/30/25/38/28/37/22/23/19/9/1/-/-
WEIGHT FOR AGE 3yo-4lb

3535 PRESTWOLD STKS (3-Y.O+) (Class C) £5,156.00 (£1,856.00: £888.00: £360.00: £140.00) **5f 2y** Stalls: High GOING minus 0.46 sec per fur (F) 4-15 (4-16)

3103* **Mr Oscar** *(101+) (MJohnston)* 3-8-12 MRoberts(3) (lw: led after 1f: hung rt over 1f out: unchal) ....— **1**
3316[3] Lucky Parkes **(103)***(90)*(Fav)*(JBerry)* 5-9-5 JCarroll(5) (lw: led 1f: one pce fnl 2f) 5 **2**
3376[11] Millesime (IRE) **(70)***(80) (BHanbury)* 3-8-12 LDettori(1) (prom: rdn & one pce fnl 2f) 1½ **3**
3279[2] Anzio (IRE) **(71)***(64) (BAPearce)* 4-8-7b(3) PMcCabe(2) (b.hind: spd 3f) 4 **4**
3424[15] Ballysheila *(GFHCharles-Jones)* 3-7-10v(7) RStudholme(4) (s.s: a bhd: t.o) 20 **5**

4/5 Lucky Parkes, **7/4** MR OSCAR, **9/1** Anzio (IRE), **12/1** Millesime (IRE) (8/1-14/1), **200/1** Ballysheila, CSF £3.38 TOTE £2.10: £1.50 £1.10 (£1.50) OWNER Mr W. McKeown (MIDDLEHAM) BRED Zetland Stud 5 Rn 58.3 secs (-0.20) SF: 61/52/40/26/-
WEIGHT FOR AGE 3yo-2lb

3536 REMPSTONE MAIDEN STKS (II) (2-Y.O) (Class D) £3,915.00 (£1,170.00: £560.00: £255.00) **7f 9y** Stalls: High GOING minus 0.46 sec per fur (F) 4-45 (4-46)

3174[5] **Masquerade** *(79) (LMCumani)* 2-9-0 KDarley(4) (a.p: hrd rdn 2f out: led ins fnl f: r.o) ....— **1**

3104[2] Do Not Disturb (USA) *(76) (JLDunlop)* 2-9-0 PatEddery(11) (led tl ins fnl f) 1¼ 2
3174[2] Diminutive (USA) *(71)*(Fav)*(JWHills)* 2-9-0 MHills(3) (w ldr: ev ch over 1f out: one pce)........2½ 3
Mushtak (USA) *(68+) (MajorWRHern)* 2-9-0 LDettori(2) (cmpt: prom: rdn & outpcd 3f out: styd on fnl f)..........1 4
Mountain Dream *(67+) (PFICole)* 2-9-0 TQuinn(6) (w'like: a.p: one pce fnl 2f)..........½ 5
Nardus *(64+) (MRStoute)* 2-9-0 WRSwinburn(12) (unf: scope: hld up in rr: hdwy over 1f out: nvr nrr)..........1½ 6
By A Whisker *(60) (DWPArbuthnot)* 2-9-0 SWhitworth(7) (unf: dwlt: nvr trbld ldrs)..........1½ 7
Mourne Mountains *(51) (HCandy)* 2-9-0 WNewnes(10) (wl grwn: bhd fnl 2f)..........4 8
Indian Sunset *(46) (CREgerton)* 2-9-0 BThomson(8) (unf: bkwd: n.d)..........2½ 9
2615[10] Generous Present *(45) (JWPayne)* 2-9-0 MTebbutt(1) (a bhd)..........nk 10
3346[5] Celestial Sister *(CDBroad)* 2-8-9 MPerrett(9) (sn bhd: t.o fnl 3f)..........dist 11

9/4 Diminutive (USA), **11/4** MASQUERADE (6/4-3/1), **4/1** Do Not Disturb (USA), **6/1** Nardus (op 4/1), **7/1** Mushtak (USA), **20/1** Mountain Dream, **25/1** Mourne Mountains, **50/1** By A Whisker, Indian Sunset, Generous Present, **100/1** Celestial Sister, CSF £13.67 TOTE £3.30: £1.40 £1.10 £1.60 (£4.90) Trio £3.20 OWNER Lord Carnarvon (NEWMARKET) BRED Highclere Stud Ltd 11 Rn
1m 25.5 (3.00) SF: 24/21/16/13/12/9/5/-/-/-/-

3537 LEICESTERSHIRE MAIDEN STKS (3-Y.O+) (Class D) £4,543.50 (£1,362.00: £655.00: £301.50)

1m 1f 218y Stalls: High GOING minus 0.46 sec per fur (F) 5-15 (5-17)

1526[3] **Syrian Queen** *(82)*(Fav)*(HRACecil)* 3-8-9b PatEddery(4) (mde all: hrd rdn over 1f out: r.o)...— 1
3392[3] Ranosh (USA) **(74)***(79) (EALDunlop)* 3-8-9 WRSwinburn(8) (b: b.hind: 3rd st: ev ch 2f out: one pce)..........2 2
3183[2] Sheraz (IRE) **(79)***(78) (GWragg)* 3-8-7 (7) GMilligan(7) (chsd wnr: 2nd st: one pce fnl 2f)........3½ 3
3448[2] Harlech (IRE) *(76) (JHMGosden)* 3-9-0b LDettori(5) (rdn along: 4th st: one pce fnl 3f)..........1½ 4
2977[4] Wild Palm *(73) (WAO'Gorman)* 3-9-0 EmmaO'Gorman(11) (lw: s.s: hdwy & 6th st: nvr nr to chal)..........2 5
3438[7] Our Kris *(67) (GHarwood)* 3-9-0 KDarley(2) (8th st: nvr nr to chal)..........3½ 6
2880[6] Duke Valentino *(64) (RHollinshead)* 3-9-0 TIves(1) (hld up & plld hrd: 5th st: nvr trbld ldrs)..........2 7
376[7] Noble Canonire *(51) (NPLittmoden)* 3-8-9 TGMcLaughlin(9) (s.s: a bhd)..........5 8
3461[5] Docklands Courier *(54) (BJMcMath)* 3-9-0 MTebbutt(3) (7th st: nvr nr ldrs)..........1 9
3294[10] Sungai Mas (USA) *(41) (SPCWoods)* 3-8-7 (7) CWebb(12) (a bhd)..........8 10
Gymcrak Hero (IRE) *(41) (GHolmes)* 3-9-0 KFallon(13) (b.hind: a bhd)..........hd 11
3023[10] River May *(22) (AndrewTurnell)* 3-8-9 NAdams(6) (a bhd)..........9 12

15/8 SYRIAN QUEEN, **4/1** Ranosh (USA), Harlech (IRE) (3/1-9/2), **5/1** Sheraz (IRE), **9/1** Wild Palm (op 5/1), **20/1** Our Kris, **25/1** Duke Valentino, Gymcrak Hero (IRE), **50/1** Docklands Courier, Sungai Mas (USA), **66/1** Noble Canonire, River May, CSF £9.62 TOTE £2.50: £1.30 £1.40 £1.20 (£4.70) Trio £9.90 OWNER Mr Wafic Said (NEWMARKET) BRED P. T. Tellwright 12 Rn
2m 5.0 (2.30) SF: 38/35/34/32/29/23/20/7/10/-/-/-

T/Jkpt: Not won; £2,903.72 to Doncaster 6/9/95. T/Plpt: £38.70 (436.97 Tckts). T/Qdpt: £6.60 (13.4 Tckts). Hn/

3314-LINGFIELD (L-H)
Tuesday September 5th (Turf Good to firm becoming Firm, AWT Standard)

WEATHER: fair WIND: almost nil

3538 GODSTONE RATING RELATED MAIDEN LIMITED STKS (0-70) (2-Y.O) (Class E) £3,245.00 (£968.00: £462.00: £209.00)

6f Stalls: High GOING minus 0.55 sec per fur (F) 2-00 (2-00)

3430[2] **Rebel County (IRE)** **(61)***(76) (DJSCosgrove)* 2-8-9 MRimmer(6) (lw: hld up: hrd rdn 2f out: led ins fnl f: r.o wl)..........— 1
3379[3] Step On Degas **(70)***(68)*(Fav)*(SDow)* 2-8-9 WRyan(7) (lw: led tl ins fnl f: unable qckn)..........3 2
3155[8] Delaunay (IRE) **(70)***(73) (RHannon)* 2-8-9 (5) DaneO'Neill(5) (lw: rdn over 3f out: hdwy over 1f out: r.o ins fnl f)..........hd 3
3213[8] Meranti **(70)***(72) (LJHolt)* 2-9-0 JReid(4) (lw: hld up: rdn over 3f out: r.o one pce fnl 2f)..........nk 4
3203[3] Corniche Quest (IRE) **(67)***(67) (MRChannon)* 2-8-9 WWoods(2) (w ldr: rdn over 1f out: ev ch ins fnl f: one pce)..........hd 5
3093[2] Rose of Siberia (USA) **(70)***(48) (MBell)* 2-8-9 MFenton(1) (lw: bhd fnl 3f)..........7 6
2351[12] Moving Up (IRE) **(70)***(40) (GLMoore)* 2-8-9 JFEgan(3) (b.nr hind: lw: a bhd)..........3 7

3/1 Step On Degas (2/1-100/30), **7/2** Rose of Siberia (USA), **9/2** Moving Up (IRE), **6/1** Corniche Quest (IRE), **13/2** Meranti (5/1-8/1), **7/1** REBEL COUNTY (IRE), **25/1** Delaunay (IRE), CSF £25.43 TOTE £4.90: £2.60 £1.90 (£8.10) OWNER Edermine Bloodstock (NEWMARKET) BRED C. J. Foy 7 Rn
1m 10.96 (1.96) SF: 25/17/22/21/16/-/-

3539 E.B.F. NUTFIELD MAIDEN STKS (I) (2-Y.O F) (Class D)

£3,867.50 (£1,154.00: £551.00: £249.50)
7f Stalls: High GOING minus 0.47 sec per fur (F) 2-30 (2-38)

3339[4] **Mezzogiorno** *(84+)*(Fav)*(GWragg)* 2-8-11 MHills(9) (mde all: shkn up over 1f out: comf) .....— **1**
2351[11] Jezyah (USA) *(80) (RWArmstrong)* 2-8-11 WCarson(2) (w wnr: rdn 2f out: unable qckn fnl f) 1¾ **2**
3352[4] Hilaala (USA) *(75) (PTWalwyn)* 2-8-11 RHills(6) (lw: hld up: rdn over 1f out: one pce) 2 **3**
Green Charter *(71+) (HRACecil)* 2-8-11 WRyan(1) (leggy: unf: bit bkwd: a.p: rdn over 2f out: wknd ins fnl f) 2 **4**
Della Casa (IRE) *(59) (JLDunlop)* 2-8-11 PaulEddery(8) (leggy: unf: nvr nr to chal) 5 **5**
Funky *(57) (LMCumani)* 2-8-11 JReid(3) (leggy: unf: plld hrd: swtchd lft over 4f out: bhd fnl 2f) 1 **6**
3387[6] Fancy Design (IRE) *(53) (PMitchell)* 2-8-11 GDuffield(7) (hung rt thrght: hld up: rdn over 2f out: sn wknd) 2 **7**
1690[11] Illegally Yours *(23) (LMontagueHall)* 2-8-11 JWilliams(4) (bhd fnl 4f) 13 **8**
Cast A Fly (IRE) *(MPMuggeridge)* 2-8-6 (5) DaneO'Neill(5) (w'like: bkwd: s.s: sn t.o) .....dist **9**

4/9 MEZZOGIORNO, **7/1** Jezyah (USA), Green Charter (op 5/2), **10/1** Hilaala (USA) (8/1-12/1), **20/1** Della Casa (IRE), Funky, **25/1** Fancy Design (IRE), **100/1** Illegally Yours, Cast A Fly (IRE), CSF £4.62 TOTE £1.50: £1.10 £2.20 £1.90 (£4.00) Trio £7.00 OWNER Mrs R. Philipps (NEWMARKET) BRED Exors of the late Sir Robin McAlpine 9 Rn 1m 22.24 (1.64) SF: 35/31/26/22/10/8/4/-/-

3540 TATTERSALLS NURSERY AUCTION H'CAP (0-75) (2-Y.O) (Class E)

£3,588.20 (£1,073.60: £514.80: £235.40)
7f 140y Stalls: Centre GOING minus 0.47 sec per fur (F) 3-00 (3-04)

3350* **Aussie (65)***(67)*(Fav)*(MHTompkins)* 2-9-2 PRobinson(12) (nt clr run over 2f out: hdwy to ld over 1f out: rdn out) .....— **1**
3243[3] Cherry Garden (IRE) **(63)***(60) (TJNaughton)* 2-8-9 (5) JDSmith(9) (rdn over 4f out: hdwy on ins over 1f out: r.o) 2½ **2**
*3243** Bumblefoot (IRE) **(62)***(56) (MJohnston)* 2-8-13 TWilliams(6) (chsd ldr 5f: one pce) 1½ **3**
2717* Hurricane Dancer (IRE) **(60)***(53) (SPCWoods)* 2-8-11 WWoods(8) (lw: hld up: ev ch over 1f out: one pce) .....½ **4**
3025[7] Nikita's Star (IRE) **(68)***(60) (DJGMurraySmith)* 2-9-0v(5) DaneO'Neill(4) (lw: a.p: ev ch over 1f out: one pce) .....½ **5**
3379[13] Day Tripper **(70)***(61) (GBBalding)* 2-9-7 JWilliams(10) (lw: nvr nr to chal) .....nk **6**
3225[7] Hotlips Houlihan **(68)***(59) (RJRWilliams)* 2-9-5 DBiggs(5) (led 6f) .....hd **7**
3386[3] Arlington Lady **(62)***(49) (NACallaghan)* 2-8-13 RCochrane(11) (b.hind: hdwy & nt clr run over 1f out: nt rcvr) 2 **8**
3379[17] Bailiwick **(62)***(41) (NAGraham)* 2-8-13 JReid(7) (hld up: rdn over 2f out: wknd wl over 1f out) 3½ **9**
3460[10] Evidence In Chief **(68)***(46) (PFICole)* 2-9-5 WCarson(1) (prom 6f) .....¾ **10**
3379[22] Cotytto **(50)** *(MJFetherston-Godley)* 2-8-1 JQuinn(3) (s.s: a bhd: t.o) .....dist **11**

7/2 AUSSIE, **9/2** Hurricane Dancer (IRE), **5/1** Bumblefoot (IRE), **8/1** Cherry Garden (IRE), Arlington Lady, **10/1** Evidence In Chief (7/1-11/1), **12/1** Nikita's Star (IRE), **14/1** Day Tripper (8/1-16/1), **16/1** Hotlips Houlihan, **20/1** Bailiwick, **33/1** Cotytto, CSF £28.67 CT £126.17 TOTE £4.20: £1.80 £3.40 £1.90 (£12.10) Trio £14.90 OWNER Mr T. N. Claydon (NEWMARKET) BRED Floors Farming 11 Rn
1m 31.66 (3.66) SF: 19/12/8/5/12/13/11/1/-/-/-

3541 E.B.F. NUTFIELD MAIDEN STKS (II) (2-Y.O F) (Class D)

£3,867.50 (£1,154.00: £551.00: £249.50)
7f Stalls: High GOING minus 0.47 sec per fur (F) 3-30 (3-30)

Please Suzanne *(79+)*(Fav)*(RHannon)* 2-8-11 BDoyle(8) (unf: scope: hld up: led 2f out: rdn & r.o wl) .....— **1**
3339[14] Angel Chimes *(73) (JEBanks)* 2-8-8 (3) JStack(1) (b.off hind: a.p: ev ch 2f out: unable qckn) 2½ **2**
3136[6] Somer Solo *(62) (PMitchell)* 2-8-11 GDuffield(3) (led 5f: wknd over 1f out) 5 **3**
Ski For Gold *(60) (JLDunlop)* 2-8-11 JReid(2) (unf: bit bkwd: hld up: rdn over 2f out: wknd over 1f out) 1 **4**
Tiama (IRE) *(58) (SDow)* 2-8-11 MFenton(6) (unf: a.p: ev ch over 2f out: wknd wl over 1f out) .....¾ **5**

2866[5] Dells Dream (IRE) *(57) (MRChannon)* 2-8-11 WWoods(4) (prom over 4f)....½ 6
Alreeh (IRE) *(56) (JHMGosden)* 2-8-11 WCarson(5) (w'like: scope: s.s: a bhd)....½ 7
2985[6] Martins Folly *(28) (JWhite)* 2-8-8 (3) SDrowne(7) (lw: bhd fnl 3f)....12 8

6/4 PLEASE SUZANNE, **4/1** Alreeh (IRE), **5/1** Angel Chimes (3/1-6/1), **6/1** Ski For Gold (3/1-7/1), **8/1** Tiama (IRE), **20/1** Dells Dream (IRE), **33/1** Somer Solo, Martins Folly, CSF £8.83 TOTE £2.10: £1.10 £2.00 £4.20 (£9.10) OWNER Mr Mohamed Suhail (MARLBOROUGH) BRED GAINSBOROUGH STUD MANAGEMENT LTD 8 Rn 1m 23.76 (3.16) SF: 17/11/-/-/-/-/-/-

3542 CHAMPAGNE JACQUART MAIDEN STKS (3-Y.O+) (Class D) £4,509.70 (£1,351.60: £649.80: £298.90)

7f Stalls: High GOING minus 0.47 sec per fur (F) 4-00 (4-04)

Mufarej (USA) *(81+)*(Fav)*(RWArmstrong)* 3-9-0 WCarson(13) (lw: rdn & hdwy 2f out: led ins fnl f: r.o wl)....— 1
3138[W] Another Batchworth **(54)***(71) (SMellor)* 3-8-9 JFEgan(8) (led tl ins fnl f: unable qckn)....2 2
3507[6] Yeast *(76) (WJHaggas)* 3-9-0 RCochrane(1) (lw: dwlt: hdwy 2f out: r.o ins fnl f)....hd 3
1240[8] Barriyah *(58) (HThomsonJones)* 3-8-9 RHills(14) (lw: chsd ldr over 5f)....6 4
664[6] Persian Butterfly *(54) (JEBanks)* 3-8-6 (3) JStack(6) (rdn & hdwy 2f out: wknd 1f out)....1½ 5
3347[4] Sweet Allegiance *(53) (JCPoulton)* 5-8-13 AMorris(11) (no hdwy fnl 3f)....½ 6
3347[6] Mad About The Girl (IRE) *(44) (DJSCosgrove)* 3-8-9 MRimmer(12) (nvr nrr)....4 7
Golden Touch (USA) *(45) (RChampion)* 3-8-7 (7) ADaly(4) (lw: prom over 5f)....1¾ 8
2553[15] Paddys Cherub *(33) (JRArnold)* 3-8-9 JQuinn(7) (bit bkwd: bhd fnl 3f)....3 9
1848[9] Empty Quarter **(93)***(37) (JHMGosden)* 3-9-0 GHind(5) (bhd fnl 4f)....½ 10
3023[11] Midnight Walker *(MrsSDWilliams)* 3-8-9 JWilliams(2) (dwlt: a wl bhd)....15 11
My Jazzmyn *(DCO'Brien)* 3-8-6 (3) DRMcCabe(9) (unf: s.s: a wl bhd)....15 12
Dovedon Lad *(GCBravery)* 3-9-0 MFenton(10) (bhd fnl 4f: t.o)....dist 13

5/4 MUFAREJ (USA), **3/1** Empty Quarter (7/4-7/2), **11/2** Persian Butterfly, **7/1** Yeast, **12/1** Barriyah, **33/1** Another Batchworth, Sweet Allegiance, **50/1** Golden Touch (USA), Paddys Cherub, Mad About The Girl (IRE), Midnight Walker, My Jazzmyn, Dovedon Lad, CSF £35.44 TOTE £2.40: £1.40 £2.70 £2.20 (£18.80) Trio £58.50 OWNER Mr Hamdan Al Maktoum (NEWMARKET) BRED Shadwell Farm Inc and Shadwell Estate Co Ltd 13 Rn 1m 21.44 (0.84) SF: 47/37/42/24/20/23/10/11/-/3/-/-/-
WEIGHT FOR AGE 3yo-4lb

3543 MARSH GREEN MAIDEN STKS (3-Y.O+) (Class D) £4,070.30 (£1,216.40: £582.20: £265.10) **1m 3f 106y** Stalls: High GOING minus 0.47 sec (F) 4-30 (4-32)

3190[4] **Kshessinskaya (95)***(74)*(Fav)*(CEBrittain)* 3-8-8 BDoyle(4) (lw: chsd ldr: led over 2f out tl ins fnl f: led nr fin)....— 1
3294[7] Fighting Times *(79) (CASmith)* 3-8-13 ACulhane(2) (3rd st: hrd rdn over 1f out: led ins fnl f: hdd nr fin)....nk 2
Dolliver (USA) *(67) (SDow)* 3-8-13 WRyan(6) (w'like: 5th st: nvr nr to chal)....8 3
3183[6] Our Little Lady *(59) (JEBanks)* 3-8-8 JQuinn(1) (led 9f: wknd over 1f out)....2½ 4
Jane's Super Top *(53) (JPearce)* 3-8-13 GBardwell(5) (str: scope: 4th st: a bhd)....8 5
3448[3] Moon Magic *(LadyHerries)* 3-8-8 JReid(7) (Withdrawn not under Starter's orders: ref to ent stalls).... W

4/5 KSHESSINSKAYA (Evens-11/10), **15/8** Moon Magic, **8/1** Fighting Times, **12/1** Our Little Lady (8/1-14/1), **25/1** Jane's Super Top, Dolliver (USA), CSF £3.28 TOTE £1.20: £1.10 £2.00 (£2.00) OWNER Mr W. J. Gredley (NEWMARKET) BRED Stetchworth Park Stud Ltd 5 Rn
2m 30.91 (8.91) SF: -/5/-/-/-/-

3544 KNIGHT, FRANK & RUTLEY (S) H'CAP (0-60) (3-Y.O+) (Class G) £2,646.20 (£733.20: £350.60)

1m 2f (Equitrack) Stalls: Low GOING minus 0.47 sec per fur (FST) 5-00 (5-02)

3305[6] **Watch Me Go (IRE) (41)***(55) (BobJones)* 6-9-2 MWigham(4) (b: lw: hld up: rdn over 2f out: led 1f out: drvn out)....— 1
1971[3] Tropical Jungle (USA) **(52)***(66)*(Fav)*(PJMakin)* 5-9-13b PaulEddery(2) (stdy hdwy 4f out: ev ch 1f out: r.o wl)....hd 2
3178[6] Salvatore Giuliano **(40)***(48) (AGFoster)* 5-9-1 BDoyle(14) (b.hind: a.p: led over 4f out tl over 2f out: ev ch 1f out: unable qckn)....3½ 3
3258[6] Zahran (IRE) **(52)***(56) (JMBradley)* 4-9-10 (3) SDrowne(6) (b: lw: a.p: led over 2f out to 1f out: sn wknd)....2½ 4
War Requiem (IRE) **(38)***(37) (MissGayKelleway)* 5-8-13 RCochrane(8) (hld up: hrd rdn over 2f out: sn wknd)....3½ 5
3426[2] Bronze Runner **(40)***(35) (SMellor)* 11-8-8b(7) ADaly(7) (nvr nr to chal)....2½ 6

4021° Kentavrus Way (IRE) **(38)***(26) (AMoore)* 4-8-13 CandyMorris(11) (nvr nrr) 4 7
2949⁸ Akola Angel **(45)***(33) (CREgerton)* 3-8-13 MFenton(3) (nvr nrr) ....s.h 8
1939⁹ Glitterazzi **(53)***(35) (LMontagueHall)* 4-10-0b JWilliams(1) (b: b.hind: prom 7f) 4 9
1966⁸ Bad News **(43)***(25) (RHarris)* 3-8-11 JFEgan(5) (lw: led over 5f) ....hd 10
496³ Long Furlong **(46)***(26) (JRBosley)* 7-9-4e(3) SSanders(10) (a bhd) 1 11
3108¹¹ Head For Heaven **(40)***(7) (RPCHoad)* 5-9-1 JQuinn(13) (bhd fnl 4f) 8 12
2093⁸ Sandra Dee (IRE) **(50)***(6) (BAPearce)* 3-8-13 (5) DaneO'Neill(9) (b: lw: s.s: hdwy 7f out: wknd over 4f out) 7 13
Today's Fancy **(30)** *(DCO'Brien)* 7-8-2 (3) DRMcCabe(12) (a bhd) ....¾ 14

11/4 Tropical Jungle (USA) (4/1-5/2), **6/1** WATCH ME GO (IRE), **13/2** Bronze Runner, **7/1** Zahran (IRE), **8/1** War Requiem (IRE), **9/1** Akola Angel (5/1-10/1), **12/1** Long Furlong, **14/1** Salvatore Giuliano, **16/1** Head For Heaven, **20/1** Kentavrus Way (IRE), Sandra Dee (IRE), Glitterazzi, **25/1** Bad News, **50/1** Today's Fancy, CSF £22.74 CT £214.12 TOTE £8.50: £2.50 £!.90 £6.20 (£12.90) Trio £109.70 OWNER Horses For Courses Racing Club (NEWMARKET) BRED Rosemount Stud 14 Rn
2m 6.87 (3.87) SF: 25/36/18/26/7/5/-/-/5/-/-/-/-/-
WEIGHT FOR AGE 3yo-7lb
No bid

3545 H.B.L.B. BLINDLEY HEATH H'CAP (0-80) (3-Y.O+) (Class D)
£4,306.90 (£1,289.20: £618.60: £283.30)
7f Stalls: High GOING minus 0.47 sec per fur (F) 5-30 (5-33)

3348⁴ **Mullitover (75)***(77)*(Fav)*(MJHeaton-Ellis)* 5-9-9 WWoods(14) (lw: a.p: led over 2f out: r.o wl) ....— 1
3074⁴ Crystal Heights (FR) **(63)***(60) (RJO'Sullivan)* 7-8-11 GDuffield(3) (b: lw: s.s: hdwy 2f out: r.o ins fnl f) 2 2
2468⁵ Samba Sharply **(76)***(71) (AHide)* 4-9-10 JWilliams(16) (hdwy over 1f out: r.o) 1 3
3286* Bedouin Invader **(72)***(65) (MRStoute)* 3-9-2b JReid(2) (lw: hld up: rdn over 1f out: one pce) ....¾ 4
3291³ Anonym (IRE) **(72)***(57) (JLDunlop)* 3-9-2 WRyan(15) (s.s: rdn over 2f out: hdwy fnl f: nvr nrr) 3½ 5
3268³ Dowsong **(69)***(49) (RAkehurst)* 4-9-0 (3) SSanders(5) (lw: a.p: hrd rdn over 1f out: wknd fnl f) 2½ 6
3359¹⁸ Oare Sparrow **(67)***(43) (PTWalwyn)* 5-9-1 MRimmer(8) (lost pl over 2f out: r.o one pce fnl f) 1¾ 7
1673⁹ Ffynone (IRE) **(76)***(51) (RHannon)* 3-9-1 (5) DaneO'Neill(13) (lw: prom over 4f) ....½ 8
3212⁷ Rocketeer (IRE) **(75)***(45) (WRMuir)* 4-9-9b PaulEddery(4) (lw: hld up: hrd rdn 3f out: sn wknd) 2 9
3359²¹ Wardara **(70)***(39) (MissGayKelleway)* 3-9-0 RMcGhin(7) (lw: a bhd) ....½ 10
3181* Mutabassim (IRE) **(77)***(46) (ACStewart)* 3-9-7 RHills(9) (lw: led over 4f) ....d.h 10
3175* Jolto **(75)***(43) (KOCunningham-Brown)* 6-9-6 (3) DRMcCabe(6) (prom over 5f) ....nk 12
3181⁴ Wandering Minstrel (IRE) **(63)***(30) (JMPEustace)* 3-8-7 RCochrane(11) (lw: a bhd) ....½ 13
2345⁸ Cameron Highland (IRE) **(80)***(47) (PFICole)* 4-9-7 (7) ADaly(1) (lw: prom over 4f) ....s.h 14

9/2 MULLITOVER, **11/2** Anonym (IRE), **6/1** Dowsong, **13/2** Bedouin Invader, Mutabassim (IRE), **8/1** Samba Sharply, **10/1** Wardara, Jolto, **14/1** Crystal Heights (FR), Rocketeer (IRE) (10/1-16/1), **16/1** Oare Sparrow, Cameron Highland (IRE), Wandering Minstrel (IRE), **20/1** Ffynone (IRE), CSF £68.75 CT £476.39 TOTE £6.00: £1.80 £4.80 £4.20 (£56.90) Trio £108.90 OWNER Mrs D. B. Mulley (WROUGHTON) BRED Mrs D. B. Mulley 14 Rn
1m 20.92 (0.32) SF: 62/45/56/46/38/34/28/32/30/20/27/28/11/32
WEIGHT FOR AGE 3yo-4lb

T/Plpt: £15.90 (852.05 Tckts). T/Qdpt: £9.70 (11.1 Tckts). AK

2695-DONCASTER (L-H)
Wednesday September 6th (Good to firm)
WEATHER: overcast, drizzle WIND: slt half bhd

3546 BATTLE OF BRITAIN LEVY BOARD NURSERY H'CAP (2-Y.O) (Class C)
£5,970.00 (£1,785.00: £855.00: £390.00)
1m (straight) Stalls: High GOING minus 0.43 sec per fur (F) 1-30 (1-31)

3157⁶ **No Cliches (72)***(79) (GLewis)* 2-9-0 PatEddery(10) (lw: swtchd lft s: hld up: hdwy & drvn along over 2f out: led over 1f out: drvn out) ....— 1
3147¹³ Opera **(77)***(83) (WJarvis)* 2-9-5 LDettori(6) (trckd ldrs: effrt over 1f out: styd on towards fin) ....¾ 2
3147⁹ Kingfisher Brave **(68)***(72) (SGNorton)* 2-8-10 KDarley(5) (a chsng ldrs: ev ch over 1f out: kpt on same pce) 1 3
3414* Double Diamond (IRE) **(81)***(84)*(Fav)*(MJohnston)* 2-9-9 7x JWeaver(3) (led tl over 1f out: unable qckn) ....½ 4

3160[3] Lucky Rabbit **(75)***(72) (BWHills)* 2-9-3 MHills(12) (hld up stands' side: hdwy 3f out: rdn & hung lft over 1f out: nvr rchd ldrs) 3 5
3280[5] Gumair (USA) **(75)***(70) (RHannon)* 2-9-3 JReid(17) (lw: chsd ldrs: drvn along & outpcd ½-wy: styd on over 1f out) ....¾ 6
1650[4] Whispering Dawn **(60)***(50) (MRChannon)* 2-7-11 (5) PPMurphy(11) (unruly in stalls: hdwy stands' side over 2f out: rdn & edgd bdly lft over 1f out) 2½ 7
3174[9] Bellator **(70)***(58) (GBBalding)* 2-8-12 JWilliams(9) (hld up: bhd: wl bhd ½-wy: sme hdwy over 1f out: n.d) 1 8
3394[4] Cumbrian Maestro **(69)***(57) (MHEasterby)* 2-8-11 MJKinane(16) (led stands' side tl over 3f out: sn rdn & outpcd) ....s.h 9
2958[9] Stately **(59)***(61d) (SirMarkPrescott)* 2-8-1 ow1 GDuffield(14) (b.hind: trckd ldrs stands' side tl wknd over 2f out) 1 10
3345[6] Tarry **(61)***(46) (CNWilliams)* 2-8-3 PaulEddery(7) (wl bhd fr ½-wy) 1½ 11
3369* Hoh Majestic (IRE) **(73)***(58) (MBell)* 2-9-1 MFenton(15) (trckd ldrs stands' side: effrt over 2f out: sn wknd) ....s.h 12
3089[14] Winged Prince **(70)***(54) (BJMeehan)* 2-8-12 JFEgan(1) (plld hrd: trckd ldrs: effrt over 2f out: sn wknd) ....½ 13
3414[2] Annaberg (IRE) **(73)***(54) (MrsJRRamsden)* 2-9-1 KFallon(8) (bhd & drvn along ½-wy: n.d)...1¼ 14
2541[6] Don't Forget Mikie (IRE) **(64)***(45) (MJHeaton-Ellis)* 2-8-6v JCarroll(2) (b: trckd ldrs tl wknd over 2f out) ....s.h 15
2846[10] Labeed (USA) **(79)***(60) (MajorWRHern)* 2-9-7 WCarson(4) (chsd ldrs tl lost pl 3f out) ....s.h 16
3309* Silent Soprano **(54)***(33) (DenysSmith)* 2-7-10 TWilliams(13) (lw: chsd ldrs stands' side 5f: sn lost pl) 1 17

5/1 Double Diamond (IRE), **6/1** Gumair (USA), **13/2** NO CLICHES, **9/1** Annaberg (IRE), **11/1** Tarry, **12/1** Kingfisher Brave, Stately, Opera, Lucky Rabbit, **14/1** Labeed (USA), Cumbrian Maestro, **16/1** Silent Soprano, **20/1** Hoh Majestic (IRE), Winged Prince, Bellator, **25/1** Don't Forget Mikie (IRE), Whispering Dawn, CSF £81.33 CT £855.49 TOTE £8.20: £1.80 £4.50 £3.50 £1.90 (£155.60) Trio £289.50 OWNER Mr Michael Watt (EPSOM) BRED Roldvale Ltd 17 Rn
1m 39.5 (3.00) SF: 32/36/25/37/25/23/3/11/10/-/-/9/5/5/-/11/-

3547 MALLARD H'CAP (0-105) (3-Y.O+) (Class B) £12,908.00

(£4,772.00: £2,286.00: £930.00: £365.00: £139.00)
1m 6f 132y Stalls: Low GOING minus 0.43 sec per fur (F) 2-00 (2-01)

3142[2] **Grey Shot (98)***(110) (IABalding)* 3-9-12 LDettori(4) (mde all: styd on wl fnl 2f: hld on wl)......— 1
3142* Saleel (IRE) **(90)***(102)*(Fav)*(ACStewart)* 3-9-4 MRoberts(2) (lw: chsd ldrs: drvn along 9f out: rdn & wnt lft 3f out: styd on wl) ....nk 2
3162[14] Tudor Island **(76)***(84) (CEBrittain)* 6-9-2 MJKinane(3) (chsd ldrs: rdn & kpt on same pce over 1f out) 3½ 3
1840[19] Top Cees **(80)***(86) (MrsJRRamsden)* 5-9-6 KFallon(5) (s.s: hld up: hdwy on ins over 3f out: swtchd & styd on same pce appr fnl f: nvr nr to chal) 2 4
2701[5] Torch Vert (IRE) **(75)***(79) (BWHills)* 3-8-3 MHills(6) (lw: effrt & hmpd 3f out: swtchd & styd on: nvr rchd ldrs) 1¼ 5
3336[2] Progression **(74)***(68) (PCHaslam)* 4-8-9b(5) MBaird(1) (trckd ldrs: effrt 3f out: sn wknd & bhd)..9 6

15/8 Saleel (IRE), **5/2** GREY SHOT, **11/2** Progression, **13/2** Top Cees, **7/1** Tudor Island, **9/1** Torch Vert (IRE), CSF £7.48 TOTE £3.20: £1.60 £1.50 (£2.40) OWNER Mr J. C. Smith (KINGSCLERE) BRED Littleton Stud 6 Rn 3m 6.62 (3.02) SF: 59/51/45/47/28/29
WEIGHT FOR AGE 3yo-12lb

3548 E.B.F. CARRIE RED NURSERY H'CAP (2-Y.O F) (Class C)

£19,737.50 (£5,900.00: £2,825.00: £1,287.50)
6f 110y Stalls: High GOING minus 0.43 sec per fur (F) 2-35 (2-36)

3375[2] **My Branch (88)***(97+) (BWHills)* 2-8-13 MHills(12) (lw: s.i.s: swtchd lft: hdwy & nt clr run over 2f out & over 1f out: swtchd & qcknd to ld ins fnl f: impressive) ....— 1
3271* Desert Tiger **(85)***(86)*(Fav)*(MJohnston)* 2-8-10 JWeaver(4) (lw: led: rdn: swrvd lft over 1f out: hung rt: no ch w wnr) 3 2
3210[2] Red Stream (USA) **(82)***(76) (MRStoute)* 2-8-7v LDettori(13) (lw: trckd ldrs: drvn along & outpcd over 2f out: kpt on fnl f) 2½ 3
3452[2] White Whispers **(91)***(83) (BJMeehan)* 2-9-2 JReid(3) (in tch: outpcd ½-wy: styd on fnl f) 1 4
3176[5] Windswept (IRE) **(70)***(60) (DJSffrenchDavis)* 2-7-2 (7) CAdamson(10) (in tch: outpcd & rdn ½-wy: styd on appr fnl f) ....½ 5
3471* Willow Dale (IRE) **(79)***(69) (DRCElsworth)* 2-8-4 5x PaulEddery(2) (in tch: kpt on fnl 2f: nt rch ldrs) ....nk 6
3228[3] Splicing **(71)***(52) (JRFanshawe)* 2-7-10 ow1 WCarson(8) (lw: prom: drvn along ½-wy: hung rt: kpt on fnl f) 3 7

3423[7] Elmswood (USA) **(72)***(54) (PWChapple-Hyam)* 2-7-11 NAdams(9) (chsd ldrs tl outpcd fnl 2f).½ 8
2594[7] Kossolian **(76)***(56) (BPalling)* 2-8-1 TSprake(17) (led stands' side: no imp fnl 2f)....................d.h 8
3386[2] Lucky Revenge **(68)***(46) (MartynMeade)* 2-7-2 (5) PFessey(6) (nvr nr ldrs) ....¾ 10
3386* Fenna **(73)***(49) (SPCWoods)* 2-7-7 (5)ow2 MHenry(16) (racd stands' side: rdn & edgd lft 3f out: n.d) ....s.h 11
3132* Kiss Me Again (IRE) **(80)***(56) (RHannon)* 2-8-5 PatEddery(14) (racd stands' side: effrt 3f out: n.d) ....¾ 12
3423[4] Polly Golightly **(77)***(50) (BSmart)* 2-8-2 GDuffield(7) (chsd ldrs tl wknd over 2f out) 1 13
3387[3] Fag End (IRE) **(96)***(69) (MHTompkins)* 2-9-7 RCochrane(1) (chsd ldrs tl wknd 2f out) ....hd 14
3468[3] Society Girl **(78)***(49) (CWThornton)* 2-8-3 DeanMcKeown(15) (lw: b.hind: chsd ldrs stands' side tl lost pl over 2f out) ....¾ 15
3289[2] Branston Danni **(70)***(36) (MrsJRRamsden)* 2-7-9 AMackay(11) (s.v.s: nt rcvr)..........................2 16
3086[6] Top Cat (FR) **(90)***(48) (EWeymes)* 2-9-1 KDarley(5) (chsd ldrs tl wknd qckly over 2f out) 3 17

LONG HANDICAP Lucky Revenge 7-5

9/2 Desert Tiger, **8/1** MY BRANCH, Red Stream (USA) (6/1-9/1), Splicing, Branston Danni, Kiss Me Again (IRE), **12/1** Willow Dale (IRE), **14/1** Fag End (IRE), **16/1** Fenna, **20/1** Society Girl, Elmswood (USA), **25/1** Kossolian, Polly Golightly, Top Cat (FR), **33/1** Lucky Revenge, White Whispers, Windswept (IRE), CSF £40.73 CT £272.70 TOTE £8.90: £2.00 £1.60 £2.50 £6.30 (£17.10) Trio £46.10 OWNER Mr Wafic Said (LAMBOURN) BRED Addison Racing Ltd Inc 17 Rn

1m 18.26 (7.26) SF: 58/47/37/44/21/30/13/13/17/7/10/17/11/30/10/-/9

3549 STONES BITTER PARK HILL STKS (Gp 3) (3-Y.O+ F & M) (Class A)

£22,748.20 (£8,423.80: £4,046.90: £1,659.50: £664.75: £266.85)
1m 6f 132y Stalls: Low GOING minus 0.43 sec per fur (F) 3-10 (3-12)

3161[7] **Noble Rose (IRE) (107)***(110+)*(Fav)*(LMCumani)* 4-9-3 LDettori(4) (lw: hld up: smooth hdwy to ld over 1f out: shkn up & r.o: drvn out towards fin)..— 1
3162[7] Misbelief **(97)***(110) (JRFanshawe)* 5-9-3 KFallon(8) (s.i.s: hld up: swtchd outside & gd hdwy over 2f out: ev ch over 1f out: nt qckn towards fin) ....½ 2
3162[17] Saxon Maid **(105)***(109) (LMCumani)* 4-9-3 MJKinane(6) (chsd ldrs: drvn along 3f out: swtchd ins: hrd rdn & styd on fnl f) ....s.h 3
3041a[6] Totality **(103)***(105) (HRACecil)* 4-9-3 PatEddery(5) (led to 11f out: chal 4f out: wknd over 1f out)...4 4
3338* Najmat Alshemaal (IRE) **(97)***(105) (MajorWRHern)* 3-8-5 RCochrane(3) (dwlt s: hld up: effrt over 3f out: n.m.r 2f out: one pce) ....nk 5
3479a* Honfleur (IRE) *(103) (PWChapple-Hyam)* 3-8-5 JReid(1) (led 11f out tl over 1f out: sn wknd)...1¾ 6
3223[4] Opera Lover (IRE) **(101)***(103) (MRStoute)* 3-8-5 KDarley(2) (lw: trckd ldrs: effrt u.p 3f out: wknd 2f out)..s.h 7
2563a[6] Asterita **(106)***(95) (RHannon)* 3-8-5 MRoberts(7) (lw: chsd ldrs: chal over 3f out: wknd qckly wl over 1f out) 7 8

11/4 NOBLE ROSE (IRE), **3/1** Totality, **11/2** Saxon Maid, Honfleur (IRE), **15/2** Asterita, **9/1** Misbelief, **16/1** Opera Lover (IRE), Najmat Alshemaal (IRE), CSF £24.82 TOTE £3.30: £1.40 £2.80 £1.50 (£26.20) OWNER Sheikh Mohammed (NEWMARKET) BRED Sheikh Mohammed bin Rashid al Maktoum 8 Rn

3m 11.4 (7.80) SF: 26/26/25/21/9/7/7/-
WEIGHT FOR AGE 3yo-12lb

3550 DONCASTER BLOODSTOCK SALES SCARBROUGH STKS (Listed) (Class A)

£12,378.00 (£4,602.00: £2,226.00: £930.00: £390.00: £174.00)
5f Stalls: High GOING minus 0.43 sec per fur (F) 3-40 (3-42)

2671[2] **Eveningperformance (105)***(111) (HCandy)* 4-9-2 WNewnes(10) (swtg: mde all: qcknd ½-wy: drvn out)...— 1
2888a[4] Double Quick (IRE) **(102)***(106) (MJohnston)* 3-9-3 JWeaver(8) (lw: sn chsng wnr: kpt on u.p fnl f: no imp)...2½ 2
2764[4] Espartero (IRE) **(101)***(105)*(Fav)*(SirMarkPrescott)* 3-9-5 GDuffield(7) (lw: s.i.s: bhd & drvn along 3f out: styd on wl ins fnl f)..1 3
2935* That Man Again **(100)***(101) (GLewis)* 3-9-5b PatEddery(1) (chsd ldrs: hrd rdn & nt qckn appr fnl f) 1¼ 4
3476a[2] Warning Star **(103)***(94) (BWHills)* 3-9-0 MHills(9) (swtchd lft s: hdwy ½-wy: kpt on appr fnl f: nvr nr to chal) ....½ 5
3187[2] Ya Malak **(111)***(102) (JWPayne)* 4-9-10 BThomson(2) (lw: dwlt s: sn chsng ldrs: wknd 1f out) ....s.h 6
3342[4] Saint Express **(107)***(91) (MrsMReveley)* 5-9-7 KDarley(4) (in tch: effrt ½-wy: n.d) 2½ 7
3316* Don't Worry Me (IRE) **(100)***(81) (FHLee)* 3-9-0 PaulEddery(3) (w ldrs tl wknd over 1f out) 1½ 8
3166[7] Lago Di Varano **(98)***(81) (JBerry)* 3-9-5b JCarroll(6) (lw: in tch: drvn along ½-wy: wknd over 1f out)..1½ 9

4/1 Espartero (IRE) (3/1-9/2), **9/2** EVENINGPERFORMANCE, Saint Express, Ya Malak, **11/2** Warning Star, **7/1** That Man Again, **15/2** Double Quick (IRE), **14/1** Don't Worry Me (IRE), **33/1** Lago Di Varano, CSF £36.79 TOTE £5.50: £1.90 £2.00 £2.20 (£25.50) Trio £52.40 OWNER Mrs David Blackburn (WANTAGE) BRED Mrs R. D. Peacock 9 Rn

58.8 secs (0.40) SF: 57/50/49/45/38/48/37/25/25

WEIGHT FOR AGE 3yo-2lb

3551

TOTE-PORTLAND H'CAP (0-110) (3-Y.O+) (Class B) £18,244.00 (£6,796.00: £3,298.00: £1,390.00: £595.00: £277.00)
5f 140y Stalls: High GOING minus 0.43 sec per fur (F) 4-10 (4-14)

3446[3] **Hello Mister (92)***(107)*(Fav)*(JO'Donoghue)* 4-8-7 (3) PMcCabe(3) (hld up: gd hdwy & swtchd rt over 1f out: r.o strly to ld ins fnl f: sn clr) ....— 1
3476a[9] Bold Effort (FR) **(97)***(102) (KOCunningham-Brown)* 3-8-12 TIves(5) (swtg: led far side: kpt on wl fnl f: no ch w wnr) 3½ 2
3191[8] Cool Jazz **(102)***(105) (CEBrittain)* 4-9-6 MJKinane(7) (a chsng ldrs: kpt on fnl f) ....¾ 3
1765[13] Call Me I'm Blue (IRE) **(90)***(91) (NTinkler)* 5-8-8 WNewnes(11) (sn outpcd & bhd: edgd lft: styd on wl fnl f) ....¾ 4
3087* Master of Passion **(86)***(85) (JMPEustace)* 6-8-4 JTate(8) (chsd ldrs: nt qckn appr fnl f) ....¾ 5
3446[7] Join the Clan **(90)***(89) (MrsNMacauley)* 6-8-5 (3) SDrowne(2) (lw: a chsng ldrs: kpt on same pce fnl 2f) ....s.h 6
3446[2] Venture Capitalist **(105)***(103) (DNicholls)* 6-9-9b AlexGreaves(13) (lw: s.i.s: gd hdwy over 1f out: styd on towards fin) ....hd 7
3342[5] Hard to Figure **(110)***(107) (RJHodges)* 9-10-0 RCochrane(4) (s.i.s: bhd & drvn along: styd on appr fnl f) ....½ 8
3446[6] Tabook (IRE) **(95)***(88) (EALDunlop)* 4-8-13 WRSwinburn(16) (lw: chsd ldrs tl grad wknd over 1f out) 1½ 9
3236* Name the Tune **(91)***(83) (PHowling)* 4-8-9 PaulEddery(1) (b.hind: chsd ldrs trl wknd over 1f out) ....nk 10
3359[10] Lord Olivier (IRE) **(91)***(81) (WJarvis)* 5-8-9 JReid(21) (lw: w ldr stands' side tl wknd over 1f out) ....½ 11
3446[4] Jayannpee **(97)***(87) (IABalding)* 4-9-1 LDettori(19) (lw: trckd ldrs: effrt over 2f out: n.m.r, squeezed thro & hmpd over 1f out: sn wknd) ....s.h 12
3446[11] Welsh Mist **(102)***(92) (RBoss)* 4-9-6 JCarroll(10) (swtchd lft s: n.d) ....s.h 13
3407[7] Painted Desert **(88)***(75) (RCharlton)* 3-8-3 ow1 KDarley(18) (led stands' side: n.m.r & wknd over 1f out) ....¾ 14
1895[28] Amron **(84)***(71) (JBerry)* 8-8-2 NCarlisle(14) (s.i.s: a in rr) ....½ 15
3219* Mr Bergerac (IRE) **(84)***(70) (BPalling)* 4-8-2 TSprake(6) (prom tl rdn & lost pl 2f out) ....s.h 16
3376[5] Quiz Time **(88)***(72) (SirMarkPrescott)* 3-8-3 GDuffield(12) (lw: racd centre: edgd rt ½-wy: wknd 2f out) ....¾ 17
2617[6] Inherent Magic (IRE) **(92)***(75) (WRMuir)* 6-8-10 PatEddery(20) (b: bhd: hdwy over 2f out: eased over 1f out) ....nk 18
2570[2] Sailormaite **(85)***(66) (SRBowring)* 4-8-3 ow1 SWebster(22) (in tch stands' side: sn pushed along: outpcd fr ½-wy) ....½ 19
3230* Double Blue **(108)***(88) (MJohnston)* 6-9-12 JWeaver(15) (w ldrs centre tl lost pl 2f out: eased) ....¾ 20
1756* Lord High Admiral (CAN) **(93)***(64) (CREgerton)* 7-8-11b MRoberts(17) (lw: chsd ldrs: wkng whn edgd lft & hmpd over 1f out) 3 21
3342[6] Iltimas (USA) **(95)***(59) (PTWalwyn)* 3-8-10 WCarson(9) (lw: stmbld s: a in rr) 2½ 22

7/1 HELLO MISTER, **15/2** Double Blue, **9/1** Sailormaite, **10/1** Venture Capitalist, Lord Olivier (IRE), **14/1** Name the Tune, Jayannpee, Quiz Time, Iltimas (USA), **16/1** Master of Passion, Join the Clan, Amron, Mr Bergerac (IRE), **20/1** Inherent Magic (IRE), Tabook (IRE), Hard to Figure, Lord High Admiral (CAN), **25/1** Cool Jazz, Painted Desert, Welsh Mist, Bold Effort (FR), **33/1** Call Me I'm Blue (IRE), CSF £164.85 CT £3,815.74 TOTE £7.50: £2.50 £6.60 £4.60 £20.00 (£111.80) Trio £1,395.20 OWNER Mr Brian Mitten (REIGATE) BRED B. Mitten and T. Powell 22 Rn

1m 6.62 (-0.38) SF: 64/56/62/48/42/46/60/64/45/40/38/44/49/29/28/27/26/32/23/45/21/13

WEIGHT FOR AGE 3yo-3lb

STEWARDS' ENQUIRY Dettori susp. 15-16 & 18-20/9/95 (irresponsible riding).

3552

PRINCE OF WALES LIMITED STKS (0-80) (3-Y.O) (Class D) £4,698.00 (£1,404.00: £672.00: £306.00)
1m 2f 60y Stalls: Low GOING minus 0.43 sec per fur (F) 4-40 (4-42)

2980[2] **Out on a Promise (IRE) (80)***(93) (GWragg)* 3-8-11 MHills(5) (hld up & bhd: gd hdwy on outside 2f out: wnt lft: led jst ins fnl f: drvn out) ....— 1
2638* Avignon (IRE) **(80)***(90) (PWChapple-Hyam)* 3-8-8 JReid(4) (led: hdd jst ins fnl f: kpt on wl) ....nk 2

2468[6] Green Seed (IRE) **(79)***(84)* *(JRFanshawe)* 3-8-6 KFallon(9) (lw: dwlt s: hld up & bhd: gd hdwy on ins over 2f out: styd on same pce appr fnl f) 2½ 3
3232[W] Seckar Vale (USA) **(80)***(88+)* *(BWHills)* 3-8-11 KDarley(8) (dwlt s: hld up & bhd: nt clr run over 2f out: swtchd & styd on strly ins fnl f: fin wl) ..... ¾ 4
3189[6] Pumice **(75)***(80)* *(LMCumani)* 3-8-8 LDettori(6) (sn trckng ldrs: effrt & outpcd over 2f out: kpt on same pce appr fnl f) 3 5
2738[13] Sparrowhawk (IRE) **(80)***(80)* *(BWHills)* 3-8-8 WCarson(3) (bhd & pushed along over 3f out: styd on: nvr rchd ldrs) ..... hd 6
3349[3] Lovely Lyca **(74)***(78)* *(JWHills)* 3-8-3 (5) MHenry(7) (chsd ldrs: ev ch over 2f out: sn wknd) 1 7
2766[9] Eurolink the Rebel (USA) **(80)***(81)* *(RAkehurst)* 3-8-13 RCochrane(2) (in tch: drvn along over 3f out: n.m.r 2f out: sn wknd) 1½ 8
3214[10] Kimbridge Knight (IRE) **(80)***(77)* *(PTWalwyn)* 3-9-1v PatEddery(1) (chsd ldrs: rdn & wknd over 2f out) 4 9
3320[3] Gloriana **(74)***(59)* *(LadyHerries)* 3-8-8 PaulEddery(10) (chsd ldrs: wkng whn hmpd 2f out) 7 10
2929* Never Explain (IRE) **(80)***(52)*(Fav)*(JLDunlop)* 3-8-8 MJKinane(11) (lw: chsd ldrs: wkng whn bdly hmpd 2f out: eased) 4 11

4/1 Never Explain (IRE), **9/2** Pumice, **11/2** Avignon (IRE), **13/2** Sparrowhawk (IRE), **8/1** OUT ON A PROMISE (IRE), **9/1** Green Seed (IRE), **12/1** Kimbridge Knight (IRE), Lovely Lyca, Eurolink the Rebel (USA), **14/1** Seckar Vale (USA), Gloriana, CSF £50.16 TOTE £7.60: £2.60 £1.80 £2.50 (£16.80) Trio £63.20 OWNER Mrs H. H. Morriss (NEWMARKET) BRED H. H. and Mrs Morriss 11 Rn 2m 7.01 (0.01) SF: 61/58/52/56/48/48/46/49/45/27/20

T/Jkpt: Not won; £8,927.01 to Doncaster 7/9/95. T/Plpt: £50.10 (632.93 Tckts). T/Qdpt: £15.80 (17.4 Tckts). WG

3403-EPSOM (L-H)

Wednesday September 6th (Good, 5f course Good to firm)

WEATHER: fair WIND: mod across

3553 LEATHERHEAD MAIDEN STKS (2-Y.O) (Class E) £3,302.20 (£985.60: £470.80: £213.40) 7f Stalls: Low GOING minus 0.37 sec per fur (F) 2-15 (2-15)

3174[3] **Paint It Black** *(76)*(Fav)*(RHannon)* 2-9-0 RHughes(1) (lw: chsd ldr: rdn over 2f out: led ins fnl f: r.o wl) ..... — 1
3423[6] Laughing Buccaneer **(72)***(76)* *(BJMeehan)* 2-9-0b BDoyle(8) (lw: led: clr over 4f out: hdd ins fnl f: r.o) ..... hd 2
3266[2] Vasetto **(80)***(64)* *(SirMarkPrescott)* 2-9-0 WWoods(6) (3rd st: unable qckn fnl 3f) 5 3
3337[0] Stronz (IRE) **(79)***(63)* *(RAkehurst)* 2-8-11 (3) SSanders(9) (4th st: one pce fnl 3f) ..... ¾ 4
3260[6] Even Handed *(62)* *(PFICole)* 2-9-0 TQuinn(4) (nvr nr to chal) ..... nk 5
Knave *(56)* *(RHannon)* 2-8-9 (5) DaneO'Neill(5) (unf: a bhd) 2½ 6
3025[6] Seaford Star (IRE) **(71)***(55)* *(MRChannon)* 2-8-11 (3) JStack(3) (a bhd) ..... ½ 7
3340[15] Hever Golf Eagle *(49)* *(TJNaughton)* 2-9-0 DHolland(2) (b: 5th st: wknd over 3f out) 2½ 8
3306[2] Toffee *(33)* *(JRFanshawe)* 2-8-6 (3) NVarley(7) (a bhd) 5 9

6/4 PAINT IT BLACK, **4/1** Toffee, **11/2** Vasetto, **6/1** Stronz (IRE), **10/1** Hever Golf Eagle, **20/1** Seaford Star (IRE), **25/1** Laughing Buccaneer, Even Handed, Knave, CSF £31.75 TOTE £2.30: £1.30 £12.20 £1.70 (£43.80) Trio £60.30 OWNER Mr Michael Pescod (MARLBOROUGH) BRED Brian Winn 9 Rn 1m 23.0 (2.70) SF: 33/33/21/20/19/13/12/6/-

3554 GERALD EVE H'CAP (0-90) (3-Y.O+) (Class C) £5,472.00 (£1,656.00: £808.00: £384.00) 5f Stalls: High GOING minus 0.37 sec per fur (F) 2-45 (2-47)

3407* **Crowded Avenue** **(89)***(98)*(Fav)*(PJMakin)* 3-9-11 (3) 7x SSanders(9) (hdwy over 1f out: nt clr run ins fnl f: led wl ins fnl f: r.o wl) ..... — 1
3407[4] Miami Banker **(53)***(59)* *(WRMuir)* 9-7-8b GBardwell(5) (w ldr: rdn over 2f out: led ins fnl f: sn hdd: unable qckn) 1 2
3424[3] Pearl Dawn (IRE) **(68)***(72)* *(GLMoore)* 5-8-9 SWhitworth(10) (dwlt: outpcd: gd hdwy fnl f: r.o wl) ..... ½ 3
3333[2] Hever Golf Star **(68)***(72)* *(TJNaughton)* 3-8-7 DHolland(4) (dwlt: hld up: rdn over 1f out: ev ch ins fnl f: one pce) ..... hd 4
3357* Kalar **(52)***(54)* *(DWChapman)* 6-7-7b JQuinn(3) (lw: led: rdn over 1f out: hdd & edgd lft ins fnl f: one pce) ..... ½ 5
3407[2] Insider Trader **(73)***(71)* *(RGuest)* 4-8-9v(5) DaneO'Neill(7) (b: hld up: rdn over 2f out: one pce) 1¼ 6
3407[9] Ashtina **(87)***(84)* *(RJHodges)* 10-9-7 (7) AmandaSanders(11) (nvr nr to chal) ..... ½ 7
3250[2] Bashful Brave **(73)***(69)* *(JWPayne)* 4-9-0 MRimmer(8) (lw: a.p: ev ch over 1f out: wknd ins fnl f) ..... hd 8

3359[9] Jo Maximus **(70)***(60) (SDow)* 3-8-2 (7) ADaly(6) (lw: bhd fnl 2f) 2 **9**
3453[2] Domicksky **(55)***(35) (MRChannon)* 7-7-10 FNorton(2) (lw: hld up: rdn over 2f out: wknd over 1f out) 3 **10**
3524[3] Newbury Coat **(67)***(38) (BJMeehan)* 5-8-8b 7x BDoyle(1) (hld up: hrd rdn over 1f out: sn wknd) 3 **11**

13/8 CROWDED AVENUE, **6/1** Insider Trader, **7/1** Miami Banker, **10/1** Hever Golf Star, Bashful Brave, **12/1** Pearl Dawn (IRE), **14/1** Domicksky, Jo Maximus, **16/1** Kalar, **20/1** Ashtina, **25/1** Newbury Coat, CSF £13.01 CT £95.58 TOTE £2.40: £1.20 £2.20 £3.40 (£10.30) Trio £25.10 OWNER Mr T. W. Wellard (MARLBOROUGH) BRED The Duke of Marlborough 11 Rn
54.73 secs (0.23) SF: 74/37/50/48/32/49/62/47/36/13/16
WEIGHT FOR AGE 3yo-2lb

3555 SOUTHERN MOBILE H'CAP (0-85) (3-Y.O+) (Class D) £4,143.00 (£1,254.00: £612.00: £291.00) **1m 4f 10y** Stalls: Low GOING minus 0.37 sec (F) 3-20 (3-24)

3277[4] **Daily Starlight (USA) (76)***(85) (MissGayKelleway)* 3-8-9 (3) SSanders(2) (4th st: rdn over 2f out: ev ch ins fnl f: r.o wl: fin 2nd, s.h: awrdd r) ....— **1**
3224[2] Top Lady (IRE) **(75)***(84) (MRStoute)* 3-8-11 DHolland(1) (lw: 3rd st: rdn over 2f out: led ins fnl f: all out: fin 1st: disq: plcd 2nd).... **2**
3336[3] Meant to Be **(73)***(81)*(Fav)*(LadyHerries)* 5-9-4 TQuinn(8) (led: hrd rdn over 2f out: hdd ins fnl f)....¾ **3**
3349[4] Chatham Island **(70)***(78) (CEBrittain)* 7-9-1 BDoyle(7) (lw: 2nd st: hrd rdn over 2f out: ev ch ins fnl f: one pce)....nk **4**
3406[9] Warm Spell **(74)***(81) (GLMoore)* 5-9-5 SWhitworth(5) (lw: 6th st: rdn over 2f out: r.o ins fnl f)....hd **5**
3277[6] Krayyan Dawn **(53)***(58) (RAkehurst)* 5-7-12 JQuinn(6) (lw: nvr nr to chal)....1¾ **6**
1805[3] Amancio (USA) **(83)***(81) (GHarwood)* 4-10-0 MPerrett(9) (bhd fnl 4f)....5 **7**
3237[10] Pursuit of Glory **(78)***(62) (CACyzer)* 4-9-9 DBiggs(4) (lw: 5th st: wknd over 3f out)....11 **8**
3154[4] Soviet Bride (IRE) **(63)** *(SDow)* 3-7-13 StephenDavies(3) (Withdrawn not under Starter's orders: lost rider & got loose).... **W**

3/1 Meant to Be, **7/2** Krayyan Dawn, **11/2** Top Lady (IRE), **13/2** Soviet Bride (IRE), **7/1** Chatham Island, Amancio (USA), **9/1** DAILY STARLIGHT (USA), **12/1** Warm Spell, **16/1** Pursuit of Glory, CSF £50.59 CT £160.67 TOTE £11.20: £2.70 £1.10 £1.60 (£14.30) Trio £12.80 OWNER Mr A. Al-Radi (WHITCOMBE) BRED Robert S. West Jnr 8 Rn 2m 38.77 (3.77) SF: 44/43/49/46/49/26/49/30
WEIGHT FOR AGE 3yo-9lb

3556 CHALK LANE RATED STKS H'CAP (0-105) (3-Y.O+) (Class B) £7,641.24 (£2,861.16: £1,400.58: £603.90: £271.95: £139.17) **1m 2f 18y** Stalls: Low GOING minus 0.37 sec per fur (F) 3-50 (3-57)

3030* **Sayeh (IRE) (92)***(103) (HThomsonJones)* 3-8-4 RHills(8) (mde all: drvn out) ....— **1**
3374[3] Warning Order **(94)***(105) (JLDunlop)* 3-8-6 SWhitworth(2) (6th st: hdwy & nt clr run on ins over 2f out: swtchd rt over 1f out: r.o wl ins fnl f) ....nk **2**
3336[4] Danjing (IRE) **(85)***(92) (PFICole)* 3-7-11 CRutter(4) (b.off hind: 4th st: rdn over 2f out: unable qckn)....2½ **3**
3188[4] Knave's Ash (USA) **(95)***(100)*(Fav)*(MRStoute)* 4-9-0 DHolland(6) (lw: stdy hdwy 2f out: rdn over 1f out: one pce) 1¼ **4**
2738[12] Triquetti (IRE) **(93)***(94) (LMCumani)* 3-8-5 WRyan(5) (lw: nvr nr to chal)....2 **5**
3382[2] Wakeel (USA) **(90)***(91) (SDow)* 3-7-9 (7) ADaly(1) (3rd st: wknd 2f out)....nk **6**
3164[6] Aljazzaf **(102)***(102) (RAkehurst)* 5-9-7 TQuinn(3) (b.nr fore: lw: chsd wnr: hrd rdn over 2f out: bmpd & wknd over 1f out) ....½ **7**
3382[5] Second Chance (IRE) **(85)***(72) (PMitchell)* 5-7-13 (5) DaneO'Neill(7) (lw: 5th st: wknd over 3f out) 8 **8**
LONG HANDICAP Second Chance (IRE) 8-0

9/4 Knave's Ash (USA), **5/1** Aljazzaf, Danjing (IRE), **7/1** Wakeel (USA) (5/1-15/2), **8/1** Triquetti (IRE) (6/1-9/1), SAYEH (IRE), **12/1** Warning Order (8/1-14/1), **20/1** Second Chance (IRE), CSF £79.68 CT £462.64 TOTE £6.50: £1.40 £3.30 £2.00 (£50.80) OWNER Mr Hamdan Al Maktoum (NEWMARKET) BRED Lord Harrington in Ireland 8 Rn 2m 5.3 (1.30) SF: 48/50/37/52/39/36/54/24
WEIGHT FOR AGE 3yo-7lb

3557 RUBBING HOUSE CONDITIONS STKS (3-Y.O+) (Class C) £4,739.20 (£1,772.80: £866.40: £372.00: £166.00: £83.60) **6f** Stalls: High GOING minus 0.37 sec per fur (F) 4-20 (4-23)

3279[4] **Croeso-I-Cymru** *(99)*(Fav)*(RAkehurst)* 4-8-13 TQuinn(2) (mde virtually all: rdn over 2f out: r.o wl)....— **1**

3166[10] Shamanic **(92)***(102) (RHannon)* 3-9-3 (5) DaneO'Neill(1) (lw: 2nd st: ev ch over 2f out: unable qckn) 3½ **2**
3582a[8] Katya (IRE) **(94)***(89) (MRChannon)* 3-8-13 RHughes(4) (lw: 5th st: hdwy over 1f out: r.o one pce) 1¼ **3**
3316[2] Wavian **(100)***(87) (RCharlton)* 3-8-12b(3) SSanders(3) (3rd st: rdn 2f out: wknd ins fnl f) 1¾ **4**
2823[5] Palacegate Touch **(85)***(85) (JBerry)* 5-9-8b GCarter(6) (4th st: wknd over 3f out) 2 **5**
3109[5] Red Rita (IRE) **(75)***(69) (WRMuir)* 4-8-10 DHolland(5) (lw: 6th st: a bhd) 1¾ **6**

15/8 CROESO-I-CYMRU, **9/4** Wavian, **7/2** Katya (IRE), **12/1** Palacegate Touch, **14/1** Shamanic, Red Rita (IRE), CSF £20.86 TOTE £2.80: £2.00 £4.60 (£17.90) OWNER Mrs Richard Evans (EPSOM) BRED R. R. Evans Bloodstock Ltd 6 Rn 1m 8.48 (0.48) SF: 58/58/45/43/44/28
WEIGHT FOR AGE 3yo-3lb

3558 E.B.F. LADAS MAIDEN STKS (2-Y.O) (Class D) £4,143.00 (£1,254.00: £612.00: £291.00) **6f** Stalls: High GOING minus 0.37 sec per fur (F) 4-50 (4-57)

3404[3] **Caricature (IRE) (82)***(79)*(Fav)*(GLewis)* 2-9-0b SWhitworth(1) (led: clr over 3f out: hdd over 1f out: led ins fnl f: drvn out) ....— **1**
3371[3] The Man *(79) (MRChannon)* 2-9-0 RHughes(9) (chsd ldr: led over 1f out tl ins fnl f: r.o) ....hd **2**
3337[2] Extra Hour (IRE) *(68) (WRMuir)* 2-9-0 CRutter(3) (lw: 4th st: rdn over 2f out: unable qckn) 4 **3**
3157[4] Lancashire Legend *(66) (SDow)* 2-9-0 TQuinn(8) (5th st: rdn over 2f out: one pce) ....¾ **4**
3009[3] Auriga **(84)***(61)*(Fav)*(IABalding)* 2-8-9 WRyan(6) (6th st: rdn over 2f out: one pce) ....hd **5**
2283[7] Top of The Stack *(63) (RHannon)* 2-8-9 (5) DaneO'Neill(4) (a bhd) 1¼ **6**
1653[6] Mystic Dawn *(52) (SDow)* 2-8-9 JQuinn(7) (lw: s.s: a wl bhd) 2 **7**
2442[17] Midnight Cookie *(17) (RJHodges)* 2-8-7 (7) AmandaSanders(2) (3rd st: wknd over 2f out) 15 **8**
3404[7] Almushtarak (IRE) *(MissGayKelleway)* 2-9-0 DHolland(5) (Withdrawn not under Starter's order: ref to ent stalls) .... **W**

3/1 CARICATURE (IRE), Auriga, **4/1** The Man (op 5/2), **7/1** Extra Hour (IRE) (op 9/2), **10/1** Lancashire Legend (7/1-11/1), **12/1** Top of The Stack, Almushtarak (IRE), **25/1** Mystic Dawn, **50/1** Midnight Cookie, CSF £12.59 TOTE £2.80: £1.60 £1.40 £2.00 (£6.70) Trio £10.70 OWNER White Bear Ltd (EPSOM) BRED P. Larkin 8 Rn 1m 9.57 (1.57) SF: 43/43/32/30/25/27/16/-/-

3559 DOWNS MAIDEN STKS (3-Y.O) (Class D) £4,084.50 (£1,236.00: £603.00: £286.50) **1m 114y** Stalls: Low GOING minus 0.37 sec per fur (F) 5-20 (5-22)

3105[3] **Dorothea Brooke (IRE) (70)***(94) (PWHarris)* 3-8-9 WRyan(3) (mde all: clr over 3f out: unchal) ....— **1**
1514[6] Ottavio Farnese *(82) (AHide)* 3-9-0 WWoods(6) (lw: poor 6th st: hdwy over 1f out: r.o one pce) 9 **2**
3409[2] Raise the Stakes **(75)***(79) (IABalding)* 3-8-9 (5) DGriffiths(2) (lw: mod 5th st: one pce fnl 3f) ...1¾ **3**
3016[13] Night Flare (FR) *(73) (RHannon)* 3-8-9 (5) DaneO'Neill(5) (lw: chsd wnr over 6f: 3rd st: wknd over 2f out) 3 **4**
3392[2] Afsaat *(69)*(Fav)*(MRStoute)* 3-9-0 DHolland(4) (4th st: hung lft fnl 3f: nt rcvr) 2 **5**
3023[4] Academy Life **(71)***(64) (PFICole)* 3-8-9 TQuinn(7) (lw: 2nd st: rdn over 2f out: wknd fnl f) ....s.h **6**
3409[5] Star Anise *(8) (MRChannon)* 3-8-10 ow1 RHughes(1) (s.s: a bhd: t.o) 30 **7**

7/4 Afsaat, **7/2** Raise the Stakes, **9/2** Academy Life, **5/1** Ottavio Farnese, **8/1** DOROTHEA BROOKE (IRE) (op 5/1), **16/1** Night Flare (FR), **50/1** Star Anise, CSF £42.24 TOTE £7.30: £2.20 £3.80 (£33.10) OWNER Mrs P. W. Harris (BERKHAMSTED) BRED Pendley Farm 7 Rn
1m 43.16 (1.16) SF: 51/39/36/30/26/21/-

T/Plpt: £48.50 (307.7 Tckts). T/Qdpt: £23.00 (3 Tckts). AK

3546-DONCASTER (L-H)
Thursday September 7th (Good)

WEATHER: overcast WIND: mod half bhd

3560 QUEEN'S OWN YORKSHIRE DRAGOONS STKS (2-Y.O) (Class C) £5,362.50 (£1,987.50: £956.25: £393.75: £159.38: £65.62) **7f** Stalls: High GOING minus 0.06 sec per fur (G) 2-00 (2-04)

2775* **Mawwal (USA) (100)***(96+)*(Fav)*(RWArmstrong)* 2-9-7 WCarson(6) (lw: trckd ldr: led over 2f out: qcknd: easily) ....— **1**
3174[6] Tria Kemata *(78) (JLDunlop)* 2-8-11 MJKinane(7) (plld hrd: trckd ldrs: effrt 2f out: styd on fnl f: nt pce of wnr) 3½ **2**
Rocky Oasis (USA) *(75+) (MRStoute)* 2-8-11 WRSwinburn(4) (w'like: cmpt: bit bkwd: dwlt: hdwy 2f out: styd on) 1¼ **3**

2131* Sea Dane **(100)***(76)*(Fav)*(PWHarris)* 2-9-7 PatEddery(8) (a.p: effrt over 2f out: sn rdn & no imp)....4 4
Elite Force (IRE) *(63+)* *(PWChapple-Hyam)* 2-8-11 JReid(3) (w'like: scope: chsd ldrs: rdn 3f out: btn appr fnl f)....1¼ 5
1752[10] Influence Pedler *(49)* *(CEBrittain)* 2-8-11 MRoberts(2) (pushed along thrght: nvr trbld ldrs)....6 6
2365[5] Canons Park **(98)***(42)* *(IABalding)* 2-9-1 LDettori(5) (swtg: unruly s: led tl over 2f out: sn wknd)....5 7
Torch Ochre (USA) *(BWHills)* 2-8-11 MHills(1) (unf: scope: dwlt: sn outpcd & t.o)....25 8

11/4 MAWWAL (USA), Sea Dane (2/1-3/1), **4/1** Elite Force (IRE), **13/2** Rocky Oasis (USA), **15/2** Tria Kemata, **9/1** Canons Park (op 6/1), **10/1** Torch Ochre (USA), **33/1** Influence Pedler, CSF £22.55 TOTE £3.20: £1.40 £1.90 £1.70 (£13.10) OWNER Mr Hamdan Al Maktoum (NEWMARKET) BRED Shadwell Estate Co., Ltd. and Shadwell Farm Inc. 8 Rn
1m 27.35 (3.95) SF: 52/34/31/32/19/5/-/-

3561

MAY HILL STKS (Gp 3) (2-Y.O F) (Class A) £18,052.20 (£6,679.80: £3,204.90: £1,309.50: £519.75: £203.85)
1m (round) Stalls: Low GOING minus 0.06 sec per fur (G) 2-35 (2-36)

2554[2] **Solar Crystal (IRE) (100)***(101)* *(HRACecil)* 2-8-9 WRyan(9) (lw: mde all: styd on strly fnl 2f)— 1
3578a[2] Like A Hawk (USA) **(90)***(99)* *(PFICole)* 2-8-9 TQuinn(1) (a chsng wnr: rdn 3f out: kpt on wl)....1¼ 2
3339* Ruznama (USA) *(97)*(Fav)*(BWHills)* 2-8-9 WCarson(7) (lw: a.p: rdn ½-wy: styd on wl towards fin)....¾ 3
3186[3] Sweet Robin (IRE) **(100)***(96)* *(MJohnston)* 2-8-9 MJKinane(6) (bhd & rdn ½-wy: swtchd outside 2f out: r.o wl fnl f)....¾ 4
3306* Myrtle **(92)***(93)* *(RHannon)* 2-8-9 MRoberts(4) (s.i.s: bhd tl hdwy u.p 3f out: styd on one pce: no imp fnl f)....1½ 5
2886[2] Gryada **(90)***(89)* *(WJarvis)* 2-8-9 PatEddery(11) (bhd: hdwy u.p 3f out: styd on: n.d)....1¾ 6
3216[2] Staffin **(100)***(89)* *(JRFanshawe)* 2-8-9 WRSwinburn(5) (swtg: bhd: effrt on ins ½-wy: rdn & no imp)....hd 7
2947* Bint Salsabil (USA) *(84)* *(JLDunlop)* 2-8-12 RHills(8) (in tch tl outpcd ½-wy: sn btn)....4 8
3397[2] Ailesbury Hill (USA) **(80)***(79)* *(PWChapple-Hyam)* 2-8-9 JReid(3) (b.hind: lw: effrt 4f out: sn hrd rdn: n.d)....¾ 9
2947[3] Witch of Fife (USA) *(71)* *(BWHills)* 2-8-9 MHills(10) (prom to ½-wy: sn rdn & btn)....4 10
3260* Faraway Waters *(45)* *(DWPArbuthnot)* 2-8-9 LDettori(2) (chsd ldrs tl wknd wl over 2f out)....13 11

3/1 Ruznama (USA), **4/1** Bint Salsabil (USA), **7/1** Sweet Robin (IRE), Like A Hawk (USA), **15/2** SOLAR CRYSTAL (IRE), Staffin, **8/1** Witch of Fife (USA), **10/1** Faraway Waters, **16/1** Myrtle, **20/1** Gryada, **33/1** Ailesbury Hill (USA), CSF £58.18 TOTE £13.50: £3.00 £2.20 £1.70 (£38.70) Trio £94.00 OWNER Mr Michael Poland (NEWMARKET) BRED Michael Poland 11 Rn
1m 39.44 (3.14) SF: 56/54/52/51/48/44/44/39/34/26/-

3562

KIVETON PARK STKS (Gp 3) (3-Y.O+) (Class A) £23,020.80 (£8,527.20: £4,098.60: £1,683.00: £676.50: £273.90)
1m (round) Stalls: Low GOING minus 0.06 sec per fur (G) 3-10 (3-10)

3478a[2] **Bishop of Cashel (112)***(116)* *(JRFanshawe)* 3-8-9 WRSwinburn(3) (a.p: smooth hdwy to ld 1½f out: rdn & r.o)....— 1
3067[2] Nijo **(109)***(115)* *(DRLoder)* 4-9-0 MJKinane(8) (a.p: hdwy to chal 2f out: sn rdn & outpcd: kpt on towards fin)....¾ 2
3325a* Mr Martini (IRE) **(103)***(118)* *(CEBrittain)* 5-9-4 MRoberts(7) (w ldr: slt ld 2f out: hdd over 1f out: kpt on wl)....s.h 3
3358[2] Moccasin Run (USA) **(103)***(109)* *(IABalding)* 4-9-0 LDettori(6) (lw: led 6f: sn outpcd: kpt on towards fin)....2½ 4
3360[5] Shahid **(113)***(113)* *(JLDunlop)* 3-8-13 WCarson(4) (hld up: effrt 3f out: styd on: no imp)....hd 5
3473* Bin Ajwaad (IRE) **(112)***(107)*(Fav)*(BHanbury)* 5-9-4 PatEddery(5) (lw: hld up: hdwy 3f out: sn rdn & no imp)....3 6
3067[8] Brief Glimpse (IRE) **(106)***(72)* *(MajorDNChappell)* 3-8-6 MHills(2) (swtg: plld hrd: hmpd after 1½f: a bhd)....14 7
3381[8] Indhar **(102)***(74)* *(JEBanks)* 4-9-0 JWeaver(9) (chsd lrs tl wknd fnl 2½f)....¾ 8

2/1 Bin Ajwaad (IRE), **11/4** Nijo, **9/2** BISHOP OF CASHEL, **7/1** Shahid (5/1-8/1), **11/1** Brief Glimpse (IRE) (8/1-12/1), Mr Martini (IRE) (8/1-12/1), **16/1** Moccasin Run (USA), **20/1** Indhar, CSF £16.85 TOTE £5.70: £1.60 £1.40 £2.20 (£7.10) Trio £22.00 OWNER Cheveley Park Stud (NEWMARKET) BRED Carroll Bloodstock Ltd 8 Rn
1m 40.13 (3.83) SF: 48/52/55/46/45/44/4/11
WEIGHT FOR AGE 3yo-5lb

3563

EAST COAST DONCASTER CUP STKS (Gp 3) (3-Y.O+) (Class A)
£21,019.80 (£7,768.20: £3,719.10: £1,510.50: £590.25: £222.15)
2m 2f Stalls: Low GOING minus 0.06 sec per fur (G) 3-40 (3-42)

2702* **Double Trigger (IRE) (121)***(124+)*(Fav)*(MJohnston)* 4-9-7 JWeaver(6) (lw: mde virtually all: shkn up 3f out: r.o v.strly: eased ins fnl f) ....— **1**
2702⁹ Further Flight **(107)***(117) (BWHills)* 9-9-3 MHills(3) (lw: b.hind: hld up: hdwy on bit to chal 3f out: sn rdn: r.o: no ch w wnr) 3 **2**
3146⁵ Old Rouvel (USA) **(98)***(113) (DJGMurraySmith)* 4-9-0 MJKinane(1) (hld up: hdwy 4f out: swtchd 2f out: r.o: nvr able to chal) 1½ **3**
3361* Admiral's Well (IRE) **(108)***(112) (RAkehurst)* 5-9-0 TQuinn(4) (lw: a chsng ldrs: ev ch & rdn over 3f out: r.o one pce) 1 **4**
3146² Cuff Link (IRE) **(107)***(101) (MajorWRHern)* 5-9-0 PaulEddery(5) (chsd wnr after 2f: rdn 7f out: wknd fnl 3f) 12 **5**
2219a⁶ Escarpment (USA) **(106)***(101) (PWChapple-Hyam)* 4-9-0 LDettori(2) (trckd ldrs: stdy hdwy ent st: rdn & wknd over 3f out) ....½ **6**

4/11 DOUBLE TRIGGER (IRE), **10/1** Cuff Link (IRE), Admiral's Well (IRE) (op 6/1), **11/1** Further Flight (op 7/1), **14/1** Escarpment (USA), **25/1** Old Rouvel (USA), CSF £4.88 TOTE £1.30: £1.10 £2.90 (£3.50) OWNER Mr R. W. Huggins (MIDDLEHAM) BRED Dene Investments N V 6 Rn
3m 58.74 (6.04) SF: 74/67/63/62/51/51

3564

KYOTO SCEPTRE STKS (Listed) (3-Y.O+ F & M) (Class A)
£12,030.00 (£4,470.00: £2,160.00: £900.00: £375.00: £165.00)
7f Stalls: High GOING minus 0.06 sec per fur (G) 4-10 (4-12)

3491² **Branston Abby (IRE) (105)***(117) (MJohnston)* 6-8-13 MRoberts(10) (a.p: led appr fnl f: r.o wl) ....— **1**
Lovely Millie (IRE) *(109) (DRLoder)* 3-8-6 LDettori(3) (lw: trckd ldrs: led over 2f out: edgd rt: hdd appr fnl f: no ch w wnr) 2 **2**
3191* Didina **(109)***(112)*(Fav)*(RCharlton)* 3-8-9 PatEddery(2) (a.p: effrt over 2f out: styd on: nt pce to chal) ....s.h **3**
1850⁷ Myself **(106)***(112) (PWChapple-Hyam)* 3-8-11 JReid(12) (lw: b: trckd ldrs: hmpd wl over 1f out: r.o one pce) 1¼ **4**
3582a⁷ Hoh Magic **(114)***(101) (MBell)* 3-8-6 MHills(6) (bhd: styd on u.p fnl 3f: nvr rchd ldrs) 2½ **5**
933¹⁰ Autumn Affair **(104)***(98) (CEBrittain)* 3-8-6 WCarson(11) (a.p: nt clr run & swtchd wl over 1f out: no imp) 1¼ **6**
3209⁶ She's Dynamite (IRE) **(83)***(89) (WJarvis)* 3-8-6 BThomson(5) (lw: mid div: drvn along ½-wy: no hdwy) 4 **7**
3235⁵ Mamlakah (IRE) **(100)***(86) (HThomsonJones)* 3-8-6b RHills(9) (led tl hdd & wknd over 2f out) 1¼ **8**
3373* Twilight Patrol **(94)***(84) (RHannon)* 3-8-6 MJKinane(1) (b.nr fore: outpcd fr ½-wy) ....¾ **9**
3399* Queenfisher **(88)***(81) (RHannon)* 3-8-6 SWhitworth(4) (bhd: rdn ½-wy: n.d) 1½ **10**
3451* Silent Expression **(79)***(56) (BJMeehan)* 5-8-10 RHughes(7) (bhd: rdn ½-wy: n.d) 11 **11**
2673⁹ Germane **(100)***(28) (MBell)* 3-8-6 MFenton(8) (bhd: rdn ½-wy: n.d) 12 **12**

13/8 Didina, **3/1** BRANSTON ABBY (IRE), **6/1** Hoh Magic, **7/1** Lovely Millie (IRE), **10/1** Myself, **16/1** Mamlakah (IRE), **20/1** Autumn Affair, Twilight Patrol, **33/1** Queenfisher, **50/1** Silent Expression, Germane, **66/1** She's Dynamite (IRE), CSF £23.55 TOTE £4.40: £1.70 £1.60 £1.20 (£13.20) Trio £5.90 OWNER Mr J. D. Abell (MIDDLEHAM) BRED John David Abell 12 Rn
1m 25.52 (2.12) SF: 67/55/58/58/47/44/35/32/30/27/6/-
WEIGHT FOR AGE 3yo-4lb

3565

DONCASTER FREE PRESS LADIES DAY H'CAP (0-90) (3-Y.O+) (Class C) £7,096.00 (£2,128.00: £1,024.00: £472.00)
7f Stalls: High GOING minus 0.06 sec per fur (G) 4-40 (4-46)

3411⁴ **Knobbleeneeze (70)***(82) (MRChannon)* 5-9-0v RHughes(21) (lw: trckd ldrs centre: effrt over 2f out: r.o to ld ins fnl f) ....— **1**
2531* Fame Again **(80)***(86) (MrsJRRamsden)* 3-9-6 KFallon(4) (lw: hdwy over 2f out: hrd rdn & r.o: nrst fin) 2½ **2**
3411⁵ Flashy's Son **(69)***(75) (GMMoore)* 7-8-13 LDettori(5) (b: b.hind: led far side tl ins fnl f: kpt on one pce) ....s.h **3**
3214² Russian Maid **(82)***(87) (JRFanshawe)* 3-9-8 MJKinane(2) (b.hind: chsd ldrs: chal over 1f out: no ex ins fnl f) ....¾ **4**
3396² Kid Ory **(66)***(67) (PCalver)* 4-8-10 MBirch(17) (b.hind: racd centre: a.p: styd on & hung lft fnl 2f) 1¾ **5**

2634[11] Gadge **(72)***(70) (DMorris)* 4-9-2 RCochrane(6) (effrt 3f out: edgd lft & styd on) ... 1 **6**
3373[5] French Grit (IRE) **(87)***(84) (MDods)* 3-9-13 JWeaver(18) (led centre 2f: led 3f out: hdd & btn over 1f out) ... ¾ **7**
2652[8] Queenbird **(73)***(69) (MJRyan)* 4-9-3 TQuinn(1) (chsd ldrs tl wknd over 2f out) ... nk **8**
3457* Samah **(71)***(67)*(Fav)*(DNicholls)* 5-9-1 4x NConnorton(11) (lw: trckd ldrs: smooth hdwy to chal over 2f out: sn rdn & nt qckn) ... hd **9**
3411[8] Allinson's Mate (IRE) **(77)***(72) (TDBarron)* 7-9-7b DeanMcKeown(8) (lw: s.i.s: styd on fnl 2f: n.d) ... hd **10**
3356[3] Young Benson **(66)***(52) (BAMcMahon)* 3-8-6 FNorton(12) (sn chsng ldrs: rdn ½-wy: wknd 2f out) ... 4 **11**
3103[3] Daysman (USA) **(76)***(62) (BWHills)* 3-9-2 MHills(9) (chsd ldrs 5f: sn rdn & btn) ... nk **12**
3209[5] Sotoboy (IRE) **(88)***(73) (PWHarris)* 3-10-0 SWhitworth(14) (prom 5f) ... s.h **13**
3493[13] Roseate Lodge **(58)***(42) (NBycroft)* 9-8-2 SMaloney(22) (b: racd centre: n.d) ... ½ **14**
3237[11] Allez Cyrano (IRE) **(81)***(61) (MBell)* 4-9-11v MFenton(16) (reminders after s: led after 2f to 3f out: sn lost pl) ... 2 **15**
3112[5] Courageous Dancer (IRE) **(83)***(55) (BHanbury)* 3-9-9 WRyan(13) (bhd: sme hdwy 3f out: nvr nr to chal) ... 3½ **16**
2737[6] Hawa Al Nasamaat (USA) **(83)***(53) (EALDunlop)* 3-9-9 WRSwinburn(19) (racd centre: n.d) ... ¾ **17**
1069[4] Axeman (IRE) **(88)***(50) (RHannon)* 3-10-0 PatEddery(20) (lw: racd centre: outpcd & bhd fnl 3f) ... 3½ **18**
3475[16] Rasmi (CAN) **(68)***(30) (PHowling)* 4-8-12 PaulEddery(7) (a bhd) ... hd **19**
*3396** King Rat (IRE) **(80)** *(TJEtherington)* 4-9-10b WCarson(15) (Withdrawn not under Starter's orders: lame at s) ... **W**
3373[6] Desert Harvest **(74)** *(RCharlton)* 3-9-0b JReid(3) (Withdrawn not under Starter's orders: ref to ent stalls) ... **W**

4/1 Samah, **5/1** Russian Maid, **11/2** Fame Again, **10/1** King Rat (IRE), **12/1** Gadge, Queenbird, Axeman (IRE), **14/1** Daysman (USA), **16/1** Courageous Dancer (IRE), KNOBBLEENEEZE, **20/1** Flashy's Son, Kid Ory, Hawa Al Nasamaat (USA), Desert Harvest, **25/1** French Grit (IRE), Young Benson, Roseate Lodge, Allinson's Mate (IRE), Allez Cyrano (IRE), **33/1** Sotoboy (IRE), **50/1** Rasmi (CAN), CSF £98.22 CT £1,657.50 TOTE £14.70: £2.80 £1.50 £4.50 £1.40 (£39.10) Trio £825.80 OWNER Mr Anthony Andrews (UPPER LAMBOURN) BRED A. and Mrs Andrews 19 Rn
1m 26.75 (3.35) SF: 53/53/46/54/38/41/51/40/38/43/19/29/40/13/32/22/20/17/1/-/-
WEIGHT FOR AGE 3yo-4lb

T/Jkpt: Not won; £20,841.29 to Doncaster 8/9/95. T/Plpt: £26.90 (1,366.48 Tckts). T/Qdpt: £9.50 (17.8 Tckts). AA

3135-FOLKESTONE (R-H)
Thursday September 7th (Good to firm)
WEATHER: overcast, showers WIND: str half against

3566
EAST WEAR BAY CLAIMING STKS (I) (2-Y.O) (Class F) £2,519.00 (£694.00: £329.00) **6f** Stalls: Low GOING minus 0.38 sec per fur (F) 1-45 (1-49)

3160[11] **Bozeman (IRE) (60)***(77?) (RHannon)* 2-8-5b(5) DaneO'Neill(10) (led 4f out: rdn out) ... — **1**
3423* Times of Times (IRE) **(68)***(67)*(Fav)*(DJSCosgrove)* 2-8-9 MRimmer(8) (a.p: swtchd rt over 1f out: unable qckn) ... 3½ **2**
3441[10] Boston Tea Party *(51) (IABalding)* 2-7-2 (7) MartinDwyer(1) (hdwy over 2f out: r.o one pce) ... ½ **3**
Subtle One (IRE) *(59) (GLMoore)* 2-8-7 JFEgan(2) (small: bit bkwd: dwlt: bmpd over 4f out: rdn over 3f out: hdwy 2f out: r.o one pce) ... 1¾ **4**
3468[5] Madonna da Rossi *(48) (SirMarkPrescott)* 2-8-0 CNutter(5) (led 2f: rdn over 3f out: wknd over 1f out) ... 1¼ **5**
3233[6] Spanish Luck **(53)***(46) (JWHills)* 2-8-3b GDuffield(11) (prom over 4f) ... 2 **6**
3441[9] Hurricane Horn (IRE) **(58)***(48) (WRMuir)* 2-8-12 CRutter(7) (lw: no hdwy fnl 3f) ... 2½ **7**
1841[8] Orange And Blue **(60)***(25) (MAJarvis)* 2-7-7c(3)ow1 NVarley(3) (spd over 4f) ... 2½ **8**
3378[13] A Million At Last (IRE) *(36) (MBell)* 2-8-8 PRobinson(6) (s.s: a bhd) ... ¾ **9**
3378[11] Deedeejay *(15) (JMBradley)* 2-7-9 GBardwell(4) (bhd fnl 3f) ... 3 **10**
3427[12] Masbro Bird **(46)** *(BRMillman)* 2-8-1 JLowe(9) (bhd fnl 4f) ... 9 **11**

4/6 Times of Times (IRE), **8/1** BOZEMAN (IRE) (6/1-9/1), **9/1** Orange And Blue (6/1-10/1), Spanish Luck (op 5/1), **12/1** Madonna da Rossi (op 8/1), **20/1** Subtle One (IRE), **25/1** Masbro Bird, **33/1** Hurricane Horn (IRE), A Million At Last (IRE), Deedeejay, Boston Tea Party, CSF £13.05 TOTE £10.30: £2.10 £1.10 £4.50 (£5.70) Trio £97.00 OWNER Lord Carnarvon (MARLBOROUGH) BRED Don Kelly 11 Rn
1m 14.4 (2.70) SF: 25/15/-/7/-/-/-/-/-/-/-
Boston Tea Party clmd BSmith £2,000
STEWARDS' ENQUIRY Obj. to Bozeman (IRE) by Rimmer overruled.

3567 E.B.F. MARGATE RATING RELATED MAIDEN LIMITED STKS (0-65) (2-Y.O) (Class F) £2,941.20 (£813.20: £387.60)

5f Stalls: Low GOING minus 0.38 sec per fur (F) 2-15 (2-16)

2277^{7} **Thai Morning (63)***(70)*(Fav)*(PWHarris)* 2-9-0 GHind(4) (lw: led 3f out: r.o wl) ....— 1
3284^{4} Dande Flyer **(65)***(64) (DWPArbuthnot)* 2-9-0 BDoyle(1) (b.nr hind: dwlt: hld up: chsd wnr over 1f out: unable qckn) 2 2
3093^{5} Oare Budgie **(65)***(36) (PTWalwyn)* 2-8-9 KDarley(2) (lw: hld up: rdn over 2f out: sn wknd) 7 3
2091^{6} Dancing Jack **(64)***(36) (JJBridger)* 2-9-0 GDuffield(3) (lw: a.p: hung rt 2f out: wknd over 1f out) 1½ 4
3244^{5} Poppy My Love **(42)***(19) (RHarris)* 2-8-9 DBatteate(5) (led 2f: wknd over 1f out) 4 5

13/8 THAI MORNING, **7/4** Dande Flyer (10/11-15/8), **9/2** Oare Budgie (3/1-5/1), **9/1** Dancing Jack (9/2-10/1), **50/1** Poppy My Love, CSF £4.32 TOTE £2.60: £1.60 £1.40 (£2.30) OWNER The Thai Connection (BERKHAMSTED) BRED R. G. Percival 5 Rn 60.9 secs (2.30) SF: 27/21/-/-/-

3568 SANDWICH BAY NURSERY H'CAP (0-85) (2-Y.O) (Class D) £3,980.00 (£1,190.00: £570.00: £260.00)

5f Stalls: Low GOING minus 0.38 sec per fur (F) 2-45 (2-49)

3335* **Chemcast (66)***(68) (BJMeehan)* 2-8-8 BDoyle(6) (lw: a.p: led over 2f out: rdn out) ....— 1
3149* Lady Caroline Lamb (IRE) **(60)***(61) (MRChannon)* 2-8-2 GCarter(2) (s.s: hdwy over 3f out: rdn over 2f out: ev ch ins fnl f: r.o) ....nk 2
3423^{2} Miss Carottene **(57)***(56) (MJRyan)* 2-7-8b(5) MBaird(1) (rdn over 2f out: hdwy over 1f out: r.o) ....¾ 3
3012* Supreme Power **(74)***(71) (WRMuir)* 2-9-2b CRutter(7) (lw: s.s: rdn over 3f out: hdwy over 1f out: r.o) ....½ 4
3132^{4} Goretski (IRE) **(60)***(50)*(Fav)*(NTinkler)* 2-8-2 ow1 KDarley(4) (lw: a.p: rdn over 2f out: unable qckn) 2 5
2940^{7} Heaven Sent (IRE) **(60)***(47) (PMitchell)* 2-7-11 (5) MHenry(9) (hdwy over 1f out: one pce) 1¼ 6
3434^{2} Pleasure Time **(78)***(61) (CSmith)* 2-9-6b GHind(3) (lw: hld up: shkn up 2f out: eased whn btn over 1f out) 1 7
2779^{6} Foreman **(64)***(47) (WAO'Gorman)* 2-8-6 EmmaO'Gorman(13) (hdwy over 1f out: sn wknd) ...nk 8
3314* Little Noggins (IRE) **(74)***(56) (CADwyer)* 2-8-13 (3) JStack(5) (prom over 3f) ....hd 9
2940^{4} Just Lady **(75)***(54) (WGMTurner)* 2-8-10 (7) JWilkinson(11) (led over 2f: wknd over 1f out) 1 10
3213^{4} Centurion **(79)***(52) (RHannon)* 2-9-2 (5) DaneO'Neill(12) (lw: bhd fnl 2f) 2 11
3284* No Sympathy **(61)***(33) (GLMoore)* 2-8-3 JFEgan(10) (a bhd) ....hd 12
3053* Western Venture (IRE) **(72)***(38) (JWPayne)* 2-9-0 MRimmer(8) (a bhd) 2 13

7/2 Goretski (IRE) (7/1-3/1), **4/1** Lady Caroline Lamb (IRE), **11/2** Little Noggins (IRE) (4/1-13/2), **7/1** Supreme Power (op 4/1), **12/1** Foreman (7/1-14/1), Miss Carottene, Pleasure Time (op 7/1), **14/1** Centurion, No Sympathy (8/1-16/1), **16/1** Just Lady, CHEMCAST, Western Venture (IRE), **33/1** Heaven Sent (IRE), CSF £77.55 CT £752.38 TOTE £23.50: £4.90 £1.70 £3.80 (£27.20) Trio £351.00 OWNER Mrs Kim Parker (UPPER LAMBOURN) BRED C. R. and V. M. Withers 13 Rn
60.2 secs (1.60) SF: 33/26/21/36/15/12/26/12/21/19/17/-/3

3569 DAVID CAMERON MEMORIAL H'CAP (0-70) (3-Y.O+) (Class E) £3,588.20 (£1,073.60: £514.80: £235.40)

1m 7f 92y Stalls: Low GOING minus 0.17 sec per fur (GF) 3-20 (3-22)

2812^{4} **Unchanged (62)***(75) (CEBrittain)* 3-9-0 BDoyle(4) (lw: a.p: led over 5f out: r.o wl) ....— 1
3425^{2} Chez Catalan **(45)***(57)*(Fav)*(RAkehurst)* 4-8-9b AMcGlone(3) (lw: rdn over 2f out: 3rd st: chsd wnr fnl f: r.o) 1 2
3217^{9} Chakalak **(45)***(56) (SDow)* 7-8-2 (7) ADaly(6) (lw: rdn & hdwy over 5f out: 6th st: r.o ins fnl f) 1 3
3527^{15} Iron N Gold **(48)***(58) (AMoore)* 3-7-9 (5) MHenry(1) (2nd st: rdn over 3f out: unable qckn fnl 2f) ....¾ 4
2592^{7} Coleridge **(40)***(50) (JJSheehan)* 7-8-1b(3) NVarley(9) (rdn over 4f out: hdwy over 2f out: r.o ins fnl f) ....nk 5
3140^{2} Zuiena (USA) **(67)***(76) (PFICole)* 3-9-5b KDarley(11) (lw: 4th st: hrd rdn over 1f out: one pce) ....¾ 6
Dawn Flight **(50)***(52) (JRJenkins)* 6-9-0 DHolland(14) (lw: nvr nr to chal) 7 7
3292^{4} Old Swinford (IRE) **(52)***(52) (BJMeehan)* 3-8-4 GBardwell(12) (hdwy over 5f out: 5th st: wknd wl over 1f out) 1½ 8
3303* Top Prize **(43)***(41) (MBrittain)* 7-8-7v JLowe(2) (nvr nrr) 1¾ 9
Touching Times **(36)***(28) (JJBridger)* 7-7-11 (3)ow1 SSanders(5) (b: a bhd) 5 10
737^{9} Smuggler's Point (USA) **(60)***(53) (JJBridger)* 5-9-10 GDuffield(8) (b: lw: a bhd) ....hd 11

1594[7] Mint a Million (IRE) **(31)***(22) (MBlanshard)* 4-7-4 (5)ow2 MBaird(10) (a bhd) .... ½ **12**
3137[6] Admiral's Guest (IRE) **(49)** *(GHarwood)* 3-8-1v JQuinn(13) (lw: led 10f: t.o) .... dist **13**
2530[12] High Five (IRE) **(37)** *(DAWilson)* 5-8-1 GCarter(7) (lw: a bhd: t.o) .... ¾ **14**
LONG HANDICAP Mint a Million (IRE) 7-6

11/4 Chez Catalan, **11/2** Top Prize (7/2-6/1), **6/1** Zuiena (USA), **8/1** Admiral's Guest (IRE) (6/1-9/1), **10/1** UNCHANGED (7/1-11/1), High Five (IRE) (6/1-12/1), Chakalak, **12/1** Old Swinford (IRE) (op 8/1), **20/1** Iron N Gold, **25/1** Coleridge, Smuggler's Point (USA), **33/1** Dawn Flight, **40/1** Mint a Million (IRE), Touching Times, CSF £35.69 CT £264.95 TOTE £13.40: £3.90 £1.60 £4.10 (£12.90) Trio £51.20 OWNER Mr M. J. Simmonds (NEWMARKET) BRED M. J. Simmonds 14 Rn
3m 24.9 (8.00) SF: 44/38/37/27/31/45/33/21/22/9/34/3/-/-
WEIGHT FOR AGE 3yo-12lb

3570

EAST WEAR BAY CLAIMING STKS (II) (2-Y.O) (Class F) £2,519.00 (£694.00: £329.00) **6f** Stalls: Low GOING minus 0.38 sec per fur (F) 3-50 (3-53)

3312* **Spirito Libro (USA) (64)***(65)*(Fav)*(SirMarkPrescott)* 2-8-5 GDuffield(1) (w ldr: led over 1f out: drvn out) .... — **1**
3378[2] Never Think Twice **(68)***(67) (KTIvory)* 2-8-3v(7) CScally(2) (b: hld up: rdn over 2f out: r.o ins fnl f) 1¼ **2**
2249[2] Bells of Holland *(58) (BWHills)* 2-8-3 DHolland(10) (a.p: hrd rdn over 1f out: unable qckn) .... ½ **3**
3289[8] L A Touch **(57)***(54) (CADwyer)* 2-7-13 JQuinn(6) (hld up: hrd rdn over 1f out: one pce) .... s.h **4**
2965[W] Don't Tell Vicki **(56)***(55) (JSMoore)* 2-7-12 (3) NVarley(3) (lw: led over 4f: one pce) .... nk **5**
3008[4] Arch Angel (IRE) **(56)***(53) (DJSffrenchDavis)* 2-8-3 NAdams(4) (lw: hld up: rdn over 2f out: one pce) 1½ **6**
2656[7] Baker *(24) (HCandy)* 2-9-0 WNewnes(8) (a bhd) 15 **7**
3054[4] Sally State *(MrsMMcCourt)* 2-7-6 (7) RStudholme(9) (a bhd) 7 **8**
3378[6] Moniques Venture *(DJSCosgrove)* 2-8-3 DBiggs(5) (bhd fnl 4f) 3½ **9**
2838[6] Iron And Steel *(AMoore)* 2-8-5v CandyMorris(7) (lw: bhd fnl 3f) .... ½ **10**

6/4 SPIRITO LIBRO (USA), **4/1** Bells of Holland (op 9/4), **6/1** Arch Angel (IRE), **13/2** Never Think Twice, **8/1** L A Touch (4/1-10/1), **10/1** Don't Tell Vicki (op 6/1), **25/1** Baker, Sally State, **33/1** Moniques Venture, Iron And Steel, CSF £11.87 TOTE £2.80: £1.50 £2.10 £1.60 (£3.70) Trio £8.20 OWNER Mrs Timothy Rooney (NEWMARKET) BRED T. J. Rooney 10 Rn
1m 14.5 (2.80) SF: 20/22/13/9/10/8/-/-/-/-
Spirito Libro (USA) clmd JBates £7,000

3571

LYSANDER INSURANCE BROKERS LIMITED STKS (0-70) (3-Y.O+) (Class E) £3,388.00 (£1,012.00: £484.00: £220.00)
1m 4f Stalls: Low GOING minus 0.17 sec per fur (GF) 4-20 (4-21)

3355[2] **Finlaggan (70)***(84) (SirMarkPrescott)* 3-8-9 GDuffield(5) (led 9f out: drvn out) .... — **1**
2768[5] Global Dancer **(68)***(85) (SDow)* 4-8-12 (7) ADaly(8) (2nd st: ev ch fnl 2f: r.o wl) .... s.h **2**
3317* Alaraby (IRE) **(70)***(80) (IABalding)* 3-8-0 (7) MartinDwyer(1) (b.nr hind: 6th st: hdwy over 1f out: r.o) 1½ **3**
3277[3] Frozen Sea (USA) **(67)***(72) (GPEnright)* 4-9-0 (5) DGibbs(3) (hdwy over 1f out: nvr nrr) 8 **4**
3083* Newport Knight **(66)***(72) (RAkehurst)* 4-9-7 AMcGlone(7) (lw: 4th st: wknd 2f out) 2 **5**
3291[9] College Night (IRE) **(62)***(64) (CADwyer)* 3-8-2 (3) JStack(6) (nvr nr to chal) .... ½ **6**
3294[6] Sharazi (USA) **(60)***(69) (DJSCosgrove)* 4-9-5b MRimmer(11) (lw: nvr nrr) .... s.h **7**
3320[2] Lucky Coin **(70)***(65) (CEBrittain)* 3-8-7 BDoyle(4) (5th st: wknd 2f out) .... ½ **8**
3395[2] Divina Mia **(65)***(60) (JWHills)* 3-8-0 (5) MHenry(2) (bhd fnl 3f) 2½ **9**
2863* Sweet Pavlova (USA) **(69)***(42)*(Fav)*(PFICole)* 3-8-2 (5) DaneO'Neill(9) (led 3f: 3rd st: wknd 2f out) 15 **10**
3343[4] Antiguan Flyer **(53)***(43) (RHarris)* 6-9-5 AMackay(10) (b: a bhd) 1¾ **11**

7/2 Sweet Pavlova (USA), **9/2** FINLAGGAN (op 3/1), **5/1** Lucky Coin, **6/1** Alaraby (IRE), **7/1** Newport Knight (5/1-8/1), Global Dancer, **8/1** Divina Mia, **12/1** Frozen Sea (USA), Sharazi (USA), **16/1** Antiguan Flyer, **33/1** College Night (IRE), CSF £37.20 TOTE £3.60: £1.20 £3.20 £2.20 (£56.00) Trio £55.20 OWNER Mrs C. R. Philipson (NEWMARKET) BRED Mrs C. R. Philipson 11 Rn
2m 36.4 (5.20) SF: 45/55/41/42/42/25/39/26/21/3/13
WEIGHT FOR AGE 3yo-9lb

3572

LEVY BOARD APPRENTICE H'CAP (0-70) (3-Y.O+) (Class E) £3,531.00 (£1,056.00: £506.00: £231.00)
1m 4f Stalls: Low GOING minus 0.17 sec per fur (GF) 4-50 (4-50)

1991[3] **Kaafih Homm (IRE) (54)***(69) (NACallaghan)* 4-9-7 JStack(6) (b.nr hind: lw: gd hdwy over 2f out: 6th st: led 1f out: r.o wl) .... — **1**

3470[4] Wottashambles **(40)***(53) (LMontagueHall)* 4-8-7 SSanders(12) (hdwy over 4f out: 5th st: ev ch over 1f out: unable qckn) 1¼ **2**
3287* Masuri Kabisa (USA) **(39)***(52)*(Fav)*(HJCollingridge)* 4-8-6v DaneO'Neill(4) (lw: 3rd st: led over 1f out: sn hdd: one pce) ....nk **3**
2439[8] One Off the Rail (USA) **(40)***(46) (AMoore)* 5-8-7 AWhelan(10) (4th st: hrd rdn over 1f out: one pce) 5 **4**
3302* Ruby Heights **(52)***(56) (RHannon)* 4-9-0 (5) EGreehy(8) (lw: led 9f out tl over 1f out: sn wknd)..2 **5**
3137[3] Bag of Tricks (IRE) **(51)***(54) (SDow)* 5-9-1 (3) ADaly(2) (2nd st: wknd over 1f out) ....nk **6**
3091[7] Nobby North **(65)***(64) (LordHuntingdon)* 3-9-4 (5) AimeeCook(1) (stmbld s: a bhd) 3½ **7**
2052[10] Barahin (IRE) **(42)***(30) (JJBridger)* 6-8-9 LNewton(5) (b: a bhd) 8 **8**
3311[3] Acquittal (IRE) **(59)***(31) (JRFanshawe)* 3-9-3 NVarley(7) (led 3f: wknd over 4f out) 12 **9**
2768[4] Niknaks Nephew **(68)***(7) (DJSffrenchDavis)* 3-9-12 MHenry(9) (bhd fnl 5f: t.o) 25 **10**

11/4 Masuri Kabisa (USA), **6/1** Bag of Tricks (IRE), Wottashambles (op 7/2), Ruby Heights, **7/1** KAAFIH HOMM (IRE), **9/1** Acquittal (IRE), **10/1** Niknaks Nephew (8/1-12/1), One Off the Rail (USA), **16/1** Nobby North, **20/1** Barahin (IRE), CSF £46.04 CT £131.83 TOTE £4.80: £1.50 £1.70 £1.70 (£96.00) Trio £44.30 OWNER Gallagher Materials Ltd (NEWMARKET) BRED Sheikh Ahmed bin Rashid al Maktoum 10 Rn 2m 38.5 (7.30) SF: 43/27/26/20/30/28/29/4/-/-
WEIGHT FOR AGE 3yo-9lb

3573 DEAL MAIDEN STKS (3-Y.O+ F & M) (Class D) £4,171.70 (£1,247.60: £597.80: £272.90) 1m 1f 149y Stalls: High GOING minus 0.17 sec per fur (GF) 5-20 (5-21)

2506[2] **Anna of Brunswick (75)***(65)*(Fav)*(HRACecil)* 3-8-9 AMcGlone(8) (mde virtually all: rdn out) ....— **1**
3234[4] Cyphell (IRE) **(68)***(62) (MRStoute)* 3-8-9 DHolland(5) (chsd wnr: hrd rdn over 1f out: unable qckn) 2 **2**
3428[2] Urania *(60) (MAJarvis)* 3-8-9 PRobinson(3) (3rd st: rdn over 2f out: one pce) 1 **3**
Silver Singer *(56) (DRLoder)* 3-8-9 GCarter(1) (leggy: unf: 4th st: rdn over 2f out: one pce).2½ **4**
2880[7] Sujud (IRE) *(51) (HThomsonJones)* 3-8-9 JFEgan(6) (lw: lost pl over 5f out: mod 6th st: one pce fnl 2f) 3 **5**
1290[9] Dalcross **(41)***(41) (HJCollingridge)* 4-9-2 JQuinn(4) (hdwy over 3f out: 5th st: wknd over 1f out) 6 **6**
Sagitta's Reel (HOL) *(34) (MrsJReynaert,Belgium)* 4-9-2 GHind(2) (a bhd) 4 **7**
Tapestry Rose *(JCPoulton)* 4-9-2 AMorris(7) (a bhd: t.o) ....dist **8**

13/8 ANNA OF BRUNSWICK, **4/1** Silver Singer (op 9/4), **9/2** Cyphell (IRE) (5/2-6/1), Urania (op 5/2), **9/1** Sujud (IRE), **16/1** Sagitta's Reel (HOL), **100/1** Dalcross, Tapestry Rose, CSF £8.72 TOTE £1.70: £1.10 £1.60 £1.30 (£5.00) OWNER Sheikh Mohammed (NEWMARKET) BRED Sheikh Mohammed bin Rashid al Maktoum 8 Rn 2m 2.7 (5.00) SF: 37/34/32/28/23/20/13/-
WEIGHT FOR AGE 3yo-7lb

T/Plpt: £47.30 (225.59 Tckts). T/Qdpt: Not won; £48.40 to Doncaster 8/9/95. AK

2730a-ARLINGTON PARK (Chicago, USA) (L-H) Saturday August 26th (Firm)

3574a TOLOMEO STKS (3-Y.O+) £31,923.00 1m 110y 23-40 (21-46)

Marastani (USA) *(108) (TAmoss,USA)* 5-8-3 SSellers ....— **1**
Joseph's Robe (USA) *(100) (USA)* 4-8-0 EFires 2¾ **2**
Coaxing Matt (USA) *(97) (USA)* 6-8-0 CSilva 1½ **3**
1236a[10] Port Lucaya *(92) (DRLoder)* 5-8-3 CMcCarron (btn approx 8l) **8**

P-M £7.80: PL £4.80 £5.60 SHOW £3.00 £3.20 £3.60 (£20.40) OWNER T. Webber,jnr BRED Albert G. & John W. Clay 10 Rn 1m 41.2 SF: -/-/-/-

3478a-DEAUVILLE (France) (R-H) Sunday August 27th (Good)

3575a PRIX DE LA NONETTE (Gp 3) (3-Y.O F) £26,347.00 (£9,581.00: £4,790.00: £2,395.00) 1m 2f 3-20 (3-23)

1712a[2] **Matiara (USA)** *(114) (MmeCHead,France)* 3-9-2 FHead ....— **1**
Dance Partner (JPN) *(114) (MmePBarbe,France)* 3-9-2 YTake ....s.h **2**

2561a* Garden Rose (IRE) *(114) (PBary,France)* 3-9-2 DBoeuf ....s.h 3
3040a* Angel In My Heart (FR) *(109) (JEHammond,France)* 3-9-2 CAsmussen 3 4

P-M 2.00F: 1.20F 1.40F (9.00F) OWNER Ecurie Aland (FRANCE) BRED Societe Aland 4 Rn
2m 11.3 (9.70) SF: -/-/-/-

3480a-ARLINGTON PARK (Chicago, USA) (L-H)
Sunday August 27th (Firm)

3576a
ARLINGTON MILLION (Gp 1) (3-Y.O+) £384,615.00 (£128,205.00: £70,513.00: £38,462.00) **1m 2f** 21-45 (21-44)

Awad (USA) *(126) (DDonk,USA)* 5-9-0 EMaple (hld up: hdwy st: led over 1f out: rdn out) ....— 1
Sandpit (BRZ) *(122) (RMandella,USA)* 6-9-0 CNakatani (trckd ldrs: r.o fnl 2f: wnt 2nd cl hme) 2¼ 2
The Vid (USA) *(122) (MWolfson,USA)* 5-9-0 HMcCauley (a.p: led 2f out tl over 1f out: no ex)nk 3
2894a[2] Kaldounevees(FR) *(121) (JEHammond,France)* 4-9-0 KDesormeaux (hld up: hdwy 3f out: r.o wl fnl f) ....½ 4
Tinners Way (USA) *(119) (RFrankel,USA)* 5-9-0 EDelahoussaye (mid div: nvr plcd to chal) 1¼ 5
Lassigny (USA) *(116) (WMott,USA)* 4-9-0 JBailey (hld up: nvr plcd to chal)........1¾ 6
2286[7] Prince of Andros (USA) *(114) (DRLoder)* 5-9-0 PDay (hld up: prog 4f out: nt qckn st) 1¼ 7
Kiri's Clown (USA) *(109) (PJohnson,USA)* 6-9-0 MLuzzi (trckd ldr to 2f out: sn wknd)........3½ 8
Manilaman (USA) *(109) (WHoward,USA)* 4-9-0 RRomero (led tl 2f out: wknd) ....nse 9
Northern Spur (IRE) *(102) (RMcAnally,USA)* 4-9-0 CMcCarron (mid div: wknd & bhd st) 4 10
Johann Quatz (FR) *(RMcAnally,USA)* 6-9-0 AGryder (rr whn stmbld & u.r. 2f out)........ U

P-M £13.80: PL £4.80 £3.60 SHOW £4.20 £3.00 £9.60 (SF £38.40 DF £16.60) OWNER Ryehill Farm BRED Ryehill Farm 11 Rn
1m 58.69 SF: -/-/-/-/-/-/-/-/-/-/-

3486a-BADEN-BADEN (Germany) (L-H)
Tuesday August 29th (Soft)

3577a
OETTINGEN-RENNEN (Gp 3) (3-Y.O+) £30,864.00 (£12,346.00: £6,173.00) **1m** 3-25 (3-27)

2893a* **A Magicman (FR)** *(115) (HSteguweit,Germany)* 3-8-7 NGrant ....— 1
2389a[6] Ladoni *(113) (HRemmert,Germany)* 3-8-7 KWoodburn 1 2
2389a[3] Chato (USA) *(111) (HSteinmetz,Germany)* 3-8-7 AStarke 1 3

Tote 80DM: 19DM 14DM 18DM (SF 253DM) OWNER Stall Dagobert BRED H. Voegele & Maria Koenig 8 Rn
1m 43.31 SF: -/-/-

3482a-DEAUVILLE (France) (R-H)
Tuesday August 29th (Good)

3578a
PRIX DU CALVADOS (Gp 3) (2-Y.O F) £26,347.00 (£9,581.00: £4,790.00: £2,395.00) **7f** 1-50 (1-49)

2726a[4] **Blushing Gleam** *(101) (MmeCHead,France)* 2-8-9 ODoleuze ....— 1
1769[2] Like A Hawk (USA) *(99) (PFICole)* 2-8-9 TQuinn ....¾ 2
Wedding Gift *(99) (PDemercastel,France)* 2-8-9 SGuillot ....nse 3
2554* Tamnia *(98) (JLDunlop)* 2-8-9 JReid ....½ 4

P-M 3.50F: 2.00F 2.70F (SF 16.70F) OWNER Mr J. Wertheimer (FRANCE) BRED J.Wertheimer & Frere 6 Rn
1m 28.3 SF: -/-/-/-

3579a
PRIX DU LIEUREY (Listed) (3-Y.O F) £16,766.00 (£5,748.00: £3,593.00) **1m** 2-50 (2-58)

1712a[10] **Vadlamixa (FR)** *(106) (AFabre,France)* 3-9-2 TJarnet ....— 1
3192a[2] Marie de Ken (FR) *(106) (AdeRoyerDupre,France)* 3-9-2 GMosse ....s.nk 2
2897a[6] Nagnagnag (IRE) *(104) (SDow)* 3-9-2 MRoberts ....¾ 3

P-M 4.70F: 1.90F 1.50F 2.50F (9.70F) OWNER Mr J-L. Lagardere (FRANCE) BRED S.N.C. Lagardere Elevage 10 Rn
1m 44.6 SF: -/-/-

3580a PRIX DE L'EURE (3-Y.O) £7,784.00
1m 2f 3-20 (3-31)

Grecian Dart (IRE) *(88) (JEHammond,France)* 3-9-0 CAsmussen ....— 1
Palatine Boy (FR) *(93) (France)* 3-9-6 J-RDubosc ....¾ 2
Altor *(84) (France)* 3-9-0 SGuillot 2 3
3091[4] Indonesian (IRE) *(80) (MBell)* 3-9-6 MFenton (btn approx 4¼l) 5

P-M 5.50F: 2.00F 2.10F 1.80F (9.50F) OWNER Lord Weinstock BRED Ballymacoll Stud Farm Ltd 14 Rn
2m 11.6 (10.00) SF: -/-/-/-

3577a-BADEN-BADEN (Germany) (L-H)
Wednesday August 30th (Soft)

3581a MILKA STEHER-CUP (Listed) (3-Y.O+) £20,576.00 (£8,230.00: £4,938.00) 2m
2-10 (2-21)

Lakadone *(122) (RSuerland,Germany)* 3-8-4 PSchiergen ....— 1
Pasolini *(114) (JKujath,Germany)* 4-9-0 GBocskai 4½ 2
Silver Wedge (USA) *(110) (LordHuntingdon)* 4-9-0 MHills 4 3
3146[4] Khamaseen *(112) (JLDunlop)* 4-9-6 WRSwinburn (btn approx 9l) 5

Tote 85DM: 27DM 40DM (SF 560DM) OWNER Gestut Neffeltal BRED Gestut Neffeltal 6 Rn
3m 23.59 SF: -/-/-/-

3582a JACOBS GOLDENE PEITSCHE (Gp 2) (3-Y.O+) £51,440.00 (£20,576.00: £10,288.00: £6,584.00) 6f
3-25 (3-38)

3484a* **Hever Golf Rose** *(120) (TJNaughton)* 4-8-12 JWeaver (disp ld tl qcknd clr 1½f out: r.o wl) ..— 1
3491[6] Lavinia Fontana (IRE) *(115) (JLDunlop)* 6-8-12 MRimmer (disp ld over 4f: r.o) 2 2
3042a[3] Wessam Prince *(106) (CLaffon-Parias,France)* 4-9-3 WRSwinburn (trckd ldrs: one pce fnl 2f) 5 3
2728a[2] Matula (USA) *(100) (BSchutz,Germany)* 3-8-11 THellier (mid div; nvr rchd ldrs) 1½ 4
3195a[2] Siberian Grey *(98) (CSprengel,Germany)* 3-8-11 MO'Reilly (rr to ½-way: nvr plcd to chal) 1 5
1870[7] Adjmal (IRE) *(99) (PeterLautner,Germany)* 6-9-3 DRegnard (mid-div: one pce fnl 2f) ....nk 6
3564[5] Hoh Magic *(91) (MBell)* 3-8-7 MHills (hmpd early: nvr plcd to chal) ....¾ 7
3005[3] Katya (IRE) *(84) (MRChannon)* 3-8-7 RHughes (outpcd) 2½ 8
3195a* Desidera (IRE) *(79) (HBlume,Germany)* 3-8-7 AStarke (chsd ldrs tl wknd 2f out) 2 9

Tote 52DM: 17DM 16DM 13DM (221DM) OWNER Mr M. P. Hanson (EPSOM) BRED Ronald Popely 9 Rn
1m 10.64 SF: -/-/-/-/-/-/-/-/-

BORDEAUX (France) (R-H)
Thursday August 31st (Soft)

3583a CRITERIUM DU BEQUET (Listed) (2-Y.O) £14,371.00 (£4,790.00: £2,395.00) 6f
3-20 (3-20)

3132[2] **Just Ice** *(80?) (SirMarkPrescott)* 2-8-6 OPeslier ....— 1
Sarrans *(79) (RMartin,Spain)* 2-8-9 JoseLouisMartinez 1½ 2
Volona *(71) (JBernard,France)* 2-8-9 J-BEyquem 3 3

P-M 3.40F: 1.50F 3.00F 2.40F (17.90F) OWNER Canary Thoroughbreds (NEWMARKET) BRED Prof Klaus E. Rohde 8 Rn
No Time Taken SF: -/-/-

3581a-BADEN-BADEN (Germany) (L-H)
Friday September 1st (Soft)

3584a MOET & CHANDON RENNEN (Gp 2) (2-Y.O) £41,152.00 (£16,461.00: £8,230.00: £4,115.00) 6f
3-25 (3-29)

3197a[4] **Flying Squaw** *(96) (MRChannon)* 2-8-12 RHughes (hld up: swtchd 2f out: qcknd to ld ins fnl f: comf) ....— 1
Savage (IRE) *(92) (Germany)* 2-8-12 GHuber (mid div: r.o. fnl 2f: nt rch wnr) 1½ 2

Fairlight (GER) *(89) (Germany)* 2-8-12 THellier (led tl hdd by wnr: no ex) 1¼ **3**
Henning's Boy *(87) (Germany)* 2-9-2 DRegnard (mid div: nt pce to chal) 2 **4**
2892a* Happy Boy *(84) (HJentzsch,Germany)* 2-9-2 PSchiergen (chsd ldrs: no ex fnl 2f) 1¼ **5**
2043a* Tarte Aux Pommes (FR) *(80) (JBertranDeBalanda,France)* 2-8-12 SGuillot (chsd ldrs tl rdn & wknd 2f out) ....hd **6**
Atlantic City *(80) (Germany)* 2-8-12 PHeugl (alwys rr) ....hd **7**
My Happy Guest (IRE) *(62) (Germany)* 2-9-2 AHelfenbein (prom tl wknd fnl 2f) 8 **8**

Tote 26DM: 15DM 15DM 23DM (SF 125DM) OWNER Mr Michael Foy (UPPER LAMBOURN) BRED Brook Stud Ltd 8 Rn 1m 13.12 SF: -/-/-/-/-/-/-/-

3585a PREIS DER STADT BADEN-BADEN (Listed) (3-Y.O+) £16,461.00 (£6,584.00: £4,115.00: £2,469.00) **1m 2f** 4-35 (4-41)

Thagus (GER) *(102) (CvonderRecke,Germany)* 5-8-12 PSchiergen ....— **1**
1892a[2] Dream For Future (IRE) *(107) (PRemmert,Germany)* 5-9-6 GBocskai 1¾ **2**
Mut (GB) *(101) (HJGroschel,Germany)* 4-9-2 TMundry 1¼ **3**
1224[5] Wijara (IRE) *(103) (RHannon)* 3-8-11 RHughes ....hd **4**
2738[9] Danegold (IRE) *(99) (MRChannon)* 3-8-2 FNorton (btn approx 5¼l) **8**

Tote 115DM: 29DM 25DM 60DM (SF 614DM) OWNER Mydlinghoven Horse International BRED Gestut Weidingen 13 Rn 2m 9.17 SF: -/-/-/-/-

3325a-CURRAGH (Newbridge, Ireland) (R-H) Saturday September 2nd (Good to firm)

3586a ANGLESEY STKS (Gp 3) (2-Y.O) £16,250.00 (£4,750.00: £2,250.00) **6f 63y** 3-00 (3-02)

3197a[2] **Woodborough (USA)** *(103)*(Fav)*(PWChapple-Hyam)* 2-8-10 JReid ....— **1**
Lidanna (IRE) *(96) (DHanley,Ireland)* 2-8-7 MJKinane 1½ **2**
Harghar (USA) *(94) (JOxx,Ireland)* 2-8-10 JPMurtagh 2 **3**

4/6 WOODBOROUGH (USA), **9/4** Harghar (USA), **9/1** Lidanna (IRE), Tote £1.50: £1.10 £3.70 (£12.00) OWNER Mr A. J. F. O'Reilly (MARLBOROUGH) BRED Swettenham Stud 5 Rn 1m 15.0 SF: -/-/-

3587a TATTERSALLS BREEDERS STKS (2-Y.O) £73,500.00 (£28,500.00: £13,500.00: £4,500.00) **6f** 4-00 (4-06)

No Animosity (IRE) *(86+) (APO'Brien,Ireland)* 2-8-10 CRoche ....— **1**
Troysend *(75) (APO'Brien,Ireland)* 2-8-10 PShanahan 4 **2**
2886* Key To A Million (IRE) *(70) (RHannon)* 2-8-7 MRoberts ....¾ **3**
3225[5] Therhea (IRE) *(BRMillman)* 2-8-10 AWhelan **7**
3089[2] Reinhardt (IRE) (Fav)*(PWChapple-Hyam)* 2-8-10 JReid **9**
3203* Xenophon of Cunaxa (IRE) *(MJFetherston-Godley)* 2-8-10 JJBehan **9**
2651[6] Lia Fail (IRE) *(RHollinshead)* 2-8-7 DHogan **15**
2876[5] Love Bird (IRE) *(MJohnston)* 2-8-10 JWeaver **20**
2442[5] Crocodile Shoes *(RHannon)* 2-8-10 MJKinane **21**
3337[4] South Pagoda (IRE) *(PWChapple-Hyam)* 2-8-10 RHavlin **22**
3379[6] Mam'selle Bergerac (IRE) *(PMitchell)* 2-8-7 JoannaMorgan **23**
3337[3] Dragon's Back (IRE) *(MrsJCecil)* 2-8-10 JTate **25**
3158[8] Soviet Sakti (IRE) *(PMitchell)* 2-8-10 RPerham **28**

3/1 Reinhardt (IRE), **9/1** NO ANIMOSITY (IRE), **11/1** Key To A Million (IRE), **14/1** Crocodile Shoes, Love Bird (IRE), **20/1** South Pagoda (IRE), **25/1** Dragon's Back (IRE), **33/1** Therhea (IRE), Xenophon of Cunaxa (IRE), Troysend, **40/1** Soviet Sakti (IRE), **50/1** Mam'selle Bergerac (IRE), Lia Fail (IRE), Tote £7.50: £2.60 £37.90 £3.40 (£166.80) OWNER Mr D. M. Murphy (IRELAND) BRED Leinster Stud 29 Rn 1m 11.7 (1.10 under 2y best) (1.10) SF: -/-/-/-/-/-/-/-/-/-/-/-/-

3588a FUTURITY STKS (Gp 3) (2-Y.O) £16,250.00 (£4,750.00: £2,250.00) **1m** 4-30 (4-40)

3141* **Bijou d'Inde** *(97+)*(Fav)*(MJohnston)* 2-8-10 JWeaver ....— **1**
2441[2] Axford (USA) *(92) (PWChapple-Hyam)* 2-8-10 JReid 2½ **2**

Classic Fountain (IRE) *(87) (GMLyons,Ireland)* 2-8-10 JPMurtagh 2½ 3

8/11 BIJOU D'INDE, **4/1** Axford (USA), **16/1** Classic Fountain (IRE), Tote £1.70: £1.30 £2.20 £3.40 (£3.20) OWNER Mr J. S. Morrison (MIDDLEHAM) BRED Whitsbury Manor Stud 8 Rn
1m 38.7 (2.70) SF: -/-/-

2386a-LONGCHAMP (Paris, France) (R-H)
Sunday September 3rd (Good to firm)

3589a EMIRATES PRIX DU MOULIN DE LONGCHAMP (Gp 1) (3-Y.O+ C & F)
£107,784.00 (£43,114.00: £21,557.00: £10,778.00) **1m** 3-15 (3-15)

1850* **Ridgewood Pearl** *(125) (JOxx,Ireland)* 3-8-8 JPMurtagh (a.p: 3rd st: plld out 1½f out: rdn to ld 1f out: r.o. wl)....................— 1
3199a³ Shaanxi (USA) *(124) (ELellouche,France)* 3-8-8 DBoeuf (racd in 6th: prog to chal ins fnl f: no ex cl home)....................¾ 2
3476a* Missed Flight *(125) (CFWall)* 5-9-2 GDuffield (racd in 5th: rdn 2f out: r.o)....................¾ 3
3199a² Sayyedati *(122) (CEBrittain)* 5-8-13 BDoyle (hld up: rdn 2f out: r.o fnl f: nrst fin)....................nse 4
3199a⁸ Smolensk (USA) *(120) (AFabre,France)* 3-8-8 TJarnet (disp ld tl led 2f out: hdd 1f out: fdd)....................¾ 5
3199a* Miss Satamixa (IRE) *(119) (AFabre,France)* 3-8-8 SGuillot (hld up in rr: late prog: nvr nrr)....½ 6
3199a⁵ Green Tune (USA) *(117) (MmeCHead,France)* 4-9-2 ODoleuze (prom: 4th st: rdn & wknd over 1f out)....................2½ 7
3360² Darnay *(101) (SbinSuroor)* 4-9-2 WRSwinburn (disp ld tl rdn & hdd 2f out: wknd)....................8 8

P-M 2.30F: 1.30F 2.40F 1.90F (17.30F) OWNER Mrs Anne Coughlan BRED S. Coughlan 8 Rn
1m 36.9 SF: -/-/-/-/-/-/-/-

2724a-SAN SIRO (Milan, Italy) (R-H)
Sunday September 3rd (Good)

3590a PREMIO PESARO (2-Y.O) £7,880.00
6f 2-25 (2-30)

3231* **Greek Icon** *(72#) (JLDunlop)* 2-8-8 MTellini ....— 1
Vilaine *(Italy)* 2-8-10 MEsposito 8¾ 2
Enhorabuena (IRE) *(Italy)* 2-8-9 EBotti ....s.nk 3

Tote 17L: 15L 43L (136L) OWNER Mr A. M. Cati (ARUNDEL) BRED Kirtlington Stud 7 Rn
1m 10.5 (0.60 under 2y best) SF: -/-/-

3584a-BADEN-BADEN (Germany) (L-H)
Sunday September 3rd (Soft)

3591a GROSSER PREIS VON BADEN (Gp 1) (3-Y.O+) £133,745.00
(£53,498.00: £26,749.00: £12,346.00) **1m 4f** 3-25 (3-49)

2894a* **Germany (USA)** *(126) (BSchutz,Germany)* 4-9-6 LDettori (racd in 2nd: led 2f out: sn clr: easily)....................— 1
3046a² Lecroix (GER) *(117) (MHofer,Germany)* 3-8-9 ATylicki (5th st: r.o fnl 2f: no ch w wnr)....................5 2
3088⁵ Right Win (IRE) *(115) (RHannon)* 5-9-6 MRoberts (a.p: 3rd st: r.o one pce fnl 2f)....................3½ 3
3046a⁴ Kornado *(113) (ALowe,Germany)* 5-9-6 GBocskai (6th st: r.o one pce)....................1½ 4
2890a³ Beauchamp Hero *(112) (JLDunlop)* 5-9-6 JReid (hld up: r.o one pce fnl 2f)....................nk 5
3200a² Oxalagu (GER) *(104) (BSchutz,Germany)* 3-8-11 ow2 THellier (rr early; nvr plcd to chal)....................5 6
2729a* Lando (GER) *(92) (HJentzsch,Germany)* 6-9-6 PSchiergen (mid div: 4th & rdn 3f out: sn btn)....................10 7
3046a³ Concepcion (GER) *(HJentzsch,Germany)* 5-9-6 SEccles (led tl hdd & wknd 2f out).................... 8
2595³ Strategic Choice (USA) *(PFICole)* 4-9-6 TQuinn (rr tl hdwy ½-way: wknd over 2f out).................... 9
3161⁴ Royal Ballerina (IRE) *(MKauntze,Ireland)* 5-9-2 WJO'Connor (mid div: wknd 4f out: p.u. 1f out).................... P

Tote 47DM: 19DM 21DM 60DM (SF 260DM) OWNER Mr Jaber Abdullah BRED Curative Ltd 10 Rn
2m 37.72 SF: -/-/-/-/-/-/-/-/-/-

3560-DONCASTER (L-H)
Friday September 8th (Good to soft)
WEATHER: overcast WIND: mod half against

3592 HOLLYBANK ENGINEERING MAIDEN STKS (2-Y.O) (Class D) £5,760.00 (£1,710.00: £810.00: £360.00)
1m (straight) Stalls: Low GOING: 0.15 sec per fur (G) 1-30 (1-31)

Heron Island (IRE) *(80+) (PWChapple-Hyam)* 2-9-0 JReid(3) (leggy: unf: b.nr hind: trckd ldrs: shkn up to ld over 1f out: pushed out)....— 1
3280³ Skillington (USA) **(95)***(80)*(Fav)*(IABalding)* 2-9-0 KDarley(8) (lw: mde most tl over 1f out: kpt on)....hd 2
Lonely Leader (IRE) *(70+) (RHannon)* 2-9-0 PatEddery(6) (w'like: scope: lw: s.i.s: hdwy ½-wy: sn drvn along & chsng ldrs: eased whn btn ins fnl f)....5 3
Clerkenwell (USA) *(64+) (MRStoute)* 2-9-0 KFallon(2) (w'like: scope: bkwd: s.i.s: rn green: hdwy over 2f out: kpt on fnl f)....3 4
3340¹⁶ Spanking Roger *(59) (BWHills)* 2-9-0 MJKinane(4) (chsd ldrs tl grad wknd fnl 2f)....2½ 5
3340¹³ Humourless *(59+) (LMCumani)* 2-9-0 OUrbina(16) (bit bkwd: in tch: rn green ½-wy: nvr rchd ldrs)....hd 6
Sharaf (IRE) *(57) (JLDunlop)* 2-9-0 WCarson(17) (w'like: leggy: unf: racd wd: chsd ldrs: rdn & no imp fnl 2f)....1 7
Busy Flight *(56+) (BWHills)* 2-9-0 MHills(15) (gd sort: bkwd: s.s: bhd: stdy hdwy & nt clr run over 1f out: improve)....nk 8
3266³ Suparoy *(55) (TGMills)* 2-9-0 JFEgan(5) (w ldrs tl wknd over 2f out)....¾ 9
Whitley Grange Boy *(53) (JLEyre)* 2-9-0 RLappin(13) (leggy: scope: s.i.s: sn outpcd & drvn along: n.d)....¾ 10
3463⁴ Wire Act (USA) *(43) (MartynMeade)* 2-9-0 VSlattery(10) (chsd ldrs tl lost pl 3f out)....5 11
3465¹⁵ Mister Woodstick (IRE) *(41) (MAJarvis)* 2-9-0 PRobinson(9) (chsd ldrs tl wknd over 2f out) 1¼ 12
Go With The Wind *(34) (MBell)* 2-9-0 MFenton(7) (leggy: unf: a outpcd: drvn along ½-wy) ..3½ 13
Royal Expose (USA) *(28) (RHannon)* 2-9-0 JCarroll(12) (w'like: s.s: bhd: sme hdwy over 2f out: sn wknd)....3 14
2420⁶ Dancing Cormorant *(23) (JDBethell)* 2-9-0 TIves(11) (sn outpcd)....2½ 15
2346⁸ Just Another High (IRE) *(10) (DrJDScargill)* 2-8-9 DWright(14) (bhd fr ½-wy)....4 16
Mime Time (IRE) *(5) (WJarvis)* 2-9-0 MTebbutt(1) (w'like: s.s: a bhd)....5 17

100/30 Skillington (USA), **7/2** HERON ISLAND (IRE), **5/1** Lonely Leader (IRE), **6/1** Sharaf (IRE) (op 4/1), **15/2** Clerkenwell (USA), **12/1** Busy Flight, **14/1** Humourless (10/1-16/1), Spanking Roger, Go With The Wind, **20/1** Royal Expose (USA), Mime Time (IRE), **25/1** Suparoy, Mister Woodstick (IRE), **33/1** Dancing Cormorant, Wire Act (USA), **50/1** Whitley Grange Boy, Just Another High (IRE), CSF £17.15 TOTE £4.50: £1.50 £1.80 £1.90 (£6.30) Trio £17.10 OWNER Mr R. E. Sangster (MARLBOROUGH) BRED Barronstown Stud and Roncon Ltd 17 Rn
1m 42.38 (5.88) SF: 49/49/39/33/28/28/26/25/24/22/12/10/3/-/-/-/-

3593 JOY U.K. H'CAP (0-100) (3-Y.O+) (Class C) £5,120.00 (£1,520.00: £720.00: £320.00) **1m 4f** Stalls: Low GOING: 0.15 sec per fur (G) 2-00 (2-02)

2445⁴ **Bit on the Side (IRE)** **(70)***(83)*(Fav)*(WJMusson)* 6-8-0 (3) PMcCabe(11) (dwlt: hld up & bhd: hdwy 3f out: n.m.r & swtchd over 1f out: r.o strly to ld ins fnl f)....— 1
3237³ Bencher Q C (USA) **(85)***(98) (JHMGosden)* 3-8-9 MJKinane(1) (lw: chsd ldrs: led over 1f out tl ins fnl f: r.o u.p)....nk 2
3505² Once More for Luck (IRE) **(63)***(73) (MrsMReveley)* 4-7-10 TWilliams(3) (hld up: hdwy on ins over 3f out: hmpd wl over 1f out: styd on same pce)....2 3
3349⁵ Typhoon Eight (IRE) **(76)***(84) (BWHills)* 3-8-0 WCarson(9) (hld up: effrt 3f out: swtchd 2f out: kpt on same pce)....1¾ 4
3489⁴ Tethys (USA) **(85)***(85) (JLEyre)* 4-9-4v RLappin(8) (b.nr hind: chsd ldrs: one pce fnl 2f)....6 5
3091* My Learned Friend **(86)***(85) (AHide)* 4-9-5 JWilliams(5) (trckd ldrs: outpcd 3f out: edgd lft: n.d)nk 6
3580a⁵ Indonesian (IRE) **(82)***(81) (MBell)* 3-8-6v MFenton(7) (chsd ldrs: led over 3f out tl over 1f out: sn wknd)....nk 7
3162²¹ Lombardic (USA) **(91)***(81) (MrsJCecil)* 4-9-10 JReid(2) (led tl over 3f out: wknd over 1f out)....7 8
2599³ Swallows Dream (IRE) **(81)***(69) (JLDunlop)* 4-9-0 PatEddery(12) (lw: in tch: effrt over 2f out: sn wknd)....1¼ 9
3142⁵ Crystal Blade **(88)***(75) (IABalding)* 3-8-12 KDarley(10) (chsd ldrs tl over 2f out)....½ 10
Golden Hello **(79)***(50) (MHEasterby)* 4-8-12 MBirch(13) (bit bkwd: bhd: sme hdwy 7f out: wknd over 3f out: eased)....12 11
Roll a Dollar **(95)***(66) (DRCElsworth)* 9-10-0 SWhitworth(6) (bit bkwd: b: bhd: sme hdwy 7f out: drvn along over 3f out: n.d: eased)....s.h 12
3433¹⁰ Museum (IRE) **(74)***(38) (DNicholls)* 4-8-7 AlexGreaves(4) (a in rr: eased whn no ch)....5 13

3/1 BIT ON THE SIDE (IRE), **5/1** Bencher Q C (USA), **7/1** Swallows Dream (IRE), **15/2** My Learned Friend, **8/1** Typhoon Eight (IRE), **9/1** Once More for Luck (IRE), **10/1** Lombardic (USA), **11/1** Indonesian (IRE), **12/1** Museum (IRE), **14/1** Crystal Blade, **20/1** Tethys (USA), **25/1** Golden Hello, **33/1** Roll a Dollar, CSF £19.11 CT £118.72 TOTE £3.40: £1.50 £2.10 £2.30 (£8.00) Trio £34.30 OWNER Mr Mike Hawkett (NEWMARKET) BRED Stallion Development Group in Ireland 13 Rn

2m 36.5 (5.90) SF: 60/66/50/52/62/62/49/58/46/43/27/43/15

WEIGHT FOR AGE 3yo-9lb

3594 RJB MINING PLC CONDITIONS STKS (3, 4 & 5-Y.O) (Class B)

£7,275.00 (£2,685.00: £1,282.50: £517.50: £198.75: £71.25)
1m 2f 60y Stalls: Low GOING: 0.15 sec per fur (G) 2-35 (2-37)

1611⁷ **Riyadian (113)***(116+)*(Fav)*(PFICole)* 3-8-11 WCarson(6) (trckd ldrs: nt clr run 2f out: swtchd & led over 1f out: qcknd & sn clr: easily) .... — **1**
3030² Night City **(95)***(106) (LadyHerries)* 4-9-2 KDarley(3) (trckd ldrs: led over 2f out tl over 1f out: no ch w wnr) 5 **2**
2670⁶ Indian Light **(104)***(100) (JLDunlop)* 3-8-12b PatEddery(4) (trckd ldrs: chal over 2f out: sn rdn: one pce) 6 **3**
3374⁶ Heathyards Rock **(84)***(98) (RHollinshead)* 3-8-11 TIves(5) (bhd: effrt over 3f out: no imp) .... ½ **4**
1848¹² Rambrino **(100)***(91) (PWChapple-Hyam)* 3-8-12 MHills(1) (led tl over 2f out: sn wknd) 5 **5**
Petosiva (IRE) *(76) (JLDunlop)* 3-8-9 JReid(2) (hld up: effrt over 3f out: sn wknd) 8 **6**

11/8 RIYADIAN (4/5-6/4), **11/4** Indian Light, **11/2** Night City (4/1-6/1), **7/1** Rambrino (5/1-8/1), **14/1** Petosiva (IRE), **16/1** Heathyards Rock, CSF £8.37 TOTE £1.90: £1.40 £1.90 (£3.40) OWNER Prince Fahd Salman (WHATCOMBE) BRED Newgate Stud Co. 6 Rn

2m 12.57 (5.57) SF: 63/60/47/45/38/23

WEIGHT FOR AGE 3yo-7lb

3595 O & K TROY STKS (Listed) (3-Y.O) (Class A) £15,076.00 (£4,816.00: £2,308.00)

1m 4f Stalls: High GOING: 0.15 sec per fur (G) 3-05 (3-07)

3144² **Singspiel (IRE) (121)***(108)*(Fav)*(MRStoute)* 3-8-11 MJKinane(2) (lw: trckd ldr: chal over 3f out: led over 2f out: shkn up over 1f out: styd on strly & drvn clr ins fnl f) .... — **1**
3183* Jumairah Sun (IRE) **(84)***(100) (LMCumani)* 3-8-6 KDarley(1) (lw: hld up: effrt over 2f out: edgd lft & chal over 1f out: nt qckn) 2½ **2**
2415* Tenorio **(104)***(99) (DRLoder)* 3-8-11 PatEddery(3) (lw: led tl over 2f out: wkng whn hmpd over 1f out) 4 **3**

30/100 SINGSPIEL (IRE), **7/2** Tenorio, **10/1** Jumairah Sun (IRE), CSF £2.98 **TOTE** £1.30 (£1.90) OWNER Sheikh Mohammed (NEWMARKET) BRED Sheikh Mohammed bin Rashid al Maktoum 3 Rn

2m 45.95 (15.35) SF: 7/-/-

3596 LAURENT-PERRIER CHAMPAGNE STKS (Gp 2) (2-Y.O C & G) (Class A)

£45,621.75 (£14,560.50: £6,967.75)
7f Stalls: High GOING: 0.15 sec per fur (G) 3-35 (3-35)

3216* **Alhaarth (IRE)** *(104)*(Fav)*(MajorWRHern)* 2-9-0 WCarson(1) (lw: mde all: edgd lft 1f out: drvn out) .... — **1**
2347⁴ Rio Duvida **(100)***(99) (DRLoder)* 2-8-10 PatEddery(2) (trckd wnr: effrt 2f out: ev ch fnl f: nt qckn) .... ½ **2**
3163³ Take A Left **(100)***(87) (MrsJRRamsden)* 2-8-10 KFallon(3) (lw: hld up: effrt over 2f out: nvr able to chal) 5 **3**

2/5 ALHAARTH (IRE) (1/4-4/9), **7/2** Take A Left, **11/2** Rio Duvida, CSF £2.63 TOTE £1.30 (£2.00) OWNER Mr Hamdan Al Maktoum (LAMBOURN) BRED Shadwell Estate Company Limited 3 Rn

1m 31.57 (8.17) SF: 14/9/-

3597 H. LEVERTON H'CAP (0-80) (3-Y.O+) (Class D) £3,840.00 (£1,140.00: £540.00: £240.00)

5f Stalls: High GOING: 0.15 sec per fur (G) 4-10 (4-12)

3219⁶ **General Sir Peter (IRE) (72)***(80) (PFICole)* 3-9-5 CRutter(18) (hdwy ½-wy: styd on wl u.p fnl f: led post) .... — **1**
3221⁵ Lady Sheriff **(75)***(83) (MWEasterby)* 4-9-3b(7) RuthCoulter(8) (led: clr over 1f out: jst ct) .... s.h **2**
3313⁵ Just Bob **(67)***(71) (SEKettlewell)* 6-8-13 (3) JStack(22) (lw: b.hind: dwlt: hdwy 2f out: styd on u.p fnl f) 1¼ **3**
3418⁴ Captain Carat **(65)***(65)*(Fav)*(MrsJRRamsden)* 4-9-0 KFallon(11) (bmpd s: bhd: nt clr run & hmpd over 1f out: styd on strly towards fin) 1¼ **4**

2764[21] Broadstairs Beauty (IRE) **(76)***(73) (SRBowring)* 5-9-6b(5) CTeague(9) (b: b.hind: lw: chsd ldrs: rdn & outpcd ½-wy: kpt on fnl f) ....¾ **5**
Polly Particular **(79)***(76) (TDBarron)* 3-9-12 KDarley(16) (swtg: hld up: effrt ½-wy: edgd lft over 1f out: kpt on wl towards fin) ....s.h **6**
3376[9] Shadow Jury **(72)***(65) (DWChapman)* 5-9-7b LCharnock(20) (a chsng ldrs: one pce fnl 2f)....1½ **7**
2461[11] Bold Street (IRE) **(71)***(63) (ABailey)* 5-9-3b(3) DWright(10) (b: bmpd s: hdwy ½-wy: hmpd over 1f out: kpt on towards fin) ....hd **8**
2609[6] Bollin Harry **(70)***(62) (MHEasterby)* 3-9-3 MBirch(19) (effrt ½-wy: kpt on wl fnl f: n.d) ....hd **9**
Kung Frode **(65)***(53) (BAMcMahon)* 3-8-12 JCarroll(7) (hdwy ½-wy: kpt on fnl f: nvr nr to chal) 1¼ **10**
3166[3] Nite-Owl Dancer **(70)***(57) (JAHarris)* 3-9-3 WCarson(14) (sn drvn along & outpcd: hmpd over 1f out: n.d) ....nk **11**
3418[8] Just Dissident (IRE) **(68)***(52) (RMWhitaker)* 3-9-1 DaleGibson(1) (lw: chsd ldrs 3f: sn rdn & wknd) 1 **12**
3418[7] Here Comes a Star **(73)***(56) (JMCarr)* 7-9-8 ACulhane(13) (effrt ½-wy: nvr nr ldrs) ....nk **13**
3407[6] Ann's Pearl (IRE) **(79)***(57) (JWHills)* 4-9-9 (5) MHenry(17) (in tch over 3f: sn wknd)....1½ **14**
3279[9] Beau Venture (USA) **(78)***(55) (FHLee)* 7-9-13 RLappin(5) (chsd ldrs: rdn ½-wy: wknd wl over 1f out) ....nk **15**
3466[9] Thick as Thieves **(77)***(49) (RonaldThompson)* 3-9-10 SDWilliams(2) (chsd ldrs tl lost pl 2f out) 1½ **16**
3522[8] Sound the Trumpet (IRE) **(74)***(41) (AStreeter)* 3-9-0v(7) DSweeney(3) (s.i.s: a outpcd: bhd fr ½-wy) 1¾ **17**

3/1 Captain Carat, **4/1** Broadstairs Beauty (IRE) (op 6/1), **13/2** Nite-Owl Dancer, **11/1** Bollin Harry, GENERAL SIR PETER (IRE), **14/1** Bold Street (IRE), Lady Sheriff, **16/1** Just Bob, Beau Venture (USA), Ann's Pearl (IRE), **20/1** Shadow Jury, Kung Frode, Just Dissident (IRE), Here Comes a Star, Polly Particular, **33/1** Thick as Thieves, Sound the Trumpet (IRE), CSF £152.42 CT £2,257.29 TOTE £13.20: £3.20 £4.90 £2.80 £1.20 (£290.90) Trio £932.80 OWNER Mr Yahya Nasib (WHATCOMBE) BRED Hamilton Bloodstock (UK) Ltd 17 Rn
62.43 secs (4.03) SF: 47/52/40/34/42/43/34/32/29/20/24/19/25/26/24/16/8
WEIGHT FOR AGE 3yo-2lb

3598

SUN PRINCESS CONDITIONS STKS (3-Y.O) (Class C) £4,560.00 (£1,680.00: £800.00: £320.00: £120.00: £40.00)
1m (round) Stalls: High GOING: 0.15 sec per fur (G) 4-40 (4-41)

3377* **Clan Ben (IRE)** *(101)*(Fav)*(HRACecil)* 3-9-1 PatEddery(8) (lw: sn trckng ldr: led over 1f out: drvn along & r.o strly) ....— **1**
1586[7] Royal Philosopher **(100)***(97) (KMcAuliffe)* 3-9-3 KDarley(5) (led tl over 1f out: no ch w wnr) 3 **2**
3085[7] Lipizzaner (IRE) **(94)***(101) (BWHills)* 3-9-7 MJKinane(6) (lw: hld up: effrt over 2f out: styd on u.p fnl f) ....s.h **3**
2469* Sveltana *(87) (JRFanshawe)* 3-8-7 (3) NVarley(3) (s.i.s: effrt & swtchd outside over 1f out: styd on ins fnl f) 1¼ **4**
2460* Code of Law (USA) *(89) (PWChapple-Hyam)* 3-9-1 JReid(4) (plld hrd: trckd ldrs: effrt over 2f out: one pce) 1½ **5**
3282* Starry Eyed *(83) (JHMGosden)* 3-8-10 JCarroll(9) (chsd ldrs: effrt over 2f out: edgd lft & outpcd over 1f out) ....½ **6**
2778[U] Mountgate **(71)***(76) (MPBielby)* 3-9-3 JFEgan(2) (plld hrd: hld up & bhd: effrt 3f out: sn wl outpcd) 7 **7**
Blue Ocean (USA) *(67) (MRStoute)* 3-9-1 WCarson(7) (hld up: effrt 3f out: sn wknd: eased)3½ **8**

2/1 CLAN BEN (IRE), **7/2** Starry Eyed (5/2-4/1), **9/2** Royal Philosopher, **6/1** Code of Law (USA), Lipizzaner (IRE), **8/1** Blue Ocean (USA) (6/1-9/1), **10/1** Sveltana, **33/1** Mountgate, CSF £12.12 TOTE £3.00: £1.20 £1.70 £2.10 (£8.20) Trio £22.00 OWNER Angus Dundee Ltd (NEWMARKET) BRED T. Hillman 8 Rn 1m 43.92 (7.62) SF: 33/29/33/19/21/15/8/-
T/Jkpt: £1,372.00 (20.34 Tckts). T/Plpt: £5.60 (3,861.91 Tckts). T/Qdpt: £4.60 (34.4 Tckts). WG

3384-GOODWOOD (R-H)
Friday September 8th (Good)

WEATHER: overcast WIND: mod half against

3599

RAUGHMERE CONDITIONS STKS (3-Y.O) (Class C) £5,632.00 (£2,032.00: £976.00: £400.00: £160.00)
7f Stalls: High GOING minus 0.01 sec per fur (G) 2-10 (2-10)

3334* **Inzar (USA) (107)***(119)*(Fav)*(PFICole)* 3-9-8 TQuinn(1) (mde all: qcknd over 1f out: comf) ...— **1**
3085[3] Bin Rosie **(103)***(109) (DRLoder)* 3-9-0b WRSwinburn(4) (lw: 5th st: rdn 2f out: r.o ins fnl f)......¾ **2**

1796* Hawaash (IRE) *(108) (JRFanshawe)* 3-9-0 WRyan(2) (bit bkwd: 4th st: chsd wnr over 1f out tl ins fnl f: r.o)........¾ 3
Il Trastevere (FR) *(94) (JLDunlop)* 3-9-2 MRimmer(3) (cmpt: 3rd st: rdn over 1f out: sn wknd)4 4
667⁷ Bin Nashwan (USA) **(112)***(96) (CEBrittain)* 3-8-12 BDoyle(5) (2nd st: rdn over 1f out: wknd fnl f)........s.h 5

15/8 INZAR (USA), **9/4** Bin Rosie, Bin Nashwan (USA) (7/4-11/4), **7/1** Hawaash (IRE), **33/1** Il Trastevere (FR), CSF £6.23 TOTE £2.70: £1.50 £1.10 (£3.70) OWNER Prince Fahd Salman (WHATCOMBE) BRED Newgate Stud Farm Inc in USA 5 Rn 1m 30.42 (6.02) SF: 34/24/23/9/11

3600 BELLWAY HOMES STARDOM STKS (Listed) (2-Y.O) (Class A)

£10,770.00 (£3,210.00: £1,530.00: £690.00)
1m Stalls: High GOING minus 0.01 sec per fur (G) 2-40 (2-40)

3215* **Bonarelli (IRE) (95)***(93)*(Fav)*(MRStoute)* 2-8-11 WRSwinburn(1) (chsd ldr: hrd rdn over 1f out: led wl ins fnl f: r.o wl)........— 1
3215² Mushahid (USA) **(100)***(93)*(Fav)*(JLDunlop)* 2-8-11 RHills(3) (led: rdn over 2f out: hdd wl ins fnl f: r.o wl)........hd 2
3398* Ski Academy (IRE) *(89) (PWChapple-Hyam)* 2-8-11 BThomson(4) (lw: 5th st: rdn over 1f out: r.o ins fnl f)........1¾ 3
3366* Longing (USA) *(79) (DRLoder)* 2-8-6 GCarter(2) (3rd st: rdn over 2f out: unable qckn) 2½ 4
3301² Modern Day (USA) **(92)***(77) (HRACecil)* 2-8-11 WRyan(5) (lw: 4th st: hrd rdn over 2f out: wknd over 1f out)........3½ 5

9/4 BONARELLI (IRE), Mushahid (USA), **9/2** Ski Academy (IRE), **5/1** Longing (USA), **13/2** Modern Day (USA), CSF £7.20 TOTE £2.40: £1.70 £1.40 (£2.50) OWNER Sheikh Mohammed (NEWMARKET) BRED Robert Griffin 5 Rn 1m 41.83 (4.23) SF: 51/51/47/37/35

3601 SCHRODER INVESTMENT MANAGEMENT H'CAP (0-100) (3-Y.O+) (Class C) £12,135.00 (£3,630.00: £1,740.00: £795.00)

1m 1f Stalls: High GOING minus 0.01 sec per fur (G) 3-10 (3-11)

3388² **Conspicuous (IRE) (69)***(81) (LGCottrell)* 5-8-2 JQuinn(8) (lw: hdwy 2f out: led ins fnl f: rdn out)........— 1
2703⁸ Embankment (IRE) **(83)***(92) (RHannon)* 5-8-11 (5) DaneO'Neill(2) (3rd st: hrd rdn 2f out: ev ch ins fnl f: unable qckn)........1½ 2
3556⁸ Second Chance (IRE) **(81)***(87) (PMitchell)* 5-8-11 (3) SSanders(1) (lw: 2nd st: led 2f out tl ins fnl f: one pce)........2 3
3447⁶ Reverand Thickness **(74)***(79) (SCWilliams)* 4-8-7 TQuinn(4) (7th st: hrd rdn over 1f out: r.o)........½ 4
2577⁷ Aeroking (USA) **(78)***(81) (GHarwood)* 4-8-11 MPerrett(5) (led 7f: wknd fnl f) 1¼ 5
1851²¹ Wilcuma **(81)***(84)*(Fav)*(PJMakin)* 4-9-0 JWeaver(14) (rdn & hdwy over 2f out: r.o one pce) ...hd 6
2488⁷ Misty Silks **(70)***(72) (MJRyan)* 5-8-3 DBiggs(9) (6th st: rdn over 2f out: wknd fnl f) ....hd 7
*2634*³ Segala (IRE) **(75)***(75) (SirMarkPrescott)* 4-8-8 GDuffield(6) (rdn & hdwy over 2f out: r.o one pce)........1½ 8
3388* Fieldridge **(78)***(75) (MPMuggeridge)* 6-8-11 BThomson(10) (4th st: ev ch over 1f out: eased whn btn ins fnl f)........1½ 9
2577* Special Dawn (IRE) **(91)***(88) (JLDunlop)* 5-9-10 PaulEddery(3) (lw: hdwy 1f out: eased whn btn ins fnl f)........hd 10
3362⁵ Pay Homage **(83)***(80) (IABalding)* 7-8-11 (5) DGriffiths(12) (5th st: wknd over 1f out)........hd 11
3440³ Adolescence (IRE) **(83)***(73) (KMcAuliffe)* 5-9-2 RHughes(7) (bhd fnl 6f) 3½ 12
3222¹⁴ Secret Aly (CAN) **(82)***(55) (CEBrittain)* 5-9-1 MRoberts(13) (lw: a bhd)........10 13
1507* Manabar **(83)***(55) (DMorley)* 3-8-10 RHills(11) (lw: a bhd)........½ 14

5/1 Wilcuma, **11/2** Segala (IRE), **7/1** CONSPICUOUS (IRE), **9/1** Embankment (IRE), Special Dawn (IRE), **10/1** Manabar (7/1-14/1), Adolescence (IRE), **12/1** Reverand Thickness, Misty Silks, **14/1** Fieldridge (10/1-16/1), Secret Aly (CAN), **20./1** Aeroking (USA), **25/1** Second Chance (IRE), **33/1** Pay Homage, CSF £63.73 CT £1,364.05 TOTE £9.00: £2.70 £2.80 £7.50 (£34.60) Trio £170.50 OWNER Mrs Jenny Hopkins (CULLOMPTON) BRED Gerry Canavan 14 Rn
1m 56.6 (5.90) SF: 33/44/39/31/33/36/24/27/27/40/32/25/7/1
WEIGHT FOR AGE 3yo-6lb

3602 COCKING RATED STKS H'CAP (0-105) (3-Y.O+) (Class B)

£10,498.80 (£3,889.20: £1,869.60: £768.00: £309.00: £125.40)
7f Stalls: High GOING minus 0.01 sec per fur (G) 3-40 (3-41)

3334² **Indian Fly (99)***(108)*(Fav)*(RHannon)* 4-8-10 (5) DaneO'Neill(9) (5th st: led 2f out: edgd rt ins fnl f: rdn out)........— 1

2948[12] Cadeaux Tryst **(102)***(111) (EALDunlop)* 3-9-0 WRSwinburn(7) (lw: rdn & hdwy wl over 1f out: r.o ins fnl f)....hd 2
3261* Muktabas (IRE) **(94)***(103) (JHMGosden)* 3-8-6 RHills(3) (lw: hdwy 2f out: hrd rdn over 1f out: r.o)....hd 3
3373[3] Emerging Market **(91)***(98) (JLDunlop)* 3-8-3 MRoberts(8) (lw: 6th st: nt clr run & lost pl over 2f out: swtchd lft over 1f out: r.o)....¾ 4
3334[3] Delta One (IRE) **(97)***(98) (IABalding)* 4-8-13 WRyan(2) (lw: hdwy over 2f out: hrd rdn over 1f out: unable qckn)....2½ 5
2470[5] Karayb (IRE) **(94)***(92) (DMorley)* 3-8-6 BThomson(1) (hdwy over 2f out: wknd fnl f)....1½ 6
2409[4] Carranita (IRE) **(105)***(102) (BPalling)* 5-9-7 TSprake(11) (3rd st: wknd over 1f out)....nk 7
2006[5] Dee-Lady **(91)***(88) (WGMTurner)* 3-8-3 GDuffield(4) (lw: hdwy over 2f out: wknd over 1f out)....s.h 8
3446[9] Green Perfume (USA) **(102)***(96) (PFICole)* 3-9-0 TQuinn(5) (lw: 2nd st: led over 2f out: sn hdd: wknd 1f out)....1¼ 9
3316[4] Averti (IRE) **(97)***(84) (WRMuir)* 4-8-13 DHolland(10) (4th st: wknd 2f out)....3 10
3358[4] Croft Valley **(95)***(59) (RAkehurst)* 8-8-8 (3) SSanders(6) (lw: led over 4f)....10 11
LONG HANDICAP Emerging Market 8-1 Dee-Lady 8-1

11/4 INDIAN FLY (op 9/2), **11/2** Muktabas (IRE) (op 7/2), **13/2** Croft Valley, **7/1** Cadeaux Tryst, **15/2** Carranita (IRE), **10/1** Delta One (IRE) (8/1-12/1), **11/1** Emerging Market (8/1-12/1), **12/1** Green Perfume (USA), **20/1** Averti (IRE), **25/1** Dee-Lady, Karayb (IRE), CSF £20.72 CT £87.83 TOTE £3.30: £1.20 £2.90 £2.00 (£11.90) Trio £18.10 OWNER Mrs Chris Harrington (MARLBOROUGH) BRED Mrs Chris Harrington 11 Rn 1m 28.6 (4.20) SF: 48/47/39/34/38/28/42/24/32/24/-
WEIGHT FOR AGE 3yo-4lb

3603 VICRYL* RAPIDE CONDITIONS STKS (3-Y.O+) (Class C) £7,613.10 (£2,745.60: £1,317.80: £539.00: £214.50)
1m 4f Stalls: Centre GOING minus 0.01 sec per fur (G) 4-15 (4-15)

1122a[8] **Posidonas (105)***(111) (PFICole)* 3-8-13 TQuinn(5) (3rd st: nt clr run on ins over 3f out tl over 1f out: rdn & led nr fin)....— 1
3380[2] Bal Harbour **(108)***(103) (HRACecil)* 4-9-0 WRyan(2) (lw: led: rdn over 2f out: hdd nr fin)....nk 2
3438* Fire on Ice (IRE) *(101)*(Fav)*(MRStoute)* 3-8-7 DHolland(4) (lw: 5th st: rdn over 2f out: one pce)....2½ 3
3046a[7] Ionio (USA) **(109)***(103) (CEBrittain)* 4-9-4 MRoberts(1) (b: lw: 2nd st: rdn over 2f out: one pce)....s.h 4
1611[15] Maralinga (IRE) **(98)***(100) (LadyHerries)* 3-8-11 PaulEddery(3) (4th st: rdn over 2f out: wknd over 1f out)....4 5

11/4 Fire on Ice (IRE), **3/1** Ionio (USA), **100/30** Bal Harbour (9/4-7/2), **7/2** POSIDONAS, **9/1** Maralinga (IRE) (6/1-10/1), CSF £13.44 TOTE £5.50: £2.60 £1.50 (£9.60) OWNER Mr Athos Christodoulou (WHATCOMBE) BRED A. Christodoulou 5 Rn 2m 38.75 (6.75) SF: 52/53/42/53/41
WEIGHT FOR AGE 3yo-9lb

3604 E.B.F. FOXHALL MAIDEN STKS (2-Y.O) (Class D) £5,166.00 (£1,548.00: £744.00: £342.00) 6f Stalls: Centre GOING minus 0.01 sec per fur (G) 4-50 (4-50)

1063[2] **Welville** *(84) (PJMakin)* 2-9-0 JWeaver(6) (mde all: rdn out)....— 1
2767[3] Brandon Magic *(80) (IABalding)* 2-9-0 WRyan(11) (lw: hld up: rdn over 2f out: r.o one pce)....1½ 2
2660[4] Forest Robin *(79) (RFJohnsonHoughton)* 2-9-0 BThomson(10) (lw: a.p: rdn 2f out: one pce)....nk 3
3371[6] Keiko *(68) (JHMGosden)* 2-8-9 GHind(16) (hld up: rdn over 2f out: one pce)....2½ 4
Tarneem (USA) *(61+)*(Fav)*(MRStoute)* 2-8-9 WRSwinburn(15) (unf: hld up: rdn over 2f out: eased whn btn ins fnl f)....2½ 5
3404[8] Rawi **(65)***(65) (CJBenstead)* 2-9-0 MWigham(13) (lw: nvr nr to chal)....nk 6
Mac Oates *(62) (DWPArbuthnot)* 2-9-0 BDoyle(7) (unf: s.s: hld up: rdn over 2f out: one pce) .1 7
3180[4] Unsold *(60) (JRFanshawe)* 2-9-0 TQuinn(4) (hld up: hrd rdn over 2f out: wknd over 1f out)....1 8
2615[7] Film Buff *(49) (BWHills)* 2-8-9 DHolland(8) (nvr nrr)....2 9
Roushan *(54) (KMcAuliffe)* 2-9-0 JTate(12) (leggy: unf: hld up: rdn over 2f out: one pce)....s.h 10
3260[10] Impeccable *(47) (JLDunlop)* 2-8-9 RHughes(9) (lw: bhd fnl 2f)....1 11
1592[6] Get Tough *(48) (SDow)* 2-8-7 (7) ADaly(5) (bhd fnl 4f)....1½ 12
Dazzling Star *(40) (RHannon)* 2-8-4 (5) DaneO'Neill(1) (neat: bit bkwd: s.s: hdwy over 3f out: wknd over 2f out)....1 13
Night Harmony (IRE) *(29) (RHannon)* 2-9-0 MRoberts(3) (b: str: a bhd)....6 14
3337[7] Burj *(26) (NAGraham)* 2-9-0 RHills(2) (w ldr 4f)....1¼ 15

13/8 Tarneem (USA), **11/2** WELVILLE (5/1-9/1), **6/1** Brandon Magic (op 7/2), **9/1** Keiko (5/1-10/1), Unsold (5/1-10/1), **10/1** Roushan (op 5/1), **14/1** Forest Robin (10/1-25/1), **20/1** Film Buff, Night Harmony (IRE), **33/1** Dazzling Star, Mac Oates, Burj, **50/1** Rawi, Impeccable, **66/1** Get Tough, CSF £37.37 TOTE £6.70: £1.70 £1.90 £4.50 (£15.00) Trio £62.70 OWNER Mr T. G. Warner (MARLBOROUGH) BRED Red House Stud 15 Rn 1m 14.84 (4.64) SF: 32/28/27/16/9/13/10/8/-/2/-/-/-/-/-

3605

HIGH WOOD H'CAP (0-70) (3-Y.O+) (Class E) £4,435.00 (£1,330.00: £640.00: £295.00) **1m** Stalls: High GOING minus 0.01 sec per fur (G) 5-20 (5-22)

*3075*12 **Prenonamoss (49)**(63) *(DWPArbuthnot)* 7-8-8 DHolland(21) (b.hind: hdwy over 1f out: led ins fnl f: r.o wl)........— 1
3269 2 Another Fiddle (IRE) **(62)**(73) *(RAkehurst)* 5-9-4 (3) SSanders(9) (6th st: ev ch 1f out: unable qckn)........1½ 2
3497 2 Sharpical **(69)**(80)(Fav)*(BJMeehan)* 3-9-9 RHughes(12) (b.off fore: 7th st: swtchd rt over 2f out: ev ch ins fnl f: one pce)........s.h 3
3440 8 Thatchmaster (IRE) **(46)**(56) *(CAHorgan)* 4-8-5 WNewnes(4) (lw: led tl ins fnl f: one pce)......nk 4
3125 10 Super High **(57)**(64) *(PHowling)* 3-8-11 PaulEddery(10) (4th st: hrd rdn over 2f out: one pce)1½ 5
3106 13 Roi de la Mer (IRE) **(65)**(72) *(JAkehurst)* 4-9-10 GCarter(16) (hdwy 2f out: nt clr run over 1f out: one pce)........nk 6
2317 16 Ironic (IRE) **(55)**(59) *(RHannon)* 3-8-4 (5) DaneO'Neill(7) (lw: nvr nr to chal)........1½ 7
3383 4 Pat's Splendour **(46)**(50) *(HJCollingridge)* 4-8-5 JQuinn(17) (nvr nrr)........hd 8
2342 8 Rising Spray **(54)**(57) *(CAHorgan)* 4-8-6 (7) AmandaSanders(19) (hdwy 3f out: wknd over 1f out)........nk 9
3501 4 Kestrel Forboxes (IRE) **(63)**(65) *(CMcCready,Jersey)* 7-9-8 RMcGhin(8) (hdwy over 2f out: wknd over 1f out)........nk 10
3497 13 Mo's Star **(61)**(59) *(SDow)* 3-8-8 (7) ADaly(5) (lw: a mid div)........2 11
2979 4 Vanborough Lad **(55)**(53) *(MJBolton)* 6-9-0 BThomson(1) (3rd st: wknd over 1f out)........nk 12
*2140*5 Audrey Grace **(47)**(44) *(BJMeehan)* 4-8-6v RHills(20) (hdwy over 2f out: wandered over 1f out: eased whn btn fnl f)........½ 13
1732 5 Arcatura **(67)**(63) *(CJames)* 3-9-7 AMcGlone(3) (a mid div)........nk 14
3403 2 Gentle Irony **(62)**(54) *(BJMeehan)* 3-9-2b MRimmer(15) (bhd fnl 2f)........2 15
2657 12 White Heat **(56)**(42) *(MJHeaton-Ellis)* 3-8-10v MRoberts(6) (2nd st: wknd over 2f out)........3 16
3439 4 Duello **(55)**(40) *(MBlanshard)* 4-9-0 WRyan(18) (hdwy & nt clr run over 2f out: eased fnl 2f)........¾ 17
3359 20 Jaazim **(62)**(46) *(MMadgwick)* 5-9-7 StephenDavies(22) (lw: bhd fnl 3f)........hd 18
3108 8 Daswaki (CAN) **(52)**(26) *(GLMoore)* 7-8-11 RPerham(14) (b: bhd fnl 5f)........5 19
3182 2 Cavil **(67)**(38) *(CEBrittain)* 3-9-7 BDoyle(11) (bhd fnl 3f)........1½ 20
2317 5 Crimson Shower **(57)** *(JRFanshawe)* 3-8-11 TQuinn(13) (5th st: wknd over 2f out)........15 21

11/2 Sharpical, **13/2** Crimson Shower, **8/1** Duello, **9/1** Super High (8/1-12/1), Another Fiddle (IRE), **12/1** Cavil, **14/1** PRENONAMOSS, Gentle Irony, Vanborough Lad, **16/1** Pat's Splendour, Kestrel Forboxes (IRE), **20/1** Thatchmaster (IRE), White Heat, Arcatura, Daswaki (CAN), Rising Spray, **25/1** Ironic (IRE), Audrey Grace, **33/1** Jaazim, Roi de la Mer (IRE), Mo's Star, CSF £134.07 CT £726.85 TOTE £12.10: £3.20 £2.30 £2.50 £10.00 (£73.50) Trio £100.50 OWNER Mrs W. A. Oram (COMPTON) BRED Phil Bull 21 Rn
1m 42.69 (5.09) SF: 45/55/57/38/41/54/36/32/39/47/36/35/26/40/31/19/22/28/8/15/-
WEIGHT FOR AGE 3yo-5lb

T/Plpt: £49.20 (429.4 Tckts). T/Qdpt: £78.10 (1.4 Tckts). AK

3592-DONCASTER (L-H)
Saturday September 9th (Good to soft)

WEATHER: sunny periods WIND: slt half against

3606

KEEPMOAT HOLDINGS CONDITIONS STKS (2-Y.O) (Class C) £5,362.50 (£1,987.50: £956.25: £393.75) **6f** Stalls: High GOING: 0.17 sec per fur (G) 2-00 (2-03)

3465 5 **King of The East (IRE)** (84) *(MRStoute)* 2-8-11 WRSwinburn(6) (lw: hld up: hdwy 2f out: led 1f out: edgd rt: r.o)........— 1
3185 6 Sabot (83) *(BWHills)* 2-8-11 DHolland(7) (trckd ldrs: hdwy 2f out: ev ch ins fnl f: r.o)........½ 2
2347 8 First Fiddler **(100)**(76) *(WJarvis)* 2-9-1 BThomson(4) (cl up: disp ld 2f out to 1f out: no ex)........4 3
2740 5 Shaniko (IRE) **(100)**(73) *(PWChapple-Hyam)* 2-9-1 JReid(5) (led 4f: rdn & r.o one pce)........1 4
3371 8 Sharp Pearl (69) *(RCharlton)* 2-8-11 WRyan(1) (hld up: hdwy ½-wy: disp ld 2f out to 1f out: wknd)........s.h 5
903* La Volta (62) *(JGFitzGerald)* 2-8-6 KFallon(8) (lw: hld up: effrt ½-wy: sn outpcd: sytd on fnl f)........1 6

3068[2] Yarob (IRE) *(57)(Fav)(HThomsonJones)* 2-9-1 JFEgan(3) (swtg: cl up tl rdn & wknd 2f out) ...5 **7**
1871[7] Kala Sunrise **(85)***(51) (CSmith)* 2-8-13 WWoods(2) (spd 4f) 1¾ **8**

2/1 Yarob (IRE), **7/2** Shaniko (IRE) (5/2-4/1), **9/2** KING OF THE EAST (IRE), **6/1** First Fiddler, **15/2** La Volta, **10/1** Sharp Pearl, **11/1** Sabot (8/1-12/1), **25/1** Kala Sunrise, CSF £47.13 TOTE £5.60: £1.50 £3.60 £2.00 (£44.40) OWNER Dr K. Shimizu (NEWMARKET) BRED Barronstown Stud And Ron Con Ltd 8 Rn 1m 15.3 (4.30) SF: 49/48/41/38/34/27/22/16

3607

ROTHMANS ROYALS NORTH SOUTH CHALLENGE SERIES SEMI-FINAL H'CAP (0-100) (3-Y.O+) (Class C) £19,040.00 (£5,720.00: £2,760.00: £1,280.00)
1m (round) Stalls: High GOING: 0.17 sec per fur (G) 2-30 (2-31)

3488[3] **Band on the Run (92)***(104) (BAMcMahon)* 8-9-13 LDettori(4) (a in tch: hdwy 2f out: r.o to ld cl home) .... — **1**
3368* Scaraben **(68)***(79) (SEKettlewell)* 7-8-0 (3) JStack(12) (a.p: led over 1f out: r.o: jst ct) ....½ **2**
3457[12] Karinska **(67)***(77) (MCChapman)* 5-7-9 (7) CMunday(16) (dwlt: hdwy ½-wy: swtchd over 1f out: r.o wl towards fin) ....½ **3**
3419[2] Celestial Choir **(85)***(94) (JLEyre)* 5-9-6 TWilliams(2) (a in tch: hdwy u.p 2f out: n.m.r: kpt on wl towards fin) ....½ **4**
3447[5] Master Beveled **(75)***(83)(Fav)(PDEvans)* 5-8-10 RHughes(17) (a.p: led over 2f out tl over 1f out: kpt on) ....½ **5**
3457[8] Pine Ridge Lad (IRE) **(60)***(62) (JLEyre)* 5-7-4 (5)ow2 MBaird(19) (led tl hdd over 2f out: one pce) 2 **6**
3419[6] Pride of Pendle **(78)***(82) (DNicholls)* 6-8-13 AlexGreaves(11) (hdwy ½-wy: styd on fnl 2f: nvr able to chal) ....hd **7**
3222[13] Cee-Jay-Ay **(60)***(61) (JBerry)* 8-7-4 (5) PFessey(10) (s.s: nrst fin) 1½ **8**
3368[12] Shinerolla **(75)***(69) (MrsJRRamsden)* 3-8-5 KFallon(6) (s.s: hdwy ½-wy: styd on: nvr rchd ldrs) 3½ **9**
3506* Ninia (USA) **(73)***(63) (MJohnston)* 3-8-3 JWeaver(15) (cl up tl grad wknd fnl 3f) 2 **10**
2222[9] Superoo **(68)***(53) (MrsPSly)* 9-8-3 ACulhane(8) (prom to ½-wy) 2½ **11**
3368[5] Clifton Fox **(82)***(67) (JAGlover)* 3-8-12 PatEddery(1) (chsd ldrs tl outpcd over 3f out) ....hd **12**
3368[9] Marowins **(60)***(38) (EJAlston)* 6-7-6 (3)ow2 DWright(13) (dwlt: hdwy on outside ½-wy: nvr able to chal) 2½ **13**
3393* Break the Rules **(77)***(47) (MrsMReveley)* 3-8-7 KDarley(14) (effrt on outside ½-wy: no imp) 5 **14**
3506[4] Phase One (IRE) **(63)***(27) (JLEyre)* 5-7-7 (5)ow5 MHenry(18) (chsd ldrs 5f) ....nk **15**
2117[6] Sandmoor Chambray **(72)***(40) (MHEasterby)* 4-8-7 MBirch(3) (chsd ldrs 5f: sn lost pl) ....½ **16**
3447[9] Chinour (IRE) **(69)***(37) (EJAlston)* 7-7-13 (5) LNewton(5) (s.s: hdwy ½-wy: sn wknd) ....hd **17**
3368[4] Kemo Sabo **(80)***(42) (MrsJRRamsden)* 3-8-10 JFEgan(7) (chsd ldrs 5f: wknd) 3 **18**
LONG HANDICAP Phase One (IRE) 7-3 Pine Ridge Lad (IRE) 7-2 Marowins 6-8

4/1 Master Beveled (op 6/1), **6/1** Scaraben, **7/1** Celestial Choir, **15/2** Break the Rules, Ninia (USA), **8/1** Shinerolla, **10/1** BAND ON THE RUN, **12/1** Clifton Fox, **16/1** Pride of Pendle, Kemo Sabo, **20/1** Sandmoor Chambray, Cee-Jay-Ay, **25/1** Chinour (IRE), Pine Ridge Lad (IRE), **33/1** Phase One (IRE), Superoo, **50/1** Karinska, Marowins, CSF £69.75 CT £2,681.17 TOTE £9.80: £2.30 £1.80 £18.90 £1.70 (£41.00) Trio £1,291.40 OWNER Mr D. J. Allen (TAMWORTH) BRED Mrs J. R. Hine and Miss J. Bunting 18 Rn 1m 42.41 (6.11) SF: 61/36/34/51/40/19/39/18/21/15/10/19/-/-/-/-/-/-
WEIGHT FOR AGE 3yo-5lb

3608

PORCELANOSA RATED STKS H'CAP (0-105) (3-Y.O+) (Class B) £13,905.60 (£5,150.40: £2,475.20: £1,016.00)
1m (straight) Stalls: High GOING: 0.17 sec per fur (G) 3-05 (3-07)

3348* **Akil (IRE) (87)***(95) (RWArmstrong)* 3-8-2 WCarson(6) (mde most: hld on gamely fnl f) ....— **1**
3222[12] Roving Minstrel **(87)***(95) (BAMcMahon)* 4-8-7 KDarley(4) (lw: hdwy 3f out: chal ins fnl f: nt qckn nr fin) ....s.h **2**
3487a* Hoh Express **(97)***(104) (IABalding)* 3-8-12 LDettori(3) (a chsng ldrs: effrt over 2f out: kpt on wl) ....nk **3**
2325[6] Hiwaya **(95)***(98) (HThomsonJones)* 3-8-10 WRyan(2) (cl up: effrt 3f out: one pce appr fnl f) 2 **4**
3433[5] Rambo's Hall **(87)***(90) (JAGlover)* 10-8-7 DeanMcKeown(7) (plld hrd: cl up tl outpcd fnl 2f) ..s.h **5**
3358[6] Celestial Key (USA) **(101)***(100) (MJohnston)* 5-9-7 JWeaver(11) (hld up: hdwy over 2f out: nt qckn fnl f) 2 **6**
3374[8] Sue's Return **(87)***(86) (APJarvis)* 3-7-9 (7) CAdamson(8) (plld hrd: bhd tl swtchd & hdwy 2f out: nvr rchd ldrs) ....hd **7**
1839[6] Holtye (IRE) **(102)***(101)(Fav)(HRACecil)* 3-9-3 PatEddery(9) (a.p: rdn over 2f out: no imp after) ....s.h **8**
3332a[9] Our Rita **(87)***(86) (DrJDScargill)* 6-8-7 DHolland(10) (hld up & bhd: effrt over 2f out: no imp) .hd **9**
3027* Knight Commander (USA) **(96)***(83) (RHannon)* 3-8-11 JReid(5) (lw: hld up & bhd: hdwy 3f out: rdn 2f out: sn btn) 6 **10**

1837[9] Muhab (USA) **(100)**_(77) (PTWalwyn)_ 3-9-1 WRSwinburn(1) (chsd ldrs tl wknd fnl 2f)..............5 **11**

LONG HANDICAP Rambo's Hall 8-6 Roving Minstrel 8-6 Our Rita 8-6 Akil (IRE) 8-0

5/2 Holtye (IRE) (op 4/1), **11/2** Hoh Express, **6/1** AKIL (IRE), **13/2** Rambo's Hall (9/2-7/1), **8/1** Celestial Key (USA), **9/1** Roving Minstrel, **10/1** Hiwaya, **14/1** Knight Commander (USA), Our Rita, **16/1** Sue's Return, **20/1** Muhab (USA), CSF £56.71 CT £292.47 TOTE £6.70: £2.00 £2.50 £2.10 (£79.90) Trio £58.80 OWNER Mr Hamdan Al Maktoum (NEWMARKET) BRED Denis Noonan 11 Rn

1m 42.42 (5.92) SF: 40/45/49/43/40/50/31/46/36/28/22

WEIGHT FOR AGE 3yo-5lb

3609 PERTEMPS ST LEGER STKS (Gp 1) (3-Y.O C & F) (Class A)
£166,802.00 (£61,718.00: £29,609.00: £12,095.00)
1m 6f 132y Stalls: Low GOING: 0.17 sec per fur (G) 3-40 (3-46)

2218a[5] **Classic Cliche (IRE) (118)**_(123)_(Fav)_(SbinSuroor)_ 3-9-0 LDettori(7) (lw: trckd ldrs: led wl over 3f out: r.o strly)..........— **1**

1301[2] Minds Music (USA) **(106)**_(119) (HRACecil)_ 3-9-0 WRyan(10) (a in tch: hdwy 3½f out: chsd wnr fnl 2f: no imp)..........3½ **2**

3380* Istidaad (USA) **(113)**_(116) (ACStewart)_ 3-9-0 WCarson(8) (a chsng ldrs: chal appr st: outpcd 3f out: kpt on appr fnl f)..........2½ **3**

2670[4] In Camera (IRE) **(109)**_(116) (MRStoute)_ 3-9-0v KDarley(4) (in tch: effrt over 3f out: n.m.r & swtchd 2f out: styd on wl towards fin)..........½ **4**

2898a* Affidavit (USA) _(113) (AFabre,France)_ 3-9-0 WRSwinburn(9) (lw: hld up: hdwy over 3f out: one pce fnl 2f: no imp)..........2½ **5**

2386a[3] Anchor Clever **(100)**_(113) (PAKelleway)_ 3-9-0 RHughes(3) (lw: hld up & bhd: rdn over 4f out: styd on: nvr trbld ldrs)..........hd **6**

2670[5] Kalabo (USA) **(113)**_(113) (HRACecil)_ 3-9-0 PatEddery(1) (prom tl outpcd over 3f out: no ch after)..........½ **7**

3144[3] Luso **(124)**_(112) (CEBrittain)_ 3-9-0 RCochrane(6) (lw: hld up: effrt 4f out: rdn & btn wl over 2f out)..........s.h **8**

3389* Jellaby Askhir _(110) (RAkehurst)_ 3-9-0 JReid(2) (lw: in tch tl outpcd appr st: n.d after)..........2½ **9**

3486a[2] Jural **(109)**_(105) (MJohnston)_ 3-8-11 JWeaver(5) (led tl hdd wl over 3f out: wknd 2f out)......1¾ **10**

100/30 CLASSIC CLICHE (IRE), **4/1** Affidavit (USA), **5/1** Luso, **11/2** Kalabo (USA), **7/1** Jural, **11/1** Istidaad (USA), **12/1** Minds Music (USA), **16/1** Anchor Clever, **25/1** Jellaby Askhir, **33/1** In Camera (IRE), CSF £37.89 TOTE £4.40: £1.70 £2.40 £3.10 (£17.90) Trio £88.90 OWNER Godolphin (NEWMARKET) BRED Lord Victor Matthews in Ireland 10 Rn

3m 9.74 (6.14) SF: 79/75/72/72/69/69/69/68/66/61

3610 TRIPLEPRINT FLYING CHILDERS STKS (Gp 2) (2-Y.O) (Class A)
£29,007.50 (£10,692.50: £5,096.25: £2,043.75)
5f Stalls: High GOING: 0.17 sec per fur (G) 4-15 (4-18)

2740[2] **Cayman Kai (IRE) (100)**_(100) (RHannon)_ 2-8-12 PatEddery(1) (in tch: hdwy 2f out: led 1f out: r.o u.p)..........— **1**

3165* Mubhij (IRE) **(100)**_(98) (BWHills)_ 2-8-12 WCarson(3) (led tl hdd 1f out: kpt on wl)..........¾ **2**

3330a[7] Lucky Lionel (USA) **(100)**_(99) (RHannon)_ 2-9-3 JReid(7) (rdn ½-wy: styd on wl fnl f: nrst fin)..........1¼ **3**

3499* Rambling Bear **(100)**_(90) (MBlanshard)_ 2-8-12 StephenDavies(2) (cl up: rdn over 1f out: nt qckn)..........1¼ **4**

3086* Amazing Bay **(100)**_(69) (IABalding)_ 2-8-7 LDettori(6) (bhd: effrt & wnt lft ½-wy: no imp)..........5 **5**

2740* Almaty (IRE) **(100)**_(69)_(Fav)_(CCollins,Ireland)_ 2-9-3 KDarley(8) (racd alone stands' side: cl up: effrt & hung lft ½-wy: wknd over 1f out)..........3 **6**

3324a[2] Prince Aslia **(95)**_(16) (MJohnston)_ 2-8-12 JWeaver(5) (outpcd ½-wy: sn wl bhd)..........15 **7**

3687a[7] Maggi For Margaret **(100)**_(3) (MRChannon)_ 2-8-8 ow1 RHughes(4) (outpcd ½-wy: eased appr fnl f)..........2½ **8**

5/2 Almaty (IRE), **3/1** Amazing Bay, **11/2** Mubhij (IRE), **7/1** Lucky Lionel (USA) (5/1-8/1), Rambling Bear, CAYMAN KAI (IRE) (5/1-8/1), **11/1** Maggi For Margaret (8/1-12/1), **12/1** Prince Aslia, CSF £43.55 TOTE £10.00: £2.30 £1.60 £2.40 (£34.40) OWNER Mr I. A. N. Wight (MARLBOROUGH) BRED Tommy Burns 8 Rn

61.01 secs (2.61) SF: 66/64/65/56/35/35/-/-

OFFICIAL EXPLANATION **Almaty: the colt reportedly hung left, did not act on the ground and was heard to cough before the race.**

3611 LADBROKE H'CAP (0-95) (3-Y.O+) (Class C) £16,620.00 (£6,180.00: £2,990.00: £1,250.00) **1m 2f 60y** Stalls: Low GOING: 0.17 sec per fur (G) 4-45 (4-48)

2672[10] **Sue's Artiste (79)**_(95) (BWHills)_ 4-9-2 DHolland(23) (mid div: hdwy 3f out: qcknd to ld ins fnl f: r.o wl)..........— **1**

3531[3] Braille (IRE) **(65)***(77) (MGMeagher)* 4-7-11 (5) AWhelan(26) (a.p: led over 3f out tl disp ld over 2f out: hdd ins fnl f: kpt on)....2½ **2**
3393[5] Wentbridge Lad (IRE) **(60)***(71) (PDEvans)* 5-7-11v TWilliams(25) (bhd: hdwy 3f out: styd on wl fnl f: nrst fin)....¾ **3**
3440[2] Bardon Hill Boy (IRE) **(79)***(87) (BHanbury)* 3-8-6 (3) JStack(21) (hld up: gd hdwy 4f out: disp ld over 2f out: nt qckn fnl f)....2 **4**
2457[7] Unforgiving Minute **(79)***(85) (PWHarris)* 6-9-2 BThomson(18) (gd hdwy over 3f out: sn chsng ldrs: kpt on one pce fnl f)....1½ **5**
1872[12] Kutta **(90)***(93) (RWArmstrong)* 3-9-6 WCarson(10) (bhd: gd hdwy over 2f out: bdly hmpd & snatched up 1f out: nt rcvr)....1½ **6**
2482* Moneefa **(69)***(71)*(Fav)*(HRACecil)* 4-8-6 PatEddery(22) (trckd ldrs gng wl: smooth hdwy to disp ld over 2f out: wknd appr fnl f)....¾ **7**
2444[4] Windrush Lady **(70)***(72) (MMcCormack)* 5-8-7 DeanMcKeown(15) (chsd ldrs tl outpcd fnl 2f)....hd **8**
Moon Mistress **(82)***(82) (LadyHerries)* 4-9-5 RCochrane(13) (swtg: chsd ldrs tl grad wknd fnl 2f)....1¼ **9**
3374[10] Palatial Style **(83)***(83) (PJMakin)* 8-9-6 MBirch(1) (b: bhd tl hdwy on ins 3f out: n.m.r: nvr plcd to chal)....hd **10**
3462[8] Ooh Ah Cantona **(69)***(69) (JLEyre)* 4-8-6 RLappin(9) (stmbld bdly 4f out: nt rcvr)....s.h **11**
3348[10] Monument **(75)***(73) (RCharlton)* 3-8-5 KDarley(14) (effrt 4f out: hmpd 2f out: n.d)....1¼ **12**
2457[5] Gone for a Burton (IRE) **(86)***(84) (PJMakin)* 5-9-9 JReid(6) (hld up: effrt on ins over 4f out: n.m.r: n.d)....hd **13**
3433[3] Mowlaie **(67)***(62) (DWChapman)* 4-8-4 ACulhane(12) (effrt & nt clr run 3f out: n.d)....1½ **14**
2101* Tony's Fen **(78)***(72) (DRCElsworth)* 6-9-1 RHughes(4) (b: s.s: a bhd)....¾ **15**
3469* Dont Shoot Fairies **(75)***(61) (CEBrittain)* 3-8-5 WRyan(8) (cl up: led 4f out tl over 3f out: eased whn btn over 1f out)....5 **16**
2241[16] Green Crusader **(89)***(75) (MRStoute)* 4-9-12v WRSwinburn(11) (prom tl nt clr run & lost pl fnl 3f)....d.h **16**
3419[5] Bold Amusement **(80)***(64) (WSCunningham)* 5-9-3 JCarroll(5) (chsd ldrs tl wknd 3f out)....1¼ **18**
2678[6] Colorful Ambition **(74)***(53) (MrsASwinbank)* 5-8-11 NConnorton(20) (hdwy 4f out: sn prom: wknd fnl 2f)....3½ **19**
3459[5] Deano's Beeno **(80)***(55) (MJohnston)* 3-8-10 JWeaver(16) (lw: led tl hdd & wknd 4f out)....2½ **20**
3115* Catercap (IRE) **(78)***(31) (JHMGosden)* 3-8-8 LDettori(24) (swtg: hdwy ent st: sn chsng ldrs: wknd fnl 2f)....14 **21**
3189[13] Carlito Brigante **(72)***(24) (MrsJRRamsden)* 3-8-2 JFEgan(3) (in tch: effrt 3f out: n.m.r & btn 2f out)....½ **22**
3373[9] Last Roundup **(71)***(19) (CWThornton)* 3-8-1 DaleGibson(2) (a outpcd & bhd)....3 **23**
2510[2] Greatest **(71)***(13) (RAkehurst)* 4-8-3 (5) MHenry(17) (cl up tl rdn & wknd over 3f out)....4 **24**
3393[7] Colway Rock (USA) **(65)** *(JWWatts)* 5-8-2 LCharnock(7) (a bhd: t.o)....dist **25**

11/2 Moneefa, **8/1** Gone for a Burton (IRE), **9/1** Catercap (IRE), **11/1** Windrush Lady, **12/1** Deano's Beeno (op 20/1), Kutta (op 20/1), **14/1** Unforgiving Minute, Green Crusader, **16/1** Dont Shoot Fairies, Carlito Brigante, Braille (IRE), Tony's Fen, Bardon Hill Boy (IRE), SUE'S ARTISTE, Greatest, **20/1** Monument, **25/1** Colorful Ambition, Colway Rock (USA), Moon Mistress, Ooh Ah Cantona, Mowlaie, **33/1** Wentbridge Lad (IRE), Last Roundup, Bold Amusement, **50/1** Palatial Style, CSF £254.69 CT £7,393.55 TOTE £23.10: £4.70 £4.30 £6.60 £4.80 (£330.60) OWNER Mr A. L. R. Morton (LAMBOURN) BRED Juddmonte Farms 25 Rn

2m 12.9 (5.90) SF: 68/50/44/53/58/59/44/45/55/56/42/39/57/35/45/27/48/37/26/21/-/-/-/-/-

WEIGHT FOR AGE 3yo-7lb

OFFICIAL EXPLANATION **Ooh Ah Cantona: clipped the heels of another horse and nearly fell three furlongs out.**

3612

OSTRICH FARMING NURSERY H'CAP (0-85) (2-Y.O) (Class D)
£5,127.00 (£1,536.00: £738.00: £339.00)
6f Stalls: High GOING: 0.17 sec per fur (G) 5-15 (5-18)

3465* **Some Horse (IRE) (83)***(88) (MGMeagher)* 2-9-5 RHughes(12) (s.i.s: hdwy ½-wy: led ins fnl f: r.o wl)....— **1**
3289[3] Clincher Club **(70)***(74) (MJohnston)* 2-8-6 JWeaver(16) (bhd: hdwy & swtchd 2f out: qcknd to chal wl ins fnl f: no ex nr fin)....nk **2**
3260[7] Mr Speaker (IRE) **(65)***(59) (CFWall)* 2-8-1 NCarlisle(5) (lw: s.i.s: hdwy ½-wy: styd on u.p fnl f: nrst fin)....4 **3**
3432* Dashing Blue **(84)***(76) (IABalding)* 2-9-6 PatEddery(4) (chsd ldrs: led over 2f out tl ins fnl f: no ex)....¾ **4**
3427[3] Half An Inch (IRE) **(70)***(60) (BJMeehan)* 2-8-6 LDettori(9) (in tch: kpt on u.p fnl f: nrst fin)....¾ **5**
3147[6] Soul of Honour (FR) **(70)***(58)*(Fav)*(MrsJRRamsden)* 2-8-6 KFallon(7) (lw: sn bhd: hdwy 2f out: styd on wl towards fin)....¾ **6**

3394³ Middle East **(76)***(60)* *(TDBarron)* 2-8-12 KDarley(15) (trckd ldrs: effrt & edgd lft appr fnl f: sn btn) 1½ 7
3352* Munakeb (FR) **(77)***(55)* *(RWArmstrong)* 2-8-13 WCarson(17) (dwlt: sn wl bhd: hdwy u.p 2f out: no imp) 2 8
3509⁴ Charterhouse Xpres **(64)***(39)* *(MMcCormack)* 2-8-0 StephenDavies(8) (w ldrs tl wknd 2f out) 1¼ 9
3379⁵ Napoleon's Return **(67)***(42)* *(AGFoster)* 2-8-3v TSprake(3) (lw: drvn along ½-wy: no imp) ....hd 10
3434³ U-No-Harry (IRE) **(71)***(45)* *(RHollinshead)* 2-8-2 (5) MHenry(10) (w ldrs: led 3½f out tl over 2f out: wknd over 1f out) ....hd 11
3271² Albert The Bear **(77)***(49)* *(JBerry)* 2-8-13 JCarroll(2) (in tch tl outpcd fnl 2f) ....¾ 12
3233⁹ Sphinx Levelv (IRE) **(64)***(36)* *(APJarvis)* 2-7-7 (7) CAdamson(1) (prom 4f: sn lost pl) ....nk 13
3228* Ramsey Hope **(85)***(53)* *(CWFairhurst)* 2-9-7 NKennedy(13) (lw: cl up tl wknd appr fnl f) 1½ 14
3228⁶ La Finale **(64)***(31)* *(MHEasterby)* 2-8-0 SMaloney(11) (mid div & rdn ½-wy: sn btn) ....hd 15
3284³ Montrestar **(65)***(27)* *(PDEvans)* 2-8-1v TWilliams(14) (lw: n.d) 2 16
3471² Ben'a'vachei Boy **(63)** *(JDBethell)* 2-7-13b JFEgan(6) (led 2½f: wknd qckly) 11 17

4/1 Soul of Honour (FR), **5/1** Dashing Blue, **6/1** Munakeb (FR), **7/1** Albert The Bear, **15/2** SOME HORSE (IRE), **10/1** Clincher Club, **12/1** La Finale, Half An Inch (IRE), **14/1** Ben'a'vachei Boy, **16/1** Charterhouse Xpres, U-No-Harry (IRE), Middle East, Montrestar, Ramsey Hope, **20/1** Napoleon's Return, Sphinx Levelv (IRE), **25/1** Mr Speaker (IRE), CSF £88.21 CT £1,712.97 TOTE £10.30: £2.40 £2.20 £10.10 £1.40 (£41.90) Trio £877.10 OWNER The Anfield Hombres (ORMSKIRK) BRED Luisa Salini 17 Rn 1m 15.22 (4.22) SF: 58/44/29/46/30/28/30/25/9/12/15/19/6/23/1/-/-

T/Jkpt: Not won; £3,556.12 to Nottingham 11/9/95. T/Plpt: £1,345.90 (14.3 Tckts). T/Qdpt: £56.60 (8.1 Tckts). AA

3599-GOODWOOD (R-H)
Saturday September 9th (Good)
WEATHER: sunny WIND: str half against

3613
HIGHLAND SPRING/ROA NURSERY H'CAP (2-Y.O) (Class C) £6,018.75 (£1,800.00: £862.50: £393.75)
7f Stalls: High GOING minus 0.09 sec per fur (G) 2-15 (2-15)

3174* **Alzanti (80)***(80)*(Fav)*(PFICole)* 2-8-10 (5) DaneO'Neill(10) (w ldr: led over 2f out: drvn out) ...— 1
3477a* Winter Quarters (USA) **(86)***(85)* *(IABalding)* 2-9-7 GHind(3) (lw: hdwy & nt clr run on ins over 2f out: chsd wnr over 1f out: r.o ins fnl f) ....nk 2
3289⁵ Goodwood Rocket **(69)***(64)* *(JLDunlop)* 2-8-4 GCarter(4) (lw: swtchd lft & rdn over 2f out: hdwy over 1f out: r.o) 1¾ 3
2912⁷ Tapintime (USA) **(75)***(62)* *(PFICole)* 2-8-10 TQuinn(6) (lw: 3rd st: hrd rdn over 2f out: one pce) 3½ 4
2315⁷ Daily Risk **(69)***(55)* *(SDow)* 2-7-11 (7) ADaly(11) (lw: led over 4f: wknd 1f out) ....½ 5
3516⁸ Kinnescash (IRE) **(69)***(55)* *(MSSaunders)* 2-8-4 AMcGlone(5) (b: 6th st: nt clr run over 1f out: one pce) ....s.h 6
3281² Prince of Florence (IRE) **(85)***(70)* *(LMCumani)* 2-8-13 (7) GMitchell(8) (lw: 4th st: nt clr run on ins over 1f out: one pce) ....nk 7
3208⁵ Serious Trust **(68)***(47)* *(SirMarkPrescott)* 2-8-3 GDuffield(7) (a bhd) 3 8
3375¹⁵ Eights High (USA) **(71)***(34)* *(RHannon)* 2-8-6 MRoberts(2) (lw: 5th st: wknd over 1f out) 7 9
2710² Last Token **(80)***(41)* *(JSMoore)* 2-8-12 (3) NVarley(1) (bhd fnl 3f) ....¾ 10
3267³ Vanishing Point **(76)** *(GLewis)* 2-8-11 PaulEddery(9) (Withdrawn not under Starter's orders: Veterinary advice) .... W

3/1 ALZANTI, **100/30** Winter Quarters (USA), **5/1** Prince of Florence (IRE), **8/1** Goodwood Rocket, **10/1** Tapintime (USA), **11/1** Daily Risk, **12/1** Vanishing Point, Last Token, **14/1** Serious Trust, **16/1** Eights High (USA), **33/1** Kinnescash (IRE), CSF £12.67 CT £64.73 TOTE £3.50: £1.60 £1.30 £2.00 (£3.70) Trio £12.90 OWNER Elite Racing Club (WHATCOMBE) BRED J. Weinfeld 10 Rn
1m 29.4 (5.00) SF: 33/38/17/15/8/8/23/-/-/-

3614
WESTMINSTER TAXI INSURANCE SELECT STKS (Gp 3) (3-Y.O+) (Class A) £22,242.00 (£8,322.60: £3,996.30: £1,739.10)
1m 2f Stalls: High GOING minus 0.09 sec per fur (G) 2-45 (2-46)

3458* **Triarius (USA)** *(119)*(Fav)*(SbinSuroor)* 5-9-0 GCarter(2) (lw: 3rd st: led over 1f out: rdn & r.o wl) ....— 1
2936* Fahal (USA) **(119)***(120)* *(DMorley)* 3-8-10 RHills(3) (4th st: nt clr run over 3f out to 2f out: rdn over 1f out: unable qckn) 1½ 2
3498³ Wayne County (IRE) **(108)***(116)* *(RAkehurst)* 5-9-0 TQuinn(1) (led over 8f: one pce) ....nk 3
3194a³ Richard of York *(118)* *(JHMGosden)* 5-9-3 GHind(6) (5th st: rdn 2f out: one pce) ....¾ 4

3381[3] Alriffa **(113)***(116) (RHannon)* 4-9-3 MRoberts(4) (lw: 2nd st: wknd over 1f out)........1¼ **5**
3381[6] Young Buster (IRE) **(115)***(111) (GWragg)* 7-9-0 PaulEddery(5) (lw: 6th st: a in rr)........1 **6**

7/4 TRIARIUS (USA), **2/1** Fahal (USA), **6/1** Alriffa, **7/1** Richard of York (5/1-15/2), **8/1** Young Buster (IRE), **20/1** Wayne County (IRE), CSF £5.46 TOTE £2.70: £1.90 £1.80 (£2.60) OWNER Godolphin (NEWMARKET) BRED Tyra Black and Summa Stables 6 Rn

2m 10.07 (5.07) SF: 51/45/48/50/48/43
WEIGHT FOR AGE 3yo-7lb

3615

WILLIAM HILL SPRINT CUP H'CAP (0-95) (3-Y.O+) (Class C)
£16,150.00 (£4,900.00: £2,400.00: £1,150.00)
6f Stalls: Low GOING minus 0.09 sec per fur (G) 3-20 (3-21)

3466* **Iktamal (USA) (96)***(102)*(Fav)*(EALDunlop)* 3-9-12 PaulEddery(19) (hdwy over 1f out: led ins fnl f: all out)........— **1**
2764[20] La Petite Fusee **(69)***(75) (RJO'Sullivan)* 4-8-2 GDuffield(10) (led tl ins fnl f: r.o wl)........s.h **2**
3557* Croeso-I-Cymru **(89)***(94) (RAkehurst)* 4-9-5 (3) 4x SSanders(11) (hld up: rdn over 2f out: r.o wl ins fnl f)........nk **3**
3359* No Extras (IRE) **(95)***(100) (GLMoore)* 5-10-0 SWhitworth(20) (outpcd: hdwy over 1f out: r.o)........s.h **4**
3512[4] Oggi **(67)***(71) (PJMakin)* 4-8-0b JTate(21) (hdwy over 1f out: r.o)........nk **5**
2507[3] Hakiki (IRE) **(84)***(87) (PTWalwyn)* 3-9-0 RHills(13) (lw: a.p: ev ch 1f out: unable qckn ins fnl f)........½ **6**
3442[4] Gone Savage **(65)***(67) (WJMusson)* 7-7-12 AMcGlone(18) (a.p: ev ch over 1f out: one pce)..nk **7**
3359[2] Rich Glow **(68)***(70) (NBycroft)* 4-8-1 RPrice(24) (hld up: rdn over 2f out: one pce ins fnl f)........hd **8**
3492[2] Sue Me (IRE) **(72)***(74) (WRMuir)* 3-8-2 PRobinson(15) (lw: hld up: hrd rdn & ev ch over 1f out: one pce)........hd **9**
3492[11] Craigie Boy **(62)***(56) (NBycroft)* 5-7-2b(7)ow2 MartinDwyer(14) (no hdwy fnl 2f)........2 **10**
3145[7] How's Yer Father **(84)***(80) (RJHodges)* 9-9-0 (3) SDrowne(1) (nvr nrr)........hd **11**
3286[2] Dancing Heart **(70)***(66) (BJMeehan)* 3-8-0 GBardwell(27) (a.p: ev ch over 1f out: wknd ins fnl f)........hd **12**
3212[11] Champagne Grandy **(76)***(71) (MRChannon)* 5-8-4 (5) PPMurphy(16) (lw: nvr nrr)........nk **13**
3519[6] Astral Invader (IRE) **(63)***(58) (MSSaunders)* 3-7-7v NAdams(22) (a mid div)........s.h **14**
3466[5] Montserrat **(75)***(70) (LGCottrell)* 3-8-5 MFenton(8) (a mid div)........s.h **15**
3087[2] Penny Dip **(84)***(78) (RFJohnsonHoughton)* 3-9-0 TQuinn(5) (hdwy over 2f out: wknd over 1f out)........nk **16**
3359[7] Agwa **(73)***(63) (RJO'Sullivan)* 6-8-6 DBiggs(25) (spd over 4f)........1¼ **17**
3457[7] Jato **(72)***(62) (SCWilliams)* 6-8-5 GHind(2) (lw: nvr nrr)........nk **18**
3359[5] Sea Thunder **(81)***(65) (IABalding)* 3-8-6 (5) DGriffiths(3) (lw: bhd fnl 2f)........2 **19**
3535[4] Anzio (IRE) **(71)***(54) (BAPearce)* 4-7-11b(7) JWilkinson(17) (b: lw: a bhd)........½ **20**
2551[4] Tinker Osmaston **(65)***(45) (MSSaunders)* 4-7-12 AMackay(4) (lw: prom over 3f)........1 **21**
3359[6] Petraco (IRE) **(64)***(44) (NASmith)* 7-7-8 (3) NVarley(7) (bhd fnl 2f)........s.h **22**
3466[2] Bajan Rose **(76)***(54) (MBlanshard)* 3-8-6 MRoberts(26) (hdwy 3f out: wknd 1f out)........¾ **23**
Fascination Waltz **(69)***(45) (JJSheehan)* 8-7-13 (3)ow1 PMcCabe(23) (spd 5f)........½ **24**
3333[5] Green Golightly (USA) **(60)***(35) (DAWilson)* 4-7-7 JLowe(28) (bhd fnl 2f)........¾ **25**
3359[22] Thatcherella **(76)***(43) (MajorDNChappell)* 4-8-9 GCarter(12) (hdwy over 2f out: eased whn btn ins fnl f)........3 **26**

LONG HANDICAP Astral Invader (IRE) 7-6 Green Golightly (USA) 7-1 Craigie Boy 7-0

8/1 IKTAMAL (USA), **10/1** Croeso-I-Cymru, **11/1** Sue Me (IRE), **12/1** Sea Thunder, **14/1** No Extras (IRE), Gone Savage, **16/1** Rich Glow, How's Yer Father, Montserrat, Bajan Rose, Penny Dip, **20/1** Oggi, Petraco (IRE), Agwa, Jato, **25/1** Champagne Grandy, Anzio (IRE), Dancing Heart, Thatcherella, **33/1** Astral Invader (IRE), La Petite Fusee, Hakiki (IRE), **40/1** Tinker Osmaston, **50/1** Green Golightly (USA), Craigie Boy, **66/1** Fascination Waltz, CSF £217.83 CT £2,435.58 TOTE £7.10: £2.00 £9.40 £2.30 £3.80 (£295.90) Trio £1,667.30 OWNER Maktoum Al Maktoum (NEWMARKET) BRED Green Ireland Properties Ltd 26 Rn 1m 12.56 (2.36)

SF:68/44/63/69/40/53/36/39/40/25/49/32/40/24/36/44/32/31/31/23/14/13/20/14/4/12
WEIGHT FOR AGE 3yo-3lb

3616

BARKERS TRIDENT TROPHY H'CAP (0-90) (3-Y.O+) (Class C)
£5,952.00 (£1,776.00: £848.00: £384.00)
2m Stalls: High GOING minus 0.09 sec per fur (G) 3-55 (3-58)

3406[6] **Lear Dancer (USA) (66)***(79) (PMitchell)* 4-9-0v GDuffield(4) (hrd rdn & hdwy over 1f out: led wl ins fnl f: r.o)........— **1**
3384[2] Supreme Star (USA) **(64)***(76) (PRHedger)* 4-8-7 (5) DaneO'Neill(6) (5th st: led over 2f out: hrd rdn over 1f out: hdd wl ins fnl f: unable qckn)........¾ **2**

24137 Purple Splash **(80)***(92) (PJMakin)* 5-10-0b TQuinn(8) (b: 6th st: hdwy over 2f out: ev ch ins fnl f: one pce) ....½ **3**
34702 Sea Freedom **(70)***(78) (GBBalding)* 4-9-4 JWilliams(2) (4th st: swtchd rt over 2f out: one pce) 4 **4**
35278 Ballymac Girl **(51)***(58) (JMBradley)* 7-7-13 GBardwell(10) (b: s.s: hdwy after 1f: lost pl over 4f out: one pce) ....¾ **5**
3071* Blaze Away (USA) **(80)***(80) (IABalding)* 4-9-9 (5) DGriffiths(9) (lw: led over 13f: wknd over 1f out) 7 **6**
32294 Snowy Petrel (IRE) **(76)***(75) (JLDunlop)* 3-8-11 GCarter(5) (plld hrd: 7th st: wknd over 2f out) 1 **7**
2098 12 Shadirwan (IRE) **(74)***(72)*(Fav)*(RAkehurst)* 4-9-8 JQuinn(7) (lw: 2nd st: ev ch over 2f out: sn wknd) 1¼ **8**
Honey Mount **(75)***(71) (NJHWalker)* 4-9-9 CRutter(1) (a bhd) 2 **9**
18407 Simafar (IRE) **(67)***(60) (NAGraham)* 4-9-1 PaulEddery(3) (3rd st: wknd over 2f out) 3 **10**

3/1 Shadirwan (IRE), **5/1** Blaze Away (USA), Supreme Star (USA), **11/2** Sea Freedom, **10/1** Purple Splash, Snowy Petrel (IRE) (8/1-12/1), **12/1** Simafar (IRE) (8/1-14/1), **14/1** LEAR DANCER (USA) (10/1-16/1), **16/1** Ballymac Girl, **25/1** Honey Mount, CSF £75.23 CT £668.76 TOTE £21.50: £4.60 £1.50 £3.80 (£43.60) Trio £202.20 OWNER Mrs R. A. Johnson BRED Alan S. Kline 10 Rn
3m 30.79 (6.29) SF: 61/58/74/60/40/62/44/54/53/42
WEIGHT FOR AGE 3yo-13lb

3617 MACMILLAN MAIDEN STKS (2-Y.O) (Class D) £4,386.00 (£1,308.00: £624.00: £282.00) **1m** Stalls: High GOING minus 0.09 sec per fur (G) 4-30 (4-33)

Dreamhill (USA) *(74t)*(Fav)*(PWHarris)* 2-9-0 GDuffield(5) (w'like: scope: chsd ldr: led 2f out: r.o wl) ....— **1**
Jamaican Flight (USA) *(70t) (JWHills)* 2-9-0 RHills(1) (w'like: bit bkwd: 3rd st: ev ch over 1f out: unable qckn) 2 **2**
Soviet King (IRE) *(65t) (PMitchell)* 2-9-0 RPerham(3) (b: unf: scope: 4th st: rdn 3f out: n.m.r & swtchd lft over 1f out: one pce) 2½ **3**
Galway Blade *(57t) (APJarvis)* 2-9-0 JTate(2) (leggy: 5th st: nvr nr to chal) 4 **4**
Clouds Hill (FR) *(54t)*(Fav)*(RHannon)* 2-9-0 MRoberts(6) (b.off hind: leggy: led 6f: eased whn btn over 1f out) 1¾ **5**
Ela-Yie-Mou (IRE) *(28t) (LMCumani)* 2-9-0 TQuinn(4) (leggy: scope: lw: bhd fnl 5f) 13 **6**

9/4 DREAMHILL (USA), Clouds Hill (FR) (6/4-5/2), **5/2** Ela-Yie-Mou (IRE) (6/4-11/4), **10/1** Jamaican Flight (USA) (op 5/1), **14/1** Galway Blade, **33/1** Soviet King (IRE), CSF £19.62 TOTE £3.30: £1.50 £2.80 (£18.70) OWNER Stable Minds (BERKHAMSTED) BRED Swettenham Stud 6 Rn
1m 44.02 (6.42) SF: 26/22/17/9/6/-

3618 ARCHFORM ORTHODONTIC LABORATORY MAIDEN STKS (3-Y.O) (Class D) £4,815.00 (£1,440.00: £690.00: £315.00) **1m 2f** Stalls: High GOING minus 0.09 sec per fur (G) 5-00 (5-03)

Akayid *(79) (CJBenstead)* 3-8-9 MWigham(5) (hdwy on ins over 4f out: nt clr run & swtchd lft over 2f out: led nr fin) ....— **1**
34484 Fire of London *(79) (JHMGosden)* 3-8-9 GHind(2) (b.nr hind: 5th st: led over 2f out tl over 1f out: led 1f out: edgd rt ins fnl f: hdd nr fin) ....hd **2**
13532 Secret Spring (FR) **(83)***(81)*(Fav)*(RCharlton)* 3-9-0 TQuinn(10) (3rd st: led over 1f out: sn hdd: 3rd & btn whn n.m.r wl ins fnl f) 1½ **3**
33384 Prophets Honour **(79)***(80) (CACyzer)* 3-9-0 DBiggs(8) (2nd st: led over 3f out tl over 2f out: 4th & btn whn snatched up wl ins fnl f) ....¾ **4**
Mu-Tadil *(75) (MajorWRHern)* 3-9-0 RHills(6) (w'like: bit bkwd: rdn over 3f out: hdwy over 1f out: one pce) 3 **5**
House of Dreams *(73) (BWHills)* 3-9-0 JWilliams(11) (bit bkwd: nvr nr to chal) 1¼ **6**
Sicarian *(65) (MJHeaton-Ellis)* 3-9-0 GCarter(12) (w'like: scope: sme hdwy over 2f out: sn wknd) 5 **7**
31788 Shared (IRE) **(35)***(53) (MMadgwick)* 3-9-0 MFenton(9) (led over 6f) 8 **8**
Modajjaj *(50) (MAJarvis)* 3-9-0 PRobinson(3) (w'like: scope: bit bkwd: 6th st: wknd over 3f out) 1½ **9**
Hypertension *(45) (RHannon)* 3-9-0 RPerham(1) (leggy: scope: a bhd) 3 **10**
3129 12 Swaynes Lad *(CPWildman)* 3-9-0 GDuffield(4) (bhd fnl 5f: t.o) ....dist **11**

7/4 Secret Spring (FR), **100/30** Prophets Honour, **6/1** Modajjaj (5/2-7/1), **8/1** Fire of London (5/1-9/1), **10/1** Hypertension, **14/1** Mu-Tadil (op 7/1), **20/1** House of Dreams, **33/1** AKAYID, Sicarian, **66/1** Shared (IRE), Swaynes Lad, CSF £239.53 TOTE £59.70: £6.60 £2.40 £1.30 (£91.50) Trio £110.70 OWNER Mr Hamdan Al Maktoum (EPSOM) BRED Shadwell Estate Company Limited 11 Rn
2m 12.21 (7.21) SF: 29/29/31/30/25/23/15/3/-/-/-

3619 BATTLE OF BRITAIN WESTHAMPNETT AMATEUR LIMITED STKS (0-70) (3-Y.O+) (Class E) £4,175.00 (£1,250.00: £600.00: £275.00)
7f Stalls: High GOING minus 0.09 sec per fur (G) 5-30 (5-31)

3565* **Knobbleeneeze (70)***(79)*(Fav)*(MRChannon)* 5-10-11v 2x MissJWinter(2) (lw: stdy hdwy over 2f out: shkn up ins fnl f: led nr fin) — **1**
2593[6] Polly Peculiar **(56)***(73) (BSmart)* 4-10-1 (5) MissVMarshall(8) (swtchd rt over 3f out: hdwy on ins over 2f out: led over 1f out: rdn & hdd nr fin) nk **2**
3125[3] Primo Lara **(66)***(70) (PWHarris)* 3-10-5 MissAElsey(12) (lw: 2nd st: led 2f out tl over 1f out: one pce) 3 **3**
3390* Stoppes Brow **(68)***(71) (GLMoore)* 3-10-2 (5) MrKGoble(15) (led over 5f out to 2f out: one pce fnl f) s.h **4**
2455[9] Pusey Street Boy **(52)***(69) (JRBosley)* 8-10-9 MrsSBosley(10) (lw: hld up: rdn over 1f out: r.o one pce) s.h **5**
3493[3] Chief of Staff **(63)***(67) (JPearce)* 6-10-11 MrsLPearce(6) (hdwy over 1f out: r.o wl ins fnl f) 2 **6**
3242[8] Purple Fling **(70)***(68) (SirMarkPrescott)* 4-11-1 MissDianaJones(3) (lw: nvr nr to chal) 1 **7**
3385[4] Tirollac (IRE) **(42)***(51) (LGCottrell)* 3-9-9 (5) MissLPope(13) (5th st: wknd over 2f out) 3 **8**
3510[7] Masnun (USA) **(67)***(52) (RJO'Sullivan)* 10-10-9 MrsAPerrett(1) (a mid div) 1½ **9**
3094[4] Top Pet (IRE) **(51)***(50) (RAkehurst)* 5-10-9 MrTMcCarthy(17) (nvr nrr) ¾ **10**
3455* Kindergarten Boy (IRE) **(62)***(50) (RBoss)* 4-10-13 MrsMCowdrey(5) (3rd st: wknd over 1f out) 2 **11**
3385[5] Starlight Flyer **(19)***(45) (JELong)* 8-10-4b(5) MrTWaters(7) (b.hind: s.s: a bhd) ½ **12**
3426[8] False Pretences (IRE) **(30)***(41) (BAPearce)* 3-10-0 (5) MrRBlyth(14) (lw: s.s: a bhd) 1½ **13**
3348[8] Kingchip Boy **(68)***(42) (MJRyan)* 6-10-6v(5) MrSJLavallin(4) (s.s: a bhd) ½ **14**
3439[15] Shepherd Market (IRE) **(63)***(35) (DAWilson)* 4-10-11 MrRJohnson(16) (4th st: wknd over 2f out) 3 **15**
2144[3] Scissor Ridge **(43)***(32) (JJBridger)* 3-10-0 (5) MrDBridger(11) (swtg: led over 1f: 6th st: wknd over 3f out) ½ **16**
3426[14] Portland Way **(33)***(28) (APJarvis)* 3-10-0 (5) MrsEBurke(9) (bhd fnl 3f) 2 **17**

5/2 KNOBBLEENEEZE, **7/1** Shepherd Market (IRE), **8/1** Stoppes Brow, Primo Lara, **10/1** Kindergarten Boy (IRE), Chief of Staff, **11/1** Purple Fling (8/1-12/1), **12/1** Top Pet (IRE), Kingchip Boy, **16/1** Masnun (USA), **20/1** Polly Peculiar, **25/1** Pusey Street Boy, **50/1** Scissor Ridge, Tirollac (IRE), **66/1** Starlight Flyer, False Pretences (IRE), Portland Way, CSF £49.73 TOTE £2.90: £1.50 £9.60 £4.30 (£110.20) Trio £628.60 OWNER Mr Anthony Andrews (UPPER LAMBOURN) BRED A. and Mrs Andrews 17 Rn 1m 29.77 (5.37) SF: 51/45/38/39/41/39/40/19/24/22/22/17/9/14/7/-/-
WEIGHT FOR AGE 3yo-4lb

T/Plpt £176.70 (43.06 Tckts). T/Qdpt £242.90 (4.3 Tckts). AK

3258-NOTTINGHAM (L-H)
Monday September 11th (Good to soft, soft patches)
WEATHER: fine WIND: almost nil

3620 E.B.F. NOTTINGHAM MAIDEN STKS (2-Y.O) (Class D) £4,435.00 (£1,330.00: £640.00: £295.00) **1m 54y** Stalls: Low GOING minus 0.14 sec (G) 2-00 (2-00)

3416[2] **Storm Trooper (USA)** *(83+)*(Fav)*(HRACecil)* 2-9-0 PatEddery(8) (led after 1f: qcknd clr appr fnl f: unchal) — **1**
3089[16] Dark Waters (IRE) *(71) (MRStoute)* 2-9-0 WRSwinburn(13) (chsd ldrs: hdwy 4f out: styd on appr fnl f: no ch w wnr) 6 **2**
Sweetness Herself *(64) (MJRyan)* 2-8-4 (5) DGibbs(6) (neat: unf: swtg: chsd ldrs: 6th st: chal 3f out: outpcd appr fnl f) 1¼ **3**
1418[2] Classic Lover (IRE) *(54) (SCWilliams)* 2-8-9 AMackay(7) (bhd tl styd on fnl 2f) 5 **4**
3340[11] Select Few *(54) (LMCumani)* 2-9-0 KDarley(15) (in tch: styd on fnl 2f: nvr nrr) 2½ **5**
3397[7] Needwood Epic *(46) (BAMcMahon)* 2-8-9 GCarter(17) (chsd ldrs: 5th st: one pce fnl 2f) 2 **6**
3553[6] Knave *(50) (RHannon)* 2-8-9 (5) DaneO'Neill(3) (hld up & bhd: shkn up & r.o fnl 2f) ½ **7**
3089[12] Amber Fort *(49) (PFICole)* 2-9-0 TQuinn(12) (chsd ldrs: 2nd st: wknd over 2f out) hd **8**
Arctic Fancy (USA) *(46) (PWHarris)* 2-9-0 GHind(10) (w'like: scope: bkwd: bhd tl styd on fnl 2f) 1½ **9**
3266[4] Autumn (FR) *(41) (PCHaslam)* 2-8-9 MTebbutt(1) (hdwy 4f out: nvr nr ldrs) ½ **10**
2846[7] General Macarthur *(44) (JLDunlop)* 2-9-0 MRoberts(19) (mid div: no hdwy fnl 2f) ¾ **11**
3231[11] Forgie (IRE) *(41) (PCalver)* 2-9-0 MBirch(4) (s.s: stdy late hdwy: nvr nrr) 1½ **12**
Alzotic (IRE) *(40) (SGNorton)* 2-9-0 KFallon(2) (cmpt: bkwd: nvr nr to chal) ½ **13**
Siege Perilous (IRE) *(40) (BobJones)* 2-9-0 JReid(16) (w'like: unf: scope: s.s: a in rr) nk **14**

3503[5] Swish **(50)***(38) (NTinkler)* 2-9-0 LCharnock(5) (prom: 4th st: rdn & wknd over 2f out)...............1 **15**
3215[5] Minsterbeach *(36) (CEBrittain)* 2-9-0 BDoyle(20) (led 1f: 3rd st: rdn & wknd over 1f out).........1 **16**
3523[11] Arrogant Heir *(28) (SGNorton)* 2-9-0 TWilliams(18) (bit bkwd: m.n.s).......................................4 **17**
3463[12] Young Saffy *(18) (MrsMReveley)* 2-9-0 JFanning(14) (bit bkwd: s.i.s: a in rr: t.o).....................5 **18**
2294[6] Lucky Lees (IRE) *(17) (PGMurphy)* 2-8-7 (7) RWaterfield(9) (t.o)...¾ **19**
3463[14] Gunner B Special *(16) (SRBowring)* 2-8-9 (5) CTeague(11) (b: b.hind: prom tl wknd over 3f out: t.o)...½ **20**

1/3 STORM TROOPER (USA) (op 4/5), **7/1** Amber Fort (op 9/2), **10/1** Dark Waters (IRE) (op 5/1), Select Few, General Macarthur (op 6/1), Alzotic (IRE), **12/1** Classic Lover (IRE) (op 7/1), **16/1** Knave, Arctic Fancy (USA), **20/1** Sweetness Herself, **25/1** Forgie (IRE), **33/1** Needwood Epic, Autumn (FR), Siege Perilous (IRE), Young Saffy, Minsterbeach, Arrogant Heir, **50/1** Swish, Lucky Lees (IRE), Gunner B Special, CSF £10.16 TOTE £1.60: £1.30 £2.40 £31.10 (£6.00) Trio £158.90 OWNER Prince Fahd Salman (NEWMARKET) BRED Robert N. Clay and Airlie Stud 20 Rn

1m 44.8 (5.20) SF: 35/23/16/6/6/-/2/1/-/-/-/-/-/-/-/-/-/-/-/-

3621 TRENT LIMITED STKS (0-70) (3-Y.O+) (Class E) £3,759.80 (£1,126.40: £541.20: £248.60) **1m 1f 213y** Stalls: Low GOING minus 0.14 sec per fur (G) 2-30 (2-31)

3278[4] **Emily-Mou (IRE) (70)***(83) (BJMeehan)* 3-8-12 BDoyle(3) (b: mde all: drvn along 2f out: styd on strly)..— **1**
3395[4] Posing (IRE) **(63)***(74) (JRFanshawe)* 3-8-6v TQuinn(10) (chsd wnr: 2nd st: effrt u.p appr fnl f: nt pce to chal)...1¾ **2**
2747[2] Pass Mark **(62)***(71) (JRFanshawe)* 3-8-6 WRyan(6) (chsd ldng pair: 3rd st: rdn over 1f out: unable qckn)..1¾ **3**
3462[5] Sweet Mignonette **(70)***(66)*(Fav)*(MrsMReveley)* 7-8-13 KDarley(13) (lw: hld up: hdwy & 6th st: rdn 2f out: no imp)...3½ **4**
3059[4] Mansur (IRE) **(70)***(66) (DRLoder)* 3-8-11 PatEddery(12) (hld up in rr: styd on fnl 2f: nvr nrr)....3 **5**
974[10] Matamoros **(69)***(63) (JLDunlop)* 3-8-11 JReid(11) (chsd ldrs: 5th st: wknd over 2f out)..........1¾ **6**
Secret Service (IRE) **(70)***(57) (JHanson)* 3-8-11 WRSwinburn(4) (chsd ldrs: 4th st: shkn up 2f out: eased whn btn)...4 **7**
2979[10] Just Harry **(68)***(56) (MJRyan)* 4-8-13 (5) MBaird(8) (lw: a in rr)..nk **8**
2279[10] Feinte **(68)***(49) (WJarvis)* 3-8-6 MHills(1) (nvr bttr than mid div).......................................1½ **9**
2310[7] River Wye (IRE) **(41)***(49) (JMCarr)* 3-8-11 SMorris(7) (lw: plld hrd: hld up in rr: effrt ent st: no imp)..3 **10**
The Deaconess **(32)***(22) (MrsALMKing)* 4-8-10 (3) SDrowne(5) (a bhd: rdn over 3f out: no rspnse: t.o)...14 **11**
3433[11] Hunters' Heaven (USA) **(52)***(26) (JMackie)* 4-9-4 JQuinn(2) (a in rr: t.o)...............................nk **12**
2433[7] Divertimiento **(54)** *(JMackie)* 4-9-4 GCarter(9) (unruly stalls: uns rdr leaving stalls).................. **U**

7/2 Sweet Mignonette, **9/2** Matamoros, EMILY-MOU (IRE), **13/2** Pass Mark, **7/1** Mansur (IRE), **8/1** Feinte, Secret Service (IRE), **10/1** Just Harry, Posing (IRE), **33/1** River Wye (IRE), Hunters' Heaven (USA), Divertimiento, **40/1** The Deaconess, CSF £50.98 TOTE £5.50: £2.20 £3.70 £2.10 (£20.10) Trio £43.40 OWNER Mr A. S. Reid (UPPER LAMBOURN) BRED W. and R. Barnett Ltd 13 Rn

2m 8.2 (5.70) SF: 38/29/26/28/21/18/12/18/4/4/-/-/-

WEIGHT FOR AGE 3yo-7lb

3622 MIRROR 4 PUNTERS CLUB H'CAP (0-70) (3-Y.O+) (Class E) £4,108.50 (£1,233.00: £594.00: £274.50) **5f 13y** Stalls: High GOING: 0.02 sec per fur (G) 3-00 (3-01)

3072[2] **Chadwell Hall (48)***(61++)*(Fav)*(SRBowring)* 4-8-1b(5) CTeague(18) (b.off hind: mde virtually all stands' side: clr over 1f out: drvn out)...— **1**
3072[13] Endless Wave **(57)***(64) (MBell)* 3-8-13 MFenton(2) (a.p: far side: rdn appr fnl f: r.o wl).............2 **2**
3453* Bangles **(70)***(71) (LordHuntingdon)* 5-10-0 WWoods(8) (w ldrs far side: rdn & one pce appr fnl f)..1¾ **3**
2992[9] The Fed **(49)***(50) (RMWhitaker)* 5-8-7v MHills(15) (a.p stands' side: rdn over 1f out: one pce)..s.h **4**
3396[8] Bargash **(65)***(64) (PDEvans)* 3-9-7b GHind(6) (hdwy far side bel dist: nrst fin)..........................¾ **5**
3357[10] Able Sheriff **(46)***(44+) (MWEasterby)* 3-7-11b(5) PFessey(24) (racd stands' side: r.o appr fnl f: nvr nrr)...nk **6**
3051[6] High Domain (IRE) **(64)***(62) (TDBarron)* 4-9-8b KDarley(4) (chsd ldrs far side: no hdwy fnl 2f)..s.h **7**
3554[10] Domicksky **(56)***(53) (MRChannon)* 7-9-0 RHughes(14) (swtg: chsd ldrs stands' side: one pce appr fnl f)...s.h **8**
3467[10] Invigilate **(55)***(50) (MartynWane)* 6-8-13 KFallon(11) (nvr nr ldrs)..¾ **9**
3134[6] Rocky Two **(51)***(45) (PHowling)* 4-8-9b JQuinn(5) (lw: nvr nrr)...nk **10**
3376[4] Moujeeb (USA) **(54)***(46) (PatMitchell)* 5-8-7v(5) DaneO'Neill(16) (dwlt: nvr nrr)........................¾ **11**

2973[3] Hannah's Usher **(66)**_(57) (PCHaslam)_ 3-9-8 MTebbutt(9) (nvr trbld ldrs) ....hd **12**
3442[18] Featherstone Lane **(48)**_(39) (MissLCSiddall)_ 4-8-6v DeanMcKeown(21) (m.n.s) ....hd **13**
3442[12] Jucea **(62)**_(48) (JLSpearing)_ 6-9-6 PaulEddery(23) (m.n.s) 1½ **14**
2680[8] Pursuance (IRE) **(53)**_(36) (JBalding)_ 3-8-2b(7)ow2 JEdmunds(1) (prom far side over 3f) ....½ **15**
3134[7] Miriam **(50)**_(29) (MJFetherston-Godley)_ 4-8-8b PatEddery(10) (led far side over 3f) 1¾ **16**
_3073[7]_ Cool Tactician **(52)**_(25) (RHollinshead)_ 3-8-3 (5) MHenry(19) (m.n.s) 2 **17**
3442* Classic Pet (IRE) **(46)**_(18) (CAHorgan)_ 3-8-2 NAdams(17) (lw: m.n.s) ....nk **18**
3376[2] Robellion **(70)**_(42) (DWPArbuthnot)_ 4-10-0 TQuinn(12) (chsd ldrs stands' side: eased whn btn appr fnl f) ....s.h **19**
3357[4] The Institute Boy **(42)**_(14) (MissJFCraze)_ 5-8-0 JO'Reilly(3) (s.s: a outpcd & bhd) ....s.h **20**
3535[3] Millesime (IRE) **(70)**_(38) (BHanbury)_ 3-9-9 (3) JStack(22) (s.s: a bhd & outpcd) 1 **21**
_2295[11]_ Statomist **(45)**_(13) (RHarris)_ 3-8-1b StephenDavies(13) (swtg: m.n.s) ....hd **22**
3313[8] Daily Starshine (IRE) **(51)**_(14) (JBerry)_ 3-8-7b JCarroll(26) (prom stands' side over 3f: wknd qckly) 1½ **23**
3357[9] Kabcast **(46)**_(8) (DWChapman)_ 10-8-4b LCharnock(25) (swtg: spd 3f) ....nk **24**

7/1 CHADWELL HALL, **11/1** Classic Pet (IRE), Bangles, The Fed, Domicksky, **12/1** Robellion, High Domain (IRE), Invigilate, Moujeeb (USA), Millesime (IRE), **14/1** Miriam, Able Sheriff, Hannah's Usher, **16/1** Daily Starshine (IRE), Jucea, Featherstone Lane, Endless Wave, **20/1** Kabcast, Rocky Two, **25/1** Pursuance (IRE), Cool Tactician, The Institute Boy, **33/1** Bargash, **50/1** Statomist, CSF £122.29 CT £1,178.24 TOTE £9.30: £2.10 £4.60 £2.80 £3.40 (£136.20) Trio £1,718.20 OWNER Mr D. H. Bowring (EDWINSTOWE) BRED J. C. and Mrs C. L. Owen 24 Rn
62.0 secs (3.30) SF: 36/37/46/25/37/17/37/28/25/20/21/30/14/23/9/4/-/-/17/-/11/-/-/-
WEIGHT FOR AGE 3yo-2lb

3623

COLWICK NURSERY H'CAP (0-75) (2-Y.O F) (Class E) £3,931.40 (£1,179.20: £567.60: £261.80)
6f 15y Stalls: High GOING: 0.02 sec per fur (G) 3-30 (3-30)

3432[6] **Antonias Melody (62)**_(66)_(Fav)_(SRBowring)_ 2-8-8 SWebster(8) (mde all far side: clr appr fnl f: readily) ....— **1**
3404[5] Sheilana (IRE) **(72)**_(68) (TGMills)_ 2-9-4 JReid(1) (a.p far side: rdn over 1f out: kpt on) 3 **2**
3423[3] Morning Surprise **(61)**_(57) (APJarvis)_ 2-8-0 (7) CAdamson(2) (a.p far side: rdn & one pce fnl f) ....hd **3**
3314[7] Lunar Mist **(62)**_(54) (MartynMeade)_ 2-8-8 VSlattery(9) (a.p: rdn & hung lft over 1f out: kpt on) 1½ **4**
3379[14] Little Kenny **(58)**_(49) (MJFetherston-Godley)_ 2-8-4 FNorton(6) (bhd & outpcd tl r.o ins fnl f) ....½ **5**
3471[4] Dil Dil **(71)**_(59) (RHannon)_ 2-8-12 (5) DaneO'Neill(7) (chsd ldrs far side over 4f) 1 **6**
3414[7] Gladys Althorpe (IRE) **(72)**_(59) (JLEyre)_ 2-9-4 KFallon(20) (hld up stands' side: rdn & r.o fnl 2f) ....½ **7**
3430[9] Lawn Order **(54)**_(33) (MrsJRRamsden)_ 2-8-0 JFEgan(17) (hdwy stands' side 2f out: hung lft: nvr rchd ldrs) 3 **8**
3568[3] Miss Carottene **(59)**_(34) (MJRyan)_ 2-8-0b(5) MBaird(14) (prom centre: rdn wl over 1f out: sn btn) 1¼ **9**
2847[5] Croeso Cynnes **(66)**_(41) (BPalling)_ 2-8-12 TSprake(11) (w ldrs centre: rdn over 1f out: sn btn) ....nk **10**
2750[5] Victoria Sioux **(57)**_(30) (JWharton)_ 2-8-3 JQuinn(3) (in tch far side 4f) ....¾ **11**
2911[4] Crimson And Clover **(56)**_(25) (RAkehurst)_ 2-7-11 (5) MHenry(10) (a mid div) 1¼ **12**
2855[5] Thorntoun Jewel (IRE) **(60)**_(28) (JBalding)_ 2-8-6 TWilliams(4) (swvd rt s: a bhd) ....½ **13**
_3077[5]_ Peters Folly **(49)**_(12) (JLEyre)_ 2-7-6 (3)ow2 NVarley(22) (led stands' side: no ch fnl 2f) 1¼ **14**
_3528[2]_ Image Maker (IRE) **(53)**_(17) (DWPArbuthnot)_ 2-7-13 WCarson(5) (chsd ldrs far side over 4f) hd **15**
_1758[5]_ Magical Midnight **(56)**_(19) (NTinkler)_ 2-8-2 KimTinkler(18) (m.n.s) ....½ **16**
3417* Mystic Times **(56)**_(15) (MissSEHall)_ 2-8-2 ow1 MRoberts(15) (swtg: outpcd) 1¼ **17**
3378* Lilli Claire **(68)**_(23) (AGFoster)_ 2-9-0 BDoyle(19) (a in rr) 2 **18**
2399[4] Lila Pedigo (IRE) **(60)**_(13) (JBerry)_ 2-8-6 JCarroll(12) (outpcd) ....¾ **19**
3465[10] Wild Humour (IRE) **(70)**_(7) (WRMuir)_ 2-9-2 TIves(13) (lw: a bhd: t.o) 6 **20**
3400* Gagajulu **(78)**_(10) (PDEvans)_ 2-9-10 GHind(21) (swtg: prom stands' side: rdn & outpcd fnl 2f: t.o) 1¾ **21**
3434[4] Doug's Folly **(70)** _(MWEasterby)_ 2-9-2b KDarley(16) (sn drvn along: bhd fr ½-wy: t.o) 1½ **22**
LONG HANDICAP Peters Folly 7-6

5/1 ANTONIAS MELODY, **8/1** Dil Dil, **10/1** Crimson And Clover, Image Maker (IRE), Gagajulu, Miss Carottene, **12/1** Gladys Althorpe (IRE), Lilli Claire, Lawn Order, Croeso Cynnes, Mystic Times, **14/1** Morning Surprise, **16/1** Lunar Mist, Doug's Folly, **20/1** Peters Folly, Wild Humour (IRE), Sheilana (IRE), Thorntoun Jewel (IRE), Lila Pedigo (IRE), Victoria Sioux, **25/1** Little Kenny, **33/1** Magical Midnight, CSF £111.68 CT £1,299.35 TOTE £5.60: £1.90 £4.10 £3.50 £10.60 (£132.10) Trio £412.90 OWNER Mrs B. D. Georgiou (EDWINSTOWE) BRED B. D. Georgiou 22 Rn
1m 15.7 (4.70) SF: 28/30/19/16/11/21/21/-/-/3/-/-/-/-/-/-/-/-/-/-/-/-

3624

BURTON JOYCE H'CAP (0-70) (3-Y.O+ F & M) (Class E) £4,045.80 (£1,214.40: £585.20: £270.60)
6f 15y Stalls: High GOING: 0.02 sec per fur (G) 4-00 (4-02)

3534[2] **It's Academic (61)***(71)*(Fav)*(MrsJRRamsden)* 3-9-2 KFallon(5) (in tch far side: hdwy 2f out: n.m.r 1f out: led wl ins fnl f: r.o wl) .... — **1**
3028[10] Poyle Jezebelle **(49)***(56) (MBlanshard)* 4-8-7 JQuinn(1) (chsd ldrs far side: led ins fnl f: hung st: sn hdd & btn) 1¼ **2**
3072[11] Tael of Silver **(65)***(68) (KRBurke)* 3-9-6 JTate(3) (mde most far side tl hdd ins fnl f) 1½ **3**
3293[9] Beveled Edge **(46)***(42) (BPalling)* 6-8-4 TSprake(6) (w ldrs far side: rdn over 2f out: one pce) 2½ **4**
3359[11] Patsy Grimes **(66)***(61) (LJHolt)* 5-9-10 AMcGlone(9) (racd far side: in tch: kpt on fnl 2f) .... nk **5**
3293[*] Irchester Lass **(40)***(35) (SRBowring)* 3-7-9 NKennedy(10) (racd far side: in tch: one pce appr fnl f) .... nk **6**
3519[7] Prima Silk **(70)***(64) (MJRyan)* 4-10-0 TIves(22) (racd stands' side: styd on fnl 2f: nrst fin) .... nk **7**
3524[9] Arasong **(61)***(48) (EWeymes)* 3-8-13 (3) PMcCabe(7) (hdwy far side over 2f out: no imp) 2½ **8**
3492[5] Miss Aragon **(58)***(45) (MissLCSiddall)* 7-9-2 NCarlisle(4) (chsd ldrs far side over 4f) .... hd **9**
3442[7] Followmegirls **(44)***(30) (MrsALMKing)* 6-8-2 AGarth(12) (racd far side: n.d) .... nk **10**
3492[16] Indiahra **(42)***(27) (RHollinshead)* 4-7-9v(5) MHenry(20) (racd stands' side: a.p: no imp fnl 2f) ... ½ **11**
3453[5] Midnight Break **(64)***(49) (PTWalwyn)* 3-9-5 PatEddery(15) (chsd ldrs stands' side 4f) .... hd **12**
3372[3] Rosa Bonheur **(54)***(38) (MAJarvis)* 3-8-6 (3) NVarley(19) (b.hind: racd stands' side: n.d) .... nk **13**
3467[2] Brookhead Lady **(58)***(39) (PDEvans)* 4-9-2 GHind(16) (racd centre: spd 4f) 1 **14**
3333[4] Lugana Vision **(53)***(33) (RHarris)* 3-8-8b StephenDavies(13) (racd stands' side: n.d) .... ½ **15**
3512[13] Mixed Mood **(48)***(21) (BJLlewellyn)* 3-7-10b(7)ow4 JWilkinson(14) (racd centre: n.d) 1 **16**
3497[11] Sylvandra **(68)***(42) (PGMurphy)* 3-9-9 JWilliams(24) (racd stands' side: n.d) 1¼ **17**
3359[17] Rambold **(59)***(30) (NEBerry)* 4-9-3 RPerham(21) (cl up stands' side 4f) 1¼ **18**
1883[13] Noor El Houdah (IRE) **(59)***(28) (JBerry)* 3-9-0 JCarroll(25) (chsd ldrs stands' side 4f) .... ¾ **19**
3534[11] Cavatina **(65)***(26) (TWDonnelly)* 5-9-9b CRutter(23) (racd stands' side: bhd fr ½-wy) 3 **20**
1414[11] Hi Rock **(55)***(11) (MJCamacho)* 3-8-10 LCharnock(18) (racd stands' side: n.d) 1¾ **21**
Macaroon Lady **(40)** *(NBycroft)* 4-7-12 TWilliams(11) (racd far side: n.d) 6 **22**
2609[8] Twice in Bundoran (IRE) **(52)** *(PSFelgate)* 4-8-7 (3) DWright(8) (racd far side: outpcd fr ½-wy) .... ½ **23**
3179[2] Charnwood Queen **(59)** *(RWArmstrong)* 3-9-0 WCarson(26) (led stands' side 4f: wknd) 1½ **24**

4/1 IT'S ACADEMIC (op 8/1), **5/1** Charnwood Queen, **8/1** Miss Aragon, Patsy Grimes, **9/1** Irchester Lass, **10/1** Brookhead Lady, **12/1** Midnight Break, **16/1** Sylvandra, Tael of Silver, Followmegirls, Indiahra, **20/1** Poyle Jezebelle, Rosa Bonheur, Arasong, Lugana Vision, Mixed Mood, Prima Silk, Rambold, Hi Rock, Beveled Edge, **25/1** Noor El Houdah (IRE), Twice in Bundoran (IRE), **33/1** Cavatina, **50/1** Macaroon Lady, CSF £95.52 CT £1,188.50 TOTE £6.10: £1.80 £6.50 £6.30 £9.50 (£83.80) Trio £244.90 OWNER Mr J. R. Chester (THIRSK) BRED W. H. F. Carson 24 Rn
1m 14.6 (3.60) SF: 51/39/48/25/44/15/47/28/28/13/10/29/18/22/13/1/22/13/8/9/-/-/-/-
WEIGHT FOR AGE 3yo-3lb

3625

LEVY BOARD MAIDEN STKS (I) (2-Y.O) (Class D) £4,240.00 (£1,270.00: £610.00: £280.00) **6f 15y** Stalls: High GOING: 0.02 sec per fur (G) 4-30 (4-32)

3364[4] **Ocean Grove (IRE)** *(79) (PWChapple-Hyam)* 2-8-9 JReid(6) (mde most: r.o wl appr fnl f) .... — **1**
3525[4] Quality (IRE) *(80) (WAO'Gorman)* 2-9-0 EmmaO'Gorman(5) (chsd ldrs: hdwy 2f out: kpt on fnl f) 1½ **2**
Carburton *(80+)*(Fav)*(JAGlover)* 2-9-0 PaulEddery(8) (gd sort: bit bkwd: a chsng ldrs: rdn 2f out: styd on wl towards fin) .... hd **3**
Eastern Paradise *(69+) (MRStoute)* 2-9-0 WRSwinburn(9) (lt-f: in tch: effrt & hung lft over 1f out: nt qckn) 4 **4**
Thordis *(68) (PJMakin)* 2-9-0 KDarley(2) (lt-f: unf: bkwd: in tch: styd on wl fnl f) .... ½ **5**
3397[4] Time of Night (USA) *(58) (RGuest)* 2-8-9 JCarroll(17) (prom over 4f) 2 **6**
3405[6] Galapino **(85)***(62) (CEBrittain)* 2-9-0 BDoyle(1) (disp ld 4f: grad wknd) .... nk **7**
Shady Girl (IRE) *(52) (BWHills)* 2-8-9 PatEddery(16) (w'like: scope: in tch: eased whn btn ins fnl f) 2 **8**
Le Teteu (FR) *(55) (BobJones)* 2-9-0 MWigham(4) (leggy: unf: nvr plcd to chal) .... ½ **9**
3157[8] Classic Artiste (USA) *(48) (SCWilliams)* 2-8-9 AMackay(12) (chsd ldrs tl grad wknd fnl 2f) 1 **10**
3441[6] Righteous Gent *(48) (KMcAuliffe)* 2-9-0 JTate(21) (racd alone stands' side: no ch fnl 2f) 1¾ **11**
2025[10] Primelta *(40) (RAkehurst)* 2-8-9 TQuinn(11) (in tch tl wknd fnl 2f) 1¼ **12**
Princely Affair *(43) (MBell)* 2-9-0 MFenton(7) (w'like: scope: bkwd: nvr trbld ldrs) .... ½ **13**
3353[10] Go-Go-Power-Ranger *(43) (BEllison)* 2-9-0 NKennedy(14) (n.d) .... nk **14**
3379[21] Quiet Moments (IRE) *(41) (PGMurphy)* 2-8-7 (7) RWaterfield(19) (n.d) .... ¾ **15**
3558[6] Top of The Stack *(35) (RHannon)* 2-8-9 (5) DaneO'Neill(13) (nvr trbld ldrs) 2 **16**
Gilling Dancer (IRE) *(34) (PCalver)* 2-9-0 MBirch(20) (w'like: leggy: bkwd: s.i.s: a bhd) .... ½ **17**

Known Secret (USA) *(31) (MrsJRRamsden)* 2-9-0 KFallon(15) (str: bkwd: shkn up ½-wy: n.d) 1¼ **18**
3012[6] Toe Tappin Music (USA) *(18) (MartynMeade)* 2-9-0 VSlattery(10) (spd 4f: wknd qckly) 5 **19**
Mutahassin (USA) *(12) (RWArmstrong)* 2-9-0 WCarson(18) (small: cmpt: bkwd: bhd & rdn ½-wy: n.d) 2 **20**

15/8 Carburton, **11/4** OCEAN GROVE (IRE) (op 7/4), **13/2** Galapino, **8/1** Mutahassin (USA) (op 4/1), Shady Girl (IRE) (op 4/1), **9/1** Quality (IRE), **10/1** Eastern Paradise (op 5/1), Known Secret (USA) (op 5/1), **12/1** Princely Affair (op 7/1), **14/1** Top of The Stack, Time of Night (USA), Classic Artiste (USA) (op 7/1), Primelta (op 8/1), **16/1** Thordis, **20/1** Gilling Dancer (IRE), Le Teteu (FR), **33/1** Go-Go-Power-Ranger, **50/1** Righteous Gent, Toe Tappin Music (USA), Quiet Moments (IRE), CSF £39.78 TOTE £4.50: £1.70 £2.90 £1.50 (£21.20) Trio £41.30 OWNER Mr R.E.Sangster (MARLBOROUGH) BRED Swettenham Stud 20 Rn
1m 15.6 (4.60) SF: 31/32/32/21/20/10/14/4/7/-/-/-/-/-/-/-/-/-/-/-

3626 LEVY BOARD MAIDEN STKS (II) (2-Y.O) (Class D) £4,207.50 (£1,260.00: £605.00: £277.50) 6f 15y Stalls: High GOING: 0.02 sec per fur (G) 5-00 (5-01)

3069[8] **Keepers Dawn (IRE)** *(80) (RFJohnsonHoughton)* 2-8-9 JReid(10) (a.p: rdn to ld ins fnl f: r.o wl) ....— **1**
2615[6] Wee Hope (USA) *(77)(Fav)(MRStoute)* 2-9-0 WRSwinburn(9) (mde most tl hdd ins fnl f: kpt on) 3 **2**
Papaha (FR) *(72+) (HRACecil)* 2-8-9 WRyan(5) (small: lt-f: b.nr fore: in tch: hdwy 2f out: styd on wl fnl f) ....hd **3**
2487[4] Maristax *(59) (PJMakin)* 2-8-9 MRoberts(2) (in tch: styd on fnl 2f: nvr able chal) 5 **4**
3456[4] Ocean Stream (IRE) *(64) (JLEyre)* 2-9-0 KDarley(6) (bhd tl styd on wl fnl 2f) ....s.h **5**
3436[6] Lay The Blame *(60) (WJarvis)* 2-9-0 TQuinn(12) (w ldrs over 4f: grad wknd) 1¼ **6**
Agent *(56+) (WJHaggas)* 2-9-0 MHills(13) (w'like: leggy: hmpd ½-wy: sme late hdwy) 1½ **7**
Magic Melody *(51) (JLSpearing)* 2-8-6 (3) SDrowne(1) (leggy: lt-f: chsd ldrs tl wknd fnl 2f) ....nk **8**
3499[4] Abundant *(55) (BGubby)* 2-9-0b RHughes(19) (swtchd lft after s: n.m.r ½-wy: n.d) ....nk **9**
Smarter Charter *(51+) (MrsJRRamsden)* 2-9-0 KFallon(11) (leggy: scope: dwlt: bhd & swtchd lft ½-wy: stdy late hdwy) 1½ **10**
3022[5] Holloway Melody *(44) (BAMcMahon)* 2-8-9 GCarter(8) (wnt lft ½-wy: n.d after) ....½ **11**
3509[2] Forest Boy *(46) (KMcAuliffe)* 2-9-0 JCarroll(18) (n.d) 1¼ **12**
Ashik (IRE) *(44) (PTWalwyn)* 2-9-0 WCarson(14) (w'like: bkwd: prom 4f: eased whn btn) ....¾ **13**
3436[10] Skram *(43) (RDickin)* 2-9-0 PRobinson(3) (plld hrd: wandered bdly over 2f out: n.d) ....½ **14**
Chalice *(34) (JBalding)* 2-8-9 JWilliams(20) (w'like: bit bkwd: n.d) 1½ **15**
3523[7] Maiteamia *(35) (SRBowring)* 2-8-9b(5) CTeague(4) (hung lft after 2f: n.d) 1½ **16**
3465[14] Kiwud **(58)***(27) (GMMoore)* 2-8-9 GHind(16) (n.d) 1 **17**
Smiling Bess *(24) (KRBurke)* 2-8-9 JTate(7) (lt-f: bit bkwd: cl up 4f: wknd) 1¼ **18**
2970[5] Redbrook Lady *(SGNorton)* 2-8-9 StephenDavies(17) (bolted gng to s: spd 2½f: sn bhd: t.o) 25 **19**

7/4 Wee Hope (USA), **5/2** Papaha (FR) (Evens-7/2), **4/1** Abundant, **8/1** Maristax (op 5/1), **10/1** Ashik (IRE) (op 6/1), **12/1** Lay The Blame (op 6/1), Forest Boy, Ocean Stream (IRE) (op 8/1), **14/1** Smarter Charter (op 7/1), **16/1** KEEPERS DAWN (IRE), Agent, **20/1** Smiling Bess, Chalice, **25/1** Holloway Melody, **33/1** Skram, Maiteamia, Kiwud, Magic Melody, Redbrook Lady, CSF £55.73 TOTE £35.60: £6.60 £1.60 £1.80 (£45.10) Trio £57.00 OWNER Mr Bob Lanigan (DIDCOT) BRED Tullamaine Castle Stud 19 Rn 1m 15.1 (4.10) SF: 37/34/29/16/21/17/13/8/12/8/1/6/4/2/-/-/-/-/-

3627 CARLTON H'CAP (0-70) (3-Y.O+) (Class E) £4,017.20 (£1,205.60: £580.80: £268.40) 2m 9y Stalls: Low GOING minus 0.14 sec per fur (G) 5-30 (5-31)

3245[3] **En Vacances (IRE) (61)***(76) (AGFoster)* 3-9-0 TSprake(1) (trckd ldrs: led 1½f out: r.o wl) ....— **1**
3435[10] Amiarge **(32)***(46) (MBrittain)* 5-7-9 (3) DWright(16) (hld up: stdy hdwy over 3f out: disp ld over 1f out: rdn & nt qckn) 1¼ **2**
3202[2] Rose of Glenn **(47)***(57) (BPalling)* 4-8-10 (3) SSanders(8) (a in tch: kpt on u.p fnl 2f: nt pce to chal) 4 **3**
2854[4] Kilernan **(42)***(51) (TDBarron)* 4-8-8 DeanMcKeown(10) (led tl hdd 1½f out: one pce) 1¼ **4**
3140[4] Carnbrea Belle (IRE) **(67)***(75) (MBell)* 3-9-6 MFenton(17) (lw: styd on fnl 4f: nvr able chal) ....½ **5**
3435[2] Inn At the Top **(57)***(65) (JNorton)* 3-8-10 DaleGibson(9) (cl up tl grad wknd fnl 2½f) ....s.h **6**
2834[3] Hong Kong Designer **(50)***(57) (SGNorton)* 3-8-3 TWilliams(20) (plld hrd: cl up: chal 3f out: wknd fnl 2f) ....¾ **7**
3435[5] Romalito **(39)***(46) (MBlanshard)* 5-8-5 KFallon(3) (lw: outpcd & bhd tl styd on fnl 2f) ....s.h **8**
3217[6] Tommy Cooper **(43)***(50) (MrsBarbaraWaring)* 4-8-6 (3) SDrowne(12) (b.hind: chsd ldrs: effrt over 3f out: grad wknd) ....nk **9**
3470[5] Silver Hunter (USA) **(56)***(62) (GCBravery)* 4-9-8v MHills(6) (a chsng ldrs: nt clr run 2½f out: one pce after) ....½ **10**

3263* Bellara **(53)**_(52) (NMBabbage)_ 3-8-6 JQuinn(19) (effrt appr st: nvr trbld ldrs)..........7 **11**
3435[4] Jalcanto **(58)**_(57)_(Fav)_(MrsMReveley)_ 5-9-10 KDarley(15) (lw: dwlt: hdwy ½-wy: hung lft & wknd fnl 2½f)..........½ **12**
3521[7] Chanson D'Avril **(41)**_(39) (DAWilson)_ 4-8-7 JWilliams(5) (n.d)..........1 **13**
Full Quiver **(46)**_(43) (MrsBarbaraWaring)_ 10-8-12v NAdams(4) (b: a bhd)..........½ **14**
3435[9] Nahri (USA) **(44)**_(37) (JMackie)_ 4-8-10 GCarter(11) (lw: chsd ldrs tl outpcd 4f out: sn btn)..........4 **15**
3140[6] Vanola **(40)**_(28) (PHowling)_ 3-7-7 NCarlisle(13) (a bhd)..........5 **16**
3262[4] Kanat Lee (IRE) **(32)**_(18) (DonEnricoIncisa)_ 4-7-12 KimTinkler(2) (a bhd)..........2 **17**
2990[5] Charmed Life **(36)**_(19) (MrsALMKing)_ 6-8-2 AGarth(18) (a bhd)..........3 **18**
_259_[11] Jolis Absent **(50)**_(31) (MJRyan)_ 5-9-2 GBardwell(7) (bit bkwd: bhd fr ½-wy)..........2 **19**
Parks Pride **(30)** _(MrsLAMurphy)_ 4-7-7 (3) NVarley(14) (a bhd: t.o)..........30 **20**

LONG HANDICAP Vanola 7-4

5/1 Jalcanto, **6/1** Bellara, **7/1** Inn At the Top, **8/1** Kileman, **10/1** Carnbrea Belle (IRE), Silver Hunter (USA), **12/1** Rose of Glenn (op 8/1), Amiarge, Tommy Cooper, EN VACANCES (IRE), Nahri (USA), **14/1** Romalito, Hong Kong Designer, **20/1** Chanson D'Avril, Full Quiver, Jolis Absent, **25/1** Kanat Lee (IRE), Charmed Life, **50/1** Vanola, Parks Pride, CSF £158.12 CT £1,661.15 TOTE £20.10: £4.70 £2.80 £3.70 £3.30 (£241.50) Trio £363.50 OWNER Lambourn Valley Racing (LAMBOURN) BRED The Woodhaven Stud 20 Rn

3m 33.0 (8.60) SF: 45/28/39/33/44/34/26/28/32/44/21/39/21/25/19/-/-/1/13/-

WEIGHT FOR AGE 3yo-13lb

T/Jkpt: £7,100.00 (0.5 Tckts); £3,528.27 to Sandown 12/9/95. T/Plpt: £416.00 (48.84 Tckts). T/Qdpt: £51.10 (1.2 Tckts). IM/AA

3436-SANDOWN (R-H)

Tuesday September 12th (Rnd Good to Soft, St Good, Good to soft patches)

Race 5 hand-timed

WEATHER: sunny spells WIND: almost nil

3628

'AHEAD OF THE FIELD' MAIDEN AUCTION STKS (2-Y.O) (Class D)
£3,696.25 (£1,120.00: £547.50: £261.25)
5f 6y Stalls: High GOING minus 0.22 sec per fur (GF) 2-15 (2-21)

3430[3] **Air Wing** _(88?) (MHTompkins)_ 2-8-0 PRobinson(19) (lw: mde all: rdn out)..........— **1**
Music Gold (IRE) _(85?) (WAO'Gorman)_ 2-8-10 EmmaO'Gorman(18) (w'like: bit bkwd: s.s: hdwy 3f out: chsd wnr over 1f out: unable qckn)..........4 **2**
2740[W] Village Native (FR) _(70) (KOCunningham-Brown)_ 2-8-6b RCochrane(12) (chsd wnr over 3f out tl over 1f out: one pce)..........3½ **3**
3379[9] Daffodil Express (IRE) _(48) (MJRyan)_ 2-7-4 (5) MBaird(15) (lost pl 3f out: one pce fnl 2f)..........3½ **4**
3025[10] Longhill Boy _(59) (BJMeehan)_ 2-8-6 BDoyle(20) (a.p: hrd rdn over 1f out: sn wknd)..........hd **5**
2791[2] Second Time Lucky (IRE) _(48)_(Fav)_(LordHuntingdon)_ 2-8-6 LDettori(14) (bmpd s: nvr nr to chal)..........3½ **6**
Divina Luna _(43) (JWHills)_ 2-8-5 DHolland(10) (unf: bit bkwd: s.s: outpcd: nvr nrr)..........1¼ **7**
3471[3] Rowlandsons Charm (IRE) **(65)**_(30) (GLMoore)_ 2-7-4 (7)ow2 CAdamson(17) (nvr nr to chal)..........¾ **8**
3260[3] Impington (IRE) _(31) (MAJarvis)_ 2-8-2 ow1 MRoberts(7) (a mid div)..........1¾ **9**
3379[15] Eskimo Kiss (IRE) _(29) (MJFetherston-Godley)_ 2-8-1 DaleGibson(16) (nvr nrr)..........½ **10**
2508[2] Sweet Nature (IRE) _(27) (WJarvis)_ 2-8-5 BThomson(1) (racd centre: outpcd)..........2 **11**
2970[2] Baroness Blixen _(21) (DJGMurraySmith)_ 2-7-10 (5) MHenry(13) (a mid div)..........½ **12**
2666[4] Wrays (USA) _(15) (MJohnston)_ 2-7-12 TWilliams(8) (outpcd)..........1 **13**
3025[8] Efficacious (IRE) **(60)**_(17) (CJBenstead)_ 2-8-1 JLowe(9) (lw: a bhd)..........nk **14**
3379[16] Absolutelystunning _(1) (MrsBarbaraWaring)_ 2-8-1 JFEgan(4) (racd centre: a bhd)..........5 **15**
3520[4] Simply Miss Chief (IRE) _(DWPArbuthnot)_ 2-7-12 AMackay(11) (prom 3f)..........1¾ **16**
3110[4] My Millie _(RBoss)_ 2-8-1 WCarson(5) (racd centre: a bhd)..........3 **17**
3379[23] Soul Risk _(JARToller)_ 2-8-3 (3) SSanders(6) (lw: racd centre: outpcd)..........4 **18**
Magical Mill _(RGuest)_ 2-7-12 FNorton(3) (unf: racd centre: a bhd)..........1½ **19**
Prosarch (IRE) _(RFJohnsonHoughton)_ 2-8-3 ow2 AClark(2) (str: bit bkwd: racd centre: a bhd)..........8 **20**

3/1 Second Time Lucky (IRE), **5/1** Rowlandsons Charm (IRE), **11/2** AIR WING, **10/1** Baroness Blixen, Village Native (FR) (op 6/1), Sweet Nature (IRE) (7/1-11/1), **11/1** Wrays (USA) (7/1-12/1), **12/1** My Millie (8/1-14/1), **16/1** Impington (IRE), Prosarch (IRE), **20/1** Simply Miss Chief (IRE), Daffodil Express (IRE), Music Gold (IRE), Magical Mill, Divina Luna, **33/1** Eskimo Kiss (IRE), **50/1** Longhill Boy, Soul Risk, Efficacious (IRE), Absolutelystunning, CSF £114.50 TOTE £5.00: £1.90 £13.80 £2.70 (£63.80) Trio £122.90 OWNER P H Betts (Holdings) Ltd (NEWMARKET) BRED Miss J. Curtis 20 Rn

62.0 secs (2.20) SF: 30/27/12/-/1/-/-/-/-/-/-/-/-/-/-/-/-/-/-/-

3629 WEATHERBYS 'NEWCOMERS' SERIES H'CAP (0-80) (3-Y.O+) (Class D)

£4,474.50 (£1,356.00: £663.00: £316.50)
7f 16y Stalls: High GOING: 0.13 sec per fur (G) 2-50 (2-56)

3043a7 **Comanche Companion (68)**(84)(Fav)(TJNaughton) 5-9-2 PatEddery(16) (3rd st: n.m.r & swtchd lft 2f out: led over 1f out: r.o wl) — **1**
3493* Gymcrak Flyer **(62)**(69) (GHolmes) 4-8-10 LDettori(15) (b.hind: 6th st: led over 2f out tl over 1f out: unable qckn) 4 **2**
3605 17 Duello **(55)**(59) (MBlanshard) 4-8-3 MRoberts(14) (lw: rdn & hdwy over 2f out: r.o one pce) 1¼ **3**
34392 Dancing Lawyer **(69)**(69) (BJMeehan) 4-9-3 BDoyle(4) (5th st: ev ch over 1f out: sn wknd) 1¾ **4**
31597 Soaking **(62)**(58) (PBurgoyne) 5-8-10 MWigham(7) (hdwy over 2f out: rdn over 1f out: one pce) 1¾ **5**
3534 19 Great Hall **(60)**(56) (PDCundell) 6-8-1b(7) MartinDwyer(5) (s.s: hdwy over 1f out: nvr nrr) nk **6**
30115 Helios **(72)**(63) (NJHWalker) 7-9-6 RCochrane(6) (hdwy over 2f out: wknd over 1f out) 2 **7**
3545 14 Cameron Highland (IRE) **(80)**(65) (PFICole) 4-9-9 (5) AWhelan(1) (lw: nvr nrr) 2½ **8**
3439 14 Milos **(62)**(47) (TJNaughton) 4-8-5 (5) JDSmith(8) (b.nr hind: lw: a bhd) nk **9**
34513 Winsome Wooster **(64)**(43) (PGMurphy) 4-8-12 MFenton(11) (4th st: wknd over 1f out) 2½ **10**
1131 12 Fawj (USA) **(80)**(58) (RWArmstrong) 3-9-10 WCarson(9) (plld hrd: stdy hdwy 2f out: eased whn btn over 1f out) ½ **11**
35658 Queenbird **(73)**(48) (MJRyan) 4-9-7 AClark(2) (a bhd) 1½ **12**
34574 Napoleon Star (IRE) **(69)**(41) (MSSaunders) 4-9-3 NAdams(12) (2nd st: wknd over 2f out) 1¼ **13**
10659 Lidhama (USA) **(62)**(22) (GLewis) 3-8-6 SWhitworth(13) (bit bkwd: a bhd) 5 **14**
*3529*16 Bon Secret (IRE) **(60)**(19) (TJNaughton) 3-8-1 (3) SSanders(3) (lw: a bhd) ½ **15**
*3510*12 Aljaz **(65)**(16) (RHarris) 5-8-13 AMackay(10) (led over 4f) 3½ **16**

9/2 COMANCHE COMPANION, **5/1** Dancing Lawyer, **6/1** Gymcrak Flyer, **15/2** Napoleon Star (IRE), **8/1** Duello, **10/1** Queenbird, Lidhama (USA) (8/1-12/1), **12/1** Fawj (USA), **14/1** Winsome Wooster, **16/1** Soaking, Great Hall, Helios, **20/1** Cameron Highland (IRE), Bon Secret (IRE), Aljaz, **33/1** Milos, CSF £33.78 CT £207.80 TOTE £4.70: £1.40 £1.30 £1.60 £2.00 (£7.60) Trio £35.50 OWNER The Allstars Club (EPSOM) BRED The National Stud 16 Rn
1m 32.31 (5.71) SF: 45/30/20/30/19/17/24/26/8/4/15/9/2/-/-/-
WEIGHT FOR AGE 3yo-4lb

3630 WOODCHESTER CREDIT LYONNAIS H'CAP (0-95) (3-Y.O F) (Class C)

£5,654.00 (£1,712.00: £836.00: £398.00)
1m 14y Stalls: High GOING: 0.13 sec per fur (G) 3-25 (3-28)

34194 **Donna Viola (83)**(97) (CFWall) 3-9-2 (5) LNewton(10) (lw: hrd rdn & hdwy 2f out: led 1f out: r.o wl) — **1**
32045 La Gran Senorita (USA) **(74)**(84) (PFICole) 3-8-9 (3) SSanders(2) (b.hind: 5th st: led wl over 1f out to 1f out: unable qckn) 2 **2**
17703 Rosy Hue (IRE) **(72)**(81) (RCharlton) 3-8-10 PatEddery(8) (bit bkwd: led 1f: 2nd st: ev ch 1f out: one pce) ½ **3**
33889 Ron's Secret **(75)**(83) (JWPayne) 3-8-13 RCochrane(7) (4th st: rdn over 2f out: nt clr run on ins ins fnl f: one pce) nk **4**
3559* Dorothea Brooke (IRE) **(75)**(74)(Fav)(PWHarris) 3-8-13 5x GHind(1) (led 7f out tl wl over 1f out: 3rd & wkng whn bmpd over 1f out) 5 **5**
34085 Hujjab (USA) **(79)**(70) (JLDunlop) 3-9-3b WCarson(6) (rdn over 3f out: nvr nrr) 4 **6**
32378 Bring on the Choir **(79)**(66) (RBoss) 3-9-3 DHolland(12) (6th st: wknd over 2f out) 1¾ **7**
3383* Aldaneh **(74)**(61) (RHannon) 3-8-12 LDettori(3) (lw: nvr nrr) s.h **8**
1617 10 Brave Princess **(68)**(50) (MAJarvis) 3-8-6 PRobinson(11) (a bhd) 2½ **9**
32143 Pennycairn **(81)**(61) (HRACecil) 3-9-5 WRyan(4) (3rd st: rdn over 2f out: eased whn btn over 1f out) 1¼ **10**
902a6 Queen's Ransom (IRE) **(79)**(49) (PWChapple-Hyam) 3-8-12 (5) RHavlin(5) (swtg: a bhd) 5 **11**
30314 Cap And Gown (IRE) **(78)** (PFICole) 3-8-11 (5) AWhelan(9) (a bhd: t.o) dist **12**

100/30 Dorothea Brooke (IRE), **4/1** Pennycairn, **6/1** Rosy Hue (IRE), **15/2** Aldaneh, **10/1** DONNA VIOLA, Bring on the Choir, **11/1** Ron's Secret, **12/1** Hujjab (USA), Cap And Gown (IRE), **14/1** La Gran Senorita (USA), **16/1** Queen's Ransom (IRE), Brave Princess, CSF £133.33 CT £844.90 TOTE £14.70: £3.50 £3.50 £2.80 (£84.80) Trio £449.30 OWNER Mr Kieran Scott (NEWMARKET) BRED Lady Juliet de Chair 12 Rn 1m 45.51 (6.31) SF: 52/39/36/38/29/25/21/16/5/16/4/-

3631 ZANUSSI FUTURITY CONDITIONS STKS (2-Y.O) (Class C) £4,808.80 (£1,799.20: £879.60: £378.00) **1m 14y** Stalls: High GOING: 0.13 sec per fur (G) 4-00 (4-02)

31585 **Inchrory (100)**(83) (HRACecil) 2-9-1 PatEddery(8) (lw: mde virtually all: pushed out) — **1**

3340* Even Top (IRE) *(80)*(Fav)*(MHTompkins)* 2-9-1 PRobinson(4) (chsd wnr 5f out: hrd rdn & ev ch 1f out: unable qckn) 1¾ **2**
3437³ Diego *(70) (CEBrittain)* 2-8-11 BDoyle(6) (3rd st: rdn over 2f out: one pce) 3 **3**
3437* Night Watch (USA) **(92)***(70) (IABalding)* 2-9-1 LDettori(2) (lw: 4th st: rdn over 2f out: one pce) 1¾ **4**
3437⁵ Zaforum *(50) (LMontagueHall)* 2-8-11 BThomson(5) (6th st: wknd over 2f out) 8 **5**
3136* Expensive Taste *(29) (MRStoute)* 2-8-10 WRSwinburn(3) (s.s: bmpd over 3f out: sme hdwy over 2f out: eased whn btn over 1f out) 10 **6**
760* High Hope Henry (USA) *(29) (PFICole)* 2-9-1 WCarson(7) (lw: 5th st: wknd over 3f out) 2½ **7**
3437⁷ Hencarlam (IRE) *(MRChannon)* 2-8-11 RHughes(1) (a bhd) 30 **8**

2/1 Even Top (IRE), **9/4** Night Watch (USA), **5/1** Expensive Taste (3/1-11/2), **6/1** INCHRORY, **7/1** High Hope Henry (USA) (5/1-8/1), **25/1** Diego, **33/1** Zaforum, Hencarlam (IRE), CSF £17.94 TOTE £8.60: £1.70 £1.30 £3.60 (£23.40) OWNER Sir David Wills (NEWMARKET) BRED Sir David Wills 8 Rn
1m 45.64 (6.44) SF: 45/42/32/32/12/-/-/-

3632 WILLOW CLAIMING STKS (3-Y.O+) (Class E) £3,615.00 (£1,095.00: £535.00: £255.00) 5f 6y Stalls: High GOING minus 0.22 sec per fur (GF) 4-30 (4-40)

*3522** **Spaniards Close (90)***(76)*(Fav)*(PJMakin)* 7-8-11 LDettori(13) (a.p: rdn over 1f out: led ins fnl f: r.o wl) ....— **1**
3407⁵ Halbert **(60)***(65) (MRChannon)* 6-7-11v(7) DSweeney(6) (led tl ins fnl f: unable qckn) 1¼ **2**
3519⁴ John O'Dreams **(47)***(65) (MrsALMKing)* 10-8-5 AGarth(11) (b: s.s: rdn over 2f out: hdwy over 1f out: r.o) ....nk **3**
Soldier Cove (USA) *(70) (MartynMeade)* 5-8-11 VSlattery(14) (a.p: rdn over 1f out: one pce) ....nk **4**
1615⁷ Barranak (IRE) *(72) (MrsMMcCourt)* 3-9-0 BThomson(10) (hdwy over 1f out: r.o) 1 **5**
3551²¹ Lord High Admiral (CAN) **(93)***(70) (CREgerton)* 7-9-1b MRoberts(5) (plld hrd: a.p: ev ch over 1f out: eased whn btn ins fnl f) ....nk **6**
3522² King Rambo **(64)***(53) (RHollinshead)* 4-8-4 WRyan(12) (hld up: rdn over 1f out: one pce) 2 **7**
3554³ Pearl Dawn (IRE) **(68)***(51) (GLMoore)* 5-8-2 JFEgan(1) (nvr nrr) ....s.h **8**
3551¹⁸ Inherent Magic (IRE) **(92)***(50) (WRMuir)* 6-8-11 PatEddery(9) (b: lw: no ch fnl 2f) 3 **9**
3439¹⁶ Rocky Waters (USA) **(62)***(46) (PBurgoyne)* 6-8-9 MWigham(7) (b.hind: a bhd) ....¾ **10**
3268⁵ Blurred Image (IRE) **(71)***(44) (MissGayKelleway)* 4-9-0 (3) SSanders(2) (swtg: a bhd) 3 **11**
3424⁹ Thehillsarealive (IRE) **(55)***(28) (DRCElsworth)* 3-8-7 WNewnes(3) (s.s: a bhd) 2½ **12**
Roxanian (IRE) **(70)***(19) (MJohnston)* 4-8-6 DHolland(4) (prom 3f) 1¾ **13**
*3177** Norling (IRE) **(53)** *(KOCunningham-Brown)* 5-8-7 RCochrane(8) (Withdrawn not under Starter's orders: Veterinary advice) .... **W**

6/4 SPANIARDS CLOSE, **7/2** Inherent Magic (IRE), **9/2** Lord High Admiral (CAN) (5/2-5/1), **9/1** King Rambo, **12/1** Pearl Dawn (IRE) (8/1-14/1), **20/1** Halbert, Roxanian (IRE), **25/1** Blurred Image (IRE), **33/1** Barranak (IRE), John O'Dreams, Soldier Cove (USA), Norling (IRE), **50/1** Thehillsarealive (IRE), Rocky Waters (USA), CSF £30.85 TOTE £2.80: £1.50 £3.40 £3.80 (£40.00) Trio £219.10 OWNER Avon Industries Ltd (MARLBOROUGH) BRED Avon Industries Bath Ltd 13 Rn
60.9 secs (1.10) SF: 58/47/47/52/52/52/35/33/32/28/26/8/1/-
WEIGHT FOR AGE 3yo-2lb

3633 E.B.F. WEY MAIDEN STKS (2-Y.O F) (Class D) £4,065.00 (£1,230.00: £600.00: £285.00) 1m 14y Stalls: High GOING: 0.13 sec per fur (G) 5-00 (5-10)

3364³ **Scarlet Plume** *(90?) (JLDunlop)* 2-8-11 WCarson(4) (lw: mde all: pushed out) ....— **1**
3339⁶ Inchyre *(86)*(Fav)*(RCharlton)* 2-8-11 PatEddery(6) (4th st: chsd wnr over 2f out: rdn: unable qckn) 2 **2**
3010⁹ Veiled Dancer (IRE) *(74) (JLDunlop)* 2-8-11 MRoberts(1) (lw: 2nd st: rdn over 2f out: one pce) 6 **3**
Classic Ballet (FR) *(73) (SCWilliams)* 2-8-11 AMackay(2) (w'like: bit bkwd: 5th st: hdwy over 2f out: one pce) ....½ **4**
2705⁵ Eccola *(65) (IABalding)* 2-8-11 LDettori(3) (lw: 3rd st: wknd 3f out) 4 **5**
3397⁵ Threesocks *(62) (BSmart)* 2-8-11 RPerham(8) (lw: 6th st: a bhd) 1¾ **6**
3474⁴ Mischief Star *(59) (DRCElsworth)* 2-8-11 RHughes(7) (bhd fnl 6f) 1½ **7**
Beverly Hills *(JWHills)* 2-8-11 DHolland(5) (Withdrawn not under Starter's orders: ref to ent stalls) .... **W**

8/13 Inchyre, **5/2** SCARLET PLUME, **12/1** Eccola (op 8/1), **20/1** Classic Ballet (FR), **25/1** Beverly Hills, **33/1** Threesocks, Mischief Star, Veiled Dancer (IRE), CSF £4.14 TOTE £3.00: £1.80 £1.50 (£1.50) OWNER Mrs Nigel Elwes (ARUNDEL) BRED Exors of the late Sir Robin McAlpine 7 Rn
1m 46.47 (7.27) SF: 33/29/17/16/8/5/2/-

3634

SURREY RACING H'CAP (0-70) (3-Y.O) (Class E) £3,468.75 (£1,050.00: £512.50: £243.75) **1m 3f 91y** Stalls: High GOING: 0.13 sec per fur (G) 5-35 (5-43)

2919[7] **Leading Spirit (IRE) (60)***(72) (CFWall)* 3-9-1 PatEddery(7) (lw: mde all: clr over 2f out: r.o wl) — **1**
3363[5] Tonka **(59)***(66) (PJMakin)* 3-8-11 (3) SSanders(8) (hdwy 3f out: chsd wnr over 2f out: unable qckn) 3½ **2**
2026[9] George Bull **(65)***(71) (MajorWRHern)* 3-9-6 WRyan(6) (lw: 6th st: nt clr run on ins over 3f out tl over 2f out: swtchd lft: r.o one pce) 1 **3**
2969[2] Paradise Waters **(62)***(63) (RFJohnsonHoughton)* 3-9-3 BThomson(1) (2nd st: rdn over 2f out: wknd wl over 1f out) 3½ **4**
3320[5] Marchant Ming (IRE) **(60)***(60) (MAJarvis)* 3-9-1b PRobinson(11) (hdwy over 1f out: nvr nrr) nk **5**
3440[10] Cuba **(65)***(61) (MRStoute)* 3-9-6 WRSwinburn(3) (lw: 3rd st: hrd rdn over 3f out: eased whn btn over 1f out) 3 **6**
1498[4] Battleship Bruce **(64)***(53)*(Fav)*(NACallaghan)* 3-9-5 MRoberts(5) (b.hind: lw: rdn over 3f out: sme hdwy over 2f out: sn wknd) 5 **7**
3501[6] Hadabet **(65)***(54) (MissJacquelineDoyle)* 3-9-1 (5) AWhelan(10) (lw: a mid div) hd **8**
1529[3] Green Land (BEL) **(66)***(55) (SCWilliams)* 3-9-7 LDettori(4) (lw: 5th st: wknd over 2f out) nk **9**
2350[6] Praglia (IRE) **(66)***(39) (JLDunlop)* 3-9-7 WCarson(9) (a bhd) 11 **10**
3438[11] Rainelle **(65)***(17) (CEBrittain)* 3-9-6 BDoyle(13) (a bhd) 15 **11**
3363[4] Night Time **(61)***(12) (RHannon)* 3-9-2 RPerham(2) (lw: 4th st: wknd over 2f out) 1 **12**
2145[9] Lucky Quest **(65)***(15) (NAGraham)* 3-9-6 DHolland(15) (a bhd) ½ **13**
3521[5] Special Beat **(60)***(4) (PFICole)* 3-9-1 RCochrane(14) (bhd fnl 3f) 4 **14**
1859[6] Almuhtaram **(64)***(6) (MissGayKelleway)* 3-9-5 MTebbutt(12) (bit bkwd: a bhd) 1½ **15**

3/1 Battleship Bruce, **11/2** Green Land (BEL), **7/1** Paradise Waters, **15/2** LEADING SPIRIT (IRE), **10/1** Praglia (IRE) (7/1-12/1), **12/1** Marchant Ming (IRE), Tonka, Special Beat, **14/1** Cuba, George Bull (8/1-16/1), Hadabet, **16/1** Night Time, Almuhtaram, **20/1** Rainelle, **33/1** Lucky Quest, CSF £94.81 CT £1,160.09 TOTE £9.80: £2.30 £3.90 £3.90 (£46.10) Trio £527.40 OWNER Induna Racing Partners Two (NEWMARKET) BRED Sir Peter Nugent and Ascot Stables 15 Rn
2m 30.69 (8.99) SF: 46/40/45/37/34/35/27/28/29/13/-/-/-/-/-

T/Jkpt: Not won; £8,411.00 to Sandown 13/9/95. T/Plpt: £454.50 (47.42 Tckts). T/Qdpt: £148.50 (0.5 Tckts). AK

3179-YARMOUTH (L-H)
Tuesday September 12th (Good)

WEATHER: fine WIND: fresh half against

3635

BROOKE CLAIMING STKS (3-Y.O) (Class E) £3,416.60 (£1,020.80: £488.40: £222.20) **1m 3f 101y** Stalls: Low GOING minus 0.14 sec per fur (G) 2-00 (2-01)

3184[4] **Fresh Look (IRE) (50)***(59)*(Fav)*(RFJohnsonHoughton)* 3-8-2 RHills(9) (led 1f: 3rd st: n.m.r over 1f out: swtchd rt & r.o to ld cl home) — **1**
3254[3] Last Corner **(50)***(70)*(Fav)*(RHollinshead)* 3-8-13 KDarley(1) (hld up: hdwy 4f out: rdn to disp ld wl ins fnl f: r.o) nk **2**
2621[6] Sea Victor **(74)***(78) (JLHarris)* 3-9-7 JWeaver(11) (lw: a.p: shkn up to ld 2f out: hrd rdn & hdd cl home) s.h **3**
3401[2] Born to Please (IRE) **(44)***(65) (PWHarris)* 3-8-11 GDuffield(8) (lw: s.i.s: led after 1f tl rdn & hdd 2f out: styd on) 1½ **4**
2994[4] Hello Peter (IRE) **(48)***(58) (MHTompkins)* 3-8-5 SMulvey(13) (prom: 4th st: rdn over 2f out: grad faded) 1¼ **5**
Alioli *(55) (MJRyan)* 3-8-6 DBiggs(10) (dwlt: rdn over 3f out: styd on one pce) 2½ **6**
3403[5] Birthday Boy (IRE) **(56)***(62) (RHannon)* 3-8-8v(5) DaneO'Neill(7) (hld up: effrt 3f out: sn rdn: kpt on one pce) nk **7**
3438[9] Greenway Lady *(53) (CNAllen)* 3-8-8 GCarter(5) (b.hind: hld up in rr: sme hdwy fnl 2f: nvr nrr) 2½ **8**
Kim Tate (IRE) *(41) (CNAllen)* 3-7-10 NCarlisle(2) (lt-f: a in rr) nk **9**
3410[3] Lindisfarne Lady **(41)***(48) (MrsMReveley)* 3-8-4 WWoods(3) (hld up: hdwy over 3f out: sn rdn: no imp) nk **10**
2851[4] Bunker (IRE) **(53)***(50) (JPearce)* 3-8-9 GBardwell(4) (hld up: 6th st: rdn 3f out: sn btn) 2½ **11**
2524[8] Dalysnicelitlerner *(41) (JRJenkins)* 3-8-3 AMcGlone(12) (bit bkwd: chsd ldrs: 5th st: wknd 3f out) 2½ **12**
3074[11] Chili Lass **(36)** *(JWharton)* 3-8-0 JQuinn(6) (bit bkwd: chsd ldrs tl wknd 5f out: t.o) dist **13**

6/1 FRESH LOOK (IRE), Last Corner, **13/2** Born to Please (IRE), **7/1** Hello Peter (IRE), Birthday Boy (IRE), **15/2** Bunker (IRE), **9/1** Sea Victor, **10/1** Lindisfarne Lady, **25/1** Alioli, Kim Tate (IRE), **33/1** Chili Lass, **40/1** Greenway Lady, **50/1** Dalysnicelitlerner, CSF £36.35 TOTE £7.50: £2.40 £2.00 £2.10 (£15.80) Trio £34.50 OWNER Mr C. W. Sumner (DIDCOT) 13 Rn

2m 30.9 (7.90) SF: 21/32/40/27/20/17/24/15/3/10/12/3/-

Fresh Look (IRE) clmd J Purcell £5,000.

OFFICIAL EXPLANATION Chili Lass: was reported to have gurgled.

3636 JOHN MUSKER STKS (Listed) (3-Y.O+ F & M) (Class A) £13,402.50 (£4,020.00: £1,935.00: £892.50)

1m 2f 21y Stalls: Low GOING minus 0.14 sec per fur (G) 2-35 (2-35)

3278* **Poppy Carew (IRE) (106)***(113) (PWHarris)* 3-8-6 JQuinn(2) (chsd ldrs: 5th st: swtchd rt 2f out: led ins fnl f: r.o wl) ....— **1**
3278[3] Jumilla (USA) **(85)***(111) (GWragg)* 3-8-6b MHills(12) (hld up: 6th st: hdwy over 2f out: rdn & ev ch ins fnl f: r.o) 1¼ **2**
3239* Goalwah **(87)***(110) (HThomsonJones)* 3-8-6 RHills(4) (chsd ldrs: 4th st: led over 2f out tl hdd & no ex ins fnl f) ....½ **3**
3331a[11] Western Reel (USA) **(107)***(107) (PFICole)* 3-8-6 TQuinn(1) (lw: chsd ldrs: 7th st: ev ch wl over 1f out: rdn & no ex fnl f) 2 **4**
3331a[2] Tillandsia (IRE) **(109)***(105)*(Fav)*(DRLoder)* 3-8-6 JWeaver(9) (led tl hdd over 2f out: sn hrd rdn: wknd fnl f) 1¼ **5**
1729[6] Pitcroy **(93)***(101) (JRFanshawe)* 3-8-6 KFallon(8) (lw: hld up in rr: hdwy whn bdly hmpd 2f out: nt rcvr) 2½ **6**
2763[6] Subya **(107)***(97) (JLDunlop)* 3-8-10 JReid(7) (lw: hld up: effrt & drvn along 3f out: carried rt 2f out: nt rch ldrs) 5 **7**
2329* Temora (IRE) *(92) (HRACecil)* 3-8-6 AMcGlone(3) (prom: 3rd st: wknd wl over 1f out) ....½ **8**
1867[6] Strutting (IRE) **(97)***(92) (RHannon)* 3-8-6 PaulEddery(6) (in rr: effrt 3f out: no imp) ....s.h **9**
3413[8] Red Azalea **(97)***(89) (SirMarkPrescott)* 3-8-6b GDuffield(5) (prom: 2nd st: rdn & wknd over 2f out) 2 **10**
3595[2] Jumairah Sun (IRE) **(84)***(85) (LMCumani)* 3-8-6 KDarley(10) (s.s: hdwy ent st: rdn 3f out: sn btn) 2½ **11**
3413[6] Pearl Venture **(90)***(83) (SPCWoods)* 3-8-6b WWoods(11) (a wl bhd) 1¼ **12**

3/1 Tillandsia (IRE), **4/1** POPPY CAREW (IRE), **6/1** Jumairah Sun (IRE), **7/1** Temora (IRE), **15/2** Goalwah, **9/1** Subya (op 6/1), **14/1** Western Reel (USA), **16/1** Pitcroy, **20/1** Strutting (IRE), Jumilla (USA), **33/1** Red Azalea, Pearl Venture, CSF £71.24 TOTE £5.10: £1.90 £4.10 £3.10 (£30.10) Trio £111.60 OWNER Mrs P. W. Harris (BERKHAMSTED) BRED Pendley Farm 12 Rn

2m 8.4 (4.00) SF: 47/45/44/41/39/35/31/26/26/23/19/17

3637 BRIAN TAYLOR MEMORIAL H'CAP (0-90) (3-Y.O+) (Class C) £6,992.00 (£2,096.00: £1,008.00: £464.00)

6f 3y Stalls: High GOING: 0.23 sec per fur (G) 3-10 (3-10)

3145[18] **Be Warned (70)***(78)*(Fav)*(NACallaghan)* 4-8-9b PaulEddery(14) (lw: hld up: hdwy over 1f out: str run to ld nr fin) ....— **1**
3411[11] Cyrano's Lad (IRE) **(86)***(94) (CADwyer)* 6-9-11 CDwyer(6) (led stands' side: hrd rdn fnl f: ct cl home) ....hd **2**
3451[7] First Veil **(71)***(75) (JRFanshawe)* 5-8-10 KFallon(12) (hld up: hdwy bel dist: rdn & edgd lft fnl f: r.o wl) 1¼ **3**
1305[8] The Jotter **(90)***(94) (WJarvis)* 3-9-12 TQuinn(17) (bit bkwd: hld up: hdwy over 2f out: hrd rdn & r.o ins fnl f) ....hd **4**
3179* Awayil (USA) **(80)***(83) (HThomsonJones)* 3-9-2 RHills(10) (lw: hld up: hdwy u.p bel dist: r.o wl fnl f) ....½ **5**
3359[13] So Intrepid (IRE) **(73)***(73) (JMBradley)* 5-8-9 (3) SDrowne(15) (hdwy 2f out: hrd rdn fnl f: nvr able chal) 1¼ **6**
2240[15] Twice as Sharp **(82)***(80) (PWHarris)* 3-9-4 GDuffield(18) (bit bkwd: prom stands' side over 4f) ....¾ **7**
3212[10] Highborn (IRE) **(80)***(71) (PSFelgate)* 6-9-2 (3) PMcCabe(13) (lw: s.i.s: bhd & rdn along ½-wy: n.d) 2½ **8**
2827[2] Veuve Hoornaert (IRE) **(85)***(73) (RHannon)* 3-9-7 JReid(16) (prom: rdn whn hmpd ent fnl f: sn btn) 1 **9**
3624[7] Prima Silk **(70)***(55) (MJRyan)* 4-8-9 TIves(9) (nvr nrr) 1¼ **10**
2206[2] Second Cello **(67)***(43) (DMorris)* 3-8-3 RPrice(8) (prom stands' side tl rdn & wknd bel dist) 3½ **11**
2240[12] Lynton Lad **(86)***(58) (CPEBrooks)* 3-9-8 JWilliams(11) (chsd ldrs over 4f) 1½ **12**
3551[6] Join the Clan **(89)***(55) (MrsNMacauley)* 6-10-0 JWeaver(4) (lw: led far side: rdn over 2f out: sn no ch) 2 **13**

3065³ Face the Future **(62)**_(18) (LJHolt)_ 6-8-1 AMcGlone(7) (chsd ldrs over 3f: sn lost tch) 4 **14**
3145¹⁹ Croft Pool **(81)**_(33) (JAGlover)_ 4-9-6 KDarley(5) (chsd ldr far side: rdn wl over 2f out: sn lost tch) 1½ **15**
3451⁴ Delight of Dawn **(74)**_(23) (KTIvory)_ 3-8-3 (7)ow2 CScally(1) (b: racd far side: spd over 3f).........nk **16**
3250³ Prolific Lady (IRE) **(72)**_(14) (MBrittain)_ 3-8-8v JQuinn(3) (racd far side: a in rr)........................3½ **17**
2507⁴ Mousehole **(71)**_(11) (RGuest)_ 3-8-7 MHills(2) (bit bkwd: racd far side: a bhd & outpcd)...........¾ **18**

6/1 BE WARNED, **13/2** Awayil (USA), **15/2** Twice as Sharp (op 14/1), **10/1** Veuve Hoornaert (IRE), **11/1** Croft Pool, Face the Future, **12/1** Highborn (IRE), **14/1** Join the Clan, **16/1** So Intrepid (IRE), The Jotter, First Veil, **20/1** Prolific Lady (IRE), Cyrano's Lad (IRE), Second Cello, Mousehole, Delight of Dawn, **25/1** Lynton Lad, Prima Silk, CSF £110.70 CT £1,672.03 TOTE £4.80: £2.30 £6.60 £7.00 £4.40 (£270.60) Trio £537.40 OWNER Midcourts (NEWMARKET) BRED Patrick Eddery Ltd 18 Rn 1m 14.6 (4.00) SF: 56/72/53/69/58/51/55/49/48/33/18/33/33/-/11/-/-/-
WEIGHT FOR AGE 3yo-3lb

3638 CAISTER (S) STKS (3-Y.O+) (Class G) £2,847.80 (£790.80: £379.40)
7f 3y Stalls: High GOING: 0.23 sec per fur (G) 3-45 (3-46)

3443⁶ **First Gold (54)**_(70) (JWharton)_ 6-9-1b KFallon(2) (hld up in rr: hdwy 2f out: n.m.r ins fnl f: swtchd & qcknd to ld cl home) ....— **1**
3443³ Guesstimation (USA) **(62)**_(74) (JPearce)_ 6-9-6 MHills(15) (hld up gng wl: led ins fnl f: edgd lft: ct nr fin)...............½ **2**
3431⁴ Cape Colony _(65)_(Fav)_(CFWall)_ 3-8-11 GDuffield(10) (hdwy ½-wy: led over 1f out tl ins fnl f: unable qckn) 1¾ **3**
3492¹⁷ Here Comes Risky **(67)**_(62) (MJohnston)_ 3-8-11 JWeaver(4) (a.p: led 2f out: sn hdd: one pce fnl f)...............1¼ **4**
3365* Winter Scout (USA) **(62)**_(60) (MrsMReveley)_ 7-9-1 KDarley(14) (hld up: hdwy over 1f out: r.o ins fnl f: nvr nrr) 1 **5**
3344⁷ Keys Seminar **(41)**_(55) (JohnBerry)_ 3-8-11 CDwyer(8) (chsd ldrs: rdn wl over 1f out: nt pce to chal)...............2 **6**
Harvest Reaper **(57)**_(50) (JLHarris)_ 3-8-8 (3) DRMcCabe(3) (b.nr fore: prom: rdn whn hmpd & snatched up ins fnl f)...............2½ **7**
3363⁸ Western Valley **(26)**_(41) (CPWildman)_ 5-8-10 StephenDavies(5) (bkwd: chsd ldr 4f: sn rdn & wknd) 1¾ **8**
3249² See You Again **(56)**_(44) (RHannon)_ 3-8-6 (5) DaneO'Neill(1) (in tch on outside: rdn 2f out: no imp) ....¾ **9**
_3510⁵_ Rakis (IRE) **(65)**_(44) (MBrittain)_ 5-9-1b JWilliams(6) (b: chsd ldrs: rdn along 2f out: sn lost tch)...............hd **10**
_3319⁹_ Our Shadee (USA) **(45)**_(45) (KTIvory)_ 5-8-13v(7) CScally(11) (hdwy ½-wy: rdn 2f out: wknd appr fnl f)...............1½ **11**
3542⁷ Mad About The Girl (IRE) _(33) (DJSCosgrove)_ 3-8-6 MRimmer(7) (nvr nr ldrs) ....¾ **12**
3504⁶ Magication **(28)**_(32) (CNAllen)_ 5-8-10 GBardwell(9) (b: effrt u.p 3f out: no imp) ....¾ **13**
3515¹¹ Titanium Honda (IRE) **(30)**_(41) (CEBrittain)_ 4-9-6 WWoods(13) (chsd ldrs over 5f: wknd qckly)...............nk **14**
Jolly Hokey _(27) (JWharton)_ 3-8-11 JQuinn(12) (bit bkwd: led to 2f out: wknd qckly) 4 **15**
_3510⁹_ Sapphire Son (IRE) **(54)**_(24) (CNWilliams)_ 3-8-11v PaulEddery(16) (spd over 4f) 1½ **16**

4/1 Cape Colony (op 6/1), **5/1** Here Comes Risky, Guesstimation (USA), Winter Scout (USA) (op 3/1), **7/1** FIRST GOLD, **12/1** See You Again, Sapphire Son (IRE), Rakis (IRE), **20/1** Magication, **25/1** Our Shadee (USA), Titanium Honda (IRE), **33/1** Mad About The Girl (IRE), Western Valley, Keys Seminar, Jolly Hokey, Harvest Reaper, CSF £41.14 TOTE £8.80: £2.00 £2.20 £1.70 (£18.80) Trio £33.70 OWNER Mr K. D. Standen (MELTON MOWBRAY) BRED Messinger Stud Ltd 16 Rn 1m 28.8 (6.00) SF: 46/50/37/34/36/27/22/17/16/20/21/5/8/17/-/-
WEIGHT FOR AGE 3yo-4lb
No bid.

3639 JACK LEADER MEMORIAL CHALLENGE TROPHY NURSERY H'CAP (2-Y.O F) (Class D) £4,659.00 (£1,392.00: £666.00: £303.00)
7f 3y Stalls: High GOING: 0.23 sec per fur (G) 4-15 (4-16)

3450⁴ **Consordino (76)**_(86) (LMCumani)_ 2-9-1 KDarley(6) (mde all: qcknd clr 2f out: unchal).........— **1**
3090² Green Bentley (IRE) **(71)**_(75) (RHannon)_ 2-8-5 (5) DaneO'Neill(14) (bhd: hdwy over 2f out: rdn & r.o ins fnl f) 2½ **2**
3289⁴ Deerly **(65)**_(59) (DMorris)_ 2-8-4 ow1 PaulEddery(8) (chsd ldrs: drvn along ½-wy: kpt on fnl f) 4 **3**
2783² Marjaana (IRE) **(81)**_(72) (PTWalwyn)_ 2-9-6 RHills(11) (hld up: effrt & swtchd lft over 2f out: nvr able chal)...............2 **4**
3306⁵ La Fandango (IRE) **(65)**_(53) (MWEasterby)_ 2-8-1 (3) PMcCabe(12) (hmpd ½-wy: swtchd lft bel dist: rdn: r.o) 1 **5**

3271[3] Frezeliere **(82)***(70) (JLDunlop)* 2-9-7 JReid(10) (lw: hld up: hdwy 3f out: rdn whn bdly hmpd bel dist: nt rcvr) ....nk 6
3516[3] Balpare **(62)***(48) (NACallaghan)* 2-8-1 GCarter(7) (mid div: rdn over 2f out: no imp) ....¾ 7
3546[11] Tarry **(60)***(37) (CNWilliams)* 2-7-13 GBardwell(1) (chsd ldrs over 4f) 4 8
3366[2] Fikra (USA) **(76)***(53) (DMorley)* 2-9-1 MHills(5) (prom: rdn over 2f out: grad wknd) ....hd 9
3495[11] Petite Heritiere **(62)***(37) (MJRyan)* 2-8-1v DBiggs(13) (chsd ldrs over 5f: sn lost tch) ....¾ 10
3540[4] Hurricane Dancer (IRE) **(60)***(32) (SPCWoods)* 2-7-13 AMcGlone(4) (lw: prom over 4f) 1¼ 11
3460[7] Down The Yard **(56)***(25) (MCChapman)* 2-7-6 (3)ow2 NVarley(2) (chsd ldrs over 4f: sn wknd) ..½ 12
*2143** Itsinthepost **(60)***(29)*(Fav)*(MJohnston)* 2-7-13 JFanning(3) (spd 5f: sn rdn & wknd) ....¾ 13
1779[4] Lady Eclat **(63)***(32) (JAGlover)* 2-8-2 JQuinn(9) (bit bkwd: in tch: rdn 3f out: sn lost pl) ....nk 14

LONG HANDICAP Down The Yard 7-3

11/2 Itsinthepost, **6/1** CONSORDINO, Green Bentley (IRE), Frezeliere, **13/2** Marjaana (IRE), **8/1** Tarry, **10/1** Balpare, **14/1** Hurricane Dancer (IRE), **16/1** Deerly, Fikra (USA), Lady Eclat, **20/1** Petite Heritiere, **25/1** La Fandango (IRE), **33/1** Down The Yard, CSF £41.04 CT £515.38 TOTE £5.90: £2.20 £1.80 £5.10 (£14.60) Trio £101.90 OWNER Sheikh Mohammed (NEWMARKET) BRED Lord Rotherwick 14 Rn 1m 28.8 (6.00) SF: 46/35/19/32/13/30/8/-/13/-/-/-/-

3640 REGENT MAIDEN STKS (3-Y.O+) (Class D) £3,698.50 (£1,102.00: £525.00: £236.50) 5f 43y Stalls: High GOING: 0.23 sec per fur (G) 4-45 (4-46)

3023[12] **Unfuwaanah** *(73) (HThomsonJones)* 3-8-7 MHills(8) (lw: hld up & bhd: rapid hdwy appr fnl f: qcknd to ld nr fin) ....— 1
3492[4] Intiaash (IRE) **(70)***(72) (PTWalwyn)* 3-8-7 RHills(3) (swvd lft s: sn chsng ldrs: ev ch ins fnl f: r.o) ....½ 2
Forever Roses *(68) (PFICole)* 3-8-7 TQuinn(6) (leggy: lt-f: hld up: hdwy over 2f out: rdn & ev ch ins fnl f: unable qckn) 1¼ 3
2430[2] Glorious Aragon **(88)***(60)*(Fav)*(RFJohnsonHoughton)* 3-8-7 JReid(9) (led over 2f out: rdn appr fnl f: sn hdd & outpcd) 2½ 4
772[12] Black Boy (IRE) **(33)***(57) (RFMarvin)* 6-9-0b TGMcLaughlin(7) (prom: rdn wl over 1f out: sn outpcd) 2½ 5
3466[3] Midnight Spell **(75)***(37) (MrsJCecil)* 3-8-7 PaulEddery(1) (led over 2f: eased whn btn appr fnl f) 5 6
3179[4] Merrie le Bow **(43)***(35) (PatMitchell)* 3-8-4v(3) NVarley(2) (prom: rdn over 1f out: sn outpcd) ....½ 7
2692[8] Taylord **(64)***(39) (RHannon)* 3-8-7 (5) DaneO'Neill(5) (lw: spd 3f) ....½ 8
3138[4] Fiery Footsteps **(46)***(25) (PHowling)* 3-8-7 JQuinn(4) (w ldr to ½-wy: wknd wl over 1f out) 3 9

13/8 Glorious Aragon, **3/1** Intiaash (IRE), Midnight Spell, **10/1** Forever Roses (6/1-12/1), **14/1** UNFUWAANAH (10/1-16/1), **20/1** Taylord, **33/1** Merrie le Bow, **40/1** Fiery Footsteps, **50/1** Black Boy (IRE), CSF £52.36 TOTE £18.80: £3.40 £1.10 £1.60 (£27.30) Trio £77.70 OWNER Mr Hadi Al-Tajir (NEWMARKET) BRED Hadi Al Tajir 9 Rn 64.0 secs (3.70) SF: 50/49/45/37/36/14/12/16/2

WEIGHT FOR AGE 3yo-2lb

3641 HORSEY LADIES' H'CAP (0-75) (3-Y.O+) (Class G) £3,071.20 (£853.20: £409.60) 1m 3f 101y Stalls: High GOING minus 0.14 sec per fur (G) 5-15 (5-22)

3303[7] **Scenic Dancer (33)***(55)*(Fav)*(AHide)* 7-9-0 MissLHide(3) (s.s: hdwy 3f out: led wl over 1f out: sn clr: unchal) ....— 1
3344[11] Buckley Boys **(46)***(57) (ABailey)* 4-9-13 MissBridgetGatehouse(6) (hld up: hdwy over 3f out: kpt on appr fnl f: no ch w wnr) 8 2
2811[3] Paper Cloud **(62)***(71) (CEBrittain)* 3-10-3 (4) MrsSFaber(7) (hld up in tch: hdwy 3f out: styd on one pce) 1¼ 3
3288[5] Smocking **(33)***(39) (JPearce)* 5-9-0 MrsLPearce(10) (swtg: styd on fnl 2f: nvr nr ldrs) 2½ 4
3288* Don't Drop Bombs (USA) **(38)***(43)*(Fav)*(DTThom)* 6-9-5v MissJFeilden(4) (led: clr ent st: wknd & hdd wl over 1f out: sn btn) ....¾ 5
3435[8] Modest Hope (USA) **(44)***(46)*(Fav)*(BRichmond)* 8-9-11 MissDianaJones(15) (mid div: rdn & effrt 3f out: nvr nr to chal: t.o) 2 6
3056[4] Faustino **(49)***(50) (PFICole)* 3-9-8b MrsMCowdrey(12) (prom: 2nd st: rdn over 2f out: sn wknd) ....½ 7
332[10] Binlaboon (IRE) **(39)***(35) (KGWingrove)* 4-9-6 ow4 MrsHNoonan(17) (bit bkwd: hdwy over 3f out: nvr nr ldrs) ....¾ 8
3229[7] New Inn **(55)***(54) (SGollings)* 4-10-4 (4) MrsJMGollings(9) (hld up: effrt over 3f out: nvr nrr) ....¾ 9
2678[3] Teen Jay **(68)***(64) (MJRyan)* 5-11-7b MissJAllison(14) (s.s: nvr nr to chal) 2½ 10
87[5] Gold Surprise (IRE) **(50)***(45) (SEKettlewell)* 6-10-3 MrsDKettlewell(1) (bit bkwd: a in rr) ....½ 11
3047[5] Dots Dee **(33)***(24) (JMBradley)* 6-9-0 MissEJJones(16) (chsd ldrs: 3rd st: effrt & c wd over 3f out: grad wknd) 2½ 12
3017[7] Dolly Dolittle **(35)***(24) (HJCollingridge)* 4-9-2 ow2 MrsDMcHale(8) (a in rr) ....hd 13
3515[2] Mighty Kingdom (IRE) **(43)***(26) (CADwyer)* 4-9-10 MissVMarshall(5) (t.o) 6 14

3521⁶ Jean de Florette (USA) **(39)***(15) (CADwyer)* 4-9-2 (4)ow5 MissLPurcell(2) (t.o)....1½ **15**
3159¹² Scorpius **(65)***(33) (CNWilliams)* 5-11-4 MissYHaynes(11) (b: chsd ldrs: 5th st: wknd over 3f out: nvr nrr)....9 **16**
*3513*⁸ Karon Beach **(38)** *(JRBostock)* 4-9-5 MissKWright(19) (lw: hdwy 6f out: 6th st: wknd over 3f out: t.o)....25 **17**
Kindakoola **(45)** *(MCChapman)* 4-9-12 MrsSBosley(18) (bkwd: chsd ldrs: 4th st: wknd over 3f out: t.o)....15 **18**
3076⁸ Fen Terrier **(54)** *(WJHaggas)* 3-9-13 MrsAPerrett(13) (Withdrawn not under Starter's orders: ref to ent stalls).... **W**
LONG HANDICAP Dots Dee 8-8 Dolly Dolittle 7-10 Scenic Dancer 8-13

6/1 SCENIC DANCER, Don't Drop Bombs (USA), Modest Hope (USA), **7/1** Smocking, Faustino, Teen Jay, **9/1** Fen Terrier, **12/1** New Inn, **16/1** Paper Cloud, Buckley Boys, Gold Surprise (IRE), Dots Dee, Mighty Kingdom (IRE), Jean de Florette (USA), **20/1** Karon Beach, **25/1** Scorpius, **33/1** Binlaboon (IRE), **40/1** Kindakoola, Dolly Dolittle, CSF £90.44 CT £1,037.70 TOTE £7.30: £1.70 £10.00 £3.90 £1.90 (£175.90) Trio £298.90 OWNER Mr Anthony Hide (NEWMARKET) BRED Alan Gibson 18 Rn 2m 30.2 (7.20) SF: 37/39/45/21/25/28/24/17/36/46/27/6/6/8/-/15/-/-/-
WEIGHT FOR AGE 3yo-8lb

T/Plpt: £1,145.40 (14.45 Tckts). T/Qdpt: £82.90 (1.5 Tckts). IM

3302-BEVERLEY (R-H)
Wednesday September 13th (Good, Good to soft patches)
WEATHER: showers WIND: almost nil

3642
HUMBER ESTUARY NURSERY (S) H'CAP (0-65) (2-Y.O) (Class G)
£2,635.00 (£735.00: £355.00)
7f 100y Stalls: High GOING minus 0.17 sec per fur (GF) 2-10 (2-11)

3415⁸ **Domoor (52)***(49) (MJohnston)* 2-8-13 JWeaver(11) (swtg: mde most: hld on wl fnl f)....— **1**
3430⁷ The Wad **(55)***(52) (MWEasterby)* 2-9-2 GHind(6) (cl up: disp ld over 1f out tl ins fnl f: kpt on)....hd **2**
3533⁵ Anna Settic **(56)***(51) (DrJDScargill)* 2-9-3 RCochrane(8) (b.hind: prom: hdwy to chal 2f out: no ex ins fnl f)....¾ **3**
*3528*¹¹ Concert Party (IRE) **(50)***(37) (DWChapman)* 2-8-11 ACulhane(17) (lw: chsd ldrs: ev ch 3f out: outpcd fnl 2f)....4 **4**
3460¹¹ Kratz (IRE) **(55)***(41) (BSRothwell)* 2-8-13b(3) JStack(16) (hdwy 2f out: nvr rchd ldrs)....nk **5**
3386⁶ Red Misty (IRE) **(50)***(34)*(Fav)*(MRChannon)* 2-8-11 JFEgan(9) (hmpd & stumbled 6f out: bhd tl styd on wl fnl 3f)....¾ **6**
3417¹³ Mels Baby (IRE) **(50)***(32) (JLEyre)* 2-8-11 RLappin(15) (chsd ldrs: effrt 3f out: grad wknd) ...1¼ **7**
3018⁶ Lawnswood Captain (IRE) **(56)***(32) (RHollinshead)* 2-9-3 KFallon(5) (bhd tl sme late hdwy) .2½ **8**
3533¹² Priddy Fair **(56)***(32) (RBoss)* 2-9-3 AMcGlone(10) (unruly s: s.s: nvr rchd ldrs)....nk **9**
3434⁸ Theatre Magic **(60)***(34) (TJEtherington)* 2-9-7v KDarley(13) (effrt 3f out: hung rt: n.d)....¾ **10**
3533¹¹ Shanoora (IRE) **(56)***(30) (BPalling)* 2-9-3 DHolland(7) (in tch: one pce fnl 3f)....hd **11**
3533⁶ How Could-I (IRE) **(52)***(21) (MHEasterby)* 2-8-13 SMaloney(3) (chsd ldrs tl rdn & btn over 2f out)....2½ **12**
3468⁸ Larrylukeathugh **(56)***(21) (JJO'Neill)* 2-9-3 DeanMcKeown(2) (in tch: rdn appr st: sn wknd)..1½ **13**
*3528*¹⁰ Marketeer Magic **(58)** *(JBerry)* 2-9-5 JCarroll(12) (b: dwlt: sme hdwy on outside 3f out: sn btn)....13 **14**
3456⁵ Hobbs Choice **(59)** *(MissJFCraze)* 2-9-6v SWebster(1) (effrt on outside appr st: sn wknd & wl bhd)....½ **15**
3048⁶ Sovitaka (IRE) **(60)** *(MHEasterby)* 2-9-7 MBirch(4) (s.i.s: a bhd)....4 **16**
3019⁹ Pat's Choice (IRE) **(51)** *(MHEasterby)* 2-8-12 BThomson(14) (in tch to ½-wy: sn wknd)....4 **17**

9/2 Red Misty (IRE), **5/1** Anna Settic, Priddy Fair (op 10/1), **10/1** Shanoora (IRE), Lawnswood Captain (IRE), **12/1** DOMOOR, How Could-I (IRE), Theatre Magic, Pat's Choice (IRE), **14/1** Kratz (IRE), Sovitaka (IRE), **16/1** Marketeer Magic, Mels Baby (IRE), **20/1** The Wad, Larrylukeathugh, **25/1** Hobbs Choice, Concert Party (IRE), CSF £229.47 CT £1,258.02 TOTE £13.80: £2.40 £7.40 £1.50 £14.60 (£622.20) Trio £232.20 OWNER Mark Johnston Racing Ltd (MIDDLEHAM) BRED Greenland Park Stud 17 Rn 1m 38.2 (6.20) SF: 17/20/19/5/9/2/-/-/-/2/-/-/-/-/-/-/-
Bt in 5,200 gns

3643
E.B.F. GARROWBY MAIDEN STKS (2-Y.O F) (Class D) £4,211.00
(£1,268.00: £614.00: £287.00)
7f 100y Stalls: High GOING minus 0.17 sec per fur (GF) 2-40 (2-42)

Wavey *(78+) (JHMGosden)* 2-8-11 GHind(12) (w'like: disp ld tl led 2½f out: clr over 1f out: kpt on wl)....— **1**

Degree *(75) (HRACecil)* 2-8-11 AMcGlone(10) (lengthy: unf: lw: dwlt: sn chsng ldrs: rdn over 2f out: styd on strly towards fin) 1¼ 2
3069[11] Sabaah Elfull *(73)*(Fav)*(ACStewart)* 2-8-11 RCochrane(8) (lw: chsd ldrs: ev ch 2f out: nt qckn fnl f) 1¼ 3
1246[4] Chalamont (IRE) *(49) (PWChapple-Hyam)* 2-8-6 (5) RHavlin(9) (disp ld tl wknd fnl 2½f) 11 4
3523[4] Classic Delight (USA) *(40) (SCWilliams)* 2-8-11 AMackay(13) (bhd tl styd on fnl 3f) 4 5
3306[6] Candy's Delight *(37) (JLEyre)* 2-8-11 RLappin(3) (nvr bttr than mid div) 1½ 6
3495[5] Mighty Phantom (USA) *(36) (JWHills)* 2-8-11 BThomson(5) (prom to st) ....½ 7
3452[3] Temptress *(32) (PTWalwyn)* 2-8-11 DHolland(11) (w ldrs to st: sn wknd) 2 8
2940[3] Fyors Gift (IRE) *(13) (BHanbury)* 2-8-8 (3) JStack(1) (s.i.s: a bhd) 9 9
2666[5] Needwood Fantasy *(4) (BAMcMahon)* 2-8-11 SDWilliams(4) (a bhd) 4 10
3495[W] Sweet Amoret *(RCSpicer)* 2-8-11 DeanMcKeown(6) (unruly leaving paddock: a bhd) 3½ 11
3306[7] Ann's Music *(JMJefferson)* 2-8-11 KFallon(2) (a bhd: wl t.o) ....dist 12

6/4 Sabaah Elfull, **3/1** Degree (op 2/1), **5/1** Chalamont (IRE), **13/2** Mighty Phantom (USA) (op 4/1), **8/1** WAVEY (op 5/1), **16/1** Temptress, **20/1** Fyors Gift (IRE), **33/1** Classic Delight (USA), **40/1** Candy's Delight, **50/1** Needwood Fantasy, Sweet Amoret, Ann's Music, CSF £32.56 TOTE £15.00: £3.00 £1.90 £1.30 (£16.80) Trio £35.20 OWNER Mr George Strawbridge (NEWMARKET) BRED T. D. Holland-Martin and The Kris Syndicate 12 Rn 1m 36.4 (4.40) SF: 34/31/29/5/-/-/-/-/-/-/-/-

3644

TATTERSALLS MAIDEN AUCTION STKS (2-Y.O) (Class E) £4,016.00 (£1,208.00: £584.00: £272.00) **7f 100y** Stalls: High GOING minus 0.17 sec (GF) 3-10 (3-17)

3463[3] **Weet-A-Minute (IRE)** **(87)***(78)*(Fav)*(RHollinshead)* 2-8-5 KFallon(8) (a.p: r.o wl fnl f to ld cl home) ....— 1
3339[9] Lovely Prospect *(73) (RGuest)* 2-8-0 (3)ow2 JStack(15) (led: clr 2f out: hdd & no ex nr fin) ....nk 2
3468[4] Addie Pray (IRE) *(69) (MAJarvis)* 2-7-13 JTate(16) (a chsng ldrs: effrt over 2f out: nt qckn ins fnl f) 1 3
3502[2] Yuppy Girl (IRE) **(63)***(50) (CaptJWilson)* 2-7-11 AMackay(5) (bhd: hdwy 3f out: styd on: nrst fin) 8 4
Perpetual Light *(47) (JJQuinn)* 2-7-11 DaleGibson(14) (unf: in tch: styd on one pce fnl 3f) ...1¼ 5
Killmessan-Town (IRE) *(46) (JMCarr)* 2-8-4 NKennedy(17) (cmpt: bkwd: unruly s: s.s: bhd tl styd on wl fnl 3f) 4 6
3460[4] Exactly (IRE) **(48)***(42) (JLEyre)* 2-8-1 TWilliams(6) (bhd tl styd on fnl 2f) ....½ 7
3398[4] Verulam (IRE) *(50) (JARToller)* 2-8-9 GHind(2) (chsd ldrs tl outpcd fnl 2½f) ....hd 8
3436[8] Classic Defence (IRE) *(42) (JWHills)* 2-8-7 DHolland(1) (chsd ldrs: chal appr st: wknd over 2f out) 2½ 9
3502[3] Current Leader **(70)***(34) (RHannon)* 2-8-3 KDarley(4) (in tch: effrt 3f out: no imp) 2 10
3260[5] Our Albert (IRE) *(22) (JAGlover)* 2-8-5 ow1 SDWilliams(12) (w ldrs tl wknd fnl 2½f) 6 11
Fisiostar *(22) (MDods)* 2-8-4 NConnorton(13) (leggy: unf: a bhd) ....hd 12
3502[4] Cerise (IRE) **(50)***(14) (CWCElsey)* 2-7-6 (5) PFessey(9) (lw: bhd tl sme late hdwy) ....½ 13
2498[8] Mill End Lady *(13) (MWEasterby)* 2-8-0 JFanning(3) (a rr div) 1¾ 14
Marsayas (IRE) *(18) (MJCamacho)* 2-8-8 LCharnock(10) (str: cmpt: bkwd: drvn along 4f out: a rr div) 1½ 15
1540[11] Royal Rapport *(16) (BAMcMahon)* 2-8-6b JFEgan(7) (chsd ldrs to st: sn lost pl) ....hd 16
Friendly Dreams (IRE) *(4) (PTDalton)* 2-7-13 ow1 SMaloney(11) (bkwd: a outpcd & wl bhd)..1¾ 17

2/1 WEET-A-MINUTE (IRE), **9/2** Addie Pray (IRE), **6/1** Lovely Prospect, Current Leader (9/2-7/1), **7/1** Yuppy Girl (IRE), **15/2** Verulam (IRE) (9/2-8/1), **9/1** Classic Defence (IRE) (op 6/1), **10/1** Perpetual Light, **12/1** Marsayas (IRE) (op 25/1), **14/1** Royal Rapport, **16/1** Our Albert (IRE), **20/1** Cerise (IRE), **25/1** Fisiostar, Mill End Lady, Killmessan-Town (IRE), Exactly (IRE), Friendly Dreams (IRE), CSF £19.42 TOTE £3.00: £1.50 £2.60 £1.90 (£12.10) Trio £20.50 OWNER Ed Weetman (Haulage & Storage) Ltd (UPPER LONGDON) BRED Cyclades Farming Co 17 Rn
1m 36.6 (4.60) SF: 26/21/17/-/-/-/-/-/-/-/-/-/-/-/-/-/-

3645

JOHN MANGLES MEMORIAL H'CAP (0-80) (3-Y.O+) (Class D) £3,855.00 (£1,155.00: £555.00: £255.00)
1m 100y Stalls: High GOING: 0.20 sec per fur (G) 3-40 (3-52)

3393[6] **Three Arch Bridge** **(58)***(71) (MJohnston)* 3-8-1b TWilliams(18) (lw: disp ld: led ent st: r.o wl)— 1
3101[8] Racing Brenda **(55)***(63) (BAMcMahon)* 4-8-3 JFEgan(13) (chsd ldrs: effrt over 2f out: nt qckn fnl f) 2½ 2
3611[14] Mowlaie **(67)***(72) (DWChapman)* 4-9-1 ACulhane(17) (lw: a.p: kpt on u.p fnl f: nvr able to chal) 1¾ 3
3506[2] Michellisa **(60)***(64) (JDBethell)* 4-8-8 KFallon(19) (lw: in tch: styd on fnl 2f: nrst fin) ....½ 4
3621[8] Just Harry **(68)***(69) (MJRyan)* 4-8-11 (5) DGibbs(16) (lw: chsd ldrs: one pce fnl 2f) 1¾ 5
2922[5] Evan 'elp Us **(62)***(60) (JLEyre)* 3-8-5b JTate(2) (racd wd: swtchd stands' side ent st: kpt on: no imp) 1½ 6

*3075*7 Sandmoor Denim **(66)***(54)*(Fav)*(SRBowring)* 8-8-9 (5) CTeague(14) (b: hdwy 3f out: sn rdn: no ex appr fnl f)........1½ **7**
3443 5 Lorelei Lee (IRE) **(61)***(47) (JohnBerry)* 3-8-4 ow1 DHolland(4) (chsd ldrs tl grad wknd fnl 2f)....nk **8**
3611 18 Bold Amusement **(80)***(66) (WSCunningham)* 5-10-0 DeanMcKeown(11) (drvn along appr st: styd on: n.d)........¾ **9**
3534 7 Kilnamartyra Girl **(52)***(36) (JParkes)* 5-8-0 JFanning(12) (lw: nvr nrr)........¾ **10**
3431 2 Night Wink (USA) **(61)***(34) (DNicholls)* 3-8-4 JCarroll(5) (hld up & bhd: effrt 3f out: n.d)........6 **11**
3396 7 Murphy's Gold (IRE) **(57)***(11) (RAFahey)* 4-8-5 SMaloney(6) (lw: b: prom to st)........10 **12**
3443 2 Blaze of Oak (USA) **(66)***(19) (WJHaggas)* 4-9-0 RCochrane(3) (racd wd: in tch to st)........nk **13**
3531 11 Lancashire Life (IRE) **(51)** *(EJAlston)* 4-7-13 AMackay(1) (racd wd: prom to st)........3½ **14**
3457 5 Ochos Rios (IRE) **(62)***(9) (BSRothwell)* 4-8-7 (3) JStack(9) (a bhd)........s.h **15**
988 3 Alabang **(50)***(40) (MJCamacho)* 4-7-12 LCharnock(15) (lw: s.i.s: n.d)........4 **16**
*3240*11 Dance King **(69)***(15) (DNicholls)* 3-8-12 AlexGreaves(8) (disp ld to st: sn wknd)........hd **17**
3411 12 Impulsive Air (IRE) **(77)** *(EWeymes)* 3-9-6 GHind(10) (lw: s.s: a bhd)........20 **18**
3294 4 Troubadour Song **(70)** *(IABalding)* 3-8-13b KDarley(7) (racd wd: bhd tl gd hdwy appr st: sn wknd & eased)........2½ **19**

6/1 Sandmoor Denim, **13/2** Night Wink (USA) (4/1-7/1), **7/1** Troubadour Song, **8/1** Michellisa, **17/2** Blaze of Oak (USA), **9/1** Lorelei Lee (IRE) (16/1-8/1), Ochos Rios (IRE) (op 6/1), Alabang (6/1-10/1), **11/1** Mowlaie, **14/1** THREE ARCH BRIDGE, Racing Brenda, **16/1** Bold Amusement, Murphy's Gold (IRE), Kilnamartyra Girl, Dance King, **20/1** Evan 'elp Us, Just Harry, Impulsive Air (IRE), Lancashire Life (IRE), CSF £209.11 CT £2,068.87 TOTE £27.70: £3.80 £4.40 £4.00 £2.80 (£87.20) Trio not won; £770.95 to Ayr 14/9/95 OWNER Mr R. N. Pennell (MIDDLEHAM) BRED R. Taylor 19 Rn 1m 50.5 (6.50) SF: 45/42/51/43/48/34/33/21/45/15/8/-/-/-/-/19/-/-/-
WEIGHT FOR AGE 3yo-5lb

3646 RAMBO DANCER H'CAP (0-75) (3-Y.O+) (Class D) £4,849.50 (£1,461.00: £708.00: £331.50)

1m 3f 216y Stalls: High GOING: 0.20 sec per fur (G) 4-10 (4-17)

3462 U **Ashover (55)***(69) (TDBarron)* 5-8-9 DeanMcKeown(15) (chsd ldrs: led over 1f out: wandered: drvn out)........— **1**
3469 9 Hand Woven **(73)***(84) (WJHaggas)* 3-9-4 RCochrane(9) (a in tch: drvn along 5f out: styd on wl u.p fnl 2f: nt rch wnr)........2 **2**
3505 7 Sariyaa **(55)***(66) (MBrittain)* 4-8-9 JCarroll(14) (a chsng ldrs: kpt on same pce appr fnl f)........½ **3**
3388 8 El Bailador (IRE) **(61)***(70) (JDBethell)* 4-9-1 JWeaver(10) (led tl over 1f out: kpt on same pce) 1 **4**
3445 4 Floating Line **(62)***(71)*(Fav)*(EJAlston)* 7-9-2 SDWilliams(12) (w ldr: chal over 3f out: styd on same pce fnl 2f)........hd **5**
2878 2 Hullbank **(63)***(70) (WWHaigh)* 5-9-3 DaleGibson(13) (b: hld up: hdwy 4f out: styd fnl 2f: nvr rchd ldrs)........1½ **6**
3505 9 Faal Mario (USA) **(70)***(60) (MrsJRRamsden)* 4-9-10 KFallon(11) (hld up: effrt over 4f out: sn outpcd)........13 **7**
3255 5 Mca Below the Line **(53)***(40) (JLEyre)* 7-8-7 RLappin(4) (bhd: drvn along 4f out: sme hdwy 2f out: n.d)........2½ **8**
*3245*4 Stevie's Wonder (IRE) **(56)***(28) (MJRyan)* 5-8-5 (5) DGibbs(3) (in tch to ½-wy: bhd & rdn along 4f out)........11 **9**
3066 11 Kilcoran Bay **(72)***(42) (IABalding)* 3-9-3 KDarley(2) (bhd & drvn along 5f out: n.d)........1½ **10**
*3245** Barti-Ddu **(52)***(19) (SCWilliams)* 4-8-6 JTate(6) (chsd ldrs tl lost pl over 3f out)........2½ **11**
Five to Seven (USA) **(67)***(18) (CWThornton)* 6-9-4 (3)ow1 OPears(5) (b: t.o fr ½-wy)........11 **12**
3571 6 College Night (IRE) **(63)***(12) (CADwyer)* 3-8-8 ow1 CDwyer(7) (swtg: racd wd: prom tl lost pl over 3f out: sn bhd: t.o)........1½ **13**
Crowther Homes **(48)** *(EJAlston)* 5-8-2 TWilliams(8) (bkwd: dwlt: a bhd: t.o)........2 **14**
3395 5 Hatta River (USA) **(58)** *(JAHarris)* 5-8-12b DHolland(1) (racd wd: chsd ldrs tl lost pl over 3f out: sn wl bhd: t.o)........9 **15**

9/2 Floating Line, **5/1** Kilcoran Bay, **11/2** Barti-Ddu, **7/1** Stevie's Wonder (IRE), Hullbank, **9/1** ASHOVER, Faal Mario (USA), **10/1** El Bailador (IRE), Hand Woven, **16/1** Sariyaa, **20/1** Five to Seven (USA), **25/1** Mca Below the Line, College Night (IRE), Crowther Homes, Hatta River (USA), CSF £97.06 CT £1,309.97 TOTE £11.40: £2.80 £3.80 £5.20 (£100.60) Trio £227.10; £227.19 to Ayr 14/9/95 OWNER Mr Timothy Cox (THIRSK) BRED Bridge End Bloodstock 15 Rn
2m 44.7 (13.20) SF: 30/36/27/31/32/31/21/1/-/-/-/-/-/-/-
WEIGHT FOR AGE 3yo-9lb

3647 JACKSONS BAKERY MAIDEN STKS (I) (2-Y.O) (Class D) £3,704.00 (£1,112.00: £536.00: £248.00)

5f Stalls: Centre GOING: 0.20 sec per fur (G) 4-45 (4-45)

3541 2 **Angel Chimes** *(77) (JEBanks)* 2-8-6 (3) JStack(5) (dwlt: sn outpcd & drvn along: hdwy on outside whn sltly hmpd over 1f out: styd on strly to ld nr fin)........— **1**

30865 Repatriate (AUS) *(73)*(Fav)*(PWChapple-Hyam)* 2-8-5 (5)ow1 RHavlin(8) (w ldr: led ½-wy tl wl ins fnl f)....1¼ 2
Polar Refrain *(65) (MrsJRRamsden)* 2-8-9 KFallon(10) (unf: bit bkwd: s.i.s: hdwy & pushed along ½-wy: nvr able to chal)....2½ 3
28172 Answers-To-Thomas *(70) (JMJefferson)* 2-9-0 GHind(2) (led to ½-wy: hung rt & one pce fr over 1f out)....hd 4
28207 Miletrian City *(70) (JBerry)* 2-9-0 JCarroll(9) (sn outpcd: hdwy & hung lft over 1f out: styd on towards fin)....s.h 5
*3509*12 Castle Governor *(54) (PCHaslam)* 2-8-7 (7) CarolDavison(11) (sn outpcd: wandered 2f out: nvr nr ldrs)....5 6
34306 Power Princess *(48) (RMWhitaker)* 2-8-9 ACulhane(12) (in tch: kpt on fr ½-wy: nvr able to chal)....hd 7
Queens Check *(43) (MissJFCraze)* 2-8-9 SWebster(3) (neat: chsd ldrs: hung rt & wknd over 1f out)....1½ 8
Arctic Zipper (USA) *(37) (WAO'Gorman)* 2-9-0 RCochrane(6) (str: scope: s.s: sme hdwy ½-wy: sn wknd)....3½ 9
31705 Polish Saga *(27) (MDods)* 2-8-9 LCharnock(7) (w ldrs tl wknd 2f out)....1¾ 10
Green Barries *(6) (MJohnston)* 2-9-0 JWeaver(4) (cmpt: str: scope: bit bkwd: unruly: sn chsng ldrs: rn green & lost pl ½-wy: hmpd over 1f out: eased)....8 11

6/4 Repatriate (AUS), **9/2** Green Barries (op 7/4), Answers-To-Thomas (op 10/1), **5/1** Arctic Zipper (USA), **6/1** ANGEL CHIMES (op 3/1), **8/1** Polar Refrain, **20/1** Miletrian City, **25/1** Power Princess, Queens Check, Polish Saga, Castle Governor, CSF £17.07 TOTE £8.40: £2.60 £1.40 £3.40 (£6.10) Trio £22.20 OWNER Mr Giles Pritchard-Gordon (NEWMARKET) BRED Giles W. Pritchard-Gordon 11 Rn
66.4 secs (4.90) SF: 36/32/24/29/29/13/7/2/-/-/-

3648 JACKSONS BAKERY MAIDEN STKS (II) (2-Y.O) (Class D) £3,678.00 (£1,104.00: £532.00: £246.00)
5f Stalls: Centre GOING: 0.20 sec per fur (G) 5-15 (5-16)

*3525*9 **First Maite** *(70) (SRBowring)* 2-9-0b SWebster(10) (chsd ldrs: rdn & outpcd 2f out: styd on u.p to ld wl ins fnl f)....— 1
32318 Gymcrak Gem (IRE) *(62) (GHolmes)* 2-8-9 KFallon(11) (unruly s: w ldrs: led ins fnl f: hdd & nt qckn nr fin)....1 2
20856 Literary Society (USA) *(57)*(Fav)*(JARToller)* 2-9-0 DHolland(8) (lw: mde most tl ins fnl f: nt qckn)....3 3
Gotla Bird *(51) (MJohnston)* 2-8-9 JWeaver(1) (neat: sn outpcd & pushed along: edgd rt & styd on fnl f)....½ 4
346511 Amington Lass *(49) (BAMcMahon)* 2-8-9 SDWilliams(9) (w ldr tl wknd jst ins fnl f)....½ 5
24124 Chelsea Classic (IRE) *(38) (MRChannon)* 2-8-9 KDarley(2) (chsd ldrs: wkng whn carried rt ins fnl f)....3½ 6
167015 Turbo North *(38) (MDods)* 2-9-0 DaleGibson(3) (lw: sn outpcd: rdn along & sme hdwy 2f out: n.d)....1½ 7
Sizzling Serenade *(29) (SGNorton)* 2-8-9 JTate(5) (leggy: neat: s.i.s: bhd: sme hdwy over 1f out: n.d)....1¼ 8
*3077*10 General Equation *(29) (JBalding)* 2-8-7 (7) JEdmunds(6) (outpcd fr ½-wy)....1½ 9
Ya Marhaba *(13) (JWPayne)* 2-9-0 BThomson(4) (str: scope: unruly: s.i.s: a outpcd)....5 10
30936 Penny Ghent *(PSFelgate)* 2-8-9 DeanMcKeown(7) (s.i.s: a outpcd & bhd)....4 11

7/4 Literary Society (USA), **7/2** Chelsea Classic (IRE) (op 9/4), **5/1** Ya Marhaba, **6/1** Gotla Bird (op 4/1), Amington Lass (op 4/1), **9/1** Gymcrak Gem (IRE), **16/1** FIRST MAITE, Sizzling Serenade, **20/1** Turbo North, **25/1** General Equation, Penny Ghent, CSF £155.50 TOTE £36.10: £5.20 £2.20 £1.40 (£66.80) Trio £130.10 OWNER Mr S. R. Bowring (EDWINSTOWE) BRED S. R. Bowring 11 Rn
66.7 secs (5.20) SF: 46/38/33/27/25/14/14/5/5/-/-

3649 END OF SEASON MAIDEN STKS (3-Y.O+) (Class D) £4,263.00 (£1,284.00: £622.00: £291.00)
5f Stalls: Centre GOING: 0.20 sec per fur (G) 5-45 (5-47)

35072 **Allyana (IRE) (70)***(76)*(Fav)*(IABalding)* 3-8-7 KDarley(6) (hld up & plld hrd: n.m.r after 1½f: styd on appr fnl f: led towards fin: readily)....— 1
31382 Dancing Sioux **(63)***(77) (RGuest)* 3-8-12 LCharnock(3) (chsd ldrs: led ½-wy tl ins fnl f)....1¼ 2
27864 Quilling **(69)***(66) (MDods)* 3-8-12v JWeaver(14) (sn outpcd: hdwy over 1f out: styd on towards fin)....3½ 3
269817 Anytime Baby **(35)***(61) (PTDalton)* 3-8-7 JFEgan(4) (led to ½-wy: hung rt: nt qckn appr fnl f)....hd 4
350815 Skiptamaloo **(25)***(56) (DonEnricoIncisa)* 4-8-9b KimTinkler(5) (in tch: n.m.r & outpcd ½-wy: styd on appr fnl f)....1½ 5

2084[12] Never Say so **(54)***(40) (CSmith)* 3-8-7 GHind(1) (w ldrs tl wknd over 1f out) 5 6
3357[14] Silk Cottage **(63)***(44) (RMWhitaker)* 3-8-12 RCochrane(11) (chsd ldrs tl wknd over 1f out).....nk 7
2290[9] Marsh Arab **(54)***(42) (JBalding)* 4-8-7 (7) JEdmunds(9) (in tch: outpcd ½-wy: n.d after) ....½ 8
Adamton *(34) (MrsJCecil)* 3-8-12 JTate(13) (cmpt: sme hdwy ½-wy: wknd over 1f out)........2½ 9
3293[15] Mr Moriarty (IRE) **(20)***(33) (SRBowring)* 4-8-9b(5) CTeague(10) (bhd & rdn ½-wy)....nk 10
3428[6] Graceful Lady *(15) (EJAlston)* 5-8-9 SDWilliams(2) (s.i.s: outpcd fr ½-wy)....4 11
3524[15] Sundries *(11) (DWChapman)* 5-9-0 ACulhane(12) (s.i.s: a outpcd & bhd)....3 12
2236[11] Fred Said Right (IRE) *(10) (MJHeaton-Ellis)* 3-8-12 DHolland(15) (chsd ldrs tl wknd 2f out)..hd 13
482[15] Lotties Bid **(40)** *(PSFelgate)* 3-8-7 DeanMcKeown(7) (outpcd fr ½-wy) 1¾ 14
Dancing Jazztime *(JSWainwright)* 4-8-9 NConnorton(8) (w'like: bkwd: sn outpcd: wl bhd fr ½-wy) 15 15

11/8 ALLYANA (IRE), **4/1** Quilling (3/1-9/2), **6/1** Dancing Sioux, **7/1** Silk Cottage, Adamton, **12/1** Mr Moriarty (IRE) (op 20/1), **20/1** Never Say so, **25/1** Dancing Jazztime, Graceful Lady, Fred Said Right (IRE), **33/1** Skiptamaloo, Anytime Baby, Sundries, Lotties Bid, Marsh Arab, CSF £11.62 TOTE £2.20: £1.30 £2.80 £2.00 (£5.20) Trio £3.60 OWNER Mr George Strawbridge (KINGSCLERE) BRED Yeomanstown Lodge Stud 15 Rn 65.6 secs (4.10) SF: 36/37/26/21/18/-/4/4/-/-/-/-/-/-/-
WEIGHT FOR AGE 3yo-2lb

T/Plpt: £573.60 (18.8 Tckts). T/Qdpt: £90.10 (0.5 Tckts); £60.90 to Ayr 14/9/95. AA/WG

3628-SANDOWN (R-H)
Wednesday September 13th (Good to soft, Soft patches)
WEATHER: warm, sunny WIND: almost nil

3650
E.B.F. 'GRASS WIDOWS' MAIDEN STKS (I) (2-Y.O) (Class D)
£4,240.50 (£1,284.00: £627.00: £298.50)
7f 16y Stalls: High GOING: 0.19 sec per fur (G) 1-45 (1-48)

1184[3] **Masehaab (IRE)** *(86)*(Fav)*(JLDunlop)* 2-9-0 WCarson(3) (lw: led over 2f: 2nd st: rdn 2f out: led ins fnl f: r.o wl)....— 1
3208[4] Acharne **(89)***(85) (CEBrittain)* 2-9-0 BDoyle(1) (lw: s.s: hdwy 6f out: led over 4f out: c centre st: hdd ins fnl f: r.o) ....nk 2
3339[3] Victoria Regia (IRE) *(78) (RCharlton)* 2-8-9 TQuinn(5) (b.off hind: lw: 3rd st: rdn over 1f out: ev ch ins fnl f: unable qckn)....1¼ 3
3494[7] Majdak Jereeb (IRE) *(69) (MajorWRHern)* 2-9-0 WRyan(8) (rdn & hdwy over 2f out: one pce) 6 4
3280[6] Flyfisher (IRE) *(61) (GLewis)* 2-9-0 PaulEddery(7) (4th st: wknd over 2f out) 3½ 5
Fort de France (USA) *(45) (MRStoute)* 2-9-0 WNewnes(2) (w'like: scope: a bhd)....7 6
Clemente *(37) (RHannon)* 2-9-0 RPerham(4) (w'like: bit bkwd: 6th st: a bhd) 3½ 7
3494[11] Three Weeks *(26) (WRMuir)* 2-9-0 JReid(6) (lw: bhd fnl 2f) 5 8
859[6] Sharp Night *(10) (MSSaunders)* 2-9-0 ADicks(9) (lw: 5th st: wknd over 3f out) 7 9

10/11 MASEHAAB (IRE) (4/6-Evens), **2/1** Victoria Regia (IRE), **14/1** Acharne (7/1-16/1), Majdak Jereeb (IRE) (7/1-16/1), Flyfisher (IRE), **16/1** Fort de France (USA), **33/1** Clemente, **50/1** Three Weeks, Sharp Night, CSF £14.01 TOTE £1.90: £1.10 £2.70 £1.30 (£11.60) Trio £3.80 OWNER Mr Hamdan Al Maktoum (ARUNDEL) BRED T. Newman and Mellon Stud 9 Rn
1m 33.31 (6.71) SF: 36/35/28/19/11/-/-/-/-

3651
'1845 INAUGURATION' CLAIMING STKS (2-Y.O) (Class E) £3,273.75
(£990.00: £482.50: £228.75)
5f 6y Stalls: High GOING minus 0.23 sec per fur (GF) 2-15 (2-18)

2706[9] **Standown (71)***(73) (JBerry)* 2-8-7 LDettori(9) (rdn over 3f out: hdwy on ins over 2f out: led over 1f out: r.o wl)....— 1
3568[11] Centurion **(79)***(72)*(Fav)*(RHannon)* 2-8-9 JReid(13) (lw: led over 3f: unable qckn fnl f)....1 2
3570[7] Baker *(57) (HCandy)* 2-8-7 WNewnes(14) (hdwy on ins over 1f out: r.o one pce)....4 3
2176[6] Golden Silver **(46)***(42) (JSMoore)* 2-7-9 (3) NVarley(8) (outpcd: hdwy over 1f out: nvr nrr).........2 4
852[9] Hi Hoh (IRE) *(41) (MBell)* 2-7-11 FNorton(12) (b.hind: a.p: hrd rdn over 1f out: one pce)......s.h 5
2859* Tymeera **(60)***(44) (BPalling)* 2-8-1 (3) SSanders(10) (b: chsd ldr 3f) 1¼ 6
3378[4] Killatty Lark (IRE) *(36) (WJMusson)* 2-7-11 CRutter(4) (lw: nvr nrr)....hd 7
3520[6] Poly By Staufan (IRE) *(20) (MRChannon)* 2-8-0 BDoyle(3) (lw: outpcd)....6 8
3570[3] Bells of Holland *(17) (BWHills)* 2-7-12 NAdams(2) (a bhd) ....½ 9
3314[2] Arctic Romancer (IRE) **(81)***(24) (GLewis)* 2-8-13b PaulEddery(6) (lw: prom 3f) 2½ 10
2826[5] Nameless **(51)** *(DJSCosgrove)* 2-7-12 JQuinn(5) (lw: prom over 2f)....4 11
3587a[28] Soviet Sakti (IRE) **(61)** *(PMitchell)* 2-8-9 RPerham(1) (lw: a bhd) 5 12
Dancing Man *(MrsMELong)* 2-8-9 ow2 JWilliams(11) (w'like: bit bkwd: s.s: a wl bhd) ....½ 13

3/1 Centurion, **4/1** Arctic Romancer (IRE) (op 5/2), Tymeera, **11/2** STANDOWN, **10/1** Bells of Holland (8/1-12/1), **12/1** Hi Hoh (IRE), **14/1** Baker (20/1-12/1), **16/1** Killatty Lark (IRE), **20/1** Nameless, Golden Silver, **33/1** Poly By Staufan (IRE), **40/1** Dancing Man, **50/1** Soviet Sakti (IRE), CSF £22.19 TOTE £4.90: £1.80 £1.70 £4.00 (£8.60) Trio £65.70 OWNER Mrs Chris Deuters (COCKERHAM) BRED Alan Gibson 13 Rn 62.5 secs (2.70) SF: 27/26/11/-/-/-/-/-/-/-/-/-/-

3652 E.B.F. 'GRASS WIDOWS' MAIDEN STKS (II) (2-Y.O) (Class D) £4,221.00 (£1,278.00: £624.00: £297.00) 7f 16y Stalls: High GOING: 0.19 sec (G) 2-50 (2-51)

22002 **Lomberto** *(84+) (RHannon)* 2-8-9 (5) DaneO'Neill(1) (lw: 3rd st: qcknd & led 1f out: r.o wl)....— 1
Sunley Secure *(76) (MRChannon)* 2-9-0 RHughes(3) (w'like: scope: 2nd st: led 2f out to 1f out: unable qckn)....3½ 2
23207 D'naan (IRE) *(73)*(Fav)*(WJHaggas)* 2-9-0 LDettori(8) (lw: 4th st: rdn over 2f out: one pce fnl f)....1¼ 3
27676 Nakhal *(73) (DJGMurraySmith)* 2-9-0 PaulEddery(9) (led 5f: one pce)....nk 4
Law Dancer (IRE) *(70) (TGMills)* 2-9-0 JReid(7) (w'like: lw: hdwy over 2f out: rdn over 1f out: wknd ins fnl f)....1 5
334014 One Pound *(65) (BWHills)* 2-9-0 JWilliams(6) (sme hdwy over 2f out: wknd over 1f out)....2½ 6
Iamus *(61) (PTWalwyn)* 2-9-0 TQuinn(5) (str: scope: bit bkwd: hdwy over 2f out: wknd over 1f out)....1½ 7
337924 Forliando *(50) (MSSaunders)* 2-9-0 NAdams(4) (6th st: wknd over 2f out)....5 8
Carwyn's Choice *(31) (PCClarke)* 2-8-9 FNorton(2) (unf: scope: 5th st: wknd over 3f out)....6 9

15/8 D'naan (IRE) (op 5/4), **11/4** LOMBERTO, **11/2** Iamus (3/1-6/1), Law Dancer (IRE), **14/1** Nakhal, **16/1** Sunley Secure, **25/1** One Pound, **50/1** Forliando, Carwyn's Choice, CSF £37.81 TOTE £3.30: £1.40 £1.70 £1.20 (£27.50) Trio £15.10 OWNER Mr Saleh Al Homeizi (MARLBOROUGH) BRED C. R. and V. M. Withers 9 Rn 1m 35.01 (8.41) SF: 18/10/7/7/4/-/-/-/-

3653 'CRICKET DEVELOPMENT' MAIDEN STKS (3-Y.O) (Class D) £4,065.00 (£1,230.00: £600.00: £285.00) 1m 2f 7y Stalls: High GOING: 0.19 sec (G) 3-20 (3-27)

66310 **Coburg** *(84) (HRACecil)* 3-9-0 WRyan(6) (hld up: led over 2f out: r.o wl)....— 1
33772 Prickwillow (USA) *(75)*(Fav)*(JHMGosden)* 3-8-9 LDettori(15) (6th st: chsd wnr over 1f out: unable qckn)....2½ 2
77911 Love The Blues *(69) (DNicholson)* 3-8-9 JWilliams(1) (hdwy over 1f out: r.o)....3½ 3
18342 Meghdoot **(69)***(65) (HJCollingridge)* 3-8-9 MRimmer(7) (bit bkwd: 4th st: ev ch over 2f out: wknd fnl f)....3 4
19274 Drum Battle *(66) (RCharlton)* 3-9-0 TQuinn(2) (hdwy over 2f out: wknd over 1f out)....2½ 5
22086 Big Treat (IRE) *(55) (PAKelleway)* 3-9-0 BDoyle(16) (led 1f: led 8f out tl over 6f out: led over 5f out tl over 2f out: wknd over 1f out)....7 6
109711 Volunteer (IRE) *(51) (RJO'Sullivan)* 3-9-0 WNewnes(13) (lw: led 9f out to 8f out: led over 6f out tl over 5f out: 2nd st: wknd over 2f out)....2½ 7
33386 King of Babylon (IRE) *(50) (LadyHerries)* 3-9-0 JQuinn(18) (5th st: wknd over 2f out)....nk 8
114711 What's Secreto (USA) *(50) (PAKelleway)* 3-9-0 MWigham(4) (bit bkwd: nvr nrr)....s.h 9
Printers Quill *(48) (MajorDNChappell)* 3-9-0 JReid(11) (unf: bit bkwd: nvr nrr)....1½ 10
27906 Maftun (USA) *(45) (MajorWRHern)* 3-9-0 WCarson(5) (lw: nvr plcd to chal)....1¾ 11
32398 Jilly Beveled *(29) (RHannon)* 3-8-6 (3) SSanders(8) (swtg: prom over 3f)....7 12
My Darlingdaughter *(24) (RCharlton)* 3-8-9 PaulEddery(10) (w'like: scope: bhd fnl 6f)....3 13
17177 Bala Monaafis (IRE) *(23) (WRMuir)* 3-8-6 (3) SSanders(14) (bit bkwd: 3rd st: wknd over 3f out)....½ 14
340110 Most Becoming *(13) (JRArnold)* 3-8-9 CRutter(9) (a bhd)....6 15
27603 Woodlands Lad Too *(11) (PAPritchard)* 3-9-0 NAdams(12) (bhd fnl 3f)....5 16
Bagby Boy *(3) (PRHedger)* 3-9-0 MPerrett(17) (leggy: s.s: a bhd)....5 17

Evens Prickwillow (USA), **9/2** COBURG, **10/1** Maftun (USA) (op 6/1), Meghdoot, **11/1** Drum Battle (7/1-12/1), **14/1** My Darlingdaughter, **20/1** King of Babylon (IRE), **25/1** Volunteer (IRE), Printers Quill, Love The Blues, **33/1** Bala Monaafis (IRE), Jilly Beveled, **50/1** Big Treat (IRE), What's Secreto (USA), Bagby Boy, **100/1** Most Becoming, Woodlands Lad Too, CSF £9.27 TOTE £5.80: £1.70 £1.20 £10.10 (£3.70) Trio £142.10 OWNER Sheikh Mohammed (NEWMARKET) BRED Sheikh Mohammed bin Rashid al Maktoum 17 Rn
2m 11.0 (6.70) SF: 59/50/44/40/41/30/26/25/25/23/20/4/-/-/-/-/-

3654 SURREY COUNTY CRICKET CLUB 150TH ANNIVERSARY H'CAP (0-80) (3-Y.O) (Class D) £4,591.50 (£1,392.00: £681.00: £325.50) 1m 14y Stalls: High GOING: 0.19 sec per fur (G) 3-55 (4-03)

3585a8 **Danegold (IRE) (78)***(87+) (MRChannon)* 3-9-7v RHughes(10) (6th st: swtchd rt 2f out: qcknd & led 1f out: comf)....— 1

6947 Noble Sprinter (IRE) **(76)***(84) (RHannon)* 3-9-5 JReid(9) (hld up: rdn 2f out: r.o ins fnl f).........½ 2
34976 Cyrus the Great (IRE) **(72)***(79) (MBell)* 3-9-1 TQuinn(3) (rdn over 2f out: hdwy over 1f out: r.o)........½ 3
34756 Twice Purple (IRE) **(59)***(63) (BJMeehan)* 3-7-13 (3) SSanders(1) (lost pl over 4f out: rallied over 1f out: unable qckn)........1½ 4
3227* Strumming (IRE) **(78)***(80) (JHMGosden)* 3-9-7 LDettori(13) (lw: led over 6f out tl over 2f out: led over 1f out: sn hdd: one pce)........1¼ 5
307912 Pedaltothemetal (IRE) **(52)***(49) (PMitchell)* 3-7-2 (7)ow2 CAdamson(2) (b.off hind: rdn over 2f out: hdwy over 1f out r.o one pce)........1½ 6
34979 Norsong **(54)***(53) (RAkehurst)* 3-7-11 JQuinn(7) (7th st: ev ch over 1f out: one pce)........s.h 7
34295 Fastini Gold **(60)***(58) (MDIUsher)* 3-8-3 AClark(4) (lw: nvr nr to chal)........s.h 8
30664 Mister Fire Eyes (IRE) **(74)***(69)*(Fav)*(CEBrittain)* 3-9-3 BDoyle(8) (led over 1f: 2nd st: led over 2f out tl over 1f out: sn wknd)........1½ 9
24147 Jigadee Creek **(57)***(46) (GHarwood)* 3-8-0 CRutter(11) (lw: 5th st: wknd over 2f out)........3½ 10
*3514*12 Brown Eyed Girl **(60)***(31) (RHannon)* 3-8-3 PaulEddery(12) (3rd st: wknd over 2f out)........9 11
*3075*13 Lees Please (IRE) **(55)***(16) (KOCunningham-Brown)* 3-7-12 FNorton(6) (hdwy 3f out: wknd over 2f out)........5 12
*1366*16 Amboyna Burl (IRE) **(50)** *(DAWilson)* 3-7-7 NAdams(5) (Withdrawn not under Starter's orders on veterinary advice)........ W

LONG HANDICAP Pedaltothemetal (IRE) 6-9 Amboyna Burl (IRE) 7-3

11/4 Mister Fire Eyes (IRE) (4/1-5/2), **4/1** Strumming (IRE) (op 5/2), **13/2** DANEGOLD (IRE), **9/1** Twice Purple (IRE), **10/1** Cyrus the Great (IRE), **11/1** Norsong (8/1-12/1), **12/1** Brown Eyed Girl, **16/1** Noble Sprinter (IRE), Lees Please (IRE), **20/1** Jigadee Creek, **25/1** Fastini Gold, **50/1** Pedaltothemetal (IRE), Amboyna Burl (IRE), CSF £90.70 CT £931.57 TOTE £6.30: £1.80 £4.90 £3.60 (£37.60) Trio £133.40 OWNER The Dream Team (UPPER LAMBOURN) BRED Barronstown Stud and Ron Con Ltd 12 Rn 1m 45.06 (5.86) SF: 61/58/53/37/54/23/27/32/43/20/5/-/-

3655 'KENNINGTON OVAL' NURSERY H'CAP (2-Y.O) (Class D) £4,201.50 (£1,272.00: £621.00: £295.50)

5f 6y Stalls: High GOING minus 0.23 sec per fur (GF) 4-25 (4-31)

31602 **White Emir (80)***(80) (BJMeehan)* 2-8-11 BDoyle(8) (lw: a.p: chsd ldr over 1f out: led ins fnl f: r.o wl)........— 1
34002 Comic Fantasy (AUS) **(89)***(85)*(Fav)*(PWChapple-Hyam)* 2-9-6b JReid(9) (lw: led tl ins fnl f: unable qckn)........1¼ 2
32135 Erupt **(70)***(60) (GBBalding)* 2-7-12v(3) NVarley(6) (hld up: rdn & n.m.r on ins over 2f out: r.o ins fnl f)........2 3
35682 Lady Caroline Lamb (IRE) **(64)***(41) (MRChannon)* 2-7-9 JQuinn(2) (chsd ldr over 3f: wknd fnl f)........4 4
22812 Gi La High **(77)***(41) (JBerry)* 2-8-8 LDettori(5) (nvr nr to chal)........4 5
26745 Proud Monk **(74)***(32) (GLMoore)* 2-8-5 SWhitworth(4) (lw: a bhd)........2 6
3434* Bedside Mail **(90)***(40) (JMPEustace)* 2-9-2 (5) DaneO'Neill(7) (lw: hld up: rdn over 2f out: sn wknd)........2½ 7
3566* Bozeman (IRE) **(66)***(12) (RHannon)* 2-7-11b 6x FNorton(3) (a bhd)........1¼ 8
16345 Mystery Matthias **(65)** *(MissBSanders)* 2-7-10 NAdams(1) (a bhd)........5 9

7/2 Comic Fantasy (AUS), **5/1** WHITE EMIR, Bozeman (IRE) (op 3/1), **13/2** Lady Caroline Lamb (IRE), Bedside Mail, **7/1** Gi La High, **9/1** Erupt, **10/1** Proud Monk (7/1-12/1), **33/1** Mystery Matthias, CSF £21.62 CT £138.85 TOTE £6.70: £2.00 £1.80 £2.60 (£7.40) Trio £34.30 OWNER Mr Nigel Stafford (UPPER LAMBOURN) BRED G. Dickinson 9 Rn 61.5 secs (1.70) SF: 47/52/27/8/8/-/7/-/-

OFFICIAL EXPLANATION Bozeman (IRE): was bumped leaving the stalls and reluctant to race thereafter.

3656 'CRICKET CELEBRATION' LIMITED STKS (0-75) (3-Y.O) (Class D) £3,694.50 (£1,116.00: £543.00: £256.50)

7f 16y Stalls: High GOING: 0.19 sec per fur (G) 5-00 (5-00)

33472 **Summer Retreat (USA) (72)***(81)*(Fav)*(JHMGosden)* 3-8-7 LDettori(5) (3rd st: rdn over 2f out: chsd ldr over 1f out: led ins fnl f: r.o)........— 1
3488* South Rock **(75)***(83)*(Fav)*(JAGlover)* 3-8-13 WRyan(8) (led: qcknd over 2f out: hdd ins fnl f: unable qckn)........1¾ 2
33473 Zahwa **(72)***(75) (RWArmstrong)* 3-8-7 WCarson(3) (lw: 4th st: rdn over 2f out: r.o ins fnl f)......1 3
23613 African-Pard (IRE) **(70)***(71) (DHaydnJones)* 3-8-12 JReid(4) (5th st: rdn over 2f out: one pce) 4 4
*1882*8 Denbrae (IRE) **(72)***(65) (DJGMurraySmith)* 3-9-1 RHughes(1) (nvr nr to chal)........4 5
27085 Millazure (USA) **(70)***(56) (RCharlton)* 3-8-7 PaulEddery(6) (lw: 6th st: wknd over 1f out)........½ 6
31758 Scharnhorst **(71)***(57) (SDow)* 3-9-1 TQuinn(2) (2nd st: wknd over 1f out)........3 7
31757 Masruf (IRE) **(72)***(29) (TThomsonJones)* 3-8-12 SWhitworth(7) (a bhd)........11 8

11/4 SUMMER RETREAT (USA) (2/1-3/1), South Rock, **10/3** Zahwa, **7/1** Scharnhorst, **15/2** Millazure (USA), **14/1** Masruf (IRE), African-Pard (IRE), **33/1** Denbrae (IRE), CSF £10.47 TOTE £3.40: £1.50 £1.70 £1.10 (£5.00) OWNER Mr K. Abdullah (NEWMARKET) BRED Juddmonte Farms 8 Rn 1m 31.87 (5.27) SF: 46/48/40/36/30/21/22/-

3657 '150TH SEASON CLOSES' APPRENTICE H'CAP (0-70) (3-Y.O+) (Class F) £2,721.75 (£834.00: £414.50: £204.75)

1m 2f 7y Stalls: High GOING: 0.19 sec per fur (G) 5-30 (5-33)

3462[2] **Kandyan (66)***(82) (MHTompkins)* 4-9-2 (8) JGotobed(5) (lw: hdwy over 4f out: led wl over 1f out: r.o wl) — 1
3611[2] Braille (IRE) **(65)***(77)*(Fav)*(MGMeagher)* 4-9-4 (5) SBuckley(15) (hld up: rdn over 1f out: r.o one pce) 2½ 2
3440[6] Lady Lacey **(45)***(55) (GBBalding)* 8-8-3v IonaWands(3) (hdwy over 1f out: r.o) 1½ 3
3302[2] Broughton's Pride (IRE) **(49)***(56) (JAGlover)* 4-8-1 (6) VictoriaAppleby(10) (lw: 2nd st: ev ch over 1f out: wknd ins fnl f) 1¾ 4
3501* Lady Sabina **(42)***(48) (WJMusson)* 5-8-0 JWilkinson(7) (lw: s.s: hdwy over 2f out: one pce) ½ 5
3154[2] Music Maker **(56)***(59) (SirMarkPrescott)* 3-8-7 DToole(13) (led 7f out tl wl over 1f out: wknd) 2 6
3531[4] Curtelace **(54)***(56) (LadyHerries)* 5-8-12 CWebb(16) (lw: hdwy on ins 3f out: one pce fnl 2f) ½ 7
3406[4] Roisin Clover **(67)***(69) (SDow)* 4-9-1 (10) PBrookwood(14) (nvr nr to chal) nk 8
2568[3] Spread The Word **(63)***(64) (LGCottrell)* 3-8-9 (5) CScudder(17) (lw: no hdwy fnl 2f) nk 9
2993[3] Tajar (USA) **(62)***(62) (DMorley)* 3-8-13 GFaulkner(18) (swtg: 5th st: wknd over 1f out) ½ 10
3024[6] Emma Grimes (IRE) **(40)***(32) (JSMoore)* 4-7-5 (7) TThomas(6) (lw: nvr nrr) 5 11
2979[8] Astral Weeks (IRE) **(67)***(59) (RHannon)* 4-9-3 (8) EGreehy(4) (lw: a mid div) hd 12
990[6] Chita Rivera **(44)***(30) (PJMakin)* 4-8-2v AEddery(2) (led 1f: 3rd st: wknd over 2f out) 4 13
3336[5] Dancing Sensation (USA) **(70)***(51) (RAkehurst)* 8-9-6 (8) TAshley(20) (a mid div) 3 14
406[14] Ebony Blaze **(56)***(36) (CPWildman)* 4-8-9 (5) JBramhill(12) (6th st: wknd over 2f out) ½ 15
3383[9] Maybe Today **(51)***(30) (BRMillman)* 3-7-11 (5) RStudholme(1) (bhd fnl 5f) ½ 16
3515[6] Astrojoy (IRE) **(50)***(21) (SGKnight)* 3-8-1b AimeeCook(9) (b.off fore: dwlt: a bhd) 5 17
3544[5] War Requiem (IRE) **(44)***(12) (MissGayKelleway)* 5-7-11 (5)ow3 FLynch(19) (lw: bhd fnl 2f) s.h 18
2522[5] Sound Trick (USA) **(50)***(10) (GCBravery)* 3-7-10 (5) BHalligan(11) (led 9f out to 7f out: 4th st: wknd over 3f out) 7 19

4/1 Braille (IRE), **5/1** KANDYAN, **15/2** Lady Sabina, **8/1** Lady Lacey, Curtelace (6/1-9/1), **12/1** Broughton's Pride (IRE), **14/1** Music Maker, Dancing Sensation (USA) (10/1-16/1), **16/1** Roisin Clover, Tajar (USA), Spread The Word, **20/1** Maybe Today, **25/1** Astral Weeks (IRE), Chita Rivera, Astrojoy (IRE), **33/1** War Requiem (IRE), Emma Grimes (IRE), Sound Trick (USA), **50/1** Ebony Blaze, CSF £25.69 CT £155.85 TOTE £6.30: £1.30 £1.60 £2.00 £3.50 (£8.50) Trio £58.00 OWNER Mr B. W. Gaule (NEWMARKET) BRED Sheikh Mohammed bin Rashid al Maktoum 19 Rn
2m 13.97 (9.67) SF: 45/40/18/19/11/15/19/32/20/18/-/22/-/14/-/-/-/-/-
WEIGHT FOR AGE 3yo-7lb

T/Jkpt: £10,311.40 (0.1 Tckts); £13,070.88 to Ayr 14/9/95. T/Plpt: £53.00 (323.42 Tckts). T/Qdpt: £50.20 (4.35 Tckts). AK

3635-YARMOUTH (L-H)
Wednesday September 13th (Good)

WEATHER: sunny WIND: mod across

3658 COURAGE EAST ANGLIA (S) STKS (3-Y.O+) (Class G) £2,959.80 (£822.80: £395.40) 1m 2f 21y Stalls: Low GOING minus 0.20 sec per fur (GF) 2-30 (2-31)

3363[6] **Lunar Mission (IRE) (54)***(69) (JMPEustace)* 4-9-3 MTebbutt(12) (lw: hld up: 4th st: led over 2f out: sn drvn clr: hld on wl) — 1
3254[4] Hard Love **(62)***(67) (SPCWoods)* 3-8-10 WWoods(9) (chsd ldr: 2nd st: rdn bel dist: kpt on ins fnl f) 1¼ 2
3529[5] Rival Bid (USA) **(55)***(67) (MrsNMacauley)* 7-8-10 (7) AmandaSanders(13) (lw: hld up: hdwy 3f out: effrt 2f out: rdn & r.o wl fnl f) hd 3
3514[6] Shooter **(60)***(63) (PFICole)* 3-8-10 MHills(2) (a.p: 3rd st: rdn over 2f out: one pce) 2½ 4
2979[20] Bobanlyn (IRE) **(59)***(56) (DMorris)* 3-8-5 CNutter(17) (hld up: effrt 3f out: sn rdn: nt pce to chal) 1 5
3544[4] Zahran (IRE) **(46)***(66) (JMBradley)* 4-9-5 (3) SDrowne(14) (b: chsd ldrs: 6th st: rdn over 2f out: styd on) hd 6
3641[2] Buckley Boys **(46)***(55) (ABailey)* 4-8-9 (3) DWright(7) (led tl hdd over 2f out: sn rdn & impeded: nt rcvr) ¾ 7
3129* Latin Leader **(63)***(64)*(Fav)*(CREgerton)* 5-9-8 MRoberts(16) (hld up: hdwy ½-wy: rdn along 3f out: sn btn) ¾ 8
3402[7] Queens Stroller (IRE) **(54)***(57) (CCElsey)* 4-9-3 PatEddery(10) (hld up: hdwy on ins 3f out: rdn & btn whn hmpd appr fnl f) 1¼ 9

3344[15] Watch My Lips **(39)***(55) (MHTompkins)* 3-8-10 PRobinson(4) (nvr nr to chal) 1¼ 10
3272[2] Wordsmith (IRE) **(41)***(53) (JLHarris)* 5-9-3 GDuffield(1) (lw: hld up in tch: rdn & outpcd 3f out: sn wknd) 1¼ 11
3258[5] Premier Blues (FR) **(18)***(48) (RJRWilliams)* 5-8-12 DBiggs(15) (a in rr) ....s.h 12
3638[13] Magication **(28)***(48) (CNAllen)* 5-8-12 GBardwell(5) (a bhd) ....hd 13
Water Diviner **(35)***(48) (KGWingrove)* 5-9-0 (3) PMcCabe(3) (chsd ldrs: 5th st: wknd over 3f out) 3 14
3410[6] Straw Thatch **(45)***(52) (RBastiman)* 6-9-3 (5) HBastiman(6) (a bhd) ....¾ 15
3426[6] Pop to Stans **(44)***(44) (JPearce)* 6-9-1 (7) MNutter(18) (a in rr: t.o) 5 16
1606[4] Pewter Lass **(38)***(32) (MBlanshard)* 3-8-5 TSprake(8) (swtg: mid div tl wknd over 3f out: t.o) 1¼ 17

4/1 Latin Leader, **5/1** Hard Love, **6/1** Bobanlyn (IRE), **8/1** Queens Stroller (IRE), **9/1** Rival Bid (USA), **12/1** LUNAR MISSION (IRE), Shooter, **16/1** Buckley Boys, Pop to Stans, **33/1** Watch My Lips, Zahran (IRE), Premier Blues (FR), Magication, Straw Thatch, Wordsmith (IRE), **50/1** Water Diviner, Pewter Lass, CSF £64.11 TOTE £16.70: £4.40 £1.80 £3.50 (£36.40) Trio £98.00 OWNER R and S Partnership (NEWMARKET) BRED Miss Ann Marie Crowley 17 Rn

2m 10.3 (5.90) SF: 37/28/35/24/17/34/23/32/25/16/21/16/16/16/20/12/-

WEIGHT FOR AGE 3yo-7lb

Bt in 4,000 gns

3659 GOLDEN JUBILEE CHALLENGE TROPHY H'CAP (0-90) (3-Y.O+) (Class C) £6,836.00 (£2,048.00: £984.00: £452.00)
1m 2f 21y Stalls: Low GOING minus 0.20 sec per fur (GF) 3-00 (3-05)

Domappel (65)*(73) (MrsJCecil)* 3-8-1 (5) MHenry(14) (a.p: 3rd st: rdn to ld over 1f out: sn hdd: one pce: fin 2nd, 3l: awrdd r) ....— 1
3501[2] Myfontaine **(62)***(70) (KTIvory)* 8-8-10 GBardwell(2) (hld up in tch: nt clr run over 2f out: swtchd outside over 1f out: fin wl: fin 3rd, s.h: plcd 2nd) 2
2780[7] Virtual Reality **(77)***(82) (AHide)* 4-9-11 WWoods(6) (hld up & bhd: stdy hdwy 3f out: nrst fin: fin 4th, 2l: plcd 3rd) 3
3459[4] Vindaloo **(87)***(91) (JLHarris)* 3-10-0 MRoberts(5) (lw: a.p: 4th st: rdn & n.m.r 2f out: kpt on one pce: fin 5th, 3/4l: plcd 4th) 4
1865[4] Beaumont (IRE) **(61)***(64) (JEBanks)* 5-8-6 (3) SDrowne(8) (hld up: hdwy over 3f out: rdn over 1f out: one pce: fin 6th, 1 1/4l: plcd 5th) 5
3368[13] Hakika (USA) **(85)***(87) (DMorley)* 3-9-12 RHills(4) (hld up in tch: effrt 3f out: ev ch 2f out: hmpd & wknd ins fnl f) ....½ 7
3461* Delta Soleil (USA) **(86)***(84)*(Fav)*(PWHarris)* 3-9-13 PatEddery(1) (lw: chsd ldr: 2nd st: led over 4f out tl over 1f out: sn rdn & no ex) 2½ 8
3156[3] Grand Selection (IRE) **(82)***(72) (MBell)* 3-9-9 MFenton(9) (swtg: hld up mid div: effrt 3f out: nvr nr to chal) 5 9
3500[10] Yet Again **(60)***(44) (BHanbury)* 3-7-10 (5) AWhelan(10) (a in rr) 4 10
3119* Roseberry Ray (IRE) **(77)***(55) (GWragg)* 3-9-4 MHills(12) (hld up: hdwy 4f out: wknd over 2f out) 3½ 11
3496[2] Quivira **(77)***(47) (TTClement)* 4-9-11 EGuest(7) (a in rr) 5 12
2980[8] Just Flamenco **(54)***(21) (MJRyan)* 4-8-2 DBiggs(16) (s.i.s: hdwy 6f out: 6th st: wknd 3f out) .1¾ 13
2707[11] River Keen (IRE) **(79)***(43) (RWArmstrong)* 3-9-6 RPrice(15) (a in rr) 2 14
1103[7] Eight Sharp (IRE) **(80)***(42) (BWHills)* 3-9-7 GDuffield(18) (a bhd) 1¼ 15
3382[4] Mackook (USA) **(85)***(41) (MRStoute)* 3-9-12 WRSwinburn(17) (chsd ldrs 6f: sn lost tch: t.o) 4 16
3445[12] Non Vintage (IRE) **(52)** *(MCChapman)* 4-7-7 (7)ow4 CMunday(3) (led tl hdd & wknd over 4f out: t.o) 2½ 17
2438* Quandary (USA) **(80)***(93) (HRACecil)* 4-10-0 PRobinson(13) (hld up gng wl: 5th st: n.m.r wl over 1f out: barged thro to ld ins fnl f: sn clr: fin 1st: disq: plcd last) 0

4/1 Delta Soleil (USA), **6/1** Vindaloo, **8/1** Roseberry Ray (IRE), Beaumont (IRE), **9/1** Grand Selection (IRE) (op 6/1), **10/1** Mackook (USA) (8/1-12/1), **11/1** Virtual Reality, **12/1** Quandary (USA) (8/1-14/1), **16/1** Myfontaine, Hakika (USA), Quivira, **20/1** River Keen (IRE), **33/1** Yet Again, Eight Sharp (IRE), DOMAPPEL, Non Vintage (IRE), Just Flamenco, CSF £432.60 CT £5,456.17 TOTE £46.80: £6.20 £3.20 £2.80 £1.40 (£993.50) Trio £615.00; £779.67 to Yarmouth 14/9/95 OWNER Mr M. C. Banks (NEWMARKET) BRED Bolton Grange 17 Rn

2m 7.4 (3.00) SF: 44/48/60/62/42/58/55/43/15/26/25/-/14/13/12/-/71

WEIGHT FOR AGE 3yo-7lb

STEWARDS' ENQUIRY Robinson susp. 22-25/9/95 (irresponsible riding).

3660 DANNY WRIGHT MEMORIAL CONDITIONS STKS (3-Y.O+) (Class C) £5,116.80 (£1,891.20: £905.60: £368.00: £144.00: £54.40)
6f 3y Stalls: High GOING minus 0.20 sec per fur (GF) 3-30 (3-34)

3602[7] **Carranita (IRE) (105)***(109)*(Fav)*(BPalling)* 5-9-9 TSprake(7) (a.p: led over 2f out: drvn clr)...— 1

3557³ Katya (IRE) **(94)***(95) (MRChannon)* 3-9-0 MHills(4) (hld up: hdwy 2f out: kpt on fnl f: no ch w wnr) 3 2
Subzero **(98)***(89) (MRStoute)* 3-8-13 WRSwinburn(3) (bhd: effrt u.p wl over 1f out: r.o ins fnl f) 2 3
3279* Coffee 'n Cream **(95)***(93) (RHannon)* 3-9-5 MRoberts(6) (prom tl outpcd over 1f out: eased ins fnl f) ....¾ 4
3637¹³ Join the Clan **(89)***(90) (MrsNMacauley)* 6-9-6 (3) SDrowne(5) (lw: chsd ldrs: rdn over 1f out: nt pce to chal) 1¼ 5
2013* Christmas Kiss **(84)***(80) (RHannon)* 3-9-0 PatEddery(2) (chsd ldrs 4f: sn outpcd) 1¾ 6
2677³ Bahith (USA) **(96)***(65) (HThomsonJones)* 3-9-1b RHills(1) (lw: led over 3f: wknd appr fnl f: t.o) 6 7

2/1 CARRANITA (IRE), **3/1** Coffee 'n Cream, **5/1** Bahith (USA), **13/2** Katya (IRE), **10/1** Subzero, **12/1** Christmas Kiss, **20/1** Join the Clan, CSF £13.51 TOTE £3.10: £1.90 £2.80 (£7.70) OWNER Lamb Lane Associates (COWBRIDGE) BRED Mrs Anita Quinn 7 Rn

1m 11.8 (1.20) SF: 73/56/50/54/54/41/26
WEIGHT FOR AGE 3yo-3lb

3661

SHADWELL STUD SERIES APPRENTICE H'CAP (0-70) (3-Y.O+) (Class E) £3,600.00 (£1,080.00: £520.00: £240.00)
7f 3y Stalls: High GOING minus 0.20 sec per fur (GF) 4-00 (4-01)

3457¹¹ **Thunder River (IRE) (60)***(70) (MJHeaton-Ellis)* 5-9-9v DRMcCabe(10) (mde all: hrd rdn fnl f: hld on wl) ....— 1
*3510** Bentico **(57)***(66) (MrsNMacauley)* 6-9-6b AmandaSanders(20) (w wnr: ev ch fnl 2f: unable qckn) ....nk 2
2685³ Racing Telegraph **(42)***(49) (JWPayne)* 5-8-5 SDrowne(9) (hld up: hdwy 2f out: rdn & r.o wl fnl f) 1¼ 3
2843³ Amany (IRE) **(44)***(48) (GLewis)* 3-8-3 AWhelan(18) (lw: hdwy wl over 1f out: nrst fin) 1¼ 4
2414¹¹ Ahjay **(48)***(49) (DAWilson)* 5-8-11 JDSmith(15) (bit bkwd: hdwy 2f out: rdn & r.o wl ins fnl f).1¼ 5
3295⁵ Upex le Gold Too **(40)***(39) (LRLloyd-James)* 3-7-8 (5)ow2 KSked(13) (hdwy ½-wy: rdn bel dist: r.o one pce) ....s.h 6
3475* Cuban Reef **(44)***(40)*(Fav)*(WJMusson)* 3-8-3 PMcCabe(16) (hld up: hdwy 2f out: rdn & r.o wl fnl f) 2 7
3291⁸ Mr Cube (IRE) **(60)***(50) (JMBradley)* 5-9-6v(3) RWaterfield(3) (in tch: rdn over 2f out: no imp)2½ 8
3365⁴ Passion Sunday **(37)***(23) (LRLloyd-James)* 4-8-0 DWright(17) (b.hind: prom tl rdn & wknd wl over 1f out) 2 9
3455¹¹ Chancey Fella **(54)***(36) (KTIvory)* 4-9-0 (3) CScally(7) (b: nvr trbld ldrs) 1¾ 10
3372² Flyaway Blues **(59)***(40) (MrsMReveley)* 3-9-4v GParkin(14) (lw: effrt & rdn over 2f out: no rspnse) ....nk 11
2786⁶ Hot Snap **(55)***(25) (CFWall)* 3-9-0 LNewton(11) (prom: rdn over 2f out: sn btn) 5 12
3167* Highspeed (IRE) **(52)***(22) (SEKettlewell)* 3-8-11 MHenry(4) (a in rr) ....hd 13
3638⁸ Western Valley **(30)** *(CPWildman)* 5-7-7 MartinDwyer(1) (chsd ldrs over 4f) 3 14
3310* Legal Issue (IRE) **(67)***(29) (SirMarkPrescott)* 3-9-12 HBastiman(5) (lw: bhd: effrt 3f out: nvr plcd to chal) ....½ 15
3428* Dunloe (IRE) **(61)***(17) (GWragg)* 3-9-3 (3) GMilligan(12) (chsd ldrs: rdn 3f out: sn btn) 2½ 16
2361⁷ Triple Tricks (IRE) **(67)***(21) (WJHaggas)* 3-9-7 (5) ElizabethTurner(6) (a in rr) ....¾ 17
3034⁵ Hylters Girl **(39)** *(MJRyan)* 3-7-12 MBaird(2) (a bhd) 2 18
3275⁶ Awesome Venture **(46)** *(MCChapman)* 5-8-9 CMunday(8) (prom 5f) ....s.h 19

LONG HANDICAP Western Valley 7-3

11/2 Cuban Reef, **7/1** Legal Issue (IRE), **8/1** Dunloe (IRE) (op 5/1), **9/1** Bentico, **10/1** Highspeed (IRE), **11/1** Flyaway Blues, **12/1** Racing Telegraph, Ahjay, **14/1** Passion Sunday, Awesome Venture, Chancey Fella, **16/1** Mr Cube (IRE), Hot Snap, THUNDER RIVER (IRE), Amany (IRE), **20/1** Upex le Gold Too, **25/1** Triple Tricks (IRE), **33/1** Hylters Girl, Western Valley, CSF £154.12 CT £1,665.03 TOTE £27.50: £4.80 £2.00 £3.60 £3.20 (£101.30) Trio £1,452.80; £818.50 to Yarmouth 14/9/95 OWNER Mr T. H. Luckock (WROUGHTON) BRED Clifton Lodge Stud 19 Rn

1m 25.9 (3.10) SF: 52/48/31/26/31/17/18/32/5/18/18/3/-/-/7/-/-/-/-
WEIGHT FOR AGE 3yo-4lb

3662

E.B.F. HALVERGATE MAIDEN STKS (2-Y.O) (Class D) £4,142.50 (£1,240.00: £595.00: £272.50)
6f 3y Stalls: High GOING minus 0.20 sec per fur (GF) 4-35 (4-36)

3495² **Obsessive (USA)** *(85+)*(Fav)*(MRStoute)* 2-8-9 WRSwinburn(8) (hld up in tch: swtchd lft appr fnl f: qcknd to ld fnl 100y: readily) ....— 1
3432² Dark Deed (USA) *(77) (BWHills)* 2-8-9 PatEddery(1) (disp ld: ev ch ins fn f: unable qckn) 3 2

3371[5] Hoh Returns (IRE) *(79) (MBell)* 2-9-0 MFenton(5) (lw: mde most tl hdd & no ex wl ins fnl f) 1¼ 3
Apple Musashi *(73) (JHMGosden)* 2-9-0 WWoods(9) (w'like: scope: hld up: hdwy over 2f out: one pce fnl f) 2 4
Tsarskaya (USA) *(58) (MrsJCecil)* 2-8-9 MRoberts(2) (lt-f: unf: lost pl after 2f: shkn up & rallied appr fnl f: nvr nrr) 4 5
3180[8] A-Aasem *(59) (HThomsonJones)* 2-9-0 RHills(4) (bit bkwd: prom tl wknd wl over 1f out) 1¼ 6
3104[3] White Settler *(53) (RHannon)* 2-9-0 PRobinson(6) (prom on outside over 4f) 2½ 7
School Clock *(51) (CNAllen)* 2-9-0 GCarter(7) (w'like: leggy: a bhd & outpcd) ....¾ 8
Ageeb (IRE) *(49) (WJHaggas)* 2-9-0 MHills(10) (neat: a in rr: rdn 2f out: no imp) ....¾ 9
2135[11] Bouton d'Or *(PHowling)* 2-8-9 NCarlisle(3) (bit bkwd: chsd ldrs: rdn & wknd 3f out: t.o) ....dist 10

11/10 OBSESSIVE (USA) (5/4-evens), **5/2** Dark Deed (USA), **8/1** A-Aasem (op 3/1), **11/1** Hoh Returns (IRE), **16/1** Apple Musashi, **20/1** Tsarskaya (USA), **25/1** White Settler, **33/1** Ageeb (IRE), **50/1** School Clock, **66/1** Bouton d'Or, CSF £4.13 TOTE £2.20: £1.10 £1.40 £2.60 (£1.80) Trio £3.80 OWNER Cheveley Park Stud (NEWMARKET) BRED Cheveley Park Stud Ltd 10 Rn
1m 12.7 (2.10) SF: 46/38/40/34/19/20/14/12/10/-

3663 E.B.F. FLEGGBOROUGH MAIDEN STKS (2-Y.O) (Class D) £5,478.00 (£1,644.00: £792.00: £366.00)
7f 3y Stalls: High GOING minus 0.20 sec per fur (GF) 5-05 (5-07)

Shawanni *(78+) (BWHills)* 2-8-9 MHills(18) (w'like: scope: hld up: hdwy & n.m.r over 2f out: rdn to ld wl ins fnl f: r.o strly) ....— 1
3340[4] Hal's Pal *(80) (DRLoder)* 2-9-0 GCarter(12) (a w ldrs: disp ld ins fnl f: unable qckn cl home) 1¼ 2
3340[5] Dabka Dancer *(80) (ACStewart)* 2-9-0 MRoberts(6) (chsd ldrs: effrt & rdn over 1f out: slt ld ins fnl f: sn hdd: r.o) ....hd 3
Ali-Royal (IRE) *(78)*(Fav)*(HRACecil)* 2-9-0 PatEddery(14) (leggy: scope: a.p: drvn along 2f out: ev ch tl unable qckn fnl f) ....¾ 4
Insatiable (IRE) *(75) (MRStoute)* 2-9-0 KBradshaw(13) (leggy: lt-f: hld up: gd hdwy over 1f out: rn green: no ex ins fnl f) 1¼ 5
Final Stab (IRE) *(74) (PWHarris)* 2-8-9 (5) MHenry(8) (leggy: unf: bit bkwd: led tl hdd & n.m.r ins fnl f) ....½ 6
3340[7] Hamlet (IRE) *(70) (MBell)* 2-9-0 MFenton(15) (chsd ldrs: kpt on one pce fnl 2f) 2 7
Missile *(64) (WJHaggas)* 2-9-0 RMcGhin(7) (leggy: unf: s.s: hdwy over 2f out: nt rch ldrs) ...2½ 8
Shady Link (IRE) *(64) (MRStoute)* 2-9-0 WRSwinburn(11) (unf: chsd ldrs tl wknd appr fnl f) ....hd 9
Passing Strangers (USA) *(60) (PWHarris)* 2-9-0 GDuffield(2) (w'like: bkwd: prom 5f) 1½ 10
3340[11] Fursan (USA) *(57) (NAGraham)* 2-9-0 RHills(5) (chsd ldrs: rdn over 1f out: sn btn) 1¼ 11
Winter Romance *(54) (EALDunlop)* 2-9-0 NCarlisle(10) (w'like: scope: bit bkwd: a in rr) 1½ 12
Fly Fishing (USA) *(52) (MrsJCecil)* 2-9-0 EGuest(20) (w'like: bit bkwd: s.s: nvr trbld ldrs) ....¾ 13
My Lewicia (IRE) *(47) (PWHarris)* 2-8-9 RPrice(16) (b.off hind: rangy: unf: s.s: a bhd) ....s.h 14
School Boy *(45) (CNAllen)* 2-9-0 StephenDavies(9) (w'like: bkwd: sn lost pl: rdn along: n.d) ...3 15
Compass Pointer *(42) (JMPEustace)* 2-9-0 MTebbutt(17) (lt-f: a in rr) 1½ 16
3379[19] Soldier Mak *(35) (AHide)* 2-9-0 WWoods(4) (outpcd: a bhd) 3 17
Spillo *(32) (LMCumani)* 2-9-0 OUrbina(3) (leggy: lt-f: bkwd: m.n.s) 1¼ 18
Naval Hunter (USA) *(5) (PWHarris)* 2-9-0 PRobinson(1) (leggy: lt-f: outpcd: t.o) 12 19

5/2 Ali-Royal (IRE), **7/2** Hal's Pal, SHAWANNI, **5/1** Dabka Dancer, **14/1** Passing Strangers (USA), **16/1** Shady Link (IRE), **20/1** Hamlet (IRE), **33/1** Fursan (USA), **40/1** Fly Fishing (USA), **50/1** Insatiable (IRE), Final Stab (IRE), Winter Romance, Missile, My Lewicia (IRE), School Boy, Compass Pointer, Soldier Mak, Spillo, Naval Hunter (USA), CSF £15.50 TOTE £4.70: £2.00 £1.70 £1.80 (£10.90) Trio £11.10 OWNER Sheikh Mohammed (LAMBOURN) BRED Sheikh Mohammed bin Rashid al Maktoum 19 Rn 1m 26.7 (3.90) SF: 30/32/32/30/27/26/22/16/16/12/9/6/4/-/-/-/-/-/-

3664 NORTH SEA H'CAP (0-80) (3-Y.O+) (Class D) £4,374.50 (£1,310.00: £629.00: £288.50)
1m 3y Stalls: High GOING minus 0.20 sec per fur (GF) 5-40 (5-42)

3248[2] **Confronter (70)***(83) (SDow)* 6-9-9 MRoberts(7) (hld up: hdwy 3f out: led ins fnl f: drvn clr) ....— 1
3222[6] Mr Rough **(63)***(71)*(Fav)*(DMorris)* 4-9-2 StephenDavies(8) (hld up: hdwy to ld 2f out: rdn & hdd ins fnl f) 2½ 2
*3514** Hatta Breeze **(60)***(63) (MAJarvis)* 3-8-5b(3) DRMcCabe(12) (lw: a.p: ev ch over 1f out: kpt on one pce) 2½ 3
3497[5] My Gina **(72)***(74) (MRStoute)* 3-9-6 WRSwinburn(3) (hld up: hdwy & n.m.r over 1f out: nvr nrr) ....nk 4

3373[8] Distant Princess **(67)***(64) (BWHills)* 3-9-1 MHills(5) (hld up: effrt & n.m.r over 1f out: nvr able to chal)........2½ 5
3181[6] Midnight Jazz (IRE) **(73)***(67) (WAO'Gorman)* 5-9-12 EmmaO'Gorman(6) (hld up & bhd: effrt & nt clr run over 1f out: swtchd outside: nt pce to chal)........1½ 6
3475[7] By The Bay **(60)***(53) (CCElsey)* 3-8-8 PatEddery(2) (nvr bttr than mid div)........½ 7
3173* Oozlem (IRE) **(42)***(32) (JCPoulton)* 6-7-9b NCarlisle(1) (lw: reluctant to r: sn drvn along: n.d)1½ 8
3319[2] Sooty Tern **(71)***(60) (JMBradley)* 8-9-7 (3) SDrowne(10) (chsd ldr over 5f: wknd fnl 2f)........¾ 9
3488[12] Bassmaat (USA) **(70)***(56) (WJHaggas)* 4-9-9 RHills(14) (chsd ldrs 5f: eased whn btn wl over 1f out)........1¼ 10
3402[6] Runic Symbol **(41)***(11) (MBlanshard)* 4-7-3b(5)ow1 MBaird(9) (prom tl wknd over 3f out: t.o)......8 11
2928[3] Admirals Flame (IRE) **(74)***(29) (CFWall)* 4-9-13 GDuffield(4) (b: chsd ldrs over 5f: wknd qckly: t.o)........8 12
1830[10] Sea Spouse **(41)** *(MBlanshard)* 4-7-8 GBardwell(11) (bit bkwd: led: rdn & drifted lft 3f out: sn hdd & wknd: t.o)........1¾ 13
3504* Another Time **(53)** (Fav)*(SPCWoods)* 3-7-10 (5) MHenry(13) (hld up: rdn along & hdwy whn crashed thro rail & fell 3f out)........ F

LONG HANDICAP Runic Symbol 7-1

11/2 Another Time, Mr Rough, **13/2** Distant Princess, **8/1** Admirals Flame (IRE), CONFRONTER, My Gina, **9/1** Hatta Breeze, **10/1** Oozlem (IRE), **12/1** Sooty Tern, **16/1** Midnight Jazz (IRE), **20/1** Bassmaat (USA), By The Bay, Sea Spouse, **33/1** Runic Symbol, CSF £50.31 CT £379.83 TOTE £8.80: £2.10 £2.10 £4.10 (£21.50) Trio £327.20; £13.83 to Yarmouth 14/9/95 OWNER Hatfield Ltd (EPSOM) BRED Hamilton Bloodstock (UK) Ltd 14 Rn

1m 39.8 (4.50) SF: 43/31/18/29/19/27/8/-/20/16/-/-/-/-

WEIGHT FOR AGE 3yo-5lb

T/Plpt: £127.40 (114.31 Tckts). T/Qdpt: £10.50 (12.8 Tckts). IM

3167-**AYR (L-H)**

Thursday September 14th (Good)

WEATHER: sunny WIND: almost nil

3665 BRITISH RED CROSS 125TH BIRTHDAY INVITATION AMATEUR H'CAP

(0-70) (3-Y.O+) (Class G) £2,560.00 (£760.00: £360.00: £160.00)
1m 2f 192y Stalls: Low GOING minus 0.21 sec per fur (GF) 2-10 (2-11)

3308* **Keep Your Distance (60)***(71) (MrsMReveley)* 5-11-9 MissHDudgeon(10) (hld up: stdy hdwy 3f out: led 1f out: r.o)........— 1
3464[2] Contrafire (IRE) **(68)***(77) (WJarvis)* 3-11-9 MrCPlatts(6) (lw: a.p: led over 2f out to 1f out: kpt on)........1¼ 2
3059[2] Mentalasanythin **(65)***(57)*(Fav)*(ABailey)* 6-12-0 MissBridgetGatehouse(9) (in tch: styd on fnl 3f: nvr able to chal)........12 3
3276[7] Chantry Bellini **(38)***(29) (MrsSMAustin)* 6-10-1 MrsDWilkinson(5) (b: b.hind: cl up: led 7f out tl over 2f out: wknd)........s.h 4
3367[3] Imperial Bid (FR) **(55)***(43) (DenysSmith)* 7-11-4 MrJCartner(4) (lw: a.p: effrt 2f out: one pce)2½ 5
2835[4] Manful **(64)***(44) (JHetherton)* 3-11-5 MissAElsey(14) (sn pushed along: hdwy 3f out: nvr rchd ldrs)........5 6
839[20] Steadfast Elite (IRE) **(43)***(19) (JJO'Neill)* 4-10-6 MarthaGoldie(1) (chsd ldrs tl wknd fnl 3f).......3 7
3311[2] Thisonesforalice **(37)***(6) (JSGoldie)* 7-10-0 MrKSantana(15) (nvr trbld ldrs)........5 8
2379[11] All on **(42)***(5) (JHetherton)* 4-10-5 RowenaRamsay(11) (a bhd)........4 9
3531[10] Jubran (USA) **(63)***(25) (MJohnston)* 9-11-12 MrSLove(12) (lw: chsd ldrs tl outpcd fnl 3f)........nk 10
Sharp At Six (IRE) **(40)** *(TDyer)* 5-10-3 MrsAFarrell(2) (chsd ldrs: rdn ent st: sn wknd)........6 11
1581[7] Absolute Folly **(50)***(3) (JBerry)* 3-10-5 SallySyms(8) (bhd fnl 5f)........nk 12
1960[4] Kirkie Cross **(45)** *(RMMcKellar)* 3-10-0 AmandaCreedon(13) (dwlt: a bhd: t.o)........15 13
1464[4] Homecrest **(55)** *(MrsAMNaughton)* 3-10-10 ow6 MrJDelahunt(7) (lw: led to 7f out: sn wknd: t.o)........15 14

LONG HANDICAP Kirkie Cross 9-9

4/1 Mentalasanythin (op 6/1), **9/2** Contrafire (IRE), **6/1** KEEP YOUR DISTANCE (op 4/1), Jubran (USA), **9/1** Imperial Bid (FR), **12/1** Manful, Thisonesforalice (op 8/1), **14/1** Chantry Bellini (op 8/1), **20/1** Absolute Folly, **25/1** All on, **33/1** Steadfast Elite (IRE), **66/1** Sharp At Six (IRE), **100/1** Kirkie Cross, Homecrest, CSF £28.95 CT £107.74 TOTE £5.40: £1.80 £1.80 £1.90 (£7.10) Trio £8.70 OWNER Mr P. D. Savill (SALTBURN) BRED Cedric Ford 14 Rn

2m 23.99 (7.79) SF: 59/57/45/17/31/24/7/-/-/13/-/-/-/-

WEIGHT FOR AGE 3yo-8lb

3666 E.B.F. 'WELCOME TO TIMEFORM' MAIDEN STKS (2-Y.O) (Class D)

£4,807.00 (£1,441.00: £693.00: £319.00)
7f Stalls: Low GOING minus 0.21 sec per fur (GF) 2-40 (2-43)

3416[4] **Jo Mell** *(85+) (MHEasterby)* 2-9-0 MBirch(3) (mde all: qcknd over 2f out: r.o wl)........— 1

3587a9 Reinhardt (IRE) *(79)*(Fav)*(PWChapple-Hyam)* 2-9-0 PatEddery(8) (lw: chsd ldrs: pushed along appr st: sme late hdwy)....2½ **2**
21824 Desert Bell (IRE) *(75) (MRStoute)* 2-9-0 KDarley(11) (in tch: hdwy 2f out: one pce appr fnl f)....2 **3**
Karisma (IRE) *(72) (DenysSmith)*2-9-0 DHolland(5) (wl grwn: cl up: effrt over 2f out: one pce)....1 **4**
Portuguese Lil *(65) (DNicholls)* 2-8-9 AlexGreaves(15) (w'like: mid div tl styd on wl fnl f).....1¼ **5**
34167 Mister Aspecto (IRE) *(68) (MJohnston)* 2-9-0 JWeaver(2) (mid div: hdwy u.p 2f out: no imp) .¾ **6**
Desert Frolic (IRE) *(61+) (MJohnston)* 2-8-9 MJKinane(9) (w'like: dwlt: hdwy appr st: rdn over 2f out: no imp)....1 **7**
34635 Eric's Bett **(74)***(64) (MrsSMAustin)* 2-9-0v JMarshall(4) (b: cl up tl wknd fnl 2f)....¾ **8**
Seattle Alley (USA) *(64+) (MrsJRRamsden)* 2-9-0 KFallon(13) (w'like: str: bit bkwd: s.i.s: n.d)....hd **9**
Mustang *(60) (CWThornton)* 2-9-0 DeanMcKeown(1) (w'like: str: bit bkwd: s.i.s: n.d)....1½ **10**
33525 Szloto *(56) (TDBarron)* 2-9-0 LCharnock(10) (s.i.s: a bhd)....2 **11**
350210 General Glow *(47) (NBycroft)* 2-9-0 GHind(12) (a outpcd & bhd)....4 **12**
14944 Dancing Dot (IRE) *(21) (MissLAPerratt)* 2-8-9 NConnorton(14) (a bhd)....9 **13**
All In Good Time *(17) (CWThornton)* 2-9-0 ACulhane(7) (w'like: bkwd: a rr div)....4 **14**
33664 Time For A Glass *(WTKemp)* 2-8-9 TWilliams(6) (Withdrawn not under Starter's orders: Veterinary advice).... **W**

4/5 Reinhardt (IRE) (tchd Evens), **9/2** JO MELL, **5/1** Desert Bell (IRE), **10/1** Mister Aspecto (IRE) (8/1-12/1), **12/1** Portuguese Lil (10/1-16/1), **16/1** Seattle Alley (USA), **20/1** Desert Frolic (IRE), **50/1** Karisma (IRE), Szloto, All In Good Time, **66/1** Mustang, **100/1** General Glow, Eric's Bett, **200/1** Dancing Dot (IRE), Time For A Glass, CSF £8.39 TOTE £6.20: £1.50 £1.30 £1.90 (£3.80) Trio £3.20 OWNER C H Newton Jnr Ltd (MALTON) BRED D.B. Lamplough 14 Rn
1m 28.63 (4.63) SF: 26/20/16/13/6/9/2/5/5/1/-/-/-/-

3667 LADBROKE SPRINT H'CAP (0-75) (3-Y.O+) (Class D) £7,200.00 (£2,160.00: £1,040.00: £480.00)

5f Stalls: High GOING minus 0.21 sec per fur (GF) 3-10 (3-16)

3508* **Portelet (67)***(79) (RGuest)* 3-9-5 LCharnock(26) (mde all stands' side: r.o wl fnl f)....— **1**
31665 Stolen Kiss (IRE) **(70)***(74) (MWEasterby)* 3-9-8b MJKinane(27) (in tch stands' side: kpt on fnl f: nvr able to chal)....2½ **2**
296311 Runs in the Family **(55)***(54) (PGMurphy)* 3-8-0b(7) RWaterfield(2) (chsd ldr far side: chal ½-wy: no ch w stands' side ldrs fnl f)....1½ **3**
35545 Kalar **(52)***(51) (DWChapman)* 6-8-6b DHolland(1) (lw: led far side: rdn 2f out: nt qckn)....hd **4**
35973 Just Bob **(67)***(58) (SEKettlewell)* 6-9-7 JFEgan(29) (lw: hdwy stands' side 2f out: nrst fin)....2½ **5**
32793 Lepine (IRE) **(74)***(63)*(Fav)*(JWWatts)* 4-10-0v PatEddery(23) (chsd ldrs stands' side: sn drvn along: no imp fr ½-wy)....½ **6**
26272 Freckles Kelly **(46)***(27) (MHEasterby)* 3-7-12 SMaloney(22) (lw: cl up stands' side tl wknd over 1f out)....2½ **7**
35245 Primula Bairn **(62)***(42) (DNicholls)* 5-9-2b JLowe(24) (hdwy stands' side 2f out: nvr trbld ldrs)....nk **8**
35089 Kenesha (IRE) **(47)***(25) (DANolan)* 5-8-1bow1 VHalliday(13) (prom centre over 3f)....nk **9**
335712 Murray's Mazda (IRE) **(39)***(17) (JLEyre)* 6-7-2 (5) PFessey(20) (b: racd stands' side: n.d)....½ **10**
31507 Knayton Lass **(56)***(34) (MWEasterby)* 4-8-10 MBirch(7) (n.d far side)....s.h **11**
327510 Diet **(55)***(31) (MissLAPerratt)* 9-8-2v(7) CAdamson(5) (nvr trbld ldrs far side)....½ **12**
33104 Southern Dominion **(61)***(27) (MJohnston)* 3-8-13 JWeaver(8) (lw: chsd ldrs far side 3f)....3 **13**
19534 Lord Sky **(58)***(24) (ABailey)* 4-8-9 (3) DWright(18) (lw: chsd ldrs stands' side 3f)....s.h **14**
28774 Breakfast Creek **(57)***(22) (JBerry)* 3-8-9 ow1 JCarroll(3) (b: cl up far side 3f: sn lost pl)....s.h **15**
180918 Rankaidade **(41)***(7) (DonEnricoIncisa)* 4-7-9 KimTinkler(12) (swtchd stands' side after s: n.d)....hd **16**
35192 Giggleswick Girl **(63)***(27) (MRChannon)* 4-8-10 (7) JDennis(17) (n.d stands' side)....½ **17**
36227 High Domain (IRE) **(64)***(27) (TDBarron)* 4-9-4b DeanMcKeown(16) (n.d stands' side)....½ **18**
33136 Ramborette **(47)***(6) (DenysSmith)* 3-7-13 JFanning(21) (spd stands' side to ½-wy)....1 **19**
34186 Ned's Bonanza **(71)***(30) (MDods)* 6-9-11 KFallon(11) (n.d far side)....s.h **20**
24755 Petite-D-Argent **(60)***(15) (TDyer)* 6-8-7 (7) GFaulkner(28) (a bhd stands' side)....1¼ **21**
359712 Just Dissident (IRE) **(67)***(17) (RMWhitaker)* 3-9-5 ACulhane(15) (lw: n.d stands' side)....1½ **22**
14388 Strathtore Dream (IRE) **(42)** *(MissLAPerratt)* 4-7-10 AMackay(25) (a bhd stands' side)....hd **23**
36228 Domicksky **(56)***(5) (MRChannon)* 7-8-10 KDarley(4) (prom far side 3f)....½ **24**
31505 Pallium (IRE) **(59)***(5) (MrsAMNaughton)* 7-8-13 NConnorton(10) (a bhd far side)....¾ **25**
176510 Tenor **(61)***(7) (DNicholls)* 4-9-1 AlexGreaves(14) (n.d stands' side)....hd **26**
34244 My Abbey **(55)** *(EJAlston)* 6-8-9 GHind(6) (chsd ldrs far side to ½-wy: wknd qckly)....¾ **27**
15663 Mamma's Due **(59)** *(JBerry)* 3-8-4 (7) CLowther(9) (unruly s: sn bhd far side)....1 **28**
Live Project (IRE) **(75)***(6) (MJohnston)* 3-9-13 TWilliams(19) (no imp fr ½-wy)....3 **29**

7/1 Lepine (IRE), **10/1** Just Bob, **14/1** PORTELET, Kalar, Lord Sky (12/1-20/1), Freckles Kelly, **16/1** Giggleswick Girl, Stolen Kiss (IRE), Domicksky, Southern Dominion, Ned's Bonanza, **20/1** My Abbey, High Domain (IRE), Knayton Lass, Tenor, **25/1** Breakfast Creek, Primula Bairn, Petite-D-Argent, Ramborette, Diet, **33/1** Just Dissident (IRE), Mamma's Due, Pallium (IRE), Runs in the Family, **50/1** Rankaidade, Strathtore Dream (IRE), Kenesha (IRE), Murray's Mazda (IRE), Live Project (IRE), CSF £204.46 CT £6,413.54 TOTE £12.10: £2.80 £2.70 £15.50 £3.10 (£78.10) Trio £2,580.10 OWNER Lord Matthews (NEWMARKET) BRED Lord Victor Matthews 29 Rn
58.64 secs (1.64) SF: 55/50/30/29/36/41/3/20/3/-/12/9/3/2/-/-/5/5/-/8/-/-/-/-/-/-/-/-/-
WEIGHT FOR AGE 3yo-2lb

3668 TIMEFORM HARRY ROSEBERY TROPHY STKS (Listed) (2-Y.O) (Class A) £10,290.00 (£3,810.00: £1,830.00: £750.00)
5f Stalls: High GOING minus 0.21 sec per fur (GF) 3-40 (3-43)

3444² **Westcourt Magic (98)***(107)*(Fav)*(MWEasterby)* 2-8-11 MJKinane(11) (lw: cl up: led 2f out: rdn & r.o wl fnl f) — **1**
3086⁴ Kunucu (IRE) **(93)***(102) (TDBarron)* 2-8-9 KDarley(9) (sn pushed along: hdwy ½-wy: chal ins fnl f: nt qckn towards fin) 1 **2**
3434⁵ Tadeo **(99)***(94) (MJohnston)* 2-8-11 JWeaver(12) (lw: led 3f: r.o one pce) 3 **3**
3210³ Whittle Rock **(78)***(81?) (EJAlston)* 2-8-6 KFallon(13) (s.i.s: hdwy ½-wy: nrst fin) 2½ **4**
3420⁵ Dovebrace **(100)***(88) (ABailey)* 2-9-2 AMackay(1) (sn pushed along: hdwy ½-wy: nvr rchd ldrs) 1 **5**
3086³ Hear The Music (IRE) **(91)***(76) (BWHills)* 2-8-6b DHolland(5) (chsd ldrs over 3f) ¾ **6**
1868⁶ Whicksey Perry **(95)***(77) (JBerry)* 2-9-0 JCarroll(10) (lw: chsd ldrs over 3f) 2 **7**
3176* Tarf (USA) **(91)***(69) (PTWalwyn)* 2-8-9 MBirch(8) (s.i.s: hld up: effrt & nt clr run ½-wy: swtchd & nt qckn) 1 **8**
3548¹⁷ Top Cat (FR) **(90)***(69) (EWeymes)* 2-8-11b DeanMcKeown(3) (spd 3f) ½ **9**
3465⁷ Johayro **(73)***(68) (WGMTurner)* 2-8-11 PMcCabe(2) (prom tl outpcd ½-wy: n.d) ½ **10**
3444³ Soviet Style (AUS) **(98)***(68) (PWChapple-Hyam)* 2-9-0 RHavlin(7) (chsd lrds tl outpcd fnl 2f) ¾ **11**
3499² Eastern Prophets **(100)***(62) (GLewis)* 2-9-2 PatEddery(6) (in tch: outpcd ½-wy: sn no ch) 2½ **12**
3371⁴ Man of Wit (IRE) *(49) (APJarvis)* 2-8-11 JTate(4) (s.i.s: n.d) 2½ **13**

2/1 WESTCOURT MAGIC, **5/1** Eastern Prophets, **6/1** Tarf (USA), **7/1** Tadeo, Soviet Style (AUS), **11/1** Kunucu (IRE), **14/1** Hear The Music (IRE), Dovebrace, **20/1** Whicksey Perry, Man of Wit (IRE), **50/1** Top Cat (FR), **66/1** Whittle Rock, Johayro, CSF £24.21 TOTE £2.80: £1.20 £5.40 £2.30 (£32.40) Trio £55.80 OWNER Mr K. Hodgson (SHERIFF HUTTON) BRED C. R. and V. M. Withers 13 Rn
59.16 secs (2.16) SF: 39/34/26/13/20/8/9/1/1/-/-/-/-

3669 ROCK STEADY SECURITY H'CAP (0-75) (3-Y.O+) (Class D) £6,836.00 (£2,048.00: £984.00: £452.00)
1m 7f Stalls: Low GOING minus 0.21 sec per fur (GF) 4-10 (4-11)

3445² **Istabraq (IRE) (75)***(90)*(Fav)*(JHMGosden)* 3-9-7 PatEddery(20) (b: cl up: led 11f out: rdn & r.o wl fnl 3f) — **1**
3464* Boundary Express **(56)***(67) (EJAlston)* 3-8-2 ow1 GHind(2) (a cl up: chal 3f out: r.o: nt pce of wnr fnl f) 2½ **2**
*3526*⁶ Hotspur Street **(66)***(73) (MJohnston)* 3-8-12 JWeaver(17) (hld up & bhd: hdwy appr st: styd on wl: nrst fin) 5 **3**
2622³ Eau de Cologne **(70)***(77) (CWThornton)* 3-9-2 DeanMcKeown(4) (a.p: effrt appr st: styd on: nt pce to chal) nk **4**
3299⁷ Bark'n'bite **(50)***(56) (MrsMReveley)* 3-7-10 JLowe(1) (a chsng ldrs: rdn along 7f out: styd on: no imp) ¾ **5**
2993⁴ Court Joker (IRE) **(50)***(55) (MHTompkins)* 3-7-10 DaleGibson(18) (hdwy 6f out: sn drvn along: swtchd 2f out: styd on: nvr rchd ldrs) 1 **6**
1730⁴ Bowcliffe Court (IRE) **(62)***(66) (BWHills)* 3-8-8 DHolland(7) (bhd: effrt appr st: nrst fin) ¾ **7**
*3318** Claireswan (IRE) **(60)***(58) (SCWilliams)* 3-8-6 JTate(3) (lw: led tl hdd 11f out: cl up tl rdn & btn 3f out) 6 **8**
1825⁵ Final Fling **(52)***(45) (JWWatts)* 3-7-12 JFanning(8) (nvr trbld ldrs) 4 **9**
3299⁴ Punch **(52)***(43) (NTinkler)* 3-7-12b JFEgan(5) (chsd ldrs tl rdn & wknd fnl 3f) 2½ **10**
*3527*⁷ Noble Ballerina (USA) **(49)***(36) (APJarvis)* 3-7-6 (3)ow2 DWright(9) (n.d) 1¾ **11**
3470³ Greycoat Boy **(64)***(50) (BJMeehan)* 3-8-10 MJKinane(19) (nvr trbld ldrs) 2½ **12**
3299⁶ Island Cascade **(47)***(27) (DonEnricoIncisa)* 3-7-7 KimTinkler(6) (bhd tl sme late hdwy) 6 **13**
3189¹² Royal York **(72)***(51) (MissSEHall)* 3-9-4 KDarley(13) (chsd ldrs fr ½-wy tl rdn & wknd ent st) ¾ **14**
*3527*⁵ Philmist **(48)***(26) (CWCElsey)* 3-7-8 NKennedy(15) (a bhd) ½ **15**
3224⁵ Victoria Day **(48)***(12) (JWWatts)* 3-7-8 LCharnock(16) (chsd ldrs: rdn 7f out: wknd appr st:) 14 **16**
2774³ Jackmanii **(49)***(7) (WTKemp)* 3-7-9 ow2 TWilliams(10) (n.d) 3 **17**
Monaco Gold (IRE) **(55)***(14) (RMMcKellar)* 3-7-8 (7) KSked(11) (b.nr hind: bhd & rn wd st: n.d) 1 **18**

3217[2] Swivel **(70)***(29)* *(JRFanshawe)* 3-9-2 KFallon(12) (chsd ldrs: drvn along appr st: wknd over 3f out)........hd 19
3462[6] Ballard Lady (IRE) **(50)***(6)* *(JSWainwright)* 3-7-10 ow3 AMackay(14) (n.d)........s.h 20

LONG HANDICAP Jackmanii 7-6 Island Cascade 6-13 Noble Ballerina (USA) 7-5 Ballard Lady (IRE) 7-3

6/4 ISTABRAQ (IRE), **13/2** Claireswan (IRE), **7/1** Bowcliffe Court (IRE), **10/1** Swivel, **12/1** Greycoat Boy, **14/1** Royal York, **16/1** Eau de Cologne, Boundary Express, **20/1** Court Joker (IRE), **25/1** Bark'n'bite, Punch, Victoria Day, Hotspur Street, Jackmanii, **33/1** Final Fling, Philmist, **40/1** Ballard Lady (IRE), **100/1** Island Cascade, Noble Ballerina (USA), **200/1** Monaco Gold (IRE), CSF £27.83 CT £463.63 TOTE £2.10: £1.50 £4.30 £6.50 £4.60 (£26.10) Trio £181.20 OWNER Mr Hamdan Al Maktoum (NEWMARKET) BRED Shadwell Estate Company Limited 20 Rn
3m 17.69 (7.59) SF: 48/25/31/35/14/13/24/16/3/1/-/8/-/9/-/-/-/-/-/-

3670 WILLIAMS DE BROE (S) STKS (2-Y.O) (Class E) £4,142.50 (£1,240.00: £595.00: £272.50) 5f Stalls: High GOING minus 0.21 sec per fur (GF) 4-40 (4-46)

2859[5] **Swynford Dream** *(67)* *(JFBottomley)* 2-8-11 JLowe(4) (lw: mde all: shkn up & r.o wl fnl f)....— 1
3415[3] Hickleton Miss **(55)***(61)* *(MrsMReveley)* 2-8-11 KDarley(16) (s.i.s: gd hdwy 2f out: chsng wnr appr fnl f: nt qckn)........2 2
3417[6] Bee Health Boy **(50)***(57)* *(MWEasterby)* 2-8-11b MBirch(17) (cl up: rdn ½-wy: r.o one pce)......1 3
3538[5] Corniche Quest (IRE) **(67)***(52)* *(MRChannon)* 2-8-6 JFEgan(8) (lw: in tch: rdn ½-wy: kpt on fnl f)........hd 4
3417[3] Power Don **(58)***(57)* *(WGMTurner)* 2-8-8v(3) PMcCabe(14) (lw: a.p: hdwy & n.m.r over 1f out: nt qckn ins fnl f)........hd 5
3434[6] Krystal Max (IRE) **(84)***(57)*(Fav)*(TDBarron)* 2-9-2 DeanMcKeown(15) (bmpd s: nt clr run 2f out: rdn & no imp appr fnl f)........1½ 6
3369[7] Pathaze **(70)***(39)* *(NBycroft)* 2-8-11 SMaloney(10) (in tch: hrd rdn ½-wy: kpt on: no imp)........4 7
3064[10] Natural Key **(73)***(38)*(Fav)*(DHaydnJones)* 2-8-11 AMackay(11) (chsd ldrs: hrd rdn ½-wy: btn appr fnl f)........½ 8
3124[7] Taurean Fire *(34)* *(MrsMReveley)* 2-8-4 (7) DDenby(3) (rdn ½-wy: nvr trbld ldrs)........1 9
Sly's Fancy *(25)* *(JBerry)* 2-8-6 SDWilliams(13) (leggy: unruly bef s: in tch 3f)........1¼ 10
2773[5] Ready Teddy (IRE) *(24)* *(MissLAPerratt)* 2-8-1 (5) CTeague(6) (n.d)........½ 11
2962[8] Monsieur Culsyth **(62)***(31)* *(JBerry)* 2-9-2 JCarroll(12) (cl up tl rdn & btn over 1f out)........1 12
Fernway *(17)* *(RMWhitaker)* 2-8-6 ACulhane(9) (leggy: scope: dwlt: nt rcvr)........1 13
3271[7] Yougoa **(48)***(13)* *(MWEasterby)* 2-8-6 MJKinane(2) (in tch: hrd rdn ½-wy: sn btn)........1½ 14
3243[10] What Jim Wants (IRE) *(14)* *(JJO'Neill)* 2-8-11 KFallon(7) (outpcd & wl bhd fr ½-wy)........1¼ 15
3468[13] So Select *(5)* *(APJarvis)* 2-8-6 JTate(1) (n.d)........1 16
3415[5] Ultra Power *(2)* *(PCHaslam)* 2-8-11 JWeaver(5) (nvr wnt pce)........2½ 17
3231[7] Nuclear Jewel *(RMWhitaker)* 2-8-6 DaleGibson(18) (lw: s.s: a wl bhd)........dist 18

7/2 Krystal Max (IRE), Natural Key, **6/1** Corniche Quest (IRE), **9/1** Power Don, SWYNFORD DREAM (5/1-10/1), **11/1** Fernway, **12/1** Hickleton Miss, **14/1** Pathaze, **16/1** Yougoa, **20/1** Monsieur Culsyth, Ultra Power, **33/1** So Select, Sly's Fancy, Taurean Fire, Bee Health Boy, **50/1** What Jim Wants (IRE), Ready Teddy (IRE), Nuclear Jewel, CSF £109.86 TOTE £14.30: £3.10 £2.90 £16.80 (£73.40) Trio £380.20, £390.97 to Ayr 15/09/95. OWNER Qualitair Holdings Ltd (MALTON) BRED Qualitair Stud Ltd 18 Rn
59.93 secs (2.93) SF: 26/20/16/11/16/16/-/-/-/-/-/-/-/-/-/-/-/-
Bt in 8,800 gns

OFFICIAL EXPLANATION **Ultra Power: the jockey stated the gelding was never travelling, kept changing his legs and moved badly.**

3671 TATTERSALLS MAIDEN AUCTION STKS (2-Y.O) (Class E) £4,045.00 (£1,210.00: £580.00: £265.00) 6f Stalls: High GOING minus 0.21 sec per fur (GF) 5-10 (5-14)

2914[2] **Diminuet (79)***(76)* *(JWWatts)* 2-7-13 JFanning(5) (lw: a.p: effrt 2f out: led ins fnl f: r.o)........— 1
3309[5] Craignairn **(53)***(82)* *(JBerry)* 2-8-6 JCarroll(6) (led tl hdd ins fnl f: r.o)........½ 2
2453[4] Gulf of Siam *(69)*(Fav)*(MissSEHall)* 2-8-7 NConnorton(7) (s.i.s: sn trckng ldrs pllng hrd: rdn over 2f out: styd on one pce)........5 3
2424[5] Termon **(61)***(63)* *(MissLAPerratt)* 2-8-2 JLowe(4) (swtg: outpcd ½-wy: hdwy 2f out: r.o)........½ 4
3463[10] Principal Boy (IRE) **(70)***(62)* *(TJEtherington)* 2-8-6 KDarley(9) (a chsng ldrs: rdn 2f out: one pce)........1¾ 5
3502[5] Distinctlyfoster's (IRE) *(48)* *(MJohnston)* 2-7-12 TWilliams(10) (chsd ldrs tl rdn & btn appr fnl f)........2½ 6
2773[3] Valise *(41)* *(MrsMReveley)* 2-7-12 LCharnock(12) (outpcd fr ½-wy)........2½ 7
3430[4] Cocoon (IRE) *(35)* *(CWThornton)* 2-7-13 AMackay(2) (lw: s.i.s: sn prom: rdn ½-wy: wknd over 1f out)........2½ 8
Goldrill *(42)* *(MissSEHall)* 2-8-6 JMarshall(3) (str: cmpt: b: bhd: rdn ½-wy: rn green & no imp)........s.h 9

3415[4] Rattle *(38) (JJO'Neill)* 2-8-4 KFallon(1) (outpcd & bhd after 2f)....¾ 10
Aye Ready *(31) (MissLAPerratt)* 2-8-5 MBirch(11) (cmpt: bit bkwd: dwlt: a outpcd & wl bhd) ..3 11
3502[14] Bold Future (IRE) *(27) (JWWatts)* 2-8-3 JFEgan(8) (lw: prom to ½-wy: sn bhd)....1 12

15/8 Gulf of Siam, **3/1** DIMINUET (2/1-7/2), **5/1** Cocoon (IRE), **10/1** Principal Boy (IRE), Distinctlyfoster's (IRE), **12/1** Valise, **14/1** Craignairn, **20/1** Termon, **25/1** Rattle, **33/1** Goldrill, **40/1** Bold Future (IRE), **50/1** Aye Ready, CSF £42.39 TOTE £3.50: £1.60 £3.80 £1.30 (£30.20) Trio £25.40 OWNER Mrs S. Cunliffe-Lister (RICHMOND) BRED Mrs N. Cunliffe-Lister 12 Rn
1m 12.73 (2.93) SF: 24/30/17/11/10/-/-/-/-/-/-/-

T/Jkpt: Not won; £19,658.48 to Ayr 15/9/95. T/Plpt: £82.20 (322.29 Tckts). T/Qdpt: £88.10 (1.2 Tckts). AA

3538-LINGFIELD (L-H)
Thursday September 14th (Turf Good becoming Soft, AWT Standard)
WEATHER: almost nil WIND: rain

3672
LEVY BOARD MAIDEN STKS (I) (2-Y.O) (Class D) £4,239.30 (£1,268.40: £608.20: £278.10) **7f 140y** Stalls: Centre GOING minus 0.02 sec per fur (G) 1-50 (1-51)

Najm Mubeen (IRE) *(85+) (ACStewart)* 2-9-0 MRoberts(3) (leggy: a.p: led over 1f out: rdn out)....— 1
3436[2] Glenrazie (IRE) *(80) (PWChapple-Hyam)* 2-9-0 JReid(4) (lw: hld up: rdn over 3f out: unable qckn fnl f)....2½ 2
2846[6] Mystic Knight *(79)*(Fav)*(RCharlton)* 2-9-0 TSprake(1) (rdn over 4f out: hdwy 2f out: r.o wl ins fnl f)....nk 3
3472[4] Trojan Risk *(78) (GLewis)* 2-9-0 SWhitworth(12) (lw: plld hrd: led over 4f out tl over 1f out: one pce)....½ 4
Beas River (IRE) *(78) (WRMuir)* 2-9-0 WWoods(8) (unf: a.p: nt clr run 2f out: rdn over 1f out: one pce)....hd 5
Dirab *(72+) (HRACecil)* 2-9-0 AMcGlone(2) (scope: lw: hld up: rdn over 4f out: wknd over 2f out)....3 6
3441[W] Ben Bowden *(72) (MBlanshard)* 2-9-0 StephenDavies(13) (led 3f: wkng whn squeezed out 2f out)....s.h 7
Questionaire *(41) (RAkehurst)* 2-8-6 (3) SSanders(7) (unf: bit bkwd: bhd fnl 3f)....12 8
3450[9] Bianca Cappello (IRE) *(39) (JLDunlop)* 2-8-9 TQuinn(9) (bhd fnl 3f)....1¼ 9
3587a[23] Mam'selle Bergerac (IRE) *(30) (PMitchell)* 2-8-9 AClark(11) (b.hind: bhd fnl 3f)....4 10
Sterling Fellow *(32) (RHannon)* 2-9-0 RPerham(5) (str: bit bkwd: a bhd)....1¾ 11
3441[7] Safecracker *(JWHills)* 2-9-0 RHughes(6) (a bhd)....15 12

6/4 Mystic Knight, **7/4** Glenrazie (IRE), **8/1** Dirab (3/1-9/1), **12/1** NAJM MUBEEN (IRE) (6/1-14/1), **16/1** Trojan Risk, Sterling Fellow, **33/1** Mam'selle Bergerac (IRE), Safecracker, Bianca Cappello (IRE), Questionaire, **50/1** Ben Bowden, Beas River (IRE), CSF £32.37 TOTE £16.90: £3.40 £1.30 £1.50 (£27.10) Trio £15.80 OWNER Sheikh Ahmed Al Maktoum (NEWMARKET) BRED Kilfrush Stud Ltd 12 Rn
1m 33.76 (5.76) SF: 31/26/25/24/24/18/18/-/-/-/-/-

3673
LEVY BOARD MAIDEN STKS (II) (2-Y.O) (Class D) £4,205.50 (£1,258.00: £603.00: £275.50) **7f 140y** Stalls: Centre GOING minus 0.02 sec per fur (G) 2-20 (2-27)

Patria (USA) *(78+) (MRStoute)* 2-8-9 WCarson(7) (neat: rdn 3f out: hdwy over 1f out: str run fnl f: led nr fin)....— 1
Crazy Chief *(82+) (PFICole)* 2-9-0 TQuinn(2) (w'like: a.p: led on bit over 2f out: edgd lft over 1f out: rdn: hdd nr fin)....½ 2
1481[4] Secret Pleasure (IRE) *(72) (RHannon)* 2-8-9 RHughes(5) (lw: hld up: swtchd lft over 1f out: one pce fnl f)....2½ 3
The Swan *(71+) (JLDunlop)* 2-8-9 SWhitworth(10) (unf: s.s: hdwy over 1f out: r.o wl ins fnl f)....nk 4
Little Black Dress (USA) *(69) (RCharlton)* 2-8-9 SRaymont(3) (w'like: bit bkwd: a.p: ev ch over 1f out: wknd ins fnl f)....1¼ 5
Lady Isabell *(63) (TGMills)* 2-8-9 JReid(8) (leggy: lt-f: hld up: rdn over 2f out: wknd over 1f out)....2½ 6
Snowpoles *(62) (MrsJCecil)* 2-8-9 EGuest(1) (leggy: unf: led 5f: wknd fnl f)....½ 7
2801[5] Budding Annie *(56) (JRBosley)* 2-8-9 RPerham(11) (swtchd lft over 1f out: nvr nr to chal)......3 8
Sally's Twins *(53) (JSMoore)* 2-8-6 (3) NVarley(4) (w'like: hld up: rdn over 3f out: wknd over 1f out)....1½ 9

3157[7] Craven Cottage *(39)* *(CJames)* 2-9-0 AMcGlone(13) (bhd whn bdly hmpd & stmbld over 1f out) 9 **10**
Henry Cooper *(DrJDScargill)* 2-9-0 MRimmer(6) (str: a bhd) 20 **11**
Rowlandsons Links *(BJMeehan)* 2-9-0 AClark(9) (unf: s.s: hdwy over 5f out: wknd over 3f out) 6 **12**
3463[2] Double Bluff (IRE) (Fav)*(IABalding)* 2-8-9 (5) DGriffiths(12) (Withdrawn not under Starter's orders: ref to ent stalls) .... **W**

8/11 Double Bluff (IRE), **4/1** Crazy Chief, **6/1** PATRIA (USA) (op 3/1), **16/1** Secret Pleasure (IRE), **20/1** Lady Isabell, **25/1** Little Black Dress (USA), The Swan, Snowpoles, **50/1** Budding Annie, Sally's Twins, Henry Cooper, Rowlandsons Links, Craven Cottage, CSF £8.04 TOTE £2.70: £1.40 £1.30 £1.90 (£3.70) Trio £5.60 OWNER Hesmonds Stud (NEWMARKET) BRED Mr and Mrs John C. Mabee 12 Rn 1m 34.12 (6.12) SF: 23/27/17/16/14/8/7/1/-/-/-/-

3674

DIBB LUPTON BROOMHEAD LIMITED STKS (0-80) (3-Y.O+) (Class D) £3,913.25 (£1,166.00: £555.50: £250.25)
7f 140y Stalls: Centre GOING minus 0.02 sec per fur (G) 2-50 (2-53)

2840[4] **Sharp 'n Smart (66)***(82)* *(BSmart)* 3-8-10 (3) SSanders(3) (lw: chsd ldr: rdn over 1f out: led ins fnl f: r.o wl) ....— **1**
3619* Knobbleeneeze **(70)***(79)* *(MRChannon)* 5-9-6v RHughes(6) (lw: hld up: hrd rdn over 1f out: unable to qckn ins fnl f) 2½ **2**
3109[9] Waikiki Beach (USA) **(77)***(70)* *(GLMoore)* 4-8-7 (7) ALakeman(7) (lw: led: clr over 2f out: hdd ins fnl f: one pce) 1½ **3**
3457[10] Dontforget Insight (IRE) **(68)***(64)* *(PFICole)* 4-9-0 TQuinn(2) (hdwy over 2f out: one pce)....2½ **4**
3214[7] Captain's Day **(79)***(62)* *(TGMills)* 3-8-10 JReid(8) (lw: hld up: rdn over 3f out: wknd wl over 1f out) 1½ **5**
3451[8] Anam **(78)***(61)* *(PTWalwyn)* 3-8-11 MRoberts(4) (lw: a bhd) 1¼ **6**
3201* Sejaal (IRE) **(80)***(50)*(Fav)*(JLDunlop)* 3-8-13 WCarson(5) (lw: a bhd) 6 **7**
3079[5] Real Madrid **(34)***(36)* *(GPEnright)* 4-9-0b VJanssen(1) (lw: bhd fnl 3f) 5 **8**

6/4 Sejaal (IRE), **11/4** Captain's Day, **3/1** Knobbleeneeze, **8/1** Anam (5/1-10/1), **14/1** Waikiki Beach (USA), **25/1** Dontforget Insight (IRE), **33/1** SHARP 'N SMART, **66/1** Real Madrid, CSF £123.09 TOTE £21.60: £2.20 £1.50 £2.70 (£28.90) OWNER Mr K. H. Burks (LAMBOURN) BRED Aston Park Stud 8 Rn 1m 33.58 (5.58) SF: 32/34/25/19/12/11/-/-
WEIGHT FOR AGE 3yo-5lb

OFFICIAL EXPLANATION **Sejaal (IRE): failed to act on the rain-softened ground.**

3675

DIBB LUPTON BROOMHEAD (S) STKS (2-Y.O) (Class G) £2,691.00 (£746.00: £357.00) **6f** Stalls: Low GOING minus 0.02 sec (STD) 3-20 (3-22)

3335[4] **Where's Margaret (63)***(61)*(Fav)*(GLewis)* 2-8-6b MRoberts(10) (lw: a.p: led 2f out: r.o wl)....— **1**
3528[8] Ghostly Apparition **(59)***(50)* *(JohnUpson)* 2-8-4 (7) DSweeney(4) (hld up: rdn over 1f out: r.o ins fnl f) 6 **2**
3570[5] Don't Tell Vicki **(56)***(48)* *(JSMoore)* 2-8-8 (3) NVarley(3) (lw: led 4f: one pce) ....¾ **3**
3077[4] The Imps (IRE) **(58)***(53)* *(BWHills)* 2-9-2b TQuinn(8) (swtg: a.p: ev ch wl over 1f out: one pce)s.h **4**
3570[4] L A Touch **(57)***(40)* *(CADwyer)* 2-8-8 (3) DRMcCabe(11) (nvr nr to chal) 3 **5**
3290[7] Trible Pet **(48)***(34)* *(BGubby)* 2-8-1 (5) MHenry(5) (lw: outpcd) ....½ **6**
2601[3] Latzio **(51)***(27)* *(BAPearce)* 2-8-6 StephenDavies(1) (b.hind: outpcd) 2½ **7**
3528[7] Red Simba **(59)***(35)* *(JBerry)* 2-8-9 (7) PRoberts(14) (lw: a mid div) ....¾ **8**
1073[4] Cool Caper *(22)* *(AGFoster)* 2-8-11v TSprake(13) (outpcd) 3 **9**
3314[10] Golden Wedding *(17)* *(DCO'Brien)* 2-8-11v AClark(6) (a bhd) 1¾ **10**
3533[8] Multi Franchise **(61)***(19)* *(BGubby)* 2-9-2b RHughes(9) (swtg: a bhd) 1¼ **11**
3541[6] Dells Dream (IRE) *(4)* *(MRChannon)* 2-8-6 WWoods(12) (a wl bhd) 1¾ **12**
2135[13] Malice Corner *(8)* *(LGCottrell)* 2-8-11 MFenton(7) (lw: a bhd) ....½ **13**

9/4 WHERE'S MARGARET, **6/1** L A Touch, **7/1** Don't Tell Vicki, The Imps (IRE) (op 9/2), Latzio (14/1-6/1), **10/1** Multi Franchise (6/1-12/1), **12/1** Dells Dream (IRE), **14/1** Cool Caper, Trible Pet, **16/1** Red Simba, **20/1** Malice Corner, **25/1** Ghostly Apparition, Golden Wedding, CSF £55.58 TOTE £2.40: £1.20 £5.70 £2.80 (£588.60) Trio £207.80, £263.43 to Ayr 15/09/95. OWNER Mr G. H. P. Pritchard (EPSOM) BRED The Woodhaven Stud 13 Rn 1m 13.44 (4.44) SF: 6/-/-/-/-/-/-/-/-/-/-/-/-
Bt in 5,200 gns

3676

FERN HOWARD H'CAP (0-70) (3-Y.O+) (Class E) £3,874.20 (£1,161.60: £558.80: £257.40) **1m 6f** Stalls: High GOING minus 0.02 sec per fur (G) 3-50 (3-53)

3287[2] **All the Joys (38)***(53)* *(CACyzer)* 4-7-13 DBiggs(9) (hdwy over 6f out: 5th st: chsd ldr over 1f out: led last strides) ....— **1**

3056[5] Euro Singer **(52)***(67) (RAkehurst)* 3-7-13 (3) SSanders(3) (lw: led: clr 6f out: rdn over 2f out: hdd last strides)....hd **2**
3425[5] Harry Welsh (IRE) **(58)***(68) (KMcAuliffe)* 3-8-8v MRoberts(5) (hdwy over 2f out: r.o one pce)...4 **3**
938[9] Chief's Song **(60)***(67)*(Fav)*(SDow)* 5-9-7 TQuinn(15) (hdwy over 2f out: r.o)....3 **4**
1997[4] Much Too High **(51)***(56) (TJNaughton)* 3-8-1 AMcGlone(2) (4th st: rdn over 2f out: one pce) 1¾ **5**
3571[3] Alaraby (IRE) **(70)***(73) (IABalding)* 3-8-13 (7) MartinDwyer(6) (b.nr hind: 2nd st: hrd rdn over 2f out: wknd over 1f out)....2 **6**
3238[3] Disputed Call (USA) **(46)***(38) (JFfitch-Heyes)* 6-8-7 RPrice(1) (3rd st: rdn over 2f out: eased whn btn over 1f out)....9 **7**
3401[3] Delicious **(52)***(42) (MajorDNChappell)* 3-8-2 WCarson(14) (bhd fnl 6f)....2 **8**
3217[5] Persian Smoke **(40)***(27) (AHide)* 4-7-10 (5) MHenry(11) (6th & rn wd st: wknd over 2f out).....2½ **9**
Tour Leader (NZ) **(42)***(26) (RHBuckler)* 6-8-3 MFenton(7) (nvr nrr)....2½ **10**
3569[4] Iron N Gold **(48)***(31) (AMoore)* 3-7-12 NAdams(8) (lw: prom 10f)....1¼ **11**
3569[12] Mint a Million (IRE) **(34)***(4) (MBlanshard)* 4-7-4 (5)ow2 MBaird(4) (prom 7f)....10 **12**
3470[7] Quest Again **(65)***(14) (DWPArbuthnot)* 4-9-12 RHughes(19) (a bhd)....20 **13**
506[11] Bandar Perak **(55)***(3) (MJHaynes)* 4-9-2 JReid(10) (lw: bhd fnl 8f)....nk **14**
*1784** Cavina **(45)** *(NAGraham)* 5-8-6 MRimmer(20) (a bhd)....¾ **15**
1210[11] Laabas **(38)** *(JELong)* 12-7-6 (7)ow6 TField(18) (b: bkwd: a bhd)....1¼ **16**
2177[7] Toat Chieftain **(47)** *(GHarwood)* 3-7-11 ow3 CRutter(16) (bhd fnl 6f)....¾ **17**
3351[3] Dixiemelody **(65)***(10) (RHannon)* 3-9-1 RPerham(17) (a bhd)....nk **18**
2280[9] Prosequendo (USA) **(47)** *(GLMoore)* 8-8-8 AClark(13) (b.hind: a bhd)....¾ **19**
LONG HANDICAP Mint a Million (IRE) 7-3 Laabas 7-1

6/1 Chief's Song (op 10/1), **13/2** Alaraby (IRE) (4/1-7/1), **8/1** Euro Singer (6/1-9/1), Cavina (6/1-9/1), Disputed Call (USA), **10/1** Harry Welsh (IRE), Iron N Gold, Delicious (6/1-11/1), Dixiemelody (op 6/1), **12/1** Much Too High, Prosequendo (USA), Persian Smoke, **14/1** ALL THE JOYS (12/1-20/1), Quest Again (op 8/1), **20/1** Bandar Perak, **33/1** Tour Leader (NZ), Toat Chieftain, Mint a Million (IRE), **100/1** Laabas, CSF £130.18 CT £1,114.96 TOTE £22.50: £2.90 £3.10 £2.70 £2.10 (£44.50) Trio £287.60, £222.82 to Ayr 15/09/95. OWNER Mrs G. M. Gooderham (HORSHAM) BRED Mrs G. Gooderham 19 Rn
3m 9.95 (14.65) SF: 1/4/5/15/-/10/-/-/-/-/-/-/-/-/-/-/-/-/-
WEIGHT FOR AGE 3yo-11lb

3677 C & H (HAULIERS) H'CAP (0-70) (3-Y.O+) (Class E) £3,845.60 (£1,152.80: £554.40: £255.20) **7f** Stalls: High GOING minus 0.02 sec per fur (G) 4-20 (4-27)

3365[9] **Blow Dry (IRE) (54)***(65) (MartynWane)* 5-9-0 RPrice(4) (racd far side: mde all: hrd rdn over 2f out: r.o wl)....— **1**
3512[8] Pharaoh's Dancer **(68)***(74) (PBurgoyne)* 8-9-9 (5) DGibbs(1) (racd far side: chsd wnr: ev ch over 1f out: unable qckn)....2 **2**
3439[8] Morocco (IRE) **(57)***(57) (MRChannon)* 6-9-3 RHughes(8) (hld up: swtchd far side over 5f out: hrd rdn over 1f out: one pce)....3 **3**
2295[2] Canovas Heart **(61)***(61) (BobJones)* 6-9-7 WCarson(13) (hld up: rdn over 2f out: one pce)...s.h **4**
3545[10] Wardara **(70)***(68)*(Fav)*(MissGayKelleway)* 3-9-9b(3) SSanders(11) (a.p: rdn over 2f out: one pce)....¾ **5**
2624[9] Best of Bold **(65)***(61) (NAGraham)* 3-9-7 JReid(2) (lw: racd far side: hld up: rdn over 3f out: one pce)....¾ **6**
2010[13] Deeply Vale (IRE) **(62)***(55) (GLMoore)* 4-9-8 SWhitworth(3) (racd far side: hld up: rdn over 2f out: wknd fnl f)....1½ **7**
3182[6] South Eastern Fred **(54)***(43) (HJCollingridge)* 4-9-0 MRimmer(16) (nvr nrr)....1½ **8**
3534[6] Paddy's Rice **(60)***(47) (LJHolt)* 4-8-13 (7) IonaWands(7) (lw: prom 4f)....1 **9**
3390[10] Sally Weld **(58)***(42) (CJBenstead)* 3-9-0 MWigham(10) (prom 5f)....1¼ **10**
3173[8] I'm Outa Here (IRE) **(63)***(41) (RHannon)* 3-9-5 MRoberts(5) (racd far side: a bhd)....2½ **11**
3605[9] Rising Spray **(54)***(32) (CAHorgan)* 4-8-7 (7) AmandaSanders(12) (s.s: hld up: rdn over 2f out: wknd over 1f out)....nk **12**
3605[5] Super High **(57)***(23) (PHowling)* 3-8-13 StephenDavies(6) (prom 4f)....5 **13**
3293[7] Robo Magic (USA) **(58)***(24) (LMontagueHall)* 3-9-0 TQuinn(14) (b: hdwy over 2f out: wknd over 1f out)....hd **14**
2141[5] Dream Carrier (IRE) **(60)***(18) (REPeacock)* 7-9-3 (3) NVarley(15) (bhd fnl 4f)....3½ **15**
3615[25] Green Golightly (USA) **(54)***(10) (DAWilson)* 4-9-0 NGwilliams(9) (bhd fnl 3f)....¾ **16**

4/1 Wardara, **11/2** Canovas Heart, **8/1** Super High (6/1-9/1), **9/1** I'm Outa Here (IRE) (op 6/1), Paddy's Rice (6/1-10/1), Robo Magic (USA) (6/1-10/1), **12/1** Sally Weld (op 8/1), Deeply Vale (IRE), Green Golightly (USA) (7/1-14/1), Morocco (IRE), **14/1** Best of Bold, **16/1** South Eastern Fred, **20/1** Rising Spray, BLOW DRY (IRE), **25/1** Dream Carrier (IRE), Pharaoh's Dancer, CSF £411.31 CT £5,553.88 TOTE £31.10: £7.20 £18.90 £2.60 £1.40 (£1,208.30) Trio not won; £586.29 to Ayr 4.05 15/09/95. OWNER Mr Gerard Moran (RICHMOND) BRED Miss Janet Mehigan 16 Rn
1m 25.94 (5.34) SF: 31/40/23/27/30/23/21/9/13/4/3/-/-/-/-/-
WEIGHT FOR AGE 3yo-4lb

3678 TRAVIS PERKINS MAIDEN H'CAP (0-70) (3-Y.O+) (Class E) £3,445.20 (£1,029.60: £492.80: £224.40) **5f** Stalls: High GOING minus 0.02 sec(G) 4-50 (4-55)

3467[7] **Secret Miss (45)***(62) (APJarvis)* 3-8-3 TSprake(7) (lw: racd far side: hdwy over 2f out: led 1f out: r.o wl) — **1**
3442[3] Just Like Me **(61)***(59)*(Fav)*(RGuest)* 3-9-5 WCarson(3) (racd far side: rdn over 2f out: hdwy over 1f out: r.o) 6 **2**
1419[5] Bajan Frontier (IRE) **(45)***(38) (FHLee)* 3-8-3 AMcGlone(1) (b.hind: racd far side: led 4f: unable qckn) 1½ **3**
3508[5] Pemley **(37)***(24) (RMWhitaker)* 3-7-6 (3)ow2 NVarley(2) (lw: racd far side: last pl over 2f out: r.o one pce fnl f) 1¼ **4**
3467[17] Granmas Delight **(40)***(25) (MMcCormack)* 4-8-0 StephenDavies(5) (racd far side: outpcd: nvr nrr) 1¼ **5**
2512[5] Supreme Thought **(66)***(51) (LGCottrell)* 3-9-10 MFenton(14) (a.p: rdn over 1f out: one pce) .d.h **5**
3508[7] Last World **(42)***(21) (JAPickering)* 3-8-0 DBiggs(4) (lw: racd far side: a.p: rdn over 2f out: wknd over 1f out) 1¾ **7**
3508[4] China Hand (IRE) **(46)***(24) (MartynWane)* 3-8-4 MRoberts(13) (prom 4f) nk **8**
3293[10] Woodlands Electric **(37)** *(PAPritchard)* 5-7-4 (7)ow4 JoHunnam(8) (bhd fnl 2f) 4 **9**
3519[8] Lovely Me (IRE) **(63)***(19) (RFJohnsonHoughton)* 4-9-9 JReid(12) (a bhd) 3 **10**
Wychwood Sandy **(56)***(2) (HJCollingridge)* 4-9-2 MRimmer(10) (a bhd) 3 **11**
1909[7] Logie Pert Lad **(36)** *(JJBridger)* 3-7-8 ow1 NAdams(15) (a bhd) nk **12**
3640[8] Taylord **(64)** *(RHannon)* 3-9-8v RHughes(9) (bhd fnl 2f) 11 **13**
3508[2] Northern Grey **(52)** *(JBerry)* 3-8-3 (7) PRoberts(6) (lw: racd far side: bhd whn stmbld & uns rdr 3f out) **U**

LONG HANDICAP Woodlands Electric 6-3 Logie Pert Lad 7-2 Pemley 6-12

5/2 Just Like Me, **6/1** Northern Grey, **8/1** Bajan Frontier (IRE), **9/1** Lovely Me (IRE) (6/1-10/1), **10/1** Supreme Thought (6/1-11/1), **12/1** China Hand (IRE) (op 7/1), Pemley, Taylord (op 7/1), **14/1** SECRET MISS (op 8/1), **20/1** Granmas Delight, Last World, **33/1** Logie Pert Lad, Wychwood Sandy, **40/1** Woodlands Electric, CSF £45.73 CT £284.08 TOTE £27.20: £4.00 £1.60 £4.90 (£23.20) Trio £206.10 OWNER Mr N. Coverdale (ASTON UPTHORPE) BRED J. R. C. and Mrs Wren 14 Rn

59.48 secs (2.48) SF: 42/39/18/4/7/31/1/4/-/1/-/-/-/-

WEIGHT FOR AGE 3yo-2lb

3679 PUTNEY H'CAP (0-75) (3-Y.O+) (Class D) £4,239.30 (£1,268.40: £608.20: £278.10) **1m 2f** Stalls: Low GOING minus 0.02 sec per fur (G) 5-20 (5-23)

3572* **Kaafih Homm (IRE) (54)***(68)*(Fav)*(NACallaghan)* 4-8-7 WCarson(10) (b.hind: hdwy & nt clr run over 2f out: swtchd rt: led over 1f out: r.o wl) — **1**
3373[4] Domitia (USA) **(62)***(70) (MBell)* 3-8-8 MFenton(4) (6th st: hrd rdn over 2f out: led wl over 1f out: sn hdd: unable qckn) 4 **2**
3440[4] Zeetaro **(74)***(80) (MajorWRHern)* 4-9-13v TSprake(6) (lw: hdwy over 2f out: hrd rdn over 1f out: r.o one pce) ¾ **3**
3384[6] Bookcase **(67)***(71) (DRCElsworth)* 8-9-6 MRoberts(8) (hdwy over 2f out: ev ch over 1f out: one pce) 1½ **4**
2571[9] Braydon Forest **(65)***(66) (CJDrewe)* 3-8-11b RHughes(7) (lw: led over 2f: led over 4f out to wl over 1f out: sn wknd) 1¾ **5**
3377[6] Arzani (USA) **(65)***(60) (DJSCosgrove)* 4-9-4 MRimmer(5) (nvr nr to chal) 4 **6**
3531[9] Tribal Peace (IRE) **(68)***(60) (BGubby)* 3-9-0 SWhitworth(1) (lw: 3rd st: wknd over 1f out) 1½ **7**
1367[3] Koathary (USA) **(66)***(54) (LGCottrell)* 4-9-2 (3) SSanders(3) (nvr nrr) 3 **8**
3501[9] Caerle Lad (IRE) **(63)***(48) (GHarwood)* 4-9-2 AClark(14) (led over 7f out tl over 4f out: 2nd st: wknd over 2f out) 1½ **9**
3294[9] Woodlands Energy **(52)***(31) (PAPritchard)* 4-8-5 NAdams(16) (nvr nrr) 4 **10**
2460[7] Top Skipper (IRE) **(64)***(40) (BHanbury)* 3-8-5 (5) MHenry(12) (5th st: wknd over 3f out) 1¾ **11**
3214[9] Yeath (IRE) **(61)***(23) (RAkehurst)* 3-8-7 TQuinn(2) (lw: plld hrd: 4th st: wknd over 2f out) 9 **12**
3388[7] Fairy Knight **(74)***(29) (RHannon)* 3-9-6 JReid(9) (lw: bhd fnl 4f) 4 **13**
*3511** Shanghai Venture (USA) **(72)***(13) (SPCWoods)* 4-9-11 WWoods(11) (prom 6f) 9 **14**
3362[4] Thames Side **(56)** *(MMadgwick)* 4-8-6v(3) DRMcCabe(15) (a bhd) 1¾ **15**
3108[9] Khalyani (IRE) **(75)***(7) (RRowe)* 5-10-0 MPerrett(13) (bhd fnl 6f) 3½ **16**

2/1 KAAFIH HOMM (IRE), **4/1** Yeath (IRE), **7/1** Bookcase (5/1-9/1), **15/2** Fairy Knight, **12/1** Zeetaro (7/1-14/1), Shanghai Venture (USA) (7/1-14/1), **14/1** Arzani (USA), Domitia (USA) (10/1-16/1), **20/1** Thames Side, Koathary (USA), **25/1** Caerle Lad (IRE), Top Skipper (IRE), Tribal Peace (IRE), Braydon Forest, **50/1** Khalyani (IRE), **66/1** Woodlands Energy, CSF £31.98 CT £278.14 TOTE £2.40: £1.50 £2.80 £3.20 £1.60 (£26.10) Trio £72.90 OWNER Gallagher Materials Ltd (NEWMARKET) BRED Sheikh Ahmed bin Rashid al Maktoum 16 Rn 2m 14.09 (11.09) SF: 2/-/14/5/-/-/-/-/-/-/-/-

WEIGHT FOR AGE 3yo-7lb

T/Plpt: £32.60 (263.71 Tckts). T/Qdpt: £74.30 (0.5 Tckts); £50.25 to Ayr 15/9/95. AK

3658-**YARMOUTH (L-H)**
Thursday September 14th (Good)
WEATHER: sunny, warm WIND: mod across

3680 TED PILLAR CONDITIONS STKS (2-Y.O F) (Class C) £4,927.50 (£1,822.50: £873.75: £356.25)
6f 3y Stalls: High GOING minus 0.12 sec per fur (G) 2-30 (2-31)

2128* **Anthelia** *(88) (GWragg)* 2-8-10 MHills(2) (hld up & bhd: hdwy 2f out: r.o to ld nr fin) ....— 1
3022* Prancing *(89)*(Fav)*(DRLoder)* 2-8-12 LDettori(6) (a.p: led ½-wy: hrd rdn fnl f: hdd cl home) ....nk 2
2322⁷ Beautiful Ballad (IRE) **(88)***(83) (BWHills)* 2-8-7 (5) JDSmith(3) (b.hind: sn pushed along: hdwy 2f out: one pce ins fnl f) 2½ 3
3371* My Mariam *(73) (CREgerton)* 2-8-12 BThomson(1) (prom on outside: rdn wl over 1f out: sn outpcd) 3½ 4
3427* Just Millie (USA) *(65+) (JEBanks)* 2-8-7 JQuinn(5) (slt ld to ½-wy: rdn over 2f out: sn bhd) 1¼ 5
1627⁴ Galine *(60) (WAO'Gorman)* 2-8-7 EmmaO'Gorman(4) (bkwd: prom: rdn 2f out: wknd appr fnl f) 1¾ 6

4/5 Prancing, **9/2** ANTHELIA, **8/1** Just Millie (USA), **10/1** My Mariam (7/1-12/1), **14/1** Beautiful Ballad (IRE) (8/1-16/1), **16/1** Galine, CSF £7.82 TOTE £5.60: £2.40 £1.10 (£2.70) OWNER Mrs Claude Lilley (NEWMARKET) BRED Whitsbury Manor Stud 6 Rn 1m 15.0 (4.40) SF: 23/24/18/8

3681 BREYDON WATER H'CAP (0-70) (3-Y.O+) (Class E) £3,931.40 (£1,179.20: £567.60: £261.80)
6f 3y Stalls: High GOING minus 0.12 sec per fur (G) 3-00 (3-03)

3293⁸ **Double Splendour (IRE)** **(51)***(67+)*(Fav)*(PSFelgate)* 5-8-11 WRyan(19) (lw: s.s: sn bhd: gd hdwy 2f out: led ins fnl f: qcknd clr) ....— 1
3638¹¹ Our Shadee (USA) **(45)***(50) (KTIvory)* 5-8-5v BDoyle(14) (hdwy ½-wy: ev ch ins fnl f: sn outpcd) 4 2
3179⁵ Hello Hobson's (IRE) **(51)***(55) (RBastiman)* 5-8-6 (5) GParkin(17) (hdwy over 2f out: ev ch ent fnl f: unable qckn) ....½ 3
3442² Jobie **(66)***(63) (BWHills)* 5-9-12 MHills(18) (a.p stands' side: led over 1f out tl hdd & outpcd ins fnl f) 2½ 4
3442¹¹ Judgement Call **(49)***(45) (PHowling)* 8-8-9 NCarlisle(16) (b: lw: chsd ldrs stands' side: rdn & kpt on appr fnl f) ....½ 5
3293³ To the Roof (IRE) **(64)***(55+) (PWHarris)* 3-9-7 GDuffield(2) (lw: a wl plcd far side: rdn wl over 1f out: no ex) 2 6
3341² Squire Corrie **(61)***(45) (JEBanks)* 3-9-1 (3) JStack(10) (lw: hld up: hdwy u.p wl over 1f out: nt rch ldrs) 2½ 7
3661¹⁹ Awesome Venture **(46)***(29) (MCChapman)* 5-7-13b(7) CMunday(20) (led & clr stands' side tl hdd & wknd over 1f out) ....nk 8
3057⁶ Sarasonia **(33)***(7) (JWPayne)* 4-7-7 GBardwell(15) (prom: rdn 2f out: sn btn) 3½ 9
2659¹⁰ Lough Erne **(70)***(43) (CFWall)* 3-9-13 LDettori(3) (lw: prom far side over 4f) ....nk 10
3293⁶ Waders Dream (IRE) **(47)***(16) (PatMitchell)* 6-8-2v(5) DaneO'Neill(12) (prom 4f) 1½ 11
3177² Dahiyah (USA) **(61)***(29) (GLMoore)* 4-9-0v(7) LSuthern(9) (chsd ldrs tl rdn & wknd 2f out) ....nk 12
3522⁴ Sir Tasker **(58)***(18) (JLHarris)* 7-9-4 RCochrane(5) (lw: spd far side over 3f) 3 13
3341⁸ Green Dollar **(51)***(11) (PHowling)* 12-8-8 (3) SDrowne(11) (m.n.s) ....nk 14
3637¹⁴ Face the Future **(62)***(16) (LJHolt)* 6-9-8 WNewnes(6) (prom far side over 3f) 2 15
3524¹³ High Holme **(56)***(4) (DTThom)* 4-9-2 PRobinson(13) (outpcd) 2½ 16
3242⁷ White Sorrel **(65)***(2) (AHarrison)* 4-9-6b(5) JDSmith(7) (outpcd) 4 17
2784² Dante's Rubicon (IRE) **(48)** *(JDBethell)* 4-8-8 RHills(4) (outpcd) ....nk 18
3475¹⁷ Miss Electra **(40)** *(MBlanshard)* 3-7-11 JQuinn(1) (outpcd) ....¾ 19
1909⁵ Tiheros **(59)** *(JCPoulton)* 3-9-2 AMorris(8) (bkwd: prom centre to ½-wy: sn wknd: t.o) 20 20

LONG HANDICAP Sarasonia 7-0

5/1 DOUBLE SPLENDOUR (IRE), **11/2** Jobie, **8/1** To the Roof (IRE), **12/1** Dante's Rubicon (IRE), Lough Erne, **14/1** Hello Hobson's (IRE), Sir Tasker, Squire Corrie, Dahiyah (USA), Judgement Call, Waders Dream (IRE), Face the Future, **16/1** White Sorrel, Tiheros, **20/1** Awesome Venture, **25/1** Our Shadee (USA), **33/1** High Holme, Green Dollar, **50/1** Miss Electra, Sarasonia, CSF £118.20 CT £1,545.39 TOTE £6.50: £1.80 £3.90 £4.30 £1.70 (£94.90) Trio £485.40 OWNER Yorkshire Racing Club Owners Group 1990 (MELTON MOWBRAY) BRED R. McQuillan 20 Rn
1m 13.9 (3.30) SF: 38/21/26/34/16/23/13/-/-/11/-/-/-/-/-/-/-/-/-/-
WEIGHT FOR AGE 3yo-3lb

3682
GREAT YARMOUTH STAYERS H'CAP (0-95) (3-Y.O+) (Class C) £5,900.00 (£1,760.00: £840.00: £380.00)
2m 2f 51y Stalls: High GOING minus 0.12 sec per fur (G) 3-30 (3-30)

3391* **Invest Wisely (83)***(97) (JMPEustace)* 3-9-6 RCochrane(2) (lw: led 2f: 2nd st: led 3f out: sn drvn clr: rdn out fnl f) — 1
3425[4] Upper Mount Clair **(55)***(68)*(Fav)*(CEBrittain)* 5-8-7 BDoyle(3) (lw: drppd rr 7f out: 5th st: rdn & hdwy over 2f out: styd on strly) 1 2
3091[5] Dawlah **(87)***(100) (HThomsonJones)* 3-9-10 RHills(5) (hld up: 4th st: hdwy over 2f out: rdn & no ex ins fnl f) nk 3
3351[2] Nanton Point (USA) **(71)***(80)*(Fav)*(LadyHerries)* 3-8-8 JQuinn(6) (lw: led after 2f to 3f out: sn rdn & wknd) 5 4
3616[5] Ballymac Girl **(51)***(57) (JMBradley)* 7-8-0 (3) SDrowne(4) (hdwy 10f out: 3rd st: sn rdn: grad wknd) 3 5
3571[11] Antiguan Flyer **(53)** *(RHarris)* 6-7-12 (7) PClarke(1) (b: chsd ldrs 12f: sn lost tch: 6th st: t.o) .dist 6

5/2 Nanton Point (USA), Upper Mount Clair, **7/2** INVEST WISELY, **11/2** Dawlah, **10/1** Ballymac Girl, **25/1** Antiguan Flyer, CSF £11.41 TOTE £4.30: £1.60 £1.80 (£5.70) OWNER Mr J. C. Smith (NEWMARKET) BRED Littleton Stud 6 Rn 4m 1.8 (5.20 under best) (7.80) SF: 61/47/64/44/36/-
WEIGHT FOR AGE 3yo-15lb

3683
E.B.F. HASTINGS MAIDEN STKS (2-Y.O) (Class D) £4,581.00 (£1,368.00: £654.00: £297.00) **1m 3y** Stalls: High GOING minus 0.12 sec per fur (G) 4-00 (4-00)

3494[2] **Danesman (IRE)** *(82)*(Fav)*(JHMGosden)* 2-9-0 LDettori(1) (lw: a.p: hrd rdn over 1f out: styd on to ld nr fin) — 1
3280[2] Bright Heritage (IRE) *(81) (DRLoder)* 2-9-0 GCarter(3) (led: qcknd 2f out: hrd drvn fnl f: ct cl home) ½ 2
3416[6] Cheerful Aspect (IRE) *(67) (EALDunlop)* 2-9-0 RHills(5) (hld up: effrt over 2f out: kpt on one pce) 7 3
3494[9] Burnt Offering *(67) (CEBrittain)* 2-9-0 BDoyle(8) (bit bkwd: bhd: effrt & rdn wl over 2f out: nvr nr ldrs) hd 4
3437[2] Canon Can (USA) *(59) (HRACecil)* 2-9-0 WRyan(6) (chsd ldrs: rdn over 2f out: sn btn) 4 5
3472[3] Callaloo *(59) (MrsJCecil)* 2-9-0 PaulEddery(4) (prom: rdn 2f out: outpcd over 1f out) s.h 6
3371[12] Old School House *(58) (CNAllen)* 2-9-0 PRobinson(7) (bkwd: chsd ldrs: sn drvn along: wknd over 2f out) ½ 7
3340[18] Umberston (IRE) *(53) (LMCumani)* 2-9-0 OUrbina(2) (bkwd: a bhd) 2½ 8

6/4 DANESMAN (IRE), **2/1** Bright Heritage (IRE) (op 5/4), **4/1** Callaloo, **8/1** Canon Can (USA), **25/1** Cheerful Aspect (IRE), **50/1** Burnt Offering, Umberston (IRE), **66/1** Old School House, CSF £4.67 TOTE £2.60: £1.20 £1.30 £2.00 (£2.70) OWNER Sheikh Mohammed (NEWMARKET) BRED Bernard Cooke 8 Rn 1m 39.9 (4.60) SF: 40/39/25/25/17/17/16/11

3684
LOTTIE AND ALBERT BOTTON MEMORIAL NURSERY H'CAP (0-85) (2-Y.O) (Class D) £3,752.50 (£1,120.00: £535.00: £242.50)
1m 3y Stalls: High GOING minus 0.12 sec per fur (G) 4-30 (4-31)

3546[2] **Opera (77)***(86)*(Fav)*(WJarvis)* 2-9-4 LDettori(11) (lw: hld up gng wl: led over 1f out: drew clr fnl f: readily) — 1
3174[11] Decision Maker (IRE) **(80)***(82) (RHannon)* 2-9-2 (5) DaneO'Neill(4) (chsd ldrs: effrt 2f out: kpt on: no ch w wnr) 3½ 2
3228[5] Crackernat (IRE) **(78)***(77) (LMCumani)* 2-9-5 WRyan(8) (led tl over 1f out: rdn & one pce) 1½ 3
2192[7] Mellors (IRE) **(69)***(66) (JARToller)* 2-8-10b WNewnes(10) (stumbled s: hld up: effrt 2f out: nvr nr to chal) 1 4
3516[4] Nostoi **(73)***(70) (SirMarkPrescott)* 2-9-0 GDuffield(5) (chsd ldrs: rdn 3f out: one pce) s.h 5
3180* Uncle George **(79)***(68) (MHTompkins)* 2-9-6 PRobinson(6) (lw: hld up: hdwy over 3f out: rdn & wknd over 1f out) 4 6
3414[5] Kernof (IRE) **(65)***(46) (MDHammond)* 2-8-6 MHills(1) (lw: in tch tl rdn & wknd over 2f out) 4 7
3168[5] Miss Offset **(58)***(34) (MJohnston)* 2-7-13b NCarlisle(9) (a bhd) 2½ 8
2526[14] Be My Bird **(70)***(41) (BJMeehan)* 2-8-11 BDoyle(7) (prom tl wknd qckly over 2f out) 2½ 9
3540[2] Cherry Garden (IRE) **(65)***(16) (TJNaughton)* 2-8-1 (5)ow2 JDSmith(3) (lw: s.i.s: racd centre: a bhd: t.o) 9 10

6/4 OPERA, **6/1** Nostoi, **7/1** Uncle George, Cherry Garden (IRE), **10/1** Decision Maker (IRE), Crackernat (IRE), **11/1** Kernof (IRE), **14/1** Miss Offset, **20/1** Mellors (IRE), **33/1** Be My Bird, CSF £16.59 CT £107.39 TOTE £2.20: £1.50 £5.30 £4.70 (£29.50) Trio £48.80 OWNER Mrs Doris Allen (NEWMARKET) BRED Stowell Hill Ltd 10 Rn 1m 41.3 (6.00) SF: 29/25/20/9/13/11/-/-/-/-

3685 YARMOUTH ROADS MAIDEN H'CAP (0-60) (3-Y.O+) (Class F) £3,614.90 (£1,006.40: £484.70) **1m 3y** Stalls: High GOING minus 0.12 sec (G) 5-00 (5-04)

3383 10 **Bibliotheque (USA) (60)***(71)*(Fav)*(JHMGosden)* 3-9-12v LDettori(16) (b: hld up in rr: hdwy 2f out: led wl ins fnl f: comf)........— **1**
3182 4 Sovereigns Parade **(60)***(69) (JEBanks)* 3-9-9 (3) JStack(11) (led: clr fr ½-wy: wknd appr fnl f: hdd nr fin)........1 **2**
3605 13 Audrey Grace **(47)***(55) (BJMeehan)* 4-9-4v PaulEddery(15) (hdwy 3f out: rdn & ev ch appr fnl f: kpt on)........¾ **3**
3475 3 Saltando (IRE) **(52)***(59) (PatMitchell)* 4-9-9 RCochrane(9) (lw: hld up: hdwy over 2f out: rdn appr fnl f: kpt on)........nk **4**
3288 8 Total Rach (IRE) **(53)***(58) (RIngram)* 3-9-2 (3) SDrowne(20) (in tch stands' side: effrt over 1f out: rdn & r.o fnl f)........¾ **5**
3534 9 Takeshi (IRE) **(60)***(63) (EALDunlop)* 3-9-7b(5) AWhelan(18) (hld up: hdwy over 2f out: styd on ins fnl f)........1 **6**
3455 14 Sporting Risk **(46)***(48) (PWHarris)* 3-8-12 MHills(12) (in tch stands' side: effrt u.p 2f out: kpt on)........½ **7**
1326 4 H'Ani **(50)***(47) (WJHaggas)* 3-9-2 RHills(5) (bit bkwd: swtchd to r stands' side: rdn 2f out: nvr nrr)........2½ **8**
Lonesome Train (USA) **(46)***(43) (CWeedon)* 6-9-3 BPowell(13) (b: swtg: bkwd: prom stands' side tl rdn & wknd appr fnl f)........nk **9**
3605 7 Ironic (IRE) **(55)***(44) (RHannon)* 3-9-2 (5) DaneO'Neill(19) (chsd ldrs stands' side over 5f)........4 **10**
3461 3 Our Robert **(60)***(48) (JGFitzGerald)* 3-9-12 WNewnes(2) (led far side: outpcd fnl 2f)........½ **11**
3451 5 Agoer **(54)***(40) (CEBrittain)* 3-9-6 BDoyle(14) (hdwy over 2f out: sn hrd rdn & wknd)........1 **12**
3455 2 Saucy Maid (IRE) **(57)***(40) (MajorDNChappell)* 4-10-0 BThomson(7) (racd far side: no ch fnl 2f)........1½ **13**
3152 5 Opera Fan (IRE) **(54)***(36) (SirMarkPrescott)* 3-9-6 GDuffield(4) (lw: no ch far side fr ½-wy)....½ **14**
3396 5 Star Performer (IRE) **(49)***(29) (MrsMReveley)* 4-9-1 (5) GParkin(6) (n.d far side)........1 **15**
3475 9 Arnie (IRE) **(47)***(27) (GLMoore)* 3-8-13 WRyan(17) (chsd ldrs stands' side over 4f)........hd **16**
Broughton's Port **(42)***(20) (WJMusson)* 5-8-13 GCarter(1) (bkwd: racd far side: a bhd)........¾ **17**
2319 14 Fern's Governor **(49)***(26) (WJMusson)* 3-9-1 JQuinn(3) (racd far side: n.d)........½ **18**
3641 18 Kindakoola **(45)***(2) (MCChapman)* 4-8-9 (7) CMunday(10) (bit bkwd: prom to ½-wy: wknd: t.o)10 **19**
2993 7 Dancing Destiny **(60)***(3) (RBastiman)* 3-9-7 (5) HBastiman(8) (prom centre to ½-wy: wknd: t.o) 7 **20**

6/1 BIBLIOTHEQUE (USA), **7/1** Saucy Maid (IRE), Agoer, **8/1** Opera Fan (IRE), Our Robert, Dancing Destiny, **9/1** Fern's Governor, **10/1** Saltando (IRE), **12/1** Ironic (IRE), Star Performer (IRE), **14/1** Takeshi (IRE), **16/1** Sovereigns Parade, **25/1** Sporting Risk, Total Rach (IRE), **33/1** Audrey Grace, Arnie (IRE), Broughton's Port, H'Ani, **50/1** Kindakoola, Lonesome Train (USA), CSF £100.84 CT £2,754.11 TOTE £8.30: £2.20 £5.80 £6.70 £4.00 (£153.80) Trio not won; £596.04 to Ayr 15/09/95. OWNER Sheikh Mohammed (NEWMARKET) BRED Darley Stud Management Inc 20 Rn 1m 40.7 (5.40) SF: 43/41/32/36/30/35/20/19/20/16/20/12/17/8/6/-/-/-/-/-

WEIGHT FOR AGE 3yo-5lb

T/Plpt: £24.00 (534.44 Tckts). T/Qdpt: £8.60 (8.1 Tckts). IM

0257a-LES LANDES (Jersey) (L-H)
Monday August 28th (Good to firm)

3686a MIDLAND BANK H'CAP (3-Y.O+) £720.00 **2m** 4-50 (4-57)

3321a* **Fortensky (USA)** *(CMcCready,Jersey)* 5-10-12 RMcGhin........— **1**
3322a* Our Topsie *(JSOArthur,Jersey)* 8-8-5 SWhitelam........4 **2**
1289 7 Al Corniche (IRE) *(CPBillot,Jersey)* 3-8-5 ATucker........7 **3**
3202 R Bee Beat *(AJChamberlain)* 7-10-3 MissDOlding (btn over 31l)........ **5**
Tote £3.00: £2.40 £3.40 (£2.10) OWNER E Goody & J Wheeler (JERSEY) 5 Rn 3m 38.0

2210a-CHANTILLY (France) (R-H)
Tuesday September 5th (Good)

3687a PRIX D'ARENBERG (Gp 3) (2-Y.O) £26,347.00 (£9,581.00: £4,790.00) **5f 110y (straight)** 2-20 (2-12)

2896a 3 **Titus Livius (FR)** *(108+) (JEPease,France)* 2-8-11 CAsmussen........— **1**
Ella Nico (IRE) *(93) (NClement,France)* 2-8-8 ODoleuze........4 **2**

3444* Branston Jewel (IRE) *(93) (MJohnston)* 2-8-8 JWeaver ....nk 3
3324a* Maggi For Margaret *(83) (MRChannon)* 2-8-8 RHughes (btn 10 3/4l).... 7

P-M 5.20F: 2.80F 6.40F (SF 108.80F) OWNER Mr S. S. Niarchos BRED S.Niarchos 7 Rn 1m 5.8

3589a-LONGCHAMP (Paris, France) (R-H) Wednesday September 6th (Good)

3688a PRIX GLADIATEUR (Gp 3) (3-Y.O+) £26,347.00 (£9,581.00: £4,790.00) **1m 7f 110y** 2-20 (2-21)

3482a6 **L'ile Tudy (IRE)** *(113) (MmeMBollack-Badel,France)* 5-9-1 ABadel ....— 1
3146³ Always Aloof (USA) *(114) (MRStoute)* 4-9-2 CAsmussen ....½ 2
3329a³ Epaphos (GER) *(115) (PBary,France)* 5-9-4 DBoeuf ....nk 3
3361² The Flying Phantom *(MHTompkins)* 4-9-2 PRobinson 6

P-M 4.20F: 2.50F 2.80F (SF 30.00F) OWNER G. Halphen BRED Swettenham Stud & Partners 6 Rn 3m 21.8 SF: -/-/-/-

3481a-LEOPARDSTOWN (Dublin, Ireland) (L-H) Saturday September 9th (Good to firm)

3689a ARTHUR GUINNESS FLYING FIVE (Gp 3) £16,250.00 (£4,750.00: £2,250.00) **5f** 2-55 (3-00)

3198a6 **Bunty Boo** *(109) (RHannon)* 6-9-7 MHills ....— 1
3198a2 Petite Fantasy *(106)(Fav)(APO'Brien,Ireland)* 3-9-5 CRoche 1 2
3187⁵ Millyant *(113) (RGuest)* 5-10-0 CAsmussen ....hd 3
2671⁶ Palacegate Episode (IRE) *(JBerry)* 5-9-7 SCraine (btn over 5½l).... 6
3446¹² Ziggy's Dancer (USA) *(EJAlston)* 4-9-10 SDWilliams (btn approx 14 3/4l) 9

9/4 Petite Fantasy, **6/1** Millyant, **15/2** Palacegate Episode (IRE), **10/1** BUNTY BOO, **20/1** Ziggy's Dancer (USA), Tote £10.90: £3.20 £1.10 £3.00 (£15.80) OWNER Mrs R. C. Mayall (MARLBOROUGH) BRED Mrs J. McMahon 10 Rn 58.7 secs (0.20) SF: -/-/-/-/-

3690a GUINNESS CHAMPION STKS (Gp 1) (3-Y.O+ C & F) £87,300.00 (£28,800.00: £13,800.00: £4,800.00) **1m 2f** 4-00 (4-02)

3144* **Pentire** *(128)(Fav)(GWragg)* 3-8-11 MHills (hld up: 6th st: rdn over 1f out: r.o wl to ld cl home)....— 1
3327a2 Freedom Cry *(127) (AFabre,France)* 4-9-4 OPeslier (a.p: 4th st: rdn to ld ins fnl f: ct cl home)....½ 2
2211a* Flagbird (USA) *(121) (SbinSuroor)* 4-9-1 JPMurtagh (a.p: wnt 2nd over 3f out: led 2f out tl hdd ins fnl f: one pce)....2 3
2894a4 Definite Article *(123) (DKWeld,Ireland)* 3-8-11b MJKinane (w.w: 5th st: r.o up fnl 2f: no imp) ..½ 4
3143⁴ Needle Gun (IRE) *(121) (CEBrittain)* 5-9-4 BDoyle (led tl rdn & hdd 2f out: no ex)....1½ 5
2044a* Valanour(IRE) *(105) (AdeRoyerDupre,France)* 3-8-11 GMosse (chsd ldr to 3f out: 3rd st: sn rdn, wknd & eased)....10 6
3327a* Hernando (FR) *(105) (JEHammond,France)* 5-9-4 CAsmussen (hld up: 7th & rdn st: no imp)....s.h 7
2891a3 Kayaara (IRE) *(NoelFurlong,Ireland)* 3-8-11 PShanahan (s.i.s: sn t.o)....dist 8

9/4 PENTIRE, **5/2** Hernando (FR), **6/1** Valanour(IRE), Definite Article, **8/1** Flagbird (USA), **9/1** Freedom Cry, **20/1** Needle Gun (IRE), **50/1** Kayaara (IRE), Tote £3.30: £1.30 £3.90 £3.40 (£16.20) OWNER Mollers Racing (NEWMARKET) BRED Lord Halifax 8 Rn 2m 4.4 (0.40) SF: -/-/-/-/-/-/-/-

3586a-CURRAGH (Newbridge, Ireland) (R-H) Sunday September 10th (Rnd Good, St Good to firm)

3691a GO AND GO ROUND TOWER STKS (Listed) (2-Y.O) £9,675.00 (£2,775.00: £1,275.00) **6f** 3-00 (3-01)

3186⁴ **Thrilling Day** *(88)(Fav)(NAGraham)* 2-8-7 DHolland ....— 1
High Target (IRE) *(89) (DKWeld,Ireland)* 2-8-10 MJKinane ....¾ 2
Nashcash (IRE) *(93) (CCollins,Ireland)* 2-9-1 PVGilson ....½ 3

3/1 THRILLING DAY, **100/30** High Target (IRE), **5/1** Nashcash (IRE), tOTE £4.00: £1.90 £2.80 (£10.70) OWNER Bloomsbury Stud (NEWMARKET) BRED Bloomsbury Stud 6 Rn
1m 13.5 (2.90) SF: -/-/-

3692a MOYGLARE STUD STKS (Gp 1) (2-Y.O F) £56,100.00 (£19,100.00: £9,100.00: £3,100.00) 7f
4-30 (4-37)

	Priory Belle (IRE) *(101) (JSBolger,Ireland)* 2-8-11 PVGilson (trckd ldrs: hdwy 2f out: r.o to ld ins fnl f)	—	1
3578a4	Tamnia *(99) (JLDunlop)* 2-8-11 WCarson (mid div: hdwy 2f out: r.o wl fnl f: nrst fin)	¾	2
31862	My Melody Parkes *(98) (JBerry)* 2-8-11 JCarroll (chsd ldrs: r.o u.p fnl 2f)	½	3
	Dance Design (IRE) *(98) (DKWeld,Ireland)* 2-8-11 MJKinane (trckd ldrs: n.m.r 2f out: r.o fnl f: nvr nrr)	s.h	4
2351*	Rouge Rancon (USA) *(96) (PFICole)* 2-8-11 TQuinn (slt ld wl over 1f out tl no ex ins fnl f)	¾	5
	Rithab *(96) (KPrendergast,Ireland)* 2-8-11 WJSupple (hdwy ½-wy: chal over 1f out: wknd ins fnl f)	hd	6
	Ceirseach (IRE) *(93) (JSBolger,Ireland)* 2-8-11 JAHeffernan (led tl wl over 1f out: wknd)	1½	7
24422	Needham Star (USA) *(92) (PAKelleway)* 2-8-11 JPMurtagh (nvr plcd to chal)	hd	8
	Orange Walk (IRE) *(83) (APO'Brien,Ireland)* 2-8-11 CRoche (prom tl rdn & wknd 2f out)	4	9
2441*	Zelzelah (USA) *(81)*(Fav)*(PAKelleway)* 2-8-11 JWeaver (prom tl rdn & wknd over 2f out)	1	10
3197a3	Catch A Glimpse (USA) *(78) (DKWeld,Ireland)* 2-8-11 PShanahan (bhd fnl 3f)	1½	11
	In Generosity (IRE) *(78) (DKWeld,Ireland)* 2-8-11 DO'Donohoe (prom early: bhd fr ½-wy)	s.h	12
3197a7	Rockcorry Rose (IRE) *(73) (KPrendergast,Ireland)* 2-8-11 SCraine (a bhd)	2	13

3/1 Zelzelah (USA), **7/2** Dance Design (IRE), Rouge Rancon (USA), **5/1** Tamnia, **10/1** My Melody Parkes, **14/1** Orange Walk (IRE), **16/1** PRIORY BELLE (IRE), Needham Star (USA), Catch A Glimpse (USA), **20/1** Ceirseach (IRE), **25/1** Rithab, **40/1** In Generosity (IRE), **50/1** Rockcorry Rose (IRE), Tote £61.90: £16.40 £2.10 £5.30 (£883.50) OWNER Ballylinch Stud (IRELAND) BRED Ballylinch Stud 13 Rn
1m 25.2 (2.00) SF: -/-/-/-/-/-/-/-/-/-/-/-/-

3693a TRUSTED PARTNER MATRON STKS (Gp 3) (3-Y.O+ F) £16,250.00 (£4,750.00: £2,250.00: £750.00) 1m
5-00 (5-06)

3325a3	**Timarida (IRE)** *(112) (JOxx,Ireland)* 3-8-9 JPMurtagh	—	1
34733	Lap of Luxury *(111) (WJarvis)* 6-9-0 JWeaver	nk	2
34984	Warning Shadows (IRE) *(110)*(Fav)*(CEBrittain)* 3-8-9 MJKinane	½	3
2727a7	With the Fairies *(103) (RHannon)* 3-8-9 WCarson	3½	4
32352	Louis' Queen (IRE) *(JLDunlop)* 3-8-9 TQuinn (btn approx 6½l)		6
3235*	Private Line (USA) *(HRACecil)* 3-8-9 WJO'Connor (btn approx 7¼l)		8

6/4 Warning Shadows (IRE), **7/2** TIMARIDA (IRE), **9/2** Private Line (USA), **8/1** Louis' Queen (IRE), **10/1** Lap of Luxury, **25/1** With the Fairies, Tote £3.50: £1.60 £3.00 £1.30 (£25.20) OWNER Aga Khan BRED H.H. Aga Khan's Studs S.C. 9 Rn
1m 38.1 (2.10) SF: -/-/-/-/-/-

3688a-LONGCHAMP (Paris, France) (R-H)
Sunday September 10th (Soft)

3694a PRIX VERMEILLE (Gp 1) (3-Y.O F) £95,808.00 (£38,323.00: £19,162.00: £9,581.00) 1m 4f
3-10 (3-11)

3199a9	**Carling (FR)** *(115) (MmePBarbe,France)* 3-9-2 TThulliez (trckd ldrs: 5th st: rdn to ld over 1f out: r.o wl)	—	1
2563a3	Valley of Gold (FR) *(114) (AFabre,France)* 3-9-2 TJarnet (mid div: 7th st: rdn & styd on wl fnl 2f)	1	2
3190*	Larrocha (IRE) *(113) (LMCumani)* 3-9-2 LDettori (a.p: 2nd st: led 2f out tl over 1f out: r.o)	s.nk	3
3575a*	Matiara (USA) *(113) (MmeCHead,France)* 3-9-2 FHead (mid div: hdwy 2f out: chal & n.m.r over 1f out: no ex ins fnl f)	s.nk	4
1712a5	Muncie (IRE) *(113) (AFabre,France)* 3-9-2 OPeslier (hld up in rr: hdwy fnl 2f: fin wl)	s.h	5
3575a2	Dance Partner (JPN) *(112) (MmePBarbe,France)* 3-9-2 YTake (hld up: 9th st: r.o fnl f: nvr nrr)	¾	6
3041a2	Fanjica (IRE) *(112) (JLDunlop)* 3-9-2 PatEddery (prom: 3rd st: rdn over 2f out: wknd)	s.h	7
2045a*	Privity (USA) *(112) (PBary,France)* 3-9-2 DBoeuf (hld up in rr: plld wd & rdn 2f out: no imp)	s.nk	8
29367	Musetta (IRE) *(104) (CEBrittain)* 3-9-2 BDoyle (led tl hdd 2f out: wknd)	6	9
2763*	Caramba *(104) (RHannon)* 3-9-2 MRoberts (chsd ldrs pllng hrd: 4th st: wknd)	hd	10

P-M 7.60F: 2.00F 2.90F 2.20F (32.60F) OWNER Ecurie Delbart BRED Ecurie Delbart in France 10 Rn
2m 32.8 SF: -/-/-/-/-/-/-/-/-/-

3695a PRIX FOY (Gp 3) (4-Y.O+ C & F) £26,347.00 (£9,581.00: £4,790.00) **1m 4f** 3-40 (0-34)

2595[6] **Carnegie (IRE)** *(124) (AFabre,France)* 4-9-2 TJarnet ....— 1
1836[5] Balanchine (USA) *(121) (SbinSuroor)* 4-8-13 LDettori ....s.h 2
2213a[7] Tot Ou Tard (IRE) *(120) (SWattel,France)* 5-9-2 ESaint-Martin 3 3

P-M 1.10F: 1.10F 1.10F (SF 2.60F) OWNER Sheikh Mohammed (FRANCE) BRED Swettenham Stud 4 Rn 2m 35.8 SF: -/-/-

3696a PRIX NIEL (Gp 2) (3-Y.O C & F) £47,904.00 (£19,162.00: £9,581.00: £4,790.00) **1m 4f** 4-10 (4-14)

1007a[2] **Housamix (FR)** *(121) (AFabre,France)* 3-9-2 TJarnet (hld up: last st: swtchd over 1f out: r.o wl to ld post) ....— 1
2044a[5] Poliglote *(121) (MmeCHead,France)* 3-9-2 FHead (chsd ldr tl led 6f out: qcknd st: hdd 1f out: rallied to ld ins fnl f: ct post) ....hd 2
2595[4] Winged Love (IRE) *(121) (AFabre,France)* 3-9-2 OPeslier (led to 6f out: 2nd st: led 1f out: hdd ins fnl f: no ex cl home) ....nk 3
2722a* Song of Tara (IRE) *(117) (PWChapple-Hyam)* 3-9-2 JReid (hld up: hdwy & 3rd st: rdn 2f out: btn fnl f) 2½ 4

P-M 4.80F: 2.20F 1.80F (22.20F) OWNER Mr J-L. Lagardere (FRANCE) BRED SNC Lagadere Elevage in France 4 Rn 2m 36.1 SF: -/-/-/-

HANOVER (Germany) (R-H)
Sunday September 10th (Good)

3697a PREIS DER HANNOVERSCHEN (Gp 3) (3-Y.O+ F & M) £29,835.00 (£11,934.00: £5,967.00) **1m 4f** 4-00 (4-04)

2215a[17] **Alpha City (GER)** *(113) (HJentzsch,Germany)* 3-8-9 PSchiergen ....— 1
2729a[6] Flying Dream *(115) (BSchutz,Germany)* 4-9-6 THellier ....s.h 2
Purple Rain (FR) *(115) (BSchutz,Germany)* 4-9-6 MRimmer ....nk 3

Tote 18DM: 11DM 12DM 14DM (SF 37DM) OWNER Gestut Haus Ittlingen BRED Gestut Hof Ittlingen 7 Rn 2m 40.7 SF: -/-/-

3590a-SAN SIRO (Milan, Italy) (R-H)
Sunday September 10th (Good to soft)

3698a PREMIO FEDERICO TESIO (Gp 3) (4-Y.O+) £25,012.00 (£11,430.00: £6,359.00) **1m 3f** 4-10 (4-27)

Sternkonig (IRE) *(118) (HBlume,Germany)* 5-8-11 AStarke ....— 1
Caballo (GER) *(115) (HJentzsch,Germany)* 4-8-11 WNewnes 2¼ 2
3327a[5] Erin Bird (FR) *(111) (PWChapple-Hyam)* 4-8-8 BThomson ....¾ 3

Tote 17L: 11L 15L 12L (71L) OWNER Gestut Rottgen BRED Gestut Rottgen 8 Rn 2m 17.0

3665-AYR (L-H)
Friday September 15th (Good)

2nd race hand-timed
WEATHER: sunny WIND: almost nil

3699 SAM HALL CONDITIONS STKS (2-Y.O) (Class D) £4,581.00 (£1,368.00: £654.00: £297.00) **5f** Stalls: High GOING minus 0.06 sec per fur (G) 2-00 (2-03)

3444[4] **Oh Whataknight** *(83) (RMWhitaker)* 2-8-7 MHills(9) (lw: trckd ldrs: led over 1f out: edgd lft: r.o) ....— 1
3300* Babsy Babe *(87) (JJQuinn)* 2-8-13 DaleGibson(8) (dwlt: hdwy ½-wy: r.o wl fnl f) ....¾ 2
3176[2] Cross The Border **(88)***(88) (RHannon)* 2-9-4 KDarley(5) (led tl hdd over 1f out: one pce) 1¼ 3
3465[2] Norwegian Blue (IRE) **(82)***(81) (APJarvis)* 2-8-12 MJKinane(6) (lw: cl up tl rdn & btn appr fnl f) ....nk 4

2619[2] Sepoy (IRE) *(74) (CWThornton)* 2-8-12 DeanMcKeown(7) (lw: b: in tch: outpcd 2f out: kpt on towards fin)....2 **5**
3465[3] Kazimiera (IRE) *(68)*(Fav)*(MJohnston)* 2-8-7 JWeaver(4) (cl up tl wknd 1½f out)....½ **6**
3369[5] Everyone Can Dream **(57)***(54) (DenysSmith)* 2-9-2 KFallon(3) (outpcd & bhd fr ½-wy)....7 **7**
3289* Arajaan (USA) **(88)***(43) (BHanbury)* 2-9-4 RHills(2) (sn drvn along: bhd fr ½-wy)....4 **8**
1448* Shafir (IRE) **(70)***(32) (JBerry)* 2-8-11 JCarroll(1) (a outpcd & bhd)....1¼ **9**

2/1 Kazimiera (IRE), **3/1** Norwegian Blue (IRE) (9/4-7/2), **4/1** OH WHATAKNIGHT, **10/1** Arajaan (USA), Cross The Border, **12/1** Babsy Babe, **16/1** Shafir (IRE), **25/1** Sepoy (IRE), **66/1** Everyone Can Dream, CSF £44.01 TOTE £5.40: £1.50 £1.80 £1.90 (£25.60) Trio £103.10 OWNER Mr Derek Clee (LEEDS) BRED Normanby Stud Ltd 9 Rn 59.99 secs (2.99) SF: 34/38/39/32/25/19/5/-/-

3700 FAUCETS MEYNELL SAFEMIX H'CAP (0-90) (3-Y.O+ F & M) (Class C)

£6,316.00 (£1,888.00: £904.00: £412.00)
1m 2f Stalls: Low GOING minus 0.06 sec per fur (G) 2-35 (2-37)

Tulu (71)*(83) (MrsJRRamsden)* 4-9-3 KFallon(10) (lw: bhd: hdwy ent st: swtchd over 1f out: r.o to ld wl ins fnl f)....— **1**
3395* Locorotondo (IRE) **(65)***(77) (MBell)* 4-8-11 MFenton(2) (lw: a cl up: led over 1f out: hdd wl ins fnl f: r.o)....nk **2**
2333[6] Ballard Ring (IRE) **(48)***(57) (JSWainwright)* 4-7-8 AMackay(5) (led tl hdd appr fnl f: no ex)...1¾ **3**
3511[6] Ayunli **(55)***(62) (SCWilliams)* 4-8-1 GHind(11) (lw: cl up: effrt 3f out: nt qckn fnl 2f)....1 **4**
3097* Debutante Days **(65)***(72) (ACStewart)* 3-8-4 RHills(6) (a chsng ldrs: effrt 3f out: one pce)....nk **5**
3462* Rasayel (USA) **(52)***(55) (PDEvans)* 5-7-12 JFEgan(4) (s.s: styd on u.p fnl 3f: nrst fin)....2 **6**
2752[4] Champagne N Dreams **(54)***(52) (DNicholls)* 3-7-7 JLowe(1) (lw: in tch: effrt ent st: sn btn)...3½ **7**
3392* Chief Bee **(75)***(72)*(Fav)*(JLDunlop)* 4-9-7 KDarley(9) (lw: s.i.s: rdn over 3f out: no imp)....nk **8**
3211[4] No Comebacks **(60)***(57) (EJAlston)* 7-8-6 JWeaver(14) (hld up & bhd: effrt ent st: n.d)....½ **9**
2117[11] Promise Fulfilled (USA) **(71)***(61) (ABailey)* 4-9-0 (3) DWright(12) (lw: nvr bttr than mid div)....4 **10**
3206* Aqua Rigia (IRE) **(60)***(39) (HCandy)* 3-7-13 ow2 AMcGlone(13) (lw: rdn 2f out: lost tch fnl 3f)....6 **11**
3665[9] All on **(47)***(21) (JHetherton)* 4-7-7 NKennedy(7) (chsd ldrs to st: sn btn)....4 **12**
3602[8] Dee-Lady **(89)***(60) (WGMTurner)* 3-9-7 (7) JWilkinson(8) (cl up tl wknd 3f out)....2 **13**
*3529** Prudent Pet **(68)***(35) (CWFairhurst)* 3-8-7 5x JTate(3) (nvr trbld ldrs)....2½ **14**

LONG HANDICAP All on 7-2

3/1 Chief Bee, **9/2** Rasayel (USA), **7/1** Locorotondo (IRE), Aqua Rigia (IRE), **9/1** Debutante Days, **12/1** No Comebacks, TULU (op 8/1), **14/1** Prudent Pet, **20/1** Promise Fulfilled (USA), Dee-Lady, Ayunli, Champagne N Dreams, **33/1** Ballard Ring (IRE), **100/1** All on, CSF £87.30 CT £2,460.61 TOTE £13.60: £3.10 £2.40 £14.80 (£38.00) Trio £607.40 OWNER Mr Mark Houlston (THIRSK) BRED M. Houlston 14 Rn 2m 8.75 (4.15) SF: 63/57/37/42/45/35/25/52/37/41/12/1/33/8

WEIGHT FOR AGE 3yo-7lb

3701 LADBROKE RACING MILE NURSERY H'CAP (2-Y.O) (Class C)

£7,830.00 (£2,340.00: £1,120.00: £510.00)
1m Stalls: Low GOING minus 0.06 sec per fur (G) 3-05 (3-10)

3546[7] **Whispering Dawn (60)***(68) (MRChannon)* 2-7-9 AMackay(3) (chsd ldrs: disp ld over 1f out: r.o wl fnl f)....— **1**
3460[2] Disallowed (IRE) **(74)***(79) (MBell)* 2-8-9 MFenton(10) (chsd ldrs: disp ld over 1f out: nt qckn ins fnl f)....1¾ **2**
3546[9] Cumbrian Maestro **(69)***(70) (MHEasterby)* 2-8-4b SMaloney(5) (led tl hdd over 1f out: no ex)....1¾ **3**
3345[5] Carmentalia **(86)***(84) (SirMarkPrescott)* 2-9-7 GDuffield(2) (a chsng ldrs: rdn 2f out: styd on: nt pce to chal)....1½ **4**
3533* In Paradisum (USA) **(59)***(56) (MrsJRRamsden)* 2-7-8 5x LCharnock(1) (bhd tl hdwy on ins 3f out: nrst fin)....½ **5**
2995[11] Welcome Royale (IRE) **(73)***(66) (MHTompkins)* 2-8-8 PRobinson(4) (lw: in tch: kpt on fnl 2f: no imp)....2 **6**
3416[3] Crystal Falls (IRE) **(76)***(68)*(Fav)*(JJO'Neill)* 2-8-11 KFallon(9) (mid div: hmpd appr st & over 3f out: no imp)....½ **7**
3468[2] Oriel Lad **(72)***(63) (PDEvans)* 2-8-7b GHind(8) (in tch: hdwy u.p 3f out: sn btn)....½ **8**
3309[4] Alfayza **(66)***(45) (JDBethell)* 2-8-1 TWilliams(7) (cl up tl wknd fnl 2½f)....6 **9**
3307* Belana **(83)***(55) (JWWatts)* 2-9-4 MJKinane(12) (in tch to st: sn wknd)....3½ **10**
3503* Nabhaan (IRE) **(84)***(55) (DMorley)* 2-9-5 RHills(14) (lw: s.i.s: racd wd: hdwy ent st: sn rdn & btn)....¾ **11**
2075[2] State Approval **(65)***(35) (APJarvis)* 2-8-0 JTate(11) (lw: a bhd)....nk **12**

3546[5] Lucky Rabbit **(74)***(38) (BWHills)* 2-8-9 MHills(6) (lw: bhd & rdn ent st: n.d) 3 **13**
1857[6] Percy Park (USA) **(72)***(20) (MJohnston)* 2-8-7 JWeaver(13) (a bhd) 8 **14**
2059[5] Royal Ceilidh (IRE) **(74)***(22) (DenysSmith)* 2-8-9 JCarroll(15) (in tch: gd hdwy appr st: sn wknd) ....hd **15**

4/1 Crystal Falls (IRE), **13/2** Nabhaan (IRE), **7/1** Belana, **8/1** Disallowed (IRE), In Paradisum (USA), Welcome Royale (IRE), Lucky Rabbit, **12/1** Carmentalia, **14/1** Percy Park (USA), **16/1** WHISPERING DAWN, **20/1** Alfayza, **25/1** Oriel Lad, **33/1** State Approval, **50/1** Cumbrian Maestro, Royal Ceilidh (IRE), CSF £130.10 CT £5,584.86 TOTE £30.50: £6.00 £2.90 £16.30 (£93.80) Trio £260.90 OWNER Mr W. H. Ponsonby (UPPER LAMBOURN) BRED R. Barber 15 Rn
1m 41.34 (4.54) SF: 28/39/30/44/16/26/28/23/5/15/15/-/-/-/-

3702 SHADWELL STUD FIRTH OF CLYDE STKS (Listed) (2-Y.O F) (Class A) £18,883.20 (£6,988.80: £3,354.40: £1,372.00)
6f Stalls: High GOING minus 0.06 sec per fur (G) 3-35 (3-39)

3548* **My Branch (88)***(103+)*(Fav)*(BWHills)* 2-8-11 MHills(5) (lw: hld up & bhd: swtchd & hdwy 2f out: led 1f out: sn clr) ....— **1**
3186[9] Home Shopping **(100)***(100) (KMcAuliffe)* 2-8-13 JWeaver(4) (s.i.s: bhd tl hdwy 2f out: r.o) 2 **2**
2783* Amaniy (USA) **(84)***(96) (HThomsonJones)* 2-8-11 RHills(6) (lw: in tch: hdwy over 1f out: styd on wl) ....½ **3**
3692a[3] My Melody Parkes **(100)***(91) (JBerry)* 2-8-8 JCarroll(1) (led tl hdd 1f out: sn btn) ....¾ **4**
3186[6] Forentia **(100)***(83) (JRFanshawe)* 2-8-8 KFallon(2) (in tch: hdwy & ev ch over 1f out: rdn & no ex) 3 **5**
3548[4] White Whispers **(91)***(82) (BJMeehan)* 2-8-8 MJKinane(9) (chsd ldrs: rdn over 2f out: grad wknd appr fnl f) ....½ **6**
3583a* Just Ice **(89)***(87) (SirMarkPrescott)* 2-8-13 GDuffield(8) (cl up tl wknd fnl 1½f) ....hd **7**
3337* Astuti (IRE) **(96)***(78) (APJarvis)* 2-8-8 JTate(3) (lw: a.p: rdn 2f out: wknd appr fnl f) 1¼ **8**
2991[5] Arrhythmic (IRE) **(79)***(69) (MBrittain)* 2-8-8 MFenton(7) (b.hind: lw: chsd ldrs 4f: n wknd) 3½ **9**

6/5 MY BRANCH, **9/4** My Melody Parkes, **9/1** Just Ice, **11/1** Amaniy (USA), White Whispers, **16/1** Forentia, **20/1** Astuti (IRE), **33/1** Home Shopping, **100/1** Arrhythmic (IRE), CSF £33.04 TOTE £2.20: £1.10 £3.20 £2.30 (£21.80) Trio £38.30 OWNER Mr Wafic Said (LAMBOURN) BRED Addison Racing Ltd Inc 9 Rn 1m 12.29 (2.49) SF: 54/51/47/42/34/33/38/29/20

3703 LADBROKES AYRSHIRE H'CAP (0-90) (3-Y.O+) (Class C) £22,337.50 (£6,700.00: £3,225.00: £1,487.50)
1m Stalls: Low GOING minus 0.06 sec per fur (G) 4-05 (4-10)

3607[2] **Scaraben (68)***(82)*(Fav)*(SEKettlewell)* 7-8-8 (3) JStack(2) (trckd ldrs: led ins fnl f: r.o) ....— **1**
3488[2] Cool Edge (IRE) **(75)***(87) (MHTompkins)* 4-9-4 PRobinson(14) (cl up: led over 2f out tl over 1f out: kpt on) 1 **2**
3565[2] Fame Again **(80)***(92) (MrsJRRamsden)* 3-9-4 KFallon(4) (hdwy ent st: swtchd & ev ch over 1f out: kpt on) ....hd **3**
3607[8] Cee-Jay-Ay **(60)***(72) (JBerry)* 8-8-3 JCarroll(11) (dwlt: hdwy 3f out: styd on wl fnl f) ....s.h **4**
3447[2] Sheer Danzig (IRE) **(80)***(85) (RWArmstrong)* 3-9-4 MHills(5) (chsd ldrs: outpcd 2f out: no imp after) 3½ **5**
3607[5] Master Beveled **(75)***(79) (PDEvans)* 5-9-4 GHind(8) (bhd tl styd on fnl 3f: nrst fin) ....½ **6**
3368[10] Current Speech (IRE) **(69)***(71) (MHEasterby)* 4-8-12 SMaloney(6) (bhd tl r.o fnl 2f) 1 **7**
3565[9] Samah **(73)***(74)*(Fav)*(DNicholls)* 5-9-2 NConnorton(10) (in tch: rdn 3f out: no real hdwy) ....½ **8**
3488[5] Legal Fiction **(68)***(68) (MJohnston)* 4-8-11 JWeaver(1) (lw: led tl hdd over 2f out: grad wknd) nk **9**
3607[4] Celestial Choir **(85)***(84) (JLEyre)* 5-9-9 (5) DGriffiths(3) (lw: bhd: sme hdwy 3f out: n.d) ....¾ **10**
3511[5] Calder King **(57)***(52) (JLEyre)* 4-8-0b JTate(19) (bhd tl sme late hdwy) 2 **11**
3419* Spanish Verdict **(72)***(65) (DenysSmith)* 8-8-10 (5) CTeague(9) (nvr bttr than mid div) 1 **12**
3462[9] Durham Drapes **(60)***(52) (MHEasterby)* 4-7-12 (5)ow1 LNewton(7) (in tch 5f) ....s.h **13**
3411[10] Tawafij (USA) **(81)***(52) (TDyer)* 6-9-3 (7) GFaulkner(12) (lw: prom tl wknd fnl 3f) 11 **14**
3601[14] Manabar **(83)***(52) (DMorley)* 3-9-7 RHills(16) (chsd ldrs tl wknd fnl 2½f) 1 **15**
2419[6] Tregaron (USA) **(72)***(36) (PCalver)* 4-9-1 MBirch(17) (sn chsng ldrs: c wd st: sn btn) 2½ **16**
2737[2] Three Stops (USA) **(83)***(40) (MRStoute)* 3-9-7 KDarley(15) (in tch tl rdn & wknd 3f out) 3½ **17**
3514[5] Snake Plissken (IRE) **(50)** *(DHaydnJones)* 4-7-7 AMackay(13) (chsd ldrs to st: wknd qckly) .15 **18**
LONG HANDICAP Snake Plissken (IRE) 7-4

6/1 SCARABEN, Samah (8/1-5/1), **13/2** Master Beveled, **7/1** Fame Again, **8/1** Sheer Danzig (IRE), **10/1** Celestial Choir, Cool Edge (IRE), **14/1** Three Stops (USA), **16/1** Legal Fiction, **20/1** Spanish Verdict, **25/1** Tregaron (USA), Manabar, **33/1** Snake Plissken (IRE), Calder King, Cee-Jay-Ay, Current Speech (IRE), **50/1** Tawafij (USA), Durham Drapes, CSF £59.41 CT £395.45 TOTE £5.10: £1.10 £2.10 £1.90 £5.70 (£25.60) Trio £105.20 OWNER Mr J.Tennant (MIDDLEHAM) BRED Burton Agnes Stud Co Ltd 18 Rn 1m 40.1 (3.30) SF: 56/61/61/46/54/53/45/48/42/58/26/39/26/26/21/10/9
WEIGHT FOR AGE 3yo-5lb

3704

GODWINS CLAIMING STKS (3-Y.O+) (Class E) £4,305.00 (£1,290.00: £620.00: £285.00) **1m** Stalls: Low GOING minus 0.06 sec per fur (G) 4-35 (4-41)

*3510*3 **High Premium (74)***(82) (RAFahey)* 7-9-6 ACulhane(1) (b: in tch: hdwy on ins to ld over 1f out: r.o) — **1**
3488 10 Bold Angel **(70)***(69)*(Fav)*(MHEasterby)* 8-8-10 MBirch(12) (hld up: hdwy on ins 3f out: r.o fnl f: nrst fin) 1½ **2**
3565 14 Roseate Lodge **(58)***(60) (NBycroft)* 9-8-4 KFallon(7) (b: mid div tl hdwy on ins 2f out: nt clr run over 1f out: r.o wl towards fin) 1½ **3**
3396 11 Striffolino **(70)***(73) (TDBarron)* 3-8-13 DeanMcKeown(3) (led tl hdd over 1f out: one pce) ½ **4**
*3074*12 Benjarong **(27)***(56) (RMMcKellar)* 3-7-12 TWilliams(10) (bhd: hdwy 3f out: r.o wl) 1 **5**
3443* Second Colours (USA) **(66)***(67)*(Fav)*(MrsMReveley)* 5-9-4 KDarley(4) (in tch: effrt 3f out: r.o one pce) 2 **6**
3605 15 Gentle Irony **(57)***(51) (BJMeehan)* 3-8-1bow1 GDuffield(11) (lw: trckd ldrs: effrt over 1f out: nt r.o) 1¾ **7**
1742 5 Borrowby **(43)***(50) (MWEasterby)* 3-8-1 LCharnock(6) (chsd ldrs tl wknd fnl 2f) ¾ **8**
3151 4 Simand **(58)***(51) (EWeymes)* 3-8-2 GHind(2) (in tch: rdn 3f out: no imp) hd **9**
2873 2 Dr Caligari (IRE) **(64)***(53) (JBerry)* 3-8-7 JCarroll(18) (effrt ent st: no imp) 1¼ **10**
3497 8 Verde Luna **(67)***(60) (MHTompkins)* 3-9-1 PRobinson(9) (cl up tl wknd 2f out: eased whn btn) ½ **11**
2540 10 Pash **(30)***(39) (CWFairhurst)* 3-7-8v NKennedy(16) (lw: nvr rchd ldrs) nk **12**
3493 10 Hand of Straw (IRE) **(60)***(45) (JWWatts)* 3-8-3b NConnorton(14) (in tch 5f) 1¼ **13**
3492 13 Gondo **(40)***(44) (EJAlston)* 8-8-7v SDWilliams(20) (s.i.s: n.d) nk **14**
3621 7 Secret Service (IRE) **(70)***(55) (JHanson)* 3-9-7 MHills(5) (in tch: rdn 3f out: sn btn) 4 **15**
Walk In The Wild *(26) (ABailey)* 3-7-9 (3) DWright(17) (dwlt: a bhd) 3 **16**
3311 5 Spirituelle **(54)***(16) (JJO'Neill)* 3-8-0b SMaloney(8) (b.off fore: cl up tl wknd 3f out) 6 **17**
3079 10 Dragonflight **(28)***(17) (DHaydnJones)* 4-8-10 AMackay(15) (n.d) 2 **18**
1930 3 Harrken Heights (IRE) *(JSGoldie)* 3-8-2 AMcGlone(19) (a wl bhd) 12 **19**
Time Again *(TDyer)* 5-8-6 JWeaver(13) (cl up tl c wd st: sn wknd) 4 **20**

4/1 Second Colours (USA), Bold Angel, **7/1** Verde Luna, **8/1** Striffolino, Time Again, Simand, **12/1** Gentle Irony, HIGH PREMIUM, Dr Caligari (IRE), **16/1** Secret Service (IRE), **25/1** Roseate Lodge, Spirituelle, **33/1** Borrowby, Hand of Straw (IRE), Walk In The Wild, **100/1** Harrken Heights (IRE), Gondo, Dragonflight, **200/1** Benjarong, Pash, CSF £58.78 TOTE £12.00: £3.30 £2.30 £6.80 (£30.40) Trio £48.60 OWNER Mr J. C. Parsons (MALTON) BRED M.E Wates 20 Rn
1m 41.16 (4.36) SF: 54/41/32/40/23/39/18/17/18/20/27/6/12/16/22/-/-/-/-/-
WEIGHT FOR AGE 3yo-5lb

3705

ROBERT WYPER MOTORS H'CAP (0-75) (3-Y.O+) (Class D) £4,737.00 (£1,416.00: £678.00: £309.00)
2m 1f 105y Stalls: Low GOING minus 0.06 sec per fur (G) 5-05 (5-10)

2026 5 **Turquoise Sea (USA) (72)***(87)*(Fav)*(JLDunlop)* 3-8-12 JWeaver(7) (a.p: led 3f out: styd on strly & sn clr) — **1**
3412 2 Good Hand (USA) **(75)***(86) (JWWatts)* 9-10-0 NConnorton(10) (pushed along 10f out: hdwy 3f out: styd on wl: no ch w wnr) 4 **2**
2196 4 Cumbrian Rhapsody **(60)***(71) (MHEasterby)* 5-8-13 MBirch(2) (trckd ldrs: effrt 3f out: one pce appr fnl f) s.h **3**
Old Red (IRE) **(66)***(77) (MrsMReveley)* 5-9-5 KDarley(12) (hld up & bhd: styd on fnl 3f: nrst fin) s.h **4**
Bang in Trouble (IRE) **(63)***(64) (JJO'Neill)* 4-9-2 KFallon(3) (hld up: hdwy appr st: sn chsng ldrs & rdn: eased whn btn fnl f) 11 **5**
3425* Brumon (IRE) **(60)***(58) (TDyer)* 4-8-13v MFenton(4) (hdwy appr st: c wd & ev ch 3f out: hung lft & sn btn) 3 **6**
3435 3 Arian Spirit (IRE) **(40)***(38) (JLEyre)* 4-7-2 (5) PFessey(5) (nvr trbld ldrs) s.h **7**
3304* Tabdeel **(72)***(65) (ACStewart)* 3-8-12 MJKinane(13) (prom: hdwy u.p to chse ldrs 7f out: wknd over 3f out) 6 **8**
3569 9 Top Prize **(43)***(30) (MBrittain)* 7-7-10v JLowe(11) (in tch tl rdn & btn 3f out) 6 **9**
*3527** Who's the Best (IRE) **(42)***(24) (APJarvis)* 5-7-6 (3)ow2 3x DWright(9) (effrt ent st: sn btn) 4 **10**
2439 16 Medway (IRE) **(60)***(44) (MHTompkins)* 3-8-0 PRobinson(1) (cl up: led 10f out: clr 7f out: c wd st: hdd & wknd 3f out) s.h **11**
1817 9 Memorable **(40)** *(JHetherton)* 4-7-7v NKennedy(14) (led tl hdd 10f out: rdn & wknd qckly 6f out: t.o) 30 **12**
2931 4 Dawn Rock **(43)** *(RMMcKellar)* 4-7-3 (7)ow3 CAdamson(6) (bhd fr ½-wy: t.o) 7 **13**
*87*4 Marco Magnifico (USA) **(65)***(11) (TDyer)* 5-8-11 (7) GFaulkner(8) (chsd ldrs tl wknd appr st: t.o) 4 **14**

LONG HANDICAP Who's the Best (IRE) 6-12 Memorable 7-0 Dawn Rock 6-4 Arian Spirit (IRE) 7-0

7/2 TURQUOISE SEA (USA), **9/2** Good Hand (USA), Tabdeel, **7/1** Who's the Best (IRE), **10/1** Brumon (IRE), **12/1** Medway (IRE), Cumbrian Rhapsody, **20/1** Bang in Trouble (IRE), Top Prize, Old Red (IRE), **25/1** Memorable, **33/1** Arian Spirit (IRE), Marco Magnifico (USA), **100/1** Dawn Rock, CSF £18.37 CT £156.95 TOTE £4.80: £1.40 £2.30 £3.30 (£13.90) Trio £53.10 OWNER Exors of the late Mrs E Ogden White (ARUNDEL) BRED Kiltinan Castle Stud 14 Rn

3m 51.54 (9.04) SF: 51/63/48/54/41/35/15/29/7/1/8/-/-/-

WEIGHT FOR AGE 3yo-13lb

OFFICIAL EXPLANATION **Old Red (IRE): the jockey explained that the horse needs to be held up and come as late as possible.**

T/Jkpt: Not won; £28,937.56 to Ayr 16/9/95. T/Plpt: £1,210.00 (23.02 Tckts). T/Qdpt: £137.10 (1.45 Tckts). AA

3085-NEWBURY (L-H)
Friday September 15th (Good to soft)

WEATHER: fair WIND: slt half bhd

3706

WINCHESTER ASSET MANAGEMENT H'CAP (0-95) (3-Y.O+) (Class C)
£6,388.00 (£1,924.00: £932.00: £436.00)
7f 64y (round) Stalls: Low GOING: 0.11 sec per fur (G) 2-10 (2-12)

3615[13] **Champagne Grandy (76)**_(86) (MRChannon)_ 5-8-12 RHughes(8) (lw: barged thro & hdwy 2f out: led over 1f out: r.o wl) — 1
1467* Mister Rm **(75)**_(82) (RGuest)_ 3-8-7 DHolland(9) (bit bkwd: hdwy & nt clr run on ins over 2f out: swtchd rt & nt clr run over 1f out: r.o) 1¼ 2
2414[5] Sharp Rebuff **(75)**_(76) (PJMakin)_ 4-8-11 RCochrane(20) (hdwy over 1f out: r.o) 3 3
3439* Broughtons Turmoil **(62)**_(59) (WJMusson)_ 6-7-12 JQuinn(4) (4th st: rdn over 2f out: unable qckn) 1½ 4
3062[2] Shefoog **(90)**_(87) (RWArmstrong)_ 3-9-8 RPrice(1) (lw: 7th st: nt clr run on ins over 2f out tl over 1f out: swtchd rt: one pce ins fnl f) nk 5
2933[3] Bagshot **(77)**_(74)_(Fav)_(RHannon)_ 4-8-13 MRoberts(14) (hdwy over 1f out: nvr nrr) s.h 6
3028* Law Commission **(79)**_(72) (DRCElsworth)_ 5-9-1 TQuinn(11) (hdwy & hmpd over 2f out: wknd ins fnl f) 1¾ 7
3457[3] Safey Ana (USA) **(74)**_(65) (BHanbury)_ 4-8-10 WRyan(22) (b: b.hind: hdwy 2f out: wknd fnl f) ¾ 8
2598[7] Belfry Green (IRE) **(92)**_(82) (CAHorgan)_ 5-10-0 WWoods(18) (s.s: hdwy over 1f out: nvr nrr) ¾ 9
2477[5] Tom Morgan **(81)**_(69) (PTWalwyn)_ 4-9-3 PaulEddery(6) (swtg: 5th st: led wl over 1f out: sn hdd & wknd) ½ 10
2746[6] Saseedo (USA) **(86)**_(74) (WAO'Gorman)_ 5-9-8 EmmaO'Gorman(7) (swtg: nvr nrr) s.h 11
3439[12] Chili Heights **(58)**_(45) (GBBalding)_ 5-7-3v(5)ow1 MBaird(19) (b.hind: nvr nrr) s.h 12
_3242_[12] Leigh Crofter **(68)**_(56) (PDCundell)_ 6-8-4b WNewnes(17) (6th st: wknd over 1f out) hd 13
2946[6] Mislemani (IRE) **(63)**_(39) (AGNewcombe)_ 5-7-8 (5)ow4 MHenry(13) (a mid div) 3½ 14
3013[4] Scenic Heights (IRE) **(85)**_(64) (RWArmstrong)_ 3-9-3 PatEddery(5) (lw: hdwy over 2f out: wknd over 1f out) ¾ 15
3565[18] Axeman (IRE) **(88)**_(58) (RHannon)_ 3-9-1 (5) DaneO'Neill(21) (bhd fnl 2f) 4 16
1839[25] Tertium (IRE) **(81)**_(51) (PWChapple-Hyam)_ 3-8-13 JReid(12) (bit bkwd: hdwy 2f out: sn wknd) d.h 16
3534[13] Sharp Consul (IRE) **(69)**_(35) (HCandy)_ 3-8-1 NAdams(10) (2nd st: wkng whn hmpd wl over 1f out) 1¾ 18
870[12] Ertlon **(85)**_(31) (CEBrittain)_ 5-9-7 BDoyle(2) (led over 6f out tl wl over 1f out: sn wknd) 9 19
1183[24] Highland Magic (IRE) **(62)**_(4) (MJFetherston-Godley)_ 7-7-12 FNorton(16) (bhd fnl 4f) 1¾ 20
Sing Up **(74)**_(15) (MMcCormack)_ 3-8-6 AClark(3) (bhd fnl 3f) ½ 21
3212[6] Elite Hope (USA) **(82)**_(22) (CREgerton)_ 3-9-0 BThomson(15) (led 1f: 3rd st: wkng whn hmpd 2f out) ½ 22

LONG HANDICAP Chili Heights 7-5

7/1 Bagshot, **8/1** Scenic Heights (IRE), **10/1** Broughtons Turmoil, CHAMPAGNE GRANDY (op 16/1), **12/1** Law Commission, **14/1** Mislemani (IRE), Mister Rm, **16/1** Safey Ana (USA), Belfry Green (IRE), Shefoog, Elite Hope (USA), Chili Heights, Sharp Rebuff, Tertium (IRE), **20/1** Sharp Consul (IRE), Ertlon, **25/1** Tom Morgan, Axeman (IRE), **33/1** Highland Magic (IRE), Saseedo (USA), **50/1** Leigh Crofter, Sing Up, CSF £132.37 CT £2,035.12 TOTE £11.70: £2.30 £4.70 £4.50 £2.30 (£276.40) Trio £852.80 OWNER Grandy Girls (UPPER LAMBOURN) BRED J. B. and Mrs N. G. Stafford 22 Rn 1m 32.9 (4.40) SF: 55/47/45/28/52/43/41/34/51/38/43/14/25/8/29/23/16/-/-/-/-/-

WEIGHT FOR AGE 3yo-4lb

3707

TONY STRATTON SMITH MEMORIAL CONDITIONS STKS (3-Y.O+) (Class B) £8,156.00 (£3,044.00: £1,482.00: £630.00: £275.00: £133.00)
5f 34y Stalls: High GOING: 0.11 sec per fur (G) 2-40 (2-42)

1475[4] **Easy Option (IRE) (105)***(117+)*(Fav)*(SbinSuroor)* 3-8-10 WRSwinburn(4) (lw: a gng wl: hld up: led over 1f out: v.easily)......— 1
3660[2] Katya (IRE) **(94)***(97) (MRChannon)* 3-8-12 RHughes(5) (lw: led over 3f out tl over 1f out: unable qckn)......7 2
1119a[11] Sharp Prod (USA) **(107)***(97) (LordHuntingdon)* 5-9-9 JReid(2) (lw: outpcd: nvr nr to chal)......3 3
3446[5] Lennox Lewis **(98)***(81) (APJarvis)* 3-9-2 MRoberts(6) (led over 1f: wknd over 1f out)......3½ 4
3535[2] Lucky Parkes **(103)***(73) (JBerry)* 5-9-7 GCarter(1) (outpcd)......3½ 5
2430[5] Risky **(105)***(50) (RHannon)* 4-8-9 PatEddery(3) (b: outpcd)......3½ 6

5/4 EASY OPTION (IRE), **9/4** Risky, **9/1** Sharp Prod (USA), **10/1** Lucky Parkes (op 6/1), **11/1** Lennox Lewis (op 6/1), **12/1** Katya (IRE) (op 8/1), CSF £13.58 TOTE £1.80: £1.40 £2.70 (£9.30) OWNER Godolphin (NEWMARKET) BRED J. Davis in Ireland 6 Rn
62.56 secs (2.26) SF: 66/46/48/30/24/1
WEIGHT FOR AGE 3yo-2lb

3708

HMV UK CONDITIONS STKS (2-Y.O F) (Class B) £7,228.00 (£2,692.00: £1,306.00: £550.00) **7f** Stalls: High GOING: 0.11 sec per fur (G) 3-10 (3-14)

Wild Rumour (IRE) *(82+)*(Fav)*(PWChapple-Hyam)* 2-8-8 JReid(11) (w'like: scope: a.p: led 2f out: rdn out)......— 1
3541* Please Suzanne *(86) (RHannon)* 2-8-13 BDoyle(4) (lw: led 1f: rdn over 1f out: r.o)......½ 2
Supamova (USA) *(77+) (PFICole)* 2-8-8 PatEddery(14) (leggy: unf: scope: plld hrd: led over 5f out to 2f out: r.o)......1½ 3
El Opera (IRE) *(66+) (PFICole)* 2-8-8 TQuinn(13) (str: a.p: rdn over 1f out: wknd fnl f)......5 4
Reiterate *(59) (GBBalding)* 2-8-8 JWilliams(10) (unf: bit bkwd: led 6f out tl over 5f out: wknd over 3f out)......3 5
Ashanti Dancer (IRE) *(59) (MJHaynes)* 2-8-8 RCochrane(1) (leggy: nvr nr to chal)......hd 6
3532[10] Home Cookin' *(57) (DrJDScargill)* 2-8-8 MRimmer(6) (lost pl over 4f out: rallied over 2f out: wknd over 1f out)......¾ 7
Circled (USA) *(56) (BWHills)* 2-8-8 DHolland(5) (leggy: scope: bit bkwd: bhd fnl f)......½ 8
Bodfari Lass *(54) (BWHills)* 2-8-8 JDSmith(2) (w'like: bit bkwd: a bhd)......1 9
Flame of Hope *(20) (JLDunlop)* 2-8-8 WRyan(7) (w'like: scope: bit bkwd: hdwy over 3f out: wknd over 2f out)......15 10

11/4 WILD RUMOUR (IRE), **3/1** Please Suzanne (op 6/4), **7/2** El Opera (IRE) (op 2/1), **9/2** Supamova (USA) (op 3/1), **14/1** Flame of Hope (op 8/1), Circled (USA) (7/1-16/1), **25/1** Ashanti Dancer (IRE), **33/1** Reiterate, Bodfari Lass, **50/1** Home Cookin', CSF £10.89 TOTE £3.60: £1.60 £1.70 £1.10 (£4.90) Trio £5.00 OWNER Mr R. E. Sangster (MARLBOROUGH) BRED Swettenham Stud 10 Rn
1m 30.29 (5.79) SF: 33/37/28/17/10/10/8/7/5/-

3709

HAYNES, HANSON AND CLARK CONDITIONS STKS (2-Y.O C & G) (Class B) £7,042.40 (£2,621.60: £1,270.80: £534.00)
1m Stalls: High GOING: 0.11 sec per fur (G) 3-40 (3-41)

3463* **Mick's Love (IRE)** *(93+) (MJohnston)* 2-8-10 MRoberts(5) (a.p: led over 2f out: rdn out)......— 1
3592[8] Busy Flight *(92) (BWHills)* 2-8-10 PatEddery(2) (hdwy over 1f out: r.o ins fnl f)......¾ 2
3449[2] Sasuru *(89) (GWragg)* 2-8-10 PaulEddery(3) (a.p: ev ch over 1f out: unable qckn)......1½ 3
Lear Jet (USA) *(87) (PFICole)* 2-8-10 TQuinn(4) (w'like: scope: hld up: rdn over 3f out: r.o one pce fnl 2f)......¾ 4
3449[5] Terdad (USA) *(83) (MRStoute)* 2-8-10 WRSwinburn(6) (lw: hld up: rdn 2f out: wknd fnl f)......2 5
3588a[2] Axford (USA) *(82)*(Fav)*(PWChapple-Hyam)* 2-8-10 JReid(8) (lw: led over 5f: wknd over 1f out)......nk 6
Sovereign Prince (IRE) *(NACallaghan)* 2-8-10 WCarson(1) (b.off hind: w'like: scope: a wl bhd: t.o)......dist 7
3560[8] Torch Ochre (USA) *(BWHills)* 2-8-10 DHolland(7) (bhd fnl 4f: t.o)......½ 8

2/1 Axford (USA), **7/2** MICK'S LOVE (IRE), **4/1** Lear Jet (USA) (op 5/2), **9/2** Sasuru, **15/2** Terdad (USA), **10/1** Busy Flight (5/1-12/1), **20/1** Sovereign Prince (IRE), **50/1** Torch Ochre (USA), CSF £35.02 TOTE £3.40: £1.30 £2.30 £1.80 (£25.00) OWNER Mr M. Doyle (MIDDLEHAM) BRED Collinstown Stud Farm Ltd 8 Rn
1m 42.47 (5.47) SF: 47/46/43/41/37/36/-/-

3710 HEART 106.2 FM SILVER CLEF LADIES' H'CAP (0-70) (3-Y.O+) (Class E) £6,287.50 (£1,900.00: £925.00: £437.50)

1m 4f 5y Stalls: Low GOING: 0.11 sec per fur (G) 4-10 (4-13)

2792[3] **Witney-de-Bergerac (IRE) (57)***(69) (JSMoore)* 3-9-8 (5) MrsSMoore(18) (hld up: stdy hdwy over 3f out: led ins fnl f: r.o wl) — 1
*3078** Nordic Mine (IRE) **(44)***(55) (PJHobbs)* 5-9-9 MrsSHobbs(5) (hdwy over 3f out: led over 1f out tl ins fnl f: unable qckn) ¾ 2
3521[4] Grand Applause (IRE) **(45)***(54) (MPMuggeridge)* 5-9-10 MrsSBosley(11) (hdwy over 2f out: r.o wl ins fnl f: too much to do) 1½ 3
3401[5] Strat's Legacy **(46)***(50) (DWPArbuthnot)* 8-9-11 MrsDArbuthnot(2) (b.hind: hdwy over 2f out: r.o) 3½ 4
3388[10] Exemption **(70)***(69) (HCandy)* 4-11-2 (5) MrsCDunwoody(3) (lw: 6th st: hrd rdn over 1f out: one pce) 4 5
2145[5] Polish Consul **(62)***(61) (MajorWRHern)* 4-10-13 MissEJohnsonHoughton(6) (lw: rn wd st: hdwy fnl 2f: nvr nrr) nk 6
2745[3] Gold Blade **(47)***(45) (JPearce)* 6-9-12 MrsLPearce(7) (lw: 4th st: led 3f out tl over 1f out: sn wknd) ¾ 7
3470[12] Fruitful Affair (IRE) **(42)***(35) (TThomsonJones)* 6-9-2 (5)ow1 MrsSFaber(8) (nvr nrr) 2½ 8
3526[4] Streaky Hawk (USA) **(57)***(46) (PFICole)* 3-9-13 MissJWinter(16) (lw: a mid div) 4 9
3521* Missed the Boat (IRE) **(42)***(30)*(Fav)*(AGNewcombe)* 5-9-7 5x MrsMCowdrey(13) (lw: nvr nrr) 1 10
3263[4] Outstayed Welcome **(51)***(37) (MJHaynes)* 3-9-7 MissYHaynes(15) (3rd st: led over 4f out to 3f out: sn wknd) 1 11
3544[6] Bronze Runner **(40)***(26) (SMellor)* 11-9-5b MissEJoyce(10) (nvr nrr) hd 12
3189[4] Lord Hastie (USA) **(53)***(35) (CWThornton)* 7-10-4 MrsDKettlewell(20) (lw: 7th st: hung lft over 2f out: sn wknd) 3½ 13
2845[5] General Mouktar **(62)***(40) (MCPipe)* 5-10-13v MissDianaJones(22) (a mid div) 2½ 14
Wick Pound **(47)***(5) (JABOld)* 9-9-12 MrsMGrantham(1) (bit bkwd: bhd fnl 5f: t.o) 15 15
1513[13] Platini (IRE) **(51)***(6) (GBBalding)* 4-9-11 (5) MrsKTierney(19) (bhd fnl 8f: t.o) 2½ 16
3440[7] Achilles Heel **(49)** *(CNAllen)* 4-9-9 (5)ow9 MrsRAllen(9) (a bhd: t.o) 7 17
3462[12] Toshiba Talk (IRE) **(49)** *(BEllison)* 3-9-0 (5) MrsJSpeight(14) (lw: led over 7f: t.o) 1¼ 18
3207[8] Fair Flyer (IRE) **(51)** *(PJBevan)* 6-10-2 MrsDMcHale(21) (prom 6f: t.o) ¾ 19
3004[5] Chocolate Charlie **(60)***(2) (RCharlton)* 4-10-11 MrsAPerrett(4) (5th st: wknd over 4f out: t.o) ¾ 20
3658[9] Queens Stroller (IRE) **(54)** *(CCElsey)* 4-10-5 MissAElsey(12) (2nd st: wknd over 3f out: t.o) 1 21

5/1 Missed the Boat (IRE), **13/2** Lord Hastie (USA), **15/2** Gold Blade, **11/1** Nordic Mine (IRE), **12/1** Grand Applause (IRE), **14/1** Outstayed Welcome (op 8/1), Chocolate Charlie, Strat's Legacy, Exemption (10/1-16/1), General Mouktar, **16/1** Queens Stroller (IRE), **20/1** Bronze Runner, Polish Consul, WITNEY-DE-BERGERAC (IRE), Streaky Hawk (USA), Achilles Heel, Platini (IRE), **25/1** Fruitful Affair (IRE), **33/1** Toshiba Talk (IRE), **50/1** Fair Flyer (IRE), Wick Pound, CSF £216.87 CT £2,525.74 TOTE £39.50: £6.40 £2.90 £3.10 £4.00 (£279.90) Trio £718.30 OWNER Mr Ernie Houghton (EAST GARSTON) BRED Niall Creighton 21 Rn

2m 43.85 (14.55) SF: 23/18/17/13/32/24/8/-/-/-/-/-/3/-/-/-/-/-/-/-/-

WEIGHT FOR AGE 3yo-9lb

3711 VICTOR CHANDLER NURSERY H'CAP (2-Y.O) (Class C) £5,907.00 (£1,776.00: £858.00: £399.00)

7f 64y (round) Stalls: Low GOING: 0.11 sec per fur (G) 4-40 (4-42)

3460* **Ramooz (USA) (88)***(100)*(Fav)*(BHanbury)* 2-8-10 WRyan(5) (stdy hdwy over 2f out: led over 1f out: comf) — 1
3315[2] Sava River (IRE) **(90)***(91) (MRStoute)* 2-8-12 WRSwinburn(8) (lw: swtchd rt 2f out: hdwy over 1f out: r.o) 5 2
2779[4] Rhumba Dancer **(83)***(79) (RHannon)* 2-8-0 (5) DaneO'Neill(1) (hdwy over 2f out: nt clr run over 1f out: r.o) 2½ 3
3225* Champagne Prince **(93)***(86) (PWHarris)* 2-8-10 (5) MHenry(10) (4th st: ev ch over 1f out: unable qckn) 1¼ 4
3490[3] Brilliant Red **(99)***(89) (PFICole)* 2-9-7 TQuinn(6) (3rd st: rdn over 2f out: one pce) 1½ 5
3587a[7] Therhea (IRE) **(84)***(70) (BRMillman)* 2-8-1 (5) AWhelan(13) (led over 3f: rdn over 2f out: wknd over 1f out) 1¾ 6
3404[6] Snow Falcon **(76)***(61) (MBell)* 2-7-12 DBiggs(14) (5th st: wknd 2f out) nk 7
3375[5] Amaretto Bay (IRE) **(87)***(69) (BJMeehan)* 2-8-9b BDoyle(15) (2nd st: led 4f out tl over 1f out: sn wknd) 1¼ 8
2809* Al Shafa **(82)***(51) (JLDunlop)* 2-8-4 WCarson(12) (a mid div) 6 9
2965* Time Clash (IRE) **(76)***(42) (BPalling)* 2-7-12 ow2 TSprake(9) (nvr nrr) nk 10

3281[4] Shock-A-Lot (IRE) **(71)***(36) (GLewis)* 2-7-7 JQuinn(3) (bhd fnl 2f)....1½ **11**
3405[2] Vola Via (USA) **(88)***(53) (IABalding)* 2-8-10 PatEddery(2) (a bhd)....hd **12**
3538[3] Delaunay (IRE) **(73)***(25) (RHannon)* 2-7-4 (5)ow2 MBaird(4) (lw: bhd fnl 4f)....5 **13**
3540[5] Nikita's Star (IRE) **(71)***(7) (DJGMurraySmith)* 2-7-7 NAdams(7) (a bhd)....8 **14**
3375[14] Satellite Star (IRE) **(76)***(4) (MRChannon)* 2-7-12 FNorton(16) (5th st: wknd over 2f out)....4 **15**
LONG HANDICAP Shock-A-Lot (IRE) 7-5 Delaunay (IRE) 7-1 Nikita's Star (IRE) 7-4

7/2 RAMOOZ (USA), **13/2** Amaretto Bay (IRE), **7/1** Champagne Prince, **8/1** Al Shafa, **10/1** Sava River (IRE), Vola Via (USA), **12/1** Therhea (IRE), Snow Falcon, Brilliant Red, Shock-A-Lot (IRE), **14/1** Rhumba Dancer, **16/1** Time Clash (IRE), **20/1** Delaunay (IRE), **25/1** Nikita's Star (IRE), **33/1** Satellite Star (IRE), CSF £38.93 CT £423.33 TOTE £4.30: £2.00 £4.00 £4.60 (£44.90) Trio £129.10 OWNER Mr Hilal Salem (NEWMARKET) BRED Gainsborough Stud Management Ltd 15 Rn
1m 33.05 (4.55) SF: 52/43/31/38/41/22/13/21/3/-/-/5/-/-/-

3712 KINTBURY MAIDEN STKS (3-Y.O) (Class D) £4,272.50 (£1,280.00: £615.00: £282.50) **1m (straight)** Stalls: High GOING: 0.11 sec per fur (G) 5-10 (5-14)

1186[8] **Tarawa (IRE)** *(83) (NACallaghan)* 3-9-0 WCarson(6) (rdn & hdwy over 1f out: led ins fnl f: r.o wl)....— **1**
3105[4] Mr Medley *(80) (RHannon)* 3-8-9 (5) DaneO'Neill(16) (a.p: hrd rdn over 1f out: ev ch ins fnl f: unable qckn)....1½ **2**
1675[5] Zelda Zonk *(69) (BJMeehan)* 3-8-9 BDoyle(19) (bit bkwd: led: rdn over 2f out: hdd ins fnl f: one pce)....3 **3**
1701[8] Lancerette *(68) (NAGraham)* 3-8-9 MRimmer(9) (hld up: rdn 4f out: r.o one pce fnl 2f)....¾ **4**
3618[3] Secret Spring (FR) **(83)***(68)*(Fav)*(RCharlton)* 3-9-0 TQuinn(1) (hld up: rdn over 2f out: eased whn btn ins fnl f)....2½ **5**
Coeur Francais (FR) *(66) (MajorDNChappell)* 3-9-0 BThomson(12) (w'like: scope: hld up: ev ch wl over 1f out: wknd fnl f)....1 **6**
3537[2] Ranosh (USA) **(74)***(49) (EALDunlop)* 3-8-9 WRSwinburn(2) (b: b.hind: lw: a.p: rdn over 2f out: wknd over 1f out)....6 **7**
1168[9] Frankly Fran *(48) (DWPArbuthnot)* 3-8-9 JReid(5) (bit bkwd: lost pl over 4f out: r.o one pce fnl 2f)....nk **8**
3618[10] Hypertension *(52) (RHannon)* 3-9-0 RPerham(13) (lw: prom over 3f)....nk **9**
3461[4] Fatehalkhair (IRE) *(47) (BEllison)* 3-9-0 GCarter(3) (b: prom over 5f)....2½ **10**
Justfortherecord *(42) (BRMillman)* 3-8-9 JWilliams(11) (w'like: bit bkwd: a mid iv)....s.h **11**
Hopeful Sign *(39) (BWHills)* 3-8-9 PaulEddery(14) (leggy: unf: scope: nvr nrr)....1¾ **12**
1905[5] Mafuta (IRE) *(29) (JJSheehan)* 3-8-9 JQuinn(20) (prom over 5f)....5 **13**
Indian Spice *(26) (DJGMurraySmith)* 3-8-9 CRutter(17) (bit bkwd: a bhd)....1¼ **14**
Oscilights Gift *(21) (PBurgoyne)* 3-8-6 (3) DRMcCabe(10) (leggy: unf: prom over 3f)....2½ **15**
Wise Brave *(20) (HCandy)* 3-9-0 WNewnes(7) (w'like: scope: bit bkwd: s.s: a bhd)....3 **16**
2794[10] Fataana (USA) *(12) (BWHills)* 3-8-9 DHolland(8) (prom over 5f)....1¾ **17**
Safwan *(MissGayKelleway)* 3-9-0 RCochrane(15) (str: bkwd: a bhd: t.o)....dist **18**
Governors Fortune *(AJChamberlain)* 3-9-0 MPerrett(18) (str: bit bkwd: s.s: a bhd: t.o fnl 5f)....dist **19**

9/4 Secret Spring (FR), **3/1** Ranosh (USA), **4/1** Coeur Francais (FR) (op 8/1), **5/1** TARAWA (IRE), **12/1** Mr Medley (op 7/1), **16/1** Fataana (USA), **20/1** Zelda Zonk, Hopeful Sign, **25/1** Hypertension, **33/1** Fatehalkhair (IRE), Wise Brave, Safwan, **50/1** Lancerette, Indian Spice, Oscilights Gift, Justfortherecord, Frankly Fran, Mafuta (IRE), Governors Fortune, CSF £64.87 TOTE £9.40: £2.20 £4.60 £6.10 (£53.50) Trio £411.60 OWNER Mrs J. Callaghan (NEWMARKET) BRED Patrick Eddery Ltd 19 Rn
1m 43.31 (6.31) SF: 42/39/28/27/27/25/8/7/11/6/1/-/-/-/-/-/-/-/-

T/Plpt: £303.30 (72.7 Tckts). T/Qdpt: £43.10 (3.85 Tckts). AK

3699-AYR (L-H)
Saturday September 16th (Good)
WEATHER: sunny WIND: almost nil

3713 E.B.F. TOP FLIGHT LEISURE MAIDEN STKS (2-Y.O) (Class D) £4,503.00 (£1,344.00: £642.00: £291.00) **1m** Stalls: Low GOING minus 0.15 sec per fur (GF) 1-55 (2-07)

Ladykirk *(78+) (JWWatts)* 2-8-9 NConnorton(10) (w'like: unf: sn pushed along & bhd: hdwy over 2f out: r.o wl to ld cl home)....— **1**
3307[2] Maid For Baileys (IRE) **(79)***(77) (MJohnston)* 2-8-9 TWilliams(5) (lw: cl up: led 3f out: r.o: hdd & no ex nr fin)....½ **2**
3416[8] Mental Pressure *(80) (MRChannon)* 2-9-0 KDarley(4) (trckd ldrs: ev ch over 1f out: kpt on one pce)....1 **3**

2705[3] Salty Girl (IRE) *(75) (BWHills)* 2-8-9 DHolland(6) (chsd ldrs: ev ch over 1f out: no ex)..........s.h **4**
3587a[20] Love Bird (IRE) *(78) (MJohnston)* 2-9-0 DeanMcKeown(1) (in tch: outpcd over 2f out: hdwy over 1f out: r.o nr fin)..........1 **5**
3352[2] Juicy *(77) (WJHaggas)* 2-9-0 RCochrane(12) (a in tch: effrt u.p 2f out: btn 1f out)..........½ **6**
3280[4] Muhtadi (IRE) *(77)*(Fav)*(JLDunlop)* 2-9-0 MRoberts(2) (lw: slt ld tl hdd 3f out: ev ch tl wknd appr fnl f)..........hd **7**
3416[10] Oisin An Oir (IRE) **(50)***(51) (JBerry)* 2-9-0 JCarroll(3) (lw: cl up tl wknd over 2f out)..........13 **8**
1413[10] Village Opera *(41) (GMMoore)* 2-8-9 JTate(8) (outpcd & lost tch fnl 3f)..........2½ **9**
Phar Closer *(WTKemp)* 2-8-9 KFallon(7) (leggy: bkwd: sn outpcd & t.o)..........dist **10**
Lennox Lady *(RMMcKellar)* 2-8-9 DaleGibson(9) (b.hind: leggy: s.i.s: sn t.o)..........1 **11**
Son of Anshan *(MrsASwinbank)* 2-9-0 JFEgan(11) (Withdrawn not under Starter's orders: ref to ent stalls).......... **W**

7/4 Muhtadi (IRE), **7/2** Salty Girl (IRE) (5/2-4/1), **4/1** Maid For Baileys (IRE), **8/1** Juicy, **16/1** Love Bird (IRE), Mental Pressure, **25/1** LADYKIRK, **50/1** Village Opera, **66/1** Oisin An Oir (IRE), **200/1** Phar Closer, Lennox Lady, Son of Anshan, CSF £105.98 TOTE £36.30: £4.90 £1.30 £2.80 (£87.40) Trio £340.70 OWNER Duke of Sutherland (RICHMOND) BRED Duke of Sutherland 11 Rn
1m 41.51 (4.71) SF: 33/32/35/30/33/32/32/6/-/-/-/-

3714

SAAB NURSERY H'CAP (2-Y.O) (Class D) £5,010.00 (£1,500.00: £720.00: £330.00) **6f** Stalls: High GOING minus 0.15 sec per fur (GF) 2-25 (2-31)

3375[12] **King of Peru (77)***(82) (APJarvis)* 2-8-4 JTate(5) (cl up: led over 2f out: hld on wl fnl f)..........— **1**
3548[16] Branston Danni **(70)***(74) (MrsJRRamsden)* 2-7-11 JFEgan(12) (b.hind: trckd ldrs: chal appr fnl f: nt qckn nr fin)..........½ **2**
3147[15] Amanita **(75)***(73) (JWWatts)* 2-8-2 MRoberts(14) (a.p: rdn over 2f out: styd on: nt pce to chal)..........2 **3**
3414[6] Too Hasty **(80)***(78)*(Fav)*(MHEasterby)* 2-8-7 MBirch(15) (lw: led tl over 2f out: kpt on u.p).....nk **4**
2182[7] Deadline Time (IRE) **(72)***(66) (MHTompkins)* 2-7-13 AMcGlone(11) (b.off hind: bhd tl hdwy over 1f out: styd on nr fin)..........1¼ **5**
3375[3] Atraf **(94)***(88) (DMorley)* 2-9-7 RCochrane(4) (cl up: rdn over 2f out: r.o one pce)..........hd **6**
3612[14] Ramsey Hope **(83)***(76) (CWFairhurst)* 2-8-10 NKennedy(13) (w ldrs tl rdn & btn over 1f out).nk **7**
3670[8] Natural Key **(73)***(66) (DHaydnJones)* 2-8-0b AMackay(17) (hdwy 2f out: rdn & one pce appr fnl f)..........hd **8**
3225[9] Flood's Fancy **(66)***(58) (ABailey)* 2-7-7 NCarlisle(16) (effrt ½-wy: nvr trbld ldrs)..........nk **9**
3379[8] Duralock Fencer **(72)***(58) (PGMurphy)* 2-7-8 (5)ow6 PPMurphy(7) (b.hind: s.i.s: sme late hdwy)..........hd **10**
3375[11] Myttons Mistake **(80)***(68) (ABailey)* 2-8-4 (3) DWright(8) (bhd: hdwy over 2f out: wknd over 1f out)..........1½ **11**
2934[4] Willisa **(77)***(65) (JDBethell)* 2-8-1 (3) PMcCabe(9) (s.s: nt rcvr)..........s.h **12**
2779[5] Ned Al Sheeba **(88)***(74) (WJHaggas)* 2-9-1 KDarley(6) (in tch: rdn over 2f out: wknd wl over 1f out)..........¾ **13**
3335[3] Imp Express (IRE) **(78)***(42) (GMMoore)* 2-8-5 DeanMcKeown(10) (lost tch fr ½-wy)..........8 **14**
3394[2] Shontaine **(80)***(36) (MJohnston)* 2-8-7 DHolland(2) (in tch tl rdn & wknd over 2f out)..........3 **15**
3354[2] Red River Valley **(88)***(42) (DenysSmith)* 2-9-1 KFallon(1) (lw: a bhd)..........¾ **16**
*3244** Chilibang Bang **(66)***(10) (JBerry)* 2-7-2 (5) PFessey(3) (prom 3f: sn bhd)..........4 **17**

LONG HANDICAP Flood's Fancy 7-1 Duralock Fencer 7-4 Chilibang Bang 7-2

4/1 Too Hasty, **7/1** Ned Al Sheeba, **8/1** Branston Danni, Shontaine, **10/1** Red River Valley, **12/1** Atraf, Myttons Mistake, Amanita, **14/1** Chilibang Bang, Deadline Time (IRE) (10/1-16/1), KING OF PERU, Natural Key, **16/1** Willisa, Ramsey Hope, **20/1** Flood's Fancy, Imp Express (IRE), **25/1** Duralock Fencer, CSF £123.79 CT £1,300.12 TOTE £18.50: £4.40 £1.90 £3.80 £1.80 (£291.80) Trio £396.70 OWNER Mr L. Fust (ASTON UPTHORPE) BRED C. R. Black 17 Rn
1m 12.46 (2.66) SF: 38/30/29/34/22/44/32/22/14/14/24/21/30/-/-/-/-

3715

LADBROKE (AYR) SILVER CUP H'CAP (3-Y.O+) (Class B) £12,427.50 (£3,720.00: £1,785.00: £817.50)
6f Stalls: High GOING minus 0.15 sec per fur (GF) 3-05 (3-08)

3534* **Keston Pond (IRE) (66)***(77) (DAWilson)* 5-8-5 ow1 RCochrane(25) (a.p stands' side: hrd rdn to ld ins fnl f: r.o)..........— **1**
3492[14] Colway Rake **(69)***(78) (JWWatts)* 4-8-8b NConnorton(22) (lw: chsd ldrs stands' side: chal over 1f out: kpt on wl)..........1 **2**
3667[2] Stolen Kiss (IRE) **(70)***(79) (MWEasterby)* 3-7-13b(7) MartinDwyer(26) (lw: led stands' side tl ins fnl f: kpt on wl)..........hd **3**
3492[8] Cumbrian Waltzer **(73)***(80) (MHEasterby)* 10-8-7 (5) LNewton(23) (b.nr fore: hdwy stands' side over 1f out: r.o wl nr fin)..........¾ **4**
3492* Double Bounce **(73)***(79)*(Fav)*(PJMakin)* 5-8-12 3x DHolland(20) (hdwy stands' side over 1f out: nvr able to chal)..........nk **5**

3597[4] Captain Carat **(64)***(66) (MrsJRRamsden)* 4-8-3 JFEgan(18) (hdwy stands' side 2f out: nvr rchd ldrs) 1¾ **6**
3212[9] Selhurstpark Flyer (IRE) **(79)***(78) (JBerry)* 4-9-4e JCarroll(3) (eyeshield: racd far side: hdwy 2f out: styd on wl: nrst fin) 1 **7**
3703[8] Samah **(72)***(71) (DNicholls)* 5-8-11 5x AlexGreaves(12) (lw: racd far side: in tch: styd on wl fnl 2f: nrst fn) ....hd **8**
3492[7] Dawalib (USA) **(68)***(64) (DHaydnJones)* 5-8-7 SWhitworth(28) (lw: racd stands' side: styd on fnl 2f: nvr rchd ldrs) 1 **9**
3638[4] Here Comes Risky **(78)***(77) (MJohnston)* 3-9-0 TWilliams(27) (lw: racd stands' side: rdn ½-wy: styd on one pce: no imp) ....d.h **9**
3230[4] Statius **(77)***(73) (TDBarron)* 3-8-13 DeanMcKeown(11) (chsd ldrs far side: led far side 2f out: no ex fnl f) ....hd **11**
3359[19] Tiler (IRE) **(84)***(80) (MJohnston)* 3-9-6 MRoberts(29) (chsd ldrs stands' side tl wknd over 1f out) ....hd **12**
3597[5] Broadstairs Beauty (IRE) **(76)***(70) (SRBowring)* 5-8-10b(5) CTeague(8) (b: b.hind: led & clr far side tl wknd 2f out) ....½ **13**
3411[6] Tedburrow **(85)***(77) (MrsAMNaughton)* 3-9-7 StephenDavies(16) (racd stands' side: hdwy u.p ½-wy: wknd appr fnl f) ....¾ **14**
2848[7] Q Factor **(71)***(63) (DHaydnJones)* 3-8-7 AMackay(19) (racd stands' side: prom: hrd rdn ½-wy: grad wknd) ....s.h **15**
2410[3] Macfarlane **(69)***(59) (MJFetherston-Godley)* 7-8-5 (3) SSanders(13) (b: racd far side: outpcd fr ½-wy) ....¾ **16**
3359[3] My Best Valentine **(82)***(71) (JWhite)* 5-9-4 (3) SDrowne(2) (racd far side: n.d) ....nk **17**
3376[3] Ansellman **(74)***(62) (JBerry)* 5-8-8 (5) PFessey(7) (chsd ldrs far side 4f) ....½ **18**
1441[9] Garnock Valley **(70)***(57) (JBerry)* 5-8-9 NCarlisle(14) (racd stands' side: n.d) ....½ **19**
3615[8] Rich Glow **(64)***(48) (NBycroft)* 4-8-0 (3) PMcCabe(4) (racd far side: n.d) 1 **20**
3677[5] Wardara **(73)***(55) (MissGayKelleway)* 3-8-9b MBirch(21) (racd stands' side: n.d) ....¾ **21**
3279[8] Barato **(71)***(52) (MrsJRRamsden)* 4-8-10 KFallon(1) (b.nr hind: racd far side: n.d) ....nk **22**
3667[22] Just Dissident (IRE) **(68)***(48) (RMWhitaker)* 3-8-4 DaleGibson(6) (lw: prom far side 4f) ....nk **23**
3166[8] Karina Heights (USA) **(77)***(56) (JWWatts)* 3-8-13 TIves(15) (racd stands' side: bhd fr ½-wy) ..½ **24**
823[10] Best of All (IRE) **(72)***(51) (JBerry)* 3-8-8 AMcGlone(24) (racd stands' side: n.d) ....hd **25**
3565[3] Flashy's Son **(69)***(46) (GMMoore)* 7-8-8 JTate(10) (b: b.hind: gd spd far side 4f) ....¾ **26**
3597[8] Bold Street (IRE) **(71)***(47) (ABailey)* 5-8-7b(3) DWright(9) (racd far side: n.d) ....hd **27**
2324[2] Actual Fact (USA) **(85)***(45) (GHarwood)* 3-9-7 KDarley(5) (racd far side: bhd fr ½-wy) 6 **28**

4/1 Double Bounce, **10/1** KESTON POND (IRE), **11/1** Captain Carat, **14/1** Actual Fact (USA), My Best Valentine, Stolen Kiss (IRE), Tiler (IRE), **20/1** Statius, Samah, Barato, Wardara, Dawalib (USA), Rich Glow, **25/1** Colway Rake, Ansellman, Flashy's Son, Cumbrian Waltzer, Broadstairs Beauty (IRE), Bold Street (IRE), **33/1** Macfarlane, Here Comes Risky, Tedburrow, Selhurstpark Flyer (IRE), Karina Heights (USA), **50/1** Q Factor, **66/1** Just Dissident (IRE), Garnock Valley, Best of All (IRE), CSF £219.94 CT £3,185.39 TOTE £10.60: £2.60 £11.10 £3.50 £5.50 (£204.40) Trio £579.10 OWNER Mr T. S. M. S. Riley-Smith (EPSOM) BRED John Harrington in Ireland 28 Rn

1m 11.85 (2.05)

SF:46/47/45/49/48/35/47/40/33/43/39/46/39/43/29/28/40/31/26/17/21/21/14/22/17/15/16/11

WEIGHT FOR AGE 3yo-3lb

3716 STAKIS CASINOS DOONSIDE CUP STKS (Listed) (3-Y.O+) (Class A)

£11,826.00 (£4,374.00: £2,097.00: £855.00: £337.50: £130.50)
1m 2f 192y Stalls: Low GOING minus 0.15 sec per fur (GF) 3-35 (3-36)

3143[3] **Annus Mirabilis (FR) (119)***(95++)*(Fav)*(MRStoute)* 3-8-4 DHolland(4) (a gng wl: led on bit 2f out: shkn up appr fnl f: qcknd: easily) ....— **1**
3381[2] Captain Horatius (IRE) **(113)***(92+) (JLDunlop)* 6-9-1 KDarley(5) (hld up: hdwy 3f out: ev ch 2f out: nt pce of wnr fnl f) 5 **2**
3381[4] Salt Lake **(105)***(80) (PWChapple-Hyam)* 4-8-11 JCarroll(7) (led 1f: cl up: led over 2f out: sn hdd & one pce) 5 **3**
3700[9] No Comebacks **(60)***(75) (EJAlston)* 7-8-6 KFallon(1) (hld up: hdwy 3f out: styd on: no imp)...hd **4**
2616[11] Done Well (USA) **(93)***(65) (PMonteith)* 3-8-4 MRoberts(3) (led after 1f tl over 2f out: sn outpcd) 10 **5**
3549[5] Najmat Alshemaal (IRE) **(97)***(44) (MajorWRHern)* 3-7-13 AMcGlone(6) (chsd ldrs tl rdn & wknd 3f out) 11 **6**
3392[6] Caribbean Surfer (USA) *(48) (JSGoldie)* 6-8-11 JStack(2) (b: swtg: a bhd) 1 **7**

8/11 ANNUS MIRABILIS (FR), **7/2** Captain Horatius (IRE), **9/2** Salt Lake, **9/1** Najmat Alshemaal (IRE), **50/1** Done Well (USA), **100/1** No Comebacks, **250/1** Caribbean Surfer (USA), CSF £3.57 TOTE £1.70: £1.30 £1.80 (£1.90) OWNER Sheikh Mohammed (NEWMARKET) BRED Darley Stud Management Co Ltd 7 Rn 2m 17.04 (0.84) SF: 71/75/63/58/41/20/31

WEIGHT FOR AGE 3yo-7lb

3717 LADBROKE (AYR) GOLD CUP H'CAP (3-Y.O+) (Class B) £51,792.50 (£15,590.00: £7,545.00: £3,522.50) **6f** Stalls: High GOING minus 0.15 sec (GF) 4-15 (4-17)

3342² **Royale Figurine (IRE) (95)***(109) (MJFetherston-Godley)* 4-8-9 DHolland(27) (lw: chsd ldrs stands' side: led ins fnl f: r.o wl)........— 1
3615⁴ No Extras (IRE) **(96)***(109) (GLMoore)* 5-8-10 7x SWhitworth(20) (racd stands' side: hdwy 2f out: r.o wl fnl f)........nk 2
2001* Patto (USA) **(95)***(108) (WJHaggas)* 4-8-9 RCochrane(28) (chsd ldrs stands' side: kpt on wl fnl f)........hd 3
3551⁵ Master of Passion **(86)***(96) (JMPEustace)* 6-8-0 NKennedy(26) (led stands' side ½-wy tl ins fnl f: no ex)........1¼ 4
3551³ Cool Jazz **(102)***(108) (CEBrittain)* 4-9-2 MBirch(1) (lw: racd far side: chsd ldrs: led over 1f out: hrd rdn & nt qckn)........1¼ 5
3551⁸ Hard to Figure **(110)***(111) (RJHodges)* 9-9-7 (3) SDrowne(29) (lw: racd stands' side: hdwy 2f out: r.o)........2 6
3145⁴ Benzoe (IRE) **(83)***(84) (MrsJRRamsden)* 5-7-11 JFEgan(23) (lw: racd stands' side: chsd ldrs: rdn ½-wy: no imp)........hd 7
3551² Bold Effort (FR) **(97)***(97) (KOCunningham-Brown)* 3-8-8 TIves(17) (racd stands' side: s.i.s: nrst fin)........hd 8
3551⁷ Venture Capitalist **(105)***(100) (DNicholls)* 6-9-5b AlexGreaves(2) (lw: plld hrd: led far side ½-wy tl over 1f out: wknd)........2 9
3564* Branston Abby (IRE) **(112)***(106)*(Fav)*(MJohnston)* 6-9-12 7x MRoberts(18) (racd stands' side: bhd & drvn along: nrst fin)........nk 10
2764¹⁴ Astrac (IRE) **(94)***(88) (RAkehurst)* 4-8-5 (3) SSanders(7) (swtchd stands' side after s: rdn ½-wy: no imp)........nk 11
3342¹⁰ Fire Dome (IRE) **(101)***(93) (RHannon)* 3-8-12 KDarley(25) (led stands' side to ½-wy: wknd over 1f out)........¾ 12
3230⁶ Perryston View **(89)***(79) (PCalver)* 3-8-0v DaleGibson(11) (racd stands' side: in tch tl rdn & btn over 2f out)........¾ 13
3230³ Top Banana **(89)***(78) (HCandy)* 4-8-3 WNewnes(13) (lw: racd stands' side: rdn ½-wy: no imp)........nk 14
3551¹⁵ Amron **(84)***(72) (JBerry)* 8-7-12 NCarlisle(6) (racd stands' side: hdwy ½-wy: no imp)........hd 15
3342⁷ Paris Babe **(95)***(81) (DMorris)* 3-8-6 DeanMcKeown(14) (racd stands' side: rdn & one pce fr ½-wy)........¾ 16
3551¹⁰ Name the Tune **(91)***(73) (PHowling)* 4-8-5 AMackay(19) (b.hind: lw: racd stands' side: n.d) .1½ 17
3359⁸ Mister Jolson **(85)***(65) (RJHodges)* 6-7-8 (5)ow2 PPMurphy(8) (racd far side: a bhd)........hd 18
3557⁵ Palacegate Touch **(85)***(66) (JBerry)* 5-7-8b(5) PFessey(21) (gd spd stands' side over 4f)........½ 19
3279⁵ Sir Joey (USA) **(86)***(65) (PGMurphy)* 6-7-11 (3) DWright(10) (lw: racd stands' side: n.d)........¾ 20
3565⁷ French Grit (IRE) **(88)***(67) (MDods)* 3-7-13 AMcGlone(24) (lw: racd stands' side: outpcd fr ½-wy)........hd 21
3551¹⁹ Sailormaite **(84)***(59) (SRBowring)* 4-7-12 StephenDavies(12) (lw: uns rdr & bolted bef s: racd stands' side: nvr trbld ldrs)........1¼ 22
3551¹¹ Lord Olivier (IRE) **(92)***(65) (WJarvis)* 5-8-3 (3) JStack(22) (lw: racd stands' side: spd over 4f) ..¾ 23
803a⁶ Sir Silver Sox (USA) **(108)***(79) (TStack,Ireland)* 3-9-5v KFallon(15) (racd stands' side: rdn & bhd fr ½-wy)........1 24
3476a³ Alzianah **(100)***(68) (JDBethell)* 4-8-11 (3) PMcCabe(4) (lw: chsd ldrs far side to ½-wy)........1 25
3411⁹ Ashgore **(84)***(44) (MJohnston)* 5-7-9 (3) DarrenMoffatt(9) (racd stands' side: t.o ½-wy)........3 26
3145⁸ Loveyoumillions (IRE) **(91)***(32) (MJohnston)* 3-8-2b TWilliams(3) (led far side to ½-wy: wknd)..7 27
2764¹⁸ Daring Destiny **(100)***(38) (KRBurke)* 4-9-0b JTate(5) (racd far side: outpcd & bhd fr ½-wy)....1¼ 28
3358⁷ Shikari's Son **(96)** *(JWhite)* 8-8-10 JCarroll(16) (dwlt: hdwy whn hmpd & fell wl over 1f out)...... F

7/1 Branston Abby (IRE), **15/2** Patto (USA), **8/1** ROYALE FIGURINE (IRE), **12/1** Top Banana, Benzoe (IRE), **14/1** Astrac (IRE), **16/1** No Extras (IRE), Hard to Figure, **20/1** Alzianah, Venture Capitalist, **25/1** Cool Jazz, Sailormaite, Daring Destiny, Bold Effort (FR), Master of Passion, Lord Olivier (IRE), **33/1** Sir Silver Sox (USA), French Grit (IRE), Perryston View, **40/1** Loveyoumillions (IRE), Shikari's Son, Name the Tune, **50/1** Sir Joey (USA), Paris Babe, Palacegate Touch, Amron, Fire Dome (IRE), Mister Jolson, **66/1** Ashgore, CSF £116.57 CT £927.63 TOTE £7.20: £1.70 £4.30 £2.20 £5.00 (£57.30) Trio £132.20 OWNER Mr Craig Pearman (EAST ILSLEY) BRED Craig Pearman
29Rn 1m11.11 (1.31)
SF:62/62/61/49/61/64/37/47/53/59/41/43/29/31/25/31/26/18/19/18/17/12/18/29/21
WEIGHT FOR AGE 3yo-3lb

3718 JOHNNIE WALKER WHISKY H'CAP (0-90) (3-Y.O+) (Class C) £6,784.00 (£2,032.00: £976.00: £448.00) **1m 5f 13y** Stalls: Low GOING minus 0.15 sec per fur (GF) 4-45 (4-47)

3547⁵ **Torch Vert (IRE) (73)***(89) (BWHills)* 3-9-0 DHolland(5) (lw: mde all: rdn & r.o wl fnl 2f)........— 1

3505* Kalou **(65)***(79) (CWCElsey)* 4-8-10 (5) PFessey(10) (a.p: chsd wnr fnl 3f: nvr able chal)............2 **2**
879* Embryonic (IRE) **(75)***(88)*(Fav)*(RFFisher)* 3-9-2 KFallon(1) (lw: bhd: pushed along 7f out: hdwy 3f out: hrd rdn & no ex fnl f)..........¾ **3**
2478⁴ Flash of Realm (FR) **(55)***(67) (PMonteith)* 9-8-2 (3) DWright(2) (chsd ldrs: rdn 3f out: kpt on same pce)..........½ **4**
3130* Woodcrest **(78)***(83) (HCandy)* 3-9-5 WNewnes(6) (chsd ldrs: rdn 3f out: one pce)..........6 **5**
3459⁶ Ahla **(83)***(88) (RWArmstrong)* 3-9-10 KDarley(3) (lw: chsd ldrs: one pce fnl 3f)..........s.h **6**
2445⁵ Pembridge Place **(70)***(70) (JLDunlop)* 4-9-6b TIves(4) (hld up & bhd: c wd st: nvr trbld ldrs)..........4 **7**
3406⁵ Latvian **(72)***(67) (RAllan)* 8-9-8 RCochrane(8) (hld up: effrt ent st: sn rdn & btn)..........4 **8**
2550⁴ Tonnerre **(76)***(64) (CWFairhurst)* 3-9-3 DeanMcKeown(11) (prom tl wknd over 3f out)..........6 **9**
3351⁴ Eelious (USA) **(80)***(67) (CEBrittain)* 3-9-7 MRoberts(7) (lw: in tch: effrt ent st: sn btn)..........nk **10**
3665⁶ Manful **(64)***(50) (JHetherton)* 3-8-5v NKennedy(9) (outpcd appr st: sn no ch)..........1¼ **11**
3162⁹ Askern **(70)***(37) (DHaydnJones)* 4-9-6 AMackay(13) (lw: hld up & bhd: gd hdwy on outside appr st: wknd 3f out)..........15 **12**

3/1 Embryonic (IRE), **11/2** TORCH VERT (IRE), Woodcrest, Pembridge Place, **8/1** Kalou, **10/1** Ahla, **11/1** Askern (8/1-12/1), **12/1** Eelious (USA), **14/1** Latvian, **16/1** Manful, **20/1** Tonnerre, **66/1** Flash of Realm (FR), CSF £47.65 CT £146.01 TOTE £6.10: £1.80 £2.50 £1.80 (£23.20) Trio £30.20 OWNER Mr J. Hanson (LAMBOURN) BRED Pegasus Securities Leasing (Pty) Ltd 12 Rn

2m 49.04 (4.24) SF: 60/59/59/47/54/59/50/47/35/38/21/17

WEIGHT FOR AGE 3yo-9lb

3719 SPH PROPERTY SEARCH H'CAP (0-80) (3-Y.O+) (Class D) £5,244.00 (£1,572.00: £756.00: £348.00)

7f Stalls: Low GOING minus 0.15 sec per fur (GF) 5-15 (5-26)

3529² **Mary's Case (IRE) (53)***(63) (MJohnston)* 5-8-1b MRoberts(14) (bhd: hdwy 3f out: hrd rdn & r.o fnl f to ld nr fin)..........— **1**
2428⁴ Sagebrush Roller **(80)***(90) (JWWatts)* 7-10-0 NConnorton(2) (lw: hdwy on ins 3f out: led appr fnl f: jst ct)..........s.h **2**
3492³ Rossini Blue **(69)***(78) (MrsJRRamsden)* 4-9-3 KFallon(12) (bhd tl hdwy over 1f out: styd on u.p)..........nk **3**
3172⁵ Miss Pigalle **(48)***(45) (MissLAPerratt)* 4-7-3b(7)ow3 MartinDwyer(3) (lw: chsd ldrs tl rdn & btn appr fnl f)..........4 **4**
3072¹² My Gallery (IRE) **(50)***(47) (ABailey)* 4-7-9 (3) DWright(16) (sme hdwy u.p 2f out: nvr rchd ldrs)..........1½ **5**
3467⁹ Panther (IRE) **(55)***(52) (JHetherton)* 5-8-3 NKennedy(7) (chsd ldrs: rdn 3f out: one pce)..........s.h **6**
3169⁶ Keep Battling **(48)***(41) (JSGoldie)* 5-7-7 (3)ow3 DarrenMoffatt(1) (chsd ldrs: rdn over 2f out: wknd fnl f)..........nk **7**
3370⁸ Teejay'n'aitch (IRE) **(49)***(45) (JSGoldie)* 3-7-7 NCarlisle(8) (bhd: styd on u.p fnl 3f: n.d)..........hd **8**
3447* Chairmans Choice **(55)***(48)*(Fav)*(APJarvis)* 5-8-3 JTate(4) (lw: led: rdn & hdd appr fnl f: no ex)..........1¼ **9**
1193⁷ Stephensons Rocket **(74)***(65) (JBerry)* 4-9-8 JFEgan(17) (hrd rdn 3f out: grad wknd)..........¾ **10**
2928⁶ Celebration Cake (IRE) **(60)***(49) (MissLAPerratt)* 3-8-4v MBirch(6) (prom: rdn ent st: wknd over 2f out)..........1 **11**
3310⁶ Mister Westsound **(61)***(45) (MissLAPerratt)* 3-8-2b(3) JStack(13) (s.i.s: c wd st: sn no ch)..........2 **12**
3344* Indian Rhapsody **(52)***(28) (ABailey)* 3-7-5 (5) PFessey(11) (mid div: bhd fr 3f out)..........3½ **13**
3112⁷ Don Pepe **(69)***(45) (RBoss)* 4-9-3 DHolland(5) (lw: hld up: rdn over 2f out: eased whn btn fnl f)..........hd **14**
3488⁸ Persian Affair (IRE) **(62)***(24) (DHaydnJones)* 4-8-10 AMackay(9) (lw: c wd st: sn no h)..........6 **15**
3565¹⁰ Allinson's Mate (IRE) **(76)** *(TDBarron)* 7-9-10b KDarley(15) (Withdrawn not under Starter's orders: Veterinary advice).......... **W**

LONG HANDICAP Miss Pigalle 6-11 Teejay'n'aitch (IRE) 7-3 Keep Battling 7-2

5/2 Chairmans Choice, **5/1** Rossini Blue, **8/1** Sagebrush Roller, Don Pepe, Indian Rhapsody, **10/1** Persian Affair (IRE), Allinson's Mate (IRE), **12/1** MARY'S CASE (IRE), **14/1** Mister Westsound, **16/1** Celebration Cake (IRE), My Gallery (IRE), **20/1** Keep Battling, **25/1** Panther (IRE), **33/1** Teejay'n'aitch (IRE), Stephensons Rocket, **50/1** Miss Pigalle, CSF £101.87 CT £507.20 TOTE £7.50: £2.00 £2.90 £1.70 (£41.90) Trio £64.40 OWNER Mr M. Doyle (MIDDLEHAM) BRED Paul Callan 15 Rn 1m 26.35 (2.35) SF: 45/72/60/27/29/34/23/23/30/47/27/23/6/27/6/-

WEIGHT FOR AGE 3yo-4lb

T/Jkpt: Not won; £40,058.58 to Leicester 18/9/95. T/Plpt: £390.40 (96.29 Tckts). T/Qdpt: £26.20 (6.05 Tckts). AA

3047-**CATTERICK (L-H)**
Saturday September 16th (Good, Good to firm patches)
WEATHER: fine WIND: fresh half against

3720 E.B.F. MAIDEN STKS (2-Y.O) (Class D) £3,850.00 (£1,150.00: £550.00: £250.00)
5f 212y Stalls: Low GOING minus 0.30 sec per fur (GF) 2-20 (2-20)

3558[2] **The Man (89)***(77+)*(Fav)*(MRChannon)* 2-9-0 TSprake(10) (lw: trckd ldrs: styd on to ld jst ins fnl f: pushed out)......— **1**
3032[4] Red Nose (IRE) **(76)***(74) (MHTompkins)* 2-9-0v GCarter(7) (led: rdn & hung lft over 1f out: hdd jst ins fnl f: nt qckn)......1 **2**
2710[5] Muhandam (IRE) *(74) (MRStoute)* 2-9-0 FNorton(8) (lw: trckd ldrs: chal & hung lft over 1f out: kpt on same pce)......nk **3**
3432[10] Simply Silly (IRE) **(55)***(59) (WLBarker)* 2-8-9 LCharnock(6) (swtg: chsd ldrs: grad wknd fnl 2f)......3½ **4**
2633[6] Rhythmic Ball *(59) (TRWatson)* 2-8-9 KBradshaw(9) (chsd ldrs tl lost pl over 2f out)......hd **5**
3495[10] Fiddes (IRE) *(54) (JLDunlop)* 2-8-9 GDuffield(1) (s.i.s: bhd & drvn along: sme hdwy 2f out: n.d)......2 **6**
3604[13] Dazzling Star *(53) (RHannon)* 2-8-9 JLowe(2) (s.i.s: sn in tch: outpcd fr ½-wy)......nk **7**
3149[4] Two Timer *(48) (MJohnston)* 2-8-9 (5) RHavlin(3) (in tch: sn drvn along: outpcd fnl 2f)......3½ **8**
Needwood Limelight *(43) (BAMcMahon)* 2-9-0 SDWilliams(5) (unf: a outpcd & bhd)......2 **9**
1031[8] Margi Boo **(40)***(17) (GMMoore)* 2-8-9 JFanning(4) (swtg: sn drvn along: nvr wnt pce)......8 **10**

4/5 THE MAN (5/4-4/7), **3/1** Red Nose (IRE) (tchd 9/2), **17/2** Muhandam (IRE) (5/1-9/1), **9/1** Dazzling Star (7/1-12/1), Fiddes (IRE) (op 9/2), **12/1** Two Timer (op 8/1), **25/1** Needwood Limelight, **33/1** Rhythmic Ball, Simply Silly (IRE), Margi Boo, CSF £4.41 TOTE £1.40: £1.10 £1.60 £2.30 (£2.20) Trio £6.30 OWNER Mrs A. V. Ferguson (UPPER LAMBOURN) BRED Mrs A. Ferguson 10 Rn 1m 13.3 (2.80) SF: 33/30/30/15/15/10/9/4/-/-

3721 'GO RACING IN YORKSHIRE' ESPECIALLY AT CATTERICK NURSERY H'CAP (0-75) (2-Y.O) (Class E) £3,886.00 (£1,168.00: £564.00: £262.00)
7f Stalls: High GOING minus 0.30 sec per fur (GF) 2-50 (2-51)

3546[10] **Stately (53)***(55)*(Fav)*(SirMarkPrescott)* 2-8-4 GDuffield(9) (b.hind: sn drvn along & chsng ldrs: styd on wl to ld wl ins fnl f: hld on nr fin)......— **1**
3471[6] Emperegrine (USA) **(70)***(71) (CFWall)* 2-9-7v JLowe(14) (in tch: hrd rdn & styd on over 1f out: edgd lft & nt qckn nr fin)......nk **2**
3533[10] Ned's Contessa (IRE) **(50)***(47) (MDods)* 2-8-1 VHalliday(13) (hdwy & n.m.r 2f out: kpt on)...1¾ **3**
*3528** Harsh Times **(55)***(51) (MHEasterby)* 2-8-6 SMaloney(1) (led tl wl ins fnl f: hmpd nr fin)......¾ **4**
2904[4] Jimjareer (IRE) **(68)***(60) (CaptJWilson)* 2-9-5 SDWilliams(6) (a chsng ldrs: kpt on same pce fnl 2f)......1½ **5**
2958[5] Pendley Rose **(64)***(49) (PWHarris)* 2-9-1 FNorton(10) (b.off hind: bhd: gd hdwy on outside 2f out: nrst fin)......3 **6**
3353* Ginger Glint **(63)***(45) (MJHeaton-Ellis)* 2-9-0 TSprake(12) (mid div: effrt 2f out: sn chsng ldrs: wandered & wknd over 1f out)......1½ **7**
3570* Spirito Libro (USA) **(66)***(45) (CNAllen)* 2-8-12 (5) MBaird(17) (hdwy 2f out: styd on fnl f: n.d)..1½ **8**
3243[6] La Haye Sainte **(52)***(30) (DJSCosgrove)* 2-8-3 RLappin(8) (sme hdwy 2f out: n.d)......nk **9**
3168[4] Silverdale Knight **(70)***(48) (KWHogg)* 2-9-0 (7) ADaly(15) (in tch: effrt 2f out: nvr rchd ldrs)......hd **10**
3353[2] Euro Express **(62)***(33) (MHEasterby)* 2-8-13b JFanning(7) (sn drvn along: sme hdwy on ins over 2f out: sn wknd)......3 **11**
3405[4] It's A Ripper **(60)***(28) (GLewis)* 2-8-6 (5) AWhelan(4) (hld up & a bhd)......1¼ **12**
3642[4] Concert Party (IRE) **(50)***(16) (DWChapman)* 2-7-8 (7) JoHunnam(16) (a bhd)......1 **13**
3309[6] China Castle **(60)***(25) (PCHaslam)* 2-8-11 GCarter(5) (s.i.s: a bhd)......hd **14**
2991[7] Briganoone **(50)***(13) (SRBowring)* 2-7-8b(7) CAdamson(20) (chsd ldrs tl wknd over 2f out)......1 **15**
3623[13] Thorntoun Jewel (IRE) **(56)***(18) (JBalding)* 2-8-7 ClaireBalding(3) (swtg: unruly s: s.s: a wl bhd)......nk **16**
3502[7] Northern Falcon **(57)***(16) (MWEasterby)* 2-8-8 LCharnock(2) (s.i.s: a bhd)......1½ **17**
2371[7] Ginger Hodgers **(58)***(17) (RMWhitaker)* 2-8-9 ACulhane(11) (sn drvn along: chsd ldrs to ½-wy: sn lost pl)......hd **18**
3502[15] Good To Talk **(58)***(17) (MHEasterby)* 2-8-6 (3) NVarley(19) (w ldrs tl wknd over 2f out)......hd **19**

9/2 STATELY (op 8/1), **5/1** It's A Ripper (op 8/1), **6/1** Pendley Rose, **9/1** Euro Express, **10/1** Harsh Times, Spirito Libro (USA), Ginger Glint, Emperegrine (USA), **12/1** Ned's Contessa (IRE), China Castle, Northern Falcon, **14/1** Jimjareer (IRE), **16/1** Silverdale Knight, Briganoone, La Haye Sainte, **20/1** Concert Party (IRE), Thorntoun Jewel (IRE), **25/1** Ginger Hodgers, **33/1** Good To Talk, CSF £58.09 CT £517.74 TOTE £6.80: £2.20 £2.60 £4.00 £2.70 (£34.50) Trio £189.80 OWNER Cheveley Park Stud (NEWMARKET) BRED Cheveley Park Stud Ltd 19 Rn
1m 26.9 (3.70) SF: 20/36/12/16/25/14/10/10/-/13/-/-/-/-/-/-/-/-/-

3722 JACK RANDALL 18TH BIRTHDAY (S) STKS (3-Y.O) (Class G) £2,770.00 (£770.00: £370.00) **1m 5f 175y** Stalls: High GOING minus 0.30 sec (GF) 3-20 (3-20)

2953[5] **Durgams First (IRE) (58)**_(63)_(Fav)_(MrsMReveley)_ 3-8-9 (5) GParkin(4) (hld up gng wl: nt clr run on ins wl over 2f out: swtchd rt over 1f out: qcknd to ld jst ins fnl f: readily)...........— 1
3184[6] Try Omnipotent **(36)**_(56) (CNAllen)_ 3-8-5 (5) MBaird(8) (b: chsd ldrs: kpt on same pce appr fnl f)........2½ 2
3422[10] Skedaddle **(53)**_(50) (JGFitzGerald)_ 3-8-5 ACulhane(3) (sn drvn along: chsd ldrs: sltly hmpd over 2f out: kpt on one pce ins fnl f)........1 3
3265[2] Royal Rabbit **(44)**_(58) (GLMoore)_ 3-8-7 (7) ALakeman(6) (chsd ldrs: led 5f out to 3f out: kpt on one pce)........½ 4
3410* Trumble **(49)**_(58) (CWThornton)_ 3-9-0 SMaloney(10) (swtg: led to 5f out: led 3f out tl jst ins fnl f: one pce)........hd 5
3464[4] Never Time (IRE) **(39)**_(53) (MrsVAAconley)_ 3-8-10 MDeering(12) (hld up: effrt over 3f out: hung lft: n.d)........1½ 6
3303[6] Fools of Pride (IRE) **(36)**_(49) (RHollinshead)_ 3-8-2 (7) AEddery(2) (swtg: hdwy 7f out: effrt & outpcd over 3f out: n.d after)........2 7
3421[5] Victor Laszlo _(48) (JDBethell)_ 3-8-10 GCarter(9) (bhd: drvn 5f out: sme hdwy 2f out: n.d)....1¾ 8
3302[6] Milltown Classic (IRE) **(32)**_(39) (JParkes)_ 3-8-5 LCharnock(7) (in tch tl wknd over 2f out).....3½ 9
3504[8] Ruby Rock **(36)**_(16) (BWMurray)_ 3-8-0 (5) AWhelan(5) (chsd ldrs: rn wd bnd 8f out: t.o 4f out)20 10
Newgate Hush _(BWMurray)_ 3-8-5 JFanning(11) (bit bkwd: s.i.s: bhd & drvn along whn hmpd bnd 8f out: t.o 4f out)........25 11

5/4 DURGAMS FIRST (IRE), **7/2** Skedaddle, **5/1** Trumble, **8/1** Royal Rabbit, **10/1** Fools of Pride (IRE), **12/1** Never Time (IRE), Victor Laszlo, **16/1** Try Omnipotent, **25/1** Milltown Classic (IRE), Ruby Rock, Newgate Hush, CSF £24.70 TOTE £2.20: £1.20 £6.50 £1.40 (£24.10) Trio £21.30 OWNER The Mary Reveley Racing Club (SALTBURN) BRED William McGladdery in Ireland 11 Rn

3m 2.1 (6.90) SF: 35/28/22/30/30/25/21/20/11/-/-
Bt in 7,000 gns

3723 CONSTANT SECURITY SERVICES H'CAP (0-85) (3-Y.O+) (Class D) £4,110.00 (£1,230.00: £590.00: £270.00) **1m 3f 214y** Stalls: High GOING minus 0.30 sec per fur (GF) 3-50 (3-50)

3500[8] **Loki (IRE) (77)**_(88) (GLewis)_ 7-9-5 (5) AWhelan(7) (b: hld up: hdwy over 2f out: edgd lft jst ins fnl f: styd on wl to ld nr fin)........— 1
3657* Kandyan **(66)**_(76)_(Fav)_(MHTompkins)_ 4-8-13 GCarter(10) (chsd ldrs: led 2f out tl nr fin).........½ 2
3505[8] Hasta la Vista **(48)**_(54) (MWEasterby)_ 5-7-9bow1 LCharnock(11) (b.nr hind: led to 2f out: one pce whn hmpd jst ins fnl f)........2½ 3
3021[9] Sherqy (IRE) **(83)**_(87) (JLDunlop)_ 3-9-8 TSprake(2) (hld up: effrt 2f out: hung lft: styd on u.p: nvr nr to chal)........2 4
3470[8] Admirals Secret (USA) **(65)**_(69) (CFWall)_ 6-8-9 (3) NVarley(9) (in tch: drvn along & outpcd 4f out: kpt on fnl 2f)........hd 5
3421* Iridal **(81)**_(81) (HRACecil)_ 3-9-6 JLowe(6) (lw: trckd ldrs: drvn along 4f out: wknd over 1f out: eased nr fin)........3 6
3505[4] Jadwal (USA) **(77)**_(76) (DMorley)_ 3-9-2 GDuffield(5) (rr div: drvn along 4f out: kpt on fnl 2f: n.d)........1¼ 7
1552[2] Sunday News'n'echo (USA) **(56)**_(47) (WStorey)_ 4-8-3 JFanning(4) (plld hrd: trckd ldrs tl wknd 2f out)........6 8
1022[9] Slmaat **(69)**_(59) (MrsMReveley)_ 4-9-2 ACulhane(3) (hld up & bhd: sme late hdwy: n.d)..........¾ 9
_1880_[6] Prince Equiname **(64)**_(51) (DEddy)_ 3-8-3 SMaloney(1) (plld hrd: trckd ldrs tl lost pl 4f out).......2 10

13/8 Kandyan, **5/2** Iridal (op 9/2), **7/1** Admirals Secret (USA), **15/2** Jadwal (USA), **9/1** LOKI (IRE), **10/1** Sherqy (IRE), **11/1** Hasta la Vista, **12/1** Sunday News'n'echo (USA), **14/1** Slmaat, **20/1** Prince Equiname, CSF £26.90 CT £170.78 TOTE £14.30: £3.90 £1.50 £3.00 (£46.00) Trio £144.90 OWNER Mr Michael Watt (EPSOM) BRED Abbey Lodge Stud 10 Rn

2m 34.8 (3.80) SF: 62/50/28/53/43/47/42/21/33/17
WEIGHT FOR AGE 3yo-8lb
STEWARDS' ENQUIRY Whelan susp. 25-27/9/95 (careless riding).

3724 SKYRAM H'CAP (0-65) (3-Y.O+) (Class F) £3,353.00 (£933.00: £449.00) **1m 7f 177y** Stalls: High GOING minus 0.30 sec per fur (GF) 4-25 (4-28)

_3513_[3] **Greek Night Out (IRE) (30)**_(46) (JLEyre)_ 4-7-12 (3) NVarley(17) (in tch: drvn along 8f out: styd on fnl 2f: led jst ins fnl f: rdn out)........— 1
3303[3] Can She Can Can **(42)**_(56) (MJohnston)_ 3-8-1 FNorton(12) (a chsng ldrs: drvn along 6f out: nt qckn fnl f)........2½ 2

3435[6] Bobby's Dream **(43)***(56) (MHTompkins)* 3-8-2 GCarter(4) (a chsng ldrs: drvn along 4f out: kpt on same pce appr fnl f)....s.h **3**
3627[4] Kilernan **(42)***(54) (TDBarron)* 4-8-13 LCharnock(11) (swtg: led tl jst ins fnl f: one pce)....1¼ **4**
295[7] Moonshine Dancer **(40)***(52) (MrsMReveley)* 5-8-4 (7) DDenby(7) (bhd: hdwy 5f out: styd on fnl 2f: nvr nr ldrs)....nk **5**
3318[3] Deceit the Second **(44)***(55) (GLewis)* 3-7-12b(5)ow1 AWhelan(2) (b: hdwy 6f out: kpt on fnl 2f: nvr nr to chal)....hd **6**
3527[2] Ijab (CAN) **(26)***(36) (JParkes)* 5-7-11b JMarshall(16) (lw: bhd: hdwy on outside over 2f out: hung lft u.p: nvr nr ldrs)....2 **7**
3435[7] Izza **(33)***(43) (WStorey)* 4-8-4 JFanning(18) (s.s: bhd: stdy hdwy 5f out: no imp fnl 2f)....hd **8**
3229[6] Kinoko **(41)***(47) (KWHogg)* 7-8-5 (7) ADaly(9) (in tch: drvn along 5f out: no imp fnl 3f)....4 **9**
1840[9] Uncle Doug **(53)***(58)*(Fav)*(MrsMReveley)* 4-9-10 GDuffield(8) (lw: hld up: hdwy 8f out: drvn along over 4f out: no imp)....nk **10**
2495[6] Jarrow **(34)***(39) (MrsAMNaughton)* 4-8-5 JLowe(13) (hld up & plld hrd: drvn along 7f out: n.d)¾ **11**
3092[2] Leap in the Dark (IRE) **(30)***(32) (MissLCSiddall)* 6-8-1 ow2 RLappin(20) (effrt 5f out: wknd 2f out)....nk **12**
598[5] Zamhareer (USA) **(50)***(50) (WStorey)* 4-9-4 (3)ow2 OPears(3) (b: a in rr)....2 **13**
3311[4] Milngavie (IRE) **(28)***(29) (MJohnston)* 5-7-6 (7) BHalligan(19) (chsd ldrs: drvn along 6f out: lost pl 3f out)....1 **14**
3435[12] King of the Horse (IRE) **(28)***(18) (WStorey)* 4-7-6 (7)ow1 CAdamson(6) (a bhd)....10 **15**
2922[7] Persistent (IRE) **(53)***(37) (MHEasterby)* 3-8-12 SMaloney(1) (a bhd)....7 **16**
3292[2] Bushehr (IRE) **(65)***(34) (SCoathup)* 3-9-5 (5) RHavlin(10) (b: prom: drvn along 6f out: wknd over 3f out)....15 **17**
2495[11] Lone Risk **(46)***(14) (CNAllen)* 4-8-12 (5) MBaird(14) (t.o fnl 4f)....¾ **18**
3410[5] Doctor's Remedy **(30)** *(MrsJJordan)* 9-7-8 (7) JoHunnam(5) (bhd: t.o 5f out)....6 **19**

9/4 Uncle Doug (op 7/2), **6/1** Ijab (CAN) (8/1-5/1), Kilernan, **8/1** Bobby's Dream, **12/1** Izza, Deceit the Second, Can She Can Can, Leap in the Dark (IRE), **14/1** Milngavie (IRE), Doctor's Remedy, **16/1** Persistent (IRE), Kinoko, GREEK NIGHT OUT (IRE), Bushehr (IRE), **20/1** Zamhareer (USA), Lone Risk, Jarrow, Moonshine Dancer, **50/1** King of the Horse (IRE), CSF £217.83 CT £1,558.47 TOTE £60.70: £6.40 £3.30 £1.70 £1.70 (£270.90) Trio Not won; £211.87 to 18/9/95 OWNER . Sunpak Potatoes (HAMBLETON) BRED Airlie Stud 19 Rn

3m 27.7 (6.70) SF: 29/27/27/37/35/26/19/26/30/41/22/15/33/12/1/8/5/-/-

WEIGHT FOR AGE 3yo-12lb

3725

SUNDAY SUN 'SILVER SPUR' WALTER GLYNN MAIDEN STKS (3-Y.O) (Class D) £4,077.50 (£1,220.00: £585.00: £267.50)
7f Stalls: High GOING minus 0.30 sec per fur (GF) 5-00 (5-01)

3356[2] **Azdihaar (USA) (72)***(81)*(Fav)*(JLDunlop)* 3-8-9 GCarter(10) (chsd ldrs: drvn along ½-wy: led over 1f out: sn drew clr)....— **1**
Cashmere Lady *(73) (JLEyre)* 3-8-9 RLappin(4) (unf: mid div: effrt 2f out: edgd lft & styd on wl ins fnl f: no ch w wnr)....3½ **2**
3409[3] Masaafaat (USA) **(68)***(64) (MRStoute)* 3-8-9 FNorton(9) (led tl over 1f out: one pce)....4 **3**
3544[10] Bad News **(36)***(60) (RHarris)* 3-8-9 SWebster(6) (in tch: drvn along ½-wy: one pce)....1½ **4**
Fallal (IRE) *(55) (KMcAuliffe)* 3-8-9 GDuffield(12) (chsd ldr tl wknd over 1f out)....2½ **5**
Caddican (IRE) *(55) (RBoss)* 3-8-6 (3) NVarley(3) (leggy: bit bkwd: s.i.s: hld up & bhd: sme hdwy over 2f out: n.d)....s.h **6**
1065[3] Ramsdens (IRE) *(57) (WJHaggas)* 3-9-0 JLowe(1) (chsd ldr: drvn along ½-wy: wknd & eased over 1f out)....1 **7**
3392[5] Supreme (USA) *(52) (MDHammond)* 3-8-2 (7) DHayden(5) (bhd: sme hdwy 2f out: nvr nr ldrs)....nk **8**
2522[7] Enchanted Cottage **(37)***(45) (MDHammond)* 3-9-0 JMarshall(11) (bhd & outpcd fr ½-wy)....5 **9**
Petrico *(13) (JBerry)* 3-9-0 SDWilliams(2) (wl grwn: bit bkwd: sn drvn along: t.o ½-wy)....14 **10**
Karaylar (IRE) *(13) (WStorey)* 3-9-0 JFanning(7) (bit bkwd: s.i.s: a bhd)....nk **11**

4/5 AZDIHAAR (USA) (op 11/8), **4/1** Ramsdens (IRE), Masaafaat (USA), **10/1** Fallal (IRE), **12/1** Cashmere Lady, Caddican (IRE), **16/1** Petrico, **20/1** Bad News, **25/1** Supreme (USA), **33/1** Enchanted Cottage, Karaylar (IRE), CSF £14.58 TOTE £1.90: £1.10 £2.80 £1.80 (£30.20) Trio £30.50 OWNER Mr Hamdan Al Maktoum (ARUNDEL) BRED Shadwell Farm Inc 11 Rn

1m 26.2 (3.00) SF: 32/24/15/11/6/6/8/3/-/-/-

3726

'COME TO CATTERICK'S OPEN MORNING' H'CAP (0-70) (3-Y.O+ F & M) (Class E) £3,886.00 (£1,168.00: £564.00: £262.00)
7f Stalls: High GOING minus 0.30 sec per fur (GF) 5-30 (5-31)

3534[3] **Heathyards Lady (USA) (51)***(64) (RHollinshead)* 4-8-6 (7) FLynch(6) (lost pl after 1f: hdwy over 2f out: swtchd lft over 1f out: styd on to ld ins fnl f: sn clr)....— **1**

3507[3] Flirty Gertie **(67)***(73)*(Fav)*(RBoss)* 3-9-11 TSprake(3) (led tl ins fnl f) 3 **2**
3507[5] Kira **(45)***(51) (JLEyre)* 5-8-7 RLappin(10) (b.off hind: a chsng ldrs: ev ch over 1f out: kpt on same pce) ....s.h **3**
*3075** Kinnegad Kid **(43)***(43) (RIngram)* 6-8-5v NGwilliams(13) (a chsng ldrs: styd on one pce appr fnl f) 2½ **4**
3506[3] Formidable Liz **(58)***(58) (MDHammond)* 5-9-6 GDuffield(18) (racd wd: effrt & n.m.r 2f out: kpt on appr fnl f) ....nk **5**
2709[3] Linger **(68)***(67) (LordHuntingdon)* 3-9-7 (5) AWhelan(4) (in tch: effrt 2f out: kpt on one pce) ....½ **6**
3403[6] Owdbetts (IRE) **(60)***(58) (GLMoore)* 3-8-11 (7) ALakeman(17) (bhd & racd wd: hung lft over 2f out: styd on appr fnl f) ....s.h **7**
3121* Suedoro **(49)***(45) (RMMcKellar)* 5-8-4 (7) CAdamson(8) (in tch: effrt over 2f out: nvr able to chal) 1 **8**
3298[6] Question Ali **(57)***(52) (JBerry)* 3-9-1 GCarter(5) (sme hdwy ½-wy: nvr nr to chal) ....nk **9**
3310[2] Caltha **(45)***(40) (PCalver)* 3-8-0b(3) NVarley(16) (b.hind: nvr bttr than mid div) ....hd **10**
3467[21] Aquiletta **(44)***(28) (CBBBooth)* 5-7-13 (7)ow6 AEddery(1) (s.i.s: bhd: sme hdwy & n.m.r 2f out: n.d) 2½ **11**
2187[3] Nordan Raider **(65)***(52) (MJCamacho)* 7-9-8 (5) GParkin(20) (lw: hld up & plld hrd: racd wd: effrt over 2f out: sn wknd) 1 **12**
2795[4] Hey Up Dolly (IRE) **(67)***(53) (JBerry)* 3-9-11 SDWilliams(2) (sn drvn along & chsng ldrs: wknd over 2f out) ....½ **13**
2923[10] Miss Iron Heart (USA) **(44)***(27) (DJSCosgrove)* 3-8-2 FNorton(19) (bhd: stdy hdwy on ins 2f out: styng on same pce whn hmpd ins fnl f: eased) 1¼ **14**
1571[10] Euphyllia **(46)***(29) (BobJones)* 3-8-4 JFanning(11) (hdwy ½-wy: hung lft & n.m.r 2f out: sn wknd) ....s.h **15**
3542[6] Sweet Allegiance **(57)***(37) (JCPoulton)* 5-9-5 AMorris(12) (mid div whn hmpd over 4f out: n.d after) 1¼ **16**
3506[5] Royal Comedian **(46)***(24) (BWMurray)* 6-8-3 (5)ow2 RHavlin(15) (a bhd: drvn along ½-wy) ....nk **17**
766[7] Rainbows Rhapsody **(40)***(14) (MJCamacho)* 4-8-2 LCharnock(9) (chsd ldrs tl wknd over 2f out) 2½ **18**
2818[4] Komlucky **(43)** *(FJO'Mahony)* 3-7-10b(5) MBaird(7) (s.i.s: a wl bhd) 8 **19**

9/2 Flirty Gertie (op 3/1), **5/1** Kinnegad Kid, **7/1** HEATHYARDS LADY (USA), **8/1** Linger, Formidable Liz (op 5/1), Caltha, **10/1** Owdbetts (IRE), **12/1** Nordan Raider, Suedoro (op 7/1), **14/1** Royal Comedian, Hey Up Dolly (IRE), **16/1** Kira, **20/1** Question Ali, Sweet Allegiance, Rainbows Rhapsody, Komlucky, **25/1** Miss Iron Heart (USA), Euphyllia, **33/1** Aquiletta, CSF £43.95 CT £493.78 TOTE £7.50: £2.00 £2.30 £2.50 £1.50 (£19.10) Trio £200.50 OWNER Mr L. A. Morgan (UPPER LONGDON) BRED S A'Long Farm and Dennis Swartz 19 Rn

1m 26.2 (3.00) SF: 36/41/23/15/30/35/26/17/20/8/-/24/21/-/-/9/-/-/-

WEIGHT FOR AGE 3yo-4lb

T/Plpt: £51.30 (166.5 Tckts). T/Qdpt: £47.00 (0.6 Tckts). WG

3706-NEWBURY (L-H)

Saturday September 16th (Good to soft)

WEATHER: overcast WIND: slt half bhd

3727 FIRST IN, LAST OUT, PUB AT WINCHESTER NURSERY H'CAP (2-Y.O) (Class C) £5,312.50 (£1,600.00: £775.00: £362.50)

5f 34y Stalls: Centre GOING: 0.23 sec per fur (G) 1-30 (1-31)

3548[6] **Willow Dale (IRE) (79)***(84) (DRCElsworth)* 2-9-3 PaulEddery(6) (hld up: rdn over 2f out: led ins fnl f: r.o wl) ....— **1**
3132[5] Polish Bear (IRE) **(67)***(72) (BJMeehan)* 2-8-5 BDoyle(5) (outpcd: hdwy over 1f out: ev ch ins fnl f: r.o) ....hd **2**
3465[6] Fond Embrace **(73)***(75) (HCandy)* 2-8-11 WCarson(1) (lw: racd far side: a.p: rdn over 1f out: ev ch ins fnl f: unable qckn) ....¾ **3**
3132[8] Martara (IRE) **(66)***(67) (MRChannon)* 2-8-4 DHarrison(10) (chsd ldr: rdn over 2f out: led over 1f out tl ins fnl f: one pce) ....½ **4**
2442[12] Veesey **(63)***(58) (JohnBerry)* 2-8-1 MFenton(12) (s.s: hdwy 4f out: rdn over 2f out: one pce) ...2 **5**
3655[4] Lady Caroline Lamb (IRE) **(67)***(58) (MRChannon)* 2-7-12 (7) DSweeney(7) (led over 3f) 1¼ **6**
3558[3] Extra Hour (IRE) **(83)***(66) (WRMuir)* 2-9-7 JReid(9) (lw: hld up: rdn over 2f out: sn wknd) 2½ **7**
3520[3] Sunset Harbour (IRE) **(59)***(40) (DAWilson)* 2-7-11 JQuinn(8) (hld up: rdn over 2f out: wknd over 1f out) ....¾ **8**
3375[10] Safio **(82)***(55) (CSmith)* 2-9-6 WWoods(2) (lw: racd far side: outpcd) 2½ **9**
3655* White Emir **(87)***(58)*(Fav)*(BJMeehan)* 2-9-6 (5) 7x DaneO'Neill(3) (lw: racd far side: prom over 3f) ....¾ **10**
3080* Phoenix House **(68)***(17) (GLMoore)* 2-8-6v AClark(11) (swtg: bhd fnl 3f) 7 **11**
1919[4] Elfin Queen (IRE) **(64)** *(MJohnston)* 2-8-2 RHills(4) (racd far side: a bhd) 10 **12**

7/2 White Emir, **5/1** Martara (IRE), Fond Embrace, **8/1** Elfin Queen (IRE), Lady Caroline Lamb (IRE), WILLOW DALE (IRE), **10/1** Sunset Harbour (IRE) (14/1-8/1), **12/1** Polish Bear (IRE) (8/1-14/1), **14/1** Phoenix House (10/1-16/1), **16/1** Safio, **20/1** Extra Hour (IRE), **50/1** Veesey, CSF £92.96 CT £487.80 TOTE £8.50: £2.60 £8.60 £1.60 (£121.10) Trio £183.20 OWNER Michael Jackson Bloodstock Ltd (WHITCOMBE) BRED Shunya Seki 12 Rn

64.9 secs (4.60) SF: 44/32/35/27/18/18/26/-/15/18/-/-

3728 ARLINGTON CONDITIONS STKS (3-Y.O+) (Class C) £5,345.60 (£1,990.40: £965.20: £406.00: £173.00: £79.80)

1m 1f Stalls: Low GOING: 0.23 sec per fur (G) 2-00 (2-02)

3585a4 **Wijara (IRE) (98)**_(110) (RHannon)_ 3-9-2 RPerham(4) (lw: mde all: rdn 2f out: r.o wl) ....— 1
3598* Clan Ben (IRE) _(104)_(Fav)_(HRACecil)_ 3-9-1 WRyan(6) (lw: 4th st: chsd wnr 3f out: ev ch 2f out: unable qckn) 3 2
24573 Yoush (IRE) **(98)**_(106) (MAJarvis)_ 3-9-5 PRobinson(9) (rdn & hdwy 2f out: r.o one pce) ....¾ 3
27622 First Island (IRE) **(107)**_(100) (GWragg)_ 3-9-1 MHills(10) (5th st: rdn over 2f out: one pce) 1½ 4
18528 Nash Terrace (IRE) **(98)**_(94) (RCharlton)_ 3-8-11 WCarson(11) (lw: 2nd st: rdn over 2f out: one pce) ....¾ 5
Final Appearance (IRE) _(93) (PWChapple-Hyam)_ 3-8-11 JReid(7) (rdn over 3f out: nvr nr to chal) 1 6
17826 Pesce D'Aprile _(88) (JLDunlop)_ 3-8-8 WWoods(12) (s.s: nvr nrr) ....¾ 7
Frogmarch (USA) _(80) (MajorWRHern)_ 5-9-0 MPerrett(5) (bit bkwd: nvr nrr) 5 8
35982 Royal Philosopher **(100)**_(82) (KMcAuliffe)_ 3-8-13 DHarrison(2) (hld up: rdn over 3f out: wknd over 1f out) 1½ 9
21212 Ten Past Six **(92)**_(53) (BWHills)_ 3-8-11 RHills(1) (6th st: wknd over 3f out) 15 10
3023* Polar Queen _(36) (JHMGosden)_ 3-8-6 GHind(3) (lw: 3rd st: wknd over 3f out) 7 11
35994 Il Trastevere (FR) _(40) (JLDunlop)_ 3-8-13 MRimmer(8) (lw: bhd fnl 2f) 1¼ 12

2/1 Clan Ben (IRE), **9/2** First Island (IRE), **7/1** Yoush (IRE), **10/1** WIJARA (IRE), Nash Terrace (IRE) (7/1-11/1), Royal Philosopher, Ten Past Six, Polar Queen, **14/1** Final Appearance (IRE) (10/1-16/1), **33/1** Il Trastevere (FR), **50/1** Pesce D'Aprile, **66/1** Frogmarch (USA), CSF £29.40 TOTE £12.80: £3.10 £1.20 £2.20 (£15.20) Trio £27.20 OWNER Mr Mohamed Suhail (MARLBOROUGH) BRED Barronstown Stud and Ron Con Ltd in Ireland 12 Rn

1m 58.24 (46.44) SF: 37/31/33/27/21/20/15/12/9/-/-/-

WEIGHT FOR AGE 3yo-5lb

3729 COURAGE H'CAP (0-105) (3-Y.O+) (Class B) £16,550.00 (£6,200.00: £3,037.50: £1,312.50: £593.75: £306.25)

1m 2f 6y Stalls: Low GOING: 0.23 sec per fur (G) 2-30 (2-32)

36116 **Kutta (90)**_(102)_(Fav)_(RWArmstrong)_ 3-9-5 WCarson(2) (lw: hdwy & nt clr run on ins over 2f out: hrd rdn over 1f out: led ins fnl f: r.o wl) ....— 1
29503 Ball Gown **(75)**_(85) (DTThom)_ 5-8-10 MPerrett(12) (s.s: hdwy 2f out: led over 1f out tl ins fnl f: unable qckn) 1 2
33747 Show Faith (IRE) **(83)**_(93) (RHannon)_ 5-8-13 (5) DaneO'Neill(10) (nt clr run over 3f out tl over 2f out: hdwy wl over 1f out: r.o wl) ....½ 3
35003 Country Star (IRE) **(82)**_(88) (HCandy)_ 4-9-3 NAdams(7) (5th st: ev ch 1f out: one pce) 2 4
33883 Silver Groom (IRE) **(77)**_(77) (RAkehurst)_ 5-8-7 (5) MHenry(1) (6th st: ev ch over 1f out: sn wknd) 4 5
361115 Tony's Fen **(78)**_(77) (DRCElsworth)_ 6-8-8 (5) DGriffiths(3) (b: hdwy & nt clr run over 1f out: r.o) ....½ 6
35524 Seckar Vale (USA) **(82)**_(79) (BWHills)_ 3-8-11 RHills(16) (nt clr run over 2f out: hdwy over 1f out: nvr nrr) 1½ 7
33743 Ringmaster (IRE) **(88)**_(84) (MHTompkins)_ 4-9-9 PRobinson(15) (lw: hdwy over 1f out: nvr nrr) ....nk 8
360110 Special Dawn (IRE) **(90)**_(85) (JLDunlop)_ 5-9-11 PaulEddery(19) (hdwy over 1f out: nvr nrr) 1 9
35566 Wakeel (USA) **(89)**_(83) (SDow)_ 3-9-4 JWilliams(4) (lw: nvr nrr) ....¾ 10
33742 Amrak Ajeeb (IRE) **(88)**_(80) (BHanbury)_ 3-9-3 MRimmer(9) (b: swtg: led over 8f) 1 11
26724 Sadler's Walk **(79)**_(71) (GWragg)_ 4-9-0 MHills(5) (a mid div) ....s.h 12
26727 Star Manager (USA) **(79)**_(69) (PFICole)_ 5-9-0 CRutter(6) (lw: a mid div) 1 13
361113 Gone for a Burton (IRE) **(86)**_(70) (PJMakin)_ 5-9-7 WRyan(13) (a bhd) 4 14
3440* Tykeyvor (IRE) **(79)**_(63) (LadyHerries)_ 5-9-0 GBardwell(8) (b.hind: 4th st: wknd over 2f out) .hd 15
361116 Green Crusader **(88)**_(64) (MRStoute)_ 4-9-9v WWoods(14) (lw: 7th st: wknd over 2f out) 5 16
26726 Legendary Leap **(75)**_(50) (LordHuntingdon)_ 5-8-10 DHarrison(11) (2nd st: wknd over 1f out) ....nk 17
31314 Bernard Seven (IRE) **(90)**_(61) (CEBrittain)_ 3-9-5b BDoyle(18) (3rd st: wknd wl over 1f out) ...2½ 18
29105 Fragrant Belle (USA) **(88)**_(19) (LGCottrell)_ 4-9-9 JQuinn(17) (s.s: bhd fnl 4f) 25 19
3654* Danegold (IRE) **(82)**_(11) (MRChannon)_ 3-8-11v 4x AClark(20) (bhd fnl 4f) 1½ 20

4/1 KUTTA, **11/2** Seckar Vale (USA), **10/1** Ringmaster (IRE), Danegold (IRE), **12/1** Silver Groom (IRE), Star Manager (USA) (8/1-14/1), **14/1** Tony's Fen, Gone for a Burton (IRE), Sadler's Walk, Special Dawn (IRE), **16/1** Amrak Ajeeb (IRE), Tykeyvor (IRE), **20/1** Ball Gown, Green Crusader, **25/1** Show Faith (IRE), Country Star (IRE), Legendary Leap, **33/1** Bernard Seven (IRE), **40/1** Wakeel (USA), **50/1** Fragrant Belle (USA), CSF £80.12 CT £1,695.75 TOTE £5.10: £1.70 £5.70 £7.60 £5.10 (£86.10) Trio £1,063.60; £913.80 to 18/9/95 OWNER Mr Hamdan Al Maktoum (NEWMARKET) BRED Shadwell Estate Company Limited 20 Rn

2m 13.26 (10.26) SF: 38/27/35/30/19/19/15/26/27/19/16/13/11/12/5/6/-/-/-/-

WEIGHT FOR AGE 3yo-6lb

3730

TOTE AUTUMN CUP H'CAP (0-100) (3-Y.O+) (Class C) £15,393.75 (£4,650.00: £2,262.50: £1,068.75)
1m 5f 61y Stalls: Low GOING: 0.23 sec per fur (G) 3-00 (3-07)

3162[13] **Whitechapel (USA) (83)***(96) (LordHuntingdon)* 7-9-0 ow3 DHarrison(18) (3rd st: led 3f out: rdn out) ....— **1**
3489[6] Arctic Thunder (USA) **(93)***(105) (LadyHerries)* 4-9-10 MHills(19) (b: 6th st: chsd wnr fnl 2f: no imp) 3½ **2**
1764[4] Taklif (IRE) **(86)***(93) (BWHills)* 3-8-8 WCarson(21) (lw: led 10f out to 3f out: one pce) 4 **3**
703a[5] Fire Worshipper (IRE) **(97)***(104) (JHMGosden)* 4-10-0 GHind(22) (b: b.hind: lw: 2nd st: ev ch 3f out: one pce) ....s.h **4**
3555[5] Warm Spell **(73)***(63)*(Fav)*(GLMoore)* 5-8-4 AClark(8) (hdwy over 3f out: wknd over 2f out) 14 **5**
3616[3] Purple Splash **(80)***(68) (PJMakin)* 5-8-11v PaulEddery(4) (hdwy over 3f out: wknd over 2f out) 2 **6**
3556[3] Danjing (IRE) **(84)***(71) (PFICole)* 3-8-6 CRutter(9) (hdwy over 3f out: wknd over 2f out) ....½ **7**
3555* Daily Starlight (USA) **(79)***(66) (MissGayKelleway)* 3-7-10 (5) MHenry(11) (lw: 8th st: wknd over 2f out) ....nk **8**
3406[3] Flight Lieutenant (USA) **(73)***(59) (RHannon)* 6-7-13 (5) DaneO'Neill(20) (lw: nvr nrr) ....¾ **9**
3517* Persian Saint (IRE) **(80)***(61) (DRCElsworth)* 4-8-11 JWilliams(12) (swtg: led over 3f: 5th st: wknd over 3f out) 4 **10**
3489[5] Johns Act (USA) **(73)***(53) (DHaydnJones)* 5-8-1 (3) DRMcCabe(13) (lw: prom over 9f) ....½ **11**
3189[2] Jameel Asmar **(80)***(44) (CREgerton)* 3-8-2 GBardwell(6) (lw: a mid div) 14 **12**
3489[3] Shadow Leader **(81)***(41) (DJSffrenchDavis)* 4-8-12 MPerrett(1) (nvr nrr) 3 **13**
3406[8] Golden Arrow (IRE) **(82)***(36) (IABalding)* 4-8-13 WRyan(7) (nvr nrr) 5 **14**
3406* Proton **(79)***(31) (RAkehurst)* 5-8-10 RPerham(10) (prom 8f) 1¾ **15**
3445[5] Midyan Blue (IRE) **(80)***(31) (JMPEustace)* 5-8-11 MTebbutt(17) (nvr nrr) ....¾ **16**
3343[2] Shonara's Way **(93)***(44) (RCharlton)* 4-9-10 JReid(2) (bhd fnl 5f) ....hd **17**
3336* Jandeel (IRE) **(93)***(43) (ACStewart)* 3-9-1 RHills(3) (b: b.hind: lw: 4th st: wknd over 3f out) ....½ **18**
2559a[S] Greenspan (IRE) **(83)***(27) (WRMuir)* 3-8-5 JQuinn(5) (lw: 7th st: wknd over 3f out) 5 **19**
3593[12] Roll a Dollar **(92)***(35) (DRCElsworth)* 9-9-4 (5) DGriffiths(16) (b: a bhd) 1 **20**
1127[5] Tira Heights (USA) **(92)***(30) (RWArmstrong)* 3-9-0 WWoods(15) (a bhd) 4 **21**
2386a[6] Lord Jim (IRE) **(96)***(10) (MissGayKelleway)* 3-9-4 BDoyle(23) (bhd fnl 5f) 20 **22**
3489[8] Linpac West **(97)** *(CWCElsey)* 9-10-0 MRimmer(14) (bhd fnl 5f: t.o) ....dist **23**

13/2 Warm Spell, **15/2** Shonara's Way, Jandeel (IRE), **9/1** Proton, **12/1** WHITECHAPEL (USA), **14/1** Jameel Asmar, Midyan Blue (IRE), Fire Worshipper (IRE), **16/1** Taklif (IRE), Flight Lieutenant (USA), Purple Splash, Arctic Thunder (USA), **20/1** Shadow Leader, Daily Starlight (USA), Danjing (IRE), Golden Arrow (IRE), Linpac West, **25/1** Johns Act (USA), Persian Saint (IRE), Lord Jim (IRE), Tira Heights (USA), **50/1** Greenspan (IRE), Roll a Dollar, CSF £187.23 CT £2,828.79 TOTE £13.90: £3.20 £6.20 £4.00 £6.80 (£65.00) Trio £1,156.90 OWNER The Queen (WEST ILSLEY) BRED The Queen 23 Rn 2m 56.77 (11.47) SF: 44/53/32/52/11/16/10/5/7/9/1/-/-/-/-/-/-/-/-/-/-/-/-

WEIGHT FOR AGE 3yo-9lb

3731

BONUSPRINT MILL REEF STKS (Gp 2) (2-Y.O) (Class A) £32,018.00 (£11,980.65: £5,752.83: £2,503.52) **6f 8y** Stalls: Centre GOING: 0.23 sec per fur (G) 3-30 (3-38)

3420* **Kahir Almaydan (IRE) (100)***(109)*(Fav)*(JLDunlop)* 2-8-12 WCarson(3) (lw: mde all: rdn out) ....— **1**
2704[6] Kuantan (USA) *(93) (PFICole)* 2-8-12 MHills(1) (rdn over 2f out: hdwy over 1f out: r.o one pce) 6 **2**
2710* Warning Time **(93)***(93) (BJMeehan)* 2-8-12 BDoyle(6) (lw: hdwy over 2f out: hrd rdn over 1f out: one pce) ....hd **3**
2029[2] Resounder (USA) **(100)***(93) (JHMGosden)* 2-8-12 GHind(2) (lw: a.p: hrd rdn over 1f out: one pce) ....s.h **4**
3606* King of The East (IRE) *(85) (MRStoute)* 2-8-12 PaulEddery(4) (lw: hld up: rdn over 2f out: wknd over 1f out) 3 **5**
3185* Desert Boy (IRE) *(53)*(Fav)*(PWChapple-Hyam)* 2-8-12 JReid(5) (prom over 3f) 12 **6**

2/1 KAHIR ALMAYDAN (IRE), Desert Boy (IRE), **13/2** King of The East (IRE), **8/1** Kuantan (USA) (6/1-10/1), Warning Time, **11/1** Resounder (USA) (8/1-12/1), CSF £15.43 TOTE £2.00: £1.20 £3.00 (£7.70) OWNER Mr Mirza Al Sayegh (ARUNDEL) BRED B. Ryan 6 Rn

1m 16.28 SF: 53/37/37/37/29/-

OFFICIAL EXPLANATION **Desert Boy (IRE): the colt was reportedly uncharacteristically worked up in the parade ring, but his jockey could offer nothing futher as to his poor performance.**

3732

ROTHMANS ROYALS NORTH SOUTH CHALLENGE SERIES SEMI-FINAL H'CAP (0-100) (3-Y.O+) (Class C) £18,910.00 (£5,680.00: £2,740.00: £1,270.00)
1m 7y (round) Stalls: Low GOING: 0.23 sec per fur (G) 4-00 (4-08)

3368 3 **Almond Rock (79)***(94) (JRFanshawe)* 3-8-6 DHarrison(14) (hdwy over 3f out: led over 2f out: drvn out) ....— 1
3113 7 Country Lover **(73)***(88) (LordHuntingdon)* 4-8-4 MHills(13) (lw: hdwy over 2f out: rdn over 1f out: r.o wl) ....hd 2
3497 12 Elpidos **(73)***(83) (CEBrittain)* 3-8-0 BDoyle(18) (hdwy over 1f out: r.o) 2½ 3
3674 2 Knobbleeneeze **(76)***(78) (MRChannon)* 5-8-7v WWoods(17) (lw: 4th st: led over 4f out tl over 2f out: one pce) 4 4
3222 11 Ma Petite Anglaise **(81)***(77) (WJarvis)* 3-8-3 (5) MHenry(16) (rdn over 3f out: hdwy over 1f out: r.o) 3 5
3601 7 Misty Silks **(69)***(64+) (MJRyan)* 5-8-0 DBiggs(4) (hdwy over 3f out: wknd over 1f out) ....½ 6
3214 5 Stone Ridge (IRE) **(84)***(75) (RHannon)* 3-8-11b JReid(10) (lw: hdwy over 2f out: sn wknd) 2 7
3368 8 Crumpton Hill (IRE) **(84)***(75++) (NAGraham)* 3-8-11 PaulEddery(6) (lw: nvr nrr) ....s.h 8
3113 6 Easy Jet (POL) **(75)***(65) (LordHuntingdon)* 3-8-2 MFenton(20) (3rd st: wknd over 2f out) ....nk 9
3113* Mo-Addab (IRE) **(73)***(63) (ACStewart)* 5-7-13 (5) MHumphries(3) (lw: hdwy & nt clr run 2f out: swtchd rt: nvr nrr) ....hd 10
3358 5 Desert Green (FR) **(97)***(83) (RHannon)* 6-10-0 RPerham(19) (lw: nvr nrr) 2 11
3565 6 Gadge **(71)***(43)*(Fav)*(DMorris)* 4-8-2 RPrice(1) (6th st: wknd over 2f out) 7 12
3497* Concer Un **(79)***(50) (SCWilliams)* 3-8-6 GHind(12) (b.nr fore: hld up: rdn over 2f out: wknd over 1f out) ....¾ 13
3291* Saifan **(78)***(43) (DMorris)* 6-8-9b AClark(11) (lw: s.s: a bhd) 3 14
3664 9 Sooty Tern **(71)***(32) (JMBradley)* 8-7-9 (7) AmandaSanders(2) (2nd st: wknd over 2f out) 1¾ 15
3348 2 Fionn de Cool (IRE) **(75)***(36) (RAkehurst)* 4-8-6 RHills(9) (7th st: wknd over 2f out) ....s.h 16
3429* Risky Romeo **(66)***(9) (GCBravery)* 3-7-7 JQuinn(15) (a bhd) 9 17
3368 11 Desert Time **(75)***(18) (MRChannon)* 5-8-6 CRutter(7) (a bhd) ....s.h 18
3408* Apollono **(82)***(11) (RAkehurst)* 3-8-4 (5) DaneO'Neill(8) (5th st: wknd over 2f out) 7 19
3222 10 Artful Dane (IRE) **(73)** *(MJHeaton-Ellis)* 3-8-0 WCarson(5) (led over 3f: wknd 2f out) 20 20

LONG HANDICAP Risky Romeo 7-5

5/1 Gadge, **7/1** Apollono, **15/2** Knobbleeneeze, **8/1** Concer Un, **9/1** Misty Silks, **10/1** Country Lover, **12/1** ALMOND ROCK, Fionn de Cool (IRE), **14/1** Mo-Addab (IRE), **16/1** Easy Jet (POL), Artful Dane (IRE), Saifan, **20/1** Desert Green (FR), Crumpton Hill (IRE), Stone Ridge (IRE), **25/1** Ma Petite Anglaise, Desert Time, **33/1** Risky Romeo, Elpidos, Sooty Tern, CSF £128.72 CT £3,535.08 TOTE £16.40: £3.30 £2.90 £12.00 £1.60 (£169.00) Trio £959.50; £1,216.30 to 18/9/95 OWNER C I T Racing Ltd (NEWMARKET) BRED Lord Halifax 20 Rn

1m 41.95 (5.95) SF: 48/46/37/36/31/22/29/29/19/21/41/1/4/1/-/-/-/-/-/-

WEIGHT FOR AGE 3yo-4lb

3733

E.B.F. HARWELL MAIDEN STKS (2-Y.O) (Class D) £4,874.00 (£1,472.00: £716.00: £338.00) **6f 8y** Stalls: Centre GOING: 0.23 sec per fur (G) 4-30 (4-46)

1551 3 **Sovereign's Crown (USA)** *(92+) (JHMGosden)* 2-9-0 GHind(15) (lw: chsd ldr: led over 1f out: rdn out) ....— 1
Dwingeloo (IRE) *(76) (MajorDNChappell)* 2-8-9 WWoods(7) (w'like: bit bkwd: led over 4f: unable qckn) 4 2
2690 6 Oberons Boy (IRE) **(94)***(79) (BJMeehan)* 2-9-0 JQuinn(16) (hld up: rdn over 2f out: r.o one pce) 1 3
3560 5 Elite Force (IRE) *(78) (PWChapple-Hyam)* 2-9-0 JReid(13) (hld up: rdn over 2f out: one pce) ....nk 4
3371 10 Diamond Beach *(70+) (BWHills)* 2-9-0 JWilliams(17) (rdn over 2f out: hdwy over 1f out: nvr nrr) 3 5
Brandonville *(67) (IABalding)* 2-8-9 (5) DGriffiths(18) (leggy: scope: nvr nr to chal) 1¼ 6
Courting Danger *(64) (DRGandolfo)* 2-9-0 MFenton(8) (leggy: hld up: rdn over 2f out: wknd over 1f out) 1 7
Blue Flyer (IRE) *(61) (IABalding)* 2-9-0 RHills(12) (w'like: scope: bit bkwd: no hdwy fnl 2f) 1 8
Don Micheletto *(61) (GWragg)* 2-9-0 MHills(19) (str: scope: bit bkwd: nvr nrr) ....s.h 9
Pleading *(60) (HCandy)* 2-9-0 NAdams(6) (wl grwn: hld up: hmpd 4f out: rdn over 1f out: sn wknd) ....½ 10

Samara (IRE) *(53) (JLDunlop)* 2-8-9 WRyan(1) (w'like: bit bkwd: s.s: hdwy over 1f out: eased whn btn ins fnl f: bttr for r)........¾ **11**
Miss Universal (IRE) *(52) (CEBrittain)* 2-8-9 BDoyle(9) (w'like: nvr nrr)........nk **12**
3495⁶ Beauchamp Kate *(51) (HCandy)* 2-8-9 CRutter(21) (b.hind: lw: nvr nrr)........½ **13**
Mazcobar *(53) (PJMakin)* 2-9-0 PaulEddery(25) (leggy: scope: nvr nrr)........1¼ **14**
Newlands Corner *(45) (JAkehurst)* 2-8-9 RPrice(26) (leggy: scope: lw: reard s: nvr nrr)........1 **15**
1856⁷ Bright Diamond *(45) (JRArnold)* 2-8-6 (3) DRMcCabe(22) (hld up: rdn over 2f out: wknd over 1f out)........s.h **16**
Ballpoint *(48) (RHannon)* 2-9-0 RPerham(23) (w'like: nvr nrr)........¾ **17**
1511¹² Ed's Folly (IRE) *(43) (SDow)* 2-9-0 DHarrison(2) (lw: hld up: rdn over 2f out: sn wknd)........1¾ **18**
Country Thatch *(42) (CAHorgan)* 2-9-0 MPerrett(4) (w'like: hld up: rdn over 2f out: sn wknd)........½ **19**
3337⁵ Philistar *(41) (JMPEustace)* 2-9-0 MTebbutt(20) (a bhd)........nk **20**
3604¹⁴ Night Harmony (IRE) *(40) (RHannon)* 2-8-9 (5) DaneO'Neill(5) (b: prom over 4f)........nk **21**
Florentino (IRE) *(38) (BWHills)* 2-9-0 RStreet(27) (b.nr hind: leggy: scope: s.s: a bhd)........¾ **22**
Darby Flyer *(30) (WRMuir)* 2-9-0 MRimmer(14) (leggy: bhd fnl 2f)........3 **23**
3427⁸ Brave Maisie (IRE) **(55)***(19) (MMcCormack)* 2-8-9 AClark(24) (bhd fnl 2f)........2½ **24**
3536⁹ Indian Sunset *(2) (CREgerton)* 2-9-0 GBardwell(3) (a bhd)........8 **25**
Dramatic Act *(CRBarwell)* 2-8-4 (5) MHenry(11) (Withdrawn not under Starter's orders: uns rdr & bolted bef s)........ **W**
Insiyabi (USA) (Fav)*(JLDunlop)* 2-9-0 WCarson(10) (Withdrawn not under Starter's orders: ref to ent stalls)........ **W**

100/30 Insiyabi (USA), **7/2** Don Micheletto (op 2/1), **4/1** SOVEREIGN'S CROWN (USA), **8/1** Elite Force (IRE) (5/1-9/1), **12/1** Oberons Boy (IRE) (8/1-14/1), Dwingeloo (IRE) (7/1-14/1), **14/1** Blue Flyer (IRE) (20/1-12/1), Philistar (10/1-16/1), **20/1** Night Harmony (IRE), Miss Universal (IRE), Samara (IRE), **33/1** Pleading, Brandonville, Beauchamp Kate, Diamond Beach, Bright Diamond, Ballpoint, Newlands Corner, Country Thatch, Courting Danger, Ed's Folly (IRE), Florentino (IRE), Darby Flyer, Brave Maisie (IRE), Indian Sunset, Dramatic Act, Mazcobar, CSF £34.55 TOTE £4.40: £2.00 £4.60 £3.70 (£55.20) Trio £249.50; £319.81 to 18/9/95 OWNER Hesmonds Stud (NEWMARKET) BRED J Mack Robinson 25 Rn
1m 16.65 (4.85) SF: 50/34/37/36/28/25/22/19/19/18/11/10/9/11/3/3/6/1/-/-/-/-/-/-/-

T/Plpt: £1,279.80 (21.88 Tckts). T/ Qdpt: £208.20 (1 Tckt). AK

3509-WOLVERHAMPTON (L-H)
Saturday September 16th (Standard)

Racing delayed 1hr after race 2 - Floodlight failure
WEATHER: showery WIND: almost nil

3734

TANZANIA MAIDEN H'CAP (0-70) (3-Y.O+) (Class E) £3,236.00 (£968.00: £464.00: £212.00) **7f (Fibresand)** Stalls: High GOING: 0.12 sec (SLW) 7-00 (7-01)

3097⁵ **Jalmaid (50)***(61) (BAMcMahon)* 3-8-11 DBiggs(12) (a.p: 4th st: led over 1f out: r.o.wl)........— **1**
3514² Penmar **(55)***(65)*(Fav)*(TJEtherington)* 3-9-2 ACulhane(11) (a.p: rdn over 3f out: 3rd st: ev ch over 1f out: r.o)........½ **2**
3514³ Md Thompson **(52)***(54) (SCWilliams)* 3-8-13 JQuinn(4) (a.p: 2nd st: ev ch over 1f out: btn whn hung rt ins fnl f)........3½ **3**
3138³ Prudent Princess **(63)***(60) (AHide)* 3-9-10 MTebbutt(7) (lw: led after 1f: hdd over 1f out: btn whn hmpd & swtchd lft ins fnl f)........2 **4**
3522⁷ Anotherone to Note **(45)***(35) (NPLittmoden)* 4-8-10b TGMcLaughlin(8) (stdd s: hdwy fnl 2f: nvr nrr)........3 **5**
1498¹⁹ Callonescy (IRE) **(52)***(41) (CEBrittain)* 3-8-13 BDoyle(9) (hdwy 3f out: 5th st: nvr nr ldrs)........¾ **6**
3514¹¹ Mason (IRE) **(55)***(39) (SMellor)* 3-9-2 MWigham(1) (chsd ldrs 4f)........2 **7**
2492¹⁰ Sabella **(50)***(34) (RHarris)* 4-9-1 DBatteate(10) (led 1f: edgd rt 2f out: 6th & wkng st)........hd **8**
3442¹⁶ Merlin's Fancy **(62)***(45) (WJarvis)* 3-9-9 WWoods(3) (s.i.s: sn rcvrd: wknd 3f out)........nk **9**
3097⁶ Coryana Dancer (IRE) **(56)***(35) (RHollinshead)* 3-9-3 DHarrison(5) (chsd ldrs: pushed along over 5f out: wknd over 3f out)........2 **10**
1950⁸ Pacific Spirit **(45)***(15) (MTate)* 5-8-10 JWilliams(6) (a bhd)........4 **11**
1377⁹ Nafta **(54)***(5) (SEKettlewell)* 3-9-1 AClark(2) (prom tl wknd over 3f out: t.o)........8 **12**

5/2 Penmar, **5/1** Md Thompson, **13/2** Prudent Princess (4/1-7/1), **7/1** Coryana Dancer (IRE), Merlin's Fancy (op 9/2), **8/1** JALMAID (6/1-9/1), **10/1** Callonescy (IRE), **14/1** Pacific Spirit, **25/1** Nafta, Mason (IRE), **33/1** Sabella, Anotherone to Note, CSF £27.75 CT £103.82 TOTE £9.00: £2.50 £1.40 £1.80 (£12.40) Trio £9.10 OWNER Breeson (TAMWORTH) BRED W. H. F. Carson 12 Rn
1m 29.7 (5.70) SF: 38/42/31/37/16/18/16/15/22/12/-/-
WEIGHT FOR AGE 3yo-4lb

3735

TIPTON BRIGHT BAR LIMITED STKS (0-60) (3-Y.O+) (Class F)
£2,381.00 (£656.00: £311.00)
1m 6f 166y (Fibresand) Stalls: High GOING: 0.12 sec per fur (SLW) 7-30 (7-38)

935[14] **Elpida (USA) (59)***(71) (JPearce)* 3-8-7 GBardwell(10) (plld hrd: chsd ldrs: led 5f out: clr over 2f out: v.easily)....— 1
3635[2] Last Corner **(59)***(70) (RHollinshead)* 3-8-11 WWoods(4) (hld up: hdwy 5f out: 5th st: styd on fnl f: no ch w wnr)....5 2
2296* Hydrofoil **(60)***(65)*(Fav)*(BWHills)* 3-8-3 (5) JDSmith(12) (hld up: hdwy 5f out: 3rd st: btn whn edgd rt ins fnl f)....1¾ 3
3527[4] Environmentalist (IRE) **(47)***(63) (RHarris)* 4-9-4 DBatteate(11) (hdwy 8f out: outpcd 4f out: 6th st: styd on appr fnl f)....nk 4
3402[3] Tadellal (IRE) **(60)***(62) (WGMTurner)* 4-8-10 (7) JWilkinson(3) (dwlt: plld hrd: sn rcvrd: 2nd st: wknd over 1f out)....½ 5
3002[3] Opus One **(58)***(53) (MissSEHall)* 4-9-1 DHarrison(2) (swtg: led over 9f: 4th & wkng st: eased whn btn)....6 6
3527[11] Jaraab **(57)***(54) (GLewis)* 4-9-8v JWilliams(6) (wl bhd 8f out: sme late hdwy)....6 7
3511[10] Golden Torque **(54)***(44) (RBastiman)* 8-8-13 (5) HBastiman(5) (hld up & bhd: sme hdwy 3f out: n.d)....5 8
3641[11] Gold Surprise (IRE) **(50)***(42) (SEKettlewell)* 6-9-4 AClark(1) (dropped rr 7f out)....2½ 9
3082[5] Ultimate Warrior **(60)***(20) (CACyzer)* 5-9-4 DBiggs(7) (bhd fnl 6f: t.o)....20 10
3646[15] Hatta River (USA) **(58)** *(JAHarris)* 5-9-4b JQuinn(9) (prom over 9f: t.o)....20 11
1452[10] Riva-Deva **(25)** *(BPreece)* 3-8-7 VSlattery(8) (plld hrd: prom tl wknd qckly 7f out: sn t.o)....dist 12

4/1 Hydrofoil (3/1-9/2), **9/2** Environmentalist (IRE), **5/1** Last Corner, Opus One, **8/1** Tadellal (IRE) (op 5/1), **12/1** Ultimate Warrior, **14/1** ELPIDA (USA), **16/1** Jaraab, **20/1** Gold Surprise (IRE), **33/1** Golden Torque, Hatta River (USA), **50/1** Riva-Deva, CSF £74.09 TOTE £12.10: £3.10 £1.70 £2.40 (£32.50) Trio £30.50 OWNER Mr A. J. Thompson (NEWMARKET) BRED Bluefield Farms Corp 12 Rn 3m 19.6 (12.20) SF: 36/35/30/39/38/29/30/20/18/-/-/-
WEIGHT FOR AGE 3yo-11lb

3736

E.B.F. MALI MAIDEN STKS (2-Y.O) (Class D) £3,655.00 (£1,090.00: £520.00: £235.00) **1m 100y (Fibresand)** Stalls: Low GOING: 0.12 sec (SLW) 8-00 (8-59)

3525[2] **Nose No Bounds (IRE) (76)***(74)*(Fav)*(MJohnston)* 2-9-0 BDoyle(3) (lw: led over 3f: rdn 3f out: 2nd st: led ins fnl f: sn hdd: edgd lft & led cl home)....— 1
2924[3] Two Socks **(56)***(73) (MMcCormack)* 2-9-0 AClark(7) (a.p: 4th st: led ins fnl f: hdd cl home)...nk 2
3604[9] Film Buff **(68)***(68) (BWHills)* 2-8-9 JWilliams(2) (a.p: led over 3f out tl ins fnl f: btn whn n.m.r nr fin)....hd 3
3463[9] Larry Lambrusco *(68) (MAJarvis)* 2-9-0 WWoods(4) (led 5f out tl over 3f out: 3rd st: ev ch over 1f out: wknd fnl f)....3 4
Thorntoun Estate (IRE) *(56) (MJohnston)* 2-9-0 NAdams(8) (bit bkwd: bhd & rdn thrght: sme hdwy over 2f out: n.d)....6 5
3350[3] Colour Counsellor **(54)***(54) (KMcAuliffe)* 2-9-0b JQuinn(1) (prom 5f: poor 6th st)....1 6
Dancing Cavalier *(53) (RHollinshead)* 2-9-0 DHarrison(5) (lt-f: hld up: hdwy 4f out: 5th & wkng st)....¾ 7
3502[9] Cottage Prince (IRE) *(42) (JJQuinn)* 2-9-0 JLowe(6) (lw: plld hrd: prom 5f)....6 8

4/11 NOSE NO BOUNDS (IRE), **7/1** Film Buff (op 7/2), **12/1** Two Socks (10/1-16/1), **16/1** Larry Lambrusco, Thorntoun Estate (IRE), Colour Counsellor, **25/1** Dancing Cavalier, **66/1** Cottage Prince (IRE), CSF £6.05 TOTE £1.40: £1.10 £1.60 £1.70 (£4.00) OWNER Ridings Racing (MIDDLEHAM) BRED David Barry 8 Rn 1m 53.3 (9.30) SF: 19/18/13/13/1/-/-/-
STEWARDS' ENQUIRY Doyle susp. 25-28/9/95 (misuse of whip).

3737

MICK MILLARD 50TH BIRTHDAY H'CAP (0-70) (3-Y.O+) (Class E)
£2,976.00 (£888.00: £424.00: £192.00)
1m 4f (Fibresand) Stalls: Low GOING: 0.12 sec per fur (SLW) 8-30 (9-22)

3245[9] **Canton Venture (60)***(73) (SPCWoods)* 3-8-12 WWoods(12) (a.p: rdn 5f out: led over 2f out: r.o wl)....— 1
*3513** Tovarich **(62)***(72) (RonaldThompson)* 4-9-8 SDWilliams(6) (hld up: stdy hdwy 5f out: 3rd st: styd on fnl f: nvr trbld wnr)....2½ 2
2379[6] Sommersby (IRE) **(57)***(64) (MrsNMacauley)* 4-9-3 DHarrison(4) (b: hld up: stdy hdwy 5f out: 4th st: one pce)....2 3
3511[3] Charlie Bigtime **(48)***(54) (RHarris)* 5-8-8 DBatteate(3) (a.p: 5th st: one pce)....½ 4
3505[6] Instantaneous **(55)***(61)*(Fav)*(MHEasterby)* 3-8-7 JLowe(10) (plld hrd: a.p: led over 4f out tl over 2f out: wknd fnl f)....hd 5

3511[2] Sudden Spin **(59)***(62) (SGNorton)* 5-9-5 JQuinn(1) (hld up: hdwy 4f out: 6th st: one pce)......2½ **6**
2921* Mad Militant (IRE) **(68)***(58) (AStreeter)* 6-9-7 (7) DDenby(8) (b: a bhd)......10 **7**
3511[12] Palacegate Jo (IRE) **(50)***(38) (DWChapman)* 4-8-10 ACulhane(11) (hld up & bhd: stdy hdwy over 5f out: wknd 3f out)......1½ **8**
Latch Key Lady (USA) **(55)***(41) (MJohnston)* 3-8-7 BDoyle(7) (wl bhd fnl 6f)......1¼ **9**
3511[11] Erlking (IRE) **(43)***(26) (SMellor)* 5-7-10 (7) ADaly(9) (plld hrd: prom tl wknd over 3f out)......2½ **10**
3402[8] Celestial Dollar **(45)***(13) (OO'Neill)* 4-8-5 AClark(5) (led over 7f: sn wknd: t.o)......11 **11**
3513[2] Awestruck **(46)** *(BPreece)* 5-8-6 ow4 VSlattery(2) (a bhd: t.o fnl 5f)......12 **12**

5/2 Instantaneous (op 6/1), **9/2** Charlie Bigtime, **5/1** Sommersby (IRE) (7/2-11/2), **7/1** Tovarich (5/1-8/1), Sudden Spin, **8/1** Mad Militant (IRE), **12/1** Awestruck (8/1-14/1), **20/1** CANTON VENTURE, **25/1** Palacegate Jo (IRE), Erlking (IRE), Latch Key Lady (USA), **40/1** Celestial Dollar, CSF £146.69 CT £750.39 TOTE £24.50: £4.70 £2.30 £2.80 (£53.10) Trio Not won; £122.78 to 18/9/95 OWNER Dr Frank Chao (NEWMARKET) BRED High Point B/stock Ltd & Chao Racing & B/stock Ltd 12 Rn

2m 40.2 (9.20) SF: 45/52/44/34/33/42/38/18/13/6/-/-

WEIGHT FOR AGE 3yo-8lb

3738 CONGO (S) STKS (2-Y.O) (Class G) £2,174.00 (£599.00: £284.00)
7f (Fibresand) Stalls: High GOING: 0.12 sec per fur (SLW) 9-00 (9-46)

3533[17] **Pinocchio Boy (IRE) (57)***(66) (BJMeehan)* 2-9-2 BDoyle(2) (a.p: 2nd st: led ins fnl f: drvn out)......— **1**
3533[13] Victoria Venture **(55)***(59)*(Fav)*(SPCWoods)* 2-8-11 WWoods(9) (a.p: led 2f out tl ins fnl f: r.o)......¾ **2**
3509[5] Still Here (IRE) **(59)***(51) (MJHeaton-Ellis)* 2-8-11 AClark(7) (chsd ldrs: 4th st: r.o one pce fnl f)......3½ **3**
3533[19] Pulga Circo **(54)***(43) (BAMcMahon)* 2-8-6 FNorton(8) (led 5f: 3rd st: btn whn hung rt ins fnl f)......1½ **4**
3671[10] Rattle *(43) (JJO'Neill)* 2-8-11 SDWilliams(10) (hdwy & 5th st: no imp)......2 **5**
2962[10] Welsh Melody **(61)***(32) (KRBurke)* 2-8-11 MTebbutt(6) (hld up: hmpd 3f out: hrd rdn & 6th st: no hdwy)......5 **6**
3243[2] Rozel Bay *(20) (JLSpearing)* 2-8-6 NAdams(5) (nvr trbld ldrs)......3 **7**
3054[5] Touch of Snow *(14) (JABennett)* 2-8-6 TSprake(12) (prom 4f)......2½ **8**
3312[4] Jenny's Charmer *(17) (SEKettlewell)* 2-8-11 GBardwell(4) (dwlt: sn rcvrd: wknd 2f out)......1 **9**
3243[11] Ricochet (IRE) *(SGNorton)* 2-8-11v JQuinn(11) (b.off hind: outpcd: a wl bhd: t.o)......15 **10**
836[5] Prime Connections *(MPBielby)* 2-8-11 ACulhane(1) (sn outpcd: t.o)......10 **11**
Casnic (IRE) *(CASmith)* 2-8-6 VSlattery(3) (unf: dwlt: a bhd: t.o)......2½ **12**

15/8 Victoria Venture, **100/30** Still Here (IRE), **11/2** Rozel Bay (4/1-6/1), **8/1** Pulga Circo (5/1-9/1), **12/1** Rattle (op 6/1), Welsh Melody (op 8/1), PINOCCHIO BOY (IRE) (op 5/1), Jenny's Charmer (op 7/1), **25/1** Casnic (IRE), **40/1** Touch of Snow, Ricochet (IRE), Prime Connections, CSF £34.80 TOTE £14.10: £4.00 £1.40 £1.70 (£30.40) Trio £87.10; £61.40 to 18/9/95 OWNER Mr K. C. Gomm (UPPER LAMBOURN) BRED Owen Bourke 12 Rn

1m 31.5 (1.70 under 2y best) (7.50) SF: 22/15/7/-/-/-/-/-/-/-/-/-

No bid

3739 IVORY COAST H'CAP (0-70) (3-Y.O+) (Class E) £3,184.00 (£952.00: £456.00: £208.00) **6f (Fibresand)** Stalls: Low GOING: 0.12 sec per fur (SLW) 9-30 (10-11)

3622[15] **Pursuance (IRE) (61)***(68) (JBalding)* 3-8-9v(7) JEdmunds(5) (mde all: all out)......— **1**
3622[13] Featherstone Lane **(60)***(67) (MissLCSiddall)* 4-9-4v MWigham(11) (a.p: hrd rdn & 2nd st: edgd rt 1f out: r.o wl)......hd **2**
3510[2] Maple Bay (IRE) **(56)***(63)*(Fav)*(ABailey)* 6-9-0 GBardwell(13) (bhd & rdn along: hdwy 3f out: 5th st: r.o wl ins fnl f)......hd **3**
3293[11] Cretan Gift **(58)***(64) (NPLittmoden)* 4-9-2 TGMcLaughlin(2) (hld up: hdwy on ins & 3rd st: hrd rdn & ev ch fnl f: r.o)......s.h **4**
1676[11] Jigsaw Boy **(61)***(65) (PGMurphy)* 6-8-12 (7) RWaterfield(8) (hld up: lost pl 2f out: rallied over 1f out: r.o wl ins fnl f)......¾ **5**
3512* Desert Invader (IRE) **(66)***(70) (DWChapman)* 4-9-10 ACulhane(4) (hdwy & 8th st: r.o ins fnl f)......s.h **6**
3524[12] Dark Shot (IRE) **(64)***(67) (JBerry)* 3-8-12 (7) CLowther(7) (prom: 4th st: nt qckn fnl f)......½ **7**
3512[6] Montague Dawson (IRE) **(63)***(65) (MrsNMacauley)* 3-8-11 (7) AmandaSanders(6) (prom: 6th st: no imp)......nk **8**
3529[7] Jamaica Bridge **(57)***(55) (SGNorton)* 5-9-1 JQuinn(9) (prom over 3f)......1½ **9**
3622[17] Cool Tactician **(65)***(59) (RHollinshead)* 3-9-6 DHarrison(10) (hld up & bhd: hdwy & 7th st: wknd over 1f out)......1½ **10**
3492[10] Souperficial **(67)***(61) (JAGlover)* 4-9-11v SDWilliams(1) (bhd: effrt whn hmpd over 1f out: n.d)......hd **11**

*3512*5 Anita's Contessa (IRE) **(67)***(61) (BPalling)* 3-9-8 TSprake(3) (prom over 3f) ....s.h **12**
*3522*6 Nineacres **(57)** *(CASmith)* 4-9-1v VSlattery(12) (s.s: t.o) ....dist **13**

11/8 Maple Bay (IRE), **11/2** Desert Invader (IRE), **8/1** Montague Dawson (IRE), Souperficial, **10/1** Jigsaw Boy, **12/1** Cretan Gift (op 8/1), **14/1** Dark Shot (IRE), Featherstone Lane, Anita's Contessa (IRE), **16/1** Cool Tactician, **20/1** PURSUANCE (IRE), Jamaica Bridge, Nineacres, CSF £265.81 CT £588.42 TOTE £43.20: £12.60 £5.90 £1.30 (£222.90) Trio Not won £177.60 to 18/9/95 OWNER Spring Hill Stud (DONCASTER) BRED Michael Coogan 13 Rn
1m 15.0 (3.80) SF: 50/52/48/49/50/55/49/47/40/41/46/43/-
WEIGHT FOR AGE 3yo-3lb

T/Plpt: £25.50 (426.22 Tckts). T/Qdpt: £6.10 (15.1 Tckts). KH

3308-EDINBURGH (R-H)
Monday September 18th (Good)
WEATHER: sunny WIND: almost nil

3740
E.B.F. RATING RELATED MAIDEN LIMITED STKS (0-60) (2-Y.O F) (Class F) £3,048.00 (£924.00: £452.00: £216.00)
5f Stalls: High GOING minus 0.19 sec per fur (GF) 2-00 (2-04)

33946 **Katy-Q (IRE) (60)***(70) (PCalver)* 2-8-11b MBirch(10) (b.hind: led after 2f: kpt on wl u.p fnl f)..— **1**
29855 Gracious Gretclo **(60)***(65)*(Fav)*(CJHill)* 2-8-11 JWeaver(1) (plld hrd early: w ldrs: rdn 2f out: one pce fnl f) 1½ **2**
33785 Apartments Abroad **(53)***(60) (KMcAuliffe)* 2-8-8v(3) JStack(5) (lw: dwlt: r.o fnl f: nrst fin)....1¾ **3**
32719 Meeting Point **(55)***(59) (MrsMReveley)* 2-8-11b KDarley(7) (lw: dwlt: hrd rdn ½-wy: styd on: nvr able to chal) ....s.h **4**
367014 Yougoa **(48)***(54) (MWEasterby)* 2-8-11b JQuinn(2) (led 2f: cl up tl wknd over 1f out) 1¾ **5**
346517 Madam Zando **(56)***(47) (JBalding)* 2-8-4b(7) JEdmunds(6) (prom: rdn & no imp fr ½-wy)....2 **6**
*3523*6 Tallulah Belle **(53)***(46) (NPLittmoden)* 2-8-11 TGMcLaughlin(4) (sn outpcd & bhd)....½ **7**
27734 Monkey Zanty (IRE) **(54)***(38) (JBerry)* 2-8-11 GCarter(9) (prom tl wknd fr ½-wy) 2½ **8**
346518 Fancy Clancy **(50)***(37) (MissLCSiddall)* 2-8-11 DeanMcKeown(8) (dwlt: n.d) ....nk **9**
29329 Maysimp (IRE) **(56)** *(BPJBaugh)* 2-8-4 (7) IonaWands(3) (b: sddle slipped & uns rdr after 1½f) .... **U**

7/4 Gracious Gretclo, **9/2** KATY-Q (IRE) (op 3/1), **6/1** Apartments Abroad (op 10/1), Meeting Point, **10/1** Monkey Zanty (IRE) (6/1-11/1), **14/1** Madam Zando, **16/1** Yougoa, **25/1** Tallulah Belle, Maysimp (IRE), **33/1** Fancy Clancy, CSF £11.96 TOTE £4.80: £2.40 £1.20 £1.80 (£6.70) Trio £8.00 OWNER Lord Zetland (RIPON) BRED Mrs S. O'Riordan 10 Rn
61.0 secs (3.30) SF: 22/17/12/11/6/-/-/-/-/-

3741
LINKS CLAIMING STKS (3-Y.O+) (Class F) £2,843.00 (£798.00: £389.00)
1m 7f 16y Stalls: High GOING minus 0.19 sec per fur (GF) 2-30 (2-30)

1555* **Elementary (76)***(82) (NJHWalker)* 12-9-7 (3) JStack(6) (hld up: hdwy on bit ent st: slt ld over 2f out: r.o) ....— **1**
3296* Brodessa **(61)***(74)*(Fav)*(MrsMReveley)* 9-9-4 KDarley(2) (lw: a.p: jnd ldr 6f out: led appr st tl over 2f out: kpt on)....1½ **2**
36353 Sea Victor **(74)***(77) (JLHarris)* 3-8-13 JWeaver(7) (chsd ldrs: effrt 3f out: one pce)....3 **3**
36277 Hong Kong Designer **(50)***(53) (SGNorton)* 3-8-5 TWilliams(5) (prom: effrt ent st: sn outpcd)..15 **4**
20207 Battery Boy **(38)***(30) (CWCElsey)* 3-8-3b JQuinn(4) (led tl hdd appr st: sn wknd) 20 **5**
25456 Sallyoreally (IRE) **(37)***(18) (WStorey)* 4-8-9 JFanning(3) (hld up: wl outpcd fnl 3f) 7 **6**

11/8 Brodessa, **2/1** ELEMENTARY, **7/2** Sea Victor, **9/1** Hong Kong Designer, **25/1** Battery Boy, **50/1** Sallyoreally (IRE), CSF £5.04 TOTE £2.90: £2.00 £1.50 (£2.30) OWNER Mr Paul Green (WANTAGE) BRED Ballymaglassan Stud 6 Rn 3m 20.6 (10.10) SF: 40/32/24/-/-/-
WEIGHT FOR AGE 3yo-11lb

3742
SEPTEMBER HOLIDAY NURSERY H'CAP (0-75) (2-Y.O) (Class E) £3,113.00 (£944.00: £462.00: £221.00)
5f Stalls: High GOING minus 0.19 sec per fur (GF) 3-00 (3-05)

36234 **Lunar Mist (62)***(66+)*(Fav)*(MartynMeade)* 2-8-8 VSlattery(4) (lw: cl up: led 2f out: shkn up & qcknd clr fnl f) ....— **1**
34003 Amy Leigh (IRE) **(72)***(63) (CaptJWilson)* 2-9-4 KDarley(5) (hdwy ½-wy: styd on fnl f: no ch w wnr) 4 **2**
27736 Superfrills **(52)***(42) (MissLCSiddall)* 2-7-12 TWilliams(1) (in tch: kpt on fnl f: no imp) ....nk **3**

3253[3] Doubleyoubeay **(58)***(45) (JBerry)* 2-8-4 GCarter(3) (bhd tl styd on wl fnl f)....1 4
2783[3] Born A Lady **(75)***(60) (NPLittmoden)* 2-9-7 TGMcLaughlin(6) (in tch: rdn ½-wy: no imp)....½ 5
3623[14] Peters Folly **(49)***(30) (JLEyre)* 2-7-4 (5)ow2 MBaird(7) (cl up: led after 1½f to 2f out: wknd)....¾ 6
3468* Boffy (IRE) **(72)***(55) (BPJBaugh)* 2-8-11 (7) IonaWands(8) (bhd: hdwy ½-wy: wknd fnl f)....s.h 7
3415[2] April's Joy **(58)***(35) (JNorton)* 2-8-4 DaleGibson(2) (led over 1f: wl outpcd fr ½-wy)....2 8

LONG HANDICAP Peters Folly 7-6

5/2 LUNAR MIST, **7/2** Amy Leigh (IRE), **4/1** Boffy (IRE), **7/1** April's Joy, **10/1** Born A Lady, Peters Folly (tchd 16/1), **14/1** Doubleyoubeay (op 8/1), **50/1** Superfrills, CSF £10.54 CT £273.72 TOTE £2.90: £1.20 £1.50 £6.00 (£5.30) OWNER Ladyswood Racing Club (MALMESBURY) BRED T. Barratt 8 Rn

59.8 secs (2.10) SF: 40/37/16/19/34/4/29/9

3743

EDINBURGH FESTIVAL H'CAP (0-70) (3-Y.O+) (Class E) £3,308.00 (£1,004.00: £492.00: £236.00)
1m 4f 31y Stalls: High GOING minus 0.19 sec per fur (GF) 3-30 (3-31)

3445[8] **Chantry Beath (47)***(60) (CWThornton)* 4-8-6 DeanMcKeown(5) (a.p: led over 2f out: sn clr)....— 1
2147[6] Tremendisto **(51)***(59) (CaptJWilson)* 5-8-10 VSlattery(7) (chsd ldrs: effrt over 2f out: one pce)....3½ 2
3710[17] Achilles Heel **(40)***(47) (CNAllen)* 4-7-8 (5) MBaird(15) (lw: bhd tl hdwy over 2f out: sn wknd)..1¼ 3
3189[14] North Ardar **(60)***(65) (MrsMReveley)* 5-8-12 (7) SCopp(14) (lost pl appr st: c wd & hdwy over 2f out: rdn & nt qckn appr fnl f)....1 4
3719[7] Keep Battling **(43)***(45) (JSGoldie)* 5-8-2 ow3 GCarter(8) (styd on fnl 3f: nvr rchd ldrs)....½ 5
3076[6] Oleron **(42)***(47) (JNorton)* 3-7-7 JLowe(16) (prom: effrt ent st: one pce fnl 2f)....hd 6
3412[5] Master Hyde (USA) **(58)***(62) (WStorey)* 6-8-12 (5) RHavlin(4) (hld up: effrt on outside over 2f out: nvr able to chal)....¾ 7
3272* Pine Essence (USA) **(57)***(59) (JLEyre)* 4-9-2 TWilliams(10) (sme hdwy 3f out: no imp)....1¼ 8
3311* Lord Advocate **(42)***(34) (DANolan)* 7-8-1bow7 VHalliday(6) (led tl hdd & wknd over 3f out)....2½ 9
3572[3] Masuri Kabisa (USA) **(39)***(37)*(Fav)*(HJCollingridge)* 4-7-12v JQuinn(13) (hdwy ½-wy: sn in tch: one pce fnl 2f)....½ 10
3665[10] Jubran (USA) **(62)***(58) (MJohnston)* 9-9-7 JWeaver(3) (lw: nvr nr ldrs)....1¾ 11
1205[6] Stormless **(37)***(31) (PMonteith)* 4-7-7 (3)ow1 DarrenMoffatt(9) (chsd lds tl wknd fnl 3f)....nk 12
2921[6] Goodbye Millie **(45)***(39) (JLEyre)* 5-8-4v RLappin(11) (sn pushed along: hdwy appr st: sn wknd)....1¼ 13
3500[11] Big Pat **(69)***(63) (KMcAuliffe)* 6-9-11 (3) JStack(12) (s.s: a bhd)....s.h 14
3189[15] Our Main Man **(55)***(41) (RMWhitaker)* 5-9-0 DaleGibson(1) (cl up: led over 3f out tl over 2f out: sn wknd)....6 15

LONG HANDICAP Oleron 7-4

5/1 Masuri Kabisa (USA), **6/1** North Ardar, Big Pat, **13/2** CHANTRY BEATH, **8/1** Master Hyde (USA), **9/1** Achilles Heel, **10/1** Jubran (USA), **12/1** Lord Advocate, Keep Battling, Pine Essence (USA), **16/1** Our Main Man, **20/1** Goodbye Millie, Tremendisto, **50/1** Oleron, Stormless, CSF £121.39 CT £1,086.54 TOTE £10.20: £2.40 £7.30 £3.30 (£87.90) Trio £258.00 OWNER Racegoers Club Spigot Lodge Owners Group (MIDDLEHAM) BRED Mrs Josphine Kirk Scott 15 Rn

2m 40.0 (7.50) SF: 27/26/14/32/12/6/29/26/1/4/25/-/6/30/8

WEIGHT FOR AGE 3yo-8lb

3744

PINKIE CLAIMING STKS (2-Y.O) (Class F) £2,983.00 (£838.00: £409.00)
7f 15y Stalls: High GOING minus 0.19 sec per fur (GF) 4-00 (4-04)

3415[6] **Princess Pamgaddy (48)***(64) (JBerry)* 2-7-13 JQuinn(12) (lw: hdwy 3f out: led ins fnl f: r.o)....— 1
3566[5] Madonna da Rossi **(57)***(61)*(Fav)*(SirMarkPrescott)* 2-8-0 CNutter(10) (lw: cl up: led over 2f out tl ins fnl f: no ex)....1¾ 2
3666[13] Dancing Dot (IRE) *(66) (MissLAPerratt)* 2-8-7 JLowe(13) (hdwy 3f out: styd on: nrst fin)....1 3
2294[5] In A Tizzy **(40)***(55) (PCHaslam)* 2-7-10 DaleGibson(5) (bhd tl styd on fnl 3f: nrst fin)....hd 4
3528[12] Swing Mania (IRE) **(49)***(59) (SGNorton)* 2-8-3 VHalliday(11) (chsd ldrs: hmpd appr st: hdwy 3f out: hrd rdn & one pce appr fnl f)....1 5
3525[7] Craigmore Magic (USA) **(55)***(51) (MissMKMilligan)* 2-8-8 JFanning(8) (chsd ldrs tl wknd fnl 2½f)....6 6
3120[4] Autofyr *(44) (JSWainwright)* 2-8-7 MBirch(7) (nvr trbld ldrs)....2½ 7
3546[17] Silent Soprano **(54)***(36) (DenysSmith)* 2-8-3 TWilliams(6) (chsd ldrs tl wknd fnl 2f)....2 8
2965[5] Copper Bright **(39)***(35) (PCHaslam)* 2-8-0 (3) JStack(4) (prom over 4f)....nk 9
1213[2] Merlin's Honour **(43)***(37) (PCHaslam)* 2-8-7 JWeaver(1) (led tl hdd & wknd over 2f out)....1 10

3721[13] Concert Party (IRE) **(50)***(22)* *(DWChapman)* 2-7-11 (3) DMoffatt(9) (bdly hmpd appr st: no ch after) 3½ 11
Eastern Sunrise *(23)* *(MrsMReveley)* 2-8-8 DeanMcKeown(3) (w'like: bkwd: a bhd) 3 12
3713[11] Lennox Lady *(RMMcKellar)* 2-7-12 (5) MBaird(2) (b.hind: sn wl bhd) 13 13
3528[3] Efipetite **(48)** *(NBycroft)* 2-8-7 GCarter(14) (s.s: sn wl t.o & virtually p.u) ....dist 14

9/4 Madonna da Rossi, **3/1** Silent Soprano, **11/2** Merlin's Honour, **12/1** Concert Party (IRE), PRINCESS PAMGADDY, Copper Bright (op 7/1), **14/1** Efipetite, Swing Mania (IRE), **16/1** Craigmore Magic (USA), **25/1** In A Tizzy, Eastern Sunrise, **33/1** Dancing Dot (IRE), Autofyr, **100/1** Lennox Lady, CSF £38.82 TOTE £12.90: £4.40 £1.50 £8.70 (£20.30) Trio £214.60; £244.86 to 19/9/95 OWNER Theobalds Stud (COCKERHAM) BRED K. Panos 14 Rn
1m 31.9 (5.90) SF: 2/-/4/-/-/-/-/-/-/-/-/-/-/-

3745 HONEST TOUN MAIDEN H'CAP (0-60) (3-Y.O+) (Class F) £2,918.00 (£884.00: £432.00: £206.00) 7f 15y Stalls: High GOING minus 0.19 sec (GF) 4-30 (4-32)

2377[5] **Friar Street (IRE) (43)***(54)* *(EJAlston)* 5-9-8 SDWilliams(9) (mde all: hld on wl fnl f) ....— 1
3475[4] Bedazzle **(32)***(41)* *(MBrittain)* 4-8-11 JLowe(8) (in tch: hdwy over 2f out: ev ch ins fnl f: nt qckn towards fin) ....¾ 2
3370[2] Matisse **(41)***(46)* *(JDBethell)* 4-9-6 JWeaver(6) (lw: hdwy over 3f out: kpt on wl fnl f: nrst fin) 1¾ 3
3305[2] Chalky Dancer **(43)***(48)*(Fav)*(HJCollingridge)* 3-9-4 JQuinn(10) (lw: chsd ldrs: rdn over 2f out: one pce appr fnl f) ....nk 4
3493[11] Reed My Lips (IRE) **(34)***(33)* *(BPJBaugh)* 4-8-13 RLappin(13) (lw: styd on fnl 3f: nrst fin) 2½ 5
3719[8] Teejay'n'aitch (IRE) **(45)***(44)* *(JSGoldie)* 3-9-6 VHalliday(3) (lw: styd on fnl 3f: nrst fin) ....s.h 6
3508[8] Chloella **(40)***(38)* *(CBBBooth)* 3-9-1 SMorris(11) (chsd ldrs: rdn 3f out: one pce) ....½ 7
1598[7] Percy Parrot **(41)***(33)* *(RMWhitaker)* 3-9-2 MBirch(4) (nvr trbld ldrs) 2½ 8
3431[6] Delightful Dancer (IRE) **(48)***(39)* *(JNorton)* 3-9-9 DaleGibson(5) (prom: effrt over 2f out: one pce) ....½ 9
Hadi (IRE) **(33)***(16)* *(WStorey)* 4-8-12 JFanning(14) (in tch: hmpd 2f out: n.d after) 3½ 10
2968[6] Thwaab **(49)***(32)* *(FWatson)* 3-9-10 GCarter(7) (lw: n.d) ....s.h 11
3514[8] Memory's Music **(47)***(24)* *(IABalding)* 3-9-8v DeanMcKeown(1) (lw: chsd ldrs tl wknd qckly fnl 3f) 2½ 12
3667[23] Strathtore Dream (IRE) **(42)***(18)* *(MissLAPerratt)* 4-9-7 TWilliams(2) (bhd: sme hdwy whn hmpd 2f out: n.d) ....¾ 13

6/4 Chalky Dancer, **9/2** Matisse, **7/1** Bedazzle, **8/1** Thwaab, **12/1** Teejay'n'aitch (IRE), **14/1** FRIAR STREET (IRE), Reed My Lips (IRE), **16/1** Memory's Music, **20/1** Chloella, Strathtore Dream (IRE), **33/1** Percy Parrot, Delightful Dancer (IRE), **50/1** Hadi (IRE), CSF £103.99 CT £475.94 TOTE £22.00: £3.70 £2.60 £1.40 (£64.60) Trio £121.90 OWNER Mrs S. Y. Alston (PRESTON) BRED William Flood 13 Rn 1m 30.7 (4.70) SF: 36/23/28/26/15/22/16/11/17/-/10/2/-
WEIGHT FOR AGE 3yo-4lb

T/Plpt: £170.30 (85.52 Tckts). T/Qdpt: £17.80 (1.7 Tckts). AA

3530-LEICESTER (R-H)
Monday September 18th (Soft)
WEATHER: sunny WIND: fresh half against

3746 KEGWORTH CONDITIONS STKS (2-Y.O) (Class C) £5,580.80 (£2,067.20: £993.60: £408.00: £164.00: £66.40) 7f 9y Stalls: Low GOING: 0.40 sec per fur (GS) 2-15 (2-16)

3560[2] **Tria Kemata (100)***(84)* *(JLDunlop)* 2-8-11 PatEddery(5) (lw: plld hrd: mde all centre: rdn over 1f out: r.o wl) ....— 1
3104* Quakers Field *(86)* *(GLMoore)* 2-9-2 SWhitworth(8) (lw: hld up: hdwy 2f out: rdn & r.o wl fnl f) 1¼ 2
3216[3] Dismissed (USA) *(86)* *(PFICole)* 2-9-2 TQuinn(1) (hld up: hdwy over 2f out: rdn appr fnl f: r.o nr fin) ....s.h 3
2912[2] Wilawander *(79)*(Fav)*(BWHills)* 2-8-11 WRSwinburn(3) (led stands' side: rdn 2f out: no ex ins fnl f) 1 4
3141[4] Believe Me **(96)***(79)* *(RHannon)* 2-8-9 (5) DaneO'Neil(7) (lw: chsd wnr: rdn 2f out: one pce appr fnl f) 1¼ 5
3441* Bullfinch *(73)* *(PTWalwyn)* 2-9-0 RCochrane(2) (hld up pllng hrd: effrt wl over 1f out: no imp) 2½ 6
Gee Gee Tee *(48)* *(JAkehurst)* 2-8-11 WNewnes(6) (lt-f: unf: bkwd: b: a in rr: t.o) 10 7
3606[8] Kala Sunrise **(79)***(41)* *(CSmith)* 2-9-0 WWoods(4) (lw: prom stands' side over 4f: sn wknd: t.o) 4 8

5/2 Wilawander, **11/4** Bullfinch (2/1-3/1), **7/2** Dismissed (USA) (5/2-4/1), **4/1** TRIA KEMATA (op 6/1), **12/1** Quakers Field, **14/1** Believe Me, **50/1** Kala Sunrise, **66/1** Gee Gee Tee, CSF £43.03 TOTE £5.10: £1.50 £3.90 £1.30 (£23.50) OWNER Hesmonds Stud (ARUNDEL) BRED Hesmonds Stud Ltd 8 Rn
1m 30.6 (8.10) SF: 32/34/34/27/27/21/-/-

3747 GOLDEN HAND (S) STKS (3-Y.O) (Class G) £2,959.80 (£822.80: £395.40)
1m 1f 218y Stalls: Low GOING: 0.40 sec per fur (GS) 2-45 (2-46)

3429[8] **Mill Dancer (IRE) (40)***(63) (EJAlston)* 3-8-6 KFallon(6) (plld hrd: mde virtually all: rdn & hld on wl fnl f) ....— 1
3111[5] Born To Be Wild *(61) (WGMTurner)* 3-8-3 (3) PMcCabe(4) (hld up: hdwy over 3f out: chsd wnr fnl 2f: rdn & kpt on) 1¼ 2
3635[7] Birthday Boy (IRE) **(56)***(60)*(Fav)*(RHannon)* 3-8-6b(5) DaneO'Neill(10) (lw: hld up: hdwy over 3f out: rdn & one pce fnl f) 4 3
2922[9] Kristal Breeze **(45)***(50) (WRMuir)* 3-8-6 DHarrison(14) (hdwy over 2f out: hrd rdn bel dist: styd on) 3 4
3383[7] Fairelaine **(53)***(42) (APJarvis)* 3-8-6 JTate(19) (prom: 3rd st: rdn 2f out: sn btn) 5 5
3537[8] Noble Canonire **(49)***(41) (NPLittmoden)* 3-8-6 MFenton(1) (swtg: prom tl lost pl ent st: styd on again fnl 2f) ....½ 6
2296[4] Saterne Lady **(54)***(39) (PFICole)* 3-8-6 TQuinn(15) (prom: 2nd st: rdn & wknd over 1f out) ...1¼ 7
3426[4] Pacific Girl (IRE) **(51)***(34) (BPalling)* 3-8-6 TSprake(16) (hld up pllng hrd: nvr trbld ldrs).......3 8
3515[10] Chastleton **(30)***(30) (MRChannon)* 3-8-6 CandyMorris(2) (chsd ldrs: 6th st: wknd over 2f out) 2½ 9
2812[5] Ruddigore **(44)***(34) (KRBurke)* 3-8-11 RCochrane(7) (chsd ldrs: 5th st: rdn & wknd 2f out) .....¾ 10
2141[11] Knotty Scot **(30)***(7) (JJBridger)* 3-8-6 NAdams(5) (b: a bhd: t.o) 14 11
3504[11] Katy Koo *(7) (PJBevan)* 3-8-6 NCarlisle(13) (a bhd: t.o) ....s.h 12
2650[3] Alpine Storm (IRE) **(28)***(1) (MDIUsher)* 3-7-13b(7) CAdamson(3) (racd wd: w wnr: 4th st: wknd over 3f out: t.o) 3½ 13
3514[13] Port Hedland **(45)** *(MMcCormack)* 3-8-6 GDuffield(11) (lw: in tch: 7th st: wknd 3f out: t.o) ....½ 14
3099[16] Nebrangus (IRE) **(23)** *(NBycroft)* 3-8-11 SMaloney(8) (plld hrd: a bhd: t.o) 15 15
1691[14] Morning Master *(RMFlower)* 3-8-11b AMorris(18) (nvr plcd to chal: t.o) 1¼ 16
3504[13] Legal Brief **(30)** *(JSWainwright)* 3-8-11 LCharnock(12) (mid div tl wknd over 4f out: t.o).......6 17

4/1 Birthday Boy (IRE), **5/1** Saterne Lady, Fairelaine, **6/1** MILL DANCER (IRE) (op 12/1), **13/2** Pacific Girl (IRE), **12/1** Ruddigore, **16/1** Born To Be Wild, **20/1** Chastleton, Kristal Breeze, Alpine Storm (IRE), **25/1** Noble Canonire, Port Hedland, **50/1** Katy Koo, Knotty Scot, Nebrangus (IRE), Morning Master, Legal Brief, CSF £88.67 TOTE £7.50: £2.00 £3.70 £2.20 (£34.50) Trio £79.30 OWNER Mrs Dot Jones (PRESTON) BRED William Flood 17 Rn
2m 14.0 (11.30) SF: 31/29/28/18/10/9/7/2/-/2/-/-/-/-/-/-/-
Bt in 11,000 gns Birthday Boy (IRE) clmd DPearson £6,000 Born To Be Wild clmd CBarnes £6,000

3748 LEICESTER SOUND H'CAP (0-80) (3-Y.O+) (Class D) £4,813.90 (£1,445.20: £696.60: £322.30)
5f 2y Stalls: Low GOING: 0.40 sec per fur (GS) 3-15 (3-18)

3624[10] **Followmegirls (45)***(56) (MrsALMKing)* 6-7-8bow1 AGarth(10) (s.i.s: hdwy 2f out: led ins fnl f: edgd rt: r.o strly).......— 1
3706[13] Leigh Crofter **(68)***(75) (PDCundell)* 6-9-3b WNewnes(12) (hdwy over 1f out: rdn & r.o wl ins fnl f) 1½ 2
3622* Chadwell Hall **(55)***(61)*(Fav)*(SRBowring)* 4-7-13b(5) 7x CTeague(18) (lw: led over 2f out tl ins fnl f: no ex) ....½ 3
3597[2] Lady Sheriff **(79)***(83) (MWEasterby)* 4-9-9b(5) PFessey(16) (chsd ldrs: efftrt & hung rt 2f out: btn whn squeezed for room ins fnl f) ....½ 4
3597[10] Kung Frode **(62)***(65) (BAMcMahon)* 3-8-6 (3) SSanders(11) (hdwy 2f out: rdn & r.o wl ins fnl f).......nk 5
1604[5] Palo Blanco **(73)***(75) (TDBarron)* 4-9-8 WRyan(17) (hmpd s: hdwy bel dist: nrst fin).......nk 6
3632[2] Halbert **(60)***(57) (MRChannon)* 6-8-2v(7) DSweeney(14) (w ldrs: rdn & one pce appr fnl f) 1¾ 7
3554[6] Insider Trader **(74)***(64) (RGuest)* 4-9-9b GDuffield(9) (b: led to ½-wy: rdn & wknd over 1f out) 2 8
3442[14] Rotherfield Park (IRE) **(46)***(34) (CSmith)* 3-7-7 NAdams(24) (prom: rdn over 1f out: eased whn btn fnl f) ....¾ 9
3615[23] Bajan Rose **(75)***(62) (MBlanshard)* 3-9-8 KFallon(15) (wnt rt s: sn prom centre: no hdwy fnl 2f) ....nk 10
3622[2] Endless Wave **(57)***(42) (MBell)* 3-8-4 MFenton(19) (lw: chsd ldrs: effrt 2f out: no imp) ....½ 11
3554[8] Bashful Brave **(71)***(56) (JWPayne)* 4-9-6 MTebbutt(13) (lw: nvr nr to chal) ....hd 12
3597[7] Shadow Jury **(70)***(49) (DWChapman)* 5-9-5b LCharnock(23) (chsd ldrs far side over 3f) 1¾ 13

3442[17] Nordico Princess **(69)***(45) (MBrittain)* 4-9-4 RCochrane(22) (lw: b.off fore: spd to ½-wy) 1 **14**
3622[4] The Fed **(49)***(23) (RMWhitaker)* 5-7-12v JFEgan(3) (spd stands' side 3f) ....¾ **15**
3357[5] Miss Movie World **(57)***(23) (MDHammond)* 6-7-13 (7) DHayden(8) (n.d) 2½ **16**
2686[8] Royal Carlton (IRE) **(66)***(19) (RAkehurst)* 3-8-13 TQuinn(6) (outpcd) 4 **17**
3624[15] Lugana Vision **(53)***(2) (RHarris)* 3-8-0 StephenDavies(4) (lw: a in rr) 1¼ **18**
3554[2] Miami Banker **(55)** *(WRMuir)* 9-8-4b GBardwell(5) (spd stands' side 3f) 1¼ **19**
3624[23] Twice in Bundoran (IRE) **(52)** *(PSFelgate)* 4-8-1 AMackay(20) (m.n.s) ....hd **20**
3624[22] Macaroon Lady **(44)** *(NBycroft)* 4-7-7 NKennedy(21) (dwlt: a bhd) 2 **21**
3597[13] Here Comes a Star **(72)***(2) (JMCarr)* 7-9-7 ACulhane(7) (a bhd) 2½ **22**
3242[9] Prime Match (IRE) **(75)** *(PWHarris)* 3-9-8 PatEddery(1) (spd stands' side 3f: sn wknd) 1½ **23**

LONG HANDICAP Rotherfield Park (IRE) 7-0 Macaroon Lady 7-3

100/30 Chadwell Hall, **7/1** Endless Wave (4/1-8/1), Miami Banker, **9/1** Kung Frode (14/1-8/1), **12/1** Lady Sheriff, Leigh Crofter, **14/1** Palo Blanco, Halbert, Nordico Princess, The Fed, **16/1** Bashful Brave, Prime Match (IRE), Shadow Jury, Twice in Bundoran (IRE), Bajan Rose, Insider Trader, Royal Carlton (IRE), **20/1** FOLLOWMEGIRLS, Miss Movie World, Here Comes a Star, **25/1** Lugana Vision, **50/1** Macaroon Lady, Rotherfield Park (IRE), CSF £269.31 CT £947.24 TOTE £39.60: £7.20 £1.80 £2.30 £4.90 (£123.20) Trio £832.90 OWNER Exors of the late Mr J Martin (STRATFORD-UPON-A) BRED Haddon Stud 23 Rn

62.9 secs (4.40) SF: 37/56/42/64/44/56/38/45/13/41/21/37/30/26/4/4/-/-/-/-/-/-/-

WEIGHT FOR AGE 3yo-2lb

3749 MARION SHAW NURSERY H'CAP (0-75) (2-Y.O) (Class E) £4,500.00 (£1,350.00: £650.00: £300.00)

5f 218y Stalls: Low GOING: 0.40 sec per fur (GS) 3-45 (3-47)

3180[7] **Warming Trends (65)***(69) (SirMarkPrescott)* 2-9-0 GDuffield(13) (hld up: hdwy bel dist: hrd rdn to ld wl ins fnl f) ....— **1**
2542[3] Nilgiri Hills (IRE) **(72)***(75)*(Fav)*(JLDunlop)* 2-9-7 WCarson(12) (a.p: rdn to ld ent fnl f: hdd & no ex nr fin) ....nk **2**
3203[4] Bold Enough **(63)***(57) (BWHills)* 2-8-12 TQuinn(3) (lw: hdwy over 1f out: fin wl) 3½ **3**
3309[2] Magic Lake **(52)***(43) (EJAlston)* 2-8-1 StephenDavies(5) (a.p: ev ch over 1f out: one pce fnl f) 1 **4**
3290[6] Red Acuisle (IRE) **(57)***(47) (MBell)* 2-8-6 MFenton(10) (lw: hld up: hdwy bel dist: nt rch ldrs) ....½ **5**
3612[3] Mr Speaker (IRE) **(67)***(57) (CFWall)* 2-9-2 NCarlisle(8) (lw: hdwy ½-wy: ev ch tl rdn & unable qckn ins fnl f) ....s.h **6**
3623[6] Dil Dil **(71)***(58) (RHannon)* 2-9-1 (5) DaneO'Neill(15) (lw: rdn & effrt 2f out: r.o fnl f) 1 **7**
3623[10] Croeso Cynnes **(66)***(45) (BPalling)* 2-9-1 TSprake(11) (disp ld: ev ch tl wknd over 1f out: eased whn btn bel dist) 3 **8**
3233[10] Lindas Delight **(54)***(32) (JSMoore)* 2-8-3 JFEgan(7) (chsd ldrs stands' side: nvr able to chal) ....½ **9**
3019[10] Northern Clan **(51)***(28) (MWEasterby)* 2-8-0 LCharnock(9) (nvr trbld ldrs) ....hd **10**
3012[8] Grey Legend **(66)***(40) (RMFlower)* 2-9-1 DBiggs(14) (w ldrs: hrd rdn 2f out: sn wknd)...........1¼ **11**
3405[5] Pharaoh's Joy **(69)***(43) (JWPayne)* 2-9-4 RCochrane(17) (led over 1f: led wl over 1f out tl ent fnl f: wknd) ....s.h **12**
3423[5] My Kind **(61)***(34) (KMcAuliffe)* 2-8-10 DHarrison(18) (b: gd hdwy over 2f out: wknd ins fnl f) ....½ **13**
3260[8] Maraschino **(60)***(31) (MJHeaton-Ellis)* 2-8-9 WNewnes(6) (m.n.s) ....½ **14**
3290[2] Rothley Imp (IRE) **(58)***(13) (JWharton)* 2-8-7 PRobinson(16) (a in rr)..6 **15**
3528[5] Northern Saga (IRE) **(53)***(6) (AndrewTurnell)* 2-8-2 NAdams(1) (prom stands' side over 3f) 1 **16**
3568[8] Foreman **(59)***(7) (WAO'Gorman)* 2-8-8b EmmaO'Gorman(20) (lw: led over 2f out tl wl over 1f out: sn rdn & wknd) 1¾ **17**
2523[9] Incapol **(70)***(13) (MJRyan)* 2-9-5 AClark(22) (lw: a bhd) 2 **18**
2958[3] Serif (USA) **(64)***(1)*(Fav)*(JHMGosden)* 2-8-13 GHind(19) (led over 4f out tl over 2f out: sn lost tch) 2 **19**
3558[7] Mystic Dawn **(68)** *(SDow)* 2-9-3 WRyan(21) (lw: a bhd)..2½ **20**
3289[9] Classic Victory **(72)** *(SCWilliams)* 2-9-7 AMackay(2) (lw: prom stands' side over 3f: sn lost tch: t.o) 5 **21**

6/1 Nilgiri Hills (IRE), Serif (USA), **8/1** Mr Speaker (IRE), **10/1** Foreman, WARMING TRENDS, **11/1** Dil Dil, **12/1** Rothley Imp (IRE), **14/1** Red Acuisle (IRE), My Kind, Magic Lake, Pharaoh's Joy, Croeso Cynnes, Incapol, **16/1** Grey Legend, Northern Clan, Mystic Dawn, Bold Enough, **20/1** Classic Victory, **25/1** Lindas Delight, Northern Saga (IRE), **33/1** Maraschino, CSF £75.87 CT £932.51 TOTE £17.40: £3.30 £1.40 £5.60 £1.40 (£75.00) Trio £339.20 OWNER Hesmonds Stud (NEWMARKET) BRED Hesmonds Stud Ltd 21 Rn

1m 16.1 (6.10) SF: 45/51/33/19/23/33/34/21/8/4/16/19/10/7/-/-/-/-/-/-/-

3750 CHARNWOOD CLAIMING STKS (3 & 4-Y.O) (Class F) £3,451.40 (£960.40: £462.20) **5f 218y** Stalls: Low GOING: 0.40 sec per fur (GS) 4-15 (4-16)

3615[20] **Anzio (IRE) (70)***(66) (BAPearce)* 4-8-10b TIves(10) (b: led after 1f: clr over 1f out: hld on wl) .... — **1**
3545[8] Ffynone (IRE) **(73)***(66) (RHannon)* 3-8-5 (5) DaneO'Neill(5) (hdwy wl over 1f out: hung rt & r.o wl ins fnl f) 1¼ **2**
3637[16] Delight of Dawn **(72)***(64) (KTIvory)* 3-8-3 (7) CScally(1) (racd stands' side: gd hdwy over 1f out: fin wl) .... ½ **3**
3632[7] King Rambo **(64)***(53) (RHollinshead)* 4-8-2 WRyan(21) (hld up: hdwy over 2f out: ev ch over 1f out: rdn & one pce fnl f) .... nk **4**
3467[5] Bold Aristocrat (IRE) **(38)***(47) (RHollinshead)* 4-7-10 (7)ow1 FLynch(9) (hdwy 2f out: nt rch ldrs) 2 **5**
2879[5] Sweet Mate **(44)***(55) (SRBowring)* 3-8-2b(5) CTeague(19) (prom: rdn & hmpd over 2f out: styd on again ins fnl f) .... d.h **5**
Relentless (IRE) *(62) (BAMcMahon)* 3-8-12 (3) SSanders(6) (in tch: no hdwy fnl 2f) .... ½ **7**
2301[7] Havana Miss **(38)***(42) (BPalling)* 3-8-2 TSprake(12) (prom: hrd rdn 2f out: sn wknd) 2½ **8**
2628[2] Cheerful Groom (IRE) **(43)***(35) (JMackie)* 4-8-2 GHind(2) (lw: stdd s: hdwy ½-wy: wknd over 1f out) 1½ **9**
3534[18] Penny's Wishing **(62)***(41) (JPLeigh)* 3-8-6 KFallon(17) (lw: led 1f: rdn & wknd bel dist) .... nk **10**
3508[11] Undawaterscubadiva **(28)***(40) (MPBielby)* 3-8-4 (3) PMcCabe(15) (lw: bhd fnl 2f) 1 **11**
3451[6] Gallows Corner (IRE) **(82)***(51) (RHannon)* 3-9-4 TQuinn(16) (lw: chsd ldrs tl wknd over 1f out: eased whn btn) .... s.h **12**
3365[2] Non Dimenticar Me (IRE) **(65)***(31)*(Fav)*(SirMarkPrescott)* 3-8-2 GDuffield(7) (rdn 2f out: no imp) 1¼ **13**
3372[6] Cats Bottom **(60)***(29) (DJSCosgrove)* 3-7-11b(5) AWhelan(4) (prom stands' side over 3f) .... ¾ **14**
2337[6] Wendals Touch *(36) (RMFlower)* 4-8-13 AMorris(13) (lw: a in rr) .... nk **15**
3508[10] Young Ben (IRE) **(48)***(25) (JSWainwright)* 3-8-3 LCharnock(11) (m.n.s) 1½ **16**
3365[5] Baileys Sunset (IRE) **(61)***(21) (MJohnston)* 3-7-13 JFEgan(20) (lw: spd to ½-wy: sn rdn & wknd) .... s.h **17**
Desert Water (IRE) *(25) (JJBridger)* 3-9-5 PRobinson(14) (lengthy: bkwd: dwlt: a bhd: t.o) 6 **18**
2766[8] Great Bear **(85)** *(DWChapman)* 3-9-5 ACulhane(22) (s.s: a wl bhd: t.o) 25 **19**

5/1 Non Dimenticar Me (IRE), **11/2** Gallows Corner (IRE), **13/2** Baileys Sunset (IRE), **8/1** Cats Bottom, **10/1** ANZIO (IRE), King Rambo, Delight of Dawn, **12/1** Ffynone (IRE), Great Bear, **16/1** Bold Aristocrat (IRE), Young Ben (IRE), **20/1** Cheerful Groom (IRE), Sweet Mate, Penny's Wishing, **25/1** Relentless (IRE), Desert Water (IRE), Havana Miss, **50/1** Wendals Touch, Undawaterscubadiva, CSF £125.94 TOTE £12.70: £4.00 £5.70 £5.40 (£51.50) Trio £245.10; £113.97 to 19/9/95 OWNER Mr Richard Gray (LIMPSFIELD) BRED Rathduff Stud 19 Rn
1m 16.6 (6.60) SF: 34/31/29/21/15/20/27/7/3/6/5/16/-/-/4/-/-/-/-
WEIGHT FOR AGE 3yo-3lb

3751 HIGHFIELDS LIMITED STKS (0-60) (3-Y.O+) (Class F) £3,401.00 (£946.00: £455.00) **5f 218y** Stalls: Low GOING: 0.40 sec per fur (GS) 4-45 (4-50)

3418[3] **Maid O'Cannie (59)***(61)*(Fav)*(MWEasterby)* 4-8-9b SMaloney(10) (w ldr: led bel dist: rdn out) .... — **1**
3492[12] Petomi **(58)***(60) (SirMarkPrescott)* 3-8-6 GDuffield(16) (swtg: hld up: hdwy 2f out: hrd rdn & hung rt fnl f: r.o strly) .... ½ **2**
3615[10] Craigie Boy **(53)***(61) (NBycroft)* 5-9-0b KFallon(8) (a.p: effrt u.p appr fnl f: r.o) 1¼ **3**
3341[4] Blushing Grenadier (IRE) **(53)***(64) (MJFetherston-Godley)* 3-9-0b PatEddery(12) (hdwy fnl 2f: hrd rdn: r.o wl) .... hd **4**
3512[3] Ism **(55)***(65) (MajorWRHern)* 3-9-3 TSprake(19) (lw: hld up: hdwy over 2f out: rdn & one pce fnl f) .... ¾ **5**
3370[11] Rinus Manor (IRE) **(38)***(56) (EJAlston)* 4-9-0 MFenton(11) (swtg: hld up in tch: effrt 2f out: nt pce to chal) 1¼ **6**
3424[13] Superbit **(48)***(51) (BAMcMahon)* 3-8-11 (3) SSanders(4) (chsd ldrs: rdn over 2f out: no hdwy) ..3 **7**
3677[16] Green Golightly (USA) **(53)***(47) (DAWilson)* 4-9-0 RCochrane(13) (lw: in tch: rdn & one pce fnl 2f) .... nk **8**
3619[16] Scissor Ridge **(43)***(46) (JJBridger)* 3-8-11 GBardwell(14) (hdwy over 1f out: nvr nrr) .... nk **9**
3177[12] Pride of Hayling (IRE) **(55)***(44) (PRHedger)* 4-9-1 TQuinn(21) (lw: nvr plcd to chal) 1¼ **10**
3624[4] Beveled Edge **(46)***(33) (BPalling)* 6-8-4 (5) DaneO'Neill(9) (nvr trbld ldrs) 1¾ **11**
3542[2] Another Batchworth **(64)***(32) (SMellor)* 3-8-6 JFEgan(7) (led tl hdd & wknd bel dist) .... ½ **12**
3344[2] Chief's Lady **(52)***(28) (RHarris)* 3-8-6 StephenDavies(2) (outpcd fr ½-wy) 1½ **13**
2527[5] Sharp Holly (IRE) **(55)***(17) (JABennett)* 3-8-6 WNewnes(6) (lw: a bhd) 4 **14**
3629[6] Great Hall **(59)***(22) (PDCundell)* 6-9-3b DHarrison(15) (b.hind: a bhd & outpcd) 1 **15**
3457[18] Barik (IRE) **(60)***(22) (MrsASwinbank)* 5-9-3 NConnorton(18) (prom 4f) .... hd **16**

3681[14] Green Dollar **(51)***(17) (PHowling)* 12-9-0 MTebbutt(5) (nvr trbld ldrs)....¾ **17**
3179[7] Medieval Miss **(60)***(10) (MrsNMacauley)* 3-8-3 (3) SDrowne(3) (outpcd)....1 **18**
Strip Cartoon (IRE) **(47)** *(SRBowring)* 7-8-9b(5) CTeague(20) (bkwd: outpcd: t.o)....6 **19**
575[6] Raindeer Quest **(45)** *(CSmith)* 3-8-6 WWoods(1) (swtg: s.s: a bhd & outpcd: t.o)....9 **20**

15/8 MAID O'CANNIE, **6/1** Craigie Boy, **13/2** Petomi, **7/1** Blushing Grenadier (IRE), **11/1** Another Batchworth (6/1-12/1), **14/1** Great Hall (8/1-16/1), Beveled Edge, **16/1** Green Golightly (USA), Medieval Miss, Ism, Pride of Hayling (IRE), Chief's Lady, **25/1** Strip Cartoon (IRE), **33/1** Rinus Manor (IRE), Scissor Ridge, Barik (IRE), Green Dollar, Superbit, Sharp Holly (IRE), Raindeer Quest, CSF £16.47 TOTE £3.00: £1.80 £2.60 £1.60 (£10.60) Trio £26.90 OWNER Mrs E. Rhind (SHERIFF HUTTON) BRED E. Landi 20 Rn
1m 15.9 (5.90) SF: 43/39/43/43/44/38/30/29/25/26/15/11/7/-/4/4/-/-/-/-
WEIGHT FOR AGE 3yo-3lb

T/Jkpt: Not won; £49,846.79 to Nottingham 19/9/95. T/Plpt: £428.80 (44.61 Tckts). T/Qdpt: £102.80 (1.8 Tckts). IM

3553-EPSOM (L-H)
Tuesday September 19th (Good to soft, Soft patches becoming Soft)

WEATHER: overcast WIND: mod half bhd

3752 WALTER NIGHTINGALL MAIDEN STKS (2-Y.O) (Class D) £3,420.00 (£1,035.00: £505.00: £240.00)
1m 114y Stalls: Low GOING: 0.50 sec per fur (GS) 1-45 (1-46)

3536[2] **Do Not Disturb (USA) (84)***(84+)*(Fav)*(JLDunlop)* 2-9-0 PatEddery(7) (lw: hdwy over 4f out: 4th & c stands' side st: led over 1f out: easily)....— **1**
3345[3] Roman Gold (IRE) **(78)***(65) (RHannon)* 2-8-9 (5) DaneO'Neill(3) (lw: 2nd st: led 2f out tl over 1f out: unable qckn)....10 **2**
3155[2] Nosey Native *(62) (JPearce)* 2-9-0 GBardwell(2) (lost pl over 4f out: 5th st: rallied over 1f out: r.o one pce)....2 **3**
3398[2] East India (IRE) *(52) (RCharlton)* 2-9-0 JWeaver(9) (6th & c centre st: rdn over 3f out: nvr nr to chal)....5 **4**
3553[2] Laughing Buccaneer **(82)***(52) (BJMeehan)* 2-9-0b RHughes(6) (lw: led: clr over 6f out: hdd 2f out: wknd over 1f out)....hd **5**
424[11] Yellow Dragon (IRE) *(44) (MissGayKelleway)* 2-9-0 RCochrane(8) (c stands' side st: a bhd)..4 **6**
2912[12] Vague Spirit *(39) (CEBrittain)* 2-9-0 JQuinn(1) (lw: a bhd)....3 **7**
3436[9] Mon Pere *(1) (KMcAuliffe)* 2-9-0 DHarrison(4) (3rd st: wknd over 2f out)....20 **8**

7/4 DO NOT DISTURB (USA), **9/4** East India (IRE), **5/1** Nosey Native (3/1-11/2), **6/1** Roman Gold (IRE), **8/1** Laughing Buccaneer, **20/1** Yellow Dragon (IRE), **33/1** Vague Spirit, **40/1** Mon Pere, CSF £12.57 TOTE £2.70: £1.20 £1.50 £2.00 (£9.60) Trio £10.40 OWNER Eurolink Group Plc (ARUNDEL) BRED Helene Gonzalez 8 Rn 1m 51.63 (9.63) SF: 45/26/23/13/13/5/-/-

3753 STAFF INGHAM NURSERY H'CAP (0-85) (2-Y.O) (Class D) £3,452.50 (£1,045.00: £510.00: £242.50)
5f Stalls: High GOING: 0.30 sec per fur (G) 2-15 (2-16)

3335[2] **Miss Bigwig (78)***(84) (JBerry)* 2-9-1 (5) PFessey(5) (a.p: led 1f out: r.o wl)....— **1**
3727[4] Martara (IRE) **(66)***(66)*(Fav)*(MRChannon)* 2-8-8 RHughes(4) (a.p: led 2f out to 1f out: unable qckn)....2 **2**
3284[5] Wingnut (IRE) **(60)***(56) (GLewis)* 2-7-11 (5)ow1 AWhelan(1) (lw: outpcd: hdwy over 1f out: r.o)....¾ **3**
3568[4] Supreme Power **(79)***(75) (WRMuir)* 2-9-7b JWeaver(3) (lw: outpcd: hdwy fnl f: nvr nrr)....½ **4**
3567[2] Dande Flyer **(66)***(55) (DWPArbuthnot)* 2-8-5 (3) DRMcCabe(2) (b.nr hind: s.s: outpcd: nvr nrr)....2 **5**
2335[5] Mister Sean (IRE) **(66)***(46) (JWPayne)* 2-8-8 RCochrane(6) (led 3f)....3 **6**
3568* Chemcast **(74)***(15) (BJMeehan)* 2-9-2 PatEddery(7) (lw: prom over 2f)....12 **7**

9/4 Martara (IRE), **7/2** Chemcast, **11/2** MISS BIGWIG (4/1-6/1), Supreme Power, **15/2** Wingnut (IRE) (5/1-8/1), **10/1** Dande Flyer (8/1-12/1), **14/1** Mister Sean (IRE), CSF £16.98 TOTE £5.10: £2.30 £1.80 (£6.70) OWNER Bigwigs Entertainments (COCKERHAM) BRED Ravenstonedale Fold and Bloodstock 7 Rn 58.68 secs (4.18) SF: 54/36/26/45/25/16/-

OFFICIAL EXPLANATION **Chemcast: reportedly hung badly and did not handle the softer ground.**

3754

STANLEY WOOTTON CONDITIONS STKS (3-Y.O+) (Class C) £4,855.20 (£1,816.80: £888.40: £382.00: £171.00)
1m 2f 18y Stalls: Low GOING: 0.50 sec per fur (GS) 2-45 (2-46)

3556[2] **Warning Order (97)***(104)*(Fav)*(JLDunlop)* 3-8-13 PatEddery(3) (2nd st: led over 2f out: shkn up over 1f out: r.o wl) ....— 1
3473[6] That Old Feeling (IRE) **(94)***(92) (RHannon)* 3-8-5 (5) DaneO'Neill(2) (lw: 3rd st: nt clr run & swtchd over 2f out: chsd wnr over 1f out: unable qckn) 6 2
3380[3] Green Green Desert (FR) **(98)***(80) (MRStoute)* 4-9-2 WRSwinburn(4) (led over 7f: 2nd & btn whn n.m.r on ins wl over 1f out) 7 3
764[10] Jagellon (USA) *(73) (WRMuir)* 4-9-0 JWeaver(5) (chsd ldr over 6f: 4th st: wknd 3f out).......3½ 4
3632[4] Soldier Cove (USA) *(69) (MartynMeade)* 5-9-0 VSlattery(1) (lw: 5th st: a bhd).......2½ 5

6/4 WARNING ORDER, **2/1** Green Green Desert (FR), **100/30** That Old Feeling (IRE), **10/1** Jagellon (USA), **14/1** Soldier Cove (USA) (10/1-16/1), CSF £6.55 TOTE £2.10: £1.40 £1.50 (£3.50) OWNER Mr Ian Cameron (ARUNDEL) BRED Giles W. Pritchard-Gordon 5 Rn
2m 15.37 (11.37) SF: 46/34/28/21/17
WEIGHT FOR AGE 3yo-6lb

3755

RON SMYTH RATED STKS H'CAP (0-100) (3-Y.O+) (Class B) £7,765.80 (£2,902.20: £1,416.10: £605.50: £267.75: £132.65)
1m 114y Stalls: Low GOING: 0.50 sec per fur (GS) 3-20 (3-20)

3268* **Takhlid (USA) (79)***(90) (HThomsonJones)* 4-8-11 RHills(2) (lw: mde all: drvn out) ....— 1
3601[11] Pay Homage **(81)***(92) (IABalding)* 7-8-8 (5) DGriffiths(5) (lw: 4th st: ev ch fnl f: r.o).......hd 2
2616[6] Te Amo (IRE) **(82)***(87) (RAkehurst)* 3-8-4 (5) MHenry(8) (3rd st: rdn over 3f out: unable qckn fnl 2f) 3 3
3611[20] Deano's Beeno **(78)***(76) (MJohnston)* 3-8-5 JWeaver(3) (lw: 2nd st: rdn over 3f out: wknd over 1f out).......4 4
3602[4] Emerging Market **(90)***(87) (JLDunlop)* 3-9-3 PatEddery(4) (lw: hdwy over 3f out: wknd fnl f).......nk 5
3601[2] Embankment (IRE) **(86)***(78)*(Fav)*(RHannon)* 5-8-13 (5) DaneO'Neill(9) (6th st: wknd over 2f out) 3 6
3565[13] Sotoboy (IRE) **(84)***(75) (PWHarris)* 3-8-11 RCochrane(1) (a bhd) ....hd 7
3598[3] Lipizzaner (IRE) **(94)***(82) (BWHills)* 3-9-7b PaulEddery(7) (5th st: rdn over 3f out: wknd 1f out).......1¾ 8
Stolen Melody **(81)***(12) (SDow)* 3-8-8 ow1 RHughes(6) (s.s: a bhd) 30 9

2/1 Embankment (IRE), **9/2** Emerging Market (op 3/1), Te Amo (IRE), **13/2** Deano's Beeno, TAKHLID (USA), **9/1** Lipizzaner (IRE) (op 5/1), **14/1** Sotoboy (IRE), **25/1** Pay Homage, Stolen Melody, CSF £119.72 CT £727.04 TOTE £7.70: £2.00 £5.80 £2.00 (£52.00) Trio £104.40 OWNER Mr Hamdan Al Maktoum (NEWMARKET) BRED Cheveley Park Stud Ltd 9 Rn
1m 49.98 (7.98) SF: 59/61/51/40/51/47/39/46/-
WEIGHT FOR AGE 3yo-5lb

3756

NATIONAL STARCH & CHEMICAL CENTENARY MAIDEN STKS (3-Y.O) (Class D) £3,761.25 (£1,140.00: £557.50: £266.25)
1m 4f 10y Stalls: Low GOING: 0.50 sec per fur (GS) 3-50 (3-57)

3555[2] **Top Lady (IRE) (77)***(86) (MRStoute)* 3-8-9 WRSwinburn(13) (a.p: led over 4f out: rdn: r.o wl).......— 1
3016[2] Step Aloft **(77)***(83)*(Fav)*(LordHuntingdon)* 3-8-9 DHarrison(4) (lw: 4th st: chsd wnr over 2f out: unable qckn).......2 2
2863[6] Mighty Squaw **(53)***(82) (MissGayKelleway)* 3-8-6 (3) SSanders(7) (hdwy over 5f out: 5th st: hrd rdn over 2f out: one pce) 1 3
3224[4] Pampas Breeze (IRE) **(75)***(70) (WJarvis)* 3-8-9 RHills(8) (led over 1f: 3rd st: wknd over 2f out) 9 4
3438[2] Anchorena *(61) (RCharlton)* 3-8-9 PatEddery(1) (swtg: led over 10f out tl over 4f out: wknd over 2f out).......7 5
2316[6] Zine Lane **(69)***(61) (MajorWRHern)* 3-9-0 PaulEddery(6) (lw: 6th st: wknd over 3f out) 3½ 6
2314[15] Jovie King (IRE) **(53)***(47) (SDow)* 3-9-0 JWeaver(2) (lw: nvr nr to chal) 11 7
Portscatho (IRE) *(43) (MissJacquelineDoyle)* 3-8-9 (5) AWhelan(9) (str: bit bkwd: nvr nrr).....2½ 8
My Dutch Girl **(54)***(35) (MissBSanders)* 3-8-9 WNewnes(5) (a bhd) 2½ 9
3543[3] Dolliver (USA) *(35) (SDow)* 3-9-0 RHughes(12) (hdwy 7f out: wknd over 3f out).......4 10
Adaloaldo (USA) *(29) (PAKelleway)* 3-9-0 MWigham(11) (lw: bhd fnl 6f) 4 11
2193[5] Zalament **(57)***(20) (APJarvis)* 3-8-9 JTate(10) (prom over 6f) 3 12
2093[4] Kreef **(45)** *(RCurtis)* 3-9-0 AClark(3) (bkwd: bhd fnl 5f: t.o) 30 13

11/8 Step Aloft, **5/2** TOP LADY (IRE), **5/1** Anchorena (op 5/2), **8/1** Pampas Breeze (IRE) (6/1-9/1), **14/1** Mighty Squaw (op 25/1), **16/1** Zine Lane, Adaloaldo (USA), **25/1** Zalament, **50/1** Jovie King (IRE), Dolliver (USA), Portscatho (IRE), My Dutch Girl, Kreef, CSF £6.58 TOTE £3.60: £1.60 £1.20 £2.50 (£2.50) Trio £13.10 OWNER Lord Weinstock & The Hon Simon Weinstock (NEWMARKET) BRED Ballymacoll Stud Farm Ltd 13 Rn 2m 48.15 (13.15) SF: 47/44/43/31/22/22/8/4/-/-/-/-/-

3757

LADBROKE H'CAP (0-75) (3-Y.O+) (Class D) £4,650.00 (£1,410.00: £690.00: £330.00) **1m 114y** Stalls: Low GOING: 0.50 sec per fur (GS) 4-20 (4-26)

3629[3] **Duello (55)***(68) (MBlanshard)* 4-8-13 RCochrane(7) (6th st: led over 1f out: all out) — 1
3455[12] Double Rush (IRE) **(48)***(61) (TGMills)* 3-8-1 RHills(17) (lw: hdwy over 2f out: ev ch wl ins fnl f: r.o wl) s.h 2
3082[3] Waldo **(65)***(76) (LordHuntingdon)* 4-9-9v DHarrison(5) (w ldr: led over 4f out tl over 1f out: unable qckn ins fnl f) 1¼ 3
3638[2] Guesstimation (USA) **(62)***(68)*(Fav)*(JPearce)* 6-9-6 JWeaver(6) (hdwy over 3f out: rdn over 2f out: one pce) 2½ 4
2317[2] Court Nap (IRE) **(55)***(58) (SMellor)* 3-8-8 MWigham(13) (lw: hdwy over 2f out: one pce) 1¾ 5
3497[7] Tomal **(49)***(50) (RIngram)* 3-8-2 RPrice(8) (hdwy over 2f out: ev ch over 1f out: sn wknd) ¾ 6
3402[2] It'sthebusiness **(55)***(55) (SDow)* 3-8-8 RHughes(14) (hdwy over 2f out: hrd rdn over 1f out: sn wknd) ½ 7
1568[0] Ocean Park **(62)***(56) (LadyHerries)* 4-9-6 PaulEddery(18) (lw: nvr nr to chal) 3½ 8
3020[6] Shift Again (IRE) **(69)***(58) (WJarvis)* 3-9-8 PatEddery(2) (3rd st: wknd over 1f out) 2½ 9
3544[3] Salvatore Giuliano **(40)***(21) (AGFoster)* 5-7-5 (7) MartinDwyer(9) (4th st: wknd over 2f out) 4 10
1883[5] Doodies Pool (IRE) **(51)***(30) (PBurgoyne)* 5-8-6 (3) DRMcCabe(16) (nvr nrr) 1¼ 11
3726[4] Kinnegad Kid **(43)***(19) (RIngram)* 6-7-12v(3) DWright(10) (lw: 5th st: wknd 3f out) 1½ 12
Delpiombo **(51)***(16) (MRChannon)* 9-8-4 (5) PPMurphy(3) (nvr nrr) 6 13
3545[2] Crystal Heights (FR) **(65)***(28) (RJO'Sullivan)* 7-9-6 (3) SSanders(19) (b: s.s: sme hdwy over 4f out: wknd over 3f out) 1¼ 14
3125[7] Anistop **(45)***(5) (RAkehurst)* 3-7-12 JQuinn(20) (bhd fnl 6f) 1¼ 15
3515* Commander Glen (IRE) **(58)***(17) (MartynMeade)* 3-8-11b VSlattery(12) (bhd fnl 3f) ½ 16
3529[9] Indescent Blue **(46)** *(DWPArbuthnot)* 3-7-13 GBardwell(15) (bhd fnl 4f) 6 17
3544[9] Glitterazzi **(46)** *(LMontagueHall)* 4-7-13 (5) AWhelan(4) (b: b.hind: a bhd) ¾ 18
3611[24] Greatest **(70)** *(RAkehurst)* 4-9-9 (5) MHenry(1) (lw: led 4f: styd centre st: wknd over 2f out) 15 19

7/2 Guesstimation (USA), **13/2** DUELLO, **7/1** It'sthebusiness, **8/1** Kinnegad Kid, Ocean Park (op 5/1), **10/1** Anistop, **11/1** Double Rush (IRE) (16/1-10/1), Crystal Heights (FR), **14/1** Shift Again (IRE), Court Nap (IRE) (10/1-16/1), Waldo (10/1-16/1), **16/1** Greatest, Commander Glen (IRE), **25/1** Doodies Pool (IRE), Tomal, Salvatore Giuliano, **33/1** Indescent Blue, Glitterazzi, Delpiombo, CSF £82.10 CT £927.97 TOTE £8.70: £2.40 £3.30 £4.20 £1.60 (£80.40) Trio £358.60 OWNER H C Promotions Ltd (UPPER LAMBOURN) BRED P. D. and Mrs Player 19 Rn
1m 51.18 (9.18) SF: 49/37/57/49/34/26/31/37/34/2/11/-/-/9/-/-/-/-/-
WEIGHT FOR AGE 3yo-5lb

T/Plpt: £57.90 (319.96 Tckts). T/Qdpt: £32.20 (4.3 Tckts). AK

3620-NOTTINGHAM (L-H)
Tuesday September 19th (Good to soft, Good patches)
WEATHER: fair WIND: mod bhd

3758

E.B.F. COLWICK MAIDEN STKS (2-Y.O F) (Class D) £3,935.10 (£1,174.80: £561.40: £254.70) **1m 54y** Stalls: Low GOING minus 0.06 sec (G) 2-00 (2-03)

3532[5] **Pine Needle** *(82) (DMorley)* 2-8-11 BThomson(10) (4th st: shkn up 3f out: led ins fnl f: pushed out) — 1
3561[9] Ailesbury Hill (USA) **(90)***(80)*(Fav)*(PWChapple-Hyam)* 2-8-11 JReid(4) (b.hind: led: hrd rdn & hdd ins fnl f: r.o) 1 2
3539[6] Funky *(67) (LMCumani)* 2-8-11 KFallon(11) (lw: 6th st: rdn & wknd 2f out) 7 3
3532[7] Flahuil *(65) (RHannon)* 2-8-11 MRoberts(5) (dwlt: rdn 5f out: hdwy 3f out: hung lft 2f out: one pce) 1 4
3136[2] Smile Forever (USA) *(64) (PFICole)* 2-8-11 TQuinn(7) (3rd st: wknd over 1f out) hd 5
3136[3] Primrose Path *(57) (CEBrittain)* 2-8-11 BDoyle(9) (b: w'like: leggy: bkwd: chsd ldr: 2nd st: rdn & wknd 2f out) 4 6
3339[11] Ship's Dancer *(51) (JLDunlop)* 2-8-11 WCarson(1) (5th st: wknd over 3f out) 3 7
Sister Kit (IRE) *(47) (BPalling)* 2-8-11 TSprake(6) (s.i.s: 9th st: a bhd) 2 8
Hot Dogging *(40) (MrsPSly)* 2-8-11 ACulhane(3) (unf: scope: bit bkwd: 8th st: a bhd) 3½ 9
3570[8] Sally State *(1) (MrsMMcCourt)* 2-8-11 MHills(8) (7th & wkng st: t.o) 20 10
3174[15] Peggy Ess *(APJames)* 2-8-11 NAdams(2) (bkwd: s.s: a in rr: t.o) 3 11

6/4 Ailesbury Hill (USA), **4/1** Smile Forever (USA) (5/2-5/1), **6/1** PINE NEEDLE, Ship's Dancer (op 4/1), **11/1** Primrose Path (8/1-12/1), **14/1** Funky, Flahuil, **50/1** Sister Kit (IRE), Hot Dogging, Sally State, **66/1** Peggy Ess, CSF £14.52 TOTE £8.70: £1.70 £1.00 £3.30 (£5.90) Trio £39.50 OWNER Lord Halifax (NEWMARKET) BRED Lord Halifax 11 Rn 1m 45.7 (6.10) SF: 29/27/14/12/11/4/-/-/-/-/-

3759 BOLLINGER CHAMPAGNE CHALLENGE SERIES GENTLEMENS' H'CAP (0-70) (3-Y.O+) (Class E) £3,817.00 (£1,144.00: £550.00: £253.00)

1m 1f 213y Stalls: Low GOING minus 0.06 sec per fur (G) 2-30 (2-32)

3288[4] **Aljawab (USA) (54)***(72) (JLDunlop)* 4-11-4 (4) MrKSantana(20) (hld up: 7th st: hdwy 3f out: led over 1f out: r.o wl) ....— 1
3658[3] Rival Bid (USA) **(55)***(67)*(Fav)*(MrsNMacauley)* 7-11-9 MrRJohnson(1) (3rd st: ev ch 2f out: one pce) 3½ 2
3659[17] Non Vintage (IRE) **(48)***(57) (MCChapman)* 4-10-12 (4) MrMMackley(16) (led tl hdd over 1f out: one pce) 2 3
3061[4] Slapy Dam **(48)***(57) (JMackie)* 3-10-10 MrGRyan(18) (lw: rdn & hdwy over 3f out: one pce fnl 2f) ....hd 4
3531[8] Salska **(43)***(51) (AStreeter)* 4-10-7 (4) MrPClinton(17) (hdwy 3f out: styd on fnl 2f) ....½ 5
3429[4] Jobber's Fiddle **(45)***(49) (DLWilliams)* 3-10-3 (4) MrRBarrett(3) (chsd ldr: 2nd st: wknd 3f out)2½ 6
3529[12] Moultazim (USA) **(37)***(37) (RJPrice)* 5-10-5 MrJLLlewellyn(2) (nvr nr to chal) 2½ 7
Saint Ciel (USA) **(44)***(43) (FJordan)* 7-10-8 (4) MrGShenkin(11) (lw: plld hrd: hdwy 3f out: no imp fnl 2f) ....½ 8
*3319** Able Choice (IRE) **(48)***(47)*(Fav)*(RWArmstrong)* 5-11-2 MrPPritchard-Gordon(21) (nvr nr to chal) ....½ 9
2329[5] Reaganesque (USA) **(66)***(57) (EALDunlop)* 3-11-10 (4) MrJPortman(23) (dwlt: hld up & bhd: nvr nrr) 5 10
1555[8] Scorched Air **(50)***(33) (JGMO'Shea)* 5-11-0 (4) MrNBradley(7) (n.d) 5 11
3725[9] Enchanted Cottage **(37)***(18) (MDHammond)* 3-9-13 MrCBonner(4) (lw: n.d) 1¼ 12
3464[6] Grate British (IRE) **(54)***(31) (EWeymes)* 3-10-12 (4) MrJWeymes(13) (5th st: wknd over 2f out) 2½ 13
Prussia **(57)***(33) (WClay)* 4-11-11 MrPHenley(6) (bkwd: lost pl 5f out: n.d after) ....nk 14
3258* Threshfield (USA) **(48)***(24) (BJCurley)* 9-10-12 (4) MrCCurley(12) (b: plld hrd: 4th st: wknd over 2f out) ....nk 15
1254[13] Peveril Princess **(37)***(13) (GBBalding)* 4-10-5 MrJCulloty(5) (bit bkwd: a bhd) ....s.h 16
Poly Screen **(43)***(13) (CASmith)* 4-10-7 (4) MrCAppleby(15) (a bhd) 3½ 17
3526[13] Forest Mill **(55)***(22) (DWPArbuthnot)* 3-10-13 (4) MrEJames(9) (b.hind: a bhd) 2 18
2503[12] Intendant **(60)***(23) (JGFitzGerald)* 3-11-8 MrCWardThomas(14) (lw: plld hrd: 6th st: wknd over 2f out) 2½ 19
Assembly Dancer **(39)** *(DLWilliams)* 8-10-3 (4) MrWGreatrex(22) (bkwd: a bhd) 4 20
3527[12] Shared Risk **(53)** *(SGNorton)* 3-11-1b MrMHNaughton(19) (bhd fnl 5f: t.o) 10 21
3493[6] Beauman **(60)** *(PDEvans)* 5-11-10v(4) MrWMcLaughlin(10) (hmpd & lost pl after 1f: sn bhd: t.o) 2 22

6/1 Able Choice (IRE), Rival Bid (USA), **7/1** Slapy Dam, **8/1** Threshfield (USA), **9/1** ALJAWAB (USA), Beauman, **12/1** Grate British (IRE) (op 8/1), Saint Ciel (USA), **14/1** Non Vintage (IRE), Intendant, **16/1** Salska, Reaganesque (USA), **20/1** Forest Mill, Peveril Princess, Shared Risk, **25/1** Enchanted Cottage, Jobber's Fiddle, **33/1** Poly Screen, Prussia, Assembly Dancer, Moultazim (USA), Scorched Air, CSF £65.38 CT £718.56 TOTE £9.30: £1.80 £2.20 £6.30 £2.60 (£18.00) Trio £367.20 OWNER Mr S. Khaled (ARUNDEL) BRED Mandysland Farm 22 Rn
2m 11.5 (9.00) SF: 54/49/39/33/33/25/19/25/29/33/15/-/7/15/6/-/-/-/-/-/-/-
WEIGHT FOR AGE 3yo-6lb

3760 NOTTINGHAM GOOSE FAIR NURSERY H'CAP (0-75) (2-Y.O) (Class D) £4,240.00 (£1,270.00: £610.00: £280.00)

1m 1f 213y Stalls: Low GOING minus 0.06 sec per fur (G) 3-05 (3-08)

3613[6] **Kinnescash (IRE) (65)***(67) (MSSaunders)* 2-8-12 AMcGlone(20) (3rd st: led wl over 1f out: all out) ....— 1
3460[3] Jackson Park **(50)***(52) (MHEasterby)* 2-7-11 JLowe(1) (led 6f out: hrd rdn & hdd wl over 1f out: r.o wl) ....s.h 2
3540* Aussie **(74)***(75) (MHTompkins)* 2-9-7 PRobinson(18) (hld up: hdwy 3f out: r.o wl ins fnl f) ....¾ 3
3538[6] Rose of Siberia (USA) **(66)***(66) (MBell)* 2-8-13 MFenton(11) (hld up: 7th st: stdy hdwy 4f out: r.o wl ins fnl f) ....½ 4
3233* Homeland **(64)***(62) (TJNaughton)* 2-8-6 (5) JDSmith(15) (lw: hdwy over 2f out: hrd rdn & nt clr run over 1f out: swtchd rt ins fnl f: r.o) 1½ 5
3546[8] Bellator **(65)***(62) (GBBalding)* 2-8-12 JWilliams(16) (hld up: hdwy over 2f out: nt rch ldrs) ....hd 6
3516[6] Queen's Music (USA) **(60)***(55) (PFICole)* 2-8-7 TQuinn(13) (b.nr hind: hdwy on ins over 2f out: eased whn btn ins fnl f) 1½ 7

3530[7] Jerry Cutrona (IRE) **(65)***(56) (NACallaghan)* 2-8-12 GCarter(7) (hld up: 8th st: hdwy 3f out: wknd wl over 1f out) 2½ 8
3639[12] Down The Yard **(54)***(37) (MCChapman)* 2-7-8 (7)ow4 CMunday(10) (nvr nr to chal)....2½ 9
3651[12] Soviet Sakti (IRE) **(61)***(47) (PMitchell)* 2-8-8 RPerham(14) (led 1f: 2nd st: wknd over 2f out) ..¾ 10
846[3] Royal Rigger **(48)***(27) (CSmith)* 2-7-6 (3)ow2 NVarley(3) (nvr nr ldrs)....3 11
3417[5] Lucky Bea **(50)***(29) (MWEasterby)* 2-7-11 TWilliams(12) (hdwy over 4f out: wknd 3f out)....1 12
3350[4] Fortuitious (IRE) **(46)***(24) (JRJenkins)* 2-7-7 NCarlisle(8) (n.d) 1 13
3530[9] Chik's Secret **(53)***(28) (BPalling)* 2-8-0 ow3 TSprake(2) (bhd fnl 4f)....hd 14
3701* Whispering Dawn **(60)***(31)*(Fav)*(MRChannon)* 2-8-7 5x AMackay(19) (s.s: sn rcvrd: 5th st: wknd qckly 2f out)....4 15
3089[21] Shamand (USA) **(60)***(29) (BJMeehan)* 2-8-7 BDoyle(6) (bit bkwd: n.d) 1¼ 16
3684[9] Be My Bird **(70)***(39) (BJMeehan)* 2-9-3 KFallon(21) (a bhd)....s.h 17
3592[9] Suparoy **(67)***(36) (TGMills)* 2-9-0 JFEgan(5) (swtg: bhd fnl 3f) ....nk 18
3533[9] Dish The Dosh **(46)** *(PGMurphy)* 2-7-7b NAdams(17) (6th st: wknd 3f out: t.o)....15 19
3736[6] Colour Counsellor **(51)** *(KMcAuliffe)* 2-7-12b WCarson(4) (4th st: wknd 3f out: t.o)....3½ 20
3566[10] Deedeejay **(48)** *(JMBradley)* 2-7-4v(5)ow2 MBaird(9) (led after 1f: sddle slipped: hdd 6f out: wknd qckly: p.u over 2f out).... P

LONG HANDICAP Royal Rigger 7-1 Fortuitious (IRE) 7-2 Dish The Dosh 7-1 Deedeejay 7-6

7/2 Whispering Dawn (3/1-9/2), **7/1** Jackson Park, Aussie, Jerry Cutrona (IRE), **8/1** Bellator, **11/1** Homeland, **12/1** Rose of Siberia (USA) (op 20/1), **14/1** Colour Counsellor, **16/1** Lucky Bea, Queen's Music (USA), Shamand (USA), Suparoy, **20/1** KINNESCASH (IRE), **25/1** Be My Bird, Fortuitious (IRE), **33/1** Royal Rigger, Chik's Secret, Soviet Sakti (IRE), Down The Yard, Deedeejay, **50/1** Dish The Dosh, CSF £160.23 CT £1,025.16 TOTE £42.50: £7.20 £1.10 £2.40 £4.50 (£112.50) Trio £301.60 OWNER Mr Chris Scott (WELLS) BRED Frank Barry 21 Rn
2m 11.3 (8.80) SF: 20/5/28/19/15/15/8/9/-/-/-/-/-/-/-/-/-/-/-/-

3761 BRISTOL STREET MOTORS (SHERWOOD) MAIDEN STKS (I) (3-Y.O+)
(Class D) £4,002.70 (£1,195.60: £571.80: £259.90)
1m 54y Stalls: Low GOING minus 0.06 sec per fur (G) 3-35 (3-37)

2460[2] **Far Ahead** *(81) (JLEyre)* 3-9-0 RLappin(1) (4th st: led over 1f out: edgd rt 1f out: drvn out) ....— 1
907[2] Northern Fan (IRE) **(74)***(79) (ACStewart)* 3-9-0 MRoberts(2) (b: bit bkwd: plld hrd: led 6f out: rdn 3f out: hdd over 1f out: r.o) 1¼ 2
3292[7] Alzoomo (IRE) *(73) (JAGlover)* 3-9-0 SDWilliams(3) (lw: hld up: stdy hdwy 4f out: styd on fnl 2f)....3 3
Angus-G *(71) (MrsMReveley)* 3-8-9 (5) GParkin(4) (leggy: lt-f: s.s: gd hdwy fnl 2f: nrst fin) ....¾ 4
936[5] Nero Kris **(68)***(69) (PAKelleway)* 3-9-0 JFEgan(6) (swtg: bit bkwd: 5th st: rdn over 2f out: no hdwy)....1 5
3537[7] Duke Valentino *(67) (RHollinshead)* 3-9-0 TIves(9) (swtg: 6th st: no hdwy fnl 2f)....1¼ 6
Yaverland (IRE) *(66) (CADwyer)* 3-9-0 JReid(13) (h.d.w: bkwd: hdwy 3f out: nt trble ldrs)....¾ 7
864[9] Bataan (USA) **(73)***(59)*(Fav)*(MrsJCecil)* 4-9-4 TQuinn(11) (bkwd: 3rd st: wknd 2f out: eased whn btn ins fnl f) 3½ 8
Taroucca (IRE) *(27) (CEBrittain)* 3-8-9 BDoyle(10) (lt-f: led 2f: 2nd st: wknd wl over 2f out: t.o) 14 9
Crowning Tino *(26) (MrsNMacauley)* 3-8-4 (5) CTeague(8) (lt-f: unf: bhd fnl 4f: t.o)....½ 10
1554[6] Rock Rambler *(23) (LadyHerries)* 3-8-7 (7) JMcAuley(12) (bkwd: a bhd: t.o) 4 11
3537[10] Sungai Mas (USA) *(23) (SPCWoods)* 3-9-0 WWoods(5) (a bhd: t.o)....hd 12
1564[8] Oh Dearie Me *(JGMO'Shea)* 3-8-9 KFallon(7) (a bhd: t.o fnl 3f) 25 13

2/1 Bataan (USA) (op 7/2), **11/4** Northern Fan (IRE) (7/4-7/2), **6/1** FAR AHEAD (op 4/1), **8/1** Duke Valentino, **10/1** Yaverland (IRE), Taroucca (IRE), **14/1** Nero Kris, **16/1** Sungai Mas (USA), **20/1** Angus-G, **33/1** Crowning Tino, Rock Rambler, Alzoomo (IRE), Oh Dearie Me, CSF £23.60 TOTE £8.10: £1.60 £1.50 £11.40 (£6.70) Trio £149.60 OWNER . Sunpak Potatoes (HAMBLETON) BRED Sir John Astor 13 Rn 1m 45.6 (6.00) SF: 33/31/25/23/21/19/18/15/-/-/-/-/-
WEIGHT FOR AGE 3yo-4lb

3762 BRISTOL STREET MOTORS (SHERWOOD) MAIDEN STKS (II) (3-Y.O+)
(Class D) £3,968.90 (£1,185.20: £566.60: £257.30)
1m 54y Stalls: Low GOING minus 0.06 sec per fur (G) 4-05 (4-09)

3537[5] **Wild Palm** *(84) (WAO'Gorman)* 3-9-0 EmmaO'Gorman(2) (hld up: 6th st: hdwy 3f out: led 1f out: r.o wl)....— 1
3645[13] Blaze of Oak (USA) **(66)***(79) (WJHaggas)* 4-9-4 WCarson(10) (3rd st: led 2f out to 1f out: nt qckn)....2½ 2
3542[8] Golden Touch (USA) *(76) (RChampion)* 3-8-7 (7) ADaly(12) (plld hrd: 5th st: ev ch 2f out: one pce fnl f)....1½ 3

3030[4] Al Baha **(70)***(62)*(Fav)*(HRACecil)* 3-8-9 WRyan(11) (led: hrd rdn & hdd 2f out: sn wknd) 5 **4**
3537[11] Gymcrak Hero (IRE) *(66) (GHolmes)* 3-9-0 KFallon(3) (b: b.hind: 4th st: no hdwy fnl 3f) ....hd **5**
3438[10] Your Most Welcome *(58) (DJSffrenchDavis)* 4-8-8 (5) GParkin(13) (nvr nrr) 2 **6**
Out of The Blue *(56) (MWEckley)* 3-8-9 TWilliams(8) (w'like: str: bkwd: plld hrd: chsd ldr: 2nd st: wknd 2f out) .... ¾ **7**
3621[11] The Deaconess **(32)***(56) (MrsALMKing)* 4-8-13 GHind(9) (bit bkwd: nvr nr ldrs) ....s.h **8**
Green Divot *(52) (GWragg)* 4-8-13 MHills(4) (lengthy: unf: plld hrd: 8th st: hdwy over 3f out: wknd over 2f out) 2 **9**
Buffalo Girl *(47) (LadyHerries)* 3-8-9 DeanMcKeown(5) (w'like: scope: bkwd: plld hrd: 7th & c wd st: wknd 3f out) 2½ **10**
3542[11] Midnight Walker *(41) (MrsSDWilliams)* 3-8-9 JWilliams(6) (bit bkwd: a bhd) 3 **11**
Sun Circus *(41) (JLSpearing)* 3-8-6 (3) SDrowne(1) (scope: bkwd: dwlt: a bhd).......................nk **12**

15/8 Al Baha (Evens-2/1), **100/30** Blaze of Oak (USA), WILD PALM, **6/1** Green Divot (7/2-7/1), **12/1** Gymcrak Hero (IRE) (9/1-14/1), **14/1** Buffalo Girl (8/1-16/1), **16/1** Your Most Welcome, **40/1** Sun Circus, **50/1** Out of The Blue, Golden Touch (USA), **66/1** The Deaconess, Midnight Walker, CSF £14.83 TOTE £4.50: £1.40 £1.30 £10.00 (£5.10) Trio £222.80; £100.44 to 20/09/95. OWNER Mr S. Fustok (NEWMARKET) BRED Deerfield Farm 12 Rn 1m 46.0 (6.40) SF: 29/28/21/7/11/7/1/5/1/-/-/-
WEIGHT FOR AGE 3yo-4lb

3763 DYNASTY INTERNATIONAL MAIDEN STKS (2-Y.O F) (Class D)
£4,597.50 (£1,380.00: £665.00: £307.50)
6f 15y Stalls: High GOING minus 0.21 sec per fur (GF) 4-35 (4-40)

2675[6] **Thracian** *(80) (JLDunlop)* 2-8-11 JReid(13) (lw: racd centre: a.p: rdn to ld wl ins fnl f: r.o) ....— **1**
3643[4] Chalamont (IRE) *(78) (PWChapple-Hyam)* 2-8-6 (5) RHavlin(12) (racd centre: a.p: led 2f out tl wl ins fnl f)..¾ **2**
Ma Belle Poule *(65) (PFICole)* 2-8-11 TQuinn(4) (leggy: unf: chsd ldrs: rdn & edgd rt 3f out: r.o one pce fnl 2f) 5 **3**
3185[5] Naissant **(92)***(58) (CEBrittain)* 2-8-11 BDoyle(8) (led 4f: one pce)...2½ **4**
Desert Lynx (IRE) *(57) (TRWatson)* 2-8-11 DeanMcKeown(14) (lt-f: unf: a.p: no hdwy fnl 2f) ....½ **5**
3495[3] Star And Garter *(54) (GWragg)* 2-8-11 MHills(21) (lw: led stands' side: rdn 2f out: sn wknd) 1¼ **6**
3495[4] Petit Point (IRE) *(53) (RHannon)* 2-8-11 MRoberts(1) (prom: rdn 2f out: sn wknd)................hd **7**
Commin' Up *(53) (JWHills)* 2-8-11 GDuffield(9) (wl grwn: bkwd: prom 4f) ....s.h **8**
3539[4] Green Charter *(51)*(Fav)*(HRACecil)* 2-8-11 WRyan(10) (w ldr over 3f: wknd over 1f out) 1 **9**
The Jolly Barmaid (IRE) *(30) (PCalver)* 2-8-11 MBirch(20) (leggy: lt-f: s.s: nvr nrr) 8 **10**
Flighty *(28) (LMCumani)* 2-8-11 KFallon(6) (lt-f: unf: nvr nr to chal)...½ **11**
Tina Katerina *(27) (RChampion)* 2-8-11 AMcGlone(11) (w'like: bkwd: bhd fnl 2f)..................nk **12**
3069[17] Flash In The Pan (IRE) *(25) (MBell)* 2-8-11 MFenton(22) (s.s: a bhd) ....¾ **13**
3626[15] Chalice *(25) (JBalding)* 2-8-11 JWilliams(19) (a bhd)...nk **14**
Daydream Island *(21) (RJBaker)* 2-8-11 GCarter(23) (small: lt-f: unf: prom: hung lft over 2f out: sn wknd) 1¼ **15**
3541[7] Alreeh (IRE) *(18) (JHMGosden)* 2-8-11 WCarson(3) (a bhd)...1¼ **16**
3495[12] Astra Martin *(16) (PGMurphy)* 2-8-4 (7) RWaterfield(5) (bit bkwd: a bhd)..................................¾ **17**
Unspoken Prayer *(13) (JRArnold)* 2-8-11 CRutter(7) (lt-f: a bhd)...1 **18**
3628[19] Magical Mill *(7) (RGuest)* 2-8-11 FNorton(16) (a bhd)...2½ **19**
Miss Roberto (IRE) *(6) (MrsMMcCourt)* 2-8-11 BThomson(18) (b: cmpt: bkwd: a bhd) ....nk **20**
3648[11] Penny Ghent *(PSFelgate)* 2-8-11 GHind(2) (a bhd) 2½ **21**
Eternally Grateful *(MrsNMacauley)* 2-8-6 (5) CTeague(15) (lt-f: unf: s.s: a bhd: t.o).................7 **22**
Napier Star *(MrsNMacauley)* 2-8-8 (3) SDrowne(17) (w'like: scope: bkwd: s.s: a t.o) 6 **23**

5/2 Green Charter, **5/1** THRACIAN, **6/1** Petit Point (IRE) (op 4/1), Naissant, **7/1** Star And Garter (op 4/1), **10/1** Flighty (8/1-12/1), **14/1** Alreeh (IRE) (op 8/1), Ma Belle Poule (op 8/1), **16/1** Chalamont (IRE), **20/1** Flash In The Pan (IRE), **25/1** Commin' Up, **33/1** The Jolly Barmaid (IRE), **50/1** Tina Katerina, Chalice, Daydream Island, Desert Lynx (IRE), Astra Martin, Unspoken Prayer, Magical Mill, Miss Roberto (IRE), Penny Ghent, Eternally Grateful, Napier Star, CSF £82.31 TOTE £7.90: £1.90 £5.00 £5.80 (£609.30) Trio £279.00; £322.53 to 20/09/95 OWNER Hesmonds Stud (ARUNDEL) BRED Hesmonds Stud Ltd 23 Rn
1m 12.7 (1.70) SF: 53/51/38/31/30/27/26/26/24/3/1/-/-/-/-/-/-/-/-/-/-/-/-

3764 RNIB LIMITED STKS (0-60) (3-Y.O+) (Class F) £2,519.00 (£694.00: £329.00)
6f 15y Stalls: High GOING minus 0.21 sec per fur (GF) 5-05 (5-08)

3751[2] **Petomi (58)***(66) (SirMarkPrescott)* 3-8-6 GDuffield(3) (lw: a.p: led appr fnl f: drvn out) ....— **1**
3739[4] Cretan Gift **(52)***(71) (NPLittmoden)* 4-9-3 TGMcLaughlin(6) (hdwy over 1f out: rdn & r.o ins fnl f)...1¼ **2**

3751* Maid O'Cannie **(59)**(57)(Fav)*(MWEasterby)* 4-8-9b SMaloney(7) (chsd ldrs centre: rdn over 1f out: r.o one pce) 2 **3**
3681* Double Splendour (IRE) **(51)***(68) (PSFelgate)* 5-9-6 3x WRyan(12) (prom stands' side: one pce fnl 2f) ....nk **4**
*3242*5 Malibu Man **(57)***(64) (SMellor)* 3-9-3 TSprake(9) (lw: chsd ldr: led over 1f out: sn hdd: one pce) 1¼ **5**
3615 14 Astral Invader (IRE) **(60)***(53) (MSSaunders)* 3-8-11 AMcGlone(13) (led stands' side: one pce fnl 2f) 2 **6**
3418 10 Bells of Longwick **(56)***(42) (WWHaigh)* 6-8-9b DaleGibson(17) (nvr nr to chal) 2½ **7**
3624 9 Miss Aragon **(58)***(47) (MissLCSiddall)* 7-8-8 (7) TSiddall(10) (lw: prom: rdn & wknd 2f out) ....s.h **8**
3638* First Gold **(54)***(49) (JWharton)* 6-9-3b KFallon(11) (nvr trbld ldrs) ....nk **9**
*3524*10 Rapier Point (IRE) **(60)***(39) (PCHaslam)* 4-9-0b MTebbutt(1) (led over 4f) 2½ **10**
3751 4 Blushing Grenadier (IRE) **(53)**(42)(Fav)*(MJFetherston-Godley)* 3-9-0b MRoberts(8) (lw: chsd ldrs far side: rdn over 2f out: no rspnse) ....s.h **11**
3622 9 Invigilate **(55)***(36) (MartynWane)* 6-9-0 BThomson(18) (lw: prom stands' side 4f) 1¼ **12**
3622 11 Moujeeb (USA) **(54)***(35) (PatMitchell)* 5-9-0v BDoyle(2) (lw: bhd fnl 2f) ....nk **13**
3230 12 Plum First **(60)***(31) (LRLloyd-James)* 5-8-10 (7) RuthCoulter(15) (b.hind: bit bkwd: a bhd) 2½ **14**
*845*11 South Forest (IRE) **(60)***(23) (SRBowring)* 4-8-12b(5) CTeague(5) (b: a bhd) 3 **15**
3014 9 Diebiedale **(54)***(11) (RBoss)* 3-8-6 WCarson(14) (a bhd) 1¾ **16**
2576 12 Bold Revival **(56)** *(MrsPSly)* 3-8-6 ACulhane(4) (stdd s: a bhd: t.o) 25 **17**

4/1 Blushing Grenadier (IRE), Maid O'Cannie (op 5/2), **9/2** Double Splendour (IRE) (3/1-5/1), **6/1** First Gold, **8/1** PETOMI (op 7/2), **12/1** Diebiedale, South Forest (IRE), **14/1** Malibu Man, Astral Invader (IRE), **16/1** Miss Aragon, **20/1** Plum First, Invigilate, Moujeeb (USA), **25/1** Cretan Gift, Bells of Longwick, **33/1** Rapier Point (IRE), Bold Revival, CSF £193.15 TOTE £4.40: £1.90 £8.40 £1.90 (£252.20) Trio £180.90 OWNER Mr A. E. T. Mines (NEWMARKET) BRED Bacton Stud 17 Rn
1m 12.7 (1.70) SF: 48/56/42/53/46/35/27/32/34/24/24/21/20/16/8/-/-
WEIGHT FOR AGE 3yo-3lb

T/Jkpt: Not won; £63.292.17 to Brighton 20/9/95. T/Plpt: £875.00 (82 Tckts). T/Qdpt: Not won; £42.20 to Brighton 20/9/95. KH

3283-BRIGHTON (L-H)
Wednesday September 20th (Good)
WEATHER: sunny WIND: slt bhd

3765
E.B.F. KEMP TOWN MAIDEN STKS (2-Y.O) (Class D) £4,110.00 (£1,230.00: £590.00: £270.00)
5f 213y Stalls: Low GOING minus 0.46 sec per fur (F) 2-00 (2-01)

3625 4 **Eastern Paradise** *(78)*(Fav)*(MRStoute)* 2-9-0 KDarley(4) (2nd st: led over 2f out: edgd lft 1f out: rdn out) ....— **1**
3003 3 Surtees **(85)***(71) (RCharlton)* 2-9-0 JReid(15) (lw: 6th st: rdn over 3f out: r.o wl ins fnl f) 2½ **2**
Pride of Brixton *(71) (GLewis)* 2-9-0 SWhitworth(3) (scope: 4th st: rdn over 1f out: ev ch ins fnl f: unable qckn) ....s.h **3**
3538 4 Meranti **(74)***(66) (LJHolt)* 2-9-0 MPerrett(16) (rdn over 2f out: hdwy over 1f out: r.o ins fnl f) 2 **4**
3628 3 Village Native (FR) **(84)***(66) (KOCunningham-Brown)* 2-9-0 PaulEddery(2) (led over 3f: one pce) ....s.h **5**
3604 6 Rawi **(79)***(56) (CJBenstead)* 2-9-0 MWigham(12) (lw: 5th st: wknd over 1f out) 3½ **6**
Maple Burl *(56) (SDow)* 2-9-0 MRoberts(7) (str: bkwd: s.s: hdwy 2f out: one pce) ....s.h **7**
3472 7 Flagstaff (USA) *(45) (RHannon)* 2-8-9 (5) DaneO'Neill(5) (nvr nrr) 4 **8**
3628 5 Longhill Boy *(42) (BJMeehan)* 2-9-0 BDoyle(14) (3rd st: wknd over 2f out) ....¾ **9**
3441 11 Spa Lane *(44) (CJDrewe)* 2-8-11 (3) SSanders(11) (a mid div) ....d.h **9**
3520 2 Meg's Memory (IRE) *(34) (JohnBerry)* 2-8-9 MFenton(8) (bhd fnl 3f) 1 **11**
Traci's Castle (IRE) *(24) (RAkehurst)* 2-8-9 TQuinn(9) (leggy: bit bkwd: s.s: a bhd) 4 **12**
3157 13 Spiral Flyer (IRE) *(22) (MDIUsher)* 2-8-9 RPrice(1) (lw: bhd fnl 3f) ....½ **13**
3450 10 Silhouette (IRE) *(22) (DRCElsworth)* 2-8-9 DHarrison(10) (a bhd) ....nk **14**
Young Mazaad (IRE) *(21) (RCurtis)* 2-9-0 GBardwell(13) (w'like: bkwd: a bhd) 2 **15**
3652 9 Carwyn's Choice *(PCClarke)* 2-8-9 NAdams(6) (a bhd) 6 **16**

7/4 EASTERN PARADISE, **5/2** Surtees, **9/1** Village Native (FR), **10/1** Pride of Brixton, **12/1** Meg's Memory (IRE), **16/1** Meranti, Traci's Castle (IRE), Flagstaff (USA), Rawi, **25/1** Maple Burl, **33/1** Spa Lane, **50/1** Longhill Boy, Spiral Flyer (IRE), Silhouette (IRE), Young Mazaad (IRE), Carwyn's Choice, CSF £6.78 TOTE £2.80: £1.20 £1.60 £3.60 (£2.90) Trio £69.90 OWNER Maktoum Al Maktoum (NEWMARKET) BRED Gainsborough Stud Management Ltd 16 Rn
1m 9.4 (1.00) SF: 43/36/36/31/31/21/21/10/10/8/1/-/-/-/-/-

3766

PATCHAM CONDITIONS STKS (2-Y.O) (Class D) £3,850.00 (£1,150.00: £550.00: £250.00) **5f 213y** Stalls: Low GOING minus 0.46 sec per fur (F) 2-30 (2-35)

3558W **Almushtarak (IRE)** *(86?) (MissGayKelleway)* 2-8-9 (3) SSanders(4) (4th st: led over 2f out: all out)........— 1
3339^7 Tsarnista *(81)*(Fav)*(JLDunlop)* 2-8-7 JReid(1) (5th st: rdn over 1f out: r.o wl ins fnl f)........s.h 2
3699^3 Cross The Border **(88)***(73) (RHannon)* 2-9-4 KDarley(6) (led 4f out tl over 2f out: wknd 1f out) 7 3
3289^7 Nellie North **(80)***(57) (MrsMMcCourt)* 2-8-13 TQuinn(3) (2nd st: wknd over 1f out)........4 4
3651^10 Arctic Romancer (IRE) **(81)***(56) (GLewis)* 2-9-4 PaulEddery(2) (led 2f: 3rd st: wknd over 1f out)........2½ 5
Banzhaf (USA) *(50) (GLMoore)* 2-8-12 SWhitworth(5) (w'like: scope: lw: s.i.s: 6th st: a bhd)s.h 6

5/4 Tsarnista (Evens-6/4), **15/8** Cross The Border, **9/2** Banzhaf (USA) (5/2-5/1), **14/1** Nellie North (7/1-16/1), **16/1** Arctic Romancer (IRE), **20/1** ALMUSHTARAK (IRE), CSF £44.69 TOTE £23.50: £4.80 £1.40 (£35.40) OWNER Mr A. Al-Radi (WHITCOMBE) BRED Stonethorn Stud Farms Ltd 6 Rn
1m 9.5 (1.10) SF: 40/35/27/11/10/4

3767

STEINE CLAIMING STKS (2-Y.O) (Class F) £3,149.00 (£874.00: £419.00) **6f 209y** Stalls: Low GOING minus 0.46 sec per fur (F) 3-00 (3-03)

3566^2 **Times of Times (IRE) (73)***(69)*(Fav)*(DJSCosgrove)* 2-8-12 MRimmer(12) (4th st: led over 2f out: rdn out)........— 1
2908^3 Again Together **(59)***(63) (NACallaghan)* 2-8-5 (3) JStack(1) (b.hind: 3rd st: ev ch over 1f out: unable qckn)........¾ 2
*3738** Pinocchio Boy (IRE) **(57)***(63) (BJMeehan)* 2-8-9 BDoyle(13) (hdwy 2f out: r.o wl ins fnl f)........¾ 3
3533^3 Velvet Jones **(58)***(66) (GFHCharles-Jones)* 2-8-6 (7) ADaly(17) (6th st: rdn 2f out: one pce) ...nk 4
3509^6 Real Gem *(56) (PJMakin)* 2-8-8 GCarter(2) (5th st: rdn over 2f out: one pce)........2 5
3613^9 Eights High (USA) **(68)***(56) (RHannon)* 2-9-1b MRoberts(9) (2nd st: led over 3f out tl over 2f out: wknd qckly 1f out)........3 6
3285* Dhulikhel **(60)***(51) (DMarks)* 2-8-12 JReid(14) (no hdwy fnl 2f)........1 7
3548^8 Kossolian **(70)***(49) (BPalling)* 2-8-12 TSprake(4) (led over 3f: wknd over 2f out)........1 8
3285^5 Fair To Middling (IRE) *(39) (GLMoore)* 2-8-2 MFenton(7) (nvr nrr)........s.h 9
3650^9 Sharp Night *(49) (MSSaunders)* 2-9-0 (3) SDrowne(6) (a mid div)........2 10
The Frog Princess *(39) (KMcAuliffe)* 2-8-8 DHarrison(10) (leggy: unf: swvd rt s: nvr nrr)........½ 11
3339^17 Fit To Ski *(41) (MHTompkins)* 2-8-12 PRobinson(16) (s.s: nvr nrr)........1 12
3566^3 Boston Tea Party **(58)***(27) (AMoore)* 2-8-0 (3)ow3 SSanders(8) (a bhd)........¾ 13
3518^4 Bellapais (IRE) **(60)***(20) (WRMuir)* 2-7-12b CRutter(18) (a bhd)........2 14
3566^4 Subtle One (IRE) *(23) (GLMoore)* 2-8-2 JFEgan(15) (a bhd)........¾ 15
Public Offering *(21) (MBlanshard)* 2-7-11 (5) MBaird(3) (neat: bit bkwd: a bhd)........¾ 16
La Femme Francaise (IRE) *(12) (MRChannon)* 2-8-2 FNorton(5) (leggy: bit bkwd: s.s: a bhd) 4 17
3675^7 Latzio **(51)***(2) (BAPearce)* 2-7-11 (5) MHenry(11) (bhd fnl 2f)........4 18

4/1 TIMES OF TIMES (IRE), **11/2** Again Together, Kossolian, **7/1** Subtle One (IRE), **8/1** Eights High (USA), Real Gem, **10/1** Pinocchio Boy (IRE) (6/1-11/1), **14/1** Fit To Ski, La Femme Francaise (IRE) (6/1-16/1), **16/1** Dhulikhel, **20/1** The Frog Princess, **25/1** Velvet Jones, Latzio, Boston Tea Party, Public Offering, **33/1** Fair To Middling (IRE), Bellapais (IRE), **50/1** Sharp Night, CSF £28.25 TOTE £3.80: £1.80 £2.60 £3.50 (£16.90) Trio £35.80 OWNER Mrs M. Schneider (NEWMARKET) BRED E. Moloney 18 Rn
1m 23.9 (3.90) SF: 9/3/3/6/-/-/-/-/-/-/-/-/-/-/-/-/-/-
Times of Times (IRE) clmd Miss J Allison £10,000

3768

WATERHALL CONDITIONS STKS (3-Y.O+) (Class C) £5,302.40 (£1,961.60: £940.80: £384.00: £152.00: £59.20) **6f 209y** Stalls: Low GOING minus 0.46 sec per fur (F) 3-30 (3-30)

3382^10 **Mandarina (USA) (92)***(98) (LMCumani)* 3-8-8 KDarley(4) (lw: 4th st: led over 1f out: all out)— 1
1639^8 Crystal Cavern (USA) **(89)***(101) (RCharlton)* 3-8-11 TQuinn(3) (lw: 5th st: hrd rdn & ev ch fnl f: r.o wl)........hd 2
3599^5 Bin Nashwan (USA) **(107)***(89)*(Fav)*(CEBrittain)* 3-8-13 BDoyle(5) (led over 5f)........6 3
3282^2 Fresh Fruit Daily **(74)***(77) (PAKelleway)* 3-8-5 JFEgan(7) (3rd st: hrd rdn 2f out: sn wknd)....1¾ 4
3706^16 Axeman (IRE) **(86)***(84) (RHannon)* 3-8-8b(5) DaneO'Neill(1) (lost pl over 3f out: one pce fnl 2f)nk 5
2795^3 Emirates Express **(85)***(76) (JWHills)* 3-9-2 MHills(2) (2nd st: wknd over 1f out)........5 6
3674* Sharp 'n Smart **(66)***(62) (BSmart)* 3-8-13 (3) SSanders(6) (lw: 6th st: wknd over 2f out)........6 7

6/4 Bin Nashwan (USA), **11/4** MANDARINA (USA) (op 7/4), **9/2** Fresh Fruit Daily, **15/2** Emirates Express, **10/1** Crystal Cavern (USA) (6/1-11/1), Axeman (IRE), **20/1** Sharp 'n Smart, CSF £26.98 TOTE £4.90: £2.50 £6.00 (£19.40) OWNER Fittocks Stud Ltd (NEWMARKET) BRED Fittocks Stud 7 Rn
1m 21.4 (1.40) SF: 35/38/26/14/21/13/-

3769 FRIEND-JAMES MEMORIAL LIMITED STKS (0-65) (3-Y.O+) (Class F) £3,174.20 (£881.20: £422.60) **1m 3f 196y** Stalls: High GOING minus 0.46 sec (F) 4-00 (4-00)

2411[8] **Wild Rita (65)***(75+) (WRMuir)* 3-8-5 MRoberts(11) (hdwy over 2f out: led wl over 1f out: r.o wl)........ — 1
3083[5] Prince Danzig (IRE) **(60)***(75) (DJGMurraySmith)* 4-9-6 PaulEddery(5) (lw: hdwy 4f out: 6th st: rdn over 2f out: unable qckn)........5 2
2439[6] Wild Strawberry **(57)***(70) (MissBSanders)* 6-8-12 (3) SSanders(13) (hdwy over 5f out: led 4f out tl wl over 1f out: one pce)........½ 3
3555[W] Soviet Bride (IRE) **(63)***(69) (SDow)* 3-8-0 (7) ADaly(8) (5th st: rdn over 2f out: n.m.r on ins 1f out: one pce)........½ 4
3679* Kaafih Homm (IRE) **(57)***(73)*(Fav)*(NACallaghan)* 4-9-3 (3) JStack(6) (b.hind: lw: hdwy over 2f out: hung lft over 1f out: one pce)........¾ 5
3641[3] Paper Cloud **(62)***(54) (CEBrittain)* 3-8-5 BDoyle(3) (prom over 7f)........9 6
3572[10] Niknaks Nephew **(65)***(53) (DJSffrenchDavis)* 3-8-10b WNewnes(1) (s.s: hdwy 11f out: wknd 5f out)........4 7
3184[2] Innocence **(64)***(48) (GWragg)* 3-8-5 MHills(4) (led 8f: 2nd st: wknd over 2f out)........½ 8
3531[6] Regal Fanfare (IRE) **(65)***(41) (JWHills)* 3-8-0 (5) MHenry(9) (3rd st: wknd 2f out)........5 9
3572[7] Nobby North **(60)***(45) (LordHuntingdon)* 3-8-10v DHarrison(10) (prom 7f)........½ 10
3676[14] Bandar Perak **(55)***(41) (MJHaynes)* 4-9-4 JReid(2) (lw: bhd fnl 7f)........3½ 11
3572[4] One Off the Rail (USA) **(38)***(43) (AMoore)* 5-9-8 CandyMorris(7) (hdwy over 4f out: wknd over 3f out)........1 12
3500[9] Exhibit Air (IRE) **(63)** *(RAkehurst)* 5-8-13b TQuinn(12) (4th st: wknd over 2f out: t.o)........dist 13

5/2 Kaafih Homm (IRE), **4/1** Soviet Bride (IRE), **5/1** Innocence, **11/2** Exhibit Air (IRE), **9/1** Regal Fanfare (IRE) (6/1-10/1), **11/1** Wild Strawberry (8/1-12/1), Paper Cloud, **12/1** WILD RITA, **14/1** Prince Danzig (IRE), **25/1** Nobby North, **33/1** Bandar Perak, Niknaks Nephew, **66/1** One Off the Rail (USA), CSF £162.33 TOTE £17.40: £2.40 £4.70 £2.70 (£83.10) Trio £151.30 OWNER Mr T. Brady (LAMBOURN) BRED Terry Brady 13 Rn 2m 29.5 (0.50) SF: 49/57/52/43/55/28/27/22/15/19/23/25/-
WEIGHT FOR AGE 3yo-8lb

3770 ERIC SIMMS MEMORIAL H'CAP (0-80) (3-Y.O+) (Class D) £4,340.70 (£1,299.60: £623.80: £285.90) **7f 214y** Stalls: Low GOING minus 0.46 sec per fur (F) 4-30 (4-30)

3664* **Confronter (75)***(92) (SDow)* 6-9-12 5x MRoberts(9) (lw: hdwy over 2f out: led ins fnl f: r.o wl)........ — 1
3348[7] Yaa Wale **(72)***(89) (JHMGosden)* 3-9-5 GHind(6) (3rd st: led over 2f out tl ins fnl f: r.o)........hd 2
3619[2] Polly Peculiar **(60)***(70)*(Fav)*(BSmart)* 4-8-11 DHarrison(14) (b.hind: s.s: hdwy & swtchd lft wl over 1f out: hrd rdn: r.o one pce)........3½ 3
3559[3] Raise the Stakes **(74)***(83) (IABalding)* 3-9-2 (5) DGriffiths(13) (lw: 6th st: ev ch over 1f out: one pce)........nk 4
3403[3] Charm Dancer **(54)***(61) (MCPipe)* 3-8-1 GCarter(5) (hdwy over 1f out: r.o)........1¼ 5
3664[8] Oozlem (IRE) **(42)***(45) (JCPoulton)* 6-7-7b GBardwell(7) (s.s: rdn thrght: nvr nr to chal)........1¾ 6
3493[2] Eden's Star (IRE) **(66)***(63) (MHTompkins)* 3-8-13 PRobinson(8) (lw: 2nd st: wknd wl over 1f out)........3 7
2778[8] Sheama (USA) **(62)***(58) (WJarvis)* 3-8-9 MHills(10) (led over 5f)........½ 8
*3073** Sweet Supposin (IRE) **(62)***(58) (CADwyer)* 4-8-10b(3) SSanders(1) (lw: sme hdwy over 2f out: wknd over 1f out)........hd 9
3629[12] Queenbird **(71)***(57) (MJRyan)* 4-9-8 BDoyle(12) (4th st: wknd over 2f out)........5 10
3390[3] Landlord **(66)***(51) (JARToller)* 3-8-13b WNewnes(2) (lw: bhd fnl 3f)........nk 11
3383[3] Never so Rite (IRE) **(60)***(38) (DWPArbuthnot)* 3-8-4 (3) DRMcCabe(4) (bhd fnl 3f)........3½ 12
3545[6] Dowsong **(68)** *(RAkehurst)* 4-9-5 TQuinn(11) (lw: 5th st: ev ch wl over 1f out: p.u ins fnl f: lame)........ P

4/1 Polly Peculiar, **9/2** CONFRONTER, **5/1** Eden's Star (IRE), **9/1** Yaa Wale (6/1-10/1), **10/1** Dowsong, Landlord (8/1-12/1), Sweet Supposin (IRE) (8/1-12/1), **11/1** Charm Dancer (7/1-12/1), Never so Rite (IRE), **12/1** Raise the Stakes, **14/1** Oozlem (IRE), **20/1** Sheama (USA), **25/1** Queenbird, CSF £45.25 CT £167.58 TOTE £4.40: £3.30 £2.10 £1.50 (£35.80) Trio £45.10 OWNER Hatfield Ltd (EPSOM) BRED Hamilton Bloodstock (UK) Ltd 13 Rn
1m 33.8 (1.60) SF: 52/45/30/39/17/5/19/14/18/17/7/-/-
WEIGHT FOR AGE 3yo-4lb

3771 PAVILION H'CAP (0-70) (3-Y.O+) (Class E) £3,702.60 (£1,108.80: £532.40: £244.20) **6f 209y** Stalls: Low GOING minus 0.46 sec per fur (F) 5-00 (5-01)

3554[9] **Jo Maximus (68)***(81) (SDow)* 3-9-1 (7) ADaly(11) (mde all: r.o wl)........ — 1

3706[14] Mislemani (IRE) **(59)***(65) (AGNewcombe)* 5-8-12 (5) DGriffiths(13) (7th st: rdn over 1f out: unable qckn)....3 **2**
3619[4] Stoppes Brow **(68)***(71) (GLMoore)* 3-9-8 SWhitworth(6) (2nd st: ev ch over 1f out: one pce) 1¼ **3**
2317[13] Present Situation **(56)***(59) (LordHuntingdon)* 4-9-0 DHarrison(16) (lw: rdn over 2f out: hdwy over 1f out: r.o)....nk **4**
3677[10] Sally Weld **(58)***(56) (CJBenstead)* 3-8-12 MWigham(2) (rdn & hdwy over 2f out: one pce)....2 **5**
3268[4] Walnut Burl (IRE) **(58)***(56)*(Fav)*(LJHolt)* 5-9-2 JReid(18) (s.s: hdwy over 1f out: nvr nrr)....s.h **6**
3677[3] Morocco (IRE) **(57)***(53) (MRChannon)* 6-9-1 AClark(10) (lw: rdn & hdwy over 2f out: one pce)....¾ **7**
3409* Tonys Gift **(70)***(64) (RHannon)* 3-9-5 (5) DaneO'Neill(1) (4th st: rdn over 2f out: wknd 1f out)....1 **8**
3619[15] Shepherd Market (IRE) **(61)***(53) (DAWilson)* 4-9-5 GCarter(14) (5th st: wknd over 1f out)....1 **9**
3455[7] North Esk (USA) **(57)***(43) (CADwyer)* 6-8-12 (3) DRMcCabe(4) (lw: 3rd st: wknd over 1f out)....2½ **10**
3629[13] Napoleon Star (IRE) **(69)***(55) (MSSaunders)* 4-9-10 (3) SDrowne(12) (lw: nvr nrr)....s.h **11**
3390[9] Crystal Gift **(63)***(49) (DWPArbuthnot)* 3-9-3 MFenton(8) (6th st: wknd over 2f out)....s.h **12**
3677[6] Best of Bold **(65)***(47) (NAGraham)* 3-9-5b PaulEddery(5) (lw: s.s: bhd fnl 2f)....1½ **13**
3634[15] Almuhtaram **(64)***(46) (MissGayKelleway)* 3-9-4 MTebbutt(15) (lw: a bhd)....hd **14**
3619[10] Top Pet (IRE) **(51)***(25)*(Fav)*(RAkehurst)* 5-8-9 TQuinn(9) (styd far side st: a bhd)....3½ **15**
3512[11] Evening Falls **(53)***(21) (CJames)* 4-8-11 CRutter(3) (bhd fnl 2f)....2½ **16**
2793* Grand Chapeau (IRE) **(61)***(28) (RHannon)* 3-9-1 MRoberts(17) (bhd fnl 3f)....½ **17**
3615[24] Fascination Waltz **(64)** *(JJSheehan)* 8-9-5 (3) PMcCabe(7) (lw: bhd fnl 3f)....20 **18**

11/2 Walnut Burl (IRE), Top Pet (IRE), **13/2** Tonys Gift, **7/1** North Esk (USA) (5/1-8/1), **8/1** Grand Chapeau (IRE), **10/1** Napoleon Star (IRE), Stoppes Brow, **11/1** Mislemani (IRE), **14/1** Shepherd Market (IRE), Morocco (IRE) (10/1-16/1), **16/1** Sally Weld, Present Situation, Best of Bold, **20/1** Almuhtaram, JO MAXIMUS, Evening Falls, Crystal Gift, **25/1** Fascination Waltz, CSF £235.84 CT £2,167.71 TOTE £21.90: £2.60 £3.80 £2.90 £2.50 (£314.30) Trio £759.40 OWNER Mr John Kelly (EPSOM) BRED Capt A. L. Smith-Maxwell 18 Rn

1m 21.7 (1.70) SF: 44/32/34/26/19/23/20/27/20/10/22/12/10/9/-/-/-/-
WEIGHT FOR AGE 3yo-4lb

T/Jkpt: Not won; £100,640.65 to Pontefract 21/9/95. T/Plpt: £368.60 (52.53 Tckts). T/Qdpt: £95.30 (1.2 Tckts). AK

3220-CHESTER (L-H)
Wednesday September 20th (Good to soft)
WEATHER: cloudy & dry WIND: slt half against

3772
CARDEN MAIDEN STKS (3-Y.O+) (Class D) £4,055.00 (£1,220.00: £590.00: £275.00) **1m 5f 89y** Stalls: Low GOING: 0.12 sec per fur (G) 2-20 (2-23)

1672[4] **General Assembly (IRE) (95)***(88+)*(Fav)*(HRACecil)* 3-8-12 PatEddery(3) (chsd ldr: led 2f out: sn pushed clr: unchal)....— **1**
929[4] Dato Star (IRE) *(80+) (JMJefferson)* 4-9-7 KFallon(10) (swtg: hld up & bhd: hdwy 3f out: 5th st: styd on fnl f: no ch w wnr)....7 **2**
3304[3] Yougo *(79) (MJohnston)* 3-8-12 JWeaver(11) (led to 2f out: 2nd st: sn rdn & outpcd)....¾ **3**
3618[4] Prophets Honour **(79)***(78) (CACyzer)* 3-8-12 DBiggs(5) (hld up: effrt & 4th st: one pce)....¾ **4**
3294[2] Dtoto *(77) (MRStoute)* 3-8-12 WRSwinburn(6) (hld up in tch: hdwy 3f out: rdn & 3rd st: wknd fnl f)....1 **5**
3421[3] Darter (IRE) *(70) (LMCumani)* 3-8-12 OUrbina(1) (lw: hld up & bhd: effrt on ins over 3f out: 6th st: nvr able to chal)....6 **6**
2568[4] Bint Zamayem (IRE) **(89)***(59) (BWHills)* 3-8-7 BThomson(2) (prom: pushed along & hmpd & checked 3f out: sn lost tch: t.o)....5 **7**
Little Serena *(56) (WMBrisbourne)* 5-9-2 SMaloney(8) (a in rr: t.o)....2½ **8**
2901[4] Malihabad (IRE) *(56) (RHollinshead)* 6-9-7 TIves(9) (hld up: rdn along over 5f out: no imp: t.o)....4 **9**
Royrace *(56) (WMBrisbourne)* 3-8-12 RCochrane(12) (mid div tl rdn & wknd 3f out: t.o)....hd **10**
3521[2] Western Horizon (USA) **(37)***(49) (CEBrittain)* 3-8-7 MBirch(7) (lw: s.i.s: hdwy ½-wy: wknd over 2f out: eased: t.o)....1¼ **11**
3618[5] Mu-Tadil *(42) (MajorWRHern)* 3-8-12 RHills(4) (bhd: rdn & dropped rr 6f out: t.o)....10 **12**

5/6 GENERAL ASSEMBLY (IRE) (4/5-Evens), **6/1** Dtoto, **13/2** Bint Zamayem (IRE), **9/1** Dato Star (IRE), **12/1** Darter (IRE), **14/1** Yougo, **16/1** Mu-Tadil, **20/1** Prophets Honour, **33/1** Western Horizon (USA), **50/1** Malihabad (IRE), **100/1** Royrace, Little Serena, CSF £9.68 TOTE £1.80: £1.20 £2.30 £3.50 (£6.20) Trio £69.40 OWNER H R H Prince Fahd Salman (NEWMARKET) BRED E. J. Loder 12 Rn

3m 1.39 (11.39) SF: 39/40/30/29/28/21/10/16/16/7/-/-
WEIGHT FOR AGE 3yo-9lb

3773

MARFORD MAIDEN STKS (2-Y.O) (Class D) £4,536.00 (£1,368.00: £664.00: £312.00) **7f 2y** Stalls: Low GOING: 0.12 sec per fur (G) 2-50 (2-54)

3208² **Hidden Oasis** *(89)*(Fav)*(MRStoute)* 2-9-0 WRSwinburn(4) (b: a.p: led 3f out: drvn clr appr fnl f: unchal)........— 1
3647⁹ Arctic Zipper (USA) *(69) (WAO'Gorman)* 2-9-0 RCochrane(3) (hld up: hdwy on ins over 2f out: 3rd st: one pce fnl f)........9 2
3432³ Baileys First (IRE) *(63) (MJohnston)* 2-8-9 JWeaver(6) (a.p: rdn over 3f out: 2nd st: one pce appr fnl f)........hd 3
3472² Ashjar (USA) *(64) (HThomsonJones)* 2-9-0 RHills(7) (lw: hld up in tch: effrt & 4th st: kpt on one pce)........1¾ 4
Three Hills *(48) (BWHills)* 2-9-0 PatEddery(1) (w'like: str: bkwd: outpcd: a bhd: 7th st)........7 5
3620¹³ Alzotic (IRE) *(48) (SGNorton)* 2-9-0 KFallon(2) (bkwd: outpcd & a wl bhd: 6th st)........nk 6
My Archie *(20) (RDEWoodhouse)* 2-9-0 NConnorton(8) (small: lt-f: outpcd: a bhd: 8th st).....12 7
3612⁹ Charterhouse Xpres **(60)***(15) (MMcCormack)* 2-9-0v BThomson(5) (led 4f: wknd qckly & 5th st)........2½ 8

4/6 HIDDEN OASIS, **4/1** Ashjar (USA) (op 5/2), **6/1** Three Hills (4/1-13/2), **7/1** Baileys First (IRE), **25/1** Arctic Zipper (USA), Charterhouse Xpres, **33/1** Alzotic (IRE), **50/1** My Archie, CSF £17.16 TOTE £1.70: £1.10 £3.00 £1.60 (£32.40) OWNER Sheikh Mohammed (NEWMARKET) BRED Sheikh Mohammed bin Rashid al Maktoum 8 Rn 1m 29.52 (4.32) SF: 57/37/31/32/16/16/-/-

3774

DAVID MCLEAN GROUP H'CAP (0-80) (3-Y.O+) (Class D) £5,702.50 (£1,720.00: £835.00: £392.50) **1m 7f 195y** Stalls: Low GOING: 0.12 sec per fur (G) 3-20 (3-23)

3569* **Unchanged (66)***(80) (CEBrittain)* 3-8-2 RHills(1) (hld up: rdn over 4f out: hdwy & 6th st: styd on to ld cl home)........— 1
3071⁴ French Ivy (USA) **(61)***(75)*(Fav)*(FMurphy)* 8-8-9 RCochrane(3) (b: hld up & bhd: hdwy 3f out: 5th st: rdn to ld ins fnl f: sn hdd: r.o)........½ 2
3571* Finlaggan **(74)***(87) (SirMarkPrescott)* 3-8-10 GDuffield(10) (led after 3f: clr over 1f out: hrd rdn & hdd ins fnl f)........nk 3
3445⁷ Star Rage (IRE) **(80)***(88) (MJohnston)* 5-10-0 JWeaver(4) (hld up & bhd: hdwy over 2f out: nvr nrr)........5 4
Bean King **(80)***(88) (MrsJCecil)* 9-10-0 TIves(2) (bkwd: led 3f: prom tl 4th & wkng st)........nk 5
3425⁸ Northern Law **(74)***(82) (BWHills)* 3-8-10 PatEddery(9) (prom: rdn & n.m.r over 2f out: swtchd rt fnl f: r.o)........nk 6
3627* En Vacances (IRE) **(65)***(71) (AGFoster)* 3-7-12 (3) 4x DWright(6) (prom early: lost pl ½-wy: sme late hdwy: n.d)........1½ 7
3676* All the Joys **(45)***(50) (CACyzer)* 4-7-7 4x JLowe(12) (hld up: hdwy 3f out: wnt 2nd st: rdn & wknd fnl f)........1 8
3425⁷ Welshman **(53)***(57) (MBlanshard)* 9-8-1 JQuinn(7) (chsd ldrs: rdn 8f out: 4th st: sn lost tch) .1¼ 9
3445⁹ Cuango (IRE) **(60)***(49) (RHollinshead)* 4-8-8 WRyan(8) (lw: hld up in rr: hdwy 4f out: no rspnse: t.o)........15 10
Champagne Gold **(53)** *(JCMcConnochie)* 8-8-1 TWilliams(11) (b: bit bkwd: s.s: a in rr: t.o fnl 3f)........dist 11
3223³ Soba Up **(76)** *(TJEtherington)* 5-9-10 ACulhane(5) (withdrawn not under Starter's orders: veterinary advice)........ W

LONG HANDICAP All the Joys 7-0

9/2 French Ivy (USA), **5/1** En Vacances (IRE), **11/2** Cuango (IRE), Star Rage (IRE), **6/1** Finlaggan, **13/2** Northern Law, **7/1** UNCHANGED, **8/1** Soba Up, **10/1** Welshman, **12/1** All the Joys, **14/1** Bean King, **33/1** Champagne Gold, CSF £40.21 CT £192.52 TOTE £7.60: £2.00 £1.70 £2.90 (£24.20) Trio £39.30 OWNER Mr M. J. Simmonds (NEWMARKET) BRED M. J. Simmonds 11 Rn 3m 34.79 (11.89) SF: 37/44/44/57/57/39/28/19/26/18/-/-

WEIGHT FOR AGE 3yo-12lb

3775

BEESTON CASTLE NURSERY H'CAP (2-Y.O) (Class C) £5,410.00 (£1,630.00: £790.00: £370.00) **7f 2y** Stalls: Low GOING: 0.12 sec per fur (G) 3-50 (3-52)

3701⁸ **Oriel Lad (72)***(80) (PDEvans)* 2-8-7b KFallon(5) (hld up: hdwy 3f out: 3rd st: led ins fnl f: sn clr)........— 1
3548³ Red Stream (USA) **(82)***(83) (MRStoute)* 2-9-3v WRSwinburn(2) (lw: hld up in rr: hdwy over 2f out: 4th st: rdn & r.o ins fnl f)........3 2
3613* Alzanti **(86)***(87)*(Fav)*(PFICole)* 2-9-2 (5) AWhelan(4) (led after 1f tl hdd & outpcd ins fnl f).......nk 3
3281* Rock Sharp **(78)***(77) (RHannon)* 2-8-13 PatEddery(6) (lw: led 1f: ev ch & 2nd st: rdn & one pce fnl f)........¾ 4
3427² Scenicris (IRE) **(67)***(64) (RHollinshead)* 2-8-2 NCarlisle(1) (hld up & bhd: effrt over 2f out: 5th & rdn st: nt trble ldrs)........1 5

3502* Silver Welcome (69)(54) (MHEasterby) 2-8-4 SMaloney(3) (plld hrd: prom over 4f: 6th & btn st) 5 6

2/1 Alzanti, **5/2** Rock Sharp, **7/2** Red Stream (USA), **7/1** Silver Welcome, **9/1** Scenicris (IRE), **14/1** ORIEL LAD, CSF £56.61 TOTE £16.40: £3.70 £1.90 (£23.00) OWNER Kendall White & Co Ltd (WELSHPOOL) BRED D. J. Watkins 6 Rn 1m 30.42 (5.22) SF: 40/43/47/37/24/14

3776 HESWALL CONDITIONS STKS (2-Y.O) (Class C) £4,803.30 (£1,750.80: £855.40: £367.00: £163.50) 7f 122y Stalls: Low GOING: 0.12 sec per fur (G) 4-20 (4-20)

*3523** **Wood Magic** *(86)*(Fav)*(DRLoder)* 2-9-0 PatEddery(4) (lw: a.p: 3rd st: shkn up to ld ent fnl f: r.o wl) ....— 1
2573⁸ Henry The Fifth *(78) (CEBrittain)* 2-8-11 JWeaver(2) (lw: led tl over 1f out: rallied u.p fnl f) 2½ 2
3720* The Man **(89)***(79) (MRChannon)* 2-9-0 3x RHughes(1) (b.nr hind: chsd ldr: slt ld over 1f out: sn hdd & swtchd: one pce fnl f) 1 3
3612* Some Horse (IRE) **(92)***(74) (MGMeagher)* 2-9-3 KFallon(5) (lw: sn drvn along: 4th & rdn st: nvr nr to chal) 3½ 4
3736² Two Socks **(52)***(51) (MMcCormack)* 2-8-11 RCochrane(3) (lw: outpcd: a bhd: t.o) 8 5

11/8 WOOD MAGIC, **7/4** Some Horse (IRE), **4/1** The Man, **16/1** Two Socks, **20/1** Henry The Fifth, CSF £17.72 TOTE £2.10: £1.40 £3.40 (£18.80) OWNER Sheikh Mohammed (NEWMARKET) BRED Sheikh Mohammed bin Rashid al Maktoum 5 Rn 1m 37.61 (5.91) SF: 43/35/36/31/8

3777 TARPORLEY H'CAP (0-85) (3-Y.O+) (Class D) £5,312.50 (£1,600.00: £775.00: £362.50) 5f 16y Stalls: Low GOING: 0.12 sec per fur (G) 4-50 (4-52)

3715¹⁶ **Macfarlane (69)***(73+)*(Fav)*(MJFetherston-Godley)* 7-8-13 WRSwinburn(9) (b: bhd: gd hdwy wl over 1f out: str run on outside to ld ins fnl f) ....— 1
3624¹¹ Indiahra **(50)***(51) (RHollinshead)* 4-7-8v^ow1 NCarlisle(4) (hdwy on ins over 1f out: str run fnl f: jst failed) ....½ 2
3704¹⁴ Gondo **(51)***(48) (EJAlston)* 8-7-2v(7)ow2 MartinDwyer(1) (chsd ldrs: led over 1f out tl ins fnl f: kpt on) 1 3
1560⁷ Little Ibnr **(63)***(62) (PDEvans)* 4-8-7 KFallon(3) (lw: a.p: led ½-wy tl over 1f out: hrd rdn fnl f: r.o wl) ....s.h 4
3279⁷ Takadou (IRE) **(80)***(77) (MissLCSiddall)* 4-9-10 RCochrane(2) (lw: bhd: gd hdwy over 1f out: fin wl) ....¾ 5
3359¹⁵ Elle Shaped (IRE) **(82)***(66) (ABailey)* 5-9-9 (3) DWright(10) (mid div: effrt u.p 2f out: nvr nr to chal) 4 6
3466⁸ Super Park **(73)***(52) (MHEasterby)* 3-9-1b MBirch(5) (led after 1f tl over 2f out: wknd appr fnl f) 1¾ 7
3667⁸ Primula Bairn **(62)***(39) (DNicholls)* 5-8-6b JLowe(13) (hdwy fnl 2f: nvr nrr) ....½ 8
3376⁶ Spender **(73)***(49) (PWHarris)* 6-9-3 RHills(8) (nvr trbld ldrs) ....nk 9
3376* Crystal Loop **(67)***(38) (ABailey)* 3-8-9 PatEddery(7) (chsd ldrs 3f: sn outpcd) 1½ 10
Local Heroine **(54)***(25) (JBerry)* 5-7-7 (5) PFessey(11) (lw: nvr nr ldrs) ....d.h 10
3667¹⁴ Lord Sky **(58)***(24) (ABailey)* 4-8-2b GDuffield(6) (led 1f: wknd 2f out) 1¾ 12
2925¹¹ The Real Whizzbang (IRE) **(50)***(4) (PSFelgate)* 4-7-5b(3)ow1 NVarley(12) (lw: spd on outside 3f) 3½ 13

LONG HANDICAP Gondo 6-12 Indiahra 7-0 The Real Whizzbang (IRE) 6-13

9/4 MACFARLANE, **5/1** Crystal Loop, **7/1** Elle Shaped (IRE), **8/1** Takadou (IRE), **10/1** Spender, **11/1** Gondo (20/1-10/1), **14/1** Little Ibnr, Primula Bairn, **16/1** Lord Sky, Super Park, **20/1** The Real Whizzbang (IRE), **25/1** Local Heroine, Indiahra, CSF £53.32 CT £488.28 TOTE £3.30: £1.90 £5.20 £2.40 (£79.00) Trio £119.20 OWNER Mr P. Fetherston-Godley (EAST ILSLEY) BRED P. Fetherston-Godley and Partners 13 Rn 64.24 secs (4.24) SF: 37/15/12/26/41/30/14/3/13/-/-/-/-

WEIGHT FOR AGE 3yo-2lb

T/Plpt: £109.60 (158.91 Tckts). T/Qdpt: £20.90 (7.5 Tckts). IM

3271-PONTEFRACT (L-H)
Thursday September 21st (Good)
WEATHER: overcast WIND: mod half bhd

3778 PONTEFRACT APPRENTICE SERIES ROUND 4 LIMITED STKS (0-70) (3-Y.O+) (Class E) £3,045.00 (£930.00: £460.00: £225.00) 1m 2f 6y Stalls: Low GOING minus 0.25 sec per fur (GF) 2-30 (2-31)

3621⁴ **Sweet Mignonette (70)***(75) (MrsMReveley)* 7-8-11 MHenry(1) (sn trckng ldrs: led over 3f out: sn rdn clr: eased towards fin) ....— 1

3723² Kandyan (66)*(72)*(Fav)*(MHTompkins)* 4-8-13 (5) JGotobed(11) (a.p: effrt over 2f out: styd on fnl f: no ch w wnr)....6 2
*3737*⁶ Sudden Spin **(42)***(63) (SGNorton)* 5-8-11 (7) SarahSenior(5) (a chsng ldrs: one pce fnl 2f) 6 3
2967⁵ Zacaroon **(67)***(56) (LordHuntingdon)* 4-8-13 AimeeCook(2) (hld up: hmpd 7f out: effrt 3f out: one pce) 1½ 4
*3737*⁷ Mad Militant (IRE) **(64)***(48) (AStreeter)* 6-9-6 DDenby(3) (b: hld up: effrt on outside 3f out: sn rdn & no imp) 9 5
3669²⁰ Ballard Lady (IRE) **(43)***(36) (JSWainwright)* 3-8-4 (3) FLynch(4) (led tl over 3f out: wknd wl over 1f out) 3 6
3645¹⁷ Dance King **(69)***(39) (DNicholls)* 3-8-12 GFaulkner(6) (w ldrs tl wknd over 2f out) 1¾ 7
3129⁸ Malindi Bay **(30)***(31) (BJMcMath)* 7-9-2 MartinDwyer(8) (sn bhd)....3½ 8
3537⁹ Docklands Courier **(50)***(15) (BJMcMath)* 3-8-6 (5)ow1 RMoogan(7) (prom tl lost pl over 3f out: sn bhd) 10 9
*225** Forgotten Empress **(69)***(6) (AHarrison)* 3-8-5 GMilligan(10) (bhd & drvn along 4f out: n.d)....2½ 10
3665¹⁴ Homecrest **(49)***(11) (MrsAMNaughton)* 3-8-10 PFessey(9) (bhd & drvn along 4f out)....hd 11
3464⁹ Ranger Sloane **(33)** *(GFierro)* 3-8-10 AEddery(12) (sn trckng ldrs: drvn along 5f out: sn lost pl & bhd)....12 12

6/4 Kandyan, **3/1** SWEET MIGNONETTE, **100/30** Zacaroon, **10/1** Forgotten Empress, **16/1** Mad Militant (IRE), Dance King, **20/1** Sudden Spin, **33/1** Docklands Courier, **50/1** Malindi Bay, Ballard Lady (IRE), Homecrest, Ranger Sloane, CSF £7.85 TOTE £3.00: £1.30 £1.30 £3.10 (£3.80) Trio £29.10 OWNER Mr Ron Whitehead (SALTBURN) BRED Countess of Durham 12 Rn
2m 13.2 (4.90) SF: 38/35/26/19/11/-/-/-/-/-/-/-
WEIGHT FOR AGE 3yo-6lb

3779

E.B.F. SIMPSON COULSON MAIDEN STKS (I) (2-Y.O) (Class D)£4,260.00 (£1,290.00: £630.00: £300.00) **6f** Stalls: Low GOING minus 0.25 sec(GF) 3-00 (3-01)

3465⁴ **Sketchbook (88)***(85+)*(Fav)*(GLewis)* 2-9-0 PatEddery(12) (lw: trckd ldrs: effrt over 2f out: shkn up & qcknd to ld over 1f out: sn clr: eased towards fin) ....— 1
Priolo Prima *(78+) (SirMarkPrescott)* 2-9-0 GDuffield(6) (wl grwn: lengthy: trckd ldr: led 2f out tl over 1f out: no ch w wnr) 2½ 2
Babinda *(76+) (CEBrittain)* 2-9-0 BDoyle(9) (w'like: wl grwn: in tch: outpcd 2f out: styd on fnl f)....1 3
3604¹¹ Impeccable *(49) (JLDunlop)* 2-8-9 WCarson(4) (led to 2f out: wknd & eased 1f out)....8 4
3662⁹ Ageeb (IRE) *(54) (WJHaggas)* 2-9-0 MHills(1) (s.i.s: bhd: nt clr run ½-wy: styd on fnl f) ....nk 5
3625² Quality (IRE) **(90)***(53) (WAO'Gorman)* 2-9-0 EmmaO'Gorman(10) (chsd ldrs: rdn & hung lft over 1f out: no imp)....nk 6
3417⁸ Mister Joel *(43) (MWEasterby)* 2-9-0 LCharnock(2) (prom tl wknd 2f out) 3½ 7
Appeal Again (IRE) *(42) (MrsJRRamsden)* 2-9-0 KFallon(11) (w'like: rangy: bit bkwd: s.i.s: bhd: sme hdwy 2f out: nvr nr ldrs)....½ 8
3416⁹ Sheemore (IRE) *(39) (JDBethell)* 2-9-0 TIves(3) (sn outpcd: bhd fr ½-wy) 1¼ 9
3536⁷ By A Whisker *(39) (DWPArbuthnot)* 2-9-0 SWhitworth(7) (nvr wnt pce) ....hd 10
3432¹³ One Life To Live (IRE) *(32) (AHarrison)* 2-8-11 (3) JStack(5) (lw: outpcd & drvn along) 2½ 11
3018¹³ Lugana Boy *(ASmith)* 2-9-0 DeanMcKeown(8) (ref to r: virtually t.n.p) .... R

5/4 SKETCHBOOK, **7/2** Quality (IRE), **4/1** Babinda, **5/1** Priolo Prima, **16/1** Impeccable, Appeal Again (IRE), By A Whisker, **20/1** Ageeb (IRE), **33/1** Sheemore (IRE), **50/1** Mister Joel, One Life To Live (IRE), **66/1** Lugana Boy, CSF £9.31 TOTE £2.40: £1.20 £2.10 £1.50 (£8.30) Trio £14.60 OWNER Highclere Thoroughbred Racing Ltd (EPSOM) BRED Lord Halifax 12 Rn
1m 16.3 (2.00) SF: 51/44/42/15/20/19/9/8/5/5/-/-

3780

ROBERT R. ROBERTS NURSERY H'CAP (0-85) (2-Y.O) (Class D) £4,045.00 (£1,210.00: £580.00: £265.00)
1m 4y Stalls: Low GOING minus 0.25 sec per fur (GF) 3-30 (3-30)

3613W **Vanishing Point (76)***(82) (GLewis)* 2-9-0 PatEddery(3) (lw: w ldrs: led over 4f out: drvn clr over 1f out: hld on wl towards fin)....— 1
3436³ Warbrook **(80)***(84) (IABalding)* 2-9-4 LDettori(2) (chsd ldrs: rdn 2f out: styd on u.p fnl f: nt qckn wl ins fnl f)....1 2
3516⁷ Munketh (USA) **(83)***(79) (JLDunlop)* 2-9-7 WCarson(4) (stdd s: hld up: stdy hdwy ½-wy: effrt & n.m.r 2f out: edgd rt & kpt on same pce appr fnl f) 4 3
3612⁶ Soul of Honour (FR) **(69)***(64) (MrsJRRamsden)* 2-8-7 KFallon(8) (hld up: hdwy ½-wy: effrt & n.m.r over 2f out: kpt on: nvr able chal) ....¾ 4
3540⁹ Bailiwick **(55)***(44) (NAGraham)* 2-7-7 GBardwell(7) (hdwy on outside over 2f out: kpt on appr fnl f: nvr nr ldrs)....3 5
3546³ Kingfisher Brave **(72)***(55)*(Fav)*(SGNorton)* 2-8-10 KDarley(10) (in tch: drvn along ½-wy: outpcd over 2f out: n.d after)....3 6

2926[5] Sticks Mckenzie **(65)***(43) (BWHills)* 2-8-3 MHills(13) (in tch: outpcd & drvn along ½-wy: sme hdwy over 1f out: nvr nr to chal)....2½ **7**
3463[11] Noir Esprit **(60)***(38) (JMCarr)* 2-7-12 NKennedy(5) (sn drvn along & outpcd: n.d)....s.h **8**
3744[11] Concert Party (IRE) **(56)***(21) (DWChapman)* 2-7-8 ow1 LCharnock(12) (sn bhd & drvn along)...6 **9**
3642[11] Shanoora (IRE) **(55)***(19) (BPalling)* 2-7-7 JLowe(1) (mde most tl over 4f out: wknd 3f out).......1 **10**
3523[3] Boundary Bird (IRE) **(65)***(26) (MJohnston)* 2-8-3 JWeaver(6) (chsd ldrs: drvn along ½-wy: lost pl over 2f out)....1¼ **11**
3642[16] Sovitaka (IRE) **(61)** *(MHEasterby)* 2-7-13bow1 SMaloney(9) (chsd ldrs tl wknd qckly over 2f out: sn wl bhd & eased)....15 **12**
3019[2] Russian Rascal (IRE) **(68)** *(MHEasterby)* 2-8-6 MBirch(11) (racd wd: p.u 3f out: b.b.v).... **P**

LONG HANDICAP Concert Party (IRE) 7-2 Shanoora (IRE) 7-3

9/4 Kingfisher Brave (op 7/2), **4/1** Soul of Honour (FR), **6/1** Warbrook, Munketh (USA), **15/2** VANISHING POINT, **17/2** Russian Rascal (IRE), **12/1** Sticks Mckenzie, **16/1** Boundary Bird (IRE), **20/1** Noir Esprit, **25/1** Sovitaka (IRE), Bailiwick, **33/1** Shanoora (IRE), **40/1** Concert Party (IRE), CSF £53.31 CT £274.41 TOTE £9.10: £2.30 £2.20 £1.90 (£26.70) Trio £23.40 OWNER Mr John Manley (EPSOM) BRED J. G. Fitzgerald 13 Rn 1m 46.1 (4.10) SF: 38/40/35/20/-/11/-/-/-/-/-/-/-

3781 DALBY SCREW-DRIVER RATED STKS H'CAP (0-95) (3-Y.O+) (Class B) £9,400.40 (£3,503.60: £1,701.80: £719.00: £309.50: £145.70) **1m 2f 6y** Stalls: Low GOING minus 0.25 sec per fur (GF) 4-00 (4-01)

3556[4] **Knave's Ash (USA) (94)***(104)*(Fav)*(MRStoute)* 4-9-7 WRSwinburn(8) (swtg: trckd ldr: shkn up & qcknd to ld over 1f out: hld on wl towards fin)....— **1**
3659[4] Vindaloo **(87)***(95) (JLHarris)* 3-8-8 JWeaver(4) (hld up: effrt over 2f out: styd on fnl f: nt rch wnr)....1 **2**
3433[6] Silently **(80)***(86) (IABalding)* 3-7-8 (7) MartinDwyer(5) (hld up: effrt 3f out: kpt on appr fnl f: nvr nr to chal)....1¾ **3**
3552[8] Eurolink the Rebel (USA) **(80)***(82) (RAkehurst)* 3-8-1 WCarson(7) (sn prom: rdn & outpcd 3f out: kpt on fnl f)....2½ **4**
Blair Castle (IRE) **(80)***(78) (GBBalding)* 4-8-7 JWilliams(3) (hld up: hdwy on outside ½-wy: sn prom: outpcd over 1f out)....2½ **5**
3408[8] Peutetre **(80)***(73) (CEBrittain)* 3-8-1 BDoyle(6) (led tl over 1f out: sn wknd)....3 **6**
3593[7] Indonesian (IRE) **(80)***(72) (MBell)* 3-8-1v MFenton(2) (trckd ldrs: effrt over 3f out: wknd over 1f out)....¾ **7**

2/1 KNAVE'S ASH (USA), **9/4** Vindaloo, **5/1** Indonesian (IRE), **7/1** Eurolink the Rebel (USA), **8/1** Blair Castle (IRE), **10/1** Silently, **33/1** Peutetre, CSF £6.87 CT £30.95 TOTE £2.60: £1.70 £1.80 (£2.50) OWNER Sheikh Mohammed (NEWMARKET) BRED Farfellow Farms Ltd in USA 7 Rn
2m 14.0 (5.70) SF: 41/26/17/13/15/4/3
WEIGHT FOR AGE 3yo-6lb

3782 EASDALE LANE CONDITIONS STKS (2-Y.O) (Class C) £5,588.00 (£1,808.00: £884.00) **1m 4y** Stalls: Low GOING minus 0.25 sec per fur (GF) 4-30 (4-30)

3631[4] **Night Watch (USA) (92)***(94+)*(Fav)*(IABalding)* 2-9-0 LDettori(4) (lw: mde all: pushed clr over 1f out: v.easily)....— **1**
3490[5] Dublin River (USA) **(100)***(91) (HThomsonJones)* 2-9-5 GCarter(1) (a chsng wnr: pushed along ½-wy: no imp)....4 **2**
2432[5] Lagan *(65) (CEBrittain)* 2-8-11 BDoyle(2) (bit bkwd: chsd ldrs: drvn along ½-wy: wknd wl over 1f out: eased)....9 **3**

4/6 NIGHT WATCH (USA), **13/8** Dublin River (USA), **12/1** Lagan, CSF £1.91 TOTE £1.40 (£1.10) OWNER The Queen (KINGSCLERE) BRED The Queen 3 Rn 1m 46.4 (4.40) SF: 36/33/7

3783 JOHN GOODCHILD H'CAP (0-70) (3-Y.O+) (Class E) £3,769.00 (£1,132.00: £546.00: £253.00) **5f** Stalls: Low GOING minus 0.25 sec per fur (GF) 5-00 (5-02)

3150[2] **Royal Dome (IRE) (64)***(70) (MartynWane)* 3-9-6 LDettori(8) (a chsng ldrs: styd on to ld ins fnl f: all out)....— **1**
3242[3] Sing With the Band **(55)***(61) (BAMcMahon)* 4-8-10 (3) SSanders(18) (a chsng ldrs: r.o wl ins fnl f: jst failed)....s.h **2**
3622[14] Jucea **(62)***(68) (JLSpearing)* 6-9-6 JWeaver(3) (hdwy ½-wy: effrt & swtchd rt over 1f out: styd on wl towards fin)....hd **3**
3615[22] Petraco (IRE) **(62)***(67) (NASmith)* 7-9-6 SDWilliams(7) (chsd ldrs: drvn along ½-wy: nt qckn ins fnl f)....hd **4**
3649[7] Silk Cottage **(63)***(67) (RMWhitaker)* 3-9-5 ACulhane(1) (led tl ins fnl f: no ex)....½ **5**
3524[4] Ninety-Five **(65)***(65) (JGFitzGerald)* 3-9-0 (7) MartinDwyer(14) (a chsng ldrs: kpt on same pce appr fnl f)....1¼ **6**

*3512*7 Pageboy **(62)***(60) (PCHaslam)* 6-9-6 MTebbutt(6) (lw: mid div: hdwy on ins over 1f out: nt clr run: eased towards fin) .... ½ **7**
3715 6 Captain Carat **(65)***(63)*(Fav)*(MrsJRRamsden)* 4-9-9 KFallon(15) (swtchd lft s: hld up: hdwy 2f out: nt clr run ins fnl f: nvr nr to chal) .... hd **8**
3418 11 Lochon **(57)***(55) (JLEyre)* 4-9-1 RLappin(12) (lw: bkwd: mid div: hdwy 2f out: kpt on: nvr nr to chal) .... s.h **9**
3622 19 Robellion **(70)***(67) (DWPArbuthnot)* 4-10-0 SWhitworth(4) (lw: s.i.s: bhd: sme hdwy over 1f out: n.d) .... s.h **10**
*3522*5 Nadwaty (IRE) **(52)***(49) (MCChapman)* 3-8-1 (7) CMunday(13) (chsd ldrs tl wknd over 1f out) s.h **11**
3492 18 Stand Tall **(52)***(47) (CWThornton)* 3-8-8 DeanMcKeown(16) (in tch: outpcd & drvn along ½-wy: sme hdwy over 1f out: n.d) .... ¾ **12**
2949 7 Utr (USA) **(55)***(50) (HThomsonJones)* 3-8-11 GCarter(17) (swtg: unruly s: bhd: sme hdwy over 1f out: n.d) .... hd **13**
3777 8 Primula Bairn **(62)***(50) (DNicholls)* 5-9-6b JLowe(5) (chsd ldrs tl wknd over 1f out: eased towards fin) 2 **14**
1723 7 Rymer's Rascal **(66)***(54) (EJAlston)* 3-9-8 StephenDavies(9) (lw: sn outpcd & drvn along: n.d) .... hd **15**
3667 26 Tenor **(61)***(45) (DNicholls)* 4-9-5 AlexGreaves(11) (a in rr) 1¼ **16**
3222 17 Monis (IRE) **(65)***(47) (JBalding)* 4-9-2 (7) JEdmunds(10) (nvr nr ldrs) .... ½ **17**
*3522*3 Most Uppitty **(52)***(29) (JBerry)* 3-8-1 (7) JoanneWebster(2) (a bhd) 1½ **18**

9/4 Captain Carat (4/1-2/1), **6/1** ROYAL DOME (IRE), **8/1** Sing With the Band (op 5/1), **10/1** Petraco (IRE), Jucea, **12/1** Lochon, Pageboy, Robellion, **14/1** Ninety-Five, **16/1** Primula Bairn, Tenor, Rymer's Rascal, Utr (USA), **20/1** Silk Cottage, **25/1** Stand Tall, Nadwaty (IRE), Most Uppitty, **33/1** Monis (IRE), CSF £58.24 CT £464.32 TOTE £5.40: £1.60 £2.30 £2.30 £3.00 (£18.60) Trio £137.10 OWNER Mr G. W. Jones (RICHMOND) BRED Michael F. Fogarty 18 Rn
63.4 secs (1.90) SF: 52/45/52/51/49/47/44/47/39/51/31/29/32/34/36/29/31/11
WEIGHT FOR AGE 3yo-2lb

3784

E.B.F. SIMPSON COULSON MAIDEN STKS (II) (2-Y.O) (Class D)
£4,240.50 (£1,284.00: £627.00: £298.50)
6f Stalls: Low GOING minus 0.25 sec per fur (GF) 5-30 (5-31)

3604 2 **Brandon Magic** *(80)*(Fav)*(IABalding)* 2-9-0 LDettori(6) (lw: a chsng ldrs: styd on to ld jst ins fnl f: drvn out) .... — **1**
3530 2 Singing Patriarch (IRE) *(77) (JLDunlop)* 2-9-0 PatEddery(11) (hld up: effrt over 2f out: qcknd to chal jst ins fnl f: no ex towards fin) 1 **2**
3626 2 Wee Hope (USA) *(64) (MRStoute)* 2-9-0 WRSwinburn(7) (lw: trckd ldrs: qcknd to ld over 1f out: hung lft & hdd jst ins fnl f: sn wl outpcd) 5 **3**
3604 3 Forest Robin **(90)***(57) (RFJohnsonHoughton)* 2-9-0 BThomson(3) (lw: a chsng ldrs: effrt over 2f out: nt clr run: kpt on same pce) 2½ **4**
3626 7 Agent *(57) (WJHaggas)* 2-9-0 MHills(2) (hld up & plld hrd: effrt 2f out: nvr nr to chal) .... hd **5**
Kenilworth Dancer *(44) (MrsMReveley)* 2-9-0 KDarley(8) (cmpt: bit bkwd: unruly s: outpcd & bhd: sme hdwy 2f out: sn wknd) 5 **6**
3465 9 Angus McCoatup (IRE) *(39) (BAMcMahon)* 2-9-0 GCarter(1) (bit bkwd: led over 2f out: hdd over 1f out: grad wknd & eased) 1¾ **7**
3432 8 Escobar (IRE) *(34) (PCalver)* 2-9-0 MBirch(5) (led tl over 2f out: sn wknd) 1¾ **8**
3536 10 Generous Present *(24) (JWPayne)* 2-9-0 MTebbutt(9) (b.hind: s.i.s: a in rr) 4 **9**
3626 16 Maiteamia *(22) (SRBowring)* 2-8-9b(5) CTeague(12) (racd wd: sn bhd) .... ½ **10**
3432 15 Glorious Sound *(1) (JHanson)* 2-9-0 ACulhane(10) (b.off hind: s.i.s: a in rr) 8 **11**

9/4 BRANDON MAGIC, **5/2** Wee Hope (USA) (7/4-11/4), **7/2** Forest Robin, **6/1** Singing Patriarch (IRE) (3/1-7/1), **11/1** Agent, **16/1** Angus McCoatup (IRE), **20/1** Kenilworth Dancer, Escobar (IRE), **50/1** Generous Present, Maiteamia, Glorious Sound, CSF £16.53 TOTE £3.40: £1.20 £1.40 £1.50 (£8.60) Trio £4.40 OWNER Mr R. P. B. Michaelson (KINGSCLERE) BRED Highclere Stud Ltd 11 Rn
1m 16.7 (2.40) SF: 46/43/30/23/23/10/5/-/-/-/-

T/Jkpt: £2,278.90 (62.02 Tckts). T/Plpt: £14.30 (2,156.68 Tckts). T/Qdpt: £6.20 (24.45 Tckts). WG

3687a-CHANTILLY (France) (R-H)
Monday September 11th (Soft)

3785a

PRIX SEINE-ET-OISE (Gp 3) (3-Y.O+) £26,347.00 (£9,581.00: £4,790.00) **6f (straight)** 2-45 (2-37)

3582a* **Hever Golf Rose** *(121) (TJNaughton)* 4-9-1 JWeaver .... — **1**
1116a 10 Tereshkova (USA) *(118) (AFabre,France)* 3-8-10 TJarnet .... nk **2**

3195a3 Glenlivet (SWE) *(114) (LKelp,Sweden)* 7-9-0 JohnFortune 2 3

P-M 2.10F: 1.10F 1.20F 2.50F (2.50F) OWNER Mr M. P. Hanson (EPSOM) BRED Ronald Popely 9 Rn
1m 12.4 SF: -/-/-

3694a-LONGCHAMP (Paris, France) (R-H) Thursday September 14th (Very Soft)

3786a PRIX D'AUMALE (Gp 3) (2-Y.O F) £26,347.00 (£9,581.00: £4,790.00) **1m** 3-15 (3-22)

Shake the Yoke *(108) (ELellouche,France)* 2-8-9 DBoeuf ....— 1
Miss Tahiti (IRE) *(104) (AFabre,France)* 2-8-9 OPeslier 2 2
Raisonnable *(101) (DSepulchre,France)* 2-8-9 ESaint-Martin 1½ 3

P-M 11.10F: 3.20F 2.60F 4.70F (67.30F) OWNER S. Brunswick BRED Sussex Stud & Calogo Bloodstock 11 Rn
1m 43.6 SF: -/-/-

3691a-CURRAGH (Newbridge, Ireland) (R-H) Saturday September 16th (Good)

3787a MACDONAGH & BOLAND STKS (Listed) (3-Y.O+) £9,579.00 (£2,748.00: £1,262.00) **7f** 2-45 (2-46)

3191 11 **Wizard King** *(119) (SirMarkPrescott)* 4-9-4 TQuinn ....— 1
1234a4 Burden Of Proof (IRE) *(113) (CO'Brien,Ireland)* 3-8-10 CRoche 1 2
3193a3 Park Charger *(99) (APO'Brien,Ireland)* 3-8-7 WJSupple 4½ 3
1837 7 Adjareli (IRE) *(106)*(Fav)*(JOxx,Ireland)* 3-9-0 JPMurtagh ....hd 4
3325a2 Ivory Frontier (IRE) *(102) (JSBolger,Ireland)* 5-9-0 JAHeffernan ....s.h 5

11/10 Adjareli (IRE), **9/2** Burden Of Proof (IRE), Ivory Frontier (IRE), **5/1** WIZARD KING, **16/1** Park Charger, Tote £7.30: £2.40 £1.20 £5.90 (£14.30) OWNER Sheikh Ahmed bin Saeed Al Maktoum (NEWMARKET) BRED Sheikh Mohammed bin Rashid al Maktoum 9 Rn 1m 23.1 (-0.10)

3788a NATIONAL STKS (Gp 1) (2-Y.O C & F) £58,515.00 (£18,911.00: £9,010.00: £3,069.00) **7f** 3-15 (3-17)

3197a* **Danehill Dancer (IRE)** *(104)*(Fav)*(NACallaghan)* 2-9-0 PatEddery (hld up: hdwy ½-wy: rdn to ld 1f out: r.o wl) ....— 1
2704* Polaris Flight (USA) *(101) (PWChapple-Hyam)* 2-9-0 WRSwinburn (trckd ldrs: rdn & hmpd 1½f out: styd.on wl) 1½ 2
Force of Will (USA) *(99) (DKWeld,Ireland)* 2-9-0 MJKinane (hld up: hdwy 2f out: rdn 1½f out: r.o fnl f) ....¾ 3
3197a9 Deed of Love (USA) *(99) (JSBolger,Ireland)* 2-9-0 JAHeffernan (a.p: led 3f out to 1f out: one pce) ....s.h 4
3586a3 Harghar (USA) *(93) (JOxx,Ireland)* 2-9-0 JPMurtagh (hld up: nvr plcd to chal) 2½ 5
Roi Estate (IRE) *(89) (DHanley,Ireland)* 2-9-0 WJSupple (prom tl wknd over 2f out) 2 6
3273 4 Double Oscar (IRE) *(78) (MJohnston)* 2-9-0 JWeaver (led tl rdn & hdd 3f out: sn wknd) 4½ 7

4/5 DANEHILL DANCER (IRE), **2/1** Polaris Flight (USA), **13/2** Force of Will (USA), **8/1** Harghar (USA), **16/1** Deed of Love (USA), Double Oscar (IRE), **66/1** Roi Estate (IRE), Tote £1.80: £1.40 £1.80 (£1.80) OWNER Mr M. Tabor (NEWMARKET) BRED L. K. and K. McCreery 7 Rn
1m 24.1 (0.90) SF: -/-/-/-/-/-/-

3789a JEFFERSON SMURFIT MEMORIAL IRISH ST LEGER (Gp 1) (3-Y.O+) £87,921.00 (£28,515.00: £13,663.00: £4,752.00) **1m 6f** 4-25 (4-29)

3591a9 **Strategic Choice (USA)** *(125) (PFICole)* 4-9-8 TQuinn (hld up: hdwy & 4th st: led on bit 1½f out: rdn out) ....— 1
1869 2 Moonax (IRE) *(125) (BWHills)* 4-9-8 PatEddery (trckd ldrs: 3rd st: rdn to chal 2f out: r.o gamely u.p) ....hd 2
2218a4 Oscar Schindler (IRE) *(122) (KPrendergast,Ireland)* 3-8-12 WJSupple (hld up: 6th st: prog to chal over 1f out: no ex u.p) 3 3
3481a* Vintage Crop *(119)*(Fav)*(DKWeld,Ireland)* 8-9-8 MJKinane (a.p: 2nd st: rdn to ld over 2f out: sn hdd & btn) 2 4
2211a6 Double On (IRE) *(115) (PJFlynn,Ireland)* 4-9-5 MDuffy (5th st: rdn over 2f out: one pce) ....¾ 5

3481a2 Johansson (USA) *(113) (JOxx,Ireland)* 3-8-12 JPMurtagh (a bhd) 4½ 6
3482a2 Zilzal Zamaan (USA) *(113) (MRStoute)* 4-9-8 WRSwinburn (led tl rdn & hdd over 2f out: sn wknd) ....nk 7

11/10 Vintage Crop, **9/4** Moonax (IRE), **6/1** STRATEGIC CHOICE (USA), **10/1** Oscar Schindler (IRE), Zilzal Zamaan (USA), **33/1** Johansson (USA), **40/1** Double On (IRE), Tote £8.20: £3.80 £2.10 (£11.80) OWNER Mr M. Arbib (WHATCOMBE) BRED M. Arbib 7 Rn 3m 0.9 (5.50) SF: -/-/-/-/-/-/-

3698a-SAN SIRO (Milan, Italy) (R-H)
Saturday September 16th (Very Soft)

3790a GRAN PREMIO D'ITALIA (Gp 1) (3-Y.O) £88,751.00 (£45,799.00: £26,960.00: £13,480.00) 1m 4f 3-15 (3-23)

3603* **Posidonas** *(114) (PFICole)* 3-9-2 RHughes (trckd ldr tl led 2f out: r.o wl: comf) ....— 1
Slicious *(109) (VCaruso,Italy)* 3-9-2 MEsposito (4th st: r.o fnl 2f: nt rch wnr) 3½ 2
2218a9 Court of Honour (IRE) *(107) (PWChapple-Hyam)* 3-9-2 BThomson (led to 2f out: one pce) .1½ 3
2218a11 Humbel (USA) *(106) (DKWeld,Ireland)* 3-9-2 GMosse (trckd ldrs: 3rd st: rdn 2f out: no ex) ....¾ 4
Valsodo (USA) *(102) (LMariani,Italy)* 3-9-2 LSorrentino (a bhd) 3¼ 5
Tarhelm (ITY) *(102) (GColleo,Italy)* 3-9-2 MLatorre (mid div: 5th st: nvr plcd to chal) ....hd 6
Golden Glenstal (IRE) *(90) (GFratini,Italy)* 3-9-2 FJovine (a bhd: t.o) 9 7

Tote 45L: 24L 40L (134L) OWNER Mr Athos Christodoulou (WHATCOMBE) BRED A. Christodoulou 7 Rn 2m 33.0 SF: -/-/-/-/-/-/-

3791a PREMIO BOLDINASCO H'CAP (3-Y.O) £7,880.00 1m 2f 4-10 (4-25)

1886a2 **Suranom (IRE)** *(75+) (LMCumani)* 3-8-12 FJovine ....— 1
Trillo (ITY) *(63) (Italy)* 3-8-7 ACarboni 4½ 2
Donful (IRE) *(60) (Italy)* 3-8-5 MLatorre ....nk 3

Tote 26L: 16L 37L 18L (337L) OWNER Scuderia Rencati (NEWMARKET) 8 Rn 2m 6.7 SF: -/-/-

2890a-MAISONS-LAFFITTE (France)
Saturday September 16th (Very Soft)

3792a LA COUPE DE MAISONS-LAFFITTE (Gp 3) (4-Y.O+) £26,347.00 (£9,581.00: £4,790.00) 1m 2f 3-30 (3-40)

Gunboat Diplomacy (FR) *(124) (ELellouche,France)* 4-8-11 OPeslier ....— 1
1394a7 Dernier Empereur (USA) *(119) (AFabre,France)* 5-8-11 TJarnet 3 2
Northern Spy (FR) *(118) (DSepulchre,France)* 4-8-11 ODoleuze 1 3

P-M 3.40F: 1.40F 1.10F (SF 8.10F) OWNER Mr D. Wildenstein BRED London T'bred Serv. & George Strawbridge in France 6 Rn 2m 6.2 SF: -/-/-

3786a-LONGCHAMP (Paris, France) (R-H)
Sunday September 17th (Very Soft)

3793a PRIX DE LA SALAMANDRE (Gp 1) (2-Y.O C & F) £47,904.00 (£19,162.00: £9,581.00: £4,790.00) 7f 2-40 (2-43)

3315* **Lord of Men** *(108+) (JHMGosden)* 2-8-11 LDettori (trckd ldr: chal over 1f out: led ins fnl f: r.o wl) ....— 1
3330a2 With Fascination (USA) *(103) (JEPease,France)* 2-8-8 OPeslier (led tl ins fnl f: r.o wl u.p) 1 2
3586a* Woodborough (USA) *(101) (PWChapple-Hyam)* 2-8-11 JReid (plld hrd: 3rd st: swtchd over 1f out: r.o one pce u.p) 2 3
3687a* Titus Livius (FR) *(99) (JEPease,France)* 2-8-11 CAsmussen (hld up: rdn 2f out: one pce) 1 4
3330a3 Barricade (USA) *(94) (AFabre,France)* 2-8-11 TJarnet (hld up: effrt 2f out: unable qckn) 2 5
3483a3 Restless Carl (IRE) *(94) (AFabre,France)* 2-8-11 GMosse (4th st: nvr plcd to chal) ....s.h 6

Star Finch (FR) *(60) (PBourgoin,France)* 2-8-11 RO'Brien (a bhd) 15 7

P-M 7.00F: 3.00F 2.30F (SF 33.90F) OWNER Sheikh Mohammed (NEWMARKET) BRED Sheikh Mohammed bin Rashid al Maktoum 7 Rn 1m 27.0 SF: -/-/-/-/-/-/-

3794a PRIX DU PRINCE D'ORANGE (Gp 3) (3-Y.O) £26,347.00 (£9,581.00: £4,790.00) **1m 2f** 3-10 (3-10)

1611[2] **Tamure (IRE)** *(118) (JHMGosden)* 3-8-11 LDettori ....— 1
1611[13] Spectrum (IRE) *(125) (PWChapple-Hyam)* 3-9-4 JReid ....nk 2
3486a[3] Rifapour (IRE) *(120) (AdeRoyerDupre,France)* 3-9-2 GMosse 1½ 3

P-M 1.70F: 1.20F 2.10F (SF 4.80F) OWNER Sheikh Mohammed (NEWMARKET) BRED Sheikh Mohammed bin Rashid al Maktoum 5 Rn 2m 25.9 SF: -/-/-

3795a PRIX DU PIN (Listed) (3-Y.O+) £16,766.00 (£5,748.00: £3,593.00) **7f** 4-10 (4-07)

2040a[3] **Poplar Bluff (IRE)** *(119) (AFabre,France)* 3-8-11 OPeslier ....— 1
3042a[2] Young Ern *(116) (SDow)* 5-9-1 TQuinn 1½ 2
3042a[9] Nec Plus Ultra (FR) *(117) (AdeRoyerDupre,France)* 4-9-4 GMosse ....¾ 3

P-M 5.00F: 1.50F 1.10F (SF 14.20F) OWNER Mr D. Wildenstein (FRANCE) 6 Rn 1m 28.2 SF: -/-/-

3790a-SAN SIRO (Milan, Italy) (R-H) Sunday September 17th (Heavy)

3796a PREMIO MOLVEDO (3-Y.O+) £31,445.00 **7f 110y** 1-30 (1-30)

900a[3] **Robins (IRE)** *(106) (AColella,Italy)* 3-9-1 FJovine ....— 1
1396a[11] Thomire *(104) (Italy)* 3-9-1 BJovine ....¾ 2
El Paesa (IRE) *(99) (Italy)* 5-9-0 GForte ....nse 3
3039a[2] Albinor (IRE) *(89) (JLDunlop)* 3-8-9 MTellini 4½ 4

Tote 21L: 11L 17L 13L (63L) OWNER San Paolo Agricola Stud 11 Rn 1m 34.3 SF: -/-/-/-

3797a PREMIO HAVRESAC II (2-Y.O C & G) £33,415.00 **7f 110y** 2-00 (2-10)

Coral Reef (ITY) *(GColleo,Italy)* 2-8-12 MLatorre ....— 1
Brave Indigo *(Italy)* 2-8-12 SDettori ....¾ 2
Trood *(Italy)* 2-8-12 LSorrentino 3½ 3
3530[5] Robamaset (IRE) *(LMCumani)* 2-8-12 FJovine (btn approx 17l) 11

Tote 78L: 15L 18L 43L (105L) OWNER Scuderia Andy Capp BRED A. Rampa 13 Rn 1m 38.4

2567a-FRANKFURT (Germany) (L-H) Sunday September 17th (Good)

3798a MADE IN EUROPE VAL DES PRES-TROPHY (Gp 2) (3-Y.O+) £49,383.00 (£19,753.00: £9,053.00: £4,115.00) **1m 2f** 3-10 (3-12)

2891a[2] **Hushang (IRE)** *(119) (JOxx,Ireland)* 5-9-0 JPMurtagh (mde most: r.o wl u.p)....— 1
Sylvan Point *(119) (HRemmert,Germany)* 4-9-0b KWoodburn (4th tl hdwy over 1f out: r.o wl)hd 2
2729a[4] Manzoni (GER) *(117) (AWohler,Germany)* 3-8-9 ABoschert (a.p: 2nd st: chal over 1f out: no ex ins fnl f)....2 3
2894a[5] Hondero (GER) *(112) (BoerjeOlsson,Sweden)* 5-9-2 DRegnard (a.p: no ex fnl 2f)....3½ 4
Latmos (GER) *(107) (Germany)* 5-9-0 GHuber (hld up: nvr plcd to chal)....1¾ 5
2567a[3] No Dancer (GER) *(105) (Germany)* 4-9-0b ATylicki (5th st: wknd over 1f out) 1½ 6
Mr Woodman (GER) *(95) (Germany)* 3-8-5 ASuborics (a bhd)....4 7
2729a[8] Bad Bertrich (IRE) *(84) (Germany)* 4-9-0b GBocskai (prom tl wknd over 4f out) 9 8
Upper Heights (GER) *(71) (Germany)* 7-9-0 LMader (a bhd)....8 9

Tote 24DM: 12DM 17DM 11DM (SF 333DM) OWNER Aga Khan BRED H H Aga Khan Stud S C 9 Rn 2m 9.74 SF: -/-/-/-/-/-/-/-/-

3488-HAYDOCK (L-H)
Friday September 22nd (Good)
WEATHER: drizzle WIND: mod half against

3799 STANLEY SPORTSLINE MAIDEN STKS (3-Y.O) (Class D) £4,242.00 (£1,281.00: £623.00: £294.00)
1m 2f 120y Stalls: High GOING minus 0.15 sec per fur (GF) 2-00 (2-03)

3183[4] **Merry Festival (USA)** *(83) (JHMGosden)* 3-8-9 LDettori(17) (prom: 4th st: led wl over 1f out: r.o wl)......— **1**
1167[3] Lion Tower *(85)*(Fav)*(HRACecil)* 3-9-0 WRyan(3) (bit bkwd: prom: 6th st: rdn over 2f out: chsd wnr bel dist: no imp)......2 **2**
3505[3] High Patriarch (IRE) **(77)***(83) (JLDunlop)* 3-9-0b WCarson(2) (hld up & plld hrd: 7th st: styd on appr fnl f: nvr nrr)......1¼ **3**
3573[4] Silver Singer *(71) (DRLoder)* 3-8-9 GCarter(6) (chsd ldng pair: 3rd st: wknd over 1f out)......5 **4**
Witchfinder (USA) *(75) (JHMGosden)* 3-9-0 GHind(7) (b.hind: bkwd: nvr plcd to chal)......½ **5**
635[7] Snow Princess (IRE) *(69) (LordHuntingdon)* 3-8-9 JReid(15) (bit bkwd: hld up: hdwy on ins over 2f out: no ex appr fnl f)......nk **6**
3618[7] Sicarian *(67) (MJHeaton-Ellis)* 3-9-0 RHughes(16) (bit bkwd: chsd ldr: 2nd st: rdn & wkng whn n.m.r appr fnl f)......5 **7**
3653[5] Drum Battle *(66) (RCharlton)* 3-9-0 JWeaver(5) (swtg: led: rdn over 3f out: hdd & wknd wl over 1f out)......½ **8**
3618[6] House of Dreams *(66) (BWHills)* 3-9-0 MHills(14) (in tch tl wknd over 3f out)......nk **9**
3447[10] Mr Christie **(49)***(64) (MissLCSiddall)* 3-9-0 WNewnes(12) (s.s: a in rr)......1 **10**
3239[10] Ozubeck (USA) *(56) (BHanbury)* 3-8-9 RHills(13) (a bhd)......2 **11**
Three Wild Days *(52) (TPTate)* 3-9-0 ACulhane(4) (wl grwn: bit bkwd: a bhd: t.o)......6 **12**
3421[4] New Broom (IRE) *(43) (MHEasterby)* 3-8-9 SMaloney(11) (mid div tl wknd 3f out: t.o)......2½ **13**
3653[15] Most Becoming *(26) (JRArnold)* 3-8-9 CRutter(9) (a in rr: t.o)......11 **14**
3227[2] Golden Pound (USA) **(79)***(31) (EALDunlop)* 3-9-0 JTate(10) (lw: chsd ldrs: 5th st: drvn along over 3f out: sn wknd: t.o)......s.h **15**
On The Off Chance *(GHolmes)* 3-9-0b JFEgan(8) (w'like: bkwd: a bhd: t.o fnl 3f)......dist **16**

3/1 Lion Tower, **9/2** High Patriarch (IRE), **6/1** MERRY FESTIVAL (USA) (op 4/1), Golden Pound (USA), **8/1** Snow Princess (IRE), **10/1** Silver Singer, Witchfinder (USA), **12/1** House of Dreams, **14/1** Drum Battle, **25/1** Sicarian, **50/1** Ozubeck (USA), Mr Christie, New Broom (IRE), **100/1** Most Becoming, Three Wild Days, On The Off Chance, CSF £23.69 TOTE £6.30: £2.20 £1.30 £1.80 (£7.30) Trio £6.20 OWNER Sheikh Mohammed (NEWMARKET) BRED Darley Stud Management Co Ltd 16 Rn 2m 14.39 (2.89) SF: 59/61/59/47/51/45/43/42/42/40/32/28/19/2/7/-

3800 STANLEY CREDIT CLAIMING H'CAP (0-70) (3-Y.O+) (Class E) £3,582.50 (£1,085.00: £530.00: £252.50)
6f Stalls: High GOING minus 0.15 sec per fur (GF) 2-30 (2-35)

3467* **Densben (48)***(57) (DenysSmith)* 11-8-8 KFallon(7) (lw: hld up: gd hdwy bel dist: str run to ld wl ins fnl f)......— **1**
3667[13] Southern Dominion **(61)***(67) (MJohnston)* 3-9-4 RHills(22) (led tl rdn & hdd wl ins fnl f)......1¼ **2**
3467[16] Princess Maxine (IRE) **(53)***(57) (JJO'Neill)* 6-8-13 AMackay(19) (lw: gd hdwy over 1f out: fin wl)......½ **3**
3681[3] Hello Hobson's (IRE) **(51)***(54) (RBastiman)* 5-8-6 (5) GParkin(15) (hld up: hdwy bel dist: swtchd lft 1f out: r.o wl fnl f)......½ **4**
3624[8] Arasong **(61)***(59) (EWeymes)* 3-9-4 SMaloney(20) (chsd ldrs: rdn over 1f out: one pce)......1¾ **5**
3457[6] Mustn't Grumble (IRE) **(62)***(60) (WSCunningham)* 5-9-8 LDettori(2) (racd far side: rdn & r.o wl ins fnl f)......hd **6**
3715[9] Here Comes Risky **(67)***(64) (MJohnston)* 3-9-10 JWeaver(9) (chsd ldrs stands' side: rdn wl over 1f out: no imp)......nk **7**
3615[7] Gone Savage **(64)***(61) (WJMusson)* 7-9-7 (3) PMcCabe(17) (nvr nr to chal)......s.h **8**
3678[U] Northern Grey **(52)***(49) (JBerry)* 3-8-9 GCarter(13) (hdwy over 1f out: nt rch ldrs)......hd **9**
3739[6] Desert Invader (IRE) **(56)***(50) (DWChapman)* 4-9-2 ACulhane(12) (lw: nvr trbld ldrs)......1¼ **10**
3649[8] Marsh Arab **(54)***(47) (JBalding)* 4-8-7 (7) JEdmunds(21) (lw: nvr nrr)......s.h **11**
3519[5] Random **(52)***(45) (CJames)* 4-8-12 JWilliams(3) (prom far side 4f)......hd **12**
2202[2] Friendly Brave (USA) **(66)***(58) (MissGayKelleway)* 5-9-12 MHills(10) (prom stands' side: ev ch over 1f out: wknd fnl f)......½ **13**
3677* Blow Dry (IRE) **(60)***(49) (MartynWane)* 5-9-6 6x RPrice(16) (prom over 4f)......1¼ **14**
3678[2] Just Like Me **(61)***(48)*(Fav)*(RGuest)* 3-9-4 MRoberts(24) (prom over 4f: sn rdn & wknd)......½ **15**
3681[18] Dante's Rubicon (IRE) **(48)***(32) (JDBethell)* 4-8-8 WCarson(23) (m.n.s)......1¼ **16**
3739[5] Jigsaw Boy **(61)***(43) (PGMurphy)* 6-9-7 RHughes(8) (effrt & rdn over 1f out: nt trble ldrs)......¾ **17**

2828[2] Blasted **(62)***(39) (RHannon)* 3-9-5 JReid(18) (lw: bhd fnl 2f)....1¾ **18**
3624[3] Tael of Silver **(65)***(37) (KRBurke)* 3-9-8 JTate(6) (b.nr hind: racd far side: n.d)....2 **19**
3649[6] Never Say so **(54)***(26) (CSmith)* 3-8-11 WWoods(5) (a bhd far side)....s.h **20**
3734[5] Anotherone to Note **(48)***(20) (NPLittmoden)* 4-8-8b StephenDavies(14) (outpcd)....s.h **21**
838[11] Bella Parkes **(63)***(34) (DNicholls)* 4-9-9 AlexGreaves(4) (bit bkwd: racd far side: prom over 4f)....s.h **22**
3622[5] Bargash **(65)***(34) (PDEvans)* 3-9-8b GHind(11) (m.n.s)....1 **23**
3624[14] Brookhead Lady **(58)***(13) (PDEvans)* 4-8-13 (5) CTeague(1) (b.nr fore: lw: led far side over 4f: sn wknd: t.o)....5 **24**

7/1 Just Like Me, **8/1** Gone Savage, **10/1** Blow Dry (IRE), **12/1** Jigsaw Boy, Hello Hobson's (IRE), Mustn't Grumble (IRE), Here Comes Risky, Blasted, DENSBEN, **14/1** Random, Dante's Rubicon (IRE), **16/1** Southern Dominion, Friendly Brave (USA), Brookhead Lady, Tael of Silver, Bargash, **20/1** Northern Grey, Desert Invader (IRE), Bella Parkes, **25/1** Arasong, Princess Maxine (IRE), **33/1** Anotherone to Note, Never Say so, **50/1** Marsh Arab, CSF £198.32 CT £4,324.77 TOTE £21.70: £3.10 £12.60 £5.00 £6.70 (£1,033.90) OWNER Janet Pike (BISHOP AUCKLAND) BRED D. W. Pike
24 Rn 1m 14.67 (2.97) SF: 38/45/38/35/37/41/42/42/27/31/28/26/39/30/26/13/24/17/15/4/1/15/12/-
WEIGHT FOR AGE 3yo-3lb

3801 STANLEY RACING H'CAP (0-90) (3-Y.O+) (Class C) £6,092.50 (£1,840.00: £895.00: £422.50)

1m 3f 200y Stalls: High GOING minus 0.15 sec per fur (GF) 3-00 (3-03)

3469[2] **Lucayan Sunshine (USA) (77)***(87)*(Fav)*(LadyHerries)* 3-9-1 LDettori(11) (hld up in tch: 6th st: hdwy & rdn 3f out: styd on to ld post)....— **1**
3646[5] Floating Line **(62)***(72) (EJAlston)* 7-8-8 GHind(1) (chsd ldrds: 4th st: led over 2f out: hrd rdn fnl f: ct fnl stride)....s.h **2**
3657[2] Braille (IRE) **(69)***(78) (MGMeagher)* 4-8-10 (5) AWhelan(15) (hld up: hdwy over 3f out: sn hrd rdn: r.o wl ins fnl f)....½ **3**
2555[3] Haniya (IRE) **(85)***(92) (JLDunlop)* 3-9-9 WCarson(16) (prom: 3rd st: rdn 2f out: one pce fnl f)....1¾ **4**
3021[6] Hazard a Guess (IRE) **(76)***(83) (MrsJRRamsden)* 5-9-8 KFallon(4) (lw: hld up: hdwy on ins 3f out: kpt on fnl f)....nk **5**
3500[6] Danesrath (IRE) **(76)***(81) (ACStewart)* 3-9-0 MRoberts(5) (led after 3f tl over 2f out: wknd ins fnl f)....1½ **6**
1505[7] Shakiyr (FR) **(62)***(66) (RHollinshead)* 4-8-8 WRyan(3) (bhd tl hdwy fnl 2f: nvr nrr)....¾ **7**
3388[13] Slaney Project (IRE) **(69)***(71) (WRMuir)* 3-8-7 JWeaver(2) (led 3f: 2nd st: wknd 2f out)....1¼ **8**
2392[7] Sunderland Echo **(67)***(68) (MrsMReveley)* 6-8-13 ACulhane(12) (plld hrd: hld up: nvr nrr)....½ **9**
1617[11] In Good Faith **(73)***(72) (JJQuinn)* 3-8-11 JFEgan(7) (plld hrd: hld up: effrt 3f out: eased whn btn fnl f)....1¾ **10**
3091[3] Riparius (USA) **(78)***(76) (HCandy)* 4-9-10b WNewnes(13) (lw: a bhd)....nk **11**
3705[3] Cumbrian Rhapsody **(60)***(54) (MHEasterby)* 5-8-6 SMaloney(6) (chsd ldrs: 5th st: wknd wl over 2f out)....3 **12**
Welsh Mill (IRE) **(72)***(66) (MrsMReveley)* 6-8-13 (5) GParkin(9) (bkwd: plld hrd: a bhd)....s.h **13**
3593[3] Once More for Luck (IRE) **(65)***(46) (MrsMReveley)* 4-8-11 MHills(10) (lw: plld hrd: hdwy ent st: wknd 3f out: t.o)....10 **14**
3611[8] Windrush Lady **(68)***(48) (MMcCormack)* 5-9-0 OUrbina(8) (chsd ldrs: 7th & rdn st: sn wknd: t.o)....¾ **15**
3634[10] Praglia (IRE) **(66)***(43) (JLDunlop)* 3-8-4 GCarter(14) (a wl bhd: t.o)....2½ **16**

9/2 LUCAYAN SUNSHINE (USA) (7/1-4/1), **11/2** Danesrath (IRE), **7/1** Braille (IRE), **15/2** Haniya (IRE), **8/1** Once More for Luck (IRE), **9/1** Hazard a Guess (IRE), **10/1** Cumbrian Rhapsody, **12/1** Floating Line, Windrush Lady, **14/1** Riparius (USA), In Good Faith, **16/1** Sunderland Echo, **20/1** Slaney Project (IRE), **25/1** Praglia (IRE), Shakiyr (FR), **50/1** Welsh Mill (IRE), CSF £59.10 CT £361.49 TOTE £5.40: £1.50 £3.40 £1.60 £2.20 (£90.50) Trio £65.60 OWNER Lucayan Stud (LITTLEHAMPTON) BRED Foxfield 16 Rn
2m 33.25 (5.25) SF: 51/44/50/56/55/45/38/35/40/36/48/26/38/18/20/7
WEIGHT FOR AGE 3yo-8lb

3802 STANLEY LEISURE ORGANISATION DREAM MILE H'CAP (0-85) (3-Y.O+) (Class D) £4,796.00 (£1,448.00: £704.00: £332.00)

1m 30y Stalls: Low GOING minus 0.15 sec per fur (GF) 3-30 (3-34)

3601[6] **Wilcuma (80)***(92) (PJMakin)* 4-9-13 JWeaver(13) (hld up: hdwy & n.m.r bel dist: swtchd rt over 1f out: str run to ld cl home)....— **1**
3703[11] Calder King **(57)***(67) (JLEyre)* 4-8-4v JTate(12) (in tch: hdwy to ld bel dist: hdd nr fin)....1 **2**
3654[2] Noble Sprinter (IRE) **(76)***(85) (RHannon)* 3-9-5 JReid(6) (hld up: hdwy over 2f out: ev ch ins fnl f: no ex)....nk **3**

3497³ Atlaal (USA) **(73)***(82) (HThomsonJones)* 3-9-2 RHills(3) (chsd ldrs: 6th st: rdn & ev ch ins fnl f: unable qckn)....s.h **4**
3656* Summer Retreat (USA) **(77)***(83)*(Fav)*(JHMGosden)* 3-9-6 5x LDettori(8) (lw: prom: 4th st: ev ch over 1f out: rdn & nt qckn)....1½ **5**
3431³ Parliament Piece **(74)***(77) (DNicholls)* 9-9-7 AlexGreaves(10) (rdn over 3f out: nvr nrr)....1½ **6**
3607³ Karinska **(69)***(72) (MCChapman)* 5-8-9 (7) CMunday(2) (nvr nr to chal)....nk **7**
3408⁶ Noble Neptune **(60)***(60) (WJMusson)* 3-8-3 RPrice(9) (b: nt clr run bel dist: nvr nrr)....1¼ **8**
3534⁸ Rood Music **(57)***(56) (MGMeagher)* 4-8-4 AMackay(14) (nvr trbld ldrs)....¾ **9**
3685¹¹ Our Robert **(60)***(52) (JGFitzGerald)* 3-8-3 JFEgan(7) (lw: prom: 3rd st: wknd over 3f out)....3½ **10**
3447³ Bollin Frank **(59)***(50) (MHEasterby)* 3-8-2 MRoberts(17) (led over 6f: wknd appr fnl f)....½ **11**
3433⁸ Shayim (USA) **(80)***(61) (RWArmstrong)* 3-9-9b WCarson(11) (plld hrd: w ldr: 2nd st: led wl over 1f out: sn hdd & wknd)....5 **12**
3611³ Wentbridge Lad (IRE) **(63)***(43) (PDEvans)* 5-8-10v GHind(15) (chsd ldrs: 5th st: wknd over 2f out)....½ **13**
3611²² Carlito Brigante **(70)***(42) (MrsJRRamsden)* 3-8-13 KFallon(5) (mid div: sn rdn: bhd fnl 3f)....4 **14**
3706* Champagne Grandy **(80)***(50) (MRChannon)* 5-9-13 5x RHughes(1) (hld up: hdwy over 2f out: eased whn n.m.r appr fnl f)....1 **15**
2415⁸ Oneoftheoldones **(75)***(44) (SGNorton)* 3-9-4 StephenDavies(18) (lw: drvn along ent st: a bhd)½ **16**
2928² Nordic Breeze (IRE) **(76)***(34) (ABailey)* 3-9-2 (3) DWright(16) (dwlt: a bhd: t.o)....6 **17**
3703⁴ Cee-Jay-Ay **(59)** *(JBerry)* 8-8-6 GCarter(4) (s.v.s: a t.o)....20 **18**

11/4 Summer Retreat (USA) (op 9/2), **7/1** Noble Sprinter (IRE), **8/1** WILCUMA, Shayim (USA), Champagne Grandy, **10/1** Cee-Jay-Ay, **11/1** Karinska, **12/1** Wentbridge Lad (IRE), Atlaal (USA), Carlito Brigante, **14/1** Nordic Breeze (IRE), Bollin Frank, **20/1** Our Robert, Noble Neptune, Parliament Piece, **25/1** Rood Music, **33/1** Oneoftheoldones, Calder King, CSF £245.55 CT £1,820.41 TOTE £9.10: £2.50 £8.50 £2.10 £3.10 (£254.00) Trio £597.30 OWNER Mr T. G. Warner (MARLBOROUGH) BRED Red House Stud 18 Rn
1m 44.55 (4.15) SF: 57/32/46/43/44/42/37/21/21/13/11/22/8/3/15/5/-/-
WEIGHT FOR AGE 3yo-4lb
OFFICIAL EXPLANATION **Champagne Grandy: the trainer's representative reported that the mare failed to stay the trip.**

3803

STANLEY SNOOKER NURSERY H'CAP (0-85) (2-Y.O) (Class D) £3,805.00 (£1,150.00: £560.00: £265.00) **6f** Stalls: High GOING minus 0.15 sec(GF) 4-00 (4-02)

3742* **Lunar Mist (69)***(74)*(Fav)*(MartynMeade)* 2-8-5 (5) 7x RHavlin(12) (lw: hld up: hdwy & n.m.r appr fnl f: qcknd to ld wl ins fnl f)....— **1**
3612¹¹ U-No-Harry (IRE) **(66)***(68) (RHollinshead)* 2-8-7 WRyan(8) (hld up: hdwy over 1f out: ev ch wl ins fnl f: unable qckn)....1 **2**
1860² Playmaker **(76)***(78) (JBerry)* 2-9-3 LDettori(2) (lw: a w ldrs: ev ch 1f out: r.o)....hd **3**
2964⁸ Careful (IRE) **(61)***(60) (BWHills)* 2-8-2 RHills(9) (s.i.s: rdn ½-wy: hdwy & nt clr run & swtchd lft ins fnl f: r.o strly)....1 **4**
3271⁵ Missile Toe (IRE) **(70)***(69) (JEBanks)* 2-8-11 JReid(11) (w ldrs: led over 1f out tl wl ins fnl f)..nk **5**
2982³ Bearnaise (IRE) **(64)***(63) (RHannon)* 2-8-5 MRoberts(13) (lw: hld up: hdwy & nt clr run over 1f out: fin fast)....s.h **6**
2615* Akalim **(80)***(76) (DMorley)* 2-9-7 WCarson(10) (lw: led tl over 1f out: sn rdn & btn)....1 **7**
3612¹⁶ Montrestar **(65)***(58) (PDEvans)* 2-8-6 GHind(4) (nvr trbld ldrs)....1¼ **8**
3460⁸ Camionneur (IRE) **(60)***(52) (MHEasterby)* 2-8-1 SMaloney(7) (hld up: effrt 2f out: sn ev ch: wknd ins fnl f)....hd **9**
3546¹² Hoh Majestic (IRE) **(73)***(62) (MBell)* 2-9-0v MFenton(6) (prom: rdn 2f out: btn whn hmpd ent fnl f)....1¼ **10**
3158⁷ Fervent Fan (IRE) **(80)***(48) (MBell)* 2-9-7 MHills(1) (lw: outpcd: t.o)....8 **11**
3612² Clincher Club **(78)***(42) (MJohnston)* 2-9-5 JWeaver(3) (lw: plld hrd: prom over 3f: t.o)....1½ **12**
3644¹⁶ Royal Rapport **(55)***(15) (BAMcMahon)* 2-7-10v FNorton(5) (lw: rdn over 3f out: sn bhd: t.o)...1¼ **13**

100/30 LUNAR MIST (9/2-3/1), **9/2** Clincher Club, Akalim, **7/1** Playmaker, Bearnaise (IRE), **10/1** Missile Toe (IRE), **12/1** Hoh Majestic (IRE), **14/1** Camionneur (IRE), **16/1** Careful (IRE), **20/1** Fervent Fan (IRE), U-No-Harry (IRE), **25/1** Montrestar, Royal Rapport, CSF £65.59 CT £418.01 TOTE £4.70: £2.00 £3.80 £2.30 (£104.40) Trio £115.30 OWNER Ladyswood Racing Club (MALMESBURY) BRED T. Barratt 13 Rn 1m 15.17 (3.47) SF: 34/28/38/20/29/23/36/18/12/22/8/2/-

3804

STANLEY CLUBS CONDITIONS STKS (3-Y.O+) (Class C) £4,996.00 (£1,864.00: £907.00: £385.00: £167.50: £80.50)
1m 6f Stalls: Centre GOING minus 0.15 sec per fur (GF) 4-30 (4-30)

2799⁴ **New Reputation (88)***(103) (BWHills)* 4-9-6 MHills(3) (mde most: hrd rdn fnl f: styd on strly).— **1**
Bahamian Sunshine (USA) *(100)*(Fav)*(DRLoder)* 4-9-4 LDettori(1) (2nd st: jnd wnr over 2f out: rdn over 1f out: no ex nr fin)....½ **2**

1912[5] Rainfest (FR) **(86)**(79) (RCharlton) 4-8-11 JReid(8) (bkwd: chsd wnr 9f: 3rd st: wknd over 3f out) 13 **3**
3262* Wannaplantatree **(57)**(79) (NMBabbage) 4-8-12 RHughes(4) (hld up in rr: 6th st: nvr nr ldrs) .¾ **4**
Katie Oliver (76) (BSmart) 3-8-2 ow2 JTate(7) (lengthy: bkwd: s.s: hdwy 7f out: 5th st: wknd over 3f out) ....½ **5**
1470[2] Moshaajir (USA) **(73)**(71) (CSmith) 5-9-6 WWoods(5) (bkwd: chsd ldrs: 4th st: sn lost tch: t.o) 13 **6**
1289[4] Doddington Flyer **(65)**(58) (RHollinshead) 3-8-7 WRyan(6) (bit bkwd: plld hrd: hld up: a bhd: t.o) 9 **7**
Trainglot **(83)**(47) (JGFitzGerald) 8-9-1 WCarson(2) (b: swtg: bkwd: hld up: a bhd: t.o) 8 **8**

6/5 Bahamian Sunshine (USA) (Evens-10/11), **2/1** NEW REPUTATION, **11/2** Rainfest (FR), **12/1** Trainglot, **16/1** Moshaajir (USA), **20/1** Doddington Flyer, **33/1** Wannaplantatree, **66/1** Katie Oliver, CSF £4.70 TOTE £3.10: £1.50 £1.50 £1.60 (£1.70) OWNER Mr R. E. Sangster (LAMBOURN) BRED Seahorse Investments 8 Rn
3m 1.5 (3.30) SF: 73/70/49/49/36/41/18/17
WEIGHT FOR AGE 3yo-10lb

T/Jkpt: Not won; £4,433.60 to Ascot 23/9/95. T/Plpt: £426.00 (50.9 Tckts). T/Qdpt: £17.70 (10.2 Tckts). IM

3391-REDCAR (L-H)
Friday September 22nd (Good, Good to firm patches)
WEATHER: cloudy & rain WIND: fresh across

3805 SCARBOROUGH (S) MAIDEN STKS (3-Y.O) (Class G) £2,917.00 (£812.00: £391.00) 1m 3f Stalls: Low GOING minus 0.02 sec per fur (G) 2-10 (2-12)

3462[11] **Highfield Fizz (55)**(63)(Fav)(CWFairhurst) 3-8-9 RCochrane(10) (b.off hind: trckd ldrs: led 2f out: rdn clr ins fnl f) ....— **1**
2719[5] Maronetta **(35)**(56) (MJRyan) 3-8-4 (5) DGibbs(5) (swtg: a chsng ldrs: chal over 3f out: edgd rr & kpt on same pce appr fnl f) 5 **2**
3153[4] Remontant (IRE) **(38)**(50) (RHollinshead) 3-8-2 (7) FLynch(6) (a.p: one pce fnl 3f) 4 **3**
509[7] Simposa (IRE) **(50)**(55) (EJAlston) 3-9-0 SDWilliams(8) (trckd ldrs: led over 6f out: clr over 3f out: hdd 2f out: one pce) ....nk **4**
3669[13] Island Cascade **(39)**(41) (DonEnricoIncisa) 3-8-9 KimTinkler(7) (s.i.s: bhd: hdwy & nt clr run over 3f out: edgd lft & kpt on) 6 **5**
2582[9] Magical Bid (IRE) **(44)**(44) (JMBradley) 3-8-11v(3) SDrowne(9) (b: chsd ldrs: rdn over 3f out: sn wknd) 1½ **6**
3638[6] Keys Seminar **(41)**(25) (JohnBerry) 3-9-0 CDwyer(15) (prom whn stumbled bdly after 1f: sn lost pl) 13 **7**
2874[4] Highbank **(48)**(24)(Fav)(MrsMReveley) 3-9-0 KDarley(4) (hld up & bhd: drvn along 6f out: n.d) ....¾ **8**
3722[6] Never Time (IRE) **(39)**(23) (MrsVAAconley) 3-9-0 MDeering(14) (hld up: hdwy & hung lft over 2f out: nvr nr ldrs) ....¾ **9**
Haido'hart **(69)**(20) (BSRothwell) 3-8-11 (3) JStack(2) (chsd ldrs: effrt 3f out: hung rt: wknd qckly wl over 1f out) 1¾ **10**
3422[13] Mr Eglantine **(30)**(7) (ASmith) 3-9-0 JLowe(16) (chsd ldrs tl lost pl over 3f out) 9 **11**
3543[5] Jane's Super Top (2) (JPearce) 3-9-0 GBardwell(11) (lw: chsd ldrs: drvn along over 4f out: lost pl 3f out) 3½ **12**
477[6] Robellina **(34)** (MDods) 3-9-0 DaleGibson(13) (sn in tch: lost pl 5f out) 1¼ **13**
Blotoft (MrsSMAustin) 3-9-0 JMarshall(3) (b: prom early: bhd fnl 4f) 4 **14**
3722[11] Newgate Hush (BWMurray) 3-8-9 TWilliams(1) (b.off hind: s.i.s: a bhd) 6 **15**
3115[5] Stray Rein (JJQuinn) 3-8-9 MBirch(17) (bit bkwd: s.i.s: a bhd: eased fnl f) 7 **16**
3507[7] Sheroot (DMoffatt) 3-8-11 (3) DarrenMoffatt(12) (led tl over 6f out: sn lost pl) ....nk **17**

3/1 HIGHFIELD FIZZ, Highbank, **11/2** Simposa (IRE), **6/1** Haido'hart, **7/1** Remontant (IRE), **12/1** Maronetta, **14/1** Magical Bid (IRE), Keys Seminar, Never Time (IRE), Island Cascade (12/1-6/1), Jane's Super Top, **33/1** Stray Rein, **100/1** Robellina, Blotoft, Newgate Hush, Mr Eglantine, Sheroot, CSF £41.67 TOTE £3.80: £1.60 £3.40 £2.00 (£28.50) Trio £102.40 OWNER Mrs P. J. Taylor-Garthwaite (MIDDLEHAM) BRED K. and P. J. Garthwaite 17 Rn
2m 23.0 (7.30) SF: 38/31/25/30/16/19/-/-/-/-/-/-/-/-/-/-/-
Bt in 9,200 gns

3806 NEWBY MEDIAN AUCTION MAIDEN STKS (2-Y.O F) (Class E) £3,302.75 (£992.00: £478.50: £221.75) 7f Stalls: Centre GOING minus 0.02 sec(G) 2-40 (2-42)

3450[3] **Cebwob** (85)(Fav)(PFICole) 2-8-11 TQuinn(2) (lw: trckd ldrs: pushed along ½-wy: styd on wl to ld ins fnl f: readily) ....— **1**

3495[8] Manderella (76) (JAkehurst) 2-8-11 SWhitworth(8) (b.off hind: chsd ldrs: led ½-wy tl ins fnl f: unable qckn) 4 2
Divine (75+) (ACStewart) 2-8-11 KDarley(13) (unf: scope: lw: s.i.s: sn chsng ldrs: ev ch over 2f out: nt qckn over 1f out) ....½ 3
3468[6] Nutcracker (67) (CBBBooth) 2-8-11 MBirch(1) (bhd: drvn along ½-wy: styd on fnl f) 3½ 4
3644[14] Mill End Lady (63) (MWEasterby) 2-8-11 LCharnock(4) (chsd ldrs: outpcd fnl 2f) 1¾ 5
3417[12] Mysterious Times (45)(51) (BWMurray) 2-8-11 TWilliams(10) (w ldrs over 4f: sn hrd rdn & outpcd) 5 6
3022[4] Forest Fantasy (51) (JWharton) 2-8-11 SDWilliams(6) (s.i.s: bhd tl sme hdwy 2f out: n.d) ....hd 7
2161[5] Bear To Dance (49) (JohnBerry) 2-8-8 (3) JStack(9) (swtg: led to ½-wy: sn wknd) ....¾ 8
3502[8] Sassetta (IRE) (50)(47) (NTinkler) 2-8-11 KimTinkler(11) (s.i.s: bhd: rdn along ½-wy: hmpd over 1f out: n.d) 1 9
3744[14] Efipetite (48)(43) (NBycroft) 2-8-8 (3) NVarley(15) (w ldr tl wknd over 2f out) 2 10
3672[9] Bianca Cappello (IRE) (37) (JLDunlop) 2-8-11 NConnorton(5) (sn outpcd: sme hdwy ½-wy: sn lost pl) 2½ 11
Dona Filipa (36) (MissLCSiddall) 2-8-11 DeanMcKeown(3) (cmpt: bkwd: s.s: a bhd) ....nk 12
1190[13] Elle Mac (13) (MPBielby) 2-8-8 (3) DRMcCabe(12) (chsd ldrs: drvn along ½-wy: edgd rt & sn wknd) 10 13
3253[8] Princess Briana (6) (DMoffatt) 2-8-8 (3) DarrenMoffatt(7) (w ldrs tl wknd 3f out: sn wl bhd) 3 14
Chavin Point (MissLCSiddall) 2-8-11 DHarrison(14) (small: s.s: a wl bhd) 6 15

5/4 CEBWOB (op Evens), **3/1** Divine, **4/1** Manderella, **10/1** Forest Fantasy, **14/1** Bianca Cappello (IRE), Nutcracker, **25/1** Bear To Dance, **33/1** Sassetta (IRE), Dona Filipa, Mill End Lady, **50/1** Mysterious Times, Chavin Point, **66/1** Efipetite, **100/1** Elle Mac, Princess Briana, CSF £7.38 TOTE £1.60: £1.20 £1.30 £1.60 (£4.70) Trio £3.00 OWNER Mr C. M. Budgett (WHATCOMBE) BRED Kirtlington Stud Ltd 15 Rn 1m 27.2 (5.20) SF: 30/21/20/12/8/-/-/-/-/-/-/-/-/-/-

3807 G + H MCGILL H'CAP (0-85) (3-Y.O+) (Class D) £4,516.50 (£1,362.00: £661.00: £310.50) 7f Stalls: Centre GOING minus 0.02 sec per fur (G) 3-10 (3-21)

3565[5] **Kid Ory (65)**(76) (PCalver) 4-8-7 (3) NVarley(2) (b.hind: w ldrs: led ½-wy: jst hld on) ....— 1
3719[3] Rossini Blue (69)(80) (MrsJRRamsden) 4-9-0 DHarrison(4) (dwlt: hld up & bhd: gd hdwy over 2f out: styd on wl towards fin) ....hd 2
3637[8] Highborn (IRE) (80)(88) (PSFelgate) 6-9-11 TQuinn(11) (a chsng ldrs: kpt on same pce fnl f) 1¼ 3
3719[12] Mister Westsound (61)(63) (MissLAPerratt) 3-8-2b JLowe(12) (dwlt: bhd tl hdwy ½-wy: rdn & edgd rt over 1f out: kpt on same pce) 2½ 4
3645[15] Ochos Rios (IRE) (62)(60) (BSRothwell) 4-8-4 (3) JStack(15) (in tch: effrt over 2f out: kpt on same pce) 2 5
3661[5] Ahjay (48)(40) (DAWilson) 5-7-7 GBardwell(8) (in tch: sn drvn along: kpt on fnl 2f: nvr nr ldrs) 2½ 6
984[12] Shaffishayes (63)(55) (MrsMReveley) 3-8-4 DeanMcKeown(10) (s.i.s: hld up & bhd: hdwy over 2f out: wandered: nvr nr to chal) ....hd 7
3607[16] Sandmoor Chambray (71)(59) (MHEasterby) 4-9-2b MBirch(9) (chsd ldrs tl wknd 2f out) 1½ 8
3431[5] Battle Colours (IRE) (53)(41) (DonEnricoIncisa) 6-7-12 KimTinkler(16) (bhd: gd hdwy & wnt lft ½-wy: nvr nr ldrs) ....s.h 9
3382[8] Thabit (USA) (78)(55) (PTWalwyn) 4-9-9 RCochrane(18) (hld up: effrt 3f out: sn wknd) 5 10
3545[5] Anonym (IRE) (71)(48) (JLDunlop) 3-8-12 NConnorton(14) (s.i.s: bhd: sme hdwy ½-wy: sn wknd) ....hd 11
3565[W] King Rat (IRE) (80)(54)(Fav)(TJEtherington) 4-9-11b KDarley(17) (lw: trckd ldrs: effrt ½-wy: wknd over 2f out) 1¼ 12
3704[3] Roseate Lodge (54)(22) (NBycroft) 9-7-13 LCharnock(3) (b: chsd ldrs 4f: sn wknd) 2½ 13
2963[9] Peacefull Reply (USA) (49)(14) (FHLee) 5-7-8b[ow1] NKennedy(5) (w ldrs tl wknd 3f out) 1 14
3050[3] What a Nightmare (IRE) (63)(28) (JAGlover) 3-8-4v SDWilliams(6) (led to ½-wy: wknd qckly over 2f out: eased) ....½ 15
Crystado (FR) (62) (JSHaldane) 6-8-7 DaleGibson(1) (swtg: b: uns rdr gng to s: sn bhd: t.o ½-wy) ....dist 16
3649[3] Quilling (69) (MDods) 3-8-10 SWhitworth(13) (Withdrawn not under Starter's orders: broke out of stalls & bolted) .... W

LONG HANDICAP Peacefull Reply (USA) 6-13

3/1 King Rat (IRE), **11/2** Rossini Blue, **7/1** Ahjay, **8/1** KID ORY, **9/1** Anonym (IRE), **12/1** What a Nightmare (IRE), Quilling, **14/1** Mister Westsound (12/1-20/1), Sandmoor Chambray, Thabit (USA), Roseate Lodge, **16/1** Highborn (IRE), Ochos Rios (IRE), **20/1** Shaffishayes, Battle Colours (IRE), **33/1** Peacefull Reply (USA), **200/1** Crystado (FR), CSF £49.50 CT £571.12 TOTE £13.20: £2.20 £1.10 £3.50 £5.50 (£24.00) Trio £111.00 OWNER Mrs C. Calver (RIPON) BRED G. A. Bosley and T. H. Clarkin 16 Rn 1m 25.9 (3.90) SF: 45/49/57/28/29/9/20/28/10/24/13/23/-/-/-/-

WEIGHT FOR AGE 3yo-4lb

3808

MISSISSIPPI AMATEUR H'CAP (0-70) (3-Y.O+) (Class E) £3,871.50 (£1,167.00: £566.00: £265.50) **1m** Stalls: Centre GOING minus 0.02 sec per fur (G) 3-40 (3-51)

*3529*10 **Bold Habit (57)***(71) (JPearce)* 10-11-3 MrsLPearce(12) (in tch: effrt over 2f out: styd on wl to ld ins fnl f: r.o) — 1
31019 Shining Edge **(52)***(62) (MHEasterby)* 3-10-8 MrsAFarrell(20) (prom early: sn outpcd: hdwy & hrd rdn over 1f out: styd on wl) 2 2
36574 Broughton's Pride (IRE) **(49)***(59) (JAGlover)* 4-10-4 (5) MrsMMorris(4) (chsd ldrs: wandered over 1f out: kpt on wl) s.h 3
353410 Love Legend **(51)***(60) (DWPArbuthnot)* 10-10-11 MrsDArbuthnot(11) (in tch: effrt & n.m.r 2f out: styd on wl ins fnl f) ½ 4
34579 Ashdren **(52)***(60) (AHarrison)* 8-10-12 MrNWilson(19) (hdwy over 2f out: styd on fnl f: nt rch ldrs) nk 5
31185 Lord Vivienne (IRE) **(40)***(44) (BSRothwell)* 6-10-0 MissAElsey(24) (a in tch: kpt on same pce fnl 2f) 2 6
3661* Thunder River (IRE) **(60)***(64) (MJHeaton-Ellis)* 5-11-6v MrsAPerrett(5) (led tl over 1f out: grad wknd) nk 7
36455 Just Harry **(68)***(72) (MJRyan)* 4-12-0 MissJAllison(29) (hdwy ½-wy: sn chsng ldrs: wknd over 1f out) s.h 8
28225 Bulsara **(57)***(61) (CWFairhurst)* 3-10-13 MrsSBosley(6) (lw: a chsng ldrs: sn drvn along: one pce fnl 2f) s.h 9
33964 Legend Dulac (IRE) **(44)***(47) (JAHarris)* 6-10-4 MrRJohnson(9) (lw: b.off fore: w ldr: led over 1f out tl hdd & wknd ins fnl f) s.h 10
29056 Make the Break **(44)***(45) (MWEasterby)* 4-9-13 (5) MrsSHardy(28) (bhd: hdwy over 1f out: styd on towards fin) 1¼ 11
Major Snugfit **(43)***(41) (MWEasterby)* 3-9-8 (5) MrCAppleby(21) (in tch: hrd rdn & edgd lft over 2f out: styd on fnl f) 1¼ 12
353417 King Chestnut **(60)***(58)*(Fav)*(MDods)* 4-11-6 MrsDKettlewell(13) (lw: mid div: sme hdwy ½-wy: n.d) hd 13
353415 Johnnie the Joker **(51)***(49) (JPLeigh)* 4-10-6b(5) MrRThornton(7) (w ldrs tl wknd over 2f out) nk 14
36415 Don't Drop Bombs (USA) **(38)***(34)*(Fav)*(DTThom)* 6-9-12v MissJFeilden(22) (lw: w ldrs tl wknd over 2f out) ¾ 15
34478 Avishayes (USA) **(46)***(41) (MrsMReveley)* 8-10-6 MrCBonner(23) (nvr bttr than mid div) ½ 16
*3529*13 Breezed Well **(40)***(33) (BRCambidge)* 9-9-9 (5) MrsHNoonan(1) (in tch tl outpcd fnl 3f) 1¼ 17
33103 Tinklers Folly **(46)***(32) (DenysSmith)* 3-9-11 (5) MissMCarson(18) (chsd ldrs tl wknd over 2f out) 3½ 18
368515 Star Performer (IRE) **(49)***(31) (MrsMReveley)* 4-10-4 (5) MissHDudgeon(17) (nvr bttr than mid div) 2 19
Suselja (IRE) **(42)***(23) (JMJefferson)* 4-9-11 (5) MissMCheyne(14) (prom 5f: sn lost pl) hd 20
343812 Good (IRE) **(45)***(25) (DTThom)* 3-10-1v MissDianaJones(2) (sn drvn along: n.d) ¾ 21
339616 Ballyhays (IRE) **(40)***(19) (JAHarris)* 6-9-9 (5) MrDTRobinson(15) (n.d) ½ 22
364514 Lancashire Life (IRE) **(49)***(27) (EJAlston)* 4-10-9 MrRHale(10) (bhd fr ½-wy) ½ 23
Express Gift **(62)***(35) (MrsMReveley)* 6-11-8 MrMHNaughton(27) (nvr nr ldrs) 2½ 24
33055 Tolls Choice (IRE) **(53)***(21) (MWEasterby)* 6-10-13 MrKWhelan(25) (w ldrs: hrd rdn & edgd lft over 2f out: sn lost pl) 2½ 25
*3514*9 Saatchmo **(60)***(27) (JLSpearing)* 3-10-11 (5) MissCSpearing(16) (s.s: a bhd) nk 26
35067 Doo Han (IRE) **(49)***(9) (MDHammond)* 3-10-0 (5)ow6 MrJDavies(30) (a in rr) ¾ 27
348811 Move Smartly (IRE) **(56)***(20) (FHLee)* 5-10-11v(5) MrsCWilliams(26) (lw: chsd ldrs tl wknd over 2f out) ¾ 28
349315 Miss Springtime **(57)***(21) (JJO'Neill)* 4-10-12 (5) MrLCorcoran(3) (bhd fr ½-wy) s.h 29

8/1 Don't Drop Bombs (USA), King Chestnut, **10/1** Thunder River (IRE), **11/1** Legend Dulac (IRE), **12/1** Express Gift, Avishayes (USA), Broughton's Pride (IRE), **14/1** Johnnie the Joker, BOLD HABIT, Bulsara, **16/1** Love Legend, Tolls Choice (IRE), Shining Edge, Tinklers Folly, **20/1** Major Snugfit, Star Performer (IRE), Ashdren, Just Harry, Lancashire Life (IRE), Move Smartly (IRE), **25/1** Lord Vivienne (IRE), Make the Break, **33/1** Doo Han (IRE), Breezed Well, Ballyhays (IRE), **50/1** Saatchmo, Suselja (IRE), Good (IRE), Miss Springtime, CSF £233.27 CT £2,570.37 TOTE £17.50: £4.00 £6.40 £3.30 £3.90 (£203.90) OWNER Mr Arthur Old (NEWMARKET) BRED R. Butters 29 Rn
1m 42.5 (7.50) SF: 47/34/35/36/36/20/40/48/33/23/21/13/34/25/10/17/9/4/7/-/-/-/3/11/-/-/-/-/-
WEIGHT FOR AGE 3yo-4lb

3809

MICHAELMAS NURSERY H'CAP (0-85) (2-Y.O) (Class D) £4,250.00 (£1,280.00: £620.00: £290.00)
7f Stalls: Centre GOING minus 0.02 sec per fur (G) 4-10 (4-16)

33073 **Samim (USA) (75)***(86) (JLDunlop)* 2-9-2 TQuinn(14) (lw: a chsng ldrs: hung lft & led ins fnl f: drvn out) — 1

3639* Consordino **(83)***(92)*(Fav)*(LMCumani)* 2-9-3 (7) 7x GMitchell(6) (lw: a chsng ldrs: nt qckn ins fnl f) ... ¾ **2**
3701[3] Cumbrian Maestro **(64)***(70) (MHEasterby)* 2-8-5b DHarrison(1) (led far side: rdn & edgd rt 2f out: nt qckn fnl f) ... 1½ **3**
3471[8] Golden Pond (IRE) **(65)***(71) (RFJohnsonHoughton)* 2-8-6 AMcGlone(5) (lw: led centre: kpt on same pce fnl f) ... s.h **4**
2681[4] Khabar **(77)***(79) (DMorley)* 2-9-4 RCochrane(10) (trckd ldrs: effrt over 2f out: kpt on same pce fnl f) ... 1¾ **5**
3546[16] Labeed (USA) **(68)***(68) (MajorWRHern)* 2-8-9 MPerrett(13) (in tch: effrt & hung lft 2f out: nvr nr to chal) ... 1 **6**
*3525** Taufan Boy **(80)***(79) (PWHarris)* 2-9-2 (5) MHenry(11) (a chsng ldrs: kpt on same pce fnl 2f) .s.h **7**
3460[6] Oriole **(62)***(43) (NTinkler)* 2-8-3 KimTinkler(3) (chsd ldrs far side tl lost pl 2f out) ... 8 **8**
3019[7] Contradictory **(55)***(31) (MWEasterby)* 2-7-3 (7)ow3 MartinDwyer(8) (outpcd fr ½-wy) ... ¾ **9**
3460[5] Aztec Flyer (USA) **(62)***(39) (MrsMReveley)* 2-8-3 KDarley(7) (a in rr) ... 1¼ **10**
3671[4] Termon **(61)***(33) (MissLAPerratt)* 2-8-2 JLowe(9) (bhd fr ½-wy) ... 2 **11**
3642[5] Kratz (IRE) **(55)***(27) (BSRothwell)* 2-7-7v(3) NVarley(15) (sn drvn along: bhd fr ½-wy) ... s.h **12**
2424* Precious Girl **(76)***(42) (DMoffatt)* 2-9-0 (3) DarrenMoffatt(4) (lw: racd far side: chsd ldrs tl lost pl ½-wy) ... 2½ **13**
2483* The Butterwick Kid **(72)***(32) (RAFahey)* 2-8-13 MBirch(12) (hld up: a in rr) ... 2½ **14**
3620[15] Swish **(53)***(1) (NTinkler)* 2-7-8 ow1 LCharnock(2) (lw: sn chsng ldrs: lost pl ½-wy: sn wl bhd) ... 5 **15**

LONG HANDICAP Contradictory 7-5 Swish 7-5

5/4 Consordino, **4/1** Taufan Boy, **8/1** Cumbrian Maestro, Khabar, **9/1** Precious Girl, **10/1** Golden Pond (IRE), **12/1** SAMIM (USA), The Butterwick Kid, **14/1** Aztec Flyer (USA), Labeed (USA), **20/1** Termon, **25/1** Oriole, **33/1** Contradictory, Kratz (IRE), Swish, CSF £31.93 CT £144.21 TOTE £9.70: £2.10 £1.50 £2.10 (£12.00) Trio £42.80 OWNER Mr Hamdan Al Maktoum (ARUNDEL) BRED Shadwell Estate Company Limited 15 Rn 1m 27.2 (5.20) SF: 35/41/19/20/28/17/28/-/-/-/-/-/-/-/-

3810 HORNSEA H'CAP (0-80) (3-Y.O+) (Class D) £4,360.50 (£1,314.00: £637.00: £298.50) 1m 2f Stalls: Low GOING minus 0.02 sec per fur (G) 4-40 (4-42)

3679[3] **Zeetaro (74)***(87) (MajorWRHern)* 4-9-10v MPerrett(4) (trckd ldrs: swtchd rt over 2f out: led over 1f out: drvn clr) ... — **1**
3297[2] Essayeffsee **(55)***(63) (MrsMReveley)* 6-8-5 NConnorton(8) (hld up: hdwy 3f out: styd on fnl f) ... 3 **2**
3703[7] Current Speech (IRE) **(69)***(76) (MHEasterby)* 4-9-5 MBirch(9) (lw: hld up & bhd: stdy hdwy on ins over 3f out: n.m.r & snatched up: styd on wl ins fnl f) ... ½ **3**
3657[7] Curtelace **(54)***(59) (LadyHerries)* 5-8-4 KDarley(17) (hld up in tch: smooth hdwy to ld 2f out: hdd over 1f out: kpt on one pce) ... 1¼ **4**
3611[5] Unforgiving Minute **(78)***(80) (PWHarris)* 6-9-9 (5) MHenry(5) (rr div: drvn along & outpcd over 3f out: styd on appr fnl f) ... 2 **5**
3700[2] Locorotondo (IRE) **(65)***(67)*(Fav)*(MBell)* 4-8-8 (7) GFaulkner(11) (lw: trckd ldrs: led 3f out: hdd 2f out: one pce) ... nk **6**
Efizia **(67)***(66) (MrsMReveley)* 5-8-10 (7) DDenby(7) (dwlt: hld up & bhd: styd on fnl f) ... 1¾ **7**
3320[6] Larn Fort **(57)***(45) (CWFairhurst)* 5-8-7v RCochrane(12) (lw: hld up: sme hdwy over 3f out: sn wknd) ... 7 **8**
3601[5] Aeroking (USA) **(77)***(58) (GHarwood)* 4-9-13 AClark(2) (lw: mde most to 3f out: sn wknd) ... 4 **9**
3276[4] Tilaal (USA) **(73)***(53) (EALDunlop)* 3-9-3v SWhitworth(10) (w ldrs: wknd over 2f out) ... 1 **10**
3646[8] Mca Below the Line **(53)***(32) (JLEyre)* 7-8-3v TWilliams(1) (b: sn bhd & drvn along: sme hdwy over 3f out: sn wknd) ... ¾ **11**
3605[20] Cavil **(65)***(40) (CEBrittain)* 3-8-6 (3) DRMcCabe(13) (prom tl lost pl 3f out) ... 2 **12**
3601[4] Reverand Thickness **(73)***(44) (SCWilliams)* 4-9-9 TQuinn(3) (lw: a chsng ldrs: close 3f out: sn wknd & eased) ... 3 **13**
3641[10] Teen Jay **(68)***(37) (MJRyan)* 5-8-13v(5) DGibbs(16) (chsd ldrs: rdn & edgd rt 3f out: sn wknd) ... 1¼ **14**
3030[5] Tafia (IRE) **(72)***(25) (JPearce)* 4-9-8 GBardwell(6) (b.off hind: hld up: effrt over 4f out: sn bhd) ... 10 **15**
Bridge of Fire (FR) **(73)***(2) (DonEnricoIncisa)* 3-9-3 KimTinkler(14) (plld hrd: trckd ldrs tl lost pl over 3f out: sn wl bhd) ... 15 **16**

9/4 Locorotondo (IRE), **9/2** Unforgiving Minute, **11/2** Curtelace, **8/1** Reverand Thickness, **10/1** Current Speech (IRE), **12/1** ZEETARO, Aeroking (USA), **14/1** Essayeffsee, Teen Jay, **16/1** Tilaal (USA), **25/1** Cavil, Larn Fort, **33/1** Efizia, Mca Below the Line, **40/1** Tafia (IRE), **66/1** Bridge of Fire (FR), CSF £166.69 CT £1,613.83 TOTE £13.90: £2.50 £2.20 £7.20 £1.40 (£85.60) Trio £329.60 OWNER The Dayspring Company Ltd (LAMBOURN) BRED D. Aykroyd 16 Rn
2m 9.0 (6.50) SF: 53/29/42/25/46/33/32/11/24/13/-/-/10/3/-/-
WEIGHT FOR AGE 3yo-6lb

T/Plpt: £264.00 (47.14 Tckts). T/Qdpt: £70.70 (0.5 Tckts). WG

3277-**ASCOT (R-H)**

Saturday September 23rd (Good, Good to soft patches)

WEATHER: warm WIND: nil

3811

CUMBERLAND LODGE STKS (Gp 3) (3-Y.O+) (Class A) £31,550.00 (£11,940.00: £5,845.00: £2,665.00) **1m 4f** Stalls: High GOING: 0.10 sec per fur (G) 2-15 (2-16)

3594* **Riyadian (113)***(122)*(Fav)*(PFICole)* 3-8-6 TQuinn(2) (lw: 2nd st: led on bit 2f out: shkn up: easily).......— 1
3614⁴ Richard of York *(118) (JHMGosden)* 5-9-3b LDettori(6) (hdwy 5f out: 4th st: ev ch wl over 1f out: unable qckn).......5 2
3498* Burooj **(110)***(113) (DMorley)* 5-9-3 WCarson(7) (7th st: rdn & hdwy over 1f out: one pce).......4 3
3614³ Wayne County (IRE) **(111)***(108) (RAkehurst)* 5-9-0 JWeaver(5) (lw: chsd ldr: led over 3f out to 2f out: wknd over 1f out).......1¼ 4
3164* Medaille Militaire **(99)***(108) (JLDunlop)* 3-8-6 JReid(4) (5th st: rdn over 2f out: wknd over 1f out).......nk 5
3581a³ Silver Wedge (USA) **(104)***(108) (LordHuntingdon)* 4-9-3v MHills(1) (swtg: led over 8f: 3rd st: wknd over 2f out).......2 6
3603³ Fire on Ice (IRE) **(103)***(97) (MRStoute)* 3-8-6 RHills(9) (lw: rdn over 3f out: 6th st: wknd over 2f out).......6 7
3576a⁷ Prince of Andros (USA) **(113)** *(DRLoder)* 5-9-5 MJKinane(8) (swtg: 8th st: bhd fnl 3f: t.o: lame).......dist 8

2/1 RIYADIAN, **9/2** Medaille Militaire, **11/2** Prince of Andros (USA) (7/2-6/1), Richard of York, **7/1** Burooj, **11/1** Wayne County (IRE) (8/1-12/1), **20/1** Fire on Ice (IRE), **40/1** Silver Wedge (USA), CSF £12.00 TOTE £2.60: £1.20 £1.40 £1.70 (£4.00) Trio £8.70 OWNER H R H Prince Fahd Salman (WHATCOMBE) BRED Newgate Stud Co. 8 Rn 2m 32.28 (2.78) SF: 80/84/79/74/66/74/55/-

WEIGHT FOR AGE 3yo-8lb

OFFICIAL EXPLANATION **Prince of Andros: finished lame.**

3812

ROYAL LODGE STKS (Gp 2) (2-Y.O C & G) (Class A) £63,730.00 (£23,890.25: £11,507.63: £5,047.12)
1m (round) Stalls: High GOING: 0.10 sec per fur (G) 2-50 (2-52)

3068* **Mons (100)***(106+) (LMCumani)* 2-8-11 LDettori(6) (w ldr: led over 5f out: clr over 1f out: comf).......— 1
3483a* More Royal (USA) **(100)***(96) (IABalding)* 2-8-11 WRSwinburn(5) (lw: 3rd st: chsd wnr over 2f out: no imp).......5 2
3490⁴ Jack Jennings **(95)***(95?) (BAMcMahon)* 2-8-11 JReid(7) (lw: rdn over 3f out: 5th st: r.o one pce fnl 2f).......nk 3
3141² Hammerstein *(87) (MRStoute)* 2-8-11 MJKinane(1) (lw: hdwy over 3f out: 6th st: rdn over 2f out: wknd over 1f out).......4 4
3588a* Bijou d'Inde **(100)***(90) (MJohnston)* 2-9-0 JWeaver(2) (lw: 2nd st: rdn over 2f out: wknd over 1f out).......nk 5
3650² Acharne **(89)***(83) (CEBrittain)* 2-8-11 BDoyle(4) (lw: bmpd over 3f out: 7th & rd wd st: nvr nr to chal).......2 6
3560* Mawwal (USA) **(100)***(77)*(Fav)*(RWArmstrong)* 2-8-11 WCarson(8) (lw: hdwy over 3f out: 4th st: wknd 2f out).......3 7
3215³ Oblomov **(86)***(57) (GLewis)* 2-8-11 PaulEddery(3) (led over 2f: wknd over 3f out: 8th st).......10 8

2/1 Mawwal (USA), **5/2** Bijou d'Inde, **7/2** MONS, **6/1** More Royal (USA) (4/1-13/2), **8/1** Hammerstein, **50/1** Acharne, **66/1** Jack Jennings, Oblomov, CSF £22.54 TOTE £4.60: £1.10 £1.70 £6.30 (£12.00) OWNER Mrs E. H. Vestey (NEWMARKET) BRED Sir Eric Parker 8 Rn

1m 42.74 (3.14) SF: 72/62/61/53/56/49/43/23

OFFICIAL EXPLANATION **Mawwal: the trainer reported that the colt had got upset in the stalls, missed the break and was unable to to be up with the pace.**

3813

TOTE FESTIVAL H'CAP (3-Y.O+) (Class B) £52,913.75 (£15,935.00: £7,717.50: £3,608.75)
7f Stalls: Centre GOING: 0.10 sec per fur (G) 3-25 (3-39)

3109² **Night Dance (84)***(97) (GLewis)* 3-7-10 (5)ow3 AWhelan(6) (lw: racd stands' side: hdwy over 1f out: led wl ins fnl f: drvn out).......— 1
3085² Decorated Hero **(102)***(115)*(Fav)*(JHMGosden)* 3-9-5 LDettori(1) (racd stands' side: a.p: rdn over 1f out: ev ch ins fnl f: unable qckn).......1¼ 2
3411* Western Fame (USA) **(85)***(98) (JLDunlop)* 3-8-2 5x JQuinn(18) (lw: hld up: led wl over 1f out tl wl ins fnl f: unable qckn).......s.h 3

3703[3] Fame Again **(80)***(91) (MrsJRRamsden)* 3-7-11 JFEgan(16) (rdn & hdwy over 1f out: r.o ins fnl f)....¾ 4
3411[7] Gymcrak Premiere **(88)***(99) (GHolmes)* 7-8-9v WNewnes(25) (b.nr hind: lw: hdwy over 1f out: r.o)....s.h 5
3602[2] Cadeaux Tryst **(102)***(112) (EALDunlop)* 3-9-5 WRSwinburn(20) (b: rdn & hdwy over 1f out: r.o)....½ 6
3715[8] Samah **(74)***(82) (DNicholls)* 5-7-2 (7)ow2 5x MartinDwyer(11) (racd stands' side: hdwy over 2f out: rdn over 1f out: one pce)....hd 7
3717[2] No Extras (IRE) **(95)***(103) (GLMoore)* 5-9-2 SWhitworth(4) (racd stands' side: hdwy over 1f out: one pce ins fnl f)....¾ 8
3212[12] Chickawicka (IRE) **(87)***(93) (MCPipe)* 4-8-8v DBiggs(30) (lw: led over 5f)....¾ 9
3608* Akil (IRE) **(90)***(94) (RWArmstrong)* 3-8-7 5x WCarson(15) (racd stands' side: a.p: rdn over 2f out: one pce)....1¼ 10
3637* Be Warned **(75)***(78) (NACallaghan)* 4-7-10b 5x EJohnson(9) (racd stands' side: nvr nrr)....nk 11
3348[5] Quintus Decimus **(78)***(79) (LordHuntingdon)* 3-7-2 (7)ow1 CAdamson(29) (lw: hld up: rdn over 2f out: one pce)....½ 12
3382[7] Classic Sky (IRE) **(97)***(97) (EALDunlop)* 4-9-4 RHills(7) (racd stands' side: a mid div)....¾ 13
3706[19] Ertlon **(85)***(82) (CEBrittain)* 5-8-6 BDoyle(28) (lw: a.p: rdn over 2f out: wknd fnl f)....1¼ 14
2948[8] Kayvee **(101)***(98) (GHarwood)* 6-9-8 AClark(8) (racd stands' side: s.s: hdwy over 1f out: eased whn btn ins fnl f)....hd 15
2948* Verzen (IRE) **(97)***(93) (DRLoder)* 3-9-0 MJKinane(17) (lw: nvr nrr)....nk 16
3607* Band on the Run **(95)***(91) (BAMcMahon)* 8-8-13 (3) 5x SSanders(23) (lw: prom over 5f)....s.h 17
3717[3] Patto (USA) **(95)***(91) (WJHaggas)* 4-9-2 RCochrane(13) (lw: racd stands' side: hdwy over 2f out: wknd over 1f out)....hd 18
3608[6] Celestial Key (USA) **(101)***(94) (MJohnston)* 5-9-8 JWeaver(21) (a.p: ev ch over 1f out: sn wknd)....1¼ 19
3562[4] Moccasin Run (USA) **(103)***(95) (IABalding)* 4-9-10 PatEddery(10) (racd stands' side: bhd fnl 2f)....nk 20
3706[9] Belfry Green (IRE) **(92)***(84) (CAHorgan)* 5-8-13 WWoods(2) (racd stands' side: hld up: rdn over 2f out: wknd over 1f out)....nk 21
3411[2] Somerton Boy (IRE) **(76)***(68) (PCalver)* 5-7-11 NCarlisle(22) (lw: bhd fnl 2f)....s.h 22
3579a[3] Nagnagnag (IRE) **(100)***(85) (SDow)* 3-9-3 MRoberts(12) (racd stands' side: hld up: hrd rdn over 2f out: wknd over 1f out)....3 23
3564[7] She's Dynamite (IRE) **(83)***(65) (WJarvis)* 3-7-9 (5) MHenry(3) (racd stands' side: prom over 3f)....1¼ 24
3419[7] Scotsky (IRE) **(95)***(74) (JLDunlop)* 3-8-12 TQuinn(24) (lw: s.s: a bhd)....1¼ 25
3209* Wild Rice **(90)***(63)*(Fav)*(GWragg)* 3-8-7 MHills(19) (b: lw: bhd fnl 2f)....2½ 26
3706[2] Mister Rm **(77)***(42) (RGuest)* 3-7-3 (5)ow1 MBaird(27) (lw: a bhd)....3 27
3706[7] Law Commission **(79)** *(DRCElsworth)* 5-7-11 (3) NVarley(26) (Withdrawn not under Starter's orders: broke out of stalls & bolted).... W

LONG HANDICAP Mister Rm 7-6

10/1 Wild Rice, Decorated Hero, **11/1** Western Fame (USA), Verzen (IRE), Cadeaux Tryst, **12/1** Patto (USA), Akil (IRE), **14/1** No Extras (IRE) (20/1-2/1), **16/1** Fame Again, Mister Rm, Quintus Decimus, **20/1** NIGHT DANCE, Samah, Belfry Green (IRE), Nagnagnag (IRE), Band on the Run, **25/1** Moccasin Run (USA), Kayvee, **33/1** Celestial Key (USA), Classic Sky (IRE), Gymcrak Premiere, Somerton Boy (IRE), Be Warned, **50/1** Law Commission, **66/1** Scotsky (IRE), Chickawicka (IRE), She's Dynamite (IRE), Ertlon, CSF £193.63 CT £2,121.36 TOTE £48.00: £9.80 £2.90 £3.50 £5.90 (£335.30) Trio £1,240.10 OWNER Mr G. V. Wright (EPSOM) BRED Miss J. A. Challen 27 Rn 1m 30.57 (4.07)

SF:44/62/45/38/50/59/33/54/44/41/29/26/48/33/49/40/42/42/45/46/35/19/32/12/21/10/-/-

WEIGHT FOR AGE 3yo-4lb

STEWARDS' ENQUIRY Egan susp. 2-3/10/95 (Improper use of the whip).

3814 QUEEN ELIZABETH II STKS (Gp 1) (3-Y.O+) (Class A) £194,760.00 (£72,345.50: £34,297.75: £14,446.75)

1m (round) Stalls: High GOING: 0.10 sec per fur (G) 4-05 (4-19)

3143[2] **Bahri (USA) (125)***(134) (JLDunlop)* 3-8-11 WCarson(1) (lw: racd wd bk st: led 7f out: clr over 1f out: comf)....— 1
3589a* Ridgewood Pearl *(119)*(Fav)*(JOxx,Ireland)* 3-8-8 JPMurtagh(5) (b: lw: hld up: chsd wnr over 3f out: ev ch over 2f out: rdn wl over 1f out: unable qckn)....6 2
2689[5] Soviet Line (IRE) **(121)***(112) (MRStoute)* 5-9-1 WRSwinburn(3) (5th st: rdn & hdwy over 2f out: one pce)....5 3
3562* Bishop of Cashel **(114)***(110) (JRFanshawe)* 3-8-11 LDettori(6) (3rd st: wknd wl over 1f out)....1 4
3562[3] Mr Martini (IRE) **(111)***(80) (CEBrittain)* 5-9-1 BDoyle(4) (lw: 4th st: wknd over 2f out)....15 5
3608[11] Muhab (USA) **(100)***(40) (PTWalwyn)* 3-8-11 RHills(2) (led 1f: wknd over 3f out: 6th st)....20 6

8/13 Ridgewood Pearl, **5/2** BAHRI (USA), **13/2** Soviet Line (IRE) (op 10/1), **14/1** Bishop of Cashel, **40/1** Mr Martini (IRE), **100/1** Muhab (USA), CSF £4.35 TOTE £3.50: £1.40 £1.10 (£1.60) OWNER Mr Hamdan Al Maktoum (ARUNDEL) BRED Shadwell Farm Inc 6 Rn

1m 40.54 (0.94) SF: 95/80/77/71/45/1
WEIGHT FOR AGE 3yo-4lb

3815 ASCOT RATED STKS H'CAP (0-105) (3-Y.O+) (Class B) £15,622.00 (£5,848.00: £2,861.50: £1,232.50)
5f Stalls: Centre GOING: 0.10 sec per fur (G) 4-40 (4-46)

3632* **Spaniards Close (90)**(*102*) (*PJMakin*) 7-8-11 MJKinane(4) (hdwy over 1f out: led ins fnl f: rdn out) ....— **1**
426⁸ Leap for Joy **(89)**(*101*) (*JHMGosden*) 3-8-8 LDettori(3) (lw: a.p: led 1f out tl ins fnl f: r.o) ....hd **2**
3236⁹ Brave Edge **(99)**(*103*) (*RHannon*) 4-9-6 PatEddery(11) (rdn & hdwy over 1f out: unable qckn ins fnl f) 2½ **3**
3551⁴ Call Me I'm Blue (IRE) **(89)**(*90*) (*NTinkler*) 5-8-10 WNewnes(9) (nt clr run & swtchd over 1f out: hdwy fnl f: r.o) 1 **4**
3706¹¹ Saseedo (USA) **(86)**(*86*) (*WAO'Gorman*) 5-8-7 EmmaO'Gorman(13) (lw: nt clr run over 1f out: hdwy fnl f: r.o wl) ....nk **5**
3550² Double Quick (IRE) **(102)**(*101*)(Fav)(*MJohnston*) 3-9-7 JWeaver(12) (a.p: led over 2f out to 1f out: one pce) ....nk **6**
3717⁸ Bold Effort (FR) **(99)**(*97*) (*KOCunningham-Brown*) 3-9-4 TQuinn(10) (a.p: rdn over 2f out: one pce) ....s.h **7**
3717⁴ Master of Passion **(86)**(*76*) (*JMPEustace*) 6-8-7 MTebbutt(1) (a.p: rdn over 2f out: wknd fnl f) 2½ **8**
3551¹⁷ Quiz Time **(87)**(*68*) (*SirMarkPrescott*) 3-8-6 WWoods(8) (prom over 3f) 3 **9**
3597¹⁴ Ann's Pearl (IRE) **(86)**(*67*) (*JWHills*) 4-8-2 (5) MHenry(5) (hld up: rdn over 2f out: wknd over 1f out) ....hd **10**
3554⁷ Ashtina **(86)**(*60*) (*RJHodges*) 10-8-7 JReid(2) (led over 2f: wkng whn n.m.r over 1f out) 2 **11**
3551¹² Jayannpee **(96)**(*70*) (*IABalding*) 4-8-10 (7) MartinDwyer(7) (lw: s.s: a bhd) ....hd **12**
3550⁴ That Man Again **(100)**(*72*) (*GLewis*) 3-9-5b PaulEddery(6) (lw: dwlt: a bhd) ....½ **13**

LONG HANDICAP Saseedo (USA) 8-6 Ashtina 8-5 Ann's Pearl (IRE) 7-12

9/2 Double Quick (IRE), **6/1** Master of Passion, **7/1** SPANIARDS CLOSE, That Man Again, **8/1** Brave Edge, Call Me I'm Blue (IRE) (6/1-9/1), **9/1** Jayannpee, **10/1** Bold Effort (FR), **14/1** Leap for Joy, Quiz Time, **25/1** Ashtina, **33/1** Saseedo (USA), **66/1** Ann's Pearl (IRE), CSF £89.76 CT £729.73 TOTE £5.90: £1.70 £3.70 £2.40 (£29.70) Trio £130.80 OWNER Avon Industries Ltd (MARLBOROUGH) BRED Avon Industries Bath Ltd 13 Rn

62.38 secs (2.88) SF: 55/52/56/43/39/52/48/29/19/20/13/23/23
WEIGHT FOR AGE 3yo-2lb

3816 BLUE SEAL CONDITIONS STKS (2-Y.O F) (Class B) £12,022.00 (£4,498.00: £2,199.00: £945.00: £422.50: £213.50)
6f Stalls: Centre GOING: 0.10 sec per fur (G) 5-15 (5-15)

Polska (USA) (*86+*)(Fav)(*DRLoder*) 2-8-8 MJKinane(5) (neat: lw: mde virtually all: rdn out) .— **1**
3604⁵ Tarneem (USA) (*83*) (*MRStoute*) 2-8-8 WRSwinburn(6) (hld up: rdn & faltered 1f out: r.o)...1¼ **2**
3708² Please Suzanne **(85)**(*86*) (*RHannon*) 2-8-11 BDoyle(7) (w wnr: rdn over 1f out: ev ch ins fnl f: unable qckn) ....s.h **3**
Seirenes (*79*) (*PTWalwyn*) 2-8-8 JReid(8) (cmpt: bit bkwd: hld up: rdn 2f out: one pce) 1¼ **4**
*3509*³ Miss Pickpocket (IRE) (*74*) (*PAKelleway*) 2-8-8 RCochrane(1) (s.s: plld hrd: hdwy 5f out: rdn over 1f out: one pce) 2 **5**
Madame Steinlen (*74*) (*BWHills*) 2-8-8 MHills(3) (cmpt: bit bkwd: nvr nr to chal) ....s.h **6**
3625⁸ Shady Girl (IRE) (*66*) (*BWHills*) 2-8-8 PatEddery(2) (hld up: hung rt over 1f out: sn wknd) 3 **7**
Ewar Sunrise (*50*) (*CEBrittain*) 2-8-8 JQuinn(4) (neat: bit bkwd: bhd fnl 2f) 6 **8**

7/4 POLSKA (USA) (5/4-2/1), **9/4** Please Suzanne (3/1-2/1), **4/1** Tarneem (USA), **10/1** Shady Girl (IRE) (8/1-12/1), **16/1** Madame Steinlen, **20/1** Seirenes, **40/1** Miss Pickpocket (IRE), Ewar Sunrise, CSF £8.49 TOTE £2.80: £1.40 £1.50 £1.40 (£4.80) OWNER Sheikh Mohammed (NEWMARKET) BRED Darley Stud Management Inc 8 Rn 1m 18.08 (4.48) SF: 40/37/40/33/28/28/20/4

3817 GORDON CARTER H'CAP (0-95) (3-Y.O+) (Class C) £14,525.00 (£4,400.00: £2,150.00: £1,025.00)
2m 45y Stalls: High GOING: 0.10 sec per fur (G) 5-50 (5-50)

3351* **Fujiyama Crest (IRE) (79)**(*95*) (*MRStoute*) 3-8-8 LDettori(10) (mde all: clr 2f out: r.o wl) ....— **1**

3500[5] Benfleet **(82)***(95) (RWArmstrong)* 4-9-9 RHills(11) (lw: stdy hdwy over 5f out: 8th st: chsd wnr over 1f out: no imp) 3 **2**
3616[2] Supreme Star (USA) **(65)***(76) (PRHedger)* 4-8-1 (5) DaneO'Neill(8) (stdy hdwy over 5f out: 4th st: rdn over 2f out: one pce) 2½ **3**
3555[3] Meant to Be **(73)***(83) (LadyHerries)* 5-9-0 JReid(5) (3rd st: rdn over 2f out: one pce) ....¾ **4**
2413* Kristal's Paradise (IRE) **(87)***(93) (JLDunlop)* 3-9-2 PatEddery(6) (lw: chsd wnr: rdn over 2f out: wknd over 1f out) 4 **5**
3616* Lear Dancer (USA) **(68)***(73) (PMitchell)* 4-8-6v(3) SSanders(2) (hdwy over 4f out: 6th st: wknd wl over 1f out) 1¼ **6**
3616[4] Sea Freedom **(68)***(73) (GBBalding)* 4-8-9 JWilliams(15) (lost pl over 6f out: one pce fnl 2f) ...hd **7**
Pistol River (IRE) **(87)***(90) (NJHWalker)* 5-10-0 RCochrane(14) (nvr nrr) 1¼ **8**
1840[17] Star Player **(60)***(57) (RJBaker)* 9-8-1 JQuinn(1) (lw: stdy hdwy over 5f out: 9th st: wknd over 2f out) 6 **9**
3616[10] Simafar (IRE) **(62)***(57) (NAGraham)* 4-8-3 BDoyle(9) (lw: nvr nrr) 2 **10**
3669* Istabraq (IRE) **(82)***(76)*(Fav)*(JHMGosden)* 3-8-11 WCarson(4) (b: bhd fnl 7f) 1½ **11**
3412[3] Red Bustaan **(81)***(73) (ACStewart)* 3-8-10 MRoberts(13) (lw: 7th st: wknd over 2f out) 2 **12**
3616[8] Shadirwan (IRE) **(73)***(64) (RAkehurst)* 4-9-0 TQuinn(3) (5th st: wknd over 2f out) ....¾ **13**
3710* Witney-de-Bergerac (IRE) **(67)***(53) (JSMoore)* 3-7-3 (7)ow3 MDwyer(16) (lw: a bhd) 2 **14**
3593[4] Typhoon Eight (IRE) **(77)***(65) (BWHills)* 3-8-6 MHills(7) (10th st: wknd over 2f out) 1 **15**
3142[4] Great Crusader **(90)***(77) (CACyzer)* 3-9-5b DBiggs(12) (lw: s.s: hdwy 14f out: wknd over 5f out) 1 **16**

LONG HANDICAP Witney-de-Bergerac (IRE) 7-5

5/2 Istabraq (IRE) (9/4-11/2), **9/2** Kristal's Paradise (IRE), **8/1** FUJIYAMA CREST (IRE), Red Bustaan, **9/1** Typhoon Eight (IRE), **10/1** Shadirwan (IRE), **14/1** Supreme Star (USA), **16/1** Great Crusader, Sea Freedom, Lear Dancer (USA), **20/1** Meant to Be, Benfleet, **33/1** Star Player, **40/1** Witney-de-Bergerac (IRE), Simafar (IRE), **66/1** Pistol River (IRE), CSF £147.18 CT £2,027.79 TOTE £8.10: £1.50 £5.40 £2.70 £3.20 (£194.60) Trio £1,448.00 OWNER Mr Seisuke Hata (NEWMARKET) BRED B. Kennedy 16 Rn

3m 33.75 (7.25) SF: 65/77/58/65/63/55/55/72/39/39/46/43/46/23/35/47

WEIGHT FOR AGE 3yo-12lb

T/Jkpt: Not won; £20,662.14 to Ascot 24/9/95. T/Plpt: £82.30 (651.28 Tckts). T/Qdpt: £16.50 (40.85 Tckts). AK

3799-HAYDOCK (L-H)
Saturday September 23rd (Good)

WEATHER: fine & dry WIND: slt half against

3818

SEPTEMBER MAIDEN H'CAP (0-70) (3-Y.O+) (Class E) £3,629.50 (£1,096.00: £533.00: £251.50) **1m 6f** Stalls: Low GOING minus 0.24 sec (GF) 2-15 (2-17)

3759[5] **Salska** **(43)***(56) (AStreeter)* 4-8-7 TSprake(10) (hld up in tch: lost pl ent st: hdwy u.p 3f out: styd on to ld cl home) ....— **1**
1767[3] Sugar Mill **(60)***(73) (MrsMReveley)* 5-9-10 KFallon(6) (chsd ldrs: 5th st: led 1f out: hrd rdn & ct last stride) ....s.h **2**
3061[7] Thrower **(38)***(49) (PDEvans)* 4-8-2 NAdams(11) (a.p: 4th st: led over 3f out to 1f out: rdn & no ex fnl f) 1½ **3**
3526[5] Pretoria Dancer **(64)***(75) (JHMGosden)* 3-9-4 GHind(17) (hld up: hdwy 5f out: hrd rdn over 1f out: styd on) ....nk **4**
3627[6] Inn At the Top **(56)***(67) (JNorton)* 3-8-10 DaleGibson(18) (lw: hld up: hdwy on ins over 2f out: n.m.r appr fnl f: nvr nrr) ....nk **5**
3724[13] Zamhareer (USA) **(45)***(54) (WStorey)* 4-8-4 (5) PFessey(14) (hld up: hdwy on outside 3f out: nvr nrr) 1½ **6**
3710[3] Grand Applause (IRE) **(46)***(53) (MPMuggeridge)* 5-8-10 GBardwell(15) (hld up & bhd: hdwy over 3f out: nt rch ldrs) 1½ **7**
1439[0] True Bird (IRE) **(60)***(61) (JDBethell)* 3-9-0 TIves(4) (bit bkwd: nvr nr to chal) 5 **8**
1966[6] Benjamins Law **(49)***(48) (JAPickering)* 4-8-13 DeanMcKeown(8) (led 4f: 2nd st: slt ld 4f out: sn hdd & wknd) 2 **9**
3304[2] Torreglia (IRE) **(65)***(63) (JLDunlop)* 3-9-5 MRimmer(7) (unruly stalls: nvr bttr than mid div) ....¾ **10**
3669[6] Court Joker (IRE) **(47)***(44)*(Fav)*(MHTompkins)* 3-8-1 FNorton(16) (a in rr) 1 **11**
3710[9] Streaky Hawk (USA) **(53)***(44) (PFICole)* 3-8-7 AMcGlone(1) (hdwy 9f out: 3rd st: wknd over 2f out) 5 **12**
3537[6] Our Kris **(65)***(56) (GHarwood)* 3-9-5 CRutter(19) (a in rr) ....s.h **13**
3217[3] Southampton **(36)***(25) (GBBalding)* 5-7-11v(3) DWright(20) (sn drvn along: nvr nr to chal) 1¾ **14**
3635[8] Greenway Lady **(49)***(36) (CNAllen)* 3-8-0 (3)ow2 DRMcCabe(12) (a in rr) ....s.h **15**
3685[19] Kindakoola **(38)***(4) (MCChapman)* 4-7-9 (7) CMunday(3) (led 6f out to 4f out: sn wknd: t.o) 20 **16**

3646[14] Crowther Homes **(46)***(12) (EJAlston)* 5-8-10 SDWilliams(13) (a bhd: t.o)......s.h **17**
3421[2] Twilight Hour (USA) **(67)***(21)*(Fav)*(BWHills)* 3-9-7 DHolland(9) (led 10f out to 6f out: 6th & wkng st: t.o)......11 **18**
Waking (CAN) **(50)** *(JGFitzGerald)* 4-9-0 MWigham(5) (bkwd: chsd ldrs 8f: sn lost tch: t.o) ..20 **19**
3448[5] Sunoma Valley **(52)** *(JMPEustace)* 3-8-6 NKennedy(2) (a bhd: t.o)......25 **20**

7/1 Court Joker (IRE), Twilight Hour (USA), **8/1** Sugar Mill, Torreglia (IRE), **9/1** Southampton (op 6/1), Grand Applause (IRE), Our Kris (op 6/1), **14/1** Zamhareer (USA), True Bird (IRE), **16/1** Pretoria Dancer, Streaky Hawk (USA), Inn At the Top, **20/1** Sunoma Valley, Thrower, Greenway Lady, **25/1** Waking (CAN), Crowther Homes, SALSKA, Benjamins Law, **50/1** Kindakoola, CSF £215.46 CT £3,750.42 TOTE £43.60: £5.30 £2.30 £8.30 £2.80 (£193.90) Trio £412.80 OWNER Mr P. L. Clinton (UTTOXETER) BRED J. A. Haverhals 20 Rn

3m 3.49 (5.29) SF: 43/60/36/52/44/41/40/38/35/40/21/21/33/12/13/-/-/-/-/-

WEIGHT FOR AGE 3yo-10lb

STEWARDS' ENQUIRY Munday susp. 2-6/10/95 (excessive use of whip).

OFFICIAL EXPLANATION **Twilight Hour: had swallowed her tongue and was choking. Court Joker: the jockey reported that his instructions were to drop the gelding in and get him settled and, in the race, he was stopped twice in running.**

3819

SALE CONDITIONS STKS (2-Y.O F) (Class B) £7,497.60 (£2,421.60: £1,180.80)
7f 30y Stalls: Low GOING minus 0.24 sec per fur (GF) 2-45 (2-46)

3561[10] **Witch of Fife (USA) (100)***(88)*(Fav)*(BWHills)* 2-8-11 DHolland(2) (lw: chsd ldr: 2nd st: pushed along & bmpd over 2f out: sn rdn: one pce: fin 2nd, 2½l: awrdd r)......— **1**
3518[2] Parrot Jungle (IRE) **(91)***(94?) (JLDunlop)* 2-8-11 KFallon(3) (hld up: 3rd st: shkn up & chal between horses: led 2f out: r.o strly: fin 1st: disq: plcd 2nd)...... **2**
1833[4] Miss Waterline *(71) (PDEvans)* 2-8-11 GHind(1) (led 5f: rdn & outpcd appr fnl f)......8 **3**

4/7 WITCH OF FIFE (USA), **2/1** Parrot Jungle (IRE), **8/1** Miss Waterline, CSF £1.94 TOTE £1.50 (£1.10) OWNER Sheikh Mohammed (LAMBOURN) BRED Darley Stud Management Inc 3 Rn

1m 31.67 (4.37) SF: 20/26/3

STEWARDS' ENQUIRY Fallon susp. 2-7 & 9 &10/10/95 (irresponsible riding).

3820

AKZO NOBEL GROUP H'CAP (0-90) (3-Y.O+) (Class C) £6,157.50 (£1,860.00: £905.00: £427.50) **1m 2f 120y** Stalls: High GOING minus 0.24 sec (GF) 3-15 (3-16)

3156[5] **Haroldon (IRE) (72)***(82) (BPalling)* 6-9-0 TSprake(15) (b: hld up in tch: gd hdwy to ld 1f out: hld on gamely)......— **1**
1851[22] Serious **(79)***(89) (LadyHerries)* 5-9-7 DHolland(7) (hld up: hdwy & swtchd rt to chal 3f out: hrd rdn fnl f: r.o)......nk **2**
Home Counties (IRE) **(68)***(76) (DMoffatt)* 6-8-7 (3) DarrenMoffatt(10) (bit bkwd: hld up & bhd: hdwy 2f out: styd on strly fnl f)......1¼ **3**
3422[3] Komreyev Dancer **(67)***(71) (ABailey)* 3-7-13 (3) DWright(6) (hld up: hdwy over 2f out: nrst fin)2½ **4**
3382[9] Zermatt (IRE) **(68)***(61) (MDIUsher)* 5-8-10 NAdams(4) (prom: 3rd st: led 2f out: sn hdd: btn whn squeezed out ent fnl f)......7 **5**
3700* Tulu **(75)***(68)*(Fav)*(MrsJRRamsden)* 4-9-3 KFallon(8) (lw: hld up: hdwy & bmpd 3f out: rdn & hung lft appr fnl f: nt pce to chal)......½ **6**
3601[9] Fieldridge **(78)***(70) (MPMuggeridge)* 6-9-3 (3) DRMcCabe(13) (lw: led 1f: 5th st: rdn over 2f out: one pce)......hd **7**
3730[19] Greenspan (IRE) **(78)***(70) (WRMuir)* 3-8-13 CRutter(1) (lw: chsd ldrs: 6th st: wknd 2f out)......½ **8**
661[16] Dreams End **(83)***(71) (JMBradley)* 7-9-8 (3) JStack(14) (b: chsd ldrs: 4th st: wknd over 2f out)2½ **9**
3700[3] Ballard Ring (IRE) **(51)***(37) (JSWainwright)* 4-7-2 (5) PFessey(9) (led after 1f to 6f out: 2nd st: wknd over 2f out)......1½ **10**
2006[6] Marguerite Bay (IRE) **(78)***(61) (EALDunlop)* 3-8-13 TIves(3) (bkwd: hld up: effrt & rdn 3f out: wknd over 2f out)......2 **11**
3700[6] Rasayel (USA) **(52)***(27) (PDEvans)* 5-7-8 GBardwell(2) (lw: led 6f out to 2f out: sn rdn & wknd)......5 **12**
Rafters **(63)***(36) (JMBradley)* 6-8-2 (3) SDrowne(11) (b: bkwd: a bhd)......1½ **13**
1022[10] Mamnoon (USA) **(72)***(7) (WClay)* 4-9-0 DaleGibson(5) (bkwd: bhd fr ½-wy: t.o)......25 **14**

LONG HANDICAP Ballard Ring (IRE) 7-4

2/1 Tulu, **11/2** Rasayel (USA), **7/1** Marguerite Bay (IRE), **8/1** Komreyev Dancer, **10/1** Serious, **12/1** HAROLDON (IRE), Ballard Ring (IRE), Fieldridge, **14/1** Zermatt (IRE), Home Counties (IRE), **16/1** Dreams End, **20/1** Greenspan (IRE), **25/1** Rafters, Mamnoon (USA), CSF £127.43 CT £1,572.55 TOTE £20.70: £3.60 £4.60 £3.40 (£111.20) Trio £316.00 OWNER Lamb Brook Associates (COWBRIDGE) BRED Owen Bourke in Ireland 14 Rn

2m 14.29 (2.79) SF: 57/64/51/39/36/43/45/38/46/12/29/2/11/-

WEIGHT FOR AGE 3yo-7lb

3821 E.B.F. KNUTSFORD MAIDEN STKS (2-Y.O) (Class D) £4,495.50 (£1,359.00: £662.00:£156.75:£156.75) **7f 30y** Stalls: Low GOING minus 0.24 sec(GF) 3-45 (3-49)

3441[2] **Polar Prince (IRE) (90)***(76+)*(Fav)*(MAJarvis)* 2-9-0 TIves(2) (lw: led 1f: 2nd st: disp ld 3f out: slt ld bel dist: rdn & r.o wl) ....— **1**
3494[4] Stellar Line (USA) *(72) (BWHills)* 2-9-0 DHolland(7) (a.p: led 3f out to bel dist: sn hrd rdn: one pce) 1¾ **2**
3398[3] Prince of My Heart **(77)***(67) (BWHills)* 2-8-9 (5) JDSmith(13) (hld up: hdwy on outside over 2f out: hung lft u.p: kpt on ins fnl f) 2½ **3**
3339[15] Steal 'Em *(37) (ABailey)* 2-8-6 (3) DWright(14) (chsd ldrs: 5th st: rdn & wknd wl over 1f out) 11 **4**
849[7] Pride of Kashmir *(42) (PWHarris)* 2-9-0 GHind(16) (hdwy over 2f out: nvr nr to chal) ....d.h **4**
Dance On A Cloud (USA) *(33) (MRStoute)* 2-8-9 DeanMcKeown(8) (tall: s.s: nvr nrr) 1½ **6**
Alpine Hideaway (IRE) *(38) (BHanbury)* 2-8-11 (3) JStack(4) (chsd ldrs: 4th st: wknd fnl 2f) ....hd **7**
3539[5] Della Casa (IRE) *(32) (JLDunlop)* 2-8-9 MRimmer(11) (nvr plcd to chal) ....¾ **8**
3620[14] Siege Perilous (IRE) *(35) (BobJones)* 2-9-0 MWigham(12) (a in rr) ....¾ **9**
Ameer Alfayaafi (IRE) *(32) (ACStewart)* 2-8-11 (3) DRMcCabe(3) (small: cmpt: bkwd: nvr nr ldrs) 1¼ **10**
Northern Motto *(32) (MrsJRRamsden)* 2-9-0 MDeering(6) (w'like: a bhd) ....s.h **11**
Alpine Joker *(31) (MrsJRRamsden)* 2-9-0 KFallon(10) (lengthy: bkwd: s.s: a in rr) ....nk **12**
3366[3] Islay Brown (IRE) **(77)***(18) (CWCElsey)* 2-8-4 (5) PFessey(15) (chsd ldrs: 6th st: wknd over 2f out) 3½ **13**
Joe Shaw *(12) (MrsMReveley)* 2-9-0 FNorton(1) (leggy: bkwd: a in rr: t.o) 5 **14**
2820[9] Dino's Mistral *(11) (FHLee)* 2-9-0 AMcGlone(5) (led after 1f to 3f out: wknd over 2f out: t.o) ....½ **15**
Storm Wind (IRE) *(KRBurke)* 2-9-0 SDWilliams(9) (neat: bkwd: outpcd: t.o) 8 **16**

15/8 POLAR PRINCE (IRE), **7/2** Stellar Line (USA), **13/2** Dance On A Cloud (USA), **10/1** Ameer Alfayaafi (IRE), Prince of My Heart, **12/1** Della Casa (IRE) (op 8/1), **20/1** Steal 'Em, Alpine Hideaway (IRE), Alpine Joker, Northern Motto, **25/1** Pride of Kashmir, Islay Brown (IRE), **33/1** Siege Perilous (IRE), Joe Shaw, Dino's Mistral, **50/1** Storm Wind (IRE), CSF £9.49 TOTE £2.70: £1.40 £1.80 £2.70 (£3.40) Trio £15.60 OWNER Mrs Christine Stevenson (NEWMARKET) BRED Michael Morrin 16 Rn 1m 30.72 (3.42) SF: 39/35/30/-/5/-/1/-/-/-/-/-/-/-/-/-

3822 LEIGH H'CAP (0-90) (3-Y.O+) (Class C) £6,255.00 (£1,890.00: £920.00: £435.00) **5f** Stalls: High GOING minus 0.24 sec per fur (GF) 4-15 (4-17)

3637[15] **Croft Pool (80)***(90) (JAGlover)* 4-9-7 SDWilliams(11) (lw: a.p: led over 1f out: rdn & edgd lft: all out) ....— **1**
3748[7] Halbert **(65)***(74) (MRChannon)* 6-7-13v(7) DSweeney(14) (a.p stands' side: rdn & ev ch over 1f out: unable qckn) ....nk **2**
3551[16] Mr Bergerac (IRE) **(84)***(91) (BPalling)* 4-9-11 TSprake(3) (racd centre: hdwy over 1f out: fin wl) ....½ **3**
3492[15] Louisville Belle (IRE) **(54)***(58) (MDIUsher)* 6-7-9 NAdams(6) (b: lw: chsd ldrs centre: rdn & kpt on wl ins fnl f) 1 **4**
3677[4] Canovas Heart **(61)***(63) (BobJones)* 6-8-2 CRutter(13) (led stands' side over 3f: hrd rdn: no ex fnl f) ....¾ **5**
3764[7] Bells of Longwick **(56)***(57) (WWHaigh)* 6-7-11v DaleGibson(15) (hdwy wl over 1f out: nrst fin) ....nk **6**
3512[2] Four of Spades **(61)***(59) (PDEvans)* 4-8-2 ow3 GHind(7) (lw: swtchd rt s: hdwy appr fnl f: nvr nrr) ....hd **7**
3715[13] Broadstairs Beauty (IRE) **(75)***(75) (SRBowring)* 5-8-11b(5) CTeague(10) (b: led centre: rdn wl over 1f out: one pce) ....nk **8**
3715[18] Ansellman **(74)***(73) (JBerry)* 5-8-8 (7) PRoberts(12) (in tch: rdn whn hmpd 2f out: sn btn) ....s.h **9**
3622[3] Bangles **(70)***(69)*(Fav)*(LordHuntingdon)* 5-8-11 KFallon(18) (chsd ldrs stands' side: rdn over 1f out: one pce) ....s.h **10**
2659[9] I'm Your Lady **(69)***(67) (BAMcMahon)* 4-8-10 FNorton(9) (lw: hdwy 2f out: sn rdn: nt rch ldrs) ....nk **11**
3640[4] Glorious Aragon **(83)***(81) (RFJohnsonHoughton)* 3-9-8 AMcGlone(16) (hdwy 2f out: rdn over 1f out: no imp) ....s.h **12**
3777[6] Elle Shaped (IRE) **(82)***(75) (ABailey)* 5-9-6 (3) DWright(19) (sn drvn: nvr gng pce of ldrs) 1½ **13**
3637[6] So Intrepid (IRE) **(72)***(64) (JMBradley)* 5-8-10 (3) SDrowne(8) (lw: hdwy 2f out: rdn & kpt on same pce fr bel dist) ....½ **14**
3597[6] Polly Particular **(78)***(66) (TDBarron)* 3-9-3 DeanMcKeown(4) (lw: prom centre tl rdn & wknd wl over 1f out) 1¼ **15**
3597[15] Beau Venture (USA) **(77)***(64) (FHLee)* 7-9-4 RLappin(5) (lw: chsd ldrs: rdn 2f out: sn btn) .....nk **16**

3777[10] Crystal Loop **(67)***(51) (ABailey)* 3-8-6 GBardwell(17) (chsd ldrs stands' side over 3f)..............¾ **17**
3667* Portelet **(77)***(58) (RGuest)* 3-8-13 (3) JStack(1) (w ldr centre over 3f: sn wknd)..........................1 **18**

5/1 Bangles, **13/2** Portelet, **8/1** Canovas Heart, Broadstairs Beauty (IRE), Polly Particular, **9/1** Ansellman, **12/1** Mr Bergerac (IRE), Glorious Aragon, **14/1** Elle Shaped (IRE), Halbert, So Intrepid (IRE), Crystal Loop, CROFT POOL, **16/1** I'm Your Lady, Four of Spades, **25/1** Louisville Belle (IRE), Beau Venture (USA), **33/1** Bells of Longwick, CSF £201.00 CT £2,244.15 TOTE £34.90: £6.20 £3.70 £3.70 £12.30 (£120.90) Trio £2,397.30 OWNER Countrywide Classics Ltd (WORKSOP) BRED J. S. Bell 18 Rn 60.26 secs (1.26) SF: 63/47/64/31/36/30/32/48/46/42/40/52/48/37/37/37/22/29

WEIGHT FOR AGE 3yo-2lb

3823

CASTLE IRWELL H'CAP (0-80) (3-Y.O+) (Class D) £4,082.75 (£1,232.00: £598.50: £281.75) **7f 30y** Stalls: Low GOING minus 0.24 sec per fur (GF) 4-45 (4-47)

3656[2] **South Rock (79)***(94) (JAGlover)* 3-9-7 MRimmer(1) (lw: mde all: drvn clr appr fnl f: unchal).— **1**
3624* It's Academic **(68)***(74) (MrsJRRamsden)* 3-8-10 KFallon(12) (lw: hld up: hdwy 3f out: rdn & r.o ins fnl f: no ch w wnr)..4 **2**
3034[2] Make Time **(66)***(69) (JPearce)* 3-8-8 GBardwell(8) (in tch: 6th st: rdn over 2f out: kpt on fnl f)1¼ **3**
3451[2] Splintercat (USA) **(73)***(76)*(Fav)*(JHMGosden)* 3-9-1 GHind(3) (lw: chsd ldrs: 4th st: wnt 2nd over 1f out: rdn & one pce fnl f)..nk **4**
3597[9] Bollin Harry **(69)***(67) (MHEasterby)* 3-8-11 DeanMcKeown(5) (chsd ldrs: 3rd st: rdn 2f out: kpt on one pce)..2 **5**
3656[4] African-Pard (IRE) **(70)***(60) (DHaydnJones)* 3-8-12 DHolland(15) (hdwy 2f out: nt rch ldrs) ..3½ **6**
3645[18] Impulsive Air (IRE) **(68)***(58) (EWeymes)* 3-8-10v TIves(7) (s.i.s: hld up: effrt u.p over 2f out: nvr nrr)...s.h **7**
3739[12] Anita's Contessa (IRE) **(64)***(50) (BPalling)* 3-8-6 TSprake(6) (chsd ldrs: 5th st: rdn over 2f out: sn lost tch)..1¾ **8**
3726[13] Hey Up Dolly (IRE) **(64)***(49) (JBerry)* 3-8-1 (5) PFessey(11) (lw: rdn over 3f out: nvr nr ldrs).....½ **9**
3598[7] Mountgate **(71)***(56) (MPBielby)* 3-8-10 (3) DRMcCabe(16) (lw: nvr nr to chal)..........................hd **10**
3679[11] Top Skipper (IRE) **(61)***(42) (BHanbury)* 3-8-0 (3)ow2 JStack(4) (a in rr) 1 **11**
2500[7] Barrel of Hope **(70)***(49) (JLEyre)* 3-8-12 RLappin(13) (a bhd)..1½ **12**
2536[8] Indian Jockey **(65)***(44) (MCPipe)* 3-8-7 AMcGlone(14) (chsd wnr: ev ch 3f out: sn rdn & wknd)..nk **13**
3545[13] Wandering Minstrel (IRE) **(60)***(34) (JMPEustace)* 3-8-2 NKennedy(10) (lw: hdwy 3f out: sn rdn: wknd fnl f)...2 **14**
1951[4] Gulf Shaadi **(72)***(42) (EJAlston)* 3-9-0 SDWilliams(2) (a bhd)..1¾ **15**

9/4 Splintercat (USA), **100/30** It's Academic, **8/1** Make Time, **10/1** SOUTH ROCK, Indian Jockey, **11/1** Mountgate, **12/1** Bollin Harry, **14/1** Gulf Shaadi, **16/1** Hey Up Dolly (IRE), African-Pard (IRE), **20/1** Wandering Minstrel (IRE), Barrel of Hope, Impulsive Air (IRE), **25/1** Top Skipper (IRE), Anita's Contessa (IRE), CSF £46.21 CT £274.47 TOTE £11.00: £3.50 £1.70 £2.00 (£12.50) Trio £37.50 OWNER Mr B. H. Farr (WORKSOP) BRED Worksop Manor Stud Farm 15 Rn

1m 30.04 (2.74) SF: 54/34/29/36/27/20/18/10/9/16/2/9/4/-/2

T/Plpt: £4,259.00 (3.48 Tckts). T/Qdpt: Not won; £200.30 to Ascot 24/9/95. IM

3805-REDCAR (L-H)
Saturday September 23rd (Good)

WEATHER: overcast WIND: fresh half bhd

3824

NORTHERN LIGHTS NURSERY H'CAP (0-75) (2-Y.O) (Class E) £3,575.75 (£1,076.00: £520.50: £242.75) **5f** Stalls: Centre GOING minus 0.10 sec per fur (G) 1-50 (1-53)

3670* **Swynford Dream (65)***(70+)*(Fav)*(JFBottomley)* 2-9-2 JLowe(9) (lw: mde all: wnt rt over 1f out: kpt on strly: comf) ....— **1**
3509[8] Rustic Song (IRE) **(52)***(51) (JWharton)* 2-8-3 SMaloney(10) (a chsng ldrs: kpt on u.p fnl f: no imp)...2 **2**
3430* Secret Voucher **(67)***(65) (BAMcMahon)* 2-8-13 (5) LNewton(3) (a chsng ldrs: nt qckn over 1f out) ....s.h **3**
3567* Thai Morning **(70)***(67) (PWHarris)* 2-9-4 (3) PMcCabe(1) (outpcd & wandered ½-wy: hdwy over 1f out: styd on towards fin) ....½ **4**
*3509** Vax New Way **(68)***(63) (JLSpearing)* 2-9-5 MFenton(7) (in tch: effrt 2f out: styd on ins fnl f)....½ **5**
3727[6] Lady Caroline Lamb (IRE) **(65)***(60) (MRChannon)* 2-9-2 WRyan(12) (n.m.r after s: bhd tl styd on fnl 2f)..hd **6**
3415* Opening Chorus **(68)***(61) (MrsMReveley)* 2-9-5 KDarley(6) (chsd ldrs: effrt over 2f out: kpt on same pce)..½ **7**

3670² Hickleton Miss **(61)***(53) (MrsMReveley)* 2-8-7 (5) GParkin(17) (hmpd s: sn wl bhd: hdwy over 1f out: styd on wl towards fin) ..... ½ **8**
3369⁴ Mystique Smile **(59)***(51) (JBerry)* 2-8-10 GCarter(2) (nvr nr to chal) ..... s.h **9**
3742³ Superfrills **(52)***(42) (MissLCSiddall)* 2-8-3 TWilliams(5) (chsd ldrs 3f: sn wknd) ..... ½ **10**
3568⁵ Goretski (IRE) **(59)***(46) (NTinkler)* 2-8-10 KimTinkler(16) (in tch: effrt & swtchd lft over 1f out: sn wknd) 1 **11**
3647⁷ Power Princess **(54)***(36) (RMWhitaker)* 2-8-5 AMackay(14) (b: chsd ldrs tl lost pl ½-wy) 1½ **12**
3639¹⁴ Lady Eclat **(60)***(42) (JAGlover)* 2-8-11 MBirch(11) (nvr wnt pce) ..... hd **13**
3626¹⁹ Redbrook Lady **(55)***(36) (SGNorton)* 2-8-6 JTate(13) (nvr nr ldrs) ..... nk **14**
3670³ Bee Health Boy **(59)***(35) (MWEasterby)* 2-8-3b(7) RuthCoulter(15) (sn bhd) 1½ **15**
3430⁸ Harriet's Beau **(58)***(29) (MWEasterby)* 2-8-9b RPrice(18) (swvd lft s: bhd: sme hdwy ½-wy: sn wknd) 1½ **16**
2606⁶ Darerock **(50)***(18) (MDods)* 2-8-1 LCharnock(8) (sn wl outpcd: wl bhd fr ½-wy) 1 **17**

5/2 SWYNFORD DREAM, **11/2** Opening Chorus, **6/1** Lady Caroline Lamb (IRE), **7/1** Mystique Smile, **8/1** Thai Morning, **9/1** Secret Voucher, **10/1** Hickleton Miss, **12/1** Vax New Way (10/1-16/1), **16/1** Rustic Song (IRE), Lady Eclat, **20/1** Harriet's Beau, Bee Health Boy, Superfrills, **25/1** Power Princess, Goretski (IRE), **33/1** Redbrook Lady, **66/1** Darerock, CSF £47.80 CT £329.45 TOTE £4.30: £1.20 £3.80 £4.20 (£60.50) Trio not won; £360.07 to Ascot 24/9/95 OWNER Qualitair Holdings Ltd (MALTON) BRED Qualitair Stud Ltd 17 Rn
59.4 secs (2.70) SF: 44/25/39/41/37/34/35/27/25/16/20/10/16/10/9/3/-

3825 REYNARD (S) H'CAP (0-60) (3-Y.O+) (Class G) £2,959.00 (£824.00: £397.00)
1m 2f Stalls: Low GOING minus 0.10 sec per fur (G) 2-25 (2-25)

3658⁵ **Bobanlyn (IRE) (53)***(65) (DMorris)* 3-8-12 (3) PMcCabe(12) (bhd: effrt u.p 3f out: swtchd outside: styd on wl to ld wl ins fnl f) ..... — **1**
3505¹⁰ Antartictern (USA) **(43)***(53) (GROldroyd)* 5-8-11 AMackay(6) (hdwy over 3f out: led 1f out: edgd lft, hdd & no ex wl ins fnl f) 1¼ **2**
3402¹⁰ Mhemeanles **(40)***(49) (CaptJWilson)* 5-8-8 GCarter(5) (b.hind: chsd ldrs: led 2f out: sn hdd & nt qckn) ..... ½ **3**
3658¹⁶ Pop to Stans **(44)***(48) (JPearce)* 6-8-12v JLowe(1) (hld up: effrt 3f out: hung lft: kpt on same pce appr fnl f) 3½ **4**
*3511*⁶ Level Edge **(40)***(34) (MDHammond)* 4-8-8 MFenton(3) (chsd ldrs tl wknd over 1f out) 6 **5**
3658* Lunar Mission (IRE) **(63)***(55) (JMPEustace)* 4-10-3 JTate(7) (chsd ldrs: effrt 2f out: sn wknd) .. 1 **6**
3658¹⁵ Straw Thatch **(46)***(37) (RBastiman)* 6-8-9b(5)ow1 HBastiman(15) (in tch: no imp fnl 3f) ..... ½ **7**
3422¹¹ Orchidarma **(51)***(41) (JJQuinn)* 3-8-13v NConnorton(13) (sn bhd: sme hdwy 3f out: n.d) 1 **8**
3422⁶ Cumbrian Minstrel **(46)***(35) (MHEasterby)* 3-8-8 MBirch(14) (in tch: effrt 3f out: sn ev ch: wknd wl over 1f out) ..... ½ **9**
*3526*¹⁰ Just-Mana-Mou (IRE) **(47)***(34)*(Fav)*(GLewis)* 3-8-9 WRyan(2) (bhd: effrt & swtchd ins 3f out: nvr nr ldrs) 1¼ **10**
3534¹⁶ Lady-Bo-K **(46)***(31) (CaptJWilson)* 4-9-0 DHarrison(4) (b.hind: s.i.s: a in rr) 1½ **11**
3504¹⁰ Resolute Bay **(41)***(24) (RMWhitaker)* 9-8-2v(7) FLynch(9) (mid div: effrt on ins 5f out: wknd over 3f out) 1 **12**
1027¹⁰ Waterlord (IRE) **(44)***(21) (DNicholls)* 5-8-5 (7)ow1 SCopp(8) (led 2f: led over 2f out: sn hdd & wknd qckly) 3 **13**
3462¹⁴ Samaka Hara (IRE) **(52)***(30) (WSCunningham)* 3-9-0 KDarley(10) (sn bhd) ..... s.h **14**
*3241*⁷ No Submission (USA) **(42)***(20) (DWChapman)* 9-8-10 ACulhane(11) (lw: chsd ldrs tl lost pl 3f out) ..... ½ **15**
1285¹⁵ Greek Gold (IRE) **(44)***(14) (DNicholls)* 6-8-12 AlexGreaves(17) (lw: led after 2f tl over 2f out: wknd qckly) 5 **16**
Elegant Friend **(50)** *(DWChapman)* 7-9-4 LCharnock(16) (s.i.s: a bhd: t.o fnl 2f) 20 **17**

7/2 Just-Mana-Mou (IRE) (5/1-3/1), **11/2** Lunar Mission (IRE), **7/1** Samaka Hara (IRE), **8/1** Cumbrian Minstrel, Antartictern (USA), BOBANLYN (IRE), **9/1** Greek Gold (IRE), **10/1** Mhemeanles, Straw Thatch, **14/1** Level Edge, Orchidarma, No Submission (USA), **16/1** Pop to Stans, Resolute Bay, **20/1** Waterlord (IRE), **33/1** Lady-Bo-K, **50/1** Elegant Friend, CSF £79.94 CT £632.98 TOTE £10.40: £2.10 £2.20 £4.00 £3.40 (£64.00) Trio £253.80 OWNER Mrs Sheila Walker (NEWMARKET) BRED Mrs S. A. Pfeiffer and Partners in Ireland 17 Rn
2m 8.9 (6.40) SF: 39/33/29/28/14/35/17/15/9/8/11/4/1/4/-/-/-
WEIGHT FOR AGE 3yo-6lb
No bid

3826 TOTE BOOKMAKERS RATED STKS H'CAP (0-95) (3-Y.O+) (Class B)
£7,801.32 (£2,921.88: £1,430.94: £617.70: £278.85: £143.31)
1m 6f 19y Stalls: Low GOING minus 0.10 sec per fur (G) 3-00 (3-00)

3262³ **Trazl (IRE) (78)***(89)*(Fav)*(JLDunlop)* 3-8-7 GCarter(4) (chsd ldrs: effrt over 3f out: styd on to ld wl ins fnl f) ..... — **1**

2902[6] Executive Design **(77)***(88) (MrsMReveley)* 3-8-6 JTate(3) (unruly & reard s: effrt on outside over 3f out: led 2f out: hdd, hrd rdn & nt qckn wl ins fnl f)....nk **2**
3593[5] Tethys (USA) **(82)***(87) (JLEyre)* 4-9-7v WRyan(1) (led to 2f out: kpt on same pce)....5 **3**
3189[8] Boloardo **(65)***(68) (CEBrittain)* 6-8-4 MBirch(6) (hld up & plld hrd: stdy hdwy 4f out: rdn & outpcd over 2f out: kpt on appr fnl f)....1½ **4**
3391[2] Batabanoo **(80)***(77) (MrsMReveley)* 6-9-5 KDarley(7) (wnt 2nd 11f out: drvn along over 4f out: wknd 3f out)....6 **5**

5/2 TRAZL (IRE) (op 6/4), **11/4** Batabanoo (2/1-3/1), **3/1** Tethys (USA) (9/2-11/4), **7/2** Executive Design, **11/2** Boloardo, CSF £11.24 TOTE £2.90: £1.90 £2.80 (£12.90) OWNER Hesmonds Stud (ARUNDEL) BRED Hesmonds Stud Ltd 5 Rn 3m 8.0 (10.00) SF: 28/27/36/17/26
WEIGHT FOR AGE 3yo-10lb

3827 E.B.F. REG BOYLE BOOKMAKERS MAIDEN STKS (2-Y.O) (Class D) £3,938.00 (£1,184.00: £572.00: £266.00)

1m 1f Stalls: Low GOING minus 0.10 sec per fur (G) 3-35 (3-36)

2107[2] **House of Riches** *(77)*(Fav)*(LMCumani)* 2-9-0 KDarley(9) (lw: mde virtually all: styd on wl u.p fnl f)....— **1**
3620[9] Arctic Fancy (USA) *(77) (PWHarris)* 2-9-0 RPrice(4) (chsd ldrs: chal over 1f out: nt qckn towards fin)....nk **2**
3620[4] Classic Lover (IRE) *(68) (SCWilliams)* 2-8-9 AMackay(6) (in tch: effrt 3f out: styd on appr fnl f: nvr able chal)....2 **3**
2579[5] Silver Wing (USA) *(68) (MBell)* 2-8-9 MFenton(12) (b.off hind: stdy hdwy on outside over 3f out: edgd lft & kpt on fnl 2f: nvr nr to chal)....hd **4**
3592[7] Sharaf (IRE) *(73) (JLDunlop)* 2-9-0 GCarter(3) (chsd ldrs: effrt 3f out: n.m.r over 1f out: kpt on one pce)....hd **5**
Tissue of Lies (USA) *(57) (MJohnston)* 2-9-0 WRyan(8) (w'like: leggy: bit bkwd: s.i.s: bhd: sme hdwy 3f out: n.d)....9 **6**
3666[6] Mister Aspecto (IRE) *(57) (MJohnston)* 2-9-0 TWilliams(11) (chsd ldrs: chal 3f out: sn wknd)s.h **7**
Hallikeld *(51) (TJEtherington)* 2-8-9 JLowe(13) (lengthy: bit bkwd: nvr nr ldrs)....hd **8**
2995[10] No More Hassle (IRE) *(52) (MrsMReveley)* 2-9-0 ACulhane(14) (s.i.s: a in rr)....2½ **9**
Young Dalesman *(49) (AStreeter)* 2-8-9 (5) LNewton(7) (unf: bkwd: s.i.s: sme hdwy whn rn wd ent st: sn bhd)....1¾ **10**
2283[5] Double Agent *(42) (MJohnston)* 2-9-0 JTate(5) (sn pushed along: chsd ldrs: outpcd over 3f out: sn lost pl)....4 **11**
3523[9] Irish Oasis (IRE) *(31) (BSRothwell)* 2-9-0 LCharnock(10) (bit bkwd: chsd ldrs tl lost pl over 3f out)....6 **12**
2195[8] Song Song Blue (IRE) *(NTinkler)* 2-9-0 DHarrison(1) (bit bkwd: a bhd: t.o)....20 **13**

5/4 HOUSE OF RICHES, **5/1** Sharaf (IRE) (op 3/1), Mister Aspecto (IRE), **6/1** Classic Lover (IRE), Double Agent, **10/1** Silver Wing (USA), **12/1** Tissue of Lies (USA), **16/1** Arctic Fancy (USA), **50/1** No More Hassle (IRE), Young Dalesman, Hallikeld, **100/1** Song Song Blue (IRE), **1000/1** Irish Oasis (IRE), CSF £24.76 TOTE £2.00: £1.50 £3.80 £1.10 (£24.60) Trio £83.30 OWNER Sheikh Mohammed (NEWMARKET) BRED Sheikh Mohammed bin Rashid al Maktoum 13 Rn
1m 57.0 (8.00) SF: 18/18/9/9/14/-/-/-/-/-/-/-/-

3828 TETLEY TEA MAIDEN STKS (2-Y.O F) (Class D) £3,782.00 (£1,136.00: £548.00: £254.00) 6f Stalls: Centre GOING minus 0.10 sec per fur (G) 4-10 (4-11)

Last Second (IRE) *(80+) (SirMarkPrescott)* 2-8-11 KDarley(4) (w'like: leggy: scope: s.i.s: sn trckng ldrs: led ½-wy: pushed out)....— **1**
2934[2] Dimakya (USA) *(80)*(Fav)*(DRLoder)* 2-8-11 GCarter(8) (lw: trckd ldrs: disp ld ½-wy: rdn & nt qckn ins fnl f)....hd **2**
3626[8] Magic Melody *(61) (JLSpearing)* 2-8-11 JTate(1) (disp ld to ½-wy: wl outpcd over 1f out)....7 **3**
3647[10] Polish Saga *(61?) (MDods)* 2-8-11 NConnorton(6) (trckd ldrs: wl outpcd fnl 2f)....hd **4**
Dungeon Princess (IRE) *(58) (MRChannon)* 2-8-11 AMackay(5) (w'like: cmpt: chsd ldrs: effrt ½-wy: edgd lft & wknd over 1f out)....1¼ **5**
Any Colour *(51) (MJCamacho)* 2-8-11 LCharnock(9) (cmpt: bkwd: s.s: sn trckng ldrs: wl outpcd fr ½-wy)....2½ **6**
3509[7] The Barnsley Belle (IRE) *(51) (SGNorton)* 2-8-11 TWilliams(7) (sn wl outpcd & bhd)....hd **7**
2143[6] Amoeba (IRE) **(80)***(45) (JBerry)* 2-8-11 MBirch(3) (mde most to ½-wy: lost pl 2f out)....2 **8**
Mishaweer *(24) (JRFanshawe)* 2-8-11 DHarrison(2) (cmpt: unf: outpcd after 2f: sn bhd)....8 **9**

4/5 Dimakya (USA) (Evens-11/10), **3/1** LAST SECOND (IRE), **5/1** Dungeon Princess (IRE), **7/1** Mishaweer (op 9/2), **14/1** Amoeba (IRE), **25/1** The Barnsley Belle (IRE), Magic Melody, **66/1** Any Colour, Polish Saga, CSF £6.14 TOTE £4.00: £1.30 £1.40 £10.00 (£3.00) Trio £94.10 OWNER Mr Faisal Salman (NEWMARKET) BRED Miss K. Rausing and Mrs S. M. Rogers 9 Rn
1m 12.6 (3.30) SF: 39/39/20/20/17/10/10/4/-

3829

TRANSMORE VAN HIRE MAIDEN STKS (3-Y.O+) (Class D) £4,074.50 (£1,226.00: £593.00: £276.50)
7f Stalls: Centre GOING minus 0.10 sec per fur (G) 4-40 (4-41)

Dreamboat (USA) *(79)*(Fav)*(JHMGosden)* 3-8-9 WRyan(10) (trckd ldrs: led over 1f out: drvn out towards fin).........— 1
3542[3] Yeast *(83) (WJHaggas)* 3-9-0 KDarley(6) (lw: trckd ldr: led ½-wy tl over 1f out: kpt on wl u.p cl home).........nk 2
Neuwest (USA) **(85)***(83) (HThomsonJones)* 3-9-0 JLowe(9) (lw: trckd ldrs: ev ch over 1f out: kpt on u.p towards fin).........s.h 3
Ducking *(71) (JRFanshawe)* 3-8-9 MFenton(3) (chsd ldrs: outpcd over 2f out: kpt on ins fnl f).........3 4
Sombreffe *(70) (DRLoder)* 3-8-9 GCarter(7) (w'like: cmpt: w ldrs: ev ch tl wknd over 1f out)..½ 5
Aswaat (IRE) *(72) (JHMGosden)* 3-9-0 StephenDavies(5) (small: bit bkwd: b: s.i.s: sn chsng ldrs: effrt & hung rt 2f out: sn wknd).........1¼ 6
442[3] Mistress Thames *(61) (JRFanshawe)* 3-8-9 DHarrison(1) (prom: effrt over 2f out: sn outpcd) .3 7
Crees Sqaw *(60) (BAMcMahon)* 3-8-4 (5) LNewton(2) (leggy: unf: sn pushed along: nvr wnt pce).........hd 8
3357[15] Ladys Promise **(25)***(15) (GROldroyd)* 3-8-9v AMackay(4) (led to ½-wy: sn wl bhd: t.o).........20 9
3649[12] Sundries *(1) (DWChapman)* 5-9-4 ACulhane(8) (hld up: outpcd after 2f: sn t.o).........8 10

4/5 DREAMBOAT (USA), **9/2** Yeast, Sombreffe (op 3/1), **7/1** Neuwest (USA), **9/1** Mistress Thames (op 5/1), **12/1** Ducking, **20/1** Aswaat (IRE), **100/1** Crees Sqaw, Ladys Promise, **200/1** Sundries, CSF £5.82 TOTE £1.60: £1.10 £1.40 £2.00 (£4.40) Trio £6.20 OWNER Sheikh Mohammed (NEWMARKET) BRED Robert N. Clay 10 Rn 1m 24.7 (2.70) SF: 52/56/56/44/43/45/34/33/-/-
WEIGHT FOR AGE 3yo-4lb

3830

CLEVELAND APPRENTICE H'CAP (0-80) (3-Y.O+) (Class E) £3,395.50 (£1,024.00: £497.00: £233.50)
6f Stalls: Centre GOING minus 0.10 sec per fur (G) 5-10 (5-12)

3667[11] **Knayton Lass (54)***(61) (MWEasterby)* 4-8-2 (5) RuthCoulter(5) (chsd ldrs: carried lft ½-wy: led over 1f out: hung rt & drvn out).........— 1
3751[3] Craigie Boy **(53)***(57)*(Fav)*(NBycroft)* 5-8-6b PMcCabe(7) (lw: bmpd s: sn in tch: effrt 2f out: styd on wl ins fnl f).........1 2
3715[22] Barato **(69)***(73) (MrsJRRamsden)* 4-9-3 (5) TFinn(3) (b.nr hind: trckd ldrs: led over 3f out tl over 1f out: kpt on wl towards fin).........hd 3
3715[4] Cumbrian Waltzer **(73)***(77) (MHEasterby)* 10-9-12 LNewton(13) (b.nr hind: hld up: hdwy over 2f out: sn rdn: styd on wl ins fnl f).........s.h 4
3467[13] Mu-Arrik **(46)***(49) (GROldroyd)* 7-7-8v(5) KSked(9) (swvd lft s: hdwy ½-wy: kpt on ins fnl f)......½ 5
3275[3] Birchwood Sun **(61)***(62) (MDods)* 5-8-9b(5) GFaulkner(12) (in tch: hrd rdn 2f out: edgd lft & styd on same pce fnl f).........¾ 6
3622[6] Able Sheriff **(45)***(44) (MWEasterby)* 3-7-4b(5) RMullen(6) (in tch: ev ch over 1f out: kpt on one pce).........½ 7
3519[10] Fantasy Racing (IRE) **(78)***(76) (MRChannon)* 3-9-9 (5) JDennis(10) (bmpd after s: bhd tl styd on appr fnl f).........½ 8
3764[8] Miss Aragon **(57)***(53) (MissLCSiddall)* 7-8-3 (7) TSiddall(14) (s.v.s: bhd tl hdwy fnl 2f: nt rch ldrs).........¾ 9
Evanro (IRE) **(47)***(38) (TDBarron)* 4-7-11 (3) GMitchell(1) (nvr wnt pce).........2 10
2278[10] Pc's Cruiser (IRE) **(53)***(39) (JLEyre)* 3-7-12b(5) DDenby(4) (s.i.s: a in rr).........1¾ 11
3118[6] Ragazzo (IRE) **(50)***(13) (JSWainwright)* 5-7-12b(5)ow10 FLynch(11) (b.hind: swvd lft s: chsd ldrs to ½-wy: sn lost pl).........5 12
1876[5] We're Joken **(57)***(19) (JBerry)* 3-8-2 (5) CLowther(2) (b.nr hind: led over 2f: hung lft & wknd 2f out).........4 13
3726[12] Nordan Raider **(62)** *(MJCamacho)* 7-8-12 (3) GParkin(8) (Withdrawn not under Starter's orders: b.b.v going to s)......... W

LONG HANDICAP Ragazzo (IRE) 6-13

5/2 Craigie Boy, **4/1** Cumbrian Waltzer, Birchwood Sun (tchd 6/1), **5/1** Nordan Raider, **8/1** Barato, **9/1** Able Sheriff, KNAYTON LASS, Miss Aragon (8/1-14/1), **10/1** Fantasy Racing (IRE), Evanro (IRE), **14/1** Mu-Arrik, **16/1** We're Joken, **33/1** Pc's Cruiser (IRE), **50/1** Ragazzo (IRE), CSF £36.16 CT £193.72 TOTE £17.00: £3.20 £1.70 £3.00 (£27.30) Trio £271.40 OWNER Mrs J. M. Davenport (SHERIFF HUTTON) BRED E. J. B. Maude 13 Rn
1m 12.0 (2.70) SF: 44/40/56/60/32/45/24/56/36/21/19/-/-/-
WEIGHT FOR AGE 3yo-3lb

T/Plpt: £42.70 (239.92 Tckts). T/Qdpt: £5.50 (17.45 Tckts). WG

3811-ASCOT (R-H)
Sunday September 24th (Good to soft becoming Soft)
WEATHER: sunny WIND: str half against

3831 HARVEST STKS (Listed) (3-Y.O+ F & M) (Class A) £24,281.25 (£7,350.00: £3,587.50: £1,706.25) **1m 4f** Stalls: High GOING: 0.32 sec per fur (G) 2-25 (2-26)

1729[3] **Spout (109)***(111) (RCharlton)* 3-8-9 PatEddery(5) (lw: s.s: 5th st: hdwy over 2f out: swtchd lft over 1f out: led ins fnl f: r.o wl)........— 1
3549[3] Saxon Maid **(105)***(109)*(Fav)*(LMCumani)* 4-9-3 MJKinane(1) (rdn over 7f out: hdwy on ins over 3f out: 3rd st: hrd rdn over 1f out: ev ch ins fnl f: unable qckn)........1¾ 2
1729[5] Snowtown (IRE) **(97)***(105) (PWChapple-Hyam)* 3-8-6 WCarson(9) (lw: led: hrd rdn over 1f out: hdd ins fnl f: one pce)........¾ 3
3088[6] Royal Circle **(97)***(85) (RCharlton)* 3-8-6 KDarley(8) (lw: lost pl over 6f out: 9th st: one pce fnl 2f)........15 4
3549[7] Opera Lover (IRE) **(95)***(84) (MRStoute)* 3-8-6 DHolland(3) (hdwy over 4f out: 2nd st: wknd 2f out)........nk 5
2614* Hagwah (USA) **(102)***(77) (BHanbury)* 3-8-9 MRoberts(6) (4th st: wknd over 2f out)........8 6
2891a[4] Ballykett Nancy (IRE) *(66) (JSBolger,Ireland)* 4-9-3 JAHeffernan(2) (a bhd)........8 7
3496* Tinashaan (IRE) **(98)***(47) (JRFanshawe)* 3-8-6 DHarrison(4) (lw: 7th st: wknd over 2f out)....12 8
1729[4] Alessia **(97)***(27) (BWHills)* 3-8-6 RHills(7) (6th st: wknd over 2f out)........15 9

13/8 Saxon Maid (9/4-6/4), **4/1** Ballykett Nancy (IRE), **15/2** Tinashaan (IRE), **8/1** SPOUT (5/1-9/1), Hagwah (USA) (5/1-9/1), **11/1** Royal Circle (8/1-12/1), **25/1** Alessia, **33/1** Opera Lover (IRE), Snowtown (IRE), CSF £19.35 TOTE £9.20: £2.30 £1.10 £2.60 (£7.30) Trio £30.10 OWNER Lady Rothschild (BECKHAMPTON) BRED Exors of the late Mrs D. M. de Rothschild 9 Rn
2m 36.05 (6.55) SF: 75/81/69/49/48/41/38/11/-
WEIGHT FOR AGE 3yo-8lb

3832 SUNDAY CONDITIONS STKS (2-Y.O) (Class B) £12,370.00 (£4,630.00: £2,265.00: £975.00: £437.50: £222.50) **7f** Stalls: Centre GOING: 0.32 sec per fur (G) 3-00 (3-01)

Story Line *(97+) (BWHills)* 2-8-6 DHolland(3) (b.hind: unf: scope: lw: hdwy over 1f out: led ins fnl f: pushed out)........— 1
3472* Double Leaf *(101)*(Fav)*(MRStoute)* 2-9-0 WRSwinburn(7) (lw: stdy hdwy 2f out: led 1f out tl ins fnl f: unable qckn)........1¾ 2
3339[2] Ta Rib (USA) *(90) (EALDunlop)* 2-8-6 WCarson(1) (lw: hld up: led over 1f out: sn hdd: one pce ins fnl f)........1½ 3
3643* Wavey *(81) (JHMGosden)* 2-8-9 GHind(2) (w ldr: led over 2f out tl over 1f out: sn wknd)........5 4
3449[7] Eagle Canyon (IRE) *(77) (BHanbury)* 2-8-11 WRyan(4) (led over 4f)........2½ 5
3530[3] Lasseman *(44) (RBoss)* 2-8-11 PatEddery(6) (lw: a bhd)........3½ 6
3494[3] Van Gurp *(61) (BAMcMahon)* 2-8-11 GCarter(8) (hld up: rdn over 2f out: sn wknd)........3½ 7
Sorbie Tower (IRE) *(60) (MissGayKelleway)* 2-8-11 RCochrane(5) (str: scope: lw: hld up: rdn over 2f out: wknd over 1f out)........¾ 8

9/4 Double Leaf, **3/1** Ta Rib (USA) (op 2/1), **7/2** Wavey, **5/1** Van Gurp (6/1-10/1), **14/1** Lasseman (10/1-16/1), **16/1** Sorbie Tower (IRE), STORY LINE, **50/1** Eagle Canyon (IRE), CSF £49.38 TOTE £15.30: £2.90 £1.50 £1.30 (£30.50) OWNER Broughton Homes Ltd (LAMBOURN) BRED Filletts Farm Stud and Darley Stud Management 8 Rn 1m 33.94 (7.44) SF: 31/35/24/15/11/3/-/-

3833 ROSEMARY RATED STKS H'CAP (0-105) (Listed) (3-Y.O+ F & M) (Class A) £18,537.60 (£6,938.40: £3,394.20: £1,461.00: £655.50: £333.30) **1m (straight)** Stalls: Centre GOING: 0.32 sec per fur (G) 3-35 (3-36)

3608[4] **Hiwaya (94)***(107)*(Fav)*(HThomsonJones)* 3-8-13 RHills(9) (lw: mde virtually all: clr over 1f out: pushed out)........— 1
3565[16] Courageous Dancer (IRE) **(84)***(90) (BHanbury)* 3-8-3 WRyan(5) (rdn & hdwy 2f out: chsd wnr over 1f out: r.o)........3½ 2
3261[3] Hedera (USA) **(89)***(87) (MRStoute)* 3-8-8 MJKinane(1) (lw: rdn over 3f out: hdwy over 1f out: r.o one pce)........4 3
3235[3] A la Carte (IRE) **(101)***(98)*(Fav)*(JLDunlop)* 3-9-6 TQuinn(2) (lw: hdwy 3f out: rdn over 2f out: one pce)........nk 4
3630* Donna Viola **(88)***(80)*(Fav)*(CFWall)* 3-8-7 LNewton(3) (a.p: rdn over 2f out: wknd over 1f out)........2½ 5
3552[2] Avignon (IRE) **(84)***(71) (PWChapple-Hyam)* 3-8-3 WCarson(10) (w wnr 5f)........2½ 6

3564[6] Autumn Affair **(102)***(86) (CEBrittain)* 3-9-7 BDoyle(7) (b.off hind: hld up: rdn over 2f out: sn wknd) 1¾ **7**
1588[8] All Time Great **(85)***(57) (LMCumani)* 3-8-4 KDarley(6) (prom 5f) 6 **8**
3611[9] Moon Mistress **(84)***(52) (LadyHerries)* 4-8-7 RCochrane(8) (hld up: ev ch over 2f out: wknd over 1f out) 2 **9**

LONG HANDICAP Moon Mistress 8-5 Courageous Dancer (IRE) 8-0 Avignon (IRE) 8-0

5/1 HIWAYA, Donna Viola, A la Carte (IRE), **7/1** Hedera (USA), Moon Mistress, **8/1** Autumn Affair, All Time Great, Avignon (IRE), **25/1** Courageous Dancer (IRE), CSF £89.25 CT £778.78 TOTE £5.50: £2.00 £4.70 £2.40 (£175.10) Trio £129.40 OWNER Mr Hamdan Al Maktoum (NEWMARKET) BRED Shadwell Estate Company Limited 9 Rn 1m 47.99 (8.79) SF: 39/22/19/30/12/3/18/-/-

WEIGHT FOR AGE 3yo-4lb

3834

DIADEM STKS (Gp 3) (3-Y.O+) (Class A) £40,560.00 (£15,363.00: £7,531.50: £3,445.50) **6f** Stalls: Centre GOING: 0.32 sec per fur (G) 4-10 (4-17)

3717[5] **Cool Jazz (102)***(121) (CEBrittain)* 4-9-0 CNakatani(1) (hld up: nt clr run over 2f out tl over 1f out: swtchd lft: led ins fnl f: all out) .... — **1**
3795a[2] Young Ern **(118)***(121)*(Fav)*(SDow)* 5-9-0 TQuinn(15) (hld up: led over 1f out tl ins fnl f: r.o wl) .... s.h **2**
3717[10] Branston Abby (IRE) **(113)***(118) (MJohnston)* 6-8-11 MRoberts(6) (lw: rdn 4f out: hdwy & squeezed thro over 1f out: r.o wl ins fnl f) .... s.h **3**
3360* Harayir (USA) **(118)***(122) (MajorWRHern)* 3-9-0 WCarson(13) (hdwy over 1f out: unable qckn ins fnl f) .... ¾ **4**
3582a[3] Wessam Prince *(118) (CLaffon-Parias,France)* 4-9-0 FHead(8) (lw: a.p: led over 2f out tl over 1f out: one pce ins fnl f) .... nk **5**
2443[4] Montendre **(106)***(117) (MMcCormack)* 8-9-0 RCochrane(2) (nt clr run over 2f out: hdwy over 1f out: r.o ins fnl f) .... nk **6**
3198a* Desert Style (IRE) *(109) (JSBolger,Ireland)* 3-8-11 WRSwinburn(12) (str: scope: lw: a.p: rdn over 3f out: ev ch over 2f out: wknd fnl f) 3 **7**
3551[20] Double Blue **(108)***(108) (MJohnston)* 6-9-0 JWeaver(4) (lw: lost pl 4f out: nt clr run 1f out: one pce) .... nk **8**
3551* Hello Mister **(102)***(104) (JO'Donoghue)* 4-9-0 PMcCabe(16) (nvr nrr) 1½ **9**
3191[2] Foxhound (USA) *(98) (SbinSuroor)* 4-9-0 MJKinane(10) (lw: a.p: ev ch over 2f out: wkng whn bmpd over 1f out) 2½ **10**
3660* Carranita (IRE) **(102)***(87) (BPalling)* 5-8-11 TSprake(9) (bhd fnl 2f) 3 **11**
3707[3] Sharp Prod (USA) **(107)***(84) (LordHuntingdon)* 5-9-0 DHarrison(5) (lw: a.p: ev ch over 2f out: wknd over 1f out) 2 **12**
3473[5] Easy Dollar **(107)***(84) (BGubby)* 3-8-11b PaulEddery(14) (lw: hdwy 2f out: sn wknd) .... nk **13**
Hill Hopper (IRE) **(111)***(74) (JHMGosden)* 4-8-11 PatEddery(7) (led 5f out tl over 2f out: sn wknd) 2½ **14**
3707[2] Katya (IRE) **(94)***(73) (MRChannon)* 3-8-8 RHughes(3) (lw: led 1f: wknd over 2f out) .... nk **15**

7/2 Young Ern, **5/1** Desert Style (IRE), **6/1** Branston Abby (IRE), Harayir (USA) (4/1-13/2), **8/1** Foxhound (USA), **14/1** Wessam Prince (10/1-16/1), **16/1** Carranita (IRE), Hill Hopper (IRE), **20/1** Montendre, Double Blue, **25/1** Sharp Prod (USA), **33/1** Hello Mister, COOL JAZZ, **40/1** Easy Dollar, **66/1** Katya (IRE), CSF £133.18 TOTE £31.90: £4.60 £1.80 £2.60 (£49.30) Trio £238.00 OWNER Mr Saeed Manana (NEWMARKET) BRED Saeed Manana 15 Rn

1m 18.56 (4.96) SF: 57/57/54/55/54/53/42/44/40/34/23/20/17/10/6

WEIGHT FOR AGE 3yo-3lb

3835

FILLIES MILE STKS (Gp 1) (2-Y.O F) (Class A) £90,495.00 (£33,764.75: £16,132.38: £6,932.87) **1m (round)** Stalls: High GOING: 0.32 sec (G) 4-45 (4-48)

3069* **Bosra Sham (USA)** *(118+)*(Fav)*(HRACecil)* 2-8-10 PatEddery(5) (lw: 3rd st: led over 1f out: shkn up: r.o wl) .... — **1**
3387* Bint Shadayid (USA) *(111) (JLDunlop)* 2-8-10 WCarson(1) (lw: chsd ldr: led over 2f out tl over 1f out: unable qckn) 3½ **2**
3490[2] Matiya (IRE) **(98)***(104) (BHanbury)* 2-8-10 RHills(4) (led over 5f: one pce) 3½ **3**
3692a[5] Rouge Rancon (USA) *(96) (PFICole)* 2-8-10 TQuinn(2) (5th st: wknd wl over 1f out) 4 **4**
3663* Shawanni *(95) (BWHills)* 2-8-10 MJKinane(3) (4th st: rdn over 2f out: wknd over 1f out) .... ½ **5**
3692a[10] Zelzelah (USA) *(77d) (PAKelleway)* 2-8-10 PaulEddery(6) (lw: 6th st: a bhd) 9 **6**

10/11 BOSRA SHAM (USA), **5/2** Shawanni, **5/1** Bint Shadayid (USA) (4/1-6/1), **10/1** Rouge Rancon (USA) (8/1-12/1), **16/1** Zelzelah (USA), **20/1** Matiya (IRE), CSF £6.11 TOTE £2.10: £1.40 £2.40 (£3.50) OWNER Mr Wafic Said (NEWMARKET) BRED Gerald W. Leigh 6 Rn

1m 43.13 (3.53) SF: 85/78/71/63/62/44

3836 TOTE SUNDAY SPECIAL H'CAP (3-Y.O+) (Class B) £46,836.25 (£14,065.00: £6,782.50: £3,141.25)
1m 4f Stalls: High GOING: 0.32 sec per fur (G) 5-20 (5-20)

3164² **Taufan's Melody (100)***(115) (LadyHerries)* 4-9-1 RCochrane(2) (2nd st: led 2f out: drvn out) ....— 1
3489² Better Offer (IRE) **(92)***(105) (GHarwood)* 3-7-13 JQuinn(1) (5th st: hrd rdn & ev ch over 1f out: unable qckn ins fnl f) 1¼ 2
2691* Pilsudski (IRE) **(95)***(108) (MRStoute)* 3-8-2 KDarley(7) (b.hind: lw: hdwy over 2f out: hrd rdn over 1f out: r.o) ....nk 3
3730* Whitechapel (USA) **(85)***(94) (LordHuntingdon)* 7-8-0 ow1 4x DHarrison(15) (nt clr run over 2f out: swtchd lft: hdwy over 1f out: str run fnl f: fin wl) 2½ 4
3489* Inquisitor (USA) **(103)***(113)*(Fav)*(JHMGosden)* 3-8-10 4x PatEddery(17) (lw: 4th st: hrd rdn over 1f out: one pce) ....s.h 5
3593* Bit on the Side (IRE) **(78)***(87) (WJMusson)* 6-7-7 4x GBardwell(5) (hdwy over 3f out: 6th st: wknd over 1f out) ....hd 6
3459* Mezaan (IRE) **(92)***(100) (MRStoute)* 3-7-13 4x WCarson(12) (lw: a.p: led over 5f out to 2f out: wknd fnl f) ....¾ 7
3107* Mystic Hill **(89)***(96) (RCharlton)* 4-8-4 TQuinn(16) (hdwy over 2f out: hrd rdn over 1f out: one pce) ....¾ 8
3162⁴ Son of Sharp Shot (IRE) **(102)***(105) (JLDunlop)* 5-9-3 PaulEddery(4) (lw: nvr nrr) 3½ 9
3459² Rokeby Bowl **(95)***(97) (IABalding)* 3-8-2 MRoberts(19) (lw: 3rd st: wknd over 1f out) ....¾ 10
3729⁸ Ringmaster (IRE) **(88)***(87) (MHTompkins)* 4-8-3 WRyan(6) (lw: a mid div) 2 11
2069⁴ Sharp Falcon (IRE) **(79)***(76) (JWharton)* 4-7-1 (7)ow1 MartinDwyer(14) (s.s: hdwy over 3f out: sn wknd) ....½ 12
3486a⁷ Bob's Ploy **(92)***(89) (RAkehurst)* 3-7-13 AMcGlone(8) (lw: 7th st: wknd over 2f out) 1¼ 13
3500⁴ Artic Courier **(81)***(74) (DJSCosgrove)* 4-7-10 AMackay(10) (lw: a bhd) 3 14
2559a* Munif (IRE) **(104)***(87) (DKWeld,Ireland)* 3-8-11 4x MJKinane(18) (lw: bhd fnl 2f) 7 15
3547⁶ Progression **(78)***(52) (PCHaslam)* 4-7-2b(5) MBaird(13) (s.s: a bhd) 7 16
3603⁴ Ionio (USA) **(109)***(78) (CEBrittain)* 4-9-10 WRSwinburn(9) (b: lw: led over 6f: wknd over 3f out) 4 17
3676¹³ Quest Again **(80)***(33) (DWPArbuthnot)* 4-7-2 (7)ow2 CAdamson(20) (lw: bhd fnl 3f) 10 18

LONG HANDICAP Bit on the Side (IRE) 6-13 Progression 7-3 Sharp Falcon (IRE) 7-1 Quest Again 6-10

3/1 Inquisitor (USA), **6/1** Whitechapel (USA), Better Offer (IRE), **9/1** Mezaan (IRE), **12/1** Bob's Ploy, Ringmaster (IRE), Bit on the Side (IRE), **14/1** Pilsudski (IRE) (10/1-16/1), Rokeby Bowl, **16/1** Son of Sharp Shot (IRE), Munif (IRE), Mystic Hill, **20/1** TAUFAN'S MELODY, **40/1** Progression, **50/1** Artic Courier, Sharp Falcon (IRE), **66/1** Ionio (USA), **100/1** Quest Again, CSF £130.84 CT £1,619.39 TOTE £28.00: £6.70 £2.00 £4.20 £1.40 (£273.40) Trio £841.40 OWNER All At Sea (LITTLEHAMPTON) BRED Midhurst Farm Inc 18 Rn

2m 35.52 (6.02) SF: 85/67/70/64/75/57/62/66/75/59/57/46/51/44/49/22/48/3

WEIGHT FOR AGE 3yo-8lb

3837 MAIL ON SUNDAY MILE FINAL H'CAP (3-Y.O+) (Class B) £28,920.00 (£8,760.00: £4,280.00: £2,040.00)
1m (straight) Stalls: Centre GOING: 0.32 sec per fur (G) 5-50 (5-58)

3732¹⁰ **Mo-Addab (IRE) (73)***(86) (ACStewart)* 5-8-13 MRoberts(9) (lw: hld up: nt clr run over 2f out: led over 1f out: drvn out) ....— 1
3601³ Second Chance (IRE) **(81)***(93) (PMitchell)* 5-9-4 (3) SSanders(4) (lw: led over 6f: rdn: r.o wl)..nk 2
3629* Comanche Companion **(75)***(87)*(Fav)*(TJNaughton)* 5-9-1 PatEddery(1) (rdn over 2f out: hdwy over 1f out: r.o wl ins fnl f) ....hd 3
3382⁶ Toujours Riviera **(84)***(96) (JPearce)* 5-9-10 GBardwell(18) (lw: hdwy over 2f out: hung lft & ev ch over 1f out: r.o) ....s.h 4
3802¹³ Wentbridge Lad (IRE) **(63)***(74) (PDEvans)* 5-8-3v GHind(2) (lw: hdwy on ins over 1f out: nt clr run on ins fnl f: r.o) ....¾ 5
3703⁶ Master Beveled **(74)***(84)*(Fav)*(PDEvans)* 5-9-0 TQuinn(10) (lw: lost pl 5f out: nt clr run over 2f out: rallied over 1f out: r.o) ....nk 6
3703⁹ Legal Fiction **(66)***(73) (MJohnston)* 4-8-6 JWeaver(6) (lw: nt clr run 2f out: hdwy over 1f out: r.o) 1½ 7
1926⁸ Zajko (USA) **(78)***(78) (LadyHerries)* 5-9-4 RCochrane(7) (lw: hld up: nt clr run over 2f out: wknd over 1f out) 3½ 8
3605* Prenonamoss **(58)***(54) (DWPArbuthnot)* 7-7-7 (5)ow4 MHenry(17) (b.hind: prom over 6f) ....hd 9
3645* Three Arch Bridge **(65)***(63) (MJohnston)* 3-8-1b WCarson(19) (hdwy over 1f out: sn wknd) 1 10
3729²⁰ Danegold (IRE) **(86)***(76) (MRChannon)* 3-9-8v RHughes(11) (lw: hdwy over 2f out: wknd over 1f out) 4 11

3629[2] Gymcrak Flyer **(63)***(53) (GHolmes)* 4-8-3 JFEgan(13) (b.hind: prom over 6f)....hd **12**
3545[3] Samba Sharply **(76)***(62) (AHide)* 4-9-2 JWilliams(5) (hld up: nt clr run over 2f out: wknd over 1f out)....2 **13**
3619[14] Kingchip Boy **(67)***(52) (MJRyan)* 6-8-7v AClark(15) (hld up: rdn over 2f out: sn wknd)....hd **14**
3393[2] Mukhatab **(82)***(67) (HThomsonJones)* 3-9-4 RHills(16) (lw: prom 6f)....nk **15**
1183[20] Set the Fashion **(66)***(1) (LordHuntingdon)* 6-8-6v DHarrison(21) (a bhd: t.o)....25 **16**
3348[9] Deevee **(73)** *(CJBenstead)* 6-8-13 WRSwinburn(20) (a bhd: virtually p.u over 1f out: t.o)....5 **17**
Kurdistan (IRE) **(84)** *(EdwardLynam,Ireland)* 5-9-10 MJKinane(14) (lw: stumbled s: prom over 5f: bhd whn bdly hmpd wl over 1f out: t.o)....25 **18**
3634[7] Battleship Bruce **(61)** *(NACallaghan)* 3-7-11 AMackay(3) (bhd whn stumbled & fell wl over 1f out).... **F**
1183[16] Broughton Singer (IRE) **(55)** *(WJMusson)* 4-7-9 JQuinn(12) (Withdrawn not under Starter's orders: veterinary advice).... **W**

9/2 Master Beveled, Comanche Companion (6/1-4/1), **11/1** Samba Sharply, Set the Fashion, **12/1** Second Chance (IRE), **14/1** Mukhatab, Gymcrak Flyer (12/1-20/1), Zajko (USA) (10/1-16/1), **16/1** Prenonamoss, Kurdistan (IRE), Deevee, Three Arch Bridge, **20/1** Danegold (IRE), Battleship Bruce, **25/1** Broughton Singer (IRE), MO-ADDAB (IRE), **33/1** Wentbridge Lad (IRE), Legal Fiction, Kingchip Boy, Toujours Riviera, CSF £272.21 CT £1,453.96 TOTE £23.60: £5.20 £3.10 £1.90 £7.50 (£185.60) Trio £490.70 OWNER Mr S. J. Hammond (NEWMARKET) BRED Mrs M. Upsdell 19 Rn
1m 48.97 (9.77) SF: 29/36/30/39/17/27/16/21/-/2/15/-/5/-/6/-/-/-/-/-
WEIGHT FOR AGE 3yo-4lb

T/Jkpt; Not won: £36,841.62 to Bath 25/9/95. T/Plpt: £42.90 (956.89 Tckts). T/Qdpt: £33.10 (25.6 Tckts). AK

3117-HAMILTON (R-H)
Sunday September 24th (Good, Good to firm patches)
WEATHER: sunny periods WIND: fresh against

3838
E.B.F. VARIETY CLUB MEDIAN AUCTION MAIDEN STKS (2-Y.O) (Class E) £3,615.00 (£1,095.00: £535.00: £255.00)
6f 5y Stalls: Low GOING minus 0.20 sec per fur (GF) 2-15 (2-16)

3699[5] **Sepoy (IRE) (88)***(84)*(Fav)*(CWThornton)* 2-9-0 DeanMcKeown(6) (lw: b: trckd ldrs: led 2f out: rdn & r.o wl)....— **1**
3809[11] Termon **(58)***(58) (MissLAPerratt)* 2-8-9 MBirch(3) (bhd: hdwy 2f out: styd on: no ch w wnr)....8 **2**
3468[9] Power Game **(67)***(63) (JBerry)* 2-9-0 KFallon(7) (prom: effrt & ch 2f out: r.o one pce)....hd **3**
3670[4] Corniche Quest (IRE) **(65)***(51) (MRChannon)* 2-8-4 (5) PPMurphy(4) (bhd: hdwy u.p 2f out: nvr able chal)....2½ **4**
3647[8] Queens Check *(40) (MissJFCraze)* 2-8-9 SWebster(5) (lw: cl up tl rdn & wknd wl over 1f out)....4 **5**
Silent Guest (IRE) *(39) (SirMarkPrescott)* 2-9-0 WWoods(9) (w'like: leggy: unf: in tch: rdn ½-wy: no imp)....2½ **6**
3720[5] Rhythmic Ball *(31) (TRWatson)* 2-8-6 (3) JStack(2) (chsd ldrs tl rdn & wknd fnl 2f)....1 **7**
3670[11] Ready Teddy (IRE) *(27) (MissLAPerratt)* 2-8-9 TWilliams(1) (led 4f: wknd qckly)....1½ **8**

7/4 SEPOY (IRE), **7/2** Corniche Quest (IRE) (op 6/1), **4/1** Silent Guest (IRE) (op 2/1), **9/1** Power Game, **14/1** Rhythmic Ball, **16/1** Queens Check, **20/1** Termon, **50/1** Ready Teddy (IRE), CSF £27.65 TOTE £2.40: £1.20 £4.10 £3.30 (£33.40) Trio £14.90 OWNER Mr J. Hanson (MIDDLEHAM) BRED Gay O'Callaghan 8 Rn 1m 12.6 (2.60) SF: 44/18/23/11/-/-/-/-

3839
E.B.F. ADRENALINN MAIDEN STKS (2-Y.O) (Class D) £4,260.00 (£1,290.00: £630.00: £300.00)
6f 5y Stalls: Low GOING minus 0.20 sec per fur (GF) 2-45 (2-45)

Marcomir (USA) *(71+)*(Fav)*(MJohnston)* 2-9-0 TWilliams(4) (w'like: scope: trckd ldrs: led wl over 1f out: rn green: rdn & r.o fnl f)....— **1**
3626[5] Ocean Stream (IRE) **(73)***(68) (JLEyre)* 2-9-0 DeanMcKeown(2) (lw: s.i.s: sn pushed along: hdwy ½-wy: ev ch 1f out: r.o)....1¼ **2**
3472[5] Johnny Jones (USA) *(61) (PWChapple-Hyam)* 2-8-9 (5) RHavlin(1) (lw: cl up: rdn over 2f out: nt qckn)....2½ **3**
3647[5] Miletrian City **(67)***(48) (JBerry)* 2-9-0 KFallon(3) (led over 4f: wknd 1f out)....5 **4**

8/13 MARCOMIR (USA), **4/1** Johnny Jones (USA) (2/1-5/1), **9/2** Ocean Stream (IRE), **9/1** Miletrian City, CSF £3.58 TOTE £1.40 (£2.20) OWNER Sheikh Mohammed (MIDDLEHAM) BRED Darley Stud Management Co Ltd 4 Rn
1m 14.5 (4.50) SF: 18/15/8/-

3840

EVENING TIMES H'CAP (0-90) (3-Y.O+) (Class C) £7,295.00 (£2,210.00: £1,080.00: £515.00) **1m 1f 36y** Stalls: High GOING minus 0.20 sec (GF) 3-20 (3-20)

3664[4] **My Gina (71)***(83) (MRStoute)* 3-8-10 KFallon(8) (lw: in tch: hdwy to ld 2f out: hld on wl) — 1
3469[6] Nigel's Lad (IRE) **(79)***(88) (PCHaslam)* 3-9-4 LCharnock(6) (a.p: chal 3f out: r.o: no ex nr fin) 1½ 2
3781[2] Vindaloo **(86)***(91) (JLHarris)* 3-9-11 MBirch(11) (trckd ldrs: effrt 3f out: styd on: nt pce to chal) 2½ 3
3601[8] Segala (IRE) **(73)***(72) (SirMarkPrescott)* 4-9-3 WWoods(7) (bhd: hdwy over 3f out: styd on one pce fnl f: nvr able chal) 3½ 4
3433[7] Thaleros **(57)***(54) (GMMoore)* 5-8-1 DaleGibson(2) (led tl hdd 3f out: one pce) 1 5
3393[3] Master Ofthe House **(62)***(57) (MDHammond)* 9-8-6 JMarshall(3) (hld up & bhd: stdy hdwy over 2f out: nvr rchd ldrs) 1½ 6
3255[4] Talented Ting (IRE) **(68)***(61) (PCHaslam)* 6-8-12 MTebbutt(4) (cl up: slt ld 3f out: hdd 2f out: wknd over 1f out) ¾ 7
3611[4] Bardon Hill Boy (IRE) **(79)***(69)*(Fav)*(BHanbury)* 3-9-1 (3) JStack(1) (lw: hld up: rdn 3f out: no hdwy) 2 8
3704[20] Time Again **(70)***(46) (TDyer)* 5-9-0 MFenton(10) (bhd: rdn over 3f out: n.d) 8 9
3368[2] Thatched (IRE) **(58)***(30) (REBarr)* 5-7-11 (5) PFessey(5) (prom: rdn 4f out: wknd 3f out) 2 10

7/2 Bardon Hill Boy (IRE), **4/1** Segala (IRE), Vindaloo, **6/1** Thatched (IRE), **15/2** MY GINA, **8/1** Master Ofthe House, **12/1** Talented Ting (IRE) (op 7/1), Nigel's Lad (IRE) (op 8/1), **20/1** Thaleros, **66/1** Time Again, CSF £83.88 CT £376.10 TOTE £10.10: £2.50 £3.60 £2.00 (£53.10) Trio £37.10 OWNER Mr A. Al Khalifa (NEWMARKET) BRED P. T. and Mrs Tellwright 10 Rn
1m 56.4 (2.10) SF: 60/65/68/54/36/39/43/46/28/12
WEIGHT FOR AGE 3yo-5lb

3841

GTX PROTECTION PLUS CLAIMING STKS (3-Y.O) (Class E) £3,052.50 (£924.00: £451.00: £214.50) **1m 65y** Stalls: High GOING minus 0.20 sec (GF) 3-55 (3-58)

3704[5] **Benjarong (27)***(50) (RMMcKellar)* 3-8-8 TWilliams(9) (hld up: gd hdwy ½-wy: disp ld 1f out: r.o u.p to ld nr fin) — 1
1407[8] Jackatack (IRE) **(42)***(55) (MRChannon)* 3-8-13 WWoods(3) (lw: led: rdn 2f out: r.o: hdd & no ex towards fin) hd 2
3704[12] Pash **(30)***(39) (CWFairhurst)* 3-8-2v NKennedy(6) (lw: sn pushed along: a in tch: outpcd 4f out: styd on wl fnl 2f) 2½ 3
3704[10] Dr Caligari (IRE) **(64)***(51) (JBerry)* 3-8-12 (7) PRoberts(1) (lw: cl up: effrt 3f out: one pce appr fnl f) 2½ 4
2873[4] Salduba **(29)***(29) (TDyer)* 3-8-2 MFenton(7) (chsd ldrs tl rdn & btn over 1f out) 2½ 5
3747[9] Chastleton **(30)***(29) (MRChannon)* 3-7-11 (5) PPMurphy(2) (bhd: hdwy on outside 4f out: ch 2f out: wknd 1f out) nk 6
3645[8] Lorelei Lee (IRE) **(59)***(20)*(Fav)*(JohnBerry)* 3-9-2 KFallon(4) (in tch: rdn 3f out: wknd over 1f out) 12 7
3060[4] Merger Mania *(8) (MissJFCraze)* 3-8-11 SWebster(5) (b: unruly s: a bhd) 3½ 8

9/4 Lorelei Lee (IRE) (op 6/4), **3/1** BENJARONG, Dr Caligari (IRE), **7/1** Jackatack (IRE), **16/1** Pash, Chastleton, **25/1** Salduba, **100/1** Merger Mania, CSF £20.96 TOTE £5.60: £1.60 £1.40 £3.00 (£15.90) Trio £47.80 OWNER Mrs Margaret Brown (LESMAHAGOW) BRED Wheelersland Stud 8 Rn
1m 48.9 (5.60) SF: 23/28/12/24/2/2/-/-

3842

PEUGEOT FLEET CONDITIONS STKS (2-Y.O) (Class C) £5,695.20 (£1,843.20: £901.60) **1m 65y** Stalls: High GOING minus 0.20 sec per fur (GF) 4-30 (4-30)

3561[6] **Gryada (100)***(89) (WJarvis)* 2-8-11 MTebbutt(1) (lw: mde all: r.o gamely fnl f) — 1
3068[4] Latin Reign (USA) *(87?) (PWChapple-Hyam)* 2-8-5 (5) RHavlin(4) (lw: trckd wnr: chal over 2f out: r.o) ½ 2
3711[2] Sava River (IRE) **(94)***(88)*(Fav)*(MRStoute)* 2-9-2 KFallon(2) (hld up: swtchd & effrt over 2f out: btn appr fnl f) 2½ 3

11/8 Sava River (IRE), **7/4** GRYADA, **9/4** Latin Reign (USA), CSF £5.06 TOTE £2.20 (£2.40) OWNER Lord Howard de Walden (NEWMARKET) BRED Lord Howard de Walden 3 Rn
1m 49.8 (6.50) SF: 17/15/16

3843

EAGLE TAVERNS H'CAP (0-70) (3-Y.O) (Class E) £3,934.10 (£1,191.80: £582.40: £277.70) **1m 4f 17y** Stalls: High GOING minus 0.20 sec per fur (GF) 5-05 (5-06)

3634* **Leading Spirit (IRE) (66)***(80)*(Fav)*(CFWall)* 3-9-7 WWoods(5) (lw: mde all: r.o wl fnl 2f) — 1

3096[3] Colosse **(52)**_(62) (JLEyre)_ 3-8-7 RLappin(6) (lw: hld up: hdwy 3f out: hung rt: ev ch over 1f out: no ex) 3 **2**
3464[7] Khan **(49)**_(52) (CWThornton)_ 3-8-4 DeanMcKeown(8) (a.p: effrt 4f out: r.o one pce) 5 **3**
909[10] Hamilton Silk **(54)**_(57) (MGMeagher)_ 3-8-9 KFallon(1) (bhd: rdn & hdwy over 3f out: nvr rchd ldrs) .....hd **4**
_3735_[2] Last Corner **(59)**_(62) (RHollinshead)_ 3-9-0 MTebbutt(3) (hld up: effrt 4f out: rdn & nvr rchd ldrs) .....½ **5**
3635* Fresh Look (IRE) **(50)**_(45) (RCSpicer)_ 3-8-2 (3) JStack(4) (nvr trbld ldrs) 6 **6**
3725[8] Supreme (USA) **(48)**_(32) (MDHammond)_ 3-8-3 DaleGibson(9) (chsd ldrs tl wknd wl over 2f out) 8 **7**
3669[10] Punch **(50)**_(33) (NTinkler)_ 3-8-5b LCharnock(2) (lw: chsd ldrs: rdn 6f out: wknd wl over 2f out) .....½ **8**
3669[18] Monaco Gold (IRE) **(45)**_(13) (RMMcKellar)_ 3-7-7 (7) KSked(7) (prom tl wknd 4f out) 12 **9**

6/4 LEADING SPIRIT (IRE) (op 9/4), **5/1** Fresh Look (IRE) (op 5/2), **6/1** Last Corner (op 4/1), **7/1** Khan, **9/1** Punch, **12/1** Colosse (7/1-14/1), **16/1** Hamilton Silk, **20/1** Supreme (USA), **66/1** Monaco Gold (IRE), CSF £17.72 CT £87.62 TOTE £2.70: £1.90 £2.90 £1.80 (£17.30) Trio £23.70 OWNER Induna Racing Partners Two (NEWMARKET) BRED Sir Peter Nugent and Ascot Stables 9 Rn
2m 36.1 (4.10) SF: 62/44/34/39/44/27/14/15/-

T/Plpt: £437.60 (22.5 Tckts). T/Qdpt: £48.60 (0.5 Tckts). AA

3515-BATH (L-H)
Monday September 25th (Good to firm)
WEATHER: overcast WIND: mod against

3844
ALDIE MAIDEN APPRENTICE H'CAP (0-75) (3-Y.O+) (Class E)
£3,415.00 (£1,030.00: £500.00: £235.00)
1m 5y Stalls: Low GOING minus 0.28 sec per fur (GF) 2-00 (2-03)

3679[15] **Thames Side (51)**_(65) (MMadgwick)_ 4-8-11 (3) AEddery(14) (bhd: gd hdwy & wandered over 2f out: str run to ld ins fnl f: r.o wl) .....— **1**
3383[2] The Mestral **(44)**_(50) (MJRyan)_ 3-8-0 (3) NicolaHowarth(17) (led after 2f: clr over 2f out: hdd ins fnl f) 4 **2**
3677[12] Rising Spray **(51)**_(57) (CAHorgan)_ 4-9-0 AmandaSanders(4) (lw: hld up: hdwy over 2f out: r.o one pce fnl f) .....s.h **3**
3475[8] Speedy Snaps Pride **(46)**_(48) (PDCundell)_ 3-8-2 (3)ow2 GFaulkner(18) (plld hrd: 6th st: r.o one pce fnl f) 1 **4**
3757[10] Salvatore Giuliano **(40)**_(40) (AGFoster)_ 5-8-3 GMitchell(10) (hdwy fnl 2f: nt rch ldrs) 1¾ **5**
3657[15] Ebony Blaze **(52)**_(52) (CPWildman)_ 4-8-10 (5) JBramhill(12) (lw: hdwy over 2f out: one pce fnl f) .....nk **6**
3657[17] Astrojoy (IRE) **(45)**_(44) (SGKnight)_ 3-7-13b(5) DSweeney(11) (s.s: sn rcvrd: 5th st: no hdwy fnl 2f) .....½ **7**
3294[8] Florismart **(63)**_(57) (JARToller)_ 3-9-8 DGibbs(5) (nvr nrr) 2½ **8**
3455[15] Howqua River **(46)**_(38) (PWChapple-Hyam)_ 3-7-12 (7) RCody-Boutcher(8) (led 2f: 3rd st: wknd over 2f out) .....¾ **9**
3654[8] Fastini Gold **(57)**_(49) (MDIUsher)_ 3-9-2 CAdamson(1) (nvr trbld ldrs) .....nk **10**
3645[19] Troubadour Song **(65)**_(54) (IABalding)_ 3-9-5 (5) CScudder(13) (lw: prom 4f) 1¼ **11**
3428[3] Fragaria **(51)**_(33)_(Fav)_(IABalding)_ 3-8-10 MartinDwyer(3) (s.i.s: a bhd) 3½ **12**
3710[20] Chocolate Charlie **(54)**_(36) (RCharlton)_ 4-8-10 (7) RBrisland(15) (prom: rn wd 5f out: 4th st: wknd over 2f out) .....s.h **13**
3537[12] River May **(45)**_(25) (AndrewTurnell)_ 3-7-13 (5) RStudholme(7) (plld hrd: 6th st: wknd over 2f out) 1 **14**
_381_[4] Considerable Charm **(50)**_(26) (LordHuntingdon)_ 3-8-6 (3) AimeeCook(9) (bit bkwd: a bhd) 2 **15**
3747[7] Saterne Lady **(54)**_(30) (PFICole)_ 3-8-6 (7) DavidO'Neill(6) (2nd st: wknd over 2f out) .....nk **16**
3747[8] Pacific Girl (IRE) **(51)**_(23) (BPalling)_ 3-8-10 ADaly(16) (a bhd) 1¾ **17**

11/4 Fragaria (4/1-9/4), **11/2** Fastini Gold, **7/1** The Mestral, **12/1** Saterne Lady, THAMES SIDE (op 8/1), Considerable Charm (op 8/1), Troubadour Song (op 7/1), **14/1** Speedy Snaps Pride, Rising Spray (op 7/1), **16/1** Ebony Blaze, Pacific Girl (IRE), Chocolate Charlie, Astrojoy (IRE), **20/1** Salvatore Giuliano, Florismart, **33/1** Howqua River, **40/1** River May, CSF £94.85 CT £1,1225.25 TOTE £16.90: £2.90 £1.70 £4.30 £2.60 (£47.20) Trio £345.30 OWNER Mr D. Knight (DENMEAD) BRED Miss D. M. Green 17 Rn 1m 42.3 (3.80) SF: 37/18/29/16/12/24/12/25/6/17/22/1/8/-/-/-/-
WEIGHT FOR AGE 3yo-4lb

OFFICIAL EXPLANATION Thames Side: his improved form was due to the fact that on his previous run he had worn a visor which had not suited him and he was unable to act on the soft ground coming down the hill at Lingfield.

3845 MORRIS DANCER CONDITIONS STKS (3-Y.O+) (Class C) £5,191.10 (£1,934.90: £939.95: £397.25) 1m 5y Stalls: Low GOING minus 0.28 sec (GF) 2-30 (2-31)

3473[4] **Star of Zilzal (USA) (102)***(101)*(Fav)*(MRStoute)* 3-9-2 WRSwinburn(2) (hld up & bhd: 5th st: hdwy over 2f out: rdn to ld wl ins fnl f: r.o) ....— 1
3732[11] Desert Green (FR) **(96)***(101) (RHannon)* 6-9-7 RPerham(4) (chsd ldr: 2nd st: rdn to ld over 1f out: hdd wl ins fnl f) ....½ 2
3399[2] Miasma (USA) **(88)***(90) (JARToller)* 3-8-6 JReid(5) (led: hrd rdn & hdd over 1f out: r.o) ....s.h 3
3700[13] Dee-Lady **(85)***(85) (WGMTurner)* 3-8-6 TSprake(8) (hld up: 3rd st: rdn & ev ch over 1f out: wknd ins fnl f) 2½ 4
3602[3] Muktabas (IRE) **(95)***(64) (JHMGosden)* 3-9-1 WCarson(7) (4th & rdn st: wknd over 2f out)....15 5
3706[21] Sing Up **(70)***(19) (MMcCormack)* 3-8-10 AClark(1) (a bhd: last st: t.o fnl 3f) 20 6

6/4 STAR OF ZILZAL (USA), **7/4** Muktabas (IRE) (6/4-9/4), **9/2** Miasma (USA) (3/1-5/1), **7/1** Desert Green (FR) (op 9/2), **14/1** Dee-Lady, **50/1** Sing Up, CSF £11.54 TOTE £2.20: £1.50 £2.30 (£7.20) OWNER Mr Mana Al Maktoum (NEWMARKET) BRED Gainsborough Farm Inc 6 Rn
1m 40.3 (1.80) SF: 59/63/48/43/22/-
WEIGHT FOR AGE 3yo-4lb

3846 E.B.F. DODINGTON MAIDEN STKS (2-Y.O) (Class D) £4,510.00 (£1,360.00: £660.00: £310.00) 1m 2f 46y Stalls: Low GOING minus 0.28 sec (GF) 3-00 (3-08)

2420[3] **Gentilhomme (90)***(69)*(Fav)*(PFICole)* 2-9-0 TQuinn(3) (3rd st: hrd rdn over 2f out: r.o to ld last strides) ....— 1
3650[5] Flyfisher (IRE) *(69) (GLewis)* 2-9-0 PaulEddery(7) (led: rdn over 2f out: hdd last strides) ....s.h 2
3666[2] Reinhardt (IRE) **(84)***(61) (PWChapple-Hyam)* 2-9-0 JReid(5) (lw: hld up: stdy hdwy over 5f out: 4th & rdn st: one pce fnl 2f) 5 3
3463[7] Magic Ron *(56) (MBell)* 2-9-0v MFenton(8) (2nd st: rdn & ev ch over 2f out: wknd over 1f out) 3½ 4
3650[6] Fort de France (USA) *(38) (MRStoute)* 2-9-0 WRSwinburn(4) (hld up: stdy hdwy over 5f out: lost pl bnd over 4f out: 5th & hrd rdn st: sn wknd) 11 5
3617[3] Soviet King (IRE) *(37) (PMitchell)* 2-9-0 RPerham(6) (b: prom 5f: poor 6th st) ....¾ 6
2529[8] Louisiana Purchase *(MrsBarbaraWaring)* 2-9-0 WNewnes(2) (s.i.s: sn rcvrd: wknd 4f out: t.o fnl 3f) ....dist 7
3620[19] Lucky Lees (IRE) *(PGMurphy)* 2-9-0 JWilliams(9) (lw: a bhd: t.o fnl 3f) 25 8

4/5 GENTILHOMME, **7/4** Reinhardt (IRE) (op 4/5), **10/1** Flyfisher (IRE) (8/1-12/1), Fort de France (USA), **25/1** Magic Ron, Soviet King (IRE), **100/1** Louisiana Purchase, Lucky Lees (IRE), CSF £9.78 TOTE £2.00: £1.30 £1.90 £1.10 (£11.10) Trio £3.00 OWNER H R H Prince Fahd Salman (WHATCOMBE) BRED M. A. Kirby and E. Kessly 8 Rn 2m 11.6 (3.90) SF: 45/45/37/32/14/13/-/-
STEWARDS' ENQUIRY Quinn susp. 4-5/10/95 (excessive use of whip).

3847 STEVE VICK INTERNATIONAL MAIDEN STKS (3-Y.O+) (Class D) £4,173.75 (£1,260.00: £612.50: £288.75) 1m 2f 46y Stalls: Low GOING minus 0.28 sec per fur (GF) 3-30 (3-36)

3653[2] **Prickwillow (USA) (78)***(69++)*(Fav)*(JHMGosden)* 3-8-7 LDettori(7) (3rd st: led on bit wl over 1f out: v.easily) ....— 1
3377[5] Kalamata *(71) (ACStewart)* 3-8-12 PaulEddery(5) (2nd st: ev ch 2f out: nt qckn) 1¾ 2
3653[10] Printers Quill *(59) (MajorDNChappell)* 3-8-12 JReid(4) (led tl hdd wl over 1f out: sn wknd) 8 3
3712[13] Mafuta (IRE) *(51) (JJSheehan)* 3-8-7 JQuinn(8) (stdy hdwy 6f out: 6th st: one pce fnl 2f)....1½ 4
3635[6] Alioli *(39) (MJRyan)* 3-8-7 WCarson(9) (7th st: nvr nr ldrs) 8 5
Expansive Runner (USA) *(42) (PWHarris)* 3-8-12 GHind(2) (8th st: a bhd) 1¼ 6
Lady Kate (USA) *(13) (KOCunningham-Brown)* 3-8-7 TQuinn(1) (plld hrd: 4th st: wknd qckly 3f out) 15 7
3653[16] Woodlands Lad Too *(PAPritchard)* 3-8-12 NAdams(6) (plld hrd: rdn 4f out: 5th & wkng st: t.o) ....dist 8
Sun Dreamer *(JLSpearing)* 6-8-10 (3) SDrowne(3) (a bhd: t.o fnl 3f) ....dist 9
3712[19] Governors Fortune *(AJChamberlain)* 3-8-5 (7) MartinDwyer(10) (sn bhd: t.o fnl 3f)....dist 10

2/7 PRICKWILLOW (USA), **6/1** Expansive Runner (USA) (op 4/1), **11/1** Alioli (20/1-10/1), **12/1** Kalamata, Printers Quill (op 20/1), **40/1** Lady Kate (USA), **50/1** Mafuta (IRE), **66/1** Sun Dreamer, **100/1** Woodlands Lad Too, Governors Fortune, CSF £5.98 TOTE £1.30: £1.10 £1.50 £2.00 (£3.50) Trio £23.60 OWNER Sheikh Mohammed (NEWMARKET) BRED Darley Stud Management Co Ltd 10 Rn
2m 10.8 (3.10) SF: 45/47/35/27/15/18/-/-/-/-
WEIGHT FOR AGE 3yo-6lb

3848 E.B.F. TORMARTON MAIDEN STKS (2-Y.O) (Class D) £4,848.00 (£1,464.00: £712.00: £336.00)
5f 161y Stalls: High GOING minus 0.28 sec per fur (GF) 4-00 (4-02)

2876[3] **Celandine** *(83)*(Fav)*(RCharlton)* 2-8-9 TQuinn(2) (hld up: rdn & edgd rt over 2f out: led over 1f out: r.o wl) ....— 1
3711[6] Therhea (IRE) **(78)***(77) (BRMillman)* 2-9-0 LDettori(10) (rdn & hdwy wl over 1f out: r.o ins fnl f) 4 2
Incatinka *(65) (JLSpearing)* 2-8-6 (3) SDrowne(3) (w'like: chsd ldrs: r.o one pce fnl f) 2½ 3
3727[7] Extra Hour (IRE) **(80)***(63) (WRMuir)* 2-9-0 JReid(7) (a.p: one pce fnl 2f) 2½ 4
3668[10] Johayro **(80)***(59) (WGMTurner)* 2-8-11b(3) PMcCabe(9) (led tl hdd over 1f out: wknd ins fnl f) 1½ 5
Realms of Glory (IRE) *(59) (PMitchell)* 2-9-0 PaulEddery(8) (w'like: nvr nrr) ....s.h 6
1443[8] Queen Emma (IRE) *(44) (JSMoore)* 2-8-9 JFEgan(1) (w ldrs over 3f) 3½ 7
3626[13] Ashik (IRE) *(13) (PTWalwyn)* 2-9-0 WCarson(4) (spd 3f: t.o) 13 8
2114[4] Heights of Love **(55)** *(MSSaunders)* 2-8-9 AMcGlone(5) (s.s: a bhd: t.o) 10 9
People Direct *(KMcAuliffe)* 2-8-9 DHarrison(6) (unf: reluctant to r: uns rdr sn after s) .... U

2/1 CELANDINE (6/4-9/4), **3/1** Therhea (IRE), **11/2** Extra Hour (IRE), **13/2** Johayro, **15/2** Ashik (IRE), **10/1** Incatinka (op 20/1), **11/1** Realms of Glory (IRE) (8/1-12/1), **16/1** People Direct, **25/1** Heights of Love, **50/1** Queen Emma (IRE), CSF £9.08 TOTE £2.90: £1.20 £1.90 £1.90 (£4.00) Trio £27.30 OWNER Mr K. Abdullah (BECKHAMPTON) BRED Juddmonte Farms 10 Rn
1m 12.6 (3.30) SF: 23/17/5/3/-/-/-/-/-/-

3849 CHUCKLESTONE H'CAP (0-80) (3-Y.O+) (Class D) £3,969.00 (£1,197.00: £581.00: £273.00) **2m 1f 34y** Stalls: High GOING minus 0.28 sec (GF) 4-30 (4-31)

3669[12] **Greycoat Boy (61)***(76) (BJMeehan)* 3-7-11b JFEgan(4) (lw: 4th st: led over 2f out: clr 1f out: r.o wl) ....— 1
2996[5] Paradise Navy **(68)***(81) (CREgerton)* 6-9-2 RHughes(13) (hld up: 9th st: stdy hdwy over 2f out: rdn over 1f out: r.o one pce) 2½ 2
3569[3] Chakalak **(46)***(58) (SDow)* 7-7-8 JQuinn(14) (hld up: 5th st: ev ch 2f out: nt qckn) ....nk 3
3774[4] Star Rage (IRE) **(80)***(91) (MJohnston)* 5-10-0 JReid(5) (hld up: stdy hdwy & 8th st: styd on fnl 2f) 1¾ 4
3627[8] Romalito **(46)***(55) (MBlanshard)* 5-7-1 (7)ow1 MartinDwyer(12) (bhd tl styd on fnl 2f: nvr nrr) .....½ 5
3627[9] Tommy Cooper **(45)***(50) (MrsBarbaraWaring)* 4-7-7v NAdams(8) (b.hind: plld hrd: hdwy & 7th st: wknd over 2f out) 6 6
3616[6] Blaze Away (USA) **(80)***(83) (IABalding)* 4-10-0 LDettori(7) (led tl hdd over 2f out: sn wknd) ..1¾ 7
3705* Turquoise Sea (USA) **(79)***(80)*(Fav)*(JLDunlop)* 3-9-1 WCarson(1) (lw: hld up: 6th st: hrd rdn over 2f out: wknd wl over 1f out) 2½ 8
3425[3] Kriva **(64)***(62) (RJRWilliams)* 3-8-0 DBiggs(3) (b.hind: 3rd st: wknd over 2f out) 3½ 9
3627[11] Bellara **(67)***(52) (NMBabbage)* 3-7-10 (7)ow10 SallySandes(6) (swtg: bhd fnl 4f) 2½ 10
3616[9] Honey Mount **(70)***(58) (NJHWalker)* 4-9-4b CRutter(9) (2nd st: wknd over 2f out) 8 11
Rustavi (IRE) **(73)** *(RCurtis)* 4-9-7 WNewnes(2) (a bhd: t.o fnl 4f) ....dist 12
589[9] Ballad Ruler **(51)** *(PAPritchard)* 9-7-6 (7)ow6 JoHunnam(11) (a bhd: t.o fnl 3f) 15 13
3676[16] Laabas **(47)** *(JELong)* 12-7-2 (7)ow2 CAdamson(10) (sn prom: dropped rr 9f out: sn t.o) 20 14
LONG HANDICAP Tommy Cooper 7-3 Bellara 7-1 Romalito 6-13 Ballad Ruler 5-10 Laabas 6-2

5/4 Turquoise Sea (USA), **11/2** Blaze Away (USA), **13/2** Star Rage (IRE), **8/1** Paradise Navy, Chakalak, **14/1** Kriva, **20/1** GREYCOAT BOY, Honey Mount, Tommy Cooper, **25/1** Bellara, **33/1** Romalito, Rustavi (IRE), **150/1** Ballad Ruler, Laabas, CSF £163.28 CT £1,279.69 TOTE £25.20: £3.90 £2.40 £1.90 (£58.00) Trio £200.20 OWNER Mr N. W. Rimington (UPPER LAMBOURN) BRED N. W. Rimington 14 Rn 3m 49.6 (8.60) SF: 22/39/16/49/13/8/41/26/8/-/16/-/-/-
WEIGHT FOR AGE 3yo-12lb

T/Jkpt: £14,980.30 (3.1 Tckts). T/Plpt: £59.30 (334.05 Tckts). T/Qdpt: £10.70 (8.7 Tckts). KH

3838-HAMILTON (R-H)
Monday September 25th (Good)
WEATHER: showers WIND: fresh across

3850 E.B.F. BOTHWELL BRIDGE MEDIAN AUCTION MAIDEN STKS (2-Y.O) (Class F) £3,203.30 (£970.40: £474.20: £226.10)
1m 65y Stalls: High GOING minus 0.17 sec per fur (GF) 2-15 (2-16)

3666[8] **Eric's Bett (70)***(77) (MrsSMAustin)* 2-9-0 JMarshall(1) (b: hld up: n.m.r 2f out: hdwy over 1f out: styd on strly to ld last strides) ....— 1

3672[2] Glenrazie (IRE) *(77)*(Fav)*(PWChapple-Hyam)* 2-8-9 (5) RHavlin(9) (lw: bhd: gd hdwy ½-wy: led over 1f out: clr ent fnl f: hdd & no ex towards fin)....hd 2
3523[5] Daira *(66) (JDBethell)* 2-8-9 KFallon(5) (prom: outpcd ½-wy: styd on wl appr fnl f: nrst fin).....3 3
3736[5] Thorntoun Estate (IRE) *(70) (MJohnston)* 2-9-0 JWeaver(4) (cl up tl outpcd 2f out: kpt on fnl f)....½ 4
3652[2] Sunley Secure *(68) (MRChannon)* 2-9-0 KDarley(6) (led tl hdd over 1f out: wknd ins fnl f)......1 5
3427[9] Cry Baby **(55)***(60) (NTinkler)* 2-9-0 LCharnock(7) (chsd ldrs: rdn 5f out: outpcd fnl 3f)..............4 6
3170[4] She's Simply Great (IRE) *(54) (JJO'Neill)* 2-8-9 DeanMcKeown(10) (effrt ½-wy: nvr trbld ldrs)....¾ 7
3744[3] Dancing Dot (IRE) *(41) (MissLAPerratt)* 2-8-9 JLowe(3) (chsd ldrs: pushed along 5f out: sn wknd)....7 8
3643[6] Candy's Delight *(31) (JLEyre)* 2-8-9 RLappin(2) (chsd ldrs tl wknd fnl 3f)....5 9
3744[13] Lennox Lady *(RMMcKellar)* 2-8-9 TWilliams(8) (b.hind: t.o fr ½-wy)....dist 10

6/5 Glenrazie (IRE) (op 4/5), **5/4** Sunley Secure, **20/1** ERIC'S BETT, Daira, Dancing Dot (IRE), **25/1** Thorntoun Estate (IRE), **33/1** Candy's Delight, **40/1** Cry Baby, **50/1** She's Simply Great (IRE), **100/1** Lennox Lady, CSF £42.16 TOTE £74.70: £9.40 £1.50 £4.10 (£52.20) Trio £123.10 OWNER Mr Eric Fowler (MALTON) BRED G. Amey 10 Rn 1m 50.2 (6.90) SF: 19/19/8/12/10/2/-/-/-/-

3851 LORD HAMILTON OF DALZELL NURSERY H'CAP (0-75) (2-Y.O) (Class E) £3,615.00 (£1,095.00: £535.00: £255.00)

1m 65y Stalls: High GOING minus 0.17 sec per fur (GF) 2-45 (2-48)

3760[5] **Homeland (64)***(62) (TJNaughton)* 2-8-12 (5) JDSmith(7) (sn cl up: slt ld over 2f out: hld on wl fnl f)....— 1
3642* Domoor **(54)***(51)*(Fav)*(MJohnston)* 2-8-7 JWeaver(10) (led tl hdd over 2f out: rallied fnl f)......½ 2
3749[4] Magic Lake **(52)***(48) (EJAlston)* 2-8-5 KFallon(6) (lw: in tch: hdwy ½-wy: ch & hrd rdn over 1f out: r.o one pce)....½ 3
3744[4] In A Tizzy **(40)***(33) (PCHaslam)* 2-7-7 NKennedy(1) (unruly s: bhd tl hdwy ½-wy: styd on wl: edgd rt: nrst fin)....1¾ 4
3625[10] Classic Artiste (USA) **(68)***(47) (SCWilliams)* 2-9-7 AMackay(9) (lw: unruly s: in tch: rdn over 4f out: sn wknd)....7 5
3744* Princess Pamgaddy **(54)***(32) (JBerry)* 2-8-7 6x GCarter(8) (lw: pushed along & bhd: hdwy ½-wy: nvr able to chal)....½ 6
3639[5] La Fandango (IRE) **(60)***(36) (MWEasterby)* 2-8-13 KDarley(5) (wl bhd tl styd on fnl 3f)............1 7
2192[10] Reef Raider **(50)***(1) (NTinkler)* 2-8-3 LCharnock(4) (prom: rdn over 3f out: sn outpcd) 13 8
3721[10] Silverdale Knight **(66)***(4) (KWHogg)* 2-9-0 (5) MBaird(2) (cl up tl wknd fnl 3f)....7 9
2230[3] Vales Ales **(49)** *(RMMcKellar)* 2-7-9 (7) KSked(3) (b.hind: in tch to ½-wy: sn wknd: t.o) ....dist 10

4/1 Domoor, **9/2** HOMELAND, **11/2** Magic Lake, **6/1** La Fandango (IRE), **7/1** In A Tizzy, **8/1** Classic Artiste (USA) (op 5/1), Princess Pamgaddy, **12/1** Reef Raider, Silverdale Knight, **66/1** Vales Ales, CSF £21.91 CT £92.76 TOTE £4.50: £2.10 £2.30 £2.80 (£7.90) Trio £24.20 OWNER Mrs E. Jackman (EPSOM) BRED P. D. and Mrs Player 10 Rn 1m 49.6 (6.30) SF: 27/16/13/-/12/-/1/-/-/-

3852 BILL MCHARG MEMORIAL H'CAP (0-70) (4-Y.O+) (Class E) £4,004.30 (£1,213.40: £593.20: £283.10)

1m 4f 17y Stalls: High GOING minus 0.17 sec per fur (GF) 3-15 (3-16)

3700[4] **Ayunli (54)***(67) (SCWilliams)* 4-9-1 GCarter(16) (lw: chsd ldrs: led 4f out: hld on wl)............— 1
3710[13] Lord Hastie (USA) **(50)***(62) (CWThornton)* 7-8-11 JWeaver(6) (lw: in tch: hdwy over 3f out: ch ins fnl f: kpt on)....1 2
3743[12] Stormless **(38)***(43) (PMonteith)* 4-7-10 (3)ow2 DarrenMoffatt(1) (chsd ldrs: c wd st: ev ch 3f out: wandered u.p: nt qckn fnl f)....3½ 3
3743[3] Achilles Heel **(40)***(44) (CNAllen)* 4-8-1 GBardwell(2) (lw: hdwy 3f out: styd on wl: nrst fin) 2 4
3665[3] Mentalasanythin **(65)***(69) (ABailey)* 6-9-12 AMackay(13) (lw: mid div: outpcd over 3f out: styd on appr fnl f)....nk 5
3743[5] Keep Battling **(40)***(41) (JSGoldie)* 5-8-1 TWilliams(15) (hld up: hdwy 4f out: chsd ldrs 2f out: sn btn)....2½ 6
1109[12] Pharly Dancer **(57)***(56) (WWHaigh)* 6-9-4 DaleGibson(4) (led tl hdd 4f out: sn btn) 1½ 7
3274[3] Diamond Crown (IRE) **(47)***(36) (MartynWane)* 4-8-8 RLappin(7) (bhd: hdwy on ins & hmpd over 2f out: nt rcvr)....7 8
2465[5] Cutthroat Kid (IRE) **(64)***(53) (MrsMReveley)* 5-9-11v KDarley(17) (lw: sn in tch: effrt 4f out: no imp)....nk 9
3716[4] No Comebacks **(65)***(49) (EJAlston)* 7-9-12 KFallon(10) (bhd: effrt 4f out: no imp) 4 10
3627[17] Kanat Lee (IRE) **(32)***(16) (DonEnricoIncisa)* 4-7-7 KimTinkler(12) (lw: nvr nrr)....hd 11
1817[8] Pendolino (IRE) **(48)***(29) (MBrittain)* 4-8-9 JLowe(14) (b.hind: prom tl wknd fnl 3½f) 1¾ 12
3743* Chantry Beath **(52)***(31)*(Fav)*(CWThornton)* 4-8-13 5x DeanMcKeown(11) (a.p: rdn over 3f out: r.o one pce)....1½ 13

3743[9] Lord Advocate **(40)***(14) (DANolan)* 7-8-1bow5 VHalliday(9) (lw: chsd ldrs tl wknd fnl 3½f).......s.h **14**
3724[9] Kinoko **(38)***(15) (KWHogg)* 7-7-8 (5) MBaird(3) (bhd: hdwy on outside 5f out: sn wknd)..........1¾ **15**
2931[5] Kalko **(32)***(6) (JSGoldie)* 6-7-2 (5) PFessey(5) (b: dwlt: a bhd)..........2½ **16**

LONG HANDICAP Kanat Lee (IRE) 7-3 Kalko 7-3

3/1 Chantry Beath, **9/2** Mentalasanythin, **6/1** Achilles Heel, **7/1** AYUNLI, **9/1** Lord Hastie (USA), Cutthroat Kid (IRE), **12/1** Keep Battling, **14/1** No Comebacks, Kinoko, **20/1** Lord Advocate, Pharly Dancer, **25/1** Diamond Crown (IRE), **50/1** Stormless, Pendolino (IRE), **100/1** Kanat Lee (IRE), Kalko, CSF £66.74 CT £2,696.62 TOTE £14.50: £2.80 £1.60 £11.30 £2.10 (£69.30) Trio not won; £402.69 to Newmarket 26/09/95. OWNER Mr I. A. Southcott (NEWMARKET) BRED I. A. Southcott
16 Rn 2m 37.5 (5.50) SF: 49/44/25/26/51/23/38/18/35/31/-/11/13/-/-/-

3853

SHAWFIELD CLAIMING STKS (3-Y.O+) (Class E) £3,166.90 (£959.20: £468.60: £223.30) **1m 3f 16y** Stalls: High GOING minus 0.17 sec per fur (GF) 3-45 (3-45)

3665* **Keep Your Distance (65)***(72)*(Fav)*(MrsMReveley)* 5-9-7 KDarley(10) (lw: hld up: stdy hdwy 4f out: led 2f out: rdn & qcknd: eased ins fnl f)..........— **1**
3718[8] Latvian **(70)***(68) (RAllan)* 8-9-7 JWeaver(3) (hld up: c wd st: chsd wnr over 1f out: no imp)...2½ **2**
3743[13] Goodbye Millie **(45)***(52) (JLEyre)* 5-8-6v RLappin(4) (pushed along & hdwy after 4f: led over 3f out to 2f out: kpt on one pce)..........1 **3**
3735[9] Gold Surprise (IRE) **(46)***(53) (SEKettlewell)* 6-8-10 (3) JStack(13) (lw: chsd ldrs: chal over 3f out: one pce fnl 2f)..........4 **4**
Silverdale Fox *(40) (KWHogg)* 8-8-2 (5) MBaird(5) (nvr nrr)..........5 **5**
3272[3] Bardia **(33)***(39) (DonEnricoIncisa)* 5-8-6 KimTinkler(9) (s.i.s: styd on fnl 3f: n.d)..........nk **6**
3723[10] Prince Equiname **(59)***(37) (DEddy)* 3-8-12 DaleGibson(6) (nvr bttr than mid div)..........10 **7**
3295[8] Juice Plus **(21)***(24) (JParkes)* 4-8-11 DeanMcKeown(12) (in tch tl outpcd fnl 3½f)..........3½ **8**
2772[9] Hutchies Lady **(37)***(12) (RMMcKellar)* 3-7-8 (7) KSked(1) (b.hind: prom tl wknd 4f out)..........6 **9**
1420[4] Karibu (GER) **(45)***(21) (PMonteith)* 4-9-0 (3) DWright(2) (plld hrd: led tl hdd over 3f out: sn btn)..........½ **10**
3370[U] Malzoom **(33)** *(SEKettlewell)* 3-8-3 LCharnock(7) (cl up tl wknd over 3f out)..........20 **11**
Swift Move *(PMonteith)* 3-8-6 (3) DarrenMoffatt(11) (bkwd: s.s: t.o)..........dist **12**

11/10 KEEP YOUR DISTANCE (op Evens), **4/1** Latvian (3/1-9/2), **7/1** Goodbye Millie, **12/1** Gold Surprise (IRE), **14/1** Malzoom (op 25/1), **16/1** Bardia, **25/1** Prince Equiname, Karibu (GER), **50/1** Silverdale Fox, Juice Plus, **66/1** Hutchies Lady, **100/1** Swift Move, CSF £5.51 TOTE £2.20: £1.20 £2.20 £2.50 (£2.60) Trio £9.40 OWNER Mr P. D. Savill (SALTBURN) BRED Cedric Ford 12 Rn
2m 26.5 (7.50) SF: 37/33/17/18/5/4/-/-/-/-/-/-
WEIGHT FOR AGE 3yo-7lb

3854

TENNENT'S LAGER CONDITIONS STKS (3-Y.O+) (Class C) £4,901.60 (£1,834.40: £897.20: £386.00)
6f 5y Stalls: Low GOING minus 0.17 sec per fur (GF) 4-15 (4-16)

713[9] **Art of War (109)***(116) (RCharlton)* 3-9-3 JWeaver(6) (lw: hld up: smooth hdwy to ld wl over 1f out: shkn up & r.o)..........— **1**
3660[3] Subzero **(95)***(101) (MRStoute)* 3-8-13 KDarley(1) (b: b.hind: cl up: led over 2f out tl wl over 1f out: hung rt & no ex)..........4 **2**
3717[25] Alzianah **(100)***(88)*(Fav)*(JDBethell)* 4-8-12 KFallon(5) (lw: chsd ldrs: sn pushed along: ev ch 2f out: one pce)..........3½ **3**
3550[9] Lago Di Varano **(95)***(87) (JBerry)* 3-9-5b GCarter(2) (lw: w ldrs tl wknd fnl 2f)..........4 **4**
1723[8] Six for Luck **(60)***(58) (DANolan)* 3-8-11 VHalliday(4) (led tl hdd & wknd over 2f out)..........8 **5**
Nordisk Legend *(45?) (MrsDThomson)* 3-8-11 JLowe(3) (dwlt: a bhd)..........5 **6**

11/10 Alzianah, **5/2** ART OF WAR (2/1-100/30), **3/1** Subzero, **9/1** Lago Di Varano, **150/1** Six for Luck, **500/1** Nordisk Legend, CSF £9.78 TOTE £3.10: £2.40 £2.10 (£3.30) OWNER Sir Philip Oppenheimer (BECKHAMPTON) BRED Hascombe and Valiant Studs 6 Rn
1m 11.9 (1.90) SF: 59/44/34/30/1/-
WEIGHT FOR AGE 3yo-3lb

3855

TENNENT'S 80/- APPRENTICE H'CAP (0-70) (3-Y.O+) (Class F) £3,043.50 (£933.00: £464.00: £229.50)
6f 5y Stalls: Low GOING minus 0.17 sec per fur (GF) 4-45 (4-47)

2997[7] **Leading Princess (IRE) (39)***(51) (MissLAPerratt)* 4-7-10b(5)ow4 AngelaGallimore(6) (mde all stands' side: kpt on wl fnl f)..........— **1**
3807[4] Mister Westsound **(60)***(71) (MissLAPerratt)* 3-9-5b CLowther(14) (lw: dwlt: hdwy far side ½-wy: edgd lft: ev ch over 1f out: hrd drvn & one pce)..........2 **2**
3172[8] Seconds Away **(31)***(35) (JSGoldie)* 4-7-2b(5) JMcAuley(13) (racd far side: chsd ldrs: ev ch 2f out: one pce)..........2½ **3**

3783[7] Pageboy **(62)***(65) (PCHaslam)* 6-9-7v(3) CarolDavison(9) (lw: s.i.s: hdwy stands' side 2f out: nrst fin) ....½ 4
3719[6] Panther (IRE) **(53)***(53) (JHetherton)* 5-9-1 ALakeman(2) (lw: in tch stands' side: styd on fnl 2f: nvr able chal) 1 5
3050[5] The Happy Loon (IRE) **(51)***(46)*(Fav)*(DenysSmith)* 4-8-13 FLynch(16) (racd far side 4f: wknd)2 6
3313[7] Sunday Mail Too (IRE) **(42)***(26) (MissLAPerratt)* 3-7-10 (5)ow8 RSmith(5) (racd centre: prom tl wknd over 1f out) 1 7
3745[13] Strathtore Dream (IRE) **(36)***(28) (MissLAPerratt)* 4-7-12 TFinn(1) (s.i.s: n.d racd stands' side) ....hd 8
3467[15] Cronk's Courage **(42)***(33) (MGMeagher)* 9-8-4v SBuckley(10) (nvr trbld ldrs) ....nk 9
3726[8] Suedoro **(49)***(35) (RMMcKellar)* 5-8-6 (5) TSiddall(3) (s.i.s: hdwy centre ½-wy: n.d) 1¾ 10
3507[8] Respect A Secret **(45)***(20) (SEKettlewell)* 3-7-13 (5)ow10 JoanneWebster(4) (chsd ldrs stands' side over 4f) ....½ 11
3667[12] Diet **(54)***(32) (MissLAPerratt)* 9-9-2v JEdmunds(12) (chsd ldrs centre over 4f) 2½ 12
3667[21] Petite-D-Argent **(58)***(34) (TDyer)* 6-9-6 RMullen(7) (cl up centre: edgd lft fr ½-wy: grad wknd) 1 13
3313[2] Serious Hurry **(53)***(20) (RMMcKellar)* 7-9-1b KSked(8) (led far side 4f: wknd) 3½ 14
Ca Ira (IRE) **(31)** *(RCSpicer)* 4-7-7 BHalligan(15) (racd far side: s.i.s: n.d) 5 15
3678[4] Pemley **(34)** *(RMWhitaker)* 3-7-2 (5) CraigHalliwell(11) (racd far side: bhd fr ½-wy) 2½ 16
LONG HANDICAP Seconds Away 7-1 Sunday Mail Too (IRE) 7-6 Ca Ira (IRE) 7-3 Pemley 6-13

5/1 The Happy Loon (IRE), **6/1** Pageboy, **7/1** Mister Westsound, Diet, **8/1** Panther (IRE), **9/1** Suedoro, Pemley, Serious Hurry (6/1-10/1), **12/1** Cronk's Courage, **20/1** Petite-D-Argent, **25/1** Seconds Away, **33/1** LEADING PRINCESS (IRE), Strathtore Dream (IRE), Respect A Secret, Ca Ira (IRE), Sunday Mail Too (IRE), CSF £231.20 CT £5,228.57 TOTE £46.80: £7.30 £2.20 £6.90 £1.40 (£81.10) Trio £586.70 OWNER Mrs Ruth Wyllie (AYR) BRED Woodford Stud 16 Rn

1m 12.9 (2.90) SF: 26/43/10/40/28/21/-/3/8/10/-/7/9/-/-/-

WEIGHT FOR AGE 3yo-3lb

STEWARDS' ENQUIRY Lowther susp. 4-5/10/95 (excessive use of whip).

T/Plpt: £60.50 (237.2 Tckts). T/Qdpt: £30.30 (0.3 Tckts); £28.70 to Newmarket 26/9/95. AA

3765-BRIGHTON (L-H)
Tuesday September 26th (Good)

vis: v.bad races 5, 6 &7
WEATHER: raining WIND: v str across

3856 FINAL (S) STKS (2-Y.O) (Class G) £2,243.00 (£618.00: £293.00)
5f 59y Stalls: Low GOING: 0.04 sec per fur (G) 1-45 (1-46)

3417[2] **Miletrian Refurb (IRE) (59)***(65) (MRChannon)* 2-8-11 RHughes(9) (4th st: led over 1f out: drvn out) ....— 1
3651[8] Poly By Staufan (IRE) **(52)***(60) (MRChannon)* 2-8-6 WWoods(11) (lw: hdwy over 1f out: r.o wl ins fnl f) ....hd 2
3670[5] Power Don **(58)***(62) (WGMTurner)* 2-8-8v(3) PMcCabe(8) (lw: 2nd st: ev ch over 1f out: unable qckn) 1 3
3612[10] Napoleon's Return **(62)***(59) (AGFoster)* 2-8-11 TSprake(10) (6th st: bmpd wl over 1f out: swtchd rt: one pce fnl f) ....¾ 4
3675[5] L A Touch **(56)***(52) (CADwyer)* 2-8-11 CDwyer(2) (hdwy over 2f out: rdn over 1f out: one pce) 2½ 5
3765[14] Silhouette (IRE) *(41) (DRCElsworth)* 2-8-4 (5)ow3 DaneO'Neill(4) (lw: hrd rdn over 2f out: hdwy over 1f out: one pce) 2 6
3740[3] Apartments Abroad **(53)***(35) (KMcAuliffe)* 2-8-7 ow1 MTebbutt(12) (nvr nrr) 2 7
3727[11] Phoenix House **(65)***(37) (GLMoore)* 2-9-2 SWhitworth(5) (lw: 3rd st: wknd over 2f out) 2½ 8
3753[6] Mister Sean (IRE) **(66)***(31)*(Fav)*(JWPayne)* 2-8-11b RCochrane(7) (lw: led over 3f) ....½ 9
3753[5] Dande Flyer **(66)***(25) (DWPArbuthnot)* 2-8-11 AClark(1) (b.hind: s.s: hdwy over 2f out: wknd fnl f) 2 10
3528[15] Caveat Emptor (IRE) **(50)***(17) (SDow)* 2-8-4v(7) ADaly(6) (5th st: wknd over 3f out) 2½ 11
Further Future (IRE) *(17) (JohnBerry)* 2-8-4 (7) RMullen(3) (str: bkwd: s.s: a bhd) ....s.h 12

11/4 Mister Sean (IRE), **4/1** Dande Flyer, **5/1** MILETRIAN REFURB (IRE) (4/1-6/1), **6/1** Power Don, **10/1** Phoenix House, **11/1** Napoleon's Return (8/1-12/1), **14/1** L A Touch, Caveat Emptor (IRE) (8/1-16/1), **16/1** Apartments Abroad, **20/1** Silhouette (IRE), **25/1** Poly By Staufan (IRE), **33/1** Further Future (IRE), CSF £106.82 TOTE £4.30: £1.50 £7.10 £2.00 (£54.60) Trio £129.00 OWNER Miletrian Plc (UPPER LAMBOURN) BRED Rosebank Stud 12 Rn

63.7 secs (3.70) SF: 37/32/34/31/24/13/7/9/3/-/-/-

No bid

3857 E.B.F. SOMPTING MAIDEN STKS (2-Y.O) (Class D) £3,882.50 (£1,160.00: £555.00: £252.50) **6f 209y** Stalls: Low GOING: 0.04 sec per fur (G) 2-20 (2-20)

Nador *(85+) (DRLoder)* 2-9-0 GCarter(5) (neat: lw: 5th st: led 2f out: r.o wl)........................— 1
3339[5] Threesome (USA) *(73)*(Fav)*(LMCumani)* 2-8-9 GHind(6) (lw: 4th st: swtchd lft 2f out: unable qckn fnl f)........................3 2
3495[7] Ecstatic Madam (IRE) *(67) (BWHills)* 2-8-4 (5) JDSmith(7) (6th st: hrd rdn over 1f out: one pce)........................2½ 3
3721[2] Emperegrine (USA) **(74)***(71) (CFWall)* 2-8-9v(5) LNewton(3) (3rd st: rdn over 2f out: wknd fnl f)........................½ 4
3713[6] Juicy **(77)***(62) (WJHaggas)* 2-9-0b RCochrane(4) (led over 1f: 2nd st: wknd over 1f out)..........4 5
3672[5] Beas River (IRE) *(56) (WRMuir)* 2-9-0 WWoods(2) (lw: led over 5f out tl 2f out: wknd over 1f out)........................2½ 6
2534[6] Honestly *(28) (BSmart)* 2-8-9 RPerham(1) (bhd fnl 4f)........................10 7

8/11 Threesome (USA), **7/2** NADOR (9/4-4/1), **15/2** Juicy, **8/1** Beas River (IRE), Emperegrine (USA) (7/1-12/1), **20/1** Ecstatic Madam (IRE), **50/1** Honestly, CSF £6.68 TOTE £4.60: £1.60 £1.10 (£2.00) OWNER Sheikh Mohammed (NEWMARKET) BRED Sheikh Mohammed Bin Rashid Al Maktoum 7 Rn
1m 25.5 (5.50) SF: 33/21/15/19/10/4/-

3858 A.R. DENNIS BOOKMAKERS SEPTEMBER NURSERY H'CAP (0-75) (2-Y.O) (Class E) £3,702.60 (£1,108.80: £532.40: £244.20) **6f 209y** Stalls: Low GOING: 0.04 sec per fur (G) 2-55 (2-56)

3749* **Warming Trends (70)***(75)*(Fav)*(SirMarkPrescott)* 2-9-6 5x WWoods(8) (lw: hdwy over 2f out: led over 1f out: hung lft: r.o wl)........................— 1
3612[5] Half An Inch (IRE) **(70)***(73) (BJMeehan)* 2-9-6b RHughes(5) (6th st: hrd drvn fnl 2f: r.o)...........1 2
3655[6] Proud Monk **(71)***(74) (GLMoore)* 2-9-7 SWhitworth(4) (3rd st: ev ch over 1f out: one pce) ....s.h 3
3749[13] My Kind **(61)***(60) (KMcAuliffe)* 2-8-11v RCochrane(7) (b: rdn over 2f out: hdwy over 1f out: r.o)........................1¾ 4
3775* Oriel Lad **(73)***(71) (PDEvans)* 2-9-9b 5x KFallon(9) (hdwy over 2f out: hrd rdn over 1f out: 4th & btn whn n.m.r wl ins fnl f)........................nk 5
3655[9] Mystery Matthias **(56)***(47) (MissBSanders)* 2-8-6 GCarter(14) (n.m.r & lost pl over 2f out: r.o one pce)........................3 6
3767[4] Velvet Jones **(58)***(46) (GFHCharles-Jones)* 2-8-1 (7) ADaly(1) (2nd st: wknd over 1f out).......1½ 7
3267[5] Takapuna (IRE) **(58)***(44) (TJNaughton)* 2-8-3 (5) JDSmith(11) (lw: nvr nrr)........................½ 8
3749[16] Northern Saga (IRE) **(53)***(36) (AndrewTurnell)* 2-7-10 (7) RStudholme(15) (lw: 7th st: wknd over 2f out)........................1½ 9
3133[8] Sunrise Special (IRE) **(58)***(35) (GLewis)* 2-8-8 GHind(10) (prom 3f)........................2½ 10
3174[13] Etterby Park (USA) **(52)***(29) (MDIUsher)* 2-8-2 NAdams(13) (lw: a bhd)........................s.h 11
3378[3] Music Mistress (IRE) **(62)***(38) (RHannon)* 2-8-7 (5) DaneO'Neill(3) (b.hind: 5th st: wknd over 2f out)........................½ 12
*1954** Subfusk **(61)***(28) (WGMTurner)* 2-8-8 (3) PMcCabe(6) (led over 5f)........................4 13
3623[9] Miss Carottene **(61)***(9) (MJRyan)* 2-8-11v AClark(2) (4th st: rdn over 2f out: wknd over 1f out)........................8 14
3623[5] Little Kenny **(58)** *(MJFetherston-Godley)* 2-8-8 FNorton(12) (bhd fnl 5f: t.o)........................dist 15

11/4 WARMING TRENDS, **7/2** Oriel Lad (5/1-3/1), **15/2** Half An Inch (IRE), **10/1** Little Kenny, **14/1** Takapuna (IRE), Velvet Jones, Miss Carottene, **16/1** Subfusk, My Kind, Music Mistress (IRE), Etterby Park (USA), **20/1** Sunrise Special (IRE), Proud Monk, Mystery Matthias, **40/1** Northern Saga (IRE), CSF £24.07 CT £336.75 TOTE £4.30: 2.30 £2.50 £7.70 (£32.70) Trio £166.90 OWNER Hesmonds Stud (NEWMARKET) BRED Hesmonds Stud Ltd 15 Rn
1m 25.6 (5.60) SF: 37/35/36/22/33/9/8/6/-/-/-/-/-/-/-
STEWARDS' ENQUIRY Hughes susp. 6-17/10/95 (unreasonable frequency).

3859 SALTDEAN MAIDEN STKS (3-Y.O+) (Class D) £3,833.70 (£1,143.60: £545.80: £246.90) **7f 214y** Stalls: Low GOING: 0.04 sec per fur (G) 3-25 (3-26)

3542[10] **Empty Quarter (85)***(92) (JHMGosden)* 3-9-3 GHind(7) (3rd st: led over 1f out: comf)...........— 1
3362[3] Balasara (IRE) **(75)***(86) (DRCElsworth)* 5-9-2b(5) DaneO'Neill(1) (led: clr 5f out: hdd over 1f out: unable qckn)........................3 2
3514[4] Rockusa **(47)***(67) (PRHedger)* 3-8-12 GCarter(4) (lw: hdwy over 4f out: 4th st: wknd over 1f out)........................7 3
3023[5] Swiss Bank *(61) (LordHuntingdon)* 3-8-12 KFallon(5) (hdwy over 3f out: 5th st: wknd over 1f out)........................3 4
3573[2] Cyphell (IRE) **(68)***(59)*(Fav)*(MRStoute)* 3-8-12 RCochrane(8) (2nd st: rdn over 2f out: wknd over 1f out)........................1 5

3725[5] Fallal (IRE) *(35) (KMcAuliffe)* 3-8-12 RHughes(3) (hdwy over 4f out: 6th st: wknd 2f out)......12 **6**
3750[15] Wendals Touch *(15) (RMFlower)* 4-9-2 AMorris(2) (bhd fnl 3f)..........10 **7**
First Shot *(RCurtis)* 4-9-4 (3) PMcCabe(6) (bit bkwd: bhd fnl 4f)..........25 **8**

15/8 Cyphell (IRE), **2/1** EMPTY QUARTER (op 11/10), **9/4** Swiss Bank, **13/2** Balasara (IRE), **16/1** Rockusa, Fallal (IRE), **33/1** Wendals Touch, First Shot, CSF £16.62 TOTE £2.70: £1.10 £2.10 £1.50 (£6.80) OWNER Abdullah Saeed Bul Hab (NEWMARKET) BRED R. H. Cowell 8 Rn
1m 37.4 (5.20) SF: 48/46/23/17/15/-/-/-
WEIGHT FOR AGE 3yo-4lb

3860 EDDIE HIGHAM MEMORIAL LIMITED STKS (0-65) (3-Y.O) (Class F) £3,073.40 (£852.40: £408.20)
7f 214y Stalls: Low GOING: 0.04 sec per fur (G) 4-00 (4-01)

3664[F] **Another Time (53)***(74)*(Fav)*(SPCWoods)* 3-9-3 WWoods(2) (4th st: led ins fnl f: rdn out).....— **1**
3685[8] H'Ani **(48)***(65) (WJHaggas)* 3-8-9 KFallon(7) (3rd st: swtchd lft 1f out: r.o)..........nk **2**
3429[6] Shady Deed (USA) **(62)***(63) (JWHills)* 3-8-12v RCochrane(6) (led to ins fnl f: unable qckn) ...2½ **3**
3771[14] Almuhtaram **(59)***(53) (MissGayKelleway)* 3-9-0 MTebbutt(1) (hdwy over 4f out: 5th st wknd 2f out)..........6 **4**
3618[8] Shared (IRE) **(35)***(43) (MMadgwick)* 3-9-0 AClark(8) (6th st: wknd over 2f out)..........5 **5**
3026[7] Prince of Spades **(62)***(46) (CACyzer)* 3-9-6 DBiggs(4) (a bhd)..........1½ **6**
3619[8] Tirollac (IRE) **(42)***(5) (LGCottrell)* 3-8-9 GCarter(3) (2nd st: wknd over 3f out)..........15 **7**
3654[W] Amboyna Burl (IRE) **(46)** *(DAWilson)* 3-9-0 RHughes(5) (virtually ref to r: a t.o)..........dist **8**

2/1 ANOTHER TIME (3/1-7/4), **4/1** H'Ani, Shady Deed (USA) (op 5/2), **9/2** Almuhtaram (8/1-12/1), **5/1** Prince of Spades (7/2-11/2), **12/1** Tirollac (IRE) (op 7/1), **20/1** Shared (IRE), **40/1** Amboyna Burl (IRE), CSF £10.86 TOTE £3.20: £1.50 £1.50 £1.80 (£6.60) OWNER Mr D. Sullivan (NEWMARKET) BRED W. G. Barker 8 Rn 1m 37.8 (5.60) SF: 44/35/33/23/13/16/-/-

3861 STEYNING CONDITIONS STKS (2-Y.O) (Class D) £3,817.50 (£1,140.00: £545.00: £247.50) 6f 209y Stalls: Low GOING: 0.04 sec per fur (G) 4-30 (4-31)

3733[3] **Oberons Boy (IRE) (94)***(89)*(Fav)*(BJMeehan)* 2-8-11 RHughes(1) (mde all: clr over 1f out: r.o wl)..........— **1**
3613[7] Prince of Florence (IRE) **(80)***(73?) (LMCumani)* 2-8-11 KFallon(4) (chsd wnr fnl 4f: no imp) 7 **2**
940[6] Al's Alibi *(64) (WRMuir)* 2-8-11 CRutter(3) (4th st: wknd over 1f out)..........4 **3**
3773[2] Arctic Zipper (USA) *(43) (WAO'Gorman)* 2-8-11 RCochrane(2) (3rd st: eased whn btn over 1f out)..........9 **4**

11/10 OBERONS BOY (IRE) (5/4-Evens), **6/4** Prince of Florence (IRE), **7/2** Arctic Zipper (USA) (op 2/1), **20/1** Al's Alibi, CSF £3.21 TOTE £1.90 (£1.50) OWNER Mr Edward Winfield (UPPER LAMBOURN) BRED M. A. O'Toole and Ron Con Ltd 4 Rn 1m 24.5 (4.50) SF: 42/26/17/-

3862 LEVY BOARD MAIDEN H'CAP (0-70) (3-Y.O+) (Class E) £3,874.20 (£1,161.60: £558.80: £257.40)
1m 3f 196y Stalls: High GOING: 0.04 sec per fur (G) 5-00 (5-04)

3513[5] **Aviator's Dream (32)***(43) (JPearce)* 5-7-12 CRutter(6) (hdwy over 1f out: rdn: led nr fin).....— **1**
3805[2] Maronetta **(36)***(46) (MJRyan)* 3-7-3 (5)ow1 MBaird(17) (lw: led 4f out: hrd rdn over 1f out: hdd nr fin)..........nk **2**
3621[6] Matamoros **(68)***(78) (JLDunlop)* 3-9-12 SWhitworth(4) (hdwy over 1f out: r.o wl ins fnl f) ....¾ **3**
3384[10] Ginger Jim **(57)***(63) (PRHedger)* 4-9-6 (3) SDrowne(15) (lw: 4th st: hrd rdn over 1f out: one pce)..........2½ **4**
3621[5] Mansur (IRE) **(68)***(72) (DRLoder)* 3-9-12 GCarter(1) (lw: 5th st: rdn over 2f out: wknd fnl f)..........2 **5**
3288[7] Guest Alliance (IRE) **(48)***(51) (AMoore)* 3-8-6 CandyMorris(3) (lw: nvr nr to chal)..........½ **6**
3646[13] College Night (IRE) **(56)***(54) (CADwyer)* 3-9-0 CDwyer(2)..........3½ **7**
3756[3] Mighty Squaw **(53)***(50)*(Fav)*(MissGayKelleway)* 3-8-8 (3) SSanders(13) (6th st: wknd over 2f out)..........1¼ **8**
3526[12] Junior Ben (IRE) **(60)***(56) (PHowling)* 3-9-4 RCochrane(11)..........¾ **9**
2961[5] Delgarth Lady **(31)***(18) (JLSpearing)* 4-7-11 ow2 FNorton(9) (3rd st: wknd over 2f out) 5 **10**
3573[5] Sujud (IRE) **(57)***(19) (HThomsonJones)* 3-9-1 MTebbutt(5)..........20 **11**
3756[7] Jovie King (IRE) **(53)***(15) (SDow)* 3-8-4 (7) ADaly(10) (lw: bhd fnl 3f)..........hd **12**
3521[3] Santella Boy (USA) **(60)***(22) (GHarwood)* 3-9-4v AClark(16) (led 8f: 2nd st: wknd 3f out)..........hd **13**
3526[3] Northern Highlight **(53)***(13) (TPMcGovern)* 4-9-5 KFallon(12) (b: lw: bhd fnl 3f)..........1½ **14**
3402[5] Marzipan (IRE) **(58)** *(JWHills)* 3-9-2 RHughes(7) (bhd fnl 3f)..........20 **15**
3426[10] Moonlight Air **(28)** *(JLSpearing)* 4-7-8 NAdams(14)..........hd **16**

6/4 Mighty Squaw (op 3/1), **7/1** AVIATOR'S DREAM, Northern Highlight, Santella Boy (USA) (5/1-8/1), **9/1** Maronetta, **10/1** Matamoros (op 6/1), **12/1** Marzipan (IRE), Mansur (IRE) (op 7/1), Sujud (IRE) (op 8/1), **14/1** Ginger Jim, **16/1** Guest Alliance (IRE), **20/1** Junior Ben (IRE), **25/1** Delgarth Lady, Jovie King (IRE), **33/1** College Night (IRE), Moonlight Air, CSF £76.92 CT £612.01 TOTE £14.40: £2.40 £2.40 £2.40 £3.80 (£74.10) Trio £248.50 OWNER Mr P. Bottomley (NEWMARKET) BRED Qualitair Stud Ltd 16 Rn No Time Taken

WEIGHT FOR AGE 3yo-8lb

T/Plpt: £28.40 (322.47 Tckts). T/Qdpt: £8.50 (5.75 Tckts). AK

3371-NEWMARKET (R-H)
Tuesday September 26th (Good)

WEATHER: rain WIND: slt half bhd

3863

SHADWELL STUD SERIES FINAL APPRENTICE H'CAP (0-85) (3-Y.O+) (Class E) £7,425.00 (£2,250.00: £1,100.00: £525.00)
1m 2f (Rowley) Stalls: High GOING minus 0.05 sec per fur (G) 1-55 (1-57)

3757[4] **Guesstimation (USA) (62)***(73) (JPearce)* 6-8-8 SDrowne(18) (hld up: hdwy 2f out: led ent fnl f: rdn & hld on wl) — **1**
3654[3] Cyrus the Great (IRE) **(74)***(85) (MBell)* 3-9-0 SSanders(11) (hld up mid div: hdwy over 2f out: ev ch fnl f: r.o) nk **2**
3659* Domappel **(67)***(76)*(Fav)*(MrsJCecil)* 3-8-7 MartinDwyer(2) (a.p: led over 3f out to 1f out: rdn & no ex fnl f) 1¼ **3**
3685[2] Sovereigns Parade **(61)***(67) (JEBanks)* 3-8-1 JStack(14) (hld up: hdwy over 2f out: fin wl) 1½ **4**
3657[3] Lady Lacey **(47)***(51) (GBBalding)* 8-7-4v(3) IonaWands(9) (hdwy 2f out: rdn & r.o wl towards fin) 1¼ **5**
3704* High Premium **(79)***(81) (RAFahey)* 7-9-11 GParkin(15) (b: lw: chsd ldrs: rdn & outpcd 2f out: kpt on appr fnl f) 1½ **6**
3621[3] Pass Mark **(62)***(63) (JRFanshawe)* 3-8-2 NVarley(7) (chsd ldrs: rdn bel dist: r.o one pce) ¾ **7**
3723* Loki (IRE) **(82)***(81)*(Fav)*(GLewis)* 7-10-0 AWhelan(10) (b: hld up: hdwy 3f out: wknd over 1f out) 1¼ **8**
3552[7] Lovely Lyca **(75)***(70) (JWHills)* 3-9-1 ow3 HBastiman(1) (nvr nrr) hd **9**
3469[3] Harry Browne (IRE) **(69)***(65)*(Fav)*(MrsJRRamsden)* 3-8-6 (3) GMilligan(4) (bhd: hdwy over 2f out: nvr nr to chal) 1½ **10**
3433[9] Game Ploy (POL) **(72)***(68) (FMurphy)* 3-8-12 CAdamson(6) (chsd ldrs tl wknd 2f out) hd **11**
3469[4] Blue Nile (IRE) **(68)***(64) (ACStewart)* 3-8-8 MHumphries(20) (chsd ldrs: effrt wl over 1f out: wknd appr fnl f) s.h **12**
2086[2] Yarrow (IRE) **(79)***(72)*(Fav)*(JHMGosden)* 3-9-5 PRoberts(13) (bit bkwd: nvr plcd to chal) 1¾ **13**
3659[2] Myfontaine **(64)***(46) (KTIvory)* 8-8-7 (3) CScally(3) (b: bhd: effrt & rdn 3f out) 7 **14**
3531[13] Vin St Koola **(63)***(43) (MCChapman)* 3-8-3 CMunday(16) (led tl hdd & wknd over 3f out: t.o) 1¼ **15**
2792[5] Trade Wind **(72)***(48) (DRCElsworth)* 4-9-4b DGibbs(8) (prom over 7f: sn wknd: t.o) 2½ **16**
3214[13] Iktasab **(83)***(59) (EALDunlop)* 3-9-9 DRMcCabe(17) (lw: a bhd: t.o) s.h **17**
3685[4] Saltando (IRE) **(51)***(19) (PatMitchell)* 4-7-11 DarrenMoffatt(19) (lw: prom 6f: sn wknd: t.o) 5 **18**
3294* Western Sal **(72)***(38) (WJarvis)* 3-8-12 MBaird(5) (a in rr: t.o) ¾ **19**

LONG HANDICAP Lady Lacey 7-5

8/1 Harry Browne (IRE), Loki (IRE), Domappel, Yarrow (IRE), **10/1** Cyrus the Great (IRE), Blue Nile (IRE), **11/1** Pass Mark, **12/1** Western Sal, **14/1** High Premium, Lady Lacey, Trade Wind, Lovely Lyca, Sovereigns Parade, Myfontaine, GUESSTIMATION (USA), **20/1** Saltando (IRE), Iktasab, Game Ploy (POL), **33/1** Vin St Koola, CSF £150.60 CT £1,124.97 TOTE £21.00: £4.60 £2.80 £1.90 £4.70 (£115.00) Trio £631.70 OWNER Quintet Partnership (NEWMARKET) BRED Oak Crest Farm 19 Rn 2m 6.4 (3.80) SF: 55/61/52/43/33/63/39/63/46/41/44/40/48/28/19/30/35/1/14

WEIGHT FOR AGE 3yo-6lb

3864

HUNTER PRICE PARTNERSHIP RATED STKS H'CAP (0-100) (3-Y.O+) (Class B) £8,435.44 (£3,118.96: £1,494.48: £608.40)
1m 4f (Rowley) Stalls: High GOING minus 0.05 sec per fur (G) 2-30 (2-32)

3729[7] **Seckar Vale (USA) (82)***(94+) (BWHills)* 3-7-13 WCarson(4) (lw: hld up & bhd: hdwy on ins & rdn 2f out: r.o to ld ins fnl f: comf) — **1**
3730[12] Jameel Asmar **(82)***(94+) (CREgerton)* 3-7-13 NCarlisle(5) (lw: a.p: ev ch 2f out: hrd rdn & kpt on strly towards fin) nk **2**
3593[2] Bencher Q C (USA) **(90)***(102)*(Fav)*(JHMGosden)* 3-8-7 LDettori(8) (hld up: hdwy to ld 2f out: hdd ins fnl f: rallied cl home) s.h **3**
3500* Persian Elite (IRE) **(85)***(91) (PFICole)* 4-8-10 TQuinn(3) (led to 2f out: r.o one pce appr fnl f) 4 **4**

3164[9] Penny a Day (IRE) **(96)***(102) (MrsMReveley)* 5-9-7 KDarley(1) (hld up: hdwy 3f out: rdn bel dist: sn btn)....½ 5
3593[8] Lombardic (USA) **(90)***(94) (MrsJCecil)* 4-9-1 JReid(6) (lw: chsd ldr: drvn along over 2f out: sn btn)....1¼ 6
3594[4] Heathyards Rock **(84)***(86) (RHollinshead)* 3-8-1 PaulEddery(2) (lw: a rr div)....1¼ 7
3162[20] Burning (USA) **(98)***(100) (GHarwood)* 3-9-1 WRSwinburn(7) (hld up & bhd: hdwy over 3f out: rdn 2f out: wknd appr fnl f)....½ 8

LONG HANDICAP Jameel Asmar 7-11

3/1 Bencher Q C (USA), **4/1** SECKAR VALE (USA) (3/1-9/2), **9/2** Penny a Day (IRE) (6/1-4/1), **5/1** Burning (USA), **13/2** Persian Elite (IRE) (9/2-7/1), **10/1** Jameel Asmar (8/1-12/1), **20/1** Lombardic (USA), **25/1** Heathyards Rock, CSF £36.26 CT £116.11 TOTE £5.50: £1.60 £3.50 £1.30 (£36.70) OWNER Mr J. Hanson (LAMBOURN) BRED S. Patrick Terry in USA 8 Rn

2m 34.5 (5.20) SF: 45/45/53/50/61/53/37/51

WEIGHT FOR AGE 3yo-8lb

3865 TATTERSALLS HOUGHTON SALES CONDITIONS STKS (2-Y.O) (Class B)

£13,011.70 (£4,780.30: £2,265.15: £893.25)

7f (Rowley) Stalls: High GOING minus 0.05 sec per fur (G) 3-05 (3-08)

3596[2] **Rio Duvida (100)***(99)*(Fav)*(DRLoder)* 2-9-0 LDettori(18) (a.p: led wl over 1f out: r.o wl)....— 1
3539* Mezzogiorno *(92) (GWragg)* 2-8-9 MHills(16) (a w ldrs: led 3f out tl wl over 1f out: rdn & kpt on fnl f)....1 2
2947[4] Honest Guest (IRE) **(100)***(87) (MHTompkins)* 2-8-9 PRobinson(29) (hld up in tch: hdwy 2f out: rdn & one pce ins fnl f)....2 3
3626[3] Papaha (FR) *(87) (HRACecil)* 2-8-9 WRyan(2) (racd stands' side: rdn & kpt on fnl f: nvr nrr)....hd 4
3692a[2] Tamnia **(100)***(87) (JLDunlop)* 2-8-9 WCarson(6) (hld up: led stands' side 2f out: rdn & nt pce to chal)....s.h 5
3436* Al Abraq (IRE) *(85) (JWHills)* 2-9-0 RHills(19) (hdwy fnl 2f: nrst fin)....3 6
3561[11] Faraway Waters *(79) (DWPArbuthnot)* 2-8-9 JWilliams(20) (b.hind: hdwy u.p bel dist: nt rch ldrs)....nk 7
3404[2] Roses In The Snow (IRE) **(86)***(77) (JWHills)* 2-8-9 CNakatani(7) (effrt stands' side over 1f out: nt rch ldrs)....1 8
3784[2] Singing Patriarch (IRE) *(82) (JLDunlop)* 2-9-0 WNewnes(17) (lw: spd over 4f: kpt on one pce)....hd 9
3711[12] Vola Via (USA) **(88)***(82) (IABalding)* 2-9-0 TIves(28) (prom tl wknd over 1f out)....s.h 10
3691a[2] High Target (IRE) *(80) (DKWeld,Ireland)* 2-9-0 MJKinane(13) (gd sort: lw: nvr trbld ldrs)....¾ 11
3733[12] Miss Universal (IRE) *(75) (CEBrittain)* 2-8-9 DRMcCabe(27) (nvr nr ldrs)....hd 12
3281[2] Royal Mark (IRE) **(88)***(80) (JWWatts)* 2-9-0 MRoberts(21) (nvr trbld ldrs)....hd 13
His Excellence (USA) *(79) (APO'Brien,Ireland)* 2-9-0 CRoche(9) (w'like: scope: a mid div)...hd 14
2846[2] Flying Green (FR) *(76) (RCharlton)* 2-9-0 PaulEddery(15) (lw: prom over 4f)....1½ 15
3420[4] Red Nymph **(96)***(69) (WJarvis)* 2-8-9 JWeaver(14) (spd 4f)....1 16
2995* Pleasant Surprise **(91)***(73) (MJohnston)* 2-9-0 WRSwinburn(11) (led 4f: wknd 2f out)....nk 17
3663[7] Hamlet (IRE) *(73) (MBell)* 2-9-0 MFenton(3) (chsd ldrs stands' side over 4f)....s.h 18
3763[3] Ma Belle Poule *(64) (PFICole)* 2-8-9 TQuinn(4) (led stands' side: hrd rdn 2f out: wknd qckly)1½ 19
Sarah's Guest (IRE) *(63) (VictorBowens,Ireland)* 2-8-9 DeanMcKeown(22) (a in rr)....½ 20
3339[12] Ceilidh Star (IRE) *(63) (BWHills)* 2-8-9 DHolland(12) (chsd ldrs centre 4f)....nk 21
2932* Crissem (IRE) **(73)***(60) (RHollinshead)* 2-8-9 MRimmer(2) (outpcd)....1¼ 22
3652[3] D'naan (IRE) *(64) (WJHaggas)* 2-9-0 AMcGlone(24) (outpcd)....½ 23
3650[4] Majdak Jereeb (IRE) *(63) (MajorWRHern)* 2-9-0 MBirch(25) (chsd ldrs to ½-wy: sn wknd)....hd 24
2775[5] Classic Flyer (IRE) **(82)***(54) (SCWilliams)* 2-8-9 AMackay(1) (s.s: a in rr)....2 25
3536* Masquerade *(57) (LMCumani)* 2-9-0 KDarley(10) (chsd ldrs over 4f: sn wknd)....¾ 26
3763[5] Desert Lynx (IRE) *(50) (TRWatson)* 2-8-9 JTate(8) (a in rr)....1 27
2467[2] Kalao Tua (IRE) *(42) (JRFanshawe)* 2-8-9 DHarrison(30) (chsd ldrs 4f: wknd over 2f out)...3½ 28
3600[3] Ski Academy (IRE) *(46) (PWChapple-Hyam)* 2-9-0 JReid(26) (prom tl wknd qckly over 2f out)....½ 29
3280[8] Hever Golf Hero *(18) (TJNaughton)* 2-9-0 StephenDavies(5) (t.o)....12 30

2/1 RIO DUVIDA, **13/2** Tamnia, **11/1** Mezzogiorno, **12/1** High Target (IRE), Ski Academy (IRE), **14/1** Royal Mark (IRE), Masquerade, His Excellence (USA), Papaha (FR), **16/1** Honest Guest (IRE), **20/1** Al Abraq (IRE), Red Nymph, **25/1** Pleasant Surprise, **33/1** Flying Green (FR), **40/1** Roses In The Snow (IRE), **50/1** Faraway Waters, Vola Via (USA), Hamlet (IRE), Singing Patriarch (IRE), D'naan (IRE), Kalao Tua (IRE), Ma Belle Poule, Classic Flyer (IRE), **66/1** Majdak Jereeb (IRE), **100/1** Sarah's Guest (IRE), Miss Universal (IRE), Desert Lynx (IRE), Ceilidh Star (IRE), Crissem (IRE), Hever Golf Hero, CSF £25.82 TOTE £3.70: £2.00 £3.70 £7.90 (£20.60) Trio £543.60 OWNER Lady Harrison (NEWMARKET) BRED Limestone Stud 30 Rn 1m 26.39 (2.69)

SF:62/55/50/50/50/48/42/40/45/45/43/38/43/42/39/32/36/36/27/26/26/23/27/26/17/20/13/5/9/-

3866

SHADWELL STUD CHEVELEY PARK STKS (Gp 1) (2-Y.O F) (Class A)
£84,680.00 (£30,680.00: £14,840.00: £6,200.00)
6f (Rowley) Stalls: High GOING minus 0.05 sec per fur (G) 3-40 (3-40)

2594* **Blue Duster (USA) (100)***(113+)*(Fav)*(DRLoder)* 2-8-11 MJKinane(5) (lw: chsd ldrs: led over 1f out: qcknd clr: impressive)........— **1**
3702* My Branch *(106) (BWHills)* 2-8-11 MHills(3) (hld up: hdwy & ev ch over 1f out: kpt on fnl f: no ch w wnr)........2½ **2**
3452* Najiya **(98)***(98) (JLDunlop)* 2-8-11 WCarson(1) (a.p: jnd ldr over 2f out: ev ch appr fnl f: one pce)........3 **3**
3186* Dance Sequence (USA) **(100)***(97) (MRStoute)* 2-8-11 WRSwinburn(4) (led tl over 1f out: rdn & outpcd fnl f)........½ **4**
3708[3] Supamova (USA) *(86) (PFICole)* 2-8-11 TQuinn(2) (stdd s: effrt 2f out: outpcd appr fnl f).......4 **5**

4/5 BLUE DUSTER (USA), **100/30** My Branch, **7/1** Najiya, Dance Sequence (USA) (5/1-8/1), **12/1** Supamova (USA) (10/1-16/1), CSF £3.79 TOTE £1.60: £1.20 £1.60 (£2.70) OWNER Sheikh Mohammed (NEWMARKET) BRED Darley Stud Management Inc 5 Rn
1m 12.78 (1.48) SF: 71/64/56/55/44

3867

E.B.F. JERSEY LILY NURSERY H'CAP (2-Y.O F) (Class C)
£23,490.00 (£7,020.00: £3,360.00: £1,530.00)
7f (Rowley) Stalls: High GOING minus 0.05 sec per fur (G) 4-15 (4-17)

3516* **Pacific Grove (83)***(85) (PFICole)* 2-8-1 (5) AWhelan(14) (hld up: gd hdwy appr fnl f: hrd rdn to ld last stride)........— **1**
3346[4] Rumpipumpy **(83)***(85) (LordHuntingdon)* 2-8-6 TQuinn(11) (a.p: led ins fnl f tl ct last stride)..s.h **2**
3702[8] Astuti (IRE) **(88)***(90) (APJarvis)* 2-8-11 JTate(7) (hld up in rr: hdwy over 1f out: str run appr fnl f: jst failed)........hd **3**
3714[3] Amanita **(77)***(75) (JWWatts)* 2-8-0 JFEgan(4) (lw: a.p: led over 2f out tl ins fnl f: no ex)........1¾ **4**
3631[6] Expensive Taste **(85)***(83) (MRStoute)* 2-8-8 WRSwinburn(1) (prom on outside: rdn 1f out: one pce)........s.h **5**
3147[2] Tabriz **(76)***(73) (JDBethell)* 2-7-13 TWilliams(16) (led tl over 2f out: kpt on one pce)........s.h **6**
3639[6] Frezeliere **(82)***(78) (JLDunlop)* 2-8-5b WRyan(9) (hld up & bhd: hdwy bel dist: fin wl)........½ **7**
3450[7] Lyzia (IRE) **(86)***(77) (CEBrittain)* 2-8-9 MJKinane(10) (sme late hdwy: nvr nrr)........2½ **8**
3680[4] My Mariam **(90)***(81) (CREgerton)* 2-8-13 JReid(18) (lw: chsd ldrs far side over 5f)........s.h **9**
3639[4] Marjaana (IRE) **(81)***(68) (PTWalwyn)* 2-8-4 WCarson(3) (chsd ldrs: rdn over 1f out: eased whn btn fnl f)........1½ **10**
3553[9] Toffee **(71)***(54) (JRFanshawe)* 2-7-5 (3)ow1 NVarley(5) (prom tl wknd fnl 2f)........1¼ **11**
3495* Prima Volta **(80)***(64) (RHannon)* 2-8-3 MRoberts(15) (prom tl wknd 2f out: eased whn btn) ..s.h **12**
3315[3] Baltic Dream (USA) **(81)***(64) (KRBurke)* 2-8-4 MFenton(6) (hld up mid div: swtchd far side 2f out: wknd qckly appr fnl f)........nk **13**
3432[9] Ancestral Jane **(70)***(53) (MrsJRRamsden)* 2-7-7 JLowe(17) (m.n.s)........nk **14**
3387[5] React **(98)***(81) (WJarvis)* 2-9-7 LDettori(8) (lw: hld up mid div: effrt 2f out: no imp)........hd **15**
3736[3] Film Buff **(70)***(52) (BWHills)* 2-7-7 GBardwell(2) (chsd ldrs: rdn over 2f out: sn wknd)........nk **16**
3558[5] Auriga **(78)***(56) (IABalding)* 2-8-1 PaulEddery(12) (a in rr)........1½ **17**
3647* Angel Chimes **(70)***(47)*(Fav)*(JEBanks)* 2-7-7 NCarlisle(13) (a in rr)........¾ **18**
LONG HANDICAP Toffee 7-5 Film Buff 7-5

4/1 Angel Chimes, **5/1** Prima Volta, **15/2** React, **11/1** Ancestral Jane (6/1-12/1), **12/1** PACIFIC GROVE, Tabriz, Amanita, **14/1** Rumpipumpy, Baltic Dream (USA), Frezeliere, Marjaana (IRE), **16/1** Toffee, Film Buff, **20/1** Expensive Taste, Astuti (IRE), Lyzia (IRE), Auriga, My Mariam, CSF £162.99 CT £2,999.01 TOTE £13.90: £3.20 £4.30 £12.60 £4.70 (£166.20) Trio £457.80 OWNER Elite Racing Club (WHATCOMBE) BRED Tarworth Bloodstock Investments Ltd 18 Rn
1m 26.96 (3.26) SF: 48/48/53/38/46/36/41/40/44/31/17/27/27/16/44/15/19/10

3868

E.B.F. SOLTYKOFF MAIDEN STKS (2-Y.O C & G) (Class D)
£5,845.00 (£1,750.00: £840.00: £385.00)
1m (Rowley) Stalls: High GOING minus 0.05 sec per fur (G) 4-45 (4-47)

Helicon (IRE) *(95+) (HRACecil)* 2-8-11 MJKinane(16) (neat: dwlt: hld up & bhd: hdwy 2f out: led ins fnl f: r.o wl)........— **1**
2283[3] Committal (IRE) *(93)*(Fav)*(JHMGosden)* 2-8-11 LDettori(8) (lw: led tl ins fnl f: rdn & no ex) 1 **2**
Sapiston *(92+) (DRLoder)* 2-8-11 DHolland(2) (w'like: leggy: s.s: hld up: hdwy over 2f out: jnd ldr ent fnl f: kpt on one pce nr fin)........¾ **3**
Shaamit (IRE) *(88+) (WJHaggas)* 2-8-11 MHills(1) (leggy: scope: s.i.s: hdwy ½-wy: ev ch 1f out: unable qckn)........2 **4**
Athenry *(87) (JPearce)* 2-8-11 GBardwell(14) (w'like: leggy: chsd ldrs: kpt on ins fnl f: nrst fin)........½ **5**

Palamon (USA) *(86) (RCharlton)* 2-8-11 KDarley(7) (w'like: s.i.s: sn wnt prom: ev ch tl one pce appr fnl f) ....nk 6
Orinoco River (USA) *(85) (PWChapple-Hyam)* 2-8-11 MRoberts(4) (w'like: hdwy over 3f out: one pce appr fnl f) ....½ 7
3663[18] Spillo *(84+) (LMCumani)* 2-8-11 JWeaver(13) (nvr nrr) ....½ 8
State Theatre (IRE) *(80+) (PWChapple-Hyam)* 2-8-11 JReid(18) (w'like: leggy: in tch: rdn over 2f out: nvr nr ldrs) 2 9
3436[4] Energy Man *(74) (JRFanshawe)* 2-8-11 DHarrison(12) (prom over 5f) 3 10
Lydhurst (USA) *(74) (DRLoder)* 2-8-8 (3) DRMcCabe(17) (w'like: scope: prom tl wknd wl over 1f out) ....hd 11
Chief Mouse *(72) (RCharlton)* 2-8-11 PaulEddery(10) (wl grwn: bit bkwd: sn rdn along: a in rr) 1 12
3617[6] Ela-Yie-Mou (IRE) *(72) (LMCumani)* 2-8-11 TQuinn(3) (lw: w ldr 5f: sn lost tch) ....s.h 13
Mr Speculator *(65) (PAKelleway)* 2-8-11 MWigham(9) (w'like: scope: nvr nr ldrs) 3½ 14
3592[13] Go With The Wind *(63) (MBell)* 2-8-11 MFenton(6) (m.n.s) ....¾ 15
Billaddie *(63) (RBoss)* 2-8-11 WRyan(19) (cmpt: scope: a in rr) ....nk 16
Tomba La Bomba (USA) *(62) (PAKelleway)* 2-8-11 MRimmer(15) (wl grwn: bkwd: m.n.s) ....½ 17
3617[4] Galway Blade *(56) (APJarvis)* 2-8-11 JTate(11) (lw: a bhd) 3 18
1913[7] Sign From Heaven *(50) (NCWright)* 2-8-11 RPrice(5) (bkwd: chsd ldrs 5f: sn wknd) 3 19
3536[4] Mushtak (USA) *(47) (MajorWRHern)* 2-8-11 WCarson(20) (lw: nvr bttr than mid div: lost tch fnl 2f) 1½ 20

9/4 Committal (IRE), **4/1** State Theatre (IRE) (5/2-9/2), **7/1** HELICON (IRE) (4/1-8/1), Mushtak (USA), **12/1** Sapiston (7/1-14/1), Palamon (USA) (8/1-14/1), Chief Mouse (8/1-16/1), Spillo (op 6/1), **14/1** Ela-Yie-Mou (IRE) (8/1-16/1), **16/1** Orinoco River (USA), Energy Man, **20/1** Lydhurst (USA), Shaamit (IRE), **25/1** Go With The Wind, Galway Blade, **33/1** Mr Speculator, Sign From Heaven, Tomba La Bomba (USA), **50/1** Billaddie, Athenry, CSF £26.32 TOTE £6.30: £2.70 £1.40 £8.50 (£7.40) Trio £95.90 OWNER Sheikh Mohammed (NEWMARKET) BRED Sheikh Mohammed bin Rashid al Maktoum 20 Rn

1m 40.5 (3.50) SF: 55/53/52/48/47/46/45/44/40/34/34/32/32/25/23/23/22/16/10/7

T/Jkpt: Not won; £4,551.50 to Salisbury 27/9/95. T/Plpt: £133.80 (209.01 Tckts). T/Qdpt: £162.20 (1.3 Tckts). IM

3566-FOLKESTONE (R-H)
Wednesday September 27th (Soft)

WEATHER: sunny WIND: str half bhd

3869 STEVE MARSH BENEFIT MAIDEN AUCTION STKS (I) (2-Y.O) (Class F)
£2,947.40 (£816.40: £390.20)
6f 189y Stalls: High GOING: 0.49 sec per fur (GS) 1-50 (1-51)

Salmis *(80) (JRFanshawe)* 2-7-10 (3) NVarley(8) (neat: hdwy over 3f out: 5th st: led over 1f out: rdn: r.o wl) ....— 1
3663[8] Missile *(83) (WJHaggas)* 2-8-5 RMcGhin(5) (hdwy over 4f out: led 3f out tl over 1f out: unable qckn) 1¼ 2
3626[9] Abundant *(68) (BGubby)* 2-8-4 WWoods(4) (lw: rdn & hdwy over 1f out: r.o) 6 3
3672[4] Trojan Risk *(61)*(Fav)*(GLewis)* 2-8-4 PaulEddery(10) (lw: 4th st: one pce fnl 2f) 3 4
Apicella *(61) (RBoss)* 2-8-4 WRyan(7) (neat: s.i.s: hdwy over 1f out: nvr nrr) ....s.h 5
3644[3] Addie Pray (IRE) *(51) (MAJarvis)* 2-8-0 PRobinson(3) (lw: led 4f: 2nd st: wknd over 1f out) .2½ 6
3628[8] Rowlandsons Charm (IRE) **(65)***(43) (GLMoore)* 2-7-10 TWilliams(1) (lw: 3rd st: wknd over 1f out) 2 7
3643[8] Temptress *(36) (PTWalwyn)* 2-7-13v DaleGibson(2) (bhd fnl 2f) 4 8
3746[7] Gee Gee Tee *(22) (JAkehurst)* 2-8-3 CRutter(9) (b: lw: 5th whn hmpd & lost pl over 4f out)....8 9
Music In Motion *(12) (PHowling)* 2-7-12 FNorton(6) (neat: bkwd: a bhd) 2 10
3628[4] Daffodil Express (IRE) *(4) (MJRyan)* 2-7-5 (5) MBaird(11) (prom over 3f: 6th st) 2½ 11

11/8 Trojan Risk, **7/2** Addie Pray (IRE), **5/1** Missile (10/1-9/2), **11/2** Abundant (5/2-6/1), **16/1** SALMIS, **20/1** Daffodil Express (IRE), Rowlandsons Charm (IRE), **33/1** Apicella, Gee Gee Tee, Music In Motion, Temptress, CSF £89.12 TOTE £18.20: £4.90 £1.10 £3.50 (£15.40) Trio £63.60 OWNER Sally Vere Nicoll, Dexa'tex and Partners (NEWMARKET) BRED The Overbury Stud 11 Rn

1m 28.3 (6.70) SF: 43/46/31/24/24/14/6/-/-/-/-

3870 STEVE MARSH BENEFIT MAIDEN AUCTION STKS (II) (2-Y.O) (Class F)
£2,922.20 (£809.20: £386.60)
6f 189y Stalls: High GOING: 0.49 sec per fur (GS) 2-20 (2-20)

3644[2] **Lovely Prospect** *(76)*(Fav)*(RGuest)* 2-8-2 PaulEddery(4) (lw: 2nd st: led over 2f out: r.o wl)— 1

3427[5] Zdenka **(59)***(71) (MBlanshard)* 2-7-6 (7) MartinDwyer(10) (4th st: rdn over 2f out: r.o) 1 2
1968[2] Singoalla (IRE) **(73)***(68)*(Fav)*(JLDunlop)* 2-7-13 WCarson(5) (led over 5f: unable qckn) 1¼ 3
3525[W] Eurobox Boy *(71) (APJarvis)* 2-8-2 JTate(3) (cmpt: lw: s.s: 6th st: hdwy over 1f out: 4th whn nt clr run wl ins fnl f) ....hd 4
3779[6] Quality (IRE) **(90)***(70) (WAO'Gorman)* 2-8-6 EmmaO'Gorman(2) (5th st: one pce fnl 2f) 1¾ 5
3523[2] Kings Harmony (IRE) *(68) (PJMakin)* 2-8-5 RCochrane(1) (3rd st: wknd over 1f out) ....¾ 6
3711[13] Delaunay (IRE) **(72)***(56) (RHannon)* 2-8-7 JFEgan(6) (lw: bhd fnl 4f) 6 7
Double Check (IRE) *(43) (MJohnston)* 2-7-9 NCarlisle(7) (w'like: lw: s.s: a bhd) ....½ 8
1690[10] Matthias Mystique *(44) (MissBSanders)* 2-8-0 (3)ow4 SSanders(9) (bhd fnl 3f) 1¼ 9

2/1 LOVELY PROSPECT, Singoalla (IRE) (5/4-85/40), **9/2** Kings Harmony (IRE) (op 3/1), **10/1** Zdenka (op 6/1), Quality (IRE) (op 6/1), Double Check (IRE) (op 5/1), **25/1** Eurobox Boy, Delaunay (IRE), **33/1** Matthias Mystique, CSF £21.81 TOTE £3.00: £1.50 £3.50 £1.30 (£24.40) Trio £18.70 OWNER Mr R. Axford (NEWMARKET) BRED Green Park Investments Ltd 9 Rn

1m 28.9 (7.30) SF: 38/33/30/33/32/30/18/5/6

3871 KENT CHAMBER CLAIMING STKS (3-Y.O+) (Class F) £3,300.20 (£917.20: £440.60) 1m 1f 149y Stalls: High GOING: 0.49 sec per fur (GS) 2-50 (2-52)

3619[6] **Chief of Staff (63)***(78) (JPearce)* 6-9-5 GBardwell(2) (hdwy over 3f out: led over 2f out: rdn out) ....— 1
3605[2] Another Fiddle (IRE) **(64)***(64)*(Fav)*(RAkehurst)* 5-8-6 (3) SSanders(14) (lw: 6th st: hrd rdn over 4f out: r.o ins fnl f) 2½ 2
3344[4] Equilibrium **(47)***(58) (JWHills)* 3-7-12 TWilliams(7) (a.p: led 4f out tl over 2f out: 2nd st: hrd rdn over 1f out: unable qckn) ....nk 3
3658[8] Latin Leader **(62)***(63) (CREgerton)* 5-8-10b CRutter(9) (3rd st: hrd rdn over 1f out: one pce) ...¾ 4
3082[10] Captain Marmalade **(42)***(56) (DTThom)* 6-8-11 WWoods(1) (b: lw: hdwy over 1f out: nvr nrr) ..5 5
3658[13] Magication **(28)***(42) (CNAllen)* 5-8-0 NCarlisle(8) (lw: hdwy over 1f out: nvr nrr) 2 6
3076[5] Sparkling Roberta **(37)***(45) (MDIUsher)* 4-8-1 (7) CAdamson(4) (hld up: rdn over 2f out: sn wknd) 3 7
3529[3] Rockstine (IRE) **(42)***(43) (PMitchell)* 4-8-10v PaulEddery(10) (b.hind: nvr nr to chal) 2 8
2450[9] Swinging Tich **(40)***(33) (ICampbell)* 6-8-0 DaleGibson(6) (nvr nrr) ....hd 9
Absolutely Fact (USA) **(47)***(29) (FCalaerts,Belgium)* 5-8-7 RCochrane(15) (4th st: wknd wl over 1f out) 7 10
2638[5] Anjomajasa *(34) (JFfitch-Heyes)* 3-8-8 RPrice(5) (bhd fnl 3f) 1 11
Happy Hostage **(67)***(22) (JWhite)* 4-8-12 (5) LNewton(13) (lw: bhd fnl 4f) 9 12
Amir's Blue (BEL) *(9) (FCalaerts,Belgium)* 4-8-4 (5) MBaird(11) (led over 5f: wknd over 2f out) 3 13
3679[16] Khalyani (IRE) **(67)** *(RRowe)* 5-8-7 PRobinson(3) (prom 5f) 13 14

9/4 Another Fiddle (IRE), **6/1** CHIEF OF STAFF, Absolutely Fact (USA) (4/1-7/1), **7/1** Latin Leader (9/2-8/1), Happy Hostage (10/1-16/1), **12/1** Rockstine (IRE) (op 8/1), **14/1** Amir's Blue (BEL) (10/1-20/1), **16/1** Equilibrium, **20/1** Captain Marmalade, Anjomajasa, **25/1** Sparkling Roberta, **33/1** Swinging Tich, Magication, Khalyani (IRE), CSF £19.56 TOTE £6.40: £2.20 £1.50 £2.90 (£7.10) Trio £22.20 OWNER The Exclusive Partnership (NEWMARKET) BRED Lord Halifax 14 Rn

2m 9.5 (11.80) SF: 43/29/17/28/21/7/10/8/-/-/-/-/-/-

WEIGHT FOR AGE 3yo-6lb

3872 SCOTTISH EQUITABLE LIMITED STKS (0-60) (3-Y.O+) (Class F) £3,350.60 (£931.60: £447.80) 1m 1f 149y Stalls: High GOING: 0.49 sec (GS) 3-20 (3-21)

3770[3] **Polly Peculiar (60)***(71) (BSmart)* 4-8-13 JTate(12) (b.hind: swtchd lft over 4f out: hdwy over 2f out: 6th st: led 1f out: drvn out) ....— 1
3677[13] Super High **(56)***(75) (PHowling)* 3-9-0 RCochrane(9) (hdwy over 2f out: 5th st: ev ch 1f out: unable qckn) 1¾ 2
3634[2] Tonka **(60)***(71) (PJMakin)* 3-8-9 (3) SSanders(6) (hld up: led 3f out to 1f out: one pce) 1½ 3
2687[7] Uncharted Waters **(53)***(50) (CACyzer)* 4-8-11 DBiggs(10) (hdwy over 1f out: nvr nrr) 8 4
3657[10] Tajar (USA) **(60)***(47) (DMorley)* 3-8-10 WCarson(7) (lw: nt clr run over 3f out: 4th st: wknd over 1f out) 5 5
3511[9] Can Can Charlie **(55)***(44) (JPearce)* 5-9-4 PaulEddery(13) (nvr nr to chal) 3 6
3726[7] Owdbetts (IRE) **(58)***(40) (GLMoore)* 3-8-2 (7) ALakeman(3) (hdwy 7f out: wknd over 2f out) ....¾ 7
3384[8] Bold Look **(57)***(36) (PWHarris)* 4-9-4 WNewnes(8) (s.s: nvr nrr) 4 8
2980[7] Song of Years (IRE) **(56)***(26) (JWHills)* 4-8-11 CRutter(15) (prom over 2f) 1¾ 9
3403* Harvey White (IRE) **(56)***(30) (JPearce)* 3-8-12 GBardwell(1) (bhd fnl 3f) 2 10
3128[7] Almasi (IRE) **(59)***(21) (CFWall)* 3-8-0 (5) LNewton(2) (lw: 3rd st: wknd over 2f out) 1½ 11
2974[6] Biya (IRE) **(60)***(9) (MJohnston)* 3-8-10 TWilliams(14) (lw: prom over 6f) 10 12

2319[7] My Brave Girl **(59)** (Fav)*(HRACecil)* 3-8-5 WRyan(5) (bhd fnl 3f) 15 **13**
3641[16] Scorpius **(60)** *(CNWilliams)* 5-9-2b PRobinson(11) (b: b.off hind: lw: led over 6f: 2nd st: wknd qckly over 2f out: t.o) 30 **14**

4/1 My Brave Girl, **9/2** POLLY PECULIAR (op 3/1), **13/2** Tonka, **15/2** Biya (IRE), **8/1** Harvey White (IRE) (5/1-9/1), Tajar (USA), **10/1** Scorpius, **12/1** Can Can Charlie (op 8/1), **14/1** Bold Look (op 8/1), Almasi (IRE) (6/1-16/1), **16/1** Owdbetts (IRE), **20/1** Song of Years (IRE), **25/1** Super High, Uncharted Waters, CS £105.25 TOTE £5.10: £2.20 £5.40 £2.60 (£66.80) Trio £146.60; £55.76 to 28/9/95 OWNER Mr B. Smart (LAMBOURN) BRED Aston Park Stud 14 Rn
2m 8.8 (11.10) SF: 43/41/37/22/13/16/6/8/-/-/-/-/-/-
WEIGHT FOR AGE 3yo-6lb

OFFICIAL EXPLANATION **My Brave Girl: lost her action five furlongs out and was never travelling thereafter.**
Scorpius: choked during the race and finished distressed.

3873

E.B.F. ASHFORD MAIDEN STKS (2-Y.O) (Class D) £4,664.00 (£1,034.00: £1,034.00: £308.00) **6f** Stalls: Low GOING minus 0.35 sec per fur (F) 3-50 (3-51)

3404[4] **Sylva Paradise (IRE) (83)***(77) (CEBrittain)* 2-9-0 WRyan(5) (lw: w ldr: led wl over 1f out: rdn out) ....— **1**
3604[4] Keiko *(67) (JHMGosden)* 2-8-9 PaulEddery(10) (a.p: rdn over 2f out: r.o ins fnl f) 2 **2**
3663[15] School Boy *(72) (CNAllen)* 2-9-0 StephenDavies(6) (lw: led over 4f: unable qckn fnl f) ....d.h **2**
3733[7] Courting Danger *(56) (DRGandolfo)* 2-9-0 AMcGlone(4) (hld up: rdn over 2f out) 6 **4**
3553[4] Stronz (IRE) **(72)***(45) (RAkehurst)* 2-8-11 (3) SSanders(9) (a.p: rdn over 2f out: wknd over 1f out) 4 **5**
Alakhluki *(33) (GLewis)* 2-8-9 CRutter(1) (w'like: bit bkwd: outpcd) 2½ **6**
2767[2] Raed *(33)*(Fav)*(PTWalwyn)* 2-9-0 WCarson(7) (lw: a.p: rdn over 3f out: eased whn btn over 1f out) 2 **7**
3644[9] Classic Defence (IRE) *(31) (JWHills)* 2-9-0 PRobinson(3) (lw: a bhd) ....¾ **8**
Steamroller Stanly *(CACyzer)* 2-9-0 DBiggs(8) (str: scope: swvd rt s: a bhd) 15 **9**

1/2 Raed, **9/2** Keiko (op 3/1), **9/1** Stronz (IRE) (9/2-10/1), **12/1** SYLVA PARADISE (IRE) (op 9/2), **25/1** Classic Defence (IRE), Alakhluki, Courting Danger, **33/1** School Boy, Steamroller Stanly, CSF SP & SB £121.66, SP & K £31.03 TOTE £21.30: £2.50 SB £6.60, K £1.40 (SP & SB £272.10, SP & K £21.00) Trio £149.20; £189.25 to Newmarket 28/9/95 OWNER Eddy Grimstead Honda Ltd (NEWMARKET) BRED Mrs J. Costelloe 9 Rn 1m 13.6 (1.90) SF: 42/32/37/21/10/-/-/-/-

OFFICIAL EXPLANATION **Raed: no explanation offered**

3874

KENT ENTERPRISE OFFICE H'CAP (0-65) (3-Y.O+) (Class F) £3,375.80 (£938.80: £451.40) **6f** Stalls: Low GOING minus 0.35 sec per fur (F) 4-20 (4-22)

3545[7] **Oare Sparrow (64)***(75) (PTWalwyn)* 5-10-0 PaulEddery(14) (racd far side: chsd ldr: led over 2f out: pushed out) ....— **1**
3783[4] Petraco (IRE) **(62)***(72)*(Fav)*(NASmith)* 7-9-12 MRimmer(16) (racd far side: led over 3f: hrd rdn fnl f: r.o) ....½ **2**
3624[24] Charnwood Queen **(58)***(57) (RWArmstrong)* 3-9-5 RPrice(11) (lw: a.p: rdn over 2f out: unable qckn) 4 **3**
3624[2] Poyle Jezebelle **(53)***(47) (MBlanshard)* 4-9-3 StephenDavies(9) (hdwy over 2f out: one pce) ..2 **4**
3771[18] Fascination Waltz **(64)***(58) (JJSheehan)* 8-9-11 (3) PMcCabe(5) (lw: nvr nr to chal) ....s.h **5**
3771[9] Shepherd Market (IRE) **(61)***(54) (DAWilson)* 4-9-6 (5) LNewton(12) (lw: no hdwy fnl 2f) ....s.h **6**
3293[5] Dashing Dancer (IRE) **(59)***(50) (RAkehurst)* 4-9-6 (3) SSanders(1) (lw: spd over 4f) ....¾ **7**
3751[10] Pride of Hayling (IRE) **(55)***(30) (PRHedger)* 4-9-2 (3) NVarley(10) (lw: a mid div) 6 **8**
3764[13] Moujeeb (USA) **(53)***(28) (PatMitchell)* 5-9-3v PRobinson(7) (lw: nvr nrr) ....s.h **9**
3522[9] Tyrian Purple (IRE) **(58)***(32) (TJNaughton)* 7-9-3b(5) JDSmith(13) (racd far side: outpcd) ....½ **10**
3681[15] Face the Future **(60)***(33) (LJHolt)* 6-9-10b AMcGlone(4) (a bhd) ....½ **11**
1792[5] Canary Falcon **(62)***(31) (JohnBerry)* 4-9-12 VSmith(6) (b: lw: outpcd) 1¼ **12**
3632[W] Norling (IRE) **(53)***(14) (KOCunningham-Brown)* 5-9-3 RCochrane(8) (lw: prom 3f) 3 **13**
3751[15] Great Hall **(59)***(15) (PDCundell)* 6-9-9b WNewnes(15) (racd far side: s.s: a wl bhd) 2 **14**
3542[4] Barriyah **(58)***(9) (HThomsonJones)* 3-9-5 WRyan(2) (lw: bhd fnl 3f) 2 **15**
3519[13] Dark Menace **(59)** *(SMellor)* 3-8-13b(7) ADaly(3) (prom 4f) 8 **16**

5/1 Petraco (IRE), **11/2** Dashing Dancer (IRE), **13/2** Poyle Jezebelle, **15/2** Norling (IRE), **8/1** Barriyah, **10/1** Charnwood Queen, Face the Future, **12/1** Great Hall, **14/1** Moujeeb (USA), OARE SPARROW, **16/1** Tyrian Purple (IRE), Canary Falcon, Pride of Hayling (IRE), Shepherd Market (IRE), **33/1** Fascination Waltz, Dark Menace, CSF £84.68 CT £696.41 TOTE £16.30: £3.00 £1.20 £4.70 £1.50 (£42.30) Trio £50.80 OWNER Mrs Henry Keswick (LAMBOURN) BRED Mrs Henry Keswick 16 Rn 1m 13.6 (1.90) SF: 55/52/34/27/38/34/30/10/8/12/13/11/-/-/-/-
WEIGHT FOR AGE 3yo-3lb

3875

ROBERTSBRIDGE H'CAP (0-70) (3-Y.O) (Class E) £3,817.00 (£1,144.00: £550.00: £253.00) **1m 4f** Stalls: High GOING: 0.49 sec per fur (GS) 4-50 (4-52)

3759[4] **Slapy Dam (49)***(65) (JMackie)* 3-7-13 (3)ow1 SSanders(2) (stdy hdwy 5f out: 5th st: led wl over 1f out: sn clr: r.o wl) — 1
3705[11] Medway (IRE) **(55)***(63) (MHTompkins)* 3-8-8 PRobinson(6) (lw: hdwy over 3f out: 6th st: hrd rdn over 1f out: unable qckn) 7 2
3318[4] Euro Forum **(54)***(61) (GLMoore)* 3-8-7 PaulEddery(5) (lw: 3rd st: hrd rdn over 1f out: one pce) ½ 3
3641[W] Fen Terrier **(54)***(61) (WJHaggas)* 3-8-7 RMcGhin(15) (lw: 2nd st: ev ch wl over 1f out: one pce) s.h 4
3526[8] Nautical Jewel **(48)***(55) (MDIUsher)* 3-8-1 RPrice(16) (hld up: led 3f out to wl over 1f out: one pce) nk 5
3497[15] Victory Team (IRE) **(64)***(51) (JRFanshawe)* 3-9-0 (3) NVarley(11) (lw: 4th st: wknd 2f out) 15 6
La Brief **(54)***(40) (MJRyan)* 3-8-2 (5) MBaird(9) (hdwy over 1f out: nvr nrr) ½ 7
774[4] Imlak (IRE) **(65)***(48)*(Fav)*(DMorley)* 3-9-4 WCarson(4) (lw: nvr nrr) 2 8
3294[11] Tap On Tootsie **(49)***(32) (ICampbell)* 3-8-2 DBiggs(1) (lw: nvr nrr) s.h 9
3808[21] Good (IRE) **(45)***(27) (DTThom)* 3-7-12 FNorton(3) (nvr nrr) 1 10
3501[7] Shining Dancer **(60)***(39) (SDow)* 3-8-6 (7) ADaly(14) (a mid div) 2½ 11
3395[3] First Bite (IRE) **(67)***(42) (JLDunlop)* 3-9-6 RCochrane(17) (b.nr fore: swtg: a mid div) 3 12
3531[15] Keen To The Last (FR) **(67)***(38) (GHarwood)* 3-9-6 CRutter(7) (lw: a mid div) 2½ 13
1979[18] Bakheta **(54)***(17) (KTIvory)* 3-8-2 (5) LNewton(12) (b: b.hind: prom 9f) 6 14
3571[8] Lucky Coin **(68)***(21) (CEBrittain)* 3-9-7 WRyan(18) (led 9f) 8 15
3756[9] My Dutch Girl **(54)** *(MissBSanders)* 3-8-7 WNewnes(10) (prom over 5f) 15 16
3475[11] Zuno Flyer (USA) **(43)** *(GLewis)* 3-7-10 GBardwell(8) (prom 8f) 2 17
3722[2] Try Omnipotent **(42)** *(CNAllen)* 3-7-9 NCarlisle(13) (b: bhd fnl 5f) 15 18

7/2 Imlak (IRE) (6/1-3/1), **11/2** SLAPY DAM, **8/1** First Bite (IRE), **9/1** Fen Terrier, Euro Forum (op 6/1), **10/1** Lucky Coin, Keen To The Last (FR), Try Omnipotent, **12/1** Victory Team (IRE), Medway (IRE), **16/1** Shining Dancer, La Brief, Nautical Jewel, Zuno Flyer (USA), **20/1** Tap On Tootsie, Bakheta, **25/1** My Dutch Girl, **33/1** Good (IRE), CSF £77.72 CT £576.68 TOTE £7.00: £1.50 £3.90 £2.50 £2.40 (£79.20) Trio £111.60 OWNER Rose And Crown, Boylestone (CHURCH BROUGHTON) BRED Hesmonds Stud Ltd 18 Rn
2m 44.5 (13.30) SF: 37/35/33/33/27/23/12/20/4/-/11/14/10/-/-/-/-/-

3876

LEVY BOARD MAIDEN APPRENTICE STKS (3-Y.O+) (Class F) £2,947.40 (£816.40: £390.20)
1m 4f Stalls: High GOING: 0.49 sec per fur (GS) 5-20 (5-21)

3277[2] **Edan Heights (68)***(77)*(Fav)*(SDow)* 3-8-8 ADaly(5) (lw: a.p: led 3f out: r.o wl) — 1
3754[4] Jagellon (USA) *(76) (WRMuir)* 4-9-2 MartinDwyer(2) (plld hrd: stdy hdwy 5f out: 3rd st: chsd wnr over 1f out: r.o) ½ 2
Couchant (IRE) **(62)***(68) (JWhite)* 4-9-2 RHavlin(11) (lw: 6th st: hrd rdn over 1f out: one pce) 6 3
3571[7] Sharazi (USA) **(60)***(66) (DJSCosgrove)* 4-9-2b DGibbs(9) (lw: 4th st: hrd rdn over 1f out: one pce) 2 4
357[3] Anjou *(63) (JPearce)* 3-8-1 (7) MNutter(8) (5th st: wknd over 1f out) 2 5
Abinger *(60) (LadyHerries)* 3-8-1 (7) RSmith(3) (bit bkwd: s.s: nvr nr to chal) 2½ 6
1950[3] Nivasha **(37)***(52) (RPCHoad)* 3-8-3 GMitchell(1) (hdwy 5f out: 2nd st: wknd over 1f out) 1¾ 7
1189[8] Sails Legend **(43)***(31) (MrsMELong)* 4-8-9 (7) TField(10) (bit bkwd: prom 8f) 20 8
3653[17] Bagby Boy *(30) (PRHedger)* 3-8-3 (5) ALakeman(4) (led 9f) ¾ 9
3747[16] Morning Master *(20) (RMFlower)* 3-8-8b CAdamson(6) (bhd fnl 4f) 7 10
3573[8] Tapestry Rose *(JCPoulton)* 4-8-8 (3) GFaulkner(7) (a bhd) 13 11

Evens EDAN HEIGHTS, **100/30** Jagellon (USA), **11/2** Anjou (5/1-8/1), **10/1** Abinger (5/1-12/1), Sharazi (USA), **16/1** Couchant (IRE), **20/1** Nivasha, **33/1** Sails Legend, **50/1** Bagby Boy, Morning Master, Tapestry Rose, CSF £5.24 TOTE £2.50: £1.50 £1.80 £1.20 (£1.50) Trio £26.30 OWNER Mr T. R. Mountain (EPSOM) BRED T. R. Mountain 11 Rn 2m 47.5 (16.30) SF: 24/31/23/21/10/7/-/-/-/-/-
WEIGHT FOR AGE 3yo-8lb
T/Plpt: £146.70 (65.85 Tckts). T/Qdpt: £32.50 (1.1 Tckts). AK

3410-NEWCASTLE (L-H)
Wednesday September 27th (Good)
All races hand-timed
WEATHER: sunny WIND: str half bhd

3877 E.B.F. POLWARTH MAIDEN STKS (2-Y.O) (Class D) £3,615.00 (£1,095.00: £535.00: £255.00) **6f** Stalls: High GOING: 0.12 sec per fur (G) 2-00 (2-01)

Meldorf *(87+)*(Fav)*(DRLoder)* 2-9-0 KDarley(9) (w'like: leggy: trckd ldrs: shkn up & qcknd to ld jst ins fnl f: pushed clr) — 1
3662³ Hoh Returns (IRE) **(87)***(76) (MBell)* 2-9-0 GHind(5) (lw: trckd ldrs: led over 2f out tl jst ins fnl f: no ch w wnr) 4 2
3625⁶ Time of Night (USA) **(77)***(55) (RGuest)* 2-8-9 DHolland(10) (a chsng ldrs: one pce fnl 2f) 6 3
1722³ River Tern *(57) (JBerry)* 2-9-0 JCarroll(11) (hld up: hdwy to trck ldrs ½-wy: kpt on fnl 2f: n.d) 1¼ 4
3625¹⁷ Gilling Dancer (IRE) *(48) (PCalver)* 2-9-0 MBirch(7) (sn chsng ldrs: outpcd fnl 2f) 3½ 5
3666⁹ Seattle Alley (USA) *(48+) (MrsJRRamsden)* 2-9-0 KFallon(2) (bit bkwd: hld up & bhd: stdy hdwy 2f out: styd on towards fin) s.h 6
3647⁴ Answers-To-Thomas **(67)***(46) (JMJefferson)* 2-9-0 TIves(8) (led tl over 2f out: sn wknd) ½ 7
3806¹² Dona Filipa *(39) (MissLCSiddall)* 2-8-9 DeanMcKeown(4) (outpcd fr ½-wy) 1 8
3784⁶ Kenilworth Dancer *(37) (MrsMReveley)* 2-9-0 NConnorton(6) (nvr wnt pce) 2½ 9
3415⁷ Petrefuz (IRE) **(50)***(29) (EWeymes)* 2-9-0 ACulhane(1) (plld hrd: trckd ldrs tl lost pl ½-wy: hung rt & sn bhd) 3 10
3720⁴ Simply Silly (IRE) **(59)***(13) (WLBarker)* 2-8-9 LCharnock(3) (chsd ldrs tl lost pl over 2f out) 4 11

11/10 MELDORF (4/5-5/4), **2/1** Hoh Returns (IRE), **9/1** Time of Night (USA), **10/1** Answers-To-Thomas, **12/1** Seattle Alley (USA), **16/1** River Tern, **20/1** Kenilworth Dancer, **25/1** Simply Silly (IRE), **33/1** Gilling Dancer (IRE), **50/1** Petrefuz (IRE), Dona Filipa, CSF £4.11 TOTE £2.10: £1.10 £1.10 £1.80 (£1.70) Trio £5.90 OWNER Sheikh Mohammed (NEWMARKET) BRED Mrs S. M. Sands and M. Yiapatos 11 Rn 1m 17.0 (5.50) SF: 32/21/-/2/-/-/-/-/-/-/-

OFFICIAL EXPLANATION Seattle Alley (USA): his jockey felt that the colt was likely to become unbalanced if subjected to great pressure.

3878 JARROW SPRINT H'CAP (0-85) (3-Y.O+) (Class D) £4,011.80 (£1,216.40: £595.20: £284.60) **5f** Stalls: High GOING: 0.12 sec per fur (G) 2-30 (2-33)

3637⁷ **Twice as Sharp (81)***(90) (PWHarris)* 3-9-10 GHind(6) (lw: mde all far side: clr 2f out: drvn out) — 1
3748²² Here Comes a Star **(72)***(80) (JMCarr)* 7-9-3 ACulhane(4) (racd far side: hdwy over 1f out: styd on wl cl home) nk 2
1806² Coastal Bluff **(83)***(90) (TDBarron)* 3-9-12 KDarley(12) (hld up stands' side: gd hdwy over 1f out: styd on strly towards fin) nk 3
3632³ John O'Dreams **(51)***(50) (MrsALMKing)* 10-7-10 ow3 AGarth(19) (b: s.i.s: bhd on stands' side: hdwy over 1f out: styd on wl towards fin) 1½ 4
3783⁵ Silk Cottage **(58)***(60) (RMWhitaker)* 3-7-12 (3) DWright(20) (lw: led stands' side: hung bdly lft over 1f out: kpt on same pce) hd 5
3830² Craigie Boy **(53)***(55) (NBycroft)* 5-7-12b NKennedy(5) (racd far side: hdwy over 1f out: styd on nr fin) s.h 6
3748²⁰ Twice in Bundoran (IRE) **(51)***(53) (PSFelgate)* 4-7-10 AMackay(1) (racd far side: bhd: styd on wl appr fnl f: nt rch ldrs) s.h 7
3783⁸ Captain Carat **(64)***(65)*(Fav)*(MrsJRRamsden)* 4-8-9 KFallon(9) (hld up stands' side: effrt & swtchd lft over 1f out: styd on nr fin) nk 8
3667¹⁷ Giggleswick Girl **(64)***(62) (MRChannon)* 4-8-9 DHolland(13) (s.s: bhd stands' side tl hdwy fnl f) 1 9
3777⁷ Super Park **(73)***(70) (MHEasterby)* 3-9-2b MBirch(7) (chsd ldrs far side: rdn ½-wy: grad wknd) hd 10
3279¹⁰ Super Rocky **(76)***(70) (RBastiman)* 6-9-2 (5) HBastiman(17) (chsd ldrs stands' side: rdn 2f out: wknd appr fnl f) 1 11
3783¹⁶ Tenor **(60)***(54) (DNicholls)* 4-8-5 SDWilliams(15) (in tch stands' side: effrt over 1f out: sn wknd) hd 12
3715²⁰ Rich Glow **(67)***(58) (NBycroft)* 4-8-12 SMaloney(3) (racd far side: sme hdwy ½-wy: n.d) ¾ 13
3667²⁰ Ned's Bonanza **(70)***(56) (MDods)* 6-9-1 JCarroll(2) (chsd ldrs far side 3f: sn wknd) 1½ 14
3715³ Stolen Kiss (IRE) **(72)***(58) (MWEasterby)* 3-8-10b(5) PFessey(14) (lw: chsd ldr stands' side over 3f) nk 15
3777¹⁰ Local Heroine **(54)***(39) (JBerry)* 5-7-6b(7) BHalligan(16) (in tch stands' side tl wknd over 1f out) s.h 16

3717[21] French Grit (IRE) **(85)***(70) (MDods)* 3-10-0 JWeaver(11) (chsd ldrs stands' side tl wknd 2f out)....hd **17**
3748[13] Shadow Jury **(70)***(49) (DWChapman)* 5-9-1b LCharnock(18) (w ldrs stands' side to ½-wy: sn lost pl)....2 **18**
3649[4] Anytime Baby **(51)***(16) (PTDalton)* 3-7-8 ow1 JLowe(8) (swtchd rt s: sme hdwy stands' side ½-wy: sn wknd)....4 **19**
3640[6] Midnight Spell **(72)***(30) (MrsJCecil)* 3-9-1b TIves(10) (chsd ldrs stands' side tl rdn & wknd qckly 2f out)....2½ **20**

LONG HANDICAP Anytime Baby 6-12

5/1 Captain Carat, **6/1** Stolen Kiss (IRE), **7/1** Silk Cottage, **8/1** John O'Dreams, **10/1** Coastal Bluff, Craigie Boy, **11/1** TWICE AS SHARP, **12/1** Super Rocky, **14/1** Giggleswick Girl, Tenor, Midnight Spell, **16/1** Rich Glow, **20/1** Ned's Bonanza, French Grit (IRE), **25/1** Here Comes a Star, Local Heroine, Shadow Jury, **33/1** Twice in Bundoran (IRE), Super Park, **50/1** Anytime Baby, CSF £254.04 CT £2,615.35 TOTE £16.50: £3.90 £11.50 £2.20 £2.00 (£417.40) Trio £645.50; £818.24 to Newmarket 28/9/95 OWNER Formula Twelve (BERKHAMSTED) BRED R. and A. Craddock 20 Rn

61.7 secs (3.30) SF: 61/53/61/23/31/28/26/38/35/41/43/27/31/29/29/12/41/22/-/1

WEIGHT FOR AGE 3yo-2lb

3879

BOLLINGER CHAMPAGNE CHALLENGE SERIES GENTLEMENS' H'CAP (0-70) (3-Y.O+) (Class E) £3,209.80 (£972.40: £475.20: £226.60)
7f Stalls: Low GOING: 0.12 sec per fur (G) 3-00 (3-06)

3830[6] **Birchwood Sun (61)***(75)*(Fav)*(MDods)* 5-11-11b MrSSwiers(3) (hdwy far side over 2f out: led 1f out: drvn clr)....— **1**
3667[10] Murray's Mazda (IRE) **(43)***(41) (JLEyre)* 6-10-3 (4)ow7 MrRWakley(4) (trckd ldrs far side: chal 1f out: kpt on same pce)....4 **2**
3745[6] Teejay'n'aitch (IRE) **(45)***(43) (JSGoldie)* 3-10-1 (4) MrKSantana(6) (led far side to 1f out: one pce)....3 **3**
3841* Benjarong **(47)***(38)*(Fav)*(RMMcKellar)* 3-10-3 (4) 5x MrCAppleby(1) (hdwy far side over 2f out: styd on same pce fnl f)....3 **4**
3665[4] Chantry Bellini **(39)***(29) (MrsSMAustin)* 6-9-13 (4)ow1 MrAManners(7) (b: b.hind: lost pl ½-wy: styd on u.p appr fnl f)....s.h **5**
3275* Prime Property (IRE) **(38)***(23) (MWEasterby)* 3-9-12b MrJCulloty(2) (chsd ldrs far side: hrd rdn over 2f out: grad wknd)....2½ **6**
Blue Domain **(41)***(21) (MDods)* 4-10-1 (4)ow1 MrJDavies(5) (racd far side: hdwy over 2f out: nvr nr to chal)....2 **7**
2946[8] Twin Creeks **(52)***(32) (MDHammond)* 4-11-2 MrCBonner(8) (racd far side: in tch tl outpcd fnl 2f)....nk **8**
3750[9] Cheerful Groom (IRE) **(43)***(23) (JMackie)* 4-10-3 (4) MrKGreen(20) (in tch stands' side: hdwy over 2f out: styd on fnl f)....s.h **9**
3719[4] Miss Pigalle **(43)***(19) (MissLAPerratt)* 4-10-3b(4)ow2 MrJWeymes(17) (w ldrs stands' side: led 3f out tl over 1f out: sn wknd)....¾ **10**
2377[15] Corona Gold **(43)***(8) (JGFitzGerald)* 5-10-7 MrRHale(16) (led stands' side 4f: sn wknd)....6 **11**
3808[10] Legend Dulac (IRE) **(44)***(4) (JAHarris)* 6-10-8 MrRJohnson(10) (bolted gng to s: chsd ldrs far side tl wknd over 2f out)....2 **12**
3726[11] Aquiletta **(40)** *(CBBBooth)* 5-10-0 (4)ow2 MrSBrown(13) (racd stands' side: a bhd)....7 **13**
3762[2] Blaze of Oak (USA) **(64)***(6)*(Fav)*(WJHaggas)* 4-12-0 MrPPritchard-Gordon(18) (hld up stands' side: effrt & edgd lft over 2f out: no imp)....¾ **14**
3529[8] Langtonian **(30)** *(JLEyre)* 6-9-4v(4) MrRBarrett(19) (s.i.s: hdwy stands' side ½-wy: edgd lft: n.d)....s.h **15**
3504[2] My Godson **(41)** *(FJO'Mahony)* 5-10-1b(4) MrVLukaniuk(14) (chsd ldrs stands' side 4f: sn hmpd & wknd)....nk **16**
2753[8] General Gubbins **(55)** *(JHetherton)* 4-11-5 MrMHNaughton(11) (s.s: racd far side: a bhd)....1¼ **17**
3661[9] Passion Sunday **(35)** *(LRLloyd-James)* 4-9-9b(4) MrSRutherford(15) (w ldrs stands' side 4f: sn hmpd & wknd)....4 **18**
3726[9] Question Ali **(54)** *(JBerry)* 3-11-0 MrCWardThomas(12) (b.nr hind: swtchd lft s: racd far side: a in rr)....5 **19**

7/1 BIRCHWOOD SUN, Blaze of Oak (USA), Benjarong, **8/1** Prime Property (IRE), **9/1** Legend Dulac (IRE), **12/1** Teejay'n'aitch (IRE), Twin Creeks, **14/1** Corona Gold, Chantry Bellini, Miss Pigalle, Question Ali, My Godson, Langtonian, **16/1** Passion Sunday, Murray's Mazda (IRE), Cheerful Groom (IRE), General Gubbins, **25/1** Aquiletta, **33/1** Blue Domain, CSF £117.67 CT £1,257.77 TOTE £10.10: £3.30 £4.80 £8.30 £2.00 (£120.90) Trio £273.10; £196.23 to Newmarket 28/9/95 OWNER Mr A. G. Watson (DARLINGTON) BRED The Hall Stud Ltd 19 Rn

1m 32.3 (8.00) SF: 50/16/14/9/4/-/-/7/-/-/-/-/-/-/-/-/-/-/-

WEIGHT FOR AGE 3yo-4lb

3880
GATESHEAD CONDITIONS STKS (3-Y.O+) (Class C) £4,918.25 (£1,787.00: £868.50: £367.50) **5f** Stalls: High GOING: 0.12 sec per fur (G) 3-30 (3-30)

3777[5] **Takadou (IRE) (80)***(94?) (MissLCSiddall)* 4-9-4 JWeaver(1) (lw: hld up: stdy hdwy 2f out: styd on wl to ld ins fnl f: drvn out) — 1
3707[5] Lucky Parkes **(99)***(92) (JBerry)* 5-9-7 GHind(3) (led: qcknd over 1f out: hdd & no ex ins fnl f) 1½ 2
3550[7] Saint Express **(106)***(80)*(Fav)*(MrsMReveley)* 5-9-4 KDarley(4) (lw: chsd ldrs: hrd drvn 2f out: edgd rt & one pce 1f out) 3 3
3717[19] Palacegate Touch **(81)***(67) (JBerry)* 5-9-4b JCarroll(5) (trckd ldrs: effrt 2f out: hung lft & fnd nil) 4 4
1924[8] Musica **(79)***(36) (MRChannon)* 3-8-8 DHolland(2) (w ldr to ½-wy: sn wknd & eased) 7 5

4/7 Saint Express, **11/2** TAKADOU (IRE), **6/1** Lucky Parkes, **8/1** Palacegate Touch, Musica, CSF £31.47 TOTE £4.50: £2.10 £2.00 (£14.80) OWNER Mr F. Tyldesley (TADCASTER) BRED Woodford Stud and St. Simon Foundation 5 Rn 62.4 secs (4.00) SF: 44/41/29/16/-

WEIGHT FOR AGE 3yo-2lb

3881
E.B.F. HEBBURN MAIDEN STKS (2-Y.O) (Class D) £3,745.00 (£1,135.00: £555.00: £265.00) **7f** GOING: 0.12 sec per fur (G) 4-00 (4-02)

3663[5] **Insatiable (IRE)** *(78+)*(Fav)*(MRStoute)* 2-9-0 KDarley(3) (lw: trckd ldrs: nt clr run over 2f out: swtchd ins & qcknd to ld over 1f out: drvn out) — 1
3733[5] Diamond Beach *(69) (BWHills)* 2-9-0 DHolland(7) (trckd ldrs: ev ch over 1f out: kpt on same pce) 4 2
Magic Mill (IRE) *(66+) (FJO'Mahony)* 2-9-0 SDWilliams(2) (cmpt: hld up: hdwy on ins & n.m.r over 1f out: shkn up & styd on wl towards fin) 1¼ 3
3666[10] Mustang *(55+) (CWThornton)* 2-9-0 DeanMcKeown(1) (led: hung rt & hdd over 1f out: grad wknd) 5 4
Strategic Ploy *(49) (MrsJRRamsden)* 2-8-9 KFallon(10) (lengthy: unf: s.i.s: bhd tl kpt on wl appr fnl f: nvr nr ldrs) nk 5
Nasrudin (USA) *(48) (DRLoder)* 2-8-11 (3) DRMcCabe(4) (w'like: w ldrs: chal over 2f out: wknd over 1f out) 2½ 6
3633[4] Classic Ballet (FR) *(43) (SCWilliams)* 2-8-9 AMackay(11) (sn in tch: drvn along ½-wy: nvr nr to chal) nk 7
3773[6] Alzotic (IRE) *(46) (SGNorton)* 2-9-0 SMaloney(9) (mid div: kpt on fnl 2f: nvr nr to chal) ½ 8
Sing And Dance *(30) (EWeymes)* 2-8-9 GHind(8) (lengthy: bkwd: dwlt s: a outpcd & bhd) 5 9
Two Four Sports (IRE) *(34) (JAHarris)* 2-9-0 JWeaver(5) (small: lt-f: unf: sn outpcd & pushed along) ½ 10
3494[6] Firle Phantasy *(25) (PCalver)* 2-9-0 MBirch(6) (bit bkwd: chsd ldrs tl wknd over 2f out) 4 11

8/13 INSATIABLE (IRE) (op Evens), **9/2** Diamond Beach, Nasrudin (USA) (op 3/1), **9/1** Classic Ballet (FR) (6/1-10/1), **14/1** Firle Phantasy, **20/1** Strategic Ploy, **33/1** Sing And Dance, Mustang, **50/1** Magic Mill (IRE), Two Four Sports (IRE), Alzotic (IRE), CSF £4.88 TOTE £1.70: £1.10 £1.70 £10.00 (£2.20) Trio £83.50 OWNER Sir Evelyn de Rothschild (NEWMARKET) BRED W. Maxwell Ervine 11 Rn 1m 29.5 (5.20) SF: 46/37/34/23/17/16/11/14/-/2/-

3882
BRUNTON LANE RATING RELATED MAIDEN LIMITED STKS (0-65) (2-Y.O) (Class F) £2,801.60 (£787.60: £384.80)
7f Stalls: Low GOING: 0.12 sec per fur (G) 4-30 (4-31)

3749[3] **Bold Enough (63)***(63)*(Fav)*(BWHills)* 2-8-9 DHolland(3) (trckd ldrs: shkn up to ld over 1f out: swvd bdly rt ins fnl f: drvn out) — 1
3612[15] La Finale **(60)***(60) (MHEasterby)* 2-8-9 KFallon(4) (prom: effrt over 1f out: styng on same pce whn sltly hmpd wl ins fnl f) 1¼ 2
3463[6] Sedbergh (USA) **(65)***(63) (MrsMReveley)* 2-9-0 KDarley(2) (w ldrs: led over 2f out tl over 1f out: kpt on same pce) 1 3
3354[5] Mooncusser **(54)***(59) (JGFitzGerald)* 2-9-0 JCarroll(5) (trckd ldrs: effrt 2f out: hung rt: kpt on same pce) 1½ 4
3780[11] Boundary Bird (IRE) **(65)***(59) (MJohnston)* 2-9-0 JWeaver(1) (sn outpcd & bhd: hdwy over 2f out: no imp appr fnl f) nk 5
3780[8] Noir Esprit **(60)***(50) (JMCarr)* 2-9-0 SMorris(9) (outpcd & drvn along ½-wy: n.d) 4 6
3666[11] Szloto **(65)***(47) (TDBarron)* 2-9-0 DeanMcKeown(6) (disp ld tl over 2f out: sn wknd) 1 7
3503[2] Arc of The Diver (IRE) **(64)***(20) (JBerry)* 2-9-0 SDWilliams(8) (chsd ldrs: pushed along ½-wy: hung lft & sn wknd) 12 8
3671[5] Principal Boy (IRE) **(60)***(15) (TJEtherington)* 2-9-0 TIves(7) (disp ld tl over 2f out: wknd qckly over 1f out) 2 9

4/6 BOLD ENOUGH, **11/2** La Finale, **6/1** Sedbergh (USA), **7/1** Szloto, **12/1** Arc of The Diver (IRE), Principal Boy (IRE), **20/1** Noir Esprit, Boundary Bird (IRE), **33/1** Mooncusser, CSF £6.07 TOTE £1.60: £1.70 £1.50 £1.90 (£2.40) Trio £12.70 OWNER Mr Ray Richards (LAMBOURN) BRED Berkshire Equestrian Services Ltd 9 Rn 1m 32.7 (8.40) SF: 6/3/6/2/2/-/-/-/-

T/Plpt: £107.30 (105.51 Tckts). T/Qdpt: £22.20 (1.65 Tckts). WG

3450-SALISBURY (R-H)
Wednesday September 27th (Good to soft)

Flip start: race 2
WEATHER: sunny WIND: mod against

3883 E.B.F. MARLBOROUGH MAIDEN STKS (2-Y.O) (Class D) £4,783.00 (£1,444.00: £702.00: £331.00)
1m Stalls: Centre GOING: 0.18 sec per fur (G) 2-10 (2-12)

3672[3] **Mystic Knight** *(85) (RCharlton)* 2-9-0 TSprake(3) (w ldrs: led over 4f out: r.o wl) — 1
3684[2] Decision Maker (IRE) **(82)***(82) (RHannon)* 2-8-9 (5) DaneO'Neill(6) (a.p: r.o ins fnl f) 1¾ 2
Annaba (IRE) *(76) (JHMGosden)* 2-8-9 LDettori(15) (w'like: hdwy 2f out: rdn over 1f out: r.o one pce) hd 3
A Likely Tale (USA) *(80) (MBell)* 2-9-0 MFenton(4) (leggy: bit bkwd: hdwy over 2f out: nvr nrr) ¾ 4
3683[3] Cheerful Aspect (IRE) *(79) (EALDunlop)* 2-9-0 RHills(13) (gd hdwy 2f out: one pce fnl f) ½ 5
Foreign Judgement (USA) *(77) (PWChapple-Hyam)* 2-9-0 JReid(10) (unf scope: nvr nr to chal) ¾ 6
3709[4] Lear Jet (USA) *(74)*(Fav)*(PFICole)* 2-9-0 TQuinn(12) (a.p: ev ch 2f out: sn rdn & wknd) 1¾ 7
2995[6] Shu Gaa (IRE) *(72) (WJHaggas)* 2-9-0 MHills(5) (nvr nrr) ¾ 8
3673[4] The Swan *(65) (JLDunlop)* 2-8-9 SWhitworth(17) (nvr plcd to chal) 1 9
Agile *(63) (IABalding)* 2-8-9 (5) DGriffiths(14) (w'like: str: bkwd: w ldrs: ev ch over 2f out: sn wknd) 3½ 10
3532[7] Just Nuisance *(57) (CEBrittain)* 2-8-9 MRoberts(11) (sme hdwy whn nt clr run ins fnl f) ½ 11
3436[7] Flint And Steel *(58) (RHannon)* 2-9-0 RPerham(9) (a.p: veered rt over 2f out: no hdwy) 2 12
Bronhallow *(58) (MrsBarbaraWaring)* 2-9-0 NAdams(8) (unf: b.nr.hind: s.s: a bhd) hd 13
Washington Reef (USA) *(53) (JHMGosden)* 2-9-0 AClark(1) (gd sort: str: bkwd: prom over 5f) 2½ 14
Ruby Two Shoes *(47) (BRMillman)* 2-8-9 JWilliams(18) (w'like: bit bkwd: outpcd) ½ 15
Dashing Invader (USA) *(42) (PWHarris)* 2-9-0 GCarter(2) (str: scope: bkwd: a bhd) 5 16
Sliparis *(7) (KOCunningham-Brown)* 2-8-9 DHarrison(7) (lengthy: unf: led over 3f: t.o) 15 17
Super Baron *(RHannon)* 2-9-0 RHughes(16) (cmpt: bit bkwd: hung bdly rt 3f out: sn wknd: t.o) dist 18

Evens Lear Jet (USA), **7/2** Annaba (IRE), **9/1** MYSTIC KNIGHT, Foreign Judgement (USA) (op 7/2), **12/1** The Swan (8/1-14/1), **16/1** Cheerful Aspect (IRE), Decision Maker (IRE), **25/1** Dashing Invader (USA), **33/1** A Likely Tale (USA), Agile, Shu Gaa (IRE), Flint And Steel, Bronhallow, Washington Reef (USA), Ruby Two Shoes, Just Nuisance, Sliparis, Super Baron, CSF £130.85 TOTE £9.80: £2.40 £2.90 £2.00 (£55.60) Trio £83.60 OWNER Sir Philip Oppenheimer (BECKHAMPTON) BRED Hascombe and Valiant Studs 18 Rn 1m 50.82 (11.52) SF: -/-/-/-/-/-/-/-/-/-/-/-/-/-/-/-/-/-

3884 HURDLERS CLAIMING H'CAP (0-60) (3-Y.O+) (Class F) £3,197.00 (£892.00: £431.00) **1m 6f** GOING: 0.18 sec per fur (G) 2-40 (2-42)

3646[9] **Stevie's Wonder (IRE) (54)***(69) (MJRyan)* 5-9-10v MHills(19) (led after 2f: r.o wl) — 1
2511[6] Opera Buff (IRE) **(50)***(64) (MissGayKelleway)* 4-9-6 DHarrison(15) (hld up & bhd: gd hdwy over 2f out: hrd rdn over 1f out: r.o ins fnl f) 1 2
3818[3] Thrower **(38)***(50)*(Fav)*(PDEvans)* 4-8-8 NAdams(20) (lw: plld hrd: hdwy 6f out: ev ch 2f out: nt qckn) 2 3
3627[14] Full Quiver **(42)***(53) (MrsBarbaraWaring)* 10-8-9 (3) SDrowne(14) (b: b.off hind: stdy hdwy 4f out: hrd rdn 2f out: one pce) ¾ 4
3676[8] Delicious **(48)***(58) (MajorDNChappell)* 3-8-8 JReid(11) (a.p: r.o one pce fnl 2f) nk 5
3634[13] Lucky Quest **(60)***(64) (NAGraham)* 3-9-6b MRoberts(8) (led 2f: hrd rdn & no hdwy fnl 2f) 6 6
3627[3] Rose of Glenn **(48)***(51) (BPalling)* 4-9-4 TSprake(6) (bhd & plld hrd: hdwy fnl 2f: r.o) ½ 7
El Volador **(51)***(53) (RJO'Sullivan)* 8-9-7 RHughes(7) (hdwy 3f out: eased whn btn over 1f out) 1 8
3657[13] Chita Rivera **(40)***(40) (PJMakin)* 4-8-10 LDettori(4) (a mid div) 2 9
3470[13] Excelled (IRE) **(39)***(28) (CJDrewe)* 6-8-6 (3) JStack(9) (chsd ldrs: eased whn btn over 1f out) 9 10

2676[2] Call Me Albi (IRE) **(47)***(33) (GLMoore)* 4-9-3 MFenton(10) (lw: prom tl wknd 2f out)....3 **11**
2284[5] Requested **(58)***(42) (PBurgoyne)* 8-10-0 TQuinn(2) (b: a bhd)....1¼ **12**
3569[8] Old Swinford (IRE) **(50)***(30) (BJMeehan)* 3-8-10 SWhitworth(17) (lw: nvr bttr than mid div)...3½ **13**
Ejtaaz (USA) **(50)***(20) (MCPipe)* 4-9-6 GCarter(18) (nvr nr ldrs)....9 **14**
3759[20] Assembly Dancer **(39)***(6) (DLWilliams)* 8-8-4 (5) DGriffiths(1) (swtchd rt 3f out: nvr nr ldrs)....3 **15**
3757[18] Glitterazzi **(46)***(12) (LMontagueHall)* 4-9-2 AMorris(16) (b: a bhd)....½ **16**
3401[6] Manila Bay (USA) **(44)***(10) (JSKing)* 5-9-0 JWilliams(12) (lw: a bhd)....hd **17**
3759[18] Forest Mill **(55)***(21) (DWPArbuthnot)* 3-9-1 AClark(5) (b.hind: prom tl rdn & wknd 4f out)....hd **18**
Calgary Redeye **(50)** *(MrsJGRetter)* 8-9-6 MTebbutt(13) (bkwd: a wl bhd: hrd rdn 7f out: t.o)....dist **19**
343[5] Quick Million **(38)** *(JWMullins)* 4-8-3 (5) DaneO'Neill(3) (p.u 6f out: sddle slipped).... **P**

6/1 Thrower, **13/2** Requested, **10/1** Old Swinford (IRE), Chita Rivera (7/1-12/1), STEVIE'S WONDER (IRE), **12/1** Delicious, **14/1** Call Me Albi (IRE), Opera Buff (IRE), Rose of Glenn, **16/1** El Volador, **20/1** Manila Bay (USA), Full Quiver, Excelled (IRE), Quick Million, **25/1** Ejtaaz (USA), Calgary Redeye, **33/1** Lucky Quest, Forest Mill, Glitterazzi, Assembly Dancer, CSF £127.92 CT £828.17 TOTE £8.60: £2.10 £3.90 £2.10 £7.40 (£42.30) Trio £90.00 OWNER Newmarket Consortium (NEWMARKET) BRED Ovidstown Investments Ltd in Ireland 20 Rn

3m 10.89 (12.69) SF: 50/45/31/34/29/35/32/34/21/9/14/23/1/1/-/-/-/-/-/-

WEIGHT FOR AGE 3yo-10lb

3885 GOLDING CHALKE H'CAP (0-70) (3-Y.O+) (Class E) £3,834.00 (£1,152.00: £556.00: £258.00)

1m Stalls: Centre GOING: 0.18 sec per fur (G) 3-10 (3-12)

3685* **Bibliotheque (USA) (65)***(77+)*(Fav)*(JHMGosden)* 3-9-7v LDettori(2) (b: hld up: squeezed thro 1f out: qcknd to ld ins fnl f: comf)....— **1**
3757* Duello **(60)***(68) (MBlanshard)* 4-9-6 6x MRoberts(3) (a.p: ev ch over 1f out: nt qckn)....2 **2**
3605[14] Arcatura **(64)***(71) (CJames)* 3-9-6 JWilliams(4) (hdwy & wnt rt over 1f out: r.o ins fnl f)....½ **3**
3808[8] Just Harry **(66)***(72) (MJRyan)* 4-9-12 AClark(17) (b.hind: hdwy over 2f out: led over 1f out tl ins fnl f)....½ **4**
3605[6] Roi de la Mer (IRE) **(64)***(69) (JAkehurst)* 4-9-10 GCarter(13) (hdwy fnl 2f: nrst fin)....s.h **5**
3706[12] Chili Heights **(55)***(59) (GBBalding)* 5-9-1v TSprake(5) (hdwy whn nt clr run over 1f out: nrst fin)....¾ **6**
2994[8] Nashaat (USA) **(63)***(49) (NJHWalker)* 7-9-4 (5) DGriffiths(10) (nvr bttr than mid div)....9 **7**
3679[5] Braydon Forest **(63)***(46) (CJDrewe)* 3-9-5b RHughes(1) (w ldrs: ev ch over 1f out: wknd fnl f)....1½ **8**
3629[5] Soaking **(61)***(24) (PBurgoyne)* 5-9-7 TQuinn(7) (nvr nr to chal)....10 **9**
3619[5] Pusey Street Boy **(54)***(16) (JRBosley)* 8-8-7 (7) AimeeCook(15) (w ldrs tl wknd over 1f out)....nk **10**
3757[5] Court Nap (IRE) **(55)***(12) (SMellor)* 3-8-11 MWigham(6) (led tl wknd over 1f out)....2½ **11**
450[14] Duckey Fuzz **(68)***(22) (RMFlower)* 7-10-0 AMorris(16) (bit bkwd: bhd fnl 2f)....1¼ **12**
3659[10] Yet Again **(57)***(9) (BHanbury)* 3-8-10 (3) JStack(9) (w ldrs: wkng whn hmpd over 1f out)....1 **13**
3621[2] Posing (IRE) **(64)***(14) (JRFanshawe)* 3-9-6v DHarrison(18) (prom tl wknd 2f out)....1¼ **14**
1911[3] Autumn Cover **(54)***(3) (RMFlower)* 3-8-7 (3) SDrowne(11) (b: bit bkwd: bhd fnl 3f)....nk **15**
3664[10] Bassmaat (USA) **(66)** *(WJHaggas)* 4-9-12 RHills(12) (ev ch over 1f out: sn wknd: t.o)....12 **16**

9/4 BIBLIOTHEQUE (USA), **7/1** Duello, Posing (IRE), **10/1** Chili Heights, **14/1** Roi de la Mer (IRE), **16/1** Arcatura, Nashaat (USA), Court Nap (IRE), Soaking, Pusey Street Boy, **20/1** Braydon Forest, Just Harry, **25/1** Yet Again, Bassmaat (USA), **33/1** Duckey Fuzz, Autumn Cover, CSF £17.74 CT £190.55 TOTE £2.90: £1.60 £2.10 £6.00 £3.40 (£9.20) Trio £56.60 OWNER Sheikh Mohammed (NEWMARKET) BRED Darley Stud Management Inc 16 Rn

1m 50.16 (10.86) SF: 12/7/6/11/8/-/-/-/-/-/-/-/-/-/-/-

WEIGHT FOR AGE 3yo-4lb

3886 CRANBORNE CONDITIONS STKS (2-Y.O) (Class C) £4,658.00 (£1,742.00: £851.00: £365.00) 6f

Stalls: Centre GOING: 0.18 sec per fur (G) 3-40 (3-42)

3784* **Brandon Magic** *(92+)*(Fav)*(IABalding)* 2-9-1 LDettori(7) (hdwy over 2f out: led over 1f out: r.o wl)....— **1**
3163[5] Tamhid (USA) *(85) (HThomsonJones)* 2-9-1 RHills(1) (lw: hld up: hdwy 2f out: r.o ins fnl f)....2½ **2**
3776[3] The Man **(85)***(81) (MRChannon)* 2-9-1 RHughes(10) (hdwy & swtchd rt over 1f out: nt qckn ins fnl f)....1½ **3**
3625* Ocean Grove (IRE) **(90)***(76) (PWChapple-Hyam)* 2-8-10 JReid(3) (hld up: ev ch over 1f out: wknd ins fnl f)....s.h **4**
3702[6] White Whispers **(90)***(71) (BJMeehan)* 2-8-7 DHarrison(2) (a.p: led over 2f out tl wknd over 1f out)....1 **5**
3553* Paint It Black **(83)***(68) (RHannon)* 2-8-7 (5) DaneO'Neill(4) (gd spd over 4f)....3 **6**

3398[8] Samara Song *(57) (RJBaker)* 2-8-12 GCarter(6) (a bhd) 4 **7**
3727* Willow Dale (IRE) **(87)***(31) (DRCElsworth)* 2-9-4 TQuinn(5) (lw: in tch tl wknd 2f out: t.o)....12 **8**
3560[4] Sea Dane **(100)***(29) (PWHarris)* 2-9-6 MHills(9) (prom tl wknd 2f out: t.o)....1½ **9**
3819[3] Miss Waterline *(12) (PDEvans)* 2-8-10 AClark(8) (led over 3f: t.o)....2½ **10**

7/2 BRANDON MAGIC, **4/1** Tamhid (USA), **5/1** Ocean Grove (IRE), White Whispers, **6/1** Sea Dane (op 4/1), **12/1** Willow Dale (IRE), Paint It Black, **14/1** The Man, **50/1** Miss Waterline, **66/1** Samara Song, CSF £16.59 TOTE £4.10: £1.70 £1.70 £2.80 (£9.00) Trio £25.40 OWNER Mr R. P. B. Michaelson (KINGSCLERE) BRED Highclere Stud Ltd 10 Rn
1m 18.43 (6.13) SF: 30/23/19/14/9/6/-/-/-/-

3887 LEVY BOARD MEDIAN AUCTION MAIDEN STKS (2-Y.O F) (Class F)
£2,903.00 (£808.00: £389.00)
1m Stalls: Centre GOING: 0.18 sec per fur (G) 4-10 (4-13)

3441[3] **White Sea (IRE) (79)***(83) (PFICole)* 2-8-11 TQuinn(10) (w ldr: led on bit over 1f out: hrd rdn & hdd ins fnl f: led post)....— **1**
3733[W] Dramatic Act *(83) (CRBarwell)* 2-8-11 JWilliams(6) (leggy: lt-f: unf: bit bkwd: hld up & bhd: stdy hdwy & swtchd rt over 2f out: led ins fnl f: hdd post)....s.h **2**
3397[3] Swift Maiden *(75) (MrsLAMurphy)* 2-8-11 JReid(4) (a.p: rdn & ev ch over 1f out: nt qckn)....4 **3**
3758[8] Sister Kit (IRE) *(72) (BPalling)* 2-8-11 TSprake(1) (b: bhd: hdwy over 1f out: nvr nrr)....1½ **4**
3701[2] Disallowed (IRE) **(77)***(72)*(Fav)*(MBell)* 2-8-11 MFenton(7) (led: hrd rdn & hdd over 1f out: wknd fnl f)....s.h **5**
3673[9] Sally's Twins *(72) (JSMoore)* 2-8-11 DHarrison(5) (bhd tl hdwy fnl f: nvr plcd to chal)....hd **6**
3673[3] Secret Pleasure (IRE) **(76)***(71) (RHannon)* 2-8-11 RHughes(3) (hld up & bhd: nvr nr to chal)....½ **7**
Double Up *(63) (LadyHerries)* 2-8-11 AClark(8) (cmpt: scope: nvr nr ldrs)....4 **8**
Lovely Morning *(61) (RHannon)* 2-8-6 (5) DaneO'Neill(2) (w'like: prom 6f)....1 **9**
2939[2] Whalley Abbey **(71)***(56) (GLMoore)* 2-8-11 SWhitworth(9) (prom tl wknd over 1f out)....2½ **10**
1977[16] Gemolly (IRE) *(16) (MartynMeade)* 2-8-11 VSlattery(12) (rdn over 3f out: t.o fnl 2f)....20 **11**
1253[11] Petros Pride *(MJBolton)* 2-8-8 (3) SDrowne(11) (lw: plld hrd: prom: rdn over 3f out: sn t.o)....20 **12**

5/4 Disallowed (IRE), **100/30** WHITE SEA (IRE), **7/1** Secret Pleasure (IRE) (op 4/1), **9/1** Double Up, **10/1** Swift Maiden, **14/1** Lovely Morning, **20/1** Whalley Abbey, **33/1** Sister Kit (IRE), **50/1** Sally's Twins, Dramatic Act, Gemolly (IRE), Petros Pride, CSF £124.92 TOTE £3.70: £1.60 £5.30 £2.00 (£152.90) Trio £282.50; £238.78 to Newmarket 28/9/95 OWNER Mr T. M. Hely-Hutchinson (WHAT-COMBE) BRED Rathbarry Stud 12 Rn 1m 49.95 (10.65) SF: 5/5/-/-/-/-/-/-/-/-/-/-

3888 AUTUMN MAIDEN STKS (I) (2-Y.O) (Class D) £4,068.00 (£1,224.00: £592.00: £276.00) 6f 212y Stalls: Centre GOING: 0.18 sec per fur (G) 4-40 (4-43)

3663[6] **Final Stab (IRE)** *(74) (PWHarris)* 2-9-0 MFenton(8) (a.p: led wl over 1f out: all out)....— **1**
3652[7] Iamus *(74) (PTWalwyn)* 2-9-0 JReid(1) (hdwy over 1f out: r.o wl ins fnl f: jst failed)....s.h **2**
3617[5] Clouds Hill (FR) *(74) (RHannon)* 2-9-0 RHughes(11) (b.off hind: hdwy 2f out: hrd rdn & ev ch fnl f: r.o)....hd **3**
Name of Our Father (USA) *(65) (JHMGosden)* 2-9-0 LDettori(10) (unf: lw: hdwy over 2f out: one pce fnl f)....4 **4**
3155[6] Dancing Image *(53) (IABalding)* 2-9-0 MHills(3) (lw: led over 5f: sn wknd)....5 **5**
Indian Nectar *(45) (GBBalding)* 2-8-6 (3) SDrowne(6) (unf: nvr nrr)....1½ **6**
Hard News (USA) *(47) (RCharlton)* 2-9-0 TSprake(7) (cmpt: nvr nr ldrs)....1 **7**
The Dilettanti (USA) *(39) (JARToller)* 2-9-0 MRoberts(9) (w'like: prom tl rdn & wknd 2f out).3½ **8**
1977[6] Hank-a-chief *(38) (MMcCormack)* 2-9-0 RStreet(13) (a bhd)....½ **9**
3494[8] Alfahaal (IRE) *(37) (HThomsonJones)* 2-9-0 RHills(4) (lw: prom 5f: eased whn btn fnl f)....nk **10**
Present Arms (USA) *(37)*(Fav)*(PFICole)* 2-9-0 TQuinn(2) (w'like: scope: w ldrs: hrd rdn over 2f out: sn wknd)....nk **11**
Sandpiper *(9) (KOCunningham-Brown)* 2-8-9 DHarrison(12) (unf: sn t.o)....10 **12**
Parsa (USA) *(JLDunlop)* 2-8-9 SWhitworth(5) (Withdrawn not under Starter's orders: ref to ent stalls).... **W**

3/1 Present Arms (USA) (13/8-7/2), **9/2** Alfahaal (IRE) (8/1-12/1), **11/2** The Dilettanti (USA) (8/1-5/1), **6/1** Name of Our Father (USA) (op 5/2), **7/1** FINAL STAB (IRE) (6/1-10/1), **10/1** Dancing Image (7/1-11/1), **12/1** Hard News (USA), **16/1** Clouds Hill (FR), **25/1** Parsa (USA), Iamus, **33/1** Hank-a-chief, Sandpiper, Indian Nectar, CSF £139.93 TOTE £10.60: £3.00 £6.70 £3.00 (£127.70) Trio £203.40 OWNER Mrs P. W. Harris (BERKHAMSTED) BRED Pendley Farm 12 Rn
1m 34.67 (8.97) SF: 10/10/10/1/-/-/-/-/-/-/-/-

3889

FONTHILL H'CAP (0-70) (3-Y.O+) (Class E) £3,756.00 (£1,128.00: £544.00: £252.00) **1m 1f 209y** Stalls: Centre GOING: 0.18 sec per fur (G) 5-10 (5-16)

3095[3] **Princess Danielle (54)***(68) (CCElsey)* 3-8-10 MHills(3) (styd far side ent st: led over 4f out: all out)........— 1
3757[7] It'sthebusiness **(55)***(69) (SDow)* 3-8-11 TQuinn(4) (bhd tl swtchd far side & hdwy 5f out: ev ch fnl f: r.o)........nk 2
3572[5] Ruby Heights **(51)***(60) (RHannon)* 4-8-8 (5) DaneO'Neill(15) (prom: led stands' side 3f out: r.o one pce fnl f)........3 3
3653[7] Volunteer (IRE) **(63)***(71) (RJO'Sullivan)* 3-9-5 RHills(1) (lw: bhd tl hdwy fnl 2f: nvr nrr)........½ 4
3384[4] Father Dan (IRE) **(57)***(60) (MissGayKelleway)* 6-9-5 DHarrison(16) (hld up: no hdwy fnl 2f)....3 5
3094[8] Lady Highfield **(54)***(57) (MJRyan)* 4-9-2 AClark(11) (hdwy over 3f out: one pce fnl 2f)........nk 6
3526[W] Fabillion **(62)***(64) (CASmith)* 3-9-4 VSlattery(8) (no hdwy fnl 3f)........½ 7
1771* Spitfire Bridge (IRE) **(50)***(52) (MMcCormack)* 3-8-3 (3) JStack(7) (prom tl wknd over 2f out)...s.h 8
2654[5] El Don **(53)***(54) (MJRyan)* 3-8-9 GCarter(18) (prom tl wknd over 2f out)........½ 9
3679[8] Koathary (USA) **(64)***(63) (LGCottrell)* 4-9-12 LDettori(14) (led 2f: wknd over 1f out)........1 10
3679[4] Bookcase **(66)***(61) (DRCElsworth)* 8-10-0 MRoberts(2) (lw: stdd s: a bhd)........2½ 11
2361[6] Nessun Doro **(65)***(60) (SMellor)* 3-9-7 MWigham(13) (a bhd)........s.h 12
3759[22] Beauman **(60)***(52) (PDEvans)* 5-9-8 RHughes(6) (a bhd)........2 13
3388[14] Araboybill **(58)***(48) (RSimpson)* 4-9-6b SWhitworth(10) (prom tl wknd qckly over 1f out)........1 14
3529[14] Off the Air (IRE) **(47)***(28) (BJLlewellyn)* 4-8-2b(7) JWilkinson(9) (prom tl rdn & wknd over 2f out)........6 15
Nordansk **(45)***(23) (MMadgwick)* 6-8-7 MFenton(17) (rdn over 3f out: a bhd)........2 16
3461[2] Viyapari (IRE) **(70)***(25)*(Fav)*(LMCumani)* 3-9-12 JReid(5) (lw: led after 2f: hdd over 4f out: wknd over 2f out: t.o)........14 17
3422[5] Bellateena **(52)** *(HJCollingridge)* 3-8-8 MTebbutt(12) (prom: hrd rdn & wknd over 2f out: t.o)........6 18

7/2 Viyapari (IRE), **7/1** Beauman, Bookcase, **8/1** Koathary (USA), **10/1** Father Dan (IRE), **12/1** It'sthebusiness, Ruby Heights, **14/1** Volunteer (IRE), Lady Highfield, **20/1** Bellateena, Spitfire Bridge (IRE), PRINCESS DANIELLE, **25/1** Nordansk, Araboybill, El Don, **33/1** Fabillion, Nessun Doro, Off the Air (IRE), CSF £227.12 CT £2,722.17 TOTE £21.30: £4.30 £3.30 £2.20 £2.80 (£105.00) Trio £179.10 OWNER Mrs Marion Wickham (LAMBOURN) BRED Mrs Wickham 18 Rn

2m 14.67 (9.97) SF: 29/30/27/32/27/24/25/13/15/30/28/21/19/15/-/-/-/-

WEIGHT FOR AGE 3yo-6lb

3890

AUTUMN MAIDEN STKS (II) (2-Y.O) (Class D) £4,068.00 (£1,224.00: £592.00: £276.00) **6f 212y** Stalls: Centre GOING: 0.18 sec per fur (G) 5-40 (5-45)

Centre Stalls (IRE) *(89+) (RFJohnsonHoughton)* 2-9-0 JReid(10) (w'like: a.p: led 1f out: qckn clr)........— 1
3673[2] Crazy Chief *(81)*(Fav)*(PFICole)* 2-9-0 TQuinn(7) (plld hrd: a.p: led 3f out tl 1f out: nt qckn)........3½ 2
3663[12] Winter Romance *(77+) (EALDunlop)* 2-9-0 SWhitworth(5) (hld up & bhd: gd hdwy fnl f: bttr for r)........1¾ 3
3650[7] Clemente *(76) (RHannon)* 2-9-0 MRoberts(13) (plld hrd: a.p: r.o one pce fnl 2f)........½ 4
Punkah (USA) *(76) (LordHuntingdon)* 2-9-0 RPerham(4) (neat: w ldrs tl wknd 1f out)........s.h 5
Chalcuchima *(71) (RCharlton)* 2-9-0 SRaymont(8) (unf: nvr nrr)........2 6
3525[5] Pleasureland (IRE) *(67) (PJMakin)* 2-9-0 AClark(12) (nvr nr to chal)........1¾ 7
Jelali (IRE) *(66) (DJGMurraySmith)* 2-9-0 RHughes(1) (unf: c stands' side 4f out: hrd rdn 3f out: n.d)........nk 8
1977[10] Bold Patriot (IRE) *(66) (JWHills)* 2-9-0 MHills(6) (prom over 4f)........hd 9
3663[10] Passing Strangers (USA) *(66) (PWHarris)* 2-9-0 MFenton(2) (bhd fnl 3f)........s.h 10
2681[9] Poetic Dance (USA) *(52) (JLDunlop)* 2-9-0 GCarter(9) (bhd fnl 3f)........6 11
Jona Holley *(39) (IABalding)* 2-9-0 LDettori(11) (unf: led 4f: sn wknd)........6 12
Alambar (IRE) *(25) (PTWalwyn)* 2-9-0 RHills(3) (w'like: scope: c stands' side 4f out: bhd fnl 3f: t.o)........6 13

6/4 Crazy Chief, **6/1** CENTRE STALLS (IRE), Poetic Dance (USA), **8/1** Jona Holley (op 5/1), **12/1** Passing Strangers (USA) (op 8/1), Chalcuchima (op 8/1), Alambar (IRE) (7/1-14/1), **14/1** Bold Patriot (IRE), Winter Romance, **20/1** Jelali (IRE), **25/1** Punkah (USA), Pleasureland (IRE), **33/1** Clemente, CSF £15.95 TOTE £7.20: £2.30 £1.60 £3.30 (£6.40) Trio £71.30 OWNER Mr Anthony Pye-Jeary (DIDCOT) BRED Limestone Stud 13 Rn

1m 31.75 (6.05) SF: 42/34/30/29/29/24/20/19/19/19/5/-/-

T/Jkpt: Not won; £8,018.30 to LIngfield 28/9/95. T/Plpt: £1,139.80 (12.12 Tckts). T/Qdpt: £81.70 (1 Tckt). KH

3672-LINGFIELD (L-H)
Thursday September 28th (Soft)

6th race: hand-timed
WEATHER: fair WIND: almost nil

3891 E.B.F. SLEEPING PARTNER MAIDEN STKS (I) (2-Y.O) (Class D) £4,205.50 (£1,258.00: £603.00: £275.50)
6f Stalls: High GOING: 0.32 sec per fur (G) 1-20 (1-21)

3699[4] **Norwegian Blue (IRE) (92)***(77+)*(Fav)*(APJarvis)* 2-9-0 JTate(3) (mde all: clr over 1f out: easily) ....— **1**
3625[20] Mutahassin (USA) *(64) (RWArmstrong)* 2-9-0 WWoods(1) (lw: chsd wnr: rdn over 3f out: unable qckn fnl 2f) 5 **2**
Bowled Over *(63) (CACyzer)* 2-9-0 DBiggs(11) (leggy: bit bkwd: rdn over 4f out: swtchd lft 3f out: hdwy over 2f out: r.o one pce) ....nk **3**
Superior Force *(58) (MissBSanders)* 2-8-9 (5) AWhelan(10) (str: scope: bit bkwd: rdn over 4f out: hdwy over 1f out: one pce) 1¾ **4**
Classic Affair (USA) *(51) (SCWilliams)* 2-8-9 AMackay(8) (b.hind: unf: bit bkwd: dwlt: hld up: rdn over 2f out: one pce) 1 **5**
Royal Diversion (IRE) *(47) (JLDunlop)* 2-8-9 GCarter(9) (neat: nvr nr to chal) 1¼ **6**
3379[12] Indira *(46) (HCandy)* 2-8-9 CRutter(5) (prom over 2f) ....½ **7**
3541[5] Tiama (IRE) *(30) (SDow)* 2-8-2 (7) ADaly(6) (stdd s: hld up: a bhd) 6 **8**
1779[7] Governors Dream *(25) (MrsNMacauley)* 2-8-6 (3) SDrowne(4) (bit bkwd: hld up: rdn over 2f out: wknd over 1f out) 1¾ **9**
2277[5] Impetuous Lady (USA) *(24) (WJMusson)* 2-8-6 (3) PMcCabe(7) (a bhd) ....nk **10**
3672[8] Questionaire *(24) (RAkehurst)* 2-8-6 (3) SSanders(2) (bhd fnl 3f) ....nk **11**

5/4 NORWEGIAN BLUE (IRE), **6/1** Tiama (IRE), **7/1** Royal Diversion (IRE) (op 3/1), **8/1** Impetuous Lady (USA) (6/1-10/1), **11/1** Classic Affair (USA) (7/1-12/1), **12/1** Indira (op 8/1), **14/1** Mutahassin (USA) (op 8/1), **20/1** Bowled Over, Governors Dream, Superior Force, Questionaire, CSF £18.54 TOTE £2.00: £1.20 £3.90 £3.00 (£22.30) Trio £81.60 OWNER Mr Ambrose Turnbull (ASTON UPTHORPE) BRED Martyn J. McEnery 11 Rn 1m 16.04 (7.04) SF: 25/12/11/6/-/-/-/-/-/-/-
OFFICIAL EXPLANATION Tiama (IRE): reportedly still weak, was not suited by the soft ground.

3892 JARDINE INSURANCE MAIDEN STKS (2-Y.O) (Class D) £4,110.00 (£1,230.00: £590.00: £270.00)
5f Stalls: High GOING: 0.32 sec per fur (G) 1-50 (1-52)

Angaar (IRE) *(78)*(Fav)*(ACStewart)* 2-9-0 MRoberts(7) (unf: lw: a.p: led over 2f out tl ins fnl f: hrd rdn: led last strides) ....— **1**
3628[2] Music Gold (IRE) *(78)*(Fav)*(WAO'Gorman)* 2-9-0 EmmaO'Gorman(14) (hld up: hrd rdn over 1f out: led ins fnl f: stumbled: hdd last strides) ....s.h **2**
3733[18] Ed's Folly (IRE) *(70) (SDow)* 2-9-0 WRyan(5) (racd far side: a.p: rdn over 2f out: one pce)..2½ **3**
Need You Badly *(65) (SPCWoods)* 2-8-9 WWoods(2) (neat: racd far side: hdwy 2f out: rdn over 1f out: one pce) ....s.h **4**
2487[10] Tahya (USA) *(62) (HThomsonJones)* 2-8-9 GCarter(3) (racd far side: a.p: rdn over 1f out: one pce) 1 **5**
3495[9] Wildwood Flower *(57) (RHannon)* 2-8-4 (5) DaneO'Neill(12) (no hdwy fnl 2f) 1½ **6**
3733[19] Country Thatch *(52) (CAHorgan)* 2-9-0 DHolland(13) (swtchd lft over 1f out: nvr plcd to chal) 3 **7**
3625[13] Princely Affair *(49) (MBell)* 2-8-7 (7) GFaulkner(1) (racd far side: nvr nrr) 1 **8**
Inaminit *(43) (HJCollingridge)* 2-9-0 KFallon(6) (unf: no hdwy fnl 2f) 1¾ **9**
3648[10] Ya Marhaba *(43) (JWPayne)* 2-9-0 MTebbutt(10) (prom over 2f) ....hd **10**
3432[14] Forzara *(36) (JBerry)* 2-8-9 JCarroll(15) (led over 2f) ....¾ **11**
3558[8] Midnight Cookie **(55)***(33) (RJHodges)* 2-8-11 (3) SDrowne(16) (a bhd) 2½ **12**
3848[9] Heights of Love **(55)***(20) (MSSaunders)* 2-8-9 JFEgan(8) (prom over 2f) 2½ **13**
3648[4] Gotla Bird *(8) (MJohnston)* 2-8-9 TWilliams(9) (s.s: rdn & hdwy over 2f out: wknd wl over 1f out) 3½ **14**
3668[13] Man of Wit (IRE) **(88)***(2) (APJarvis)* 2-9-0 JTate(4) (lw: racd far side: spd 3f) 3½ **15**
Lord Ellangowan (IRE) *(RIngram)* 2-9-0 AMackay(11) (unf: s.s: a bhd) 3 **16**

9/4 ANGAAR (IRE) (op 6/4), Music Gold (IRE), **5/1** Man of Wit (IRE) (4/1-6/1), **7/1** Need You Badly, **10/1** Gotla Bird (op 5/1), **12/1** Wildwood Flower (op 5/1), **20/1** Forzara, Country Thatch, **25/1** Princely Affair, Tahya (USA), Heights of Love, Ya Marhaba, **50/1** Ed's Folly (IRE), Inaminit, Midnight Cookie, Lord Ellangowan (IRE), CSF £8.58 TOTE £2.50: £1.10 £1.70 £2.80 (£3.70) Trio £134.80 OWNER Sheikh Ahmed Al Maktoum (NEWMARKET) BRED Ron Con Ltd 16 Rn
62.08 secs (5.08) SF: 37/37/29/24/21/16/11/8/2/2/-/-/-/-/-/-

3893 E.B.F. SLEEPING PARTNER MAIDEN STKS (II) (2-Y.O) (Class D) £4,171.70 (£1,247.60: £597.80: £272.90)
6f Stalls: High GOING: 0.32 sec per fur (G) 2-20 (2-21)

3662⁴ **Apple Musashi** *(87+)*(Fav)*(JHMGosden)* 2-9-0 GHind(1) (lw: a.p: led over 1f out: comf)......— **1**
3765³ Pride of Brixton *(66) (GLewis)* 2-9-0 SWhitworth(2) (lw: led over 4f: eased whn btn ins fnl f)........8 **2**
2335⁶ Mrs McBadger **(50)***(50) (BSmart)* 2-8-9 JTate(3) (chsd ldr over 3f: wknd over 1f out)........4 **3**
3606⁵ Sharp Pearl *(48) (RCharlton)* 2-9-0 WRyan(4) (lw: hld up: rdn over 2f out: wknd over 1f out)........2½ **4**
3765⁴ Meranti **(71)***(35) (LJHolt)* 2-9-0 DHolland(8) (hdwy 2f out: rdn over 1f out: eased whn btn ins fnl f)........5 **5**
3733⁸ Blue Flyer (IRE) *(24) (IABalding)* 2-8-9 (5) DGriffiths(5) (nvr nrr)........4 **6**
3733¹¹ Samara (IRE) *(19) (JLDunlop)* 2-8-9 GCarter(6) (a bhd)........hd **7**
3763¹⁸ Unspoken Prayer *(16) (JRArnold)* 2-8-9 CRutter(9) (bhd fnl 4f)........1 **8**
Goldsearch (IRE) *(12) (WAO'Gorman)* 2-8-9 EmmaO'Gorman(10) (str: scope: bit bkwd: hld up: rdn over 2f out: sn wknd)........1½ **9**
Condor Ridge *(BJMeehan)* 2-9-0 RPerham(7) (unf: s.s: a bhd)........20 **10**

Evens APPLE MUSASHI, **2/1** Sharp Pearl, **7/1** Pride of Brixton (op 4/1), **12/1** Samara (IRE) (op 5/1), **16/1** Meranti, **25/1** Mrs McBadger, Goldsearch (IRE), **33/1** Blue Flyer (IRE), **50/1** Unspoken Prayer, Condor Ridge, CSF £9.22 TOTE £2.50: £1.10 £2.10 £2.40 (£7.60) Trio £46.30 OWNER Mr Kazuhiro Taiwa Hasegawa (NEWMARKET) BRED Cheveley Park Stud Ltd 10 Rn
1m 14.47 (5.47) SF: 47/26/10/8/-/-/-/-/-/-
STEWARDS' ENQUIRY Hind susp. 7 & 9/10/95 (improper riding).

3894 HERTFORD OFFSET NURSERY H'CAP (0-75) (2-Y.O) (Class E) £4,074.40 (£1,223.20: £589.60: £272.80)
7f Stalls: High GOING: 0.32 sec per fur (G) 2-55 (3-04)

3858* **Warming Trends (72)***(81?)*(Fav)*(SirMarkPrescott)* 2-9-9 7x WWoods(4) (lw: racd far side: mde all: clr over 2f out: unchal)........— **1**
3639¹¹ Hurricane Dancer (IRE) **(60)***(51) (SPCWoods)* 2-8-4 (7) CWebb(3) (lw: racd far side: hld up: rdn over 3f out: chsd wnr fnl 2f: no imp)........8 **2**
3714⁵ Deadline Time (IRE) **(70)***(56) (MHTompkins)* 2-9-7 PRobinson(6) (lw: hld up: rdn over 3f out: one pce)........2 **3**
3721⁶ Pendley Rose **(60)***(46) (PWHarris)* 2-8-11 GHind(16) (b.off hind: hdwy 3f out: one pce fnl 2f)........hd **4**
2204² Asking For Kings (IRE) **(63)***(31) (SDow)* 2-8-7 (7) ADaly(5) (hld up: rdn over 2f out: wknd over 1f out)........8 **5**
*3675** Where's Margaret **(63)***(30) (GLewis)* 2-8-9b(5) AWhelan(2) (lw: racd far side: chsd wnr 5f)......½ **6**
3592¹¹ Wire Act (USA) **(65)***(31) (MartynMeade)* 2-8-11 (5) RHavlin(7) (prom over 5f)........nk **7**
3623³ Morning Surprise **(63)***(17) (APJarvis)* 2-9-0 JTate(13) (nvr nrr)........5 **8**
3553⁷ Seaford Star (IRE) **(64)***(18) (MRChannon)* 2-9-1 AClark(11) (lw: hdwy over 3f out: wknd over 1f out)........hd **9**
3643⁵ Classic Delight (USA) **(57)***(8) (SCWilliams)* 2-8-8 AMackay(9) (bhd fnl 3f)........1½ **10**
3721⁸ Spirito Libro (USA) **(66)** *(CNAllen)* 2-9-3 MRimmer(15) (bhd fnl 3f)........10 **11**
3628¹⁰ Eskimo Kiss (IRE) **(64)** *(MJFetherston-Godley)* 2-8-10 (5) DaneO'Neill(12) (bhd fnl 3f)........nk **12**
2651⁵ Pearls of Thought (IRE) **(63)** *(PTWalwyn)* 2-9-0 DHolland(10) (a bhd)........2½ **13**
3620¹⁶ Minsterbeach **(60)** *(CEBrittain)* 2-8-8v(3) DRMcCabe(8) (swvd lft s: bhd fnl 3f)........½ **14**
3132¹⁰ All She Surveys **(65)** *(JAkehurst)* 2-9-2b GCarter(14) (Withdrawn not under Starter's orders: did not wear blinkers on wy to s)........ **W**

7/4 WARMING TRENDS, **5/1** Pendley Rose, **7/1** Deadline Time (IRE) (10/1-6/1), **8/1** Where's Margaret, **12/1** Asking For Kings (IRE), Morning Surprise, Pearls of Thought (IRE), **14/1** Wire Act (USA), Classic Delight (USA) (8/1-16/1), **16/1** Spirito Libro (USA), **20/1** Seaford Star (IRE), Hurricane Dancer (IRE), **25/1** Eskimo Kiss (IRE), Minsterbeach, All She Surveys, CSF £39.32 CT £207.61 TOTE £2.80: £1.60 £8.00 £1.70 (£33.10) Trio £35.00 OWNER Hesmonds Stud (NEWMARKET) BRED Hesmonds Stud Ltd 14 Rn 1m 28.07 (7.47) SF: 42/12/17/7/-/-/-/-/-/-/-/-/-/-

3895 ORIGIN CLAIMING STKS (2-Y.O) (Class F) £3,123.80 (£866.80: £415.40)
6f Stalls: High GOING: 0.32 sec per fur (G) 3-25 (3-32)

3548¹¹ **Fenna (71)***(80?)*(Fav)*(SPCWoods)* 2-8-8 WWoods(4) (a.p: led over 1f out: pushed out).......— **1**
3538* Rebel County (IRE) **(68)***(75) (DJSCosgrove)* 2-9-2 MRimmer(3) (lw: a.p: hrd rdn 2f out: unable qckn)........5 **2**
2434⁷ Midas Gold *(65) (BJMeehan)* 2-9-3 MTebbutt(5) (led over 4f: one pce)........4 **3**

3628[13] Wrays (USA) **(66)***(49) (MJohnston)* 2-8-2 TWilliams(2) (a.p: rdn over 2f out: one pce) ....nk 4
3386[4] Moi Canard **(62)***(50) (JBerry)* 2-8-13 JCarroll(8) (lw: rdn & hdwy over 2f out: wknd over 1f out) ...4 5
3509[10] Paper Maze **(48)***(31) (JAHarris)* 2-8-0 DaleGibson(6) (hld up: rdn over 2f out: wknd over 1f out) ...2 6
3651[7] Killatty Lark (IRE) *(22) (WJMusson)* 2-8-1 (3) PMcCabe(10) (lw: hdwy 2f out: wknd over 1f out) ...5 7
3675[3] Don't Tell Vicki **(56)***(16) (JSMoore)* 2-8-2 JFEgan(15) (racd stands' side: prom over 3f)........1½ 8
2801[6] Stand Your Ground *(16) (GLMoore)* 2-8-7 SWhitworth(14) (lw: racd stands' side: nvr nrr).......2 9
3628[12] Baroness Blixen *(10) (DJGMurraySmith)* 2-8-12 KFallon(13) (racd stands' side: nvr nrr).........4 10
3516[10] Emei Shan **(45)** *(PGMurphy)* 2-7-11 (7)ow2 RWaterfield(7) (b.nr hind: nvr nrr)........................s.h 11
3520* Jessica's Song **(61)** *(WGMTurner)* 2-8-1 (7) ADaly(11) (racd stands' side: prom over 3f)..........6 12
3290[12] Fantasy Fair *(RBoss)* 2-8-4 WRyan(9) (lw: a bhd) ...6 13
Swingalong Girl *(TMJones)* 2-8-6 RPerham(1) (b: str: a bhd) ...½ 14
3651[13] Dancing Man *(MrsMELong)* 2-8-13 CRutter(16) (lw: racd stands' side: dwlt: bhd fnl 3f).........6 15
3767[16] Public Offering *(MBlanshard)* 2-8-0 StephenDavies(12) (racd stands' side: bhd fnl 3f) 6 16

2/1 FENNA (6/4-9/4), **7/2** Rebel County (IRE), **7/1** Wrays (USA), **8/1** Jessica's Song, Baroness Blixen, Killatty Lark (IRE), **10/1** Don't Tell Vicki, Moi Canard (8/1-12/1), **14/1** Stand Your Ground, **20/1** Paper Maze, Fantasy Fair, **25/1** Emei Shan, Midas Gold, Swingalong Girl, Dancing Man, **33/1** Public Offering, CSF £11.98 TOTE £2.30: £1.60 £1.50 £4.30 (£3.00) Trio £24.30 OWNER Mr S. P. C. Woods (NEWMARKET) BRED High Point Bloodstock Ltd and Nigel Fenner Fownes 16 Rn
1m 14.28 (5.28) SF: 44/39/29/13/14/-/-/-/-/-/-/-/-/-/-/-

3896 MG CALOR MAIDEN STKS (3-Y.O+) (Class D) £4,137.90 (£1,237.20: £592.60: £270.30) **1m 6f** Stalls: High GOING: 0.81 sec per fur (S) 3-55 (3-57)

1175[8] **Harbour Island** *(81) (MRStoute)* 3-8-11b KFallon(1) (5th st: hrd rdn over 2f out: led wl ins fnl f: r.o wl) ...— 1
3730[3] Taklif (IRE) **(86)***(80)*(Fav)*(BWHills)* 3-8-11 DHolland(13) (lw: a.p: led 4f out: hrd rdn over 2f out: hdd wl ins fnl f: unable qckn) ...1 2
Bimsey (IRE) *(79) (RAkehurst)* 5-9-7 RPerham(5) (rdn over 5f out: 4th st: ev ch over 1f out: one pce ins fnl f) ...1 3
3676[18] Dixiemelody **(60)***(75) (RHannon)* 3-8-6 (5) DaneO'Neill(6) (hdwy over 2f out: r.o one pce)......3½ 4
3804[5] Katie Oliver *(69) (BSmart)* 3-8-6 JTate(3) (hdwy 6f out: 2nd st: ev ch over 2f out: wknd over 1f out) ...½ 5
3772[11] Western Horizon (USA) **(37)***(59) (CEBrittain)* 3-8-3b(3) DRMcCabe(2) (lw: no hdwy fnl 3f) 9 6
3317[2] Snow Valley **(74)***(47) (LMCumani)* 3-8-11 GCarter(4) (prom 10f) ...15 7
2494[2] Racing Hawk (USA) *(44) (HRACecil)* 3-8-11 WRyan(12) (lw: led 3f: 6th st: wknd over 3f out) ...2½ 8
3772[3] Yougo *(39) (MJohnston)* 3-8-11 TWilliams(15) (led 11f out to 4f out: 3rd st: wknd over 3f out) ...4 9
3178[7] Fortunes Rose (IRE) *(18) (JSKing)* 3-8-3 (3) SDrowne(7) (bhd fnl 5f) ...14 10
3178[9] Andre's Affair *(23) (DJSffrenchDavis)* 4-9-7 MTebbutt(8) (a bhd) ...½ 11
Credit Controller (IRE) *(6) (JFfitch-Heyes)* 6-9-7 AMackay(14) (a bhd) ...15 12
Miss Parkes **(38)** *(PCClarke)* 6-9-2 NAdams(9) (a bhd) ...20 13
3438[8] Wassl Street (IRE) *(JHMGosden)* 3-8-11b GHind(10) (prom 8f) ...10 14
3627[16] Vanola **(32)** *(PHowling)* 3-8-6 PRobinson(11) (bhd fnl 8f) ...8 15

6/5 Taklif (IRE) (4/5-5/4), **9/4** Bimsey (IRE), **7/1** Snow Valley, **15/2** Yougo, **14/1** Racing Hawk (USA), Wassl Street (IRE), **20/1** Dixiemelody, HARBOUR ISLAND, **33/1** Western Horizon (USA), **50/1** Fortunes Rose (IRE), Katie Oliver, Credit Controller (IRE), Miss Parkes, Andre's Affair, Vanola, CSF £47.14 TOTE £28.70: £6.70 £1.10 £1.80 (£36.20) Trio £100.50 OWNER Mr R. Barnett (NEWMARKET) BRED W. and R. Barnett Ltd 15 Rn 3m 19.2 (23.90) SF: 24/23/32/18/12/2/-/-/-/-/-/-/-/-/-
WEIGHT FOR AGE 3yo-10lb

3897 LEVY BOARD H'CAP (0-70) (3-Y.O) (Class E) £3,588.20 (£1,073.60: £514.80: £235.40) **7f** Stalls: High GOING: 0.32 sec per fur (G) 4-25 (4-28)

3706[18] **Sharp Consul (IRE) (65)***(78) (HCandy)* 3-9-2 CRutter(5) (lw: bmpd s: hld up: rdn over 2f out: led wl ins fnl f: r.o wl) ...— 1
3747[5] Fairelaine **(53)***(65) (APJarvis)* 3-8-4 JTate(2) (hdwy 2f out: led over 1f out tl wl ins fnl f: unable qckn) ...½ 2
3615[12] Dancing Heart **(70)***(75) (BJMeehan)* 3-9-7 JFEgan(9) (lw: a.p: led wl over 1f out: sn hdd: one pce) ...3 3
3475[12] Saltis (IRE) **(53)***(55) (DWPArbuthnot)* 3-8-4 ow1 AClark(3) (rdn & hdwy over 2f out: one pce)....1 4
3764[11] Blushing Grenadier (IRE) **(56)***(52) (MJFetherston-Godley)* 3-8-2 (5)ow3 DaneO'Neill(11) (hdwy over 1f out: nvr nrr) ...1½ 5

3732[20] Artful Dane (IRE) **(70)**_(62) (MJHeaton-Ellis)_ 3-9-4 (3) DRMcCabe(10) (a.p: led over 2f out tl wl over 1f out: sn wknd)....3 6
3751[5] Ism **(55)**_(47)_(Fav)_(MajorWRHern)_ 3-8-6 TSprake(4) (a.p: hrd rdn over 1f out: sn wknd)....s.h 7
3681[10] Lough Erne **(67)**_(50) (CFWall)_ 3-8-13 (5) LNewton(12) (racd stands' side: nvr nrr)....4 8
3764[6] Astral Invader (IRE) **(60)**_(41) (MSSaunders)_ 3-8-11v NAdams(8) (hdwy over 4f out: wknd over 2f out)....1 9
3347[5] Jareer Do (IRE) **(65)**_(40) (BPalling)_ 3-8-13 (3) SDrowne(7) (hld up: rdn over 3f out: sn wknd).2½ 10
3685[12] Agoer **(50)**_(21) (CEBrittain)_ 3-8-1 DaleGibson(1) (bhd fnl 4f)....2 11
3654[7] Norsong **(53)**_(20) (RAkehurst)_ 3-8-1 (3) SSanders(15) (racd stands' side: prom over 3f)....1½ 12
3751[13] Chief's Lady **(52)**_(6) (RHarris)_ 3-8-3 StephenDavies(6) (led over 4f)....6 13
3725[7] Ramsdens (IRE) **(69)**_(17) (WJHaggas)_ 3-9-6 WWoods(13) (racd stands' side: bhd fnl 4f)....2½ 14
3664[7] By The Bay **(56)**_(4) (CCElsey)_ 3-8-7 WRyan(14) (racd stands' side: a bhd)....s.h 15
3704[11] Verde Luna **(67)**_(12) (MHTompkins)_ 3-9-4v PRobinson(16) (racd stands' side: prom 4f)....1¼ 16

7/4 Ism, **8/1** Norsong, **9/1** Astral Invader (IRE), **10/1** Dancing Heart, **12/1** Blushing Grenadier (IRE) (8/1-14/1), By The Bay, SHARP CONSUL (IRE), Chief's Lady (op 20/1), Fairelaine, **16/1** Lough Erne, Jareer Do (IRE), Agoer, Saltis (IRE), Artful Dane (IRE), **20/1** Ramsdens (IRE), Verde Luna, CSF £154.27 CT £1,393.46 TOTE £30.70: £5.40 £5.10 £1.80 £8.40 (£101.60) Trio £292.00 OWNER Mrs David Blackburn (WANTAGE) BRED B. Barnwell 16 Rn

1m 27.34 (6.74) SF: 44/31/41/21/18/28/13/16/7/6/-/-/-/-/-/-

3898 LEWES AMATEUR LIMITED STKS (0-65) (3-Y.O+) (Class F) £3,199.40 (£888.40: £426.20)

1m 3f 106y Stalls: High GOING: 0.81 sec per fur (S) 4-55 (4-56)

3853* **Keep Your Distance (65)**_(74)_(Fav)_(MrsMReveley)_ 5-10-7 (6) MissHDudgeon(1) (4th st: led over 1f out: r.o wl)....— 1
3657[9] Spread The Word **(61)**_(67) (LGCottrell)_ 3-9-11 (6)ow3 MrLJefford(5) (lw: 6th st: rdn over 2f out: ev ch ins fnl f: r.o)....½ 2
3571[5] Newport Knight **(65)**_(68) (RAkehurst)_ 4-10-7 (6) MrKGoble(9) (lw: led 7f out: clr over 3f out: hdd over 1f out: wknd fnl f)....4 3
_3735*_ Elpida (USA) **(65)**_(58)_(Fav)_(JPearce)_ 3-10-5 MrsLPearce(2) (lw: led over 4f: 2nd st: wknd over 1f out)....6 4
3759* Aljawab (USA) **(54)**_(59) (JLDunlop)_ 4-10-7 (6) MrKSantana(3) (lw: 3rd st: wknd over 1f out)....hd 5
3808[17] Breezed Well **(40)**_(57) (BRCambidge)_ 9-10-7 (6) MrsHNoonan(11) (hdwy over 2f out: wknd over 1f out)....1¾ 6
3097[3] Toskano **(62)**_(55) (DLWilliams)_ 3-10-5 MrCBonner(6) (hdwy over 3f out: 7th st: wknd over 1f out)....½ 7
3710[8] Fruitful Affair (IRE) **(40)**_(46) (TThomsonJones)_ 6-10-2 (6) MrsSFaber(8) (lost pl over 6f out: no hdwy fnl 3f)....4 8
2810[4] Hong Kong Dollar **(49)**_(47) (BAPearce)_ 3-9-13 (6) MrRBlyth(12) (nvr nrr)....1½ 9
1339[10] Yahmi (IRE) **(61)**_(43) (JABOld)_ 5-10-7 (6) MrGBaines(13) (nvr nrr)....4 10
Great Simplicity **(52)**_(15) (AJChamberlain)_ 8-10-7 (6) MrSHowe(4) (b: bhd fnl 8f)....20 11
1937[6] Phanan **(35)** _(REPeacock)_ 9-10-7 (6) MrsCPeacock(14) (b: bit bkwd: prom 5f)....11 12
Regal Aura (IRE) **(38)** _(DCO'Brien)_ 5-10-7 (6) MrVLukaniuk(16) (a bhd)....1¼ 13
3759[9] Able Choice (IRE) **(48)** _(RWArmstrong)_ 5-10-9 (4) MrPPritchard-Gordon(15) (5th st: wknd over 3f out)....1½ 14
_1955_[12] Manolete **(37)** _(JFfitch-Heyes)_ 4-10-7b(6) MissJEwer(10) (lw: a bhd)....1½ 15

9/4 KEEP YOUR DISTANCE, Elpida (USA), **100/30** Aljawab (USA), **10/1** Newport Knight (op 5/1), **20/1** Spread The Word, Hong Kong Dollar, Able Choice (IRE), Fruitful Affair (IRE), Yahmi (IRE), **25/1** Phanan, **33/1** Toskano, Regal Aura (IRE), **50/1** Breezed Well, **66/1** Manolete, **100/1** Great Simplicity, CSF £46.91 TOTE £2.20: £1.50 £5.40 £2.80 (£213.20) Trio £95.40 OWNER Mr P. D. Savill (SALTBURN) BRED Cedric Ford 15 Rn

2m 42.41 (20.41) SF: 46/32/40/23/31/29/20/18/12/15/-/-/-/-/-

WEIGHT FOR AGE 3yo-7lb

T/Jkpt: Not won; £12,465.58 to Newmarket 29/9/95. T/Plpt: £6.40 (1,517.25 Tckts). T/Qdpt: £7.90 (8.05 Tckts). AK

3863-NEWMARKET (R-H)
Thursday September 28th (Good)

WEATHER: sunny WIND: fresh bhd

3899 MELVILLE HOMES CLAIMING STKS (3-Y.O+) (Class D) £4,542.00 (£1,356.00: £648.00: £294.00)

1m 4f (Rowley) Stalls: High GOING minus 0.32 sec (GF) 1-30 (1-34)

3730[7] **Danjing (IRE) (83)**_(88)_(Fav)_(PFICole)_ 3-9-6b TQuinn(13) (a.p: led 4f out: styd on wl fnl f)....— 1

3517³ Berkeley Bounder (USA) **(75)***(75) (MCPipe)* 3-8-10 PatEddery(2) (cl up: chal 3f out: no ex ins fnl f)....2 **2**
3756⁴ Pampas Breeze (IRE) **(75)***(74) (WJarvis)* 3-9-1 LDettori(3) (lw: in tch: outpcd 4f out: styd on fnl 2f)....5 **3**
*3735*⁴ Environmentalist (IRE) **(56)***(68) (RHarris)* 4-9-4 RPrice(15) (in tch: outpcd 4f out: styd on fnl 2f)....nk **4**
*2072** Old Provence **(85)***(64) (RHarris)* 5-9-0 DBatteate(7) (b: led: hung bdly lft fnl 8f: hdd 4f out: one pce)....½ **5**
*3513*⁴ Kismetim **(39)***(58) (BJMeehan)* 5-8-13 RHughes(16) (chsd ldrs tl hrd rdn & wknd 3f out)......3½ **6**
2391⁵ Viardot (IRE) **(74)***(63) (MrsMReveley)* 6-9-4 KDarley(4) (hld up & bhd: hdwy over 4f out: nvr rchd ldrs)....nk **7**
3756¹¹ Adaloaldo (USA) *(62) (PAKelleway)* 3-8-10 MWigham(11) (lw: bhd: sme hdwy 4f out: n.d)....¾ **8**
3635¹¹ Bunker (IRE) **(48)***(57) (JPearce)* 3-8-6 GBardwell(10) (in tch tl wknd fnl 3f)....½ **9**
3646² Hand Woven **(74)***(66) (WJHaggas)* 3-9-4 RCochrane(12) (in tch: drvn along 4f out: one pce)..2 **10**
3127⁴ Pharamineux **(64)***(52) (RAkehurst)* 9-9-0 JWeaver(8) (s.i.s: hdwy on ins over 4f out: no imp)....1½ **11**
3653⁹ What's Secreto (USA) *(62) (PAKelleway)* 3-9-4 JReid(1) (in tch: outpcd over 4f out: n.d after)....1¾ **12**
3757¹⁶ Commander Glen (IRE) **(58)***(54) (MartynMeade)* 3-8-10b VSlattery(5) (a bhd)....nk **13**
1985⁴ Lexus (IRE) **(27)***(39) (RJRWilliams)* 7-9-0 MHills(9) (bhd fr ½-wy)....8 **14**
*3318*⁸ Premazing **(27)***(33) (JPearce)* 3-8-5v AMcGlone(6) (chsd ldrs tl wknd 5f out)....4 **15**
Ballysokerry (IRE) *(JParkes)* 4-9-6 DHarrison(14) (bkwd: in tch to ½-wy: sn lost pl)....30 **16**

6/4 DANJING (IRE), **5/1** Hand Woven, **8/1** Viardot (IRE), Berkeley Bounder (USA) (op 9/2), **9/1** Pampas Breeze (IRE) (op 5/1), **10/1** Pharamineux (6/1-12/1), Old Provence (op 6/1), **33/1** Ballysokerry (IRE), **50/1** Bunker (IRE), Environmentalist (IRE), Adaloaldo (USA), What's Secreto (USA), Commander Glen (IRE), Lexus (IRE), Premazing, Kismetim, CSF £13.30 TOTE £2.50: £1.40 £1.80 £2.40 (£8.70) Trio £36.30 OWNER Mrs Linda Gardiner (WHATCOMBE) BRED J. P. McManus 16 Rn 2m 33.18 (3.88) SF: 52/39/38/40/36/30/35/26/21/30/24/26/18/11/-/-
WEIGHT FOR AGE 3yo-8lb
Danjing clmd HonBCLeigh £20,000

3900 E.B.F. JOCELYN HAMBRO MAIDEN STKS (2-Y.O) (Class D)
£7,983.00 (£2,394.00: £1,152.00: £531.00)
7f (Rowley) Stalls: High GOING minus 0.32 sec per fur (GF) 2-00 (2-08)

3449⁴ **Astor Place (IRE)** *(91+)*(Fav)*(PWChapple-Hyam)* 2-9-0 JReid(18) (b: a cl up: led ins fnl f: r.o wl)....— **1**
Legal Right (USA) *(85+) (PWChapple-Hyam)* 2-9-0 PaulEddery(23) (w'like: scope: lw: w ldrs: led 3f out tl ins fnl f: kpt on)....2½ **2**
Santillana (USA) *(82+) (JHMGosden)* 2-9-0 LDettori(22) (leggy: bkwd: chsd ldrs: effrt 2f out: styd on wl fnl f)....1½ **3**
Dombey *(80+) (RCharlton)* 2-9-0 TQuinn(20) (w'like: in tch: styd on fnl 2f: nvr able chal)....¾ **4**
Raise A Prince (FR) *(80+) (RWArmstrong)* 2-9-0 RPrice(15) (w'like: unf: a chsng ldrs)....s.h **5**
Seeking Fortune (USA) *(71+) (JRFanshawe)* 2-8-9 DHarrison(1) (lt-f: unf: hld up: hdwy over 2f out: nvr nr to chal)....2 **6**
Germano *(74) (GWragg)* 2-9-0 MHills(16) (gd sort: chsd ldrs: effrt 2f out: no imp)....¾ **7**
Fahim *(70) (ACStewart)* 2-9-0 WCarson(2) (w'like: scope: s.s: hld up: stdy hdwy 2f out: nvr plcd to chal)....1½ **8**
Hayaain *(69) (MajorWRHern)* 2-9-0 RHills(17) (gd sort: bkwd: a.p: no hdwy fnl 2f)....½ **9**
Green Bopper (USA) *(68) (MBell)* 2-9-0 MFenton(13) (cmpt: prom tl outpcd fnl 2f)....½ **10**
Migwar *(65) (LMCumani)* 2-9-0 OUrbina(9) (str: cmpt: hld up: stdy hdwy over 2f out: n.d)....1¼ **11**
Rossel (USA) *(65) (MRStoute)* 2-9-0 WRSwinburn(21) (neat: scope: chsd ldrs over 5f)....hd **12**
Dance Star *(59) (MAJarvis)* 2-8-9 TIves(6) (w'like: scope: lw: hld up: effrt 3f out: nvr trbld ldrs)....nk **13**
Tintara (IRE) *(58) (BWHills)* 2-8-9 JWilliams(3) (leggy: scope: nvr plcd to chal)....½ **14**
Giddy *(58) (DMorley)* 2-8-9 RCochrane(14) (gd sort: leggy: dwlt: hdwy & in tch ½-wy: wknd wl over 1f out)....hd **15**
Reveuse de Jour (IRE) *(57) (RCharlton)* 2-8-9 JWeaver(5) (small: dwlt: shkn up 3f out: sme late hdwy)....½ **16**
State of Caution *(58) (JLDunlop)* 2-9-0 RHughes(8) (w'like: leggy: s.i.s: bhd & shkn up 3f out: n.d)....1¾ **17**
3763¹² Tina Katerina *(52) (RChampion)* 2-8-9 AMcGlone(19) (led 4f: sn wknd)....½ **18**
Roseberry Avenue (IRE) *(54) (LadyHerries)* 2-9-0 KDarley(12) (cmpt: sn wl bhd: n.d)....1 **19**
Flamands (IRE) *(48) (LMCumani)* 2-8-9 PatEddery(4) (neat: a rr div)....¾ **20**
White Plains (IRE) *(52) (MBell)* 2-9-0 CNakatani(7) (cmpt: bkwd: outpcd & bhd fr ½-wy)....½ **21**
Persephone *(39) (BHanbury)* 2-8-9 JStack(11) (neat: in tch 4f)....3½ **22**
Tashjir (USA) *(33) (DMorley)* 2-8-9 JLowe(10) (w'like: sn bhd)....2½ **23**

3/1 ASTOR PLACE (IRE), **13/2** Fahim, **8/1** Germano (5/1-10/1), Santillana (USA) (op 5/1), **9/1** Flamands (IRE) (6/1-12/1), **10/1** Seeking Fortune (USA), **12/1** Rossel (USA) (8/1-14/1), Dombey (6/1-14/1), **16/1** Reveuse de Jour (IRE), Legal Right (USA), **20/1** Tintara (IRE), **25/1** Tashjir (USA), Raise A Prince (FR), Migwar, Roseberry Avenue (IRE), State of Caution, **33/1** Hayaain, White Plains (IRE), Persephone, **50/1** Dance Star, Giddy, Green Bopper (USA), Tina Katerina, CSF £54.40 TOTE £3.40: £1.90 £5.70 £2.50 (£29.10) Trio £94.40 OWNER Mr R. E. Sangster (MARLBOROUGH) BRED Roncon Ltd 23 Rn

1m 26.36 (2.66) SF: 40/34/31/29/29/20/23/19/18/17/14/14/8/7/7/6/7/1/3/-/1/-/-

3901

BAILEY'S HORSE FEEDS NURSERY H'CAP (2-Y.O) (Class C) £8,090.00 (£2,420.00: £1,160.00: £530.00)
5f (Rowley) Stalls: High GOING minus 0.32 sec per fur (GF) 2-35 (2-37)

3803* **Lunar Mist (69)***(74+) (MartynMeade)* 2-8-2 (5) 7x PFessey(4) (a.p: hdwy over 1f out: r.o wl to ld cl home) ....— **1**
3824* Swynford Dream **(72)***(75)*(Fav)*(JFBottomley)* 2-8-10 7x JLowe(7) (led: rdn over 1f out: r.o: jst ct) ....½ **2**
3568⁹ Little Noggins (IRE) **(74)***(73) (CADwyer)* 2-8-12 CDwyer(5) (chsd ldrs: effrt over 1f out: kpt on wl) 1¼ **3**
3651* Standown **(71)***(61) (JBerry)* 2-8-9 LDettori(2) (outpcd & bhd tl r.o fnl f) 3 **4**
3471⁵ Jolis Present **(65)***(52) (MJRyan)* 2-8-3b WCarson(1) (dwlt: outpcd & wl bhd tl r.o wl fnl f) 1 **5**
3753⁷ Chemcast **(72)***(56) (BJMeehan)* 2-8-10 GBardwell(9) (chsd ldrs: rdn ½-wy: wknd appr fnl f) ....¾ **6**
3655⁷ Bedside Mail **(83)***(66) (JMPEustace)* 2-9-7 RCochrane(8) (lw: sn drvn along: bhd tl sme late hdwy) ....½ **7**
3711¹⁵ Satellite Star (IRE) **(70)***(51) (MRChannon)* 2-8-8 PatEddery(11) (prom tl rdn & wknd over 1f out) ....½ **8**
3824² Rustic Song (IRE) **(57)***(35) (JWharton)* 2-7-2 (7)ow2 MartinDwyer(10) (chsd ldrs: sn drvn along: wknd appr fnl f) ....nk **9**
3727⁵ Veesey **(64)***(43) (JohnBerry)* 2-7-13 (3) NVarley(3) (prom tl wl outpcd fnl 2f) ....nk **10**
3568⁷ Pleasure Time **(71)***(50) (CSmith)* 2-8-9b NCarlisle(6) (lw: unruly s: chsd ldrs tl rdn & btn wl over 1f out) ....d.h **10**

LONG HANDICAP Rustic Song (IRE) 7-4

2/1 Swynford Dream, **5/2** LUNAR MIST, **15/2** Standown, **10/1** Jolis Present, **14/1** Satellite Star (IRE), Pleasure Time (8/1-16/1), **16/1** Rustic Song (IRE), **20/1** Veesey, **25/1** Little Noggins (IRE), Bedside Mail, Chemcast, CSF £7.54 CT £81.84 TOTE £4.00: £1.80 £1.50 £4.30 (£2.80) Trio £29.70 OWNER Ladyswood Racing Club (MALMESBURY) BRED T. Barratt 11 Rn

59.76 secs (1.06) SF: 46/47/45/33/24/28/38/23/7/15/23

3902

NEWARK INTERNATIONAL ANTIQUES & COLLECTORS FAIR 10TH ANNIVERSARY ROUS STKS (Listed) (3-Y.O+) (Class A) £12,034.80 (£4,453.20: £2,136.60: £873.00)
5f (Rowley) Stalls: Low GOING minus 0.32 sec per fur (GF) 3-05 (3-07)

2888a² **Dairine's Delight (IRE)** *(104) (MCunningham,Ireland)* 5-8-10 LDettori(1) (mde most: hld on wl fnl f) ....— **1**
3815⁶ Double Quick (IRE) **(102)***(105) (MJohnston)* 3-8-8 JWeaver(8) (lw: chsd ldrs: hdwy to disp ld ins fnl f: no ex towards fin) ....¾ **2**
3834¹⁵ Katya (IRE) **(95)***(99) (MRChannon)* 3-8-5 TQuinn(9) (prom: hdwy over 1f out: styd on wl towards fin) ....¾ **3**
952⁵ Ginger Tree (USA) **(92)***(91) (PWChapple-Hyam)* 3-8-6 ow1 JReid(3) (lw: prom: rdn 2f out: r.o one pce) 2½ **4**
3768³ Bin Nashwan (USA) **(107)***(88) (CEBrittain)* 3-8-10 CNakatani(2) (chsd wnr over 3f: sn btn) ..2½ **5**
1364⁵ El Yasaf (IRE) **(105)***(80) (RHarris)* 7-9-1 MWigham(7) (b.nr hind: rdn ½-wy: no imp) 3½ **6**
3554* Crowded Avenue **(97)***(77)*(Fav)*(PJMakin)* 3-8-10 PaulEddery(5) (trckd ldrs: effrt 2f out: rdn & btn over 1f out) ....s.h **7**
2671⁸ Loch Patrick **(106)***(72) (LJHolt)* 5-8-12 AMcGlone(4) (s.i.s: nvr wnt pce) 1½ **8**
3067⁷ Raah Algharb (USA) **(109)***(71) (MRStoute)* 3-8-10 WRSwinburn(6) (lw: s.i.s: bhd & hrd rdn over 2f out: n.d) ....nk **9**

5/2 Crowded Avenue, **100/30** DAIRINE'S DELIGHT (IRE), **5/1** Loch Patrick, Double Quick (IRE), **7/1** Raah Algharb (USA), **14/1** Bin Nashwan (USA), El Yasaf (IRE) (12/1-20/1), **33/1** Katya (IRE), **40/1** Ginger Tree (USA), CSF £19.06 TOTE £3.70: £1.40 £1.80 £4.00 (£9.90) Trio £51.00 OWNER Seamus Maccrosain 9 Rn

58.61 secs (-0.09) SF: 66/65/59/51/48/42/37/34/31

WEIGHT FOR AGE 3yo-2lb

OFFICIAL EXPLANATION **Crowded Avenue: never picked up in the race and was thought to be feeling the effects of a hard season.**

3903

MIDDLE PARK STKS (Gp 1) (2-Y.O C) (Class A) £72,928.75 (£26,335.00: £12,667.50: £5,212.50)
6f (Rowley) Stalls: Low GOING minus 0.32 sec per fur (GF) 3-40 (3-42)

3163* **Royal Applause (100)***(115) (BWHills)* 2-8-11 WRSwinburn(5) (lw: led after 1½f: shkn up & r.o fnl f)........—— **1**
3793a[3] Woodborough (USA) *(104) (PWChapple-Hyam)* 2-8-11 JReid(2) (lw: a chsng ldrs: kpt on fnl f: nt pce to chal)........4 **2**
3731* Kahir Almaydan (IRE) **(100)***(100)*(Fav)*(JLDunlop)* 2-8-11 WCarson(1) (led 1½f: sn pushed along: hrd rdn appr fnl f: no ex)........1¾ **3**
3610[3] Lucky Lionel (USA) **(100)***(94) (RHannon)* 2-8-11 PatEddery(4) (s.i.s: effrt u.p ½-wy: no imp)...2 **4**
3731[4] Resounder (USA) **(100)***(91) (JHMGosden)* 2-8-11 LDettori(3) (chsd ldrs tl outpcd fnl 2f).......1¼ **5**

8/11 Kahir Almaydan (IRE), **3/1** ROYAL APPLAUSE (2/1-100/30), **11/2** Woodborough (USA), **9/1** Lucky Lionel (USA) (8/1-12/1), **25/1** Resounder (USA), CSF £16.70 TOTE £3.20: £1.70 £2.20 (£8.90) OWNER Maktoum Al Maktoum (LAMBOURN) BRED Gainsborough Stud Management Ltd 5 Rn 1m 11.14 (-0.16) SF: 71/60/56/50/47

3904

NGK SPARK PLUGS JOEL STKS (Listed) (3-Y.O+) (Class A) £12,243.60 (£4,532.40: £2,176.20: £891.00)
1m (Rowley) Stalls: High GOING minus 0.32 sec per fur (GF) 4-15 (4-17)

3599[2] **Bin Rosie (103)***(118) (DRLoder)* 3-8-10b KDarley(2) (prom: led wl over 1f out: qcknd clr: r.o u.p)........—— **1**
660[3] Red Carnival (USA) **(112)***(109)*(Fav)*(MRStoute)* 3-8-5 WCarson(5) (hld up: nt clr run over 2f out: hdwy over 1f out: r.o: nrst fin)........2 **2**
1135[7] Airport (USA) **(102)***(116) (JHMGosden)* 4-9-4 LDettori(4) (hld up: hdwy 2f out: r.o: nrst fin) 1 **3**
Pater Noster (USA) **(106)***(111) (MrsJCecil)* 6-9-0 PaulEddery(13) (b: led tl hdd wl over 1f out: r.o one pce)........nk **4**
3473[2] Realities (USA) **(111)***(111) (GHarwood)* 5-9-0 WRSwinburn(10) (lw: hdwy ½-wy: ev ch 2f out: no ex fnl f)........s.h **5**
3693a[2] Lap of Luxury **(108)***(101) (WJarvis)* 6-8-9 TQuinn(7) (prom: effrt & ch 2f out: rdn & nt qckn) .2½ **6**
3562[8] Indhar **(100)***(103) (JEBanks)* 4-9-0 RHughes(11) (hld up & bhd: rdn 2f out: nvr able to chal) 1½ **7**
3608[8] Holtye (IRE) **(101)***(100) (HRACecil)* 3-8-10 PatEddery(8) (effrt ½-wy: nvr trbld ldrs)..............1½ **8**
3360[6] Dance Turn **(108)***(98) (RWArmstrong)* 4-9-0 JReid(9) (lw: swtg: chsd ldrs tl wknd fnl f)............1 **9**
3413[5] Shemaq (USA) **(96)***(91) (HThomsonJones)* 3-8-5 RHills(3) (cl up tl wknd wl over 1f out) 1¼ **10**
3458[4] Be Mindful **(100)***(92) (JRFanshawe)* 3-8-10v DHarrison(12) (in tch 6f)........1¾ **11**
2762[5] Solar Flight **(100)***(89) (BWHills)* 3-8-10 CNakatani(6) (chsd ldrs 6f: wknd)........1½ **12**
3599[3] Hawaash (IRE) *(86) (JRFanshawe)* 3-8-10 MHills(1) (bhd: rdn over 2f out: n.d) 1½ **13**

5/2 Red Carnival (USA), **4/1** Realities (USA), **6/1** Lap of Luxury, **15/2** Holtye (IRE), **10/1** Dance Turn, **12/1** Hawaash (IRE) (tchd 8/1), BIN ROSIE (op 8/1), Airport (USA), **14/1** Pater Noster (USA) (10/1-16/1), Shemaq (USA), **20/1** Be Mindful, Solar Flight, **33/1** Indhar, CSF £43.61 TOTE £9.60: £2.20 £1.70 £3.00 (£20.30) Trio £80.10 OWNER Mr Wafic Said (NEWMARKET) BRED Addison Racing Ltd Inc 13 Rn 1m 36.24 (-0.76) SF: 76/67/78/73/73/63/65/58/60/49/50/47/44
WEIGHT FOR AGE 3yo-4lb

3905

PORT OF FELIXSTOWE H'CAP (0-80) (3-Y.O) (Class D) £5,088.00 (£1,524.00: £732.00: £336.00) **5f** Stalls: High GOING minus 0.32 sec per fur (GF) 4-50 (4-53)

3681[7] **Squire Corrie (60)***(70) (JEBanks)* 3-8-0b(3)ow1 JStack(18) (mde all far side: clr over 1f out: r.o)........—— **1**
3783* Royal Dome (IRE) **(71)***(76) (MartynWane)* 3-9-0 7x MRoberts(7) (led stands' side: kpt on same pce fnl f)........2 **2**
3298[4] Latching (IRE) **(73)***(77) (RFJohnsonHoughton)* 3-9-2 JReid(8) (prom stands' side: hdwy 2f out: kpt on wl)........nk **3**
3649* Allyana (IRE) **(70)***(74) (IABalding)* 3-8-13 LDettori(2) (trckd ldrs stands' side: swtchd 2f out: r.o fnl f)........s.h **4**
3748[10] Bajan Rose **(75)***(72) (MBlanshard)* 3-9-4 RCochrane(14) (chsd wnr far side: rdn over 2f out: wknd fnl f)........2 **5**
3830[7] Able Sheriff **(50)***(44) (MWEasterby)* 3-7-0b(7) RMullen(1) (lw: chsd ldrs stands' side: ev ch 2f out: no ex fnl f)........1 **6**
2686[3] Lloc **(54)***(48) (CADwyer)* 3-7-8 (3) NVarley(13) (b: chsd ldrs far side over 3f) ....hd **7**
3750[17] Baileys Sunset (IRE) **(61)***(54) (MJohnston)* 3-8-4 JWeaver(9) (s.i.s: racd stands' side: nrst fin)........s.h **8**
3624[12] Midnight Break **(63)***(55) (PTWalwyn)* 3-8-6v PaulEddery(6) (s.i.s: hdwy u.p stands' side ½-wy: n.d)........nk **9**

2867[7] Shashi (IRE) **(74)***(64) (DMorley)* 3-9-3 WCarson(3) (prom stands' side over 3f) ....¾ **10**
3830[8] Fantasy Racing (IRE) **(78)***(67) (MRChannon)* 3-9-7 RHughes(10) (racd stands' side: nvr wnt pce) ....nk **11**
2112[3] Moody **(65)***(52) (MissGayKelleway)* 3-8-8 DHarrison(16) (b.hind: nvr wnt pce far side) ....¾ **12**
3822[17] Crystal Loop **(67)***(54) (ABailey)* 3-8-7 (3) DWright(5) (racd stands' side: in tch over 3f) ....s.h **13**
1741[6] Ultra Beet **(73)***(56) (PCHaslam)* 3-8-11 (5) MBaird(15) (a outpcd far side) 1¼ **14**
2071[4] Blue Sioux **(58)***(36) (JWharton)* 3-7-8 (7) MartinDwyer(4) (cl up stands' side 3f) 1½ **15**
3640* Unfuwaanah **(73)***(44)*(Fav)*(HThomsonJones)* 3-9-2 RHills(17) (nvr wnt pce far side) 2 **16**
3649[2] Dancing Sioux **(66)***(35) (RGuest)* 3-8-9 PatEddery(11) (spd far side to ½-wy: sn wknd) ....¾ **17**
2708[9] Marwell Indigo **(57)***(26) (PDCundell)* 3-8-0 JLowe(12) (s.s: a bhd far side) ....hd **18**

LONG HANDICAP Able Sheriff 7-2

4/1 Unfuwaanah, **11/2** Allyana (IRE), **7/1** Dancing Sioux, **10/1** Lloc, Royal Dome (IRE) (7/1-12/1), **12/1** Shashi (IRE), **16/1** Bajan Rose, Latching (IRE), Ultra Beet, Crystal Loop, **20/1** Baileys Sunset (IRE), SQUIRE CORRIE, **25/1** Able Sheriff, Midnight Break, Blue Sioux, Fantasy Racing (IRE), Moody, **33/1** Marwell Indigo, CSF £193.87 CT £2,983.24 TOTE £46.80: £6.70 £1.70 £4.50 £1.40 (£206.50) Trio £1,474.50 OWNER Mr Giles Pritchard-Gordon (NEWMARKET) BRED Whitsbury Manor Stud 18 Rn 58.9 secs SF: 57/63/64/61/59/31/35/41/42/51/54/39/41/43/23/31/22/13
T/Plpt: £57.50 (409.73 Tckts). T/Qdpt: £11.70 (13.8 Tckts). AA

3484a-TABY (Stockholm, Sweden) (L-H)
Tuesday September 5th (Soft)

3906a LANSFORSAKRINGAR SVEALANDLOPN (2-Y.O) £8,598.00 **6f**
6-55 (6-55)

Turfman (IRE) *(BNeuman,Sweden)* 2-9-2 RMuggeridge ....— **1**
Secret Optimist (IRE) *(MKahn,Sweden)* 2-9-2 FDiaz 1 **2**
Blue Collar (FR) *(WNeuroth,Norway)* 2-9-2 MLarsen 2½ **3**
2876[7] Hever Golf Queen *(TJNaughton)* 2-8-12 JohnFortune (btn approx 16l) **8**
Tote 23.6SKr: 12SKr 14SKr 12SKr (100.8SKr) OWNER R.Tradgard BRED Airlie Stud 9 Rn 1m 15.3

3785a-CHANTILLY (France) (R-H)
Monday September 18th (Very Soft)

3907a PRIX DES CHENES (Gp 3) (2-Y.O C & G) £26,347.00 (£9,581.00: £4,790.00) **1m**
2-20 (2-17)

Manninamix *(97) (AFabre,France)* 2-9-2 TJarnet ....— **1**
3613[2] Winter Quarters (USA) *(96) (IABalding)* 2-9-2 MHills ....nk **2**
Martiniquais (IRE) *(91) (AFabre,France)* 2-9-2 OPeslier 2½ **3**
P-M 3.40F: 2.10F 2.70F (SF 26.60F) OWNER Mr J-L. Lagardere (FRANCE) BRED J-L Lagardere 6 Rn 1m 46.7 (12.10) SF: -/-/-

1710a-BELMONT PARK (New York, USA) (L-H)
Thursday September 21st (Firm)

3908a CLAIMING RACE (3-Y.O+) £13,077.00 **1m 110y**
21-40 (21-42)

Wave Your Flag (USA) *(100) (EFisher,USA)* 8-8-1 SSellers ....— **1**
Reason Prevails (USA) *(97) (FSchulhofer,USA)* 4-8-5 JulieKrone 4 **2**
L'Hermine *(95) (MHushion,USA)* 6-8-5 RMigliore ....¾ **3**
2455[7] Dune River *(DRLoder)* 6-8-1 RDavis (btn over 31l) **9**
P-M £31.60: PL £12.40 £10.80 SHOW £8.00 £4.70 £2.70 (£313.50) OWNER J. A. Schettino BRED A.N.W. Enterprises & Swettenham Stud 9 Rn 1m 42.6 SF: -/-/-/-

3906a-TABY (Stockholm, Sweden) (L-H)
Saturday September 23rd (Good)

3909a TVAARSLOPNING (2-Y.O) £1,806.00 **7f 110y**
12-00 (12-00)

3906a[8] **Hever Golf Queen** *(68?) (TJNaughton)* 2-8-10 JohnFortune ....— **1**

Steinway (SWE) *(71) (CStromberg,Sweden)* 2-9-0 GNordling ....½ 2
Lions Queen (DEN) *(61) (BFriberg,Sweden)* 2-8-10 RSkrzydlo 3 3
Tote 15.32SKr: 60SKr 25SKr OWNER Mr M. P. Hanson (EPSOM) BRED Hever Castle Stud 5 Rn
1m 33.5 SF: -/-/-

2892a-COLOGNE (Germany) (R-H)
Saturday September 23rd (Good)

3910a GROSSER KAUFHOF PREIS (Gp 2) (3-Y.O+) £29,835.00 (£11,934.00: £5,967.00: £3,704.00) **1m** 3-40 (3-49)

3577a* **A Magicman (FR)** *(112) (HSteguweit,Germany)* 3-8-11 NGrant (hld up: gd hdwy to ld over 1f out: r.o wl)....— 1
3577a3 Chato (USA) *(111) (HSteinmetz,Germany)* 3-8-11 AStarke (trckd ldrs: 4th st: led 2f out tl over 1f out: r.o wl)....¾ 2
3577a2 Ladoni *(104) (HRemmert,Germany)* 3-8-11 KWoodburn (mid div: hmpd st: r.o wl ins fnl f)...3½ 3
Orfijar (FR) *(103) (Germany)* 5-9-2 ABond (a cl up: no ex fnl 2f) ....¾ 4
1121a7 Sinyar *(99) (Germany)* 3-8-9 THellier (rr early: hmpd st: nvr plcd to chal)....nk 5
Oktan (IRE) *(97) (Germany)* 3-8-9 ATylicki (prom: 3rd st: sn led: hdd 2f out: wknd)....1 6
Perfect Vintage *(97) (Germany)* 5-9-2 DRegnard (led tl over 2f out: rdn & wknd)....1½ 7
Grappolo (GER) *(88) (Germany)* 3-8-9b WMongil (a bhd) 3 8
2015* Moon King (IRE) *(RHannon)* 3-8-9 RPerham (w ldr: rdn & wknd over 2f out: btn over 11l) 9
Tote 32DM: 15DM 21DM 16DM (SF 161DM) OWNER Stall Dagobert BRED H. Voegele & Maria Koenig 11 Rn
1m 34.95 SF: -/-/-/-/-/-/-/-/-

3908a-BELMONT PARK (New York, USA) (L-H)
Saturday September 23rd (Soft)

3911a FLOWER BOWL INVITATIONAL (Gp 1) (3-Y.O+ F & M) £76,923.00 (£25,641.00: £7,692.00) **1m 2f** 21-45 (21-45)

Northern Emerald (USA) *(116) (WMott,USA)* 5-8-1 RPerez ....— 1
Danish (IRE) *(117) (CClement,USA)* 4-8-4 JSantos 1 2
Duda (USA) *(113) (WMott,USA)* 4-8-1 JBailey ....¾ 3
3694a7 Fanjica (IRE) *(114) (JLDunlop)* 3-8-0 HMcCauley (btn approx 3½l).... 5
3480a4 La Confederation *(101) (DRLoder)* 4-8-7 RDavis (btn approx 10½l).... 8
P-M £17.20: PL £7.40 £7.10 SHOW £5.20 £4.50 £4.50 (£125.50) OWNER H Polk & D Richardson 10 Rn
2m 6.68 SF: -/-/-/-/-

3910a-COLOGNE (Germany) (R-H)
Sunday September 24th (Good)

3912a PREIS VON KOLN (Listed) (3-Y.O+ F & M) £24,691.00 (£9,876.00: £4,938.00) **1m** 2-05 (0-21)

1004a* **Penny Drops** *(107) (LordHuntingdon)* 6-9-6 JReid ....— 1
Lara (GER) *(104) (BSchutz,Germany)* 3-9-0 ASuborics ....nk 2
Prime Lady (GER) *(102) (RSuerland,Germany)* 4-9-2 WMongil ....nk 3
Tote 45DM: 28DM 37DM 68DM (SF 700DM) OWNER Mr Stanley Sharp (WEST ILSLEY) BRED T. M. Saud 15 Rn
1m 31.23 SF: -/-/-

3913a IDUNA/NOVA-FLIEGER PREIS (Listed) (3-Y.O+) £8,230.00 (£3,292.00: £1,646.00) **5f** 3-15 (3-18)

3689a6 **Palacegate Episode (IRE)** *(102) (JBerry)* 5-9-8 LDettori ....— 1
Auenadler (GER) *(101) (UOstmann,Germany)* 3-9-10 GBocskai 1½ 2
Property Man *(95) (BHellier,Germany)* 3-9-10 PSchiergen 2 3
Tote 17DM: 12DM 16DM 18DM (SF 74DM) OWNER Palacegate Corporation Ltd (COCKERHAM) BRED Brendan and Sheila Powell 10 Rn
56.15 secs SF: -/-/-

3914a EMS-KURIERPOST-EUROPA-PREIS (Gp 1) (3-Y.O+) £123,457.00 (£49,383.00: £24,691.00: £12,346.00) **1m 4f** 3-55 (3-58)

3486a* **Solon (GER)** *(124) (HJentzsch,Germany)* 3-8-10 PSchiergen (a.p: 3rd st: led 2f out: sn clr: r.o wl u.p) ....— 1

3698a* Sternkonig (IRE) *(123) (HBlume,Germany)* 5-9-6 OSchick (mid div: 5th st: chsd wnr fr 2f out: no imp) 2½ 2
3046a[6] Protektor (GER) *(120) (ALowe,Germany)* 6-9-6 THellier (hld up: 8th st: styd on wl fnl f: nvr nrr) 2 3
3591a* Germany (USA) *(117) (BSchutz,Germany)* 4-9-6 LDettori (a cl up: 4th st: rdn 2f out: nt qckn).2 4
3591a[4] Kornado *(115) (ALowe,Germany)* 5-9-6 GBocskai (mid div: nvr plcd to chal)....2 5
3482a[8] Broadway Flyer (USA) *(114) (JWHills)* 4-9-6b MHills (trckd ldr: 2nd st: sn rdn & wknd)....¾ 6
Almaz (SU) *(106) (JSchawujew,Poland)* 3-8-10 ATschugujewez (bhd tl sme hdwy fnl 3f) 4½ 7
3698a[2] Caballo (GER) *(104) (HJentzsch,Germany)* 4-9-6 LHammer-Hansen (a bhd: 7th st)....2½ 8
3482a[4] Laroche (GER) *(104) (HJentzsch,Germany)* 4-9-6b SEccles (led to 2f out: wknd qckly) ....nk 9
3591a[5] Beauchamp Hero *(96) (JLDunlop)* 5-9-6 JReid (a bhd)....6 10

Tote 43DM: 19DM 23DM 53DM (SF 243DM) OWNER Gestut Schlenderhan BRED Gestut Schlenderhan 10 Rn 2m 27.06 SF: -/-/-/-/-/-/-/-/-/-

3613-GOODWOOD (R-H)
Friday September 29th (Rnd Good, St Good to soft)
WEATHER: sunny WIND: almost nil

3915 SEPTEMBER (S) STKS (2-Y.O) (Class E) £4,272.50 (£1,280.00: £615.00: £282.50)
7f Stalls: High GOING minus 0.04 sec per fur (G) 2-15 (2-16)

3623[18] **Lilli Claire (68)***(72) (AGFoster)* 2-8-6 DHolland(12) (hdwy over 2f out: led over 1f out: pushed out)....— 1
3553[5] Even Handed **(70)***(68) (PFICole)* 2-8-6 (5) DaneO'Neill(19) (2nd st: led over 2f out tl over 1f out: unable qckn)....4 2
3680[5] Just Millie (USA) **(82)***(65)*(Fav)*(JEBanks)* 2-8-13 JTate(8) (b: hdwy over 2f out: hrd rdn over 1f out: one pce) 2 3
3528[6] Young Butt **(58)***(47) (JFfitch-Heyes)* 2-8-6 (5) AWhelan(17) (6th st: wknd over 1f out) 7 4
3838[4] Corniche Quest (IRE) **(65)***(42) (MRChannon)* 2-8-1 (5) PPMurphy(20) (led over 5f out tl over 2f out: wknd over 1f out) ....nk 5
3538[7] Moving Up (IRE) **(66)***(39) (GLMoore)* 2-8-6 SWhitworth(5) (b.nr hind: rdn over 3f out: hdwy over 1f out: nvr nrr) 1¼ 6
3379[11] Dragonjoy **(62)***(44) (LJHolt)* 2-8-11 WNewnes(10) (lw: hdwy over 1f out: nvr nrr) ....hd 7
3721[7] Ginger Glint **(59)***(43) (MJHeaton-Ellis)* 2-8-11 WWoods(4) (hdwy over 3f out: wknd over 1f out) ....s.h 8
3711[10] Time Clash (IRE) **(71)***(38) (BPalling)* 2-8-6 TSprake(13) (a mid div)....hd 9
3767[5] Real Gem **(60)***(35) (PJMakin)* 2-8-6 GCarter(14) (swtg: a mid div) 1½ 10
3767[7] Dhulikhel **(60)***(32) (DMarks)* 2-8-2 (7)ow3 GFaulkner(1) (4th st: wknd over 2f out)....1¼ 11
3733[15] Newlands Corner *(29) (JAkehurst)* 2-8-6 RPerham(16) (b.nr hind: lw: 3rd st: wknd over 1f out) 1½ 12
3673[12] Rowlandsons Links *(32) (BJMeehan)* 2-8-11 MTebbutt(3) (a bhd) ....½ 13
3767[15] Subtle One (IRE) *(21) (GLMoore)* 2-8-6 AMackay(18) (a bhd)....3 14
2035[10] Ebony T-A-P-S *(20) (JSMoore)* 2-8-6 JFEgan(2) (bit bkwd: a bhd)....hd 15
Lakeside Express *(12) (JSMoore)* 2-8-3 (3) NVarley(7) (unf: bit bkwd: bhd fnl 3f)....3½ 16
3767[11] The Frog Princess *(12) (KMcAuliffe)* 2-8-6 JWeaver(6) (led over 1f: 5th st: wknd over 3f out) ....nk 17
Topical (USA) *(5) (GHarwood)* 2-8-11b CRutter(9) (str: bit bkwd: a wl bhd) 5 18

5/2 Just Millie (USA), **7/1** Time Clash (IRE), **8/1** Even Handed, Corniche Quest (IRE), **9/1** Real Gem, **10/1** LILLI CLAIRE, **11/1** Topical (USA) (op 7/1), Newlands Corner, **12/1** Moving Up (IRE) (op 8/1), **14/1** Ginger Glint, **16/1** Dhulikhel, **20/1** Subtle One (IRE), Lakeside Express, The Frog Princess, **25/1** Dragonjoy, **33/1** Young Butt, **50/1** Ebony T-A-P-S, Rowlandsons Links, CSF £92.70 TOTE £9.30: £2.70 £3.10 £1.60 (£47.10) Trio £18.40 OWNER Miss Juliet Reed (LAMBOURN) BRED Roger C. Denton 18 Rn 1m 29.54 (5.14) SF: 27/23/20/2/-/-/-/-/-/-/-/-/-/-/-/-/-/-
Bt in 4,500 gns

3916 JACOBS BAKERY MAIDEN STKS (2-Y.O) (Class D) £4,337.50 (£1,300.00: £625.00: £287.50)
1m Stalls: High GOING minus 0.04 sec per fur (G) 2-45 (2-46)

3620[5] **Select Few** *(89)*(Fav)*(LMCumani)* 2-9-0 JWeaver(9) (3rd st: rdn over 3f out: led wl over 1f out: r.o wl)....— 1
3708[6] Ashanti Dancer (IRE) *(78) (MJHaynes)* 2-8-9 RCochrane(12) (led over 6f out tl over 3f out: led over 2f out tl wl over 1f out: unable qckn)....3 2
Altamura (USA) *(75+) (JHMGosden)* 2-8-9 GHind(4) (unf: s.s: styd far side st: hdwy over 2f out: rdn over 1f out: unable qckn)....1¾ 3

3672[6] Dirab *(73) (HRACecil)* 2-9-0 WRyan(3) (lw: 5th st: rdn over 3f out: one pce)....................3½ 4
3868[18] Galway Blade *(72) (APJarvis)* 2-9-0 JTate(10) (nvr nr to chal)....................nk 5
3541[4] Ski For Gold *(62) (JLDunlop)* 2-8-9 GCarter(1) (no hdwy fnl 3f)....................2½ 6
3672[7] Ben Bowden *(66) (MBlanshard)* 2-9-0 TSprake(11) (6th st: wknd over 2f out)....................nk 7
Classy Chief *(65) (RBoss)* 2-8-11 (3) NVarley(7) (str: bkwd: s.s: nvr nrr)....................½ 8
3280[7] Oliver Rock *(62) (MajorDNChappell)* 2-9-0 WWoods(2) (bhd fnl 2f)....................1¾ 9
Premier Generation (IRE) *(58) (DWPArbuthnot)* 2-9-0 DHolland(13) (neat: s.s: styd far side st: disp ld over 3f out tl over 2f out: eased whn btn over 1f out)....................1¾ 10
3733[14] Mazcobar *(58) (PJMakin)* 2-9-0 PaulEddery(14) (lw: 2nd & styd far side st: disp ld over 3f out tl over 2f out: eased whn btn over 1f out)....................s.h 11
Amadour (IRE) *(57) (PMitchell)* 2-9-0 RPerham(6) (cmpt: lw: s.s: sme hdwy over 3f out: wknd over 2f out)....................1¾ 12
3765[15] Young Mazaad (IRE) *(RCurtis)* 2-9-0 WNewnes(8) (led over 1f: 4th st: wknd over 3f out: t.o)....................dist 13

11/4 SELECT FEW, **100/30** Dirab, **9/2** Oliver Rock (3/1-5/1), **5/1** Altamura (USA) (op 3/1), **6/1** Ski For Gold, **10/1** Ashanti Dancer (IRE), **20/1** Galway Blade, Ben Bowden, Classy Chief, Premier Generation (IRE), Mazcobar, **40/1** Amadour (IRE), **66/1** Young Mazaad (IRE), CSF £32.52 TOTE £4.00: £1.40 £2.50 £2.30 (£49.40) Trio £314.20 OWNER Sheikh Mohammed (NEWMARKET) BRED Sheikh Mohammed bin Rashid al Maktoum 13 Rn
1m 43.32 (5.72) SF: 36/25/22/20/19/9/13/12/9/5/5/2/-

3917 LIMEKILN AUCTION STKS (2-Y.O) (Class C) £6,680.00 (£2,000.00: £960.00: £440.00) 7f Stalls: High GOING minus 0.04 sec per fur (G) 3-20 (3-21)

3746[2] **Quakers Field (100)***(99) (GLMoore)* 2-8-10 SWhitworth(6) (5th st: led over 1f out: drvn out)— 1
3867[3] Astuti (IRE) **(90)***(89)*(Fav)*(APJarvis)* 2-8-0 JTate(9) (lw: hdwy over 3f out: ev ch fnl f: r.o wl)....................hd 2
3405[3] General Rose **(72)***(75) (RHannon)* 2-8-1 ow1 GCarter(1) (3rd st: lost pl 3f out: one pce fnl 2f)...6 3
3869[3] Abundant *(75) (BGubby)* 2-7-9 (5) PPMurphy(2) (lw: hdwy on ins over 2f out: hrd rdn over 1f out: sn wknd)....................s.h 4
3788a[7] Double Oscar (IRE) **(100)***(81) (MJohnston)* 2-8-7 JWeaver(8) (led over 5f)....................½ 5
3652[5] Law Dancer (IRE) *(81) (TGMills)* 2-8-9 DHolland(4) (lw: 4th st: rdn over 3f out: wknd fnl f).....¾ 6
3345[4] She's My Love **(85)***(71) (JEBanks)* 2-8-0 AMackay(7) (lw: nvr nrr)....................nk 7
1003a* Coyote Bluff(IRE) *(80) (PWChapple-Hyam)* 2-8-4 (5) RHavlin(5) (neat: bit bkwd: hdwy over 2f out: wknd wl over 1f out)....................nk 8
3536[5] Mountain Dream *(75) (PFICole)* 2-8-12 CRutter(10) (sme hdwy over 2f out: sn wknd) 3½ 9
3765[7] Maple Burl *(56) (SDow)* 2-7-8 (7)ow1 ADaly(3) (6th st: wknd over 2f out)....................3 10
Texas Tramp *(17) (MajorDNChappell)* 2-7-6 (3) NVarley(11) (neat: bit bkwd: 2nd & styd centre st: wknd over 2f out)....................15 11

11/4 Astuti (IRE), **9/2** Double Oscar (IRE), **5/1** QUAKERS FIELD (op 3/1), **6/1** She's My Love, **13/2** Coyote Bluff(IRE) (op 4/1), **8/1** Law Dancer (IRE), **12/1** Mountain Dream (8/1-14/1), **14/1** Abundant (op 8/1), **25/1** General Rose, **33/1** Texas Tramp, **50/1** Maple Burl, CSF £18.94 TOTE £7.10: £2.10 £1.50 £2.20 (£9.20) Trio £32.60 OWNER Pennine Partners (EPSOM) BRED Summertree Stud 11 Rn
1m 29.47 (5.07) SF: 31/21/7/7/13/13/3/12/7/-/-

3918 HOSHIZAKI ICE MAKERS H'CAP (0-80) (3-Y.O) (Class D) £4,413.75 (£1,320.00: £632.50: £288.75) 1m 4f Stalls: Low GOING minus 0.04 sec per fur (G) 3-50 (3-50)

3653[4] **Meghdoot (69)***(79) (HJCollingridge)* 3-8-12 MRimmer(7) (4th st: led 2f out: hrd rdn: r.o wl)..— 1
3616[7] Snowy Petrel (IRE) **(75)***(84) (JLDunlop)* 3-9-4 GCarter(5) (led 10f: hrd rdn & ev ch fnl f: r.o)...½ 2
3552[10] Gloriana **(73)***(82) (LadyHerries)* 3-9-2 RCochrane(2) (rdn over 4f out: 5th st: r.o ins fnl f).......nk 3
3459[3] Eurolink Mischief **(78)***(84)*(Fav)*(LMCumani)* 3-9-7 JWeaver(4) (b.hind: 2nd st: hrd rdn & ev ch 2f out: unable qckn)....................2½ 4
3653[11] Maftun (USA) **(66)***(72) (MajorWRHern)* 3-8-9 WRyan(3) (lw: 6th st: rdn over 3f out: one pce)....................s.h 5
3500[7] Courbaril **(60)***(62) (SDow)* 3-7-10 (7) ADaly(8) (swtg: hdwy 7f out: 3rd & styd centre st: wknd over 1f out)....................3 6
3537[4] Harlech (IRE) **(74)***(76) (JHMGosden)* 3-9-3b GHind(1) (s.s: a bhd)....................s.h 7
3571[9] Divina Mia **(62)***(44) (JWHills)* 3-8-5 DHolland(6) (a bhd)....................15 8
3875[13] Keen To The Last (FR) **(67)***(44) (GHarwood)* 3-8-10v WWoods(9) (lw: bhd fnl 3f)....................3½ 9

9/4 Eurolink Mischief, **4/1** Courbaril (op 7/1), **9/2** MEGHDOOT, **13/2** Harlech (IRE) (op 4/1), **8/1** Gloriana (op 5/1), **10/1** Snowy Petrel (IRE) (op 5/1), **12/1** Maftun (USA) (op 8/1), **14/1** Keen To The Last (FR) (op 7/1), **16/1** Divina Mia, CSF £45.39 CT £324.19 TOTE £6.30: £2.00 £3.10 £1.70 (£32.20) Trio £82.10 OWNER CSGJ Racing Syndicate (NEWMARKET) BRED L. Audus 9 Rn
2m 41.49 (9.49) SF: 31/36/34/36/24/14/28/-/-

3919

FRIALATOR INTERNATIONAL H'CAP (0-70) (3-Y.O+) (Class E)
£4,565.00 (£1,370.00: £660.00: £305.00)
5f Stalls: Low GOING minus 0.04 sec per fur (G) 4-25 (4-32)

*3524** **Rhythmic Dancer (62)***(71) (AStreeter)* 7-9-3 (3) SDrowne(17) (reard s: hdwy over 1f out: led ins fnl f: r.o wl)......— **1**
3764[5] Malibu Man **(57)***(61) (SMellor)* 3-8-13 TSprake(26) (swtg: a.p: led over 1f out tl ins fnl f: unable qckn)......1½ **2**
3442[15] Half Tone **(40)***(44) (RMFlower)* 3-7-7b(3) NVarley(13) (a.p: rdn over 2f out: ev ch ins fnl f: one pce)......s.h **3**
3615[21] Tinker Osmaston **(63)***(67) (MSSaunders)* 4-9-7 JFEgan(14) (lw: hrd rdn & hdwy over 1f out: r.o one pce)......s.h **4**
2120[5] Hickory Blue **(68)***(64) (MrsNMacauley)* 5-9-7b(5) RHavlin(9) (a.p: rdn over 2f out: one pce)...2½ **5**
3014[4] Sizzling **(61)***(55) (RHannon)* 3-8-12 (5) DaneO'Neill(20) (hdwy over 1f out: nvr nrr)......¾ **6**
3800[2] Southern Dominion **(60)***(53) (MJohnston)* 3-9-2 JWeaver(25) (lw: a.p: hrd rdn over 1f out: sn wknd)......s.h **7**
3822[4] Louisville Belle (IRE) **(54)***(46) (MDIUsher)* 6-8-12 MRimmer(5) (b: nvr nr to chal)......½ **8**
3822[2] Halbert **(65)***(56) (MRChannon)* 6-9-4v(5) PPMurphy(12) (hld up: hrd rdn over 1f out: sn wknd)......nk **9**
3177[7] Correspondence (CAN) **(40)***(30) (MartynMeade)* 5-7-7 (5) PFessey(6) (nvr nrr)......nk **10**
1164[14] Hi Kiki **(44)***(34) (MartynMeade)* 4-8-2 FNorton(10) (outpcd: hdwy fnl f: r.o)......s.h **11**
3467[11] Bonny Melody **(42)***(31) (PDEvans)* 4-7-7 (7) AmandaSanders(18) (hld up: hrd rdn 2f out: wknd over 1f out)......nk **12**
3748[14] Nordico Princess **(69)***(58) (MBrittain)* 4-9-13 RCochrane(19) (led over 3f)......s.h **13**
3800[13] Friendly Brave (USA) **(66)***(54) (MissGayKelleway)* 5-9-10 SWhitworth(11) (nvr nrr)......s.h **14**
3748[18] Lugana Vision **(51)***(35) (RHarris)* 3-8-0 (7) ADaly(2) (no hdwy fnl 2f)......1½ **15**
3678* Secret Miss **(55)***(38) (APJarvis)* 3-8-11 JTate(7) (lw: s.s: nvr nrr)......s.h **16**
3681[16] High Holme **(50)***(30) (DTThom)* 4-8-5v(3) DRMcCabe(16) (lw: s.s: a bhd)......1 **17**
3667[3] Runs in the Family **(55)***(32) (PGMurphy)* 3-8-4b(7) RWaterfield(8) (prom over 2f)......1 **18**
3622[16] Miriam **(48)***(23) (MJFetherston-Godley)* 4-8-6 CRutter(23) (hdwy 2f out: wknd fnl f)......½ **19**
2024[4] Swan At Whalley **(66)***(37) (MartynWane)* 3-9-8 GCarter(4) (prom over 3f)......1¼ **20**
2692[10] Mazzarello (IRE) **(43)***(10) (RCurtis)* 5-7-10 (5) AWhelan(21) (lw: hung rt over 3f out: a bhd)...1¼ **21**
3678[5] Supreme Thought **(65)***(28) (LGCottrell)* 3-9-7 PaulEddery(22) (swtg: bhd fnl 3f)......1¼ **22**
3667[4] Kalar **(52)***(14)*(Fav)*(DWChapman)* 6-8-10b DHolland(1) (lw: prom over 2f)......nk **23**
2943[11] Tachycardia **(50)***(11) (RJO'Sullivan)* 3-8-6 WWoods(24) (prom over 2f)......½ **24**
2239[13] Deardaw **(43)** *(MDIUsher)* 3-7-6 (7) CAdamson(3) (b: bhd fnl 2f)......5 **25**

5/1 Kalar (op 8/1), **8/1** Runs in the Family, **10/1** Southern Dominion (7/1-12/1), Halbert, **11/1** RHYTHMIC DANCER, Secret Miss (8/1-12/1), **14/1** Sizzling (10/1-16/1), Malibu Man (op 8/1), Correspondence (CAN), **16/1** Louisville Belle (IRE), Friendly Brave (USA), **20/1** Supreme Thought, Hickory Blue, **25/1** Tinker Osmaston, Bonny Melody, Swan At Whalley, Half Tone, Mazzarello (IRE), **33/1** Miriam, Tachycardia, Hi Kiki, Lugana Vision, Nordico Princess, Deardaw, **40/1** High Holme, CSF £154.92 CT £3,466.43 TOTE £8.90: £1.80 £3.10 £7.50 £8.00 (£101.30) Trio £961.70 OWNER Mr K. Nicholls (UTTOXETER) BRED Heathavon Stables Ltd 25 Rn
60.73 secs (4.03) SF: 30/18/1/26/23/12/10/5/15/-/-/-/17/13/-/-/-/-/-/-/-/-/-/-/-
WEIGHT FOR AGE 3yo-2lb

3920

MERBURY CATERING CONSULTANTS CLAIMING H'CAP (0-60) (3-Y.O+) (Class E) £4,630.00 (£1,390.00: £670.00: £310.00)
1m Stalls: High GOING minus 0.04 sec per fur (G) 4-55 (5-06)

3079[9] **Swinging Sixties (IRE) (53)***(65) (GLMoore)* 4-9-8 SWhitworth(7) (hdwy 3f out: swtchd lft over 2f out: led over 1f out: r.o wl)......— **1**
3837[9] Prenonamoss **(54)***(64) (DWPArbuthnot)* 7-9-9 DHolland(10) (b.hind: rdn & hdwy over 1f out: r.o)......1 **2**
3863[18] Saltando (IRE) **(51)***(58) (PatMitchell)* 4-9-1 (5) DaneO'Neill(15) (hrd rdn over 2f out: hdwy over 1f out: r.o)......1½ **3**
Labudd (USA) **(58)***(64) (RIngram)* 5-9-13 WRSwinburn(20) (b: hdwy over 3f out: led wl over 1f out: sn hdd: unable qckn)......nk **4**
3757[11] Doodies Pool (IRE) **(51)***(53) (PBurgoyne)* 5-9-3 (3) DRMcCabe(12) (rdn over 3f out: hdwy over 1f out: one pce fnl f)......2 **5**
3800[14] Blow Dry (IRE) **(59)***(58) (MartynWane)* 5-10-0 MTebbutt(21) (4th st: led over 2f out tl wl over 1f out: wknd fnl f)......1¾ **6**
3645[11] Night Wink (USA) **(59)***(54) (DNicholls)* 3-9-10 GHind(18) (5th st: ev ch over 1f out: sn wknd)1¾ **7**
3661[2] Bentico **(59)***(51)*(Fav)*(MrsNMacauley)* 6-9-7b(7) AmandaSanders(13) (2nd st: wknd over 1f out)......1¾ **8**
2342[9] Access Carnival (IRE) **(50)***(38) (RBoss)* 4-9-2 (3) NVarley(14) (6th st: wknd over 2f out)......1¾ **9**

3807[13] Roseate Lodge **(57)***(44) (NBycroft)* 9-9-12b TIves(4) (b: a mid div) .... ¾ **10**
3771[15] Top Pet (IRE) **(51)***(37) (RAkehurst)* 5-9-6 PaulEddery(6) (rdn over 3f out: hdwy over 2f out: wkng whn hmpd over 1f out) .... ½ **11**
3363[3] Alerting **(60)***(46) (IABalding)* 3-9-11 WRyan(5) (hdwy over 2f out: wknd over 1f out) .... s.h **12**
3654[12] Lees Please (IRE) **(49)***(32) (KOCunningham-Brown)* 3-9-0 JTate(2) (nvr nrr) 1½ **13**
1591[7] Miss Jemmima **(57)***(39) (LordHuntingdon)* 3-9-8 RPerham(3) (bhd fnl 3f) .... nk **14**
3605[4] Thatchmaster (IRE) **(47)***(25) (CAHorgan)* 4-9-2 WNewnes(22) (led 7f out tl over 2f out: sn wknd) 2 **15**
3152[3] Miss Laughter **(53)***(30) (JWHills)* 3-9-4 CRutter(19) (3rd st: wknd over 2f out) .... ½ **16**
3455[8] Kevasingo **(60)***(35) (SDow)* 3-9-4 (7) ADaly(17) (7th st: wknd over 3f out) 1¼ **17**
3770[5] Charm Dancer **(54)***(27) (MCPipe)* 3-9-5 GCarter(9) (bhd fnl 3f) .... ¾ **18**
3159[4] Quillon Rose **(52)***(25) (CFWall)* 3-8-12 (5) LNewton(8) (swtg: bhd fnl 3f) .... nk **19**
3751[8] Green Golightly (USA) **(51)***(23) (DAWilson)* 4-9-6 RCochrane(1) (led 1f: wknd over 5f out) .... nk **20**
3685[14] Opera Fan (IRE) **(51)***(18) (SirMarkPrescott)* 3-9-2 WWoods(16) (bhd fnl 3f) 2½ **21**
3654[10] Jigadee Creek **(51)***(14) (GHarwood)* 3-9-2v JWeaver(11) (8th st: wknd over 3f out) 2 **22**

9/2 Bentico, **6/1** Labudd (USA), Prenonamoss, **7/1** Charm Dancer, **10/1** Quillon Rose, **12/1** Opera Fan (IRE), Alerting, Kevasingo, Thatchmaster (IRE), **14/1** Saltando (IRE), Top Pet (IRE), Jigadee Creek, Night Wink (USA), Miss Laughter, **16/1** Miss Jemmima, Blow Dry (IRE), **20/1** Access Carnival (IRE), Lees Please (IRE), SWINGING SIXTIES (IRE), Green Golightly (USA), **25/1** Roseate Lodge, **33/1** Doodies Pool (IRE), CSF £161.55 CT £1,689.65 TOTE £63.50: £9.10 £2.50 £5.80 £2.10 (£282.50) Trio £776.40 OWNER K.Higson (EPSOM) BRED Ron Con Ltd & Swettenham Stud 22 Rn 1m 43.05 (5.45) SF: 47/46/40/46/35/40/32/33/20/26/19/24/10/17/7/8/13/5/3/5/-/-
WEIGHT FOR AGE 3yo-4lb

3921

PHEASANTRY MAIDEN STKS (3-Y.O) (Class D) £4,270.75 (£1,276.00: £610.50: £277.75)
1m 2f Stalls: High GOING minus 0.04 sec per fur (G) 5-25 (5-40)

3630[3] **Rosy Hue (IRE) (72)***(77) (RCharlton)* 3-8-9 JWeaver(12) (mde all: clr over 4f out: rdn out) ... — **1**
3016[17] Devon Peasant *(77) (LGCottrell)* 3-8-9 GCarter(9) (hrd rdn over 3f out: hdwy over 2f out: chsd wnr over 1f out: r.o wl) .... s.h **2**
Roussi (USA) *(72) (MRStoute)* 3-9-0 WRSwinburn(8) (str: bkwd: dwlt: rdn over 2f out: hdwy over 1f out: r.o) 6 **3**
2604[3] Quillwork (USA) **(56)***(67) (MrsJCecil)* 3-8-9 TIves(10) (hdwy over 2f out: hrd rdn over 1f out: one pce) .... s.h **4**
3438[6] Timeless *(59)*(Fav)*(HRACecil)* 3-8-9 WRyan(13) (lw: 2nd st: rdn over 2f out: wknd fnl f) 5 **5**
3653[3] Love The Blues *(58) (DNicholson)* 3-8-9 JWilliams(1) (lw: nvr nr to chal) .... ½ **6**
3756[10] Dolliver (USA) *(60) (SDow)* 3-8-7 (7) ADaly(6) (styd far side st: nvr nrr) 2 **7**
1514[4] Zidac **(72)***(59) (PJMakin)* 3-9-0 DHolland(5) (3rd st: wknd over 2f out) .... ½ **8**
3559[4] Night Flare (FR) **(70)***(57) (RHannon)* 3-8-9 (5) DaneO'Neill(14) (7th st: wknd 3f out) 1¾ **9**
552[8] Barbason *(56) (JRFanshawe)* 3-8-11 (3) NVarley(7) (bit bkwd: 4th st: wknd 2f out) .... nk **10**
3517[2] Mayreau **(78)***(48) (GHarwood)* 3-8-9 WWoods(4) (5th st: wknd over 2f out) 2 **11**
3653[8] King of Babylon (IRE) *(51) (LadyHerries)* 3-9-0 PaulEddery(15) (lw: bhd fnl 3f) 1¼ **12**
3618[2] Fire of London **(78)***(36) (JHMGosden)* 3-8-9 GHind(3) (b.hind: 6th st: wknd over 3f out) 6 **13**
Mamlouk *(25) (JWPayne)* 3-9-0 MTebbutt(11) (bhd fnl 8f) 10 **14**
Readypower *(JJBridger)* 3-9-0 JFEgan(2) (b: bkwd: dwlt: a bhd: t.o fnl 4f) .... dist **15**

3/1 Timeless (op 6/1), **4/1** ROSY HUE (IRE), **9/2** Roussi (USA) (op 5/4), **5/1** Mayreau (9/2-7/1), Fire of London, **8/1** Love The Blues (op 5/1), **16/1** Zidac, **25/1** Quillwork (USA), King of Babylon (IRE), **33/1** Barbason, Night Flare (FR), **66/1** Devon Peasant, Dolliver (USA), Mamlouk, **100/1** Readypower, CSF £192.95 TOTE £6.20: £1.60 £7.80 £2.00 (£134.00) Trio £259.60 OWNER Lord Weinstock & The Hon Simon Weinstock (BECKHAMPTON) BRED Ballymacoll Stud Farm Ltd 15 Rn 2m 12.19 (7.19) SF: 33/33/28/23/15/14/16/15/13/12/4/7/-/-/-

T/Plpt: £302.80 (50.61 Tckts). T/Qdpt: £125.20 (0.4 Tckts); £101.58 to Goodwood 30/9/95. AK

3899-NEWMARKET (R-H)
Friday September 29th (Good)

WEATHER: cloudy WIND: fresh half bhd

3922

NGK SPARK PLUGS RATED STKS H'CAP (0-105) (3-Y.O+ F & M) (Class B) £8,646.56 (£3,199.04: £1,534.52: £626.60: £248.30: £96.98)
6f (Rowley) Stalls: High GOING minus 0.38 sec per fur (F) 1-45 (1-46)

2848[2] **Doctor's Glory (USA) (86)***(96) (RHannon)* 3-8-4 MRoberts(8) (chsd ldrs: rdn over 2f out: str run to ld wl ins fnl f) .... — **1**

3342* Cheyenne Spirit **(103)***(112) (BHanbury)* 3-9-4 (3) JStack(4) (lw: a.p: led ins fnl f: sn hdd: unable qckn) ....nk 2
3446[8] Jawlaat (USA) **(89)***(96) (JLDunlop)* 3-8-7 RHills(10) (led tl ins fnl f: no ex) ....¾ 3
Fleet Petite (IRE) **(86)***(92) (ALeahy,Ireland)* 3-8-4b MFenton(1) (w'like: leggy: hld up: hdwy 2f out: rdn & nt qckn fnl f) ....nk 4
3615[3] Croeso-I-Cymru **(90)***(95)*(Fav)*(RAkehurst)* 4-8-11 TQuinn(3) (hld up & bhd: hdwy 2f out: sn rdn: nt pce to chal) ....½ 5
3637[4] The Jotter **(90)***(94) (WJarvis)* 3-8-8 JReid(5) (lw: hld up: effrt 2f out: sn rdn: nvr nr to chal) ....½ 6
3706[5] Shefoog **(90)***(92) (RWArmstrong)* 3-8-8 RPrice(6) (prom: rdn 2f out: outpcd appr fnl f) ....¾ 7
3717[16] Paris Babe **(95)***(95) (DMorris)* 3-8-13 RHughes(12) (in tch: effrt over 2f out: btn appr fnl f) ....¾ 8
3565[4] Russian Maid **(86)***(78) (JRFanshawe)* 3-8-4 DHarrison(2) (b.hind: dwlt: effrt & rdn over 2f out: no imp) 3 9
3235[4] Amanah (USA) **(100)***(88) (JHMGosden)* 3-9-4 WCarson(11) (swtg: chsd ldrs far side 4f: sn wknd) 1½ 10
3660[6] Christmas Kiss **(86)***(60) (RHannon)* 3-8-4 KDarley(7) (a in rr: t.o) 5 11
1848[15] Baaderah (IRE) **(102)***(68) (LMCumani)* 3-9-6 LDettori(9) (bit bkwd: in tch 3f: sn outpcd: eased whn btn fnl f: t.o) 3 12

LONG HANDICAP Doctor's Glory (USA) 8-2 Fleet Petite (IRE) 8-3 Christmas Kiss 8-2 Russian Maid 8-0

5/1 Croeso-I-Cymru, **11/2** Cheyenne Spirit, **6/1** The Jotter, **7/1** Amanah (USA), Baaderah (IRE), **8/1** Russian Maid, **12/1** Paris Babe, **16/1** Shefoog, **20/1** Fleet Petite (IRE), DOCTOR'S GLORY (USA), Jawlaat (USA), Christmas Kiss, CSF £109.66 CT £2,006.17 TOTE £18.00: £3.20 £2.20 £4.90 (£84.50) Trio £336.10 OWNER Cheveley Park Stud (MARLBOROUGH) BRED Cheveley Park Stud in USA 12 Rn 1m 11.49 (0.19) SF: 54/70/54/50/56/52/50/53/36/46/18/26

WEIGHT FOR AGE 3yo-3lb

3923 RACING POST GODOLPHIN STKS (Listed) (3-Y.O+) (Class A)

£11,617.20 (£4,294.80: £2,057.40: £837.00: £328.50: £125.10)
1m 4f (Rowley) Stalls: High GOING minus 0.38 sec per fur (F) 2-20 (2-20)

3609[2] **Minds Music (USA) (115)***(113)*(Fav)*(HRACecil)* 3-8-6 PatEddery(3) (lw: chsd ldng pair: pushed along ½-wy: led 3f out: styd on strly fnl f) ....— 1
Mack the Knife **(106)***(110) (MCPipe)* 6-9-0 MRoberts(5) (hld up & bhd: hdwy 3f out: chsd wnr wl over 1f out: one pce fnl f) 2½ 2
3754* Warning Order **(97)***(107) (JLDunlop)* 3-8-6 LDettori(2) (hld up: hdwy 3f out: n.m.r 2f out: one pce fnl f) 2 3
3609[9] Jellaby Askhir **(104)***(108) (RAkehurst)* 3-8-10 TQuinn(6) (w ldr 9f: rdn & edgd rt ent fnl f: one pce) 2 4
Hawker's News (IRE) *(102) (MRStoute)* 4-9-0 WCarson(4) (bit bkwd: chsd ldrs: drvn along 2f out: sn btn) 2 5
3728[6] Final Appearance (IRE) **(95)***(101) (PWChapple-Hyam)* 3-8-6 JReid(1) (hld up in tch: effrt 3f out: nvr able chal) ....nk 6
3162[15] Blushing Flame (USA) **(89)***(100) (MRStoute)* 4-9-0 WRSwinburn(7) (lw: mde most 9f: rdn & btn whn squeezed for room 1f out) 1 7

1/2 MINDS MUSIC (USA) (49/1-8/15), **17/2** Warning Order, **11/1** Jellaby Askhir (8/1-12/1), Final Appearance (IRE), **12/1** Hawker's News (IRE) (op 7/1), **20/1** Mack the Knife, Blushing Flame (USA), CSF £10.10 TOTE £1.60: £1.20 £3.20 (£9.40) OWNER Mr S. S. Niarchos (NEWMARKET) BRED Flaxman Holdings Ltd 7 Rn 2m 30.36 (1.06) SF: 53/58/47/48/50/41/48

WEIGHT FOR AGE 3yo-8lb

3924 CHARLES WELLS BOMBARDIER BITTER RATED STKS H'CAP (0-100)

(3-Y.O+) (Class B) £8,827.52 (£3,267.68: £1,568.84: £642.20: £256.10: £101.66)
7f (Rowley) Stalls: High GOING minus 0.38 sec per fur (F) 2-50 (2-52)

3637[2] **Cyrano's Lad (IRE) (89)***(100) (CADwyer)* 6-8-10 CDwyer(7) (mde all: clr appr fnl f: rdn out) ....— 1
3488[7] Kabil **(87)***(96) (HThomsonJones)* 3-8-4 RHills(13) (lw: hld up: gd hdwy on rail 2f out: kpt on wl fnl f) ....¾ 2
3813[5] Gymcrak Premiere **(88)***(96) (GHolmes)* 7-8-9v KFallon(6) (b.hind: bhd: rdn along ½-wy: hdwy on rail over 1f out: fin wl) ....¾ 3
3815[5] Saseedo (USA) **(86)***(93) (WAO'Gorman)* 5-8-7 EmmaO'Gorman(12) (bhd: rdn over 2f out: r.o wl fnl f: nvr nrr) ....nk 4
3598[8] Blue Ocean (USA) **(86)***(90) (MRStoute)* 3-8-3 PRobinson(4) (chsd ldrs: drvn along 2f out: kpt on one pce) 1½ 5
3717[11] Astrac (IRE) **(93)***(93) (RAkehurst)* 4-8-11 (3) SSanders(11) (a chsng ldrs: effrt & rdn bel dist: wknd ins fnl f) 1¾ 6

1895[22] Sheppard's Cross **(86)***(83) (PTWalwyn)* 4-8-7 PatEddery(2) (chsd ldrs: rdn wl over 1f out: sn btn) 1 **7**
3419[8] Moving Arrow **(90)***(87) (MissSEHall)* 4-8-11 KDarley(3) (in tch: sn pushed along: n.d) ....hd **8**
3542* Mufarej (USA) **(86)***(82)*(Fav)*(RWArmstrong)* 3-8-3 WCarson(9) (mid div: pushed along over 2f out: nvr rchd ldrs) ....nk **9**
3755[8] Lipizzaner (IRE) **(94)***(87) (BWHills)* 3-8-11b MHills(8) (lw: prom over 5f) 1½ **10**
941[7] New Century (USA) **(88)***(72) (DNicholls)* 3-8-5 AlexGreaves(5) (a in rr) 4 **11**
3358[8] En Attendant (FR) **(100)***(83) (BHanbury)* 7-9-7 JReid(1) (hld up: effrt 3f out: no imp) ....nk **12**
3729[18] Bernard Seven (IRE) **(88)***(55) (CEBrittain)* 3-8-5b MRoberts(14) (lw: a bhd: t.o) 7 **13**
3602[5] Delta One (IRE) **(94)***(57) (IABalding)* 4-9-1 LDettori(10) (chsd ldrs 4f: sn lost tch: t.o) 1¾ **14**

LONG HANDICAP Sheppard's Cross 8-4 Saseedo (USA) 8-6 Mufarej (USA) 8-1 Blue Ocean (USA) 8-2

9/2 Mufarej (USA), **5/1** Gymcrak Premiere, **9/1** Astrac (IRE) (11/2-10/1), **10/1** CYRANO'S LAD (IRE), Delta One (IRE) (7/1-11/1), Kabil, **14/1** En Attendant (FR), Saseedo (USA), Moving Arrow, Sheppard's Cross, **16/1** Lipizzaner (IRE), Bernard Seven (IRE), **20/1** Blue Ocean (USA), **33/1** New Century (USA), CSF £94.06 CT £509.23 TOTE £16.60: £3.90 £3.10 £2.00 (£101.10) Trio £248.20
OWNER Mr M. M. Foulger (NEWMARKET) BRED J. C. Condon 14 Rn
1m 23.58 (-0.12) SF: 64/56/60/57/50/57/47/51/42/47/32/47/15/21
WEIGHT FOR AGE 3yo-4lb

3925 SOMERVILLE TATTERSALL STKS (Listed) (2-Y.O C & G) (Class A) £10,048.00 (£3,712.00: £1,776.00: £720.00)

7f (Rowley) Stalls: High GOING minus 0.38 sec per fur (F) 3-25 (3-26)

3631[2] **Even Top (IRE) (100)***(104) (MHTompkins)* 2-8-9 PRobinson(8) (lw: mde all: r.o u.p fnl f) ....— **1**
3163[2] Tumbleweed Ridge **(100)***(101)*(Fav)*(BJMeehan)* 2-8-9 RHughes(4) (lw: hld up: hdwy gng wl 2f out: sn rdn: unable qckn nr fin) 1½ **2**
3733* Sovereign's Crown (USA) *(99) (JHMGosden)* 2-8-9 LDettori(3) (a.p: shkn up ent fnl f: r.o) ....½ **3**
3592* Heron Island (IRE) *(99) (PWChapple-Hyam)* 2-8-9 JReid(7) (lw: a chsng ldrs: drvn along 2f out: kpt on fnl f: nt pce to chal) ....hd **4**
3494* Kings Witness (USA) **(90)***(99) (WJHaggas)* 2-8-9 KDarley(6) (s.i.s: sn chsng ldrs: rdn appr fnl f: kpt on) ....nk **5**
1856* Truancy *(85) (MBell)* 2-8-9 MFenton(5) (bit bkwd: prom tl wknd qckly ins fnl f) 6 **6**
3672* Najm Mubeen (IRE) *(79) (ACStewart)* 2-8-9 MRoberts(1) (stdd s: sn prom: wknd over 1f out) 2½ **7**
3731[2] Kuantan (USA) **(100)***(75) (PFICole)* 2-8-9 TQuinn(2) (lw: bolted gng to s: a bhd: rdn along 3f out: no imp) 1¾ **8**

9/4 Tumbleweed Ridge, **5/2** Heron Island (IRE) (7/2-9/4), **4/1** Sovereign's Crown (USA), **8/1** Kuantan (USA) (6/1-9/1), **12/1** EVEN TOP (IRE) (8/1-14/1), **14/1** Kings Witness (USA) (10/1-16/1), **20/1** Najm Mubeen (IRE), **33/1** Truancy, CSF £36.44 TOTE £22.20: £4.20 £1.60 £1.80 (£19.00)
OWNER Mr B. Schmidt-Bodner (NEWMARKET) BRED M. Dwan 8 Rn
1m 24.51 (0.81) SF: 52/49/47/47/47/33/27/23

3926 SNOWDENS MARQUEES H'CAP (0-100) (3-Y.O) (Class C) £8,285.00 (£2,480.00: £1,190.00: £545.00)

1m 2f (Rowley) Stalls: High GOING minus 0.38 sec per fur (F) 3-55 (3-57)

3840[2] **Nigel's Lad (IRE) (79)***(93) (PCHaslam)* 3-8-4 (5) MBaird(6) (hmpd & lost pl after 2f: hdwy over 2f out: led bel dist: clr fnl f) ....— **1**
3214* Alkateb **(90)***(98) (MissGayKelleway)* 3-9-6 MHills(20) (lw: hld up: stdy hdwy over 2f out: sn rdn: nt pce of wnr) 4 **2**
3500[2] State Law **(91)***(95) (GHarwood)* 3-9-7 AClark(11) (hld up: hdwy 3f out: ev ch over 1f out: unable qckn fnl f) 2½ **3**
3621* Emily-Mou (IRE) **(73)***(74) (BJMeehan)* 3-8-3 GBardwell(19) (b: led 6f out: rdn 3f out: hdd bel dist: kpt on one pce) 1¾ **4**
3820[4] Komreyev Dancer **(67)***(66) (ABailey)* 3-7-8 (3) DWright(17) (hld up in tch: effrt 2f out: one pce fnl f) 1 **5**
Indigo Time (IRE) **(80)***(76) (PFICole)* 3-8-10 TQuinn(10) (in tch: hrd drvn over 2f out: one pce) 2 **6**
3863[2] Cyrus the Great (IRE) **(74)***(68) (MBell)* 3-8-4 MFenton(15) (hld up: hdwy 3f out: wknd over 1f out) 1¼ **7**
3864[7] Heathyards Rock **(84)***(75) (RHollinshead)* 3-9-0 KFallon(4) (bhd: sn drvn along: hdwy 3f out: styd on appr fnl f) 2 **8**
3840[3] Vindaloo **(86)***(75) (JLHarris)* 3-9-2 PRobinson(18) (chsd ldrs: rdn over 2f out: one pce fr bel dist) 1¼ **9**
Failte Ro **(65)***(52) (JEBanks)* 3-7-2 (7)ow1 MartinDwyer(14) (in tch: rdn 3f out: grad wknd) ....nk **10**

3598⁴ Sveltana **(80)***(68) (JRFanshawe)* 3-8-10 DHarrison(2) (in tch tl outpcd over 2f out) ....½ **11**
3611²¹ Catercap (IRE) **(76)***(59) (JHMGosden)* 3-8-6v LDettori(16) (chsd ldrs tl outpcd 3f out: sn bhd) .3 **12**
3598⁵ Code of Law (USA) **(83)***(65) (PWChapple-Hyam)* 3-8-13 JReid(7) (a in rr) ....nk **13**
3459⁷ Prize Pupil (IRE) **(76)***(53) (CFWall)* 3-8-6 MRoberts(12) (prom over 6f: sn pushed along & outpcd) 3½ **14**
3755³ Te Amo (IRE) **(82)***(59) (RAkehurst)* 3-8-9 (3) SSanders(9) (bhd fnl 4f)......................................s.h **15**
3107³ Major Change **(86)***(62) (RHannon)* 3-9-2 PatEddery(5) (led 4f: rdn along 2f out: sn wknd)......½ **16**
3602⁶ Karayb (IRE) **(91)***(63) (DMorley)* 3-9-7 WCarson(13) (lw: chsd ldrs tl outpcd over 1f out: eased whn btn)..2½ **17**
2411² Goonda **(75)***(44)*(Fav)*(HRACecil)* 3-8-5 AMcGlone(8) (outpcd & wl bhd fr ½-wy) 1¾ **18**
3552⁹ Kimbridge Knight (IRE) **(78)***(39) (PTWalwyn)* 3-8-8v KDarley(3) (prom tl wknd qckly 3f out: t.o) 5 **19**
3730²¹ Tira Heights (USA) **(88)** *(RWArmstrong)* 3-9-4 RPrice(1) (prom 6f: wknd qckly: t.o)............dist **20**

7/1 Goonda, **8/1** Cyrus the Great (IRE), **10/1** Sveltana, Emily-Mou (IRE), Vindaloo, Alkateb, **11/1** NIGEL'S LAD (IRE), **12/1** Prize Pupil (IRE), Code of Law (USA), Catercap (IRE) (8/1-14/1), **14/1** Major Change, Te Amo (IRE) (10/1-16/1), **16/1** Karayb (IRE), State Law, **20/1** Indigo Time (IRE), **25/1** Kimbridge Knight (IRE), Komreyev Dancer, **33/1** Failte Ro, Heathyards Rock, Tira Heights (USA), CSF £115.51 CT £1,625.90 TOTE £17.10: £3.00 £3.10 £5.10 £2.00 (£85.30) Trio £1,769.40 OWNER Mr N. C. Dunnington (MIDDLEHAM) BRED Nikita Investments 20 Rn
2m 2.67 (0.07) SF: 62/67/64/43/35/45/37/44/44/21/37/28/34/22/28/31/32/13/8/-

3927

STAYERS' H'CAP (0-90) (3-Y.O+) (Class C) £6,576.00 (£1,968.00: £944.00: £432.00) **1m 6f (Rowley)** Stalls: High GOING minus 0.38 sec (F) 4-30 (4-34)

3801² **Floating Line (61)***(74) (EJAlston)* 7-8-9 KFallon(6) (mde virtually all: drvn clr appr fnl f: styd on strly) ....— **1**
3669⁷ Bowcliffe Court (IRE) **(59)***(69) (BWHills)* 3-7-11 WCarson(10) (hld up in tch: effrt & ev ch 2f out: sn rdn: one pce)..2½ **2**
3445* Celeric **(89)***(99)*(Fav)*(DMorley)* 3-9-13 LDettori(5) (hld up: stdy hdwy fnl 3f: rdn ent fnl f: nt pce of wnr) ....nk **3**
3634⁴ Paradise Waters **(59)***(64) (RFJohnsonHoughton)* 3-7-11 DaleGibson(1) (disp ld tl rdn & outpcd appr fnl f) 4 **4**
3730⁸ Daily Starlight (USA) **(79)***(84) (MissGayKelleway)* 3-9-0 (3) SSanders(4) (hld up: hdwy 3f out: hrd drvn over 1f out: one pce) ....hd **5**
3292* Make a Stand **(62)***(63) (MCPipe)* 4-8-10 PatEddery(13) (s.i.s: hld up & bhd: effrt & n.m.r 3f out: r.o one pce) 4 **6**
3676⁴ Chief's Song **(58)***(54) (SDow)* 5-8-6 TQuinn(12) (lw: hld up in tch: rdn & lost pl 4f out: n.d after)..4 **7**
3669³ Hotspur Street **(64)***(59) (MJohnston)* 3-8-2 TWilliams(3) (chsd ldrs: rdn 3f out: wknd fnl 2f) ....½ **8**
3470⁶ Broughtons Formula **(52)***(47) (WJMusson)* 5-8-0b RPrice(11) (in tch: sn rdn along: eased whn btn appr fnl f)..½ **9**
3445³ Cherrington **(86)***(80) (GWragg)* 3-9-10 MHills(8) (hld up: nvr plcd to chal) ....½ **10**
3552⁶ Sparrowhawk (IRE) **(77)***(70) (BWHills)* 3-9-1 JReid(9) (lw: chsd ldrs 10f: sn lost tch) 1½ **11**
Broctune Bay **(58)***(44) (MrsMReveley)* 6-8-6 KDarley(2) (s.s: hld up: a bhd: t.o)......................6 **12**
3676⁷ Disputed Call (USA) **(45)***(27) (JFfitch-Heyes)* 6-7-7 JLowe(7) (chsd ldrs10f: sn lost pl: t.o) ...3½ **13**
LONG HANDICAP Disputed Call (USA) 7-6

9/4 Celeric, **6/1** Cherrington (op 4/1), Bowcliffe Court (IRE), **13/2** FLOATING LINE, **7/1** Make a Stand, **11/1** Chief's Song, **12/1** Paradise Waters, **16/1** Hotspur Street, Sparrowhawk (IRE), Broughtons Formula, **25/1** Daily Starlight (USA), **33/1** Broctune Bay, Disputed Call (USA), CSF £44.95 CT £107.05 TOTE £10.40: £2.40 £2.50 £1.60 (£57.40) Trio £46.80 OWNER Mr G.Lowe (PRESTON) BRED R.Kalman 13 Rn 2m 56.19 (0.19) SF: 62/47/77/42/62/51/42/37/35/58/48/32/15
WEIGHT FOR AGE 3yo-10lb

T/Jkpt: Not won £22.524.54 to Newmarket 30/9/95. T/Plpt: £72.80 (418.32 Tckts). T/Qdpt: £65.90 (5.15 Tckts). IM

3915-GOODWOOD (R-H)

Saturday September 30th (Rnd Good becoming Good to soft, St Good to soft becoming Soft)

Vis: race 6 poor, race 7 less than 1f
WEATHER: wet WIND: almost nil

3928

GROUP TRAVEL ORGANISER NURSERY H'CAP (0-85) (2-Y.O) (Class D) £3,720.00 (£1,110.00: £530.00: £240.00)
1m Stalls: High GOING: 0.27 sec per fur (G) 2-15 (2-16)

1829* **Queen's Insignia (USA) (61)***(67) (PFICole)* 2-7-12 DBiggs(2) (2nd st: led 3f out: rdn out) ...— **1**

3613[3] Goodwood Rocket **(71)***(71)*(Fav)*(JLDunlop)* 2-8-8 RCochrane(4) (lw: hmpd over 2f out: hdwy over 1f out: r.o) 3 **2**
3701[6] Welcome Royale (IRE) **(68)***(67) (MHTompkins)* 2-8-5 RHills(10) (lw: dwlt: hdwy over 2f out: hrd rdn over 1f out: unable qckn) ....¾ **3**
3701[4] Carmentalia **(84)***(80) (SirMarkPrescott)* 2-9-7 WWoods(7) (5th st: rdn over 3f out: one pce) .1¼ **4**
3613[4] Tapintime (USA) **(72)***(67) (PFICole)* 2-8-9 TQuinn(6) (led 5f: hrd rdn over 2f out: one pce) .....¾ **5**
3604[12] Get Tough **(62)***(51) (SDow)* 2-7-13 FNorton(5) (rdn & hdwy over 3f out: wknd over 1f out) 3 **6**
3281[5] The Legions Pride **(62)***(47) (JWHills)* 2-7-8 (5)ow1 PPMurphy(8) (6th st: hmpd over 2f out: wknd over 1f out) 1½ **7**
3541[3] Somer Solo **(60)***(44) (PMitchell)* 2-7-4 (7) CAdamson(11) (s.s: a bhd) ....¾ **8**
3760* Kinnescash (IRE) **(68)***(44) (MSSaunders)* 2-8-5 AMcGlone(3) (b: 3rd st: wkng whn hmpd over 2f out) 4 **9**
3010[10] Atlantic Mist **(65)** *(BRMillman)* 2-7-9 (7)ow2 JWilkinson(9) (lw: sddle slipped s: bhd fnl 3f: t.o) ....dist **10**

9/4 Goodwood Rocket, **5/1** Carmentalia, **11/2** QUEEN'S INSIGNIA (USA), **8/1** Tapintime (USA) (6/1-9/1), **9/1** Kinnescash (IRE), **12/1** Welcome Royale (IRE), **14/1** The Legions Pride (10/1-16/1), Somer Solo (op 8/1), **20/1** Atlantic Mist, **33/1** Get Tough, CSF £16.61 CT £125.93 TOTE £5.70: £1.90 £1.20 £2.80 (£5.10) Trio £36.10 OWNER Mr W. H. Ponsonby (WHATCOMBE) BRED Stephen E. Johnson and Mrs Johnson 10 Rn 1m 44.85 (7.25) SF: 31/35/31/44/31/15/11/8/8/-
STEWARDS' ENQUIRY Quinn susp. 9-12/10/95 (careless riding).

3929

ROYAL NAVY H'CAP (0-90) (3-Y.O) (Class C) £6,368.00 (£1,904.00: £912.00: £416.00) **7f** Stalls: High GOING: 0.27 sec per fur (G) 2-45 (2-49)

1862[2] **Neverending (USA) (83)***(95) (HRACecil)* 3-9-2 WRyan(8) (b.off hind: lw: hdwy 2f out: led 1f out: drvn out) ....— **1**
2556[5] Youdontsay **(77)***(89) (RCurtis)* 3-8-5 (5) PPMurphy(6) (lw: hdwy over 1f out: r.o wl ins fnl f) ....s.h **2**
3615[19] Sea Thunder **(80)***(84) (IABalding)* 3-8-8 (5) DGriffiths(11) (lw: hdwy 3f out: led over 1f out: sn hdd: unable qckn) 3½ **3**
3565[17] Hawa Al Nasamaat (USA) **(82)***(80) (EALDunlop)* 3-9-1 TQuinn(10) (lw: hdwy over 1f out: r.o one pce) 2½ **4**
3715[28] Actual Fact (USA) **(83)***(79)*(Fav)*(GHarwood)* 3-9-2 MRimmer(9) (plld hrd: 6th st: hrd rdn over 1f out: wknd fnl f) 1 **5**
3359[14] Balance of Power **(69)***(61) (RAkehurst)* 3-8-2 AMcGlone(4) (b: nt clr run over 2f out: nvr nr to chal) 1¾ **6**
3712[3] Zelda Zonk **(68)***(58) (BJMeehan)* 3-8-1 DBiggs(7) (2nd st: led 3f out tl over 1f out: sn wknd) ...1 **7**
3656[7] Scharnhorst **(70)***(55) (SDow)* 3-8-3 FNorton(1) (3rd st: wknd over 1f out) 2 **8**
3674[6] Anam **(75)***(58) (PTWalwyn)* 3-8-8 RHills(5) (led 4f: wknd over 1f out) ....¾ **9**
3715[12] Tiler (IRE) **(82)***(65) (MJohnston)* 3-9-1 RCochrane(2) (4th st: wknd over 2f out) ....hd **10**
Wigberto (IRE) **(88)***(48) (MajorDNChappell)* 3-9-7 WWoods(3) (lw: 5th st: wknd 3f out) 10 **11**

4/1 Actual Fact (USA) (op 6/1), **11/2** NEVERENDING (USA), **13/2** Zelda Zonk, **7/1** Sea Thunder, Tiler (IRE), **10/1** Anam, **11/1** Hawa Al Nasamaat (USA) (8/1-12/1), **14/1** Scharnhorst, **16/1** Balance of Power, Youdontsay, **25/1** Wigberto (IRE), CSF £74.50 CT £557.36 TOTE £4.10: £1.90 £3.10 £2.50 (£25.70) Trio £200.10 OWNER Mr S. Khaled (NEWMARKET) BRED Palides Investments N. V. 11 Rn 1m 30.38 (5.98) SF: 51/45/40/36/35/17/14/11/14/21/4

3930

CITY OF PORTSMOUTH RATED STKS H'CAP (0-100) (3-Y.O+) (Class B) £8,103.68 (£2,993.12: £1,431.56: £579.80: £224.90: £82.94) **2m** Stalls: High GOING: 0.27 sec per fur (G) 3-20 (3-20)

3817[5] **Kristal's Paradise (IRE) (87)***(98)*(Fav)*(JLDunlop)* 3-8-3 WCarson(7) (lw: led 14f out tl over 1f out: unable qckn: fin 2nd, 1 3/4l: awrdd r) ....— **1**
3730[17] Shonara's Way **(93)***(100) (RCharlton)* 4-9-7 RCochrane(1) (lw: 5th & c stands' side st: hrd rdn over 2f out: hung rt over 1f out: one pce: fin 3rd, 4l: plcd 2nd) **2**
3211[5] Moonlight Quest **(79)***(86) (BHanbury)* 7-8-7 MRimmer(6) (rdn & hdwy 3f out: bmpd over 2f out: one pce: fin 4th, 3/4l : plcd 3rd) **3**
2218a[13] Daraydan (IRE) **(98)***(102) (LadyHerries)* 3-9-0 WRyan(5) (w'like: 6th st: hdwy over 3f out: wknd over 1f out: fin 5th, 3l: plcd 4th) **4**
3682[3] Dawlah **(88)***(90) (HThomsonJones)* 3-8-4 RHills(3) (led 2f: 4th st: wknd 3f out: fin 6th, 2l: plcd 5th) **5**
3343* Latahaab (USA) **(89)***(77) (RAkehurst)* 4-9-3 TQuinn(4) (lw: 2nd st: bdly hmpd over 2f out: nt rcvr: fin 7th, 14l: plcd 6th) **6**
3406[7] Seasonal Splendour (IRE) **(85)***(98) (MCPipe)* 5-8-13 DBiggs(2) (3rd st: barged thro over 2f out: led over 1f out: rdn out: fin 1st: disq: plcd last) **0**

LONG HANDICAP Moonlight Quest 8-3

9/4 KRISTAL'S PARADISE (IRE), **11/4** Latahaab (USA), **5/1** Dawlah, **11/2** Shonara's Way (4/1-6/1), **10/1** Seasonal Splendour (IRE) (7/1-11/1), **12/1** Moonlight Quest, Daraydan (IRE), CSF £13.89 TOTE £2.30: £1.50 £4.10 (£6.40) OWNER Windflower Overseas Holdings Inc (ARUNDEL) BRED Windflower Overseas 7 Rn 3m 32.45 (7.95) SF: 68/82/68/72/60/59/80

WEIGHT FOR AGE 3yo-12lb

STEWARDS' ENQUIRY Biggs susp. 9-14 & 16/10/95 (irresponsible riding).

3931 CHARLTON HUNT SUPREME STKS (Gp 3) (3-Y.O+) (Class A) £23,232.00 (£8,702.10: £4,186.05: £1,829.85)

7f Stalls: High GOING: 0.27 sec per fur (G) 3-55 (3-57)

3599* **Inzar (USA) (107)***(120) (PFICole)* 3-8-8 TQuinn(7) (led over 1f: 2nd st: led over 3f out to 2f out: rdn: led nr fin) ....— 1
2105 8 Mutakddim (USA) **(111)***(120) (JHMGosden)* 4-8-12 WCarson(9) (lw: 5th st: led 2f out: rdn: hdd nr fin) ....s.h 2
3564 4 Myself **(109)***(119) (PWChapple-Hyam)* 3-8-9 FNorton(10) (b: lw: 6th st: rdn over 2f out: nt clr run on ins 1f out: swtchd lft: r.o) ....¾ 3
3562 6 Bin Ajwaad (IRE) **(116)***(122) (BHanbury)* 5-9-2 MRimmer(8) (hdwy over 1f out: hrd rdn: r.o)..nk 4
3834 3 Branston Abby (IRE) **(113)***(103)*(Fav)*(MJohnston)* 6-8-9 RCochrane(3) (rdn over 2f out: nvr nr to chal) 5 5
2673 3 Epagris **(105)***(102) (HRACecil)* 3-8-5 WRyan(1) (3rd st: rdn over 2f out: wknd fnl f) ....½ 6
3562 5 Shahid **(113)***(106) (JLDunlop)* 3-8-12 RHills(4) (4th st: rdn 2f out: wknd fnl f) 1¼ 7
3834 13 Easy Dollar **(107)***(95) (BGubby)* 3-8-8b AMcGlone(2) (lw: led over 5f out tl over 3f out: wknd over 1f out) 3 8
3562 7 Brief Glimpse (IRE) **(106)***(83) (MajorDNChappell)* 3-8-5 WWoods(5) (a bhd) 4 9
3834 9 Hello Mister **(102)***(79) (JO'Donoghue)* 4-8-12 DBiggs(6) (a bhd) 3 10

7/4 Branston Abby (IRE), **3/1** INZAR (USA) (9/2-11/4), **6/1** Mutakddim (USA), **13/2** Bin Ajwaad (IRE), **10/1** Epagris (8/1-12/1), **11/1** Myself (8/1-12/1), **12/1** Shahid (op 8/1), **16/1** Brief Glimpse (IRE), **40/1** Easy Dollar, Hello Mister, CSF £21.47 TOTE £4.10: £1.50 £2.10 £3.20 (£11.40) Trio £53.20 OWNER H R H Prince Fahd Salman (WHATCOMBE) BRED Newgate Stud Farm Inc in USA 10 Rn 1m 28.77 (4.37) SF: 63/67/62/69/50/45/49/38/26/26

WEIGHT FOR AGE 3yo-4lb

3932 R.O.A. FOUNDATION STKS (Listed) (3-Y.O+) (Class A) £15,400.00 (£4,600.00: £2,200.00: £1,000.00)

1m 2f Stalls: High GOING: 0.27 sec per fur (G) 4-25 (4-26)

2936 6 **Revere (IRE) (112)***(114)*(Fav)*(PFICole)* 5-9-3 TQuinn(3) (b: mde all: clr over 1f out: r.o wl) ..— 1
3728 5 Nash Terrace (IRE) **(98)***(109) (RCharlton)* 3-8-8 RCochrane(9) (lw: hdwy 3f out: chsd wnr over 2f out: no imp) 1½ 2
3278 2 Ninette (USA) *(94) (JHMGosden)* 3-8-3 WCarson(8) (5th st: rdn over 3f out: one pce) 6 3
619 7 Al Widyan (IRE) **(106)***(97) (HRACecil)* 3-8-8 WRyan(5) (lw: 6th st: rdn over 3f out: one pce) 1½ 4
3728 4 First Island (IRE) **(106)***(96) (GWragg)* 3-8-8 WWoods(4) (lw: c stands' side st: nvr nr to chal) ....hd 5
3636 9 Strutting (IRE) **(93)***(86) (RHannon)* 3-8-4 ow1 RPerham(6) (4th st: wknd over 1f out) 3½ 6
3556* Sayeh (IRE) **(96)***(87) (HThomsonJones)* 3-8-8 RHills(10) (3rd st: wknd over 2f out) 2½ 7
3556 7 Aljazzaf **(100)***(77) (RAkehurst)* 5-9-0 AMcGlone(1) (2nd st: wknd over 2f out) 6 8
3813 23 Nagnagnag (IRE) **(100)***(32) (SDow)* 3-8-3 FNorton(2) (s.i.s: c stands' side st: bhd fnl 5f) 25 9

2/1 REVERE (IRE), **3/1** Ninette (USA), **9/2** Sayeh (IRE), **6/1** First Island (IRE) (op 4/1), **8/1** Al Widyan (IRE), **11/1** Nagnagnag (IRE) (6/1-12/1), **14/1** Nash Terrace (IRE) (12/1-20/1), Aljazzaf, **33/1** Strutting (IRE), CSF £29.24 TOTE £3.60: £1.70 £3.00 £1.40 (£39.60) Trio £42.30 OWNER H R H Prince Fahd Salman (WHATCOMBE) BRED Newgate Stud Co 9 Rn

2m 11.08 (6.08) SF: 74/63/48/51/50/40/41/37/-

WEIGHT FOR AGE 3yo-6lb

3933 E.B.F. OCEAN FM MAIDEN STKS (2-Y.O) (Class D) £4,163.50 (£1,243.00: £594.00: £269.50)

6f Stalls: Low GOING: 0.27 sec per fur (G) 4-55 (4-56)

2351 W **Trafalgar Lady (USA)** *(75+) (RCharlton)* 2-8-9 TQuinn(7) (bit bkwd: s.s: hdwy over 3f out: led over 1f out: rdn out) ....— 1
2552 11 Mimosa *(72) (LJHolt)* 2-8-9 FNorton(4) (a.p: led wl over 1f out : sn hdd: unable qckn) 1 2
Muhandis *(73+)*(Fav)*(JHMGosden)* 2-9-0 WCarson(1) (b.hind: cmpt: hld up: n.m.r over 1f out: hung rt fnl f: one pce) 1¾ 3
Mansab (USA) *(71) (JLDunlop)* 2-9-0 RHills(5) (cmpt: hdwy over 2f out: ev ch wl over 1f out: one pce) ....½ 4

3604[7] Mac Oates *(63) (DWPArbuthnot)* 2-9-0 AMcGlone(2) (s.s: nt clr run on ins over 2f out: nvr nr to chal) 3 **5**
3733[20] Philistar *(63) (JMPEustace)* 2-9-0 RCochrane(3) (led over 4f) ....nk **6**
3558[4] Lancashire Legend *(SDow)* 2-9-0 WRyan(6) (bhd fnl 4f: t.o) ....dist **7**

4/6 Muhandis (op 11/8), **6/1** Mansab (USA) (5/2-13/2), **7/1** TRAFALGAR LADY (USA) (4/1-8/1), **12/1** Philistar, **14/1** Lancashire Legend, **16/1** Mac Oates, **25/1** Mimosa, CSF £104.95 TOTE £7.40: £2.80 £3.20 (£68.90) OWNER Mr W. L. Armitage (BECKHAMPTON) BRED Swettenham Stud 7 Rn
1m 15.98 (5.78) SF: 34/31/32/30/22/22/-

3934

GEORGE TODD APPRENTICE H'CAP (0-80) (3-Y.O+) (Class E)
£3,752.50 (£1,120.00: £535.00: £242.50)
1m 1f Stalls: High GOING: 0.27 sec per fur (G) 5-25 (5-28)

3679[7] **Tribal Peace (IRE) (65)***(77) (BGubby)* 3-9-0 PPMurphy(13) (lw: 5th 3f out: in ld ins fnl f: r.o wl) ....— **1**
3657[5] Lady Sabina **(46)***(51) (WJMusson)* 5-7-9 (5)ow4 JWilkinson(3) (lw: 4th 3f out: 2nd ins fnl f: unable qckn) 1½ **2**
3844[3] Rising Spray **(51)***(59) (CAHorgan)* 4-8-2 (3) AmandaSanders(9) (lw: 3rd ins fnl f: one pce) 1 **3**
3605[8] Pat's Splendour **(44)***(51) (HJCollingridge)* 4-7-7 (5) JoHunnam(6) (r.o ins fnl f) ....hd **4**
3757[3] Waldo **(65)***(70) (LordHuntingdon)* 4-9-0v(5) AimeeCook(4) (mid div 3f out: nrst fin) 1½ **5**
3810[9] Aeroking (USA) **(74)***(77) (GHarwood)* 4-9-9 (5) GayeHarwood(10) (in ld 3f out: wkng ins fnl f) ..1 **6**
3863[5] Lady Lacey **(45)***(47)*(Fav)*(GBBalding)* 8-7-8v(5) IonaWands(1) ....nk **7**
3820[5] Zermatt (IRE) **(66)***(65) (MDIUsher)* 5-9-3 (3) CAdamson(11) (lw: 2nd 3f out) 2 **8**
3844[6] Ebony Blaze **(52)***(50) (CPWildman)* 4-8-1 (5) JBramhill(8) (6th 3f out) ....½ **9**
3770[6] Oozlem (IRE) **(45)***(32) (JCPoulton)* 6-7-10b(3)ow5 MHumphries(7) 3½ **10**
Another Monk (IRE) **(43)***(25) (RCurtis)* 4-7-4 (7)ow4 RachaelMoody(2) (lw: 3rd 3f out) 3½ **11**
3885[12] Duckey Fuzz **(68)***(20) (RMFlower)* 7-9-8 DGriffiths(12) (bhd fnl f) 4 **12**
3703[15] Manabar **(78)** *(DMorley)* 3-9-8 (5) GFaulkner(5) (lw: bhd fnl 2f: t.o) 25 **13**
LONG HANDICAP Another Monk (IRE) 6-10

3/1 Lady Lacey, **5/1** Waldo (3/1-11/1), **13/2** Lady Sabina, **7/1** TRIBAL PEACE (IRE) (op 14/1), **8/1** Zermatt (IRE), **9/1** Duckey Fuzz, **10/1** Oozlem (IRE), **12/1** Pat's Splendour, **14/1** Aeroking (USA), Rising Spray, **16/1** Manabar, **20/1** Ebony Blaze, **33/1** Another Monk (IRE), CSF £52.91 CT £588.34 TOTE £10.20: £2.90 £3.20 £7.50 (£35.20) Trio £220.00 OWNER Brian Gubby Ltd (BAGSHOT) BRED Mrs P. H. Burns in Ireland 13 Rn 2m 0.6 (9.90) SF: 31/10/18/10/29/36/6/24/9/-/-/5/-
WEIGHT FOR AGE 3yo-5lb

T/Plpt: £362.10 (35.2 Tckts). T/Qdpt: £212.70 (1.3 Tckts). AK

3818-HAYDOCK (L-H)
Saturday September 30th (Soft, Heavy patches)
WEATHER: overcast WIND: slt bhd

3935

MULBERRY H'CAP (0-80) (3-Y.O) (Class D) £3,969.00 (£1,197.00: £581.00: £273.00) **1m 2f 120y** Stalls: High GOING: 0.37 sec per fur (GS) 2-05 (2-08)

2555[5] **Dance So Suite (71)***(86) (PFICole)* 3-9-4 CRutter(14) (in tch: 6th st: led over 2f out: r.o) ....— **1**
3805* Highfield Fizz **(52)***(63) (CWFairhurst)* 3-7-6 (7) PDoe(3) (b.off hind: hld up: bhd: hdwy over 4f out: sn drvn along: chsd wnr appr fnl f: one pce) 2½ **2**
1097[2] Heboob Alshemaal (IRE) **(74)***(80) (JHMGosden)* 3-9-2 (5) JDSmith(2) (a.p: led after 4f: hdd over 3f out: sn rdn: wknd over 1f out) 3½ **3**
3505[5] Tessajoe **(73)***(78) (MJCamacho)* 3-9-6 LCharnock(1) (in tch: 3rd st: led over 3f out: hdd over 2f out: wknd appr fnl f) ....¾ **4**
3820[8] Greenspan (IRE) **(73)***(78) (WRMuir)* 3-9-3 (3) SSanders(4) (lw: hld up: hdwy over 3f out: sn ev ch: rdn over 2f out: one pce) ....hd **5**
3747* Mill Dancer (IRE) **(48)***(51)*(Fav)*(EJAlston)* 3-7-9 ow1 AMackay(9) (hld up: bhd: drvn along 4f out: styd on fnl 2f: n.d) ....½ **6**
3734[2] Penmar **(55)***(55) (TJEtherington)* 3-8-2 MFenton(12) (lw: mid div: rdn & no hdwy fr wl over 1f out) 2½ **7**
3843[4] Hamilton Silk **(53)***(43) (MGMeagher)* 3-8-0 ow1 SMaloney(7) (in tch: 5th st: rdn over 3f out: btn 2f out) 6 **8**
3802[14] Carlito Brigante **(68)***(59) (MrsJRRamsden)* 3-8-8 (7) SBuckley(6) (hld up in rr: effrt over 3f out: wknd 2f out) ....nk **9**
3462[4] Westcourt Princess **(56)***(39) (MWEasterby)* 3-8-0 (3) SDrowne(13) (led 4f: chsd ldr: 2nd st: wknd over 2f out) 5 **10**
2356[7] Thatcher's Era (IRE) **(61)***(41) (TDBarron)* 3-8-8 SDWilliams(15) (in tch: rdn 3f out: eased whn btn wl over 1f out) 2 **11**

3469[10] Swandale Flyer **(47)***(19) (NBycroft)* 3-7-3 (5) PFessey(8) (a towards rr) 5 **12**
3759[13] Grate British (IRE) **(50)***(20) (EWeymes)* 3-7-11 DaleGibson(16) (mid div: dropped rr over 3f out) 1½ **13**
3719[11] Celebration Cake (IRE) **(58)***(16) (MissLAPerratt)* 3-8-5 MBirch(11) (prom: plld hrd: 7th st: sn rdn & wknd) 8 **14**
3700[7] Champagne N Dreams **(52)***(8) (DNicholls)* 3-7-13 KimTinkler(10) (mid div tl rdn & wknd 4f out) 1 **15**
3704[8] Borrowby **(48)***(1) (MWEasterby)* 3-7-4 (5)ow2 MBaird(17) (chsd ldrs: 4th st: rdn over 3f out: sn btn) ....¾ **16**
2189* Cross Talk (IRE) **(70)***(23) (RHollinshead)* 3-8-10 (7) AEddery(5) (a bhd) 1½ **17**

LONG HANDICAP Borrowby 7-4

6/1 Mill Dancer (IRE), **13/2** Highfield Fizz, Heboob Alshemaal (IRE), **15/2** Westcourt Princess, **8/1** Tessajoe, DANCE SO SUITE, **14/1** Penmar, Cross Talk (IRE), Carlito Brigante, **16/1** Greenspan (IRE), Champagne N Dreams, Grate British (IRE), **20/1** Celebration Cake (IRE), Hamilton Silk, **25/1** Thatcher's Era (IRE), **33/1** Borrowby, Swandale Flyer, CSF £58.27 CT £336.82 TOTE £6.90: £2.00 £2.50 £1.70 £2.50 (£37.20) Trio £337.50 OWNER J.S.Gutkin (WHATCOMBE) BRED Genesis Green Stud and Walter Swinburn Ltd 17 Rn 2m 20.92 (9.42) SF: 60/37/54/52/52/25/29/17/33/13/15/-/-/-/-

3936

RACING SCHOOLS' APPRENTICE H'CAP (0-70) (3-Y.O+) (Class E) £3,371.25 (£1,020.00: £497.50: £236.25)
1m 6f Stalls: Low GOING: 0.37 sec per fur (GS) 2-40 (2-41)

3682[5] **Ballymac Girl (46)***(62) (JMBradley)* 7-8-10 SDrowne(2) (b: lw: in tch: 5th st: led 2f out: clr 1f out: comf) ....— **1**
3627[2] Amiarge **(37)***(44) (MBrittain)* 5-8-1 AEddery(14) (mid div: gd hdwy over 2f out: hung lft over 1f out: kpt on: no ch w wnr) 8 **2**
My Rossini **(51)***(56) (PJBevan)* 6-9-1 DDenby(12) (bit bkwd: chsd ldrs: 4th st: drvn & hung lft over 2f out: styd on fnl f) 2 **3**
3676[2] Euro Singer **(55)***(58) (RAkehurst)* 3-8-9 SSanders(13) (lw: led after 2f: rdn whn hdd 2f out: sn wknd) 1¾ **4**
3818[6] Zamhareer (USA) **(44)***(46) (WStorey)* 4-8-8 PFessey(8) (lw: mid div: hdwy 5f out: rdn & no hdwy fnl 2f) ....½ **5**
3669[2] Boundary Express **(59)***(60)*(Fav)*(EJAlston)* 3-8-13 CTeague(6) (led 2f: styd prom: 2nd st: wknd over 1f out) ....¾ **6**
3801[8] Slaney Project (IRE) **(66)***(67) (WRMuir)* 3-9-6 GMitchell(9) (lw: in tch: 6th st: sn drvn along: wknd over 2f out) ....½ **7**
3705[5] Bang in Trouble (IRE) **(59)***(58) (JJO'Neill)* 4-9-9 RHavlin(5) (lw: lost tch over 6f out: drvn 4f out: n.d) 1¼ **8**
3759[12] Enchanted Cottage **(47)***(35) (MDHammond)* 3-7-12 (3)ow8 MSemple(16) (nvr on terms) 2½ **9**
3774[10] Cuango (IRE) **(55)***(43) (RHollinshead)* 4-9-2 (3) FLynch(3) (lw: mid div: drvn 3f out: btn 2f out) 7 **10**
3435[11] Record Lover (IRE) **(29)***(13) (MCChapman)* 5-7-1 (6) RhonaGent(11) (bhd: rdn over 4f out: no imp) 3½ **11**
3092[3] Bresil (USA) **(33)** *(KRBurke)* 6-7-11 RWaterfield(4) (a bhd: t.o) 15 **12**
3759[14] Prussia **(55)***(22) (WClay)* 4-9-5 GMilligan(10) (in tch tl rdn & wknd fr over 3f out: t.o) ....hd **13**
1948[3] Great Easeby (IRE) **(53)***(20) (WStorey)* 5-9-0 (3) KSked(17) (bit bkwd: t.o fr ½-wy) ....½ **14**
2612[7] Belgran (USA) **(29)** *(PDEvans)* 6-7-4 (3) PDoe(1) (bit bkwd: a in rr: t.o) 4 **15**
3801[12] Cumbrian Rhapsody **(60)***(21) (MHEasterby)* 5-9-10 RPainter(15) (bhd: hrd rdn 3f out: sn btn & eased: t.o) 1 **16**
3127[5] Triple Tie (USA) **(47)***(3) (MBlanshard)* 4-8-11 MBaird(7) (chsd ldrs: 3rd st: sn rdn: wknd qckly: t.o) 4 **17**

LONG HANDICAP Belgran (USA) 7-4 Record Lover (IRE) 7-5 Enchanted Cottage 6-13

6/1 Boundary Express, **13/2** My Rossini, **7/1** Euro Singer, **8/1** Zamhareer (USA), **10/1** Cumbrian Rhapsody, Cuango (IRE), **11/1** Slaney Project (IRE), **12/1** Amiarge, Triple Tie (USA), BALLYMAC GIRL, Bang in Trouble (IRE), **14/1** Great Easeby (IRE), **16/1** Bresil (USA), Belgran (USA), **25/1** Prussia, Record Lover (IRE), **50/1** Enchanted Cottage, CSF £146.72 CT £949.83 TOTE £14.30: £2.20 £2.40 £2.10 £1.80 (£51.00) Trio £255.60 OWNER Mr Lee Bowles (CHEPSTOW) BRED Miss K. Rausing and Mrs S.M. Rogers 17 Rn 3m 12.37 (14.17) SF: 44/26/38/30/28/32/39/40/7/25/-/-/4/2/-/3

WEIGHT FOR AGE 3yo-10lb

3937

MAPLE NURSERY (S) H'CAP (0-65) (2-Y.O) (Class G) £2,759.00 (£774.00: £377.00)
6f Stalls: High GOING: 0.37 sec per fur (GS) 3-10 (3-13)

3824[15] **Bee Health Boy (59)***(64) (MWEasterby)* 2-9-1b(5) CTeague(21) (mde all: rdn & jnd over 1f out: r.o wl) ....— **1**

3779[7] Mister Joel **(55)***(56) (MWEasterby)* 2-9-2 SMaloney(19) (chsd ldrs: rdn & ev ch over 1f out: edgd rt & outpcd: r.o ins fnl f) 1½ 2
3675[4] The Imps (IRE) **(58)***(56) (BWHills)* 2-9-0 (5) JDSmith(23) (chsd ldrs: rdn 2f out: kpt on fnl f) 1 3
3738[5] Rattle **(55)***(49) (JJO'Neill)* 2-9-2 AMackay(3) (outpcd: sn drvn along: styd on fnl 2f: nvr nrr)..1½ 4
3623[16] Magical Midnight **(50)***(39) (NTinkler)* 2-8-11 KimTinkler(8) (in tch: hrd rdn 2f out: one pce fnl f)2 5
3353[4] Phantom Dancer (IRE) **(53)***(35) (JBerry)* 2-9-0 JWilliams(5) (hdwy 2f out: nvr nrr)....2½ 6
3642[8] Lawnswood Captain (IRE) **(56)***(38) (RHollinshead)* 2-8-10 (7) FLynch(9) (towards rr: kpt on u.p fr over 1f out) ....nk 7
3856[5] L A Touch **(56)***(36) (CADwyer)* 2-9-0 (3) SDrowne(13) (mid div: rdn & no hdwy fr over 1f out) ..½ 8
3566[6] Spanish Luck **(49)***(28) (JWHills)* 2-8-10b CRutter(7) (prom centre tl rdn & wknd over 1f out)...nk 9
3528[14] Ticka Ticka Timing **(50)***(29) (BWMurray)* 2-8-6 (5) PFessey(4) (in rr: effrt 2f out: nt pce to chal) ....nk 10
3642[6] Red Misty (IRE) **(50)***(28) (MRChannon)* 2-8-11 TSprake(14) (chsd ldrs 4f centre) ....nk 11
3721[19] Good To Talk **(52)***(27) (MHEasterby)* 2-8-13 MBirch(6) (sn drvn along: nvr on terms) 1 12
2204[3] Bites **(52)***(17) (JAHarris)* 2-8-13 SDWilliams(22) (prom tl wknd 2f out) 4 13
3749[5] Red Acuisle (IRE) **(56)***(20)*(Fav)*(MBell)* 2-9-3v MFenton(12) (nvr nr ldrs) ....nk 14
3824[12] Power Princess **(50)***(10) (RMWhitaker)* 2-8-11 ACulhane(1) (sn drvn along: nvr trbld ldrs) ...1¼ 15
2251[5] Chilly Looks **(51)***(9) (MWEasterby)* 2-8-5 (7) GMitchell(24) (sn drvn along: nvr on terms) ....¾ 16
2820[8] Sonya Marie **(50)***(8) (JGFitzGerald)* 2-8-4 (7) KSked(16) (a in rr) ....hd 17
3738[6] Welsh Melody **(56)***(12) (KRBurke)* 2-9-3 MTebbutt(2) (chsd ldrs centre: rdn over 2f out: sn btn) ....¾ 18
3738[9] Jenny's Charmer **(56)***(10) (SEKettlewell)* 2-9-3 LCharnock(10) (spd to ½-wy) ....¾ 19
3738[3] Still Here (IRE) **(58)***(7) (MJHeaton-Ellis)* 2-9-0 (5) RHavlin(17) (dwlt: a bhd) 1¾ 20
3675[2] Ghostly Apparition **(60)***(9) (JohnUpson)* 2-9-4 (3) OPears(11) (in tch: rdn whn nt clr run wl over 1f out: sn btn) ....hd 21
3300[4] Stealth Attack (IRE) **(59)***(6) (JBerry)* 2-8-13 (7) PRoberts(20) (a in rr) 1 22
3721[16] Thorntoun Jewel (IRE) **(55)** *(JBalding)* 2-8-13 (3) SSanders(18) (prom: rdn over 2f out: sn btn) ....½ 23
3740[U] Maysimp (IRE) **(50)** *(BPJBaugh)* 2-8-11 RLappin(15) (b: b.hind: bhd fr ½-wy) 1½ 24

6/1 Red Acuisle (IRE), **7/1** The Imps (IRE), Red Misty (IRE), **11/1** Stealth Attack (IRE), **14/1** L A Touch, **16/1** Mister Joel, Chilly Looks, Spanish Luck, **20/1** Welsh Melody, Lawnswood Captain (IRE), Rattle, Phantom Dancer (IRE), Ticka Ticka Timing, BEE HEALTH BOY, Good To Talk, Bites, Maysimp (IRE), Power Princess, Still Here (IRE), Thorntoun Jewel (IRE), **25/1** Ghostly Apparition, Jenny's Charmer, **33/1** Magical Midnight, Sonya Marie, CSF £301.54 CT £2,260.06 TOTE £28.30: £5.30 £3.20 £2.00 £7.40 (£204.80) Trio £129.50 OWNER Bee Health Ltd (SHERIFF HUTTON) BRED Roger and Mrs Margaret Lightfoot 24 Rn

1m 18.28 (6.58) SF: 43/35/35/28/18/14/17/15/7/8/7/6/-/-/-/-/-/-/-/-/-/-/-/-

3938

HOLLY CONDITIONS STKS (3-Y.O+) (Class C) £4,832.00 (£1,808.00: £884.00: £380.00) **5f** Stalls: High GOING: 0.37 sec per fur (GS) 3-40 (3-40)

3632[9] **Inherent Magic (IRE) (85)***(98) (WRMuir)* 6-8-13 (3) SSanders(1) (b: lw: chsd ldrs: led wl over 1f out: jnd ent fnl f: rdn out) ....— 1
3717[12] Fire Dome (IRE) **(99)***(98) (RHannon)* 3-9-0 JWilliams(6) (lw: hdwy to chse wnr appr fnl f: sn ev ch: rdn & r.o) ....hd 2
3880* Takadou (IRE) **(80)***(90) (MissLCSiddall)* 4-9-7 4x RLappin(2) (outpcd: sn pushed along: hdwy over 1f out: sn rdn: one pce fnl f) 4 3
3902[3] Katya (IRE) **(95)***(79)*(Fav)*(MRChannon)* 3-8-10 TSprake(3) (chsd ldr: ev ch over 2f out: rdn & kpt on same pce fr over 1f out) ....½ 4
1909[2] Palacegate Jack (IRE) **(88)***(75) (JBerry)* 4-9-1b(5) PFessey(5) (led tl rdn & hdd wl over 1f out: sn wknd) 4 5
3689a[9] Ziggy's Dancer (USA) **(90)***(61) (EJAlston)* 4-9-8 SDWilliams(4) (chsd ldrs tl rdn & wknd appr fnl f) 5 6

9/4 Katya (IRE), **5/2** Takadou (IRE), **7/2** Palacegate Jack (IRE), **6/1** Fire Dome (IRE), **9/1** Ziggy's Dancer (USA), **16/1** INHERENT MAGIC (IRE), CSF £89.95 TOTE £18.80: £4.60 £2.80 (£42.10) OWNER Mrs Danita Winstanly (LAMBOURN) BRED Mrs M. McStay 6 Rn

63.07 secs (4.07) SF: 62/60/54/41/39/25
WEIGHT FOR AGE 3yo-2lb

3939

WHITEBEAM MAIDEN STKS (2-Y.O F) (Class D) £3,454.00 (£1,042.00: £506.00: £238.00) **7f 30y** Stalls: Low GOING: 0.37 sec per fur (GS) 4-15 (4-16)

Classic Romance *(80+) (SCWilliams)* 2-8-11 AMackay(4) (w'like: s.s: sn prom: 4th st: led appr fnl f: r.o) ....— 1
3713[4] Salty Girl (IRE) **(75)***(77) (BWHills)* 2-8-11 JWilliams(2) (led tl hdd over 1f out: rdn & unable qckn fnl f) 1¼ 2

Meribel (IRE) *(73+)*(Fav)*(PWChapple-Hyam)* 2-8-6 (5) RHavlin(5) (w'like: chsd ldrs: 3rd st: sn pushed along: r.o one pce)....2 3
3666[7] Desert Frolic (IRE) *(70) (MJohnston)* 2-8-11 DaleGibson(1) (chsd ldr: 2nd st: pushed along 3f out: r.o one pce)....1¼ 4
1671[9] Madam Marash (IRE) *(59) (AGFoster)* 2-8-11 TSprake(7) (bhd: 7th st: effrt over 2f out: btn bel dist)....5 5
3708[9] Bodfari Lass *(53) (BWHills)* 2-8-6 (5) JDSmith(6) (sn drvn along: 6th st: btn over 2f out)....2½ 6
3740[9] Fancy Clancy **(48)***(8) (MissLCSiddall)* 2-8-11 RLappin(3) (plld hrd: hld up: 5th st: wknd over 3f out: t.o)....20 7

7/4 Meribel (IRE), **3/1** Salty Girl (IRE) (2/1-100/30), **5/1** Desert Frolic (IRE), **13/2** Bodfari Lass, **7/1** CLASSIC ROMANCE, **33/1** Madam Marash (IRE), Fancy Clancy, CSF £25.52 TOTE £7.60: £2.70 £1.80 (£18.50) OWNER Classic Bloodstock Plc (NEWMARKET) BRED Barrettstown Stud Farms Ltd 7 Rn
1m 36.42 (9.12) SF: 22/19/15/12/1/-/-

3940 WALNUT MAIDEN STKS (2-Y.O) (Class D) £3,649.00 (£1,102.00: £536.00: £253.00) 5f Stalls: High GOING: 0.37 sec per fur (GS) 4-50 (4-55)

3647[2] **Repatriate (AUS)** *(74)*(Fav)*(PWChapple-Hyam)* 2-8-4 (5) RHavlin(10) (chsd ldrs: led 2 out: sn clr: pushed out)....— 1
3763[14] Chalice *(68) (JBalding)* 2-8-9 JWilliams(5) (in tch: pushed along wl over 1f out: r.o)....2 2
3699[6] Kazimiera (IRE) *(64) (MJohnston)* 2-8-9 ACulhane(6) (reluctant to ent stalls: bhd: hdwy 2f out: rdn & r.o one pce fnl f)....1¼ 3
3465[16] Finisterre (IRE) *(46) (JJO'Neill)* 2-9-0 AMackay(7) (sn outpcd & drvn along: kpt on u.p fnl f)...7 4
1203[7] Swifty Nifty (IRE) *(36) (JBerry)* 2-8-4 (5) PFessey(8) (led 3f: sn rdn & wknd)....1¾ 5
2629[9] Farida Seconda *(26) (JBalding)* 2-8-9 SDWilliams(4) (chsd ldrs tl wknd over 1f out)....3 6
3626[18] Smiling Bess *(24) (KRBurke)* 2-8-9 MFenton(2) (in tch tl wknd 2f out)....¾ 7
3647[3] Polar Refrain *(14) (MrsJRRamsden)* 2-8-6 (3) SDrowne(9) (towards rr: sn drvn along: no imp) 3 8
3626[10] Smarter Charter *(13) (MrsJRRamsden)* 2-9-0 MDeering(1) (a in rr)....1¾ 9
1781[8] Seeking Destiny (IRE) *(MCChapman)* 2-8-7 (7) CMunday(3) (sn drvn along: drppd rr ½-wy)..6 10

85/40 REPATRIATE (AUS), **9/4** Kazimiera (IRE), **7/2** Polar Refrain, **10/1** Smarter Charter (7/1-12/1), **16/1** Finisterre (IRE), **20/1** Swifty Nifty (IRE), **25/1** Chalice, **33/1** Smiling Bess, Seeking Destiny (IRE), **50/1** Farida Seconda, CSF £44.54 TOTE £2.70: £1.60 £4.60 £1.30 (£53.60) Trio £67.80 OWNER Mr R. E. Sangster (MARLBOROUGH) BRED Swettenham Stud 10 Rn
65.27 secs (6.27) SF: 19/13/9/-/-/-/-/-/-/-

3941 HAWTHORN H'CAP (0-80) (3-Y.O+ F & M) (Class D) £3,991.75 (£1,204.00: £584.50: £274.75) 7f 30y Stalls: Low GOING: 0.37 sec per fur (GS) 5-20 (5-21)

3725* **Azdihaar (USA)** **(72)***(90)*(Fav)*(JLDunlop)* 3-9-5 TSprake(11) (chsd ldrs: 3rd st: led over 2f out: clr appr fnl f: comf)....— 1
3879[5] Chantry Bellini **(49)***(54) (MrsSMAustin)* 6-7-7 (7)ow7 DDenby(5) (b: b.hind: a.p: 4th st: chsd wnr appr fnl f: one pce)....2½ 2
3802[7] Karinska **(67)***(74) (MCChapman)* 5-8-11 (7) CMunday(10) (mid div: kpt on wl fnl 2f: nrst fin)....2½ 3
3645[4] Michellisa **(59)***(61) (JDBethell)* 4-8-5 (5) JDSmith(3) (styd on fr over 2f out: nvr nr to chal)....2 4
3879[4] Benjarong **(48)***(48) (RMMcKellar)* 3-7-4 (5)ow2 MBaird(6) (led tl hdd & racd alone far side ent st: rdn 2f out: sn btn)....hd 5
3373[7] Alarming **(80)***(73) (JHMGosden)* 3-9-13 DaleGibson(1) (mid div: 6th & drvn ent st: sn outpcd: kpt on appr fnl f)....4 6
3800[3] Princess Maxine (IRE) **(54)***(46)*(Fav)*(JJO'Neill)* 6-8-5 AMackay(2) (lw: hld up towards rr: stdy hdwy fr over 2f out: drvn appr fnl f: eased whn btn)....nk 7
3726[17] Royal Comedian **(42)***(33) (BWMurray)* 6-7-2 (5) PFessey(12) (chsd ldrs: led ent st: hdd over 2f out: sn wknd)....¾ 8
3377[4] Darcey Bussell **(58)***(40) (BWHills)* 3-8-5 MFenton(7) (b: a in rr)....4 9
2915[3] Four Lane Flyer **(50)***(21) (EJAlston)* 3-7-11 LCharnock(4) (a bhd)....5 10
3700[10] Promise Fulfilled (USA) **(69)***(28) (ABailey)* 4-9-3b(3) SDrowne(9) (a bhd)....5 11
3559[6] Academy Life **(68)***(21) (PFICole)* 3-9-1 CRutter(8) (in tch: 5th st: wknd over 2f out)....3 12

LONG HANDICAP Chantry Bellini 7-3 Benjarong 7-3

5/1 AZDIHAAR (USA), Princess Maxine (IRE), **11/2** Alarming, **8/1** Academy Life, Michellisa, **9/1** Karinska, **10/1** Darcey Bussell, Benjarong (8/1-12/1), **12/1** Promise Fulfilled (USA), Chantry Bellini, **20/1** Royal Comedian, **25/1** Four Lane Flyer, CSF £58.98 CT £485.71 TOTE £3.70: £1.80 £4.80 £3.00 (£48.60) Trio £213.80 OWNER Mr Hamdan Al Maktoum (ARUNDEL) BRED Shadwell Farm Inc 12 Rn
1m 36.58 (9.28) SF: 27/-/15/2/-/10/-/-/-/-/-/-
WEIGHT FOR AGE 3yo-4lb

T/Plpt: £732.00 (13.6 Tckts). T/Qdpt: £142.40 (0.2 Tckts); £154.00 to Haydock 1/10/95. J

3922-NEWMARKET (R-H)
Saturday September 30th (Good to firm)
WEATHER: sunny spells WIND: almost nil

3942
MARY REVELEY RACING CLUB OH SO SHARP STKS (Listed) (2-Y.O F) (Class A) £9,594.00 (£3,546.00: £1,698.00: £690.00)
7f (Rowley) Stalls: High GOING minus 0.19 sec per fur (GF) 1-50 (1-51)

3561[3] **Ruznama (USA) (100)***(98+)*(Fav)*(BWHills)* 2-8-9 WCarson(3) (lw: trckd ldr: led on bit over 2f out: r.o: comf) — 1
3662* Obsessive (USA) *(92) (MRStoute)* 2-8-9 DHolland(5) (hld up: hdwy 2f out: r.o: no ch w wnr) 2½ 2
3548[14] Fag End (IRE) **(96)***(85) (MHTompkins)* 2-8-9 PRobinson(4) (chsd ldrs: rdn 3f out: one pce) 3 3
3590a* Greek Icon *(84) (JLDunlop)* 2-8-9 KDarley(6) (hld up: hdwy & ev ch over 1f out: rdn & nt qckn) ½ 4
3702[2] Home Shopping **(100)***(88) (KMcAuliffe)* 2-8-13 CNakatani(2) (swtg: hld up: effrt & hung lft 2f out: rdn & no imp) nk 5
3518* La Modiste **(92)***(76) (SDow)* 2-8-9 MRoberts(1) (led tl hdd over 2f out: sn wknd) 3½ 6

11/8 RUZNAMA (USA), **5/2** Obsessive (USA), **7/1** Greek Icon, **15/2** Home Shopping (5/1-8/1), **14/1** Fag End (IRE) (10/1-16/1), **16/1** La Modiste, CSF £4.73 TOTE £2.00: £1.40 £1.60 (£2.10) OWNER Mr Hamdan Al Maktoum (LAMBOURN) BRED Shadwell Estate Co., Ltd. and Shadwell Farm Inc. 6 Rn 1m 25.33 (1.63) SF: 58/52/45/44/48/36

3943
HAMELLS DIAMOND JUBILEE H'CAP (0-90) (3-Y.O+) (Class C) £8,740.00 (£2,620.00: £1,260.00: £580.00)
7f (Rowley) Stalls: High GOING minus 0.19 sec per fur (GF) 2-20 (2-23)

3813[7] **Samah (73)***(83) (DNicholls)* 5-8-11 CNakatani(18) (lw: chsd ldrs: led over 2f out tl over 1f out: rallied to ld ins fnl f) — 1
3706[4] Broughtons Turmoil **(62)***(71) (WJMusson)* 6-8-0 GHind(11) (lw: smooth hdwy ½-wy: ev ch over 1f out: r.o) nk 2
3703[2] Cool Edge (IRE) **(79)***(87) (MHTompkins)* 4-9-3v PRobinson(6) (lw: hld up & bhd: hdwy 3f out: led over 1f out tl ins fnl f: no ex) ½ 3
3659[8] Delta Soleil (USA) **(86)***(94) (PWHarris)* 3-9-6 MHills(9) (lw: a cl up: chal 3f out: kpt on) hd 4
3545* Mullitover **(81)***(89) (MJHeaton-Ellis)* 5-9-2 (3) DRMcCabe(5) (hdwy over 1f out: r.o wl towards fin) s.h 5
3715[5] Double Bounce **(77)***(83) (PJMakin)* 5-9-1 DHolland(7) (b: hld up: bhd: hdwy whn hmpd & swtchd 2f out: r.o wl fnl f) 1 6
3615[18] Jato **(70)***(74) (SCWilliams)* 6-8-8 JTate(13) (bhd: hdwy 3f out: styd on: nt pce to chal) ½ 7
2613[7] Cutpurse Moll **(75)***(75) (JRFanshawe)* 3-8-6v(3) NVarley(23) (chsd ldrs: chal 3f out: wknd over 1f out) 2 8
3750* Anzio (IRE) **(73)***(70) (BAPearce)* 4-8-11b TIves(25) (b: chsd ldrs: ev ch 2½f out: wknd over 1f out) 1¼ 9
3771[2] Mislemani (IRE) **(60)***(57) (AGNewcombe)* 5-7-12 JFEgan(17) (in tch: outpcd 3f out: hdwy 2f out: styd on: n.d) hd 10
3615[2] La Petite Fusee **(71)***(67) (RJO'Sullivan)* 4-8-9 AClark(26) (lw: a in tch: rdn over 2f out: r.o one pce) nk 11
694[5] Willie Conquer **(78)***(74) (RAkehurst)* 3-8-7 (5) DaneO'Neill(21) (b.off fore: bkwd: sme hdwy u.p 2f out: nvr rchd ldrs) hd 12
3706[8] Safey Ana (USA) **(73)***(68) (BHanbury)* 4-8-8 (3) JStack(14) (b: swtg: nvr trbld ldrs) nk 13
3813[11] Be Warned **(74)***(66) (NACallaghan)* 4-8-12b PaulEddery(27) (bhd: hdwy u.p over 2f out: n.d) 1½ 14
3719[2] Sagebrush Roller **(81)***(72) (JWWatts)* 7-9-5 NConnorton(2) (effrt 3f out: hung rt over 2f out: sn btn) nk 15
3732[4] Knobbleeneeze **(76)***(64) (MRChannon)* 5-9-0v RHughes(20) (in tch: effrt 3f out: no imp) 1¼ 16
Field of Vision (IRE) **(65)***(53) (MJohnston)* 5-8-3 TWilliams(12) (s.i.s: hdwy u.p 2f out: swtchd 1f out: n.d) nk 17
3703[17] Three Stops (USA) **(81)***(68) (MRStoute)* 3-9-1v KDarley(15) (lw: cl up tl rdn & btn 2f out) s.h 18
3214[12] Jibereen **(72)***(59)*(Fav)*(GLewis)* 3-8-6 SWhitworth(16) (chsd ldrs: hrd rdn 3f out: wknd 2f out) nk 19
3674[5] Captain's Day **(77)***(62) (TGMills)* 3-8-4 (7) JCornally(4) (lw: bhd fnl 3f) ¾ 20
3534[4] Whatever's Right (IRE) **(70)***(55) (MDIUsher)* 6-8-8 DeanMcKeown(30) (chsd ldrs: hrd rdn 3f out: sn wknd) hd 21
3551[9] Tabook (IRE) **(90)***(74) (EALDunlop)* 4-9-9 (5) MHenry(3) (lw: hld up: hdwy ½-wy: sn prom: wknd fnl 2f) ½ 22
3715* Keston Pond (IRE) **(73)***(52) (DAWilson)* 5-8-11 GCarter(29) (chsd ldrs 5f) 2 23
3615[11] How's Yer Father **(83)***(60) (RJHodges)* 9-9-7 WNewnes(1) (bhd fnl 3f) 1 24

3411³ Halmanerror **(72)***(48) (MrsJRRamsden)* 5-8-10 KFallon(19) (bhd: hdwy u.p 3f out: btn whn hmpd 1f out) ....nk **25**
3557⁶ Red Rita (IRE) **(75)***(51) (WRMuir)* 4-8-8 (5) AWhelan(24) (unruly gng to s: led tl hdd & wknd over 2f out) ....hd **26**
3706¹⁰ Tom Morgan **(79)***(52) (PTWalwyn)* 4-9-3 JCarroll(8) (outpcd fr ½-wy) 1¼ **27**
3755⁹ Stolen Melody **(74)***(47) (SDow)* 3-8-1 (7) ADaly(10) (n.d) ....s.h **28**
3347* Nottash (IRE) **(74)***(47) (JRFanshawe)* 3-8-8 DHarrison(28) (n.d) ....s.h **29**
3654⁹ Mister Fire Eyes (IRE) **(71)***(38) (CEBrittain)* 3-8-5b MRoberts(22) (lw: spd over 4f) 2½ **30**

9/2 Jibereen, **11/1** SAMAH, **12/1** Delta Soleil (USA), Cool Edge (IRE), Keston Pond (IRE), Double Bounce, **14/1** Mullitover (3/1-16/1), **16/1** Be Warned, Broughtons Turmoil, Halmanerror, **20/1** Three Stops (USA), Knobbleeneeze, Willie Conquer, Whatever's Right (IRE), Sagebrush Roller, Nottash (IRE), **25/1** La Petite Fusee, Tabook (IRE), **33/1** Field of Vision (IRE), Safey Ana (USA), Captain's Day, Anzio (IRE), Cutpurse Moll, How's Yer Father, Mislemani (IRE), Red Rita (IRE), Tom Morgan, Jato, Mister Fire Eyes (IRE), **66/1** Stolen Melody, CSF £178.62 CT £2,014.62 TOTE £22.80: £5.80 £7.90 £2.20 £3.20 (£334.80) Trio £1,932.30 OWNER Mr S. Aitken (THIRSK) BRED Shadwell Estate Company Limited 30 Rn 1m 24.83 (1.13)
SF:66/54/70/73/72/66/57/54/53/40/50/53/51/49/55/47/36/47/38/41/38/57/35/43/31/34/35/26/26/17
WEIGHT FOR AGE 3yo-4lb

3944 SUN CHARIOT STKS (Gp 2) (3-Y.O+ F & M) (Class A) £33,691.00 (£12,469.00: £5,984.50: £2,447.50)
1m 2f (Rowley) Stalls: Low GOING minus 0.19 sec per fur (GF) 2-55 (2-56)

3693a³ **Warning Shadows (IRE) (111)***(116) (CEBrittain)* 3-8-8 KDarley(5) (trckd ldrs: stdy hdwy 3f out: led over 1f out: rdn & r.o wl) ....— **1**
3690a³ Flagbird (USA) *(122)*(Fav)*(SbinSuroor)* 4-9-6 CNakatani(6) (gd sort: lw: trckd ldr: led over 3f out tl over 1f out: rallied fnl f: jst failed) ....hd **2**
3636* Poppy Carew (IRE) **(106)***(111) (PWHarris)* 3-8-8 PaulEddery(7) (lw: hld up: hdwy 3f out: sn rdn: styd on: nt pce to chal) 3 **3**
3636⁶ Pitcroy **(93)***(105) (JRFanshawe)* 3-8-8 KFallon(4) (swtg: hld up: effrt 3f out: one pce fnl 2f) 4 **4**
3413³ Ellie Ardensky **(94)***(98) (JRFanshawe)* 3-8-8 DHarrison(3) (lw: trckd ldrs tl rdn & btn wl over 1f out) 4 **5**
Cosy Corner (IRE) *(97) (ErichPils)* 3-8-8 JTate(1) (w'like: hld up: effrt 3f out: rdn & nvr able chal) 1 **6**
3694a⁹ Musetta (IRE) **(110)***(85) (CEBrittain)* 3-8-8 MRoberts(2) (lw: led tl hdd over 3f out: sn wknd) ...7 **7**

4/6 Flagbird (USA), **9/2** Poppy Carew (IRE), **6/1** WARNING SHADOWS (IRE), **10/1** Musetta (IRE), **20/1** Ellie Ardensky, **33/1** Pitcroy, **66/1** Cosy Corner (IRE), CSF £9.85 TOTE £6.90: £2.40 £1.30 (£3.30) OWNER Sheikh Marwan Al Maktoum (NEWMARKET) BRED Sheikh Marwan al Maktoum 7 Rn 2m 4.91 (2.31) SF: 58/70/53/47/40/39/27
WEIGHT FOR AGE 3yo-6lb

3945 WILLIAM HILL CAMBRIDGESHIRE H'CAP (3-Y.O+) (Class B) £55,716.50 (£20,823.50: £10,161.75: £4,346.25: £1,923.13: £953.87)
1m 1f (Rowley) Stalls: High GOING minus 0.19 sec per fur (GF) 3-35 (3-38)

3188* **Cap Juluca (IRE) (107)***(122+) (RCharlton)* 3-9-10 RHughes(26) (lw: mde all: r.o gamely fnl f) ....— **1**
3729² Ball Gown **(79)***(90) (DTThom)* 5-7-10 (5)ow4 AWhelan(22) (hdwy 2f out: r.o wl fnl f: jst failed) ....nk **2**
3413⁷ Hunters of Brora (IRE) **(91)***(102) (JDBethell)* 5-8-13 TIves(2) (lw: hdwy 3f out: chsng ldrs over 1f out: r.o) 1¾ **3**
3729³ Show Faith (IRE) **(84)***(95) (RHannon)* 5-8-1 (5) DaneO'Neill(15) (in tch: hdwy 4f out: chsng ldrs 2f out: r.o) ....hd **4**
3703¹⁰ Celestial Choir **(78)***(87) (JLEyre)* 5-7-11 (3) NVarley(13) (chsd ldrs: rdn over 2f out: kpt on one pce) 1¼ **5**
3611* Sue's Artiste **(84)***(92) (BWHills)* 4-8-6 5x DHolland(27) (a.p: effrt 3f out: kpt on wl) ....nk **6**
3732⁸ Crumpton Hill (IRE) **(85)***(93) (NAGraham)* 3-8-2 DHarrison(25) (lw: hdwy over 2f out: edgd lft appr fnl f: nvr rchd ldrs) ....nk **7**
3813¹⁵ Kayvee **(101)***(108) (GHarwood)* 6-9-9 AClark(21) (hld up & bhd: hdwy 3f out: prom 2f out: one pce after) ....nk **8**
3382* Weaver Bird **(88)***(95) (HCandy)* 5-8-10 5x WNewnes(11) (hld up & bhd: hdwy over 2f out: nvr able to chal) ....nk **9**
3433* Mellottie **(90)***(97) (MrsMReveley)* 10-8-12 KDarley(9) (bhd tl styd on wl fnl 2f: nrst fin) ....hd **10**
3607⁷ Pride of Pendle **(78)***(85) (DNicholls)* 6-7-7 (7) MartinDwyer(39) (lw: bhd: hdwy over 2f out: edgd lft appr fnl f: nvr rchd ldrs) ....hd **11**

1853[15] Smart Generation **(83)***(89) (LordHuntingdon)* 4-8-5 MHills(19) (n.m.r 3f out: hdwy u.p over 2f out: nvr rchd ldrs)....nk **12**
3729[5] Silver Groom (IRE) **(75)***(79) (RAkehurst)* 5-7-6 (5) MHenry(35) (lw: in tch: hdwy over 2f out: nt pce to chal)....1¼ **13**
3601[13] Secret Aly (CAN) **(82)***(86) (CEBrittain)* 5-8-4 JFEgan(17) (lw: effrt & n.m.r 4f out: styd on: n.d)....hd **14**
3594[2] Night City **(95)***(98) (LadyHerries)* 4-9-3 SWhitworth(4) (lw: in tch: rdn ½-wy: no imp)....nk **15**
3810[13] Reverand Thickness **(74)***(76) (SCWilliams)* 4-7-10b NKennedy(18) (chsd ldrs tl wknd wl over 1f out)....½ **16**
3802* Wilcuma **(81)***(81) (PJMakin)* 4-8-3 PaulEddery(33) (effrt 4f out: nvr trbld ldrs)....1¼ **17**
3608[7] Sue's Return **(88)***(88) (APJarvis)* 3-8-5 JTate(40) (in tch: hdwy u.p 3f out: wknd over 1f out)....hd **18**
3608[3] Hoh Express **(102)***(102) (IABalding)* 3-9-5 5x GHind(6) (lw: prom tl outpcd fnl 3f)....hd **19**
2738[2] Blisland **(94)***(93) (RCharlton)* 3-8-11 CNakatani(3) (chsd ldrs tl wknd fnl 2f)....s.h **20**
3608[2] Roving Minstrel **(86)***(84) (BAMcMahon)* 4-8-3 (5) LNewton(37) (lw: hdwy over 3f out: hrd rdn & in tch 2f out: sn wknd)....¾ **21**
3729[15] Tykeyvor (IRE) **(75)***(72) (LadyHerries)* 5-7-11 GBardwell(31) (b.hind: bhd tl sme late hdwy)...¾ **22**
3188[8] Bettergeton **(93)***(89) (PJBevan)* 3-8-10 NCarlisle(30) (hld up: effrt 3f out: n.d)....nk **23**
3608[5] Rambo's Hall **(87)***(82) (JAGlover)* 10-8-9 DeanMcKeown(28) (swtg: prom tl wknd fnl 2f)....¾ **24**
3729[11] Amrak Ajeeb (IRE) **(87)***(81) (BHanbury)* 3-8-1 (3) JStack(12) (hld up: rdn 3f out: n.d)....nk **25**
3813[2] Decorated Hero **(102)***(96) (JHMGosden)* 3-9-5 JCarroll(1) (chsd ldrs tl wknd wl over 1f out)....½ **26**
3729[10] Wakeel (USA) **(87)***(80) (SDow)* 3-7-11 (7) ADaly(32) (prom 6f)....hd **27**
3188[9] Billy Bushwacker **(87)***(78) (MrsMReveley)* 4-8-9 KFallon(23) (lw: bhd: effrt 3f out: n.d)....1½ **28**
3837[6] Master Beveled **(75)***(66) (PDEvans)* 5-7-8 (3) DarrenMoffatt(24) (chsd ldrs 6f: sn wknd)....hd **29**
Tartan Gem (IRE) **(78)***(68) (JARToller)* 4-7-11 (3) DWright(34) (bkwd: hrd rdn 3f out: no imp) .nk **30**
3728[3] Yoush (IRE) **(98)***(86)*(Fav)*(MAJarvis)* 3-9-1 PRobinson(8) (swtg: rdn ½-wy: sn bhd)....1 **31**
3813[19] Celestial Key (USA) **(101)***(89) (MJohnston)* 5-9-9 TWilliams(36) (lw: hdwy & in tch ½-wy: rdn & btn over 1f out: eased)....s.h **32**
3458[3] Naked Welcome **(96)***(84) (MJFetherston-Godley)* 3-8-13b MRoberts(5) (lw: drvn along thrght: a bhd)....hd **33**
3603[5] Maralinga (IRE) **(98)***(84) (LadyHerries)* 3-8-12 (3) DRMcCabe(20) (chsd ldrs tl wknd 3f out) ..1¼ **34**
3732[12] Gadge **(72)***(56) (DMorris)* 4-7-8 JLowe(29) (bhd most of wy)....1 **35**
3608[9] Our Rita **(86)***(69) (DrJDScargill)* 6-8-8 NConnorton(16) (mid div & rdn ½-wy: n.m.r & n.d)....nk **36**
3413[2] Vena (IRE) **(90)***(70) (JLDunlop)* 3-8-7 GCarter(14) (chsd ldrs tl wknd over 2f out)....2 **37**
3729[17] Legendary Leap **(75)***(49) (LordHuntingdon)* 5-7-11 NAdams(38) (chsd ldrs 6f: sn wknd)....3½ **38**
3659[3] Virtual Reality **(77)***(38) (AHide)* 4-7-13 RPrice(10) (swtg: in tch: rdn over 3f out: sn wknd)....7 **39**

8/1 Yoush (IRE), **11/1** CAP JULUCA (IRE), Sue's Artiste, **12/1** Naked Welcome, **14/1** Vena (IRE), Celestial Choir, **16/1** Ball Gown, Mellottie, Wilcuma, Billy Bushwacker, **20/1** Blisland, Rambo's Hall, Decorated Hero, Master Beveled, **25/1** Hunters of Brora (IRE), Roving Minstrel, Silver Groom (IRE), Smart Generation, Hoh Express, **33/1** Crumpton Hill (IRE), Maralinga (IRE), Show Faith (IRE), Bettergeton, Night City, Weaver Bird, **40/1** Kayvee, Virtual Reality, Tykeyvor (IRE), **50/1** Gadge, Secret Aly (CAN), **66/1** Pride of Pendle, Celestial Key (USA), Wakeel (USA), Amrak Ajeeb (IRE), Reverand Thickness, Our Rita, Sue's Return, Legendary Leap, **100/1** Tartan Gem (IRE), CSF £172.93 CT £3,970.49 TOTE £12.60: £4.00 £3.20 £7.40 £11.10 (£100.10) Trio £2,214.80 OWNER Mr Martin Myers (BECKHAMPTON) BRED Mrs N. Myers 39 Rn 1m 50.71 (1.01)
SF:83/56/68/61/53/58/54/74/61/63/51/55/45/52/64/42/47/49/63/54/50/38/50/48/42/57/41/44/32/34/47/55/45/45/22/35/31/15/4 WEIGHT FOR AGE 3yo-5lb

3946

JOCKEY CLUB CUP STKS (Gp 3) (3-Y.O+) (Class A) £22,995.00 (£8,505.00: £4,077.50: £1,662.50)
2m (Rowley) Stalls: High GOING minus 0.19 sec per fur (GF) 4-10 (4-13)

3563[2] **Further Flight (107)***(120) (BWHills)* 9-9-3 MHills(3) (b.hind: hld up: effrt over 4f out: led 1½f out: r.o v.wl)....— **1**
Assessor (IRE) *(115) (RHannon)* 6-9-0 RHughes(1) (b: bit bkwd: stdy hdwy 6f out: rdn over 2f out: r.o: no ch w wnr)....2½ **2**
3146* Double Eclipse (IRE) **(115)***(114)*(Fav)*(MJohnston)* 3-8-2 TWilliams(7) (lw: chsd ldrs: rdn 6f out: led over 2f out: hdd 1½f out: no ex)....nk **3**
3563[3] Old Rouvel (USA) **(100)***(113) (DJGMurraySmith)* 4-9-0 MRoberts(8) (lw: bhd: drvn along 7f out: hdwy over 2f out: nt clr run & swtchd 1f out: styd on)....1 **4**
3563[5] Cuff Link (IRE) **(107)***(113) (MajorWRHern)* 5-9-0 PaulEddery(2) (in tch: effrt 4f out: ch 2f out: one pce)....hd **5**
3454* Source of Light **(104)***(103) (RCharlton)* 6-9-0 CNakatani(5) (plld hrd: led & qcknd 7f out: hdd & wknd over 2f out)....10 **6**
3389[2] Wot-If-We (IRE) **(100)***(95) (TGMills)* 3-8-2 GCarter(4) (lw: led tl hdd 7f out: wknd fnl 3f)....8 **7**
3543* Kshessinskaya **(95)***(72) (CEBrittain)* 3-7-13 JFEgan(6) (lw: chsd ldrs tl wknd fnl 6f)....20 **8**

6/4 Double Eclipse (IRE), **5/2** FURTHER FLIGHT, **9/2** Source of Light, **14/1** Assessor (IRE) (10/1-16/1), Cuff Link (IRE) (10/1-16/1), **16/1** Old Rouvel (USA), **33/1** Wot-If-We (IRE), **40/1** Kshessinskaya, CSF £30.31 TOTE £3.20: £1.40 £2.60 £1.20 (£29.50) OWNER Mr S. WingfieldDigby (LAMBOURN) BRED S. Wingfield Digby 8 Rn

3m 28.14 (4.84) SF: 62/57/44/55/55/45/25/2
WEIGHT FOR AGE 3yo-12lb

3947 NGK SPARK PLUGS PERFORMANCE NURSERY H'CAP (2-Y.O) (Class C)

£8,350.00 (£2,500.00: £1,200.00: £550.00)
6f (Rowley) Stalls: High GOING minus 0.19 sec per fur (GF) 4-45 (4-45)

3714* **King of Peru (86)***(93) (APJarvis)* 2-9-3 JTate(12) (lw: a cl up: led over 1f out: hung lft & r.o wl)......— 1
3620⁸ Amber Fort **(69)***(69) (PFICole)* 2-7-9b(5) MHenry(11) (led tl hdd over 1f out: no ex)......2½ 2
3803⁵ Missile Toe (IRE) **(70)***(70) (JEBanks)* 2-7-10 (5) AWhelan(7) (hdwy 2f out: r.o: nrst fin)......s.h 3
3604⁸ Unsold **(75)***(74) (JRFanshawe)* 2-8-6 DHarrison(5) (bhd tl hdwy over 1f out: r.o wl)......½ 4
3375* Creative Account (USA) **(90)***(88+)*(Fav)*(MrsJRRamsden)* 2-9-7 KFallon(6) (bhd: nt clr run 2f out: swtchd over 1f out: fin wl)......½ 5
3803⁷ Akalim **(78)***(70) (DMorley)* 2-8-9 MHills(9) (cl up tl wknd over 1f out)......2 6
2978⁷ Jaleel **(75)***(65) (RHannon)* 2-8-6 MRoberts(13) (in tch: rdn ½-wy: no hdwy)......¾ 7
3714¹² Willisa **(73)***(61) (JDBethell)* 2-8-4 CNakatani(14) (lw: outpcd & bhd tl sme late hdwy)......¾ 8
3655³ Erupt **(68)***(55) (GBBalding)* 2-7-10v(3) NVarley(8) (chsd ldrs tl wknd over 1f out)......nk 9
3684⁶ Uncle George **(75)***(62) (MHTompkins)* 2-8-6 PRobinson(1) (a outpcd & bhd)......hd 10
3623² Sheilana (IRE) **(74)***(61) (TGMills)* 2-8-5 GCarter(10) (nvr wnt pce)......hd 11
3548⁵ Windswept (IRE) **(68)***(55) (DJSffrenchDavis)* 2-7-13 NAdams(4) (chsd ldrs 4f: wknd)......s.h 12
3465¹³ Awafeh **(65)***(48) (JWPayne)* 2-7-10 GBardwell(15) (swtg: sn outpcd & bhd)......1¼ 13
3714¹¹ Myttons Mistake **(76)***(59) (ABailey)* 2-8-4b(3) DWright(3) (in tch: hdwy over 2f out: sn btn)......s.h 14
3766* Almushtarak (IRE) **(89)***(71) (MissGayKelleway)* 2-9-1 (5) DaneO'Neill(2) (lw: in tch 4f)......½ 15
3626* Keepers Dawn (IRE) **(84)***(45) (RFJohnsonHoughton)* 2-9-1 KDarley(16) (swtg: prom 4f: sn wknd)......8 16

7/2 Creative Account (USA), **6/1** Keepers Dawn (IRE), Amber Fort, **9/1** KING OF PERU, **12/1** Akalim, Myttons Mistake, Sheilana (IRE), **14/1** Missile Toe (IRE), Almushtarak (IRE), **16/1** Unsold, Erupt, Uncle George, **20/1** Jaleel, Willisa, Windswept (IRE), **66/1** Awafeh, CSF £61.04 CT £707.64 TOTE £10.10: £2.40 £1.70 £3.70 £3.30 (£39.40) Trio £282.20 OWNER Mr L. Fust (ASTON UPTHORPE) BRED C. R. Black 16 Rn

1m 13.13 (1.83) SF: 59/35/36/40/54/36/31/27/21/28/27/21/14/25/37/11

3948 ALINGTON MAIDEN STKS (2-Y.O F) (Class D) £5,708.50 (£1,708.00: £819.00: £374.50) 6f (Rowley)

Stalls: High GOING minus 0.19 sec per fur (GF) 5-15 (5-17)

Polish Spring (IRE) *(87+) (BWHills)* 2-8-11 MHills(16) (lw: wl grwn: w ldrs: led wl over 1f out: r.o)......— 1
Oneforthediteh (USA) *(84+) (JHMGosden)* 2-8-11 JCarroll(14) (lt-f: unf: in tch: swtchd & effrt over 1f out: r.o wl towards fin)......1 2
3539² Jezyah (USA) *(78) (RWArmstrong)* 2-8-11 RPrice(9) (reard s: sn rcvrd & cl up: nt qckn fnl f)2½ 3
Mua-Tab *(76+) (PTWalwyn)* 2-8-11 DHarrison(12) (leggy: lt-f: sn drvn along: in tch: kpt on fnl f)......½ 4
Indian Relative *(76+) (RGuest)* 2-8-6 (5) MHenry(8) (unf: scope: bkwd: in tch: hdwy over 1f out: r.o)......nk 5
3639² Green Bentley (IRE) **(78)***(75) (RHannon)* 2-8-6 (5) DaneO'Neill(4) (chsd ldrs: effrt 2f out: r.o one pce)......hd 6
2322⁶ Phantom Creek *(71)*(Fav)*(SbinSuroor)* 2-8-11 GHind(7) (swtg: plld hrd: led tl hdd wl over 1f out: r.o)......1½ 7
Petite Juliette *(70+) (WJarvis)* 2-8-8 (3) JStack(5) (cmpt: bkwd: bhd: shkn up over 1f out: r.o wl towards fin)......½ 8
Budby *(69+) (ACStewart)* 2-8-11 MRoberts(3) (w'like: bkwd: dwlt: hld up & bhd: stdy hdwy on bit 2f out: nvr plcd to chal)......½ 9
3733¹³ Beauchamp Kate *(66) (HCandy)* 2-8-11 WNewnes(11) (lw: b.hind: mid div: shkn up over 2f out: n.d)......1 10
Fairywings *(64) (MrsJRRamsden)* 2-8-11 KFallon(1) (b.hind: lt-f: s.s: sme hdwy fnl 2f)......¾ 11
Smithereens *(60) (PTWalwyn)* 2-8-11 DHolland(17) (w'like: scope: gd spd 4f)......1½ 12
Sylvella *(59) (MAJarvis)* 2-8-8 (3) DRMcCabe(10) (leggy: lt-f: bhd: hmpd over 1f out: n.d)......½ 13
Fiona Shann (USA) *(58) (JLDunlop)* 2-8-11 KDarley(2) (leggy: lt-f: unf: n.d)......nk 14
Miss Pravda *(50) (PTWalwyn)* 2-8-11 GCarter(6) (w'like: bkwd: rdn ½-wy: sn bhd)......3 15
Starfida *(45) (CADwyer)* 2-8-11 MWigham(13) (lt-f: nvr nr ldrs)......1¾ 16
Shirlaty *(44) (EALDunlop)* 2-8-11 PaulEddery(15) (w'like: s.i.s: sn rcvrd & chsd ldrs: wknd appr fnl f)......½ 17

11/8 Phantom Creek, **6/1** Green Bentley (IRE), **13/2** Jezyah (USA), **7/1** Onefortheditch (USA) (5/1-9/1), **8/1** POLISH SPRING (IRE), **12/1** Budby, **14/1** Fiona Shann (USA), **20/1** Petite Juliette, Smithereens, **33/1** Beauchamp Kate, Fairywings, Mua-Tab, Sylvella, Indian Relative, Miss Pravda, Starfida, Shirlaty, CSF £62.03 TOTE £14.40: £3.20 £2.90 £2.00 (£56.80) Trio £177.20 OWNER Marston Stud (LAMBOURN) BRED Lady Richard Wellesley and Grange Nominees 17 Rn
1m 14.84 (3.54) SF: 30/27/21/19/19/18/14/13/12/9/7/3/2/1/-/-/-

T/Jkpt: Not won; £33,212.80 to Haydock 1/10/95. T/Plpt: £78.50 (473.71 Tckts). T/Qdpt: £11.10 (26.9 Tckts). AA

3734-WOLVERHAMPTON (L-H)
Saturday September 30th (Standard)
WEATHER: drizzle WIND: almost nil

3949 PINK ICE MEDIAN AUCTION MAIDEN STKS (2-Y.O) (Class F) £2,519.00 (£694.00: £329.00) **6f** **(Fibresand)** Stalls: Low GOING: 0.12 sec (SLW) 7-00 (7-04)

3628 11 **Sweet Nature (IRE)** *(74+) (WJarvis)* 2-8-6 (3) SSanders(4) (a.p: led wl over 1f out: edgd rt ins fnl f: rdn out) — **1**
3625 5 Thordis *(71)*(Fav)*(PJMakin)* 2-9-0 TIves(7) (sn rdn: 7th st: hdwy over 1f out: r.o ins fnl f) 3 **2**
3894 7 Wire Act (USA) **(65)***(67) (MartynMeade)* 2-9-0 VSlattery(9) (sn rdn & outpcd: hdwy over 1f out: nvr nrr) 1½ **3**
3626 12 Forest Boy *(65) (KMcAuliffe)* 2-9-0v MTebbutt(11) (prom: 4th & rdn st: one pce) ¾ **4**
3740 7 Tallulah Belle **(53)***(59) (NPLittmoden)* 2-8-2 (7) ADaly(2) (chsd ldrs: 5th & rdn st: no hdwy) nk **5**
3828 7 The Barnsley Belle (IRE) *(58) (SGNorton)* 2-8-9 NConnorton(1) (led over 4f: 2nd st: wknd over 1f out) nk **6**
3623 15 Image Maker (IRE) **(55)***(48) (DWPArbuthnot)* 2-8-9 AClark(5) (bhd tl hdwy 2f out: wknd over 1f out) 4 **7**
3720 8 Two Timer *(39) (MJohnston)* 2-9-0 TWilliams(8) (prom: 6th, hrd rdn & wkng st) 5 **8**
3352 7 Mullagh Hill Lad (IRE) *(35) (BAMcMahon)* 2-9-0 SDWilliams(6) (s.i.s: a bhd) 1¾ **9**
3628 9 Impington (IRE) **(66)***(27) (MAJarvis)* 2-8-9 PRobinson(3) (b.off hind: w ldrs: 3rd & rdn st: wknd over 1f out) 1 **10**
Andsome Boy *(28) (CRBarwell)* 2-9-0 JWilliams(12) (unf: a bhd) 1½ **11**
3379 20 Fairly Sure (IRE) *(12) (NEBerry)* 2-8-4 (5) RPainter(10) (bhd fnl 3f) 4 **12**

9/4 Thordis, **4/1** SWEET NATURE (IRE) (3/1-9/2), **6/1** Forest Boy (4/1-7/1), **8/1** Impington (IRE), The Barnsley Belle (IRE) (6/1-10/1), **12/1** Image Maker (IRE), **14/1** Two Timer, Wire Act (USA), **16/1** Tallulah Belle, Mullagh Hill Lad (IRE), **25/1** Andsome Boy, **33/1** Fairly Sure (IRE), CSF £13.60 TOTE £3.60: £1.60 £2.10 £3.30 (£7.10) Trio £44.40 OWNER Mrs Doris Allen (NEWMARKET) BRED S. W. D. McIlveen 12 Rn
1m 15.6 (4.40) SF: 45/42/38/36/30/29/19/10/6/-/-/-

3950 LIFTING GEAR & TOOL HIRE CLAIMING STKS (3-Y.O+) (Class F) £2,415.00 (£665.00: £315.00) **7f** **(Fibresand)** Stalls: High GOING: 0.12 sec (SLW) 7-30 (7-36)

1255* **Spencer's Revenge (73)***(80) (MJRyan)* 6-9-2 GBardwell(6) (a.p: 4th st: led ins fnl f: qcknd clr) — **1**
3704 7 Gentle Irony **(55)***(59) (BJMeehan)* 3-8-5b JFEgan(4) (a.p: 5th st: ev ch over 1f out: hung rt: one pce fnl f) 6 **2**
3807 15 What a Nightmare (IRE) **(70)***(64) (JAGlover)* 3-8-5b(5) AWhelan(3) (led: rdn 3f out: hdd 2f out: 3rd st: one pce fnl f) s.h **3**
3739 9 Jamaica Bridge **(54)***(52) (SGNorton)* 5-8-5 ow1 KFallon(7) (a.p: led 2f out tl ins fnl f) 1 **4**
3677 15 Dream Carrier (IRE) **(60)***(61) (REPeacock)* 7-9-0 TSprake(10) (lw: nvr nr to chal) nk **5**
3681 13 Sir Tasker **(80)***(62) (JLHarris)* 7-9-1 (3) SSanders(5) (w ldrs: 2nd st: ev ch wl over 1f out: wknd fnl f) 1¼ **6**
3770 9 Sweet Supposin (IRE) **(87)***(65)*(Fav)*(CADwyer)* 4-9-8b SWhitworth(12) (lw: hdwy over 3f out: 7th st: no imp) ½ **7**
3800 6 Mustn't Grumble (IRE) **(75)***(54) (WSCunningham)* 5-9-4 AClark(8) (chsd ldrs: 6th st: wknd over 1f out) 3 **8**
3629 9 Milos **(68)***(57) (TJNaughton)* 4-9-8 PaulEddery(11) (b.nr hind: racd wd: hld up & bhd: nvr plcd to chal) ½ **9**
3510 11 Chadleigh Lane (USA) **(62)***(36) (RHollinshead)* 3-8-10 TIves(9) (a bhd) 6 **10**
3624 16 Mixed Mood **(63)** *(BJLlewellyn)* 3-8-5b TWilliams(1) (a bhd: t.o) 20 **11**

5/4 Sweet Supposin (IRE), **7/2** Mustn't Grumble (IRE) (op 7/1), **6/1** SPENCER'S REVENGE, **13/2** What a Nightmare (IRE), **14/1** Jamaica Bridge, **16/1** Sir Tasker, **20/1** Dream Carrier (IRE), Milos, **25/1** Gentle Irony, Mixed Mood, **33/1** Chadleigh Lane (USA), CSF £124.33 TOTE £5.40: £1.40 £7.20 £1.60 (£72.20) Trio £105.00 OWNER Mr A. S. Reid (NEWMARKET) BRED Lord Crawshaw 11 Rn
1m 29.3 (5.30) SF: 46/21/26/18/27/28/31/20/23/-/-
WEIGHT FOR AGE 3yo-4lb

3951

TOTE PLACEPOT H'CAP (0-60) (3-Y.O+) (Class F) £3,073.40 (£852.40: £408.20)
1m 4f (Fibresand) Stalls: Low GOING: 0.12 sec per fur (SLW) 8-00 (8-06)

*3737*3 **Sommersby (IRE) (58)***(73)*(Fav)*(MrsNMacauley)* 4-9-9 (3) SDrowne(8) (a.p: led on bit wl over 1f out: easily) ....— 1
38994 Environmentalist (IRE) **(52)***(64)*(Fav)*(RHarris)* 4-9-6 AMackay(11) (hdwy 6f out: 5th st: hrd rdn & r.o ins fnl f) 2 2
37432 Tremendisto **(45)***(57) (CaptJWilson)* 5-8-13 JFEgan(1) (hld up: rdn 5f out: hdwy & 6th st: r.o ins fnl f) ....nk 3
*600*3 Sleeptite (FR) **(60)***(71) (WGMTurner)* 5-9-7 (7) ADaly(12) (a.p: led over 3f out: hdd & 2nd st: one pce) ....¾ 4
36463 Sariyaa **(55)***(64) (MBrittain)* 4-9-9 JCarroll(9) (a.p: led 5f out: hrd rdn & hdd over 3f out: 4th st: one pce) 1½ 5
364611 Barti-Ddu **(58)***(66) (SCWilliams)* 4-9-12 JTate(5) (led after 3f to 5f out: 3rd st: wknd fnl f) ....½ 6
36416 Modest Hope (USA) **(46)***(53) (BRichmond)* 8-9-0 JWilliams(6) (hld up & bhd: hdwy 4f out: 7th st: no imp) 1 7
*3245*5 Rolling Waters **(56)***(36) (JARToller)* 5-9-7 (3) SSanders(3) (led 3f: wknd 5f out: t.o) 20 8
375921 Shared Risk **(53)***(31) (SGNorton)* 3-8-13b KFallon(10) (b.hind: hdwy 7f out: wknd over 2f out: t.o) 2 9
37434 North Ardar **(57)***(34)*(Fav)*(MrsMReveley)* 5-9-4 (7) SCopp(7) (a bhd: t.o fnl 3f) ....½ 10
38718 Rockstine (IRE) **(51)***(15) (PMitchell)* 4-9-5v PaulEddery(4) (rdn 6f out: sn bhd: t.o) 10 11
22484 Surprise Guest (IRE) **(47)** *(APJames)* 4-9-1b TWilliams(2) (s.i.s: sn prom: rdn & dropped rr 8f out: sn t.o) ....dist 12

5/1 SOMMERSBY (IRE), Environmentalist (IRE), North Ardar, **11/2** Tremendisto, **6/1** Barti-Ddu, **10/1** Sariyaa, Rockstine (IRE), **14/1** Rolling Waters, **16/1** Shared Risk, Modest Hope (USA), Sleeptite (FR), **25/1** Surprise Guest (IRE), CSF £29.92 CT £134.33 TOTE £5.30: £1.90 £2.60 £2.60 (£21.10) Trio £40.00 OWNER Mr A. J. Peake (MELTON MOWBRAY) BRED Campbell Stud 12 Rn
2m 41.8 (10.80) SF: 48/39/32/46/39/41/28/11/-/9/-/-
WEIGHT FOR AGE 3yo-8lb

3952

TOTE DUAL FORECAST H'CAP (0-70) (3-Y.O+) (Class E) £3,616.80 (£1,082.40: £519.20: £237.60)
1m 1f 79y (Fibresand) Stalls: Low GOING: 0.12 sec per fur (SLW) 8-30 (8-31)

37783 **Sudden Spin (58)***(70)*(Fav)*(SGNorton)* 5-9-6 KFallon(11) (a.p: hrd rdn 5f out: 2nd st: led over 1f out: drvn out) ....— 1
36309 Brave Princess **(64)***(74) (MAJarvis)* 3-9-7 PRobinson(6) (b.off hind: hld up: hdwy over 4f out: 3rd st: rdn & r.o ins fnl f) 1 2
3726* Heathyards Lady (USA) **(57)***(63) (RHollinshead)* 4-8-12 (7) FLynch(13) (jnd ldrs 6f out: led over 2f out tl over 1f out: one pce) 2½ 3
25439 Asmarina **(45)***(46) (SRBowring)* 5-8-2b(5) CTeague(7) (wl bhd tl hdwy fnl 2f: nrst fin) 3 4
377011 Landlord **(63)***(60) (JARToller)* 3-9-3b(3) SSanders(10) (chsd ldr: led over 4f out tl over 2f out: 4th & wkng st) 2½ 5
38715 Captain Marmalade **(49)***(46) (DTThom)* 6-8-11 JTate(9) (outpcd: hdwy over 4f out: one pce fnl 2f) ....s.h 6
*3529*11 Certain Way (IRE) **(53)***(39) (NPLittmoden)* 5-9-1 MFenton(5) (prom: wknd over 2f out: 6th & btn st) 6 7
*2292*10 Shareoftheaction **(54)***(32) (MrsAMNaughton)* 4-9-2v NConnorton(8) (a bhd) 5 8
27615 Bella Sedona **(60)***(37) (LadyHerries)* 3-9-3 DeanMcKeown(3) (chsd ldrs tl wknd 4f out) ....nk 9
38108 Larn Fort **(51)***(28) (CWFairhurst)* 5-8-13v LCharnock(12) (hrd rdn 4f out: sn bhd) ....nk 10
33904 Caddy's First **(61)***(36) (SMellor)* 3-9-4 MWigham(1) (led tl over 4f out: 5th & wkng st) 1 11
380829 Miss Springtime **(62)***(3) (JJO'Neill)* 4-9-10 JCarroll(2) (prom tl rdn & wknd 5f out: t.o) 20 12
*414*12 Slip a Coin **(60)** *(DBurchell)* 4-9-5 (3) SDrowne(4) (bhd fnl 5f: t.o) 11 13

11/4 SUDDEN SPIN (8/1-5/2), **9/2** Heathyards Lady (USA), **6/1** Asmarina, **13/2** Brave Princess, **10/1** Landlord, Larn Fort, **12/1** Caddy's First, **14/1** Captain Marmalade, Bella Sedona (op 8/1), **16/1** Certain Way (IRE), Slip a Coin, **25/1** Miss Springtime, **33/1** Shareoftheaction, CSF £21.76 CT £76.68 TOTE £4.30: £2.30 £3.40 £1.40 (£16.20) Trio £20.90 OWNER Mr Billy Parker (BARNSLEY) BRED The Arrow Farm and Stud 13 Rn 2m 3.1 (7.10) SF: 52/51/45/28/37/28/21/14/14/10/13/-/-
WEIGHT FOR AGE 3yo-5lb

3953

AKELER HOLDING NURSERY (S) H'CAP (0-65) (2-Y.O) (Class F) £2,519.00 (£694.00: £329.00)
5f (Fibresand) Stalls: Low GOING: 0.12 sec per fur (SLW) 9-00 (9-04)

33122 **Don't Tell Anyone (50)***(55) (JBerry)* 2-8-1 (5) PFessey(10) (hdwy & 5th st: led ins fnl f: r.o wl) ....— 1

*3528*4 Frances Mary **(49)***(52) (CWFairhurst)* 2-8-2 (3) SSanders(13) (lw: hdwy & 6th st: r.o wl ins fnl f)....½ 2
37738 Charterhouse Xpres **(64)***(65) (MMcCormack)* 2-9-1v(5) DaneO'Neill(11) (a.p: 3rd st: led over 1f out tl ins fnl f)....¾ 3
2706 12 Touch of Fantasy **(49)***(37) (CADwyer)* 2-8-2 (3) SDrowne(12) (b.hind: a.p: 4th st: ev ch over 1f out: wknd ins fnl f)....4 4
37424 Doubleyoubeay **(65)***(49) (JBerry)* 2-9-7 JCarroll(4) (bhd tl hdwy over 1f out: nrst fin)....1¼ 5
37427 Boffy (IRE) **(58)***(34) (BPJBaugh)* 2-8-7 (7) ADaly(1) (b: lw: led over 3f: wknd fnl f)....2½ 6
36489 General Equation **(53)***(29) (JBalding)* 2-8-9 NAdams(2) (lw: a.p: 2nd st: ev ch over 1f out: wknd fnl f)....s.h 7
37533 Wingnut (IRE) **(50)***(24)*(Fav)*(GLewis)* 2-8-6 PaulEddery(3) (sn rdn along: chsd ldrs 3f)....½ 8
27354 Sporting Fantasy **(57)***(22) (JBalding)* 2-8-6 (7) JEdmunds(8) (bdly hmpd over 3f out: sn bhd)....3 9
3824 10 Superfrills **(49)***(10) (MissLCSiddall)* 2-8-5 TWilliams(9) (chsd ldrs: rdn & wknd over 2f out)...1¼ 10
30185 Melos **(56)***(12) (RonaldThompson)* 2-8-12 AMackay(6) (s.i.s: a bhd)....1½ 11
3824 14 Redbrook Lady **(50)***(5) (SGNorton)* 2-8-6 KFallon(7) (prom over 3f)....nk 12

9/4 Wingnut (IRE), **5/1** Charterhouse Xpres (op 10/1), **7/1** Boffy (IRE) (op 4/1), **8/1** Superfrills (op 5/1), **9/1** DON'T TELL ANYONE (op 6/1), **10/1** Touch of Fantasy, **12/1** Doubleyoubeay (op 8/1), **14/1** Frances Mary, Sporting Fantasy (10/1-16/1), **16/1** General Equation, Redbrook Lady, **20/1** Melos, CSF £119.43 CT £646.92 TOTE £8.00: £2.50 £3.80 £2.20 (£83.00) Trio £75.60 OWNER Manny Bernstein (Racing) Ltd (COCKERHAM) BRED C. G. Reid 12 Rn

64.2 secs (6.20) SF: -/-/6/-/-/-/-/-/-/-/-/-

No bid

3954 RUBY H'CAP (0-65) (3-Y.O+) (Class F) £2,174.00 (£599.00: £284.00)
6f (Fibresand) Stalls: Low GOING: 0.12 sec per fur (SLW) 9-30 (9-31)

37642 **Cretan Gift (59)***(70) (NPLittmoden)* 4-9-8v MFenton(4) (hdwy 2f out: hung lft over 1f out: led ins fnl f: r.o)....— 1
37504 King Rambo **(65)***(72)*(Fav)*(RHollinshead)* 4-10-0 TIves(9) (a.p: wnt 2nd st: ev ch ins fnl f: nt qckn)....1½ 2
*3739** Pursuance (IRE) **(64)***(64) (JBalding)* 3-9-3v(7) JEdmunds(5) (led: sn clr: hdd ins fnl f)....2½ 3
3800 17 Jigsaw Boy **(60)***(54) (PGMurphy)* 6-9-2 (7) RWaterfield(10) (bhd tl hdwy over 2f out: edgd lft fnl f: nrst fin)....2½ 4
35199 Bold Gem **(65)***(45) (BJMeehan)* 4-9-7b(7) GHannon(3) (sn rdn along: chsd ldrs: 6th st: no hdwy)....5 5
3629 16 Aljaz **(56)***(34) (RHarris)* 5-9-5 AMackay(2) (prom: 3rd & rdn st: wknd over 1f out)....¾ 6
37398 Montague Dawson (IRE) **(62)***(37) (MrsNMacauley)* 3-9-1b(7) AmandaSanders(8) (prom: 5th st: wknd over 1f out)....1¼ 7
3751 16 Barik (IRE) **(54)***(27) (MrsASwinbank)* 5-9-3 NConnorton(12) (chsd ldr tl 4th & wkng st)....¾ 8
3624 18 Rambold **(60)***(32) (NEBerry)* 4-9-9 PaulEddery(13) (prom 4f)....nk 9
36818 Awesome Venture **(62)***(34) (MCChapman)* 5-9-4b(7) CMunday(6) (bhd fnl 3f)....hd 10
2685 12 Media Express **(64)***(25) (MBrittain)* 3-9-10 JCarroll(11) (a bhd)....4 11
37392 Featherstone Lane **(61)***(19) (MissLCSiddall)* 4-9-10v MWigham(7) (bhd fnl 4f)....1¼ 12

3/1 King Rambo, **9/2** CRETAN GIFT, **5/1** Jigsaw Boy, **6/1** Aljaz (8/1-5/1), **13/2** Featherstone Lane, **7/1** Pursuance (IRE), **14/1** Montague Dawson (IRE), Media Express, **20/1** Rambold, Awesome Venture, Barik (IRE), **25/1** Bold Gem, CSF £19.31 CT £91.61 TOTE £5.00: £1.80 £1.80 £1.80 (£12.90) Trio £35.90 OWNER R A M Racecourses Ltd (NEWARK) BRED Hesmonds Stud Ltd 12 Rn

1m 15.9 (4.70) SF: 50/52/41/34/25/14/14/7/12/14/2/-

WEIGHT FOR AGE 3yo-3lb

T/Plpt: £50.00 (167.32 Tckts). T/Qdpt: £26.20 (3.9 Tckts). KH

3856-BRIGHTON (L-H)
Sunday October 1st (Good)
WEATHER: sunny WIND: str across

3955 LEVY BOARD MAIDEN STKS (2-Y.O) (Class D) £4,856.25 (£1,470.00: £717.50: £341.25) **7f 214y** Stalls: Low GOING: 0.02 sec per fur (G) 2-15 (2-15)

Naval Gazer (IRE) *(72+)*(Fav)*(DRLoder)* 2-8-6 (3) DRMcCabe(7) (leggy: dwlt: hdwy over 3f out: 5th st: led over 1f out: rdn out)....— 1
The Boozing Brief (USA) *(74) (MAJarvis)* 2-9-0 PRobinson(4) (wl grwn: 2nd st: led over 2f out tl over 1f out: unable qckn)....1½ 2
3888 11 Present Arms (USA) *(73) (PFICole)* 2-9-0 CRutter(8) (lw: 3rd st: wandered & ev ch over 1f out: one pce)....½ 3

3371[11] Prince Zizim *(65) (CADwyer)* 2-8-11 (3) SSanders(5) (lw: hdwy 2f out: 6th st: wknd over 1f out)4 **4**
3652[8] Forliando *(35) (MSSaunders)* 2-8-11 (3) SDrowne(3) (bhd fnl 4f) 15 **5**
3763[20] Miss Roberto (IRE) *(29) (MrsMMcCourt)* 2-8-9 SWhitworth(2) (b: lw: led over 5f) ....nk **6**
3617[2] Jamaican Flight (USA) *(34) (JWHills)* 2-9-0 AClark(1) (lw: s.s: hdwy 7f out: 4th st: wknd over 1f out) ....s.h **7**

7/4 NAVAL GAZER (IRE) (11/10-2/1), **9/4** Jamaican Flight (USA), **4/1** Present Arms (USA) (5/2-9/2), **7/1** The Boozing Brief (USA) (6/1-9/1), **20/1** Prince Zizim, **40/1** Miss Roberto (IRE), **50/1** Forliando, CSF £12.49 TOTE £3.10: £1.70 £2.30 (£17.50) OWNER Mr William Fox (NEWMARKET) BRED Barronstown Bloodstock Ltd 7 Rn 1m 38.3 (6.10) SF: 29/31/30/22/-/-/-

OFFICIAL EXPLANATION Jamaican Flight (USA): failed to handle the track.

3956 PUBLICAN NEWSPAPER BEER TAX NURSERY H'CAP (2-Y.O) (Class C) £6,243.00 (£2,337.00: £1,143.50: £492.50)

6f 209y Stalls: Low GOING: 0.02 sec per fur (G) 2-45 (2-46)

3711[9] **Al Shafa (77)***(89) (JLDunlop)* 2-8-5 (3) DRMcCabe(3) (rdn 2f out: hdwy over 1f out: led ins fnl f: r.o wl) ....— **1**
3613[5] Daily Risk **(65)***(70) (SDow)* 2-7-5 (5) MHenry(7) (lw: 4th st: ev ch over 1f out: unable qckn)....3 **2**
3858[3] Proud Monk **(71)***(74)*(Fav)*(GLMoore)* 2-7-9 (7) CAdamson(9) (led 1f: 2nd st: ev ch over 1f out: one pce) 1 **3**
3684[5] Nostoi **(72)***(74) (SirMarkPrescott)* 2-8-3b WWoods(5) (lw: led 6f out: hung lft wl over 1f out: hdd ins fnl f: sn wknd)....nk **4**
3714[13] Ned Al Sheeba **(83)***(76) (WJHaggas)* 2-9-0 PRobinson(2) (dwlt: 5th st: rdn over 2f out: swtchd lft wl over 1f out: wknd fnl f)....4 **5**
3767* Times of Times (IRE) **(71)***(62) (MJRyan)* 2-8-2 GBardwell(8) (3rd st: carried lft & ev ch over 1f out: sn wknd) 1 **6**
2106[5] Cyrillic **(90)***(73) (PAKelleway)* 2-9-7 MWigham(1) (6th st: wknd over 2f out) 3½ **7**

11/4 Proud Monk, **100/30** Times of Times (IRE), **5/1** AL SHAFA, Ned Al Sheeba, **13/2** Nostoi, **11/1** Daily Risk, **16/1** Cyrillic, CSF £46.30 CT £153.86 TOTE £4.60: £2.90 £3.00 (£52.50) Trio £41.30 OWNER Prince A. A. Faisal (ARUNDEL) BRED Fonthill Stud 7 Rn

1m 24.4 (4.40) SF: 39/20/24/24/26/12/23

3957 DAILY MIRROR H'CAP (0-100) (3-Y.O+) (Class C) £11,394.00 (£4,266.00: £2,088.00: £900.00) **1m 3f 196y** Stalls: High GOING: 0.02 sec (G) 3-15 (3-16)

3406[2] **Casual Water (IRE) (68)***(79) (AGNewcombe)* 4-7-9 (5) MHenry(6) (3rd st: n.m.r & swtchd lft over 1f out: led nr fin)....— **1**
3836[2] Better Offer (IRE) **(96)***(107)*(Fav)*(GHarwood)* 3-9-6 MPerrett(10) (lw: 5th st: led 2f out: rdn: hdd nr fin) ....nk **2**
3388[5] Silktail (IRE) **(69)***(79) (CADwyer)* 3-7-7 NKennedy(2) (lw: rdn over 2f out: hdwy over 1f out: ev ch ins fnl f: one pce) ....¾ **3**
3769[2] Prince Danzig (IRE) **(63)***(72) (DJGMurraySmith)* 4-7-4 (5) MBaird(11) (lw: 2nd st: rdn over 2f out: ev ch over 1f out: one pce)....½ **4**
3769* Wild Rita **(71)***(77) (WRMuir)* 3-7-2 (7)ow2 MartinDwyer(7) (6th st: carried lft over 1f out: one pce) 1 **5**
3571[2] Global Dancer **(74)***(81) (SDow)* 4-7-13 (7) ADaly(8) (led 10f) ....¾ **6**
3756* Top Lady (IRE) **(77)***(79) (MRStoute)* 3-8-1 PRobinson(5) (4th st: rdn over 2f out: wknd over 1f out)....3½ **7**
3820[7] Fieldridge **(77)***(78) (MPMuggeridge)* 6-8-4 (5) DaneO'Neill(9) (lw: bhd fnl 3f) ....¾ **8**
3485a* Glide Path (USA) **(96)***(93) (JWHills)* 6-10-0 AClark(4) (lw: hdwy over 2f out: n.m.r wl over 1f out: sn wknd)....3 **9**
3730[5] Warm Spell **(73)***(69) (GLMoore)* 5-8-5 SWhitworth(1) (lw: bhd fnl 4f) ....nk **10**
3817[6] Lear Dancer (USA) **(68)***(38) (PMitchell)* 4-8-0v GBardwell(3) (a bhd)....20 **11**

LONG HANDICAP Wild Rita 7-6 Silktail (IRE) 7-5

7/2 Better Offer (IRE), **4/1** Top Lady (IRE), **5/1** Warm Spell, **7/1** Wild Rita, **9/1** CASUAL WATER (IRE), **10/1** Glide Path (USA), **14/1** Silktail (IRE), Global Dancer, **16/1** Fieldridge, Prince Danzig (IRE), Lear Dancer (USA), CSF £39.06 CT £408.82 TOTE £10.60: £2.60 £1.60 £6.90 (£18.90) Trio £128.30 OWNER Mr G. H. Leatham (BARNSTAPLE) BRED Dunderry Stud 11 Rn

2m 34.9 (5.90) SF: 47/67/39/40/37/49/39/46/61/37/6

WEIGHT FOR AGE 3yo-8lb

3958 TOTE LADIES IN RED MEDIAN AUCTION MAIDEN STKS (3-Y.O) (Class E) £4,123.50 (£1,248.00: £609.00: £289.50)

1m 1f 209y Stalls: High GOING: 0.02 sec per fur (G) 4-00 (4-01)

3559[2] **Ottavio Farnese** *(82)*(Fav)*(AHide)* 3-9-0 WWoods(2) (lw: 2nd st: led 3f out: r.o wl) ....— **1**

3573[3] Urania **(66)***(71) (MAJarvis)* 3-8-9 PRobinson(7) (led 7f: unable qckn fnl 2f) 3½ 2
3862[6] Guest Alliance (IRE) **(48)***(70) (AMoore)* 3-9-0 CandyMorris(6) (lw: lost pl 4f out: 5th st: r.o one pce) 4 3
3712[2] Mr Medley **(79)***(70) (RHannon)* 3-8-9 (5) DaneO'Neill(5) (b.nr hind: rdn over 4f out: one pce fnl 3f) ....nk 4
2623[2] Reefa's Mill (IRE) **(69)***(58) (JWHills)* 3-9-0 AClark(1) (3rd st: rdn over 2f out: wknd fnl f) 7 5
South Sea Bubble (IRE) *(32) (LMCumani)* 3-8-2 (7) JoHunnam(3) (w'like: bkwd: s.s: styd far side st: a bhd) 13 6
1974[20] Stoneham Girl **(26)** *(PButler)* 3-8-6 (3) SDrowne(4) (s.s: a bhd: t.o fnl 4f) 25 7

15/8 OTTAVIO FARNESE (op 3/1), **5/2** Mr Medley (op 6/4), **11/2** South Sea Bubble (IRE) (7/2-6/1), **13/2** Urania (op 4/1), **8/1** Reefa's Mill (IRE), **33/1** Guest Alliance (IRE), **99/1** Stoneham Girl, CSF £12.41 TOTE £3.40: £2.00 £2.70 (£8.80) OWNER Mr Cyril Humphris (NEWMARKET) BRED Rykneld Thoroughbred Co Ltd 7 Rn 2m 5.1 (7.10) SF: 40/29/28/28/16/-/-

3959 REID MINTY RED ROSE LADIES' H'CAP (0-75) (3-Y.O) (Class E)

£4,182.00 (£1,266.00: £618.00: £294.00)
1m 1f 209y Stalls: High GOING: 0.02 sec per fur (G) 4-30 (4-31)

3679[2] **Domitia (USA) (63)***(75) (MBell)* 3-10-10 MrsAPerrett(5) (lw: led 1f: 4th st: led over 1f out: edgd lft: rdn out) ....— 1
3288[3] Water Hazard (IRE) **(49)***(59) (SDow)* 3-9-10 MissYHaynes(7) (led 7f out tl over 1f out: hung lft: unable qckn) 1¼ 2
3130[4] No Pattern **(74)***(84) (GLMoore)* 3-11-3 (4) MrsJMoore(1) (lw: hdwy & swtchd lft over 1f out: n.m.r on ins ins fnl f: r.o) ....nk 3
3654[6] Pedaltothemetal (IRE) **(43)***(52) (PMitchell)* 3-9-4 MrsLPearce(6) (b.hind: 3rd st: hung lft 1f out: one pce) ....hd 4
3747[13] Alpine Storm (IRE) **(39)***(44) (MDIUsher)* 3-8-10 (4) MrsAUsher(8) (nvr nr to chal) 2½ 5
3214[6] Red Light **(74)***(76)*(Fav)*(LordHuntingdon)* 3-11-7 MrsMCowdrey(4) (5th st: wknd over 2f out) 2 6
3771[12] Crystal Gift **(60)***(61) (DWPArbuthnot)* 3-10-7 MrsDArbuthnot(3) (s.s: led 9f out to 7f out: 2nd st: rdn over 1f out: 5th & btn whn n.m.r ins fnl f) ....¾ 7
3619[13] False Pretences (IRE) **(39)***(30) (BAPearce)* 3-8-7 (7) MrsSColville(2) (lw: s.s: 6th st: wknd over 1f out) 6 8
LONG HANDICAP Alpine Storm (IRE) 8-0 False Pretences (IRE) 8-5

9/4 Red Light, **7/2** DOMITIA (USA), **4/1** Pedaltothemetal (IRE), **9/2** No Pattern (3/1-5/1), **6/1** Water Hazard (IRE), **20/1** Crystal Gift, **66/1** Alpine Storm (IRE), False Pretences (IRE), CSF £22.28 CT £84.22 TOTE £4.40: £1.70 £1.30 £2.10 (£9.30) OWNER Mr Desmond Fitzgerald (NEWMARKET) BRED Wakefield Farm 8 Rn 2m 11.2 (13.20) SF: 13/-/22/-/-/14/-/-

3960 KEITH MCDOWALL ASSOCIATES ROLLING ROSE LIMITED STKS (0-70) (3-Y.O+) (Class E) £4,221.00 (£1,278.00: £624.00: £297.00)

6f 209y Stalls: Low GOING: 0.02 sec per fur (G) 5-00 (5-00)

3757[14] **Crystal Heights (FR) (64)***(77) (RJO'Sullivan)* 7-9-1 (3) SSanders(1) (b: lw: s.s: hdwy over 2f out: led over 1f out: all out) ....— 1
3771[7] Morocco (IRE) **(56)***(79) (MRChannon)* 6-9-1 (5) PPMurphy(3) (lw: hdwy 2f out: ev ch fnl f: r.o wl) ....hd 2
3726[6] Linger **(66)***(67) (LordHuntingdon)* 3-8-10 WWoods(6) (lw: hdwy 2f out: rdn: one pce) 2 3
3771* Jo Maximus **(75)***(74)*(Fav)*(SDow)* 3-8-10 (7) ADaly(11) (3rd st: led 2f out tl over 1f out: one pce) ....nk 4
3677[2] Pharaoh's Dancer **(70)***(67) (PBurgoyne)* 8-8-11 (5) DGibbs(10) (hdwy over 3f out: 5th st: rdn over 2f out: one pce) 1¼ 5
2538[7] Mutinique **(41)***(50) (BAPearce)* 4-8-6 (5) MHenry(8) (nvr nr to chal) 5 6
3674[3] Waikiki Beach (USA) **(70)***(53) (GLMoore)* 4-8-9 (7) ALakeman(4) (lw: led over 4f out: styd centre st: hdd 2f out: wknd over 1f out) 1 7
3771[6] Walnut Burl (IRE) **(57)***(55) (LJHolt)* 5-9-4 MPerrett(9) (s.s: a bhd) ....hd 8
3770[10] Queenbird **(65)***(31) (MJRyan)* 4-8-11b GBardwell(12) (led over 2f: 2nd st: wknd over 2f out) 7 9
3519[12] Colston-C **(70)***(27) (RJHodges)* 3-8-12 (3) SDrowne(5) (4th st: wknd 3f out) 5 10
3747[14] Port Hedland **(36)***(12) (MMcCormack)* 3-8-8 AClark(2) (6th & styd centre st: wknd 3f out) 3½ 11

15/8 Jo Maximus, **5/1** Pharaoh's Dancer, **11/2** Waikiki Beach (USA), **8/1** Linger (6/1-9/1), Queenbird, **9/1** Colston-C, **14/1** CRYSTAL HEIGHTS (FR) (op 9/1), Walnut Burl (IRE), **20/1** Morocco (IRE), **66/1** Mutinique, Port Hedland, CSF £219.82 TOTE £10.70: £2.50 £5.60 £2.10 (£54.40) Trio £38.00 OWNER Mr Jack Joseph (BOGNOR REGIS) BRED Ahmad Fustok 11 Rn 1m 24.1 (4.10) SF: 52/54/39/46/42/25/28/30/6/-/-
WEIGHT FOR AGE 3yo-3lb

3961

BMP DDB NEEDHAM H'CAP (0-80) (3-Y.O+) (Class D) £5,197.50 (£1,575.00: £770.00: £367.50)
5f 59y Stalls: Low GOING: 0.02 sec per fur (G) 5-30 (5-31)

3519[3] **Bowden Rose (79)***(89)*(Fav)*(MBlanshard)* 3-9-7b(5) MBaird(10) (lw: outpcd: swtchd lft 2f out: gd hdwy to ld over 1f out: r.o wl)......— 1
3667[24] Domicksky **(54)***(58) (MRChannon)* 7-7-11 (5) PPMurphy(9) (lw: hdwy over 2f out: ev ch over 1f out: unable qckn)......2 2
3632[8] Pearl Dawn (IRE) **(69)***(73)*(Fav)*(GLMoore)* 5-9-3 SWhitworth(7) (lw: dwlt: hdwy 2f out: ev ch over 1f out: one pce)......hd 3
3717[18] Mister Jolson **(80)***(72) (RJHodges)* 6-9-11 (3) SDrowne(11) (hdwy over 1f out: r.o one pce)......4 4
3615[26] Thatcherella **(73)***(61) (MajorDNChappell)* 4-9-7 WWoods(1) (hld up: ev ch over 1f out: sn wknd)......1 5
1241[8] Invocation **(59)***(47) (AMoore)* 8-8-4 (3) SSanders(8) (b.nr hind: lw: 5th st: wknd 2f out)......s.h 6
3919[9] Halbert **(67)***(53)*(Fav)*(MRChannon)* 6-8-8v(7) JDennis(4) (lw: 3rd st: led 3f out tl over 1f out: sn wknd)......¾ 7
3751[12] Another Batchworth **(60)***(42) (SMellor)* 3-8-7 RPerham(6) (2nd st: wknd 2f out)......1¼ 8
3748[19] Miami Banker **(55)***(37)*(Fav)*(WRMuir)* 9-8-3b GBardwell(2) (led: styd far side st: hdd 3f out: ev ch wl over 1f out: wknd fnl f)......hd 9
3376[7] Windrush Boy **(65)***(47) (JRBosley)* 5-8-6 (7) AimeeCook(5) (4th st: wknd over 2f out)......s.h 10
3622[10] Rocky Two **(51)***(20) (PHowling)* 4-7-13bow1 DBiggs(3) (6th st: wknd 2f out)......4 11
446[7] Dolly Face **(68)***(27) (WRMuir)* 3-8-10 (5) MHenry(12) (nt clr run over 1f out: a bhd)......3½ 12

6/1 BOWDEN ROSE, Miami Banker, Pearl Dawn (IRE), Halbert, **10/1** Domicksky, Mister Jolson, **12/1** Thatcherella (7/1-14/1), Another Batchworth, Windrush Boy (op 8/1), **14/1** Dolly Face (10/1-16/1), **20/1** Invocation, **25/1** Rocky Two, CSF £55.81 CT £336.44 TOTE £7.60: £2.80 £2.90 £1.30 (£28.40) Trio £105.50 OWNER The Lower Bowden Syndicate (UPPER LAMBOURN) BRED E. A. Badger 12 Rn 62.4 secs (2.40) SF: 71/41/56/55/44/30/36/24/20/30/3/9

WEIGHT FOR AGE 3yo-1lb

T/Plpt: £834.70 (15.57 Tckts). T/Qdpt: Not won; £141.20 to Pontefract 2/10/95. AK

3935-HAYDOCK (L-H)
Sunday October 1st (Soft, Heavy patches)

WEATHER: sunny periods WIND: str against

3962

AUTEUIL CONDITIONS STKS (2-Y.O F) (Class C) £4,565.20 (£1,706.80: £833.40: £357.00)
5f Stalls: High GOING: 0.83 sec per fur (S) 2-00 (2-01)

3668[6] **Hear The Music (IRE) (90)***(95) (BWHills)* 2-8-11 RHughes(3) (mde virtually all: clr appr fnl f: unchal)......— 1
3668[4] Whittle Rock **(91)***(73) (EJAlston)* 2-8-11 KFallon(6) (lw: bhd & pushed along: hdwy over 1f out: kpt on fnl f: no ch w wnr)......7 2
3702[3] Amaniy (USA) **(100)***(77)*(Fav)*(HThomsonJones)* 2-9-2 RHills(5) (chsd ldrs: rdn ½-wy: no imp)......hd 3
3753* Miss Bigwig **(82)***(70) (JBerry)* 2-8-9 (5) PFessey(1) (disp ld 2f: reminders ½-wy: wknd over 1f out)......1¾ 4
3668[9] Top Cat (FR) **(85)***(55) (EWeymes)* 2-9-4 TIves(4) (lw: dwlt: sn drvn along: a bhd: t.o)......6 5

11/8 Amaniy (USA), **11/4** Miss Bigwig, **9/2** HEAR THE MUSIC (IRE), **6/1** Whittle Rock, **12/1** Top Cat (FR), CSF £24.90 TOTE £5.60: £2.20 £2.40 (£16.10) OWNER Lady Harrison (LAMBOURN) BRED Gay O'Callaghan 5 Rn 1m 7.15 (8.15) SF: 28/6/10/3/-

3963

LONGCHAMP H'CAP (0-85) (3-Y.O+) (Class D) £3,826.25 (£1,160.00: £567.50: £271.25) **1m 3f 200y** Stalls: High GOING: 0.83 sec per fur (S) 2-30 (2-30)

3852[2] **Lord Hastie (USA) (50)***(68) (CWThornton)* 7-7-13 SMaloney(7) (chsd ldrs: 4th st: led 2f out: sn clr: v.easily)......— 1
3718[2] Kalou **(66)***(77) (CWCElsey)* 4-8-10 (5) PFessey(6) (chsd ldr: 2nd st: remained far side: rdn & one pce fnl 2f)......5 2
3801[9] Sunderland Echo **(65)***(68) (MrsMReveley)* 6-9-0 KDarley(13) (lw: stdd s: plld hrd: sn prom: 3rd st: led 3f out to 2f out: sn rdn & btn)......6 3
3820* Haroldon (IRE) **(76)***(78) (BPalling)* 6-9-11 TSprake(3) (b: hld up in tch: hdwy over 2f out: sn hrd rdn: nt rch ldrs)......1¼ 4
3718[9] Tonnerre **(73)***(74) (CWFairhurst)* 3-9-0 DeanMcKeown(8) (led to 3f out: sn drvn along & wknd)......hd 5

3837[5] Wentbridge Lad (IRE) **(64)***(59) (PDEvans)* 5-8-13v GHind(4) (hld up: effrt over 2f out: sn rdn: no imp) 5 **6**
3820[9] Dreams End **(78)***(72) (JMBradley)* 7-9-13 RHughes(11) (b: hld up: racd alone centre fnl 4f: rdn over 2f out: no imp) ....¾ **7**
3801[10] In Good Faith **(70)***(48) (JJQuinn)* 3-8-11 MBirch(1) (chsd ldrs: 6th st: drvn along over 3f out: sn btn: t.o) 12 **8**
3801[5] Hazard a Guess (IRE) **(75)***(43) (MrsJRRamsden)* 5-9-10 KFallon(9) (lw: hld up in tch: rdn & effrt 3f out: no imp: t.o) 7 **9**
1527[2] Advance East **(71)***(24) (MrsJRRamsden)* 3-8-12 JFEgan(5) (hld up: a in rr: t.o fnl 3f) 11 **10**
Talos (IRE) **(59)***(11) (DMoffatt)* 7-8-5 (3) DarrenMoffatt(10) (bkwd: a bhd: remained far side st: t.o) ....¾ **11**
2392[3] Twice the Groom (IRE) **(64)***(12) (RLee)* 5-8-13 NCarlisle(12) (b: bit bkwd: chsd ldrs: 5th st: wknd 3f out: t.o) 3½ **12**
3718[3] Embryonic (IRE) **(75)***(21)*(Fav)*(RFFisher)* 3-9-2 NConnorton(2) (mid div tl wknd over 3f out: t.o) 1 **13**

4/1 Embryonic (IRE), **11/2** LORD HASTIE (USA), **7/1** In Good Faith, **8/1** Kalou, Sunderland Echo, Hazard a Guess (IRE), **10/1** Haroldon (IRE), Advance East, Wentbridge Lad (IRE), **14/1** Dreams End, **20/1** Tonnerre, Twice the Groom (IRE), **33/1** Talos (IRE), CSF £48.00 CT £329.67 TOTE £5.80: £1.50 £2.90 £2.30 (£20.30) Trio £36.40 OWNER Mrs Joy Bendall (MIDDLEHAM) BRED Upland Park Stud 13 Rn 2m 42.8 (14.80) SF: 50/59/50/60/48/41/54/22/25/-/-/-/-
WEIGHT FOR AGE 3yo-8lb

3964 D.H. WELTON AND COMPANY LTD. H'CAP (0-90) (3-Y.O) (Class C)
£6,356.00 (£1,928.00: £944.00: £452.00)
6f Stalls: High GOING: 0.83 sec per fur (S) 3-00 (3-01)

3492[6] **Charlie Sillett (69)***(80) (BWHills)* 3-8-1 (5)ow1 JDSmith(11) (b: b.hind: hdwy 2f out: led ins fnl f: hung bdly lft: rdn clr) ....— **1**
3777[4] Little Ibnr **(61)***(64) (PDEvans)* 4-8-0 ow1 GHind(10) (led ½-wy tl ins fnl f: no ex) 3 **2**
3637[3] First Veil **(72)***(76) (JRFanshawe)* 5-8-8 (3) NVarley(2) (hdwy 2f out: hrd rdn & impeded ins fnl f: r.o) ....hd **3**
3823[2] It's Academic **(70)***(70)*(Fav)*(MrsJRRamsden)* 3-8-7 KFallon(19) (chsd ldrs: nt clr run 2f out: swtchd centre: r.o ins fnl f) 1¼ **4**
2659[4] Brockton Flame **(70)***(66) (JMPEustace)* 3-8-7 MTebbutt(24) (chsd ldrs stands' side: rdn & kpt on fnl f) 1¾ **5**
3615[15] Montserrat **(72)***(68) (LGCottrell)* 3-8-9 MFenton(1) (racd wd: spd over 4f) ....hd **6**
3715[27] Bold Street (IRE) **(69)***(63) (ABailey)* 5-8-5b(3) DWright(3) (b: hdwy 2f out: rdn & r.o ins fnl f) ....½ **7**
3830[4] Cumbrian Waltzer **(73)***(65) (MHEasterby)* 10-8-7 (5) LNewton(20) (lw: hdwy bel dist: nvr nrr) 1 **8**
3823[7] Impulsive Air (IRE) **(65)***(54) (EWeymes)* 3-8-2v DaleGibson(16) (n.m.r 2f out: nvr nr to chal) ...1 **9**
3637[12] Lynton Lad **(80)***(61) (CPEBrooks)* 3-9-3 TIves(12) (nvr trbld ldrs) 3 **10**
3830* Knayton Lass **(58)***(32) (MWEasterby)* 4-7-11 JLowe(17) (in tch: rdn & btn whn squeezed out 2f out) 2½ **11**
3830[3] Barato **(69)***(42) (MrsJRRamsden)* 4-8-1 (7) TFinn(8) (nvr nr to chal) ....½ **12**
594[6] Red Five **(56)***(25) (DMoffatt)* 4-7-6 (3)ow2 DarrenMoffatt(23) (nvr trbld ldrs) ....¾ **13**
3717[15] Amron **(77)***(48) (JBerry)* 8-9-2 NCarlisle(13) (spd 4f) ....hd **14**
3823[5] Bollin Harry **(68)***(35) (MHEasterby)* 3-8-5 MBirch(5) (chsd ldrs over 4f) 1½ **15**
3783[15] Rymer's Rascal **(65)***(31) (EJAlston)* 3-8-2 TWilliams(14) (outpcd) ....nk **16**
3615[5] Oggi **(67)***(27) (PJMakin)* 4-8-6b PaulEddery(15) (hdwy ½-wy: rdn & wknd wl over 1f out) 2 **17**
3807[12] King Rat (IRE) **(80)***(39) (TJEtherington)* 4-9-5b JCarroll(7) (chsd ldrs centre over 4f) ....½ **18**
3615[6] Hakiki (IRE) **(83)***(41) (PTWalwyn)* 3-9-6 DeanMcKeown(22) (mde most to ½-wy: rdn & wknd wl over 1f out) ....nk **19**
3822[3] Mr Bergerac (IRE) **(85)***(43) (BPalling)* 4-9-10 TSprake(6) (m.n.s) ....hd **20**
3298[3] Nawaasi **(74)***(31) (HThomsonJones)* 3-8-11 RHills(18) (chsd ldrs: rdn & n.m.r wl over 1f out: eased whn btn appr fnl f) ....nk **21**
3822[7] Four of Spades **(59)***(11) (PDEvans)* 4-7-5 (7)ow1 AmandaSanders(4) (rdn 2f out: a in rr) 1½ **22**
3298[2] Showery **(74)***(21) (JWWatts)* 3-8-11 NConnorton(21) (w ldrs over 3f: wknd fnl 2f) 2½ **23**
3802[15] Champagne Grandy **(83)** *(MRChannon)* 5-9-8 RHughes(9) (Withdrawn not under Starter's orders: inj in parade ring) .... **W**

9/2 It's Academic (6/1-4/1), **10/1** Oggi, CHARLIE SILLETT, **11/1** Hakiki (IRE), **12/1** Cumbrian Waltzer, Bold Street (IRE), Showery, **14/1** Little Ibnr, Montserrat, Barato, Nawaasi, **16/1** King Rat (IRE), Mr Bergerac (IRE), Knayton Lass, Brockton Flame, First Veil, **20/1** Four of Spades, Rymer's Rascal, Lynton Lad, Bollin Harry, Amron, **33/1** Impulsive Air (IRE), Red Five, CSF £151.54 CT £2,090.02 TOTE £16.40: £3.20 £3.80 £9.80 £1.80 (£268.30) Trio £2,356.70 OWNER Mr John Sillett (LAMBOURN) BRED J. Sillett 23 Rn
1m 19.39 (7.69) SF: 52/38/50/42/38/40/37/39/26/33/6/16/-/22/7/3/1/13/13/17/3/-/-/-
WEIGHT FOR AGE 3yo-2lb

3965

SAINT-CLOUD LIMITED STKS (0-70) (3-Y.O+) (Class E) £3,126.00 (£948.00: £464.00: £222.00)
1m 2f 120y Stalls: High GOING: 0.83 sec per fur (S) 3-30 (3-32)

3799⁶ **Snow Princess (IRE) (69)***(71) (LordHuntingdon)* 3-8-6 RHills(9) (chsd ldrs: 5th st: led ins fnl f: all out) — 1
3526² Shining Example **(67)***(76) (PJMakin)* 3-8-11 PaulEddery(7) (hld up: hdwy over 2f out: str chal fnl f: jst failed) s.h 2
3710⁵ Exemption **(69)***(77) (HCandy)* 4-9-6 NAdams(4) (chsd ldrs: 3rd st: led over 2f out tl ins fnl f: kpt on) ½ 3
3801³ Braille (IRE) **(70)***(71) (MGMeagher)* 4-9-1 (5) AWhelan(10) (lw: hld up: 4th st: slt ld 3f out: sn hdd: rdn appr fnl f: one pce) 4 4
3646⁴ El Bailador (IRE) **(60)***(69) (JDBethell)* 4-9-8 KFallon(8) (mde most over 7f: sn rdn: btn appr fnl f) 2½ 5
3810⁷ Efizia **(67)***(53) (MrsMReveley)* 5-8-13 KDarley(6) (lw: hld up: 6th st: hdwy 4f out: wknd wl over 1f out) 5 6
3810³ Current Speech (IRE) **(71)***(52)*(Fav)*(MHEasterby)* 4-9-4 MBirch(2) (hld up in tch: c centre st: wknd over 2f out) 4 7
3745⁵ Reed My Lips (IRE) **(32)***(21) (BPJBaugh)* 4-8-11 (7) IonaWands(1) (a bhd: t.o) 20 8
222⁸ Doon Ridge **(47)** *(JJO'Neill)* 4-9-4 SDWilliams(5) (lw: w ldr: 2nd st: wknd 3f out: t.o) 20 9

9/4 Current Speech (IRE), **7/2** Braille (IRE), **9/2** Efizia, SNOW PRINCESS (IRE), **6/1** Shining Example, **10/1** Exemption, **20/1** El Bailador (IRE), **25/1** Doon Ridge, **50/1** Reed My Lips (IRE), CSF £30.92 TOTE £5.50: £2.10 £1.40 £3.40 (£10.40) Trio £82.10 OWNER Lord Weinstock & The Hon Simon Weinstock (WEST ILSLEY) BRED Ballymacoll Stud Co 9 Rn

2m 27.53 (16.03) SF: 35/40/48/42/40/24/23/-/-
WEIGHT FOR AGE 3yo-7lb

3966

SKY TELEVISION H'CAP (0-90) (3-Y.O) (Class C) £6,092.00 (£1,712.00: £836.00)
1m 30y Stalls: High GOING: 0.83 sec per fur (S) 4-15 (4-15)

3630⁴ **Ron's Secret (75)***(86)*(Fav)*(JWPayne)* 3-9-3 RHughes(5) (stdd s: 3rd st: led on bit 1f out: canter) — 1
3802¹¹ Bollin Frank **(57)***(67) (MHEasterby)* 3-7-13 LCharnock(4) (led: c stands' side: rdn & hdd ent fnl f: kpt on) ¾ 2
3607¹⁰ Ninia (USA) **(72)***(58) (MJohnston)* 3-9-0 TWilliams(1) (lw: chsd ldr: 2nd st: rdn over 2f out: sn btn) 12 3

Evens RON'S SECRET, **5/2** Ninia (USA), **11/4** Bollin Frank, CSF £3.30 TOTE £1.80 (£1.80) OWNER Mrs Linda Popely (NEWMARKET) BRED Mrs L.Popely 3 Rn 1m 54.39 (13.99) SF: 29/10/1

3967

DEAUVILLE MAIDEN STKS (2-Y.O C & G) (Class D) £3,582.50 (£1,085.00: £530.00: £252.50)
7f 30y Stalls: Low GOING: 0.83 sec per fur (S) 4-45 (4-47)

3625³ **Carburton** *(80+)*(Fav)*(JAGlover)* 2-8-11 PaulEddery(5) (lw: mde all: drvn along ent fnl f: r.o wl) — 1
3701⁷ Crystal Falls (IRE) **(76)***(79) (JJO'Neill)* 2-8-11 KFallon(14) (chsd ldrs: 4th st: effrt & ev ch ins fnl f: unable qckn) ½ 2
3416⁵ Desert Cat (IRE) *(76) (HThomsonJones)* 2-8-11 RHills(10) (bit bkwd: hld up: 6th st: effrt & ev ch ins fnl f: one pce) 1½ 3
Backdrop (IRE) *(72) (PWChapple-Hyam)* 2-8-6 (5) RHavlin(3) (w'like: scope: bkwd: hld up: hdwy centre 3f out: kpt on one pce appr fnl f) 1¾ 4
Kamari (USA) *(69) (ACStewart)* 2-8-11 MBirch(11) (gd sort: bit bkwd: stdd s: hdwy 3f out: shkn up & rn green 2f out: one pce) 1¼ 5
Doctor Bravious (IRE) *(64) (MBell)* 2-8-11 MFenton(9) (leggy: lw: hld up: hdwy over 2f out: nt rch ldrs) 2 6
3821¹¹ Northern Motto *(55) (MrsJRRamsden)* 2-8-11 MDeering(6) (bkwd: nvr nr to chal) 4 7
Bashtheboards *(55) (JJQuinn)* 2-8-11 SDWilliams(12) (lt-f: unf: hld up: sme hdwy fnl 2f: nvr nrr) nk 8
3827⁷ Mister Aspecto (IRE) *(51) (MJohnston)* 2-8-11 TWilliams(16) (in tch tl wknd over 2f out) 1½ 9
3821¹² Alpine Joker *(49) (MrsJRRamsden)* 2-8-11 JFEgan(7) (bit bkwd: a in rr) 1¼ 10
3625¹⁸ Known Secret (USA) *(43) (MrsJRRamsden)* 2-8-11 RHughes(15) (bit bkwd: a in rr) 2½ 11
3736⁷ Dancing Cavalier *(40) (RHollinshead)* 2-8-11 KDarley(1) (prom: 2nd st: wknd 3f out) 1½ 12
Rinus Magic *(EJAlston)* 2-8-11 GHind(13) (gd sort: bkwd: s.s: a bhd: t.o) 20 13
Chillington *(WMBrisbourne)* 2-8-11 AGarth(2) (w'like: bkwd: chsd ldrs: 5th st: wknd over 3f out: t.o) 14 14

9/4 CARBURTON, **3/1** Desert Cat (IRE), **11/2** Crystal Falls (IRE) (4/1-6/1), **13/2** Backdrop (IRE), **7/1** Kamari (USA), **14/1** Doctor Bravious (IRE), Mister Aspecto (IRE), **20/1** Known Secret (USA), **25/1** Alpine Joker, Dancing Cavalier, **33/1** Northern Motto, Rinus Magic, **50/1** Bashtheboards, Chillington, CSF £16.07 TOTE £3.20: £1.40 £2.10 £1.80 (£8.10) Trio £7.70 OWNER Mr B. H. Farr (WORKSOP) BRED Worksop Manor Stud Farm 14 Rn 1m 37.6 (10.30) SF: 45/44/41/37/34/29/20/20/16/14/8/5/-/-

T/Jkpt: £30,853.20 (0.48 Tckts); £22,596.76 to Pontefract 2/10/95. T/Plpt: £264.90 (61.6 Tckts). T/Qdpt: £22.20 (16.8 Tckts). IM

3778-PONTEFRACT (L-H)
Monday October 2nd (Good to firm)

WEATHER: sunny periods WIND: almost nil

3968

E.B.F. CLAXTON BAY MAIDEN STKS (2-Y.O) (Class D) £4,260.00 (£1,290.00: £630.00: £300.00)
1m 2f 6y Stalls: Low GOING minus 0.33 sec per fur (GF) 2-15 (2-17)

3780[2] **Warbrook (84)**(84)(Fav)*(IABalding)* 2-9-0 LDettori(12) (lw: a.p: qcknd to ld wl over 1f out: r.o wl)........ — **1**
3155[7] Benatom (USA) *(81) (HRACecil)* 2-9-0 WRyan(6) (led tl hdd wl over 1f out: kpt on wl)........1¾ **2**
3827[2] Arctic Fancy (USA) *(76) (PWHarris)* 2-9-0 GHind(3) (lw: in tch: effrt 3f out: hung lft over 1f out: styd on wl towards fin)........3½ **3**
3644[7] Exactly (IRE) **(50)***(71) (JLEyre)* 2-8-9 RLappin(4) (a chsng ldrs: one pce fnl 3f)........hd **4**
3827[6] Tissue of Lies (USA) *(72) (MJohnston)* 2-9-0 TWilliams(9) (bit bkwd: in tch: hdwy 4f out: ev ch over 2f out: wknd appr fnl f)........2½ **5**
Double Dash (IRE) *(64) (MJohnston)* 2-9-0 JWeaver(11) (wl grwn: bhd: shkn up over 4f out: styd on fnl 2f)........5 **6**
3821[9] Siege Perilous (IRE) *(49) (BobJones)* 2-9-0 MWigham(14) (in tch tl outpcd fnl 3½f)........9 **7**
Siberian Henry *(43) (BSmart)* 2-9-0 RCochrane(7) (w'like: bhd tl styd on fnl 3f)........4 **8**
3713[8] Oisin An Oir (IRE) **(50)***(40) (JBerry)* 2-9-0 JCarroll(2) (bhd & rdn 4f out: n.d)........1½ **9**
3683[7] Old School House *(36) (CNAllen)* 2-9-0 StephenDavies(8) (cl up tl wknd wl over 1f out)......2½ **10**
3560[6] Influence Pedler *(34) (CEBrittain)* 2-9-0 MRoberts(13) (chsd ldrs tl wknd 2f out)........1½ **11**
3827[9] No More Hassle (IRE) *(30) (MrsMReveley)* 2-9-0 KDarley(5) (hld up: nvr nr to chal)........2½ **12**
3620[17] Arrogant Heir *(SGNorton)* 2-9-0 PaulEddery(10) (bit bkwd: bhd fnl 4f: t.o)........20 **13**
3436[12] Sylvan Princess *(CNAllen)* 2-8-9 TIves(1) (b.hind: lost tch 4f out: t.o)........20 **14**

10/11 WARBROOK, **7/2** Benatom (USA), **9/2** Arctic Fancy (USA), **12/1** Double Dash (IRE) (op 6/1), **16/1** Tissue of Lies (USA), **20/1** Influence Pedler, Old School House, **33/1** Exactly (IRE), No More Hassle (IRE), **50/1** Siege Perilous (IRE), Siberian Henry, Oisin An Oir (IRE), Arrogant Heir, Sylvan Princess, CSF £5.09 TOTE £2.00: £1.10 £1.50 £1.30 (£2.20) Trio £2.50 OWNER Mr J. C. Smith (KINGSCLERE) BRED Littleton Stud 14 Rn
2m 13.0 (2.50 under 2y best) (4.70) SF: 36/33/28/23/24/16/1/-/-/-/-/-/-/-

3969

LEVY BOARD NURSERY H'CAP (0-75) (2-Y.O) (Class E) £3,756.00 (£1,128.00: £544.00: £252.00)
6f Stalls: Low GOING minus 0.33 sec per fur (GF) 2-45 (2-46)

3809[4] **Golden Pond (IRE) (68)***(71) (RFJohnsonHoughton)* 2-9-2 AMcGlone(3) (hdwy to ld ½-wy: kpt on wl towards fin)........ — **1**
3271[6] Weetman's Weigh (IRE) **(65)***(68) (RHollinshead)* 2-8-13 TIves(17) (cl up: disp ld wl ins fnl f: no ex towards fin)........hd **2**
3639[3] Deerly **(67)***(68) (DMorris)* 2-9-1 LDettori(10) (mid div: effrt 2f out: swtchd twice fnl f: r.o)........¾ **3**
3080[2] Vera's First (IRE) **(73)***(70) (GLewis)* 2-9-7b PaulEddery(16) (b.hind: hdwy over 2f out: ev ch ins fnl f: nt qckn)........1¼ **4**
3714[10] Duralock Fencer **(63)***(59) (PGMurphy)* 2-8-4 (7) RWaterfield(14) (hdwy 2f out: styd on: nrst fin)........½ **5**
3749[18] Incapol **(66)***(61) (MJRyan)* 2-8-9 (5) MBaird(12) (cl up: rdn 2f out: r.o one pce)........nk **6**
3623[7] Gladys Althorpe (IRE) **(70)***(59) (JLEyre)* 2-9-4 RLappin(18) (cl up: rdn 2f out: wknd over 1f out)........2½ **7**
3851[9] Silverdale Knight **(66)***(48) (KWHogg)* 2-8-7 (7) ADaly(8) (outpcd & bhd tl sme late hdwy)........2½ **8**
3824[7] Opening Chorus **(67)***(41) (MrsMReveley)* 2-9-1 KDarley(9) (hld up: nvr plcd to chal)........3 **9**
3779[4] Impeccable **(72)***(44)*(Fav)*(JLDunlop)* 2-9-6 RHughes(4) (chsd ldrs: rdn wl over 1f out: btn & eased ins fnl f)........¾ **10**
3651[3] Baker **(61)***(32) (HCandy)* 2-8-9 WNewnes(15) (nvr nr ldrs)........nk **11**
3828[4] Polish Saga **(64)***(34) (MDods)* 2-8-12 TWilliams(6) (s.i.s: n.d)........½ **12**
3604[15] Burj **(60)***(29) (NAGraham)* 2-8-8 JReid(7) (outpcd fr ½-wy)........nk **13**
3612[7] Middle East **(72)***(38) (TDBarron)* 2-9-6 DeanMcKeown(11) (swtg: s.i.s: nvr plcd to chal)........1 **14**

3369[6] Dancing Rainbow **(62)**(22) *(MJCamacho)* 2-8-10 LCharnock(1) (led to ½-wy: wknd wl over 1f out)....2½ **15**
2932[5] Globe Runner **(72)**(18) *(JJO'Neill)* 2-9-6 SDWilliams(2) (s.i.s: hmpd appr st: a bhd)....5 **16**
2926[4] Rapid Liner **(66)**(10) *(AHarrison)* 2-9-0 RCochrane(5) (swtg: sn drvn along & bhd: hmpd appr st: n.d)....1 **17**
3809[14] The Butterwick Kid **(62)**(4) *(RAFahey)* 2-8-10 ACulhane(13) (s.i.s: hmpd appr st: a bhd)....½ **18**

5/1 Impeccable, **13/2** Opening Chorus, **8/1** GOLDEN POND (IRE), **10/1** Deerly, Vera's First (IRE), Middle East, **11/1** The Butterwick Kid, **12/1** Incapol, Burj, **14/1** Baker, Rapid Liner, Gladys Althorpe (IRE), **16/1** Globe Runner, Duralock Fencer, Polish Saga, **20/1** Weetman's Weigh (IRE), **25/1** Dancing Rainbow, **33/1** Silverdale Knight, CSF £157.24 CT £1,515.31 TOTE £9.20: £2.30 £4.90 £2.00 £1.90 (£270.60) Trio £155.50 OWNER Mr John Horgan (DIDCOT) BRED Tullamaine Castle Stud and Partners 18 Rn 1m 17.7 (3.40) SF: 28/25/25/27/16/18/16/5/-/1/-/-/-/-/-/-/-/-

STEWARDS' ENQUIRY Daly susp. 11-14/10/95 (careless riding).

OFFICIAL EXPLANATION Impeccable: lost her action coming up the hill and was unsuited by the ground.

3970 PONTEFRACT APPRENTICE SERIES FINAL H'CAP (0-70) (3-Y.O+) (Class E) £3,149.00 (£962.00: £476.00: £233.00)

1m 4f 8y Stalls: Low GOING minus 0.33 sec per fur (GF) 3-15 (3-17)

3704[15] **Secret Service (IRE) (68)**(80) *(JHanson)* 3-9-8 GFaulkner(15) (trckd ldrs: led 3f out: hld on wl fnl 2f)....— **1**
2917* Turnpole (IRE) **(66)**(77)(Fav)*(MrsMReveley)* 4-10-0 MHenry(9) (swtg: chsd ldrs: chal 3f out: kpt on wl towards fin)....½ **2**
3808[24] Express Gift **(60)**(70) *(MrsMReveley)* 6-9-1 (7) KPrendergast(2) (bit bkwd: hld up: gd hdwy 3f out: styd on: nrst fin)....1¼ **3**
3737[5] Instantaneous **(50)**(52) *(MHEasterby)* 3-8-4 GMitchell(4) (in tch: hdwy on outside 5f out: one pce fnl 2f)....6 **4**
3852[4] Achilles Heel **(39)**(39) *(CNAllen)* 4-8-1 MartinDwyer(17) (bhd: hdwy 3f out: hmpd appr st: styd on: nrst fin)....1 **5**
2495[8] Winn's Pride (IRE) **(47)**(45) *(RHollinshead)* 4-8-6 (3) FLynch(16) (lw: styd on fnl 3f: n.d)....1¾ **6**
*3737** Canton Venture **(55)**(40) *(SPCWoods)* 3-8-2 (7) JMoon(13) (nvr nrr)....10 **7**
Fair and Fancy (FR) **(40)**(23) *(DNicholls)* 4-7-13 (3) JoHunnam(1) (bit bkwd: cl up: led after 3f to 5f out: grad wknd)....1½ **8**
3778[5] Mad Militant (IRE) **(63)**(42) *(AStreeter)* 6-9-11 DDenby(11) (b: hdwy after 4f: wknd over 3f out)....3 **9**
3863[15] Vin St Koola **(63)**(38) *(MCChapman)* 3-9-3 CScally(7) (a rr div)....3 **10**
3469[8] On a Pedestal (IRE) **(52)**(27) *(MrsJRRamsden)* 3-8-1 (5) TFinn(3) (lw: bhd: sme hdwy 4f out: n.d)....hd **11**
3705[14] Marco Magnifico (USA) **(55)**(27) *(TDyer)* 5-8-12 (5) RMullen(12) (chsd ldrs tl wknd over 3f out)....1¾ **12**
3951[7] Modest Hope (USA) **(42)**(12) *(BRichmond)* 8-8-1 (3) GayeHarwood(14) (effrt on outside 6f out: wknd 3f out)....2 **13**
3572[2] Wottashambles **(40)**(2) *(LMontagueHall)* 4-8-2 ADaly(5) (w ldrs 4f: grad lost pl)....6 **14**
3843[2] Colosse **(55)**(15) *(JLEyre)* 3-8-4 (5) KSked(6) (cl up: led 5f out to 3f out: sn wknd)....1 **15**
Altoby **(42)** *(EJAlston)* 4-7-13 (5) BHalligan(8) (led 3f: wknd 4f out)....15 **16**
1029[15] Fred's Delight (IRE) **(37)** *(MrsVAAconley)* 4-7-8v(5) JBramhill(18) (s.i.s: racd wd & a bhd)....6 **17**
3723[5] Admirals Secret (USA) **(63)** *(CFWall)* 6-9-6 (5) PClarke(10) (bhd & racd wd 7f out: n.d)....20 **18**

3/1 Turnpole (IRE), **6/1** Admirals Secret (USA), **15/2** Colosse, **8/1** Wottashambles, Achilles Heel, **9/1** On a Pedestal (IRE) (op 6/1), **10/1** Instantaneous, **12/1** Modest Hope (USA), **14/1** Canton Venture, **16/1** Mad Militant (IRE), **20/1** Express Gift, SECRET SERVICE (IRE), **25/1** Marco Magnifico (USA), Fair and Fancy (FR), **33/1** Vin St Koola, Altoby, Winn's Pride (IRE), **50/1** Fred's Delight (IRE), CSF £82.59 CT £1,200.61 TOTE £33.90: £4.70 £1.60 £6.80 £2.60 (£94.70) Trio £510.20 OWNER Mr J. Hanson (WETHERBY) BRED E. O'Leary 18 Rn

2m 38.3 (4.00) SF: 54/59/52/26/21/27/14/5/24/12/1/9/-/-/-/-/-/-

WEIGHT FOR AGE 3yo-8lb

3971 TRINIDAD & TOBAGO H'CAP (0-70) (3-Y.O+) (Class E) £3,991.50 (£1,197.00: £576.00: £265.50) **2m 1f 22y** Stalls: Centre GOING minus 0.33 sec (GF)3-45 (3-46)

3705[7] **Arian Spirit (IRE) (34)**(48) *(JLEyre)* 4-7-8 ow1 LCharnock(11) (hdwy 6f out: styd on u.p to ld wl ins fnl f)....— **1**
3774* Unchanged **(69)**(83)(Fav)*(CEBrittain)* 3-9-4 MRoberts(18) (hdwy & prom ½-wy: rdn 3f out: ev ch ins fnl f: styd on)....¾ **2**
3724* Greek Night Out (IRE) **(35)**(48) *(JLEyre)* 4-7-6 (3) NVarley(15) (prom: led 5f out tl hdd & no ex wl ins fnl f)....1 **3**

3849² Paradise Navy **(68)***(81) (CREgerton)* 6-10-0 RHughes(1) (lw: hld up: hdwy over 2f out: r.o towards fin)....nk **4**
3724³ Bobby's Dream **(44)***(55) (MHTompkins)* 3-7-7 NCarlisle(5) (a chsng ldrs: outpcd 5f out: hdwy over 2f out: one pce fnl f)....1¾ **5**
3724⁵ Moonshine Dancer **(40)***(49) (MrsMReveley)* 5-7-7 (7)ow1 DDenby(16) (b.nr fore: hld up: hdwy 7f out: ch 2f out: no ex ins fnl f)....1½ **6**
3705⁶ Brumon (IRE) **(59)***(63) (TDyer)* 4-9-5v MFenton(6) (nvr nrr)....7 **7**
3818¹³ Our Kris **(62)***(65) (GHarwood)* 3-8-11 AClark(14) (effrt 4f out: nvr rchd ldrs)....1 **8**
1444* Inchcailloch (IRE) **(63)***(64) (JSKing)* 6-9-9 PaulEddery(12) (lw: bhd tl sme hdwy fnl 3f)....2 **9**
3676¹⁰ Tour Leader (NZ) **(38)***(38) (RHBuckler)* 6-7-12 DaleGibson(4) (hld up: effrt 4f out: n.d)....½ **10**
Alcian Blue **(45)***(45) (MDHammond)* 4-8-2 (3) DRMcCabe(19) (a in rr)....hd **11**
751* Roberty Lea **(68)***(67) (MrsMReveley)* 7-10-0 KDarley(8) (bit bkwd: hld up & bhd: nvr plcd to chal)....1 **12**
3296² Don't Cry **(33)***(32) (DonEnricoIncisa)* 7-7-7 KimTinkler(20) (bhd tl sme late hdwy)....s.h **13**
3676³ Harry Welsh (IRE) **(58)***(55) (KMcAuliffe)* 3-8-7v JWeaver(17) (n.d)....2½ **14**
3741² Brodessa **(63)***(56) (MrsMReveley)* 9-9-2 (7) SCopp(13) (chsd ldrs: ev ch 5f out: wknd fnl 2½f)..4 **15**
3705⁹ Top Prize **(40)***(27) (MBrittain)* 7-8-0v JLowe(3) (chsd ldrs: hmpd 5f out: sn wknd)....7 **16**
3818¹⁷ Crowther Homes **(40)***(26) (EJAlston)* 5-8-0 TWilliams(7) (in tch: hmpd ½-wy: sn wknd)....¾ **17**
3722⁷ Fools of Pride (IRE) **(46)***(28) (RHollinshead)* 3-7-4 (5)ow2 MHenry(9) (chsd ldrs tl wknd 5f out)....2 **18**
3438⁵ Reem Dubai (IRE) **(69)***(50) (JHMGosden)* 3-9-4 LDettori(2) (led 4f: chsd ldrs tl wknd fnl 3f)....3 **19**
3646¹² Five to Seven (USA) **(64)***(44) (CWThornton)* 6-9-7 (3) OPears(10) (b: led after 4f: sn clr: hdd 5f out: wknd qckly)....1½ **20**

LONG HANDICAP Don't Cry 6-6 Fools of Pride (IRE) 6-13

9/4 Unchanged, **13/2** Paradise Navy, **8/1** Reem Dubai (IRE), Inchcailloch (IRE), **12/1** Brodessa, **14/1** Roberty Lea, Brumon (IRE), Greek Night Out (IRE), Bobby's Dream, **16/1** Moonshine Dancer, Harry Welsh (IRE), Tour Leader (NZ), Our Kris, **25/1** Top Prize, ARIAN SPIRIT (IRE), **50/1** Don't Cry, Crowther Homes, Fools of Pride (IRE), Alcian Blue, Five to Seven (USA), CSF £83.60 CT £818.02 TOTE £55.30: £5.70 £1.70 £2.30 £1.80 (£149.30) Trio £1,006.90 OWNER Mr Martin West (HAMBLETON) BRED M. Ervine in Ireland 20 Rn

3m 46.2 (6.20) SF: 25/49/25/58/21/26/40/31/41/15/22/44/9/21/33/4/3/-/16/21

WEIGHT FOR AGE 3yo-11lb

3972 BUCCOO REEF CLAIMING STKS (3-Y.O) (Class F) £3,230.50 (£898.00: £431.50)

6f Stalls: Low GOING minus 0.33 sec per fur (GF) 4-15 (4-17)

3905¹¹ **Fantasy Racing (IRE) (75)***(86)*(Fav)*(MRChannon)* 3-8-9 RHughes(1) (trckd ldrs: led appr fnl f: qcknd & sn clr)....— **1**
3750³ Delight of Dawn **(72)***(77) (KTIvory)* 3-8-1 (7) CScally(18) (b: hdwy over 2f out: r.o: no ch w wnr)3 **2**
3624²¹ Hi Rock **(53)***(62) (MJCamacho)* 3-7-12 LCharnock(4) (a chsng ldrs: rdn over 2f out: kpt on: no imp)....2 **3**
3624¹⁷ Sylvandra **(66)***(66) (PGMurphy)* 3-8-6 JWilliams(6) (lw: mid div: styd on fnl 2f: nvr nrr)....1¼ **4**
3637¹¹ Second Cello **(65)***(65) (DMorris)* 3-8-6 LDettori(3) (swtg: effrt on ins whn hmpd 2f out: styd on: nrst fin)....½ **5**
1677¹¹ Never Such Bliss **(60)***(54) (JDBethell)* 3-7-13 NCarlisle(11) (bhd: nt clr run & swtchd over 1f out: styd on)....1½ **6**
3467⁸ Saint Amigo **(44)***(57) (JLEyre)* 3-8-5 MRoberts(8) (bhd: hdwy over 1f out: nvr rchd ldrs)....1¼ **7**
3624¹³ Rosa Bonheur **(52)***(50) (MAJarvis)* 3-7-10 (3) NVarley(12) (b.hind: bhd tl hdwy on ins over 1f out: nvr rchd ldrs)....hd **8**
3750¹⁰ Penny's Wishing **(61)***(48) (JPLeigh)* 3-7-9 (5) PFessey(2) (chsd ldrs tl wknd over 1f out)....1¼ **9**
524⁵ Rockcracker (IRE) **(63)***(51) (RCharlton)* 3-8-8b KDarley(16) (lw: cl up: led 2f out tl over 1f out: sn btn)....1¾ **10**
*1883*³ Komiamaite **(58)***(43) (SRBowring)* 3-7-13 (5) CTeague(7) (nvr trbld ldrs)....1½ **11**
3638¹⁵ Jolly Hokey **(35)***(45) (JWharton)* 3-8-6 AClark(9) (nvr rchd ldrs)....s.h **12**
3750⁸ Havana Miss **(38)***(31) (BPalling)* 3-7-7 (5) MHenry(13) (n.d)....2½ **13**
3748⁹ Rotherfield Park (IRE) **(39)***(29) (CSmith)* 3-7-13 NAdams(17) (cl up tl wknd 1½f out)....1 **14**
3457¹⁶ Russian Heroine **(73)***(29) (MJohnston)* 3-8-2 TWilliams(5) (led 4f: sn rdn & wknd)....1¼ **15**
3624¹⁹ Noor El Houdah (IRE) **(57)***(28) (JBerry)* 3-8-3 JCarroll(14) (bhd fr ½-wy)....½ **16**
3597¹⁶ Thick as Thieves **(69)***(36) (RonaldThompson)* 3-8-11 SDWilliams(10) (lw: chsd ldrs tl wknd qckly over 1f out)....s.h **17**
*3739*¹⁰ Cool Tactician **(49)***(26) (RHollinshead)* 3-8-7 WRyan(15) (n.d)....2½ **18**

5/2 FANTASY RACING (IRE), **9/2** Russian Heroine, **11/2** Delight of Dawn, **7/1** Second Cello, **9/1** Rockcracker (IRE), **12/1** Sylvandra, **16/1** Rosa Bonheur, Saint Amigo, **20/1** Komiamaite, Penny's Wishing, Noor El Houdah (IRE), **25/1** Hi Rock, Thick as Thieves, Never Such Bliss, **33/1** Rotherfield Park (IRE), **50/1** Havana Miss, Jolly Hokey, Cool Tactician, CSF £17.97 TOTE £4.00: £1.70 £2.10 £4.00 (£8.20) Trio £158.10 OWNER Aldridge Racing Ltd (UPPER LAMBOURN) BRED Barronstown Stud and Ron Con Ltd 18 Rn 1m 16.1 (1.80) SF: 42/33/18/22/21/10/13/6/4/7/-/1/-/-/-/-/-/-

3973 MARAVAL H'CAP (0-80) (3-Y.O) (Class D) £5,845.00 (£1,750.00: £840.00: £385.00) 1m 4y Stalls: Low GOING minus 0.33 sec per fur (GF) 4-45 (4-51)

3607[9] **Shinerolla (75)***(85) (MrsJRRamsden)* 3-9-4 JReid(15) (lw: racd wd: hld up: smooth hdwy to ld wl over 1f out: rdn & r.o) ....— **1**
3761* Far Ahead **(74)***(82) (JLEyre)* 3-9-3 RLappin(5) (in tch: outpcd 2f out: hdwy over 1f out: r.o towards fin) 1 **2**
3286[6] Seventeens Lucky **(67)***(73) (BobJones)* 3-8-10 RCochrane(4) (hdwy 2f out: styd on wl: nrst fin) 1 **3**
3645[6] Evan 'elp Us **(60)***(63) (JLEyre)* 3-8-0b(3) NVarley(13) (prom: effrt & ev ch over 1f out: r.o one pce) 1½ **4**
3808[2] Shining Edge **(52)***(50) (MHEasterby)* 3-7-9 JLowe(16) (a chsng ldrs: rdn over 2f out: styd on one pce) 2½ **5**
3837[10] Three Arch Bridge **(64)***(54) (MJohnston)* 3-8-7b TWilliams(9) (in tch: effrt u.p 2f out: no imp) 4 **6**
3732[3] Elpidos **(75)***(64) (CEBrittain)* 3-9-4 MRoberts(10) (lw: effrt on outside over 2f out: rdn & no imp appr fnl f) ....¾ **7**
3512[12] Forzair **(68)***(55) (SRBowring)* 3-8-6 (5) CTeague(1) (hdwy 2f out: styd on wl: nrst fin) 1 **8**
3889[9] El Don **(53)***(36) (MJRyan)* 3-7-5 (5) MBaird(6) (nvr trbld ldrs) 1¾ **9**
3659[11] Roseberry Ray (IRE) **(76)***(59) (GWragg)* 3-9-5b MHills(12) (in tch tl outpcd fnl 2½f) ....hd **10**
3820[11] Marguerite Bay (IRE) **(76)***(45) (EALDunlop)* 3-9-5v JTate(11) (s.i.s: effrt ½-wy: n.d) 7 **11**
3383[6] Elite Racing **(61)***(23) (NTinkler)* 3-7-11 (7) ADaly(7) (prom to ½-wy: sn hrd rdn & bhd) 3½ **12**
3761[3] Alzoomo (IRE) **(67)***(29) (JAGlover)* 3-8-10 SDWilliams(2) (lw: n.d) ....s.h **13**
3497[3] Nordinex (IRE) **(78)***(36)*(Fav)*(RWArmstrong)* 3-9-7 LDettori(8) (cl up: led 3f out tl wl over 1f out: sn wknd & eased) 2 **14**
True Ballad **(59)** *(TDyer)* 3-8-2 MFenton(3) (led 5f: wknd qckly: p.u 1f out) .... **P**
3823[10] Mountgate **(70)** *(MPBielby)* 3-8-10 (3) DRMcCabe(14) (Withdrawn not under Starter's orders: uns rdr & bolted gng to s) .... **W**

7/2 Nordinex (IRE), **4/1** SHINEROLLA, **7/1** Elpidos, **9/1** Shining Edge, **10/1** Far Ahead, **12/1** Roseberry Ray (IRE), **14/1** Alzoomo (IRE), **16/1** Elite Racing, Three Arch Bridge, **20/1** Evan 'elp Us, Marguerite Bay (IRE), Seventeens Lucky, Mountgate, El Don, **25/1** True Ballad, Forzair, CSF £42.06 CT £661.96 TOTE £4.40: £2.60 £2.90 £4.20 (£42.30) Trio £226.30 OWNER Mrs Alison Iles (THIRSK) BRED Lord Vestey 15 Rn 1m 46.0 (4.00) SF: 37/34/25/15/2/6/16/7/-/11/-/-/-/-/-
OFFICIAL EXPLANATION Nordinex (IRE): reportedly ran too free in the early stages.

3974 CARONI MAIDEN STKS (3-Y.O) (Class D) £3,810.00 (£1,155.00: £565.00: £270.00) 1m 4y Stalls: Low GOING minus 0.33 sec per fur (GF) 5-15 (5-18)

3712[4] **Lancerette** *(80) (NAGraham)* 3-8-9 MRimmer(3) (bhd: swtchd & hmpd over 2f out: hdwy over 1f out: r.o wl to ld nr fin) ....— **1**
Clearly Devious *(80+)*(Fav)*(JRFanshawe)* 3-8-9 DHarrison(7) (lengthy: scope: sn trckng ldrs gng wl: led 2f out: qcknd clr: rdn ins fnl f: jst ct) ....hd **2**
3725[2] Cashmere Lady *(74) (JLEyre)* 3-8-9 RLappin(5) (a chsng ldrs: kpt on one pce fnl 2f) 3 **3**
3761[6] Duke Valentino **(62)***(78) (RHollinshead)* 3-9-0 TIves(9) (mid div: effrt whn hmpd over 2f out: kpt on wl fnl f) ....nk **4**
3761[4] Angus-G *(76) (MrsMReveley)* 3-9-0 KDarley(11) (s.i.s: stdy hdwy over 2f out: nvr plcd to chal) 1¼ **5**
La Alla Wa Asa (IRE) *(69) (JHMGosden)* 3-8-9 LDettori(15) (leggy: unf: s.i.s: outpcd & bhd: hdwy whn bdly hmpd appr st: r.o) 1 **6**
3761[5] Nero Kris **(64)***(71) (PAKelleway)* 3-9-0 MWigham(1) (swtg: styd on fnl 2f: nvr nrr) 1¼ **7**
3761[2] Northern Fan (IRE) **(72)***(68) (ACStewart)* 3-9-0 MRoberts(16) (chsd ldrs tl wknd fnl 2½f) 1½ **8**
3770[4] Raise the Stakes **(73)***(68) (IABalding)* 3-9-0 RCochrane(12) (lw: led tl hdd 2f out: sn wknd) ....s.h **9**
3761[7] Yaverland (IRE) **(61)***(60) (CADwyer)* 3-9-0 JReid(13) (nvr trbld ldrs) 4 **10**
Fire The Anvil *(60) (JLDunlop)* 3-9-0 RHughes(10) (lengthy: bkwd: s.i.s: shkn up over 1f out: n.d) ....hd **11**
2770[8] Ihtimaam (FR) **(64)***(46) (MrsASwinbank)* 3-9-0 NConnorton(8) (b: b.hind: unruly bef s: in tch tl wknd over 2f out) 7 **12**
1085[8] Beauchief *(39) (RFMarvin)* 3-8-11 (3) SDrowne(17) (n.d) 3½ **13**
3712[10] Fatehalkhair (IRE) *(38) (BEllison)* 3-9-0 TWilliams(2) (b: trckd ldrs tl wknd over 2f out) ....½ **14**
1990[6] Lady Nash **(58)***(32) (CEBrittain)* 3-8-9 SHatakeyama(6) (chsd ldrs 5f) ....½ **15**
3761[10] Crowning Tino *(24) (MrsNMacauley)* 3-8-4 (5) CTeague(14) (a bhd: hmpd appr st) 4 **16**
3725[6] Caddican (IRE) *(10) (RBoss)* 3-8-9 WRyan(18) (n.d) 7 **17**
Shamokin *(10) (FWatson)* 3-9-0 JWeaver(4) (bit bkwd: dwlt: a wl bhd) 2½ **18**

3/1 Clearly Devious, **11/2** Northern Fan (IRE), **6/1** La Alla Wa Asa (IRE), Raise the Stakes, Cashmere Lady, **13/2** Angus-G, **11/1** LANCERETTE, **20/1** Nero Kris, Duke Valentino, Yaverland (IRE), Fire The Anvil, Caddican (IRE), Lady Nash, **25/1** Ihtimaam (FR), **50/1** Beauchief, Crowning Tino, Fatehalkhair (IRE), Shamokin, CSF £23.85 TOTE £3.20: £1.90 £1.80 39.60 (£17.50) Trio £562.50 OWNER Sir John Swaine (NEWMARKET) BRED Corvette Paddocks Ltd 18 Rn
1m 45.3 (3.30) SF: 35/35/29/33/31/24/26/23/23/15/15/1/-/-/-/-/-/-
T/Jkpt; Not won: £29,792.47 to Warwick 3/10/1995. T/Plpt: £49.30 (441.02 Tckts). T/Qdpt: £69.70 (3.25 Tckts). AA

3824-REDCAR (L-H)
Tuesday October 3rd (Firm)
WEATHER: overcast WIND: fresh bhd

3975
MALTON CLAIMING STKS (2-Y.O) (Class F) £3,449.00 (£964.00: £467.00)
7f Stalls: Centre GOING minus 0.56 sec per fur (F) 2-10 (2-13)

3856[4] **Napoleon's Return (62)***(66)*(Fav)*(AGFoster)* 2-7-11 (5) AWhelan(14) (a chsng ldrs: led ins fnl f: r.o)........— **1**
3937[2] Mister Joel **(55)***(71) (MWEasterby)* 2-8-10b TIves(11) (led & clr centre: hdd ins fnl f: kpt on same pce)........1¼ **2**
3856[7] Apartments Abroad **(53)***(64) (KMcAuliffe)* 2-8-3 JTate(22) (hdwy stands' side 2f out: styd on wl towards fin)........nk **3**
3851[6] Princess Pamgaddy **(49)***(53) (JBerry)* 2-7-6 (5) PFessey(15) (chsd ldrs: rdn ½-wy: one pce).....2 **4**
3760[12] Lucky Bea **(44)***(59) (MWEasterby)* 2-8-5bow1 ACulhane(7) (hdwy 3f out: styd on: nvr rchd ldrs)........nk **5**
3721[4] Harsh Times **(55)***(56) (MHEasterby)* 2-8-3b SMaloney(9) (chsd ldrs: rdn over 2f out: one pce).1 **6**
3721[11] Euro Express **(62)***(53) (MHEasterby)* 2-8-8b LDettori(1) (b.nr hind: racd far side: spd over 5f)........3½ **7**
3740[4] Meeting Point **(53)***(50) (MrsMReveley)* 2-8-9b KDarley(23) (effrt ½-wy: nvr trbld ldrs)............1¾ **8**
3642[7] Mels Baby (IRE) **(45)***(47) (JLEyre)* 2-8-6 RLappin(21) (in tch & wandered u.p 3f out: no imp)s.h **9**
3647[6] Castle Governor *(52) (PCHaslam)* 2-8-5 (7) CarolDavison(18) (in tch: outpcd ½-wy: styd on fnl 2f)........nk **10**
3895[4] Wrays (USA) **(66)***(37) (MJohnston)* 2-8-1 StephenDavies(24) (in tch: rdn ½-wy: eased whn btn appr fnl f)........1¾ **11**
3309[3] Veshca Lady (IRE) **(61)***(35) (EWeymes)* 2-8-0 (3) PMcCabe(4) (sme hdwy 3f out: nvr nr to chal)........1¾ **12**
3468[11] Hannahs Bay *(29) (MGMeagher)* 2-7-13 AMackay(26) (nvr trbld ldrs)........1 **13**
3744[5] Swing Mania (IRE) **(45)***(27) (SGNorton)* 2-7-10 (3) NVarley(28) (n.d)........¾ **14**
3744[7] Autofyr *(33) (JSWainwright)* 2-8-5 NConnorton(25) (n.d)........hd **15**
3744[10] Merlin's Honour **(43)***(22) (PCHaslam)* 2-7-4 (5) MBaird(16) (prom tl wknd fnl 3f)........½ **16**
3809[12] Kratz (IRE) **(47)***(27) (BSRothwell)* 2-8-2v MFenton(8) (n.d)........¾ **17**
3720[10] Margi Boo **(40)***(20) (GMMoore)* 2-7-10 (3) DarrenMoffatt(13) (n.d)........2 **18**
3767[9] Fair To Middling (IRE) **(52)***(14) (GLMoore)* 2-7-7 (5)ow3 PPMurphy(10) (n.d)........½ **19**
3648[8] Sizzling Serenade *(17) (SGNorton)* 2-8-1 NKennedy(5) (bit bkwd: n.d)........1½ **20**
3806[9] Sassetta (IRE) **(50)***(16) (NTinkler)* 2-8-1 KimTinkler(27) (a outpcd & bhd)........½ **21**
3850[8] Dancing Dot (IRE) **(52)***(13) (MissLAPerratt)* 2-8-0 (3)ow2 JStack(3) (swtg; nvr wnt pce)........1¼ **22**
3644[12] Fisiostar *(25) (MDods)* 2-9-0 JCarroll(20) (dwlt: a outpcd & bhd)........½ **23**
3670[15] What Jim Wants (IRE) *(17) (JJO'Neill)* 2-8-6 SDWilliams(6) (n.d)........hd **24**
3821[15] Dino's Mistral *(17) (FHLee)* 2-8-8 JWeaver(17) (dwlt: a bhd)........½ **25**
3738[11] Prime Connections *(13) (MPBielby)* 2-8-1b(5) CTeague(12) (n.d)........1¼ **26**
3824[17] Darerock **(46)***(6) (MDods)* 2-8-6 LCharnock(19) (a bhd)........3 **27**
Snow Domino (IRE) *(JMJefferson)* 2-8-8 SWhitworth(29) (cmpt: bkwd: s.i.s: a bhd)........8 **28**

13/2 NAPOLEON'S RETURN, **8/1** Veshca Lady (IRE), **9/1** Wrays (USA) (op 6/1), Mister Joel, **10/1** Meeting Point, **12/1** Apartments Abroad, Harsh Times (op 8/1), Euro Express (op 8/1), Fair To Middling (IRE), **14/1** Princess Pamgaddy, **16/1** Swing Mania (IRE), **25/1** Castle Governor, Mels Baby (IRE), Sizzling Serenade, Margi Boo, Merlin's Honour, Darerock, Sassetta (IRE), Lucky Bea, **33/1** Kratz (IRE), Dancing Dot (IRE), Dino's Mistral, Hannahs Bay, **50/1** Fisiostar, Autofyr, What Jim Wants (IRE), Snow Domino (IRE), **66/1** Prime Connections, CSF £65.80 TOTE £7.20: £2.40 £3.00 £29.70 (£43.40) Trio £54.00 OWNER Bonapartes Partnership (LAMBOURN) BRED T. K. Knox 28 Rn 1m 23.1 (1.10) SF: 26/31/24/13/19/16/13/10/7/12/-/-/-/-/-/-/-/-/-/-/-/-/-/-/-/-/-/-
Napoleon's Return clmd S.Moore £3,000

3976
E.B.F. PICKERING MAIDEN STKS (2-Y.O F) (Class D) £4,003.00 (£1,204.00: £582.00: £271.00) **6f** Stalls: Centre GOING minus 0.56 sec per fur (F) 2-40 (2-41)

3763[2] **Chalamont (IRE) (95)***(82+) (PWChapple-Hyam)* 2-8-11 KDarley(2) (b.off fore: mde all: qcknd 3f out: r.o wl)........— **1**

Hulm (IRE) *(58+) (HThomsonJones)* 2-8-11 RHills(6) (lengthy: chsd ldrs: rdn 3f out: r.o: no ch w wnr)....9 2
1176[8] Eccentric Dancer *(53) (MPBielby)* 2-8-8 (3) DRMcCabe(4) (outpcd & wandered ½-wy: r.o fnl f)....2 3
Lavanda *(53)*(Fav)*(DRLoder)* 2-8-11 LDettori(5) (leggy: unf: plld hrd: cl up tl rdn & hung lft 3f out: sn btn)....s.h 4
Frog *(51) (SirMarkPrescott)* 2-8-11 MFenton(3) (rangy: bit bkwd: sn outpcd & bhd: r.o fnl f)..¾ 5
3806[15] Chavin Point *(16) (MissLCSiddall)* 2-8-11 DeanMcKeown(7) (bit bkwd: sn outpcd & bhd)....13 6
Welcome Lu *(PSFelgate)* 2-8-11 AMackay(1) (cmpt: bkwd: s.s: a wl bhd)....14 7

11/10 Lavanda, **13/8** Hulm (IRE), **7/2** CHALAMONT (IRE) (5/2-4/1), **20/1** Frog, **66/1** Eccentric Dancer, **150/1** Welcome Lu, **300/1** Chavin Point, CSF £9.38 TOTE £3.30: £1.50 £1.60 (£3.80) OWNER Mr R. E. Sangster (MARLBOROUGH) BRED Swettenham Stud 7 Rn

1m 9.9 (0.60) SF: 38/14/9/9/7/-/-

3977

BARCLAYS BANK H'CAP (0-70) (3-Y.O+) (Class E) £3,964.00 (£1,192.00: £576.00: £268.00)
1m 1f Stalls: Low GOING minus 0.40 sec per fur (F) 3-10 (3-12)

3860[4] **Almuhtaram (59)***(73) (MissGayKelleway)* 3-8-7b(5) AWhelan(9) (in tch: hrd rdn to ld appr fnl f: styd on)....— 1
3810[4] Curtelace **(53)***(66)*(Fav)*(LadyHerries)* 5-8-11 KDarley(16) (hld up: smooth hdwy to chal appr fnl f: rdn & nt r.o)....½ 2
3082[11] Roman Reel (USA) **(67)***(77) (GLMoore)* 4-9-11 SWhitworth(2) (lw: led tl hdd appr fnl f: one pce)....1¾ 3
3531* Hawkish (USA) **(51)***(60)*(Fav)*(DMorley)* 6-8-9 MFenton(7) (outpcd 4f out: styd on appr fnl f: nrst fin)....¾ 4
3810[2] Essayeffsee **(57)***(63) (MrsMReveley)* 6-9-1 NConnorton(4) (chsd ldrs: rdn 3f out: one pce)..1¾ 5
3840[6] Master Ofthe House **(60)***(64) (MDHammond)* 9-8-11 (7) SCopp(1) (mid div: effrt over 3f out: styd on: no imp)....¾ 6
3703[12] Spanish Verdict **(70)***(72) (DenysSmith)* 8-9-9 (5) CTeague(11) (lw: cl up tl grad wknd fnl 3f) ..1½ 7
3593[13] Museum (IRE) **(70)***(70) (DNicholls)* 4-10-0 AlexGreaves(5) (lw: led tl hdd appr fnl f: one pce).¾ 8
3759[19] Intendant **(58)***(58) (JGFitzGerald)* 3-8-11 TIves(6) (chsd ldrs tl wknd fnl 3f)....s.h 9
3808[9] Bulsara **(57)***(56) (CWFairhurst)* 3-8-10 DeanMcKeown(13) (a chsng ldrs: outpcd 3f out: grad wknd)....½ 10
3802[9] Rood Music **(56)***(54) (MGMeagher)* 4-9-0 AMackay(10) (bhd & drvn along ½-wy: n.d)....1 11
3607[6] Pine Ridge Lad (IRE) **(55)***(52) (JLEyre)* 5-8-13 RLappin(15) (bhd: effrt on outside 3f out: no imp)....hd 12
3889[6] Lady Highfield **(54)***(51) (MJRyan)* 4-8-7 (5) MBaird(14) (a rr div)....1 13
3825* Bobanlyn (IRE) **(59)***(55) (DMorris)* 3-8-9 (3) PMcCabe(3) (nvr trbld ldrs)....d.h 13
3808[13] King Chestnut **(60)***(38) (MDods)* 4-9-4 JCarroll(8) (n.d)....10 15
3762[5] Gymcrak Hero (IRE) **(57)***(29) (GHolmes)* 3-8-10 LDettori(12) (b: b.hind: mid div: effrt over 3f out: btn over 2f out)....3½ 16

5/1 Hawkish (USA), Curtelace, **8/1** Gymcrak Hero (IRE), Essayeffsee, **9/1** Bobanlyn (IRE) (8/1-12/1), Bulsara, **10/1** Pine Ridge Lad (IRE), **12/1** King Chestnut, **14/1** Rood Music, ALMUHTARAM, Master Ofthe House, Spanish Verdict, **16/1** Lady Highfield, **25/1** Intendant, Roman Reel (USA), **50/1** Museum (IRE), CSF £83.30 CT £1,638.33 TOTE £18.40: £3.50 £1.60 £9.30 £1.60 (£19.60) Trio £367.00 OWNER Mr A. M. Al-Midani (WHITCOMBE) BRED A. M. Midani 16 Rn

1m 51.5 (2.50) SF: 40/38/49/32/35/36/44/42/25/23/26/24/23/22/10/-

WEIGHT FOR AGE 3yo-5lb

STEWARDS' ENQUIRY Whelan susp. 12-14 & 16-17/10/95 (improper use of whip).

3978

BEVERLEY H'CAP (0-80) (3-Y.O+) (Class D) £4,074.50 (£1,226.00: £593.00: £276.50)
1m 6f 19y Stalls: Low GOING minus 0.40 sec per fur (F) 3-40 (3-41)

3818[4] **Pretoria Dancer (65)***(79) (JHMGosden)* 3-8-4b LDettori(2) (set stdy pce: qcknd over 4f out: hdd appr fnl f: sn led again: r.o)....— 1
3723[7] Jadwal (USA) **(75)***(89) (DMorley)* 3-9-0 RHills(4) (trckd ldrs: swtchd ins over 2f out: hung rt appr fnl f: sn led: hdd & no ex ins fnl f)....nk 2
3799[3] High Patriarch (IRE) **(77)***(87)*(Fav)*(JLDunlop)* 3-9-2v SWhitworth(8) (trckd ldrs: hdwy & ev ch 3f out: hung lft: btn appr fnl f)....3 3
3849[4] Star Rage (IRE) **(80)***(86) (MJohnston)* 5-10-0 JWeaver(7) (trckd wnr: rdn over 3f out: btn whn n.m.r over 1f out)....4 4
3804[6] Moshaajir (USA) **(72)***(73) (CSmith)* 5-9-3 (3) JStack(9) (hld up: effrt 4f out: no imp)....4 5
3935[2] Highfield Fizz **(54)***(55) (CWFairhurst)* 3-7-0 (7) PDoe(1) (b.off hind: hld up: hdwy 4f out: outpcd fnl 2½f)....½ 6

1535⁹ Rolling the Bones (USA) **(48)***(41) (PSFelgate)* 6-7-10 ow3 AMackay(6) (hld up: outpcd fnl 4f) 4 7

LONG HANDICAP Highfield Fizz 7-5 Rolling the Bones (USA) 7-4

2/1 High Patriarch (IRE), **4/1** PRETORIA DANCER, **9/2** Star Rage (IRE), **11/2** Highfield Fizz, **7/1** Moshaajir (USA), **8/1** Jadwal (USA), **40/1** Rolling the Bones (USA), CSF £30.68 CT £72.43 TOTE £3.80: £2.50 £3.80 (£16.80) Trio £13.00 OWNER Sheikh Ahmed bin Saeed Al Maktoum (NEWMARKET) BRED Sheikh Mohammed bin Rashid al Maktoum 7 Rn 3m 7.6 (9.60) SF: 5/15/13/21/8/-/-

WEIGHT FOR AGE 3yo-9lb

3979

CASTLETON CONDITIONS STKS (3-Y.O+) (Class C) £5,420.80 (£1,884.80: £912.40: £382.00)
7f Stalls: Centre GOING minus 0.56 sec per fur (F) 4-10 (4-14)

3859* **Empty Quarter (85)***(104) (JHMGosden)* 3-9-1 LDettori(4) (chsd ldrs: rdn 3f out: chal 2f out: r.o to ld nr fin) ....— 1
3191⁹ Monaassib (IRE) **(100)***(105)*(Fav)*(EALDunlop)* 4-9-5 RHills(2) (b.hind: led: rdn & edgd lft fnl 2f: jst ct) ....hd 2
3854² Subzero **(95)***(84) (MRStoute)* 3-8-13 KDarley(3) (b: b.hind: a.p: hdwy over 2f out: btn over 1f out) 8 3
3728¹² Il Trastevere (FR) *(81) (JLDunlop)* 3-9-3 MRimmer(1) (lw: cl up tl wknd appr fnl f) 3 4

11/8 Monaassib (IRE), **2/1** EMPTY QUARTER, Subzero (11/8-9/4), **25/1** Il Trastevere (FR), CSF £5.06 TOTE £2.80 (£2.50) OWNER Abdullah Saeed Bul Hab (NEWMARKET) BRED R. H. Cowell 4 Rn 1m 21.0 (1.10 under best) (-1.00) SF: 63/67/43/40

WEIGHT FOR AGE 3yo-3lb

3980

SETTRINGTON H'CAP (0-70) (3-Y.O) (Class E) £3,803.25 (£1,146.00: £555.50: £260.25)
7f Stalls: Centre GOING minus 0.56 sec per fur (F) 4-40 (4-43)

3807W **Quilling (66)***(77) (MDods)* 3-9-3 JWeaver(5) (mde all: r.o wl fnl 2f) ....— 1
3855² Mister Westsound **(60)***(67) (MissLAPerratt)* 3-8-11b LDettori(2) (trckd ldrs: chal on bit 2f out: hrd rdn & nt run on) 1¾ 2
3661⁷ Cuban Reef **(44)***(50) (WJMusson)* 3-7-9 AMackay(17) (a in tch: styd on fnl 2f: nrst fin) ....nk 3
3750⁵ Sweet Mate **(44)***(50) (SRBowring)* 3-7-9b ClaireBalding(30) (hdwy ½-wy: kpt on fnl 2f: nrst fin) ....nk 4
3757⁶ Tomal **(49)***(47) (RIngram)* 3-8-0 ow1 JTate(18) (hdwy 3f out: kpt on fnl f: nrst fin) 3 5
3370¹⁰ Boost **(48)***(35) (CWThornton)* 3-7-6 (7)ow6 KSked(24) (prom: rdn ½-wy: styd on fnl f) 2½ 6
3667⁷ Freckles Kelly **(46)***(37) (MHEasterby)* 3-7-11 LCharnock(7) (a chsng ldrs: rdn & no imp fnl 3f) ....¾ 7
3830¹¹ Pc's Cruiser (IRE) **(51)***(39) (JLEyre)* 3-8-2bow1 RLappin(8) (chsd ldrs: rdn & one pce fnl 2½f) 1 8
3844² The Mestral **(44)***(33) (MJRyan)* 3-7-4 (5) MBaird(15) (cl up tl wknd fnl 2½f) ....hd 9
3704¹³ Hand of Straw (IRE) **(55)***(43) (JWWatts)* 3-8-6 NConnorton(19) (styd on fnl 3f: n.d) ....½ 10
2788⁶ Euro Sceptic (IRE) **(49)***(36) (MHEasterby)* 3-8-0b SMaloney(25) (in tch: no hdwy fnl 3f) ....nk 11
3515⁴ Prince Pellinore **(43)***(29) (CADwyer)* 3-7-5 (3)ow1 NVarley(11) (nvr rchd ldrs) ....s.h 12
3732¹⁷ Risky Romeo **(64)***(49) (GCBravery)* 3-9-1 MFenton(13) (in tch tl outpcd fnl 2½f) ....¾ 13
2331⁶ Master Charter **(59)***(43)*(Fav)*(MrsJRRamsden)* 3-8-10 KDarley(14) (lw: sn drvn along & bhd: hdwy over 2f out: wknd over 1f out) ....½ 14
3638¹² Mad About The Girl (IRE) **(47)***(27) (DJSCosgrove)* 3-7-12 ow1 StephenDavies(29) (s.s: sme late hdwy) 1¼ 15
3439⁶ Star of Gold **(64)***(44) (CREgerton)* 3-9-1 RHills(22) (sme hdwy ½-wy: n.d) ....½ 16
3823¹⁵ Gulf Shaadi **(68)***(48) (EJAlston)* 3-9-5 SWhitworth(4) (s.s: n.d) ....hd 17
3879³ Teejay'n'aitch (IRE) **(45)***(21) (JSGoldie)* 3-7-3 (7)ow2 JMcAuley(23) (sn drvn along: n.d) 1 18
3745⁴ Chalky Dancer **(48)***(19) (HJCollingridge)* 3-7-6 (7)ow6 JoHunnam(21) (chsd ldrs over 4f) ....nk 19
3810¹⁶ Bridge of Fire (FR) **(70)***(47) (DonEnricoIncisa)* 3-9-7 KimTinkler(10) (in tch to ½-wy) ....hd 20
3879⁶ Prime Property (IRE) **(42)***(18) (MWEasterby)* 3-7-2b(5) PFessey(3) (n.d) ....hd 21
1467⁵ Donna Fugata (IRE) **(42)***(18) (CBBBooth)* 3-7-7 NKennedy(16) (a in rr) ....hd 22
3879¹⁹ Question Ali **(54)***(27) (JBerry)* 3-8-5 JCarroll(20) (b.nr hind: prom 4f: sn wknd) 1½ 23
3657¹⁹ Sound Trick (USA) **(48)***(13) (GCBravery)* 3-7-8 (5)ow5 PPMurphy(12) (lw: a outpcd & bhd) 1 24
2502¹⁴ Carol Again **(44)** *(NBycroft)* 3-7-2 (7)ow2 BHalligan(1) (t.o fr ½-wy) 10 25
2959⁸ All Honour **(42)** *(DWChapman)* 3-7-0 (7) PDoe(6) (sn wl bhd) ....hd 26
591¹³ Semi Serious **(45)** *(DWChapman)* 3-7-7 (3) DarrenMoffatt(26) (wl bhd fr ½-wy: t.o) 25 27

LONG HANDICAP Prince Pellinore 7-4 Donna Fugata (IRE) 7-3 Prime Property (IRE) 7-3 Carol Again 7-0 All Honour 7-0

7/2 Master Charter, **8/1** Mister Westsound, **9/1** QUILLING, **10/1** Cuban Reef, The Mestral, Star of Gold, **12/1** Freckles Kelly, Risky Romeo, **14/1** Tomal, Sweet Mate, Euro Sceptic (IRE), **16/1** Mad About The Girl (IRE), Pc's Cruiser (IRE), Teejay'n'aitch (IRE), **20/1** Chalky Dancer, Prince Pellinore, Prime Property (IRE), **25/1** Boost, **33/1** Gulf Shaadi, Hand of Straw (IRE), Sound Trick (USA), **50/1** Semi Serious, Question Ali, **66/1** Donna Fugata (IRE), **100/1** Carol Again, All Honour, Bridge of Fire (FR), CSF £86.89 CT £718.41 TOTE £11.20: £2.00 £2.30 £3.70 £1.90 (£23.90) Trio £258.60 OWNER Mr A. G. Watson (DARLINGTON) BRED Hesmonds Stud Ltd 27 Rn

1m 21.7 (0.40 under best) (-0.30) SF: 57/47/30/30/27/15/17/19/13/23/16/9/29/23/7/24/28/1/-/27/-/-/7/-/-/-/-

3981 GUISBOROUGH MAIDEN STKS (3-Y.O) (Class D) £4,048.50 (£1,218.00: £589.00: £274.50)

6f Stalls: Centre GOING minus 0.56 sec per fur (F) 5-10 (5-13)

3640² **Intiaash (IRE) (70)***(78) (PTWalwyn)* 3-8-9 RHills(3) (trckd ldrs gng wl: effrt & hung lft 2f out: led over 1f out: hung lft: r.o) — 1
3829⁵ Sombreffe *(71) (DRLoder)* 3-8-9 LDettori(7) (lw: sn chsng ldrs: qcknd to ld 2f out: hdd over 1f out: btn whn hmpd ins fnl f) 2½ 2
3829⁷ Mistress Thames *(61) (JRFanshawe)* 3-8-6 (3) NVarley(9) (lw: hld up: hdwy ½-wy: styd on: no imp) 4 3
3000⁴ Cemaes Bay **(67)***(56) (JBerry)* 3-9-0 JCarroll(8) (a in tch: styd on: one pce fnl 2f) 3½ 4
3226³ Dictation (USA) **(82)***(48)*(Fav)*(RCharlton)* 3-9-0 KDarley(1) (chsd ldrs: effrt over 2f out: sn btn) 3 5
Margaretrose Anna **(65)***(37) (EJAlston)* 3-8-9 SDWilliams(10) (bit bkwd: w ldrs tl wknd 2f out) 2½ 6
3678³ Bajan Frontier (IRE) **(43)***(31) (FHLee)* 3-8-9 JWeaver(5) (b.hind: hld up & bhd: n.d) 2 7
It Is Now *(33) (SGollings)* 3-9-0 MFenton(6) (nvr wnt pce) 1¼ 8
3649¹³ Fred Said Right (IRE) *(30) (MJHeaton-Ellis)* 3-9-0 TIves(4) (led tl hdd 2f out: sn wknd) 1¼ 9

13/8 Dictation (USA), **2/1** Sombreffe, **7/2** INTIAASH (IRE), **13/2** Mistress Thames, **12/1** Cemaes Bay, **25/1** Margaretrose Anna, **33/1** Bajan Frontier (IRE), **50/1** It Is Now, **100/1** Fred Said Right (IRE), CSF £11.30 TOTE £4.60: £1.30 £1.10 £2.60 (£5.70) Trio £28.30 OWNER Mr Hamdan Al Maktoum (LAMBOURN) BRED Shadwell Estate Company Limited 9 Rn

1m 9.8 (0.50) SF: 38/31/21/16/8/-/-/-/-

T/Plpt: £777.20 (14.24 Tckts). T/Qdpt: £46.60 (1.1 Tckts). AA

3423-WARWICK (L-H)
Tuesday October 3rd (Good to soft)
WEATHER: cloudy WIND: fresh across

3982 TATTERSALLS MAIDEN AUCTION STKS (I) (2-Y.O) (Class E) £3,915.00 (£1,170.00: £560.00: £255.00)

6f Stalls: Low GOING minus 0.34 sec per fur (GF) 1-30 (1-33)

3628⁶ **Second Time Lucky (IRE) (76)***(73)*(Fav)*(LordHuntingdon)* 2-8-5 DHarrison(13) (chsd ldrs: 3rd st: c stands' side: rdn to ld ins fnl f: r.o) — 1
3832⁸ Sorbie Tower (IRE) *(72) (MissGayKelleway)* 2-8-9 RCochrane(6) (chsd ldrs: led over 4f out: hdd & unable qckn ins fnl f) 2 2
3901¹⁰ Veesey **(64)***(61) (JohnBerry)* 2-8-0 TWilliams(12) (chsd ldrs: 4th st: rdn over 2f out: no ex fnl f) ½ 3
3644⁴ Yuppy Girl (IRE) **(56)***(58) (CaptJWilson)* 2-7-11 (7)ow7 FLynch(5) (s.i.s: hdwy over 2f out: r.o ins fnl f: nrst fin) s.h 4
3784⁷ Angus McCoatup (IRE) **(75)***(62) (BAMcMahon)* 2-8-5 GCarter(7) (chsd ldrs: outpcd & 5th st: n.d after) 1½ 5
3337⁹ Beldray Park (IRE) *(61) (MrsALMKing)* 2-8-4 AGarth(11) (led over 1f: 2nd st: c stands' side ent st: wknd over 1f out) s.h 6
3763⁸ Commin' Up *(54) (JWHills)* 2-7-8 (5) MHenry(3) (bit bkwd: s.i.s: styd on appr fnl f: nvr nrr) ¾ 7
Rocket Grounds (IRE) *(50) (JJQuinn)* 2-7-12 DaleGibson(2) (lt-f: unf: bkwd: s.i.s: nvr nrr) 1 8
Quinntessa *(49) (BPalling)* 2-8-0 ow3 TSprake(9) (small: bkwd: prom: plld hrd: 6th st: wknd over 1f out) nk 9
3765¹¹ Meg's Memory (IRE) **(60)***(40) (JohnBerry)* 2-7-12b GBardwell(1) (outpcd fr ½-wy) 3½ 10
Commons Wheel (IRE) *(46) (DJSCosgrove)* 2-8-5 CRutter(10) (small: cmpt: bkwd: s.i.s: n.d) ½ 11
3427⁶ Lavender Della (IRE) *(39) (MJFetherston-Godley)* 2-7-12 FNorton(14) (prom 3f) s.h 12
3628¹⁶ Simply Miss Chief (IRE) *(36) (DWPArbuthnot)* 2-7-12 JLowe(15) (hld up: rdn ½-wy: grad wknd) 1¼ 13
3857⁶ Beas River (IRE) *(45) (WRMuir)* 2-8-9 WCarson(4) (lw: s.i.s: a in rr) ½ 14

2/1 SECOND TIME LUCKY (IRE) (6/4-9/4), **6/1** Sorbie Tower (IRE) (5/1-8/1), Commin' Up (op 4/1), **8/1** Beas River (IRE) (5/1-10/1), **10/1** Yuppy Girl (IRE), **12/1** Angus McCoatup (IRE), **16/1** Beldray Park (IRE), **20/1** Meg's Memory (IRE), Rocket Grounds (IRE), **25/1** Quinntessa, Veesey, **33/1** Lavender Della (IRE), **40/1** Simply Miss Chief (IRE), Commons Wheel (IRE), CSF £13.79 TOTE £3.10: £1.70 £2.80 £3.70 (£9.50) Trio £32.70 OWNER Mr G. W. Mooratoff (WEST ILSLEY) BRED Lodge Park Stud 14 Rn 1m 13.9 (1.90) SF: 35/34/23/20/24/23/16/12/11/2/8/1/-/7

3983

E.B.F. MAIDEN STKS (2-Y.O F) (Class D) £4,370.00 (£1,310.00: £630.00: £290.00) **7f** Stalls: Low GOING minus 0.34 sec per fur (GF) 2-00 (2-03)

Sil Sila (IRE) *(78) (BSmart)* 2-8-8 (3) SSanders(6) (w'like: bit bkwd: chsd ldrs: 4th st: led ins fnl f: r.o wl)...— **1**
3539[3] Hilaala (USA) *(75) (PTWalwyn)* 2-8-11 WCarson(11) (led 6f out: rdn & hdd ins fnl f: no ex)...1¼ **2**
West Humble *(74) (LadyHerries)* 2-8-11 GCarter(14) (w'like: hld up: hdwy & 7th st: styd on ins fnl f)...½ **3**
3620[3] Sweetness Herself *(68) (MJRyan)* 2-8-11 AClark(12) (hld up in tch: rdn 2f out: nt pce to chal)...2½ **4**
Medieval Lady *(67) (LadyHerries)* 2-8-11 RCochrane(1) (w'like: scope: bkwd: hld up: hdwy & nt clr run fnl 2f: nt plcd to chal)...¾ **5**
3532[2] Fijon (IRE) *(66)*(Fav)*(BWHills)* 2-8-11 MHills(13) (swtg: hld up: hdwy u.p over 1f out: nt rch ldrs)...nk **6**
3758[4] Flahuil *(60) (RHannon)* 2-8-6 (5) DaneO'Neill(7) (led 1f: 3rd st: wknd fnl f)...2½ **7**
Caribbean Dancer *(55) (MRStoute)* 2-8-11 PRobinson(10) (lt-f: unf: b.hind: prom: 5th st: wknd over 1f out)...2½ **8**
3633[W] Beverly Hills *(53) (JWHills)* 2-8-6b(5) MHenry(2) (scope: chsd ldrs: 6th st: rdn & wknd over 1f out)...¾ **9**
3352[3] Basood (USA) *(53) (EALDunlop)* 2-8-11 PatEddery(15) (hld up: hdwy over 2f out: wknd fnl f)...hd **10**
Kitty Kitty Cancan *(51) (LadyHerries)* 2-8-11 PaulEddery(9) (lt-f: sn pushed along: hdwy over 3f out: wknd & eased over 1f out)...½ **11**
Sweet Times *(49) (PFICole)* 2-8-11 TQuinn(17) (w'like: leggy: chsd ldrs: 2nd st: wknd wl over 1f out)...1 **12**
3283[5] Janies Girl (IRE) *(48) (KRBurke)* 2-8-11 TSprake(16) (swtg: n.d)...½ **13**
Uplift *(34) (SirMarkPrescott)* 2-8-11 GDuffield(4) (leggy: a in rr)...6 **14**
Dance Across (IRE) *(27) (HCandy)* 2-8-11 WNewnes(18) (w'like: scope: bkwd: bhd fr ½-wy).3 **15**
Northern Sky *(24) (RDickin)* 2-8-11 JLowe(5) (small: lt-f: unf: s.s: a in rr)...1½ **16**
3765[16] Carwyn's Choice *(24) (PCClarke)* 2-8-11 NAdams(3) (s.s: a in rr)...hd **17**

5/2 Fijon (IRE) (op 5/1), **9/2** Sweetness Herself, **7/1** Hilaala (USA), Basood (USA), **8/1** Sweet Times (4/1-10/1), **14/1** Caribbean Dancer (op 6/1), **16/1** Flahuil, Uplift, Beverly Hills, **20/1** Dance Across (IRE), Kitty Kitty Cancan, West Humble, **25/1** Janies Girl (IRE), Medieval Lady, **50/1** SIL SILA (IRE), Northern Sky, Carwyn's Choice, CSF £361.49 TOTE £88.80: £15.10 £1.80 £15.50 (£227.40) Trio not won; £304.20 to York 04/10/95 OWNER Mr Alvarez Cervera (LAMBOURN) BRED L A C 17 Rn 1m 26.9 (2.70) SF: 35/32/31/25/24/23/17/12/10/10/8/6/5/-/-/-/-

3984

MOP FAIR LIMITED STKS (0-70) (3-Y.O+) (Class E) £3,582.00 (£1,071.00: £513.00: £234.00) **1m** Stalls: Low GOING minus 0.34 sec per fur (GF) 2-30 (2-34)

3241[11] **Northern Celadon (IRE) (68)***(75) (MJHeaton-Ellis)* 4-9-2 GDuffield(19) (mde all: rdn out)....— **1**
3960[3] Linger **(66)***(69) (LordHuntingdon)* 3-8-4 (5) MHenry(4) (hld up: hdwy & 6th st: chsd wnr over 1f out: r.o)...1¾ **2**
3771[8] Tonys Gift **(69)***(65) (RHannon)* 3-8-4 (5) DaneO'Neill(17) (hld up: hdwy over 2f out: nt pce to chal)...2 **3**
3519* Master Millfield (IRE) **(69)***(69) (RJHodges)* 3-9-0 MRoberts(15) (a.p: 4th st: rdn 2f out: r.o one pce)...nk **4**
3319[10] Kintwyn **(41)***(65) (CCElsey)* 5-9-2 MHills(20) (lw: chsd ldrs: 5th & rdn st: no hdwy)...¾ **5**
3762* Wild Palm **(69)***(66) (WAO'Gorman)* 3-9-0 EmmaO'Gorman(7) (hld up: hdwy over 2f out: no imp fnl f)...½ **6**
2979[9] Robsera (IRE) **(67)***(64) (GLewis)* 4-9-2 PaulEddery(9) (chsd ldrs: 3rd & rdn st: eased whn btn fnl f)...nk **7**
3645[7] Sandmoor Denim **(65)***(64) (SRBowring)* 8-9-2 GHind(18) (b: chsd wnr: rdn 3f out: 7th & wkng st)...hd **8**
3704[2] Bold Angel **(69)***(64) (MHEasterby)* 8-9-4 MBirch(1) (lw: bhd: styd on u.p appr fnl f: nrst fin)...¾ **9**
3829[4] Ducking **(69)***(55) (JRFanshawe)* 3-8-7 DHarrison(3) (hld up: hdwy u.p over 2f out: nt rch ldrs)...1¼ **10**

3747[10] Ruddigore **(42)***(59) (KRBurke)* 3-8-12 RCochrane(11) (hld up: effrt over 1f out: n.d) ....hd **11**
3674[8] Real Madrid **(34)***(56) (GPEnright)* 4-9-2v NAdams(6) (n.d) 1½ **12**
3757[19] Greatest **(68)***(57) (RAkehurst)* 4-9-1 (3) SSanders(2) (chsd ldrs: 8th & rdn st: sn wknd) ....½ **13**
2449[3] Incha **(68)***(47) (HThomsonJones)* 3-8-7 GCarter(16) (prom: rdn over 3f out: grad wknd) 1¾ **14**
3732[6] Misty Silks **(69)***(39)*(Fav)*(MJRyan)* 5-8-11 AClark(10) (lw: hld up in tch: rdn 3f out: eased whn btn) 4 **15**
3667[29] Live Project (IRE) **(70)***(44) (MJohnston)* 3-8-12 TWilliams(5) (swtg: a in rr) ....hd **16**
3621[9] Feinte **(64)***(29) (WJarvis)* 3-8-7b PatEddery(12) (chsd ldrs: 2nd st: wknd qckly) 5 **17**
3621[12] Hunters' Heaven (USA) **(49)***(26) (JMackie)* 4-9-2 JWilliams(8) (a in rr) 4 **18**
Proud Brigadier (IRE) **(64)***(19) (PBurgoyne)* 7-9-2 TQuinn(14) (b: hld up: effrt over 3f out: grad wknd) 3½ **19**
3871* Chief of Staff **(63)** *(JPearce)* 6-9-6 GBardwell(13) (in rr whn b.b.v & fell 5f out) .... **F**

100/30 Misty Silks, **4/1** Wild Palm, **6/1** Ducking, **10/1** Tonys Gift, Bold Angel (8/1-12/1), Master Millfield (IRE), **12/1** Incha (op 8/1), NORTHERN CELADON (IRE) (10/1-16/1), **14/1** Greatest, Robsera (IRE) (10/1-16/1), **16/1** Sandmoor Denim, Chief of Staff, Linger, **20/1** Live Project (IRE), Feinte, Proud Brigadier (IRE), Kintwyn, **33/1** Hunters' Heaven (USA), Ruddigore, **50/1** Real Madrid, CSF £208.64 TOTE £17.90: £4.70 £3.80 £4.70 (£316.90) Trio not won; £513.70 to York 04/10/95 OWNER The Over The Bridge Partnership (WROUGHTON) BRED A. F. O'Callaghan 20 Rn

1m 38.4 (1.40) SF: 57/47/43/47/47/44/46/46/46/33/37/38/39/25/21/22/7/8/1/-

WEIGHT FOR AGE 3yo-4lb

OFFICIAL EXPLANATION **Misty Silks: was reportedly never travelling throughout the race and would have preferred softer ground.**

3985 SKETCHLEY TEXTILE SERVICES NURSERY H'CAP (0-85) (2-Y.O) (Class D) £4,402.50 (£1,320.00: £635.00: £292.50)

1m Stalls: High GOING minus 0.34 sec per fur (GF) 3-00 (3-03)

3894[3] **Deadline Time (IRE) (70)***(77) (MHTompkins)* 2-8-9v PRobinson(13) (lw: hld up: hdwy & 6th st: led ins fnl f: sn clr) ....— **1**
3713[2] Maid For Baileys (IRE) **(76)***(77) (MJohnston)* 2-9-1 TWilliams(17) (a.p: 2nd st: led over 2f out: hdd & outpcd ins fnl f) 3 **2**
3721* Stately **(58)***(56)*(Fav)*(SirMarkPrescott)* 2-7-11 JLowe(15) (b: hld up in tch: chal over 1f out: unable qckn) 1¾ **3**
3290[8] Makaskamina **(57)***(52) (PMitchell)* 2-7-3 (7)ow1 CAdamson(20) (hld up: hdwy over 1f out: r.o) ...1 **4**
3639[7] Balpare **(63)***(55) (NACallaghan)* 2-8-2 ow1 DHarrison(8) (hld up: hdwy over 2f out: nvr able to chal) 1½ **5**
3870[2] Zdenka **(59)***(51) (MBlanshard)* 2-7-5 (7) MartinDwyer(14) (hld up: hdwy 3f out: rdn over 1f out: no ex) ....hd **6**
3775[6] Silver Welcome **(65)***(54) (MHEasterby)* 2-8-1 (3)ow3 SSanders(19) (led over 5f: no ex) ....nk **7**
3784[10] Maiteamia **(55)***(45) (SRBowring)* 2-7-8 NCarlisle(18) (chsd ldrs: 5th st: wknd over 1f out) ....¾ **8**
3620[11] General Macarthur **(65)***(53) (JLDunlop)* 2-8-4 MRoberts(16) (hld up: nvr plcd to chal) 1¼ **9**
3821[4] Pride of Kashmir **(60)***(48) (PWHarris)* 2-7-13 FNorton(7) (hld up: nvr plcd to chal) ....hd **10**
3701[12] State Approval **(60)***(42) (APJarvis)* 2-7-10 (3) DWright(12) (swtg: disp ld: 2nd st: sn rdn & wknd) 3 **11**
3721[5] Jimjareer (IRE) **(65)***(44) (CaptJWilson)* 2-8-4 GCarter(3) (lw: mid div: drvn along ½-wy: nvr trbld ldrs) 1¼ **12**
3633[5] Eccola **(75)***(49) (IABalding)* 2-9-0 MHills(11) (n.d) 2½ **13**
3758[2] Ailesbury Hill (USA) **(78)***(51) (PWChapple-Hyam)* 2-8-12 (5) RHavlin(9) (chsd ldrs: 3rd & ev ch st: sn rdn & wknd) ....nk **14**
3780[7] Sticks Mckenzie **(60)***(33) (BWHills)* 2-7-8 (5) MHenry(2) (mid div: outpcd 4f out: sn bhd) ....s.h **15**
3570[6] Arch Angel (IRE) **(56)***(28) (DJSffrenchDavis)* 2-7-9 NAdams(1) (prom tl 7th & wkng st) ....¾ **16**
3780* Vanishing Point **(82)***(38) (GLewis)* 2-9-7 PatEddery(6) (chsd ldrs over 4f) 8 **17**
3765[6] Rawi **(70)***(18) (CJBenstead)* 2-8-9 WCarson(10) (lw: prom to ½-wy) 4 **18**
3760[17] Be My Bird **(60)** *(BJMeehan)* 2-7-13b GBardwell(4) (hld up: rdn 4f out: sn wknd) 8 **19**

5/2 Stately (op 4/1), **9/2** General Macarthur, **6/1** Vanishing Point (op 4/1), **8/1** Zdenka, **10/1** Maid For Baileys (IRE) (6/1-12/1), DEADLINE TIME (IRE) (7/1-12/1), Ailesbury Hill (USA) (7/1-12/1), **12/1** Silver Welcome, **16/1** Eccola, Sticks Mckenzie, Jimjareer (IRE), Rawi, **20/1** Be My Bird, Pride of Kashmir, **25/1** State Approval, Arch Angel (IRE), Makaskamina, Balpare, **33/1** Maiteamia, CSF £120.96 CT £317.45 TOTE £21.40: £2.90 £2.30 £2.30 £27.90 (£96.60) Trio £88.80 OWNER Mr P. D. Savill (NEWMARKET) BRED Johnny Kelly 19 Rn

1m 39.0 (2.00) SF: 45/45/24/20/23/19/22/13/21/16/10/12/17/19/1/-/6/-/-

OFFICIAL EXPLANATION **General Macarthur: got outpaced early on and lost his action and it was later on in the straight, when he was balanced, that he was able to run on. It was added that he may benefit from a more galloping track and from softer ground.**

3986 RACING SCHOOLS' APPRENTICE H'CAP (0-70) (3-Y.O+) (Class F)
£3,206.00 (£891.00: £428.00)
2m 20y Stalls: High GOING minus 0.34 sec per fur (GF) 3-30 (3-30)

3569⁵ **Coleridge (39)***(55) (JJSheehan)* 7-8-0b CWebb(14) (hld up: hdwy 10f out: led 4f out: drifted rt appr fnl f: rdn & r.o wl) — 1
1929¹⁰ Soojama (IRE) **(41)***(52) (RMFlower)* 5-8-2 ow2 DGriffiths(11) (hld up: hdwy ½-wy: 3rd st: str chal bel dist: unable qckn) 3½ 2
3936* Ballymac Girl **(51)***(60)*(Fav)*(JMBradley)* 7-8-12 5x SDrowne(13) (b: chsd ldrs: wnt far side & led 7f out: hdd 4f out: 2nd st: one pce fr bel dist) 3½ 3
2569⁶ Head Turner **(41)***(49) (CPWildman)* 7-8-2 AEddery(18) (swtg: hld up in tch: effrt & 5th st: wknd over 1f out) 1½ 4
3724⁶ Deceit the Second **(43)***(45) (GLewis)* 3-7-3b(4) RMullen(6) (styd on fnl 3f: nvr nrr) 6 5
3849¹⁰ Bellara **(51)***(51) (NMBabbage)* 3-7-8 (7) RFfrench(9) (swtg: mid div: rdn 7f out: wknd fnl 3f) 1¼ 6
2768⁷ Well Arranged (IRE) **(67)***(67) (RAkehurst)* 4-10-0 SSanders(7) (chsd ldrs: 4th st: wknd wl over 1f out) s.h 7
3676⁵ Much Too High **(48)***(46) (TJNaughton)* 3-7-12 GMitchell(19) (plld hrd: prom tl 6th & wknd st: sddle slipped) 2 8
1349⁷ Springtime Affair **(40)***(38) (MrsNMacauley)* 4-8-1 IonaWands(17) (bit bkwd: hld up: hdwy ½-wy: wknd over 3f out) hd 9
2592² Flashman **(41)***(37) (BJLlewellyn)* 5-8-2 JWilkinson(1) (n.d) 2 10
3849⁵ Romalito **(37)***(32) (MBlanshard)* 5-7-12 RWaterfield(3) (nvr trbld ldrs) 1 11
3627¹⁸ Charmed Life **(37)***(25) (MrsALMKing)* 6-7-8b(4)ow5 MSemple(5) (b: nvr nr to chal) 2 12
3686a³ Al Corniche (IRE) **(53)***(35) (KOCunningham-Brown)* 3-7-13 (4)ow8 FLynch(2) (m.n.s) 3½ 13
Patroclus **(36)***(23) (JMackie)* 10-7-11 DDenby(20) (bit bkwd: prom over 12f) 3 14
Decided (CAN) **(40)***(23) (RLee)* 12-8-1 KimberleyHart(4) (b: bkwd: w ldrs early: prom tl wknd over 5f out) 3½ 15
3876⁸ Sails Legend **(43)***(25) (MrsMELong)* 4-7-11 (7) TField(10) (chsd ldrs 10f) 1¼ 16
3774¹¹ Champagne Gold **(47)***(18) (JCMcConnochie)* 8-8-8 RHavlin(15) (hld up: hdwy ½-wy: wknd over 4f out: t.o) 11 17
3884¹⁵ Assembly Dancer **(39)***(5) (DLWilliams)* 8-7-10 (4)ow4 RStudholme(8) (led 3f: wknd over 4f out: t.o) ¾ 18
3669¹¹ Noble Ballerina (USA) **(50)***(13) (APJarvis)* 3-7-7 (7)ow7 RBrisland(16) (led after 3f: sn clr: hdd & wknd 7f out: t.o) d.h 18
Fadi **(56)***(7) (FJordan)* 4-9-3 RPainter(12) (bkwd: hdwy 10f out: wknd over 5f out: t.o) 20 20
LONG HANDICAP Noble Ballerina (USA) 7-4 Charmed Life 7-5

2/1 Ballymac Girl, **6/1** Well Arranged (IRE), **8/1** Flashman, **12/1** Romalito, Head Turner, Soojama (IRE), Much Too High (op 8/1), Deceit the Second, **14/1** COLERIDGE, Springtime Affair, Bellara, Patroclus, **16/1** Decided (CAN), Al Corniche (IRE), **25/1** Fadi, **33/1** Charmed Life, Sails Legend, Assembly Dancer, Noble Ballerina (USA), Champagne Gold, CSF £182.54 CT £450.18 TOTE £26.50: £4.10 £2.50 £1.90 £2.20 (£81.80) Trio £72.80 OWNER Mr P. J. Sheehan (FINDON) BRED W. and R. Barnett Ltd 20 Rn 3m 32.0 (6.00) SF: 29/26/34/23/8/14/41/9/12/11/6/-/-/-/-/-/-/-/-/-
WEIGHT FOR AGE 3yo-11lb

3987 GERALD EVE CHARTERED SURVEYORS CLAIMING H'CAP (0-60) (3-Y.O+) (Class F) £3,353.00 (£933.00: £449.00)
1m 2f 169y Stalls: High GOING minus 0.34 sec per fur (GF) 4-00 (4-00)

3759² **Rival Bid (USA) (57)***(72) (MrsNMacauley)* 7-9-12 PatEddery(19) (hld up: hdwy 2f out: str run u.p to ld cl home) — 1
3735⁸ Golden Torque **(50)***(65)*(Fav)*(RBastiman)* 8-9-0 (5) HBastiman(4) (s.i.s: hdwy 4f out: 5th st: led bel dist tl wl ins fnl f) nk 2
3889⁸ Spitfire Bridge (IRE) **(50)***(60) (MMcCormack)* 3-8-12 RCochrane(8) (a.p: 3rd st: rdn & one pce fnl f) 3 3
3635⁴ Born to Please (IRE) **(50)***(59) (PWHarris)* 3-8-12 GHind(9) (led over 2f: 2nd st: sn rdn: one pce appr fnl f) ½ 4
3743⁸ Pine Essence (USA) **(52)***(60) (JLEyre)* 4-9-7 TWilliams(5) (hld up: hdwy & 6th st: hrd rdn appr fnl f: kpt on) ¾ 5
3825³ Mhemeanles **(42)***(48) (CaptJWilson)* 5-8-11 GCarter(6) (b.hind: hld up: hdwy over 2f out: nvr able chal) 1¼ 6
3659¹³ Just Flamenco **(52)***(56) (MJRyan)* 4-9-7 MHills(12) (chsd ldrs: 4th st: ev ch 2f out: rdn & one pce fnl f) 1½ 7
3685⁵ Total Rach (IRE) **(51)***(53) (RIngram)* 3-8-10 (3) SDrowne(17) (hdwy ent st: nvr nr to chal) 1¾ 8
3238⁶ No Speeches (IRE) **(51)***(50) (CACyzer)* 4-9-6 DBiggs(7) (hld up: hdwy 5f out: 7th st: sn rdn & wknd) 1½ 9

3679[9] Caerle Lad (IRE) **(59)***(55) (GHarwood)* 4-10-0 AClark(3) (swtg: prom: rdn 4f out: wknd wl over 1f out)....2 **10**
1539[5] Jemima Puddleduck **(50)***(46) (DWPArbuthnot)* 4-9-5 TQuinn(13) (b.hind: led 8f out tl hdd & wknd bel dist: eased whn btn)....s.h **11**
Johns Joy **(44)***(37) (JJBridger)* 10-8-13 JWilliams(11) (b: bkwd: nvr trbld ldrs)....2 **12**
3852[8] Diamond Crown (IRE) **(47)***(40) (MartynWane)* 4-9-2 MTebbutt(15) (a in rr)....nk **13**
1776[6] Silks and Studs **(50)***(40) (JWhite)* 3-8-12b FNorton(16) (bit bkwd: m.n.s)....2 **14**
Lord Glenvara (IRE) **(44)***(24) (TPMcGovern)* 7-8-13b PaulEddery(18) (led far side over 7f out tl wknd 3f out: t.o)....7 **15**
1858[13] Preston Guild (IRE) **(46)***(23) (AStreeter)* 5-8-10 (5) LNewton(20) (jnd ldrs ½-wy: wknd over 3f out: t.o)....1¾ **16**
*3734** Jalmaid **(50)***(27) (BAMcMahon)* 3-8-12 WCarson(14) (prom tl wknd over 3f out: t.o)....hd **17**
3679[10] Woodlands Energy **(45)***(20) (PAPritchard)* 4-9-0 NAdams(2) (s.s: a bhd: t.o)....1¼ **18**
Irrepressible (IRE) **(42)***(15) (KBishop)* 4-8-11 RPerham(10) (bkwd: a bhd: t.o)....1 **19**
3658[7] Buckley Boys **(48)** *(ABailey)* 4-9-0 (3) DWright(1) (chsd ldrs 6f: wknd & p.u ent st).... **P**

3/1 Golden Torque (op 7/1), **7/2** RIVAL BID (USA), **6/1** Just Flamenco (op 3/1), **8/1** Jemima Puddleduck, **10/1** Jalmaid, No Speeches (IRE) (op 5/1), **12/1** Diamond Crown (IRE), Pine Essence (USA), Born to Please (IRE) (op 8/1), Preston Guild (IRE), **14/1** Spitfire Bridge (IRE), Mhemeanles (10/1-16/1), Buckley Boys, Total Rach (IRE), **16/1** Johns Joy, Caerle Lad (IRE), **20/1** Silks and Studs, **33/1** Woodlands Energy, Irrepressible (IRE), Lord Glenvara (IRE), CSF £19.12 CT £151.30 TOTE £4.90: £2.20 £2.40 £7.40 £2.10 (£35.30) Trio £311.30; £43.85 to York 04/10/95 OWNER Mr Ralph Peters (MELTON MOWBRAY) BRED Marvin L. Warner Jnr. 20 Rn

2m 18.7 (5.20) SF: 43/36/24/23/31/19/27/17/21/26/17/8/11/4/-/-/-/-/-/-

WEIGHT FOR AGE 3yo-7lb

STEWARDS' ENQUIRY Bastiman susp. 12 & 16/10/95 (excessive & improper use of whip).

3988 TATTERSALLS MAIDEN AUCTION STKS (II) (2-Y.O) (Class E)
£3,915.00 (£1,170.00: £560.00: £255.00)
6f Stalls: High GOING minus 0.34 sec per fur (GF) 4-30 (4-33)

3626[6] **Lay The Blame** *(73) (WJarvis)* 2-8-10 TQuinn(5) (in tch: rdn & 5th st: led over 1f out: drvn clr)....— **1**
3626[4] Maristax *(60) (PJMakin)* 2-8-2 MRoberts(6) (a.p: 3rd st: led 2f out: sn hdd: one pce fnl f)....1¾ **2**
3775[5] Scenicris (IRE) **(65)***(55) (RHollinshead)* 2-7-11 NCarlisle(7) (hdwy & nt clr run 2f out: r.o strly fnl f: nvr nrr)....s.h **3**
3733[6] Brandonville *(63) (IABalding)* 2-8-7 MHills(12) (sn pushed along: effrt & 6th st: styd on appr fnl f)....1 **4**
Minoletti *(60) (EALDunlop)* 2-8-6 PaulEddery(9) (w'like: bkwd: s.i.s: hdwy fnl 2f: nrst fin)....½ **5**
3816[5] Miss Pickpocket (IRE) *(48)*(Fav)*(PAKelleway)* 2-7-13 FNorton(11) (hdwy u.p 2f out: nt rch ldrs)....2 **6**
2633[4] Nkapen Rocks (SPA) *(52) (CaptJWilson)* 2-8-4 GCarter(13) (bit bkwd: chsd ldrs: 2nd st: ev ch over 1f out: unable qckn)....nk **7**
2523[8] Members Welcome (IRE) **(59)***(50) (PGMurphy)* 2-7-11 (7)ow2 RWaterfield(1) (chsd ldrs: 4th st: wknd over 1f out)....s.h **8**
Lady Bankes (IRE) *(45) (WGMTurner)* 2-7-5 (7) CAdamson(3) (small: s.i.s: a in rr)....nk **9**
3441[5] Ice Pick (IRE) **(80)***(43)*(Fav)*(RHannon)* 2-8-9 PatEddery(8) (prom: rdn 4f out: grad lost pl)....5 **10**
3628[20] Prosarch (IRE) *(31) (RFJohnsonHoughton)* 2-8-2 DHarrison(2) (led 4f: sn rdn & wknd)....1¾ **11**
3891[10] Impetuous Lady (USA) *(20) (WJMusson)* 2-8-1 TWilliams(10) (outpcd)....4 **12**
3763[10] The Jolly Barmaid (IRE) *(5) (PCalver)* 2-8-0 DaleGibson(14) (sn outpcd: t.o)....5 **13**
1336[2] Natatarl (IRE) *(2) (MCPipe)* 2-7-12 DBiggs(15) (bit bkwd: prom tl wknd ent st: t.o)....½ **14**
3856[12] Further Future (IRE) *(JohnBerry)* 2-7-9 (7) RMullen(4) (bkwd: s.i.s: a bhd & outpcd: t.o)....4 **15**

3/1 Ice Pick (IRE), Miss Pickpocket (IRE), **7/2** Maristax, **9/2** Brandonville, **10/1** LAY THE BLAME (op 6/1), **11/1** Scenicris (IRE), **12/1** Minoletti (op 8/1), **14/1** Natatarl (IRE) (10/1-16/1), **20/1** Nkapen Rocks (SPA), The Jolly Barmaid (IRE), **25/1** Lady Bankes (IRE), Impetuous Lady (USA), **33/1** Members Welcome (IRE), Prosarch (IRE), **50/1** Further Future (IRE), CSF £50.51 TOTE £17.60: £4.10 £2.40 £2.10 (£39.80) Trio £217.20; £183.59 to York 04/10/95 OWNER Mr Anthony Foster (NEWMARKET) BRED Wheelersland Stud 15 Rn

1m 14.0 (2.00) SF: 38/25/20/28/25/13/17/15/10/8/-/-/-/-/-

3989 E.B.F. BRINKLOW MAIDEN STKS (2-Y.O C & G) (Class D) £4,305.00 (£1,290.00: £620.00: £285.00) **7f** Stalls: High GOING minus 0.34 sec per fur (GF) 5-00 (5-03)

3663[4] **Ali-Royal (IRE)** *(87+)*(Fav)*(HRACecil)* 2-8-11 PatEddery(10) (swtg: led over 3f: 2nd st: led over 2f out: sn clr)....— **1**
3784[4] Forest Robin **(79)***(78) (RFJohnsonHoughton)* 2-8-11 MHills(3) (chsd wnr: led over 3f out tl over 2f out: sn outpcd)....4 **2**

3494[5] Danish Circus (IRE) *(74) (MJHeaton-Ellis)* 2-8-11 AClark(4) (chsd ldrs: 3rd st: one pce appr fnl f) 1½ **3**
Fourdaned (IRE) *(72) (PWHarris)* 2-8-11 GHind(11) (unf: hld up: styd on appr fnl f: nvr nrr)....1 **4**
Veni Vidi Vici (IRE) *(68) (MJHeaton-Ellis)* 2-8-8 (3) SSanders(16) (lt-f: unf: hdwy fnl 2f: nrst fin)....1¾ **5**
Infamous (USA) *(68) (PFICole)* 2-8-11 TQuinn(6) (lt-f: unf: s.i.s: bhd: rdn ent st: styd on fnl f)....hd **6**
3089[10] Hal Hoo Yaroom *(68) (MajorWRHern)* 2-8-11 WCarson(8) (chsd ldrs: rdn over 3f out: sn btn)....s.h **7**
3861[3] Al's Alibi *(67) (WRMuir)* 2-8-11 CRutter(7) (mid div: drvn along ½-wy: 6th st: wknd wl over 1f out)....nk **8**
Circus Star *(65) (SirMarkPrescott)* 2-8-11 GDuffield(13) (w'like: leggy: bit bkwd: hld up: nvr plcd to chal)....¾ **9**
3398[5] Montecristo *(65) (RGuest)* 2-8-11 MRoberts(14) (bit bkwd: bhd: rdn over 2f out: no imp)....hd **10**
3733[17] Ballpoint *(62) (RHannon)* 2-8-6 (5) DaneO'Neill(12) (a in rr)....1¼ **11**
3626[14] Skram *(56) (RDickin)* 2-8-11 PRobinson(17) (w ldrs tl 4th & wkng st)....3 **12**
3888[9] Hank-a-chief *(53) (MMcCormack)* 2-8-11 RCochrane(5) (bhd fr ½-wy)....1 **13**
3536[6] Nardus *(51) (MRStoute)* 2-8-11 KBradshaw(9) (prom over 3f)....1 **14**
Blue Suede Hoofs *(46) (BJMeehan)* 2-8-11 DHarrison(2) (small: w'like: n.d)....2 **15**
3821[16] Storm Wind (IRE) *(28) (KRBurke)* 2-8-11 GCarter(18) (sn outpcd: t.o)....8 **16**
Come On In *(RDickin)* 2-8-11 JLowe(1) (small: bkwd: s.s: a bhd: t.o)....15 **17**

8/15 ALI-ROYAL (IRE), **6/1** Hal Hoo Yaroom, **11/1** Danish Circus (IRE) (8/1-12/1), Forest Robin, **14/1** Montecristo, Infamous (USA) (6/1-16/1), **16/1** Fourdaned (IRE), Nardus, **25/1** Ballpoint, Circus Star, Veni Vidi Vici (IRE), Blue Suede Hoofs, **33/1** Al's Alibi, **50/1** Hank-a-chief, Skram, Storm Wind (IRE), Come On In, CSF £10.68 TOTE £1.60: £1.10 £2.40 £2.10 (£6.20) Trio £49.00 OWNER Greenbay Stables Ltd (NEWMARKET) BRED C. H. WACKER III 17 Rn
1m 26.0 (1.80) SF: 45/36/32/30/26/26/26/25/23/23/20/14/11/9/4/-/-

T/Jkpt: Not won; £35,343.91 to York 4/10/95. T/Plpt: £947.20 (13.74 Tckts). T/Qdpt: £60.60 (0.7 Tckts); £24.60 to York 4/10/95. CR

3456-YORK (L-H)
Wednesday October 4th (Good, Good to firm patches)
WEATHER: overcast WIND: str half bhd

3990
LEOPARDSTOWN NURSERY H'CAP (2-Y.O) (Class C) £6,472.00 (£1,936.00: £928.00: £424.00)
6f Stalls: High GOING minus 0.32 sec per fur (GF) 2-00 (2-01)

3612[4] **Dashing Blue (86)***(91) (IABalding)* 2-8-13 LDettori(3) (lw: b.nr fore: trckd ldrs gng wl: led appr fnl f: r.o)....— **1**
3749[2] Nilgiri Hills (IRE) **(77)***(79)*(Fav)*(JLDunlop)* 2-8-4 MRoberts(13) (drvn along thrght: hdwy ½-wy: edgd lft: kpt on fnl f)....1¼ **2**
3394[7] Pharmacy **(80)***(72) (JWWatts)* 2-8-7 NConnorton(2) (lw: led after 1½f tl hdd appr fnl f: no ex)....3½ **3**
3375[9] No Monkey Nuts **(83)***(73) (JBerry)* 2-8-10 JCarroll(1) (led 1½f: cl up: outpcd over 2f out: styd on fnl f)....¾ **4**
3824[5] Vax New Way **(68)***(58) (JLSpearing)* 2-7-4 (5) PFessey(6) (swtg: chsd ldrs: outpcd over 2f out: kpt on fnl f)....s.h **5**
3901[4] Standown **(71)***(61) (JBerry)* 2-7-12 LCharnock(14) (spd stands' side: drvn along thrght: kpt on towards fin)....hd **6**
3699[8] Arajaan (USA) **(94)***(83) (BHanbury)* 2-9-4 (3) JStack(5) (sn pushed along: hdwy 2f out: nvr able to chal)....nk **7**
3714[7] Ramsey Hope **(80)***(67) (CWFairhurst)* 2-8-7 NKennedy(9) (chsd ldrs over 3f)....1 **8**
3803[2] U-No-Harry (IRE) **(69)***(50) (RHollinshead)* 2-7-5 (5) MHenry(4) (sn pushed along: sme hdwy ½-wy: wknd fnl f)....2 **9**
3858[5] Oriel Lad **(79)***(58) (PDEvans)* 2-8-6b GHind(10) (a outpcd)....¾ **10**
3773[3] Baileys First (IRE) **(76)***(52) (MJohnston)* 2-8-3 TWilliams(7) (nvr wnt pce)....1¼ **11**
3648* First Maite **(76)***(49) (SRBowring)* 2-8-3b MFenton(12) (sn drvn along & bhd)....1 **12**
3809[3] Cumbrian Maestro **(70)***(37) (MHEasterby)* 2-7-11b JLowe(8) (sn outpcd & bhd)....2½ **13**
3612[8] Munakeb (FR) **(80)***(31) (RWArmstrong)* 2-8-7 WCarson(11) (lw: sn outpcd & bhd)....6 **14**

7/4 Nilgiri Hills (IRE), **13/2** DASHING BLUE, **12/1** Standown, No Monkey Nuts, Vax New Way, U-No-Harry (IRE), Munakeb (FR), First Maite, Cumbrian Maestro, **14/1** Baileys First (IRE), Arajaan (USA), Pharmacy, Oriel Lad, **16/1** Ramsey Hope, CSF £19.37 CT £159.33 TOTE £5.80: £2.10 £1.20 £3.40 (£3.70) Trio £22.40 OWNER Mrs Duncan Allen (KINGSCLERE) BRED Mrs I. A. Balding 14 Rn
1m 10.56 (0.96) SF: 56/44/37/38/23/26/48/32/15/23/17/14/2/-

3991

MICKLEGATE RATED STKS H'CAP (0-100) (3-Y.O+) (Class B)
£8,154.50 (£3,015.50: £1,445.25: £588.75)
7f 202y Stalls: Low GOING minus 0.32 sec per fur (GF) 2-30 (2-30)

3924[8] **Moving Arrow (90)***(100) (MissSEHall)* 4-9-1 JWeaver(2) (mde all: rdn & r.o wl fnl 3f) ....— 1
3813[10] Akil (IRE) **(90)***(98)*(Fav)*(RWArmstrong)* 3-8-11 WCarson(4) (lw: hld up: hdwy over 3f out: rdn fnl 2f: styd on: nrst fin)..........1 2
3813[16] Verzen (IRE) **(96)***(103) (DRLoder)* 3-9-3v LDettori(5) (chsd wnr: effrt over 2f out: one pce).....nk 3
3770* Confronter **(82)***(84) (SDow)* 6-8-7 MRoberts(6) (lw: hld up & bhd: effrt over 3f out: nrst fin)...2½ 4
3943[3] Cool Edge (IRE) **(82)***(84) (MHTompkins)* 4-8-7v PRobinson(7) (lw: hld up & bhd: effrt over 3f out: nvr rchd ldrs)..........nk 5
3924[11] New Century (USA) **(88)***(85) (DNicholls)* 3-8-9 AlexGreaves(3) (prom: effrt 3f out: wknd over 1f out)..........2½ 6
3755[2] Pay Homage **(84)***(73) (IABalding)* 7-8-4 (5) DGriffiths(1) (cl up tl wknd 3f out)..........4 7
622[2] Blomberg (IRE) **(100)***(77) (JRFanshawe)* 3-9-7 DHarrison(8) (in tch tl rdn & wknd fnl 3f) 6 8
LONG HANDICAP Confronter 8-5 Cool Edge (IRE) 8-4

3/1 Akil (IRE), **7/2** Verzen (IRE), **4/1** Cool Edge (IRE), **6/1** Confronter, Pay Homage, **7/1** Blomberg (IRE), **8/1** MOVING ARROW, **25/1** New Century (USA), CSF £32.46 CT £93.76 TOTE £9.10: £2.10 £1.40 £1.80 (£23.00) OWNER Mr G. W. Westgarth (MIDDLEHAM) BRED W. G. Barker 8 Rn
1m 35.12 (-0.88) SF: 82/76/81/66/66/63/55/55
WEIGHT FOR AGE 3yo-4lb

3992

NEWINGTON HOTEL YORK RACEGOERS H'CAP (0-80) (3-Y.O+) (Class D) £7,044.00 (£2,112.00: £1,016.00: £468.00)
5f Stalls: High GOING minus 0.32 sec per fur (GF) 3-00 (3-02)

3905[2] **Royal Dome (IRE) (67)***(76) (MartynWane)* 3-9-1 MRoberts(18) (prom: hdwy to ld appr fnl f: hung lft: r.o)..........— 1
3748[3] Chadwell Hall **(56)***(65) (SRBowring)* 4-8-0b(5) CTeague(13) (chsd ldrs: ev ch 1f out: edgd lft: r.o) ....hd 2
3878[2] Here Comes a Star **(70)***(76) (JMCarr)* 7-9-5 ACulhane(16) (hdwy over 1f out: r.o towards fin)..........¾ 3
3878[5] Silk Cottage **(62)***(68) (RMWhitaker)* 3-8-10b MHills(20) (lw: chsd ldrs: hdwy over 1f out: kpt on) ....hd 4
3822[9] Ansellman **(74)***(78) (JBerry)* 5-9-2 (7) PRoberts(3) (chsd ldrs: outpcd ½-wy: kpt on fnl f) ....½ 5
3748[8] Insider Trader **(73)***(77) (RGuest)* 4-9-8b GDuffield(15) (a chsng ldrs: hmpd 2f out: kpt on wl fnl f) ....s.h 6
3783[3] Jucea **(63)***(66) (JLSpearing)* 6-8-12 JWeaver(9) (led & sn clr: hdd over 1f out: sn btn)...........½ 7
3783[6] Ninety-Five **(63)***(62) (JGFitzGerald)* 3-8-6 (5) DaneO'Neill(8) (chsd ldrs tl wknd appr fnl f)......1¼ 8
3822[15] Polly Particular **(76)***(73) (TDBarron)* 3-9-10 KDarley(14) (prom: rdn ½-wy: one pce) ....½ 9
3878[13] Rich Glow **(67)***(63) (NBycroft)* 4-8-9 (7) MartinDwyer(10) (in tch: drvn along ½-wy: no imp) .....nk 10
3878[12] Tenor **(59)***(54) (DNicholls)* 4-8-8 AlexGreaves(19) (a outpcd & bhd) ....nk 11
3919[5] Hickory Blue **(68)***(62) (MrsNMacauley)* 5-9-0b(3) SDrowne(22) (racd stands' side: outpcd fr ½-wy) ....½ 12
3830[9] Miss Aragon **(55)***(47) (MissLCSiddall)* 7-8-4 NCarlisle(4) (bhd tl sme late hdwy) ....½ 13
3822[16] Beau Venture (USA) **(75)***(67) (FHLee)* 7-9-10 RLappin(21) (nvr trbld ldrs)..........hd 14
1847[2] Stuffed **(55)***(46) (MWEasterby)* 3-8-3 WCarson(7) (lw: in tch: drvn along ½-wy: no imp) ....hd 15
3667[5] Just Bob **(67)***(52) (SEKettlewell)* 6-8-13 (3) JStack(11) (s.i.s: n.d)..........2 16
3905[15] Blue Sioux **(58)***(40) (JWharton)* 3-8-6b PRobinson(6) (nvr wnt pce)..........1 17
3783[10] Robellion **(69)***(45) (DWPArbuthnot)* 4-9-4 RHughes(2) (n.d) 1¾ 18
3905[4] Allyana (IRE) **(70)***(36)*(Fav)*(IABalding)* 3-9-4 LDettori(5) (outpcd & bhd ½-wy: eased fnl 2f) 3 19
3878[6] Craigie Boy **(54)***(15) (NBycroft)* 5-8-3b SMaloney(17) (s.i.s: a bhd)..........1¾ 20
3777* Macfarlane **(72)***(30) (MJFetherston-Godley)* 7-9-7 PatEddery(23) (b: racd stands' side: n.d)..........1 21
3919[20] Swan At Whalley **(66)** *(MartynWane)* 3-9-0v MTebbutt(12) (in tch: rdn ½-wy: sn btn) 14 22

13/2 Allyana (IRE), **8/1** ROYAL DOME (IRE), **9/1** Macfarlane, Stuffed, Here Comes a Star, **12/1** Jucea, Chadwell Hall, **14/1** Just Bob, **16/1** Ansellman, Polly Particular, Silk Cottage, Robellion, **20/1** Insider Trader, Craigie Boy, Hickory Blue, Tenor, **25/1** Ninety-Five, Rich Glow, **33/1** Beau Venture (USA), Blue Sioux, Miss Aragon, Swan At Whalley, CSF £97.90 CT £819.44 TOTE £7.40: £2.10 £2.60 £2.30 £6.30 (£41.20) Trio £120.40 OWNER Mr G. W. Jones (RICHMOND) BRED Michael F. Fogarty 22 Rn
57.91 secs (0.91) SF: 55/45/56/47/58/57/46/41/52/43/34/42/27/47/25/32/19/25/15/-/10/-
WEIGHT FOR AGE 3yo-1lb
STEWARDS' ENQUIRY Obj. to Royal Dome (IRE) by Teague overruled.

3993 BOOKER CHEF'S LARDER H'CAP (0-85) (3-Y.O+) (Class D) £6,264.00 (£1,872.00 £896.00: £408.00) **1m 2f 85y** Stalls: Low GOING minus 0.32 sec (GF) 3-35 (3-35)

3703[5] **Sheer Danzig (IRE) (80)***(93) (RWArmstrong)* 3-9-4 LDettori(5) (lw: a.p: led 1½f out: r.o wl) .— 1
3729[12] Sadler's Walk **(78)***(85) (GWragg)* 4-9-8 MHills(13) (lw: chsd ldrs: styd on u.p fnl 3f: nvr able to chal)....4 2
2159[5] Mbulwa **(51)***(54) (RAFahey)* 9-7-9 ow2 LCharnock(11) (chsd ldrs: hrd rdn to ld wl over 1f out: sn hdd & one pce)....1½ 3
3778* Sweet Mignonette **(74)***(75)*(Fav)*(MrsMReveley)* 7-9-4 KDarley(6) (hld up: effrt 4f out: nrst fin)....2½ 4
3781[3] Silently **(79)***(80) (IABalding)* 3-9-3 PatEddery(4) (lw: mid div: hdwy 4f out: rdn & wandered 2f out: nvr able to chal)....s.h 5
1862[5] Percy Braithwaite (IRE) **(83)***(81) (MJohnston)* 3-9-7b JWeaver(2) (led & sn clr: hdd wl over 1f out: sn btn)....2 6
Magic Junction (USA) **(77)***(74) (LordHuntingdon)* 4-9-7 DHarrison(12) (mid div: effrt 4f out: no imp)....½ 7
3963[6] Wentbridge Lad (IRE) **(64)***(61) (PDEvans)* 5-8-8v GHind(9) (bhd: effrt 4f out: nvr rchd ldrs)...s.h 8
1558[7] Clouded Elegance **(78)***(69) (LadyHerries)* 5-9-8 JReid(8) (nvr nr ldrs)....4 9
Cumbrian Challenge (IRE) **(84)***(74) (MHEasterby)* 6-10-0 MBirch(10) (s.i.s: sme hdwy fnl 3f: nrst fin)....nk 10
721[3] Surrey Dancer **(70)***(54) (MrsMReveley)* 7-8-7 (7) SCopp(1) (s.i.s: a bhd)....4 11
1801[6] Unprejudice **(65)***(44) (MDHammond)* 4-8-9 RHughes(7) (a bhd)....3 12
3781[7] Indonesian (IRE) **(76)***(49) (MBell)* 3-9-0v MFenton(3) (chsd ldr to st: sn wknd)....4 13

LONG HANDICAP Mbulwa 7-2

100/30 Sweet Mignonette, **7/2** SHEER DANZIG (IRE), **7/1** Sadler's Walk, **15/2** Silently, **8/1** Clouded Elegance, **10/1** Percy Braithwaite (IRE), Wentbridge Lad (IRE), **12/1** Magic Junction (USA), Indonesian (IRE), **14/1** Surrey Dancer, **20/1** Cumbrian Challenge (IRE), **25/1** Unprejudice, **33/1** Mbulwa, CSF £29.38 CT £674.06 TOTE £4.00: £1.70 £2.40 £10.60 (£11.40) Trio £699.30 OWNER Mr R. J. Arculli (NEWMARKET) BRED Mrs Max Morris 13 Rn

2m 8.45 (0.95) SF: 68/66/35/56/55/56/55/42/50/55/35/25/24

WEIGHT FOR AGE 3yo-6lb

3994 MONKGATE MEDIAN AUCTION MAIDEN STKS (2-Y.O) (Class E) £6,004.00 (£1,792.00: £856.00: £388.00) **7f 202y** Stalls: Low GOING minus 0.32 sec per fur (GF) 4-05 (4-10)

3821[3] **Prince of My Heart (77)***(77)*(Fav)*(BWHills)* 2-9-0 PatEddery(10) (trckd ldrs: rdn to ld over 1f out: r.o)....— 1
3888[2] Iamus *(74) (PTWalwyn)* 2-9-0 JReid(14) (sn cl up: led wl over 1f out: sn hdd & no ex)....1¾ 2
Northern Soul (USA) *(61+) (MJohnston)* 2-9-0 JWeaver(3) (w'like: str: bit bkwd: chsd ldrs: outpcd 3f out: kpt on fnl f)....6 3
3436[5] Spring Campaign (IRE) *(60) (MCPipe)* 2-9-0 MRoberts(2) (led tl wl over 1f out: sn btn)....¾ 4
Society Magic (USA) *(53+) (IABalding)* 2-9-0 LDettori(6) (wl grwn: lw: trckd ldrs: effrt 3f out: wknd wl over 1f out)....3½ 5
3868[10] Energy Man *(52) (JRFanshawe)* 2-9-0 DHarrison(9) (in tch: hdwy 4f out: no imp fnl 2f)....nk 6
2422[3] Los Alamos *(41) (CWThornton)* 2-8-9 DeanMcKeown(13) (rdn ½-wy: nvr bttr than mid div)....3 7
3663[16] Compass Pointer *(38) (JMPEustace)* 2-9-0 MTebbutt(1) (prom to ½-wy)....4 8
2681[8] Oversman **(81)***(36) (JGFitzGerald)* 2-9-0 RHughes(11) (bhd & hmpd appr st: n.d)....1 9
3644[13] Cerise (IRE) **(48)***(30) (CWCElsey)* 2-8-4 (5) PFessey(5) (nvr nr ldrs)....¾ 10
Bright Eclipse (USA) *(34) (JWHills)* 2-9-0 MHills(8) (a rr div)....nk 11
3779[10] By A Whisker *(30) (DWPArbuthnot)* 2-9-0 SWhitworth(4) (in tch: rdn ent st: sn wknd)....2 12
3806[4] Nutcracker *(20) (CBBBooth)* 2-8-9 MBirch(7) (hung bdly rt appr st: a bhd)....2½ 13
3644[6] Killmessan-Town (IRE) *(JMCarr)* 2-9-0 SMorris(12) (Withdrawn not under Starter's orders: ref to ent stalls).... W

7/4 PRINCE OF MY HEART (9/4-6/4), **11/4** Iamus (2/1-3/1), **17/2** Society Magic (USA), **9/1** Energy Man, Bright Eclipse (USA), **12/1** Spring Campaign (IRE), **14/1** Northern Soul (USA), Los Alamos, **20/1** Oversman, Nutcracker, **25/1** By A Whisker, **33/1** Compass Pointer, Cerise (IRE), Killmessan-Town (IRE), CSF £7.75 TOTE £2.40: £1.30 £1.30 £3.90 (£1.90) Trio £29.40 OWNER Mr G. J. Hicks (LAMBOURN) BRED George Joseph Hicks 13 Rn

1m 37.43 (1.08 under 2y best) (1.43) SF: 57/54/41/40/33/32/21/18/16/10/14/10/-/-

3995 GILLYGATE CONDITIONS STKS (3-Y.O+) (Class C) £7,337.00 (£2,342.00: £1,121.00) **1m 5f 194y** Stalls: High GOING minus 0.32 sec per fur (GF) 4-35 (4-35)

3804[2] **Bahamian Sunshine (USA)** *(95) (DRLoder)* 4-9-4 LDettori(1) (hld up: smooth hdwy to ld 1½f out: shkn up & r.o)....— 1

1764* Corradini *(90)*(Fav)*(HRACecil)* 3-8-9 PatEddery(2) (lw: chsd ldrs: rdn over 4f out: chal 3f out: slt ld wl over 1f out: sn hdd & one pce)....4 **2**
3826[3] Tethys (USA) **(79)***(79) (JLEyre)* 4-9-3 JWeaver(3) (led tl wl over 1f out: sn btn)....9 **3**

5/6 Corradini, **6/4** BAHAMIAN SUNSHINE (USA), **6/1** Tethys (USA), CSF £2.97 TOTE £2.00 (£1.10) OWNER Lucayan Stud (NEWMARKET) 3 Rn 2m 57.58 (3.98) SF: 54/40/38
WEIGHT FOR AGE 3yo-9lb

3996 E.B.F. SPURRIERGATE MAIDEN STKS (2-Y.O) (Class D) £5,744.00 (£1,712.00: £816.00: £368.00)
6f Stalls: High GOING minus 0.32 sec per fur (GF) 5-05 (5-06)

3650[3] **Victoria Regia (IRE) (94)***(82+)*(Fav)*(RCharlton)* 2-8-9 PatEddery(4) (b.off hind: lw: mde all: r.o wl fnl 2f)....— **1**
3337[8] Sihafi (USA) *(74+) (EALDunlop)* 2-9-0 WCarson(1) (hld up: smooth hdwy over 2f out: no ch w wnr: eased)....5 **2**
Lachesis *(50) (RHollinshead)* 2-8-9 KDarley(6) (cmpt: chsd ldrs: no imp fnl 2f)....7 **3**
3839[2] Ocean Stream (IRE) **(75)***(51) (JLEyre)* 2-9-0b LDettori(3) (lw: chsd ldrs: rdn 2½f out: sn btn) 1½ **4**
3671[3] Gulf of Siam *(46) (MissSEHall)* 2-9-0 JWeaver(5) (unruly s: cl up tl outpcd fnl 2f)....1¾ **5**
Manoy *(28) (JHetherton)* 2-9-0 NKennedy(2) (w'like: bit bkwd: dwlt: a outpcd & bhd)....7 **6**

1/2 VICTORIA REGIA (IRE), **5/1** Sihafi (USA), Ocean Stream (IRE), **10/1** Gulf of Siam, **20/1** Lachesis, **33/1** Manoy, CSF £3.82 TOTE £1.50: £1.20 £1.80 (£2.30) OWNER Dr Carlos Stelling (BECKHAMPTON) BRED Cambremont Ltd Partnership 6 Rn 1m 10.98 (1.38) SF: 46/38/14/15/10/-

T/Jkpt: £37,265.40 (0.59 Tckts); £21, 519.47 to York 5/10/95. T/Plpt: £27.50 (925.87 Tckts). T/Qdpt: £8.00 (22.1 Tckts). AA

3990-YORK (L-H)
Thursday October 5th (Good to firm, good patches)
WEATHER: fine & cloudy WIND: fresh half bhd

3997 BADGER HILL CONDITIONS STKS (2-Y.O F) (Class C) £6,472.00 (£1,768.00)
6f 214y Stalls: High GOING minus 0.27 sec per fur (GF) 2-00 (2-01)

3763* **Thracian** *(103+)*(Fav)*(JLDunlop)* 2-8-12 WCarson(2) (lw: trckd ldr gng wl: led on bit over 1f out: pushed clr ins fnl f: easily)....— **1**
3828[2] Dimakya (USA) **(75)***(89) (DRLoder)* 2-8-9 LDettori(1) (led: drvn along 3f out: hdd over 1f out: eased whn no ch w wnr)....5 **2**

4/6 THRACIAN, **5/4** Dimakya (USA), TOTE £1.40 OWNER Hesmonds Stud (ARUNDEL) BRED Hesmonds Stud Ltd 2 Rn 1m 25.92 (4.42) SF: 20/6

3998 E.B.F. SANCTON MAIDEN STKS (2-Y.O) (Class D) £5,536.00 (£1,648.00: £784.00: £352.00)
5f Stalls: High GOING minus 0.27 sec per fur (GF) 2-30 (2-31)

3892[2] **Music Gold (IRE)** *(87)*(Fav)*(WAO'Gorman)* 2-9-0 EmmaO'Gorman(2) (lw: chsd ldrs: effrt 2f out: led jst ins fnl f: edgd rt: r.o)....— **1**
Songsheet *(79) (RGuest)* 2-8-9 GDuffield(1) (lengthy: scope: w ldrs: led over 1f out tl jst ins fnl f: nt qckn ins fnl f)....1 **2**
Magic Mail *(76) (JMPEustace)* 2-9-0 RCochrane(3) (gd sort: trckd ldrs: led ½-wy tl over 1f out: kpt on same pce fnl f)....2½ **3**
3832[5] Eagle Canyon (IRE) *(68) (BHanbury)* 2-8-11 (3) JStack(4) (chsd ldrs: rdn & outpcd 2f out: edgd lft & no imp)....2½ **4**
3891[9] Governors Dream *(MrsNMacauley)* 2-8-6 (3) SDrowne(5) (swtg: led to ½-wy: rdn & wkng whn edgd rt, hit rails & fell wl over 1f out).... **F**

5/4 MUSIC GOLD (IRE) (op 8/11), **9/4** Songsheet (op 4/1), **6/1** Eagle Canyon (IRE) (op 4/1), **7/1** Magic Mail, **33/1** Governors Dream, CSF £3.95 TOTE £1.90: £1.30 £1.10 (£1.70) OWNER Mr N. S. Yong (NEWMARKET) BRED Denis Noonan 5 Rn 59.23 secs (2.23) SF: 35/27/24/16/-

3999 ALLIED DUNBAR RATED STKS H'CAP (0-105) (3-Y.O+) (Class B) £7,951.50 (£2,938.50: £1,406.75: £571.25)
6f 214y Stalls: High GOING minus 0.27 sec per fur (GF) 3-00 (3-01)

3188[12] **Hi Nod (93)***(102) (MJCamacho)* 5-9-0 LCharnock(6) (lw: trckd ldrs: effrt over 2f out: styd on u.p to ld ins fnl f: r.o wl)....— **1**

3813[3] Western Fame (USA) **(88)***(96)*(Fav)*(JLDunlop)* 3-8-6 PatEddery(7) (sn chsng ldrs: hrd rdn over 2f out: ev ch ins fnl f: unable qckn)....½ **2**
3924* Cyrano's Lad (IRE) **(92)***(94) (CADwyer)* 6-8-13 3x CDwyer(3) (lw: trckd ldrs: led 2f out tl ins fnl f: kpt on same pce)....2½ **3**
3768[6] Emirates Express **(86)***(87) (JWHills)* 3-7-13 (5) MHenry(8) (chsd ldrs: led ½-wy to 2f out: nt qckn appr fnl f)....nk **4**
3334[4] Everglades (IRE) **(100)***(92) (RCharlton)* 7-9-7 PaulEddery(4) (hld up: effrt over 2f out: nvr nr to chal)....4 **5**
Orange Place (IRE) **(90)***(36) (TJNaughton)* 4-8-11 MHills(2) (led to ½-wy: sn lost pl & bhd)...20 **6**
LONG HANDICAP Emirates Express 8-1

6/5 Western Fame (USA) (4/5-5/4), **7/2** Cyrano's Lad (IRE), **4/1** HI NOD, **11/2** Everglades (IRE), **16/1** Emirates Express, **20/1** Orange Place (IRE), CSF £9.05 CT £15.58 TOTE £5.60: £1.80 £1.30 (£3.60) OWNER Mr Brian Nordan (MALTON) BRED B. Nordan 6 Rn
1m 23.3 (1.80) SF: 53/44/45/35/43/-
WEIGHT FOR AGE 3yo-3lb

4000 INTERNATIONAL FACTORS APPRENTICE H'CAP (0-70) (3-Y.O+) (Class E) £6,888.00 (£2,064.00: £992.00: £456.00)
1m 3f 195y Stalls: Low GOING minus 0.27 sec per fur (GF) 3-30 (3-31)

3852* **Ayunli (59)***(70)*(Fav)*(SCWilliams)* 4-9-3 5x ADaly(13) (lw: a chsng ldrs: styd on to ld over 1f out: all out)....— **1**
3863[10] Harry Browne (IRE) **(69)***(80) (MrsJRRamsden)* 3-9-0 (5) SBuckley(2) (s.i.s: hld up & bhd: hdwy over 3f out: ev ch ins fnl f: r.o)....s.h **2**
3646* Ashover **(59)***(65) (TDBarron)* 5-9-0 (3) KimberleyHart(22) (lw: sn chsng ldrs: led over 3f out tl over 1f out: kpt on same pce)....3½ **3**
3970[5] Achilles Heel **(42)***(45) (CNAllen)* 4-7-11 (3)ow3 RWaterfield(1) (lw: in tch: effrt over 3f out: hung lft: kpt on appr fnl f)....s.h **4**
3723[3] Hasta la Vista **(48)***(53) (MWEasterby)* 5-8-6b MartinDwyer(9) (lw: chsd ldrs: chal over 3f out: kpt on one pce appr fnl f)....1 **5**
3852[3] Stormless **(38)***(37) (PMonteith)* 4-7-7 (3)ow3 DDenby(14) (sn chsng ldrs: wandered & kpt on same pce fnl 3f)....2 **6**
3871[7] Sparkling Roberta **(37)***(36) (MDIUsher)* 4-7-9 CAdamson(3) (mid div whn hmpd on ins 6f out: hdwy 3f out: nvr nr ldrs)....2½ **7**
*3951** Sommersby (IRE) **(56)***(48) (MrsNMacauley)* 4-9-0 5x RHavlin(18) (b: rr div: hdwy u.p over 2f out: hung lft: n.d)....5 **8**
312[6] Eurotwist **(43)***(33) (SEKettlewell)* 6-7-10 (5) PDoe(11) (in tch: sn pushed along: outpcd fnl 3f)....1¼ **9**
3970[8] Fair and Fancy (FR) **(40)***(29) (DNicholls)* 4-7-7 (5) JoHunnam(16) (chsd ldrs tl lost pl 3f out)..1¼ **10**
3852[15] Kinoko **(38)***(26) (KWHogg)* 7-7-5 (5) JBramhill(8) (bhd: sme hdwy over 3f out: n.d)....½ **11**
3799[10] Mr Christie **(49)***(36) (MissLCSiddall)* 3-7-13 PFessey(6) (mid div: effrt over 3f out: n.d)....½ **12**
1506[12] Farfields Prince **(48)***(32) (DNicholls)* 3-7-7 (5) KSked(10) (chsd ldrs tl wknd 3f out)....2½ **13**
3825[5] Level Edge **(48)***(17) (MDHammond)* 4-7-13 (7)ow11 DHayden(7) (led tl over 3f out: wknd 2f out)....3 **14**
2845[3] Rock The Barney (IRE) **(56)***(29) (PBurgoyne)* 6-9-0 DGibbs(12) (rr div: effrt over 3f out: sn btn)....5 **15**
3843[6] Fresh Look (IRE) **(48)***(21) (RCSpicer)* 3-7-7 (5) RMullen(4) (a in rr)....s.h **16**
3862* Aviator's Dream **(37)***(8) (JPearce)* 5-7-4 (5) 5x BHalligan(19) (s.i.s: racd wd: hdwy to chse ldrs ½-wy: wknd over 2f out)....1½ **17**
3723[8] Sunday News'n'echo (USA) **(55)***(26) (WStorey)* 4-8-10 (3) JWilkinson(15) (in tch: outpcd & drvn along ½-wy: sme hdwy 3f out: sn wknd)....s.h **18**
1767[6] Strictly Personal (USA) **(53)***(24) (MABarnes)* 5-8-11 GMitchell(5) (unruly s: sn bhd)....nk **19**
3801[13] Welsh Mill (IRE) **(70)***(39) (MrsMReveley)* 6-10-0 GParkin(17) (hdwy ½-wy: wknd 3f out)....1½ **20**
3756[12] Zalament **(54)***(19) (APJarvis)* 3-8-1v(3) GFaulkner(20) (racd wd: sn chsng ldrs: wknd over 3f out)....2½ **21**
LONG HANDICAP Stormless 7-6

5/1 AYUNLI, **6/1** Sommersby (IRE), **9/1** Hasta la Vista, **10/1** Rock The Barney (IRE), Harry Browne (IRE), Aviator's Dream, Ashover, **11/1** Achilles Heel, **16/1** Eurotwist, Sunday News'n'echo (USA), Stormless, **20/1** Fresh Look (IRE), Mr Christie, Zalament, Welsh Mill (IRE), **25/1** Farfields Prince, Kinoko, Sparkling Roberta, Strictly Personal (USA), Fair and Fancy (FR), **33/1** Level Edge, CSF £57.23 CT £473.65 TOTE £6.10: £1.80 £2.40 £2.00 £2.70 (£41.90) Trio £84.90 OWNER Mr I. A. Southcott (NEWMARKET) BRED I. A. Southcott 21 Rn
2m 30.99 (3.99) SF: 52/54/47/27/35/19/18/30/15/11/8/10/6/-/11/-/-/8/6/21/-
WEIGHT FOR AGE 3yo-8lb

4001 GREEN HOWARDS CUP (NURSERY) H'CAP (2-Y.O) (Class C) £6,212.00 (£1,856.00: £888.00: £404.00)
7f 202y Stalls: Low GOING minus 0.27 sec per fur (GF) 4-00 (4-01)

3644* **Weet-A-Minute (IRE) (84)***(94) (RHollinshead)* 2-9-3 LDettori(11) (hld up: smooth hdwy to ld over 1f out: pushed clr: readily) ....— 1
3271[11] Scathebury **(62)***(64) (SPCWoods)* 2-7-4 (5)ow2 MBaird(10) (hld up & plld hrd: effrt & swtchd rt over 2f out: hung lft: kpt on ins fnl f) 3 2
3666* Jo Mell **(85)***(89) (MHEasterby)* 2-9-4 MBirch(9) (lw: s.i.s: sn trckng ldrs: led 3f out tl over 1f out: kpt on same pce) ....hd 3
3809* Samim (USA) **(82)***(84)*(Fav)*(JLDunlop)* 2-9-1 WCarson(1) (lw: a chsng ldrs: sn drvn along: n.m.r 2f out: kpt on one pce) 1 4
*3736** Nose No Bounds (IRE) **(76)***(74) (MJohnston)* 2-8-9 JWeaver(6) (sn bhd & pushed along: styd on fnl 2f: nvr nr to chal) 1¾ 5
3701[5] In Paradisum (USA) **(60)***(58) (MrsJRRamsden)* 2-7-4 (3) NVarley(2) (s.i.s: bhd: drvn along over 3f out: kpt on: n.d) ....s.h 6
3642[2] The Wad **(62)***(56) (DNicholls)* 2-7-2 (7)ow2 MartinDwyer(5) (led 1f: led over 3f out: sn hdd: wknd 2f out) 1 7
3147[7] Urgent Swift **(72)***(63) (APJarvis)* 2-7-12 (7) CAdamson(8) (led after 1f tl over 3f out: sn wknd) 2½ 8
3231[3] Six Clerks (IRE) **(73)***(63) (JGFitzGerald)* 2-8-6 PatEddery(12) (chsd ldrs: effrt over 3f out: sn wl outpcd) ....¾ 9
3721[17] Northern Falcon **(60)***(43) (MWEasterby)* 2-7-2 (5) PFessey(7) (sn bhd & pushed along: n.d) 3 10
3806[6] Mysterious Times **(63)***(29) (BWMurray)* 2-7-10bow3 TWilliams(4) (s.i.s: a bhd & sn drvn along) 7 11

LONG HANDICAP The Wad 7-3 Scathebury 7-2 In Paradisum (USA) 7-5 Northern Falcon 7-2 Mysterious Times 6-12

15/8 Samim (USA), **100/30** Jo Mell, **13/2** WEET-A-MINUTE (IRE), **8/1** Nose No Bounds (IRE), Six Clerks (IRE), **10/1** In Paradisum (USA), **12/1** Urgent Swift, **14/1** The Wad, **20/1** Scathebury, **33/1** Northern Falcon, Mysterious Times, CSF £114.28 CT £467.81 TOTE £6.10: £1.60 £3.70 £1.70 (£63.60) Trio £84.40 OWNER Ed Weetman (Haulage & Storage) Ltd (UPPER LONGDON) BRED Cyclades Farming Co 11 Rn 1m 38.29 (2.29) SF: 55/25/50/45/35/19/17/24/24/4/-

4002 WALMGATE CLAIMING STKS (3-Y.O+) (Class D) £6,160.00 (£1,840.00: £880.00: £400.00)
1m 2f 85y Stalls: Low GOING minus 0.27 sec per fur (GF) 4-30 (4-34)

3945[10] **Mellottie (94)***(95)*(Fav)*(MrsMReveley)* 10-9-7 KDarley(8) (lw: hld up: effrt & chsd ldr 3f out: hung rt: styd on u.p to ld ins fnl f) ....— 1
2117[7] Western General **(78)***(84) (MissSEHall)* 4-8-6 (5) MHenry(10) (hld up: hdwy 3f out: swtchd lft & styd on fnl f) 1 2
3801[14] Once More for Luck (IRE) **(65)***(78) (MrsMReveley)* 4-8-6 JWeaver(3) (led: qcknd clr over 3f out: hdd & no ex ins fnl f) ....s.h 3
3863[6] High Premium **(79)***(77) (RAFahey)* 7-8-8 ACulhane(6) (b: hdwy 3f out: kpt on same pce u.p: nvr nr to chal) 2½ 4
1999* Katy's Lad **(65)***(61) (BAMcMahon)* 8-8-1 (5) LNewton(2) (b: unruly gng to s: dwlt: sn chsng ldrs: lost pl 3f out) 9 5
3852[12] Pendolino (IRE) **(48)***(60) (MBrittain)* 4-8-6b JCarroll(13) (nvr nr ldrs) ....¾ 6
3754[5] Soldier Cove (USA) *(61) (MartynMeade)* 5-8-8 VSlattery(1) (trckd ldrs tl lost pl 3f out) ....½ 7
3462[7] Bold Top **(40)***(60) (BSRothwell)* 3-8-2 MFenton(4) (chsd ldrs: drvn along 4f out: sn lost pl) ....½ 8
Peep O Day *(55) (JLEyre)* 4-8-3 RLappin(9) (sn bhd: pushed along 6f out: n.d) ....s.h 9
3531[7] Course Fishing **(42)***(49) (BAMcMahon)* 4-8-6 LDettori(5) (prom tl lost pl over 3f out) 6 10
3853[10] Karibu (GER) **(45)***(32) (PMonteith)* 4-8-6 SDWilliams(7) (hld up & bhd: plld hrd: n.d) 11 11
3899[16] Ballysokerry (IRE) *(JParkes)* 4-8-6 DHarrison(12) (chsd ldrs tl lost pl over 3f out: sn bhd: t.o) 30 12

10/11 MELLOTTIE (Evens-4/5), **5/1** Western General, **11/2** High Premium (4/1-6/1), **9/1** Once More for Luck (IRE), **11/1** Katy's Lad, **12/1** Course Fishing, **25/1** Peep O Day, Soldier Cove (USA), **33/1** Pendolino (IRE), **50/1** Bold Top, Karibu (GER), Ballysokerry (IRE), CSF £6.63 TOTE £1.90: £1.30 £2.00 £2.00 (£6.40) Trio £17.50 OWNER Mrs J. G. Fulton (SALTBURN) BRED Mrs G. R. Reveley and Partners 12 Rn 2m 9.37 (1.87) SF: 68/57/51/50/34/33/34/27/28/22/5/-

WEIGHT FOR AGE 3yo-6lb

4003 AINSTY MAIDEN STKS (3-Y.O) (Class D) £6,108.00 (£1,824.00: £872.00: £396.00) **1m 2f 85y** Stalls: Low GOING minus 0.27 sec per fur (GF) 5-00 (5-01)

485[2] **Motakabber (IRE)** *(90++)*(Fav)*(JHMGosden)* 3-9-0 LDettori(4) (lw: trckd ldrs: smooth hdwy on bit over 2f out: led over 1f out: impressive) ....— **1**
3756[2] Step Aloft **(75)***(82) (LordHuntingdon)* 3-8-9 DHarrison(9) (lw: trckd ldrs: rdn to ld over 2f out: hdd over 1f out: no ch w wnr) 1¾ **2**
3772[7] Bint Zamayem (IRE) **(80)***(68) (BWHills)* 3-8-9 MHills(7) (led tl over 2f out: eased ins fnl f) 9 **3**
3618[9] Modajjaj *(68) (MAJarvis)* 3-9-0 PRobinson(2) (bit bkwd: chsd ldrs: sn drvn along: hung lft over 3f out: sn wl outpcd) 3½ **4**
657[7] Solatium (IRE) *(64+) (MCPipe)* 3-9-0 PaulEddery(3) (lw: hld up & bhd: hung rt ½-wy: stdy hdwy 3f out: nvr plcd to chal) 2½ **5**
1600[7] Telmo (IRE) *(57) (CFWall)* 3-9-0 OUrbina(5) (s.i.s: a in rr) 5 **6**
797[9] All The Time *(51) (PFICole)* 3-8-9 WCarson(6) (lw: chsd ldrs: drvn along 6f out: outpcd fnl 4f) s.h **7**
1691[10] Brick Court (IRE) *(RFJohnsonHoughton)* 3-8-9 PatEddery(8) (sn bhd: t.o 3f out) ....dist **8**

Evens MOTAKABBER (IRE), **2/1** Step Aloft, **8/1** All The Time, **10/1** Bint Zamayem (IRE), **11/1** Solatium (IRE), **14/1** Brick Court (IRE), **20/1** Modajjaj, **25/1** Telmo (IRE), CSF £3.90 TOTE £1.90: £1.40 £1.10 £1.90 (£1.60) Trio £3.30 OWNER Sheikh Ahmed Al Maktoum (NEWMARKET) BRED Stackallen Stud and Calogo Bloodstock Ag 8 Rn 2m 10.37 (2.87) SF: 53/45/31/31/27/20/14/-

STEWARDS' ENQUIRY Paul Eddery susp. 14 & 16-18/10/95 (failure to obtain best possible placing).

T/Jkpt: £3,792.90 (9 Tckts). T/Plpt: £17.90 (1,002.17 Tckts). T/Qdpt: £10.50 (19.05 Tckts). WG

3796a-SAN SIRO (Milan, Italy) (R-H)
Saturday September 30th (Soft)

4004a PREMIO CASCINA CROCE (2-Y.O F) £4,925.00 **7f** 3-20 (3-20)

Wight *(RHannon)* 2-9-0 GBietolini ....— **1**
Fleet Key *(MCiciarelli,Italy)* 2-9-0 VVarchetta 4¼ **2**
Paola (USA) *(FTurner,Italy)* 2-9-0 MTellini 1¾ **3**
On the Carpet (IRE) *(JLDunlop)* 2-9-0 VMezzatesta (btn 16l) **10**

Tote 39L: 19L 55L 27L (535L) OWNER Scuderia Erasec (MARLBOROUGH) BRED G.B. Turnbull Ltd 14 Rn 1m 29.2 SF: -/-/-/-

4005a PREMIO GORNATE (2-Y.O C & G) £4,925.00 **7f** 4-15 (4-15)

Jilmez (ITY) *(?) (GBotti,Italy)* 2-9-0 MBotti ....— **1**
De Albertis (IRE) *(VCaruso,Italy)* 2-9-0 MEsposito ....½ **2**
Oberon's Dart (IRE) *(JLDunlop)* 2-9-0 VMezzatesta ....nk **3**

Tote 44L: 22L 21L 13L (362L) OWNER Scuderia Siba (ITALY) BRED L. Luciani 11 Rn 1m 31.1

1892a-DORTMUND (Germany) (R-H)
Saturday September 30th (Good to soft)

4006a CONTINENTALE FLIEGER-PREIS (Listed) (3-Y.O+) £20,576.00 (£8,230.00: £6,173.00) **5f** 3-05 (3-08)

3407[11] **Windmachine (SWE)** *(100) (MKahn,Sweden)* 4-8-10 JohnFortune ....— **1**
3913a[2] Auenadler (GER) *(101) (UOstmann,Germany)* 3-8-11 GBocskai ....¾ **2**
1707a* Troon *(97) (RHaugen,Norway)* 5-9-0 MSantos 1½ **3**
3913a* Palacegate Episode (IRE) *(86) (JBerry)* 5-8-10 KWoodburn (btn 9 3/4l) **6**

Tote 54DM: 31DM 24DM 60DM (SF 289DM) OWNER Stall Fagernes BRED S. Pilroth & J. Engelbrektsson in Sweden 11 Rn 58.3 secs SF: -/-/-/-

3793a-LONGCHAMP (Paris, France) (R-H)
Saturday September 30th (Very Soft)

4007a PRIX DOLLAR (Gp 2) (3-Y.O+) £35,928.00 (£14,371.00: £7,186.00: £3,593.00) **1m 1f 165y** 2-25 (2-20)

1837[6] **Flemensfirth (USA)** *(128) (JHMGosden)* 3-9-2 LDettori (mde most: qcknd 2f out: r.o wl) .....— **1**

1118a5 Volochine (IRE) *(119) (RCollet,France)* 4-9-0 TJarnet (hld up in rr: prog fr 2f out: nt rch wnr).½ **2**
3614* Triarius (USA) *(114) (SbinSuroor)* 5-9-0 MJKinane (trckd wnr: 3rd st: rdn 2f out: one pce fnl f)3 **3**
Madrileno (IRE) *(115) (RMartin-Sanchez,Spain)* 3-8-10 JMartinez (rr early: last st: prog fnl 2f: nt rch ldrs)....½ **4**
3036a* Marildo (FR) *(113) (DSmaga,France)* 8-9-0b GGuignard (2nd early: chal 2f out: outpcd fnl f) hd **5**
1836[4] Just Happy (USA) *(113) (MRStoute)* 4-9-0 WRSwinburn (5th st: outpcd fnl 2f) ....s.nk **6**
Vetheuil (USA) *(99) (AFabre,France)* 3-8-10 OPeslier (4th tl st: fdd)....10 **7**

P-M 1.60F: 2.00F 2.40F (SF 34.50F) OWNER Sheikh Mohammed (NEWMARKET) BRED Mill Ridge Farm Ltd in USA 7 Rn
2m 7.8 (9.30) SF: -/-/-/-/-/-/-

4008a PRIX DU CADRAN (Gp 1) (4-Y.O+) £59,880.00 (£23,952.00: £11,976.00: £5,988.00) **2m 4f** 2-55 (2-50)

1001a3 **Always Earnest (USA)** *(124) (MmeMBollack-Badel,France)* 7-9-2 ABadel (hld up in rr: hdwy 2f out: hrd rdn to ld ins fnl f: r.o)....— **1**
3789a2 Moonax (IRE) *(124) (BWHills)* 4-9-2 PatEddery (racd in 3rd: led 2f out: hdd ins fnl f: r.o u.p)s.h **2**
3329a2 Nononito (FR) *(122) (JLesbordes,France)* 4-9-2 GMosse (4th st: chal 2f out: one pce fnl f) .2½ **3**
3563* Double Trigger (IRE) *(120) (MJohnston)* 4-9-2 JWeaver (led: qcknd 3f out: hdd 2f out: outpcd)....3 **4**
3563[4] Admiral's Well (IRE) *(113) (RAkehurst)* 5-9-2 LDettori (trckd ldr: 2nd st: rdn 2f out: wknd) 8 **5**
3688a3 Epaphos (GER) *(97) (PBary,France)* 5-9-2 DBoeuf (3rd early: rdn & bhd st: t.o) 20 **6**

P-M 9.50F: 3.00F 1.90F (SF 35.80F) OWNER Mme M. Bollack-Badel BRED M. Stevens 6 Rn
4m 36.5 SF: -/-/-/-/-/-

4009a PRIX DE ROYALLIEU (Gp 2) (3-Y.O+ F & M) £35,928.00 (£14,371.00: £7,186.00: £3,593.00) **1m 4f 110y** 4-00 (4-02)

3326a2 **Russian Snows (IRE)** *(117) (JOxx,Ireland)* 3-8-7 MJKinane (bhd: hdwy st: qcknd to ld 1f out: sn clr)....— **1**
3196a2 Daraydala (IRE) *(113) (AdeRoyerDupre,France)* 3-8-7 GMosse (3rd st: hdwy to ld over 2f out: hdd 1f out: outpcd)....3 **2**
3041a4 Genovefa (USA) *(112) (AFabre,France)* 3-8-7 TJarnet (rr early: effrt 2f out: r.o fnl f) ....¾ **3**
3549* Noble Rose (IRE) *(110) (LMCumani)* 4-9-1 LDettori (mid div: rdn over 2f out: outpcd fnl f)......2 **4**
3697a2 Flying Dream *(109) (BSchutz,Germany)* 4-9-1 THellier (mid div: prog 2f out: rdn & one pce)s.nk **5**
3549[6] Honfleur (IRE) *(102) (PWChapple-Hyam)* 3-8-7 JReid (led to 3f out: 2nd st: wknd) 6 **6**
3688a* L'ile Tudy (IRE) *(94) (MmeMBollack-Badel,France)* 5-9-1 ABadel (a bhd)....6 **7**
3329a5 Lafille du General (FR) *(92) (PLenogue,France)* 4-9-1 OPeslier (trckd ldr tl led 3f out: hdd 2f out: wknd)....1½ **8**
Syvanie (FR) *(92) (FDoumen,France)* 3-8-7 GGuignard (4th st: sn rdn & btn) ....hd **9**

Tote 1.70F: 1.80F 1.60F 1.90F (12.50F) OWNER Sheikh Mohammed BRED Kilfrush Stud Ltd 9 Rn
2m 45.0 SF: -/-/-/-/-/-/-/-/-

4010a PRIX DE LA ROCHETTE (Gp 3) (2-Y.O C & G) £26,347.00 (£9,581.00: £4,790.00) **1m** 4-30 (4-35)

Le Triton (USA) *(108) (MmeCHead,France)* 2-8-11 WRSwinburn ....— **1**
Cliptomania (USA) *(103) (J-CRouget,France)* 2-8-11 CAsmussen 2½ **2**
Radevore *(100) (AFabre,France)* 2-8-11 TJarnet 1½ **3**
3812[2] More Royal (USA) *(96) (IABalding)* 2-8-11 LDettori (btn 6l) **5**

P-M 6.40F: 2.20F 2.50F (SF 30.00F) OWNER Maktoum Al Maktoum (FRANCE) BRED West Star Bloodstock 6 Rn
1m 46.4 SF: -/-/-/-

4011a PRIX DE LUTECE (Gp 3) (3-Y.O) £26,347.00 (£9,581.00: £4,790.00: £2,395.00) **1m 7f** 5-05 (5-02)

3547* **Grey Shot** *(118) (IABalding)* 3-8-9 LDettori ....— **1**
3790a3 Court of Honour (IRE) *(117) (PWChapple-Hyam)* 3-8-11 JReid 2½ **2**
Periple (FR) *(115) (AFabre,France)* 3-8-9 TJarnet ....s.h **3**
3162* Sanmartino (IRE) *(110) (BWHills)* 3-8-9 PatEddery 5 **4**
3609[4] In Camera (IRE) *(104) (MRStoute)* 3-8-11 MJKinane (btn approx 14l) **6**

P-M 7.60F: 3.00F 2.90F (14.90F) OWNER Mr J. C. Smith (KINGSCLERE) BRED Littleton Stud 7 Rn
3m 20.6 SF: -/-/-/-/-
DS

4007a-LONGCHAMP (Paris, France) (R-H) Sunday October 1st (Soft)

4012a PRIX DE L'ABBAYE DE LONGCHAMP (Gp 1) (C & F) £59,880.00 (£23,952.00: £11,976.00: £5,988.00) 5f 2-30 (2-26)

3785a* **Hever Golf Rose** *(126) (TJNaughton)* 4-9-7 JWeaver (chsd ldr tl led 2f out: rdn clr: r.o wl)...— 1
3491* Cherokee Rose (IRE) *(118) (JEHammond,France)* 4-9-7 CAsmussen (outpcd early: r.o fnl f: nrst fin)....2½ 2
3550* Eveningperformance *(117) (HCandy)* 4-9-7 WNewnes (led to 2f out: r.o u.p)....nk 3
3707* Easy Option (IRE) *(117) (SbinSuroor)* 3-9-7 LDettori (sn cl up: chsd wnr 2f out: no ex fnl f)s.nk 4
3491⁶ Lavinia Fontana (IRE) *(113) (JLDunlop)* 6-9-7 CNakatani (outpcd tl r.o fnl 2f: nvr nrr)....1 5
3689a³ Millyant *(113) (RGuest)* 5-9-7 MRoberts (a mid div: nt pce to chal)....hd 6
3834* Cool Jazz *(115) (CEBrittain)* 4-9-10 MJKinane (chsd ldrs: one pce fnl 2f)....s.nk 7
3491⁵ Mind Games *(111) (JBerry)* 3-9-10 WCarson (prom tl ½-wy: wknd)....1½ 8
3689a* Bunty Boo *(101) (RHannon)* 6-9-7 MHills (a bhd)....2 9
3793a² With Fascination (USA) *(90) (JEPease,France)* 2-8-4 OPeslier (outpcd)....4 10
Bruttina *(76) (MmePBarbe,France)* 3-9-7b TThulliez (sn outpcd)....4 11
901a² Late Parade (IRE) *(59) (ASpanu,France)* 4-9-10 JReid (bhn whn hmpd after 2f: nt rcvr)....6 12

P-M 4.10F: 1.60F 1.30F 3.00F (4.50F) OWNER Mr M. P. Hanson (EPSOM) BRED Ronald Popely
12 Rn 57.7 secs (2.70) SF: -/-/-/-/-/-/-/-/-/-/-/-

4013a PRIX MARCEL BOUSSAC (Gp 1) (2-Y.O F) £95,808.00 (£38,323.00: £19,162.00: £9,581.00) 1m 3-05 (3-03)

3786a² **Miss Tahiti (IRE)** *(105) (AFabre,France)* 2-8-11 OPeslier (mid div: 5th st: rdn over 2f out: led ins fnl f: r.o wl)....— 1
3786a* Shake the Yoke *(101) (ELellouche,France)* 2-8-11 DBoeuf (a.p: 2nd st: rdn to ld 1f out: sn hdd & no ex)....2 2
3561* Solar Crystal (IRE) *(101) (HRACecil)* 2-8-11 WRyan (led to 1f out: styd on)....hd 3
3692a⁴ Dance Design (IRE) *(98) (DKWeld,Ireland)* 2-8-11 MJKinane (in tch: 4th st: nt qckn fnl 2f) ..1½ 4
3578a* Blushing Gleam *(92) (MmeCHead,France)* 2-8-11 ODoleuze (6th st: rdn 2f out: no imp fnl f)..3 5
3584a⁶ Tarte Aux Pommes (FR) *(91) (JBertranDeBalanda,France)* 2-8-11 CAsmussen (rr early: nvr plcd to chal)....½ 6
Wedding Gift (FR) *(89) (PDemercastel,France)* 2-8-11 TJarnet (hld up in rr: 7th st: no imp)....1 7
Clever Dorothy (USA) *(86) (DSepulchre,France)* 2-8-11 ESaint-Martin (nvr plcd to chal)....1½ 8
3280* Moody's Cat (IRE) *(80) (BWHills)* 2-8-11 MHills (prom: 3rd st: sn rdn & wknd)....3 9
3474* Sea Spray (IRE) *(79) (PWChapple-Hyam)* 2-8-11 JReid (a bhd: nt pce to chal)....½ 10
3532* Caribbean Quest *(74) (BHanbury)* 2-8-11 WRSwinburn (5th early: hmpd appr st: nt rcvr)....2½ 11

P-M 11.60F: 2.60F 1.70F 2.40F (17.60F) OWNER Mr D. Wildenstein (FRANCE) BRED Dayton Ltd
11 Rn 1m 40.2 SF: -/-/-/-/-/-/-/-/-/-/-

4014a FORTE PRIX DE L'ARC DE TRIOMPHE (Gp 1) (3-Y.O+ C & F) £479,042.00 (£191,617.00: £95,808.00: £23,952.00) 1m 4f 3-50 (3-50)

2595* **Lammtarra (USA)** *(132+) (SbinSuroor)* 3-8-11 LDettori (chsd ldr tl led over 2f out: r.o u.p: all out)....— 1
3690a² Freedom Cry *(131) (AFabre,France)* 4-9-5 OPeslier (hld up: 10th st: gd prog to chal ins fnl f: no ex cl home)....¾ 2
3482a* Swain (IRE) *(128) (AFabre,France)* 3-8-11 MJKinane (mid div: 7th st: hdwy to chal over 1f out: no ex)....2 3
3591a⁷ Lando (GER) *(126) (HJentzsch,Germany)* 5-9-5 MRoberts (bhd to st: hdwy fnl 2f: nt pce to chal)....1½ 4
3161* Pure Grain *(120) (MRStoute)* 3-8-8 JReid (trckd ldrs: chal over 2f out: one pce)....2½ 5
3695a* Carnegie (IRE) *(122) (AFabre,France)* 4-9-5 TJarnet (lw: racd in 6th: rdn 2f out: no imp)....½ 6
3482a⁵ Partipral (USA) *(121) (ELellouche,France)* 6-9-5 GGuignard (s.s: bhd tl sme prog st)....1 7
3792a* Gunboat Diplomacy (FR) *(120) (ELellouche,France)* 4-9-5 DBoeuf (in tch: 9th st: effrt 2f out: wknd fnl f)....1 8
3694a* Carling (FR) *(106) (MmePBarbe,France)* 3-8-8 TThulliez (prom: 4th st: sn rdn & wknd)....8 9
3695a² Balanchine (USA) *(106) (SbinSuroor)* 4-9-2 WRSwinburn (nvr plcd to chal)....s.nk 10
1008a³ El Tenor(FR) *(106) (ASpanu,France)* 3-8-11 SCoerette (a bhd)....2 11
3695a³ Tot Ou Tard (IRE) *(102) (SWattel,France)* 5-9-5 ESaint-Martin (nvr bttr than mid div)....3 12
3609⁸ Luso *(98) (CEBrittain)* 3-8-11b CAsmussen (led tl over 2f out: wknd qckly)....3 13
3789a* Strategic Choice (USA) *(95) (PFICole)* 4-9-5 TQuinn (prom: 3rd st: rdn & wknd over 2f out)....2½ 14

El Sembrador (ARG) *(94) (JLPalacios,Argentina)* 4-9-5 GSena (s.i.s: a bhd)....½ 15
3482a3 Sunrise Song (FR) *(84) (FDoumen,France)* 4-9-2 GMosse (a bhd: eased fnl f)....5 16

P-M 3.10F: 2.20F 3.90F 4.10F (29.10F) OWNER Mr Saeed Maktoum Al Maktoum (NEWMARKET) BRED Gainsborough Farm Inc. in USA 16 Rn 2m 31.8 SF: -/-/-/-/-/-/-/-/-/-/-/-/-/-/-/-

4015a SUNSET & VINE PRIX DE L'OPERA (Gp 2) (3-Y.O+ F & M) £47,904.00 (£19,162.00: £9,581.00: £4,790.00) **1m 1f 55y** 4-40 (4-39)

3693a* **Timarida (IRE)** *(118) (JOxx,Ireland)* 3-8-9 JPMurtagh (hld up: 9th st: rdn to ld 1f out: sn clr)....— 1
3575a4 Angel In My Heart (FR) *(114) (JEHammond,France)* 3-8-9 CAsmussen (8th st: nt clr run tl over 1f out: r.o wl: nrst fin)....2½ 2
3331a* Balanka (IRE) *(113) (AdeRoyerDupre,France)* 3-8-9 GMosse (mid div: rdn to chal 1f out: no ex)....nk 3
3575a3 Garden Rose (IRE) *(112) (PBary,France)* 3-8-9 DBoeuf (mid div: 7th st: chal over 1f out: no imp fnl f)....¾ 4
3579a* Vadlamixa (FR) *(111) (AFabre,France)* 3-8-9 TJarnet (5th st: rdn 2f out: one pce)....nk 5
3698a3 Erin Bird (FR) *(109) (MmePBarbe,France)* 4-8-12 TThulliez (2nd early: rdn to ld 2f out: hdd 1f out: fdd)....½ 6
3579a2 Marie de Ken (FR) *(107) (AdeRoyerDupre,France)* 3-8-9 OPeslier (led tl hdd 2f out: wknd)....2 7
2894a3 Tryphosa (IRE) *(109) (AWohler,Germany)* 3-8-11 ABoschert (3rd st: rdn & no imp fnl 2f)...s.nk 8
3041a5 Truly a Dream (IRE) *(102) (RCollet,France)* 4-8-12 ESaint-Martin (a rr)....1½ 9
2389a* Kill the Crab (IRE) *(104) (WNeuroth,Norway)* 3-8-11 MLarsen (prom: 4th st: wknd)....1½ 10
2214a3 Coco Passion (FR) *(100) (JEHammond,France)* 3-8-9 WRSwinburn (a last)....1 11

P-M 3.50F: 2.40F 2.70F 2.60F (40.90F) OWNER Aga Khan BRED H.H. Aga Khan's Studs S.C. 11 Rn 1m 55.7 (3.70) SF: -/-/-/-/-/-/-/-/-/-/-

4016a PRIX DU ROND-POINT (Gp 2) (3-Y.O+) £47,904.00 (£19,162.00: £9,581.00: £4,790.00) **1m** 5-20 (5-18)

3589a2 **Shaanxi (USA)** *(120) (ELellouche,France)* 3-8-9 ow1 DBoeuf (5th early: hdwy to ld ins fnl f: r.o wl)....— 1
1848 10 Petit Poucet *(119) (NClement,France)* 3-8-11 CAsmussen (6th st: rdn 2f out: r.o fnl f: nrst fin)2 2
3795a3 Nec Plus Ultra (FR) *(118) (AdeRoyerDupre,France)* 4-9-1 GMosse (4th early: hdwy 2f out: one pce fnl f)....nk 3
3042a7 Atticus (USA) *(117) (MmeCHead,France)* 3-8-11 ODoleuze (a.p: 3rd st: rdn 2f out: outpcd fnl f)....½ 4
Signoretto (FR) *(115) (DSmaga,France)* 8-9-1 GGuignard (rr early: rdn 3f out: styd on fnl f: nvr plcd to chal)....1 5
3478a4 Pollen Count (USA) *(113) (SbinSuroor)* 6-9-1 LDettori (led tl ins fnl f: wknd)....1 6
2040a2 Bashaayeash (IRE) *(73) (CLaffon-Parias,France)* 3-8-11 WRSwinburn (2nd early: rdn 2f out: wknd)....20 7

P-M 1.80F: 1.30F 2.10F (8.80F) OWNER Mr T. Yoshida. BRED Fares Farm Inc 7 Rn 1m 39.5 SF: -/-/-/-/-/-/-

4017a PRIX FORTE H'CAP (4-Y.O+) £23,952.00 **1m 2f** 5-55 (5-53)

Rainbow Reef *(94) (LAudon,France)* 7-7-12 PBruneau....— 1
Parme (USA) *(105) (ELellouche,France)* 4-8-11 OPeslier....1½ 2
3374 9 Cedez le Passage (FR) *(96) (CEBrittain)* 4-8-4 MHills....¾ 3
P-M 15.20F: 3.50F 2.00F 5.50F (42.60F) OWNER J-P Van Horenbeke BRED Balidar Ltd 16 Rn 2m 7.6 SF: -/-/-
DS

4006a-DORTMUND (Germany) (R-H)
Sunday October 1st (Heavy)

4018a BMW DEUTSCHES ST LEGER (Gp 2) (3-Y.O C & F) £49,383.00 (£19,753.00: £9,876.00: £4,938.00) **1m 6f** 3-55 (3-55)

First Hello (GER) *(108) (PRau,Germany)* 3-9-2 TMundry (a.p: 3rd st: led 2f out: r.o wl)....— 1
1705a2 Tascilla (GER) *(102) (HRemmert,Germany)* 3-8-12 KWoodburn (hld up in rr: gd hdwy fnl 2f: nt rch wnr)....1¾ 2
3200a6 Moltaire (GER) *(104) (BSchutz,Germany)* 3-9-2 ASuborics (led to 2f out: r.o)....2 3
3591a6 Oxalagu (GER) *(103) (BSchutz,Germany)* 3-9-2 THellier (trckd ldrs: chal 2f out: no ex)....nk 4

Taylor (GER) *(103) (Germany)* 3-9-2 PSchiergen (a cl up: 2nd st: one pce fnl f)....................½ 5
El Society (GER) *(95) (Germany)* 3-9-2 NGrant (nvr plcd to chal)..7 6
Little Smart (GER) *(92) (Germany)* 3-9-2 ManfredHofer (trckd ldrs: 5th st: sn wknd)............2½ 7
2215a[4] Sir King (GER) *(85) (Germany)* 3-9-2 GBocskai (a bhd)..6 8
3609[6] Anchor Clever *(PAKelleway)* 3-9-2 MRimmer (a bhd: btn over 20l)................................ 9
Tote 107DM: 29DM 46DM 42DM (SF 1451DM) OWNER Gestut Ittlingen BRED Gestut Hof Ittlingen 13 Rn 3m 5.5 SF: -/-/-/-/-/-/-/-/-

4004a-SAN SIRO (Milan, Italy) (R-H)
Sunday October 1st (Good to soft)

4019a PREMIO PIETRO BESSARO (Listed) (3-Y.O+ F & M) £17,730.00 (£7,801.00: £3,617.00) 1m 4-40 (4-48)

3912a* **Penny Drops** *(102) (LordHuntingdon)* 6-8-13 DHarrison...— 1
3768* Mandarina (USA) *(98) (LMCumani)* 3-8-7 ow1 FJovine...nk 2
2566a[3] Senebrova *(95) (VValiani,Italy)* 4-8-8 SLandi...¾ 3

Tote 13L: 11L 14L 13L (29L) OWNER Mr Stanley Sharp (WEST ILSLEY) BRED T. M. Saud 9 Rn 1m 38.0 SF: -/-/-

1395a-CAPANNELLE (Rome, Italy) (R-H)
Sunday October 1st (Good)

4020a PREMIO LYDIA TESIO (Gp 2) (3-Y.O+ F & M) £38,103.00 (£17,584.00: £9,832.00: £4,916.00) 1m 2f 4-30 (4-46)

Pourquoi Pas (IRE) *(101) (MGasparini,Italy)* 3-8-8 AHerrera (4th st: hdwy to ld over 1f out: r.o wl)...— 1
2566a* Olimpia Dukakis (ITY) *(100) (GBotti,Italy)* 3-8-8 GForte (3rd st: w wnr 2f out: r.o u.p)............½ 2
1704a[4] De Puntillas *(95) (Ld'Auria,Italy)* 3-8-8 MPasquale (mid div: hdwy fnl 2f: nrst fin)..................3½ 3
2566a[2] Rosi Zambotti (IRE) *(92) (BGrizzetti,Italy)* 3-8-8 ACarboni (hld up: prog 2f out: no ex fnl f)...1½ 4
3697a* Alpha City (GER) *(90) (HJentzsch,Germany)* 3-8-8 LHammer-Hansen (a.p: 2nd st: led over 2f out: sn hdd: wknd)...1½ 5
1237a[10] Love Secret (USA) *(80) (Italy)* 3-8-8 RCangiano (nvr plcd to chal)..6 6
Streisand *(74) (Italy)* 4-8-11 BJovine (a bhd)...1¾ 7
3537* Syrian Queen *(76) (HRACecil)* 3-8-8b AMcGlone (led tl hdd over 2f out: sn wknd)....................¾ 8
Dama Grande *(72) (Italy)* 6-8-11 OFrancera (a rr)..1 9
Tote 172L: 22L 12L 19L (75L) OWNER Miss F. Turri BRED G. Canavan 9 Rn2m 0.9 SF: -/-/-/-//-/-/-

2888a-TIPPERARY (Ireland) (L-H)
Sunday October 1st (Firm)

4021a COOLMORE STUD HOME OF CHAMPIONS CONCORDE STKS (Gp 3) (3-Y.O+) £16,089.00 (£4,703.00: £2,228.00) 7f 3-00 (3-02)

Wild Bluebell (IRE) *(116) (JSBolger,Ireland)* 3-8-6 JAHeffernan...— 1
3787a* Wizard King *(119)*(Fav)*(SirMarkPrescott)* 4-8-12 GDuffield...s.h 2
1848[6] Mediation (IRE) *(111) (JOxx,Ireland)* 3-8-6 DHogan..2 3

8/11 Wizard King, **15/2** Mediation (IRE), **11/1** WILD BLUEBELL (IRE), Tote £13.40: £3.60 £1.20 (£9.60) OWNER Ballylinch Stud (IRELAND) BRED T.F. Lacy 7 Rn 1m 32.9 SF: -/-/- NR

3831-ASCOT (R-H)
Friday October 6th (Good to soft becoming Soft)
WEATHER: raining WIND: mod across

4022 BOLLINGER CHAMPAGNE CHALLENGE SERIES FINAL GENTLEMENS' H'CAP (0-80) (3-Y.O+) (Class E) £4,299.00 (£1,302.00: £636.00:£303.00) 1m 4f Stalls: High GOING: 0.50 sec per fur (GS) 2-00 (2-00)

3700[8] **Chief Bee (76)***(92) (JLDunlop)* 4-11-10 MrJDurkan(11) (hdwy over 2f out: led wl over 1f out: hrd rdn: hung lft ins fnl f: r.o wl)...— 1

3029[7] Minnesota Viking **(55)***(62)*(Fav)*(LadyHerries)* 4-10-3 MrPPritchard-Gordon(3) (swtg: a.p: led over 5f out tl wl over 1f out: unable qckn)....7 **2**
3889[5] Father Dan (IRE) **(57)***(63) (MissGayKelleway)* 6-10-5 MrRJohnson(5) (lw: 4th st: hrd rdn over 1f out: one pce)....½ **3**
3818[7] Grand Applause (IRE) **(45)***(46) (MPMuggeridge)* 5-9-3 (4) MrSRutherford(12) (gd hdwy over 1f out: fin wl)....3½ **4**
3863[16] Trade Wind **(72)***(70) (DRCElsworth)* 4-11-6b MrSSwiers(4) (lw: nvr nr to chal)....2½ **5**
Cuban Nights (USA) **(60)***(54) (BJLlewellyn)* 3-10-0 ow1 MrJLLlewellyn(2) (hdwy over 5f out: 3rd st: wknd 2f out)....2 **6**
3875[3] Euro Forum **(55)***(48) (GLMoore)* 3-9-5 (4)ow1 MrKGoble(1) (6th st: wknd over 2f out)....¾ **7**
2658[9] Backview **(64)***(58) (BJLlewellyn)* 3-10-0 (4) MrKSantana(10) (lw: led over 6f: 2nd st: wknd 2f out)....nk **8**
3555[6] Krayyan Dawn **(52)***(39) (RAkehurst)* 5-10-0 MrTMcCarthy(8) (lw: 5th st: wknd over 2f out)....5 **9**
3730[14] Golden Arrow (IRE) **(80)***(66) (IABalding)* 4-12-0 MrABalding(7) (lw: prom over 8f)....1 **10**
1998[4] Air Command (BAR) **(58)***(22) (CTNash)* 5-10-2 (4)ow9 MrPPhillips(6) (a bhd)....10 **11**
3898[13] Regal Aura (IRE) **(45)***(6) (DCO'Brien)* 5-9-3 (4) MrVLukaniuk(9) (lw: prom over 7f)....9 **12**

LONG HANDICAP Regal Aura (IRE) 9-0

5/1 Minnesota Viking, **11/2** Father Dan (IRE), **6/1** Krayyan Dawn (op 4/1), **7/1** CHIEF BEE, Euro Forum, **15/2** Grand Applause (IRE), **10/1** Golden Arrow (IRE), **12/1** Trade Wind (op 7/1), **20/1** Backview, Cuban Nights (USA), **33/1** Air Command (BAR), **66/1** Regal Aura (IRE), CSF £37.18 CT £185.79 TOTE £6.70: £2.80 £1.60 £2.10 (£20.50) Trio £19.90 OWNER Mrs Mark Burrell (ARUNDEL) BRED Mrs M. Burrell 12 Rn 2m 46.22 (16.72) SF: 63/33/34/17/41/17/11/21/10/37/-/-

WEIGHT FOR AGE 3yo-8lb

4023 TRIPLEPRINT MAIDEN STKS (2-Y.O) (Class D) £7,067.50 (£2,140.00: £1,045.00: £497.50)

6f Stalls: Low GOING: 0.50 sec per fur (GS) 2-30 (2-31)

Midnight Blue *(86+t) (WJarvis)* 2-8-9 JReid(10) (neat: a.p: led over 1f out: rdn out)....— **1**
Mutamanni (USA) *(83t) (HThomsonJones)* 2-9-0 RHills(9) (neat: hld up: n.m.r 2f out: chsd wnr fnl f: no imp)....3 **2**
3733[W] Insiyabi (USA) *(72+t) (JLDunlop)* 2-9-0 WCarson(11) (unf: scope: lw: hld up: rdn over 2f out: one pce)....4 **3**
Cornish Snow (USA) *(68t)*(Fav)*(DRLoder)* 2-9-0b LDettori(4) (cmpt: plld hrd: chsd ldr: ev ch wl over 1f out: wknd fnl f)....1½ **4**
Old Hat (IRE) *(64t) (RHannon)* 2-9-0 PatEddery(6) (w'like: scope: rdn over 4f out: hdwy over 1f out: eased whn btn ins fnl f)....1¾ **5**
Little Pilgrim *(63t) (TMJones)* 2-9-0 RPerham(3) (w'like: scope: lw: led over 4f)....hd **6**
Tawaaded (IRE) *(57t) (PTWalwyn)* 2-8-9 DHarrison(2) (leggy: hld up: rdn over 2f out: wknd over 1f out)....½ **7**
Northern Judge *(57t) (BHanbury)* 2-9-0 WRyan(1) (w'like: scope: lw: a bhd)....2 **8**
Warren Knight *(55t) (CAHorgan)* 2-9-0 WNewnes(5) (unf: a bhd)....½ **9**
Bandit Girl *(37t) (IABalding)* 2-8-9 MHills(7) (unf: scope: bit bkwd: dwlt: a bhd)....5 **10**
Valjess *(DCO'Brien)* 2-8-9 DaneO'Neill(8) (leggy: a bhd)....14 **11**

11/10 Cornish Snow (USA), **9/2** Insiyabi (USA) (9/4-5/1), **7/1** Mutamanni (USA) (op 4/1), **8/1** Northern Judge (op 5/1), **14/1** Bandit Girl (8/1-16/1), Old Hat (IRE) (10/1-16/1), **16/1** MIDNIGHT BLUE, Tawaaded (IRE), **40/1** Warren Knight, **50/1** Valjess, **66/1** Little Pilgrim, CSF £114.02 TOTE £27.50: £3.60 £1.90 £1.70 (£112.10) Trio £145.60 OWNER Sussex-Essex Racing (NEWMARKET) BRED P. V. And Mrs J. P. Jackson 11 Rn

1m 18.9 (5.30) SF: 62/59/48/44/40/39/33/33/31/13/-

4024 BONUSPRINT OCTOBER STKS (Listed) (3-Y.O+ F & M) (Class A) £17,018.75 (£5,150.00: £2,512.50: £1,193.75)

1m (round) Stalls: High GOING: 0.50 sec per fur (GS) 3-05 (3-06)

3833[4] **A la Carte (IRE) (100)***(104) (JLDunlop)* 3-8-7 TQuinn(1) (lw: 5th st: led wl over 1f out: rdn out)— **1**
3833[7] Autumn Affair **(98)***(102) (CEBrittain)* 3-8-7 MRoberts(6) (b.off hind: 3rd st: chsd wnr over 1f out: r.o)....1 **2**
3833[5] Donna Viola **(87)***(97) (CFWall)* 3-8-7 LDettori(8) (lw: rdn over 2f out: hdwy over 1f out: r.o one pce)....2½ **3**
3833[2] Courageous Dancer (IRE) **(87)***(96) (BHanbury)* 3-8-7 WRyan(10) (rdn over 2f out: hdwy over 1f out: one pce)....½ **4**
3693a[6] Louis' Queen (IRE) *(91) (JLDunlop)* 3-8-7 JReid(5) (plld hrd: chsd ldr: led 3f out tl wl over 1f out: sn wknd)....2½ **5**
3611[7] Moneefa **(69)***(90) (HRACecil)* 4-8-11 PatEddery(9) (nvr nr to chal)....nk **6**
3636[12] Pearl Venture **(88)***(90) (SPCWoods)* 3-8-7 WWoods(3) (lw: 6th st: rdn over 2f out: one pce).hd **7**
3768[2] Crystal Cavern (USA) **(94)***(84) (RCharlton)* 3-8-7 DHarrison(4) (lw: no hdwy fnl 2f)....3 **8**
3831[9] Alessia **(95)***(74) (BWHills)* 3-8-7 MHills(2) (4th st: wknd wl over 1f out)....5 **9**

3636[3] Goalwah **(99)***(74)*(Fav)*(HThomsonJones)* 3-8-7 RHills(7) (led 5f: 2nd st: wkng whn hmpd 2f out) ....nk **10**

5/2 Goalwah, **4/1** Louis' Queen (IRE), **5/1** A LA CARTE (IRE), **8/1** Crystal Cavern (USA) (9/2-9/1), **10/1** Courageous Dancer (IRE), **12/1** Autumn Affair, Donna Viola, **14/1** Moneefa, **16/1** Alessia, **50/1** Pearl Venture, CSF £54.81 TOTE £6.10: £1.70 £2.80 £2.40 (£23.10) Trio £72.70 OWNER Mrs Patrick Darling-Susan Abbott Racing (ARUNDEL) BRED Dene Investments N V 10 Rn
1m 45.45 (5.85) SF: 69/67/62/61/56/59/55/49/39/39
WEIGHT FOR AGE 3yo-4lb

4025 AIM AVIATION (NURSERY) H'CAP (2-Y.O) (Class C) £9,758.00 (£2,954.00: £1,442.00: £686.00)
7f Stalls: Low GOING: 0.50 sec per fur (GS) 3-40 (3-40)

2106[7] **Prends Ca (IRE) (82)***(86) (RHannon)* 2-9-3 PatEddery(6) (hdwy over 1f out: led 1f out: drvn out) ....— **1**
3867[7] Frezeliere **(82)***(85) (JLDunlop)* 2-9-3b LDettori(5) (hdwy over 2f out: edgd lft over 1f out: ev ch ins fnl f: r.o) ....½ **2**
3711[3] Rhumba Dancer **(83)***(83) (RHannon)* 2-8-13 (5) DaneO'Neill(7) (lw: hld up: led 2f out to 1f out: unable qckn) 1¼ **3**
3803[4] Careful (IRE) **(62)***(54) (BWHills)* 2-7-11 WCarson(2) (hld up: rdn over 3f out: wknd 1f out) ...3½ **4**
3546[4] Double Diamond (IRE) **(86)***(77) (MJohnston)* 2-9-7 JWeaver(1) (led 1f: led over 2f out: sn hdd: wknd over 1f out) ....½ **5**
3882* Bold Enough **(68)***(59)*(Fav)*(BWHills)* 2-8-3 5x RHills(3) (lw: hld up: nt clr run over 2f out: wknd over 1f out) ....hd **6**
3858[2] Half An Inch (IRE) **(69)***(25) (BJMeehan)* 2-8-4b JFEgan(4) (led 6f out tl over 2f out: sn wknd) 15 **7**

7/2 Bold Enough (op 11/2), **4/1** Careful (IRE) (5/2-9/2), **9/2** Frezeliere, Half An Inch (IRE), **5/1** Rhumba Dancer, **9/1** Double Diamond (IRE) (5/1-10/1), **12/1** PRENDS CA (IRE), CSF £58.32 TOTE £15.00: £4.10 £2.60 (£49.40) OWNER Mr P. B. Adams (MARLBOROUGH) BRED Sheikh Mohammed Bin Rashid Al Maktoum 7 Rn 1m 34.73 (8.23) SF: 46/45/43/14/37/19/-

4026 WYNDHAM H'CAP (0-90) (3-Y.O+) (Class C) £9,849.00 (£2,982.00: £1,456.00: £693.00)
2m 45y Stalls: High GOING: 0.50 sec per fur (GS) 4-15 (4-15)

3817[4] **Meant to Be (75)***(90) (LadyHerries)* 5-9-1 JReid(9) (a.p: led over 5f out: all out) ....— **1**
3849* Greycoat Boy **(64)***(79) (BJMeehan)* 3-7-7b 3x NCarlisle(8) (4th st: nt clr run 2f out: ev ch ins fnl f: r.o wl) ....s.h **2**
3774[2] French Ivy (USA) **(64)***(75) (FMurphy)* 8-8-4 ow2 RCochrane(7) (b: lw: 5th st: rdn over 2f out: unable qckn wl ins fnl f) 1¾ **3**
3817[7] Sea Freedom **(68)***(75) (GBBalding)* 4-8-8 JWilliams(3) (nvr nr to chal) 6 **4**
3817[2] Benfleet **(86)***(93)*(Fav)*(RWArmstrong)* 4-9-12 LDettori(5) (lw: nt clr run over 2f out: swtchd lft & hdwy over 1f out: wknd fnl f) ....¾ **5**
3817[3] Supreme Star (USA) **(68)***(72) (PRHedger)* 4-8-3 (5) DaneO'Neill(6) (3rd st: wknd over 1f out) 2½ **6**
3849[8] Turquoise Sea (USA) **(79)***(68) (JLDunlop)* 3-8-8 WCarson(10) (led 8f: 2nd st: wknd 2f out) ...15 **7**
3817[9] Star Player **(53)***(42) (RJBaker)* 9-7-4 (3) NVarley(2) (lw: hdwy over 3f out: sn wknd) ....nk **8**
3986[4] Head Turner **(54)***(41) (CPWildman)* 7-7-8 ow1 NAdams(4) (bhd fnl 3f) 1¼ **9**
3801[11] Riparius (USA) **(77)***(65) (HCandy)* 4-9-3b WNewnes(11) (lw: led 8f out tl over 5f out: 6th st: wknd over 2f out) ....nk **10**
3774[5] Bean King **(80)***(60) (MrsJCecil)* 9-9-6 TIves(1) (bhd fnl 6f) 8 **11**
3884[12] Requested **(59)***(35) (PBurgoyne)* 8-7-13 ow1 JFEgan(12) (lw: s.s: a bhd) 3 **12**
LONG HANDICAP Head Turner 6-9

9/2 Benfleet, **5/1** French Ivy (USA), **11/2** Turquoise Sea (USA), **7/1** Greycoat Boy, **9/1** Supreme Star (USA), **10/1** MEANT TO BE (8/1-12/1), Bean King (8/1-12/1), **11/1** Star Player, **14/1** Sea Freedom, **20/1** Head Turner, Riparius (USA), Requested, CSF £72.26 CT £351.95 TOTE £11.70: £2.90 £2.40 £1.60 (£83.30) Trio £107.50 OWNER Lady Mary Mumford (LITTLEHAMPTON) BRED Mrs B. V. Chennells 12 Rn 3m 41.4 (14.90) SF: 66/44/51/51/69/48/33/18/17/41/36/11
WEIGHT FOR AGE 3yo-11lb

4027 MAYFLOWER CONDITIONS APPRENTICE STKS (3-Y.O+) (Class E) £4,041.00 (£1,233.00: £609.00: £297.00)
1m (straight) Stalls: Low GOING: 0.50 sec per fur (GS) 4-45 (4-46)

King of Tunes (FR) *(81) (JJSheehan)* 3-8-7 PPMurphy(3) (w'like: s.s: hdwy over 2f out: led over 1f out: hrd rdn: r.o wl) ....— **1**
2703[20] Beauchamp Jazz **(100)***(75)*(Fav)*(JLDunlop)* 3-9-1 AWhelan(1) (lw: led over 6f: unable qckn) ..7 **2**

3920[3] Saltando (IRE) **(51)***(64) (PatMitchell)* 4-8-11 DaneO'Neill(7) (hrd rdn & hdwy 2f out: one pce)1½ **3**
3630[2] La Gran Senorita (USA) **(75)***(43) (PFICole)* 3-7-10 (7)ow1 DavidO'Neill(5) (swtg: a.p: hrd rdn over 2f out: wknd over 1f out)....8 **4**
586[12] Precious Wonder **(37)***(46) (PButler)* 6-8-8 (3) GMitchell(4) (nvr nr to chal)....1 **5**
3762[9] Green Divot *(GWragg)* 4-8-1 (5) GMilligan(2) (lw: prom over 4f)....25 **6**
3712[6] Coeur Francais (FR) *(MajorDNChappell)* 3-8-7 MHenry(6) (lw: prom over 5f)....¾ **7**
3885[15] Autumn Cover **(54)** *(RMFlower)* 3-8-7 DGriffiths(9) (b: a bhd)....8 **8**
Emperors Wood *(PHayward)* 4-8-8 (3) PFessey(8) (Withdrawn not under Starter's orders: ref to ent stalls).... **W**

4/7 Beauchamp Jazz (4/11-4/6), **9/2** La Gran Senorita (USA) (6/1-4/1), Coeur Francais (FR), **20/1** Saltando (IRE), Green Divot, **33/1** Autumn Cover, KING OF TUNES (FR), **50/1** Precious Wonder, Emperors Wood, CSF £52.25 TOTE £42.80: £4.30 £1.20 £2.30 (£37.20) Trio £159.40 OWNER Mrs Eileen Sheehan (FINDON) BRED Thierry Storme 8 Rn 1m 48.02 (8.82) SF: 43/37/30/5/12/-/-/-/-
WEIGHT FOR AGE 3yo-4lb

4028

TANKERVILLE H'CAP (0-90) (3-Y.O+) (Class C) £7,327.50 (£2,220.00: £1,085.00: £517.50) **1m 4f** Stalls: High GOING: 0.50 sec per fur (GS) 5-15 (5-16)

3926[6] **Indigo Time (IRE) (80)***(91) (PFICole)* 3-9-0 TQuinn(11) (3rd st: led over 1f out: rdn out)......— **1**
3801* Lucayan Sunshine (USA) **(80)***(87)*(Fav)*(LadyHerries)* 3-9-0 LDettori(2) (4th st: ev ch over 1f out: unable qckn)....3 **2**
3836[12] Sharp Falcon (IRE) **(72)***(77) (JWharton)* 4-9-0 JWeaver(10) (s.s: rdn over 2f out: hdwy over 1f out: r.o)....1¾ **3**
Reimei **(67)***(72) (RAkehurst)* 6-8-9 DHarrison(1) (b: rdn over 2f out: hdwy 1f out: one pce)...d.h **3**
3659[14] River Keen (IRE) **(77)***(80) (RWArmstrong)* 3-8-11b RPrice(6) (lw: hdwy over 3f out: 6th st: rdn over 2f out: one pce)....1 **5**
3836[14] Artic Courier **(80)***(81) (DJSCosgrove)* 4-9-8 MRimmer(15) (5th st: wknd over 1f out)....2 **6**
3729[4] Country Star (IRE) **(82)***(73) (HCandy)* 4-9-10 WNewnes(5) (led 9f: 2nd st: ev ch over 1f out: sn wknd)....7 **7**
3593[9] Swallows Dream (IRE) **(79)***(70) (JLDunlop)* 4-9-7b WCarson(14) (lw: nvr nrr)....hd **8**
3384* Mr Browning (USA) **(73)***(62) (RAkehurst)* 4-9-1b SSanders(13) (a.p: led 3f out tl over 1f out: sn wknd)....1½ **9**
3987[9] No Speeches (IRE) **(51)***(39) (CACyzer)* 4-7-4 (3) NVarley(7) (bhd fnl 3f)....1¼ **10**
3963[2] Kalou **(66)***(52) (CWCElsey)* 4-8-3 (5) PFessey(8) (bhd fnl 3f)....1¼ **11**
3863[8] Loki (IRE) **(82)***(68) (GLewis)* 7-9-10 JReid(4) (b: s.s: bhd fnl 2f)....s.h **12**
3810[5] Unforgiving Minute **(76)***(59) (PWHarris)* 6-8-13 (5) MHenry(3) (lw: hld up: rdn 3f out: sn wknd) .2 **13**
3836[6] Bit on the Side (IRE) **(77)** *(WJMusson)* 6-9-5 PatEddery(9) (a bhd: t.o)....dist **14**
1840[16] Bayrak (USA) **(73)** *(MJRyan)* 5-9-1 RCochrane(12) (lw: bhd fnl 5f: t.o)....5 **15**

100/30 Lucayan Sunshine (USA), **4/1** Bit on the Side (IRE), **9/1** Unforgiving Minute, **10/1** INDIGO TIME (IRE) (8/1-12/1), Country Star (IRE) (8/1-12/1), Kalou, **11/1** Mr Browning (USA) (7/1-12/1), **12/1** Swallows Dream (IRE), **14/1** Sharp Falcon (IRE), Loki (IRE), Reimei (10/1-16/1), **20/1** Artic Courier, Bayrak (USA), **33/1** No Speeches (IRE), River Keen (IRE), CSF £43.63 CT IT, LS & SF £223.88 IT, LS & R £223.88 TOTE £16.30: £3.50 £2.20 SF £2.60 R £3.90 (£46.80) Trio £40.00(SF), £171.40(R) OWNER Mr Terry Neill (WHATCOMBE) BRED Miss Mary Davison 15 Rn
2m 40.54 (11.04) SF: 65/61/59/54/54/63/55/52/44/21/34/50/41/-/-
WEIGHT FOR AGE 3yo-8lb

T/Jkpt: Not won; £6,796.67 to York 7/10/95. T/Plpt: £238.60 (116.01 Tckts). T/Qdpt: £263.00 (1.1 Tckts). AK

4022-ASCOT (R-H)
Saturday October 7th (Soft)

4029

ANGLO AFRICAN HOLDINGS AUTUMN STKS (Listed) (2-Y.O) (Class A) £14,005.00 (£4,240.00: £2,070.00: £985.00)
1m (round) Stalls: High GOING: 0.69 sec per fur (GS) 1-45 (1-46)

3490* **Beauchamp King (100)***(102) (JLDunlop)* 2-8-11 JReid(4) (3rd st: led over 1f out: r.o wl) .....— **1**
3620* Storm Trooper (USA) **(90)***(100)*(Fav)*(HRACecil)* 2-8-11 PatEddery(1) (lw: led over 4f: 2nd st: ev ch over 1f out: unable qckn ins fnl f)....1¼ **2**
3683[2] Bright Heritage (IRE) *(90) (DRLoder)* 2-8-11 GCarter(3) (lw: chsd ldrs: led over 3f out tl over 1f out: wknd fnl f)....5 **3**
3711* Ramooz (USA) **(100)***(85) (BHanbury)* 2-8-11 WRSwinburn(2) (lw: led over 4f: 2nd st: ev ch over 1f out: unable qckn ins fnl f)....2½ **4**
3942[6] La Modiste **(92)***(60) (SDow)* 2-8-6 TQuinn(5) (s.s: 5th st: a in rr)....10 **5**

15/8 Storm Trooper (USA), **2/1** Ramooz (USA), **3/1** BEAUCHAMP KING, **8/1** Bright Heritage (IRE) (7/2-9/1), **40/1** La Modiste, CSF £8.21 TOTE £3.50: £2.00 £1.10 (£3.60) OWNER Mr E. Penser (ARUNDEL) BRED E. Penser 5 Rn 1m 48.16 (8.56) SF: 60/58/48/43/18

4030

PRINCESS ROYAL STKS (Gp 3) (3-Y.O+ F & M) (Class A)
£30,950.00 (£11,710.00: £5,730.00: £2,610.00)
1m 4f Stalls: High GOING: 0.69 sec per fur (GS) 2-15 (2-16)

3223[2] **Labibeh (USA) (86)***(111) (JLDunlop)* 3-8-6 WCarson(5) (chsd ldr: led over 3f out: all out)....— 1
3831[2] Saxon Maid **(106)***(106) (LMCumani)* 4-9-0 WRSwinburn(1) (hrd rdn over 4f out: 5th st: hdwy on ins over 2f out: unable qckn fnl f)....3½ 2
3831[*] Spout **(109)***(97)*(Fav)*(RCharlton)* 3-8-6 PatEddery(6) (4th st: wknd over 1f out)....7 3
3831[4] Royal Circle **(97)***(96) (RCharlton)* 3-8-6 KDarley(3) (lw: 3rd st: wknd wl over 1f out)....¾ 4
3831[3] Snowtown (IRE) **(102)***(83) (PWChapple-Hyam)* 3-8-7 ow1 JReid(4) (lw: led over 8f: 2nd st: wknd over 1f out)....10 5

5/4 Spout (4/5-11/8), **15/8** Saxon Maid, **6/1** Snowtown (IRE) (op 4/1), **11/1** Royal Circle, **16/1** LABIBEH (USA), CSF £41.86 TOTE £6.70: £1.70 £1.50 (£9.10) OWNER Mr Hamdan Al Maktoum (ARUNDEL) BRED Shadwell Farm Estate Co Ltd and Shadwell Farm Inc 5 Rn
2m 41.86 (12.36) SF: 64/67/50/49/36
WEIGHT FOR AGE 3yo-8lb

4031

MITRE RATED STKS H'CAP (0-105) (3-Y.O+) (Class B) £12,555.60
(£4,700.40: £2,300.20: £991.00: £445.50: £227.30)
1m 2f Stalls: High GOING: 0.69 sec per fur (GS) 2-50 (2-53)

3659[0] **Quandary (USA) (86)***(98+)*(Fav)*(HRACecil)* 4-8-7 PatEddery(5) (2nd st: led on bit over 2f out: pushed out)....— 1
2348[10] Romios (IRE) **(86)***(95) (PFICole)* 3-8-1 CRutter(4) (plld hrd: hdwy over 2f out: hung lft over 1f out & ins fnl f: unable qckn)....2 2
3945[19] Hoh Express **(99)***(104) (IABalding)* 3-9-0 WRSwinburn(11) (lw: 4th st: rdn 2f out: one pce)..2½ 3
3945[12] Smart Generation **(86)***(91) (LordHuntingdon)* 4-8-2 (5) MHenry(1) (lw: rdn over 2f out: hdwy over 1f out: one pce)....s.h 4
3836[10] Rokeby Bowl **(95)***(96) (IABalding)* 3-8-5 (5) DGriffiths(3) (lw: hdwy over 1f out: nvr nrr)....2½ 5
3200a[4] Korambi **(93)***(88) (CEBrittain)* 3-8-8 MRoberts(6) (lw: led over 7f: wknd over 1f out)....3½ 6
3836[8] Mystic Hill **(88)***(75) (RCharlton)* 4-8-9 TQuinn(12) (5th st: wknd over 1f out)....5 7
3945[2] Ball Gown **(86)***(68) (DTThom)* 5-8-2 (5) AWhelan(2) (hdwy over 2f out: wknd wl over 1f out)....3 8
3729[16] Green Crusader **(86)***(66) (MRStoute)* 4-8-7v JReid(10) (hdwy over 3f out: wknd 2f out)....1¼ 9
3864[8] Burning (USA) **(96)***(62) (GHarwood)* 3-8-11 MPerrett(14) (a bhd)....9 10
3820[2] Serious **(86)***(46) (LadyHerries)* 5-8-7 KDarley(7) (lw: hdwy 5f out: 3rd st: wknd over 2f out)..3½ 11
3729[9] Special Dawn (IRE) **(90)***(50) (JLDunlop)* 5-8-11 PaulEddery(9) (lw: hdwy over 4f out: wknd over 2f out)....nk 12
3932[8] Aljazzaf **(100)***(58) (RAkehurst)* 5-9-7 MHills(15) (swtg: 6th st: wkng whn hmpd over 2f out)....1 13
Caerphilly (IRE) **(90)** *(DMorley)* 3-8-5 WCarson(13) (prom 6f)....30 14

LONG HANDICAP Green Crusader 8-6 Ball Gown 8-3 Serious 8-3 Smart Generation 8-4

9/2 QUANDARY (USA) (op 3/1), **11/2** Ball Gown, **9/1** Smart Generation, Mystic Hill, **10/1** Green Crusader, **11/1** Special Dawn (IRE), **12/1** Hoh Express, Romios (IRE), Rokeby Bowl, **14/1** Korambi, **16/1** Serious, **20/1** Burning (USA), Aljazzaf, **33/1** Caerphilly (IRE), CSF £51.51 CT £553.35 TOTE £3.70: £2.00 £2.40 £4.20 (£22.20) Trio £92.70 OWNER Mr K. Abdullah (NEWMARKET) BRED Juddmonte Farms 14 Rn 2m 14.51 (10.21) SF: 65/56/65/58/57/49/42/35/33/23/13/17/25/-
WEIGHT FOR AGE 3yo-6lb

4032

WILLMOTT DIXON CORNWALLIS STKS (Gp 3) (2-Y.O) (Class A)
£22,295.00 (£8,438.50: £4,131.75: £1,884.75)
5f Stalls: Low GOING: 0.69 sec per fur (GS) 3-20 (3-21)

3610[2] **Mubhij (IRE) (100)***(108)*(Fav)*(BWHills)* 2-8-12 WCarson(1) (mde all: comf)....— 1
3668[*] Westcourt Magic **(100)***(97) (MWEasterby)* 2-8-12 JReid(2) (wnt rt s: chsd wnr: rdn over 2f out: unable qckn)....3½ 2
3886[3] The Man **(89)***(86) (MRChannon)* 2-8-12 PatEddery(6) (outpcd: hdwy over 1f out: one pce)..3½ 3
3668[2] Kunucu (IRE) **(100)***(78) (TDBarron)* 2-8-7 KDarley(3) (hmpd s: outpcd: sme hdwy over 1f out: one pce)....¾ 4
3668[12] Eastern Prophets **(100)***(83) (GLewis)* 2-8-12 PaulEddery(7) (swtg: hld up: rdn over 2f out: wknd fnl f)....s.h 5
3699[*] Oh Whataknight **(92)***(30) (RMWhitaker)* 2-8-7 MHills(4) (lw: bhd fnl 3f)....15 6
2726a[8] Sacramento (IRE) *(27) (BTevels,Belgium)* 2-8-12b RVindevogel(5) (lt-f: bhd fnl 2f)....2½ 7

6/5 MUBHIJ (IRE), **7/2** Westcourt Magic, **6/1** Kunucu (IRE) (4/1-13/2), **8/1** Oh Whataknight, **11/1** The Man, **12/1** Eastern Prophets (op 8/1), **33/1** Sacramento (IRE), CSF £5.55 TOTE £1.90: £1.40 £2.40 (£2.80) OWNER Mr Hamdan Al Maktoum (LAMBOURN) BRED Shadwell Estate Company Limited 7 Rn 65.36 secs (5.86) SF: 55/44/33/25/30/-/-

4033

WILLMOTT DIXON H'CAP (0-110) (3-Y.O+) (Class B) £15,500.00 (£4,700.00: £2,300.00: £1,100.00) **5f** Stalls: Low GOING: 0.69 sec per fur (GS) 3-50 (3-52)

3878[3] **Coastal Bluff** **(84)***(94)*(Fav)*(TDBarron)* 3-8-7 KDarley(22) (hdwy over 1f out: led wl ins fnl f: rdn out)........ — 1
3938[2] Fire Dome (IRE) **(96)***(105) (RHannon)* 3-9-5 JReid(7) (lw: hdwy over 1f out: led ins fnl f: sn hdd: r.o)........nk 2
3813[8] No Extras (IRE) **(100)***(107) (GLMoore)* 5-9-10 SWhitworth(10) (gd hdwy over 1f out: str run fnl f: fin wl)........¾ 3
3931[10] Hello Mister **(102)***(106) (JO'Donoghue)* 4-9-9 (3) PMcCabe(6) (rdn & hdwy over 1f out: r.o ins fnl f)........¾ 4
3748[4] Lady Sheriff **(79)***(82) (MWEasterby)* 4-8-3b WCarson(14) (a.p: rdn over 2f out: led over 1f out tl ins fnl f: one pce)........½ 5
3924[4] Saseedo (USA) **(87)***(86) (WAO'Gorman)* 5-8-11 EmmaO'Gorman(5) (swtg: s.s: nt clr run 2f out: gd hdwy fnl f: r.o wl)........1¼ 6
3615[17] Agwa **(71)***(68) (RJO'Sullivan)* 6-7-6 (3) NVarley(1) (led over 3f)........½ 7
3992[21] Macfarlane **(77)***(63) (MJFetherston-Godley)* 7-7-10 (5)ow3 AWhelan(3) (b: nt clr run 2f out to 1f out: hdwy fnl f: nvr nrr)........2½ 8
3854[4] Lago Di Varano **(92)***(75) (JBerry)* 3-9-1v GCarter(9) (lw: nvr nrr)........2 9
3717[20] Sir Joey (USA) **(84)***(66) (PGMurphy)* 6-8-8 JWilliams(24) (hmpd s: hdwy wl over 1f out: sn wknd)........hd 10
1277[5] Chewit **(80)***(59) (AMoore)* 3-8-3 CandyMorris(11) (swtg: hld up: hrd rdn wl over 1f out: eased whn btn fnl f)........1 11
3929[2] Youdontsay **(82)***(59) (RCurtis)* 3-8-0 (5) PPMurphy(4) (a mid div)........¾ 12
3815[10] Ann's Pearl (IRE) **(77)***(47) (JWHills)* 4-7-10 (5) MHenry(2) (spd over 3f)........2 13
3878[15] Stolen Kiss (IRE) **(72)***(42) (MWEasterby)* 3-7-2b(7) MartinDwyer(17) (prom over 3f)........hd 14
1489[10] Seigneurial **(90)***(58) (GHarwood)* 3-8-13 AClark(13) (s.s: a mid div)........¾ 15
3961* Bowden Rose **(85)***(52) (MBlanshard)* 3-8-3b(5) MBaird(8) (s.s: outpcd: nt clr run over 1f out: nvr nrr)........s.h 16
3815[4] Call Me I'm Blue (IRE) **(88)***(51) (NTinkler)* 5-8-12 WNewnes(15) (prom over 2f: bhd whn hmpd ins fnl f)........1¼ 17
3815[12] Jayannpee **(94)***(53) (IABalding)* 4-9-4 MHills(18) (a mid div)........1¼ 18
3938* Inherent Magic (IRE) **(91)***(49)*(Fav)*(WRMuir)* 6-9-1 PatEddery(12) (b: lw: bhd fnl 2f)........½ 19
3938[3] Takadou (IRE) **(88)***(46) (MissLCSiddall)* 4-8-12 WRSwinburn(20) (hdwy over 1f out: eased whn btn fnl f)........s.h 20
3632[6] Lord High Admiral (CAN) **(90)***(44) (CREgerton)* 7-9-0b TQuinn(23) (racd alone: bhd fnl 3f) ...1¼ 21
3815[11] Ashtina **(82)***(25) (BAPearce)* 10-7-13 (7) JWilkinson(16) (prom 3f)........3½ 22
3717[17] Name the Tune **(89)***(30) (PHowling)* 4-8-13 PaulEddery(19) (b.hind: a bhd)........½ 23
3878* Twice as Sharp **(84)***(15) (PWHarris)* 3-8-7 PRobinson(21) (hdwy over 3f out: wknd 2f out)......3 24

8/1 COASTAL BLUFF (6/1-9/1), Inherent Magic (IRE), **9/1** Bowden Rose, **10/1** Macfarlane, **12/1** Call Me I'm Blue (IRE), Lady Sheriff, Twice as Sharp, **14/1** Takadou (IRE), Youdontsay, Saseedo (USA), Fire Dome (IRE), **16/1** No Extras (IRE), Agwa, **20/1** Hello Mister, Name the Tune, **25/1** Jayannpee, Stolen Kiss (IRE), Lord High Admiral (CAN), Sir Joey (USA), **33/1** Ann's Pearl (IRE), Seigneurial, Ashtina, Lago Di Varano, **50/1** Chewit, CSF £114.13 CT £1,646.13 TOTE £7.50: £2.20 £4.30 £4.80 £8.70 (£72.00) Trio £225.10 OWNER Mrs D. E. Sharp (THIRSK) BRED R. M. West 24 Rn 65.59 secs (6.09) SF: 47/58/61/60/36/40/22/17/28/20/12/12/1/-/11/5/5/7/3/-/-/-/-/-

WEIGHT FOR AGE 3yo-1lb

4034

HYPERION CONDITIONS STKS (2-Y.O) (Class B) £7,282.80 (£2,725.20: £1,332.60: £573.00: £256.50: £129.90) **7f** Stalls: Low GOING: 0.69 sec per fur (GS) 4-25 (4-27)

3886* **Brandon Magic** **(100)***(98)*(Fav)*(IABalding)* 2-8-13 WRSwinburn(3) (rdn 2f out: hdwy over 1f out: led ins fnl f: r.o wl)........ — 1
3776[2] Henry The Fifth **(90)***(95) (CEBrittain)* 2-8-11 KDarley(4) (led: clr over 4f out: rdn over 1f out: hdd ins fnl f: r.o)........nk 2
3861* Oberons Boy (IRE) **(94)***(89) (BJMeehan)* 2-8-11 PatEddery(2) (chsd ldr: rdn over 2f out: unable qckn ins fnl f)........3 3
1838[9] What Fun **(99)***(72) (RHannon)* 2-9-1 WCarson(5) (bhd fnl 2f)........9 4
3925[8] Kuantan (USA) **(100)** *(PFICole)* 2-9-1 TQuinn(6) (Withdrawn not under Starter's orders: ref to ent stalls)........ **W**

10/11 BRANDON MAGIC (Evens-11/10), **4/1** Oberons Boy (IRE) (3/1-9/2), **5/1** Kuantan (USA), **9/1** Henry The Fifth (5/1-10/1), **12/1** What Fun (op 8/1), CSF £5.08 TOTE £1.40: £2.20 (£4.70) OWNER Mr R. P. B. Michaelson (KINGSCLERE) BRED Highclere Stud Ltd 4 Rn

1m 37.28 (10.78) SF: 29/26/20/3/-

4035 DUKE OF EDINBURGH H'CAP (0-90) (3-Y.O+) (Class C) £11,917.50 (£3,615.00: £1,770.00: £847.50)
1m (straight) Stalls: Low GOING: 0.69 sec per fur (GS) 5-00 (5-03)

3813* **Night Dance (90)***(107) (GLewis)* 3-9-9 (5) AWhelan(14) (hdwy on ins 3f out: led over 2f out: rdn out) — 1
3601* Conspicuous (IRE) **(74)***(90) (LGCottrell)* 5-9-2 MRoberts(4) (hdwy 2f out: r.o wl ins fnl f) ½ 2
3712* Tarawa (IRE) **(80)***(92)*(Fav)*(NACallaghan)* 3-8-13 (5) MHenry(21) (a.p: ev ch over 2f out: hrd rdn over 1f out: one pce) 2 3
3813[12] Quintus Decimus **(76)***(76) (LordHuntingdon)* 3-9-0 MHills(22) (hdwy over 2f out: hrd rdn over 1f out: one pce) 6 4
3959[6] Red Light **(71)***(70) (LordHuntingdon)* 3-8-9v JWilliams(15) (hdwy 1f out: nvr nrr) ¾ 5
3729[13] Star Manager (USA) **(78)***(76) (PFICole)* 5-9-6 TQuinn(9) (swtg: hdwy 4f out: wknd 2f out) nk 6
3837[4] Toujours Riviera **(86)***(83) (JPearce)* 5-9-11 (3) NVarley(6) (lw: a.p: ev ch over 2f out: wknd over 1f out) ½ 7
2531[7] Crested Knight (IRE) **(65)***(59) (CAHorgan)* 3-8-3 CRutter(3) (hdwy over 1f out: nvr nrr) 1¼ 8
3885[4] Just Harry **(65)***(54) (MJRyan)* 4-8-7 AClark(17) (lw: nvr nrr) 2½ 9
3885[2] Duello **(61)***(42) (MBlanshard)* 4-7-12 (5) MBaird(8) (a.p: led 4f out tl over 2f out: wknd 1f out) 4 10
3837[14] Kingchip Boy **(64)***(45) (MJRyan)* 6-8-6v DBiggs(20) (prom over 4f) hd 11
3706[3] Sharp Rebuff **(76)***(56) (PJMakin)* 4-9-4 KDarley(11) (hdwy over 3f out: wknd 2f out) ¾ 12
3728[8] Frogmarch (USA) **(85)***(63) (MajorWRHern)* 5-9-13 PaulEddery(10) (lw: a mid div) ¾ 13
3813[27] Mister Rm **(79)***(56) (RGuest)* 3-9-3 WCarson(12) (lw: s.s: hdwy over 2f out: sn wknd) ¾ 14
3781[4] Eurolink the Rebel (USA) **(77)***(47) (RAkehurst)* 3-9-1 PatEddery(23) (prom over 5f) 3½ 15
3629[7] Helios **(70)***(34) (NJHWalker)* 7-8-12 GCarter(16) (bhd fnl 4f) 3 16
3945[35] Gadge **(68)***(26) (DMorris)* 4-8-10v RPrice(18) (bhd fnl 3f: bmpd over 2f out) 3 17
3139[2] Spectacle Jim **(51)***(7) (JO'Donoghue)* 6-7-7b NCarlisle(19) (bhd fnl 3f: bmpd over 2f out) 1 18
3393[8] Flag Fen (USA) **(80)***(33) (MartynMeade)* 4-9-8 VSlattery(1) (bhd fnl 4f) 1¼ 19
3768[7] Sharp 'n Smart **(77)***(26) (BSmart)* 3-9-1 WNewnes(13) (swtg: led 4f) 2 20
2602[8] Green City **(68)** *(JAkehurst)* 3-8-6 ow2 SWhitworth(7) (prom over 3f) 12 21
2056[3] Ever so Lyrical **(74)** *(PWHarris)* 5-9-2 WRSwinburn(5) (a bhd) ½ 22

LONG HANDICAP Spectacle Jim 7-3

5/1 Tarawa (IRE), **13/2** Conspicuous (IRE), **15/2** Star Manager (USA), **9/1** Quintus Decimus, NIGHT DANCE, **10/1** Duello, **14/1** Toujours Riviera, Ever so Lyrical, Mister Rm, Sharp Rebuff (12/1-20/1), **16/1** Eurolink the Rebel (USA), Gadge, **20/1** Frogmarch (USA), Red Light, Just Harry, Sharp 'n Smart, **33/1** Crested Knight (IRE), Helios, Spectacle Jim, Flag Fen (USA), Green City, Kingchip Boy, CSF £67.49 CT £307.17 TOTE £8.70: £2.40 £2.20 £2.70 £2.20 (£25.90) Trio £78.70 OWNER Mr G. V. Wright (EPSOM) BRED Miss J. A. Challen 22 Rn

1m 50.24 (11.04) SF: 56/43/41/25/19/29/36/8/7/-/-/9/16/5/-/-/-/-/-/-/-/-
WEIGHT FOR AGE 3yo-4lb
T/Plpt: £44.70 (599.66). T/Qdpt: £12.20 (29.2 Tckts). AK

3997-YORK (L-H)
Saturday October 7th (Good)
WEATHER: drizzle WIND: slt half bhd

4036 BRAMHAM MOOR H'CAP (0-85) (3-Y.O+) (Class D) £7,635.00 (£2,280.00: £1,090.00: £247.50: £247.50)
1m 5f 194y Stalls: Low GOING: 0.03 sec per fur (G) 2-15 (2-15)

3547[3] **Tudor Island (76)***(89) (CEBrittain)* 6-9-6 LDettori(8) (trckd ldrs: effrt over 3f out: led over 1f out: hld on wl) — 1
3927* Floating Line **(67)***(80)*(Fav)*(EJAlston)* 7-8-11 JCarroll(5) (swtg: trckd ldrs: led over 3f out tl over 1f out: r.o) nk 2
3978[4] Star Rage (IRE) **(79)***(86) (MJohnston)* 5-9-9 JWeaver(1) (hld up: stdy hdwy over 3f out: nt qckn appr fnl f) 5 3
3730[16] Midyan Blue (IRE) **(79)***(85) (JMPEustace)* 5-9-9 RCochrane(11) (in tch: effrt over 3f out: styd on one pce fnl 2f) ½ 4
3936[2] Amiarge **(50)***(55) (MBrittain)* 5-7-5 (3)ow1 DWright(9) (bhd: hdwy over 3f out: styd on wl ins fnl f) d.h 4
3445[6] Faugeron **(60)***(64) (NTinkler)* 6-8-4 KimTinkler(13) (s.i.s: drvn along 7f out: kpt on fnl 3f: nvr nr ldrs) 1¾ 6
3801[7] Shakiyr (FR) **(61)***(65) (RHollinshead)* 4-8-5 WRyan(12) (hld up & bhd: styd on fnl 3f: nvr nr to chal) hd 7
3682[4] Nanton Point (USA) **(68)***(68) (LadyHerries)* 3-8-3 DHarrison(7) (chsd ldrs: drvn along 6f out: one pce fnl 3f) 4 8
3705[2] Good Hand (USA) **(75)***(72) (JWWatts)* 9-9-5 NConnorton(10) (b.hind: s.i.s: a bhd) 2½ 9

3669[4] Eau de Cologne **(68)***(59) (CWThornton)* 3-8-3 DeanMcKeown(4) (lw: trckd ldrs: led over 4f out tl over 3f out: sn lost pl) 5 **10**
3801[4] Haniya (IRE) **(84)***(60) (JLDunlop)* 3-9-5 RHills(2) (chsd ldrs tl wknd over 2f out: eased whn no ch: t.o) 13 **11**
3864[4] Persian Elite (IRE) **(84)***(53) (PFICole)* 4-9-9 (5) DaneO'Neill(3) (led tl over 4f out: sn lost pl: t.o)6 **12**
3774[W] Soba Up **(76)***(11) (TJEtherington)* 5-9-6 ACulhane(6) (in tch: pushed along 8f out: lost pl over 3f out: eased: t.o) 30 **13**

LONG HANDICAP Amiarge 6-12

4/1 Floating Line, **9/2** TUDOR ISLAND, **6/1** Haniya (IRE), **13/2** Nanton Point (USA), **9/1** Persian Elite (IRE), **10/1** Midyan Blue (IRE), **11/1** Good Hand (USA), **12/1** Star Rage (IRE), Shakiyr (FR), Soba Up, Eau de Cologne, **20/1** Amiarge, Faugeron, CSF £24.05 CT £194.20 TOTE £4.50: £2.00 £2.20 £4.70 (£7.40) Trio £36.80 OWNER Mr D. Sieff (NEWMARKET) BRED David Sieff 13 Rn

3m 1.46 (7.86) SF: 61/52/58/57/27/36/37/31/44/22/23/25/-
WEIGHT FOR AGE 3yo-9lb

4037 COLDSTREAM GUARDS ASSOCIATION CUP MAIDEN STKS (2-Y.O) (Class D) £6,108.00 (£1,824.00: £872.00: £396.00)

7f 202y Stalls: Low GOING: 0.03 sec per fur (G) 2-45 (2-46)

3868[2] **Committal (IRE)** *(85+)*(Fav)*(JHMGosden)* 2-9-0 LDettori(7) (trckd ldrs: led on bit over 3f out: pushed clr over 1f out: comf) ....— **1**
3827[4] Silver Wing (USA) *(72) (MBell)* 2-8-9 MFenton(2) (b.off hind: trckd ldrs: kpt on fnl 2f: no ch w wnr) 4 **2**
3666[4] Karisma (IRE) *(72) (DenysSmith)* 2-9-0 TWilliams(8) (trckd ldrs: effrt over 3f out: kpt on same pce) 2½ **3**
Rusk *(72) (JPearce)* 2-9-0 MWigham(1) (w'like: dwlt: hdwy over 3f out: styd on fr over 1f out: nvr nr to chal) ....hd **4**
3592[10] Whitley Grange Boy *(62) (JLEyre)* 2-9-0 RLappin(6) (swtg: chsd ldrs: sn drvn along: lost pl over 3f out) 5 **5**
Private Audience (USA) *(52) (HRACecil)* 2-9-0 WRyan(3) (w'like: leggy: sn pushed along: sme hdwy over 3f out: sn wknd) 5 **6**
Bluebeard (IRE) *(44) (JHMGosden)* 2-9-0 JCarroll(4) (wl grwn: rangy: bit bkwd: s.i.s: bhd & rn green: drvn along & hung lft over 3f out) 3½ **7**
3503[3] Anchor Venture *(44) (SPCWoods)* 2-9-0 WWoods(5) (led tl over 3f out: wknd over 2f out)....hd **8**

1/2 COMMITTAL (IRE), **100/30** Private Audience (USA) (9/4-7/2), **12/1** Silver Wing (USA) (op 8/1), **14/1** Bluebeard (IRE) (op 8/1), **16/1** Karisma (IRE), **20/1** Anchor Venture, **33/1** Rusk, **50/1** Whitley Grange Boy, CSF £7.98 TOTE £1.60: £1.10 £1.70 £1.90 (£4.50) OWNER Sheikh Mohammed (NEWMARKET) BRED Sheikh Mohammed bin Rashid al Maktoum 8 Rn

1m 40.85 (4.85) SF: 50/37/37/37/27/17/9/9

4038 CROWTHER HOMES H'CAP (0-80) (3-Y.O+) (Class D) £11,580.00 (£3,480.00: £1,680.00: £780.00)

1m 205y Stalls: Low GOING: 0.03 sec per fur (G) 3-15 (3-16)

3973[3] **Seventeens Lucky (67)***(77) (BobJones)* 3-8-10 MWigham(9) (in tch: hdwy to ld over 1f out: r.o u.p) ....— **1**
3935[9] Carlito Brigante **(65)***(73) (MrsJRRamsden)* 3-8-8 JFEgan(23) (mid div: hdwy over 2f out: r.o fnl f: nt rch wnr) 1 **2**
3802[3] Noble Sprinter (IRE) **(79)***(87)*(Fav)*(RHannon)* 3-9-8 LDettori(25) (racd wd: in tch: effrt over 3f out: styd on wl fnl f) ....nk **3**
3447[4] Nobby Barnes **(45)***(52) (DonEnricoIncisa)* 6-7-7 KimTinkler(13) (bhd: gd hdwy over 2f out: edgd lft & styd on wl fnl f) ....nk **4**
3863* Guesstimation (USA) **(66)***(73) (JPearce)* 6-8-11 (3) SDrowne(6) (hld up: stdy hdwy 3f out: kpt on fnl f: nt rch ldrs) ....hd **5**
2593[5] Rory **(78)***(84) (MrsJCecil)* 4-9-5 (7) AmandaSanders(18) (a chsng ldrs: kpt on same pce fnl 2f) ....¾ **6**
3945[14] Secret Aly (CAN) **(80)***(81) (CEBrittain)* 5-10-0 MBirch(4) (bhd tl styd on wl fnl 2f: nt rch ldrs) 2½ **7**
3935[10] Westcourt Princess **(53)***(50) (MWEasterby)* 3-7-10 TWilliams(12) (led tl over 1f out: sn wknd) 2½ **8**
3993[8] Wentbridge Lad (IRE) **(63)***(59) (PDEvans)* 5-8-11v SSanders(24) (in tch: hdwy 3f out: sn hmpd, hung lft & kpt on appr fnl f) ....nk **9**
2222[3] Coureur **(67)***(60) (JDBethell)* 6-9-1 TIves(19) (racd wd: in tch: effrt on outside 3f out: nvr rchd ldrs) 1½ **10**
3945[11] Pride of Pendle **(77)***(67) (DNicholls)* 6-9-11 AlexGreaves(26) (hld up on outside: effrt over 3f out: n.d) 2 **11**
2848[5] Tranquillity **(70)***(59) (LordHuntingdon)* 3-8-13 DHarrison(15) (swtg: chsd ldrs tl outpcd fnl 2f) nk **12**

3852[6] Keep Battling **(46)**_(33)_ _(JSGoldie)_ 5-7-1 (7)ow1 RMullen(16) (swtg: mid div: hdwy 2f out: styd on fnl f)..........1 **13**

3840[10] Thatched (IRE) **(55)**_(39)_ _(REBarr)_ 5-7-12 (5) PFessey(1) (s.i.s: bhd tl hdwy over 2f out: n.d)..1¾ **14**

3825[2] Antarcticern (USA) **(48)**_(30)_ _(GROldroyd)_ 5-7-10 ow2 AMackay(8) (s.i.s: a bhd)..........½ **15**

3664[2] Mr Rough **(65)**_(48)_ _(DMorris)_ 4-8-13 RCochrane(10) (mid div & drvn along 6f out: sn chsng ldrs: wknd over 1f out)..........½ **16**

3630[5] Dorothea Brooke (IRE) **(75)**_(57)_ _(PWHarris)_ 3-9-4 JWeaver(21) (racd wd: hld up: hdwy on outside over 3f out: nvr rchd ldrs)..........½ **17**

3182[8] Prizefighter **(65)**_(42)_ _(JLEyre)_ 4-8-13 JTate(17) (chsd ldrs tl wknd over 2f out)..........2½ **18**

3743[15] Our Main Man **(52)**_(27)_ _(RMWhitaker)_ 5-7-11 (3) DWright(3) (chsd ldrs tl wknd qckly 2f out)......1 **19**

3659[12] Quivira **(77)**_(52)_ _(TTClement)_ 4-9-11v RHills(7) (swtg: a bhd)..........½ **20**

3840[5] Thaleros **(55)**_(27)_ _(GMMoore)_ 5-8-3 DaleGibson(22) (racd wd: chsd ldrs tl lost pl 3f out)......1¼ **21**

Nizaal (USA) **(80)**_(42)_ _(DNicholls)_ 4-10-0 JCarroll(14) (swtg: a in rr)..........6 **22**

3926[7] Cyrus the Great (IRE) **(77)**_(38)_ _(MBell)_ 3-9-6 MFenton(5) (b.nr fore: swtg: in tch tl wknd 3f out)..........½ **23**

3820[10] Ballard Ring (IRE) **(47)**_(2)_ _(JSWainwright)_ 4-7-9 LCharnock(2) (rr div: sn drvn along: bhd fnl 4f)..........3 **24**

Lord Lambson **(45)** _(JPearce)_ 6-7-7 JLowe(11) (a wl last: t.o)..........dist **25**

LONG HANDICAP Keep Battling 7-1 Nobby Barnes 7-3 Lord Lambson 7-0

11/2 Noble Sprinter (IRE), **13/2** Guesstimation (USA) (op 10/1), **7/1** Pride of Pendle, **9/1** Dorothea Brooke (IRE), **12/1** Mr Rough, **14/1** SEVENTEENS LUCKY, Carlito Brigante, Coureur, Tranquillity, Cyrus the Great (IRE), Westcourt Princess, **20/1** Rory, Secret Aly (CAN), Thatched (IRE), Nizaal (USA), Wentbridge Lad (IRE), Thaleros, **25/1** Quivira, Antarcticern (USA), Ballard Ring (IRE), Prizefighter, **33/1** Nobby Barnes, **40/1** Keep Battling, **50/1** Our Main Man, **66/1** Lord Lambson, CSF £204.24 CT £1,138.87 TOTE £42.30: £6.70 £4.70 £2.00 £8.60 (£515.40) Trio £1,439.00 OWNER Mr D. M. Cameron (NEWMARKET) BRED D. E. Weeden 25 Rn

1m 53.89 (4.89) SF: 52/48/62/32/53/64/61/25/39/40/47/34/13/19/10/28/32/22/7/32/7/22/13/-/-

WEIGHT FOR AGE 3yo-5lb

4039 EAST COAST ROCKINGHAM STKS (Listed) (2-Y.O) (Class A)

£10,113.75 (£3,645.00: £1,747.50: £712.50: £281.25)

6f Stalls: High GOING: 0.03 sec per fur (G) 3-45 (3-46)

3903[5] **Resounder (USA) (100)**_(97)_(Fav)_(JHMGosden)_ 2-8-11 LDettori(4) (trckd ldrs: effrt on ins 2f out: led over 1f out: r.o strly)..........— **1**

3731[3] Warning Time **(100)**_(92)_ _(BJMeehan)_ 2-8-11 JFEgan(1) (hld up: hdwy on outside 2f out: rdn & hung bdly rt ins fnl f: no ch w wnr)..........2 **2**

3680[3] Beautiful Ballad (IRE) **(96)**_(82)_ _(BWHills)_ 2-8-6 RHills(2) (lw: trckd ldrs: rdn & edgd rt over 1f out: kpt on same pce: hmpd ins fnl f)..........1¾ **3**

3668[3] Tadeo **(96)**_(82)_ _(MJohnston)_ 2-8-11 JWeaver(5) (led: hung lft & hdd over 1f out: kpt on same pce)..........2 **4**

3925[6] Truancy _(80)_ _(MBell)_ 2-8-11 MFenton(3) (lw: trckd ldrs: effrt over 2f out: outpcd over 1f out: wkng whn hmpd ins fnl f)..........¾ **5**

6/4 RESOUNDER (USA), **2/1** Warning Time, **5/1** Truancy, **6/1** Tadeo, **9/1** Beautiful Ballad (IRE), CSF £4.90 TOTE £2.40: £1.30 £1.50 (£1.80) OWNER Mr Herbert Allen (NEWMARKET) BRED Gainesway Thoroughbreds Ltd 5 Rn 1m 12.89 (3.29) SF: 50/45/35/35/33

4040 CORAL SPRINT TROPHY H'CAP (0-100) (3-Y.O+) (Class C)

£18,130.00 (£5,440.00: £2,620.00: £1,210.00)

6f Stalls: High GOING: 0.03 sec per fur (G) 4-15 (4-16)

3943[6] **Double Bounce (77)**_(87)_(Fav)_(PJMakin)_ 5-8-8 LDettori(19) (swtg: sn pushed along: hdwy & swtchd rt over 2f out: r.o wl to ld wl ins fnl f)..........— **1**

3807[3] Highborn (IRE) **(80)**_(90)_ _(PSFelgate)_ 6-8-11 WRyan(20) (swtg: hdwy over 2f out: ev ch ins fnl f: edgd lft nr fin: r.o)..........hd **2**

3748[6] Palo Blanco **(72)**_(80)_ _(TDBarron)_ 4-8-3 LCharnock(3) (chsd ldrs: led jst ins fnl f: edgd rt & styd on: hdd wl ins fnl f)..........¾ **3**

2973* Brecongill Lad **(79)**_(80)_ _(MissSEHall)_ 3-8-8b WWoods(12) (s.i.s: hdwy to chse ldrs ½-wy: ev ch over 1f out: kpt on same pce)..........2½ **4**

3815[7] Bold Effort (FR) **(98)**_(95)_ _(KOCunningham-Brown)_ 3-9-13 JWeaver(15) (chsd ldr: led over 1f out: edgd lft & hdd jst ins fnl f: grad wknd)..........1½ **5**

3557[2] Shamanic **(92)**_(88)_ _(RHannon)_ 3-9-2 (5) DaneO'Neill(16) (a in tch: kpt on u.p fnl 2f)..........nk **6**

3717[13] Perryston View **(87)**_(82)_ _(PCalver)_ 3-9-2v MBirch(6) (led tl over 1f out: kpt on same pce ins fnl f)..........½ **7**

3715[11] Statius **(76)**_(71)_ _(TDBarron)_ 3-8-5 DeanMcKeown(21) (lw: hdwy ½-wy: sn chsng ldrs: edgd lft & nt qckn over 1f out)..........s.h **8**

3964[W] Champagne Grandy **(83)***(75) (MRChannon)* 5-8-9 (5) RPainter(9) (outpcd & bhd tl styd on wl appr fnl f)....1 **9**
3815[8] Master of Passion **(86)***(77) (JMPEustace)* 6-9-3 MTebbutt(1) (chsd ldrs far side: kpt on fnl 2f)....nk **10**
3943[24] How's Yer Father **(81)***(68) (RJHodges)* 9-8-12 RCochrane(13) (hdwy over 2f out: kpt on fnl f)....1¾ **11**
3964[17] Oggi **(67)***(54) (PJMakin)* 4-7-12b JLowe(10) (in tch tl outpcd fnl 2f)....s.h **12**
3717[7] Benzoe (IRE) **(80)***(66) (MrsJRRamsden)* 5-8-11 JFEgan(11) (lw: sn chsng ldrs: rdn 2f out: sn wknd)....hd **13**
3964[14] Amron **(73)***(58) (JBerry)* 8-7-13 (5) PFessey(18) (s.i.s: bhd: sme hdwy 2f out: n.d)....½ **14**
3964[10] Lynton Lad **(75)***(52) (CPEBrooks)* 3-8-4 DHarrison(4) (chsd ldrs far side over 3f)....3 **15**
3938[6] Ziggy's Dancer (USA) **(88)***(60) (EJAlston)* 4-9-5 JCarroll(2) (chsd ldrs far side: wknd over 2f out)....1¾ **16**
3905[3] Latching (IRE) **(73)***(44) (RFJohnsonHoughton)* 3-8-2 RHills(5) (chsd ldrs far side over 3f: sn wknd)....½ **17**
3715[2] Colway Rake **(72)***(40) (JWWatts)* 4-8-3bow1 NConnorton(22) (lw: chsd ldrs over 3f)....¾ **18**
3922[5] Croeso-I-Cymru **(90)***(58) (RAkehurst)* 4-9-7 SSanders(7) (swtg: chsd ldrs over 3f: sn wknd) .nk **19**
3359[4] Samsolom **(73)***(39) (PHowling)* 7-8-4 JTate(17) (sn bhd)....¾ **20**
3457[13] Encore M'Lady (IRE) **(67)***(28) (FHLee)* 4-7-12 AMackay(14) (chsd ldrs to ½-wy: sn wknd)......2 **21**
3717[23] Lord Olivier (IRE) **(89)***(43) (WJarvis)* 5-9-3 (3) JStack(23) (chsd ldrs stands' side over 3f: sn lost pl)....2½ **22**
3984[4] Master Millfield (IRE) **(69)***(7) (RJHodges)* 3-7-12 StephenDavies(8) (sn drvn along & outpcd).6 **23**

3/1 DOUBLE BOUNCE (op 5/1), **6/1** Benzoe (IRE), **10/1** Colway Rake, **12/1** Statius, Latching (IRE), Croeso-I-Cymru, **14/1** Palo Blanco, Brecongill Lad, Perryston View, **16/1** Bold Effort (FR), How's Yer Father, Highborn (IRE), Master of Passion, Champagne Grandy, **20/1** Oggi, Shamanic, Samsolom, Master Millfield (IRE), **25/1** Lord Olivier (IRE), Lynton Lad, **33/1** Ziggy's Dancer (USA), Encore M'Lady (IRE), Amron, CSF £58.27 CT £606.20 TOTE £4.40: £1.60 £4.20 £5.20 £3.70 (£61.20) Trio £475.40 OWNER Mrs P. Scott-Dunn (MARLBOROUGH) BRED Mrs P. Scott-Dunn 23 Rn
1m 12.19 (2.59) SF: 58/61/51/49/64/57/51/40/46/48/39/25/37/29/21/31/13/11/29/10/-/14/-
WEIGHT FOR AGE 3yo-2lb

4041 NAPOLEONS CASINO H'CAP (0-85) (3-Y.O+) (Class D) £10,644.00 (£3,192.00: £1,536.00: £708.00) **6f 214y** Stalls: High GOING: 0.03 sec per fur (G) 4-45 (4-46)

3837[3] **Comanche Companion** **(77)***(88) (TJNaughton)* 5-9-3 (5) JDSmith(10) (hdwy u.p ½-wy: styd on wl to ld ins fnl f)....— **1**
3823[12] Barrel of Hope **(67)***(75) (JLEyre)* 3-8-9b SDWilliams(1) (led tl ins fnl f)....1¼ **2**
3545[12] Jolto **(74)***(79) (KOCunningham-Brown)* 6-9-5 JWeaver(19) (w ldr tl nt qckn fnl f)....1½ **3**
3943[2] Broughtons Turmoil **(65)***(69)*(Fav)*(WJMusson)* 6-8-10 LDettori(18) (hdwy to chse ldrs ½-wy: kpt on same pce appr fnl f)....½ **4**
3807[5] Ochos Rios (IRE) **(60)***(60) (BSRothwell)* 4-8-5 LCharnock(12) (hdwy u.p over 2f out: kpt on: nvr rchd ldrs)....1½ **5**
3813[14] Ertlon **(83)***(83) (CEBrittain)* 5-10-0 RHills(23) (racd wd: hmpd after 1f: sn in tch: styd on fnl 2f)....hd **6**
3800* Densben **(54)***(52) (DenysSmith)* 11-7-13 TWilliams(6) (bhd: hdwy ½-wy: styd on appr fnl f) ...¾ **7**
3837[8] Zajko (USA) **(77)***(73) (LadyHerries)* 5-9-8 RCochrane(5) (lw: hld up: hdwy 2f out: r.o: nt rch ldrs)....1 **8**
3943[25] Halmanerror **(71)***(65) (MrsJRRamsden)* 5-9-2 DHarrison(7) (s.i.s: bhd tl hdwy over 2f out: n.m.r & styd on ins fnl f)....¾ **9**
3534[5] Pelleman **(69)***(62) (RBoss)* 3-8-11 WRyan(4) (chsd ldrs: rdn over 2f out: sn outpcd)....nk **10**
3943[15] Sagebrush Roller **(80)***(72) (JWWatts)* 7-9-11 NConnorton(14) (bhd tl styd on appr fnl f: n.d) ..½ **11**
3807[2] Rossini Blue **(71)***(63) (MrsJRRamsden)* 4-9-2 JFEgan(9) (s.i.s: bhd: hdwy & hung rt 2f out: swtchd lft & n.m.r: styd on nr fin)....s.h **12**
3943[16] Knobbleeneeze **(76)***(67) (MRChannon)* 5-9-2v(5) RPainter(13) (mid div: effrt ½-wy: nvr nr to chal)....½ **13**
3878[17] French Grit (IRE) **(83)***(73) (MDods)* 3-9-11 WWoods(20) (chsd ldrs tl wknd over 2f out).........nk **14**
3813[22] Somerton Boy (IRE) **(79)***(69) (PCalver)* 5-9-10 MBirch(2) (lw: prom: effrt over 2f out: wknd) ..nk **15**
3964[8] Cumbrian Waltzer **(71)***(60) (MHEasterby)* 10-8-11 (5) LNewton(8) (b: sn bhd: sme hdwy over 1f out: n.d)....½ **16**
3771[11] Napoleon Star (IRE) **(68)***(51) (MSSaunders)* 4-8-10 (3) SDrowne(11) (sn bhd & rdn along)....2½ **17**
3943* Samah **(77)***(59) (DNicholls)* 5-9-8 AlexGreaves(21) (lw: swtchd rt s: racd v.wd: chsd ldrs tl hung lft & wknd 2f out)....½ **18**
3964[18] King Rat (IRE) **(78)***(57) (TJEtherington)* 4-9-9 TIves(16) (chsd ldrs: drvn along ½-wy: sn lost pl)....1¼ **19**
3719[10] Stephensons Rocket **(70)***(48) (JBerry)* 4-9-1 JCarroll(3) (b.hind: trckd ldrs tl wknd 2f out).......½ **20**
3719[W] Allinson's Mate (IRE) **(76)***(53) (TDBarron)* 7-9-7b DeanMcKeown(17) (s.i.s: a bhd)....½ **21**
3802[6] Parliament Piece **(74)***(44) (DNicholls)* 9-9-5 MTebbutt(22) (sn bhd)....3 **22**

3715[23] Just Dissident (IRE) **(63)***(30) (RMWhitaker)* 3-8-5 ACulhane(15) (a rr div) 1 **23**

11/4 Broughtons Turmoil, **7/1** Samah, **15/2** COMANCHE COMPANION, **8/1** Zajko (USA), Rossini Blue, **14/1** Pelleman, Sagebrush Roller, Halmanerror, **16/1** Densben, Cumbrian Waltzer, Parliament Piece, Knobbleeneeze, Somerton Boy (IRE), **20/1** Jolto, Ertlon, Allinson's Mate (IRE), French Grit (IRE), **25/1** Ochos Rios (IRE), King Rat (IRE), Napoleon Star (IRE), **33/1** Stephensons Rocket, **50/1** Barrel of Hope, Just Dissident (IRE), CSF £338.28 CT £6,571.89 TOTE £8.60: £2.30 £9.60 £4.60 £1.60 (£1,181.90) Trio Not won; £2,464.38 to Leicester 9/10/95. OWNER The Allstars Club (EPSOM) BRED The National Stud 23 Rn

1m 25.01 (3.51) SF: 65/49/56/46/37/60/29/50/42/36/49/40/44/47/46/37/28/36/34/25/30/21/4

WEIGHT FOR AGE 3yo-3lb

4042 STAMFORD BRIDGE CONDITIONS STKS (2-Y.O C & G) (Class C)

£5,376.00 (£1,856.00: £888.00: £360.00)
6f 214y Stalls: High GOING: 0.03 sec per fur (G) 5-15 (5-15)

3746[5] **Believe Me (90)***(82) (RHannon)* 2-8-4 (5) DaneO'Neill(3) (chsd ldr: led jst ins fnl f: jst hld on) — **1**
3746[6] Bullfinch **(90)***(81) (PTWalwyn)* 2-8-9 DHarrison(1) (swvd bdly lft s: hld up & effrt over 2f out: styd on wl ins fnl f: fin wl)..........nk **2**
3746* Tria Kemata **(100)***(85)*(Fav)*(JLDunlop)* 2-9-0 RCochrane(2) (led tl jst ins fnl f: no ex)..............½ **3**
2131[7] Sualtach (IRE) **(93)** *(RHollinshead)* 2-8-12 LDettori(4) (bit bkwd: trckd ldrs: effrt over 2f out: sn wknd: virtually p.u appr fnl f) ....dist **4**

Evens Tria Kemata, **5/2** Bullfinch, **9/2** BELIEVE ME, **5/1** Sualtach (IRE), CSF £14.46 TOTE £5.10 (£8.80) OWNER Mr Bruce Adams (MARLBOROUGH) BRED Derek R. Price 4 Rn

1m 25.43 (3.93) SF: 48/47/51/-

T/Jkpt: Not won; £14,647.89 to 9/10/95. T/Plpt: £14.70 (2,399.06 Tckts). T/Qdpt: £19.60 (14.1 Tckts). WG

3746-LEICESTER (R-H)
Monday October 9th (Good)

WEATHER: fine & dry WIND: strong across

4043 SHELDUCK H'CAP (0-70) (3-Y.O+ F & M) (Class E) £3,817.00(£1,144.00: £550.00: £253.00) **1m 8y** Stalls: High GOING minus 0.28 sec per fur (GF) 2-00 (2-02)

3664[3] **Hatta Breeze (59)***(73) (MAJarvis)* 3-8-13b WCarson(19) (lw: a.p: led over 4f out: drvn clr appr fnl f: comf)..........— **1**
3984[15] Misty Silks **(69)***(80)*(Fav)*(MJRyan)* 5-9-13 AClark(5) (hld up: rdn & hdwy over 2f out: r.o ins fnl f)..........1¾ **2**
3808[3] Broughton's Pride (IRE) **(51)***(57)*(Fav)*(JAGlover)* 4-8-4 (5)ow2 DaneO'Neill(20) (a.p: rdn over 1f out: r.o one pce)..........1¼ **3**
3897[2] Fairelaine **(57)***(62) (APJarvis)* 3-8-11 JTate(17) (hdwy over 2f out: nt rch ldrs) 1½ **4**
3935[11] Thatcher's Era (IRE) **(57)***(61) (TDBarron)* 3-8-11 RCochrane(15) (hld up & bhd: hdwy over 1f out: nrst fin) ....½ **5**
3987[8] Total Rach (IRE) **(51)***(52) (RIngram)* 3-8-5b WWoods(10) (w ldrs: rdn over 1f out: one pce)..1½ **6**
3734[9] Merlin's Fancy **(59)***(58) (WJarvis)* 3-8-13 WRyan(13) (hdwy 3f out: rdn & one pce fnl 2f).........1 **7**
2053[4] French Ginger **(66)***(63) (IABalding)* 4-9-10 WRSwinburn(14) (mid div: no hdwy fnl 2f) 1¼ **8**
2488[9] Mnemonic **(53)***(50) (HCandy)* 3-8-7 WNewnes(11) (prom tl rdn & wknd over 2f out)..........s.h **9**
3645[10] Kilnamartyra Girl **(51)***(40) (JParkes)* 5-8-6 (3) PMcCabe(3) (nvr plcd to chal) 4 **10**
3607[15] Phase One (IRE) **(54)***(41) (JLEyre)* 5-8-12 RLappin(16) (w ldrs 5f: sn lost tch)..........¾ **11**
3469[11] Lucidity **(53)***(39) (CWThornton)* 3-8-7 DeanMcKeown(8) (rdn 3f out: no imp) ....½ **12**
3952[3] Heathyards Lady (USA) **(57)***(33) (RHollinshead)* 4-8-8 (7) FLynch(12) (chsd ldrs 5f) 5 **13**
2181[7] Glowing Jade **(70)***(43) (JAGlover)* 5-10-0 SDWilliams(4) (bit bkwd: a bhd) 1½ **14**
3941[2] Chantry Bellini **(49)***(22) (MrsSMAustin)* 6-8-7 JWeaver(6) (b: b.hind: prom over 5f)..........s.h **15**
3645[2] Racing Brenda **(58)***(21) (BAMcMahon)* 4-9-2 GCarter(1) (chsd ldrs 4f: sn wknd)..........5 **16**
3726[16] Sweet Allegiance **(54)***(17) (JCPoulton)* 5-8-12 AMorris(9) (chsd ldrs over 5f)..........s.h **17**
3605[16] White Heat **(52)***(11) (MJHeaton-Ellis)* 3-8-6v MRoberts(2) (led over 3f: sn wknd) 1¾ **18**
1644[9] Mazilla **(53)** *(AStreeter)* 3-8-2 (5) LNewton(7) (b: a bhd: t.o)..........14 **19**
2037[16] Run-Do-Run **(54)** *(HJCollingridge)* 3-8-8 JQuinn(18) (ref to r: t.n.p) .... **R**

7/1 Misty Silks (5/1-8/1), Broughton's Pride (IRE), **9/1** Chantry Bellini, Racing Brenda, **10/1** HATTA BREEZE, Heathyards Lady (USA), **11/1** Fairelaine (8/1-12/1), **12/1** Total Rach (IRE), Glowing Jade (10/1-16/1), **16/1** French Ginger, Mnemonic, **20/1** Lucidity, Merlin's Fancy, Phase One (IRE), Kilnamartyra Girl, Thatcher's Era (IRE), Run-Do-Run, **25/1** White Heat, Mazilla, **33/1** Sweet Allegiance, CSF £78.47 CT £497.71 TOTE £11.60: £2.70 £1.50 £2.10 £2.70 (£49.00) Trio £268.20 OWNER Sheikh Ahmed Al Maktoum (NEWMARKET) BRED Grange Stud (UK) 20 Rn

1m 37.5 (2.50) SF: 47/58/35/36/35/26/32/41/24/18/19/13/11/21/-/-/-/-/-/-

WEIGHT FOR AGE 3yo-4lb

4044 BADGER LIMITED STKS (0-60) (3-Y.O+) (Class F) £3,678.20 (£1,025.20: £494.60)
1m 8y Stalls: High GOING minus 0.28 sec per fur (GF) 2-30 (2-34)

3920[8] **Bentico (59)***(76) (MrsNMacauley)* 6-9-6 JWeaver(15) (lw: a.p: led wl over 1f out: pushed clr: unchal) .....— 1
3860* Another Time **(59)***(72)*(Fav)*(SPCWoods)* 3-9-4 WWoods(8) (lw: hld up: hdwy over 2f out: r.o one pce fnl f) 3 2
3941[4] Michellisa **(58)***(64) (JDBethell)* 4-9-1 WCarson(16) (hld up: hdwy 3f out: kpt on one pce ins fnl f) .....½ 3
3920* Swinging Sixties (IRE) **(58)***(67) (GLMoore)* 4-9-6 SWhitworth(1) (lw: hld up & bhd: gd hdwy 2f out: r.o wl fnl f) 1¼ 4
3802[2] Calder King **(60)***(64) (JLEyre)* 4-9-4v JTate(3) (hld up: hdwy 3f out: rdn & one pce appr fnl f) ..½ 5
3654[4] Twice Purple (IRE) **(59)***(63) (BJMeehan)* 3-9-0 PatEddery(9) (prom: led over 2f out tl wl over 1f out: no ex fnl f) .....nk 6
2276[3] Hawwam **(54)***(55) (EJAlston)* 9-9-4 KDarley(14) (bit bkwd: hdwy ½-wy: ev ch 2f out: sn rdn & wknd) 4 7
3638[7] Harvest Reaper **(53)***(53) (JLHarris)* 3-8-11 (3) PMcCabe(13) (plld hrd: led tl hdd over 2f out: sn wknd) 1¼ 8
3972[11] Komiamaite **(58)***(52) (SRBowring)* 3-8-9 (5) CTeague(17) (prom: no hdwy fnl 2f) .....nk 9
3860[2] H'Ani **(50)***(46) (WJHaggas)* 3-8-9 RHills(20) (w ldrs tl wknd 2f out) .....nk 10
3802[10] Our Robert **(55)***(51) (JGFitzGerald)* 3-9-0 LCharnock(11) (prom over 5f) .....nk 11
3771[13] Best of Bold **(60)***(47) (NAGraham)* 3-9-0b PaulEddery(19) (prom over 5f) 1¾ 12
3823[14] Wandering Minstrel (IRE) **(57)***(47) (JMPEustace)* 3-9-0b RCochrane(10) (lw: plld hrd: jnd ldrs ½-wy: rdn & wknd over 2f out) .....nk 13
647[12] Our Tom **(58)***(44) (JWharton)* 3-9-0 JQuinn(7) (lw: nvr trbld ldrs) 1½ 14
3808[28] Move Smartly (IRE) **(54)***(43) (FHLee)* 5-9-6v GCarter(6) (s.s: a bhd) 1¼ 15
4027[8] Autumn Cover **(54)***(40) (RMFlower)* 3-9-0b GDuffield(4) (b: dwlt: a bhd) .....½ 16
3739[11] Souperficial **(60)***(43) (JAGlover)* 4-9-3v(5) DaneO'Neill(2) (racd alone stands' side: rdn 2f out: no imp) .....¾ 17
3920[4] Labudd (USA) **(58)***(38)*(Fav)*(RIngram)* 5-9-4 WRSwinburn(5) (b: lw: mid div: hrd rdn over 2f out: no imp) .....nk 18
3363* Tragic Hero **(58)***(39) (MCPipe)* 3-9-4 MRoberts(18) (prom 5f) 1¾ 19
3706[20] Highland Magic (IRE) **(56)***(25) (MJFetherston-Godley)* 7-9-4 CRutter(12) (bhd fnl 3f: t.o) 5 20

7/1 Labudd (USA), Another Time, **8/1** Tragic Hero, BENTICO, **9/1** Swinging Sixties (IRE), **10/1** Calder King, Twice Purple (IRE), H'Ani, **11/1** Souperficial, **12/1** Michellisa, **14/1** Autumn Cover (12/1-20/1), **16/1** Hawwam, **20/1** Wandering Minstrel (IRE), Our Robert, **25/1** Our Tom, Komiamaite, Best of Bold, Move Smartly (IRE), **33/1** Harvest Reaper, Highland Magic (IRE), CSF £66.07 TOTE £9.30: £3.90 £3.60 £4.10 (£92.80) Trio £220.60 OWNER Mr G. Wiltshire (MELTON MOWBRAY) BRED Britton House Stud 20 Rn

1m 37.0 (2.00) SF: 59/51/47/50/47/42/38/32/31/25/30/26/26/23/26/19/26/21/18/8

WEIGHT FOR AGE 3yo-4lb

OFFICIAL EXPLANATION **Labudd(USA): no explanation could be offered for the horse's poor performance.**

4045 STOAT (S) STKS (2-Y.O) (Class G) £2,825.40 (£784.40: £376.20)
1m 1f 218y Stalls: High GOING minus 0.28 sec per fur (GF) 3-00 (3-03)

3533[4] **Willie Rushton (58)***(62)*(Fav)*(GLMoore)* 2-8-6 SWhitworth(18) (hld up: 7th st: led 2f out: edgd lft: clr fnl f) .....— 1
3915[4] Young Butt **(58)***(59) (JFfitch-Heyes)* 2-8-6 (5) AWhelan(4) (lw: chsd ldrs: 6th st: led over 3f out to 2f out: no ch w wnr) 5 2
3752[6] Yellow Dragon (IRE) *(57) (MissGayKelleway)* 2-8-11 PatEddery(11) (bhd: hdwy 3f out: styd on wl fnl f) 1¼ 3
3850[4] Thorntoun Estate (IRE) *(55) (MJohnston)* 2-8-11 JWeaver(8) (swtg: led 3f: 2nd st: led over 3f out: sn hdd: kpt on ins fnl f) 1½ 4
3749[9] Lindas Delight **(50)***(50) (JSMoore)* 2-8-10 JFEgan(17) (lw: in tch: 8th st: hdwy 3f out: no hdwy fnl 2f) 2 5
3858[7] Velvet Jones **(68)***(49) (GFHCharles-Jones)* 2-8-4 (7) ADaly(10) (hdwy 4f out: one pce fnl 2f) .1½ 6
3738[4] Pulga Circo **(53)***(44) (BAMcMahon)* 2-8-6 FNorton(9) (lw: chsd ldrs: 5th st: hrd rdn 2f out: no hdwy) .....s.h 7
Belle's Boy *(48) (BPalling)* 2-8-11 TSprake(14) (lengthy: unf: hdwy fnl 2f: nt rch ldrs) .....½ 8
3592[16] Just Another High (IRE) **(55)***(42) (DrJDScargill)* 2-8-6 MFenton(16) (lw: nvr trbld ldrs) 1 9
3955[5] Forliando **(58)***(46) (MSSaunders)* 2-8-11 AMcGlone(6) (lw: hdwy over 2f out: wknd bel dist) ..½ 10
3915[14] Subtle One (IRE) **(47)***(33) (GLMoore)* 2-8-6 JQuinn(15) (prom: 4th st: wknd over 3f out) 5 11
3642[9] Priddy Fair **(46)***(27) (RBoss)* 2-8-6 WRyan(1) (prom: 3rd st: rdn & wknd over 2f out) 3½ 12
3721[9] La Haye Sainte **(48)***(23) (DJSCosgrove)* 2-8-1 (5) LNewton(13) (a bhd) 2½ 13

2029⁵ Moylough Rebel *(19) (MrsMELong)* 2-8-11 MPerrett(19) (b.nr fore: prom to ½-wy: sn wknd: t.o)......6 **14**
3539⁸ Illegally Yours **(50)***(10) (LMontagueHall)* 2-8-6 KDarley(7) (a bhd: t.o)......2 **15**
3983¹⁶ Northern Sky *(10) (RDickin)* 2-8-6 DaleGibson(3) (a bhd: t.o)......s.h **16**
3983¹⁷ Carwyn's Choice *(PCClarke)* 2-8-6 NAdams(12) (mid div tl wknd over 3f out: t.o)......12 **17**
3989¹⁷ Come On In *(RDickin)* 2-8-11 JLowe(2) (lw: a bhd: t.o)......4 **18**
3975²⁶ Prime Connections *(MPBielby)* 2-8-8b(3) PMcCabe(5) (led after 3f tl over 3f out: wknd qckly: t.o)......7 **19**

7/2 WILLIE RUSHTON, **4/1** Thorntoun Estate (IRE), **5/1** Velvet Jones (4/1-6/1), **6/1** Yellow Dragon (IRE), **10/1** Priddy Fair, La Haye Sainte, **14/1** Young Butt, Lindas Delight, Moylough Rebel, Pulga Circo, **16/1** Subtle One (IRE), Just Another High (IRE), **20/1** Belle's Boy, **25/1** Illegally Yours, **33/1** Forliando, Northern Sky, Carwyn's Choice, Come On In, Prime Connections, CSF £57.79 TOTE £4.00: £1.90 £5.70 £2.50 (£29.90) Trio £97.20 OWNER Pennine Partners (EPSOM) BRED K. Higson 19 Rn 2m 10.3 (7.60) SF: 8/5/3/1/-/-/-/-/-/-/-/-/-/-/-/-/-/-/-
Bt in 5,000 gns

4046 HEDGEHOG CONDITIONS STKS (2-Y.O) (Class C) £4,971.00 (£1,839.00: £882.00: £360.00)
1m 1f 218y Stalls: High GOING minus 0.28 sec per fur (GF) 3-30 (3-33)

3846² **Flyfisher (IRE) (85)***(84) (GLewis)* 2-8-11 PaulEddery(3) (w ldr: 2nd st: rdn over 2f out: styd on gamely to ld nr fin)......— **1**
3746³ Dismissed (USA) **(100)***(88) (PFICole)* 2-9-1 WCarson(4) (lw: led tl hdd cl home)......s.h **2**
3752* Do Not Disturb (USA) **(92)***(78)*(Fav)*(JLDunlop)* 2-9-1 PatEddery(1) (chsd ldrs: 4th st: effrt & rdn wl over 1f out: sn btn)......6 **3**
3631³ Diego **(90)***(74) (CEBrittain)* 2-8-11 BDoyle(9) (lw: chsd ldrs: 3rd st: outpcd 3f out: styd on appr fnl f)......½ **4**
3631⁵ Zaforum *(71) (LMontagueHall)* 2-8-11 MRoberts(7) (chsd ldrs: 6th st: outpcd 4f out: n.d after)......1½ **5**
3900¹⁹ Roseberry Avenue (IRE) *(67) (LadyHerries)* 2-8-11 KDarley(8) (hld up in rr: nvr nr to chal)..2½ **6**
3887⁶ Sally's Twins *(59) (JSMoore)* 2-8-6 JFEgan(2) (a bhd)......2 **7**
3683⁵ Canon Can (USA) *(63) (HRACecil)* 2-8-11 WRyan(5) (s.s: a bhd: drvn along 3f out: no imp) .¾ **8**
3928⁹ Kinnescash (IRE) **(68)***(60) (MSSaunders)* 2-9-1 AMcGlone(6) (chsd ldrs: 5th st: rdn & wknd over 2f out)......4 **9**

6/4 Do Not Disturb (USA), **7/2** Dismissed (USA) (3/1-9/2), **9/2** FLYFISHER (IRE), Diego, **8/1** Canon Can (USA) (op 5/1), **16/1** Roseberry Avenue (IRE), **25/1** Kinnescash (IRE), **33/1** Zaforum, **50/1** Sally's Twins, CSF £20.92 TOTE £4.90: £1.20 £1.80 £1.30 (£10.30) Trio £5.70 OWNER Highclere Thoroughbred Racing Ltd (EPSOM) BRED P. D. and Mrs Player 9 Rn
2m 8.1 (5.40) SF: 29/33/23/19/16/12/4/8/5

4047 RABBIT H'CAP (0-85) (3-Y.O) (Class D) £4,509.70 (£1,351.60: £649.80: £298.90)
1m 3f 183y Stalls: High GOING minus 0.28 sec per fur (GF) 4-00 (4-01)

3875* **Slapy Dam (57)***(66) (JMackie)* 3-7-2 (5) PFessey(5) (hld up: hdwy over 2f out: led over 1f out: r.o wl)......— **1**
1717³ Beauchamp Jade **(75)***(82) (HCandy)* 3-8-11 WNewnes(2) (hld up: 9th st: hdwy over 2f out: rdn & r.o ins fin f)......1¼ **2**
1872³ Monarch **(85)***(92)*(Fav)*(PFICole)* 3-9-7 LDettori(1) (bit bkwd: racd wd: 7th st: ev ch over 1f out: nt qckn)......s.h **3**
3769⁴ Soviet Bride (IRE) **(66)***(70) (SDow)* 3-7-9 (7)ow3 ADaly(17) (5th st: hung lft & led 2f out: hdd over 1f out: one pce)......½ **4**
3927¹¹ Sparrowhawk (IRE) **(72)***(78) (BWHills)* 3-8-8 JWeaver(16) (hld up & bhd: stdy hdwy on ins & 10th st: one pce fnl 2f)......½ **5**
3843* Leading Spirit (IRE) **(74)***(76) (CFWall)* 3-8-10 PatEddery(15) (6th st: no hdwy fnl 2f)......3 **6**
3634³ George Bull **(65)***(67) (MajorWRHern)* 3-8-1 WCarson(13) (8th st: rdn & no hdwy fnl 2f)......hd **7**
3921⁶ Love The Blues **(68)***(70) (DNicholson)* 3-8-4 MRoberts(4) (hld up & bhd: stdy hdwy & 11th st: no imp fnl 2f)......hd **8**
3611¹⁶ Dont Shoot Fairies **(75)***(74) (CEBrittain)* 3-8-11 BDoyle(14) (led 2f: 4th st: ev ch 2f out: wknd over 1f out)......1¾ **9**
3927⁴ Paradise Waters **(58)***(48) (RFJohnsonHoughton)* 3-7-8 JQuinn(3) (3rd st: led over 3f out tl 2f out: sn wknd)......7 **10**
3772¹⁰ Royrace **(59)***(43) (WMBrisbourne)* 3-7-2 (7)ow2 MartinDwyer(10) (rdn 8f out: a bhd)......2½ **11**
881⁶ Merit (IRE) **(61)***(45) (PFICole)* 3-7-11 ow1 CRutter(7) (lw: a bhd)......¾ **12**
3935¹⁷ Cross Talk (IRE) **(69)***(54) (RHollinshead)* 3-8-5 WRyan(9) (dwlt: a bhd)......s.h **13**
3936⁷ Slaney Project (IRE) **(64)***(45) (WRMuir)* 3-8-0 JFEgan(11) (led after 2f tl over 3f out: wknd qckly)......3 **14**
3772⁵ Dtoto **(78)***(57) (MRStoute)* 3-9-0 WRSwinburn(12) (hrd rdn 4f out: sn bhd)......1¾ **15**

3237[7] Grooms Gold (IRE) **(64)***(41) (PWHarris)* 3-8-0 GDuffield(6) (2nd st: ev ch 2f out: sn wknd)...1¾ **16**
3611[23] Last Roundup **(67)***(37) (CWThornton)* 3-8-3 DeanMcKeown(8) (hld up: a bhd) 5 **17**
1478[7] United Front **(77)***(20) (RJO'Sullivan)* 3-8-13 KDarley(18) (bkwd: a bhd: t.o)............................20 **18**

LONG HANDICAP Royrace 6-11

13/8 Monarch, **13/2** Leading Spirit (IRE), **8/1** SLAPY DAM, **10/1** George Bull, Merit (IRE), Dtoto, **14/1** Dont Shoot Fairies, Love The Blues, Beauchamp Jade, Paradise Waters, **16/1** Soviet Bride (IRE), Sparrowhawk (IRE), **20/1** Grooms Gold (IRE), United Front, Slaney Project (IRE), **25/1** Cross Talk (IRE), **33/1** Last Roundup, **100/1** Royrace, CSF £124.11 CT £260.07 TOTE £10.00: £1.40 £2.60 £1.40 £3.30 (£103.10) Trio £215.90 OWNER Rose And Crown, Boylestone (CHURCH BROUGHTON) BRED Hesmonds Stud Ltd 18 Rn

2m 32.8 (4.00) SF: 29/45/55/33/41/39/30/33/37/11/6/8/17/8/20/4/-/-

4048 E.B.F. HARE MAIDEN STKS (I) (2-Y.O F) (Class D) £4,077.50 (£1,220.00: £585.00: £267.50)

7f 9y Stalls: High GOING minus 0.28 sec per fur (GF) 4-30 (4-40)

Oleana (IRE) *(84) (PFICole)* 2-8-11 KDarley(13) (w'like: b.hind: w ldr: led over 2f out: clr over 1f out: easily) ....— **1**
3346[2] Introducing *(80)*(Fav)*(JHMGosden)* 2-8-11 LDettori(1) (unruly s: a.p: rdn over 2f out: hung rt: chsd wnr over 1f out: r.o) 2 **2**
2083[7] Peppers (IRE) *(68) (LMCumani)* 2-8-4 (7) RFfrench(12) (bit bkwd: led over 4f: wknd fnl f) 5 **3**
3673[5] Little Black Dress (USA) *(67) (RCharlton)* 2-8-11 PatEddery(2) (hdwy 3f out: eased whn btn fnl f) ....nk **4**
3816[6] Madame Steinlen *(62) (BWHills)* 2-8-11 MHills(17) (hld up: hdwy over 2f out: nt rch ldrs) 2½ **5**
Fancy Heights *(58) (LadyHerries)* 2-8-11 WRSwinburn(15) (tall: hld up & bhd: sme hdwy fnl 2f: nvr nrr)..1¾ **6**
Polar Spirit *(57) (WJHaggas)* 2-8-11 RMcGhin(7) (b.nr fore: leggy: no hdwy fnl 2f) ....½ **7**
Inca Bird *(56) (MMcCormack)* 2-8-11 RCochrane(6) (small: lt-f: unf: s.s: nvr nrr)....................½ **8**
Conwy *(53) (NAGraham)* 2-8-11 BDoyle(10) (small: lengthy: no hdwy fnl 2f).........................1¼ **9**
3900[23] Tashjir (USA) *(49) (DMorley)* 2-8-11 WCarson(18) (lw: hld up: pushed along over 3f out: n.d) 1½ **10**
3891[8] Tiama (IRE) *(49) (SDow)* 2-8-11 MRoberts(11) (rdn over 3f out: sn bhd) ....s.h **11**
3983[15] Dance Across (IRE) *(48) (HCandy)* 2-8-11 WNewnes(9) (bit bkwd: prom 4f) ....½ **12**
Stolen Music (IRE) *(47) (MajorDNChappell)* 2-8-11 WWoods(5) (lt-f: bit bkwd: a bhd)...........nk **13**
Shirley Sue *(44) (MJohnston)* 2-8-11 JWeaver(4) (w'like: scope: s.s: a bhd)..........................1½ **14**
3136[5] Mignonnette (FR) *(35) (IABalding)* 2-8-11 WRyan(14) (chsd ldrs over 3f) 4 **15**
3983[14] Uplift *(35) (SirMarkPrescott)* 2-8-11 GDuffield(16) (a bhd)..hd **16**
Kings Nightclub *(26) (JWhite)* 2-8-11 DaleGibson(8) (w'like: bkwd: bhd fnl 3f)..........................4 **17**
2801[9] Mogin *(18) (JFfitch-Heyes)* 2-8-6 (5) AWhelan(3) (bit bkwd: unruly stalls: s.s: a bhd) 3½ **18**

5/4 Introducing, **4/1** Madame Steinlen (3/1-9/2), **9/2** OLEANA (IRE), **13/2** Little Black Dress (USA), **12/1** Fancy Heights, **20/1** Shirley Sue, Mignonnette (FR), **33/1** Conwy, Peppers (IRE), Tashjir (USA), **50/1** Polar Spirit, Inca Bird, Stolen Music (IRE), Tiama (IRE), Dance Across (IRE), Uplift, **66/1** Kings Nightclub, **100/1** Mogin, CSF £10.72 TOTE £7.90: £1.80 £1.30 £14.50 (£12.70) Trio £342.30 OWNER H R H Prince Fahd Salman (WHATCOMBE) BRED Newgate Stud Co 18 Rn

1m 25.3 (2.80) SF: 37/33/21/20/15/11/10/9/6/2/2/1/-/-/-/-/-/-

STEWARDS' ENQUIRY Eddery susp. 18-20/10/95 (failure to obtain best possible placing).

4049 DORMOUSE MAIDEN APPRENTICE STKS (3-Y.O) (Class G) £3,049.40 (£848.40: £408.20)

7f 9y Stalls: High GOING minus 0.28 sec per fur (GF) 5-00 (5-09)

3920[7] **Night Wink (USA) (57)***(78) (DNicholls)* 3-8-12 MartinDwyer(16) (lw: a.p: led over 1f out: hung lft: r.o wl)...— **1**
1731[2] Godmersham Park **(79)***(69)*(Fav)*(MJHeaton-Ellis)* 3-8-12 RHavlin(13) (prom: led over 4f out: hung lft over 2f out: hdd over 1f out: nt qckn)...4 **2**
3734[4] Prudent Princess **(63)***(59) (AHide)* 3-8-4 (3) CWebb(8) (hdwy over 2f out: rdn over 1f out: r.o one pce) 2 **3**
3640[7] Merrie le Bow **(43)***(48) (PatMitchell)* 3-8-7 AmandaSanders(2) (hdwy over 2f out: hrd rdn over 1f out: one pce) 5 **4**
3859[3] Rockusa **(47)***(45) (PRHedger)* 3-8-7 ADaly(17) (prom: rdn over 2f out: no hdwy) 1¼ **5**
2623[3] Karaar **(69)***(50) (JHMGosden)* 3-8-12 MarkDenaro(9) (hdwy over 2f out: rdn & wknd over 1f out) ....s.h **6**
3475[5] Barbrallen **(39)***(37) (DJSffrenchDavis)* 3-8-7 CAdamson(5) (prom over 4f) 3½ **7**
3750[7] Relentless (IRE) **(64)***(41) (BAMcMahon)* 3-8-9 (3) GMilligan(6) (no hdwy fnl 2f) ....nk **8**
2977[8] Arecibo (FR) *(30) (GLMoore)* 3-8-7 (5) ALakeman(19) (prom over 4f)..5 **9**
3678[12] Logie Pert Lad **(30)***(16) (JJBridger)* 3-8-9 (3) IonaWands(12) (prom over 4f) 6 **10**
Rolling Settlement (IRE) *(9) (JAHarris)* 3-8-2 (5) CLowther(3) (n.d)..1¼ **11**

3762[12] Sun Circus *(9) (JLSpearing)* 3-8-4 (3) AEddery(4) (rdn over 3f out: sn bhd)....s.h **12**
3974[16] Crowning Tino *(8) (MrsNMacauley)* 3-8-4 (3) AimeeCook(1) (sn bhd)....s.h **13**
3981[8] It Is Now *(12) (SGollings)* 3-8-12 GParkin(20) (prom: hrd rdn & wknd 3f out)....½ **14**
3712[15] Oscilights Gift *(7) (PBurgoyne)* 3-8-7 DGibbs(11) (led over 2f: wknd 3f out)....s.h **15**
3544[13] Sandra Dee (IRE) **(47)***(6) (BAPearce)* 3-8-4 (3) JWilkinson(7) (b: s.s: a bhd)....½ **16**
2836[5] Axed Again *(1) (NBycroft)* 3-8-7 GMitchell(15) (chsd ldrs over 3f)....2 **17**
3847[7] Lady Kate (USA) **(38)***(1) (KOCunningham-Brown)* 3-8-7b SCopp(18) (bhd fnl 3f)....nk **18**
3750[18] Desert Water (IRE) *(JJBridger)* 3-8-7 (5) CScudder(14) (a bhd: t.o)....9 **19**

11/4 Godmersham Park, **7/2** Karaar (6/4-4/1), **5/1** Prudent Princess, **7/1** Relentless (IRE), **8/1** NIGHT WINK (USA), **10/1** Rockusa, **12/1** Barbrallen, **25/1** It Is Now, Sandra Dee (IRE), Rolling Settlement (IRE), **33/1** Merrie le Bow, Sun Circus, Logie Pert Lad, Arecibo (FR), Oscilights Gift, Crowning Tino, Axed Again, Lady Kate (USA), Desert Water (IRE), CSF £30.45 TOTE £8.30: £2.20 £1.60 £2.00 (£17.50) Trio £27.00 OWNER Mrs Dyanne Benjamin (THIRSK) BRED Gainsborough Farm Inc 19 Rn 1m 24.7 (2.20) SF: 46/37/27/16/13/18/5/9/-/-/-/-/-/-/-/-/-/-/-

4050 E.B.F. HARE MAIDEN STKS (II) (2-Y.O F) (Class D) £4,045.00 (£1,210.00: £580.00: £265.00)
7f 9y Stalls: High GOING minus 0.28 sec per fur (GF) 5-30 (5-35)

Fairlight Down (USA) *(80+) (PFICole)* 2-8-11 LDettori(2) (a.p: led over 1f out: r.o wl)....— **1**
Academy of Dance (IRE) *(74) (MJohnston)* 2-8-11 JWeaver(12) (leggy: bit bkwd: s.s: hdwy over 2f out: r.o wl ins fnl f)....2½ **2**
Tasdik *(74)(Fav)(RWArmstrong)* 2-8-11 WCarson(17) (w ldrs: ev ch whn edgd lft over 1f out: nt qckn)....s.h **3**
3450[6] High Note *(74) (RCharlton)* 2-8-11 PatEddery(11) (a.p: bmpd over 1f out: sn swtchd rt & ev ch: nt qckn)....s.h **4**
3763[16] Alreeh (IRE) *(70) (JHMGosden)* 2-8-11b RHills(10) (b.hind: a.p: led 3f out: hdd & wandered over 1f out: one pce)....1¾ **5**
Opalette *(66) (LadyHerries)* 2-8-11 KDarley(9) (w'like: leggy: bit bkwd: stdy hdwy fnl 2f: bttr for r)....2 **6**
My Emma *(64) (RGuest)* 2-8-11 GDuffield(13) (lt-f: chsd ldrs: rdn 2f out: no hdwy)....¾ **7**
3532[6] Age of Reality (USA) *(64) (HCandy)* 2-8-11 WNewnes(1) (no hdwy fnl 2f)....s.h **8**
Another Quarter (IRE) *(62) (SPCWoods)* 2-8-11 WWoods(6) (b: w'like: leggy: nvr nrr)....¾ **9**
3628[17] My Millie *(51) (RBoss)* 2-8-11 WRyan(16) (mde most 4f: wkng whn bmpd 2f out)....5 **10**
3765[13] Spiral Flyer (IRE) *(49) (MDIUsher)* 2-8-11 RPrice(8) (prom over 4f)....¾ **11**
Sandicliffe (USA) *(46) (BWHills)* 2-8-11 MHills(5) (tall: unf: bhd fnl 3f)....1¼ **12**
Driftholme *(46) (GLMoore)* 2-8-11 SWhitworth(7) (w'like: bkwd: a bhd)....hd **13**
Turia *(37) (MajorDNChappell)* 2-8-11 PaulEddery(18) (lt-f: s.s: sn rcvrd: bhd fnl 3f)....4 **14**
3364[5] Miss Prism *(37) (JLDunlop)* 2-8-11 GCarter(15) (bhd fnl 3f)....hd **15**
Shareda (IRE) *(31) (WJHaggas)* 2-8-11 RCochrane(3) (leggy: lt-f: s.s: a bhd)....2½ **16**
Amelanchier *(30) (GBBalding)* 2-8-11 JWilliams(14) (cmpt: bkwd: hld up & plld hrd: rdn 2f out: wknd qckly)....½ **17**
570[7] Alistover *(RDickin)* 2-8-4 (7) MichelleThomas(4) (s.s: a bhd)....4 **18**

3/1 Tasdik, **7/2** FAIRLIGHT DOWN (USA) (op 7/4), **9/2** High Note, **10/1** Sandicliffe (USA) (op 6/1), Opalette (op 6/1), **12/1** Academy of Dance (IRE) (op 7/1), **14/1** Alreeh (IRE), Age of Reality (USA), My Emma, **16/1** Shareda (IRE), Turia, **20/1** My Millie, Another Quarter (IRE), **25/1** Driftholme, Miss Prism, **33/1** Spiral Flyer (IRE), Amelanchier, **50/1** Alistover, CSF £50.48 TOTE £4.20: £2.10 £5.30 £1.40 (£50.60) Trio £23.30 OWNER Sir Andrew Lloyd Webber (WHATCOMBE) BRED Maylands Stud Co Ltd 18 Rn 1m 25.3 (2.80) SF: 37/31/31/31/27/23/21/21/19/8/6/3/3/-/-/-/-/-
T/Jkpt: Not won; £20,991.33 to Leicester 10/10/95. T/Plpt: £16.70 (1,182.19 Tckts). T/Qdpt: £2.70 (12.7 Tckts). KH

3397-CHEPSTOW (L-H)
Tuesday October 10th (Good to soft, Soft patches)
WEATHER: sunny WIND: nil

4051 FONTHILL H'CAP (0-80) (3-Y.O+) (Class D) £4,060.00 (£1,225.00: £595.00: £280.00) 1m 4f 23y Stalls: Low GOING: 0.38 sec per fur (GS) 2-15 (2-16)

3876[2] **Jagellon (USA) (68)***(80) (WRMuir)* 4-9-9 JReid(1) (swtg: plld hrd: 2nd st: led over 3f out: drvn out)....— **1**
763[14] Granby Bell **(48)***(60) (PHayward)* 4-7-12 (5) PFessey(18) (swtg: 3rd st: hrd rdn over 1f out: r.o ins fnl f)....hd **2**
3936[10] Cuango (IRE) **(50)***(60) (RHollinshead)* 4-8-5 WRyan(4) (hld up & bhd: hdwy over 2f out: r.o ins fnl f)....1¼ **3**
3889[12] Nessun Doro **(61)***(71) (SMellor)* 3-8-8 RPerham(6) (hdwy over 3f out: hung lft & r.o ins fnl f)..½ **4**

3918² Snowy Petrel (IRE) **(77)***(86) (JLDunlop)* 3-9-10 KDarley(12) (led over 8f: one pce fnl f) ....½ **5**
3469⁷ Tappeto **(73)***(82) (HCandy)* 3-9-6 WNewnes(9) (swtg: hld up: 10th st: rdn & hdwy on ins 3f out: swtchd rt 2f out: wandered over 1f out: r.o ins fnl f) ....s.h **6**
3918³ Gloriana **(74)***(72)*(Fav)*(LadyHerries)* 3-9-7v RCochrane(13) (8th st: wknd over 1f out)..........8 **7**
3884⁸ El Volador **(48)***(45) (RJO'Sullivan)* 8-8-3 ow1 GHind(2) (nvr nr to chal) ....nk **8**
3963⁷ Dreams End **(73)***(70) (JMBradley)* 7-9-9 (5) JDSmith(16) (b: swtg: plld hrd: 4th st: wknd fnl f) s.h **9**
454⁷ Morstock **(48)***(44) (RJHodges)* 5-8-0 (3)ow1 SDrowne(8) (hdwy & 9th st: wknd over 1f out)......nk **10**
Fabulous Mtoto **(50)***(39) (MSSaunders)* 5-8-5 JFEgan(3) (lw: plld hrd & bhd: nvr nrr) 6 **11**
3936¹⁷ Triple Tie (USA) **(42)***(31) (MBlanshard)* 4-7-11 JQuinn(14) (swtg: 6th st: wknd over 2f out)....nk **12**
2199⁸ Ballynakelly **(56)***(43) (RAkehurst)* 3-8-3 SSanders(7) (a bhd)..........1¼ **13**
3889¹⁰ Koathary (USA) **(61)***(46) (LGCottrell)* 4-9-2 JCarroll(15) (lw: 5th st: wknd over 2f out) 1½ **14**
3872⁴ Uncharted Waters **(50)***(30) (CACyzer)* 4-8-5 StephenDavies(10) (bhd fnl 3f)..........4 **15**
3641¹⁵ Jean de Florette (USA) **(38)***(8) (CADwyer)* 4-7-7 NKennedy(17) (rdn & hdwy over 5f out: 7th st: wknd over 2f out)..........7 **16**
676¹⁹ Colonel Colt **(53)***(4) (RDickin)* 4-8-3 (5)ow1 DaneO'Neill(11) (bhd fnl 4f: t.o)..........14 **17**
3987¹⁹ Irrepressible (IRE) **(42)** *(KBishop)* 4-7-11 NAdams(5) (a bhd: t.o fnl 4f)..........6 **18**

LONG HANDICAP Jean de Florette (USA) 7-2

5/1 Gloriana, **11/2** JAGELLON (USA), Snowy Petrel (IRE), **13/2** Ballynakelly (9/2-7/1), **9/1** Cuango (IRE), El Volador, **10/1** Tappeto, **12/1** Dreams End, **14/1** Granby Bell (12/1-11/2), **16/1** Morstock, Koathary (USA), Uncharted Waters, **25/1** Nessun Doro, **33/1** Fabulous Mtoto, **50/1** Triple Tie (USA), Jean de Florette (USA), Colonel Colt, **66/1** Irrepressible (IRE), CSF £79.76 CT £649.65 TOTE £7.30: £2.00 £3.30 £1.50 £13.60 (£79.00) Trio £356.60 OWNER Mr D. J. Deer (LAMBOURN) BRED John Deer 18 Rn 2m 45.3 (14.00) SF: 45/25/25/28/43/39/29/10/35/9/4/-/-/11/-/-/-/-
WEIGHT FOR AGE 3yo-8lb

4052 SWETTENHAM CONDITIONS STKS (3-Y.O F) (Class C) £5,177.80 (£1,801.80: £873.40: £367.00) 1m 2f 36y Stalls: Low GOING: 0.38 sec per fur (GS) 2-45 (2-45)

3932⁶ **Strutting (IRE) (93)***(98+)*(Fav)*(RHannon)* 3-8-11 JReid(3) (chsd ldr: 2nd st: led on bit over 3f out: pushed out)..........— **1**
2694⁹ Celtic Fringe **(80)***(86) (HRACecil)* 3-8-12 WRyan(2) (led over 6f: wknd fnl f)..........8 **2**
3239² Miss Haversham **(79)***(82) (CACyzer)* 3-8-10 KDarley(4) (3rd st: rdn over 4f out: one pce fnl 3f)..........1¼ **3**
3799¹¹ Ozubeck (USA) *(43) (BHanbury)* 3-8-5 (5) AWhelan(1) (dwlt: 4th st: rdn & wknd 3f out: t.o)....25 **4**

10/11 STRUTTING (IRE) (Evens-4/5), **7/4** Celtic Fringe, **9/2** Miss Haversham, **50/1** Ozubeck (USA), CSF £2.74 TOTE £1.70 (£1.60) OWNER Mr M. W. Grant (MARLBOROUGH) BRED Scuderia Milano 4 Rn 2m 17.9 (13.60) SF: 18/6/2/-

4053 ANNUAL FLAT V JUMP JOCKEYS CHALLENGE H'CAP (0-70) (3-Y.O+) (Class G) £2,468.00 (£698.00: £344.00) 7f 16y Stalls: High GOING: 0.38 sec per fur (GS) 3-15 (3-18)

3943¹⁹ **Jibereen (69)***(83)*(Fav)*(GLewis)* 3-11-5 (5) DJMurphy(10) (lw: mde all: qcknd clr over 2f out: rdn out) ....— **1**
3802¹⁸ Cee-Jay-Ay **(59)***(71) (JBerry)* 8-10-12 (5) CLlewellyn(9) (s.s: hdwy 2f out: hrd rdn & r.o wl ins fnl f) ....¾ **2**
3874⁶ Shepherd Market (IRE) **(59)***(66) (DAWilson)* 4-11-3 RCochrane(8) (swtg: a.p: one pce fnl 2f)2½ **3**
3885⁶ Chili Heights **(54)***(58) (GBBalding)* 5-10-12v KDarley(2) (b.hind: hld up & bhd: hdwy over 1f out: r.o) 1¼ **4**
3764⁹ First Gold **(59)***(62) (JWharton)* 6-11-3b JReid(7) (hld up & plld hrd: no hdwy fnl 2f) ....nk **5**
3493⁷ Warning Shot **(60)***(58) (MartynMeade)* 3-10-10 (5) JOsborne(5) (swtg: prom tl wknd over 1f out) 2½ **6**
Kelly Mac **(61)***(58) (DCO'Brien)* 5-11-0 (5) GMcCourt(12) (s.s: sn rcvrd: rdn over 3f out: wknd over 2f out) ....nk **7**
3874¹⁴ Great Hall **(55)***(51) (PDCundell)* 6-10-8 (5) GBradley(6) (nvr nrr) ....½ **8**
3879* Birchwood Sun **(66)***(61) (MDods)* 5-11-10b JWilliams(11) (a bhd)..........nk **9**
3897⁹ Astral Invader (IRE) **(58)***(53) (MSSaunders)* 3-10-13 WRyan(3) (lw: hld up: wknd over 1f out)s.h **10**
876* Comeonup **(61)***(47) (JMBradley)* 4-11-0 (5) BPowell(1) (b: rdn over 3f out: a bhd) 4 **11**
2613¹² Try-Haitai (IRE) **(53)***(31) (RAkehurst)* 4-10-11 TWilliams(4) (b.off hind: hld up: rdn over 2f out: sn wknd)..........3½ **12**

3/1 JIBEREEN, **5/1** Birchwood Sun, **11/2** Chili Heights, **13/2** First Gold, **8/1** Comeonup (6/1-9/1), **10/1** Shepherd Market (IRE), **14/1** Cee-Jay-Ay, Astral Invader (IRE), Great Hall, **16/1** Try-Haitai (IRE), **25/1** Warning Shot, **50/1** Kelly Mac, CSF £41.42 CT £349.62 TOTE £3.20: £1.60 £3.30 £2.10 (£23.30) Trio £194.80 OWNER Mr Peter Skelton (EPSOM) BRED Mrs J. Everitt 12 Rn 1m 28.1 (8.10) SF: 66/57/52/44/48/41/44/37/47/36/33/17
WEIGHT FOR AGE 3yo-3lb

4054
GAINSBOROUGH (S) STKS (3-Y.O+) (Class G) £2,745.00 (£770.00:£375.00)
1m 14y Stalls: High GOING: 0.38 sec per fur (GS) 3-45 (3-48)

3954[11] **Media Express (64)***(70) (MBrittain)* 3-9-3 RCochrane(11) (hld up: hdwy over 2f out: led ins fnl f: drvn out) — 1
3770[P] Dowsong **(68)***(65) (RAkehurst)* 4-9-7 RPerham(15) (led 2f: led 3f out tl ins fnl f) 2½ 2
3531[17] Daring Ryde **(40)***(58) (JPSmith)* 4-9-2 (5) JDSmith(13) (bhd: hrd rdn & hdwy 2f out: r.o) 3½ 3
3841[3] Pash **(30)***(52) (CWFairhurst)* 3-8-12v NKennedy(10) (lw: hdwy fnl 2f: r.o) ¾ 4
3841[2] Jackatack (IRE) **(46)***(55) (MRChannon)* 3-9-3 JFEgan(12) (w ldrs: rdn 3f out: ev ch over 1f out: wknd fnl f) ¾ 5
3510[6] Best Kept Secret **(58)***(50) (JBerry)* 4-8-11 (5) PFessey(2) (hld up: no hdwy fnl 2f) nk 6
3664[13] Sea Spouse **(39)***(47) (MBlanshard)* 4-9-2 JQuinn(6) (lw: led 6f out to 3f out: wknd fnl f) 1½ 7
3422[8] Hunza Story **(36)***(45) (NPLittmoden)* 3-8-5 (7) CAdamson(17) (b.hind: nvr nr to chal) 1 8
3889[15] Off the Air (IRE) **(43)***(33) (BJLlewellyn)* 4-9-2 TWilliams(20) (prom: sn rdn along: wknd 4f out) 6 9
3950[11] Mixed Mood **(43)***(32) (BJLlewellyn)* 3-8-12 VSlattery(3) (prom over 5f) nk 10
3426[13] Causley **(60)***(30) (DMHyde)* 10-9-2 BPowell(7) (a mid div) 1¼ 11
3972[18] Cool Tactician **(49)***(34) (RHollinshead)* 3-9-3 WRyan(5) (lw: hld up: hdwy over 2f out: wknd over 1f out) ½ 12
1801[5] Yubralee (USA) **(72)***(32)*(Fav)*(MCPipe)* 3-9-3 JReid(16) (swtg: hld up: rdn over 3f out: sn wknd) ¾ 13
3799[14] Most Becoming **(38)***(17) (JRArnold)* 3-8-7v JCarroll(18) (a bhd) 2½ 14
3402[13] Pacific Overture **(41)***(17) (CRBarwell)* 3-8-7b JWilliams(14) (a bhd) s.h 15
2946[11] Kissavos **(39)***(15) (CCElsey)* 9-9-2 SSanders(1) (lw: bhd fnl 3f) 3½ 16
Celestial Waters *(10) (APJames)* 3-8-7 GHind(9) (unf: bit bkwd: a bhd) s.h 17
Air of Mystery **(36)** *(NEBerry)* 3-8-7 NAdams(8) (a bhd: t.o) 10 18
3542[12] My Jazzmyn *(DCO'Brien)* 3-8-2 (5) DaneO'Neill(4) (plld hrd: prom over 4f: t.o) 7 19

6/5 Yubralee (USA) (4/5-5/4), **11/2** Dowsong (op 7/2), Jackatack (IRE) (4/1-6/1), **11/1** Best Kept Secret, **14/1** MEDIA EXPRESS, **16/1** Off the Air (IRE), **20/1** Causley, **25/1** Kissavos, Pash, **33/1** Mixed Mood, Daring Ryde, Cool Tactician, Hunza Story, Sea Spouse, **50/1** Pacific Overture, **66/1** Most Becoming, Celestial Waters, Air of Mystery, My Jazzmyn, CSF £86.44 TOTE £21.20: £3.20 £1.90 £35.10 (£33.60) Trio £225.40 OWNER Consultco Ltd (WARTHILL) BRED Fulling Mill Farm and Stud 19 Rn 1m 40.4 (7.90) SF: 49/48/41/31/34/33/30/24/16/11/13/13/11/-/-/-/-/-/-
WEIGHT FOR AGE 3yo-4lb
No bid

4055
LESTER PIGGOTT ALL-AGED CONDITIONS STKS (Class C) £5,223.00 (£1,947.00: £946.00: £400.00)
6f 16y Stalls: High GOING: 0.38 sec per fur (GS) 4-15 (4-19)

3979[3] **Subzero (95)***(87)*(Fav)*(MRStoute)* 3-9-5 KDarley(1) (b: b.hind: hld up: rdn & hdwy over 2f out: nt clr run over 1f out: swtchd lft & led ins fnl f: qcknd clr: easily) — 1
3990[4] No Monkey Nuts **(83)***(84) (JBerry)* 2-8-4 JCarroll(2) (led 3f: led ins fnl f: sn hdd: nt qckn) 2½ 2
3660[4] Coffee 'n Cream **(95)***(80) (RHannon)* 3-9-6 (5) DaneO'Neill(6) (w ldr: led 3f out tl ins fnl f: one pce) 2½ 3
Monty *(53) (MajorDNChappell)* 3-9-3 TSprake(8) (b.off hind: leggy: unf: nvr nr to chal) 7 4
Cassimere *(42) (MajorDNChappell)* 3-8-12 RCochrane(7) (unf: bit bkwd: hld up & plld hrd: nvr nr ldrs) 2½ 5
3949[11] Andsome Boy *(38) (CRBarwell)* 2-7-12 NAdams(4) (lw: hld up: rdn over 2f out: sn bhd) 3½ 6
3632[5] Barranak (IRE) *(28) (MrsMMcCourt)* 3-9-3 WNewnes(5) (bhd fnl 2f) 3½ 7
3847[10] Governors Fortune *(AJChamberlain)* 3-9-3 BPowell(3) (bhd fnl 4f: t.o) 25 8

6/4 SUBZERO (Evens-13/8), **7/4** Coffee 'n Cream, **9/2** No Monkey Nuts, **6/1** Barranak (IRE), **16/1** Cassimere, **33/1** Monty, **66/1** Andsome Boy, **100/1** Governors Fortune, CSF £8.91 TOTE £2.50: £1.10 £1.30 £1.60 (£5.40) OWNER Mr P. D. Savill (NEWMARKET) BRED Mrs C. F. Van Straubenzee and Partners 8 Rn 1m 14.5 (5.50) SF: 56/34/49/22/11/-/-/-
WEIGHT FOR AGE 2yo-21lb, 3yo-2lb

4056
WHITSBURY MANOR CONDITIONS STKS (2-Y.O F) (Class C) £4,648.00 (£1,732.00: £841.00: £355.00)
6f 16y Stalls: High GOING: 0.38 sec per fur (GS) 4-45 (4-46)

3976* **Chalamont (IRE) (95)***(89)*(Fav)*(PWChapple-Hyam)* 2-8-13 JReid(1) (b: lw: mde all: edgd lft over 1f out: hrd rdn ins fnl f: r.o) — 1
3933* Trafalgar Lady (USA) *(88) (RCharlton)* 2-8-13 KDarley(3) (s.i.s: sn prom: ev ch ins fnl f: hrd rdn: r.o) ½ 2
3892[6] Wildwood Flower *(82) (RHannon)* 2-8-4 (5) DaneO'Neill(5) (chsd wnr: hung lft over 1f out: hrd rdn: r.o) ½ 3

3948* Polish Spring (IRE) *(68) (BWHills)* 2-8-8 (5) JDSmith(6) (b.hind: outpcd: rdn over 3f out: nvr nr to chal) 7 **4**
1977 11 Little Millie *(63) (PHayward)* 2-8-4 (5) PFessey(7) (outpcd) ....½ **5**
Charlton Imp (USA) *(44) (RJHodges)* 2-8-9 JWilliams(2) (str: bit bkwd: s.i.s: a bhd) 7 **6**
3858 13 Subfusk **(54)***(15) (WGMTurner)* 2-8-2 (7) ADaly(4) (s.i.s: bhd fnl 3f: t.o) 11 **7**

10/11 CHALAMONT (IRE) (5/4-5/6), **9/4** Polish Spring (IRE), **9/2** Trafalgar Lady (USA), **20/1** Wildwood Flower, **33/1** Charlton Imp (USA), Subfusk, **66/1** Little Millie, CSF £5.35 TOTE £1.90: £1.10 £2.50 (£2.70) OWNER Mr R. E. Sangster (MARLBOROUGH) BRED Swettenham Stud 7 Rn

1m 16.0 (7.00) SF: 30/29/23/9/4/-/-

4057 BLOOMSBURY H'CAP (0-70) (3-Y.O+) (Class E) £3,473.50 (£1,048.00: £509.00: £239.50)

5f 16y Stalls: High GOING: 0.38 sec per fur (GS) 5-15 (5-16)

3919 4 **Tinker Osmaston (65)***(76) (MSSaunders)* 4-9-9 JFEgan(10) (hld up: gd hdwy over 1f out: str run to ld ins fnl f: r.o) ....— **1**
3681 6 To the Roof (IRE) **(64)***(72) (PWHarris)* 3-9-7 GHind(3) (lw: a.p: led over 2f out tl ins fnl f) 1 **2**
3961 2 Domicksky **(54)***(57) (MRChannon)* 7-8-7 (5) PPMurphy(8) (lw: hdwy over 1f out: r.o ins fnl f) 1½ **3**
3748 2 Leigh Crofter **(70)***(70) (PDCundell)* 6-9-9b(5) DGriffiths(12) (a.p: ev ch over 1f out: nt qckn) 1 **4**
2686 5 Halliard **(56)***(56) (TMJones)* 4-9-0 RPerham(9) (swtg: led over 2f: ev ch over 1f out: nt qckn) s.h **5**
3919 2 Malibu Man **(59)***(59) (SMellor)* 3-9-2 TSprake(11) (swtg: w ldrs: ev ch 2f out: one pce) ....hd **6**
3905 7 Lloc **(52)***(49) (CADwyer)* 3-8-9 CDwyer(4) (b: swtg: prom: outpcd over 2f out: r.o ins fnl f) ....¾ **7**
3637 10 Prima Silk **(67)***(64) (MJRyan)* 4-9-6 (5) MBaird(1) (chsd ldrs: no hdwy fnl f) ....hd **8**
3905 17 Dancing Sioux **(65)***(61) (RGuest)* 3-9-8 LCharnock(2) (b: prom over 3f) ....nk **9**
3919 14 Friendly Brave (USA) **(62)***(57) (MissGayKelleway)* 5-9-6 SSanders(17) (hld up: ev ch over 1f out: wknd ins fnl f) ....nk **10**
3783 2 Sing With the Band **(57)***(48)*(Fav)*(BAMcMahon)* 4-9-1 JReid(19) (w ldrs tl wknd over 1f out) 1¼ **11**
3954 5 Bold Gem **(51)***(42) (BJMeehan)* 4-8-2b(7) GHannon(18) (s.s: nvr nrr) ....s.h **12**
3960 5 Pharaoh's Dancer **(70)***(61) (PBurgoyne)* 8-9-9 (5) DGibbs(7) (n.d) ....s.h **13**
3919 18 Runs in the Family **(54)***(43) (PGMurphy)* 3-8-11b KDarley(16) (lw: hdwy 2f out: wknd over 1f out) ....½ **14**
Risky Royal **(52)***(40) (TJNaughton)* 3-8-4 (5) JDSmith(14) (a bhd) ....½ **15**
3524 7 My Cherrywell **(53)***(35) (LRLloyd-James)* 5-8-11 TWilliams(15) (b.hind: a bhd) 1¾ **16**
3874 4 Poyle Jezebelle **(51)***(28) (MBlanshard)* 4-8-9 JQuinn(5) (swtg: s.s: a bhd) 1½ **17**
3771 17 Grand Chapeau (IRE) **(60)***(36) (RHannon)* 3-8-12 (5) DaneO'Neill(13) (bhd fnl 2f) ....½ **18**
2997 4 Walk the Beat **(64)***(32) (MartynMeade)* 5-9-8 VSlattery(20) (a bhd) 2½ **19**

5/2 Sing With the Band, **5/1** Malibu Man, **7/1** Domicksky (6/1-10/1), **9/1** Leigh Crofter, **12/1** TINKER OSMASTON (op 6/1), **14/1** Lloc, **16/1** Runs in the Family, Prima Silk, Poyle Jezebelle, Friendly Brave (USA), To the Roof (IRE), Pharaoh's Dancer, **20/1** Dancing Sioux, Halliard, Grand Chapeau (IRE), Walk the Beat, **25/1** My Cherrywell, **50/1** Bold Gem, Risky Royal, CSF £193.38 CT £1,349.65 TOTE £13.70: £2.70 £3.80 £2.50 £3.30 (£114.00) Trio £330.30 OWNER Mr John Luff (WELLS) BRED Mrs R. D. Peacock 19 Rn

62.0 secs (5.00) SF: 53/48/34/47/33/35/25/41/37/34/25/19/38/19/16/12/5/12/9

WEIGHT FOR AGE 3yo-1lb

T/Plpt: £586.10 (24.61 Tckts). T/Qdpt: £44.20 (0.5 Tckts). KH

4043-LEICESTER (R-H)
Tuesday October 10th (Good)

WEATHER: sunny WIND: almost nil

4058 E.B.F. REFERENCE POINT MAIDEN STKS (I) (2-Y.O C & G) (Class D) £4,012.50 (£1,200.00: £575.00: £262.50)

7f 9y Stalls: High GOING minus 0.26 sec per fur (GF) 1-30 (1-31)

3733 9 **Don Micheletto** *(91+) (GWragg)* 2-8-11 MHills(14) (a.p: led appr fnl f: rdn & r.o wl) ....— **1**
3890 3 Winter Romance *(90) (EALDunlop)* 2-8-11 WRSwinburn(4) (lw: hld up & bhd: hdwy over 2f out: chal 1f out: nt qckn towards fin) ....nk **2**
Balladur (USA) *(81+)*(Fav)*(HRACecil)* 2-8-11 PatEddery(2) (lt-f: unf: trckd ldrs: led over 2f out tl over 1f out: sn btn) 4 **3**
3773 4 Ashjar (USA) *(77) (HThomsonJones)* 2-8-11 RHills(10) (plld hrd: cl up: chal 2f out: wknd fnl f) 2 **4**
3900 17 State of Caution *(71) (JLDunlop)* 2-8-11 JWeaver(11) (sn outpcd & bhd: hdwy over 2f out: ev ch over 1f out: sn rdn & btn) 2½ **5**
Jackson Hill *(71+) (RCharlton)* 2-8-11 DHarrison(12) (gd sort: bkwd: s.i.s: shkn up ½-wy: styd on: no imp) ....hd **6**

2320⁴ Ironheart (64) *(JHMGosden)* 2-8-11 LDettori(6) (bit bkwd: hld up: hdwy over 2f out: sn btn & eased) 3 7
3989¹⁰ Montecristo (58) *(RGuest)* 2-8-11 PaulEddery(1) (prom over 4f) 2½ 8
3683⁶ Callaloo (54) *(MrsJCecil)* 2-8-11 PRobinson(13) (led tl hdd & wknd over 2f out) 1¾ 9
3620⁷ Knave (50) *(RHannon)* 2-8-11 MRoberts(7) (cl up over 4f) 2 10
3371¹³ Night of Glass (36) *(DMorris)* 2-8-11 DeanMcKeown(9) (a bhd) 6 11
3869⁹ Gee Gee Tee (35) *(JAkehurst)* 2-8-11 SWhitworth(3) (b: cl up: rdn 3f out: sn wknd) ....nk 12
Night Silence (22) *(SirMarkPrescott)* 2-8-11 GDuffield(5) (lt-f: bit bkwd: dwlt: a wl bhd) 6 13
Below The Red Line *(MrsNMacauley)* 2-8-11v SDWilliams(8) (small: bit bkwd: s.s: a wl bhd)25 14

7/4 Balladur (USA), **7/2** DON MICHELETTO, **4/1** Ironheart (2/1-5/1), **9/2** Winter Romance, **14/1** Ashjar (USA) (8/1-16/1), **20/1** Jackson Hill, Callaloo, **33/1** State of Caution, Montecristo, Knave, Night of Glass, **50/1** Gee Gee Tee, Night Silence, Below The Red Line, CSF £20.13 TOTE £7.90: £1.10 £1.30 £1.50 (£20.30) Trio £35.00 OWNER Exors of the late Sir Philip Oppenheimer (NEWMARKET) BRED Hascombe and Valiant Studs 14 Rn
1m 24.3 (1.80) SF: 51/50/41/37/31/31/24/18/14/10/-/-/-/-

4059 WYMESWOLD CONDITIONS STKS (2-Y.O) (Class C) £5,365.50 (£1,855.50: £890.25: £363.75)
7f 9y Stalls: High GOING minus 0.26 sec per fur (GF) 2-00 (2-01)

3650* **Masehaab (IRE)** (67+)(Fav) *(JLDunlop)* 2-9-2 WCarson(4) (trckd ldrs: led over 2f out: shkn up & qcknd ins fnl f: easily) ....— 1
3851³ Magic Lake **(54)***(52)* *(EJAlston)* 2-8-5 MRoberts(2) (hld up: qcknd to disp ld 1f out: hung lft: no ch w wnr) 1¾ 2
Baloustar (USA) (32) *(SPCWoods)* 2-8-5 WWoods(1) (lengthy: unf: trckd ldrs: effrt 2f out: sn btn) 9 3
3502¹² Mulhollande Lad (IRE) (28) *(MCChapman)* 2-8-3 ⁽⁷⁾ CMunday(3) (led tl hdd over 2f out: sn btn) 4 4

2/15 MASEHAAB (IRE), **10/1** Baloustar (USA) (op 5/1), **12/1** Magic Lake, **66/1** Mulhollande Lad (IRE), CSF £2.31 TOTE £1.10 (£1.40) OWNER Mr Hamdan Al Maktoum (ARUNDEL) BRED T. Newman and Mellon Stud 4 Rn 1m 26.7 (4.20) SF: 28/13/-/-

4060 WHISSENDINE (S) H'CAP (0-60) (3-Y.O+) (Class G) £2,937.40 (£816.40: £392.20)
7f 9y Stalls: High GOING minus 0.26 sec per fur (GF) 2-30 (2-33)

3885⁷ **Nashaat (USA) (60)***(74)* *(NJHWalker)* 7-9-11 ⁽³⁾ JStack(12) (swtg: in tch: hdwy to ld over 2f out: drvn out) ....— 1
3719* Mary's Case (IRE) **(55)***(68)* *(MJohnston)* 5-9-9b JWeaver(2) (wl bhd tl hdwy 3f out: r.o wl fnl f: jst failed) ....½ 2
3677⁷ Deeply Vale (IRE) **(60)***(68)* *(GLMoore)* 4-10-0 SWhitworth(1) (s.s: hdwy ½-wy: ev ch over 1f out: nt qckn) 2 3
3897⁵ Blushing Grenadier (IRE) **(53)***(60)* *(MJFetherston-Godley)* 3-9-4b WRSwinburn(18) (rdn ½-wy: hdwy 2f out: swtchd lft: r.o wl towards fin) ....¾ 4
3638³ Cape Colony **(54)***(59)*(Fav) *(CFWall)* 3-9-5 GDuffield(13) (hdwy 3f out: ch & hrd rdn over 1f out: no ex) ....¾ 5
3941⁷ Princess Maxine (IRE) **(54)***(58)* *(JJO'Neill)* 6-9-8 DeanMcKeown(17) (a chsng ldrs: one pce fnl 2½f) ....½ 6
3385* Southern Memories (IRE) **(56)***(60)* *(WJMusson)* 5-9-7 ⁽³⁾ PMcCabe(9) (w ldrs: led 2½f out: sn hdd: wknd fnl f) ....hd 7
3885¹⁰ Pusey Street Boy **(52)***(50)* *(JRBosley)* 8-9-6 MHills(4) (t: drvn along ½-wy: nvr trbld ldrs) 2½ 8
2540² Dowdency **(54)***(51)* *(JAPickering)* 3-8-12 ⁽⁷⁾ SCopp(11) (bhd tl styd on fnl 3f: nrst fin) ....nk 9
3808⁴ Love Legend **(51)***(44)* *(DWPArbuthnot)* 10-9-5 AClark(3) (b: nvr trbld ldrs) 1¾ 10
3807⁹ Battle Colours (IRE) **(51)***(42)* *(DonEnricoIncisa)* 6-9-5 KimTinkler(6) (sn pushed along: outpcd fnl 3f) 1 11
3152⁴ Frans Lad **(57)***(47)* *(JBerry)* 3-9-8b GCarter(8) (a in tch: rdn 3f out: one pce) ....½ 12
3920⁶ Blow Dry (IRE) **(58)***(47)* *(MartynWane)* 5-9-12 MRoberts(10) (w ldrs tl wknd fnl 2½f) ....½ 13
3808⁵ Ashdren **(52)***(36)* *(AHarrison)* 8-9-6 PatEddery(19) (bhd tl sme hdwy 2f out: n.d) 2 14
230⁵ Faez **(56)***(36)* *(RSimpson)* 5-9-7b⁽³⁾ NVarley(5) (bit bkwd: plld hrd: cl up tl wknd over 2f out) 1¾ 15
3920²⁰ Green Golightly (USA) **(49)***(29)* *(DAWilson)* 4-8-12 ⁽⁵⁾ LNewton(16) (chsd ldrs tl wknd fnl 2½f) ....nk 16
3467¹⁸ Annie Fay (IRE) **(54)***(31)* *(JLHarris)* 3-9-5 RHills(15) (chsd ldrs tl wknd over 2f out) 1 17
3241⁸ Legatee **(59)***(31)* *(AStreeter)* 4-9-13 FNorton(14) (b: led tl hdd 2½f out: sn wknd) 2½ 18
3751¹⁴ Sharp Holly (IRE) **(53)** *(JABennett)* 3-9-4 BDoyle(20) (in tch: rdn ½-wy: sn wknd) 20 19
3638⁹ See You Again **(53)** *(RHannon)* 3-9-4 LDettori(7) (swtg: n.d) ....¾ 20

5/2 Cape Colony (op 4/1), **7/1** Mary's Case (IRE) (5/1-8/1), **8/1** Southern Memories (IRE), **9/1** Blushing Grenadier (IRE), **10/1** Ashdren, Blow Dry (IRE), **12/1** See You Again, Green Golightly (USA) (tchd 20/1), Pusey Street Boy, **14/1** Love Legend, **16/1** Princess Maxine (IRE), Dowdency, **20/1** NASHAAT (USA), **25/1** Deeply Vale (IRE), Frans Lad, Battle Colours (IRE), Faez, Legatee, **33/1** Sharp Holly (IRE), Annie Fay (IRE), CSF £166.69 CT £3,285.55 TOTE £41.50: £11.70 £1.80 £4.60 £2.10 (£226.60) Trio £433.20 OWNER Mrs Christine Painting (WANTAGE) BRED Echo Valley Horse Farm and Swettenham Stud 20 Rn

1m 26.0 (3.50) SF: 47/41/41/30/29/31/33/23/21/17/15/17/20/9/9/2/1/4/-/-

WEIGHT FOR AGE 3yo-3lb

No bid

Cape Colony clmd Mr JO'Shea £6,000

4061 STEWARDS H'CAP (0-70) (3-Y.O+) (Class E) £4,017.20 (£1,205.60: £580.80: £268.40) **1m 1f 218y** GOING minus 0.26 sec per fur (GF) 3-00 (3-05)

3898[5] **Aljawab (USA) (61)***(75) (JLDunlop)* 4-9-8 GCarter(4) (hdwy 3f out: swtchd over 2f out: led ins fnl f: r.o u.p) — **1**
3977[2] Curtelace **(53)***(64)*(Fav)*(LadyHerries)* 5-8-9 (5) GParkin(7) (hld up & bhd: hdwy on outside 3f out: ev ch ins fnl f: nt qckn: fin 3rd, hd: plcd 2nd) **2**
3977[13] Lady Highfield **(52)***(63) (MJRyan)* 4-8-13 AClark(6) (hdwy 4f out: led 1½f out tl ins fnl f: no ex: fin 4th, nk: plcd 3rd) **3**
3987* Rival Bid (USA) **(62)***(70) (MrsNMacauley)* 7-9-9 5x PatEddery(18) (b.hind: bhd: hdwy over 3f out: styd on: fin 5th, 2l: plcd 4th) **4**
3872* Polly Peculiar **(60)***(65) (BSmart)* 4-9-7 DHarrison(10) (b.hind: chsd ldrs: chal over 2f out: wknd over 1f out: fin 6th, 2l: plcd 5th) **5**
1643[4] Cliburnel News (IRE) **(58)***(61) (AStreeter)* 5-8-12 (7) DDenby(16) (hdwy 3f out: styd on: no imp) 1 **7**
771[3] Hattaafeh (IRE) **(56)***(56) (MAJarvis)* 4-9-0 (3) NVarley(5) (in tch: rdn ent st: no imp after) 1¾ **8**
3889[7] Fabillion **(60)***(60) (CASmith)* 3-9-1 DeanMcKeown(17) (nvr trbld ldrs) s.h **9**
3837[W] Broughton Singer (IRE) **(55)***(55) (WJMusson)* 4-9-2 RPrice(15) (hdwy 3f out: sn prom: wknd wl over 1f out) nk **10**
3934[3] Rising Spray **(51)***(50) (CAHorgan)* 4-8-5 (7) AmandaSanders(13) (s.i.s: hdwy on outside 3f out: no imp) ½ **11**
3889[14] Araboybill **(57)***(48) (RSimpson)* 4-9-4b LDettori(12) (chsd ldrs tl wknd fnl 2f) 5 **12**
3965[6] Efizia **(66)***(54) (MrsMReveley)* 5-9-13 ACulhane(9) (nvr nr ldrs) 1½ **13**
3810[6] Locorotondo (IRE) **(67)***(54) (MBell)* 4-10-0 MFenton(8) (led tl hdd & wknd over 1f out) 1 **14**
1446[5] Shahrani **(60)***(45) (MCPipe)* 3-9-1 MRoberts(11) (bit bkwd: bhd fnl 3f) 1¼ **15**
3810[12] Cavil **(62)***(45) (CEBrittain)* 3-9-3 BDoyle(3) (prom tl wknd fnl 2½f) 1¼ **16**
3875[8] Imlak (IRE) **(64)***(42) (DMorley)* 3-9-5 WCarson(14) (chsd ldrs: wkng whn hmpd wl over 1f out) 3 **17**
3825[6] Lunar Mission (IRE) **(60)***(32) (JMPEustace)* 4-9-7 MTebbutt(1) (cl up tl wknd wl over 2f out) 4 **18**
3987[7] Just Flamenco **(52)***(23) (MJRyan)* 4-8-13 MHills(2) (lost tch fnl 3f) nk **19**
3844* Thames Side **(58)***(70) (MMadgwick)* 4-8-12 (7) AEddery(19) (hdwy over 2f out: hung lft & r.o u.p: nrst fin: fin 2nd, 1½l: disq: plcd last) **0**

11/2 Curtelace, **6/1** Imlak (IRE), Polly Peculiar (op 4/1), **7/1** Rival Bid (USA), **10/1** ALJAWAB (USA), **11/1** Shahrani, **12/1** Lunar Mission (IRE), Locorotondo (IRE), **14/1** Thames Side, **16/1** Hattaafeh (IRE), Broughton Singer (IRE), Lady Highfield, **20/1** Efizia, Cliburnel News (IRE), Just Flamenco, Rising Spray, **25/1** Cavil, Araboybill, **33/1** Fabillion, CSF £67.42 CT £844.99 TOTE £10.90: £4.00 £1.80 £3.50 £3.10 (£37.00) Trio £254.20 OWNER Mr S. Khaled (ARUNDEL) BRED Mandysland Farm 19 Rn 2m 6.8 (4.10) SF: 51/40/39/46/41/37/32/30/31/26/24/30/30/15/15/12/8/-/46

WEIGHT FOR AGE 3yo-6lb

STEWARDS' ENQUIRY A.Eddery susp. 19-21 & 23/10/95 (irresponsible riding).

4062 PADDOCK CLAIMING STKS (3-Y.O+) (Class F) £3,375.80 (£938.80: £451.40) **1m 3f 183y** Stalls: High GOING minus 0.26 sec per fur (GF) 3-30 (3-34)

3899[2] **Berkeley Bounder (USA) (70)***(81)*(Fav)*(MCPipe)* 3-9-4 PatEddery(4) (chsd ldrs: led over 2f out: rdn clr fnl f) — **1**
3741* Elementary **(76)***(78) (NJHWalker)* 12-9-9 (3) JStack(9) (chsd ldrs: led over 4f out tl over 2f out: rdn & one pce fnl f) 2½ **2**
3741[3] Sea Victor **(67)***(77) (JLHarris)* 3-9-4 PRobinson(22) (a.p: rdn 2f out: kpt on ins fnl f) ¾ **3**
3641* Scenic Dancer **(42)***(59) (AHide)* 7-9-0 WWoods(13) (s.i.s: hdwy over 2f out: fin wl) 4 **4**
3735[11] Hatta River (USA) **(53)***(57) (JAHarris)* 5-9-0 JWeaver(11) (hld up: swtchd ins over 2f out: nrst fin) 1¾ **5**
3884[18] Forest Mill **(48)***(52) (DWPArbuthnot)* 3-8-4v AClark(12) (b.hind: hdwy ent st: rdn & kpt on appr fnl f) 2 **6**

3987[6] Mhemeanles **(42)***(55) (CaptJWilson)* 5-9-3 GCarter(15) (b.hind: hdwy over 3f out: sn rdn along: no imp) 1¾ **7**
3899[6] Kismetim **(39)***(49) (BJMeehan)* 5-8-11 BDoyle(10) (mid div: effrt 3f out: nt trble ldrs)....s.h **8**
Affordable Dora *(45) (JRFanshawe)* 3-8-4 DHarrison(18) (b.hind: chsd ldrs tl wknd fnl 3f) ...3½ **9**
2830* Glow Forum **(34)***(44) (GLMoore)* 4-8-12 MFenton(6) (lw: mid div: effrt over 2f out: no imp appr fnl f) 1 **10**
Ciracusa (IRE) *(51) (JMackie)* 3-8-9 (3) NVarley(21) (w'like: scope: bkwd: s.s: sn drvn along: n.d)....nk **11**
3825[7] Straw Thatch **(43)***(50) (RBastiman)* 6-9-1 (5) HBastiman(8) (a in rr) ....d.h **12**
Woodmans Lady *(46) (JJSheehan)* 3-8-4 (3) PMcCabe(16) (w'like: leggy: b: nvr nr ldrs) ....½ **12**
3871[12] Happy Hostage **(64)***(55) (JWhite)* 4-9-7 (5) LNewton(2) (nvr plcd to chal)....1¼ **14**
3096[6] Nushka Babushka **(38)***(33) (BobJones)* 3-7-12 FNorton(14) (bhd fnl 3f) 1½ **15**
598[8] Joyrider **(40)***(31) (MissMKMilligan)* 4-9-9 GDuffield(19) (t.o)....14 **16**
3292[11] Sonny Place *(24) (JLHarris)* 4-9-3 RPrice(3) (bit bkwd: in tch: drvn along 4f out: sn wknd: t.o)....½ **17**
Zadok *(19) (RTPhillips)* 3-9-1 MRoberts(20) (w'like: scope: bit bkwd: a bhd: t.o) 8 **18**
3665[12] Absolute Folly **(47)***(22) (JBerry)* 3-8-11 (7) PRoberts(1) (led to ½-wy: wknd 3f out: t.o) ....hd **19**
3401[7] Peter Monamy **(60)***(14) (MCPipe)* 3-9-4 LDettori(17) (prom tl outpcd ent st: sn bhd: t.o) 6 **20**
Morski *(TTBill)* 6-8-11 NCarlisle(5) (a bhd: t.o)....2 **21**
3805[4] Simposa (IRE) **(47)***(4) (EJAlston)* 3-9-1 SDWilliams(7) (led ½-wy tl over 4f out: sn wknd: t.o) ..3 **22**

11/8 BERKELEY BOUNDER (USA), **3/1** Elementary, **7/1** Sea Victor, **10/1** Scenic Dancer, **14/1** Peter Monamy, Affordable Dora (op 7/1), **20/1** Mhemeanles, Kismetim, Forest Mill, Hatta River (USA), Simposa (IRE), Glow Forum, Happy Hostage, **25/1** Zadok, Absolute Folly, **33/1** Straw Thatch, **50/1** Sonny Place, Woodmans Lady, Joyrider, Nushka Babushka, Ciracusa (IRE), **66/1** Morski, CSF £7.59 TOTE £2.70: £1.20 £1.90 £1.80 (£2.80) Trio £7.00 OWNER Mr B. A. Kilpatrick (WELLINGTON) BRED Gainesway Thoroughbreds Ltd 22 Rn

2m 34.4 (5.60) SF: 44/49/40/30/28/15/26/20/8/15/14/22/9/26/-/2/-/-/-/-/-/-

WEIGHT FOR AGE 3yo-8lb

Berkeley Bounder (USA) clmd RMcKellar £8,000

4063 E.B.F. SOAR MAIDEN STKS (2-Y.O) (Class D) £4,467.50 (£1,340.00: £645.00: £297.50)

1m 8y Stalls: High GOING minus 0.26 sec per fur (GF) 4-00 (4-03)

Forest Buck (USA) *(94+)*(Fav)*(HRACecil)* 2-9-0 PatEddery(3) (w'like: unf: hld up: hdwy ½-wy: led bel dist: rn green: comf) ....— **1**
Jiyush *(92) (HThomsonJones)* 2-9-0 RHills(16) (w'like: w ldrs: led wl over 1f out: sn hdd: kpt on)....1¼ **2**
Lakeline Legend (IRE) *(86) (MAJarvis)* 2-9-0 JWeaver(17) (cmpt: bkwd: w ldrs: led over 2f out: sn hdd: one pce fnl f)....3 **3**
3592[6] Humourless *(85) (LMCumani)* 2-9-0 MHills(5) (slt ld over 5f: rdn & one pce appr fnlf)....hd **4**
3865[21] Ceilidh Star (IRE) *(70) (BWHills)* 2-8-9 PaulEddery(7) (hld up: effrt & rdn over 2f out: nvr able to chal)....5 **5**
Halebid *(72) (SPCWoods)* 2-9-0 WWoods(11) (w'like: bit bkwd: chsd ldrs: effrt 2f out: nvr able to chal)....1½ **6**
Persuasion *(65) (LordHuntingdon)* 2-8-9 DHarrison(1) (lt-f: bkwd: chsd ldrs: no hdwy fnl 2f) 1¼ **7**
Salsian *(61) (SCWilliams)* 2-8-9 GDuffield(10) (lengthy: unf: b.nr hind: bhd: sn pushed along: sme late hdwy: nvr nrr) 1¾ **8**
Atienza (USA) *(58) (SCWilliams)* 2-8-9 JTate(15) (unf: scope: sme hdwy 2f out: nvr nrr) 1¾ **9**
3758[7] Ship's Dancer *(46) (JLDunlop)* 2-8-9 GCarter(14) (nvr nr ldrs) 6 **10**
1671[7] Lady of The Mist (IRE) *(43) (JSMoore)* 2-8-6 (3) NVarley(6) (m.n.s) 1¾ **11**
3765[9] Spa Lane *(44) (CJDrewe)* 2-8-11 (3) JStack(8) (w ldrs tl wknd fnl 2f) 1¾ **12**
Tawafek (USA) *(42) (DMorley)* 2-9-0 WCarson(13) (w'like: unf: s.i.s: sn drvn along: a bhd) .1¼ **13**
3887[4] Sister Kit (IRE) *(36) (BPalling)* 2-8-9 BDoyle(12) (b: a in rr) ....s.h **14**
Red Tie Affair (USA) *(39) (MBell)* 2-9-0 MFenton(2) (unf: scope: a in rr) 1¼ **15**
3827[10] Young Dalesman *(21) (AStreeter)* 2-8-9 (5) LNewton(4) (b.hind: bhd fr ½-wy: t.o)....9 **16**
3883[14] Washington Reef (USA) *(19) (JHMGosden)* 2-9-0 LDettori(9) (b: bkwd: sn pushed along: a bhd: t.o) 1 **17**

4/1 FOREST BUCK (USA) (2/1-9/2), **5/1** Lakeline Legend (IRE) (op 14/1), Humourless, **11/2** Tawafek (USA), **7/1** Washington Reef (USA) (5/1-8/1), **8/1** Jiyush, **10/1** Ceilidh Star (IRE), **14/1** Persuasion, **16/1** Sister Kit (IRE), Ship's Dancer, **25/1** Red Tie Affair (USA), **33/1** Lady of The Mist (IRE), Salsian, Atienza (USA), Halebid, **50/1** Young Dalesman, Spa Lane, CSF £38.13 TOTE £4.40: £2.70 £3.70 £2.80 (£14.10) Trio £96.60 OWNER Buckram Oak Holdings (NEWMARKET) BRED Buckram Oak Farm 17 Rn

1m 38.0 (3.00) SF: 44/42/36/35/20/22/15/11/8/-/-/-/-/-/-/-/-

4064 E.B.F. REFERENCE POINT MAIDEN STKS (II) (2-Y.O C & G) (Class D) £4,012.50 (£1,200.00: £575.00: £262.50)
7f 9y Stalls: High GOING minus 0.26 sec per fur (GF) 4-30 (4-31)

Gold Disc (USA) *(81+)*(Fav)*(BWHills)* 2-8-11 PatEddery(2) (w'like: stdd s: hdwy ½-wy: led over 1f out: r.o wl) — 1
3890 13 Alambar (IRE) *(75) (PTWalwyn)* 2-8-11 WCarson(4) (mde most 5f: kpt on ins fnl f) 2½ 2
Domak Amaam (IRE) *(74+) (JHMGosden)* 2-8-11 LDettori(8) (cmpt: a.p: led 2f out tl over 1f out: one pce) ¾ 3
3890 8 Jelali (IRE) *(73) (DJGMurraySmith)* 2-8-11 PaulEddery(13) (hdwy 3f out: hrd rdn appr fnl f: kpt on) ½ 4
Rififi *(67) (JLDunlop)* 2-8-11 MRimmer(6) (small: cmpt: bkwd: s.s: hdwy 3f out: sn rdn: nt plcd to chal) 2½ 5
3890 6 Chalcuchima *(61) (RCharlton)* 2-8-11 DHarrison(3) (chsd ldrs: rdn over 2f out: sn btn) 2½ 6
3877 6 Seattle Alley (USA) *(61+) (MrsJRRamsden)* 2-8-11 MDeering(10) (bkwd: hdwy ½-wy: rdn 2f out: sn lost tch) s.h 7
3848 6 Realms of Glory (IRE) *(58) (PMitchell)* 2-8-11 GDuffield(9) (b.nr hind: w ldr tl wknd over 2f out) 1½ 8
2380 8 African Sun (IRE) *(44) (BHanbury)* 2-8-8 (3) JStack(11) (bit bkwd: hld up: hdwy & ev ch 2f out: sn rdn & wknd: eased: t.o) 6 10
Hill Climber *(30) (MBell)* 2-8-11 MFenton(5) (w'like: scope: s.s: a in rr: t.o) 6 11
3881 10 Two Four Sports (IRE) *(14) (JAHarris)* 2-8-11 SDWilliams(1) (spd over 4f: sn wknd: t.o) 7 11
Backtiari *(SGollings)* 2-8-11 CRutter(7) (unf: bkwd: a bhd: t.o) 25 12

13/8 GOLD DISC (USA), **9/4** Domak Amaam (IRE) (6/4-5/2), **6/1** Chalcuchima (4/1-13/2), **12/1** Rififi (op 7/1), Seattle Alley (USA) (7/1-14/1), **14/1** Jelali (IRE), **16/1** Alambar (IRE), **20/1** Hill Climber, **33/1** Realms of Glory (IRE), **50/1** African Sun (IRE), **100/1** Two Four Sports (IRE), Backtiari, CSF £26.95 TOTE £2.30: £1.20 £3.90 £1.60 (£33.40) Trio £12.00 OWNER Mr K. Abdullah (LAMBOURN) BRED Juddmonte Farms 12 Rn 1m 27.1 (4.60) SF: 18/12/11/10/4/-/-/-/-/-/-

4065 WREAKE CONDITIONS STKS (3-Y.O F) (Class C) £5,116.80 (£1,891.20: £905.60: £368.00)
1m 8y Stalls: High GOING minus 0.26 sec per fur (GF) 5-00 (5-02)

3904 10 **Shemaq (USA) (96)***(95)*(Fav)*(HThomsonJones)* 3-9-1 RHills(4) (lw: a.p: led over 1f out: rdn out) — 1
3926 17 Karayb (IRE) **(88)***(94) (DMorley)* 3-9-1 WCarson(1) (a w ldrs: ev ch fnl f: unable qckn) ½ 2
3966* Ron's Secret **(79)***(99) (JWPayne)* 3-9-7 LDettori(6) (hld up: shkn up 2f out: str run fnl f: r.o) ½ 3
3845 4 Dee-Lady **(84)***(86) (WGMTurner)* 3-8-9 GDuffield(2) (a.p: led over 3f out tl over 1f out: rdn & no ex fnl f) ¾ 4
3932 9 Nagnagnag (IRE) **(100)***(92) (SDow)* 3-9-2 MRoberts(8) (s.i.s: hdwy stands' side wl over 1f out: rdn & nt qckn fnl f) hd 5
1105 7 Mary's Way (GR) **(84)***(48) (RCharlton)* 3-8-11 JWeaver(5) (dwlt: a in rr: t.o) 20 6
1811 9 Pinkerton Polka **(47)***(38) (CEBrittain)* 3-8-7 BDoyle(3) (bit bkwd: led over 4f: wknd fnl 2f: t.o) 3 7
3768 4 Fresh Fruit Daily **(74)***(36) (PAKelleway)* 3-8-7 PatEddery(7) (disp ld 5f: rdn over 2f out: sn btn: t.o) ¾ 8

11/4 SHEMAQ (USA), **9/2** Ron's Secret, **5/1** Karayb (IRE), Nagnagnag (IRE) (op 5/2), **11/2** Dee-Lady, **8/1** Mary's Way (GR), **10/1** Fresh Fruit Daily, **50/1** Pinkerton Polka, CSF £15.90 TOTE £3.10: £2.00 £3.20 £1.20 (£20.60) OWNER Mr Hamdan Al Maktoum (NEWMARKET) BRED Thomas P. Whitney in USA 8 Rn 1m 38.1 (3.10) SF: 44/43/48/35/41/-/-/-
T/Jkpt: Not won; £31,140.25 to Haydock 11/10/95. T/Plpt: £25.50 (540.1 Tckts). T/Qdpt: £19.10 (1.6 Tckts). AA

3962-HAYDOCK (L-H)
Wednesday October 11th (Good to soft, Good patches)
WEATHER: overcast WIND: slt half bhd

4066 SYCAMORE NURSERY H'CAP (2-Y.O) (Class D) £3,785.50 (£1,144.00: £557.00: £263.50) **5f** Stalls: High GOING minus 0.01 sec per fur (G) 2-00 (2-02)

3953 3 **Charterhouse Xpres (66)***(78) (MMcCormack)* 2-7-4v(3) NVarley(6) (w ldr: hung lft ½-wy: led over 1f out: drvn out) — 1
3809 13 Precious Girl **(70)***(76) (DMoffatt)* 2-7-8 (3) DarrenMoffatt(3) (lw: in tch: hdwy & hung lft over 1f out: styd on wl towards fin) 2 2
3962* Hear The Music (IRE) **(90)***(92)*(Fav)*(BWHills)* 2-9-3 PatEddery(1) (racd alone centre: led tl over 1f out: kpt on one pce) 1¼ 3

3937* Bee Health Boy **(66)**_(61) (MWEasterby)_ 2-7-2b(5) PFessey(8) (chsd ldrs: hung lft ½-wy: kpt on) 2 **4**
3940[2] Chalice **(78)**_(72) (JBalding)_ 2-8-5 JWilliams(9) (lw: outpcd & bhd: styd on appr fnl f) ....nk **5**
3892[3] Ed's Folly (IRE) **(74)**_(59) (SDow)_ 2-7-10 (5)ow1 AWhelan(11) (lw: chsd ldrs 3f: sn wknd)....2½ **6**
699[4] Tropical Beach **(68)**_(50) (JBerry)_ 2-7-9 LCharnock(4) (bit bkwd: s.i.s: bhd: sme hdwy over 1f out: n.d) 1¼ **7**
3668[7] Whicksey Perry **(94)**_(74) (JBerry)_ 2-9-0 (7) PRoberts(5) (lw: chsd ldrs tl wknd ½-wy) ....¾ **8**
3990[12] First Maite **(71)**_(49) (SRBowring)_ 2-7-12b TWilliams(2) (sn outpcd & drvn along) ....½ **9**
3940[4] Finisterre (IRE) **(68)**_(19) (JJO'Neill)_ 2-7-9bow2 JQuinn(10) (sn bhd)....8 **10**
3623[20] Wild Humour (IRE) **(68)** _(WRMuir)_ 2-7-2 (7)ow2 MartinDwyer(7) (b: outpcd) 7 **11**
LONG HANDICAP Charterhouse Xpres 7-1 Bee Health Boy 7-6 Finisterre (IRE) 7-3 Wild Humour (IRE) 7-1

5/4 Hear The Music (IRE), **6/1** Ed's Folly (IRE), Bee Health Boy (op 7/2), **7/1** Precious Girl, **12/1** Chalice, **14/1** Tropical Beach, Whicksey Perry, **16/1** First Maite, Finisterre (IRE), **20/1** CHARTERHOUSE XPRES, Wild Humour (IRE), CSF £148.80 CT £280.90 TOTE £42.80: £4.60 £2.70 £1.10 (£132.20) Trio £45.80 OWNER Charterhouse Holdings Plc (WANTAGE) BRED I and F Yorkshire Holdings 11 Rn 61.85 secs (2.85) SF: 29/27/43/12/23/10/1/25/-/-/-

4067 MARTON INSTITUTE CENTENARY CONDITIONS STKS (2-Y.O) (Class C)
£4,907.60 (£1,715.60: £837.80: £359.00)
1m 30y Stalls: Low GOING: 0.19 sec per fur (G) 2-30 (2-30)

3631* **Inchrory (100)**_(97)_(Fav)_(HRACecil)_ 2-9-7 PatEddery(2) (lw: mde all: drvn out) ....— **1**
3869* Salmis _(81) (JRFanshawe)_ 2-8-6 DHarrison(1) (trckd ldrs: ev ch over 1f out: hung lft & nt qckn ins fnl f) ....¾ **2**
3939* Classic Romance _(67) (SCWilliams)_ 2-8-10 AMackay(3) (trckd ldrs: effrt over 3f out: ev ch over 1f out: wknd & eased jst ins fnl f) 9 **3**
3773[7] My Archie _(RDEWoodhouse)_ 2-8-11 NConnorton(4) (chsd ldr tl rdn & lost pl over 3f out: sn bhd & eased: t.o) ....dist **4**

4/6 INCHRORY, **9/4** Salmis, **9/2** Classic Romance, **66/1** My Archie, CSF £2.51 TOTE £1.60 (£1.60) OWNER Sir David Wills (NEWMARKET) BRED Sir David Wills 4 Rn 1m 46.86 (6.46) SF: 56/40/26/-

4068 TOMMY WALLIS H'CAP (0-80) (3-Y.O+) (Class D) £4,240.50
(£1,284.00: £627.00: £298.50)
6f Stalls: High GOING minus 0.01 sec per fur (G) 3-00 (3-03)

3764[4] **Double Splendour (IRE) (60)**_(70) (PSFelgate)_ 5-8-10 WRyan(8) (lw: hld up: stdy hdwy ½-wy: swtchd rt over 1f out: led ins fnl f: r.o wl) ....— **1**
3943[14] Be Warned **(74)**_(79) (NACallaghan)_ 4-9-10b PaulEddery(20) (s.i.s: bhd: hdwy & nt clr run over 1f out: styd on wl ins fnl f) 1¾ **2**
4040[3] Palo Blanco **(72)**_(77) (TDBarron)_ 4-9-8 LCharnock(19) (swtg: a chsng ldrs: kpt on wl fnl f)....s.h **3**
3964[11] Knayton Lass **(58)**_(59) (MWEasterby)_ 4-8-8 MBirch(11) (chsd ldrs: led over 1f out: hung lft & hdd jst ins fnl f) 1½ **4**
3905[5] Bajan Rose **(71)**_(70) (MBlanshard)_ 3-9-5 MRoberts(3) (chsd ldrs: kpt on same pce appr fnl f) ....¾ **5**
3800[8] Gone Savage **(63)**_(62) (WJMusson)_ 7-8-10 (3) PMcCabe(21) (hld up: hdwy over 1f out: nvr nr to chal)....s.h **6**
3822[6] Bells of Longwick **(54)**_(48) (WWHaigh)_ 6-8-4v DaleGibson(6) (hdwy over 1f out: nt rch ldrs)..1¾ **7**
3964* Charlie Sillett **(76)**_(70) (BWHills)_ 3-9-10 MHills(1) (b: b.hind: dwlt: sn swtchd rt: hdwy & nt clr run over 1f out: eased fnl f) ....s.h **8**
3964[5] Brockton Flame **(68)**_(59) (JMPEustace)_ 3-9-2 RCochrane(9) (lw: hld up & bhd: hdwy & nt clr run over 1f out: n.d) 1¼ **9**
3822[8] Broadstairs Beauty (IRE) **(74)**_(65) (SRBowring)_ 5-9-10 SDWilliams(4) (b: b.hind: chsd ldrs tl outpcd ½-wy: styd on fnl f) ....hd **10**
3615[9] Sue Me (IRE) **(71)**_(61)_(Fav)_(WRMuir)_ 3-9-5 WCarson(7) (in tch: effrt 2f out: nvr nr to chal)....nk **11**
4041[12] Rossini Blue **(71)**_(61) (MrsJRRamsden)_ 4-9-7 KFallon(15) (s.i.s: bhd tl sme hdwy over 1f out: n.d) ....hd **12**
3964[3] First Veil **(73)**_(61) (JRFanshawe)_ 5-9-6 (3) NVarley(14) (outpcd & drvn along ½-wy: n.d)....½ **13**
3964[2] Little Ibnr **(62)**_(48) (PDEvans)_ 4-8-12 GHind(23) (lw: chsd ldrs tl wknd over 1f out) ....¾ **14**
3980* Quilling **(72)**_(57) (MDods)_ 3-9-6 6x JWeaver(12) (lw: chsd ldrs tl wknd over 1f out: eased) ....½ **15**
4041[7] Densben **(54)**_(38) (DenysSmith)_ 11-8-4 TWilliams(5) (sn outpcd & pushed along: n.d)....nk **16**
3964[12] Barato **(68)**_(49) (MrsJRRamsden)_ 4-8-11 (7) TFinn(17) (lw: s.i.s: a in rr) 1¼ **17**
3929[3] Sea Thunder **(80)**_(58) (IABalding)_ 3-10-0 LDettori(18) (hld up: sme hdwy over 2f out: wknd over 1f out: eased) 1¼ **18**
3715[7] Selhurstpark Flyer (IRE) **(76)**_(53) (JBerry)_ 4-9-5 (7) PRoberts(16) (led to ½-wy: sn wknd)....s.h **19**
3764[3] Maid O'Cannie **(58)**_(35) (MWEasterby)_ 4-8-8b SMaloney(2) (s.i.s: hld up: a bhd)....hd **20**
3783[17] Monis (IRE) **(58)**_(34) (JBalding)_ 4-8-8 JWilliams(10) (chsd ldrs 3f: sn wknd) ....nk **21**

18068 Superpride **(72)***(46) (MrsMReveley)* 3-9-6 KDarley(13) (bkwd: mid div & drvn along ½-wy: sn bhd) ......¾ **22**
366728 Mamma's Due **(57)***(29) (JBerry)* 3-8-5 JCarroll(24) (led ½-wy: hdd & wknd qckly over 1f out) ..1 **23**
39614 Mister Jolson **(78)***(36) (RJHodges)* 6-10-0 PatEddery(22) (b.nr fore: chsd ldrs: wkng whn hmpd & eased over 1f out) 5 **24**

7/1 Sue Me (IRE), **15/2** Be Warned (op 12/1), **8/1** DOUBLE SPLENDOUR (IRE), Little Ibnr, **9/1** Palo Blanco, **10/1** Charlie Sillett, **12/1** Gone Savage, Brockton Flame, **14/1** Sea Thunder, First Veil, **16/1** Rossini Blue, Mister Jolson, Quilling, Selhurstpark Flyer (IRE), **20/1** Maid O'Cannie, Broadstairs Beauty (IRE), Densben, **25/1** Barato, Bajan Rose, Bells of Longwick, Superpride, **33/1** Knayton Lass, **50/1** Mamma's Due, Monis (IRE), CSF £72.94 CT £540.54 TOTE £10.90: £2.10 £3.50 £2.30 £15.00 (£196.90) Trio £334.10 OWNER Yorkshire Racing Club Owners Group 1990 (MELTON MOWBRAY) BRED R. McQuillan 24 Rn
1m 14.66 (2.96) SF: 52/61/59/41/50/44/30/50/39/47/41/43/43/30/37/20/31/38/35/17/16/26/9/18
WEIGHT FOR AGE 3yo-2lb

4069 KING'S REGIMENT CUP CONDITIONS STKS (3-Y.O+) (Class C)
£4,981.80 (£1,816.80: £888.40: £382.00: £171.00)
1m 3f 200y Stalls: High GOING: 0.19 sec per fur (G) 3-30 (3-31)

1127* **Sebastian (112)***(122+)*(Fav)*(HRACecil)* 3-9-1 PatEddery(2) (lw: mde all: rdn & styd on strly over 1f out: readily) ......— **1**
39232 Mack the Knife **(106)***(115) (MCPipe)* 6-9-7 MRoberts(4) (hld up: pushed along over 5f out: chsd wnr fnl 3f: nt qckn fnl f) 4 **2**
39322 Nash Terrace (IRE) **(100)***(109) (RCharlton)* 3-8-10 JReid(5) (trckd ldrs: effrt over 3f out: n.m.r: hung lft over 1f out: one pce) 1¾ **3**
38645 Penny a Day (IRE) **(94)***(105) (MrsMReveley)* 5-9-13 KDarley(3) (lw: chsd ldrs: effrt over 2f out: wknd & eased fnl f) 10 **4**
39268 Heathyards Rock **(81)***(70) (RHollinshead)* 3-8-11v WRyan(1) (hld up: wknd 3f out: sn bhd)....20 **5**

1/2 SEBASTIAN, **4/1** Mack the Knife, **5/1** Nash Terrace (IRE), **16/1** Penny a Day (IRE), **50/1** Heathyards Rock, CSF £2.94 TOTE £1.40: £1.10 £1.90 (£2.00) OWNER Lord Howard de Walden (NEWMARKET) BRED Lord Howard de Walden 5 Rn 2m 37.9 (9.90) SF: 47/48/34/38/-
WEIGHT FOR AGE 3yo-8lb

4070 E.B.F. HAWTHORN MAIDEN STKS (I) (2-Y.O) (Class D) £4,320.00 (£1,305.00: £635.00: £300.00) 7f 30y Stalls: Low GOING: 0.19 sec per fur (G) 4-00 (4-01)

Polar Eclipse *(89+) (MJohnston)* 2-9-0 JWeaver(8) (leggy: scope: mde all: shkn up 2f out: r.o wl) ......— **1**
30685 Alessandra *(80) (BWHills)* 2-8-9 MHills(5) (b: chsd wnr: 2nd st: effrt & ev ch over 2f out: one pce) 1¾ **2**
38688 Spillo *(65)*(Fav)*(LMCumani)* 2-9-0 KDarley(7) (lw: s.i.s: sn chsng ldrs: 3rd st: pushed along 3f out: wknd appr fnl f) 9 **3**
Harbour Dues *(63+) (LadyHerries)* 2-9-0 RCochrane(1) (gd sort: bit bkwd: dwlt: hld up: 5th st: hdwy over 2f out: nt rch ldrs) 1 **4**
38386 Silent Guest (IRE) *(54) (SirMarkPrescott)* 2-9-0 GDuffield(4) (plld hrd: 4th st: wknd over 2f out) 4 **5**
Waypoint *(43) (RCharlton)* 2-8-9 TSprake(2) (unf: scope: bkwd: in tch tl wknd over 2f out) ..2½ **6**
3713W Son of Anshan *(40) (MrsASwinbank)* 2-9-0 NConnorton(9) (b.hind: bkwd: chsd ldrs: 6th st: wknd 3f out) 3½ **7**
Batoutoftheblue *(37) (WWHaigh)* 2-9-0 DaleGibson(3) (w'like: bkwd: s.i.s: a bhd) 1¼ **8**
Present 'n Correct *(CBBBooth)* 2-9-0 MBirch(6) (cmpt: bkwd: a bhd: t.o) 25 **9**

13/8 Spillo, **2/1** Alessandra, **7/1** POLAR ECLIPSE, **8/1** Waypoint (op 5/1), **10/1** Harbour Dues, **12/1** Silent Guest (IRE), **25/1** Present 'n Correct, **33/1** Batoutoftheblue, **40/1** Son of Anshan, CSF £21.27 TOTE £7.30: £2.10 £1.20 £1.30 (£7.60) Trio £7.40 OWNER Mr J. R. Good (MIDDLEHAM) BRED J. R. and Mrs P. Good 9 Rn 1m 33.99 (6.69) SF: 37/28/13/11/2/-/-/-/-

4071 HORNBEAM H'CAP (0-80) (3-Y.O F) (Class D) £3,811.50
(£1,152.00: £561.00: £265.50)
1m 2f 120y Stalls: High GOING: 0.19 sec per fur (G) 4-30 (4-30)

37005 **Debutante Days (64)***(77) (ACStewart)* 3-8-10 MRoberts(16) (a.p: 3rd st: led over 3f out: rdn over 1f out: r.o wl) ......— **1**
7176 Mistinguett (IRE) **(73)***(82) (DRLoder)* 3-9-5 GCarter(6) (chsd ldrs: sn drvn along: 4th st: jnd wnr 2f out: rdn & one pce fnl f) 2½ **2**
39575 Wild Rita **(71)***(79) (WRMuir)* 3-9-3 MHills(7) (hld up: hdwy 4f out: styd on ins fnl f) ......¾ **3**

3757[9] Shift Again (IRE) **(66)**_(70) (WJarvis)_ 3-8-12 JReid(10) (hld up: hdwy 2f out: styd on fnl f: nvr nrr) 2½ **4**
3935[3] Heboob Alshemaal (IRE) **(75)**_(76)_(Fav)_(JHMGosden)_ 3-9-7 LDettori(13) (hld up: effrt over 3f out: nt rch ldrs) 2½ **5**
3935[6] Mill Dancer (IRE) **(48)**_(47) (EJAlston)_ 3-7-5 (3)ow1 DWright(4) (chsd ldrs: 5th st: rdn 3f out: kpt on same pce) ....hd **6**
3921* Rosy Hue (IRE) **(73)**_(61) (RCharlton)_ 3-9-5 PatEddery(9) (lw: chsd ldrs: 6th st: rdn 3f out: sn btn) 8 **7**
3552[5] Pumice **(73)**_(58) (LMCumani)_ 3-9-5 KDarley(5) (hld up & bhd: effrt & n.m.r over 2f out: no imp)2 **8**
3970[4] Instantaneous **(51)**_(31) (MHEasterby)_ 3-7-11 ow1 WCarson(12) (nvr bttr than mid div) 3 **9**
3959* Domitia (USA) **(67)**_(32) (MBell)_ 3-8-13 MFenton(11) (b.off hind: mid div tl wknd wl over 2f out: t.o) 10 **10**
_3734_[10] Coryana Dancer (IRE) **(56)**_(21) (RHollinshead)_ 3-7-11 (5) MHenry(1) (nvr nr to ldrs) ....hd **11**
_3952_[2] Brave Princess **(64)**_(22) (MAJarvis)_ 3-8-10 PRobinson(2) (chsd ldrs: rdn along 3f out: sn wknd: t.o) 5 **12**
1916[4] Sadly Sober (IRE) **(66)**_(19) (PFICole)_ 3-8-12 JWeaver(14) (bit bkwd: led over 4f: 2nd st: wknd over 3f out: t.o) 3 **13**
1702[4] Boldly So **(48)** _(WJMusson)_ 3-7-8 ow1 JQuinn(15) (racd wd: sn pushed along: a bhd: t.o) 6 **14**
3700[14] Prudent Pet **(63)**_(5) (CWFairhurst)_ 3-8-9 JTate(3) (lw: hld up: effrt 3f out: sn no imp: t.o) 1¼ **15**
3926[4] Emily-Mou (IRE) **(71)** _(BJMeehan)_ 3-9-3 BDoyle(8) (b: chsd ldr: led 6f out tl hdd & wknd over 3f out: t.o) 15 **16**

LONG HANDICAP Boldly So 7-1

9/2 Heboob Alshemaal (IRE), **13/2** Rosy Hue (IRE), **8/1** Pumice, **9/1** Emily-Mou (IRE), Instantaneous, Mistinguett (IRE), **10/1** DEBUTANTE DAYS, **12/1** Sadly Sober (IRE), Domitia (USA), **14/1** Brave Princess, Boldly So, **16/1** Wild Rita, **20/1** Shift Again (IRE), Mill Dancer (IRE), Prudent Pet, **33/1** Coryana Dancer (IRE), CSF £95.97 CT £1,333.40 TOTE £12.30: £3.10 £3.50 £2.70 £6.50 (£128.90) Trio £798.70; £798.70 to Newmarket 12/10/95 OWNER Lady McAlpine (NEWMARKET) BRED Lady McAlpine 16 Rn 2m 20.28 (8.78) SF: 43/48/45/36/42/13/27/24/-/-/-/-/-/-/-/-

4072 HOLLY MAIDEN STKS (3-Y.O+) (Class D) £4,026.00 (£1,218.00: £594.00: £282.00) 1m 3f 200y Stalls: High GOING: 0.19 sec per fur (G) 5-00 (5-05)

2151[2] **Richelieu (IRE)** _(94) (HRACecil)_ 3-8-11 WRyan(8) (lw: hdwy ½-wy: sn chsng ldrs: styd on u.p to ld nr fin) ....— **1**
3896[2] Taklif (IRE) **(86)**_(94)_(Fav)_(BWHills)_ 3-8-11 WCarson(5) (lw: hdwy ½-wy: sn chsng ldrs: led ins fnl f tl ct cl home) ....nk **2**
950[10] Autumn Wings (FR) _(86) (BWHills)_ 3-8-6 PatEddery(3) (chsd ldrs: 5th st: led over 3f out tl ins fnl f) 1¾ **3**
4003[7] All The Time _(66) (PFICole)_ 3-8-6 JWeaver(15) (led 1f: 3rd st: rdn 3f out: sn outpcd) 15 **4**
3772[6] Darter (IRE) _(63) (LMCumani)_ 3-8-11 KDarley(20) (chsd ldrs: led 6f out to 3f out: sn rdn & grad wknd) 6 **5**
Clear Attraction (USA) _(55) (LordHuntingdon)_ 3-8-6 DHarrison(1) (tall: unf: hld up: sme hdwy fnl 2f: nvr nrr) 2 **6**
3799[12] Three Wild Days _(58) (TPTate)_ 3-8-11 ACulhane(7) (sn prom: c wd st: one pce fnl 3f) 1½ **7**
4003[4] Modajjaj _(56) (MAJarvis)_ 3-8-11 PRobinson(6) (mid div: effrt 6f out: wknd fnl f) 1½ **8**
3921[3] Roussi (USA) _(54) (MRStoute)_ 3-8-11 WRSwinburn(4) (chsd ldrs: 4th st: c stands' side: sn rdn & wknd) 2 **9**
3844[12] Fragaria **(48)**_(48) (IABalding)_ 3-8-6b PaulEddery(14) (nvr nr ldrs) ....½ **10**
3256[7] Palace River (IRE) _(45) (DMoffatt)_ 7-8-11 (3) DarrenMoffatt(10) (a bhd) 2½ **11**
1555[7] Lawful Love (IRE) **(35)**_(50) (TWDonnelly)_ 5-9-5 SDWilliams(17) (a bhd) ....s.h **12**
3847[6] Expansive Runner (USA) _(46) (PWHarris)_ 3-8-11 GHind(2) (bit bkwd: s.i.s: a in rr) 3 **13**
3756[8] Portscatho (IRE) _(41) (MissJacquelineDoyle)_ 3-8-6 (5) AWhelan(12) (bit bkwd: m.n.s) 3½ **14**
3716[7] Caribbean Surfer (USA) _(40) (JSGoldie)_ 6-9-0 (5) RHavlin(11) (b: swtg: s.s: a bhd) ....½ **15**
3799[4] Silver Singer _(30) (DRLoder)_ 3-8-6 LDettori(16) (led after 1f to 6f out: 2nd st: wknd qckly 3f out) 4 **16**
2331[9] Calcando _(EWeymes)_ 3-8-6 DaleGibson(19) (bkwd: sn pushed along: a in rr: t.o) 30 **17**
Damarita _(LadyHerries)_ 4-8-7 (7) ShonaCrombie(18) (bit bkwd: plld hrd: chsd ldrs 8f: sn wknd: t.o) 7 **18**
Livio (USA) _(LLungo)_ 4-9-5 MBirch(9) (bkwd: a bhd: t.o) 1 **19**
Kirkadian _(NBycroft)_ 5-8-7 (7) GWright(13) (Withdrawn not under Starter's orders: ref to ent stalls) .... **W**

2/1 Taklif (IRE), **3/1** Roussi (USA), **6/1** RICHELIEU (IRE), **9/1** Darter (IRE), **10/1** Autumn Wings (FR), Clear Attraction (USA), Silver Singer, **16/1** Modajjaj, **20/1** Fragaria, All The Time, Expansive Runner (USA), **33/1** Livio (USA), **50/1** Calcando, **66/1** Three Wild Days, Caribbean Surfer (USA), Palace River (IRE), Lawful Love (IRE), Damarita, Portscatho (IRE), Kirkadian, CSF £19.76 TOTE £5.00: £2.10 £1.70 £4.00 (£7.50) Trio £40.70 OWNER Cliveden Stud (NEWMARKET) BRED Cliveden Stud Ltd 19 Rn 2m 37.52 (9.52) SF: 46/46/38/18/15/7/10/8/6/-/5/10/-/-/-/-/-/-/-

WEIGHT FOR AGE 3yo-8lb

4073 E.B.F. HAWTHORN MAIDEN STKS (II) (2-Y.O) (Class D) £4,320.00 (£1,305.00: £635.00: £300.00)
7f 30y Stalls: Low GOING: 0.19 sec per fur (G) 5-30 (5-31)

3708[8] **Circled (USA)** *(84+) (BWHills)* 2-8-9 MHills(5) (mde all: styd on strly to go clr fnl f)...............— 1
3888[4] Name of Our Father (USA) *(76) (JHMGosden)* 2-9-0 LDettori(6) (a.p: 3rd st: rdn & one pce fnl f)..........6 2
3441[4] Fog City *(72) (WJarvis)* 2-9-0 PatEddery(8) (hld up: 6th st: hdwy & ev ch 2f out: wknd fnl f).1¾ 3
3900[4] Dombey *(71)*(Fav)*(RCharlton)* 2-9-0 JReid(9) (dwlt: hld up: hdwy 3f out: sn rdn: hmpd 1f out: no imp)..........nk 4
Classic Colours (USA) *(58) (SCWilliams)* 2-9-0 AMackay(4) (unf: scope: swvd lft s: sn chsng ldrs: hung lft & wknd over 1f out)..........6 5
3975[24] What Jim Wants (IRE) **(40)***(44) (JJO'Neill)* 2-9-0 SDWilliams(2) (prom: 2nd st: wknd over 2f out)..........6 6
Rain Cloud *(38) (WWHaigh)* 2-8-9 DaleGibson(3) (b.hind: bkwd: s.s: a in rr)..........nk 7
3620[18] Young Saffy *(43) (MrsMReveley)* 2-9-0 ACulhane(7) (bit bkwd: a bhd)..........s.h 8
1935[7] Ballykissangel *(NBycroft)* 2-9-0 KFallon(1) (bit bkwd: prom to ½-wy: t.o)..........30 9

5/4 Dombey, **100/30** Fog City, **7/2** Name of Our Father (USA), **7/1** Classic Colours (USA), **10/1** CIRCLED (USA), **33/1** Rain Cloud, **50/1** What Jim Wants (IRE), Young Saffy, **66/1** Ballykissangel, CSF £43.32 TOTE £13.70: £1.90 £1.70 £1.30 (£24.50) Trio £19.70 OWNER Mrs J. M. Corbett (LAMBOURN) BRED Mrs Harry W. Stone 9 Rn 1m 34.22 (6.92) SF: 30/22/18/17/4/-/-/-/-
T/Jkpt: Not won; £54,317.39 to Newmarket 12/10/95. T/Plpt: £63.90 (286.86 Tckts). T/Qdpt: £80.60 (2.75 Tckts). WG

3942-NEWMARKET (R-H)
Thursday October 12th (Good to firm)
WEATHER: overcast WIND: almost nil

4074 NGK SPARK PLUGS CONDITIONS STKS (3-Y.O+) (Class B) £8,767.20 (£3,244.80: £1,557.40: £637.00)
1m 2f Stalls: Centre GOING minus 0.38 sec per fur (F) 1-30 (1-32)

3603[2] **Bal Harbour (106)***(107)*(Fav)*(HRACecil)* 4-9-0 PatEddery(4) (mde all: qcknd over 3f out: hld on wl fnl f)..........— 1
3923[3] Warning Order **(102)***(111) (JLDunlop)* 3-9-0 KDarley(7) (hld up & bhd: gd hdwy 2f out: chal ins fnl f: hung rt & nt qckn towards fin)..........1 2
3811[3] Burooj **(110)***(116) (DMorley)* 5-9-12 WCarson(8) (lw: hld up: hmpd over 2f out: hdwy over 1f out: r.o wl towards fin)..........1 3
3813[6] Cadeaux Tryst **(103)***(108) (EALDunlop)* 3-9-1 WRSwinburn(3) (lw: b: hld up: hdwy over 3f out: ch over 1f out: nt qckn)..........1½ 4
3945[25] Amrak Ajeeb (IRE) **(85)***(105) (BHanbury)* 3-8-12 MRimmer(2) (in tch: hdwy 3f out: ch 1½f out: no ex)..........½ 5
3944[4] Pitcroy **(96)***(91) (JRFanshawe)* 3-8-5 DHarrison(6) (lw: in tch: hrd rdn 2f out: no imp)..........4 6
3552* Out on a Promise (IRE) **(85)***(96) (GWragg)* 3-8-12 WWoods(1) (chsd ldrs tl wknd fnl 2f)..........1¼ 7
3923[6] Final Appearance (IRE) **(95)***(83) (PWChapple-Hyam)* 3-8-10 JReid(9) (chsd ldrs tl wknd over 2f out)..........7 8
3754[2] That Old Feeling (IRE) **(90)***(81) (RHannon)* 3-8-9 RCochrane(5) (chsd ldrs tl rdn & btn over 2f out)..........¾ 9

5/2 BAL HARBOUR, **3/1** Burooj (op 2/1), **13/2** Cadeaux Tryst, Pitcroy, **8/1** Warning Order (6/1-9/1), **9/1** Final Appearance (IRE), **12/1** Out on a Promise (IRE), **20/1** That Old Feeling (IRE), **33/1** Amrak Ajeeb (IRE), CSF £21.11 TOTE £2.50: £1.30 £2.30 £1.40 (£12.00) Trio £5.20 OWNER Mr K. Abdullah (NEWMARKET) BRED Juddmonte Farms 9 Rn 2m 3.03 SF: 64/62/73/59/56/42/47/34/32
WEIGHT FOR AGE 3yo-6lb

4075 BUCKENHAM (S) STKS (2-Y.O) (Class E) £7,815.00 (£2,370.00: £1,160.00: £555.00) **7f (Rowley)** Stalls: Centre GOING minus 0.38 sec per fur (F) 2-00 (2-05)

2656[5] **Domettes (IRE) (64)***(72) (RHannon)* 2-8-6 (5) DaneO'Neill(27) (in tch centre: hdwy over 2f out: r.o to ld cl home)..........— 1
3379[18] Sharp Shuffle (IRE) *(72) (RHannon)* 2-8-11 JReid(18) (chsd ldrs centre: led wl ins fnl f: hdd & no ex nr fin)..........s.h 2
3870[4] Eurobox Boy *(71) (APJarvis)* 2-8-8 (3) JStack(17) (chsd ldrs: led centre over 2f out tl wl ins fnl f: r.o)..........nk 3
3975[3] Apartments Abroad **(49)***(62) (KMcAuliffe)* 2-8-6 RCochrane(16) (b.hind: hdwy centre over 2f out: hrd rdn & styd on: nrst fin)..........2 4

3915[2] Even Handed **(70)**_(66) (PFICole)_ 2-8-11 AClark(13) (swtg: racd centre: chsd ldrs: rdn 2f out: kpt on one pce)....hd 5
3533[15] Herald Angel (IRE) **(40)**_(59) (MHTompkins)_ 2-8-3 (7)ow4 JGotobed(2) (chsd ldrs stands' side tl rdn & btn over 1f out)....1¼ 6
3894[11] Spirito Libro (USA) **(64)**_(60) (CNAllen)_ 2-8-6 (5) MHenry(5) (b: chsd ldrs stands' side: hdwy over 2f out: no imp)....1½ 7
3868[11] Lydhurst (USA) _(59)_(Fav)_(DRLoder)_ 2-8-11v PatEddery(11) (sn drvn along centre: hdwy ½-wy: ev ch wl over 1f out: sn btn)....½ 8
3752[5] Laughing Buccaneer **(78)**_(50) (BJMeehan)_ 2-8-11b WRSwinburn(1) (lw: swtg: led & clr stands' side tl hdd & wknd wl over 1f out)....4 9
3975[4] Princess Pamgaddy **(49)**_(49) (JBerry)_ 2-8-6 (5) PFessey(26) (in tch centre: rdn & no imp fnl 2½f)....½ 10
3530[8] Sheath Kefaah _(49) (WJHaggas)_ 2-8-11 WCarson(7) (racd stands' side: nvr trbld ldrs)....s.h 11
Mandapan _(41) (SPCWoods)_ 2-7-13 (7) CWebb(20) (small: lt-f: bhd tl hdwy centre over 1f out: n.d)....1¼ 12
3868[16] Billaddie _(46) (RBoss)_ 2-8-8 (3) NVarley(22) (b: racd centre: nvr trbld ldrs)....s.h 13
3968[12] No More Hassle (IRE) **(50)**_(45) (MrsMReveley)_ 2-8-11 KDarley(4) (racd stands' side: n.d)....hd 14
3894[2] Hurricane Dancer (IRE) **(60)**_(44) (SPCWoods)_ 2-8-11 WWoods(12) (swtg: outpcd fr ½-wy)....½ 15
3937[11] Red Misty (IRE) **(47)**_(39) (MRChannon)_ 2-8-6 PaulEddery(19) (led centre: clr ½-wy: sn hdd & wknd)....hd 16
3540[8] Arlington Lady **(60)**_(43) (NACallaghan)_ 2-8-11 GHind(15) (racd centre: prom to ½-wy)....½ 17
On The Wildside _(37) (MRChannon)_ 2-8-1 (5) PPMurphy(9) (leggy: lt-f: s.i.s: racd centre: n.d)....½ 18
3894[12] Eskimo Kiss (IRE) **(60)**_(36) (MJFetherston-Godley)_ 2-8-6 MTebbutt(6) (racd stands'side: n.d)....nk 19
Isitoff _(35) (CADwyer)_ 2-8-11 CDwyer(23) (w'like: racd centre: n.d)....2½ 20
3651[4] Golden Silver **(48)**_(28) (JSMoore)_ 2-8-6 JFEgan(25) (racd centre: n.d)....1¼ 21
3883[18] Super Baron _(23) (RHannon)_ 2-8-11 SWhitworth(14) (racd centre: n.d)....4 22
2128[8] Esperto _(17) (JPearce)_ 2-8-11 GBardwell(10) (racd stands' side: outpcd & bhd fr ½-wy)....3 23
3895[15] Dancing Man _(15) (MrsMELong)_ 2-8-11 NAdams(24) (b: racd centre: bhd fr ½-wy)....¾ 24
3988[15] Further Future (IRE) _(12) (JohnBerry)_ 2-8-11 MRimmer(8) (lw: racd stands' side: sn bhd)...1¼ 25
3430[10] Signs R Us (IRE) _(11) (DrJDScargill)_ 2-8-8 (3) DWright(3) (racd stands' side: sn bhd)....½ 26
3873[5] Stronz (IRE) **(69)** _(RAkehurst)_ 2-8-11 DHarrison(21) (lost tch centre ½-wy: p.u over 2f out)...... P

9/4 Lydhurst (USA), **6/1** Eurobox Boy, **7/1** Laughing Buccaneer (5/1-8/1), **10/1** Sheath Kefaah (6/1-12/1), Even Handed, **12/1** Esperto (8/1-14/1), **16/1** Hurricane Dancer (IRE), DOMETTES (IRE), Super Baron, Stronz (IRE), Arlington Lady, **20/1** Sharp Shuffle (IRE), Spirito Libro (USA), Apartments Abroad, **25/1** Isitoff, Golden Silver, **33/1** Herald Angel (IRE), Mandapan, Red Misty (IRE), Billaddie, On The Wildside, Eskimo Kiss (IRE), Princess Pamgaddy, No More Hassle (IRE), Further Future (IRE), Signs R Us (IRE), **50/1** Dancing Man, CSF £330.45 TOTE £33.70: £9.30 £8.10 £2.80 (£146.80) Trio £590.30 OWNER Albion Investments (MARLBOROUGH) BRED Sandville Stud 27 Rn 1m 26.24 (2.54) SF: 33/33/32/23/27/20/21/20/11/10/10/2/7/6/5/-/4/-/-/-/-/-/-/-/-/-/-

No bid

Even Handed clmd Mme M Bollack-Badell £8,000.

4076 GREENE KING RATED STKS H'CAP (0-100) (3-Y.O+) (Class B)

£8,510.84 (£3,147.56: £1,508.78: £614.90)

1m 4f (Rowley) Stalls: Centre GOING minus 0.38 sec per fur (F) 2-35 (2-38)

3945[33] **Naked Welcome (96)**_(110) (MJFetherston-Godley)_ 3-8-9 JReid(9) (hld up & bhd: hdwy over 3f out: r.o wl to ld wl ins fnl f)....— 1
3864* Seckar Vale (USA) **(86)**_(100)_(Fav)_(BWHills)_ 3-7-13 WCarson(5) (plld hrd early: hdwy over 2f out: led appr fnl f: hung lft & r.o: nt qckn towards fin)....nk 2
3836[4] Whitechapel (USA) **(88)**_(98) (LordHuntingdon)_ 7-8-9 DHarrison(1) (chsd ldr: chal over 3f out: led wl over 1f out: sn hdd & one pce)....2½ 3
3930[4] Daraydan (IRE) **(96)**_(106) (LadyHerries)_ 3-8-9 KDarley(6) (in tch: hdwy & ev ch 2f out: btn whn hmpd ins fnl f)....hd 4
3836[9] Son of Sharp Shot (IRE) **(100)**_(106) (JLDunlop)_ 5-9-7 PatEddery(2) (lw: hld up: effrt over 2f out: nvr able chal)....3½ 5
3899* Danjing (IRE) **(86)**_(88) (SESherwood)_ 3-7-8b(5) MHenry(4) (plld hrd: led after 3f tl wl over 1f out: grad wknd)....2½ 6
3016* Polydamas **(86)**_(84) (MRStoute)_ 3-7-13 JFEgan(7) (lw: chsd ldrs: effrt 3f out: wknd fnl 2f)....3½ 7
3454[2] Edbaysaan (IRE) **(95)**_(88) (RAkehurst)_ 5-9-2b RCochrane(3) (led 3f: chsd ldr tl wknd fnl 3½f)....3½ 8
2012[5] Acting Brave **(92)**_(77) (GHarwood)_ 4-8-13 AClark(8) (bhd: shkn up & hdwy 4f out: wknd fnl 2f)....6 9
3957[9] Glide Path (USA) **(94)**_(76) (JWHills)_ 6-9-1 WRSwinburn(10) (lw: hld up: effrt 4f out:n.d)....2½ 10

LONG HANDICAP Danjing (IRE) 7-10 Polydamas 7-11

3/1 Seckar Vale (USA), **7/2** Son of Sharp Shot (IRE), **11/2** Polydamas, **7/1** Whitechapel (USA), **10/1** NAKED WELCOME, Danjing (IRE), Daraydan (IRE) (8/1-12/1), **11/1** Glide Path (USA) (8/1-12/1), **20/1** Acting Brave, **25/1** Edbaysaan (IRE), CSF £38.43 CT £208.87 TOTE £12.70: £3.30 £1.40 £3.00 (£16.80) Trio £45.00 OWNER The Most Welcome Partnership (EAST ILSLEY) BRED W. H. Joyce 10 Rn
2m 29.58 (0.28) SF: 61/51/57/57/65/39/35/47/36/35
WEIGHT FOR AGE 3yo-8lb

4077 SPORTING LIFE NURSERY H'CAP (2-Y.O) (Class C) £8,155.00 (£2,440.00: £1,170.00: £535.00)
6f (Rowley) Stalls: Centre GOING minus 0.38 sec per fur (F) 3-10 (3-11)

3901* **Lunar Mist (76)***(83)*(Fav)*(MartynMeade)* 2-8-7 (5) RHavlin(3) (a.p: led ins fnl f: r.o wl)........— 1
2991³ Stop Play (IRE) **(74)***(76) (MHTompkins)* 2-8-10 RCochrane(14) (lw: s.i.s: hdwy 2f out: r.o wl)1¾ 2
3727¹⁰ White Emir **(84)***(86) (BJMeehan)* 2-9-6 WRSwinburn(18) (cl up: led over 1f out tl ins fnl f: kpt on)........nk 3
3990⁶ Standown **(69)***(69) (JBerry)* 2-8-0 (5) PFessey(13) (lw: a.p: rdn over 2f out: nt qckn ins fnl f)....¾ 4
3901³ Little Noggins (IRE) **(77)***(75) (CADwyer)* 2-8-6 (7) MartinDwyer(1) (racd stands' side: cl up tl rdn & btn over 1f out: sn bhd)........¾ 5
3894⁶ Where's Margaret **(63)***(57) (GLewis)* 2-7-13b NAdams(16) (led tl hdd over 1f out: sn btn)......1¼ 6
3867¹² Prima Volta **(85)***(79) (RHannon)* 2-9-2 (5) DaneO'Neill(10) (styd on fnl 2f: nvr trbld ldrs)........hd 7
3803¹² Clincher Club **(78)***(72) (MJohnston)* 2-9-0 WWoods(12) (swtg: outpcd & bhd tl styd on appr fnl f)........hd 8
3969² Weetman's Weigh (IRE) **(65)***(58) (RHollinshead)* 2-7-10 (5) MHenry(4) (swtg: prom: effrt & ev ch over 1f out: wknd ins fnl f)........nk 9
3824⁶ Lady Caroline Lamb (IRE) **(62)***(54) (MRChannon)* 2-7-12 FNorton(11) (chsd ldrs: hdwy u.p 2f out: sn wknd)........½ 10
3969³ Deerly **(66)***(54) (DMorris)* 2-8-2 PaulEddery(17) (nvr wnt pce)........1½ 11
3767² Again Together **(63)***(47) (NACallaghan)* 2-7-13 GBardwell(6) (drvn along thrght: n.d)........1¼ 12
3749¹⁷ Foreman **(59)***(41) (WAO'Gorman)* 2-7-4b(5)ow2 MBaird(9) (lw: s.i.s: n.d)........d.h 12
3894⁵ Asking For Kings (IRE) **(63)***(47) (SDow)* 2-7-13 JFEgan(5) (sn pushed along: n.d)........s.h 14
3940* Repatriate (AUS) **(84)***(68) (PWChapple-Hyam)* 2-9-6 JReid(8) (lw: chsd ldrs 4f)........hd 15
3887⁷ Secret Pleasure (IRE) **(76)***(59) (RHannon)* 2-8-12 PatEddery(15) (sn bhd)........½ 16
3848⁴ Extra Hour (IRE) **(77)***(56) (WRMuir)* 2-8-13 KDarley(7) (s.i.s: plld hrd: n.d)........1¼ 17
*3949** Sweet Nature (IRE) **(70)***(48) (WJarvis)* 2-8-6 WCarson(2) (lw: racd stands' side: spd to ½-wy: sn rdn & btn)........nk 18

LONG HANDICAP Foreman 7-5

4/1 LUNAR MIST, **11/2** Sweet Nature (IRE), **11/1** Little Noggins (IRE), Standown, **12/1** Deerly, Weetman's Weigh (IRE), Repatriate (AUS), **14/1** Lady Caroline Lamb (IRE), Where's Margaret, **16/1** Again Together, Secret Pleasure (IRE), Stop Play (IRE), Foreman, **20/1** Asking For Kings (IRE), White Emir, Prima Volta, Clincher Club, **25/1** Extra Hour (IRE), CSF £66.10 CT £1,098.71 TOTE £4.50: £2.00 £3.50 £4.10 £3.10 (£59.20) Trio £371.90 OWNER Ladyswood Racing Club (MALMESBURY) BRED T. Barratt 18 Rn
1m 12.26 (0.96) SF: 51/44/54/37/43/25/47/40/26/22/22/15/9/15/36/27/24/16

4078 CHALLENGE STKS (Gp 2) (3-Y.O+) (Class A) £35,721.00(£13,239.00: £6,369.50: £2,622.50) **7f (Rowley)** Stalls: Centre GOING minus 0.38 sec (F) 3-40 (3-41)

3834⁴ **Harayir (USA) (118)***(124)*(Fav)*(MajorWRHern)* 3-8-12 WCarson(8) (lw: trckd ldrs: qcknd to ld over 1f out: r.o wl)........— 1
3814³ Soviet Line (IRE) **(121)***(126) (MRStoute)* 5-9-4 WRSwinburn(6) (lw: hld up: hdwy over 2f out: ev ch ins fnl f: hrd rdn & r.o)........½ 2
3904² Red Carnival (USA) **(112)***(115) (MRStoute)* 3-8-8 JReid(5) (h.d.w: swtg: trckd ldrs: effrt & n.m.r 2f out: ch ins fnl f: kpt on)........1½ 3
3195a¹⁰ Mistle Cat (USA) **(111)***(117) (SPCWoods)* 5-9-0 WWoods(4) (led: rdn & qcknd over 2f out: hdd over 1f out: kpt on)........½ 4
3931⁷ Shahid **(113)***(106) (JLDunlop)* 3-8-11 RCochrane(1) (hld up & bhd: hdwy 2f out: nvr able chal)5 5
4024² Autumn Affair **(102)***(102) (CEBrittain)* 3-8-8 DHarrison(2) (b.off hind: bhd tl styd on towards fin)........nk 6
3360⁴ Emperor Jones (USA) **(118)***(105) (SbinSuroor)* 5-9-0 PatEddery(3) (lw: chsd ldrs tl wknd fnl 2f)........nk 7
4012a⁷ Cool Jazz **(102)***(100) (CEBrittain)* 4-9-0 KDarley(7) (lw: trckd ldrs: effrt 2f out: sn btn)........2 8

13/8 HARAYIR (USA), **3/1** Red Carnival (USA), **6/1** Emperor Jones (USA) (4/1-13/2), **7/1** Soviet Line (IRE), **10/1** Cool Jazz, **16/1** Shahid, **25/1** Mistle Cat (USA), **40/1** Autumn Affair, CSF £12.07 TOTE £2.10: £1.10 £2.10 £1.70 (£6.00) OWNER Mr Hamdan Al Maktoum (LAMBOURN) BRED Shadwell Farm Inc in USA 8 Rn
1m 23.79 (-0.61) SF: 72/77/63/68/54/50/56/51
WEIGHT FOR AGE 3yo-3lb

4079 MILCARS LEASING H'CAP (0-85) (3-Y.O+) (Class D) £3,890.00 (£1,190.00: £590.00: £290.00)

1m (Rowley) Stalls: Centre GOING minus 0.38 sec per fur (F) 4-15 (4-18)

4035[3] **Tarawa (IRE) (80)**(96)(Fav)(NACallaghan) 3-9-10 PatEddery(12) (lw: prom: led wl over 1f out: r.o wl)........— **1**
3934[6] Aeroking (USA) **(73)**(86) (GHarwood) 4-9-7 AClark(16) (a chsng ldrs: kpt on u.p fnl 2f: nt pce of wnr)........1½ **2**
3973[W] Mountgate **(70)**(75) (MPBielby) 3-9-0 RCochrane(19) (a.p: effrt 3f out: hrd rdn & one pce appr fnl f)........4 **3**
3929[7] Zelda Zonk **(66)**(69) (BJMeehan) 3-8-10 PaulEddery(22) (b.hind: bhd tl hdwy 2f out: r.o towards fin)........1 **4**
3945[16] Reverand Thickness **(71)**(73) (SCWilliams) 4-9-5b KDarley(20) (swtg: led & sn clr: hdd wl over 1f out: sn wknd)........½ **5**
3755[7] Sotoboy (IRE) **(80)**(81) (PWHarris) 3-9-10 GHind(4) (hdwy over 2f out: nrst fin)........nk **6**
4027[3] Saltando (IRE) **(51)**(52) (PatMitchell) 4-7-13 JFEgan(7) (bhd tl r.o u.p fnl 2f)........s.h **7**
3808[16] Avishayes (USA) **(45)**(45) (MrsMReveley) 8-7-7 GBardwell(21) (dwlt: r.o fnl 2f: nvr nrr)........¾ **8**
3726[2] Flirty Gertie **(67)**(61) (RBoss) 3-8-11 JReid(9) (in tch: rdn 3f out: no imp)........3 **9**
3685[17] Broughton's Port **(45)**(39) (WJMusson) 5-7-7 NAdams(15) (chsd ldrs tl rdn & wknd fnl 2½f) .s.h **10**
3941[5] Benjarong **(50)**(41) (RMMcKellar) 3-7-3 (5)ow1 PFessey(10) (lw: chsd ldrs tl wknd fnl 3f)........¾ **11**
3605[21] Crimson Shower **(57)**(45) (JRFanshawe) 3-7-12 (3) NVarley(6) (nvr trbld ldrs)........2 **12**
4038[5] Guesstimation (USA) **(66)**(53) (JPearce) 6-8-11 (3) SDrowne(8) (b.off hind: in tch: effrt 3f out: wknd 2f out)........¾ **13**
3641[14] Mighty Kingdom (IRE) **(47)**(30) (CADwyer) 4-7-2 (7)ow2 MartinDwyer(5) (rdn over 3f out: n.d) ..¾ **14**
2486[13] Ballestro (IRE) **(50)**(34) (JFfitch-Heyes) 3-7-5 (3)ow1 DWright(18) (drvn along & bhd most of wy)........hd **15**
3762[3] Golden Touch (USA) **(62)**(46) (RChampion) 3-8-3 (3) PMcCabe(17) (chsd ldrs tl wknd 2f out)........¾ **16**
3934[5] Waldo **(64)**(47) (LordHuntingdon) 4-8-12v DHarrison(3) (n.d)........hd **17**
3657[12] Astral Weeks (IRE) **(61)**(30) (RHannon) 4-8-4b(5) DaneO'Neill(1) (lw: sn pushed along: nvr trbld ldrs)........7 **18**
3941* Azdihaar (USA) **(78)**(45) (JLDunlop) 3-9-8 WCarson(11) (prom tl wknd over 2f out)........1 **19**
3984[10] Ducking **(69)** (JRFanshawe) 3-8-13 WRSwinburn(2) (lost tch fr ½-wy: t.o)........30 **20**

LONG HANDICAP Benjarong 7-1 Mighty Kingdom (IRE) 7-5 Broughton's Port 7-2 Ballestro (IRE) 6-7
3/1 TARAWA (IRE) (2/1-100/30), **9/2** Azdihaar (USA), **7/1** Guesstimation (USA), **8/1** Reverand Thickness, **10/1** Flirty Gertie, **12/1** Waldo, **16/1** Saltando (IRE), Mountgate, Ducking, **20/1** Avishayes (USA), Golden Touch (USA), Crimson Shower, **25/1** Aeroking (USA), Zelda Zonk, Sotoboy (IRE), **33/1** Astral Weeks (IRE), Mighty Kingdom (IRE), **50/1** Broughton's Port, Benjarong, **100/1** Ballestro (IRE), CSF £76.13 CT £1,023.97 TOTE £3.60: £1.60 £4.50 £4.90 £5.20 (£78.00) Trio £615.00 OWNER Mrs J. Callaghan (NEWMARKET) BRED Patrick Eddery Ltd 20 Rn
1m 38.17 (1.17) SF: 64/58/43/37/45/49/24/17/29/11/9/13/25/2/2/14/19/2/13/-
WEIGHT FOR AGE 3yo-4lb

4080 E.B.F. CHESTERTON MAIDEN STKS (2-Y.O) (Class D) £7,924.50 (£2,376.00: £1,143.00: £526.50)

1m (Rowley) Stalls: Centre GOING minus 0.38 sec per fur (F) 4-50 (4-54)

Silver Dome (USA) (96+)(Fav)(HRACecil) 2-9-0 PatEddery(15) (wl grwn: bit bkwd: disp ld tl led 3f out: r.o wl fnl f)........— **1**
Sacho (IRE) (93+) (JHMGosden) 2-9-0 WRSwinburn(11) (neat: scope: lw: hdwy over 2f out: r.o wl towards fin)........1½ **2**
3773[5] Three Hills (92) (BWHills) 2-9-0 AClark(2) (w ldrs: effrt 2f out: wknd ins fnl f)........nk **3**
3797a[11] Robamaset (IRE) (87) (LMCumani) 2-9-0 KDarley(14) (unruly in stalls: a chsng ldrs: kpt on one pce fnl 2f)........2½ **4**
3900[9] Hayaain (86) (MajorWRHern) 2-9-0 MPerrett(9) (bit bkwd: in tch tl outpcd 3f out: styd on appr fnl f)........½ **5**
3868[7] Orinoco River (USA) (84) (PWChapple-Hyam) 2-9-0 JReid(13) (lw: disp ld 5f: grad wknd)...1¼ **6**
Village King (IRE) (84) (RHannon) 2-9-0 SWhitworth(12) (w'like: prom: outpcd over 2f out: no imp after)........s.h **7**
3089[9] Prince Kinsky (83) (LordHuntingdon) 2-9-0 DHarrison(4) (bhd tl shkn up & r.o fnl 2f)........nk **8**
Censor (83) (HRACecil) 2-9-0 AMcGlone(7) (w'like: leggy: dwlt: hdwy 3f out: nvr able chal) .nk **9**
Mohannad (IRE) (79) (JWHills) 2-9-0 WNewnes(3) (leggy: scope: lw: nvr trbld ldrs)........2 **10**
Flocheck (USA) (78) (JLDunlop) 2-9-0 RCochrane(8) (gd sort: scope: dwlt: hld up & bhd: stdy hdwy 2f out: nvr nr to chal)........nk **11**
Prospero (70) (IABalding) 2-9-0 DGriffiths(6) (w'like: scope: hld up & bhd: n.d)........4 **12**
Elashath (USA) (64) (JHMGosden) 2-9-0 WCarson(10) (wl grwn: outpcd: bhd fr ½-wy)........3 **13**
Suitor (58) (WJarvis) 2-9-0 MTebbutt(1) (gd sort: bit bkwd: a in rr)........3 **14**

4/6 SILVER DOME (USA), **4/1** Sacho (IRE) (5/2-9/2), **8/1** Orinoco River (USA) (5/1-9/1), **14/1** Elashath (USA) (8/1-16/1), Censor (12/1-25/1), **16/1** Three Hills, **25/1** Suitor, **33/1** Hayaain, Prince Kinsky, Robamaset (IRE), Flocheck (USA), Mohannad (IRE), Village King (IRE), **50/1** Prospero, CSF £4.68 TOTE £1.70: £1.10 £1.30 £3.90 (£3.30) Trio £38.30 OWNER Buckram Oak Holdings (NEWMARKET) BRED Buckram Oak Farm 14 Rn

1m 40.78 (3.78) SF: 28/25/24/19/18/16/16/15/15/11/10/2/-/-

T/Jkpt: £50,309.30 (0.1 Tckts); £63,772.42 to Catterick 13/10/95. T/Plpt: £113.30 (222.75 Tckts). T/Qdpt: £4.90 (26.25 Tckts). AA

3975-REDCAR (L-H)
Thursday October 12th (Firm, Good to firm patches)
WEATHER: overcast WIND: slt across

4081 CUB HUNTERS RATING RELATED MAIDEN LIMITED STKS (0-70) (2-Y.O) (Class E) £3,234.50 (£971.00: £468.00: £216.50)
1m Stalls: Centre GOING minus 0.41 sec per fur (F) 1-45 (1-46)

3870[5] **Quality (IRE) (70)***(77) (WAO'Gorman)* 2-9-0 JCarroll(5) (lw: chsd ldrs: drvn along over 3f out: nt clr run 2f out: styd on to ld wl ins fnl f) — 1
3809[6] Labeed (USA) **(66)***(76) (MajorWRHern)* 2-9-0 RHills(2) (lw: trckd ldrs: rdn & ev ch over 1f out: nt qckn ins fnl f) ½ 2
3711[14] Nikita's Star (IRE) **(64)***(76) (DJGMurraySmith)* 2-9-0b MJKinane(10) (sn chsng ldrs: ev ch over 1f out: hung rt: styd on) s.h 3
3928[3] Welcome Royale (IRE) **(68)***(76)*(Fav)*(MHTompkins)* 2-9-0 PRobinson(9) (w ldrs: led over 1f out tl wl ins fnl f) s.h 4
3928[5] Tapintime (USA) **(70)***(69) (PFICole)* 2-9-0 LDettori(7) (hld up: effrt over 2f out: sn wknd) 3½ 5
3857[3] Ecstatic Madam (IRE) **(70)***(63)*(Fav)*(BWHills)* 2-8-9 MHills(8) (led after 3f tl over 1f out: sn wknd) nk 6
3877[10] Petrefuz (IRE) **(50)***(66) (EWeymes)* 2-9-0 WRyan(4) (led 3f: wknd 2f out) 1¼ 7
3851[7] La Fandango (IRE) **(60)***(59) (MWEasterby)* 2-8-9 LCharnock(12) (sn bhd: kpt on fnl 2f: n.d) ¾ 8
2192[6] Needle Knot (IRE) **(62)***(63) (MJohnston)* 2-9-0 JWeaver(3) (hld up: hdwy over 2f out: edgd lft & sn wknd) ½ 9
3949[3] Wire Act (USA) **(65)***(63) (MartynMeade)* 2-9-0 VSlattery(6) (sn outpcd & drvn along) s.h 10
3916[5] Galway Blade **(70)***(53) (APJarvis)* 2-9-0 JTate(1) (lw: s.i.s: outpcd & drvn along ½-wy) 5 11
3307[4] Recall To Mind **(70)***(49) (MHEasterby)* 2-9-0 MBirch(11) (chsd ldrs: rdn ½-wy: sn lostpl) 2 12

9/2 Welcome Royale (IRE), Ecstatic Madam (IRE), **5/1** Tapintime (USA), **11/2** QUALITY (IRE), Labeed (USA), **9/1** Galway Blade (14/1-8/1), **12/1** Nikita's Star (IRE), Recall To Mind (op 8/1), **14/1** Wire Act (USA), **25/1** Needle Knot (IRE), **33/1** La Fandango (IRE), **50/1** Petrefuz (IRE), CSF £34.89 TOTE £6.80: £2.10 £2.10 £4.60 (£56.00) Trio £66.40 OWNER Mr N. S. Yong (NEWMARKET) BRED Major C.R. Philipson 12 Rn 1m 37.1 (2.10) SF: 41/40/40/40/33/27/30/23/27/27/17/13

4082 LESLIE PETCH MEMORIAL H'CAP (0-95) (3-Y.O+) (Class C) £5,702.50 (£1,720.00: £835.00: £392.50)
1m 6f 19y Stalls: Low GOING minus 0.41 sec per fur (F) 2-20 (2-21)

3957[7] **Top Lady (IRE) (77)***(87) (MRStoute)* 3-9-5 LDettori(1) (lw: led: drvn along over 3f out: all out) — 1
3826* Trazl (IRE) **(82)***(92)*(Fav)*(JLDunlop)* 3-9-10 GCarter(4) (lw: effrt on ins & nt clr run 3f out: swtchd & ev ch ins fnl f: edgd lft nr fin: r.o) s.h 2
3772[4] Prophets Honour **(79)***(82) (PCHaslam)* 3-9-2 (5) JDSmith(3) (unruly s: plld hrd: trckd ldrs: pushed along over 4f out: sn ev ch: bmpd over 1f out: sn wl outpcd) 6 3
4036[6] Faugeron **(60)***(63) (NTinkler)* 6-8-11 MJKinane(2) (chsd ldrs: outpcd 3f out: n.d after) hd 4

13/8 Trazl (IRE), **9/4** TOP LADY (IRE), **3/1** Faugeron, **6/1** Prophets Honour, CSF £5.84 TOTE £2.50 (£1.80) OWNER Lord Weinstock & The Hon Simon Weinstock (NEWMARKET) BRED Ballymacoll Stud Farm Ltd 4 Rn 3m 5.0 (7.00) SF: 32/37/27/17
WEIGHT FOR AGE 3yo-9lb

4083 TEES COMPONENTS H'CAP (0-85) (3-Y.O+) (Class D) £4,412.50 (£1,330.00: £645.00: £302.50)
1m Stalls: Centre GOING minus 0.41 sec per fur (F) 2-55 (2-56)

3993[3] **Mbulwa (51)***(63) (RAFahey)* 9-7-8 ow1 LCharnock(8) (mde all: styd on wl u.p appr fnl f) — 1
3664[12] Admirals Flame (IRE) **(72)***(83) (CFWall)* 4-9-1 GDuffield(6) (b: hld up: swtchd & hdwy over 2f out: r.o wl fnl f: nt rch wnr) 1¼ 2
3659[7] Hakika (USA) **(83)***(93) (DMorley)* 3-9-8 RHills(12) (trckd ldrs: effrt 2f out: nt qckn fnl f) nk 3

4038 14 Thatched (IRE) **(55)**_(62)_ _(REBarr)_ 5-7-12 AMackay(7) (s.i.s: sn in tch: edgd lft: styd on same pce appr fnl f)....1¼ **4**
3979* Empty Quarter **(91)**_(93)_(Fav)_(JHMGosden)_ 3-10-2 6x LDettori(3) (lw: trckd ldrs: effrt over 2f out: kpt on same pce)....2½ **5**
3706 16 Tertium (IRE) **(78)**_(79)_ _(PWChapple-Hyam)_ 3-9-3 BDoyle(4) (bhd: hdwy over 2f out: nvr nr ldrs)....¾ **6**
3799 15 Golden Pound (USA) **(75)**_(69)_ _(EALDunlop)_ 3-9-0 MHills(5) (swtg: s.i.s: effrt over 2f out: sn wknd)....3½ **7**
3964 9 Impulsive Air (IRE) **(61)**_(52)_ _(EWeymes)_ 3-8-0v DaleGibson(9) (s.i.s: bhd tl styd on fnl 2f)....1¼ **8**
3977 7 Spanish Verdict **(70)**_(61)_ _(DenysSmith)_ 8-8-8 (5) CTeague(13) (lw: chsd ldrs tl lost pl 2f out)...hd **9**
3973 12 Elite Racing **(62)**_(38)_ _(NTinkler)_ 3-8-1 ow1 GCarter(2) (in tch tl outpcd fr ½-wy)....7 **10**
3715 26 Flashy's Son **(70)**_(47)_ _(GMMoore)_ 7-8-13 JTate(14) (b: b.hind: chsd ldrs tl wknd over 2f out)s.h **11**
3630 10 Pennycairn **(80)**_(53)_ _(HRACecil)_ 3-9-5 WRyan(15) (s.i.s: sn chsng ldrs: lost pl over 2f out)......2 **12**
3993 6 Percy Braithwaite (IRE) **(83)**_(56)_ _(MJohnston)_ 3-9-8b JWeaver(1) (racd far side: chsd ldrs: edgd lft 3f out: sn wknd)....s.h **13**
3980 20 Bridge of Fire (FR) **(70)**_(36)_ _(DonEnricoIncisa)_ 3-8-9 KimTinkler(11) (sn chsng ldrs: lost pl 3f out)....3½ **14**

LONG HANDICAP Mbulwa 7-1

6/4 Empty Quarter, **8/1** Pennycairn, **10/1** Hakika (USA), Percy Braithwaite (IRE) (7/1-11/1), **11/1** MBULWA, **12/1** Spanish Verdict, **14/1** Thatched (IRE), Tertium (IRE), **16/1** Flashy's Son, Golden Pound (USA), Admirals Flame (IRE), **20/1** Impulsive Air (IRE), **33/1** Elite Racing, **100/1** Bridge of Fire (FR), CSF £158.05 CT £1,654.95 TOTE £16.50: £2.60 £4.80 £2.10 (£164.50) Trio £462.10 OWNER Northumbria Leisure Ltd (MALTON) BRED Hascombe and Valiant Studs 14 Rn

1m 35.0 (equals standard) SF: 43/63/69/42/69/55/45/28/41/14/27/29/32/12

WEIGHT FOR AGE 3yo-4lb

4084 REDCAR TWO-YEAR-OLD TROPHY STKS (2-Y.O) (Class B) £81,824.00 (£30,416.00: £14,708.00: £6,140.00: £2,570.00: £1,142.00)
6f Stalls: Centre GOING minus 0.41 sec per fur (F) 3-25 (3-30)

2442* **Blue Iris** _(96+)_ _(MAJarvis)_ 2-8-2 PRobinson(14) (lw: trckd ldr: led ½-wy: rdn over 1f out: r.o strly ins fnl f)....— **1**
3610* Cayman Kai (IRE) **(100)**_(100)_ _(RHannon)_ 2-8-9 MRoberts(5) (lw: chsd ldrs: ev ch 2f out: nt qckn ins fnl f)....1¼ **2**
3680* Anthelia _(91+)_ _(GWragg)_ 2-8-2 MHills(26) (lw: s.s: hdwy ½-wy: styd on wl u.p fnl f: nt rch ldrs)....½ **3**
3186 5 Baize **(100)**_(86)_ _(RFJohnsonHoughton)_ 2-7-13 TSprake(3) (in tch: effrt over 2f out: kpt on same pce appr fnl f)....1 **4**
3680 2 Prancing **(100)**_(88)_ _(DRLoder)_ 2-8-2 GCarter(18) (a chsng ldrs: effrt over 2f out: unable qckn)....hd **5**
3714 16 Red River Valley **(85)**_(78)_ _(DenysSmith)_ 2-7-12 LCharnock(23) (a chsng ldrs: kpt on same pce fnl 2f)....2½ **6**
2442 13 Kandavu **(100)**_(79)_ _(MMcCormack)_ 2-7-13 NCarlisle(12) (in tch: outpcd ½-wy: styd on fnl 2f)s.h **7**
3610 7 Prince Aslia **(100)**_(86)_ _(MJohnston)_ 2-8-7 TWilliams(24) (chsd ldrs: sn drvn along: no imp fnl 2f)....nk **8**
3925 3 Sovereign's Crown (USA) _(89)_ _(JHMGosden)_ 2-9-0 LDettori(19) (lw: hld up: effrt & n.m.r over 2f out: swtchd & styd on: nt rch ldrs)....1½ **9**
3606 6 La Volta **(90)**_(71)_ _(JGFitzGerald)_ 2-7-10 JQuinn(2) (chsd ldrs: edgd rt & kpt on same pce fnl 2f)....hd **10**
3163 4 Gothenberg (IRE) **(100)**_(86)_ _(MJohnston)_ 2-8-13 JWeaver(8) (in tch to ½-wy)....¾ **11**
3714 6 Atraf **(94)**_(72)_ _(DMorley)_ 2-8-4 RHills(21) (chsd ldrs: n.m.r over 2f out: sn wknd)....1¾ **12**
3606 4 Shaniko (IRE) **(100)**_(75)_ _(PWChapple-Hyam)_ 2-8-7 WRyan(1) (b: chsd ldrs tl lost pl 2f out)..s.h **13**
3877* Meldorf _(80)_(Fav)_(DRLoder)_ 2-8-12 MJKinane(16) (lw: chsd ldrs: drvn along ½-wy: sn wl outpcd: hmpd over 1f out: eased)....s.h **14**
3692a 8 Needham Star (USA) _(74)_ _(PAKelleway)_ 2-8-7 GDuffield(11) (sn outpcd & drvn along: hdwy over 1f out: n.d)....nk **15**
3699 2 Babsy Babe _(72)_ _(JJQuinn)_ 2-8-5 DaleGibson(20) (hld up & bhd: effrt & n.m.r over 2f out: swtchd: n.d)....s.h **16**
3375 7 Flying North (IRE) **(82)**_(67)_ _(MrsMReveley)_ 2-8-4 DeanMcKeown(15) (bhd: effrt over 2f out: hung lft: n.d)....1½ **17**
3848 2 Therhea (IRE) **(78)**_(67)_ _(BRMillman)_ 2-8-4b KFallon(10) (chsd ldrs: sn drvn along: wknd 3f out)....s.h **18**
3753 4 Supreme Power **(77)**_(59)_ _(WRMuir)_ 2-7-12b CRutter(7) (chsd ldrs: rdn over 2f out: sn wknd)....¾ **19**
3387 4 Bewitching (USA) **(95)**_(55)_ _(JARToller)_ 2-8-1 ow2 SSanders(4) (lw: chsd ldrs tl wknd 2f out)...1¾ **20**
3861 4 Arctic Zipper (USA) _(63)_ _(WAO'Gorman)_ 2-8-7b JCarroll(13) (led to ½-wy: wknd over 2f out)....hd **21**
4034 4 What Fun **(99)**_(60)_ _(RHannon)_ 2-8-7 RPerham(6) (prom: drvn along ½-wy: sn lost pl)....1 **22**

3625[7] Galapino **(82)***(53) (CEBrittain)* 2-8-1 BDoyle(17) (s.i.s: a bhd)....½ **23**
3301* Dankeston (USA) **(92)***(53) (MBell)* 2-8-4v MFenton(9) (chsd ldrs: sn drvn along: lost pl ½-wy)....1 **24**
3873[2] School Boy *(55) (CNAllen)* 2-8-7 StephenDavies(22) (prom early: sn drvn along: outpcd fr ½-wy)....½ **25**
3989[5] Veni Vidi Vici (IRE) *(45) (MJHeaton-Ellis)* 2-8-7 JTate(25) (s.i.s: a bhd)....3½ **26**

9/2 Meldorf, **5/1** Cayman Kai (IRE), **6/1** Anthelia, BLUE IRIS, **9/1** Prancing, **10/1** Baize, **11/1** Sovereign's Crown (USA), **16/1** Atraf, Babsy Babe, **25/1** Needham Star (USA), Dankeston (USA), Bewitching (USA), Kandavu, **33/1** Gothenberg (IRE), Shaniko (IRE), **50/1** Prince Aslia, La Volta, What Fun, Red River Valley, **66/1** Therhea (IRE), Flying North (IRE), Supreme Power, **100/1** Galapino, School Boy, Veni Vidi Vici (IRE), **200/1** Arctic Zipper (USA), CSF £35.42 TOTE £7.00: £2.40 £2.60 £2.70 (£14.30) Trio £40.20 OWNER Mr M. A. Jarvis (NEWMARKET) BRED North Cheshire Trading and Storage Ltd 26 Rn 1m 9.7 (0.10 under 2y best)(0.40)
SF: 45/49/40/35/37/27/28/35/38/20/35/21/24/29/23/21/16/16/8/4/12/9/2/2/4/-

4085 E.B.F. MAIDEN STKS (2-Y.O F) (Class D) £4,549.00 (£1,372.00: £666.00: £313.00)

7f Stalls: Centre GOING minus 0.41 sec per fur (F) 3-55 (3-59)

3763[9] **Green Charter** *(79) (HRACecil)* 2-8-11 WRyan(5) (w ldr: led over 1f out: jst hld on)....— **1**
Jamrat Jumairah (IRE) *(79+) (EALDunlop)* 2-8-11 MJKinane(11) (w'like: scope: sn in tch: effrt over 2f out: edgd lft & styd on ins fnl f: jst failed)....s.h **2**
Awaamir *(79+) (JHMGosden)* 2-8-11 RHills(1) (w'like: trckd ldrs: ev ch over 1f out: edgd rt: r.o)....s.h **3**
3763[6] Star And Garter **(82)***(75)*(Fav)*(GWragg)* 2-8-11 MHills(2) (b.nr hind: chsd ldrs: ev ch over 1f out: btn whn squeezed out towards fin)....1¾ **4**
3816[7] Shady Girl (IRE) *(67) (BWHills)* 2-8-11 JWeaver(9) (mde most tl over 1f out: sn wknd)....3½ **5**
3948[11] Fairywings *(63) (MrsJRRamsden)* 2-8-11 KFallon(10) (b.hind: v.unruly s: s.s: bhd: sn drvn along: kpt on fnl 2f: nvr nr ldrs)....1½ **6**
3763[11] Flighty *(63) (LMCumani)* 2-8-11 LDettori(7) (nvr nr ldrs)....nk **7**
3891[5] Classic Affair (USA) *(62) (SCWilliams)* 2-8-11 AMackay(3) (in tch: drvn along ½-wy: sn wl outpcd)....nk **8**
3821[8] Della Casa (IRE) *(61) (JLDunlop)* 2-8-11 GDuffield(6) (s.i.s: bhd tl kpt on appr fnl f)....nk **9**
3881[5] Strategic Ploy *(53) (MrsJRRamsden)* 2-8-11 MDeering(4) (unruly s: s.s: a in rr)....3½ **10**
Domusky *(51) (FJO'Mahony)* 2-8-11 ACulhane(8) (cmpt: bkwd: chsd ldrs 3f: sn bhd)....1 **11**
2380[10] Kudos Blue *(35) (JDBethell)* 2-8-11 JCarroll(12) (trckd ldrs tl lost pl ½-wy: sn wl bhd)....7 **12**

11/4 Star And Garter, **3/1** Awaamir, **4/1** GREEN CHARTER, **6/1** Shady Girl (IRE), **8/1** Jamrat Jumairah (IRE) (6/1-9/1), Fairywings (op 5/1), **10/1** Flighty, **20/1** Classic Affair (USA), Della Casa (IRE), **33/1** Strategic Ploy, **100/1** Kudos Blue, **200/1** Domusky, CSF £36.85 TOTE £4.90: £2.60 £2.60 £1.90 (£16.40) Trio £22.40 OWNER Mr Eduardo Hinojosa (NEWMARKET) BRED W. and R. Barnett Ltd 12 Rn 1m 24.4 (2.40) SF: 31/31/31/27/19/15/15/14/13/5/3/-
STEWARDS' ENQUIRY Fallon susp. 21 & 23-28/10/95 (improper riding).

4086 LEVY BOARD H'CAP (0-70) (3-Y.O+) (Class E) £3,939.75 (£1,188.00: £576.50: £270.75)

1m 5f 135y Stalls: Low GOING minus 0.41 sec per fur (F) 4-25 (4-25)

3634[9] **Green Land (BEL) (62)***(75) (SCWilliams)* 3-9-2 KFallon(13) (b.nr fore: hld up: wnt prom 7f out: drvn along & outpcd over 3f out: styd on strly to ld over 1f out: readily)...— **1**
3862[3] Matamoros **(70)***(81) (JLDunlop)* 3-9-10 MJKinane(1) (in tch: outpcd & lost pl over 3f out: hrd rdn: styd on wl appr fnl f)....2 **2**
3896[6] Western Horizon (USA) **(40)***(49) (CEBrittain)* 3-7-8 ow1 JQuinn(9) (swtg: chsd ldrs: led over 2f out tl over 1f out: one pce)....1 **3**
3635[10] Lindisfarne Lady **(41)***(48) (MrsMReveley)* 3-7-9 LCharnock(8) (hld up & bhd: hdwy over 3f out: sn prom: hung lft & no imp fnl 2f)....2½ **4**
3724[7] Ijab (CAN) **(30)***(35) (JParkes)* 5-7-7 JLowe(11) (chsd ldr: drvn along & outpcd 5f out: kpt on one pce fnl 3f)....1 **5**
3978* Pretoria Dancer **(70)***(75)*(Fav)*(JHMGosden)* 3-9-10b 5x LDettori(12) (led tl over 3f out: wknd over 1f out)....½ **6**
3805[5] Island Cascade **(39)***(43) (DonEnricoIncisa)* 3-7-7 KimTinkler(4) (s.i.s: bhd tl kpt on fnl 2f)....1 **7**
2501[5] Lightning Quest (IRE) **(33)***(31) (JSWainwright)* 4-7-10bow3 AMackay(6) (bhd: drvn along 7f out: sme hdwy 3f out: n.d)....2½ **8**
3759[10] Reaganesque (USA) **(63)***(62) (EALDunlop)* 3-9-3 RHills(2) (trckd ldr: led over 3f out: hdd over 2f out: sn wknd)....1½ **9**
3669[15] Philmist **(41)***(28) (CWCElsey)* 3-7-9 NKennedy(5) (bhd & drvn along 8f out)....10 **10**

Pepitist **(48)***(29) (MDHammond)* 4-8-11 JCarroll(10) (a bhd) 5 **11**

LONG HANDICAP Island Cascade 7-5 Western Horizon (USA) 7-5 Ijab (CAN) 7-1 Lightning Quest (IRE) 7-4

9/4 Pretoria Dancer, **5/2** Matamoros, **9/2** GREEN LAND (BEL), **6/1** Reaganesque (USA), **10/1** Western Horizon (USA), **14/1** Lindisfarne Lady, **16/1** Ijab (CAN), **20/1** Pepitist, **25/1** Philmist, Lightning Quest (IRE), **33/1** Island Cascade, CSF £16.82 CT £104.24 TOTE £5.40: £2.20 £1.70 £1.70 (£15.60) Trio £31.10 OWNER Mrs V. Vilain (NEWMARKET) BRED Patrick Madelein 11 Rn
2m 58.1 (7.10) SF: 27/33/1/-/-/27/-/-/14/-/-
WEIGHT FOR AGE 3yo-9lb

4087 EGTON CONDITIONS STKS (3-Y.O) (Class C) £5,862.80 (£1,884.80: £912.40)
7f Stalls: Centre GOING minus 0.41 sec per fur (F) 5-00 (5-00)

3910a⁹ **Moon King (IRE) (100)***(108) (RHannon)* 3-9-3 JWeaver(2) (lw: trckd ldr: qcknd to ld over 1f out: drvn out) ....— **1**
3931⁶ Epagris **(105)***(104)*(Fav)*(HRACecil)* 3-9-2 MJKinane(3) (led: hdd over 1f out: kpt on wl towards fin) 1¼ **2**
3945¹⁸ Sue's Return **(85)***(87) (APJarvis)* 3-8-8 JTate(1) (trckd ldrs: effrt & ev ch over 2f out: wl outpcd over 1f out) 4 **3**

4/6 Epagris, **6/4** MOON KING (IRE), **11/1** Sue's Return, CSF £2.74 TOTE £2.90 (£1.20) OWNER Mr Mohamed Suhail (MARLBOROUGH) BRED Gainsborough Stud Management Ltd 3 Rn
1m 24.6 (2.60) SF: 35/31/14
T/Plpt: £1,320.90 (9.68 Tckts). T/Qdpt: £30.80 (3.2 Tckts). WG

3200a-HOPPEGARTEN (Berlin, Germany) (R-H)
Tuesday October 3rd (Soft)

4088a PREIS DER DEUTSCHEN EINHEIT (Gp 3) (3-Y.O+) £35,391.00 (£14,815.00: £7,407.00) 1m 2f 3-05 (3-13)

3591a⁸ **Concepcion (GER)** *(116) (HJentzsch,Germany)* 5-9-7 SEccles ....— **1**
3798a² Sylvan Point *(115) (HRemmert,Germany)* 4-9-7 KWoodburn ....½ **2**
3914a⁷ Almaz (SU) *(111) (AMSavujev,Slovakia)* 3-8-13 ATschugujewez 1¼ **3**
3716² Captain Horatius (IRE) *(104) (JLDunlop)* 6-9-7 JReid (btn approx 6l) **8**

Tote 152DM: 39DM 19DM 37DM (SF 799DM) (3rd place dividend relates to fourth horse Hondero, as third horse was originally a reserve and not included for betting purposes) OWNER Gestut Haus Ittlingen BRED Gestut Fahrhof 14 Rn 2m 6.1 SF: -/-/-/-

4012a-LONGCHAMP (Paris, France) (R-H)
Thursday October 5th (Soft)

4089a PRIX DE CONDE (Gp 3) (2-Y.O) £26,347.00 (£9,581.00: £4,790.00) 1m 1f 2-45 (2-48)

Go Between (FR) *(ASpanu,France)* 2-9-2 ESaint-Martin ....— **1**
Battle Dore (USA) *(AFabre,France)* 2-9-2 TJarnet ....¾ **2**
Esquive *(PBary,France)* 2-8-13 GMosse ....nk **3**

P-M 3.10F: 1.20F 1.10F (SF 6.60) OWNER Mr N. Pharaon BRED Sir R. McAlpine 5 Rn
2m 2.5 SF: -/-/-

2560a-SAINT-CLOUD (France) (L-H)
Friday October 6th (Good)

4090a PRIX EUGENE DE SAVOIE (Listed) (3-Y.O+) £16,766.00 (£5,748.00: £3,593.00) 1m 3-40 (3-51)

Alamtara (IRE) *(113) (CLaffon-Parias,France)* 4-9-1 ODoleuze ....— **1**
3038a³ Super Gascon *(114) (TLallie,France)* 3-8-12 DRegnard ....s.h **2**
3904⁴ Pater Noster (USA) *(109) (MrsJCecil)* 6-9-1 PaulEddery 2 **3**

P-M 4.20F: 1.50F 3.50F 1.40F (69.70F) OWNER Maktoum Al Maktoum BRED Mount Coote Stud 9 Rn
1m 38.9 SF: -/-/-

3787a-CURRAGH (Newbridge, Ireland) (R-H)
Saturday October 7th (Yielding)

4091a
C.L. WELD PARK STKS (Gp 3) (2-Y.O F) £14,773.00 (£4,318.00: £2,045.00) **7f** 4-00 (4-01)

3828* **Last Second (IRE)** (Fav)*(SirMarkPrescott)* 2-8-9 GDuffield ....— 1
Super Gift (IRE) (Fav)*(DKWeld,Ireland)* 2-8-9 MJKinane ....hd 2
3692a7 Ceirseach (IRE) *(JSBolger,Ireland)* 2-8-9b JAHeffernan 1 3

4/1 LAST SECOND (IRE), Super Gift (IRE), **7/1** Ceirseach (IRE), Tote £3.70: £2.90 £2.00 (£15.30) OWNER Mr Faisal Salman (NEWMARKET) BRED Miss K. Rausing and Mrs S. M. Rogers 7 Rn
1m 28.2 (5.00) SF: -/-/-

4019a-SAN SIRO (Milan, Italy) (R-H)
Sunday October 8th (Soft)

4092a
PREMIO DUCA D'AOSTA (Listed) (4-Y.O+) £17,730.00 (£7,801.00: £3,617.00) **1m 7f** 2-55 (3-00)

My Irish *(118) (MCiciarelli,Italy)* 5-9-5 AParravani ....— 1
3581a5 Khamaseen *(116) (JLDunlop)* 4-9-5 JReid 1¾ 2
1392a4 Puerto Escondido (USA) *(109) (OPessi,Italy)* 4-9-0b OFancera 2¼ 3

Tote 123L: 30L 14L (77L) OWNER Scuderia Briantea BRED Norton Brookes 6 Rn 3m 16.4

4093a
PREMIO VITTORIO DI CAPUA (Gp 1) (3-Y.O+ C & F) £56,172.00 (£28,502.00: £16,637.00: £8,397.00) **1m** 4-40 (5-00)

3199a7 **Nicolotte** *(121) (GWragg)* 4-8-11 MHills (a.p: 2nd st: led 2f out: r.o wl).......— 1
3199a6 Prince Arthur (IRE) *(120) (PWChapple-Hyam)* 3-8-9 JReid (prom: 3rd st: outpcd 3f out: styd on fnl f).......1¾ 2
Morigi *(117) (ITellini,Italy)* 4-8-11 MTellini (mid div: 7th st: chsd wnr 1f out: no ex fnl f).......s.h 3
1577a* Les Boyer *(112) (GBotti,Italy)* 4-8-11 MBotti (mid div: 6th st: nvr plcd to chal).......2½ 4
4019a3 Senebrova *(108) (VValiani,Italy)* 4-8-8 GBietolini (5th st: no imp fnl 2f).......¾ 5
Bartok (IRE) *(111) (ARenzoni,Italy)* 4-8-11 JacquelineFreda (led to 2f out: wknd).......s.nk 6
1577a5 Lear White (USA) *(106) (FBrogi,Italy)* 4-8-11 JCaro (bhd tl hdwy st: nvr plcd to chal).......2½ 7
1577a3 New Herald (IRE) *(101) (MCiciarelli,Italy)* 6-8-11b AParravani (m.n.s).......2¼ 8
3796a* Robins (IRE) *(100) (AColella,Italy)* 3-8-9 BJovine (cl up: 4th st: sn wknd).......1¾ 9
Ravier (ITY) *(93) (EBorromeo,Italy)* 4-8-11 BJovine (a bhd).......2½ 10
Action Mutante (USA) *(87) (OPessi,Italy)* 3-8-9b OFancera (a bhd).......4 11

Tote 27L: 16L 17L 28L (35L) OWNER Mollers Racing (NEWMARKET) BRED Crescent (UK) Ltd 11 Rn
1m 39.6 SF: -/-/-/-/-/-/-/-/-/-/-

2728a-DUSSELDORF (Germany) (R-H)
Sunday October 8th (Heavy)

4094a
GROSSER PREIS VON DUSSELDORF (Gp 2) (3-Y.O+) £32,922.00 (£13,169.00: £6,584.00: £3,292.00) **1m 2f** 4-40 (4-50)

Tres Heureux (GER) *(115) (FrauEMader,Germany)* 5-9-0 LHammer-Hansen (hld up: gd hdwy 2f out: led wl ins fnl f).......— 1
3487a2 Devil River Peek (USA) *(113) (BSchutz,Germany)* 3-8-7 StephenDavies (a.p: 4th st: led ins fnl f: sn hdd & no ex).......¾ 2
Ostwahl (IRE) *(105) (PeterLautner,Germany)* 5-8-9b ABond (a.p: 3rd st: chal over 1f out: one pce fnl f).......2½ 3
3910a2 Chato (USA) *(110) (HSteinmetz,Germany)* 3-8-9 AStarke (hdwy & 5th st: chal over 1f out: no ex fnl f).......½ 4
3798a7 Mr Woodman (GER) *(106) (Germany)* 3-8-7b ASuborics (hdwy 2f out: nt pce to chal).......1½ 5
3045a3 Fiello (GER) *(105) (Germany)* 5-9-0 TMundry (prom tl wknd wl over 1f out).......1¼ 6
1705a3 Anna Domani(FR) *(98) (Germany)* 3-8-3 SEccles (hld up: sme hdwy st).......¾ 7
3910a4 Orfijar (FR) *(102) (Germany)* 5-9-0 ATylicki (w ldr tl led 2f out: hdd & wknd 1f out).......1 8
Nautiker (GER) *(99) (Germany)* 4-9-0 AHelfenbein (m.n.s).......1¾ 9

Tote 236DM: 54DM 28DM 50DM (SF 1981) OWNER Stall Mucos BRED Frau E. Hofer-Janker 13 Rn
1m 49.45 SF: -/-/-/-/-/-/-/-/-

2894a-MUNICH (Germany) (L-H)
Sunday October 8th (Good to soft)

4095a GROSSER BUCHMACHER SPRINGER SPRINT-PREIS (Listed) (3-Y.O+)
£12,346.00 (£4,938.00: £2,469.00) **6f 110y** 3-45 (3-59)

2895a* **Macanal (USA)** *(115) (HJentzsch,Germany)* 3-8-11 PSchiergen ....— 1
3834[12] Sharp Prod (USA) *(111) (LordHuntingdon)* 5-8-12 DHarrison 1¼ 2
Liftoff (FR) *(111) (RStadelmann,Germany)* 4-9-1b FSanchez 1¼ 3

Tote 20DM: 10DM 11DM 12DM (SF 109DM) OWNER Gestut Fahrhof BRED Bruce Hundley in USA
8 Rn 1m 18.3 SF: -/-/-

3720-CATTERICK (L-H)
Friday October 13th (Good to firm, Firm patches)
WEATHER: overcast WIND: almost nil

4096 CRAVEN MAIDEN APPRENTICE STKS (3-Y.O) (Class G) £2,322.50
(£660.00: £327.50)
1m 3f 214y Stalls: Low GOING minus 0.35 sec per fur (F) 2-15 (2-16)

3876[5] **Anjou** **(56)***(75) (JPearce)* 3-8-5 (7) MNutter(5) (lw: trckd ldrs: led over 4f out: styd on wl fnl f) ....— 1
3847[2] Kalamata *(72)*(Fav)*(ACStewart)* 3-8-12 GFaulkner(4) (plld hrd: trckd ldrs: effrt over 2f out: styd on ins fnl f) 2½ 2
3799[9] House of Dreams **(68)***(72) (BWHills)* 3-8-5 (7) GBrace(3) (plld hrd: racd wd: led tl over 4f out: disp ld 3f out: nt qckn appr fnl f) ....s.h 3
3862[8] Mighty Squaw **(58)***(60) (MissGayKelleway)* 3-8-3 (4) KSked(1) (chsd ldrs: pushed along 5f out: outpcd fnl 3f) 5 4
2953[4] Soupreme *(MrsMReveley)* 3-8-7 DDenby(2) (bit bkwd: hld up: drvn & lost tch over 5f out: t.o) ....dist 5

11/8 Kalamata (10/11-6/4), **11/4** House of Dreams, **4/1** Mighty Squaw, **7/1** Soupreme (tchd 12/1), **8/1** ANJOU, CSF £18.82 TOTE £13.30: £2.10 £1.50 (£7.50) OWNER Mr G. H. Tufts (NEWMARKET) BRED Sheikh Mohammed bin Rashid al Maktoum 5 Rn 2m 35.8 (4.80) SF: 37/34/34/22/-

4097 ILKLEY NURSERY H'CAP (0-85) (2-Y.O) (Class D) £4,272.50 (£1,280.00: £615.00: £282.50) **5f** Stalls: Low GOING minus 0.35 sec per fur (F) 2-45 (2-45)

3901[2] **Swynford Dream** **(77)***(84+)*(Fav)*(JFBottomley)* 2-9-6 JLowe(5) (lw: mde all: clr over 1f out: eased towards fin) ....— 1
3803[9] Camionneur (IRE) **(54)***(56) (MHEasterby)* 2-7-11b JQuinn(11) (in tch: styd on appr fnl f: no ch w wnr) 1½ 2
3949[9] Mullagh Hill Lad (IRE) **(54)***(51) (BAMcMahon)* 2-7-8 (3)ow4 DarrenMoffatt(3) (dwlt s: hdwy ½-wy: kpt on same pce appr fnl f) ....nk 3
3714[14] Imp Express (IRE) **(75)***(75) (GMMoore)* 2-9-4 JWeaver(17) (hdwy on outside ½-wy: kpt on same pce appr fnl f) ....½ 4
3856* Miletrian Refurb (IRE) **(58)***(54) (MRChannon)* 2-8-1 JFEgan(18) (dwlt s: styd on appr fnl f: n.m.r & eased nr fin) 1 5
3623[21] Gagajulu **(78)***(74) (PDEvans)* 2-9-7 GHind(13) (a chsng ldrs: nt qckn fnl 2f) ....nk 6
3149[3] Time To Fly **(59)***(52) (BWMurray)* 2-8-2 TWilliams(10) (chsd ldrs: sn drvn along: one pce fnl 2f) ....¾ 7
3953[2] Frances Mary **(50)***(43) (CWFairhurst)* 2-7-2 (5) PFessey(2) (in tch: effrt ½-wy: nvr nr to chal)..hd 8
3824[11] Goretski (IRE) **(56)***(43) (NTinkler)* 2-7-13 KimTinkler(15) (mid div: drvn along ½-wy: n.d) 1¾ 9
3434[7] Limerick Princess (IRE) **(66)***(50) (JBerry)* 2-8-9 JCarroll(1) (chsd ldrs tl wknd 1f out: eased)....1 10
3877[7] Answers-To-Thomas **(66)***(48) (JMJefferson)* 2-8-9 DeanMcKeown(8) (hld up: effrt ½-wy: sn wknd) ....½ 11
3882[9] Principal Boy (IRE) **(52)***(34) (TJEtherington)* 2-7-9 LCharnock(16) (rr div whn bdly hmpd 1f out) ....hd 12
3824[8] Hickleton Miss **(61)***(40) (MrsMReveley)* 2-8-4 KDarley(4) (s.i.s: a in rr) 1 13
3937[19] Jenny's Charmer **(54)***(29) (SEKettlewell)* 2-7-6 (5) MHenry(6) (in tch: wkng whn sltly hmpd 1f out) 1¼ 14
3623[22] Doug's Folly **(65)***(39) (MWEasterby)* 2-8-8 MBirch(9) (sn wl bhd) ....nk 15
3824[9] Mystique Smile **(58)***(31) (JBerry)* 2-8-1 ow1 GCarter(14) (swtg: a bhd) ....s.h 16
3806[5] Mill End Lady **(61)***(28) (MWEasterby)* 2-7-13 (5)ow3 LNewton(7) (s.i.s: a wl bhd) 1¼ 17
2185[2] Snitch **(56)***(20) (CSmith)* 2-7-13b NCarlisle(12) (b: prom: wknd & wandered over 1f out) 1¾ 18
LONG HANDICAP Frances Mary 7-6 Mullagh Hill Lad (IRE) 7-2

6/4 SWYNFORD DREAM, **8/1** Miletrian Refurb (IRE), **10/1** Mullagh Hill Lad (IRE), Hickleton Miss, **11/1** Gagajulu, **12/1** Camionneur (IRE), Limerick Princess (IRE), **14/1** Frances Mary, Mystique Smile, Imp Express (IRE), **25/1** Goretski (IRE), Answers-To-Thomas, Mill End Lady, Doug's Folly, Snitch, **33/1** Jenny's Charmer, Time To Fly, Principal Boy (IRE), CSF £22.97 CT £146.53 TOTE £2.20: £1.10 £3.90 £1.90 £3.00 (£48.30) Trio £115.20 OWNER Qualitair Holdings Ltd (MALTON) BRED Qualitair Stud Ltd 18 Rn 59.3 secs (1.80) SF: 42/14/9/33/12/32/10/1/1/8/6/-/-/-/-/-/-/-

4098 E.B.F. RIPLEY MAIDEN STKS (2-Y.O) (Class D) £4,402.50 (£1,320.00: £635.00: £292.50)

5f 212y Stalls: High GOING minus 0.35 sec per fur (F) 3-15 (3-16)

3865[9] **Singing Patriarch (IRE) (100)***(82)*(Fav)*(JLDunlop)* 2-9-0 KDarley(9) (lw: trckd ldrs: chal 1f out: rdn to ld nr fin) — 1
3671[2] Craignairn **(70)***(82) (JBerry)* 2-9-0 GCarter(2) (led: hung lft u.p fnl f: hdd nr fin) hd 2
3838[3] Power Game **(64)***(72) (JBerry)* 2-9-0 JCarroll(7) (a chsng ldrs: kpt on same pce appr fnl f) 3½ 3
Classic Beauty (IRE) *(65) (SCWilliams)* 2-8-9 AMackay(6) (w'like: cmpt: dwlt s: sn trckng ldrs: effrt over 2f out: hung lft: nvr able to chal) 1 4
3989[9] Circus Star *(62+) (SirMarkPrescott)* 2-9-0 GDuffield(4) (bit bkwd: hld up: stdy hdwy 2f out: r.o ins fnl f: nvr nr ldrs) 3 5
3967[10] Alpine Joker *(55) (MrsJRRamsden)* 2-9-0 JFEgan(3) (bhd: sme hdwy 2f out: n.d) 2½ 6
3784[8] Escobar (IRE) *(54) (PCalver)* 2-9-0 MBirch(12) (in tch tl outpcd fnl 2f) ½ 7
Lapu-Lapu *(46+) (MJCamacho)* 2-8-9 LCharnock(13) (cmpt: bit bkwd: s.i.s: stdy hdwy 2f out: nt clr run 1f out: nvr plcd to chal) 1 8
3976[5] Frog *(45) (SirMarkPrescott)* 2-8-9 JLowe(5) (a bhd) ½ 9
Arabian Heights *(48) (MrsJRRamsden)* 2-9-0 MDeering(11) (unf: s.i.s: a bhd: rn wd ent st) ½ 10
3806[14] Princess Briana *(DMoffatt)* 2-8-6 (3) DarrenMoffatt(1) (chsd ldrs tl wknd over 2f out: eased & sn wl bhd) 25 11
Hawksley Hill (IRE) *(MrsJRRamsden)* 2-9-0 NConnorton(8) (Withdrawn not under Starter's orders: lame at s) W

8/13 SINGING PATRIARCH (IRE), **5/1** Circus Star, **10/1** Craignairn, **12/1** Classic Beauty (IRE), **14/1** Power Game, Alpine Joker, Frog, **16/1** Hawksley Hill (IRE), **20/1** Escobar (IRE), **50/1** Arabian Heights, **100/1** Lapu-Lapu, **300/1** Princess Briana, CSF £8.38 TOTE £1.50: £1.10 £2.50 £2.30 (£5.20) Trio £7.00 OWNER Mr Peter Winfield (ARUNDEL) BRED Gestut Romerhof 11 Rn 1m 12.2 (1.70) SF: 44/44/34/27/24/17/16/8/7/10/-/-

4099 BRETTANBY H'CAP (0-80) (3-Y.O) (Class D) £3,915.00 (£1,170.00: £560.00: £255.00)

1m 7f 177y Stalls: Low GOING minus 0.35 sec per fur (F) 3-50 (3-51)

4062[3] **Sea Victor (67)***(81) (JLHarris)* 3-8-13 KDarley(1) (lw: sn trckng ldr: led over 4f out: r.o wl u.p fnl 2f: eased nr fin) — 1
3818[8] True Bird (IRE) **(57)***(69) (JDBethell)* 3-8-3 JCarroll(2) (chsd ldrs: pushed along over 4f out: hdwy & ev ch over 2f out: nt qckn) 1¾ 2
3774[3] Finlaggan **(75)***(87)*(Fav)*(SirMarkPrescott)* 3-9-7 GDuffield(5) (hld up: effrt over 4f out: sn ev ch: rdn over 2f out: kpt on same pce) nk 3
3896[9] Yougo **(75)***(75) (MJohnston)* 3-9-7 JWeaver(6) (led tl over 4f out: sn lost pl) 12 4
3843[3] Khan **(47)***(38) (CWThornton)* 3-7-7 JLowe(3) (trckd ldrs: pushed along 6f out: lost pl over 3f out) 9 5
3761[12] Sungai Mas (USA) **(48)** *(SPCWoods)* 3-7-8 ow1 NAdams(4) (reminders 8f out: sn lost pl: t.o 3f out) dist 6

LONG HANDICAP Sungai Mas (USA) 7-6

11/8 Finlaggan, **7/2** SEA VICTOR, **9/2** Khan (op 8/1), **9/1** Yougo (op 7/2), **10/1** True Bird (IRE) (op 6/1), **20/1** Sungai Mas (USA), CSF £28.63 TOTE £3.70: £2.50 £2.70 (£22.00) OWNER Mr David Abell (MELTON MOWBRAY) BRED Juddmonte Farms 6 Rn 3m 24.5 (3.50) SF: 52/40/58/46/9/-

4100 E.B.F. ZETLAND MEDIAN AUCTION MAIDEN STKS (2-Y.O F) (Class E) £3,405.00 (£1,020.00: £490.00: £225.00)

7f Stalls: Low GOING minus 0.35 sec per fur (F) 4-25 (4-27)

3983[2] **Hilaala (USA) (71)***(76)*(Fav)*(PTWalwyn)* 2-8-11 KDarley(13) (trckd ldrs: led 2f out: hung lft u.p: kpt on) — 1
3948[5] Indian Relative *(75) (RGuest)* 2-8-6 (5) MHenry(7) (led 2f: led over 2f out: sn hdd: nt qckn towards fin) ½ 2
Ground Game *(61+) (DRLoder)* 2-8-11 GCarter(1) (lengthy: scope: s.i.s: sn chsng ldrs: sltly hmpd & swtchd lft 2f out: rn green: kpt on) 6 3
3733[16] Bright Diamond *(55) (JRArnold)* 2-8-11 JQuinn(8) (in tch: effrt over 2f out: kpt on one pce) 2½ 4

*3949*6 The Barnsley Belle (IRE) **(55)***(46) (SGNorton)* 2-8-11 TWilliams(11) (chsd ldrs: drvn along ½-wy: sn outpcd) 4 5
3828 6 Any Colour *(46) (MJCamacho)* 2-8-11 LCharnock(5) (bit bkwd: s.i.s: hdwy on ins over 2f out: nt clr run: swtchd & wandered: n.d) ....s.h 6
3870 8 Double Check (IRE) *(41) (MJohnston)* 2-8-11 JWeaver(9) (bit bkwd: sme hdwy 2f out: n.d).2½ 7
3432 7 Ma Bulsie *(39) (BAMcMahon)* 2-8-6 (5) LNewton(6) (s.i.s: a in rr) ....½ 8
3806 10 Efipetite **(47)***(39) (NBycroft)* 2-8-11 SMaloney(4) (chsd ldrs tl lost pl over 2f out) ....nk 9
Polish Lady (IRE) *(38) (WLBarker)* 2-8-11 JLowe(10) (leggy: unf: bit bkwd: s.s: a bhd) ....nk 10
2063 6 Champagne Warrior (IRE) *(37) (MJCamacho)* 2-8-11 MBirch(12) (bit bkwd: a bhd) ....½ 11
2951 8 Spring Silhouette **(45)***(9) (MrsVAAconley)* 2-8-11v MDeering(2) (plld hrd: led after 2f tl over 2f out: wandered & sn wknd) 12 12
*3806*8 Bear To Dance **(51)** *(JohnBerry)* 2-8-11 GHind(3) (Withdrawn not under Starter's orders: uns rdr at s: jockey inj) .... W

2/1 HILAALA (USA), **5/2** Indian Relative, **3/1** Ground Game (op 2/1), **8/1** Bright Diamond (op 14/1), **10/1** Ma Bulsie, **20/1** Double Check (IRE), The Barnsley Belle (IRE), **25/1** Any Colour, **50/1** Bear To Dance, Champagne Warrior (IRE), **150/1** Efipetite, **200/1** Spring Silhouette, Polish Lady (IRE), CSF £7.48 TOTE £2.90: £1.30 £1.70 £1.30 (£3.40) Trio £2.20 OWNER Mr Hamdan Al Maktoum (LAMBOURN) BRED Shadwell Estate Company 12 Rn
1m 24.7 (1.50) SF: 48/47/33/27/18/18/13/11/11/10/9/-/-

4101

HORNBY CASTLE H'CAP (0-75) (3-Y.O+) (Class D) £4,597.50 (£1,380.00: £665.00: £307.50) **1m 3f 214y** Stalls: Low GOING minus 0.35 sec (F) 4-55 (5-00)

3898* **Keep Your Distance (70)***(79)*(Fav)*(MrsMReveley)* 5-9-10 KDarley(11) (lw: hld up & bhd: hmpd & rn wd bnd 8f out: hdwy 5f out: effrt 2f out: r.o wl to ld jst ins fnl f: eased nr fin) ....— 1
3934 4 Pat's Splendour **(44)***(52) (HJCollingridge)* 4-7-12 JQuinn(12) (in tch: effrt & hmpd over 2f out: swtchd & styd on appr fnl f: no ch w wnr) 1 2
4000 5 Hasta la Vista **(50)***(55) (MWEasterby)* 5-7-13b(5)ow2 LNewton(6) (lw: led tl jst ins fnl f: one pce) ....nk 3
*3951*3 Tremendisto **(52)***(59) (CaptJWilson)* 5-8-6 JFEgan(8) (plld hrd: trckd ldrs: effrt over 2f out: kpt on same pce) ....s.h 4
3808 20 Suselja (IRE) **(42)***(43) (JMJefferson)* 4-7-5 (5) PFessey(9) (hdwy 5f out: outpcd over 3f out: kpt on appr fnl f) 5 5
3852 13 Chantry Beath **(52)***(52) (CWThornton)* 4-8-6 DeanMcKeown(2) (chsd ldrs: effrt over 2f out: wknd appr fnl f) ....½ 6
3665 5 Imperial Bid (FR) **(55)***(54) (DenysSmith)* 7-8-9v TWilliams(5) (lw: chsd ldrs: sn drvn along: wknd over 1f out: eased) 1 7
905 6 Supertop **(55)***(52) (LLungo)* 7-8-9 MBirch(3) (b: hld up & bhd: stdy hdwy over 2f out: nvr plcd to chal) 1½ 8
*3526*9 Dally Boy **(50)***(43) (MHEasterby)* 3-7-10 LCharnock(13) (swtg: w ldr tl wknd over 2f out) 3 9
1359 8 Escape Talk **(42)***(31) (JDooler)* 8-7-3 (7)ow3 JBramhill(7) (bhd & drvn along 5f out) ....nk 10
*422*5 Comtec's Legend **(39)***(23) (JFBottomley)* 5-7-7 JLowe(4) (in tch: effrt on ins & bmpd 3f out: sn lost pl) 6 11
3936 15 Belgran (USA) **(40)***(16) (PDEvans)* 6-7-8bow1 NAdams(10) (chsd ldrs tl wknd 3f out) 5 12
3305 9 Embezzler **(49)** *(SGollings)* 3-7-6 (3)ow2 NVarley(1) (uns rdr gng to s: rn wd bnd 8f out: racd v.wd after: t.o 3f out) ....dist 13
LONG HANDICAP Escape Talk 5-12 Comtec's Legend 7-2 Belgran (USA) 6-4 Embezzler 7-0

2/1 KEEP YOUR DISTANCE, **4/1** Hasta la Vista, **6/1** Chantry Beath, **7/1** Tremendisto, **8/1** Imperial Bid (FR), **9/1** Pat's Splendour, **20/1** Supertop, **25/1** Dally Boy, **33/1** Comtec's Legend, Embezzler, **66/1** Suselja (IRE), Belgran (USA), **100/1** Escape Talk, CSF £19.28 CT £62.13 TOTE £2.60: £1.30 £1.80 £1.90 (£13.40) Trio £16.80 OWNER Mr P. D. Savill (SALTBURN) BRED Cedric Ford 13 Rn
2m 34.1 (0.70 under best) (3.10) SF: 59/32/35/39/23/32/34/32/15/11/3/-/-
WEIGHT FOR AGE 3yo-8lb
T/Jkpt: £5,638.10 (14.14 Tckts). T/Plpt: £18.80 (923.22 Tckts). T/Qdpt: £17.30 (8.6 Tckts). WG

4074-NEWMARKET (R-H)
Friday October 13th (Good to firm)

WEATHER: warm & sunny WIND: slt against

4102

NEWMARKET CHALLENGE CUP MAIDEN STKS (2-Y.O) (Class G) **7f (Rowley)** Stalls: Centre GOING minus 0.33 sec per fur (GF) 1-30 (1-30)

Shemozzle (IRE) *(67+)*(Fav)*(JHMGosden)* 2-8-9 LDettori(3) (leggy: unf: chsd ldr: slt ld over 3f out: drvn out) ....— 1

3437[4] Martha Quest **(77)***(60) (BWHills)* 2-8-9 PatEddery(1) (led to ½-wy: shkn up appr fnl f: r.o one pce) 3 **2**
3948[15] Miss Pravda *(58) (PTWalwyn)* 2-8-9 RCochrane(2) (hld up in rr: effrt over 2f out: no imp) 1 **3**

4/11 SHEMOZZLE (IRE), **9/4** Martha Quest (Evens-5/2), **12/1** Miss Pravda (8/1-14/1), CSF £1.61 TOTE £1.30 (£1.10) OWNER Lord Hartington (NEWMARKET) BRED Side Hill Stud 3 Rn
1m 29.24 (5.54) SF: 2/-/-

4103 E.B.F. TRAVIS PERKINS MAIDEN STKS (2-Y.O) (Class D)

£6,618.50 (£1,988.00: £959.00: £444.50)
6f (Rowley) Stalls: Centre GOING minus 0.33 sec per fur (GF) 2-00 (2-01)

Projection (USA) *(91+) (BWHills)* 2-9-0 PatEddery(16) (w'like: scope: in tch: drvn along ½-wy: hdwy to ld ins fnl f: all out) ....— **1**
Mutadarra (IRE) *(91+)*(Fav)*(RWArmstrong)* 2-9-0 WCarson(17) (gd sort: lw: a.p: led over 1f out: hdd ins fnl f: r.o) ....s.h **2**
1597[4] Inverlochy *(80) (JLDunlop)* 2-9-0b WNewnes(14) (a chsng ldrs stands' side: kpt on u.p fnl f) ...4 **3**
3606[2] Sabot *(80) (BWHills)* 2-9-0 KFallon(3) (chsd ldrs stands' side: rdn over 1f out: r.o one pce) .s.h **4**
Polish Widow *(75) (GWragg)* 2-8-9 FNorton(19) (w'like: effrt & rdn 2f out: styd on ins fnl f) ...hd **5**
Flying Flowers *(74) (RHannon)* 2-8-9 RPerham(2) (w'like: leggy: hdwy over 1f out: kpt on wl ins fnl f) ....nk **6**
3877[2] Hoh Returns (IRE) **(88)***(79) (MBell)* 2-9-0 MFenton(6) (a.p stands' side: led over 2f out tl over 1f out: hrd rdn fnl f: one pce) ....s.h **7**
Antarctic Storm *(76) (EALDunlop)* 2-9-0 PaulEddery(12) (cmpt: lw: bhd: hdwy fnl 2f: nvr nrr)..1 **8**
1964[7] Tasliya (USA) *(70) (JLDunlop)* 2-8-9 TQuinn(13) (sme hdwy appr fnl f: nvr nrr) ....nk **9**
Nunsharpa *(70) (JRFanshawe)* 2-8-9 DHarrison(15) (leggy: scope: mid div: rdn 2f out: no imp) ....nk **10**
3821[7] Alpine Hideaway (IRE) *(75) (BHanbury)* 2-8-11 (3) JStack(1) (lw: hdwy 2f out: rdn & kpt on fnl f) ....d.h **10**
Blessed Spirit *(70) (CFWall)* 2-8-9 WWoods(4) (lt-f: scope: nvr nr to chal) ....s.h **12**
3893[9] Goldsearch (IRE) *(64) (WAO'Gorman)* 2-8-9 JWilliams(7) (led tl hdd over 2f out: sn lost tch)..2 **13**
3989[15] Blue Suede Hoofs *(68) (BJMeehan)* 2-9-0 BDoyle(21) (effrt 3f out: n.d) ....nk **14**
3933[3] Muhandis *(68) (JHMGosden)* 2-9-0 RHills(9) (b.hind: lw: chsd ldrs 4f) ....hd **15**
Doctor Green (FR) *(68) (LordHuntingdon)* 2-9-0 LDettori(18) (w'like: nvr trbld ldrs) ....hd **16**
Stately Dancer *(62) (GWragg)* 2-8-9 MHills(20) (w'like: leggy: nvr bttr than mid div) ....nk **17**
3828[5] Dungeon Princess (IRE) *(59) (MRChannon)* 2-8-9 MRoberts(10) (prom to ½-wy) 1 **18**
2320[15] Red Raja *(62) (PMitchell)* 2-9-0 PRobinson(5) (s.s: a bhd) 1 **19**
Mr Teddy *(58) (WJarvis)* 2-9-0 SSanders(11) (neat: a in rr) 1½ **20**
Enamel Tiger *(50) (JEBanks)* 2-9-0 AClark(8) (leggy: scope: b: b.hind: dwlt: a bhd) 3 **21**

5/2 Mutadarra (IRE), **4/1** PROJECTION (USA), Sabot (9/4-9/2), **12/1** Muhandis (op 6/1), Hoh Returns (IRE) (8/1-14/1), **14/1** Stately Dancer (op 7/1), **20/1** Nunsharpa, Doctor Green (FR), **33/1** Dungeon Princess (IRE), Inverlochy, Polish Widow, Flying Flowers, Enamel Tiger, **50/1** Mr Teddy, Tasliya (USA), **66/1** Antarctic Storm, Blue Suede Hoofs, Goldsearch (IRE), Red Raja, Blessed Spirit, Alpine Hideaway (IRE), CSF £13.40 TOTE £7.00: £2.50 £1.70 £5.90 (£6.40) Trio £159.20 OWNER Mr K. Abdullah (LAMBOURN) BRED Juddmonte Farms 21 Rn
1m 13.31 (2.01) SF: 42/42/31/31/26/25/30/27/21/21/26/21/15/19/19/19/13/10/13/9/1

4104 BARING INTERNATIONAL DARLEY STKS (Listed) (3-Y.O+) (Class A)

£11,826.00 (£4,374.00: £2,097.00: £855.00: £337.50: £130.50)
1m 1f (Rowley) Stalls: Centre GOING minus 0.33 sec per fur (GF) 2-35 (2-36)

3164[3] **Restructure (IRE) (99)***(116)*(Fav)*(MrsJCecil)* 3-8-9 PaulEddery(3) (lw: hld up: hdwy 3f out: led over 1f out: hrd rdn & hld on gamely cl home) ....— **1**
3904[6] Lap of Luxury **(108)***(111) (WJarvis)* 6-8-9 TQuinn(2) (hld up: hdwy over 2f out: chal ins fnl f: r.o) ....s.h **2**
3728* Wijara (IRE) **(104)***(112) (RHannon)* 3-8-9 RPerham(1) (a.p: led over 2f out tl over 1f out: rdn & one pce fnl f) 2½ **3**
3932[3] Ninette (USA) *(106) (JHMGosden)* 3-8-4 LDettori(4) (swtg: hld up & bhd: hdwy 3f out: rdn bel dist: nvr able to chal) ....nk **4**
3381[7] Munwar **(114)***(106) (PTWalwyn)* 3-9-2v WCarson(6) (plld hrd: led tl hdd over 2f out: grad wknd) 7 **5**
3932[4] Al Widyan (IRE) **(100)***(93) (HRACecil)* 3-8-9 PatEddery(7) (lw: prom over 6f: sn rdn & wknd) ..3 **6**
4035[7] Toujours Riviera **(86)***(81) (JPearce)* 5-9-0 GBardwell(5) (prom tl rdn & wknd wl over 1f out: t.o) 7 **7**
2215a[11] Kulshee Mashee (USA) *(67) (BSchutz,Germany)* 3-8-9 WRSwinburn(8) (w'like: prom tl rdn along ½-wy: wknd over 3f out: t.o) 8 **8**

11/4 RESTRUCTURE (IRE), **4/1** Lap of Luxury, **9/2** Wijara (IRE), **13/2** Munwar, **7/1** Al Widyan (IRE), **9/1** Ninette (USA) (6/1-10/1), **20/1** Kulshee Mashee (USA), **40/1** Toujours Riviera, CSF £12.40 TOTE £3.90: £1.50 £1.60 £1.70 (£7.20) OWNER Mr Martin Myers (NEWMARKET) BRED J. H. Stone 8 Rn 1m 50.23 (0.53) SF: 61/61/57/51/51/38/31/12

WEIGHT FOR AGE 3yo-5lb

STEWARDS' ENQUIRY Quinn susp. Oct 23-24/10/95 (excessive use of the whip).

4105 GREENE KING ROCKFEL STKS (Gp 3) (2-Y.O F) (Class A)

£19,362.00 (£7,158.00: £3,429.00: £1,395.00: £547.50: £208.50)
7f (Rowley) Stalls: Low GOING minus 0.33 sec per fur (GF) 3-05 (3-06)

3561[8] **Bint Salsabil (USA) (100)***(99) (JLDunlop)* 2-8-12 WCarson(7) (swtg: mde all: qcknd whn chal ent fnl f: r.o wl) — 1
3819[2] Parrot Jungle (IRE) **(95)***(94) (JLDunlop)* 2-8-9 JReid(1) (lw: hld up & bhd: hdwy wl over 1f out: swvd bdly rt ins fnl f: r.o) ¾ 2
3866[2] My Branch **(100)***(93)*(Fav)*(BWHills)* 2-8-12 MHills(2) (hld up: hdwy bel dist: rdn & unable qckn fnl f) 2 3
3942[5] Home Shopping **(100)***(87) (KMcAuliffe)* 2-8-12 JTate(6) (swtg: chsd ldrs: rdn bel dist: sn outpcd) 2½ 4
3865[4] Papaha (FR) *(83) (HRACecil)* 2-8-9 PatEddery(5) (prom tl outpcd & wknd over 1f out) nk 5
3691a* Thrilling Day **(100)***(86) (NAGraham)* 2-8-12 WRSwinburn(8) (lw: chsd ldrs: rdn over 1f out: sn outpcd) nk 6
3886[8] Willow Dale (IRE) **(87)***(75) (DRCElsworth)* 2-8-9 TQuinn(4) (hld up: effrt over 2f out: sn rdn: no imp) 3½ 7
3832[4] Wavey *(52) (JHMGosden)* 2-8-9 LDettori(3) (chsd ldrs over 4f: sn wknd: t.o) 10 8

5/4 My Branch (tchd Evens), **9/4** Papaha (FR), **15/2** BINT SALSABIL (USA) (6/1-9/1), **12/1** Thrilling Day, **14/1** Parrot Jungle (IRE), **20/1** Wavey, **25/1** Home Shopping, **50/1** Willow Dale (IRE), CSF £83.89 TOTE £5.40: £1.30 £2.40 £1.20 (£42.70) OWNER Mr Hamdan Al Maktoum (ARUNDEL) BRED Shadwell Estate Company Limited 8 Rn 1m 26.05 (2.35) SF: 41/36/35/29/25/28/17/-

4106 GENEROUS DEWHURST STKS (Gp 1) (2-Y.O C & F) (Class A)

£82,390.00 (£28,590.00: £13,795.00: £5,725.00)
7f (Rowley) Stalls: Low GOING minus 0.33 sec per fur (GF) 3-40 (3-40)

3596* **Alhaarth (IRE) (100)***(121+)*(Fav)*(MajorWRHern)* 2-9-0 WCarson(1) (h.d.w: chsd ldr: led wl over 2f out: r.o strly: impressive) — 1
3788a* Danehill Dancer (IRE) *(115) (NACallaghan)* 2-9-0 PatEddery(3) (lw: hld up: hdwy over 2f out: rdn to chal ent fnl f: nt pce of wnr) 2½ 2
3330a* Tagula (IRE) **(100)***(112) (IABalding)* 2-9-0 WRSwinburn(4) (hld up: hdwy 2f out: rdn appr fnl f: nt pce to chal) 1½ 3
3449[6] Albaha (USA) *(55) (RWArmstrong)* 2-9-0 RHills(2) (led tl hdd wl over 2f out: sn lost tch: t.o) 25 4

4/7 ALHAARTH (IRE), **2/1** Danehill Dancer (IRE), **13/2** Tagula (IRE), **100/1** Albaha (USA), CSF £2.10 TOTE £1.50 (£1.30) OWNER Mr Hamdan Al Maktoum (LAMBOURN) BRED Shadwell Estate Company Limited 4 Rn 1m 24.64 (0.94) SF: 59/53/50/-

4107 H & K COMMISSIONS NURSERY H'CAP (2-Y.O) (Class C) £8,025.00

(£2,400.00: £1,150.00: £525.00)
1m (Rowley) Stalls: Centre GOING minus 0.33 sec per fur (GF) 4-15 (4-15)

3883* **Mystic Knight (85)***(90+) (RCharlton)* 2-9-2 PatEddery(5) (lw: a.p: shkn up to ld wl ins fnl f: comf) — 1
4059[2] Magic Lake **(64)***(65?) (EJAlston)* 2-7-4 (5)ow2 MBaird(10) (a.p: led & qcknd wl over 1f out: edgd lft & ct wl ins fnl f) 1 2
4025[3] Rhumba Dancer **(83)***(83) (RHannon)* 2-8-9 (5) DaneO'Neill(8) (lw: bhd: hdwy over 2f out: styd on u.p fnl f) 1½ 3
3883[5] Cheerful Aspect (IRE) **(80)***(73) (EALDunlop)* 2-8-11 WRSwinburn(1) (lw: chsd ldrs: rdn over 1f out: one pce) 3½ 4
3758* Pine Needle **(80)***(71) (DMorley)* 2-8-11 WRyan(2) (hld up: hdwy over 2f out: rdn & hung rt over 1f out: nvr nrr) 1¼ 5
3809[2] Consordino **(89)***(79) (LMCumani)* 2-9-6 LDettori(7) (chsd ldrs: rdn wl over 1f out: one pce) hd 6
3947[5] Creative Account (USA) **(90)***(75)*(Fav)*(MrsJRRamsden)* 2-9-7 KFallon(4) (hld up: effrt & n.m.r 3f out: eased whn btn fnl f) 2½ 7
3985[4] Makaskamina **(64)***(46) (PMitchell)* 2-7-2 (7)ow2 CAdamson(6) (nvr nr to chal) ½ 8
3985[5] Balpare **(62)***(41) (NACallaghan)* 2-7-7 GBardwell(12) (led tl hdd wl over 1f out: sn wknd) 2½ 9
3821* Polar Prince (IRE) **(90)***(69) (MAJarvis)* 2-9-7 PRobinson(3) (hld up in rr: effrt & hmpd bel dist: n.d) hd 10

3812[8] Oblomov **(86)**_(62) (GLewis)_ 2-9-3 PaulEddery(11) (drvn along ½-wy: sn btn) 1½ **11**
3870* Lovely Prospect **(78)**_(54) (RGuest)_ 2-8-6 (3) JStack(9) (chsd ldrs over 5f) ....nk **12**
LONG HANDICAP Magic Lake 6-13 Makaskamina 7-1 Balpare 7-5

11/4 Creative Account (USA), **9/2** MYSTIC KNIGHT, **5/1** Consordino, **15/2** Polar Prince (IRE), **8/1** Pine Needle, **12/1** Cheerful Aspect (IRE) (8/1-14/1), **14/1** Magic Lake, Rhumba Dancer (10/1-16/1), **16/1** Balpare, Lovely Prospect, **20/1** Oblomov, **33/1** Makaskamina, CSF £61.41 CT £759.26 TOTE £5.60: £2.30 £4.00 £3.20 (£61.60) Trio £177.90 OWNER Exors of the late Sir Philip Oppenheimer (BECKHAMPTON) BRED Hascombe and Valiant Studs 12 Rn
1m 39.6 (2.60) SF: 46/21/39/29/27/35/31/2/-/25/18/10

4108 NGK SPARK PLUGS H'CAP (0-95) (3-Y.O) (Class C) £6,160.00 (£1,840.00: £880.00: £400.00)
1m 6f (Rowley) Stalls: High GOING minus 0.33 sec per fur (GF) 4-50 (4-51)

3971[8] **Our Kris (62)**_(76) (GHarwood)_ 3-8-13 AClark(4) (lw: hld up: hdwy to ld 3f out: hrd rdn fnl f: hld on gamely) ....— **1**
3676[6] Alaraby (IRE) **(68)**_(80) (IABalding)_ 3-8-12 (7) MartinDwyer(7) (b.nr hind: hld up: hdwy u.p 3f out: kpt on fnl f: nvr able to chal) 1½ **2**
3876* Edan Heights **(70)**_(78) (SDow)_ 3-9-7 LDettori(3) (chsd ldr: drvn along wl over 1f out: one pce) 4 **3**
3936[6] Boundary Express **(57)**_(63) (EJAlston)_ 3-8-8 JReid(1) (lw: led to 3f out: rdn & wknd over 1f out) 1¼ **4**
4000[2] Harry Browne (IRE) **(69)**_(68) (MrsJRRamsden)_ 3-9-6 KFallon(6) (hld up & bhd: rdn over 2f out: no imp) 6 **5**
3927[2] Bowcliffe Court (IRE) **(61)**_(58)_(Fav)_(BWHills)_ 3-8-12 WCarson(5) (hld up: hdwy on ins 4f out: sn rdn along & btn) 1¾ **6**
3896[4] Dixiemelody **(65)** _(RHannon)_ 3-9-2 MRoberts(2) (swtg: chsd ldrs tl broke hind leg & fell 9f out: dead) .... **F**

2/1 Bowcliffe Court (IRE), **3/1** Boundary Express (op 5/1), **9/2** Harry Browne (IRE) (op 3/1), **11/2** Edan Heights, **10/1** Dixiemelody, **12/1** Alaraby (IRE) (op 8/1), **25/1** OUR KRIS, CSF £223.84 TOTE £26.80: £6.50 £4.40 (£80.00) OWNER Mr K. J. Buchanan (PULBOROUGH) BRED K. J. and Mrs Buchanan 7 Rn
2m 59.89 (3.89) SF: 49/53/51/36/41/31/-
T/Plpt: £47.20 (380.99 Tckts). T/Qdpt: £25.90 (14.85 Tckts). IM

4096-CATTERICK (L-H)
Saturday October 14th (Good to firm, Firm patches)
WEATHER: misty WIND: slt half bhd

4109 E.B.F. PROSPECT HILL MAIDEN STKS (2-Y.O) (Class D) £4,012.50 (£1,200.00: £575.00: £262.50)
5f Stalls: Low GOING minus 0.41 sec per fur (F) 2-05 (2-05)

3848[5] **Johayro (78)**_(73+)_(Fav)_(WGMTurner)_ 2-8-7b(7) CAdamson(6) (led over 3f out: styd on wl fnl f) ....— **1**
3647[11] Green Barries _(62) (MJohnston)_ 2-9-0 TWilliams(2) (led over 1f: chsd wnr: nt qckn appr fnl f) 3½ **2**
3856[2] Poly By Staufan (IRE) **(52)**_(55) (MRChannon)_ 2-8-9 WNewnes(13) (mid div: sn drvn along on outside: styd on appr fnl f) ....½ **3**
3892[4] Need You Badly _(52)_(Fav)_(SPCWoods)_ 2-8-9 WWoods(14) (mid div: hdwy on outside 2f out: styd on) 1 **4**
Time To Tango _(47+) (GMMoore)_ 2-8-9 DeanMcKeown(8) (small: bkwd: s.s: bhd tl styd on fnl 2f) 1½ **5**
3838[5] Queens Check _(44) (MissJFCraze)_ 2-8-9 SWebster(15) (b.hind: chsd ldrs tl wknd over 1f out) 1 **6**
1842[12] Sandblaster **(46)**_(34+) (MrsJRRamsden)_ 2-8-9 NConnorton(5) (hld up: stdy hdwy 2f out: nvr plcd to chal) 3 **7**
3940[8] Polar Refrain _(32+) (MrsJRRamsden)_ 2-8-9 MDeering(9) (sn bhd: drvn along ½-wy: sme late hdwy) ....¾ **8**
3651[5] Hi Hoh (IRE) _(32) (MBell)_ 2-8-9 MFenton(12) (in tch tl outpcd fr ½-wy) ....hd **9**
3892[5] Tahya (USA) _(31) (HThomsonJones)_ 2-8-9 GDuffield(10) (in tch: outpcd ½-wy: sn wknd) ....hd **10**
3940[5] Swifty Nifty (IRE) **(54)**_(30) (JBerry)_ 2-8-9 NCarlisle(1) (in tch to ½-wy: sn lost pl) ....½ **11**
2932[8] Katie Komaite **(60)**_(27) (CaptJWilson)_ 2-8-4 (5) PFessey(7) (in tch to ½-wy: sn lost pl) ....¾ **12**
3892[8] Princely Affair _(10) (MBell)_ 2-9-0 FNorton(3) (sn bhd) 7 **13**
977[2] Il Doria (IRE) _(4) (JBerry)_ 2-8-9 JCarroll(11) (sn outpcd & drvn along: eased fnl f) ....nk **14**
3110[7] Jive Baby _(NBycroft)_ 2-9-0 SMaloney(4) (bit bkwd: in tch early: bhd fr ½-wy) 6 **15**

3/1 JOHAYRO, Need You Badly, **9/2** Il Doria (IRE) (op 2/1), **5/1** Green Barries, **7/1** Tahya (USA), **12/1** Polar Refrain, Poly By Staufan (IRE), **14/1** Hi Hoh (IRE), **16/1** Katie Komaite, **20/1** Swifty Nifty (IRE), **25/1** Queens Check, Time To Tango, Princely Affair, **33/1** Sandblaster, **50/1** Jive Baby, CSF £21.43 TOTE £5.60: £2.30 £2.20 £3.30 (£28.30) Trio £197.30 OWNER Mr Frank Brady (SHERBORNE) BRED R. M. Whitaker 15 Rn 58.3 secs (0.80) SF: 48/37/30/27/22/19/9/7/7/6/5/2/-/-/-

OFFICIAL EXPLANATION **Sandblaster: the jockey reported that his orders were to do his best without knocking the filly about, but she got outpaced early on and then just stayed on, changing her legs and giving the impression that she might need further.**

4110

PLODMIRE WOOD CLAIMING STKS (3-Y.O+) (Class F) £3,083.50 (£856.00: £410.50) **1m 3f 214y** Stalls: Low GOING minus 0.41 sec per fur (F) 2-40 (2-40)

4002³ **Once More for Luck (IRE) (65)***(67+) (MrsMReveley)* 4-9-2 ACulhane(6) (lw: hld up: hdwy 6f out: shkn up & led over 2f out: sn clr: eased towards fin) .....— **1**
3853³ Goodbye Millie **(45)***(52) (JLEyre)* 5-8-6v RLappin(10) (chsd ldrs: kpt on fnl 2f: no ch w wnr).....4 **2**
3899⁸ Adaloaldo (USA) *(61) (PAKelleway)* 3-8-10 DeanMcKeown(4) (s.i.s: sn drvn along: sn trckng ldrs: rdn 2f out: r.o one pce) 2 **3**
3825¹⁶ Greek Gold (IRE) **(40)***(48) (DNicholls)* 6-8-10 AlexGreaves(3) (led tl over 2f out: wknd over 1f out).....3½ **4**
3047⁹ Le Temeraire **(17)***(47) (DonEnricoIncisa)* 9-8-9 KimTinkler(5) (chsd ldrs tl lost pl 5f out: hrd rdn 2f out: styd on towards fin).....nk **5**
3853² Latvian **(69)***(55)*(Fav)*(RAllan)* 8-9-4 GDuffield(2) (bhd & pushed along 8f out: hdwy 5f out: rdn over 2f out: no imp) 1 **6**
3431⁸ Here Comes Herbie **(30)***(45) (WStorey)* 3-7-10 ⁽⁵⁾ PFessey(7) (sn bhd: kpt on fnl 2f: n.d).......hd **7**
2501⁷ Baroski **(20)***(13) (JLHarris)* 4-8-10 RPrice(1) (chsd ldrs: drvn along & lost pl 5f out: sn bhd) ..25 **8**
2994⁷ Moofaji **(48)***(13) (FWatson)* 4-8-11 SMaloney(8) (bhd & drvn along 6f out) .....½ **9**
3741⁶ Sallyoreally (IRE) **(32)** *(WStorey)* 4-8-4 JCarroll(9) (chsd ldrs tl wknd over 2f out) 15 **10**

Evens Latvian, **7/4** ONCE MORE FOR LUCK (IRE), **6/1** Goodbye Millie, **10/1** Adaloaldo (USA), **14/1** Moofaji, **20/1** Sallyoreally (IRE), Greek Gold (IRE), **33/1** Le Temeraire, **50/1** Baroski, Here Comes Herbie, CSF £14.30 TOTE £3.10: £1.70 £2.10 £2.60 (£8.20) Trio £20.70 OWNER The Mary Reveley Racing Club (SALTBURN) BRED Kerr and Co Ltd 10 Rn
2m 34.3 (0.50 under best) (3.30) SF: 46/31/32/27/26/34/16/-/-/-
WEIGHT FOR AGE 3yo-8lb

4111

CAMP PLANTATION NURSERY H'CAP (0-85) (2-Y.O) (Class D) £4,565.00 (£1,370.00: £660.00: £305.00)
7f Stalls: Low GOING minus 0.41 sec per fur (F) 3-15 (3-19)

3701¹⁵ **Royal Ceilidh (IRE) (67)***(73) (DenysSmith)* 2-8-2 ⁽⁵⁾ CTeague(9) (chsd ldrs: rdn & outpcd 2f out: styd on wl to ld jst ins fnl f).....— **1**
3867¹⁴ Ancestral Jane **(63)***(67+) (MrsJRRamsden)* 2-8-3 JCarroll(17) (sn bhd: hdwy over 2f out: nt clr run over 1f out: swtchd & styd on strly towards fin) .....¾ **2**
3969* Golden Pond (IRE) **(69)***(72)*(Fav)*(RFJohnsonHoughton)* 2-8-9 AMcGlone(4) (w ldrs: led over 3f out tl jst ins fnl f: unable qckn).....¾ **3**
3857⁵ Juicy **(65)***(67) (WJHaggas)* 2-8-5 WWoods(1) (lw: chsd ldrs: sn drvn along: one pce fnl 2f) ...nk **4**
3985⁷ Silver Welcome **(60)***(60) (MHEasterby)* 2-8-0 SMaloney(8) (led tl over 3f out: kpt on one pce appr fnl f) 1 **5**
4001⁷ The Wad **(56)***(55) (DNicholls)* 2-7-5 ⁽⁵⁾ PFessey(7) (chsd ldrs: ev ch over 2f out: sn rdn & hung lft: nt qckn fnl f) .....hd **6**
3975* Napoleon's Return **(54)***(49) (GMMoore)* 2-7-8 NAdams(15) (s.i.s: hdwy ½-wy: kpt on fnl 2f).1¾ **7**
3985¹⁰ Pride of Kashmir **(56)***(50) (PWHarris)* 2-7-10 ow1 FNorton(16) (sn bhd: styd on fnl 2f: nvr nr ldrs) .....s.h **8**
1871⁸ Worldwide Elsie (USA) **(70)***(65) (RHarris)* 2-8-10 DBatteate(18) (hdwy on outside to chse ldrs 5f out: outpcd fnl 2f) .....s.h **9**
3714¹⁵ Shontaine **(78)***(73) (MJohnston)* 2-9-4 TWilliams(2) (lw: chsd ldrs: sn drvn along: outpcd fnl 2f).....s.h **10**
3809⁷ Taufan Boy **(78)***(70) (PWHarris)* 2-9-4 WNewnes(13) (sn pushed along: chsd ldrs to ½-wy: wknd over 1f out) 1½ **11**
3975¹² Veshca Lady (IRE) **(60)***(52) (EWeymes)* 2-8-0 NKennedy(14) (nvr nr ldrs) .....s.h **12**
3857⁴ Emperegrine (USA) **(74)***(64) (CFWall)* 2-9-0v JLowe(5) (lw: mid div: effrt over 2f out: n.m.r jst ins fnl f: eased) .....½ **13**
3714⁴ Too Hasty **(81)***(71) (MHEasterby)* 2-9-7 MBirch(19) (mid div: effrt over 2f out: sn wknd) ....s.h **14**
3969⁷ Gladys Althorpe (IRE) **(64)***(54) (JLEyre)* 2-8-4 RLappin(6) (stumbled after s: hld up: stdy hdwy 2f out: nt clr run & eased ins fnl f).....hd **15**
3613⁸ Serious Trust **(61)***(48) (SirMarkPrescott)* 2-8-1 ow1 GDuffield(20) (a in rr) 1 **16**
3267⁶ Distant Storm **(62)***(21) (MBell)* 2-8-2 ow1 MFenton(11) (sn wl bhd) 12 **17**
3976³ Eccentric Dancer **(65)** *(MPBielby)* 2-8-5 ACulhane(3) (s.i.s: a bhd: virtually p.u 2f out).........20 **18**

5/1 Golden Pond (IRE), **8/1** Napoleon's Return, **9/1** Juicy, **10/1** Gladys Althorpe (IRE), Emperegrine (USA), Taufan Boy, Ancestral Jane, **12/1** Silver Welcome, Too Hasty, The Wad, Shontaine, **14/1** Serious Trust, **16/1** Eccentric Dancer, Pride of Kashmir, **20/1** Veshca Lady (IRE), ROYAL CEILIDH (IRE), Distant Storm, Worldwide Elsie (USA), CSF £206.73 CT £1,064.97 TOTE £47.70: £7.90 £3.30 £2.20 £3.20 (£317.60) Trio £381.30 OWNER Carlton Appointments (Aberdeen) Ltd (BISHOP AUCKLAND) BRED Thomas and Mary Shirley 18 Rn

1m 25.4 (2.20) SF: 31/25/30/25/18/13/7/8/23/31/28/10/22/29/12/6/-/-

4112

SOUR BECK CONDITIONS STKS (2-Y.O) (Class D) £3,817.50 (£1,140.00: £545.00: £247.50) **5f** Stalls: Low GOING minus 0.41 sec per fur (F) 3-50 (3-51)

3733[2] **Dwingeloo (IRE)** *(71+)*(Fav)*(MajorDNChappell)* 2-8-6 WWoods(4) (unruly: mde virtually all: shkn up over 1f out: pushed out) — **1**
3742[2] Amy Leigh (IRE) **(72)***(70) (CaptJWilson)* 2-8-5 (5) PFessey(3) (lw: chsd ldrs: hdwy u.p & ev ch over 1f out: nt qckn) 1½ **2**
3742[5] Born A Lady **(75)***(51) (NPLittmoden)* 2-8-10 NCarlisle(2) (sn outpcd & bhd: hdwy over 1f out: styd on towards fin) 6 **3**
3702[9] Arrhythmic (IRE) **(79)***(46) (MBrittain)* 2-8-10b MFenton(8) (b.nr hind: chsd wnr: rdn ½-wy: sn outpcd) 1½ **4**
3699[9] Shafir (IRE) **(70)***(38) (JBerry)* 2-8-10 JCarroll(1) (chsd ldrs tl lost pl & wknd ½-wy) 2½ **5**
3018[4] Colway Bridge *(10) (MrsMReveley)* 2-8-11 ACulhane(6) (bit bkwd: bolted going to s: sn wl bhd) 9 **6**
Call Me Jendie *(JPLeigh)* 2-8-6 DeanMcKeown(5) (unf: scope: s.i.s: a wl bhd) 3 **7**

8/15 DWINGELOO (IRE) (2/5-4/6), **6/1** Arrhythmic (IRE), **7/1** Amy Leigh (IRE), **8/1** Born A Lady (6/1-9/1), **10/1** Shafir (IRE), **12/1** Colway Bridge, **25/1** Call Me Jendie, CSF £5.79 TOTE £1.40: £1.30 £2.40 (£3.50) OWNER Mrs G. C. Maxwell (WHITSBURY) BRED J. C. Condon 7 Rn

58.1 secs (0.60) SF: 44/43/24/19/11/-/-

4113

CROW HOLE BANK H'CAP (0-85) (3-Y.O+) (Class D) £4,565.00 (£1,370.00: £660.00: £305.00) **5f** Stalls: Low GOING minus 0.41 sec per fur (F) 4-25 (4-29)

3992[6] **Insider Trader (72)***(83)*(Fav)*(RGuest)* 4-9-4b GDuffield(12) (w ldrs: led 3f out: drvn along & styd on fnl f) — **1**
4033[5] Lady Sheriff **(78)***(85) (MWEasterby)* 4-9-5b(5) PFessey(17) (led 2f: effrt over 1f out: nt qckn ins fnl f) 1¼ **2**
3293[17] Slivovitz **(53)***(54) (MJHeaton-Ellis)* 5-7-6v(7)ow6 AmandaSanders(10) (a chsng ldrs: kpt on wl fnl f) hd **3**
4057[3] Domicksky **(54)***(56) (MRChannon)* 7-7-9 (5) PPMurphy(6) (bhd tl hdwy 2f out: styd on ins fnl f) 1½ **4**
3878[11] Super Rocky **(74)***(75) (RBastiman)* 6-9-1 (5) HBastiman(5) (hld up: hdwy ½-wy: kpt on appr fnl f: nvr rchd ldrs) nk **5**
3783[9] Lochon **(56)***(55) (JLEyre)* 4-8-2 RLappin(16) (bhd: hdwy ½-wy: kpt on appr fnl f: nt rch ldrs) ½ **6**
3667[6] Lepine (IRE) **(73)***(72)*(Fav)*(JWWatts)* 4-9-5b NConnorton(7) (a chsng ldrs: nt qckn appr fnl f) hd **7**
3777[9] Spender **(72)***(68) (PWHarris)* 6-9-4 WNewnes(2) (hdwy far side 2f out: kpt on ins fnl f: nvr nr to chal) 1 **8**
3961[5] Thatcherella **(71)***(63) (MajorDNChappell)* 4-9-3 WWoods(19) (lw: bhd: hdwy 2f out: nvr nr ldrs) 1¼ **9**
3992[9] Polly Particular **(73)***(64) (TDBarron)* 3-9-4 AMcGlone(4) (chsd ldrs tl rdn & wknd 1f out) nk **10**
3667[9] Kenesha (IRE) **(50)***(38) (DANolan)* 5-7-3b(7)ow3 CAdamson(8) (chsd ldrs tl lost pl ½-wy) hd **11**
3748[15] The Fed **(48)***(33) (RMWhitaker)* 5-7-8v JLowe(3) (chsd ldrs to ½-wy: sn lost pl) 1¾ **12**
3878[16] Local Heroine **(51)***(31) (JBerry)* 5-7-11b NCarlisle(11) (nvr nr ldrs) 1½ **13**
3783[11] Nadwaty (IRE) **(50)***(30) (MCChapman)* 3-7-9b NKennedy(14) (in tch tl outpcd ½-wy) s.h **14**
3640[5] Black Boy (IRE) **(47)***(25) (RFMarvin)* 6-7-7b ClaireBalding(9) (b: sn bhd) ¾ **15**
3878[10] Super Park **(68)***(43) (MHEasterby)* 3-8-13 MBirch(18) (bhd: sme hdwy on outside 2f out: n.d) ¾ **16**
3992[3] Here Comes a Star **(74)***(47)*(Fav)*(JMCarr)* 7-9-6 ACulhane(15) (lw: s.i.s: a bhd) ¾ **17**
3667[15] Breakfast Creek **(55)***(17) (JBerry)* 3-8-0 NAdams(1) (b: in tch early: bhd fr ½-wy) 3½ **18**
3855[14] Serious Hurry **(53)***(3) (RMMcKellar)* 7-7-6b(7) KSked(13) (in tch tl lost pl ½-wy: sn bhd: b.b.v) 3½ **19**

LONG HANDICAP Slivovitz 7-5 Black Boy (IRE) 6-7 Kenesha (IRE) 7-5

11/2 INSIDER TRADER, Lepine (IRE), Here Comes a Star, **15/2** Domicksky (op 12/1), Polly Particular, Lady Sheriff, **10/1** Spender, **12/1** Super Rocky, **14/1** The Fed, **16/1** Lochon, Super Park, **20/1** Thatcherella, Serious Hurry, Nadwaty (IRE), Slivovitz, **25/1** Black Boy (IRE), **33/1** Local Heroine, Breakfast Creek, Kenesha (IRE), CSF £51.06 CT £750.54 TOTE £5.90: £2.20 £3.00 £5.60 £1.30 (£34.60) Trio £382.60 OWNER Lord Matthews (NEWMARKET) BRED Lord Victor Matthews 19 Rn 58.1 secs (0.60) SF: 56/58/27/29/48/28/45/41/36/36/11/6/4/2/-/15/20/-/-

WEIGHT FOR AGE 3yo-1lb

4114 THIEVES GILL LIMITED STKS (0-60) (3-Y.O+) (Class F) £3,279.50(£912.00: £438.50) **1m 5f 175y** Stalls: Low GOING minus 0.41 sec per fur (F) 4-55 (4-55)

*3527*13 **Zanzara (IRE) (48)***(64) (MrsVAAconley)* 4-9-1 MDeering(1) (chsd ldrs: pushed along 6f out: outpcd over 2f out: hrd rdn & styd on to ld ins fnl f)....—— 1
40617 Cliburnel News (IRE) **(58)***(61)*(Fav)*(AStreeter)* 5-8-6 (7) DDenby(2) (b: hld up: hdwy to chse ldrs 5f out: led over 1f out: hdd & nt qckn ins fnl f)....1¼ 2
38059 Never Time (IRE) **(35)***(62) (MrsVAAconley)* 3-8-9 ACulhane(4) (hld up: hdwy on ins over 2f out: effrt & styng on whn bdly hmpd jst ins fnl f: fin 4th, nk: plcd 3rd).... 3
398713 Diamond Crown (IRE) **(43)***(64) (MartynWane)* 4-9-6 JCarroll(6) (swtg: plld hrd: trckd ldrs: effrt 2f out: rdn, hung lft & hmpd jst ins fnl f: fin 3rd, 3l: disq: plcd 4th).... 4
40029 Peep O Day **(55)***(55) (JLEyre)* 4-8-13 RLappin(5) (w ldrs: led 7f out tl over 1f out: btn whn hmpd jst ins fnl f)....1¼ 5
23297 Bold Joker **(30)***(31) (GROldroyd)* 4-9-4 JLowe(3) (led to 7f out: lost pl 3f out: sn bhd)....25 6

8/11 Cliburnel News (IRE), **3/1** Peep O Day, **11/2** ZANZARA (IRE), Diamond Crown (IRE), **16/1** Never Time (IRE), **25/1** Bold Joker, CSF £10.72 TOTE £6.90: £2.40 £1.20 (£4.60) OWNER Mr J. Chan (WESTOW) BRED Miss Ruth Lonergan 6 Rn 3m 8.1 (12.90) SF: -/-/-/-/-/-
WEIGHT FOR AGE 3yo-9lb
STEWARDS' ENQUIRY Carroll susp. 23-25/10/95 (careless riding).

4115 'CLOSE OF PLAY' H'CAP (0-70) (3-Y.O+) (Class E) £3,925.00(£1,180.00: £570.00: £265.00) **7f** Stalls: Low GOING minus 0.41 sec per fur (F) 5-30 (5-34)

*2943*12 **Blue Bomber (65)***(80) (TDBarron)* 4-9-9 WNewnes(20) (mde virtually all: styd on strly ins fnl f)....—— 1
37263 Kira **(45)***(55) (JLEyre)* 5-8-3 RLappin(9) (b.off hind: chsd ldrs: ev ch over 1f out: unable qckn)....2 2
4049* Night Wink (USA) **(57)***(62)*(Fav)*(DNicholls)* 3-8-12 AlexGreaves(19) (lw: trckd ldrs: ev ch over 2f out: nt qckn appr fnl f)....2½ 3
36193 Primo Lara **(66)***(68) (PWHarris)* 3-9-7 MFenton(17) (chsd ldrs: effrt & edgd lft over 1f out: unable qckn)....1¼ 4
38555 Panther (IRE) **(52)***(50) (JHetherton)* 5-8-10 NKennedy(8) (lw: mid div: styd on fnl 2f: nt rch ldrs)....1½ 5
394317 Field of Vision (IRE) **(65)***(62) (MJohnston)* 5-9-9 TWilliams(16) (a chsng ldrs: nt qckn fnl 2f)....½ 6
387211 Almasi (IRE) **(59)***(55) (CFWall)* 3-9-0 GDuffield(2) (chsd ldrs: outpcd ½-wy: kpt on appr fnl f)....¾ 7
361911 Kindergarten Boy (IRE) **(62)***(56) (RBoss)* 4-9-6 AMcGlone(3) (in tch: outpcd over 2f out: kpt on appr fnl f)....½ 8
380814 Johnnie the Joker **(49)***(42) (JPLeigh)* 4-8-7b FNorton(1) (chsd ldrs tl lost pl ½-wy: sme hdwy over 1f out: n.d)....½ 9
38305 Mu-Arrik **(44)***(29) (GROldroyd)* 7-8-2 NCarlisle(7) (lw: s.i.s: bhd tl sme late hdwy)....3½ 10
383010 Evanro (IRE) **(44)***(29) (TDBarron)* 4-7-9 (7) CAdamson(13) (s.i.s: bhd: sme hdwy 2f out: n.d)....s.h 11
360711 Superoo **(67)***(51) (MrsPSly)* 9-9-11 ACulhane(4) (hld up & bhd: n.d)....½ 12
39602 Morocco (IRE) **(60)***(43) (MRChannon)* 6-8-13 (5) PPMurphy(11) (a in rr)....½ 13
3807* Kid Ory **(68)***(50) (PCalver)* 4-9-12 MBirch(5) (b.hind: prom early: lost pl ½-wy: n.d after)....nk 14
371519 Garnock Valley **(66)***(47) (JBerry)* 5-9-10 JCarroll(10) (prom tl rn wd & lost pl 2f out: sn bhd)...½ 15
39729 Penny's Wishing **(58)***(35) (JPLeigh)* 3-8-8 (5) PFessey(12) (chsd ldrs tl wknd 2f out)....2 16
38004 Hello Hobson's (IRE) **(51)***(16) (RBastiman)* 5-8-9 DeanMcKeown(18) (hld up: hdwy to chse ldrs ½-wy: sn lost pl)....5 17
38787 Twice in Bundoran (IRE) **(49)** *(PSFelgate)* 4-8-7 JLowe(15) (swtg: hmpd & lost pl sn after s: n.d)....6 18
389713 Chief's Lady **(50)** *(CNAllen)* 3-8-5 StephenDavies(6) (w ldrs tl wknd over 2f out)....3 19

3/1 Night Wink (USA) (tchd 7/4), **4/1** Field of Vision (IRE), **8/1** Kid Ory, **9/1** Morocco (IRE), **10/1** Hello Hobson's (IRE) (8/1-12/1), Primo Lara, **12/1** Kindergarten Boy (IRE), **14/1** Twice in Bundoran (IRE), Kira, **16/1** Superoo, Garnock Valley, **20/1** Panther (IRE), Mu-Arrik, Almasi (IRE), Chief's Lady, **25/1** Penny's Wishing, Evanro (IRE), Johnnie the Joker, BLUE BOMBER, CSF £348.92 CT £1,253.69 TOTE £60.40: £8.50 £3.50 £1.60 £3.80 (£522.40) OWNER Mr Geoffrey Martin (THIRSK) BRED R. H. Cowell and Mrs R. B. Collie 19 Rn
1m 24.0 (0.80) SF: 62/37/41/47/32/44/34/38/24/11/11/33/25/32/29/14/-/-/-
WEIGHT FOR AGE 3yo-3lb
OFFICIAL EXPLANATION **Blue Bomber: had broken a blood vessel on his last run.**
T/Plpt: £36.40 (296.34 Tckts). T/Qdpt: £8.90 (22.5 Tckts). WG

4102-NEWMARKET (R-H)
Saturday October 14th (Good to firm)
WEATHER: sunny & warm WIND: slt against

4116 ROTHMANS ROYALS NORTH SOUTH CHALLENGE SERIES FINAL H'CAP (3-Y.O+) (Class B) £29,570.00 (£8,960.00: £4,380.00: £2,090.00)
1m (Rowley) Stalls: Centre GOING minus 0.18 sec per fur (GF) 1-45 (1-46)

3732⁷ **Stone Ridge (IRE) (82)***(95) (RHannon)* 3-8-5 (5) DaneO'Neill(21) (chsd ldrs far side: led 3f out: hld on wl)........— 1
3837* Mo-Addab (IRE) (76)*(88) (ACStewart)* 5-8-8 MRoberts(16) (swtg: hld up far side: swtchd & hdwy 3f out: chal ins fnl f: r.o)........nk 2
3973* Shinerolla **(81)***(91) (MrsJRRamsden)* 3-8-9 KFallon(7) (hld up: gd hdwy 2f out: ch ins fnl f: kpt on)........1¼ 3
3607¹² Clifton Fox **(81)***(88) (JAGlover)* 3-8-9 SDWilliams(23) (chsd ldrs far side: effrt over 2f out: r.o one pce)........1½ 4
3732² Country Lover **(79)***(85) (LordHuntingdon)* 4-8-11 MHills(24) (racd far side: hdwy ½-wy: sn chsng ldrs: kpt on one pce fnl 2f)........nk 5
3732¹⁶ Fionn de Cool (IRE) **(75)***(81) (RAkehurst)* 4-8-7 TQuinn(12) (prom: chal over 3f out: one pce fnl 2f)........hd 6
3945²⁹ Master Beveled **(74)***(80) (PDEvans)* 5-8-6 KDarley(3) (in tch stands' side: hdwy over 2f out: rdn & nvr able chal)........s.h 7
3732¹⁹ Apollono **(80)***(83) (JRFanshawe)* 3-8-8 DHarrison(2) (swtg: racd stands' side: effrt 3f out: nvr able chal)........1½ 8
3732¹⁴ Saifan **(77)***(80) (DMorris)* 6-8-9b RCochrane(1) (dwlt & swtchd rt s: racd stands' side: hdwy 2f out: r.o)........s.h 9
4038¹¹ Pride of Pendle **(76)***(78) (DNicholls)* 6-8-1 (7) MartinDwyer(19) (mid div far side: effrt over 2f out: n.d)........nk 10
3941³ Karinska **(67)***(68) (MCChapman)* 5-7-6 (7) CMunday(22) (in tch far side: no hdwy fnl 3f)........½ 11
3966³ Ninia (USA) **(70)***(71) (MJohnston)* 3-7-12 GBardwell(4) (swtg: cl up stands' side: rdn & nt qckn fnl 2½f)........nk 12
3977¹² Pine Ridge Lad (IRE) **(61)***(62) (JLEyre)* 5-7-4 (3) NVarley(14) (cl up far side tl wknd over 2f out)........s.h 13
4053² Cee-Jay-Ay **(62)***(60) (JBerry)* 8-7-8 ow1 LCharnock(13) (mid div far side: effrt 3f out: no imp)....1 14
3703* Scaraben **(74)***(73)*(Fav)*(SEKettlewell)* 7-8-3 (3) JStack(5) (trckd ldrs stands' side: effrt 3f out: sn btn)........s.h 15
3945⁵ Celestial Choir **(82)***(80) (JLEyre)* 5-9-0 WRSwinburn(18) (bhd far side: effrt over 2f out: hdwy whn hmpd appr fnl f: eased)........nk 16
3802⁸ Noble Neptune **(65)***(61) (WJMusson)* 3-7-7 JQuinn(10) (racd stands' side: n.d)........¾ 17
3732⁵ Ma Petite Anglaise **(80)***(74) (WJarvis)* 3-8-3 (5) MHenry(17) (racd far side: effrt ½-wy: n.d)........1 18
3945⁷ Crumpton Hill (IRE) **(85)***(78) (NAGraham)* 3-8-13 PatEddery(9) (lw: dwlt: racd stands' side: n.d)........¾ 19
3813¹⁷ Band on the Run **(96)***(86) (BAMcMahon)* 8-10-0 JWeaver(20) (lw: led far side 5f: sn lost pl) 1¼ 20
3973⁷ Elpidos **(73)***(61) (CEBrittain)* 3-8-1 BDoyle(8) (lw: chsd ldrs stands' side 5f)........1 21
3732⁹ Easy Jet (POL) **(73)***(55) (LordHuntingdon)* 3-8-1 RHills(11) (racd stands' side: prom 5f)........3 22
4041¹³ Knobbleeneeze **(75)***(55) (MRChannon)* 5-8-7v JFEgan(6) (lw: led stands' side tl edgd rt & wknd fnl 2½f: btn whn hmpd over 1f out)........1¼ 23

LONG HANDICAP Cee-Jay-Ay 7-5 Noble Neptune 7-1 Pine Ridge Lad (IRE) 6-12
6/1 Scaraben, **9/1** Country Lover, Crumpton Hill (IRE), Celestial Choir, **11/1** Mo-Addab (IRE), Shinerolla (8/1-12/1), **16/1** Fionn de Cool (IRE), Master Beveled, Saifan, **20/1** Pride of Pendle, Band on the Run, **25/1** STONE RIDGE (IRE), Ma Petite Anglaise, Cee-Jay-Ay, Ninia (USA), Karinska, Clifton Fox, Apollono, **33/1** Knobbleeneeze, Easy Jet (POL), Elpidos, **66/1** Noble Neptune, Pine Ridge Lad (IRE), CSF £249.40 CT £2,899.09 TOTE £40.90: £6.60 £2.70 £3.30 £5.00 (£212.80) Trio £1,615.60 OWNER Mrs Chris Harrington (MARLBOROUGH) BRED Mrs Chris Harrington 23 Rn
1m 38.71 (1.71) SF: 62/59/58/55/56/52/51/50/51/49/39/38/33/31/44/51/28/41/45/57/28/22/26
WEIGHT FOR AGE 3yo-4lb

4117 HOUGHTON CONDITIONS STKS (2-Y.O) (Class B) £7,805.40 (£2,810.40: £1,345.20: £546.00: £213.00)
7f (Rowley) Stalls: Centre GOING minus 0.18 sec per fur (GF) 2-20 (2-20)

3779³ **Babinda** *(85+)*(Fav)*(CEBrittain)* 2-8-12 BDoyle(5) (lw: mde all: shkn up & qcknd over 1f out: comf)........— 1
4048⁵ Madame Steinlen *(75) (BWHills)* 2-8-7 MHills(2) (lw: w wnr: rdn 2f out: nt qckn fnl f)........2 2
4004a* Wight *(67) (RHannon)* 2-8-10 TQuinn(3) (trckd ldrs: effrt over 2f out: r.o one pce)........5 3
Samraan (USA) *(66) (JLDunlop)* 2-8-12 WCarson(1) (w'like: leggy: rn green & outpcd 3f out: styd on towards fin)........1½ 4

3900[11] Migwar *(65) (LMCumani)* 2-8-12 KDarley(4) (bit bkwd: a chsng ldrs: rdn over 2f out: wknd 1½f out)....hd **5**

2/1 BABINDA, **11/4** Migwar, **4/1** Wight, Samraan (USA), **10/1** Madame Steinlen (6/1-12/1), CSF £16.40 TOTE £2.70: £1.50 £2.70 (£12.90) OWNER Mr Saeed Manana (NEWMARKET) BRED Saeed Manana 5 Rn 1m 27.18 (3.48) SF: 40/30/22/21/20

4118 TOTE CESAREWITCH H'CAP (3-Y.O+) (Class B) £46,170.00 (£13,860.00: £6,680.00: £3,090.00)
2m 2f (Rowley) Stalls: High GOING minus 0.18 sec per fur (GF) 3-00 (3-01)

3705[4] **Old Red (IRE)** **(66)***(80) (MrsMReveley)* 5-7-11 LCharnock(18) (hld up & bhd: hdwy 5f out: rdn to ld 1f out: r.o u.p)....— **1**
4036[8] Nanton Point (USA) **(75)***(88) (LadyHerries)* 3-7-7 JQuinn(21) (chsd ldrs: led over 3f out tl hdd 1f out: r.o)....1 **2**
3547[4] Top Cees **(80)***(93)*(Fav)*(MrsJRRamsden)* 5-8-11 KFallon(14) (lw: hld up: effrt over 4f out: hdwy over 2f out: r.o towards fin)....nk **3**
3971[9] Inchcailloch (IRE) **(63)***(75) (JSKing)* 6-7-8 GBardwell(2) (bhd: hdwy 4f out: styd on: nrst fin) ..¾ **4**
3547[2] Saleel (IRE) **(90)***(100) (ACStewart)* 3-8-8 MRoberts(8) (in tch: hdwy over 3f out: ev ch over 1f out: sn btn)....3 **5**
3718* Torch Vert (IRE) **(76)***(84) (BWHills)* 3-7-3 (5)ow1 MHenry(13) (chsd ldrs: chal 3f out: hrd drvn & wknd fnl f)....s.h **6**
3849[7] Blaze Away (USA) **(80)***(89) (IABalding)* 4-8-11 WRyan(16) (b.off hind: prom: outpcd & lost pl 4f out: styd on fnl 2f)....s.h **7**
4026[4] Sea Freedom **(67)***(74) (GBBalding)* 4-7-9 (3) NVarley(11) (lw: chsd ldrs tl wknd fnl 2½f) 2½ **8**
3817[8] Pistol River (IRE) **(87)***(93) (NJHWalker)* 5-9-1v(3) JStack(19) (effrt 5f out: sn outpcd & lost tch: styd on fnl 2f)....1 **9**
3930[2] Shonara's Way **(93)***(92) (RCharlton)* 4-9-10 KDarley(5) (chsd ldrs: effrt u.p 4f out: wknd fnl 2f)8 **10**
3274* Salaman (FR) **(83)***(82) (JLDunlop)* 3-8-1 WCarson(10) (lw: hld up & bhd: hdwy 4f out: rdn & no imp)....hd **11**
3217[7] Imad (USA) **(65)***(62) (JWhite)* 5-7-10 ow2 DaleGibson(20) (rdn & gd hdwy 4f out: wknd fnl 2f)s.h **12**
4036[3] Star Rage (IRE) **(82)***(81) (MJohnston)* 5-8-13 4x JWeaver(9) (hld up & bhd: hdwy over 4f out: rdn & btn 2f out: hmpd over 1f out)....nk **13**
3343[7] Sun of Spring **(80)***(77) (JWhite)* 5-8-8 (3) SDrowne(3) (hld up: hdwy on outside 4f out: rdn & wknd fnl 2f)....1½ **14**
3817[13] Shadirwan (IRE) **(74)***(71) (RAkehurst)* 4-8-5b TQuinn(12) (swtg: chsd ldrs tl wknd fnl 3½f)......½ **15**
3971[12] Roberty Lea **(68)***(61) (MrsMReveley)* 7-7-13 SSanders(7) (lw: bhd: hdwy on outside 6f out: rdn & btn over 3f out)....4 **16**
3412[8] Shining High **(86)***(78) (JLDunlop)* 3-8-4 RCochrane(6) (led tl hdd & wknd over 3f out) 1¼ **17**
3769[3] Wild Strawberry **(63)***(52) (MissBSanders)* 6-7-5 (3)ow1 DWright(4) (cl up tl wknd fnl 3½f)...........2 **18**
3971[7] Brumon (IRE) **(64)***(52) (TDyer)* 4-7-4 (5)ow2 MBaird(17) (a wl bhd) ....¾ **19**
3971[20] Five to Seven (USA) **(66)***(46) (CWThornton)* 6-7-11 AMackay(15) (b: chsd ldrs tl wknd u.p fnl 4f)....11 **20**
3804* New Reputation **(88)** *(BWHills)* 4-9-5 MHills(1) (prom tl wknd over 3f out: p.u lame 2f out)........ **P**
LONG HANDICAP Nanton Point (USA) 7-3 Brumon (IRE) 7-1 Wild Strawberry 7-2

4/1 Top Cees, **5/1** Saleel (IRE), **11/2** Salaman (FR), **15/2** New Reputation, **10/1** Torch Vert (IRE), **11/1** OLD RED (IRE), **14/1** Imad (USA), **16/1** Shadirwan (IRE), Sea Freedom, **25/1** Inchcailloch (IRE), Star Rage (IRE), Shonara's Way, **33/1** Blaze Away (USA), **40/1** Shining High, Wild Strawberry, Nanton Point (USA), Roberty Lea, **50/1** Sun of Spring, **100/1** Pistol River (IRE), Brumon (IRE), Five to Seven (USA), CSF £334.96 CT £1,873.97 TOTE £12.90: £2.60 £9.60 £2.50 £4.00 (£354.70) Trio £1,654.30 OWNER Mr A. Flannigan (SALTBURN) BRED Oldtown Stud in Ireland 21 Rn 3m 52.62 (2.62) SF: 56/51/69/51/63/47/65/50/69/68/45/38/57/53/47/37/41/28/28/22/-
WEIGHT FOR AGE 3yo-13lb
OFFICIAL EXPLANATION **New Reputation: broke down four furlongs out.**

4119 OLIVIER DOUIEB MEMORIAL RATED STKS H'CAP (0-100) (3-Y.O+) (Class B) £9,924.60 (£3,671.40: £1,760.70: £718.50: £284.25:£110.55)
5f (Rowley) Stalls: Low GOING minus 0.18 sec per fur (GF) 3-35 (3-36)

3822* **Croft Pool** **(84)***(94) (JAGlover)* 4-8-7 SDWilliams(2) (cl up stands' side: led ins fnl f: drvn out)....— **1**
4033[20] Takadou (IRE) **(88)***(97) (MissLCSiddall)* 4-8-11 JWeaver(3) (lw: swtg: bhd stands' side: hdwy over 1f out: r.o wl)....nk **2**
Snowing **(86)***(93) (TStack,Ireland)* 4-8-9 JReid(12) (w'like: a.p centre: styd on u.p fnl f: nrst fin)....¾ **3**
3922[3] Jawlaat (USA) **(89)***(95) (JLDunlop)* 3-8-11 WCarson(11) (racd centre: led tl hdd ins fnl f: kpt on)....hd **4**

4040[16] Ziggy's Dancer (USA) **(86)***(92) (EJAlston)* 4-8-9 KFallon(8) (a chsng ldrs stands' side: hrd rdn 2f out: r.o one pce) ....hd 5
3550[8] Don't Worry Me (IRE) **(98)***(103) (FHLee)* 3-9-6 MRoberts(1) (swtg: disp ld stands' side: qcknd over 2f out: wknd ins fnl f) ....nk 6
3964[20] Mr Bergerac (IRE) **(84)***(88) (BPalling)* 4-8-7 TSprake(9) (racd stands' side: hdwy u.p 2f out: styd on wl) ....nk 7
3230[7] Rock Symphony **(89)***(85) (WJHaggas)* 5-8-12 MHills(6) (s.i.s: sn in tch: effrt ½-wy: wknd over 1f out) 2½ 8
3815[3] Brave Edge **(98)***(94)*(Fav)*(RHannon)* 4-9-7 PatEddery(10) (chsd ldrs centre: rdn 2f out: btn appr fnl f) ....hd 9
4033[22] Ashtina **(84)***(80) (BAPearce)* 10-8-7 KDarley(7) (lw: chsd ldrs stands' side: rdn ½-wy: wknd over 1f out) ....s.h 10
4033[6] Saseedo (USA) **(87)***(82) (WAO'Gorman)* 5-8-10 JWilliams(5) (swtg: s.s: t.o tl r.o wl fnl f)....s.h 11
3938[5] Palacegate Jack (IRE) **(86)***(37) (JBerry)* 4-8-9b GCarter(4) (chsd ldrs stands' side to ½-wy: sn wknd & eased) 14 12

LONG HANDICAP Ashtina 8-3 Croft Pool 8-5

10/3 Brave Edge, **11/2** Jawlaat (USA) (op 7/2), Saseedo (USA), **9/1** CROFT POOL, Rock Symphony (6/1-10/1), **11/1** Don't Worry Me (IRE) (8/1-12/1), **12/1** Snowing, **14/1** Mr Bergerac (IRE) (10/1-16/1), Takadou (IRE), Palacegate Jack (IRE) (10/1-16/1), **20/1** Ziggy's Dancer (USA), **40/1** Ashtina, CSF £110.53 CT £1,366.90 TOTE £12.10: £2.80 £3.70 £3.20 (£101.50) Trio £193.00 OWNER Countrywide Classics Ltd (WORKSOP) BRED J. S. Bell 12 Rn

59.95 secs (1.25) SF: 55/58/54/55/53/63/49/46/55/41/43/-

WEIGHT FOR AGE 3yo-1lb

4120 DUBAI CHAMPION STKS (Gp 1) (3-Y.O+) (Class A) £179,520.00

(£66,480.00: £31,940.00: £13,100.00: £5,250.00: £2,110.00)
1m 2f (Rowley) Stalls: Low GOING minus 0.18 sec per fur (GF) 4-15 (4-17)

3794a[2] **Spectrum (IRE) (119)***(128) (PWChapple-Hyam)* 3-8-10 JReid(1) (lw: hld up: hdwy 3f out: led over 1f out: edgd rt & r.o u.p) ....— 1
3811* Riyadian *(125) (PFICole)* 3-8-10 TQuinn(4) (lw: trckd ldrs: disp ld over 2f out: hdd over 1f out: r.o) 2 2
3323a* Montjoy (USA) **(110)***(125) (PFICole)* 3-8-10 PatEddery(6) (lw: hld up: hdwy to chal 2f out: r.o u.p) ....hd 3
3794a* Tamure (IRE) **(120)***(122) (JHMGosden)* 3-8-10 WRSwinburn(8) (swtg: trckd ldrs: chal 3f out: outpcd 2f out: no imp after) 1½ 4
3814* Bahri (USA) **(125)***(122)*(Fav)*(JLDunlop)* 3-8-10 WCarson(3) (lw: hld up: smooth hdwy to disp ld over 2f out: hung rt & wknd appr fnl f) ....s.h 5
3614[2] Fahal (USA) **(119)***(113) (DMorley)* 3-8-10 RHills(7) (lw: swtg: cl up: led 4f out tl over 2f out: wknd over 1f out) 6 6
3914a[4] Germany (USA) *(110) (BSchutz,Germany)* 4-9-2 JWeaver(5) (nice c: w ldrs tl wknd fnl 3f) ..1¾ 7
2595[7] Environment Friend **(112)***(86) (CEBrittain)* 7-9-2 MRoberts(2) (led 6f: sn wknd: b.b.v) 15 8

5/2 Bahri (USA), **11/4** Tamure (IRE), **7/2** Riyadian, **5/1** SPECTRUM (IRE), **10/1** Fahal (USA), **25/1** Montjoy (USA), Germany (USA), **66/1** Environment Friend, CSF £20.91 TOTE £6.20: £2.00 £1.80 £2.60 (£14.00) OWNER Lord Weinstock & The Hon Simon Weinstock (MARLBOROUGH) BRED Ballymacoll Stud Farm Ltd. in Ireland 8 Rn 2m 2.55 (-0.05) SF: 80/77/77/74/74/65/68/44

WEIGHT FOR AGE 3yo-6lb

4121 BEDFORD LODGE HOTEL BENTINCK STKS (Listed) (3-Y.O+) (Class A)

£14,068.00 (£5,212.00: £2,506.00: £1,030.00: £415.00: £169.00)
6f (Rowley) Stalls: Low GOING minus 0.18 sec per fur (GF) 4-45 (4-46)

3717* **Royale Figurine (IRE) (102)***(104) (MJFetherston-Godley)* 4-8-8 JReid(7) (hld up: hdwy 2f out: led ins fnl f: hung rt: r.o) ....— 1
4033[4] Hello Mister **(102)***(106) (JO'Donoghue)* 4-8-13 PMcCabe(6) (bhd: hdwy 2f out: r.o u.p fnl f) 1¼ 2
3904[7] Indhar **(100)***(104) (JEBanks)* 4-8-13 JQuinn(9) (bhd: hdwy 2f out: hrd rdn & r.o fnl f) ....¾ 3
3615* Iktamal (USA) **(99)***(103)*(Fav)*(EALDunlop)* 3-8-11 WRSwinburn(10) (lw: in tch: drvn along over 2f out: styd on wl fnl f) ....hd 4
3823* South Rock **(88)***(98) (JAGlover)* 3-8-6 SDWilliams(11) (swtg: mde most tl hdd & no ex ins fnl f) ....hd 5
3602* Indian Fly **(101)***(102) (RHannon)* 4-8-13 PatEddery(12) (chsd ldrs: ev ch over 1f out: nt qckn)nk 6
3880[3] Saint Express **(103)***(96) (MrsMReveley)* 5-8-13 KDarley(8) (w ldrs: rdn over 1f out: grad wknd) 2½ 7
2205[5] Stylish Ways (IRE) **(98)***(95) (GWragg)* 3-8-11 MHills(5) (bhd: rdn over 2f out: styd on one pce) ....nk 8
3902[6] El Yasaf (IRE) **(104)***(92) (CNAllen)* 7-8-13 GCarter(2) (trckd ldrs: effrt 2f out: nt qckn) 1¼ 9

3922* Doctor's Glory (USA) **(89)***(86) (RHannon)* 3-8-6 MRoberts(4) (cl up tl wknd 1f out)................hd 10
3550[5] Warning Star **(103)***(82) (BWHills)* 3-8-6 RHills(1) (hdwy ½-wy: rdn & btn over 1f out)............1½ 11
3834[8] Double Blue **(106)***(85) (MJohnston)* 6-8-13 JWeaver(3) (lw: disp ld over 3f: sn wknd).............¾ 12

7/2 Iktamal (USA), **9/2** ROYALE FIGURINE (IRE) (op 3/1), **7/1** Hello Mister, Indian Fly, **8/1** Double Blue, Warning Star, **11/1** Saint Express (8/1-12/1), **12/1** Stylish Ways (IRE), **20/1** Doctor's Glory (USA), **25/1** El Yasaf (IRE), South Rock, **33/1** Indhar, CSF £33.30 TOTE £5.00: £1.90 £2.00 £7.20 (£16.70) Trio £246.00 OWNER Mr Craig Pearman (EAST ILSLEY) BRED Craig Pearman 12 Rn
1m 11.53 (0.23) SF: 74/76/74/71/66/72/66/63/62/54/50/55
WEIGHT FOR AGE 3yo-2lb

4122 NGK SPARK PLUGS H'CAP (0-95) (3-Y.O+) (Class C) £6,732.00 (£2,016.00: £968.00: £444.00)

7f (Rowley) Stalls: Low GOING minus 0.18 sec per fur (GF) 5-20 (5-20)

3943[5] **Mullitover (83)***(93)*(Fav)*(MJHeaton-Ellis)* 5-9-4 MRoberts(2) (a cl up: led over 2f out: hld on gamely).......................— 1
3755[5] Emerging Market **(89)***(99) (JLDunlop)* 3-9-7 PatEddery(1) (chsd ldrs: effrt 2f out: disp ld ins fnl f: hrd rdn & no ex towards fin).......................hd 2
3904[13] Hawaash (IRE) **(91)***(99) (JRFanshawe)* 3-9-9 DHarrison(8) (w ldrs: rdn 2f out: kpt on wl)........1 3
3972[2] Delight of Dawn **(72)***(79) (KTIvory)* 3-8-1 (3) JStack(4) (b: bhd & drvn along over 2f out: styd on strly fnl f).......................nk 4
3943[28] Stolen Melody **(70)***(74) (SDow)* 3-8-2 SSanders(5) (cl up: hrd rdn over 1f out: one pce).......1¼ 5
3964[4] It's Academic **(70)***(73) (MrsJRRamsden)* 3-8-2 JFEgan(6) (trckd ldrs: effrt over 2f out: nvr able chal).......................nk 6
3874[9] Moujeeb (USA) **(59)***(58) (PatMitchell)* 5-7-8vow1 JQuinn(9) (hdwy u.p 2f out: one pce fnl f)....1¼ 7
3837[16] Set the Fashion **(60)***(60) (LordHuntingdon)* 6-7-4v(5) MHenry(10) (hld up: hdwy u.p over 2f out: no imp).......................hd 8
4033[12] Youdontsay **(82)***(82) (RCurtis)* 3-8-11 (3) DWright(12) (chsd ldrs centre: ev ch over 1f out: sn wknd).......................s.h 9
Ethbaat (USA) **(89)***(89) (WRMuir)* 4-9-10 JReid(11) (lw: plld hrd: led tl hdd over 2f out: sn btn).......................s.h 10
3488[9] Midwich Cuckoo **(86)***(83) (PTWalwyn)* 3-9-4v RCochrane(3) (trckd ldrs: rdn over 2f out: wknd over 1f out).......................1¼ 11
4040[4] Brecongill Lad **(79)***(72) (MissSEHall)* 3-8-11b RHills(7) (hld up: effrt over 2f out: no imp)..........2 12
LONG HANDICAP Moujeeb (USA) 6-13

2/1 MULLITOVER, **11/2** Emerging Market, **6/1** It's Academic (7/2-13/2), **7/1** Hawaash (IRE), **10/1** Delight of Dawn, Brecongill Lad (7/1-11/1), Set the Fashion, **14/1** Midwich Cuckoo, **16/1** Youdontsay, **25/1** Ethbaat (USA), **33/1** Moujeeb (USA), **50/1** Stolen Melody, CSF £13.56 CT £62.35 TOTE £3.10: £1.60 £2.10 £2.60 (£7.00) Trio £17.10 OWNER Mrs D. B. Mulley (WROUGHTON) BRED Mrs D. B. Mulley 12 Rn
1m 26.59 (2.89) SF: 52/55/55/35/30/29/17/19/38/48/39/28
WEIGHT FOR AGE 3yo-3lb

T/Jkpt: Not won; £8,422.21 to Pontefract 16/10/95. T/Plpt: £4,463.10 (9.44 Tckts). T/Qdpt: £454.90 (1.2 Tckts). AA

3949-WOLVERHAMPTON (L-H)
Saturday October 14th (Standard)

WIND: nil

4123 LADBROKES WIN AND SHOW H'CAP (0-65) (3-Y.O) (Class F) £2,856.00 (£791.00: £378.00)

5f (Fibresand) Stalls: Low GOING: 0.21 sec per fur (SLW) 7-00 (7-00)

3992[17] **Blue Sioux (55)***(63) (JWharton)* 3-8-11b AMackay(8) (b.off fore: chsd ldrs: rdn & led 1f out: edged lft & r.o).......................— 1
3992[4] Silk Cottage **(63)***(66) (RMWhitaker)* 3-9-5 MTebbutt(7) (lw: led 4f: unable qckn)..................1½ 2
3919[7] Southern Dominion **(53)***(52) (MJohnston)* 3-8-9 JWeaver(11) (lw: w ldr tl no ex appr fnl f).....1¼ 3
3954[7] Montague Dawson (IRE) **(60)***(59) (MrsNMacauley)* 3-8-13 (3) SDrowne(4) (b hind: bhd tl r.o fnl 2f).......................s.h 4
3961[8] Another Batchworth **(54)***(49) (SMellor)* 3-8-10 RPerham(5) (nt clr run wl over 1f out: hdwy over 1f out: nrst fin).......................1¼ 5
3941[12] Academy Life **(65)***(56) (PFICole)* 3-9-7b CRutter(13) (swtg: chsd ldrs: no hdwy fnl 2f)...........1¼ 6
3357[6] Dominelle **(49)***(32) (MHEasterby)* 3-8-5 SMaloney(3) (lw: prom over 3f)..............................2½ 7
3954[3] Pursuance (IRE) **(63)***(46)*(Fav)*(JBalding)* 3-8-12v(7) JEdmunds(6) (lw: dwlt: rdn 2f out: nvr nr ldrs).......................hd 8

3333[9] Flashing Sabre **(60)***(42) (JBerry)* 3-8-9 (7) PRoberts(10) (prom 3f) ....hd **9**
4057[7] Lloc **(53)***(33) (CADwyer)* 3-8-6v(3) NVarley(9) (dwlt: a bhd) ....¾ **10**
Vocal Command **(60)***(32) (WWHaigh)* 3-9-2 DaleGibson(1) (bit bkwd: sn bhd) 2½ **11**
3467[12] Time Is Money (IRE) **(50)** *(MHTompkins)* 3-8-6 GBardwell(2) (lw: stumbled s: a bhd) 10 **12**

7/2 Pursuance (IRE), **9/2** Southern Dominion, **11/2** Academy Life (8/1-5/1), **7/1** Silk Cottage (op 4/1), **8/1** Lloc, **12/1** BLUE SIOUX (op 8/1), **14/1** Montague Dawson (IRE), **16/1** Time Is Money (IRE), Flashing Sabre, Dominelle, **20/1** Another Batchworth, **25/1** Vocal Command, CSF £85.99 CT £400.01 TOTE £15.40: £2.80 £2.60 £2.00 (£75.40) Trio £88.90 OWNER Mr J.L.Ashby (MELTON MOWBRAY) BRED R. T. and Mrs Watson 12 Rn

62.7 secs (4.70) SF: 33/36/22/29/19/26/2/16/12/3/2/-

4124 HERA CLAIMING STKS (2-Y.O) (Class F) £2,415.00 (£665.00: £315.00)
6f (Fibresand) Stalls: Low GOING: 0.21 sec per fur (SLW) 7-30 (7-31)

3468[7] **Ultra Barley (79)***(87+) (PCHaslam)* 2-8-12 GCarter(12) (chsd ldrs: led 2f out: clr fnl f: comf)— **1**
3895* Fenna **(72)***(71)*(Fav)*(SPCWoods)* 2-8-7 WWoods(9) (lw: a.p: ev ch wl over 1f out: kpt on) 4 **2**
3917[8] Coyote Bluff(IRE) *(78) (PWChapple-Hyam)* 2-8-9 (5) RHavlin(2) (hdwy 2f out: r.o fnl f) ....nk **3**
3655[5] Gi La High **(62)***(58) (JBerry)* 2-8-1b LCharnock(13) (led 4f) 2½ **4**
3623[19] Lila Pedigo (IRE) **(62)***(51) (JBerry)* 2-7-13 GBardwell(8) (s.i.s: hdwy & edged lft over 1f out: nrst fin) 2 **5**
3895[3] Midas Gold **(68)***(69) (BJMeehan)* 2-9-4 JWeaver(7) (hdwy 3f out: no imp appr fnl f) ....nk **6**
3975[6] Harsh Times **(55)***(48) (MHEasterby)* 2-7-13 SMaloney(5) (effrt over 1f out: nvr plcd to chal)...¾ **7**
3721[14] China Castle **(60)***(62) (PCHaslam)* 2-9-0 MTebbutt(4) (lw: nvr plcd to chal) ....nk **8**
3077[11] Potenza *(36) (RHollinshead)* 2-8-5 ow1 KFallon(10) (bit bkwd: n.d) 6 **9**
3901[6] Chemcast **(58)***(45) (BJMeehan)* 2-9-4 BDoyle(6) (chsd ldrs tl wknd over 2f out: eased fnl f) 2 **10**
3767[18] Latzio **(46)***(24) (BAPearce)* 2-7-10 (3) DWright(11) (prom: rdn 3f out: sn wknd) ....¾ **11**
3969[6] Incapol **(60)***(29) (MJRyan)* 2-8-10 AClark(1) (lw: in tch: rdn over 2f out: sn btn & eased) 2 **12**

9/4 Fenna, **9/2** Coyote Bluff(IRE), **5/1** ULTRA BARLEY, **8/1** Midas Gold (12/1-7/1), **9/1** Gi La High (op 6/1), Harsh Times, **11/1** Chemcast (op 7/1), **12/1** Lila Pedigo (IRE), **14/1** China Castle, Incapol (op 8/1), **25/1** Latzio, Potenza, CSF £17.82 TOTE £9.30: £2.10 £1.80 £2.20 (£8.10) Trio £8.90 OWNER Pet Express Ltd T/A Nutrimix (MIDDLEHAM) BRED Benham Stud 12 Rn

1m 16.3 (5.10) SF: 41/25/32/12/5/23/2/16/-/-/-/-

4125 ALLSPORTS H'CAP (0-70) (3-Y.O+) (Class E) £3,080.00 (£920.00: £440.00: £200.00) **6f (Fibresand)** Stalls: Low GOING: 0.21 sec per fur (SLW) 8-00 (8-00)

*3954** **Cretan Gift (66)***(76) (NPLittmoden)* 4-9-10v TGMcLaughlin(7) (trckd ldrs: rdn over 1f out: led ins fnl f: r.o) ....— **1**
4057[11] Sing With the Band **(70)***(77) (BAMcMahon)* 4-10-0 GCarter(13) (lw: prom: led 3f out tl ins fnl f: no ex) 1 **2**
3954[2] King Rambo **(68)***(65)*(Fav)*(RHollinshead)* 4-9-5 (7) AEddery(12) (lw: a.p: rdn over 1f out: one pce) 4 **3**
2793[6] Speedy Classic (USA) **(65)***(56) (MJHeaton-Ellis)* 6-9-9 AClark(10) (a.p: one pce fnl 2f) 2 **4**
3554[11] Newbury Coat **(64)***(51) (BPreece)* 5-9-8b JWeaver(9) (lw: led 3f: wknd fnl f) 1½ **5**
3897[3] Dancing Heart **(70)***(55) (BJMeehan)* 3-9-12 BDoyle(5) (bhd: hdwy 3f out: nvr rchd ldrs) ....¾ **6**
3897[10] Jareer Do (IRE) **(61)***(40) (BPalling)* 3-9-3 TSprake(6) (b: prom tl rdn & btn over 2f out) 2½ **7**
2659[3] Taffeta Silk (USA) **(66)***(41) (WJarvis)* 4-9-10 SSanders(11) (lw: sn rdn along: bhd fnl 3f) 1¼ **8**
4068[21] Monis (IRE) **(58)***(23) (JBalding)* 4-8-9v(7) JEdmunds(4) (effrt & c wd 2f out: a bhd) 4 **9**
3964[16] Rymer's Rascal **(62)***(21) (EJAlston)* 3-9-4 KFallon(2) (lw: a bhd) 2 **10**
3492[20] Boursin (IRE) **(62)***(17) (NPLittmoden)* 6-9-6 DaleGibson(1) (prom 3f) 1½ **11**

3/1 King Rambo, **7/2** CRETAN GIFT, **9/2** Sing With the Band, **8/1** Dancing Heart, **9/1** Taffeta Silk (USA) (op 6/1), **14/1** Speedy Classic (USA), **16/1** Jareer Do (IRE), Newbury Coat, Rymer's Rascal, Boursin (IRE), **25/1** Monis (IRE), CSF £18.91 CT £48.31 TOTE £4.70: £2.00 £1.80 £1.80 (£12.10) Trio £9.50 OWNER R A M Racecourses Ltd (NEWARK) BRED Hesmonds Stud Ltd 11 Rn

1m 16.0 (4.80) SF: 58/59/47/38/33/35/20/23/5/1/-

WEIGHT FOR AGE 3yo-2lb

4126 FOLEY STEELSTOCK H'CAP (0-70) (3-Y.O+) (Class E) £3,080.00 (£920.00: £440.00: £200.00) **1m 4f (Fibresand)** Stalls: Low GOING: 0.21 sec(SLW) 8-30 (8-33)

3156[8] **Carpathian (60)***(73) (LordHuntingdon)* 4-9-5 RPerham(12) (lw: trckd ldrs: 2nd st: ev ch fnl f: led last stride) ....— **1**
3884* Stevie's Wonder (IRE) **(63)***(76)*(Fav)*(MJRyan)* 5-9-8v GCarter(11) (lw: led after 2f: rdn fnl f: hdd last stride) ....s.h **2**
3735[7] Jaraab **(55)***(66) (GLewis)* 4-9-0v SWhitworth(6) (sn pushed along: hdwy 5f out: 3rd st: r.o appr fnl f: no imp wl ins fnl f) 1¼ **3**

3810[14] Teen Jay **(65)***(63) (MJRyan)* 5-9-10 BDoyle(5) (a.p: 4th st: one pce) 10 **4**
3898[4] Elpida (USA) **(65)***(58) (JPearce)* 3-9-2 GBardwell(2) (prom tl 5th st: sn btn) 3½ **5**
3245[2] Premier Dance **(62)***(55) (DHaydnJones)* 8-9-7 AMackay(8) (chsd ldrs: pushed along 7f out: 6th st: no imp) ....nk **6**
4002[5] Katy's Lad **(62)***(40) (BAMcMahon)* 8-9-2 (5) LNewton(9) (b: in tch: rdn 5f out: sn btn) 11 **7**
3863[7] Pass Mark **(60)***(36) (JRFanshawe)* 3-8-11 DHarrison(10) (prom tl rdn & wknd over 3f out) ...1½ **8**
4000[8] Sommersby (IRE) **(65)***(33) (MrsNMacauley)* 4-9-7 (3) SDrowne(3) (b: trckd ldrs tl wknd 3f out) .6 **9**
234[2] Castle Secret **(52)***(8) (DBurchell)* 9-8-11 TWilson(7) (sn wl bhd) 9 **10**
3970[7] Canton Venture **(66)***(6) (SPCWoods)* 3-9-3 WWoods(4) (sn pushed along & bhd) 12 **11**
3737[2] Tovarich **(65)***(1) (RonaldThompson)* 4-9-10b JWeaver(1) (led 2f: wknd 6f out) 3 **12**

9/2 Stevie's Wonder (IRE), **11/2** Tovarich, **6/1** Sommersby (IRE), **13/2** Premier Dance, **7/1** CARPATHIAN, Canton Venture, **8/1** Elpida (USA), **9/1** Jaraab, **12/1** Pass Mark, **16/1** Katy's Lad, **25/1** Teen Jay, **33/1** Castle Secret, CSF £38.54 CT £271.01 TOTE £9.10: £2.80 £2.40 £4.80 (£20.30) Trio Not won; £160.98 to 16/10/95. OWNER The Queen (WEST ILSLEY) BRED Sheikh Mohammed bin Rashid al Maktoum 12 Rn 2m 41.3 (10.30) SF: 52/55/45/42/29/34/19/7/12/-/-/-
WEIGHT FOR AGE 3yo-8lb

4127 BULLSMOOR DEVELOPMENTS (S) STKS (2-Y.O F) (Class G) £2,415.00 (£665.00: £315.00)

1m 100y (Fibresand) Stalls: Low GOING: 0.21 sec per fur (SLW) 9-00 (9-02)

3949[7] **Image Maker (IRE) (53)***(65) (DWPArbuthnot)* 2-8-7 AClark(8) (in tch: 4th st: plld out appr fnl f: rdn to ld ins fnl f) ....— **1**
3540[3] Bumblefoot (IRE) **(63)***(69)*(Fav)*(MJohnston)* 2-8-12 JWeaver(12) (led tl hdd & unable qckn ins fnl f) ....¾ **2**
3985[19] Be My Bird **(54)***(62) (BJMeehan)* 2-8-7 BDoyle(5) (bhd: hdwy & 6th st: r.o wl appr fnl f) 1 **3**
3744[2] Madonna da Rossi **(47)***(61) (SirMarkPrescott)* 2-8-7 CNutter(3) (stdd s: plld hrd: hdwy & 2nd st: wknd appr fnl f) ....nk **4**
3738[7] Rozel Bay **(56)***(46) (JLSpearing)* 2-8-4 (3) SDrowne(4) (chsd ldrs 3f: rallied & 5th st: no imp) 8 **5**
3780[10] Shanoora (IRE) **(54)***(49) (BPalling)* 2-8-12v TSprake(13) (chsd ldrs tl rdn & wknd 2f out) 1 **6**
3738[2] Victoria Venture **(63)***(49) (SPCWoods)* 2-8-12 WWoods(10) (lw: chsd ldrs: rdn & 3rd st: sn wknd: eased fnl f) ....hd **7**
3642[3] Anna Settic **(56)***(36) (DrJDScargill)* 2-8-7 MFenton(9) (lw: bhd fnl 4f) 4 **8**
3937[18] Welsh Melody **(56)***(22) (KRBurke)* 2-8-12 MTebbutt(11) (prom 5f) 10 **9**
4045[7] Pulga Circo **(51)***(15) (BAMcMahon)* 2-8-7 SSanders(1) (lw: bhd fnl 4f) 1¼ **10**
3290[13] Zuno Princess (IRE) **(45)***(14) (GLewis)* 2-8-7b SWhitworth(6) (prom tl wknd 3f out) ....¾ **11**
3353[8] Sikosarki (USA) *(RonaldThompson)* 2-8-7 GBardwell(2) (a bhd) 8 **12**
2382[7] Chamber Music *(JBerry)* 2-8-7 GCarter(7) (a bhd) ....½ **13**

7/4 Bumblefoot (IRE), **7/2** Victoria Venture, **4/1** Anna Settic, **7/1** Madonna da Rossi, **10/1** Rozel Bay, **12/1** Pulga Circo, Chamber Music (op 8/1), **14/1** IMAGE MAKER (IRE) (op 8/1), **16/1** Welsh Melody, Be My Bird, **20/1** Zuno Princess (IRE), Shanoora (IRE), **33/1** Sikosarki (USA), CSF £44.42 TOTE £15.70: £3.90 £1.70 £5.50 (£42.40) Trio Not won; £129.30 to 16/10/95. OWNER Mr Stephen Crown (COMPTON) BRED Mellon Stud 13 Rn 1m 54.2 (10.20) SF: 12/16/9/8/-/-/-/-/-/-/-/-/-
Sold BPreece 5,400gns

4128 APHRODITE H'CAP (0-60) (3-Y.O+) (Class F) £2,415.00 (£665.00: £315.00)

1m 100y (Fibresand) Stalls: Low GOING: 0.21 sec per fur (SLW) 9-30 (9-30)

4043[13] **Heathyards Lady (USA) (57)***(72) (RHollinshead)* 4-9-4 (7) FLynch(9) (a gng wl: 2nd st: shkn up & led over 1f out: sn clr: easily) ....— **1**
3952[5] Landlord **(60)***(64) (JARToller)* 3-9-10b JWeaver(13) (lw: bhd: hdwy over 3f out: nrst fin) 6 **2**
3935[7] Penmar **(59)***(63) (TJEtherington)* 3-9-9b LCharnock(8) (lw: prom: 3rd st: one pce) ....hd **3**
3778[4] Zacaroon **(60)***(59)*(Fav)*(LordHuntingdon)* 4-10-0 DHarrison(5) (lw: in tch: rdn over 2f out: nt trble ldrs) 2½ **4**
3871[4] Latin Leader **(59)***(52) (CREgerton)* 5-9-8b(5) DaneO'Neill(11) (prom tl 6th & btn st) 3 **5**
3950[2] Gentle Irony **(60)***(52) (BJMeehan)* 3-9-10b BDoyle(12) (chsd ldr tl led 3f out: hdd over 1f out: sn wknd) ....¾ **6**
3952[7] Certain Way (IRE) **(52)***(42) (NPLittmoden)* 5-9-6 TGMcLaughlin(3) (prom: 4th st: sn wknd) 1 **7**
Tryst (IRE) **(60)***(47) (DrJDScargill)* 4-10-0 MFenton(10) (b.hind: bit bkwd: led over 5f: 5th & wkng st) 1¼ **8**
3987[17] Jalmaid **(55)***(39) (BAMcMahon)* 3-9-5 SSanders(4) (nvr nr to chal) 2 **9**
3898[9] Hong Kong Dollar **(56)***(33) (BAPearce)* 3-8-13 (7) PRoberts(7) (hmpd after 1f: sn rdn & bhd) .3½ **10**
1931[3] Halfabob (IRE) **(55)***(9) (DHaydnJones)* 3-9-5 AMackay(6) (swtg: a bhd) 12 **11**
3543[4] Our Little Lady **(59)***(11) (JEBanks)* 3-9-2 (7) MBridge(1) (a bhd) 1 **12**

9/4 Zacaroon, **4/1** Latin Leader (7/1-7/2), **6/1** Gentle Irony, HEATHYARDS LADY (USA), **8/1** Landlord, Penmar, **10/1** Jalmaid, **16/1** Certain Way (IRE), Tryst (IRE), Hong Kong Dollar, Halfabob (IRE), Our Little Lady, CSF £57.36 CT £374.35 TOTE £5.50: £2.00 £3.30 £2.40 (£28.90) Trio £90.80; £12.79 to 16/10/95. OWNER Mr L. A. Morgan (UPPER LONGDON) BRED S A'Long Farm and Dennis Swartz 12 Rn 1m 52.4 (8.40) SF: 45/33/32/32/25/21/15/20/8/2/-/-

WEIGHT FOR AGE 3yo-4lb

T/Plpt: £110.60 (90.21 Tckts).T/Qdpt: £87.30 (1.2 Tckts). Dk

3869-FOLKESTONE (R-H)
Monday October 16th (Good)

WEATHER: fair WIND: almost nil

4129 WESTENHANGER MAIDEN AUCTION STKS (I) (2-Y.O) (Class E)

£3,388.00 (£1,012.00: £484.00: £220.00)
6f 189y Stalls: Low GOING: 0.17 sec per fur (G) 1-15 (1-19)

3779[5] **Ageeb (IRE)** *(67) (WJHaggas)* 2-8-8 WWoods(14) (led 5f out: all out)........— 1
3989[8] Al's Alibi **(75)***(67) (WRMuir)* 2-8-8 JWeaver(12) (5th st: hrd rdn over 1f out: ev ch wl ins fnl f: r.o wl)........s.h 2
Poetry (IRE) *(58) (MHTompkins)* 2-8-1 ow2 PRobinson(1) (w'like: bkwd: hdwy over 3f out: 6th st: hrd rdn over 1f out: r.o wl ins fnl f)........s.h 3
3988[4] Brandonville *(66) (IABalding)* 2-8-7 DHarrison(5) (lw: lost pl over 3f out: rallied 2f out: r.o wl ins fnl f)........s.h 4
4050[2] Academy of Dance (IRE) *(53)*(Fav)*(MJohnston)* 2-7-13 JFEgan(6) (7th st: rdn over 2f out: unable qckn)........2 5
3939[2] Salty Girl (IRE) **(75)***(46) (BWHills)* 2-8-4 MFenton(13) (led 2f: 2nd st: wknd over 1f out)........5 6
3891[4] Superior Force *(51) (MissBSanders)* 2-8-10 SSanders(4) (3rd st: wknd over 1f out)........½ 7
3776[5] Two Socks **(52)***(44) (MMcCormack)* 2-8-5 BDoyle(8) (4th st: wknd 2f out)........1 8
3890[7] Pleasureland (IRE) *(43) (PJMakin)* 2-8-10 RCochrane(10) (lw: hdwy over 3f out: wknd 2f out)........2½ 9
3587a[22] South Pagoda (IRE) *(39) (PWChapple-Hyam)* 2-8-7 JReid(11) (lw: bhd fnl 3f)........nk 10
Baron Hrabovsky *(36) (PFICole)* 2-8-8 TQuinn(3) (b: b.hind: w'like: a bhd)........2 11
3892[16] Lord Ellangowan (IRE) *(29) (RIngram)* 2-8-6 ow2 WNewnes(9) (a bhd)........1¼ 12
3570[10] Iron And Steel **(50)***(19) (AMoore)* 2-8-8 CandyMorris(7) (a bhd)........6 13
3738[8] Touch of Snow *(4) (JABennett)* 2-7-6 (5) MHenry(2) (a bhd)........1¾ 14

7/4 Academy of Dance (IRE) (op Evens), **5/1** South Pagoda (IRE) (op 3/1), Salty Girl (IRE), **15/2** Brandonville (5/1-8/1), **12/1** Baron Hrabovsky (op 6/1), **14/1** AGEEB (IRE) (op 6/1), Pleasureland (IRE) (12/1-20/1), **16/1** Superior Force, **20/1** Al's Alibi, **33/1** Poetry (IRE), Two Socks, Iron And Steel, **40/1** Lord Ellangowan (IRE), **66/1** Touch of Snow, CSF £235.83 TOTE £12.10: £2.60 £5.50 £8.20 (£163.80) Trio not won; £27.95 to Chepstow 17/10/95 OWNER Mr Ahmed Al Shafar (NEWMARKET) BRED Belmont Stud 14 Rn 1m 27.1 (5.50) SF: 39/39/30/38/25/18/23/16/15/11/8/1/-/-

4130 WESTENHANGER MAIDEN AUCTION STKS (II) (2-Y.O) (Class E)

£3,388.00 (£1,012.00: £484.00: £220.00)
6f 189y Stalls: Low GOING: 0.17 sec per fur (G) 1-45 (1-48)

3988[2] **Maristax (70)***(77) (PJMakin)* 2-8-2 SSanders(12) (hmpd & sddle slipped over 2f out: 5th st: rdr kicked irons out over 1f out: led last stride)........— 1
3869[4] Trojan Risk **(80)** *(GLewis)* 2-8-4 DHarrison(8) (chsd ldr: led over 2f out: hrd rdn fnl f: hdd last stride)........hd 2
3982[7] Commin' Up *(JWHills)* 2-7-8 (5) MHenry(7) (3rd st: hrd rdn over 1f out: r.o)........nk 3
3471[7] Daunting Destiny (BEL) **(70)** *(RHannon)* 2-8-2 (5)ow4 DaneO'Neill(5) (6th st: hrd rdn over 1f out: r.o)........1¾ 4
4001[8] Urgent Swift **(65)** *(APJarvis)* 2-8-3 JTate(11) (hdwy over 1f out: nvr nrr)........1 5
3672[10] Mam'selle Bergerac (IRE) *(PMitchell)* 2-7-10 (3) DWright(2) (nvr nrr)........2½ 6
Farmost *(SirMarkPrescott)* 2-8-10 WWoods(6) (leggy: bit bkwd: nvr nr to chal)........1¼ 7
4064[5] Rififi (Fav)*(JLDunlop)* 2-8-7 JWeaver(13) (lw: led over 4f: 2nd st: hrd rdn over 1f out: wknd fnl f)........nk 8
3869[7] Rowlandsons Charm (IRE) **(65)** *(GLMoore)* 2-7-6v(5) MBaird(3) (nvr nrr)........s.h 9
3982[10] Meg's Memory (IRE) **(55)** *(JohnBerry)* 2-7-12b GBardwell(1) (s.i.s: a bhd)........2 10
Young Frederick (IRE) *(KRBurke)* 2-8-6 SWhitworth(9) (leggy: bhd fnl 4f)........2½ 11
3917[11] Texas Tramp *(MajorDNChappell)* 2-7-12 NAdams(4) (4th st: wknd over 2f out)........1¾ 12
Ajkuit (IRE) *(JJSheehan)* 2-8-6 JQuinn(10) (unf: bit bkwd: s.s: bhd fnl 4f)........4 13

11/4 Rififi (6/4-3/1), **100/30** MARISTAX, **9/2** Trojan Risk (6/1-4/1), **6/1** Daunting Destiny (BEL), **8/1** Urgent Swift, **10/1** Farmost (5/1-12/1), **14/1** Commin' Up (10/1-16/1), **20/1** Rowlandsons Charm (IRE), Texas Tramp, **25/1** Meg's Memory (IRE), Young Frederick (IRE), Ajkuit (IRE), **33/1** Mam'selle Bergerac (IRE), CSF £19.84 TOTE £5.40: £1.60 £2.00 £5.80 (£9.20) Trio £39.70 OWNER Mr T. G. Warner (MARLBOROUGH) BRED Red House Stud 13 Rn

1m 27.7 (6.10) SF: 27/29/23/23/21/11/19/15/5/1/4/-/-

4131

BIDDENDEN (S) STKS (3-Y.O) (Class F) £2,519.00 (£694.00: £329.00)
6f 189y Stalls: Low GOING: 0.17 sec per fur (G) 2-15 (2-17)

3823⁸ **Anita's Contessa (IRE) (60)***(52) (BPalling)* 3-8-9 TSprake(5) (3rd st: led over 1f out: all out) — **1**
3800⁷ Here Comes Risky **(65)***(57)*(Fav)*(MJohnston)* 3-9-0 JWeaver(8) (gd hdwy & hung lft over 1f out: str run fnl f: fin wl) s.h **2**
4044⁸ Harvest Reaper **(53)***(57) (JLHarris)* 3-9-0 PRobinson(3) (hdwy over 5f out: 4th st: hrd rdn over 1f out: r.o wl ins fnl f) hd **3**
3972¹³ Havana Miss **(38)***(49) (BPalling)* 3-8-4 (5) MHenry(2) (lw: hdwy over 1f out: r.o) 1¼ **4**
3980⁵ Tomal **(48)***(48) (RIngram)* 3-9-0 WWoods(9) (hdwy over 1f out: hung rt ins fnl f: nt qckn) 2½ **5**
3751⁹ Scissor Ridge **(43)***(44) (JJBridger)* 3-9-0 GBardwell(11) (rdn over 3f out: 6th st: one pce fnl 2f) 1¾ **6**
3531¹⁴ Shot the Sheriff **(48)***(41) (PFICole)* 3-9-0b TQuinn(15) (led 6f out tl over 1f out: sn wknd) 1¼ **7**
2363¹⁰ Nuthatch (IRE) **(34)***(36) (MDIUsher)* 3-8-9 RPrice(1) (hdwy 5f out: 5th st: hrd rdn over 1f out: wknd fnl f) hd **8**
3980¹² Prince Pellinore **(39)***(40) (CADwyer)* 3-9-0 CDwyer(10) (nvr nrr) ½ **9**
3542⁹ Paddys Cherub *(26) (JRArnold)* 3-8-9 JQuinn(6) (hdwy 5f out: 7th st: wknd over 1f out) 3½ **10**
1719⁸ Steepholme **(40)***(23) (BRMillman)* 3-8-6 (3) SDrowne(12) (lw: a bhd) 1¼ **11**
*2142*⁷ Ganador **(51)***(9) (JBerry)* 3-8-9 JReid(14) (swtg: led 1f: 2nd st: wknd 2f out) 6 **12**
3876¹⁰ Morning Master **(23)***(3) (RMFlower)* 3-9-0b AMorris(16) (swtg: a bhd) 5 **13**
4049¹⁰ Logie Pert Lad **(30)** *(JJBridger)* 3-9-0 NAdams(13) (bhd fnl 3f) 15 **14**
Elraas (USA) **(40)** *(JohnBerry)* 3-9-0 MWigham(4) (bit bkwd: bhd fnl 5f) 6 **15**
3860⁸ Amboyna Burl (IRE) **(46)** *(DAWilson)* 3-9-0 MPerrett(7) (ref to r: t.n.p) **R**

9/4 Here Comes Risky (6/4-5/2), **7/2** Shot the Sheriff, Harvest Reaper, **11/2** Tomal (op 3/1), **9/1** ANITA'S CONTESSA (IRE) (6/1-10/1), **12/1** Ganador (7/1-14/1), **16/1** Prince Pellinore, **20/1** Nuthatch (IRE), Scissor Ridge, Elraas (USA), **25/1** Logie Pert Lad, **33/1** Steepholme, Havana Miss, Paddys Cherub, **50/1** Morning Master, Amboyna Burl (IRE), CSF £32.58 TOTE £9.30: £2.10 £1.70 £2.00 (£9.20) Trio £34.60 OWNER Mrs Anita Quinn (COWBRIDGE) 16 Rn

1m 27.8 (6.20) SF: 32/37/37/29/28/24/21/16/20/6/3/-/-/-/-/-

No bid

OFFICIAL EXPLANATION **Amboyna Burl: was reluctant to leave the stalls and to race.**

4132

CLIFF MEDIAN AUCTION MAIDEN STKS (2-Y.O) (Class F) £2,947.40 (£816.40: £390.20) **5f** Stalls: Low GOING minus 0.21 sec per fur (GF) 2-45 (2-51)

3856¹⁰ **Dande Flyer (60)***(66) (DWPArbuthnot)* 2-9-0 TQuinn(12) (b.nr hind: hld up: swtchd lft over 1f out: led ins fnl f: drvn out) — **1**
Sharp Stock *(65)*(Fav)*(BJMeehan)* 2-9-0 BDoyle(10) (w'like: hld up: led over 1f out tl ins fnl f: r.o) nk **2**
May Queen Megan *(50) (MrsALMKing)* 2-8-9 AGarth(5) (unf: rdn & hdwy over 1f out: r.o one pce) 3 **3**
3733²¹ Night Harmony (IRE) *(44) (RHannon)* 2-9-0 JReid(7) (lw: a.p: led 2f out tl over 1f out: wknd fnl f) 3½ **4**
3567⁴ Dancing Jack **(54)***(41) (JJBridger)* 2-9-0 SSanders(3) (lw: nt clr run over 1f out: nvr nr to chal) 1 **5**
*3523*⁸ Mindrace *(35) (KTIvory)* 2-8-7 (7) CScally(2) (hld up: rdn 2f out: sn wknd) 1¾ **6**
2204⁸ Noon (IRE) *(26) (MHTompkins)* 2-8-9 PRobinson(8) (hld up: rdn over 1f out: sn wknd) 1½ **7**
3856⁶ Silhouette (IRE) **(48)***(22) (DRCElsworth)* 2-8-4 (5) DaneO'Neill(6) (bhd fnl 2f) 1¼ **8**
3625¹⁹ Toe Tappin Music (USA) *(21) (MartynMeade)* 2-9-0b VSlattery(11) (led 3f: wknd over 1f out) 1¾ **9**
3567⁵ Poppy My Love **(42)***(5) (RHarris)* 2-8-9 DBatteate(1) (lw: spd 3f) 3½ **10**
Musical Heights (IRE) *(1) (CADwyer)* 2-8-6 (3) SDrowne(4) (neat: a bhd) 1¼ **11**

15/8 Sharp Stock, **100/30** DANDE FLYER (2/1-7/2), **7/2** Night Harmony (IRE) (5/2-4/1), **9/1** Silhouette (IRE) (5/1-10/1), Dancing Jack (6/1-10/1), **14/1** Noon (IRE) (7/1-16/1), **25/1** Mindrace, Musical Heights (IRE), Toe Tappin Music (USA), **33/1** Poppy My Love, May Queen Megan, CSF £10.06 TOTE £2.90: £1.20 £1.40 £9.30 (£5.80) Trio £262.60 OWNER Dandelion Distribution Ltd (COMPTON) BRED G. Syvrett 11 Rn 61.2 secs (2.60) SF: 36/35/20/14/11/5/-/-/-/-/-

STEWARDS' ENQUIRY Batteate susp. 25-27/10/95 (excessive use of whip).

4133

LEVY BOARD RATING RELATED MAIDEN LIMITED STKS (0-60) (2-Y.O) (Class F) £3,149.00 (£874.00: £419.00)
6f Stalls: Low GOING minus 0.21 sec per fur (GF) 3-15 (3-19)

3982 14 **Beas River (IRE) (60)***(78) (WRMuir)* 2-9-0 WWoods(2) (hdwy over 2f out: led 1f out: rdn out)— **1**
3651 9 Bells of Holland **(59)***(65)*(Fav)*(BWHills)* 2-8-9 RHills(4) (hld up: nt clr run over 1f out: swtchd rt: hrd rdn: unable qckn)....3 **2**
3314 6 Silver Harrow **(60)***(63) (SirMarkPrescott)* 2-9-0 CNutter(6) (led over 4f: hrd rdn: one pce).....2½ **3**
3721 12 It's A Ripper **(57)***(61)*(Fav)*(GLewis)* 2-9-0 SWhitworth(3) (hdwy over 1f out: nvr nrr)....¾ **4**
3915 5 Corniche Quest (IRE) **(53)***(56) (MRChannon)* 2-8-9 JFEgan(9) (a.p: led wl over 1f out to 1f out: btn ins fnl f)....nk **5**
3267 7 Classic Daisy **(56)***(49) (MissGayKelleway)* 2-8-9v RCochrane(7) (b.hind: a.p: ev ch over 1f out: sn wknd)....2½ **6**
3533 14 Island Victory **(47)***(50) (IABalding)* 2-8-9v(5) DGriffiths(12) (lw: hld up: rdn over 2f out: wknd over 1f out)....1½ **7**
3869 11 Daffodil Express (IRE) **(59)***(44) (MJRyan)* 2-8-9 AClark(1) (hdwy over 2f out: wknd over 1f out)....nk **8**
3675 13 Malice Corner **(45)***(40) (LGCottrell)* 2-9-0 JQuinn(5) (nvr nr to chal)....3½ **9**
3670 16 So Select **(45)***(31) (APJarvis)* 2-8-9 JTate(10) (lw: prom 3f)....1½ **10**
3671 6 Distinctlyfoster's (IRE) **(48)***(25) (MJohnston)* 2-8-9 JWeaver(15) (a bhd)....2 **11**
3767 13 Boston Tea Party **(45)***(19) (AMoore)* 2-8-9 CandyMorris(8) (bhd fnl 2f)....2½ **12**
2047 5 Jemsilverthorn (IRE) **(52)***(22) (JJBridger)* 2-9-0 NAdams(14) (outpcd)....½ **13**
3895 10 Baroness Blixen **(56)***(16) (DJGMurraySmith)* 2-8-9 TQuinn(13) (outpcd)....½ **14**
2259 W Trickledown **(60)***(12) (MartynWane)* 2-8-9 RPrice(11) (spd over 2f)....1½ **15**
1981 10 Red Sky Delight (IRE) **(51)** *(PButler)* 2-8-2 (7) GMitchell(16) (outpcd)....6 **16**

7/2 It's A Ripper (5/2-4/1), Bells of Holland, **13/2** Silver Harrow (4/1-7/1), **7/1** BEAS RIVER (IRE), **15/2** Trickledown, **8/1** Corniche Quest (IRE), **12/1** Classic Daisy (6/1-14/1), **14/1** Distinctlyfoster's (IRE), **16/1** Baroness Blixen, Daffodil Express (IRE), So Select, **20/1** Island Victory, **33/1** Jemsilverthorn (IRE), Malice Corner, Boston Tea Party, Red Sky Delight (IRE), CSF £33.88 TOTE £9.40: £2.00 £2.20 £2.50 (£27.30) Trio £60.90 OWNER Mr A. J. de V Patrick (LAMBOURN) BRED Mrs Carole Douglas 16 Rn 1m 13.8 (2.10) SF: 51/38/36/34/29/22/23/17/13/4/-/-/-/-/-/-
OFFICIAL EXPLANATION Beas River: had run badly on his previous run at Warwick due to getting upset in the stalls and not settling.

4134

HERSTMONCEUX LIMITED STKS (0-70) (3-Y.O+) (Class E) £3,731.20 (£1,117.60: £536.80: £246.40) **6f** Stalls: Low GOING minus 0.21 sec per fur (GF) 3-45 (3-48)

3874 * **Oare Sparrow (70)***(77)*(Fav)*(PTWalwyn)* 5-8-12 JWeaver(15) (mde virtually all: rdn over 1f out: r.o wl)....— **1**
3771 3 Stoppes Brow **(68)***(77) (GLMoore)* 3-9-1v SWhitworth(9) (swtchd rt s: hdwy over 2f out: ev ch over 1f out: unable qckn)....1¾ **2**
3929 6 Balance of Power **(67)***(71) (RAkehurst)* 3-8-12b TQuinn(13) (b: hld up: hrd rdn over 1f out: one pce)....1¼ **3**
4057 8 Prima Silk **(67)***(70) (MJRyan)* 4-9-1 AClark(3) (racd stands' side: hld up: hrd rdn over 1f out: one pce)....¾ **4**
1832 15 Efra **(68)***(68) (RHannon)* 6-9-0 SRaymont(14) (bit bkwd: hdwy over 1f out: one pce)....½ **5**
4057 4 Leigh Crofter **(70)***(67) (PDCundell)* 6-9-0b WNewnes(1) (racd stands' side: a.p: hrd rdn over 2f out: one pce)....hd **6**
3981 3 Mistress Thames **(64)***(60) (JRFanshawe)* 3-8-7 DHarrison(8) (racd stands' side: hrd rdn & hdwy over 1f out: nvr nrr)....¾ **7**
2923 5 Tyrone Flyer **(47)***(63) (CNAllen)* 6-9-0 GBardwell(16) (w wnr 4f)....1 **8**
3822 10 Bangles **(70)***(59) (LordHuntingdon)* 5-8-7 (5) MHenry(12) (hld up: hrd rdn over 1f out: wknd)...¾ **9**
3961 6 Invocation **(56)***(50) (AMoore)* 8-8-9 (5) DaneO'Neill(2) (b.nr hind: racd stands' side: prom 4f)....4 **10**
4035 18 Spectacle Jim **(47)***(49) (JO'Donoghue)* 6-9-0v MPerrett(7) (a bhd)....½ **11**
3681 4 Jobie **(64)***(42) (BWHills)* 5-9-0 JReid(5) (racd stands' side: a bhd)....2½ **12**
3637 18 Mousehole **(69)***(34) (RGuest)* 3-9-1 RCochrane(4) (racd stands' side: prom over 3f)....4 **13**
3874 13 Norling (IRE) **(53)***(18) (KOCunningham-Brown)* 5-9-3 MWigham(10) (a bhd)....6 **14**
3681 20 Tiheros **(57)***(15) (JCPoulton)* 3-8-12b AMorris(11) (a bhd)....nk **15**
3874 15 Barriyah **(54)***(2) (HThomsonJones)* 3-8-7 RHills(6) (lw: racd stands' side: bhd fnl 3f)....3 **16**

100/30 OARE SPARROW, **6/1** Leigh Crofter, **13/2** Efra, **7/1** Bangles, Jobie, **9/1** Mousehole, **12/1** Stoppes Brow (op 8/1), Balance of Power, Prima Silk, **14/1** Invocation, Mistress Thames (10/1-16/1), **20/1** Spectacle Jim, Tyrone Flyer, Barriyah, **25/1** Norling (IRE), Tiheros, CSF £47.41 TOTE £3.40: £2.30 £6.10 £3.60 (£45.20) Trio £280.40 OWNER Mrs Henry Keswick (LAMBOURN) BRED Mrs Henry Keswick 16 Rn 1m 13.1 (1.40) SF: 59/57/51/52/50/49/40/45/41/32/31/24/14/-/-/-
WEIGHT FOR AGE 3yo-2lb

4135 LEEDS AMATEUR H'CAP (0-75) (3-Y.O+) (Class G) £2,243.00 (£618.00: £293.00) **1m 4f** Stalls: Low GOING: 0.17 sec per fur (G) 4-15 (4-16)

4022[2] **Minnesota Viking (55)***(69)*(Fav)*(LadyHerries)* 4-10-6 (3) MrPPritchard-Gordon(12) (3rd st: led wl over 1f out: sn hdd: led ins fnl f: r.o wl) — **1**
3986[2] Soojama (IRE) **(44)***(57) (RMFlower)* 5-9-12 MrRJohnson(3) (hdwy over 3f out: 6th st: led over 1f out tl ins fnl f: unable qckn) 1 **2**
3774[8] All the Joys **(43)***(55) (CACyzer)* 4-9-6 (5)ow1 MissBridgetGatehouse(7) (hdwy over 3f out: 4th st: ev ch over 1f out: one pce) hd **3**
3959[3] No Pattern **(74)***(81) (GLMoore)* 3-11-2 (5) MrKGoble(15) (lw: hmpd over 8f out: 5th st: rdn over 1f out: one pce) 4 **4**
3657[11] Emma Grimes (IRE) **(38)***(43) (JSMoore)* 4-9-1 (5) MrsSMoore(5) (lost pl over 9f out: rallied over 1f out: one pce) 2 **5**
4022[11] Air Command (BAR) **(49)***(53) (CTNash)* 5-9-12 (5) MrPPhillips(2) (nvr nr to chal) ½ **6**
3710[2] Nordic Mine (IRE) **(47)***(51) (PJHobbs)* 5-9-12 (3) MrsSHobbs(6) (nvr nrr) nk **7**
3384[13] Nothing Doing (IRE) **(38)***(41) (WJMusson)* 6-9-6 MissYHaynes(1) (a mid div) hd **8**
3987[11] Jemima Puddleduck **(45)***(48) (DWPArbuthnot)* 4-9-13 MrsDArbuthnot(13) (b.hind: hdwy 6f out: led over 2f out tl wl over 1f out: sn wknd) ½ **9**
3710[4] Strat's Legacy **(45)***(46) (DWPArbuthnot)* 8-9-13 MrsAPerrett(14) (nvr nrr) 1¼ **10**
4000[15] Rock The Barney (IRE) **(53)***(50) (PBurgoyne)* 6-10-0 (7) MissMO'Sullivan(4) (lw: nvr nrr) 3 **11**
3627[10] Silver Hunter (USA) **(53)***(49) (GCBravery)* 4-10-2v(5) MrKSantana(9) (lw: led over 9f: 2nd st: wknd wl over 1f out) 1 **12**
3735[3] Hydrofoil **(60)***(52) (BWHills)* 3-10-0 (7) MrCBHills(17) (chsd ldr 6f) 3 **13**
3898[2] Spread The Word **(65)***(41) (LGCottrell)* 3-10-7 (5) MrLJefford(10) (lw: prom 7f) 12 **14**
2177[3] Fattash (USA) **(52)***(27) (RPCHoad)* 3-9-6 (7) MissLMcIntosh(8) (a bhd) nk **15**
4027[5] Precious Wonder **(37)***(7) (PButler)* 6-9-0 (5) MrVLukaniuk(11) (bhd fnl 4f) 4 **16**
3927[13] Disputed Call (USA) **(42)** *(JFfitch-Heyes)* 6-9-10 MrPHenley(16) (bhd fnl 5f) 20 **17**

3/1 MINNESOTA VIKING, **5/1** Soojama (IRE), **6/1** Hydrofoil, **9/1** Nordic Mine (IRE), **10/1** Spread The Word, **12/1** Silver Hunter (USA), Jemima Puddleduck, **14/1** Disputed Call (USA), Fattash (USA) (10/1-16/1), Strat's Legacy, All the Joys, No Pattern (10/1-16/1), **16/1** Rock The Barney (IRE), Nothing Doing (IRE), **25/1** Precious Wonder, Emma Grimes (IRE), **33/1** Air Command (BAR), CSF £20.99 CT £191.81 TOTE £3.90: £1.80 £1.90 £7.80 £2.30 (£16.70) Trio £147.80 OWNER Mr Charles Green (LITTLEHAMPTON) BRED W. H. Joyce 17 Rn

2m 45.0 (13.80) SF: 42/30/28/47/16/26/24/14/21/19/23/22/18/7/-/-/-

WEIGHT FOR AGE 3yo-7lb

4136 HARDRES H'CAP (0-70) (3-Y.O) (Class E) £3,702.60 (£1,108.80: £532.40: £244.20) **1m 1f 149y** Stalls: Low GOING: 0.17 sec per fur (G) 4-45 (4-46)

2804[2] **Dr Edgar (64)***(78) (GWragg)* 3-9-3 FNorton(15) (lw: chsd ldr: led over 2f out: hrd rdn over 1f out: r.o wl) — **1**
3837[F] Battleship Bruce **(61)***(73) (NACallaghan)* 3-8-9 (5) DaneO'Neill(14) (b.hind: lw: 3rd st: chsd wnr over 1f out: r.o) 1 **2**
3629[14] Lidhama (USA) **(58)***(66) (GLewis)* 3-8-11 SWhitworth(11) (5th st: drvn over 1f out: one pce) 2½ **3**
3872[2] Super High **(58)***(62) (PHowling)* 3-8-11 RCochrane(2) (hdwy 3f out: 6th st: rdn over 1f out: one pce) 2½ **4**
3862[13] Santella Boy (USA) **(57)***(58) (GHarwood)* 3-8-10v JQuinn(7) (lw: led 7f: 2nd st: wknd fnl f) 2 **5**
3872[3] Tonka **(60)***(59) (PJMakin)* 3-8-13 SSanders(12) (nvr nr to chal) 1¼ **6**
4047[12] Merit (IRE) **(60)***(58) (PFICole)* 3-8-13 TQuinn(5) (nvr nrr) ½ **7**
3521[12] Victoria's Secret (IRE) **(60)***(57) (DRCElsworth)* 3-8-10b(3) SDrowne(10) (a mid div) ½ **8**
3844[10] Fastini Gold **(54)***(51) (MDIUsher)* 3-8-7 TSprake(4) (lw: nvr nrr) hd **9**
3863[4] Sovereigns Parade **(61)***(58)*(Fav)*(JEBanks)* 3-9-0 JTate(13) (lw: 4th st: wknd over 1f out) s.h **10**
4035[8] Crested Knight (IRE) **(63)***(59) (CAHorgan)* 3-9-2 CRutter(9) (a bhd) ½ **11**
4022[6] Cuban Nights (USA) **(56)***(49) (BJLlewellyn)* 3-8-9 JWeaver(1) (a bhd) 2 **12**
3934* Tribal Peace (IRE) **(68)***(49) (BGubby)* 3-9-2 (5) MHenry(8) (lw: bhd fnl 2f) 7 **13**
3889[2] It'sthebusiness **(58)***(26) (SDow)* 3-8-11 JReid(6) (lw: bhd fnl 3f) 8 **14**
3974[7] Nero Kris **(64)** *(PAKelleway)* 3-9-3 JFEgan(3) (bhd fnl 4f) 25 **15**

3/1 Sovereigns Parade, **9/2** Lidhama (USA) (6/1-7/2), **6/1** Battleship Bruce, **7/1** Super High (op 4/1), **8/1** Merit (IRE) (6/1-10/1), **9/1** Crested Knight (IRE), **10/1** It'sthebusiness (8/1-12/1), **12/1** Tribal Peace (IRE), **14/1** DR EDGAR (op 8/1), Santella Boy (USA), Tonka (10/1-16/1), **20/1** Victoria's Secret (IRE), **33/1** Fastini Gold, Cuban Nights (USA), Nero Kris, CSF £101.44 CT £416.88 TOTE £14.90: £3.80 £2.60 £2.30 (£27.20) Trio £107.30 OWNER Exors of the late Sir Philip Oppenheimer (NEWMARKET) BRED Hascombe and Valiant Studs 15 Rn

2m 5.8 (8.10) SF: 46/41/34/30/26/27/26/25/19/26/27/17/17/-/-

T/Plpt: £1,410.60 (8.08 Tckts). T/Qdpt: £18.40 (4.7 Tckts). AK

3968-PONTEFRACT (L-H)
Monday October 16th (Firm)
WEATHER: overcast WIND: fresh half bhd

4137 BROCKADALE MAIDEN AUCTION STKS (2-Y.O) (Class F) £2,983.00 (£838.00: £409.00) **6f** Stalls: Low GOING minus 0.35 sec per fur (F) 2-00 (2-02)

3869^{2} **Missile** *(68)*(Fav)*(WJHaggas)* 2-8-7 MHills(10) (lw: trckd ldrs: hung rt appr st: led ins fnl f: r.o)........— **1**
3988^{9} Lady Bankes (IRE) *(60) (WGMTurner)* 2-7-9 (7) CAdamson(2) (bhd: c wd st: r.o wl: nrst fin)....1 **2**
3283^{4} Time For Tea (IRE) **(76)***(60) (CACyzer)* 2-8-2 GDuffield(7) (led tl hdd ins fnl f: no ex) ....s.h **3**
3982^{4} Yuppy Girl (IRE) **(61)***(51) (CaptJWilson)* 2-8-2 GCarter(8) (bhd: hdwy ½-wy: hung lft over 1f out: nt qckn ins fnl f) 3½ **4**
3848^{U} People Direct *(43) (KMcAuliffe)* 2-8-7 ow5 MTebbutt(11) (in tch: hung lft wl over 1f out: styd on: no imp)........3 **5**
3975^{9} Mels Baby (IRE) **(45)***(47) (JLEyre)* 2-8-7b RLappin(13) (in tch: styd on fnl 2f: no imp)..........nk **6**
3877^{11} Simply Silly (IRE) **(59)***(34) (WLBarker)* 2-8-2 LCharnock(5) (nvr trbld ldrs) 3 **7**
4100^{9} Efipetite **(47)***(33) (NBycroft)* 2-8-2 SMaloney(4) (swtg: chsd ldrs tl wknd over 1f out)..........½ **8**
Bowlers Boy *(32) (JJQuinn)* 2-8-7 MBirch(9) (wl grwn: chsd ldrs: n.m.r & wknd over 1f out)....2 **9**
4023^{6} Little Pilgrim *(26) (TMJones)* 2-8-7 RPerham(16) (nvr trbld ldrs) 2½ **10**
3587a^{15} Lia Fail (IRE) *(20) (RHollinshead)* 2-8-3 ow1 WRyan(1) (swtg: effrt whn hmpd over 1f out: n.d)nk **11**
3895^{14} Swingalong Girl *(20) (TMJones)* 2-8-2 NCarlisle(6) (b: s.i.s: n.d)..........s.h **12**
3806^{2} Manderella **(72)***(17) (JAkehurst)* 2-8-2 TWilliams(14) (swtg: b.off hind: cl up tl wknd wl over 1f out) 1¼ **13**
3533^{18} Double Vintage (IRE) **(40)***(14) (MCChapman)* 2-8-0b(7) CMunday(12) (sn outpcd & bhd) 3 **14**
Laid Back Lucy *(7) (JAHarris)* 2-8-2 DaleGibson(3) (unf: dwlt: a outpcd & wl bhd)..........½ **15**

1/2 MISSILE, **7/1** Manderella, **9/1** Little Pilgrim (6/1-10/1), **10/1** Yuppy Girl (IRE), **12/1** Lia Fail (IRE), **14/1** Time For Tea (IRE) (op 8/1), **25/1** Lady Bankes (IRE), **33/1** Bowlers Boy, **40/1** People Direct, **50/1** Simply Silly (IRE), **100/1** Laid Back Lucy, Swingalong Girl, Mels Baby (IRE), **200/1** Double Vintage (IRE), Efipetite, CSF £16.81 TOTE £1.50: £1.30 £3.80 £2.40 (£17.70) Trio £107.70 OWNER Mr J. W. Bogie (NEWMARKET) BRED The Duke of Marlborough 15 Rn

1m 17.7 (3.40) SF: 18/10/10/1/-/-/-/-/-/-/-/-/-/-/-

STEWARDS' ENQUIRY Lappin susp. 25-28/10/95 (irresponsible riding).

4138 PACKSADDLE H'CAP (0-70) (3-Y.O+) (Class E) £3,938.00 (£1,184.00: £572.00: £266.00) **1m 2f 6y** Stalls: Low GOING minus 0.35 sec per fur (F) 2-30 (2-33)

4038^{19} **Our Main Man (49)***(62) (RMWhitaker)* 5-8-7 ACulhane(5) (hld up: hdwy 3f out: led over 1f out: r.o wl)..........— **1**
3977^{4} Hawkish (USA) **(51)***(62) (DMorley)* 6-8-9 WCarson(15) (lw: bhd: hdwy 4f out: kpt on fnl f: nt pce to chal)..........1¼ **2**
3993^{12} Unprejudice **(62)***(73) (MDHammond)* 4-9-6 MTebbutt(9) (in tch: hdwy 2f out: styd on wl).......hd **3**
3818^{9} Benjamins Law **(44)***(52) (JAPickering)* 4-8-2 RLappin(16) (led tl hdd over 1f out: one pce) 2 **4**
4061^{2} Curtelace **(57)***(64)*(Fav)*(LadyHerries)* 5-9-1b KDarley(4) (hld up: effrt appr st: n.m.r & nvr rchd ldrs)..........½ **5**
3718^{11} Manful **(59)***(65) (JHetherton)* 3-8-12 NKennedy(2) (chsd ldr tl wknd fnl 2f)..........¾ **6**
3977^{5} Essayeffsee **(56)***(58) (MrsMReveley)* 6-9-0 NConnorton(17) (lw: hld up: effrt on ins 2f out: nt clr run over 1f out: n.d)..........2½ **7**
3852^{10} No Comebacks **(60)***(60) (EJAlston)* 7-9-4 KFallon(13) (swtg: hld up & bhd: effrt 4f out: nvr able chal)..........1 **8**
3860^{6} Prince of Spades **(60)***(58) (CACyzer)* 3-8-13 WRyan(18) (nvr trbld ldrs)..........1¼ **9**
4043^{3} Broughton's Pride (IRE) **(49)***(45) (JAGlover)* 4-8-0 (7) VictoriaAppleby(6) (nvr nr to chal) 1¼ **10**
3677^{8} South Eastern Fred **(51)***(46) (HJCollingridge)* 4-8-9 MRimmer(11) (chsd ldrs tl wknd 2f out)....1 **11**
4079^{8} Avishayes (USA) **(45)***(38) (MrsMReveley)* 8-8-3 LCharnock(19) (lw: dwlt: effrt 4f out: n.d).......1 **12**
3685^{20} Dancing Destiny **(57)***(49) (RBastiman)* 3-8-10 DeanMcKeown(1) (hld up: n.m.r 2f out: n.d) ....¾ **13**
3987^{5} Pine Essence (USA) **(51)***(39) (JLEyre)* 4-8-9 TWilliams(8) (hdwy ½-wy: wknd over 2f out) ...2½ **14**
3659^{5} Beaumont (IRE) **(59)***(45) (JEBanks)* 5-9-0 (3) JStack(14) (in tch tl wknd over 3f out) 1¼ **15**
3977^{8} Museum (IRE) **(68)***(53) (DNicholls)* 4-9-12 AlexGreaves(7) (lw: chsd ldr tl wknd over 3f out) .nk **16**
2090^{7} Horsetrader **(48)***(14) (BPJBaugh)* 3-7-8 (7) IonaWands(3) (b: b.off hind: bhd fr ½-wy) 12 **17**

3/1 Curtelace, **7/2** Hawkish (USA), **6/1** Beaumont (IRE), **9/1** Broughton's Pride (IRE), **10/1** Essayeffsee, **12/1** No Comebacks, **14/1** Pine Essence (USA), **16/1** Avishayes (USA), Prince of Spades, **20/1** Museum (IRE), South Eastern Fred, **25/1** Dancing Destiny, Benjamins Law, **33/1** Unprejudice, Manful, **50/1** OUR MAIN MAN, **100/1** Horsetrader, CSF £215.02 CT £5,476.86 TOTE £70.30: £11.00 £1.50 £8.00 £4.40 (£84.40) Trio £703.90 OWNER Mr Christopher Cooke (LEEDS) BRED Pinfold Stud and Farms Ltd 17 Rn

2m 12.3 (4.00) SF: 33/33/44/23/35/31/29/31/24/16/17/9/15/10/16/24/-

WEIGHT FOR AGE 3yo-5lb

4139 TOTE SILVER TANKARD STKS (Listed) (2-Y.O) (Class A) £13,016.00 (£4,844.00: £2,347.00: £985.00)
1m 4y Stalls: Low GOING minus 0.35 sec per fur (F) 3-00 (3-00)

4001* **Weet-A-Minute (IRE) (90)**(101) (RHollinshead) 2-9-0 KFallon(4) (bhd: rdn & hdwy over 2f out: led appr fnl f: hung lft: r.o)...— 1
3968* Warbrook **(84)**(93) (IABalding) 2-8-11 WRyan(1) (chsd ldrs: effrt 3f out: styd on fnl f: nt pce to chal)...2½ 2
3600² Mushahid (USA) **(100)**(93)(Fav)(JLDunlop) 2-9-0 WCarson(6) (lw: led tl hdd appr fnl f: no ex)...1¾ 3
3746⁸ Kala Sunrise **(75)**(89?) (CSmith) 2-8-11 KDarley(3) (bhd: styd on fnl 2f: nvr able chal)...nk 4
3928⁴ Carmentalia **(82)**(68) (SirMarkPrescott) 2-8-6 GDuffield(5) (chsd ldrs tl outpcd fnl 2f)...8 5
3994* Prince of My Heart **(85)**(68) (BWHills) 2-8-11 PatEddery(2) (w ldr tl wknd appr fnl f)...2½ 6

4/6 Mushahid (USA), **4/1** WEET-A-MINUTE (IRE), **5/1** Prince of My Heart, **10/1** Carmentalia, **11/1** Warbrook (op 7/1), **100/1** Kala Sunrise, CSF £36.76 TOTE £4.10: £1.80 £3.80 (£33.70) OWNER Ed Weetman (Haulage & Storage) Ltd (UPPER LONGDON) BRED Cyclades Farming Co 6 Rn
1m 43.5 (1.50) SF: 56/48/48/44/23/23

4140 BLUFF COVE H'CAP (0-70) (3-Y.O+) (Class E) £3,574.00 (£1,072.00: £516.00: £238.00) **2m 1f 216y** Stalls: Low GOING minus 0.35 sec per fur (F) 3-30 (3-32)

3971¹¹ **Alcian Blue (40)**(55) (MDHammond) 4-8-6 (3) PMcCabe(6) (lw: a.p: hdwy to ld wl over 1f out: styd on wl)...— 1
4099* Sea Victor **(72)**(87) (JLHarris) 3-10-1 5x KDarley(4) (lw: cl up: led 2f out: sn hdd: styd on wl towards fin)...hd 2
3971³ Greek Night Out (IRE) **(37)**(50) (JLEyre) 4-8-3 (3) NVarley(9) (in tch: effrt 3f out: styd on: nt pce to chal)...2 3
3936¹¹ Record Lover (IRE) **(24)**(36) (MCChapman) 5-7-7 NKennedy(1) (led tl hdd 2f out: one pce).1¼ 4
3971⁶ Moonshine Dancer **(39)**(50) (MrsMReveley) 5-8-8 ACulhane(7) (lw: hld up: stdy hdwy 4f out: effrt over 2f out: no rspnse)...1¼ 5
3971* Arian Spirit (IRE) **(38)**(41)(Fav)(JLEyre) 4-8-7 LCharnock(5) (effrt 4f out: no imp)...9 6
3986¹⁰ Flashman **(38)**(39) (BJLlewellyn) 5-8-7 TWilliams(10) (cl up: hrd drvn 4f out: wknd 3f out)....1¾ 7
3641⁹ New Inn **(53)**(53)(Fav)(SGollings) 4-9-8 WCarson(8) (chsd ldrs tl rdn & wknd fnl 3f)...1¾ 8
3971¹⁷ Crowther Homes **(38)** (EJAlston) 5-8-7 ow4 KFallon(2) (plld hrd: sddle slipped & p.u after 3f)..... P
295⁹ Mrs Jawleyford (USA) **(43)** (CSmith) 7-8-12 GDuffield(3) (Withdrawn not under Starter's orders: lame at s)... W

4/1 Arian Spirit (IRE), New Inn, **9/2** Sea Victor, **5/1** Greek Night Out (IRE), **11/2** Flashman, **7/1** Moonshine Dancer, **16/1** Record Lover (IRE), **25/1** ALCIAN BLUE, **50/1** Mrs Jawleyford (USA), **66/1** Crowther Homes, CSF £120.52 CT £600.39 TOTE £23.80: £3.80 £1.90 £1.60 (£39.10) Trio £95.60 OWNER Rykneld Thoroughbred Co Ltd (MIDDLEHAM) BRED Rykneld Thoroughbred Co Ltd 9 Rn
3m 59.7 (7.70) SF: 33/53/28/14/28/19/17/31/-/-
WEIGHT FOR AGE 3yo-12lb

4141 BROOMFIELD NURSERY H'CAP (0-75) (2-Y.O) (Class E) £3,990.00 (£1,200.00: £580.00: £270.00)
1m 4y Stalls: Low GOING minus 0.35 sec per fur (F) 4-00 (4-02)

4111² **Ancestral Jane (63)**(74+)(Fav)(MrsJRRamsden) 2-9-0 KFallon(10) (hld up & bhd: hdwy 2f out: str run fnl f to ld wl ins fnl f)...— 1
3639⁸ Tarry **(55)**(63) (CNWilliams) 2-8-6b GCarter(7) (swtg: in tch: effrt 2f out: styd on: nt pce of wnr)1½ 2
3867¹⁸ Angel Chimes **(70)**(77) (JEBanks) 2-9-4 (3) JStack(3) (chsd ldrs: led appr fnl f: hdd & no ex towards fin)...½ 3
3850* Eric's Bett **(68)**(72) (MrsSMAustin) 2-8-12 (7) DDenby(5) (b: a.p: effrt 3f out: styd on one pce)1¾ 4
3937⁷ Lawnswood Captain (IRE) **(57)**(45) (RHollinshead) 2-8-1 (7)ow6 FLynch(9) (prom: effrt over 2f out: styd on one pce)...5 5
3468¹⁰ Saturiba (USA) **(47)**(39) (MJohnston) 2-7-12 TWilliams(16) (led & sn clr: hdd appr fnl f: sn btn)...1 6
3760⁹ Down The Yard **(48)**(39) (MCChapman) 2-7-13 NKennedy(17) (in tch: effrt 3f out: no imp).....½ 7
3975⁵ Lucky Bea **(48)**(38) (MWEasterby) 2-7-6 (7) MartinDwyer(6) (prom: rdn over 2f out: one pce) .nk 8
3858⁴ My Kind **(59)**(41) (KMcAuliffe) 2-8-10 JCarroll(11) (bhd: sme hdwy fnl 2f: n.d)...4 9
3881⁸ Alzotic (IRE) **(58)**(39) (SGNorton) 2-8-9 NConnorton(13) (hld up & plld hrd: nvr nr to chal) .....¾ 10
3850⁶ Cry Baby **(55)**(31) (NTinkler) 2-8-6 LCharnock(19) (dwlt: hdwy ½-wy: wknd 2f out)...2½ 11
3937⁴ Rattle **(54)**(29) (JJO'Neill) 2-8-5 SDWilliams(2) (chsd ldrs tl wknd fnl 2f)...hd 12
3809¹⁰ Aztec Flyer (USA) **(58)**(33) (MrsMReveley) 2-8-9 DeanMcKeown(14) (bhd fr ½-wy)...nk 13
3721¹⁵ Briganoone **(45)**(16) (SRBowring) 2-7-10 NCarlisle(1) (hld up & plld hrd: a bhd)...2 14

3975[2] Mister Joel **(58)***(28) (MWEasterby)* 2-8-9 SMaloney(4) (lw: plld v.hrd: n.d)....nk **15**
4001[11] Mysterious Times **(50)***(20) (BWMurray)* 2-7-10 (5) PFessey(18) (lw: bhd & drvn along: n.d) ....nk **16**
3502[11] Dispol Conqueror (IRE) **(50)***(6) (GROldroyd)* 2-7-12v(3) NVarley(12) (in tch 5f) 7 **17**
3720[6] Fiddes (IRE) **(55)***(6) (JLDunlop)* 2-8-6 WCarson(20) (s.i.s: a bhd)....2½ **18**

5/2 ANCESTRAL JANE, **8/1** Tarry, Angel Chimes, **9/1** Fiddes (IRE), Alzotic (IRE), **11/1** Mister Joel, **12/1** My Kind, **14/1** Eric's Bett, **20/1** Saturiba (USA), Lucky Bea, Aztec Flyer (USA), **25/1** Down The Yard, Lawnswood Captain (IRE), **33/1** Briganoone, Rattle, **40/1** Cry Baby, **50/1** Mysterious Times, Dispol Conqueror (IRE), CSF £22.28 CT £134.88 TOTE £2.80: £1.20 £2.30 £2.40 £2.10 (£15.40) Trio £64.40 OWNER Mr Paul Locke (THIRSK) 18 Rn

1m 47.0 (5.00) SF: 22/11/25/20/-/-/-/-/-/-/-/-/-/-/-/-/-/-

4142 STAPLETON H'CAP (0-80) (3-Y.O+) (Class D) £4,565.00(£1,370.00: £660.00: £305.00) 5f Stalls: Low GOING minus 0.35 sec per fur (F) 4-30 (4-32)

4040[8] **Statius (75)***(83) (TDBarron)* 3-9-10 DeanMcKeown(5) (lw: trckd ldrs: led ins fnl f: r.o) ....— **1**
3992[15] Stuffed **(55)***(61) (MWEasterby)* 3-8-4 GDuffield(3) (lw: chsd ldrs: hdwy to chal ins fnl f: nt qckn)....¾ **2**
3905* Squire Corrie **(66)***(69) (JEBanks)* 3-8-12b(3) JStack(7) (cl up: led over 2f out tl ins fnl f: kpt on)¾ **3**
3992[19] Allyana (IRE) **(69)***(68) (IABalding)* 3-9-4 KDarley(6) (in tch: gd hdwy over 2f out: sn chsng ldrs: kpt on one pce fnl f)....1¼ **4**
4068[16] Densben **(55)***(53) (DenysSmith)* 11-8-5 ow1 KFallon(11) (bhd tl hdwy 2f out: r.o towards fin)..s.h **5**
3992[7] Jucea **(63)***(59) (JLSpearing)* 6-8-13 PatEddery(4) (mid div: hdwy u.p ½-wy: nt qckn appr fnl f) 1 **6**
4068[7] Bells of Longwick **(54)***(47) (WWHaigh)* 6-8-4v DaleGibson(12) (nvr bttr than mid div) ....¾ **7**
3992[2] Chadwell Hall **(60)***(42)*(Fav)*(SRBowring)* 4-8-5b(5) CTeague(1) (w ldrs tl wknd 1f out) 3½ **8**
1900[7] Two Moves in Front (IRE) **(64)***(45) (JBerry)* 5-9-0 GCarter(10) (bhd tl sme late hdwy) ....½ **9**
4113[6] Lochon **(56)***(27) (JLEyre)* 4-8-6v RLappin(8) (led tl hdd over 2f out: wknd) 3 **10**
3905[8] Baileys Sunset (IRE) **(59)***(27) (MJohnston)* 3-8-8 TWilliams(17) (s.i.s: sn drvn along: n.d) 1 **11**
3874[2] Petraco (IRE) **(66)***(34) (NASmith)* 7-9-2 SDWilliams(13) (mid div: drvn along ½-wy: no imp).s.h **12**
3777[2] Indiahra **(50)***(12) (RHollinshead)* 4-8-0 NCarlisle(9) (dwlt: n.d)....1¾ **13**
3950[6] Sir Tasker **(57)***(18) (JLHarris)* 7-8-4 (3) PMcCabe(15) (nvr wnt pce) ....nk **14**
2748[6] Magic Pearl **(72)***(14) (EJAlston)* 5-9-8 ACulhane(16) (chsd ldrs 3f: sn lost pl)....6 **15**
3878[9] Giggleswick Girl **(63)** *(MRChannon)* 4-8-13 LCharnock(2) (lost tch fr ½-wy & eased: sddle slipped) 15 **16**

7/2 Chadwell Hall, **11/2** Jucea, **6/1** Squire Corrie, **8/1** Allyana (IRE), STATIUS, **9/1** Petraco (IRE), **11/1** Stuffed, **12/1** Lochon, **14/1** Bells of Longwick, Indiahra, Giggleswick Girl, **20/1** Densben, **25/1** Sir Tasker, Magic Pearl, Baileys Sunset (IRE), **40/1** Two Moves in Front (IRE), CSF £95.14 CT £536.64 TOTE £13.10: £3.40 £3.20 £2.20 £2.30 (£72.90) Trio £252.30 OWNER Mr Alex Gorrie (THIRSK) BRED Will Edmeades Bloodstock 16 Rn

62.4 secs (0.90) SF: 64/42/50/49/35/41/29/24/27/9/8/16/-/-/-/-

WEIGHT FOR AGE 3yo-1lb

OFFICIAL EXPLANATION Giggleswick Girl: her saddle had slipped soon after the start.

T/Jkpt: Not won; £14,352.21 to Chepstow 17/10/95. T/Plpt: £317.30 (59.3 Tckts). T/Qdpt: £48.30 (2.2 Tckts). AA

4051-CHEPSTOW (L-H)
Tuesday October 17th (Soft)

WEATHER: rain becoming bright later WIND: slt half against

4143 PAT EDDERY 200-IN-A-SEASON MAIDEN STKS (I) (2-Y.O) (Class D) £3,855.25 (£1,162.00: £563.50: £264.25) 1m 14y Stalls: High GOING: 0.43 sec per fur (GS) 1-30 (1-32)

Classic Eagle *(85?) (SCWilliams)* 2-9-0 AMackay(4) (w'like: mde all: clr 3f out: rdn & hld on wl cl home)....— **1**
Smilin N Wishin (USA) *(79?) (PWChapple-Hyam)* 2-8-9 JReid(1) (lt-f: unf: hld up: rdn to chse wnr appr fnl f: r.o wl nr fin)....¾ **2**
3890[4] Clemente *(58) (RHannon)* 2-8-9 (5) DaneO'Neill(5) (swtg: prom: rdn over 2f out: wknd fnl f)...13 **3**
2995[3] Faateq *(58)*(Fav)*(JLDunlop)* 2-9-0 WCarson(3) (bit bkwd: chsd wnr fr ½-wy: rdn & wknd over 1f out)....hd **4**
Kissing Gate (USA) *(47) (RCharlton)* 2-8-9 TQuinn(10) (leggy: wl bhd tl styd on fnl 3f) 3 **5**
3994[5] Society Magic (USA) *(22)*(Fav)*(IABalding)* 2-9-0 PatEddery(9) (hld up & plld hrd: swtchd lft over 3f out: wknd over 2f out: t.o)....15 **6**
2924[10] Topaglow (IRE) **(45)***(10) (PTDalton)* 2-9-0 RCochrane(2) (stdd s: plld hrd: a in rr: t.o)....6 **7**
Beacontree *(7) (MJohnston)* 2-9-0 JWeaver(8) (w'like: leggy: swtg: prom: rdn over 3f out: sn btn: t.o) 1½ **8**
4045[10] Forliando **(58)***(7) (MSSaunders)* 2-9-0b JFEgan(6) (rdn along 5f out: sn bhd: t.o)....s.h **9**

3883[15] Ruby Two Shoes *(BRMillman)* 2-8-9 JWilliams(11) (sn wl bhd: t.o) 1 **10**
3868[20] Mushtak (USA) *(MajorWRHern)* 2-9-0 RHills(7) (sn wl bhd: t.o) 4 **11**

4/1 Society Magic (USA), Faateq (op 5/2), **5/1** Smilin N Wishin (USA) (op 5/2), Beacontree, CLASSIC EAGLE, **7/1** Clemente, **8/1** Kissing Gate (USA) (op 5/1), **16/1** Mushtak (USA), **33/1** Ruby Two Shoes, **50/1** Forliando, Topaglow (IRE), CSF £30.23 TOTE £7.20: £1.90 £1.70 £1.70 (£33.90) Trio £108.60 OWNER Classic Bloodstock Plc (NEWMARKET) BRED A. B. Phipps 11 Rn

1m 40.2 (7.70) SF: 52/46/25/25/14/-/-/-/-/-/-

4144 COPSE NURSERY H'CAP (0-75) (2-Y.O) (Class E) £3,415.00 (£1,030.00: £500.00: £235.00) **6f 16y** Stalls: High GOING: 0.43 sec per fur (GS) 2-00 (2-03)

3947[9] **Erupt (66)***(73) (GBBalding)* 2-8-12v JWilliams(20) (lw: hld up: hdwy over 2f out: led fnl 100y: r.o wl) ....— **1**
3639[13] Itsinthepost **(60)***(65) (MJohnston)* 2-8-6 JWeaver(4) (led 1f: rdn & ev ch ins fnl f: r.o) ....¾ **2**
3893[3] Mrs McBadger **(64)***(68) (BSmart)* 2-8-10 SSanders(1) (a.p: led over 1f out tl ins fnl f) ....nk **3**
3969[4] Vera's First (IRE) **(69)***(67)*(Fav)*(GLewis)* 2-9-1b SWhitworth(15) (bhd: gd hdwy 1f out: fin wl)2½ **4**
2674[9] Mystic Tempo (USA) **(75)***(71) (PWChapple-Hyam)* 2-9-7 JReid(18) (chsd ldrs: rdn bel dist: one pce) ....½ **5**
3947[7] Jaleel **(72)***(60) (RHannon)* 2-8-13b(5) DaneO'Neill(19) (lw: hdwy 2f out: nt rch ldrs) 3 **6**
4025[4] Careful (IRE) **(62)***(50) (BWHills)* 2-8-8 RHills(9) (swtchd lft & hdwy bel dist: nvr nrr) ....hd **7**
3892[12] Midnight Cookie **(56)***(39) (BAPearce)* 2-8-2 ow1 BDoyle(8) (in tch: no hdwy fnl 2f) 1½ **8**
3749[8] Croeso Cynnes **(62)***(42) (BPalling)* 2-8-8v TSprake(3) (b: led after 1f tl over 1f out: sn wknd) ..¾ **9**
3988[8] Members Welcome (IRE) **(60)***(38) (PGMurphy)* 2-7-13 (7)ow1 RWaterfield(7) (prom over 4f) ...hd **10**
3915[9] Time Clash (IRE) **(68)***(47) (BPalling)* 2-8-9 (5) MHenry(12) (b: a in rr) ....nk **11**
3423[8] Prime Partner **(66)***(41) (WRMuir)* 2-8-12 WWoods(6) (rdn over 2f out: sn bhd) 1¼ **12**
3625[15] Quiet Moments (IRE) **(55)***(28) (PGMurphy)* 2-8-1 NAdams(17) (a in rr) ....¾ **13**
3990[5] Vax New Way **(65)***(17) (JLSpearing)* 2-8-8 (3) SDrowne(5) (plld hrd: chsd ldrs far side 4f: sn wknd: t.o) 8 **14**
1443[4] Mono Lady (IRE) **(60)***(9) (DHaydnJones)* 2-8-6 AMackay(16) (prom stands' side over 3f: sn lost tch: t.o) 1¼ **15**
3870[7] Delaunay (IRE) **(66)***(4) (RHannon)* 2-8-12b JFEgan(13) (prom tl lost pl over 2f out: t.o) 4 **16**
3969[10] Impeccable **(66)** *(JLDunlop)* 2-8-12 PatEddery(11) (prom over 3f: sn wknd: t.o) 7 **17**
3969[13] Burj **(54)** *(NAGraham)* 2-8-0b WCarson(14) (lw: prom over 3f: sn wknd & eased: t.o) 10 **18**
2857[2] Saint Rosalina **(61)** *(CJHill)* 2-8-7c DHarrison(10) (eyecover: swtg: w ldrs 3f: sn wknd: t.o)......8 **19**

13/2 Vera's First (IRE), **7/1** Itsinthepost, Croeso Cynnes, **8/1** Careful (IRE), **10/1** Vax New Way, Impeccable (op 6/1), **12/1** Burj (8/1-14/1), **14/1** ERUPT, Jaleel (op 8/1), Mystic Tempo (USA) (op 8/1), **16/1** Mrs McBadger, **20/1** Saint Rosalina, Delaunay (IRE), **25/1** Prime Partner, Mono Lady (IRE), Time Clash (IRE), Members Welcome (IRE), **33/1** Midnight Cookie, **50/1** Quiet Moments (IRE), CSF £104.06 CT £1,474.50 TOTE £14.90: £3.80 £1.80 £8.20 £1.70 (£22.60) Trio £485.50 OWNER Mr P. Richardson (ANDOVER) BRED Dodford Stud 19 Rn

1m 18.1 (9.10) SF: 5/-/-/-/3/-/-/-/-/-/-/-/-/-/-/-/-/-/-

4145 RICHARD HOLDER H'CAP (0-85) (3-Y.O+) (Class D) £4,173.75 (£1,260.00: £612.50: £288.75) **6f 16y** Stalls: High GOING: 0.43 sec per fur (GS) 2-30 (2-33)

4068[5] **Bajan Rose (71)***(77) (MBlanshard)* 3-8-12 RCochrane(13) (a.p: led 3f out: sn clr: rdn fnl f: jst hld on) ....— **1**
4057* Tinker Osmaston **(72)***(78) (MSSaunders)* 4-9-1 7x JFEgan(17) (lw: hdwy bel dist: str chal nr fin: jst failed) ....s.h **2**
3972* Fantasy Racing (IRE) **(80)***(86) (MRChannon)* 3-9-7 DHarrison(2) (hld up: hdwy wl over 1f out: hung rt fnl f: fin strly) ....s.h **3**
3943[9] Anzio (IRE) **(73)***(75) (BAPearce)* 4-9-2b TIves(6) (b: mde most to ½-wy: r.o one pce fnl f).....1½ **4**
3964[6] Montserrat **(70)***(71) (LGCottrell)* 3-8-11 MFenton(11) (lw: a.p: kpt on u.p ins fnl f) ....½ **5**
3715[15] Q Factor **(70)***(69) (DHaydnJones)* 3-8-11 AMackay(18) (lw: a.p: rdn over 1f out: r.o one pce) ¾ **6**
4040[9] Champagne Grandy **(81)***(79) (MRChannon)* 5-9-5 (5) PPMurphy(4) (b.nr hind: hdwy 2f out: rdn & r.o wl fnl f) ....nk **7**
4040[11] How's Yer Father **(79)***(71) (RJHodges)* 9-9-8 JWeaver(20) (hdwy 2f out: rdn & edgd lft: kpt on fnl f) 2 **8**
4125[6] Dancing Heart **(70)***(52) (BJMeehan)* 3-8-11 BDoyle(5) (swtg: hdwy ½-wy: eased whn btn ins fnl f) 4 **9**
4033[10] Sir Joey (USA) **(82)***(63) (PGMurphy)* 6-9-11 JWilliams(8) (lw: dwlt: a in rr) ....½ **10**
4033[8] Macfarlane **(73)***(51) (MJFetherston-Godley)* 7-9-2 JReid(7) (lw: b: outpcd) 1 **11**
3813[9] Chickawicka (IRE) **(85)***(61) (MCPipe)* 4-9-9v(5) LNewton(1) (w ldrs: sn rdn along: wknd over 2f out) ....¾ **12**
3981* Intiaash (IRE) **(75)***(44) (PTWalwyn)* 3-9-2 WCarson(3) (prom 4f) 2½ **13**

4068[24] Mister Jolson **(78)***(43) (RJHodges)* 6-9-4 (3) SDrowne(15) (lw: rdn along ½-wy: sn bhd) 1¾ **14**
4068[11] Sue Me (IRE) **(71)***(36) (WRMuir)* 3-8-12 WWoods(12) (chsd ldrs stands' side 4f)...................hd **15**
3943[11] La Petite Fusee **(71)***(32)*(Fav)*(RJO'Sullivan)* 4-9-0 AClark(14) (prom stands' side over 3f) ...1¼ **16**
3964[21] Nawaasi **(72)***(15) (HThomsonJones)* 3-8-13 RHills(9) (a bhd: t.o) 7 **17**
3929[5] Actual Fact (USA) **(82)***(23) (GHarwood)* 3-9-9 PatEddery(10) (lw: prom over 3f: wknd qckly fnl 2f: t.o) .....½ **18**
3750[2] Ffynone (IRE) **(73)***(14) (RHannon)* 3-8-9 (5) DaneO'Neill(16) (a bhd: t.o) ....nk **19**
3992[18] Robellion **(67)** *(DWPArbuthnot)* 4-8-10v TQuinn(19) (a bhd & outpcd: t.o) 3 **20**

7/1 La Petite Fusee, **8/1** How's Yer Father, Actual Fact (USA), **10/1** Intiaash (IRE), Sir Joey (USA), **12/1** Montserrat, **14/1** BAJAN ROSE, Tinker Osmaston (10/1-20/1), Sue Me (IRE), Macfarlane, **16/1** Ffynone (IRE), Chickawicka (IRE), Fantasy Racing (IRE), **20/1** Robellion, Anzio (IRE), Nawaasi, Champagne Grandy, Mister Jolson, **25/1** Q Factor, Dancing Heart, CSF £189.94 CT £2,887.09 TOTE £18.60: £4.20 £3.00 £7.70 £5.30 (£106.00) Trio £2,722.40 OWNER Mr C. McKenna (UPPER LAMBOURN) BRED E. A. Badger 20 Rn

1m 15.5 (6.50) SF: 40/43/49/40/34/32/44/36/15/28/16/26/7/8/-/-/-/-/-/-

WEIGHT FOR AGE 3yo-2lb

4146 PAT EDDERY 200-IN-A-SEASON MAIDEN STKS (II) (2-Y.O) (Class D) £3,855.25 (£1,162.00: £563.50: £264.25)

1m 14y Stalls: High GOING: 0.43 sec per fur (GS) 3-00 (3-02)

3842[2] **Latin Reign (USA) (96)***(87)*(Fav)*(PWChapple-Hyam)* 2-9-0 JReid(6) (lw: a.p: led 4f out: rdn ent fnl f: r.o wl) .....— **1**
3827[5] Sharaf (IRE) *(84) (JLDunlop)* 2-9-0 WCarson(8) (lt-f: led to ½-wy: hrd rdn & rn green 2f out: kpt on) .....½ **2**
3955[3] Present Arms (USA) *(74) (PFICole)* 2-9-0 TQuinn(3) (lw: w ldrs centre: ev ch & rdn appr fnl f: outpcd) 5 **3**
2741[8] Minnisam *(52) (JLDunlop)* 2-9-0 TSprake(2) (hdwy appr fnl f: nvr nrr)....................................11 **4**
Future's Trader *(50) (RHannon)* 2-8-9 (5) DaneO'Neill(1) (str: scope: w ldr tl wknd 3f out) 1 **5**
Morning Sir *(38) (CRBarwell)* 2-9-0 JWilliams(10) (w'like: plld hrd: hung lft: a in rr)..................6 **6**
1829[11] Carmarthen Bay *(21) (GLMoore)* 2-9-0 AClark(7) (bit bkwd: plld hrd: hdwy 3f out: wknd 2f out: t.o) 9 **7**
He's Got Wings (IRE) *(7) (CDBroad)* 2-9-0 NAdams(4) (neat: s.s: rdn along ½-wy: t.o)...........7 **8**
2683[6] Bellacardia *(1) (GLewis)* 2-8-9 PatEddery(5) (prom over 4f: sn wknd: t.o) ....nk **9**
3644[8] Verulam (IRE) **(65)** *(JARToller)* 2-9-0 WNewnes(9) (disp ld over 4f: sn wknd: t.o) 8 **10**

4/5 LATIN REIGN (USA), **4/1** Sharaf (IRE), **6/1** Present Arms (USA) (4/1-7/1), **8/1** Bellacardia, **16/1** Future's Trader, Verulam (IRE), **25/1** Minnisam, **40/1** Morning Sir, **50/1** He's Got Wings (IRE), **100/1** Carmarthen Bay, CSF £4.81 TOTE £1.80: £1.30 £1.40 £1.80 (£2.00) Trio £6.80 OWNER Mr R. E. Sangster (MARLBOROUGH) BRED Ballenger, Campion and Swettenham Stud 10 Rn

1m 41.1 (8.60) SF: 43/40/30/8/6/-/-/-/-/-

4147 SPINNEY CONDITIONS STKS (3-Y.O+) (Class C) £4,904.00 (£1,826.00: £885.50: £372.50: £158.75: £73.25)

1m 14y Stalls: High GOING: 0.43 sec per fur (GS) 4-00 (4-03)

3945[15] **Night City (95)***(104) (LadyHerries)* 4-9-0 SWhitworth(2) (stdd s: rdn & hdwy over 3f out: hrd rdn & edgd rt wl ins fnl f: led last strides) .....— **1**
3945[26] Decorated Hero **(105)***(114) (JHMGosden)* 3-9-7 GHind(3) (hld up: hdwy 3f out: led 1f out: hrd rdn & edgd lft ins fnl f: bmpd & hdd last strides) .....hd **2**
3929[11] Wigberto (IRE) **(85)***(102?) (MajorDNChappell)* 3-8-13 RHills(6) (led: clr 5f out: hdd 1f out: no ex) 1¾ **3**
3728[2] Clan Ben (IRE) **(98)***(104)*(Fav)*(HRACecil)* 3-9-7 PatEddery(1) (chsd ldr tl rdn 2f out: sn btn)...3 **4**
4027* King of Tunes (FR) *(55) (JJSheehan)* 3-8-11 JReid(4) (lw: a bhd: t.o).................................20 **5**
3302[5] Diamond Market **(42)***(43) (RHollinshead)* 3-8-11 RCochrane(5) (bit bkwd: bhd fnl 4f: t.o) 6 **6**

6/5 Clan Ben (IRE), **3/1** Decorated Hero (op 11/8), NIGHT CITY, **6/1** King of Tunes (FR), **25/1** Wigberto (IRE), **100/1** Diamond Market, CSF £11.89 TOTE £4.70: £1.60 £1.90 (£5.90) OWNER Dexam International Ltd (LITTLEHAMPTON) 6 Rn 1m 40.1 (7.60) SF: 53/60/48/50/1/-

WEIGHT FOR AGE 3yo-3lb

4148 E.B.F. MEADOW MAIDEN STKS (2-Y.O F) (Class D) £4,472.75 (£1,352.00: £658.50: £311.75) **7f 16y** Stalls: High GOING: 0.43 sec per fur (GS) 4-30 (4-34)

3916[6] **Ski For Gold** *(65) (JLDunlop)* 2-8-11 TSprake(20) (swtg: a.p: led ins fnl f: all out)...............— **1**
Lothlorien (USA) *(65+) (PWChapple-Hyam)* 2-8-11 JReid(11) (w'like: scope: a.p: rdn 3f out: rallied fnl f: r.o wl) .....hd **2**

2958[4] Capilano Princess **(56)**(60) (DHaydnJones) 2-8-11 AMackay(17) (led tl ins fnl f) 2 3
Reploy (56) (LordHuntingdon) 2-8-11 JWeaver(16) (lt-f: s.s: rdn & hdwy over 2f out: one pce fnl f) 2 4
Crystal Warrior (42) (IABalding) 2-8-6 (5) DGriffiths(10) (leggy: lt-f: bit bkwd: hdwy 3f out: one pce fnl 2f) 6 5
Chalk Dust (USA) (42)(Fav)(PFICole) 2-8-11 TQuinn(1) (wl grwn: bkwd: prom: ev ch over 2f out: wknd over 1f out) ....nk 6
3873[6] Alakhluki (41) (GLewis) 2-8-11 GHind(4) (prom tl wknd over 1f out) ....nk 7
Alisura (39) (JRFanshawe) 2-8-11 DHarrison(19) (unf: scope: bkwd: hdwy 3f out: wknd wl over 1f out) 1 8
Bullpen Belle (33) (PTWalwyn) 2-8-11 RHills(15) (w'like: str: bkwd: s.s: nvr nrr) 2½ 9
Alwarqa (32) (RWArmstrong) 2-8-11 WCarson(3) (neat: bit bkwd: nvr trbld ldrs) ....½ 10
3988[14] Natatarl (IRE) (32) (MCPipe) 2-8-6 (5) LNewton(14) (prom over 4f) ....hd 11
3888[W] Parsa (USA) (23) (JLDunlop) 2-8-11 WNewnes(18) (leggy: lt-f: bkwd: s.s: a bhd) 4 12
4048[8] Inca Bird (20) (MMcCormack) 2-8-11 RCochrane(8) (hdwy over 3f out: wknd over 2f out) ...1¼ 13
2351[6] Carmosa (USA) (19) (WJarvis) 2-8-11 PatEddery(6) (bit bkwd: hld up: stdy hdwy 4f out: wknd 2f out: eased whn btn fnl f) ....nk 14
Dangerous Waters (10) (PGMurphy) 2-8-4 (7) RWaterfield(12) (w'like: b.nr hind: bhd most of wy) 4 15
4050[13] Driftholme (2) (GLMoore) 2-8-11 SWhitworth(7) (s.s: a bhd) 3½ 16
Kentford Conquista (JWMullins) 2-8-11 JQuinn(2) (leggy: unf: prom 4f) 2 17
3763[15] Daydream Island (RJBaker) 2-8-11 NAdams(5) (dwlt: bhd fnl 4f) 4 18
3767[17] La Femme Francaise (IRE) (MRChannon) 2-8-11 JFEgan(9) (t.o) 20 19

9/4 Chalk Dust (USA) (3/1-2/1), **4/1** Lothlorien (USA) (5/2-9/2), **5/1** Carmosa (USA), **10/1** Alwarqa (op 6/1), **14/1** Reploy, Parsa (USA), SKI FOR GOLD, Alisura, **20/1** Bullpen Belle, Natatarl (IRE), Crystal Warrior, **25/1** Inca Bird, **33/1** Capilano Princess, **40/1** Alakhluki, **50/1** Dangerous Waters, Driftholme, Daydream Island, La Femme Francaise (IRE), **100/1** Kentford Conquista, CSF £69.00 TOTE £16.60: £3.20 £2.70 £5.80 (£54.80) Trio £146.70 OWNER Windflower Overseas Holdings Inc (ARUNDEL) BRED Gerald W. Leigh 19 Rn 1m 30.3 (10.30) SF: 7/7/2/-/-/-/-/-/-/-/-/-/-/-/-/-/-/-/-

4149 PASTURE H'CAP (0-80) (3-Y.O) (Class D) £4,060.00 (£1,225.00: £595.00: £280.00) **1m 4f 23y** Stalls: Low GOING: 0.43 sec per fur (GS) 5-00 (5-05)

3965* **Snow Princess (IRE) (65)**(78) (LordHuntingdon) 3-8-6 RHills(3) (lw: prom: rdn & 5th st: led over 1f out: r.o wl) ....— 1
4061[9] Fabillion **(60)**(70) (CASmith) 3-8-1 CRutter(11) (hld up: gd hdwy 3f out: led wl over 1f out: sn hdd: nt qckn) 2 2
4071[4] Shift Again (IRE) **(66)**(71) (WJarvis) 3-8-7 SSanders(5) (lw: hld up & bhd: hdwy over 3f out: rdn & swtchd lft over 1f out: r.o one pce) 4 3
4071[3] Wild Rita **(71)**(71) (WRMuir) 3-8-12 WWoods(13) (lw: bhd: rdn & hdwy 3f out: one pce fnl f) ...4 4
3935* Dance So Suite **(79)**(78) (PFICole) 3-9-6 TQuinn(9) (swtg: 6th st: ev ch over 2f out: wknd over 1f out) ....½ 5
4047* Slapy Dam **(62)**(60)(Fav)(JMackie) 3-7-12 (5) 5x PFessey(4) (hld up: hdwy on ins 3f out: hrd rdn over 1f out: one pce) 1 6
4047[4] Soviet Bride (IRE) **(63)**(60) (SDow) 3-7-11 (7) ADaly(16) (2nd st: led over 3f out tl wl over 1f out: wknd fnl f) ....nk 7
2691[6] Vaugrenier (IRE) **(80)**(67) (RHannon) 3-9-7 JReid(1) (4th st: wknd wl over 1f out) 8 8
3863[11] Game Ploy (POL) **(70)**(56) (FMurphy) 3-8-8 (3) JStack(8) (swtg: nvr nrr) ....½ 9
3921[8] Zidac **(69)**(43) (PJMakin) 3-8-10 JWeaver(18) (b: plld hrd: 3rd st: wknd over 2f out) 9 10
3756[6] Zine Lane **(64)**(37) (MajorWRHern) 3-8-5 TSprake(19) (bhd fnl 3f) 1¼ 11
4047[6] Leading Spirit (IRE) **(74)**(46) (CFWall) 3-9-1 PatEddery(12) (led over 8f: sn wknd) ....nk 12
3401* Last Laugh (IRE) **(60)**(32) (MCPipe) 3-8-1 AMcGlone(7) (sme hdwy on ins 3f out: n.d) ....s.h 13
3804[7] Doddington Flyer **(66)**(37) (RHollinshead) 3-8-7 ow1 RCochrane(2) (a bhd) ....½ 14
3957[3] Silktail (IRE) **(69)**(34) (CADwyer) 3-8-10 CDwyer(17) (hdwy over 4f out: rdn 3f out: sn wknd) ..5 15
4022[8] Backview **(59)** (BJLlewellyn) 3-8-0 TWilliams(15) (prom tl rdn & 7th st: virt p.u ins fnl f: t.o) ..30 16
4028[5] River Keen (IRE) **(76)** (RWArmstrong) 3-9-3b WCarson(10) (8th st: wknd over 3f out: t.o) 5 17
3921[11] Mayreau **(73)** (GHarwood) 3-9-0 AClark(14) (lw: t.o fnl 4f: virt p.u fnl f) ....dist 18

3/1 Slapy Dam (op 6/1), **11/2** Leading Spirit (IRE), SNOW PRINCESS (IRE), **10/1** Silktail (IRE), River Keen (IRE), **11/1** Dance So Suite, **14/1** Wild Rita, Soviet Bride (IRE), Last Laugh (IRE), **16/1** Mayreau, Zidac, Vaugrenier (IRE), **20/1** Doddington Flyer, Shift Again (IRE), **25/1** Game Ploy (POL), **33/1** Zine Lane, Fabillion, **40/1** Backview, CSF £168.05 CT £3,173.64 TOTE £6.00: £1.90 £20.80 £7.10 £2.70 (£700.90) OWNER Lord Weinstock & The Hon Simon Weinstock (WEST ILSLEY) BRED Ballymacoll Stud Co 18 Rn 2m 49.1 (17.80) SF: 9/1/2/2/9/-/-/-/-/-/-/-/-/-/-/-/-/-

T/Jkpt: £14,990.70 (0.1 Tckts); £19,002.34 to Yarmouth 18/10/95. T/Plpt: £294.80 (66.43 Tckts). T/Qdpt: Not won; £265.60 to Yarmouth 18/10/95. IM

3680-YARMOUTH (L-H)
Wednesday October 18th (Good to firm becoming Firm)
WEATHER: bright WIND: slt across

4150
RUNHAM MAIDEN STKS (3-Y.O) (Class D) £3,968.90 (£1,185.20: £566.60: £257.30) **1m 3y** Stalls: Low GOING minus 0.38 sec per fur (F) 2-00 (2-00)

3829 3 **Neuwest (USA)** **(80)***(87) (HThomsonJones)* 3-9-0 RHills(4) (lw: mde all: drvn out) .....— **1**
3941 9 Darcey Bussell **(55)***(78) (BWHills)* 3-8-9 MHills(10) (b: racd stands' side: ev ch 1f out: one pce) 2 **2**
3921 5 Timeless *(77) (HRACecil)* 3-8-9 WRyan(6) (a.p: chsd wnr fnl 3f: one pce fr over 1f out) .....½ **3**
1486 3 Bend Wavy (IRE) *(74)*(Fav)*(LMCumani)* 3-9-0 JWeaver(7) (plld hrd early: prom over 5f) 4 **4**
Cheeky Charm (USA) *(65) (MRStoute)* 3-8-9 WRSwinburn(8) (nt grwn: chsd ldrs: one pce fnl 3f) 2 **5**
3974 4 Duke Valentino **(71)***(69) (RHollinshead)* 3-9-0 TIves(9) (hld up: hdwy 3f out: one pce fr wl over 1f out) .....½ **6**
3974 2 Clearly Devious *(63) (JRFanshawe)* 3-8-9 DHarrison(5) (effrt over 2f out: sn rdn & btn) .....¾ **7**
1486 12 Errant *(63) (DJSCosgrove)* 3-9-0 GCarter(3) (plld hrd early: bhd fnl 3f) 2½ **8**
3974 11 Fire The Anvil *(37) (JLDunlop)* 3-9-0 WCarson(1) (a bhd: t.o fnl 2f) 13 **9**
Sadarah (USA) *(CSmith)* 3-8-11 (3) JStack(2) (mid div 5f: t.o fr wl over 1f out) 25 **10**
Etoile du Nord *(HJCollingridge)* 3-9-0 MRimmer(11) (b: hmpd s: prom 3f: t.o fnl 3f) 15 **11**

5/4 Bend Wavy (IRE), **7/2** NEUWEST (USA), **4/1** Clearly Devious, **8/1** Timeless (op 4/1), **20/1** Cheeky Charm (USA), **25/1** Duke Valentino, Darcey Bussell, Fire The Anvil, **50/1** Errant, Etoile du Nord, **100/1** Sadarah (USA), CSF £72.36 TOTE £4.70: £1.30 £7.40 £2.40 (£46.70) Trio £95.90 OWNER Mr Hamdan Al Maktoum (NEWMARKET) BRED Robert Bloomer and Sharon L. Bloomer 11 Rn 1m 36.4 (1.10) SF: 55/46/45/42/33/37/31/31/5/-/-

4151
BILLOCKBY NURSERY H'CAP (0-85) (2-Y.O) (Class D) £4,110.00 (£1,230.00: £590.00: £270.00)
1m 3y Stalls: Low GOING minus 0.38 sec per fur (F) 2-30 (2-32)

3752 3 **Nosey Native** **(74)***(82) (JPearce)* 2-8-13 GBardwell(14) (sn bhd & rdn along: hdwy over 2f out: carried lft ins fnl f: hrd rdn to ld cl home) .....— **1**
3861 2 Prince of Florence (IRE) **(80)***(87) (LMCumani)* 2-9-5 JWeaver(10) (lw: a.p: led 4f out: clr 2f out: rdn & hung lft ins fnl f: ct cl home) .....nk **2**
3760 8 Jerry Cutrona (IRE) **(59)***(63) (NACallaghan)* 2-7-12 JFEgan(2) (hdwy far side over 2f out: styd on one pce u.p fnl f) 1½ **3**
3985 17 Vanishing Point **(82)***(86) (GLewis)* 2-9-2 (5) AWhelan(6) (led far side: styd on one pce fnl 2f) .....hd **4**
3865 23 D'naan (IRE) **(80)***(81) (WJHaggas)* 2-9-5 MHills(15) (chsd ldrs: rdn 2f out: one pce) 1¾ **5**
3827 3 Classic Lover (IRE) **(76)***(73) (SCWilliams)* 2-9-1 AMackay(3) (hdwy far side over 3f out: wknd 1f out) 2 **6**
4081* Quality (IRE) **(76)***(72) (WAO'Gorman)* 2-9-1 6x EmmaO'Gorman(11) (hld up: hdwy 3f out: one pce fr wl over 1f out) .....½ **7**
3883 11 Just Nuisance **(65)***(51) (CEBrittain)* 2-8-4 BDoyle(9) (n.d) 5 **8**
3749 20 Mystic Dawn **(64)***(49) (SDow)* 2-8-3 MRoberts(12) (prom 5f) .....½ **9**
3780 3 Munketh (USA) **(82)***(66) (JLDunlop)* 2-9-7 RHills(19) (a outpcd) .....½ **10**
3763 13 Flash In The Pan (IRE) **(60)***(41) (MBell)* 2-7-13 FNorton(4) (plld early far side: prom to ½-wy) 1½ **11**
3701 11 Nabhaan (IRE) **(78)***(59) (DMorley)* 2-9-3 WCarson(5) (prom far side over 5f) .....s.h **12**
3928* Queen's Insignia (USA) **(67)***(46)*(Fav)*(PFICole)* 2-8-1 (5) DaneO'Neill(18) (b.hind: prom stands' side 4f: wknd qckly) .....¾ **13**
3869 6 Addie Pray (IRE) **(72)***(49) (MAJarvis)* 2-8-6 (5) MHenry(7) (prom far side 5f) 1 **14**
3985 3 Stately **(58)***(30) (SirMarkPrescott)* 2-7-11b JLowe(17) (b.hind: led 4f: wknd qckly 2f out) 2½ **15**
3947 13 Awafeh **(57)***(21) (JWPayne)* 2-7-10b JQuinn(13) (plld hrd: prom over 4f) 4 **16**
3968 10 Old School House **(55)***(17) (CNAllen)* 2-7-8 ow1 NAdams(1) (t.o fnl 3f) .....½ **17**
4001 2 Scathebury **(62)***(22) (SPCWoods)* 2-7-10 (5) MBaird(8) (plld early: prom 5f: wl bhd fnl 2f) 1¾ **18**
3760 10 Soviet Sakti (IRE) **(55)** *(PMitchell)* 2-7-8 ow1 RWoodworth(16) (spd 3f: hrd rdn ½-wy: sn t.o) .15 **19**
LONG HANDICAP Old School House 7-3 Soviet Sakti (IRE) 7-5

11/4 Queen's Insignia (USA), **13/2** Stately, **9/1** Prince of Florence (IRE), **11/1** Nabhaan (IRE), Scathebury (8/1-12/1), **12/1** Classic Lover (IRE) (op 8/1), Quality (IRE) (7/1-14/1), **14/1** Vanishing Point, Munketh (USA), **16/1** D'naan (IRE), Jerry Cutrona (IRE), **20/1** Addie Pray (IRE), NOSEY NATIVE, **25/1** Just Nuisance, Old School House, **33/1** Awafeh, Flash In The Pan (IRE), Mystic Dawn, Soviet Sakti (IRE), CSF £183.95 CT £2,690.60 TOTE £22.30: £3.60 £3.10 £9.40 £8.30 (£62.40) Trio £411.60 OWNER Mr James Furlong (NEWMARKET) BRED Lady Jennifer Green 19 Rn 1m 37.6 (2.30) SF: 42/47/23/46/41/33/32/11/9/26/1/19/6/9/-/-/-/-/-

4152
MARTHAM (S) H'CAP (0-60) (3-Y.O+) (Class G) £2,982.20 (£829.20: £398.60)
1m 3y Stalls: Low GOING minus 0.38 sec per fur (F) 3-00 (3-01)

4043[6] **Total Rach (IRE) (48)***(63) (RIngram)* 3-8-13b WWoods(15) (s.i.s: hdwy over 3f out: led 1f out: drvn out).................— 1
4028[10] No Speeches (IRE) **(46)***(59) (CACyzer)* 4-8-11 (3) NVarley(3) (hdwy far side to ld 2f out: hdd 1f out: r.o one pce).................1 2
835[8] Cicerone **(42)***(50) (JLHarris)* 5-8-10 RCochrane(8) (hdwy fnl 2f: nrst fin).................2½ 3
4060[2] Mary's Case (IRE) **(55)***(61)*(Fav)*(MJohnston)* 5-9-9b JWeaver(19) (lw: bhd early: hdwy 3f out: styd on fnl 2f: nrst fin).................1¾ 4
4079[14] Mighty Kingdom (IRE) **(43)***(45) (CADwyer)* 4-8-6 (5) MHenry(16) (a.p: one pce fnl 2f).................1¾ 5
3825[4] Pop to Stans **(42)***(44) (JPearce)* 6-8-10v JLowe(10) (sme hdwy fnl 2f: nvr nrr).................hd 6
3759[15] Threshfield (USA) **(47)***(47) (BJCurley)* 9-9-1 WRyan(5) (b: led far side 5f out to 2f out).................¾ 7
3272[4] Rad **(45)***(42) (SPCWoods)* 5-8-6 (7) CWebb(2) (prom far side 6f).................1½ 8
3057[8] Just Lucky (IRE) **(43)***(35) (RWArmstrong)* 3-8-8 RPrice(7) (led far side 3f: wknd 2f out).................2½ 9
1513[20] Vladivostok **(40)***(30) (BdeHaan)* 5-8-3 (5) DaneO'Neill(13) (led 5f out to 2f out).................1 10
4079[10] Broughton's Port **(40)***(29) (WJMusson)* 5-8-8v JReid(4) (prom far side 5f).................½ 11
2684[4] Kellaire Girl (IRE) **(44)***(31) (GLewis)* 3-8-4b(5) AWhelan(20) (a bhd).................1 12
2862[6] Fiaba **(40)***(23) (MrsNMacauley)* 7-8-8 SDWilliams(18) (chsd ldrs 6f).................2 13
4054[5] Jackatack (IRE) **(46)***(28) (MRChannon)* 3-8-11 JFEgan(9) (in tch 5f).................½ 14
3682[6] Antiguan Flyer **(46)***(27) (RHarris)* 6-9-0 JQuinn(17) (b: a bhd).................¾ 15
3959[7] Crystal Gift **(57)***(34) (DWPArbuthnot)* 3-9-8b TQuinn(12) (prom tl wknd 3f out).................2 16
2968[7] Okay Baby (IRE) **(51)***(26) (MHTompkins)* 3-9-2 PRobinson(6) (a bhd).................1 17
3823[11] Top Skipper (IRE) **(57)***(27) (BHanbury)* 3-9-5b(3) JStack(14) (a bhd: t.o).................2½ 18
Sea God **(56)***(18) (MCChapman)* 4-9-3 (7) CMunday(11) (sn led: hdd 5f out: wknd qckly).................4 19
3725[4] Bad News **(47)***(5) (CNAllen)* 3-8-12 GCarter(1) (t.o ½-wy).................1¾ 20

3/1 Mary's Case (IRE), **8/1** Kellaire Girl (IRE) (op 5/1), **10/1** Threshfield (USA) (8/1-12/1), Jackatack (IRE) (8/1-12/1), Okay Baby (IRE) (8/1-12/1), TOTAL RACH (IRE) (7/1-11/1), **11/1** Broughton's Port (8/1-12/1), **12/1** Pop to Stans, **14/1** No Speeches (IRE), **16/1** Crystal Gift, Mighty Kingdom (IRE), **20/1** Just Lucky (IRE), Bad News, Rad, Top Skipper (IRE), Fiaba, Cicerone, **33/1** Vladivostok, Antiguan Flyer, **50/1** Sea God, CSF £145.05 CT £2,554.35 TOTE £13.50: £2.60 £6.30 £3.00 £1.30 (£120.20) Trio £977.20 OWNER Mrs A. V. Cappuccini (EPSOM) BRED Oldtown Stud 20 Rn
1m 37.4 (2.10) SF: 44/43/34/45/29/28/31/26/16/14/13/12/7/9/11/15/7/8/2/-
WEIGHT FOR AGE 3yo-3lb
No bid.

4153
MAUTBY CONDITIONS STKS (2-Y.O) (Class C) £4,840.50 (£1,789.50: £857.25: £348.75) **6f 3y** Stalls: Low GOING minus 0.38 sec per fur (F) 3-30 (3-30)

3886[2] **Tamhid (USA) (100)***(95) (HThomsonJones)* 2-9-2 RHills(4) (mde all: qcknd 2f out: r.o wl).................— 1
Farhana *(80) (WJarvis)* 2-8-6 TQuinn(3) (b.off hind: leggy: unf: hld up: hdwy over 2f out: chsd wnr fr over 1f out: r.o one pce).................1¾ 2
Inner Circle (USA) *(74+)*(Fav)*(PWChapple-Hyam)* 2-8-6 JReid(6) (lt-f: w wnr 2f: pushed along & wknd over 1f out).................2½ 3
3848* Celandine **(87)***(73) (RCharlton)* 2-8-11 WRSwinburn(2) (trckd wnr tl wknd qckly 2f out).................2 4
4039[3] Beautiful Ballad (IRE) **(96)***(64) (BWHills)* 2-8-11 MHills(1) (stdd s: nvr gng wl: a bhd).................3½ 5

7/4 Inner Circle (USA), **15/8** TAMHID (USA), **4/1** Celandine, **7/1** Beautiful Ballad (IRE), **12/1** Farhana (op 6/1), CSF £17.59 TOTE £2.50: £1.40 £3.20 (£17.50) OWNER Mr Hamdan Al Maktoum (NEWMARKET) BRED Shadwell Farm 5 Rn 1m 12.6 (2.00) SF: 40/25/19/18/9

4154
WICKHAMPTON MAIDEN STKS (I) (2-Y.O) (Class D) £3,882.50 (£1,160.00: £555.00: £252.50) **7f 3y** Stalls: Low GOING minus 0.38 sec per fur (F) 4-00 (4-00)

3340[3] **Prize Giving (87)***(74)*(Fav)*(GWragg)* 2-9-0 MHills(1) (mde all: qcknd 2f out: put hd in air appr fnl f: drvn out).................— 1
Unreal City (IRE) *(73+) (HRACecil)* 2-9-0 WRyan(6) (a.p: pushed along over 2f out: ev ch ins fnl f: unable qckn cl home).................nk 2
2351[8] Al Shadeedah (USA) *(66+) (LMCumani)* 2-8-9 JWeaver(2) (trckd ldrs: n.m.r fr dist: nvr able chal).................1¼ 3
Alsahib (USA) *(67) (HThomsonJones)* 2-9-0 RHills(11) (wl grwn: hld up: hdwy over 2f out: kpt on one pce).................1½ 4
Pasternak *(53+) (SirMarkPrescott)* 2-9-0 GDuffield(5) (leggy: scope: bkwd: s.i.s: last ½-wy: sme hdwy fnl 2f: nvr nrr).................6 5
Crimson Rosella *(46) (WJHaggas)* 2-8-9 RMcGhin(4) (leggy: lt-f: chsd ldrs tl wknd over 2f out).................1¼ 6
1842[8] Ret Frem (IRE) *(50) (MAJarvis)* 2-9-0 PRobinson(12) (n.d).................hd 7
Charisse Dancer *(42) (CFWall)* 2-8-4 (5) LNewton(3) (lt-f: bhd fnl 3f).................1¼ 8

Sea Danzig (46) (PHowling) 2-9-0 RCochrane(9) (leggy: scope: unf: a outpcd) ½ 9
3940[10] Seeking Destiny (IRE) (40)(37) (MCChapman) 2-8-7 (7) CMunday(7) (prom over 4f) 4 10
Tom Swift (IRE) (33) (RCSpicer) 2-9-0 TQuinn(8) (cmpt: bit bkwd: in tch over 4f) 2 11

4/6 PRIZE GIVING (op 5/4), **5/1** Unreal City (IRE) (op 5/2), Al Shadeedah (USA), Alsahib (USA) (7/2-11/2), **16/1** Pasternak, **20/1** Ret Frem (IRE), **33/1** Crimson Rosella, Charisse Dancer, Sea Danzig, Tom Swift (IRE), **50/1** Seeking Destiny (IRE), CSF £5.83 TOTE £2.00: £1.10 £1.90 £1.60 (£2.10) Trio £7.60 OWNER Exors of the late Sir Philip Oppenheimer (NEWMARKET) BRED Hascombe and Valiant Studs 11 Rn 1m 26.6 (3.80) SF: 22/21/14/15/1/-/-/-/-/-/-

4155 WICKHAMPTON MAIDEN STKS (II) (2-Y.O) (Class D) £3,882.50 (£1,160.00: £555.00: £252.50) 7f 3y Stalls: Low GOING minus 0.38 sec per fur (F) 4-30 (4-31)

Brighstone (72+)(Fav)(HRACecil) 2-9-0 WRyan(6) (cmpt: b.hind: a.p: rdn to ld over 2f out: r.o wl) — 1
3881[6] Nasrudin (USA) (68) (DRLoder) 2-9-0 WRSwinburn(10) (lw: a.p: chal over 1f out: one pce) 1¾ 2
3916[8] Classy Chief (64) (RBoss) 2-9-0 MRoberts(7) (chsd ldrs: hrd rdn & outpcd wl over 1f out: rallied ins fnl f) 1¾ 3
4023[8] Northern Judge (60) (BHanbury) 2-8-11 (3) JStack(1) (led tl over 2f out: wknd fnl f) 2 4
3955[2] The Boozing Brief (USA) (48) (MAJarvis) 2-9-0 WWoods(8) (in tch tl wknd over 1f out) 5 5
Faith Alone (32) (CFWall) 2-8-9 NCarlisle(2) (lt-f: a bhd) 5 6
Capstone (32) (WJarvis) 2-8-9 JReid(4) (lt-f: b.off hind: a bhd) s.h 7
Belmarita (IRE) (30) (MHTompkins) 2-8-9 PRobinson(11) (scope: bit bkwd: carried rt s: a outpcd) ½ 8
4058[13] Night Silence (35) (SirMarkPrescott) 2-9-0 GDuffield(9) (plld early: bhd fnl 3f) nk 9
4050[16] Shareda (IRE) (27) (WJHaggas) 2-8-9 RMcGhin(3) (bhd fnl 3f) 1 10
604[6] Static Love (TTClement) 2-8-9 JQuinn(5) (w ldrs tl wknd qckly 3f out: t.o) 20 11

5/2 BRIGHSTONE (6/4-11/4), **3/1** Nasrudin (USA), **4/1** The Boozing Brief (USA) (5/2-9/2), **11/2** Northern Judge (5/1-8/1), **10/1** Capstone (op 6/1), **12/1** Belmarita (IRE) (7/1-14/1), Faith Alone (op 7/1), **16/1** Classy Chief, **20/1** Night Silence, **33/1** Shareda (IRE), **50/1** Static Love, CSF £11.08 TOTE £3.90: £1.50 £1.70 £2.30 (£4.60) Trio £61.30 OWNER Mr Michael Poland (NEWMARKET) BRED Michael Poland 11 Rn 1m 25.7 (2.90) SF: 32/28/24/20/8/-/-/-/-/-/-

4156 THRIGBY H'CAP (0-85) (3-Y.O+) (Class D) £4,509.70 (£1,351.60: £649.80: £298.90) 7f 3y Stalls: Low GOING minus 0.38 sec per fur (F) 5-00 (5-01)

*3950** **Spencer's Revenge (67)**(76) (MJRyan) 6-8-13 GBardwell(19) (bhd ½-wy: hdwy wl over 1f out: r.o strly to ld wl ins fnl f) — 1
4041[10] Pelleman (68)(74) (RBoss) 3-8-11 WRyan(15) (lw: hdwy over 2f out: led 1f out tl wl ins fnl f) 1¼ 2
3545[10] Mutabassim (IRE) (76)(79) (ACStewart) 3-9-5 RHills(18) (led to 1f out: r.o one pce) 1½ 3
4041[6] Ertlon (82)(85) (CEBrittain) 5-10-0 BDoyle(10) (racd centre: ev ch 2f out: one pce) s.h 4
4115[13] Morocco (IRE) (60)(58) (MRChannon) 6-8-6 JFEgan(13) (hld up: hdwy over 1f out: one pce) 2 5
4040[20] Samsolom (72)(68) (PHowling) 7-9-4 JQuinn(8) (racd centre: nvr able chal) ¾ 6
3837[7] Legal Fiction (65)(53) (MJohnston) 4-8-11b JWeaver(20) (prom: ev ch 2f out: one pce) 3½ 7
1845[6] Flight Soundly (IRE) (65)(51) (MRStoute) 3-8-8 JTate(9) (chsd ldrs tl wknd 2f out) 1 8
4122[5] Stolen Melody (70)(52) (SDow) 3-8-13 MRoberts(5) (led far side 3f out: eased whn btn wl over 1f out) 1¾ 9
3807[6] Ahjay (48)(29) (DAWilson) 5-7-8 ow1 NAdams(4) (prom far side 4f) d.h 9
3664[6] Midnight Jazz (IRE) (72)(48) (WAO'Gorman) 5-9-4b EmmaO'Gorman(11) (lw: n.d) 2½ 11
3943[23] Keston Pond (IRE) (73)(48) (DAWilson) 5-9-5 GCarter(6) (lw: prom far side over 4f) ½ 12
1745[7] Magnate's Point (62)(36) (PWHarris) 3-8-5 GHind(2) (bhd whn hmpd over 5f out: a in rr) ½ 13
2654[6] Spumante (64)(36) (RChampion) 3-8-7 AMcGlone(14) (a bhd) 1 14
3573[6] Dalcross (49)(18) (HJCollingridge) 4-7-6 (3)ow2 NVarley(12) (bhd fnl 3f) nk 15
4115[19] Chief's Lady (52)(14) (CNAllen) 3-7-4 (5)ow2 MBaird(16) (bhd fnl 3f) 3 16
3656[3] Zahwa (71)(28)(Fav)(RWArmstrong) 3-9-0 WCarson(1) (wknd qckly far side 3f out) 3 17
3929[9] Anam (73)(30) (PTWalwyn) 3-9-2 MHills(7) (led far side 4f) s.h 18

LONG HANDICAP Ahjay 7-6 Dalcross 7-1

100/30 Zahwa, **7/1** Ertlon, Keston Pond (IRE), **10/1** SPENCER'S REVENGE (op 6/1), Legal Fiction, Mutabassim (IRE), **12/1** Stolen Melody, Pelleman, **14/1** Morocco (IRE), Ahjay, Flight Soundly (IRE), **16/1** Samsolom, Anam, Midnight Jazz (IRE), **20/1** Magnate's Point, **25/1** Chief's Lady, **33/1** Spumante, Dalcross, CSF £128.33 CT £1,156.42 TOTE £10.30: £2.00 £4.20 £3.00 £1.50 (£82.20) Trio £146.00 OWNER Mr A. S. Reid (NEWMARKET) BRED Lord Crawshaw 18 Rn
1m 24.0 (1.20) SF: 51/46/51/60/33/43/28/23/24/4/23/23/8/8/-/-/-/2
WEIGHT FOR AGE 3yo-3lb

OFFICIAL EXPLANATION Zahwa: did not act on the ground.

T/Jkpt: £19,622.10 (0.18 Tckts). £22,662.15 to Newbury 19/10/95. T/Plpt: £83.10 (213.64 Tckts). T/Qdpt: £24.20 (14.5 Tckts). RC

3727-NEWBURY (L-H)
Thursday October 19th (Good to soft)

WEATHER: sunny WIND: almost nil

4157

VODAFONE BRITISH & NORTHERN RACING SCHOOLS APPRENTICE H'CAP (0-80) (3-Y.O+) (Class F) £3,475.50 (£968.00: £466.50)
7f Stalls: Centre GOING: 0.46 sec per fur (GS) 2-05 (2-05)

4041[2] **Barrel of Hope (70)**(78)(Fav)*(JLEyre)* 3-9-0b(4) DSweeney(18) (lw: a.p: led over 2f out: rdn out)......— 1
4040[15] Lynton Lad **(70)**(75) *(CPEBrooks)* 3-9-4b SCopp(27) (hld up: hrd rdn over 2f out: ev ch over 1f out: unable qckn)......1¼ 2
4053[4] Chili Heights **(54)**(57)(Fav)*(GBBalding)* 5-8-5v DGriffiths(15) (hdwy over 1f out: r.o ins fnl f)....¾ 3
3661[3] Racing Telegraph **(42)**(41) *(JWPayne)* 5-7-7 IonaWands(25) (hdwy 3f out: r.o ins fnl f)......2 4
3771[4] Present Situation **(56)**(55) *(LordHuntingdon)* 4-8-7 GMitchell(14) (lw: a.p: rdn over 2f out: one pce)......s.h 5
4131[8] Nuthatch (IRE) **(45)**(37) *(MDIUsher)* 3-7-0 (7) RhonaGent(21) (rdn over 2f out: hdwy over 1f out: r.o)......3 6
4134[6] Leigh Crofter **(70)**(59) *(PDCundell)* 6-9-0b(7) NLovelock(5) (rdn & hdwy 2f out: eased whn btn ins fnl f)......1½ 7
3808[7] Thunder River (IRE) **(63)**(47) *(MJHeaton-Ellis)* 5-9-0 SDrowne(4) (lw: prom over 5f)......2 8
1542[4] Zatopek **(63)**(46) *(RHannon)* 3-8-11 MarkDenaro(10) (lw: hdwy over 2f out: wknd fnl f)......½ 9
4043[17] Sweet Allegiance **(54)**(36) *(JCPoulton)* 5-7-12 (7) TField(17) (nvr nr to chal)......nk 10
3011[8] Mr Nevermind (IRE) **(65)**(46) *(GLMoore)* 5-9-2 LSuthern(16) (nvr nrr)......nk 11
3984[12] Real Madrid **(42)**(18) *(GPEnright)* 4-7-3v(4) PDoe(24) (nvr nrr)......2½ 12
3905[18] Marwell Indigo **(51)**(26) *(PDCundell)* 3-7-13 DDenby(20) (b.hind: a mid div)......½ 13
4054[11] Causley **(60)**(34) *(DMHyde)* 10-8-7 (4) KSked(3) (prom 4f)......nk 14
2807[8] Tower Green **(65)**(37) *(LadyHerries)* 4-8-9 (7) RSmith(13) (t: b.hind: a mid div)......1 15
3874[12] Canary Falcon **(60)**(31) *(JohnBerry)* 4-8-11 CWebb(1) (lw: hdwy over 2f out: wknd fnl f)......s.h 16
3980[16] Star of Gold **(62)**(33) *(CREgerton)* 3-8-10 RHavlin(19) (a mid div)......s.h 17
4041[3] Jolto **(75)**(45)(Fav)*(KOCunningham-Brown)* 6-9-12 CTeague(2) (led over 4f)......½ 18
Peggotty **(49)**(12) *(PHayward)* 7-7-7 (7)ow7 RCody-Boutcher(26) (nvr nrr)......nk 19
3972[4] Sylvandra **(65)**(34) *(PGMurphy)* 3-8-13 RWaterfield(8) (dwlt: a bhd)......s.h 20
3960[6] Mutinique **(42)**(9) *(BAPearce)* 4-7-7 PFessey(6) (bhd fnl 2f)......1 21
3934[9] Ebony Blaze **(49)**(12) *(CPWildman)* 4-7-10 (4) RMullen(12) (bhd fnl 2f)......2 22
3929[8] Scharnhorst **(68)**(30) *(SDow)* 3-8-9 (7) PBrookwood(7) (prom over 4f)......nk 23
2377[12] Key Pitch (USA) **(70)**(11) *(LordHuntingdon)* 3-9-4v JWilkinson(23) (bhd fnl 3f)......9 24
4060[4] Blushing Grenadier (IRE) **(53)** *(MJFetherston-Godley)* 3-8-1v MBaird(11) (lw: hld up: rdn over 3f out: wknd 2f out)......1¼ 25
3515[14] Sobeloved **(50)** *(NEBerry)* 3-7-12 ow4 KimberleyHart(22) (s.s: a bhd)......1½ 26
3844[13] Chocolate Charlie **(50)** *(RCharlton)* 4-7-8v(7) RBrisland(9) (a bhd: t.o)......dist 27

LONG HANDICAP Mutinique 7-6 Real Madrid 6-13 Peggotty 6-6 Nuthatch (IRE) 6-10

7/1 BARREL OF HOPE, Jolto, Chili Heights, **11/1** Thunder River (IRE), **14/1** Racing Telegraph, Blushing Grenadier (IRE), Sylvandra, **16/1** Zatopek, Leigh Crofter, Scharnhorst, Mr Nevermind (IRE), Present Situation, Star of Gold, **20/1** Tower Green, Chocolate Charlie, **25/1** Sweet Allegiance, Lynton Lad, Key Pitch (USA), **33/1** Marwell Indigo, Sobeloved, Causley, Ebony Blaze, Canary Falcon, Mutinique, Real Madrid, **50/1** Nuthatch (IRE), **66/1** Peggotty, CSF £168.91 CT £1,206.91 TOTE £8.00: £1.80 £6.00 £1.80 £3.80 (£82.60) Trio £339.00 OWNER Mr Peter Watson (HAMBLETON) BRED Bolton Grange 27 Rn

1m 32.6 (8.10) SF: 44/41/26/10/24/3/28/16/12/5/15/-/-/3/6/-/-/14/-/-/-/-/-/-/-/-/-
WEIGHT FOR AGE 3yo-3lb

4158

VODAFONE GROUP H'CAP (0-90) (3-Y.O+) (Class C) £6,176.50 (£1,852.00: £891.00: £410.50)
2m Stalls: Low GOING: 0.46 sec per fur (GS) 2-40 (2-41)

3774[7] **En Vacances (IRE) (70)**(84) *(AGFoster)* 3-7-12 ow5 TSprake(2) (4th st: led over 4f out: rdn out)......— 1
3817[11] Istabraq (IRE) **(82)**(96) *(JHMGosden)* 3-8-10 WCarson(8) (b: led over 11f: rdn over 2f out: ev ch ins fnl f: r.o)......nk 2
3730[6] Purple Splash **(80)**(92) *(PJMakin)* 5-9-4v WRSwinburn(1) (6th st: rdn over 3f out: ev ch ins fnl f: unable qckn)......1¾ 3
4036[10] Eau de Cologne **(65)**(71) *(CWThornton)* 3-7-7 GBardwell(9) (rdn over 4f out: hdwy over 2f out: one pce)......6 4
3971[4] Paradise Navy **(72)**(69) *(CREgerton)* 6-8-10 ow3 RHughes(6) (hdwy over 3f out: hrd rdn 2f out: eased whn btn over 1f out)......6 5
4026[2] Greycoat Boy **(67)**(66)(Fav)*(BJMeehan)* 3-7-9b NCarlisle(7) (lw: nvr nr to chal)......¾ 6

4026[7] Turquoise Sea (USA) **(75)***(72) (JLDunlop)* 3-8-3 KDarley(3) (2nd st: wknd over 3f out).........2½ 7
4026[11] Bean King **(75)***(68) (MrsJCecil)* 9-8-13 TIves(11) (3rd st: wknd 4f out).......................................4 8
1840[14] Sweet Glow (FR) **(74)***(60) (MCPipe)* 8-8-12 MRoberts(4) (a bhd)...7 9
3930[0] Seasonal Splendour (IRE) **(88)***(72) (MCPipe)* 5-9-12 TQuinn(5) (5th st: wknd over 3f out)....1½ 10
4047[18] United Front **(77)** *(RJO'Sullivan)* 3-8-5 DBiggs(10) (bhd fnl 7f: t.o) ....dist 11

7/2 Greycoat Boy, **4/1** Istabraq (IRE), **9/2** Seasonal Splendour (IRE), **8/1** Purple Splash, Paradise Navy, **9/1** Turquoise Sea (USA), **16/1** EN VACANCES (IRE), Eau de Cologne, **20/1** Bean King, Sweet Glow (FR), **33/1** United Front, CSF £72.69 CT £507.88 TOTE £12.90: £2.20 £2.00 £3.50 (£52.90) Trio £311.20 OWNER Lambourn Valley Racing (LAMBOURN) BRED The Woodhaven Stud 11 Rn 3m 37.56 (11.06) SF: 60/77/83/52/60/47/53/59/51/63/-
WEIGHT FOR AGE 3yo-10lb

4159 VODAFONE HORRIS HILL STKS (Gp 3) (2-Y.O C & G) (Class A)
£21,840.00 (£8,187.00: £3,943.50: £1,729.50)
7f 64y (round) Stalls: Low GOING: 0.46 sec per fur (GS) 3-10 (3-10)

3925[2] **Tumbleweed Ridge (100)***(100)*(Fav)*(BJMeehan)* 2-8-9 BDoyle(9) (lw: hdwy wl over 1f out: led ins fnl f: r.o wl)...— 1
3709[2] Busy Flight *(99)*(Fav)*(BWHills)* 2-8-9 MHills(8) (lw: led tl ins fnl f: one pce) ....½ 2
4034* Brandon Magic **(100)***(98) (IABalding)* 2-8-9 KDarley(6) (2nd st: rdn over 1f out: ev ch ins fnl f: unable qckn)...nk 3
3779* Sketchbook **(91)***(96) (GLewis)* 2-8-9 PaulEddery(5) (5th st: rdn over 1f out: one pce) 1 4
3652* Lomberto **(90)***(96) (RHannon)* 2-8-10 ow1 RHughes(4) (lw: rdn over 2f out: hdwy fnl f: nvr nrr)s.h 5
3917* Quakers Field **(100)***(96) (GLMoore)* 2-8-9 SWhitworth(3) (6th st: rdn over 2f out: one pce)....hd 6
3947* King of Peru **(94)***(91) (APJarvis)* 2-8-9 JTate(1) (3rd st: rdn 2f out: wknd fnl f)..........................2 7
3890* Centre Stalls (IRE) *(91) (RFJohnsonHoughton)* 2-8-9 JReid(7) (4th st: ev ch wl over 1f out: sn wknd)...nk 8
3857* Nador *(75) (DRLoder)* 2-8-9 WRSwinburn(2) (lw: reard s: hld up: rdn 2f out: sn wknd)............7 9

7/2 TUMBLEWEED RIDGE, Busy Flight (5/2-4/1), **4/1** Brandon Magic, **5/1** Centre Stalls (IRE), **7/1** Nador, **10/1** Sketchbook, **16/1** King of Peru, Lomberto, **20/1** Quakers Field, CSF £15.76 TOTE £3.60: £1.60 £1.60 £1.40 (£11.10) Trio £10.00 OWNER The Tumbleweed Partnership (UPPER LAMBOURN) BRED R. A. Dalton 9 Rn 1m 34.74 (6.24) SF: 61/60/59/57/57/57/52/52/36

4160 GARDNER MERCHANT RATED STKS H'CAP (0-110) (3-Y.O+) (Class B)
£8,739.20 (£3,252.80: £1,576.40: £662.00: £281.00: £128.60)
6f 8y Stalls: Centre GOING: 0.46 sec per fur (GS) 3-40 (3-42)

1766[8] **Domulla (96)***(107) (RAkehurst)* 5-8-2 (5) DGriffiths(7) (hld up: led over 1f out: r.o wl) ....— 1
3815* Spaniards Close **(96)***(99) (PJMakin)* 7-8-7 MRoberts(2) (rdn & hdwy over 1f out: r.o one pce).3 2
3924[6] Astrac (IRE) **(96)***(98) (RAkehurst)* 4-8-0 (7) TAshley(10) (hld up: led over 2f out tl over 1f out: one pce)...nk 3
3602[9] Green Perfume (USA) **(99)***(97) (PFICole)* 3-8-8 TQuinn(1) (rdn & hdwy over 1f out: one pce)1½ 4
3854[3] Alzianah **(99)***(96) (JDBethell)* 4-8-10 WCarson(12) (hld up: rdn over 2f out: one pce) ....½ 5
3943[22] Tabook (IRE) **(96)***(93) (EALDunlop)* 4-8-2 (5) MHenry(14) (lw: hld up: rdn over 2f out: wknd over 1f out)...s.h 6
4033[3] No Extras (IRE) **(102)***(99)*(Fav)*(GLMoore)* 5-8-13 SWhitworth(9) (hdwy & nt clr run over 1f out: nvr nrr)..d.h 7
4033[16] Bowden Rose **(96)***(93) (MBlanshard)* 3-7-12b(7) MartinDwyer(13) (rdn over 3f out: nvr nr to chal)...hd 7
3834[11] Carranita (IRE) **(108)***(102) (BPalling)* 5-9-5 TSprake(3) (a mid div)...1 9
3834[6] Montendre **(110)***(104) (MMcCormack)* 8-9-7 JReid(15) (a mid div)..s.h 10
4012a[9] Bunty Boo **(107)***(93) (RHannon)* 6-8-13 (5) DaneO'Neill(16) (spd over 4f) 3 11
4121[9] El Yasaf (IRE) **(104)***(79) (CNAllen)* 7-9-1 TIves(11) (a bhd)...4 12
3999[6] Orange Place (IRE) **(96)***(67) (TJNaughton)* 4-8-2 (5) JDSmith(4) (bhd fnl 3f)............................1½ 13
3999[3] Cyrano's Lad (IRE) **(96)***(61) (CADwyer)* 6-8-7 CDwyer(8) (led over 3f) 2½ 14
4040[5] Bold Effort (FR) **(97)***(27) (KOCunningham-Brown)* 3-8-6 KDarley(5) (prom over 3f) 13 15
3707[4] Lennox Lewis **(96)** *(APJarvis)* 3-8-5 JTate(6) (lw: prom over 2f)..10 16
LONG HANDICAP Orange Place (IRE) 7-13 Tabook (IRE) 7-13 Domulla 7-13 Spaniards Close 8-6 Astrac (IRE) 8-3 Cyrano's Lad (IRE) 8-4 Bowden Rose 7-8

7/2 No Extras (IRE), **5/1** Montendre, **8/1** Spaniards Close (6/1-9/1), **10/1** Astrac (IRE), Alzianah, Bold Effort (FR) (8/1-12/1), **12/1** Bunty Boo (op 8/1), **16/1** Green Perfume (USA), Cyrano's Lad (IRE), Lennox Lewis, **20/1** Carranita (IRE), **33/1** El Yasaf (IRE), DOMULLA, Bowden Rose, Tabook (IRE), Orange Place (IRE), CSF £245.81 CT £2,547.30 TOTE £65.20: £9.50 £1.80 £2.30 £2.70 (£581.40) Trio £1,134.70 OWNER Mr A. W. Boon (EPSOM) BRED Alan Boon 16 Rn
1m 16.63 (4.83) SF: 63/55/54/51/52/49/55/47/58/60/49/35/23/17/-/-
WEIGHT FOR AGE 3yo-2lb

4161

E.B.F. THEALE MAIDEN STKS (2-Y.O) (Class D) £4,890.00 (£1,470.00: £710.00: £330.00) **6f 8y** Stalls: Centre GOING: 0.46 sec per fur (GS) 4-10 (4-11)

Fly Tip (IRE) *(84+) (BWHills)* 2-8-9 MHills(14) (neat: a.p: led wl over 1f out: hld on wl) ......— 1
Herodian (USA) *(88+) (JHMGosden)* 2-9-0 WRSwinburn(7) (unf: scope: hdwy over 1f out: r.o wl ins fnl f) ......½ 2
3890[2] Crazy Chief *(86)*(Fav)*(PFICole)* 2-9-0 TQuinn(4) (a.p: ev ch 2f out: r.o) ......½ 3
3733[10] Pleading *(85) (HCandy)* 2-9-0 WNewnes(10) (a.p: ev ch over 1f out: hrd rdn: r.o one pce) ....½ 4
Marawis (USA) *(83) (HThomsonJones)* 2-9-0 RHills(19) (str: scope: bkwd: w ldr: led 4f out tl wl over 1f out: one pce) ......¾ 5
Catch The Lights *(75) (RHannon)* 2-8-9 JReid(12) (unf: scope: bit bkwd: hdwy fnl 2f: nvr nrr) 1¼ 6
3917[10] Maple Burl *(77) (SDow)* 2-9-0 JWilliams(6) (hdwy 2f out: nvr nr to chal) 1 7
3828[3] Magic Melody *(72) (JLSpearing)* 2-8-6 (3) SDrowne(16) (hdwy 2f out: nt rch ldrs) ......hd 8
Pivotal *(74) (SirMarkPrescott)* 2-9-0 CNutter(15) (str: scope: bkwd: s.s: wl bhd tl gd hdwy over 1f out: r.o) 1¼ 9
4023[5] Old Hat (IRE) *(72) (RHannon)* 2-9-0 MRoberts(13) (led 2f: wknd 2f out) ......¾ 10
Last But Not Least *(66) (RFJohnsonHoughton)* 2-8-9 RPerham(5) (unf: nvr bttr than mid div) ......nk 11
Flying Harold *(67) (MRChannon)* 2-9-0 RHughes(18) (unf: bhd whn rdn & edgd lft over 1f out: nvr on terms) 1½ 12
3948[14] Fiona Shann (USA) *(60) (JLDunlop)* 2-8-9 WCarson(1) (sme hdwy & edgd rt over 1f out: nvr nr ldrs) ......½ 13
3890[12] Jona Holley *(65) (IABalding)* 2-9-0 KDarley(3) (hrd rdn over 2f out: no hdwy) ......nk 14
Bella's Legacy *(59) (RJHodges)* 2-8-9 TSprake(9) (neat: outpcd) ......nk 15
Naked Emperor *(57) (MJFetherston-Godley)* 2-9-0 DaleGibson(17) (str: scope: bkwd: a wl bhd) 2½ 16
4056[5] Little Millie *(48) (PHayward)* 2-8-4 (5) PFessey(8) (b.hind: spd over 3f) 1½ 17
3890[5] Punkah (USA) *(53) (LordHuntingdon)* 2-9-0 DHarrison(11) (prom over 3f) ......hd 18
Rock Daisy *(46) (BJMeehan)* 2-8-9 PaulEddery(20) (unf: a wl bhd) ......¾ 19
3893[10] Condor Ridge *(42) (BJMeehan)* 2-9-0 BDoyle(2) (no ch whn hmpd over 1f out) 3½ 20

3/1 Crazy Chief (5/2-4/1), **6/1** Punkah (USA), Herodian (USA) (op 4/1), Marawis (USA), **11/1** FLY TIP (IRE) (6/1-12/1), Old Hat (IRE) (op 20/1), Fiona Shann (USA), **12/1** Catch The Lights (op 8/1), **16/1** Pivotal, Pleading, Last But Not Least, **25/1** Flying Harold, **33/1** Magic Melody, Jona Holley, Bella's Legacy, Naked Emperor, Little Millie, Maple Burl, Rock Daisy, Condor Ridge, CSF £75.97 TOTE £18.50: £3.40 £2.40 £1.90 (£69.30) Trio £63.00 OWNER Mr D.E.McDowell (LAMBOURN) BRED David Commins 20 Rn
1m 18.64 (6.84) SF: 37/41/39/38/36/28/30/25/27/25/19/20/13/18/12/10/1/6/-/-

4162

ROSALIE MONBIOT BIRTHDAY MAIDEN STKS (I) (3-Y.O) (Class D) £3,840.50 (£1,154.00: £557.00: £258.50)
1m 2f 6y Stalls: Low GOING: 0.46 sec per fur (GS) 4-40 (4-41)

4003[3] **Bint Zamayem (IRE) (73)***(80) (BWHills)* 3-8-9 RPerham(4) (trckd ldr: 2nd st: led over 3f out: r.o wl) ......— 1
1339[3] Main Offender **(87)***(79)*(Fav)*(HRACecil)* 3-9-0 SDWilliams(8) (lw: 8th st: hdwy 3f out: ev ch over 1f out: hung lft & no imp fnl f) 3½ 2
3921[4] Quillwork (USA) **(60)***(66) (MrsJCecil)* 3-8-9 CDwyer(5) (led tl over 3f out: one pce) 5 3
4072[9] Roussi (USA) *(64) (MRStoute)* 3-9-0 KBradshaw(11) (hdwy over 2f out: nvr nr to chal) 5 4
3030[6] Persian Flower *(56) (GCBravery)* 3-8-9 NCarlisle(3) (5th st: no hdwy fnl 2f) 1½ 5
4049[12] Sun Circus *(48) (JLSpearing)* 3-8-9 MPerrett(2) (nvr nr to chal) 5 6
3958[4] Mr Medley **(72)***(45) (RHannon)* 3-9-0 MTebbutt(7) (4th st: wknd 2f out) 5 7
3712[5] Secret Spring (FR) **(79)***(44) (RCharlton)* 3-9-0 SRaymont(10) (3rd st: wknd over 2f out) ......½ 8
3712[11] Justfortherecord *(39) (BRMillman)* 3-8-9 CNutter(6) (nvr trbld ldrs) ......½ 9
Pointer *(34) (MrsPNDutfield)* 3-9-0 JWilliams(9) (a bhd) 6 10
Palace Guard *(15) (GPEnright)* 3-9-0 NAdams(12) (sn t.o) 12 11
4003[8] Brick Court (IRE) *(4) (RFJohnsonHoughton)* 3-8-9 RPrice(13) (7th st: wknd 4f out: t.o) 3½ 12
Questrill *(2) (JHMGosden)* 3-8-9 DaleGibson(1) (6th st: poor 4th whn faltered & virtually p.u over 1f out: t.o) 1¼ 13

13/8 Main Offender, **3/1** Questrill (op 2/1), **15/2** Secret Spring (FR), **9/1** BINT ZAMAYEM (IRE) (6/1-10/1), **11/1** Mr Medley, **14/1** Roussi (USA), **16/1** Quillwork (USA), **33/1** Pointer, **50/1** Persian Flower, Justfortherecord, Palace Guard, Brick Court (IRE), Sun Circus, CSF £22.20 TOTE £9.90: £2.00 £1.30 £4.40 (£12.20) Trio £49.90 OWNER Sir Eric Parker (LAMBOURN) BRED Charlton Down Stud 13 Rn
2m 14.65 (11.65) SF: 36/35/22/20/12/4/1/-/-/-/-/-/-

4163 ROUND OAK H'CAP (0-90) (3-Y.O+) (Class C) £6,950.00 (£2,090.00: £1,010.00: £470.00) **1m 2f 6y** Stalls: Low GOING: 0.46 sec per fur (GS) 5-10 (5-14)

4051* **Jagellon (USA)** **(73)***(88) (WRMuir)* 4-8-13 5x JReid(1) (4th st: led on bit 2f out: r.o)..............— **1**
1498* Kings Assembly **(72)***(84) (PWHarris)* 3-8-7 GHind(2) (5th st: swtchd rt over 1f out: r.o).........1¾ **2**
4074[7] Out on a Promise (IRE) **(85)***(93) (GWragg)* 3-9-6 MHills(6) (hdwy over 2f out: styd on: nvr nrr)..........2½ **3**
3945[13] Silver Groom (IRE) **(75)***(81) (RAkehurst)* 5-8-10 (5) MHenry(10) (hdwy over 2f out: r.o ins fnl f)..........1¼ **4**
3926[16] Major Change **(84)***(90) (RHannon)* 3-9-0 (5) DaneO'Neill(3) (2nd st: ev ch 2f out: one pce).....nk **5**
4061* Aljawab (USA) **(66)***(70) (JLDunlop)* 4-8-6 5x TQuinn(22) (wl bhd tl gd hdwy on ins over 2f out: nvr nr to chal)..........1¼ **6**
4028[7] Country Star (IRE) **(81)***(85) (HCandy)* 4-9-7 RHills(19) (3rd st: led over 3f out to 2f out).........hd **7**
3863[3] Domappel **(68)***(69)*(Fav)*(MrsJCecil)* 3-8-0 (3) JStack(11) (6th st: ev ch over 2f out: wknd over 1f out)..........1½ **8**
4035[4] Quintus Decimus **(76)***(73) (LordHuntingdon)* 3-8-11 DHarrison(20) (wl bhd tl gd hdwy over 2f out: wknd over 1f out)..........2½ **9**
3945[24] Rambo's Hall **(85)***(81) (JAGlover)* 10-9-11 DeanMcKeown(15) (mde most to 3f out: wknd).....½ **10**
3965[3] Exemption **(69)***(64) (HCandy)* 4-8-9 WNewnes(5) (a mid div)..........1 **11**
3945[39] Virtual Reality **(76)***(72) (AHide)* 4-9-2 MTebbutt(9) (nvr nr to chal)..........d.h **11**
Summerhill Special (IRE) **(73)***(68) (MrsPNDutfield)* 4-8-13 JWilliams(21) (nvr nr ldrs)...........s.h **13**
4028[8] Swallows Dream (IRE) **(77)***(65) (JLDunlop)* 4-9-3b WCarson(14) (wl bhd tl hdwy over 2f out: wknd over 1f out)..........4 **14**
3863[13] Yarrow (IRE) **(77)***(57) (JHMGosden)* 3-8-12 PaulEddery(13) (a bhd)..........5 **15**
4038* Seventeens Lucky **(70)***(49) (BobJones)* 3-8-5 FNorton(17) (prom tl wknd 3f out)..........1 **16**
1367[11] Camden's Ransom (USA) **(58)***(35) (HGRowsell)* 8-7-12 ow1 TSprake(16) (outpcd)..........½ **17**
3993* Sheer Danzig (IRE) **(88)***(56) (RWArmstrong)* 3-9-9 WRSwinburn(7) (rdn along: prom tl wknd 3f out)..........6 **18**
4051[14] Koathary (USA) **(61)***(28) (LGCottrell)* 4-8-1 DaleGibson(18) (prom tl wknd 3f out)..........1 **19**
3945[30] Tartan Gem (IRE) **(76)***(42) (JARToller)* 4-9-2 KDarley(4) (bhd fnl 3f)..........½ **20**
3837[11] Danegold (IRE) **(84)** *(MRChannon)* 3-9-5v RHughes(8) (t.o)..........dist **21**
3974* Lancerette **(74)** *(NAGraham)* 3-8-9 MRimmer(12) (t.o)..........15 **22**

6/1 Domappel, **13/2** Sheer Danzig (IRE), **9/1** Aljawab (USA), **10/1** Quintus Decimus, **12/1** Out on a Promise (IRE), JAGELLON (USA), Country Star (IRE), Exemption, **14/1** Yarrow (IRE), Lancerette, Seventeens Lucky, **16/1** Tartan Gem (IRE), Swallows Dream (IRE), **20/1** Kings Assembly, Rambo's Hall, Major Change, Silver Groom (IRE), Danegold (IRE), Koathary (USA), **33/1** Virtual Reality, Summerhill Special (IRE), **40/1** Camden's Ransom (USA), CSF £232.58 CT £2,715.47 TOTE £15.10: £4.00 £4.30 £2.90 £4.10 (£139.30) Trio £386.30 OWNER Mr D. J. Deer (LAMBOURN) BRED John Deer 22 Rn

2m 12.39 (9.39) SF: 58/49/58/51/55/40/55/34/38/51/34/42/38/35/22/14/5/21/-/12/-/-
WEIGHT FOR AGE 3yo-5lb

4164 ROSALIE MONBIOT BIRTHDAY MAIDEN STKS (II) (3-Y.O) (Class D) £3,814.50 (£1,146.00: £553.00: £256.50) **1m 2f 6y** Stalls: Low GOING: 0.46 sec per fur (GS) 5-40 (5-43)

3422[14] **Fasih** **(68)***(90) (ACStewart)* 3-9-0 CDwyer(3) (lw: 9th st: hdwy & swtchd rt 3f out: led over 1f out: cleverly)..........— **1**
3921[2] Devon Peasant **(72)***(85)*(Fav)*(LGCottrell)* 3-8-9 SRaymont(2) (3rd st: led wl over 1f out: sn hdd: r.o)..........nk **2**
3183[5] Almuhimm (USA) *(87) (EALDunlop)* 3-9-0 JWilliams(8) (10th st: gd hdwy over 1f out: ev ch ins fnl f: nt qckn)..........1½ **3**
1990[5] Rival Queen (IRE) *(67) (HRACecil)* 3-8-9 SDWilliams(7) (2nd st: led over 3f out tl wl over 1f out: wknd fnl f: fin 5th, 3½l: plcd 4th).......... **4**
3974[6] La Alla Wa Asa (IRE) *(61) (JHMGosden)* 3-8-9 DaleGibson(4) (8th st: nvr nr to chal: fin 6th, 3½l: plcd 5th).......... **5**
3875[14] Bakheta **(45)***(59) (KTIvory)* 3-8-9 VHalliday(11) (4th st: wknd over 1f out)..........1¼ **7**
3712[9] Hypertension *(55) (RHannon)* 3-9-0 MTebbutt(1) (6th st: wknd over 2f out)..........6 **8**
3847[3] Printers Quill *(50) (MajorDNChappell)* 3-9-0 MPerrett(5) (led tl wknd over 3f out)..........3 **9**
3845[6] Sing Up **(67)***(50) (MMcCormack)* 3-9-0 RPerham(9) (5th st: wknd 3f out)..........nk **10**
Calgary Girl *(38) (PCRitchens)* 3-8-9 NRodgers(13) (unf: a wl bhd)..........4 **11**
3712[16] Wise Brave *(42) (HCandy)* 3-9-0 NAdams(10) (a wl bhd)..........1 **12**
Silver Sleeve (IRE) **(64)***(39) (JARToller)* 3-9-0 NCarlisle(12) (7th st: wknd over 3f out).........1½ **13**
2929[2] Venice Beach **(72)***(78) (BWHills)* 3-9-0 RStreet(6) (sddle slipped sn after s: lost weight cloth 4f out: hdwy 3f out: nvr nrr: fin 4th, 6l: disq: plcd last).......... **D**

2/1 Devon Peasant, **4/1** La Alla Wa Asa (IRE) (9/4-9/2), **5/1** Venice Beach, **11/2** Rival Queen (IRE) (7/2-6/1), **7/1** Almuhimm (USA), **16/1** FASIH, **20/1** Printers Quill, **25/1** Hypertension, **33/1** Sing Up, Silver Sleeve (IRE), **50/1** Bakheta, Wise Brave, **66/1** Calgary Girl, CSF £46.60 TOTE £19.70: £4.00 £1.40 £2.00 (£23.20) Trio £78.30 OWNER Mr Hamdan Al Maktoum (NEWMARKET) BRED Ranston (Bloodstock) Ltd 13 Rn 2m 13.9 (10.90) SF: 47/42/44/24/18/16/12/7/7/-/-/-/35

T/Jkpt: Not won; £31,148.15 to Doncaster 20/10/95. T/Plpt: £58.10 (35,351.13 Tckts). T/Qdpt: £27.80 (10.1 Tckts). AK/Hn

3758-NOTTINGHAM (L-H)
Thursday October 19th (Good to firm, Good patches)

4165 KEGWORTH LIMITED STKS (0-65) (3-Y.O+) (Class F) £2,519.00 (£694.00: £329.00) 5f 13y GOING minus 0.22 sec per fur (GF) 2-00 (2-00)

4068 14 **Little Ibnr (62)***(68) (PDEvans)* 4-9-1 KFallon(3) (lw: a.p: rdn to ld ins fnl f: hld on gamely)....— 1
4122 7 Moujeeb (USA) **(50)***(67) (PatMitchell)* 5-9-1v JQuinn(5) (lw: chsd ldrs: rdn over 1f out: led ins fnl f: sn hdd: r.o) ....nk 2
3992 12 Hickory Blue **(65)***(68) (MrsNMacauley)* 5-9-4v JWeaver(9) (lw: led tl hdd over 1f out: rallied u.p towards fin) ....¾ 3
4057 10 Friendly Brave (USA) **(62)***(63) (MissGayKelleway)* 5-8-10 (5) AWhelan(26) (a.p: stands' side: rdn & unable qckn ins fnl f) ....½ 4
4142 6 Jucea **(63)***(60) (JLSpearing)* 6-8-13b SSanders(11) (a chsng ldrs: ev ch appr fnl f: unable qckn) ....½ 5
4113 4 Domicksky **(54)***(61) (MRChannon)* 7-8-10 (5) PPMurphy(2) (hld up: hdwy appr fnl f: nrst fin)...hd 6
4123 2 Silk Cottage **(63)***(60) (RMWhitaker)* 3-9-0v AClark(4) (lw: a.p: led over 1f out tl hdd and no ex ins fnl f) ....nk 7
3919 15 Lugana Vision **(48)***(57) (CNAllen)* 3-8-12 MFenton(15) (hld up: hdwy stands' side over 1f out: nvr nrr) ....nk 8
4041 23 Just Dissident (IRE) **(60)***(62) (RMWhitaker)* 3-9-3 ACulhane(16) (lw: chsd ldrs stands' side: kpt on ins fnl f) ....hd 9
4057 6 Malibu Man **(59)***(64) (SMellor)* 3-8-13 (7) ADaly(18) (chsd ldrs stands' side over 3f) ....nk 10
3919 13 Nordico Princess **(65)***(53) (MBrittain)* 4-8-10 RCochrane(22) (led stands' side over 3f) ....hd 11
4057 18 Grand Chapeau (IRE) **(60)***(60) (RHannon)* 3-9-3 GCarter(6) (lw: nvr trbld ldrs) ....hd 12
3667 18 High Domain (IRE) **(62)***(52) (JLSpearing)* 4-9-1 AlexGreaves(8) (m.n.s) 1¾ 13
4142 16 Giggleswick Girl **(63)***(54) (MRChannon)* 4-8-12 (7) JDennis(25) (s.i.s: nvr nrr) ....½ 14
3748 5 Kung Frode **(62)***(50) (BAMcMahon)* 3-8-9 (5) LNewton(19) (m.n.s) ....hd 15
3800 19 Tael of Silver **(65)***(51) (KRBurke)* 3-8-12b(3) PMcCabe(1) (prom 3f) ....s.h 16
3972 10 Rockcracker (IRE) **(60)***(48) (RCharlton)* 3-9-0b WRyan(24) (led stands' side over 3f) ....½ 17
4113 12 The Fed **(48)***(42) (RMWhitaker)* 5-9-1v JLowe(10) (led over 3f) 2 18
3878 4 John O'Dreams **(48)***(40) (MrsALMKing)* 10-9-1 AGarth(7) (s.s: a bhd) ....¾ 19
4145 2 Tinker Osmaston **(65)***(39)*(Fav)*(MSSaunders)* 4-9-2 JFEgan(21) (outpcd) ....½ 20
3981 4 Cemaes Bay **(65)***(35) (JBerry)* 3-9-0 JCarroll(12) (a bhd) 1 21
4134 8 Tyrone Flyer **(47)***(30) (CNAllen)* 6-9-1b StephenDavies(23) (sn outpcd) 1½ 22
4053 6 Warning Shot **(60)***(30) (MartynMeade)* 3-9-0 VSlattery(14) (swtg: outpcd) ....hd 23
3919 17 High Holme **(45)***(27) (DTThom)* 4-9-1v GDuffield(17) (m.n.s) 1 24
4123 12 Time Is Money (IRE) **(50)***(26) (MHTompkins)* 3-9-0 PRobinson(13) (m.n.s) ....nk 25
4125 11 Boursin (IRE) **(62)***(25) (NPLittmoden)* 6-9-1 TGMcLaughlin(20) (outpcd) ....hd 26

4/1 Tinker Osmaston, **7/1** Nordico Princess, **11/1** Jucea (8/1-12/1), Silk Cottage, **12/1** Kung Frode, Hickory Blue, LITTLE IBNR, **14/1** Cemaes Bay, Domicksky, **16/1** Tael of Silver, **20/1** Rockcracker (IRE), Malibu Man, Giggleswick Girl, Warning Shot, **25/1** Grand Chapeau (IRE), Time Is Money (IRE), Friendly Brave (USA), John O'Dreams, High Domain (IRE), **33/1** Moujeeb (USA), Lugana Vision, Tyrone Flyer, Just Dissident (IRE), High Holme, The Fed, Boursin (IRE), CSF £355.86 TOTE £17.70: £6.40 £29.70 £5.10 (£1,151.90) Trio £340.70 OWNER Swinnerton Transport Ltd (WELSHPOOL) BRED R. E. Waugh 26 Rn

61.4 secs (2.70) SF: 34/33/34/29/26/27/25/22/27/29/19/25/18/20/15/16/13/8/6/5/-/-/-/-/-/-
WEIGHT FOR AGE 3yo-1lb

4166 WOODBOROUGH H'CAP (0-80) (3-Y.O+) (Class D) £4,857.50 (£1,460.00: £705.00: £327.50) 2m 9y GOING minus 0.22 sec per fur (GF) 2-30 (2-30)

4140 2 **Sea Victor (71)***(86) (JLHarris)* 3-9-1 4x PRobinson(13) (lw: chsd ldrs: 6th st: led 3f out: clr appr fnl f: hld on wl) ....— 1
4026 6 Supreme Star (USA) **(67)***(82) (PRHedger)* 4-9-4 (3) NVarley(3) (led 2f: 2nd st: outpcd 3f out: styd on strly fnl f) ....s.h 2
3986* Coleridge **(47)***(61) (JJSheehan)* 7-8-1b JQuinn(8) (a.p: 7th st: chal 3f out: hrd rdn & one pce fnl f) 1 3

3114* Great Oration (IRE) **(41)***(54) (FWatson)* 6-7-9 LCharnock(9) (lw: hdwy 6f out: styd on wl appr fnl f)....¾ **4**
4026⁸ Star Player **(46)***(59) (RJBaker)* 9-8-0 AMcGlone(19) (a.p: 4th st: nt clr run fr 2f out: nt rcvr)....½ **5**
3849³ Chakalak **(47)***(58) (SDow)* 7-7-8 (7)ow1 ADaly(16) (lw: led after 2f to 3f out: wknd appr fnl f)...1¼ **6**
3936⁸ Bang in Trouble (IRE) **(56)***(66) (JJO'Neill)* 4-8-10 KFallon(7) (lw: hld up: hdwy 2f out: nvr able chal)....1¾ **7**
3986¹⁷ Champagne Gold **(43)***(50) (JCMcConnochie)* 8-7-11 ow3 TWilliams(11) (hld up mid div: effrt 3f out: no ex appr fnl f)....s.h **8**
2352³ Thunderheart **(68)***(77) (LMCumani)* 4-9-8 JWeaver(4) (hld up: hdwy & hmpd 3f out: nt rcvr)...½ **9**
3963¹¹ Talos (IRE) **(52)***(61) (DMoffatt)* 7-8-3 (3) DarrenMoffatt(10) (b: nvr plcd to chal)....½ **10**
4051¹¹ Fabulous Mtoto **(50)***(58) (MSSaunders)* 5-8-4 JFEgan(15) (lw: nvr nrr)....¾ **11**
*45*⁷ Tilty (USA) **(56)***(63) (AStreeter)* 5-8-5 (5) LNewton(5) (bhd: effrt 4f out: nvr nrr)....½ **12**
4026⁹ Head Turner **(40)***(47) (CPWildman)* 7-7-8 JLowe(6) (hdwy 4f out: sn rdn: wknd & eased fnl 2f)....½ **13**
4026¹² Requested **(53)***(60) (PBurgoyne)* 8-8-4 (3) PMcCabe(12) (hld up mid div: effrt 4f out: no imp) .nk **14**
4086² Matamoros **(70)***(76)*(Fav)*(JLDunlop)* 3-9-0v GCarter(17) (plld hrd: prom: 3rd st: wknd over 3f out)....nk **15**
3978⁵ Moshaajir (USA) **(70)***(73) (CSmith)* 5-9-10 GDuffield(14) (hld up mid div: effrt 3f out: nvr trbld ldrs)....3½ **16**
3818* Salska **(47)***(49) (AStreeter)* 4-8-1 AMackay(18) (hld up: hdwy ½-wy: 5th st: wknd 3f out)....¾ **17**
1773⁵ Sophism (USA) **(44)***(34) (MCPipe)* 6-7-9 (3) DWright(1) (bit bkwd: a in rr)....12 **18**
Tigersong (USA) **(64)** *(MissMKMilligan)* 5-9-4 JCarroll(2) (swtg: bkwd: plld hrd: prom 10f: t.o)....dist **19**
3898⁸ Fruitful Affair (IRE) **(44)** *(TThomsonJones)* 6-7-12 ow4 StephenDavies(20) (t.o fr ½-wy)....dist **20**

4/1 Matamoros, **11/2** Thunderheart, SEA VICTOR, **9/1** Supreme Star (USA), Salska, **10/1** Chakalak, Coleridge, **14/1** Star Player, Head Turner, Great Oration (IRE), **16/1** Requested, Sophism (USA), **20/1** Moshaajir (USA), **25/1** Bang in Trouble (IRE), Fruitful Affair (IRE), **33/1** Fabulous Mtoto, Tilty (USA), Champagne Gold, Tigersong (USA), Talos (IRE), CSF £57.61 CT £463.10 TOTE £5.50: £1.30 £4.50 £1.60 £4.60 (£54.80) Trio Not won; £218.78 to Doncaster 20/10/95. OWNER Mr David Abell (MELTON MOWBRAY) BRED Juddmonte Farms 20 Rn

3m 33.5 (9.10) SF: 37/43/22/15/20/19/27/11/38/22/19/24/8/21/27/34/10/-/-/-

WEIGHT FOR AGE 3yo-10lb

4167 ST ANNS MAIDEN STKS (I) (3-Y.O+) (Class D) £4,012.50 (£1,200.00: £575.00: £262.50)

1m 6f 15y Stalls: Low GOING minus 0.22 sec per fur (GF) 3-00 (3-00)

3896³ **Bimsey (IRE)** *(71+)*(Fav)*(RAkehurst)* 5-9-7 SSanders(9) (lw: chsd ldrs: led over 5f out: clr 3f out: unchal)....— **1**
3862¹¹ Sujud (IRE) **(52)***(56) (HThomsonJones)* 3-8-7 GCarter(10) (swtg: a.p: lost pl 5f out: 6th st: styd on again fnl 2f: no ch w wnr)....9 **2**
4062¹¹ Ciracusa (IRE) *(54) (JMackie)* 3-8-9 (3) NVarley(2) (s.s: hdwy 4f out: styd on one pce fnl 2f)....6 **3**
*3513*⁶ Ever Friends **(42)***(51) (RHarris)* 3-8-12 DBatteate(4) (swtg: chsd ldrs tl lost pl 6f out: sme late hdwy: n.d)....2½ **4**
3756⁵ Anchorena *(43) (RCharlton)* 3-8-7 WRyan(5) (swtg: plld hrd: chsd ldrs: 4th st: wknd 2f out).2½ **5**
3805³ Remontant (IRE) **(35)***(40) (RHollinshead)* 3-8-0 (7) FLynch(1) (hld up: hdwy & 5th st: wknd fnl 2f)....3 **6**
2331⁴ Eurolink Shadow **(70)***(45) (LMCumani)* 3-8-12 JWeaver(11) (bit bkwd: plld hrd: led over 8f: 2nd st: wknd below dist)....s.h **7**
Fortunes Course (IRE) *(39) (JSKing)* 6-9-2 AMackay(3) (bit bkwd: hld up: shkn up 7f out: t.o) 1 **8**
4003⁵ Solatium (IRE) **(66)***(30) (MCPipe)* 3-8-12 AMcGlone(7) (hld up: hdwy & 3rd st: lost pl over 3f out: t.o)....12 **9**
4003⁶ Telmo (IRE) *(19) (CFWall)* 3-8-12 OUrbina(8) (a in rr: t.o)....10 **10**
4062¹² Woodmans Lady *(JJSheehan)* 3-8-7 JQuinn(6) (bit bkwd: a bhd: t.o)....30 **11**

13/8 BIMSEY (IRE), **4/1** Eurolink Shadow, Anchorena (op 5/2), **5/1** Solatium (IRE), **16/1** Fortunes Course (IRE), Telmo (IRE), **20/1** Sujud (IRE), **25/1** Remontant (IRE), **33/1** Ciracusa (IRE), **50/1** Ever Friends, Woodmans Lady, CSF £31.92 TOTE £2.20: £1.30 £2.00 £16.20 (£33.90) Trio; Not won £145.79 to Doncaster 20/10/95. OWNER Mr Aidan Ryan (EPSOM) BRED Golden Vale Stud 11 Rn

3m 2.1 (3.60) SF: 67/43/41/38/30/27/32/35/17/6/-

WEIGHT FOR AGE 3yo-9lb

4168 ST ANNS MAIDEN STKS (II) (3-Y.O+) (Class D) £3,980.00 (£1,190.00: £570.00: £260.00)

1m 6f 15y Stalls: Low GOING minus 0.22 sec per fur (GF) 3-30 (3-30)

3884² **Opera Buff (IRE) (54)***(76+) (MissGayKelleway)* 4-9-2 (5) AWhelan(2) (lw: hld up: hdwy & 5th st: rdn to ld over 1f out: easily)....— **1**

3899³ Pampas Breeze (IRE) **(66)**(67)(Fav)*(WJarvis)* 3-8-7 WWoods(8) (a.p: 4th st: led 3f out tl over 1f out: one pce)....4 **2**
3862⁷ College Night (IRE) **(51)**(63) *(CADwyer)* 3-8-4 (3) PMcCabe(6) (swtg: mid div: 6th st: hdwy & ev ch 2f out: no ex appr fnl f)....3½ **3**
3862⁴ Ginger Jim **(57)**(66) *(PRHedger)* 4-9-4 (3) NVarley(3) (a.p: 3rd st: rdn over 1f out: kpt on same pce)....1 **4**
4000¹⁰ Fair and Fancy (FR) **(34)**(66) *(DNicholls)* 4-9-7 AlexGreaves(9) (plld hrd: chsd ldrs: 7th st: styd on wl fnl 3f)....nk **5**
3156⁶ Karttikeya (FR) **(75)**(61) *(MrsNMacauley)* 4-9-7 JWeaver(4) (b: lw: led over 11f: wknd 2f out) .4 **6**
3896⁵ Katie Oliver (50) *(BSmart)* 3-8-7 RCochrane(5) (bhd: effrt 4f out: sn rdn: no imp)....6 **7**
4047¹¹ Royrace **(47)**(52) *(WMBrisbourne)* 3-8-12 AGarth(10) (a bhd)....2½ **8**
3849¹³ Ballad Ruler **(20)**(51) *(PAPritchard)* 9-9-0 (7) JoHunnam(1) (hld up: lost pl over 4f out)....¾ **9**
3820¹⁴ Mamnoon (USA) **(64)** *(WClay)* 4-9-7v JCarroll(7) (chsd ldr: 2nd st: wknd 3f out: virtually p.u fnl f)....dist **10**

9/4 Pampas Breeze (IRE) (op 6/4), **7/2** Katie Oliver, **4/1** Karttikeya (FR) (op 5/2), **5/1** Ginger Jim (7/1-9/2), **6/1** OPERA BUFF (IRE), **12/1** Mamnoon (USA), **16/1** College Night (IRE), **25/1** Fair and Fancy (FR), **50/1** Royrace, Ballad Ruler, CSF £20.25 TOTE £8.00: £2.20 £2.10 £4.30 (£5.20) Trio £63.90 OWNER Mr D. C. Toogood (WHITCOMBE) BRED Juddmonte Farms 10 Rn

3m 5.9 (7.40) SF: 46/28/24/36/36/31/11/13/21/-

WEIGHT FOR AGE 3yo-9lb

4169

E.B.F. MAIDEN STKS (2-Y.O) (Class D) £5,310.75 (£1,596.00: £770.50: £357.75)
1m 54y Stalls: Low GOING minus 0.22 sec per fur (GF) 4-00 (4-01)

Dushyantor (USA) (82+)(Fav)*(HRACecil)* 2-9-0 WRyan(11) (neat: trckd ldrs: 7th str: shkn up 2f out: r.o to ld ins fnl f)....— **1**
3916³ Altamura (USA) (76) *(JHMGosden)* 2-8-9 AGarth(17) (chsd ldrs: 5th str: led 3f out: qcknd 2f out: hdd ins fnl f: nt qckn)....¾ **2**
3663¹³ Fly Fishing (USA) (67) *(MrsJCecil)* 2-9-0 RCochrane(10) (b: s.s: hdwy fnl 2f: fin wl)....7 **3**
3983⁸ Caribbean Dancer (56) *(MRStoute)* 2-8-9 PRobinson(12) (swtg: prom: 3rd st: ev ch 3f out: sn outpcd)....3 **4**
4037⁷ Bluebeard (IRE) (58) *(JHMGosden)* 2-9-0v JCarroll(7) (bit bkwd: led over 5f)....1¾ **5**
*2635*⁶ Richard House Lad (57) *(RHollinshead)* 2-9-0 ACulhane(15) (in tch: styd on one pce fnl 3f) ..½ **6**
3968¹¹ Influence Pedler **(50)**(54) *(CEBrittain)* 2-9-0 WWoods(14) (swtg: in tch: effrt 3f out: no imp)..1½ **7**
3883⁹ The Swan (47) *(JLDunlop)* 2-8-9 GCarter(5) (s.i.s: bhd tl styd on fnl 3f)....¾ **8**
Spinning Mouse (47) *(DMorley)* 2-8-9 MFenton(1) (unf: scope: bkwd: in tch 5f)....nk **9**
Old Irish (49) *(LMCumani)* 2-9-0 OUrbina(9) (lt-f: scope: s.i.s: nvr trbld ldrs)....1¼ **10**
3916¹⁰ Premier Generation (IRE) (47) *(DWPArbuthnot)* 2-9-0 AClark(13) (hdwy 4f out: wknd 2f out)1½ **11**
3003⁹ Tablets of Stone (IRE) (43) *(JRBosley)* 2-9-0 CRutter(4) (prom: 6th str: sn wknd)....1¾ **12**
3620¹² Forgie (IRE) (42) *(PCalver)* 2-9-0 MBirch(16) (w ldrs: 4th str: wknd 3f out)....½ **13**
3626¹¹ Holloway Melody (35) *(BAMcMahon)* 2-8-4 (5) LNewton(2) (a bhd)....1¾ **14**
3883¹⁶ Dashing Invader (USA) (38) *(PWHarris)* 2-9-0 JQuinn(18) (still bkwd: a bhd)....¾ **15**
Pearl Anniversary (IRE) (38) *(MJohnston)* 2-9-0 TWilliams(8) (w'like: leggy: prom: rdn & 2nd st: wknd 3f out)....nk **16**
Charming Admiral (IRE) (36) *(CFWall)* 2-9-0 GDuffield(3) (w'like: str: bkwd: sn rdn & bhd) 1 **17**
Firbur (35) *(NAGraham)* 2-9-0 AMcGlone(6) (w'like: leggy: effrt 3f out: a bhd)....½ **18**
Balios (IRE) (34) *(MJohnston)* 2-9-0 JWeaver(19) (wl grwn: bkwd: chsd ldrs 4f)....½ **19**

1/3 DUSHYANTOR (USA), **7/1** Altamura (USA), **14/1** The Swan, Caribbean Dancer, Bluebeard (IRE), Old Irish, **20/1** Spinning Mouse, Fly Fishing (USA), Balios (IRE), **33/1** Influence Pedler, Firbur, **40/1** Premier Generation (IRE), Pearl Anniversary (IRE), **50/1** Tablets of Stone (IRE), Dashing Invader (USA), Richard House Lad, Charming Admiral (IRE), Forgie (IRE), Holloway Melody, CSF £5.54 TOTE £1.30: £1.10 £1.40 £4.20 (£3.80) Trio £27.60 OWNER Mr K. Abdullah (NEWMARKET) BRED Juddmonte Farms 19 Rn

1m 43.9 (4.30) SF: 37/31/22/11/13/12/9/2/2/4/2/-/-/-/-/-/-/-/-

4170

RAINWORTH CLAIMING STKS (3-Y.O+) (Class F) £2,519.00 (£694.00: £329.00)
1m 54y Stalls: Low GOING minus 0.22 sec per fur (GF) 4-30 (4-32)

*4128*⁶ **Gentle Irony (55)**(68) *(BJMeehan)* 3-8-7b JFEgan(17) (hdwy over 3f out: rdn & hmpd wl over 1f out: rallied fnl f: fin 2nd, 1l: awrdd r)....— **1**
4035¹¹ Kingchip Boy **(63)**(73) *(MJRyan)* 6-8-8v(5) DGibbs(15) (chsd ldrs: 6th st: led 3f out: went lft wl over 1f out: hld on wl fnl f: fin 1st: disq: plcd 2nd).... **2**
4002⁴ High Premium **(75)**(79)(Fav)*(RAFahey)* 7-9-7 ACulhane(19) (b: hdwy 3f out: rdn over 1f out: r.o)....s.h **3**
4060¹⁰ Love Legend **(51)**(61) *(DWPArbuthnot)* 10-8-5 AClark(10) (hdwy over 2f out: staying on whn n.m.r ins fnl f)....1¼ **4**

3984[9] Bold Angel **(68)***(64) (MHEasterby)* 8-8-9 MBirch(12) (lw: chsd ldrs: 7th st: rdn & btn appr fnl f) ... ½ **5**
4054[8] Hunza Story **(36)***(58) (NPLittmoden)* 3-7-8 (7) JoHunnam(20) (b.hind: bhd: rdn & hdwy 3f out: nrst fin) ... hd **6**
3920[5] Doodies Pool (IRE) **(49)***(62) (PBurgoyne)* 5-8-8 (3) PMcCabe(2) (bhd effrt 4f out: nvr rchd ldrs) 2 **7**
2755[7] Care And Comfort **(62)***(61) (KMcAuliffe)* 3-8-9 RCochrane(14) (nvr nrr) ... 1 **8**
3825[13] Waterlord (IRE) **(40)***(55) (DNicholls)* 5-8-9 AlexGreaves(5) (lw: led over 5f) ... 1½ **9**
3396[10] Swynford Flyer **(21)***(45) (JAHarris)* 6-7-11 (3) DarrenMoffatt(4) (chsd ldrs: rdn over 3f out: wknd 2f out) ... nk **10**
4060[11] Battle Colours (IRE) **(51)***(53) (DonEnricoIncisa)* 6-8-9 KimTinkler(11) (prom: 4th str: wknd over 2f out) ... ½ **11**
3871[6] Magication **(28)***(44) (CNAllen)* 5-8-0 CRutter(16) (stdd st: wl bhd tl r.o fnl 2f) ... nk **12**
4054[7] Sea Spouse **(39)***(52) (MBlanshard)* 4-8-11 JQuinn(6) (prom: 3rd st: n.m.r over 2f out: sn btn) ... 1½ **13**
3771[10] North Esk (USA) **(55)***(59) (CADwyer)* 6-9-2 (5) LNewton(3) (reard s: a bhd) ... 1¼ **14**
3825[12] Resolute Bay **(38)***(40) (RMWhitaker)* 9-8-5v JLowe(9) (s.i.s: a bhd) ... 1¾ **15**
3762[8] The Deaconess **(32)***(37) (MrsALMKing)* 4-8-8 AGarth(8) (hdwy & 5th st: wknd over 2f out) ... 3 **16**
4054[3] Daring Ryde **(40)***(45) (JPSmith)* 4-9-3 GDuffield(1) (s.i.s: a bhd) ... ½ **17**
3026[8] Prussian Flag **(82)***(48) (RHannon)* 3-9-4 GCarter(7) (swtg: chsd ldr: 2nd st: wknd 3f out) ... ¾ **18**
3972[7] Saint Amigo **(44)***(14) (JLEyre)* 3-8-8 WRyan(18) (chsd ldrs 4f) ... 12 **19**

9/4 High Premium, **4/1** Bold Angel, **7/1** Prussian Flag, **9/1** Kingchip Boy (6/1-10/1), **12/1** GENTLE IRONY, **14/1** Love Legend, **16/1** Battle Colours (IRE), **20/1** Doodies Pool (IRE), Care And Comfort, North Esk (USA), **25/1** Saint Amigo, Magication, Resolute Bay, **33/1** Sea Spouse, Hunza Story, The Deaconess, Daring Ryde, Waterlord (IRE), Swynford Flyer, CSF £110.99 TOTE £13.40: £3.60 £2.50 £1.70 (£69.40) Trio £56.50 OWNER Mr A. S. Reid (UPPER LAMBOURN) BRED Red House Stud 19 Rn 1m 44.4 (4.80) SF: 23/31/37/19/22/13/20/16/13/3/11/2/10/17/-/-/3/3/-

WEIGHT FOR AGE 3yo-3lb

STEWARDS' ENQUIRY Gibbs susp. 28&30/10/95 (careless riding).

4171 GAMSTON H'CAP (0-75) (3-Y.O+) (Class D) £4,695.00 (£1,410.00: £680.00: £315.00) 1m 54y Stalls: Low GOING minus 0.22 sec per fur (GF) 5-00 (5-01)

3837[13] **Samba Sharply (74)***(86) (AHide)* 4-9-13 WWoods(3) (trckd ldrs: 7th st: rdn to ld wl ins fnl f) ... — **1**
3943[30] Mister Fire Eyes (IRE) **(70)***(81) (CEBrittain)* 3-9-6 MBirch(16) (lw: w ldrs: 3rd st: led over 3f out tl wl ins fnl f) ... nk **2**
3757[8] Ocean Park **(60)***(70) (LadyHerries)* 4-8-13 TWilliams(17) (b.off hind: hld up: hdwy over 2f out: r.o fnl f) ... 1 **3**
3984[7] Robsera (IRE) **(66)***(75) (GLewis)* 4-9-0 (5) AWhelan(6) (chsd ldrs: 5th st: rdn & ev ch 3f out: no ex fnl f) ... nk **4**
3885[5] Roi de la Mer (IRE) **(64)***(72) (JAkehurst)* 4-9-3 GCarter(19) (hdwy wl over 1f out: no ex ins fnl f) ... nk **5**
4044* Bentico **(64)***(69)*(Fav)*(MrsNMacauley)* 6-9-3 5x JWeaver(15) (hdwy over 1f out: r.o) ... 1½ **6**
3679[13] Fairy Knight **(71)***(73) (RHannon)* 3-9-7b JFEgan(11) (sn in tch: no imp fnl 3f) ... 1¾ **7**
4035[10] Duello **(60)***(58) (MBlanshard)* 4-8-13 RCochrane(7) (led after 1f tl over 3f out: eased whn btn ins fnl f) ... 2 **8**
4044[3] Michellisa **(58)***(56) (JDBethell)* 4-8-11 KFallon(1) (in tch: effrt over 2f out: no imp) ... hd **9**
4035[9] Just Harry **(64)***(59) (MJRyan)* 4-8-12 (5) DGibbs(14) (nvr nrr) ... 1½ **10**
3973[8] Forzair **(66)***(56) (SRBowring)* 3-8-11 (5) CTeague(12) (effrt 3f out: nvr rchd ldrs) ... 2½ **11**
3926[10] Failte Ro **(63)***(50) (JEBanks)* 3-8-13 JQuinn(10) (in tch over 4f) ... 1¾ **12**
3984[13] Greatest **(67)***(53) (RAkehurst)* 4-9-6 SSanders(5) (led 1f: 2nd st: wknd over 2f out) ... ½ **13**
3645[3] Mowlaie **(67)***(49) (DWChapman)* 4-9-6 ACulhane(20) (a bhd) ... 1¾ **14**
2293[7] Children's Choice (IRE) **(60)***(42) (PJMcBride)* 4-8-13 JLowe(2) (bit bkwd: s.i.s: a bhd) ... hd **15**
3565[11] Young Benson **(63)***(43) (BAMcMahon)* 3-8-8 (5) LNewton(8) (chsd ldrs over 5f) ... 1¼ **16**
3719[14] Don Pepe **(67)***(46) (RBoss)* 4-9-6 WRyan(18) (chsd ldrs: 6th st: rdn 3f out: sn wknd) ... ½ **17**
4071[15] Prudent Pet **(63)***(37) (CWFairhurst)* 3-8-10 (3) PMcCabe(13) (a bhd) ... 2½ **18**
4035[22] Ever so Lyrical **(70)***(40) (PWHarris)* 5-9-9 GDuffield(9) (lw: a bhd) ... 2 **19**
4038[22] Nizaal (USA) **(75)***(45) (DNicholls)* 4-10-0 AlexGreaves(4) (plld hrd: prom: 4th st: wknd 3f out) nk **20**

4/1 Bentico, **5/1** Ocean Park, **8/1** Robsera (IRE), **10/1** SAMBA SHARPLY, **12/1** Fairy Knight, Roi de la Mer (IRE), Just Harry, Duello, Michellisa, **14/1** Greatest, Mowlaie, Ever so Lyrical, **16/1** Failte Ro, Don Pepe, Nizaal (USA), **20/1** Prudent Pet, Forzair, Young Benson, **25/1** Mister Fire Eyes (IRE), **50/1** Children's Choice (IRE), CSF £246.07 CT £1,317.88 TOTE £15.20: £4.00 £7.40 £2.20 £2.90 (£210.10) Trio Not won; £403..82 to Doncaster 20/10/95. OWNER Miss V. R. Jarvis (NEWMARKET) BRED Summerhill Stud Ltd 20 Rn

1m 43.5 (3.90) SF: 53/45/37/42/39/36/37/25/23/26/20/14/20/16/9/7/13/1/7/12

WEIGHT FOR AGE 3yo-3lb

4172 HORSERACE BETTING LEVY BOARD MEDIAN AUCTION MAIDEN STKS (2-Y.O) (Class F) £3,224.60 (£895.60: £429.80)
1m 1f 213y Stalls: Low GOING minus 0.22 sec per fur (GF) 5-30 (5-31)

3760[4] **Rose of Siberia (USA) (67)***(66)*(Fav)*(MBell)* 2-8-9 MFenton(13) (chsd ldr: 2nd st: led over 3f out: rdn out) ....— 1
3994[3] Northern Soul (USA) *(69) (MJohnston)* 2-9-0 TWilliams(4) (hdwy over 4f out: sn rdn: edgd lft fnl 2f: r.o) 1½ 2
3530[6] Not Quite Grey *(69) (KMcAuliffe)* 2-9-0 RCochrane(6) (b.off hind: chsd ldrs: 6th st: kpt on fnl 2f) ....s.h 3
3994[4] Spring Campaign (IRE) *(68) (MCPipe)* 2-9-0 AMcGlone(5) (prom: 3rd st: ev ch 2f out: one pce) ....½ 4
4075[2] Sharp Shuffle (IRE) *(65) (RHannon)* 2-9-0 JFEgan(3) (rdn 4f out: nvr rchd ldrs) 2 5
3525[8] Jump The Lights *(53) (SPCWoods)* 2-9-0 WWoods(8) (bit bkwd: in tch: no hdwy fnl 3f) 7 6
3683[8] Umberston (IRE) *(52) (LMCumani)* 2-9-0 OUrbina(10) (chsd ldrs: 4th st: one pce fnl 3f) ....¾ 7
3666[12] General Glow *(51) (NBycroft)* 2-9-0 GCarter(14) (swtg: s.s: nvr trbld ldrs) 1 8
4073[6] What Jim Wants (IRE) **(40)***(50) (JJO'Neill)* 2-9-0 JCarroll(2) (a bhd) ....s.h 9
Brighter Byfaah (IRE) *(50) (NAGraham)* 2-9-0 WRyan(11) (w'like: str: bkwd: s.i.s: a bhd) .....hd 10
4100[7] Double Check (IRE) *(45) (MJohnston)* 2-8-9 JWeaver(12) (led over 6f: wknd & eased 1f out) ....hd 11
3846[6] Soviet King (IRE) *(47) (PMitchell)* 2-9-0 RWoodworth(1) (b.hind: chsd ldrs: 5th st: wknd 3f out) 1¾ 12
3851[8] Reef Raider **(43)***(38) (NTinkler)* 2-9-0b KimTinkler(9) (a bhd) 6 13
4064[12] Backtiari *(SGollings)* 2-9-0 CRutter(7) (chsd ldrs 5f: t.o) ....dist 14

5/2 ROSE OF SIBERIA (USA), **4/1** Northern Soul (USA) (op 5/2), Sharp Shuffle (IRE) (3/1-9/2), **9/2** Not Quite Grey (5/1-10/1), **5/1** Spring Campaign (IRE) (op 3/1), **8/1** Double Check (IRE), **14/1** Jump The Lights, Umberston (IRE), **16/1** Soviet King (IRE), Brighter Byfaah (IRE), **25/1** Reef Raider, **33/1** General Glow, **66/1** What Jim Wants (IRE), Backtiari, CSF £15.81 TOTE £3.70: £1.60 £1.60 £2.40 (£6.70) Trio £49.40 OWNER Mrs J. M. Corbett (NEWMARKET) BRED Poole Investments 14 Rn
2m 9.8 (7.30) SF: 17/20/20/19/16/4/3/2/1/1/-/-/-/-

T/Plpt: £189.30 (57.8 Tckts). T/Qdpt: £16.50 (9.75 Tckts). Dk

4091a-CURRAGH (Newbridge, Ireland) (R-H) Saturday October 14th (Good to soft)

4173a BLANDFORD STKS (Gp 2) (3-Y.O+) £23,636.00 (£6,909.00: £3,273.00: £1,091.00) 1m 3f
3-00 (3-03)

3790a[4] **Humbel (USA)** *(112) (DKWeld,Ireland)* 3-8-7 MJKinane (mde all: rdn 2f out: r.o strly) ....— 1
3831[7] Ballykett Nancy (IRE) *(108) (JSBolger,Ireland)* 4-8-11 JAHeffernan (3rd st: chal 2f out: no ex fnl f) 1 2
3193a[2] Idris (IRE) *(108) (JSBolger,Ireland)* 5-9-0 CRoche (4th st: hrd rdn wl over 1f out: no imp) 2 3
3811[2] Richard of York *(103)*(Fav)*(JHMGosden)* 5-9-0b GHind (2nd st: rdn & wknd fr 2f out) 3 4
2218a[6] Damancher *(102) (PMullins,Ireland)* 3-8-7 WJO'Connor (sn bhd: styd on fnl 2f: nvr nrr) ....¾ 5

Evens Richard of York, **3/1** HUMBEL (USA), **13/2** Idris (IRE), **7/1** Ballykett Nancy (IRE), **12/1** Damancher, Tote £3.00: £1.50 £3.30 (£7.50) OWNER Dr Michael Smurfit BRED A. E. Paulson 5 Rn
2m 25.6 (9.60) SF: -/-/-/-/-

4174a JUDDMONTE BERESFORD STKS (Gp 3) (2-Y.O) £17,727.00 (£5,182.00: £2,455.00: £818.00) 1m
4-00 (4-03)

Ahkaam (USA) *(101) (DKWeld,Ireland)* 2-8-11 MJKinane ....— 1
Sheraka (IRE) *(98)*(Fav)*(JOxx,Ireland)* 2-8-8 JPMurtagh ....hd 2
4091a[3] Ceirseach (IRE) *(93) (JSBolger,Ireland)* 2-8-8b JAHeffernan 2½ 3
3587a* No Animosity (IRE) *(96)*(Fav)*(APO'Brien,Ireland)* 2-8-11 CRoche ....hd 4
Red Robin (IRE) *(92) (JOxx,Ireland)* 2-8-11 WJO'Connor 2 5

11/4 No Animosity (IRE), Sheraka (IRE), **7/2** Ceirseach (IRE), AHKAAM (USA), **7/1** Red Robin (IRE), Tote £3.80: £1.90 £2.30 (£4.30) OWNER Mr Hamdan Al Maktoum BRED Flaxman Holdings Ltd 5 Rn
1m 46.1 (10.10) SF: -/-/-/-/-
NR

3911a-BELMONT PARK (New York, USA) (L-H)
Saturday October 14th (Fast)

4175a MAID OF THE MIST STKS (2-Y.O F) £38,462.00 1m 22-00 (-)

Light Up New York (USA) *(WTerrill,USA)* 2-8-2 MSmith .... — 1
Talent Lady (USA) *(CDomino,USA)* 2-8-2 JChavez 6½ 2
Gracie Allen (USA) *(TKelly,USA)* 2-8-2 DianeNelson .... nk 3
2554³ Lac Dessert (USA) *(DRLoder)* 2-8-4 RDavis (btn 11¼l) 6

P-M £5.40: PL £3.50 £10.00 SHOW £2.70 £5.50 £3.50 (£64.50) OWNER Mr Seymour Cohn BRED Stonewall Farm 9 Rn 1m 39.01 SF: -/-/-/-

4089a-LONGCHAMP (Paris, France) (R-H)
Sunday October 15th (Good to firm)

4176a PRIX DE CONSEIL DE PARIS (Gp 2) (3-Y.O+) £35,928.00 (£14,371.00: £7,186.00: £3,593.00) 1m 4f 2-35 (2-35)

De Quest *(113) (AFabre,France)* 3-8-9 TJarnet (4th st: hdwy to ld 1f out: qcknd clr: impressive) .... — 1
3790a² Slicious *(110) (VCaruso,Italy)* 3-8-9 CAsmussen (hld up in rr: effrt 2f out: r.o) 2 2
1709a⁵ Rainbow Dancer (FR) *(107) (PBary,France)* 4-9-2 DBoeuf (rr early: swtchd & rdn 2f out: r.o: nrst fin) 2 3
1574a⁹ Walk on Mix (FR) *(112) (AFabre,France)* 3-9-0 SGuillot (mid div: 6th st: 3rd 1f out: one pce) s.nk 4
3790a* Posidonas *(111) (PFICole)* 3-9-2 TQuinn (3rd st: hmpd 2f out: one pce) 2½ 5
2219a² Capias (USA) *(103) (JHMGosden)* 4-9-2b MJKinane (5th st: rdn & outpcd 2f out) .... s.h 6
4014a¹¹ El Tenor(FR) *(102) (ASpanu,France)* 3-8-9 ESaint-Martin (led tl 1f out: wknd) 1½ 7
4009a² Daraydala (IRE) *(95) (AdeRoyerDupre,France)* 3-8-6 GMosse (prom: 2nd st: rdn over 2f out: wknd) 3 8

P-M 4.20F: 1.70F 2.70F 3.00F (27.60F) OWNER Mr K. Abdullah (FRANCE) BRED Juddmonte Farms 8 Rn 2m 27.4 SF: -/-/-/-/-/-/-/-

4177a GRAND CRITERIUM (Gp 1) (2-Y.O C & F) £119,760.00 (£47,904.00: £23,952.00: £11,976.00) 1m 3-45 (3-44)

Loup Solitaire (USA) *(110) (AFabre,France)* 2-8-11 OPeslier (racd in 3rd: hdwy fr over 1f out to ld ins fnl f: r.o) .... — 1
3907a* Manninamix *(110) (AFabre,France)* 2-8-11 TJarnet (hld up: plld out 2f out: r.o strly fnl f: jst failed) .... s.h 2
Eternity Range (USA) *(108) (PBary,France)* 2-8-11 DBoeuf (5th early: r.o fnl f: nrst fin) 1 3
4010a* Le Triton (USA) *(108) (MmeCHead,France)* 2-8-11 WRSwinburn (led: rdn over 2f out: hdd ins fnl f: no ex) .... nse 4
3900* Astor Place (IRE) *(104) (PWChapple-Hyam)* 2-8-11 JReid (4th st: rdn 2f out: unable qckn) 2 5
4037* Committal (IRE) *(104) (JHMGosden)* 2-8-11 MJKinane (trckd ldr: 2nd st: rdn over 2f out: wknd ins fnl f) .... s.h 6
Dark Nile (USA) *(103) (MmeCHead,France)* 2-8-11 PatEddery (a bhd) .... nk 7

P-M 11.30F: 2.70F 1.40F (SF 35.70) OWNER Mr D. Wildenstein (FRANCE) BRED Allez France Stables Ltd 7 Rn 1m 37.6 SF: -/-/-/-/-/-/-

4178a PRIX DE LA FORET (Gp 1) (3-Y.O+ C & F) £59,880.00 (£23,952.00: £11,976.00: £5,988.00) 7f 4-15 (4-15)

3795a* **Poplar Bluff (IRE)** *(123) (AFabre,France)* 3-9-0 OPeslier (3rd early: effrt to ld ins fnl f: r.o wl) .... — 1
3931⁴ Bin Ajwaad (IRE) *(122) (BHanbury)* 5-9-2 PatEddery (hld up: rdn & qcknd 2f out: chal ins fnl f: jst failed) .... s.nk 2
3931* Inzar (USA) *(119) (PFICole)* 3-9-0 TQuinn (2nd early: rdn to ld 1f out: hdd ins fnl f: r.o) 1½ 3
3931² Mutakddim (USA) *(118) (JHMGosden)* 4-9-2 WCarson (racd in 5th: n.m.r over 1f out: fin wl) .... s.h 4
608a² Neverneyev (USA) *(116) (MmeCHead,France)* 5-9-2 ODoleuze (led: rdn over 2f out: hdd 1f out: no ex) 1 5
Anabaa (USA) *(113) (MmeCHead,France)* 3-9-0 DBoeuf (hld up: r.o one pce fnl 2f) 1½ 6
3834⁵ Wessam Prince *(109) (CLaffon-Parias,France)* 4-9-2 WRSwinburn (racd in 4th: rdn 2f out: eased fnl f) 1½ 7

3931[5] Branston Abby (IRE) *(102) (MJohnston)* 6-8-13 MRoberts (a bhd) 1½ **8**
3931[3] Myself *(103) (PWChapple-Hyam)* 3-8-11 TJarnet (nvr plcd to chal) ....nse **9**
3834[2] Young Ern *(102) (SDow)* 5-9-2 MJKinane (8th st: m.n.s) 1½ **10**

P-M 5.00F: 1.90F 4.20F 2.20F (49.90F) OWNER Mr D. Wildenstein (FRANCE) 10 Rn 1m 18.4
DS

4092a-SAN SIRO (Milan, Italy) (R-H)
Sunday October 15th (Good to soft)

4179a PREMIO THE IRISH NATIONAL STUD (3-Y.O+ F & M) £7,880.00 (£3,467.00: £1,891.00) **1m 3f** 2-25 (2-27)

Valclub (IRE) *(91) (MCiciarelli,Italy)* 6-9-2 AParravani ....— **1**
Rain and Hail (ITY) *(88) (Italy)* 5-9-0 GForte ....½ **2**
3728[7] Pesce D'Aprile *(88) (JLDunlop)* 3-8-7 WRyan ....hd **3**

Tote 26L: 14L 14L (29L) OWNER Scuderia Briantea BRED Azienda Agricola Valtaro SAS 5 Rn
2m 20.6 SF: -/-/-

4180a PREMIO DORMELLO (Gp 3) (2-Y.O F) £26,312.00 (£12,405.00: £7,009.00) **1m** 2-50 (3-10)

3633* **Scarlet Plume** *(96+) (JLDunlop)* 2-8-11 KDarley ....— **1**
Beauty Dancer (IRE) *(91) (AColella,Italy)* 2-8-11 MEsposito 2½ **2**
3842* Gryada *(89) (WJarvis)* 2-8-11 WRyan 1¼ **3**

Tote 26L: 14L 22L 17L (223L) OWNER Mr Nigel Elwes (ARUNDEL) BRED Exors of the late Sir Robin McAlpine 11 Rn 1m 39.9 SF: -/-/-

4181a PREMIO OMENONI (Gp 3) (3-Y.O+) £29,760.00 (£16,607.00: £7,709.00: £3,854.00) **5f** 3-45 (4-12)

3815[2] **Leap for Joy** *(108) (JHMGosden)* 3-8-4 GHind ....— **1**
4006a[6] Palacegate Episode (IRE) *(105) (JBerry)* 5-8-4 GCarter ....½ **2**
Reinaldo (FR) *(105) (GBotti,Italy)* 3-8-7 GForte 1¼ **3**
3902* Dairine's Delight (IRE) *(MCunningham,Ireland)* 5-8-4 JoannaMorgan (btn approx 1½l).... **5**

Tote 43L: 18L 17L 41L (92L) OWNER Mr Seisuke Hata (NEWMARKET) BRED The Overbury Stud 9 Rn 57.9 secs SF: -/-/-/-

4182a GRAN PREMIO DEL JOCKEY CLUB ITALIANO (Gp 1) (3-Y.O+ C & F) £185,066.00 (£96,050.00: £56,678.00: £28,339.00) **1m 4f** 4-15 (4-44)

4011a[2] **Court of Honour (IRE)** *(122) (PWChapple-Hyam)* 3-8-12 WRyan (mde all: jst hld on)....— **1**
3591a[P] Royal Ballerina (IRE) *(116) (MKauntze,Ireland)* 5-9-0 WJO'Connor (a.p: str chal fnl f: jst failed) ....s.h **2**
3914a[2] Sternkonig (IRE) *(119) (HBlume,Germany)* 5-9-3 OSchick (hld up: n.m.r over 2f out: r.o wl fnl f) ....hd **3**
1890a[5] Linney Head (USA) *(118) (JHMGosden)* 4-9-3 GHind (chsd wnr: r.o wl u.p) ....nk **4**
3789a[7] Zilzal Zamaan (USA) *(118) (MRStoute)* 4-9-3 KDarley (mid div: outpcd 2f out: fin wl)....nk **5**
1890a[4] Scribano *(107) (GBotti,Italy)* 5-9-3 FJovine (in rr: effrt 2f out: no imp)....8½ **6**
3591a[3] Right Win (IRE) *(102) (RHannon)* 5-9-3b MHills (prom tl wknd qckly over 1f out)....3½ **7**
896a[6] Close Conflict (USA) *(85) (PWChapple-Hyam)* 4-9-3 JCarroll (a rr: t.o)....13 **8**

Tote 83L: 15L 15L 11L (328L) OWNER Mr R. E. Sangster (MARLBOROUGH) BRED Swettenham Stud 8 Rn 2m 28.7 SF: -/-/-/-/-/-/-/-

3912a-COLOGNE (Germany) (R-H)
Sunday October 15th (Soft)

4183a BUCHMACHER SPRINGER STEHER-PREIS (Listed) (3-Y.O+) £8,230.00 (£3,292.00: £1,646.00) **1m 6f 110y** 4-15 (4-25)

4018a[7] **Little Smart (GER)** *(111) (RPrinzinger,Germany)* 3-8-6 LHammer-Hansen ....— **1**

3581a2 Pasolini *(109) (WKujath,Germany)* 4-9-4 GBocskai 4½ 2
Kaytibos (GER) *(107) (HBlume,Germany)* 4-9-2 AStarke ....nk 3
21196 Castle Courageous *(LadyHerries)* 8-9-0 DHarrison 8

Tote 59DM: 21DM 26DM 22DM (SF 418DM) OWNER H & W Lowke BRED H. & W. Lowke 10 Rn
3m 8.26 SF: -/-/-/-

WOODBINE (Toronto, Canada) (L-H)
Sunday October 15th (Good)

4184a E.P. TAYLOR STKS (Gp 2) (3-Y.O+ F & M) £97,315.00 **1m 2f** 19-33 (19-34)

4015a* **Timarida (IRE)** *(120) (JOxx,Ireland)* 3-8-5 LDettori ....— 1
3694a4 Matiara (USA) *(114) (MmeCHead,France)* 3-8-5 FHead 3½ 2
Bold Ruritania (CAN) *(114) (MsBMinshell,USA)* 5-8-11 PDay ....½ 3
3944* Warning Shadows (IRE) *(CEBrittain)* 3-8-5 CNakatani (btn 7¼l) 7

P-M £13.00: PL £6.20 £3.80 SHOW £4.20 £2.80 £4.20 (SF £36.40) OWNER Aga Khan BRED H.H. Aga Khan's Studs S.C. 13 Rn
2m 3.6 SF: -/-/-/-

4185a ROTHMANS INTERNATIONAL (Gp 1) (3-Y.O+) £298,288.00 **1m 4f** 22-15 (22-15)

3576a6 **Lassigny (USA)** *(121) (WMott,USA)* 4-9-0 PDay ....— 1
2730a4 Mecke (USA) *(120) (ETortora,USA)* 3-8-6 JBailey ....½ 2
Hasten to Add (USA) *(118) (JDay,Canada)* 5-9-0 CNakatani 2 3
34982 Commoner (USA) *(RHannon)* 3-8-7 RHughes (btn 8 3/4l) 6
4007a2 Volochine (IRE) *(RCollet,France)* 4-9-0 TKabel (btn 13¼l) 7
3088* Presenting *(JHMGosden)* 3-8-6 LDettori (btn over 25l) 14
3696a2 Poliglote *(MmeCHead,France)* 3-8-6 FHead (btn over 30l) 15

P-M £17.40: PL £8.10 £8.10 SHOW £6.60 £7.30 £11.40 (SF £135.40) OWNER Sultan Al Kabeer BRED Haras du Mezeray 15 Rn
2m 29.8 SF: -/-/-/-/-/-/-

4020a-CAPANNELLE (Rome, Italy) (R-H)
Sunday October 15th (Good)

4186a PREMIO CAMPIDOGLIO (3-Y.O+) £9,850.00 (£4,334.00: £2,364.00: £1,182.00) **1m** 2-00 (2-00)

1118a8 **Bemont Park (ITY)** *(94) (RBrogi,Italy)* 3-8-8 GBietolini ....— 1
Welsh Liberty (IRE) *(89) (DDucci,Italy)* 6-8-11 MPasquale 2 2
4093a11 Action Mutante (USA) *(95) (OPessi,Italy)* 3-9-0 OFancera ....½ 3
3796a4 Albinor (IRE) *(89) (JLDunlop)* 3-8-9 JacquelineFreda ....nk 4

Tote 69L: 35L 26L (157L) OWNER L. Barnardini BRED M. Barnardini 7 Rn 1m 38.6 SF: -/-/-/-

LYON PARILLY (Lyon, France)
Sunday October 15th (Good)

4187a PRIX DU GRAND CAMP (Listed) (3-Y.O+) £14,371.00 (£4,790.00: £2,395.00) **1m 4f** 4-45 (4-45)

3836* **Taufan's Melody** *(114) (LadyHerries)* 4-9-3 RCochrane ....— 1
Reve Parisien (USA) *(113) (France)* 4-9-3 FSanchez ....½ 2
Perche No (FR) *(114) (France)* 3-8-10 DBouland ....½ 3

P-M 4.50F: 1.50F 1.30F 1.60F (11.40F) OWNER All At Sea Partnership (LITTLEHAMPTON) BRED Midhurst Farm Inc 8 Rn
2m 30.6 SF: -/-/-
DS

3606-DONCASTER (L-H)
Friday October 20th (Good to firm)
WEATHER: overcast WIND: almost nil

4188
E.B.F. CISWO MAIDEN STKS (2-Y.O) (Class D) £5,361.00 (£1,608.00: £774.00: £357.00) **7f** Stalls: High GOING minus 0.31 sec per fur (GF) 2-00 (2-04)

3900⁷ **Germano** *(90) (GWragg)* 2-9-0 MHills(3) (lw: a.p: led wl over 1f out: edgd rt: r.o wl)............— 1
3816² Tarneem (USA) *(83)*(Fav)*(MRStoute)* 2-8-9 WRSwinburn(14) (chsd ldrs: chal 2f out: r.o) 1 2
Dawawin (USA) *(79+) (EALDunlop)* 2-8-9 RHills(4) (w'like: unf: scope: hdwy 3f out: r.o wl fnl 2f)............1¾ 3
3989⁴ Fourdaned (IRE) *(82) (PWHarris)* 2-9-0 GHind(5) (trckd ldrs: effrt & ch over 1f out: kpt on wl)............¾ 4
4023³ Insiyabi (USA) *(81) (JLDunlop)* 2-9-0 WCarson(12) (lw: cl up tl grad wknd fnl 2f) ....½ 5
3989² Forest Robin **(84)***(78) (RFJohnsonHoughton)* 2-9-0 AMcGlone(1) (lw: w ldrs: led ½-wy tl wl over 1f out: one pce)............1¼ 6
Melt The Clouds (CAN) *(76+) (PWHarris)* 2-9-0 GDuffield(6) (w'like: lengthy: scope: hdwy ½-wy: shkn up & r.o appr fnl f)............1 7
3883⁶ Foreign Judgement (USA) *(70) (PWChapple-Hyam)* 2-9-0 JReid(13) (chsd ldrs tl outpcd fnl 2½f)............2½ 8
3900¹⁴ Tintara (IRE) *(62) (BWHills)* 2-8-9 JWilliams(15) (bit bkwd: a.p: no imp fnl 2½f)....................1½ 9
Milford Sound *(63) (JRFanshawe)* 2-9-0 DHarrison(2) (cmpt: bit bkwd: in tch tl outpcd fnl 2½f)............1¾ 10
4070⁵ Silent Guest (IRE) *(61) (SirMarkPrescott)* 2-9-0 CNutter(20) (hld up & bhd: sme late hdwy)...¾ 11
3967⁸ Bashtheboards *(58) (JJQuinn)* 2-9-0 SDWilliams(19) (s.i.s: n.d)............1¼ 12
Windyedge (USA) *(58) (BWHills)* 2-9-0 RStreet(16) (unf: bit bkwd: stdd s: hld up & bhd: nvr nr to chal)............s.h 13
1485⁹ Gympie *(58) (JHMGosden)* 2-9-0 JCarroll(21) (disp ld to ½-wy: grad lost pl) ....hd 14
Highfield Pet *(55) (MJohnston)* 2-9-0 JWeaver(8) (leggy: unf: chsd ldrs 4f)............1¼ 15
3996⁶ Manoy *(51) (JHetherton)* 2-9-0 NKennedy(9) (disp ld tl wknd ½-wy) 1½ 16
4098^W Hawksley Hill (IRE) *(50) (MrsJRRamsden)* 2-9-0 KFallon(10) (lengthy: scope: a bhd & pushed along)............½ 17
4070⁸ Batoutoftheblue *(47) (WWHaigh)* 2-9-0 DaleGibson(7) (bit bkwd: in tch: pushed along ½-wy: sn wknd) 1½ 18
3877⁹ Kenilworth Dancer *(44) (MrsMReveley)* 2-9-0 KDarley(18) (s.i.s: a bhd) 1¼ 19
Veronica Franco *(38) (JLDunlop)* 2-8-9 TQuinn(22) (unf: rn green: a outpcd & bhd) ....nk 20
3877⁸ Dona Filipa *(27) (MissLCSiddall)* 2-8-9 DeanMcKeown(17) (s.i.s: a bhd) 5 21

7/2 Tarneem (USA), **4/1** GERMANO, **11/2** Insiyabi (USA), **6/1** Fourdaned (IRE) (10/1-5/1), **7/1** Dawawin (USA) (op 4/1), **8/1** Forest Robin, **9/1** Foreign Judgement (USA) (op 6/1), **14/1** Melt The Clouds (CAN), **16/1** Tintara (IRE), Milford Sound, Veronica Franco, **25/1** Silent Guest (IRE), Windyedge (USA), Gympie, Hawksley Hill (IRE), Highfield Pet, **50/1** Manoy, Batoutoftheblue, Kenilworth Dancer, Bashtheboards, Dona Filipa, CSF £21.74 TOTE £5.10: £2.30 £1.90 £4.30 (£9.30) Trio £61.90 OWNER Baron G Von Ullmann (NEWMARKET) BRED Cambremont Ltd Partnership 21 Rn 1m 25.22 (1.82) SF: 50/43/39/42/41/38/36/30/22/23/21/18/18/18/15/11/10/7/4

4189
GIBSON BOOTH H'CAP (0-85) (3-Y.O+) (Class D) £4,771.25 (£1,430.00: £687.50: £316.25)
1m 6f 132y Stalls: Low GOING minus 0.31 sec per fur (GF) 2-30 (2-33)

3818² **Sugar Mill (63)***(79) (MrsMReveley)* 5-8-8 KDarley(7) (lw: chsd ldrs: led over 3f out: hld on wl fnl f) ....— 1
3759³ Non Vintage (IRE) **(51)***(64) (MCChapman)* 4-7-3 (7)ow3 MartinDwyer(10) (cl up: swtchd 3f out: chal 2f out: nt qckn nr fin) ....nk 2
4051³ Cuango (IRE) **(51)***(61) (RHollinshead)* 4-7-5 (5)ow1 MHenry(13) (lw: s.i.s: hdwy 4f out: styd on: nvr able to chal) 4 3
4036⁹ Good Hand (USA) **(72)***(81) (JWWatts)* 9-9-3 NConnorton(12) (b.hind: bhd: hdwy over 3f out: r.o: nrst fin)............1¾ 4
3978² Jadwal (USA) **(78)***(86) (DMorley)* 3-9-0 WCarson(9) (hld up & bhd: hdwy over 3f out: hmpd over 2f out: nvr nr to chal) 1¾ 5
3970³ Express Gift **(62)***(67)*(Fav)*(MrsMReveley)* 6-8-7 JWilliams(1) (hld up: effrt appr st: styd on fnl 3f: nvr able to chal) 2½ 6
4086* Green Land (BEL) **(66)***(69) (SCWilliams)* 3-8-2 4x JTate(3) (b.nr fore: lw: in tch: effrt over 4f out: no imp) 1½ 7
4051⁵ Snowy Petrel (IRE) **(77)***(67) (JLDunlop)* 3-8-13 JWeaver(11) (led tl over 3f out: sn wknd)......12 8
1866³ Cante Chico **(70)***(49) (TThomsonJones)* 3-8-6 ow4 SWhitworth(4) (s.i.s: n.d) 6 9
4036* Tudor Island **(81)***(62) (CEBrittain)* 6-9-12 BDoyle(8) (in tch tl wknd fnl 4f) 1¾ 10

3849[9] Kriva **(63)***(42) (RJRWilliams)* 3-7-13 SSanders(2) (in tch tl wknd over 3f out) 2½ **11**
4036[2] Floating Line **(71)***(49) (EJAlston)* 7-9-2 KFallon(5) (sn chsng ldrs: effrt ent st: wknd fnl 3f) 1 **12**
4062* Berkeley Bounder (USA) **(74)***(37) (RMMcKellar)* 3-8-10 4x TSprake(6) (lost tch fnl 5f) 13 **13**

7/2 Express Gift, **11/2** Floating Line, **7/1** SUGAR MILL, Green Land (BEL), Cuango (IRE), Tudor Island, **11/1** Snowy Petrel (IRE), Jadwal (USA), **14/1** Berkeley Bounder (USA), **16/1** Good Hand (USA), **20/1** Kriva, **25/1** Cante Chico, **33/1** Non Vintage (IRE), CSF £182.78 CT £1,541.70 TOTE £8.70: £2.70 £8.30 £2.40 (£219.20) Trio £392.80 OWNER Mr C. C. Buckley (SALTBURN) BRED Snailwell Stud Co Ltd 13 Rn 3m 5.33 (1.73) SF: 58/43/40/60/56/46/39/37/19/41/12/28/7
WEIGHT FOR AGE 3yo-9lb

4190 E.B.F. CO-OPERATIVE BANK PLC MAIDEN STKS (2-Y.O F) (Class D) £4,699.75 (£1,408.00: £676.50: £310.75)

1m (round) Stalls: High GOING minus 0.31 sec per fur (GF) 3-00 (3-02)

3339[10] **Overruled (IRE)** *(78+) (DRLoder)* 2-8-11 RHughes(6) (led 1f: led 4f out: r.o: eased ins fnl f) — **1**
Naseem Alsahar *(76) (MajorWRHern)* 2-8-11 TSprake(9) (w'like: unf: a.p: r.o wl fnl f: no ch w wnr) 1¼ **2**
Annecy (USA) *(70)*(Fav)*(HRACecil)* 2-8-11 WRyan(11) (leggy: scope: led after 1f to 4f out: one pce) 3 **3**
Trilby *(68+) (PFICole)* 2-8-11 TQuinn(1) (lengthy: scope: outpcd & bhd: hdwy 2f out: r.o nr fin) ....¾ **4**
Sinking Sun *(65) (BWHills)* 2-8-11b JWilliams(7) (unf: s.i.s: sn in tch: outpcd ½-wy: styd on nr fin) 1¼ **5**
3939[6] Bodfari Lass *(64) (BWHills)* 2-8-11 MHills(10) (a.p: one pce fnl 3f) ....½ **6**
3983[10] Basood (USA) *(57) (EALDunlop)* 2-8-11 WRSwinburn(5) (chsd ldrs tl rdn & wknd fnl 2f) 3½ **7**
4048[14] Shirley Sue *(53) (MJohnston)* 2-8-11 JWeaver(4) (outpcd ½-wy: n.d after) 2 **8**
3666[5] Portuguese Lil *(45) (DNicholls)* 2-8-11 AlexGreaves(2) (bit bkwd: nvr nr to chal) 4 **9**
Dalwhinnie *(45) (JWHills)* 2-8-11 RHills(3) (cmpt: s.i.s: n.d) ....s.h **10**
4048[16] Uplift *(17) (SirMarkPrescott)* 2-8-11 GDuffield(8) (a bhd) 14 **11**

7/4 Annecy (USA) (5/4-5/2), **3/1** OVERRULED (IRE) (7/2-9/4), **11/2** Naseem Alsahar, **6/1** Trilby, **10/1** Sinking Sun, **12/1** Bodfari Lass, Basood (USA), **14/1** Shirley Sue, **16/1** Portuguese Lil, **20/1** Dalwhinnie, **33/1** Uplift, CSF £21.92 TOTE £3.20: £1.30 £2.40 £1.70 (£12.40) Trio £10.00 OWNER Mr E. J. Loder (NEWMARKET) BRED E. J. Loder 11 Rn
1m 39.66 (3.36) SF: 35/33/27/25/22/21/14/10/2/2/-

4191 RJB MINING CONDITIONS STKS (3-Y.O+) (Class C) £5,601.60 (£1,785.60: £852.80)

2m 110y Stalls: Low GOING minus 0.31 sec per fur (GF) 3-30 (3-31)

3946[4] **Old Rouvel (USA) (103)***(82+)*(Fav)*(DJGMurraySmith)* 4-9-4 MRoberts(1) (hld up: rdn to ld over 2f out: eased ins fnl f) .... — **1**
3896* Harbour Island *(82) (MRStoute)* 3-8-8b KFallon(2) (led early: led over 4f out tl over 2f out: r.o u.p nr fin) ....nk **2**
1596[18] Tanah Merah (IRE) **(46)** *(EJAlston)* 4-9-0 KDarley(3) (bit bkwd: dwlt: plld hrd: sn led & clr: hdd over 4f out: sn btn) ....dist **3**

4/9 OLD ROUVEL (USA), **2/1** Harbour Island, **20/1** Tanah Merah (IRE), CSF £1.59 TOTE £1.40 (£1.10) OWNER Mrs R. D. Cowell (LAMBOURN) BRED The Bloodstock Agency in USA 3 Rn
3m 40.32 (11.32) SF: 24/14/-
WEIGHT FOR AGE 3yo-10lb

4192 CPL HOMEFIRE NURSERY H'CAP (2-Y.O) (Class D) £4,045.00 (£1,210.00: £580.00: £265.00)

1m (round) Stalls: High GOING minus 0.31 sec per fur (GF) 4-00 (4-01)

3967[2] **Crystal Falls (IRE) (77)***(79) (JJO'Neill)* 2-8-8 KFallon(2) (sn pushed along & bhd: hdwy on ins over 2f out: led ins fnl f: drvn out) .... — **1**
3775[3] Alzanti **(86)***(87)*(Fav)*(PFICole)* 2-8-12 (5) DaneO'Neill(1) (w ldrs: led over 2f out tl ins fnl f: r.o)nk **2**
2775[3] Exalted (IRE) **(90)***(87) (SirMarkPrescott)* 2-9-7 GDuffield(3) (lw: plld hrd early: trckd ldrs: effrt over 2f out: styd on) 2 **3**
3231[12] Phantom Haze **(62)***(59) (MissSEHall)* 2-7-4 (3) NVarley(5) (swtg: hld up & bhd: hdwy on outside over 2f out: nrst fin) ....hd **4**
3760[3] Aussie **(76)***(70) (MHTompkins)* 2-8-7 WRyan(7) (hld up: hdwy 3f out: sn prom: one pce fnl f)1½ **5**
3867[6] Tabriz **(79)***(73) (JDBethell)* 2-8-10 JReid(10) (led tl over 2f out: grad wknd) ....nk **6**
3851* Homeland **(68)***(59) (TJNaughton)* 2-7-13 SSanders(4) (lw: cl up tl outpcd 3f out: styd on fnl f)1¼ **7**

3983[6] Fijon (IRE) **(70)***(60) (BWHills)* 2-8-1 RHills(6) (trckd ldrs: effrt over 2f out: n.m.r & sn btn)....¾ **8**
3894[14] Minsterbeach **(62)***(36) (CEBrittain)* 2-7-7 JLowe(8) (cl up tl wknd fnl 2f)....8 **9**
3713[7] Muhtadi (IRE) **(77)***(41) (JLDunlop)* 2-8-8 WCarson(9) (hld up: hdwy 3f out: wknd wl over 1f out)....5 **10**
LONG HANDICAP Minsterbeach 7-0 Phantom Haze 7-1

9/2 Alzanti, **5/1** CRYSTAL FALLS (IRE), Exalted (IRE), **6/1** Muhtadi (IRE), **13/2** Homeland, Aussie, Fijon (IRE), **10/1** Tabriz, **16/1** Phantom Haze, **33/1** Minsterbeach, CSF £27.47 CT £110.71 TOTE £5.10: £1.50 £2.10 £1.70 (£14.60) Trio £16.50 OWNER Mr C. H. Stevens (PENRITH) BRED Russlson 10 Rn 1m 39.06 (2.76) SF: 38/46/46/18/29/32/18/19/-/-

4193 BRITISH COAL ENTERPRISE CLAIMING STKS (3, 4 & 5-Y.O) (Class E) £3,845.60 (£1,152.80: £554.40: £255.20)
7f Stalls: High GOING minus 0.31 sec per fur (GF) 4-30 (4-36)

3726[15] **Euphyllia (42)***(85) (BobJones)* 3-7-13 FNorton(11) (a.p: led ins fnl f: r.o)....— **1**
2766[10] Reprehend **(75)***(92) (RHannon)* 4-8-11 JReid(18) (lw: a.p: led 2f out tl ins fnl f: kpt on)....¾ **2**
3717[27] Loveyoumillions (IRE) **(88)***(84) (MJohnston)* 3-9-2b JWeaver(16) (lw: chsd ldrs tl led ½-wy: hdd 2f out: sn btn)....7 **3**
4068[12] Rossini Blue **(71)***(74)*(Fav)*(MrsJRRamsden)* 4-8-9 KFallon(9) (b.nr hind: styd on u.p fnl 2½f: nrst fin)....nk **4**
4122[4] Delight of Dawn **(72)***(75) (KTIvory)* 3-8-2 (7) CScally(2) (b: outpcd ½-wy: hdwy 2f out: nvr rchd ldrs)....¾ **5**
4054[2] Dowsong **(68)***(61) (RAkehurst)* 4-8-9 TQuinn(14) (lw: prom: effrt over 2f out: one pce)....5 **6**
3972[6] Never Such Bliss **(55)***(49) (JDBethell)* 3-8-0 WCarson(12) (spd 4f: sn wknd)....2½ **7**
3319[4] Bogart **(55)***(55) (CWFairhurst)* 4-8-13 MRoberts(15) (s.i.s: hdwy u.p & hung lft ½-wy: n.d)...1½ **8**
2455[11] Daawe (USA) **(68)***(53) (MrsVAAconley)* 4-8-11v MDeering(13) (drvn along ½-wy: n.d)....hd **9**
3805[17] Sheroot **(30)***(50) (DMoffatt)* 3-8-5 TWilliams(6) (sn bhd & pushed along: sme late hdwy)....s.h **10**
3954[10] Awesome Venture **(43)***(52) (MCChapman)* 5-8-3 (7) CMunday(3) (led & sn clr: hdd ½-wy: sn wknd)....s.h **11**
4043[8] French Ginger **(66)***(48) (IABalding)* 4-8-8 KDarley(1) (in tch 4f)....1 **12**
155[9] Cyprus Point **(44)***(42) (SWCampion)* 4-8-4 DeanMcKeown(17) (swtg: chsd ldrs tl wknd over 2f out)....½ **13**
3920[9] Access Carnival (IRE) **(48)***(44) (RBoss)* 4-8-8 WRyan(19) (sn bhd)....1¼ **14**
3964[13] Red Five **(50)***(42) (DMoffatt)* 4-8-7 (3) DarrenMoffatt(5) (sn outpcd)....1½ **15**
3935[16] Borrowby **(43)***(32) (MWEasterby)* 3-8-3b LCharnock(8) (lw: chsd ldrs 4f: sn wknd)....2½ **16**
3879[9] Cheerful Groom (IRE) **(41)***(29) (JMackie)* 4-8-6 GHind(10) (dwlt: a bhd)....1½ **17**
3667[16] Rankaidade **(36)***(3) (DonEnricoIncisa)* 4-8-1 KimTinkler(7) (nvr wnt pce)....9 **18**
4049[19] Desert Water (IRE) *(JJBridger)* 3-8-1b(5) MBaird(4) (bolted gng to s: sn t.o)....dist **19**

9/2 Rossini Blue, **5/1** Delight of Dawn, Loveyoumillions (IRE) (op 3/1), **11/2** Dowsong, Reprehend, **9/1** French Ginger, **12/1** Never Such Bliss, **16/1** Bogart, **20/1** Daawe (USA), Access Carnival (IRE), **33/1** Red Five, EUPHYLLIA, **50/1** Cyprus Point, Awesome Venture, Sheroot, Borrowby, Cheerful Groom (IRE), Rankaidade, Desert Water (IRE), CSF £199.97 TOTE £95.20: £11.60 £1.80 £2.30 (£123.30) Trio £980.50 OWNER Mr J. G. Vaughan (NEWMARKET) BRED J. Vaughan 19 Rn
1m 23.82 (0.42) SF: 53/63/52/45/43/32/17/26/24/18/23/19/13/15/13/-/-/-/-
WEIGHT FOR AGE 3yo-3lb

4194 S.I.A. APPRENTICE H'CAP (0-70) (3-Y.O) (Class E) £3,759.80 (£1,126.40: £541.20: £248.60)
7f Stalls: High GOING minus 0.31 sec per fur (GF) 5-00 (5-03)

3980[14] **Master Charter (56)***(67)*(Fav)*(MrsJRRamsden)* 3-8-7 SSanders(11) (hld up: stdy hdwy over 2f out: rdn to ld wl ins fnl f)....— **1**
4131[6] Scissor Ridge **(43)***(53) (JJBridger)* 3-7-8 MBaird(2) (led over 5f: edgd rt & kpt on wl)....½ **2**
2788[7] Nordic Doll (IRE) **(67)***(77) (BWHills)* 3-9-4 JDSmith(17) (a in tch: kpt on wl fnl f)....hd **3**
3973[4] Evan 'elp Us **(59)***(68) (JLEyre)* 3-8-10b NVarley(13) (lw: outpcd & bhd tl hdwy ½-wy: led wl over 1f out: hdd & no ex wl ins fnl f)....½ **4**
4049[4] Merrie le Bow **(43)***(49) (PatMitchell)* 3-7-5 (3) MartinDwyer(15) (chsd ldrs: effrt & n.m.r over 2f out: kpt on fnl f)....1 **5**
3257[3] So Amazing **(58)***(61) (MissSEHall)* 3-8-9 LNewton(21) (chsd ldrs: rdn 2f out: kpt on fnl f)....1¼ **6**
3980[4] Sweet Mate **(45)***(46) (SRBowring)* 3-7-10b DarrenMoffatt(7) (cl up tl wknd fnl f)....1¼ **7**
3800[18] Blasted **(62)***(61) (RHannon)* 3-8-13 DaneO'Neill(19) (styd on fnl 2f: nvr trbld ldrs)....½ **8**
739[10] Dissentor (IRE) **(49)***(47) (JAGlover)* 3-8-0 JStack(14) (in tch: swtchd over 2f out: nt qckn)....½ **9**
3897[4] Saltis (IRE) **(52)***(50) (DWPArbuthnot)* 3-8-3 SDrowne(1) (b.hind: prom: effrt over 2f out: r.o one pce)....nk **10**
4123[8] Pursuance (IRE) **(54)***(45) (JBalding)* 3-8-0v(5)ow5 JEdmunds(12) (cl up 5f)....½ **11**

4079[3] Mountgate **(70)**(66) *(MPBielby)* 3-9-7 PMcCabe(9) (lw: unruly s: s.i.s: wl bhd tl late hdwy)....s.h **12**
3390[7] Bella Coola **(49)**(41) *(CAHorgan)* 3-7-11 (3) AmandaSanders(10) (chsd ldrs over 4f)..............1¾ **13**
4057[15] Risky Royal **(52)**(40) *(TJNaughton)* 3-8-3 AWhelan(3) (in tch tl wknd fnl 2f)..............................2 **14**
3980[6] Boost **(47)**(27) *(CWThornton)* 3-7-7 (5)ow5 KSked(18) (drvn along & no imp fr ½-wy)..............1¼ **15**
3310[5] Persian Fayre **(64)**(48) *(JBerry)* 3-8-12 (3) PFessey(20) (sn outpcd)..nk **16**
2166[8] Ambidextrous (IRE) **(60)**(44) *(EJAlston)* 3-8-11 PPMurphy(6) (n.d)..nk **17**
3514[10] Northern Trove (USA) **(62)**(45) *(RonaldThompson)* 3-8-10 (3) ADaly(16) (nvr wnt pce)............hd **18**
1033[8] Polli Pui **(56)**(35) *(PDEvans)* 3-8-4 (3) GMitchell(22) (outpcd & bhd fr ½-wy)...........................1¾ **19**
4049[14] It Is Now **(42)**(10) *(SGollings)* 3-7-7 MHenry(4) (prom: sn drvn along: wknd ½-wy)...................5 **20**
3980[15] Mad About The Girl (IRE) **(43)** *(DJSCosgrove)* 3-7-8 DWright(8) (spd 4f: wknd qckly)...........12 **21**

LONG HANDICAP It Is Now 7-5

5/1 MASTER CHARTER, **6/1** Mountgate, **7/1** Evan 'elp Us, Sweet Mate, **8/1** Blasted, **10/1** Saltis (IRE), Nordic Doll (IRE), **12/1** So Amazing, **14/1** Dissentor (IRE), Persian Fayre, Boost, **16/1** Merrie le Bow, Bella Coola, **20/1** Scissor Ridge, Ambidextrous (IRE), **25/1** Pursuance (IRE), Polli Pui, **33/1** Northern Trove (USA), Risky Royal, It Is Now, Mad About The Girl (IRE), CSF £108.83 CT £935.00 TOTE £5.80: £2.00 £5.20 £2.80 £1.50 (£178.60) Trio £1,499.80 OWNER Mr Jonathan Ramsden (THIRSK) BRED Carlton Consultants Ltd 21 Rn

1m 25.2 (1.80) SF: 44/30/54/45/26/38/23/38/24/27/22/43/18/17/4/25/21/22/12/-/-

T/Jkpt: Not won; £46, 206.04 to Newbury 21/10/95. T/Plpt: £82.30 (219.74 Tckts). T/Qdpt: £10.10 (18.7 Tckts). AA

4188-DONCASTER (L-H)
Saturday October 21st (Good to firm)

WEATHER: sunny WIND: almost nil

4195 'JOCK MURRAY MEMORIAL' NURSERY H'CAP (2-Y.O) (Class C)

£6,311.25 (£1,890.00: £907.50: £416.25)
7f Stalls: High GOING minus 0.30 sec per fur (GF) 1-40 (1-41)

3967* **Carburton (80)**(89)(Fav)*(JAGlover)* 2-8-9 PaulEddery(1) (lw: a.p: rdn 3f out: led over 1f out: r.o wl)..— **1**
4141[3] Angel Chimes **(70)**(77) *(JEBanks)* 2-7-13 JQuinn(5) (hld up: hdwy over 2f out: r.o u.p ins fnl f)..¾ **2**
3988[3] Scenicris (IRE) **(65)**(67) *(RHollinshead)* 2-7-8 NCarlisle(7) (hdwy u.p over 1f out: nvr nrr).....2½ **3**
3776[4] Some Horse (IRE) **(92)**(94) *(MGMeagher)* 2-9-7 JCarroll(11) (lw: chsd ldrs: rdn wl over 1f out: r.o one pce)..s.h **4**
3720[2] Red Nose (IRE) **(74)**(74) *(MHTompkins)* 2-8-3v PRobinson(2) (led tl over 1f out: rdn & no ex fnl f)..½ **5**
3988[10] Ice Pick (IRE) **(70)**(67) *(RHannon)* 2-7-13v GBardwell(10) (s.i.s: bhd tl r.o appr fnl f).............1½ **6**
4107[2] Magic Lake **(71)**(63) *(EJAlston)* 2-7-9 (5) MBaird(3) (lw: chsd ldrs: chal 2f out: wknd fnl f).........2 **7**
3990[7] Arajaan (USA) **(90)**(82) *(BHanbury)* 2-9-2 (3) JStack(9) (prom 5f: sn rdn & outpcd)..................hd **8**
4097[15] Doug's Folly **(64)**(52) *(MWEasterby)* 2-7-2 (5) PFessey(4) (a bhd)..2 **9**
4084[23] Galapino **(79)**(59) *(CEBrittain)* 2-8-8 KDarley(8) (a bhd)..3½ **10**
3671* Diminuet **(68)**(47) *(JWWatts)* 2-7-11 LCharnock(6) (drvn along ½-wy: wl bhd fnl 2f: b.b.v).....nk **11**

LONG HANDICAP Doug's Folly 7-3

5/4 CARBURTON, **7/1** Angel Chimes, Diminuet, Magic Lake, **8/1** Red Nose (IRE), Some Horse (IRE), **12/1** Arajaan (USA), **16/1** Scenicris (IRE), Ice Pick (IRE), **20/1** Galapino, **33/1** Doug's Folly, CSF £11.96 CT £103.15 TOTE £2.00: £1.20 £2.60 £3.20 (£9.70) Trio £116.10 OWNER Mr B. H. Farr (WORKSOP) BRED Worksop Manor Stud Farm 11 Rn

1m 26.27 (2.87) SF: 34/22/12/39/19/12/8/27/-/4/-

4196 BERNARD MANNING ON THE JOB CLAIMING STKS (3-Y.O+) (Class D)

£4,475.90 (£1,341.20: £644.60: £296.30)
1m 2f 60y Stalls: Low GOING minus 0.30 sec per fur (GF) 2-10 (2-11)

4035[15] **Eurolink the Rebel (USA) (75)**(88) *(RAkehurst)* 3-8-10b PatEddery(10) (chsd ldrs: 2nd st: led over 2f out: sn clr: unchal)..— **1**
4061[18] Lunar Mission (IRE) **(59)**(71) *(JMPEustace)* 4-8-7 MTebbutt(14) (lw: a.p: 4th st: styd on fnl 2f: no ch w wnr)..6 **2**
3292[3] Oakbury (IRE) **(62)**(74) *(RHannon)* 3-8-6 ow1 JReid(2) (b.nr fore: chsd ldrs: 3rd st: outpcd over 3f out: styd on fnl f)..hd **3**
4002[2] Western General **(78)**(81)(Fav)*(MissSEHall)* 4-9-5 JWeaver(12) (hld up in tch: 7th st: hdwy over 3f out: rdn & btn appr fnl f)..¾ **4**
3977[13] Bobanlyn (IRE) **(56)**(65) *(DMorris)* 3-8-0 JQuinn(7) (prom: 6th st: effrt over 3f out: rdn & btn fnl f)..1¾ **5**

3986[5] Deceit the Second **(39)***(68) (GLewis)* 3-8-1b(5) AWhelan(4) (chsd ldrs: 5th st: one pce fnl 2f) 1¾ **6**
4110[4] Greek Gold (IRE) **(45)***(56) (DNicholls)* 6-8-8 AlexGreaves(3) (led tl over 2f out: wknd qckly)....6 **7**
4062[5] Hatta River (USA) **(51)***(51) (JAHarris)* 5-8-7 KDarley(16) (lw: mid div: effrt 3f out: no imp) 2½ **8**
4062[6] Forest Mill **(48)***(48) (DWPArbuthnot)* 3-8-4vow1 AClark(5) (b.hind: nvr nr to chal)....................2½ **9**
4072[10] Fragaria **(48)***(42) (IABalding)* 3-8-3bow2 PaulEddery(11) (a rr div)...2½ **10**
Bahamian King (IRE) *(44) (SEKettlewell)* 3-8-3 (3) JStack(6) (leggy: bkwd: s.s: a bhd)..........1¾ **11**
4110[5] Le Temeraire **(25)***(35) (DonEnricoIncisa)* 9-8-6 KimTinkler(8) (s.i.s: a bhd) 3 **12**
3635[9] Kim Tate (IRE) *(28) (CNAllen)* 3-7-10 NCarlisle(9) (nvr trbld ldrs) ....¾ **13**
3778[8] Malindi Bay **(30)***(28) (BJMcMath)* 7-8-7 ow1 WNewnes(15) (a bhd) 3½ **14**
3974[17] Caddican (IRE) *(28) (RBoss)* 3-8-2 GBardwell(13) (rdn & bhd fnl 4f).....................................nk **15**
Green's Moillon (USA) *(MBrittain)* 7-8-5 JCarroll(1) (Withdrawn not under Starter's orders: veterinary advice) .... **W**

13/8 Western General, **11/4** EUROLINK THE REBEL (USA), **5/1** Oakbury (IRE), **10/1** Bobanlyn (IRE), **12/1** Lunar Mission (IRE), **16/1** Fragaria, **20/1** Deceit the Second, **25/1** Hatta River (USA), **33/1** Forest Mill, Greek Gold (IRE), Bahamian King (IRE), Le Temeraire, Kim Tate (IRE), Malindi Bay, Caddican (IRE), **50/1** Green's Moillon (USA), CSF £33.82 TOTE £3.80: £1.60 £3.50 £1.50 (£22.80) Trio £30.80 OWNER Eurolink Group Plc (EPSOM) BRED Joseph Bryan Jnr 15 Rn

2m 8.63 (1.63) SF: 57/45/43/55/34/37/30/25/17/11/13/9/-/2/-/-

WEIGHT FOR AGE 3yo-5lb

Eurolink the Rebel (USA) clmd MHammond £12,000. Oakbury (IRE) clmd DBooth £7,000.

4197 DONCASTER WRITERS RATED STKS H'CAP (0-100) (3-Y.O+) (Class B)

£8,445.40 (£3,124.60: £1,498.80: £612.00: £242.50: £94.70)
5f Stalls: High GOING minus 0.30 sec per fur (GF) 2-40 (2-41)

4119* **Croft Pool (88)***(96)*(Fav)*(JAGlover)* 4-8-10 SDWilliams(8) (lw: chsd ldrs: led over 1f out: drvn out) ....— **1**
4055[3] Coffee 'n Cream **(95)***(101) (RHannon)* 3-9-2 JReid(5) (lw: sn drvn along: hdwy over 1f out: r.o wl nr fin)...½ **2**
3815[13] That Man Again **(100)***(105) (GLewis)* 3-9-2b(5) AWhelan(2) (a.p: led 2f out tl over 1f out: unable qckn fnl f) ....½ **3**
3466[4] The Happy Fox (IRE) **(85)***(89) (BAMcMahon)* 3-8-1 (5) LNewton(6) (swtchd lft ½-wy: rdn & hdwy appr fnl f: nvr nrr)..nk **4**
4033[23] Name the Tune **(88)***(91) (PHowling)* 4-8-10 PaulEddery(7) (b.hind: lw: s.i.s: bhd: hdwy over 1f out: rdn & r.o wl fnl f) ....nk **5**
4119[5] Ziggy's Dancer (USA) **(86)***(87) (EJAlston)* 4-8-8 GHind(4) (led 3f: rdn & outpcd appr fnl f)......¾ **6**
4119[2] Takadou (IRE) **(91)***(91)*(Fav)*(MissLCSiddall)* 4-8-13 JWeaver(3) (lw: dwlt: drvn along & bhd tl r.o wl fnl f)...s.h **7**
4033[15] Seigneurial **(85)***(84) (GHarwood)* 3-8-6 AClark(1) (prom: rdn 2f out: sn btn) ....½ **8**
4033[17] Call Me I'm Blue (IRE) **(86)***(82) (NTinkler)* 5-8-8 WNewnes(10) (a bhd & outpcd)......................¾ **9**
4119[10] Ashtina **(85)***(56) (BAPearce)* 10-8-7 KDarley(9) (spd to ½-wy: sn lost tch: t.o)...........................8 **10**
LONG HANDICAP Ashtina 8-2 Seigneurial 8-1 The Happy Fox (IRE) 8-1

7/2 CROFT POOL, Takadou (IRE), **5/1** That Man Again, **6/1** Ziggy's Dancer (USA), **13/2** Name the Tune, **7/1** Call Me I'm Blue (IRE), **9/1** Coffee 'n Cream, **16/1** The Happy Fox (IRE), **33/1** Seigneurial, Ashtina, CSF £33.49 CT £144.79 TOTE £4.10: £1.90 £1.50 £2.20 (£17.50) Trio £30.50 OWNER Countrywide Classics Ltd (WORKSOP) BRED J. S. Bell 10 Rn

58.98 secs (0.58) SF: 59/63/67/51/54/50/54/46/45/19

WEIGHT FOR AGE 3yo-1lb

4198 RACING POST CONDITIONS STKS (3-Y.O+) (Class B) £9,116.58 (£3,152.98: £1,512.99: £618.45) 7f Stalls: High GOING minus 0.30 sec per fur (GF) 3-10 (3-10)

3979[2] **Monaassib (IRE) (98)***(106) (EALDunlop)* 4-9-0 WRSwinburn(1) (b.hind: mde all: rdn & edgd rt 2f out: hld on wl nr fin)...— **1**
3991[8] Blomberg (IRE) **(95)***(101) (JRFanshawe)* 3-8-9 DHarrison(4) (lw: a.p: rdn over 1f out: styng on whn n.m.r ins fnl f: nt rcvr) 1¼ **2**
2889a[6] Prince of India **(108)***(104)*(Fav)*(LordHuntingdon)* 3-8-12 PatEddery(2) (a.p: rdn 2f out: sn ev ch: one pce fnl f) ....s.h **3**
4087* Moon King (IRE) **(100)***(108) (RHannon)* 3-9-3 JReid(3) (hld up: pushed along ½-wy: swtchd outside & ev ch over 1f out: unable qckn)...½ **4**

8/11 Prince of India, **4/1** MONAASSIB (IRE), Moon King (IRE) (op 5/2), **9/1** Blomberg (IRE), CSF £23.92 TOTE £4.40 (£14.50) OWNER Maktoum Al Maktoum (NEWMARKET) BRED Side Hill Stud in Ireland 4 Rn

1m 25.75 (2.35) SF: 45/37/40/44

WEIGHT FOR AGE 3yo-3lb

STEWARDS' ENQUIRY Obj. to Monaassib (IRE) by Harrison overruled.

4199

RACING POST TROPHY STKS (Gp 1) (2-Y.O C & F) (Class A)
£87,736.50 (£30,406.50: £14,640.75: £6,041.25)
1m (round) Stalls: Low GOING minus 0.30 sec per fur (GF) 3-40 (3-40)

4029* **Beauchamp King** *(107) (JLDunlop)* 2-9-0 JReid(3) (lw: plld hrd: hld up: 3rd st: led over 1f out: r.o wl)............— 1
3925* Even Top (IRE) **(100)***(104) (MHTompkins)* 2-9-0 PRobinson(4) (lw: plld hrd: 2nd st: led over 2f out tl over 1f out: rdn & kpt on fnl f)............1¼ 2
3812* Mons **(100)***(103)*(Fav)*(LMCumani)* 2-9-0 PatEddery(1) (lw: led tl over 2f out: sn hrd rdn: one pce fnl f)............nk 3
3994² Iamus *(99?) (PTWalwyn)* 2-9-0 WRSwinburn(2) (hld up & bhd: 4th st: outpcd 3f out: styd on appr fnl f)............2 4

4/5 Mons, **11/4** BEAUCHAMP KING, **3/1** Even Top (IRE), **33/1** Iamus, CSF £9.88 TOTE £3.20 (£3.50) OWNER Mr E. Penser (ARUNDEL) BRED E. Penser 4 Rn 1m 38.89 (2.59) SF: 46/43/42/38

4200

CHARLES SIDNEY MERCEDES BENZ DONCASTER STKS (Listed) (2-Y.O) (Class A) £9,952.50 (£3,697.50: £1,786.25: £743.75: £309.38: £135.62)
6f Stalls: High GOING minus 0.30 sec per fur (GF) 4-15 (4-16)

4105⁶ **Thrilling Day (100)***(94) (NAGraham)* 2-8-10 DHarrison(5) (s.i.s: hld up & bhd: hdwy 2f out: r.o strly to ld cl home)............— 1
4039* Resounder (USA) **(100)***(97)*(Fav)*(JHMGosden)* 2-9-1 WRSwinburn(7) (hld up: hdwy to ld over 1f out: hrd rdn & hdd nr fin)............¾ 2
3942⁴ Greek Icon *(79) (JLDunlop)* 2-8-4 KDarley(1) (a.p: led over 1f out: hdd & no ex ins fnl f)......2½ 3
4066³ Hear The Music (IRE) **(91)***(73) (BWHills)* 2-8-5 ow1 PatEddery(3) (swtg: led over 4f: rdn & one pce appr fnl f)............2½ 4
4056⁴ Polish Spring (IRE) **(86)***(65) (BWHills)* 2-8-4 PaulEddery(2) (chsd ldrs: drvn along 2f out: sn btn)............3 5
4084²² What Fun **(88)***(66) (RHannon)* 2-8-12 JReid(4) (a bhd)............2½ 6
4042⁴ Sualtach (IRE) **(88)***(47) (RHollinshead)* 2-8-9 PRobinson(6) (lw: racd alone stands' side: outpcd ½-wy: t.o)............6 7

11/10 Resounder (USA), **7/2** Greek Icon, **11/2** THRILLING DAY, Hear The Music (IRE) (op 7/2), **8/1** Polish Spring (IRE), **25/1** What Fun, **33/1** Sualtach (IRE), CSF £12.11 TOTE £5.90: £2.70 £1.50 (£4.80) OWNER Bloomsbury Stud (NEWMARKET) BRED Bloomsbury Stud 7 Rn
1m 12.81 (1.81) SF: 43/46/28/22/14/15/-

4201

LADBROKE H'CAP (0-100) (3-Y.O+) (Class C) £12,720.00 (£3,810.00: £1,830.00: £840.00)
1m 4f Stalls: Low GOING minus 0.30 sec per fur (GF) 4-45 (4-49)

3923⁷ **Blushing Flame (USA) (89)***(102) (MRStoute)* 4-9-13 PatEddery(7) (lw: chsd ldrs: 4th & rdn st: str run to ld cl home)............— 1
4003² Step Aloft **(75)***(88) (LordHuntingdon)* 3-8-6 DHarrison(13) (lw: chsd ldrs: 6th st: led wl over 1f out tl ct nr fin)............nk 2
3957* Casual Water (IRE) **(71)***(84) (AGNewcombe)* 4-8-4 (5) AWhelan(9) (hld up: hdwy 2f out: bdly hmpd & checked over 1f out: swtchd rt: fin strly)............s.h 3
4026⁵ Benfleet **(83)***(94) (RWArmstrong)* 4-9-7 RPrice(1) (lw: hld up: swtchd rt & hdwy 2f out: hung lft appr fnl f: fin wl)............1½ 4
3945²² Tykeyvor (IRE) **(77)***(87) (LadyHerries)* 5-9-1 JReid(6) (b.hind: lw: hld up in tch: 7th st: hdwy over 2f out: rdn appr fnl f: nt qckn)............¾ 5
3963* Lord Hastie (USA) **(59)***(69) (CWThornton)* 7-7-11 JQuinn(18) (prom: 3rd st: led 3f out tl wl over 1f out: no ex fnl f)............s.h 6
4028¹⁴ Bit on the Side (IRE) **(77)***(80) (WJMusson)* 6-8-12 (3) PMcCabe(5) (hld up mid div: effrt on ins over 2f out: nvr able to chal)............5 7
3593⁶ My Learned Friend **(86)***(89) (AHide)* 4-9-10 JWilliams(10) (hld up: hdwy & nt clr run over 2f out: nvr nrr)............hd 8
3718¹² Askern **(68)***(71) (DHaydnJones)* 4-8-6 AMackay(17) (chsd ldrs: 5th st: sn rdn & wknd fnl 2f) s.h 9
3772² Dato Star (IRE) **(84)***(85) (JMJefferson)* 4-9-8 JWeaver(3) (lw: hld up: nt clr run 3f out: nt rcvr)............1¼ 10
3935⁴ Tessajoe **(73)***(72) (MJCamacho)* 3-8-4 LCharnock(12) (hld up: effrt & n.m.r 4f out: hdwy 3f out: no imp)............1¼ 11
4031¹⁰ Burning (USA) **(94)***(92) (GHarwood)* 3-9-11 MPerrett(15) (hld up in rr: effrt 2f out: no imp) ...1¼ 12
3723⁹ Slmaat **(68)***(62) (MrsMReveley)* 4-8-6 ACulhane(11) (lw: hld up in tch: effrt & rdn wl over 1f out: sn outpcd)............2½ 13
4036⁷ Shakiyr (FR) **(58)***(50) (RHollinshead)* 4-7-10 NCarlisle(8) (a bhd)............2 14
1170² High Standard **(82)***(70) (MRStoute)* 3-8-13 WRSwinburn(4) (mde most 8f: wknd over 2f out) ..3 15

4101* Keep Your Distance **(76)***(62)*(Fav)*(MrsMReveley)* 5-9-0 KDarley(2) (s.s: effrt on outside ent st: sn rdn & no imp)....1½ **16**
4028[9] Mr Browning (USA) **(72)***(44)* *(RAkehurst)* 4-8-10b SSanders(19) (w ldr: 2nd st: led 4f out to 3f out: sn wknd: t.o)....10 **17**
3963[4] Haroldon (IRE) **(76)***(40)* *(BPalling)* 6-9-0 TSprake(16) (b: chsd ldrs: rdn ent st: sn lost tch: t.o) 6 **18**
3958* Ottavio Farnese **(74)***(38)* *(AHide)* 3-8-2 (3) JStack(14) (bhd fnl 3f: t.o)....½ **19**

100/30 Keep Your Distance, **8/1** BLUSHING FLAME (USA), Casual Water (IRE), Step Aloft, Dato Star (IRE), High Standard, **10/1** Ottavio Farnese, **12/1** Benfleet, **14/1** My Learned Friend, Tykeyvor (IRE), Tessajoe, Mr Browning (USA), Lord Hastie (USA), **16/1** Burning (USA), **20/1** Bit on the Side (IRE), Shakiyr (FR), Haroldon (IRE), **25/1** Askern, Slmaat, CSF £80.71 CT £518.09 TOTE £13.40: £3.50 £2.10 £2.40 £3.50 (£96.70) Trio £702.60 OWNER Cheveley Park Stud (NEWMARKET) BRED Cheveley Park Stud 19 Rn

2m 31.01 (0.41) SF: 84/63/66/76/69/51/62/71/53/67/47/67/44/32/45/44/26/22/13

WEIGHT FOR AGE 3yo-7lb

T/Plpt: £336.20 (67.84 Tckts). T/Qdpt: £84.70 (2.3 Tckts). IM

4157-NEWBURY (L-H)
Saturday October 21st (Good to soft)

WEATHER: sunny WIND: almost nil

4202

1995 NEWBURY BREEDERS CUP GALA EVENT H'CAP (0-100) (3-Y.O+) (Class B) £8,518.80 (£3,169.20: £1,534.60: £643.00: £271.50: £122.90)
1m 1f Stalls: Low GOING: 0.22 sec per fur (G) 1-30 (1-31)

4031[4] **Smart Generation (85)***(102)* *(LordHuntingdon)* 4-8-11 MHills(3) (lw: hld up: led over 1f out: all out)....— **1**
3945[17] Wilcuma **(85)***(102)* *(PJMakin)* 4-8-11 RCochrane(4) (lw: nt clr run over 2f out: hdwy over 1f out: r.o wl ins fnl f)....s.h **2**
3945[3] Hunters of Brora (IRE) **(95)***(92)* *(JDBethell)* 5-9-7 TIves(9) (hdwy over 1f out: r.o one pce)....11 **3**
3837[2] Second Chance (IRE) **(83)***(80)* *(PMitchell)* 5-8-9 GDuffield(2) (led over 7f: one pce)....hd **4**
3991[7] Pay Homage **(81)***(74)* *(IABalding)* 7-8-2 (5) DGriffiths(5) (lw: 2nd st: ev ch over 1f out: sn wknd)....2½ **5**
4136[13] Tribal Peace (IRE) **(81)***(71)* *(BGubby)* 3-7-12 (5) PPMurphy(6) (3rd st: wknd over 1f out)....1½ **6**
3487a[5] Hardy Dancer **(87)***(76)* *(GLMoore)* 3-8-9 SWhitworth(1) (4th st: wknd over 1f out)....¾ **7**
3926[15] Te Amo (IRE) **(81)***(68)* *(RAkehurst)* 3-8-3b BDoyle(10) (6th st: wknd 2f out)....1¼ **8**
3991[2] Akil (IRE) **(91)***(70)*(Fav)*(RWArmstrong)* 3-8-13 WCarson(8) (5th st: rdn over 2f out: ev ch over 1f out: sn wknd)....4 **9**
1188[7] Risk Master **(88)***(66)* *(CAHorgan)* 6-9-0 RHills(12) (a bhd)....1 **10**
3945[4] Show Faith (IRE) **(88)***(55)* *(RHannon)* 5-8-9 (5) DaneO'Neill(11) (a bhd)....6 **11**
4074[5] Amrak Ajeeb (IRE) **(90)***(53)* *(BHanbury)* 3-8-12 MRimmer(7) (plld hrd: bhd fnl 2f)....2½ **12**

LONG HANDICAP Te Amo (IRE) 8-2 Tribal Peace (IRE) 7-4

3/1 Akil (IRE), **7/1** SMART GENERATION, Second Chance (IRE) (op 9/2), Show Faith (IRE), **8/1** Wilcuma, **9/1** Hunters of Brora (IRE) (op 6/1), **14/1** Te Amo (IRE), **16/1** Hardy Dancer, Amrak Ajeeb (IRE), Pay Homage, **25/1** Risk Master, **66/1** Tribal Peace (IRE), CSF £53.80 CT £455.39 TOTE £8.00: £2.30 £2.20 £2.90 (£37.80) Trio £62.10 OWNER Mr George Ward (WEST ILSLEY) BRED Lord Halifax 12 Rn 1m 55.67 (6.47) SF: 54/54/44/32/26/19/24/16/18/18/7/1

WEIGHT FOR AGE 3yo-4lb

4203

NEWGATE STUD RADLEY STKS (Listed) (2-Y.O F) (Class A) £10,690.00 (£3,220.00: £1,560.00: £730.00)
7f 64y (round) Stalls: Low GOING: 0.22 sec per fur (G) 2-00 (2-00)

3983* **Sil Sila (IRE)** *(101)* *(BSmart)* 2-8-8 RCochrane(1) (6th st: led over 1f out: rdn out)....— **1**
3867* Pacific Grove **(90)***(93)* *(PFICole)* 2-8-8 MHills(9) (3rd & c wd st: led over 2f out tl over 1f out: unable qckn)....3½ **2**
4084[15] Needham Star (USA) **(96)***(89)* *(PAKelleway)* 2-8-8b BDoyle(4) (4th st: lost pl 3f out: rallied over 1f out: r.o)....2 **3**
4025* Prends Ca (IRE) **(90)***(86)* *(RHannon)* 2-8-8 JFEgan(7) (nt clr run 3f out: hdwy over 2f out: hrd rdn & n.m.r over 1f out: one pce)....1½ **4**
4048* Oleana (IRE) *(82)* *(PFICole)* 2-8-8 TQuinn(8) (lw: plld hrd: 2nd st: led over 2f out tl over 1f out: wknd fnl f)....1½ **5**
3917[2] Astuti (IRE) **(94)***(74)* *(APJarvis)* 2-8-8 JTate(6) (hdwy over 3f out: wknd over 1f out)....4 **6**
3997* Thracian **(95)***(47)*(Fav)*(JLDunlop)* 2-8-8 WCarson(2) (5th st: rdn over 2f out: wknd over 1f out)....12 **7**
3587a[3] Key To A Million (IRE) **(96)***(23)* *(RHannon)* 2-8-8 MRoberts(5) (led 4f)....11 **8**
3420[3] Persian Secret (FR) **(100)***(21)* *(JWWatts)* 2-8-8 WRyan(3) (lw: a bhd)....1 **9**

11/10 Thracian, **4/1** Oleana (IRE), **11/1** Prends Ca (IRE), **12/1** Key To A Million (IRE) (op 8/1), Astuti (IRE), Persian Secret (FR) (op 8/1), **14/1** Needham Star (USA), **20/1** Pacific Grove, **25/1** SIL SILA (IRE), CSF £338.56 TOTE £29.40: £4.20 £2.30 £3.00 (£125.30) Trio £197.70 OWNER Mr Alvarez Cervera (LAMBOURN) BRED L A C 9 Rn 1m 33.21 (4.71) SF: 57/49/45/42/38/30/3/-/-

4204 PERPETUAL ST SIMON STKS (Gp 3) (3-Y.O+) (Class A) £22,380.00 (£8,394.00: £4,047.00: £1,779.00) **1m 4f 5y** Stalls: Low GOING: 0.22 sec per fur (G) 2-30 (2-33)

3161[8] **Phantom Gold (109)***(115) (LordHuntingdon)* 3-8-9 RHills(1) (5th st: led over 3f out: hrd rdn & hung lft 1f out: r.o wl) — 1
3549[8] Asterita **(106)***(108) (RHannon)* 3-8-4 GCarter(3) (6th st: swtchd rt & hdwy over 3f out: chsd wnr over 1f out: r.o one pce) 1½ 2
4076[3] Whitechapel (USA) **(88)***(109) (LordHuntingdon)* 7-9-0 TIves(7) (a.p: led over 4f out tl over 3f out: one pce) 1¼ 3
4030* Labibeh (USA) **(108)***(101) (JLDunlop)* 3-8-7 WCarson(12) (racd wd bk st: led tl over 4f out: 2nd st: wknd over 3f out) 6 4
1611[10] Salmon Ladder (USA) **(104)***(99) (PFICole)* 3-8-7 RCochrane(9) (bit bkwd: nvr nr to chal) 2 5
3614[5] Alriffa **(113)***(100) (RHannon)* 4-9-3 JFEgan(5) (nvr nrr) 1½ 6
3836[17] Ionio (USA) **(107)***(94) (CEBrittain)* 4-9-0 BDoyle(8) (b: nvr nrr) 2 7
3831[6] Hagwah (USA) **(102)***(87) (BHanbury)* 3-8-4 MRoberts(4) (4th st: wknd 2f out) 3 8
3932* Revere (IRE) **(112)***(85)*(Fav)*(PFICole)* 5-9-3 TQuinn(2) (lw: led 1f: 3rd st: eased whn btn fnl 2f) 6 9
3946* Further Flight **(110)***(83) (BWHills)* 9-9-3 MHills(6) (a bhd) 1¾ 10
3594[3] Indian Light **(104)***(60) (JLDunlop)* 3-8-7 WRyan(11) (bhd fnl 4f) 15 11
3995* Bahamian Sunshine (USA) *(DRLoder)* 4-9-0 RHughes(10) (a bhd: t.o) dist 12

100/30 Revere (IRE), **5/1** Labibeh (USA), **6/1** PHANTOM GOLD, **8/1** Further Flight, **9/1** Alriffa, **10/1** Salmon Ladder (USA), Bahamian Sunshine (USA), **20/1** Ionio (USA), Hagwah (USA), Indian Light, Asterita, **25/1** Whitechapel (USA), CSF £99.27 TOTE £7.50: £2.00 £5.70 £4.80 (£103.60) Trio £1,110.80 OWNER The Queen (WEST ILSLEY) BRED The Queen 12 Rn
2m 39.71 (10.41) SF: 41/34/42/27/25/33/27/13/18/16/-/-
WEIGHT FOR AGE 3yo-7lb

4205 PADDOCK PAVILIONS CLAIMING STKS (3-Y.O+) (Class D) £4,562.00 (£1,376.00: £668.00: £314.00) **1m 4f 5y** Stalls: Low GOING: 0.22 sec per fur (G) 3-00 (3-03)

3818[11] **Court Joker (IRE) (45)***(69) (MHTompkins)* 3-8-6 WRyan(4) (3rd st: led over 3f out: all out) — 1
3993[7] Magic Junction (USA) **(76)***(74) (LordHuntingdon)* 4-9-4 MHills(6) (brought wd st: hdwy 3f out: hrd rdn over 1f out: r.o wl ins fnl f) hd 2
3440[5] Knotally Wood (USA) **(64)***(65) (JWHills)* 3-8-2 GDuffield(1) (led after 2f tl over 3f out: no ch fnl f: r.o) hd 3
3963[3] Sunderland Echo **(65)***(62)*(Fav)*(MrsMReveley)* 6-8-8 RCochrane(15) (hdwy 6f out: brought wd st: hrd rdn & no hdwy fnl 2f) 1¼ 4
3825[10] Just-Mana-Mou (IRE) **(44)***(60) (GLewis)* 3-8-0b BDoyle(5) (2nd st: r.o one pce fnl 2f) 1 5
4035[5] Red Light **(70)***(61) (LordHuntingdon)* 3-8-4 RHills(13) (hdwy fnl 2f: nvr nrr) 1¾ 6
3817[14] Witney-de-Bergerac (IRE) **(62)***(47) (JSMoore)* 3-8-6 JFEgan(17) (nrst fin) 12 7
2687[9] Blue And Royal (IRE) **(60)***(35) (RHannon)* 3-8-3b(5) DaneO'Neill(10) (nvr nr to chal) 11 8
2486[4] Brown Carpet **(26)***(25) (CAHorgan)* 8-8-7 NAdams(2) (b.hind: 5th st: wknd 3f out) 1¼ 9
3899[12] What's Secreto (USA) **(56)***(30) (PAKelleway)* 3-8-6 JTate(8) (nvr trbld ldrs) 1¼ 10
4035[19] Flag Fen (USA) **(75)***(32) (MartynMeade)* 4-9-5 VSlattery(12) (6th st: wknd over 3f out) 2½ 11
3899[11] Pharamineux **(64)***(19) (RAkehurst)* 9-8-7 TQuinn(3) (a bhd) ¾ 12
3006[6] Huish Cross **(51)***(14) (SGKnight)* 3-7-8 (3) NVarley(7) (bhd fnl 3f) 1¼ 13
Kristal Diva **(55)** *(AGNewcombe)* 4-8-4 (5) DGriffiths(14) (bit bkwd: a wl bhd: t.o) 20 14
2291[12] Phlirty *(RFJohnsonHoughton)* 3-8-0 AMcGlone(11) (4th st: wknd 4f out: t.o) 5 15
4049[18] Lady Kate (USA) **(30)** *(KOCunningham-Brown)* 3-8-7 GCarter(16) (led 2f: wknd 6f out: t.o) 11 16

11/4 Sunderland Echo, **11/2** Red Light, **6/1** Magic Junction (USA), **7/1** Pharamineux, **8/1** Knotally Wood (USA), Witney-de-Bergerac (IRE), **14/1** Blue And Royal (IRE), **20/1** Just-Mana-Mou (IRE), **25/1** COURT JOKER (IRE), **33/1** What's Secreto (USA), Flag Fen (USA), Kristal Diva, Huish Cross, Phlirty, **40/1** Brown Carpet, Lady Kate (USA), CSF £158.18 TOTE £30.80: £6.00 £2.30 £2.80 (£116.90) Trio £334.40 OWNER Oceala Ltd (NEWMARKET) BRED Mellon Stud 16 Rn
2m 41.91 (12.61) SF: 24/36/20/24/15/16/2/-/-/-/-/-/-/-/-/-
WEIGHT FOR AGE 3yo-7lb

4206 DICK DAWSON NURSERY H'CAP (2-Y.O) (Class C) £5,985.00 (£1,800.00: £870.00: £405.00) **6f 8y** Stalls: High GOING: 0.22 sec per fur (G) 3-30 (3-32)

4077* **Lunar Mist (83)***(90)*(Fav)*(MartynMeade)* 2-8-6 (5) RHavlin(12) (stdd s: hdwy 4f out: hrd rdn over 1f out: led wl ins fnl f) — 1

3711[8] Amaretto Bay (IRE) **(87)***(91) (BJMeehan)* 2-9-1b TQuinn(4) (led: hrd rdn over 1f out: hdd wl ins fnl f) 1¼ **2**
3548[13] Polly Golightly **(75)***(77) (BSmart)* 2-8-3b JFEgan(8) (w ldr: ev ch 1f out: r.o) .... ½ **3**
3727[2] Polish Bear (IRE) **(74)***(74) (BJMeehan)* 2-8-2b BDoyle(10) (chsd ldrs: r.o one pce fnl 2f) 1 **4**
4077[2] Stop Play (IRE) **(78)***(75) (MHTompkins)* 2-8-6 RCochrane(11) (nvr nrr) 1 **5**
3766[5] Arctic Romancer (IRE) **(70)***(65) (GLewis)* 2-7-12 WCarson(9) (a.p: no hdwy fnl 2f) .... ¾ **6**
3623* Antonias Melody **(70)***(57) (SRBowring)* 2-7-12 JLowe(3) (nvr nr to chal) 3 **7**
3766[4] Nellie North **(76)***(63) (MrsMMcCourt)* 2-7-11 (7) RStudholme(6) (prom tl hrd rdn & wknd 2f out) .... hd **8**
3867[9] My Mariam **(88)***(70) (CREgerton)* 2-9-2 CRutter(5) (nvr trbld ldrs) 1¾ **9**
4084[19] Supreme Power **(77)***(59) (WRMuir)* 2-8-5b MHills(2) (outpcd) .... hd **10**
3893[4] Sharp Pearl **(92)***(58) (RCharlton)* 2-9-6 RHughes(14) (outpcd) 6 **11**
2435[3] Castan (IRE) **(76)***(37) (JLDunlop)* 2-8-4 GCarter(13) (a wl bhd) 2 **12**
4084[7] Kandavu **(93)***(53) (MMcCormack)* 2-9-7 OUrbina(1) (a bhd) .... nk **13**
4144[12] Prime Partner **(68)***(10) (WRMuir)* 2-7-3b(7)ow2 MartinDwyer(7) (a bhd) 6 **14**

11/4 LUNAR MIST, **9/2** Antonias Melody, **11/2** Arctic Romancer (IRE) (10/1-5/1), **13/2** Stop Play (IRE), **11/1** Polish Bear (IRE), **12/1** Polly Golightly (20/1-10/1), **16/1** Amaretto Bay (IRE), **20/1** Castan (IRE), Supreme Power, Kandavu, **25/1** Nellie North, Sharp Pearl, My Mariam, **33/1** Prime Partner, CSF £43.54 CT £431.44 TOTE £3.90: £1.90 £4.00 £4.20 (£27.40) Trio £314.70 OWNER Ladyswood Racing Club (MALMESBURY) BRED T. Barratt 14 Rn
1m 15.84 (4.04) SF: 57/58/44/41/42/32/24/30/37/26/25/4/20/-

4207 WHATCOMBE CONDITIONS STKS (2-Y.O) (Class C) £4,706.00
(£1,754.00: £852.00: £360.00: £155.00: £73.00)
1m Stalls: High GOING: 0.22 sec per fur (G) 4-00 (4-00)

4034[2] **Henry The Fifth (100)***(95) (CEBrittain)* 2-8-11 BDoyle(4) (a.p: led over 2f out: r.o wl) .... — **1**
3450* More Than You Know (IRE) *(91) (RHannon)* 2-8-4 (5) DaneO'Neill(5) (hld up: ev ch fnl 2f: r.o) 1¼ **2**
4042* Believe Me **(97)***(90) (RHannon)* 2-9-2 MRoberts(1) (wnt lft s: plld hrd: led over 5f) 4 **3**
4034[3] Oberons Boy (IRE) **(98)***(87) (BJMeehan)* 2-9-0 TQuinn(6) (prom tl wknd over 1f out) .... s.h **4**
3449* Red Robbo (CAN) *(79)*(Fav)*(HRACecil)* 2-9-0 WRyan(3) (prom tl hrd rdn & wknd 2f out) 4 **5**

4/5 Red Robbo (CAN), **4/1** More Than You Know (IRE), **11/2** HENRY THE FIFTH, **13/2** Believe Me, **10/1** Oberons Boy (IRE) (op 5/1), CSF £24.29 TOTE £5.70: £1.90 £2.00 (£12.30) OWNER Mr A. J. Richards (NEWMARKET) BRED Ewar Stud Farms 5 Rn 1m 44.38 (7.38) SF: 37/33/32/29/21

4208 LEVY BOARD NURSERY H'CAP (0-85) (2-Y.O) (Class D) £4,146.00
(£1,248.00: £604.00: £282.00)
7f 64y (round) Stalls: Low GOING: 0.22 sec per fur (G) 4-30 (4-33)

3956[3] **Proud Monk (72)***(78) (GLMoore)* 2-8-10 SWhitworth(6) (swtchd rt s: 9th st: hdwy over 2f out: led over 1f out: r.o wl) .... — **1**
3982* Second Time Lucky (IRE) **(74)***(78) (LordHuntingdon)* 2-8-12 RHills(17) (7th st: led over 2f out tl over 1f out: r.o) 1 **2**
3985* Deadline Time (IRE) **(74)***(77)*(Fav)*(MHTompkins)* 2-8-12v WRyan(3) (5th st: ev ch over 1f out: r.o ins fnl f) .... nk **3**
3956[2] Daily Risk **(66)***(69) (SDow)* 2-8-4 GDuffield(13) (led tl over 2f out: hrd rdn: r.o) .... s.h **4**
4075[9] Laughing Buccaneer **(64)***(64) (BJMeehan)* 2-8-2b BDoyle(14) (6th st: r.o one pce fnl 2f) 1½ **5**
2911[5] Brecon **(66)***(65) (PFICole)* 2-8-4 TQuinn(9) (3rd st: ev ch over 1f out: eased whn btn ins fnl f) .... nk **6**
4100[4] Bright Diamond **(60)***(59) (JRArnold)* 2-7-12 JFEgan(5) (nvr nrr) .... ½ **7**
3969[5] Duralock Fencer **(58)***(56) (PGMurphy)* 2-7-7 (3) DWright(18) (4th st: ev ch over 1f out:nt qckn) d.h **7**
3887* White Sea (IRE) **(80)***(78) (PFICole)* 2-8-13 (5) DaneO'Neill(4) (2nd st: ev ch over 1f out: wknd ins fnl f) .... s.h **9**
3947[8] Willisa **(71)***(64) (JDBethell)* 2-8-9 ow1 RHughes(2) (nvr nr to chal) 2 **10**
3956* Al Shafa **(83)***(71) (JLDunlop)* 2-9-7 WCarson(8) (sme hdwy on ins over 2f out: nvr nr ldrs) ... 2½ **11**
4081[3] Nikita's Star (IRE) **(68)***(55) (DJGMurraySmith)* 2-8-6b MHills(16) (nvr trbld ldrs) .... ½ **12**
3887[3] Swift Maiden **(75)***(61) (MrsLAMurphy)* 2-8-10 (3) SDrowne(15) (8th st: wknd 2f out) .... ½ **13**
3891[7] Indira **(60)***(43) (HCandy)* 2-7-12 CRutter(20) (nvr on terms) 1½ **14**
3939[5] Madam Marash (IRE) **(60)***(41) (AGFoster)* 2-7-9 (3) NVarley(7) (a bhd) .... ½ **15**
3803[6] Bearnaise (IRE) **(64)***(43) (RHannon)* 2-8-2 MRoberts(10) (a bhd) 1¼ **16**
3628[14] Efficacious (IRE) **(60)***(23) (CJBenstead)* 2-7-12 JLowe(19) (a bhd) 7 **17**
4103[19] Red Raja **(72)***(32) (PMitchell)* 2-8-10 TIves(12) (a wl bhd) 1¾ **18**
3969[11] Baker **(59)***(10) (HCandy)* 2-7-11 NAdams(1) (bhd fnl 4f) 4 **19**
3765[5] Village Native (FR) **(66)** *(KOCunningham-Brown)* 2-8-4 GCarter(11) (Withdrawn not under Starter's orders: veterinary advice) .... **W**

100/30 Deadline Time (IRE) (5/1-3/1), **5/1** Bearnaise (IRE), **17/2** Al Shafa (6/1-9/1), **11/1** Second Time Lucky (IRE) (8/1-12/1), **12/1** White Sea (IRE), PROUD MONK, **14/1** Laughing Buccaneer, Daily Risk, **16/1** Nikita's Star (IRE), Village Native (FR), Duralock Fencer, **20/1** Bright Diamond, Brecon, Willisa, **25/1** Swift Maiden, **33/1** Indira, Madam Marash (IRE), Red Raja, Baker, **50/1** Efficacious (IRE), CSF £130.26 CT £501.29 TOTE £16.70: £3.10 £2.00 £1.50 £3.70 (£71.50) Trio £123.30 OWNER Pennine Partners (EPSOM) BRED K. Higson 19 Rn

1m 33.91 (5.41) SF: 51/51/50/42/37/38/32/29/51/37/44/28/34/16/14/16/-/5/-/-

T/Jkpt: Not won; £60,305.16 to Leicester 23/10/95. T/Plpt: £5,808.60 (5.7 Tckts). T/Qdpt: £127.30 (2.9 Tckts). AK

4058-LEICESTER (R-H)

Monday October 23rd (Firm, Good to firm patches)

visibility poor 6 & 7

WEATHER: cloudy & dull WIND: mod half bhd

4209 SEAGRAVE CLAIMING APPRENTICE H'CAP (0-70) (3-Y.O+) (Class G) £2,427.50 (£690.00: £342.50)

1m 8y Stalls: High GOING minus 0.53 sec per fur (F) 1-15 (1-20)

4152[3] **Cicerone (42)***(53)*(Fav)*(JLHarris)* 5-8-3 (5) DSweeney(6) (lw: a.p: jnd ldr 3f out: led 2f out: r.o wl) — 1
4152[5] Mighty Kingdom (IRE) **(42)***(53) (CADwyer)* 4-8-3 (5) RMullen(4) (lw: a.p: led over 3f out to 2f out: ev ch fnl f: r.o) hd 2
4115[11] Evanro (IRE) **(39)***(45) (TDBarron)* 4-8-5 KimberleyHart(1) (led over 4f out tl over 3f out: kpt on one pce appr fnl f) 2½ 3
3800[21] Anotherone to Note **(42)***(47) (NPLittmoden)* 4-8-3b(5) JBramhill(5) (plld hrd: chsd ldrs: rdn & styd on fnl f) nk 4
4060[8] Pusey Street Boy **(49)***(52) (JRBosley)* 8-8-12 (3) FLynch(18) (t: a.p: rdn over 2f out: edgd lft appr fnl f: one pce) 1 5
3745[3] Matisse **(40)***(43) (JDBethell)* 4-8-1 (5) TFinn(17) (bhd: hdwy ½-wy: kpt on u.p ins fnl f) hd 6
4152[8] Rad **(45)***(43) (SPCWoods)* 5-8-4 (7) JMoon(2) (nvr nr to chal) 2½ 7
855[8] Ladybower (IRE) **(42)***(40) (LordHuntingdon)* 3-8-5 JWilkinson(13) (in tch: no hdwy fnl 2f) nk 8
4152[6] Pop to Stans **(42)***(38) (JPearce)* 6-8-3v(5) MNutter(20) (lw: hdwy 3f out: rdn bel dist: no imp) 1 9
4152[13] Fiaba **(40)***(35) (MrsNMacauley)* 7-8-6 IonaWands(7) (chsd ldrs: rdn 3f out: sn wknd) s.h 10
1991[11] Shaynes Domain **(44)***(37) (RMFlower)* 4-8-5b(5)ow2 CScudder(9) (bkwd: nvr trbld ldrs) hd 11
3504[3] Golden Fish **(41)***(30) (JLEyre)* 3-8-4b GMilligan(11) (prom over 5f) 3 12
3934[10] Oozlem (IRE) **(40)***(29)*(Fav)*(JCPoulton)* 6-8-6b GFaulkner(3) (s.s: bhd: rdn 3f out: no imp) hd 13
Tauten (IRE) **(40)***(26) (PBurgoyne)* 5-8-3 (3) DebbieBiggs(14) (bkwd: hdwy 3f out: sn ev ch: wknd fnl 2f) 1¾ 14
3879[12] Legend Dulac (IRE) **(43)***(26) (JAHarris)* 6-8-4 (5) CLowther(12) (led over 3f: wknd over 2f out) 1½ 15
481[3] Forgetful **(42)***(15) (DBurchell)* 6-8-3 (5) KSked(19) (bit bkwd: chsd ldrs 5f: sn rdn & wknd: t.o) 5 16
4157[14] Causley **(55)***(24) (DMHyde)* 10-9-0 (7) RBrisland(10) (prom over 4f: sn rdn & wknd: t.o) 2 17
1351[12] Rafter-J **(58)***(23) (JAHarris)* 4-9-5 (5) JEdmunds(16) (bkwd: s.s: a in rr) 1¾ 18
3984[11] Ruddigore **(42)** *(KRBurke)* 3-7-12b(7) RFfrench(15) (prom over 4f: sn lost pl: t.o) 15 19

7/1 CICERONE, Oozlem (IRE), **15/2** Ruddigore (op 12/1), **8/1** Matisse, **10/1** Mighty Kingdom (IRE), Ladybower (IRE), Pusey Street Boy, **11/1** Pop to Stans (8/1-12/1), **14/1** Golden Fish, Legend Dulac (IRE), **16/1** Rad, Forgetful, Rafter-J, **20/1** Evanro (IRE), Shaynes Domain, Anotherone to Note, **33/1** Tauten (IRE), Causley, Fiaba, CSF £75.59 CT £1,249.32 TOTE £6.00: £1.30 £5.00 £10.00 £4.70 (£33.80) Trio not won; £764.52 to Leicester 24/10/95. OWNER Dr C. W. Ashpole (MELTON MOWBRAY) BRED Aldershawe Stud Farm 19 Rn

1m 36.4 (1.40) SF: 33/33/25/27/32/23/23/17/18/15/17/7/9/6/6/-/4/3/-

WEIGHT FOR AGE 3yo-3lb

4210 E.B.F. WIDMERPOOL MAIDEN STKS (2-Y.O) (Class D) £4,142.50 (£1,240.00: £595.00: £272.50)

7f 9y Stalls: High GOING minus 0.53 sec per fur (F) 1-45 (1-46)

3821[6] **Dance On A Cloud (USA)** *(76+) (MRStoute)* 2-8-9 MHills(4) (s.s: sn rcvrd: hdwy to ld over 1f out: sn clr: comf) — 1
3472[6] Apache Len (USA) *(77) (RHannon)* 2-9-0 RHughes(5) (hdwy over 2f out: sn rdn: kpt on fnl f: no ch w wnr) 2 2
3989[3] Danish Circus (IRE) *(74) (MJHeaton-Ellis)* 2-9-0 WWoods(11) (plld hrd: a.p: led over 2f out tl over 1f out: one pce) 1¼ 3
4070[4] Harbour Dues *(65) (LadyHerries)* 2-9-0 RCochrane(10) (lw: plld hrd: chsd ldrs tl wknd appr fnl f) 4 4

Natal Ridge (53) (DHaydnJones) 2-9-0 TIves(2) (w'like: scope: bkwd: nvr nr to chal) 5 5
4155[9] Night Silence (50) (SirMarkPrescott) 2-9-0 CNutter(7) (nvr gng pce of ldrs) 1¼ 6
Disc of Gold (USA) (40) (MJohnston) 2-8-9 TWilliams(3) (w'like: bkwd: outpcd) 2½ 7
4073[2] Name of Our Father (USA) (41)(Fav)(JHMGosden) 2-9-0 PatEddery(6) (swtg: led over 4f: sn rdn: wknd bel dist) 1¾ 8
3779[8] Appeal Again (IRE) (37) (MrsJRRamsden) 2-9-0 JFEgan(8) (bhd: effrt & rn green 3f out: no imp) 1¾ 9
Laazim Afooz (29) (RTPhillips) 2-9-0 MFenton(9) (unf: scope: bkwd: s.i.s: a in rr) 3½ 10
2534[7] North Star (IRE) (RHannon) 2-9-0 GCarter(1) (lw: prom: rdn along ½-wy: sn wknd: t.o) 15 11

9/4 Name of Our Father (USA) (7/4-3/1), **3/1** Danish Circus (IRE), **5/1** Harbour Dues, **6/1** Apache Len (USA), **10/1** DANCE ON A CLOUD (USA), Disc of Gold (USA) (op 9/2), **16/1** Appeal Again (IRE), **25/1** North Star (IRE), **33/1** Natal Ridge, Laazim Afooz, Night Silence, CSF £65.98 TOTE £7.20: £2.10 £2.10 £1.60 (£31.20) Trio £32.30 OWNER Hesmonds Stud (NEWMARKET) BRED Joseph Allen 11 Rn
1m 23.4 (0.90) SF: 37/38/35/26/14/11/1/2/-/-/-

4211 JOHN O'GAUNT NURSERY H'CAP (0-85) (2-Y.O) (Class E) £3,845.60 (£1,152.80: £554.40: £255.20)

7f 9y Stalls: High GOING minus 0.53 sec per fur (F) 2-15 (2-18)

4111[9] **Worldwide Elsie (USA) (66)**(74) (RHarris) 2-8-7 AMackay(13) (a.p: rdn 2f out: styd on to ld wl ins fnl f) ....— 1
4130[4] Daunting Destiny (BEL) **(70)**(76) (RHannon) 2-8-6 (5) DaneO'Neill(12) (lw: chsd ldrs: rdn & r.o ins fnl f) 1 2
3806* Cebwob **(80)**(85)(Fav)(PFICole) 2-9-2 (5) MHenry(5) (lw: b.hind: a.p: led over 2f out tl wl ins fnl f) ....nk 3
4058[10] Knave **(65)**(66) (RHannon) 2-8-6 GCarter(10) (lw: hld up: mid div: hdwy over 2f out: drifted lft fnl f: nt rch ldrs) 1¾ 4
4208[W] Village Native (FR) **(66)**(67) (KOCunningham-Brown) 2-8-4 (3) PMcCabe(11) (plld hrd: led over 4f: one pce fnl f) ....hd 5
4133[4] It's A Ripper **(57)**(50) (GLewis) 2-7-12 TWilliams(6) (lw: s.s: rdn 3f out: nvr nr ldrs) 3½ 6
4064[7] Seattle Alley (USA) **(70)**(56) (MrsJRRamsden) 2-8-11 MDeering(8) (unruly s: s.s: hdwy 2f out: nt pce to chal) 3 7
3895[2] Rebel County (IRE) **(73)**(59) (DJSCosgrove) 2-9-0 MRimmer(3) (nvr trbld ldrs)....................d.h 7
3858[14] Miss Carottene **(54)**(36) (MJRyan) 2-7-4v(5) MBaird(9) (hld up: rdn over 2f out: wknd bel dist)..2 9
3988[12] Impetuous Lady (USA) **(55)**(36) (WJMusson) 2-7-7 (3) NVarley(7) (rdn along ½-wy: a bhd) ....hd 10
3894[13] Pearls of Thought (IRE) **(60)**(33) (PTWalwyn) 2-8-1 FNorton(2) (a in rr) 3½ 11
3752[8] Mon Pere **(55)**(28) (KMcAuliffe) 2-7-10 JLowe(4) (prom: rdn 3f out: sn wknd)..........................nk 12

9/2 Cebwob (3/1-5/1), **11/2** Seattle Alley (USA), Daunting Destiny (BEL), **6/1** WORLDWIDE ELSIE (USA), **7/1** Rebel County (IRE), **8/1** Knave, **10/1** It's A Ripper, **12/1** Village Native (FR), Impetuous Lady (USA), **16/1** Miss Carottene, **20/1** Pearls of Thought (IRE), Mon Pere, CSF £38.57 CT £150.38 TOTE £7.30: £2.60 £2.50 £2.40 (£29.30) Trio £45.60 OWNER Mr Dawson Inner Circle (NEWMARKET) BRED Lantern Hill Farm and Dr. M. G. Marenchic 12 Rn
1m 23.5 (1.00) SF: 34/36/45/26/27/10/16/26/-/-/-/-

4212 E.B.F. FLECKNEY MAIDEN STKS (2-Y.O F) (Class D) £4,337.50 (£1,300.00: £625.00: £287.50)

5f 218y Stalls: High GOING minus 0.53 sec per fur (F) 2-45 (2-49)

4056[3] **Wildwood Flower (72)**(82) (RHannon) 2-8-6 (5) DaneO'Neill(14) (a.p: led over 2f out: edgd lft: clr fnl f) ....— 1
3893[7] Samara (IRE) (73) (JLDunlop) 2-8-11 RHughes(11) (hdwy over 2f out: rdn bel dist: r.o) 3½ 2
4103[17] Stately Dancer (69)(Fav)(GWragg) 2-8-11 MHills(17) (chsd ldrs: ev ch 2f out: r.o one pce)..1½ 3
Asmahaan (USA) (68) (HThomsonJones) 2-8-11 GCarter(16) (scope: s.s: bhd & outpcd tl r.o fnl 2f) ....hd 4
Charlotte Corday (66) (GWragg) 2-8-11 FNorton(10) (scope: hld up: swtchd rt & hdwy appr fnl f: nvr nrr) ....¾ 5
3450[8] Faraway Lass (66) (LordHuntingdon) 2-8-11 PatEddery(9) (w ldrs: rdn & one pce fnl 2f)......s.h 6
4048[3] Peppers (IRE) (66) (LMCumani) 2-8-4 (7) RFfrench(13) (chsd ldrs: rdn over 2f out: one pce) s.h 7
Rainy Day Song (64) (MissGayKelleway) 2-8-11 RCochrane(12) (w'like: bkwd: b.hind: nvr nr to chal) ....¾ 8
1098[7] Oatey (64) (MrsJRRamsden) 2-8-11 JFEgan(8) (stdd s: nvr nrr) ....hd 9
Patrio (IRE) (61) (MJohnston) 2-8-11 TWilliams(3) (lt-f: chsd ldrs over 4f) 1 10
4109[4] Need You Badly (59) (SPCWoods) 2-8-11 WWoods(4) (led over 4f: hung lft & wknd over 1f out) ....¾ 11
Truth (59) (SirMarkPrescott) 2-8-11 CNutter(18) (scope: a in rr)..........hd 12
3865[27] Desert Lynx (IRE) (57) (TRWatson) 2-8-11 SSanders(6) (chsd ldrs: rdn along 2f out: sn wknd) ....¾ 13

4098⁹ Frog *(54) (SirMarkPrescott)* 2-8-11 MBirch(5) (chsd ldrs 4f: sn wknd)....1¼ **14**
Sharp 'n' Shady *(47) (CFWall)* 2-8-11 WLord(2) (w'like: bkwd: s.s: a bhd)....2½ **15**
3848⁷ Queen Emma (IRE) *(44) (JSMoore)* 2-8-8 (3) NVarley(7) (prom to ½-wy)....1 **16**
Perrywinkle Way (IRE) *(35) (MrsALMKing)* 2-8-11 JWilliams(15) (unf: a bhd)....3½ **17**
Florrie'm *(14) (JLHarris)* 2-8-11 AMackay(1) (w'like: scope: s.s: a outpcd & t.o)....8 **18**

3/1 Stately Dancer, **4/1** Need You Badly (op 12/1), **6/1** WILDWOOD FLOWER (3/1-13/2), **7/1** Asmahaan (USA) (5/1-8/1), Peppers (IRE), **8/1** Faraway Lass, **14/1** Samara (IRE), **16/1** Charlotte Corday, Oatey, Patrio (IRE), Rainy Day Song, **20/1** Desert Lynx (IRE), **25/1** Truth, Frog, Sharp 'n' Shady, **33/1** Florrie'm, **50/1** Queen Emma (IRE), Perrywinkle Way (IRE), CSF £94.31 TOTE £6.70: £1.90 £6.40 £2.00 (£84.20) Trio £93.90 OWNER Mr G. Howard-Spink (MARLBOROUGH) BRED Sir Stephen Hastings and G. Howard-Spink 18 Rn
1m 10.5 (0.50) SF: 43/34/30/29/27/27/27/25/25/22/20/20/18/15/8/5/-/-

4213 SQUIRREL CONDITIONS STKS (3-Y.O+) (Class C) £5,163.20
(£1,908.80: £914.40: £372.00: £146.00: £55.60)
1m 3f 183y Stalls: Low GOING minus 0.53 sec per fur (F) 3-15 (3-17)

4104⁶ **Al Widyan (IRE) (94)***(99) (HRACecil)* 3-8-12 RCochrane(1) (lw: stdd s: 5th st: hdwy wl over 1f out: led ins fnl f: r.o wl)....— **1**
4047² Beauchamp Jade **(77)***(86) (HCandy)* 3-8-2 GCarter(6) (hld up: led over 5f out tl ins fnl f: no ex)....2 **2**
2208² Speed to Lead (IRE) *(82) (HRACecil)* 3-8-2 AMcGlone(3) (hld up: 6th st: hdwy 2f out: kpt on u.p fnl f)....3½ **3**
Dacha (IRE) *(86) (HRACecil)* 3-8-7 PatEddery(4) (bit bkwd: led after 2f tl 8f out: 2nd st: rdn & hung rt over 2f out: sn btn & eased)....nk **4**
1018² Sanoosea (USA) **(106)***(83)*(Fav)*(MRStoute)* 3-8-11 WRSwinburn(2) (bit bkwd: hld up: 4th st: shkn up 2f out: no imp)....5 **5**
4047⁵ Sparrowhawk (IRE) **(72)***(45) (BWHills)* 3-8-6 MHills(5) (lw: led 2f: led 8f out: stmbld, hdd & 3rd st: wknd over 2f out: t.o)....25 **6**

Evens Sanoosea (USA), **7/2** Dacha (IRE), **6/1** Beauchamp Jade, **7/1** AL WIDYAN (IRE) (5/1-15/2), **12/1** Speed to Lead (IRE) (op 8/1), **20/1** Sparrowhawk (IRE), CSF £40.76 TOTE £9.90: £2.40 £2.30 (£19.70) OWNER Prince A. A. Faisal (NEWMARKET) BRED Nawara Stud Co Ltd 6 Rn
2m 27.9 (0.60 under best) (-0.90) SF: 60/47/43/47/44/6

4214 WYSALL CONDITIONS STKS (3-Y.O+) (Class C) £5,209.60
(£1,926.40: £923.20: £376.00: £148.00: £56.80)
7f 9y Stalls: High GOING minus 0.53 sec per fur (F) 3-45 (3-49)

3922⁷ **Shefoog (88)***(93) (RWArmstrong)* 3-8-6 RPrice(6) (plld hrd: w ldr centre: led over 2f out: r.o wl)....— **1**
4065² Karayb (IRE) **(85)***(95) (DMorley)* 3-8-12 RCochrane(2) (lw: a.p: ev ch 2f out: sn rdn: kpt on) 1¾ **2**
4024⁸ Crystal Cavern (USA) **(94)***(78)*(Fav)*(RCharlton)* 3-8-6 PatEddery(7) (hld up: hdwy u.p over 2f out: nt pce to chal)....5 **3**
Miss Ticklepenny *(42) (MajorDNChappell)* 3-8-4 WWoods(3) (leggy: bkwd: chsd ldrs 4f: sn outpcd: t.o)....15 **4**
Cuckmere Venture **(21)***(34) (JCPoulton)* 5-8-3 (7)ow3 GFaulkner(4) (bkwd: plld hrd: led centre over 4f: wknd fnl 2f: t.o)....3½ **5**
Marjan (IRE) *(9) (THCaldwell)* 4-8-7 JLowe(1) (bkwd: s.s: a bhd: t.o fnl 3f)....11 **6**

7/4 Crystal Cavern (USA), **2/1** Karayb (IRE), **9/4** SHEFOOG, **20/1** Miss Ticklepenny, **150/1** Marjan (IRE), **400/1** Cuckmere Venture, CSF £6.40 TOTE £3.20: £1.40 £1.20 (£3.20) OWNER Mr Ahmed Al Shafar (NEWMARKET) BRED Ahmed Shufaar 6 Rn 1m 23.1 (0.60) SF: 38/40/23/-/-/-
WEIGHT FOR AGE 3yo-3lb

4215 THRUSSINGTON H'CAP (0-70) (3-Y.O+) (Class E) £4,360.40
(£1,311.20: £633.60: £294.80)
5f 218y Stalls: High GOING minus 0.53 sec per fur (F) 4-15 (4-16)

3919⁶ **Sizzling (59)***(69) (RHannon)* 3-8-10 (5) DaneO'Neill(6) (lw: a.p stands' side: rdn over 1f out: r.o to ld wl ins fnl f)....— **1**
3874⁷ Dashing Dancer (IRE) **(58)***(68) (RAkehurst)* 4-9-2 SSanders(16) (a.p: ev ch ins fnl f: r.o)....hd **2**
4115² Kira **(49)***(59) (JLEyre)* 5-8-7 RLappin(4) (b.off hind: hld up: hdwy wl over 1f out: ev ch ins fnl f: unable qckn)....s.h **3**
4134⁴ Prima Silk **(65)***(73)*(Fav)*(MJRyan)* 4-9-9 TIves(18) (chsd ldrs: led over 1f out tl wl ins fnl f)....½ **4**
*4125** Cretan Gift **(60)***(64) (NPLittmoden)* 4-9-4v TGMcLaughlin(3) (hld up stands' side: hdwy over 1f out: nvr nrr)....1½ **5**

4142[12] Petraco (IRE) **(66)***(68) (NASmith)* 7-9-10 SDWilliams(14) (led centre ½-wy tl over 1f out).......¾ 6
4068[9] Brockton Flame **(66)***(66) (JMPEustace)* 3-9-8 MTebbutt(17) (chsd ldrs: nt clr run 2f out: rdn over 1f out: eased whn btn ins fnl f).......¾ 7
4165[4] Friendly Brave (USA) **(60)***(56) (MissGayKelleway)* 5-9-4 MHills(8) (lw: hld up mid div: nvr trbld ldrs).......1¾ 8
4145[20] Robellion **(67)***(62) (DWPArbuthnot)* 4-9-11v RHughes(13) (hld up: hdwy 2f out: rdn & one pce appr fnl f).......hd 9
3954[9] Rambold **(54)***(47) (NEBerry)* 4-8-12 TWilliams(15) (led to ½-wy: grad wknd fnl 2f).......¾ 10
4057[17] Poyle Jezebelle **(49)***(38) (MBlanshard)* 4-8-7 RCochrane(1) (m.n.s).......1¾ 11
4068[17] Barato **(67)***(55) (MrsJRRamsden)* 4-9-4 (7) TFinn(5) (s.s: nvr nrr).......nk 12
4002[7] Soldier Cove (USA) **(66)***(49) (MartynMeade)* 5-9-5 (5) MHenry(19) (m.n.s).......2 13
4053[3] Shepherd Market (IRE) **(59)***(41) (DAWilson)* 4-9-3 GCarter(7) (lw: prom 4f).......nk 14
4068[6] Gone Savage **(62)***(40)*(Fav)*(WJMusson)* 7-9-6 PatEddery(12) (bhd fnl 2f).......1½ 15
3777[3] Gondo **(48)***(23) (EJAlston)* 8-7-13v(7) MartinDwyer(22) (lw: chsd ldrs far side 4f).......1 16
4134[14] Norling (IRE) **(53)***(27) (KOCunningham-Brown)* 5-8-11 LCharnock(2) (w ldrs stands' side 4f) nk 17
4142[13] Indiahra **(50)***(21) (RHollinshead)* 4-8-1 (7) FLynch(9) (a in rr).......1¼ 18
4060[18] Legatee **(56)***(26) (AStreeter)* 4-8-9 (5) LNewton(11) (b: prom: rdn ½-wy: sn wknd).......½ 19
4123[10] Lloc **(50)***(17) (CADwyer)* 3-8-3 (3) NVarley(10) (outpcd).......1 20
3678[11] Wychwood Sandy **(50)** *(HJCollingridge)* 4-8-8 MRimmer(20) (b: a bhd: t.o).......10 21
Cobblers Hill **(52)** *(CRBarwell)* 6-8-7 (3) PMcCabe(21) (bkwd: bhd: broke leg & p.u over 1f out: dead)....... P

6/1 Prima Silk, Gone Savage, **7/1** Friendly Brave (USA), **8/1** Cretan Gift, Brockton Flame, **10/1** Shepherd Market (IRE) (7/1-11/1), **12/1** Kira, **14/1** Dashing Dancer (IRE), **16/1** Petraco (IRE), SIZZLING, Poyle Jezebelle, Barato, Robellion, Norling (IRE), **20/1** Soldier Cove (USA), Rambold, Gondo, Lloc, **25/1** Indiahra, Legatee, **33/1** Wychwood Sandy, **50/1** Cobblers Hill, CSF £236.62 CT £2,584.52 TOTE £24.50: £6.50 £3.60 £2.90 £2.00 (£85.80) Trio £377.90 OWNER Mrs P. Jubert (MARLBOROUGH) BRED Lord Victor Matthews 22 Rn
1m 10.3 (0.30) SF: 49/50/41/55/46/50/46/38/44/29/20/37/31/23/22/5/9/3/8/-/-/-
WEIGHT FOR AGE 3yo-2lb
T/Jkpt: £67,213.50 (0.1 Tckts); £85,200.34 to Leicester 24/10/95. T/Plpt: £172.70 (99.31 Tckts).
T/Qdpt: £178.40 (0.2 Tckts); £192.88 to Leicester 24/10/95. IM

3891-LINGFIELD (L-H)
Monday October 23rd (Turf Good, AWT Standard)

5th race: hand timed
WEATHER: sunny WIND: almost nil

4216

E.B.F. CEDAR MAIDEN STKS (I) (2-Y.O F) (Class D) £4,012.50 (£1,200.00: £575.00: £262.50)
7f Stalls: High GOING minus 0.03 sec per fur (G) 1-00 (1-05)

3948[3] **Jezyah (USA) (86)***(80)*(Fav)*(RWArmstrong)* 2-8-11 WCarson(4) (lw: racd far side: mde virtually all: rdn over 1f out: r.o wl).......— 1
3816[8] Ewar Sunrise *(75) (CEBrittain)* 2-8-11 BDoyle(2) (racd far side: a.p: hrd rdn over 1f out: unable qckn).......2 2
3976[2] Hulm (IRE) *(74) (HThomsonJones)* 2-8-11 RHills(8) (lw: hld up: rdn over 1f out: one pce).....¾ 3
Always Happy *(74) (JRFanshawe)* 2-8-11 DHarrison(7) (neat: rdn over 2f out: hdwy over 1f out: r.o one pce).......s.h 4
Ninotchka (USA) *(70) (JLDunlop)* 2-8-11 KDarley(10) (unf: bit bkwd: a.p: hrd rdn wl over 1f out: one pce).......1¾ 5
3983[12] Sweet Times *(64) (PFICole)* 2-8-11 WRyan(9) (lw: a.p: rdn over 2f out: wknd fnl f).......2½ 6
Farfeste *(58) (DMorris)* 2-8-11 AClark(1) (unf: bit bkwd: racd far side: a.p: rdn over 2f out: wknd wl over 1f out).......2½ 7
4103[6] Flying Flowers *(53) (RHannon)* 2-8-11 RPerham(13) (lw: prom over 4f).......2½ 8
Alicia (IRE) *(48) (JLDunlop)* 2-8-11 JReid(11) (unf: nvr nrr).......2 9
3915[12] Newlands Corner *(48) (JAkehurst)* 2-8-11 WNewnes(12) (bhd fnl 4f).......s.h 10
Sheilas Dream *(39) (RSimpson)* 2-8-8 (3) SDrowne(3) (w'like: bit bkwd: s.s far side: prom 4f)..4 11
3763[22] Eternally Grateful *(23) (MrsNMacauley)* 2-8-4 (7) AmandaSanders(6) (bhd fnl 3f).......7 12
Diasafina *(16) (SCWilliams)* 2-8-11 JQuinn(5) (neat: s.s: a wl bhd).......3 13
3948[17] Shirlaty *(15) (EALDunlop)* 2-8-11 JTate(14) (bhd fnl 4f).......½ 14

9/4 JEZYAH (USA), **5/2** Flying Flowers, **4/1** Hulm (IRE) (11/4-5/1), **10/1** Ninotchka (USA), **16/1** Always Happy, Alicia (IRE), **20/1** Sweet Times, Ewar Sunrise, **33/1** Farfeste, Diasafina, Shirlaty, **50/1** Eternally Grateful, Newlands Corner, Sheilas Dream, CSF £43.96 TOTE £2.90: £1.30 £5.70 £1.80 (£44.20) Trio £50.50 OWNER Mr Hamdan Al Maktoum (NEWMARKET) BRED G. Watts Humphrey & Pierce & Pierce Inc. 14 Rn 1m 25.46 (4.86) SF: 33/28/27/27/23/17/11/6/1/1/-/-/-/-

4217

FALLING LEAF LIMITED STKS (0-65) (3-Y.O+) (Class F)
£3,224.60 (£895.60: £429.80)
7f (Equitrack) Stalls: Low GOING minus 0.03 sec (STD) 1-30 (1-33)

4122[8] **Set the Fashion (63)***(65) (LordHuntingdon)* 6-9-2v DHarrison(2) (hld up: rdn over 3f out: led ins fnl f: drvn out) — 1
3984[16] Live Project (IRE) **(65)***(64) (MJohnston)* 3-8-13 KDarley(3) (a.p: led over 1f out tl ins fnl f: r.o) ½ 2
1049[8] Maid Welcome **(59)***(56) (MrsNMacauley)* 8-8-4v(7) AmandaSanders(15) (led 1f: led over 3f out tl over 2f out: ev ch ins fnl f: unable qckn) 1¼ 3
3681[2] Our Shadee (USA) **(57)***(58) (KTIvory)* 5-9-2v DBiggs(5) (hdwy & n.m.r on ins over 1f out: r.o) 1¼ 4
702* African Chimes **(63)***(54)*(Fav)*(WAO'Gorman)* 8-9-2 EmmaO'Gorman(12) (b: rdn 3f out: nt clr run wl over 1f out: hdwy over 1f out: r.o one pce) 1¾ 5
3619[9] Masnun (USA) **(65)***(54) (RJO'Sullivan)* 10-9-2 AClark(8) (rdn thrght: hdwy over 1f out: nvr nrr) s.h 6
4194[2] Scissor Ridge **(49)***(54) (JJBridger)* 3-8-13 GBardwell(9) (prom over 4f) hd 7
3950[5] Dream Carrier (IRE) **(60)***(52) (REPeacock)* 7-8-13 (3) DRMcCabe(6) (nvr nrr) ¾ 8
3510[4] Dusk in Daytona **(60)***(46) (CJames)* 3-8-5 (5) AWhelan(1) (led 6f out tl over 3f out: led over 2f out tl over 1f out: sn wknd) 1½ 9
4060[15] Faez **(56)***(45) (RSimpson)* 5-8-13 (3) SDrowne(10) (b.hind: hld up: hrd rdn over 2f out: sn wknd) 1½ 10
3664[5] Distant Princess **(65)***(41) (BWHills)* 3-8-12 JReid(14) (a bhd) 1¼ 11
4123[6] Academy Life **(62)***(32) (PFICole)* 3-8-8b RHills(4) (lw: bhd fnl 2f) 2½ 12
3874[8] Pride of Hayling (IRE) **(51)***(17) (PRHedger)* 4-9-1 MPerrett(7) (lw: a bhd) 8 13
4035[21] Green City **(61)***(8) (JAkehurst)* 3-8-8 WNewnes(11) (a bhd) 2½ 14

7/2 African Chimes, **4/1** Distant Princess (op 5/2), **6/1** SET THE FASHION, **10/1** Maid Welcome, Dusk in Daytona, Masnun (USA) (op 6/1), Our Shadee (USA) (6/1-12/1), Academy Life (5/1-12/1), **16/1** Scissor Ridge, Pride of Hayling (IRE), **20/1** Dream Carrier (IRE), Live Project (IRE), **33/1** Faez, **50/1** Green City, CSF £110.04 TOTE £6.90: £2.20 £8.40 £3.60 (£84.80) Trio £290.40; £257.70 to Leicester 24/10/95 OWNER The Queen (WEST ILSLEY) BRED The Queen 14 Rn
1m 25.47 (2.47) SF: 33/29/24/26/22/22/19/20/11/13/6/-/-/-
WEIGHT FOR AGE 3yo-3lb

4218

E.B.F. CEDAR MAIDEN STKS (II) (2-Y.O F) (Class D) £3,980.00
(£1,190.00: £570.00: £260.00)
7f Stalls: High GOING minus 0.03 sec per fur (G) 2-00 (2-04)

3766[2] **Tsarnista (84)***(73+)*(Fav)*(JLDunlop)* 2-8-11 JReid(7) (mde virtually all: rdn out) — 1
3891[6] Royal Diversion (IRE) *(68) (JLDunlop)* 2-8-11 KDarley(12) (racd stands' side: hdwy over 1f out: r.o wl ins fnl f) 2 2
Ruwy *(67) (CJBenstead)* 2-8-11 WCarson(5) (str: scope: bkwd: s.s: nt clr run & swtchd rt over 2f out: hdwy over 1f out: r.o: bttr for r) ¾ 3
4130[6] Mam'selle Bergerac (IRE) *(66) (PMitchell)* 2-8-8 (3) DWright(6) (w wnr 5f: one pce) ½ 4
Alpine Twist (USA) *(64) (PWChapple-Hyam)* 2-8-6 (5) RHavlin(9) (w'like: bkwd: racd stands' side: a.p: rdn over 1f out: one pce) ½ 5
Love Bateta (IRE) *(62) (RHannon)* 2-8-11 RPerham(2) (unf: rdn over 3f out: hdwy 2f out: nt clr run on ins 1f out tl ins fnl f: one pce) 1¼ 6
3887[12] Petros Pride *(61) (MJBolton)* 2-8-11 JQuinn(4) (hld up: rdn over 3f out: one pce) nk 7
3069[13] Arcady *(59) (PTWalwyn)* 2-8-11 DHarrison(13) (racd stands' side: a.p: rdn over 3f out: wknd fnl f) 1 8
Sweet Wilhelmina *(55) (LordHuntingdon)* 2-8-6 (5) AWhelan(11) (w'like: bit bkwd: racd stands' side: hld up: rdn over 3f out: wknd fnl f) 1¾ 9
Liberatrice (FR) *(51) (JLDunlop)* 2-8-11 WNewnes(1) (unf: a bhd) 1¾ 10
3933[2] Mimosa **(79)***(42) (SDow)* 2-8-11 WRyan(3) (lw: hdwy over 2f out: wknd over 1f out) 4 11
Rising Stream *(28) (SirMarkPrescott)* 2-8-11 GDuffield(10) (b.hind: unf: racd stands' side: a bhd) 6 12
4137[12] Swingalong Girl *(20) (TMJones)* 2-8-11 NCarlisle(8) (b: bhd fnl 3f) 3½ 13

Evens TSARNISTA, **9/2** Mimosa, **10/1** Sweet Wilhelmina, **12/1** Royal Diversion (IRE), Rising Stream (7/1-14/1), **14/1** Ruwy, Alpine Twist (USA) (op 5/1), **16/1** Arcady, Love Bateta (IRE), **25/1** Liberatrice (FR), **33/1** Swingalong Girl, Mam'selle Bergerac (IRE), **50/1** Petros Pride, CSF £15.18 TOTE £2.20: £1.30 £2.70 £2.30 (£10.70) Trio £61.10 OWNER Mr I. H. Stewart-Brown (ARUNDEL) BRED I. Stewart-Brown and M. Meacock 13 Rn 1m 26.72 (6.12) SF: 18/13/12/11/9/7/6/4/-/-/-/-/-

4219

JARDINE INSURANCE BROKERS BURR CONDITIONS STKS (2-Y.O) (Class C) £4,971.00 (£1,839.00: £882.00: £360.00: £142.50: £55.50)
5f Stalls: High GOING minus 0.03 sec per fur (G) 2-30 (2-30)

4039[4] **Tadeo (96)***(95+)*(Fav)*(MJohnston)* 2-9-1 JReid(3) (lw: mde all: pushed out)................— **1**
3998[2] Songsheet *(75) (RGuest)* 2-8-6 GDuffield(2) (lw: a.p: chsd wnr over 2f out: unable qckn) 3½ **2**
3655[2] Comic Fantasy (AUS) **(90)***(76)*(Fav)*(PWChapple-Hyam)* 2-8-5b(5) RHavlin(6) (lw: n.m.r over 3f out: rdn over 2f out: hdwy over 1f out: r.o one pce)................1 **3**
4132[2] Sharp Stock *(67) (BJMeehan)* 2-8-11 BDoyle(1) (a.p: rdn over 2f out: wknd over 1f out).........3 **4**
4103[13] Goldsearch (IRE) *(60) (WAO'Gorman)* 2-8-6 EmmaO'Gorman(7) (a.p: hung lft 4f out: rdn over 2f out: wknd over 1f out)................½ **5**
4132[5] Dancing Jack **(54)***(62) (JJBridger)* 2-8-11 GBardwell(4) (a.p: rdn over 2f out: wknd over 1f out)................1 **6**
4144[8] Midnight Cookie **(48)***(27) (BAPearce)* 2-8-8 (3) DRMcCabe(5) (bhd fnl 4f)................11 **7**

2/1 TADEO (6/4-9/4), Comic Fantasy (AUS) (6/4-9/4), **5/2** Songsheet (2/1-3/1), **7/1** Sharp Stock (4/1-8/1), **25/1** Goldsearch (IRE), **33/1** Dancing Jack, **66/1** Midnight Cookie, CSF £7.33 TOTE £3.20: £1.90 £2.30 (£4.80) OWNER Mr J. R. Good (MIDDLEHAM) BRED J. R. and Mrs P. Good 7 Rn 58.99 secs (1.99) SF: 61/41/42/33/26/28/-

4220

MCDOWELLS MAIDEN STKS (3-Y.O) (Class D) £4,104.10 (£1,226.80: £587.40: £267.70)
1m 6f Stalls: High GOING minus 0.03 sec per fur (G) 3-00 (3-00)

3978[3] **High Patriarch (IRE) (78)***(94) (JLDunlop)* 3-9-0v KDarley(10) (bmpd s: hdwy 11f out: 2nd st: led over 2f out: drvn out)................— **1**
2413[2] Tibetan **(72)***(92) (LadyHerries)* 3-9-0 JQuinn(2) (lw: led 7f out tl over 2f out: ev ch ins fnl f: unable qckn)................2 **2**
4072[2] Taklif (IRE) **(86)***(77)*(Fav)*(BWHills)* 3-9-0 WCarson(4) (lw: hdwy 7f out: mod 3rd st: eased whn btn fnl 2f)................13 **3**
4096[4] Mighty Squaw **(55)***(62) (MissGayKelleway)* 3-8-4v(5) AWhelan(8) (bmpd s: hdwy over 6f out: poor 4th st: no hdwy fnl 3f)................9 **4**
2366[5] Cypress Avenue (IRE) **(94)***(59) (RHannon)* 3-9-0 JReid(11) (poor 5th st: no hdwy fnl 3f).........7 **5**
4062[18] Zadok *(58) (RTPhillips)* 3-9-0 GDuffield(5) (lw: prom over 4f: poor 6th st)................½ **6**
Lost Realm *(44) (MartynMeade)* 3-9-0 VSlattery(9) (unf: bit bkwd: s.s: nvr nr to chal) 12 **7**
3896[10] Fortunes Rose (IRE) *(22) (JSKing)* 3-8-6 (3) SDrowne(6) (led 10f out to 7f out: sn wknd)................15 **8**
Dutch *(10) (GPEnright)* 3-9-0 NAdams(1) (str: scope: bkwd: a bhd: t.o)................15 **9**
3154[8] Dazzler **(49)** *(MarkCampion)* 3-9-0 RHills(3) (led 4f: wknd 8f out: t.o)................dist **10**
3876[9] Bagby Boy *(PRHedger)* 3-9-0 MPerrett(7) (bhd fnl 10f: t.o)................2½ **11**

Evens Taklif (IRE), **7/2** Cypress Avenue (IRE) (op 9/4), **4/1** HIGH PATRIARCH (IRE) (3/1-5/1), **8/1** Tibetan (6/1-9/1), **10/1** Mighty Squaw, **50/1** Zadok, Dazzler, Dutch, **66/1** Fortunes Rose (IRE), Lost Realm, Bagby Boy, CSF £34.45 TOTE £5.30: £1.80 £2.00 £1.10 (£9.00) Trio £5.20 OWNER Mr Peter Winfield (ARUNDEL) BRED Lord Rotherwick 11 Rn 3m 8.6 (13.30) SF: 21/19/4/-/-/-/-/-/-/-/-

4221

E.B.F. WILLOW MAIDEN STKS (I) (2-Y.O C & G) (Class D) £3,785.00 (£1,130.00: £540.00: £245.00)
7f Stalls: High GOING minus 0.03 sec per fur (G) 3-30 (3-30)

Alhawa (USA) *(78) (CJBenstead)* 2-8-11 RHills(5) (leggy: scope: a.p: led over 1f out: r.o wl)— **1**
4064[2] Alambar (IRE) *(71)*(Fav)*(PTWalwyn)* 2-8-11 WCarson(8) (a.p: rdn over 2f out: unable qckn)................3 **2**
4075[3] Eurobox Boy *(71) (APJarvis)* 2-8-11 JTate(7) (lw: a.p: ev ch wl over 1f out: one pce)............nk **3**
3989[11] Ballpoint *(67) (RHannon)* 2-8-11 KDarley(2) (racd far side: chsd ldr: led over 2f out to over 1f out: one pce)................1½ **4**
2529[6] Rayner (IRE) *(67) (PWChapple-Hyam)* 2-8-11 JReid(4) (lw: racd far side: dwlt: hld up: rdn over 3f out: one pce fnl f)................s.h **5**
3782[3] Lagan *(59) (CEBrittain)* 2-8-11 BDoyle(1) (racd far side: led over 4f: wknd fnl f) 3½ **6**
3663[19] Naval Hunter (USA) *(48) (PWHarris)* 2-8-11 GHind(10) (lw: dwlt: a bhd)................5 **7**
3652[4] Nakhal *(47) (DJGMurraySmith)* 2-8-11 DHarrison(6) (prom over 4f)................hd **8**
4103[8] Antarctic Storm *(2) (EALDunlop)* 2-8-11 WRyan(9) (a bhd) 20 **9**

9/4 Alambar (IRE) (6/4-5/2), **4/1** Antarctic Storm (3/1-9/2), **5/1** Eurobox Boy, Rayner (IRE) (4/1-6/1), **7/1** Nakhal (5/1-8/1), **11/1** Lagan, **14/1** ALHAWA (USA), **20/1** Ballpoint, **33/1** Naval Hunter (USA), CSF £44.44 TOTE £23.20: £4.60 £1.40 £1.50 (£15.30) Trio £54.90 OWNER Mr Hamdan Al Maktoum (EPSOM) BRED Shadwell Farm Inc 9 Rn 1m 24.66 (4.06) SF: 42/35/35/31/31/23/12/11/-

4222 E.B.F. WILLOW MAIDEN STKS (II) (2-Y.O C & G) (Class D) £3,785.00 (£1,130.00: £540.00: £245.00) **7f** Stalls: High GOING minus 0.03 sec per fur (G) 4-00 (4-01)

4058 4 **Ashjar (USA) (75)***(79) (HThomsonJones)* 2-8-11 RHills(1) (lw: racd far side: mde all: clr over 1f out: unchal)........— **1**
Glen Parker (IRE) *(72+) (HRACecil)* 2-8-11 WRyan(8) (unf: scope: a.p: hung lft 2f out: chsd wnr over 1f out: no imp)........3 **2**
3340 9 Parsis (USA) *(58) (LadyHerries)* 2-8-11 DHarrison(7) (lw: hdwy over 2f out: one pce)........6 **3**
3916 11 Mazcobar *(57) (PJMakin)* 2-8-11 JReid(3) (racd far side: hld up: rdn over 2f out: wknd over 1f out)........¾ **4**
3672 11 Sterling Fellow *(45) (RHannon)* 2-8-11 RPerham(4) (bit bkwd: a.p: rdn over 4f out: wknd over 2f out)........5 **5**
4133 13 Jemsilverthorn (IRE) **(52)***(41) (JJBridger)* 2-8-11 NAdams(2) (racd far side: chsd wnr over 4f) 2 **6**
4154 5 Pasternak *(36) (SirMarkPrescott)* 2-8-11 GDuffield(6) (lw: a bhd)........2 **7**
4005a 3 Oberon's Dart (IRE) *(34)*(Fav)*(JLDunlop)* 2-8-11 KDarley(5) (unf: scope: lw: hld up: rdn 3f out: sn wknd)........¾ **8**
Casino Chip *(TTClement)* 2-8-8 (3) SDrowne(9) (w'like: bhd fnl 3f: t.o)........30 **9**

15/8 Oberon's Dart (IRE) (6/4-9/4), **3/1** Glen Parker (IRE) (5/4-100/30), **7/2** ASHJAR (USA) (3/1-5/1), **6/1** Pasternak, **13/2** Parsis (USA), **16/1** Mazcobar, **33/1** Sterling Fellow, **50/1** Casino Chip, **100/1** Jemsilverthorn (IRE), CSF £14.41 TOTE £4.30: £1.30 £1.60 £2.10 (£6.40) Trio £9.70 OWNER Mr Hamdan Al Maktoum (NEWMARKET) BRED Shadwell Estate Company Limited 9 Rn
1m 24.56 (3.96) SF: 43/36/22/21/9/5/-/-/-

4223 ELM H'CAP (0-70) (3-Y.O+) (Class E) £3,388.00 (£1,012.00: £484.00: £220.00) **1m 4f (Equitrack)** Stalls: Low GOING minus 0.45 sec per fur (FST) 4-30 (4-32)

4136 7 **Merit (IRE) (58)***(78) (PFICole)* 3-8-11b CRutter(1) (lw: led 2f: led over 3f out to over 2f out: led ins fnl f: all out)........— **1**
4028 12 Loki (IRE) **(60)***(79)*(Fav)*(GLewis)* 7-9-1 (5) AWhelan(3) (b: lw: hdwy 7f out: led over 2f out: hrd rdn: hdd ins fnl f: r.o)........½ **2**
4099 3 Finlaggan **(70)***(83) (SirMarkPrescott)* 3-9-9 GDuffield(4) (a.p: rdn 9f out: one pce fnl 2f)........5 **3**
3735 5 Tadellal (IRE) **(58)***(70) (WGMTurner)* 4-9-1 (3) DRMcCabe(2) (lw: no hdwy fnl 3f)........½ **4**
3769 13 Exhibit Air (IRE) **(61)***(70) (RAkehurst)* 5-9-7b DHarrison(14) (a.p: rdn 5f out: wknd over 2f out) 2 **5**
3957 6 Global Dancer **(68)***(76) (SDow)* 4-9-7 (7) ADaly(8) (lw: led 10f out to over 3f out: wknd over 2f out)........¾ **6**
3843 5 Last Corner **(59)***(62) (RHollinshead)* 3-8-12 KDarley(15) (nvr nr to chal)........4 **7**
3844 5 Salvatore Giuliano **(42)***(33) (AGFoster)* 5-8-2 ow3 BDoyle(5) (b.hind: prom 3f)........7 **8**
3970 14 Wottashambles **(38)***(30) (LMontagueHall)* 4-7-12 ow1 StephenDavies(11) (b: b.hind: prom 3f).½ **9**
3884 10 Excelled (IRE) **(35)***(28) (CJDrewe)* 6-7-9 NAdams(10) (nvr nrr)........nk **10**
3207 6 Studio Thirty **(47)***(30) (DMorris)* 3-8-0 JTate(6) (a bhd)........7 **11**
4086 3 Western Horizon (USA) **(41)***(22) (CEBrittain)* 3-7-8 ow1 JQuinn(13) (a bhd)........1 **12**
673 4 Analogue (IRE) **(69)***(38) (MRStoute)* 3-9-8v JReid(9) (s.s: a bhd)........10 **13**
3810 15 Tafia (IRE) **(65)***(28) (JPearce)* 4-9-11 GBardwell(7) (bhd fnl 9f)........4 **14**
High Melody **(47)***(7) (GCBravery)* 3-8-0 NCarlisle(12) (bhd fnl 9f)........2½ **15**

9/2 Loki (IRE) (op 3/1), **5/1** Exhibit Air (IRE), **11/2** Finlaggan, Analogue (IRE), **9/1** Global Dancer, **10/1** Last Corner, **11/1** MERIT (IRE) (5/1-12/1), Salvatore Giuliano, **12/1** Tadellal (IRE) (8/1-14/1), **14/1** Western Horizon (USA) (10/1-16/1), **20/1** Wottashambles, **33/1** Studio Thirty, Excelled (IRE), High Melody, **40/1** Tafia (IRE), CSF £60.02 CT £288.48 TOTE £11.70: £3.10 £2.70 £2.50 (£29.50) Trio £32.00 OWNER H R H Prince Fahd Salman (WHATCOMBE) BRED Newgate Stud Co 15 Rn
2m 30.93 (1.53) SF: 49/57/54/48/48/54/33/11/8/6/1/-/9/6/-
WEIGHT FOR AGE 3yo-7lb
T/Plpt: £72.10 (154.7 Tckts). T/Qdpt: £5.80 (38.9 Tckts). AK

4209-LEICESTER (R-H)
Tuesday October 24th (Firm)
WEATHER: fair WIND: str bhd

4224 TUGBY MEDIAN AUCTION MAIDEN STKS (2-Y.O) (Class F) £3,527.00 (£982.00: £473.00) **5f 218y** Stalls: High GOING minus 0.66 sec per fur (HD) 1-45 (1-48)

3949 2 **Thordis** *(71) (PJMakin)* 2-9-0 KDarley(15) (lw: rdn to ld ins fnl f: r.o wl)........— **1**
4103 14 Blue Suede Hoofs *(67) (BJMeehan)* 2-9-0 BDoyle(17) (led: rdn & hung rt over 1f out: hdd ins fnl f)........1½ **2**
4132 6 Mindrace *(67) (KTIvory)* 2-9-0 DBiggs(6) (a.p: ev ch over 1f out: r.o one pce)........s.h **3**
3848 3 Incatinka *(57) (JLSpearing)* 2-8-6 (3) SDrowne(8) (a.p: rdn & wandered over 1f out: one pce)..2 **4**

4137[11] Lia Fail (IRE) *(43) (RHollinshead)* 2-8-9 AMcGlone(7) (no hdwy fnl 2f) 5 **5**
4132[3] May Queen Megan *(30) (MrsALMKing)* 2-8-9 JWilliams(9) (hdwy 2f out: nvr nr to chal) 5 **6**
1318[10] Hadadabble *(30) (PatMitchell)* 2-8-9 RCochrane(10) (swtg: s.s: hdwy fnl 2f: nvr nrr) ....s.h **7**
3933[5] Mac Oates *(35) (DWPArbuthnot)* 2-9-0 SWhitworth(11) (chsd ldrs over 3f) ....s.h **8**
3881[2] Diamond Beach **(84)***(34)*(Fav)*(BWHills)* 2-9-0 MHills(3) (hmpd & stumbled after s: hdwy 3f out: eased whn btn fnl f) ....s.h **9**
4100[W] Bear To Dance **(51)***(24) (JohnBerry)* 2-8-9 CDwyer(5) (swtg: n.d) 2 **10**
3763[17] Astra Martin *(21) (PGMurphy)* 2-8-2 (7) RWaterfield(4) (sn rdn: a bhd) 1¼ **11**
3436[11] Dauphin (IRE) *(24) (WJMusson)* 2-8-11 (3) PMcCabe(19) (bit bkwd: a bhd) ....½ **12**
4055[6] Andsome Boy *(21) (CRBarwell)* 2-9-0 NAdams(12) (prom 3f) 1¼ **13**
3937[13] Bites **(52)***(11) (JAHarris)* 2-8-9 PaulEddery(20) (a bhd) 2 **14**
Mrs Keen *(10) (MrsMMcCourt)* 2-8-9 WNewnes(13) (w'like: bkwd: a bhd) ....nk **15**
3314[11] Lunar Gris *(7) (JEBanks)* 2-8-9 AClark(16) (swtg: a bhd) 1 **16**
4063[12] Spa Lane **(52)***(10) (CJDrewe)* 2-8-9 (5) DaneO'Neill(2) (chsd ldrs 3f) 1 **17**
3915[16] Lakeside Express *(JSMoore)* 2-8-9 JFEgan(14) (lw: sn bhd) 3 **18**
3976[7] Welcome Lu *(PSFelgate)* 2-8-9 AMackay(1) (bit bkwd: s.s: a bhd) 5 **19**

10/11 Diamond Beach (8/11-11/10), **6/1** Incatinka (tchd 9/1), **7/1** THORDIS, **8/1** Mac Oates (op 5/1), **14/1** Blue Suede Hoofs, **16/1** May Queen Megan, **20/1** Lia Fail (IRE), **50/1** Lunar Gris, Mindrace, Bites, Dauphin (IRE), Spa Lane, **66/1** Mrs Keen, Hadadabble, **100/1** Andsome Boy, Bear To Dance, Astra Martin, Lakeside Express, Welcome Lu, CSF £91.37 TOTE £7.50: £2.10 £2.50 £6.60 (£78.70) Trio £213.20; £189.23 to Yarmouth 25/10/95 OWNER Mr Barrie Whitehouse (MARLBOROUGH) BRED B. Whitehouse 19 Rn

1m 10.1 (0.10 under 2y best) (0.10) SF: 41/37/37/27/13/-/-/5/4/-/-/-/-/-/-/-/-/-/-

4225

FOSSE WAY CLAIMING STKS (3-Y.O) (Class F) £3,401.00 (£946.00: £455.00)
1m 8y Stalls: High GOING minus 0.66 sec per fur (HD) 2-15 (2-21)

3984[3] **Tonys Gift (65)***(76)*(Fav)*(RHannon)* 3-8-7 (5) DaneO'Neill(15) (a.p: led wl over 1f out: comf).— **1**
3841[4] Dr Caligari (IRE) **(55)***(70) (JBerry)* 3-8-10 GCarter(11) (led over 6f: r.o one pce) 2 **2**
3079[3] Burnt Sienna (IRE) **(35)***(63) (JSMoore)* 3-7-13 (5) PPMurphy(20) (lw: a.p: rdn & ev ch over 2f out: r.o one pce) ....½ **3**
4170* Gentle Irony **(55)***(60) (BJMeehan)* 3-8-4b JFEgan(16) (hld up: hdwy over 2f out: one pce fnl f) 1½ **4**
4057[9] Dancing Sioux **(62)***(64) (RGuest)* 3-8-11 GDuffield(3) (hld up: rdn & hung rt 2f out: no hdwy)1½ **5**
4196[5] Bobanlyn (IRE) **(56)***(56) (DMorris)* 3-8-6 JQuinn(9) (hdwy over 2f out: rdn over 1f out: one pce) 1½ **6**
3515[8] L'Eglise Belle **(37)***(48) (MrsALMKing)* 3-7-13b(3)ow2 SDrowne(6) (nvr nr to chal) 1¼ **7**
4060[9] Dowdency **(53)***(50) (JAPickering)* 3-8-1 (3) JStack(8) (nvr nr to chal) ....¾ **8**
4131[4] Havana Miss **(38)***(36) (BPalling)* 3-8-2 TSprake(5) (nvr trbld ldrs) 6 **9**
Broughtons Champ *(42) (WJMusson)* 3-8-6 (3) PMcCabe(7) (leggy: w'like: bkwd: s.s: nvr nr ldrs) ....½ **10**
3685[16] Arnie (IRE) **(42)***(34) (GLMoore)* 3-8-4 AClark(4) (n.d) 1¾ **11**
3860[5] Shared (IRE) **(35)***(37) (MMadgwick)* 3-8-9 AMcGlone(17) (w ldrs: one pce fnl 2f) ....¾ **12**
4062[22] Simposa (IRE) **(39)***(34) (EJAlston)* 3-8-9 SWhitworth(2) (prom: wkng whn hung rt wl over 1f out) 1¾ **13**
Begger's Opera *(33) (PatMitchell)* 3-8-11 GBardwell(10) (cmpt: bkwd: a bhd) 1½ **14**
4054[14] Most Becoming **(30)** *(JRArnold)* 3-7-12b AMackay(19) (prom tl rdn & wknd over 2f out) 11 **15**
4049[11] Rolling Settlement (IRE) *(JAHarris)* 3-7-11 (5) MBaird(14) (bit bkwd: s.s: a bhd) 2½ **16**
3871[11] Anjomajasa **(40)** *(JFfitch-Heyes)* 3-7-11 (3) DWright(13) (a bhd: t.o) 10 **17**
3515[18] Bills Ploughgirl **(32)** *(JSMoore)* 3-7-12 NAdams(18) (plld hrd: prom over 4f: t.o) ....s.h **18**
4049[15] Oscilights Gift *(PBurgoyne)* 3-8-3 (3) DRMcCabe(1) (a bhd: t.o) 2½ **19**
4131[R] Amboyna Burl (IRE) **(46)** *(DAWilson)* 3-8-3 DBiggs(12) (ref to r: t.n.p) .... **R**

2/1 TONYS GIFT, **7/2** Gentle Irony, **11/2** Bobanlyn (IRE), **12/1** Dancing Sioux (op 7/1), **14/1** Dowdency, Burnt Sienna (IRE), **16/1** Dr Caligari (IRE), **20/1** Havana Miss, **25/1** Simposa (IRE), **33/1** Anjomajasa, Broughtons Champ, **50/1** Rolling Settlement (IRE), L'Eglise Belle, Begger's Opera, **66/1** Bills Ploughgirl, Arnie (IRE), Shared (IRE), Oscilights Gift, **100/1** Most Becoming, Amboyna Burl (IRE), CSF £32.48 TOTE £2.30: £1.20 £2.40 £4.80 (£11.50) Trio £51.90 OWNER Mr A. F. Harrington (MARLBOROUGH) BRED Mrs Sean Kelly and West Lodge Stud 20 Rn

1m 34.7 (-0.30) SF: 44/38/31/28/32/24/16/18/4/10/2/5/2/1/-/-/-/-/-/-

Tonys Gift clmd D.Richmond £10,000

4226

E.B.F. HOBY MAIDEN STKS (2-Y.O) (Class D) £4,402.50 (£1,320.00: £635.00: £292.50) **1m 8y** Stalls: High GOING minus 0.66 sec per fur (HD) 2-45 (2-46)

Lady Carla *(79+) (HRACecil)* 2-8-9 PatEddery(10) (leggy: scope: a.p: rdn over 3f out: led wl over 1f out: easily) ....— **1**

3985⁹ General Macarthur **(60)***(76) (JLDunlop)* 2-9-0 GDuffield(7) (a.p: rdn & ev ch over 2f out: no imp) 4 **2**
4063¹³ Tawafek (USA) *(69) (DMorley)* 2-9-0 RCochrane(13) (hdwy fnl 2f: r.o) 3½ **3**
3967³ Desert Cat (IRE) *(69) (HThomsonJones)* 2-9-0 RHills(12) (w ldr: led on bit over 2f out: hdd wl over 1f out: sn btn) ....hd **4**
4046⁶ Roseberry Avenue (IRE) *(69) (LadyHerries)* 2-9-0 KDarley(1) (prom tl rdn & wknd 2f out) ....hd **5**
2957³ Flaming June (USA) *(61) (HRACecil)* 2-8-9 WRyan(3) (led over 5f: edgd lft & wknd over 1f out) 1¼ **6**
3989⁷ Hal Hoo Yaroom *(59) (MajorWRHern)* 2-9-0 TSprake(11) (chsd ldrs tl wknd over 2f out) 3½ **7**
4080⁵ Hayaain *(58)*(Fav)*(MajorWRHern)* 2-9-0 WCarson(2) (hdwy 4f out: wknd over 2f out) ....½ **8**
3449⁸ Jean-Pierre *(38) (JPearce)* 2-8-11 (3) SDrowne(6) (a bhd: t.o) 10 **9**
Spartan Heartbeat *(38) (CEBrittain)* 2-9-0 BDoyle(5) (gd sort: bit bkwd: t.o fnl 4f) ....nk **10**
4146⁸ He's Got Wings (IRE) *(36) (CDBroad)* 2-9-0 NAdams(4) (t.o fnl 5f) ....¾ **11**
4129¹¹ Baron Hrabovsky *(22) (PFICole)* 2-9-0 PaulEddery(8) (b.hind: bit bkwd: bhd fnl 3f: t.o) 7 **12**

9/4 Hayaain, **5/2** LADY CARLA, **3/1** Desert Cat (IRE) (op 2/1), **8/1** Flaming June (USA), **14/1** Roseberry Avenue (IRE), **16/1** Spartan Heartbeat, General Macarthur, **20/1** Hal Hoo Yaroom, **25/1** Tawafek (USA), **33/1** Baron Hrabovsky, **66/1** He's Got Wings (IRE), Jean-Pierre, CSF £41.36 TOTE £3.40: £1.50 £6.00 £9.00 (£66.90) Trio £192.40; £67.77 to Yarmouth 25/10/95 OWNER Mr Wafic Said (NEWMARKET) BRED Meon Valley Stud 12 Rn

1m 34.6 (1.20 under 2y best) (-0.40) SF: 42/39/32/32/32/24/22/21/1/1/-/-

4227 ERMINE STREET H'CAP (0-85) (3-Y.O+) (Class D) £4,678.70 (£1,403.60: £675.80: £311.90) **1m 8y** Stalls: High GOING minus 0.66 sec per fur (HD) 3-15 (3-16)

4038⁷ **Secret Aly (CAN) (78)***(89) (CEBrittain)* 5-9-10 BDoyle(8) (lw: a.p: rdn 2f out: r.o to ld last strides) ....— **1**
4041⁸ Zajko (USA) **(76)***(87)*(Fav)*(LadyHerries)* 5-9-8 RCochrane(12) (a.p: led 2f out: hdd last strides) ....hd **2**
4035⁶ Star Manager (USA) **(77)***(85) (PFICole)* 5-9-9 MHills(4) (hld up & bhd: hdwy over 1f out: fin wl) 1½ **3**
3630⁸ Aldaneh **(74)***(81) (RHannon)* 3-8-12 (5) DaneO'Neill(1) (hld up: hdwy 4f out: ev ch over 1f out: nt qckn ins fnl f) ....½ **4**
4024⁶ Moneefa **(69)***(76) (HRACecil)* 4-9-1 PatEddery(2) (a.p: ev ch 1f out: eased whn btn cl home)s.h **5**
4038⁶ Rory **(78)***(80) (MrsJCecil)* 4-9-10 TIves(13) (hld up: hdwy 2f out: one pce fnl f) 2½ **6**
3897* Sharp Consul (IRE) **(70)***(70) (HCandy)* 3-8-13 WNewnes(9) (bhd: rdn 3f out: nvr nr to chal)...¾ **7**
3977³ Roman Reel (USA) **(67)***(64) (GLMoore)* 4-8-13 SWhitworth(6) (lw: w ldrs: led over 2f out: sn hdd: wknd fnl f) 1¾ **8**
4043² Misty Silks **(71)***(61) (MJRyan)* 5-9-3 AClark(3) (hld up: rdn over 2f out: eased whn btn fnl f) .3½ **9**
4061¹² Araboybill **(56)***(44) (RSimpson)* 4-7-13b(3) SDrowne(10) (led over 5f) ....¾ **10**
4116⁹ Saifan **(76)***(62) (DMorris)* 6-9-5b(3) JStack(7) (hld up: rdn 2f out: eased whn btn fnl f) 1¼ **11**
3980¹⁷ Gulf Shaadi **(64)***(28) (EJAlston)* 3-8-7 GHind(11) (s.s: hdwy over 4f out: wknd qckly fnl f)....11 **12**
3455⁶ Rock Oyster **(50)***(7) (BJMeehan)* 3-7-7b GBardwell(5) (rdn 3f out: a bhd) 3½ **13**

LONG HANDICAP Rock Oyster 7-5

11/4 Zajko (USA), **4/1** Misty Silks (tchd 6/1), **5/1** Moneefa (op 9/4), **8/1** Saifan, **9/1** Rory (6/1-10/1), **10/1** SECRET ALY (CAN), **11/1** Sharp Consul (IRE), **14/1** Star Manager (USA), **16/1** Aldaneh, **20/1** Roman Reel (USA), **33/1** Araboybill, Gulf Shaadi, Rock Oyster, CSF £37.64 CT £363.92 TOTE £15.30: £5.20 £1.70 £4.50 (£23.50) Trio £81.90 OWNER Mr B. H. Voak (NEWMARKET) BRED Northern Equine Thoroughbred Productions 13 Rn

1m 34.0 (0.40 under best) (-1.00) SF: 63/61/59/52/50/54/41/38/35/18/36/-/-

WEIGHT FOR AGE 3yo-3lb

4228 BARSBY LIMITED STKS (0-70) (3-Y.O) (Class E) £3,330.80 (£994.40: £475.20: £215.60) **1m 3f 183y** Stalls: High GOING minus 0.32 sec per fur (GF) 3-45 (3-45)

3863⁹ **Lovely Lyca (70)***(74) (JWHills)* 3-8-11 RHills(9) (4th st: led over 2f out: rdn & r.o wl) ....— **1**
4108³ Edan Heights **(70)***(76)*(Fav)*(SDow)* 3-8-7 (7) ADaly(8) (chsd ldr: 2nd st: led wl over 2f out: sn hdd: hrd rdn & rallied cl home) ....½ **2**
4072⁵ Darter (IRE) **(67)***(71) (LMCumani)* 3-9-0 KDarley(3) (lw: 3rd st: rdn over 3f out: styd on one pce fnl 2f) 4 **3**
4065⁷ Pinkerton Polka **(47)***(59) (CEBrittain)* 3-8-9 BDoyle(6) (lw: 7th st: styd on fnl 2f) 5 **4**
4047¹³ Cross Talk (IRE) **(66)***(65) (RHollinshead)* 3-9-2 TIves(4) (5th st: rdn & wknd over 3f out) ....¾ **5**
4096³ House of Dreams **(66)***(61) (BWHills)* 3-9-0 MHills(2) (lw: led over 9f: rdn & wknd fnl2f) 1¼ **6**
4096* Anjou **(70)***(59) (JPearce)* 3-9-0 GBardwell(5) (plld hrd: 8th st: a bhd) 1¾ **7**
*1329*⁵ Northern Charmer **(41)***(51) (EJAlston)* 3-9-0 GHind(7) (bit bkwd: s.i.s: 6th st: wknd over 3f out) 6 **8**
4061¹⁵ Shahrani **(56)***(37) (MCPipe)* 3-9-0 PatEddery(1) (hld up: last st: rdn 4f out: a bhd: t.o) 10 **9**

2/1 Edan Heights, **9/2** Anjou (op 3/1), **5/1** LOVELY LYCA (op 5/2), **11/2** Darter (IRE), **13/2** House of Dreams (4/1-7/1), **14/1** Cross Talk (IRE), Shahrani, **33/1** Pinkerton Polka, **50/1** Northern Charmer, CSF £14.56 TOTE £6.10: £1.70 £1.40 £1.40 (£7.70) Trio £28.10 OWNER The Losers Owners Group (LAMBOURN) BRED Stowell Hill Ltd 9 Rn 2m 32.2 (3.40) SF: 47/49/44/32/38/34/32/24/10

STEWARDS' ENQUIRY Daly susp. 2-3/11/95 (improper use of whip).

OFFICIAL EXPLANATION **Anjou: had been unsuited by the slow early pace and his jockey was unable to get him into a prominent position. He then did not pick up when they quickened into the straight.**

4229

CASTLE H'CAP (0-70) (3-Y.O+) (Class E) £4,360.40 (£1,311.20: £633.60: £294.80)
1m 1f 218y Stalls: High GOING minus 0.32 sec per fur (GF) 4-15 (4-17)

4061[4] **Rival Bid (USA) (62)***(74) (MrsNMacauley)* 7-9-2 (7) AmandaSanders(13) (lw: 4th st: qcknd to ld wl ins fnl f: r.o)........— 1
3965[5] El Bailador (IRE) **(60)***(71) (JDBethell)* 4-9-7 RHills(6) (led over 7f: ev ch ins fnl f: r.o)........¾ 2
4079[20] Ducking **(64)***(74) (JRFanshawe)* 3-9-6 DHarrison(16) (chsd ldr: 2nd st: led over 2f out tl wl ins fnl f)........nk 3
4079[13] Guesstimation (USA) **(65)***(72) (JPearce)* 6-9-9 (3) SDrowne(8) (plld hrd: hdwy & 6th st: one pce fnl 2f)........2 4
4061[0] Thames Side **(61)***(68)*(Fav)*(MMadgwick)* 4-9-1 (7) AEddery(14) (hld up: 8th st: rdn & hdwy over 2f out: one pce fnl f)........nk 5
4116[17] Noble Neptune **(59)***(64) (WJMusson)* 3-9-1 GCarter(2) (hld up & plld hrd: hdwy over 2f out: nvr nr to chal)........1 6
4079[7] Saltando (IRE) **(50)***(53) (PatMitchell)* 4-8-6 (5) DaneO'Neill(11) (lw: s.i.s: no hdwy fnl 2f)........1¼ 7
3984[5] Kintwyn **(50)***(51) (CCElsey)* 5-8-11 MHills(15) (lw: hdwy on ins 3f out: wknd over 1f out)........1 8
2648[4] Wonderful Day **(67)***(62) (TTClement)* 4-10-0 TIves(3) (bkwd: hld up & bhd: nvr trbld ldrs)........4 9
3108[5] Yo Kiri-B **(51)***(41) (JFfitch-Heyes)* 4-8-12 GDuffield(5) (plld hrd: a bhd)........3 10
3960[9] Queenbird **(62)***(49) (MJRyan)* 4-9-9 AClark(1) (3rd st: rdn over 2f out: sn wknd)........2 11
Harding **(66)***(52) (SMellor)* 4-9-13 MPerrett(9) (bkwd: 5th st: wknd over 2f out)........½ 12
1144[5] Dvorak (IRE) **(67)***(49) (RHarris)* 4-10-0 AMackay(12) (bkwd: s.i.s: a bhd)........2½ 13
18[8] Bold Acre **(45)** *(DBurchell)* 5-8-6 RPrice(10) (bkwd: plld hrd: prom tl 7th & lost pl st: sddle slipped: t.o)........dist 14

9/2 Thames Side, **5/1** El Bailador (IRE), **6/1** RIVAL BID (USA), Guesstimation (USA), **9/1** Wonderful Day, Saltando (IRE) (op 6/1), **12/1** Dvorak (IRE), Kintwyn, **14/1** Yo Kiri-B, Noble Neptune, **16/1** Bold Acre, Ducking, **20/1** Harding, Queenbird, CSF £37.16 CT £432.87 TOTE £5.00: £2.50 £1.60 £8.30 (£27.00) Trio £388.50 OWNER Mr G. Wiltshire (MELTON MOWBRAY) BRED Marvin L. Warner Jnr. 14 Rn 2m 6.2 (3.50) SF: 52/49/47/50/46/37/31/29/40/19/27/30/27/-

WEIGHT FOR AGE 3yo-5lb

T/Jkpt: £86,849.10 (0.5 Tckts); £60,907.87 to Yarmouth 25/10/95. T/Plpt: £2,862.30 (7.05 Tckts). T/Qdpt: Not won; £285.88 to Yarmouth 25/10/95. KH

4081-REDCAR (L-H)
Tuesday October 24th (Firm)

WEATHER: sunny WIND: str bhd

4230

E.B.F. WILTON MEDIAN AUCTION MAIDEN STKS (2-Y.O) (Class F) £3,020.00 (£905.00: £435.00: £200.00)
5f Stalls: Centre GOING minus 0.73 sec per fur (HD) 1-30 (1-31)

4141[15] **Mister Joel (62)***(71) (MWEasterby)* 2-9-0b SMaloney(9) (cl up: led after 2f: hld on wl fnl f)....— 1
4109[5] Time To Tango *(66)*(Fav)*(GMMoore)* 2-8-9 DeanMcKeown(7) (sn chsg ldrs: ev ch ins fnl f: nt qckn)........hd 2
4133[5] Corniche Quest (IRE) **(53)***(62) (MRChannon)* 2-8-10 ow1 RHughes(11) (swtg: outpcd & bhd tl hdwy 2f out: nvr able chal)........1¼ 3
3982[6] Beldray Park (IRE) **(65)***(66) (MrsALMKing)* 2-9-0 AGarth(3) (cl up: rdn ½-wy: nt qckn appr fnl f)........hd 4
3300[3] Niteowl Raider (IRE) *(58) (JAHarris)* 2-8-7 (7) MartinDwyer(5) (lw: chsd ldrs: ch 2f out: one pce)........2½ 5
3824[13] Lady Eclat **(56)***(50) (JAGlover)* 2-8-9v SDWilliams(2) (led 2f: wknd over 1f out)........¾ 6
3982[3] Veesey **(64)***(39) (JohnBerry)* 2-8-9 MFenton(1) (spd 3f: sn wknd)........3½ 7
4100[12] Spring Silhouette **(35)***(29) (MrsVAAconley)* 2-8-9v ACulhane(10) (nvr wnt pce)........3 8
4109[15] Jive Baby *(NBycroft)* 2-9-0b LCharnock(6) (nvr wnt pce)........12 9
3953[10] Superfrills **(49)** *(MissLCSiddall)* 2-8-9 TWilliams(8) (a outpcd & bhd: sddle slipped & eased fnl 2f)........2½ 10
3779[R] Lugana Boy *(ASmith)* 2-9-0 MBirch(4) (ref to r: t.n.p)........ R

7/4 Time To Tango, **9/2** MISTER JOEL, Veesey, **5/1** Corniche Quest (IRE), **6/1** Beldray Park (IRE) (op 4/1), **12/1** Lady Eclat, **14/1** Superfrills, **20/1** Niteowl Raider (IRE), **66/1** Spring Silhouette, Lugana Boy, **200/1** Jive Baby, CSF £13.05 TOTE £6.10: £1.90 £1.80 £1.40 (£7.90) Trio £16.10
OWNER Mr Philip Jarvis (SHERIFF HUTTON) BRED Roldvale Ltd 11 Rn
56.9 secs (0.20 under 2y best) (0.20) SF: 31/26/22/26/18/11/-/-/-/-/-
STEWARDS' ENQUIRY Maloney susp. 2-4 & 6/11/95 (improper use of whip).

4231 LEVY BOARD NURSERY H'CAP (0-75) (2-Y.O) (Class E) £3,644.00 (£1,097.00: £531.00: £248.00)

6f Stalls: Centre GOING minus 0.73 sec per fur (HD) 2-00 (2-03)

3956[6] **Times of Times (IRE) (68)***(81) (MJRyan)* 2-9-7 CRutter(12) (cl up: led over 2f out: r.o. wl) ..— **1**
4097[7] Time To Fly **(57)***(62) (BWMurray)* 2-8-10 TWilliams(6) (led tl hdd over 2f out: kpt on) 3 **2**
4133* Beas River (IRE) **(67)***(72)*(Fav)*(WRMuir)* 2-9-6 7x WWoods(17) (lw: dwlt: hdwy over 2f out: nrst fin)..............s.h **3**
4109[7] Sandblaster **(48)***(50) (MrsJRRamsden)* 2-8-1 SSanders(14) (chsd ldrs: outpcd 2f out: kpt on fnl f)..............1¼ **4**
4097[2] Camionneur (IRE) **(58)***(59) (MHEasterby)* 2-8-11b MBirch(16) (chsd ldrs: effrt 2f out: edgd lft & nt qckn)..............nk **5**
4109[12] Katie Komaite **(56)***(49) (CaptJWilson)* 2-8-4 (5) PFessey(19) (prom tl outpcd fnl 2f)..............3 **6**
4100[5] The Barnsley Belle (IRE) **(55)***(44) (SGNorton)* 2-8-8 DeanMcKeown(5) (n.d) 1½ **7**
3850[9] Candy's Delight **(45)***(32) (JLEyre)* 2-7-9 (3) NVarley(4) (chsd ldrs: ev ch over 2f out: wknd over 1f out)..............½ **8**
4109[3] Poly By Staufan (IRE) **(60)***(46) (MRChannon)* 2-8-13 RHughes(18) (bhd tl hdwy 2f out: nrst fin) ....½ **9**
3809[8] Oriole **(56)***(42) (NTinkler)* 2-8-9 KimTinkler(15) (outpcd: sme hdwy 2f out: n.d)..............s.h **10**
3949[5] Tallulah Belle **(48)***(29) (NPLittmoden)* 2-7-10 (5) MHenry(2) (in tch: rdn & no imp fnl 2f) 1¾ **11**
3670[9] Taurean Fire **(48)***(29) (MrsMReveley)* 2-7-8 (7) DDenby(11) (a outpcd & bhd) ....s.h **12**
3953[6] Boffy (IRE) **(68)***(48) (BPJBaugh)* 2-9-0 (7) IonaWands(9) (nvr trbld ldrs) ....hd **13**
4137[8] Efipetite **(46)***(25) (NBycroft)* 2-7-13 ow1 SMaloney(20) (nvr wnt pce) ....s.h **14**
4066[7] Tropical Beach **(65)***(38) (JBerry)* 2-8-11 (7) PRoberts(7) (n.d)..............2½ **15**
3699[7] Everyone Can Dream **(57)***(24) (DenysSmith)* 2-8-10 LCharnock(8) (lw: in tch: drvn along ½-wy: sn btn)..............2½ **16**
3701[14] Percy Park (USA) **(65)***(29) (MWEasterby)* 2-9-4 JFanning(1) (a outpcd & bhd) 1 **17**
4097[13] Hickleton Miss **(58)***(21) (MrsMReveley)* 2-8-6 (5) GParkin(3) (a outpcd & bhd)..............nk **18**
4111[18] Eccentric Dancer **(60)***(23) (MPBielby)* 2-8-13 SDWilliams(13) (dwlt: a bhd)..............hd **19**
3969[12] Polish Saga **(60)***(22) (MDods)* 2-8-13 NConnorton(10) (a bhd) ....½ **20**

9/4 Beas River (IRE), **6/1** Camionneur (IRE), **8/1** TIMES OF TIMES (IRE), Sandblaster (op 5/1), Poly By Staufan (IRE), **10/1** Everyone Can Dream, **12/1** Hickleton Miss, **14/1** Oriole, **16/1** Boffy (IRE), Tropical Beach, **20/1** Time To Fly, Percy Park (USA), **25/1** Polish Saga, **33/1** Candy's Delight, Taurean Fire, Tallulah Belle, Eccentric Dancer, The Barnsley Belle (IRE), Katie Komaite, **66/1** Efipetite, CSF £161.49 CT £454.15 TOTE £8.70: £2.50 £5.70 £1.30 £2.00 (£78.70) Trio £257.50
OWNER Mr A. S. Reid (NEWMARKET) BRED E. Moloney 20 Rn
1m 9.5 (0.30 under 2y best) (0.20) SF: 39/20/30/8/17/7/2/-/4/-/-/-/7/-/-/-/-/-/-/-

4232 BRASS CASTLE CLAIMING STKS (3-Y.O+) (Class F) £2,987.00 (£832.00: £401.00)

1m 3f Stalls: Low GOING minus 0.18 sec per fur (GF) 2-30 (2-32)

3426* **Shabanaz (60)***(65)*(Fav)*(WRMuir)* 10-8-13 CRutter(1) (lw: hld up: hdwy 3f out: led 1f out: r.o. u.p) ....— **1**
4170[6] Hunza Story **(36)***(54) (NPLittmoden)* 3-7-7 (5) MHenry(8) (hld up: hdwy on bit to ld 3f out: hdd 1f out: kpt on) 1¾ **2**
4110[2] Goodbye Millie **(49)***(50) (JLEyre)* 5-8-6v RLappin(3) (hdwy 4f out: sn rdn & r.o: nrst fin) 4 **3**
3853[6] Bardia **(33)***(46) (DonEnricoIncisa)* 5-8-6 KimTinkler(7) (dwlt: hdwy 3f out: hrd rdn & nvr able chal)..............2½ **4**
4138[6] Manful **(59)***(52) (JHetherton)* 3-9-1 NKennedy(2) (a chsg ldrs: rdn 4f out: one pce)..............6 **5**
874[16] Marble **(33)***(32) (MGMeagher)* 4-7-13 (3) NVarley(10) (led 2f: chsd ldrs: one pce fnl 3f) 1¼ **6**
Stamshaw *(21) (WStorey)* 6-8-2 DaleGibson(4) (b: bit bkwd: nvr trbld ldrs) 7 **7**
4110[3] Adaloaldo (USA) **(59)***(36) (PAKelleway)* 3-9-1 DeanMcKeown(9) (dwlt: hdwy 8f out: wknd fnl 3½f) 3 **8**
3805[15] Newgate Hush *(18) (BWMurray)* 3-7-5 (7) MartinDwyer(5) (nvr nr ldrs)..............1 **9**
1846[7] Handsome Squaw *(2) (BWMurray)* 3-7-12 TWilliams(13) (b.hind: led after 2f to 3f out: wknd)..............11 **10**
4110[7] Here Comes Herbie **(30)** *(WStorey)* 3-7-10 (5) PFessey(12) (chsd ldrs tl wknd fnl 3½f) 6 **11**
School of Science *(RMMcKellar)* 5-8-9 JFanning(6) (prom tl wknd appr st)..............9 **12**
4114[6] Bold Joker **(25)** *(GROldroyd)* 4-8-11 JLowe(11) (prom tl lost pl appr st: sn wl bhd)..............hd **13**

6/5 SHABANAZ (11/10-Evens), **4/1** Manful, Goodbye Millie, **5/1** Adaloaldo (USA), **9/1** Hunza Story, **25/1** Bardia, **66/1** Marble, School of Science, Here Comes Herbie, **100/1** Stamshaw, Handsome Squaw, Bold Joker, **200/1** Newgate Hush, CSF £12.92 TOTE £2.00: £1.30 £2.30 £1.20 (£16.60) Trio £9.40 OWNER Fayzad Thoroughbred Ltd (LAMBOURN) BRED The Overbury Stud 13 Rn

2m 22.5 (6.80) SF: 33/16/18/14/14/-/-/-/-/-/-/-/-

WEIGHT FOR AGE 3yo-6lb

4233

TELEPROMPTER LIMITED STKS (0-65) (3-Y.O+) (Class F) £2,966.00 (£826.00: £398.00) **1m 2f** Stalls: Low GOING minus 0.18 sec per fur (GF) 3-00 (3-02)

4044[2] **Another Time (65)***(83)*(Fav)*(SPCWoods)* 3-9-2 WWoods(3) (hld up & bhd: gd hdwy to ld over 1f out: rdn & r.o)........— **1**
4071[10] Domitia (USA) **(65)***(74) (MBell)* 3-8-9 MFenton(4) (b: trckd ldrs: led over 2f out: hdd over 1f out: kpt on wl)........1 **2**
4171[3] Ocean Park **(60)***(74)*(Fav)*(LadyHerries)* 4-9-3 DeanMcKeown(1) (b.off hind: bhd: hdwy 4f out: rdn & one pce appr fnl f)........2 **3**
3977* Almuhtaram **(64)***(72) (MissGayKelleway)* 3-8-9b(5) AWhelan(2) (trckd ldrs: effrt 3f out: one pce)........2½ **4**
4128[4] Zacaroon **(65)***(62)*(Fav)*(LordHuntingdon)* 4-8-12 SSanders(6) (in tch: effrt over 3f out: no imp)2 **5**
4061[13] Efizia **(62)***(62) (MrsMReveley)* 5-8-12 LCharnock(8) (bhd: rdn 4f out: nvr nrr)........nk **6**
4115[9] Johnnie the Joker **(47)***(62) (JPLeigh)* 4-9-3b MBirch(5) (cl up tl wknd fnl 3f)........3 **7**
4110* Once More for Luck (IRE) **(65)***(59)*(Fav)*(MrsMReveley)* 4-9-5 ACulhane(9) (lw: led tl hdd over 2f out: sn wknd)........3 **8**
4038[24] Ballard Ring (IRE) **(44)** *(JSWainwright)* 4-8-12 RHughes(7) (s.i.s: sn prom: wknd 4f out: t.o)........dist **9**

7/2 ANOTHER TIME, Zacaroon, Ocean Park, Once More for Luck (IRE), **11/2** Almuhtaram, **9/1** Efizia, **12/1** Domitia (USA) (op 8/1), **50/1** Ballard Ring (IRE), **100/1** Johnnie the Joker, CSF £42.08 TOTE £5.10: £1.70 £2.40 £1.60 (£27.40) Trio £71.20 OWNER Mr D. Sullivan (NEWMARKET) BRED W. G. Barker 9 Rn

2m 6.3 (3.80) SF: 55/46/51/44/39/39/39/36/-

WEIGHT FOR AGE 3yo-5lb

4234

ELLERBY H'CAP (0-75) (3-Y.O+) (Class D) £4,178.50 (£1,258.00: £609.00: £284.50) **1m** Stalls: Centre GOING minus 0.73 sec per fur (HD) 3-30 (3-33)

4115[3] **Night Wink (USA) (70)***(89) (DNicholls)* 3-9-5 (7) MartinDwyer(8) (lw: cl up: led ½-wy: shkn up & qcknd clr fnl 2f)........— **1**
4116[13] Pine Ridge Lad (IRE) **(54)***(63) (JLEyre)* 5-8-13 SDWilliams(13) (a chsng ldrs: rdn ½-wy: kpt on fnl f)........5 **2**
4083* Mbulwa **(55)***(62)*(Fav)*(RAFahey)* 9-9-0 LCharnock(12) (trckd ldrs: effrt over 2f out: one pce)1¼ **3**
3276[6] Piquant **(66)***(68) (LordHuntingdon)* 8-9-11 SSanders(11) (outpcd & bhd ½-wy: styd on fnl 2f: nrst fin)........2½ **4**
4083[4] Thatched (IRE) **(54)***(55) (REBarr)* 5-8-8 (5) PFessey(2) (bhd: styd on fnl 3f: nvr able chal)........½ **5**
3977[15] King Chestnut **(58)***(58) (MDods)* 4-9-3b DeanMcKeown(4) (lw: dwlt: sn prom: one pce fnl 3f).hd **6**
3980[11] Euro Sceptic (IRE) **(47)***(42) (MHEasterby)* 3-8-3b SMaloney(7) (bhd tl sme late hdwy)........2½ **7**
4038[4] Nobby Barnes **(45)***(39) (DonEnricoIncisa)* 6-8-4 KimTinkler(5) (dwlt: a bhd)........½ **8**
4083[9] Spanish Verdict **(69)***(63) (DenysSmith)* 8-9-9 (5) CTeague(3) (lw: chsd ldrs tl wknd fnl 3f)......s.h **9**
3941[8] Royal Comedian **(40)***(22) (BWMurray)* 6-7-13 TWilliams(6) (led to ½-wy: sn lost pl)........6 **10**
4101[9] Dally Boy **(45)***(26) (MHEasterby)* 3-8-1 JLowe(14) (a in rr)........hd **11**
3974[12] Ihtimaam (FR) **(59)***(24) (MrsASwinbank)* 3-9-1 NConnorton(1) (b: b.hind: unruly s: nvr wnt pce)........8 **12**
4110[10] Sallyoreally (IRE) **(36)** *(WStorey)* 4-7-6 (3)ow2 NVarley(10) (chsd ldrs: rdn ½-wy: sn wknd)........4 **13**
2543[8] My Handy Man **(51)** *(RAllan)* 4-8-10 ACulhane(9) (a bhd)........7 **14**

LONG HANDICAP Sallyoreally (IRE) 7-1

7/2 Mbulwa, **9/2** Thatched (IRE), **6/1** Piquant, **9/1** Ihtimaam (FR), **11/1** Nobby Barnes, Pine Ridge Lad (IRE), Euro Sceptic (IRE), **12/1** NIGHT WINK (USA) (op 8/1), King Chestnut, Spanish Verdict, **16/1** My Handy Man, **33/1** Royal Comedian, Dally Boy, **100/1** Sallyoreally (IRE), CSF £127.73 CT £516.07 TOTE £10.40: £3.30 £3.10 £1.90 (£65.50) Trio £57.00 OWNER Mrs Dyanne Benjamin (THIRSK) BRED Gainsborough Farm Inc 14 Rn

1m 33.1 (1.70 under best) (-1.90) SF: 68/45/44/50/37/40/21/21/45/4/5/3/-/-

WEIGHT FOR AGE 3yo-3lb

4235

CAPTAIN COOK CONDITIONS STKS (2-Y.O) (Class D) £3,470.00 (£1,040.00: £500.00: £230.00)
7f Stalls: Centre GOING minus 0.73 sec per fur (HD) 4-00 (4-01)

4084[10] **La Volta (86)***(81) (JGFitzGerald)* 2-8-10 RHughes(5) (lw: made virtually all: hld on wl fnl f)........— **1**

3865[8] Roses In The Snow (IRE) **(98)***(77)*(Fav)*(JWHills)* 2-8-1 (5) MHenry(3) (trckd ldrs: effrt over 2f out: disp ld & hung lft ins fnl f: nt qckn nr fin)....hd 2
4037[3] Karisma (IRE) *(57) (DenysSmith)* 2-8-11 TWilliams(2) (lw: cl up: rdn over 2f out: wknd over 1f out)....11 3
Sleepy Boy *(11) (WStorey)* 2-8-11 JFanning(1) (unf: bkwd: sn outpcd & bhd)....20 4
4112[7] Call Me Jendie *(JPLeigh)* 2-8-6 DeanMcKeown(4) (swtg: plld hrd early: sn outpcd & wl bhd)....13 5

4/5 Roses In The Snow (IRE) (tchd Evens), **9/4** LA VOLTA (6/4-5/2), **4/1** Karisma (IRE), **100/1** Call Me Jendie, **200/1** Sleepy Boy, CSF £4.16 TOTE £3.60: £2.50 £1.00 (£2.20) OWNER Sir Andrew Lloyd Webber (MALTON) BRED K. G. Bridges 5 Rn 1m 22.8 (0.80) SF: 23/19/-/-/-

4236 GANTON H'CAP (0-85) (3-Y.O+) (Class D) £3,970.50 (£1,194.00: £577.00: £268.50) 7f Stalls: Centre GOING minus 0.73 sec per fur (HD) 4-30 (4-32)

4068[15] **Quilling (72)***(83) (MDods)* 3-9-2 DeanMcKeown(6) (lw: mde all: hld on wl fnl f)....— 1
4041[19] King Rat (IRE) **(77)***(87) (TJEtherington)* 4-9-10b CRutter(12) (chsd ldrs: chal over 1f out: nt qckn towards fin)....½ 2
3411[13] Super Benz **(60)***(64) (FJO'Mahony)* 9-8-2 (5) MHenry(3) (b: chsd ldrs: drvn alng ½-wy: kpt on)....2½ 3
4115[6] Field of Vision (IRE) **(63)***(66) (MJohnston)* 5-8-10 TWilliams(13) (lw: chsd ldrs: effrt over 2f out: edgd lft & styd on)....½ 4
3645[16] Alabang **(48)***(50) (MJCamacho)* 4-7-9 LCharnock(10) (bhd: stdy hdwy over 2f out: r.o. towards fin)....nk 5
3980[2] Mister Westsound **(62)***(63)*(Fav)*(MissLAPerratt)* 3-7-13b(7) MartinDwyer(1) (dwlt: hdwy ½-wy: sn chsng ldrs: rdn & btn over 1f out)....¾ 6
4115[14] Kid Ory **(67)***(61) (PCalver)* 4-8-11 (3) NVarley(9) (b.hind: chsd ldrs: drvn along ½-wy: grad wknd)....3 7
3973[2] Far Ahead **(77)***(65) (JLEyre)* 3-9-7 RLappin(14) (in tch: effrt 3f out: no imp)....2½ 8
4043[14] Glowing Jade **(68)***(54) (JAGlover)* 5-9-1 SDWilliams(4) (in tch: effrt 3f out: n.d)....¾ 9
4115[10] Mu-Arrik **(46)***(31) (GROldroyd)* 7-7-7v JLowe(5) (a bhd)....½ 10
4113[16] Super Park **(65)***(49) (MHEasterby)* 3-8-9 MBirch(15) (n.d)....¾ 11
4115[16] Penny's Wishing **(54)***(34) (JPLeigh)* 3-7-7 (5) PFessey(8) (w wnr tl wknd over 3f out)....1½ 12
3991[6] New Century (USA) **(84)***(63) (DNicholls)* 3-10-0 RHughes(11) (a in rr)....nk 13
4068[22] Superpride **(70)***(48) (MrsMReveley)* 3-9-0 ACulhane(2) (a bhd)....½ 14
4041[22] Parliament Piece **(71)***(46) (DNicholls)* 9-9-4 NConnorton(7) (lw: hld up & a bhd)....1½ 15

LONG HANDICAP Mu-Arrik 7-5

9/2 Mister Westsound (op 8/1), **11/2** Far Ahead, **6/1** Parliament Piece (8/1-5/1), Field of Vision (IRE), **7/1** Glowing Jade, New Century (USA), **10/1** QUILLING, Superpride, **11/1** Kid Ory, **12/1** Alabang (op 7/1), **20/1** King Rat (IRE), **25/1** Super Benz, **33/1** Mu-Arrik, Super Park, Penny's Wishing, CSF £189.06 CT £4,384.16 TOTE £12.30: £4.40 £7.00 £5.60 (£118.20) Trio £544.30; £552.00 to Yarmouth 25/10/95 OWNER Mr A. G. Watson (DARLINGTON) BRED Hesmonds Stud Ltd 15 Rn 1m 21.1 (1.00 under best) (-0.90) SF: 49/56/33/35/19/29/30/31/23/-/15/-/29/14/15

WEIGHT FOR AGE 3yo-3lb

T/Plpt: £12.70 (1,029.13 Tckts). T/Qdpt: £6.50 (8.2 Tckts). AA

4150-YARMOUTH (L-H)
Wednesday October 25th (Firm)

WEATHER: cloudy WIND: fresh slt against

4237 LOUND NURSERY H'CAP (0-85) (2-Y.O) (Class E) £3,655.00 (£1,090.00: £520.00: £235.00) 5f 43y Stalls: Low GOING minus 0.31 sec per fur (GF) 1-25 (1-26)

4132* **Dande Flyer (67)***(74) (DWPArbuthnot)* 2-8-10 7x BDoyle(1) (b.nr hind: hld up: qcknd thro gap 1f out: led 150y out: r.o wl)....— 1
4097[6] Gagajulu **(77)***(72) (PDEvans)* 2-9-6 GHind(4) (led 2f out: sn hrd rdn: hdd 150y out: one pce)..4 2
4137[3] Time For Tea (IRE) **(76)***(70) (CACyzer)* 2-9-5 MRoberts(3) (a.p: led wl over 2f out: hdd 2f out: ev ch 1f out: one pce)....hd 3
4077[5] Little Noggins (IRE) **(78)***(69)*(Fav)*(CADwyer)* 2-9-7 CDwyer(5) (prom: ev ch 2f out: rdn & hung lft appr fnl f: no ex)....1 4
3998[F] Governors Dream **(55)** *(MrsNMacauley)* 2-7-12v GBardwell(2) (lw: led over 2f: wknd qckly: t.o)....25 5

10/11 Little Noggins (IRE), **7/2** Gagajulu, DANDE FLYER, **13/2** Time For Tea (IRE), **33/1** Governors Dream, CSF £14.65 TOTE £5.10: £2.50 £2.50 (£12.20) OWNER Dandelion Distribution Ltd (COMPTON) BRED G. Syvrett 5 Rn 62.6 secs (2.30) SF: 30/28/26/25/-

4238

CORTON CONDITIONS STKS (3-Y.O+) (Class C) £5,108.40 (£1,838.40: £879.20: £356.00) **6f 3y** Stalls: Low GOING minus 0.31 sec per fur (GF) 2-00 (2-00)

4119[11] **Saseedo (USA)** **(86)***(81)*(Fav)*(WAO'Gorman)* 5-9-5 EmmaO'Gorman(1) (lw: hld up: hdwy over 1f out: led 100y out: r.o wl) ....— **1**
4165[2] Moujeeb (USA) **(50)***(71) (PatMitchell)* 5-9-0v JQuinn(2) (lw: led 1f: trckd ldr: hrd rdn wl over 1f out: outpcd bel dist: rallied cl home) 2 **2**
4160[7] Bowden Rose **(85)***(77) (MBlanshard)* 3-9-4b RCochrane(3) (led 5f out: qcknd over 2f out: hdd 100y out: no ex) ....s.h **3**
4068[13] First Veil **(72)***(61) (JRFanshawe)* 5-8-8 DHarrison(4) (hld up: styd on u.p fnl 2f) 1¼ **4**
4145[3] Fantasy Racing (IRE) **(80)***(55) (MRChannon)* 3-9-4 RHughes(5) (cl up tl rdn & wknd appr fnl f) 7 **5**

2/1 SASEEDO (USA), **5/2** Bowden Rose (op 6/4), **100/30** Fantasy Racing (IRE), **9/2** First Veil (op 3/1), **14/1** Moujeeb (USA), CSF £19.97 TOTE £2.30: £1.50 £2.50 (£8.20) OWNER Mr S. Fustok (NEWMARKET) BRED Audley Farm Incorporated 5 Rn 1m 12.7 (2.10) SF: 47/37/41/27/19
WEIGHT FOR AGE 3yo-2lb

4239

E.B.F. HERRINGFLEET MAIDEN STKS (2-Y.O) (Class D) £4,932.00 (£1,476.00: £708.00: £324.00)
7f 3y Stalls: Low GOING minus 0.31 sec per fur (GF) 2-35 (2-35)

Mawjud *(88) (HThomsonJones)* 2-9-0 RHills(3) (str: scope: led after 1f: rdn 1f out: r.o wl) ....— **1**
3983[5] Medieval Lady *(82) (LadyHerries)* 2-8-9 RCochrane(6) (a.p: ev ch over 1f out: rallied u.p ins fnl f) ....nk **2**
Royal Canaska *(86) (DRLoder)* 2-9-0 RHughes(7) (unf: lw: led 1f: a.p: hrd rdn & ev ch 1f out: one pce) ....¾ **3**
4058[3] Balladur (USA) *(81)*(Fav)*(HRACecil)* 2-9-0 PatEddery(8) (lw: hld up: hdwy ½-wy: ev ch 2f out: sn btn) 2 **4**
Menoo Hal Batal (USA) *(80) (MRStoute)* 2-9-0 KBradshaw(1) (unf: scope: prom: ev ch wl over 1f out: one pce fr dist) ....nk **5**
Distinct Beauty (IRE) *(71) (WAO'Gorman)* 2-8-9 EmmaO'Gorman(5) (leggy: lt-f: s.i.s: nvr nr to chal) 2 **6**
Extremely Friendly *(68) (CEBrittain)* 2-9-0 BDoyle(10) (cmpt: a outpcd) 3½ **7**
3948[8] Petite Juliette *(62) (WJarvis)* 2-8-9 WRyan(9) (sn bhd) ....nk **8**
Hanbitooh (USA) *(53) (EALDunlop)* 2-9-0 PaulEddery(2) (gd sort: leggy: scope: a outpcd) 6 **9**
Go Too Moor (IRE) *(53) (GCBravery)* 2-9-0 MHills(4) (leggy: scope: in tch to ½-wy) ....hd **10**

4/6 Balladur (USA), **4/1** Royal Canaska (3/1-9/2), **8/1** MAWJUD (6/1-9/1), **10/1** Menoo Hal Batal (USA) (6/1-4/1), **12/1** Medieval Lady, **20/1** Hanbitooh (USA), Extremely Friendly, **25/1** Petite Juliette, **50/1** Distinct Beauty (IRE), Go Too Moor (IRE), CSF £91.83 TOTE £6.90: £2.00 £1.80 £1.50 (£27.80) Trio £36.60 OWNER Mr Hamdan Al Maktoum (NEWMARKET) BRED Shadwell Estate Company Limited 10 Rn 1m 26.4 (3.60) SF: 29/23/27/22/21/12/9/3/-/-

4240

NEWPORT CLAIMING STKS (3-Y.O+) (Class F) £3,098.60 (£859.60: £411.80)
7f 3y Stalls: Low GOING minus 0.31 sec per fur (GF) 3-10 (3-15)

4060* **Nashaat (USA)** **(65)***(70) (NJHWalker)* 7-8-1 (3)ow2 JStack(10) (hdwy 3f out: led wl over 1f out: drvn out) ....— **1**
4156* Spencer's Revenge **(67)***(79)*(Fav)*(MJRyan)* 6-9-2 GBardwell(6) (hrd rdn & hdwy wl over 1f out: chsd wnr fnl f: no imp) 2 **2**
*1087** Berge (IRE) **(64)***(60) (WAO'Gorman)* 4-8-8b EmmaO'Gorman(11) (a.p: led 4f out to wl over 1f out: one pce) 5 **3**
4193[11] Awesome Venture **(43)***(57) (MCChapman)* 5-7-13 (7) CMunday(5) (reard s: sn disp ld: wknd wl over 1f out) ....½ **4**
Framed (IRE) *(60) (SCWilliams)* 5-8-10 JTate(2) (b.off fore: hdwy 3f out: styd on one pce fnl f) ....nk **5**
4217[4] Our Shadee (USA) **(46)***(52) (KTIvory)* 5-8-4v BDoyle(4) (lw: m.n.s) 1 **6**
4131[5] Tomal **(48)***(53) (RIngram)* 3-8-4 ow1 WWoods(12) (stmbld s: nvr btr than mid div) ....½ **7**
3511[13] Action Jackson **(64)***(50) (BJMcMath)* 3-8-7 RCochrane(3) (b.hind: in tch 4f) 3 **8**
3681[11] Waders Dream (IRE) **(45)***(40) (PatMitchell)* 6-8-2v PRobinson(1) (prom 4f) ....¾ **9**
3875[17] Zuno Flyer (USA) **(34)***(42) (GLewis)* 3-7-12b(5)ow2 AWhelan(8) (led 3f: wknd qckly over 2f out) ....d.h **9**
4156[6] Samsolom **(72)***(49) (PHowling)* 7-9-10 JQuinn(13) (lw: a outpcd: wl bhd fnl 2f) 6 **11**
2065[7] Magic Leader (IRE) **(33)***(6) (TTClement)* 3-8-1v AMackay(9) (b: prom over 4f: t.o) 10 **12**
Missal (IRE) **(30)** *(PatMitchell)* 6-7-5b(7)ow1 AmandaSanders(14) (prom 4f: t.o fnl 2f) 1 **13**

3524[14] Polhymnia **(30)** *(GCBravery)* 4-7-11v NCarlisle(7) (reluctant to leave paddock: reluctant to r: sn t.o) 15 **14**

7/4 Spencer's Revenge, **3/1** NASHAAT (USA), **6/1** Berge (IRE) (op 10/1), **10/1** Tomal, **11/1** Our Shadee (USA), **12/1** Action Jackson, **14/1** Samsolom, **16/1** Zuno Flyer (USA), **25/1** Framed (IRE), **33/1** Waders Dream (IRE), Awesome Venture, **50/1** Magic Leader (IRE), **66/1** Missal (IRE), Polhymnia, CSF £8.70 TOTE £4.60: £1.90 £1.40 £2.60 (£5.00) Trio £5.10 OWNER Mrs Christine Painting (WANTAGE) BRED Echo Valley Horse Farm and Swettenham Stud 14 Rn

1m 24.8 (2.00) SF: 39/48/29/26/29/21/19/16/9/8/18/-/-/-

WEIGHT FOR AGE 3yo-3lb

Nashaat(USA) clmd M Chapman £4,000

4241 RANWORTH MAIDEN STKS (2-Y.O) (Class D) £4,628.25 (£1,386.00: £665.50: £305.25) 1m 3y Stalls: Low GOING minus 0.31 sec per fur (GF) 3-45 (3-48)

Bright Water *(93)*(Fav)*(HRACecil)* 2-9-0 PatEddery(5) (cmpt: a.p: rdn 2f out: led ins fnl f: hrd rdn & hung rt) ....— **1**
Aethra (USA) *(87) (LadyHerries)* 2-8-9 RCochrane(9) (scope: bit bkwd: dwlt: hdwy over 3f out: led over 1f out: hdd ins fnl f: r.o wl) ....nk **2**
4048[2] Introducing *(79) (JHMGosden)* 2-8-9 GHind(13) (a in tch: styd on one pce fnl 2f) 4 **3**
4063[2] Jiyush *(81) (HThomsonJones)* 2-9-0 RHills(8) (a.p: led wl over 2f out: rdn 2f out: hdd over 1f out: ev ch whn squeezed out jst ins fnl f: nt rcvr) 1½ **4**
3900[12] Rossel (USA) *(67) (MRStoute)* 2-9-0 KBradshaw(10) (s.i.s: sn in tch: nvr able chal) 7 **5**
4063[6] Halebid *(67) (SPCWoods)* 2-9-0 WWoods(4) (ev ch 2f out: sn btn) ....hd **6**
3663[17] Soldier Mak *(64) (AHide)* 2-9-0 AMcGlone(1) (n.d) 1½ **7**
4080[14] Suitor *(62) (WJarvis)* 2-9-0 MTebbutt(12) (lw: s.s: a bhd) 1¼ **8**
4155[7] Capstone *(55) (WJarvis)* 2-8-9 WRyan(2) (a outpcd) ....¾ **9**
St Adele (USA) *(55) (DRLoder)* 2-8-6 (3) DRMcCabe(3) (leggy: lt-f: in tch to ½-wy) ....s.h **10**
4073[5] Classic Colours (USA) *(58) (SCWilliams)* 2-9-0 AMackay(11) (lw: led to wl over 2f out: wknd qckly) 1¼ **11**
3887[8] Double Up *(43) (LadyHerries)* 2-8-9 JQuinn(7) (a outpcd) 5 **12**
3928[8] Somer Solo **(57)***(36) (PMitchell)* 2-8-9 GDuffield(6) (prom over 4f: t.o) 3½ **13**

7/4 BRIGHT WATER, **5/2** Jiyush, **11/4** Introducing, **11/1** St Adele (USA) (5/1-12/1), **16/1** Rossel (USA), **20/1** Aethra (USA), **25/1** Capstone, Double Up, **33/1** Suitor, Soldier Mak, Classic Colours (USA), Halebid, Somer Solo, CSF £35.83 TOTE £2.60: £1.60 £3.70 £1.20 (£35.70) Trio £47.10 OWNER Mr K. Abdulla (NEWMARKET) BRED Juddmonte Farms 13 Rn

1m 37.2 (1.90) SF: 52/46/38/40/26/26/23/21/14/14/17/2/-

4242 CALIFORNIA H'CAP (0-70) (3-Y.O+) (Class E) £3,915.00 (£1,170.00: £560.00: £255.00) 7f 3y Stalls: Low GOING minus 0.31 sec per fur (GF) 4-15 (4-16)

4156[9] **Ahjay (46)***(59) (DAWilson)* 5-8-9 MRoberts(9) (a.p stands' side: led wl over 1f out: drvn out)— **1**
3897[11] Agoer **(46)***(55) (CEBrittain)* 3-8-6 BDoyle(12) (b.hind: racd stands' side: hdwy 2f out: ev ch dist: unable qckn fnl f) 1¾ **2**
4165[3] Hickory Blue **(65)***(67) (MrsNMacauley)* 5-9-11v(3) SDrowne(13) (led tl wl over 1f out: one pce) 3 **3**
4170[4] Love Legend **(50)***(52) (DWPArbuthnot)* 10-8-13 TIves(10) (racd stands' side: hrd rdn 2f out: one pce) ....s.h **4**
4150[2] Darcey Bussell **(55)***(53)*(Fav)*(NCWright)* 3-8-10 (5) DaneO'Neill(4) (effrt over 2f out: sn hrd rdn: one pce) 2 **5**
4156[5] Morocco (IRE) **(57)***(53) (MRChannon)* 6-9-6 RHughes(11) (hld up: gd hdwy over 2f out: hrd rdn & ev ch over 1f out: sn one pce) ....¾ **6**
3020[5] Spanish Stripper (USA) **(63)***(56) (MCChapman)* 4-9-5 (7) CMunday(2) (n.d) 1¼ **7**
4194[5] Merrie le Bow **(43)***(33) (PatMitchell)* 3-7-10 (7) MartinDwyer(8) (prom: led far side 3f out: ev ch 2f out: sn wknd) 1¼ **8**
3661[18] Hylters Girl **(34)***(10) (MJRyan)* 3-7-8 GBardwell(5) (wl bhd fnl 3f) 6 **9**
2180* Move With Edes **(63)***(38) (WGMTurner)* 3-9-2 (7) AEddery(1) (in tch tl hrd rdn & wknd over 2f out) ....½ **10**
4044[18] Labudd (USA) **(58)***(10) (RIngram)* 5-9-7 RHills(7) (led far side 4f: wknd qckly) 10 **11**
4043[7] Merlin's Fancy **(56)** *(WJarvis)* 3-9-2 WRyan(6) (a bhd: t.o) 5 **12**

4/1 Darcey Bussell, **9/2** AHJAY (op 7/1), **6/1** Morocco (IRE), **13/2** Labudd (USA), **7/1** Move With Edes, **8/1** Love Legend, **9/1** Hickory Blue, **10/1** Merrie le Bow, **12/1** Merlin's Fancy, Agoer, **20/1** Spanish Stripper (USA), **33/1** Hylters Girl, CSF £57.14 CT £444.49 TOTE £7.10: £1.90 £2.80 £2.70 (£22.00) Trio £143.60 OWNER Mr R. J. Thomas (EPSOM) BRED Robert J. Thomas 12 Rn

1m 25.0 (2.20) SF: 41/34/49/34/32/35/38/12/-/17/-/-

WEIGHT FOR AGE 3yo-3lb

T/Jkpt: £15,941.00 (5.2 Tckts). T/Plpt: £251.90 (67.06 Tckts). T/Qdpt: £56.40 (7.55 Tckts). RC

4165-NOTTINGHAM (L-H)
Thursday October 26th (Good to firm)
WEATHER: cloudy WIND: mod against

4243 RUSHCLIFFE NURSERY H'CAP (0-85) (2-Y.O) (Class E) £3,559.60 (£1,064.80: £510.40: £233.20)
6f 15y Stalls: High GOING: 0.06 sec per fur (G) 1-20 (1-22)

3947^6 **Akalim (76)***(78) (DMorley)* 2-9-5 RHills(2) (hld up in tch: shkn up to ld over 1f out: drvn out)........— 1
4144* Erupt **(73)***(74) (GBBalding)* 2-9-2v 7x JWilliams(5) (dwlt: hdwy 2f out: fin wl)........nk 2
4144^14 Vax New Way **(65)***(61) (JLSpearing)* 2-8-5b(3) SDrowne(1) (led & sn clr: wknd & hdd appr fnl f)........2 3
4097^3 Mullagh Hill Lad (IRE) **(54)***(47)*(Fav)*(BAMcMahon)* 2-7-11 FNorton(10) (hld up: hdwy & edgd lft 2f out: no imp fnl f)........1 4
4144^4 Vera's First (IRE) **(69)***(62) (GLewis)* 2-8-12b PaulEddery(4) (s.i.s: effrt over 1f out: nvr nrr)....nk 5
4066^2 Precious Girl **(74)***(66) (DMoffatt)* 2-9-0 (3) DarrenMoffatt(8) (chsd ldrs: hung lft bel dist: wknd ins fnl f)........hd 6
4206^5 Stop Play (IRE) **(78)***(70) (MHTompkins)* 2-9-7 PRobinson(13) (prom: sn pushed along stands' side: one pce fnl 2f)........hd 7
3901^5 Jolis Present **(61)***(46) (MJRyan)* 2-8-4b GBardwell(3) (rdn along & bhd ½-wy: n.d)........2½ 8
4077^11 Deerly **(66)***(49) (DMorris)* 2-8-6 (3) JStack(9) (mid div: rdn over 2f out: one pce)........1 9
4077^8 Clincher Club **(78)***(61) (MJohnston)* 2-9-7 TWilliams(11) (swtg: chsd ldrs: rdn over 2f out: sn btn)........s.h 10
3567^3 Oare Budgie **(52)***(35) (PTWalwyn)* 2-7-9 NAdams(14) (sn rdn along: a in rr)........s.h 11
3858^12 Music Mistress (IRE) **(66)***(43) (RHannon)* 2-8-4 (5)ow4 DaneO'Neill(12) (swtg: nvr nr to chal)...½ 12
3901^9 Rustic Song (IRE) **(54)***(32) (JWharton)* 2-7-11 JQuinn(6) (prom over 3f)........1¼ 13
*3953** Don't Tell Anyone **(56)***(25) (JBerry)* 2-7-8 (5) PFessey(7) (spd 3f: sn wknd)........3½ 14

9/2 Mullagh Hill Lad (IRE), **5/1** Stop Play (IRE), **11/2** Jolis Present, **9/1** Erupt, Vera's First (IRE), **12/1** Precious Girl, Deerly, AKALIM, **14/1** Clincher Club, Don't Tell Anyone, **16/1** Vax New Way, **20/1** Music Mistress (IRE), Rustic Song (IRE), Oare Budgie, CSF £109.74 CT £1,565.34 TOTE £16.30: £3.90 £3.70 £5.00 (£195.80) Trio £137.00 OWNER Mr Hamdan Al Maktoum (NEWMARKET) BRED R. Powell-Tuck and Partners 14 Rn
1m 15.9 (4.90) SF: 41/37/24/10/25/29/33/9/12/24/-/6/-/-

4244 SHERWOOD CONDITIONS STKS (2-Y.O) (Class D) £3,915.00 (£1,170.00: £560.00: £255.00) **6f 15y** Stalls: High GOING: 0.06 sec per fur (G) 1-50 (1-52)

3988* **Lay The Blame (80)***(86) (WJarvis)* 2-9-3 TQuinn(10) (lw: hld up: hdwy 2f out: led ins fnl f: rdn out)........— 1
4023^2 Mutamanni (USA) *(80)*(Fav)*(HThomsonJones)* 2-8-11 RHills(3) (lw: a.p: led ½-wy: edgd rt appr fnl f: sn hdd: no ex nr fin)........hd 2
4146^7 Carmarthen Bay *(56) (GLMoore)* 2-8-11 JWilliams(8) (hld up: hdwy 2f out: nt rch ldrs)........9 3
4112^3 Born A Lady **(75)***(54) (NPLittmoden)* 2-8-10 NCarlisle(7) (spd stands' side 4f: sn outpcd)........½ 4
3474^2 Kirov Lady (IRE) **(83)***(52) (RHannon)* 2-8-5 (5) DaneO'Neill(2) (led 3f: rdn & hung rt 2f out: sn btn)........½ 5
3955^6 Miss Roberto (IRE) *(39) (MrsMMcCourt)* 2-8-6 MFenton(4) (rdn after 2f: nvr nr to chal)........3½ 6
1964^8 Roc de Fer (IRE) *(41) (WAO'Gorman)* 2-8-11 EmmaO'Gorman(1) (chsd ldrs: rdn wl over 1f out: wknd)........1¼ 7
Thenorthernplayboy (IRE) *(22) (BAMcMahon)* 2-8-11 KDarley(9) (lt-f: unf: bkwd: s.s: a bhd: t.o)........7 8
4059^3 Baloustar (USA) *(7) (SPCWoods)* 2-8-6 WWoods(5) (unruly in stalls: a bhd: t.o)........4 9
3432^16 Gresham Flyer **(50)** *(BRichmond)* 2-8-11 SDWilliams(6) (bkwd: spd over 3f out: sn wknd: t.o)........14 10

8/13 Mutamanni (USA), **4/1** Kirov Lady (IRE) (3/1-9/2), **9/2** LAY THE BLAME, **14/1** Born A Lady (8/1-16/1), **20/1** Baloustar (USA), **25/1** Thenorthernplayboy (IRE), Roc de Fer (IRE), **50/1** Miss Roberto (IRE), **66/1** Carmarthen Bay, Gresham Flyer, CSF £7.75 TOTE £6.50: £1.10 £1.10 £9.30 (£4.20) Trio £111.20 OWNER Mr Anthony Foster (NEWMARKET) BRED Wheelersland Stud 10 Rn
1m 15.7 (4.70) SF: 39/33/9/7/5/-/-/-/-/-

4245 SNEINTON CONDITIONS STKS (3-Y.O+) (Class C) £5,054.00 (£1,886.00: £918.00: £390.00) **1m 1f 213y** Stalls: Low GOING: 0.06 sec per fur (G) 2-20 (2-21)

4162^2 **Main Offender (87)***(91) (HRACecil)* 3-8-11 WRyan(6) (b.hind: led tl hdd ent fnl f: rallied u.p to ld nr fin)........— 1

4051[9] Dreams End **(70)***(95) (JMBradley)* 7-9-3 (3) SDrowne(4) (t: b: hld up: 6th st: led ent fnl f: hrd rdn: ct cl home)....hd 2
3958[6] South Sea Bubble (IRE) *(79) (LMCumani)* 3-8-6 KDarley(5) (hld up: 4th st: hdwy over 2f out: r.o wl fnl f)....4 3
2415[2] Time for Action (IRE) **(89)***(84) (MHTompkins)* 3-9-0 PRobinson(1) (bit bkwd: a.p: 3rd st: rdn 2f out: kpt on same pce)....2 4
4162* Bint Zamayem (IRE) **(73)***(80)*(Fav)*(BWHills)* 3-8-10 RHills(10) (lw: w ldr: 2nd st: ev ch over 2f out: wknd appr fnl f)....nk 5
3820[3] Home Counties (IRE) **(69)***(67) (DMoffatt)* 6-9-1 (3) DarrenMoffatt(8) (bit bkwd: hld up: hdwy 4f out: nt rch ldrs)....10 6
Tarian (USA) *(58) (GBBalding)* 3-8-11 NCarlisle(7) (w'like: neat: bit bkwd: hld up & bhd: nvr nr to chal)....4 7
Vicenza *(53) (GWragg)* 3-8-6 FNorton(2) (neat: s.s: a bhd)....nk 8
4027[6] Green Divot *(43) (GWragg)* 4-8-11 MHills(9) (swtg: dwlt: sn chsng ldrs: 5th st: wknd 3f out: t.o)....6 9

7/4 Bint Zamayem (IRE), **5/2** MAIN OFFENDER, **7/2** Time for Action (IRE), **10/1** Home Counties (IRE), **14/1** Dreams End, **20/1** South Sea Bubble (IRE), Tarian (USA), Vicenza, Green Divot, CSF £32.03 TOTE £3.30: £1.30 £3.60 £6.70 (£24.50) Trio £276.90; £234.00 to Newmarket 27/10/95 OWNER Mr L. Marinopoulos (NEWMARKET) BRED Stilvi Compania Financiera S A 9 Rn

2m 8.4 (5.90) SF: 51/60/39/44/40/32/18/13/8
WEIGHT FOR AGE 3yo-5lb

4246 E.B.F. NETHERFIELD MAIDEN STKS (I) (2-Y.O) (Class D)

£3,492.50 (£1,040.00: £495.00: £222.50)
1m 54y Stalls: Low GOING: 0.06 sec per fur (G) 2-50 (2-52)

4080[9] **Censor** *(83) (HRACecil)* 2-9-0 WRyan(11) (hld up: hdwy & 3rd st: led over 2f out: pushed out)....— 1
4050[3] Tasdik *(75)*(Fav)*(RWArmstrong)* 2-8-9 RHills(2) (a.p: 4th st: chsd wnr 2f out: swished tail: no imp fnl f)....1¾ 2
4063[9] Atienza (USA) *(65) (SCWilliams)* 2-8-9 JTate(6) (chsd ldrs: 6th st: effrt over 2f out: nt pce to chal)....5 3
Dancing Debut *(58) (JHMGosden)* 2-8-9 GHind(5) (scope: bit bkwd: hld up & bhd: plld out & hdwy 2f out: nrst fin)....3½ 4
4050[9] Another Quarter (IRE) *(57) (SPCWoods)* 2-8-9 WWoods(9) (b.nr fore: hld up: hdwy over 3f out: nvr nr ldrs)....½ 5
Magic Heights *(57) (JEBanks)* 2-9-0 JQuinn(7) (w'like: scope: bkwd: s.s: sme late hdwy: n.d)2½ 6
4063[16] Young Dalesman *(56) (AStreeter)* 2-8-9 (5) LNewton(8) (b.hind: plld hrd: 5th st: wknd over 2f out)....½ 7
3868[12] Chief Mouse *(56) (RCharlton)* 2-9-0 PaulEddery(1) (bit bkwd: s.i.s: led after 1f tl over 3f out: wknd fnl 2f)....nk 8
4146[4] Minnisam *(48) (JLDunlop)* 2-9-0 TSprake(3) (lw: s.i.s: mid div tl wknd 3f out)....4 9
2198[12] Another Picea *(9) (NTinkler)* 2-9-0 LCharnock(10) (led 1f: 2nd st: led over 3f out: eased whn btn bel dist: t.o)....20 10

10/11 Tasdik (Evens-5/4), **4/1** CENSOR (2/1-9/2), **8/1** Dancing Debut (7/2-10/1), **9/1** Chief Mouse (4/1-10/1), Magic Heights (4/1-10/1), **12/1** Minnisam, **20/1** Another Quarter (IRE), **25/1** Atienza (USA), **100/1** Young Dalesman, Another Picea, CSF £7.97 TOTE £3.90: £1.40 £1.10 £11.50 (£2.70) Trio £81.20 OWNER Lord Howard de Walden (NEWMARKET) BRED Lord Howard de Walden 10 Rn 1m 47.0 (7.40) SF: 30/22/12/5/4/4/3/3/-/-

4247 E.B.F. NETHERFIELD MAIDEN STKS (II) (2-Y.O) (Class D)

£3,460.00 (£1,030.00: £490.00: £220.00)
1m 54y Stalls: Low GOING: 0.06 sec per fur (G) 3-20 (3-23)

3900[13] **Dance Star** *(79) (MAJarvis)* 2-8-9 EmmaO'Gorman(7) (stdd s: hdwy on bit 2f out: edgd lft & led ins fnl f: sn clr)....— 1
4148[9] Bullpen Belle *(74) (PTWalwyn)* 2-8-9 KDarley(8) (led: rdn wl over 1f out: hdd & no ex ins fnl f)....2½ 2
Pencilled In *(76+)*(Fav)*(PWChapple-Hyam)* 2-9-0 JReid(4) (unf: scope: lw: a.p: 2nd st: rdn over 2f out: kpt on same pce)....1¾ 3
Viridis (USA) *(70) (HRACecil)* 2-8-9 WRyan(6) (rangy: unf: bit bkwd: chsd ldrs: 3rd st: rdn & outpcd 3f out: styd on fnl f)....½ 4
3868[13] Ela-Yie-Mou (IRE) *(74) (LMCumani)* 2-9-0 TQuinn(5) (hld up: hdwy wl 2f out: nt rch ldrs) .....nk 5
Sadler's Realm *(74) (MRStoute)* 2-9-0 KBradshaw(2) (w'like: scope: bkwd: a.p: 4th st: effrt over 2f out: kpt on u.p fnl f)....s.h 6

4080[11] Flocheck (USA) *(67) (JLDunlop)* 2-9-0 RCochrane(3) (chsd ldrs: 5th st: rdn & btn over 2f out) 3½ 7
4172[6] Jump The Lights *(63) (SPCWoods)* 2-9-0 WWoods(10) (in tch: 6th st: drvn along over 2f out: sn btn) 2 8
4063[8] Salsian *(58) (SCWilliams)* 2-8-9 JTate(9) (a in rr) ....s.h 9
4048[10] Tashjir (USA) *(55) (DMorley)* 2-8-9 RHills(11) (a bhd) 2 10
4172[13] Reef Raider **(43)***(54) (NTinkler)* 2-9-0b LCharnock(1) (in tch tl wknd over 2f out) 3 11

9/4 Pencilled In, **4/1** Viridis (USA) (op 5/4), **11/2** Flocheck (USA) (4/1-6/1), **6/1** Sadler's Realm (3/1-13/2), **7/1** Ela-Yie-Mou (IRE), **12/1** DANCE STAR, **20/1** Bullpen Belle, Salsian, **25/1** Jump The Lights, Tashjir (USA), **50/1** Reef Raider, CSF £190.54 TOTE £45.40: £4.60 £4.40 £1.10 (£274.50) Trio £300.90 OWNER Mr N. S. Yong (NEWMARKET) BRED F. C. T. Wilson 11 Rn

1m 47.8 (8.20) SF: 17/12/14/8/12/12/5/1/-/-/-

4248

MIX-IT PRODUCTS H'CAP (0-80) (3-Y.O+) (Class D) £4,857.50 (£1,460.00: £705.00: £327.50)
1m 6f 15y Stalls: Low GOING: 0.06 sec per fur (G) 3-50 (3-51)

4189[3] **Cuango (IRE) (51)***(65)*(Fav)*(RHollinshead)* 4-7-10 (5) MHenry(16) (hld up: 6th st: led 3f out: edgd lft ent fnl f: r.o) ....— 1
4149[2] Fabillion **(58)***(71) (CASmith)* 3-7-13 CRutter(14) (chsd ldrs: 4th st: outpcd 3f out: r.o strly u.p fnl f) 1 2
3836[18] Quest Again **(62)***(74) (DWPArbuthnot)* 4-8-12 TQuinn(6) (hld up: hdwy 4f out: chal over 2f out: swtchd rt fnl f: r.o) ....½ 3
3971[14] Harry Welsh (IRE) **(55)***(67) (KMcAuliffe)* 3-7-10v JQuinn(9) (hld up mid div: gd hdwy 2f out: fin wl) ....nk 4
4118[8] Sea Freedom **(65)***(75) (GBBalding)* 4-9-1 JWilliams(4) (chsd ldrs: led ent st to 3f out: rdn & one pce) 2 5
4166[14] Requested **(53)***(59) (PBurgoyne)* 8-8-0 (3) DRMcCabe(11) (stdd s: hdwy over 3f out: nvr nrr) 3½ 6
4071[8] Pumice **(73)***(77) (LMCumani)* 3-9-0 KDarley(10) (mid div: effrt over 2f out: nt rch ldrs) 1¼ 7
4166[11] Fabulous Mtoto **(50)***(49) (MSSaunders)* 5-8-0 ow4 JFEgan(8) (hld up & bhd: styd on fnl 2f: nvr nrr) 1½ 8
4166[12] Tilty (USA) **(56)***(58) (AStreeter)* 5-8-1 (5) LNewton(18) (nvr plcd to chal) ....¾ 9
4036[13] Soba Up **(74)***(70) (TJEtherington)* 5-9-10 ACulhane(7) (chsd ldrs tl lost pl 5f out: rdn over 3f out: no imp) 5 10
4038[15] Antartictern (USA) **(45)***(38) (GROldroyd)* 5-7-9 ow2 LCharnock(2) (lw: chsd ldrs: effrt 3f out: hung rt & sn btn) 1¼ 11
3936[13] Prussia **(50)***(42) (WClay)* 4-8-0 NCarlisle(5) (chsd ldrs: 5th st: wknd 3f out) 2 12
3986[12] Charmed Life **(43)***(29) (MrsALMKing)* 6-7-2b(5) PFessey(3) (lw: chsd ldrs: drvn along ½-wy: wknd 3f out) 6 13
3710[14] General Mouktar **(57)***(42) (MCPipe)* 5-8-7b PaulEddery(1) (led tl hdd & 2nd st: sn wknd) ....nk 14
3759[17] Poly Screen **(43)***(18) (CASmith)* 4-7-7 JLowe(12) (bit bkwd: chsd ldrs: 3rd st: wknd over 3f out: t.o) 9 15
4166[19] Tigersong (USA) **(64)** *(MissMKMilligan)* 5-9-0 DeanMcKeown(19) (a bhd: t.o fnl 4f) ....dist 16

LONG HANDICAP Charmed Life 6-8 Poly Screen 7-3

7/2 CUANGO (IRE), **11/2** Sea Freedom, **6/1** Fabillion (op 3/1), **8/1** Requested, Pumice, **10/1** Fabulous Mtoto, **12/1** Harry Welsh (IRE), General Mouktar, **14/1** Quest Again, **16/1** Soba Up, Tilty (USA), **20/1** Prussia, Antartictern (USA), **33/1** Poly Screen, **50/1** Charmed Life, Tigersong (USA), CSF £25.50 CT £254.90 TOTE £3.60: £1.10 £2.80 £5.10 £3.10 (£17.60) Trio £136.90 OWNER Barouche Stud Ltd (UPPER LONGDON) BRED Citadel Stud Establishment 16 Rn

3m 6.3 (7.80) SF: 47/44/56/40/57/41/50/31/40/52/20/24/11/24/-/-

WEIGHT FOR AGE 3yo-9lb

4249

WOODTHORPE H'CAP (0-70) (3-Y.O) (Class E) £3,960.00 (£1,188.00: £572.00: £264.00) **1m 54y** Stalls: Low GOING: 0.06 sec per fur (G) 4-20 (4-21)

3889[18] **Bellateena (49)***(61) (HJCollingridge)* 3-8-0 JQuinn(19) (a.p: 2nd st: led over 3f out: sn clr: hld on cl home) ....— 1
3980[3] Cuban Reef **(45)***(57) (WJMusson)* 3-7-10 AMackay(12) (hld up & bhd: plld hrd & rapid hdwy appr fnl f: jst failed) ....s.h 2
4136[4] Super High **(58)***(70) (PHowling)* 3-8-9 RCochrane(14) (hld up in tch: effrt over 2f out: styd on fnl f) ....s.h 3
4157* Barrel of Hope **(70)***(79) (JLEyre)* 3-9-7b SDWilliams(18) (lw: chsd ldrs: 5th st: rdn over 2f out: one pce fnl f) 1¼ 4
4157[2] Lynton Lad **(70)***(79) (CPEBrooks)* 3-9-0b(7) SCopp(15) (lw: hld up mid div: hdwy u.p over 2f out: r.o wl fnl f) ....s.h 5
4194* Master Charter **(56)***(63) (MrsJRRamsden)* 3-8-7 SSanders(9) (lw: hld up: hdwy on ins over 3f out: no ex fnl f) 1¼ 6

4043* Hatta Breeze **(65)***(72)*(Fav)*(MAJarvis)* 3-8-13b(3) DRMcCabe(2) (led tl hdd over 3f out: sn wknd: eased whn btn)....s.h 7
3980 13 Risky Romeo **(62)***(66) (GCBravery)* 3-8-13 MHills(3) (bhd: hdwy 2f out: nvr nrr)....1¼ 8
4043 9 Mnemonic **(50)***(52) (HCandy)* 3-8-1 NAdams(17) (lw: chsd ldrs: rdn & nt qckn appr fnl f)....1¼ 9
4156 2 Pelleman **(68)***(66) (RBoss)* 3-9-5 WRyan(10) (lw: hld up mid div: effrt & rdn over 2f out: kpt on u.p fnl f)....2 10
4052 4 Ozubeck (USA) **(52)***(46) (BHanbury)* 3-8-0 (3)ow3 JStack(20) (s.s: n.d)....¾ 11
3973 9 El Don **(48)***(41) (MJRyan)* 3-7-13 GBardwell(13) (prom: 4th st: wknd 3f out)....1¾ 12
3980 8 Pc's Cruiser (IRE) **(49)***(42) (JLEyre)* 3-7-11v(3) NVarley(1) (sn drvn along: 6th st: sn lost tch) .nk 13
4115 7 Almasi (IRE) **(57)***(49) (CFWall)* 3-8-8 WWoods(6) (in tch over 5f)....nk 14
3653 12 Jilly Beveled **(46)***(37) (RHannon)* 3-7-11 NCarlisle(5) (swtg: bhd: effrt & nt clr run over 2f out: n.d)....½ 15
1547 4 Farmer's Tern (IRE) **(60)***(51) (WJarvis)* 3-8-11 MTebbutt(8) (hld up: plld hrd: effrt 3f out: nvr nr ldrs)....s.h 16
732 13 La Dama (USA) **(48)***(36) (FJO'Mahony)* 3-7-13 TWilliams(11) (s.s: a bhd)....1¾ 17
Storm Flash **(68)***(55) (LordHuntingdon)* 3-9-5 DHarrison(16) (lw: nvr nr ldrs)....nk 18
4156 14 Spumante **(64)***(34) (RChampion)* 3-9-1 AMcGlone(4) (prom: 3rd st: wknd 3f out: t.o)....9 19
4043 R Run-Do-Run **(56)***(21) (HJCollingridge)* 3-8-7 ow2 MRimmer(7) (b.off hind: s.v.s: a t.o)....1¼ 20

11/4 Hatta Breeze, **4/1** Master Charter (5/2-9/2), **5/1** Barrel of Hope, **10/1** Pelleman, **11/1** Cuban Reef, **12/1** Lynton Lad (op 8/1), **16/1** Super High, **20/1** El Don, Risky Romeo, Almasi (IRE), Farmer's Tern (IRE), Jilly Beveled, Pc's Cruiser (IRE), Storm Flash, **25/1** Mnemonic, BELLATEENA, **33/1** Ozubeck (USA), Run-Do-Run, Spumante, **50/1** La Dama (USA), CSF £284.53 CT £4,135.24 TOTE £59.60: £7.70 £1.80 £3.70 £1.80 (£172.60) Trio £527.50; £445.79 to Newmarket 27/10/95 OWNER Mr N. H. Gardner (NEWMARKET) BRED N. H. Gardner 20 Rn
1m 45.9 (6.30) SF: 27/23/36/45/45/29/38/32/18/32/12/7/8/15/3/17/2/21/-/-

T/Jkpt: Not won; £3,984.97 to Bangor 27/10/95. T/Plpt: £105.70 (154.6 Tckts). T/Qdpt: £37.00 (3.2 Tckts). IM

3578a-DEAUVILLE (France) (R-H)
Tuesday October 17th (Good to soft)

4250a PRIX ECLIPSE (Gp 3) (2-Y.O) £26,347.00 (£9,581.00: £4,790.00: £2,395.00) 6f 110y
3-10 (3-11)

3793a 4 **Titus Livius (FR)** *(101) (JEPease,France)* 2-9-2 CAsmussen....— 1
3483a 2 Starmaniac (USA) *(96) (CLaffon-Parias,France)* 2-8-11 GMosse....nse 2
Seattle Special (USA) *(88) (MmeCHead,France)* 2-8-8 ODoleuze....2 3
3893* Apple Musashi *(89) (JHMGosden)* 2-8-11 OPeslier....1 4
3375 4 Rabican (IRE) *(74) (GCBravery)* 2-8-11 MHills (btn approx 11¼l).... 9

P-M 2.40F: 1.30F 2.00F 1.70F (DF 11.10F) OWNER Mr S. S. Niarchos BRED S. Niarchos 9 Rn
1m 15.2 SF: -/-/-/-/-

4176a-LONGCHAMP (Paris, France) (R-H)
Sunday October 22nd (Firm)

4251a PRIX DES RESERVOIRS (Gp 3) (2-Y.O F) £26,347.00 (£9,581.00: £4,790.00) 7f 110y
1-35 (1-33)

Occupandiste (IRE) *(MmeCHead,France)* 2-8-9 ODoleuze....— 1
3786a 3 Raisonnable *(DSepulchre,France)* 2-8-9 CAsmussen....2 2
Prevail (USA) *(PBary,France)* 2-8-9 DBoeuf....1½ 3

P-M 3.80F: 1.40F 1.10F (SF 8.30F) OWNER Mr J. Wertheimer (FRANCE) BRED J. Wertheimer & Frere 5 Rn
1m 38.0 SF: -/-/-

4252a PRIX ROYAL-OAK (Gp 1) (3-Y.O+) £47,904.00 (£19,162.00: £9,581.00: £4,790.00) 1m 7f 110y
2-40 (2-47)

2213a 5 **Sunshack** *(122) (AFabre,France)* 4-9-4 TJarnet (5th early: swtchd & hdwy to ld 1½f out: qckd clr: impressive)....— 1
Shrewd Idea *(119) (CLaffon-Parias,France)* 5-9-4 ODoleuze (led tl hdd by wnr: r.o gamely u.p)....2½ 2
4014a 16 Sunrise Song (FR) *(116) (FDoumen,France)* 4-9-1 GMosse (4th early: chal over 1f out: no ex cl hme)....s.nk 3

4014a[7] Partipral (USA) *(118) (ELellouche,France)* 6-9-4 OPeslier (racd in 3rd: rdn 4f out: r.o one pce) 1½ 4
3946[2] Assessor (IRE) *(116) (RHannon)* 6-9-4 RHughes (rr early: 6th st: styd on fnl f) 2 5
3329a* Peckinpah's Soul (FR) *(107) (DSmaga,France)* 3-8-9 FHead (trckd ldr: 2nd st: chal 2f out: wknd over 1f out) 8 6
4014a[12] Tot Ou Tard (IRE) *(101) (JForesi,France)* 5-9-4 ESaint-Martin (m.n.s) 6 7

P-M 1.90F: 1.60F 4.70F (23.70F) OWNER Mr K. Abdullah (FRANCE) BRED Juddmonte Farms 7 Rn 3m 16.2 SF: -/-/-/-/-/-/-

4253a PRIX DU PETIT COUVERT (Gp 3) £26,347.00 (£9,581.00: £4,790.00) **5f** 3-10 (3-14)

4012a[6] **Millyant** *(115) (RGuest)* 5-10-0 CAsmussen ....— 1
4121* Royale Figurine (IRE) *(107) (MJFetherston-Godley)* 4-9-7 JReid (fin 3rd btn s.nk & nse: plcd 2nd) 2
4012a[11] Bruttina *(106) (MmePBarbe,France)* 3-9-7b TThulliez (fin 4th btn snk, nse & 3/4l: plcd 3rd) 3
4033[2] Fire Dome (IRE) *(102) (RHannon)* 3-9-11 RHughes (btn approx 3 3/4l) 6

P-M 2.80F: 1.20F 1.20F (SF 5.40F) OWNER Mr C. Mills (NEWMARKET) BRED Jim and Mrs Strange 7 Rn 66.9 secs (1.90) SF: -/-/-/-
STEWARDS' ENQUIRY Windmachine (SWE) finished second, but was disqualified for interference and placed fifth.

4094a-DUSSELDORF (Germany) (R-H)
Sunday October 22nd (Soft)

4254a PREIS DER SPIELBANKEN DES LANDES (Gp 3) (3-Y.O+) £20,576.00 (£8,230.00: £4,938.00) **1m 4f** 3-10 (3-11)

3914a[8] **Caballo (GER)** *(119) (HJentzsch,Germany)* 4-9-0 PSchiergen ....— 1
4018a[8] Sir King (GER) *(119) (RSuerland,Germany)* 3-8-8 TMundry ....½ 2
4009a[9] Syvanie (FR) *(107) (FDoumen,France)* 3-7-13 PBruneau 2½ 3

Tote 43DM: 21DM 30DM 55DM (SF 370DM) OWNER Gestut Fahrhof BRED Gestut Fahrhof in Germany 12 Rn 2m 37.21 SF: -/-/-

4116-NEWMARKET (R-H)
Friday October 27th (Good to firm)
WEATHER: cloudy WIND: mod half bhd

4255 E.B.F. RED LODGE MAIDEN STKS (2-Y.O) (Class D) £4,620.00 (£1,380.00: £660.00: £300.00) **6f** Stalls: Low GOING minus 0.39 sec per fur (F) 1-00 (1-00)

4153[2] **Farhana** *(64+)*(Fav)*(WJarvis)* 2-8-9 TQuinn(3) (b.off hind: trckd ldrs: led 2f out: rdn out) ....— 1
3996[4] Ocean Stream (IRE) **(73)***(68) (JLEyre)* 2-9-0 DeanMcKeown(8) (trckd ldrs: ev ch 2f out: unable qckn ins fnl f) ....½ 2
Cerdan (USA) *(67) (MRStoute)* 2-9-0 JReid(6) (w'like: scope: hld up: hdwy 2f out: no ex ins fnl f) ....hd 3
4154[9] Sea Danzig *(57) (PHowling)* 2-9-0 RCochrane(7) (led after 2f to 2f out) 4 4
3900[21] White Plains (IRE) *(55) (MBell)* 2-9-0 MFenton(4) (bhd tl r.o fnl 2f) ....½ 5
Ballymoney (IRE) *(49) (WAO'Gorman)* 2-9-0 EmmaO'Gorman(1) (w'like: leggy: ev ch 2f out: sn btn) 2½ 6
4154[7] Ret Frem (IRE) *(48) (MAJarvis)* 2-9-0 PRobinson(5) (led 2f: wknd 2f out) ....nk 7
Needle Match *(39) (CFWall)* 2-9-0 GDuffield(2) (unf: bit bkwd: outpcd) 3½ 8

1/2 FARHANA (op 4/5), **4/1** Cerdan (USA) (op 5/2), **10/1** Ocean Stream (IRE) (6/1-11/1), **20/1** Ret Frem (IRE), Needle Match, Ballymoney (IRE), **25/1** White Plains (IRE), **33/1** Sea Danzig, CSF £6.56 TOTE £1.50: £1.10 £2.30 £1.40 (£5.10) OWNER Mr A. Foustok (NEWMARKET) BRED Ahmed M. Foustok 8 Rn 1m 13.08 SF: 36/40/39/29/27/21/20/11

4256 NGK SPARK PLUGS SOHAM HOUSE CONDITIONS STKS (2-Y.O) (Class C) £5,156.00 (£1,856.00: £888.00: £360.00) **1m (Rowley)** Stalls: Low GOING minus 0.39 sec per fur (F) 1-30 (1-30)

4207[3] **Believe Me (97)***(99?) (RHannon)* 2-8-10 (5) DaneO'Neill(3) (mde all: rdn & hld on wl fnl f) ....— 1

4203[6] Astuti (IRE) **(94)***(87) (APJarvis)* 2-8-6 JTate(1) (hld up: hdwy 3f out: ev ch over 1f out: no ex fnl f)....................1¾ 2
4042[2] Bullfinch **(96)***(91)*(Fav)*(PTWalwyn)* 2-8-11 DHarrison(5) (hld up & plld hrd: hdwy & ev ch wl over 1f out: r.o ins fnl f)....................hd 3
Northern Fleet *(88) (GHarwood)* 2-8-11 AClark(4) (gd sort: chsd ldrs: ev ch 3f out: no ex appr fnl f)....................1¾ 4
Candle Smoke (USA) *(58) (GHarwood)* 2-8-11 TQuinn(2) (lengthy: scope: prom 4f: sn rdn & wknd)....................15 5

11/8 Bullfinch, **3/1** Astuti (IRE), **4/1** BELIEVE ME, **7/1** Candle Smoke (USA) (4/1-15/2), **11/1** Northern Fleet (5/1-12/1), CSF £14.42 TOTE £4.40: £1.80 £1.50 (£7.40) OWNER Mr Bruce Adams (MARLBOROUGH) BRED Derek R. Price 5 Rn 1m 38.74 (1.74) SF: 49/37/41/38/8

4257 JAMES SEYMOUR STKS (Listed) (3-Y.O+) (Class A) £11,872.80 (£4,096.80: £1,958.40: £792.00)

1m 2f Stalls: Low GOING minus 0.39 sec per fur (F) 2-05 (2-06)

4031* **Quandary (USA) (95)***(103)*(Fav)*(HRACecil)* 4-8-9 WRyan(3) (mde all: shkn up 2f out: clr fnl f)....................— 1
4163* Jagellon (USA) **(72)***(98) (WRMuir)* 4-9-0 TQuinn(1) (chsd wnr: rdn over 2f out: kpt on same pce)....................6 2
3845* Star of Zilzal (USA) **(102)***(98) (MRStoute)* 3-8-9 JReid(2) (hld up & plld hrd: hdwy 3f out: chsd wnr 2f out: sn rdn: wknd fnl f)....................s.h 3
3926[2] Alkateb **(91)***(97) (MissGayKelleway)* 3-8-9 RCochrane(4) (hld up: rdn over 3f out: nvr able chal)....................¾ 4

5/6 QUANDARY (USA), **7/2** Star of Zilzal (USA) (7/4-4/1), **4/1** Alkateb, **11/2** Jagellon (USA), CSF £5.25 TOTE £1.70 (£3.00) OWNER Mr K. Abdulla (NEWMARKET) BRED Juddmonte Farms 4 Rn
2m 3.53 SF: 54/49/44/43
WEIGHT FOR AGE 3yo-5lb

4258 GEORGE STUBBS RATED STKS H'CAP (0-105) (Listed) (3-Y.O+) (Class A) £11,053.44 (£4,080.96: £1,950.48: £788.40)

2m (Rowley) Stalls: High GOING minus 0.39 sec per fur (F) 2-40 (2-40)

4076[4] **Daraydan (IRE) (96)***(112) (LadyHerries)* 3-8-4 KDarley(5) (trckd ldrs: rdn 3f out: disp ld fnl f: led last strides)....................— 1
3930* Kristal's Paradise (IRE) **(89)***(105) (JLDunlop)* 3-7-11 JQuinn(1) (trckd ldr tl led over 3f out: rdn fnl f: ct nr fin)....................hd 2
4191* Old Rouvel (USA) **(103)***(113) (DJGMurraySmith)* 4-9-7 MHills(6) (hdwy 3f out: r.o wl fnl f).......6 3
4118[5] Saleel (IRE) **(93)***(102)*(Fav)*(ACStewart)* 3-8-1 RHills(4) (hdwy 6f out: rdn 3f out: sn ev ch: one pce appr fnl f)....................¾ 4
4118[10] Shonara's Way **(89)***(98) (RCharlton)* 4-8-7 JReid(3) (bhd: pushed along 6f out: nvr rchd ldrs)....................½ 5
3930[6] Latahaab (USA) **(89)***(97) (RAkehurst)* 4-8-7 TQuinn(2) (chsd ldrs 12f)....................¾ 6
3995[3] Tethys (USA) **(89)***(96) (JLEyre)* 4-8-7 DeanMcKeown(7) (led over 12f: wknd 2f out)..............¾ 7
LONG HANDICAP Tethys (USA) 7-11 Latahaab (USA) 8-5

5/2 Saleel (IRE) (2/1-3/1), **9/2** Kristal's Paradise (IRE), **5/1** DARAYDAN (IRE), **11/2** Shonara's Way, **6/1** Latahaab (USA) (4/1-7/1), **7/1** Old Rouvel (USA) (10/1-6/1), **33/1** Tethys (USA), CSF £24.13 TOTE £5.80: £2.40 £2.90 (£14.70) OWNER Mr P. D. Savill (LITTLEHAMPTON) BRED H.H.Aga Khan Stud Farms S.C. 7 Rn 3m 24.52 (1.22) SF: 52/45/63/42/48/47/46
WEIGHT FOR AGE 3yo-10lb

4259 NGK SPARK PLUGS H'CAP (0-70) (3-Y.O+ F & M) (Class E) £5,283.00 (£1,584.00: £762.00: £351.00)

1m 4f (Rowley) Stalls: High GOING minus 0.39 sec per fur (F) 3-15 (3-19)

4149* **Snow Princess (IRE) (69)***(86)*(Fav)*(LordHuntingdon)* 3-9-8 4x RHills(8) (pushed along 4f out: hdwy 2f out: led ins fnl f: rdn out)....................— 1
4136[3] Lidhama (USA) **(58)***(73) (GLewis)* 3-8-11 SWhitworth(12) (hdwy 3f out: led 1f out: sn hdd & unable qckn)....................1¼ 2
3531[2] Douce Maison (IRE) **(54)***(67) (APJarvis)* 4-9-0 JTate(14) (chsd ldrs: n.m.r appr fnl f: r.o)....................1½ 3
3889[3] Ruby Heights **(51)***(62) (RHannon)* 4-8-6 (5) DaneO'Neill(19) (trckd ldrs: rdn to ld wl over 1f out: hdd 1f out: nt qckn)....................2 4
4126[8] Pass Mark **(60)***(70) (JRFanshawe)* 3-8-13 WRyan(18) (prom 10f)....................½ 5
4135[3] All the Joys **(42)***(50) (CACyzer)* 4-8-2 DBiggs(17) (gd hdwy over 1f out: nrst fin)..................1½ 6

3743[10] Masuri Kabisa (USA) **(37)***(41) (HJCollingridge)* 4-7-11v JQuinn(10) (hdwy 5f out: ev ch over 2f out: wknd over 1f out) 3 **7**
4135[5] Emma Grimes (IRE) **(39)***(42) (JSMoore)* 4-7-13 ow1 JFEgan(24) (chsd ldrs: pushed along 6f out: kpt on fnl 2f) ....s.h **8**
3464[8] Tirolette (IRE) **(59)***(62) (RJRWilliams)* 3-8-12b RCochrane(13) (hld up: rdn over 3f out) 1 **9**
3676[9] Persian Smoke **(39)***(42) (AHide)* 4-7-8 (5) MHenry(1) (prom 9f) ....hd **10**
4000* Ayunli **(64)***(66) (SCWilliams)* 4-9-10 KDarley(3) (prom: ev ch tl wknd over 1f out: eased ins fnl f) ....¾ **11**
3875[7] La Brief **(49)***(49) (MJRyan)* 3-7-11 (5) MBaird(6) (bhd: hdwy 4f out: nvr rchd ldrs) 1¼ **12**
4061[8] Hattaafeh (IRE) **(55)***(55) (MAJarvis)* 4-9-1 WWoods(23) (rdn 4f out: n.d) ....hd **13**
3641[4] Smocking **(33)***(31) (JPearce)* 5-7-7 GBardwell(2) (prom: led 2f out: sn hdd & wknd) 1 **14**
3847[4] Mafuta (IRE) **(47)***(44) (JJSheehan)* 3-7-9 (5) PPMurphy(11) (stdd s: nvr nr ldrs) ....¾ **15**
3710[21] Queens Stroller (IRE) **(52)***(45) (CCElsey)* 4-8-12 MHills(22) (led 10f: sn wknd) 3 **16**
4168[3] College Night (IRE) **(51)***(36) (CADwyer)* 3-8-1 (3) PMcCabe(15) (a bhd) 6 **17**
3971[5] Bobby's Dream **(44)***(28) (MHTompkins)* 3-7-11 DaleGibson(9) (chsd ldrs 9f) 1 **18**
4171[12] Failte Ro **(63)***(46) (JEBanks)* 3-8-11 (5) AWhelan(5) (hld up: plld hrd: effrt 4f out) ....½ **19**
4000[16] Fresh Look (IRE) **(45)***(28) (RCSpicer)* 3-7-9 (3) NVarley(16) (chsd ldrs tl wknd 3f out) ....½ **20**
4138[8] No Comebacks **(60)***(42) (EJAlston)* 7-9-6 JCarroll(21) (a bhd) ....¾ **21**
4101[2] Pat's Splendour **(47)***(26) (HJCollingridge)* 4-8-7 ow1 MRimmer(4) (in tch 7f) 1¼ **22**
4101[11] Comtec's Legend **(34)***(14) (JFBottomley)* 5-7-8 JLowe(7) (rdn 4f out: a bhd) ....s.h **23**

7/2 SNOW PRINCESS (IRE), **7/1** Ayunli, **8/1** Lidhama (USA), **11/1** Masuri Kabisa (USA) (8/1-12/1), **12/1** Douce Maison (IRE) (op 8/1), **14/1** Bobby's Dream (10/1-16/1), Ruby Heights, All the Joys, Pat's Splendour (10/1-16/1), **16/1** Hattaafeh (IRE), Tirolette (IRE), **20/1** Pass Mark, No Comebacks, Smocking, Mafuta (IRE), **25/1** Queens Stroller (IRE), College Night (IRE), Failte Ro, Fresh Look (IRE), **33/1** Emma Grimes (IRE), Persian Smoke, La Brief, Comtec's Legend, CSF £33.65 CT £300.66 TOTE £4.70: £1.70 £3.50 £2.50 £2.70 (£22.10) Trio £116.40 OWNER Lord Weinstock & The Hon Simon Weinstock (WEST ILSLEY) BRED Ballymacoll Stud Co 23 Rn
2m 30.23 (0.93) SF: 68/55/56/51/52/39/30/31/44/31/55/31/44/20/26/34/18/10/28/10/31/15/3
WEIGHT FOR AGE 3yo-7lb

4260 POTTER NURSERY H'CAP (2-Y.O) (Class D) £4,347.00 (£1,296.00: £618.00: £279.00)

5f Stalls: Low GOING minus 0.39 sec per fur (F) 3-50 (3-51)

4237* **Dande Flyer (67)***(73+)*(Fav)*(DWPArbuthnot)* 2-8-3 7x BDoyle(6) (lw: b.nr hind: hld up: hdwy & n.m.r over 1f out: led 1f out: rdn & qknd clr) ....— **1**
4077[10] Lady Caroline Lamb (IRE) **(60)***(58) (MRChannon)* 2-7-10 FNorton(5) (chsd ldrs: led over 1f out: sn hdd & outpcd) 2½ **2**
4206[7] Antonias Melody **(70)***(64) (SRBowring)* 2-8-1 (5) CTeague(2) (led over 3f: wknd ins fnl f) 1¼ **3**
3824[4] Thai Morning **(71)***(61) (PWHarris)* 2-8-7 GHind(8) (chsd ldrs 3f) 1¼ **4**
3990[9] U-No-Harry (IRE) **(69)***(53) (RHollinshead)* 2-8-0 (5) MHenry(4) (sn rdn along: outpcd) 1¾ **5**
3803[3] Playmaker **(79)***(52) (JBerry)* 2-9-1 JCarroll(7) (w ldrs 3f) 3½ **6**
4097* Swynford Dream **(85)***(56) (JFBottomley)* 2-9-7 JLowe(1) (w ldrs over 3f) ....¾ **7**
4112[2] Amy Leigh (IRE) **(82)***(14) (CaptJWilson)* 2-9-4 GCarter(3) (chsd ldrs: rdn 2f out: no imp) 12 **8**

15/8 DANDE FLYER (5/2-4/1), **11/4** Swynford Dream, **6/1** Playmaker, Thai Morning, **8/1** Lady Caroline Lamb (IRE), **14/1** Amy Leigh (IRE) (8/1-16/1), Antonias Melody (7/1-16/1), **33/1** U-No-Harry (IRE), CSF £16.31 CT £149.65 TOTE £2.50: £1.30 £2.00 £4.10 (£9.40) OWNER Dandelion Distribution Ltd (COMPTON) BRED G. Syvrett 8 Rn 59.58 secs SF: 33/18/24/21/13/12/16/-

4261 AVENUE APPRENTICE H'CAP (0-70) (3-Y.O) (Class E) £4,402.50 (£1,320.00: £635.00: £292.50)

1m 1f (Rowley) Stalls: Low GOING minus 0.39 sec per fur (F) 4-25 (4-26)

3965[2] **Shining Example (67)***(83) (PJMakin)* 3-9-4 (3) RHavlin(15) (trckd ldrs: rdn to ld ins fnl f: rdn out) ....— **1**
3897[14] Ramsdens (IRE) **(65)***(81) (WJHaggas)* 3-9-0 (5) ElizabethTurner(4) (led tl hdd & no ex ins fnl f) ....nk **2**
3959[4] Pedaltothemetal (IRE) **(44)***(54) (PMitchell)* 3-7-7 (5)ow1 DSweeney(6) (hld up: hdwy 2f out: kpt on wl u.p fnl f) 2½ **3**
4164[7] Bakheta **(45)***(55) (KTIvory)* 3-7-10 (3) MartinDwyer(13) (trckd ldrs: ev ch over 1f out: one pce) ½ **4**
4136[2] Battleship Bruce **(61)***(70)*(Fav)*(NACallaghan)* 3-9-1 DaneO'Neill(5) (lw: b.hind: chsd ldrs: ev ch 2f out: no ex appr fnl f) ....¾ **5**
3872[10] Harvey White (IRE) **(56)***(64) (JPearce)* 3-8-5 (5) MNutter(11) (hdwy 4f out: nt qckn appr fnl f) ....nk **6**

3685[18] Fern's Governor **(46)***(52) (WJMusson)* 3-7-9 (5)ow2 JWilkinson(3) (dwlt: hdwy 2f out: kpt on wl fnl f) ....nk **7**
4233[4] Almuhtaram **(64)***(70) (MissGayKelleway)* 3-9-4b AWhelan(16) (in tch: n.m.r 3f out: rdn & kpt on fnl 2f) 1 **8**
3889* Princess Danielle **(58)***(60) (CCElsey)* 3-8-12 JDSmith(19) (prom tl wknd appr fnl f) 2½ **9**
4152[12] Kellaire Girl (IRE) **(44)***(45) (GLewis)* 3-7-9 (3) PFessey(12) (in tch tl rdn & btn 2f out) ....s.h **10**
3959[5] Alpine Storm (IRE) **(39)***(38) (MDIUsher)* 3-7-4 (3) CAdamson(17) (bhd: effrt 3f out: nvr rchd ldrs) 1¼ **11**
3920[14] Miss Jemmima **(54)***(50) (LordHuntingdon)* 3-8-8 MHenry(1) (w ldr tl wknd wl over 1f out) 2 **12**
4170[8] Care And Comfort **(62)***(52) (KMcAuliffe)* 3-8-13 (3) ADaly(10) (w ldrs 6f) 3 **13**
3531[5] Wet Patch (IRE) **(61)***(51) (RHannon)* 3-8-12 (3) MarkDenaro(8) (rdn 4f out: nvr nr ldrs) ....hd **14**
2789[W] Nyali Beach (IRE) **(42)***(31) (DrJDScargill)* 3-7-10 PPMurphy(2) (trckd ldrs: rdn 2f out: sn btn) ½ **15**
3099[4] Kirov Protege (IRE) **(43)***(31) (HJCollingridge)* 3-7-6 (5) JoHunnam(9) (in tch 6f) ....¾ **16**
4044[16] Autumn Cover **(50)***(34) (RMFlower)* 3-8-4b LNewton(7) (in tch 5f: sn rdn & btn) 2½ **17**
4044[14] Our Tom **(58)***(38) (JWharton)* 3-8-12 MBaird(18) (chsd ldrs tl wknd 3f out) 2 **18**
4049[5] Rockusa **(48)***(18) (PRHedger)* 3-8-2 ow1 DGriffiths(14) (prom 4f: sn bhd: wknd appr fnl f) 5 **19**

LONG HANDICAP Alpine Storm (IRE) 6-10

3/1 Battleship Bruce, **5/1** Wet Patch (IRE), **11/2** SHINING EXAMPLE, **11/1** Princess Danielle, **12/1** Kirov Protege (IRE), **14/1** Almuhtaram (10/1-16/1), **16/1** Kellaire Girl (IRE), Pedaltothemetal (IRE), Rockusa, **20/1** Harvey White (IRE), Our Tom, **25/1** Miss Jemmima, Ramsdens (IRE), Autumn Cover, Nyali Beach (IRE), **33/1** Fern's Governor, Alpine Storm (IRE), Care And Comfort, Bakheta, CSF £125.68 CT £1,899.52 TOTE £5.00: £1.60 £11.10 £3.40 £15.30 (£108.80) Trio £1,159.20 OWNER Mr D. M. Ahier (MARLBOROUGH) BRED Stetchworth Park Stud Ltd 19 Rn

1m 51.71 (2.01) SF: 55/53/26/27/42/36/24/42/32/17/10/22/24/23/3/3/6/10/-

T/Plpt: £66.80 (218.25 Tckts). T/Qdpt: £28.10 (5.2 Tckts). Dk

4255-NEWMARKET (R-H)
Saturday October 28th (Good to firm)

WEATHER: fine WIND: slt across

4262 E.B.F. BALATON LODGE MAIDEN STKS (2-Y.O F) (Class D)

£5,166.00 (£1,548.00: £744.00: £342.00)
7f (Rowley) Stalls: Centre GOING minus 0.39 sec per fur (F) 1-00 (1-00)

4085[3] **Awaamir** *(84+)*(Fav)*(JHMGosden)* 2-8-11 RHills(7) (trckd ldrs: qcknd to ld 1f out: easily) ....— **1**
4148[6] Chalk Dust (USA) *(79) (PFICole)* 2-8-11 TQuinn(13) (lw: wnt rt s: prom: led over 1f out: sn hdd & unable qckn) 2 **2**
3867[8] Lyzia (IRE) **(84)***(77) (CEBrittain)* 2-8-11 BDoyle(4) (led after 2f tl over 1f out: one pce) 1¼ **3**
Really A Dream (IRE) *(74+) (MRStoute)* 2-8-11 JReid(12) (w'like: leggy: trckd ldrs: rdn 2f out: kpt on one pce) 1¼ **4**
Bathilde (IRE) *(71+) (MRStoute)* 2-8-11 KBradshaw(20) (leggy: lt-f: in tch: rdn & edgd lft 2f out: r.o fnl f) 1 **5**
Lady Joshua (IRE) *(69) (JLDunlop)* 2-8-11 GCarter(1) (leggy: unf: chsd ldrs: one pce fnl 2f) ..1 **6**
Mountain Holly *(68) (DRLoder)* 2-8-11 RHughes(8) (leggy: scope: dwlt: hdwy over 1f out: nrst fin) ....½ **7**
On Fair Stage (IRE) *(66) (MRStoute)* 2-8-11 KDarley(19) (lt-f: unf: prom 4f) ....¾ **8**
3379[7] Fran Godfrey *(65) (PTWalwyn)* 2-8-11 DHarrison(17) (prom tl wknd appr fnl f) ....½ **9**
Passage Creeping (IRE) *(65) (LMCumani)* 2-8-11 WRyan(10) (leggy: scope: nvr nr to chal) s.h **10**
Wolf Cleugh (IRE) *(64) (AHide)* 2-8-11 JWilliams(18) (lt-f: n.d) ....½ **11**
4103[12] Blessed Spirit *(63) (CFWall)* 2-8-11 WWoods(14) (in tch over 4f) ....nk **12**
Tart *(60) (RFJohnsonHoughton)* 2-8-11 AMcGlone(2) (lengthy: scope: in tch: pushed along over 3f out: sn btn) 1¼ **13**
3948[13] Sylvella *(57) (MAJarvis)* 2-8-8 (3) DRMcCabe(3) (bhd fnl 3f) 1½ **14**
3758[5] Smile Forever (USA) *(56) (PFICole)* 2-8-11 CRutter(9) (nvr plcd to chal) ....½ **15**
4155[8] Belmarita (IRE) *(56) (MHTompkins)* 2-8-11 PRobinson(5) (led 2f: eased whn btn fnl f) ....hd **16**
Bellaphento *(54) (RJRWilliams)* 2-8-11 RCochrane(15) (leggy: unf: hmpd & s.i.s: a bhd) ....½ **17**
Victim of Love *(54) (RCharlton)* 2-8-11 TSprake(6) (cmpt: a bhd) ....nk **18**
Antiguan Jane *(33) (RWArmstrong)* 2-8-11 RPrice(11) (unf: scope: bkwd: reluctant to r fr ½-wy: t.o) 9 **19**

2/1 AWAAMIR, **11/4** Really A Dream (IRE), **7/1** Chalk Dust (USA) (5/1-8/1), **8/1** Lyzia (IRE) (6/1-9/1), **10/1** Mountain Holly (op 6/1), **20/1** Passage Creeping (IRE), Victim of Love, Blessed Spirit, **25/1** On Fair Stage (IRE), Fran Godfrey, Smile Forever (USA), **33/1** Belmarita (IRE), Lady Joshua (IRE), Bellaphento, Tart, **50/1** Wolf Cleugh (IRE), Sylvella, Bathilde (IRE), Antiguan Jane, CSF £17.69 TOTE £3.40: £1.60 £2.50 £3.00 (£11.30) Trio £40.30 OWNER Mr Hamdan Al Maktoum (NEWMARKET) BRED Shadwell Estate Company Limited 19 Rn

1m 26.4 (2.70) SF: 31/26/24/21/18/16/15/13/12/12/11/10/7/4/3/3/1/1/-

4263 NGK SPARK PLUGS (S) STKS (2-Y.O) (Class E) £4,012.50 (£1,200.00: £575.00: £262.50) **1m (Rowley)** Stalls: Centre GOING minus 0.39 sec per fur (F) 1-35 (1-35)

4048[7] **Polar Spirit** *(68) (WJHaggas)* 2-8-6 RHills(10) (trckd ldrs: led over 1f out: rdn & hld on wl ins fnl f)...— 1
4172[5] Sharp Shuffle (IRE) **(64)***(73)*(Fav)*(RHannon)* 2-8-11 JReid(1) (rdn 4f out: rdn over 2f out: ev ch over 1f out: r.o)..hd 2
3985[11] State Approval **(55)***(69) (APJarvis)* 2-8-11 JTate(11) (w ldrs: led over 2f out to over 1f out: kpt on)..2 3
4107[9] Balpare **(57)***(59) (NACallaghan)* 2-8-10 ow1 RHughes(15) (hld up: hdwy 2f out: no imp fnl 2f)..4 4
4081[9] Needle Knot (IRE) **(56)***(56) (MJohnston)* 2-8-11 KDarley(3) (chsd ldrs: no hdwy fnl 2f).........2½ 5
3625[11] Righteous Gent *(51) (KMcAuliffe)* 2-8-11b JCarroll(4) (w ldrs: rdn over 2f out: sn btn)...........2½ 6
4075[18] On The Wildside *(43) (MRChannon)* 2-8-1 (5) PPMurphy(8) (dwlt: rdn & r.o fnl 2f: nvr nr)......1½ 7
4064[11] Hill Climber *(43) (MBell)* 2-8-11b MFenton(14) (lw: plld hrd & in tch tl wknd 3f out)...............2½ 8
4045[5] Lindas Delight **(52)***(41) (JSMoore)* 2-8-9 JFEgan(9) (b.hind: prom tl wknd 2f out)..................nk 9
4111[5] Silver Welcome **(60)***(45) (MHEasterby)* 2-9-0 MBirch(5) (led over 5f: sn wknd).......................½ 10
3780[5] Bailiwick **(51)***(34) (NAGraham)* 2-8-11 PaulEddery(12) (nvr nr to chal)....................................4 11
4127[2] Bumblefoot (IRE) **(63)***(29) (MJohnston)* 2-8-9 TWilliams(7) (in tch 5f: sn rdn & btn)...............1¼ 12
Glowing Reeds *(19) (PJMcBride)* 2-8-6 GCarter(6) (leggy: lt-f: s.i.s: a bhd)..........................3½ 13
3915[7] Dragonjoy **(53)***(24) (JWPayne)* 2-8-11 AMcGlone(2) (racd alone: a bhd)...............................nk 14

11/4 Sharp Shuffle (IRE), **100/30** POLAR SPIRIT (5/1-3/1), **13/2** Bumblefoot (IRE), **7/1** Silver Welcome (5/1-15/2), **10/1** Balpare (5/1-11/1), **12/1** Needle Knot (IRE), **16/1** State Approval, **20/1** Bailiwick, Lindas Delight, **33/1** Hill Climber, Righteous Gent, **40/1** On The Wildside, Glowing Reeds, Dragonjoy, CSF £12.16 TOTE £4.10: £1.90 £1.60 £6.00 (£5.40) Trio £47.10 OWNER Cheveley Park Stud (NEWMARKET) BRED Miss E. Drax 14 Rn

1m 39.14 (2.14) SF: 37/42/38/28/25/20/12/12/10/14/3/-/-/-
Bt in 8,000 gns

4264 ASKO APPLIANCES ZETLAND STKS (Listed) (2-Y.O) (Class A) £9,246.00 (£3,414.00: £1,632.00: £660.00) **1m 2f** Stalls: Centre GOING minus 0.39 sec per fur (F) 2-10 (2-10)

3846* **Gentilhomme (98)***(102)*(Fav)*(PFICole)* 2-8-11 TQuinn(4) (mde all: rdn wl over 1f out: sn drew clr)...— 1
4139* Weet-A-Minute (IRE) **(90)***(99)*(Fav)*(RHollinshead)* 2-9-2 TIves(6) (hld up: hdwy over 3f out: chsd wnr over 2f out: rdn & btn appr fnl f).......................5 2
4070* Polar Eclipse *(94) (MJohnston)* 2-8-11 JReid(2) (plld hrd: trckd ldrs: lost pl over 2f out: r.o fnl f).......................................s.h 3
4046[5] Zaforum **(86)***(94+) (LMontagueHall)* 2-8-11 BDoyle(3) (chsd ldrs tl drppd rr 4f out: r.o again appr fnl f).......................................hd 4
3858[5] Athenry *(92) (JPearce)* 2-8-11 GBardwell(1) (chsd wnr: rdn 3f out: sn outpcd)........................1 5
4192[3] Exalted (IRE) **(90)***(76) (SirMarkPrescott)* 2-8-11 GDuffield(5) (lw: chsd ldrs 7f).......................10 6

5/2 GENTILHOMME, Weet-A-Minute (IRE), **3/1** Polar Eclipse (op 2/1), **6/1** Exalted (IRE), **7/1** Athenry (op 12/1), **33/1** Zaforum, CSF £8.67 TOTE £3.60: £1.70 £1.50 (£4.40) OWNER H R H Prince Fahd Salman (WHATCOMBE) BRED M. A. Kirby and E. Kessly 6 Rn

2m 6.87 SF: 30/27/22/22/20/4

4265 ASKO APPLIANCES MARSHALL STKS (Listed) (3-Y.O+) (Class A) £11,512.80 (£4,255.20: £2,037.60: £828.00) **1m (Rowley)** Stalls: Centre GOING minus 0.39 sec per fur (F) 2-45 (2-45)

3945[32] **Celestial Key (USA) (100)***(111) (MJohnston)* 5-8-12 PRobinson(6) (lw: hld up: hdwy 2f out: r.o wl to ld last strides)..— 1
3932[5] First Island (IRE) **(106)***(111)*(Fav)*(GWragg)* 3-8-9 MHills(7) (lw: chsd ldrs: swtchd lft wl over 1f out: led wl ins fnl f: ct last strides)..............................s.h 2
3904* Bin Rosie **(104)***(111) (DRLoder)* 3-8-12b KDarley(4) (lw: trckd ldrs: led & qcknd clr over 2f out: hdd & no ex wl ins fnl f).......................................1¼ 3
4121[6] Indian Fly **(101)***(106) (RHannon)* 4-8-12 JReid(1) (lw: plld hrd: trckd ldrs tl hmpd wl over 1f out: n.d after).......................................1¼ 4
4147[4] Clan Ben (IRE) **(98)***(103) (HRACecil)* 3-8-9 WRyan(3) (lw: chsd ldrs: rdn over 2f out: one pce).......................................1¼ 5
4024[5] Louis' Queen (IRE) **(96)***(90) (JLDunlop)* 3-8-4 TQuinn(2) (plld hrd: bhd fnl 3f)............................4 6
4052* Strutting (IRE) **(93)***(68) (RHannon)* 3-8-4 RHills(5) (led over 5f: btn whn bdly hmpd wl over 1f out).......................................11 7

9/4 First Island (IRE), **5/2** Bin Rosie (7/4-11/4), **9/2** Indian Fly, **11/2** Clan Ben (IRE), **9/1** Louis' Queen (IRE), **20/1** Strutting (IRE), **25/1** CELESTIAL KEY (USA), CSF £74.76 TOTE £20.70: £4.90 £2.10 (£30.20) OWNER Mr M. J. Brodrick (MIDDLEHAM) BRED Pillar Stud Inc 7 Rn
1m 36.91 (-0.09) SF: 65/62/62/60/54/41/19
WEIGHT FOR AGE 3yo-3lb

4266 ASKO APPLIANCES QUALITY CONDITIONS STKS (2 & 3-Y.O) (Class C)
£6,744.00 (£2,496.00: £1,198.00: £490.00: £195.00: £77.00)
6f (Rowley) Stalls: Centre GOING minus 0.39 sec per fur (F) 3-20 (3-22)

2597[2] **Elshabiba (USA)** *(88+)*(Fav)*(JLDunlop)* 2-8-5 TQuinn(7) (lw: pushed along in tch: rdn 1f out: led ins fnl f: r.o) — **1**
3273[2] Laafee **(99)***(88) (HThomsonJones)* 2-8-8 RHills(5) (lw: led tl hdd & nt qckn ins fnl f) 1 **2**
4040[17] Latching (IRE) **(72)***(72) (RFJohnsonHoughton)* 3-9-2 JReid(2) (chsd ldr: rdn over 2f out: one pce) 2½ **3**
4145[5] Montserrat **(70)***(72) (LGCottrell)* 3-9-5v MFenton(6) (trckd ldrs: rdn 2f out: kpt on) 1 **4**
4055[4] Monty *(58) (MajorDNChappell)* 3-9-7 WWoods(1) (b.off hind: bhd fnl 3f) 6 **5**
4055[5] Cassimere *(MajorDNChappell)* 3-9-2 RCochrane(4) (wl bhd fnl 4f: eased) dist **6**

4/6 ELSHABIBA (USA), **9/4** Laafee (op 6/4), **8/1** Latching (IRE) (7/1-11/1), **16/1** Montserrat, **33/1** Cassimere, **50/1** Monty, CSF £2.54 TOTE £1.80: £1.40 £1.20 (£1.50) OWNER Mr Hamdan Al Maktoum (ARUNDEL) BRED Shadwell Farm Inc 6 Rn 1m 12.05 (0.75) SF: 47/47/49/49/35/-
WEIGHT FOR AGE 2yo-20lb, 3yo-2lb

4267 LADBROKE AUTUMN H'CAP (0-100) (3-Y.O+) (Class C) £24,083.50
(£9,026.50: £4,425.75: £1,916.25)
1m (Rowley) Stalls: Centre GOING minus 0.39 sec per fur (F) 3-55 (3-59)

4079* **Tarawa (IRE) (91)***(104) (NACallaghan)* 3-9-2 RHughes(21) (lw: trckd ldrs: led over 2f out: rdn & hld on wl fnl f) — **1**
4031[11] Serious **(80)***(91) (LadyHerries)* 5-8-8 PaulEddery(28) (lw: hdwy 2f out: r.o wl fnl f) 1¼ **2**
3943[4] Delta Soleil (USA) **(88)***(98) (PWHarris)* 3-8-13 GHind(9) (hld up: hdwy 3f out: ev ch over 1f out: no ex ins fnl f) ½ **3**
3945[28] Billy Bushwacker **(85)***(94) (MrsMReveley)* 4-8-13b KDarley(4) (hdwy fnl 2f: fin wl) nk **4**
4156[4] Ertlon **(82)***(88) (CEBrittain)* 5-8-10 BDoyle(26) (led 2f: led 4f out tl over 2f out: kpt on) 1½ **5**
4038[3] Noble Sprinter (IRE) **(80)***(86) (RHannon)* 3-8-5b RPerham(13) (led after 2f to 4f out: kpt on fnl 2f) hd **6**
3999[2] Western Fame (USA) **(90)***(95) (JLDunlop)* 3-9-1 TQuinn(18) (lw: hdwy 3f out: ev ch over 1f out: sn hmpd & nt rcvr) ½ **7**
4035[2] Conspicuous (IRE) **(79)***(81) (LGCottrell)* 5-8-7 JQuinn(24) (chsd ldrs: lost pl ½-wy: r.o wl fnl 2f) 1½ **8**
4116[16] Celestial Choir **(81)***(82) (JLEyre)* 5-8-6 (3) NVarley(25) (lw: chsd ldrs: no hdwy fnl 2f) nk **9**
3945[8] Kayvee **(100)***(101) (GHarwood)* 6-10-0 AClark(17) (hld up: hdwy 2f out: r.o) nk **10**
4116[5] Country Lover **(79)***(77) (LordHuntingdon)* 4-8-7 MHills(27) (rdn over 2f out: nvr trbld ldrs) 1½ **11**
4116[8] Apollono **(79)***(76) (JRFanshawe)* 3-8-4 DHarrison(22) (chsd ldrs 6f) s.h **12**
4116* Stone Ridge (IRE) **(88)***(85) (RHannon)* 3-8-8 (5) DaneO'Neill(10) (chsd ldrs over 5f) hd **13**
3945[9] Weaver Bird **(88)***(82) (HCandy)* 5-9-2 WNewnes(3) (stdd s: effrt 3f out: nvr trbld ldrs) 1½ **14**
4227[11] Saifan **(76)***(70) (DMorris)* 6-8-1b(3) JStack(6) (nvr nr to chal) hd **15**
4035* Night Dance **(96)***(88)*(Fav)*(GLewis)* 3-9-2 (5) AWhelan(29) (lw: prom 5f) 1¼ **16**
3945[27] Wakeel (USA) **(87)***(77) (SDow)* 3-8-12 GDuffield(16) (chsd ldrs: rdn over 3f out: sn btn) ¾ **17**
4052[2] Celtic Fringe **(80)***(69) (HRACecil)* 3-8-5 WRyan(11) (prom 5f) ½ **18**
4116[2] Mo-Addab (IRE) **(81)***(70) (ACStewart)* 5-8-9 RHills(12) (lw: chsd ldrs 5f) hd **19**
3945[36] Our Rita **(81)***(66) (DrJDScargill)* 6-8-9 RCochrane(15) (a bhd) 1¾ **20**
4202[5] Pay Homage **(80)***(62) (IABalding)* 7-8-3 (5) DGriffiths(7) (in tch over 4f) 1½ **21**
4041* Comanche Companion **(83)***(65) (TJNaughton)* 5-8-6 (5) JDSmith(30) (prom tl wknd 3f out) hd **22**
4171* Samba Sharply **(77)***(59) (AHide)* 4-8-5 WWoods(8) (swtg: chsd ldrs 4f: sn rdn & btn) nk **23**
3991[5] Cool Edge (IRE) **(81)***(61) (MHTompkins)* 4-8-9 PRobinson(1) (racd alone: spd 5f) ¾ **24**
4122[10] Ethbaat (USA) **(87)***(62) (WRMuir)* 4-9-1 JTate(23) (prom 6f) 2½ **25**
4065[3] Ron's Secret **(90)***(63) (JWPayne)* 3-8-10 (5) MHenry(19) (prom 6f) 1 **26**
4031[8] Ball Gown **(82)***(55) (DTThom)* 5-8-10 JReid(5) (a bhd) s.h **27**
4116[18] Ma Petite Anglaise **(79)***(51) (WJarvis)* 3-8-4 JCarroll(14) (bhd fnl 3f) nk **28**
4116[4] Clifton Fox **(81)***(52) (JAGlover)* 3-8-6 SDWilliams(20) (in tch 5f: eased whn btn) ½ **29**
Sharp Review (IRE) **(88)***(54) (JRJenkins)* 7-9-2 AMcGlone(2) (in tch 5f) 2½ **30**

15/2 Night Dance, **17/2** Delta Soleil (USA), **9/1** TARAWA (IRE), **10/1** Celestial Choir (op 16/1), **11/1** Conspicuous (IRE) (16/1-10/1), **12/1** Western Fame (USA), **14/1** Mo-Addab (IRE), Ball Gown, **16/1** Comanche Companion, **20/1** Samba Sharply, Clifton Fox, Stone Ridge (IRE), Billy Bushwacker, **25/1** Kayvee, Country Lover, Noble Sprinter (IRE), Cool Edge (IRE), Celtic Fringe, Ertlon, Apollono, Weaver Bird, Ron's Secret, **33/1** Serious, Saifan, **40/1** Pay Homage, **50/1** Wakeel (USA), Ethbaat (USA), Our Rita, Ma Petite Anglaise, Sharp Review (IRE), CSF £267.15 CT £2,415.56 TOTE £14.40: £3.80 £7.50 £4.00 £5.00 (£706.40) Trio £5,711.90 OWNER Mrs J. Callaghan (NEWMARKET) BRED Patrick Eddery Ltd 30 Rn 1m 37.16 (0.16)
SF:67/57/61/60/54/49/58/47/48/67/43/39/48/48/36/51/40/32/36/32/28/31/25/27/28/26/21/14/15/20
WEIGHT FOR AGE 3yo-3lb
STEWARDS' ENQUIRY Eddery susp. 6, 8, 10-11 & 16/11/95 (careless riding).

4268

BURROUGH GREEN H'CAP (0-80) (3-Y.O+) (Class D) £5,322.00 (£1,596.00: £768.00: £354.00)
7f (Rowley) Stalls: Centre GOING minus 0.39 sec per fur (F) 4-25 (4-28)

4194 12 **Mountgate (70)***(82) (MPBielby)* 3-9-7 JFEgan(10) (lw: trckd ldrs: qcknd to ld ins fnl f: rdn & r.o wl) — **1**
4236* Quilling **(77)***(88) (MDods)* 3-10-0 5x KDarley(8) (prom: led 2f out tl ins fnl f: unable qckn) ½ **2**
4079 4 Zelda Zonk **(66)***(71) (BJMeehan)* 3-9-3 BDoyle(2) (b.hind: lw: bhd: effrt & n.m.r over 2f out: rdn & r.o wl appr fnl f) 2½ **3**
4157 16 Canary Falcon **(58)***(63) (JohnBerry)* 4-8-12 MWigham(6) (hdwy over 1f out: r.o wl fnl f) hd **4**
3629 10 Winsome Wooster **(62)***(64) (PGMurphy)* 4-8-13 (3) SDrowne(3) (bhd: hdwy over 1f out: kpt on fnl f) 1½ **5**
4157 8 Thunder River (IRE) **(62)***(63) (MJHeaton-Ellis)* 5-9-2v TIves(11) (lw: led 5f) s.h **6**
4215 5 Cretan Gift **(60)***(60) (NPLittmoden)* 4-9-0v MFenton(7) (s.i.s: hdwy 2f out: nvr rchd ldrs) ½ **7**
4234* Night Wink (USA) **(75)***(74)*(Fav)*(DNicholls)* 3-9-5 (7) 5x MartinDwyer(14) (lw: prom: ev ch 2f out: sn rdn & btn) ½ **8**
3919 8 Louisville Belle (IRE) **(52)***(47) (MDIUsher)* 6-8-6 NAdams(13) (b: in tch: n.m.r over 2f out: sn btn) 1¾ **9**
4113 9 Thatcherella **(70)***(64) (MajorDNChappell)* 4-9-10 JReid(4) (chsd ldrs 4f) nk **10**
4193* Euphyllia **(68)***(62) (BobJones)* 3-9-5 FNorton(12) (chsd ldrs over 4f) nk **11**
4134* Oare Sparrow **(70)***(52) (PTWalwyn)* 5-9-10 PaulEddery(5) (prom 5f) 5 **12**
4134 11 Spectacle Jim **(47)***(25) (JO'Donoghue)* 6-8-1b NCarlisle(16) (chsd ldrs tl rdn & wknd over 2f out) 2 **13**
3748 17 Royal Carlton (IRE) **(62)***(37) (RAkehurst)* 3-8-13 TQuinn(15) (prom tl wknd over 2f out) 1 **14**
4157 4 Racing Telegraph **(41)***(12) (JWPayne)* 5-7-4 (5) MBaird(9) (lw: plld hrd: in tch over 4f) 1¾ **15**
Jahangir (IRE) **(62)***(32) (PatMitchell)* 6-8-11 (5) DaneO'Neill(1) (a bhd) ¾ **16**

9/4 Night Wink (USA), **6/1** Oare Sparrow (op 4/1), **7/1** Royal Carlton (IRE) (8/1-12/1), **9/1** Euphyllia (12/1-8/1), **10/1** Quilling (op 6/1), **12/1** Cretan Gift (op 8/1), Thunder River (IRE), **14/1** Louisville Belle (IRE) (10/1-16/1), Zelda Zonk, Thatcherella (10/1-16/1), MOUNTGATE, Racing Telegraph, **16/1** Winsome Wooster, **20/1** Spectacle Jim, **25/1** Canary Falcon, **50/1** Jahangir (IRE), CSF £151.91 CT £1,863.59 TOTE £22.90: £4.00 £2.90 £2.40 £9.00 (£238.80) Trio £541.80 OWNER Mr J. F. Coupland (GRIMSBY) BRED Llety Stud 16 Rn
1m 25.32 (1.62) SF: 53/59/42/37/38/37/34/45/21/38/33/26/-/8/-/6
WEIGHT FOR AGE 3yo-3lb

T/Jkpt: Not won; £15,931.81 to Newcastle 30/10/95. T/Plpt: £112.80 (227.77 Tckts). T/Qdpt: £27.80 (8.6 Tckts). Dk

4123-WOLVERHAMPTON (L-H)
Saturday October 28th (Standard)

WEATHER: misty WIND: nil

4269

PENDEFORD MEDIAN AUCTION MAIDEN STKS (2-Y.O) (Class E) £3,106.00 (£928.00: £444.00: £202.00)
6f (Fibresand) Stalls: Low GOING minus 0.02 sec per fur (STD) 7-00 (7-07)

4073 3 **Fog City** *(83) (WJarvis)* 2-9-0 EmmaO'Gorman(3) (dwlt: hdwy over 3f out: nt clr run 2f out: 2nd st: led ins fnl f: r.o) — **1**
4100 2 Indian Relative *(75)*(Fav)*(RGuest)* 2-8-4 (5) MHenry(10) (led tl hdd & no ex ins fnl f) 1 **2**
3857 7 Honestly **(50)***(65) (BSmart)* 2-8-9 SSanders(12) (a.p: 4th st: one pce fnl f) 4 **3**
4130 2 Trojan Risk **(80)***(66) (GLewis)* 2-8-9 (5) AWhelan(7) (a.p: 3rd st: wknd over 1f out) 1½ **4**
4212 12 Truth *(45) (SirMarkPrescott)* 2-8-9 CNutter(13) (bhd: poor 6th st: nvr nr ldrs) 6 **5**
4137 5 People Direct *(38) (KMcAuliffe)* 2-8-9 MTebbutt(1) (prom: hrd rdn over 2f out: 5th & wkng st) 2½ **6**

4161[8] Magic Melody *(37) (JLSpearing)* 2-8-6 (3) SDrowne(4) (rdn 4f out: bhd fnl 3f) ....nk **7**
3763[19] Magical Mill *(35) (RGuest)* 2-8-9 GHind(11) (sn bhd)....¾ **8**
4130[7] Farmost *(40) (SirMarkPrescott)* 2-9-0 RPerham(6) (lw: a bhd) ....hd **9**
Embroidered *(28) (SirMarkPrescott)* 2-8-9 GDuffield(8) (unf: prom: rdn 4f out: sn wknd)....2½ **10**
Wyedean *(12) (WRMuir)* 2-9-0 GCarter(5) (neat: s.i.s: sn wl bhd) 8 **11**
3104[6] Clint *(JFfitch-Heyes)* 2-9-0 AClark(9) (a bhd: t.o) 15 **12**
3892[14] Gotla Bird *(MJohnston)* 2-8-9 TWilliams(2) (Withdrawn not under Starter's orders: bolted bef s).... **W**

9/4 Indian Relative, **7/2** Trojan Risk (3/1-9/2), **9/2** FOG CITY (5/1-8/1), **12/1** Embroidered (op 5/1), **14/1** Farmost (op 7/1), **16/1** Magical Mill, Magic Melody, People Direct, Gotla Bird, **20/1** Wyedean, **25/1** Truth, **33/1** Clint, Honestly, CSF £14.23 TOTE £4.90: £1.80 £1.50 £13.10 (£4.90) Trio £79.10 OWNER Mr Jerry Sung (NEWMARKET) BRED Jerry Sung 12 Rn
1m 15.3 (4.10) SF: 39/31/21/22/1/-/-/-/-/-/-/-

4270 SHIFNAL CLAIMING STKS (3-Y.O+) (Class F) £2,243.00 (£618.00: £293.00)
1m 4f (Fibresand) Stalls: Low GOING minus 0.02 sec per fur (STD) 7-30 (7-33)

4062[8] **Kismetim (39)***(63) (BJMeehan)* 5-8-8 MTebbutt(12) (lw: hld up: stdy hdwy 5f out: led over 2f out: drvn out) ....— **1**
3852[7] Pharly Dancer **(82)***(77) (WWHaigh)* 6-9-10 DaleGibson(8) (plld hrd: a.p: led over 3f out tl over 2f out: 2nd st: r.o one pce)....1¼ **2**
4196[6] Deceit the Second **(41)***(72) (GLewis)* 3-8-8b(5) AWhelan(9) (prom: rdn 5f out: 3rd st: r.o one pce) 1 **3**
4126[2] Stevie's Wonder (IRE) **(67)***(69)*(Fav)*(MJRyan)* 5-9-10v GCarter(1) (led over 8f: 4th st: wknd over 1f out)....5 **4**
120[2] Rousitto *(58) (RHollinshead)* 7-9-2 TIves(11) (lw: hld up: stdy hdwy over 5f out: outpcd over 4f out: 6th st: no hdwy) 2½ **5**
3884[7] Rose of Glenn **(42)***(49) (BPalling)* 4-8-9 TSprake(7) (chsd ldr over 8f: wknd over 2f out: 5th & btn st)....1½ **6**
4079[15] Ballestro (IRE) **(35)***(31) (JFfitch-Heyes)* 3-7-12 (5) MHenry(10) (a bhd: t.o fnl 4f) 14 **7**
4167[6] Remontant (IRE) **(38)***(24) (RHollinshead)* 3-7-10 (7)ow3 FLynch(3) (a bhd: t.o fnl 4f) 3½ **8**
3737[12] Awestruck **(40)***(21) (BPreece)* 5-8-10b VSlattery(6) (nvr gng wl: t.o fnl 4f) 4 **9**
3073[10] Princethorpe *(10) (BRCambidge)* 8-8-12 ACulhane(4) (hld up & bhd: rdn & hdwy 6f out: wknd over 4f out: sn t.o)....10 **10**
4131[11] Steepholme **(36)** *(BRMillman)* 3-7-12 JLowe(2) (s.i.s: plld hrd: sn prom: wknd over 5f out: sn t.o) 15 **11**

6/4 Stevie's Wonder (IRE), **5/2** Pharly Dancer, **6/1** Rousitto, **14/1** Deceit the Second, Rose of Glenn, **16/1** KISMETIM, Remontant (IRE), Awestruck, **33/1** Ballestro' (IRE), Princethorpe, Steepholme, CSF £54.65 TOTE £21.10: £3.00 £1.60 £3.40 (£65.40) Trio £65.40 OWNER Mr Stephen Molloy (UPPER LAMBOURN) BRED Mrs M. Christian 11 Rn 2m 41.8 (10.80) SF: 21/35/23/27/16/7/-/-/-
WEIGHT FOR AGE 3yo-7lb
Kismetim clmd TBrown £2,000

4271 CHARLECOTE MEDIAN AUCTION MAIDEN STKS (3-Y.O) (Class E)
£2,872.00 (£856.00: £408.00: £184.00)
1m 100y (Fibresand) Stalls: High GOING minus 0.02 sec per fur (STD) 8-00 (8-00)

Saracen Prince (USA) (53)*(60) (PAKelleway)* 3-9-0 MWigham(9) (lw: chsd ldrs: led over 2f out: rdn out) ....— **1**
4147[6] Diamond Market **(48)***(52) (RHollinshead)* 3-9-0 TIves(5) (hdwy over 4f out: 2nd st: no imp).....4 **2**
4162[5] Persian Flower *(38) (GCBravery)* 3-8-9 MFenton(2) (outpcd 5f out: poor 6th st: late hdwy: r.o)....5 **3**
3649[9] Adamton *(36) (MrsJCecil)* 3-9-0 JTate(4) (led over 2f: hrd rdn over 2f out: 4th & wkng st) 3½ **4**
Dannistar *(31) (PDEvans)* 3-8-9 GHind(3) (leggy: lt-f: led 6f out tl over 2f out: 3rd st: wknd qckly over 1f out)....nk **5**
Geolly (IRE) *(32) (DrJDScargill)* 3-9-0 RPerham(8) (poor 5th st: n.d)....2 **6**
Unforeseen **(69)***(23)*(Fav)*(SirMarkPrescott)* 3-9-0 GDuffield(6) (bkwd: a bhd) 5 **7**
Guardsman (IRE) *(9) (THCaldwell)* 3-9-0 ACulhane(7) (a bhd) 7 **8**
4128[11] Halfabob (IRE) **(48)***(6) (DHaydnJones)* 3-9-0 AMackay(1) (prom: rdn 6f out: sn wknd)....½ **9**

9/4 Unforeseen (op 6/4), **3/1** SARACEN PRINCE (USA), **9/2** Diamond Market, **6/1** Persian Flower, **7/1** Adamton, **12/1** Halfabob (IRE) (op 8/1), **14/1** Dannistar, **25/1** Geolly (IRE), **33/1** Guardsman (IRE), CSF £16.84 TOTE £5.80: £2.00 £1.80 £1.60 (£50.50) Trio £30.50 OWNER Mr P. A. Kelleway (NEWMARKET) BRED Arthur I. Appleton 9 Rn 1m 52.7 (8.70) SF: 15/7/-/-/-/-/-/-/-

4272

CASTLECROFT H'CAP (0-70) (3-Y.O+) (Class E) £3,080.00 (£920.00: £440.00: £200.00) **7f (Fibresand)** Stalls: High GOING minus 0.02 sec (STD) 8-30 (8-30)

*4128** **Heathyards Lady (USA) (67)***(77) (RHollinshead)* 4-9-6 (7) FLynch(5) (lw: s.i.s: hdwy 3f out: led 1f out: r.o) — 1
4044 5 Calder King **(61)***(69) (JLEyre)* 4-9-7b TIves(4) (hld up: hdwy & 7th st: ev ch whn hung lft over 1f out: r.o) 1 2
3739 3 Maple Bay (IRE) **(57)***(64)*(Fav)*(ABailey)* 6-9-0 (3) DWright(7) (lw: hdwy 3f out: rdn & 5th st: ev ch whn carried lft over 1f out: r.o) ½ 3
3800 10 Desert Invader (IRE) **(66)***(68) (DWChapman)* 4-9-12 ACulhane(11) (sn prom: led 2f out to 1f out: one pce) 2 4
4057 12 Bold Gem **(62)***(58) (BJMeehan)* 4-9-1b(7) GHannon(1) (hld up: 6th st: ev ch over 1f out: wknd ins fnl f) 2½ 5
4217 8 Dream Carrier (IRE) **(60)***(55) (REPeacock)* 7-9-6 TSprake(12) (nvr nr to chal) ½ 6
4217 2 Live Project (IRE) **(65)***(59) (MJohnston)* 3-9-8 TWilliams(2) (w ldrs: 3rd st: wknd over 1f out) ½ 7
3950 3 What a Nightmare (IRE) **(70)***(60) (JAGlover)* 3-9-8b(5) AWhelan(10) (led 5f: 2nd st: wknd over 1f out) 1¾ 8
3390 8 David James' Girl **(62)***(44) (ABailey)* 3-9-5 SSanders(3) (bhd fnl 3f) 3½ 9
4115 12 Superoo **(65)***(41) (MrsPSly)* 9-9-11 DeanMcKeown(8) (chsd ldrs 3f) 2½ 10
4125 5 Newbury Coat **(63)***(35) (BPreece)* 5-9-9b NAdams(9) (prom: n.m.r over 3f out: 8th & wkng st) 1¾ 11
3534 12 Belleminette (IRE) **(66)***(35) (DHaydnJones)* 4-9-12 AMackay(6) (s.s: a bhd) 1½ 12

5/2 Maple Bay (IRE), **6/1** HEATHYARDS LADY (USA), Calder King, Live Project (IRE), **7/1** What a Nightmare (IRE), **8/1** Desert Invader (IRE), **12/1** Dream Carrier (IRE), **14/1** David James' Girl, **20/1** Belleminette (IRE), Superoo, Newbury Coat, **25/1** Bold Gem, CSF £41.58 CT £106.31 TOTE £6.60: £2.10 £2.40 £1.80 (£33.60) Trio £48.40 OWNER Mr L. A. Morgan (UPPER LONGDON) BRED S A'Long Farm and Dennis Swartz 12 Rn 1m 30.0 (6.00) SF: 38/30/25/29/19/16/17/18/2/2/-/-
WEIGHT FOR AGE 3yo-3lb

4273

MIDLAND BAR NURSERY (S) H'CAP (0-65) (2-Y.O) (Class F) £2,415.00 (£665.00: £315.00) **1m 100y (Fibresand)** Stalls: Low GOING minus 0.02 sec (STD) 9-00 (9-00)

4045 2 **Young Butt (54)***(65) (JFfitch-Heyes)* 2-8-8 (5) MHenry(7) (bhd: rdn over 4f out: gd hdwy & 7th st: led ins fnl f: r.o wl) — 1
3937 14 Red Acuisle (IRE) **(55)***(63) (MBell)* 2-9-0 MFenton(10) (lw: a.p: 2nd st: led over 1f out tl ins fnl f) 1½ 2
4045 4 Thorntoun Estate (IRE) **(56)***(63) (MJohnston)* 2-9-1 TWilliams(11) (lw: a.p: hrd rdn 5f out: 3rd st: ev ch over 1f out: edgd lft ins fnl f: nt qckn) ¾ 3
*4127** Image Maker (IRE) **(59)***(64) (BPreece)* 2-9-4 AClark(5) (hld up: 4th st: ev ch 2f out: one pce) 1 4
3858 10 Sunrise Special (IRE) **(51)***(50) (GLewis)* 2-8-5b(5) AWhelan(4) (b: lw: a.p: led 5f out tl over 1f out: eased whn btn ins fnl f) 3 5
4111 7 Napoleon's Return **(57)***(54) (GMMoore)* 2-9-2 JTate(8) (bhd tl hdwy over 2f out: 5th st: ev ch over 1f out: wknd ins fnl f) 1 6
4169 6 Richard House Lad **(62)***(55)*(Fav)*(RHollinshead)* 2-9-7 ACulhane(9) (chsd ldrs: no hdwy fnl 2f) 2½ 7
4127 5 Rozel Bay **(52)***(44) (JLSpearing)* 2-8-8b(3) SDrowne(12) (b: dwlt: hdwy & 6th st: wknd over 1f out) nk 8
4063 11 Lady of The Mist (IRE) **(55)***(45) (JSMoore)* 2-8-9 (5) PPMurphy(2) (n.d) 1 9
3566 7 Hurricane Horn (IRE) **(55)***(44) (WRMuir)* 2-9-0 SSanders(1) (led over 3f: hrd rdn & wknd over 2f out) ¾ 10
4222 6 Jemsilverthorn (IRE) **(49)***(32) (JJBridger)* 2-8-1 (7) ADaly(3) (plld hrd: w ldrs tl wknd over 4f out) 3 11
4127 10 Pulga Circo **(49)***(27) (BAMcMahon)* 2-8-8 GCarter(13) (sn bhd) 2½ 12
4141 9 My Kind **(59)***(36) (KMcAuliffe)* 2-9-4b GDuffield(6) (b: b.hind: a bhd) ¾ 13

9/2 Richard House Lad, **5/1** Image Maker (IRE), **6/1** YOUNG BUTT, **7/1** Red Acuisle (IRE), Thorntoun Estate (IRE), My Kind, **8/1** Napoleon's Return, **14/1** Sunrise Special (IRE), Rozel Bay, Hurricane Horn (IRE), **16/1** Lady of The Mist (IRE), Pulga Circo, **33/1** Jemsilverthorn (IRE), CSF £48.57 CT £286.54 TOTE £5.80: £2.40 £3.20 £3.10 (£41.90) Trio £60.50 OWNER Mr G. R. Butterfield (LEWES) BRED Llety Stud 13 Rn 1m 54.0 (10.00) SF: 3/1/1/2/-/-/-/-/-/-/-/-/-
Bt in 4,000gns

4274

WEST MIDLANDS H'CAP (0-60) (3-Y.O+) (Class F) £2,208.00 (£608.00: £288.00) **6f (Fibresand)** Stalls: Low GOING minus 0.02 sec per fur (STD) 9-30 (9-30)

4123 5 **Another Batchworth (53)***(64+) (SMellor)* 3-9-6 RPerham(11) (led early: led over 2f out: easily) — 1

3954[4] Jigsaw Boy **(59)***(65)*(Fav)*(PGMurphy)* 6-9-11 (3) SDrowne(10) (a.p: 3rd st: r.o ins fnl f)............2 **2**
2084[14] Peggy Spencer **(55)***(59) (CWThornton)* 3-9-8 DeanMcKeown(3) (sn led: hdd over 2f out: 2nd st: one pce)............½ **3**
4131[3] Harvest Reaper **(52)***(43) (JLHarris)* 3-9-5 SSanders(7) (prom: rdn & 5th st: no hdwy)............5 **4**
3919[16] Secret Miss **(55)***(44) (APJarvis)* 3-9-8 JTate(6) (hdwy 4f out: rdn & 6th st: one pce)............¾ **5**
3950[4] Jamaica Bridge **(54)***(40) (SGNorton)* 5-9-6 (3) OPears(4) (hdwy & 4th st: wknd over 1f out)...1¼ **6**
3512[9] Lady Silk **(58)***(43) (MissJFCraze)* 4-9-13 SWebster(12) (nvr trbld ldrs)............nk **7**
4115[5] Panther (IRE) **(54)***(31) (JHetherton)* 5-9-9 NKennedy(13) (n.d)............3 **8**
3954[6] Aljaz **(52)***(18) (RHarris)* 5-9-7 AMackay(8) (a bhd)............4 **9**
4128[9] Jalmaid **(55)***(15) (BAMcMahon)* 3-9-8 DBiggs(5) (sn outpcd)............2½ **10**
3830[13] We're Joken **(56)***(10) (JBerry)* 3-9-2 (7) CLowther(9) (a bhd)............2 **11**
Al Shaati (FR) **(52)** *(RJO'Sullivan)* 5-9-7 GDuffield(2) (a bhd)............5 **12**
3597[17] Sound the Trumpet (IRE) **(60)** *(AStreeter)* 3-9-8 (5) LNewton(1) (a bhd: t.o)............8 **13**

7/2 Jigsaw Boy (op 6/1), **5/1** Harvest Reaper (7/2-11/2), **7/1** Secret Miss (op 4/1), **8/1** Panther (IRE), We're Joken, **10/1** Jamaica Bridge (op 6/1), Aljaz, ANOTHER BATCHWORTH, **12/1** Jalmaid (op 8/1), Peggy Spencer (op 7/1), **20/1** Al Shaati (FR), **25/1** Lady Silk, **33/1** Sound the Trumpet (IRE), CSF £44.70 CT £405.36 TOTE £10.70: £2.70 £1.90 £3.10 (£10.70) OWNER Mrs Diana Price (SWINDON) BRED Mrs D. Price 13 Rn 1m 15.0 (3.80) SF: 49/52/44/28/29/27/30/18/5/-/-/-/-
WEIGHT FOR AGE 3yo-2lb

T/Plpt: £258.10 (39.43 Tckts). T/Qdpt: £52.10 (1.4 Tckts). KH

3877-NEWCASTLE (L-H)
Monday October 30th (Good to firm)
WEATHER: sunny periods WIND: slt across

4275

BEDLINGTON CLAIMING H'CAP (0-60) (3-Y.O+) (Class F) £3,028.40 (£852.40: £417.20) **7f** Stalls: Low GOING minus 0.23 sec per fur (GF) 1-30 (1-33)

3467[4] **Northern Spark (43)***(58) (MissLAPerratt)* 7-8-11 GDuffield(10) (sn pushed along far side: hdwy 2f out: led ins fnl f: r.o wl)............— **1**
4234[3] Mbulwa **(55)***(67)*(Fav)*(RAFahey)* 9-9-2 (7) MartinDwyer(13) (lw: cl up far side: led over 2f out: hdd & one pce ins fnl f)............1¼ **2**
4209[6] Matisse **(40)***(46) (JDBethell)* 4-8-8 KFallon(7) (lw: racd far side: hdwy & nt clr run 2f out & 1f out: r.o ins fnl f)............2½ **3**
3745[11] Thwaab **(46)***(51) (FWatson)* 3-8-11 MFenton(9) (racd far side: a.p: effrt 2f out: kpt on one pce fnl f)............½ **4**
4225[2] Dr Caligari (IRE) **(55)***(60) (JBerry)* 3-9-6 JCarroll(19) (cl up stands side: kpt on wl fnl f)............hd **5**
4194[15] Boost **(42)***(46) (CWThornton)* 3-8-7 DeanMcKeown(2) (cl up far side: rdn & one pce fnl 2f)....½ **6**
3807[14] Peacefull Reply (USA) **(40)***(43) (FHLee)* 5-8-8 GCarter(12) (dwlt: racd far side: hdwy 2f out: nvr able chal)............½ **7**
4054[6] Best Kept Secret **(55)***(57) (JBerry)* 4-9-4 (5) PFessey(1) (racd far side: hdwy over 2f out: nt qckn fnl f)............½ **8**
4060[13] Blow Dry (IRE) **(57)***(58) (MartynWane)* 5-9-11 AMackay(14) (plld hrd: racd stands side: n.d).nk **9**
3800[16] Dante's Rubicon (IRE) **(46)***(47) (JDBethell)* 4-9-0 WCarson(11) (racd far side: effrt ½-wy: no imp)............hd **10**
4044[15] Move Smartly (IRE) **(52)***(50) (FHLee)* 5-9-6v NCarlisle(4) (s.i.s: hdwy & ev ch 2f out: sn wknd)............1¼ **11**
3172[7] King of Show (IRE) **(46)***(41) (RAllan)* 4-8-9 (5) CTeague(17) (cl up stands side tl wknd appr fnl f)............1¼ **12**
4193[10] Sheroot **(42)***(33) (DMoffatt)* 3-8-4 (3) DarrenMoffatt(18) (b.off fore: racd stands side: n.d)......1¾ **13**
4170[19] Saint Amigo **(44)***(33) (JLEyre)* 3-8-9 TWilliams(15) (s.i.s: racd stands side & n.d)............1 **14**
4110[9] Moofaji **(42)***(12) (FWatson)* 4-8-10 SMaloney(20) (racd stands' side: outpcd fr ½-wy)............8 **15**
4249[17] La Dama (USA) **(48)***(2) (FJO'Mahony)* 3-8-13 MMcAndrew(5) (racd far side: led tl hdd over 2f out: sn wknd)............7 **16**
3879[13] Aquiletta **(38)** *(CBBBooth)* 5-8-6 MBirch(8) (racd far side: dwlt: effrt ½-wy: sn wknd)............12 **17**
4165[24] High Holme **(39)** *(DTThom)* 4-8-7 LDettori(3) (chsd ldrs far side 5f: easd whn btn)............2½ **18**
Natural Path **(50)** *(MrsVAAconley)* 4-9-4 MDeering(16) (sn bhd stands side)............2½ **19**
3980[27] Semi Serious **(40)** *(DWChapman)* 3-8-5 ACulhane(6) (early spd far side: sn t.o)............25 **20**

9/4 Mbulwa, **5/1** Dr Caligari (IRE), **8/1** Matisse, **12/1** NORTHERN SPARK, Dante's Rubicon (IRE) (op 8/1), **14/1** Blow Dry (IRE), **16/1** Boost, Best Kept Secret, Thwaab, High Holme, Move Smartly (IRE), King of Show (IRE), Saint Amigo, **25/1** Peacefull Reply (USA), Moofaji, **33/1** Aquiletta, **50/1** La Dama (USA), Sheroot, Natural Path, Semi Serious, CSF £40.12 CT £230.03 TOTE £10.00: £2.00 £1.10 £1.90 £6.60 (£25.30) Trio £33.00 OWNER Scottish Daily Record & Sunday Mail Ltd (AYR) BRED I. Thoday 20 Rn 1m 27.38 (3.08) SF: 40/49/28/30/39/25/25/39/40/29/32/23/12/12/-/-/-
WEIGHT FOR AGE 3yo-3lb

4276 E.B.F. AMBLE MAIDEN STKS (2-Y.O) (Class D) £3,696.25 (£1,120.00: £547.50: £261.25)
6f Stalls: High GOING minus 0.23 sec per fur (GF) 2-00 (2-02)

4161⁹ **Pivotal** *(86) (SirMarkPrescott)* 2-9-0 GDuffield(4) (trckd ldrs gng wl: swtchd over 1f out: r.o to ld wl ins fnl f)......— **1**
4064³ Domak Amaam (IRE) *(79) (JHMGosden)* 2-9-0 LDettori(9) (b.hind: cl up: led & qcknd over 1f out: hdd & no ex wl ins fnl f)......2½ **2**
3933⁴ Mansab (USA) *(66)*(Fav)*(JLDunlop)* 2-9-0 WCarson(3) (chsd ldrs: outpcd 2f out: kpt on fnl f)......5 **3**
3877⁵ Gilling Dancer (IRE) *(57) (PCalver)* 2-9-0 MBirch(8) (swtg: plld hrd: in tch: kpt on one pce fnl 2f)......3½ **4**
4097¹¹ Answers-To-Thomas **(64)***(56) (JMJefferson)* 2-9-0 DeanMcKeown(5) (hld up: hdwy & n.m.r 2f out: r.o fnl f)......nk **5**
4219⁷ Midnight Cookie **(48)***(54) (BAPearce)* 2-8-9 ⁽⁵⁾ DaneO'Neill(11) (led tl hdd 1½f out: sn btn)......¾ **6**
4188¹⁶ Manoy *(49) (JHetherton)* 2-9-0 NKennedy(12) (bhd: shkn up & hdwy over 2f out: n.d)......1¾ **7**
4188¹⁵ Highfield Pet *(49) (MJohnston)* 2-9-0 TWilliams(7) (sn pushed along & bhd: n.d)......hd **8**
4098⁸ Lapu-Lapu *(44+) (MJCamacho)* 2-8-9 LCharnock(2) (hld up & bhd: nvr plcd to chal)......hd **9**
*4127*¹³ Chamber Music **(53)***(30) (JBerry)* 2-8-9 JCarroll(6) (spd to ½-wy: sn btn)......5 **10**
Insideout *(11) (FWatson)* 2-9-0 MFenton(10) (w'like: leggy: s.i.s: a bhd)......9 **11**
4073⁹ Ballykissangel *(11) (NBycroft)* 2-9-0 KFallon(1) (in tch over 3f)......s.h **12**

7/4 Mansab (USA), **2/1** PIVOTAL, Domak Amaam (IRE), **20/1** Answers-To-Thomas, **25/1** Highfield Pet, **33/1** Gilling Dancer (IRE), Lapu-Lapu, Chamber Music, **50/1** Midnight Cookie, Manoy, Insideout, **100/1** Ballykissangel, CSF £6.66 TOTE £2.90: £1.60 £1.10 £1.40 (£6.20) Trio £1.20 OWNER Cheveley Park Stud (NEWMARKET) BRED Cheveley Park Stud Ltd 12 Rn
1m 13.57 (2.07) SF: 50/43/30/21/20/18/13/13/8/-/-/-

4277 ALNWICK MAIDEN STKS (2-Y.O F) (Class D) £3,761.25 (£1,140.00: £557.50: £266.25)
7f Stalls: Low GOING minus 0.23 sec per fur (GF) 2-30 (2-31)

4102* **Shemozzle (IRE)** *(73)*(Fav)*(JHMGosden)* 2-8-11 LDettori(2) (b.hind: trckd ldrs: led over 1f out: r.o)......— **1**
Abir *(70+) (HThomsonJones)* 2-8-11 GCarter(15) (w'like: hld up: hdwy 3f out: chal 1f out: nt qckn)......1¼ **2**
4218⁸ Arcady *(66) (PTWalwyn)* 2-8-11 KDarley(12) (led tl hdd over 1f out: no ex)......2 **3**
3449⁹ Sis Garden *(54) (MHEasterby)* 2-8-11 MBirch(14) (trckd ldrs: nt qckn appr fnl f)......5 **4**
3850³ Daira *(48) (JDBethell)* 2-8-11 JCarroll(3) (chsd ldrs: hung lft over 1f out: sn btn)......2½ **5**
The Fullbangladesh *(46) (JLEyre)* 2-8-11 RLappin(4) (lengthy: unf: in tch 5f)......1¼ **6**
4212¹⁸ Florrie'm *(44) (JLHarris)* 2-8-11 AMackay(5) (cl up over 5f)......¾ **7**
River Divine (USA) *(44) (MRStoute)* 2-8-11 KFallon(9) (tall: dwlt: plld hrd & sn in tch: shkn up ½-wy: btn whn hmpd 1½f out)......hd **8**
Radmore Brandy *(41) (SGNorton)* 2-8-11 TWilliams(8) (small: bkwd: hld up & bhd: shkn up over 2f out: n.d)......1¼ **9**
3881⁹ Sing And Dance *(37) (EWeymes)* 2-8-11 DaleGibson(1) (bit bkwd: in tch over 4f)......1½ **10**
3827⁸ Hallikeld *(34) (TJEtherington)* 2-8-11 JLowe(10) (n.d)......1½ **11**
Blossom Dearie *(32) (GMMoore)* 2-8-11 DeanMcKeown(6) (small: bkwd: a bhd)......¾ **12**
4100¹¹ Champagne Warrior (IRE) *(32) (MJCamacho)* 2-8-11 LCharnock(11) (a bhd)......hd **13**
Gildoran Sound *(32) (MHEasterby)* 2-8-11 SMaloney(13) (unf: b.hind: sn outpcd & bhd)......hd **14**

15/8 SHEMOZZLE (IRE), **9/4** River Divine (USA), **5/2** Abir (op 5/4), **14/1** Arcady, Daira, **33/1** Gildoran Sound, **40/1** Hallikeld, **50/1** The Fullbangladesh, Radmore Brandy, Sing And Dance, Sis Garden, Blossom Dearie, Champagne Warrior (IRE), **66/1** Florrie'm, CSF £7.03 TOTE £2.20: £1.60 £1.60 £1.90 (£4.30) Trio £10.00 OWNER Lord Hartington (NEWMARKET) BRED Side Hill Stud 14 Rn
1m 28.08 (3.78) SF: 32/29/25/13/7/5/3/3/-/-/-/-/-/-

4278 ASHINGTON H'CAP (0-85) (3-Y.O+) (Class D) £3,978.00 (£1,206.00: £590.00: £282.00) **5f** Stalls: High GOING minus 0.23 sec per fur (GF) 3-00 (3-04)

3855* **Leading Princess (IRE) (45)***(55) (MissLAPerratt)* 4-7-2b⁽⁵⁾ PFessey(1) (racd far side: cl up: led ½-wy: r.o)......— **1**
4165⁵ Jucea **(61)***(66) (JLSpearing)* 6-8-9 KFallon(7) (outpcd & bhd: hdwy u.p 2f out: r.o nr fin)......1½ **2**
4165⁶ Domicksky **(53)***(57) (MRChannon)* 7-7-10 ⁽⁵⁾ PPMurphy(14) (in tch: hdwy 2f out: nt qckn fnl f)......nk **3**
4113² Lady Sheriff **(80)***(84)*(Fav)*(MWEasterby)* 4-10-0b LDettori(9) (chsd ldrs: outpcd 2f out: kpt on fnl f)......hd **4**

3748* Followmegirls **(50)***(52) (MrsALMKing)* 6-7-12b AGarth(6) (dwlt: hdwy fnl 2f: nrst fin) ....¾ 5
3878 18 Shadow Jury **(68)***(69) (DWChapman)* 5-9-2b LCharnock(8) (chsd ldrs: nt qckn fnl f) ....hd 6
3981 7 Bajan Frontier (IRE) **(46)***(39) (FHLee)* 3-7-7 NCarlisle(3) (b.hind: led tl hdd ½-wy: wknd over 1f out) 2½ 7
Serious Fact **(46)***(39) (SirMarkPrescott)* 3-7-7 JLowe(4) (hdwy ½-wy: no imp) ....hd 8
3854 5 Six for Luck **(60)***(52) (DANolan)* 3-8-7 VHalliday(11) (b: b.hind: in tch 3f: sn outpcd) ....nk 9
4197 10 Ashtina **(78)***(67) (BAPearce)* 10-9-7 (5) DaneO'Neill(10) (in tch to ½-wy: sn outpcd) 1 10
2124 11 Another Nightmare (IRE) **(46)***(31) (JSGoldie)* 3-7-7 JQuinn(2) (racd far side: gd spd 3f) 1¼ 11
2753 3 Metal Boys **(62)***(43) (MissLCSiddall)* 8-8-10 GHind(5) (nvr wnt pce) 1¼ 12
3298 5 Princess Sadie **(76)***(53) (MJohnston)* 3-9-9 TWilliams(13) (s.i.s: a bhd) 1¼ 13
4040 21 Encore M'Lady (IRE) **(64)***(38) (FHLee)* 4-8-12b GCarter(12) (s.i.s: n.d) ....¾ 14
LONG HANDICAP Serious Fact 7-1 Another Nightmare (IRE) 7-2 Leading Princess (IRE) 7-6 Bajan Frontier (IRE) 7-4

5/2 Lady Sheriff, **6/1** Jucea, Followmegirls, **13/2** Domicksky, **9/1** Princess Sadie, **12/1** LEADING PRINCESS (IRE), Metal Boys, **16/1** Encore M'Lady (IRE), Serious Fact, Shadow Jury, **20/1** Ashtina, **25/1** Bajan Frontier (IRE), **33/1** Six for Luck, Another Nightmare (IRE), CSF £80.09 CT £474.03 TOTE £21.00: £4.50 £2.30 £1.50 (£62.20) Trio £91.80 OWNER Mrs Ruth Wyllie (AYR) BRED Woodford Stud 14 Rn 59.73 secs (1.33) SF: 36/47/38/65/33/50/19/19/32/48/11/24/33/19
WEIGHT FOR AGE 3yo-1lb

4279 BLYTH NURSERY H'CAP (0-85) (2-Y.O) (Class D) £3,566.25 (£1,080.00: £527.50: £251.25)
7f Stalls: Low GOING minus 0.23 sec per fur (GF) 3-30 (3-31)

4151 7 **Quality (IRE) (69)***(73+)*(Fav)*(WAO'Gorman)* 2-8-10b EmmaO'Gorman(6) (lw: hld up: smooth hdwy to ld ins fnl f: r.o) ....— 1
4107 11 Oblomov **(80)***(77)*(Fav)*(GLewis)* 2-9-7b KDarley(1) (lw: led tl hdd ins fnl f: r.o) 3 2
4103 9 Tasliya (USA) **(80)***(71) (JLDunlop)* 2-9-7 WCarson(5) (hld up: hdwy 2f out: r.o towards fin) 2½ 3
3838 2 Termon **(59)***(49) (MissLAPerratt)* 2-8-0 TWilliams(8) (trckd ldrs: chal 2f out: rdn & wknd ins fnl f) ....½ 4
4141 4 Eric's Bett **(68)***(58) (MrsSMAustin)* 2-8-2 (7) DDenby(4) (b: sn pushed along: styd on fnl 2f: nvr able chal) ....nk 5
3548 15 Society Girl **(70)***(58) (CWThornton)* 2-8-11 DeanMcKeown(2) (b.hind: chsd ldrs: rdn over 2f out: wknd over 1f out) ....¾ 6
4077 4 Standown **(71)***(52)*(Fav)*(JBerry)* 2-8-7 (5) PFessey(3) (lw: chsd ldrs tl outpcd fnl 2½f) 3 7
4066 4 Bee Health Boy **(66)***(27)*(Fav)*(MWEasterby)* 2-8-7b LDettori(7) (lw: cl up 5f: sn wknd) 9 8

9/2 QUALITY (IRE), Oblomov, Bee Health Boy, Standown, **6/1** Tasliya (USA), **13/2** Society Girl, **8/1** Termon, Eric's Bett, CSF £24.81 CT £114.10 TOTE £5.30: £1.90 £2.40 £1.80 (£14.50) OWNER Mr N. S. Yong (NEWMARKET) BRED Major C.R. Philipson 8 Rn
1m 26.95 (2.65) SF: 44/48/42/20/29/29/23/-

4280 MORPETH H'CAP (0-70) (3-Y.O+) (Class E) £3,467.20 (£1,051.60: £514.80: £246.40) 6f Stalls: High GOING minus 0.23 sec per fur (GF) 4-00 (4-01)

4068* **Double Splendour (IRE) (66)***(76)*(Fav)*(PSFelgate)* 5-9-10 GHind(15) (lw: hld up & bhd: hdwy 2f out: r.o to ld nr fin) ....— 1
4142 2 Stuffed **(58)***(67) (MWEasterby)* 3-9-0 LDettori(18) (lw: chsd ldrs centre: styd on to disp ld wl ins fnl f: no ex nr fin) ....nk 2
4113 3 Slivovitz **(54)***(61) (MJHeaton-Ellis)* 5-8-5v(7) AmandaSanders(1) (lw: racd far side: led tl ct nr fin) ....¾ 3
3783 12 Stand Tall **(48)***(53) (CWThornton)* 3-8-4 DeanMcKeown(2) (a chsng ldrs: effrt over 2f out: r.o one pce) 1 4
3972 3 Hi Rock **(57)***(58) (MJCamacho)* 3-8-13 LCharnock(4) (a chsg ldrs: effrt over 2f out: r.o one pce) 1¼ 5
4215 3 Kira **(49)***(49) (JLEyre)* 5-8-7 RLappin(12) (cl up centre: nt qckn appr fnl f) ....½ 6
4236 6 Mister Westsound **(62)***(61) (MissLAPerratt)* 3-9-4b GDuffield(6) (lw: hmpd over 2f out: r.o fnl f: nrst fin) ....nk 7
4165 14 Giggleswick Girl **(61)***(57) (MRChannon)* 4-9-0 (5) PPMurphy(3) (chsd ldrs: rdn & no imp fnl 2f) 1 8
1434 11 Light Movement (IRE) **(44)***(32) (WSCunningham)* 5-8-2 DaleGibson(8) (chsd ldrs tl rdn & btn over 1f out) 3 9
4142 5 Densben **(54)***(40) (DenysSmith)* 11-8-7 (5) CTeague(16) (outpcd & bhd tl r.o. fnl f) ....¾ 10
3859 6 Fallal (IRE) **(47)***(31) (KMcAuliffe)* 3-8-3 ow1 MFenton(7) (in tch over 3f) ....½ 11
3879 2 Murray's Mazda (IRE) **(43)***(27) (JLEyre)* 6-8-1 JQuinn(11) (b: prom 4f) ....nk 12
3855 12 Diet **(53)***(36) (MissLAPerratt)* 9-8-4v(7) KSked(10) (chsd ldrs 4f) ....½ 13
4165 18 The Fed **(47)***(27) (RMWhitaker)* 5-8-5vow2 ACulhane(17) (n.d) ....½ 14

4215 6 Petraco (IRE) **(64)***(42) (NASmith)* 7-9-8 SDWilliams(20) (n.d) 1¼ **15**
3878 8 Captain Carat **(62)***(37) (MrsJRRamsden)* 4-9-6 KFallon(19) (hld up & bhd: n.d) 1¼ **16**
3442 9 Always Grace **(66)***(38) (MissGayKelleway)* 3-9-3 (5) DaneO'Neill(9) (cl up centre 4f) 1¼ **17**
4053 9 Birchwood Sun **(66)***(34) (MDods)* 5-9-10b KDarley(5) (sn t.o: sme late hdwy) 1½ **18**
4142 14 Sir Tasker **(56)***(20) (JLHarris)* 7-9-0 AMackay(14) (cl up centre over 3f) 1½ **19**
3992 20 Craigie Boy **(53)***(12) (NBycroft)* 5-8-11b SMaloney(13) (b.off hind: dwlt: a bhd) 1¾ **20**

5/2 DOUBLE SPLENDOUR (IRE), **5/1** Captain Carat, **13/2** Stuffed, **10/1** Slivovitz, **12/1** Mister Westsound, Kira, **14/1** Birchwood Sun, Hi Rock, **16/1** Giggleswick Girl, Always Grace, **20/1** Petraco (IRE), Craigie Boy, Densben, Murray's Mazda (IRE), **25/1** Sir Tasker, The Fed, **33/1** Stand Tall, Diet, Fallal (IRE), **50/1** Light Movement (IRE), CSF £21.28 CT £148.69 TOTE £3.40: £1.70 £2.20 £3.20 £6.60 (£9.50) Trio £181.50 OWNER Yorkshire Racing Club Owners Group 1990 (MELTON MOWBRAY) BRED R. McQuillan 20 Rn
1m 13.65 (2.15) SF: 58/47/43/33/38/31/41/39/14/22/11/9/18/9/24/19/18/16/2/-
WEIGHT FOR AGE 3yo-2lb

T/Jkpt: Not won; £24,386.46 to Redcar 31/10/95. T/Plpt: £39.00 (485.06 Tckts). T/Qdpt: £26.90 (3 Tckts). AA

4230-REDCAR (L-H)
Tuesday October 31st (Firm, Good to firm patches)
WEATHER: overcast WIND: mod half bhd

4281 OAK LIMITED STKS (0-85) (3-Y.O+) (Class D) £3,788.50 (£1,138.00: £549.00: £254.50) 6f Stalls: Centre GOING: minus 0.31 sec per fur (GF) 1-45 (1-48)

4040 2 **Highborn (IRE) (83)***(87)*(Fav)*(PSFelgate)* 6-9-0 KDarley(3) (lw: dwlt: jnd ldrs ½-wy: r.o u.p to ld nr fin) ....— **1**
4197 8 Seigneurial **(80)***(87) (GHarwood)* 3-8-12 AClark(11) (cl up: led ½-wy: r.o: jst ct) ....hd **2**
3929 10 Tiler (IRE) **(80)***(86) (MJohnston)* 3-9-1 JReid(7) (lw: led to ½-wy: ev ch tl nt qckn fnl f) 1½ **3**
4145 4 Anzio (IRE) **(73)***(83) (BAPearce)* 4-9-6 TIves(2) (b: w ldrs 3f: one pce) 2 **4**
4236 2 King Rat (IRE) **(77)***(81) (TJEtherington)* 4-9-6b CRutter(5) (lw: chsd ldrs tl outpcd fnl 2f) 1 **5**
4041 14 French Grit (IRE) **(81)***(73) (MDods)* 3-9-1 DeanMcKeown(9) (in tch: rdn ½-wy: no imp) 1¾ **6**
4197 9 Call Me I'm Blue (IRE) **(84)***(70) (NTinkler)* 5-9-0 KimTinkler(4) (bhd: hdwy u.p over 1f out: n.d) ....s.h **7**
4145 7 Champagne Grandy **(80)***(67) (MRChannon)* 5-8-13 (5) PPMurphy(10) (sn drvn along: nvr trbld ldrs) 2½ **8**
3880 4 Palacegate Touch **(81)***(60) (JBerry)* 5-9-0b JCarroll(6) (w ldrs 4f: sn wknd) 1¼ **9**
3637 5 Awayil (USA) **(80)***(47) (HThomsonJones)* 3-8-10 GCarter(1) (nvr wnt pce) 4 **10**
2463 10 Dauntless Fort **(37)***(28) (MrsVAAconley)* 4-8-9 MDeering(8) (sn outpcd & bhd) 6 **11**

15/8 HIGHBORN (IRE), **5/2** Awayil (USA), **7/1** Tiler (IRE), **9/1** Call Me I'm Blue (IRE), **10/1** Seigneurial, **12/1** French Grit (IRE), **14/1** Palacegate Touch, Champagne Grandy, King Rat (IRE), **25/1** Anzio (IRE), **500/1** Dauntless Fort, CSF £21.52 TOTE £3.10: £1.20 £2.20 £2.80 (£20.90) Trio £84.30 OWNER Yorkshire Racing Club Owners Group 1990 (MELTON MOWBRAY) BRED Mrs P. F. McQuillan 11 Rn 1m 10.1 (0.80) SF: 60/58/57/56/54/44/43/40/33/18/1
WEIGHT FOR AGE 3yo-2lb

4282 E.B.F. BIRCH MAIDEN STKS (2-Y.O) (Class D) £4,042.00 (£1,216.00: £588.00: £274.00) 7f Stalls: Centre GOING: minus 0.31 sec per fur (GF) 2-15 (2-17)

3881 3 **Magic Mill (IRE)** *(82+) (FJO'Mahony)* 2-9-0 SDWilliams(2) (trckd ldrs: disp ld ½-wy: led over 1f out: r.o) ....— **1**
4210 2 Apache Len (USA) *(76)*(Fav)*(RHannon)* 2-9-0 JReid(9) (lw: disp ld tl hdd over 1f out: no ex)2½ **2**
3967 6 Doctor Bravious (IRE) *(72) (MBell)* 2-9-0 MFenton(4) (lw: in tch: effrt ½-wy: styd on: no imp) .2 **3**
4098 4 Classic Beauty (IRE) *(64) (SCWilliams)* 2-8-9 AMackay(5) (in tch: drvn along ½-wy: styd on fnl f) 1¼ **4**
4212 10 Patrio (IRE) *(60) (MJohnston)* 2-8-9 TWilliams(1) (cl up tl outpcd fnl 2f) 1½ **5**
Green Gem (BEL) *(51) (SCWilliams)* 2-8-9 KDarley(8) (lenthy: unf: chsd ldrs tl wknd over 1f out) 4 **6**
3644 15 Marsayas (IRE) *(48) (MJCamacho)* 2-9-0 LCharnock(3) (disp ld to ½-wy: sn outpcd) 3½ **7**
4085 10 Strategic Ploy *(35) (MrsJRRamsden)* 2-8-9 SSanders(7) (outpcd fr ½-wy) 3½ **8**
3967 7 Northern Motto *(27) (MrsJRRamsden)* 2-9-0 KFallon(6) (unruly s: s.s: a wl bhd) 6 **9**

4/5 Apache Len (USA), **7/2** MAGIC MILL (IRE), **6/1** Doctor Bravious (IRE), **13/2** Classic Beauty (IRE), **9/1** Northern Motto (6/1-10/1), **14/1** Patrio (IRE), Green Gem (BEL) (op 8/1), **33/1** Strategic Ploy, **66/1** Marsayas (IRE), CSF £7.49 TOTE £4.00: £1.50 £1.60 £1.50 (£4.80) Trio £5.70 OWNER Mr A. S. Scott (HAMBLETON) BRED Sean Madigan 9 Rn
1m 24.3 (2.30) SF: 44/38/34/26/22/13/10/-/-

4283

SYCAMORE H'CAP (0-80) (3-Y.O) (Class D) £3,970.50 (£1,194.00: £577.00: £268.50) **1m 3f** Stalls: Low GOING: minus 0.31 sec per fur (GF) 2-45 (2-45)

3899 10 **Hand Woven (74)***(84) (WJHaggas)* 3-9-3 JCarroll(4) (lw: a cl up: led over 1f out: all out) .....— 1
3918 4 Eurolink Mischief **(77)***(87)*(Fav)*(LMCumani)* 3-9-6b KDarley(1) (hld up: nt clr run over 2f out tl ins fnl f: r.o towards fin)........nk 2
4149 8 Vaugrenier (IRE) **(78)***(87) (RHannon)* 3-9-7 JReid(2) (b.hind: a.p: hdwy over 2f out: ev ch ins fnl f: nt qckn towards fin) ....nk 3
3665 2 Contrafire (IRE) **(72)***(78) (WJarvis)* 3-9-1 SSanders(6) (lw: a.p: ev ch & edgd lft 2f out: btn 1f out) 2 4
3722 5 Trumble **(50)***(49) (CWThornton)* 3-7-2 (5) PFessey(3) (led tl hdd over 1f out: sn btn) 5 5
4096 2 Kalamata **(67)***(66) (ACStewart)* 3-8-10 SWhitworth(5) (cl up tl outpcd over 2f out)........s.h 6
4138 13 Dancing Destiny **(55)***(32) (RBastiman)* 3-7-12 LCharnock(7) (a bhd: lost tch fnl 4f) 15 7

LONG HANDICAP Trumble 7-5

11/4 Eurolink Mischief, **3/1** Contrafire (IRE), **4/1** Vaugrenier (IRE), **11/2** Kalamata, **6/1** HAND WOVEN, **14/1** Trumble, Dancing Destiny, CSF £21.69 TOTE £9.40: £3.20 £2.70 (£30.90) OWNER Mrs M. M. Haggas (NEWMARKET) BRED Waverton Farm (Stow) 7 Rn

2m 19.2 (3.50) SF: 50/53/53/44/15/32/-

4284

POPLAR H'CAP (0-70) (3-Y.O+) (Class E) £3,712.25 (£1,118.00: £541.50: £253.25) **1m 2f** Stalls: Low GOING: minus 0.31 sec per fur (GF) 3-15 (3-16)

4171 7 **Fairy Knight (69)***(80) (RHannon)* 3-9-12 JReid(8) (lw: mid div: hdwy 2f out: led ins fnl f: r.o)— 1
169 7 Wahem (IRE) **(35)***(45) (CEBrittain)* 5-7-6 (5) MHenry(12) (led after 2f: rdn over 2f out: hdd ins fnl f: kpt on) ....½ 2
4229 4 Guesstimation (USA) **(65)***(73) (JPearce)* 6-9-10 (3) SDrowne(1) (a.p: chal over 1f out: no ex ins fnl f) 1½ 3
3952 10 Larn Fort **(55)***(61) (CWFairhurst)* 5-9-3v LCharnock(6) (in tch: effrt 4f out: styd on fnl f) 1 4
4138 7 Essayeffsee **(56)***(62) (MrsMReveley)* 6-9-4 KDarley(13) (lw: styd on fnl 4f: nrst fin) ....hd 5
4138 14 Pine Essence (USA) **(48)***(50) (JLEyre)* 4-8-10 RLappin(14) (s.i.s: swtchd & hdwy over 2f out: nrst fin) 2½ 6
4225 6 Bobanlyn (IRE) **(55)***(57) (DMorris)* 3-8-12 SMaloney(16) (bhd: rdn 4f out: styd on fnl 2f) ....hd 7
4233 6 Efizia **(62)***(61) (MrsMReveley)* 5-9-3 (7) SCopp(17) (s.i.s: sme late hdwy: n.d) 2 8
4038 10 Coureur **(66)***(58) (JDBethell)* 6-10-0 TIves(7) (mid div: effrt 4f out: no imp) 4 9
4138 3 Unprejudice **(63)***(53)*(Fav)*(MDHammond)* 4-9-11 MTebbutt(15) (lw: bhd: hdwy 3f out: nvr rchd ldrs) 1¼ 10
4232 4 Bardia **(33)***(23) (DonEnricoIncisa)* 5-7-9 KimTinkler(4) (dwlt: bhd tl sme late hdwy) ....nk 11
4232 2 Hunza Story **(40)***(26) (NPLittmoden)* 3-7-6 (5) CAdamson(11) (b.hind: trckd ldrs tl rdn & btn over 2f out) 2½ 12
1180 16 Himalayan Blue **(65)***(49) (JEBanks)* 3-9-8 JQuinn(10) (lw: b: n.d) 1¼ 13
4209 18 Rafter-J **(58)***(23) (JAHarris)* 4-9-6 KFallon(9) (lw: a bhd) 12 14
4194 18 Northern Trove (USA) **(57)***(9) (RonaldThompson)* 3-9-0 TWilliams(2) (led 2f: cl up tl wknd 3f out) 8 15
4061 17 Imlak (IRE) **(63)** *(JLHarris)* 3-9-6 JFEgan(3) (w ldrs tl wknd 4f out: p.u & crashed thro rails over 3f out: b.b.v) .... F
3987 10 Caerle Lad (IRE) **(55)** *(DNicholls)* 4-9-3 AlexGreaves(5) (trckd ldrs: chal 2f out: broke down & p.u ent fnl f: dead) .... P

9/2 Unprejudice, **6/1** FAIRY KNIGHT, **13/2** Guesstimation (USA), Essayeffsee, **8/1** Hunza Story, Coureur, **14/1** Larn Fort, Efizia, Bobanlyn (IRE), **16/1** Imlak (IRE), Wahem (IRE), **20/1** Pine Essence (USA), **25/1** Himalayan Blue, Rafter-J, Bardia, **33/1** Northern Trove (USA), Caerle Lad (IRE), CSF £96.59 CT £605.36 TOTE £6.40: £2.20 £5.40 £1.00 £8.40 (£105.80) Trio £353.00 OWNER P & S Lever Partners (MARLBOROUGH) BRED Peter McCalmont 17 Rn

2m 5.8 (3.30) SF: 57/27/55/43/44/32/34/43/40/35/5/3/26/5/-/-/-

WEIGHT FOR AGE 3yo-5lb

4285

BEECH NURSERY H'CAP (0-75) (2-Y.O) (Class E) £3,666.75 (£1,104.00: £534.50: £249.75) **1m** Stalls: Centre GOING: minus 0.31 sec per fur (GF) 3-45 (3-48)

4211 2 **Daunting Destiny (BEL) (72)***(79) (RHannon)* 2-9-2 (5) DaneO'Neill(14) (lw: a cl up: led wl over 2f out: hld on wl) ....— 1
4151 3 Jerry Cutrona (IRE) **(60)***(67)*(Fav)*(NACallaghan)* 2-8-9 JFEgan(1) (lw: trckd ldrs: effrt 2f out: sn ev ch: r.o) ....hd 2

4141² Tarry **(58)***(65) (CNWilliams)* 2-8-7v GCarter(8) (trckd ldrs: swtchd & hdwy over 1f out: fin fast)........hd 3
3994¹⁰ Cerise (IRE) **(48)***(52) (CWCElsey)* 2-7-6b(5) PFessey(2) (in tch: jnd ldrs ½-wy: rdn & btn appr fnl f)........1½ 4
3882² La Finale **(60)***(59) (MHEasterby)* 2-8-9 KFallon(6) (hld up: effrt 3f out styd on one pce appr fnl f)........2½ 5
4192⁴ Phantom Haze **(63)***(62) (MissSEHall)* 2-8-12 MBirch(4) (s.i.s: hdwy ½-wy: sn in tch: rdn & no imp fnl 2f)........s.h 6
4169⁷ Influence Pedler **(60)***(53) (CEBrittain)* 2-8-9 JQuinn(3) (chsd ldrs: effrt 3f out: grad wknd)........3 7
3985¹² Jimjareer (IRE) **(60)***(51) (CaptJWilson)* 2-8-9 SDWilliams(15) (lw: trckd ldrs tl grad wknd fnl 2f)........¾ 8
4075¹⁴ No More Hassle (IRE) **(44)***(33) (MrsMReveley)* 2-7-7 LCharnock(5) (led tl hdd & wknd wl over 2f out)........1 9
4141⁵ Lawnswood Captain (IRE) **(55)***(34) (RHollinshead)* 2-7-11 (7)ow4 FLynch(12) (prom to ½-wy)...3 10
4172¹¹ Double Check (IRE) **(50)***(31) (MJohnston)* 2-7-13 TWilliams(11) (dwlt: hdwy over 2f out: wknd over 1f out)........1¼ 11
4169¹² Tablets of Stone (IRE) **(53)***(31) (JRBosley)* 2-8-2 CRutter(13) (lw: in tch tl rdn & wknd fnl 3f)........1¼ 12
3975¹⁵ Autofyr **(44)***(20) (JSWainwright)* 2-7-7 NKennedy(16) (s.i.s: n.d)........1¼ 13
4188¹⁹ Kenilworth Dancer **(55)***(29) (MrsMReveley)* 2-8-4 KDarley(9) (s.i.s: a bhd)........¾ 14
4081⁸ La Fandango (IRE) **(51)***(24) (MWEasterby)* 2-8-0 SMaloney(7) (hld up & bhd: n.d)........nk 15
4141¹³ Aztec Flyer (USA) **(53)***(23) (MrsMReveley)* 2-8-2 DaleGibson(10) (a bhd)........1½ 16

LONG HANDICAP Autofyr 7-5

100/30 Jerry Cutrona (IRE), **4/1** DAUNTING DESTINY (BEL), **5/1** Tarry, La Finale, **10/1** Phantom Haze, **12/1** La Fandango (IRE) (op 8/1), **14/1** Jimjareer (IRE), Lawnswood Captain (IRE), **16/1** Kenilworth Dancer, **20/1** Influence Pedler, Double Check (IRE), **25/1** No More Hassle (IRE), Tablets of Stone (IRE), **33/1** Aztec Flyer (USA), Cerise (IRE), **66/1** Autofyr, CSF £18.73 CT £68.48 TOTE £5.40: £2.10 £1.90 £1.90 £3.00 (£8.30) Trio £10.30 OWNER The Gold Buster Syndicate (MARLBOROUGH) BRED Patrick Madelein 16 Rn

1m 38.47 (3.47) SF: 42/30/28/15/22/25/16/14/-/-/-/-/-/-/-/-

4286

ASH CONDITIONS STKS (3-Y.O+) (Class C) £5,383.60 (£1,871.60: £905.80: £379.00) **5f** Stalls: Centre GOING: minus 0.31 sec per fur (GF) 4-15 (4-15)

4160¹¹ **Bunty Boo (106)***(109)*(Fav)*(RHannon)* 6-9-2 (5) DaneO'Neill(1) (lw: cl up: led wl over 1f out: r.o wl)........— 1
4119⁶ Don't Worry Me (IRE) **(97)***(92) (FHLee)* 3-8-13 KDarley(4) (swtg: led over 3f: kpt on same pce)........3 2
3822¹⁸ Portelet **(75)***(78) (RGuest)* 3-8-8 GDuffield(2) (wnt rt s: cl up tl outpcd fnl 2f)........3 3
4033⁹ Lago Di Varano **(88)***(61) (JBerry)* 3-9-3b JCarroll(3) (sltly hmpd s: a outpcd & bhd)........8 4

Evens BUNTY BOO, **13/8** Don't Worry Me (IRE) (5/4-15/8), **7/1** Lago Di Varano, **10/1** Portelet, CSF £2.89 TOTE £1.80 (£1.50) OWNER Mrs R. C. Mayall (MARLBOROUGH) BRED Mrs J. McMahon 4 Rn 58.0 secs (1.30) SF: 54/36/22/5

WEIGHT FOR AGE 3yo-1lb

T/Jkpt: £15,840.30 (1.96 Tckts). T/Plpt: £21.00 (949.36 Tckts). T/Qdpt: £28.50 (2.4 Tckts). AA

3740-EDINBURGH (R-H)
Thursday November 2nd (Soft)

WEATHER: sunny WIND: almost nil

4287

E.B.F. TENNENTS 80 SHILLING ALE RATING RELATED MAIDEN LIMITED STKS (0-70) (2-Y.O) (Class E) £3,078.75 (£930.00: £452.50: £213.75) **5f** Stalls: High GOING: 0.40 sec per fur (GS) 1-40 (1-40)

4109⁶ **Queens Check (53)***(69?) (MissJFCraze)* 2-8-9b SWebster(2) (cl up: led ½-wy: kpt on wl).....— 1
4097⁸ Frances Mary **(48)***(67?) (CWFairhurst)* 2-8-9 RCochrane(8) (in tch: hdwy over 1f out: kpt on towards fin)........½ 2
3828⁸ Amoeba (IRE) **(54)***(59) (JBerry)* 2-8-9 JCarroll(1) (led to ½-wy: rdn & r.o one pce)........2½ 3
4230³ Corniche Quest (IRE) **(53)***(54)*(Fav)*(MRChannon)* 2-8-9 KDarley(7) (w ldrs tl rdn & btn over 1f out)........1¾ 4
3939⁷ Fancy Clancy **(46)***(51) (MissLCSiddall)* 2-8-9 DeanMcKeown(3) (unruly s: swvd rt & s.s: rdn & bhd tl r.o fnl f)........1 5
4097¹² Principal Boy (IRE) **(50)***(49) (TJEtherington)* 2-9-0b LCharnock(4) (chsd ldrs: rdn ½-wy: btn over 1f out)........2 6

4066[10] Finisterre (IRE) **(62)***(38) (JJO'Neill)* 2-9-0 KFallon(5) (lw: chsd ldrs over 3f: sn wknd)............3½ **7**
4151[16] Awafeh **(53)***(32) (JWPayne)* 2-9-0b LDettori(6) (cl up 3f: sn btn)............1¾ **8**

2/1 Corniche Quest (IRE), **9/2** Amoeba (IRE), **5/1** Awafeh (op 5/2), **8/1** Principal Boy (IRE), Frances Mary, **9/1** Finisterre (IRE), **11/1** QUEENS CHECK (8/1-12/1), **40/1** Fancy Clancy, CSF £80.62 TOTE £32.30: £1.50 £1.40 £3.10 (£31.10) OWNER Mr W. Cooper (YORK) BRED Mrs Sandra Cooper 8 Rn
62.7 secs (5.00) SF: 41/39/31/26/23/21/10/4

4288 TENNENTS NOVEMBER H'CAP (0-70) (3-Y.O+) (Class E) £4,396.50 (£1,332.00: £651.00: £310.50) **1m 7f 16y** Stalls: High GOING: 0.40 sec per fur (GS) 2-10 (2-14)

*4223** **Merit (IRE) (61)***(78+)*(Fav)*(PFICole)* 3-9-1 4x TQuinn(15) (lw: a.p: led 3f out: rdn clr: eased fnl f)............— **1**
4101[4] Tremendisto **(52)***(64) (CaptJWilson)* 5-9-1 LDettori(5) (a chsng ldrs: chal 3f out: one pce appr fnl f)............5 **2**
4158[4] Eau de Cologne **(62)***(74) (CWThornton)* 3-9-2 DeanMcKeown(12) (in tch: hdwy to chse ldrs 3f out: hrd drvn & one pce)............s.h **3**
4168* Opera Buff (IRE) **(64)***(74) (MissGayKelleway)* 4-9-13 RCochrane(17) (lw: mid div: effrt 4f out: sn chsng ldrs: one pce appr fnl f)............1¼ **4**
4166[7] Bang in Trouble (IRE) **(53)***(63) (JJO'Neill)* 4-9-2 KFallon(16) (prom: effrt over 3f out: styd on one pce)............hd **5**
4248[2] Fabillion **(64)***(73) (CASmith)* 3-9-4 VSlattery(8) (bhd: hdwy 4f out: nt qckn appr fnl f)............¾ **6**
4248* Cuango (IRE) **(55)***(64) (RHollinshead)* 4-8-13 (5) 4x MHenry(7) (hld up & bhd: effrt 5f out: rdn & no imp fnl 3f)............nk **7**
3986[3] Ballymac Girl **(54)***(63)*(Fav)*(JMBradley)* 7-9-0 (3) SDrowne(6) (lw: b: a.p: rdn 3f out: one pce)s.h **8**
4118[20] Five to Seven (USA) **(58)***(62) (CWThornton)* 6-9-4 (3)ow1 OPears(13) (b: led to 3f out: sn btn)..4 **9**
4000[18] Sunday News'n'echo (USA) **(51)***(56) (WStorey)* 4-8-9 (5) PFessey(10) (nvr trbld ldrs)............nk **10**
4114[5] Peep O Day **(48)***(37) (JLEyre)* 4-8-11 RLappin(2) (n.d)............15 **11**
4110[6] Latvian **(65)***(50) (RAllan)* 8-9-9 (5) CTeague(4) (in tch tl lost pl 6f out)............3 **12**
4072[15] Caribbean Surfer (USA) **(45)***(30) (JSGoldie)* 6-8-5 (3) NVarley(14) (b: prom to st)............¾ **13**
4166[4] Great Oration (IRE) **(42)***(25) (FWatson)* 6-8-5 LCharnock(11) (hld up: effrt appr st: sn btn)............1¼ **14**
4166[10] Talos (IRE) **(47)***(30) (DMoffatt)* 7-8-7 (3) DarrenMoffatt(3) (b: a bhd)............½ **15**
4114* Zanzara (IRE) **(48)** *(MrsVAAconley)* 4-8-11 MDeering(1) (a bhd: wl t.o)............dist **16**
4099[2] True Bird (IRE) **(60)** *(JDBethell)* 3-9-0 JCarroll(9) (Withdrawn not under Starter's orders: veterinary advice at s)............ **W**

5/1 MERIT (IRE), Ballymac Girl, **6/1** Fabillion, **7/1** Cuango (IRE), **9/1** Bang in Trouble (IRE), **12/1** Opera Buff (IRE), Eau de Cologne, **14/1** Tremendisto (10/1-16/1), True Bird (IRE), **20/1** Sunday News'n'echo (USA), Great Oration (IRE), **25/1** Zanzara (IRE), Five to Seven (USA), Talos (IRE), Latvian, **40/1** Caribbean Surfer (USA), **50/1** Peep O Day, CSF £62.78 CT £638.08 TOTE £4.50: £1.10 £3.90 £4.30 £1.20 (£33.30) Trio £234.60 OWNER H R H Prince Fahd Salman (WHATCOMBE) BRED Newgate Stud Co 16 Rn
3m 28.4 (17.90) SF: 37/32/33/42/31/32/32/31/30/24/5/18/-/-/-/-/-
WEIGHT FOR AGE 3yo-9lb

4289 LEONARD THOMSON BITES THE DUST H'CAP (0-80) (3-Y.O+ F & M) (Class D) £3,826.25 (£1,160.00: £567.50: £271.25) **1m 4f 31y** Stalls: High GOING: 0.40 sec per fur (GS) 2-40 (2-43)

4259[12] **La Brief (51)***(63) (MJRyan)* 3-7-7 GBardwell(8) (bhd: hdwy appr st: rdn to ld ins fnl f: r.o) ....— **1**
4189[7] Green Land (BEL) **(64)***(75) (SCWilliams)* 3-8-6 KFallon(3) (in tch: hdwy to ld over 1f out: hdd & no ex ins fnl f)............1 **2**
4028[11] Kalou **(68)***(72) (CWCElsey)* 4-8-12 (5) PFessey(6) (a.p: led over 2f out tl over 1f out: no ex).....5 **3**
4248[10] Soba Up **(74)***(77) (TJEtherington)* 5-9-9 ACulhane(13) (chsd ldrs tl lost pl appr st: hdwy & ev ch over 2f out: one pce fnl f)............1 **4**
4259[21] No Comebacks **(59)***(53) (EJAlston)* 7-8-8 JCarroll(11) (mid div: effrt 3f out: nvr able chal).......7 **5**
4258[7] Tethys (USA) **(79)***(70) (JLEyre)* 4-10-0v DeanMcKeown(14) (led tl hdd over 2f out: grad wknd)............2 **6**
3918* Meghdoot **(72)***(56)*(Fav)*(HJCollingridge)* 3-9-0 MRimmer(10) (a.p: effrt ent st: one pce fnl 3f) .5 **7**
3978[6] Highfield Fizz **(54)***(23) (CWFairhurst)* 3-7-10 LCharnock(12) (in tch: effrt appr st: sn btn).......12 **8**
2769[4] Ricana **(56)** *(WTKemp)* 3-7-9 (3)ow5 DarrenMoffatt(2) (chsd ldrs tl wknd appr st)............15 **9**
4228* Lovely Lyca **(75)***(20) (JWHills)* 3-9-3 5x LDettori(5) (chsd ldrs tl wknd over 3f out)............3 **10**
4249[11] Ozubeck (USA) **(52)** *(BHanbury)* 3-7-3 (5)ow1 MBaird(7) (a rr div)............20 **11**
4228[4] Pinkerton Polka **(55)** *(CEBrittain)* 3-7-6 (5)ow4 MHenry(4) (n.d)............3 **12**
4201[13] Slmaat **(66)** *(MrsMReveley)* 4-9-1 KDarley(1) (s.s: a wl t.o)............14 **13**
3704[19] Harrken Heights (IRE) **(54)** *(JSGoldie)* 3-7-7 (3)ow3 NVarley(9) (t.o fnl 6f)............dist **14**

LONG HANDICAP La Brief 7-5 Ricana 6-9 Ozubeck (USA) 7-5 Pinkerton Polka 7-3 Harrken Heights (IRE) 6-0

7/2 Meghdoot, **4/1** Slmaat, **9/2** Lovely Lyca, **9/1** Green Land (BEL), **10/1** Kalou, Pinkerton Polka, **12/1** Highfield Fizz, Tethys (USA), **14/1** LA BRIEF, **20/1** Ozubeck (USA), **25/1** No Comebacks, Soba Up, **100/1** Ricana, Harrken Heights (IRE), CSF £125.51 CT £1,208.43 TOTE £23.50: £3.20 £2.90 £3.60 (£149.50) Trio not won; £517.67 to Doncaster 3/11/95 OWNER Four Jays Racing Partnership (NEWMARKET) BRED Stud-On-The-Chart 14 Rn 2m 45.9 (13.40) SF: 22/34/38/43/19/36/15/-/-/-
WEIGHT FOR AGE 3yo-7lb
OFFICIAL EXPLANATION Slmaat: was left at the start and never recovered.

4290 PETERBOROUGH SOFTWARE MAIDEN AUCTION STKS (2-Y.O) (Class F)
£2,776.40 (£780.40: £381.20)
7f 15y Stalls: High GOING: 0.40 sec per fur (GS) 3-10 (3-15)

Prospector's Cove *(83+) (JPearce)* 2-8-7 GBardwell(13) (w'like: scope: lw: a.p: rdn to ld 1f out: r.o) ....— 1
4195[3] Scenicris (IRE) **(64)***(68) (RHollinshead)* 2-7-8 (5) MHenry(1) (mid div: hdwy u.p 3f out: nrst fin) 3 2
4231[6] Katie Komaite **(56)***(69) (CaptJWilson)* 2-7-11 (5) PFessey(14) (cl up: led ent st: hdd 1f out: no ex) 1 3
4192[6] Tabriz **(77)***(68)*(Fav)*(JDBethell)* 2-8-5 ow3 KFallon(3) (a.p: rdn over 3f out: styd on one pce) ....½ 4
4129[5] Academy of Dance (IRE) *(57)*(Fav)*(MJohnston)* 2-8-2 TWilliams(9) (chsd ldrs: rdn 3f out: styd on one pce) 5 5
4137[2] Lady Bankes (IRE) *(54)*(Fav)*(WGMTurner)* 2-7-11 (5) CAdamson(7) (sme hdwy fnl 3f: nvr rchd ldrs) 1 6
4133[6] Classic Daisy **(53)***(43) (MissGayKelleway)* 2-7-11 (5) MBaird(8) (b.hind: s.i.s: n.d) 5 7
4100[10] Polish Lady (IRE) *(26) (WLBarker)* 2-7-10 (3) NVarley(6) (rdn ½-wy: n.d) 6 8
3018[10] Brogans Brush **(45)***(30) (JSHaldane)* 2-8-4 DeanMcKeown(10) (in tch tl wknd fnl 3f) ....½ 9
3502[6] Contract Bridge (IRE) **(65)***(28) (CWThornton)* 2-8-2 AMackay(5) (nvr trbld ldrs) ....hd 10
4172[9] What Jim Wants (IRE) **(40)***(29) (JJO'Neill)* 2-8-4 JCarroll(2) (mid div: effrt ent st: no imp) ......nk 11
3528[16] Derek's Bo **(40)***(24) (NBycroft)* 2-7-13 LCharnock(11) (led tl hdd ent st: sn wknd) ....hd 12
3975[22] Dancing Dot (IRE) **(40)***(18) (MissLAPerratt)* 2-7-10 (3) DarrenMoffatt(12) (sn outpcd & bhd) ..2½ 13
2971[10] Goldmart (IRE) *(TJEtherington)* 2-8-7 KDarley(4) (wl bhd fr ½-wy) 20 14

7/2 Tabriz, Academy of Dance (IRE), Lady Bankes (IRE), **5/1** Scenicris (IRE), **6/1** PROSPECTOR'S COVE, **16/1** Contract Bridge (IRE), **20/1** Classic Daisy, **25/1** Katie Komaite, **50/1** Goldmart (IRE), Dancing Dot (IRE), **66/1** Polish Lady (IRE), **100/1** Derek's Bo, What Jim Wants (IRE), **200/1** Brogans Brush, CSF £33.27 TOTE £7.70: £2.40 £1.70 £4.20 (£37.30) Trio £174.60 OWNER Saracen Racing (NEWMARKET) BRED Southcourt Stud 14 Rn
1m 33.4 (7.40) SF: 38/23/24/23/12/9/-/-/-/-/-/-/-/-

4291 E.B.F. TENNENTS LAGER MAIDEN STKS (2-Y.O) (Class D)
£3,972.50 (£1,205.00: £590.00: £282.50)
1m 16y Stalls: High GOING: 0.40 sec per fur (GS) 3-40 (3-43)

3900[3] **Santillana (USA)** *(82+)*(Fav)*(JHMGosden)* 2-9-0 LDettori(2) (lw: a gng wl: led over 1f out: easily) ....— 1
3881[7] Classic Ballet (FR) *(74) (SCWilliams)* 2-8-9 AMackay(1) (led tl over 1f out: no ch w wnr) 1¾ 2
4169[3] Fly Fishing (USA) *(73) (MrsJCecil)* 2-9-0 RCochrane(4) (s.i.s: hdwy 3f out: nvr able chal) 3 3
3994[7] Los Alamos *(65) (CWThornton)* 2-8-9 DeanMcKeown(8) (a chsng ldrs: outpcd ent st: no imp after) 1½ 4
4172[3] Not Quite Grey **(69)***(52) (KMcAuliffe)* 2-9-0 KFallon(5) (b.off hind: chsd ldrs tl outpcd over 3f out: sn wknd) 9 5
4190[9] Portuguese Lil *(46) (DNicholls)* 2-8-9 AlexGreaves(3) (sme hdwy whn hmpd over 1f out: n.d) ....½ 6
Chauvelin (IRE) *(46) (MJohnston)* 2-9-0 TWilliams(7) (cmpt: str: rn green & sn pushed along: n.d) 2½ 7
Tonto *(CWThornton)* 2-9-0 LCharnock(6) (leggy: scope: dwlt: a wl bhd) 25 8

2/5 SANTILLANA (USA), **4/1** Fly Fishing (USA), **8/1** Not Quite Grey, **14/1** Portuguese Lil, **25/1** Chauvelin (IRE), Classic Ballet (FR), **33/1** Los Alamos, **66/1** Tonto, CSF £12.60 TOTE £1.30: £1.00 £2.00 £1.40 (£9.00) OWNER Sheikh Mohammed (NEWMARKET) BRED Mr David Caldwell 8 Rn
1m 46.6 (8.00) SF: 50/42/41/33/20/14/14/-

4292 LADBROKE ON-COURSE H'CAP (0-70) (3-Y.O+) (Class E) £3,631.25
(£1,100.00: £537.50: £256.25)
1m 16y Stalls: High GOING: 0.40 sec per fur (GS) 4-10 (4-11)

3715[25] **Best of All (IRE) (67)***(81) (JBerry)* 3-9-11 JCarroll(1) (racd wd: cl up: led over 3f out: r.o wl) ....— 1

4128[3] Penmar **(53)***(64) (TJEtherington)* 3-8-11b LCharnock(14) (a chsng ldrs: ev ch over 3f out: nt qckn appr fnl f)....1½ **2**
4236[4] Field of Vision (IRE) **(63)***(66) (MJohnston)* 5-9-10b TWilliams(2) (racd wd: a chsng ldrs: one pce fnl 3f)....4 **3**
4275* Northern Spark **(48)***(51) (MissLAPerratt)* 7-8-4 (5) 5x PFessey(12) (hdwy ent st: racd far side: kpt on wl: nvr able chal)....nk **4**
4234[2] Pine Ridge Lad (IRE) **(54)***(54) (JLEyre)* 5-9-1 SDWilliams(10) (led early: chsd ldrs: racd far side st & one pce fnl 3f)....1¼ **5**
3977[11] Rood Music **(55)***(53) (MGMeagher)* 4-9-2 AMackay(8) (styd on u.p fnl 3f: nvr able chal)....1¼ **6**
2610[3] Frontiersman **(52)***(38) (JWWatts)* 3-8-10b LDettori(3) (racd wd: led after 1f tl over 3f out: sn btn)....6 **7**
4272[2] Calder King **(60)***(42) (JLEyre)* 4-9-4b(3) OPears(9) (bhd tl hdwy u.p 3f out: n.d)....1¾ **8**
4249[3] Super High **(56)***(37)*(Fav)*(PHowling)* 3-9-0 RCochrane(6) (nvr trbld ldrs)....¾ **9**
4193[9] Daawe (USA) **(60)***(33) (MrsVAAconley)* 4-9-7v MDeering(7) (prom 5f)....4 **10**
3823[9] Hey Up Dolly (IRE) **(61)***(27) (JBerry)* 3-9-5b KDarley(13) (racd far side st: outpcd & bhd fnl 3f)....3½ **11**
4280[13] Diet **(53)***(18) (MissLAPerratt)* 9-9-0v KFallon(4) (chsd ldrs: racd far side & wknd fnl 3f)....½ **12**
4043[15] Chantry Bellini **(49)***(11) (MrsSMAustin)* 6-8-3b(7) DDenby(11) (b: b.hind: racd far side: bhd fnl 3f)....1½ **13**
4193[8] Bogart **(55)***(13) (CWFairhurst)* 4-9-2 MRimmer(5) (in tch tl wknd fnl 3½f)....2 **14**

3/1 Super High, **9/2** Frontiersman, **6/1** Calder King, Pine Ridge Lad (IRE), **8/1** Northern Spark, **10/1** Field of Vision (IRE), **12/1** Rood Music, **14/1** Chantry Bellini, **16/1** Penmar, **20/1** Diet, **25/1** Bogart, **33/1** BEST OF ALL (IRE), Hey Up Dolly (IRE), **50/1** Daawe (USA), CSF £439.17 CT £5,046.21 TOTE £33.80: £4.90 £6.30 £4.40 (£195.00) Trio £504.20 OWNER Mr Robert Aird (COCKERHAM) BRED Mrs D. Hutch 14 Rn 1m 46.6 (8.00) SF: 60/43/48/33/36/35/17/24/16/15/6/-/-/-
WEIGHT FOR AGE 3yo-3lb

T/Jkpt: Not won; £8,927.20 to Doncaster 3/11/95. T/Plpt: £1,829.20 (8.22 Tckts). T/Qdpt: £58.00 (0.8 Tckts); £15.70 to Doncaster 3/11/95. AA

4216-LINGFIELD (L-H)
Thursday November 2nd (Standard)

4293 LEO CLAIMING STKS (3-Y.O+) (Class F) £2,997.80 (£830.80: £397.40)
1m 4f (Equitrack) Stalls: Low GOING minus 0.47 sec per fur (FST) 1-30 (1-32)

4062[2] **Elementary (70)***(73)*(Fav)*(NJHWalker)* 12-9-7 (3) JStack(6) (lw: a.p: led 4f out: clr 3f out: r.o wl)....— **1**
2174[7] Sir Norman Holt (IRE) **(70)***(66) (RJO'Sullivan)* 6-9-10b DBiggs(3) (chsd ldr: led over 5f out to 4f out: unable qckn)....5 **2**
4205[10] What's Secreto (USA) **(50)***(58) (PAKelleway)* 3-8-12v(5) AWhelan(10) (hdwy over 6f out: rdn over 4f out: one pce)....6 **3**
Tamandu *(45) (CJames)* 5-8-13 AMcGlone(5) (lost pl 5f out: r.o one pce fnl 2f)....1½ **4**
3384[14] Don't Give Up **(33)***(38) (PBurgoyne)* 7-8-3b(3) DRMcCabe(8) (hdwy over 1f out: nvr nrr)....hd **5**
4232* Shabanaz **(60)***(53) (WRMuir)* 10-9-7 CRutter(12) (hdwy over 6f out: hrd rdn over 3f out: wknd over 1f out)....nk **6**
158[4] Night Edition *(39) (SDow)* 5-8-12 GDuffield(9) (b: b.hind: hld up: rdn over 5f out: wknd over 2f out)....3½ **7**
3743[14] Big Pat **(65)***(42) (JGMO'Shea)* 6-9-1 JTate(2) (b: hdwy over 4f out: wknd over 2f out)....½ **8**
2090[6] Cone Lane **(15)***(23) (BGubby)* 9-8-1 (5) PPMurphy(4) (bit bkwd: bhd fnl 6f)....7 **9**
813[18] Good so Fa (IRE) **(55)***(37) (CNAllen)* 3-9-3 TIves(1) (dwlt: a bhd)....3½ **10**
Presidential (FR) *(21) (KOCunningham-Brown)* 4-9-1b RHughes(11) (a bhd)....5 **11**
1012[11] More Bills (IRE) **(40)***(15) (AMoore)* 3-8-5b CandyMorris(7) (b.hind: plld hrd: led: sn clr: hdd over 5f out: sn wknd)....2 **12**

10/11 ELEMENTARY, **9/4** Shabanaz, **9/1** Big Pat (6/1-10/1), **10/1** Sir Norman Holt (IRE), **20/1** Night Edition, **33/1** Good so Fa (IRE), Presidential (FR), Don't Give Up, **50/1** Cone Lane, What's Secreto (USA), Tamandu, More Bills (IRE), CSF £11.10 TOTE £2.00: £1.10 £2.20 £4.50 (£12.70) Trio £232.70; £262.23 to Doncaster 3/11/95 OWNER Mr Paul Green (WANTAGE) BRED Ballymaglassan Stud 12 Rn 2m 32.27 (2.87) SF: 50/43/28/22/15/30/16/19/-/7/-/-
WEIGHT FOR AGE 3yo-7lb

4294 SCORPIO NURSERY H'CAP (0-75) (2-Y.O) (Class E) £3,159.20 (£941.60: £448.80: £202.40)
5f (Equitrack) Stalls: High GOING minus 0.47 sec per fur (FST) 2-00 (2-03)

2859[4] **Beeny (60)***(64) (APJarvis)* 2-8-7 JTate(6) (a.p: led over 1f out: rdn out)....— **1**

4237[3] Time For Tea (IRE) **(71)***(67) (CACyzer)* 2-9-4 DBiggs(2) (hld up: rdn over 2f out: r.o ins fnl f)........2½ **2**
4077[12] Foreman **(59)***(48) (WAO'Gorman)* 2-8-6v[ow4] EmmaO'Gorman(7) (lw: hdwy over 1f out: str run fnl f: fin wl)........1 **3**
4219[6] Dancing Jack **(54)***(44) (JJBridger)* 2-8-1 GDuffield(3) (led 1f: ev ch over 1f out: one pce)........1 **4**
3662[10] Bouton d'Or **(50)***(36) (PHowling)* 2-7-11 JQuinn(4) (hld up: rdn over 2f out: one pce)........1 **5**
4260[2] Lady Caroline Lamb (IRE) **(60)***(42)*(Fav)*(MRChannon)* 2-8-2 (5) PPMurphy(1) (led 4f out tl over 1f out: wknd fnl f)........1¼ **6**
4144[5] Mystic Tempo (USA) **(74)***(56) (PWChapple-Hyam)* 2-9-2 (5) RHavlin(5) (lw: bhd fnl 3f)........hd **7**
3982[13] Simply Miss Chief (IRE) **(55)***(36) (DWPArbuthnot)* 2-8-2 SSanders(8) (b: b.hind: bhd fnl 3f)...½ **8**
4056[7] Subfusk **(61)***(41) (WGMTurner)* 2-8-5 (3) PMcCabe(9) (a.p: rn v.wd bnd wl over 1f out: wknd) nk **9**
3651[11] Nameless **(64)***(40) (DJSCosgrove)* 2-8-6b(5) AWhelan(10) (b.hind: lw: bhd fnl 3f)........1 **10**

15/8 Lady Caroline Lamb (IRE), **9/2** Time For Tea (IRE), **6/1** BEENY, Mystic Tempo (USA) (4/1-13/2), **11/1** Subfusk, Dancing Jack, **12/1** Nameless (8/1-14/1), **14/1** Foreman (10/1-16/1), **33/1** Simply Miss Chief (IRE), Bouton d'Or, CSF £31.25 TOTE £8.40: £2.60 £2.20 £3.40 (£14.70) Trio £110.90 OWNER Mr J. D. Rogers (ASTON UPTHORPE) BRED Miss S. E. Jarvis 10 Rn
59.82 secs (1.62) SF: 24/27/8/4/-/2/16/-/1/-

4295

TAURUS H'CAP (0-70) (3-Y.O+) (Class E) £3,273.60 (£976.80: £466.40: £211.20)
5f (Equitrack) Stalls: High GOING minus 0.47 sec per fur (FST) 2-30 (2-31)

4215[8] **Friendly Brave (USA) (60)***(67)*(Fav)*(MissGayKelleway)* 5-9-0 (5) AWhelan(8) (lost pl over 2f out: rallied over 1f out: led wl ins fnl f: rdn out)........— **1**
4125[4] Speedy Classic (USA) **(61)***(64) (MJHeaton-Ellis)* 6-9-6 AClark(7) (rdn & hdwy over 2f out: ev ch ins fnl f: unable qckn)........1¼ **2**
3333[8] Tee-Emm **(56)***(55) (PHowling)* 5-9-1 JQuinn(5) (b.hind: a.p: led over 1f out tl ins fnl f: one pce)........1¼ **3**
4142[3] Squire Corrie **(67)***(64) (GHarwood)* 3-9-5b(7) GayeHarwood(3) (a.p: ev ch ins fnl f: one pce)...½ **4**
3919[23] Kalar **(69)***(66) (DWChapman)* 6-10-0b RHughes(1) (led over 3f: one pce fnl f)........hd **5**
3524[11] Lift Boy (USA) **(60)***(51) (AMoore)* 6-9-5 CandyMorris(6) (b.hind: lost pl 3f out: rallied over 1f out: one pce)........2 **6**
4057[5] Halliard **(58)***(47) (TMJones)* 4-9-3 RPerham(10) (b: no hdwy fnl 2f)........½ **7**
4215[9] Robellion **(65)***(50) (DWPArbuthnot)* 4-9-10v GCarter(2) (b: b.hind: dwlt: a bhd)........1¼ **8**
3424[10] Cork Street Girl (IRE) **(52)***(29) (GBBalding)* 3-8-6b(5) DaneO'Neill(9) (a bhd)........2½ **9**
3961[10] Windrush Boy **(64)***(36) (JRBosley)* 5-9-9 CRutter(4) (a bhd)........1¾ **10**

100/30 FRIENDLY BRAVE (USA), **9/2** Squire Corrie (3/1-5/1), **5/1** Speedy Classic (USA), **11/2** Kalar, Halliard, **12/1** Tee-Emm (op 8/1), Robellion, Windrush Boy, **14/1** Cork Street Girl (IRE), **16/1** Lift Boy (USA), CSF £20.44 CT £168.41 TOTE £5.80: £2.30 £2.20 £2.00 (£32.80) Trio £62.80 OWNER Grid Thoroughbred Racing Partnership (WHITCOMBE) BRED Foxfield 10 Rn
58.95 secs (0.75) SF: 49/46/37/46/48/33/29/32/11/18

4296

LIBRA MAIDEN STKS (3-Y.O) (Class D) £3,968.90 (£1,185.20: £566.60: £257.30)
7f (Equitrack) Stalls: Low GOING minus 0.47 sec per fur (FST) 3-00 (3-02)

2265[5] **Joyful (IRE)** *(63) (JHMGosden)* 3-8-9 GHind(3) (bit bkwd: hld up: hung lft over 1f out: rdn fnl f: led last stride)........— **1**
3981[2] Sombreffe *(63)*(Fav)*(DRLoder)* 3-8-9 RHughes(5) (a.p: led over 2f out: hrd rdn fnl f: hdd last stride)........s.h **2**
4225[5] Dancing Sioux **(62)***(59) (RGuest)* 3-9-0 GDuffield(11) (hld up: rdn 2f out: one pce)........4 **3**
4152[16] Crystal Gift **(56)***(57) (DWPArbuthnot)* 3-8-9b(5) PPMurphy(4) (rdn over 2f out: hdwy over 1f out: nvr nrr)........¾ **4**
3282[5] Awasha (IRE) *(49) (MissGayKelleway)* 3-8-4 (5) AWhelan(10) (a.p: ev ch over 2f out: wknd fnl f)........1¼ **5**
1654[4] Komodo (USA) **(65)***(49) (KOCunningham-Brown)* 3-9-0 WWoods(6) (led 4f out tl over 2f out: sn wknd)........2½ **6**
4193[19] Desert Water (IRE) **(35)***(45) (JJBridger)* 3-9-0b JQuinn(9) (s.s: nvr nrr)........1¾ **7**
2786[8] Sooty (IRE) **(51)***(37) (HThomsonJones)* 3-8-9 GCarter(8) (bhd fnl 3f)........1 **8**
3960[11] Port Hedland **(36)***(8) (MMcCormack)* 3-8-9v AClark(7) (dwlt: a bhd)........13 **9**
Royal Dancer **(40)***(7) (RJWeaver)* 3-8-4 (5) DaneO'Neill(2) (led 3f: wknd over 2f out)........nk **10**
Chapel Annie *(CPWildman)* 3-8-9 StephenDavies(1) (unf: s.s: a wl bhd)........3 **11**

Evens Sombreffe, **9/2** Awasha (IRE), **5/1** JOYFUL (IRE), **7/1** Komodo (USA), **14/1** Sooty (IRE) (8/1-16/1), **16/1** Dancing Sioux, **50/1** Crystal Gift, Royal Dancer, Chapel Annie, **66/1** Port Hedland, Desert Water (IRE), CSF £9.89 TOTE £6.80: £2.10 £1.10 £3.00 (£3.20) Trio £10.60 OWNER Sheikh Mohammed (NEWMARKET) BRED Sheikh Mohammed bin Rashid al Maktoum 11 Rn
1m 24.83 (1.83) SF: 32/32/28/26/18/18/14/6/-/-/-

4297

DICK AND DENYSE MYSON 45TH ANNIVERSARY H'CAP (0-75) (3-Y.O+) (Class D) £4,070.30 (£1,216.40: £582.20: £265.10)
1m (Equitrack) Stalls: High GOING minus 0.47 sec per fur (FST) 3-30 (3-31)

*4217** **Set the Fashion (69)***(80) (DLWilliams)* 6-9-11v 6x DHarrison(4) (rdn over 3f out: hdwy over 2f out: swtchd rt over 1f out: led wl ins fnl f: r.o wl)— 1
4157⁵ Present Situation **(68)***(77)*(Fav)*(LordHuntingdon)* 4-9-5 (5) AWhelan(5) (lw: a.p: led over 2f out tl wl ins fnl f: unable qckn)1 2
4171⁶ Bentico **(72)***(78) (MrsNMacauley)* 6-9-7b(7) AmandaSanders(6) (a.p: led 4f out tl over 2f out: one pce)1½ 3
4145⁹ Dancing Heart **(67)***(68) (BJMeehan)* 3-9-6 RHughes(1) (led 4f: rdn wl over 1f out: one pce).2½ 4
3268⁷ Digpast (IRE) **(69)***(67) (RJO'Sullivan)* 5-9-11b DBiggs(8) (lost pl over 2f out: r.o one pce)1¾ 5
4071¹² Brave Princess **(67)***(62) (MAJarvis)* 3-9-6 WWoods(7) (b.nr hind: lost pl over 2f out: one pce)1½ 6
3960⁷ Waikiki Beach (USA) **(67)***(60) (GLMoore)* 4-9-9 SWhitworth(9) (lw: prom 5f)¾ 7
4038¹⁶ Mr Rough **(63)***(55) (DMorris)* 4-9-5 TIves(2) (prom over 4f)nk 8
4157²³ Scharnhorst **(66)***(55) (SDow)* 3-9-5 GDuffield(12) (b.hind: lost pl 5f out: rallied over 3f out: wknd over 2f out)1½ 9
4134¹⁰ Invocation **(70)***(54) (AMoore)* 8-9-9 (3) JStack(3) (b.hind: lw: bhd fnl 4f)2½ 10
4194³ Nordic Doll (IRE) **(69)***(45) (BWHills)* 3-9-3 (5) JDSmith(10) (b: b.hind: hdwy over 3f out: wknd over 2f out)4 11
3630¹¹ Queen's Ransom (IRE) **(75)***(48) (PWChapple-Hyam)* 3-9-9 (5) RHavlin(11) (a bhd)1½ 12

5/2 Present Situation, **6/1** Digpast (IRE), **7/1** Nordic Doll (IRE), **8/1** Bentico, SET THE FASHION (5/1-9/1), **9/1** Mr Rough, **11/1** Brave Princess (7/1-12/1), Dancing Heart, **16/1** Waikiki Beach (USA), Queen's Ransom (IRE), **20/1** Scharnhorst, **25/1** Invocation, CSF £27.89 CT £158.29 TOTE £8.70: £3.10 £1.70 £3.70 (£8.70) Trio £17.50 OWNER Mr R. J. Matthews (NEWBURY) BRED The Queen
12 Rn 1m 37.34 (0.94) SF: 60/57/58/45/47/39/40/35/32/34/22/25
WEIGHT FOR AGE 3yo-3lb

4298

ARIES AMATEUR H'CAP (0-65) (3-Y.O+) (Class F) £3,048.20 (£845.20: £404.60)
1m 2f (Equitrack) Stalls: Low GOING minus 0.47 sec per fur (FST) 4-00 (4-01)

4152² **No Speeches (IRE) (51)***(63) (SDow)* 4-10-7 MrTMcCarthy(10) (b.hind: a.p: led over 2f out: r.o wl)— 1
4223⁴ Tadellal (IRE) **(58)***(67) (WGMTurner)* 4-10-9 (5) MrEJames(9) (lw: a.p: rdn 3f out: nt qckn)....1¾ 2
4217⁶ Masnun (USA) **(65)***(74) (RJO'Sullivan)* 10-11-7 MrMArmytage(4) (lw: stdy hdwy 4f out: hrd rdn over 1f out: one pce)s.h 3
3288⁶ Montone (IRE) **(50)***(57) (JRJenkins)* 5-10-1 (5) MrMMannish(14) (chsd ldr over 5f: one pce)..1¼ 4
3808* Bold Habit **(51)***(53)*(Fav)*(JPearce)* 10-10-7 MrsLPearce(12) (hdwy over 1f out: nvr nrr)3 5
3182⁷ Star Fighter **(50)***(51) (MJHaynes)* 3-10-1b MissYHaynes(3) (b.hind: nvr nr to chal)¾ 6
4272³ Maple Bay (IRE) **(57)***(57) (ABailey)* 6-10-8 (5) MissBridgetGatehouse(13) (nvr nrr)1 7
4227⁸ Roman Reel (USA) **(58)***(57) (GLMoore)* 4-10-9 (5) MrKGoble(6) (lw: led over 7f)½ 8
3952⁶ Captain Marmalade **(48)***(46) (DTThom)* 6-10-4 MissDianaJones(8) (b: lw: nvr nrr)nk 9
4163¹⁷ Camden's Ransom (USA) **(57)***(51) (HGRowsell)* 8-10-13 MrMRimell(5) (hld up: rdn over 3f out: sn wknd)2½ 10
4171¹⁴ Mowlaie **(65)***(58) (DWChapman)* 4-11-2 (5) MissRClark(11) (lw: bhd fnl 5f)½ 11
4152* Total Rach (IRE) **(54)***(46) (RIngram)* 3-10-0b(5) MrsSIngram(7) (a bhd)¾ 12
1974¹⁹ Awesome Power **(58)***(46) (JWHills)* 9-11-0 MissEJohnsonHoughton(2) (hld up: rdn over 3f out: sn wknd)2½ 13
4170² Kingchip Boy **(53)***(1) (MJRyan)* 6-10-4v(5) MrSLavallin(1) (bhd fnl 5f)25 14

4/1 Bold Habit, **11/2** Maple Bay (IRE), Kingchip Boy, **6/1** NO SPEECHES (IRE), Tadellal (IRE), **8/1** Masnun (USA), **12/1** Captain Marmalade, Camden's Ransom (USA), Total Rach (IRE) (8/1-14/1), Roman Reel (USA) (op 8/1), **14/1** Star Fighter, **20/1** Montone (IRE), **25/1** Awesome Power, Mowlaie, CSF £45.23 CT £280.55 TOTE £6.50: £2.20 £3.20 £2.30 (£28.60) Trio £204.00 OWNER Mr S. Dow (EPSOM) BRED Lyonstown Stud and Swettenham Stud 14 Rn
2m 6.32 (3.32) SF: 53/57/64/47/43/36/47/47/36/41/48/31/36/-
WEIGHT FOR AGE 3yo-5lb
T/Plpt: £99.10 (98.26 Tckts). T/Qdpt: £47.40 (1.2 Tckts). AK

2889a-EVRY (France) (R-H)
Monday October 23rd (Good)

4299a

PRIX DE SAINT-CYR (Listed) (3-Y.O F) £16,766.00 (£5,748.00: £3,593.00) **7f** 2-40 (2-38)

4121⁵ **South Rock** *(103) (JAGlover)* 3-8-12 PaulEddery — 1

Karliyka (IRE) *(103) (AdeRoyerDupre,France)* 3-8-12 GMosse ....hd 2
Tousle (FR) *(94) (JEHammond,France)* 3-8-12 FSanchez 4 3

P-M 4.40F: 1.80F 1.30F 1.80F (4.30F) OWNER Mr B. H. Farr (WORKSOP) BRED Worksop Manor Stud Farm 8 Rn 1m 25.95 SF: -/-/-

4187a-LYON PARILLY (Lyon, France)
Thursday October 26th (Good)

4300a PRIX ANDRE BABOIN-GRAND PRIX DES PROVINCES (Gp 3) (3-Y.O+) £26,347.00 (£7,185.00: £7,185.00) **1m 2f** 2-30 (2-30)

4017a[2] **Parme (USA)** *(116) (ELellouche,France)* 4-8-10 RLaplanche ....— 1
Bulington (FR) *(116) (H-APantall,France)* 3-8-6 JBoisnard ....¾ 2
4016a[5] Signoretto (FR) *(115) (DSmaga,France)* 8-8-10 GGuignard ....d.h 2
P-M 4.80F: 1.40F 2.70F (Bulington) 1.40F (Signoretto) (11.40F 3.90F) OWNER Mr D. Wildenstein BRED Allez France Stables 12 Rn 2m 6.3 SF: -/-/-

LE CROISE-LAROCHE (Lille, France) (L-H)
Saturday October 28th (Soft)

4301a GRAND PRIX DU NORD (Listed) (3-Y.O) £14,371.00 (£4,790.00: £2,395.00) **1m 2f 165y** 2-30 (2-30)

Karamiyna (IRE) *(98) (AdeRoyerDupre,France)* 3-8-8 GMosse ....— 1
3945[34] Maralinga (IRE) *(100) (LadyHerries)* 3-8-11 SWhitworth 1 2
Egipcio *(94) (MmeMBollack-Badel,France)* 3-8-11 ABadel 4 3

P-M 2.60F: 1.30F 2.00F 1.90F (12.80F) OWNER Aga Khan BRED H.H. Aga Khan's Studs S.C. 8 Rn

4175a-BELMONT PARK (New York, USA) (L-H)
Saturday October 28th (Turf Soft, Dirt Muddy)

4302a BREEDERS' CUP JUVENILE FILLIES (Gp 1) (2-Y.O F) £333,333.00 (£128,205.00: £76,923.00) **1m 110y** 3-55 (3-55)

My Flag (USA) *(110t) (CMcGaughey,USA)* 2-8-7b JBailey (bhd early: hdwy & 3rd st: led u.p wl ins fnl f) ....— 1
Cara Rafaela (USA) *(109t) (DWLukas,USA)* 2-8-7 PDay (trckd ldr: chal on ins & led ins fnl f: hdd cl home) ....½ 2
Golden Attraction (USA) *(106t) (DWLukas,USA)* 2-8-7 GStevens (led tl ins fnl f: one pce) ...1½ 3

P-M £9.00: PL £5.00 £5.90 SHOW £2.80 £2.90 £2.30 (SF £42.40) OWNER Mr O. Phipps BRED Ogden Phipps 8 Rn 1m 42.55 SF: -/-/-

4303a BREEDERS' CUP SPRINT (Gp 1) (3-Y.O+) £333,333.00 (£128,205.00: £76,923.00: £35,897.00: £12,820.00) **6f (Dirt)** 4-27 (4-29)

Desert Stormer (USA) *(127) (FLyons,USA)* 5-8-11 KDesormeaux (mde vitually all: r.o wl fnl f) ....— 1
Mr. Greeley (USA) *(128) (NZito,USA)* 3-8-11 JulieKrone (disp ld thrght: hrd rdn ins fnl f: r.o) ....nk 2
Lit de Justice (USA) *(124) (JenineSahadi,USA)* 5-9-0b CNakatani (bhd tl r.o strly fnl 2f: fin wl) 2 3
Not Surprising (USA) *(123) (JVanWorp,USA)* 5-9-0 RDavis (mid div: hdwy & 6th st: r.o) ....nk 4
Friendly Lover (USA) *(118) (JHPierce,USA)* 7-9-0b RWilson (mid div: nvr able to chal) 2 5
Our Emblem (USA) *(118) (CMcGaughey,USA)* 4-9-0 PDay (in rr tl r.o fnl 2f: nrst fin) ....hd 6
3491[3] Owington *(117) (GWragg)* 4-9-0 LDettori (dwlt: hdwy & 5th st: nvr able to chal) ....nk 7
4012a* Hever Golf Rose *(111) (TJNaughton)* 4-8-11 JWeaver (trckd ldrs: 3rd st: sn rdn & wknd) 1 8
Golden Gear (USA) *(109) (NHickey,USA)* 4-9-0 CPerret (a mid div) 2 9
You and I (USA) *(108) (RFrankel,USA)* 4-9-0 JChavez (a bhd) ....hd 10
Track Gal (USA) *(79) (JSadler,USA)* 4-8-11 CMcCarron (prom early: 4th st: wknd) 10 11
3491[4] Lake Coniston (IRE) *(60) (GLewis)* 4-9-0 PatEddery (5th early: rdn & lost pl ½-wy: t.o) 8 12
Da Hoss (USA) *(57) (MWDickinson,America)* 3-8-11 JBailey (prom early: wknd) 1 13

P-M £31.00: PL £15.60 £28.00 SHOW £16.40 £15.80 £16.40 (SF £733.00) OWNER Joanne Nor
BRED Joanne H. Nor 13 Rn 1m 9.14 SF: -/-/-/-/-/-/-/-/-/-/-/-/-

4304a BREEDERS' CUP DISTAFF (Gp 1) (3-Y.O+ F & M) £333,333.00 (£128,205.00: £76,923.00) **1m 1f (Dirt)** 4-59 (4-59)

Inside Information (USA) *(130+) (CMcGaughey,USA)* 4-8-11 MSmith (trckd ldrs: hdwy to ld over 4f out: clr ent st: v.easily) — 1
Heavenly Prize (USA) *(106) (CMcGaughey,USA)* 4-8-11 PDay (sn wl bhd: 8th st: r.o wl fnl f: no ch w wnr) 13½ 2
Lakeway (USA) *(102) (GJones,USA)* 4-8-11b KDesormeaux (led tl over 4f out: one pce) 2¼ 3

P-M £3.60: PL £3.20 £3.20 SHOW £2.20 £2.20 £4.80 (SF £34.20) OWNER Mr Ogden Mills Phipps
BRED Ogden Mills Phipps 10 Rn 1m 46.0 SF: -/-/-

4305a BREEDERS' CUP MILE (Gp 1) (3-Y.O+) £333,333.00 (£128,205.00: £76,923.00: £35,897.00: £12,820.00) **1m (Turf)** 5-31 (5-32)

3814[2] **Ridgewood Pearl** *(132) (JOxx,Ireland)* 3-8-7 JPMurtagh (sn cl up: 2nd st: rdn to ld over 1f out: r.o wl) — 1
Fastness (IRE) *(132) (JenineSahadi,USA)* 5-9-0 GStevens (a.p: led ent st: hdd over 1f out: r.o u.p) 2 2
3589a[4] Sayyedati *(115) (CEBrittain)* 5-8-11 CNakatani (dwlt: rr early: gd hdwy over 2f out: r.o ins fnl f) 7 3
Dove Hunt (USA) *(118) (WHoward,USA)* 4-9-0 PDay (cl up: 5th st: one pce) nse 4
Savinio (USA) *(117) (WGreenman,USA)* 5-9-0 CMcCarron (a.p: 4th st: wknd over 1f out) nk 5
4078[2] Soviet Line (IRE) *(115) (MRStoute)* 5-9-0 WRSwinburn (rr early: hdwy ent st: nvr nr to chal) 1 6
Fourstars Allstar (USA) *(105) (LO'Brien,USA)* 7-9-0 JSantos (led early: led briefly 3f out: sn wknd) 5 7
4012a[2] Cherokee Rose (IRE) *(101) (JEHammond,France)* 4-8-11 CAsmussen (bhd early: hdwy & 8th st: nt rch ldrs) ½ 8
Mighty Forum *(103) (MHennig,USA)* 4-9-0 EDelahoussaye (a bhd) ½ 9
Earl of Barking (IRE) *(102) (RCross,USA)* 5-9-0 LDettori (nvr rchd ldrs) ½ 10
4016a* Shaanxi (USA) *(97) (ELellouche,France)* 3-8-7 DBoeuf (mid div: hdwy appr st: no imp) ¾ 11
3576a[3] The Vid (USA) *(98) (MWolfson,USA)* 5-9-0 JBailey (m.n.s) 1½ 12
4178a* Poplar Bluff (IRE) *(57) (AFabre,France)* 3-8-10 OPeslier (2nd early: led after 2f: hdd 3f out: sn wknd) 20 13

P-M £7.10: PL £4.40 £6.20 SHOW £3.60 £4.60 £7.00 (SF £47.60) OWNER Mrs Anne Coughlan
BRED S. Coughlan 13 Rn 1m 43.65 SF: -/-/-/-/-/-/-/-/-/-/-/-/-

4306a BREEDERS' CUP JUVENILE (Gp 1) (2-Y.O C & G) £333,333.00 (£128,205.00: £76,923.00) **1m 110y (Dirt)** 6-03 (6-04)

Unbridled's Song (USA) *(124t) (JRyerson,USA)* 2-8-10 MSmith (chsd ldrs: hdwy to ld ent st: r.o gamely fnl f) — 1
Hennessy (USA) *(123t) (DWLukas,USA)* 2-8-10 DonnaBarton (w ldrs: led ½-wy tl hdd by wnr: rallied u.p ins fnl f) nk 2
Editor's Note (USA) *(116t) (DWLukas,USA)* 2-8-10b JBailey (rr early: hdwy st: r.o wl fnl f) 4 3
3907a[2] Winter Quarters (USA) *(95t) (RFrankel,USA)* 2-8-10 CMcCarron (chsd ldrs: 4th st: rdn & wknd over 1f out: btn 14½l) 6

P-M £12.40: PL £8.10 £8.50 SHOW £6.70 £6.70 £7.90 (SF £108.50) OWNER Paraneck Stable
BRED Mandysland Farm 13 Rn 1m 41.6 SF: -/-/-/-

4307a BREEDERS' CUP TURF (Gp 1) (3-Y.O+) £666,667.00 (£256,410.00: £153,846.00: £71,795.00: £25,641.00) **1m 4f (Turf)** 6-35 (6-35)

3576a[10] **Northern Spur (IRE)** *(132) (RMcAnally,USA)* 4-9-0 CMcCarron (3rd early: led 3f out: r.o wl) — 1
4014a[2] Freedom Cry *(132) (AFabre,France)* 4-9-0 OPeslier (trckd ldrs: 2nd st: chal over 1f out: r.o) nk 2
4014a[6] Carnegie (IRE) *(130) (AFabre,France)* 4-9-0 TJarnet (trckd ldrs: 4th st: r.o one pce fnl f) 1½ 3
4120[4] Tamure (IRE) *(128) (JHMGosden)* 3-8-9 LDettori (dwlt: hdwy & 6th st: r.o fnl f) 2½ 4
3690a[7] Hernando (FR) *(126) (JEHammond,France)* 5-9-0 CAsmussen (mid div: 9th st: r.o u.p) nk 5
3576a* Awad (USA) *(117) (DDonk,USA)* 5-9-0b EMaple (rr early: r.o st: nvr plcd to chal) 6¾ 6
Alice Springs (USA) *(109) (JonathanSheppard,USA)* 5-8-11 JulieKrone (hdwy ½-wy: 4th over 4f out: wknd) 3½ 7
Flitch (USA) *(113) (WBadgett,USA)* 3-8-9 MSmith (mid div: gd hdwy 3f out: 7th & rdn st: sn wknd) 1 8

Turk Passer (USA) *(104) (FSchulhofer,USA)* 5-9-0 JVelasquez (led to 3f out: 3rd & rdn st: sn wknd) 5 9
Celtic Arms (FR) *(104) (RRash,USA)* 4-9-0 GStevens (a bhd) ....nk 10
Signal Tap (USA) *(99) (FSchulhofer,USA)* 4-9-0 JSantos (chsd ldrs early: bhd st) 4 11
4014a[4] Lando (GER) *(95) (HJentzsch,Germany)* 5-9-0 MRoberts (a.p: rdn appr st: sn btn) 3 12
Talloires (USA) *(94) (RMandella,USA)* 5-9-0b KDesormeaux (a in rr) ....nk 13

P-M £9.90: PL £4.70 £5.00 SHOW £3.80 £3.50 £3.70 (SF £52.50) OWNER C. Cella BRED Swettenham Stud in Ireland 13 Rn 2m 42.07 SF: -/-/-/-/-/-/-/-/-/-/-/-/-

4308a BREEDERS' CUP CLASSIC (Gp 1) (3-Y.O+) £1,000,000.00 (£348,615.00: £230,769.00: £107,692.00: £38,461.00) **1m 2f (Dirt)** 7-10 (7-10)

Cigar (USA) *(138+) (WMott,USA)* 5-9-0 JBailey (a.p: led 3f out: r.o strly) ....— 1
L'Carriere (USA) *(134) (HJBond,USA)* 4-9-0b JChavez (2nd early: led ½-wy to 3f out: rallied fnl f) 2½ 2
Unaccounted For (USA) *(132) (FSchulhofer,USA)* 4-9-0b PDay (trckd ldrs: hdwy & 2nd st: r.o u.p) 1 3
Soul of the Matter (USA) *(131) (RMandella,USA)* 4-9-0 KDesormeaux (chsd ldrs: effrt & 4th st: no ex) ....¾ 4
1710a[2] Star Standard (USA) *(122) (NZito,USA)* 3-8-9 CMcCarron (led to ½-wy: 5th st: wknd) 6 5
Peaks and Valleys (USA) *(119) (JDay,Canada)* 3-8-9 JulieKrone (4th early: rdn & bhd st)...1¾ 6
3576a[5] Tinners Way (USA) *(116) (RFrankel,USA)* 5-9-0 EDelahoussaye (bhd: r.o st: nvr plcd to chal) 2 7
Concern (USA) *(114) (RSmall,USA)* 4-9-0b MSmith (rr early: sme late hdwy) ....¾ 8
French Deputy (USA) *(108) (NDrysdale,USA)* 3-8-9 GStevens (6th early: rdn & btn st) 4 9
Jed Forest (USA) *(103) (ACallejas,USA)* 4-9-0 RDouglas (dwlt: a bhd) 3 10
3143* Halling (USA) *(62) (SbinSuroor)* 4-9-0 WRSwinburn (mid div: hdwy ½-wy: rdn & lost pl 3f out: eased) 26 11

P-M £3.40: PL £3.60 £22.20 SHOW £2.90 £10.00 £3.50 (SF £85.50) OWNER Mr Allen Paulson BRED A. E. Paulson 11 Rn 1m 59.58 SF: -/-/-/-/-/-/-/-/-/-/-
AR

4090a-SAINT-CLOUD (France) (L-H)
Sunday October 29th (Good to soft)

4309a PRIX DE FLORE (Gp 3) (3-Y.O+ F & M) £26,347.00 (£9,581.00: £4,790.00) **1m 2f 110y** 1-40 (1-41)

1712a[11] **Tamise** *(114) (AFabre,France)* 3-8-7 OPeslier ....— 1
Suivez La (USA) *(110) (JCunnington,France)* 3-8-7 FSanchez 2½ 2
1712a[9] Loretta Gianni (FR) *(110) (DSmaga,France)* 3-8-7 GGuignard ....nk 3
P-M 1.70F: 1.20F 2.40F (SF 13.80F) OWNER Mr D. Wildenstein (FRANCE) 7 Rn 2m 15.1 SF: -/-/-

4310a CRITERIUM DE SAINT-CLOUD (Gp 1) (2-Y.O C & F) £47,904.00 (£19,162.00: £6,581.00: £4,790.00) **1m 2f** 2-40 (2-38)

3788a[2] **Polaris Flight (USA)** *(PWChapple-Hyam)* 2-9-0 JReid (4th early: hdwy 7f out: led ent st: r.o gamely u.p) ....— 1
Ragmar (FR) *(PBary,France)* 2-9-0 DBoeuf (hld up: rdn & hdwy over 1f out: str chal fnl f: jst failed) ....s.h 2
Oliviero (FR) *(AMauchamp,France)* 2-9-0b ABadel (led 3f: hrd rdn 2f out: r.o) 1 3
4089a* Go Between (FR) *(ASpanu,France)* 2-9-0 ESaint-Martin (trckd ld tl led 7f out: hdd ent st: r.o u.p: no ex cl home) ....nse 4
Quorum *(AFabre,France)* 2-9-0 TJarnet (4th st: rdn 2f out: no ex fnl f) ....nk 5

P-M 3.10F: 2.30F 3.10F (SF 29.80F) OWNER Mr Richard Kaster (MARLBOROUGH) BRED Bill Van Den Dool 5 Rn 2m 13.7 (10.20) SF: -/-/-/-/-

4179a-SAN SIRO (Milan, Italy) (R-H)
Sunday October 29th (Very heavy)

4311a PREMIO CARLO PORTA (Gp 3) (3-Y.O+) £26,005.00 (£12,175.00) **1m 2f** 2-45 (2-55)

4088a* **Concepcion (GER)** *(118) (AWohler,Germany)* 5-9-0 SEccles ....— 1

4030[5] Snowtown (IRE) *(105) (PWChapple-Hyam)* 3-8-4 KDarley 4¾ 2
4088a[2] Sylvan Point *(107) (HRemmert,Germany)* 4-8-11b KWoodburn ....½ 3

Tote 29L: 16L 26L (130L) OWNER Gestut Fahrhof BRED Gestut Fahrhof 6 Rn 2m 7.8 SF: -/-/-

4195-DONCASTER (L-H)
Friday November 3rd (Good to firm, Good patches)
WEATHER: cloudy & cold WIND: mod half bhd

4312 E.B.F. FLANDERS MAIDEN STKS (I) (2-Y.O) (Class D) £4,280.50 (£1,279.00: £612.00: £278.50) **7f** Stalls: High GOING minus 0.23 sec per fur (GF) 12-50 (12-53)

Wahiba Sands *(84+) (JLDunlop)* 2-9-0 WCarson(7) (w'like: leggy: hld up: hdwy 3f out: led ent fnl f: r.o wl) ....— 1
Private Song (USA) *(83+) (RCharlton)* 2-9-0 WRyan(11) (unf: scope: a.p: rdn & kpt on wl ins fnl f) ....½ 2
Marigliano (USA) *(80+) (MRStoute)* 2-9-0 KBradshaw(18) (b.hind: rangy: a.p: led over 1f out: hdd ent fnl f: unable qckn fnl f) 1¼ 3
Hippy *(70) (CEBrittain)* 2-8-9 KDarley(1) (neat: a w ldrs: ev ch 1f out: unable qckn) 2 4
Mattimeo (IRE) *(73) (APJarvis)* 2-9-0 JTate(15) (leggy: unf: a chsng ldrs: one pce appr fnl f) 1¼ 5
Mawingo (IRE) *(70) (GWragg)* 2-9-0 MHills(9) (leggy: hld up: effrt ½-wy: nt pce to chal) 1¼ 6
Ragsak Jameel (USA) *(66) (MajorWRHern)* 2-9-0 TSprake(3) (w'like: leggy: bit bkwd: bhd tl styd on fnl 2f) 1½ 7
4161[12] Flying Harold *(65) (MRChannon)* 2-9-0 RHughes(6) (led tl over 1f out: wknd appr fnl f) ....½ 8
My Mother's Local (USA) *(60) (KOCunningham-Brown)* 2-8-9 SWhitworth(8) (leggy: lt-f: s.i.s: hdwy fnl 2f: nvr nrr) ....hd 9
3708[10] Flame of Hope *(57) (JLDunlop)* 2-8-9 TQuinn(2) (bit bkwd: chsd ldrs 5f: sn lost pl) 1¼ 10
Liefling (USA) *(55) (JHMGosden)* 2-8-9 JCarroll(16) (b.hind: lt-f: prom stands' side 5f) ....¾ 11
Philosopher (IRE) *(56) (RHannon)* 2-9-0 JReid(13) (leggy: unf: sn drvn along: a in rr) 1¾ 12
4216[7] Farfeste *(33) (DMorris)* 2-8-9 RCochrane(14) (spd over 4f) 8 13
Lituus (USA) *(38)*(Fav)*(JHMGosden)* 2-9-0 LDettori(10) (unf: scope: bkwd: s.s: sn drvn along: n.d) ....s.h 14
Public Reproof *(32) (PCHaslam)* 2-9-0 VHalliday(4) (lt-f: outpcd) 2½ 15
One Dream *(28) (BSmart)* 2-9-0 SSanders(17) (cmpt: outpcd) 1¾ 16
1943[12] Totally Different *(17) (GROldroyd)* 2-9-0 LCharnock(5) (bkwd: w ldrs over 4f: sn lost tch: t.o) 5 17
Northern Miracle (IRE) *(CFWall)* 2-8-9 GDuffield(12) (neat: outpcd fr ½-wy: sn bhd: t.o) 7 18

4/1 Lituus (USA) (5/2-9/2), **9/2** Mawingo (IRE) (op 3/1), **6/1** Philosopher (IRE), WAHIBA SANDS, **8/1** Ragsak Jameel (USA) (op 12/1), Private Song (USA), **10/1** Liefling (USA), Marigliano (USA), **12/1** One Dream, **14/1** Hippy, Flying Harold, Flame of Hope, **25/1** Northern Miracle (IRE), Mattimeo (IRE), **33/1** Public Reproof, Farfeste, Totally Different, My Mother's Local (USA), CSF £60.57 TOTE £7.50: £2.30 £3.70 £6.90 (£43.50) Trio £277.40 OWNER Mr J. L. Dunlop (ARUNDEL) BRED Fares Stables Ltd 18 Rn 1m 27.1 (3.70) SF: 35/34/31/21/24/21/17/16/11/8/6/7/-/-/-/-/-/-

4313 E.B.F. FLANDERS MAIDEN STKS (II) (2-Y.O) (Class D) £4,280.50 (£1,279.00: £612.00: £278.50) **7f** Stalls: High GOING minus 0.23 sec per fur (GF) 1-20 (1-29)

4058[6] **Jackson Hill** *(91+)*(Fav)*(RCharlton)* 2-9-0 TSprake(4) (a.p: led ins fnl f: readily) ....— 1
Kerry Ring *(83+) (JHMGosden)* 2-8-9 LDettori(1) (neat: s.s: hdwy ½-wy: kpt on ins fnl f: unlucky) 1¼ 2
4222[7] Pasternak *(85+) (SirMarkPrescott)* 2-9-0 GDuffield(9) (hld up: stdy hdwy 2f out: r.o towards fin) 1½ 3
3662[6] A-Aasem *(84) (HThomsonJones)* 2-9-0 RHills(2) (chsd ldrs: led 2f out tl hdd & no ex ins fnl f) ....nk 4
Formidable Partner *(78) (RWArmstrong)* 2-9-0 JReid(11) (scope: a.p: kpt on one pce fnl 2f) 2½ 5
Arterxerxes *(72) (MJHeaton-Ellis)* 2-9-0 AClark(5) (w'like: led 5f: one pce appr fnl f) 3 6
4239[6] Distinct Beauty (IRE) *(63) (WAO'Gorman)* 2-8-9 EmmaO'Gorman(14) (hdwy over 2f out: kpt on appr fnl f) 1½ 7
Radiant Star *(66) (GWragg)* 2-9-0 MHills(12) (unf: scope: s.s: hdwy 3f out: nvr nr to chal) ....¾ 8
4154[11] Tom Swift (IRE) *(58) (RCSpicer)* 2-9-0 DeanMcKeown(10) (chsd ldrs over 5f) 3½ 9
Daydreamer (USA) *(58) (JHMGosden)* 2-9-0 JCarroll(13) (w'like: scope: unruly s: hld up in tch: effrt & one pce fnl 2f) ....hd 10
4216[2] Ewar Sunrise *(52) (CEBrittain)* 2-8-9 KDarley(17) (prom stands' side: ev ch 2f out: wknd appr fnl f) ....nk 11

4148[12] Parsa (USA) *(51) (JLDunlop)* 2-8-9 WCarson(7) (s.i.s: mid div: drvn along 3f out: nvr nr ldrs) ....½ 12
Charlie Chang (IRE) *(55) (RHannon)* 2-9-0 RPerham(16) (hld up: hdwy 3f out: wknd wl over 1f out) ....½ 13
4155[6] Faith Alone *(47) (CFWall)* 2-8-9 NCarlisle(18) (nvr trbld ldrs) 1½ 14
Persian Dawn *(46) (MajorDNChappell)* 2-8-9 WWoods(15) (leggy: chsd ldrs over 4f)....nk 15
3967[12] Dancing Cavalier *(50) (RHollinshead)* 2-9-0 TIves(3) (prom tl wknd fnl 2f) ....½ 16
Irish Kinsman *(45) (PTWalwyn)* 2-9-0 DHarrison(8) (leggy: unf: spd over 4f) 2 17
High Atlas *(BWHills)* 2-8-9 KFallon(6) (Withdrawn not under Starter's orders: unruly in stalls) .... W

4/1 JACKSON HILL, **9/2** Kerry Ring (5/2-5/1), **5/1** Radiant Star, **7/1** Formidable Partner, **8/1** Ewar Sunrise, **9/1** Pasternak, **10/1** High Atlas, **12/1** Daydreamer (USA), A-Aasem, **14/1** Distinct Beauty (IRE), Parsa (USA), **16/1** Charlie Chang (IRE), **20/1** Persian Dawn, Irish Kinsman, **33/1** Arterxerxes, Dancing Cavalier, Faith Alone, Tom Swift (IRE), CSF £23.56 TOTE £4.70: £1.90 £1.80 £9.00 (£7.70) Trio £42.70 OWNER Mr James Wolfensohn (BECKHAMPTON) BRED S. Tindall and Stowell Hill Ltd 17 Rn
1m 27.16 (3.76) SF: 34/26/28/27/21/15/6/9/1/1/-/-/-/-/-/-/-

4314

E.B.F. DUNKIRK MAIDEN STKS (2-Y.O) (Class D) £5,021.50 (£1,507.00: £726.00: £335.50) **6f** Stalls: High GOING minus 0.23 sec per fur (GF) 1-50 (2-02)

Miss Riviera *(90+) (GWragg)* 2-8-9 MHills(13) (neat: chsd ldrs: chal 1f out: r.o to ld fnl 50y) — 1
4109[2] Green Barries *(94) (MJohnston)* 2-9-0 TWilliams(12) (a w ldrs: led bel dist: hung rt: hdd wl ins fnl f: swvd left nr fin) ....½ 2
Major Quality *(86) (JRFanshawe)* 2-9-0 DHarrison(8) (neat: hld up: hdwy over 2f out: rdn & one pce fnl f) 3 3
4161[5] Marawis (USA) *(86) (HThomsonJones)* 2-9-0 RHills(5) (led tl bel dist: rdn & one pce fnl f) ...s.h 4
Yezza (IRE) *(67) (APJarvis)* 2-8-9 JTate(18) (mid div: rdn along ½-wy: styd on appr fnl f).......5 5
4255[4] Sea Danzig *(68) (PHowling)* 2-9-0 RCochrane(16) (prom over 4f)....1¾ 6
4098[5] Circus Star *(66) (SirMarkPrescott)* 2-9-0 GDuffield(1) (s.i.s: hdwy over 2f out: nvr nrr) ....½ 7
4212[9] Oatey *(60) (MrsJRRamsden)* 2-8-9 JFEgan(15) (mid div: drvn along ½-wy: nvr nrr) ....nk 8
4212[15] Sharp 'n' Shady *(60) (CFWall)* 2-8-9 WLord(17) (prom over 4f)....s.h 9
Sahhar *(63) (RWArmstrong)* 2-9-0 RPrice(19) (lt-f: hdwy ½-wy: nvr able to chal) ....¾ 10
4137[9] Bowlers Boy *(60) (JJQuinn)* 2-9-0 MBirch(14) (plld hrd: chsd ldrs over 4f) 1¼ 11
4161[13] Fiona Shann (USA) *(55) (JLDunlop)* 2-8-10 ow1 RHughes(7) (a in rr) ....s.h 12
4239[7] Extremely Friendly *(60) (CEBrittain)* 2-9-0 KDarley(9) (sn pushed along: a bhd)....s.h 13
4188[17] Hawksley Hill (IRE) *(56) (MrsJRRamsden)* 2-9-0 KFallon(2) (s.i.s: stdy hdwy 2f out: nvr plcd to chal)....1½ 14
4210[5] Natal Ridge *(55) (DHaydnJones)* 2-9-0 TIves(4) (prom tl wknd over 2f out) ....nk 15
Attarikh (IRE) *(55)(Fav)(JHMGosden)* 2-9-0 WCarson(3) (s.s: a in rr) ....s.h 16
4210[9] Appeal Again (IRE) *(55) (MrsJRRamsden)* 2-9-0 JReid(10) (pushed along ½-wy: n.d) ....s.h 17
1399[5] Autobabble (IRE) *(54) (RHannon)* 2-9-0 RPerham(21) (chsd ldrs tl wknd over 2f out) ....hd 18
Backwoods *(41) (GWragg)* 2-9-0 WWoods(22) (unf: scope: nvr wnt pce: t.o) 5 19
3976[6] Chavin Point *(7) (MissLCSiddall)* 2-8-9 DeanMcKeown(20) (a bhd: t.o) 11 20
Lead Him On (USA) *(PWHarris)* 2-9-0 GHind(11) (Withdrawn not under Starter's orders: unruly in stalls) .... W

7/2 Attarikh (IRE), **4/1** Marawis (USA), **9/2** MISS RIVIERA, **9/1** Green Barries, Sahhar, **10/1** Circus Star, **12/1** Fiona Shann (USA), **14/1** Major Quality, Backwoods, Sea Danzig, Autobabble (IRE), Extremely Friendly, **16/1** Lead Him On (USA), Appeal Again (IRE), Oatey, Natal Ridge, **20/1** Hawksley Hill (IRE), **25/1** Yezza (IRE), Sharp 'n' Shady, **33/1** Chavin Point, Bowlers Boy, CSF £55.26 TOTE £7.70: £3.10 £2.60 £10.20 (£41.50) Trio £419.90 OWNER Mr J. L. C. Pearce (NEWMARKET) BRED J. L. C. Pearce 20 Rn
1m 13.37 (2.37) SF: 40/44/36/36/17/18/16/10/10/13/10/5/10/6/5/5/5/4/-/-/-

4315

ROYAL BRITISH LEGION CONDITIONS STKS (3-Y.O+) (Class C) £5,024.00 (£1,856.00: £888.00: £360.00: £140.00: £52.00) **1m 6f 132y** Stalls: Low GOING minus 0.23 sec per fur (GF) 2-20 (2-27)

4022* **Chief Bee (83)***(87++)(Fav)(JLDunlop)* 4-9-1 KDarley(2) (hld up gng wl: 2nd st: led on bit over 2f out: pushed clr fnl f) ....— 1
3718[6] Ahla **(80)***(81) (RWArmstrong)* 3-8-4 WCarson(5) (led tl over 2f out: sn hrd drvn: no ch w wnr)....4 2
4149[14] Doddington Flyer **(64)***(81) (RHollinshead)* 3-8-11 WRyan(3) (hld up & bhd: 7th st: effrt over 2f out: nvr nrr)....6 3
Outset (IRE) **(52)***(74) (MDHammond)* 5-8-11 (3) SDrowne(4) (prom: 3rd st: rdn over 2f out: sn outpcd)....1 4
Campaign **(85)***(73) (MDHammond)* 4-9-2 LDettori(7) (bkwd: prom tl 5th & outpcd ent st)......2½ 5

3543[2] Fighting Times *(70) (CASmith)* 3-8-5 ACulhane(1) (hld up: 4th st: rdn over 3f out: sn btn)......¾ 6
2433[5] Kings Cay (IRE) **(59)***(54) (THCaldwell)* 4-9-5 JCarroll(6) (bkwd: hld up: 6th st: effrt & rdn 3f out: sn outpcd & eased: t.o)..20 7

5/4 CHIEF BEE, **7/4** Ahla, **8/1** Fighting Times, Campaign, **20/1** Doddington Flyer, **25/1** Outset (IRE), **33/1** Kings Cay (IRE), CSF £3.76 TOTE £2.20: £1.40 £1.50 (£1.70) OWNER Mrs Mark Burrell (ARUNDEL) BRED Mrs M. Burrell 7 Rn
3m 11.17 (7.57) SF: 40/25/25/27/26/14/7
WEIGHT FOR AGE 3yo-9lb

4316

UNKNOWN SOLDIER CONDITIONS STKS (3-Y.O+ F & M) (Class C)
£5,116.80 (£1,891.20: £905.60: £368.00: £144.00: £54.40)
1m 2f 60y Stalls: Low GOING minus 0.23 sec per fur (GF) 2-50 (2-54)

3945[6] **Sue's Artiste (85)***(98+) (BWHills)* 4-9-8 MHills(4) (lw: trckd ldrs: led over 2f out: r.o. wl)..— 1
4265[7] Strutting (IRE) **(93)***(92) (RHannon)* 3-8-10 (5) DaneO'Neill(3) (hld up: effrt 3f out: styd on u.p: nt pce of wnr)..2½ 2
4038[20] Quivira **(74)***(80) (TTClement)* 4-8-12 MRimmer(2) (sn w ldr: led 3f out: sn hdd & one pce) ...2½ 3
1175* Mountains of Mist (IRE) *(79)*(Fav)*(RCharlton)* 3-8-11 JReid(6) (a.p: effrt 3f out: rdn & btn appr fnl f)..3½ 4
4079[12] Crimson Shower **(55)***(65) (JRFanshawe)* 3-8-7 LDettori(5) (in tch: hdwy 3f out: rdn & btn over 1f out)..6 5
2553[6] Regal Portrait (IRE) *(58) (HRACecil)* 3-8-7 WRyan(1) (led tl hdd & wknd 3f out)......................5 6
3726[14] Miss Iron Heart (USA) **(41)***(50) (DJSCosgrove)* 3-8-2b(5) LNewton(7) (swtg: dwlt: a bhd)..........5 7

6/4 Mountains of Mist (IRE), **3/1** SUE'S ARTISTE, **4/1** Strutting (IRE), **9/2** Regal Portrait (IRE), **14/1** Quivira, **16/1** Crimson Shower, **50/1** Miss Iron Heart (USA), CSF £14.93 TOTE £3.70: £1.60 £2.40 (£6.20) OWNER Mr A. L. R. Morton (LAMBOURN) BRED Juddmonte Farms 7 Rn
2m 11.75 (4.75) SF: 50/39/32/26/12/5/-
WEIGHT FOR AGE 3yo-5lb

4317

NORMANDY BEACHES NURSERY H'CAP (0-85) (2-Y.O) (Class D)
£3,882.50 (£1,160.00: £555.00: £252.50)
5f Stalls: High GOING minus 0.23 sec per fur (GF) 3-20 (3-21)

4206[3] **Polly Golightly (77)***(80) (BSmart)* 2-9-0b RCochrane(6) (led stands' side: r.o u.p to ld cl home)..— 1
3998* Music Gold (IRE) **(84)***(87) (WAO'Gorman)* 2-9-7 EmmaO'Gorman(4) (lw: s.i.s: hdwy centre ½-wy: led wl over 1f out: hung rt: nt qckn towards fin) ....s.h 2
4260* Dande Flyer **(73)***(69)*(Fav)*(DWPArbuthnot)* 2-8-7 (3) 7x DRMcCabe(1) (b.nr hind: racd centre & sn wl bhd: gd hdwy 2f out: kpt on fnl f)..2 3
4231[5] Camionneur (IRE) **(58)***(53) (MHEasterby)* 2-7-9b JQuinn(7) (racd stands' side: a.p: sn drvn along: kpt on one pce fnl 2f)..½ 4
4260[3] Antonias Melody **(70)***(64) (SRBowring)* 2-8-7 SWebster(10) (b: racd stands' side: a chsng ldrs: nt qckn fnl 2f)..nk 5
4055[2] No Monkey Nuts **(83)***(75) (JBerry)* 2-9-6 JCarroll(9) (s.i.s: racd stands' side: bhd tl r.o wl fnl f)..½ 6
3947[2] Amber Fort **(71)***(57) (PFICole)* 2-8-8 TQuinn(11) (racd stands' side: hdwy u.p 2f out: nvr able chal)..2 7
4077[15] Repatriate (AUS) **(80)***(66) (PWChapple-Hyam)* 2-9-3 JReid(5) (cl up centre tl wknd over 1f out) ....s.h 8
4230* Mister Joel **(69)***(47) (MWEasterby)* 2-8-6b 7x LDettori(3) (led centre tl hdd wl over 1f out: edgd lft & sn btn)..2½ 9
4237[2] Gagajulu **(77)***(48) (PDEvans)* 2-9-0 GHind(8) (racd stands' side: outpcd fr ½-wy) 2 10
4097[18] Snitch **(56)***(8) (CSmith)* 2-7-7v NCarlisle(2) (w ldrs centre to ½-wy: sn wknd)............................6 11
LONG HANDICAP Snitch 6-13

13/8 Dande Flyer, **9/2** Amber Fort, **7/1** POLLY GOLIGHTLY, **9/1** Mister Joel, Music Gold (IRE), **10/1** Antonias Melody, **11/1** No Monkey Nuts, **12/1** Repatriate (AUS), Gagajulu, **16/1** Camionneur (IRE), **33/1** Snitch, CSF £67.89 CT £141.32 TOTE £10.80: £2.40 £2.60 £1.50 (£44.30) Trio £32.50 OWNER Mr David Sykes (LAMBOURN) BRED Aston Park Stud and T. R. Lock 11 Rn
59.99 secs (1.59) SF: 51/58/40/24/35/46/28/37/18/19/-

4318

WESTERN DESERT CONDITIONS STKS (2-Y.O) (Class C) £5,058.00
(£1,872.00: £898.50: £367.50: £146.25: £57.75)
1m (straight) Stalls: High GOING minus 0.23 sec per fur (GF) 3-50 (3-50)

4155* **Brighstone** *(89+)*(Fav)*(HRACecil)* 2-9-1 WRyan(5) (cl up: led 2f out: pushed out fnl f).........— 1

4235* La Volta **(86)***(83) (JGFitzGerald)* 2-8-10 RHughes(1) (lw: led tl hdd 2f out: r.o towards fin) .....½ **2**
1311³ Corporal Nym (USA) *(82) (PFICole)* 2-8-11 TQuinn(3) (bit bkwd: hld up: hdwy 3f out: r.o towards fin)........................1 **3**
4207* Henry The Fifth **(100)***(85) (CEBrittain)* 2-9-3 KDarley(4) (hld up: hdwy ½-wy: nt qckn appr fnl f) 1½ **4**
4244⁵ Kirov Lady (IRE) **(83)***(74?) (RHannon)* 2-8-2 (5)ow1 DaneO'Neill(2) (trckd ldrs: outpcd 2f out: r.o towards fin)........................hd **5**
4218* Tsarnista **(84)***(71) (JLDunlop)* 2-8-10 JReid(6) (prom tl wknd fnl 2f) 3½ **6**

6/4 BRIGHSTONE (tchd 9/4), **7/2** Corporal Nym (USA), **4/1** Henry The Fifth, **9/2** Tsarnista, **8/1** La Volta, **12/1** Kirov Lady (IRE), CSF £13.12 TOTE £2.40: £1.60 £3.10 (£14.20) OWNER Mr Michael Poland (NEWMARKET) BRED Michael Poland 6 Rn 1m 40.28 (3.78) SF: 41/35/34/37/26/23

4319 POPPY H'CAP (0-80) (3-Y.O+) (Class D) £5,050.50 (£1,518.00: £733.00: £340.50)
7f Stalls: High GOING minus 0.23 sec per fur (GF) 4-20 (4-24)

4068⁸ **Charlie Sillett (76)***(90) (BWHills)* 3-9-8 MHills(7) (a gng wl: qcknd to ld ins fnl f: hng lft & sn clr)........................— **1**
3598⁶ Starry Eyed **(77)***(88) (JHMGosden)* 3-9-9 LDettori(15) (a.p: chal over 1f out: nt qckn)...........1½ **2**
4236³ Super Benz **(60)***(69) (FJO'Mahony)* 9-8-3 (5) MHenry(14) (b: w ldrs centre: kpt on wl fnl 2f).....¾ **3**
4268⁵ Winsome Wooster **(62)***(70) (PGMurphy)* 4-8-7 (3) SDrowne(19) (in tch: hdwy over 1f out: styd on wl) ....nk **4**
3706²² Elite Hope (USA) **(80)***(87) (CREgerton)* 3-9-12 RHughes(17) (hld up & bhd: hdwy 2f out: nvr rchd ldrs) ....¾ **5**
4041¹⁵ Somerton Boy (IRE) **(77)***(83) (PCalver)* 5-9-11 TIves(2) (lw: a chsng ldrs: kpt on fnl f) ....nk **6**
4041¹⁶ Cumbrian Waltzer **(70)***(75) (MHEasterby)* 10-9-4 MBirch(11) (b: prom: rdn 3f out: no imp) .....½ **7**
4157¹⁸ Jolto **(75)***(76) (KOCunningham-Brown)* 6-9-9 RCochrane(8) (mde most tl hdd & wknd ins fnl f) 1¾ **8**
4171² Mister Fire Eyes (IRE) **(72)***(72)*(Fav)*(CEBrittain)* 3-9-4 KDarley(21) (lw: outpcd & bhd: hdwy over 2f out: nvr rchd ldrs) ....hd **9**
4268¹¹ Euphyllia **(68)***(68) (BobJones)* 3-9-0v FNorton(4) (w ldrs: outpcd whn hmpd ent fnl f) ....hd **10**
4157²⁰ Sylvandra **(63)***(63) (PGMurphy)* 3-8-9v JWilliams(9) (lw: in tch: rdn 3f out: grad wknd)............nk **11**
4145⁶ Q Factor **(69)***(67) (DHaydnJones)* 3-9-1 AMackay(6) (chsd ldrs tl wknd fnl 2f)........................¾ **12**
4268² Quilling **(78)***(76) (MDods)* 3-9-10 6x DeanMcKeown(3) (lw: w ldr tl wknd fnl 2f)........................hd **13**
3943⁸ Cutpurse Moll **(74)***(69) (JRFanshawe)* 3-9-6v DHarrison(12) (nvr trbld ldrs) 1¼ **14**
4041¹¹ Sagebrush Roller **(79)***(74) (JWWatts)* 7-9-13 GDuffield(13) (effrt over 2f out: no imp) ....hd **15**
4116⁶ Fionn de Cool (IRE) **(75)***(69) (RAkehurst)* 4-9-9 TQuinn(10) (drvn alng ½-wy: nvr trbld ldrs)..nk **16**
4049² Godmersham Park **(70)***(64) (MJHeaton-Ellis)* 3-9-2 JReid(22) (racd stands' side tl swvd lft after 3f: nvr trbld ldrs) ....hd **17**
3645⁹ Bold Amusement **(78)***(69) (WSCunningham)* 5-9-12 JFEgan(1) (chsd ldrs tl wknd fnl 2f)......1¼ **18**
4171²⁰ Nizaal (USA) **(71)***(61) (DNicholls)* 4-8-12 (7) BPeel(20) (lw: a outpcd & bhd)........................½ **19**
4041⁹ Halmanerror **(70)***(59) (MrsJRRamsden)* 5-9-4 KFallon(18) (nvr wnt pce) ....nk **20**
4035¹⁷ Gadge **(63)***(51) (DMorris)* 4-8-11 JCarroll(16) (bhd fr ½-wy) ....nk **21**
3552¹¹ Never Explain (IRE) **(80)** *(JLDunlop)* 3-9-12 WCarson(5) (Withdrawn not under Starter's orders: spread plate at s) .... **W**

9/2 Mister Fire Eyes (IRE) (op 10/1), **7/1** Starry Eyed, **8/1** Quilling, **9/1** CHARLIE SILLETT, Sagebrush Roller, **11/1** Fionn de Cool (IRE), **12/1** Jolto, **14/1** Halmanerror (12/1-20/1), **16/1** Godmersham Park, Super Benz, Never Explain (IRE), **20/1** Gadge, Somerton Boy (IRE), Cutpurse Moll, Winsome Wooster, **25/1** Cumbrian Waltzer, Euphyllia, Q Factor, **33/1** Bold Amusement, Nizaal (USA), Elite Hope (USA), Sylvandra, CSF £70.04 CT £928.94 TOTE £10.80: £2.90 £1.90 £5.30 £6.00 (£45.80) Trio £723.30 OWNER Mr John Sillett (LAMBOURN) BRED J. Sillett 21 Rn
1m 26.29 (2.89) SF: 52/50/33/34/49/47/39/40/34/30/25/29/38/31/38/33/26/33/25/23/15/-
WEIGHT FOR AGE 3yo-2lb

T/Jkpt: Not won; £13,762.97 to Doncaster 4/11/95. T/Plpt: £157.60 (81.16 Tckts). T/Qdpt: £17.40 (7.1 Tckts). AA/IM

4312-DONCASTER (L-H)
Saturday November 4th (Good to firm, Good patches)
WEATHER: fine & sunny WIND: almost nil

4320 B.O.C. SUREFLOW MEDIAN AUCTION MAIDEN STKS (2-Y.O) (Class E) £4,188.80 (£1,258.40: £607.20: £281.60)
1m (straight) Stalls: High GOING minus 0.16 sec per fur (GF) 12-50 (12-54)

3868⁴ **Shaamit (IRE)** *(85+)*(Fav)*(WJHaggas)* 2-9-0 MHills(6) (lw: hld up far side: hdwy to ld over 1f out: r.o wl)........................— **1**

4155[3] Classy Chief *(78) (RBoss)* 2-9-0 RHughes(24) (w ldrs stands' side: rdn & kpt on fnl f) 3½ 2
4172[2] Northern Soul (USA) *(78) (MJohnston)* 2-9-0 KDarley(18) (lw: led stands' side: styd on ins fnl f) ....s.h 3
4216[4] Always Happy *(73) (JRFanshawe)* 2-8-9 WWoods(21) (a.p stands' side: rdn & r.o ins fnl f) ..hd 4
2741[5] Serendipity (FR) *(77) (JLDunlop)* 2-9-0 RCochrane(13) (racd far side: hdwy 3f out: styd on fnl f) ....nk 5
Thea (USA) *(72) (JRFanshawe)* 2-8-6 (3) NVarley(1) (w'like: leggy: bit bkwd: a.p far side: led over 3f out: sn clr: hdd over 1f out: wknd) ....s.h 6
4080[7] Village King (IRE) *(71) (RHannon)* 2-8-9 (5) DaneO'Neill(8) (bit bkwd: chsd ldrs far side: kpt on one pce fnl 2f) 3 7
In The Band *(65) (LordHuntingdon)* 2-8-9 RHills(20) (lt-f: sme hdwy fnl 2f: nvr nrr) ....¾ 8
Misky Bay *(62) (JHMGosden)* 2-9-0 LDettori(19) (unf: scope: bkwd: nvr nr to chal) 4 9
Hoofprints (IRE) *(58) (GHarwood)* 2-9-0 AClark(5) (wl grwn: in tch tl outpcd fnl 3f) 2 10
Sawa-Id *(57) (JHMGosden)* 2-9-0 WCarson(22) (w'like: leggy: bkwd: chsd ldrs stands' side: no hdwy fnl 2f) ....s.h 11
4004a[10] On the Carpet (IRE) *(52) (JLDunlop)* 2-8-9 GDuffield(4) (bit bkwd: racd far side: nvr nr ldrs) s.h 12
4247[3] Pencilled In *(56) (PWChapple-Hyam)* 2-9-0 JReid(2) (lw: led far side over 4f) ....½ 13
3994[8] Compass Pointer *(55) (JMPEustace)* 2-9-0 MTebbutt(23) (chsd ldrs stands' side over 5f) .....½ 14
3708[7] Home Cookin' *(48) (DrJDScargill)* 2-8-9 DaleGibson(9) (a bhd) 1 15
4169[9] Spinning Mouse *(48) (DMorley)* 2-8-9 MFenton(3) (bit bkwd: chsd ldrs far side over 5f) ....hd 16
Squandamania *(52) (PFICole)* 2-9-0 TQuinn(14) (lengthy: unf: in tch far side: rdn 2f out: sn wknd) ....½ 17
1597[11] Le Sport *(51) (ABailey)* 2-8-11 (3) DWright(11) (plld hrd: racd centre: a in rr) ....½ 18
4226[10] Spartan Heartbeat *(50) (CEBrittain)* 2-9-0 MBirch(10) (bkwd: dwlt: a in rr) ....¾ 19
Stunning Prospect (USA) *(49) (PFICole)* 2-9-0 CRutter(17) (rangy: chsd ldrs stands' side 5f: sn wknd) ....½ 20
4148[16] Driftholme *(26) (GLMoore)* 2-8-9 SWhitworth(16) (prom stands' side to ½-wy: sn wknd: t.o)...9 21
Shooting Light (IRE) *(30) (MAJarvis)* 2-9-0 PRobinson(15) (leggy: lt-f: bkwd: s.i.s: a outpcd & bhd) ....nk 22
War Shanty *(15) (JRArnold)* 2-8-9 JQuinn(12) (lt-f: b.off fore: outpcd: t.o) 5 23

13/8 SHAAMIT (IRE) (9/4-6/4), **4/1** Serendipity (FR), **6/1** Pencilled In (op 4/1), **10/1** Northern Soul (USA), Misky Bay (7/1-11/1), Classy Chief, **12/1** Squandamania (op 8/1), Village King (IRE), **14/1** Always Happy, Sawa-Id, **16/1** Shooting Light (IRE), **20/1** Hoofprints (IRE), In The Band, **25/1** Home Cookin', **33/1** Spartan Heartbeat, Spinning Mouse, On the Carpet (IRE), War Shanty, Thea (USA), Stunning Prospect (USA), **50/1** Driftholme, Compass Pointer, Le Sport, CSF £25.59 TOTE £2.50: £1.40 £4.40 £2.60 (£19.80) Trio £48.50 OWNER Mr Khalifa Dasmal (NEWMARKET) BRED Khalifa Abdulla Dasmal 23 Rn

1m 39.2 (2.70) SF: 57/50/50/45/49/44/43/37/34/30/29/24/28/27/20/20/24/23/22/21/-/2/-

4321

WEMBLEY NURSERY H'CAP (2-Y.O) (Class D) £4,402.50 (£1,320.00: £635.00: £292.50) **7f** Stalls: High GOING minus 0.16 sec per fur (GF) 1-20 (1-22)

4148[3] **Capilano Princess (66)***(68) (DHaydnJones)* 2-8-1 AMackay(12) (a.p: led over 1f out: r.o wl) ....— 1
4025[5] Double Diamond (IRE) **(86)***(84) (MJohnston)* 2-9-7 TWilliams(7) (led tl hdd over 1f out: kpt on u.p) 1¾ 2
4208* Proud Monk **(77)***(69) (GLMoore)* 2-8-12 SWhitworth(10) (a.p: rdn over 1f out: one pce) 2½ 3
3917[3] General Rose **(78)***(67) (RHannon)* 2-8-8 (5) DaneO'Neill(11) (hld up: hdwy 2f out: rdn & r.o ins fnl f) 1½ 4
4243[7] Stop Play (IRE) **(76)***(64) (MHTompkins)* 2-8-11v PRobinson(6) (hld up: hdwy 2f out: unable qckn fnl f) ....½ 5
4243[6] Precious Girl **(74)***(58) (DMoffatt)* 2-8-6 (3) DarrenMoffatt(13) (bhd tl styd on fnl 2f) 1¾ 6
4100[8] Ma Bulsie **(58)***(38) (BAMcMahon)* 2-7-7 GBardwell(4) (s.i.s: plld hrd: nvr on terms) 1¾ 7
4279* Quality (IRE) **(76)***(53)*(Fav)*(WAO'Gorman)* 2-8-11b 7x EmmaO'Gorman(5) (lw: hmpd s: hld up gng wl: outpcd & wnt rt over 2f out: sn bhd) 1 8
3281[6] Capture The Moment **(75)***(20) (RJRWilliams)* 2-8-10 RHills(1) (b.nr hind: hld up in rr: outpcd fr ½-wy) 5 9
4208[13] Swift Maiden **(71)***(36) (MrsLAMurphy)* 2-8-3 (3) SDrowne(3) (outpcd: a bhd) ....nk 10
4231[17] Percy Park (USA) **(60)***(23) (MWEasterby)* 2-7-4 (5) PFessey(9) (spd 3f: sn lost pl) 1¼ 11
3983[7] Flahuil **(65)***(27) (RHannon)* 2-8-0 JQuinn(8) (chsd ldrs over 4f) ....nk 12

LONG HANDICAP Ma Bulsie 6-8

5/2 Quality (IRE), **9/2** Stop Play (IRE), **11/2** Proud Monk, **15/2** Double Diamond (IRE), **8/1** Flahuil, **10/1** CAPILANO PRINCESS, **11/1** General Rose, **12/1** Precious Girl, **14/1** Percy Park (USA) (op 25/1), **20/1** Capture The Moment, **25/1** Ma Bulsie, Swift Maiden, CSF £81.74 CT £422.07 TOTE £15.90: £3.20 £2.00 £2.00 (£61.80) Trio £102.30 OWNER Mr H. G. Collis (PONTYPRIDD) BRED Mrs O. M. Collis 12 Rn 1m 26.76 (3.36) SF: 32/48/33/31/28/22/2/17/5/-/-/-

4322

C.I.U. N.S.P.C.C. APPEAL H'CAP (0-80) (3-Y.O+) (Class D)
£4,712.50 (£1,414.00: £681.00: £314.50)
5f Stalls: High GOING minus 0.16 sec per fur (GF) 1-50 (1-54)

3822 13 **Elle Shaped (IRE) (79)***(89) (ABailey)* 5-9-10 (3) DWright(11) (lw: hdwy far side 2f out: str run to ld cl home)........— **1**
4286 3 Portelet **(75)***(85) (RGuest)* 3-9-4 (5) DaneO'Neill(19) (led stands' side: clr fr ½-wy: r.o)........hd **2**
3822 11 I'm Your Lady **(66)***(74) (BAMcMahon)* 4-8-7 (7) MartinDwyer(4) (hdwy far side over 1f out: rdn & r.o nr fin)........½ **3**
4278 4 Lady Sheriff **(80)***(88) (MWEasterby)* 4-10-0b LDettori(10) (lw: a.p far side: led 2f out: hrd rdn & hdd wl ins fnl f)........hd **4**
4165 7 Silk Cottage **(62)***(67) (RMWhitaker)* 3-8-10 ACulhane(8) (lw: hdwy 2f out: kpt on wl towards fin)........1 **5**
4278 6 Shadow Jury **(68)***(72) (DWChapman)* 5-9-2b LCharnock(5) (prom far side: ev ch tl wknd ins fnl f)........hd **6**
4215 4 Prima Silk **(65)***(69) (MJRyan)* 4-8-13 TIves(1) (hdwy over 1f out: n.m.r: r.o wl cl home)........hd **7**
4033 7 Agwa **(69)***(73) (RJO'Sullivan)* 6-9-3 TQuinn(9) (hdwy over 1f out: fin wl)........s.h **8**
4165* Little Ibnr **(63)***(64) (PDEvans)* 4-8-8 (3) SDrowne(18) (lw: rdn & r.o fnl f: nvr nrr)........1 **9**
4068 19 Selhurstpark Flyer (IRE) **(73)***(73) (JBerry)* 4-9-7e JCarroll(3) (eyeshield: nvr trbld ldrs)........nk **10**
4165 20 Tinker Osmaston **(74)***(74) (MSSaunders)* 4-9-8 JFEgan(14) (racd stands' side: nvr nr ldrs)..d.h **10**
4113* Insider Trader **(77)***(74) (RGuest)* 4-9-11b GDuffield(6) (led far side 3f: rdn over 1f out: sn btn)........¾ **12**
4145 11 Macfarlane **(72)***(68) (MJFetherston-Godley)* 7-9-6 JReid(17) (b: sn drvn along: nvr nr to chal)........½ **13**
3961 3 Pearl Dawn (IRE) **(69)***(64) (GLMoore)* 5-9-3 SWhitworth(7) (s.i.s: a bhd & outpcd)........s.h **14**
4236 14 Superpride **(68)***(63) (MrsMReveley)* 3-9-2 KDarley(22) (a in rr)........nk **15**
4278 12 Metal Boys **(62)***(56) (MissLCSiddall)* 8-8-10 GHind(13) (outpcd)........nk **16**
4040 13 Benzoe (IRE) **(78)***(65) (MrsJRRamsden)* 5-9-12 KFallon(12) (lw: reard s: a bhd)........2 **17**
4281 2 Seigneurial **(80)***(66)*(Fav)*(GHarwood)* 3-10-0 AClark(15) (lw: chsd ldr stands' side over 3f)...nk **18**
3992 14 Beau Venture (USA) **(72)***(57) (FHLee)* 7-9-6 RLappin(16) (spd stands' side over 3f)........½ **19**
4278 13 Princess Sadie **(76)***(48) (MJohnston)* 3-9-10 PRobinson(2) (w ldrs far side 3f)........4 **20**
4134 9 Bangles **(67)***(37) (LordHuntingdon)* 5-9-1 WWoods(20) (swtg: outpcd)........½ **21**
4278 10 Ashtina **(78)***(26) (BAPearce)* 10-9-12 RHughes(21) (t.o)........7 **22**

5/1 Seigneurial, **8/1** Insider Trader, **10/1** Benzoe (IRE), Lady Sheriff, Portelet, **11/1** Prima Silk, Agwa, Little Ibnr, **12/1** Bangles, **14/1** Pearl Dawn (IRE), **16/1** Tinker Osmaston, Macfarlane, Silk Cottage, **20/1** Shadow Jury, ELLE SHAPED (IRE), Selhurstpark Flyer (IRE), Princess Sadie, Superpride, **25/1** Beau Venture (USA), I'm Your Lady, **33/1** Metal Boys, Ashtina, CSF £216.55 CT £4,580.00 TOTE £61.90: £11.10 £2.90 £9.40 £2.20 (£259.30) Trio not won; £1,865.94 to Folkestone 6/11/95 OWNER Simple Technology UK Ltd (TARPORLEY) BRED Dan Daly 22 Rn
60.14 secs (1.74) SF: 67/63/52/66/45/50/47/51/42/51/52/52/46/42/41/34/43/44/35/26/15/4

4323

COOPERATIVE BANK SERLBY STKS (Listed) (3-Y.O+) (Class A)
£11,421.00 (£4,239.00: £2,044.50: £847.50)
1m 4f Stalls: Low GOING minus 0.16 sec per fur (GF) 2-20 (2-22)

4201* **Blushing Flame (USA) (93)***(110) (MRStoute)* 4-9-0 MHills(1) (a.p: 4th st: rdn to ld over 1f out: r.o wl)........— **1**
4176a 6 Capias (USA) **(109)***(113)*(Fav)*(JHMGosden)* 4-9-5 LDettori(5) (lw: chsd ldr: 2nd st: led over 3f out tl appr fnl f: unable qckn)........1¼ **2**
4213* Al Widyan (IRE) **(94)***(108) (HRACecil)* 3-8-7 RCochrane(6) (hld up: 6th st: hdwy 2f out: kpt on u.p ins fnl f)........½ **3**
4076* Naked Welcome **(101)***(105) (MJFetherston-Godley)* 3-8-7 JReid(7) (hld up & bhd: last st: hdwy over 2f out: sn rdn: no imp)........1¾ **4**
4030 4 Royal Circle **(97)***(96) (RCharlton)* 3-8-3 ow1 KDarley(3) (lw: chsd ldrs: 5th st: rdn & one pce fnl 2f)........3 **5**
4204 4 Labibeh (USA) **(108)***(95) (JLDunlop)* 3-8-10 WCarson(2) (led over 8f: rdn & outpcd whn hmpd 2f out)........7 **6**
3923 4 Jellaby Askhir **(103)***(93) (RAkehurst)* 3-8-12 RHughes(4) (chsd ldrs: 3rd st: rdn over 3f out: sn btn)........3 **7**
4245 2 Dreams End **(70)***(85) (JMBradley)* 7-9-0 GHind(8) (t: b: hld up: 7th st: effrt 3f out: wknd fnl 2f) 2 **8**

5/2 Capias (USA), **100/30** Naked Welcome, **7/2** Al Widyan (IRE), **6/1** Labibeh (USA), **8/1** BLUSHING FLAME (USA), **9/1** Jellaby Askhir, **12/1** Royal Circle, **33/1** Dreams End, CSF £27.97 TOTE £10.60: £2.30 £1.40 £1.90 (£15.30) OWNER Cheveley Park Stud (NEWMARKET) BRED Cheveley Park Stud 8 Rn
2m 31.26 (0.66) SF: 81/84/72/69/60/59/57/56
WEIGHT FOR AGE 3yo-7lb

4324

KEEPMOAT HOLDINGS STKS (Listed) (3-Y.O+) (Class A) £12,030.00 (£4,470.00: £2,160.00: £900.00)
6f Stalls: High GOING minus 0.16 sec per fur (GF) 2-50 (2-52)

4160⁹ **Carranita (IRE) (105)***(110) (BPalling)* 5-8-6 TSprake(1) (mde all: pushed clr appr fnl f) ....— 1
4178a⁸ Branston Abby (IRE) **(113)***(110) (MJohnston)* 6-8-9 PRobinson(5) (hld up & bhd: hdwy & n.m.r 2f out: r.o strly ins fnl f) 1¼ 2
4253a² Royale Figurine (IRE) **(102)***(103) (MJFetherston-Godley)* 4-8-9 JReid(6) (hld up: hdwy 2f out: sn rdn: nt pce to chal) 2½ 3
4197* Croft Pool **(93)***(105) (JAGlover)* 4-8-11 SDWilliams(3) (lw: hdwy over 2f out: rdn appr fnl f: nt pce of wnr) ....hd 4
4253a⁶ Fire Dome (IRE) **(99)***(103) (RHannon)* 3-8-10 MHills(7) (bhd: rdn & effrt over 2f out: kpt on fnl f) ....½ 5
4078⁴ Mistle Cat (USA) **(111)***(100) (SPCWoods)* 5-8-11 WWoods(10) (w wnr over 4f: sn outpcd) ..1¼ 6
4040⁶ Shamanic **(90)***(100) (RHannon)* 3-8-10 TQuinn(4) (lw: prom: ev ch 2f out: hrd rdn: one pce) .hd 7
4197⁷ Takadou (IRE) **(91)***(97) (MissLCSiddall)* 4-8-11 WNewnes(8) (hld up: hdwy 2f out: nvr able to chal) 1 8
4160¹⁰ Montendre **(108)***(99) (MMcCormack)* 8-9-0 RCochrane(11) (bhd: effrt over 2f out: no imp) ....nk 9
3854* Art of War **(109)***(96)*(Fav)*(RCharlton)* 3-8-10 KDarley(2) (lw: stdd s: effrt over 2f out: sn rdn & wknd) ....s.h 10
4181a* Leap for Joy **(100)***(96) (JHMGosden)* 3-8-11 LDettori(12) (chsd ldrs: rdn whn hmpd bel dist: eased) ....½ 11
3230⁵ Bayin (USA) **(73)***(79) (MDIUsher)* 6-8-11 RStreet(9) (b: s.i.s: a bhd: t.o) 6 12

5/2 Art of War, **4/1** Royale Figurine (IRE), Branston Abby (IRE), **5/1** Mistle Cat (USA), **7/1** Leap for Joy, **12/1** Croft Pool, Montendre, **16/1** Fire Dome (IRE), **20/1** CARRANITA (IRE), **40/1** Shamanic, Takadou (IRE), **100/1** Bayin (USA), CSF £98.88 TOTE £46.50: £5.70 £2.10 £1.60 (£96.10) Trio £96.40 OWNER Lamb Lane Associates (COWBRIDGE) BRED Mrs Anita Quinn 12 Rn
1m 12.42 (1.42) SF: 57/57/50/52/49/47/46/44/46/42/42/26
WEIGHT FOR AGE 3yo-1lb

4325

TOTE CREDIT NOVEMBER H'CAP (3-Y.O+) (Class B) £24,843.00 (£9,237.00: £4,468.50: £1,867.50)
1m 4f Stalls: Low GOING minus 0.16 sec per fur (GF) 3-25 (3-29)

4259* **Snow Princess (IRE) (73)***(90)*(Fav)*(LordHuntingdon)* 3-8-2 8x RHills(10) (chsd ldrs: 4th st: led 2f out: drvn out) ....— 1
4201¹⁰ Dato Star (IRE) **(84)***(99) (JMJefferson)* 4-9-6 KFallon(9) (hld up & bhd: swtchd rt & hdwy 3f out: hung bdly lft u.p ins fnl f: r.o) 1½ 2
3970* Secret Service (IRE) **(73)***(83) (CWThornton)* 3-8-2 GDuffield(18) (lw: hld up: hdwy 3f out: rdn whn hmpd ent fnl f: nt rcvr) 3½ 3
4201⁶ Lord Hastie (USA) **(59)***(69) (CWThornton)* 7-7-9 JQuinn(6) (lw: chsd ldrs: 7th st: hdwy over 2f out: styd on u.p) ....nk 4
3412⁴ Foundry Lane **(80)***(89) (MrsMReveley)* 4-9-2 KDarley(1) (lw: hld up in tch: effrt on ins over 2f out: kpt on) 1 5
3730¹¹ Johns Act (USA) **(72)***(80) (DHaydnJones)* 5-8-8 JReid(12) (chsd ldrs: 5th st: n.m.r 2f out: styd on fnl f) ....¾ 6
2415⁴ Royal Scimitar (USA) **(94)***(101) (PFICole)* 3-9-9 TQuinn(8) (chsd ldrs: 6th st: effrt & ev ch 2f out: sn rdn: no ex) ....¾ 7
4031⁶ Korambi **(92)***(97) (CEBrittain)* 3-9-2 (5) MHenry(3) (lw: prom: 3rd st: led wl over 2f out: sn hdd: one pce) 1¼ 8
4204³ Whitechapel (USA) **(88)***(91) (LordHuntingdon)* 7-9-10 TIves(14) (prom: 2nd st: rdn & outpcd fnl 2f) 1¼ 9
4213² Beauchamp Jade **(75)***(78) (HCandy)* 3-8-4 WNewnes(17) (hld up: hdwy over 3f out: sn rdn: n.d) ....½ 10
4245⁴ Time for Action (IRE) **(89)***(91) (MHTompkins)* 3-9-4 PRobinson(19) (lw: led tl hdd wl over 2f out: sn rdn: wknd bel dist) ....nk 11
4038⁹ Wentbridge Lad (IRE) **(62)***(64) (PDEvans)* 5-7-12b NAdams(13) (stdd s: plld hrd: n.d) ....½ 12
4201⁹ Askern **(68)***(69) (DHaydnJones)* 4-8-4 AMackay(7) (hld up: swtchd & effrt 3f out: no imp) .....hd 13
3730¹⁵ Proton **(79)***(76) (RAkehurst)* 5-9-1 RCochrane(15) (a rr div) 3½ 14
4028³ Reimei **(68)***(63) (RAkehurst)* 6-8-4 ow1 LDettori(4) (mid div: effrt & n.m.r over 2f out: no imp) ....¾ 15
4028⁶ Artic Courier **(79)***(73) (DJSCosgrove)* 4-8-10 (5) DGibbs(2) (hdwy ent st: nt clr run over 2f out: grad wknd) 1 16
4028* Indigo Time (IRE) **(88)***(78) (PFICole)* 3-9-3 WCarson(11) (effrt & nt clr run ent st: wknd 3f out) 3 17
4028¹⁵ Bayrak (USA) **(74)***(37) (MJRyan)* 5-8-10 ow1 RHughes(5) (a bhd: t.o fnl 3f) 20 18

5/1 SNOW PRINCESS (IRE), **7/1** Royal Scimitar (USA), Reimei, Foundry Lane, **15/2** Indigo Time (IRE), **10/1** Whitechapel (USA), Beauchamp Jade, **11/1** Dato Star (IRE) (op 7/1), **12/1** Proton, **16/1** Korambi, **20/1** Lord Hastie (USA), **25/1** Secret Service (IRE), Askern, Time for Action (IRE), **33/1** Johns Act (USA), Artic Courier, Bayrak (USA), **50/1** Wentbridge Lad (IRE), CSF £58.15 CT £1,188.78 TOTE £5.40: £1.80 £3.60 £3.50 £4.30 (£63.00) Trio £396.80 OWNER Lord Weinstock & The Hon Simon Weinstock (WEST ILSLEY) BRED Ballymacoll Stud Co 18 Rn

2m 31.9 (1.30) SF: 65/81/58/51/71/62/76/72/73/53/66/46/51/58/45/55/53/19

WEIGHT FOR AGE 3yo-7lb

4326

COALITE DRAGON H'CAP (0-95) (3-Y.O+) (Class C) £8,285.00 (£2,480.00: £1,190.00: £545.00)
2m 110y Stalls: Low GOING minus 0.16 sec per fur (GF) 4-00 (4-03)

4288* **Merit (IRE) (60)**_(78+)_(Fav)_(PFICole)_ 3-7-9 3x JQuinn(3) (lw: a.p: 6th st: led 2f out: styd on strly) — 1
4158[5] Paradise Navy **(66)**_(82) (CREgerton)_ 6-8-11 RHughes(13) (hld up & bhd: styd on fnl 2f: no ch w wnr) 2½ 2
4166* Sea Victor **(75)**_(90) (JLHarris)_ 3-8-10 PRobinson(9) (chsd ldrs: 7th st: styd on u.p appr fnl f) nk 3
4189[2] Non Vintage (IRE) **(55)**_(70) (MCChapman)_ 4-7-7 (7) MartinDwyer(12) (prom tl lost pl & 8th st: effrt over 2f out: kpt on fnl f) nk 4
4189[4] Good Hand (USA) **(70)**_(83) (JWWatts)_ 9-9-1 MBirch(7) (hld up: hdwy wl over 1f out: styd on fnl f) 2 5
4118[7] Blaze Away (USA) **(79)**_(91) (IABalding)_ 4-9-10 LDettori(1) (lw: led 2f: 2nd st: led 4f out to 2f out: wknd appr fnl f) 1¼ 6
4118* Old Red (IRE) **(72)**_(83) (MrsMReveley)_ 5-9-3 LCharnock(11) (hld up & bhd: effrt & outpcd 3f out: n.d) 1 7
4166[3] Coleridge **(49)**_(57) (JJSheehan)_ 7-7-8b AMackay(10) (hld up & bhd: hdwy 7f out: 5th & rn wd st: wknd 3f out) 3 8
4118[4] Inchcailloch (IRE) **(65)**_(69) (JSKing)_ 6-8-10 GBardwell(4) (hld up in tch: rdn & outpcd over 2f out) 4 9
4158[2] Istabraq (IRE) **(84)**_(87) (JHMGosden)_ 3-9-5 WCarson(6) (b: lw: led after 2f to 4f out: wknd fnl 2f) 1 10
4166[2] Supreme Star (USA) **(70)**_(73) (PRHedger)_ 4-8-10 (5) DaneO'Neill(14) (swtg: hld up: hdwy & 4th st: wknd over 2f out) ½ 11
4189* Sugar Mill **(69)**_(43) (MrsMReveley)_ 5-9-0 KDarley(8) (hld up: hdwy 6f out: 3rd st: wknd over 3f out: t.o) 30 12
4166[9] Thunderheart **(64)** _(JJO'Neill)_ 4-8-9 GDuffield(5) (sn t.o: p.u 4f out: lame) P

2/1 MERIT (IRE) (11/4-7/4), **9/2** Istabraq (IRE), **7/1** Sugar Mill, **15/2** Old Red (IRE), **8/1** Good Hand (USA), **11/1** Thunderheart, Blaze Away (USA), **12/1** Inchcailloch (IRE), Sea Victor, **14/1** Paradise Navy, Supreme Star (USA), **25/1** Coleridge, Non Vintage (IRE), CSF £33.74 CT £280.36 TOTE £3.00: £1.60 £3.70 £3.10 (£18.10) Trio £142.00 OWNER H R H Prince Fahd Salman (WHATCOMBE) BRED Newgate Stud Co 13 Rn

3m 39.84 (10.84) SF: 16/30/28/18/31/39/31/5/17/25/21/-/-

WEIGHT FOR AGE 3yo-10lb

T/Jkpt: Not won; £21,672.38 to Folkestone 6/11/95. T/Plpt: £276.00 (111.34 Tckts). T/Qdpt: £41.30 (4.25 Tckts). IM

4129-FOLKESTONE (R-H)
Monday November 6th (Good to firm)

WEATHER: fair WIND: almost nil

4327

CUTLASS NURSERY H'CAP (0-75) (2-Y.O) (Class E) £3,616.80 (£1,082.40: £519.20: £237.60) **6f 189y** Stalls: Low GOING minus 0.18 sec (GF) 1-00 (1-01)

4285[2] **Jerry Cutrona (IRE) (60)**_(68) (NACallaghan)_ 2-8-1 (5) AWhelan(10) (lw: chsd ldrs: 4th st: led wl over 1f out: r.o) — 1
4211* Worldwide Elsie (USA) **(71)**_(73)_(Fav)_(RHarris)_ 2-9-3 AMackay(5) (10th st: rdn 2f out: hdwy over 1f out: r.o one pce fnl f) 2½ 2
4208[6] Brecon **(65)**_(66) (PFICole)_ 2-8-11 TQuinn(8) (lw: in tch: 8th st: hdwy over 1f out: r.o one pce fnl f) ½ 3
4111[8] Pride of Kashmir **(54)**_(55) (PWHarris)_ 2-8-0 FNorton(11) (mid div: rdn 3f out: 9th st: hdwy over 1f out: r.o one pce fnl f) hd 4
4129[2] Al's Alibi **(75)**_(71) (WRMuir)_ 2-9-7 JReid(16) (chsd ldrs: 3rd st: ev ch wl over 1f out: one pce) 3 5

4211[4] Knave **(64)***(57) (RHannon)* 2-8-5 (5) DaneO'Neill(1) (lw: 7th st: rdn 2f out: one pce) 1½ **6**
4221[3] Eurobox Boy **(76)***(68) (APJarvis)* 2-9-8 JTate(12) (chsd ldrs: 5th st: wknd over 1f out) ....hd **7**
3928[6] Get Tough **(60)***(52) (SDow)* 2-7-13 (7) ADaly(7) (lw: chsd ldrs: 6th st: wknd over 1f out)..........hd **8**
4206[12] Castan (IRE) **(72)***(61) (JLDunlop)* 2-9-4 SWhitworth(6) (s.i.s: nvr nrr) 1½ **9**
4241[7] Soldier Mak **(70)***(53) (AHide)* 2-9-2 WWoods(2) (a bhd) 2½ **10**
4208[7] Duralock Fencer **(57)***(40) (PGMurphy)* 2-7-10 (7) RWaterfield(13) (lw: b.nr hind: chsd ldr: 2nd st: ev ch wl over 1f out: sn wknd) ....s.h **11**
4058[8] Montecristo **(68)***(47) (RGuest)* 2-9-0 EGuest(3) (a bhd)..1½ **12**
4058[12] Gee Gee Tee **(62)***(36) (JAkehurst)* 2-8-8 ow2 WNewnes(4) (b: a bhd) 1¼ **13**
4188[11] Silent Guest (IRE) **(68)***(40) (SirMarkPrescott)* 2-9-0 GDuffield(14) (lw: s.i.s: a bhd) 1¾ **14**
4195[10] Galapino **(73)***(42) (CEBrittain)* 2-9-0 (5) MHenry(9) (led: hdd wl over 1f out: sn wknd) 1¼ **15**
4244[6] Miss Roberto (IRE) **(60)***(26) (MrsMMcCourt)* 2-8-6b MFenton(15) (a bhd) 1¼ **16**

3/1 Worldwide Elsie (USA), **9/2** JERRY CUTRONA (IRE) (11/4-5/1), **7/1** Brecon, **8/1** Al's Alibi, **10/1** Duralock Fencer, **12/1** Knave (7/1-14/1), **14/1** Castan (IRE) (10/1-16/1), Eurobox Boy, **16/1** Pride of Kashmir, Soldier Mak, Get Tough, Montecristo, Silent Guest (IRE), **20/1** Miss Roberto (IRE), Galapino, **33/1** Gee Gee Tee, CSF £19.63 CT £94.78 TOTE £4.50: £1.60 £1.90 £1.50 £3.40 (£6.40) Trio £16.30 OWNER Mr Michael Hill (NEWMARKET) BRED Dr Paschal Carmody 16 Rn
1m 25.3 (3.70) SF: 30/35/28/17/33/19/30/14/23/15/2/9/-/2/4/-

4328 EPEE CONDITIONS STKS (2-Y.O) (Class C) £5,493.00 (£2,037.00: £981.00: £405.00) **5f** Stalls: Low GOING minus 0.50 sec per fur (F) 1-30 (1-30)

4276* **Pivotal** *(95+)*(Fav)*(SirMarkPrescott)* 2-9-2 GDuffield(8) (a.p: led wl over 1f out: sn clr: easily)...— **1**
3948[12] Smithereens *(72) (PTWalwyn)* 2-8-6 DHarrison(3) (a.p: led 3f out: hdd over 1f out: one pce) 4 **2**
4098* Singing Patriarch (IRE) **(100)***(74) (JLDunlop)* 2-9-2 TQuinn(7) (s.i.s: rr: hdwy 2f out: rdn over 1f out: one pce) 2½ **3**
4206[6] Arctic Romancer (IRE) **(70)***(68) (GLewis)* 2-8-9 (5) AWhelan(4) (a.p: rdn over 2f out: one pce) 1¼ **4**
4219[2] Songsheet *(58) (RGuest)* 2-8-1 (5) MHenry(5) (sn chsd along in rr: hdwy over 2f out: hrd rdn over 1f out: one pce)...¾ **5**
4231* Times of Times (IRE) **(78)***(56) (MJRyan)* 2-8-12 CRutter(1) (chsd ldrs: swtchd rt 3f out: rdn over 2f out: one pce)...2½ **6**
1634[4] To The Whire **(75)***(52) (GLMoore)* 2-8-11 SWhitworth(9) (chsd ldrs to ½-wy) 1 **7**
4219[3] Comic Fantasy (AUS) **(90)***(46) (PWChapple-Hyam)* 2-8-11 JReid(2) (spd to ½-wy) 1¾ **8**
4276[6] Midnight Cookie **(48)***(8) (BAPearce)* 2-8-6 (5) DaneO'Neill(6) (led 2f)..12 **9**

Evens PIVOTAL, **5/1** Songsheet (3/1-6/1), Singing Patriarch (IRE), **6/1** Times of Times (IRE), **15/2** Comic Fantasy (AUS) (9/2-8/1), **25/1** Arctic Romancer (IRE), To The Whire, **40/1** Smithereens, **100/1** Midnight Cookie, CSF £33.74 TOTE £1.80: £1.10 £5.50 £1.80 (£47.30) Trio £206.90; £116.60 to Sedgefield 7/11/95 OWNER Cheveley Park Stud (NEWMARKET) BRED Cheveley Park Stud Ltd 9 Rn 58.5 secs (0.30 under best) (-0.10) SF: 59/36/38/32/22/20/16/10/-

4329 E.B.F. BROADSWORD MEDIAN AUCTION MAIDEN STKS (I) (2-Y.O) (Class E) £3,817.50 (£1,140.00: £545.00: £247.50) **6f** Stalls: Low GOING minus 0.50 sec per fur (F) 2-00 (2-01)

4255[5] **White Plains (IRE)** *(70) (MBell)* 2-9-0 MFenton(3) (lw: hld up: hdwy over 2f out: rdn ins fnl f: led last strides)...— **1**
2548[7] Blue Adelaide *(65) (PFICole)* 2-8-9 TQuinn(6) (lw: chsd ldrs: rdn & edgd lft over 1f out: led ins fnl f: hdd last strides)...hd **2**
4161[11] Last But Not Least *(61) (RFJohnsonHoughton)* 2-8-9 JReid(9) (led: hdd ins fnl f: one pce) 1½ **3**
782[5] Lady Dignity (IRE) *(53) (PJMakin)* 2-8-9 RCochrane(1) (a.p: ev ch 2f out: rdn & n.m.r over 1f out: one pce) 3 **4**
4212[6] Faraway Lass *(53) (LordHuntingdon)* 2-8-9 DHarrison(11) (lw: a.p: ev ch 2f out: wknd ins fnl f) ....hd **5**
4144[3] Mrs McBadger **(67)***(42)*(Fav)*(BSmart)* 2-8-9 SSanders(2) (prom: ev ch 2f out: wkng whn sltly hmpd over 1f out)...4 **6**
4161[7] Maple Burl **(78)***(44) (SDow)* 2-9-0 JWilliams(10) (rr: hdwy ½-wy: rdn over 2f out: one pce) 1 **7**
4212[17] Perrywinkle Way (IRE) *(26) (MrsALMKing)* 2-8-9 AGarth(4) (bhd fnl 3f).................................5 **8**
4224[15] Mrs Keen *(15) (MrsMMcCourt)* 2-8-9 WNewnes(8) (dwlt: a bhd) 4 **9**
Learning Curve (IRE) *(9) (SirMarkPrescott)* 2-8-9 GDuffield(7) (unf: bit bkwd: sn rdn along in rr: a bhd)..2½ **10**
2534[9] Dorspring (IRE) *(9) (CEBrittain)* 2-8-9 (5) MHenry(5) (bit bkwd: bhd fnl 2f)...............................1¾ **11**

7/2 Mrs McBadger, **4/1** Faraway Lass (op 5/2), **11/2** Learning Curve (IRE) (3/1-6/1), **6/1** Maple Burl (op 3/1), **13/2** WHITE PLAINS (IRE), Lady Dignity (IRE) (8/1-5/1), **7/1** Last But Not Least (5/1-8/1), **12/1** Blue Adelaide, **50/1** Perrywinkle Way (IRE), Mrs Keen, Dorspring (IRE), CSF £76.00 TOTE £8.40: £2.40 £2.90 £2.40 (£22.90) Trio £191.80; £10.81 to Sedgefield 7/11/95 OWNER Deln Ltd (NEWMARKET) BRED Howard Kaskel 11 Rn 1m 12.9 (1.20) SF: 40/35/31/23/23/12/14/-/-/-/-

4330

E.B.F. BROADSWORD MEDIAN AUCTION MAIDEN STKS (II) (2-Y.O)
(Class E) £3,817.50 (£1,140.00: £545.00: £247.50)
6f Stalls: Low GOING minus 0.18 sec per fur (GF) 2-30 (2-36)

4211[5] **Village Native (FR) (65)***(76) (KOCunningham-Brown)* 2-9-0 DBiggs(8) (mde all: rdn ins fnl f: r.o) — 1
4208[16] Bearnaise (IRE) **(64)***(68)*(Fav)*(RHannon)* 2-8-4 (5) DaneO'Neill(7) (a.p: chsd wnr over 1f out: hrd rdn ins fnl f: unable qckn) 1¼ 2
4224[6] May Queen Megan *(66) (MrsALMKing)* 2-8-9 AGarth(4) (chsd ldrs: rdn & outpcd over 2f out: styd on fnl f) ½ 3
3870[6] Kings Harmony (IRE) *(69) (PJMakin)* 2-9-0 RCochrane(3) (chsd wnr over 3f: rdn over 1f out: one pce) ¾ 4
4148[7] Alakhluki *(58) (GLewis)* 2-8-9 SWhitworth(2) (chsd ldrs: rdn over 2f out: swtchd rt over 1f out: one pce) 2½ 5
4075[13] Billaddie *(60) (RBoss)* 2-9-0 WWoods(5) (dwlt: bhd: hdwy over 1f out: styd on fnl f: nvr nrr) 1 6
4224[7] Hadadabble *(42) (PatMitchell)* 2-8-9 MFenton(6) (prom 4f) 5 7
4137[10] Little Pilgrim *(42) (TMJones)* 2-9-0 RPerham(10) (bhd fnl 2f) 1¾ 8
3892[9] Inaminit *(39) (HJCollingridge)* 2-9-0 JQuinn(9) (dwlt: a bhd) 1 9
4269[9] *Farmost (SirMarkPrescott)* 2-9-0 GDuffield(1) (Withdrawn not under Starter's orders: ref to ent stalls) W

13/8 Bearnaise (IRE), **7/2** VILLAGE NATIVE (FR) (5/2-4/1), Kings Harmony (IRE), **15/2** Alakhluki (4/1-8/1), **10/1** Little Pilgrim (8/1-12/1), **12/1** Hadadabble, May Queen Megan (8/1-14/1), **14/1** Farmost, **16/1** Inaminit, **33/1** Billaddie, CSF £9.92 TOTE £4.90: £1.80 £1.50 £2.80 (£4.90) Trio £13.10 OWNER Mr A. J. Richards (STOCKBRIDGE) BRED Ewar Stud Farms 9 Rn
1m 12.8 SF: 43/35/33/36/25/27/9/9/6/-

4331

CLAYMORE CLAIMING H'CAP (0-65)
(3-Y.O+) (Class F) £2,519.00 (£694.00: £329.00)
2m 93y Stalls: Low GOING minus 0.18 sec per fur (GF) 3-00 (3-01)

3724[14] **Milngavie (IRE) (26)***(43) (MJohnston)* 5-7-12b NAdams(5) (chsd ldr: led over 9f out: clr over 2f out: hrd rdn over 1f out: r.o wl) — 1
3884[9] Chita Rivera **(35)***(50) (PJMakin)* 4-8-7 SSanders(14) (a.p: chsd wnr 7f out: 2nd st: hrd rdn fnl f: unable qckn) 1¾ 2
3862[2] Maronetta **(39)***(53) (MJRyan)* 3-8-1 GBardwell(11) (mid div: hdwy 6f out: 3rd st: rdn 2f out: one pce) 1¼ 3
3951[2] Environmentalist (IRE) **(56)***(69) (RHarris)* 4-10-0 AMackay(13) (b: b.nr hind: hld up: hdwy 3f out: 8th st: rdn 2f out: r.o one pce) 1¼ 4
4270[3] Deceit the Second **(45)***(56)*(Fav)*(GLewis)* 3-8-2b(5) AWhelan(1) (hld up in rr: hdwy over 3f out: 6th st: rdn over 2f out: one pce) 1¾ 5
St Kitts **(40)***(48) (WGMTurner)* 4-8-5 (7) ADaly(8) (mid div: rdn over 4f out: 7th st: one pce fnl 2f) 3 6
4248[6] Requested **(50)***(55) (PBurgoyne)* 8-9-8b TQuinn(6) (hld up: hdwy 5f out: 9th st: sn rdn: eased whn btn over 1f out) 3½ 7
4270[6] Rose of Glenn **(45)***(49) (BPalling)* 4-8-12 (5) DaneO'Neill(7) (chsd ldrs: 4th st: wknd 2f out) ¾ 8
4248[13] Charmed Life **(30)***(24) (MrsALMKing)* 6-7-11b(5) MHenry(4) (a bhd) 10 9
4270[7] Ballestro (IRE) **(35)***(28) (JFfitch-Heyes)* 3-7-8v(3) NVarley(9) (a bhd) 1¼ 10
1965[9] Secret Assignment (USA) **(23)***(14) (RCurtis)* 5-7-9 ow1 JQuinn(10) (t: chsd ldrs: 5th st: wknd 2f out) 1½ 11
4135[15] Fattash (USA) **(48)***(20) (RPCHoad)* 3-8-10b RCochrane(3) (bhd fnl 6f: t.o) 20 12
1509[14] Keep Quiet **(41)** *(WJMusson)* 3-8-0b(3)ow1 PMcCabe(2) (a bhd: t.o) 30 13
1514[19] Sirius (IRE) **(41)** *(CWeedon)* 3-8-3 GDuffield(12) (led 7f: wknd over 6f out: t.o) 2 14

3/1 Deceit the Second, **5/1** Requested (op 3/1), Maronetta, **11/2** Environmentalist (IRE), **13/2** Fattash (USA), **10/1** Rose of Glenn, MILNGAVIE (IRE), **12/1** Chita Rivera, **16/1** St Kitts, Keep Quiet, **25/1** Secret Assignment (USA), Charmed Life, Sirius (IRE), **33/1** Ballestro (IRE), CSF £126.65 CT £632.36 TOTE £7.10: £2.10 £10.20 £1.80 (£122.10) Trio £303.00; £85.36 to Sedgefield 7/11/95 OWNER Mr A. S. Robertson (MIDDLEHAM) BRED D. Oldrey and D. P. Aykroyd 14 Rn
3m 40.5 (69.30) SF: 24/31/24/50/27/29/36/30/5/-/-/-/-/-
WEIGHT FOR AGE 3yo-10lb

4332 FOIL (S) H'CAP (0-60) (3-Y.O+) (Class G) £2,243.00 (£618.00: £293.00)
1m 4f Stalls: Low GOING minus 0.18 sec per fur (GF) 3-30 (3-31)

4051[8] **El Volador (45)**(62) *(RJO'Sullivan)* 8-9-2 (5) MHenry(13) (hld up mid div: hdwy 5f out: led over 2f out: drvn out)......— **1**
4135[8] Nothing Doing (IRE) **(33)**(48) *(WJMusson)* 6-8-9 RCochrane(1) (hld up: hdwy to chse ldrs 9f out: 5th st: rdn over 1f out: r.o)......1¼ **2**
4062[10] Glow Forum **(34)**(46) *(GLMoore)* 4-8-10 MFenton(11) (hdwy 4f out: 6th st: hrd rdn over 1f out: r.o one pce fnl f)......2½ **3**
3265[4] Miltak **(37)**(49) *(PJMakin)* 3-8-6 SSanders(8) (mid div: 8th st: rdn 2f out: r.o one pce fnl f)......hd **4**
245[6] Sharp Thrill **(38)**(47) *(BSmart)* 4-9-0 DHarrison(3) (hld up: hdwy 7f out: led 3f out: sn hdd: 2nd st: wknd over 1f out)......2½ **5**
4259[17] College Night (IRE) **(47)**(53) *(CADwyer)* 3-8-13 (3) PMcCabe(4) (chsd ldrs: 4th st: rdn 2f out: one pce)......2 **6**
4259[14] Smocking **(30)**(34) *(JPearce)* 5-8-6 GBardwell(18) (plld hrd: chsd ldrs tl lost pl 6f out: rdn over 3f out: one pce fnl 2f)......1½ **7**
4259[8] Emma Grimes (IRE) **(35)**(36) *(JSMoore)* 4-8-11 JFEgan(17) (chsd ldrs: 7th st: wknd 2f out)......2½ **8**
4209[14] Tauten (IRE) **(37)**(37) *(PBurgoyne)* 5-8-13 JWilliams(7) (nvr nrr)......½ **9**
4135[9] Jemima Puddleduck **(38)**(37)(Fav)*(DWPArbuthnot)* 4-9-0 TQuinn(2) (chsd ldrs: 3rd st: wknd 2f out)......¾ **10**
4261[17] Autumn Cover **(47)**(43) *(RMFlower)* 3-8-11 (5) DaneO'Neill(12) (bhd fnl 5f)......2½ **11**
4062[4] Scenic Dancer **(48)**(42) *(AHide)* 7-9-10 WWoods(5) (nvr nrr)......1½ **12**
3876[7] Nivasha **(37)**(30) *(RPCHoad)* 3-8-6 JQuinn(16) (bhd fnl 5f)......nk **13**
4293[7] Night Edition **(42)**(26) *(SDow)* 5-9-4 GDuffield(6) (bhd fnl 5f)......7 **14**
13[4] Kenyatta (USA) **(30)**(7) *(AMoore)* 6-8-6 CandyMorris(9) (led 9f)......5 **15**
3847[5] Alioli **(44)**(16) *(MJRyan)* 3-8-8 (5) MBaird(14) (prom 8f)......4 **16**
4249[20] Run-Do-Run **(52)** *(HJCollingridge)* 3-9-7 WNewnes(10) (ref to r: t.n.p)...... **R**

3/1 Jemima Puddleduck, **4/1** EL VOLADOR (3/1-5/1), **11/2** Scenic Dancer, **15/2** Nothing Doing (IRE) (5/1-10/1), **8/1** Emma Grimes (IRE), **12/1** Alioli, Glow Forum (op 8/1), Night Edition, **14/1** Smocking, **16/1** Miltak, College Night (IRE), Autumn Cover, **20/1** Tauten (IRE), Sharp Thrill, Kenyatta (USA), Nivasha, **25/1** Run-Do-Run, CSF £40.04 CT £342.27 TOTE £8.40: £2.40 £2.90 £3.60 £4.90 (£49.10) Trio £328.60 OWNER Mr A. A. J. Peirce (BOGNOR REGIS) BRED L. and Mrs Hutch 17 Rn 2m 40.8 (9.60) SF: 28/14/12/8/13/12/-/2/3/3/2/8/-/-/-/-/-

WEIGHT FOR AGE 3yo-7lb

No bid

4333 SABRE H'CAP (0-70) (3-Y.O+) (Class E) £3,960.00 (£1,188.00: £572.00: £264.00)
1m 4f Stalls: Low GOING minus 0.18 sec per fur (GF) 4-00 (4-01)

4259[11] **Ayunli (62)**(78) *(SCWilliams)* 4-9-4 (5) DaneO'Neill(11) (chsd ldrs: 3rd st: led wl over 1f out: hrd rdn fnl f: r.o)......— **1**
4284* Fairy Knight **(74)**(90) *(RHannon)* 3-10-0 5x JReid(15) (chsd ldrs: rdn 4f out: 4th st: hdwy to chse wnr over 1f out: hrd rdn fnl f: r.o)......nk **2**
4135* Minnesota Viking **(59)**(65) *(LadyHerries)* 4-9-6 RCochrane(3) (hld up: hdwy 4f out: 8th st: rdn 2f out: r.o one pce)......7 **3**
4248[3] Quest Again **(64)**(66) *(DWPArbuthnot)* 4-9-11 TQuinn(13) (hld up: hdwy 4f out: 7th st: rdn 2f out: one pce)......3½ **4**
4135[11] Rock The Barney (IRE) **(52)**(54) *(PBurgoyne)* 6-8-10 (3) PMcCabe(8) (rr: rdn 5f out: 10th st: styd on fnl 2f: nrst fin)......hd **5**
4259[3] Douce Maison (IRE) **(55)**(53) *(APJarvis)* 4-9-2 JTate(12) (chsd ldr: 2nd st: rdn & ev ch wl over 1f out: sn wknd)......2½ **6**
4259[5] Pass Mark **(59)**(57) *(JRFanshawe)* 3-8-10 (3) NVarley(4) (chsd ldrs: 5th st: rdn 2f out: sn wknd)......s.h **7**
3927[9] Broughtons Formula **(50)**(46) *(WJMusson)* 5-8-11b JQuinn(2) (nvr nrr)......1¼ **8**
668[13] Retender (USA) **(65)**(59) *(JPearce)* 6-9-12 JWilliams(10) (rr: rdn 5f out: nvr nrr)......2 **9**
4259[2] Lidhama (USA) **(61)**(52)(Fav)*(GLewis)* 3-9-1 SWhitworth(5) (hld up: hdwy on outside over 1f out: 9th st: sn wknd)......1¾ **10**
4136[6] Tonka **(59)**(49) *(PJMakin)* 3-8-13 SSanders(16) (chsd ldrs: 6th st: wknd 2f out)......¾ **11**
1048[14] Todd (USA) **(63)**(49) *(PMitchell)* 4-9-5 (5) MHenry(17) (led: hdd wl over 1f out: sn wknd)......3½ **12**
4171[15] Children's Choice (IRE) **(56)**(34) *(PJMcBride)* 4-8-12 (5) AWhelan(9) (bhd fnl 5f)......6 **13**
4229[7] Saltando (IRE) **(48)**(25) *(PatMitchell)* 4-8-9 MFenton(14) (a bhd)......nk **14**
4051[2] Granby Bell **(51)**(27) *(PHayward)* 4-8-12 DHarrison(7) (prom 8f)......¾ **15**
4261[2] Ramsdens (IRE) **(69)**(45) *(WJHaggas)* 3-9-9 WWoods(6) (chsd ldrs 7f)......½ **16**
4228[7] Anjou **(63)**(5) *(JPearce)* 3-9-3 GBardwell(1) (bhd fnl 6f: t.o)......25 **17**
Tickerty's Gift **(57)** *(GLMoore)* 5-9-4 CandyMorris(18) (bhd fnl 6f: t.o)......2½ **18**

13/8 Lidhama (USA), **11/2** Douce Maison (IRE), **7/1** Ramsdens (IRE) (op 4/1), **15/2** Minnesota Viking, **12/1** Children's Choice (IRE) (16/1-10/1), Fairy Knight, **14/1** Rock The Barney (IRE), Quest Again, Granby Bell, AYUNLI (10/1-16/1), Pass Mark, **20/1** Anjou, Broughtons Formula, **25/1** Tonka, **33/1** Saltando (IRE), Retender (USA), Todd (USA), **50/1** Tickerty's Gift, CSF £184.20 CT £1,278.40 TOTE £31.50: £3.50 £4.20 £2.10 £4.10 (£104.30) Trio £153.90 OWNER Mr I. A. Southcott (NEWMARKET) BRED I. A. Southcott 18 Rn
2m 38.2 (7.00) SF: 46/51/33/34/22/21/18/14/27/13/10/17/2/-/-/6/-/-
WEIGHT FOR AGE 3yo-7lb

TJkpt: Not won; £28,767.45 to Sedgefield 7/11/95. T/Plpt: £329.00 (41.87 Tckts). T/Qdpt: £144.60 (1 Tckt). SM

3522-SOUTHWELL (L-H)
Monday November 6th (Standard)
WEATHER: fine & sunny WIND: mod half bhd

4334
MIDWAY MAIDEN STKS (I) (2-Y.O) (Class D) £3,362.50 (£1,000.00: £465.00: £212.50) **1m (Fibresand)** Stalls: Low GOING: 0.05 sec per fur (STD) 1-10 (1-12)

4151[5] **D'naan (IRE) (78)***(76)*(Fav)*(WJHaggas)* 2-9-0b TIves(3) (lw: chsd ldrs: effrt & swtchd outside over 2f out: styd on u.p to ld over 1f out: drvn out) — 1
Milton *(75+) (PFICole)* 2-9-0 RHughes(10) (rangy: chsd ldrs: led 5f out: hung rt & hdd over 1f out: styd on wl towards fin) ½ 2
4037[5] Whitley Grange Boy *(67) (JLEyre)* 2-9-0 RLappin(8) (swtg: trckd ldrs: outpcd over 2f out: kpt on appr fnl f) 4 3
3463[8] Whothehellisharry **(63)***(51) (JBerry)* 2-9-0 SDWilliams(7) (led 3f: rdn over 3f out: wknd over 2f out) 8 4
3975[28] Snow Domino (IRE) *(43) (JMJefferson)* 2-9-0 KFallon(9) (bit bkwd: dwlt: hdwy on outside 5f out: ev ch 3f out: wknd 2f out) 4 5
4282[7] Marsayas (IRE) *(42) (MJCamacho)* 2-9-0 LCharnock(11) (chsd ldrs tl outpcd fnl 2f) ½ 6
Red Rusty (USA) *(41) (DMorris)* 2-9-0 StephenDavies(12) (bit bkwd: hld up: effrt on outside 3f out: nvr nr ldrs) ½ 7
4045[8] Belle's Boy *(39) (BPalling)* 2-9-0 TSprake(2) (sn drvn along: chsd ldrs tl lost pl over 2f out) 1¼ 8
Ivor's Deed *(14) (CFWall)* 2-8-4 (5) LNewton(6) (lengthy: bit bkwd: s.i.s: sn chsng ldrs: wknd 2f out) 1 9
4224[16] Lunar Gris **(48)***(25) (JEBanks)* 2-8-6 (3) JStack(13) (w ldrs: rdn 3f out: sn lost pl) 3½ 10
Crystal Fast (USA) *(27) (PAKelleway)* 2-9-0 MRimmer(1) (lengthy: unf: unruly s: s.i.s: n.d) 1¼ 11
Water Chestnut *(24) (MrsNMacauley)* 2-8-7 (7) AmandaSanders(5) (cmpt: b: s.i.s: a wl bhd) 1¾ 12
3093[4] Gold Kicker *(14) (MJRyan)* 2-9-0 AClark(4) (a bhd) 5 13

4/6 D'NAAN (IRE) (op 5/4), **5/1** Milton, **6/1** Gold Kicker (op 7/2), **12/1** Whitley Grange Boy (op 8/1), **16/1** Crystal Fast (USA), Lunar Gris, **20/1** Ivor's Deed, **25/1** Whothehellisharry, **33/1** Snow Domino (IRE), Marsayas (IRE), Belle's Boy, **50/1** Water Chestnut, Red Rusty (USA), CSF £5.51 TOTE £1.70: £1.10 £1.70 £2.10 (£3.40) Trio £13.70 OWNER Mr Adel Almojil (NEWMARKET) BRED Blandford Bloodstock 13 Rn
1m 48.3 (9.00) SF: 13/12/4/-/-/-/-/-/-/-/-/-/-

4335
MARIANA LIMITED STKS (0-55) (3-Y.O+) (Class F) £2,519.00 (£694.00: £329.00)
1m 3f (Fibresand) Stalls: Low GOING: 0.05 sec per fur (STD) 1-40 (1-43)

4022[3] **Father Dan (IRE) (50)***(72) (MissGayKelleway)* 6-9-5 KFallon(6) (bhd: gd hdwy 7f out: chsd ldrs 3f out: rdn to ld over 1f out: eased ins fnl f) — 1
4071[9] Instantaneous **(55)***(65)*(Fav)*(MHEasterby)* 3-8-5 (5) LNewton(8) (in tch: smooth hdwy to ld over 4f out: clr over 2f out: sn rdn: hdd over 1f out: kpt on same pce) 2½ 2
4138* Our Main Man **(53)***(62) (RMWhitaker)* 5-9-7 DaleGibson(1) (sn drvn along: hdwy 5f out: styd on fnl 2f: nvr nr to chal) 6 3
4044[10] H'Ani **(50)***(51) (WJHaggas)* 3-8-6 DeanMcKeown(4) (bhd: hdwy 4f out: kpt on fnl 2f: nvr nr to chal) 1½ 4
4061[3] Lady Highfield **(50)***(54) (MJRyan)* 4-9-2 AClark(10) (bhd: gd hdwy 6f out: one pce fnl 2f) s.h 5
4229* Rival Bid (USA) **(57)***(56) (MrsNMacauley)* 7-9-0 (7) AmandaSanders(3) (lw: hld up: hdwy to trck ldrs ½-wy: effrt over 2f out: sn rdn & no imp) 2½ 6
4271[2] Diamond Market **(49)***(39) (RHollinshead)* 3-8-11 TIves(12) (in tch: effrt over 3f out: sn lost pl) 9 7

4061 19 Just Flamenco **(50)***(34) (MJRyan)* 4-9-7 RHughes(7) (sn w ldrs: led over 5f out: sn hdd: rdn 3f out: sn wknd & eased)....6 **8**
4249 13 Pc's Cruiser (IRE) **(54)***(28) (JLEyre)* 3-8-11 RLappin(13) (a in rr)....1¼ **9**
4196 7 Greek Gold (IRE) **(54)***(21) (DNicholls)* 6-9-3 MTebbutt(9) (lw: led 2f: trckd ldrs tl lost pl 3f out)....5 **10**
4152 19 Sea God **(49)***(21) (MCChapman)* 4-8-10 (7) CMunday(14) (w ldrs: led 8f out tl over 5f out: sn lost pl)....hd **11**
771 14 Tempering **(53)** *(DWChapman)* 9-9-3 ACulhane(2) (led after 2f: sn hdd: lost pl 6f out: sn wl bhd: t.o)....25 **12**
4261 16 Kirov Protege (IRE) **(48)** *(HJCollingridge)* 3-8-11 MRimmer(5) (bhd & drvn along 5f out: t.o)....4 **13**
3737 9 *Latch Key Lady (USA)* **(48)** *(MJohnston)* 3-8-6 TWilliams(11) (Withdrawn not under Starter's orders: reard over backwards in stalls & inj rdr).... **W**

100/30 Instantaneous (5/1-3/1), **7/2** Rival Bid (USA) (op 2/1), **6/1** FATHER DAN (IRE) (op 4/1), **13/2** Greek Gold (IRE), **7/1** Lady Highfield, **9/1** H'Ani (op 6/1), **10/1** Pc's Cruiser (IRE), **12/1** Our Main Man, Tempering, **16/1** Diamond Market, **20/1** Just Flamenco, Kirov Protege (IRE), **33/1** Sea God, Latch Key Lady (USA), CSF £28.58 TOTE £4.70: £2.20 £1.50 £4.80 (£29.20) Trio £215.20; £33.34 to Sedgefield 7/11/95 OWNER Wessex Fm (Whitcombe) Racing Club Ltd (WHITCOMBE) BRED John Michael 13 Rn
2m 31.1 (9.60) SF: 39/26/29/12/21/23/-/1/-/-/-/-/-
WEIGHT FOR AGE 3yo-6lb

4336 BOUNTY AMATEUR H'CAP (0-70) (3-Y.O+) (Class E) £3,416.60 (£1,020.80: £488.40: £222.20)

1m 6f (Fibresand) Stalls: High GOING: 0.05 sec per fur (STD) 2-10 (2-12)

4168 5 **Fair and Fancy (FR) (34)***(48)*(Fav)*(DNicholls)* 4-9-9 MrsAPerrett(6) (lw: in tch: hdwy to ld 3f out: r.o u.p fnl f)....— **1**
4086 5 Ijab (CAN) **(42)***(55) (JParkes)* 5-10-3b MrMHNaughton(10) (in tch: hdwy to chal over 2f out: hrd rdn & nt qckn fnl f)....½ **2**
4140 3 Greek Night Out (IRE) **(33)***(44) (JLEyre)* 4-9-8 MissDianaJones(7) (bhd: hdwy & pushed along 6f out: styd on fnl 3f: nvr nr to chal)....2½ **3**
1840 13 Kadiri (IRE) **(60)***(71) (JRBosley)* 4-11-7 MrsSBosley(1) (bhd: swtchd wd 7f out: sn chsng ldrs: kpt on wl fnl 2f)....s.h **4**
4288 9 Five to Seven (USA) **(57)***(63) (CWThornton)* 6-11-4 MrSSwiers(3) (lw: w ldrs: one pce fnl 3f)....4 **5**
2592 4 Stalled (IRE) **(48)***(47) (PTWalwyn)* 5-10-4 (5) MarchionessBlandford(15) (trckd ldrs on outside: effrt 3f out: grad wknd)....6 **6**
4086 10 Philmist **(49)***(44) (CWCElsey)* 3-10-2b MissAElsey(11) (w ldrs: led 6f out to 3f out: grad wknd)....4 **7**
4101 5 Suselja (IRE) **(40)***(35) (JMJefferson)* 4-9-10 (5) MrWWenyon(17) (a in tch: drvn along over 3f out: no imp)....d.h **7**
3724 18 Lone Risk **(46)***(40) (CNAllen)* 4-10-2 (5) MrVLukaniuk(14) (b.nr fore: bhd: sme hdwy 3f out: n.d)....¾ **9**
4101 3 Hasta la Vista **(44)***(23) (MWEasterby)* 5-10-5b MrCBonner(4) (mde most to 6f out: lost pl over 2f out)....13 **10**
3898 12 Phanan **(33)***(9) (REPeacock)* 9-9-3 (5)ow3 MrsCPeacock(8) (b: plld hrd: w ldrs tl wknd over 4f out)....s.h **11**
3876 6 Abinger **(55)***(33) (LadyHerries)* 3-10-8 MrPPritchard-Gordon(12) (bhd & drvn along 5f out: n.d)....¾ **12**
4135 2 Soojama (IRE) **(45)***(20) (RMFlower)* 5-10-6 MrRJohnson(5) (mid div: drvn along over 5f out: n.d)....3 **13**
3245 12 Handmaiden **(47)***(17) (AHarrison)* 5-10-8 MrsDKettlewell(9) (bhd: gd hdwy on outside 5f out: sn in tch: wknd 3f out)....4 **14**
4140 P Crowther Homes **(30)** *(EJAlston)* 5-9-5 MrsAFarrell(16) (racd wd: w ldrs tl lost pl 5f out)....7 **15**
4140 W Mrs Jawleyford (USA) **(53)***(6) (CSmith)* 7-10-9 (5) MrsMMorris(13) (b: bhd: hdwy 5f out: sn lost pl)....8 **16**
4126 5 Elpida (USA) **(62)***(13) (JPearce)* 3-11-1 MrsLPearce(2) (plld hrd: prom early: sn bhd: drvn along over 5f out: sn wknd & eased)....1¼ **17**

5/1 FAIR AND FANCY (FR) (op 10/1), **6/1** Abinger (op 4/1), Soojama (IRE), **13/2** Greek Night Out (IRE), **7/1** Hasta la Vista, Elpida (USA), **9/1** Ijab (CAN), **10/1** Stalled (IRE), **12/1** Five to Seven (USA), **14/1** Kadiri (IRE), **16/1** Philmist, **20/1** Mrs Jawleyford (USA), Handmaiden, **25/1** Lone Risk, Suselja (IRE), **33/1** Crowther Homes, **50/1** Phanan, CSF £53.90 CT £292.04 TOTE £8.80: £2.10 £3.20 £2.00 £3.20 (£71.20) Trio £107.10 OWNER Mr Ron Motion (THIRSK) BRED Alec Head 17 Rn
3m 16.7 (17.00) SF: 17/24/13/40/32/16/5/4/9/-/-/-/-/-/-/-/-
WEIGHT FOR AGE 3yo-8lb

4337 FYFFES OF NOTTINGHAM H'CAP (0-80) (3-Y.O+) (Class D)
£4,104.10 (£1,226.80: £587.40: £267.70)
6f (Fibresand) Stalls: Low GOING: 0.05 sec per fur (STD) 2-40 (2-44)

4145[16] **La Petite Fusee (60)***(78+) (RJO'Sullivan)* 4-8-10 RHughes(15) (mde virtually all: drvn clr over 2f out: unchal)......— 1
4060[3] Deeply Vale (IRE) **(60)***(59) (GLMoore)* 4-8-10 AClark(11) (sn bhd: hdwy over 2f out: styd on fnl f: no ch w wnr)......7 2
4240[3] Berge (IRE) **(74)***(72)*(Fav)*(WAO'Gorman)* 4-9-10b EmmaO'Gorman(10) (lw: s.i.s: bhd: hdwy over 2f out: styd on fnl f)......½ 3
4157[7] Leigh Crofter **(76)***(74) (PDCundell)* 6-9-7b(5) DGriffiths(7) (b.nr hind: n.m.r after 1f: hdwy on outside over 2f out: kpt on fnl f)......hd 4
3964[7] Bold Street (IRE) **(68)***(56) (ABailey)* 5-9-1b(3) DWright(9) (lw: bhd: hdwy over 2f out: kpt on fnl f)......3½ 5
4280[19] Sir Tasker **(77)***(65) (JLHarris)* 7-9-6 (7) DSweeney(6) (lw: in tch: kpt on on outside fnl 2f: nvr nr to chal)......hd 6
4165[11] Nordico Princess **(72)***(54) (MBrittain)* 4-9-8 KFallon(3) (lw: w ldrs tl wknd over 2f out)......2½ 7
3344[9] At the Savoy (IRE) **(67)***(47) (TDBarron)* 4-8-10b(7) KimberleyHart(5) (a in tch: no imp fnl 2f)....¾ 8
4322[5] Silk Cottage **(64)***(43) (RMWhitaker)* 3-8-13 ACulhane(12) (lw: n.m.r after 1f: in tch: kpt on one pce fnl 2f)......s.h 9
4242[3] Hickory Blue **(60)***(33) (MrsNMacauley)* 5-8-3b(7) AmandaSanders(2) (b: chsd ldrs tl lost pl over 2f out)......2½ 10
4274[2] Jigsaw Boy **(59)***(32) (PGMurphy)* 6-8-6 (3) SDrowne(14) (lw: in tch early: outpcd fr ½-wy)......s.h 11
4145[15] Sue Me (IRE) **(63)***(32) (WRMuir)* 3-8-12 TIves(16) (sn outpcd & bhd)......1½ 12
4068[10] Broadstairs Beauty (IRE) **(75)***(33) (SRBowring)* 5-9-11 SDWilliams(1) (lw: b: b.hind: chsd ldrs tl lost pl over 2f out: eased)......4 13
4171[16] Young Benson **(59)***(17) (BAMcMahon)* 3-8-8 DaleGibson(13) (in tch: sn drvn along: outpcd fr ½-wy)......hd 14
3681[17] White Sorrel **(78)***(36) (AHarrison)* 4-9-11 (3) JStack(4) (stumbled s: n.d)......s.h 15
4055[7] Barranak (IRE) **(60)** *(MrsMMcCourt)* 3-8-2 (7) RStudholme(8) (sn outpcd, drvn along & bhd)......10 16

11/4 Berge (IRE) (op 5/1), **6/1** Bold Street (IRE), **7/1** Silk Cottage, Jigsaw Boy, **8/1** LA PETITE FUSEE, Broadstairs Beauty (IRE), **10/1** Hickory Blue, **12/1** At the Savoy (IRE), Sue Me (IRE), **14/1** Leigh Crofter, **16/1** White Sorrel, Barranak (IRE), Nordico Princess, **20/1** Young Benson, Sir Tasker, Deeply Vale (IRE), CSF £166.74 CT £520.53 TOTE £8.40: £3.00 £4.40 £1.60 £6.80 (£165.30) Trio £291.70 OWNER Skampcargo Racing Partnership (BOGNOR REGIS) BRED H. Powis 16 Rn
1m 18.2 (4.70) SF: 35/16/29/31/13/22/11/4/-/-/-/-/-/-/-/-
WEIGHT FOR AGE 3yo-1lb

4338 MIDWAY MAIDEN STKS (II) (2-Y.O) (Class D) £3,362.50
(£1,000.00: £465.00: £212.50)
1m (Fibresand) Stalls: Low GOING: 0.05 sec per fur (STD) 3-10 (3-12)

4100[3] **Ground Game** *(76)*(Fav)*(DRLoder)* 2-8-9 RHughes(10) (b.hind: trckd ldrs: led over 2f out: styd on u.p fnl f)......— 1
4141[10] Alzotic (IRE) **(55)***(80) (SGNorton)* 2-9-0 KFallon(5) (chsd ldrs: outpcd ½-wy: hdwy & ev ch 1f out: hrd rdn & nt qckn towards fin)......nk 2
2995[12] Oxgang (IRE) *(70) (JGFitzGerald)* 2-9-0 TIves(12) (bit bkwd: a chsng ldrs: kpt on same pce fnl 2f)......5 3
4143[5] Kissing Gate (USA) *(65) (RCharlton)* 2-8-9 TSprake(8) (hld up: drvn along & outpcd over 3f out: styd on appr fnl f)......s.h 4
3968[6] Double Dash (IRE) *(70) (MJohnston)* 2-9-0 SDWilliams(3) (s.i.s: sn chsng ldrs: led 3f out: sn hdd: one pce appr fnl f)......nk 5
4277[4] Sis Garden *(62) (MHEasterby)* 2-8-9 MRimmer(9) (led 1f: chsd ldrs: rdn & hung lft 2f out: sn wknd)......1½ 6
Contrarie *(32) (MJRyan)* 2-8-9 AClark(6) (leggy: unf: s.i.s: bhd tl hdwy on outside ½-wy: sn wknd)......15 7
4073[7] Rain Cloud *(16) (WWHaigh)* 2-8-9 DaleGibson(11) (bit bkwd: outpcd ½-wy: sn bhd)......8 8
4129[8] Two Socks **(69)***(17) (MMcCormack)* 2-8-11 (3) JStack(2) (led after 1f to 3f out: sn wknd)......1¾ 9
Tagatay *(16) (MJCamacho)* 2-9-0 LCharnock(7) (lengthy: unf: bit bkwd: s.i.s: a in rr)......½ 10
Maestro Time (USA) *(TDBarron)* 2-9-0 DeanMcKeown(4) (lengthy: bkwd: s.i.s: a outpcd & bhd)......10 11
4112[6] Colway Bridge *(MrsMReveley)* 2-9-0 ACulhane(1) (in tch tl lost pl ½-wy: t.o)......30 12

5/4 GROUND GAME (Evens-6/4), **9/4** Alzotic (IRE) (op 7/1), **5/1** Kissing Gate (USA), **8/1** Double Dash (IRE) (4/1-9/1), **11/1** Two Socks (8/1-12/1), **14/1** Oxgang (IRE) (10/1-16/1), **20/1** Contrarie, Maestro Time (USA), Sis Garden, **25/1** Colway Bridge, **33/1** Tagatay, Rain Cloud, CSF £4.42 TOTE £2.10: £1.80 £1.70 £7.00 (£3.60) Trio £43.30 OWNER Mrs P. T. Fenwick (NEWMARKET) BRED Michael Watt and Miss Jemima Johnson 12 Rn 1m 47.0 (7.70) SF: 21/25/15/10/15/7/-/-/-/-/-/-

4339

BONIN (S) STKS (2-Y.O) (Class E) £3,330.80 (£994.40: £475.20: £215.60)
7f (Fibresand) Stalls: Low GOING: 0.05 sec per fur (STD) 3-40 (3-48)

4263[14] **Dragonjoy (50)***(67) (JWPayne)* 2-8-11b AMcGlone(13) (reminders in stalls: mde virtually all: clr over 2f out: kpt on unchal) .....— **1**
4277[6] The Fullbangladesh *(59)*(Fav)*(JLEyre)* 2-8-6 RLappin(5) (dwlt: bhd: effrt over 2f out: styd on appr fnl f: nt qckn last 100y).....1½ **2**
3937[10] Ticka Ticka Timing **(55)***(67) (BWMurray)* 2-8-9 (7) MartinDwyer(15) (a chsng ldrs: kpt on same pce appr fnl f).....½ **3**
3566[8] Orange And Blue **(43)***(59) (MissJFCraze)* 2-8-11e SWebster(14) (eyecover: a chsng ldrs: styd on one pce fnl 2f).....1½ **4**
4273[10] Hurricane Horn (IRE) **(50)***(59) (WRMuir)* 2-8-11b MRimmer(9) (s.i.s: bhd: kpt on appr fnl f: nvr nr to chal).....s.h **5**
4127[6] Shanoora (IRE) **(54)***(56) (BPalling)* 2-8-11b TSprake(6) (a chsng ldrs: one pce fnl 2f).....1½ **6**
3612[13] Sphinx Levelv (IRE) **(47)***(55) (APJarvis)* 2-8-8v(3) DWright(11) (hld up & plld hrd: effrt 2f out: hung lft: nvr nr to chal).....hd **7**
4263[6] Righteous Gent **(60)***(54) (KMcAuliffe)* 2-8-11b RHughes(3) (bhd tl sme hdwy fnl 2f: n.d).....¾ **8**
3975[13] Hannahs Bay *(48) (MGMeagher)* 2-8-6 KFallon(10) (in tch: sn drvn along: n.d).....hd **9**
4273[7] Richard House Lad **(56)***(48) (RHollinshead)* 2-8-11 TIves(16) (sn bhd & drvn along: sme hdwy ove 2f out: n.d).....2½ **10**
3620[20] Gunner B Special *(46) (SRBowring)* 2-8-6 (5) CTeague(1) (b: sn wl bhd: t.o ½-wy: kpt on u.p fnl 2f).....½ **11**
3994[13] Nutcracker **(65)***(36) (CBBBooth)* 2-8-6 NKennedy(2) (sn bhd).....2½ **12**
3982[8] Rocket Grounds (IRE) *(30) (JJQuinn)* 2-8-6 ACulhane(7) (in tch: drvn ½-wy: sn lost pl).....2½ **13**
4269[10] Embroidered *(29) (SirMarkPrescott)* 2-8-6 CNutter(8) (chsd ldrs tl wknd over 2f out).....½ **14**
3738[10] Ricochet (IRE) *(SGNorton)* 2-8-11b DeanMcKeown(4) (sn drvn along & outpcd: t.o ½-wy)..30 **15**
2371[6] Ron's Gem *(WWHaigh)* 2-8-11 DaleGibson(12) (Withdrawn not under Starter's orders: uns rdr at stalls & bolted)..... **W**

7/2 The Fullbangladesh, **5/1** Richard House Lad, **7/1** Nutcracker, Rocket Grounds (IRE), Righteous Gent, Sphinx Levelv (IRE) (op 4/1), **10/1** Embroidered, **12/1** Shanoora (IRE), Ticka Ticka Timing, **14/1** Ron's Gem, Hurricane Horn (IRE) (op 8/1), **20/1** DRAGONJOY, Gunner B Special, Hannahs Bay, **25/1** Orange And Blue, **33/1** Ricochet (IRE), CSF £90.76 TOTE £43.40: £7.60 £1.20 £5.40 (£143.30) Trio £123.70 OWNER Mr T. H. Barma (NEWMARKET) BRED T. H. Barma 15 Rn
1m 35.8 (9.00) SF: -/-/-/-/-/-/-/-/-/-/-/-/-/-/-
No bid

STEWARDS' ENQUIRY Julie Craze fined £100 (declaring an eyeshield and using an eyecover).

4340

SOLOMAN H'CAP (0-60) (3-Y.O+) (Class F) £2,519.00 (£694.00: £329.00)
1m (Fibresand) Stalls: Low GOING: 0.05 sec per fur (STD) 4-10 (4-18)

4292[6] **Rood Music (55)***(62) (MGMeagher)* 4-9-13 KFallon(14) (mde virtually all: rdn along 3f out: styd on strly to go clr over 1f out).....— **1**
3889[13] Beauman **(56)***(49) (PDEvans)* 5-10-0 RHughes(16) (lw: a chsng ldrs: chal & rdn over 2f out: kpt on same pce).....7 **2**
4274[7] Lady Silk **(54)***(45) (MissJFCraze)* 4-9-12 SWebster(11) (rr div: hdwy 2f out: styd on fnl f).....1¼ **3**
2181[6] Lucky Tucky **(50)***(40) (JRJenkins)* 4-9-8 AMcGlone(15) (a chsng ldrs: one pce fnl 3f).....nk **4**
4240[8] Action Jackson **(57)***(39) (BJMcMath)* 3-9-12 MRimmer(10) (b: chsd ldrs: rdn over 2f out: sn outpcd).....4 **5**
835[5] Eastleigh **(55)***(35) (RHollinshead)* 6-9-13 TIves(12) (hmpd & lost pl after 1f: bhd tl sme hdwy 2f out: n.d).....1 **6**
4123[11] Vocal Command **(56)***(35) (WWHaigh)* 3-9-11 DaleGibson(5) (bhd & drvn along: kpt on fnl 2f: n.d).....½ **7**
4170[14] North Esk (USA) **(53)***(32) (CADwyer)* 6-9-11 CDwyer(9) (mid div: effrt 3f out: nvr nr ldrs).....hd **8**
4234[8] Nobby Barnes **(51)***(26) (DonEnricoIncisa)* 6-9-9 KimTinkler(13) (mid div: drvn along & outpcd 3f out: edgd lft u.p: n.d).....1¾ **9**
2923[2] Exclusive Assembly **(57)***(30) (APJames)* 3-9-7 (5) LNewton(3) (in tch: hrd rdn over 2f out: sn wknd).....1¼ **10**
4044[9] Komiamaite **(58)***(25) (SRBowring)* 3-9-8 (5) CTeague(2) (unruly s: sn bhd).....3 **11**
3511[8] Dia Georgy **(51)***(16) (MrsNMacauley)* 4-9-9 SDWilliams(6) (b: chsd ldrs tl lost pl 3f out).....¾ **12**
4271[*] Saracen Prince (USA) **(58)***(23)*(Fav)*(PAKelleway)* 3-9-10 (3) JStack(1) (lw: chsd ldrs: sn pushed along: lost pl over 3f out).....nk **13**

3952[8] Shareoftheaction **(51)***(14) (MrsAMNaughton)* 4-9-9v VHalliday(7) (sn bhd) 1 **14**
169[9] Hawaii Storm (FR) **(56)***(9) (DJSffrenchDavis)* 7-9-9 (5) AProcter(4) (hld up: hdwy on ins 3f out: sn wknd & eased) 5 **15**
4284[15] Northern Trove (USA) **(57)** *(RonaldThompson)* 3-9-12b DMcKeown(8) (s.i.s: plld hrd: sn trckng ldrs: wknd over 2f out) 7 **16**

11/4 Saracen Prince (USA), **9/2** Dia Georgy, **10/1** Nobby Barnes (8/1-12/1), **12/1** Beauman, ROOD MUSIC, Exclusive Assembly (op 8/1), Lucky Tucky, North Esk (USA), Komiamaite (op 8/1), **14/1** Action Jackson, Eastleigh, **16/1** Hawaii Storm (FR), Vocal Command, **33/1** Shareoftheaction, Lady Silk, Northern Trove (USA), CSF £144.67 CT £4,168.53 TOTE £18.20: £2.60 £5.50 £3.40 £1.30 (£58.50) Trio Not won; £614.80 to Sedgefield 7/11/95 OWNER Mr M. R. Johnson (ORMSKIRK) BRED T. R. G. Vestey 16 Rn 1m 46.3 (7.00) SF: 44/31/27/22/18/17/14/14/8/9/4/-/2/-/-/-
WEIGHT FOR AGE 3yo-3lb

OFFICIAL EXPLANATION **Saracen Prince(USA): the trainer reported that the gelding did not seem to have acted well on the inside of the course where the ground was at its deepest.**
T/Plpt: £38.10 (232.11 Tckts). T/Qdpt: Not won; £34.80 to Sedgefield 7/11/95. WG

3689a-LEOPARDSTOWN (Dublin, Ireland) (L-H)
Monday October 30th (Good to yielding)

4341a KILLAVULLAN STKS (Gp 3) (2-Y.O) £16,089.00 (£4,703.00: £2,228.00) 7f 2-45 (2-48)

Aylesbury (IRE) *(JOxx,Ireland)* 2-8-10 JPMurtagh ....— 1
Errazuriz (IRE) *(MrsFionaO'Connor,Ireland)* 2-8-7 WJO'Connor 1 2
Dance Clear (IRE) *(MichaelDalton,Ireland)* 2-8-7 CRoche 1 3

Tote £1.70: £1.30 £5.30 (£14.60) OWNER Sheikh Mohammed BRED Sheikh Mohammed 6 Rn
1m 30.0 (5.00) SF: -/-/-

TESIO (Turin, Italy) (R-H)
Wednesday November 1st (Good to soft)

4342a ST LEGER ITALIANO (Gp 3) (3-Y.O+) £29,208.00 (£13,356.00: £7,433.00) 1m 6f 110y 2-15 (2-10)

4252a[5] **Assessor (IRE)** *(112+) (RHannon)* 6-9-2 RHughes ....— 1
4092a[3] Puerto Escondido (USA) *(110) (OPessi,Italy)* 4-9-2 MTellini 2¼ 2
4092a* My Irish *(109) (MCiciarelli,Italy)* 6-9-2 AParravani ....½ 3

Tote 13L: 11L 15L (29L) OWNER Sultan Al Kabeer (MARLBOROUGH) 5 Rn 3m 21.0 SF: -/-/-

4186a-CAPANNELLE (Rome, Italy) (R-H)
Wednesday November 1st (Heavy)

4343a CRITERIUM FEMMINILE (Listed) (2-Y.O F) £17,730.00 (£7,801.00: £3,617.00) 7f 2-30 (2-30)

Blu Tuama (USA) *(96?) (AVerdesi,Italy)* 2-8-8 MVargiu ....— 1
4105[2] Parrot Jungle (IRE) *(94?) (JLDunlop)* 2-8-8 JReid ....¾ 2
Sooki Sooki (IRE) *(92?) (GDolfi,Italy)* 2-8-8 FJovine 1 3
Tote 78L: 18L 12L 20L (45L) OWNER Scuderia Blu Horse 10 Rn 1m 28.6 SF: -/-/-

4309a-SAINT-CLOUD (France) (L-H)
Saturday November 4th (Good)

4344a PRIX THOMAS BRYON (Gp 3) (2-Y.O) £26,347.00 (£9,581.00: £4,790.00) 1m 1-45 (1-41)

Ashkalani (IRE) *(AdeRoyerDupre,France)* 2-8-9 GMosse ....— 1
Mayoumbe (FR) *(JEPease,France)* 2-8-9 CAsmussen 2½ 2
Gaitero (FR) *(CLaffon-Parias,France)* 2-8-9 ESaint-Martin ....¾ 3
P-M 1.80F: 1.10F 1.20F (SF 6.00F) OWNER Aga Khan BRED Aga Khan's Studs S.C. 5 Rn
1m 42.3 SF: -/-/-

4311a-SAN SIRO (Milan, Italy) (R-H)
Saturday November 4th (Good)

4345a PREMIO CHIUSURA (Gp 3) £25,816.00 (£12,033.00: £6,760.00) **7f** 1-55 (2-01)

4012a5 **Lavinia Fontana (IRE)** *(108) (JLDunlop)* 6-9-3 GForte ....— 1
1119a4 Imprevedibile (IRE) *(110) (PCeriotti,Italy)* 5-9-6 AParravani ....½ 2
2389a4 Tristano *(110) (ALowe,Germany)* 3-9-6 AStarke 1 3
41983 Prince of India *(108) (LordHuntingdon)* 3-9-6 LSorrentino ....¾ 5
4095a2 Sharp Prod (USA) *(102) (LordHuntingdon)* 5-9-6 DHarrison 1¾ 6
Tote 20L: 15L 21L 57L (75L) OWNER Mr Cyril Humphris (ARUNDEL) BRED D. Brosnan 10 Rn
1m 24.8 SF: -/-/-/-/-

NANTES (France) (L-H)
Sunday November 5th (Good to soft)

4346a GRAND PRIX DE LA VILLE DE NANTES (Listed) (3-Y.O+) £27,545.00 (£10,060.00: £5,030.00) **1m 4f** 2-15 (2-14)

4187a* **Taufan's Melody** *(110) (LadyHerries)* 4-9-5 RCochrane ....— 1
Cinnamon (SWE) *(97) (TGustavsson,Sweden)* 5-8-8 JTandari 1½ 2
Gold Island (FR) *(98) (GMargogne,France)* 5-8-11 TLerner 1½ 3
P-M 6.80F: 2.40F 2.50F 2.50F (13.30F) OWNER All At Sea Partnership (LITTLEHAMPTON) BRED Midhurst Farm Inc 9 Rn No Time Taken SF: -/-/-

4345a-SAN SIRO (Milan, Italy) (R-H)
Sunday November 5th (Good)

4347a PREMIO SORESINA (3-Y.O+) £5,910.00 (£2,364.00) **1m 3f** 1-25 (1-28)

Capolago (IRE) *(98) (RosannaTurri,Italy)* 8-8-4 AParravani ....— 1
3791a* Suranom (IRE) *(105) (LMCumani)* 3-8-9 SDettori 2½ 2
New College *(87) (Italy)* 5-8-6 MBotti 6¾ 3
Tote 37L: 17L 13L (37L) OWNER Mr C. Turri BRED Scuderia Cesare Turri 5 Rn 2m 20.4 SF: -/-/-

4348a PREMIO VOGHERA MAIDEN (2-Y.O) £4,925.00 (£2,167.00: £1,182.00) **7f 110y** 2-25 (2-24)

Mironov *(MRChannon)* 2-8-10 RHughes ....— 1
Frequent *(LMCumani)* 2-8-10 SDettori ....½ 2
Higden *(NAGraham)* 2-8-10 MBotti 5 3
Tote 19L: 12L 12L (21L) OWNER Allevamento La Nuovo Sbarra (UPPER LAMBOURN) BRED K. Eng 6 Rn 1m 34.0 SF: -/-/-

FLEMINGTON (Melbourne, Australia) (L-H)
Tuesday November 7th (Heavy)

4349a FOSTER'S MELBOURNE CUP H'CAP (Gp 1) (3-Y.O+) £660,891.00 (£198,020.00: £89,109.00: £39,604.00) **2m** 4-20 (4-21)

Doriemus (NZ) *(116) (DLFreedman,Australia)* 5-8-8b DOliver (hdwy 5f out: ld 1f out: rdn clr)— 1
Nothin' Leica Dane (AUS) *(106) (MrsGWaterhouse,Australia)* 3-7-7 ow1 RSDye (hdwy 4f out: ev ch 1f out: wknd ins fnl f)....4 2
3789a4 Vintage Crop *(122) (DKWeld,Ireland)* 8-9-4 MJKinane (rr tl hdwy over 5f out: plld out 2f out: rdn & r.o wl)....nk 3
Quick Ransom *(106) (DLFreedman,Australia)* 7-8-3 LDittman (in tch: effrt over 2f out: styd on wl app fnl f)....½ 4
4008a4 Double Trigger (IRE) (Fav)*(MJohnston)* 4-9-7 JWeaver (prom tl rdn & wknd 6f out: easd fnl 2f: btn 51½l).... 17
7/2 Double Trigger (IRE), **8/1** Vintage Crop, **10/1** DORIEMUS (NZ), **20/1** Quick Ransom, Nothin' Leica Dane (AUS), Tote A£9.90: A£3.40 A£4.80 A£3.10 (A£93.20) OWNER Pacers Australia Syndicate BRED J. D. Corcoran 21 Rn 3m 27.6 SF: -/-/-/-/-

INDEX TO MEETINGS

† abandoned

* all-weather

A

A-Aasem 2 ch c Polish Precedent (USA)-Janbiya (IRE) (Kris) 3180^{8} 3662^{6} 4313^{4} **>84f<**

A Badge Too Far (IRE) 5 b m Heraldiste (USA)-Travel *835^{13}* 1645^{17}

Abalene 6 b g Forzando-Riva Renald (Try My Best (USA)) 1039^{7} 1295^{8} (2224) 2871^{6} 2931^{3} **>49f<**

Abbey House 3 b f Efisio-Power and Red (Skyliner) *7^{2}* *86^{4}* *(410)* *473^{5}* 1445^{14} *2144^{4}* *2402^{4}* 2642^{8} **>71a 50f<**

Abbott of Whalley 2 b g Marching On-La Pepper (Workboy) 1024^{3} 1266^{2} *(1570)* *2146^{6}* **>57a 55f<**

Abduction 2 ch c Risk Me (FR)-Spirit Away (Dominion) 533^{11} 574^{4} 1035^{5} 1266^{5} 1646^{9} **>45f<**

Abigails Boy (HOL) 6 gr h Superlative-Heartbreaker 507^{9} 594^{3} 1499^{16} *1883^{2}* *2383^{7}* *2628^{6}* **>43a 43f<**

Abinger 3 ch c Absalom-Western Singer (Chief Singer) 3876^{6} *4336^{12}* **>33a 60f<**

Abir 2 ch f Soviet Star (USA)-Nafhaat (USA) (Roberto (USA)) 4277^{2} **>70+f<**

Able Choice (IRE) 5 b h Taufan (USA)-Great Land (USA) (Friend's Choice (USA)) *318^{7}* *403^{2}* 454^{12} 545^{17} 1651^{3} 1911^{9} 3182^{5} *(3319)* 3759^{9} 3898^{14} **>79a 58f<**

Able Sheriff 3 br g Doulab (USA)-Rich Lass (Broxted) 754^{6} 1450^{3} 1582^{8} 2521^{10} 2837^{2} 2973^{5} 3357^{10} 3622^{6} 3830^{7} 3905^{6} **>23a 44f<**

Above the Cut (USA) 3 ch c Topsider (USA)-Placer Queen (Habitat) 2417^{4} 3419^{9} **>86f<**

Absalom's Pillar 5 ch g Absalom-Collapse *15^{6}* *259^{3}* 506^{6} *1029^{5}* *1332^{6}* *2919^{15}* *3245^{8}* *3527^{10}* **>70a 55f<**

Absolute Folly 3 gr g Absalom-Agreloui (Tower Walk) 521^{9} *(893)* 1059^{3} 1430^{3} 1581^{7} 3665^{12} 4062^{19} **>54a 66df<**

Absolutely Fabulus 3 gr f Absalom-Valldemosa (Music Boy) 754^{4} 904^{6} 1199^{10} 2048^{6} **>37a 43f<**

Absolutely Fact (USA) 5 ch g Known Fact (USA)-Chilly Welcome (General Assembly (USA)) 3871^{10} **>53a 29f<**

Absolutely Fayre 4 ch c Absalom-June Fayre (Sagaro) 1052^{7} 1367^{5} 2007^{10} **>75f<**

Absolutelystunning 2 br f Aragon-Dramatic Mood (Jalmood (USA)) 3379^{16} 3628^{15} **>42f<**

Absolute Magic 5 b g Doulab (USA)-Trickster 563^{10} 2428^{2} 2948^{11} 3212^{13} **>84f<**

Absolute Millions 3 ch f Absalom-Kinkajoo (Precocious) 2353^{7} **>15f<**

Abu Dancer (IRE) 5 b g Heraldiste (USA)-Ottavia Abu (Octavo (USA)) *19^{5}* *84^{7}* **>49a 46f<**

Abundant 2 ch c Rich Charlie-Cabra (Red Sunset) 2767^{5} 3499^{4} 3626^{9} 3869^{3} 3917^{4} **>88?f<**

Abu Simbel (USA) 3 ch c Seeking the Gold (USA)-Bold Flora (USA) (Bold Favorite (USA)) *418^{2}* 715^{2} (936) 1130^{4} **>72a 98f<**

Academy Life 3 ch f Royal Academy (USA)-Exclusive Life (USA) (Exclusive Native (USA)) 695^{6} 1128^{6} 3023^{4} 3559^{6} 3941^{12} *4123^{6}* *4217^{12}* **>56a 81f<**

Academy of Dance (IRE) 2 b f Royal Academy (USA)-Bold Meadows (Persian Bold) 4050^{2} 4129^{5} 4290^{5} **>74f<**

Access Adventurer (IRE) 4 b c Al Hareb (USA)-Olwyn 935^{3} 1102^{9} (2333) 2577^{3} (3234) **>83f<**

Access Carnival (IRE) 4 b c Rousillon (USA)-Flying Fairy (Bustino) 841^{6} 1502^{8} 2342^{9} 3920^{9} 4193^{14} **>62df<**

Access Sun 8 b h Pharly (FR)-Princesse du Seine (FR) 582^{11} 1444^{8} 1773^{3} 2078^{2} **>60f<**

Accuse (USA) 3 b f Alleged (USA)-Rascal Rascal (USA) (Ack Ack (USA)) 1675^{7} 1905^{4} 2086^{4} **>55f<**

Ace Chapel (IRE) 3 br g Simply Great (FR)-Sistina 908^{8} 1196^{9} 1401^{6} 1718^{14} *2626^{6}* **>39a 53f<**

Acharne 2 ch c Pharly (FR)-Sibley (Northfields (USA)) 2183^{3} 2441^{5} 3208^{4} 3650^{2} 3812^{6} **>85f<**

Achilles Heel 4 br c Superlative-Ela-Yianni-Mou (Anfield) *231^{6}* *330^{2}* *355^{3}* (423) 668^{7} 763^{6} 879^{8} 1109^{6} 1292^{8} 2452^{5} 2687^{5} 3440^{7} 3710^{17} 3743^{3} 3852^{4} 3970^{5} 4000^{4} **>56a 47f<**

Achill Princess 3 b f Dowsing (USA)-Princess Matilda 492^{6} 2927^{5} 2999^{8} 3167^{2} (3257) 3310^{7} **>50f<**

Ack's Again 3 b f Dancing Brave (USA)-Ack's Secret (USA) (Ack Ack (USA)) 1717^{10} (2506) 3391^{3} **>87f<**

Aconitum (USA) 7 b g Alleged (USA)-Autumn Glory (USA) (Graustark (USA)) 1404^{7} *1567^{6}* **>46f<**

Aconorace 3 b c Midyan (USA)-Saint Cynthia (Welsh Saint) 1038^{6} 1270^{7} 1422^{4} **>63f<**

Acquittal (IRE) 3 b c Danehill (USA)-Perfect Alibi (Law Society (USA)) *362^{4}* 492^{2} 745^{3} 1669^{6} (1816) 1978^{3} 2201^{6} 2980^{4} 3311^{3} 3572^{9} **>55a 68f<**

Across the Bay 8 ch h Krayyan-Siofra Beag (Steel Heart) *413^{10}* *471^{7}* *601^{10}* 1244^{14} 1523^{16} 2056^{9} 2310^{13} **>39a 33f<**

Acrow Line 10 b g Capricorn Line-Miss Acrow (Comedy Star (USA)) *223^{3}* 556^{14} *(1210)* *1567^{2}* **>66da 50f<**

Acting Brave 4 b c Dancing Brave (USA)-Sarah Siddons (Le Levanstell) 2012^{5} 4076^{9} **>99f<**

Action Jackson 3 ch c Hadeer-Water Woo (USA) (Tom Rolfe) 1258^{5} 1914^{2} 2207^{2} 2780^{6} 3058^{4} *3511^{13}* 4240^{8} *4340^{5}* **>39a 75f<**

Action Mutante (USA) 3 c 4093a^{11} 4186a^{3} **>95f<**

Actual Fact (USA) 3 b c Known Fact (USA)-Wistoral (USA) (Exceller (USA)) 1316^{2} 2324^{2} 3715^{28} 3929^{5} 4145^{18} **>88f<**

Adaloaldo (USA) 3 ch c Arctic Tern (USA)-Alicia's Lady (USA) (Al Nasr (FR)) 3756^{11} 3899^{8} 4110^{3} 4232^{8} **>62f<**

Adamton 3 b g Domynsky-Berwyn (Sharpo) 3649^{9} *4271^{4}* **>36a 34f<**

Addaya (IRE) 3 b f Persian Bold-Night of Stars (Sadler's Wells (USA)) 853^{14} **>45f<**

Added Dimension (IRE) 4 b c Top Ville-Lassalia (Sallust) *218^{7}* *252^{10}* **>12a 14f<**

Addie Pray (IRE) 2 b f Great Commotion (USA)-Green Wings (General Assembly (USA)) 3468^{4} 3644^{3} 3869^{6} 4151^{14} **>69f<**

Adilov 3 b c Soviet Star (USA)-Volida (Posse (USA)) *394^{5}* 973^{4} 1286^{9} **>49a 68f<**

Adjacent Too 3 gr f Prince Daniel (USA)-Tula Singh 1198^{15} *1628^{11}* *1881^{6}* 2280^{15} 2532^{11} **>16a 22f<**

Adjareli (IRE) 3 gr c Nishapour (FR)-Adjriyna (Top Ville) (708a) 1234a^{2} 1837^{7} 3787a^{4} **>124f<**

Adjmal (IRE) 6 b h Dancing Brave (USA)-Adjarida 1870^{7} 3582a^{6} **>105f<**

Admiral Hood (USA) 4 b c Devil's Bag (USA)-De la Rose (USA) (Nijinsky (CAN)) *290^{6}* *357^{4}* **>70a f<**

Admiral Jones (IRE) 2 b c Lycius (USA)-Chelsworth (Never so Bold) 1685^{6} (2431) (2706) 3165^{4} **>92+f<**

Admirals Flame (IRE) 4 b c Doulab (USA)-Fan The Flame (Grundy) *191^{8}* *249^{6}* *302^{8}* 433^{11} 749^{4} 984^{8} 1368^{6} (1830) 1995^{5} (2345) 2613^{8} 2928^{3} 3664^{12} 4083^{2} **>56a**

83f<

Admiral's Guest (IRE) **3** ch c Be My Guest (USA)-Watership (USA) (Foolish Pleasure (USA)) 715^{18} 853^{12} 1978^{9} 2781^{5} 3137^{6} 3569^{13} **>57f<**

Admirals Realm **6** gr g Another Realm-Bedeni 1257^{13} 1510^{12} **>59f<**

Admirals Secret (USA) **6** ch h Secreto (USA)-Noble Mistress (USA) (Vaguely Noble) *37^{5}* (1295) (1578) 1861^{2} 2138^{5} 2658^{2} (2835) 3211^{6} 3470^{8} 3723^{5} 3970^{18} **>63da 78df<**

Admiral's Well (IRE) **5** b h Sadler's Wells (USA)-Exotic Bride (USA) (Blushing Groom (FR)) 869^{6} 1869^{3} 2702^{5} (3361) 3563^{4} 4008a^{5} **>115f<**

Adolescence (IRE) **5** ch m Broken Hearted-Cailin d'Oir (Roi Soleil) 563^{8} 1616^{4} 1800^{4} 2068^{3} 2274^{9} 2967^{2} 3169^{2} (3362) 3440^{3} 3601^{12} **>95f<**

Adonisis **3** b c Emarati (USA)-Kind Lady (Kind of Hush) 2094^{3} 2883^{W} **>63f<**

Advance East **3** b c Polish Precedent (USA)-Startino (Bustino) 647^{6} 948^{2} 1295^{2} 1527^{2} 3963^{10} **>45+a 76f<**

Aeolian **0** S 3282^{11}

Aerial View **4** br g Sulaafah (USA)-Flying Portion *46^{4} 153^{9} 469^{5}* 874^{18} 1647^{4} 1743^{4} **>36da 50f<**

Aerleon Jane **2** ch f Caerleon (USA)-An Empress (USA) (Affirmed (USA)) 3364^{2} **>74+f<**

Aeroking (USA) **4** b c Lear Fan (USA)-Blue Grass Baby (USA) (Icecapade (USA)) 793^{8} 1753^{4} 2080^{4} 2577^{7} 3601^{5} 3810^{9} 3934^{6} 4079^{2} **>86f<**

Aethra (USA) **2** ch f Trempolino (USA)-All For Hope (USA) (Sensitive Prince (USA)) 4241^{2} **>87f<**

Affidavit (USA) **3** b c Affirmed (USA)-Narwala (Darshaan) 1574a^{7} (2386a) (2898a) 3609^{5} **>115f<**

Affordable Dora **3** b f Sharrood (USA)-Polly Packer 4062^{9} **>45f<**

Afisiak **2** b f Efisio-Maestrette (Manado) 436^{5} 574^{2} *(889)* **>59a 62f<**

African Chimes **8** b h Kampala-Rynville (Ballymore) *177^{6} 407^{6} 446^{8}* (702) *4217^{5}* **>67a 75f<**

Africannightingale (IRE) **3** ch c Ela-Mana-Mou-Glasson Lady (GER) (Priamos (GER)) 837^{4} 1430^{5} **>53f<**

African-Pard (IRE) **3** b c Don't Forget Me-Petite Realm (Realm) 955^{6} 1446^{2} 1792^{3} 2199^{6} 2361^{3} 3656^{4} 3823^{6} **>76f<**

African Sun (IRE) **2** b c Mtoto-Nuit D'Ete (USA) (Super Concorde (USA)) *2380^{8}* 4064^{10} **>44f<**

Afsaat **3** b c Efisio-Blue Jane 3227^{3} 3392^{2} 3559^{5} **>83f<**

Again Together **2** b f Then Again-Starawak (Star Appeal) 2107^{8} 2346^{2} 2717^{R} 2908^{3} 3767^{2} 4077^{12} **>63f<**

Agathe (USA) **4** ch f Manila (USA)-Albertine (FR) (Irish River (FR)) 704a^{2} 897a^{2} 1394a^{5} 1711a^{3} 2897a^{3} **>119f<**

Ageeb (IRE) **2** b c Dancing Dissident (USA)-Majesty's Nurse 3662^{9} 3779^{5} (4129) **>67f<**

Agent **2** ch c Anshan-Maria Cappuccini (Siberian Express (USA)) 3626^{7} 3784^{5} **>57f<**

Age of Reality (USA) **2** b f Alleged (USA)-Isticanna (USA) (Far North (CAN)) 3532^{6} 4050^{8} **>68f<**

Agile **2** b c Shareef Dancer (USA)-Hence (USA) (Mr Prospector (USA)) 3883^{10} **>63f<**

Agnella (IRE) **2** b f Polish Patriot (USA)-Annaberta (GER) (Alpenkonig (GER)) 1361^{4} (1536) 3090^{7} 3477a^{3} **>88f<**

Agoer **3** ch f Hadeer-Abuzz (Absalom) 2164^{2} 2337^{2} 2504^{4} 3181^{5} 3451^{5} 3685^{12} 3897^{11} 4242^{2} **>56f<**

Agwa **6** b h Local Suitor (USA)-Meissarah (USA) (Silver Hawk (USA)) 1673^{10} 1815^{6} 2288^{3} 2533^{2} 2764^{9} 3028^{6} 3359^{7} 3615^{17} 4033^{7} 4322^{8} **>75a 75f<**

Ahaalee (USA) **3** ch c Alysheba (USA)-Sans Supplement (USA) (Grey Dawn II) 552^{11} 643^{4} 777^{4} 1322^{5} 1578^{2} 1858^{10} 1986^{W} 2189^{S} **>70f<**

Ahjay **5** br h Tina's Pet-City Link Rose (Lochnager) 765^{2} 887^{7} (1126) 1255^{4} 1732^{3} 2414^{11} 3661^{5} 3807^{6} 4156^{9} (4242) **>59f<**

Ahkaam (USA) **2** ch c Riverman (USA)-Rare Mint (USA) (Key To The Mint (USA)) (4174a) **>101f<**

Ahla **3** ch f Unfuwain (USA)-Rahik (Wassl) 1128^{15} 1490^{3} (1691) 2445^{3} 3459^{6} 3718^{6} 4315^{2} **>95f<**

Ailesbury Hill (USA) **2** ch f Woodman (USA)-Golden Oriole (USA) (Northern Dancer) 2025^{4} 2705^{2} 3397^{2} 3561^{9} 3758^{2} 3985^{14} **>80f<**

Ailleacht (USA) **3** b or br f Chief's Crown-Poster Beauty (Codex) 1390a^{10} **>70f<**

Ain'tlifelikethat **8** gr h Godswalk (USA)-Blue Alicia (Wolver Hollow) 1785^{13} 2021^{7} 2641^{7} 3139^{9} 3396^{14} **>43f<**

Airbourne Ron (IRE) **3** b c Ajraas (USA)-Ching A Ling (Pampapaul) *315^{10}* 437^{15} **>15a 54tf<**

Air Command (BAR) **5** br h Concorde Hero (USA)-Hubbardair (Town And Country) *408^{7}* 586^{14} 778^{5} 1048^{6} 1323^{4} 1596^{3} 1998^{4} 4022^{11} 4135^{6} **>2a 55f<**

Air Commodore (IRE) **4** b c Elegant Air-Belle Enfant (Beldale Flutter (USA)) 793^{2} 960^{7} 1851^{12} (2080) 2287^{6} **>104f<**

Air of Mystery **3** ch f Ballad Rock-Keep Looking (USA) (Mr Prospector (USA)) 4054^{18} **>16f<**

Airport (USA) **4** b c Lear Fan (USA)-Vague Prospect (USA) (Vaguely Noble) (425) 666^{3} 872^{2} 1135^{7} 3904^{3} **>116f<**

Air Wing **2** ch c Risk Me (FR)-Greenstead Lass (Double-U-Jay) 3430^{3} (3628) **>88?f<**

Aisling's Image **3** b f Rambo Dancer (CAN)-Mrs Cullumbine (Silly Season) *90^{13} 213^{10}*

Aitch N'Bee **12** ch h Northfields (USA)-Hot Case (Upper Case (USA)) *(18) 125^{10} 212^{4} 387^{2}* 430^{26} 526^{10} (976) 1297^{6} *1631^{5}* **>74a 73f<**

Ajdar **4** b g Slip Anchor-Loucoum (FR) (Iron Duke (FR)) *894^{6}* **>44a 47f<**

Ajkuit (IRE) **2** b c Persian Heights-Hazar (IRE) (Thatching) 4130^{13}

Akabusi **4** gr c Absalom-Clarandal (Young Generation) *139^{11} 179^{9}* 526^{20} **>21da 39f<**

Akalim **2** b c Petong-Tiszta Sharok (Song) 1856^{6} 2182^{5} (2615) 3803^{7} 3947^{6} (4243) **>78f<**

Akansa (IRE) **2** ch c Cadeaux Genereux-Amerindian (Commanche Run) 2183^{8} **>38f<**

Akayid **3** b f Old Vic-Psylla (Beldale Flutter (USA)) (3618) **>79f<**

Akhiyar (IRE) **4** gr c Doyoun-Akishka (Nishapour) 1235a^{6} 1708a^{3} **>107f<**

Akil (IRE) **3** b c Cyrano de Bergerac-Nonnita (Welsh Saint) 1796^{3} (2255) 3085^{8} (3348) (3608) 3813^{10} 3991^{2} 4202^{9} **>98f<**

Akola Angel **3** ch f Indian Ridge-Heavenly Note (Chief Singer) 2236^{9} 2949^{8} *3544^{8}* **>33a 42f<**

Alabang 4 ch c Valiyar-Seleter (Hotfoot) 988^{3} 3645^{16} 4236^{5} **>58f<**

Al Abraq (IRE) 2 b c Reprimand-Dazzling Maid (IRE) (Tate Gallery (USA)) (3436) 3865^{6} **>85f<**

A la Carte (IRE) 3 b f Caerleon (USA)-Cheese Soup (USA) (Spectacular Bid (USA)) 547^{2} (868) 1850^{6} 2673^{4} 3235^{3} 3833^{4} (4024) **>104f<**

Alakhluki 2 b f Aragon-Hawaiian Bloom (USA) (Hawaii) 3873^{6} 4148^{7} 4330^{5} **>58f<**

Alambar (IRE) 2 b c Fairy King (USA)-Lightino 3890^{13} 4064^{2} 4221^{2} **>75f<**

Alamein (USA) 2 ch c Roi Danzig (USA)-Pollination (Pentotal) 2315^{9} 2796^{3} 3180^{3} 3432^{4} **>73f<**

Alami (USA) 3 br c Danzig (USA)-Alchaasibiyeh (USA) (Seattle Slew (USA)) 667^{4} **>104f<**

Alamtara (IRE) 4 b c Cadeaux Genereux-Catalonda (African Sky) (4090a) **>113f<**

Alanar (USA) 3 b c Danzig (USA)-Classic Crown (USA) (Mr Prospector (USA)) 1301^{4} 1976^{3} **>96f<**

Alanees 4 b c Cadeaux Genereux-Dabaweyaa (Shareef Dancer (USA)) 425^{3} 794^{5} **>112f<**

Alaraby (IRE) 3 b f Caerleon (USA)-Circo (High Top) 950^{9} 1526^{4} 2863^{5} (3317) 3571^{3} 3676^{6} 4108^{2} **>80f<**

Alarming 3 b f Warning-Metair (Laser Light) 658^{3} (2236) (2709) 3373^{7} 3941^{6} **>88f<**

Al Baha 3 ch f Midyan (USA)-Dafinah (USA) (Graustark (USA)) 1515^{5} 1846^{2} 3030^{4} 3762^{4} **>76df<**

Albaha (USA) 2 br c Woodman (USA)-Linda's Magic (USA) (Far North (CAN)) 2370^{3} 3449^{6} 4106^{4} **>75f<**

Albeit 5 ch m Mandrake Major-Sioux Be It (Warpath) *1458^{8}* **>48df<**

Albert The Bear 2 b c Puissance-Florentynna Bay (Aragon) 523^{8} 788^{7} 951^{5} *1454^{10}* (2023) (2988) (3049) 3220^{4} 3271^{2} 3612^{12} **>23a 91f<**

Albinor (IRE) 3 b c Danehill (USA)-Schwanensee (USA) (Mr Leader (USA)) 622^{10} 900a^{11} 2030^{2} (2724a) 3039a^{2} 3796a^{4} 4186a^{4} **>95f<**

Alcian Blue 4 b c Tina's Pet-Rhiannon (Welsh Pageant) 3971^{11} (4140) **>52a 58f<**

Al Corniche (IRE) 3 b f Bluebird (USA)-Naxos (USA) (Big Spruce (USA)) *243^{6} 273^{2} 384^{5}* 453^{3} 525^{2} 947^{11} 1289^{7} 3686a^{3} 3986^{13} **>48a 51f<**

Aldaneh 3 ch f Indian Ridge-Maiyaasah (Kris) (1425) 1845^{7} 2405^{2} 2709^{4} (3383) 3630^{8} 4227^{4} **>81f<**

Alderbrook 6 b h Ardross-Twine (Thatching) 607a^{7} 898a^{2} 1398a^{2} **>123f<**

Aldevonie 3 b f Green Desert (USA)-Kintail (Kris) 1337^{2} **>81f<**

Aldington Chapple 7 b g Creetown-Aldington Miss (Legal Eagle) *35^{8} 77^{7}* **>40da f<**

Aldwick Colonnade 8 ch m Kind of Hush-Money Supply (Brigadier Gerard) *1571^{12} 1762^{13}* 2028^{8} 2246^{11} 2747^{6} 3173^{3} 3501^{3} **>37a 49f<**

Alerting 3 b c Warning-Zalfa (Luthier (FR)) 777^{5} 1124^{10} (1512) 1792^{6} 2033^{6} 2536^{4} 2875^{9} 3363^{3} 3920^{12} **>65f<**

Alessandra 2 ch f Generous (IRE)-Kiss 2572^{2} 3068^{5} 4070^{2} **>81f<**

Alessia 3 b f Caerleon (USA)-Kiss 932^{5} 1729^{4} 3831^{9} 4024^{9} **>89f<**

Alex 18 b h Exparte-Alstermadel (Kaiseradler) 3167^{6}

Alfaaselah (GER) 3 b f Dancing Brave (USA)-Alya (GER) (Lombard (GER)) 932^{7} **>76f<**

Alfahaal (IRE) 2 b c Green Desert (USA)-Fair of the Furze (Ela-Mana-Mou) 3494^{8} 3888^{10} **>51f<**

Alfayza 2 b f Danehill (USA)-Dahlawise (IRE) (Caerleon (USA)) 1247^{6} 1579^{6} 1919^{5} 2221^{4} 2474^{2} (2855) 3309^{4} 3701^{9} **>65f<**

Alhaarth (IRE) 2 b c Unfuwain (USA)-Irish Valley (USA) (Irish River (FR)) (2320) (2690) (3216) (3596) (4106) **>121+f<**

Alhawa (USA) 2 ch c Mt Livermore (USA)-Petrava (NZ) (Imposing (AUS)) (4221) **>78f<**

Alice Springs 0 D Coronation Year 3480a^{2} **>119f<**

Alice Springs (USA) 5 b m Val de L'Orne (FR)-First Approach (USA) (Northern Fling (USA)) 4307a^{7} **>121f<**

Alicia (IRE) 2 b br f Darshaan-Tribal Rite 4216^{9} **>48f<**

A Likely Tale (USA) 2 b c Alleged (USA)-Thatsallshewrote (USA) (Graustark) 3883^{4} **>80f<**

Alilisa (USA) 7 b m Alydar (USA)-Balletomane (USA) (Nijinsky (CAN)) 2087^{10} 2238^{8} **>20f<**

Alioli 3 br f Nishapour (FR)-Allegra (Niniski (USA)) 3635^{6} 3847^{5} 4332^{16} **>55f<**

Ali-Royal (IRE) 2 b c Royal Academy (USA)-Alidiva (Chief Singer) 3663^{4} (3989) **>87+f<**

Alisidora (IRE) 3 ch f Nashwan-Christabelle (Northern Da 2211a^{5} 2563a^{10} **>106f<**

Alis Princess 2 ch f Sayf El Arab (USA)-Princess Zeddera 3306^{8}

Alistover 2 b f Zalazl (USA)-Song of Gold 508^{12} 570^{7} 4050^{18} **>22f<**

Alisura 2 br f Lead on Time (USA)-Iosifa (Top Ville) 4148^{8} **>39f<**

Alizarin 6 ch m Noalto-The Crying Game (Manor Farm Boy) *422^{11}* 549^{19}

Aljadeer (USA) 6 b or br h Alleged (USA)-Return The Roses (USA) (Carry Back) 534^{10} 751^{6} 1529^{4} **>50f<**

Aljawab (USA) 4 b or br c Alleged (USA)-Chuckles (USA) (Riverman (USA)) 549^{8} 839^{4} 1027^{2} *(1329)* 1484^{2} *2292^{7}* 2655^{3} 3288^{4} (3759) 3898^{5} (4061) 4163^{6} **>71+a 75f<**

Aljaz 5 b g Al Nasr (FR)-Santa Linda (USA) (Sir Ivor) *20^{4} 55^{3} 89^{8} 167^{3} 265^{6} 297^{3} 419^{15}* (491) 563^{13} *3510^{12}* 3629^{16} *3954^{6} 4274^{9}* **>57a 68f<**

Aljazzaf 5 b g Mtoto-Ibtisamm (USA) (Caucasus (USA)) 1225^{9} 1610^{2} 2241^{17} (2596) 3164^{6} 3556^{7} 3932^{8} 4031^{13} **>109df<**

Al Jinn 4 ch c Hadeer-Mrs Musgrove (Jalmood (USA)) 1368^{12} 1643^{8} 2695^{7} **>74a 54df<**

Alka International 3 b g Northern State (USA)-Cachucha (Gay Fandango (USA)) *156^{8} 316^{6} 444^{3}* 745^{10} 1097^{19} 1371^{5} **>51a 52f<**

Alkateb 3 ch g Rock City-Corley Moor (Habitat) (1905) 2111^{3} (3214) 3926^{2} 4257^{4} **>98f<**

Allahrakha 4 ch g Aragon-Bernigra Girl (Royal Match) 549^{11} 882^{16} **>40df<**

Allemande (IRE) 3 b c Nashwan (USA)-Dance Festival (Nureyev (USA)) *(394)* (2409) **>77a 109f<**

Allesca 5 b m Alleging (USA)-Hitesca 430^{18} 623^{10} 763^{10} (1368) (1557) 1757^{8} 2289^{8} **>74f<**

Allez Cyrano (IRE) 4 b c Alzao (USA)-Miss Bergerac (Bold Lad (IRE)) 1851^{23} 2703^{15} 3085^{10} 3237^{11} 3565^{15} **>81f<**

All Honour 3 b g Kabour-Tolly's Best (Hittite Glory)

515^{10} 591^{14} 2959^{8} 3980^{26} **>15a f<**

Allied Forces (USA) 2 ch c Miswaki (USA)-Mangala (USA) (Sharpen Up) (1134) 1838^{8} (2365) 2690^{2} **>100f<**

Allimac Nomis 6 b g Daring March-Game for a Laugh (Martinmas) 848^{15} 1292^{12} **>18f<**

All In Good Time 2 b c Shadeed (USA)-Good Thinking (USA) (Raja Baba (USA)) 3666^{14} **>17f<**

Allinson's Mate (IRE) 7 b h Fayruz-Piney Pass (Persian Bold) *117^{10} 211^{4} 281^{6} 337^{5} 627^{3}* (784) 927^{5} 1148^{5} 1421^{8} (1603) 1932^{4} (2455) 2647^{2} 2853^{3} 3222^{3} 3411^{8} 3565^{10} 3719^{W} 4041^{21} **>66a 84f<**

All in the Mind 4 b g Vision (USA)-No More Rosies (Warpath) 741^{10} **>67df<**

Allmosa 6 b m Alleging (USA)-Wimosa (Mossborough) 738^{18} 1444^{5} 1552^{4} **>69a 65f<**

All My Dreams (IRE) 3 b c Assert-Marie de Beaujeu (Kenmare (2215a) (3200a) **>114f<**

All on 4 ch f Dunbeath (USA)-Fresh Line (High Line) *53^{5} (136) 279^{6}* 866^{12} 1557^{2} 1680^{3} *2293^{5} 2379^{11}* 3665^{9} 3700^{12} **>63+a 45f<**

All She Surveys 2 b f Mazilier (USA)-Sunley Stars (Sallust) 617^{16} 725^{4} 2135^{5} (2308) 3132^{10} 3894^{W} **>60f<**

All the Joys 4 b or br f Adbass (USA)-Joytime (John de Coombe) 1013^{10} 1286^{6} 1472^{6} 1539^{12} 3137^{2} 3287^{2} (3676) 3774^{8} 4135^{3} 4259^{6} **>56f<**

All The Time 3 b f Dancing Brave (USA)-Just You Wait (Nonoalco (USA)) 695^{4} 797^{9} 4003^{7} 4072^{4} **>80df<**

Allthruthenight (IRE) 6 ch h Precocious-Time For Pleasure (Tower Walk) 565^{2} 693^{7} 1637^{3} 2168^{4} 3407^{10} **>90f<**

Alltime Dancer (IRE) 3 b g Waajib-Dance On Lady (Grundy) 431^{8} 555^{5} 758^{9} 966^{17} 1180^{9} 1358^{8} (1651) 1680^{7} 2166^{4} 2528^{2} (2881) **>64f<**

All Time Great 3 b f Night Shift (USA)-Someone Special (Habitat) 692^{4} 933^{14} 1588^{8} 3833^{8} **>104df<**

Allwight Then (IRE) 4 gr c Dancing Dissident (USA)-Abergwrle (Absalom) 1106^{16} 1376^{2} 1765^{9} 2060^{4} 2247^{3} 2609^{9} 2935^{14} 3221^{13} **>75f<**

Allyana (IRE) 3 b f Thatching-Miss Loving (Northfields (USA)) 752^{3} 1522^{2} 1786^{3} 3507^{2} (3649) 3905^{4} 3992^{19} 4142^{4} **>76f<**

Almapa 3 ch c Absalom-More Fun (Malicious) 855^{5} (1125) 1202^{15} 1541^{9} 2342^{12} 2864^{5} **>68f<**

Almasi (IRE) 3 b f Petorius-Best Niece (Vaigly Great) 1982^{8} 2318^{7} 2491^{5} 3128^{7} 3872^{11} 4115^{7} 4249^{14} **>60f<**

Almaty (IRE) 2 b c Dancing Dissident (USA)-Almaaseh (IRE) (Dancing B (2564a) (2740) 3610^{6} **>104f<**

Almaz (SU) 3 c $3914a^{7}$ $4088a^{3}$ **>111f<**

Almizaj 3 b f Ballad Rock-Salabella (Sallust) 957^{4} 1675^{4} 2332^{5} 2856^{2} 3370^{P} **>78f<**

Al Mohaajir (USA) 4 ch c Cadeaux Genereux-Lady in White (Shareef Dancer (USA)) $3326a^{3}$ **>113f<**

Almond Rock 3 b c Soviet Star (USA)-Banket (Glint of Gold) 1221^{8} 2199^{3} (2711) 3026^{2} 3368^{3} (3732) **>94f<**

Almost a Princess 7 b m Alleging (USA)-Rabab (Thatching) *19^{8} 153^{12}* **>22a f<**

Al Moulouki 5 b g Efisio-Prejudice (Young Generation) 454^{14} 749^{17} **>66f<**

Almuhimm (USA) 3 b c Diesis-Abeesh (USA) (Nijinsky (CAN)) 2794^{4} 3183^{5} 4164^{3} **>87f<**

Almuhtaram 3 b c Rambo Dancer (CAN)-Mrs Mainwaring (FR) (Home Guard (USA)) *64^{4} (168)* 1366^{7} 1676^{15} 1859^{6} 3634^{15} 3771^{14} 3860^{4} (3977) 4233^{4} 4261^{8} **>60a 73f<**

Almushtarak (IRE) 2 b c Fairy King (USA)-Exciting (Mill Reef (USA)) 3176^{6} 3404^{7} 3558^{W} (3766) 3947^{15} **>86?f<**

Al Nufooth (IRE) 3 b c Green Desert (USA)-Reine Maid (USA) (Mr Prospector (USA)) 633^{8} 883^{6} **>99f<**

Alpha City (GER) 3 ch f Unfuwain-Alpha (Frontal) (2042a) $2215a^{17}$ (3697a) $4020a^{5}$ **>113f<**

Alpheton Prince 2 b g Prince of Cill Dara-Batsam Lady (Battle Hymn) *1090^{6}* **>8a f<**

Alpine 2 b c Alzao (USA)-Pine Ridge (High Top) 919^{5} 1226^{6} **>58f<**

Alpine Hideaway (IRE) 2 b c Tirol-Arbour (USA) (Graustark (USA)) 3821^{7} 4103^{10} **>75f<**

Alpine Johnny 4 b c Salse (USA)-Alpine Sunset (Auction Ring (USA)) *63^{3} (82) 130^{3} 150^{4} 211^{W} 267^{W}* **>60a 53df<**

Alpine Joker 2 b c Tirol-Whitstar (Whitstead) 3821^{12} 3967^{10} 4098^{6} **>55f<**

Alpine Skier (IRE) 4 b c Nordico (USA)-Heather Lil (Ballymore) 430^{21} 1161^{16} 1548^{3} 2220^{8} **>43f<**

Alpine Storm (IRE) 3 b f Al Hareb (USA)-Alpine Dance (USA) (Apalachee (USA)) 730^{9} 1656^{5} *2140^{11}* 2450^{8} 2650^{3} 3747^{13} 3959^{5} 4261^{11} **>13a 44f<**

Alpine Twist (USA) 2 b f Seattle Dancer (USA)-Polar Bird (Thatching) 4218^{5} **>64f<**

Alpride (IRE) 4 b f Alzao (USA)-Roberts Pride (Roberto (USA)) $3480a^{3}$ **>119f<**

Al Rawda (FR) 3 b f Green Desert (USA)-Double Celt (Owen Dudley) 633^{7} 959^{2} (1227) 1480^{9} **>90f<**

Alreeh (IRE) 2 b f Priolo (USA)-Fleeting (USA) (Lear Fan (USA)) 3541^{7} 3763^{16} 4050^{5} **>70f<**

Alriffa 4 b c Danehill (USA)-Sweet Soprano (High Line) 631^{4} 913^{5} (1056) 1171^{4} (1385) 3381^{3} 3614^{5} 4204^{6} **>116f<**

Al Safeer (IRE) 3 b c Common Grounds-Indian Swallow (Indian King (USA)) 552^{3} (673) 941^{3} 1872^{16} 2415^{7} **>88f<**

Alsahib (USA) 2 b c Slew O' Gold (USA)-Khwlah (USA) (Best Turn (USA)) 4154^{4} **>67f<**

Al's Alibi 2 b c Alzao (USA)-Lady Kris (IRE) (Kris) 940^{6} 3861^{3} 3989^{8} 4129^{2} 4327^{5} **>71f<**

Al Shaati (FR) 5 b m Lead on Time (USA)-With You All (Free Round (USA)) *4274^{12}* **>52da 54f<**

Al Shadeedah (USA) 2 br f Nureyev (USA)-Copperama (AUS) (Comeram (FR)) 1928^{5} 2351^{8} 4154^{3} **>74f<**

Al Shafa 2 b c Midyan (USA)-Thundercloud (Electric) 1592^{3} 2058^{2} 2453^{2} (2809) 3711^{9} (3956) 4208^{11} **>89f<**

Altamura (USA) 2 b f El Gran Senor (USA)-Narwala (Darshaan) 3916^{3} 4169^{2} **>76f<**

Alternation (FR) 6 ch m Electric-Alanood (Northfields (USA)) *234^{5} 285^{7}* **>50a f<**

Althrey Leader (IRE) 5 b g Supreme Leader-Shannon Belle (Pollerton) 3282^{12}

Altoby 4 b c Tobin Lad (USA)-Natina-May (Mandrake Major) 3970^{16} **>59df<**

Altor 3 gr c Kendor-Ramonda $3580a^{3}$

Alusha 3 b f Soviet Star (USA)-Glowing With Pride (Ile de Bourbon (USA)) 3007^{4} **>96+f<**

Alute (IRE) 3 b f Last Tycoon-Pu Yi (Habitat) *418^{4} 468^{3}* 733^{11} 867^{10} **>64a 46f<**

Alwarqa 2 b f Old Vic-Ostora (USA) (Blushing Groom (FR)) 4148^{10} **>32f<**

Always Aloof (USA) **4** b c Alleged (USA)-Miranda (USA) (Forli (ARG)) (632) 998^{10} 1840^{20} 2098^{5} 3146^{3} 3688a^{2} **>114f<**
Always Earnest (USA) **7** b g Alleged (USA)-Nettie Cometti (USA) (Giacometti) 1001a^{3} (4008a) **>124f<**
Always Grace **3** b f Never so Bold-Musical Sally (USA) (The Minstrel (CAN)) *85^{4}* *232^{2}* (3138) 3442^{9} 4280^{17} **>50a 80f<**
Always Greener (IRE) **4** gr f Vision (USA)-Great Meadow (Northfields (USA)) *352^{3}* *592^{6}* *3513^{7}* **>58a f<**
Always Happy **2** ch f Sharrood (USA)-Convivial (Nordance (USA)) 4216^{4} 4320^{4} **>74f<**
Al Widyan (IRE) **3** b c Slip Anchor-Rafha (Kris) 619^{7} 3932^{4} 4104^{6} (4213) 4323^{3} **>108f<**
Al Wujud (IRE) **4** b c Polish Precedent (USA)-Alkariyh (USA) (Alydar (USA)) 876^{14} 992^{2} 1297^{W} 1421^{3} (1809) 1932^{2} (2096) 2461^{2} (2909) 3145^{P} **>75f<**
Alyeska (GER) **3** f 1705a^{9}
Alzanti **2** b c Alzao (USA)-Mumtaz Flyer (USA) (Al Hattab (USA)) 2573^{6} (3174) (3613) 3775^{3} 4192^{2} **>87f<**
Alzianah **4** b f Alzao (USA)-Ghassanah (Pas de Seul) 571^{6} 934^{2} 1233a^{5} 1895^{2} 3476a^{3} 3717^{25} 3854^{3} 4160^{5} **>108f<**
Alzoomo (IRE) **3** b c Alzao (USA)-Fandangerina (USA) (Grey Dawn II) 815^{9} 3292^{7} 3761^{3} 3973^{13} **>73f<**
Alzotic (IRE) **2** b c Alzao (USA)-Exotic Bride (USA) (Blushing Groom (FR)) 3620^{13} 3773^{6} 3881^{8} 4141^{10} *4338^{2}* **>80a 48f<**
Amaam Amaam **5** b h Last Tycoon-What A Pity (Blakeney) 1350^{15} 1623^{6} **>47f<**
Amadour (IRE) **2** b c Contract Law (USA)-Truly Flattering (Hard Fought) 3916^{12} **>57f<**
A Magicman (FR) **3** dk br c The Wonder-Ayanapa (FR) (Pharly (FR)) 1121a^{3} 1713a^{6} 2215a^{9} (2893a) (3577a) (3910a) **>112f<**
Amanah (USA) **3** ch f Mr Prospector (USA)-Cheval Volant (USA) (Kris S (USA)) 539^{2} (1804) 2006^{2} 3235^{4} 3922^{10} **>102f<**
Amancio (USA) **4** b c Manila (USA)-Kerry Ring (USA) (Ack Ack (USA)) (1635) 1805^{3} 3555^{7} **>86f<**
Amanita **2** ch f Lead on Time (USA)-Amana River (USA) (Raise A Cup (USA)) 1098^{6} (1375) 3147^{15} 3714^{3} 3867^{4} **>75f<**
Amaniy (USA) **2** b f Dayjur (USA)-Muhbubh (USA) (Blushing Groom (FR)) 1307^{3} (2000) 2432^{2} (2783) 3702^{3} 3962^{3} **>96f<**
Amany (IRE) **3** b f Waajib-Treeline (High Top) 695^{17} 1168^{13} 1326^{5} 2017^{3} 2318^{10} 2711^{7} 2843^{3} 3661^{4} **>48f<**
Amaretto Bay (IRE) **2** b c Common Grounds-Harmer (IRE) (Alzao (USA)) 523^{6} (617) 871^{4} (1384) 1868^{5} 2216a^{5} 2442^{7} 2765^{7} 3147^{8} 3375^{5} 3711^{8} 4206^{2} **>91f<**
Amazing Bay **2** b f Mazilier (USA)-Petriece (Mummy's Pet) (1169) (1769) 2322^{5} 2740^{4} (3086) 3610^{5} **>96f<**
Amazing News **4** ch f Mazilier (USA)-Glint of Silver (Sallust) *216^{5}* *247^{10}* **>40a 42f<**
Amber Fort **2** gr c Indian Ridge-Lammastide (Martinmas) 2320^{6} 3089^{12} 3620^{8} 3947^{2} 4317^{7} **>74f<**
Amber Lily **3** ch f Librate-Just Bluffing (Green Shoon) 1971^{11} 2149^{7} 2843^{10} 3424^{14} **>47f<**
Amber Nectar **9** ch h Sallust-Curtana 541^{14} 1750^{6} 2056^{10} 2789^{16} **>18f<**
Amber Valley (USA) **4** ch c Bering-Olatha (USA) (Miswaki (USA)) 454^{13} **>69f<**
Ambidextrous (IRE) **3** b c Shareef Dancer (USA)-Amber Fizz (USA) (Effervescing (USA)) 854^{11} 978^{10} 1814^{3} 2166^{8} 4194^{17} **>69f<**
Amboyna Burl (IRE) **3** b c Cyrano de Bergerac-Mind The Beat *566^{8}* 1322^{10} 1366^{16} 3654^{W} 3860^{8} 4131^{R} 4225^{R} **>20df<**
Ambuscade (USA) **9** ch h Roberto (USA)-Gurkhas Band (USA) 432^{5} 556^{12} 751^{5} 1416^{4} 1826^{2} **>66da 64f<**
Ameer Alfayaafi (IRE) **2** b g Mujtahid (USA)-Sharp Circle (IRE) (Sure Blade (USA)) 3821^{10} **>32f<**
Ameeri (USA) **3** b c Ogygian (USA)-Royal Suite (USA) (Majestic Prince) *2921^{7}* 3096^{9} **>21a 27f<**
Amelanchier **2** ch f Cigar-Frost In Summer (Busted) 4050^{17} **>30f<**
Amercius **3** ch c Old Vic-Elarrih (USA) (Sharpen Up) *17^{4}* 428^{8} 525^{3} 655^{5} 1696^{10} 3029^{9} **>9a 63f<**
America's Cup (IRE) **3** b g Fairy King (USA)-Boat Race (USA) (Seattle 1233a^{3} **>107f<**
Amiarge **5** b h Reference Point-Scotia Rose (Tap On Wood) 2087^{8} 2232^{2} 2713^{8} (2860) 3114^{3} 3435^{10} 3627^{2} 3936^{2} 4036^{4} **>55f<**
Ami Bleu (FR) **3** 808a^{7} **>64f<**
A Million At Last (IRE) **2** b g Cyrano de Bergerac-Any Price (Gunner B) 3180^{9} 3378^{13} 3566^{9} **>36f<**
A Million to One (IRE) **3** b f Common Grounds-Princess Nabila (USA) (King Pellinore (USA)) 426^{9} 681^{5} 1172^{6} 1338^{4} (1654) 1969^{5} **>79f<**
A Million Watts **4** b g Belfort (FR)-Peters Pet Girl (Norwick (USA)) *62^{2}* *203^{5}* *(378)* *512^{2}* 634^{14} *845^{2}* 1402^{11} **>75a 64f<**
Amington Lass **2** ch f Cree Song-Millfields House (Record Token) 3465^{11} 3648^{5} **>49f<**
Amir's Blue (BEL) **4** br c Amir Albadeia (USA)-Source Bleue (FR) (Lionel) 3871^{13} **>9f<**
Amlak (USA) **6** b h Riverman (USA)-Ruwiyda (USA) (In Reality (USA)) *32^{9}* *340^{7}* *416^{13}* 748^{12} 988^{16} **>14a 19f<**
Amnesia (IRE) **4** b f Don't Forget Me-Amboselli (Raga Navarro (ITY)) 1206^{6} 1422^{6} 1491^{4} 1688^{3} 1957^{10} **>40a 53df<**
Amnesty Bay **3** b f Thatching-Sanctuary Cove (Habitat) 987^{10} 1125^{11} (1625) 2278^{6} **>57f<**
Amoeba (IRE) **2** b f Distinctly North (USA)-Lady Ingrid (Taufan (USA)) 1525^{2} 1790^{2} *2143^{6}* 3828^{8} 4287^{3} **>41a 66f<**
Among Islands **4** b f Jupiter Island-Queen of The Nile (Hittite Glory) 1555^{5} 1965^{5} **>43f<**
Amrak Ajeeb (IRE) **3** b c Danehill (USA)-Noble Dust (USA) (Dust Commander (USA)) 613^{2} 987^{5} (1476) 1839^{29} 2446^{4} (2903) 3237^{2} 3374^{2} 3729^{11} 3945^{25} 4074^{5} 4202^{12} **>94f<**
Amron **8** b h Bold Owl-Sweet Minuet 441^{7} 659^{10} 1100^{6} 1766^{9} 1895^{28} 3551^{15} 3717^{15} 3964^{14} 4040^{14} **>72f<**
Amy Leigh (IRE) **2** b f Imperial Frontier (USA)-Hollyberry (IRE) (Runnett) *(1089)* 1511^{8} 2085^{3} 2800^{4} 3400^{3} 3742^{2} 4112^{2} 4260^{8} **>70+a 70f<**
Amy's Dream **4** b f Doc Marten-Dovey (Welsh Pageant) 673^{W}
Amy's Star **9** b m Touch Boy-Keep Believing (Sweet Revenge) *34^{6}* **>10a f<**
Anabaa (USA) **3** c 4178a^{6} **>113f<**
Analogue (IRE) **3** b c Reference Point-Dancing Shadow

(Dancing Image (USA)) 673[4] *4223[13]* >38a **74f**<

Anam 3 b f Persian Bold-Yaqut (USA) (Northern Dancer) 1000[7] 1474[5] 1787[3] (2362) 2679[7] (2941) 3175[4] 3451[8] 3674[6] 3929[9] 4156[18] **>86df<**

Anastina 3 ch f Thatching-Nikitina (Nijinsky (CAN)) 539[14] 2350[7] **>47f<**

Ancestral Jane 2 b f Distant Relative-Antoinette Jane (Ile de Bourbon (USA)) 2820[5] 3170[2] 3432[9] 3867[14] 4111[2] (4141) **>74+f<**

Anchor Clever 3 b c Slip Anchor-Mountain Bluebird (USA) (Clever Trick (USA)) 657[4] 912[2] 1396a[9] (1672) 1852[7] 2386a[3] 3609[6] 4018a[9] **>113f<**

Anchor Crown 3 b f Slip Anchor-Doumayna (Kouban (FR)) *893[6]* 1059[8] *2378[W]* *2626[8]* 3265[8] **>36a 53f<**

Anchorena 3 b f Slip Anchor-Canna (Caerleon (USA)) 3438[2] 3756[5] 4167[5] **>81df<**

Anchor Venture 2 b c Slip Anchor-Ski Michaela (USA) (Devil's Bag (USA)) 3503[3] 4037[8] **>64f<**

Andre's Affair 4 b c Sulaafah (USA)-Andrea Dawn (Run The Gantlet (USA)) 3178[9] 3896[11] **>26f<**

Andsome Boy 2 ch g Out of Hand-My Home (Homing) *3949[11]* 4055[6] 4224[13] **>38f<**

Anegre (IRE) 3 gr c Cyrano de Bergerac-Lady Celina (FR) (Crystal Palace (FR)) 742[6] 963[6] 1125[3] 1371[7] 1787[6] 2032[3] 2363[11] *3319[5]* 3390[6] 3515[15] **>48a 69df<**

A New Flame 4 gr g Most Welcome-Couleur de Rose (Kalaglow) *290[10]* *352[6]* *469[6]* **>42a f<**

Angaar (IRE) 2 b c Fairy King (USA)-Decadence (Vaigly Great) (3892) **>78f<**

Angel Chimes 2 ch f Most Welcome-Bell Toll (High Line) 3339[14] 3541[2] (3647) 3867[18] 4141[3] 4195[2] **>77f<**

Angel Face (USA) 2 b f Zilzal (USA)-Touching Love 3155[9] **>53f<**

Angel Falls (FR) 3 dk c Shirley Heights-Waterfall (Riverman (USA) 808a[2] 1115a[3] 3323a[7] **>111f<**

Angelic Belle 3 b f Komaite (USA)-Lucky Angel (Lucky Wednesday) *315[13]* *362[7]* *420[12]*

Angelic Dancer 4 b f Komaite (USA)-Lucky Angel (Lucky Wednesday) *182[10]* *532[6]* 646[6] 701[9] 862[12] *1032[11]* **>41a 50f<**

Angel In My Heart (FR) 3 ch f Rainbow Quest-Sweetly (Lyphard) 2723a[2] (3040a) 3575a[4] 4015a[2] **>114f<**

Anglesey Sea View 6 gr m Seymour Hicks (FR)-Lexham View (Abwah) (1623) 1898[4] **>73f<**

Angus-G 3 br g Chief Singer-Horton Line (High Line) 3761[4] 3974[5] **>76f<**

Angus McCoatup (IRE) 2 ch c Mac's Imp (USA)-In For More (Don) 2932[6] 3465[9] 3784[7] 3982[5] **>63f<**

Animation 2 ch f Superlative-What A Looker (USA) (Raise A Native) 1781[6] 2116[7] **>40f<**

Anistop 3 b c Nomination-Pounelta (Tachypous) 971[9] 1512[10] 1788[6] 2711[2] 3125[7] 3757[15] **>50f<**

Anita's Contessa (IRE) 3 b f Anita's Prince-Take More (GER) (Frontal) 547[6] 742[7] 1544[6] *3512[5]* *3739[12]* 3823[8] (4131) **>67a 62f<**

Anjomajasa 3 b f Teenoso (USA)-Captain Bonnie (Captain James) 2337[4] 2638[5] 3871[11] 4225[17] **>47f<**

Anjou 3 b c Saumarez-Bourbon Topsy (Ile de Bourbon (USA)) *256[4]* *357[3]* 3876[5] (4096) 4228[7] 4333[17] **>70a 75f<**

Anlace 6 b m Sure Blade (USA)-Ascot Strike (USA) (Mr Prospector (USA)) 762[10] 975[3] 1166[13] 1323[8] 1484[5] 1645[2] (1745) 1911[7] 2314[2] 2557[9] 2658[5] 2981[6] **>60f<**

Annaba (IRE) 2 ch f In The Wings-Anna Matrushka (Mill Reef (USA)) 3883[3] **>76f<**

Anna Bannanna 3 b f Prince Sabo-Top Berry (High Top) 648[16] 971[11] 1254[18] **>63f<**

Annabella Baggins (IRE) 4 b f Nomination-Last Detail (Dara Monarch) *22[8]* *187[11]* **>26a f<**

Annabel's Baby (IRE) 6 b m Alzao (USA)-Spyglass (Double Form) 3056[8] 3303[9] **>13f<**

Annaberg (IRE) 2 b f Tirol-Icecapped (Caerleon (USA)) 2128[5] (2498) (2750) 3168[3] 3414[2] 3546[14] **>76f<**

Anna Domani(FR) 3 f 1009a[8] 1705a[3] 4094a[7] **>100f<**

Annagh 2 b f Grey Desire-Tango Lady (Gorytus (USA)) 490[5] 638[6] 1159[7]

Anna-Jane 3 ch f Soviet Star (USA)-Aloha Jane (USA) (Hawaii) 664[10] 885[5] 1472[9] 1692[2] 2488[6] 2711[6] 3475[2] **>73f<**

Anna of Brunswick 3 b f Rainbow Quest (USA)-Anna Paola (GER) (Prince Ippi (GER)) 1270[2] 1600[2] 2506[2] (3573) **>77f<**

Anna Settic 2 b f Pharly (FR)-Gwiffina (Welsh Saint) 2683[5] 3135[2] 3285[3] 3533[5] 3642[3] *4127[8]* **>36a 51f<**

Annecy (USA) 2 b f Mr Prospector (USA)-Lake Country (CAN) (Caucasus (USA)) 4190[3] **>70f<**

Anne D'Autriche (IRE) 3 ch f Rainbow Quest (USA)-Anna Matrushka (Mill Reef (USA)) 2350[3] (2883) 3496[3] **>81+f<**

Ann Hill (IRE) 5 ch m Bob Back (USA)-Yuma (USA) (Caro) *201[5]* *260[3]* *304[10]* 569[4] 1285[8] 1427[4] *1759[7]* 2450[7] 3092[9] 3426[7] **>39a 42f<**

Annie Fay (IRE) 3 gr f Fayruz-Angie (Prince Bee) 862[4] 966[12] 1248[3] 1550[3] *1763[13]* 2018[0] 2304[4] 2870[5] 3467[18] 4060[17] **>19a 61df<**

Anniversarypresent 3 b c Puissance-Safidar 438[8] 883[4] (1131) 1839[14] 2369[3] **>105f<**

Ann's Music 2 b f Clantime-An-Go-Look (Don't Look) 2483[11] 2852[7] 3306[7] 3643[12] **>36f<**

Ann's Pearl (IRE) 4 br f Cyrano de Bergerac-Pariscene (Dragonara Palace (USA)) 565[8] 693[14] (1057) 1304[17] 1777[10] 3221[2] 3407[6] 3597[14] 3815[10] 4033[13] **>77f<**

Annus Mirabilis (FR) 3 b c Warning-Anna Petrovna (FR) (Wassl) 1107[2] 1575a[2] 1837[5] 2218a[3] 3143[3] (3716) **>122f<**

Annyban 5 b m Bairn (USA)-Mandrian *2920[5]* **>32a f<**

Anonym (IRE) 3 b g Nashamaa-Bonny Bertha 881[3] 1196[10] 1514[10] 1945[3] 2279[4] (2698) (2966) 3291[3] 3545[5] 3807[11] **>77f<**

Anorak (USA) 5 b h Storm Bird (CAN)-Someway Somehow (USA) (What Luck (USA)) *50[7]* *137[7]* *351[6]* *399[5]* 2165[2] 2400[3] 2478[2] 2544[4] **>54da 72f<**

Anotheranniversary 2 gr f Emarati (USA)-Final Call (650) (852) 1259[2] 1849[11] 2243[2] **>92f<**

Another Batchworth 3 b f Beveled (USA)-Batchworth Dancer (Ballacashtal (CAN)) 1476[9] 1783[8] 2301[W] 2642[5] 2844[2] 3138[W] 3542[2] 3751[12] 3961[8] *4123[5]* *(4274)* **>64+a 57f<**

Another Episode (IRE) 6 b g Drumalis-Pasadena Lady (Captain James) *70[6]* *188[6]* 944[5] **>56a 79f<**

Another Felix (USA) 3 ch g Miswaki-Give Her The Gun (Le Fa 2722a[2] **>82f<**

Another Fiddle (IRE) 5 b g Waajib-Elmar (Lord Gayle

(USA)) 433[23] 731[8] 1244[6] 1693[5] 2056[5] 2669[6] 3269[2] 3605[2] 3871[2] **>73f<**

Another Jade **5** ch m Beveled (USA)-Zamindara (Crofter (USA)) *(511)* 542[4] *627[8]* 726[2] 1071[3] 1265[2] 1429[2] 1510[3] 1750[2] 2027[5] 2288[13] 2692[6] *3072[9]* **>65a 70f<**

Another Monk (IRE) **4** br g Supreme Leader-Royal Demon (Tarboosh (USA)) 3934[11] **>25f<**

Another Nightmare (IRE) **3** b f Treasure Kay-Carange (Known Fact (USA)) *210[9]* 685[8] 904[10] 1157[5] 1434[8] 1721[11] 2024[6] 2124[11] 4278[11] **>1a 42f<**

Anotherone to Note **4** ch c Beveled (USA)-Dame Nellie (Dominion) *39[5]* *192[9]* *331[3]* *501[11]* 748[9] 2786[7] *2925[6]* *3522[7]* *3734[5]* 3800[21] 4209[4] **>37a 47f<**

Another Picea **2** b c Picea-Atoka 1938[15] 2198[12] 4246[10] **>9f<**

Another Quarter (IRE) **2** b f Distinctly North (USA)-Numidia (Sallust) 4050[9] 4246[5] **>62f<**

Another Time **3** ch g Clantime-Another Move (Farm Walk) 966[5] 1180[5] 3125[6] (3504) 3664[F] (3860) 4044[2] (4233) **>83f<**

Another Venture (IRE) **5** br g Tanfirion-Fitz's Buck (Master Buck) 1948[5] **>46f<**

Ansellman **5** gr h Absalom-Grace Poole (Sallust) 434[14] 1304[5] 1599[6] 2150[2] 2617[3] 2764[12] (3051) 3205[2] 3376[3] 3715[18] 3822[9] 3992[5] **>80f<**

Anshan's Deity **2** ch c Anshan-Pagan Deity (Brigadier Gerard) 615[10] 1540[8] 1798[4] 2855[8] *3523[10]* **>9a 63f<**

Answers-To-Thomas **2** b c Komaite (USA)-Launde Abbey (Absalom) 2498[6] 2817[2] 3647[4] 3877[7] 4097[11] 4276[5] **>70f<**

Antarctica (USA) **3** ch f Arctic Tern (USA)-Loved Etsu (USA) (Liloy (FR)) 428[7] 584[12] **>42f<**

Antarctic Storm **2** b g Emarati (USA)-Katie Scarlett (Lochnager) 4103[8] 4221[9] **>76f<**

Antartictern (USA) **5** b g Arctic Tern (USA)-False Image (USA) (Danzig (USA)) 569[5] 2917[5] 3101[3] 3232[2] 3367[6] 3505[10] 3825[2] 4038[15] 4248[11] **>53f<**

Anthelia **2** b f Distant Relative-Confection (Formidable) (2128) (3680) 4084[3] **>91+f<**

Antiguan Flyer **6** b h Shirley Heights-Fleet Girl 3129[9] 3343[4] 3571[11] 3682[6] 4152[15] **>58f<**

Antiguan Jane **2** b f Shirley Heights-Dabbiana (CAN) (Fappiano (USA)) 4262[19] **>33f<**

Antonias Melody **2** b f Rambo Dancer (CAN)-Ayodessa (Lochnager) 2487[8] 3022[2] 3432[6] (3623) 4206[7] 4260[3] 4317[5] **>66f<**

Any Colour **2** b f Anshan-Council Rock (General Assembly (USA)) 3828[6] 4100[6] **>51f<**

Any Minute Now (IRE) **5** b g Alzao (USA)-Miss Siddons (Cure The Blues (USA)) 1695[8] **>46f<**

Any One Line (IRE) **3** b f Contract Law (USA)-North Hut 885[11] **>61f<**

Anytime Baby **3** b f Bairn (USA)-Cindys Gold (Sonnen Gold) *72[10]* *180[8]* 2088[W] 2451[7] 2698[17] 3649[4] 3878[19] **>49a 61f<**

Anzio (IRE) **4** b c Hatim (USA)-Highdrive (Ballymore) *347[10]* 433[22] 743[3] 1071[10] 1168[4] (1538) 1909[3] 2009[6] *2402[2]* 2743[4] 3028[7] (3134) 3279[2] 3535[4] 3615[20] (3750) 3943[9] 4145[4] 4281[4] **>50a 83f<**

Anziyan (USA) **2** b c Danzig-Razyana (His Majesty) 3037a[3]

Aoife Alainn (IRE) **3** ch f Glenstal (USA)-Majestic Nurse (On Your Mark) 742[4] 1172[10] (2125) 2376[P] **>66f<**

Apache Len (USA) **2** br c Rahy (USA)-Shining Skin (USA) (Fappiano (USA)) 3472[6] 4210[2] 4282[2] **>77f<**

Apartments Abroad **2** b f Prince Sabo-La Graciosa (Comedy Star (USA)) 508[7] 1536[9] 1981[7] 2185[5] 3290[4] 3378[5] 3740[3] 3856[7] 3975[3] 4075[4] **>64f<**

Apicella **2** ch c Pharly (FR)-Sixslip (USA) (Diesis) 3869[5] **>61f<**

Apollono **3** b g Cyrano de Bergerac-Daima (Dominion) 1165[3] 1366[13] 1787[2] (2537) 3011[2] (3408) 3732[19] 4116[8] 4267[12] **>89f<**

Apollo Red **6** ch h Dominion-Woolpack (Golden Fleece (USA)) *177[5]* *237[3]* *344[6]* *400[7]* *401[7]* *447[3]* 541[2] 1013[11] 1276[7] 1785[10] **>57a 58f<**

Appeal Again (IRE) **2** br g Mujtahid (USA)-Diva Encore (Star Appeal) 3779[8] 4210[9] 4314[17] **>55f<**

Applaud (USA) **2** ch f Rahy (USA)-Band (USA) (Northern Dancer) (1497) 1893[2] (2322) **>100f<**

Apple Musashi **2** b c Never so Bold-Third Movement (Music Boy) 3662[4] (3893) 4250a[4] **>89f<**

April's Joy **2** b f Mazilier (USA)-Ziobia (Tribal Chief) 983[3] 1215[2] 1282[4] *1570[5]* 2185[4] *2382[4]* 2859[3] 3018[3] (3253) 3415[2] 3742[8] **>51a 54f<**

April The Eighth **2** b c Statoblest-Miami Melody (Miami Springs) 690[3] 1893[7] (2221) (2674) 3197a[6] **>95f<**

Aqaarid (USA) **3** b f Nashwan (USA)-Ashayer (USA) (Lomond (USA)) (692) 933[2] 1587[6] **>115f<**

Aquado **6** b h Green Desert (USA)-Meliora *55[5]* *93[10]* *129[10]* *(228)* *269[2]* *313[3]* *(354)* *378[9]* *(416)* *518[4]* 780[2] 984[5] (1157) 1297[11] 1433[6] *1571[3]* 1828[17] **>58a 57f<**

Aqua Rigia (IRE) **3** b f Last Tycoon-Crystal Fountain (Great Nephew) 1539[7] (2719) (3206) 3700[11] **>61f<**

Aquiletta **5** ch m Bairn (USA)-Emerald Eagle (Sandy Creek) 1377[12] 1738[5] 3467[21] 3726[11] 3879[13] 4275[17] **>20a 32f<**

Arabian Flight **3** ch c Sayf El Arab (USA)-Smooth Flight (Sandhurst Prince) 1979[14] 2949[9] 2977[11] **>46f<**

Arabian Heights **2** ch g Persian Heights-Arabian Rose (USA) (Lyphard (USA)) 4098[10] **>48f<**

Arabian Story **2** gr c Sharrood (USA)-Once Upon a Time (Teenoso (USA)) (2534) **>72+f<**

Araboybill **4** b c Aragon-Floral (Floribunda) 731[10] 975[7] 2052[3] (2174) 2687[10] 2861[6] 3094[6] 3288[2] 3388[14] 3889[14] 4061[12] 4227[10] **>62f<**

Arabride **3** ch f Unfuwain (USA)-Model Bride (USA) (Blushing Groom (FR)) 881[5] 1675[2] (1927) 2349[4] (3192a) 3478a[6] **>110f<**

Arafel **4** ch f Northern State (USA)-Don't Loiter (Town And Country) *317[4]* 778[8] **>40a 47f<**

Aragona **6** b m Aragon-Polly Worth (Wolver Hollow) *63[9]* **>12a f<**

Aragrove **5** b h Aragon-Grovehurst (Homing) *401[8]* *447[7]* 542[5] (726) 972[2] (1321) (1537) (1815) 2013[3] 2326[2] (2692) 2743[3] 3051[3] 3236[5] **>52a 86f<**

Arajaan (USA) **2** br c Septieme Ciel (USA)-Maid's Quarters (USA) (Sauce Boat (USA)) 1298[2] 1562[3] 2581[3] (3289) 3699[8] 3990[7] 4195[8] **>85f<**

Aramon **5** b g Aragon-Princess Mona (Prince Regent (FR)) 1937[10] 2268[10] **>22f<**

Arasong **3** b f Aragon-Songstead (Song) 674[2] 823[13] 1249[8] 1677[7] 1936[4] (2179) 2697[3] 2877[5] 3275[7] *3524[9]*

3624^{8} 3800^{5} **>44a 66f<**

Aratikos (GER) 4 b c Konigsstuhl (GER)-Aratika (FR) (Zino) 1398a^{4} 2046a^{9} 2729a^{7} **>114f<**

Arawa 5 b m Doulab (USA)-High Heather (Shirley Heights) *65^{10} 224^{8} 302^{9}* 548^{16} *627^{6} 832^{8} 1033^{7} 1457^{6}* **>34a 39f<**

Arcady 2 b f Slip Anchor-Elysian (Northfields (USA)) 3069^{13} 4218^{8} 4277^{3} **>66f<**

Arcatura 3 b c Beveled (USA)-Bar Gold 715^{10} 1136^{8} 1732^{5} 3605^{14} 3885^{3} **>71f<**

Arc Bright (IRE) 5 b h Trempolino (USA)-Brillante (FR) (Green Dancer (USA)) *9^{2} (109) 147^{3} 277^{2} 346^{3} 412^{7} 469^{2}* 556^{7} 649^{3} 840^{8} (1046) 1328^{7} 1435^{5} (1643) 1858^{3} 2355^{4} 2514^{2} 2860^{5} (2986) 3211^{3} **>73a 57f<**

Arch Angel (IRE) 2 ch f Archway (IRE)-Saintly Guest (What A Guest) 1318^{6} (1699) 2035^{2} *(2635)* 3008^{4} 3570^{6} 3985^{16} **>59a 58f<**

Arc Lamp 9 b h Caerleon (USA)-Dazzling Light *65^{5} 129^{8} 165^{6} 233^{13} 1763^{7}* 1963^{11} *2074^{5} 2383^{10}* 2698^{5} 2821^{2} (2956) (3098) 3293^{4} 3467^{19} **>56a 50f<**

Arc of The Diver (IRE) 2 ch c Archway (IRE)-Inner Pearl (Gulf Pearl) 1278^{5} 1877^{5} 2542^{6} 3503^{2} 3882^{8} **>66f<**

Arctic Charmer (USA) 3 ch c Arctic Tern (USA)-Bunch of Smiles (USA) (Graustark (USA)) 484^{2} 1601^{4} 2545^{4} 2931^{2} 3178^{4} *3527^{3}* **>74a 76f<**

Arctic Diamond 4 b c Rambo Dancer (CAN)-Falaka (Sparkler) *1091^{13}* **>36a 61f<**

Arctic Explosion (USA) 3 2730a^{7} **>93f<**

Arctic Fancy (USA) 2 ch c Arctic Tern (USA)-Fit And Fancy (USA) (Vaguely Noble) 3620^{9} 3827^{2} 3968^{3} **>77f<**

Arctic Guest (IRE) 5 ch m Arctic Tern (USA)-Sojourn (Be My Guest (USA)) *3^{5} 108^{9} 147^{5}* **>57a 68f<**

Arctic Poppy (USA) 3 ch f Arctic Tern (USA)-Nether Poppleton (USA) (Deputy Minister (CAN)) 651^{16} 857^{11} 1124^{11} 1812^{4} 2088^{14} *2587^{8}* 2843^{6} **>16a 61f<**

Arctic Romancer (IRE) 2 b c Distinctly North (USA)-Kowalski (IRE) (Cyrano de Bergerac) 617^{14} 825^{8} (1327) 1634^{2} 1893^{9} 2242^{6} 2618^{3} 3064^{9} 3314^{2} 3651^{10} 3766^{5} 4206^{6} 4328^{4} **>79f<**

Arctic Thunder (USA) 4 b g Far North (CAN)-Flying Cloud (USA) (Roberto (USA)) 931^{6} (1102) 1135^{3} 1768^{2} 3489^{6} 3730^{2} **>105f<**

Arctic Zipper (USA) 2 gr c Unzipped (USA)-Arctic Fashion (USA) (The Knack) 3647^{9} 3773^{2} 3861^{4} 4084^{21} **>69f<**

Arctiid (USA) 2 b br c Silver Hawk (USA)-Arctic Eclipse (USA) (Northern Dancer) 1913^{4} **>63f<**

Ardleigh Prince 3 b c Prince Daniel (USA)-Rising Star 1514^{14} 1983^{7} **>46f<**

Arecibo (FR) 3 ch g Dancing Spree (USA)-Anahita (FR) (Gay Mecene (USA)) 2708^{8} 2977^{8} 4049^{9} **>56f<**

Argyle Cavalier (IRE) 5 b h Simply Great (FR)-Fete Champetre (Welsh Pageant) *(3) (67) 81^{2} 147^{2}* 432^{10} 632^{16} (821) 998^{5} 1156^{2} 1313^{3} 1686^{2} 1840^{11} **>76a 72f<**

Arian Spirit (IRE) 4 b f High Estate-Astral Way (Hotfoot) *(9) 288^{5}* 534^{4} 1046^{6} 1496^{4} 1667^{2} 1957^{5} 2157^{3} 2501^{2} (2734) 3114^{4} 3303^{2} 3435^{3} 3705^{7} (3971) 4140^{6} **>44a 48f<**

Arkady (IRE) 4 ch c Tate Gallery (USA)-Veruschka (Lorenzaccio) 2038a^{3} **>74a 68f<**

Arkindale Amber 3 b c Superpower-Najat (Tender King) 2484^{14} 2821^{9} **>23f<**

Arlington Lady 2 b f Prince Sabo-Flitcham (Elegant Air) 1627^{6} (1810) 2335^{2} 2674^{6} 2982^{2} 3160^{9} 3386^{3} 3540^{8} 4075^{17} **>66f<**

Armston 3 ch c Rock City-Silka (ITY) (Lypheor) *1091^{5}* 1601^{3} *(1881) 2147^{2}* **>74a 57f<**

Arndilly 4 b f Robellino (USA)-Upper Caen (High Top) *93^{7} (150) 187^{3} 281^{7} 323^{2} 371^{6}* (848) 946^{4} (1092) 1274^{9} 1775^{2} (1969) 2057^{4} **>65a 79f<**

Arnie (IRE) 3 b c Double Schwartz-The Moneys Gone (Precocious) 2528^{16} 3475^{9} 3685^{16} 4225^{11} **>42f<**

Arrasas Lady 5 ch m Arrasas (USA)-Sharelle (Relko) *32^{5} 56^{10} 343^{6} 416^{7}* 586^{13} 1016^{12} 2789^{10} 2843^{R} 3079^{11} **>36a 13f<**

Arras Royale 5 ch h Arrasas (USA)-Sheer Class (Victor Hugo) *248^{10} 288^{12}* **>18f<**

Arrhythmic (IRE) 2 b f Broken Hearted-Gay's Flutter (Beldale Flutter (USA)) 2221^{3} 2666^{2} 2782^{2} (2918) 2991^{5} 3702^{9} 4112^{4} **>69f<**

Arrogant Boy 6 b or br g Kabour-Belhill (Beldale Flutter (USA)) *34^{9} 82^{13} 92^{6} 179^{7} 335^{5} 390^{2} 408^{6} 520^{13}* 1285^{21} *1883^{6} 1950^{7} 2076^{7} 2923^{9}* 3370^{3} **>30a 24f<**

Arrogant Heir 2 b c Henbit (USA)-Quiet Arrogance (USA) (Greek Sky (USA)) *3523^{11}* 3620^{17} 3968^{13} **>6a 28f<**

Artan (IRE) 3 c 2215a^{5} **>110f<**

Art Deco Lady 4 ch f Master Willie-Art Deco (Artaius (USA)) *266^{7}* 1058^{19} **>24a 64df<**

Arterxerxes 2 b c Anshan-Hanglands (Bustino) 4313^{6} **>72f<**

Art Form (USA) 8 b g Little Current (USA)-Christi Dawn (USA) (Grey Dawn II) *(147) (206)* 821^{8} 1189^{11} 1444^{9} 1840^{2} 2154^{3} 2569^{2} 3217^{F} **>85+a 81f<**

Artful Dane (IRE) 3 b c Danehill (USA)-Art Age (Artaius (USA)) 881^{2} 1173^{7} 2345^{3} (2794) 3222^{10} 3732^{20} 3897^{6} **>80f<**

Artic Courier 4 gr c Siberian Express (USA)-La Reine de France (Queen's Hussar) 584^{2} 668^{6} 961^{2} 1144^{8} 1612^{2} (1878) 2525^{2} 2639^{3} 3107^{2} 3500^{4} 3836^{14} 4028^{6} 4325^{16} **>86f<**

Art of War 3 b c Machiavellian (USA)-On The House (FR) (Be My Guest (USA)) 713^{9} (3854) 4324^{10} **>116f<**

Art Tatum 4 b c Tate Gallery (USA)-Rose Chanelle (Welsh Pageant) 549^{15} 744^{6} 1286^{5} **>68f<**

Arvzees (IRE) 2 ch c Magical Wonder (USA)-Zestino (Shack (USA)) 436^{3} 474^{3} 540^{2} 574^{3} 644^{2} (740) (983) 1177^{4} (1288) 1678^{2} **>69f<**

Arzani (USA) 4 ch c Shahrastani (USA)-Vie En Rose (USA) (Blushing Groom (FR)) 853^{3} 987^{9} 1314^{5} 3377^{6} 3679^{6} **>78df<**

Asaaf (USA) 12 b h Cutlass (USA)-Honky Chateau (USA) *234^{15} 402^{11}*

Ashanti Dancer (IRE) 2 b f Dancing Dissident (USA)-Shanntabariya (IRE) (Shernazar) 3708^{6} 3916^{2} **>78f<**

Ashdren 8 b h Lochnager-Stellaris (Star Appeal) 559^{13} 965^{6} 1355^{5} 1809^{13} 2220^{6} 3172^{4} 3457^{9} 3808^{5} 4060^{14} **>40a 60f<**

Ashgore 5 b h Efisio-Fair Atlanta (Tachypous) *(3074)* 3411^{9} 3717^{26} **>84a 87f<**

Ashik (IRE) 2 b c Marju (IRE)-Wakayi (Persian Bold) 3626^{13} 3848^{8} **>44f<**

Ashjar (USA) 2 b c Kris-Jathibiyah (USA) (Nureyev (USA)) 3472^{2} 3773^{4} 4058^{4} (4222) **>79f<**

Ashkalani (IRE) 2 ch c Soviet Star-Ashtarka (4344a)

Ashkernazy (IRE) 4 ch f Salt Dome (USA)-Eskaroon (Artaius (USA)) 856[6] 1257[4] 1777[9] 1972[9] 2364[4] *(2492)* 2858[2] 3134[5] **>50a 48f<**

Ashoka 4 b c Emerati (USA)-Teevano (Blakeney) 1119a[3] **>108f<**

Ashover 5 gr h Petong-Shiny Kay (Star Appeal) *(229) (266) 351[2]* 423[4] (1861) 2022[3] 2224[5] (2584) 2785[3] 2816[3] 3229[8] 3462[U] (3646) 4000[3] **>79a 69f<**

Ashtina 10 b h Tina's Pet-Mrewa (Runnymede) 693[13] (1019) 1637[7] 1765[11] 2150[4] 2418[7] 2570[8] 3407[9] 3554[7] 3815[11] 4033[22] 4119[10] 4197[10] 4278[10] 4322[22] **>80f<**

Asian Elegance 3 b f Shareef Dancer (USA)-Benazir (High Top) 3125[13] **>40a 20f<**

Askern 4 gr c Sharrood (USA)-Silk Stocking (Pardao) (1422) (1688) 1933[2] 2226[3] (3061) 3162[9] 3718[12] 4201[9] 4325[13] **>71f<**

Asking 3 b g Skyliner-Ma Famille *394[7] 515[9]* 773[10] 1812[7] 2278[7] 2540[7] 3096[5] **>37a 49f<**

Asking For Kings (IRE) 2 b c Thatching-Lady Donna (Dominion) 1726[10] 2070[4] 2204[2] 3894[5] 4077[14] **>65f<**

Asmahaan (USA) 2 br f Dayjur (USA)-Albadeeah (USA) (Nashua) 4212[4] **>68f<**

Asmarina 5 b m Ascendant-Marina Plata (Julio Mariner) *2[9] 53[10] 117[7] 416[6] 520[4] (624)* 776[6] *894[7] (2292)* 2332[3] 2543[9] *3952[4]* **>48+a 50f<**

Aspirant 7 b h High Top-Yen (AUS) (Biscay (AUS)) *254[7]*

Assembly Dancer 8 b h General Assembly (USA)-A Red Red Rose (Gulf Pearl) 3759[20] 3884[15] 3986[18] **>6f<**

Assessor (IRE) 6 b h Niniski (USA)-Dingle Bay (Petingo) 3946[2] 4252a[5] (4342a) **>116f<**

Assia (IRE) 3 b f Royal Academy-Alys (Blakeney) 3487a[3] **>98f<**

Assignment 9 b h Known Fact (USA)-Sanctuary (Welsh Pageant) *386[4] 404[4] 446[9]* 546[12] 1403[5] 1785[14] *2493[4]* **>57da 52f<**

As Such (IRE) 4 b c Ajraas (USA)-Ching A Ling (Pampapaul) *102[9]* 1276[6] 1499[13] 1855[8] 2108[7] 2718[6] 2885[7] **>59a 57f<**

Assumpsit (IRE) 3 b c Contract Law (USA)-Bridal Blush (Coquelin (USA)) 442[8] 524[11] *603[12]* 727[3] 1125[4] 1263[3] **>17a 64f<**

Assur (GER) 3 c 1713a[8] **>92f<**

Asterita 3 b f Rainbow Quest (USA)-Northshiel (Northfields (USA)) 797[5] (1067) 1587[5] 2563a[6] 3549[8] 4204[2] **>108f<**

Asterix 7 ch h Prince Sabo-Gentle Gael 646[3] 789[6] 1499[15] 1516[2] 1714[2] 1797[8] 1963[3] 2112[2] (2148) 2396[6] 2549[2] 2698[11] 3139[8] 3177[5] **>19a 61f<**

Aston Court 10 br h Tanfirion-Msida 3017[8]

Aston Manor (IRE) 3 b g Cyrano de Bergerac-Mamie's Joy (Prince Tenderfoot (USA)) 482[9] *591[2] 842[2]* **>61a 70f<**

Astor Place (IRE) 2 b c Sadler's Wells (USA)-Broadway Joan (USA) (Bold Arian (USA)) 3449[4] (3900) 4177a[5] **>104f<**

Astrac (IRE) 4 b c Nordico (USA)-Shirleen (Daring Display (USA)) 922[5] (1895) 2764[14] 3717[11] 3924[6] 4160[3] **>102f<**

Astral Invader (IRE) 3 ch c Astronef-Numidia (Sallust) 621[5] 813[7] 1052[3] 1126[13] 1483[11] 1832[12] 2512[4] 3204[3] 3519[6] 3615[14] 3764[6] 3897[9] 4053[10] **>58f<**

Astral's Chance 2 ch g Risk Me (FR)-Astral Suite (On Your Mark) 810[4] *1031[5]* **>43a 55f<**

Astral Weeks (IRE) 4 ch c Astronef-Doon Belle (Ardoon) 946[7] 1126[12] 1351[9] 1693[8] 2979[8] 3657[12] 4079[18] **>59f<**

Astra Martin 2 ch f Doc Marten-Bertrade (Homeboy) 3495[12] 3763[17] 4224[11] **>39f<**

Astrojoy (IRE) 3 ch f Astronef-Pharjoy (FR) (Pharly (FR)) 1718[10] 2712[2] 3341[7] 3515[6] 3657[17] 3844[7] **>51f<**

Astrolabe 3 b c Rainbow Quest (USA)-Sextant (Star Appeal) 428[3] 657[11] (995) 1281[3] 1973[2] 2193[3] 2688[8] **>88f<**

Astromar (ITY) 3 ch c Astronef-Maremma Amara (Ashmore (FR)) 1886a[3] **>68f<**

Astuti (IRE) 2 b f Waajib-Aunty Eileen (Ahonoora) 2675[3] 2947[W] 3186[7] (3337) 3702[8] 3867[3] 3917[2] 4203[6] 4256[2] **>90f<**

A Suitable Girl 4 b f Reprimand-No Jazz (Jaazeiro (USA)) 1058[18] **>36a 26f<**

Aswaat (IRE) 3 b c Fairy King (USA)-Native Melody 3829[6] **>72f<**

As You Like it (USA) 3 b c Nijinsky (CAN)-Asiram (USA) (Sharpen Up) 2790[7] 3016[8] **>77f<**

Ataxia 3 b f Belmez (USA)-Margamania (CAN) (Riverman (USA)) 1097[6] **>68f<**

Athenry 2 b c Siberian Express (USA)-Heresheis (Free State) 3868[5] 4264[5] **>92f<**

Atherton Green (IRE) 5 ch h Shy Groom (USA)-Primacara (Rusticaro (FR)) *91[5] 215[6]* 841[14] **>50a 63f<**

Athinar 3 b f Tina's Pet-Highland Rossie (Pablond) *156[5] 204[3]* **>35a f<**

Atienza (USA) 2 ch f Chief's Crown (USA)-Hattab Voladora (USA) (Dewan (USA)) 4063[9] 4246[3] **>65f<**

Atlaal (USA) 3 br c Machiavellian (USA)-Minifah (USA) (Nureyev (USA)) (637) 911[5] 1269[2] 2367[7] 3026[5] 3497[3] 3802[4] **>85f<**

Atlantic City 2 3584a[7] **>80f<**

Atlantic Mist 2 ch c Elmaamul (USA)-Overdue Reaction (Be My Guest (USA)) 1798[3] 2526[13] 3010[10] 3928[10] **>63f<**

At Liberty (IRE) 3 b c Danehill (USA)-Music of The Night (USA) (Blushing Groom (FR)) 437[7] 618[2] 941[2] (1478) 1589[4] 1872[4] 2691[8] **>96f<**

Atours (USA) 7 b h Chief's Crown (USA)-Ataire (USA) (What A Pleasure (USA)) 3071[6] **>86f<**

Atraf 2 b c Clantime-Flitteriss Park (Beldale Flutter (USA)) 1551[4] 1779[2] (2095) 2618[2] 3213[3] 3375[3] 3714[6] 4084[12] **>88f<**

Attarikh (IRE) 2 b c Mujtahid (USA)-Silly Tune (IRE) (Coquelin (USA)) 4314[16] **>55f<**

At the Savoy (IRE) 4 gr c Exhibitioner-Hat And Gloves (Wolver Hollow) *82[9] 119[2] 138[5] 199[2] 228[2] 268[4] (334) 354[5] 419[3] 511[3]* 578[4] *(769) 1076[6]* 1297[5] 1843[12] *2073[3]* 2156[2] 2307[2] 2390[9] 2517[2] 2832[7] 2972[6] *3074[2]* 3344[9] *4337[8]* **>73a 53f<**

Atticus (USA) 3 ch c Nureyev (IRE)-Athyka (Secretariat) (806a) 1117a[2] 1837[4] 3042a[7] 4016a[4] **>117f<**

Attimo Fuggente (IRE) 2 b c Roi Danzig-Pepi Image (National) 2387a[2]

Audrey Grace 4 b f Infantry-Fair Nic (Romancero) 731[13] 885[2] 1402[9] 1676[16] *2140[5]* 3605[13] 3685[3] **>33a 56f<**

Auenadler (GER) 3 b c Big Shuffle-Auenmaid 3913a[2] 4006a[2] **>101f<**

Backwoods 2 ch c In The Wings-Kates Cabin (Habitat) 4314^{19} **>41f<**
Bad Bertrich (IRE) 4 b c Waajib-Sweet Unison (USA) (One For All (USA)) 1398a^{7} 2046a^{6} 2729a^{8} 3798a^{8} **>115f<**
Baddi Quest 3 b c Rainbow Quest (USA)-Baddi Baddi (USA) 761^{9} 978^{9} 1339^{5} 1656^{4} 2506^{4} 2825^{2} *3084^{4}* **>64a 68f<**
Badger Bay (IRE) 2 b f Salt Dome (USA)-Legit (IRE) (Runnett) 570^{2} 782^{2} 910^{8} 1448^{2} 1652^{7} 3032^{2} **>63f<**
Bad News 3 ch f Pharly (FR)-Phylae (Habitat) 759^{16} 984^{16} 1680^{8} 1854^{9} 1966^{8} *3544^{10}* 3725^{4} 4152^{20} **>60f<**
Badri (USA) 2 b c Topsider (USA)-Hedonic (USA) (Fappiano (USA)) 3530^{10} **>50+f<**
Bagby Boy 3 b g Puissance-Miss Milton (Young Christopher) 3653^{17} 3876^{9} 4220^{11} **>30f<**
Bag of Tricks (IRE) 5 br h Chief Singer-Bag Lady (Be My Guest (USA)) *11^{6} 88^{2} 127^{3} 206^{3} 303^{6} (471)* 744^{2} 1014^{8} 1477^{9} 1788^{3} 2050^{2} 2687^{8} 3137^{3} 3572^{6} **>71a 59f<**
Bagshot 4 b c Rousillon (USA)-Czar's Bride (USA) (Northern Dancer) 439^{6} 1183^{10} 1409^{4} 2703^{17} 2933^{3} 3706^{6} **>87f<**
Bahamian King (IRE) 3 b g Fairy King (USA)-Look of Love (General Assembly (USA)) 4196^{11} **>44f<**
Bahamian Knight (CAN) 2 b br c Ascot Knight (CAN)-Muskoka Command (USA) (Top Command (USA)) 825^{2} 1134^{2} (1318) 1871^{3} **>90f<**
Bahamian Sunshine (USA) 4 ch c Sunshine Forever (USA)-Pride of Darby (USA) (Danzig (USA)) 3804^{2} (3995) 4204^{12} **>112?f<**
Bahith (USA) 3 ch c Topsider (USA)-Alghuzaylah (Habitat) 622^{9} 1138^{7} 1698^{2} 2237^{2} 2677^{3} 3660^{7} **>92f<**
Bahrain Queen (IRE) 7 ch m Caerleon (USA)-Bahrain Vee (CAN) (Blushing Groom (FR)) 1036^{5} **>44a 38?f<**
Bahri (USA) 3 b c Riverman (USA)-Wasnah (USA) (Nijinsky (CAN)) 713^{2} 920^{3} 1234a^{3} (1837) 2689^{2} 3143^{2} (3814) 4120^{5} **>127f<**
Baileys Bride (IRE) 2 ch f Shy Groom (USA)-Lacey Brief (USA) 638^{5} *846^{4}* 1665^{12} **>29a 31f<**
Baileys First (IRE) 2 b f Alzao (USA)-Maiden Concert (Condorcet (FR)) 3170^{3} 3432^{3} 3773^{3} 3990^{11} **>73f<**
Baileys Sunset (IRE) 3 b c Red Sunset-Stradey Lynn (Derrylin) *(7) 132^{6} 173^{2} 236^{2} 331^{2}* 482^{4} (581) 734^{4} 1508^{5} 1580^{7} 1822^{3} 2067^{5} 2124^{3} 2372^{3} (2463) 2680^{6} (2810) 3121^{6} 3251^{3} 3365^{5} 3750^{17} 3905^{8} 4142^{11} **>73a 61df<**
Bailiwick 2 b c Dominion-Lady Barkley (Habitat) 1977^{8} 2548^{8} 3379^{17} 3540^{9} 3780^{5} 4263^{11} **>47f<**
Bairn Glen 4 ch f Bairn (USA)-Rage Glen (Grey Mirage) 722^{13} **>13f<**
Baize 2 ch f Efisio-Bayonne (Bay Express) (1653) (1833) 2740^{3} 3186^{5} 4084^{4} **>89f<**
Bajan Affair 5 b m Bold Owl-Silvery Moon 1160^{7} 1359^{7} 2695^{8} 2875^{10} **>32f<**
Bajan Frontier (IRE) 3 ch f Imperial Frontier (USA)-Sajanjal (Dance In Time (CAN)) 555^{8} 1419^{5} 3678^{3} 3981^{7} 4278^{7} **>39f<**
Bajan (IRE) 4 b c Taufan (USA)-Thatcherite (Final Straw) 738^{5} (1048) 1612^{11} (2209) **>70f<**
Bajan Rose 3 b f Dashing Blade-Supreme Rose (Frimley Park) 939^{7} 1806^{15} 2066^{6} 2271^{7} 2909^{2} 3087^{5} 3466^{2} 3615^{23} 3748^{10} 3905^{5} 4068^{5} (4145) **>77f<**
Baker 2 b g Cigar-Bread 'N Honey (Goldhills Pride) 2656^{7} 3570^{7} 3651^{3} 3969^{11} 4208^{19} **>57f<**
Bakers Daughter 3 ch f Bairn (USA)-Tawnais (Artaius (USA)) *(270) 384^{2} 395^{4} 1209^{11}* (2524) 3455^{9} **>59a 59f<**
Bakers' Gate (USA) 3 b br c Danzig (USA)-Alydaress (USA) (Alydar (USA)) 987^{2} 1136^{3} **>83f<**
Bakheta 3 b f Persian Bold-Vielle (Ribero) 1691^{12} 1979^{18} 3875^{14} 4164^{7} 4261^{4} **>59f<**
Bala Monaafis (IRE) 3 b f In The Wings-Samya's Flame (Artaius (USA)) 1717^{7} 3653^{14} **>60f<**
Balance of Power 3 b g Ballacashtal (CAN)-Moreton's Martha (Derrylin) 1165^{4} 1639^{6} 2168^{5} 2531^{5} 3028^{5} 3359^{14} 3929^{6} 4134^{3} **>71f<**
Balanchine (USA) 4 ch f Storm Bird (CAN)-Morning Devotion (USA) (Affirmed (USA)) 1836^{5} 3695a^{2} 4014a^{10} **>133f<**
Balanka (IRE) 3 b f Alzao (USA)-Banana Peel (Green Dancer (USA)) 1712a^{4} 2561a^{3} (3331a) 4015a^{3} **>115f<**
Balasara (IRE) 5 ch g Don't Forget Me-Tameen (FR) (Pharly (FR)) 1383^{W} 1732^{2} 2100^{2} 2438^{2} 2805^{2} 3362^{3} 3859^{2} **>86f<**
Bal Harbour 4 b c Shirley Heights-Balabina (USA) (Nijinsky (CAN)) 1894^{3} 2323^{4} 3070^{4} 3380^{2} 3603^{2} (4074) **>113f<**
Balios (IRE) 2 b c Be My Guest (USA)-Clifden Bottoms (Wolver Hollow) 4169^{19} **>34f<**
Bali Tender 4 ch g Balidar-Highest Tender (Prince Tenderfoot (USA)) 777^{W} 1291^{W} 1554^{7} 1683^{8} 1878^{5} *2377^{9}* 2624^{4} 2786^{5} 3050^{8} 3508^{6} **>22a 36f<**
Ballad Dancer 10 ch h Ballad Rock-Manx Image *2^{8} 63^{5} 120^{6}* **>44a 45df<**
Ballad Ruler 9 ch h Ballad Rock-Jessamy Hall *589^{9}* 3849^{13} 4168^{9} **>51?f<**
Balladur (USA) 2 b c Nureyev (USA)-Ballinderry (Irish River (FR)) 4058^{3} 4239^{4} **>81+f<**
Ballard Lady (IRE) 3 ch f Ballad Rock-First Blush (Ela-Mana-Mou) 573^{8} 1154^{8} 1358^{10} (1598) 2425^{7} 2479^{5} 2759^{2} 3061^{8} 3462^{6} 3669^{20} 3778^{6} **>51df<**
Ballard Ring (IRE) 4 ch f Ballad Rock-Miss Victoria (Auction Ring (USA)) 559^{14} 724^{11} 1079^{5} 1251^{10} 1528^{9} 1679^{11} 2088^{11} 2333^{6} 3700^{3} 3820^{10} 4038^{24} 4233^{9} **>57f<**
Ballestro (IRE) 3 b g Astronef-Balaine (GER) (Balidar) 543^{6} *624^{9}* 848^{8} 1092^{11} 2134^{5} 2486^{13} 4079^{15} *4270^{7}* 4331^{10} **>50a 52df<**
Ballet Prince (IRE) 5 b h Sadler's Wells (USA)-Sun Princess (English Prince) 1231a^{2} **>110f<**
Ball Gown 5 b m Jalmood (USA)-Relatively Smart (Great Nephew) 1095^{2} (1347) 1612^{6} 1912^{3} 2577^{D} 2780^{4} 2950^{3} 3729^{2} 3945^{2} 4031^{8} 4267^{27} **>90f<**
Ballindalloch 3 b f Damister (USA)-Loch Spey (Formidable) 2164^{4} 3167^{4} **>39f<**
Balliol Boy 3 b c Nashwan (USA)-Fiesta Fun (Welsh Pageant) 826^{3} 1068^{4} 1396a^{4} **>104f<**
Ballpoint 2 ch c Indian Ridge-Ballaquine (Martinmas) 3733^{17} 3989^{11} 4221^{4} **>67f<**
Ballyhays (IRE) 6 ch g Glow (USA)-Relanca *18^{5} 68^{8} 269^{12} 308^{7} 343^{9} 399^{3} 416^{11} 835^{10}* (1548) 1873^{13} 2056^{8} 2207^{5} 2310^{9} 2528^{13} 3396^{16} 3808^{22} **>52a 34f<**
Ballykett Nancy (IRE) 4 b f Hero's Honor (USA)-Last Flair (Busted) 2211a^{3} 2891a^{4} 3831^{7} 4173a^{2} **>108f<**
Ballykissangel 2 ro c Hadeer-April Wind (Windjammer

(USA)) 1935^{7} 4073^{9} 4276^{12} **>29f<**

Ballymac Girl 7 gr m Niniski (USA)-Alruccaba (Crystal Palace (FR)) 432^{8} 556^{4} 582^{2} 649^{10} *3527^{8}* 3616^{5} 3682^{5} (3936) 3986^{3} 4288^{8} **>32a 63f<**

Ballymoney (IRE) 2 b c Fayruz-Blunted 4255^{6} **>49f<**

Ballynakelly 3 ch g Deploy-Musical Charm (USA) (The Minstrel (CAN)) 1244^{13} 1663^{13} 2199^{8} 4051^{13} **>57f<**

Ballyranter 6 ch h Bold Owl-Whipalash (Stephen George) *(27) 145^{4} 246^{4} 445^{5}* **>74a 68f<**

Ballysheila 3 b f Ayres Rock-Baltana (Balidar) 2968^{10} 3205^{7} 3424^{15} 3535^{5}

Ballysokerry (IRE) 4 b c Hatim (USA)-Wonder Woman (Horage) 3899^{16} 4002^{12}

Bally Wonder 3 b f Music Boy-Salacious (Sallust) *156^{3} 294^{6}* **>39a 44f<**

Balmaha 4 b f Absalom-Mo Ceri (Kampala) *387^{11}* **>58a 64f<**

Balnibarbi 6 b h Rainbow Quest (USA)-Balabina (USA) (Nijinsky (CAN)) 494^{7} **>70df<**

Baloustar (USA) 2 b f Green Forest (USA)-Ballerina Star (USA) (Forli (ARG)) 4059^{3} 4244^{9} **>32f<**

Balpare 2 ch f Charmer-Balinese (Balidar) 1913^{3} 2107^{7} *2381^{7}* (2683) 2826^{4} 3090^{8} 3375^{8} 3516^{3} 3639^{7} 3985^{5} 4107^{9} 4263^{4} **>35a 62f<**

Balrath Cross (IRE) 4 gr g Roi Danzig (USA)-Dawn Echo (Don (ITY)) *239^{7}*

Baltic Dream (USA) 2 b f Danzig Connection (USA)-Ascot Princess (USA) (Vanlandingham (USA)) (2964) 3315^{3} 3867^{13} **>77f<**

Baltic Raider 3 b or br c Polish Precedent (USA)-Sassalya 438^{7} 619^{5} 720^{4} **>98f<**

Baluteer (IRE) 2 ch c Ballad Rock-Sweetsider (USA) (Topsider (USA)) 561^{5} **>45f<**

Balzino (USA) 6 ch h Trempolino (USA)-Royal Procession (USA) (Lyphard (USA)) 1268^{8} 1420^{5} 1606^{3} 1921^{6} 1998^{5} 2465^{4}

Bambara 3 b f Old Vic-Babita (Habitat) *500^{5}* (698) 997^{6} **>51a 83f<**

Banadam (USA) 3 ch c Bering-Madame Alydar (USA) (Alydar (USA)) 553^{2} 637^{2} 936^{4} (1309) **>83f<**

Banbury Flyer 7 b g Mummy's Game-Haddon Anna (Dragonara Palace (USA)) *102^{4} 220^{13}* **>27a 42f<**

Banco Prime (IRE) 5 ch h Exactly Sharp (USA)-Bhama (FR) (Habitat) 487a^{2}

Bandar Perak 4 b c Aragon-Noire Small (USA) (Elocutionist (USA)) 506^{11} 3676^{14} 3769^{11} **>49a 54f<**

Bandita 4 ch f Chilibang-La Carlotta (Ela-Mana-Mou) *119^{5} 235^{7} 290^{4} 329^{4} 367^{5} 403^{7}* 2657^{6} 2984^{3} 3206^{6} **>51a 46f<**

Bandit Boy 2 gr c Robellino (USA)-Patraana (Nishapour (FR)) 2681^{10} **>31f<**

Bandit Girl 2 b f Robellino (USA)-Manx Millenium (Habitat) 4023^{10} **>37tf<**

Band on the Run 8 ch h Song-Sylvanecte (FR) 665^{8} 814^{7} 953^{6} 1143^{8} 1409^{3} 1617^{3} (2235) 2933^{5} 3488^{3} (3607) 3813^{17} 4116^{20} **>104f<**

Bang in Trouble (IRE) 4 b c Glenstal (USA)-Vaguely Deesse (USA) (Vaguely Noble) 3705^{5} 3936^{8} 4166^{7} 4288^{5} **>72f<**

Bangles 5 ch m Chilibang-Vague Lass (Vaigly Great) 2987^{2} 3333^{7} (3453) 3622^{3} 3822^{10} 4134^{9} 4322^{21} **>63a 75f<**

Banner (USA) 3 b f Known Fact (USA)-Abeer (USA) (Dewan (USA)) 985^{4} 1701^{6} 2519^{2} (2787) 3109^{7} 3466^{6} **>81f<**

Banny Hill Lad 5 gr g Pragmatic-Four M'S (Majestic Maharaj) 2798^{3}

Banzhaf (USA) 2 ch c Rare Performer (USA)-Hang On For Effer (USA) (Effervescing (USA)) 3766^{6} **>50f<**

Barahin (IRE) 6 b h Diesis-Red Comes Up (USA) (Blushing Groom (FR)) *158^{8} 235^{4} (497)* 2052^{10} 3572^{8} **>60a 39f<**

Barato 4 ch c Efisio-Tentraco Lady (Gay Fandango (USA)) 434^{16} 611^{2} 1271^{8} (1441) 2096^{4} 2194^{2} 2458^{4} 2652^{4} 2992^{3} 3279^{8} 3715^{22} 3830^{3} 3964^{12} 4068^{17} 4215^{12} **>73f<**

Barbaroja 4 ch c Efisio-Bias 1135^{6} 1345^{5} **>103df<**

Barbason 3 ch c Polish Precedent (USA)-Barada (USA) (Damascus (USA)) 552^{8} 3921^{10} **>56f<**

Barbezieux 8 b h Petong-Merchantmens Girl 688^{10} 1152^{12} **>47df<**

Barbrallen 3 b f Rambo Dancer (CAN)-Barrie Baby (Import) 1675^{13} 2684^{7} 3016^{16} 3475^{5} 4049^{7} **>37f<**

Bardia 5 b m Jalmood (USA)-Bauhinia (Sagaro) *771^{12}* 991^{3} 1252^{9} 1651^{2} 1854^{8} 1917^{4} 2132^{3} 2917^{2} 3094^{7} 3272^{3} 3853^{6} 4232^{4} 4284^{11} **>47f<**

Bardolph (USA) 8 b h Golden Act (USA)-Love To Barbara (USA) (Stevward) 696^{3} 998^{16} 1444^{6} 1840^{21} 2036^{3} 2154^{6} (2514) 2688^{7} 2942^{2} 3217^{12} **>86f<**

Bardon Hill Boy (IRE) 3 br g Be My Native (USA)-Star With A Glimer (Montekin) *(38) 564^{5}* 995^{6} *(1211)* 1357^{4} 1589^{8} *2589^{3}* 2902^{5} 3440^{2} 3611^{4} 3840^{8} **>85a 87f<**

Barford Lad 8 b h Nicholas Bill-Grace Poole (Sallust) 988^{5} **>74f<**

Barford Sovereign 3 b f Unfuwain (USA)-Barford Lady (Stanford) 957^{6} 1218^{2} 1514^{3} 1730^{3} 2472^{3} **>75f<**

Bargash 3 ch c Sharpo-Anchor Inn (Be My Guest (USA)) 1326^{2} *1630^{6}* 1832^{10} 2194^{4} (2448) 2652^{10} 2700^{2} 3050^{10} 3112^{13} 3212^{8} 3396^{8} 3622^{5} 3800^{23} **>38a 74f<**

Barik (IRE) 5 b h Be My Guest (USA)-Smoo (Kris) 3457^{18} 3751^{16} *3954^{8}* **>27a 22f<**

Bark'n'bite 3 b c Reprimand-Tree Mallow (Malicious) 786^{3} 947^{6} 1379^{10} 2232^{3} (2401) (2751) 2871^{4} 3299^{7} 3669^{5} **>61f<**

Barnaby Willow 3 ch g Dominion-Joli's Girl (Mansingh (USA)) 942^{11} 1368^{W} **>45f<**

Barneys Gold (IRE) 6 ch g Orchestra-Fair Corina (Menelek) 3282^{8}

Baroness Blixen 2 b f Cyrano de Bergerac-Provocation (Kings Lake (USA)) 2970^{2} 3628^{12} 3895^{10} 4133^{14} **>69f<**

Baroness Gold 2 ch f Ron's Victory (USA)-Baroness Gymcrak (Pharly (FR)) 2951^{7} 3353^{5} 3417^{11} **>37f<**

Baron Ferdinand 5 ch h Ferdinand (USA)-In Perpetuity (Great Nephew) (923) (1262) 2041a^{2} (2476) 2936^{4} **>123f<**

Baron Hrabovsky 2 ch g Prince Sabo-Joli's Girl (Mansingh (USA)) 4129^{11} 4226^{12} **>36f<**

Baroski 4 b c Petoski-Gohar (USA) (Barachois (CAN)) *1455^{4} 1567^{9} 2072^{7}* 2256^{4} 2501^{7} 4110^{8} **>33a 39f<**

Barossa Valley (IRE) 4 b c Alzao (USA)-Night of Wind (Tumble Wind (USA)) 1019^{4} 1174^{9} 2027^{4} 2692^{7} 3065^{11} **>75f<**

Barranak (IRE) 3 b g Cyrano de Bergerac-Saulonika (Saulingo) 1615^{7} 3632^{5} 4055^{7} *4337^{16}* **>72df<**

Barrel of Hope 3 b c Distant Relative-Musianica (Music Boy) 686^{2} 928^{3} 1180^{15} 1605^{5} *1953^{10}* 2500^{7} 3823^{12} 4041^{2} (4157) 4249^{4} **>69a 79f<**

Barricade (USA) 2 b c Riverman-Balletta (Lyphard) 2726a^{3} 3330a^{3} 3793a^{5} **>101f<**

Barriyah 3 b f Kris-Jathibiyah (USA) (Nureyev (USA)) 752^{9} 1240^{8} 3542^{4} 3874^{15} 4134^{16} **>60f<**

Barti-Ddu 4 b c Mister Majestic-Grugiar (Red Sunset) *(91) 186^{5} 351^{3}* (494) 1022^{6} *1332^{4}* 1552^{5} *(1955) 2293^{3} 2919^{4} (3245)* 3646^{11} *3951^{6}* **>66a 70f<**

Bartok (IRE) 4 b c Fairy King (USA)-Euromill (Shirley Heights) 4093a^{6} **>111f<**

Barton Heights 3 b g Primitive Rising (USA)-Changatre (Malinowski (USA)) 2953^{2} **>67f<**

Bashaayeash (IRE) 3 b c Fairy King (USA)-Queen Cake (Sandhurst Prince) 1573a^{2} 2040a^{2} 4016a^{7} **>117f<**

Bashful Brave 4 ch c Indian Ridge-Shy Dolly (Cajun) (583) 1050^{2} (1400) 1864^{6} (2048) (2247) 2686^{2} 3087^{8} 3250^{2} 3554^{8} 3748^{12} **>75f<**

Bashtheboards 2 b g Dancing Dissident (USA)-Vilanika (FR) (Top Ville) 3967^{8} 4188^{12} **>58f<**

Basood (USA) 2 b f Woodman (USA)-Basoof (USA) (Believe It (USA)) 3352^{3} 3983^{10} 4190^{7} **>57f<**

Bassetlaw Belle 6 b m Lucky Wednesday-Delayed Action *32^{4} 49^{6}* **>23a f<**

Bassmaat (USA) 4 b f Cadeaux Genereux-Mangayah (USA) (Spectacular Bid (USA)) *20^{11}* 481^{4} 3222^{8} 3488^{12} 3664^{10} 3885^{16} **>35a 75f<**

Bataan (USA) 4 b c Manila (USA)-Comtesse de Loir (FR) (Val de Loir) 864^{9} 3761^{8} **>81df<**

Batabanoo 6 ch h Bairn (USA)-For Instance (Busted) (2022) 2462^{4} 2816^{2} 3391^{2} 3826^{5} **>80+a 90f<**

Bathilde (IRE) 2 ch f Generous (IRE)-Bex (USA) (Explodent (USA)) 4262^{5} **>71+f<**

Bath Knight 2 b g Full Extent (USA)-Mybella Ann (Anfield) 540^{4} 781^{3} 1011^{2} 1327^{3} 1590^{11} 2515^{7} 2826^{6} 3233^{8} 3533^{2} **>45f<**

Baton Bleu 4 b c Music Boy-Fair Eleanor (Saritamer (USA)) *70^{7} 244^{4} 407^{8}* 507^{19} 1050^{15} **>38a 4f<**

Batoutoftheblue 2 br c Batshoof-Action Belle (Auction Ring (USA)) 4070^{8} 4188^{18} **>47f<**

Battery Boy 3 b g K-Battery-Bonny's Pet (Mummy's Pet) 641^{5} 1083^{12} 1596^{9} 2020^{7} 3741^{5} **>59df<**

Battle Colours (IRE) 6 b h Petorius-Streamertail (Shirley Heights) *31^{2} 117^{4} 211^{2} 267^{4} 293^{2} 336^{2}* 503^{5} *767^{9}* 1808^{13} 2321^{11} 2620^{2} 2769^{3} 3152^{2} 3431^{5} 3807^{9} 4060^{11} 4170^{11} **>69a 67df<**

Battle Dore (USA) 2 ch c Sanglamore-Nashmeel 4089a^{2}

Battleship Bruce 3 b c Mazilier (USA)-Quick Profit (Formidable) *(10) 99^{2} 151^{4}* 678^{9} 873^{8} 1183^{14} 1498^{4} 3634^{7} 3837^{F} 4136^{2} 4261^{5} **>73a 74f<**

Batty's Island 6 b g Town And Country-Just Something (Good Times (ITY)) 3304^{4} **>49f<**

Bawader (USA) 3 b f Danzig (USA)-Michelle Mon Amour (USA) (Best Turn (USA)) 804a^{3} 1895^{18} **>80f<**

Baybeejay 8 b m Buzzards Bay-Peak Condition (Mountain Call) *234^{12}*

Baydur (IRE) 4 b g Danehill (USA)-Sutton Place (Tyrant (USA)) 1851^{11} **>84f<**

Bayin (USA) 6 b h Caro-Regatela (USA) (Dr Fager) 611^{10} 765^{8} 870^{16} (1174) 1411^{14} 1809^{3} 2096^{10} 2364^{7} 2746^{2} 3145^{3} 3230^{5} 4324^{12} **>81f<**

Bay of Islands 3 b g Jupiter Island-Lawyer's Wave (USA) (Advocator) 2350^{4} 3183^{3} (3448) **>80f<**

Bayou (IRE) 4 br c Treasure Kay-Bumpity Bump (Local Suitor (USA)) 2885^{6} 2994^{2} 3344^{10} 3396^{15} **>42a 57f<**

Bayphia 7 ch h Bay Express-Sophie Avenue (Guillaume Tell (USA)) *374^{12} 496^{4}* **>36a 33f<**

Bayrak (USA) 5 b h Bering-Phydilla (FR) (Lyphard (USA)) 549^{10} (721) 763^{4} 1140^{5} (1340) 1505^{2} 1681^{4} 1840^{16} 4028^{15} 4325^{18} **>82f<**

Bdoore (IRE) 7 b m Petoski-Princess Biddy 2874^{6} **>24f<**

Beacontree 2 ch c Lycius (USA)-Beaconaire (USA) (Vaguely Noble) 4143^{8} **>7f<**

Bean King 9 gr g Ardross-Meanz Beanz (High Top) 3774^{5} 4026^{11} 4158^{8} **>88f<**

Bearall (IRE) 4 b f Al Hareb (USA)-Soxoph (Hotfoot) 1262^{4} 1585^{8} **>100f<**

Bearnaise (IRE) 2 b f Cyrano de Bergerac-Gentle Guest (IRE) (Be My Guest (USA)) 943^{4} 1448^{5} 2198^{2} 2982^{3} 3803^{6} 4208^{16} 4330^{2} **>68f<**

Bear To Dance 2 b f Rambo Dancer (CAN)-Pooh Wee (Music Boy) 671^{12} 2161^{5} 3806^{8} 4100^{W} 4224^{10} **>49f<**

Beas River (IRE) 2 b c Classic Music (USA)-Simple Annie (Simply Great (FR)) 3672^{5} 3857^{6} 3982^{14} (4133) 4231^{3} **>78f<**

Beat of Drums 4 b c Warning-Nyoka (USA) (Raja Baba (USA)) 1397a^{2} **>98f<**

Beauchamp Hero 5 b h Midyan (USA)-Buss 931^{3} 1243^{3} (1585) (1894) (2323) 2890a^{3} 3591a^{5} 3914a^{10} **>121f<**

Beauchamp Jade 3 gr f Kalaglow-Beauchamp Buzz (High Top) 1527^{4} 1717^{3} 4047^{2} 4213^{2} 4325^{10} **>86f<**

Beauchamp Jazz 3 ch c Nishapour (FR)-Afariya (FR) (Silver Shark) 504^{7} (675) 941^{5} 1839^{2} 2287^{4} 2703^{20} 4027^{2} **>107df<**

Beauchamp Kate 2 b f Petoski-Beauchamp Buzz (High Top) 3495^{6} 3733^{13} 3948^{10} **>66f<**

Beauchamp King 2 gr c Nishapour (FR)-Afariya (FR) (Silver Shark) 2005^{3} (2926) (3490) (4029) (4199) **>107f<**

Beauchief 3 br c Kind of Hush-Firdale Rosie (Town Crier) 777^{7} 1085^{8} 3974^{13} **>39f<**

Beauman 5 b h Rainbow Quest (USA)-Gliding 623^{12} 956^{3} 1141^{14} 1596^{7} 3061^{5} 3493^{6} 3759^{22} 3889^{13} *4340^{2}* **>53a 69f<**

Beau Matelot 3 ch c Handsome Sailor-Bellanoora (Ahonoora) *72^{7} 213^{2} 376^{3}* 537^{3} *626^{6}* 1083^{4} 1358^{5} 1945^{5} 2225^{5} **>61a 62f<**

Beaumont (IRE) 5 br h Be My Native (USA)-Say Yes (Junius (USA)) 1378^{8} 1616^{8} 1865^{4} 3659^{5} 4138^{15} **>64f<**

Beaumood 9 b h Jalmood (USA)-Falcon Berry (FR) (Bustino) *375^{13}* **>12a 52f<**

Beau Temps 3 br c Mtoto-Shimmer (FR) (Green Dancer (USA)) 1115a^{4} **>107f<**

Beautete 4 b c Komaite (USA)-New Central (Remainder Man) *(13) 87^{6} 403^{6}* 545^{5} 668^{10} 884^{9} 1518^{7} 1937^{9} **>73a 66f<**

Beautiful Ballad (IRE) 2 b f Ballad Rock-Delightful Time (Manado) 791^{4} (1278) 1530^{2} 1833^{3} 2322^{7} 3680^{3} 4039^{3} 4153^{5} **>84f<**

Beauty Dancer (IRE) 2 b f Alzao-Dawning Beauty 4180a^{2} **>91f<**

Beau Venture (USA) 7 ch h Explodent (USA)-Old Westbury (USA) 723^{9} 1193^{6} 1304^{7} (1864) 2120^{4} 2692^{2} 2935^{3} 3279^{9} 3597^{15} 3822^{16} 3992^{14} 4322^{19} **>67f<**

Bebe Pomme 3 b f Clantime-Orchard Road (Camden Town) *420^{8}* 522^{11} **>17a 47f<**

Becky Boo 5 b m White Mill-Aber Cothi (Dominion) 2450^{4} 2511^{2} **>26f<**

Beckyhannah 5 b m Rambling River-Munequita (Marching On) *(129) 224^{10} 348^{6}* 491^{5} 594^{9} **>36a 43df<**

Bedazzle 4 b c Formidable-Wasimah (Caerleon (USA)) 479^{3} *766^{6}* 2832^{4} 2872^{3} 3264^{5} 3475^{4} 3745^{2} **>31a 41f<**

Bedevil (USA) 5 b h Devil's Bag (USA)-Pailleron (USA) (Majestic Light (USA)) 1268^{3} 1623^{4} **>82f<**

Bedivere (USA) 3 b c El Gran Senor (USA)-Obeah (Cure The Blues (USA)) 694^{3} 980^{2} 1183^{5} 1839^{3} 2703^{21} **>99f<**

Bedouin Invader 3 b c Green Desert (USA)-La Tuerta (Hot Spark) 658^{5} 955^{7} 1296^{6} 2240^{16} 2700^{3} 3159^{6} (3286) 3545^{4} **>80f<**

Bedside Mail 2 b c Mazilier (USA)-Lucky Flinders (Free State) 436^{4} 615^{6} (1690) 2242^{4} (2435) 2779^{8} 2978^{5} 3132^{3} (3434) 3655^{7} 3901^{7} **>88f<**

Bee Beat 7 ch h Bairn (USA)-Thorny Rose (Tap On Wood) 1328^{R} 1513^{4} 1643^{R} 2109^{R} (2721a) 2713^{7} 3024^{R} 3202^{R} 3686a^{5} **>42a 58f<**

Beecham 3 ch c Superlative-Busted Harmony (Busted) *283^{2} 348^{7} 448^{6} 518^{7} 1950^{9} 2636^{9}* **>53a 76f<**

Bee Dee Best (IRE) 4 b c Try My Best (USA)-Eloquent Charm (USA) (Private Account (USA)) 839^{18} 972^{5} 2428^{7} 2789^{5} 3515^{5} **>40a 48f<**

Bee Health Boy 2 b g Superpower-Rekindle (Relkino) 1678^{10} 2185^{6} 2483^{5} 2606^{2} 2855^{6} 3271^{10} 3417^{6} 3670^{3} 3824^{15} (3937) 4066^{4} 4279^{8} **>64f<**

Beekman Street 9 b h Jalmood (USA)-Plato's Retreat (Brigadier Gerard) 879^{12} **>51f<**

Beeny 2 b c Lugana Beach-Child Star (Precocious) 2091^{7} 2299^{6} 2656^{4} 2859^{4} *(4294)* **>64a 69f<**

Befuto (FR) 4 b c Saint Andrews (FR)-Horphaly (FR) (Pharly (FR)) (1005a) **>104f<**

Begger's Opera 3 ch c North Briton-Operelle (Music Boy) 4225^{14} **>33f<**

Behaviour 3 b c Warning-Berry's Dream (Darshaan) (1947) (2419) 2703^{11} 3188^{3} 3358^{3} **>101f<**

Belana 2 br f Shaadi (USA)-Bellagio (Busted) 2083^{6} 2485^{4} 2995^{2} (3307) 3701^{10} **>77f<**

Beldray Park (IRE) 2 b br c Superpower-Ride Bold (USA) (J O Tobin (USA)) 3053^{4} 3337^{9} 3982^{6} 4230^{4} **>66f<**

Belfort Ruler 8 b h Belfort (FR)-Call Me Kate (Firestreak) *187^{10} 317^{5}* **>34a 48f<**

Belfry Green (IRE) 5 ro h Doulab (USA)-Checkers (Habat) 665^{3} 870^{8} 1143^{9} 1728^{5} 1895^{10} 2598^{7} 3706^{9} 3813^{21} **>95f<**

Belgran (USA) 6 b h El Gran Senor (USA)-Belle of Dodge Me (USA) 1349^{8} 1757^{9} 2248^{6} 2450^{15} 2612^{7} 3936^{15} 4101^{12} **>16f<**

Believe Me 2 b c Beveled (USA)-Pink Mex (Tickled Pink) (2340) 2690^{5} 3141^{4} 3746^{5} (4042) 4207^{3} (4256) **>99?f<**

Belinda Blue 3 b f Belfort (FR)-Carrula (Palm Track) 969^{11} 1847^{6} **>45f<**

Bellacardia 2 b f Law Society (USA)-Clarista (USA) (Riva Ridge (USA)) 2683^{6} 4146^{9} **>47f<**

Bella Coola 3 b f Northern State (USA)-Trigamy 937^{8} 1258^{12} 1660^{4} 3390^{7} 4194^{13} **>50f<**

Bella Michela (IRE) 2 ch f Superpower-Lumiere (Northjet) 1395a^{2}

Bellapais (IRE) 2 b f Distinctly North (USA)-Mistress Vyne 3080^{8} 3378^{7} 3518^{4} 3767^{14} **>32f<**

Bella Parkes 4 b f Tina's Pet-Summerhill Spruce (Windjammer (USA)) *69^{4} 134^{2} 182^{5} (233) 297^{2} 338^{2} (380)* 434^{12} 535^{7} 702^{5} 838^{11} 3800^{22} **>81a 59f<**

Bellaphento 2 b f Lyphento (USA)-Nautical Belle (Kind of Hush) 4262^{17} **>54f<**

Bellara 3 b f Thowra (FR)-Sicilian Vespers (Mummy's Game) *273^{6}* 557^{4} 721^{4} (3263) 3627^{11} 3849^{10} 3986^{6} **>28a 63f<**

Bella Sedona 3 ch f Belmez (USA)-My Surprise (Welsh Pageant) 1264^{6} 1533^{7} 2761^{5} *3952^{9}* **>37a 63f<**

Bellas Gate Boy 3 b c Doulab (USA)-Celestial Air (Rheingold) 618^{15} 813^{8} 1097^{22} 1472^{2} 1661^{6} 2081^{7} **>68f<**

Bella's Legacy 2 b f Thowra (FR)-Miss Lawsuit (Neltino) 4161^{15} **>59f<**

Bellateena 3 b f Nomination-Bella Travaille (Workboy) *357^{9} 418^{8}* 664^{11} 1093^{8} (2279) 2719^{3} 3422^{5} 3889^{18} (4249) **>23a 62f<**

Bellator 2 b c Simply Great (FR)-Jupiter's Message (Jupiter Island) 1597^{5} 2453^{5} 3174^{9} 3546^{8} 3760^{6} **>67f<**

Bella Vitessa (IRE) 3 b f Thatching-Burghclere 1346^{6} 1691^{8} 2082^{7} 2509^{7} 3263^{9} **>66df<**

Bell Contractors (IRE) 3 b g Jareer (USA)-Baghio (Ballymore) 1353^{4} 1658^{5} 2139^{9} 2359^{7} 2524^{7} **>62f<**

Belle Argentine (FR) 4 br f Fijar Tango (FR)-Jarlina (Pharly (FR)) 1262^{3} **>118df<**

Belleminette (IRE) 4 ch f Simply Great (FR)-Kitty's Sister (Bustino) *337^{3} 364^{7}* 481^{9} 885^{3} 1664^{13} (2088) 2549^{4} 2698^{14} 3159^{5} 3439^{9} 3534^{12} *4272^{12}* **>78a 61f<**

Belle of the Ball (IRE) 3 b f Fairy King (USA)-Commanche Belle (Shirley Heights) 1154^{4} 1504^{6} **>62f<**

Belle's Boy 2 b c Nalchik (USA)-Ty-With-Belle (Pamroy) 4045^{8} *4334^{8}* **>39a 48f<**

Bellesonnette (IRE) 3 br f Damister (USA)-Rocket Alert (Red Alert) *515^{2}* **>73a 59f<**

Bello Gallico (IRE) 4 b c Gallic League-Jeewan (Touching Wood (USA)) 2746^{10} **>81f<**

Bells of Holland 2 b f Belmez (USA)-Annie Albright (USA) (Verbatim (USA)) 1903^{5} 2249^{2} 3570^{3} 3651^{9} 4133^{2} **>65f<**

Bells of Longwick 6 b m Myjinski (USA)-Bells of St Martin (Martinmas) 639^{9} *1032^{5}* 1599^{11} *2628^{7}* 3418^{10} 3764^{7} 3822^{6} 4068^{7} 4142^{7} **>50a 57f<**

Belmarita (IRE) 2 ch f Belmez (USA)-Congress Lady (General Assembly (USA)) 4155^{8} 4262^{16} **>56f<**

Belmez Melody 3 b f Belmez (USA)-Lyphantissima (FR) (Lightning (FR)) 3239^{3} 3347^{7} **>74f<**

Belmont Princess (IRE) 5 b m Carmelite House (USA)-Silly Song *32^{10}* **>3a 42f<**

Below The Red Line 2 b c Reprimand-Good Try 4058^{14}

Belzao 2 b c Alzao (USA)-Belle Enfant (Beldale Flutter (USA)) 1104^{3} 1406^{3} 2299^{4} **>81f<**

Be Mindful 3 b c Warning-Fetlar (Pharly (FR)) 667^{9} 720^{2} 1586^{2} 2008^{5} 2762^{3} 3458^{4} 3904^{11} **>107f<**

Bemont Park (ITY) 4 br f Love the Groom (USA)-Boscher Queen (Ela-Mana-Mou) 1118a[8] (4186a) **>110f<**

Be My Bird 2 b f Be My Chief (USA)-Million Heiress (Auction Ring (USA)) 1169[W] 1318[11] 1671[5] 1968[3] 2173[5] 2526[14] 3684[9] 3760[17] 3985[19] *4127[3]* **>62a 61f<**

Be My Choice 3 ch f Be My Chief (USA)-Hence (USA) (Mr Prospector (USA)) 673[15] *1880[3] 2378[W] 2626[3]* **>57a 57f<**

Benatom (USA) 2 gr c Hawkster (USA)-Dance Til Two (USA) (Sovereign Dancer (USA)) 3155[7] 3968[2] **>81f<**

Ben'a'vachei Boy 2 gr c Rock City-Vacherin (USA) (Green Dancer (USA)) 849[4] 1327[W] 1481[7] 2660[13] 3471[2] 3612[17] **>62f<**

Ben Bowden 2 br g Sharrood (USA)-Elegant Rose (Noalto) 3009[9] 3441[W] 3672[7] 3916[7] **>72f<**

Bencher Q C (USA) 3 ch c Affirmed (USA)-Au Printemps (USA) (Dancing Champ (USA)) *(468)* 2910[4] 3237[3] 3593[2] 3864[3] **>75++a 102f<**

Bend Wavy (IRE) 3 ch c Kefaah (USA)-Prosodie (FR) (Relko) 1486[3] 4150[4] **>84f<**

Bene Erit (USA) 3 ch c Bering-Breath Taking (FR) (Nureyev (USA)) 706a[2] 1117a[5] **>98f<**

Benfleet 4 ch c Dominion-Penultimate (Final Straw) *(37) (88) 325[7]* (550) 634[3] 811[7] 981[6] 1314[2] 1612[3] 1853[4] 2241[14] 2599[2] 2768[9] 3500[5] 3817[2] 4026[5] 4201[4] **>82+a 95f<**

Ben Gunn 3 b g Faustus (USA)-Pirate Maid (Auction Ring (USA)) 1070[13] 1624[9] (2318) 2737[3] **>79f<**

Benjamins Law 4 b or br c Mtoto-Absaloute Service (Absalom) 841[3] 988[12] 1292[3] 1651[11] 1966[6] 3818[9] 4138[4] **>52f<**

Benjarong 3 ch f Sharpo-Rose And The Ring *212[5] 411[5]* 478[8] 594[13] 875[4] 992[13] 2156[9] 2540[11] *3074[12]* 3704[5] (3841) 3879[4] 3941[5] 4079[11] **>48a 50f<**

Benny Glow 2 b c Presidium-Linpac North Moor (Moorestyle) (1652) 2085[5] (2328) (2696) **>82f<**

Benten 3 b f Sharrood (USA)-Lurking (Formidable) *54[9] 258[6] 305[5] 363[4] 420[10]* 578[13] *769[11] 842[9]* 1045[4] 1528[11] 1669[12] 1847[9] 2020[5] 2190[4] 2332[9] 2818[9] **>39a 34f<**

Bentham's About 3 b c Formidable-Hawaiian Song (Henbit (USA)) *225[5] 339[12]* **>12a tf<**

Bentico 6 b h Nordico (USA)-Bentinck Hotel *18[4] 66[4] 152[3] 195[4] (269) 364[6] 406[11]* 864[7] 1351[4] 1506[7] 1644[6] 1988[6] *2291[2] 2588[3] 3073[2] 3241[2] (3510)* 3661[2] 3920[8] (4044) 4171[6] *4297[3]* **>78a 76f<**

Benzoe (IRE) 5 b h Taufan (USA)-Saintly Guest (What A Guest) 611[11] 838[9] (1151) 1271[9] 1765[2] 2060[11] 2418[6] 2758[2] 3145[4] 3717[7] 4040[13] 4322[17] **>86f<**

Bequeath 3 ch c Rainbow Quest (USA)-Balabina (USA) (Nijinsky (CAN)) 1755[3] 2350[2] **>93f<**

Berge (IRE) 4 b c Most Welcome-Miss Blitz (Formidable) *(417)* (701) 780[7] *(1087)* 4240[3] *4337[3]* **>84a 68+f<**

Bergholt 3 b g Reprimand-Kina (USA) (Bering) 677[10] 1312[9] 1786[13] **>49f<**

Berkeley Bounder (USA) 3 b c Diesis-Top Socialite (USA) (Topsider (USA)) 585[6] 730[3] 978[5] 1273[2] 1691[2] 3517[3] 3899[2] (4062) 4189[13] **>82f<**

Bernard Seven (IRE) 3 b c Taufan (USA)-Madame Nureyev (USA) (Nureyev (USA)) 539[3] 730[2] (1051) (1415) 1839[22] 3131[4] 3729[18] 3924[13] **>95f<**

Bernard Star (IRE) 3 b f Cyrano de Bergerac-Make Your Bid (Auction Ring (USA)) *283[8] 326[9]*

Bernie's Sister (IRE) 4 b f Jareer (USA)-Amorak (Wolver Hollow) *143[7] 217[12]* **>13f<**

Bescaby Boy 9 b g Red Sunset-Charo (Mariacci (FR)) 550[8] 676[8] 817[14] **>69f<**

Bescaby Girl 4 ch f Master Willie-Thatched Grove (Thatching) *49[8]* **>40f<**

Bessie's Will 4 ch f Chilibang-Empress Corina (Free State) *65[12] 92[10] 107[8] 150[8] 182[9] 233[15]* **>26a 14f<**

Best Kept Secret 4 b c Petong-Glenfield Portion (Mummy's Pet) *625[3]* 734[2] 1080[7] 1355[2] 1545[3] 1819[3] 1993[3] 2398[5] 2913[3] 3252[5] 3365[3] *3510[6]* 4054[6] 4275[8] **>59a 58f<**

Best of All (IRE) 3 b f Try My Best (USA)-Skisette (Malinowski (USA)) 823[10] 3715[25] (4292) **>81f<**

Best of Bold 3 ch c Never so Bold-I'll Try (Try My Best (USA)) 881[4] 1196[5] 1371[4] 2624[9] 3677[6] 3771[13] 4044[12] **>66f<**

Best of Times 4 ch f Handsome Sailor-Early Doors (Ballad Rock) 593[R] **>23?f<**

Betabetcorbett 4 b g Prince Sabo-Leprechaun Lady (Royal Blend) *34[8] 46[11] 153[11]* **>11a 30f<**

Bettergeton 3 ch c Rakaposhi King-Celtic Tore (IRE) (Torus) (686) 980[6] (1344) (1862) (2117) 2598[2] 3188[8] 3945[23] **>70+a 100f<**

Better Offer (IRE) 3 b g Waajib-Camden's Gift (Camden Town) 717[5] 1747[0] (2804) 2950[2] (3156) 3489[2] 3836[2] 3957[2] **>107f<**

Betty Kenwood 5 ch m Dominion-Doogali (Doon) *3[8] 53[6]* **>37a 49f<**

Bettykimvic 4 b f Reesh-Palace Pet (Dragonara Palace (USA)) 685[W] 748[15] **>34a 75df<**

Beveled Edge 6 ch m Beveled (USA)-Best Offer (Crepello) *590[2] 769[4] 2925[4]* 3293[9] 3624[4] 3751[11] **>58a 42f<**

Beverly Hills 2 b f Shareef Dancer (USA)-Debbie Harry (USA) (Alleged (USA)) 3633[W] 3983[9] **>53f<**

Beware of Agents 6 b h Tremblant-Saltation *20[7] 68[3] 187[5]* 548[2] 965[5] 1044[9] 1355[15] 1785[6] **>61a 65df<**

Be Warned 4 b g Warning-Sagar (Habitat) 665[15] 922[13] 1648[6] 2130[3] 2321[9] 2613[11] 3145[18] (3637) 3813[11] 3943[14] 4068[2] **>79f<**

Bewitching (USA) 2 ch f Imp Society (USA)-Mrs Magnum (USA) (Northjet) 791[3] 1017[4] (3003) 3387[4] 4084[20] **>86f<**

Bex Boy (IRE) 4 ch c Mon Tresor-Calcine 1647[9] 2220[5] 2586[3] 2824[6] 2972[11] 3302[3] 3370[9] **>36f<**

Bex Hill 3 ch f Grey Desire-Pour Moi (Bay Express) *1209[6] 1457[12] 2497[9] 3510[10]* **>39a 39f<**

Beyaateh 3 b f Kefaah (USA)-Keswa (Kings Lake (USA)) *350[9] 418[10] 591[10]* 698[6] 773[9] 1182[6] 1696[13] *1881[13]* 2129[9] 3099[14] **>14a 53f<**

Beyond Doubt 3 ch f Belmez (USA)-Highbrow (Shirley Heights) (1514) (2014) **>83+f<**

Beyrouth (USA) 3 b f Alleged-Lightning Fire (Kris) 3192a[3] **>86f<**

Bezirgan 4 b f Dowsing (USA)-Lomond Ring (Lomond (USA)) 812[12] 1048[13] 1274[8] **>37f<**

Bianca Cappello (IRE) 2 b f Glenstal (USA)-Idara (Top Ville) 3450[9] 3672[9] 3806[11] **>39f<**

Bianca Stella (USA) 2 b c Green Dancer (USA)-Sharmila (FR) (Blakeney) 2526[6] **>69f<**

Biased View 3 ch c Beveled (USA)-Scenic Villa (Top Ville) 867^{16} 1471^{7} 1645^{16} **>35f<**

Bibliotheque (USA) 3 ch f Woodman (USA)-Book Collector (USA) (Irish River (FR)) 915^{3} 1221^{6} 1990^{4} 3383^{10} (3685) (3885) **>77+f<**

Bide Our Time (USA) 3 b c Timeless Moment (USA)-Had To Buy (USA) (Sadair) 1728^{9} 3085^{14} 3382^{12} **>85f<**

Bid for a Rainbow 4 b c Sulaafah (USA)-Star Alert 630^{10} **>50f<**

Big Chance 6 ch g Sharpo-Cherry Ridge (Riva Ridge (USA)) *835^{4}* 1523^{13} *1762^{2}* *2292^{9}* **>37a 28f<**

Big Pat 6 b g Backchat (USA)-Fallonetta (Tachypous) 3277^{5} 3500^{11} 3743^{14} *4293^{8}* **>57a 70f<**

Big Tickle (IRE) 6 b g Colonel Godfrey (USA)-Head Scarf 2113^{6} **>32f<**

Big Treat (IRE) 3 b c Be My Guest (USA)-Cavurina (Cavo Doro) 2208^{6} 3653^{6} **>55f<**

Bijou d'Inde 2 ch c Cadeaux Genereux-Pushkar (Northfields (USA)) 2063^{2} 2693^{2} (3141) (3588a) 3812^{5} **>98f<**

Biko Alpha (JPN) 5 dk b h $805a^{2}$ **>119f<**

Billaddie 2 b g Touch of Grey-Young Lady (Young Generation) 3868^{16} 4075^{13} 4330^{6} **>63f<**

Bill and Win 4 b c Faustus (USA)-Water Folly (Sharpo) 738^{19} **>35a 32f<**

Bill Moon 9 ch h Nicholas Bill-Lunar Queen 1323^{12} 1714^{7} 1843^{6} 2784^{12} **>32da 32f<**

Bills Ploughgirl 3 gr f Risk Me (FR)-Petite Angel (Burslem) *60^{5}* 3515^{18} 4225^{18} **>10a 45f<**

Billyback 5 b g Absalom-Petit Secret 2334^{12}

Billy Bushwacker 4 b c Most Welcome-Secret Valentine (Wollow) (946) 1143^{6} 1851^{4} 2241^{15} 3188^{9} 3945^{28} 4267^{4} **>94f<**

Billy Cruncheon 4 b c Sharpo-Sorayah (Persian Bold) 541^{4} 1257^{11} **>57df<**

Billytobinslad 4 b g Tobin Lad (USA)-Sybilly (Nicholas Bill) 2990^{6} 3272^{8} **>17f<**

Bimsey (IRE) 5 b h Horage-Cut It Out (Cut Above) 3896^{3} (4167) **>79f<**

Bin Ajwaad (IRE) 5 b h Rainbow Quest (USA)-Salidar (Sallust) 425^{9} (609a) $1002a^{2}$ (3473) 3562^{6} 3931^{4} $4178a^{2}$ **>122f<**

Binlaboon (IRE) 4 b or br c Polish Precedent (USA)-Aldhabyih (General Assembly (USA)) *254^{6}* *308^{9}* *332^{10}* 3641^{8} **>24a 35f<**

Bin Nashwan (USA) 3 b c Nashwan (USA)-Dabaweyaa (Shareef Dancer (USA)) 667^{7} 3599^{5} 3768^{3} 3902^{5} **>102df<**

Bin Rosie 3 b g Distant Relative-Come on Rosi (Valiyar) 677^{3} 1051^{2} (1486) 1839^{5} 2616^{2} 3085^{3} 3599^{2} (3904) 4265^{3} **>118f<**

Bint Salsabil (USA) 2 ch f Nashwan (USA)-Salsabil (Sadler's Wells (USA)) (1928) (2947) 3561^{8} (4105) **>99f<**

Bint Shadayid (USA) 2 gr f Nashwan (USA)-Shadayid (USA) (Shadeed (USA)) (2572) (3387) 3835^{2} **>111f<**

Bint Zamayem (IRE) 3 b f Rainbow Quest (USA)-Zamayem (Sadler's Wells (USA)) 997^{5} 1139^{3} 1587^{7} 2568^{4} 3772^{7} 4003^{3} (4162) 4245^{5} **>80f<**

Birchwood Sun 5 b h Bluebird (USA)-Shapely Test (USA) (Elocutionist (USA)) 491^{3} 594^{7} 789^{5} 965^{3} 1044^{5} 1355^{6} (1493) 1828^{14} (1996) 2229^{7} 2330^{5} 2611^{2} 2870^{3} 3121^{5} 3275^{3} 3830^{6} (3879) 4053^{9} 4280^{18} **>75f<**

Bird in Blue (IRE) 3 b f Bluebird (USA)-Amata (USA) (Nodouble (USA)) 1128^{8} 1442^{7} **>65f<**

Bird Island 4 gr c Jupiter Island-Roybirdie (Mansingh (USA)) 1513^{16} 1830^{11} **>67f<**

Birequest 4 ch c Rainbow Quest (USA)-Artic Mistral (CAN) (Briartic (CAN)) *(11)* *(145)* *249^{2}* *318^{4}* *445^{13}* 505^{14} 1830^{13} **>84a 76df<**

Birthday Boy (IRE) 3 b c Scenic-Thank You Note (What A Guest) 663^{8} 851^{5} 1093^{9} 1368^{9} 1985^{2} 2406^{2} 2536^{5} 3130^{7} 3403^{5} 3635^{7} 3747^{3} **>71f<**

Bishop of Cashel 3 b c Warning-Ballet Classique (USA) (Sadler's Wells (USA)) 713^{8} $2558a^{2}$ $3478a^{2}$ (3562) 3814^{4} **>119f<**

Bitch 3 ch f Risk Me (FR)-Lightning Legend (Lord Gayle (USA)) 1355^{11} 1669^{13} 1824^{6} 1962^{9} 2258^{3} 2582^{5} **>38a 49f<**

Bites 2 b f Risk Me (FR)-Sundaysport Splash (Lord Gayle (USA)) 455^{6} 561^{3} *834^{2}* *1090^{5}* 1369^{2} 1699^{7} 2204^{3} 3937^{13} 4224^{14} **>32a 48f<**

Bite the Bullet 4 ch c Ballacashtal (CAN)-Longgoe (Lorenzaccio) *422^{10}* 1255^{11} 1714^{20}

Bit of Bother (IRE) 2 b c Millfontaine-Mother White (Jukebox) 964^{4} 1203^{2} 1899^{2} **>55f<**

Bit on the Side (IRE) 6 b m Vision (USA)-Mistress (USA) (Damascus (USA)) 423^{11} 623^{13} 931^{5} 1410^{3} 2445^{4} (3593) 3836^{6} 4028^{14} 4201^{7} **>87f<**

Bitter N Twisted 3 ch f Jalmood (USA)-Stedham (Jaazeiro (USA)) *85^{8}* *135^{8}* *368^{6}* 477^{5} 837^{6} **>27a 40f<**

Biya (IRE) 3 ch c Shadeed (USA)-Rosie Potts (Shareef Dancer (USA)) *17^{2}* *(72)* 2974^{6} 3872^{12} **>62a 48f<**

Black Boy (IRE) 6 br g Auction Ring (USA)-Relic Spirit (Relic) *55^{7}* *69^{7}* *140^{6}* 772^{12} 3640^{5} 4113^{15} **>30a 57f<**

Black Ice Boy (IRE) 4 b c Law Society (USA)-Hogan's Sister (USA) (Speak John) 929^{10} 1607^{9} 3153^{6} **>60f<**

Blackpool Festival (IRE) 3 b g Contract Law (USA)-Burkina (African Sky) *47^{8}* *171^{7}* **>43a 66f<**

Black Shadow 3 b f Forzando-Basenite (Mansingh (USA)) *7^{6}* *287^{4}* *319^{3}* *359^{6}* 580^{7} 1016^{15} 1257^{7} 1453^{5} 2190^{5} **>49a 36f<**

Blackspot (IRE) 3 b f Contract Law (USA)-Hitopah (Bustino) 722^{12} 818^{14} 1379^{14} **>19f<**

Blair Castle (IRE) 4 b c Waajib-Caimanite (Tap On Wood) 3781^{5} **>83f<**

Blakenmor 2 b g No Evil-Kinz (Great Nephew) 1829^{9} **>25f<**

Blanchland 6 gr h Bellypha-Premier Rose (Sharp Edge) 1402^{12} 1484^{8} 1745^{12} 1974^{16} 2209^{5} **>68a 53f<**

Blasted 3 ch c Statoblest-Apprila (Bustino) 572^{3} 722^{8} 971^{5} 1125^{7} (2016) 2549^{6} 2828^{2} 3800^{18} 4194^{8} **>74df<**

Blaster Bates (USA) 4 b c Bates Motel (USA)-A Society Girl (USA) (Verbatim (USA)) *335^{6}* *354^{10}* **>25a 27f<**

Blaze Away (USA) 4 b c Polish Navy (USA)-Battle Drum (USA) (Alydar (USA)) 632^{3} (938) 1189^{5} 1313^{4} 1768^{5} 2098^{14} 2569^{3} (3071) 3616^{6} 3849^{7} 4118^{7} 4326^{6} **>92f<**

Blaze of Oak (USA) 4 ch c Green Forest (USA)-Magic Robe (USA) (Grey Dawn II) 2209^{2} 2621^{4} 3294^{5} 3443^{2} 3645^{13} 3762^{2} 3879^{14} **>79f<**

Blaze of Song 3 ch c Jester-Intellect (Frimley Park) 573^{2} 813^{5} (948) (1124) (1338) 1839^{9} **>88f<**

Blazing Miracle 3 b f Shaab-Cottage Blaze (Sunyboy) 635^{20} 1053^{12} **>29f<**

Blenheim Terrace 2 b g Rambo Dancer (CAN)-

Boulevard Girl (Nicholas Bill) *2625^{3}* *2958^{10}* 3160^{7} 3460^{9} **>48a 56f<**

Blessed Spirit **2** ch f Statoblest-Kukri (Kris) 4103^{12} 4262^{12} **>70f<**

Blessingindisguise **2** b c Kala Shikari-Blowing Bubbles (Native Admiral (USA)) 671^{9} (964) 1267^{2} 1556^{2} 1893^{10} **>83f<**

Blisland **3** b c Danehill (USA)-Busca (USA) (Mr Prospector (USA)) 553^{5} (1554) 2367^{3} 2738^{2} 3945^{20} **>99f<**

Blockade (USA) **6** b g Imperial Falcon (CAN)-Stolen Date (USA) (Sadair) 503^{9} (1148) 1280^{9} 1626^{8} (2057) (2207) 2468^{4} 2766^{4} 2945^{2} (3269) 3443^{4} **>80f<**

Blomberg (IRE) **3** b c Indian Ridge-Daniella Drive (USA) (Shelter Half (USA)) (435) 622^{2} 3991^{8} 4198^{2} **>101f<**

Blossom Dearie **2** b f Landyap (USA)-Jose Collins 4277^{12} **>32f<**

Blotoft **3** b g High Kicker (USA)-Foothold (Hotfoot) 3805^{14}

Blow Dry (IRE) **5** b h Glenstal (USA)-Haco 594^{4} 877^{8} 1044^{3} 1421^{7} 1724^{6} 2156^{5} (2398) 3365^{9} (3677) 3800^{14} 3920^{6} 4060^{13} 4275^{9} **>65f<**

Blowedifiknow **5** b h Prince Rupert (FR)-Ballys Princess *35^{6}* *166^{4}* *259^{5}* **>44a 50f<**

Blue Adelaide **2** b f Puissance-Dominion Blue (Dominion) 2548^{7} 4329^{2} **>65f<**

Blue And Royal (IRE) **3** b g Bluebird (USA)-Cat Girl (USA) (Grey Dawn II) 1173^{6} 1691^{7} 2341^{3} 2687^{9} 4205^{8} **>75f<**

Blue Bay (GER) **3** f $1705a^{5}$ **>94f<**

Bluebeard (IRE) **2** b c Bluebird (USA)-Shebasis (USA) (General Holme (USA)) 4037^{7} 4169^{5} **>58f<**

Blueberry Fields **2** gr f Shernazar-Be Easy 3371^{14} **>42f<**

Blue Blazer **5** b h Bluebird (USA)-View (Shirley Heights) (967) 1102^{2} 1303^{3} 1767^{7} (2238) 2462^{3} 2882^{4} 3343^{8} **>88f<**

Blue Bomber **4** b c Tina's Pet-Warm Wind (Tumble Wind (USA)) 1244^{11} 1593^{5} 2538^{6} *2943^{12}* (4115) **>80f<**

Blue Collar (FR) **2** c $3906a^{3}$

Blue Delight (IRE) **2** b c Bluebird (USA)-Highly Delighted (USA) (Verbatim (USA)) 690^{12} **>34f<**

Blue Domain **4** b c Dominion-Blue Rag 3879^{7} **>24a 24f<**

Blue Duster (USA) **2** b f Danzig (USA)-Blue Note (FR) (Habitat) (1361) (1849) (2594) (3866) **>113+f<**

Blue Ensign **10** b h Beldale Flutter (USA)-Blue Rag *217^{7}* *343^{7}* **>38a f<**

Blue Flyer (IRE) **2** b g Bluebird (USA)-Born to Fly (IRE) (Last Tycoon) 3733^{8} 3893^{6} **>61f<**

Blue Grit **9** b h Thatching-Northern Wisdom (Northfields (USA)) 579^{5} 838^{8} 1484^{3} 1582^{9} 1828^{10} *2074^{6}* 2330^{3} 2645^{4} **>32a 60f<**

Blue Iris **2** b f Petong-Bo' Babbity (Strong Gale) (1620) (2442) (4084) **>96+f<**

Blue Judge (IRE) **5** b h Rainbow Quest (USA)-Water Splash (USA) (Little Current (USA)) 735^{6} 958^{3} **>97f<**

Blue Lugana **3** b g Lugana Beach-Two Friendly (Be Friendly) 966^{14} 1279^{11} 1936^{6} 2261^{2} 2502^{6} 3000^{8} **>44f<**

Blue Nile (IRE) **3** b f Bluebird (USA)-Angelus Chimes (Northfields (USA)) (1218) 1347^{5} 2028^{5} 3469^{4} 3863^{12} **>75f<**

Blue Ocean (USA) **3** b c Danzig (USA)-Foreign Courier (USA) 3598^{8} 3924^{5} **>99?f<**

Blue Pennant **4** b f Jupiter Island-Tudor Whisper *46^{5}* *153^{7}* *288^{7}* *588^{9}* **>27a 30f<**

Blue Sioux **3** b f Indian Ridge-Blues Indigo (Music Boy) 522^{4} 697^{8} 1660^{15} *2071^{4}* 3905^{15} 3992^{17} *(4123)* **>63a 57f<**

Blue Siren **4** ch f Bluebird (USA)-Manx Millenium (Habitat) 571^{2} 921^{13} **>116f<**

Blue Smoke (IRE) **3** b c Posen (USA)-Raubritter 484^{4} 657^{9} 787^{4} 947^{8} 2193^{7} 2481^{3} 2860^{11} 3263^{8} **>68f<**

Blue Suede Hoofs **2** br c Nomination-Massive Powder (Caerleon (USA)) 3989^{15} 4103^{14} 4224^{2} **>68f<**

Bluetong **2** b c Petong-Sculpture Bleue (Claude Monet (USA)) 2299^{7} 2876^{12} **>46f<**

Blue Zulu (IRE) **3** gr f Don't Forget Me-Aldern Stream (Godswalk (USA)) (957) 1242^{7} 2006^{3} 2616^{4} 3382^{3} **>96f<**

Bluffing (USA) **0** D $2563a^{7}$ **>70f<**

Blurred Image (IRE) **4** ch c Exactly Sharp (USA)-Bear's Affair (Gay Fandango (USA)) *249^{7}* 1261^{11} 1517^{8} 1910^{3} 2053^{3} 3175^{3} 3268^{5} 3632^{11} **>61a 82df<**

Blushing Flame (USA) **4** b c Blushing Groom (FR)-Nearctic Flame (Sadler's Wells (USA)) 634^{2} 931^{2} 1853^{11} 3162^{15} 3923^{7} (4201) (4323) **>110f<**

Blushing Gleam **2** f $2726a^{4}$ (3578a) $4013a^{5}$ **>92f<**

Blushing Grenadier (IRE) **3** ch c Salt Dome (USA)-La Duse (Junius (USA)) 733^{12} 1094^{11} 1414^{4} 1797^{4} (2084) 2342^{13} 2711^{3} 3341^{4} 3751^{4} 3764^{11} 3897^{5} 4060^{4} 4157^{25} **>64f<**

Blush Rambler (USA) **5** b h Blushing Groom (FR)-Romanette (USA) (Alleged (USA)) 827^{4} 1780^{3} 3070^{3} **>117f<**

Blu Tuama (USA) **2** b f Northern Prospect-Fulvous Gold (4343a) **>96?f<**

Bobanlyn (IRE) **3** b f Dance of Life (USA)-Sheer Innocence (Shirley Heights) 694^{12} 962^{9} 2376^{4} 2719^{7} 2979^{20} 3658^{5} (3825) 3977^{13} 4196^{5} 4225^{6} 4284^{7} **>65f<**

Bobby's Dream **3** b f Reference Point-Kiralyi (FR) (Kings Lake (USA)) 851^{10} 1372^{6} 1696^{2} 3435^{6} 3724^{3} 3971^{5} 4259^{18} **>56f<**

Bobinski **3** br c Polish Precedent-Cockade (Derring-Do) $1575a^{4}$ $2044a^{10}$ **>117f<**

Bob's Ploy **3** b c Deploy-Santa Magdalena (Hard Fought) 618^{16} 857^{2} (1314) 1589^{6} 1872^{2} 2691^{9} $3486a^{7}$ 3836^{13} **>98f<**

Bobsworthatcaspers **2** b g Risk Me (FR)-Hot Sunday Sport (Star Appeal) 863^{6} 1047^{8} 1226^{2} 1352^{2} *2143^{7}* 2403^{2} 2505^{3} 2637^{5} *2962^{4}* 3135^{6} **>36a 65f<**

Boccadirosa (IRE) **2** b f Waajib-Atreides (Simply Great) $2900a^{3}$

Bodantree **4** b c Rambo Dancer (CAN)-Snow Tree (Welsh Pageant) *279^{4}* *367^{7}* 2165^{7} 2227^{3} **>34a 52f<**

Bodfari Lass **2** b f Tirol-Sugar Loch (Lochnager) 3708^{9} 3939^{6} 4190^{6} **>64f<**

Boffy (IRE) **2** ch c Mac's Imp (USA)-No Dowry (Shy Groom (USA)) *1090^{3}* 1203^{5} 1562^{4} 2000^{4} *2146^{2}* 2399^{3} 2606^{5} (3290) (3468) 3742^{7} *3953^{6}* 4231^{13} **>49a 74f<**

Bogart **4** gr g Belfort (FR)-Lamem (Meldrum) *148^{4}* *228^{3}* 559^{15} 789^{7} 984^{2} 1374^{3} 1995^{10} 2549^{8} 2832^{3} 3172^{3} *3319^{4}* 4193^{8} 4292^{14} **>54a 62f<**

Bold Acre **5** ch h Never so Bold-Nicola Wynn (Nicholas

Bill) *18*^{8} 4229^{14} >**58da 64f**<

Bold Amusement **5** ch h Never so Bold-Hysterical (High Top) 1808^{10} 2457^{12} (2668) 2952^{5} 3419^{5} 3611^{18} 3645^{9} 4319^{18} >**85f**<

Bold Angel **8** b h Lochnager-Lobela (Lorenzaccio) 1560^{5} 1809^{9} 2099^{5} 2517^{3} (2836) *3074*^{5} 3222^{2} 3488^{10} 3704^{2} 3984^{9} 4170^{5} >**66a 78df**<

Bold Appeal (IRE) **3** b c Caerleon (USA)-La Bella Fontana (Lafontaine (USA)) *2291*^{9} >**22a f**<

Bold Aristocrat (IRE) **4** b c Bold Arrangement-Wyn Mipet (Welsh Saint) *140*^{8} *182*^{3} *233*^{3} *417*^{8} 548^{12} 1523^{19} *1883*^{4} *(2383)* *2925*^{3} *3072*^{5} 3344^{19} 3467^{5} 3750^{5} >**61a 47f**<

Bold Charlie **3** ch g Weldnaas (USA)-Flirty Lady (Never so Bold) 1731^{8} 1983^{8} *2494*^{5} *2960*^{9} >**14a 2f**<

Bold Cyrano (IRE) **4** b c Cyrano de Bergerac-Court Hussar (Queen's Hussar) *2*^{13} *129*^{11} *358*^{5} *404*^{11} *511*^{6} 739^{8} 972^{4} 1499^{8} 1975^{6} 2137^{3} 2549^{10} 3128^{4} 3467^{14} >**47da 63f**<

Bold Effort (FR) **3** b g Bold Arrangement-Malham Tarn (Riverman (USA)) *64*^{2} *(124)* *159*^{3} *(278)* *345*^{7} 621^{9} (939) 1069^{3} 1487^{2} (1806) 2764^{22} 3476a^{9} 3551^{2} 3717^{8} 3815^{7} 4040^{5} 4160^{15} >**80a 102f**<

Bold Elect **7** b h Electric-Famous Band (USA) (Banderilla (USA)) 568^{9} 1861^{4} >**60f**<

Bold Enough **2** ch f Bold Arrangement-Sweet Enough (Caerleon (USA)) 2675^{7} 3069^{12} 3203^{4} 3749^{3} (3882) 4025^{6} >**71f**<

Bold Frontier **3** gr c Chief Singer-Mumtaz Flyer (USA) (Al Hattab (USA)) *118*^{2} *170*^{4} *257*^{4} 426^{0} *473*^{2} *(629)* >**76a 57f**<

Bold Future (IRE) **2** b g Treasure Kay-Mother Courage (Busted) 3231^{15} 3502^{14} 3671^{12} >**27f**<

Bold Gait **4** ch g Persian Bold-Miller's Gait (Mill Reef (USA)) (696) 1132^{6} (2098) 2702^{4} >**121f**<

Bold Gem **4** b f Never so Bold-Precious Jade 1595^{7} 1832^{8} 2092^{6} (2364) 2659^{6} 2867^{4} 3014^{7} 3376^{10} 3519^{9} *3954*^{5} 4057^{12} *4272*^{5} >**69a 56f**<

Bold Habit **10** ch h Homing-Our Mother *240*^{2} *408*^{3} 820^{16} *3529*^{10} (3808) *4298*^{5} >**55a 71f**<

Boldina Bay **3** b f Never so Bold-Mary Martin (Be My Guest (USA)) 1467^{3} (1533) 1793^{10} 2062^{2} 2397^{P} >**84f**<

Bold Joker **4** b c Jester-Bold Difference (Bold Owl) 2329^{7} 4114^{6} 4232^{13} >**31f**<

Bold Look **4** b c Never so Bold-Madame Bovary (Ile de Bourbon (USA)) (817) 1141^{7} 1502^{9} 1966^{10} 2954^{2} 3234^{5} 3384^{8} 3872^{8} >**70f**<

Boldly So **3** b f Never so Bold-Baino Clinic (USA) (Sovereign Dancer (USA)) *43*^{7} *171*^{4} *270*^{P} (521) 1702^{4} 4071^{14} >**50a 46f**<

Bold Mick **4** b c Never so Bold-Purple Fan (Dalsaan) *2*^{4} *44*^{11} *150*^{7} 450^{8} 548^{11} 818^{2} 1350^{4} 1513^{6} >**49a 61f**<

Bold Patriot (IRE) **2** b c Polish Patriot (USA)-Don't Be Cruel (Persian Bold) 1977^{10} 3890^{9} >**66f**<

Bold Pursuit (IRE) **6** b h Thatching-Pursue (Auction Ring (USA)) *589*^{3} >**74da 64f**<

Bold Revival **3** b f Never so Bold-Convivial (Nordance (USA)) 1683^{6} 2049^{2} 2576^{12} 3764^{17} >**51f**<

Bold Ruritania (CAN) **5** m 4184a^{3} >**114f**<

Bold Sally **3** b f Bold Fox-Sally Bowles 1053^{9} 1337^{10} 1717^{8} >**51f**<

Bold Street (IRE) **5** ch h Shy Groom (USA)-Ferry Lane (Dom Racine (FR)) *281*^{9} *386*^{3} 2001^{9} 2461^{11} 3597^{8} 3715^{27} 3964^{7} *4337*^{5} >**68a 63f**<

Bold Times **2** br g Timeless Times (USA)-Spanish Bold (Tower Walk) 1278^{6} (1640) *1954*^{2} 2153^{3} 2328^{2} (2800) 3049^{P} >**59a 77f**<

Bold Top **3** ch c Bold Owl-Whirlygigger (Taufan (USA)) 1039^{8} 1379^{13} 1669^{3} 1945^{7} 2225^{2} 2875^{2} 3422^{7} 3462^{7} 4002^{8} >**60f**<

Bollin Dorothy **2** b f Rambo Dancer (CAN)-Bollin Harriet (Lochnager) 1597^{2} 1877^{3} 2095^{2} >**75f**<

Bollin Frank **3** b c Rambo Dancer (CAN)-Bollin Emily (Lochnager) 577^{4} 823^{6} 1180^{4} 1471^{5} 1920^{3} 2084^{11} (2276) 2500^{6} 2881^{8} 3447^{3} 3802^{11} 3966^{2} >**67f**<

Bollin Harry **3** b c Domynsky-Bollin Harriet (Lochnager) (966) 1249^{4} (1450) 1580^{5} 1876^{4} 2271^{2} 2609^{6} 3597^{9} 3823^{5} 3964^{15} >**67f**<

Bollin Joanne **2** b f Damister (USA)-Bollin Zola (Alzao (USA)) 1620^{2} >**70f**<

Bollin Sophie **3** b f Efisio-Bollin Zola (Alzao (USA)) 442^{18} 539^{11} 673^{11} 1598^{11} 1944^{7} 3370^{14} >**39f**<

Boloardo **6** b h Persian Bold-Northshiel (Northfields (USA)) 2433^{2} 2768^{6} 3189^{8} 3826^{4} >**75f**<

Bolshoi (IRE) **3** br c Royal Academy (USA)-Mainly Dry (The Brianstan) (555) 733^{10} 999^{2} 1181^{4} 1487^{9} 1806^{7} >**72f**<

Bonarelli (IRE) **2** b c Dancing Dissident (USA)-Sovereign Dona (Sovereign Path) 2183^{2} (2796) (3215) (3600) >**93f**<

Bonita **3** ch f Primo Dominie-Loufagh (USA) (Bering) (580) 746^{5} 862^{14} 1541^{W} (1692) 2108^{8} >**66f**<

Bon Luck (IRE) **3** ch c Waajib-Elle Va Bon (Tanfirion) 1474^{9} 1754^{2} 2010^{4} >**78f**<

Bonne Etoile **3** b f Diesis-Bonne Ile (Ile de Bourbon (USA)) 1736^{2} (1990) (2679) (3413) >**98f**<

Bonny Melody **4** b f Sizzling Melody-Bonny Quiver (Gorytus (USA)) *142*^{8} *226*^{6} 594^{12} 748^{7} 862^{13} 1080^{6} *(1331)* 1400^{4} 1565^{7} 1677^{10} *2074*^{10} *(2295)* *2492*^{7} 2753^{6} 2858^{7} 3467^{11} 3919^{12} >**42a 43f**<

Bon Secret (IRE) **3** b c Classic Secret (USA)-Bon Retour (Sallust) *(57)* *86*^{3} *146*^{3} *159*^{4} *(216)* *247*^{6} *278*^{2} *319*^{2} *(473)* *532*^{5} *560*^{2} 3529^{16} 3629^{15} >**77a 32f**<

Bookcase **8** b h Siberian Express (USA)-Colourful (FR) (Gay Mecene (USA)) 430^{14} 623^{14} (744) 884^{6} 1141^{3} 1367^{2} 1757^{7} 1908^{2} (2289) 2599^{4} (3004) 3107^{5} 3384^{6} 3679^{4} 3889^{11} >**75f**<

Boost **3** b c Superpower-Sirene Bleu Marine (USA) (Secreto (USA)) 701^{12} 2540^{5} 2761^{4} 2927^{2} 3167^{3} 3370^{10} 3980^{6} 4194^{15} 4275^{6} >**53df**<

Borana Lodge (USA) **2** b c Sabona (USA)-Dancing Danzig (USA) (Danzig (USA)) 684^{6} 788^{8} 1959^{5} 2516^{11} >**46f**<

Born A Lady **2** ch f Komaite (USA)-Lucky Candy (Lucky Wednesday) *(1031)* 1634^{6} 2085^{2} 2523^{4} 2783^{3} 3742^{5} 4112^{3} 4244^{4} >**49a 60f**<

Born To Be Wild **3** gr f Pharly (FR)-Carose 2806^{2} 3111^{5} 3747^{2} >**61f**<

Born to Please (IRE) **3** ch c Waajib-Gratify (Grundy) 888^{10} 1202^{11} 1513^{9} 1978^{6} 2244^{5} 3056^{6} 3401^{2} 3635^{4} 3987^{4} >**65f**<

Borocay **7** b g Lochnager-Maybehandy (Some Hand) *(96)* *166*^{2} *234*^{3} (476) 534^{3} >**45a 49f**<

Borrowby **3** ch c Domynsky-Close the Deal (Nicholas

Bill) 1060^{7} 1279^{9} 1506^{4} 1742^{5} 3704^{8} 3935^{16} 4193^{16} **>38a 52f<**

Bosra Sham (USA) **2** ch f Woodman (USA)-Korveya (USA) (Riverman (USA)) (3069) (3835) **>118+f<**

Boston Rock (IRE) **3** ch c Ballad Rock-Miss Boston (FR) (River River (FR)) 2236^{8} **>19f<**

Boston Tea Party **2** b f Rambo Dancer (CAN)-Tea-Pot (Ragstone) 2791^{14} 3441^{10} 3566^{3} 3767^{13} 4133^{12} **>51f<**

Bouche Bee (USA) **3** b f Naevus (USA)-Miss Henderson Co (USA) (Silver Hawk (USA)) 915^{7} 1168^{2} 1360^{2} (1549) (1915) (2325) 2737^{5} 3188^{5} **>98f<**

Boundary Bird (IRE) **2** b c Tirol-Warning Sound (Red Alert) 1722^{4} 3432^{12} *3523*^{3} 3780^{11} 3882^{5} **>54a 59f<**

Boundary Express **3** b g Sylvan Express-Addison's Jubilee (Sparkler) *133*^{2} *176*^{6} *213*^{5} 575^{4} 672^{4} 786^{4} 875^{2} 2327^{8} 2770^{5} *2961*^{8} (3111) 3299^{3} (3464) 3669^{2} 3936^{6} 4108^{4} **>51a 67f<**

Boundless (IRE) **3** b f Cyrano de Bergerac-Blink 485^{15} *893*^{3} 1427^{9} 2078^{7} **>46a 45f<**

Boursin (IRE) **6** b h Taufan (USA)-Cloven Dancer (USA) (Hurok (USA)) *93*^{13} 1151^{10} 1441^{6} 2585^{3} 2700^{5} 3492^{20} *4125*^{11} 4165^{26} **>17a 67df<**

Bouton d'Or **2** b f Mazilier (USA)-Cow Pastures (Homing) 1833^{7} 2135^{11} 3662^{10} *4294*^{5} **>36a 36f<**

Bowcliffe **4** b c Petoski-Gwiffina (Welsh Saint) 1596^{13} 2052^{5} 2439^{4} 2713^{6} **>66f<**

Bowcliffe Court (IRE) **3** b c Slip Anchor-Res Nova (USA) (Blushing Groom (FR)) 635^{18} 1219^{3} (1529) 1730^{4} 3669^{7} 3927^{2} 4108^{6} **>69f<**

Bowcliffe Grange (IRE) **3** b c Dominion Royale-Cala-Vadella *2588*^{12} 2815^{7} 3125^{12} 3275^{12} 3508^{3} **>16a 19f<**

Bowden Rose **3** ch f Dashing Blade-Elegant Rose (Noalto) 733^{15} 1124^{14} 1541^{10} 1692^{4} (2017) (2202) (2507) 2802^{2} 3065^{6} 3279^{6} 3519^{3} (3961) 4033^{16} 4160^{7} 4238^{3} **>93f<**

Bowled Over **2** b g Batshoof-Swift Linnet (Wolver Hollow) 3891^{3} **>63f<**

Bowlers Boy **2** ch g Risk Me (FR)-Snow Wonder (Music Boy) 4137^{9} 4314^{11} **>60f<**

Boxboy **5** b h Kings Lake (USA)-Majan *397*^{9} **>37da 17f<**

Bozeman (IRE) **2** b g Cyrano de Bergerac-Catherine Clare (Sallust) 690^{13} 1278^{7} (1590) 2706^{7} 3160^{11} (3566) 3655^{8} **>77?f<**

Brackenthwaite **5** ch h Faustus (USA)-Cosset *31*^{4} *66*^{5} *137*^{5} *349*^{9} 1292^{11} *1459*^{9} 1854^{21} *2076*^{2} *2292*^{5} *2588*^{10} *3529*^{4} **>67a 52f<**

Bradwell (IRE) **4** b f Taufan (USA)-Tabriya (Nishapour (FR)) *2*^{3} *82*^{3} *182*^{7} **>51a 55f<**

Braes'O'Shieldhill **2** ch f Music Maestro-Dalchroy 474^{6} 878^{8} *1213*^{4} *3244*^{9} **>13a 20f<**

Braille (IRE) **4** br c Vision (USA)-Winning Feature (Red Alert) 433^{20} 535^{21} 841^{4} 988^{4} 1205^{10} 1651^{9} 2621^{5} 2937^{8} (3059) (3169) (3207) 3531^{3} 3611^{2} 3657^{2} 3801^{3} 3965^{4} **>78f<**

Brancher **4** gr g Lyphento (USA)-Sunlit (Warpath) 3282^{4}

Brandonhurst **5** b h Elegant Air-Wolverina 526^{11} 762^{12} 1166^{7} 2439^{14} **>72f<**

Brandon Lane **4** b g Good Times (ITY)-Fauve (Dominion) 2309^{6} 2620^{11} **>45f<**

Brandon Magic **2** ch c Primo Dominie-Silk Stocking (Pardao) 2767^{3} 3604^{2} (3784) (3886) (4034) 4159^{3} **>98f<**

Brandon Prince (IRE) **7** b h Shernazar-Chanson de Paris (USA) (The Minstrel (CAN)) 432^{11} 506^{7} 696^{8} 840^{2} 1058^{9} **>81f<**

Brandonville **2** b c Never so Bold-Enduring (Sadler's Wells (USA)) 3733^{6} 3988^{4} 4129^{4} **>67f<**

Branston Abby (IRE) **6** ch m Risk Me (FR)-Tuxford Hideaway (Cawston's Clown) 571^{3} 659^{8} 814^{4} 1100^{2} 1133^{3} 1393a^{6} 1488^{2} 1618^{5} 1895^{24} (2097) 2416^{4} 2728a^{D} 2895a^{2} (3045a) 3195a^{5} (3446) 3491^{2} (3564) 3717^{10} 3834^{3} 3931^{5} 4178a^{8} 4324^{2} **>118f<**

Branston Danni **2** b f Ron's Victory (USA)-Softly Spoken (Mummy's Pet) 1017^{2} 2095^{5} (2302) 2706^{10} 2991^{6} 3289^{2} 3548^{16} 3714^{2} **>74f<**

Branston Jewel (IRE) **2** ch f Prince Sabo-Tuxford Hideaway (Cawston's Clown) (3133) (3444) 3687a^{3} **>93f<**

Branston Kristy **3** b f Hallgate-Bare Spectacle (Welsh Pageant) *118*^{9} *258*^{5} *299*^{3} *363*^{10} **>39a 53f<**

Brass Tacks **3** br f Prince Sabo-Brassy Nell (Dunbeath (USA)) 1065^{6} 1453^{3} 1660^{7} 1811^{3} (1906) *3073*^{11} 3269^{5} **>10a 71f<**

Braveboy **7** b h Never so Bold-Relkina (FR) (Relkino) *100*^{3} *152*^{5} *203*^{3} *312*^{7} *406*^{8} **>64a 59f<**

Brave Edge **4** b c Beveled (USA)-Daring Ditty (Daring March) 693^{2} (796) (1106) 1637^{4} 1895^{3} 2764^{14} 3236^{9} 3815^{3} 4119^{9} **>108f<**

Brave Fighter (USA) **3** b f Gone West (USA)-Psyched (USA) (Hagley (USA)) 2236^{4} 2393^{6} 2638^{3} 3034^{6} **>67f<**

Brave Indigo **2** b c Rainbow Quest-Nyoka 3797a^{2}

Brave Maisie (IRE) **2** b f Mazaad-London Spin 1671^{6} 2447^{4} 2846^{11} 3427^{8} 3733^{24} **>50f<**

Brave Patriarch (IRE) **4** gr c Alzao (USA)-Early Rising (USA) (Grey Dawn II) 714^{19} 960^{11} **>90f<**

Brave Princess **3** b f Dancing Brave (USA)-Princess Zena 695^{9} (1326) 1617^{10} 3630^{9} *3952*^{2} 4071^{12} *4297*^{6} **>74a 75f<**

Brave Revival **3** b f Dancing Brave (USA)-Fearless Revival (Cozzene (USA)) (911) 1242^{5} 1588^{2} **>99f<**

Brave Spy **4** b g Law Society (USA)-Contralto *357*^{5} *470*^{3} *1091*^{3} *1784*^{3} 2413^{4} *(2495)* 2942^{3} *3245*^{10} **>66a 70f<**

Braydon Forest **3** b c Presidium-Sleekit (Blakeney) 764^{8} 941^{6} 1514^{5} 1663^{3} 2094^{2} 2314^{3} 2571^{9} 3679^{5} 3885^{8} **>73f<**

Breakfast Creek **3** b f Hallgate-North Pine (Import) 1565^{4} 1822^{8} 2521^{17} 2877^{4} 3667^{15} 4113^{18} **>53f<**

Break the Rules **3** b c Dominion-Surf Bird (Shareef Dancer (USA)) 1504^{4} 2376^{2} 2770^{3} (3393) 3607^{14} **>81f<**

Breckland (IRE) **5** b h Trojan Fen-Rose Noir (Floribunda) *12*^{10} *62*^{8} *239*^{3} *332*^{2} *401*^{9} **>56a 40f<**

Brecon **2** b br c High Estate-No Can Tell (USA) (Clev Er Tell (USA)) 1856^{4} 2200^{3} 2467^{4} 2911^{5} 4208^{6} 4327^{3} **>72f<**

Brecongill Lad **3** b g Clantime-Chikala (Pitskelly) 697^{7} 823^{3} 1151^{7} 1380^{3} (1624) 2311^{3} (2973) 4040^{4} 4122^{12} **>84f<**

Breezed Well **9** b h Wolverlife-Precious Baby (African Sky) 738^{11} 1070^{8} 1323^{5} 3020^{3} 3288^{10} *3529*^{13} 3808^{17} 3898^{6} **>44a 57f<**

Bresil (USA) **6** ch h Bering-Clever Bidder (USA) (Bold Bidder (USA)) 738^{22} 1323^{17} 1622^{14} 1854^{14} 2197^{7} (2511) 2713^{4} 3029^{8} 3092^{3} 3936^{12} **>31a 43f<**

Bretton Princess 3 ch f Handsome Sailor-Cutlass Princess (USA) (Cutlass (USA)) *5[5] 54[2] 171[3] 283[4]* 482[14] *515[4] 587[7] 628[6]* 773[7] 1371[10] 1564[6] **>52a 36f<**

Brick Court (IRE) 3 ch f Bluebird (USA)-Palmyra (GER) (Arratos (FR)) 1691[10] 4003[8] 4162[12] **>64f<**

Bridge of Fire (FR) 3 b g Mtoto-Amana River (USA) (Raise A Cup (USA)) 3810[16] 3980[20] 4083[14] **>61f<**

Brief Glimpse (IRE) 3 b or br f Taufan (USA)-Mini Look (FR) (In Fijar (USA)) 1588[3] 1850[9] (2673) 3067[8] 3562[7] 3931[9] **>109df<**

Brief Respite (IRE) 4 b or br g Simply Great (FR)-No Time To Dance (Shareef Dancer (USA)) *67[8] 137[8] 255[9]* **>43da f<**

Brier Creek (USA) 6 b h Blushing Groom (FR)-Savannah Dancer (USA) (Northern Dancer) 923[3] **>112f<**

Brigadore Gold 5 br m Petong-Brigado (Brigadier Gerard) *214[10] (390) 408[8]* 478[10] *835[12]* 1081[7] *1457[8]* 1797[11] *1951[9]* 2191[7] 2390[10] 2821[8] *2961[11]* 3063[10] 3256[5] **>29a 28f<**

Briganoone 2 b g Cyrano de Bergerac-Zareeta (Free State) 684[8] *1212[4] 1454[7]* 2991[7] 3721[15] 4141[14] **>57a 26f<**

Briggs Lad (IRE) 6 ch g Be My Native (USA)-Zestino (Shack (USA)) 556[21] **>15f<**

Brighstone 2 ch c Cadeaux Genereux-High Fountain (High Line) (4155) (4318) **>89+f<**

Bright Diamond 2 b f Never so Bold-Diamond House (Habitat) 1856[7] 3733[16] 4100[4] 4208[7] **>59f<**

Bright Eclipse (USA) 2 br c Sunny's Halo (CAN)-Miss Lantana (USA) (Danzig Connection (USA)) 3994[11] **>34f<**

Brighter Byfaah (IRE) 2 ch c Kefaah (USA)-Bright Landing (Sun Prince) 4172[10] **>50f<**

Bright Heritage (IRE) 2 b c Ela-Mana-Mou-Mother of The Wind (Tumble Wind (USA)) 3280[2] 3683[2] 4029[3] **>90f<**

Bright Paragon (IRE) 6 b or br h Treasure Kay-Shining Bright (USA) (Bold Bidder (USA)) 507[7] 565[5] 726[9] 1071[7] 1483[12] 1738[4] **>38a 48f<**

Bright Water 2 b c Caerleon (USA)-Shining Water (Kalaglow) (4241) **>93f<**

Brilliant 7 ch m Never so Bold-Diamond Hill (High Top) *285[9]* **>28a 67df<**

Brilliant Red 2 b c Royal Academy (USA)-Red Comes Up (USA) (Blushing Groom (FR)) 1134[3] 2408[2] (3155) 3490[3] 3711[5] **>95f<**

Bring on the Choir 3 b f Chief Singer-Primulette (Mummy's Pet) 620[7] 933[9] 1139[7] 1500[5] 1923[9] 2240[8] 3237[8] 3630[7] **>81f<**

Brisas 8 ch h Vaigly Great-Legal Sound (Legal Eagle) *69[8] 165[4] 233[6] (348) 419[6] 590[7]* 753[10] 1043[3] 1721[6] 1996[3] 2398[3] 2821[4] 3116[4] 3252[3] 3467[6] **>51a 44f<**

Britannia Mills 4 gr f Nordico (USA)-May Fox *2[14] 34[4] 120[8] 267[6] 353[5] 379[9]* 430[25] 1854[19] 2280[14] 2719[9] 3101[10] **>37a 41f<**

Broadstairs Beauty (IRE) 5 ch h Dominion Royale-Holy Water (Monseigneur (USA)) 723[2] 994[2] (1193) (2326) 2764[21] 3597[5] 3715[13] 3822[8] 4068[10] *4337[13]* **>78a 81f<**

Broadway Flyer (USA) 4 b c Theatrical-Serena (SAF) (Jan Ekels) 712[2] 1020[3] 1890a[2] 2595[5] 3482a[8] 3914a[6] **>124f<**

Brockton Flame 3 b f Emarati (USA)-Minne Love (Homeric) 674[3] 823[8] 1094[17] (1660) 2239[4] 2507[2] 2659[4] 3964[5] 4068[9] 4215[7] **>71f<**

Brockton Light 3 b f Be My Chief (USA)-Lovers Light (Grundy) 888[7] 1053[11] 1273[4] 1601[5] **>58f<**

Brockville Bairn 2 b g Tina's Pet-Snow Chief 943[8] 1278[10] 1670[16] *3077[7]* 3417[10] *3528[9]* **>40a 40f<**

Broctune Bay 6 b g Midyan (USA)-Sweet Colleen (Connaught) 3927[12] **>72df<**

Broctune Gold 4 b c Superpower-Golden Sunlight (Ile de Bourbon (USA)) (965) (1080) 1297[14] 2913[8] 3256[3] 3504[7] **>49a 52f<**

Brodessa 9 gr g Scallywag-Jeanne du Barry (Dubassoff (USA)) *79[2] 223[4]* (1667) (1921) 2157[2] 2355[9] (3017) (3296) 3741[2] 3971[15] **>66da 74f<**

Brogans Brush 2 ch c Jendali (USA)-Sweet 'n' Sharp (Sharpo) 554[5] *770[4]* 1466[6] 1665[13] *2496[10]* 3018[10] 4290[9] **>34a 45f<**

Bronhallow 2 b g Belmez (USA)-Grey Twig (Godswalk (USA)) 3883[13] **>58f<**

Bronze Maquette (IRE) 5 b m Ahonoora-Working Model (Ile de Bourbon (USA)) 1402[8] **>37a 54f<**

Bronze Runner 11 b or ro h Gunner B-Petingalyn 1285[6] 1854[15] (1974) (2089) 2334[8] 2486[3] 2976[4] 3426[2] *3544[6]* 3710[12] **>35a 56f<**

Brooke Wood 3 b f Risk Me (FR)-Oh My Joy (Grundy) *286[5] 316[12]* 1514[20] *2090[11]* **>7a 10f<**

Brookhead Lady 4 b f Petong-Lewista (Mandrake Major) *511[5] 625[4]* (748) 972[7] 1993[9] 2018[6] 2398[3] *2493[2]* 2784[4] *3073[4]* (3256) 3467[2] 3624[14] 3800[24] **>46a 65f<**

Brooks Masquerade 4 gr f Absalom-Miss Cindy *2630[7] 2960[5]* **>14a 33df<**

Broom Isle 7 b m Damister (USA)-Vynz Girl (Tower Walk) *(412) 530[2]* 879[3] **>73a 60df<**

Brother Barnabas 4 ch g Bustino-As Blessed 539[15] 1291[7] 1533[11] 1944[9] 2478[5] 2676[5] **>51f<**

Brother Roy 2 b c Prince Sabo-Classic Heights (Shirley Heights) 1318[5] **>65f<**

Broughtons Bird (IRE) 4 b f Exhibitioner-Mo Mhuimin (Miner's Lamp) 1092[15] 1381[9] 1509[13] *2960[10]* **>18f<**

Broughtons Champ 3 b g Dowsing (USA)-Knees Up (USA) (Dancing Champ (USA)) 4225[10] **>42f<**

Broughtons Formula 5 b h Night Shift (USA)-Forward Rally (Formidable) 549[17] 763[13] 1144[6] 1502[3] 1757[3] 2289[4] 2530[7] 2792[2] (2845) (3015) 3238[4] 3470[6] 3927[9] 4333[8] **>65a 60f<**

Broughton Singer (IRE) 4 ch f Common Grounds-Unbidden Melody (USA) (Chieftain II) 780[14] 1183[16] 3837[W] 4061[10] **>55f<**

Broughton's Port 5 b g Reesh-Tawnais (Artaius (USA)) 3685[17] 4079[10] 4152[11] **>59da 39f<**

Broughton's Pride (IRE) 4 b f Superpower-French Quarter (Ile de Bourbon (USA)) *35[7]* 568[8] 738[2] 874[2] 988[18] 1368[10] 3302[2] 3657[4] 3808[3] 4043[3] 4138[10] **>36a 62f<**

Broughtons Turmoil 6 b g Petorius-Rustic Stile (Rusticaro (FR)) *(181) 255[5] (341) 501[7]* 873[14] 1070[2] 1830[6] (2108) 2342[5] *2634[7]* (3439) 3706[4] 3943[2] 4041[4] **>68a 72f<**

Brown Carpet 8 b or br h Never so Bold-Geopelia (Raffingora) 586[11] 1659[6] 1974[10] 2486[4] 4205[9] **>51f<**

Brown Eyed Girl 3 ch f Sharpo-Ella Mon Amour (Ela-Mana-Mou) 1549[2] 1701[5] 2319[8] 3218[2] *3514[12]* 3654[11] **>1a 70f<**

Brown Fairy (USA) 7 b m Northern Baby (CAN)-Chepstow Vale (USA) (Key To The Mint (USA)) 798a^{2} (2385a) **>64f<**
Brownlows 3 b c Prince Sabo-Glockenmadel (GER) (Kaiseradler) *384^{9}* 1039^{10} 2189^{4} 2481^{7} **>51a 43f<**
Brumon (IRE) 4 b c Sadler's Wells (USA)-Loveliest (USA) (Tibaldo) 1410^{10} 2154^{4} 2413^{5} 2860^{3} 3217^{4} (3425) 3705^{6} 3971^{7} 4118^{19} **>72f<**
Brunswick Blue (IRE) 7 b h Sarab-Lanata 1694^{11} 1858^{14} 2175^{5} 2439^{10} **>16f<**
Brusque (USA) 11 . g 1036^{7} 3303^{8} **>28a 23f<**
Bruttina 3 b f 4012a^{11} 4253a^{3} **>106f<**
Bruz 4 b c Risk Me (FR)-My Croft (Crofter (USA)) 3313^{9} **>43a 25df<**
Bryan Robson (USA) 4 b c Topsider (USA)-Queen's Visit (Top Command (USA)) 636^{5} 949^{8} 1354^{12} 2288^{11} 2551^{8} **>65f<**
Buckley Boys 4 gr f Grey Desire-Strip Fast (Virginia Boy) *63^{8}* 3344^{11} 3641^{2} 3658^{7} 3987^{P} **>53a 57f<**
Budby 2 ch f Rock City-Lustrous (Golden Act (USA)) 3948^{9} **>69f<**
Budding Annie 2 b f Lord Bud-Gold Paper (FR) (Rheingold) 2801^{5} 3673^{8} **>56f<**
Buddy's Friend (IRE) 7 ch h Jester-Hasta (Skymaster) *12^{6} 94^{3} (169) 212^{2} 269^{4} 373^{6}* 762^{8} 1528^{4} 1742^{7} 1911^{8} **>67a 68f<**
Bud's Bet (IRE) 7 b h Reasonable (FR)-Pearl Creek (Gulf Pearl) *375^{4} 514^{12}* 1449^{5} **>50a 36f<**
Buff 2 b f Persian Heights-Manicure Kit (USA) (J O Tobin (USA)) 2508^{6} 2715^{7} **>26f<**
Buffalo Girl 3 b f Nomination-Beretta (Moorestyle) 3762^{10} **>47f<**
Built for Comfort (IRE) 3 b f Nordico (USA)-Dewan's Niece (USA) (Dewan (USA)) 779^{5} 1015^{2} 1244^{12} 1539^{11} **>69f<**
Bulington (FR) 3 br c Sicyos-Barbra 4300a^{2} **>116f<**
Bullfinch 2 b c Anshan-Lambay (Lorenzaccio) (3441) 3746^{6} 4042^{2} 4256^{3} **>93?f<**
Bullpen Belle 2 b f Relief Pitcher-Hopeful Waters (Forlorn River) 4148^{9} 4247^{2} **>74f<**
Bulsara 3 b c Dowsing (USA)-Taiga (Northfields (USA)) 431^{11} *591^{11}* (990) 1358^{7} 1669^{2} (2375) 2822^{5} 3808^{9} 3977^{10} **>1a 67f<**
Bumblefoot (IRE) 2 b f Cyrano de Bergerac-La Vosgienne (Ashmore (FR)) 2951^{4} *(3243)* 3540^{3} *4127^{2}* 4263^{12} **>69a 56f<**
Bunker (IRE) 3 b c Scenic-Diamond Lake (Kings Lake (USA)) (2129) (2480) 2662^{4} 2851^{4} 3635^{11} 3899^{9} **>64f<**
Bunting 3 br f Shaadi (USA)-Warm Welcome (General Assembly (USA)) (557) 1067^{2} 1237a^{3} 1587^{10} **>96f<**
Bunty Boo 6 b m Noalto-Klairove (Averof) 719^{7} 921^{11} 1393a^{7} 1480^{6} (2285) 2443^{8} 3198a^{6} (3689a) 4012a^{9} 4160^{11} (4286) **>109f<**
Burden Of Proof (IRE) 3 b c Fairy King (USA)-Belle Passe (Be My Guest (USA)) 803a^{3} 1234a^{4} 3787a^{2} **>114f<**
Bures (IRE) 4 b c Bold Arrangement-Grid (FR) (Grundy) *186^{9} 259^{8} 303^{4} 370^{4}* 1552^{7} **>57a 63df<**
Burj 2 b c Aragon-Aspark (Sparkler) 2940^{8} 3337^{7} 3604^{15} 3969^{13} 4144^{18} **>67f<**
Burning (USA) 3 b c Bering-Larnica (USA) (Alydar (USA)) (663) 1127^{3} 1872^{6} 2691^{4} 3162^{20} 3864^{8} 4031^{10} 4201^{12} **>100f<**
Burnt Offering 2 b c Old Vic-Burnt Amber (Balidar) 3494^{9} 3683^{4} **>67f<**
Burnt Sienna (IRE) 3 b f Don't Forget Me-Ribot Ann (Kampala) 635^{21} 1072^{9} 1125^{10} 1426^{12} 1962^{8} 2174^{8} 2486^{9} 2661^{6} (2789) 3079^{3} 4225^{3} **>63f<**
Burntwood Melody 4 gr c Merdon Melody-Marwick (Roan Rocket) 556^{20} **>38a 8f<**
Burooj 5 br h Danzig (USA)-Princess Sucree (USA) (Roberto (USA)) (918) 1357^{3} (1610) 1926^{2} (2575) 3088^{4} (3498) 3811^{3} 4074^{3} **>116f<**
Bursul Lady 2 b f Be My Chief (USA)-Neverdown (Never so Bold) 3474^{5} **>14f<**
Bury the Hatchet 3 b g Be My Chief (USA)-Royal Agreement (USA) (Vaguely Noble) 648^{8} **>65f<**
Bushehr (IRE) 3 b c Persian Bold-Shejrah (USA) (Northjet (USA)) 1092^{8} 1412^{3} (1791) 2065^{4} 2359^{2} 2835^{3} 3292^{2} 3724^{17} **>75f<**
Buster 7 br g Macmillion-Valsette (Anfield) 1344^{8} 3092^{11} 3402^{12} **>35a 41f<**
Bustle'em (IRE) 4 b f Burslem-Speedy Action (Horage) *399^{8}* **>60df<**
Busy Banana 3 b c Insan (USA)-Linda's Design (Persian Bold) 427^{10} *(566)* (648) 736^{2} (785) **>84a 92f<**
Busy Flight 2 br c Pharly (FR)-Bustling Nelly (Bustino) 3592^{8} 3709^{2} 4159^{2} **>99f<**
Butterwick Belle (IRE) 2 b f Distinctly North (USA)-Forest Berries (IRE) (Thatching) 671^{2} 819^{3} 1293^{4} **>66f<**
By Arrangement (IRE) 6 b m Bold Arrangement-Eulalie (Queen's Hussar) 582^{3} 741^{4} 1058^{15} 1535^{6} 3361^{3} **>53f<**
By A Whisker 2 ch c Keen-Razor Blade 3536^{7} 3779^{10} 3994^{12} **>60f<**
By The Bay 3 b f Shareef Dancer (USA)-Beryl's Jewel 915^{4} 1240^{7} 1549^{3} 2776^{3} 2968^{3} 3475^{7} 3664^{7} 3897^{15} **>66df<**

C

Caballo (GER) 4 br c Konigsstuhl (GER)-Carmelita (GER) (Surumu (GER)) 3698a^{2} 3914a^{8} (4254a) **>119f<**
Cabcharge Blue 3 b f Midyan (USA)-Mashobra (Vision (USA)) 504^{8} 674^{8} 907^{7} 1639^{12} **>40a 76f<**
Cabcharge Striker 2 b c Rambo Dancer (CAN)-Ivory Bride (Domynsky) (480) 871^{3} 993^{3} 1267^{6} (1634) 1871^{5} 2059^{2} (2387a) **>87?tf<**
Caddican (IRE) 3 ch f Ballad Rock-Sweetsider (USA) (Topsider (USA)) 3725^{6} 3974^{17} 4196^{15} **>55f<**
Caddy's First 3 b c Petong-Love Scene (Carwhite) *1088^{6}* 1255^{3} 1456^{5} *1630^{3}* 1797^{12} 2137^{7} *(2587) 2963^{2}* 3390^{4} *3952^{11}* **>64a 56f<**
Cadeaux Premiere 4 b c Cadeaux Genereux-Clare Island (Connaught) 1161^{10} **>32df<**
Cadeaux Tryst 3 b c Cadeaux Genereux-Trystero (Shareef Dancer (USA)) 1839^{16} 2205^{2} (2369) 2948^{12} 3602^{2} 3813^{6} 4074^{4} **>112f<**
Ca'd'oro 2 ch c Cadeaux Genereux-Palace Street (USA) (Secreto (USA)) 825^{6} 1184^{11} **>70f<**
Caerle Lad (IRE) 4 b c Caerleon (USA)-Miss Zadig 764^{20} 853^{6} 1141^{6} 1367^{8} 1745^{2} 1908^{6} 3501^{9} 3679^{9} 3987^{10} 4284^{P} **>57f<**
Caerphilly (IRE) 3 b f Caerleon (USA)-Hooked Bid (CAN) (Spectacular Bid (USA)) 4031^{14} **>89f<**
Cafe Glace 3 b f Beldale Flutter (USA)-Little White Star

1128^{13} 1337^{9} **>44f<**
Cafe Solo 4 b or br f Nomination-Piney Lake 526^{19} 838^{12} 1079^{3} 1250^{16} 1441^{10} 1599^{5} 1809^{12} 2088^{3} (2191) 2358^{7} 2461^{5} 2477^{7} 2698^{4} 2853^{4} 3098^{9} 3457^{14} 3506^{6} **>44f<**
Caherass Court (IRE) 4 b f Taufan (USA)-Grass Court (USA) (Herbager) *65^{11} 129^{13} 306^{9} 315^{12} 2076^{12} 2141^{9} 2493^{8} 3074^{10}* **>24a 50f<**
Cahita 3 b f Northern State (USA)-Two Stroke (Malicious) 1473^{12} 2049^{8} **>11f<**
Ca Ira (IRE) 4 b f Dancing Dissident (USA)-Silver Mantle (Bustino) 3855^{15} **>30f<**
Caisson 3 b f Shaadi (USA)-Gibraltar Heights (High Top) 1264^{5} 1674^{10} **>73f<**
Cajun Cadet 4 b c Cadeaux Genereux-Petty Purse (Petingo) 1707a^{2} 3484a^{2} **>100f<**
Calcando 3 b f Teenoso (USA)-Musical Princess (Cavo Doro) 2331^{9} 4072^{17}
Calder King 4 ch c Rakaposhi King-Name the Game (Fair Season) *373^{8}* 676^{11} 749^{15} 1037^{3} 1250^{7} 1432^{7} 1506^{3} 1875^{6} *2073^{2}* 2375^{7} *3240^{4} 3511^{5}* 3703^{11} 3802^{2} 4044^{5} *4272^{2}* 4292^{8} **>69a 67f<**
Caleman 6 b h Daring March-Lillemor (Connaught) 665^{11} 960^{8} 1261^{7} 2321^{5} 2669^{3} 3113^{P} 3348^{3} **>93f<**
Calgary Girl 3 ch f Weld-Calgary 4164^{11} **>38f<**
Calgary Redeye 8 gr h Kalaglow-River Call (FR) 3884^{19}
Calisar 5 br h Mummy's Game-Maycrest (Imperial Fling (USA)) *73^{5} 155^{7}* (672) 874^{8} 909^{6} 1285^{9} 1548^{5} *1762^{4}* 1974^{12} **>45a 48f<**
Callaloo 2 b c Mtoto-Catawba (Mill Reef (USA)) 3472^{3} 3683^{6} 4058^{9} **>68f<**
Calling Collect (USA) 6 b m 665^{14} (872) **>104f<**
Calling Jamaica 3 b f Elmaamul (USA)-Tolstoya (Northfields (USA)) 654^{8} **>52f<**
Calling (USA) 4 ch c Phone Trick (USA)-Sweet Singer (USA) (Sing Sing) 972^{10} 1323^{11} 1516^{12} 1714^{8} 1994^{5} 2112^{5} *2963^{6}* **>19a 40f<**
Call Me Albi (IRE) 4 ch g Glenstal (USA)-Albeni *260^{10} 370^{3} 469^{4} 1319^{2}* 1427^{10} 2078^{8} 2486^{2} 2676^{2} 3884^{11} **>50a 65f<**
Call Me Blue 5 gr h Kalaglow-Woodfold (Saritamer (USA)) *235^{8} 329^{5} (361) 422^{6}* **>61a 64f<**
Call Me Flash 3 ch g Presidium-Relkisha (Relkino) 747^{10} 1353^{10} *1761^{3}* **>25a 51f<**
Call Me I'm Blue (IRE) 5 b h Reasonable (FR)-Bluebutton (Blue Cashmere) 441^{11} 571^{11} 700^{6} 1100^{9} 1489^{6} 1765^{13} 3551^{4} 3815^{4} 4033^{17} 4197^{9} 4281^{7} **>91f<**
Call Me Jendie 2 b f Jendali (USA)-Lady Carol (Lord Gayle (USA)) 4112^{7} 4235^{5}
Callonescy (IRE) 3 b c Royal Academy (USA)-Take Your Mark (USA) (Round Table (USA)) *256^{7} 282^{2} 372^{8}* 1498^{19} *3734^{6}* **>61a 4f<**
Call Tophorse 3 b g Today and Tomorrow-Sum Star (Comedy Star (USA)) *300^{4} 1761^{8}* 1971^{12} **>38a f<**
Call to the Bar (IRE) 6 b h Kafu-Papun (USA) (Mount Hagen (FR)) 926^{8} 1080^{5} 1827^{8} 2234^{7} 2753^{9} 3365^{8} **>52a 77f<**
Caltha 3 b f Dunbeath (USA)-Rillandel (Wolver Hollow) 786^{9} 1083^{7} 1412^{4} *1569^{13}* 1962^{4} 2425^{4} (2540) 2733^{9} (2927) 3310^{2} 3726^{10} **>53f<**
Calypso Run 2 ch f Lycius (USA)-Sea Venture (FR) 3352^{6} **>45f<**
Camden's Ransom (USA) 8 b h Hostage (USA)-Camden Court (USA) (Inverness Drive (USA)) *27^{2} 76^{5} 186^{10} (271) 312^{4} (406) 445^{8} 1091^{4}* 1367^{11} 4163^{17} *4298^{10}* **>62a 53f<**
Cameron Highland (IRE) 4 b c Night Shift (USA)-Vestal Flame (Habitat) 439^{8} 870^{19} 1409^{9} *1953^{11}* (2010) 2345^{8} 3545^{14} 3629^{8} **>41a 85f<**
Camionneur (IRE) 2 b g Cyrano de Bergerac-Fact of Time (Known Fact (USA)) 1356^{4} 1670^{7} 1877^{4} 2128^{4} 2498^{5} 2914^{4} 3460^{8} 3803^{9} 4097^{2} 4231^{5} 4317^{4} **>59f<**
Campaign 0 S 4315^{5} **>96?f<**
Campaspe 3 b f Dominion-Lady River (FR) (Sir Gaylord) *1330^{8} 1761^{4} 2141^{7}* 2784^{11} **>22a 28f<**
Camp Follower 2 b c Warrshan (USA)-Housemaid (Habitat) (2725a) **>61f<**
Canary Blue (IRE) 4 b f Bluebird (USA)-Norfolk Bonnet (Morston (FR)) *2495^{10} 2626^{7}* **>5a 45f<**
Canary Falcon 4 ch c Polish Precedent (USA)-Pumpona (USA) (Sharpen Up) *8^{5} 127^{5} (199) 344^{4}* 546^{6} 728^{3} 961^{7} 1792^{5} 3874^{12} 4157^{16} 4268^{4} **>64a 64f<**
Can Can Charlie 5 gr h Vaigly Great-Norton Princess (Wolver Hollow) *122^{3} 158^{2} 266^{5} (3240) 3511^{9}* 3872^{6} **>67a 53f<**
Candle Smile (USA) 3 b c Pleasant Colony (USA)-Silent Turn (USA) (Silent Cal (USA)) 691^{4} 1099^{3} **>94f<**
Candle Smoke (USA) 2 b br c Woodman (USA)-Light the Lights (FR) (Shirley Heights) 4256^{5} **>58f<**
Candrika 0 1887a^{2}
Candy Dancer 2 ch c Opening Run (USA)-Poly Negative 3018^{7} 3253^{5} 3353^{9} **>36f<**
Candy's Delight 2 b f Dunbeath (USA)-Simply Candy (IRE) (Simply Great (FR)) 3306^{6} 3643^{6} 3850^{9} 4231^{8} **>55f<**
Canlubang 2 ch f Mujtahid (USA)-Snug (USA) (Lyphard (USA)) 819^{9} *1031^{6}* 1466^{8} **>25a 26f<**
Cannizaro (IRE) 3 b f Gallic League-Paradise Regained (North Stoke) *(316)* 2532^{8} 2776^{7} 3501^{5} **>64a 43f<**
Canny Lad 5 b h Green Ruby (USA)-Young Whip (Bold Owl) 1297^{8} 1501^{5} *1880^{9}* 2254^{9} 2620^{7} 2755^{4} 2972^{4} 3305^{8} 3431^{7} **>39a 55f<**
Canon Can (USA) 2 ch c Green Dancer (USA)-Lady Argyle (USA) (Don B (USA)) 3437^{2} 3683^{5} 4046^{8} **>68f<**
Canons Park 2 ch c Keen-Low Line (High Line) 1752^{3} (2005) 2365^{5} 3560^{7} **>75f<**
Canovas Heart 6 b g Balidar-Worthy Venture (Northfields (USA)) (507) 583^{4} 856^{2} 1304^{4} *(1566) 2295^{2}* 3677^{4} 3822^{5} **>59a 63f<**
Can She Can Can 3 b f Sulaafah (USA)-Dominance (Dominion) 1725^{6} 2126^{4} 2305^{2} 2650^{2} 2860^{9} 3017^{3} 3092^{7} 3303^{3} 3724^{2} **>56f<**
Cante Chico 3 b c Reference Point-Flamenco Wave (USA) (Desert Wine (USA)) 1173^{10} 1526^{6} 1866^{3} 4189^{9} **>68f<**
Canton Venture 3 ch c Arctic Tern (USA)-Ski Michaela (USA) (Devil's Bag (USA)) 1167^{8} 1317^{4} 1691^{15} *(2636)* 2969^{5} *3245^{9} (3737)* 3970^{7} *4126^{11}* **>73a 62f<**
Can't Say (IRE) 3 br c Gallic League-Mixed Feelings (Junius (USA)) 648^{18} 971^{10} 1290^{14} 1353^{6} 1516^{9} 1963^{8} 2049^{6} 2642^{7} 3424^{11} **>55f<**
Cap And Gown (IRE) 3 ch f Royal Academy (USA)-Wrapping (Kris) 547^{3} (1053) 1500^{6} 2152^{4} 2679^{2} 3031^{4}

3630^{12} **>86f<**
Cape Colony 3 b g Dominion-Valiancy (Grundy) *3073^{6}* 3431^{4} 3638^{3} 4060^{5} **>58a 67f<**
Cape Pigeon (USA) 10 ch h Storm Bird (CAN)-Someway Somehow (USA) (What Luck (USA)) 848^{4} (1509) 1830^{4} (2134) **>74f<**
Capias (USA) 4 b c Alleged (USA)-Smooth Bore (USA) (His Majesty (USA)) (1408) (1780) 2219a^{2} 4176a^{6} 4323^{2} **>114f<**
Capilano Princess 2 b f Tragic Role (USA)-Lady Capilano (Nebbiolo) 480^{4} *1212^{3} 1454^{6} 2958^{4}* 4148^{3} (4321) **>61a 68f<**
Cap Juluca (IRE) 3 b c Mtoto-Tabyan (USA) (Topsider (USA)) 715^{5} (2319) (2593) (3066) (3188) (3945) **>122+f<**
Capo Bay (IRE) 2 b c Salt Dome (USA)-Trojan Honey (Trojan Fen) 533^{15} *604^{7}* **>11f<**
Capolago (IRE) 8 b h Horage-Panthere Rouge (4347a) **>98f<**
Capstone 2 b f Shirley Heights-Doumayna (Kouban (FR)) 4155^{7} 4241^{9} **>55f<**
Captain Carat 4 gr g Handsome Sailor-Gem of Gold (Jellaby) 434^{22} 535^{23} 646^{8} 812^{13} (949) 1354^{7} 1599^{10} 2096^{7} 2330^{2} 2652^{6} 3121^{3} 3275^{2} 3418^{4} 3597^{4} 3715^{6} 3783^{8} 3878^{8} 4280^{16} **>62a 70f<**
Captain Haddock (FR) 4 b c Comrade in Arms-Lorelei Lee (FR) (Rose Laurel) 3036a^{3} **>115f<**
Captain Horatius (IRE) 6 b h Taufan (USA)-One Last Glimpse (Relko) (631) 1392a^{2} 2476^{2} 3381^{2} 3716^{2} 4088a^{8} **>124f<**
Captain Marmalade 6 ch g Myjinski (USA)-Lady Seville (Orange Bay) *13^{5} 155^{4} 203^{2} 249^{4} 330^{3} 355^{2} 406^{4} 415^{5} 445^{7}* 526^{2} 586^{5} (738) 762^{16} *1078^{2}* 1484^{7} 1745^{8} *2076^{4}* 2682^{7} 2946^{5} *3082^{10}* 3871^{5} *3952^{6} 4298^{9}* **>58a 56f<**
Captain Scarlet (IRE) 4 b c Red Sunset-Shangara (Credo) 1594^{5} **>60a 86f<**
Captain's Day 3 ch c Ballacashtal (CAN)-Seymour Ann (Krayyan) 536^{7} 829^{7} 1069^{7} 1244^{2} 1941^{3} 2240^{3} 2669^{5} 3214^{7} 3674^{5} 3943^{20} **>85df<**
Captain Sinbad 3 b g Welsh Captain-Lane Patrol (Hopton Lane) *149^{7} 197^{8} 232^{8}* 3259^{9} 3424^{12} **>28a 14f<**
Captain Starlight (IRE) 4 b g Vision (USA)-Belitis (Tudor Melody) 741^{6} 1254^{17} 1513^{12} 2806^{6} **>52f<**
Capture The Moment 2 b f Keen-Shaieef (IRE) (Shareef Dancer (USA)) 669^{4} 910^{2} 1278^{2} (1481) 1893^{12} 2489^{4} 3049^{3} 3281^{6} 4321^{9} **>65df<**
Caramba 3 b f Belmez (USA)-Melodrama 1101^{2} 1712a^{7} (2349) (2763) 3694a^{10} **>117+f<**
Cara Rafaela (USA) 2 gr f Quiet American (USA)-Oil Fable (USA) 4302a^{2} **>109tf<**
Carburton 2 b c Rock City-Arminda (Blakeney) 3625^{3} (3967) (4195) **>89f<**
Care And Comfort 3 ch f Most Welcome-Whipp's Cross (Kris) 451^{6} 585^{12} 779^{8} 1124^{4} 1402^{10} 1735^{6} (2102) 2357^{4} *2588^{13}* 2755^{7} 4170^{8} 4261^{13} **>61f<**
Careful (IRE) 2 gr f Distinctly North (USA)-Caring 2487^{9} 2791^{8} 2964^{8} 3803^{4} 4025^{4} 4144^{7} **>60f<**
Carfax 10 ch h Tachypous-Montana Moss (Levmoss) *1210^{3} 1319^{11}* **>37a 46f<**
Cariad Ffol 3 b f Jupiter Island-Tearful Reunion (Pas de Seul) *2494^{7}*
Caribbean Dancer 2 b f Shareef Dancer (USA)-Deposit (Thatch (USA)) 3983^{8} 4169^{4} **>56f<**
Caribbean Expresso (IRE) 2 b f Soviet Lad (USA)-She Is The Boss (Skyliner) 1913^{8}
Caribbean Quest 2 b f Rainbow Quest (USA)-Jammaayil (IRE) (Lomond (USA)) (3532) 4013a^{11} **>87+f<**
Caribbean Surfer (USA) 6 b h Summing (USA)-Caribbean Surfing (USA) (Northjet (USA)) 3392^{6} 3716^{7} 4072^{15} 4288^{13} **>51f<**
Caricature (IRE) 2 b g Cyrano de Bergerac-That's Easy (Swing Easy (USA)) 690^{2} 1011^{3} 1298^{4} 2940^{2} 3213^{6} 3404^{3} (3558) **>86f<**
Carling (FR) 3 b f Garde Royale-Corraleja (FR) (Carvin (FR)) 807a^{3} 1116a^{2} (1712a) 3199a^{9} (3694a) 4014a^{9} **>115f<**
Carlito Brigante 3 b c Robellino (USA)-Norpella (Northfields (USA)) 616^{8} 777^{9} 955^{4} 1415^{10} 1605^{4} 1825^{3} 2333^{5} (2678) (2856) 3189^{13} 3611^{22} 3802^{14} 3935^{9} 4038^{2} **>73f<**
Carlowitz (USA) 7 b h Danzig (USA)-Aunt Carol (USA) (Big Spruce (USA)) *(58) 97^{5} 122^{0}* **>61da 31df<**
Carmarthen Bay 2 ch c Prionsaa-Pattie's Grey (Valiyar) 1829^{11} 4146^{7} 4244^{3} **>56f<**
Carmentalia 2 b f Formidable (USA)-Carmen's Joy (Chief Singer) 1697^{3} *(2381)* (3168) 3345^{5} 3701^{4} 3928^{4} 4139^{5} **>73a 84f<**
Carmosa (USA) 2 ch f Blushing John (USA)-Bobbinette (Whitstead) 2351^{6} 4148^{14} **>76f<**
Carnbrea Belle (IRE) 3 ch f Kefaah (USA)-Bright Landing (Sun Prince) 547^{11} 745^{2} 908^{5} 1289^{3} 1452^{2} (1696) (1998) 2296^{2} (2550) (2603) (2695) 2907^{5} 3140^{4} 3627^{5} **>78f<**
Carnegie Blue 4 b f Hallgate-Penumbra (Wolver Hollow) 2316^{10} *2631^{11}* 2865^{5}
Carnegie (IRE) 4 b c Sadler's Wells (USA)-Detroit (FR) (Riverman (USA)) 1609^{5} (2213a) 2595^{6} (3695a) 4014a^{6} 4307a^{3} **>130f<**
Carol Again 3 b f Kind of Hush-Lady Carol (Lord Gayle (USA)) 904^{5} 1414^{9} 1843^{10} 2502^{14} 3980^{25} **>24f<**
Carol's Dream (USA) 3 ch c Risen Star (USA)-Merle Halton (USA) (Rattle Dancer) 613^{3} 853^{5} 1038^{7} 2279^{2} 2333^{2} 2883^{2} 3227^{4} **>83f<**
Caromandoo (IRE) 7 b g Simply Great (FR)-Tanimara (Sassafras (FR)) 1799^{12} 2359^{9}
Carondra 3 ch f Good Times (ITY)-Romany Home (Gabitat) 477^{7} 2931^{7} **>4f<**
Carpathian 4 b c Danzig (USA)-Diminuendo (USA) (Diesis) *76^{4} (178)* (1014) 2138^{6} *(2379)* 2687^{2} (2829) 2981^{2} 3156^{8} *(4126)* **>73a 70f<**
Carranita (IRE) 5 b m Anita's Prince-Take More (GER) (Frontal) 1284^{4} 1618^{2} 2409^{4} 3602^{7} (3660) 3834^{11} 4160^{9} (4324) **>110f<**
Carrolls Marc (IRE) 7 b h Horage-Rare Find (Rarity) *45^{3} 131^{4} 153^{5}* **>55a 57f<**
Carte Blanche 4 b f Cadeaux Genereux-Granny's Bank (Music Boy) *220^{3} (347) 2407^{6}* 2602^{6} 2707^{9} *(2922) 3075^{8} 3240^{6}* **>69a 53f<**
Carwyn's Choice 2 b f Then Again-Over My Head (Bay Express) 3652^{9} 3765^{16} 3983^{17} 4045^{17} **>31f<**
Cascadia (IRE) 2 br f Caerleon (USA)-Flood (USA) (Riverman (USA)) 852^{3} **>72f<**
Cashmere Lady 3 b f Hubbly Bubbly (USA)-Choir (High Top) 3725^{2} 3974^{3} **>74f<**
Cashmirie 3 b f Domynsky-Betrothed (Aglojo) 1270^{W}

1956^{2} 2327^{2} 2396^{5} 2676^{4} (2901) 3259^{4} **>60f<**
Cashtal Lace 2 ch f Ballacashtal (CAN)-Chantilly Lace (FR) (Carwhite) 970^{6} 1336^{8}
Casino Chip 2 br c Daring March-Important Guest (Be My Guest (USA)) 4222^{9}
Cask 3 br f Be My Chief (USA)-Premiere Cuvee (Formidable) (547) 620^{3} 868^{4} (1923) 2561a^{6} 3007^{2} **>109f<**
Casnic (IRE) 2 b f Petorius-Romfaea (USA) (Alleged (USA)) *3738^{12}*
Casper's Risk 3 ch c Risk Me (FR)-Trip the Daisey (Touching Wood (USA)) 437^{12} 482^{7} 524^{12} *591^{3}* 890^{2} **>60a 55f<**
Caspian Gold 4 ch g Clantime-Parijoun (Manado) 611^{13} 1148^{13} **>70da 29f<**
Cassimere 3 ch f Clantime-Poshteen 4055^{5} 4266^{6} **>42f<**
Cast A Fly (IRE) 2 b f Cyrano de Bergerac-Leaping Salmon (Salmon Leap (USA)) 3539^{9}
Castan (IRE) 2 b c Persian Bold-Erzsi (Caerleon (USA)) 940^{4} 1223^{2} 1715^{8} 2435^{3} 4206^{12} 4327^{9} **>67f<**
Castel Rosselo 5 br h Rousillon (USA)-On The House (FR) (Be My Guest (USA)) *365^{2}* 439^{11} 665^{4} 927^{3} 1299^{3} 1626^{10} **>88a 90f<**
Castle Courageous 8 b g Castle Keep-Peteona 735^{4} 958^{4} 1171^{5} 2119^{6} 4183a^{8} **>113df<**
Castle Governor 2 b g Governor General-Sorcha (IRE) (Shernazar) *3509^{12}* 3647^{6} 3975^{10} **>21a 54f<**
Castlerea Lad 6 b h Efisio-Halo (Godswalk (USA)) (434) 535^{20} 611^{6} (838) 949^{5} (1241) 1648^{5} 1895^{6} 2096^{9} 2764^{W} 2935^{6} 3145^{11} 3342^{11} **>91f<**
Castle Secret 9 b h Castle Keep-Baffle (Petingo) *45^{6}* *234^{2}* *4126^{10}* **>58a 67df<**
Castletown Count 3 b g Then Again-Pepeke (Mummy's Pet) 1083^{10} 1191^{9} 1285^{12} 1596^{14} 2544^{7} 2662^{7} **>50f<**
Castoret 9 b h Jalmood (USA)-Blaskette 1659^{4} *2145^{8}* **>51a 83f<**
Casual Water (IRE) 4 b g Simply Great (FR)-Top Nurse (High Top) 1513^{5} (1622) (2109) (2248) 3238^{2} 3406^{2} (3957) 4201^{3} **>84f<**
Catawampus 4 ch c Beveled (USA)-Second Flower (Indian Ruler (USA)) 817^{17} 1290^{17} **>28f<**
Catch A Glimpse (USA) 2 ch f Gulch (USA)-Spring to Light (USA) 3197a^{3} 3692a^{11} **>96f<**
Catch The Lights 2 b f Deploy-Dream Chaser (Record Token) 4161^{6} **>75f<**
Catch the Pigeon 6 b m Wonderful Surprise-Cheeky Pigeon (Brave Invader (USA)) 2331^{7} 2520^{4} 2825^{4} 3297^{6} **>56f<**
Catempo (IRE) 5 b h Cataldi-Raise The Tempo (Relkino) 485^{8} 584^{11} 1048^{12} **>46f<**
Catercap (IRE) 3 b c Royal Academy (USA)-Catos Ridge (USA) (Cox's Ridge (USA)) 670^{8} (916) 2794^{2} (3115) 3611^{21} 3926^{12} **>80f<**
Catiche 3 b f Shavian-Catalpa 747^{7} **>47f<**
Cats Bottom 3 ch f Primo Dominie-Purple Fan (Dalsaan) 681^{4} 850^{4} 985^{6} 1487^{12} 1624^{4} 1778^{2} 2108^{9} 2776^{5} 3126^{4} 3372^{6} 3750^{14} **>71f<**
Catumbella (USA) 2 ch f Diesis-Benguela (USA) (Little Current (USA)) 3532^{3} **>75+f<**
Catwalk Girl 2 b f Skyliner-Pokey's Pet (Uncle Pokey) 1177^{5} 1466^{2} 1665^{3} 1943^{2} (2516) *2924^{11}* **>55f<**
Causley 10 br g Swing Easy (USA)-Four Lawns 3426^{13} 4054^{11} 4157^{14} 4209^{17} **>67a 34f<**
Cavalier Royal Gem 3 b f Cavalier Servente-Springfield Match (Royal Match) 1866^{5}
Cavatina 5 br m Chief Singer-Pennycuick 1679^{15} 2088^{15} 3534^{11} 3624^{20} **>55f<**
Caveat Emptor (IRE) 2 b c Distinctly North (USA)-Ellebanna (Tina's Pet) 561^{8} 725^{6} 1272^{2} 1590^{9} 1810^{7} *3528^{15}* 3856^{11} **>44f<**
Cavendish Rose 4 ch f Music Boy-Afef John (Monseigneur (USA)) 1931^{4} **>48f<**
Cavers Yangous 4 b g Daring March-Rapid Lady (Rapid River) 491^{6} 1433^{3} (1648) *1882^{2}* 1994^{2} 2130^{2} 2330^{8} 2461^{6} 2797^{11} 3411^{14} **>74a 81f<**
Cavil 3 b c Reprimand-Lagta (Kris) 1927^{5} 2438^{5} 2883^{3} 3182^{2} 3605^{20} 3810^{12} 4061^{16} **>75f<**
Cavina 5 b m Ardross-Royal Yacht (USA) (Riverman (USA)) 1036^{6} 1328^{13} *(1784)* 3676^{15} **>65a 61f<**
Cawdor Lady 2 ch f Clantime-Moon Risk (Risk Me (FR)) 1821^{2} 2023^{6} *2629^{8}* 2869^{4} 2965^{8} **>4a 60f<**
Caxton Star 2 ch c Soviet Star (USA)-Fiesta Fun (Welsh Pageant) (3530) **>81+f<**
Cayman Kai (IRE) 2 ch c Imperial Frontier (USA)-Safiya (USA) (Riverman (USA)) (1163) 1384^{2} 1584^{3} 1868^{2} 2243^{4} 2740^{2} (3610) 4084^{2} **>100f<**
Cayumanque (CHI) 6 br h El Morgon (USA)-Recoleta (CHI) (Sun Sun) 1363^{7} **>92f<**
Cd Super Targeting (IRE) 2 ch f Polish Patriot (USA)-Hazy Bird (Ballymore) 716^{6} **>50f<**
Cebwob 2 br f Rock City-Island Ruler (Ile de Bourbon (USA)) 3450^{3} (3806) 4211^{3} **>85f<**
Cedar Dancer 3 b f Rambo Dancer (CAN)-Nonasalome (Absalom) 580^{3} 733^{8} 1016^{9} 1290^{15} 1445^{8} 2054^{2} 2361^{5} 2712^{6} 3177^{9} **>39a 49f<**
Cedar Girl 3 b f Then Again-Classic Times (Dominion) 1012^{4} 1199^{7} 1429^{8} 2137^{4} 2318^{12} 3139^{13} **>36a 51f<**
Cedez le Passage (FR) 4 b c Warning-Microcosme (Golden Fleece (USA)) *106^{2}* 440^{8} 631^{5} 1005a^{4} 1610^{5} 1853^{16} 2457^{11} 2598^{8} 3374^{9} 4017a^{3} **>95a 106f<**
Cee-Jay-Ay 8 gr h Free State-Raffinrula (Raffingora) *365^{6}* 433^{8} 505^{7} 642^{6} 785^{3} 1021^{7} 1250^{10} 1560^{6} 1969^{4} 2061^{4} 2390^{5} *2634^{5}* 2797^{4} 2952^{3} 3222^{13} 3607^{8} 3703^{4} 3802^{18} 4053^{2} 4116^{14} **>62a 72f<**
Ceilidh Dancer 4 ch f Scottish Reel-Turtle Dove 3178^{10} 3438^{13} **>4f<**
Ceilidh (IRE) 2 b g Classic Music (USA)-Pourboire (Star Appeal) 1841^{11} 1943^{7} 2155^{3} 2516^{8} **>42f<**
Ceilidh Star (IRE) 2 b f Soviet Star (USA)-Highland Ball (Bold Lad (IRE)) 3339^{12} 3865^{21} 4063^{5} **>75f<**
Ceirseach (IRE) 2 br f Don't Forget Me-Beparajojo 3692a^{7} 4091a^{3} 4174a^{3} **>93f<**
Celandine 2 b f Warning-Silly Bold (Rousillon (USA)) 2572^{3} 2876^{3} (3848) 4153^{4} **>83f<**
Celcius 11 b h Ile de Bourbon (USA)-Cistus (Sun Prince) 2268^{4} **>36f<**
Celebration Cake (IRE) 3 b g Mister Majestic-My Louise (Manado) 966^{7} (1423) 1465^{3} 1904^{3} 2479^{3} 2928^{6} 3719^{11} 3935^{14} **>67f<**
Celeric 3 b c Mtoto-Hot Spice (Hotfoot) (974) (1289) 1872^{11} (2445) 3071^{2} (3445) 3927^{3} **>99f<**
Celestial Choir 5 b m Celestial Storm (USA)-Choir (High Top) *364^{4}* 439^{13} 558^{7} 724^{4} 927^{4} 1179^{8} 1468^{3} 1617^{7}

2222^{8} 2477^{4} 2707^{8} 3113^{3} (3276) 3419^{2} 3607^{4} 3703^{10} 3945^{5} 4116^{16} 4267^{9} **>78a 94f<**

Celestial Dollar 4 b g Celestial Storm (USA)-Pennies to Pounds (Ile de Bourbon (USA)) 2082^{5} 2553^{14} 2790^{12} 3402^{8} *3737^{11}* **>13a 72f<**

Celestial Faith 4 b f Celestial Storm (USA)-All Gold Rose (Rheingold) *21^{4} 96^{6} 158^{6} 201^{8}* **>35a f<**

Celestial Fire 3 gr c Celestial Storm (USA)-Fiery Gal (CAN) (Explodent (USA)) 1691^{13} 2532^{12} **>54f<**

Celestial Key (USA) 5 br h Star de Naskra (USA)-Casa Key (USA) (Cormorant (USA)) 922^{10} 1100^{5} (1179) 1299^{4} (1617) (1728) 2369^{7} 2436^{8} 2703^{14} 2948^{3} 3188^{7} 3358^{6} 3608^{6} 3813^{19} 3945^{32} (4265) **>111f<**

Celestial Sister 2 ch f Brotherly (USA)-Lunaria (USA) (Twist The Axe (USA)) 3346^{5} 3536^{11}

Celestial Waters 3 b f Monsanto (FR)-Hopeful Waters (Forlorn River) 4054^{17} **>10f<**

Celestial Way (USA) 4 ch c Diesis-Stellaria (USA) (Roberto (USA)) 162a^{3}

Celladonia (IRE) 3 b c Green Desert-Gayle Gal (Lord Gayle) 1234a^{8} **>109f<**

Celtic Arms (FR) 4 b c Comrade in Arms-Amour Celtique (Northfields (USA)) 4307a^{10} **>115f<**

Celtic Ceilidh 4 ch f Scottish Reel-Show Home (Music Boy) 481^{2} 676^{5} 776^{7} **>61f<**

Celtic Fringe 3 b f Shavian-Highland Light 865^{2} 1195^{4} (2449) 2694^{9} 4052^{2} 4267^{18} **>86f<**

Celtic Swing 3 br c Damister (USA)-Celtic Ring (Welsh Pageant) (713) 920^{2} (1574a) 2218a^{8} **>131f<**

Cemaes Bay 3 b g Statoblest-Queen And Country (Town And Country) 772^{2} 955^{10} *1882^{5}* 2624^{5} 3000^{4} 3981^{4} 4165^{21} **>46a 69f<**

Ceneketes (GER) 3 c 1713a^{7} **>92f<**

Censor 2 b c Kris-Mixed Applause (USA) 4080^{9} (4246) **>83f<**

Centaine 3 b f Royal Academy-Hi Lass (Shirley Heights) 1009a^{3} (1705a) 2215a^{12} 2894a^{6} **>106f<**

Centaur Express 3 b c Siberian Express (USA)-Gay Twenties (Lord Gayle (USA)) *133^{10} 292^{11} 350^{5}* 521^{7} *628^{7}* 1350^{3} 1645^{10} 1854^{16} **>40a 40f<**

Cent Nouvelles (USA) 3 ch f Storm Bird (CAN)-Centavos (USA) (Scout Leader (USA)) 2393^{7} 2787^{3} 3181^{W} **>79f<**

Centre Stalls (IRE) 2 b c In The Wings-Lora's Guest (Be My Guest (USA)) (3890) 4159^{8} **>91f<**

Centurion 2 ch c Presidium-Missish (Mummy's Pet) 682^{3} 760^{3} 1341^{3} (2170) 2674^{7} 2826^{3} 3064^{3} 3213^{4} 3568^{11} 3651^{2} **>73f<**

Cephista 3 br f Shirley Heights-Cephira (FR) (Abdos) 1283^{4} 1866^{2} 2152^{5} 2719^{4} *3076^{9}* 3521^{9} **>1a 62f<**

Cerbera 6 b g Caruso-Sealed Contract (Runnymede) *410^{10}* **>16a f<**

Cerdan (USA) 2 ch c Zilzal (USA)-Vie En Rose (USA) (Blushing Groom (FR)) 4255^{3} **>67f<**

Cerise (IRE) 2 b f Red Sunset-Noble Nancy (Royal And Regal (USA)) 2608^{6} 2957^{4} 3231^{10} 3502^{4} 3644^{13} 3994^{10} 4285^{4} **>52f<**

Certain Way (IRE) 5 ch h Sure Blade (USA)-Ruffling Point (Gorytus (USA)) *50^{2} 231^{4} 3529^{11} 3952^{7} 4128^{7}* **>51a 56?f<**

Certificate-X 4 b f Never so Bold-Screenable (USA) (Silent Screen (USA)) 1164^{10} 1199^{9} **>49f<**

Chadayed (USA) 3 dk b or c Woodman-Chaudenay (Assert) 1122a^{3} 1713a^{3} 2215a^{P} **>100f<**

Chadleigh Lane (USA) 3 ch c Imp Society (USA)-Beauty Hour (USA) (Bold Hour) *243^{5} 294^{5} 411^{2} (599)* 995^{8} 1294^{6} *1629^{W} 3241^{9} 3510^{11} 3950^{10}* **>52a 56f<**

Chadleigh Walk (IRE) 3 b or br c Pennine Walk-Safiya (USA) (Riverman (USA)) *326^{3} 388^{4} 893^{10} 1330^{9}* 1718^{12} 1962^{16} 2149^{8} **>53da 41f<**

Chadwell Hall 4 b c Kala Shikari-Cherrywood Blessin (Good Times (ITY)) *167^{4} (224) 268^{2} 297^{4} 353^{2} 398^{2} (602)* 688^{5} *1331^{2} 1566^{2} 1763^{5} 3072^{2}* (3622) 3748^{3} 3992^{2} 4142^{8} **>66a 65f<**

Chahaya Timor (IRE) 3 b c Slip Anchor-Roxy Hart (High Top) 584^{6} 816^{6} 947^{3} *1784^{4} (2960) 3084^{2}* **>80a 72f<**

Chairmans Choice 5 ch g Executive Man-Revida Girl (Habat) 526^{4} 976^{5} 1245^{3} 1323^{6} 1426^{2} 1797^{3} (2310) 2766^{3} (3447) 3719^{9} **>84a 88df<**

Chakalak 7 b h Damister (USA)-Wig And Gown (Mandamus) 632^{18} 866^{16} 1109^{10} 1535^{5} 1773^{2} 1929^{5} (2501) 2695^{3} 3217^{9} 3569^{3} 3849^{3} 4166^{6} **>58f<**

Chalamont (IRE) 2 ch f Kris-Durtal 1246^{4} 3643^{4} 3763^{2} (3976) (4056) **>89f<**

Chalcuchima 2 gr c Reprimand-Ica (Great Nephew) 3890^{6} 4064^{6} **>71f<**

Chaldon Herring 3 b c Sulaafah (USA)-Langton Herring (Nearly A Hand) *118^{7} 210^{5} 294^{4} 354^{8}* 427^{13} 538^{4} 575^{2} 647^{7} 875^{W} 969^{P} **>57a 71f<**

Chalice 2 b f Governor General-Eucharis (Tickled Pink) 3626^{15} 3763^{14} 3940^{2} 4066^{5} **>72f<**

Chalk Circle (IRE) 3 b c Sadler's Wells (USA)-Grace Note (FR) (Top Ville) 663^{12} **>61f<**

Chalk Dust (USA) 2 b f Unbridled-Charmie Carmie (USA) (Lyphard (USA)) 4148^{6} 4262^{2} **>79f<**

Chalky Dancer 3 br c Adbass (USA)-Tiny Feet (Music Maestro) 1514^{18} 2208^{7} 2623^{4} 2966^{2} 3305^{2} 3745^{4} 3980^{19} **>51f<**

Chamber Music 2 ch f Music Boy-Piccadilly Etta 1176^{5} 2128^{6} *2382^{7} 4127^{13}* 4276^{10} **>41a 57f<**

Champagne Gold 8 ch h Bairn (USA)-Halkissimo 3774^{11} 3986^{17} 4166^{8} **>50f<**

Champagne Grandy 5 ch m Vaigly Great-Monstrosa (Monsanto (FR)) 434^{11} 542^{6} 636^{10} 1174^{15} (1560) (1673) 2001^{8} 3212^{11} 3615^{13} (3706) 3802^{15} 3964^{W} 4040^{9} 4145^{7} 4281^{8} **>86df<**

Champagne N Dreams 3 b f Rambo Dancer (CAN)-Pink Sensation (Sagaro) 759^{10} (1207) 1423^{3} 1465^{5} 1961^{4} 2482^{7} 2752^{4} 3700^{7} 3935^{15} **>62f<**

Champagne Prince 2 b c Prince Sabo-Champagne Season (USA) (Vaguely Noble) 1697^{2} (2200) 2454^{4} (3019) (3225) 3711^{4} **>90f<**

Champagne Warrior (IRE) 2 b f Waajib-Late Swallow 2063^{6} 4100^{11} 4277^{13} **>43f<**

Chancel (USA) 4 b f Al Nasr (FR)-Christchurch (FR) *361^{2}* **>56a 53f<**

Chance Me 3 ch c Risk Me (FR)-Tuxford Hideaway (Cawston's Clown) 1822^{7} *2071^{3}* 2124^{12} *2295^{5} 2492^{9}* **>44a 43f<**

Chancey Fella 4 ch c Sylvan Express-Musical Piece 2744^{8} 2979^{17} 3173^{4} 3344^{5} 3455^{11} 3661^{10} **>38a 67f<**

Chanson D'Avril 4 br f Chief Singer-Chappelle Blanche (USA) 3287^{4} 3521^{7} 3627^{13} **>45f<**

Chantry Beath 4 ch c Dunbeath (USA)-Sallametti (USA)

(Giacometti) 1102^{8} 1359^{6} 1496^{3} 1863^{7} 2937^{4} 3238^{5} 3445^{8} (3743) 3852^{13} 4101^{6} **>60f<**

Chantry Bellini 6 ch m Efisio-Lifestyle (Jimmy Reppin) *30^{12}* (1037) 1432^{3} (1649) 2332^{10} 2668^{5} 2999^{11} 3276^{7} 3665^{4} 3879^{5} 3941^{2} 4043^{15} 4292^{13} **>54f<**

Chapel Annie 3 ch f Tinoco-The Suestan (Ballyciptic) *4296^{11}*

Chapel Haven (IRE) 5 ch m King Persian-Saybya (Sallust) *19^{7} 79^{10}* **>22a 10f<**

Chapel Hill (IRE) 7 b m The Parson-Hazy Hill (Goldhill) *104^{4} 153^{8}* **>42da f<**

Chapter Two 4 ch c Celestial Storm (USA)-Lingering (Kind of Hush) *26^{8} 84^{8} 200^{10}* **>18a 32f<**

Chardonnay Girl 4 b f Hubbly Bubbly (USA)-Chaconia Girl (Bay Express) *6^{8}* 3357^{16} 3506^{8} **>12a 37f<**

Charillus 3 803a^{4} **>103f<**

Charisse Dancer 2 b f Dancing Dissident (USA)-Cadisa (Top Ville) 4154^{8} **>42f<**

Charity Crusader 4 b c Rousillon (USA)-Height of Folly (Shirley Heights) 440^{5} 610^{4} 1109^{11} 1612^{5} 2012^{4} **>104?f<**

Charlie Bigtime 5 b g Norwick (USA)-Sea Aura (Roi Soleil) *52^{6} 215^{4} 259^{6} 321^{4} (389) 412^{4} 894^{3} 1029^{10}* 1292^{5} 1401^{2} 1622^{11} *1955^{3}* (3127) *3511^{3} 3737^{4}* **>57a 57f<**

Charlie Chang (IRE) 2 b c Don't Forget Me-East River (FR) (Arctic Tern (USA)) 4313^{13} **>55f<**

Charlie Charlie 4 b c Emarati (USA)-Hound Song 1326^{9} **>48a 32f<**

Charlie-Don't Surf 3 b c Reprimand-Miami Melody (Miami Springs) 758^{15} 1371^{12} 1501^{10} **>22f<**

Charlies Dream (IRE) 4 b f Doulab (USA)-Caithness *30^{8}* **>43da f<**

Charlie Sillett 3 ch c Handsome Sailor-Bystrouska (Gorytus (USA)) 2318^{3} 3492^{6} (3964) 4068^{8} (4319) **>54a 90f<**

Charlistiona 4 ch f Good Times (ITY)-Abigails Portrait (Absalom) *28^{11} 58^{8}* **>17a 34df<**

Charlotte Corday 2 b f Kris-Dancing Rocks (Green Dancer (USA)) 4212^{5} **>66f<**

Charlotte Penny 4 b or br f High Kicker (USA)-Affluent Lady (Billion (USA)) *28^{12} 225^{6} 334^{9}* 1037^{15} **>24da 24?f<**

Charlton Imp (USA) 2 b f Imp Society (USA)-Percentage (USA) (Vaguely Noble) 4056^{6} **>44f<**

Charm Dancer 3 b f Rambo Dancer (CAN)-Skelton (Derrylin) (1059) 1791^{6} 1984^{3} 3403^{3} 3770^{5} 3920^{18} **>61f<**

Charmed Life 6 b h Legend of France (USA)-Tanagrea (Blakeney) 2990^{5} 3627^{18} 3986^{12} 4248^{13} 4331^{9} **>31f<**

Charme Slave (FR) 7 ch h Sicyos (USA)-Irish Arms (FR) (Irish River (FR)) (208a)

Charming Admiral (IRE) 2 b c Shareef Dancer (USA)-Lilac Charm (Bustino) 4169^{17} **>36f<**

Charming Bride 2 b f Charmer-Loredana (Grange Melody) 2683^{2} *2939^{4}* **>33a 54f<**

Charnwood Forest (IRE) 3 b or br c Warning-Dance of Leaves (Sadler's Wells (USA)) (677) 1837^{2} (2417) **>118f<**

Charnwood Nell (USA) 2 ch f Arctic Tern (USA)-Aphilandra (Viceregal (CAN)) 3532^{11} **>52f<**

Charnwood Queen 3 ch f Cadeaux Genereux-Florentynna Bay (Aragon) *72^{12} 210^{6} 769^{5} 842^{3} 1032^{9}* 1660^{3} 2048^{5} 2318^{2} (2491) (2659) *2943^{10}* 3179^{2} 3624^{24} 3874^{3} **>34a 63f<**

Charterhouse Xpres 2 b c Clantime-Uptown Girl (Caruso) 1096^{5} 1511^{10} *2143^{3} 2633^{2} 3509^{4}* 3612^{9} 3773^{8} *3953^{3}* (4066) **>71a 78f<**

Charwelton 2 b f Indian Ridge-Bazaar Promise (Native Bazaar) (2767) **>76tf<**

Chase the Melody 3 b c Sizzling Melody-Odilese (Mummy's Pet) 1125^{17} 1771^{10} 2033^{9} 2640^{6} **>32a 31f<**

Chasmarella 10 b m Yukon Eric (CAN)-Miss Polly Peck (March Past) *1210^{6}* 2268^{11} **>16a 23f<**

Chastleton 3 b f Presidium-Double Stitch (Wolver Hollow) *264^{4} 310^{2} 382^{3} (513)* 596^{5} 880^{5} 1974^{7} 2282^{8} 2684^{3} 2849^{4} 3129^{7} 3206^{5} 3383^{11} 3515^{10} 3747^{9} 3841^{6} **>57a 30f<**

Chatham Island 7 ch g Jupiter Island-Floreal (Formidable) *66^{2} 325^{2}* 623^{4} 935^{8} (1303) 1502^{6} 2002^{9} 3349^{4} 3555^{4} **>99a 78f<**

Chato (USA) 3 b c Local Talent-Quick Blush (Blushing Gro (1236a) 1586^{3} 2389a^{3} 3577a^{3} 3910a^{2} 4094a^{4} **>111f<**

Chattaroy (IRE) 3 b c Persian Bold-Lady Chatterley (USA) (Roberto (USA)) 694^{13} 1222^{6} (1474) 1839^{15} 2933^{4} **>91f<**

Chauvelin (IRE) 2 ch c Durgam (USA)-Kaliala (FR) (Pharly (FR)) 4291^{7} **>46f<**

Chavin Point 2 b f Inca Chief (USA)-To The Point (Sharpen Up) 3806^{15} 3976^{6} 4314^{20} **>16f<**

Cheeky Chappy 4 b c Sayf El Arab (USA)-Guilty Guest (USA) (Be My Guest (USA)) *102^{3} 139^{5} 192^{4} 268^{5}* 1157^{10} 1377^{11} *1763^{9}* 1963^{6} *2071^{2} 2295^{6}* 2463^{2} *2627^{5}* 2821^{7} 2879^{4} 2997^{5} 3252^{2} (3313) 3442^{6} **>42a 49f<**

Cheeky Charm (USA) 3 b f Nureyev (USA)-Very Charming (USA) (Vaguely Noble) 4150^{5} **>65f<**

Cheerful Aspect (IRE) 2 b g Cadeaux Genereux-Strike Home (Be My Guest (USA)) 3416^{6} 3683^{3} 3883^{5} 4107^{4} **>79f<**

Cheerful Groom (IRE) 4 ch g Shy Groom (USA)-Carange (Known Fact (USA)) *23^{3} 78^{2} 139^{3} 167^{9} 228^{4} 297^{7}* 1433^{13} 1599^{9} *1763^{8} 1882^{6} 2383^{9} 2628^{2}* 3750^{9} 3879^{9} 4193^{17} **>44a 39f<**

Chelsea Classic (IRE) 2 b f Classic Music (USA)-Romantic Air (He Loves Me) 2412^{4} 3648^{6} **>56f<**

Chelsea My Love (USA) 2 ch f Opening Verse (USA)-Wewarrenju (USA) (Damascus (USA)) 3141^{6} **>29f<**

Chemcast 2 ch c Chilibang-Golden October (Young Generation) 1774^{5} *2143^{5}* 2431^{3} 2706^{11} 2866^{2} *3077^{2}* (3335) (3568) 3753^{7} 3901^{6} *4124^{10}* **>60a 68f<**

Cherokee Rose (IRE) 4 b f Dancing Brave (USA)-Celtic Assembly (USA) (Secretariat (USA)) (1389a) (2040a) (3042a) (3491) 4012a^{2} 4305a^{8} **>123f<**

Cherrington 3 b c Reference Point-Cherry Hinton (USA) (811) 995^{3} 1872^{5} (2701) 3445^{3} 3927^{10} **>96f<**

Cherry Garden (IRE) 2 b c Treasure Kay-Door To Door (USA) (Nureyev (USA)) 2336^{4} 2791^{11} *3243^{3}* 3540^{2} 3684^{10} **>60a 60f<**

Chevalier (USA) 3 b br c Danzig (USA)-Royal Touch (Tap On Wood) 1967^{2} 2643^{2} **>73f<**

Cheveley Dancer (USA) 7 b g Northern Baby (CAN)-Alwah (USA) (Damascus (USA)) 454^{4} 586^{8} 738^{17} 1141^{11} 1513^{18} **>49f<**

Cheveux Mitchell 8 ch h Dunbeath (USA)-Hide Out 1148^{12} **>60a 52f<**

Chewit 3 gr c Beveled (USA)-Sylvan Song (Song) *124[2]* *381[2]* *(499)* 542[2] 1069[5] 1277[5] 4033[11] **>80a 85f<**

Cheyenne Spirit 3 ch f Indian Ridge-Bazaar Promise (Native Bazaar) (681) 828[7] 1066[2] 1305[6] (1766) 1870[8] (2271) 2673[2] (3033) 3198a[3] (3342) 3922[2] **>112f<**

Chez Catalan 4 b c Niniski (USA)-Miss Saint-Cloud (Nonoalco (USA)) 866[19] 1386[9] 2186[3] 2569[10] 3425[2] 3569[2] **>61f<**

Chickawicka (IRE) 4 b c Dance of Life (USA)-Shabby Doll (Northfields (USA)) 439[17] 714[10] 1021[13] 1225[7] 1851[16] 2053[2] (2428) 3065[5] 3212[12] 3813[9] 4145[12] **>93f<**

Chicodari 3 b c Shardari-Chicobin (USA) (J O Tobin (USA)) 1831[8] (2133) **>69f<**

Chief Bee 4 b f Chief's Crown (USA)-Lady Be Mine (USA) (Sir Ivor) 3016[6] (3392) 3700[8] (4022) (4315) **>92+f<**

Chief Minister (IRE) 6 br h Rainbow Quest (USA)-Riverlily (FR) (Green Dancer (USA)) 1156[4] 1607[5] 2098[16] **>80df<**

Chief Mouse 2 b c Be My Chief (USA)-Top Mouse (High Top) 3868[12] 4246[8] **>72f<**

Chief of Staff 6 ch h Caerleon (USA)-Fanny's Cove (Mill Reef (USA)) (1534) 1843[7] 2115[6] 3106[12] 3264[W] 3493[3] 3619[6] (3871) 3984[F] **>76a 78f<**

Chief's Lady 3 b f Reprimand-Pussy Foot (Red Sunset) 1602[6] 1972[6] 2844[5] 3055[6] 3344[2] 3751[13] 3897[13] 4115[19] 4156[16] **>57f<**

Chief's Princess 3 ch f Be My Chief (USA)-Settlement (USA) (Irish River (FR)) 1682[4] **>44f<**

Chief's Song 5 b h Chief Singer-Tizzy (Formidable) 632[10] 795[9] 938[9] 3676[4] 3927[7] **>70f<**

Chieftain's Crown (USA) 4 ch c Chief's Crown (USA)-Simple Taste (USA) (Sharpen Up) 2317[9] 2789[8] **>45df<**

Chik's Secret 2 ch f Nalchik (USA)-Lana's Secret (Most Secret) *1090[2]* 1288[4] 3008[7] 3530[9] 3760[14] **>52a 49f<**

Children's Choice (IRE) 4 b f Taufan (USA)-Alice Brackloon (USA) (Melyno) (430) 668[2] 763[9] 991[9] 1635[5] *2293[7]* 4171[15] 4333[13] **>57a 69df<**

Child Star (FR) 6 gr m Bellypha-Miss Shirley (FR) (Shirley Heights) *67[3]* *108[2]* *227[11]* *279[3]* *(514)* 582[7] *833[5]* *2147[5]* *2592[5]* **>50a 38f<**

Chilibang Bang 2 b f Chilibang-Quenlyn (Welsh Pageant) (595) 1959[2] 2158[2] 2606[7] 2869[2] *(3077)* *(3244)* 3714[17] **>62+a 49df<**

Chili Heights 5 gr h Chilibang-Highest Tender (Prince Tenderfoot (USA)) 636[8] 1126[11] 1255[5] 1676[6] 2414[2] 2578[5] 3439[12] 3706[12] 3885[6] 4053[4] 4157[3] **>62f<**

Chili Lady 5 ch m Chilibang-Barbary Court (Grundy) *26[5]* *56[3]* *100[6]* **>37a 6f<**

Chili Lass 3 ch f Chilibang-City Link Lass *3074[11]* 3635[13] **>2a 14f<**

Chiliola 4 ch f Chilibang-Sisola (USA) (Coastal (USA)) *139[7]* *182[8]* **>44a 66df<**

Chillam 2 ch c Chilibang-Tissue Paper (Touch Paper) 1356[9] *1758[4]* *1879[3]* 2782[8] **>47a 33f<**

Chillington 2 gr g Chilibang-Saskia's Pride (Giacometti) 3967[14]

Chilly Billy 3 b c Master Willie-Sweet Snow (USA) (Lyphard (USA)) 680[4] 920[8] 1133[4] **>113f<**

Chilly Lad 4 ch c High Kicker (USA)-Miss Poll Flinders (Swing Easy (USA)) 2747[10] **>63a 62f<**

Chilly Looks 2 b f Siberian Express (USA)-Exceptional Beauty (Sallust) 1503[9] 1665[8] 1943[3] 2251[5] 3937[16] **>45f<**

Chilly Time 4 ch f Chilibang-Leap in Time (Dance In Time (CAN)) *519[6]* *532[12]* 646[16] **>22a 35f<**

Chimanimani 4 b c Petong-La Primavera (Northfields (USA)) 506[13] 661[15] 956[4] 1022[11] 2238[7] 2584[3] 3001[5] **>85f<**

Chimborazo 4 ch c Salse (USA)-Pale Gold (FR) *325[5]* *396[12]* 632[13] 866[14] *1075[4]* **>67a 88df<**

Chiming In 3 ch f Niniski (USA)-River Chimes 573[3] (674) 838[2] 1131[6] 1648[7] 2260[2] 2519[4] **>76f<**

China Castle 2 b g Sayf El Arab (USA)-Honey Plum (Kind of Hush) 2483[10] 2756[6] *(2924)* 3309[6] 3721[14] *4124[8]* **>64+a 58f<**

China Hand (IRE) 3 ch c Salt Dome (USA)-China Blue (Ahonoora) 1248[8] 1559[4] 1739[5] 2821[6] 3508[4] 3678[8] **>51f<**

China Mail (IRE) 3 b c Slip Anchor-Fenney Mill (Levmoss) 428[6] 635[12] 851[15] 986[5] 1219[7] 1696[5] 1986[5] 2244[6] **>68f<**

Chinese Viking 3 b g Petorius-Comhail (USA) (Nodouble (USA)) 1065[8] 1258[11] 1515[6] 1719[6] 2054[10] **>61f<**

Ching 3 b f Shaadi (USA)-Chinese Justice (USA) (Diesis) 442[14] **>84f<**

Chinour (IRE) 7 b g Dalsaan-Chishtiya (Try My Best (USA)) *20[8]* *44[6]* *130[4]* 433[14] (567) 611[5] 922[8] 1179[6] 1421[9] 1687[5] 2194[5] (2645) 2952[6] 3212[3] 3447[9] 3607[17] **>59a 75f<**

Chita Rivera 4 b f Chief Singer-Shirley Superstar (Shirley Heights) *592[11]* 990[6] 3657[13] 3884[9] 4331[2] **>50f<**

Chloella 3 b f Shaadi (USA)-Echoing (Formidable) *2383[13]* *2925[5]* 3508[8] 3745[7] **>36a 38f<**

Chloes Diamond (IRE) 7 ch m Heraldiste (USA)-Salique (Sallust) *408[9]* 503[12] 800a[5] **>40f<**

Chocolate Charlie 4 b g Cadeaux Genereux-Lady Zi (Manado) 485[12] 584[13] 2316[7] 3004[5] 3710[20] 3844[13] 4157[27] **>57df<**

Choir Master (CAN) 8 b g Assert-Choral Group (CAN) (Lord Durham (CAN)) *1319[P]* **>26a 35f<**

Chosen Man 3 br c Dowsing (USA)-Town Lady 732[16] 966[19] **>24f<**

Chowpor 4 b f Nishapour (FR)-Salchow (Niniski (USA)) 757[12] **>49f<**

Chris's Governor 2 b c Governor General-Fara (Castle Keep) *1632[7]* *1954[9]* **>13a f<**

Chris's Lad 4 b c Thowra (FR)-Stockline (Capricorn Line) 2055[4] **>65a 73f<**

Christian Flight (IRE) 6 b m Fayruz-Opening Flight *94[12]* *268[3]* *338[3]* *354[4]* *419[4]* *511[4]* *590[8]* *603[11]* (862) 1042[3] **>39a 52f<**

Christian Spirit 5 gr h Petong-Hidden Asset (Hello Gorgeous (USA)) *217[11]* *248[9]* *402[6]* 586[15] **>25a 30f<**

Christian Warrior 6 gr h Primo Dominie-Rashah (Blakeney) 1326[7] 1483[9] 1714[18] 1797[6] 1963[20] *2076[13]* 2784[16] 2983[10] **>9a 39f<**

Christmas Kiss 3 b f Taufan (USA)-Ancestry (Persepolis (FR)) 431[4] 547[7] (937) 1222[4] 1474[3] (2013) 3660[6] 3922[11] **>87f<**

Chrysalu 3 b f Distant Relative-Final Rush (Final Straw) 1116a[16] **>84f<**

Chucklestone 12 b h Chukaroo-Czar's Diamond

(Queen's Hussar) 2201^{7} 2514^{7} 2986^{4} 3217^{8} 3425^{6} **>80f**<

Cicerone 5 br h Tina's Pet-Emma Royale (Royal And Regal (USA)) *1^{7} 80^{4} 230^{2} 354^{6} 520^{6} 835^{8}* 4152^{3} (4209) **>48a 53f**<

Cigar (USA) 5 b h Palace Music-Solar Slew (USA) *(4308a)* **>138+a f**<

Cim Bom Bom (IRE) 3 b c 659^{11} 829^{4} 953^{3} 1306^{9} **>98f**<

Cinders Chance 3 ch f Beveled (USA)-Salinas (Bay Express) 1302^{8} 1580^{10} 1993^{12} **>16f**<

Cinders Pet 4 ch f Aragon-Salinas (Bay Express) 1248^{11}

Cinnamon Stick (IRE) 2 ch c Don't Forget Me-Gothic Lady (Godswalk (USA)) 671^{5} *1212^{8}* 1369^{4} **>44a 49f**<

Cinnamon (SWE) 5 br m Diaglyphard-Stone of Scone (Ragstone) 4346a^{2} **>97f**<

Ciracusa (IRE) 3 b g Kahyasi-Miranisa (Habitat) 4062^{11} 4167^{3} **>54f**<

Circa 3 ch f Risk Me (FR)-Dancing Belle (Dance In Time (CAN)) 932^{8} **>82+a 96f**<

Circled (USA) 2 gr f Cozzene (USA)-Hold The Hula (USA) (Hawaii) 3708^{8} (4073) **>84+f**<

Circle of Friends (IRE) 4 b f Taufan (USA)-Pitlessie (Hook Money) 2945^{P} **>35f**<

Circus Star 2 b c Soviet Star (USA)-Circus Act (Shirley Heights) 3989^{9} 4098^{5} 4314^{7} **>66f**<

Ciserano (IRE) 2 ch f Mujtahid (USA)-Blue Persian 1536^{2} 1746^{3} 2192^{4} 2464^{4} **>73f**<

Citadeed (USA) 3 b c Shadeed (USA)-Johanna Keene (USA) (Raise A Cup (USA)) 667^{3} 1006a^{9} 1710a^{3} **>81+a 111f**<

Citizen Darnet (USA) 4 c 2213a^{8} **>99f**<

City Rhythm 5 b g Librate-Star City (Royal Boxer) *68^{10} 172^{9}* **>42f**<

City Run (USA) 3 b c Mehmet (USA)-Sable Sham (USA) (Sham (USA)) 677^{9} 1097^{15} **>61f**<

Civil 3 b f Risk Me (FR)-Astrid Gilberto (Runnett) *587^{12}* **>58f**<

Civil Liberty 2 b c Warning-Libertine (Hello Gorgeous (USA)) 2741^{6} 3158^{2} **>84f**<

Claireswan (IRE) 3 ch g Rhoman Rule (USA)-Choclate Baby (Kashiwa) *443^{5} 628^{5} 844^{4}* 1596^{4} 1863^{6} (2232) *(2592)* (2931) 3029^{2} *(3318)* 3669^{8} **>70a 69f**<

Clan Ben (IRE) 3 ch c Bluebird (USA)-Trina's Girl (Nonoalco (USA)) 2977^{2} (3377) (3598) 3728^{2} 4147^{4} 4265^{5} **>104f**<

Clan Chief 2 b c Clantime-Mrs Meyrick (Owen Dudley) 782^{3} 1938^{3} 2128^{2} 2431^{2} 3400^{4} **>67f**<

Clancy's Express 4 b c Faustus (USA)-Pink Pumpkin (Tickled Pink) *175^{8}* 887^{15} 1092^{10} 1350^{7} 1622^{18} 1974^{6} 2115^{8} **>42df**<

Clan Scotia 3 ch f Clantime-Moorhill (Vaigly Great) 855^{16} **>52f**<

Claque 3 ch c Kris-Mixed Applause (USA) 1691^{6} 1987^{7} **>76f**<

Claret Bumble 4 ch f Absalom-Mumtaz Mayfly (Tap On Wood) *187^{6} 217^{9}* **>41a f**<

Clarion Call (IRE) 4 b c Don't Forget Me-Hillbrow (Swing Easy (USA)) 567^{7} 1092^{19} **>56f**<

Clary Sage 2 br f Sayf El Arab (USA)-Supergreen (Superlative) 638^{4} **>6f**<

Clashawan (IRE) 5 b m Strong Gale-Sheergraustark (Energist) 2798^{4}

Classic Affair (USA) 2 ch f Trempolino (USA)-Coupole (USA) (Vaguely Noble) 3891^{5} 4085^{8} **>62f**<

Classical Star 6 b h Tout Ensemble-Spic And Span 1056^{4} 1167^{13} 1446^{11} **>47f**<

Classic Artiste (USA) 2 ch f Arctic Tern (USA)-Batan Gantlet (Run The Gantlet (USA)) 1913^{5} 3157^{8} 3625^{10} 3851^{5} **>58f**<

Classic Ballet (FR) 2 b f Fabulous Dancer (USA)-Tyranesque (USA) (Key To The Mint (USA)) 3633^{4} 3881^{7} 4291^{2} **>74f**<

Classic Beauty (IRE) 2 b f Fairy King (USA)-Working Model (Ile de Bourbon (USA)) 4098^{4} 4282^{4} **>65f**<

Classic Call (IRE) 2 b c Classic Music (USA)-Queen of Wolves (Wolver Hollow) 1856^{11} *2958^{7}* **>39a 27f**<

Classic Cliche (IRE) 3 b c Salse (USA)-Pato (High Top) (1107) 1574a^{4} 1897^{2} 2218a^{5} (3609) **>123f**<

Classic Colours (USA) 2 ch c Blushing John (USA)-All Agleam (USA) (Gleaming (USA)) 4073^{5} 4241^{11} **>58f**<

Classic Daisy 2 b f Prince Sabo-Bloom of Youth (IRE) (Last Tycoon) 2198^{9} 2447^{3} 2732^{3} 3267^{7} 4133^{6} 4290^{7} **>49f**<

Classic Defence (IRE) 2 b c Cyrano de Bergerac-My Alanna (Dalsaan) 3436^{8} 3644^{9} 3873^{8} **>62f**<

Classic Delight (USA) 2 b f Green Forest (USA)-Weather Girl (USA) (One For All (USA)) 1856^{12} *3523^{4}* 3643^{5} 3894^{10} **>43a 40f**<

Classic Eagle 2 b c Unfuwain (USA)-La Lutine (My Swallow) (4143) **>85?f**<

Classic Exhibit 6 b h Tate Gallery (USA)-See The Tops (Cure The Blues (USA)) *312^{14} 367^{9} 389^{9}* **>22a 17f**<

Classic Flyer (IRE) 2 b f Alzao (USA)-Sea Harrier (Grundy) 1142^{5} (2183) 2775^{5} 3865^{25} **>68+f**<

Classic Fountain (IRE) 2 b c Classic Music (USA)-Lucky Fountain (IRE) 3588a^{3} **>87f**<

Classic Leader 2 b c Thatching-Tenderetta 1190^{2} **>76#f**<

Classic Look (IRE) 2 b br f Classic Music (USA)-Mini Look (FR) (In Fijar (USA)) 3069^{15} **>55f**<

Classic Lover (IRE) 2 b f Taufan (USA)-Sound Pet (Runnett) 1418^{2} 3620^{4} 3827^{3} 4151^{6} **>73f**<

Classic Model (IRE) 4 b g High Line-Fast Car (FR) (Carwhite) 4231^{7} **>69f**<

Classic Pet (IRE) 3 b f Petorius-Checkers (Habat) 621^{14} 850^{8} 1124^{9} 1512^{19} 1660^{9} 1963^{16} 3177^{14} (3442) 3622^{18} **>51f**<

Classic Romance 2 b f Cadeaux Genereux-What A Pity (Blakeney) (3939) 4067^{3} **>80f**<

Classic Sky (IRE) 4 b c Jareer (USA)-Nawadder (Kris) 665^{2} 870^{7} 1143^{3} (1397a) 1728^{3} 2287^{8} 2703^{12} 3085^{4} 3382^{7} 3813^{13} **>104f**<

Classic Victory 2 b c Puissance-Seattle Mama (USA) (Seattle Song (USA)) 1176^{10} 1597^{7} 2283^{10} (2771) 3049^{4} 3289^{9} 3749^{21} **>77df**<

Classicy 3 b c Cadeaux Genereux-Sauceboat (758) (980) (1130) 1839^{19} 2703^{7} **>96+f**<

Classy Chief 2 b c Be My Chief (USA)-Jalopy (Jalmood (USA)) 3916^{8} 4155^{3} 4320^{2} **>78f**<

Claudia Habibi (IRE) 3 ch f Zalazl (USA)-Choral Dancer (USA) (Night Shift (USA)) 1353^{8} *1939^{10}* 2711^{8} **>22a 56f**<

Clean Edge (USA) 3 ch c Woodman (USA)-Najidiya

(USA) (Riverman (USA)) 525^{6} **>61f<**

Clear Attraction (USA) 3 b f Lear Fan (USA)-Highclere (Queen's Hussar) 4072^{6} **>55f<**

Clear Look 5 b m Green Desert (USA)-Avoid (USA) (Buckpasser) *28^{6} 91^{12}* **>34a 43f<**

Clearly Devious 3 b f Machiavellian (USA)-Shoot Clear (Bay Express) 3974^{2} 4150^{7} **>80+f<**

Clearwater Lady (IRE) 3 ch f Nordance (USA)-Fantasise (FR) (General Assembly (USA)) 3043a^{2} **>64f<**

Cledeschamps 6 b m Doc Marten-Cape Farewell (Record Run) *55^{9}* 594^{2} 789^{16} *1034^{10} 1571^{15}* **>42da 41f<**

Clemente 2 b br c Robellino (USA)-Gravad Lax (Home Guard (USA)) 3650^{7} 3890^{4} 4143^{3} **>76f<**

Clerkenwell (USA) 2 b c Sadler's Wells (USA)-Forlene 3592^{4} **>64+f<**

Clever Dorothy (USA) 2 f Clever Trick-Dear Dorothy 4013a^{8} **>86f<**

Cliburnel News (IRE) 5 b m Horage-Dublin Millennium (Dalsaan) *97^{2} 153^{3} 200^{3} 254^{4} 329^{3} 356^{4}* (549) 811^{8} 1160^{5} (1349) 1435^{4} 1643^{4} 4061^{7} 4114^{2} **>55a 66f<**

Clifton Fox 3 b c Deploy-Loveskate (USA) (Overskate (CAN)) 427^{8} (572) 614^{3} 1130^{7} (1351) 1619^{5} 3368^{5} 3607^{12} 4116^{4} 4267^{29} **>89f<**

Clifton Game 5 b g Mummy's Game-Brave Maiden (Three Legs) *367^{2}* 549^{14} **>49a 34f<**

Clincher Club 2 b f Polish Patriot (USA)-Merry Rous (Rousillon (USA)) 1653^{8} 1938^{8} (3110) 3289^{3} 3612^{2} 3803^{12} 4077^{8} 4243^{10} **>74f<**

Clint 2 b c Colmore Row-Eastwood Heiress (Known Fact (USA)) 424^{9} 3104^{6} *4269^{12}* **>41f<**

Cliptomania (USA) 2 b c Cryptoclearance-Mary Tavy 4010a^{2} **>103f<**

Cloette 3 b f Damister (USA)-Mademoiselle Chloe (Night Shift (USA)) *(515) (847)* 1624^{5} 1778^{6} 2178^{4} 2504^{6} *2923^{4}* **>76a 69f<**

Cloghran Lad 8 ch g Millfontaine-Lady Pitt (Pitskelly) *588^{8}*

Close Conflict (USA) 4 b c High Estate-Catopetl (USA) (Northern Dancer) 896a^{6} 4182a^{8} **>117f<**

Clouded Elegance 5 b h Elegant Air-Clouded Vision (So Blessed) (864) 1141^{4} 1558^{7} 3993^{9} **>83f<**

Clouds Hill (FR) 2 b c Sarhoob (USA)-Dana Dana (FR) (Pharly (FR)) 3617^{5} 3888^{3} **>74f<**

Club Elite 3 b f Salse (USA)-Little Bittern (USA) (Riva Ridge (USA)) 867^{11} *1030^{6} 1330^{4} 1568^{11}* 1902^{5} 2450^{12} *2632^{2}* 2806^{5} 3092^{4} 3303^{5} **>47a 45f<**

Clued Up 2 b f Beveled (USA)-Scharade (Lombard (GER)) 2485^{8} *2625^{4}* 3502^{13} **>32a 44f<**

Clurican (IRE) 6 ch h Dara Monarch-Jane Bond 820^{14} 998^{18} 1295^{13} **>36f<**

Cnocma (IRE) 4 b f Tender King-Peggy Dell (Sovereign Gleam) 3515^{17} **>13f<**

Coalisland 5 br h Kind of Hush-Hit The Line (Saulingo) *100^{8} 158^{5} 203^{7} 248^{8}* 583^{7} 984^{9} 1151^{15} 1499^{17} 1940^{12} 2439^{12} 2486^{16} 2830^{4} **>38a 32f<**

Coastal Bluff 3 gr g Standaan (FR)-Combattente (Reform) 502^{9} (645) 1181^{5} 1487^{4} 1806^{2} 3878^{3} (4033) **>94+f<**

Coast Along (IRE) 3 b g Satco (FR)-Golden Flats (Sonnen Gold) 1358^{11} 1581^{4} 1667^{7} 2129^{3} 2232^{5} (2662) **>48f<**

Coastguards Haven 3 b g Superpower-Marton Maid (Silly Season) 1196^{11} 1446^{10} 1771^{7} 2177^{6} **>40f<**

Coastguards Hero 2 ch c Chilibang-Aldwick Colonnade (Kind of Hush) 1592^{W} 2264^{5} 2791^{10} **>39f<**

Coaxing Matt (USA) 6 ro h Coax Me Chad (USA)-Native Scent (USA) 3574a^{3}

Cobblers Hill 6 gr h Another Realm-Morning Miss 4215^{P}

Cobbs Cross 5 ch g Bairn (USA)-Trapani *397^{10} 1883^{14}* **>33a 24f<**

Coburg 3 ch c Old Vic-Gatchina (Habitat) 663^{10} (3653) **>84f<**

Cocoon (IRE) 2 b f Cyrano de Bergerac-Arena (Sallust) 2498^{9} 3430^{4} 3671^{8} **>43f<**

Coco Passion (FR) 3 ch f Groom Dancer (USA)-Gaiete de Coeur (Lomond (USA)) 2214a^{3} 4015a^{11} **>100f<**

Code of Law (USA) 3 b c Woodman (USA)-Eloquent Minister (USA) (Deputy Minister (CAN)) (2460) 3598^{5} 3926^{13} **>89f<**

Code of Silence 3 br c Adbass (USA)-Keep Silent (Balidar) 548^{5} 733^{4} *1033^{12}* 1445^{5} 1654^{5} 2037^{12} 2661^{5} 2712^{7} **>21a 58f<**

Coeur Francais (FR) 3 b g Hero's Honor (USA)-Marie d'Anjou (FR) (Free Round (USA)) 3712^{6} 4027^{7} **>66df<**

Coffee 'n Cream 3 ch c Handsome Sailor-Thorner Lane (Tina's Pet) 551^{5} 612^{5} 743^{4} 1614^{13} (2344) 2742^{2} 2935^{4} 3065^{4} (3279) 3660^{4} 4055^{3} 4197^{2} **>101f<**

Coggle 3 b f Kind of Hush-Packet 635^{19} 1147^{7} 1691^{5} 2189^{5} 2509^{5} (2841) 3287^{5} **>71f<**

Coigach 4 b f Niniski (USA)-Rynechra (Blakeney) 2104^{5} **>103f<**

Cold Shoulder (IRE) 2 b c Distinctly North (USA)-Shygate (Shy Groom (USA)) 2340^{8} 2791^{9} 3246^{3} **>66f<**

Coldstream 2 b c Shareef Dancer (USA)-Sea Saga (Dara Monarch) 3089^{3} (3416) **>86+f<**

Coleridge 7 gr h Bellypha-Quay Line (High Line) 795^{12} 1058^{6} 1328^{2} 1657^{6} 2284^{10} 2413^{6} *2592^{7}* 3569^{5} (3986) 4166^{3} 4326^{8} **>85a 61f<**

Collecta (FR) 3 b f Caerleon (USA)-Canaletto (USA) (Iron Duke (FR)) 1116a^{5} 1576a^{4} **>106f<**

College Don 4 gr g Kalaglow-Westerlake (Blakeney) 1295^{4} 1502^{4} (1858) 2087^{4} 2119^{4} (2612) (2907) 3162^{10} 3412^{6} **>78f<**

College Night (IRE) 3 b f Night Shift (USA)-Gertrude Lawrence (Ballymore) 557^{3} 756^{6} 935^{P} 3031^{5} 3291^{9} 3571^{6} 3646^{13} 3862^{7} 4168^{3} 4259^{17} 4332^{6} **>64f<**

Colonel Colt 4 b c Saint Andrews (FR)-Vallee des Sauges (USA) (Secretariat (USA)) 550^{17} 676^{19} 4051^{17} **>36f<**

Colorful Ambition 5 b h Slip Anchor-Reprocolor 988^{9} (1251) (1378) 1616^{2} 2427^{2} 2678^{6} 3611^{19} **>82f<**

Colosse 3 b f Reprimand-French Cutie (USA) (Vaguely Noble) *766^{15}* 2102^{2} 2279^{11} 2885^{2} 3096^{3} 3843^{2} 3970^{15} **>62f<**

Colour Counsellor 2 gr c Touch of Grey-Bourton Downs *1073^{3} 1212^{5}* 2161^{6} *2380^{7} 2635^{5} 2962^{11}* 3233^{5} 3350^{3} *3736^{6}* 3760^{20} **>56a 45df<**

Colpo Di Scena (IRE) 2 b f Scenic-Yankee Lady (Lord Gayle) (1887a)

Colston-C 3 gr c Belfort (FR)-Grand Occasion (Great Nephew) *25^{8} 331^{8}* 855^{6} 1445^{4} 1546^{4} 1719^{2} 1914^{3} (2250) 2512^{2} 2793^{2} (3204) 3519^{12} 3960^{10} **>43da 71f<**

Colt D'Or **3** ch c Beldale Lark-Nijinsgayle (FR) (Nice Havrais (USA)) 739^{11} 1317^{8} 1656^{6} **>52f<**

Colway Bridge **2** b c Colway Radial-Bell Bridge Girl (Coded Scrap) 3018^{4} 4112^{6} *4338^{12}* **>55f<**

Colway Prince (IRE) **7** b h Prince Tenderfoot (USA)-El Cerrito 2081^{10} **>64f<**

Colway Rake **4** b c Salse (USA)-Barely Hot (Bold Lad (IRE)) 535^{9} 639^{3} (877) 1174^{2} 1614^{10} 2288^{6} 3418^{2} 3492^{14} 3715^{2} 4040^{18} **>74da 78f<**

Colway Rock (USA) **5** b h Irish River (FR)-Petite Diable (USA) (Sham (USA)) 1616^{9} 2118^{6} 3393^{7} 3611^{25} **>65df<**

Comanche Companion **5** b m Commanche Run-Constant Companion (Pas de Seul) 780^{8} 876^{7} 1362^{2} 1638^{10} 2056^{2} 2310^{5} 3043a^{7} (3629) 3837^{3} (4041) 4267^{22} **>66a 88f<**

Comaneci (IRE) **7** b m Ahonoora-Church Mountain (Furry Glen) *234^{13}*

Come on Dancer (IRE) **7** ch h Ahonoora-Crimson Royale (High Line) *190^{4} 290^{3} 2600^{6}* **>58a 57f<**

Come On In **2** b c Most Welcome-Lominda (IRE) (Lomond (USA)) 3989^{17} 4045^{18}

Come on Lucy **6** b m Reesh-Her Excellency (Dragonara Palace (USA)) *130^{8}* **>55f<**

Comeonup **4** b g Most Welcome-Scarlet Veil (Tyrnavos) 702^{14} 785^{11} (876) 4053^{11} **>68f<**

Come on Winn **3** ch f Handsome Sailor-Ragusa Girl (Morston (FR)) 772^{U} 1546^{12} *1763^{U}* 3424^{U} **>7f<**

Comfortable **5** ch g Hard Fought-Key Harvest *4^{8} 50^{6} 96^{11} 417^{7}* **>19a 27f<**

Comic Fantasy (AUS) **2** b f Rory's Jester (AUS)-Enchanted Dream (NZ) (Danzatore (CAN)) 2351^{4} 2660^{6} (2985) 3176^{3} 3400^{2} 3655^{2} 4219^{3} 4328^{8} **>86f<**

Commanche Creek **5** b h Commanche Run-Vice Vixen (CAN) (Vice Regent (CAN)) 1084^{5} 1647^{12} **>57df<**

Commanche Storm (IRE) **3** b g Maelstrom Lake-Commanche Maid (Commanche Run) *133^{8}* **>10a 38f<**

Commander Glen (IRE) **3** b c Glenstal (USA)-Une Parisienne (FR) (Bolkonski) 1198^{11} 1317^{9} 1799^{11} 2016^{6} (2818) 2927^{3} 2972^{17} 3000^{2} 3344^{18} 3372^{5} (3515) 3757^{16} 3899^{13} **>66f<**

Commin' Up **2** b f Primo Dominie-Ridalia 3763^{8} 3982^{7} 4130^{3} **>54f<**

Committal (IRE) **2** b c Lycius (USA)-Just Cause (Law Society (USA)) 2283^{3} 3868^{2} (4037) 4177a^{6} **>104f<**

Commoner (USA) **3** b c Far North (CAN)-Searching Around (USA) (Round Table (USA)) 619^{2} 1068^{5} 1574a^{11} (2910) 3070^{2} 3498^{2} 4185a^{6} **>116f<**

Commons Wheel (IRE) **2** b c Common Grounds-Daisy Wheel (Doulab (USA)) 3982^{11} **>46f<**

Compass Pointer **2** gr c Mazilier (USA)-Woodleys (Tyrnavos) 3663^{16} 3994^{8} 4320^{14} **>55f<**

Compensate (IRE) **2** ch f Great Commotion (USA)-Clipping (Kris) 716^{7} 1798^{8} 2035^{5} 2908^{7} **>48f<**

Comrade Chinnery (IRE) **2** ch c Jareer (USA)-Phar Lapa (Grundy) 671^{11} 1734^{4} 2505^{5} 3233^{3} 3350^{5} **>48f<**

Comtec's Legend **5** ch m Legend of France (USA)-Comtec Princess (Gulf Pearl) *29^{6} (172) 246^{5} 304^{3} 422^{5}* 4101^{11} 4259^{23} **>40a 39f<**

Concepcion (GER) **5** br h Acatenango (GER)-Comprida (GER) (Windwurf (GER)) 2046a^{8} 3046a^{3} 3591a^{8} (4088a) (4311a) **>118f<**

Concern (USA) **4** b c Broad Brush (USA)-Fara's Team (USA) (Tunerup (USA)) *4308a^{8}* **>114a 131f<**

Concert Party (IRE) **2** b c Classic Music (USA)-Crown Class (USA) (Chief's Crown (USA)) 2408^{9} 2801^{8} 3155^{10} *3528^{11}* 3642^{4} 3721^{13} 3744^{11} 3780^{9} **>6a 58f<**

Concer Un **3** ch g Lord Bud-Drudwen (Sayf El Arab (USA)) *64^{7} 332^{4} 362^{3}* (492) 839^{2} 1028^{2} 1207^{3} 2003^{3} 2188^{3} 2437^{4} 2500^{2} (2864) (2974) 3125^{2} 3408^{2} (3497) 3732^{13} **>55a 84f<**

Concinnity (USA) **6** b h Hello Gorgeous (USA)-Cincinnity (USA) (Shareef Dancer (USA)) 2486^{11} **>27f<**

Condor Ridge **2** b c Inca Chief (USA)-Second Flower (Indian Ruler (USA)) 3893^{10} 4161^{20} **>42f<**

Cone Lane **9** ch h On Your Mark-Cee Beauty (Ribero) *13^{8} 122^{6} 200^{5} 329^{10} 1319^{8}* 1594^{8} *2090^{6} 4293^{9}* **>28a 39f<**

Coneygree **3** b f Northern State (USA)-Welsh Blossom (Welsh Saint) 537^{6} 1219^{5} 1379^{9} 2166^{6} 2574^{3} 2966^{3} 3125^{11} **>47f<**

Coney Hills **4** b f Beverley Boy-Adder Howe (Amboise) 1342^{7} 1419^{6} 1668^{11} 2084^{9} 2310^{12} 2624^{11} 2761^{3} 2955^{8} 3357^{11} 3508^{11} **>25f<**

Confronter **6** ch h Bluebird (USA)-Grace Darling (USA) (Vaguely Noble) (162a) 208a^{2} 253a^{2} 487a^{4} (546) 731^{3} 873^{21} 1517^{2} 1693^{2} 1775^{3} 2169^{7} 3248^{2} (3664) (3770) 3991^{4} **>79a 92?f<**

Conic Hill (IRE) **4** ch c Lomond (USA)-Krisalya (Kris) 653^{10} 1351^{10} **>24a 79f<**

Coniston Lake (IRE) **6** ch h Coquelin (USA)-High Lake *68^{11}* **>37a 44f<**

Conquistajade (USA) **2** b br f Conquistador Cielo (USA)-Uncut Jade (CAN) (Vice Regent (CAN)) 1746^{4} 3339^{18} **>60f<**

Considerable Charm **3** ch f Charmer-Leap in Time (Dance In Time (CAN)) *239^{4} 286^{2} 381^{4}* 3844^{15} **>44a 26f<**

Consordino **2** b f Alzao (USA)-Consolation (Troy) 2912^{9} 3180^{5} 3450^{4} (3639) 3809^{2} 4107^{6} **>92f<**

Conspicuous (IRE) **5** b h Alzao (USA)-Mystery Lady (USA) (Vaguely Noble) *195^{5} 262^{6}* 2490^{2} 2707^{2} (3106) 3388^{2} (3601) 4035^{2} 4267^{8} **>60+a 90f<**

Contrac Countess (IRE) **5** b m Thatching-Crimson Sails (Lomond (USA)) 1966^{14}

Contract Bridge (IRE) **2** b f Contract Law (USA)-Mystery Bid (Auction Ring (USA)) 1448^{8} 2932^{3} 3231^{2} 3502^{6} 4290^{10} **>60f<**

Contract Venture (IRE) **3** b g Contract Law (USA)-Ultra (Stanford) 1312^{7} 1504^{5} 2102^{8} 2776^{6} 3096^{4} 3372^{4} **>65f<**

Contradictory **2** br f Reprimand-Artistic Licence (High Top) 1177^{7} 1266^{3} 1678^{6} 2257^{3} 2914^{6} 3019^{7} 3809^{9} **>47f<**

Contrafire (IRE) **3** b g Contract Law (USA)-Fiery Song (Ballad Rock) *(17) 151^{3} (301)* 427^{2} 537^{2} 687^{6} 2557^{8} 3061^{3} (3320) 3464^{2} 3665^{2} 4283^{4} **>76a 78f<**

Contrarie **2** b f Floose-Chanita (Averof) *4338^{7}* **>32a f<**

Conwy **2** ch f Rock City-Degannwy (Caerleon (USA)) 4048^{9} **>53f<**

Cool Caper **2** b c Inca Chief (USA)-Rekindled Flame (IRE) (Kings Lake (USA)) *1073^{4} 3675^{9}* **>52a 22f<**

Cool Edge (IRE) **4** ch c Nashamaa-Mochara (Last Fandango) 646^{5} (906) 1152^{4} 1193^{4} 1738^{2} 2746^{3} 3457^{2}

3488^{2} 3703^{2} 3943^{3} 3991^{5} 4267^{24} **>87f<**

Cool Fire 2 b c Colmore Row-Into the Fire (Dominion) 2070^{5} 2681^{7} **>62f<**

Cool Jazz 4 b c Lead on Time (USA)-Amber Fizz (USA) (Effervescing (USA)) 441^{8} 652^{2} 814^{6} 1284^{3} 1480^{3} (2237) 3191^{8} 3551^{3} 3717^{5} (3834) 4012a^{7} 4078^{8} **>121f<**

Cool Luke (IRE) 6 b g Red Sunset-Watet Khet (FR) (Wittgenstein (USA)) (597) 757^{5} **>74f<**

Cool Steel (IRE) 3 gr g Absalom-Formidable Task (Formidable) 492^{5} 640^{8} 1412^{6} **>61f<**

Cool Tactician 3 gr c Petong-Thevetia (Mummy's Pet) 442^{12} *(603)* 867^{15} 999^{10} 1279^{6} 1598^{3} 1825^{12} 2003^{6} 2549^{13} 2815^{4} *3073^{7}* 3622^{17} *3739^{10}* 3972^{18} 4054^{12} **>68a 55df<**

Copent Garden(IRE) 3 b c Sadler's Wells-Ameridienne (FR) (Targowice (USA)) 1008a^{4} 1230a^{2} **>104f<**

Copper Bright 2 b g Mon Tresor-Arabian Nymph (Sayf El Arab (USA)) 863^{4} 1190^{11} 1413^{7} 2328^{11} 2644^{4} 2965^{5} 3744^{9} **>47f<**

Coral Reef (ITY) 2 b c Big Reef-All the Crown (3797a)

Corina's Glow 3 gr f Sizzling Melody-Pale Glow (Kalaglow) 548^{17} 1059^{10} **>17f<**

Corio 3 b c Sharpo-Constant Delight (Never so Bold) 985^{8} 2455^{10} **>41a 76f<**

Cork Street Girl (IRE) 3 b f Bold Arrangement-Ward of Court (IRE) (Law Society (USA)) *499^{10} 629^{4}* 727^{2} 1016^{11} 1201^{5} 1263^{8} 1719^{4} *1952^{7}* 2318^{6} 2491^{4} 2641^{5} 3134^{3} 3424^{10} *4295^{9}* **>52a 53f<**

Corky's Girl 3 b f Today and Tomorrow-Rectory Maid (Tina's Pet) *211^{7}*

Corniche Quest (IRE) 2 b f Salt Dome (USA)-Angel Divine (Ahonoora) 903^{3} 1054^{7} 1253^{2} 1671^{3} 1823^{2} 3203^{3} 3538^{5} 3670^{4} 3838^{4} 3915^{5} 4133^{5} 4230^{3} 4287^{4} **>67f<**

Cornish Snow (USA) 2 br c Storm Cat (USA)-Pleasantly Free (USA) (Pleasant Colony (USA)) 4023^{4} **>68tf<**

Corona Gold 5 b h Chilibang-Miss Alkie (Noalcoholic (FR)) 672^{6} *1034^{3} 1088^{10} 1334^{5} (1883)* 2156^{3} *2377^{15}* 3879^{11} **>45a 48f<**

Coronar (GER) 3 c 3200a^{5} **>83f<**

Corporal Nym (USA) 2 gr c Cozzene (USA)-Fiji Fan (USA) (unknown) 1104^{4} 1311^{3} 4318^{3} **>82f<**

Corradini 3 b c Rainbow Quest (USA)-Cruising Height (Shirley Heights) 691^{12} (1764) 3995^{2} **>90f<**

Correspondence (CAN) 5 br h Phone Trick (USA)-Chas' Lady (USA) (Key to the Kingdom (USA)) 3014^{2} 3134^{4} 3177^{7} 3919^{10} **>43f<**

Corrievarkie 3 ch f Dominion-Mary Bankes (USA) (Northern Baby (CAN)) 435^{10} 547^{9} *767^{11}* 2180^{3} 2524^{5} **>63f<**

Coryana Dancer (IRE) 3 b f Waajib-Fettle (Relkino) 1000^{6} 1308^{6} 1615^{8} 2393^{4} 3097^{6} *3734^{10}* 4071^{11} **>35a 80df<**

Cosy Corner (IRE) 3 b f Cyrano de Bergerac-Trysting Place (He Loves Me) 3944^{6} **>97f<**

Cottage Prince (IRE) 2 b g Classic Secret (USA)-Susan's Blues (Cure The Blues (USA)) 1035^{8} 3502^{9} *3736^{8}* **>42a 30f<**

Cotteir Chief (IRE) 4 b c Chief Singer-Hasty Key (USA) (Key To The Mint (USA)) 440^{2} 712^{6} 1108^{8} 1610^{7} **>117f<**

Cottesloe Beach 2 ch g Gabitat-Georgian Quickstep (Dubassoff (USA)) 1699^{9} 1829^{10} *2075^{7} 2962^{7}* 3080^{5} **>40a 50f<**

Cotytto 2 b br f Puissance-Drudwen (Sayf El Arab (USA)) 2135^{12} 3069^{18} 3379^{22} 3540^{11} **>47f<**

Couchant (IRE) 4 b c Petoski-Be Easy 3876^{3} **>72f<**

Country Lover 4 ch c Thatching-Fair Country (Town And Country) 439^{18} 634^{10} 1357^{5} 1808^{9} 2457^{8} 2672^{8} 3113^{7} 3732^{2} 4116^{5} 4267^{11} **>86?a 88f<**

Country Star (IRE) 4 b c Persian Bold-Sugar Plum Fairy (Sadler's Wells (USA)) 1661^{4} 2241^{11} (2790) 3106^{2} 3500^{3} 3729^{4} 4028^{7} 4163^{7} **>89f<**

Country Thatch 2 b c Thatching-Alencon (Northfields (USA)) 3733^{19} 3892^{7} **>52f<**

Courage-Mon-Brave 7 gr g Bold Owl-Bri-Ette (Brittany) *1455^{5}* **>15a f<**

Courageous Dancer (IRE) 3 b f Cadeaux Genereux-Hafwah (Gorytus (USA)) 695^{3} 865^{3} (1522) (1787) 2325^{5} 2470^{4} 3112^{5} 3565^{16} 3833^{2} 4024^{4} **>96f<**

Courbaril 3 b c Warrshan (USA)-Free on Board (Free State) 163a^{6} 207a^{5} (291a) 488a^{9} 427^{6} 717^{2} 974^{4} 1978^{5} 2172^{3} 2439^{9} (2812) 3130^{3} 3500^{7} 3918^{6} **>52a 72f<**

Coureur 6 b g Ajdal (USA)-Nihad (Alleged (USA)) 1250^{2} (1531) 1808^{W} 1946^{3} 2222^{3} 4038^{10} 4284^{9} **>74f<**

Course Fishing 4 ch c Squill (USA)-Migoletty (Oats) 1286^{4} *1459^{8}* 1799^{7} 1971^{9} (2245) 2543^{5} 2861^{5} 3259^{2} (3402) 3531^{7} 4002^{10} **>17a 54f<**

Courting Danger 2 b g Tina's Pet-Court Town (Camden Town) 3733^{7} 3873^{4} **>64f<**

Courting Newmarket 7 b h Final Straw-Warm Wind (Tumble Wind (USA)) *298^{7} 371^{8}* 882^{19} 1541^{11} 1714^{13} 1940^{6} 2148^{2} 2789^{17} **>57a 53f<**

Court Joker (IRE) 3 b c Fools Holme (USA)-Crimson Glen (Glenstal (USA)) 689^{4} 948^{5} 1970^{10} 2993^{4} 3669^{6} 3818^{11} (4205) **>69f<**

Court Minstrel 6 br h Hadeer-Sheer Bliss 873^{20} 1126^{6} 1676^{4} 2010^{5} 2345^{4} 3455^{5} **>63f<**

Court Nap (IRE) 3 ch c Waajib-Mirhar (FR) (Sharpen Up) *627^{5}* 976^{2} 1323^{15} 1512^{3} 1664^{2} 2010^{8} 2317^{2} 3757^{5} 3885^{11} **>64a 64f<**

Court of Honour (IRE) 3 b c Law Society (USA)-Captive Island (Northfields (USA)) 979^{2} 1396a^{2} 1611^{5} 2218a^{9} 3790a^{3} 4011a^{2} (4182a) **>122f<**

Courtown Boy 5 ch g Ballacashtal (CAN)-Palace Gossip (Tender King) 1814^{2} 2331^{3} **>72f<**

Coven Moon 5 ch m Crofthall-Mayspark (Stanford) *335^{2} 379^{6} 415^{8}* 2450^{13} *2961^{10}* (3259) **>36a 41f<**

Covent Garden Girl 5 b m Sizzling Melody-Azelly (Pitskelly) 688^{13} **>67da 44f<**

Cowboy Dreams (IRE) 2 b c Nashamaa-Shahrazad (Young Emperor) 2777^{5} 3157^{9} 3494^{10} **>36f<**

Coyote Bluff(IRE) 2 gr c Fayruz-Ikala (Lashkari) (1003a) 3917^{8} *4124^{3}* **>78a 80f<**

Cozzi (FR) 7 gr g Cozzene (USA)-Land Girl (USA) (Sir Ivor) 818^{7} 1048^{8} 2050^{7} **>6a 49df<**

Crab 'n Lobster (IRE) 5 b m Waajib-Storm Crest *45^{13} 2592^{11} 2960^{8}* **>33a 40f<**

Crackernat (IRE) 2 b c Classic Music (USA)-Party Piece (Thatch (USA)) 1856^{9} (2453) 2833^{2} 3228^{5} 3684^{3} **>83df<**

Cracking Prospect 4 ch g Hubbly Bubbly (USA)-Crackerjill (Sparkler) 817^{16} 1126^{16} 2037^{6} 2510^{4} 2863^{4}

3137^{8} **>50f<**

Cradle Days **6** b h Dance of Life (USA)-Dream Chaser (Record Token) *93^{8}* 565^{10} 723^{10} 812^{8} 984^{11} 1537^{10} 1909^{4} 2665^{9} 2879^{6} **>59a 64f<**

Crafty Cricketer **4** ch c Clantime-Ruby Shoes (Day Is Done) *23^{8} 39^{10} 142^{5} 341^{10} 390^{6}* 541^{12} **>21a 42f<**

Craigie Boy **5** b h Crofthall-Lady Carol (Lord Gayle (USA)) 723^{11} 877^{3} 1179^{13} 1508^{8} 1614^{6} 2930^{9} 3145^{16} 3492^{11} 3615^{10} 3751^{3} 3830^{2} 3878^{6} 3992^{20} 4280^{20} **>29a 61f<**

Craigmill **3** b f Slip Anchor-Rynechra (Blakeney) 2348^{9} 2691^{14} **>84f<**

Craigmore Magic (USA) **2** br g Simply Majestic (USA)-Some Rehearsal (USA) (Halo (USA)) *2629^{6}* 2756^{5} *3525^{7}* 3744^{6} **>43a 54f<**

Craignairn **2** b c Merdon Melody-Bri-Ette (Brittany) 1494^{3} 1935^{3} 2464^{6} 2852^{6} 3309^{5} 3671^{2} 4098^{2} **>82f<**

Cramona (IRE) **5** ch m Carmelite House (USA)-Cramond *267^{12}* **>35da 34f<**

Cranbrook Kate **3** b f Damister (USA)-Overdraft (Bustino) 736^{7} *893^{7}* **>26a 22f<**

Cranfield Cracker **4** b f Beveled (USA)-Jump to it (Double Form) *177^{11} 240^{8}* **>9a f<**

Craven Cottage **2** b g Inca Chief (USA)-Seymour Ann (Krayyan) 2340^{6} 3157^{7} 3673^{10} **>61f<**

Crazy Chief **2** b c Indian Ridge-Bizarre Lady (Dalsaan) 3673^{2} 3890^{2} 4161^{3} **>86f<**

Crazy Paving (IRE) **4** b c Danehill (USA)-Clunk Click (Star Appeal) 665^{7} **>96df<**

Creative Account (USA) **2** b br c Time For A Change (USA)-Stolie (USA) (Navajo (USA)) 1247^{5} 2473^{2} 3117^{2} (3375) 3947^{5} 4107^{7} **>88f<**

Credit Controller (IRE) **6** b g Dromod Hill-Fotopan (Polyfoto) 3896^{12} **>6f<**

Credite Risque **2** b f Risk Me (FR)-Lompoa (Lomond (USA)) 782^{8} 1017^{8} 1779^{5} **>36f<**

Credit Squeeze **5** ch h Superlative-Money Supply (Brigadier Gerard) 430^{17} (545) 738^{3} (884) 1102^{5} 1635^{4} 2022^{4} 2745^{8} 2937^{7} **>74a 85f<**

Crees Sqaw **3** b f Cree Song-Elsocko (Swing Easy (USA)) 3829^{8} **>60f<**

Crespo (IRE) **3** b c Kris-Fair Salinia (Petingo) 485^{5} 1194^{4} (1477) **>85+f<**

Crested Knight (IRE) **3** gr c Night Shift (USA)-Casual (USA) (Caro) 427^{17} 651^{4} 1907^{2} 2531^{7} 4035^{8} 4136^{11} **>72f<**

Cretan Gift **4** ch c Cadeaux Genereux-Caro's Niece (USA) (Caro) *519^{2} (590) 769^{9}* 3293^{11} *3739^{4}* 3764^{2} *(3954) (4125)* 4215^{5} 4268^{7} **>76a 71f<**

Criminal Record (USA) **5** b h Fighting Fit (USA)-Charlie's Angel (USA) (Halo (USA)) *375^{6} 516^{6}* **>66da f<**

Crimson And Clover **2** gr f Midyan (USA)-Carose 725^{3} 878^{5} 1798^{7} (2505) 2911^{4} 3623^{12} **>66f<**

Crimson Rosella **2** b br f Polar Falcon (USA)-Double Finesse 4154^{6} **>46f<**

Crimson Shower **3** b or br f Dowsing (USA)-Flaming Rose (USA) (Upper Nile (USA)) 451^{4} 753^{3} 1366^{4} (1664) 2317^{5} 3605^{21} 4079^{12} 4316^{5} **>65f<**

Crissem (IRE) **2** b f Thatching-Deer Emily 2275^{5} 2782^{3} (2932) 3865^{22} **>69f<**

Cristal Springs **4** b f Dance of Life (USA)-Cristalga (High Top) *58^{7} 260^{4} 375^{10}* 729^{4} 840^{5} 1449^{4} **>34a 45f<**

Crock d'Or **5** b g Heights of Gold-Pegleg (New Member) 3282^{6}

Crocodile Rock **3** b c Sizzling Melody-Sunley Sinner (Try My Best (USA)) *64^{10} 225^{9} 316^{11}* 887^{18} 1207^{13} 2016^{9} **>6a 20f<**

Crocodile Shoes **2** b c Emarati (USA)-Gas Only (Northfields (USA)) 1511^{2} (1977) 2442^{5} 3587a^{21} **>76f<**

Croeso Cynnes **2** ch f Most Welcome-Miss Taleca (Pharly (FR)) 1054^{9} (1540) 2315^{6} 2847^{5} 3623^{10} 3749^{8} 4144^{9} **>75f<**

Croeso-I-Cymru **4** b f Welsh Captain-Bridge of Gold (Balidar) 858^{5} 1488^{9} 1766^{10} 3279^{4} (3557) 3615^{3} 3922^{5} 4040^{19} **>99f<**

Crofters Ceilidh **3** ch f Scottish Reel-Highland Rowena (Royben) 1220^{4} 1488^{8} 1765^{12} **>100?f<**

Croft Imperial **8** ch h Crofthall-Farinara (Dragonara Palace (USA)) 723^{5} 926^{11} 1106^{8} 1304^{6} 1461^{2} 1599^{7} 1741^{4} 2120^{6} 2252^{4} (2521) 2992^{10} 3221^{4} (3418) **>77a 71f<**

Croft Pool **4** b c Crofthall-Blackpool Belle (The Brianstan) *(6) 93^{2} 184^{5} 345^{3}* 949^{2} 1106^{5} 1354^{2} 1648^{2} 2096^{11} 2458^{7} 2652^{2} 2823^{2} 3145^{19} 3637^{15} (3822) (4119) (4197) 4324^{4} **>84a 105f<**

Croft Valley **8** ch h Crofthall-Sannavally (Sagaro) 1728^{4} 2235^{2} 2436^{3} 3085^{13} 3358^{4} 3602^{11} **>103f<**

Cromayres **5** b g Ayres Rock-Cromwell Girl (Forlorn River) 3282^{15}

Cronk's Courage **9** ch h Krayyan-Iresine (GER) (Frontal) *307^{4} 354^{12}* 491^{4} 594^{16} *1334^{10}* 1565^{6} 3467^{15} 3855^{9} **>41a 36f<**

Cross Talk (IRE) **3** b c Darshaan-Liaison (USA) 539^{12} 657^{8} 1150^{6} 1495^{2} 2004^{2} (2189) 3935^{17} 4047^{13} 4228^{5} **>74f<**

Cross The Border **2** b c Statoblest-Brave Advance (USA) (Bold Laddie (USA)) 2408^{10} 2660^{2} (2970) 3176^{2} 3699^{3} 3766^{3} **>89f<**

Crowded Avenue **3** b c Sizzling Melody-Lady Bequick 1094^{19} 1201^{6} (1419) (1822) 2239^{2} (2742) 3166^{2} (3407) (3554) 3902^{7} **>98f<**

Crowned Glory (USA) **3** b c Chief's Crown (USA)-Cherry Jubilee (USA) (Coastal (USA)) 584^{3} 851^{14} 1325^{5} (1606) 2065^{2} 2244^{7} **>74f<**

Crowning Tino **3** b f Crowning Honors (CAN)-Tino Reppin (Neltino) 3761^{10} 3974^{16} 4049^{13} **>26f<**

Crown of Love (USA) **3** b f Nureyev (USA)-Hiaam (USA) (Alydar (USA)) 1476^{12} 2236^{3} 2507^{6} 2819^{2} 3128^{5} **>68f<**

Crown of Sheba (USA) **3** b f Alysheba (USA)-Belle de Jour (USA) 1701^{4} (1967) 2321^{8} **>73f<**

Crown Prosecutor **5** b g Law Society (USA)-Dance Card (Be My Guest (USA)) *53^{2} 223^{0}* **>75a f<**

Crowther Homes **5** br m Neltino-Fair Sara (McIndoe) 3646^{14} 3818^{17} 3971^{17} 4140^{P} *4336^{15}* **>30f<**

Crucis (IRE) **4** gr c Kalaglow-Brave Advance (USA) (Bold Laddie (USA)) 539^{18} 675^{4} *845^{3} 1329^{4}* **>51a 45f<**

Crumpton Hill (IRE) **3** b c Thatching-Senane (Vitiges (FR)) (694) 1306^{3} 3368^{8} 3732^{8} 3945^{7} 4116^{19} **>93f<**

Cry Baby **2** b c Bairn (USA)-Estonia (Kings Lake (USA)) 1798^{6} *3243^{8}* 3427^{9} 3850^{6} 4141^{11} **>44a 60f<**

Crystado (FR) **6** ch h Crystal Glitters (USA)-Kantado 3807^{16}

Crystal Bird (IRE) **0** ch f Ela-Mana-Mou-Irish Bird (USA)

(Sea-Bir 2563a^{9} **>66f<**

Crystal Blade 3 b c Dashing Blade-Crystal's Solo (USA) (Crystal Water (USA)) 1490^{4} 1764^{2} (2004) 2415^{3} 3142^{5} 3593^{10} **>90f<**

Crystal Cavern (USA) 3 ch f Be My Guest (USA)-Krisalya (Kris) 868^{5} 1178^{5} 1639^{8} 3768^{2} 4024^{8} 4214^{3} **>92df<**

Crystal Falls (IRE) 2 b r Alzao (USA)-Honourable Sheba (USA) (Roberto (USA)) 2485^{6} 2876^{2} 3228^{2} 3416^{3} 3701^{7} 3967^{2} (4192) **>79f<**

Crystal Fast (USA) 2 b c Fast Play (USA)-Crystal Cave (USA) (Nearctic) *4334^{11}* **>27a f<**

Crystal Gift 3 b c Dominion-Grain Lady (USA) (Greinton) 730^{4} *1034^{14}* 1949^{3} 3390^{9} 3771^{12} 3959^{7} 4152^{16} *4296^{4}* **>57a 64f<**

Crystal Heart (IRE) 4 ch f Broken Hearted-Arachosia (Persian Bold) 2327^{13} **>43f<**

Crystal Heights (FR) 7 ch h Crystal Glitters (USA)-Fahrenheit (Mount Hagen (FR)) *(192) 237^{4} 272^{2} 359^{3} 405^{4} 499^{2}* 728^{6} 1071^{4} 1276^{5} 1510^{4} 1676^{8} 2178^{2} (2538) *3074^{4}* 3545^{2} 3757^{14} (3960) **>67a 77f<**

Crystal Loop 3 b f Dowsing (USA)-Gipping (Vision (USA)) *(43) 74^{5} 196^{2} (243) 284^{4} (392)* 426^{11} 674^{12} 999^{12} 1157^{2} 1279^{2} 1565^{11} 1783^{4} 2311^{2} (2394) 2519^{5} 2935^{9} 2997^{8} (3376) 3777^{10} 3822^{17} 3905^{13} **>76a 72f<**

Crystal Magic 4 b f Mazilier (USA)-Thulium (Mansingh (USA)) 693^{5} 858^{2} 1055^{3} 1475^{8} **>93f<**

Crystal Warrior 2 b f Warrshan (USA)-Crystal's Solo (USA) (Crystal Water (USA)) 4148^{5} **>42f<**

Cuango (IRE) 4 b or br c Mtoto-Barinia 737^{3} 954^{3} 1109^{3} 1310^{5} 1794^{4} 1929^{7} 2087^{5} 2238^{3} 2612^{4} 2937^{6} 3445^{9} 3774^{10} 3936^{10} 4051^{3} 4189^{3} (4248) 4288^{7} **>65f<**

Cuba 3 b c Soviet Star (USA)-Rosetta Stone (Guillaume Tell (USA)) 1312^{6} 1755^{6} *2494^{3}* 3440^{10} 3634^{6} **>61a 76f<**

Cuban Nights (USA) 3 b g Our Native (USA)-Havana Moon (USA) (Cox's Ridge (USA)) 4022^{6} 4136^{12} **>54f<**

Cuban Reef 3 b f Dowsing (USA)-Cox's Pippin (USA) (Cox's Ridge (USA)) *38^{8} 144^{8} 2636^{8}* 3344^{3} (3475) 3661^{7} 3980^{3} 4249^{2} **>32a 57f<**

Cuckmere Venture 5 br m King of Spain-Kala Nashan (Kala Shikari) 4214^{5} **>34f<**

Cuff Link (IRE) 5 ch g Caerleon (USA)-Corinth Canal (Troy) (958) 1363^{6} (1898) 2702^{7} 3146^{2} 3563^{5} 3946^{5} **>113f<**

Cuillin Caper 3 b f Scottish Reel-That Space (Space King) 773^{6} 1059^{9} 1647^{13} **>50f<**

Culrain 4 b g Hadeer-La Vie En Primrose (Henbit (USA)) *104^{5}* **>49a 36f<**

Cumbrian Challenge (IRE) 6 ch h Be My Native (USA)-Sixpenny (English Prince) 3993^{10} **>74f<**

Cumbrian Maestro 2 b c Puissance-Flicker Toa Flame (USA) (Empery (USA)) 1597^{9} 2063^{5} 2192^{3} 2608^{4} 3394^{4} 3546^{9} 3701^{3} 3809^{3} 3990^{13} **>70f<**

Cumbrian Minstrel 3 b c Efisio-Miss Nanna (Vayrann) 969^{9} 1269^{5} 1666^{8} 2356^{6} 2610^{6} 3099^{3} 3422^{6} 3825^{9} **>57f<**

Cumbrian Rhapsody 5 ch m Sharrood (USA)-Bustellina (Busted) 1268^{5} 1621^{6} 2101^{3} 2196^{4} 3705^{3} 3801^{12} 3936^{16} **>71f<**

Cumbrian Waltzer 10 ch g Stanford-Mephisto Waltz 1468^{11} 1599^{4} 2746^{7} 3418^{5} 3492^{8} 3715^{4} 3830^{4} 3964^{8} 4041^{16} 4319^{7} **>80f<**

Cupla Focail 2 b f Inca Chief (USA)-Lizzie Bee (Kind of Hush) *1031^{7}* 2656^{6} 3378^{8} *3528^{13}* **>7a 21f<**

Cupronickel (IRE) 3 b f Distant Relative-One Half Silver (CAN) (Plugged Nickle (USA)) 613^{7} 758^{6} 924^{8} 1358^{13} 1742^{11} **>56f<**

Curie Crusader (IRE) 4 gr c Belfort (FR)-Katysue *92^{8} (306)* **>59a 62f<**

Curie Express (IRE) 3 ch f Fayruz-Windini (Windjammer (USA)) *7^{4}* **>46a 66f<**

Current Leader 2 b c Primo Dominie-Trelissick (Electric) 690^{11} 910^{7} 2741^{7} 3246^{2} 3502^{3} 3644^{10} **>76f<**

Current Speech (IRE) 4 b g Thatching-Lady Aladdin (Persian Bold) 785^{9} 3368^{10} 3703^{7} 3810^{3} 3965^{7} **>76f<**

Curtelace 5 ch h Nishapour (FR)-Khandjar (Kris) 3384^{5} 3531^{4} 3657^{7} 3810^{4} 3977^{2} 4061^{2} 4138^{5} **>66f<**

Cut Adrift 4 b f Nordico (USA)-Cut No Ice (Great Nephew) *53^{11} 347^{6}* **>36a 73df<**

Cutpurse Moll 3 b f Green Desert (USA)-Pretty Pol (Final Straw) 1476^{5} 1701^{2} (2206) 2613^{7} 3943^{8} 4319^{14} **>77f<**

Cutthroat Kid (IRE) 5 b h Last Tycoon-Get Ahead 423^{13} 495^{2} 2374^{5} 2465^{5} 3852^{9} **>45a 74f<**

C-Yer-Simmie (IRE) 3 b f Prince Rupert (FR)-Battle Queen (Kind of Hush) *132^{2} 284^{2} 342^{3}* 426^{12} 483^{5} 754^{2} 1450^{7} 1580^{6} 2024^{3} 2394^{8} 2680^{5} 2877^{2} *3524^{2}* **>63a 64f<**

Cymbalo 4 ch c Sharpo-Cynomis (Shergar) 1422^{9} 1688^{6} 2478^{7} **>4f<**

Cyphell (IRE) 3 b f Sadler's Wells (USA)-Cipriani 779^{3} 950^{8} 2449^{2} 2664^{3} 3234^{4} 3573^{2} 3859^{5} **>65f<**

Cypress Avenue (IRE) 3 b c Law Society (USA)-Flying Diva (Chief Singer) 691^{5} 942^{3} 1099^{2} 1987^{4} 2119^{3} 2366^{5} 4220^{5} **>86df<**

Cyprus Point 4 b f Unfuwain (USA)-Sunshine Coast (Posse (USA)) *63^{6} 155^{9}* 4193^{13} **>31a 57f<**

Cyrano's Lad (IRE) 6 b or br g Cyrano de Bergerac-Patiala 848^{3} 1080^{2} (1482) 1915^{3} 2703^{16} 2948^{7} 3411^{11} 3637^{2} (3924) 3999^{3} 4160^{14} **>100f<**

Cyrillic 2 ch f Rock City-Lariston Gale (Pas de Seul) 561^{2} 669^{9} (1424) 1634^{3} 2106^{5} 3956^{7} **>73f<**

Cyrus the Great (IRE) 3 ch c Persian Heights-Smart As Paint (USA) (Caerleon (USA)) 504^{10} 614^{11} 3497^{6} 3654^{3} 3863^{2} 3926^{7} 4038^{23} **>85f<**

Czarna (IRE) 4 b c Polish Precedent (USA)-Noble Dust (USA) (Dust Commander (USA)) 714^{5} 870^{11} 1143^{4} 1365^{2} 1851^{19} 2369^{13} 2746^{9} 2950^{4} **>97f<**

D

Daaniera (IRE) 5 gr h Standaan (FR)-Right Cash (Right Tack) *102^{5} 177^{9} 369^{7} 498^{7} 3524^{6}* **>49a 23f<**

Daawe (USA) 4 b c Danzig (USA)-Capo Di Monte (Final Straw) 1291^{6} 1808^{14} 2455^{11} 4193^{9} 4292^{10} **>58f<**

Dabka Dancer 2 b c Cadeaux Genereux-Lady Shipley (Shirley Heights) 3340^{5} 3663^{3} **>80f<**

Dacha (IRE) 3 b c Soviet Star (USA)-Shadywood (Habitat) 4213^{4} **>86f<**

Daffaq 3 b c Unfuwain (USA)-Awayed (USA) (Sir Ivor) 428^{5} 504^{17} 1338^{3} 1611^{14} **>80f<**

Daffodil Express (IRE) 2 b f Skyliner-Miss Henry (Blue Cashmere) 3379^{9} 3628^{4} 3869^{11} 4133^{8} **>53f<**

Dahik 3 b c Green Desert (USA)-Littlefield (Bay Express) 622^{4} 886^{2} (1103) 1636^{5} 2738^{8} 3131^{3} **>109f<**

Dahiyah (USA) **4** b c Ogygian (USA)-Sticky Prospect (USA) (Mr Prospector (USA)) *199[7]* *408[4]* 541[5] (1016) 1276[9] 1429[6] *2943[6]* 3177[2] 3681[12] **>48a 67f<**

Dahlenburg (IRE) **3** b br c Alzao (USA)-Dahsala (Top Ville) 764[15] 968[3] 1147[9] 1436[2] 1596[16] 2747[13] 3125[8] **>74f<**

Da Hoss (USA) **3** b g Gone West (USA)-Jolly Saint (USA) *4303a[13]* **>57a f<**

Daily Challenger (USA) **3** b c Moment of Hope (USA)-Goodness Sakes (USA) (The Real McCoy (USA)) *48[5]* *95[8]* *339[11]* *420[9]* *603[9]* 732[6] 1153[5] 1523[14] 2372[4] 2818[2] 3257[5] **>37a 74f<**

Daily Risk **2** ch c Risk Me (FR)-Give Me a Day (Lucky Wednesday) 562[5] 760[6] 2315[7] 3613[5] 3956[2] 4208[4] **>70f<**

Daily Sport Girl **6** b m Risk Me (FR)-Net Call (USA) (Quack (USA)) 778[2] 905[4] **>47f<**

Daily Starlight (USA) **3** br c Minshaanshu Amad (USA)-Appeal The Rule (USA) (Valid Appeal (USA)) (1204) (1725) 1817[4] (2026) 2193[4] 3277[4] (3555) 3730[8] 3927[5] **>85f<**

Daily Starshine (IRE) **3** b f Petorius-Mainly Sunset (Red Sunset) 475[10] *629[3]* *831[3]* 1157[4] 1580[3] 1721[5] 1972[10] 3313[8] 3622[23] **>65a 61f<**

Daira **2** br f Daring March-Ile de Reine (Ile de Bourbon (USA)) *3523[5]* 3850[3] 4277[5] **>43a 66f<**

Dairine's Delight (IRE) **5** b m Fairy King (USA)-Silius (Junius (USA)) 1572a[6] 2888a[2] (3902) 4181a[5] **>107f<**

Dakota Brave (IRE) **4** b c Exactly Sharp (USA)-Terrama Sioux (Relkino) *843[8]* **>70a 66f<**

Dakota Girl **4** b f Northern State (USA)-Marielou (FR) (Carwhite) 582[8] 795[W] **>54f<**

Dalcross **4** gr f Nishapour (FR)-Pomade (Luthier (FR)) 546[15] 839[10] 1290[9] 3573[6] 4156[15] **>41f<**

Daleria **4** b f Darshaan *394[4]* 987[8] 1683[2] *2379[2]* *3076[2]* *(3526)* **>63a 48f<**

Daleside **7** gr h Full Out (USA)-All Regal (Run The Gantlet (USA)) 2157[4] 2734[8] **>35f<**

Dalidjan (IRE) **3** b c Doyoun-Damana (Crystal Palace) 1575a[7] **>104f<**

Dallachio (IRE) **4** ch g Shernazar-Mafiosa (Miami Springs) 623[17] **>61f<**

Dallai (IRE) **4** b c Dance of Life (USA)-Wavetree (Realm) *4[5]* *(183)* *259[10]* **>56a 55f<**

Dally Boy **3** b c Efisio-Gay Hostess (FR) (Direct Flight) 3422[9] *3526[9]* 4101[9] 4234[11] **>70a 53f<**

Dalu (IRE) **4** br f Dancing Brave (USA)-Abhaaj (Kris) 946[6] 1251[7] **>75f<**

Dalwhinnie **2** b f Persian Bold-Land Line (High Line) 4190[10] **>45f<**

Dalysnicelitlerner **3** gr c Daily Sport Soon-Aphabel (Belfort (FR)) 2524[8] 3635[12] **>41f<**

Dama Grande **6** b m Damister (USA)-Spimpinina (Be My Guest (USA)) 4020a[9] **>101f<**

Damancher **3** b c Damister-Amalancher (USA) (Alleged (USA)) 2218a[6] 4173a[5] **>118f<**

Damarita **4** ch f Starry Night (USA)-Sirenivo (USA) 4072[18]

Damier Blanc (FR) **6** b g Damister (USA)-Roche Blanche (FR) (Great Nephew) 652[6] **>72f<**

Damocles **3** b c Dashing Blade-Madam Trilby (Grundy) 1125[14] 1445[10] 1719[5] 1962[17] **>59f<**

Danaa Minni (IRE) **3** ch c Caerleon (USA)-Ivory Home (FR) (Home Gua 2559a[2]

Danamich (IRE) **2** b c Fayruz-Galapagos (Pitskelly) 3231[17]

Dana Point (IRE) **3** br g Phardante (FR)-Wallpark Princess (Balidar) (3295) **>70f<**

Dance Across (IRE) **2** b f Nabeel Dancer (USA)-Fordes Cross (Ya Zaman (USA)) 3983[15] 4048[12] **>48f<**

Dance a Dream **3** b f Sadler's Wells (USA)-Exclusive Order (USA) (Exclusive Native (USA)) (997) 1587[2] 1867[4] 3161[6] **>114f<**

Dance and Sing (IRE) **5** b g The Noble Player (USA)-Cherlinoa (FR) (Crystal Palace (FR)) *68[9]* *129[9]* 1996[10] 2546[13] **>30a 25f<**

Dance Band (USA) **3** b c Dixieland Band (USA)-Brief Remarks (USA) (Talc (USA)) 536[3] 678[4] 980[4] 1474[2] 1839[18] 2471[3] 2593[2] (2803) 3066[6] **>98f<**

Dance Clear (IRE) **2** b f Marju (IRE)-Dance Ahead (Shareef Dancer (USA)) 4341a[3]

Dance Design (IRE) **2** b f Sadler's Wells (USA)-Elegance in Design (Habitat) 3692a[4] 4013a[4] **>98f<**

Dance King **3** b c Rambo Dancer (CAN)-Northern Venture *381[3]* *443[7]* 689[2] 1154[2] 1436[3] (2760) 2974[2] *3240[11]* 3645[17] 3778[7] **>62a 75f<**

Dance Motion **3** b g Damister (USA)-Tantalizing Song (CAN) (The Minstrel (CAN)) 1358[15] **>42a 55f<**

Dance of Joy **3** b f Shareef Dancer (USA)-Lady Habitat 648[14] 948[8] 1498[15] 2640[5] **>60f<**

Dance of The Moon **2** b f High Estate-Oh So Well (IRE) (Sadler's Wells (USA)) 523[2] 669[3] **>82f<**

Dance On A Cloud (USA) **2** b f Capote (USA)-Sharp Dance (USA) (Dancing Czar (USA)) 3821[6] (4210) **>76+f<**

Dance on Sixpence **7** b h Lidhame-Burning Ambition (Troy) *1078[8]* 2246[20] **>52f<**

Dance Partner (JPN) **3** b f Sunday Silence (USA)-Dancing Key (USA) 3575a[2] 3694a[6] **>112f<**

Dance Sequence (USA) **2** ch f Mr Prospector (USA)-Dancing Tribute (USA) (Nureyev (USA)) 1361[2] 1849[2] 2322[2] (3186) 3866[4] **>105f<**

Dance So Suite **3** b c Shareef Dancer (USA)-Three Piece (Jaazeiro (USA)) (1978) 2166[2] 2406[3] 2555[5] (3935) 4149[5] **>55a 86f<**

Dance Star **2** b f Damister (USA)-Glen Dancer (Furry Glen) 3900[13] (4247) **>79f<**

Dances With Hooves **3** b c Dancing Dissident (USA)-Princesse Legere (USA) (Alleged (USA)) 553[3] 715[11] **>74f<**

Dance To Victory **2** b f Ron's Victory (USA)-Nodolya (Niniski (USA)) 474[5] 554[6] **>25f<**

Dance Treat (USA) **3** ch f Nureyev (USA)-Office Wife (USA) (Secretariat (USA)) 3239[9]

Dance Turn **4** b c Damister (USA)-Spin Turn (Homing) 714[15] 1108[5] (1365) 1835[6] 2217a[2] 2444[2] 3325a[4] 3360[6] 3904[9] **>116df<**

Dancing Beggar **3** c 2044a[7] **>114f<**

Dancing Cavalier **2** b c Nalchik (USA)-Miss Admington (Double Jump) *3736[7]* 3967[12] 4313[16] **>53a 50f<**

Dancing Cormorant **2** b c Shareef Dancer (USA)-Cormorant Creek (Gorytus (USA)) 2420[6] 3592[15] **>37f<**

Dancing Debut **2** b f Polar Falcon (USA)-Exclusive Virtue (USA) (Shadeed (USA)) 4246[4] **>58f<**

Dancing Destiny **3** b f Dancing Brave (USA)-Tender Loving Care (Final Straw) 1128[7] 1658[2] 1922[2] 2993[7]

3685^{20} 4138^{13} 4283^{7} **>63f<**

Dancing Diamond (IRE) 5 b m Alzao (USA)-Shay Tien (Gunner B) *58^{2} 178^{3} (200) 260^{2} (288) 374^{11}* **>59a 47f<**

Dancing Dot (IRE) 2 b f Durgam (USA)-Canty's Gold (Sonnen Gold) 1494^{4} 3666^{13} 3744^{3} 3850^{8} 3975^{22} 4290^{13} **>66f<**

Dancing Heart 3 b c Thowra (FR)-Miss Lawsuit (Neltino) 971^{4} (1165) 1222^{8} 2848^{4} 3286^{2} 3615^{12} 3897^{3} *4125^{6}* 4145^{9} *4297^{4}* **>68a 78f<**

Dancing Heights (IRE) 4 b f High Estate-Alpine Symphony (Northern Dancer) 1280^{4} 1808^{5} 2028^{7} 2577^{5} **>86f<**

Dancing Image 2 ch c Salse (USA)-Reflection (Mill Reef (USA)) 2597^{3} 3155^{6} 3888^{5} **>78f<**

Dancing Jack 2 ch c Clantime-Sun Follower (Relkino) 760^{9} 1096^{3} 1384^{5} 2091^{6} 3567^{4} 4132^{5} 4219^{6} *4294^{4}* **>44a 65f<**

Dancing Jazztime 4 b f Clantime-Dance in Spain (King of Spain) 3649^{15}

Dancing Lawyer 4 b c Thowra (FR)-Miss Lawsuit (Neltino) *89^{16}* 1815^{5} 2010^{3} 2169^{4} 2342^{4} 2685^{6} 3026^{4} 3248^{3} 3439^{2} 3629^{4} **>77a 80f<**

Dancing Lottie (IRE) 2 b f Dancing Dissident (USA)-Charlotteen 455^{2} 615^{15} 910^{6} *1089^{8}* 1989^{4} 2204^{4} 2800^{5} 2965^{7} **>28a 62f<**

Dancing Man 2 ch c Executive Man-Lyne Dancer (Be My Native (USA)) 3651^{13} 3895^{15} 4075^{24} **>15f<**

Dancing Rainbow 2 b f Rambo Dancer (CAN)-Heemee (On Your Mark) (1821) 2085^{8} 2991^{4} 3369^{6} 3969^{15} **>71df<**

Dancing Reef 6 b m Miramar Reef-Facing (Quiet Fling (USA)) *120^{13}*

Dancing Sensation (USA) 8 b m Faliraki-Sweet Satina (USA) (Crimson Satan) *356^{3} 403^{10}* 423^{22} 763^{2} (961) 1410^{2} 1612^{9} 2289^{3} (2599) 3336^{5} 3657^{14} **>37a 78f<**

Dancing Sioux 3 b c Nabeel Dancer (USA)-Sutosky (Great Nephew) 1486^{9} 1786^{4} 1982^{9} *2923^{14}* 3103^{4} 3138^{2} 3649^{2} 3905^{17} 4057^{9} 4225^{5} *4296^{3}* **>59a 80df<**

Dancing Sunset (IRE) 4 br f Red Sunset-Dancing Partner (USA) (Graustark (USA)) 1235a^{5} 2211a^{10} **>112f<**

Dande Flyer 2 b br c Clantime-Lyndseylee (Swing Easy (USA)) 1054^{5} 1774^{4} 2135^{6} 2515^{3} 2826^{2} 3284^{4} 3567^{2} 3753^{5} 3856^{10} (4132) (4237) (4260) 4317^{3} **>74f<**

Danefair 3 b f Danehill-Roupala (Vaguely Noble) (2723a) **>99f<**

Danegold (IRE) 3 b c Danehill (USA)-Cistus (Sun Prince) 427^{3} *500^{3} 566^{5}* (689) 829^{10} 1124^{2} 1294^{2} (1447) 1638^{2} (1747) 1839^{13} 2062^{4} 2738^{9} 3585a^{8} (3654) 3729^{20} 3837^{11} 4163^{21} **>67a 87f<**

Danehill Chief 3 b g Dunbeath (USA)-Calafuria (Chief Singer) 1146^{11} 1405^{7} **>20f<**

Danehill Dancer (IRE) 2 b c Danehill (USA)-Mira Adonde (USA) (Sharpen Up) (2370) (3197a) (3788a) 4106^{2} **>115f<**

Danesman (IRE) 2 b c Danehill (USA)-Vernonhills (Hard Fought) 3174^{4} 3494^{2} (3683) **>82f<**

Danesrath (IRE) 3 b f Danehill (USA)-Tribal Rite 1717^{2} 2208^{4} (3224) 3500^{6} 3801^{6} **>85f<**

Dangerous Guest (IRE) 3 b c Deploy-Guest List (Be My Guest (USA)) *1211^{3}* 1872^{10} 2555^{2} **>83a 91f<**

Dangerous Waters 2 b f Risk Me (FR)-Queen's Lake (Kings Lake (USA)) 4148^{15} **>10f<**

Danico 2 ch c Most Welcome-Spica (USA) (Diesis) 2161^{4} 2971^{6} **>63f<**

Daniel's Lass 3 b f Prince Daniel (USA)-Haverhill Lass (Music Boy) 7321^{15} *844^{7}*

Danish Circus (IRE) 2 b c Danehill (USA)-Circus Maid (IRE) (High Top) 3494^{5} 3989^{3} 4210^{3} **>74f<**

Danish (IRE) 4 b f Danehill (USA)-Tea House (Sassafras (FR)) 3911a^{2} **>118f<**

Danjing (IRE) 3 b c Danehill (USA)-Beijing (USA) (Northjet (USA)) (1173) 1672^{5} 2691^{10} 3066^{9} 3336^{4} 3556^{3} 3730^{7} (3899) 4076^{6} **>92f<**

Dankeston (USA) 2 b c Elmaamul (USA)-Last Request (Dancers Image (USA)) 480^{2} (863) 2059^{3} 2434^{2} (2833) 3147^{3} (3301) 4084^{24} **>86f<**

Dannec (IRE) 3 c 2215a^{14} **>72f<**

Dannistar 3 br f Puissance-Loadplan Lass (Nicholas Bill) *4271^{5}* **>31a f<**

Danny's Gift 3 ch f Prince Daniel (USA)-Triple Bar *316^{8} 368^{4}* 521^{15} 1012^{10} **>30a 23f<**

Danseur Landais 5 b h Damister (USA)-Rise and Fall (Mill Reef 703a^{2} 1387a^{4} **>111f<**

Danson 4 b c Dancing Brave (USA)-Liaison (USA) *352^{9} 394^{12}* 1971^{8} **>25a 33f<**

Dantean 3 b c Warning-Danthonia (USA) (Northern Dancer) 1264^{7} 1490^{8} 1791^{7} **>61f<**

Dante's Rubicon (IRE) 4 ch c Common Grounds-Dromorehill (Ballymore) *520^{7} 766^{5}* 1153^{2} 1469^{11} 1603^{8} 1828^{15} (2220) 2484^{6} 2784^{2} 3681^{18} 3800^{16} 4275^{10} **>45a 52f<**

Danus Rex (IRE) 3 b c Roi Danzig (USA)-Hear Me 988^{11} 1219^{6} (1379) 1527^{9} *2147^{W}* 2860^{7} *3527^{9}* **>35a 66f<**

Daphnis (USA) 6 b h Lead on Time (USA)-Dancing Vaguely (USA) (Vaguely Noble) *46^{3} 245^{7}* **>47a f<**

Darakah 8 ch m Doulab (USA)-Ladytown (English Prince) *148^{10} 182^{11} 235^{9}* 503^{7} 1783^{5} 2246^{12} 2510^{6} **>17a 43f<**

Daraydala (IRE) 3 b f Royal Academy-Daralinsha (Empery) 2723a^{3} 3196a^{2} 4009a^{2} 4176a^{8} **>113f<**

Daraydan (IRE) 3 b c Kahyasi-Delsy (Abdos) 2218a^{13} 3930^{4} 4076^{4} (4258) **>112f<**

Darby Flyer 2 ch c Dominion Royale-Shining Wood (Touching Wood (USA)) 3733^{23} **>30f<**

Darcey Bussell 3 b f Green Desert (USA)-Docklands (On Your Mark) 2553^{8} 3023^{7} 3377^{4} 3941^{9} 4150^{2} 4242^{5} **>78f<**

Darerock 2 b g Daring March-Marock Morley 1678^{8} 2371^{5} 2606^{6} 3824^{17} 3975^{27} **>38f<**

Daring Destiny 4 b f Daring March-Raunchy Rita (Brigadier Gerard) 441^{5} 895a^{2} (1066) 1766^{2} 2212a^{11} 2673^{6} 2764^{18} 3717^{28} **>105f<**

Daring Gift 4 b or br f Never so Bold-Krameria (Kris) 748^{14} **>31f<**

Daring Ryde 4 b g Daring March-Mini Myra (Homing) 780^{19} 1290^{6} (1501) 1855^{5} 2276^{9} 2946^{10} 3531^{17} 4054^{3} 4170^{17} **>58f<**

Daring Venture 2 b f Dowsing (USA)-Berberana (Never so Bold) 1690^{13} **>23f<**

Darius The Great (IRE) 3 ch c Persian Heights-Derring Dee (Derrylin) 654^{7} *1030^{13}* 1834^{5} 2486^{14} **>32f<**

Dark Deed (USA) 2 ch f Known Fact (USA)-Sin Lucha (USA) (Northfields (USA)) 3069^{3} 3432^{2} 3662^{2} **>77f<**

Dark Eyed Lady (IRE) 5 b m Exhibitioner-Tribal Eye (Tribal Chief) *499[7]* 636[11] 2987[5] 3250[5] 3519[11] **>55a 48f<**

Dark Menace 3 br c Beveled (USA)-Sweet and Sure (Known Fact (USA)) 937[3] 1522[6] 1982[7] 2708[7] 2844[3] 3249[3] 3519[13] 3874[16] **>61df<**

Dark Nile (USA) 2 c 4177a[7] **>103f<**

Dark Robe 2 b f Timeless Times (USA)-Harem Queen (Prince Regent (FR)) 1798[11] **>13f<**

Dark Shot (IRE) 3 b c Rock City-Jeanne Avril (Music Boy) *151[5]* *(261)* *363[3]* *404[5]* *(591)* 732[2] 890[5] *3524[12]* *3739[7]* **>67a 67f<**

Dark Street (IRE) 5 b or br h Darshaan-Bay Street 1118a[9] **>101f<**

Dark Truffle 2 br f Deploy-River Dove (USA) (Riverman (USA)) 1142[8] **>54f<**

Dark Waters (IRE) 2 b c Darshaan-Grecian Sea (FR) (Homeric) 3089[16] 3620[2] **>71f<**

Darkwood Bay (USA) 4 b or br c Green Dancer (USA)-Unyielding (USA) 1408[7] **>100?f<**

Darling Clover 3 ch f Minster Son-Lady Clementine (He Loves Me) *213[4]* *376[4]* *509[2]* (1093) 1372[10] 1978[7] 2314[5] 2884[2] 3126[3] **>61a 64f<**

Darling Flame (USA) 2 b f Capote (USA)-My Darling One (USA) (Exclusive Native (USA)) 1627[2] (2025) 2322[2] 3186[8] **>99f<**

Darnay 4 br c Darshaan-Flawless Image (USA) (The Minstrel (CAN)) 1851[2] (2217a) 2689[3] 3067[3] 3360[2] 3589a[8] **>121f<**

Darren Boy (IRE) 4 ch g Ballad Rock-Trojan Relation (Trojan Fen) 693[11] 934[10] 1895[20] 2369[18] **>90f<**

Darter (IRE) 3 b c Darshaan-Mamouna (USA) (Vaguely Noble) 3421[3] 3772[6] 4072[5] 4228[3] **>71f<**

Dashing Blue 2 ch c Dashing Blade-Blubella (Balidar) 1246[2] 1620[4] 2091[2] (3432) 3612[4] (3990) **>93f<**

Dashing Dancer (IRE) 4 ch c Conquering Hero (USA)-Santa Maria (GER) (Literat) 765[5] 1016[4] 1483[2] 1756[4] 2009[3] 2578[8] *2943[2]* 3293[5] 3874[7] 4215[2] **>63a 68f<**

Dashing Invader (USA) 2 ch c Pirate Army (USA)-Cherie's Hope (USA) (Flying Paster (USA)) 3883[16] 4169[15] **>42f<**

Dashing Water 3 b f Dashing Blade-Peckitts Well (Lochnager) 660[6] 1185[4] 1370[3] 2325[7] 2737[10] 3085[12] 3316[5] **>90f<**

Das Island 3 b c Presidium-Phamilla (IRE) (Bellypha) *(274)* *319[4]* *342[4]* *447[2]* 1276[8] 1550[10] **>63a 55f<**

Daswaki (CAN) 7 b h Miswaki (USA)-Nice Manners (CAN) (Barachois (CAN)) 1754[10] 2661[8] 3108[8] 3605[19] **>47f<**

Dato Star (IRE) 4 br g Accordion-Newgate Fairy (Flair Path) 610[5] 929[4] 3772[2] 4201[10] 4325[2] **>99f<**

Daunt 3 b c Darshaan-Minute Waltz (Sadler's Wells (USA)) (552) **>90++f<**

Daunting Destiny (BEL) 2 b c Formidable (USA)-Heavy Land (FR) (Recitation (USA)) 2198[7] 2526[8] 3008[2] 3471[7] 4130[4] 4211[2] (4285) **>79f<**

Dauntless Fort 4 gr f Belfort (FR)-Dauntless Flight (Golden Mallard) *167[10]* *354[9]* 1469[7] *1571[11]* *1884[8]* 2162[5] 2463[10] 4281[11] **>42da 47f<**

Dauphin (IRE) 2 b br c Astronef-Va Toujours (Alzao (USA)) 3436[11] 4224[12] **>26f<**

David Blue (IRE) 4 b c Colmore Row-Royal Aunt (Martinmas) *28[10]* **>17a 54df<**

David James' Girl 3 b f Faustus (USA)-Eagle's Quest (Legal Eagle) *48[8]* *197[2]* *283[0]* *(411)* *528[4]* *2291[6]* 2390[2] 2815[2] *3075[9]* 3390[8] *4272[9]* **>73a 70f<**

Dawalib (USA) 5 ch h Danzig Connection (USA)-Centavos (USA) (Scout Leader (USA)) *44[5]* *93[3]* *184[4]* *281[3]* *365[3]* (780) 887[2] (1021) 1280[2] 1560[2] 2010[2] 2414[6] (3109) 3492[7] 3715[9] **>73a 75f<**

Dawawin (USA) 2 b f Dixieland Band (USA)-Stalwart Moment (USA) (Stalwart (USA)) 4188[3] **>79+f<**

Dawlah 3 b or br f Shirley Heights-Urjwan (USA) (Seattle Slew (USA)) 797[2] 1105[3] (1346) 1800[3] 2415[5] 2878[W] 3091[5] 3682[3] 3930[5] **>100df<**

Dawn Flight 6 b g Precocious-Sea Kestrel 3569[7] **>36a 52f<**

Dawn Mission 3 b g Dunbeath (USA)-Bustellina (Busted) 641[3] 787[5] 929[8] 2189[3] 2648[5] *3078[4]* 3299[5] 3464[5] **>51a 52f<**

Dawn Palace 4 ch g Dawn Johnny (USA)-Lenton Palace (Dragonara Palace (USA)) 2834[4]

Dawn Rock 4 b c Norwick (USA)-Venetian Joy (Windjammer (USA)) *79[5]* 495[6] 534[13] 597[5] 879[17] 2931[4] 3705[13] **>50a 29f<**

Dawsha (IRE) 3 b f Slip Anchor-Zarrara (USA) (Desert Wine) 715[8] 937[6] (1317) 1589[5] **>75f<**

Daydreamer (USA) 2 b c Alleged (USA)-Stardusk (USA) (Stage Door Johnny) 4313[10] **>58f<**

Daydream Island 2 ch f Never so Bold-La Belle Vie (Indian King (USA)) 3763[15] 4148[18] **>21f<**

Daysman (USA) 3 b c Dayjur (USA)-Model Village (Habitat) 442[7] 2949[4] 3103[3] 3565[12] **>83f<**

Days of Thunder 7 ch h Vaigly Great-Silent Prayer (Queen's Hussar) *214[4]* *497[5]* **>41a 49f<**

Daytime Dawn (IRE) 4 b g Rashar (USA)-Ard Clos (Ardoon) 784[5] 990[12] 1464[W] **>42f<**

Daytona Beach (IRE) 5 ch h Bluebird (USA)-Water Spirit (USA) (Riverman (USA)) *416[2]* *(520)* (762) 873[13] 1402[3] *1631[2]* 1830[5] *2634[2]* 2928[4] 3207[2] 3222[7] 3439[13] **>72a 75f<**

Day Tripper 2 b g Forzando-Solo Vacation (Pas de Seul) 2548[9] 3025[4] 3379[13] 3540[6] **>64f<**

Dazzle Me 3 ch f Kalaglow-Defy Me (Bustino) 1125[15] 1516[13] 1719[11] **>26f<**

Dazzler 3 ch g Zalazl (USA)-Mrs Danvers (Balidar) 1514[7] 1979[11] 2319[11] 3154[8] 4220[10] **>52f<**

Dazzling Star 2 gr f Thatching-Dazzlingly Radiant (Try My Best (USA)) 3604[13] 3720[7] **>53f<**

Deadline Time (IRE) 2 b c Fayruz-Cut it Fine (USA) (Big Spruce (USA)) 682[4] 1964[5] 2182[7] 3714[5] 3894[3] (3985) 4208[3] **>77f<**

Deaken Dancer 2 b f Rambo Dancer (CAN)-Une Emigree (USA) (L'Emigrant (USA)) 455[4] 540[5] 644[W] **>37f<**

De Albertis (IRE) 2 b c High Estate-Alpi Dora 4005a[2]

Deano's Beeno 3 b c Far North (CAN)-Sans Dot (Busted) 717[3] 3102[2] 3189[9] 3459[5] 3611[20] 3755[4] **>89f<**

Deardaw 3 b f Tina's Pet-Faw (Absalom) *473[8]* 855[3] 1094[24] 2239[13] 3919[25] **>45f<**

Death by Chocolate 3 b g Sayf El Arab (USA)-Mia Fillia (Formidable) *174[5]* *261[3]* *316[5]* *444[14]* *1762[10]* **>54a f<**

Deauville Dancer (IRE) 3 ch c Al Hareb (USA)-Bru Ri (FR) (Sir Gaylord) 1085[5] 1378[10] 1669[14] **>55f<**

Debacle (USA) 6 b h Raft (USA)-Kuala (USA) (Hawaii)

374[6] 412[6] >**48a** f<
Deb's Ball 9 b m Glenstal (USA)-D'eb Old Fruit (Levmoss) 879[15] 1435[8] >**52a 49f**<
Debutante Days 3 ch f Dominion-Doogali (Doon) 1097[17] 2329[3] 2653[2] (3097) 3700[5] (4071) >**77f**<
Deceit the Second 3 ch c Bairn (USA)-Bushti Music (Bustino) 580[6] 867[6] 1372[9] 2052[8] 2246[8] (2450) 2682[3] 2842[10] *3318[3]* 3724[6] 3986[5] 4196[6] *4270[3]* 4331[5] >**72a 68f**<
Deceive 3 b f Machiavellian (USA)-Talon D'Aiguille (USA) (Big Spruce (USA)) 1116a[12] 1848[W] >**93f**<
Decided (CAN) 12 b h Affirmed (USA)-Expediency (USA) (Vaguely Noble) 3986[15] >**23f**<
Decision Maker (IRE) 2 b c Taufan (USA)-Vain Deb (Gay Fandango (USA)) 2370[7] 3009[4] 3174[11] 3684[2] 3883[2] >**82f**<
Decorated Hero 3 b c Warning-Bequeath (USA) (Lyphard (USA)) (1072) (2121) 2417[3] 3085[2] 3813[2] 3945[26] 4147[2] >**115f**<
Deedeejay 2 b f Cigar-Miss Patdonna (Starch Reduced) 3135[4] 3378[11] 3566[10] 3760[P] >**15f**<
Deed of Love (USA) 2 b c Shadeed-Widaad 3197a[9] 3788a[4] >**99f**<
Dee-Lady 3 b f Deploy-Bermuda Lily (Dunbeath (USA)) 438[4] 557[2] 720[6] 1139[5] 1315[5] 2006[5] 3602[8] 3700[13] 3845[4] 4065[4] >**90f**<
Deep Divide 3 b f Nashwan (USA)-Miss Fancy That (USA) (The Minstrel (CAN)) 1346[7] 1716[7] >**80f**<
Deeply Vale (IRE) 4 b g Pennine Walk-Late Evening (USA) (Riverman (USA)) 563[12] 1071[11] 1261[9] 1537[6] 2010[13] 3677[7] 4060[3] *4337[2]* >**59a 68f**<
Deerlet 4 br f Darshaan-Roxy Hart (High Top) 1328[11] 1535[12] >**24a 67f**<
Deerly 2 b f Hadeer-Grafitti Gal (USA) (Pronto (ARG)) (1369) 1650[3] 2982[5] 3289[4] 3639[3] 3969[3] 4077[11] 4243[9] >**68f**<
Deevee 6 b h Hallgate-Lady Woodpecker (Tap On Wood) (873) 1183[9] 1626[2] 2031[6] 2321[2] 3348[9] 3837[17] >**83f**<
Defined Feature (IRE) 2 ch f Nabeel Dancer (USA)-Meissarah (USA) (Silver Hawk (USA)) (2114) 2716[2] (3032) (3273) 3499[3] >**89f**<
Definite Article 3 b c Indian Ridge-Summer Fashion (Moorestyle) 2218a[2] 2894a[4] 3690a[4] >**123f**<
Degree 2 b f Warning-Krill (Kris) 3643[2] >**75+f**<
De la Billiere (IRE) 7 b h King of Clubs-Crazyfoot (Luthier (FR)) 2334[11]
Delaunay (IRE) 2 b c Maelstrom Lake-Artlesse (Ahonoora) 910[5] 1123[4] 3025[9] 3155[8] 3538[3] 3711[13] 3870[7] 4144[16] >**73f**<
Del Deya (IRE) 5 br m Caerleon (USA)-Point of Honour (Kris) 1118a[2] 1394a[9] >**116f**<
Delgarth Lady 4 b f Scottish Reel-Pastrana (King of Spain) 526[12] *624[5] 835[6] 1630[5] 2961[5]* 3862[10] >**34a 23f**<
Delicious 3 b f Dominion-Confection (Formidable) 3006[5] 3401[3] 3676[8] 3884[5] >**59f**<
Deliffin 9 b g Wolverlife-Teletype (Guillaume Tell (USA)) *1319[13]* 2439[15] >**31a** f<
Delightful Dancer (IRE) 3 b c Dancing Dissident (USA)-Allberry (Alzao (USA)) 648[6] 813[13] 1016[5] 1377[U] 1778[10] 3256[6] 3431[6] 3745[9] >**58df**<
Delight of Dawn 3 b f Never so Bold-Vogos Angel (Song) 674[9] 971[6] 1180[11] 1366[12] 1654[2] 1906[6] 2718[5] (2776) (2968) (3372) 3451[4] 3637[16] 3750[3] 3972[2] 4122[4] 4193[5] >**79f**<
Della Casa (IRE) 2 ch f Royal Academy (USA)-Diamond Spring (USA) (Vaguely Noble) 3539[5] 3821[8] 4085[9] >**61f**<
Dells Dream (IRE) 2 b f Classic Music (USA)-Jeewan (Touching Wood (USA)) 2866[5] 3541[6] *3675[12]* >**57f**<
Delmour 4 b g Seymour Hicks (FR)-Delbounty (Bounteous) *399[7]* 1350[18] 1501[7] 2191[6] 2390[8] 2832[11] 3063[11] >**15a 29f**<
Delpiombo 9 br g Lochnager-Precious Petra (Bing II) 3757[13] >**55da 63f**<
Delrob 4 b f Reprimand-Stoneydale (Tickled Pink) *16[3] 69[5] 129[7] 154[4] 244[3] 323[3] 366[5]* (2364) 2850[3] 3442[13] >**62a 54f**<
Delta One (IRE) 4 b c Danehill (USA)-Seminar 3334[3] 3602[5] 3924[14] >**106f**<
Delta Soleil (USA) 3 b c Riverman (USA)-Sunny Roberta (USA) (Robellino (USA)) (3461) 3659[8] 3943[4] 4267[3] >**98f**<
Demokos (FR) 10 ch h Dom Racine (FR)-Eagletown (FR) (Dictus (FR)) 1578[9] 1816[8] >**28f**<
Demurrer 5 b h Dominion-Belle Enfant (Beldale Flutter (USA)) 534[15] 1854[4] 2156[8] 2307[4] 2861[8] 3118[7] >**43f**<
Denbrae (IRE) 3 b c Sure Blade (USA)-Fencing (Viking (USA)) *(315)* (524) 621[2] 823[4] 999[6] 1165[15] *1882[8]* 3656[5] >**69a 75df**<
Denebola Way (GR) 3 br c Wadood (USA)-Northern Moon (Ile de Bourbon (USA)) 680[5] >**86f**<
Densben 11 b g Silly Prices-Eliza de Rich (Spanish Gold) 491[7] 701[7] 789[9] 1043[5] 1297[7] 1828[5] 1963[2] 2229[3] 2330[7] 2698[8] 3112[6] 3275[4] 3396[9] (3467) (3800) 4041[7] 4068[16] 4142[5] 4280[10] >**57f**<
Dent's Delight (IRE) 3 b f Gallic League-Sassalin (Sassafras (FR)) *5[13]*
Denver County (USA) 3 br c Mr Prospector (USA)-Colorado Dancer (Shareef 808a[3] >**95f**<
Depreciate 2 ch c Beveled (USA)-Shiny Penny (Glint of Gold) (1592) (2432) 2978[4] >**82f**<
De Puntillas 3 f 1704a[4] 4020a[3] >**95f**<
Deputy Tim 12 ch h Crofter (USA)-Kindle *397[8] 413[13]* 493[6] 593[6] >**44a 38f**<
De Quest 3 b c Rainbow Quest-De Stael (4176a) >**113f**<
Derek's Bo 2 b f Rambo Dancer (CAN)-Mother Hubbard (Mummy's Pet) 819[7] *1089[9]* 1841[5] 2000[6] *3528[16]* 4290[12] >**27a 38f**<
Derisbay (IRE) 7 b h Gorytus (USA)-Current Bay (Tyrant (USA)) *214[8]* >**19a** f<
Dernier Empereur (USA) 5 b h Trempolino (USA)-Dear Colleen (USA) (In Reality (USA)) 1002a[7] 1394a[7] 3792a[2] >**127f**<
Derricks Refusal 4 b c Ring Bidder-Hobournes Katie (Starch Reduced) *50[5]* >**21a 33f**<
Derry Queen 3 b f Derrylin-Emerin *173[6] 236[5]* >**31a 15f**<
Desert Bell (IRE) 2 b c Green Desert (USA)-Salabella (Sallust) 1803[3] 2182[4] 3666[3] >**75f**<
Desert Boy (IRE) 2 br c Green Desert (USA)-City Fortress (Troy) (3185) 3731[6] >**87f**<
Desert Cat (IRE) 2 b c Green Desert (USA)-Mahabba (USA) (Elocutionist (USA)) 3416[5] 3967[3] 4226[4] >**76f**<

Desert Courier **3** b c Green Desert (USA)-Possessive (Posse (USA)) 930^{2} **>99f<**

Desert Fighter **4** b c Green Desert (USA)-Jungle Rose (Shirley Heights) 1192^{11} **>83?a 95df<**

Desert Force (IRE) **6** b h Lomond (USA)-St Padina *1086^{9} 2919^{13}* **>16a 51f<**

Desert Frolic (IRE) **2** b f Persian Bold-Try To Catch Me (USA) (Shareef Dancer (USA)) 3666^{7} 3939^{4} **>70f<**

Desert Green (FR) **6** b h Green Desert (USA)-Green Leaf (USA) (Alydar (USA)) 665^{10} (960) 1365^{5} 2080^{3} 2703^{3} 3358^{5} 3732^{11} 3845^{2} **>102f<**

Desert Harvest **3** b c Green Desert (USA)-Mill on the Floss (Mill Reef (USA)) 715^{6} 1186^{5} 1474^{10} 3373^{6} 3565^{W} **>82+f<**

Desert Invader (IRE) **4** br c Lead on Time (USA)-Aljood (Kris) *191^{5} 275^{6} (349) 378^{7} 417^{4}* 535^{15} 702^{8} 746^{7} 1668^{9} *1953^{8}* 2461^{4} 2607^{7} *(3512) 3739^{6}* 3800^{10} *4272^{4}* **>70a 58f<**

Desert Lynx (IRE) **2** b f Green Desert (USA)-Sweeping (Indian King (USA)) 3763^{5} 3865^{27} 4212^{13} **>57f<**

Desert Power **6** b h Green Desert (USA)-Rivers Maid 981^{7} 1166^{15} 1340^{4} 1926^{7} (2110) 2593^{9} 3021^{3} **>73f<**

Desert President **4** ch c Polish Precedent (USA)-Majestic Kahala (USA) *234^{4} 516^{5} 1210^{10}* **>38a 49f<**

Desert Shot **5** b h Green Desert (USA)-Out of Shot (Shirley Heights) (666) 827^{5} 2476^{7} (3381) 3498^{6} **>119f<**

Desert Spring **3** b c Green Desert (USA)-Little Loch Broom 815^{5} 1195^{8} **>79f<**

Desert Stormer (USA) **5** b m Storm Cat (USA)-Breezy Stories (USA) *(4303a)* **>127a f<**

Desert Style (IRE) **3** b c Green Desert (USA)-Organza (High Top) (803a) 1233a^{2} (1706a) (3198a) 3834^{7} **>124f<**

Desert Tiger **2** br f Green Desert (USA)-Desert Bride (USA) (Key to the Kingdom (USA)) 1098^{3} (1307) 2223^{2} (2399) (3271) 3548^{2} **>88f<**

Desert Time **5** b or br h Green Desert (USA)-Supper Time 1183^{8} 1409^{6} (1593) 1851^{31} 2031^{5} 3011^{3} 3175^{5} 3368^{11} 3732^{18} **>84f<**

Desert Water (IRE) **3** b g Green Desert (USA)-Ozone Friendly (USA) (Green Forest (USA)) 3750^{18} 4049^{19} 4193^{19} *4296^{7}* **>45a 25f<**

Desert Zone (USA) **6** ch h Affirmed (USA)-Deloram (CAN) (Lord Durham (CAN)) 839^{5} 1061^{5} 1351^{11} 1484^{6} **>60f<**

Desidera (IRE) **3** b f Shaadi (USA)-Diasprina (GER) (Aspros (GER)) 2212a^{2} (3195a) 3582a^{9} **>108f<**

Desiderata **4** b c Green Desert (USA)-Yldizlar (Star Appeal) 454^{11} 642^{4} 992^{11} *1457^{11}* **>11a 59f<**

Detachment (USA) **2** b c Night Shift (USA)-Mumble Peg (General Assembly (USA)) 1752^{2} 2034^{2} 2464^{3} **>81f<**

De-Veers Currie (IRE) **3** b f Glenstal (USA)-Regent Star (Prince Regent (FR)) 1866^{4} **>54f<**

Devil River Peek (USA) **3** c 1121a^{6} 1892a^{3} 2389a^{5} 3487a^{2} 4094a^{2} **>113f<**

Devilry **5** b h Faustus (USA)-Ancestry (Persepolis (FR)) 598^{4} **>60f<**

Devon Peasant **3** b f Deploy-Serration (Kris) 2532^{6} 3016^{17} 3921^{2} 4164^{2} **>85f<**

Dhulikhel **2** b f Reprimand-Travel Storm (Lord Gayle (USA)) *1954^{5} 2146^{5}* 2839^{4} *2962^{3}* (3285) 3767^{7} 3915^{11} **>40a 56f<**

Diaco **10** b h Indian King (USA)-Coral Cave 1663^{W} **>64f<**

Dia Georgy **4** b c Reesh-Carpadia (Icecapade (USA)) 450^{13} 546^{10} 731^{6} 1126^{17} *1320^{2} (1459) (1631) 2076^{8}* 2174^{3} 2557^{7} *2961^{4} 3082^{2} 3511^{8} 4340^{12}* **>60a 60f<**

Diaghilef (IRE) **3** b c Royal Academy (USA)-Miss Audimar (USA) (Mr Leader (USA)) (968) 1636^{4} (1872) 2274^{2} 3162^{5} **>118f<**

Diamond Beach **2** b c Lugana Beach-Cannon Boy (USA) (Canonero II (USA)) 3371^{10} 3733^{5} 3881^{2} 4224^{9} **>70f<**

Diamond Crown (IRE) **4** ch c Kris-State Treasure (USA) (Secretariat (USA)) 841^{11} 1161^{12} 1285^{2} 1422^{3} 1645^{14} 2126^{6} (2990) 3148^{2} 3274^{3} 3852^{8} 3987^{13} 4114^{4} **>17a 64f<**

Diamond Crown (USA) **3** b c Gone West (USA)-Elegant Champagne (USA) (Alleged (USA)) 1150^{5} 1464^{3} **>70f<**

Diamond Heart **2** b f Generous (IRE)-Chellita (Habitat) 3339^{16} **>47f<**

Diamond Market **3** gr c Absalom-The Victor Girls (Crofthall) 1532^{6} 1969^{9} 2250^{4} *2587^{2} 2960^{4}* 3302^{5} 4147^{6} *4271^{2} 4335^{7}* **>52a 57tf<**

Diamond Mix (IRE) **3** gr c Linamix (FR)-Diamond Seal (Persian Bold) (808a) 1574a^{6} 2044a^{3} **>119f<**

Diasafina **2** b f Safawan-Diana Dee (Blakeney) 4216^{13} **>16f<**

Dick Christian **3** ch g Nicholas Bill-Carolyn Christensen (Sweet Revenge) 854^{13} 1175^{11} 1407^{7} 3426^{16} **>15f<**

Dickyvearncombe **3** ch g Persian Heights-Royal Celerity (USA) (Riverman (USA)) 1446^{W}

Dictation (USA) **3** b c Dayjur (USA)-Mofida 2576^{4} 2949^{2} 3226^{3} 3981^{5} **>88df<**

Didina **3** ch f Nashwan (USA)-Didicoy (USA) (Danzig (USA)) (3062) (3191) 3564^{3} **>112f<**

Diebiedale **3** b f Dominion-Welwyn (Welsh Saint) 1602^{5} 1972^{4} 2190^{2} 3014^{9} 3764^{16} **>64f<**

Diego **2** b c Belmez (USA)-True Queen (USA) (Silver Hawk (USA)) 2839^{6} 3437^{3} 3631^{3} 4046^{4} **>74f<**

Diet **9** b g Starch Reduced-Highland Rossie (Pablond) 491^{11} 877^{12} 994^{8} (1023) 1157^{11} 1441^{7} 1461^{4} 1493^{4} 1689^{5} 1721^{2} 1819^{2} 2229^{2} (2304) 2398^{2} 2461^{7} (2870) 2930^{5} 3121^{2} 3275^{10} 3667^{12} 3855^{12} 4280^{13} 4292^{12} **>59f<**

Different Times (IRE) **5** b h Cyrano de Bergerac-Centre Travel (Godswalk (USA)) 702^{10} **>53a 58f<**

Diffident (FR) **3** b c Nureyev (USA)-Shy Princess (USA) (Irish River (FR)) (667) 920^{6} 1572a^{2} (2562a) 3042a^{4} **>117f<**

Digarah (IRE) **3** ch c Digamist (USA)-Zurarah (Siberian Express (USA)) 2724a^{2} **>83f<**

Digpast (IRE) **5** ch h Digamist (USA)-Starlit Way (Pall Mall) *41^{2} 89^{6} 160^{3} (219) 265^{2} (371) 472^{3}* 2979^{13} 3268^{7} *4297^{5}* **>72a 47df<**

Digwana (IRE) **2** b g Digamist (USA)-Siwana (IRE) (Dom Racine (FR)) 480^{8} 782^{11} 1336^{6} **>36f<**

Dil Dil **2** b f Puissance-My Croft (Crofter (USA)) 1142^{7} 1938^{6} 2135^{4} (2552) 3289^{10} 3471^{4} 3623^{6} 3749^{7} **>70f<**

Dillyetta **3** ch f Prince Sabo-Piccadilly Etta 2653^{6}

Dimakya (USA) **2** b f Dayjur (USA)-Reloy (USA) (Liloy (FR)) 2351^{2} 2934^{2} 3828^{2} 3997^{2} **>94f<**

Diminuet **2** b f Dominion-Primulette (Mummy's Pet) 819^{16} 1579^{2} 1823^{P} 2914^{2} (3671) 4195^{11} **>76df<**

Diminutive (USA) **2** b c Diesis-Graceful Darby (USA) (Darby Creek Road (USA)) 2912^{6} 3174^{2} 3536^{3} **>71f<**

Dingo Warrior 3 ch c Roman Warrior-Patsy Pennall (Celtic Cone) *72^{9} 239^{5} 273^{7} 368^{7}* 2177^{4} **>28a 38f<**
Dino's Mistral 2 b c Petong-Marquessa d'Howfen (Pitcairn) 2820^{9} 3821^{15} 3975^{25} **>17f<**
Dirab 2 ch c Groom Dancer (USA)-Double Celt (Owen Dudley) 3672^{6} 3916^{4} **>73f<**
Direct Dial (USA) 3 br c Phone Trick (USA)-Jig Jig (USA) (Never Bend) 1476^{3} 1796^{5} 2236^{7} **>65f<**
Dirty Dancer 6 b g Sizzling Melody-Stratch (FR) (Thatch (USA)) 2134^{9} 2438^{9} **>43f<**
Disallowed (IRE) 2 b f Distinctly North (USA)-Miss Allowed (USA) (Alleged (USA)) 791^{6} 1287^{3} *2381^{4}* 3345^{2} 3460^{2} 3701^{2} 3887^{5} **>62a 79f<**
Disco Boy 5 b h Green Ruby (USA)-Sweet And Shiny (Siliconn) *892^{6} 1076^{3}* 1456^{6} *2074^{8} 2383^{12} 2631^{3} 3072^{10}* **>57a 54f<**
Disc of Gold (USA) 2 ch f Silver Hawk (USA)-Equal Change (USA) 4210^{7} **>40f<**
Discorsi 3 b c Machiavellian (USA)-Bustara (Busted) 816^{7} 1417^{W} 2329^{4} 2790^{9} 3229^{10} **>71f<**
Dish The Dosh 2 b f Superpower-Taxitilly (Formidable (USA)) 1774^{8} 2198^{11} *2962^{12}* 3378^{10} 3533^{9} 3760^{19} **>22f<**
Dismissed (USA) 2 b c Dayjur (USA)-Bemissed (USA) (Nijinsky (CAN)) (2473) 3216^{3} 3746^{3} 4046^{2} **>88f<**
Dismissive (IRE) 3 ch f Digamist (USA)-Gulf Craft (IRE) (Petorius) 1146^{9} 1521^{6} 1906^{8} **>10a 22f<**
Dispol Conqueror (IRE) 2 b c Conquering Hero (USA)-Country Niece 3110^{8} 3307^{6} 3502^{11} 4141^{17} **>36f<**
Dispol Princess (IRE) 2 b f Cyrano de Bergerac-Tallow Hill (Dunphy) 2128^{12}
Dispol Sapphire 2 br f Belfort (FR)-Spring Rose (Blakeney) 671^{13} 755^{6} 964^{9}
Disputed Call (USA) 6 b h Alleged (USA)-Tennis Partner (USA) (Northern Dancer) *9^{4} 161^{7} 277^{9}* 2439^{2} (3024) 3238^{3} 3676^{7} 3927^{13} 4135^{17} **>43da 52f<**
Dissentor (IRE) 3 b c Dancing Dissident (USA)-Helen's Dynasty (Habitat) 543^{8} 739^{10} 4194^{9} **>51f<**
Dissident Dancer 6 b g The Dissident-Someway (Dublin Taxi) *63^{10} 153^{10}* **>3a 16f<**
Distant Dynasty 5 br h Another Realm-Jianna (Godswalk (USA)) *23^{2} 70^{4} 102^{2} 188^{2} 237^{9} 247^{2} 407^{3}* 507^{3} 583^{2} 726^{5} 1023^{12} 1400^{8} 1516^{11} *2925^{13}* 3079^{13} 3139^{10} **>67a 53f<**
Distant King 2 b c Distant Relative-Lindfield Belle (IRE) (Fairy King (USA)) 2904^{5}
Distant Memory 6 gr h Don't Forget Me-Canton Silk 2078^{6} **>46f<**
Distant Princess 3 b f Distant Relative-Sojourn (Be My Guest (USA)) 658^{9} *2140^{8}* 2499^{3} (3034) (3182) 3373^{8} 3664^{5} *4217^{11}* **>44a 75f<**
Distant Storm 2 ch g Pharly (FR)-Candle in the Wind (Thatching) 2346^{10} (2637) 3090^{11} 3267^{6} 4111^{17} **>66f<**
Distinct Beauty (IRE) 2 ch f Pancho Villa (USA)-Beautiful Secret (USA) (Secreto (USA)) 4239^{6} 4313^{7} **>71f<**
Distinct (IRE) 2 b g Distinctly North (USA)-Shy Jinks (Shy Groom (USA)) 1282^{5} **>21f<**
Distinctive Lady 5 ch m Primo Dominie-Kenton's Girl (Record Token) *107^{11} 198^{7} 331^{11}* **>16a f<**
Distinctlyfoster's (IRE) 2 b f Distinctly North (USA)-Amata (USA) (Nodouble (USA)) 3117^{5} 3502^{5} 3671^{6} 4133^{11} **>52f<**

Distinctly Red (IRE) 2 b c Distinctly North (USA)-Persian Mistress (IRE) (Persian Bold) 1341^{6} 1943^{13}
Distinctly Swingin (IRE) 2 b f Distinctly North (USA)-Swoon Along (Dunphy) 2158^{3} 2423^{5} **>55f<**
Divertimiento 4 b c Night Shift (USA)-Aunt Jemima (Busted) *592^{10}* 2433^{7} 3621^{U} **>23a 64f<**
Divina Luna 2 b f Dowsing (USA)-Famosa (Dancing Brave (USA)) 3628^{7} **>43f<**
Divina Mia 3 br f Dowsing (USA)-Hardihostess (Be My Guest (USA)) 813^{17} 2780^{8} 3234^{3} 3395^{2} 3571^{9} 3918^{8} **>71f<**
Divine 2 b f Dowsing (USA)-Rectitude 3806^{3} **>75+f<**
Divine Pursuit 3 ch f Kris-Dance Quest (FR) (Green Dancer (USA)) 1221^{4} 1554^{3} **>70f<**
Dixie Dynasty (USA) 3 $2730a^{5}$ **>110f<**
Dixiemelody 3 b c Rock City-Run To The Sun (Run The Gantlet (USA)) 1983^{6} 3016^{12} 3178^{2} 3351^{3} 3676^{18} 3896^{4} 4108^{F} **>83f<**
Dixit Dominus 4 b g Dominion-So True (So Blessed) 761^{13} 1092^{14} 1596^{12} **>64f<**
Djais (FR) 6 ch h Vacarme (USA)-Dame de Carreau (FR) (Targowice (USA)) 2119^{5} 2575^{4} **>117f<**
D K Reunion 5 b g Welsh Captain-Thetford Chase (Relkino) *46^{12}*
D'naan (IRE) 2 b c Royal Academy (USA)-Festive Season (USA) (Lypheor) 2320^{7} 3652^{3} 3865^{23} 4151^{5} *(4334)* **>76a 81f<**
Docklands Courier 3 b c Dominion-High Quail (USA) (Blushing Groom (FR)) *156^{4} 263^{2} 384^{4}* 3461^{5} 3537^{9} 3778^{9} **>56a 54f<**
Doc's Coat 10 b g Tower Walk-Gold Loch (Lochnager) *277^{11}* **>41da f<**
Doctor Bravious (IRE) 2 b c Priolo (USA)-Sharp Slipper (Sharpo) 3967^{6} 4282^{3} **>72f<**
Doctor Green (FR) 2 b c Green Desert (USA)-Highbrow (Shirley Heights) 4103^{16} **>68f<**
Doctor Roy 7 ch h Electric-Pushkar (Northfields (USA)) 476^{8} 534^{6} **>37f<**
Doctor's Glory (USA) 3 gr f Elmaamul (USA)-Doctor Bid (USA) (Spectacular Bid (USA)) 1362^{5} 1806^{6} 2325^{2} 2616^{7} 2848^{2} (3922) 4121^{10} **>96f<**
Doctor's Remedy 9 br h Doc Marten-Champagne Party (Amber Rama (USA)) 1946^{5} 2373^{6} 2543^{3} 2785^{5} 3017^{5} (3148) 3296^{3} 3410^{5} 3724^{19} **>50df<**
Doddington Flyer 3 b c Distant Relative-Tino-Ella (Bustino) *418^{5}* 427^{7} (525) 655^{6} (947) 1289^{4} 3804^{7} 4149^{14} 4315^{3} **>50a 81f<**
Dolliver (USA) 3 b c Northern Baby (CAN)-Mabira (Habitat) 3543^{3} 3756^{10} 3921^{7} **>67f<**
Dolly Dolittle 4 ch f Infantry-Lost Moment (Hotfoot) *4^{6} 178^{7}* 839^{16} 1347^{8} 2037^{15} 2509^{6} 3017^{7} 3641^{13} **>30a 24f<**
Dolly Face 3 gr c Chilibang-Press Corps *40^{4} 118^{4} (159) 278^{3} 284^{3} 342^{2} (407) 446^{7}* 3961^{12} **>72a 73f<**
Domak Amaam (IRE) 2 b c Dominion-La Courant (USA) (Little Current (USA)) 4064^{3} 4276^{2} **>79f<**
Domappel 3 b g Domynsky-Appelania (Star Appeal) (3659) 3863^{3} 4163^{8} **>76f<**
Dombey 2 b c Dominion-Arderelle (FR) (Pharly (FR)) 3900^{4} 4073^{4} **>80f<**
Dome Patrol 4 gr c Dominion-Tranquility Base *(62) 179^{4} 248^{5} 343^{4} 402^{5} 416^{4}* **>52a 43f<**

Domettes (IRE) **2** ch f Archway (IRE)-Superetta (Superlative) 1671^{8} (1981) 2195^{2} 2656^{5} (4075) **>72f<**
Domicksky **7** b h Dominion-Mumruffin (Mummy's Pet) 507^{10} 565^{3} 688^{6} 765^{14} 1057^{4} 1193^{5} 1265^{5} 1411^{9} 1510^{5} 1595^{8} 2013^{2} 2150^{5} 2410^{6} 2551^{5} 2686^{4} 2850^{4} 3014^{6} 3134^{8} 3333^{3} 3453^{2} 3554^{10} 3622^{8} 3667^{24} 3961^{2} 4057^{3} 4113^{4} 4165^{6} 4278^{3} **>67a 61f<**
Dominant Serenade **6** b h Dominion-Sing Softly (Luthier (FR)) 1084^{3} **>48f<**
Dominelle **3** b f Domynsky-Gymcrak Lovebird (Taufan (USA)) 674^{10} 926^{14} 1582^{4} 1847^{5} (2024) (2261) 2519^{3} 2680^{3} 2837^{7} 3150^{3} 3357^{6} *4123^{7}* **>32a 54f<**
Dominion's Dream **3** ch f Dominion-Sharp Jose (USA) (Sharpen Up) *(528) 627^{12}* 1202^{10} 1371^{3} 1719^{7} **>72a 60f<**
Domino Flyer **2** b c Warrshan (USA)-Great Dilemma (Vaigly Great) 1620^{5} 2161^{7} 2422^{2} 3160^{8} 3417^{4} **>55f<**
Domitia (USA) **3** ch f Arctic Tern (USA)-Fast Trek (FR) (Trepan (FR)) 730^{5} 1290^{2} 2189^{2} 2557^{4} 3031^{2} 3182^{3} 3373^{4} 3679^{2} (3959) 4071^{10} 4233^{2} **>75f<**
Dom One **3** b f Dominion-Mrs Musgrove (Jalmood (USA)) 868^{9} **>91f<**
Domoor **2** b c Dominion-Corley Moor (Habitat) 1041^{4} 2971^{9} 3415^{8} (3642) 3851^{2} **>51f<**
Dom Pennion **4** b f Dominion-Pennycuick 728^{5} 946^{5} 1409^{5} *1760^{4} 2073^{5}* **>56a 74f<**
Domulla **5** br h Dominion-Ulla Laing (Mummy's Pet) 434^{2} (611) 934^{5} 1614^{8} 1766^{8} (4160) **>107f<**
Domusky **2** ch f Domynsky-Roches Roost (Pauper) 4085^{11} **>51f<**
Domybly **3** ch c Domynsky-Nellie Bly (Dragonara Palace (USA)) *353^{9}* **>56f<**
Dona Filipa **2** ch f Precocious-Quisissanno (Be My Guest (USA)) 3806^{12} 3877^{8} 4188^{21} **>39f<**
Don Corleone **3** b c Caerleon (USA)-Dance by Night (Northfields (USA)) (1301) 1897^{4} (2273) 2670^{2} 3088^{3} **>117f<**
Done Well (USA) **3** b c Storm Bird (CAN)-Suspicious Toosome (USA) (Secretariat (USA)) 2015^{2} 2369^{19} 2616^{11} 3716^{5} **>77f<**
Donful (IRE) **3** b c Law Society-Don Furia 3791a^{3} **>60f<**
Donia (USA) **6** ch m Graustark (USA)-Katrinka (USA) (Sovereign Dancer (USA)) *77^{4} (222)* **>48a f<**
Donington Park **2** ch f Risk Me (FR)-Small Double (IRE) (Double Schwartz) 644^{5} *846^{2} 1089^{5}* **>45a 43f<**
Don Micheletto **2** b c Machiavellian (USA)-Circe's Isle (Be My Guest (USA)) 3733^{9} (4058) **>91+f<**
Donna Fugata (IRE) **3** br f Chief Singer-Jumra (Thatch (USA)) *844^{6}* 1296^{12} 1467^{5} 3980^{22} **>25f<**
Donna Viola **3** b f Be My Chief (USA)-Countess Olivia (Prince Tenderfoot (USA)) 724^{3} 962^{5} 1591^{2} 1747^{3} (2405) 2778^{4} (3095) 3419^{4} (3630) 3833^{5} 4024^{3} **>97f<**
Do Not Disturb (USA) **2** ro c Darn That Alarm (USA)-Little Emotion (USA) (Nonparrell (CAN)) 2615^{2} 3104^{2} 3536^{2} (3752) 4046^{3} **>84f<**
Don Pepe **4** br c Dowsing (USA)-Unique Treasure (Young Generation) (579) 780^{5} (1421) 1932^{3} 2455^{6} 3112^{7} 3719^{14} 4171^{17} **>75f<**
Dontbetalking (IRE) **5** gr m Heraldiste (USA)-Fine Flame (Le Prince) *421^{11}*
Don't Cry **7** b m Dominion-Black Veil (Blakeney) 534^{14} 1025^{5} 1149^{7} 1359^{5} 1667^{5} 1826^{5} 1965^{3} 2186^{4} 2545^{7} 3052^{4} 3153^{2} 3296^{2} 3971^{13} **>39f<**
Don't Drop Bombs (USA) **6** ch h Fighting Fit (USA)-Promised Star (USA) (Star de Naskra (USA)) *77^{5} (122) 172^{5} 285^{2} 402^{3}* 1622^{20} 1635^{6} 1745^{5} 2052^{4} 2946^{2} 3047^{3} (3288) 3641^{5} 3808^{15} **>43da 45f<**
Dont Forget Curtis (IRE) **3** b c Don't Forget Me-Norse Lady (Viking (USA)) *322^{2}* 504^{5} 618^{6} 1038^{3} 1382^{9} 1791^{2} 2279^{8} **>78a 84f<**
Dontforget Insight (IRE) **4** b c Don't Forget Me-Starlust (Sallust) 1517^{10} 1693^{6} 1915^{2} 2169^{6} 2266^{5} 2613^{5} 2766^{5} 3237^{6} 3457^{10} 3674^{4} **>78f<**
Don't Forget Mikie (IRE) **2** b c Don't Forget Me-Sokolova (Red Regent) 424^{3} 533^{9} *1212^{5}* 2277^{4} 2541^{6} 3546^{15} **>56a 69f<**
Don't Forget Ruby (IRE) **3** br f Don't Forget Me-Gaelic Jewel (Scottish Rifle) *360^{7} 444^{13}* 521^{3} (867) *891^{5}* **>41a 61f<**
Don't Give Up **7** b h Nomination-Tug Along (Posse (USA)) 3234^{12} 3384^{14} *4293^{5}* **>40a 41f<**
Don't Go Crazy (USA) **3** c Houston-Overdue Reaction (Be My G 1388a^{3} **>71f<**
Don't Look Now **3** ch f Dashing Blade-Sly Wink (Song) 2164^{5} 2337^{5} 2712^{9} **>51a 58f<**
Don't Mean a Thing (IRE) **3** b c Treasure Kay-Traminer (Status Seeker) *72^{11}* 453^{8} 521^{18} 1254^{11} **>24a 53f<**
Dont Shoot Fairies **3** ch c Vague Shot-Fairy Fans *566^{3}* 651^{6} (774) 948^{6} 1402^{2} (1527) 2691^{12} (3469) 3611^{16} 4047^{9} **>56a 81f<**
Don't Tell Anyone **2** gr c Petong-Glenfield Portion (Mummy's Pet) 684^{3} 1640^{4} *1954^{3}* 2155^{4} *2629^{5}* 2951^{3} 3124^{4} 3312^{2} *(3953)* 4243^{14} **>55a 55f<**
Don't Tell Vicki **2** b f Mazilier (USA)-Jans Contessa (Rabdan) 429^{3} 508^{8} *531^{2} 604^{5}* 1226^{3} (1272) 1734^{2} 1810^{6} 2435^{2} 2765^{9} 2965^{W} 3570^{5} *3675^{3}* 3895^{8} **>29a 58f<**
Don't Worry Me (IRE) **3** b f Dancing Dissident (USA)-Diva Encore (Star Appeal) 719^{3} 952^{3} 1220^{5} 1637^{2} 2671^{9} (3316) 3550^{8} 4119^{6} 4286^{2} **>103f<**
Doodies Pool (IRE) **5** b h Mazaad-Barncogue (Monseigneur (USA)) *217^{8} 302^{4} 341^{9} 355^{8}* 848^{10} 1255^{7} 1509^{4} 1785^{8} *1883^{5}* 3757^{11} 3920^{5} 4170^{7} **>44a 62f<**
Doo Han (IRE) **3** ch f Doulab (USA)-Valdora (High Hat) 3506^{7} 3808^{27} **>35f<**
Doon Ridge **4** ch g Indian Ridge-Quisissanno (Be My Guest (USA)) *222^{8}* 3965^{9} **>12a 50df<**
Doonyasha **3** br f Tragic Role (USA)-Sharper Still 1967^{3} 2653^{5} 3081^{2} (3270) 3493^{8} **>72f<**
Doreen's Delight **9** ch h Bay Express-Elizabeth Howard (Sharpen Up) *88^{5}* **>42a 33?f<**
Doree (USA) **3** b f Stop The Music (USA)-Autumn Glory (USA) (Graustark (USA)) 1572a^{10} 2727a^{3} **>107f<**
Doriemus (NZ) **5** ch g Norman Pentaquad (NZ)-Golden Woods (4349a)
Dormston Boyo **5** b h Sula Bula-March at Dawn (Nishapour (FR)) *2271^{0} 1075^{6}* **>38da 6f<**
Dormy Three **5** b g Morston (FR)-Dominant (Behistoun) 1260^{5} 1477^{4} 2007^{2} 2109^{2} 2530^{6} **>65a 80f<**
Dorothea Brooke (IRE) **3** b f Dancing Brave (USA)-Connaught Bridge 1346^{3} 1755^{8} 2167^{2} 2593^{4} 3105^{3} (3559) 3630^{5} 4038^{17} **>94df<**
Dorspring (IRE) **2** b c Jareer (USA)-Daniela Samuel

(USA) (No Robbery) 810^{11} *2380^{5}* 2534^{9} 4329^{11} **>28a 26f**<

Dosses Dan (IRE) 3 b c Danehill (USA)-Flyaway Bride (USA) (Blushing Groom (FR)) 616^{3} 924^{3} 1326^{3} 1933^{5} *3075^{11}* **>28a 74f**<

Dots Dee 6 ch m Librate-Dejote (Bay Express) 905^{11} 1048^{5} 1285^{4} 1350^{5} 1854^{12} (2052) 2209^{3} 2254^{7} 2842^{7} 3047^{5} 3641^{12} **>38f**<

Double Agent 2 ch c Niniski (USA)-Rexana 1903^{3} 2283^{5} 3827^{11} **>71f**<

Double Blue 6 ch h Town And Country-Australia Fair (AUS) (Without Fear (FR)) 441^{3} 659^{7} 934^{8} (3230) 3551^{20} 3834^{8} 4121^{12} **>112df**<

Double Bluff (IRE) 2 gr g Sharrood (USA)-Timely Raise (USA) (Raise A Man (USA)) 3089^{4} 3463^{2} 3673^{W} **>84f**<

Double Booking (IRE) 3 b c Cyrano de Bergerac-Holiday Regrets (Silly Season) *25^{10}* **>18f**<

Double Bounce 5 b g Interrex (CAN)-Double Gift (Cragador) (2652) 3028^{2} 3219^{4} (3492) 3715^{5} 3943^{6} (4040) **>87f**<

Double Check (IRE) 2 ch f Most Welcome-Marie de France (USA) (Diesis) 3870^{8} 4100^{7} 4172^{11} 4285^{11} **>45f**<

Double Dagger 4 b c Reference Point-Tolmi 1563^{2} 2036^{2} **>110f**<

Double Dash (IRE) 2 gr c Darshaan-Safka (USA) (Irish River (FR)) 3968^{6} *4338^{5}* **>70a 64f**<

Double Diamond (IRE) 2 b c Last Tycoon-State Treasure (USA) (Secretariat (USA)) 919^{4} 1158^{2} 1856^{10} *(2958)* (3414) 3546^{4} 4025^{5} 4321^{2} **>73a 84f**<

Double Echo (IRE) 7 br h Glow (USA)-Piculet 549^{12} 757^{11} **>72df**<

Double Eclipse (IRE) 3 b c Ela-Mana-Mou-Solac (FR) (Gay Lussac (ITY)) 1008a^{8} 1852^{2} 2218a^{10} 2702^{2} (3146) 3946^{3} **>122f**<

Double Glow 3 b f Presidium-Glow Again (The Brianstan) *284^{6} 380^{6}* 426^{13} 524^{17} 926^{17} 1151^{13} *1566^{15}* 1847^{7} 2372^{6} *3522^{11}* **>56da 66f**<

Double Jeopardy 4 b c Polish Precedent (USA)-Infamy (Shirley Heights) 2490^{11} **>77f**<

Double Leaf 2 b c Sadler's Wells (USA)-Green Leaf (USA) (Alydar (USA)) (3472) 3832^{2} **>101f**<

Double Matt (IRE) 3 b c Double Schwartz-Kasarose (Owen Dudley) 658^{4} 742^{3} 1168^{7} 2576^{4} 2708^{4} 3282^{3} (3507) **>88f**<

Double On (IRE) 0 01 f Doubletour-Nothing On (ST Chad) 1235a^{4} 2211a^{6} 3789a^{5} **>115f**<

Double Or Bust 2 ch f Presidium-Defy Me (Bustino) 429^{5} 1774^{6} 3157^{12} **>36f**<

Double Oscar (IRE) 2 ch c Royal Academy (USA)-Broadway Rosie (Absalom) (1418) 1727^{3} 3273^{4} 3788a^{7} 3917^{5} **>83f**<

Double Point (IRE) 2 b g Alzao (USA)-Batra (USA) (Green Dancer (USA)) 699^{2} 788^{3} 1011^{4} *(1212)* 1608^{3} 2432^{3} 2900a^{8} 3375^{13} **>74a 79f**<

Double Quick (IRE) 3 b f Superlative-Haraabah (USA) (Topsider (USA)) 426^{2} 483^{7} (828) (1181) (1637) 1924^{2} 2285^{5} 2888a^{4} 3550^{2} 3815^{6} 3902^{2} **>106f**<

Double Rush (IRE) 3 b c Doulab (USA)-Stanza Dancer (Stanford) (449) 648^{7} 882^{12} 2051^{6} 3159^{3} 3455^{12} 3757^{2} **>61f**<

Double Splendour (IRE) 5 b g Double Schwartz-Princess Pamela (Dragonara Palace (USA)) (646) 3123^{3} 3293^{8} (3681) 3764^{4} (4068) (4280) **>45a 76f**<

Double Trigger (IRE) 4 ch c Ela-Mana-Mou-Solac (FR) (Gay Lussac (ITY)) (869) 1132^{4} (1363) (1869) (2702) (3563) 4008a^{4} 4349a^{17} **>127f**<

Double Up 2 ch f Weldnaas (USA)-Bel Esprit (Sagaro) 3887^{8} 4241^{12} **>63f**<

Double Vintage (IRE) 2 b c Double Schwartz-Great Alexándra (Runnett) 943^{12} 1662^{13} 1893^{14} 2107^{9} 2995^{13} 3533^{18} 4137^{14} **>35f**<

Doubleyoubeay 2 ch c Beveled (USA)-Hollia (Touch Boy) *(1073)* 1226^{5} 2195^{7} 2859^{7} 3253^{3} 3742^{4} *3953^{5}* **>61a 57f**<

Doubling Dice 4 b c Jalmood (USA)-Much Too Risky (Bustino) 476^{2} 905^{13} 1161^{5} 1816^{4} **>49f**<

Douce Maison (IRE) 4 b f Fools Holme (USA)-Cardomine (Dom Racine (FR)) 676^{6} *1088^{2}* 1244^{9} 1745^{10} 2028^{2} 2707^{7} *3075^{2} 3240^{3}* 3531^{2} 4259^{3} 4333^{6} **>68a 67f**<

Doug's Folly 2 ch f Handsome Sailor-Stern Lass (Bold Lad (IRE)) 1215^{3} 1282^{2} (1678) 2328^{8} 3225^{10} 3434^{4} 3623^{22} 4097^{15} 4195^{9} **>67f**<

Doulily 3 ch f French Gondolier (USA)-Doulally (Doulab (USA)) *48^{10} 171^{11}*

Dovebrace 2 b g Dowsing (USA)-Naufrage (Main Reef) (951) (1104) 1838^{5} 2365^{3} (3220) 3420^{5} 3668^{5} **>106f**<

Dovedon Lad 3 ch c Statoblest-Miss Petella (Dunphy) 3542^{13} **>21f**<

Dove Hunt (USA) 4 b c Danzig (USA)-Hunt's Lark (USA) (Knightly Dawn (USA)) 4305a^{4} **>118f**<

Dover Patrol (IRE) 5 b h Dancing Brave (USA)-Britannia's Rule 1621^{2} 1898^{2} **>100f**<

Dowdency 3 b f Dowsing (USA)-Tendency (Ballad Rock) *43^{5} 118^{8} 258^{2} (283) 326^{4}* 482^{2} 548^{6} *628^{9}* 732^{5} *847^{6}* 2540^{2} 4060^{9} 4225^{8} **>49a 60f**<

Down The Yard 2 b f Batshoof-Sequin Lady (Star Appeal) 943^{11} *1089^{10} 1570^{6}* 1699^{3} 1823^{7} 1989^{4} 2204^{9} (2715) 3019^{8} 3460^{7} 3639^{12} 3760^{9} 4141^{7} **>25a 56f**<

Dowsong 4 br c Dowsing (USA)-Winsong Melody (Music Maestro) 2446^{7} 2685^{10} (3057) 3268^{3} 3545^{6} 3770^{P} 4054^{2} 4193^{6} **>75f**<

Doyce 6 b m Formidable-Current Raiser (Filiberto (USA)) 632^{4} **>78f**<

Dozen Dirham (USA) 3 b g Dayjur (USA)-Capades (USA) (Overskate (CAN)) 1736^{11} 3504^{9} **>42f**<

Dragon Bold (IRE) 4 ch c Bold Arrangement-Yavarro (Raga Navarro (ITY)) 731^{11} *1049^{9}* **>30a 59f**<

Dragonflight 4 b c Formidable-Lappet (Kampala) *199^{6} 269^{8} 352^{10} 409^{2} 520^{12}* 1855^{12} 3079^{10} 3704^{18} **>65a 17f**<

Dragon Green 4 gr g Green Desert (USA)-Dunoof (Shirley Heights) 1659^{8} **>50f**<

Dragonjoy 2 b c Warrshan (USA)-Nazakat (Known Fact (USA)) 1481^{11} 1662^{7} 1977^{7} 2198^{10} 3379^{11} 3915^{7} 4263^{14} *(4339)* **>67a 52f**<

Dragonmist (IRE) 5 b m Digamist (USA)-Etage (Ile de Bourbon (USA)) *288^{9} 329^{9}* 545^{14} **>30a 41df**<

Dragon Rose 3 ch g Grey Desire-The Shrew (Relko) 955^{9} 1309^{8} **>46f**<

Dragon's Back (IRE) 2 ch c Digamist (USA)-Classic Choice (Patch) 3157^{3} 3337^{3} 3587a^{25} **>70f**<

Drama King 3 b c Tragic Role (USA)-Consistent Queen (Queen's Hussar) *339^{10}* 521^{12} **>45a 19f**<

Dramatic Act 2 gr f Tragic Role (USA)-Curious Feeling

(Nishapour (FR)) 3733^{W} 3887^{2} >**83f**<
Dramatic Entry (IRE) **2** b f Persian Bold-Galatrix (Be My Guest (USA)) 2011^{3} 2299^{2} 2515^{2} 2716^{3} 2985^{3} 3520^{5} >**66df**<
Dramatic Moment **2** b f Belmez (USA)-Drama School (Young Generation) 3010^{8} 3397^{6} >**65f**<
Dr Caligari (IRE) **3** b c My Generation-Mallabee 758^{2} 924^{5} 1467^{2} 1846^{3} 2460^{5} 2755^{3} 2815^{3} 2873^{2} 3704^{10} 3841^{4} 4225^{2} 4275^{5} >**70f**<
Dreamboat (USA) **3** b f Mr Prospector (USA)-Gorgeous (USA) (Slew O' Gold (USA)) (3829) >**82f**<
Dream Carrier (IRE) **7** b h Doulab (USA)-Dream Trader (Auction Ring (USA)) *2^{2} 20^{5} (92) 150^{3} 230^{4} 267^{5} 323^{4} 413^{6} 417^{6} 1629^{6} 2141^{5}* 3677^{15} *3950^{5} 4217^{8} 4272^{6}* >**62a 52f**<
Dreamer (USA) **3** ch c Zilzal (USA)-Affection Affirmed (USA) (Affirmed (USA)) 619^{4} 756^{2} 1122a^{4} 3070^{5} >**103f**<
Dream For Future (IRE) **5** b h Shernazar-Karosa (FR) (Caro) 1892a^{2} 3585a^{2} >**108f**<
Dreamhill (USA) **2** b c Danehill (USA)-Keep the Thought (USA) (Valdez (USA)) (3617) >**74tf**<
Dream Missy **4** b f Dreams to Reality (USA)-Mrs Feathers (Pyjama Hunt) 1350^{16} 1745^{13} >**19f**<
Dreams End **7** ch h Rainbow Quest (USA)-Be Easy 440^{4} 661^{16} 3820^{9} 3963^{7} 4051^{9} 4245^{2} 4323^{8} >**95f**<
Dream Sweet Dreams (USA) **6** b m Dahar (USA)-Aronia (USA) (Grey Dawn II) 2825^{3} 3355^{4} >**23f**<
Dream Ticket (USA) **3** b f Danzig (USA)-Capo Di Monte (Final Straw) 664^{3} (1000) >**88f**<
Dream Wedding **3** ch f Soviet Star (USA)-Island Wedding (USA) (Blushing Groom (FR)) 779^{6} >**63f**<
Dr Edgar **3** b c Most Welcome-African Dancer 427^{11} 647^{8} 1022^{8} 1372^{5} (1831) 2490^{10} 2804^{2} (4136) >**78f**<
Dr Frances (IRE) **3** b f Pennine Walk-Pounding Beat (Ya Zaman (USA)) 1136^{12} 1353^{7} 1675^{10} 2532^{10} 3184^{5} 3521^{8} >**42f**<
Driftholme **2** b f Safawan-Avahra 4050^{13} 4148^{16} 4320^{21} >**46f**<
Drimard (IRE) **4** ch g Ela-Mana-Mou-Babilla (USA) (Raja Baba (USA)) 1427^{5} *(1567)* 1826^{8} 1965^{11} *2592^{6} 2919^{9}* >**51a 33f**<
Dromalane (IRE) **3** b g Vision (USA)-Clodianus (Bay Express) 4422^{20} >**24f**<
Drum Battle **3** ch c Bold Arrangement-Cannon Boy (USA) (Canonero II (USA)) 1927^{4} 3653^{5} 3799^{8} >**70f**<
Drumdonna (IRE) **5** b m Drumalis-Decoy Duck (Decoy Boy) 2396^{10} 2769^{8} >**41f**<
Drummer Hicks **6** b or br h Seymour Hicks (FR)-Musical Princess (Cavo Doro) 676^{15} 991^{2} 1251^{9} 1744^{5} 2064^{6} >**58f**<
Drumochter **3** ch c Prince Sabo-Short And Sharp (Sharpen Up) 1083^{2} 1358^{2} 1813^{3} 2282^{9} 2662^{6} >**66f**<
Drum Sergeant **8** b h Elegant Air-Cala-Vadella 748^{11} 965^{12} 1499^{11} 1528^{10} 2162^{6} >**37f**<
Dry Point **9** ch h Sharpo-X-Data 1199^{13} 1483^{8} 1673^{2} 1832^{9} (2009) 2746^{5} 3028^{4} 3204^{6} >**77f**<
Dr Zhivago **3** b c Soviet Star (USA)-Reltop 1175^{3} 1383^{2} 1872^{20} 3438^{3} >**84f**<
Dtoto **3** b g Mtoto-Deposit (Thatch (USA)) 2790^{10} 3294^{2} 3772^{5} 4047^{15} >**78f**<
Dubai College (IRE) **2** b c Old Vic-Murooj (USA) (Diesis) 1485^{10} 3180^{6} >**54f**<
Dubai Falcon (USA) **4** b c Woodman (USA)-Keeper's Charm (USA) *66^{9} 242^{6} 416^{8}* >**48a 77df**<
Dublin River (USA) **2** b c Irish River (FR)-Vivre Libre (USA) (Honest Pleasure (USA)) (2467) (3158) 3490^{5} 3782^{2} >**91f**<
Duchess of Alba **3** b f Belmez (USA)-Juliette Marny 2167^{3} (2520) 2868^{2} 3351^{6} >**80f**<
Duckey Fuzz **7** b h Ardross-Twine (Thatching) 450^{14} 3885^{12} 3934^{12} >**32f**<
Ducking **3** b f Reprimand-Gliding 3829^{4} 3984^{10} 4079^{20} 4229^{3} >**74f**<
Duda (USA) **4** f 3911a^{3} >**113f**<
Duello **4** b c Sure Blade (USA)-Royal Loft (Homing) 503^{2} *601^{3} 845^{5}* 1509^{2} 1911^{6} 2317^{8} 2490^{7} 3291^{5} 3439^{4} 3605^{17} 3629^{3} (3757) 3885^{2} 4035^{10} 4171^{8} >**71a 68f**<
Duffertoes **3** ch g High Kicker (USA)-Miss Poll Flinders (Swing Easy (USA)) 504^{15} 618^{7} 939^{10} 1183^{21} >**86f**<
Duggan **8** b h Dunbeath (USA)-Silka (ITY) (Lypheor) (1427) (2122) 2359^{6} 2734^{3} 3047^{6} >**13a 42f**<
Dugort Strand (IRE) **4** b or br g Entitled-Soltina (Sun Prince) *514^{10} 588^{7}* 649^{13} >**58da 32f**<
Duke of Dreams **5** gr g Efisio-Tame Duchess (Saritamer (USA)) 1716^{9} 2197^{9} >**47f**<
Duke Valentino **3** br c Machiavellian (USA)-Aldhabyih (General Assembly (USA)) 2880^{6} 3537^{7} 3761^{6} 3974^{4} 4150^{6} >**78f**<
Dulford Dolly **2** b f Never so Bold-High Quail (USA) (Blushing Groom (FR)) 2651^{9} >**43f**<
Dulford Lad **4** b c In Fijar (USA)-Highsplasher (USA) (Bucksplasher (USA)) 3332a^{3} >**97f**<
Dumaani (USA) **4** gr c Danzig (USA)-Desirable (Lord Gayle (USA)) (805a) >**118f**<
Duncombe Hall **2** b c Salse (USA)-Springs Welcome (Blakeney) 1223^{5} >**30f**<
Dundeelin **4** ch f Dunbeath (USA)-Iron Lass (Thatch (USA)) *233^{12}* 478^{4} 578^{8} 672^{9} 790^{3} 1161^{7} 1523^{17} *2925^{7} 3524^{8}* >**34a 41f**<
Dune River **6** b h Green Desert (USA)-River Spey (Mill Reef (USA)) *(383)* 2455^{7} 3908a^{9} >**95a 86df**<
Dungeon Dancer **3** b c Rambo Dancer (CAN)-Falcrello 1202^{3} 1447^{9} 1591^{4} 1831^{7} (1971) 2309^{3} >**50a 66f**<
Dungeon Master (IRE) **2** ch c Polish Patriot (USA)-Etty (Relko) 424^{6} (523) (683) 1391a^{2} >**84tf**<
Dungeon Princess (IRE) **2** b f Danehill (USA)-Taplow (Tap On Wood) 3828^{5} 4103^{18} >**59f**<
Dunloe (IRE) **3** b f Shaadi (USA)-Kates Cabin (Habitat) 2977^{9} (3428) 3661^{16} >**60f**<
Dunmebrains (IRE) **2** ch f Rich Charlie-Branch Out (Star Appeal) 3160^{6} >**54f**<
Duo Master **2** b c Primo Dominie-Musical Sally (USA) (The Minstrel (CAN)) 1134^{9} 1267^{3} >**66f**<
Duralock Fencer **2** b g General Wade-Madame Laffitte (Welsh Pageant) 1327^{2} 2548^{13} 3379^{8} 3714^{10} 3969^{5} 4208^{7} 4327^{11} >**68f**<
Durano **4** b c Dunbeath (USA)-Norapa (Ahonoora) 2132^{5} (2373) 2621^{3} 2917^{3} 3102^{4} >**71a 73f**<
Durgams First (IRE) **3** ch g Durgam (USA)-Miromaid (Simply Great (FR)) *(5) 241^{2} (350)* 427^{9} 575^{3} 654^{3} 773^{3} 1083^{8} (1430) 1581^{3} (2233) 2953^{5} (3722) >**75a 72f**<
Durham **4** ch c Caerleon (USA)-Sanctuary (Welsh Pageant) *214^{3}* >**42a 79f**<
Durham Drapes **4** b f Taufan (USA)-Miss Bali Beach

(Nonoalco (USA)) 839[8] 1064[5] 1192[4] 1452[9] 2375[5] 2607[4] (2955) (3151) 3255[6] 3462[9] 3703[13] **>68f<**

Durrah **4** b g Midyan (USA)-Sir Ivor's Sorrow (USA) (Sir Ivor) 2798[5]

Durshan (USA) **6** ch h Shahrastani (USA)-Dukayna (Northfields (USA)) *2591[15]* 582[5] 763[3] 1313[5] 1552[3] 1695[4] 2007[9] **>69df<**

Dushyantor (USA) **2** b c Sadler's Wells (USA)-Slightly Dangerous (USA) (Roberto (USA)) (4169) **>82+f<**

Dusk in Daytona **3** b f Beveled (USA)-Mount of Light (Sparkler) 783[4] 1141[16] *2093[2]* 2538[3] *3074[6]* (3249) *3510[4]* *4217[9]* **>63a 68f<**

Dusty Point (IRE) **5** b h Reference Point-Noble Dust (USA) (Dust Commander (USA)) 668[20] 1477[8] 2007[8] *2293[6]* 2465[2] 2695[4] 3029[3] **>58a 72f<**

Dutch **3** ch c Nicholas Bill-Dutch Princess (Royalty) 4220[9] **>10f<**

Dutosky **5** b m Doulab (USA)-Butosky (Busted) *320[4]* *355[5]* 744[7] 1166[2] (1367) (1539) 1908[3] **>53a 70f<**

Duty Sergeant (IRE) **6** b g Pennine Walk-Plainsong (FR) (Amen (FR)) 887[14] *1049[5]* 1402[7] 1518[3] 1694[2] **>36a 42f<**

Dvorak (IRE) **4** b c Darshaan-Grace Note (FR) (Top Ville) *84[2]* *252[2]* 495[3] (986) 1144[5] 4229[13] **>62a 75f<**

Dwingeloo (IRE) **2** b f Dancing Dissident (USA)-Thank One's Stars (Alzao (USA)) 3733[2] (4112) **>71+f<**

Dyanko **2** b g Midyan (USA)-Regain (Relko) 1226[4] 1690[8] *2633[W]* **>59f<**

Dynamis (IRE) **4** b f Dancing Brave (USA)-Diasprina (GER) (Aspros (GER)) *225[3]* *307[9]* *328[6]* *390[8]* 1788[9] *1955[9]* 2139[7] *2292[8]* 2547[7] **>38a 74f<**

E

Eagle Canyon (IRE) **2** b br c Persian Bold-Chrism (Baptism) 3449[7] 3832[5] 3998[4] **>77f<**

Eagle Day (USA) **4** b c Phone Trick (USA)-Ellen L (USA) (To Market) 434[19] 502[8] 693[8] 1016[2] 1057[7] 1265[8] 1595[6] **>82f<**

Earl of Barking (IRE) **5** b h Common Grounds-The Saltings (FR) (Morston (FR)) 4305a[10] **>102f<**

Early Peace (IRE) **3** b c Bluebird (USA)-Everything Nice (Sovereign Path) 1136[14] 1258[3] 2350[5] **>74f<**

Early Star **6** b h Precocious-Staritsa (USA) (Alleged (USA)) *49[3]* *138[7]* 882[15] *1091[14]* **>51a 48f<**

Early to Rise **5** b h Don't Forget Me-Foreno (Formidable) 1799[9] **>42f<**

Easby Jester **4** b g Idiot's Delight-Khatti Hawk (Hittite Glory) 2913[9] **>20f<**

East Barns (IRE) **7** gr h Godswalk (USA)-Rocket Lass (Touch Paper) 486[W] 753[7] 1037[11] (1286) **>46a 52f<**

Easter Coul (IRE) **3** br f Brush Aside (USA)-Cree's Figurine (Creetown) 695[14] 1175[10] 3270[3] **>57f<**

Eastern Paradise **2** b c Mujtahid (USA)-Bedouin Veil (USA) (Shareef Dancer (USA)) 3625[4] (3765) **>78f<**

Eastern Prophets **2** b c Emarati (USA)-Four Love (Pas de Seul) 760[5] (943) (1197) 1343[2] (1556) 1868[8] 2442[9] 2991[2] 3499[2] 3668[12] 4032[5] **>97f<**

Eastern Sunrise **2** b g Statoblest-Oriental Splendour (Runnett) 3744[12] **>23f<**

East India (IRE) **2** b c Scenic-Eastern Aura (IRE) (Ahonoora) 3010[7] 3398[2] 3752[4] **>67f<**

Eastleigh **6** b h Efisio-Blue Jane *12[5]* *41[6]* *56[2]* *169[3]* *181[4]* *205[8]* *302[2]* *(343)* *397[3]* *413[3]* *(472)* *835[5]* *4340[6]* **>68a 31f<**

East of Heaven(IRE) **0** 01 c Lyphard-Escaline (Arctic Tern) 1007a[3] 2560a[4] **>103f<**

East Sheen **3** b f Salse (USA)-Madam Cody (Hot Spark) 1052[10] 1366[11] 2032[7] **>60f<**

Easy Dollar **3** ch c Gabitat-Burglars Girl 543[5] 621[3] 853[4] 963[5] 1186[11] 1316[4] 2344[2] (2576) (2737) 3067[5] 3342[3] 3473[5] 3834[13] 3931[8] **>111f<**

Easy D'Or **4** b c Glint of Gold-Eastern Command (USA) (Far Out East (USA)) 1449[7] 1667[9] **>37f<**

Easy Jet (POL) **3** b c Robellino (USA)-Etourdie (USA) (Arctic Tern (USA)) 1186[2] 2362[2] 3113[6] 3732[9] 4116[22] **>78f<**

Easy Listening (USA) **3** b c Easy Goer (USA)-Queen of Song (USA) (His Majesty (USA)) (1198) **>89+f<**

Easy Option (IRE) **3** ch f Prince Sabo-Brazen Faced 1475[4] (3707) 4012a[4] **>117+f<**

Easy To Remember (IRE) **2** b c Mujtahid (USA)-In Unison (Bellypha) 3155[11]

Eau de Cologne **3** b c Persian Bold-No More Rosies (Warpath) 824[5] 1195[5] (1436) 1681[3] 2622[3] 3669[4] 4036[10] 4158[4] 4288[3] **>77f<**

Eben Al Habeeb (IRE) **4** ch c Nashwan (USA)-Family Style (USA) (State Dinner (USA)) 935[18] 2525[9] 2967[3] 3517[3] **>78f<**

Ebony Blaze **4** b c Aragon-Velvet Pigeon (Homing) *406[14]* 3657[15] 3844[6] 3934[9] 4157[22] **>40a 52f<**

Ebony Boy **2** bl c Sayf El Arab (USA)-Actress (Known Fact (USA)) 480[7] *1454[3]* *1758[2]* *2380[2]* *(2625)* 2991[8] 3289[11] **>64a 29f<**

Ebony T-A-P-S **2** bl f Adbass (USA)-August Seventeenth (Sharpo) 2035[10] 3915[15] **>20f<**

Eccentric Dancer **2** b f Rambo Dancer (CAN)-Lady Eccentric (IRE) (Magical Wonder (USA)) 925[4] 1176[8] 3976[3] 4111[18] 4231[19] **>53f<**

Eccola **2** b f Seattle Dancer (USA)-Evocatrice 2025[8] 2705[5] 3633[5] 3985[13] **>69f<**

Ecstatic Madam (IRE) **2** b f Statoblest-Neeran (Wollow) 3371[9] 3495[7] 3857[3] 4081[6] **>67f<**

Edan Heights **3** b g Heights of Gold-Edna (Shiny Tenth) 630[8] 888[4] 1221[5] 1747[7] 2557[3] 3277[2] (3876) 4108[3] 4228[2] **>78f<**

Edbaysaan (IRE) **5** b h Slip Anchor-Legend of Arabia (Great Nephew) (2360) 3146[6] 3454[2] 4076[8] **>109df<**

Eden Dancer **3** b c Shareef Dancer (USA)-Dash (Connaught) (576) 759[12] 2020[6] 2356[5] (2774) 2993[9] **>65f<**

Eden's Close **6** ch h Green Dancer (USA)-Royal Agreement (USA) (Vaguely Noble) 550[14] 676[7] 2138[4] 2472[4] 2612[2] **>69f<**

Eden's Star (IRE) **3** b c Fools Holme (USA)-Flinging Star (USA) (Northern Fling (USA)) 647[14] 907[3] 2881[7] 3097[4] (3356) 3429[2] 3493[2] 3770[7] **>77f<**

Edgar Kirby **4** ch c Caerleon (USA)-Martha Stevens (USA) (Super Concorde (USA)) 3063[8] **>64f<**

Editor's Note (USA) **2** ch c Forty Niner (USA)-Beware of the Cat (USA) *4306a[3]* **>116ta f<**

Edler Von Baraga (GER) **3** c 1713a[5] **>96f<**

Ed's Folly (IRE) **2** b c Fayruz-Tabriya (Nishapour (FR)) 1511[12] 3733[18] 3892[3] 4066[6] **>70f<**

Educated Pet **6** gr h Petong-School Road *30[5]* *130[6]*

228^{5} 268^{7} 314^{9} 387^{10} 646^{14} *2588^{8}* 3291^{10} 3493^{9} 3531^{16} **>56a 53f<**

Eelious (USA) 3 b c Nureyev (USA)-Maxencia (FR) (Tennyson (FR)) 1147^{3} 1490^{5} (1987) 2366^{4} 2937^{3} 3351^{4} 3718^{10} **>88f<**

Efaad (IRE) 4 b c Shaadi (USA)-Krismas River (Kris) 751^{11} 866^{17} **>68f<**

Efficacious (IRE) 2 ch f Efisio-Bushti Music (Bustino) 1938^{9} 2340^{9} 3025^{8} 3628^{14} 4208^{17} **>48f<**

Efficacy 4 b f Efisio-Lady Killane (Reform) *55^{8} 138^{8} 165^{5} 182^{4} 247^{5} (625) 769^{2} 1076^{4}* (1456) *(1633) 2074^{2} 2383^{5}* **>56a 47f<**

Efipetite 2 ch f Efisio-Petite Elite (Anfield) *1879^{5}* 2128^{11} 2302^{4} *2629^{4}* 2757^{5} 2914^{7} 3160^{12} *3528^{3}* 3744^{14} 3806^{10} 4100^{9} 4137^{8} 4231^{14} **>47a 47f<**

Efizia 5 b m Efisio-Millie Grey (Grey Ghost) 3810^{7} 3965^{6} 4061^{13} 4233^{6} 4284^{8} **>67f<**

Efosa 3 b c Efisio-Wimosa (Mossborough) *2494^{6}* **>2a f<**

Efra 6 b h Efisio-Ra Ra (Lord Gayle (USA)) 765^{6} 1071^{8} 1537^{8} 1832^{15} 4134^{5} **>74f<**

Egipcio 3 b c Java Gold-Teresa 4301a^{3} **>94f<**

Eglwys Newydd 4 ch f Gabitat-Jalna (Free Boy) *3081^{10}*

Ehtefaal (USA) 4 b c Alysheba (USA)-Bolt From The Blue (USA) (Blue Times (USA)) *1210^{4}* **>44a 89f<**

Eid (USA) 6 b h Northern Baby (CAN)-Millracer (USA) (Le Fabuleux) 1295^{7} **>59f<**

Eightandahalf (IRE) 6 b h Be My Guest (USA)-Nancy Chere (USA) (Gallant Man) *2591^{14}* 556^{19} 751^{12} 840^{14} **>64f<**

Eight Sharp (IRE) 3 b c Sure Blade (USA)-Octavia Girl (Octavo (USA)) 822^{2} 1103^{7} 3659^{15} **>82f<**

Eights High (USA) 2 b c Local Talent (USA)-Vantasy Park (USA) (Highland Park (USA)) 615^{7} 671^{6} 859^{2} 1054^{2} 2192^{2} 2435^{4} 3375^{15} 3613^{9} 3767^{6} **>69f<**

Eileen's Girl (IRE) 2 b f Cyrano de Bergerac-Beguiled (IRE) (Be My Guest (USA)) 2354^{6} **>7f<**

Eileen's Guest (IRE) 3 b f Taufan (USA)-Gentle Guest (IRE) (Be My Guest (USA)) 861^{7} 1654^{8} **>46f<**

Eire Leath-Sceal 8 b h Legend of France (USA)-Killarney Belle (USA) (Irish Castle (USA)) 2256^{2} 2501^{6} **>67f<**

Ejtaaz (USA) 4 b c Topsider (USA)-Summer Silence (USA) (Stop The Music (USA)) 3884^{14} **>41f<**

Ela-Aristokrati (IRE) 3 b c Danehill (USA)-Dubai Lady (Kris) 829^{3} (1636) 1807^{2} 3143^{6} 3381^{5} **>115f<**

Ela Man Howa 4 b c Mtoto-Top Treat (USA) (Topsider (USA)) 1254^{2} 1518^{4} 1794^{3} 2184^{3} 2530^{4} 3015^{3} 3292^{5} (3470) **>59da 65f<**

El Angelo (USA) 3 b c El Gran Senor-Angela Serra (Arctic Tern 2722a^{3} **>82f<**

Ela Palikari Mou (IRE) 4 b g Lomond (USA)-Ionian Raja (USA) (Raja Baba (USA)) *21^{6} 101^{5}* 630^{12} 1048^{9} **>33a 30f<**

Elashath (USA) 2 b c El Gran Senor (USA)-Gorgeoso (USA) (Damascus (USA)) 4080^{13} **>64f<**

Elation 3 b c Sadler's Wells (USA)-Chellita (Habitat) 484^{5} 786^{2} 974^{9} 1093^{14} 3002^{6} 3464^{3} **>58f<**

El Atrevido (FR) 5 ch g Rainbow Quest (USA)-Majestic Peck (USA) (Majestic Light (USA)) *(26) 276^{3} (470)* 634^{21} *1049^{11}* **>72a 16f<**

Ela-Yie-Mou (IRE) 2 ch c Kris-Green Lucia (Green Dancer (USA)) 3617^{6} 3868^{13} 4247^{5} **>74f<**

El Bailador (IRE) 4 b c Dance of Life (USA)-Sharp Ego (USA) (Sharpen Up) 935^{5} 1368^{8} *(1939) 2407^{5}* (2861) 3388^{8} 3646^{4} 3965^{5} 4229^{2} **>66a 71f<**

Elburg (IRE) 5 b h Ela-Mana-Mou-Iosifa (Top Ville) *87^{3} 147^{4} 277^{4}* 432^{4} 696^{6} (840) **>65a 74f<**

El Don 3 b g High Kicker (USA)-Madam Gerard (Brigadier Gerard) 813^{12} 1165^{14} 2654^{5} 3889^{9} 3973^{9} 4249^{12} **>54f<**

Election Day (IRE) 3 b c Sadler's Wells (USA)-Hellenic (Darshaan) 3016^{11} **>49f<**

Electric Committee (IRE) 5 ch g Lancastrian-Mary Black (Ardoon) 2157^{5} **>31f<**

Electrolyte 5 b h Electric-This Sensation (Balidar) *3^{7} 131^{7} 295^{12} 1086^{12}* **>25a f<**

Elegant Friend 7 ch g Music Boy-Cardinal Palace (Royal Palace) 3825^{17}

Elementary 12 b h Busted-Santa Vittoria (Ragusa) *(97) 143^{4} 496^{2}* 729^{2} (1149) (1555) (3741) 4062^{2} *(4293)* **>73a 82f<**

Elfin Laughter 3 b f Alzao (USA)-Rainbow's End 647^{2} 1382^{8} **>78f<**

Elfin Queen (IRE) 2 b f Fairy King (USA)-West of Eden (Crofter (USA)) 1579^{3} 1722^{2} 1919^{4} 3727^{12} **>70f<**

Elfland (IRE) 4 b c Fairy King (USA)-Ridge The Times (USA) (Riva Ridge (USA)) 922^{4} (1299) 2369^{9} **>88f<**

Elite Force (IRE) 2 b c Fairy King (USA)-La Petruschka (Ballad Rock) 3560^{5} 3733^{4} **>78f<**

Elite Hope (USA) 3 ch f Moment of Hope (USA)-Chervil (USA) (Greenough (USA)) 1487^{15} 2531^{2} 2948^{4} 3212^{6} 3706^{22} 4319^{5} **>88f<**

Elite Justice 3 ch c Absalom-Persian Express (Persian Bold) 1130^{9} 1447^{4} 1775^{6} 1985^{3} 2536^{2} 2711^{4} **>69f<**

Elite Number (USA) 3 ro f Elmaamul (USA)-Comicus (USA) (Northern Jove (CAN)) *59^{6} 273^{9} 1329^{7}* 1669^{W} 1824^{13} 2774^{5} **>51a 51f<**

Elite Racing 3 b f Risk Me (FR)-Hot Stone (Hotfoot) (1274) 1539^{9} 1735^{7} 2102^{4} (2171) 2537^{3} 2684^{2} 3218^{5} 3383^{6} 3973^{12} 4083^{10} **>68df<**

Ella Nico (IRE) 2 ch f Archway-Ceann-Na-Bann (Doulab (USA)) 3687a^{2} **>93f<**

Ellastyle (IRE) 4 b f Waajib-Grecian Hill (Ela-Mana-Mou) 1039^{11} 1452^{8} 1667^{8} **>41f<**

Elle Mac 2 b f Merdon Melody-Tripolitaine (FR) 863^{7} 1190^{13} 3806^{13} **>18f<**

Elle Shaped (IRE) 5 b g Treasure Kay-Mamie's Joy (Prince Tenderfoot (USA)) 434^{15} 535^{16} 790^{2} 949^{3} 1021^{8} 1151^{4} 1316^{8} (1565) 1668^{5} 1765^{3} 2001^{5} 2060^{10} 3051^{2} 3212^{2} (3221) 3359^{15} 3777^{6} 3822^{13} (4322) **>89f<**

Ellie Ardensky 3 b f Slip Anchor-Circus Ring (High Top) (1195) 1800^{2} 2614^{4} (3007) 3413^{3} 3944^{5} **>102f<**

Elly Fleetfoot (IRE) 3 b f Elmaamul (USA)-Fleetwood Fancy (Taufan (USA)) 797^{7} 1097^{10} 1372^{7} (1659) 1984^{4} **>73f<**

Elmer's Tune 3 b c Superpower-Malindi (Mansingh (USA)) 544^{7} 1381^{7} 1519^{10} 1974^{21} **>42f<**

Elmswood (USA) 2 b f Woodman (USA)-Lilian Bayliss (IRE) (Sadler's Wells (USA)) 977^{4} 1176^{3} 1460^{3} 3090^{10} 3423^{7} 3548^{8} **>72f<**

El Nido 7 ch h Adonijah-Seleter (Hotfoot) *(79) (375)* 495^{4} *588^{2} 843^{2} 1210^{9}* **>75a 53f<**

El Opera (IRE) 2 b f Sadler's Wells (USA)-Ridge The

Times (USA) (Riva Ridge (USA)) 3708^{4} **>66+f<**

El Paesa (IRE) 5 br h Doyoun-Samedi Soir (Reform) 3796a^{3} **>99f<**

Elpida (USA) 3 b c Trempolino (USA)-All For Hope (USA) (Sensitive Prince (USA)) 764^{18} 935^{14} *(3735)* 3898^{4} *4126^{5} 4336^{17}* **>71a 61f<**

Elpidos 3 ch c Bold Arrangement-Thalassa 427^{12} 537^{5} *626^{4}* 1322^{3} 1793^{3} 1988^{2} 2367^{4} 2707^{10} (3125) 3214^{11} 3497^{12} 3732^{3} 3973^{7} 4116^{21} **>62a 83f<**

Elraas (USA) 3 b c Gulch (USA)-Full Card (USA) 4131^{15} **>41f<**

El Sembrador (ARG) 4 ch c Octante-Nina Flor 4014a^{15} **>94f<**

Elshabiba (USA) 2 b br c Dayjur (USA)-Sweet Roberta (USA) (Roberto (USA)) 2597^{2} (4266) **>88+f<**

El Shitane(FR) 4 b c Fabulous Dancer-Didia Clara (Sea Break) 1005a^{2} **>96f<**

Elsies Bar 3 gr f Primo Dominie-Tabeeba (Diesis) 521^{11} **>58f<**

El Society (GER) 3 c 4018a^{6} **>95f<**

El Supremo (USA) 3 b c Storm Bird (CAN)-Sharmila (FR) (Blakeney) (504) 900a^{5} (1388a) 2596^{3} 3038a^{5} **>108f<**

El Taurus 3 b c El Conquistador-Meralto (Noalto) *350^{8}* 732^{11} **>19f<**

El Tenor(FR) 0 01 c Bon Sang (FR)-Prima Sinfonia (Acamas) 1008a^{3} 4014a^{11} 4176a^{7} **>106f<**

Eltish (USA) 3 b c Cox's Ridge (USA)-Nimble Feet (USA) (Danzig (USA)) 679^{3} 1006a^{6} 1836^{2} 2286^{5} 3143^{5} **>122f<**

Elton Ledger (IRE) 6 b h Cyrano de Bergerac-Princess of Nashua (Crowned Prince (USA)) *93^{4}* **>71a 53f<**

Eluned May 4 ch f Clantime-Arroganza (Crofthall) 1802^{6} 1972^{11} **>48df<**

El Volador 8 br h Beldale Flutter (USA)-Pharjoy (FR) (Pharly (FR)) 3884^{8} 4051^{8} (4332) **>62f<**

El Yasaf (IRE) 7 b h Sayf El Arab (USA)-Winsong Melody (Music Maestro) (571) (700) 921^{5} 1364^{5} 3902^{6} 4121^{9} 4160^{12} **>99f<**

Embankment (IRE) 5 b or br h Tate Gallery (USA)-Great Leighs (Vaigly Great) 714^{13} 918^{5} 1188^{3} 1610^{4} 1926^{11} 2287^{7} 2703^{8} 3601^{2} 3755^{6} **>71a 92f<**

Embarcadero (GER) 7 b h Vacarme (USA)-Escadrille (GER) (Frontal) 1398a^{8} 1890a^{6} **>78f<**

Embezzler 3 b c Emarati (USA)-Double Touch (FR) (Nonoalco (USA)) 648^{9} *830^{6}* 1083^{6} 1245^{7} 1403^{4} 1654^{7} 2317^{17} 2881^{6} 2993^{6} 3305^{9} 4101^{13} **>57a 43f<**

Embracing 3 b f Reference Point-Hug Me (Shareef Dancer (USA)) 929^{2} (1162) (1386) (1794) (2055) 3162^{8} 3445^{10} **>99f<**

Embroidered 2 br f Charmer-Emblazon *4269^{10} 4339^{14}* **>29a f<**

Embryonic (IRE) 3 b c Prince Rupert (FR)-Belle Viking (FR) (641) (879) 3718^{3} 3963^{13} **>88df<**

Emei Shan 2 br f Inca Chief (USA)-Tricata (Electric) 1443^{7} 1829^{7} 3174^{14} 3516^{10} 3895^{11} **>38f<**

Emerald Dream (IRE) 3 b or br f Vision (USA)-Island Mom (USA) (Our Native (USA)) *174^{6} 372^{5} 444^{10}* 2536^{6} **>43a 43f<**

Emerging Market 3 b c Emarati (USA)-Flitteriss Park (Beldale Flutter (USA)) 543^{2} (743) 1487^{8} 1806^{12} 2099^{2} 2737^{9} 3085^{6} 3373^{3} 3602^{4} 3755^{5} 4122^{2} **>99f<**

Emily-Mou (IRE) 3 b f Cadeaux Genereux-Sarajill (High Line) (1914) 2057^{2} 2171^{2} (2411) 2694^{6} (2849) 3130^{2} 3278^{4} (3621) 3926^{4} 4071^{16} **>47a 83f<**

Emirates Express 3 b c Shaadi (USA)-Les Dancelles (Pas de Seul) 504^{9} 980^{3} 1222^{2} 1639^{2} 1839^{30} 2169^{3} 2795^{3} 3768^{6} 3999^{4} **>90f<**

Emma Grimes (IRE) 4 b f Nordico (USA)-Keep the Faith (Furry Glen) 2246^{14} 2488^{5} 2657^{2} 2829^{4} 3024^{6} 3657^{11} 4135^{5} 4259^{8} 4332^{8} **>8a 45f<**

Emnala (IRE) 3 b f Contract Law (USA)-African Light (Kalaglow) *509^{5}* 584^{7} 654^{11} 837^{5} **>27a 53df<**

Emperegrine (USA) 2 b br c Imperial Falcon (CAN)-In Spate (USA) (In Reality) 1551^{8} 1697^{4} 1977^{3} 2264^{3} 2926^{2} 3225^{6} 3471^{6} 3721^{2} 3857^{4} 4111^{13} **>71f<**

Emperor Jones (USA) 5 b h Danzig (USA)-Qui Royalty (USA) 805a^{4} 3360^{4} 4078^{7} **>120f<**

Emperors Wood 4 b g Then Again-Silver Empress (Octavo (USA)) 4027^{W}

Emphatic Candidate (IRE) 3 ch c Salt Dome (USA)-Humble Mission (Shack (USA)) 739^{4} (1012) 1263^{6} 1654^{3} 2406^{4} *2959^{2} 3241^{6}* 3403^{7} **>69a 74f<**

Empower (IRE) 3 b c Tirol-Trusted Maiden 552^{5} 1273^{3} 1748^{3} 2102^{6} 2574^{6} **>75f<**

Empty Quarter 3 b c Night Shift (USA)-Infanta Real (Formidable) 1309^{3} 1486^{2} 1848^{9} 3542^{10} (3859) (3979) 4083^{5} **>104f<**

Enamel Tiger 2 ch c Risk Me (FR)-Dancing Belle (Dance In Time (CAN)) 4103^{21} **>50f<**

En Attendant (FR) 7 ch h Bairn (USA)-Vizenia (Vitiges (FR)) 953^{5} 1365^{6} 1698^{6} 2099^{8} 2369^{15} (3212) 3358^{8} 3924^{12} **>106f<**

En Cascade (FR) 4 b c Baillamont (USA)-Crystal Echo (Posse) 489a^{2}

Enchanted Cottage 3 b c Governor General-Mitsubishi Colour (Cut Above) 1150^{9} 1378^{9} 2522^{7} 3725^{9} 3759^{12} 3936^{9} **>45f<**

Enchanteur 4 b f Damister (USA)-Brown Maid (URU) (Admirals Launch) *(409) 530^{8} 605^{4}* 2088^{12} **>60a 69f<**

Encore M'Lady (IRE) 4 b f Dancing Dissident (USA)-Diva Encore (Star Appeal) 1019^{8} 1648^{10} 1895^{26} 2194^{9} 2916^{4} 3457^{13} 4040^{21} 4278^{14} **>67f<**

Endless Fantasy 3 b f Kalaglow-Headrest (Habitat) *2093^{5} 2378^{4}* 2532^{9} 2976^{5} 3140^{5} *3318^{2}* **>57a 41f<**

Endless Light (USA) 4 b c Sunshine Forever (USA)-Propositioning (USA) (Mr Prospector (USA)) 623^{7} 931^{10} 1102^{4} 1243^{5} 1612^{12} 1999^{3} **>94f<**

Endless Wave 3 b f Indian Ridge-Sound of the Sea (Windjammer (USA)) 483^{8} 581^{3} 850^{11} 1094^{16} 1802^{4} 2742^{6} *3072^{13}* 3622^{2} 3748^{11} **>64f<**

Endowment 3 ch c Cadeaux Genereux-Palm Springs (Top Ville) (854) 1127^{6} 2298^{6} 2792^{4} (2989) **>80f<**

Energy Man 2 b c Hadeer-Cataclysmic (Ela-Mana-Mou) 3436^{4} 3868^{10} 3994^{6} **>74f<**

English Invader 4 b c Rainbow Quest (USA)-Modica 958^{5} 1056^{2} 1479^{4} 2456^{4} **>103f<**

Enhorabuena (IRE) 2 b c Fairy King-Lassalla 3590a^{3}

Enquiry (FR) 3 b f Darshaan-Eloura (Top Ville) 1704a^{2} 2045a^{5} 2898a^{3} **>101f<**

En Vacances (IRE) 3 b f Old Vic-Welcome Break (Wollow) 715^{14} 886^{4} 1339^{2} 1717^{5} 2599^{8} *3078^{2} 3245^{3}* (3627) 3774^{7} (4158) **>72a 84f<**

Environmentalist (IRE) 4 b c Sure Blade (USA)-Vielle

(Ribero) *313[13]* 423[16] 549[5] 649[4] 866[2] *3245[6] 3527[4] 3735[4]* 3899[4] *3951[2]* 4331[4] >**64a 69f**<

Environment Friend 7 gr h Cozzene (USA)-Water Woo (USA) (Tom Rolfe) 1235a[3] 1609[7] 2286[4] 2595[7] 4120[8] >**117f**<

Epagris 3 ch f Zalazl (USA)-Trikymia (Final Straw) 660[2] 933[5] (1145) 1848[11] 2416[2] 2673[3] 3931[6] 4087[2] >**107f**<

Epaphos (GER) 5 br h Acatenango (GER)-Eidothea (GER) (Teotepec (GER)) 1239a[3] 3329a[3] 3688a[3] 4008a[6] >**115f**<

Epica 4 b c Picea-Aladyat (Home Guard (USA)) *(153) 412[8] 833[7] 1210[8] 1319[5]* >**54da 49f**<

Eqtesaad (USA) 4 b or br c Danzig (USA)-Last Feather (USA) (Vaguely Noble) *(21) (63) 100[5] (512)* 634[12] 873[16] 1368[14] >**80a 78f**<

Equasion (IRE) 3 b f Cyrano de Bergerac-Konigin Kate (GER) (Authi) 881[7] 1136[17] 2841[2] >**59f**<

Equerry 4 b c Midyan (USA)-Supreme Kingdom (Take A Reef) 479[2] *529[2]* 579[3] 876[6] (1061) 1250[3] *1631[4]* 2061[5] 2222[4] *(2634)* (2788) >**68a 81f**<

Equilibrium 3 b f Statoblest-Allander Girl 1146[5] 1719[3] *2093[6]* 2808[4] 3344[4] 3871[3] >**46a 58f**<

Equity's Darling (IRE) 3 b f Law Society (USA)-Curie Abu (Crofter (USA)) 553[8] 630[6] 907[4] 1194[8] *1459[2] 1569[5] (2140) 2959[4] 3241[10]* >**64a 67f**<

Eretan (IRE) 4 b g Lashkari-Eretna (Golden Fleece (USA)) 1328[P] >**74df**<

Eric's Bett 2 b c Chilibang-Mira Lady (Henbit (USA)) 1063[5] 1842[6] 2485[5] 2926[3] 3463[5] 3666[8] (3850) 4141[4] 4279[5] >**77f**<

Erin Bird (FR) 4 b f Bluebird (USA)-Maid of Erin (USA) (Irish River (FR)) 805a[13] 1120a[8] 2763[3] 3327a[5] 3698a[3] 4015a[6] >**116f**<

Erin's Lad 4 br c Bold Owl-Vernair (USA) (Super Concorde (USA)) 3440[11] >**65f**<

Erlking (IRE) 5 b h Fairy King (USA)-Cape of Storms (Fordham (USA)) *2922[6] 3240[12] 3511[11] 3737[10]* >**42a f**<

Ermbold (GER) 3 ch c Never so Bold-Ermione (Surumu) (902a) >**92f**<

Erminius (GER) 4 ch c Highest Honor (FR)-Ermione (Surumu (GER)) 1236a[2] >**108f**<

Errant 3 b c Last Tycoon-Wayward Lass (USA) (Hail the Pirates (USA)) 1486[12] 4150[8] >**63f**<

Errazuriz (IRE) 2 ch f Classic Music (USA)-Miss Lee Ann 4341a[2]

Ertlon 5 b h Shareef Dancer (USA)-Sharpina (Sharpen Up) *89[2] 242[2] 281[2] 383[3]* 433[13] (728) 870[12] 3706[19] 3813[14] 4041[6] 4156[4] 4267[5] >**95a 88f**<

Erupt 2 b c Beveled (USA)-Sparkling Sovereign (Sparkler) 943[2] 1662[9] 2077[4] 2459[6] 3213[5] 3655[3] 3947[9] (4144) 4243[2] >**74f**<

Escape Talk 8 gr m Gabitat-Getaway Girl (Capistrano) 1295[12] 1359[8] 4101[10] >**31f**<

Escarpment (USA) 4 ch c Green Dancer (USA)-Revidere (USA) (Reviewer (USA)) 712[9] 869[5] (1171) 2219a[6] 3563[6] >**115f**<

Escobar (IRE) 2 br c Cyrano de Bergerac-Gale Force Seven (Strong Gale) 3432[8] 3784[8] 4098[7] >**54f**<

Eskimo Kiss (IRE) 2 b f Distinctly North (USA)-Felicitas (Mr Fluorocarbon) 3069[20] 3379[15] 3628[10] 3894[12] 4075[19] >**48f**<

Eskimo Nel (IRE) 4 ch f Shy Groom (USA)-North Lady (Northfields (USA)) 430[7] >**24a 46f**<

Espartero (IRE) 3 ch c Ballad Rock-Elabella (Ela-Mana-Mou) 1373[4] (1924) 2764[4] 3550[3] >**112f**<

Esperer 5 b g Full of Hope-Priory Maid (Malinowski (USA)) *21[9] 187[8] 285[10] 346[12]* 1381[10] >**29a f**<

Esperto 2 b c Risk Me (FR)-Astrid Gilberto (Runnett) 1913[6] 2128[8] 4075[23] >**59f**<

Esquive 2 ch f Safawan-Edraianthus (Windjammer (USA)) 4089a[3]

Essayeffsee 6 b g Precocious-Floreal (Formidable) 1192[5] 1378[2] 1491[2] 2064[3] 2126[3] 2375[6] (2875) 3297[2] 3810[2] 3977[5] 4138[7] 4284[5] >**63f**<

Essentialselection 2 gr g Petong-Love Scene (Carwhite) 1481[2] 1662[2] 1857[7] 2077[3] 2839[3] 3160[4] >**82f**<

Essex Girl 5 b m Dominion-Valiancy (Grundy) (800a) 1228a[3] >**66df**<

Esthal (IRE) 5 b h Kalaglow-Chevrefeuille (Ile de Bourbon (USA)) 1202[14] 1659[5] 1771[14] 2280[12] >**27a 50f**<

Esther Louise 2 b f Governor General-Cuba Libre (Rum (USA)) 1503[6] 1841[9] 2251[11] >**21f**<

Estrela Castanha 3 b f Heights of Gold-Soleil Etoile (Roi Soleil) 2638[6] 3058[7] 3317[4] >**44f**<

Eternally Grateful 2 b f Picea-Carpadia (Icecapade (USA)) 3763[22] 4216[12] >**23f**<

Eternity Range (USA) 2 b c Majestic Light-Northern Eternity 4177a[3] >**108f**<

Ethbaat (USA) 4 b or br c Chief's Crown (USA)-Alchaasibiyeh (USA) (Seattle Slew (USA)) 4122[10] 4267[25] >**94f**<

Etoile du Nord 3 b or br c Tragic Role (USA)-Daisy Topper (Top Ville) 4150[11] >**52f**<

Etterby Park (USA) 2 b c Silver Hawk (USA)-Bonita Francita (USA) (Devil's Bag (USA)) 825[10] 1343[5] 3174[13] 3858[11] >**51f**<

Euchan Falls (IRE) 3 b g Durgam (USA)-Glen Maddie (Reasonable (FR)) *3513[12]* >**40a 64f**<

Eulogy (FR) 8 b or br h Esprit du Nord (USA)-Louange (Green Dancer (USA)) *375[7] 516[3]* >**59a f**<

Euphyllia 3 b f Superpower-Anse Chastanet (Cavo Doro) 813[15] 1377[8] *1571[10]* 3726[15] (4193) 4268[11] 4319[10] >**38a 85df**<

Eurobox Boy 2 ch g Savahra Sound-Princess Poquito (Hard Fought) *3243[W] 3525[W]* 3870[4] 4075[3] 4221[3] 4327[7] >**71f**<

Euro Express 2 ch c Domynsky-Teresa Deevey (Runnett) 533[14] 1190[12] 2251[8] 2516[4] 3048[2] 3225[8] 3353[2] 3721[11] 3975[7] >**60f**<

Euro Forum 3 ch c Deploy-Unique Treasure (Young Generation) 427[5] 717[7] 851[7] 947[2] 1386[3] 1695[6] 2248[5] 2603[2] *3318[4]* 3875[3] 4022[7] >**58a 67f**<

Eurolink Mischief 3 b f Be My Chief (USA)-Lady Eurolink (Kala Shikari) 865[4] 1128[3] 1264[2] (1674) 2026[2] 3459[3] 3918[4] 4283[2] >**87f**<

Eurolink Shadow 3 b c Be My Chief (USA)-Miss Top Ville (FR) (Top Ville) 1147[5] 1383[4] 2331[4] 4167[7] >**76f**<

Eurolink the Rebel (USA) 3 ch g Timeless Native (USA)-Seeing Stars (USA) (Unconscious (USA)) 1258[6] (1748) 2103[2] 2766[9] 3552[8] 3781[4] 4035[15] (4196) >**88f**<

Europex 2 bl g Dunbeath (USA)-Afrabela (African Sky) 2095[6] 2192[8] 2606[3] 2855[4] >**67f**<

Europharm Lassie 4 b f Tate Gallery (USA)-Panama

Princess (Indian King (USA)) 39^{9} 142^{7} 198^{3} 334^{8} 1164^{15} **>33a 28f<**
Euro Rebel **3** ch c Roi Danzig (USA)-Teresa Deevey (Runnett) 573^{4} 640^{7} 1151^{11} 1668^{6} **>56f<**
Euro Sceptic (IRE) **3** ch c Classic Secret (USA)-Very Seldom (Rarity) 538^{14} 759^{6} (1060) 1207^{2} (1528) 1679^{3} 2020^{2} 2484^{7} 2788^{6} 3980^{11} 4234^{7} **>59f<**
Euro Singer **3** br c Chief Singer-Crystal Gael (Sparkler) 867^{8} 1322^{2} 1498^{6} 2037^{3} 3056^{5} 3676^{2} 3936^{4} **>67f<**
Eurotwist **6** b h Viking (USA)-Orange Bowl (General Assembly (USA)) 312^{6} 4000^{9} **>40a 54?f<**
Euskara **2** ch f La Grange Music-Ciboure (Norwick (USA)) 1077^{4} 1272^{5} 2294^{2} 2496^{4} 2591^{4} 2965^{6} **>42a 23f<**
Eva Luna (IRE) **3** b f Double Schwartz-Guess Again (GER) (Stradavinsky) $707a^{4}$ 1896^{10} **>102f<**
Evan Can Wait (IRE) **3** b f Phardante (FR)-Brandywell (Skyliner) 350^{10} 2815^{6} 3504^{12} **>17f<**
Evan 'elp Us **3** ch c Executive Man-Recent Events (Stanford) 876^{15} 1528^{5} 1862^{3} 2278^{5} 2503^{9} 2922^{5} 3645^{6} 3973^{4} 4194^{4} **>43a 68f<**
Evanro (IRE) **4** ch c Common Grounds-Opening Day (Day Is Done) 3830^{10} 4115^{11} 4209^{3} **>45f<**
Evaporate **3** b f Insan (USA)-Mona (Auction Ring (USA)) 2636^{6} 3318^{7} **>35a 30f<**
Even Handed **2** b g Then Again-Trecauldah (Treboro (USA)) 3089^{22} 3260^{6} 3553^{5} 3915^{2} 4075^{5} **>68f<**
Evening Chime (USA) **2** b c Night Shift (USA)-Brattice Cloth (USA) (L'Enjoleur (CAN)) 1041^{2} 1341^{2} 1620^{3} (2371) 2779^{11} (3147) **>79f<**
Evening Falls **4** ro f Beveled (USA)-Encore L'Amour (USA) (Monteverdi) 906^{5} 1673^{7} 2288^{10} (2631) (3072) 3376^{12} 3512^{11} 3771^{16} **>61a 51f<**
Eveningperformance **4** b f Night Shift (USA)-Classic Design (Busted) 571^{9} 921^{2} 1475^{2} 1896^{6} 2430^{8} 2671^{2} (3550) $4012a^{3}$ **>117f<**
Even Top (IRE) **2** br c Topanoora-Skevena (Niniski (USA)) 1551^{6} (3340) 3631^{2} (3925) 4199^{2} **>104f<**
Ever Friends **3** ch c Crever-Cappuccilli 239^{6} 372^{7} 418^{9} 546^{14} 3513^{6} 4167^{4} **>40a 51f<**
Everglades (IRE) **7** b h Green Desert (USA)-Glowing With Pride (Ile de Bourbon (USA)) 1227^{2} 1618^{3} 1895^{19} 2436^{7} 3027^{4} 3334^{4} 3999^{5} **>103f<**
Everset (FR) **7** b h Green Desert (USA)-Eversince (USA) (Foolish Pleasure (USA)) 20^{2} 92^{2} (123) **>95a 63f<**
Ever so Lyrical **5** b h Never so Bold-Lyra (Blakeney) 1732^{7} 2056^{3} 4035^{22} 4171^{19} **>79f<**
Everyone Can Dream **2** br c Shareef Dancer (USA)-Saltation 523^{9} (1959) 3049^{5} 3369^{5} 3699^{7} 4231^{16} **>60df<**
Evezio Rufo **3** b c Blakeney-Empress Corina (Free State) 711^{7} **>85f<**
Evidence In Chief **2** b f Be My Chief (USA)-Ominous (Dominion) 716^{5} 1540^{6} (1798) 3460^{10} 3540^{10} **>69f<**
Ewar Imperial **3** b c Legend of France (USA)-Monaneigue Lady (Julio Mariner) 1983^{4} 2314^{11} 2406^{6} 2993^{8} 3455^{13} **>57df<**
Ewar Sunrise **2** ch f Shavian-Sunset Reef (Mill Reef (USA)) 3816^{8} 4216^{2} 4313^{11} **>75f<**
Exactly (IRE) **2** b f Taufan (USA)-Not Mistaken (USA) (Mill Reef (USA)) 531^{4} 684^{7} 755^{3} 1035^{7} 3460^{4} 3644^{7} 3968^{4} **>7a 71f<**
Exalted (IRE) **2** b c High Estate-Heavenward (USA) (Conquistador Cielo (USA)) (2581) 2775^{3} 4192^{3} 4264^{6} **>87f<**
Exceedingly **2** ch f 1307^{4} 1653^{7} 2204^{6} **>69f<**
Excelled (IRE) **6** gr m Treasure Kay-Excelling Miss (USA) (Exceller (USA)) 2134^{7} 2486^{6} 2976^{2} (3202) 3470^{13} 3884^{10} 4223^{10} **>28a 55f<**
Exclusion **6** ch h Ballad Rock-Great Exception (Grundy) 80^{5} 155^{6} 351^{7} 1681^{2} 1858^{5} 2122^{4} 2373^{3} 2543^{6} (3122) 3277^{7} **>43a 50f<**
Exclusive Assembly **3** ch g Weldnaas (USA)-Pretty Pollyanna (General Assembly (USA)) 411^{8} 473^{3} (518) 1034^{16} 1459^{6} 2148^{7} 2448^{3} 2698^{12} 2923^{2} 4340^{10} **>63a 54f<**
Executive Design **3** b g Unfuwain (USA)-Seven Seas (FR) (Riverman (USA)) (537) 655^{2} 1527^{5} 2193^{2} 2555^{4} 2902^{6} 3826^{2} **>88f<**
Exemption **4** ch g Ballad Rock-Great Exception (Grundy) 549^{6} 763^{7} 1340^{2} (1716) 2110^{2} 3388^{10} 3710^{5} 3965^{3} 4163^{11} **>78f<**
Exhibit Air (IRE) **5** b m Exhibitioner-Airy Queen (USA) (Sadair) 2339^{4} 2639^{2} 2829^{3} 3500^{9} 3769^{13} 4223^{5} **>70a 74f<**
Expansive Runner (USA) **3** b c Explodent (USA)-Scissors (USA) (Blade (USA)) 3847^{6} 4072^{13} **>75f<**
Expensive Taste **2** b f Cadeaux Genereux-Um Lardaff (Mill Reef (USA)) (3136) 3631^{6} 3867^{5} **>83f<**
Explore Mondial (IRE) **4** b c Alzao (USA)-Organdy (Blakeney) 495^{7} **>54f<**
Export Mondial **5** b g Night Shift (USA)-Star Face 548^{9} 817^{12} 976^{7} **>31a 44f<**
Express Gift **6** br g Bay Express-Annes Gift (Ballymoss) 3808^{24} 3970^{3} 4189^{6} **>72f<**
Express Routing **3** b c Aragon-San Marguerite 502^{12} 1072^{4} 1546^{6} **>60f<**
Extra Hour (IRE) **2** b g Cyrano de Bergerac-Renzola (Dragonara Palace (USA)) 690^{7} 3337^{2} 3558^{3} 3727^{7} 3848^{4} 4077^{17} **>71f<**
Extremely Friendly **2** ch c Generous (IRE)-Water Woo (USA) (Tom Rolfe) 4239^{7} 4314^{13} **>68f<**
Ezekiel **4** ch c Be My Guest (USA)-Judeah (Great Nephew) 100^{10} **>23da 36f<**

F

Faal Mario (USA) **4** b c Gulch (USA)-Mousseline De Soie (FR) (Riverman (USA)) 558^{8} 811^{6} 954^{5} 3505^{9} 3646^{7} **>84df<**
Faateq **2** b c Caerleon (USA)-Treble (USA) 2529^{3} 2995^{3} 4143^{4} **>72f<**
Fabillion **3** ch c Deploy-Kai (Kalamoun) 376^{6} 1198^{5} 1526^{12} 2245^{6} 3526^{W} 3889^{7} 4061^{9} 4149^{2} 4248^{2} 4288^{6} **>46a 73f<**
Fabriana **5** b m Northern State (USA)-Fashion Flow (Balidar) 481^{7} 1664^{14} **>54f<**
Fabulous Mtoto **5** b h Mtoto-El Fabulous (FR) (Fabulous Dancer (USA)) 4051^{11} 4166^{11} 4248^{8} **>58f<**
Fabulous Princess (IRE) **4** b f Jareer (USA)-Nora Yo Ya (Ahonoora) 397^{5} **>38a 72?f<**
Face the Future **6** ch h Ahonoora-Chiltern Red 765^{11} 887^{5} 1174^{11} 1411^{12} 1537^{3} 2009^{5} 2448^{5} 3065^{3} 3637^{14} 3681^{15} 3874^{11} **>67f<**
Face Up **8** br h Top Ville-Pomade (Luthier (FR)) 1126^{14}

1334[12] **>8a 34f<**

Fadi **4** b c Celestial Storm (USA)-Rachael Tennessee (USA) (Matsadoon (USA)) 3986[20] **>63f<**

Faez **5** b h Mtoto-Ghanimah (Caerleon (USA)) *6[4]* *55[11]* *230[5]* 4060[15] *4217[10]* **>53a 78?f<**

Fag End (IRE) **2** b f Treasure Kay-Gauloise Bleue (USA) (Lyphard's Wish (FR)) 1348[5] (1823) 2136[3] (2454) 2775[2] 3387[3] 3548[14] 3942[3] **>87f<**

Fahal (USA) **3** b c Silver Hawk (USA)-By Land By Sea (USA) (Sauce Boat (USA)) 1224[3] 1611[4] 2273[3] (2936) 3614[2] 4120[6] **>120f<**

Fahema **3** b f Most Welcome-Fujaiyrah (In Fijar (USA)) *25[5]* *(98)* *144[4]* *273[8]* *326[7]* **>49a 61f<**

Fahim **2** b c Green Desert (USA)-Mahrah (USA) (Vaguely Noble) 3900[8] **>70f<**

Failte Ro **3** bl f Macmillion-Safe Passage 3926[10] 4171[12] 4259[19] **>64a 52f<**

Fair and Fancy (FR) **4** b c Always Fair (USA)-Fancy Star (FR) (Bellypha) 3970[8] 4000[10] 4168[5] *(4336)* **>48a 66f<**

Fair Attraction **3** ch g Charmer-Fairfields (Sharpen Up) 1550[11] 1914[7] 2466[5] **>54f<**

Fairelaine **3** b f Zalazl (USA)-Blue and White (Busted) *443[3]* 547[10] *624[7]* 971[2] 1172[8] 1442[4] 2139[10] 2669[4] 2862[3] 3248[4] 3383[7] 3747[5] 3897[2] 4043[4] **>65a 65f<**

Fair Ella (IRE) **3** ch f Simply Great (FR)-Dance Or Burst (Try My Best (USA)) *261[4]* *444[5]* *626[8]* 1401[5] 2813[6] **>49a 43f<**

Fairey Firefly **4** b f Hallgate-Tremellick *78[7]* *139[2]* 1456[13] **>57a 54f<**

Fair Flyer (IRE) **6** b h Tilt Up (USA)-Fair Siobahn (Petingo) 3207[8] 3710[19] **>52f<**

Fairlight Down (USA) **2** b f Dayjur (USA)-Stresa (Mill Reef (USA)) (4050) **>80+f<**

Fairlight (GER) **2** dk f Big Shuffle-Frille (Shareef Dancer) 3584a[3] **>89f<**

Fairlight Magic **3** b f Mandrake Major-Magic Mover (Julio Mariner) *299[6]* **>3a f<**

Fairly Sure (IRE) **2** b f Red Sunset-Mirabiliary (USA) (Crow (FR)) 2651[7] *2939[W]* 3379[20] *3949[12]* **>12a 48f<**

Fair Rose **4** b f Fayruz-Scottish Rose (Warpath) *2291[13]*

Fair To Middling (IRE) **2** b f Midyan (USA)-Smagiada (Young Generation) 2683[8] 3285[5] 3767[9] 3975[19] **>47f<**

Fairy Fay (IRE) **3** b f Fayruz-Isa (Dance In Time (CAN)) 646[18] 1414[13] 2203[6] 2326[10] **>63a 65f<**

Fairy Highlands (IRE) **2** b f Fairy King (USA)-Breyani 1536[8] **>52f<**

Fairy Knight **3** b c Fairy King (USA)-Vestal Flame (Habitat) 873[10] (1591) 1831[2] 2289[2] 2768[8] 3106[4] 3388[7] 3679[13] 4171[7] (4284) 4333[2] **>90f<**

Fairy Path (USA) **3** ch f Irish River (FR)-Pointed Path 1116a[11] (2214a) 2897a[5] **>109f<**

Fairy Prince (IRE) **2** b c Fairy King (USA)-Danger Ahead (Mill Reef (USA)) 1511[11] 2515[5] 3231[14] **>55f<**

Fairy's Son **3** b c Belmez (USA)-Sea Fairy (Wollow) *25[9]* *98[3]* *116[7]* *292[4]* *310[6]* *409[7]* 1060[10] 1153[9] **>42a 32f<**

Fairy Story (IRE) **5** ch m Persian Bold-Certain Story (Known Fact (USA)) (2169) 2414[3] (2803) 3222[5] **>57a 81f<**

Fairy Wind (IRE) **3** b f Fairy King (USA)-Decadence (Vaigly Great) 522[5] 658[8] (772) 999[4] (1257) 1376[5] 1624[6] 1924[4] (2067) 2324[5] 2617[5] (3166) **>94f<**

Fairywings **2** b f Kris-Fairy Flax (IRE) (Dancing Brave (USA)) 3948[11] 4085[6] **>64f<**

Faith Alone **2** b f Safawan-Strapless (Bustino) 4155[6] 4313[14] **>47f<**

Faith 'n Glory (IRE) **3** b f Nordico (USA)-Amalee (Troy) 783[7] 1467[4] 1812[10] 2316[9] **>52f<**

Fajjoura (IRE) **3** b f Fairy King (USA)-Danger Ahead (Mill Reef (USA)) 1305[9] **>94f<**

Fakhira (IRE) **3** b f Jareer (USA)-Mira Adonde (USA) (Sharpen Up) 551[6] **>35f<**

Fakih (USA) **3** b c Zilzal (USA)-Barakat (Bustino) (1065) **>88f<**

Falcons Dawn **8** b h Exhibitioner-African Bloom (African Sky) *46[8]* *269[7]* **>14a f<**

Fallal (IRE) **3** b f Fayruz-Lady Bidder 3725[5] 3859[6] 4280[11] **>28a 55f<**

False Pretences (IRE) **3** ch c Al Hareb (USA)-Christle Mill (Pas de Seul) *473[6]* 543[9] 848[13] 1545[9] 2843[12] 3249[5] 3426[8] 3619[13] 3959[8] **>21a 41f<**

Fame Again **3** b f Then Again-Starawak (Star Appeal) 427[15] 572[7] 662[9] 946[2] 1131[5] 1299[5] 2117[2] (2531) 3565[2] 3703[3] 3813[4] **>92f<**

Family Rose **6** gr h Absalom-Greenhill Lass *2922[10]* **>49a f<**

Fancy Clancy **2** b f Clantime-Bold Sophie (Bold Owl) 925[3] 2302[3] 2619[11] 3465[18] 3740[9] 3939[7] 4287[5] **>51f<**

Fancy Design (IRE) **2** b f Cyrano de Bergerac-Crimson Robes (Artaius (USA)) 3387[6] 3539[7] **>53f<**

Fancy Heights **2** b f Shirley Heights-Miss Fancy That (USA) (The Minstrel (CAN)) 4048[6] **>58f<**

Fangio **6** b g Nordance (USA)-Verily Jane (Royben) 565[6] (685) 723[14] (944) 1451[2] (1909) **>86f<**

Fanion de Fete (FR) **4** b c 1709a[6] **>114f<**

Fanjica (IRE) **3** b f Law Society (USA)-Florie (FR) (Gay Mecene (USA)) 932[2] 1237a[4] (2272) 3041a[2] 3694a[7] 3911a[5] **>114f<**

Fantasy Fair **2** ch f Salt Dome (USA)-Staiconme (USA) (Pancho Villa (USA)) 3290[12] 3895[13] **>4f<**

Fantasy Racing (IRE) **3** b f Tirol-Highland Girl (USA) 504[12] 674[6] 985[5] 1172[9] (1263) 1445[2] (1564) 1639[4] 1778[5] 1906[2] (2018) (2258) 2437[7] 2712[4] 2865[2] (2987) 3204[2] (3251) 3390[5] 3519[10] 3830[8] 3905[11] (3972) 4145[3] 4238[5] **>86f<**

Far Ahead **3** b g Soviet Star (USA)-Cut Ahead (Kalaglow) 2255[3] 2460[2] (3761) 3973[2] 4236[8] **>82f<**

Farani **3** b f Distant Relative-Jhansi Ki Rani (USA) (Far North (CAN)) 695[2] 957[P] **>94f<**

Farastrada **4** b f Midyan (USA)-Dawn Redwood (Mummy's Pet) *14[2]* *107[6]* *154[10]* **>54a 40f<**

Faraway Lass **2** b f Distant Relative-Vague Lass (Vaigly Great) 3450[8] 4212[6] 4329[5] **>66f<**

Faraway Waters **2** ch f Pharly (FR)-Gleaming Water (Kalaglow) 3069[2] (3260) 3561[11] 3865[7] **>96f<**

Fard (IRE) **3** gr c Reprimand-Anneli Rose (Superlative) 1480[2] 1896[5] 2368[5] 3042a[8] **>118f<**

Farenvaros **3** 801a[5] 1230a[3] **>102f<**

Farfelu **8** b h Lyphard's Special (USA)-Spring Azure *70[5]* *123[4]* *202[3]* *305[6]* *(391)* **>68a 66f<**

Farfeste **2** b f Jester-Our Horizon (Skyliner) 4216[7] 4312[13] **>58f<**

Far Fetched (IRE) **3** b f Distant Relative-Gay Milly (FR) 883[3] 1500[2] 2287[3] **>100f<**

Farfields Prince **3** b g Weldnaas (USA)-Coca (Levmoss) 758^{10} 969^{8} 1506^{12} 4000^{13} **>40f<**
Farhana **2** b f Fayruz-Fahrenheit (Mount Hagen (FR)) 4153^{2} (4255) **>80f<**
Farida Seconda **2** gr f Green Ruby (USA)-Faridetta *2629^{9}* 3940^{6} **>26f<**
Farmer Jock **13** ch h Crofter (USA)-Some Dame *129^{5} 165^{10} (353) 400^{8} 419^{8}* 541^{7} *590^{5} 769^{3} 1034^{9} 1334^{3}* 1456^{8} *1571^{7}* 1700^{8} **>43a 48f<**
Farmer's Tern (IRE) **3** ch f Sharrood (USA)-Winter Tern (USA) (Arctic Tern (USA)) 670^{W} 1167^{7} 1317^{3} 1547^{4} 4249^{16} **>61f<**
Farmost **2** ch c Pharly (FR)-Dancing Meg (USA) (Marshua's Dancer (USA)) 4130^{7} *4269^{9}* 4330^{W} **>40a f<**
Farndale **8** gr h Vaigly Great-Beloved Mistress *71^{9} 107^{4} 129^{2} 167^{2} 202^{5} 306^{6} 602^{3} 625^{5} 892^{8} 1033^{6} 1214^{9}* 2502^{8} 2665^{8} 2821^{5} 3256^{4} **>50a 42f<**
Farringdon Hill **4** b g Minster Son-Firgrove (Relkino) 811^{3} 1140^{9} **>87f<**
Fascination Waltz **8** b m Shy Groom (USA)-Cuckoo Weir 3615^{24} 3771^{18} 3874^{5} **>58f<**
Fashionable Dancer **5** b h Lomond (USA)-Circulate *63^{7}* **>33a 37df<**
Fasih **3** b c Rock City-Nastassia (FR) (Noble Decree (USA)) 2553^{11} 2880^{5} 3422^{14} (4164) **>90f<**
Fast Food **2** gr c Petong-Respray (Rusticaro (FR)) 2346^{11} 2505^{4} 2637^{6} 3353^{11} 3533^{16} **>50f<**
Fast Forward Fred **4** gr g Sharrood (USA)-Sun Street (Ile de Bourbon (USA)) 1383^{8} 1794^{7} 2530^{13} **>62f<**
Fastini Gold **3** b c Weldnaas (USA)-La Carlotta (Ela-Mana-Mou) 2438^{8} 2794^{7} 3201^{2} 3429^{5} 3654^{8} 3844^{10} 4136^{9} **>58f<**
Fastness (IRE) **5** gr h Rousillon (USA)-City Fortress (Troy) $4305a^{2}$ **>132f<**
Fataana (USA) **3** b f El Gran Senor (USA)-Maggie O'Brien (USA) (Quadrangle) 2794^{10} 3712^{17} **>52f<**
Fata (IRE) **3** b or br c Machiavellian (USA)-Wakayi (Persian Bold) (442) 621^{6} 985^{10} 1249^{11} **>79f<**
Fatehalkhair (IRE) **3** ch c Kris-Midway Lady (USA) (Alleged (USA)) 3461^{4} 3712^{10} 3974^{14} **>58f<**
Father Dan (IRE) **6** ch h Martin John-Sonia John (Main Reef) *318^{5} (355) 445^{11}* 884^{5} 1014^{4} 1368^{4} 1502^{2} 1757^{4} 2731^{6} (2981) 3384^{4} 3889^{5} 4022^{3} *(4335)* **>72a 64f<**
Father Sky **4** b c Dancing Brave (USA)-Flamenco Wave (USA) (Desert Wine (USA)) 696^{4} **>84f<**
Father Tim (IRE) **5** ch g Montekin-Gentle Mulla *404^{8} 497^{8}* 685^{9} **>37a 32f<**
Fattash (USA) **3** ch c Tejano (USA)-Green Pompadour (USA) (Green Dancer (USA)) 1124^{8} 1322^{8} 1591^{6} 1970^{3} 2177^{3} 4135^{15} 4331^{12} **>59f<**
Faugeron **6** ch h Niniski (USA)-Miss Longchamp (Northfields (USA)) 668^{18} (1965) (2157) (2806) 2990^{2} 3171^{3} 3445^{6} 4036^{6} 4082^{4} **>69f<**
Faustino **3** gr c Faustus (USA)-Hot Case (Upper Case (USA)) *766^{3}* 1124^{6} 1834^{4} 1970^{6} 2658^{4} 2812^{3} 3056^{4} 3641^{7} **>58a 59f<**
Favourite Prince (IRE) **4** b c Prince Rupert (FR)-Fete Champetre (Welsh Pageant) $2046a^{10}$ **>120f<**
Fawj (USA) **3** b c Clever Trick (USA)-Smooch (USA) (Raise A Native) 431^{6} (630) 1131^{12} 3629^{11} **>82f<**
Faynaz **9** ch h Tumble Wind (USA)-Ceduna (FR) (Right Tack) *39^{4} 157^{6}* 909^{11} 1433^{8} 1724^{11} 2021^{9} **>32a 38f<**
Fayre Holly (IRE) **2** b f Fayruz-Holly Bird (Runnett) 2114^{3} 2552^{7} 2791^{4} **>64f<**
Fearless Dove **3** b f Nomination-Stranger to Fear (Never so Bold) *2920^{8}* **>25f<**
Fearless Venture **3** b c Darshaan-Push a Button (Bold Lad (IRE)) 584^{4} 787^{2} 1382^{10} 1801^{7} 2184^{6} **>68f<**
Fearless Wonder **4** b c Formidable-Long View (Persian Bold) *312^{2}* 986^{3} 1643^{12} *2293^{9}* 2544^{6} (2676) 2834^{2} 2990^{4} 3410^{2} **>62a 67f<**
Featherstone Lane **4** b c Siberian Express (USA)-Try Gloria (Try My Best (USA)) 789^{17} 926^{5} 1157^{7} *1331^{3}* 1565^{13} 1689^{2} 1864^{2} 2027^{3} 2234^{3} 2303^{6} *2492^{6}* 3116^{10} 3219^{7} 3442^{18} 3622^{13} *3739^{2} 3954^{12}* **>67a 60df<**
February **2** b f Full Extent (USA)-Foligno (Crofter (USA)) *889^{5}* 1646^{3} 1821^{3} 1899^{3} 2153^{5} *2294^{3} 2591^{6}* 2982^{7} 3283^{3} 3427^{10} **>32a 53f<**
Feeling Foolish (IRE) **6** ch g Fools Holme (USA)-Felin Geri *58^{6}* **>10a 28f<**
Feinte **3** b f Green Desert (USA)-Escrime (USA) (Sharpen Up) 915^{5} 1431^{2} 2279^{10} 3621^{9} 3984^{17} **>72f<**
Feline (IRE) **4** ch f Pennine Walk-Felin Geri *4^{3} 214^{2}* **>41a 45f<**
Felitza (IRE) **3** b f Soviet Star (USA)-Oh So Sharp (Kris) (1979) (2470) **>104+f<**
Fenna **2** b f Dowsing (USA)-Tasseled (USA) (Tate Gallery (USA)) 1810^{2} (2204) (2403) 2779^{10} 2982^{4} (3386) 3548^{11} (3895) *4124^{2}* **>71a 80?f<**
Fen Terrier **3** b f Emarati (USA)-Kinz (Great Nephew) *(292)* 1093^{W} 1372^{11} (1702) *1955^{6} 2292^{2} 2630^{2}* 2731^{5} *3076^{8}* 3641^{W} 3875^{4} **>62a 62f<**
Fergal (USA) **2** ch c Inishpour-Campus (USA) (Minnesota Mac) 1919^{7} 2185^{3} 2732^{5} **>44f<**
Fernhill Blaze (IRE) **2** b c High Estate-Bonnie Isle (Pitcairn) 1715^{9}
Fern's Governor **3** b f Governor General-Sharp Venita (Sharp Edge) 1072^{7} 1796^{10} 2319^{14} 3685^{18} 4261^{7} **>52f<**
Fernway **2** ch f Handsome Sailor-Redgrave Design (Nebbiolo) 3670^{13} **>17f<**
Fervent Fan (IRE) **2** b f Soviet Lad (USA)-Shannon Lady (Monsanto (FR)) 2351^{7} *(2939)* 3158^{7} 3803^{11} **>68+a 75f<**
Festive Lassie **4** b f Faustus (USA)-Truth Will Out 1878^{2} 2331^{2} 2544^{2} 3297^{7} **>71f<**
Ffynone (IRE) **3** b f Taufan (USA)-Ana Gabriella (USA) (Master Derby (USA)) 939^{4} 1362^{6} 1673^{9} 3545^{8} 3750^{2} 4145^{19} **>66f<**
Fiaba **7** b m Precocious-Historia (Northfields (USA)) *302^{3} 343^{3} 379^{4} 413^{12} 472^{5} 835^{2} 1074^{3}* 1081^{2} *1209^{5}* 1645^{12} 2862^{6} 4152^{13} 4209^{10} **>49a 49df<**
Fiddes (IRE) **2** b f Alzao (USA)-Kashteh (IRE) (Green Desert (USA)) 3069^{16} 3495^{10} 3720^{6} 4141^{18} **>55f<**
Fiddles Delight **2** b f Colmore Row-Nutwood Emma (Henbit (USA)) 983^{4} *1073^{5}* 2838^{4} 2998^{4} 3290^{9} 3335^{6} **>12a 52f<**
Field of Stars **5** b h Salse (USA)-Marseillaise (Artaius (USA)) *190^{3}* **>72da 76f<**
Field of Vision (IRE) **5** b h Vision (USA)-Bold Meadows (Persian Bold) 3943^{17} 4115^{6} 4236^{4} 4292^{3} **>66f<**
Fieldridge **6** ch h Rousillon (USA)-Final Thought (Final Straw) 1367^{6} 1661^{10} 1908^{8} 2298^{2} 3094^{3} (3388) 3601^{9} 3820^{7} 3957^{8} **>85df<**
Fiello (GER) **5** $2389a^{7}$ $3045a^{3}$ $4094a^{6}$ **>114f<**

Fiendish (USA) 3 ch f Devil's Bag (USA)-Connecting Link (USA) (Linkage (USA)) 692^{6} **>100f<**

Fiery Footsteps 3 ro f Chilibang-Dancing Daughter (Dance In Time (CAN)) *124^{4}* *173^{5}* 426^{14} 855^{13} 1521^{4} *2071^{13}* 2527^{4} 2844^{6} 3138^{4} 3640^{9} **>46a 59f<**

Fiery Sun 10 b g Sexton Blake-Melanie Jane (Lord Gayle (USA)) *3^{4}* *200^{2}* *285^{4}* **>31a 72—f<**

Fifty Four(USA) 3 c $1008a^{7}$ **>100f<**

Fighter Squadron 6 ch g Primo Dominie-Formidable Dancer (Formidable) *224^{5}* *307^{5}* 1323^{U} 1534^{10} 1714^{9} 2115^{9} **>45a 52f<**

Fighting Times 3 b g Good Times (ITY)-Duellist (Town Crier) 3294^{7} 3543^{2} 4315^{6} **>70f<**

Fijon (IRE) 2 b f Doyoun-Tasskeen (FR) (Lyphard (USA)) 3306^{3} 3532^{2} 3983^{6} 4192^{8} **>77df<**

Fikra (USA) 2 b br f Gulch (USA)-Bolt From The Blue (USA) (Blue Times (USA)) 2070^{3} 2579^{6} 3366^{2} 3639^{9} **>64f<**

Fill the Bill (IRE) 3 b c Bob Back (USA)-Neat Dish (CAN) (Stalwart (USA)) 2476^{5} $2891a^{5}$ **>103f<**

Film Buff 2 b f Midyan (USA)-Upper Circle (Shirley Heights) 1443^{6} 2615^{7} 3604^{9} *3736^{3}* 3867^{16} **>68a 52f<**

Final Appearance (IRE) 3 b c Sadler's Wells (USA)-Topping Girl 3728^{6} 3923^{6} 4074^{8} **>101f<**

Final Fling 3 b f Last Tycoon-Lady Day (FR) (Lightning (FR)) 539^{9} 643^{3} 1194^{9} 1825^{5} 3669^{9} **>50f<**

Final Stab (IRE) 2 b c Kris-Premier Rose (Sharp Edge) 3663^{6} (3888) **>74f<**

Financial Star (IRE) 2 b f Last Tycoon-Dawn Star (High Line) 3010^{6} 3306^{P}

Finisterre (IRE) 2 b g Salt Dome (USA)-Inisfail (Persian Bold) 3110^{6} 3465^{16} 3940^{4} 4066^{10} 4287^{7} **>54f<**

Finjan 8 b h Thatching-Capriconia (Try My Best (USA)) *220^{8}* 503^{4} 882^{7} 1785^{4} 2528^{7} 2842^{8} **>44a 50f<**

Finlaggan 3 b f Be My Chief (USA)-Misty Halo (High Top) *1784^{2}* (1922) 2139^{2} 2333^{3} *(3084)* 3355^{2} (3571) 3774^{3} 4099^{3} *4223^{3}* **>83a 87f<**

Fiona Shann (USA) 2 b f Phone Trick (USA)-Aminata 3948^{14} 4161^{13} 4314^{12} **>60f<**

Fionn de Cool (IRE) 4 b g Mazaad-Pink Fondant (Northfields (USA)) 636^{3} 870^{15} 1126^{7} 1409^{2} 1915^{4} 2266^{2} 2598^{9} (3026) 3348^{2} 3732^{16} 4116^{6} 4319^{16} **>84f<**

Firbur 2 b c Be My Chief (USA)-La Masse (High Top) 4169^{18} **>35f<**

Fire Blast 3 b c Statoblest-Great Aim (Great Nephew) 1136^{21} 1414^{14} 1676^{18} **>84f<**

Fire Dome (IRE) 3 ch c Salt Dome (USA)-Penny Habit (Habitat) 633^{3} 883^{2} 1145^{7} $3195a^{8}$ 3342^{10} 3717^{12} 3938^{2} 4033^{2} $4253a^{6}$ 4324^{5} **>103f<**

Fire of London 3 b f Shirley Heights-Home Fire 3239^{6} 3448^{4} 3618^{2} 3921^{13} **>79f<**

Fire on Ice (IRE) 3 b c Sadler's Wells (USA)-Foolish Lady (USA) (Foolish Pleasure (USA)) (3438) 3603^{3} 3811^{7} **>101f<**

Fire The Anvil 3 gr g Chilibang-Harlestone Lake (Riboboy (USA)) 3974^{11} 4150^{9} **>60f<**

Fire Worshipper (IRE) 4 b c Sadler's Wells (USA)-Beaconaire (USA) (Vaguely Noble) (440) $703a^{5}$ 3730^{4} **>105f<**

Firing Line (IRE) 6 b h Slip Anchor-Red Partridge (Solinus) $1118a^{3}$ $1392a^{P}$ **>115f<**

Firle Phantasy 2 ch c Pharly (FR)-Shamasiya (FR) (Vayrann) 3494^{6} 3881^{11} **>61f<**

Firm Contract (IRE) 3 b c Double Schwartz-Glass Goblet (USA) (Storm Bird (CAN)) 1296^{5} **>60f<**

First Amendment (IRE) 3 ch f Caerleon (USA)-Penultimate (USA) (Roberto (USA)) 1182^{3} **>77f<**

First Bid 8 ch h Crofthall-Redgrave Design (Nebbiolo) 1844^{7} 2373^{5} 2663^{4} 2785^{P} **>75f<**

First Bite (IRE) 3 b c Be My Native (USA)-Saga's Humour (Bustino) 745^{13} 1372^{4} (1966) 2333^{4} 2861^{10} 3395^{3} 3875^{12} **>78f<**

First Century (IRE) 6 b h Petorius-Parima (Pardao) *222^{2}* *304^{8}* **>51a 53f<**

First Crush 3 b f Primo Dominie-Fleeting Affair (Hotfoot) *300^{2}* (2376) *2605^{5}* (2828) 3096^{2} 3269^{6} **>59da 73f<**

First Fiddler 2 b c Primo Dominie-Full Orchestra (Shirley Heights) 825^{3} 1176^{2} (1511) 1868^{4} 2347^{8} 3606^{3} **>90f<**

First Gold 6 gr h Absalom-Cindys Gold (Sonnen Gold) 486^{4} 646^{4} 702^{11} 812^{3} 1299^{6} 1506^{10} *2073^{6}* *2377^{2}* *2628^{4}* 2992^{5} 3291^{6} 3443^{6} (3638) 3764^{9} 4053^{5} **>67a 70f<**

First Hello (GER) 3 dk c Nebos-First Love (4018a) **>108f<**

First Island (IRE) 3 ch c Dominion-Caymana (FR) (Bellypha) (1221) (1345) 1848^{3} 2762^{2} 3728^{4} 3932^{5} 4265^{2} **>111f<**

First Maite 2 b c Komaite (USA)-Marina Plata (Julio Mariner) 3432^{11} *3525^{9}* (3648) 3990^{12} 4066^{9} **>39a 70f<**

First Option 5 ch g Primo Dominie-Merrywren (Julio Mariner) 1042^{W} 1248^{9} 1721^{12} 3467^{U} **>62a 57f<**

First Point (IRE) 3 b c Ajraas (USA)-Fifty Grand (Ballad Rock) *146^{7}* *211^{6}* *273^{10}* **>28a 27f<**

First Shot 4 b c Emarati (USA)-First Time Over (Derrylin) 3859^{8}

First Veil 5 b m Primo Dominie-Valika (Valiyar) 2206^{3} (2743) 2948^{10} 3451^{7} 3637^{3} 3964^{3} 4068^{13} 4238^{4} **>77f<**

Fishy Affair 3 ch c Risk Me (FR)-Always on a Sunday (Star Appeal) 880^{2} 1045^{3} 1423^{5} 1465^{11} 1559^{9} **>38a 56f<**

Fisiostar 2 b g Efisio-Sweet Colleen (Connaught) 3644^{12} 3975^{23} **>25f<**

Fit To Ski 2 b f Niniski (USA)-Baino Fit (USA) (Fit To Fight (USA)) 2846^{14} 3339^{17} 3767^{12} **>46f<**

Fitzrovian (IRE) 4 b c Miller's Mate-Nuravia (Nureyev (USA)) 666^{5} **>101f<**

Fitzroy Lad 5 b h Grey Desire-My-Elane (Welsh Saint) *529^{7}* *832^{4}* 1714^{14} **>29a 30f<**

Fiveaday 3 ch c Komaite (USA)-Silently Yours (USA) (Silent Screen (USA)) *57^{4}* *124^{6}* *411^{11}* 2303^{10} 2576^{11} 2712^{10} 2885^{8} **>53a 57f<**

Five to Seven (USA) 6 br h Little Missouri (USA)-French Galaxy (USA) (Majestic Light (USA)) 3646^{12} 3971^{20} 4118^{20} 4288^{9} *4336^{5}* **>63a 76df<**

Flagbird (USA) 4 b or br f Nureyev (USA)-Up the Flagpole (USA) (Hoist The Flag (USA)) (1118a) $1394a^{6}$ (2211a) $3690a^{3}$ 3944^{2} **>122f<**

Flag Fen (USA) 4 b br c Riverman (USA)-Damascus Flag (USA) (Damascus (USA)) 3393^{8} 4035^{19} 4205^{11} **>63f<**

Flagstaff (USA) 2 b c Personal Flag (USA)-Shuffle Up (USA) (Raja Baba (USA)) 3472^{7} 3765^{8} **>45f<**

Flahuil 2 b f Generous (IRE)-Sipsi Fach (Prince Sabo) 3532^{7} 3758^{4} 3983^{7} 4321^{12} **>67f<**

'lair Lady **4** gr f Chilibang-Flair Park (Frimley Park) 037[14] 1206[2] 1274[3] 1523[12] 2134[2] 2528[6] 2885[5] **>44a 9f<**
'lamands (IRE) **2** b f Sadler's Wells (USA)-Fleur Royale Mill Reef (USA)) 3900[20] **>48f<**
'lamboro **3** ch c Handsome Sailor-Scottish Legend Legend of France (USA)) 980[12] 1249[9] 1920[4] 2188[5] **>68f<**
Flame of Athens (IRE) **2** b c Royal Academy (USA)-'lame of Tara (Artaius (U (2216a) **>98f<**
Flame of Hope **2** b f Marju (IRE)-Tweedling (USA) (Sir vor) 3708[10] 4312[10] **>57f<**
Flame Valley (USA) **2** b f Gulch (USA)-Lightning Fire 2886[4] 3474[3] **>64f<**
Flame War (USA) **3** ch f Diesis-Pocketfulof Posies (USA) (Lyphard (USA)) 824[2] 1182[2] (1983) 2525[3] 2903[4] **>85f<**
Flaming June (USA) **2** ch f Storm Bird (CAN)-Affirmative Fable (USA) (Affirmed (USA)) 2957[3] 4226[6] **>61f<**
Flamingo Paradise **4** ch c Rainbow Quest-Fabula Dancer (Northern D (1231a) **>112f<**
Flammant Rose (IRE) **3** gr f Cyrano de Bergerac-Sweet Class (Rusticaro (FR)) 1053[7] 1196[8] **>50f<**
Flash Appeal **4** b f Tate Gallery (USA)-Camomilla (Targowice (USA)) 1509[11] **>22a f<**
Flash Arrow **5** ch h Jalmood (USA)-The Firebird (Busted) 1501[8] **>34f<**
Flashfeet **5** b h Rousillon (USA)-Miellita *601[7] 624[2] 845[4] 1088[3] (1457) 1760[3] 2076[5]* 2593[10] **>64a 58df<**
Flashing Sabre **3** b c Statoblest-Placid Pet (Mummy's Pet) *892[3]* 1042[8] 1419[8] 2124[6] (2303) 2475[8] 2753[10] 2837[3] 3333[9] *4123[9]* **>58a 57f<**
Flash In The Pan (IRE) **2** ch f Bluebird (USA)-Tomona (Linacre) 1348[8] 3069[17] 3763[13] 4151[11] **>50f<**
Flashman **5** b h Flash of Steel-Proper Madam (Mummy's Pet) *(234)* 432[12] 1058[3] 1607[3] (1826) 2154[2] *2592[2]* 3986[10] 4140[7] **>51a 53f<**
Flash of Realm (FR) **9** b h Super Moment (USA)-Light of Realm 2478[4] 3718[4] **>67f<**
Flashy's Son **7** b or br h Balidar-Flashy Looker (Good Bond) 1080[3] 1248[2] 1441[3] 1668[10] 2096[8] (2231) (2461) 2645[6] 3230[13] 3411[5] 3565[3] 3715[26] 4083[11] **>75f<**
Flass Vale **7** b h Final Straw-Emblazon *108[10] 234[11]* **>26a 47f<**
Flatford Princess **3** b f Prince Daniel (USA)-Printafoil (Habat) 2535[6] **>12a 47f<**
Fleet Cadet **4** ch c Bairn (USA)-Pirogue *4[9] 103[6] 198[6]* 780[6] (984) 1202[16] 1676[9] 3181[8] **>50a 54f<**
Fleet Hill (IRE) **3** b f Warrshan (USA)-Mirkan Honey (Ballymore) 620[4] 933[13] 1139[2] 1390a[6] 1867[7] 3035a[5] **>100f<**
Fleet Key **2** ch f Afleet-Key to the Minstrel 4004a[2]
Fleet Petite (IRE) **3** b f Posen (USA)-Reet Petite (.) 3922[4] **>92f<**
Flemensfirth (USA) **3** b c Alleged (USA)-Etheldreda (USA) (Diesis) 679[2] (1115a) 1574a[5] 1837[6] (4007a) **>128f<**
Fletcher's Bounty (IRE) **6** b h Glenstal (USA)-Maimiti (Goldhill) *179[3] 231[9] 355[7] 415[13]* **>47a 54f<**
Flight Lieutenant (USA) **6** b h Marfa (USA)-Lt Golden Girl (USA) (Lt Stevens (USA)) 623[11] 795[8] 1109[8] 1243[6] 1612[7] (1749) 2530[8] 3162[12] 3406[3] 3730[9] **>87f<**
Flight Master **3** ch c Master Willie-Mumtaz Mayfly (Tap On Wood) 745[4] 1382[3] 1730[6] **>66f<**
Flight Soundly (IRE) **3** ch f Caerleon (USA)-Night of Wind (Tumble Wind (USA)) 775[7] 999[8] 1845[6] 4156[8] **>76f<**
Flighty **2** b f Reprimand-Flight of Pleasure (USA) (Roberto (USA)) 3763[11] 4085[7] **>63f<**
Flim Flam Aly (USA) **6** br h Tim Tam Aly (USA)-Okala Lass (USA) (Florida State) *45[8]* **>34a 39f<**
Flint And Steel **2** b g Rock City-Brassy Nell (Dunbeath (USA)) 3436[7] 3883[12] **>63f<**
Flirty Gertie **3** ch f Prince Sabo-Red Tapsi (Tap On Wood) 2527[3] 3103[2] 3507[3] 3726[2] 4079[9] **>74f<**
Flitch (USA) **3** b c Demons Begone (USA)-Whiffling (USA) 4307a[8] **>113f<**
Floating Line **7** ch h Bairn (USA)-County Line (High Line) 841[5] 1039[6] 1681[5] (2747) 3061[6] 3445[4] 3646[5] 3801[2] (3927) 4036[2] 4189[12] **>80f<**
Flocheck (USA) **2** ch c Hansel (USA)-Eurobird (Ela-Mana-Mou) 4080[11] 4247[7] **>78f<**
Flood's Fancy **2** b gr f Then Again-Port Na Blath (On Your Mark) 1413[9] 1670[8] 1857[8] (2195) 3225[9] 3714[9] **>60f<**
Florac (IRE) **5** b m Sayf El Arab (USA)-Marton Maid (Silly Season) *16[6]* 1508[13] **>26a 33df<**
Flora's Temple (USA) **4** b br f Halo (USA)-Kendra Road (USA) (Kennedy Road (CAN)) 3016[18] **>4f<**
Florentino (IRE) **2** b br c Machiavellian (USA)-Helens Dreamgirl (Caerleon (USA)) 3733[22] **>38f<**
Floridante (USA) **3** b c Eastern Echo (USA)-La Belle Fleur (USA) (Vaguely Noble) 637[5] 980[10] 1183[2] 1351[6] (1605) 2103[5] **>80f<**
Florid (USA) **4** ch c The Minstrel (CAN)-Kenanga (Kris) 631[6] (750) 923[2] 1408[2] 2008[4] 2739[6] **>112f<**
Florismart **3** b c Never so Bold-Spoilt Again (Mummy's Pet) 1979[4] 2553[9] 3294[8] 3844[8] **>69f<**
Florrie'm **2** ch f Tina's Pet-Rosie Dickins (Blue Cashmere) 4212[18] 4277[7] **>44f<**
Flower Miller **2** b c Formidable (USA)-Sunflower Seed (Mummy's Pet) 1685[7] **>51f<**
Flowing Ocean **5** ch h Forzando-Boswellia *(337)* 433[10] *3319[12]* **>84a 81f<**
Flutter With Life **4** b f Hubbly Bubbly (USA)-Bet Oliver (Kala Shikari) *404[10]* 541[15] **>8a f<**
Flyaway Blues **3** b c Bluebird (USA)-Voltigeuse (USA) (Filiberto (USA)) 437[11] 538[13] 687[4] 879[11] 1377[2] 1465[2] 1666[3] 1944[3] 2228[4] 2872[2] 3372[2] 3661[11] **>72f<**
Flyfisher (IRE) **2** b c Batshoof-Inveraven (Alias Smith (USA)) 3280[6] 3650[5] 3846[2] (4046) **>84f<**
Fly Fishing (USA) **2** ch c Miswaki (USA)-Sharp Flick (USA) (Sharpen Up) 3663[13] 4169[3] 4291[3] **>73f<**
Flying Anshan **4** 2894a[7] **>107f<**
Flying Dream **4** ch f Most Welcome-Finlandaise (FR) (Arctic Tern (USA)) 1231a[3] 2729a[6] 3697a[2] 4009a[5] **>115f<**
Flying Flowers **2** ch f Thatching-Flying Fairy (Bustino) 4103[6] 4216[8] **>74f<**
Flying Green (FR) **2** ch c Persian Bold-Flying Sauce (Sauce Boat (USA)) 2200[4] 2846[2] 3865[15] **>76f<**
Flying Harold **2** b c Gildoran-Anytime Anywhere (Daring March) 4161[12] 4312[8] **>67f<**

Flying Imp 4 b g Faustus (USA)-Quenlyn (Welsh Pageant) *96[14] 183[8]* **>10a f<**

Flying North (IRE) 2 b c Distinctly North (USA)-North Kildare (USA) (Northjet) 1685[2] (1992) 2779[3] 3375[7] 4084[17] **>79f<**

Flying Pennant (IRE) 2 ch c Waajib-Flying Beckee (IRE) (Godswalk (USA)) 1752[9] **>60f<**

Flying Squaw 2 b f Be My Chief (USA)-Sea Fret (Habat) (791) (1259) 2322[4] 2892a[2] 3197a[4] (3584a) **>96f<**

Fly the Eagle 3 b g Rock City-Tittlemouse (Castle Keep) 521[17] 1012[8] 3401[8] 3521[11] **>44f<**

Fly Tip (IRE) 2 b f Bluebird (USA)-Sharp Deposit (Sharpo) (4161) **>84+f<**

Fog City 2 b c Damister (USA)-Front Line Romance (Caerleon (USA)) 3441[4] 4073[3] *(4269)* **>83a 73f<**

Foist 3 b g Efisio-When The Saints *354[15]* 573[10] 759[18] 2225[7] **>10a 36+f<**

Followmegirls 6 b m Sparkling Boy-Haddon Anna (Dragonara Palace (USA)) 507[13] 796[6] 1042[4] 1827[6] 2330[9] 2692[4] 2850[7] 3123[8] 3442[7] 3624[10] (3748) 4278[5] **>56f<**

Folly Finnesse 4 b f Joligeneration-Magic Milly (Simply Great (FR)) *152[2] 242[3] 281[11]* 505[10] 634[17] 1052[8] 1225[11] 1472[16] **>78da 67f<**

Fond Embrace 2 b f Emarati (USA)-Detente (Dominion) 2660[3] 3025[3] 3465[6] 3727[3] **>76f<**

Fools Haven (IRE) 3 b c Fools Holme (USA)-Oak Queen (King of Clubs) 493[9] **>10a 46f<**

Fools Millyons (IRE) 3 ch c Fools Holme (USA)-Eloquent Charm (USA) (Private Account (USA)) *95[7] 128[4] 180[6]* **>51a 39f<**

Fools of Pride (IRE) 3 ch f Al Hareb (USA)-I'll Take Paris (USA) (Vaguely Noble) *47[6] 133[4] 180[5] 241[5] 292[3] 339[5] 376[5] 513[5]* 1219[8] 1667[3] 2166[5] 2481[6] *(2632)* 3017[2] 3303[6] 3722[7] 3971[18] **>55a 49f<**

Forbidden Gem 4 b g Formidable-Emerald Ring (Auction Ring (USA)) *101[6] 202[7]* 546[13] 2016[8] **>31a 16f<**

Force of Will (USA) 2 ch c Diesis-Clear Issue (USA) 3788a[3] **>99f<**

Forecast 2 b c Formidable (USA)-Princess Matilda *3077[9]* **>32a f<**

Foreign Judgement (USA) 2 b c El Gran Senor (USA)-Numeral (USA) (Alleged (USA)) 3883[6] 4188[8] **>77f<**

Foreman 2 b c Timeless Times (USA)-Skiddaw Bird (Bold Owl) 810[12] (910) 1096[4] 2085[7] 2779[6] 3568[8] 3749[17] 4077[12] *4294[3]* **>48a 66df<**

Foremma 4 b f Formidable-Great Dilemma (Vaigly Great) 1254[16] 1535[13] 1813[4] 1974[13] **>41f<**

Forentia 2 b f Formidable (USA)-Clarentia (Ballad Rock) (1790) 2136[2] 2779[2] 3186[6] 3702[5] **>92f<**

Foreshore (IRE) 5 b m Don't Forget Me-Krismas River (Kris) *332[11] 358[7]* **>2a 61f<**

Forest Boy 2 b c Komaite (USA)-Khadine (Astec) *3509[2]* 3626[12] *3949[4]* **>68a 46f<**

Forest Buck (USA) 2 ch c Green Forest (USA)-Perlee (FR) (Margouillat (FR)) (4063) **>94+f<**

Forest Cat (IRE) 3 b f Petorius-Forest of Arden (Tap On Wood) (1172) (1362) 2325[3] **>96f<**

Forest Fantasy 2 b f Rambo Dancer (CAN)-Another Treat (Derring Do) 2483[4] 3022[4] 3806[7] **>57+f<**

Forest Mill 3 ch f Aragon-Forest Blossom (USA) (Green Forest (USA)) 2094[4] 2653[3] 3081[3] 3320[7] *3526[13]* 3759[18] 3884[18] 4062[6] 4196[9] **>52f<**

Forest Robin 2 ch c Formidable (USA)-Blush Rambler (IRE) (Blushing Groom (FR)) 1751[3] 2660[4] 3604[3] 3784[4] 3989[2] 4188[6] **>79f<**

Foresworn (USA) 3 b c Alleged (USA)-Sybilline (FR) (Satingo) 657[5] **>76f<**

Forever Blushing 4 b f Blushing Scribe (USA)-Rheinza (Rheingold) *143[6]* **>25f<**

Forever Diamonds 8 ch h Good Times (ITY)-Mel Mira (Roi Soleil) 1415[7] 1617[5] 1808[15] 2117[8] 2994[3] 3368[6] **>88df<**

Forever Noble (IRE) 2 b c Forzando-Pagan Queen (Vaguely Noble) 825[9] **>54f<**

Forever Roses 3 b f Forzando-Red Rose Bowl (Dragonara Palace (USA)) 3640[3] **>68f<**

Forgetful 6 br m Don't Forget Me-Peak Squaw (USA) (Icecapade (USA)) 481[3] 4209[16] **>37a 38f<**

Forgie (IRE) 2 b g Don't Forget Me-Damia (Vision (USA)) 3231[11] 3620[12] 4169[13] **>42f<**

Forgotten Dancer (IRE) 4 ch c Don't Forget Me-Dancing Diana (Raga Navarro (ITY)) *61[4] 138[6] 192[8] 298[8]* **>36a 64f<**

Forgotten Empress 3 b f Dowsing (USA)-Vynz Girl (Tower Walk) *(225)* 3778[10] **>68a 68df<**

Forliando 2 b g Forzando-Lucky Orphan (Derrylin) 3379[24] 3652[8] 3955[5] 4045[10] 4143[9] **>50f<**

Formaestre (IRE) 5 b m Formidable-Maestrette (Manado) 1854[10] 2148[5] 2511[3] **>48da 32f<**

Formidable Lass 4 ch f Formidable-Stock Hill Lass (Air Trooper) 848[9] 1513[19] 3385[8] **>37f<**

Formidable Liz 5 ch m Formidable-Areej (Rusticaro (FR)) 1582[6] 1809[8] 2130[4] (2519) 2758[4] 3112[9] 3230[11] 3506[3] 3726[5] **>48a 66f<**

Formidable Partner 2 b c Formidable (USA)-Brush Away (Ahonoora) 4313[5] **>78f<**

Fort Commander (FR) 4 ch c Le Glorieux (USA)-Little Warden (Bellman (FR)) (487a)

Fort de France (USA) 2 b c Alleged (USA)-Fabrina (USA) (Storm Bird (CAN)) 3650[6] 3846[5] **>45f<**

Fortensky (USA) 5 b h Blushing Groom (FR)-Casey (Caerleon (USA)) 799a[3] 2721a[2] (3321a) (3686a) **>63f<**

For the Present 5 b h Then Again-Axe Valley (Royben) 1193[8] **>91f<**

Fort Knox (IRE) 4 b g Treasure Kay-Single Viking (Viking (USA)) 2345[5] 2602[9] (2946) 3011[7] 3079[8] 3455[16] **>61f<**

Fortuitious (IRE) 2 b f Polish Patriot (USA)-Echo Cove (Slip Anchor) 570[5] 782[9] 1288[7] 2047[3] 2176[5] 2601[6] 2674[10] 3350[4] 3760[13] **>52f<**

Fortunes Course (IRE) 6 b m Crash Course-Night Rose 4167[8] **>44f<**

Fortunes Leap 3 br c Puissance-Lucky Starkist (Lucky Wednesday) 732[12] 855[9] *2497[6] 2963[10]* **>38a 48f<**

Fortunes Rose (IRE) 3 b f Tremblant-Night Rose 3178[7] 3896[10] 4220[8] **>35f<**

Fort Vally 5 gr m Belfort (FR)-Hivally (High Line) 1292[10] 1529[11] 1666[11] 2254[4] 2375[8] 2664[7] (2972) **>53f<**

Forzair 3 b c Forzando-Persian Air (Persian Bold) 442[2] 543[4] 637[4] 1094[7] 1296[10] *1953[6] 2141[3]* 3341[5] *3512[12]* 3973[8] 4171[11] **>70a 69f<**

Forzara 2 ch f Risk Me (FR)-Valldemosa (Music Boy) 3432[14] 3892[11] **>36f<**

osters Top 3 ch g Pharly (FR)-More Sparkle (Morston FR)) *144*^{10} 1317^{10} 2171^{6} 2593^{14} 2810^{5} **>1a 44f**<

oundry Lane 4 b c Mtoto-Eider (Niniski (USA)) 1109^{2} 853^{9} 2274^{6} (2937) 3162^{3} 3412^{4} 4325^{5} **>91f**<

ourdaned (IRE) 2 b c Danehill (USA)-Pro Patria 3989^{4} 188^{4} **>82f**<

our Lane Flyer 3 b f Sayf El Arab (USA)-Collegian Stanford) 2236^{12} 2527^{6} 2915^{3} 3941^{10} **>44f**<

our of Spades 4 ch c Faustus (USA)-Fall To Pieces USA) *93*^{9} *177*^{4} *224*^{2} 579^{10} *1629*^{2} (1785) (1819) 2191^{2} 2390^{6} 2517^{4} *2923*^{6} 3098^{6} *(3242)* *3512*^{2} 3822^{7} 3964^{22} **73a 60f**<

ourstars Allstar (USA) 7 b h Compliance (USA)-Broadway Joan (USA) (Bold Arian (USA)) 4305a^{7} **>123f**<

Four Weddings (USA) 2 b c Runaway Groom-Kitty's Best (USA) (Amen (FR)) *1454*^{9} 1781^{5} 2542^{9} **>44a 49f**<

Foxhill Blue 3 b f Domynsky-Cornflower Blue (Tyrnavos) *173*^{7} **>27a 40f**<

Foxhound (USA) 4 b c Danzig (USA)-Lassie Dear (USA) (Buckpasser) 3191^{2} 3834^{10} **>109f**<

Fox Sparrow 5 b h Sharpo-Wryneck (Niniski (USA)) 505^{11} 721^{2} **>85f**<

Fraam 6 b h Lead on Time (USA)-Majestic Kahala (USA) 425^{2} 710a^{2} 1284^{2} 1711a^{2} 2217a^{4} 2703^{4} 3067^{4} **>114f**<

Fradicant 6 b g Remezzo-Elegant Star 3282^{13}

Fragaria 3 ch f Be My Chief (USA)-Strawberry Song (Final Straw) 1675^{8} 3239^{4} 3428^{3} 3844^{12} 4072^{10} 4196^{10} **>56f**<

Fragrant Belle (USA) 4 b f Al Nasr (FR)-Zolinana (FR) 2596^{6} 2910^{5} 3729^{19} **>93f**<

Fraise du Roi (IRE) 3 b f Roi Danzig (USA) *394*^{10} **>21a f**<

Framed (IRE) 5 b h Tate Gallery (USA)-Golden Thread (Glint of Gold) 4240^{5} **>60f**<

Framley Garth 3 ch f Belmez (USA)-Heavenly Abode (FR) (Habitat) *263*^{8} **>46da f**<

Frances Mary 2 ch f Sylvan Express-Maydrum (Meldrum) 2251^{4} 2516^{9} *3244*^{3} *3528*^{4} *3953*^{2} 4097^{8} 4287^{2} **>52a 67?f**<

Francfurter 3 b f Legend of France (USA)-A Priori (GER) (Prince Ippi (GER)) 630^{4} (941) 1619^{3} 3106^{5} (3237) 3388^{12} **>89f**<

Fran Godfrey 2 b f Taufan (USA)-One Last Glimpse (Relko) 3379^{7} 4262^{9} **>65f**<

Frankly Fran 3 b f Petorius-Sunita (Owen Dudley) 1168^{9} 3712^{8} **>53f**<

Frank the Swank 4 b g Dunbeath (USA)-Dark Amber (Formidable) 1878^{4} 2082^{8} 2401^{6} **>50f**<

Frans Lad 3 ch g Music Boy-Moberry (Mossberry) *830*^{2} *1034*^{8} 1279^{7} (1739) 2024^{5} *2590*^{4} 2870^{6} 3152^{4} 4060^{12} **>67a 63f**<

Freckles Kelly 3 b f Shavian-Choke Cherry (Connaught) 968^{10} 1153^{4} 2220^{2} (2372) *2627*^{2} 3667^{7} 3980^{7} **>53a 47f**<

Fred Bongusto (IRE) 4 b c Danehill (USA)-Hi Bettina (Henbit (USA)) 1119a^{2} **>115f**<

Freddie Baloo 3 b g Satin Wood-Mrs Bizz 2438^{6} *2959*^{9} **>16a 49f**<

Fred Said Right (IRE) 3 gr g Standaan (FR)-Sleeping Car (Scorpio (FR)) 2236^{11} 3649^{13} 3981^{9} **>30f**<

Fred's Delight (IRE) 4 b c Law Society (USA)-Madame Nureyev (USA) (Nureyev (USA)) *1029*^{15} 3970^{17} **>35df**<

Freedom Cry 4 b c Soviet Star (USA)-Falling Star (FR) (Mount Hagen (FR)) (607a) 898a^{4} (1398a) 3327a^{2} 3690a^{2} 4014a^{2} 4307a^{2} **>132f**<

Freedom Flame 2 b f Darshaan-Fire and Shade (USA) (Shadeed (USA)) 2464^{2} 2681^{2} **>78+f**<

Freeloader 2 ch c Be My Guest (USA)-Andy's Find (USA) (Buckfinder (USA)) 825^{12} 1226^{7} 2035^{9} **>35f**<

Free To Speak (IRE) 3 ch c Be My Guest (USA)-Love For Poetry (Lord Gay 708a^{3} **>96f**<

French Deputy (USA) 3 ch c Deputy Minister (USA)-Mitterand (USA) *4308a*^{9} **>108a f**<

French Ginger 4 ch f Most Welcome-French Plait (Thatching) 973^{5} 1168^{5} 1446^{3} 1533^{4} 2053^{4} 4043^{8} 4193^{12} **>68f**<

French Grit (IRE) 3 b c Common Grounds-Charbatte (FR) (In Fijar (USA)) 723^{4} 823^{2} (985) 1487^{3} 1806^{4} 2324^{6} 3373^{5} 3565^{7} 3717^{21} 3878^{17} 4041^{14} 4281^{6} **>84f**<

French Ivy (USA) 8 ch h Nodouble (USA)-Lierre (USA) (Gummo (USA)) 1058^{2} 1444^{2} (1929) 3071^{4} 3774^{2} 4026^{3} **>75f**<

Frequent 2 ch c Rainbow Quest-Free Guest (Be My Guest (USA)) 4348a^{2}

Fresh Fruit Daily 3 b f Reprimand-Dalmally (Sharpen Up) 1000^{5} 1242^{9} 3023^{2} 3282^{2} 3768^{4} 4065^{8} **>87df**<

Fresh Look (IRE) 3 b f Alzao (USA)-Bag Lady (Be My Guest (USA)) 722^{6} 1656^{3} 1940^{7} 2245^{8} 2884^{3} 3184^{4} (3635) 3843^{6} 4000^{16} 4259^{20} **>59f**<

Fret (USA) 5 b h Storm Bird (CAN)-Windy and Mild (USA) (Best Turn (USA)) 1606^{2} 1921^{5} 3297^{8} **>67f**<

Frezeliere 2 b f Be My Chief (USA)-Anna Karietta (Precocious) 1627^{3} 2083^{3} 2964^{4} 3271^{3} 3639^{6} 3867^{7} 4025^{2} **>85f**<

Friar's Oak 3 b c Absalom-Sunset Ray (Hotfoot) *141*^{7} *263*^{W} *292*^{7} **>25a 44f**<

Friar Street (IRE) 5 b g Carmelite House (USA)-Madam Slaney (Prince Tenderfoot (USA)) 568^{W} 874^{6} 1160^{10} *1568*^{4} *2377*^{5} (3745) **>41a 54f**<

Friday Night (USA) 2 b br f Trempolino (USA)-Assez Cuite (USA) (Graustark (USA)) 3069^{21} **>30f**<

Friendly Brave (USA) 5 b h Well Decorated (USA)-Companionship (USA) (Princely Native (USA)) *12*^{11} *89*^{12} *145*^{7} 550^{16} 731^{9} 887^{6} 1051^{3} 1499^{2} 1975^{7} 2202^{2} 3800^{13} 3919^{14} 4057^{10} 4165^{4} 4215^{8} *(4295)* **>67a 63f**<

Friendly Dreams (IRE) 2 gr f Midyan (USA)-Friendly Thoughts (USA) (Al Hattab (USA)) 3644^{17} **>4f**<

Friendly Forester (USA) 2 b c Woodman (USA)-Cameo Performance (USA) (Be My Guest (USA)) 562^{4} 690^{4} 2660^{5} 2988^{3} (3405) 3516^{2} **>84f**<

Friendly Knight 5 b h Horage-Be A Dancer (Be Friendly) 494^{6} **>40f**<

Friendly Lady (USA) 3 b f Imp Society (USA)-Icy Friend (USA) (It's Freezing (USA)) *101*^{4} **>56da 64f**<

Friendly Lover (USA) 7 b h Cutlass (USA)-Glide Along (USA) *4303a*^{5} **>118a f**<

Frisky Miss (IRE) 4 b f Fayruz-Moira My Girl (Henbit (USA)) *65*^{3} *160*^{11} *191*^{7} *224*^{4} *297*^{9} *380*^{5} 1148^{9} 1335^{7} *1633*^{6} 1692^{7} *1953*^{12} 2017^{5} 2137^{12} *2290*^{2} 2539^{8} **>66a 70f**<

Fro 2 b f Salse (USA)-Silent Sun (Blakeney) 1443^{5} 1746^{8} **>47f**<

Frog 2 b f Akarad (FR)-Best Girl Friend (Sharrood

(USA)) 3976^{5} 4098^{9} 4212^{14} **>54f<**
Frogmarch (USA) 5 ch h Diesis-La Francaise (USA) (Jim French (USA)) 3728^{8} 4035^{13} **>80f<**
Frome Lad 3 ch g Buzzards Bay-Groundsel (Reform) *72^{4}* *894^{4}* 974^{5} 1198^{12} *(1628)* *2147^{8}* **>61a 54f<**
Frontiersman 3 b g Indian Ridge-Strapless (Bustino) 442^{15} 555^{7} 772^{10} 1598^{2} 2610^{3} 4292^{7} **>56f<**
Frozen Sea (USA) 4 ch c Diesis-Ocean Ballad (Grundy) 2316^{3} 2790^{5} 3277^{3} 3571^{4} **>74f<**
Fruitful Affair (IRE) 6 b m Taufan (USA)-Lucky Engagement (USA) (What Luck (USA)) 582^{14} *1210^{12}* 1607^{2} (2745) 3029^{6} 3234^{8} 3470^{12} 3710^{8} 3898^{8} 4166^{20} **>46df<**
Frustration 4 b f Salse (USA)-Baffle (Petingo) 2008^{6} (2547) **>111f<**
Fryup Satellite 4 br g Leading Star-Comedy Imp (Import) 556^{22} *771^{6}* 874^{12} 1295^{11} **>23a 35f<**
Fujiyama Crest (IRE) 3 b c Roi Danzig (USA)-Snoozy Time (Cavo Doro) (745) (851) 995^{4} 1929^{12} 2284^{9} (3211) (3351) (3817) **>95f<**
Full Cover (IRE) 3 b c Thatching-Dead Certain (Absalom) *332^{6}* *468^{7}* 552^{7} **>44a 64f<**
Full Gloss 3 ro c Prince Sabo-Cawstons Prejudice (Cawston's Clown) 1380^{10} 1666^{10} 2191^{8} 2357^{3} 2968^{9} 3295^{7} **>54f<**
Full Quiver 10 br h Gorytus (USA)-Much Pleasure 3627^{14} 3884^{4} **>55f<**
Funky 2 ch f Classic Music (USA)-Foreno (Formidable) 3539^{6} 3758^{3} **>67f<**
Funny Rose 5 b m Belfort (FR)-Scottish Rose (Warpath) 476^{3} 578^{5} 990^{7} 1206^{4} 1819^{6} 1902^{4} (2306) 2478^{3} **>43f<**
Funny Worry 6 b g Jester-Concern 593^{11} **>24f<**
Fursan (USA) 2 b c Fred Astaire (USA)-Ancient Art (USA) (Tell (USA)) 3340^{11} 3663^{11} **>57f<**
Further Flight 9 gr g Pharly (FR)-Flying Nelly (610) 869^{8} 1132^{5} 1363^{5} (2119) 2702^{9} 3563^{2} (3946) 4204^{10} **>120f<**
Further Future (IRE) 2 br c Doubletour (USA)-Tamara's Reef (Main Reef) 3856^{12} 3988^{15} 4075^{25} **>17f<**
Future Act (USA) 3 b f Known Fact (USA)-Gamberta (USA) (Roberto (USA)) 1736^{4} (2167) (2621) 3007^{6} **>96++f<**
Future Options 4 ch f Lomond (USA)-Hemline (Sharpo) 2053^{5} 2362^{4} *2634^{10}* 3057^{10} 3173^{5} **>34a 62f<**
Future's Trader 2 b c Alzao (USA)-Awatef (Ela-Mana-Mou) 4146^{5} **>50f<**
Fuzzy 3 b c Petong-Jaydeeglen (Bay Express) 732^{14} 880^{10} 1360^{7} 1739^{10} 1993^{10} **>31f<**
Fyne Song 3 b f Chief Singer-La Reine de France (Queen's Hussar) 701^{14} *1457^{7}* 1692^{13} *2140^{4}* *2587^{4}* (2885) 3264^{7} 3344^{14} **>32a 47f<**
Fyors Gift (IRE) 2 b f Cadeaux Genereux-Miss Fyor (USA) (Danzig (USA)) 2508^{4} 2940^{3} 3643^{9} **>68f<**

G

Gabriel's Lady 4 b f Valiyar-Autumn Harvest (Martinmas) 1905^{7} 2449^{6} 2708^{10} 3055^{10} **>35f<**
Gadge 4 br g Nomination-Queenstyle (Moorestyle) 433^{3} 486^{6} 714^{3} 960^{5} 1280^{5} *2634^{11}* 3565^{6} 3732^{12} 3945^{35} 4035^{17} 4319^{21} **>35a 70f<**
Gagajulu 2 b f Al Hareb (USA)-Rion River (IRE) (Taufan (USA)) 595^{2} 788^{6} 1082^{2} 1293^{5} 1540^{12} *(1758)* 2085^{4} (2281) (2523) (2826) 3100^{4} 3213^{9} (3400) 3623^{21} 4097^{6} 4237^{2} 4317^{10} **>66a 75f<**
Gaitero (FR) 2 b c Groom Dancer-First Waltz 4344a^{3}
Galacia (IRE) 3 br f Gallic League-Little Wild Duck 2049^{3} **>46f<**
Galafron 3 ch c Nashwan (USA)-Gayane (Nureyev (USA)) 2313^{4} 2880^{8} **>53f<**
Galaka 2 b f Slip Anchor-Golden Glint (Vitiges (FR)) 3532^{9} **>61f<**
Galapino 2 b c Charmer-Carousella (Rousillon (USA)) 825^{4} 1298^{3} 2365^{4} 3405^{6} 3625^{7} 4084^{23} 4195^{10} 4327^{15} **>78f<**
Galine 2 b f Most Welcome-Tarasova (USA) (Green Forest (USA)) 1627^{4} 3680^{6} **>60f<**
Gallante 2 b c Rainbow Quest (USA)-Mary Sunley (Known Fact (USA)) 2034^{4} 2434^{5} 3266^{7} **>56f<**
Gallant Spirit (IRE) 4 br c Gallic League-So Valiant (So Blessed) 1750^{8} *1882^{7}* 2448^{7} 3055^{11} **>41a 56f<**
Gallardini (IRE) 6 b h Nordico (USA)-Sweet (Pitskelly) 430^{22} 738^{13} 1102^{10} 2621^{2} 2664^{4} **>61f<**
Gallery Artist (IRE) 7 ch h Tate Gallery (USA)-Avec L'Amour (Realm) *157^{3}* *302^{6}* *(397)* *415^{4}* **>57a 58f<**
Gallop to Glory 5 b h Petong-Merchantmens Girl *49^{7}* *130^{5}* *512^{7}* **>27a 12f<**
Gallows Corner (IRE) 3 b f Nordico (USA)-Donnarella (Dom Racine (FR)) 621^{10} 812^{7} 2324^{3} 2531^{6} 3451^{6} 3750^{12} **>87f<**
Galway Blade 2 b c Faustus (USA)-Slipperose (Persepolis (FR)) 3617^{4} 3868^{18} 3916^{5} 4081^{11} **>72f<**
Game Ploy (POL) 3 b c Deploy-Guestimate (FR) (Be My Guest (USA)) 1264^{3} 2004^{3} 3433^{9} 3863^{11} 4149^{9} **>68f<**
Gamzatti 4 gr f Midyan (USA)-Kenmara (FR) (Kenmare (FR)) *766^{13}* 1285^{14} *1458^{7}* 1647^{10} 2620^{10} 2955^{7} **>38df<**
Ganador 3 gr f Weldnaas (USA)-Shakana (Grundy) 522^{9} *599^{3}* 908^{6} 1583^{2} 1818^{7} *2142^{7}* 4131^{12} **>47a 48f<**
Ganeshaya 6 gr h Formidable-Lammastide (Martinmas) *1633^{W}*
Gant Bleu (FR) 8 ch h Crystal Glitters (USA)-Gold Honey (Artaius (USA)) 839^{11} 927^{13} 1153^{3} 1355^{7} 1506^{11} 1843^{5} 1873^{5} **>49f<**
Garboni (USA) 6 ch g Theatrical-Royal Strait Flush (USA) (Seattle Slew (USA)) *311^{4}* **>48a f<**
Garden of Heaven (USA) 6 ch h Arctic Tern (USA)-Garden of Eden (Exbury) 666^{7} 913^{6} 1135^{8} 1385^{6} 1585^{7} 2104^{4} 2596^{5} **>109f<**
Garden Rose (IRE) 3 ch f Caerleon (USA)-Gironde (USA) (Raise A Native) 1712a^{8} (2561a) 3575a^{3} 4015a^{4} **>114f<**
Garlande D'Or 3 b f Belfort (FR)-Torville Gold (Aragon) 524^{6} *832^{6}* 1414^{7} 1679^{13} 2363^{12} **>32a 47f<**
Garnock Valley 5 b h Dowsing (USA)-Sunley Sinner (Try My Best (USA)) 433^{4} 563^{9} 1441^{9} 3715^{19} 4115^{15} **>75a 68f<**
Gate of Heaven 5 b m Starry Night (USA)-Halatch (Habat) 646^{11} *769^{6}* *1076^{5}* *1214^{7}* 1377^{4} *2925^{9}* 3055^{9} 3385^{7} **>31da 21f<**
Gay Gallanta (USA) 3 ch f Woodman (USA)-Gallanta (Nureyev (USA)) 692^{5} 933^{7} 1850^{5} 2349^{2} 2673^{7} **>112f<**
Gee Gee Tee 2 ch c Superlative-Glorietta (USA) (Shadeed (USA)) 3746^{7} 3869^{9} 4058^{12} 4327^{13} **>48f<**
Geisway (CAN) 5 br h Geiger Counter (USA)-Broadway

Beauty (USA) (Chompion (USA)) 714[17] 918[10] 1558[8] 1853[19] **>105f<**
Gelsemine 2 b f Mtoto-Gelatine (Bold Lad (IRE)) 2408[10] 3010[3] 3468[14] **>68f<**
Gemolly (IRE) 2 b f Be My Native (USA)-Hayhurst (Sandhurst Prince) 1977[16] 3887[11] **>21f<**
General Assembly (IRE) 3 b c Pharly (FR)-Hastening (Shirley Heights) 657[3] 1490[2] 1672[4] (3772) **>92+f<**
General Chaos (IRE) 5 b g Taufan (USA)-Isa (Dance In Time (CAN)) 439[16] 1932[9] 2477[8] **>71f<**
General Chase 5 ch m Scottish Reel-Make A Signal (Royal Gunner (USA)) *73[4] 361[3] 403[13]* 986[9] **>53a 13f<**
General Equation 2 b c Governor General-Logarithm (King of Spain) 2221[9] *3077[10]* 3648[9] *3953[7]* **>29a 29f<**
General Glow 2 b c Presidium-Glow Again (The Brianstan) 3502[10] 3666[12] 4172[8] **>51f<**
General Gubbins 4 b c Mashhor Dancer (USA)-Crag Hall (Sharpo) 838[4] 1151[12] 2310[8] 2753[8] 3879[17] **>43f<**
General Macarthur 2 b c Alzao (USA)-Royal Climber 2408[7] 2846[7] 3620[11] 3985[9] 4226[2] **>76f<**
General Monash (USA) 3 b c Thorn Dance (USA)-Zummerudd (Habitat) 1117a[6] 3042a[10] **>106f<**
General Mouktar 5 ch h Hadeer-Fly The Coop (Kris) 423[12] 623[9] 1022[3] 1386[4] 2055[3] 2525[7] 2845[5] 3710[14] 4248[14] **>80df<**
General Rose 2 b c Governor General-Aleda Rose (Charlottown) (540) 871[5] 1634[7] 2346[3] 2847[7] 3267[2] 3405[3] 3917[3] 4321[4] **>75f<**
General Shirley (IRE) 4 b c Shirley Heights-Adjala (Northfields (USA)) *470[5]* 1092[13] **>60a 52df<**
General Sir Peter (IRE) 3 br g Last Tycoon-Nashya (Rousillon (USA)) (502) 2409[7] (2680) 3219[6] (3597) **>80f<**
Genereux 2 ch c Generous (IRE)-Flo Russell (USA) (Round Table (USA)) 3398[7] **>22f<**
Generosa 2 b f Generous (IRE)-Hotel Street (USA) (Alleged (USA)) 3450[2] **>69f<**
Generous Present 2 ch c Cadeaux Genereux-Dance Move (Shareef Dancer (USA)) 2615[10] 3536[10] 3784[9] **>45f<**
Genesis Four 5 b h Dreams to Reality (USA)-Relma (Relko) *28[2] (50) 94[8] 138[9] 227[4] 271[6] 354[2] 415[7] 520[2] 605[12]* 672[17] 2246[17] *2377[7]* 2972[3] 3275[13] **>48a 44f<**
Genovefa (USA) 3 b f Woodman-Reigning Countess (Far No (1704a) 2045a[3] 3041a[4] 4009a[3] **>112f<**
Gentilhomme 2 ch c Generous (IRE)-Bold Flawless (USA) 1184[7] 2005[2] 2420[3] (3846) (4264) **>102f<**
Gentle Friend 2 b f Dominion-Burnished (Formidable) 1536[7] 1977[18] **>57f<**
Gentle Irony 3 b f Mazilier (USA)-Irenic (Mummy's Pet) *587[11]* 773[4] 1059[2] (1325) 1581[6] 1702[5] 1791[5] 2065[3] 2532[5] (2684) 2828[5] (3096) 3218[6] 3403[2] 3605[15] 3704[7] *3950[2] 4128[6]* (4170) 4225[4] **>59a 69f<**
Gentleman Sid 5 b h Brotherly (USA)-Eugenes Chance (Flashback) 884[11] 1535[7] 1657[3] (2268) 2569[4] (3217) **>57f<**
Geolly (IRE) 3 b g Formidable-Four-Legged Friend (Aragon) *4271[6]* **>32a 39f<**
George Bull 3 b g Petoski-Firgrove (Relkino) 815[6] 1097[8] 1514[9] 2026[9] 3634[3] 4047[7] **>71f<**
George Dillingham 5 b h Top Ville-Premier Rose (Sharp Edge) 757[2] 1102[7] 1462[4] 1768[3] 2098[3] **>95f<**
George's Boy 5 b br g Sonnen Gold-Space Drama (Space King) 3282[14]
Germane 3 b f Distant Relative-Fraulein Tobin (USA) (J O Tobin (USA)) 660[4] 932[6] 1101[5] 2673[9] 3564[12] **>89df<**
Germano 2 b c Generous (IRE)-Gay Fantastic (Ela-Mana-Mou) 3900[7] (4188) **>90f<**
Germany (USA) 4 b c Trempolino (USA)-Inca Princess (USA) (Big Spruce (USA)) 2046a[2] (2894a) (3591a) 3914a[4] 4120[7] **>121f<**
Get Tough 2 b c Petong-Mrs Waddilove (Bustino) 1246[7] 1592[6] 3604[12] 3928[6] 4327[8] **>64f<**
Ghalayan 3 ch c Nashwan (USA)-Al Sylah (Nureyev (USA)) 2760[4] **>4f<**
Ghayabik (FR) 3 808a[6] **>79f<**
Ghedi (POL) 4 b g Vilnius (POL)-Ghaza (POL) (Pawiment (POL)) 2391[7] *2588[11]* **>35a 32f<**
Ghostly Apparition 2 gr g Gods Solution-Tawny (Grey Ghost) 554[3] 810[10] 1035[6] 2601[4] 2857[4] *3528[8] 3675[2]* 3937[21] **>38a 52f<**
Ghostly (IRE) 3 b f Fairy King (USA)-Gold Quest (FR) (Rainbow Quest (USA)) 1116a[6] 1390a[4] 2897a[4] **>110f<**
Giddy 2 b br f Polar Falcon (USA)-Spin Turn (Homing) 3900[15] **>58f<**
Gifted 3 b f Shareef Dancer (USA)-Rexana *1761[9]* 2225[9] 2751[4] **>18a 28f<**
Gigfy 3 b c Warrshan (USA)-Empty Purse (Pennine Walk) *105[9] 171[6] 240[5] 283[5] 326[5] 366[9]* 1718[9] 2129[7] 2546[10] **>51a 41f<**
Giggleswick Gamble 2 ch f Aragon-Persian Alexandra (Persian Bold) 3450[W]
Giggleswick Girl 4 b f Full Extent (USA)-Foligno (Crofter (USA)) *298[9] 344[7] 410[5]* 481[5] *518[11]* 646[2] 701[10] 726[4] (1042) 1157[8] 1276[3] (1434) 1538[3] 1689[8] (1741) 2092[4] 2234[6] 2260[3] 2364[3] 2533[4] 2692[3] 2867[5] 2935[10] 2987[3] 3205[4] 3453[4] 3519[2] 3667[17] 3878[9] 4142[16] 4165[14] 4280[8] **>46a 69f<**
Giggleswick Gossip 3 b f Full Extent (USA)-Foligno (Crofter (USA)) 1521[7] 1847[12] 2081[11] **>56a 51f<**
Gi La High 2 gr f Rich Charlie-Gem of Gold (Jellaby) *531[3] (604) 770[2] (1090)* 2281[2] 3655[5] *4124[4]* **>58a 66?f<**
Gildoran Sound 2 b f Gildoran-Sound of Laughter (Hasty Word) 4277[14] **>32f<**
Gilling Dancer (IRE) 2 b c Dancing Dissident (USA)-Rahwah (Northern Baby (CAN)) 3625[17] 3877[5] 4276[4] **>57f<**
Gilpa Bliss 4 b f Kabour-Wind And Reign (Tumble Wind (USA)) *3522[14]*
Gilpa Trinkets 3 b c Full Extent (USA)-Delightful Diane (Kalaglow) *473[9]* 1207[12] 1290[18] 1453[8] 1721[14] 1847[14] 3508[13] **>39a 16f<**
Gilt Throne 8 b m 1316[9] **>74f<**
Ginger Glint 2 ch c Hadeer-Sorayah (Persian Bold) *1632[6]* 1829[5] 2195[5] 2516[2] 3048[4] (3353) 3721[7] 3915[8] **>15a 61f<**
Ginger Hodgers 2 ch f Crofthall-Jarrettelle (All Systems Go) 1670[14] 1935[5] 2371[7] 3721[18] **>44f<**
Gingerillo 4 ch c Aragon-Titian Beauty (Auction Ring (USA)) *41[4] 148[8] 220[9] 237[7]* **>37a 39f<**
Ginger Jim 4 ch c Jalmood (USA)-Stratch (FR) (Thatch (USA)) *252[3] 357[6] 471[3]* 1256[3] 1594[3] 1749[3] 2201[3] 3384[10] 3862[4] 4168[4] **>62a 76f<**
Ginger Tree (USA) 3 b f Dayjur (USA)-Carotene (CAN) (Great Nephew) 952[5] 3902[4] **>91f<**

Ginka **4** b f Petoski-Pine (Supreme Sovereign) *104^{6} 280^{5}* 860^{11} 1529^{15} 2245^{11} **>31a 64f<**

Ginza Lights (IRE) **4** b c Tate Gallery (USA)-Parkeen Princess (He Loves Me) 1016^{16} **>58f<**

Girl From Ipanema **4** b f Salse (USA)-Honey Pot 631^{7} 897a^{6} 1482^{2} 1588^{6} **>108df<**

Give In **8** gr h Harlow (USA)-Moment of Weakness (Pieces of Eight) *49^{4} 73^{5} 235^{11}* **>44a 47f<**

Give Me A Ring (IRE) **2** b c Be My Guest (USA)-Annsfield Lady (Red Sunset) 1597^{12} 2473^{4} 3432^{5} **>63f<**

Gladys Althorpe (IRE) **2** b f Posen (USA)-Gortadoo (USA) (Sharpen Up) 1525^{5} 1842^{4} (2542) 3147^{14} 3414^{7} 3623^{7} 3969^{7} 4111^{15} **>71f<**

Glenlivet (SWE) **7** ch g Grant's (DEN)-Skyline (SWE) (Jimmy Reppin) 1393a^{2} 3195a^{3} 3785a^{3} **>116f<**

Glen Miller **5** b h Music Boy-Blakeney Sound (Blakeney) 548^{14} 780^{18} 882^{13} 1785^{3} 1991^{6} **>49f<**

Glen Parker (IRE) **2** ch c Bluebird (USA)-Trina's Girl (Nonoalco (USA)) 4222^{2} **>72+f<**

Glenrazie (IRE) **2** ch c Kefaah (USA)-Glendera (Glenstal (USA)) 3436^{2} 3672^{2} 3850^{2} **>80f<**

Glenrock Dancer (IRE) **3** b f Glenstal (USA)-Fourp'ny Rock (Ahonoora) 1162^{5} 1960^{3} 2400^{6} **>38f<**

Glenugie **4** b g Insan (USA)-Excavator Lady (Most Secret) 568^{14} **>59f<**

Glenvally **4** gr f Belfort (FR)-Hivally (High Line) *49^{2} 181^{8} (335) 416^{P}* **>55da 59df<**

Glide Path (USA) **6** ch h Stalwart (USA)-Jolly Polka (USA) (Nice Dancer (CAN)) 623^{3} 1853^{10} 2274^{8} 2421^{2} 2739^{7} (3485a) 3957^{9} 4076^{10} **>102df<**

Glitterazzi **4** b c Midyan (USA)-Burnt Amber (Balidar) 1593^{6} *1939^{9} 3544^{9}* 3757^{18} 3884^{16} **>37a 30f<**

Glitter Bay **4** b f Glint of Gold-Town Lady *39^{11}* **>25df<**

Glitter of Gold **4** b f Glint of Gold-Kochia (Firestreak) *592^{9}* 817^{8} 1027^{8} *2140^{7}* **>37a 62f<**

Global Dancer **4** b c Night Shift (USA)-Early Call (Kind of Hush) *11^{3} 37^{4} 145^{6} 318^{6} 403^{5}* 762^{11} (1612) 2055^{2} 2599^{6} 2768^{5} 3571^{2} 3957^{6} *4223^{6}* **>77a 85f<**

Globe Runner **2** b c Adbass (USA)-Scenic Villa (Top Ville) 1440^{5} 1935^{4} 2932^{5} 3969^{16} **>63f<**

Gloriana **3** b f Formidable-Tudor Pilgrim (Welsh Pageant) 1128^{2} 1616^{7} 1984^{6} 2356^{2} (2805) 2954^{4} 3320^{3} 3552^{10} 3918^{3} 4051^{7} **>82f<**

Glorious Aragon **3** b f Aragon-Gloria Maremmana 742^{5} 1786^{2} 2430^{2} 3640^{4} 3822^{12} **>92df<**

Glorious Bid (IRE) **3** gr f Horage-Eclipse Bid (Rusticaro (FR)) 1196^{7} **>59f<**

Glorious Sound **2** b c Music Boy-Carlton Glory (Blakeney) 3432^{15} 3784^{11} **>13f<**

Glow Forum **4** b f Kalaglow-Beau's Delight (USA) (Lypheor) *321^{10} 370^{5}* 649^{7} 744^{8} *1319^{7} (2090)* (2830) 4062^{10} 4332^{3} **>36a 46f<**

Glowing Account (IRE) **4** b g Glow (USA)-Redeem Herself (General Assembly (USA)) *177^{10} 240^{4}* 1255^{14} 1509^{9} 1963^{17} **>43a 32f<**

Glowing Jade **5** b m Kalaglow-Precious Jade (1297) 1603^{4} 1732^{6} 2181^{7} 4043^{14} 4236^{9} **>52a 79f<**

Glowing Path **5** b h Kalaglow-Top Tina (High Top) *161^{5} 200^{9}* **>49a 37f<**

Glowing Reeds **2** ch f Kalaglow-No Jazz (Jaazeiro (USA)) 4263^{13} **>19f<**

Glow of Hope **5** b m Prince Sabo-Impailand (Imperial Fling (USA)) 2124^{4} 2463^{4} 2736^{9} 2772^{4} 2997^{9} 3508^{W} **>34a 32f<**

Goalwah **3** b f Sadler's Wells (USA)-Al Bahathri (USA) (Blushing Groom (FR)) 1990^{2} 2553^{2} (3239) 3636^{3} 4024^{10} **>88f<**

Go Between (FR) **2** b c Highest Honor-Ruffle (4089a) 4310a^{4}

Godmersham Park **3** b g Warrshan (USA)-Brown Velvet (Mansingh (USA)) 630^{3} 761^{W} 1258^{2} 1731^{2} 4049^{2} 4319^{17} **>75f<**

Godwin (USA) **4** ch f Diesis-Goodbye Shelley (FR) (Home Guard (USA)) 673^{2} (816) 1102^{3} 2012^{2} 2910^{3} **>94f<**

Go-Go-Power-Ranger **2** ch c Golden Lahab (USA)-Nibelunga (Miami Springs) 424^{12} 3353^{10} 3625^{14} **>43f<**

Go Hever Golf **3** ch c Efisio-Sweet Rosina (Sweet Revenge) *(196)* 621^{8} (999) 1131^{11} 1806^{10} 2394^{3} 3044a^{7} 3407^{8} **>100+a 97+f<**

Gold and Steel (FR) **3** b c Shining Steel-Horphaly (Pharly) (1573a) 2044a^{6} (2730a) **>114f<**

Gold Blade **6** ch h Rousillon (USA)-Sharp Girl (FR) (Sharpman) *77^{2} (166)* 430^{12} 1596^{2} 1863^{8} (2226) 2396^{3} 2664^{2} 2745^{3} 3710^{7} **>69a 57f<**

Gold Desire **5** b h Grey Desire-Glory Gold (Hittite Glory) *422^{7}* 476^{5} 874^{4} 909^{5} 1161^{4} 1205^{7} 2824^{4} (3367) 3462^{3} **>18a 38f<**

Gold Disc (USA) **2** ch c Slew O' Gold (USA)-Singing (USA) (The Minstrel (CAN)) (4064) **>81+f<**

Golden Arrow (IRE) **4** ch c Glint of Gold-Sheer Luck (Shergar) 3406^{8} 3730^{14} 4022^{10} **>90f<**

Golden Attraction (USA) **2** b f Citidancer (USA)-Timeandaword (USA) 4302a^{3} **>106tf<**

Golden Ball (IRE) **4** b c Sadler's Wells (USA)-Sun Princess (English Prince) 631^{2} 1132^{7} 1479^{3} 3131^{2} **>113f<**

Golden Bechett (IRE) **5** b h Baillamont (USA)-Jiflora (FR) (Gift Card (FR)) 710a^{3} 1577a^{6} **>92f<**

Goldenberry **4** ch f Sharrood (USA)-Moberry (Mossberry) *77^{9} 172^{4} 234^{6} 311^{5} 375^{11}* 1149^{8} 1285^{11} 1557^{8} 1733^{5} 1957^{9} *3078^{8}* 3288^{11} **>34a 44f<**

Golden Chip (IRE) **7** ch g M Double M (USA)-Kimangao (Garda's Revenge (USA)) 2187^{4} 2484^{11} 3493^{14} **>70a 59df<**

Golden Digger (USA) **3** ch f Mr Prospector (USA)-Carduel (USA) (Buckpasser) 824^{7} 1431^{4} 1944^{4} **>60f<**

Golden Envoy (USA) **3** b f Dayjur (USA)-Ambassador of Luck (USA) (What Luck (USA)) 2576^{8} 2915^{2} 3390^{11} **>78f<**

Golden Fish **3** b g Efisio-Fishpond (Homing) 2220^{12} 2972^{2} 3118^{8} 3272^{5} 3504^{3} 4209^{12} **>22a 52f<**

Golden Gear (USA) **4** b c Gulch (USA)-Fineza (USA) *4303a^{9}* **>109a f<**

Golden Glenstal (IRE) **3** ch c Glenstal (USA)-Mattira (FR) (Rheffic (FR)) 3790a^{7} **>103f<**

Golden Hadeer **4** ch c Hadeer-Verchinina (Star Appeal) *76^{6} 172^{6}* **>34a 52f<**

Golden Hello **4** b g Glint of Gold-Waltz (Jimmy Reppin) 3593^{11} **>86f<**

Golden Lady (IRE) **3** b f Danehill (USA)-Gold Runner (Runnett) (542) 674^{5} 982^{2} 1241^{7} 1924^{11} **>90f<**

Golden Lucky(USA) **0** 01 c Lucky North-Here's To Us (Hold Your P 1003a^{3}

Golden Memories (IRE) **4** ch c Shernazar-Buz Kashi *413^{11}* **>69df<**

Golden Pond (IRE) **2** b f Don't Forget Me-Golden Bloom (Main Reef) 1964^{6} 2846^{3} 3089^{18} 3471^{8} 3809^{4} (3969) 4111^{3} **>72f<**

Golden Pound (USA) **3** b c Seeking the Gold (USA)-Coesse Express (USA) (Dewan (USA)) 2553^{10} 2977^{3} 3227^{2} 3799^{15} 4083^{7} **>87df<**

Golden Relation (IRE) **2** b c Marju-Rich Relation (Golden Act $1889a^{2}$

Golden Rosy (ITY) **2** b f Le Glorieux-Assertive Lass (Assert) $1395a^{3}$

Golden Silver **2** b f Precious Metal-Severals Princess (Formidable) 1590^{8} 1829^{3} 1981^{6} 2176^{6} 3651^{4} 4075^{21} **>50f<**

Golden Star (IRE) **4** ch c Salse (USA)-Tight Spin (High Top) 841^{12} **>55a 49f<**

Golden Tongue (USA) **3** ch g Nureyev (USA)-Prayers'n Promises (USA) (Foolish Pleasure (USA)) 1216^{5} 1507^{4} 1874^{2} 2310^{11} **>71f<**

Golden Torque **8** br h Taufan (USA)-Brightelmstone (Prince Regent (FR)) *367^{11} 414^{9}* 495^{5} *3511^{10} 3735^{8}* 3987^{2} **>44a 65f<**

Golden Touch (USA) **3** ch c Elmaamul (USA)-Tour D'Argent (USA) (Halo (USA)) 3542^{8} 3762^{3} 4079^{16} **>76df<**

Golden Tyke (IRE) **2** b c Soviet Lad (USA)-Golden Room (African Sky) 2619^{9} 2782^{9} **>33f<**

Golden Wedding **2** b g Today and Tomorrow-Too Familiar (Oats) *3077^{8}* 3314^{10} *3675^{10}* **>36a 20f<**

Gold Island (FR) **5** b g Noir Et Or-Djarba $4346a^{3}$ **>98f<**

Gold Kicker **2** b c High Kicker (USA)-Ship of Gold (Glint of Gold) 3093^{4} *4334^{13}* **>14a 60f<**

Goldmart (IRE) **2** ch c Waajib-Une Parisienne (FR) (Bolkonski) 2971^{10} 4290^{14} **>2f<**

Goldrill **2** ch c Never so Bold-Irish Impulse (USA) (Irish River (FR)) 3671^{9} **>42f<**

Gold Sand **3** b c Green Desert (USA)-Golden Opinion (USA) 1309^{6} **>37f<**

Goldsearch (IRE) **2** ch f Fayruz-Win For Me (Bonne Noel) 3893^{9} 4103^{13} 4219^{5} **>64f<**

Gold Surprise (IRE) **6** b or br g Petorius-Gold Piece (Golden Fleece (USA)) *(46) 87^{5}* 3641^{11} *3735^{9}* 3853^{4} **>54a 53f<**

Go Likecrazy **3** br f Dowsing (USA)-Thessaloniki (Julio Mariner) *10^{7} 95^{10}* **>24a 45f<**

Go Like West **2** b c Absalom-Wyns Vision (Vision (USA)) 436^{13} 474^{7} **>13f<**

Golina (IRE) **2** b f Polish Patriot (USA)-Las Bela (Welsh Pageant) 2660^{11} 2985^{7} **>32f<**

Gondo **8** br g Mansingh (USA)-Secret Valentine (Wollow) *244^{6} 380^{7} 398^{11}* 688^{9} 906^{6} 1157^{6} 1304^{13} 1565^{8} 1809^{17} 2234^{8} 2935^{8} 3221^{10} 3313^{3} 3467^{20} 3492^{13} 3704^{14} 3777^{3} 4215^{16} **>31a 48f<**

Gone for a Burton (IRE) **5** ch g Bustino-Crimbourne (Mummy's Pet) (505) 1140^{2} 2457^{5} 3611^{13} 3729^{14} **>97f<**

Gone Savage **7** b h Nomination-Trwyn Cilan (Import) (636) 922^{19} 1411^{10} 1614^{7} 1832^{2} 2326^{5} 2533^{5} 2909^{9} 3442^{4} 3615^{7} 3800^{8} 4068^{6} 4215^{15} **>67f<**

Goodbye Millie **5** b or br m Sayf El Arab (USA)-Leprechaun Lady (Royal Blend) *1029^{13}* 1252^{7} 1555^{2} (1743) 2280^{7} (2400) 2663^{5} *2921^{6}* 3743^{13} 3853^{3} 4110^{2} 4232^{3} **>37a 52f<**

Good Fetch **4** b f Siberian Express (USA)-Exceptional Beauty (Sallust) 3384^{16} **>44f<**

Good Hand (USA) **9** ch h Northjet (USA)-Ribonette (USA) (Ribot) 821^{7} 1084^{2} (1268) 1416^{7} 2087^{2} 2374^{4} 2937^{5} 3412^{2} 3705^{2} 4036^{9} 4189^{4} 4326^{5} **>86f<**

Good (IRE) **3** b c Persian Heights-Tres Bien (Pitskelly) 1146^{8} 1498^{7} 1696^{7} 3438^{12} 3808^{21} 3875^{10} **>26a 54f<**

Good Match (IRE) **3** br c Tirol-Vain Deb (Gay Fandango (USA)) 613^{6} 772^{11} 1154^{7} 1279^{4} 1583^{5} 1818^{6} **>63f<**

Good so Fa (IRE) **3** b c Taufan (USA)-Future Shock (Full Out (USA)) *(25) 51^{3} 144^{2} 263^{7} 384^{6}* 813^{18} *4293^{10}* **>54a 54df<**

Good To Talk **2** b c Weldnaas (USA)-Kimble Blue (Blue Refrain) 1652^{8} 2782^{7} 2970^{4} 3231^{6} 3502^{15} 3721^{19} 3937^{12} **>58?f<**

Goodwood Rocket **2** ch c Midyan (USA)-Feather-in-Her-Cap (Primo Dominie) 1246^{3} 1592^{5} 2200^{6} 3289^{5} 3613^{3} 3928^{2} **>71f<**

Goody Four Shoes **7** gr m Blazing Saddles (AUS)-Bronzamer (Saritamer (USA)) 780^{16} 1255^{6} 1499^{12} 1676^{13} **>46f<**

Googly **6** ch m Sunley Builds-Cheri Berry (Air Trooper) 432^{6} **>86f<**

Goonda **3** b f Darshaan-Grimpola (GER) (Windwurf (GER)) (1916) 2411^{2} 3926^{18} **>85f<**

Goram's Girl (IRE) **3** b f Taufan (USA)-Blue Bell Lady (Dunphy) 1155^{6} 1422^{7} 1688^{7} **>34f<**

Goretski (IRE) **2** b c Polish Patriot (USA)-Celestial Path (Godswalk (USA)) 533^{7} 2619^{7} (2951) 3132^{4} 3568^{5} 3824^{11} 4097^{9} **>66f<**

Gorinsky (IRE) **7** ch h Gorytus (USA)-Grapette (Nebbiolo) 685^{3} 1106^{11} 1248^{5} 1756^{2} 2418^{4} 2665^{3} 2935^{13} **>93df<**

Gorodenka Boy **5** ch h Then Again-Simply Jane *1566^{11}* 2952^{7} **>33a 33df<**

Go South **11** b g Thatching-Run To The Sun (Run The Gantlet (USA)) 795^{17} **>26f<**

Gospel Song **3** ch c King Among Kings-Market Blues (Porto Bello) 593^{5} 876^{9} 969^{3} (1028) (1180) 1251^{4} 1744^{3} 2123^{5} 2476^{6} 2770^{9} 2856^{3} 3002^{5} **>24a 73f<**

Gothenberg (IRE) **2** b c Polish Patriot (USA)-Be Discreet (Junius (USA)) 878^{3} (1024) (1267) (1608) 1838^{10} 3163^{4} 4084^{11} **>92f<**

Gotla Bird **2** b f Petong-Addison's Jubilee (Sparkler) 3648^{4} 3892^{14} *4269^{W}* **>51f<**

Go Too Moor (IRE) **2** b g Posen (USA)-Gulistan 4239^{10} **>53f<**

Governor George (USA) **4** b c Secreto (USA)-Sheena Native (USA) (Qui Native (USA)) (665) 1851^{30} **>110f<**

Governors Dream **2** b f Governor General-Friendly Miss 1779^{7} 3891^{9} 3998^{F} 4237^{5} **>25f<**

Governors Fortune **3** b g Governor General-Fortune's Fancy (Workboy) 3712^{19} 3847^{10} 4055^{8}

Governor's Lass **3** b f Governor General-Belle Tower (Tower Walk) *381^{7}* 482^{12} 581^{6} 732^{9} **>42a 43f<**

Go With The Wind **2** b c Unfuwain (USA)-Cominna (Dominion) 3592^{13} 3868^{15} **>63f<**

Grace Card **9** b g Ela-Mana-Mou-Val de Grace (FR) 840^{4} **>56f<**

Graceful Lady **5** br m Bold Arrangement-Northern Lady

3115^{4} 3428^{6} 3649^{11} **>39f<**

Gracie Allen (USA) **2** b f Allen's Prospect-Beseech 4175a^{3}

Gracious Gretclo **2** gr f Common Grounds-Gratclo (Belfort (FR)) 650^{3} 852^{8} 2985^{5} 3740^{2} **>67f<**

Granache (IRE) **6** br h Rousillon (USA)-Mpani (Habitat) (798a) 2385a^{2}

Granby Bell **4** b c Ballacashtal (CAN)-Betbellof 545^{9} 763^{14} 4051^{2} 4333^{15} **>60f<**

Grand Applause (IRE) **5** gr h Mazaad-Standing Ovation (Godswalk (USA)) *2293^{10}* 2490^{8} 2569^{9} 3521^{4} 3710^{3} 3818^{7} 4022^{4} **>62a 54f<**

Grand Chapeau (IRE) **3** b c Ballad Rock-All Hat (Double Form) 1094^{10} 1411^{13} 1750^{4} 2267^{2} 2513^{2} (2793) 3771^{17} 4057^{18} 4165^{12} **>64f<**

Grand du Lac (USA) **3** ch c Lac Ouimet (USA)-Vast Domain (CAN) (Vice Regent (CAN)) 1927^{2} (2553) **>93f<**

Grandee **4** b c Aragon-Bourbon Queen (Ile de Bourbon (USA)) *82^{6} 150^{9}* **>42a f<**

Grandes Oreilles (IRE) **3** b f Nordico (USA)-Top Knot (High Top) 764^{16} 1200^{5} 1674^{8} *2636^{4}* **>53a 67f<**

Grandinare (USA) **3** b or br c El Gran Senor (USA)-Hail The Lady (USA) (Hail the Pirates (USA)) 1976^{4} 2409^{8} 3066^{13} **>90f<**

Grand Salt (IRE) **4** b c Salt Dome (USA)-Fifty Grand (Ballad Rock) 454^{6} 545^{13} 1548^{6} 1745^{16} 2450^{17} 2789^{14} 3515^{13} **>22f<**

Grand Selection (IRE) **3** b c Cricket Ball (USA)-Sine Labe (USA) (Vaguely Noble) *(47) 116^{2} (141) (263) (309) 324^{3}* (1322) 1478^{2} 1589^{2} (2062) 2691^{3} 3066^{2} 3156^{3} 3659^{9} **>81+a 89f<**

Grand Time **6** ch h Clantime-Panay (Arch Sculptor) *244^{7}* 507^{6} 656^{2} 726^{6} 1199^{6} 1257^{8} *1566^{8}* 3116^{11} **>43da 34f<**

Granmas Delight **4** b f Hadeer-Miss Caro Star (Rusticaro (FR)) 3250^{4} 3467^{17} 3678^{5} **>53a 31f<**

Granny's Legacy **3** b f Most Welcome-Historical Fact (Reform) 773^{11} *893^{9}* 1252^{8} 1581^{8} **>25a 41f<**

Gransvelt (IRE) **2** b c Contract Law-Jumana (Windjammer) 1391a^{3}

Grappolo **3** ch c Sharpo-Number One Lady (Shernaza 2895a^{3} **>97f<**

Grappolo (GER) **3** c 3910a^{8} **>88f<**

Grate British (IRE) **3** b c Astronef-Stapelea (FR) (Faraway Son (USA)) 538^{9} 774^{8} 989^{4} 1269^{6} 3464^{6} 3759^{13} 3935^{13} **>54f<**

Great Bear **3** ch c Dominion-Bay Bay (Bay Express) 1138^{6} 1370^{4} 1613^{5} 2766^{8} 3750^{19} **>88f<**

Great Bond **4** b g Cree Song-May Bond (Good Bond) *92^{7}* **>41a f<**

Great Crusader **3** ch c Deploy-Shannon Princess 711^{8} 917^{3} 1099^{5} 1852^{5} 2366^{3} 2575^{3} 3142^{4} 3817^{16} **>98f<**

Great Deeds **4** b f Forzando-Deed (Derring Do) 1572a^{7} 2285^{10} **>112f<**

Great Easeby (IRE) **5** ch g Caerleon (USA)-Kasala (USA) (Blushing Groom (FR)) 1600^{8} 1878^{3} 1948^{3} 3936^{14} **>66f<**

Greatest **4** b c Superlative-Pillowing (Good Times (ITY)) *160^{5} 307^{6} 358^{3} (401)* 450^{15} 882^{2} (1426) 2187^{2} 2510^{2} 3611^{24} 3757^{19} 3984^{13} 4171^{13} **>73a 78df<**

Greatest Hopes **4** ch c Aragon-Singora (Blue Cashmere) *41^{8} 100^{9} 203^{4} 330^{11}* **>32a 38f<**

Great Expectations (FR) **4** ch g Village Star (FR)-Balnica (FR) (Nice Havrais (USA)) 764^{21} 1256^{4} 1439^{5} 1695^{7} **>61f<**

Great Hall **6** gr h Hallgate-Lily of France (Monsanto (FR)) *56^{9}* 450^{5} 486^{2} 567^{4} 887^{10} 972^{6} 1070^{9} 1354^{13} 1541^{6} 1676^{5} 1975^{4} 2108^{3} (2137) 2533^{7} 2652^{9} 2758^{8} (3065) 3175^{2} 3293^{14} 3534^{19} 3629^{6} 3751^{15} 3874^{14} 4053^{8} **>29a 56f<**

Great Inquest **3** b f Shernazar-Old Domesday Book (High Top) (1186) 1588^{9} 2240^{11} **>85f<**

Great Intent **2** gr f Aragon-Silver Berry 1790^{6} **>46f<**

Great Marquess **8** b h Touching Wood (USA)-Fruition (Rheingold) 1898^{3} **>86f<**

Great Oration (IRE) **6** b or br h Simply Great (FR)-Spun Gold (Thatch (USA)) 1435^{6} 2545^{3} 2734^{2} (3114) 4166^{4} 4288^{14} **>54f<**

Great Simplicity **8** ch g Simply Great (FR)-Affaire D'Amour (Tudor Music) 3898^{11} **>15f<**

Great Tern **3** b f Simply Great (FR)-La Neva (FR) (Arctic Tern (USA)) 1053^{6} 2449^{4} 2676^{6} **>58f<**

Grecian Dart (IRE) **3** b c Darshaan-Grecian Urn (Ela-Mana-Mou) (3580a)

Grecian Garden **4** b f Sharrood (USA)-Greek Goddess (Young Generation) 541^{13} *1032^{13}* **>37da 23f<**

Grecian Lady (IRE) **6** b m Be My Guest (USA)-Grecian Sky (African Sky) *96^{13}* **>26a f<**

Greek Gold (IRE) **6** b h Rainbow Quest (USA)-Gay Hellene (Ela-Mana-Mou) *(29) 91^{7} 120^{3} 155^{2} 175^{2} 222^{7} 296^{5} 520^{14}* 568^{15} 672^{19} 1037^{8} 1191^{4} 1285^{15} 3825^{16} 4110^{4} 4196^{7} *4335^{10}* **>64da 56f<**

Greek Icon **2** b f Thatching-Rosie Potts (Shareef Danc 1111a^{3} (3231) (3590a) 3942^{4} 4200^{3} **>84f<**

Greek Night Out (IRE) **4** b f Ela-Mana-Mou-Ce Soir (Northern Baby (CAN)) *34^{2} 120^{7} 235^{6}* 526^{9} 672^{11} 1149^{5} *1332^{9}* 1523^{8} 1647^{6} *2291^{8} 3513^{3}* (3724) 3971^{3} 4140^{3} *4336^{3}* **>46a 50f<**

Greenacres Lady **5** b m Seymour Hicks (FR)-Moon Lady (Cash And Courage) *2920^{6}* **>22a f<**

Greenacres Star **5** ch m Seymour Hicks (FR)-Greenacres Girl (Tycoon II) *79^{6} 183^{2} 280^{3}* **>51a 58f<**

Green Apache **3** b c Green Desert (USA)-Can Can Girl (Gay Fandango (USA)) 853^{20} 1257^{12} 2137^{10} 2843^{2} **>25f<**

Greenback (BEL) **4** b g Absalom-Batalya (BEL) (Boulou) 2007^{15} **>78a 63f<**

Green Barries **2** b c Green Desert (USA)-Barari (USA) (Blushing Groom (FR)) 3647^{11} 4109^{2} 4314^{2} **>94f<**

Green Bentley (IRE) **2** b f Green Desert (USA)-Lady Bentley (Bellypha) 669^{7} 1536^{3} 2515^{4} 2911^{2} 3090^{2} 3639^{2} 3948^{6} **>75f<**

Green Bopper (USA) **2** b c Green Dancer (USA)-Wayage (USA) (Mr Prospector (USA)) 3900^{10} **>68f<**

Green Charter **2** b f Green Desert (USA)-By Charter (Shirley Heights) 3539^{4} 3763^{9} (4085) **>79f<**

Green City **3** br f Rock City-Pea Green (Try My Best (USA)) 1222^{7} 1335^{8} 1673^{11} 2602^{8} 4035^{21} *4217^{14}* **>8a 74f<**

Green Crusader **4** b c Green Desert (USA)-Hysterical (High Top) 1188^{6} 1753^{5} 2241^{16} 3611^{16} 3729^{16} 4031^{9} **>86df<**

Green Divot **4** b f Green Desert (USA)-Cut Ahead (Kalaglow) 3762^{9} 4027^{6} 4245^{9} **>52f<**

Green Dollar **12** b h Tickled Pink-Burglars Girl 3341^{8}

681[14] 3751[17] >**53f**<

Greenfinch (CAN) **4** gr c Green Dancer (USA)-Princess Verna (USA) (Al Hattab (USA)) 721[6] 2186[8] >**48df**<

Green Gem (BEL) **2** b f Pharly (FR)-Batalya (BEL) (Boulou) 4282[6] >**51f**<

Green Golightly (USA) **4** b c Green Dancer (USA)-Polly Daniels (USA) (Clever Trick (USA)) 1411[15] 1614[P] 2013[5] 2288[12] 2533[11] 2764[19] 2909[8] 3065[10] 3333[5] 3615[25] 3677[16] 3751[8] 3920[20] 4060[16] >**47f**<

Green Green Desert (FR) **4** b c Green Desert (USA)-Green Leaf (USA) (Alydar (USA)) 794[4] 1408[4] 2111[2] 2593[3] 2910[2] 3380[3] 3754[3] >**104f**<

Green Green Ruby **3** b c Green Ruby (USA)-Celtic Bird (Celtic Cone) *263[11]* 521[19] 1012[5] 1381[6] 1519[8] 1974[14] 2535[5] >**35da 51f**<

Green Land (BEL) **3** b f Hero's Honor (USA)-Heavy Land (FR) (Recitation (USA)) 538[11] 908[2] (1219) (1372) 1529[3] 3634[9] (4086) 4189[7] 4289[2] >**75f**<

Green Perfume (USA) **3** b c Naevus (USA)-Pretty Is (USA) (Doonesbury (USA)) 920[11] 1613[2] 2646[6] 3067[6] 3446[9] 3602[9] 4160[4] >**106f**<

Green's Bid **5** gr h Siberian Express (USA)-Arianna Aldini (Habitat) *6[6]* *65[6]* *93[11]* *233[8]* *393[3]* *(402)* *472[6]* 820[10] *1088[15]* 1151[8] *1331[7]* 1456[2] 1809[7] 1843[2] (2021) 2358[9] *3529[15]* >**62a 64df**<

Green Seed (IRE) **3** b f Lead on Time (USA)-Lady In Green (Shareef Dancer (USA)) 1172[5] 1362[3] 1845[2] 2468[6] 3552[3] >**84f**<

Green's le Sidaner (USA) **7** b g Ziggy's Boy (USA)-Matriarchal (USA) (Pronto (ARG)) (1228a)

Green's Moillon (USA) **7** b m Hagley (USA)-My Mademoiselle (USA) (Buckaroo (USA)) 4196[W]

Greenspan (IRE) **3** b c Be My Guest (USA)-Prima Ballerina (FR) (Nonoalco (USA)) 1103[6] 1524[7] 2559a[S] 3730[19] 3820[8] 3935[5] >**78f**<

Green's Seago (USA) **7** ch h Fighting Fit (USA)-Ornamental (USA) (Triple Crown (USA)) 2280[10] 2854[7] >**27a 53f**<

Green's Wootton (USA) **3** b c Local Talent (USA)-Home Thoughts (USA) (Tom Rolfe) 1388a[2] >**65a 73f**<

Green Tune (USA) **4** ch c Green Dancer (USA)-Soundings (USA) (Mr Prospector (USA)) 607a[4] (1002a) (1394a) 3199a[5] 3589a[7] >**129f**<

Greenway Lady **3** ch f Prince Daniel (USA)-Lady Ector (USA) (King Pellinore (USA)) 2884[5] 3438[9] 3635[8] 3818[15] >**59f**<

Greenwich Again **3** b c Exodal (USA)-What a Challenge (Sallust) *333[3]* *(360)* 618[8] (1052) 1165[5] 1517[7] 2405[3] 2537[6] 3497[14] >**77a 69df**<

Gresham Flyer **2** b c Clantime-Eleanor Cross (Kala Shikari) 2221[8] 3093[7] 3432[16] 4244[10] >**12f**<

Grey Again **3** gr f Unfuwain (USA)-Grey Goddess (Godswalk (USA)) *395[3]* *528[2]* 724[7] 1060[3] 1218[6] *1457[4]* 1603[2] 2451[2] 2679[5] 2974[7] *3510[8]* 3534[20] >**58a 61f**<

Grey Blade **3** gr f Dashing Blade-High Matinee (Shirley Heights) 797[12] 1128[9] 1442[6] 1970[12] >**65f**<

Grey Charmer (IRE) **6** gr h Alzao (USA)-Sashi Woo (Rusticaro (FR)) 507[2] 656[4] 887[12] 1411[6] 1673[6] 1832[14] *2383[4]* *2925[2]* >**56a 55f**<

Greycoat Boy **3** br c Pragmatic-Sirdar Girl (Milford) 635[15] 857[8] 947[4] 1289[2] 1379[8] 2550[3] 3470[3] 3669[12] (3849) 4026[2] 4158[6] >**79f**<

Grey Galava **2** gr f Generous (IRE)-Galava (CAN) (Graustark) 2083[4] 2464[5] >**57f**<

Grey Kingdom **4** gr c Grey Desire-Miss Realm (Realm) *228[9]* 2484[13] >**31f**<

Grey Legend **2** gr c Touch of Grey-Northwold Star (USA) (Monteverdi) 2091[5] 2340[3] 2801[3] 3012[8] 3749[11] >**71f**<

Grey Shot **3** gr g Sharrood (USA)-Optaria (Song) 536[4] 711[6] 1170[3] 1281[2] 1672[2] 1852[6] (2366) 3142[2] (3547) (4011a) >**118f**<

Grey Toppa **4** gr f Belfort (FR)-Gallic Law *55[10]* *140[5]* *233[9]* *338[7]* 567[9] 734[7] *892[4]* 1042[6] 1456[7] 1499[18] *1763[3]* 1963[12] *2074[4]* 2364[6] *2627[9]* 2784[8] *2923[6]* 3344[13] >**46da 65df**<

Griffin's Girl **3** ch f Bairn (USA)-All That Crack *98[6]* *236[6]* 521[4] >**21a 31f**<

Grimstone Girl **2** b f Lochnager-Estefan (Taufan (USA)) 1035[3] 1266[4] 1503[7] 1590[10] 2185[10] *2382[9]* 2735[3] >**27a 45f**<

Grioun (FR) **4** b f Kaldoun (FR)-Griotte (USA) (Sir Ivor) 896a[2] 1239a[6] >**109f**<

Grooms Gold (IRE) **3** ch c Groom Dancer (USA)-Gortynia (FR) (My Swallow) 1736[9] 2139[11] (2356) 2546[7] 3237[7] 4047[16] >**73f**<

Ground Game **2** b f Gildoran-Running Game (Run The Gantlet (USA)) 4100[3] *(4338)*

Gryada **2** b f Shirley Heights-Grimpola (GER) (Windwurf (GER)) 1964[2] (2173) 2886[2] 3561[6] (3842) 4180a[3] >**89f**<

Guado d'Annibale (IRE) **6** ch h Glint of Gold-When Lit (Northfields (USA)) 1392a[3] 1890a[7] (2388a) >**114f**<

Guards Brigade **4** b g Bustino-Light Duty *2711[3]* 432[9] 556[5] 661[14] 879[6] 1025[3] 1160[6] 1437[6] >**30a 65f**<

Guardsman (IRE) **3** ch c Pennine Walk-Peace Princess (On Your Mark) *4271[8]* >**9a 51f**<

Guesstimation (USA) **6** b h Known Fact (USA)-Best Guess (USA) (Apalachee (USA)) 578[3] 672[5] (1404) 1509[3] (1873) 2744[4] (3108) 3443[3] 3638[2] 3757[4] (3863) 4038[5] 4079[13] 4229[4] 4284[3] >**51a 74f**<

Guest Alliance (IRE) **3** ch c Zaffaran (USA)-Alhargah (Be My Guest (USA)) 1273[5] 1534[11] *1939[5]* 2536[3] 2830[2] 3288[7] 3862[6] 3958[3] >**52a 70f**<

Gulf Bay **3** b f Reprimand-Miss Butterfield (Cure The Blues (USA)) *310[4]* 651[11] 1083[9] 1350[11] 1733[2] 1917[2] 2089[6] 2353[2] *2636[3]* 3099[9] >**37a 44f**<

Gulf of Siam **2** ch c Prince Sabo-Jussoli (Don) 2453[4] 3671[3] 3996[5] >**69f**<

Gulf Shaadi **3** b c Shaadi (USA)-Ela Meem (USA) (Kris) *(60)* *(170)* *250[3]* *301[3]* *(382)* *(405)* 563[6] 848[6] *1030[2]* *(1330)* 1589[10] 1748[4] *1951[4]* 3823[15] 3980[17] 4227[12] >**87a 62f**<

Gumair (USA) **2** ch c Summer Squall (USA)-Finisterre (AUS) (Biscay (AUS)) 2320[12] 3141[5] 3280[5] 3546[6] >**71f**<

Gun Ballad (IRE) **2** b f Ballad Rock-Machine Gun (Manado) 2725a[3] >**47f**<

Gunboat Diplomacy (FR) **4** b c Dominion-Singapore Girl (FR) (Lyphard (USA)) (3792a) 4014a[8] >**124f**<

Gunmaker **6** ch g Gunner B-Lucky Starkist (Lucky Wednesday) *234[9]* *304[7]* *1210[2]* *1567[4]* 1970[8] *2495[5]* >**41a 37f**<

Gunner B Special **2** ch g Gunner B-Sola Mia (Tolomeo) 3463[14] 3620[20] *4339[11]* >**46a 16f**<

Gunnerdale **3** b f Gunner B-Melody Moon 1085[7] 1431[5] 1846[9] >**37f**<

Gushy 9 ch h Hard Fought-Be Gustful 2713[9] 2986[6] **>15f<**
Guymichelle (IRE) 3 b f Midyan (USA)-Hemline (Sharpo) *316[9] 409[8]* **>14a f<**
Gwernymynydd 4 b f Dreams to Reality (USA)-My Valentine Card (USA) (Forli (ARG)) *1209[13]* **>27a 25f<**
Gwespyr 2 ch c Sharpo-Boozy (Absalom) 424[5] (561) 683[4] 1584[5] 2474[3] **>78tf<**
Gymcrak Diamond (IRE) 5 b g Taufan (USA)-Down The Line (Brigadier Gerard) *771[13]* 1682[3] 3052[2] **>43a 58f<**
Gymcrak Flyer 4 b f Aragon-Intellect (Frimley Park) 785[12] 1626[11] 1995[11] 2358[5] (2853) 3128[2] 3393[4] (3493) 3629[2] 3837[12] **>54a 72f<**
Gymcrak Gem (IRE) 2 b f Don't Forget Me-Santa Patricia (IRE) (Taufan (USA)) 3231[8] 3648[2] **>62f<**
Gymcrak Hero (IRE) 3 b g Taufan (USA)-Jamie's Girl (Captain James) 3537[11] 3762[5] 3977[16] **>66f<**
Gymcrak Jareer (IRE) 3 b g Jareer (USA)-Katzarah (IRE) (Pharly (FR)) 1683[3] 2255[4] 2915[4] 3370[12] **>55f<**
Gymcrak Premiere 7 ch h Primo Dominie-Oraston (Morston (FR)) 665[5] 1143[10] 1617[6] 1851[24] 2235[4] 2647[3] 2948[6] (3085) 3411[7] 3813[5] 3924[3] **>99f<**
Gymcrak Tiger (IRE) 5 b g Colmore Row-Gossip 2222[10] **>60f<**
Gymcrak Tycoon 6 b h Last Tycoon-Brazen Faced 1043[8] 1434[10] 1996[7] 2252[8] 2502[5] 3123[7] 3293[2] 3442[8] **>47f<**
Gympie 2 b c Rainbow Quest (USA)-Sunshine Coast (Posse (USA)) 1485[9] 4188[14] **>58f<**
Gypsy Love (USA) 3 b f Woodman (USA)-Pixie Erin (Golden Fleece (USA)) 1172[4] 1344[10] 2707[6] **>70f<**

H

Habeta (USA) 9 ch h Habitat-Prise 820[13] 909[4] 1205[5] (1724) 2276[7] 2375[2] 2999[2] **>49f<**
Hacketts Cross (IRE) 7 b g Rusticaro (FR)-Anglesea Market 2514[8] 3024[4] 3470[11] **>51f<**
Hadabet 3 b g Hadeer-Betsy Bay (FR) (Bellypha) 1097[14] 1372[8] 1776[4] 2138[2] (2282) 2296[3] 2657[5] 2747[3] (2980) 3154[7] 3501[6] 3634[8] **>74f<**
Hadadabble 2 ch f Hadeer-Magnifica (Sandy Creek) 1318[10] 4224[7] 4330[7] **>42f<**
Haddeyah (USA) 3 b or br f Dayjur (USA)-Albadeeah (USA) (Nashua) 2470[6] 3028[12] **>77f<**
Hadeel 3 ch f Polish Precedent (USA)-Nafhaat (USA) (Roberto (USA)) (2393) (3031) 3408[3] **>90f<**
Hadeyya Ramzeyah 3 b g Reference Point-Token Gift (USA) (Lyphard (USA)) 1308[2] (1755) **>87f<**
Hadi (IRE) 4 b c Robellino (USA)-Java Jive (Hotfoot) 3745[10] **>21f<**
Hagwah (USA) 3 b f Dancing Brave (USA)-Saraa-Ree (USA) (Caro) 816[2] 1172[2] 1473[2] (2341) (2614) 3831[6] 4204[8] **>102f<**
Haido'hart 3 b g Pharly (FR)-Try Vickers (USA) (Fuzzbuster (USA)) 3805[10] **>20f<**
Hakika (USA) 3 b f Elmaamul (USA)-Balastra (USA) (Fappiano (USA)) 1085[2] 1417[2] (1680) (2253) 2468[3] 3368[13] 3659[7] 4083[3] **>93f<**
Hakiki (IRE) 3 b c Ballad Rock-Salvationist (Mill Reef (USA)) 435[3] (585) 939[2] 1487[13] 2507[3] 3615[6] 3964[19] **>87f<**
Hala Halina 3 gr f Old Vic-Integrity 1526[13] 1736[10] 2790[11] **>50f<**
Halbert 6 b h Song-Stoneydale (Tickled Pink) *358[6] 520[16] 603[8]* 726[7] 887[9] 972[8] 1164[5] 1321[5] 1559[3] (1721) 1900[2] 2048[3] (2124) 2163[3] 2338[5] 2463[9] (3250) 3407[5] 3632[2] 3748[7] 3822[2] 3919[9] 3961[7] **>44a 74f<**
Halebid 2 b c Dowsing (USA)-Pink Robber (USA) (No Robbery) 4063[6] 4241[6] **>72f<**
Halfabob (IRE) 3 ch g Broken Hearted-Hasten (Northfields (USA)) *844[5] 1761[6]* 1931[3] *4128[11] 4271[9]* **>16a 69f<**
Half An Inch (IRE) 2 gr c Petoski-Inch 1977[17] 2340[4] 2839[2] 3427[3] 3612[5] 3858[2] 4025[7] **>73df<**
Half Tone 3 gr c Touch of Grey-Demilinga (Nishapour (FR)) *(42)* 580[4] *629[2]* 887[3] 1050[5] 1199[2] 1265[3] 1483[3] 1750[5] 3055[12] 3139[5] 3251[5] 3442[15] 3919[3] **>60a 44f<**
Hal Hoo Yaroom 2 b c Belmez (USA)-Princess Nawaal (USA) (Seattle Slew (USA)) 3089[10] 3989[7] 4226[7] **>68f<**
Halkopous 9 b h Beldale Flutter (USA)-Salamina (Welsh Pageant) 1109[5] 1300[5] **>93f<**
Halleluja Time 3 b g Risk Me (FR)-Warm Wind (Tumble Wind (USA)) 1263[9] 1538[7] **>36f<**
Halliard 4 b c Hallgate-Princess Blanco *247[7] (299)* 452[7] 583[5] (656) 726[3] 1257[5] 1595[9] 1832[13] 2247[4] 2686[5] 4057[5] *4295[7]* **>60a 57f<**
Hallikeld 2 ch f Bustino-Spring Sparkle (Lord Gayle (USA)) 3827[8] 4277[11] **>51f<**
Halling (USA) 4 ch c Diesis-Dance Machine (Green Dancer (USA)) (2286) (3143) *4308a[11]* **>62a 130+f<**
Halls Burn 7 b g Beverley Boy-Wintersgame (Game Warden) 1355[16] 1688[5] 1902[6] 2306[8] 2401[5] 2733[11] **>30f<**
Halmanerror 5 gr h Lochnager-Counter Coup (Busted) 486[11] 749[14] 1344[7] 1668[2] 1809[10] (2130) 2455[5] (3112) 3411[3] 3943[25] 4041[9] 4319[20] **>73f<**
Hal's Pal 2 br c Caerleon (USA)-Refinancing (USA) (Forli (ARG)) 3340[4] 3663[2] **>80f<**
Hamilton Gold 2 ch f Safawan-Golden Della (Glint of Gold) 1722[5]
Hamilton Silk 3 b c K-Battery-Silver's Girl (Sweet Monday) 492[4] (596) 774[10] 909[10] 3843[4] 3935[8] **>57f<**
Hamlet (IRE) 2 b c Danehill (USA)-Blasted Heath 3340[7] 3663[7] 3865[18] **>73f<**
Hammerstein 2 b c Kris-Musical Bliss (USA) (The Minstrel (CAN)) 2573[4] 3141[2] 3812[4] **>89f<**
Ham N'Eggs 4 b c Robellino (USA)-Rose And The Ring 1225[2] 1851[20] 2598[6] 3085[9] 3348[6] **>94f<**
Hamsaat (IRE) 3 b f Sadler's Wells (USA)-Steel Habit (Habitat) (1615) **>88+f<**
Hanbitooh (USA) 2 b c Hansel (USA)-Bitooh 4239[9] **>53f<**
Hancock 3 b c Jester-Fresh Line (High Line) 1581[9] **>33f<**
Hand Craft (IRE) 3 b g Dancing Dissident (USA)-Fair Flutter (Beldale Flutter (USA)) *(322)* 2362[3] (2654) (3101) **>81+a 89f<**
Handmaiden 5 gr m Shardari-Flyaway Bride (USA) (Blushing Groom (FR)) *53[3] (352)* 1858[7] *3245[12] 4336[14]* **>64a 34f<**
Hand of Straw (IRE) 3 b g Thatching-Call Me Miss (Hello Gorgeous (USA)) 1309[5] 1533[6] 1947[4] 2499[2] 3493[10] 3704[13] 3980[10] **>71df<**
Handsome Squaw 3 ch f Handsome Sailor-Brave

Squaw (High Top) 1296^{11} 1522^{W} 1846^{7} 4232^{10} **>27f<**

Handson **3** ch g Out of Hand-My Home (Homing) *282^{4} 362^{6}* 2151^{5} 2546^{14} **>20?a 45f<**

Hand Woven **3** b g Rambo Dancer (CAN)-Lifestyle (Jimmy Reppin) *362^{2}* (2623) 2770^{2} 2822^{3} 3469^{9} 3646^{2} 3899^{10} (4283) **>56a 84f<**

H'Ani **3** b f Woodman (USA)-African Dance (USA) 1065^{10} 1326^{4} 3685^{8} 3860^{2} 4044^{10} *4335^{4}* **>51a 65f<**

Hanifa **3** ch f Master Willie-Antoinette Jane (Ile de Bourbon (USA)) 942^{7} 1097^{12} 1960^{2} 2262^{2} 2841^{3} **>60f<**

Haniya (IRE) **3** ch f Caerleon (USA)-Harmless Albatross 816^{3} (1182) 2014^{2} 2555^{3} 3801^{4} 4036^{11} **>92f<**

Hank-a-chief **2** b c Inca Chief (USA)-Be Sharp (Sharpen Up) 1977^{6} 3888^{9} 3989^{13} **>53f<**

Hannahs Bay **2** b f Buzzards Bay-Hi-Hannah (Red Sunset) 3468^{11} 3975^{13} *4339^{9}* **>48a 34f<**

Hannah's Usher **3** b g Marching On-La Pepper (Workboy) *40^{2} 74^{2} (284)* 1450^{9} 1876^{6} 2973^{3} 3622^{12} **>83a 64f<**

Happy Boy **2** ch c Time For A Change-Happy Gini (Ginistrelli) (2892a) 3584a^{5} **>99f<**

Happy Brave **3** b g Daring March-Fille de Phaeton *105^{8} 176^{7} 310^{3} 394^{6} 830^{7}* 2318^{9} 2522^{4} 3177^{11} **>44a 48f<**

Happy Hostage **4** b c Beveled (USA)-Run Amber Run (Run The Gantlet (USA)) 3871^{12} 4062^{14} **>62f<**

Happy Partner (IRE) **2** b c Nabeel Dancer (USA)-Dublah (USA) (Private Account (USA)) 2354^{3} 3300^{2} **>52f<**

Happy Taipan (IRE) **2** b c Keen-Eastern View (IRE) (Persian Bold) 3266^{6} **>58f<**

Happy Tycoon (IRE) **2** br c Polish Patriot (USA)-Art Age (Artaius (USA)) (1203) 1893^{13} 2442^{15} **>60+f<**

Harayir (USA) **3** b f Gulch (USA)-Saffaanh (USA) (Shareef Dancer (USA)) 667^{2} (933) 1390a^{5} 1850^{3} 2349^{3} (3067) (3360) 3834^{4} (4078) **>124f<**

Harbour Dues **2** b c Slip Anchor-Quillotern (USA) (Arctic Tern (USA)) 4070^{4} 4210^{4} **>65f<**

Harbour Island **3** b c Rainbow Quest (USA)-Quay Line (High Line) 1175^{8} (3896) 4191^{2} **>82f<**

Hardenfast **2** ch f Clantime-Croft Original (Crofthall) 2869^{5}

Harding **4** b c Dowsing (USA)-Orange Hill (High Top) 4229^{12} **>73f<**

Harding Brown (USA) **3** ch g Strawberry Road (AUS)-Chrysilia (USA) (Tilt Up (USA)) 854^{10} 942^{9} 1382^{11} 1518^{8} 2089^{2} 2687^{6} 2812^{2} (3140) 3263^{6} **>61f<**

Hard Love **3** b f Rambo Dancer (CAN)-Djimbaran Bay 547^{12} 783^{4} (1442) 2209^{4} 2719^{2} *3076^{3}* 3254^{4} 3658^{2} **>68a 69f<**

Hard News (USA) **2** b c Lyphard (USA)-Social Column (USA) 3888^{7} **>47f<**

Hard to Figure **9** gr h Telsmoss-Count On Me (No Mercy) 441^{4} 659^{5} 870^{23} 1100^{12} (2443) 2764^{13} 3342^{5} 3551^{8} 3717^{6} **>117f<**

Hard to Get **8** b h Rousillon (USA)-Elusive (Little Current (USA)) 2078^{9} **>9f<**

Hard Try **3** ro c Sharrood (USA)-Trynova (Tyrnavos) *168^{3}* 477^{3} *592^{2}* 786^{4} *1881^{8} 2960^{7}* **>63a 62f<**

Hardy Dancer **3** ch c Pharly (FR)-Handy Dancer (Green God) (813) (962) 1170^{5} 1589^{3} 1839^{27} 2933^{2} 3214^{4} 3487a^{5} 4202^{7} **>92f<**

Harghar (USA) **2** gr c El Gran Senor (USA)-Harouniya 3586a^{3} 3788a^{5} **>94f<**

Harlech (IRE) **3** b br c Caerleon (USA)-Noble Lily (USA) (Vaguely Noble) 2460^{6} 3448^{2} 3537^{4} 3918^{7} **>77f<**

Harlequin Walk (IRE) **4** ch f Pennine Walk-Taniokey (Grundy) *(245) (329)* 741^{7} **>71a 48df<**

Harlestone Brook **5** ch g Jalmood (USA)-Harlestone Lake (Riboboy (USA)) 632^{9} 998^{2} (1840) 2688^{4} **>103f<**

Haroldon (IRE) **6** ch h Heraldiste (USA)-Cordon (Morston (FR)) *1^{9} 238^{6} 312^{10}* 549^{7} 738^{4} (975) 1324^{2} 1543^{2} 1716^{6} (2138) 2490^{5} 2967^{4} 3156^{5} (3820) 3963^{4} 4201^{18} **>49da 82f<**

Harpoon Louie (USA) **5** b h Eskimo (USA)-Twelfth Pleasure (USA) (Fappiano (USA)) 433^{16} **>83f<**

Harriet's Beau **2** b c Superpower-Pour Moi (Bay Express) 1678^{5} 2221^{5} 2498^{4} 2852^{5} 3430^{8} 3824^{16} **>64f<**

Harrken Heights (IRE) **3** b f Belmez (USA)-In High Spirits (Head for Heights) 1930^{3} 3704^{19} 4289^{14} **>39f<**

Harry Browne (IRE) **3** b g Al Hareb (USA)-Jeewan (Touching Wood (USA)) *(28) (116) 189^{3} 255^{2}* 437^{6} 648^{2} 774^{5} 1083^{5} 1286^{2} 1432^{6} 1643^{7} *1881^{3}* (2327) (2664) (2993) 3367^{2} 3469^{3} 3863^{10} 4000^{2} 4108^{5} **>68a 80f<**

Harry's Coming **11** b g Marching On-Elegant Star 452^{2} 583^{3} (734) 856^{5} 1164^{2} 1483^{10} (1545) 1756^{5} 2112^{4} 2301^{6} 3177^{13} 3424^{8} **>62f<**

Harry's Treat **3** b f Lochnager-Megara (USA) (Thatching) 758^{3} 1296^{9} 1533^{12} 1961^{3} **>57f<**

Harry Welsh (IRE) **3** gr c Treasure Kay-Excelling Miss (USA) (Exceller (USA)) 2151^{3} (2262) *2604^{4}* 2969^{3} 3140^{3} 3425^{5} 3676^{3} 3971^{14} 4248^{4} **>23a 70f<**

Harsh Times **2** ch f Efisio-Larnem (Meldrum) 699^{6} 819^{15} 1841^{6} 2516^{7} *2924^{2} (3528)* 3721^{4} 3975^{6} *4124^{7}* **>52a 56f<**

Hartfields Boy **2** b c Shavian-Fallen Angel (Quiet Fling (USA)) 2791^{13} 3012^{5} 3157^{10} **>40f<**

Harvest Dream **4** b f Primo Dominie-New Pastures (Formidable) 2016^{11}

Harvest Reaper **3** gr c Bairn (USA)-Real Silver (Silly Season) 3638^{7} 4044^{8} 4131^{3} *4274^{4}* **>43a 57f<**

Harvest Rose **6** b m Bairn (USA)-Ragtime Rose (Ragstone) 976^{12} 1811^{11} 2332^{7} 2528^{11} **>51a 57f<**

Harvey White (IRE) **3** b or br c Petorius-Walkyria (Lord Gayle (USA)) 689^{5} 1317^{6} 1788^{5} 2109^{3} 3058^{2} (3403) 3872^{10} 4261^{6} **>70f<**

Hasaid Lady (IRE) **3** b f Shaadi (USA)-Lady Ellen (Horage) 637^{12} 1240^{6} 3023^{6} **>72f<**

Hasta la Vista **5** b h Superlative-Falcon Berry (FR) (Bustino) *589^{5} 771^{10} 2379^{12}* 3102^{3} (3229) 3505^{8} 3723^{3} 4000^{5} 4101^{3} *4336^{10}* **>67da 55f<**

Hasten to Add (USA) **5** gr h Cozzene (USA)-Beau Cougar (USA) (Cougar (CHI)) 4185a^{3} **>118f<**

Hattaafeh (IRE) **4** b f Mtoto-Monongelia (Welsh Pageant) *(84) 221^{2} 374^{10} 422^{3}* 545^{3} *771^{3}* 4061^{8} 4259^{13} **>68a 60f<**

Hatta Breeze **3** b f Night Shift (USA)-Jouvencelle (Rusticaro (FR)) 950^{3} 1346^{5} 1983^{3} 2339^{7} 2969^{4} *(3514)* 3664^{3} (4043) 4249^{7} **>67a 73+f<**

Hatta River (USA) **5** b h Irish River (FR)-Fallacieuse (Habitat) 3127^{6} 3297^{4} 3395^{5} 3646^{15} *3735^{11}* 4062^{5} 4196^{8} **>57f<**

Hatta Sunshine (USA) **5** b h Dixieland Band (USA)-Mountain Sunshine (USA) (Vaguely Noble) *12^{2} 125^{4} (373)*

762^{6} *1049^{3}* 1663^{5} 1940^{4} 2557^{5} 2707^{4} *3082^{12}* 3248^{5} **>53a 50f<**

Haute Cuisine 2 b c Petong-Nevis (Connaught) 996^{5} 1751^{6} **>46f<**

Havana Heights (IRE) 2 ch f Persian Heights-Havana Blade (USA) (Blade (USA)) *1089^{7}* 1282^{6} **>27a 16f<**

Havana Miss 3 b f Cigar-Miss Patdonna (Starch Reduced) *90^{7} 236^{4} 314^{6} 353^{7} 405^{6} 420^{7}* 1199^{8} 1545^{4} 2301^{7} 3750^{8} 3972^{13} 4131^{4} 4225^{9} **>38a 49f<**

Have a Nightcap 6 ch g Night Shift (USA)-Final Orders (USA) (Prince John) *2591^{3} 375^{14}* **>2a f<**

Hawa Al Nasamaat (USA) 3 b c Houston (USA)-Barrera Miss (USA) (Barrera (USA)) 640^{3} 1366^{2} 1639^{11} (1920) 2240^{4} 2737^{6} 3565^{17} 3929^{4} **>87f<**

Hawaash (IRE) 3 b c Royal Academy (USA)-Imperial Jade (Lochnager) (1796) 3599^{3} 3904^{13} 4122^{3} **>99f<**

Hawaii Storm (FR) 7 b h Plugged Nickle (USA)-Slewvindaloo (USA) (Seattle Slew (USA)) *12^{4} 62^{4} 94^{2} 138^{3} 169^{9} 4340^{15}* **>61da 33f<**

Hawanafa 2 b f Tirol-Woodland View (Precipice Wood) 2025^{6} 2579^{7} **>56f<**

Hawker's News (IRE) 4 b c Sadler's Wells (USA)-High Hawk (Shirley Heights) 3923^{5} **>103f<**

Hawkish (USA) 6 b h Silver Hawk (USA)-Dive Royal (USA) (Inverness Drive (USA)) 1064^{4} 1368^{2} 1553^{3} (3531) 3977^{4} 4138^{2} **>41a 62f<**

Hawk's Castle 3 c 1008a^{F}

Hawksley Hill (IRE) 2 ch c Rahy (USA)-Gaijin (Caerleon (USA)) 4098^{W} 4188^{17} 4314^{14} **>56f<**

Hawwam 9 b h Glenstal (USA)-Hone (Sharpen Up) *44^{3} (80) (138) 181^{2} 242^{5} (313) 378^{4}* 493^{3} 642^{2} 873^{18} 1626^{6} *2141^{4}* 2276^{3} 4044^{7} **>77a 59f<**

Hayaain 2 b c Shirley Heights-Littlefield (Bay Express) 3900^{9} 4080^{5} 4226^{8} **>86f<**

Haya Ya Kefaah 3 b c Kefaah (USA)-Hayat (IRE) (Sadler's Wells (USA)) *128^{7} 171^{9} 225^{7} 292^{12}* **>28a f<**

Hay Dance 4 b c Shareef Dancer (USA)-Hay Reef *53^{13} 92^{9} 214^{6}* **>27a 56f<**

Haydon Hill 4 ch f Hadeer-Coppice *46^{6} 96^{12}* **>16a 46f<**

Haysong (IRE) 2 ch f Ballad Rock-Hay Knot (Main Reef) 1341^{5} **>23f<**

Hazard a Guess (IRE) 5 ch h Digamist (USA)-Guess Who (Be My Guest (USA)) 430^{13} 505^{4} (841) (1064) 1303^{7} 1558^{3} 1853^{13} 2241^{5} 2752^{3} 3021^{6} 3801^{5} 3963^{9} **>84f<**

Hazel 3 ro f Risk Me (FR)-Sir Tangs Gift (Runnett) 881^{8} 1258^{7} **>59f<**

Head For Heaven 5 b g Persian Heights-Believer (Blakeney) 848^{18} 1245^{6} 1404^{3} 1688^{2} 2050^{9} 2334^{4} 3108^{11} *3544^{12}* **>7a 62df<**

Head Turner 7 b m My Dad Tom (USA)-Top Tina (High Top) *22^{6} 75^{3} (161) (221) 238^{2} 303^{5} 346^{6} (370)* 545^{4} 661^{9} 741^{3} 795^{6} 2201^{8} 2569^{6} 3986^{4} 4026^{9} 4166^{13} **>60a 49f<**

Heart Broken 5 b m Bustino-Touch My Heart (Steel Heart) 1151^{6} 1434^{4} (1582) 1828^{8} 1996^{2} 2585^{7} *(2923)* **>73a 64f<**

Hear The Music (IRE) 2 ch f Common Grounds-Tap The Line (Tap On Wood) 669^{2} 951^{2} 1137^{4} (2782) 3086^{3} 3668^{6} (3962) 4066^{3} 4200^{4} **>95f<**

Heart Lake 4 ch c Nureyev (USA)-My Darling One (USA) (Exclusive Native (USA)) 805a^{5} (1120a) 2368^{9} **>123f<**

Heath Robinson (IRE) 3 b c In The Wings-Blasted Heath 691^{8} 978^{6} 1173^{5} 1417^{3} 1747^{9} **>83f<**

Heathyards Crusade (IRE) 4 ch c Digamist (USA)-Theda (Mummy's Pet) *75^{8}* **>40da 38f<**

Heathyards Lady (USA) 4 b f Mining (USA)-Dubiously (USA) (Jolie Jo (USA)) *44^{4} 129^{3} 224^{3} 306^{7} 400^{3} 511^{2} 627^{4} (832) 1209^{2}* 3534^{3} (3726) *3952^{3}* 4043^{13} *(4128) (4272)* **>77a 64f<**

Heathyards Magic (IRE) 3 b c Magical Strike (USA)-Idle Gossip (Runnett) *(527)* 980^{11} 1045^{2} 1504^{3} *1952^{4}* 2020^{3} 2333^{7} 3429^{9} **>64a 72f<**

Heathyards Rock 3 br c Rock City-Prudence (Grundy) *(362)* 438^{2} 536^{2} 679^{6} 1018^{5} *1211^{2}* 1619^{7} 2395^{3} *2589^{5}* 3374^{6} 3594^{4} 3864^{7} 3926^{8} 4069^{5} **>87a 86f<**

Heavenly Prize (USA) 4 b f Seeking the Gold (USA)-Oh What a Dance (USA) (Nijinsky (CAN)) *4304a^{2}* **>106a 118f<**

Heavens Above 3 br g Celestial Storm (USA)-Regal Wonder 1219^{12} 1506^{14} 3052^{7} **>50f<**

Heaven Sent (IRE) 2 b f Fayruz-Folle Remont 1833^{8} 2091^{4} 2683^{7} 2940^{7} 3568^{6} **>47f<**

Heboob Alshemaal (IRE) 3 b f Nordico (USA)-Royal Climber 553^{4} 747^{2} 1097^{2} 3935^{3} 4071^{5} **>80f<**

Hedera (USA) 3 ch f Woodman (USA)-Ivrea (Sadler's Wells (USA)) 2205^{3} 2795^{2} 3066^{10} 3261^{3} 3833^{3} **>90f<**

Hedgehog 5 b m Electric-Demderise (Vaigly Great) 1534^{14} 2052^{13} **>9f<**

Hee's a Dancer 3 b g Rambo Dancer (CAN)-Heemee (On Your Mark) 2881^{5} 3099^{7} 3370^{7} **>47f<**

Heighth of Fame 4 b g Shirley Heights-Land of Ivory (USA) (The Minstrel (CAN)) 1501^{3} 1971^{6} **>52f<**

Heights of Love 2 b f Persian Heights-Lets Fall In Love (USA) (Northern Baby (CAN)) 561^{7} 810^{5} 2114^{4} 3848^{9} 3892^{13} **>46f<**

He Knows The Rules 3 b c Tirol-Falls of Lora 485^{4} 691^{13} **>73f<**

Helicon (IRE) 2 b c Nashwan (USA)-Hebba (USA) (Nureyev (USA)) (3868) **>95+f<**

Helios 7 br h Blazing Saddles (AUS)-Mary Sunley (Known Fact (USA)) 1070^{7} 1261^{3} 1593^{3} 2169^{5} 2369^{14} 3011^{5} 3629^{7} 4035^{16} **>73f<**

Hello Hobson's (IRE) 5 b m Fayruz-Castleforbes (Thatching) *297^{8}* 1043^{7} 1582^{2} (1963) 2404^{7} 3179^{5} 3681^{3} 3800^{4} 4115^{17} **>55f<**

Hello Mister 4 b c Efisio-Ginnies Petong (Petong) 665^{21} 1475^{9} 1698^{7} 1795^{7} 1895^{12} 2150^{3} 2285^{9} 3236^{4} 3359^{12} 3446^{3} (3551) 3834^{9} 3931^{10} 4033^{4} 4121^{2} **>83a 107f<**

Hello Peter (IRE) 3 b g Taufan (USA)-Apple Rings (Godswalk (USA)) 1736^{7} 2994^{4} 3635^{5} **>59f<**

Helmsley Palace 6 b m Dominion-Queen Midas (Glint of Gold) *157^{12} 217^{10}* **>12a f<**

Helmsman (USA) 3 b c El Gran Senor (USA)-Sacred Journey (USA) (King's Bishop (USA)) 667^{8} **>102df<**

Hencarlam (IRE) 2 b c Astronef-War Ballad (FR) (Green Dancer (USA)) 3437^{7} 3631^{8} **>56f<**

Henessy (GER) 3 dk c Alkalde-Heavenly Storm (Storm Bir (2728a) **>103f<**

Hennessy (USA) 2 ch c Storm Cat (USA)-Island Song (USA) *4306a^{2}* **>123ta f<**

Henning's Boy 2 3584a^{4} **>87f<**

Henry Cooper 2 b c Distant Relative-Miss Echo (Chief

Singer) 3673^{11}

Henry Koehler 3 b c Hadeer-William's Bird (USA) (Master Willie) 431^{5} 622^{6} 713^{6} 1068^{7} 1736^{3} 1839^{26} **>90f<**

Henry The Fifth 2 b c Village Star (FR)-Microcosme (Golden Fleece (USA)) 2107^{4} 2573^{8} 3776^{2} 4034^{2} (4207) 4318^{4} **>95f<**

Henry the Hawk 4 b g Doulab (USA)-Plum Blossom (USA) (Gallant Romeo (USA)) *78^{8} 305^{7} 353^{8}* 475^{5} 688^{12} 753^{12} 1377^{3} 1419^{3} (1559) 1721^{3} 2162^{2} 2231^{4} 2502^{15} 3098^{3} 3252^{9} 3467^{22} **>39a 54f<**

Henry Weston 3 b c Statoblest-Young Tearaway (Young Generation) 1168^{15} 2491^{14} **>54f<**

Henry Will 11 b g Nicholas Bill-Silver Cygnet 1679^{9} 1873^{16} 2484^{10} 2832^{14} 2972^{15} **>24f<**

Herald Angel (IRE) 2 b f Double Schwartz-Gazettalong (Taufan (USA)) 1348^{7} *1954^{6}* 2204^{7} 3533^{15} 4075^{6} **>7a 59f<**

Here Comes a Star 7 b h Night Shift (USA)-Rapidus 1193^{14} 1376^{3} 1599^{12} 1809^{5} 1918^{4} 2096^{13} 2458^{9} 2585^{4} (2665) 2905^{3} 3051^{4} (3150) 3418^{7} 3597^{13} 3748^{22} 3878^{2} 3992^{3} 4113^{17} **>80f<**

Here Comes Herbie 3 ch g Golden Lahab (USA)-Megan's Move (Move Off) 3431^{8} 4110^{7} 4232^{11} **>45f<**

Here Comes Risky 3 b c Risk Me (FR)-Softly Spoken (Mummy's Pet) 681^{7} 3112^{11} *3319^{8}* 3492^{17} 3638^{4} 3715^{9} 3800^{7} 4131^{2} **>66a 77df<**

Hernando (FR) 5 b h Niniski (USA)-Whakilyric (USA) (Miswaki (USA)) 898a^{5} (3327a) 3690a^{7} 4307a^{5} **>128f<**

Herodian (USA) 2 b br c Housebuster (USA)-Try Something New (USA) (Hail the Pirates (USA)) 4161^{2} **>88+f<**

Heron Island (IRE) 2 b c Shirley Heights-Dalawara (IRE) (Top Ville) (3592) 3925^{4} **>99f<**

Herr Trigger 4 gr c Sharrood (USA)-Four-Legged Friend (Aragon) *11^{4} 276^{2} 445^{2}* (935) (1875) (2068) 3388^{4} **>77a 80f<**

Hershebar 5 ch h Stanford-Sugar Token (Record Token) *129^{12}* **>47a f<**

He's Got Wings (IRE) 2 b c In The Wings-Mariella (Sir Gaylord) 4146^{8} 4226^{11} **>36f<**

He's Special 3 b g Reprimand-Berylou (IRE) (Gorytus (USA)) *316^{7} 372^{9} 468^{8}* 837^{8} **>32a 37f<**

Hethers Footsteps 3 ch g Tout Ensemble-Hethermai (Pee Mai) 854^{12} >33f<

Hever Golf Eagle 2 b c Aragon-Elkie Brooks (Relkino) 3340^{15} 3553^{8} **>49f<**

Hever Golf Express 2 b c Primo Dominie-Everdene (Bustino) 617^{12} 1223^{4} (1399) 1608^{5} 2940^{6} **>78+f<**

Hever Golf Hero 2 b c Robellino (USA)-Sweet Rosina (Sweet Revenge) 2801^{4} 3280^{8} 3865^{30} **>60f<**

Hever Golf Lady 3 b f Dominion-High Run (HOL) (Runnymede) *133^{3} 292^{2} 339^{6} 368^{3} (444) 530^{5}* 654^{5} *(1319)* (1737) 2177^{2} 2854^{2} 3127^{3} *3318^{6}* **>52+a 67f<**

Hever Golf Queen 2 b f Efisio-Blue Jane 2876^{7} 3906a^{8} (3909a) **>68?f<**

Hever Golf Rose 4 b f Efisio-Sweet Rosina (Sweet Revenge) 814^{3} (1119a) 1393a^{4} 1707a^{3} (1891a) (2212a) (2671) 3187^{3} (3484a) (3582a) (3785a) (4012a) *4303a^{8}* **>111a 126f<**

Hever Golf Star 3 b c Efisio-Truly Bold (Bold Lad (IRE)) 1258^{10} (2844) 3055^{5} 3333^{2} 3554^{4} **>72f<**

Hexane (FR) 3 gr f Kendor (FR)-Texan Beauty (FR) (Vayrann) 1576a^{2} **>107f<**

Hey Up Dolly (IRE) 3 b f Puissance-I Don't Mind (Swing Easy (USA)) 697^{12} 1000^{4} (1504) 2003^{7} 2795^{4} 3726^{13} 3823^{9} 4292^{11} **>49a 67f<**

Hi-Aud 3 b f Ilium-Seragsbee (Sagaro) 618^{13} 745^{11} 974^{3} 1093^{4} (1513) (1694) 1776^{3} 2339^{5} 3351^{P} **>74f<**

Hickleton Lady (IRE) 4 br f Kala Shikari-Honest Opinion *520^{15}* **>17a 66f<**

Hickleton Miss 2 ch f Timeless Times (USA)-Honest Opinion 2308^{6} 2735^{2} (2869) 3415^{3} 3670^{2} 3824^{8} 4097^{13} 4231^{18} **>61f<**

Hickory Blue 5 ch h Clantime-Blueit (FR) (1050) 1193^{9} 1508^{9} 1765^{6} 2120^{5} 3919^{5} 3992^{12} 4165^{3} 4242^{3} *4337^{10}* **>50a 71f<**

Hidden Oasis 2 b c Green Desert (USA)-Secret Seeker (USA) (Mr Prospector (USA)) 2408^{4} 3208^{2} (3773) **>89f<**

Higden 2 b c Taufan-Hafhafhaf 4348a^{3}

High Atlas 2 b f Shirley Heights-Balliasta (USA) (Lyphard (USA)) 4313^{W}

Highbank 3 b c Puissance-Highland Daisy (He Loves Me) 1290^{13} 1412^{7} 1669^{4} 2874^{4} 3805^{8} **>56f<**

Highborn (IRE) 6 b or br g Double Schwartz-High State (Free State) *281^{8} 365^{5}* 434^{8} 611^{3} 1021^{4} 1316^{5} 2001^{7} 2458^{5} 3212^{10} 3637^{8} 3807^{3} 4040^{2} (4281) **>83a 90f<**

Highbrook (USA) 7 b m Alphabatim (USA)-Tellspot (USA) (Tell (USA)) 931^{11} 1102^{6} 1310^{3} (1462) **>80f<**

High Commotion (IRE) 3 b f Taufan (USA)-Bumble-Bee (High Line) 715^{12} 942^{5} **>67f<**

High Cut 2 b f Dashing Blade-High Habit (Slip Anchor) 1098^{2} **>82f<**

High Desire (IRE) 2 b f High Estate-Sweet Adelaide (USA) (The Minstrel (CAN)) 2526^{16} 3009^{8} 3397^{8} **>59f<**

High Domain (IRE) 4 b c Dominion Royale-Recline (Wollow) 926^{19} 1152^{9} 1508^{6} 1900^{5} 2163^{5} 2330^{11} 2521^{3} 2585^{2} 2758^{7} 3051^{6} 3622^{7} 3667^{18} 4165^{13} **>56a 64f<**

Highest Cafe (FR) 3 b c Highest Honor (FR)-Turkish Coffee (FR) (Gay Mecene (USA)) 1008a^{5} **>102f<**

Highfield Fizz 3 b f Efisio-Jendor (Condorcet (FR)) 758^{11} 924^{6} 1085^{3} 1966^{11} 2356^{3} 2774^{4} 2917^{4} 3462^{11} (3805) 3935^{2} 3978^{6} 4289^{8} **>63f<**

Highfield Pet 2 b c Efisio-Jendor (Condorcet (FR)) 4188^{15} 4276^{8} **>55f<**

High Five (IRE) 5 b g High Line-Finger Lake (Kings Lake (USA)) 423^{23} 795^{11} 938^{11} 1410^{8} 1757^{10} 1840^{22} 2530^{12} 3569^{14} **>55df<**

High Flown (USA) 3 b g Lear Fan (USA)-Isticanna (USA) (Far North (CAN)) *(48) 116^{4} 135^{9}* 837^{2} 1059^{5} 1430^{4} 1667^{6} 2129^{2} 2353^{6} 2480^{3} 2662^{2} 2851^{3} 3099^{5} *3513^{10}* **>64da 63f<**

Highflying 9 br h Shirley Heights-Nomadic Pleasure (Habitat) 821^{6} 1268^{2} (1416) 1767^{2} 2098^{6} (2462) (2569) 2907^{3} 3189^{5} 3412^{7} **>97f<**

High Flying Adored (IRE) 3 b f In The Wings-Countess Candy 1591^{3} (1984) (2172) 2701^{6} **>93f<**

High Holme 4 ch c Fools Holme (USA)-Corn Seed (Nicholas Bill) *3524^{13}* 3681^{16} 3919^{17} 4165^{24} 4275^{18} **>31a 30f<**

High Hope Henry (USA) 2 b c Known Fact (USA)-Parquill (USA) (One For All (USA)) (760) 3631^{7} **>73tf<**

Highland Flame 6 ch h Dunbeath (USA)-Blakesware Saint (Welsh Saint) *58^{9} 288^{11}* **>43da f<**

Highland Magic (IRE) 7 b h Stalker-Magic Picture 714[20] 1183[24] 3706[20] 4044[20] **>25f<**

High Melody 3 b g Sizzling Melody-Calling High (USA) *4223[15]* **>7a 31f<**

High Note 2 b f Shirley Heights-Soprano (Kris) 3089[20] 3450[6] 4050[4] **>74f<**

High Patriarch (IRE) 3 b c Alzao (USA)-Freesia (Shirley Heights) 635[6] 815[7] 3237[4] 3505[3] 3799[3] 3978[3] (4220) **>94f<**

High Premium 7 b h Forzando-High Halo (High Top) *3510[3]* (3704) 3863[6] 4002[4] 4170[3] **>57a 82f<**

High Priest 3 b c Statoblest-Intoxication (Great Nephew) 1515[2] 1942[3] 2326[11] 2649[3] 3251[4] **>74f<**

High Priority (IRE) 2 b c Marju (IRE)-Blinding (IRE) (High Top) 1592[4] (1772) 2347[7] 2726a[7] 2978[2] 3165[3] 3420[2] **>96?f<**

High Pyrenees 3 b c Shirley Heights-Twyla (Habitat) 1270[3] (1439) **>80f<**

High Ranking 3 b c Governor General-Lismore (Relkino) 754[8] 926[18] 1181[8] 2060[9] 2758[9] 2973[4] 3298[7] **>78f<**

Highspeed (IRE) 3 ch g Double Schwartz-High State (Free State) 2236[5] 2593[11] (3167) 3661[13] **>58f<**

High Standard 3 ch f Kris-Durrah (USA) (Nijinsky (CAN)) 1170[2] 4201[15] **>79f<**

High Target (IRE) 2 b c High Estate-Nice Point (Sharpen Up) 3691a[2] 3865[11] **>89f<**

High Typha 4 b f Dowsing (USA)-Zepha (Great Nephew) 1126[15] 1274[10] 1516[7] 1676[10] 1811[4] 1902[3] 2220[3] 2478[P] 2976[11] 3108[7] **>59f<**

Hi Hoh (IRE) 2 ch f Fayruz-Late Date (Goldhill) 852[9] 3651[5] 4109[9] **>41f<**

Hi Kiki 4 b f Rambo Dancer (CAN)-Hachimitsu (Vaigly Great) 753[11] 1164[14] 3919[11] **>34f<**

Hilaala (USA) 2 ch f Elmaamul (USA)-Halholah (USA) (Secreto (USA)) 3352[4] 3539[3] 3983[2] (4100) **>76f<**

Hill Climber 2 b c Danehill (USA)-Swift Pursuit (Posse (USA)) 4064[11] 4263[8] **>43f<**

Hill Farm Dancer 4 ch f Gunner B-Loadplan Lass (Nicholas Bill) *389[8] 421[6] 530[3] 600[2]* 653[2] (860) 986[4] 1324[4] 1686[7] 2022[6] 3059[3] **>66a 58f<**

Hill Farm Katie 4 b f Derrylin-Kate Brook (Nicholas Bill) *397[4] 415[12] 532[9]* 780[13] 820[12] **>42a 30f<**

Hill Hopper (IRE) 4 b f Danehill (USA)-Sea Harrier (Grundy) 3834[14] **>110f<**

Hillsdown Boy (IRE) 5 ch h Dominion Royale-Lady Mary *27[4] 203[8] 235[5] 330[8]* **>44a f<**

Hillswick 4 ch c Norwick (USA)-Quite Lucky (Precipice Wood) 545[15] 778[7] 1328[10] **>48f<**

Hillzah (USA) 7 ch h Blushing Groom (FR)-Glamour Girl (ARG) (Mysolo) *52[7] (106) 325[4] 396[5]* 597[2] 676[3] 841[7] (1435) 1858[2] (2270) 2569[5] **>86a 84f<**

Hiltons Travel (IRE) 4 b g Red Sunset-Free Rein (Sagaro) *78[9] 117[12]* 491[10] **>26a 40f<**

Himalayan Blue 3 b g Hallgate-Orange Parade (Dara Monarch) *443[4] 515[5]* (647) 857[7] 1180[16] 4284[13] **>65a 70f<**

Hinari Video 10 b h Sallust-Little Cynthia *23[7] 69[9] 102[7] 192[6] 287[7] 353[6]* **>40a 47df<**

Hindaawee (USA) 3 ch c Zilzal (USA)-Sedulous (Tap On Wood) 2237[3] 3027[3] 3261[4] **>91f<**

Hi Nod 5 b h Valiyar-Vikris (Viking (USA)) 1179[9] 1468[4] (1932) 2061[2] 2455[2] (2647) 2948[2] 3188[12] (3999) **>102f<**

Hinton Rock (IRE) 3 ch c Ballad Rock-May Hinton (Main Reef) 612[4] 952[2] 1138[9] 1475[5] 1795[5] 2324[7] 2609[5] 3051[7] 3424[2] **>94f<**

Hi Penny 4 b f Faustus (USA)-High Voltage *62[3] 155[8] 334[2] 397[7] 416[5]* 672[P] 905[10] 1534[9] 1937[15] *2076[11]* **>43a 50f<**

Hippy 2 b f Damister (USA)-Breakaway (Song) 4312[4] **>70f<**

Hi Rock 3 ch f Hard Fought-Miss Racine (Dom Racine (FR)) *519[4]* 577[2] (861) 1414[11] 3624[21] 3972[3] 4280[5] **>44a 62f<**

His Excellence (USA) 2 b c El Gran Senor (USA)-Hail The Lady (USA) (Hail the Pirates (USA)) 3865[14] **>79f<**

Hit the Canvas (USA) 4 ch c At The Threshold (USA)-Also Royal (USA) (Native Royalty (USA)) 423[19] 1359[3] 1462[3] (1934) 2127[2] 2695[5] 2854[3] **>71a 74df<**

Hiwaya 3 b f Doyoun-Himmah (USA) (Habitat) 620[8] 1588[5] 2325[6] 3608[4] (3833) **>107f<**

Hobbs Choice 2 b f Superpower-Excavator Lady (Most Secret) 533[16] *2380[9]* 2667[6] 3456[5] 3642[15] **>44f<**

Hod-Mod (IRE) 5 b h Digamist (USA)-Sallymiss (Tanfirion) 2769[9] 3118[9] **>21f<**

Hoh Express 3 b c Waajib-Tissue Paper (Touch Paper) 978[7] (1136) 1605[2] 1851[26] 2616[3] 3164[4] (3487a) 3608[3] 3945[19] 4031[3] **>105f<**

Hoh Magic 3 ch f Cadeaux Genereux-Gunner's Belle (Gunner B) 692[2] 933[4] 1116a[8] 1896[8] 2368[3] 3042a[5] 3582a[7] 3564[5] **>114f<**

Hoh Majestic (IRE) 2 b g Soviet Lad (USA)-Sevens Are Wild (Petorius) (925) 1267[7] 1772[4] 2435[W] 2618[4] 2674[8] 2859[2] 3018[2] 3284[2] (3369) 3546[12] 3803[10] **>76f<**

Hoh Returns (IRE) 2 b c Fairy King (USA)-Cipriani 690[10] 3371[5] 3662[3] 3877[2] 4103[7] **>79f<**

Hoist (IRE) 4 ch f Bluebird (USA)-Elevate (Ela-Mana-Mou) *(101) 191[6]* **>61+a 78df<**

Ho-Joe (IRE) 5 b g Burslem-Walkyria (Lord Gayle (USA)) *271[11]* 568[10] (1039) 1359[2] 1863[4] 2109[4] **>16a 58f<**

Hokuto Vega (JPN) 5 b m 805a[3] **>118f<**

Hold Your Hat on 6 ch g Celestial Storm (USA)-Thatched Grove (Thatching) *183[7]* **>14a 39?f<**

Holiday Island 6 ch h Good Times (ITY)-Green Island (St Paddy) *75[7]* 729[7] **>18a 52f<**

Holloway Melody 2 ch f Cree Song-Holloway Wonder (Swing Easy (USA)) 3022[5] 3626[11] 4169[14] **>44f<**

Hollywood Dream (GER) 4 ch f Master Willie-Holly (GER) (Cortez (GER)) (897a) **>117f<**

Holtye (IRE) 3 b c Danehill (USA)-Sacristy (Godswalk (USA)) (829) (1188) 1839[6] 3608[8] 3904[8] **>105f<**

Homebeforemidnight 4 ch f Fools Holme (USA)-Mothers Girl *53[14] 245[10]*

Home Cookin' 2 b f Salse (USA)-Home Fire 3532[10] 3708[7] 4320[15] **>57f<**

Home Counties (IRE) 6 ch h Ela-Mana-Mou-Safe Home (Home Guard (USA)) 3820[3] 4245[6] **>76f<**

Homecrest 3 b c Petoski-Homing Hill (Homing) 428[9] 1270[8] 1464[4] 3665[14] 3778[11] **>59f<**

Ho Mei Surprise 3 ch c Hadeer-By Surprise (Young Generation) *243[8] 392[9] 831[6] 892[9]* 1456[3] *1633[4] 2071[8] 2144[5]* **>44da 45f<**

Homeland 2 b c Midyan (USA)-Little Loch Broom 964[5]

1159^{3} 2195^{4} 2855^{2} 3019^{3} (3233) 3760^{5} (3851) 4192^{7} **>62f<**

Homemaker **5** b m Homeboy-Ganadora (Good Times (ITY)) *389^{4} 414^{10}* 545^{8} 860^{9} **>39a 24f<**

Home Shopping **2** b f Superpower-Shiny Kay (Star Appeal) (1443) (2243) 2442^{14} 3037a^{4} 3186^{9} 3702^{2} 3942^{5} 4105^{4} **>100f<**

Homile **7** b h Homing-Rocas (Ile de Bourbon (USA)) *588^{5}* **>23a f<**

Hondero (GER) **5** b h Damister (USA)-Hone (Sharpen Up) 2894a^{5} 3798a^{4} **>115f<**

Honest Achiever (IRE) **4** gr f Tina's Pet-Rykneld (Warpath) *103^{11} 149^{8}* 848^{17} 1291^{11}

Honest Dave **5** b g Derring Rose-Fille de Soleil (Sunyboy) *36^{5}*

Honest Guest (IRE) **2** b f Be My Guest (USA)-Good Policy (IRE) (Thatching) 1287^{2} (2242) 2947^{4} 3865^{3} **>87f<**

Honestly **2** ch f Weldnaas (USA)-Shadha (Shirley Heights) 1977^{12} 2534^{6} 3857^{7} *4269^{3}* **>65a 45f<**

Honest Woman **4** b f Petoski-Bold Polly (Bold Lad (IRE)) 976^{10} 1290^{11} *1883^{10} 2140^{9}* **>4a 31f<**

Honey Mount **4** b c Shirley Heights-Honeybeta (Habitat) 3616^{9} 3849^{11} **>84f<**

Honey Trader **3** b c Beveled (USA)-Lizzie Bee (Kind of Hush) 502^{3} 645^{8} 1342^{6} 1546^{11} 2231^{5} **>68f<**

Honfleur (IRE) **3** b f Sadler's Wells (USA)-Detroit (FR) (Riverman (USA)) 1764^{3} (2426) 3196a^{6} (3479a) 3549^{6} 4009a^{6} **>103f<**

Hong Kong Designer **3** br c Dunbeath (USA)-Pokey's Pet (Uncle Pokey) 538^{8} 786^{7} 1858^{9} 2244^{3} 2481^{4} 2834^{3} 3627^{7} 3741^{4} **>54a 65f<**

Hong Kong Dollar **3** b c Superpower-Daleside Ladybird (Tolomeo) 507^{17} 780^{11} 1146^{4} *1330^{2}* 1541^{16} *2144^{2}* 2642^{4} 2810^{4} 3898^{9} *4128^{10}* **>64a 64df<**

Honorable Estate (IRE) **2** b f High Estate-Holy Devotion (Commanche Run) 791^{6} 1017^{3} 1253^{3} (1671) **>68f<**

Hoodoo (IRE) **2** b c Danehill (USA)-Cassina (Habitat) 1751^{7} **>37f<**

Hoofprints (IRE) **2** b c Distinctly North (USA)-Sweet Reprieve (Shirley Heights) 4320^{10} **>58f<**

Hopeful Sign **3** b f Warning-Infra Green 3712^{12} **>39f<**

Horesti **3** b c Nijinsky (CAN)-Sushila 670^{5} 815^{2} 1224^{6} **>83tf<**

Hornpipe **3** b g Handsome Sailor-Snake Song (Mansingh (USA)) *3514^{7}* **>58a f<**

Horsetrader **3** b g Aragon-Grovette 848^{7} 1012^{9} 1125^{16} 1427^{6} *2090^{7}* 4138^{17} **>38a 47f<**

Hoswinoname **3** ch g Dunbeath (USA)-Miss Chrissy (Ballacashtal (CAN)) 2786^{9} **>16f<**

Hot Breeze **3** br g Hotfoot-Gunnard (Gunner B) *282^{5}*

Hot Dogging **2** b f Petoski-Mehtab (Touching Wood (USA)) 3758^{9} **>40f<**

Hotlips Houlihan **2** b f Risk Me (FR)-Lana's Pet (Tina's Pet) (782) 977^{3} 1384^{6} 1511^{9} (2756) 3225^{7} 3540^{7} **>73f<**

Hot Snap **3** gr g Chilibang-Brittle Grove (Bustino) 442^{16} 658^{7} 761^{11} 1094^{23} 2067^{8} 2318^{15} 2786^{6} 3661^{12} **>58f<**

Hotspur Street **3** b c Cadeaux Genereux-Excellent Alibi (USA) (Exceller (USA)) 640^{6} *1211^{5}* 2314^{4} 2406^{5} 3276^{3} *3526^{6}* 3669^{3} 3927^{8} **>59a 73f<**

Houghton Venture (USA) **3** ch c Groom Dancer (USA)-Perle Fine (USA) (Devil's Bag (USA)) 616^{4} 955^{3} 1507^{3} 3377^{7} **>74f<**

Housamix (FR) **3** b c Linamix (FR)-Housatonic (USA) (Riverman (USA)) 1007a^{2} (3696a) **>121f<**

House of Dreams **3** b c Darshaan-Helens Dreamgirl (Caerleon (USA)) 3618^{6} 3799^{9} 4096^{3} 4228^{6} **>73f<**

House of Riches **2** b c Shirley Heights-Pelf (USA) (Al Nasr (FR)) 1803^{2} 2107^{2} (3827) **>77f<**

How Could-I (IRE) **2** br f Don't Forget Me-Shikari Rose (Kala Shikari) 1190^{10} 1503^{4} 2756^{4} 3533^{6} 3642^{12} **>53f<**

Howqua River **3** b c *394^{3} 409^{5}* 651^{9} 2425^{5} 3455^{15} 3844^{9} **>63da 47f<**

How's it Goin (IRE) **4** ch g Kefaah (USA)-Cuirie (Main Reef) *193^{4} 280^{2} 340^{6} 375^{3}* 432^{7} *514^{7}* 2546^{8} **>62a 66f<**

How's Yer Father **9** b h Daring March-Dawn Ditty (Song) 636^{9} 812^{9} 1057^{8} 1241^{6} 1537^{2} 1766^{6} 2344^{4} 2458^{3} 2764^{17} 3065^{2} 3145^{7} 3615^{11} 3943^{24} 4040^{11} 4145^{8} **>88df<**

Hugwity **3** ch c Cadeaux Genereux-Nuit D'Ete (USA) (Super Concorde (USA)) 1186^{7} 1486^{4} 2576^{9} **>79f<**

Huish Cross **3** ch f Absalom-Sixslip (USA) (Diesis) 1824^{7} 3006^{6} 4205^{13} **>53df<**

Hujjab (USA) **3** b f Woodman (USA)-Winters' Love (USA) (Danzig (USA)) 686^{3} (885) 1415^{3} 1747^{5} 2392^{6} 3408^{5} 3630^{6} **>75f<**

Hullbank **5** b g Uncle Pokey-Dubavarna (Dubassoff (USA)) 1036^{3} (1948) 2087^{7} 2878^{2} 3646^{6} **>74f<**

Hulm (IRE) **2** ch f Mujtahid (USA)-Sunley Princess (Ballad Rock) 3976^{2} 4216^{3} **>74f<**

Humbel (USA) **3** b c Theatrical-Claxton's Slew (USA) (Sea (709a) (1113a) 1611^{8} 2218a^{11} 3790a^{4} (4173a) **>114f<**

Humbert's Landing (IRE) **4** b c Cyrano de Bergerac-Bilander (High Line) 693^{4} (1316) 1895^{30} **>97f<**

Humourless **2** ch c Nashwan (USA)-Sans Blague (USA) (The Minstrel (CAN)) 3340^{13} 3592^{6} 4063^{4} **>85f<**

Hundred Hours (IRE) **6** b h Pennine Walk-Santa Ana Wind (Busted) 162a^{2}

Hunters' Heaven (USA) **4** b c Seeking the Gold (USA)-Rose of Virginia (USA) (Northern Dancer) 676^{10} 3433^{11} 3621^{12} 3984^{18} **>47f<**

Hunters of Brora (IRE) **5** b m Sharpo-Nihad (Alleged (USA)) 960^{2} (1217) 1851^{7} 2672^{2} 3164^{7} 3413^{7} 3945^{3} 4202^{3} **>102f<**

Hunza Story **3** b f Rakaposhi King-Sense of Occasion (Artaius (USA)) *418^{12} 513^{2} 626^{7} 1762^{15}* 1962^{7} 2133^{2} 2332^{8} 2450^{6} *2630^{12}* 2972^{5} (3099) 3258^{7} 3422^{8} 4054^{8} 4170^{6} 4232^{2} 4284^{12} **>49a 58f<**

Hurricane Dancer (IRE) **2** ch f Nabeel Dancer (USA)-Raging Storm (Horage) 1163^{3} 1399^{2} 1690^{4} 2277^{2} (2717) 3540^{4} 3639^{11} 3894^{2} 4075^{15} **>63f<**

Hurricane Horn (IRE) **2** ch c Kefaah (USA)-Musical Horn (Music Boy) 1047^{7} 3314^{8} 3441^{9} 3566^{7} *4273^{10} 4339^{5}* **>59a 65f<**

Hurtleberry (IRE) **2** b f Tirol-Allberry (Alzao (USA)) 2660^{7} (3025) **>77f<**

Hushang (IRE) **5** b h Shernazar-Highest Hopes (Hethersett) (2565a) 2891a^{2} (3798a) **>119f<**

Hutchies Lady **3** b f Efisio-Keep Mum (Mummy's Pet) 539^{16} 593^{8} 758^{7} 989^{7} 1818^{5} 2478^{6} 2772^{9} 3853^{9} **>43df<**

Hydrofoil **3** gr f Sharrood (USA)-Pirogue 948^{3} 1218^{3}

(1452) (1776) 1986^{7} (2296) 3735^{3} 4135^{13} **>65a 69f<**

Hylters Girl 3 b f Dominion-Jolimo 3034^{5} 3661^{18} 4242^{9} **>26a 37f<**

Hypertension 3 ch c Roi Danzig (USA)-Sayulita (Habitat) 3618^{10} 3712^{9} 4164^{8} **>55f<**

I

Iamus 2 ch c Most Welcome-Icefern (Moorestyle) 3652^{7} 3888^{2} 3994^{2} 4199^{4} **>99?f<**

Iberian Dancer (CAN) 2 b f El Gran Senor (USA)-Cutty (USA) (Smart) 2675^{5} 3155^{3} **>77f<**

Ibiano (IRE) 6 b h Gunner B-Ilana (GER) (Windwurf (GER)) 1114a^{3} **>105f<**

Iblis (IRE) 3 b c Danehill (USA)-In Unison (Bellypha) (662) 1121a^{11} 1370^{6} 2471^{5} **>94f<**

Ibsen 7 b h Gorytus (USA)-State of Mind (Mill Reef (USA)) 108^{6} 346^{9} 1973^{4} 2569^{8} 3238^{7} **>69a 75f<**

Icanspell 4 b g Petoski-Bewitched (African Sky) 672^{18} 1161^{18} **>56da 40f<**

Ice and Glacial (IRE) 3 b c Law Society (USA)-What A Candy (USA) (Key To The Mint (USA)) 1010a^{3} 1396a^{6} **>103f<**

Ice Magic 8 ch h Red Sunset-Free Rein (Sagaro) 1596^{11} 1863^{5} 2226^{5} 2546^{4} 2695^{6} 3029^{5} 3303^{10} **>35f<**

Iceni (IRE) 2 b br f Distinctly North (USA)-Princess Galicia (Welsh Pageant) 3260^{4} **>61f<**

Ice Pick (IRE) 2 b c Distinctly North (USA)-Avril's Choice (Montelimar (USA)) 1096^{2} 1197^{3} 2034^{3} 3441^{5} 3988^{10} 4195^{6} **>75f<**

Ichor 2 b f Primo Dominie-Adeebah (USA) (Damascus (USA)) 1497^{7} 2170^{3} 2508^{5} 2991^{9} 3415^{9} **>36df<**

Idle Fancy 2 b f Mujtahid (USA)-Pizziri (Artaius (USA)) 3174^{10} **>33f<**

Idris (IRE) 5 b h Ahonoora-Idara (Top Ville) 3193a^{2} 4173a^{3} **>109f<**

I Fear Nothing 4 gr f Kalaglow-Noirmont Girl 4^{7} **>37da 76df<**

If Only 5 b g Lightning Dealer-Pentland Beauty (Remainder Man) 3282^{7}

Ihtimaam (FR) 3 b c Polish Precedent (USA)-Haebeh (USA) (Alydar (USA)) 1507^{5} 2313^{3} 2460^{3} 2770^{8} 3974^{12} 4234^{12} **>79f<**

Ihtiram (IRE) 3 b c Royal Academy (USA)-Welsh Love 694^{2} 829^{2} (1178) 1315^{2} 2008^{3} (2444) 3144^{4} 3498^{5} **>117f<**

Ijab (CAN) 5 b h Ascot Knight (CAN)-Renounce (USA) (Buckpasser) 271^{10} 422^{2} 476^{7} (592) 771^{2} 894^{2} 1921^{3} 2327^{11} (2919) 3527^{2} 3724^{7} 4086^{5} 4336^{2} **>55a 50df<**

Ikaab (USA) 3 b c Danzig (USA)-Dazzling Concorde (USA) (Super Concorde (USA)) 2746^{12} 2909^{5} 3279^{11} **>102df<**

Ikhtiraa (USA) 5 b h Imperial Falcon (CAN)-True Native (USA) (Raise A Native) 109^{4} 303^{2} 321^{3} 403^{11} 1401^{3} 1937^{12} 2175^{4} 2657^{4} 2842^{3} **>69a 69df<**

Ikis Girl 4 ch f Silver Hawk (USA)-Jealous One (USA) (Raise A Native) 481^{6} 559^{12} 738^{12} 776^{8} 1531^{7} 1826^{6} 1988^{7} 2088^{7} 2276^{10} **>53df<**

Iktamal (USA) 3 ch c Danzig Connection (USA)-Crystal Cup (USA) (Nijinsky (CAN)) 1221^{2} 2236^{6} 2583^{2} (2915) 3112^{4} (3298) (3466) (3615) 4121^{4} **>103f<**

Iktasab 3 ch c Cadeaux Genereux-Loucoum (FR) (Iron Duke (FR)) (1150) 2121^{4} 2477^{6} 2803^{6} 3214^{13} 3863^{17} **>88f<**

Il Doria (IRE) 2 ch f Mac's Imp (USA)-Pasadena Lady (Captain James) 977^{2} 4109^{14} **>50f<**

Il Fratello 4 ch g Caerleon (USA)-Miss Silca Key (Welsh Saint) 290^{9} 357^{10} 603^{10} 766^{12} 1254^{6} 1350^{2} **>30a 41f<**

Il Furetto 3 b g Emarati (USA)-Irresistable 581^{8} 861^{9} 1445^{16} 2052^{12} 2789^{15} 3055^{7} **>25f<**

Ilium Bourbon 3 b f Ilium-Little Missile (Ile de Bourbon (USA)) 2438^{10} 3023^{13}

Illegally Yours 2 br f Be My Chief (USA)-Legal Precedent (Star Appeal) 1163^{6} 1690^{11} 3539^{8} 4045^{15} **>39f<**

Illuminate 2 b c Marju - Light Bee (Majestic Light) 3530^{4} **>75f<**

Iltimas (USA) 3 b f Dayjur (USA)-Tadwin (Never so Bold) 662^{8} 1362^{8} 2066^{2} (2677) (3005) 3342^{6} 3551^{22} **>96f<**

Il Trastevere (FR) 3 b c L'Emigrant (USA)-Ideas At Work (Persepolis (FR)) 3599^{4} 3728^{12} 3979^{4} **>94f<**

Ilustre (IRE) 3 ch c Al Hareb (USA)-Time For Pleasure (Tower Walk) 580^{5} 1012^{7} 3177^{10} 3475^{10} **>56f<**

I'm a Dreamer (IRE) 5 b g Mister Majestic-Lady Wise 422^{4} **>62a 67f<**

Imad (USA) 5 b or br h Al Nasr (FR)-Blue Grass Field (Top Ville) 1840^{8} (2688) 3217^{7} 4118^{12} **>77f<**

Image Maker (IRE) 2 gr f Nordico (USA)-Dream Trader (Auction Ring (USA)) 2939^{5} 3124^{3} 3285^{4} 3528^{2} 3623^{15} 3949^{7} (4127) 4273^{4} **>65a 52f<**

Imco Glaring (IRE) 3 ch f 1237a^{7} **>86f<**

Imlak (IRE) 3 ch c Ela-Mana-Mou-Mashteen (USA) 647^{4} 774^{4} 3875^{8} 4061^{17} 4284^{F} **>69f<**

I'm Outa Here (IRE) 3 b or br c Don't Forget Me-Heavenward (USA) (Conquistador Cielo (USA)) 739^{6} 1167^{9} 1747^{8} 2032^{2} 2321^{12} 2807^{2} 3173^{8} 3677^{11} **>74f<**

Impeccable 2 ch f Mac's Imp (USA)-Ethel Knight (Thatch (USA)) 3260^{10} 3604^{11} 3779^{4} 3969^{10} 4144^{17} **>49f<**

Impending Danger 2 ch g Fearless Action (USA)-Crimson Sol (Crimson Beau) 2249^{4} 2496^{9} 2924^{5} 3423^{9} **>37a 16f<**

Imperial Bailiwick (IRE) 4 b f Imperial Frontier (USA)-Syndikos (USA) (Nashua) 608a^{4} 901a^{4} 1703a^{6} **>98f<**

Imperial Bid (FR) 7 b or br h No Pass No Sale (FR)-Tzaritsa (USA) 91^{9} 137^{3} 229^{3} 991^{4} (1205) 1437^{5} 1651^{8} 1958^{3} 2159^{4} 2226^{4} (2610) 2731^{4} 2954^{5} 3169^{8} 3367^{3} 3665^{5} 4101^{7} **>54a 63f<**

Impetuous Lady (USA) 0 D 2277^{5} 3891^{10} 3988^{12} 4211^{10} **>58f<**

Imp Express (IRE) 2 b c Mac's Imp (USA)-Fair Chance (Young Emperor) 1063^{6} 1413^{5} (1740) 2023^{2} (2474) 2706^{6} 3064^{11} 3335^{3} 3714^{14} 4097^{4} **>75f<**

Impington (IRE) 2 b f Mac's Imp (USA)-Ultra (Stanford) 2281^{4} 3260^{3} 3628^{9} 3949^{10} **>27a 68f<**

I'm Playing 3 br f Primo Dominie-Play the Game (Mummy's Game) 2590^{5} 2821^{10} **>14a 43f<**

Imprevedibile (IRE) 5 b h Bluebird (USA)-Corozal (Corvaro (USA)) (901a) 1119a^{4} 4345a^{2} **>114f<**

Imprimis (IRE) 2 b f Mac's Imp (USA)-Reasonably French 943^{6} 1035^{3} 1159^{2} 1272^{3} 1540^{13} 1699^{4} 1989^{6} 2908^{9} **>55f<**

Impromptu Melody (IRE) 2 b f Mac's Imp (USA)-Greek Music (Tachypous) 1375^{6} 1579^{8} 1877^{10} **>52f<**

Impulsive Air (IRE) 3 b c Try My Best (USA)-Tracy's

Sundown (Red Sunset) 720^{5} 914^{6} 1131^{8} 1306^{8} 3411^{12} 3645^{18} 3823^{7} 3964^{9} 4083^{8} **>58f<**

I'm Supposin (IRE) 3 b c Posen-Robinia (Roberto) 1234a^{9} 2218a^{7} 2891a^{6} **>114f<**

I'm Your Lady 4 ch f Risk Me (FR)-Impala Lass (Kampala) 1304^{3} 1604^{7} 2001^{6} 2330^{10} 2659^{9} 3822^{11} 4322^{3} **>75f<**

Inaminit 2 gr c Timeless Times (USA)-Dolly Bevan (Another Realm) 3892^{9} 4330^{9} **>43f<**

In a Moment (USA) 4 ch c Moment of Hope (USA)-Teenage Fling (USA) (Laomedonte (USA)) *229^{4} 271^{7}* 556^{13} 649^{8} **>57a 56f<**

In A Tizzy 2 b f Sizzling Melody-Tizzy (Formidable) 474^{4} *1077^{7} 2294^{5}* 3744^{4} 3851^{4} **>38a 55f<**

In Behind (IRE) 4 b f Entitled-Murroe Star (Glenstal (USA)) *37^{6} 109^{7} 277^{7} 346^{8} 374^{7}* **>45a 55f<**

Inca Bird 2 b f Inca Chief (USA)-Polly Oligant 4048^{8} 4148^{13} **>56f<**

In Camera (IRE) 3 b c Sadler's Wells (USA)-Clandestina (USA) (Secretariat (USA)) 678^{2} (815) 1068^{3} 1897^{6} 2323^{5} 2670^{4} 3609^{4} 4011a^{6} **>116f<**

Incapol 2 b c Inca Chief (USA)-Miss Poll Flinders (Swing Easy (USA)) 682^{7} 1540^{7} (1857) 2223^{3} 2523^{9} 3749^{18} 3969^{6} *4124^{12}* **>29a 66f<**

Inca Queen 2 b f Inca Chief (USA)-Albion Polka (Dance In Time (CAN)) *1954^{8}* 2176^{7} **>6a 8f<**

Incarvillea (USA) 2 b f Mr Prospector (USA)-In the Groove (Night Shift (USA)) (669) (1293) **>93?tf<**

Incatinka 2 gr f Inca Chief (USA)-Encore L'Amour (USA) (Monteverdi) 3848^{3} 4224^{4} **>65f<**

Incha 3 b f Nashwan (USA)-Idle Gossip (USA) (Lyphard (USA)) 779^{2} 1308^{3} 1736^{12} 2449^{3} 3984^{14} **>71f<**

Inchcailloch (IRE) 6 b h Lomond (USA)-Glowing With Pride (Ile de Bourbon (USA)) 795^{2} (1058) 1189^{7} (1444) 3971^{9} 4118^{4} 4326^{9} **>75f<**

Inchkeith 3 b f Reference Point-Inchmurrin (Lomond (USA)) *64^{8} 204^{2} (282)* 453^{7} *566^{4}* 1347^{3} 1702^{2} (2152) 2482^{3} **>63+a 85f<**

Inchrory 2 b c Midyan (USA)-Applecross (Glint of Gold) 1551^{5} 1856^{3} (2485) 3158^{5} (3631) (4067) **>97f<**

Inchyre 2 b f Shirley Heights-Inchmurrin (Lomond (USA)) 3339^{6} 3633^{2} **>88f<**

Indefence (IRE) 4 b c Conquering Hero (USA)-Cathryn's Song (Prince Tenderfoot (USA)) 762^{20} 882^{9} 1126^{5} 1251^{3} 1517^{6} 1775^{4} 2019^{3} **>65df<**

Inderaputeri 5 b m Bold Fort-Hello Cuddles (He Loves Me) 817^{13} 1013^{8} (2808) 3011^{4} (3248) 3439^{7} **>60da 74f<**

Indescent Blue 3 b f Bluebird (USA)-Miss Display (Touch Paper) 695^{12} 1053^{4} 1979^{13} 2794^{11} 2862^{7} *3240^{7} 3529^{9}* 3757^{17} **>41a 49f<**

Indhar 4 b c Warning-Clarista (USA) (Riva Ridge (USA)) 2409^{2} (2699) 3381^{8} 3562^{8} 3904^{7} 4121^{3} **>104f<**

Indiahra 4 b f Indian Ridge-Mavahra (Mummy's Pet) 1021^{17} 1493^{5} 1668^{12} 1828^{12} *2073^{4} 2290^{3} 2634^{13}* 2698^{10} 3275^{11} 3492^{16} 3624^{11} 3777^{2} 4142^{13} 4215^{18} **>52a 51f<**

Indian Bluff 2 b c Indian Ridge-Hannie Caulder 919^{6} **>31f<**

Indian Colours 4 b g Indian Forest (USA)-Running Rainbow (Runnett) 2309^{5} *3073^{12}* **>46f<**

Indian Crystal 4 gr f Petong-Gentle Gypsy (Junius (USA)) 1864^{5} 1996^{9} 2229^{10} *2631^{9}* 2916^{3} 3116^{8} 3252^{6} 3357^{7} **>44a 51f<**

Indian Fire 5 ch g Indian Forest (USA)-Saintly Game (Welsh Saint) *21^{8} 68^{7} 187^{12}* 853^{17} 1016^{10} **>23a 25f<**

Indian Fly 4 b c Indian Ridge-Tinas Image (He Loves Me) 439^{7} 714^{11} 870^{6} 1851^{3} 2703^{6} 3188^{2} 3334^{2} (3602) 4121^{6} 4265^{4} **>108f<**

Indian Jockey 3 b c Indian Ridge-Number Eleven (Local Suitor (USA)) (1285) (1561) 1716^{4} 2270^{3} 2536^{8} 3823^{13} **>72f<**

Indian Lament 4 b f Indian Ridge-Miss Swansong (Young Generation) 1546^{8} 2363^{5} 2709^{5} 3455^{17} **>40df<**

Indian Light 3 ch c Be My Chief (USA)-Beacon (High Top) 679^{4} 1574a^{10} 2273^{2} 2670^{6} 3594^{3} 4204^{11} **>108f<**

Indian Nectar 2 b f Indian Ridge-Sheer Nectar (Piaffer (USA)) 3888^{6} **>45f<**

Indian Relative 2 b f Distant Relative-Elegant Tern (USA) 3948^{5} 4100^{2} *4269^{2}* **>75a 76f<**

Indian Rhapsody 3 b f Rock City-Indian Love Song (Be My Guest (USA)) 435^{12} 482^{16} 576^{4} (1045) 1423^{2} 1598^{4} (1735) 1904^{5} 2225^{6} 2813^{5} 3259^{3} (3344) 3719^{13} **>62f<**

Indian Serenade 4 ch c Mansingh (USA)-La Melodie *28^{3} 129^{4} 198^{2} 371^{2} (408) 472^{U} 627^{2} 845^{8} 1049^{2}* 1323^{U} 1644^{2} **>57a 56f<**

Indian Spice 3 b f Indian Ridge-Moonlight Serenade (Crooner) 3712^{14} **>49f<**

Indian Sunset 2 ch c Indian Ridge-Alanood (Northfields (USA)) 3536^{9} 3733^{25} **>46f<**

Indian Temple 4 ch c Minster Son-Indian Flower (Mansingh (USA)) 1446^{6} 1676^{14} 1775^{7} 2037^{10} 2245^{9} **>61df<**

Indian Treasure (IRE) 3 b f Treasure Kay-Arminiya 848^{16} 1092^{17} 1625^{8} **>14f<**

Indicator 3 b g Reference Point-Comic Talent (Pharly (FR)) 1175^{6} 1339^{7} 1905^{3} **>76f<**

Indigo Time (IRE) 3 b c Ela-Mana-Mou-Majestic's Gold 3926^{6} (4028) 4325^{17} **>91+f<**

Indira 2 b f Indian Ridge-Princess Rosananti (IRE) (Shareef Dancer (USA)) 2299^{5} 3379^{12} 3891^{7} 4208^{14} **>51f<**

Indiscretion (IRE) 3 b f Kris-Foolish Dame (USA) (Foolish Pleasure (USA)) 698^{8} **>32f<**

Indonesian (IRE) 3 b or br c Alzao (USA)-Miss Garuda (Persian Bold) (678) 2348^{7} 2738^{7} 3091^{4} 3580a^{5} 3593^{7} 3781^{7} 3993^{13} **>81df<**

Indrapura (IRE) 3 b c Gallic League-Stella Ann (Ahonoora) *(443)* 971^{3} 1165^{10} 1797^{13} **>74a 70f<**

Infamous (USA) 2 ch c Diesis-Name And Fame (USA) (Arts And Letters) 3989^{6} **>68f<**

Infantry Dancer 2 ch f Infantry-Electropet (Remainder Man) 1798^{5} 2526^{5} 2839^{5} **>66f<**

Infantry Glen 5 gr h Infantry-Rage Glen (Grey Mirage) 548^{10} *767^{10}* **>37a 37f<**

Infiel 2 b f Luge-Indocina (Indian King) (1111a)

Influence Pedler 2 b c Keen-La Vie En Primrose (Henbit (USA)) 1752^{10} 3560^{6} 3968^{11} 4169^{7} 4285^{7} **>54f<**

Infrasonic 5 b h Dancing Brave (USA)-Infra Green 1239a^{5} **>109f<**

In Generosity (IRE) 2 b f Generous-Aptostar 3692a^{12} **>78f<**

In Good Faith 3 b g Beveled (USA)-Dulcidene 686^{7} 1130^{13} 1617^{11} 3801^{10} 3963^{8} **>72f<**

Inherent Magic (IRE) 6 ch m Magical Wonder (USA)-Flo Kelly 2617^{6} 3551^{18} 3632^{9} (3938) 4033^{19} **>87a 98f<**

In Love Again (IRE) 3 b f Prince Rupert (FR)-Beloved Mistress 850^{6} 1924^{12} 2194^{10} 2512^{6} **>73f<**

Inn At the Top 3 b c Top Ville-Woolpack (Golden Fleece (USA)) *51^{2} 72^{6} 189^{2}* 1452^{5} 1643^{2} *2919^{12}* 3435^{2} 3627^{6} 3818^{5} **>69a 68f<**

Inner Circle (USA) 2 ch f El Gran Senor (USA)-Conquistress (USA) (Conquistador Cielo (USA)) 4153^{3} **>74+f<**

Innocence 3 b f Unfuwain (USA)-Youthful (FR) (Green Dancer (USA)) 815^{8} 1303^{6} 2196^{2} 2509^{3} 3184^{2} 3769^{8} **>26a 74df<**

Inovar 5 b h Midyan (USA)-Princess Cinders (King of Spain) *119^{7}* 1733^{3} **>34f<**

In Paradisum (USA) 2 b c Opening Verse (USA)-Nice Noble (USA) (Vaguely Noble) 2128^{10} 2346^{7} 2516^{6} (3533) 3701^{5} 4001^{6} **>58f<**

Inquisitor (USA) 3 b c Alleged (USA)-Imperturbable Lady (CAN) (Northern Dancer) (427) 1897^{7} 2348^{6} (3489) 3836^{5} **>115+f<**

Insatiable (IRE) 2 b c Don't Forget Me-Petit Eclair (Major Portion) 3663^{5} (3881) **>78+f<**

Inside Information (USA) 4 b f Private Account (USA)-Pure Profit (USA) (Key To The Mint (USA)) *(4304a)* **>130+a f<**

Insideout 2 b c Macmillion-Parijoun (Manado) 4276^{11} **>11f<**

Insider Trader 4 b c Dowsing (USA)-Careless Whisper (Homing) 1019^{7} 1106^{14} 1489^{7} 1637^{5} 2909^{10} 3221^{8} 3407^{2} 3554^{6} 3748^{8} 3992^{6} (4113) 4322^{12} **>63a 83f<**

Insiyabi (USA) 2 b c Mr Prospector (USA)-Ashayer (USA) (Lomond (USA)) 3733^{W} 4023^{3} 4188^{5} **>81f<**

Inspiration Point 4 ch f Indian Ridge-Low Line (High Line) *218^{6}* **>36da 56f<**

Instantaneous 3 b f Rock City-Mainmast (Bustino) 1218^{8} 1669^{5} 2166^{3} 2355^{3} 2543^{2} (2759) *(3076)* 3263^{3} 3505^{6} *3737^{5}* 3970^{4} 4071^{9} *4335^{2}* **>65a 61f<**

Instant Success (USA) 3 ch f Secreto (USA)-Oath of Allegiance (USA) (Olden Times) *528^{5}* **>47a 62f<**

Intendant 3 b c Distant Relative-Bunduq 907^{6} 1180^{3} (1412) 1649^{4} 2503^{12} 3759^{19} 3977^{9} **>68a 65f<**

Intention (USA) 5 b h Shahrastani (USA)-Mimi Baker (USA) (What Luck (USA)) *75^{4} 109^{3} 183^{4} 260^{8}* **>61a 71f<**

In The Band 2 b f Sharrood (USA)-Upper Caen (High Top) 4320^{8} **>65f<**

In the Money (IRE) 6 b h Top Ville-Rensaler (USA) (Stop The Music (USA)) *37^{2} 97^{3} 178^{2} 238^{4} 303^{3} (367) 403^{4}* 423^{7} 549^{13} 757^{10} *894^{9}* 2392^{8} **>64a 71f<**

In the Zim 3 b f Mtoto-Monashee (USA) (Sovereign Dancer (USA)) 1731^{5} 2065^{6} **>58f<**

Intiaash (IRE) 3 br f Shaadi (USA)-Funun (USA) (Fappiano (USA)) 752^{2} 937^{5} 1296^{3} 1522^{4} 2067^{4} 3492^{4} 3640^{2} (3981) 4145^{13} **>78f<**

Intidab (USA) 2 b c Phone Trick (USA)-Alqwani (USA) (Mr Prospector (USA)) 1803^{4} 3449^{3} **>84+f<**

Intisab 2 b f Green Desert (USA)-Ardassine (Ahonoora) 1361^{8} **>64f<**

Intrepid Fort 6 gr h Belfort (FR)-Dauntless Flight (Golden Mallard) *334^{4} 415^{11}* 1873^{6} 2327^{10} **>28a 33f<**

Introducing 2 b f Mtoto-D'Azy (Persian Bold) 3346^{2} 4048^{2} 4241^{3} **>80f<**

Inverlochy 2 gr c Petong-Real Princess (Aragon) 1184^{6} 1597^{4} 4103^{3} **>80f<**

Invest Wisely 3 ch g Dashing Blade-Saniette (Crystal Palace (FR)) 553^{7} 747^{3} 1038^{5} 1410^{5} 2026^{4} (2509) (2882) (3391) (3682) **>97f<**

Invigilate 6 ch h Viking (USA)-Maria da Gloria (St Chad) 1151^{14} 2458^{10} 2784^{13} 2956^{5} 3116^{2} 3252^{8} 3357^{2} 3467^{10} 3622^{9} 3764^{12} **>57f<**

Invigorating 2 ch f Polar Falcon (USA)-Vitality (Young Generation) 1443^{2} 1833^{6} 2675^{4} **>70f<**

Invocation 8 ch h Kris-Royal Saint (USA) (Crimson Satan) *41^{3} 89^{10} 160^{6} 345^{4} (386) 446^{5}* 567^{2} 636^{13} 922^{14} 1071^{6} 1241^{8} 3961^{6} 4134^{10} *4297^{10}* **>71a 61f<**

In Waiting (IRE) 3 b f In The Wings-Arousal (Rousillon (USA)) 3485a^{3} **>91f<**

Inzar 4 b c Warning-Star Face *88^{6}* **>51a f<**

Inzar (USA) 3 b c Warning-Czar's Bride (USA) (Northern Dancer) 667^{5} (1185) 1618^{4} 1848^{4} 2097^{2} 2443^{2} 2764^{8} 3033^{2} (3334) (3599) (3931) 4178a^{3} **>120f<**

Ionio (USA) 4 ch c Silver Hawk (USA)-Private View (USA) (Mr Prospector (USA)) *(385)* 606a^{6} 827^{3} 1262^{2} 1609^{6} 1836^{6} 2444^{3} 2739^{2} 3046a^{7} 3603^{4} 3836^{17} 4204^{7} **>96a 107df<**

Iota 6 b or br m Niniski (USA)-Iosifa (Top Ville) *15^{2} 67^{2} 131^{3} 367^{8}* **>71a 61f<**

Irchester Lass 3 ch f Presidium-Fool's Errand (Milford) *1330^{6} 1571^{13}* 1677^{8} 1962^{5} 2220^{7} 2540^{8} 2956^{3} 3179^{3} (3293) 3624^{6} **>25a 42f<**

I Recall (IRE) 4 b g Don't Forget Me-Sable Lake (Thatching) 764^{19} 1314^{8} *2407^{4}* **>60a 73f<**

I Remember it Well (IRE) 3 ch f Don't Forget Me-Star Cream (Star Appeal) 2813^{7} 3153^{3} *3318^{10}* **>6a 50f<**

Iridal 3 ch c Rainbow Quest (USA)-Khandjar (Kris) 1127^{4} 1682^{2} 2208^{3} 2754^{2} (3421) 3723^{6} **>86f<**

Irie Mon (IRE) 3 b c Waajib-Achafalaya (USA) (Apalachee (USA)) *25^{2} 174^{2} 261^{W} (300)* 971^{7} 1541^{8} 1718^{3} 2102^{3} 2149^{2} 2524^{4} **>62a 62f<**

Irish Angel (IRE) 3 b f Cyrano de Bergerac-Sweet Finale (Sallust) 1296^{13} 1739^{7} 2162^{11} **>6a 41f<**

Irish Dominion 5 b h Dominion-Irish Cookie (Try My Best (USA)) 2984^{7} 3177^{15} **>43a 18f<**

Irish Emerald 8 b h Taufan (USA)-Gaelic Jewel (Scottish Rifle) *385^{4} 406^{13}* **>32a f<**

Irish Groom 8 b h Shy Groom (USA)-Romany Pageant (Welsh Pageant) 3426^{3} **>42da 52f<**

Irish Kinsman 2 b g Distant Relative-Inesdela (Wolver Hollow) 4313^{17} **>45f<**

Irish Oasis (IRE) 2 b c Mazaad-Alpenwind (Tumble Wind (USA)) *2924^{7} 3523^{9}* 3827^{12} **>32a 31f<**

Irish Senor (IRE) 4 ch c Al Hareb (USA)-Rivulet (USA) (Irish River (FR)) 569^{3} 1743^{3} **>75df<**

Irkutsk (USA) 4 b c Nureyev (USA)-Herb Wine (USA) (Full Pocket (USA)) 1245^{4} 1594^{2} 1749^{4} 2148^{3} **>82df<**

Iron And Steel 2 ch c Dominion-Fairy Fortune (Rainbow Quest (USA)) 429^{7} *1213^{5}* 2838^{6} 3570^{10} 4129^{13} **>16a 28f<**

Iron Gent (USA) 4 b c Greinton-Carrot Top 938^{7} 3308^{3} **>83f<**

Ironheart 2 b c Lycius (USA)-Inshirah (USA) (Caro) 2320^{4} 4058^{7} **>77f<**

Ironic (IRE) 3 b g Tirol-Allegheny River (USA) (Lear Fan (USA)) 630^{9} 888^{9} 1221^{9} 2317^{16} 3605^{7} 3685^{10} **>59df<**

Iron Man (IRE) 3 b c Conquering Hero (USA)-Doppio

Filo (Vision (USA)) *98^{2} (144) 243^{2}* **>65a 62f<**

Iron N Gold 3 b g Heights of Gold-Southern Dynasty (Gunner B) (453) 851^{4} *3527^{15}* 3569^{4} 3676^{11} **>58f<**

Irrepressible (IRE) 4 b c Don't Forget Me-Lady of Shalott (Kings Lake (USA)) 3987^{19} 4051^{18} **>37df<**

Irshad 3 ch c Soviet Star (USA)-Nahilah (Habitat) 1308^{7} 1598^{9} **>67f<**

Isitoff 2 b c Vague Shot-Plum Blossom (USA) (Gallant Romeo (USA)) 4075^{20} **>35f<**

Isla Glen 2 b f Be My Chief (USA)-Serration (Kris) 760^{7} **>45f<**

Island Blade (IRE) 6 b h Sure Blade (USA)-Queen's Eyot (Grundy) 661^{6} 1144^{3} **>72a 71f<**

Island Cascade 3 b f Hadeer-Island Mill (Mill Reef (USA)) 643^{6} 824^{9} 990^{2} 1358^{12} 1436^{4} 3099^{11} 3299^{6} 3669^{13} 3805^{5} 4086^{7} **>45f<**

Island Victory 2 ch g Ron's Victory (USA)-Island Mead (Pharly (FR)) 2200^{7} 2846^{12} 3008^{5} 3533^{14} 4133^{7} **>56f<**

Islay Brown (IRE) 2 b f Petorius-Speedy Action (Horage) 1620^{9} 2083^{5} 3366^{3} 3821^{13} **>63f<**

Ism 3 b c Petong-Brigado (Brigadier Gerard) 783^{10} *1091^{8} (1569)* 1664^{6} *2073^{9} (2628) 3512^{3}* 3751^{5} 3897^{7} **>71a 65f<**

Ismeno 4 b g Ela-Mana-Mou-Seattle Siren (USA) (Seattle Slew (USA)) 485^{13} 584^{9} 811^{11} 1144^{7} 1655^{2} 2007^{11} 2175^{2} 2359^{3} **>67f<**

Isshereal (IRE) 3 br f Durgam (USA)-Park Vision (Vision (USA)) 2016^{7} 2297^{3} 2849^{5} 3126^{6} **>74?f<**

Istabraq (IRE) 3 b c Sadler's Wells (USA)-Betty's Secret (USA) (Secretariat (USA)) 764^{12} 978^{8} 2781^{2} (3178) 3445^{2} (3669) 3817^{11} 4158^{2} 4326^{10} **>96f<**

Istidaad (USA) 3 b c Chief's Crown (USA)-Mazzei Mood (USA) (Roberto (USA)) 635^{2} (942) 1224^{2} 1897^{5} 2323^{2} 2670^{3} (3380) 3609^{3} **>117f<**

Istiwa 3 b c Statoblest-Raintree Venture (Good Times (ITY)) 2319^{12} 2794^{12} 3409^{4} **>61f<**

Itab (USA) 3 b f Dayjur (USA)-Madame Secretary (USA) (Secretariat (USA)) 1150^{2} (1520) 2003^{5} 2709^{6} **>75tf<**

Ithkurni (USA) 6 b m Green Forest (USA)-Queen's Visit (Top Command (USA)) 1335^{P} **>8a f<**

It Is Now 3 ch c Blow the Whistle-Final Game (Pardao) 3981^{8} 4049^{14} 4194^{20} **>33a 33f<**

It's Academic 3 b f Royal Academy (USA)-It's Terrific (Vaguely Noble) 752^{5} 955^{8} 1218^{4} 1251^{6} (1583) 1679^{5} 1847^{8} 2698^{3} 2832^{2} (3172) 3534^{2} (3624) 3823^{2} 3964^{4} 4122^{6} **>74f<**

It's A Ripper 2 ch c Weldnaas (USA)-Atlantic Air (Air Trooper) 1772^{5} 1977^{15} 3012^{3} 3405^{4} 3721^{12} 4133^{4} 4211^{6} **>61f<**

Itsinthepost 2 b f Risk Me (FR)-Where's the Money (Lochnager) 595^{3} 819^{12} 1375^{4} *(2143)* 3639^{13} 4144^{2} **>66a 66f<**

It's so Easy 4 b f Shaadi (USA)-Carmelina (Habitat) *2^{12} 71^{6} 219^{7}* 882^{20} 1070^{14} *1334^{6}* 1785^{15} 2539^{7} *2963^{8}* **>32a 57f<**

It'sthebusiness 3 b c Most Welcome-Douceur (USA) (Shadeed (USA)) 2491^{12} 2698^{15} 3004^{4} 3402^{2} 3757^{7} 3889^{2} 4136^{14} **>69f<**

Ivanhoe 4 b c Bairn (USA)-Ural Dancer (Corvaro (USA)) 545^{10} 988^{14} 1472^{12} **>50df<**

Ivan the Terrible (IRE) 7 ch h Siberian Express (USA)-Chrisanthy (So Blessed) *117^{6} 226^{2} 379^{3} 413^{9}* (593) (874) *1884^{6} 2961^{7}* 3443^{7} **>59a 67f<**

Ivor's Deed 0 b C Shadeed (USA)-Gena Ivor (USA) (Sir Ivor) *4334^{9}* **>14a f<**

Ivor's Flutter 6 b h Beldale Flutter (USA)-Rich Line (High Line) 1794^{8} 2098^{8} **>86f<**

Ivory Frontier (IRE) 5 ch h Imperial Frontier (USA)-Ivory Home (FR) (Home Guard (USA)) 2217a^{6} 2565a^{2} 3325a^{2} 3787a^{5} **>111f<**

Ivory's Grab Hire 2 b c Shavian-Knees Up (USA) (Dancing Champ (USA)) 1054^{8} 1288^{2} 1481^{5} 1590^{6} 1699^{2} 1989^{3} 2204^{5} 2656^{2} 2965^{4} 3135^{3} 3350^{6} **>72f<**

Ivy Lilian (IRE) 3 b f Cyrano de Bergerac-Catherine Clare (Sallust) *107^{5} 197^{6} 305^{2} 392^{6} 420^{3}* 507^{4} *602^{4} 629^{7}* 856^{14} 1042^{7} *1331^{8}* 1521^{8} 1718^{11} 2018^{9} **>52a 46f<**

Izza 4 b f Unfuwain (USA)-Wantage Park (Pas de Seul) 597^{7} 785^{14} 965^{9} 1081^{9} 1271^{11} 1649^{12} 1873^{14} 2186^{2} 2374^{6} (2545) 2854^{6} 3435^{7} 3724^{8} **>44f<**

J

Jaazim 5 ch h Night Shift (USA)-Mesmerize (Mill Reef (USA)) 3175^{10} 3359^{20} 3605^{18} **>61f<**

Jabaroot (IRE) 4 b c Sadler's Wells (USA)-Arctic Heroine (USA) (Arctic Tern (USA)) 1558^{9} **>85f<**

Jackatack (IRE) 3 b c Astronef-Redwood Hut (Habitat) *529^{6} (560) 628^{8}* 745^{8} 907^{5} 1407^{8} 3841^{2} 4054^{5} 4152^{14} **>63a 55f<**

Jack Button (IRE) 6 b h Kings Lake (USA)-Tallantire (USA) (Icecapade (USA)) 998^{6} **>96f<**

Jack Jennings 2 ch c Deploy-Lareyna *2381^{2}* (2681) 3068^{6} 3490^{4} 3812^{3} **>77a 95?f<**

Jackmanii 3 b c Most Welcome-Blue Flower (FR) (Carwhite) 575^{5} 641^{4} 1026^{3} 1161^{13} 1430^{2} 1725^{2} 1817^{10} (2126) 2306^{3} 2353^{4} 2774^{3} 3669^{17} **>60f<**

Jackson Hill 2 b c Priolo (USA)-Orange Hill (High Top) 4058^{6} (4313) **>91+f<**

Jackson Park 2 gr g Domynsky-Hysteria (Prince Bee) 788^{9} 1665^{9} 1943^{4} 3460^{3} 3760^{2} **>52f<**

Jacks to Open (USA) 4 ch g The Minstrel (CAN)-Sublime Mime (USA) (His Majesty (USA)) 2863^{7} 3129^{11} 3344^{20} **>2f<**

Jacques Point 3 b f Jester-Hill of Fare (Brigadier Gerard) 3103^{6} 3508^{16} **>17a 32f<**

Jade City 5 gr g Belfort (FR)-Dear Glenda (Gold Song) 1538^{4} **>70df<**

Jade Pet 4 b or br f Petong-Pea Green (Try My Best (USA)) 1777^{8} (2092) 2764^{11} 3065^{7} **>90df<**

Jadidh 7 b m Touching Wood (USA)-Petrol (Troy) *252^{7}* **>29a f<**

Jadwal (USA) 3 br f Woodman (USA)-Bolt From The Blue (USA) (Blue Times (USA)) 1105^{5} 1782^{4} 2101^{6} 2525^{6} 2780^{3} 3127^{2} 3505^{4} 3723^{7} 3978^{2} 4189^{5} **>89f<**

Jafeica (IRE) 4 b c Dance of Life (USA)-Moretta (Artaius (USA)) 425^{7} 666^{6} 1482^{3} 1618^{6} 2369^{10} 3067^{9} **>103f<**

Jagellon (USA) 4 b c Danzig Connection (USA)-Heavenlyspun (USA) (His Majesty (USA)) 764^{10} 3754^{4} 3876^{2} (4051) (4163) 4257^{2} **>98f<**

Jahangir (IRE) 6 ch h Ballad Rock-Marsh Benham 4268^{16} **>32f<**

Jahid (USA) 3 ch c Diesis-Hot Topic (USA) (The Minstrel (CAN)) 609a^{5} **>111f<**

Jairzinho (USA) 6 b h Robellino (USA)-B F's Sailingal (USA) 817^{15} 1095^{8} 1202^{12} *2073^{8} 2377^{11}* **>22a 46f<**

Jalcanto 5 ch h Jalmood (USA)-Bella Canto 2355^{2} 2996^{3} 3435^{4} 3627^{12} **>20a 69f<**

Jaleel 2 b c Jareer (USA)-Forest of Arden (Tap On Wood) 863^{5} (1774) 2765^{6} 2978^{7} 3947^{7} 4144^{6} **>70f<**

Jalfrezi 3 b f Jalmood (USA)-Annabrianna (Night Shift (USA)) 1053^{2} (1196) 1793^{2} 2348^{3} (2738) 3007^{5} **>94f<**

Jalmaid 3 ch f Jalmood (USA)-Misowni (Niniski (USA)) *64^{3} 149^{2} 232^{4} 306^{5} 2377^{8}* 2655^{5} 3097^{5} *(3734)* 3987^{17} *4128^{9} 4274^{10}* **>61a 60f<**

Jalore 6 gr h Jalmood (USA)-Lorelene (FR) *412^{9}* 556^{17} 598^{7} 778^{10} 840^{11} 1449^{3} 1957^{4} **>3a 41f<**

Jalwa (USA) 3 b f Northern Jove (CAN)-Outofthebluebell (USA) (Red Ryder (USA)) 1544^{7} 2776^{8} *3075^{10}* **>26a 62f<**

Jamaica Bridge 5 b g Doulab (USA)-Mill Hill (USA) (Riva Ridge (USA)) *2^{5} 82^{2} (140) 233^{5} 314^{2} 366^{2}* 578^{15} 1155^{9} *1571^{4} 2383^{8} 3073^{8} 3529^{7} 3739^{9} 3950^{4} 4274^{6}* **>55a 34f<**

Jamaican Flight (USA) 2 b c Sunshine Forever (USA)-Kalamona (USA) (Hawaii) 3617^{2} 3955^{7} **>70tf<**

Jambia 3 b f Sadler's Wells (USA)-Ala Mahlik (Ahonoora) 1346^{4} 2944^{4} **>88f<**

Jambo 2 b f Rambo Dancer (CAN)-Nicholess (Nicholas Bill) 1215^{4} 1503^{2} 1699^{6} 1841^{4} 1981^{2} (2155) **>60f<**

Jameel Asmar 3 br c Rock City-Barsham (Be My Guest (USA)) 1476^{13} (1825) (2433) 2571^{5} 3189^{2} 3730^{12} 3864^{2} **>94+f<**

Jam N Shadeed (USA) 3 b c Shadeed (USA)-Jamra (USA) (Icecapade (USA)) 616^{5} 853^{2} (973) 1222^{3} 1839^{23} 2240^{6} **>88f<**

Jamrat Jumairah (IRE) 2 b f Polar Falcon (USA)-Coryana (Sassafras (FR)) 4085^{2} **>79+f<**

Jandeel (IRE) 3 b c Last Tycoon-Pizziri (Artaius (USA)) 936^{3} (1270) (1684) 2348^{8} (3336) 3730^{18} **>106f<**

Jane's Super Top 3 ch g Superlative-Top Debutante (USA) (Monteverdi) 3543^{5} 3805^{12} **>53f<**

Janies Girl (IRE) 2 ch f Persian Heights-Lovat Spring (USA) (Storm Bird (CAN)) 2683^{3} 3283^{5} 3983^{13} **>50f<**

Jaraab 4 b c Sure Blade (USA)-Ostora (USA) (Blushing Groom (FR)) *(321) (374)* 582^{10} 649^{12} *(833) (1075) 1086^{2}* 1470^{5} 1535^{3} 1794^{10} 2942^{5} *3245^{11} 3527^{11} 3735^{7} 4126^{3}* **>67a 55f<**

Jarah (USA) 2 b c Forty Niner (USA)-Umniyatee (Green Desert (USA)) (2573) 3141^{3} **>91f<**

Jareer Do (IRE) 3 b f Jareer (USA)-Shining Bright (USA) (Bold Bidder (USA)) 1979^{6} 2265^{3} 3347^{5} 3897^{10} *4125^{7}* **>40a 67f<**

Jarrow 4 ch g Jalmood (USA)-Invite (Be My Guest (USA)) 549^{18} *771^{W}* 879^{4} 1160^{9} *2495^{6}* 3724^{11} **>31a 48f<**

Jarzon Dancer 7 br h Lidhame-Long Valley (Ribero) 1141^{10} 1622^{17} 1694^{10} 2089^{3} 2268^{13} 2439^{11} *2600^{3}* 2687^{4} 2789^{13} 2981^{7} *3078^{5}* **>31a 36f<**

Jato 6 b h Pharly (FR)-Minsden's Image (Dancers Image (USA)) 838^{3} 1179^{2} 1560^{8} 1915^{6} 2130^{6} 3457^{7} 3615^{18} 3943^{7} **>3a 74f<**

Java Red (IRE) 3 b g Red Sunset-Coffee Bean (Doulab (USA)) 818^{5} *1030^{3}* (1191) 1825^{9} **>57a 60f<**

Jawaal 5 ch h Soviet Star (USA)-Pencil Sharpener (USA) (Sharpen Up) 714^{2} (870) (1108) 1618^{8} 1851^{29} **>108+f<**

Jawani (IRE) 7 b h Last Tycoon-Fabled Lady (Bold Lad (IRE)) *109^{2}* **>62a f<**

Jawlaat (USA) 3 b or br f Dayjur (USA)-Elle Seule (USA) (Exclusive Native (USA)) 662^{4} 985^{3} 1624^{2} (2194) (2458) 2748^{5} 3446^{8} 3922^{3} 4119^{4} **>96f<**

Jayannpee 4 ch c Doulab (USA)-Amina (Brigadier Gerard) 858^{3} 1019^{2} 1637^{6} 1766^{5} 2570^{3} 2764^{3} 3236^{6} 3446^{4} 3551^{12} 3815^{12} 4033^{18} **>102df<**

J C Grey 3 gr c Grey Desire-Mazurkanova (Song) 880^{4} 1080^{9} 1377^{7} 1669^{15} 1956^{5} **>44f<**

Jean de Florette (USA) 4 b c Our Native (USA)-The Branks (USA) (Hold Your Peace (USA)) *15^{9} 166^{10}* 1502^{5} 1817^{7} 2089^{4} 2224^{2} 2658^{3} 2687^{3} *2919^{6}* 3056^{3} 3384^{7} 3521^{6} 3641^{15} 4051^{16} **>34a 43f<**

Jean-Pierre 0 S 3104^{4} 3449^{8} 4226^{9} **>47f<**

Jedaal 2 b c Soviet Star (USA)-Donya (Mill Reef (USA)) (1190) (1860) **>95+f<**

Jed Forest (USA) 4 ch c Gold Alert (USA)-What A Twist (USA) *4308a^{10}* **>103a f<**

Jehol 9 b h Teenoso (USA)-Buz Kashi 1971^{4} 2450^{14} 2976^{7} **>53f<**

Jelali (IRE) 2 b c Last Tycoon-Lautreamont (Auction Ring (USA)) 3890^{8} 4064^{4} **>73f<**

Jellaby Askhir 3 b c Salse (USA)-Circus Act (Shirley Heights) 1147^{4} (2944) (3389) 3609^{9} 3923^{4} 4323^{7} **>110f<**

Jemima Puddleduck 4 ch f Tate Gallery (USA)-Tittlemouse (Castle Keep) *266^{4}* 454^{2} 549^{3} 744^{5} 1324^{7} 1539^{5} 3987^{11} 4135^{9} 4332^{10} **>62a 52f<**

Jemsilverthorn (IRE) 2 b c Maelstrom Lake-Fairy Don (Don) 1011^{6} 1123^{8} 1481^{8} 1590^{7} 1829^{6} 2047^{5} 4133^{13} 4222^{6} *4273^{11}* **>32a 55f<**

Jemthorn Bishop 3 b c Chief Singer-Ravens Peak (High Top) *10^{8} 57^{5} 86^{6}* **>35a 49f<**

Jenaxa 2 ch f Jendali (USA)-Laxay (Laxton) 2857^{8}

Jenny's Charmer 2 ch c Charmer-Jenny Wyllie (Nishapour (FR)) 3018^{9} 3312^{4} *3738^{9}* 3937^{19} 4097^{14} **>17a 49f<**

Jenopis 2 b f Jendali (USA)-Asoness (Laxton) 2859^{10} **>16f<**

Jereed's Tut (IRE) 2 b f Mac's Imp (USA)-Jereed (IRE) (Kings Lake (USA)) *2924^{13} 3244^{7}*

Jermyn Street (USA) 4 b c Alleged (USA)-My Mother Mary (USA) (Boldnesian) 668^{19} **>79f<**

Jerry Cutrona (IRE) 2 br g Distinctly North (USA)-Foulkesmills (Tanfirion) 3185^{8} 3427^{4} 3530^{7} 3760^{8} 4151^{3} 4285^{2} (4327) **>68f<**

Jersey Belle 3 b f Distant Relative-Hong Kong Girl (Petong) *101^{2} 283^{6}* 482^{10} *591^{6} 891^{2}* 1499^{7} 1718^{8} *(2144) 2497^{3} 2963^{4}* **>56a 53f<**

Jessica's Secret (IRE) 3 ch f Classic Secret (USA)-Ferry Lane (Dom Racine (FR)) *363^{5} 830^{9}* 1000^{10} 1419^{4} 1721^{13} 1739^{9} 2018^{4} 2372^{5} **>32a 50f<**

Jessica's Song 2 b f Colmore Row-Sideloader Special (Song) *2382^{5} 2591^{5}* 2838^{3} (3520) 3895^{12} **>51a 66f<**

Jess Rebec 7 br m Kala Shikari-Laleston (Junius (USA)) 1257^{9} **>18f<**

Jet Classic 3 b f Risk Me (FR)-Sophisticated Lady (FR) (Habitat) *392^{10}* 1580^{8} 1963^{18} 2239^{11} 2582^{10} 2837^{8} **>52f<**

Jeux Interdits 3 ch c Master Willie-Priors Dean (Monsanto (FR)) 3138^{5} **>61f<**

Jewel Thief 5 b g Green Ruby (USA)-Miss Display

(Touch Paper) 1255^{10} 1714^{5} 2115^{5} **>31a 44f<**

Jewel Trader 3 b c Green Ruby (USA)-Maiden Bidder (Shack (USA)) 1165^{9} 1512^{13} 1831^{5} 2037^{4} 2245^{4} 2711^{5} 3058^{5} 3521^{10} **>52f<**

Jezyah (USA) 2 ch f Chief's Crown (USA)-Empress Jackie (USA) (Mount Hagen (FR)) 2351^{11} 3539^{2} 3948^{3} (4216) **>80f<**

Jhan Jeon 3 b f Aragon-Hala (Persian Bold) 1155^{7} *1630^{9}* **>54f<**

Jibereen 3 b c Lugana Beach-Fashion Lover (Shiny Tenth) 939^{9} 1222^{10} 1754^{9} 2616^{10} 3214^{12} 3943^{19} (4053) **>85f<**

Jigadee Creek 3 ch c Sharpo-River's Rising (FR) (Mendez (FR)) 761^{12} 2414^{7} 3654^{10} 3920^{22} **>57f<**

Jigsaw Boy 6 ch h Homeboy-Chiparia 434^{4} 567^{5} 812^{6} 1174^{6} 1354^{3} 1599^{2} 1676^{11} *3739^{5}* 3800^{17} *3954^{4} 4274^{2} 4337^{11}* **>65a 65f<**

Jihaad (USA) 5 b h Chief's Crown (USA)-Desirable (Lord Gayle (USA)) *96^{7} 121^{7}* **>46a 38f<**

Jilly Beveled 3 b f Beveled (USA)-Karens Valentine (Daring March) 3023^{8} 3239^{8} 3653^{12} 4249^{15} **>52f<**

Jilly Jaffa Cake (IRE) 3 ch f Waajib-Lady Fandet (Gay Fandango (USA)) *95^{2} 185^{4} 292^{10}* **>57a f<**

Jilmez (ITY) 2 b c Belmez-Jilt (4005a)

Jimbo 4 b c Salse (USA)-Darnelle (Shirley Heights) 485^{14} 637^{11} 1072^{8} *1568^{12}* **>39f<**

Jimjareer (IRE) 2 br c Jareer (USA)-Onthecomet (Chief Singer) *(1879)* 2696^{2} 2904^{4} 3721^{5} 3985^{12} 4285^{8} **>50+a 60f<**

Jive Baby 2 b g Crowning Honors (CAN)-Jive Music (Music Boy) 3110^{7} 4109^{15} 4230^{9} **>9f<**

Jiyush 2 b c Generous (IRE)-Urjwan (USA) (Seattle Slew (USA)) 4063^{2} 4241^{4} **>92f<**

Jobber's Fiddle 3 b f Sizzling Melody-Island Mead (Pharly (FR)) 546^{11} *847^{8}* 1664^{7} 1974^{8} 2246^{4} 2789^{6} 3429^{4} 3759^{6} **>40a 55f<**

Jobie 5 b h Precocious-Lingering (Kind of Hush) 796^{5} 922^{7} 1174^{5} 1409^{8} 2079^{3} 2288^{7} 3442^{2} 3681^{4} 4134^{12} **>71f<**

Joe Jagger (IRE) 4 b c Petorius-Seapoint (Major Point) *45^{12}* **>6a 57df<**

Joe Shaw 2 ch g Interrex (CAN)-Super Lady 3821^{14} **>12f<**

Johann Quatz (FR) 6 b h Sadler's Wells (USA)-Whakilyric (USA) (Miswaki (USA)) 3576a^{U} **>128f<**

Johansson (USA) 3 b c Seattle Dancer (USA)-Baby Grace (ARG) (Cipayo (ARG)) 1113a^{3} 2219a^{4} 3481a^{2} 3789a^{6} **>113f<**

Johayro 2 ch c Clantime-Arroganza (Crofthall) 424^{2} 617^{2} 3110^{2} 3465^{7} 3668^{10} 3848^{5} (4109) **>77f<**

John Lee Hooker 3 b c Superlative-Aunt Jemima (Busted) 618^{10} 974^{7} 1382^{6} 1695^{3} 2026^{3} (2244) 2550^{2} 3071^{3} 3351^{5} **>79f<**

Johnnie the Joker 4 gr g Absalom-Magic Tower (Tower Walk) 702^{7} 839^{6} 1297^{4} 1469^{4} 1680^{4} 3534^{15} 3808^{14} 4115^{9} 4233^{7} **>82a 62f<**

Johnny Jones (USA) 2 b c Mr Prospector (USA)-Fantastic Look (USA) (Green Dancer (USA)) 3472^{5} 3839^{3} **>61f<**

John O'Dreams 10 b g Indian King (USA)-Mississipi Shuffle 656^{7} 856^{7} 1057^{12} 2247^{6} 2410^{5} 2551^{6} 2992^{8} 3424^{5} 3519^{4} 3632^{3} 3878^{4} 4165^{19} **>65f<**

Johns Act (USA) 5 b h Late Act (USA)-Deluxe Type (USA) (Singh (USA)) *106^{4} 193^{3} 325^{3} (396)* 423^{9} (1410) 1794^{5} 3489^{5} 3730^{11} 4325^{6} **>74a 82f<**

Johns Joy 0 S 3987^{12} **>56f<**

John's Law (IRE) 2 b c Contract Law (USA)-Vieux Carre (Pas de Seul) *2958^{11}*

John-T 2 b c Thatching-Ower (IRE) (Lomond (USA)) 2846^{15} **>35f<**

Joint Effort (IRE) 4 b f Last Tycoon-Monterana (Sallust) *71^{3} 101^{3} 142^{6} 397^{6} 405^{5}* **>45a 65f<**

Join the Clan 6 ch m Clantime-Joint Reward (Netherkelly) (1354) 1614^{9} 1895^{15} (2120) 2418^{3} 2570^{7} 3005^{6} 3236^{8} 3446^{7} 3551^{6} 3637^{13} 3660^{5} **>97f<**

Joint Prospect 3 b c Midyan (USA)-Freely Given *51^{2} 32^{7} 189^{9}* **>35a 39f<**

Jolis Absent 5 b m Primo Dominie-Jolimo *259^{11}* 3627^{19} **>32a 52f<**

Jolis Present 2 b c Prince Sabo-Jolimo 617^{8} (849) 1608^{6} 2847^{6} 3471^{5} 3901^{5} 4243^{8} **>65f<**

Jolly Hokey 3 b c Dominion-Judy's Dowry (Dragonara Palace (USA)) 3638^{15} 3972^{12} **>16a 45f<**

Jolly Swagman 4 b g Governor General-Armour of Light (Hot Spark) *136^{6} 260^{12}* **>34a f<**

Jolto 6 b h Noalto-Joytime (John de Coombe) 870^{4} 1052^{6} 1261^{6} (1676) 1915^{7} 2743^{6} (3175) 3545^{12} 4041^{3} 4157^{18} 4319^{8} **>79f<**

Jo Maximus 3 b c Prince Sabo-Final Call 483^{6} 645^{3} 742^{2} 1094^{12} (1515) 1815^{3} 2168^{2} 2556^{3} 2802^{5} 3359^{9} 3554^{9} (3771) 3960^{4} **>81df<**

Jo Mell 2 b g Efisio-Militia Girl (Rarity) 2820^{4} 3416^{4} (3666) 4001^{3} **>89f<**

Jona Holley 2 b g Sharpo-Spurned (USA) (Robellino (USA)) 3890^{12} 4161^{14} **>65f<**

Jonbel 7 b h Norwick (USA)-Two Shots (Dom Racine (FR)) *229^{7} 387^{5} 414^{11}* 586^{10} **>27a 23f<**

Jo N Jack (IRE) 7 ch g Gorytus (USA)-Dancing Song (Ridan (USA)) *3082^{14}*

Jonjas Chudleigh 8 ch g Aragon-Lizabeth Chudleigh (Imperial Fling (USA)) *152^{7}* 938^{12} **>53f<**

Jon's Choice 7 b g Andy Rew-Whangarei (Gold Rod) *69^{12} 244^{5} 307^{8} 400^{5} 511^{7} 532^{7} 2492^{8} 2631^{4} 2963^{7} 3072^{6}* 3293^{12} *3511^{4}* 3534^{14} **>53a 60f<**

Joseph's Robe (USA) 4 ch c Lord At War-Cunningly 3574a^{2}

Joseph's Wine (IRE) 6 b h Smile (USA)-Femme Gendarme (USA) (Policeman (FR)) *(52) 81^{5}* 430^{2} **>86da 76f<**

Jovale 3 ch c Clantime-Cutler Heights *95^{11}* **>38da 36f<**

Jovie King (IRE) 3 ch c Salt Dome (USA)-Jovial Josie (USA) 585^{10} 1476^{10} 1731^{3} 2033^{7} 2279^{7} 2314^{15} 3756^{7} 3862^{12} **>47f<**

Joyce E Jackson 5 ch m Mansingh (USA)-Economy Pep (Jimmy Reppin) *21^{5} 109^{9} 329^{11}* **>29a f<**

Joyful (IRE) 3 b f Green Desert (USA)-Optimistic Lass (USA) (Mr Prospector (USA)) 2265^{5} *(4296)* **>63a 60f<**

Joyful Times 3 br f Doc Marten-Time for Joy (Good Times (ITY)) *48^{3} 95^{6} 171^{8} (258) 348^{4} 587^{4} 847^{4}* 1371^{6} *1760^{7}* 2088^{16} **>47a 24f<**

Joyrider 4 b c Risk Me (FR)-Villajoyosa (FR) (Satingo) *186^{8}* 598^{8} 4062^{16} **>42a 31f<**

Joys First 4 ch c Tina's Pet-Greenhills Joy (Radetzky)

884[13] 1657[5] *2960[6]* 3184[7] **>24a 53f<**

Jubilee Line 5 ch m High Line-Consistent Queen (Queen's Hussar) 860[8] *1086[8]* 2245[2] 3056[10] 3402[U] 3501[10] **>12a 40df<**

Jubilee Place (IRE) 2 br f Prince Sabo-Labelon Lady (Touching Wood (USA)) 1857[2] 2308[3] (2548) (2982) **>73f<**

Jubran (USA) 9 b h Vaguely Noble-La Vue (USA) (Reviewer (USA)) 1415[8] 1561[4] 1817[5] 1875[2] 2002[3] 2123[4] 2433[9] 2672[4] 3021[5] 3433[4] 3531[10] 3665[10] 3743[11] **>73f<**

Jucea 6 b m Bluebird (USA)-Appleby Park (Bay Express) (856) 994[4] 1023[5] 1595[4] 1777[6] 2247[7] 3442[12] 3622[14] 3783[3] 3992[7] 4142[6] 4165[5] 4278[2] **>68f<**

Judge Advocate (IRE) 3 b c Contract Law (USA)-Brigadina (Brigadier Gerard) 3091[8] 3237[9] **>71f<**

Judge and Jury 6 br h Law Society (USA)-Full of Reason (USA) (Bold Reason (USA)) 476[9] **>21f<**

Judgement Call 8 b h Alzao (USA)-Syllabub (Silly Season) 583[6] 949[9] 1265[6] 1595[5] 1832[7] 2179[5] 2502[4] (2887) 3014[3] 3219[3] 3442[11] 3681[5] **>51f<**

Juice Plus 4 ch g Kris-Highland Light 598[6] 820[9] 1037[10] 1666[6] 1854[18] 2755[6] 3295[8] 3853[8] **>25f<**

Juicy 2 b c Marju (IRE)-Seductress (Known Fact (USA)) 3110[3] 3352[2] 3713[6] 3857[5] 4111[4] **>77f<**

Ju Ju's Girl (IRE) 5 br m Fools Holme (USA)-Arctic Ford (FR) (Arctic Tern (USA)) *409[4]* *835[7]* **>53da f<**

Julgarant (IRE) 2 ch g Jareer (USA)-Naval Artiste (Captain's Gig (USA)) 1678[4] 1959[3] 2185[11] 2606[4] 3120[3] 3253[6] **>49f<**

Julia's Freebee 4 b f Interrex (CAN)-Canadian Charisma (Supreme Sovereign) 1337[7] 1509[10] 2113[3] 2404[9] 2843[8] 3344[12] **>50f<**

Jumairah Sun (IRE) 3 b f Scenic-Sun on the Spey (Glint of Gold) 544[3] (3183) 3595[2] 3636[11] **>100?f<**

Jumilla (USA) 3 b f El Gran Senor (USA)-Refill (Mill Reef (USA)) 3013[3] 3278[3] 3636[2] **>111f<**

Jump The Lights 2 b c Siberian Express (USA)-Turtle Dove *3525[8]* 4172[6] 4247[8] **>40a 63f<**

Jungle Rites (IRE) 7 b g Indian King (USA)-Spring Step (Tepukei) 1555[6] 1965[12] **>43f<**

Junior Ben (IRE) 3 b c Tirol-Piney Pass (Persian Bold) 747[4] 1439[3] 1948[4] 3130[5] *3526[12]* 3862[9] **>71f<**

Jural 3 ch f Kris-Just Cause (Law Society (USA)) 3486a[2] 3609[10] **>105f<**

Jurassic Sue 3 b f Distant Relative-Sculpture Bleue (Claude Monet (USA)) 664[9] 989[5] 1380[7] 1532[2] 2032[5] 2207[3] 3034[7] **>74?f<**

Just Another High (IRE) 2 b f High Estate-Footway (Sovereign Path) 1671[10] 2346[8] 3592[16] 4045[9] **>42f<**

Just Bob 6 b h Alleging (USA)-Diami (Swing Easy (USA)) 535[18] 723[15] 812[10] 926[12] 1152[8] 1376[8] 1689[4] 1741[2] 1827[5] 2997[2] 3313[5] 3597[3] 3667[5] 3992[16] **>56a 71f<**

Just by Chance 3 b c Teenoso (USA)-Skerryvore (Kalaglow) 3517[5] **>22f<**

Just Dissident (IRE) 3 b g Dancing Dissident (USA)-Betty Bun (St Chad) 697[9] 850[14] 1181[3] 1419[2] 1602[2] 1809[4] (1949) 2394[7] 3418[8] 3597[12] 3667[22] 3715[23] 4041[23] 4165[9] **>62f<**

Just Fizzy 3 b f Efisio-Redcross Miss (Tower Walk) 526[17] 651[3] 773[2] 974[6] 1371[2] (1718) 1962[6] (2149) 2332[2] 2586[2] 2755[2] 2862[5] **>39a 67f<**

Just Flamenco 4 ch c Scorpio (FR)-Suzannah's Song (Song) 579[9] 1649[7] *1760[5]* 1991[5] (2314) 2490[6] (2657) 2980[8] 3659[13] 3987[7] 4061[19] *4335[8]* **>46a 61f<**

Just for a Reason 3 b c Siberian Express (USA)-Artaius Rose (FR) (Artaius (USA)) 888[6] 1204[5] 1834[6] **>66f<**

Justfortherecord 3 br f Forzando-Classical Vintage (Stradavinsky) 3712[11] 4162[9] **>42f<**

Just Happy (USA) 4 b c Night Shift (USA)-Mesmerize (Mill Reef (USA)) 1235a[2] 1385[2] 1836[4] 4007a[6] **>117f<**

Just Harry 4 ch c High Kicker (USA)-Dorame (Music Boy) *(1) (44) 89[7] 195[6]* 450[2] 546[2] 1344[3] 1506[2] 1542[2] 1855[2] 2222[5] 2345[2] 2797[6] 2979[10] 3621[8] 3645[5] 3808[8] 3885[4] 4035[9] 4171[10] **>84da 72f<**

Just Ice 2 b f Polar Falcon (USA)-Justine (GER) 1579[4] (1722) 2335[4] 2706[2] (2847) 3132[2] (3583a) 3702[7] **>87f<**

Just Jesting 3 ch g Jester-Echo Chamber (Music Boy) *85[6] 124[5] 299[5] 342[6]* **>39a 65f<**

Just Lady 2 b f Emarati (USA)-Just Run (IRE) (Runnett) 508[6] (699) 977[7] 1177[2] 1833[2] 2940[4] 3568[10] **>67f<**

Just Like Me 3 b f Primo Dominie-Amina (Brigadier Gerard) 1360[3] 1602[4] 2203[4] 2344[5] 3442[3] 3678[2] 3800[15] **>66f<**

Just Lucky (IRE) 3 b c Fools Holme (USA)-Miss Victoria (Auction Ring (USA)) *250[6] 276[5]* 813[16] *1033[U]* 1649[13] 2807[5] 3057[8] 4152[9] **>72da 37f<**

Just-Mana-Mou (IRE) 3 b c Caerleon (USA)-Clarista (USA) (Riva Ridge (USA)) 1512[17] 1812[3] 2278[4] 2984[4] *3526[10]* 3825[10] 4205[5] **>51a 60f<**

Just Millie (USA) 2 ch f Elmaamul (USA)-La Plus Belle (USA) (Robellino (USA)) (3427) 3680[5] 3915[3] **>74f<**

Just Nuisance 2 b f Hadeer-Pacific Gull (USA) (Storm Bird (CAN)) 2579[4] 3532[7] 3883[11] 4151[8] **>67f<**

Just One Bid (IRE) 2 ch c Jareer (USA)-Roberts Pride (Roberto (USA)) 1726[12] **>57f<**

Just Rory 2 b g Skyliner-Judys Girl (IRE) (Simply Great (FR)) 490[4] 615[W] 996[4] 1158[6] *1954[4] 2146[8]* 2796[6] 3253[7] **>28a 54f<**

Just Whistle 3 gr f Absalom-Aunt Blue (Blue Refrain) 752[7] 1000[8] 1309[4] 1598[8] 2088[10] *2587[10]* 2769[2] **>11a 55f<**

Juweilla 3 b f Pharly (FR)-National Dress (Welsh Pageant) 1294[3] 1735[5] 2822[4] 2993[R] 3247[4] **>67df<**

Juyush (USA) 3 b c Silver Hawk (USA)-Silken Doll (USA) (Chieftain II) (438) 1107[5] 1345[3] (1925) 2366[2] 2702[8] **>110f<**

K

Kaafih Homm (IRE) 4 b g Kefaah (USA)-Shereeka (Shergar) *76[2] (100) (127) (152) 445[4]* 668[17] 935[16] 1324[3] 1531[2] 1830[3] (1911) 1991[3] (3572) (3679) 3769[5] **>69a 73f<**

Kabanova (FR) 3 b f Tropular-Karsana (FR) (Kenmare (FR)) 209a[3]

Kabcast 10 b h Kabour-Final Cast (Saulingo) 1342[8] *1566[13]* 1721[7] 2160[7] 2521[5] 2736[10] 2879[3] 3116[7] 3252[4] 3357[9] 3622[24] **>13a 48f<**

Kabil 3 b c Doyoun-Alkariyh (USA) (Alydar (USA)) 681[2] 939[3] 1915[5] 2099[4] 2471[4] 3209[3] 3488[7] 3924[2] **>96f<**

Kadiri (IRE) 4 b g Darshaan-Kadissya (USA) (Blushing Groom (FR)) *13[3] (87)* 556[8] 751[3] 840[3] 1328[4] 1607[4] 1840[13] *4336[4]* **>71a 67f<**

Kaf 3 ch c Polish Precedent (USA)-Usaylah (Siberian Express (USA)) 539^{8} 736^{3} (1944) 2115^{7} **>78+f<**

Kafani Al Widd (FR) 3 b c Royal Academy (USA)-Belle Arrivee (Bustino) 1167^{11} (1846) 2188^{8} **>70f<**

Kahir Almaydan (IRE) 2 b c Distinctly North (USA)-Kilfenora (Tribal Chief) 1184^{2} (1803) 2440^{2} 2704^{3} (3420) (3731) 3903^{3} **>109f<**

Kai's Lady (IRE) 2 b f Jareer (USA)-Rathnaleen (Scorpio (FR)) 1369^{6}

Kaitak (IRE) 4 ch g Broken Hearted-Klairelle (Klairon) 433^{19} *601*^{9} **>46a 78f<**

Kajostar 5 ch m Country Classic-Rasimareem (Golden Mallard) 2162^{7} 2698^{16} 2913^{10} 3275^{14} **>25f<**

Kalabo (USA) 3 b c Trempolino (USA)-Kalikala (Darshaan) 1897^{3} 2670^{5} 3609^{7} **>114f<**

Kalakate 10 gr h Kalaglow-Old Kate (Busted) *588*^{4} 1622^{8} *2147*^{9} **>25a 33f<**

Kalamata 3 ch c Kalaglow-Good Try 3377^{5} 3847^{2} 4096^{2} 4283^{6} **>72f<**

Kalao Tua (IRE) 2 b f Shaadi (USA)-Lisa's Favourite (Gorytus (USA)) 2467^{2} 3865^{28} **>69+f<**

Kalar 6 b h Kabour-Wind And Reign (Tumble Wind (USA)) *69*^{2} *154*^{2} *188*^{7} *327*^{3} *(369) 398*^{9} 475^{3} 491^{2} 688^{4} 701^{4} 994^{6} 1023^{3} 1271^{5} 1508^{4} *1882*^{9} 2163^{7} 2521^{2} (2837) 3123^{9} (3357) 3554^{5} 3667^{4} 3919^{23} *4295*^{5} **>71a 54f<**

Kala Star 4 gr f Kalaglow-Tantot 744^{11} 860^{10} **>57f<**

Kala Sunrise 2 ch c Kalaglow-Belle of the Dawn (Bellypha) 523^{4} (671) 1871^{7} 3606^{8} 3746^{8} 4139^{4} **>89?f<**

Kaldouneeves (FR) 4 gr c Kaldoun (FR)-Safaroa (FR) (Faraway Son (USA)) (704a) **>111f<**

Kaldounevees(FR) 4 gr c Kaldoun-Safaroa (Satingo) 1002a^{3} (1711a) 2894a^{2} 3576a^{4} **>119f<**

Kalimnos 0 S 1713a^{2} **>101f<**

Kalimnos (GER) 3 c 2215a^{16} 3200a^{3} **>91f<**

Kalko 6 b h Kalaglow-Salchow (Niniski (USA)) 568^{16} 2931^{5} 3852^{16} **>23a 13f<**

Kalou 4 b f K-Battery-Louise Moulton 558^{5} 676^{2} 988^{7} 1192^{2} 1437^{3} 2064^{8} 3367^{4} (3505) 3718^{2} 3963^{2} 4028^{11} 4289^{3} **>79f<**

Kamari (USA) 2 ch c Woodman (USA)-Karri Valley (USA) (Storm Bird (CAN)) 3967^{5} **>69f<**

Kama Simba 3 b c Lear Fan (USA)-Dance It (USA) (Believe It (USA)) *842*^{4} 1583^{4} (1962) 2132^{2} 2282^{6} 2574^{2} 2828^{4} **>43a 65f<**

Kanat Lee (IRE) 4 b f Salse (USA)-Badiya (USA) (Sir Ivor) 988^{17} 1292^{4} 1557^{6} 1966^{3} 2196^{5} 2482^{9} 2954^{6} 3262^{4} 3627^{17} 3852^{11} **>39f<**

Kandavu 2 b f Safawan-Baladee (Mummy's Pet) 508^{2} (716) 852^{5} 1137^{6} 1727^{4} 2029^{3} 2442^{13} 4084^{7} 4206^{13} **>79f<**

Kandyan 4 b g Shareef Dancer (USA)-Kandia (GER) (Luciano) 3384^{3} 3462^{2} (3657) 3723^{2} 3778^{2} **>82f<**

Kangra Valley 4 ch f Indian Ridge-Thorner Lane (Tina's Pet) 656^{11} 746^{10} *1566*^{12} **>57a 47f<**

Kanika 3 gr f Be My Chief (USA)-Kalisha (Rainbow Quest (USA)) 3448^{6}

Karaar 3 b c Efisio-Elkie Brooks (Relkino) 1186^{14} 1615^{3} 2623^{3} 4049^{6} **>83df<**

Karamiyna (IRE) 3 b f Shernazar-Karamita (Shantung) (4301a) **>98f<**

Karayb (IRE) 3 b or br f Last Tycoon-Deira (NZ) (Sir Tristram) 1145^{3} (1500) 1923^{8} 2470^{5} 3602^{6} 3926^{17} 4065^{2} 4214^{2} **>95f<**

Karayib (USA) 3 b f Danzig (USA)-Aghani (USA) (Blushing Groom (FR)) 620^{11} 1362^{7} 1588^{7} 1923^{7} **>87f<**

Karaylar (IRE) 3 b g Kahyasi-Karamana (Habitat) 3725^{11} **>13f<**

Karaysar 3 b c Bikala-Kariya (Irish River) 3479a^{2} **>83f<**

Kardelle 5 b m Kalaglow-Arderelle (FR) (Pharly (FR)) 505^{15} **>19a 37f<**

Karibu (GER) 4 b g Dancing Brave (USA)-Kaiserstadt (GER) (Dschingi's Khan) 790^{4} 1206^{8} 1420^{4} 3853^{10} 4002^{11} **>56f<**

Karina Heights (USA) 3 b f Irish Tower (USA)-Love Sick (USA) (Raise A Native) (522) 719^{5} 1641^{2} 2120^{7} 3166^{8} 3715^{24} **>79f<**

Karinska 5 b m Master Willie-Kaiserchronik (GER) (Cortez (GER)) *1*^{6} *269*^{5} 559^{8} (724) 873^{17} 1061^{6} (1468) (1663) 1845^{3} 2181^{3} 2748^{4} 2946^{12} 3457^{12} 3607^{3} 3802^{7} 3941^{3} 4116^{11} **>56a 77f<**

Karisma (IRE) 2 b c Tirol-Avra (FR) (Mendez (FR)) 3666^{4} 4037^{3} 4235^{3} **>72f<**

Karline Ka (FR) 4 ch f Franc Parler-Kadastra (FR) (Stradavinsky) 1826^{7} **>50f<**

Karliyka (IRE) 3 gr f Last Tycoon-Karlafsha 4299a^{2} **>103f<**

Karon Beach 4 ch f Handsome Sailor-Winter Resort (Miami Springs) 3083^{6} *3241*^{12} *3513*^{8} 3641^{17} **>32a 12f<**

Karttikeya (FR) 4 br c Darshaan-Karosa (FR) (Caro) 3030^{3} 3156^{6} 4168^{6} **>84f<**

Kass Alhawa 2 b c Shirley Heights-Silver Braid (USA) (Miswaki (USA)) 2912^{4} **>69+f<**

Kassbaan (USA) 5 b h Alydar (USA)-Ma Biche (USA) (Key to the Kingdom (USA)) 1227^{3} **>96f<**

Katie Komaite 2 b f Komaite (USA)-City to City (Windjammer (USA)) 1203^{6} 1448^{4} *2143*^{8} 2619^{3} 2932^{8} 4109^{12} 4231^{6} 4290^{3} **>33a 69f<**

Katie Oliver 3 b f Squill (USA)-Shih Ching (USA) (Secreto (USA)) 3804^{5} 3896^{5} 4168^{7} **>76f<**

Katie's Kid 5 br g Balidar-Khahmens Delight (Come On Grey) 1622^{2} (1788) 1937^{16} **>15a 44f<**

Katiniyd (IRE) 4 b g Kahyasi-Katiyfa 1780^{7}

Katya (IRE) 3 b f Dancing Dissident (USA)-Park Elect (Ahonoora) 437^{9} (621) 828^{2} 1305^{7} 1488^{5} 1891a^{3} 2066^{3} 2430^{4} 2895a^{5} 3005^{3} 3582a^{8} 3557^{3} 3660^{2} 3707^{2} 3834^{15} 3902^{3} 3938^{4} **>99f<**

Katy Koo 3 b f Presidium-Francis Furness (Burslem) 3060^{2} 3504^{11} 3747^{12} **>23f<**

Katy-Q (IRE) 2 b f Taufan (USA)-Swift Chorus (Music Boy) 1579^{9} 1919^{3} 2371^{2} 2914^{3} 3394^{6} (3740) **>70f<**

Katy's Lad 8 b h Camden Town-Cathryn's Song (Prince Tenderfoot (USA)) *1458*^{2} (1999) 4002^{5} *4126*^{7} **>73a 77f<**

Kausar (USA) 8 b h Vaguely Noble-Kozana (Kris) *234*^{8} *340*^{4} **>17a f<**

Kayaara (IRE) 3 2891a^{3} 3690a^{8} **>104f<**

Kayrawan (USA) 3 b c Mr Prospector (USA)-Muhbubh (USA) (Blushing Groom (FR)) 633^{6} 883^{5} 1370^{5} 2430^{7} **>94f<**

Kaytibos (GER) 4 b c Nebos-Kaytiggy (Busted) 4183a^{3} **>107f<**

Kayvee 6 gr h Kaldoun (FR)-Secret Life (USA) (Elocutionist (USA)) 870^{5} 1108^{2} 1851^{5} 2031^{4} (2598)

2948^{8} 3813^{15} 3945^{8} 4267^{10} >**108f**<

Kazaki 3 b c Sadler's Wells (USA)-Krakow (Malinowski (USA)) 670^{3} >**86tf**<

Kazimiera (IRE) 2 b f Polish Patriot (USA)-Cartier Bijoux (Ahonoora) 3465^{3} 3699^{6} 3940^{3} >**78df**<

Kealbra Lady 2 b f Petong-Greensward Blaze (Sagaro) 2077^{6}

Kebili (IRE) 2 b f Green Desert (USA)-Pebbles (Sharpen Up) 2136^{4} >**57f**<

Kedwick (IRE) 6 b g Be My Guest (USA)-Lady Pavlova *21^{2} 155^{3} 290^{5} 347^{2} 472^{2}* >**60a f**<

Keen To The Last (FR) 3 ch g Keen-Derniere Danse (Gay Mecene (USA)) 2553^{3} 3016^{7} 3294^{3} 3531^{15} 3875^{13} 3918^{9} >**76df**<

Keep Battling 5 b g Hard Fought-Keep Mum (Mummy's Pet) (991) (1437) 1687^{3} 1817^{2} 1933^{3} 2427^{4} 2610^{5} 2930^{7} 3169^{6} 3719^{7} 3743^{5} 3852^{6} 4038^{13} >**45f**<

Keepers Dawn (IRE) 2 b f Alzao (USA)-Keepers Lock (USA) (Sunny's Halo (CAN)) 2876^{6} 3069^{8} (3626) 3947^{16} >**80f**<

Keeper's Grey 3 gr c Touch of Grey-Mistress Will (USA) (Master Willie) *33^{3} 390^{5} 603^{7}* >**56a 54f**<

Keep Quiet 3 b f Reprimand-Silent Pool (Relkino) 1146^{10} 1509^{14} 4331^{13} >**31a 49f**<

Keep Your Distance 5 b h Elegant Air-Normanby Lass (Bustino) 2400^{2} (2478) (3308) (3665) (3853) (3898) (4101) 4201^{16} >**17a 79f**<

Keiko 2 ch f Generous (IRE)-Katsina (USA) (Cox's Ridge (USA)) 3371^{6} 3604^{4} 3873^{2} >**68f**<

Keith's Pride (IRE) 3 gr g Al Hareb (USA)-Zanskar (Godswalk (USA)) 593^{10} 875^{5} 990^{9} 1816^{7} >**40f**<

Kellaire Girl (IRE) 3 b f Gallic League-Frensham Manor (Le Johnstan) 451^{5} 645^{7} 1016^{6} 1263^{4} 1426^{13} *1939^{2}* 2332^{6} 2684^{4} 4152^{12} 4261^{10} >**51a 54f**<

Kelly Mac 5 b h Precocious-Ridalia 4053^{7} >**75a 68f**<

Kelly's Kite 7 br m Buzzards Bay-Bold Kelly (Pitskelly) *76^{9} 142^{10} 240^{9}* >**24da 19f**<

Kemo Sabo 3 b c Prince Sabo-Canoodle (Warpath) 504^{13} 614^{8} 774^{9} 1061^{2} 1250^{13} 1603^{5} 2117^{4} (2479) 2737^{13} 3020^{2} 3169^{3} 3368^{4} 3607^{18} >**88f**<

Kencol 3 b c Presidium-Silk Lady 581^{5} 732^{7} 855^{12} 1546^{10} 2538^{4} 2813^{8} >**66f**<

Kenesha (IRE) 5 br m Don't Forget Me-Calvino (Relkino) 479^{7} 594^{14} 790^{5} 906^{3} 1023^{7} 1042^{2} 1157^{9} 1739^{3} 1900^{6} 2475^{7} 2649^{2} 2736^{2} 2772^{5} 2997^{11} 3313^{4} 3508^{9} 3667^{9} 4113^{11} >**42f**<

Kenilworth Dancer 2 br c Shareef Dancer (USA)-Reltop 3784^{6} 3877^{9} 4188^{19} 4285^{14} >**44f**<

Kenilworth Ford 4 b f Merdon Melody-Earles-Field (Wolverlife) 1291^{12} 1469^{9} *1883^{12}* >**29a 3f**<

Kenny Davis (IRE) 2 b g Mazaad-Very Seldom (Rarity) 480^{6} 615^{13} >**42f**<

Kensington Freight 3 b f Clantime-Ascot Lass (Touching Wood (USA)) 656^{9} 856^{13} 1050^{14} 1812^{11} 2168^{6} 2491^{9} 2659^{7} 2843^{5} 3108^{6} >**48f**<

Kentavrus Way (IRE) 4 b c Thatching-Phantom Row (Adonijah) *161^{9} 402^{10} 3544^{7}* >**36a 55f**<

Kentford Conquista 2 b f El Conquistador-Notinhand (Nearly A Hand) 4148^{17}

Kentucky Flyer 4 ch f Bairn (USA)-Kentucky Air (USA) (Czaravich (USA)) *166^{8}* >**10a 23f**<

Kenyatta (USA) 6 b h Mogambo (USA)-Caranga (USA) (Caro) *13^{4}* 4332^{15} >**42a 34f**<

Kernof (IRE) 2 b g Rambo Dancer (CAN)-Empress Wu (High Line) 2542^{10} 2908^{4} 3117^{4} 3414^{5} 3684^{7} >**64f**<

Kerry Ring 2 b f Sadler's Wells (USA)-Kerrera (Diesis) 4313^{2} >**83+f**<

Kerulen 0 dk f Cadeaux Genereux-Kereolle (Riverman) (2899a) >**107f**<

Keston Pond (IRE) 5 b g Taufan (USA)-Maria Renata (Jaazeiro (USA)) (1991) 2181^{5} 3159^{8} 3181^{7} (3534) (3715) 3943^{23} 4156^{12} >**73a 84f**<

Kestrel Forboxes (IRE) 7 b h Seymour Hicks (FR)-Dance Mistress (Javelot) 3455^{3} 3501^{4} 3605^{10} >**75f**<

Ketabi (USA) 4 ch c Alydar (USA)-Ivory Fields (USA) (Sir Ivor) 505^{12} 668^{15} >**79f**<

Ketchican 3 b c Joligeneration-Fair Melys (FR) *382^{6}* 449^{6} >**30a 38f**<

Kevasingo 3 b c Superpower-Katharina *(448)* 648^{3} 867^{7} 1124^{3} 1322^{4} 1498^{11} 1745^{3} (2033) 2199^{2} 2537^{5} 2808^{6} 3455^{8} 3920^{17} >**55a 66f**<

Kewaashi (USA) 3 b f Storm Bird (CAN)-Klarifi (Habitat) 664^{12} 1195^{7} >**69+f**<

Key of Luck (USA) 4 b or br c Chief's Crown (USA)-Balbonella (FR) (Gay Mecene (USA)) 1572a^{9} 2562a^{4} >**107f**<

Key Pitch (USA) 3 ch c Dixieland Band (USA)-Gentle Persuasion (Bustino) *2377^{12}* 4157^{24} >**60a 64f**<

Keys Seminar 3 b c Pharly (FR)-Mums (Mummy's Pet) *189^{6} 273^{5} 350^{4} 448^{2} 513^{3} 766^{4}* 976^{4} *1088^{11}* 1379^{4} 1696^{11} 1854^{7} 2246^{19} 2744^{5} 3344^{7} 3638^{6} 3805^{7} >**53a 55f**<

Key To A Million (IRE) 2 b f Treasure Kay-North Lady (Northfields (USA)) 810^{6} 1287^{5} (1968) 2554^{5} (2886) 3587a^{3} 4203^{8} >**73f**<

Khabar 2 b c Forzando-Ella Mon Amour (Ela-Mana-Mou) 1964^{9} 2183^{6} 2681^{4} 3809^{5} >**79f**<

Khalidi (IRE) 6 b g Shernazar-Khaiyla (Mill Reef (USA)) 1858^{8} >**29f**<

Khalyani (IRE) 5 b h Akarad (FR)-Khaiyla (Mill Reef (USA)) 3108^{9} 3679^{16} 3871^{14} >**40f**<

Khamaseen 4 b c Slip Anchor-Tanouma (USA) (Miswaki (USA)) 440^{3} (735) (1114a) 1780^{4} 2219a^{5} 2702^{3} 3146^{4} 3581a^{5} 4092a^{2} >**118f**<

Khamseh 3 b f Thatching-Khalafiya (Darshaan) 616^{2} 865^{5} 1296^{2} (1931) 2240^{2} 2647^{7} 3209^{4} 3488^{4} >**88f**<

Khan 3 b c Be My Chief (USA)-Princess Rosananti (IRE) (Shareef Dancer (USA)) 1060^{4} 1269^{4} 1498^{13} 2499^{5} 2620^{3} 2731^{3} (2851) 3001^{2} 3229^{5} 3464^{7} 3843^{3} 4099^{5} >**59df**<

Khatim (USA) 3 b or br c Topsider (USA)-Khwlah (USA) (Best Turn (USA)) 1786^{8} (2504) 2718^{2} 3181^{2} >**75f**<

Khayrapour (IRE) 5 b h Kahyasi-Khayra (FR) 873^{7} 1183^{7} 1344^{2} (1626) 1926^{6} 2287^{2} (2703) >**95f**<

Khaytada (IRE) 3 b f Doyoun-Khaydara (Indian King (USA)) (707a) 1390a^{3} 2211a^{9} >**110f**<

Kid Ory 4 ch g Rich Charlie-Woomargama (Creetown) *139^{9} 269^{10}* 748^{3} 1355^{4} 1668^{3} 1828^{4} 2358^{2} 2698^{2} 3050^{2} 3396^{2} 3565^{5} (3807) 4115^{14} 4236^{7} >**28a 76f**<

Kierchem (IRE) 4 b c Mazaad-Smashing Gale (Lord Gayle (USA)) *2293^{4} 2495^{7}* >**63a 50f**<

Kilcoran Bay 3 b g Robellino (USA)-Catkin (USA) (Sir Ivor) 963^{3} 1221^{2} (1383) 1831^{10} 2571^{11} 3066^{11} 3646^{10}

>84df<

Kildee Lad 5 b h Presidium-National Time (USA) (Lord Avie (USA)) 434^{13} 636^{6} 796^{3} 1057^{6} 1193^{10} 1537^{7} 1777^{4} **>75f<**

Kildrummy Castle 3 b c Komaite (USA)-Khadine (Astec) 437^{10} 572^{4} 786^{6} 1219^{2} 1379^{3} 1957^{7} 2751^{2} 2875^{7} **>61f<**

Kilernan 4 ch c K-Battery-Lekuti (Le Coq d'Or) 1377^{10} 1529^{5} 1863^{2} (2186) 2545^{2} 2695^{2} 2854^{4} 3627^{4} 3724^{4} **>55f<**

Killatty Lark (IRE) 2 ch f Noalto-Killatty Sky (IRE) (Drumalis) 3378^{4} 3651^{7} 3895^{7} **>46f<**

Killick 7 b m Slip Anchor-Enthralment (USA) (Sir Ivor) *83^{2}* *106^{6}* *122^{8}* 776^{2} 981^{8} (1022) 1205^{3} *1332^{8}* 1817^{3} 2002^{2} 2196^{3} 2392^{2} 2429^{4} 2798^{5} **>54a 70f<**

Killing Time 4 b c Good Times (ITY)-Kelly's Bid (Pitskelly) *82^{8}* *(120)* *(214)* *(254)* *296^{4}* *329^{8}* *843^{5}* **>61a 55f<**

Killmessan-Town (IRE) 2 ch g Jareer (USA)-Perfect Chance (Petorius) 3644^{6} 3994^{W} **>46f<**

Kill the Crab (IRE) 3 b f Petorius-Final Decision (Tap On Wood) $1009a^{5}$ (2389a) $4015a^{10}$ **>110f<**

Killy's Filly 5 b m Lochnager-May Kells (Artaius (USA)) 646^{13} 874^{15} **>40a 57df<**

Kilnamartyra Girl 5 b m Arkan-Star Cove (Porto Bello) *518^{8}* 559^{11} 642^{7} 776^{4} 874^{13} 1297^{3} 1433^{2} 1679^{2} 2088^{8} 2276^{13} (2484) 2611^{3} 2814^{3} (3020) 3447^{7} 3534^{7} 3645^{10} 4043^{10} **>23a 59f<**

Kilvine 2 b c Shaadi (USA)-Kilavea (USA) 1184^{4} (1781) 2441^{4} 2765^{4} 3147^{5} **>89f<**

Kimberley Boy 5 b h Mtoto-Diamond House (Habitat) 503^{15} (569) 729^{3} 744^{9} 1039^{4} 1149^{4} 1245^{5} 1555^{3} 1743^{2} 1999^{5} 2165^{3} 2224^{6} **>64f<**

Kimbridge Knight (IRE) 3 b c Night Shift (USA)-Dazzling Heights (Shirley Heights) 618^{5} (857) (1382) 1872^{7} 2738^{6} 3214^{10} 3552^{9} 3926^{19} **>84f<**

Kim Tate (IRE) 3 b f Contract Law (USA)-Keen Note (Sharpo) 3635^{9} 4196^{13} **>41f<**

Kincardine Bridge (USA) 6 b g Tiffany Ice (USA)-Priestess (USA) (Time To Explode (USA)) 1420^{7}

Kindakoola 4 b or br c Kind of Hush-Nikoola Eve (Roscoe Blake) 3641^{18} 3685^{19} 3818^{16} **>46df<**

Kindergarten Boy (IRE) 4 b c Mon Tresor-High Profile (High Top) *41^{7}* *160^{9}* 984^{6} 1148^{6} 1792^{7} 1940^{3} (2317) 2602^{4} 3101^{7} (3455) 3619^{11} 4115^{8} **>52a 73f<**

Kindred Greeting 3 b c Most Welcome-Red Berry *59^{11}* *213^{6}* *292^{8}* 521^{8} 773^{5} 1026^{5} 1463^{4} 1854^{5} 2466^{2} 2884^{4} 3258^{9} **>40a 61f<**

King Balant (IRE) 3 b c Fairy King (USA)-Lassalia (Sallust) 504^{3} 1183^{19} 1831^{4} **>75f<**

King Chestnut 4 ch g Efisio-Sweet Colleen (Connaught) 1666^{12} (2358) 2504^{3} (2928) 3396^{3} 3534^{17} 3808^{13} 3977^{15} 4234^{6} **>64f<**

Kingchip Boy 6 b h Petong-Silk St James (Pas de Seul) *265^{8}* *320^{12}* 873^{25} (1244) 1638^{12} *1789^{6}* 2056^{4} 2222^{6} 2345^{7} 2669^{7} 3011^{6} 3269^{3} 3348^{8} 3619^{14} 3837^{14} 4035^{11} 4170^{2} *4298^{14}* **>57a 73f<**

King Curan (USA) 4 b c Lear Fan (USA)-Runaway Lady (USA) (Caucasus (USA)) 676^{16} 876^{3} 909^{3} (1027) 1166^{11} (1438) 1687^{12} (1933) *2292^{11}* 2397^{4} 2797^{9} 2999^{10} **>70f<**

King Etzel (IRE) 3 ch g Belmez (USA)-Kaiserblume (FR) (Viceregal (CAN)) 1403^{8} **>9f<**

Kingfisher Brave 2 b c Rock City-Lambada Style (IRE) (Dancing Brave (USA)) 1190^{5} *(2380)* 3147^{9} 3546^{3} 3780^{6} **>66a 72f<**

King of Babylon (IRE) 3 b c Persian Heights-My My Marie (Artaius (USA)) 3338^{6} 3653^{8} 3921^{12} **>76f<**

King of Peru 2 b c Inca Chief (USA)-Julie's Star (IRE) (Thatching) 1935^{2} (2192) 2674^{4} 3375^{12} (3714) (3947) 4159^{7} **>93f<**

King of Show (IRE) 4 b g Green Desert (USA)-Don't Rush (USA) (Alleged (USA)) *53^{12}* *256^{9}* 642^{13} 785^{5} 876^{16} 1251^{8} 1817^{11} 2227^{4} 2304^{2} 3172^{7} 4275^{12} **>27a 75f<**

King of The East (IRE) 2 b c Fairy King (USA)-Rising Tide (Red Alert) 1311^{4} 3465^{5} (3606) 3731^{5} **>85f<**

King of the Horse (IRE) 4 ch g Hatim (USA)-Milly Whiteway 642^{15} 3435^{12} 3724^{15} **>55a 39df<**

King of Tunes (FR) 3 b c Chief Singer-Marcotte (Nebos (GER)) (4027) 4147^{5} **>81f<**

King Optimist 6 ch h King Persian-Misoptimist (Blakeney) 569^{9} **>7f<**

King Parrot (IRE) 7 br g King of Spain-Red Lory (Bay Express) *(49)* *217^{5}* *341^{3}* *415^{6}* 882^{11} 1472^{8} 1785^{7} **>63da 55f<**

King Rambo 4 b c Rambo Dancer (CAN)-Infanta Maria (King of Spain) *398^{4}* *532^{3}* *602^{6}* 723^{8} 944^{2} *(1214)* 1304^{9} 1565^{9} 1827^{4} 2234^{4} *2492^{3}* 2665^{4} 2753^{4} (2905) 3221^{7} *3522^{2}* 3632^{7} 3750^{4} *3954^{2}* *4125^{3}* **>72a 79f<**

King Rat (IRE) 4 ch c King of Clubs-Mrs Tittlemouse (Nonoalco (USA)) 838^{13} 1174^{12} 1468^{9} 1828^{11} 2252^{6} 2521^{4} 2753^{5} (3014) 3219^{2} (3396) 3565^{W} 3807^{12} 3964^{18} 4041^{19} 4236^{2} 4281^{5} **>83a 87f<**

Kings Assembly 3 b c Presidium-To The Point (Sharpen Up) 686^{4} 873^{9} 1180^{6} (1498) 4163^{2} **>84f<**

Kings Cay (IRE) 4 b c Taufan (USA)-Provocation (Kings Lake (USA)) 1561^{6} 1844^{6} 1861^{3} 2002^{7} 2433^{5} 4315^{7} **>66f<**

King's Crown 3 ch c Lead on Time (USA)-Crystal Land (Kris) 1195^{3} (1866) 2444^{5} **>88f<**

Kingsfold Fountain 4 b g Thowra (FR)-Bella Lisa *347^{9}* *403^{14}* 884^{17} **>47a f<**

Kingsfold Pet 6 b g Tina's Pet-Bella Lisa 582^{12} **>61df<**

King's Gold 5 b g King of Spain-Goldyke (Bustino) *26^{6}* *302^{5}* *347^{7}* *447^{9}* **>41a f<**

Kings Harmony (IRE) 2 b c Nordico (USA)-Kingston Rose (Tudor Music) *3523^{2}* 3870^{6} 4330^{4} **>57+a 69f<**

Kings Nightclub 2 b f Shareef Dancer (USA)-Troy Moon (Troy) 4048^{17} **>26f<**

Kings of Canvey Is 3 ch f Hadeer-Troy Moon (Troy) *57^{6}* *286^{4}* 544^{6} *893^{8}* 1717^{9} **>26a 39f<**

King's Shilling (USA) 8 b h Fit To Fight (USA)-Pride's Crossing (USA) (Riva Ridge (USA)) *227^{9}* 1799^{6} **>52da 47f<**

Kings Vision 3 gr g Absalom-Eye Sight (Roscoe Blake) 773^{8} 969^{10} 1153^{8} 1355^{9} 1412^{5} 1523^{18} 1596^{15} **>45f<**

Kings Witness (USA) 2 b c Lear Fan (USA)-Allison's Deeds (Sassafras (FR)) 2283^{2} 2573^{3} (3494) 3925^{5} **>99f<**

Kingswood Manor 3 b c Exodal (USA)-Angelic Appeal (Star Appeal) 853^{18} **>20f<**

King Ubad (USA) 6 ch g Trempolino (USA)-Glitter (FR) 2036^{4} 2530^{9} 3470^{10} **>49f<**

King William 10 b h Dara Monarch-Norman Delight (USA) (Val de L'Orne (FR)) *87^{7}* *234^{10}* **>25a 51df<**

Kinnegad Kid 6 b m Formidable-Recamier (Reform) *(12) (56) (125) (262) 320[2] (414)* 481[8] 862[11] 1021[16] 1692[8] *1980[2] 2634[9] (3075)* 3726[4] 3757[12] **>78a 49f<**

Kinnescash (IRE) 2 ch c Persian Heights-Gayla Orchestra (Lord Gayle (USA)) 1690[3] 2198[3] *2633[5]* (2866) 3400[5] 3516[8] 3613[6] (3760) 3928[9] 4046[9] **>36a 67f<**

Kinoko 7 ch h Bairn (USA)-Octavia (Sallust) 757[9] 811[10] 866[8] 2186[7] 2427[6] 2545[8] (2663) 3229[6] 3724[9] 3852[15] 4000[11] **>47f<**

Kintavi 5 b h Efisio-Princess Tavi 1529[2] 1643[3] (1970) **>46f<**

Kintwyn 5 b h Doulab (USA)-Harriet Emma (USA) (Secretariat (USA)) *(275) (364) 406[3]* 546[4] *3319[10]* 3984[5] 4229[8] **>77a 65f<**

Kipini 6 b m Roaring Riva-Kivulini (Hotfoot) 1404[6] **>37f<**

Kira 5 b m Starry Night (USA)-Irish Limerick (Try My Best (USA)) 3507[5] 3726[3] 4115[2] 4215[3] 4280[6] **>59f<**

Kirdoun (FR) 3 b c Kaldoun (FR)-Kirova (Nijinsky (CAN)) 806a[3] 1573a[3] **>107f<**

Kiri's Clown (USA) 6 h 3576a[8]

Kirkadian 5 b m Norwick (USA)-Pushkar (Northfields (USA)) 4072[W]

Kirkie Cross 3 b f Efisio-Balgownie (Prince Tenderfoot (USA)) 1464[6] 1684[3] 1901[3] 1960[4] 3665[13] **>42f<**

Kirov Lady (IRE) 2 b f Soviet Lad (USA)-Cestrefeld (Capistrano) 2985[2] (3157) 3474[2] 4244[5] 4318[5] **>74?f<**

Kirov Protege (IRE) 3 b c Dancing Dissident (USA)-Still River (Kings Lake (USA)) *90[2] 135[5] (180) 326[2] 388[2] 448[9] 628[10]* 818[4] 988[6] 1404[2] 1825[7] 2174[5] 2640[3] 3099[4] 4261[16] *4335[13]* **>63a 63f<**

Kismetim 5 b h Dowsing (USA)-Naufrage (Main Reef) *234[14] 304[12]* 1799[10] *3513[4]* 3899[6] 4062[8] *(4270)* **>63a 58f<**

Kissavos 9 ch h Cure The Blues (USA)-Hairbrush (USA) (Sir Gaylord) *30[4] 125[8] 181[7] 601[8]* 874[7] 1484[12] 1714[5] 2538[8] 2946[11] 4054[16] **>40a 42f<**

Kissing Gate (USA) 2 ch f Easy Goer (USA)-Love's Reward (Nonoalco (USA)) 4143[5] *4338[4]* **>65a 47f<**

Kiss Kincsem 4 b f Jalmood (USA)-Horns Lodge (High Line) *9[10] 79[9]* **>43da 73df<**

Kiss Me Again (IRE) 2 b f Cyrano de Bergerac-Now Serving (Super Concorde (USA)) 2264[4] 2552[3] (2791) (3132) 3548[12] **>71f<**

Kistena (FR) 2 ro f Miswaki-Mabrova (Prince Mab) 2210a[3] 3037a[2] 3324a[3] **>89f<**

Kitty Kitty Cancan 2 b f Warrshan (USA)-Kittycatoo Katango (USA) (Verbatim (USA)) 3983[11] **>51f<**

Kitty Waterjet 3 ch f Golden Lahab (USA)-Key Harvest *350[7]* 1355[17] **>13a 22f<**

Kiwud 2 ch f Superlative-Mimining (Tower Walk) 788[11] 2619[10] 3465[14] 3626[17] **>33f<**

Kiyas 4 ch c Nashwan (USA)-Al Sylah (Nureyev (USA)) *28[4] 366[8] 410[9]* **>46a 47f<**

Klipspinger 2 ch f Formidable (USA)-Distant Relation (Great Nephew) 1356[6] 1503[5] 1678[9] **>29f<**

Knave 2 b c Prince Sabo-Royal Agnes (Royal Palace) 3553[6] 3620[7] 4058[10] 4211[4] 4327[6] **>66f<**

Knave of Diamonds 3 b c Bustomi-Kohinoor Diamond (Roman Warrior) 1755[12] 2359[8] 3475[15] **>39a 59df<**

Knave's Ash (USA) 4 ch c Miswaki (USA)-Quiet Rendezvous (USA) (Nureyev (USA)) 439[21] 960[4] 1179[12] 1851[10] (2118) 2672[3] 3188[4] 3556[4] (3781) **>104f<**

Knayton Lass 4 b f Presidium-Sister Hannah (Monseigneur (USA)) 926[15] 1271[10] 1864[8] 2358[8] 2502[2] 2858[4] 2992[6] 3150[7] 3667[11] (3830) 3964[11] 4068[4] **>62f<**

Knight Commander (USA) 3 b c Topsider (USA)-Social Registry (USA) (Raise A Native) 713[7] 2762[4] (3027) 3608[10] **>98f<**

Knightrider 4 b c Full Extent (USA)-New Street (USA) (Our Native (USA)) *11[8] 157[10] 329[7] 2961[12]* 3173[11] 3515[7] **>51da 51f<**

Knobbleeneeze 5 ch g Aragon-Proud Miss (USA) (Semi-Pro) 486[5] 563[4] 714[4] 873[24] 1070[11] 1338[2] 1468[10] 3065[9] 3411[4] (3565) (3619) 3674[2] 3732[4] 3943[16] 4041[13] 4116[23] **>78df<**

Knotally Wood (USA) 3 b f Woodman (USA)-Countess Tully (Hotfoot) 1186[6] 1675[6] 3016[9] 3440[5] 4205[3] **>72f<**

Knotty Scot 3 b f Scottish Reel-Ballyreef (Ballymore) 1905[10] *2141[11]* 3747[11] **>7a 11f<**

Known Secret (USA) 2 ch c Known Fact (USA)-Loa (USA) (Hawaii) 3625[18] 3967[11] **>43f<**

Koathary (USA) 4 b c Capote (USA)-Jeffo (USA) (Ridan (USA)) 1141[13] 1367[3] 3679[8] 3889[10] 4051[14] 4163[19] **>63f<**

Komiamaite 3 b g Komaite (USA)-Mia Scintilla (Blazing Saddles (AUS)) *591[7] 844[2] 1030[5] 1329[2]* 1527[10] *1760[9] 1883[3]* 3972[11] 4044[9] *4340[11]* **>65a 52f<**

Komlucky 3 b f Komaite (USA)-Sweet And Lucky (Lucky Wednesday) *43[4] 118[6] 197[7] 363[6]* 2620[8] 2818[4] 3726[19] **>51a 40f<**

Komodo (USA) 3 ch c Ferdinand (USA)-Platonic Interest (USA) (Drone) *372[2]* 504[6] 663[11] 1092[2] 1381[2] 1654[4] *4296[6]* **>54a 75f<**

Komreyev Dancer 3 b g Komaite (USA)-L'Ancressaan (Dalsaan) *47[2] (151) 242[4] 301[6] 324[2]* 427[4] 504[4] 774[2] 995[7] 1022[7] *1211[7]* 3207[7] 3422[3] 3820[4] 3926[5] **>82a 76f<**

Korambi 3 ch c Kris-Green Lucia (Green Dancer (USA)) 619[6] 917[4] (1170) 1611[12] 3200a[4] 4031[6] 4325[8] **>97f<**

Kornado 5 ch h Superlative-K-Sera 1398a[5] 2046a[4] 2729a[3] 3046a[4] 3591a[4] 3914a[5] **>121f<**

Kossolian 2 b f Emarati (USA)-Cwm Deri (IRE) (Alzao (USA)) 650[2] 859[7] (2264) 2594[7] 3548[8] 3767[8] **>74f<**

Kralingen 3 ch f Move Off-Elitist (Keren) 824[11] 992[9] 1598[10] 1863[13] 1944[8] 2327[12] *2630[14]* **>23f<**

Kraton Garden (USA) 3 b c Sovereign Dancer (USA)-Kenanga (Kris) 698[7] 929[9] **>56f<**

Kratz (IRE) 2 b g Prince Rupert (FR)-Some Spice (Horage) 1466[5] 1665[2] 1943[9] 2251[3] *2924[4]* 3460[11] 3642[5] 3809[12] 3975[17] **>45a 60f<**

Krayyan Dawn 5 ch h Krayyan-Tana Mist (Homeboy) *12[7] 125[5] 330[9]* 454[3] (586) 1166[5] (1401) 3277[6] 3555[6] 4022[9] **>50a 58f<**

Kreef 3 b c Kris-Pelf (USA) (Al Nasr (FR)) *448[7] 468[4]* 727[6] *830[8]* 1016[13] 1663[11] 1812[5] *2093[4]* 3756[13] **>61a 41f<**

Kriscliffe 2 ch c Kris-Lady Norcliffe (USA) (Norcliffe (CAN)) (2058) 2440[3] **>83f<**

Krishan Power 2 b c Superpower-Najat (Tender King) 2483[7] 2782[6] 2859[6] **>63f<**

Kristal Breeze 3 ch f Risk Me (FR)-Mistral's Dancer (Shareef Dancer (USA)) 648[15] 745[9] 988[13] 1442[5] *2293[11] 2636[7] 2922[9]* 3747[4] **>19a 55f<**

Kristal Diva 4 ch f Kris-Dame Ashfield (Grundy) 4205[14]

>61df<

Kristal's Paradise (IRE) **3** b f Bluebird (USA)-Kristal's Pride (Kris) 647[3] 1527[3] (2193) (2413) 3817[5] (3930) 4258[2] **>105f<**

Kristis Girl **8** ch m Ballacashtal (CAN)-Fleur d'Amour *267[11] 336[4] 399[2] 413[5] 529[3] 605[8] 843[6] 1074[5] 1087[5]* **>55a 42f<**

Kriva **3** b f Reference Point-Kraemer (USA) (Lyphard (USA)) 1987[5] 2509[4] (2868) *3084[3]* 3425[3] 3849[9] 4189[11] **>66a 78df<**

Krystallos **3** b c Polish Precedent (USA)-Dancing Crystal (Kris) 670[6] (853) 1345[2] 1839[12] 2348[2] 3066[8] **>104f<**

Krystal Max (IRE) **2** b g Classic Music (USA)-Lake Isle (IRE) (Caerleon (USA)) (1919) 2223[4] 2706[3] 3064[4] 3434[6] 3670[6] **>78f<**

Kshessinskaya **3** ch f Hadeer-Bonnie Hope (USA) (Nijinsky (CAN)) 797[6] 1067[3] 1242[4] 1587[8] 2944[6] 3190[4] (3543) 3946[8] **>92f<**

Kuantan (USA) **2** b c Gone West (USA)-Cuddly Doll (USA) (Bold Hour) (1893) 2704[6] 3731[2] 3925[8] 4034[W] **>107df<**

Kudos Blue **2** b f Elmaamul (USA)-Don't Be Shy (IRE) (Kafu) *2380[10]* 4085[12] **>35f<**

Kulshee Mashee (USA) **3** ch c With Approval (CAN)-Princess Spook (USA) (Majestic Prince) 2215a[11] 4104[8] **>87f<**

Kummel King **7** b h Absalom-Louise 2611[9] 2905[2] 3222[16] 3493[5] **>68f<**

Kung Frode **3** ch c Interrex (CAN)-Harmony Heights (Music Boy) 3597[10] 3748[5] 4165[15] **>74a 65f<**

Kunucu (IRE) **2** ch f Bluebird (USA)-Kunuz (Ela-Mana-Mou) 638[3] (819) (993) 1293[2] 1530[4] 2442[4] (2716) 3086[4] 3668[2] 4032[4] **>102f<**

Kurdistan (IRE) **5** ch g Persian Heights-Late Sally (Sallust) 3837[18]

Kush **4** b f Kind of Hush-Kasu (Try My Best (USA)) *29[9] 79[7]* **>15a 19f<**

Kustom Kit (IRE) **2** ch c Timeless Times (USA)-Friendly Song (Song) (436) 683[3] 871[7] 1343[6] 2442[11] **>77tf<**

Kutta **3** b c Old Vic-Ardassine (Ahonoora) 670[7] 764[3] 1129[4] (1526) 1872[12] 3611[6] (3729) **>102f<**

Kuwam (IRE) **2** b c Last Tycoon-Inshad (Indian King (USA)) 1298[6] 1992[5] **>42f<**

Kymin (IRE) **3** b f Kahyasi-Akila (FR) (Top Ville) 1147[2] 1275[2] **>76+f<**

Kyrenia Times **3** b c Good Times (ITY)-Kyrenia Sunset (CYP) (Lucky Look (CYP)) 942[10] 1317[5] **>53f<**

L

Laabas **12** br h Ile de Bourbon (USA)-Lyric Dance *1075[9] 1210[11]* 3676[16] 3849[14] **>43da 18f<**

Laafee **2** gr g Machiavellian (USA)-Al Sylah (Nureyev (USA)) 2182[2] (2876) 3273[2] 4266[2] **>89f<**

La Alla Wa Asa (IRE) **3** b f Alzao (USA)-Steady The Buffs (Balidar) 3974[6] 4164[5] **>69f<**

Laal (USA) **3** b c Shirley Heights-Afaff (USA) (Nijinsky (CAN)) 673[13] 1498[16] 1733[6] **>63f<**

Laazim Afooz **2** b c Mtoto-Balwa (USA) (Danzig (USA)) 4210[10] **>29f<**

Labeeb **0** 1575a[3] **>118f<**

Labeed (USA) **2** b c Riverman (USA)-Gracious Beauty (USA) (Nijinsky (CAN)) 2283[6] 2529[2] 2846[10] 3546[16] 3809[6] 4081[2] **>76f<**

La Belle Dominique **3** b f Dominion-Love Street (Mummy's Pet) *398[12]* 522[16] 856[8] 1057[14] 1201[11] 1602[3] 1942[7] 2267[3] *2492[4]* 2642[2] **>49a 65f<**

La Belle Shyanne **4** ch f Shy Groom (USA)-Defy Me (Bustino) *179[8] 238[7]* 526[15] 860[6] 1254[14] 2511[9] 2861[7] 2984[2] 3515[9] **>35f<**

Labibeh (USA) **3** gr f Lyphard (USA)-Asl (USA) (Caro) 538[W] 1093[13] (1656) 1986[4] (2339) (2543) (2785) 3223[2] (4030) 4204[4] 4323[6] **>111?f<**

La Blue **2** dk f Blue Bird-La Luganese (Surumu) 2892a[3] **>89f<**

La Bossette (IRE) **3** b f Cyrano de Bergerac-Bosquet 733[9] 1094[6] 1279[12] 1660[10] 1811[5] 2180[5] 3177[8] **>53f<**

La Brief **3** b f Law Society (USA)-Lady Warninglid (Ela-Mana-Mou) 3875[7] 4259[12] (4289) **>63f<**

Labudd (USA) **5** ch h Deputy Minister (CAN)-Delightful Vie (USA) (Barbs Delight) 3920[4] 4044[18] 4242[11] **>64f<**

Lac de Gras (IRE) **4** gr g Henbit (USA)-I've No Idea (Nishapour (FR)) *27[5] 205[W]* **>18a 25f<**

Lac Dessert (USA) **2** ch f Lac Ouimet (USA)-Tiramisu (USA) (Roberto (USA)) 925[W] (1842) (2257) 2554[3] 4175a[6] **>73f<**

Lachesis **2** ch f Lycius (USA)-Chance All (FR) (Glenstal (USA)) 3996[3] **>50f<**

Lac Ladoga **4** c 3329a[4] **>114f<**

La Confederation **4** b f Nureyev (USA)-Unite (Kris) 1385[5] 3161[5] 3480a[4] 3911a[8] **>119f<**

Lacryma Cristi (IRE) **2** b c Green Desert (USA)-L'Anno d'Oro (Habitat) (2315) 2710[3] **>91+f<**

La Dama (USA) **3** ch f Known Fact (USA)-Cypria Sacra (USA) (Sharpen Up) 732[13] 4249[17] 4275[16] **>78df<**

Ladoni **3** b c Danehill-Lilac Charm (Bustino) (1892a) 2389a[6] 3577a[2] 3910a[3] **>107f<**

Lady Bankes (IRE) **2** b f Alzao (USA)-Never so Fair (Never so Bold) 3988[9] 4137[2] 4290[6] **>60f<**

Lady-Bo-K **4** ch f Komaite (USA)-Lady Keyser (Le Johnstan) 1043[6] 1510[9] 1828[16] 1963[15] *2631[7]* 2832[9] 3534[16] 3825[11] **>28a 46f<**

Ladybower (IRE) **3** b f Pennine Walk-Eimkar (Junius (USA)) *232[6] 315[7]* 855[8] 4209[8] **>21a 40f<**

Lady Broker **5** b m Petorius-Phoenix Rose *49[9]* **>55da f<**

Lady Bunting **8** b m Well Decorated (USA)-Lady's Flag (USA) (Fifth Marine (USA)) *22[5] 285[3] 370[8]* **>29a 11f<**

Lady Carla **2** b f Caerleon (USA)-Shirley Superstar (Shirley Heights) (4226) **>79+f<**

Lady Caroline Lamb (IRE) **2** b f Contract Law (USA)-Tuft Hill (Grundy) 3012[4] (3149) 3568[2] 3655[4] 3727[6] 3824[6] 4077[10] 4260[2] *4294[6]* **>42a 61f<**

Lady Confess **5** ch m Backchat (USA)-Special Branch 988[W] **>53da f<**

Lady Davenport (IRE) **3** b f Contract Law (USA)-Sandhurst Goddess (Sandhurst Prince) *628[11]* 861[2] 1080[10] **>6a 68df<**

Lady Dignity (IRE) **2** b f Nordico (USA)-Royal Respect (Kings Lake (USA)) 782[5] 4329[4] **>53f<**

Lady Eclat **2** b f Nomination-Romantic Saga (Prince Tenderfoot (USA)) 570[6] 1287[6] 1779[4] 3639[14] 3824[13] 4230[6] **>50f<**

Lady Highfield **4** br f High Kicker (USA)-Judy Burton

672^{20} 874^{11} *1088^{14}* (1350) 1647^{2} (1854) 1966^{2} 2655^{2} 2861^{4} 3094^{8} 3889^{6} 3977^{13} 4061^{3} *4335^{5}* **>54a 63f<**

Lady Isabell 2 b f Rambo Dancer (CAN)-Warning Bell (Bustino) 3673^{6} **>63f<**

Lady Joshua (IRE) 2 ch f Royal Academy (USA)-Claretta (USA) 4262^{6} **>69f<**

Lady Kate (USA) 3 ch f Trempolino (USA)-Glitter (FR) 3847^{7} 4049^{18} 4205^{16} **>13f<**

Lady Khadija 9 b m Nicholas Bill-Chenkynowa (Connaught) *769^{14}* **>1f<**

Ladykirk 2 b f Slip Anchor-Lady Day (FR) (Lightning (FR)) (3713) **>78+f<**

Lady Kuynder 3 b f Petoski-Indian Pink (USA) (Seattle Slew (USA)) *509^{8}* 596^{6} *1458^{6} 1881^{11} 2378^{6} 2626^{5}* **>28a 9f<**

Lady Lacey 8 b m Kampala-Cecily 503^{6} 762^{15} 1323^{13} 1472^{3} 1661^{5} 2314^{6} 2657^{3} 2980^{3} 3440^{6} 3657^{3} 3863^{5} 3934^{7} **>55f<**

Lady Lancer (IRE) 3 b f Satco (FR)-Miysam (Supreme Sovereign) 773^{12} **>4f<**

Lady Lucy Linnet 3 b f Zalazl (USA)-Song Grove *133^{11} 185^{8}* **>14a 27f<**

Lady Magic (IRE) 2 b f Magical Strike (USA)-Drowsy Maggie (Tumble Wind (USA)) 1968^{5}

Lady Nash 3 b f Nashwan (USA)-Je Comprend (USA) (Caerleon (USA)) 915^{8} 1500^{7} 1990^{6} 3974^{15} **>72f<**

Lady of The Mist (IRE) 2 ch f Digamist (USA)-Stradey Lynn (Derrylin) 436^{9} 1671^{7} 4063^{11} *4273^{9}* **>45a 52f<**

Lady Ploy 3 b f Deploy-Quisissanno (Be My Guest (USA)) 722^{9} **>36f<**

Lady Pui 3 b f Puissance-Kind of Shy (Kind of Hush) *7^{5} 132^{7}* 746^{8} **>39a 62f<**

Lady Quinta (IRE) 3 b f Gallic League-Clogher Head (Sandford Lad) *602^{8}* **>56f<**

Lady Reema 4 b f Tragic Role (USA)-Garth Lady (Jalmood (USA)) *321^{11} 357^{2} 406^{6}* 545^{6} 762^{4} 975^{11} 1254^{3} 1694^{7} 1974^{2} **>66a 46f<**

Lady Roxanne 6 br m Cyrano de Bergerac-Red Lory (Bay Express) *220^{6} (338) 393^{9}* **>46a 57+f<**

Lady Sabina 5 ch m Bairn (USA)-Calibina *73^{7} 158^{7}* 1663^{4} 1974^{3} 2279^{3} 3056^{7} 3258^{2} (3501) 3657^{5} 3934^{2} **>39a 51f<**

Lady Sheriff 4 b f Taufan (USA)-Midaan (Sallust) 926^{3} (1152) (1508) 1595^{2} 1765^{8} (2163) (2418) 2609^{2} 2916^{2} 3221^{5} 3597^{2} 3748^{4} 4033^{5} 4113^{2} 4278^{4} 4322^{4} **>37++a 88f<**

Lady Silk 4 ch f Prince Sabo-Adduce (USA) (Alleged (USA)) 862^{10} *1034^{15} 2923^{13} 3512^{9} 4274^{7} 4340^{3}* **>66a 54f<**

Ladys Promise 3 b f Rakaposhi King-Acting Lady VII 875^{9} 1430^{6} 2834^{5} 3357^{15} 3829^{9} **>26f<**

Lady Thiang 2 gr f Petong-Good Woman (Good Times (ITY)) 3069^{14} (3379) **>82f<**

Lady Tjonger 4 b f Sharrood (USA)-Indian Pink (USA) (Seattle Slew (USA)) *1332^{11} 1455^{2} 2072^{8} 2630^{13}* **>50a 48f<**

Lady Valensina (IRE) 4 ch f Jareer (USA)-Coshlea (Red Alert) *103^{5} 149^{5} 240^{7}* 1444^{13} 1658^{6} 1971^{5} *2588^{9}* **>48a 48f<**

Lady Williams (IRE) 4 ch f Roi Danzig (USA)-Apple Rings (Godswalk (USA)) *320^{6} 373^{4} 406^{9}* 1542^{11} 2345^{6} 3363^{7} **>61a 71f<**

Lady Woodstock 3 b f Chilibang-Vent du Soir (Main Reef) 3401^{9} **>26f<**

La Fandango (IRE) 2 b f Taufan (USA)-Cursory Look (USA) (Nijinsky (CAN)) 2756^{7} 2971^{3} 3306^{5} 3639^{5} 3851^{7} 4081^{8} 4285^{15} **>59f<**

La Femme Francaise (IRE) 2 gr f Petong-Pear Drop (Bustino) 3767^{17} 4148^{19} **>12f<**

La Fille de Cirque 3 ch f Cadeaux Genereux-Lady of the Land (Wollow) *72^{5} 204^{4} 319^{6}* 1625^{3} 1962^{12} (2574) 2813^{2} 3125^{9} 3247^{2} 3422^{4} **>38a 61f<**

Lafille de General 4 f 3041a^{7} **>100f<**

Lafille du General (FR) 4 ch f General Holme (USA)-Blushing Bride (FR) (Raisingelle (USA)) 3329a^{5} 4009a^{8} **>110f<**

La Finale 2 ch f Dunbeath (USA)-Jamarj (Tyrnavos) 2063^{4} 2970^{3} 3228^{6} 3612^{15} 3882^{2} 4285^{5} **>60f<**

Lagan 2 b g Shareef Dancer (USA)-Lagta (Kris) 2432^{5} 3782^{3} 4221^{6} **>65f<**

Lago Di Varano 3 b c Clantime-On the Record (Record Token) 719^{2} 828^{3} 2237^{5} 3166^{7} 3550^{9} 3854^{4} 4033^{9} 4286^{4} **>91f<**

La Gran Senorita (USA) 3 br f El Gran Senor (USA)-Yanuka (Pitcairn) 1172^{11} 2708^{2} 3204^{5} 3630^{2} 4027^{4} **>84df<**

La Haye Sainte 2 ch f Rock City-Billante (USA) (Graustark (USA)) *2635^{2} 2924^{6} 3243^{6}* 3721^{9} 4045^{13} **>53a 30f<**

Lahik (IRE) 2 b c Lycius (USA)-Sangala (FR) (Jim French (USA)) 1856^{8} 2667^{7} **>40f<**

Laid Back Lucy 2 b br f Prince Daniel (USA)-Granny's Birthday (Young Generation) 4137^{15} **>7f<**

Lajadhal (FR) 6 gr h Bellypha-Rose d'Amour (USA) (Lines of Power (USA)) 649^{9} 1058^{10} 1444^{11} 2078^{5} 2154^{7} 2546^{12} 2986^{5} **>18a 35f<**

Lakadone 3 b c Horst-Herbert-Lovely Night (Armistice D (3581a)

Lake Coniston (IRE) 4 b c Bluebird (USA)-Persian Polly (Persian Bold) (659) (1133) 1870^{2} (2368) 3491^{4} *4303a^{12}* **>60a 134f<**

Lake Kariba 4 b c Persian Bold-Gold Bracelet (Golden Fleece (USA)) 3481a^{3} **>92f<**

Lakeline Legend (IRE) 2 ch c Caerleon (USA)-Bottom Line 4063^{3} **>86f<**

Lakeside Express 2 ch f Siberian Express (USA)-Jenny's Rocket 3915^{16} 4224^{18} **>12f<**

Lake Storm (IRE) 4 b c Maelstrom Lake-Our Duck (The Go-Between) 1577a^{4} **>107f<**

Lakeway (USA) 4 b f Seattle Slew (USA)-Breath Taking (USA) *4304a^{3}* **>102a f<**

Lalindi (IRE) 4 b f Cadeaux Genereux-Soemba (General Assembly (USA)) (506) 632^{5} 795^{3} 938^{5} 1189^{3} 1313^{2} (1657) 1840^{25} **>79+a 83f<**

La Menorquina (USA) 5 b m Woodman (USA)-Hail The Lady (USA) (Hail the Pirates (USA)) *238^{5} (295) 589^{2}* 866^{11} *(1086)* 1535^{4} *2495^{4} 3527^{6}* **>56a 45f<**

L'Ami Louis (USA) 2 ch c Easy Goer (USA)-Jadana (Pharly (FR)) 682^{2} (836) (1311) **>86f<**

Lammtarra (USA) 3 ch c Nijinsky (CAN)-Snow Bride (USA) (Blushing Groom (FR)) (1611) (2595) (4014a) **>132+f<**

La Modiste 2 b f Most Welcome-Dismiss (Daring March) 791^{10} 1348^{2} 1871^{4} 3158^{4} (3283) (3518) 3942^{6} 4029^{5}

>77f<
Lamp of Phoebus (USA) 3 b br f Sunshine Forever (USA)-Siala (FR) (Sharpman) 635^{16} 797^{13} **>50f<**
Lancashire Legend 2 gr c Belfort (FR)-Peters Pet Girl (Norwick (USA)) 3157^{4} 3558^{4} 3933^{7} **>66df<**
Lancashire Life (IRE) 4 b c Petorius-Parlais *766^{9}* 927^{9} 1192^{7} (1432) 1679^{4} 2123^{2} 2607^{6} 2797^{5} 3113^{9} 3305^{4} 3531^{11} 3645^{14} 3808^{23} **>28a 59f<**
Lancaster Bomber 3 b f Golden Lahab (USA)-Miami Dolphin (Derrylin) 965^{10} 1463^{6} **>22f<**
Lancerette 3 ch f Sharpo-Corvelle (Reliance II) 1701^{8} 3712^{4} (3974) 4163^{22} **>80f<**
Lancer (USA) 3 ch c Diesis-Last Bird (USA) (Sea Bird II) 536^{5} 1068^{6} 1170^{6} 1839^{17} 2253^{4} 2678^{7} **>84f<**
Landlord 3 b c Be My Chief (USA)-Pubby (Doctor Wall) 765^{16} 1069^{6} 1787^{4} 2199^{9} 3109^{8} 3390^{3} 3770^{11} *3952^{5} 4128^{2}* **>64a 67f<**
Lando (GER) 5 b h Acatenango (GER)-Laurea (Sharpman) 1398a^{3} (1890a) (2729a) 3591a^{7} 4014a^{4} 4307a^{12} **>126f<**
Lanesra Breeze 3 b g Petoski-Constant Companion (Pas de Seul) *17^{6} 443^{9}* 1519^{9} **>16a 48f<**
Langtonian 6 br h Primo Dominie-Yankee Special (Bold Lad (IRE)) *6^{3}* 1843^{9} 2156^{10} 2479^{6} 2733^{10} 3119^{5} *3529^{8}* 3879^{15} **>55a 29f<**
Languedoc 8 b h Rousillon (USA)-Can Can Girl (Gay Fandango (USA)) 478^{9} **>21a 52f<**
La Petite Fusee 4 br f Cigar-Little Missile (Ile de Bourbon (USA)) 542^{7} 636^{2} 1071^{5} (1483) 1750^{3} 2010^{7} 2404^{5} 2764^{20} 3615^{2} 3943^{11} 4145^{16} *(4337)* **>78+a 75f<**
Lap of Luxury 6 gr m Sharrood (USA)-Lap of Honour (Final Straw) 1365^{7} 1851^{28} (2287) 2673^{8} 3188^{11} 3473^{3} 3693a^{2} 3904^{6} 4104^{2} **>111f<**
Lapu-Lapu 2 b f Prince Sabo-Seleter (Hotfoot) 4098^{8} 4276^{9} **>46+f<**
Lara (GER) 3 b f Sharpo-La Salina 3912a^{2} **>104f<**
Larentia 3 ch f Salse (USA)-Clarentia (Ballad Rock) 2329^{6} 2994^{6} 3302^{7} **>72df<**
La Residence 4 b c Doulab (USA)-Ideal Home (Home Guard (USA)) *(32) 248^{4} 341^{11} 501^{2} 605^{5} 1088^{12} 1457^{9}* **>53a 60f<**
Larghetto (IRE) 2 ch c Lycius (USA)-Spoilt Again (Mummy's Pet) 993^{2} 1247^{2} 1620^{8} 2771^{2} (3117) 3394^{5} **>78f<**
Larn Fort 5 gr g Belfort (FR)-Larnem (Meldrum) *30^{3} (179)* 430^{4} (568) 738^{8} (988) 1292^{2} 1543^{4} 2327^{4} 3021^{2} 3169^{4} 3320^{6} 3810^{8} *3952^{10}* 4284^{4} **>53a 67f<**
Laroche (GER) 4 br c Nebos (GER)-Laurea (Sharpman) (1392a) 2046a^{3} 2729a^{2} 3482a^{4} 3914a^{9} **>121f<**
L'Arpege (USA) 3 b c Diesis-Tennis Partner (USA) (Northern Dancer) 164a^{3} 207a^{3}
Larrocha (IRE) 3 b f Sadler's Wells (USA)-Le Melody (1147) (1729) 2563a^{5} (3190) 3694a^{3} **>113f<**
Larry Lambrusco 2 b c Executive Man-Freudenau (Wassl) 2876^{11} 3463^{9} *3736^{4}* **>68a 47f<**
Larrylukeathugh 2 b c Prince Sabo-Hidden Asset (Hello Gorgeous (USA)) 1418^{4} 1670^{9} 2998^{5} 3468^{8} 3642^{13} **>63f<**
Lasco Blu Velvet (ITY) 2 ch f Miswaki Tern-Gallant Cadillac (My Gall 1111a^{2}
Laser Life Star 2 b f Jester-Not Alone (Pas de Seul) 1662^{10} 1981^{5} *3244^{8}* **>55f<**
La Spezia 5 b m Last Tycoon-Helenetta (Troy) 737^{7} 938^{6} 1140^{3} 1410^{P} **>72f<**
Lasseman 2 ch c Cadeaux Genereux-Lillemor (Connaught) 3530^{3} 3832^{6} **>49f<**
Lassigny (USA) 4 b c Gone West (USA)-Love Potion (BRZ) (Rio Brava (USA)) 3576a^{6} (4185a) **>121f<**
Lass of Kinloch 3 gr f Rock City-Normanby Lass (Bustino) *141^{8}* 2582^{7} 2953^{6} 3099^{13} **>34f<**
Last Ambition (IRE) 3 b f Cadeaux Genereux-Fabulous Rina (FR) (Fabulous Dancer (USA)) 1476^{14} 1905^{9} 2393^{8} 2659^{11} **>50f<**
Last But Not Least 2 b f Dominion-Almadaniyah (Dunbeath (USA)) 4161^{11} 4329^{3} **>66f<**
Last Corner 3 b c Weldnaas (USA)-Shadha (Shirley Heights) *(509) 626^{2}* 851^{8} 1194^{3} 1372^{3} 1527^{6} 1986^{6} *(2378) 2920^{2}* 3254^{3} 3635^{2} *3735^{2}* 3843^{5} *4223^{7}* **>70a 70f<**
Last Hero (FR) 2 ch c Hero's Honor-Waterford (Crystal Palace 2043a^{2}
Last Laugh (IRE) 3 b f Last Tycoon-Little Me (Connaught) 526^{3} 724^{8} 1245^{2} (1407) 1674^{7} 2546^{5} (3401) 4149^{13} **>69f<**
Lasto Adree (IRE) 4 b g Shernazar-Summer Palace (Habitat) (3282)
Last Quick (USA) 4 gr c Dixieland Band (USA)-Full Virtue (USA) (Full Out (USA)) 1888a^{3} **>105?f<**
Last Roundup 3 b c Good Times (ITY)-Washita (Valiyar) 504^{18} 1605^{7} 3209^{7} 3373^{9} 3611^{23} 4047^{17} **>71f<**
Last Second (IRE) 2 gr f Alzao (USA)-Alruccaba (Crystal Palace (FR)) (3828) (4091a) **>80+f<**
Last Spin 3 b f Unfuwain (USA)-Spin 747^{8} 1067^{5} 1587^{9} 2481^{5} *3526^{11}* **>12a 75f<**
Last Straw 7 b h Blushing Scribe (USA)-Straw Reef (Final Straw) *78^{11} 165^{8} 348^{10}* 734^{9} **>35a 35f<**
Last Token 2 b g Nomination-Beretta (Moorestyle) (2198) 2710^{2} 3613^{10} **>72f<**
Last World 3 b f Puissance-Flicker Toa Flame (USA) (Empery (USA)) 2527^{7} 3424^{6} 3508^{7} 3678^{7} **>40f<**
La Suquet 3 b f Puissance-Persian Case (Upper Case (USA)) *299^{4}* 451^{2} 522^{2} 645^{2} 772^{5} (904) 982^{7} **>34a 74f<**
Latahaab (USA) 4 b c Lyphard (USA)-Eye Drop (USA) (Irish River (FR)) *385^{3}* 440^{9} 610^{6} (1313) 2098^{7} 2799^{2} (3343) 3930^{6} 4258^{6} **>57a 98f<**
La Tansani (IRE) 2 b c High Estate-Hana Marie (Formidable) 1184^{13} 1511^{6} 1715^{7} 2693^{6} **>67f<**
Latching (IRE) 3 ch f Thatching-Keepers Lock (USA) (Sunny's Halo (CAN)) 1136^{6} 1473^{4} 2949^{3} 3298^{4} 3905^{3} 4040^{17} 4266^{3} **>79f<**
Latch Key Lady (USA) 3 b f Tejano (USA)-Key To The Heart (USA) (Arts And Letters) *3737^{9} 4335^{W}* **>41a 11f<**
Late Mail (USA) 3 b c Simply Majestic (USA)-Total Chic (USA) (Far North (CAN)) 1015^{4} 1295^{10} 1519^{11} **>70f<**
Late Parade (IRE) 4 b c Astronef-Skisette (Malinowski (USA)) 901a^{2} 4012a^{12} **>113f<**
La Thuile 3 b f Statoblest-Mild Wind 856^{12} 1125^{19} 2318^{16} 2491^{15} 2744^{9} 3333^{10} **>43f<**
Latin Beauty 2 b f Then Again-Rather Warm (Tribal Chief) 791^{9} 1011^{5} **>56f<**
Latin Leader 5 b h Primo Dominie-Ravaro (Raga Navarro (ITY)) (3129) 3658^{8} 3871^{4} *4128^{5}* **>52a 70f<**
Latin Reign (USA) 2 b br c El Gran Senor (USA)-Love

Bunny (USA) (Exclusive Native (USA)) 2320[8] 3068[4] 3842[2] (4146) **>87f<**

Latmos (GER) 5 b h Truculent (USA)-Lillebonne (GER) (Droll Role (USA)) 3798a[5] **>119f<**

L A Touch 2 b f Tina's Pet-Silvers Era (Balidar) *1758[7] 2146[7]* 2431[4] 2800[6] 2965[2] (3124) 3289[8] 3570[4] *3675[5]* 3856[5] 3937[8] **>19a 61f<**

Latvian 8 gr h Rousillon (USA)-Lorelene (FR) 967[3] 1205[2] 1462[2] 1686[6] (2544) 2648[3] (2878) 3406[5] 3718[8] 3853[2] 4110[6] 4288[12] **>76df<**

Latzio 2 b f Arrasas (USA)-Remould 1746[9] 1981[11] 2403[4] 2601[3] *3675[7]* 3767[18] *4124[11]* **>24a 49f<**

Laudation (IRE) 3 ch g Bold Arrangement-Hooray Lady (Ahonoora) 1136[13] 1353[9] 1514[17] 2278[9] **>61f<**

Laughing Buccaneer 2 ch c Weldnaas (USA)-Atlantic Line (Capricorn Line) 1123[6] 1424[3] 2534[8] 3090[9] 3423[6] 3553[2] 3752[5] 4075[9] 4208[5] **>76f<**

Laurel Crown (IRE) 2 b c Thatching-Laureon (Caerleon (USA)) 1041[3] 1460[4] 1774[2] 2063[3] 2526[7] 2756[W] **>72f<**

Lavanda 2 b f Soviet Star (USA)-One Life (USA) (L'Emigrant (USA)) 3976[4] **>53f<**

Lavender Della (IRE) 2 gr f Shernazar-All In White (FR) (Carwhite) 2447[5] 3427[6] 3982[12] **>55f<**

Lavender (IRE) 3 ch f Kris-Sailor's Mate (Shirley Heights) 950[5] 1270[4] 1814[4] **>69f<**

Lavinia Fontana (IRE) 6 ch m Sharpo-Belle Origine (USA) (Exclusive Native (USA)) 1577a[2] 3042a[6] 3582a[2] 3491[6] 4012a[5] (4345a) **>113f<**

La Volta 2 b f Komaite (USA)-Khadino (Relkino) (903) 3606[6] 4084[10] (4235) 4318[2] **>83f<**

Lawbuster (IRE) 3 b c Contract Law (USA)-Tora Tora (Home Guard (USA)) *5[2] 38[3] 128[3] 180[7] 273[4] 326[8] 368[5]* 1970[11] **>62a 47f<**

Law Commission 5 ch h Ela-Mana-Mou-Adjala (Northfields (USA)) 870[24] 1174[8] 1411[7] 2031[3] 2344[6] (3028) 3706[7] 3813[W] **>85f<**

Law Dancer (IRE) 2 b c Alzao (USA)-Judicial (USA) (Law Society (USA)) 3652[5] 3917[6] **>81f<**

Lawful Love (IRE) 5 b g Law Society (USA)-Amata (USA) (Nodouble (USA)) 673[12] 1149[6] 1555[7] 4072[12] **>50f<**

Lawn Order 2 b f Efisio-Zebra Grass 2932[7] 3231[13] 3430[9] 3623[8] **>53f<**

Lawnswood Captain (IRE) 2 ro c Maelstrom Lake-Morgiana (Godswalk (USA)) *1758[8]* 2431[7] 2750[3] 3018[6] 3642[8] 3937[7] 4141[5] 4285[10] **>58f<**

Lawnswood Junior 8 gr h Bairn (USA)-Easymede 526[18] 780[15] 1027[11] 2528[12] 2733[7] 3061[9] **>46a 46f<**

Lawnswood Lady 3 b f Lochnager-Keep Cool (FR) (Northern Treat (USA)) *64[6] 141[6] 197[5] 258[11] 392[3] 410[7] 420[5] 519[5] 591[9]* 732[8] *830[4] 2144[7]* 2818[10] **>46a 50f<**

Laxford Bridge 4 b c Lomond (USA)-Connaught Bridge 634[11] 981[3] 1192[P] 1314[6] 1926[10] 2343[3] 2664[5] 3106[10] **>90f<**

Lay The Blame 2 b c Reprimand-Rose And The Ring 3436[6] 3626[6] (3988) (4244) **>86f<**

L'Carriere (USA) 4 b g Carr de Naskra (USA)-Northern Sunset (USA) (Northfields (USA)) *4308a[2]* **>134a f<**

Lead Him On (USA) 2 b c Cahill Road (USA)-Wicked Ways (USA) (Devil's Bag (USA)) 4314[W]

Leading Princess (IRE) 4 gr f Double Schwartz-Jenny Diver (USA) (Hatchet Man (USA)) 688[3] 906[8] 994[10] 1900[8] 2231[3] 2303[7] 2463[8] 2475[10] 2736[5] 2837[5] 2930[8] 2997[7] (3855) (4278) **>10a 55f<**

Leading Spirit (IRE) 3 b c Fairy King (USA)-Shopping (FR) (Sheshoon) 435[6] 867[4] 1093[5] 2509[2] *2919[7]* (3634) (3843) 4047[6] 4149[12] **>56a 80f<**

Leap for Joy 3 ch f Sharpo-Humble Pie (Known Fact (USA)) 426[8] 3815[2] (4181a) 4324[11] **>108f<**

Leap in the Dark (IRE) 6 br h Shadeed (USA)-Star Guide (FR) (Targowice (USA)) 1268[6] 1643[11] 1921[4] 2280[2] 2355[7] 2543[7] 2860[12] 3092[2] 3724[12] **>37f<**

Leap Year Baby (IRE) 3 b f Digamist (USA)-Rahwah (Northern Baby (CAN)) 759[17] 880[7] 990[11] 1465[9] 1721[17] **>48f<**

Lear Dancer (USA) 4 b or br c Lear Fan (USA)-Green Gown (Green Dancer (USA)) 668[11] 3083[2] 3406[6] (3616) 3817[6] 3957[11] **>79f<**

Lear Jet (USA) 2 b c Lear Fan (USA)-Lajna (Be My Guest (USA)) 3709[4] 3883[7] **>87f<**

Learning Curve (IRE) 2 gr f Archway (IRE)-Children's Hour (Mummy's Pet) 4329[10] **>9f<**

Lear White (USA) 4 b c Lear Fan (USA)-White Water (FR) (Pharly (FR)) (710a) 1118a[4] 1577a[5] 4093a[7] **>114f<**

Leave it to Lib 8 b m Tender King-Nuit de Vin (Nebbiolo) 1506[9] 1966[9] 2972[13] 3462[13] **>47f<**

Le Bal 3 b f Rambo Dancer (CAN)-Skarberg (FR) (Noir Et Or) 553[10] 689[6] 862[2] 966[15] 1414[6] 1783[7] 1963[21] 2278[8] **>44f<**

Lecroix (GER) 3 b c Assert-Las Palmas (Experte) 1122a[2] (1713a) 2215a[8] 3046a[2] 3591a[2] **>114f<**

Leedons Park 3 br g Precocious-Scottish Rose (Warpath) 1647[8] 3153[5] **>47f<**

Leeds (IRE) 0 01 c 1115a[5] 1575a[5] 2044a[9] **>115f<**

Lees Please (IRE) 3 b c Glenstal (USA)-Perfect Choice (Bold Lad (IRE)) 1512[11] *3075[13]* 3654[12] 3920[13] **>42f<**

Legaitak 3 b g Rock City-Bridestones 3030[7] 3226[4] **>55f<**

Legal Brief 3 b g Law Society (USA)-Ahonita (Ahonoora) 1270[9] 1412[10] 3504[13] 3747[17] **>28f<**

Legal Fiction 4 b c Shadeed (USA)-Rally For Justice (Dominion) *(119) (195) (242) 262[4] 281[5] 364[3] 396[8]* 1638[8] 1687[10] 2099[3] (2307) 2457[13] 2477[3] 2803[4] 2928[5] 2999[7] 3419[3] 3488[5] 3703[9] 3837[7] 4156[7] **>88a 76f<**

Legal Issue (IRE) 3 b c Contract Law (USA)-Natuschka (Authi) 1207[5] 1469[3] 1541[2] (1818) 2019[2] 2425[2] 2522[2] 2864[2] 3125[4] (3310) 3661[15] **>72da 75f<**

Legally Delicious 3 b f Law Society (USA)-Bold Apple (Bold Lad (IRE)) *(90) 395[5] (767) (1030) 1330[3] 1571[8] 1880[11] 2377[10]* **>72a 9f<**

Legal Right (USA) 2 b c Alleged (USA)-Rose Red (USA) (Northern Dancer) 3900[2] **>85+f<**

Legal Train 4 ch c Siberian Express (USA)-Pushkinia (FR) (Pharly (FR)) 1014[F] **>62f<**

Legatee 4 ch f Risk Me (FR)-Legal Sound (Legal Eagle) *410[3]* 450[6] *1209[12]* 1534[6] *1951[3] 2141[2] (2963) 3073[3] 3241[8]* 4060[18] 4215[19] **>65a 58df<**

Legendary Lady 4 b f Reprimand-Sharp Celine (Sharpo) 2314[14] **>3f<**

Legendary Leap 5 b m Legend of France (USA)-Leap in Time (Dance In Time (CAN)) 1202[17] (1732) (2028) 2672[6] 3729[17] 3945[38] **>80f<**

Legend Dulac (IRE) 6 b h Legend of France (USA)-Westerlake (Blakeney) 1785[2] *2377[3]* 2698[6] 2913[2] 3396[4]

3808^{10} 3879^{12} 4209^{15} **>51da 53f<**
Legendra 5 ch m Legend of France (USA)-Obertura (USA) (Roberto (USA)) 485^{7} 1200^{4} **>57f<**
L'Eglise Belle 3 b f Minster Son-Haddon Anna (Dragonara Palace (USA)) 645^{10} 2357^{6} 2540^{9} 2968^{5} 3125^{5} 3428^{5} 3515^{8} 4225^{7} **>48f<**
Leguard Express (IRE) 7 b h Double Schwartz-All Moss (Prince Tenderfoot (USA)) 780^{9} 1199^{12} *1334*^{7} 1797^{9} **>11a 50f<**
Lehmans Lady 3 ch f Move Off-Lehmans Lot (Oats) 1724^{9} **>45f<**
Leif the Lucky (USA) 6 ch h Lemhi Gold (USA)-Corvine (USA) (Crow (FR)) 439^{4} 785^{13} 1617^{8} 1851^{17} **>93f<**
Leigh Crofter 6 ch h Son of Shaka-Ganadora (Good Times (ITY)) *14*^{4} *(69)* *154*^{3} *297*^{5} *327*^{2} *380*^{2} *398*^{6} 796^{12} 1174^{16} 1599^{13} *3242*^{12} 3706^{13} 3748^{2} 4057^{4} 4134^{6} 4157^{7} *4337*^{4} **>78a 75f<**
Leith Academy (USA) 2 b f Academy Award-Uvula (USA) (His Majesty (USA)) 1627^{5} (1935) 2257^{2} 3301^{3} **>66f<**
Lelise (IRE) 3 b f Milk of The Barley-Frolic (Good Times (ITY)) 675^{6} 861^{10} 1427^{12}
Lennox Lady 2 b f Dominion Royale-Balgownie (Prince Tenderfoot (USA)) 3713^{11} 3744^{13} 3850^{10}
Lennox Lewis 3 b c Superpower-Song's Best (Never so Bold) 633^{5} 1305^{2} 1487^{10} 2285^{4} 2443^{7} 2803^{7} 3145^{6} 3230^{2} 3446^{5} 3707^{4} 4160^{16} **>101f<**
Leona Satti (IRE) 3 f 1237a^{6} **>86f<**
Leonine (IRE) 2 gr c Danehill (USA)-Inanna (Persian Bold) 3185^{2} (3456) **>94+f<**
Leontios (IRE) 3 b c Alzao (USA)-Akamantis (Kris) 678^{5} **>70f<**
Le Pilat (USA) 3 dk b c Far North (CAN)-Sweet Shampagne (USA) (Sham (USA)) (163a)
Lepine (IRE) 4 ch c Tate Gallery (USA)-Riverine (FR) (Riverman (USA)) 1193^{13} 1441^{2} 1918^{3} 2461^{9} 2758^{3} 2935^{2} 3279^{3} 3667^{6} 4113^{7} **>77f<**
Ler Cru (IRE) 6 b h Lafontaine (USA)-Kirsova (Absalom) 2981^{9} **>70da 38df<**
Les Boyer 4 b c Midyan (USA)-Debutante 704a^{3} (1577a) 4093a^{4} **>121f<**
Le Silicon (FR) 0 b h Le Glorieux (FR)-Siliciana (Silly Season) 487a^{3}
Lesley's Fashion 4 ro f Dominion-Firelighter (Kalaglow) 981^{5} 1141^{12} 2241^{8} 2694^{8} 3106^{9} **>74f<**
Le Sorcier 3 ch g Prince des Coeurs (USA)-Pink N' Perky (Tickled Pink) 1940^{11} 2314^{12} **>35f<**
Le Sport 2 b c Dowsing (USA)-Tendency (Ballad Rock) 977^{5} 1597^{11} 4320^{18} **>59f<**
Le Temeraire 9 b h Top Ville-La Mirande (FR) (Le Fabuleux) 2824^{7} 3047^{9} 4110^{5} 4196^{12} **>40a 47f<**
Le Teteu (FR) 2 b c Saint Andrews (FR)-Nouvelle Star (USA) (Star de Naskra (USA)) 3625^{9} **>55f<**
Letluce 2 b f Aragon-Childish Prank (Teenoso (USA)) (2526) 3158^{6} **>83f<**
Le Triton (USA) 2 b c El Gran Senor-La Tritona (Touching Wood (USA)) (4010a) 4177a^{4} **>108f<**
Letsbeonestaboutit 9 b h Petong-My Bushbaby *134*^{7} *(167)* *224*^{6} *265*^{10} *314*^{3} *354*^{3} *366*^{4} *393*^{8} *518*^{6} *601*^{13} *1334*^{4} 1484^{9} *1629*^{5} **>58a 48f<**
Let's Get Lost 6 ch h Chief Singer-Lost in France (Northfields (USA)) *91*^{6} *137*^{4} *186*^{4} *304*^{5} 558^{15} 778^{11} **>58a 72f<**
Let's Hang On (IRE) 2 b f Petorius-Madam Slaney (Prince Tenderfoot (USA)) *2625*^{5}
Letterluna 3 ch f Shavian-Alteza Real (Mansingh (USA)) 1979^{5} **>55f<**
Level Edge 4 b f Beveled (USA)-Luaga (Tyrnavos) *12*^{9} *80*^{8} 1191^{6} 1291^{9} 1523^{7} 2814^{6} *2961*^{3} *3511*^{6} 3825^{5} 4000^{14} **>52da 40f<**
Le Vivarois (USA) 4 b c Local Talent (USA)-My Dear Lady (USA) (Mr Prospector (USA)) 253a^{3}
Lexus (IRE) 7 b h Gorytus (USA)-Pepi Image (USA) *73*^{3} *155*^{5} *217*^{4} *330*^{10} *1091*^{10} 1658^{3} 1985^{4} 3899^{14} **>44a 39f<**
L'Hermine 6 b h Slip Anchor-Mondialite (FR) (Habitat) 3908a^{3} **>95f<**
Lia Fail (IRE) 2 b f Soviet Lad (USA)-Sympathy (Precocious) 2308^{2} 2651^{6} 3587a^{15} 4137^{11} 4224^{5} **>60f<**
Liberatrice (FR) 2 b f Assert-Liberale (FR) (Fabulous Dancer (USA)) 4218^{10} **>51f<**
Lidanna (IRE) 2 b f Nicholas (USA)-Shapely Test 3586a^{2} **>96f<**
Lidhama (USA) 3 b f Sword Dance-Running Melody (Rheingold) 695^{15} 853^{9} 1065^{9} 3629^{14} 4136^{3} 4259^{2} 4333^{10} **>73f<**
Liefling (USA) 2 b f Alleged (USA)-Mata Cara (Storm Bird (CAN)) 4312^{11} **>55f<**
Life's a Breeze 6 b h Aragon-Zahira (What A Guest) *233*^{10} *268*^{6} 507^{14} **>41a 25f<**
Life's Too Short (IRE) 4 br f Astronef-Quality Of Life 1274^{2} 1542^{9} 1797^{7} 2052^{11} **>57f<**
Liffeyside Leader (IRE) 4 ch f Exhibitioner-Cheerleader (Floribunda) *21*^{7} *175*^{7} **>23a f<**
Lift Boy (USA) 6 b h Fighting Fit (USA)-Pressure Seat (USA) (Ginistrelli (USA)) *(65)* *107*^{3} *202*^{2} *331*^{4} 726^{7} 1070^{10} (1164) 1321^{6} *3524*^{11} *4295*^{6} **>66da 50f<**
Liftoff (FR) 4 ch c Sharpo-Lighted Glitter 4095a^{3} **>111f<**
Light Fantastic 3 gr f Deploy-La Nureyeva (USA) (Nureyev (USA)) 1428^{2} **>72f<**
Light Movement (IRE) 5 br g Thatching-Annie Albright (USA) (Verbatim (USA)) 702^{9} 789^{14} 1434^{11} 4280^{9} **>48f<**
Lightning Quest (IRE) 4 b c Rainbow Quest (USA)-Rare Roberta (USA) (Roberto (USA)) *121*^{8} 556^{18} 866^{15} 1046^{4} 1160^{8} 1435^{7} 1998^{3} 2224^{4} 2501^{5} 4086^{8} **>10a 34f<**
Light Reflections 2 b c Rainbow Quest (USA)-Tajfah (USA) (Shadeed (USA)) 3068^{7} **>45f<**
Light Up New York (USA) 2 b f Majestic Light-Pali (4175a)
Ligurian (USA) 3 b f Ogygian (USA)-Ida's Image (USA) (Alydar (USA)) 758^{8} 1471^{3} 1818^{8} **>62f<**
Like A Hawk (USA) 2 b f Silver Hawk (USA)-Like A Train (USA) (Great Sun (USA)) 1017^{5} (1253) 1769^{2} 3578a^{2} 3561^{2} **>99f<**
Lilac Rain 3 b f Petong-Dame Corley (L'Enjoleur (CAN)) 521^{13} *2963*^{3} 3154^{9} **>42a 36f<**
Lila Pedigo (IRE) 2 b f Classic Secret (USA)-Miss Goldie Locks (Dara Monarch) *889*^{3} *1031*^{3} *(1333)* (1466) 2399^{4} 3623^{19} *4124*^{5} **>51a 62f<**
Lilburne (IRE) 2 b c Lycius (USA)-Hayat (IRE) (Sadler's Wells (USA)) 1903^{6} **>48f<**
L'ile Tudy (IRE) 5 b m Wassl-Melinte (Caerleon (USA))

896a^{3} 2890a^{4} 3041a^{3} 3482a^{6} (3688a) 4009a^{7} **>113f<**
Lillibella 2 b f Reprimand-Clarandal (Young Generation) 669^{6} 3495^{13} **>71f<**
Lilli Claire 2 ch f Beveled (USA)-Lillicara (FR) (Caracolero (USA)) 2534^{3} 3136^{4} (3378) 3623^{18} (3915) **>72f<**
Limerick Princess (IRE) 2 ch f Polish Patriot (USA)-Princess of Nashua (Crowned Prince (USA)) 669^{8} 970^{3} 1413^{2} (1579) 1893^{11} 2459^{5} 3210^{4} 3434^{7} 4097^{10} **>75f<**
Limosa 4 b f Jalmood (USA)-Larive (Blakeney) 741^{9} 1084^{4} 1328^{6} 1535^{8} 3263^{7} **>49f<**
Limyski 2 b g Petoski-Hachimitsu (Vaigly Great) 2464^{7} 3463^{13} **>33f<**
Lincoln Treasure (IRE) 4 ch c Mon Tresor-Beaded Bubbles (Simply Great (FR)) 1854^{20} 2280^{11} (2744) 2945^{6} **>37a 59f<**
Lincon Twenty One 2 ch f Sharpo-Angels Are Blue (Stanford) 455^{3} 617^{18} **>45f<**
Lincstone Boy (IRE) 7 b g Kafu-Babylon (Hello Gorgeous (USA)) *407^{U}* **>48a 46f<**
Lindas Delight 2 b f Batshoof-Agreloui (Tower Walk) (2656) 3008^{9} 3233^{10} 3749^{9} 4045^{5} 4263^{9} **>54f<**
Lindisfarne Lady 3 b f Jupiter Island-Harifa (Local Suitor (USA)) 1669^{9} 2166^{7} (2353) 2650^{5} 2851^{2} 3111^{4} 3410^{3} 3635^{10} 4086^{4} **>53f<**
Line Dancer 2 b c Shareef Dancer (USA)-Note Book (Mummy's Pet) (1715) 2131^{2} 3068^{3} **>92f<**
Linger 3 b f Sharrood (USA)-Waitingformargaret (Kris) 885^{7} 1787^{7} (2451) 2709^{3} 3726^{6} 3960^{3} 3984^{2} **>69f<**
Linney Head (USA) 4 b c Lyphard (USA)-Royalivor (USA) (Sir Ivor) 712^{5} 1020^{4} 1171^{3} 1363^{3} 1890a^{5} 4182a^{4} **>120f<**
Linoise (FR) 3 b f Caerwent-LiNeo (Gift Card) (2039a) 2562a^{2} **>113f<**
Linpac West 9 b h Posse (USA)-North Page (FR) 440^{6} 735^{2} 3489^{8} 3730^{23} **>105f<**
Lionel Edwards (IRE) 2 b c Polish Patriot (USA)-Western Heights (Shirley Heights) 1485^{5} 1715^{3} 1964^{3} 2667^{3} *3525^{3}* **>74a 80f<**
Lions Queen (DEN) 2 f 3909a^{3} **>61f<**
Lion Tower 3 b c Soviet Star (USA)-Percy's Lass (Blakeney) 1167^{3} 3799^{2} **>85f<**
Lipizzaner (IRE) 3 b c Tirol-Olderfleet 694^{4} 914^{2} 1131^{2} 1839^{21} (2795) 3085^{7} 3598^{3} 3755^{8} 3924^{10} **>101f<**
Lit de Justice (USA) 5 gr h El Gran Senor (USA)-Kanmary (FR) (Kenmare (FR)) *4303a^{3}* **>124a 107f<**
Literary Society (USA) 2 ch c Runaway Groom (CAN)-Dancing Gull (USA) (Northern Dancer) 2085^{6} 3648^{3} **>62f<**
Little Black Dress (USA) 2 b f Black Tie Affair-Seattle Kat (USA) (Seattle Song (USA)) 3673^{5} 4048^{4} **>69+f<**
Little Blackfoot 7 b h Sicyos (USA)-Nip In The Air (USA) (Northern Dancer) 1523^{15} 1917^{3} 2233^{5} 3092^{10} **>30a 42f<**
Little Conker 7 ch h All Systems Go-L'Irondelle (On Your Mark) 3017^{6} **>66f<**
Little Hooligan 4 b or br c Rabdan-Nutwood Emma (Henbit (USA)) 726^{12} 882^{18} **>39a 53f<**
Little Ibnr 4 b g Formidable-Zalatia (Music Boy) *44^{2}* *(130) (184) (281) 345^{8} 365^{7}* 567^{8} 1560^{7} 3777^{4} 3964^{2} 4068^{14} (4165) 4322^{9} **>87a 68f<**
Little Kenny 2 b f Warning-Tarvie 2198^{6} 2548^{12} 3379^{14} 3623^{5} 3858^{15} **>49f<**
Little Lucky 2 b f Weldnaas (USA)-Classy Nancy (USA) (Cutlass (USA)) 716^{8} 3053^{3} **>52f<**
Little Luke (IRE) 4 b c Somethingfabulous (USA)-Yours Sincerely (USA) (Stalwart (USA)) *161^{11}* **>49da 47f<**
Little Millie 2 b f Colmore Row-Little Kraker (Godswalk (USA)) 1977^{11} 4056^{5} 4161^{17} **>63f<**
Little Miner (IRE) 4 b or br f Miner's Lamp-Hot Sauce (Hot Spark) *34^{5}* **>34a f<**
Little Miss Ribot 5 b m Lighter-Little Missile (Ile de Bourbon (USA)) *100^{7} (155) (203) 330^{4}* 3384^{12} **>38a 48f<**
Little Noggins (IRE) 2 b f Salt Dome (USA)-Calash (Indian King (USA)) (2666) (3314) 3568^{9} 3901^{3} 4077^{5} 4237^{4} **>75f<**
Little Pilgrim 2 b c Precocious-Bonny Bright Eyes (Rarity) 4023^{6} 4137^{10} 4330^{8} **>63f<**
Little Redwing 3 ch f Be My Chief (USA)-Forward Rally (Formidable) 673^{8} **>48f<**
Little Saboteur 6 ch m Prince Sabo-Shoot To Win (FR) (Rabdan) *14^{3} (70) 216^{4} 498^{2}* 565^{11} *831^{4}* 1321^{4} *1882^{3} 2142^{8} 2402^{5}* **>74a 64f<**
Little Scarlett 3 b f Mazilier (USA)-Scarlett Holly (Red Sunset) *144^{6} 270^{2} (628)* **>59+a 29f<**
Little Secret (IRE) 3 ch c Waajib-Talking Shop (General Assembly (USA)) 651^{14} 974^{12} **>20f<**
Little Serena 5 b m Primitive Rising (USA)-Navos (Tyrnavos) 3772^{8} **>56f<**
Little Shefford 3 ch g Ballacashtal (CAN)-Wolstenbury (Lochnager) 854^{9} 1173^{12} 1447^{10} 2037^{18} **>48f<**
Little Smart (GER) 3 c 4018a^{7} (4183a) **>111f<**
Little Tyson (IRE) 3 b g Gale Yaka-Avionne (Derrylin) *591^{12}* 1012^{13} **>8f<**
Little Wilma 3 b f Zalazl (USA)-Miss Sanur (Mummy's Pet) *628^{2}* 739^{W} 861^{6} *1087^{12}* **>54a 45f<**
Lituus (USA) 2 gr c El Gran Senor (USA)-Liturgism (USA) (Native Charger (USA)) 4312^{14} **>38f<**
Live Project (IRE) 3 b g Project Manager-Saturday Live (Junius (USA)) 3667^{29} 3984^{16} *4217^{2} 4272^{7}* **>64a 44f<**
Livio (USA) 4 b c Lyphard (USA)-Make Change (USA) (Roberto (USA)) 4072^{19} **>40f<**
Lixos 4 b c Soviet Star (USA)-Lypharita (FR) (Lightning (FR)) *1029^{W}* **>56f<**
Llia 3 b f Shirley Heights-Llyn Gwynant (Persian Bold) 932^{3} 1704a^{5} 2614^{5} **>92f<**
Lloc 3 b f Absalom-Nosey (Nebbiolo) 452^{8} 754^{7} *1214^{4}* 1450^{5} *1566^{9}* 1822^{5} 2326^{4} *2631^{2}* 2686^{3} 3905^{7} 4057^{7} *4123^{10}* 4215^{20} **>54a 52f<**
Lobana (IRE) 3 b f Fairy King (USA)-Sable Lake (Thatching) 695^{11} 1136^{11} **>68f<**
Lobilio (USA) 6 b h Robellino (USA)-Nabila (USA) (Foolish Pleasure (USA)) *15^{7}* **>66da 59f<**
Lobkov 3 ch f Dunbeath (USA)-Lucy Manette (Final Straw) 3129^{13} **>23f<**
Local Heroine 5 ch m Clantime-Hollia (Touch Boy) 3777^{10} 3878^{16} 4113^{13} **>54a 39f<**
Loch Mariner 3 b f Lochnager-Sky Mariner (Julio Mariner) 3508^{14} **>29f<**
Lochon 4 br g Lochnager-Sky Mariner (Julio Mariner) 1582^{10} 1689^{13} 2521^{8} (2879) 3116^{5} 3275^{5} 3418^{11} 3783^{9} 4113^{6} 4142^{10} **>63f<**
Lochore 5 b h Nordico (USA)-Hound Song 676^{18} 841^{10} *1091^{5}* 1205^{9} 1680^{5} *2292^{P}* **>63a 42f<**

Loch Patrick 5 b h Beveled (USA)-Daisy Loch (Lochnager) 1475^{6} (1795) 2285^{8} 2671^{8} 3902^{8} **>105f<**

Locorotondo (IRE) 4 b f Broken Hearted-Rahwah (Northern Baby (CAN)) 634^{19} 864^{11} 1192^{8} 1553^{2} 2068^{8} *2145^{2} 2379^{4} (2605)* (3395) 3700^{2} 3810^{6} 4061^{14} **>75a 77f<**

Logie 3 ch c Prince Sabo-Ashdown (Pharly (FR)) *64^{5} 124^{7} 261^{2}* 648^{17} *767^{5}* **>63a 37f<**

Logie Pert Lad 3 b g Green Ruby (USA)-Rhazya (Rousillon (USA)) *410^{11}* 581^{7} 742^{10} 937^{14} 1257^{10} 1445^{9} 1909^{7} 3678^{12} 4049^{10} 4131^{14} **>20f<**

Loki (IRE) 7 ch h Thatching-Sigym (Lord Gayle (USA)) *2588^{6} 3082^{8}* (3349) 3500^{8} (3723) 3863^{8} 4028^{12} *4223^{2}* **>79a 88f<**

Lomas (IRE) 4 b c Ela-Mana-Mou-Bold Miss (Bold Lad (IRE)) 793^{10} 1188^{8} 1543^{9} 1754^{4} 2031^{7} **>84f<**

Lombardic (USA) 4 b c Private Account (USA)-If Winter Comes (USA) (Dancing Champ (USA)) 1768^{4} (2274) (2421) 3162^{21} 3593^{8} 3864^{6} **>98f<**

Lombard Ships 8 ch m Orchestra-Tina's Star (Simbir) *46^{7}* **>30da 45f<**

Lomberto 2 b c Robellino (USA)-Lamees (USA) (Lomond (USA)) 1726^{4} 2200^{2} (3652) 4159^{5} **>96f<**

Lonely Leader (IRE) 2 ch c Royal Academy (USA)-Queen To Conquer (USA) (King's Bishop (USA)) 3592^{3} **>70+f<**

Lone Risk 4 b c Risk Me (FR)-Madam de Seul (Pas de Seul) *223^{2} 280^{6}* 1655^{3} *1955^{11} 2495^{11}* 3724^{18} *4336^{9}* **>68da 47f<**

Lonesome Train (USA) 6 ch h Crafty Prospector (USA)-Alaki Miss (USA) (Olden Times) 3685^{9} **>97f<**

Longcroft 3 ch f Weldnaas (USA)-Najariya (Northfields (USA)) 759^{19} *847^{9}* 867^{9} 1285^{18} 1358^{4} (1420) 2129^{8} 2280^{6} 2353^{5} 2400^{4} 2480^{4} **>12a 55f<**

Long Furlong 7 b g Castle Keep-Myrtlegrove (Scottish Rifle) *(22) 143^{3} 304^{9} 471^{5} 496^{3} 3544^{11}* **>54a 54f<**

Longhill Boy 2 b g Statoblest-Summer Eve (Hotfoot) 2660^{12} 3025^{10} 3628^{5} 3765^{9} **>59f<**

Longing (USA) 2 ch f Lyphard's Wish (FR)-Fussiness (USA) (L'Enjoleur (CAN)) (3366) 3600^{4} **>79f<**

Lon Isa 4 ch f Grey Desire-Stripanoora (Ahonoora) *82^{12} 143^{2} 201^{3} 329^{2} 403^{12} 469^{3}* **>55a 45f<**

Lookingforarainbow (IRE) 7 ch h Godswalk (USA)-Bridget Folly (Crofter (USA)) 506^{10} 668^{12} 1022^{4} 1303^{5} (1505) 1844^{3} 1912^{2} 2069^{3} 2639^{4} 2745^{5} 2909^{6} 3106^{8} 3343^{6} **>78da 86f<**

Lord Advocate 7 br h Law Society (USA)-Kereolle 1046^{3} (1161) 1435^{2} (1496) 1686^{8} 1744^{2} 1817^{6} 2159^{3} 2226^{6} 2734^{5} 2816^{4} 2871^{3} 3002^{4} 3122^{3} (3311) 3743^{9} 3852^{14} **>32a 43f<**

Lord Alfie 6 ch h Beveled (USA)-Fair Nic (Romancero) 1148^{14} 1323^{18} 1501^{9} 1785^{16} **>51df<**

Lordan Velvet (IRE) 3 br c Lord Americo-Danny's Miracle (Superlative) 2306^{7} 2518^{5} 2818^{6} **>47f<**

Lord Cornelious 2 b c Lochnager-Title (Brigadier Gerard) 2230^{4}

Lord Ellangowan (IRE) 2 ch c Astronef-Gossip 3892^{16} 4129^{12} **>29f<**

Lord Frederick 3 b g Wonderful Surprise-Romany Framboise (Amboise) *1074^{13}* 2233^{6}

Lord Glenvara (IRE) 7 ch g Millfontaine-Ishtar (Dike (USA)) 3987^{15} **>33a 48f<**

Lord Hastie (USA) 7 b h Affirmed (USA)-Sheika (USA) (Minnesota Mac (USA)) 568^{12} 879^{7} *1086^{11}* 1310^{4} 1607^{7} 2087^{3} (2648) (2824) 2871^{2} 3189^{4} 3710^{13} 3852^{2} (3963) 4201^{6} 4325^{4} **>23a 69f<**

Lord High Admiral (CAN) 7 b h Bering-Baltic Sea (CAN) (Danzig (USA)) 693^{12} 944^{3} 1106^{13} (1304) (1756) 3551^{21} 3632^{6} 4033^{21} **>95df<**

Lord Jim (IRE) 3 b c Kahyasi-Sarah Georgina (Persian Bold) (484) 717^{4} 1099^{4} 1672^{3} 1852^{10} 2119^{2} 2386a^{6} 3730^{22} **>95df<**

Lord Lambson 6 b g Today and Tomorrow-Sum Star (Comedy Star (USA)) 4038^{25} **>32df<**

Lord Oberon (IRE) 7 b h Fairy King (USA)-Vaguely Jade (Corvaro (USA)) (2266) 2446^{2} (2906) 3026^{6} 3264^{4} **>70f<**

Lord of a Dance 4 b c Night Shift (USA)-Toot Toot (Alias Smith (USA)) 550^{6} 874^{10} **>49f<**

Lord of Appeal 3 b c Sadler's Wells-Park Appeal (Ahonoora) 3194a^{2} **>103f<**

Lord of Men 2 ch c Groom Dancer (USA)-Upper Strata (Shirley Heights) 2573^{6} (2912) (3315) (3793a) **>108+f<**

Lord Olivier (IRE) 5 b g The Noble Player (USA)-Burkina (African Sky) 719^{6} 934^{7} 1100^{11} 2823^{4} 3145^{2} 3359^{10} 3551^{11} 3717^{23} 4040^{22} **>100df<**

Lord Palmerston (USA) 3 b c Hawkster (USA)-First Minister (USA) (Deputy Minister (CAN)) 815^{13} 1663^{8} 2781^{7} 2984^{6} **>73f<**

Lord Sky 4 b c Emarati (USA)-Summer Sky (Skyliner) *(327) 345^{2} 398^{7}* 639^{7} 926^{20} 1019^{9} 1304^{10} 1565^{10} *1953^{4}* 3667^{14} 3777^{12} **>76a 57f<**

Lord Vivienne (IRE) 6 b g Don't Forget Me-Lady Vivienne (Golden Fleece (USA)) *518^{10}* 2021^{8} 2254^{3} 2327^{3} 2484^{2} 2668^{4} 2784^{7} 2972^{8} 3118^{5} 3808^{6} **>17a 48f<**

Lord Wellington (IRE) 4 b c Taufan (USA)-Merrie Laughter (Morston (FR)) *352^{7}* 1014^{7} **>32a 36f<**

Lore, 3 ch f Baim (USA)-Lorelene (FR) *2093^{7}* 2344^{7} **>39a f<**

Lorelei Lee (IRE) 3 ch f Old Vic-Most Amusing (Blushing Groom (FR)) 502^{5} 739^{2} 1040^{7} 1380^{8} (1532) 1811^{8} 2139^{8} (2503) 2668^{3} 2808^{7} 3057^{9} 3218^{3} 3247^{3} 3443^{5} 3645^{8} 3841^{7} **>62df<**

Loretta Gianni (FR) 3 b f Classic Account-Seasonal Pleasure (Graust 802a^{2} 1110a^{2} 1712a^{9} 4309a^{3} **>111f<**

Lorins Gold 5 ch h Rich Charlie-Woolcana 1050^{8} 1199^{5} 1910^{5} 1975^{13} 2202^{5} 2363^{7} 2641^{8} 3385^{3} **>36f<**

Lorsanginner (IRE) 3 b f Contract Law (USA)-Castleforbes (Thatching) 695^{19} **>31f<**

Los Alamos 2 b f Keen-Washita (Valiyar) 2422^{3} 3994^{7} 4291^{4} **>65f<**

Lost Lagoon (USA) 3 ch c Riverman (USA)-Lost Virtue (USA) 3016^{4} **>83f<**

Lost Love (GER) 3 b f Acatenango (GER)-L'Oise (Alpenkonig) 2042a^{2} **>100f<**

Lost Realm 3 b g Reprimand-Clarandal (Young Generation) 4220^{7} **>44f<**

Lothlorien (USA) 2 ch f Woodman (USA)-Fairy Dancer (USA) (Nijinsky (CAN)) 4148^{2} **>65+f<**

Lotties Bid 3 b f Ring Bidder-Gleneagle *54^{6} 171^{5} 258^{4}* 482^{15} 3649^{14} **>45a f<**

Lough Erne 3 b f Never so Bold-Laugharne (Known Fact (USA)) 442^{9} 752^{4} 1094^{3} 1414^{5} 1660^{2} 2659^{10}

3681[10] 3897[8] **>72f<**
Louisiana Purchase 2 b g Macmillion-My Charade (Cawston's Clown) 2200[8] 2529[8] 3846[7] **>45f<**
Louis' Queen (IRE) 3 b f Tragic Role (USA)-Bourbon Queen (Ile de Bourbon (USA)) 3235[2] 3693a[6] 4024[5] 4265[6] **>103f<**
Louisville Belle (IRE) 6 ch m Ahonoora-Lomond Fairy (Lomond (USA)) 820[5] 1070[16] 1335[2] 1777[5] (1975) 2404[4] 2578[3] *2943[8]* 3399[3] 3492[15] 3822[4] 3919[8] 4268[9] **>42a 69f<**
Loup Solitaire (USA) 2 b c Lear Fan-Louveterie (4177a) **>110f<**
Love Bateta (IRE) 2 b br f Caerleon (USA)-Marie Noelle (FR) (Brigadier Gerard) 4218[6] **>62f<**
Love Bird (IRE) 2 b c Bluebird (USA)-Top Glad (USA) (I'm Glad (ARG)) 2693[4] 2876[5] 3587a[20] 3713[5] **>78f<**
Love Legend 10 ch h Glint of Gold-Sweet Emma (Welsh Saint) *601[4]* 838[7] 1013[4] 1426[7] 1664[11] (1714) 1969[6] 2414[8] 2549[7] 2789[4] 3020[4] 3291[2] 3534[10] 3808[4] 4060[10] 4170[4] 4242[4] **>61a 61f<**
Lovely Lyca 3 ch f Night Shift (USA)-Turban (Glint of Gold) 695[7] (1337) 1747[2] 2289[6] 2691[7] 3349[3] 3552[7] 3863[9] (4228) 4289[10] **>78f<**
Lovely Me (IRE) 4 b f Vision (USA)-Self Satisfied (Great Nephew) *256[8]* 3128[6] 3357[3] 3519[8] 3678[10] **>27a 62f<**
Lovely Millie (IRE) 3 b f Bluebird (USA)-Mother of The Wind (Tumble Wind (USA)) 3564[2] **>109f<**
Lovely Morning 2 b f Thowra (FR)-Sweet Pleasure (Sweet Revenge) 3887[9] **>61f<**
Lovely Prospect 2 b f Lycius (USA)-Lovely Lagoon (Mill Reef (USA)) 3339[9] 3644[2] (3870) 4107[12] **>76f<**
Love of the North (IRE) 4 b g Nordico (USA)-Avec L'Amour (Realm) *1074[10]* *1455[3]* 2385a[7] *2632[5]* **>49da 39f<**
Love Secret (USA) 3 b f Secreto (USA)-Lady Asterisk (USA) (J O Tobin (USA)) 809a[3] 1237a[10] 4020a[6] **>80f<**
Love The Blues 3 ch f Bluebird (USA)-Love Match (USA) (Affiliate (USA)) 779[11] 3653[3] 3921[6] 4047[8] **>70f<**
Loveyoumillions (IRE) 3 b c Law Society (USA)-Warning Sound (Red Alert) 1233a[4] 1305[4] 1639[7] 3145[8] 3717[27] 4193[3] **>91f<**
Loving Legacy 4 ch f Caerleon (USA)-Tender Loving Care (Final Straw) *2140[10]* 2719[6] **>36a 68f<**
Lowawatha 7 b h Dancing Brave (USA)-Shorthouse 935[19] 1095[5] 1225[4] 1661[7] **>86a 81f<**
Loyalize (USA) 3 b f Nureyev (USA)-Reloy (USA) (Liloy (FR)) 692[8] 921[10] 1305[5] **>102df<**
Luana Queen (IRE) 2 b f Soviet Lad-Paradise Regained (North 1887a[3]
Lucayan Cay (IRE) 4 ch c Al Hareb (USA)-Flying Melody (Auction Ring (USA)) 1543[P] **>84df<**
Lucayan Prince (USA) 2 br c Fast Play (USA)-Now That's Funny (USA) (Saratoga Six (USA)) (682) 1104[2] **>91+tf<**
Lucayan Sunshine (USA) 3 b f Sunshine Forever (USA)-Be Bop A Lu (USA) (Mr Prospector (USA)) 1283[2] 1948[2] 2506[3] 2902[3] 3469[2] (3801) 4028[2] **>87f<**
Lucidity 3 br f Vision (USA)-Boo Hoo (Mummy's Pet) 427[18] 736[5] 1194[7] 1527[7] *1881[7]* *2630[6]* 3422[2] 3469[11] 4043[12] **>31a 65f<**
Lucknam Style 7 b g Macmillion-Mrs Currie (He Loves Me) 2246[16] 2528[5] 2807[4] 3057[3] 3248[6] **>52a 54f<**
Lucky Bea 2 b c Lochnager-Knocksharry (Palm Track) 533[12] 671[8] 925[2] 1082[3] 1494[2] 2161[11] 2328[10] 2951[9] 3417[5] 3760[12] 3975[5] 4141[8] **>63f<**
Lucky Coin 3 b f Hadeer-Lucky Omen 637[8] 857[3] 1105[4] 1219[9] 1702[3] 1986[3] (2196) 3320[2] 3571[8] 3875[15] **>77f<**
Lucky Di (USA) 3 b c Diesis-Lucky Song (USA) (Seattle Song (USA)) (539) 711[2] **>98f<**
Lucky Lees (IRE) 2 b c Treasure Kay-Appiana (Prince Ippi (GER)) *2294[6]* 3620[19] 3846[8] **>17f<**
Lucky Lionel (USA) 2 ch c Mt Livermore (USA)-Crafty Nan (USA) (Crafty Prospector (USA)) (919) 1608[4] (1868) 2347[6] (2726a) 3330a[7] 3610[3] 3903[4] **>99f<**
Lucky Lucaya (USA) 3 b f Chief's Crown (USA)-Minstrelete (USA) 2010[12] *2943[9]* **>48a 53f<**
Lucky Parkes 5 b m Full Extent (USA)-Summerhill Spruce (Windjammer (USA)) 571[5] (858) (1055) 1220[3] 1795[2] 2430[3] 3005[2] 3316[3] 3535[2] 3707[5] 3880[2] **>105df<**
Lucky Peg 3 b f Komaite (USA)-Lucky Grove (Lucky Wednesday) *350[3]* *515[3]* 576[5] *1030[9]* 1721[10] 1993[7] 2162[8] **>46a 35f<**
Lucky Quest 3 b g Rainbow Quest (USA)-Pretty Lucky (Shirley Heights) 1173[9] 1526[5] 1755[11] *2145[9]* 3634[13] 3884[6] **>11a 64f<**
Lucky Rabbit 2 b c Last Tycoon-Lady Philippa (IRE) (Taufan (USA)) 2116[2] 2473[5] 2820[3] 3160[3] 3546[5] 3701[13] **>72f<**
Lucky Revenge 2 b f Komaite (USA)-Sweet And Lucky (Lucky Wednesday) 859[3] 1054[3] *2075[10]* 2548[10] 3025[2] 3260[2] 3386[2] 3548[10] **>2a 76f<**
Lucky Soph (USA) 3 b f Cozzene (USA)-Lucky Spell (USA) 915[2] 1533[3] (1930) 2510[8] 2856[4] **>75f<**
Lucky Tucky 4 b c Alleging (USA)-Romana (Roman Warrior) 454[9] 1244[10] 1542[7] 1991[4] 2181[6] *4340[4]* **>40a 68f<**
Lucy's Gold 4 b f Efisio-Hinton Rose (Frimley Park) 734[8] *892[11]* *1032[12]* 1164[12] 1499[20] 1854[17] **>25a 43df<**
Ludgate (USA) 3 b f Lyphard (USA)-Hatton Gardens (Auction Ring (USA)) (1105) **>99f<**
Lugana Boy 2 b c Lugana Beach-Mischievous Tyke (Flying Tyke) 3018[13] 3779[R] 4230[R]
Lugana Vision 3 b f Lugana Beach-Regal Look (IRE) (Vision (USA)) 685[6] 753[4] *892[2]* (1580) 1677[3] 1783[3] 1963[9] 2840[3] *2925[8]* 3123[2] 3333[4] 3624[15] 3748[18] 3919[15] 4165[8] **>42a 57f<**
Lukes Brother (IRE) 4 ch g Kirchner-Golden Baby (Sharpen Up) *590[12]* **>33a 37f<**
Lunar Gris 2 gr f Absalom-Sliprail (USA) (Our Native (USA)) 1977[9] *2382[6]* 3314[11] 4224[16] *4334[10]* **>46a 37f<**
Lunar Mission (IRE) 4 b c Waajib-Lunulae (Tumble Wind (USA)) *157[7]* 1999[2] 2468[7] 2979[18] 3129[3] 3363[6] (3658) 3825[6] 4061[18] 4196[2] **>46a 71f<**
Lunar Mist 2 b f Komaite (USA)-Sugar Token (Record Token) (1282) 3314[7] 3623[4] (3742) (3803) (3901) (4077) (4206) **>90f<**
Lunar Prince 5 b h Mansingh (USA)-Lunate (Faraway Times (USA)) *16[8]* *199[W]* *390[7]* *1568[10]* 2179[7] **>8a 12f<**
Lunar Risk 5 b h Risk Me (FR)-Moonlight Princess (Alias Smith (USA)) 582[13] 1313[6] 1612[13] 1757[2] 2007[12] 2546[6] 2687[11] **>52a 52f<**
Luso 3 b c Salse (USA)-Lucayan Princess (High Line) 438[9] 663[2] 826[4] (979) (1396a) 2213a[2] 3144[3] 3609[8]

4014a^{13} **>128df<**
Lussuria (IRE) 2 b f Last Tycoon-Shabbaba (USA) (Arctic Tern (USA)) 508^{4} 716^{2} 910^{3} (1011) 1259^{6} 2435^{5} 2637^{2} (2838) 3160^{5} 3285^{2} **>79f<**
Lydhurst (USA) 2 b c Runaway Groom (CAN)-Release The Lyd (USA) (Lydian (FR)) 3868^{11} 4075^{8} **>74f<**
Lyford Law (IRE) 3 b c Contract Law (USA)-Kilboy Concorde (African Sky) *(381)* 572^{2} 980^{7} 1366^{9} 1778^{4} **>74a 81f<**
Lynton Lad 3 b c Superpower-House Maid (Habitat) 1673^{5} 1895^{29} 2240^{12} 3637^{12} 3964^{10} 4040^{15} 4157^{2} 4249^{5} **>79f<**
Lyphard's Honour (FR) 3 b c Highest Honour-Domludge (Lyphard) 1117a^{4} **>106f<**
Lyrikos (USA) 3 b c Lyphard (USA)-Full of Fable (USA) (Devil's Bag (USA)) (715) 945^{2} 1178^{3} **>103f<**
Lyzia (IRE) 2 ch f Lycius (USA)-Zia (USA) (Shareef Dancer (USA)) 2025^{3} 2594^{5} 3450^{7} 3867^{8} 4262^{3} **>77f<**

M

Ma Belle Poule 2 b f Slip Anchor-The Kings Daughter (Indian King (USA)) 3763^{3} 3865^{19} **>65f<**
Mabthul (USA) 7 b h Northern Baby (CAN)-Persuadable (USA) (What A Pleasure (USA)) *77^{8}* **>7a f<**
Ma Bulsie 2 b f Beveled (USA)-Cool Run (Deep Run) 2660^{9} 3432^{7} 4100^{8} 4321^{7} **>56f<**
Macanal (USA) 3 b c Northern Flagship (USA)-Magnala (ARG) (Mount Athos) (2895a) (4095a) **>117f<**
Macaroon Lady 4 b f Prince Sabo-Cookie Time (Posse (USA)) 3624^{22} 3748^{21} **>34a f<**
Macedonas 7 b h Niniski (USA)-Miss Saint-Cloud (Nonoalco (USA)) 1937^{14} **>28f<**
Macfarlane 7 br h Kala Shikari-Tarvie 796^{11} 1106^{4} 1304^{15} 1411^{2} 1565^{3} 1832^{17} 2410^{3} 3715^{16} (3777) 3992^{21} 4033^{8} 4145^{11} 4322^{13} **>50a 73f<**
Mackook (USA) 3 b or br c Seeking the Gold (USA)-L'Incestueuse (USA) (Lypheor) 635^{4} 978^{4} 1927^{2} (2977) 3382^{4} 3659^{16} **>86f<**
Mack the Knife 6 b h Kris-The Dancer (FR) (Green Dancer (USA)) 3923^{2} 4069^{2} **>115f<**
Macmorris (USA) 2 b c Silver Hawk (USA)-Andover Cottage (USA) (Affiliate (USA)) 3009^{7} **>36f<**
Mac Oates 2 b c Bairn (USA)-Bit of a Lass (Wassl) 3604^{7} 3933^{5} 4224^{8} **>63f<**
Macoumba (USA) 3 b f Mr Prospector (USA)-Maximova (FR) (Green Dancer (USA)) (705a) 933^{6} 1850^{10} 2897a^{7} **>107+f<**
Mac Rambler 8 b h Hotfoot-Arkengarthdale (Sweet Story) 534^{8} 1160^{3} 1295^{5} **>41f<**
Mac's Boy 6 b g Macmillion-Tender Manx (Owen Dudley) *79^{8}* **>15a 59f<**
Macs Clan 2 ch f Clantime-Kabella (Kabour) 3018^{12}
Macs Maharanee 8 b m Indian King (USA)-High State (Free State) *337^{8} 386^{8}* 812^{5} 949^{6} 1354^{5} 1604^{3} 1918^{2} 2206^{4} 2578^{2} 2652^{3} 2935^{7} **>44a 77f<**
Mac's Taxi 3 b g Komaite (USA)-Orange Silk (Moulton) *24^{2} 85^{2} (126) 170^{5}* (759) 867^{2} *1034^{13}* 1723^{4} 1843^{4} 2188^{6} *2383^{11}* 2518^{4} **>63a 74f<**
Mad About The Girl (IRE) 3 b f Cyrano de Bergerac-Makalu (Godswalk (USA)) 3347^{6} 3542^{7} 3638^{12} 3980^{15} 4194^{21} **>44f<**
Madaiyn (IRE) 3 ch c Shernazar-Mill River (Mill Reef) 1885a^{2} **>106f<**
Madam Chairman 6 ch m Ore-Comedown (Royalty) *352^{11}*
Madame Steinlen 2 b f Steinlen-Equadif (FR) (Abdos) 3816^{6} 4048^{5} 4117^{2} **>75f<**
Madam Marash (IRE) 2 b f Astronef-Ballybannon 1253^{8} 1671^{9} 3939^{5} 4208^{15} **>59f<**
Madam Pigtails 2 ch f Rich Charlie-School Dinners (Sharpo) 1448^{7} **>24f<**
Madam Sunpak 3 b f Rambo Dancer (CAN)-Flying Hyde (Petong) *5^{6} 270^{9} 420^{11}* **>33a f<**
Madam Zando 2 ch f Forzando-Madam Trilby (Grundy) 2508^{3} 2715^{2} 3465^{17} 3740^{6} **>55f<**
Made in Heaven 3 ch f Primo Dominie-Thundercloud (Electric) 775^{8} 1619^{6} 1907^{6} 2405^{6} **>69a 74f<**
Madly Sharp 4 ch c Sharpo-Madison Girl (Last Fandango) 611^{7} (1143) 1851^{25} 2369^{4} 3145^{10} **>100f<**
Mad Militant (IRE) 6 b h Vision (USA)-Ullapool (Dominion) *(19) 296^{2} (311) 377^{3} 396^{2} 516^{2} (600)* 778^{4} 1022^{5} *(2921) 3737^{7}* 3778^{5} 3970^{9} **>79a 70f<**
Madonna da Rossi 2 b f Mtoto-Granny's Bank (Music Boy) 3246^{4} 3468^{5} 3566^{5} 3744^{2} *4127^{4}* **>61a 61f<**
Madrileno (IRE) 3 gr c Common Grounds-Legs And Things (Three Legs) 4007a^{4} **>115f<**
Madurai 4 b f Chilibang-Macarte (FR) (Gift Card (FR)) 636^{14} 1510^{8} **>69f<**
Maestro Time (USA) 2 br c Fred Astaire (USA)-Time For Muir (USA) (Sham (USA)) *4338^{11}*
Maeterlinck (IRE) 3 b c Bluebird (USA)-Entracte (Henbit (USA)) 435^{2} (824) 1872^{15} 2118^{3} (2395) 2738^{5} 3066^{12} **>95f<**
Maftun (USA) 3 ch c Elmaamul (USA)-Allesheny (Be My Guest (USA)) 2568^{2} 2790^{6} 3653^{11} 3918^{5} **>73f<**
Mafuta (IRE) 3 b f Mtoto-Chrism (Baptism) 1905^{5} 3712^{13} 3847^{4} 4259^{15} **>51f<**
Maggi For Margaret 2 b f Shavian-Feather Flower (Relkino) (455) 718^{3} (2085) 2442^{8} (2618) 3086^{2} (3324a) 3687a^{7} 3610^{8} **>96f<**
Magical Belle (IRE) 3 ch f Magical Strike (USA)-Bel Ria (Gay Fandango (USA)) 1714^{16} *2141^{6}* **>39a 38f<**
Magical Bid (IRE) 3 b c Magical Strike (USA)-Fortera (FR) (Sanctus II) 435^{8} 613^{9} 857^{10} 1290^{7} 1498^{9} 1718^{6} 1962^{2} 2582^{9} 3805^{6} **>51f<**
Magical Blues (IRE) 3 b c Magical Strike (USA)-Blue Bell Girl (Blakeney) 1154^{5} 1512^{20} 1625^{R} **>56a 65f<**
Magical Manoeuvers 3 b c Cree Song-Orbital Manoeuvers (Space King) 733^{2} 1201^{7} *2590^{2}* **>58a 57f<**
Magical Midnight 2 ch f Timeless Times (USA)-Mayor (Laxton) 436^{12} 1278^{9} *1758^{5}* 3623^{16} 3937^{5} **>34a 40f<**
Magical Mill 2 ch f Prince Sabo-Mimram Melody (Music Boy) 3628^{19} 3763^{19} *4269^{8}* **>35a 7f<**
Magical Retreat (USA) 5 b m Sir Ivor-Known Charter (Known Fact (USA)) 2104^{2} 2272^{3} 2456^{2} 3161^{2} **>118f<**
Magical Touch 3 gr f Touch of Grey-Little Enchantress (Enchantment) 2178^{W} **>5a f<**
Magication 5 b m Nomination-Gundreda (Gunner B) 1484^{11} 1548^{10} 1991^{9} 2945^{7} 3034^{4} 3206^{4} 3385^{9} 3504^{6} 3638^{13} 3658^{13} 3871^{6} 4170^{12} **>48f<**
Magic Bird (IRE) 2 b f Bluebird (USA)-Frans Cap (Captain James) 508^{11} *1213^{3} 1333^{2} 1632^{5} 2075^{8}* 3353^{6} **>35a 35f<**
Magic Galop (USA) 2 b c Seattle Dancer-Jardin De Nuit

(Raja Baba 2896a^{4}

Magic Heights 2 gr c Deploy-Lady Regent (Wolver Hollow) 4246^{6} **>57f<**

Magic Imp (IRE) 2 b f Petorius-Magic Green (Magic Mirror) 910^{4} 1652^{2} 2135^{3} 2523^{5} 2982^{8} 3335^{5} **>70f<**

Magic Junction (USA) 4 b c Danzig Connection (USA)-Sleeping Beauty (Mill Reef (USA)) 3993^{7} 4205^{2} **>80a 84f<**

Magic Lake 2 b f Primo Dominie-Magic Kingdom (Kings Lake (USA)) 2221^{6} 2431^{6} *2629^{3}* 3225^{3} 3309^{2} 3749^{4} 3851^{3} 4059^{2} 4107^{2} 4195^{7} **>47a 65?f<**

Magic Leader (IRE) 3 b or br c Architect (USA)-Magic Rotation (USA) (His Majesty (USA)) *86^{5} 135^{7}* 1023^{11} 1146^{6} 1350^{12} 1914^{6} 2065^{7} 4240^{12} **>25a 47f<**

Magic Mail 2 b c Aragon-Blue Rhythm (Blue Cashmere) 3998^{3} **>76f<**

Magic Melody 2 b f Petong-Miss Rossi (Artaius (USA)) 3626^{8} 3828^{3} 4161^{8} *4269^{7}* **>37a 72f<**

Magic Mill (IRE) 2 b c Simply Great (FR)-Rosy O'Leary 3881^{3} (4282) **>82+f<**

Magic Orb 5 b m Primo Dominie-Tricky (Song) 1489^{5} 1604^{2} 1864^{4} 2130^{5} 2288^{4} 2533^{6} 2764^{W} 3112^{8} 3376^{8} 3492^{9} **>75f<**

Magic Pearl 5 gr m Belfort (FR)-Oyster Gray (Tanfirion) 723^{7} 1019^{3} 1106^{15} 1765^{7} 2252^{W} 2609^{10} 2748^{6} 4142^{15} **>76df<**

Magic Ron 2 b g Ron's Victory (USA)-Magical Spirit (Top Ville) 2912^{8} 3463^{7} 3846^{4} **>59f<**

Magic Times 4 b g Good Times (ITY)-Young Wilkie (Callernish) *303^{8}* 494^{9} **>31a 25f<**

Magna Carta 3 b c Royal Academy (USA)-By Charter (Shirley Heights) 622^{8} 1131^{9} **>84+a 81f<**

Magnate's Point 3 b c Last Tycoon-Kindjal (Kris) 963^{7} 1380^{9} 1745^{7} 4156^{13} **>75f<**

Magnificent Devil (USA) 3 ch c Devil's Bag (USA)-Magnificent Lady (Nonoalco (USA)) (658) 930^{4} 1848^{16} 2285^{6} **>96f<**

Magnums Secret 3 b f Hubbly Bubbly (USA)-Black Veil (Blakeney) 1251^{5} 1583^{8} 2582^{12} 3099^{6} **>54f<**

Mahool (USA) 6 b h Alydar (USA)-Tax Dodge (USA) (Seattle Slew (USA)) *(365)* 439^{19} 559^{18} **>92a 82df<**

Maiandros (GR) 3 ch c Flash N Thunder (USA)-Mous Mous (GR) (Etoile Lointaine (USA)) *499^{4}* 621^{12} (971) 1130^{12} 1754^{6} (1941) 2437^{8} **>72a 90f<**

Maid For Baileys (IRE) 2 b f Marju (IRE)-Island Time (USA) (Bold Hour) 1525^{4} 2083^{2} 2320^{13} 2957^{2} 3307^{2} 3713^{2} 3985^{2} **>77f<**

Maid For The Hills 2 b f Indian Ridge-Stinging Nettle (Sharpen Up) (1627) (2106) **>87f<**

Maid for Walking 3 b or br f Prince Sabo-Stinging Nettle (Sharpen Up) 1698^{3} 2205^{4} 2436^{5} 2699^{4} **>103f<**

Maid O'Cannie 4 b f Efisio-Ichnusa (Bay Express) 535^{13} 746^{4} 1677^{6} 2194^{7} 2458^{8} 2758^{6} 3418^{3} (3751) 3764^{3} 4068^{20} **>66a 61f<**

Maid Welcome 8 br m Mummy's Pet-Carolyn Christensen (Sweet Revenge) *89^{4} (142) 160^{2} 219^{5} 281^{4} 344^{3} (447)* 542^{9} *1049^{8} 4217^{3}* **>66a 59f<**

Main Brace 4 b c Robellino (USA)-Mystery Ship (Decoy Boy) *62^{6} 226^{4} 334^{6}* 2363^{9} 2528^{14} *2587^{9}* **>39a 50f<**

Main Offender 3 ch c Be My Chief (USA)-Messaria (Ile de Bourbon (USA)) 635^{5} 978^{3} 1339^{3} 4162^{2} (4245) **>91f<**

Mai Pen Rai 7 ch g All Systems Go-Jersey Maid (On Your Mark) 1285^{16} 1542^{8} *1883^{9}* 2016^{4} 2081^{6} 2789^{9} 3173^{6} **>5a 46f<**

Maiteamia 2 ch g Komaite (USA)-Mia Scintilla (Blazing Saddles (AUS)) *3523^{7}* 3626^{16} 3784^{10} 3985^{8} **>31a 45f<**

Majal (IRE) 6 b h Caerleon (USA)-Park Special (Relkino) *(238) 321^{9}* **>60a 56f<**

Majboor Yafooz (USA) 5 b h Silver Hawk (USA)-Forced To Fly (USA) (Accipiter (USA)) 1095^{4} **>73f<**

Majdak Jereeb (IRE) 2 b c Alzao (USA)-Aunty (FR) (Riverman (USA)) 2912^{5} 3494^{7} 3650^{4} 3865^{24} **>69f<**

Majestic Role (FR) 4 ch f Theatrical-Autocratic (Tyrant) 3190^{3} **>92f<**

Major Change 3 gr c Sharrood (USA)-May the Fourteenth (Thatching) 1136^{5} (1353) 1793^{4} 2571^{3} 2738^{3} 3107^{3} 3926^{16} 4163^{5} **>92f<**

Major Dundee (IRE) 2 b c Distinctly North (USA)-Indigo Blue (IRE) (Bluebird (USA)) 3155^{4} **>81f<**

Major Mouse 7 ch g All Systems Go-Tzu-Hsi (Songedor) *117^{9} 230^{3} 313^{2} 349^{2}* 749^{16} *(845)* 1415^{5} 1666^{5} *(1884) 2922^{W}* **>67a 51f<**

Major Quality 2 b c Sizzling Melody-Bonne de Berry (Habitat) 4314^{3} **>86f<**

Major Snugfit 3 b c Tina's Pet-Sequoia 3808^{12} **>31a 48f<**

Makaskamina 2 b br g Mtoto-Flying Flo Jo (USA) (Aloma's Ruler (USA)) *2381^{8}* 2637^{4} 3048^{5} 3290^{8} 3985^{4} 4107^{8} **>15a 52f<**

Make a Stand 4 ch c Master Willie-Make A Signal (Royal Gunner (USA)) 1183^{23} 1661^{11} 2007^{14} 2314^{9} 2658^{7} (3292) 3927^{6} **>76f<**

Make the Break 4 b c Dominion-Souadah (USA) (General Holme (USA)) *82^{10} 167^{5} 220^{7} 308^{11}* 548^{15} 748^{8} *1076^{8}* 2518^{6} 2784^{15} 2905^{6} 3808^{11} **>41da 48f<**

Make Time 3 b f Sayf El Arab (USA)-Moment In Time (Without Fear (FR)) 765^{9} 922^{18} 1550^{4} 2778^{3} 3034^{2} 3823^{3} **>72f<**

Makri 3 b f Night Shift (USA)-Maria Isabella (FR) (Young Generation) 865^{6} 1053^{3} 1240^{4} 1476^{4} 2482^{4} **>81f<**

Malibu Man 3 ch c Ballacashtal (CAN)-National Time (USA) (Lord Avie (USA)) 1354^{14} 1510^{11} *1763^{4} (2074) 2295^{3} (2590) 3242^{5}* 3764^{5} 3919^{2} 4057^{6} 4165^{10} **>77+a 64f<**

Malice Corner 2 ch c Savahra Sound-Najd (St Chad) 1774^{7} 2135^{13} *3675^{13}* 4133^{9} **>40f<**

Malihabad (IRE) 6 ch g Shahrastani (USA)-Mill River (FR) (Mill Reef (USA)) 2391^{4} 2901^{4} 3772^{9} **>67f<**

Malindi Bay 7 gr h Grey Desire-Malindi (Mansingh (USA)) 1917^{5} 2309^{2} 2640^{4} 3129^{8} 3778^{8} 4196^{14} **>44f<**

Malingerer 4 gr f Petong-Crystal Gael (Sparkler) *9^{8} 22^{3} 58^{3} 83^{4} 122^{5} 200^{8} 321^{12}* 1472^{14} 1539^{2} 1970^{13} 2037^{5} 2334^{7} 2486^{8} 3056^{9} 3137^{5} **>34da 37f<**

Mallia 2 b c Statoblest-Pronetta (USA) (Mr Prospector (USA)) 533^{4} 615^{2} (878) **>78f<**

Malsisio 3 b f Efisio-Moonlight Fling (Imperial Fling (USA)) *417^{10}* 773^{13} 1412^{11} 2162^{9} 2372^{8} 2784^{14} **>30f<**

Malzoom 3 b c Statoblest-Plum Bold (Be My Guest (USA)) *362^{5} 409^{6}* 524^{14} 594^{10} 759^{7} 992^{7} 1060^{6} 1465^{7} 1742^{2} 1873^{3} 2156^{11} 2582^{3} 3370^{U} 3853^{11} **>32a 45f<**

Mamalama 7 ch m Nishapour (FR)-Gauloise *166^{9}* **>37da f<**

Mamlakah (IRE) 3 ch f Unfuwain (USA)-Narjis (USA)

(Blushing Groom (FR)) 1850^{8} 2409^{3} 2673^{5} 3235^{5} 3564^{8} **>102f<**

Mamlouk 3 gr c Distant Relative-Nelly Do Da 3921^{14} **>25f<**

Mamma's Due 3 ch f Precocious-Maple Syrup *603^{4} 768^{2}* 1040^{5} 1360^{5} *1566^{3}* 3667^{28} 4068^{23} **>63a 64f<**

Mamnoon (USA) 4 b c Nijinsky (CAN)-Continual (USA) 1022^{10} 3820^{14} 4168^{10} **>85f<**

Mam'selle Bergerac (IRE) 2 b f Cyrano de Bergerac-Miss Merryweather (Sexton Blake) 3379^{6} 3587a^{23} 3672^{10} 4130^{6} 4218^{4} **>66f<**

Mam'zelle Angot 5 b m Balidar-Ragirl *138^{2} 222^{3}* 493^{7} *1209^{9} 2292^{3} 2634^{12} 3075^{6}* **>66a 69f<**

Manabar 3 b c Reprimand-Ring of Pearl (Auction Ring (USA)) 973^{3} (1507) 3601^{14} 3703^{15} 3934^{13} **>78f<**

Mancini 2 b br g Nomination-Roman Blue 2370^{4} 2534^{2} (2839) **>84f<**

Mandalay Prince 11 b h Nishapour (FR)-Ops (Welsh Saint) 751^{13} 840^{12}

Mandapan 2 b f Rolfe (USA)-Aventina (Averof) 4075^{12} **>41f<**

Mandarina (USA) 3 ch f El Gran Senor (USA)-Oriental Mystique (Kris) 620^{6} 1242^{6} 1923^{4} 2470^{2} 3382^{10} (3768) 4019a^{2} **>99f<**

Manderella 2 b f Clantime-Ascot Lass (Touching Wood (USA)) 2277^{6} 3379^{2} 3495^{8} 3806^{2} 4137^{13} **>77f<**

Mandy's Risk 2 ch g Risk Me (FR)-Lightning Legend (Lord Gayle (USA)) 617^{19} 725^{7} 1590^{12} 1829^{12} *3077^{12}* **>17a 35f<**

Manful 3 b c Efisio-Mandrian 536^{6} 614^{9} 756^{5} 1303^{4} 1558^{4} 1872^{19} 2101^{5} 2312^{5} 2835^{4} 3665^{6} 3718^{11} 4138^{6} 4232^{5} **>70f<**

Manila Bay (USA) 5 b h Manila (USA)-Betty Money (USA) (Our Native (USA)) 2657^{14} 2989^{4} 3401^{6} 3884^{17} **>52f<**

Manilaman (USA) 4 c Manila (USA) 3576a^{9}

Manninamix 2 gr c Linamix (FR)-Mrs Annie (3907a) 4177a^{2} **>110f<**

Man of Wit (IRE) 2 b c Fayruz-Laughing Matter (Lochnager) 690^{6} 3371^{4} 3668^{13} 3892^{15} **>70f<**

Manolete 4 b c Hard Fought-Andalucia *67^{5} 172^{8} 254^{3} 311^{3} 352^{4} 1955^{12}* 3898^{15} **>61a 36f<**

Manolo (FR) 2 b c Cricket Ball (USA)-Malouna (FR) (General Holme (USA)) 671^{3} **>70f<**

Manor Adventure 5 ch m Smackover-Klairove (Averof) 812^{11} 1199^{11} **>41a 32f<**

Manoy 2 b g Precocious-Redcross Miss (Tower Walk) 3996^{6} 4188^{16} 4276^{7} **>51f<**

Mansab (USA) 2 b c Housebuster (USA)-Epitome (USA) (Summing (USA)) 3933^{4} 4276^{3} **>71f<**

Mans Passion 3 gr c Jupiter Island-Roybirdie (Mansingh (USA)) 1514^{21} 1832^{20} **>36f<**

Mansur (IRE) 3 b c Be My Chief (USA)-Moorish Idol (Aragon) 698^{3} 1083^{11} 1987^{2} 2520^{3} 3059^{4} 3621^{5} 3862^{5} **>72f<**

Manzoni (GER) 3 dk b c Solarstern-Manege (Neckar) (1121a) 1713a^{4} 2215a^{2} 2729a^{4} 3798a^{3} **>117f<**

Ma Petite Anglaise 3 b f Reprimand-Astolat (Rusticaro (FR)) (739) (907) 1306^{5} 1793^{7} (2488) 3222^{11} 3732^{5} 4116^{18} 4267^{28} **>90f<**

Maple Bay (IRE) 6 b h Bold Arrangement-Cannon Boy (USA) (Canonero II (USA)) 2276^{15} *3073^{5} 3241^{5}* 3467^{3} *3510^{2} 3739^{3} 4272^{3} 4298^{7}* **>64a 55f<**

Maple Burl 2 b g Dominion-Cam Maire (Northern Prospect (USA)) 3765^{7} 3917^{10} 4161^{7} 4329^{7} **>77f<**

Maplestead (IRE) 3 b c Shareef Dancer (USA)-Halstead (Bustino) 635^{13} 911^{6} **>60f<**

Maquina 3 b f Machiavellian (USA)-Musical Bliss (USA) (The Minstrel (CAN)) 1701^{9} **>55f<**

Maraady (USA) 6 b h Alydar (USA)-Ma Petite Jolie (USA) (Northern Dancer) 1254^{9} 1622^{16} *1759^{6}* 3234^{10} **>30a 45f<**

Maradonna (USA) 6 b g Alleged (USA)-Kiss *346^{7} 412^{2} (469)* 1189^{2} 1840^{27} 2612^{P} **>76a 75f<**

Maralinga (IRE) 3 ch c Simply Great (FR)-Bellinzona (Northfields (USA)) *(564)* 979^{3} 1103^{2} 1611^{15} 3603^{5} 3945^{34} 4301a^{2} **>98a 102f<**

Maraschino 2 ch f Lycius (USA)-Mystery Ship (Decoy Boy) 2660^{10} 3053^{5} 3260^{8} 3749^{14} **>51f<**

Marastani (USA) 5 ch g Shahrastani (USA)-Marianna's Girl (USA) (Dewan (USA)) (3574a)

Marawis (USA) 2 b c Danzig (USA)-Ra'a (USA) (Diesis) 4161^{5} 4314^{4} **>86f<**

Marble 4 b f Petong-Hymettus (Blakeney) *422^{9}* 494^{8} 818^{13} 874^{16} 4232^{6} **>22a 48df<**

Marble Falls (IRE) 3 b f Tirol-Majolique (Irish River) 899a^{2} 1238a^{2} 3040a^{4} **>100f<**

Marchant Ming (IRE) 3 br c Persian Bold-Hot Curry (USA) (Sharpen Up) *500^{4} 624^{3}* 1093^{7} 1452^{3} 1776^{2} 2245^{7} (3184) 3320^{5} 3634^{5} **>56a 75df<**

Marchman 10 b g Daring March-Saltation 864^{4} 1254^{8} 1940^{2} 2081^{3} 2490^{9} **>56f<**

Marco Magnifico (USA) 5 b or br h Bering-Viscosity (USA) (Sir Ivor) *87^{4}* 3705^{14} 3970^{12} **>70a 59df<**

Marcomir (USA) 2 b c Dayjur (USA)-Mariella (USA) (Roberto (USA)) (3839) **>71+f<**

Margaret Modes 3 b f Thatching-Avant-Garde (Pas de Seul) *332^{7}* 1012^{12} 1325^{3} 1791^{8} 2983^{8} 3096^{8} 3265^{7} **>33a 66f<**

Margaretrose Anna 3 b f Handsome Sailor-Be Bold (Bustino) 3981^{6} **>63f<**

Margi Boo 2 ch f Risk Me (FR)-Louisianalightning (Music Boy) 533^{8} 595^{4} *1031^{8}* 3720^{10} 3975^{18} **>2a 46f<**

Marguerite Bay (IRE) 3 b f Darshaan-Idrak (Young Generation) (1240) 2006^{6} 3820^{11} 3973^{11} **>90f<**

Marha 3 br f Shaadi (USA)-Balqis (USA) (Advocator) 1227^{4} (2066) 2416^{W} 3033^{4} 3342^{8} **>100f<**

Marie de Gloire (FR) 3 br or ch f Le Glorieux-Marie de Charmes (Nadjar 1238a^{4} **>75f<**

Marie de Ken (FR) 3 b f Kendor (FR)-Marie de Vez (FR) (Crystal Palace (FR)) 3192a^{2} 3579a^{2} 4015a^{7} **>107f<**

Marigliano (USA) 2 b c Riverman (USA)-Mount Holyoke (Golden Fleece (USA)) 4312^{3} **>80+f<**

Marildo (FR) 8 b h Romildo-Marike (FR) (Nasram II) 607a^{9} 898a^{9} 1394a^{3} (2041a) (3036a) 4007a^{5} **>124f<**

Marintisse (ITY) 2 b c Tisserand-Marina Bailey (Julio Mari 2900a^{2}

Mariposa Grove 3 b f Kalaglow-Feather Flower (Relkino) 813^{9} 1093^{18} 1372^{13} 1962^{15} **>48f<**

Maristax 2 b f Reprimand-Marista 2487^{4} 3626^{4} 3988^{2} (4130) **>77f<**

Marjaana (IRE) 2 b f Shaadi (USA)-Funun (USA) (Fappiano (USA)) 1928^{3} (2412) 2783^{2} 3639^{4} 3867^{10} **>80f<**

Marjan (IRE) **4** ch f Classic Secret (USA)-Powder Lass (Tap On Wood) 4214^{6} **>9f<**

Marjimel **4** b f Backchat (USA)-Mary's Double (Majetta) 866^{13} 1039^{5} 1529^{14} 1645^{6} **>54f<**

Marjons Boy **8** ch h Enchantment-Nevilles Cross (USA) *370^{10}*

Marjorie Rose (IRE) **2** b f Magical Strike (USA)-Arrapata (Thatching) 1158^{3} 1307^{2} 1460^{5} 2275^{4} **>79f<**

Marjorie's Memory (IRE) **4** b f Fairy King (USA)-Burnished Gold (Breton) 1451^{5} 2163^{9} 2772^{8} **>67df<**

Marjorie's Orchid **4** gr f Petong-Aonia (Mummy's Pet) *405^{7}* 1092^{18} **>20a 48df<**

Marketeer Magic **2** ch c Clantime-Mary From Dunlow (Nicholas Bill) 925^{7} 1082^{4} 1288^{6} 1841^{7} 3430^{5} *3528^{10}* 3642^{14} **>30a 62f<**

Marketing Man **5** b g Sizzling Melody-Best Offer (Crepello) *75^{9}* **>1a f<**

Mark of Esteem (IRE) **2** b c Darshaan-Homage (Ajdal (USA)) 2320^{2} (2741) **>89f<**

Marl **2** ch f Lycius (USA)-Pamela Peach (Habitat) 852^{2} (1137) 1849^{6} 2442^{16} **>103+f<**

Marmy **2** b f Midyan (USA)-Usaylah (Siberian Express (USA)) 2195^{3} 2447^{7} *2629^{7}* 3417^{7} 3533^{7} **>22a 51f<**

Marocco (USA) **3** ch c Diesis-Bank On Love (USA) (Gallant Romeo (USA)) 1186^{4} 1486^{5} (1683) 2015^{4} 2848^{6} **>86f<**

Maronetta **3** ch f Kristian-Suzannah's Song (Song) *156^{7}* *263^{12}* 2719^{5} 3805^{2} 3862^{2} 4331^{3} **>30a 56f<**

Marowins **6** ch h Sweet Monday-Top Cover (High Top) *269^{9}* *349^{4}* *364^{5}* *414^{7}* *(529)* *(601)* 876^{4} 1027^{6} (1506) 2276^{8} *2634^{6}* 3063^{9} 3368^{9} 3607^{13} **>73a 53f<**

Marrowfat Lady (IRE) **4** b f Astronef-Lady Topknot (High Top) 1541^{5} 1676^{7} (2051) (2178) 2488^{2} 2685^{13} **>74f<**

Marsayas (IRE) **2** ch c Classic Music (USA)-Babiana (CAN) (Sharpen Up) 3644^{15} 4282^{7} *4334^{6}* **>42a 48f<**

Marsh Arab **4** b g Night Shift (USA)-Ophrys (Nonoalco (USA)) *1078^{6}* *2074^{7}* *2290^{9}* 3649^{8} 3800^{11} **>19a 47f<**

Marsoom (CAN) **4** b c Wild Again (USA)-Sadwester (USA) (Honest Pleasure (USA)) 931^{4} 1135^{2} 1479^{2} (1563) 1853^{5} 2274^{5} 2596^{4} **>111f<**

Martara (IRE) **2** b c Marju (IRE)-Alrayhah (Habitat) 533^{6} 690^{5} (2423) 2847^{4} 3132^{8} 3727^{4} 3753^{2} **>74f<**

Martha Quest **2** ch f Rainbow Quest (USA)-Magic Flute (USA) (The Minstrel (CAN)) 2173^{4} 2796^{4} 3437^{4} 4102^{2} **>61f<**

Martiniquais (IRE) **2** ch c Simply Great-Majolique 3907a^{3} **>91f<**

Martinosky **9** b h Martinmas-Bewitched (African Sky) *386^{5}* *393^{7}* 450^{4} *590^{9}* 780^{10} **>40a 58f<**

Martins Folly **2** ch f Beveled (USA)-Millingdale (Tumble Wind (USA)) 2985^{6} 3541^{8} **>28f<**

Marwell Indigo **3** br g Interrex (CAN)-Lily of France (Monsanto (FR)) 1786^{7} 2049^{4} 2708^{9} 3905^{18} 4157^{13} **>45f<**

Mary Macblain **6** b m Damister (USA)-Tzarina (USA) (Gallant Romeo (USA)) 1037^{5} 1250^{11} 1649^{2} 1995^{6} 2307^{7} 2719^{8} **>35a 43f<**

Mary's Case (IRE) **5** b g Taufan (USA)-Second Service (Red Regent) *298^{5}* *322^{3}* *371^{3}* *415^{2}* 478^{3} *845^{7}* 928^{7} (1206) 1528^{6} 1666^{2} 1956^{4} 2156^{7} 3295^{2} 3368^{7} *3529^{2}* (3719) 4060^{2} 4152^{4} **>64a 68f<**

Mary's Way (GR) **3** b f Night Shift (USA)-Sally (DEN) (Faraway Times (USA)) (888) 1105^{7} 4065^{6} **>84df<**

Marzipan (IRE) **3** br f Green Desert (USA)-Lady Zi (Manado) 779^{9} 2411^{9} 2863^{3} 3097^{2} 3402^{5} 3862^{15} **>67f<**

Masaafaat (USA) **3** b f Woodman (USA)-Pirouette (Sadler's Wells (USA)) 1136^{10} 1533^{2} 2393^{5} 3409^{3} 3725^{3} **>78f<**

Masafah (USA) **3** ch f Cadeaux Genereux-Tatwij (USA) (Topsider (USA)) 999^{7} (1550) **>83f<**

Masai Man (USA) **4** ch c Riverman (USA)-Green Oasis (FR) (Green Dancer (USA)) *589^{10}* **>62f<**

Masbro Bird **2** b f Midyan (USA)-Grinning (IRE) (Bellypha) 782^{7} 1054^{10} 3427^{12} 3566^{11} **>39f<**

Mascalls Lady **10** b m Nicholas Bill-Whisper Gently (Pitskelly) 2148^{8} 2197^{10}

Masehaab (IRE) **2** b c Mujtahid (USA)-Firefly Night (Salmon Leap (USA)) 1184^{3} (3650) (4059) **>86f<**

Mask Flower (USA) **2** b f Dayjur (USA)-Nom de Plume (USA) (Nodouble (USA)) 1247^{4} 1460^{2} 2221^{2} **>74f<**

Masnad (USA) **4** ch c Mt Livermore (USA)-Fateful Princess (USA) (Vaguely Noble) 652^{4} 870^{25} 1143^{12} **>101f<**

Masnun (USA) **10** gr h Nureyev (USA)-Careless Kitten (USA) (Caro) *89^{13}* *(157)* *187^{2}* *(235)* *(317)* 3269^{4} *3510^{7}* 3619^{9} *4217^{6}* *4298^{3}* **>74a 68f<**

Mason (IRE) **3** ch g Simply Great (FR)-Viva Ronda (Kampala) 2337^{3} 2645^{7} *3514^{11}* *3734^{7}* **>39a 56f<**

Masquerade **2** b c Alzao (USA)-Melpomene (USA) (Lear Fan (USA)) 3174^{5} (3536) 3865^{26} **>79f<**

Masrah Dubai (USA) **4** b g Theatrical-Roycon (High Top) *190^{2}* *252^{5}* **>61a f<**

Masruf (IRE) **3** b c Taufan (USA)-Queen's Share (Main Reef) 1069^{8} 1222^{11} 1839^{28} 2271^{4} 3175^{7} 3656^{8} **>74f<**

Master Beveled **5** b g Beveled (USA)-Miss Anniversary (Tachypous) *281^{10}* *364^{8}* *406^{7}* 439^{10} 714^{7} 793^{7} 918^{7} 1280^{8} 1617^{9} 2117^{9} 3447^{5} 3607^{5} 3703^{6} 3837^{6} 3945^{29} 4116^{7} **>65a 84f<**

Master Charter **3** ch g Master Willie-Irene's Charter (Persian Bold) 772^{7} 1204^{2} 2331^{6} 3980^{14} (4194) 4249^{6} **>67f<**

Master Fiddler **5** b h Teenoso (USA)-Musical Princess (Cavo Doro) 818^{10} 990^{8} 1422^{5} 1743^{5} 2279^{6} 2955^{2} 3302^{4} **>49f<**

Master Hyde (USA) **6** gr h Trempolino (USA)-Sandspur (USA) (Al Hattab (USA)) (2816) 3189^{10} 3412^{5} 3743^{7} **>66a 68f<**

Master Lynx (USA) **2** b c Cutlass (USA)-La Ninouchka (USA) (Bombay Duck (USA)) 1184^{15} 2434^{6} **>48f<**

Master M-E-N (IRE) **3** ch c My Generation-Secret Lightning (USA) (Secretariat (USA)) 984^{17} 1201^{12} 1718^{4} 2016^{3} 2276^{11} 2524^{2} 3344^{6} 3515^{3} **>36a 62f<**

Master Millfield (IRE) **3** b c Prince Rupert (FR)-Calash (Indian King (USA)) *24^{3}* *196^{4}* *243^{3}* *(333)* *365^{4}* 524^{8} 1202^{4} 1447^{2} 1639^{5} 1778^{3} 2987^{4} 3112^{3} 3286^{3} (3519) 3984^{4} 4040^{23} **>79a 71f<**

Master of Passion **6** b h Primo Dominie-Crime of Passion (Dragonara Palace (USA)) 922^{16} 1174^{4} 1354^{4} 1895^{5} 2288^{2} 2764^{16} (3087) 3551^{5} 3717^{4} 3815^{8} 4040^{10} **>46a 96f<**

Master Ofthe House **9** b h Kind of Hush-Miss Racine (Dom Racine (FR)) 1292^{9} 1468^{5} 1808^{7} (1995) 2433^{8} 2875^{4} 3119^{3} 3295^{3} 3393^{3} 3840^{6} 3977^{6} **>70f<**

Master of Troy 7 b g Trojan Fen-Gohar (USA) (Barachois (CAN)) 840^{9} **>70df<**

Master Planner 6 b g Night Shift (USA)-Shaky Puddin (934) 1100^{3} 1480^{5} 1766^{3} 1895^{21} 2418^{5} 2617^{4} 2764^{23} 3145^{15} 3446^{10} **>106f<**

Masterplayer (GER) 3 dk c Alzao (USA)-Majoritat (Konigsstuhl) 2215a^{3} **>110f<**

Master Reach 6 br h Reach-Lady Donaro (Ardoon) *370^{6}* **>31a f<**

Master Showman (IRE) 4 b g Alzao (USA)-Arctic Winter (CAN) (Briartic (CAN)) *2961^{13}* 3259^{10}

Masuri Kabisa (USA) 4 ch f Ascot Knight (CAN)-Imperverse (USA) (Impressive (USA)) 975^{5} 1347^{7} 1694^{5} 1970^{2} 2355^{6} 2663^{3} (3056) (3287) 3572^{3} 3743^{10} 4259^{7} **>52f<**

Matamoros 3 gr c Kalaglow-Palama (USA) (Blushing Groom (FR)) 651^{2} 974^{10} 3621^{6} 3862^{3} 4086^{2} 4166^{15} **>81f<**

Matarun (IRE) 7 b h Commanche Run-Miss Mat (Matahawk) 489a^{3} 1387a^{8} 1709a^{9} **>112f<**

Match The Colour 2 b g Full Extent (USA)-Matching Lines (Thatching) 2791^{16} 2866^{4} **>25f<**

Matiara (USA) 3 b f Bering-Most Precious (USA) (Nureyev (USA)) (807a) (1116a) 1712a^{2} (3575a) 3694a^{4} 4184a^{2} **>115f<**

Matisse 4 b f Shareef Dancer (USA)-Late Matinee (Red Sunset) 1151^{16} 1433^{10} 1578^{7} 1742^{3} 2276^{14} 2479^{4} 2733^{5} 3370^{2} 3745^{3} 4209^{6} 4275^{3} **>16a 49f<**

Matiya (IRE) 2 b f Alzao (USA)-Purchasepaperchase (Young Generation) (2579) 3273^{3} 3490^{2} 3835^{3} **>104f<**

Matthew David 5 ch h Indian Forest (USA)-Mazurkanova (Song) *6^{2} 93^{5} 139^{4} 165^{7} 181^{3} 231^{3} 338^{5} 400^{6} 419^{11}* 507^{5} *2295^{7} (2925)* **>49a 34f<**

Matthias Mystique 2 gr f Sharrood (USA)-Sheznice (IRE) (Try My Best (USA)) 1690^{10} 3870^{9} **>44f<**

Mattimeo (IRE) 2 b g Prince Rupert (FR)-Herila (FR) (Bold Lad (USA)) 4312^{5} **>73f<**

Matula (USA) 3 ch c Dixieland Band-Manduria (Aloma's Ruler) 1891a^{2} 2212a^{3} 2728a^{2} 3582a^{4} **>106f<**

Maurangi 4 b c Warning-Spin Dry 526^{7} 1037^{9} 1250^{5} 1649^{6} 1808^{4} 2064^{9} 2682^{4} **>65f<**

Mawingo (IRE) 2 b c Taufan (USA)-Tappen Zee (Sandhurst Prince) 4312^{6} **>70f<**

Mawjud 2 b c Mujtahid (USA)-Elfaslah (IRE) (Green Desert (USA)) (4239) **>88f<**

Mawsam 3 ch c Nashwan (USA)-Tabdea (USA) (Topsider (USA)) 2469^{8} **>11f<**

Mawwal (USA) 2 ch c Elmaamul (USA)-Dish Dash (Bustino) 1134^{5} 1485^{4} (2283) (2775) (3560) 3812^{7} **>96+f<**

Maybank (IRE) 3 gr c Contract Law (USA)-Katysue 442^{17} 502^{13} **>34f<**

Maybe Today 3 br f Today and Tomorrow-Sonairo (Tudor Rhythm) 1510^{7} 1811^{7} 2361^{2} 3383^{9} 3657^{16} **>56f<**

Maydaan (IRE) 3 b f Alzao (USA)-Spring Reel (Mill Reef (USA)) 985^{2} 1335^{4} 3204^{8} **>82f<**

Mayday Kitty 3 ch f Interrex (CAN)-T Catty (USA) (Sensitive Prince (USA)) *5^{10} 263^{6} 368^{2} 444^{2}* 1204^{4} *1319^{4}* 1427^{3} 1581^{5} *1784^{6}* **>48a 57f<**

Maygain (IRE) 2 b g Kefaah (USA)-Sistina 1184^{18} 1369^{5} 1466^{7} 1734^{6} **>43f<**

May King Mayhem 2 ch c Great Commotion (USA)-Queen Ranavalona (Sure Blade (USA)) 3246^{5} 3530^{11} **>48f<**

Mayoumbe 2 gr c Kaldoun-Moucha 3328a^{2} **>86f<**

Mayoumbe (FR) 2 gr c Kaldoun-Moucha 4344a^{2}

May Queen Megan 2 gr f Petorius-Siva (FR) (Bellypha) 4132^{3} 4224^{6} 4330^{3} **>66f<**

Mayreau 3 b f Slip Anchor-Compton Lady (USA) (Sovereign Dancer (USA)) 3338^{2} 3517^{2} 3921^{11} 4149^{18} **>82df<**

Maysann 3 br c Shirley Heights-Tanouma (USA) (Miswaki (USA)) 453^{9} 537^{4} 947^{10} *1628^{2}* 1997^{2} 2268^{7} **>61a 62f<**

Maysimp (IRE) 2 ch f Mac's Imp (USA)-Splendid Yankee (Yankee Gold) 1597^{14} 1899^{4} 2431^{5} 2932^{9} 3740^{U} 3937^{24} **>39f<**

Mazcobar 2 ch c Mazilier (USA)-Barbary Court (Grundy) 3733^{14} 3916^{11} 4222^{4} **>58f<**

Mazeed (IRE) 2 ch c Lycius (USA)-Maraatib (IRE) (Green Desert (USA)) (2063) (2904) 3220^{2} 3499^{6} **>104f<**

Mazeeka (IRE) 4 ch f Glow (USA)-Saluti Tutti (Trojan Fen) *447^{6}* **>58da 66f<**

Maziere 3 ch f Mazilier (USA)-Good Game (Mummy's Game) 2282^{5} 2842^{9} **>36f<**

Mazilla 3 b f Mazilier (USA)-Mo Ceri (Kampala) *10^{2} (95) (171) 243^{4} 382^{2} 411^{3}* 1644^{9} 4043^{19} **>66a 54df<**

Mazirah 4 b c Mazilier (USA)-Barbary Court (Grundy) *605^{3}* 817^{10} **>58a 60f<**

Mazoski 2 b c Mazilier (USA)-Madam Petoski (Petoski) 1288^{5} 1734^{5} **>37f<**

Mazzarello (IRE) 5 ch g Hatim (USA)-Royal Demon (Tarboosh (USA)) 583^{8} *769^{12}* (1265) (1595) 1910^{4} 2692^{10} 3919^{21} **>44f<**

Mbulwa 9 ch h Be My Guest (USA)-Bundu (FR) (Habitat) 965^{2} 1323^{9} 1468^{7} 1687^{9} 2159^{5} 3993^{3} (4083) 4234^{3} 4275^{2} **>43a 67f<**

Mca Below the Line 7 ch h Lucky Wednesday-Delayed Action 1666^{7} 2621^{7} 2814^{5} 3255^{5} 3646^{8} 3810^{11} **>61f<**

Md Thompson 3 ch f Siberian Express (USA)-Zipperti Do (Precocious) 670^{10} 1405^{3} 2164^{3} *2587^{3}* 2955^{5} 3370^{4} *3514^{3} 3734^{3}* **>54a 57f<**

Meant to Be 5 b m Morston (FR)-Lady Gerardina *15^{4}* 2525^{8} 3336^{3} 3555^{3} 3817^{4} (4026) **>78a 90f<**

Me Cherokee 3 br f Persian Bold-Siouan 1296^{8} 1533^{9} 1683^{4} **>54f<**

Mecke (USA) 3 2730a^{4} 4185a^{2} **>120f<**

Medaille Militaire 3 gr c Highest Honor (FR)-Lovely Noor (USA) (Fappiano (USA)) (643) (1839) 2436^{6} (3164) 3811^{5} **>108f<**

Media Express 3 b c Sayf El Arab (USA)-Far Claim (USA) (Far North (CAN)) 450^{7} 524^{3} (733) 1411^{11} 1738^{7} 2202^{6} 2685^{12} *3954^{11}* (4054) **>25a 71f<**

Media Messenger 6 b h Hadeer-Willow Court (USA) (Little Current (USA)) *138^{12}* **>48da 40f<**

Media Nox 2 ch f Lycius-Sky Love (Nijinsky) (2210a) 2726a^{5} **>83f<**

Mediate (IRE) 3 b c Thatching-Unheard Melody (Lomond (USA)) *24^{4} 85^{3}* 1830^{12} *(2093)* 2684^{5} 2968^{2} 3177^{6} 3455^{10} **>69a 72f<**

Mediation (IRE) 3 ch f Caerleon (USA)-Redeem Herself (General Assembly (USA)) 707a^{2} 1390a^{7} 1848^{6} 4021a^{3} **>111f<**

Mediator **6** b h Valiyar-Blushing Cousin (Great Nephew) *9^{11} 143^{5}* 1427^{8} **>39a 49f<**
Medieval Lady **2** ch f Efisio-Ritsurin (Mount Hagen (FR)) 3983^{5} 4239^{2} **>82f<**
Medieval Miss **3** b f Risk Me (FR)-Dona Krista (King of Spain) 850^{13} 1094^{13} 1456^{4} *1566^{10}* 1906^{3} 2171^{3} 3179^{7} 3751^{18} **>39a 71df<**
Mediterraneo **4** ch c Be My Guest (USA)-Model Bride (USA) (Blushing Groom (FR)) 631^{9} **>100f<**
Medland (IRE) **5** ch h Imperial Frontier (USA)-Miami Dancer (Miami Springs) *77^{6} (175) 235^{3} 1087^{7} 1458^{5} 1631^{3} 1789^{4} 1951^{7}* **>58a 36f<**
Medway (IRE) **3** ch f Shernazar-Sea Port (Averof) 787^{3} 1901^{2} (1960) 2439^{16} 3705^{11} 3875^{2} **>72df<**
Meeson Times **7** b m Enchantment-National Time (USA) (Lord Avie (USA)) *78^{3} 148^{6} 228^{6} 338^{6}* 475^{9} **>46da 27f<**
Meeting Point **2** b f Common Grounds-Pastrana (King of Spain) 788^{2} 1063^{3} 1525^{3} 1670^{6} 1919^{2} 2771^{3} 2991^{10} 3271^{9} 3740^{4} 3975^{8} **>69f<**
Mega Tid **3** b g Old Vic-Dunoof (Shirley Heights) *(357)* 4381^{10} 545^{11} 851^{11} 1048^{15} 1166^{14} *1211^{4} 1320^{3}* 1745^{14} *1952^{5}* 3154^{3} *3318^{9}* **>71a 52f<**
Meghdoot **3** b f Celestial Storm (USA)-Greenhills Joy (Radetzky) 1097^{4} 1514^{2} 1834^{2} 3653^{4} (3918) 4289^{7} **>32a 79f<**
Meg's Memory (IRE) **2** b f Superlative-Meanz Beanz (High Top) 3203^{2} 3520^{2} 3765^{11} 3982^{10} 4130^{10} **>64f<**
Melasus (IRE) **3** ch g Nashamaa-Sweet Camden (Camden Town) 1474^{7} 1839^{24} **>75f<**
Meldorf **2** ch c Lycius (USA)-Melanoura (Imperial Fling (USA)) (3877) 4084^{14} **>87+f<**
Melissa's Baby **3** b f Then Again-Have Form (Haveroid) 875^{10} **>19f<**
Melling **4** b c Thowra (FR)-Miss Melmore (Nishapour (FR)) *3661^{0}* 584^{14} **>22a 25f<**
Mellors (IRE) **2** b c Common Grounds-Simply Beautiful (IRE) (Simply Great (FR)) 859^{5} 1399^{3} 2192^{7} 3684^{4} **>68f<**
Mellottie **10** b or br g Meldrum-Lottie Lehmann (Goldhill) 439^{9} 714^{6} 1108^{9} 1684^{2} 1851^{15} 2117^{5} (2766) (3021) (3433) 3945^{10} (4002) **>101f<**
Mellouise **4** ch f Handsome Sailor-Calton Colleen (Sagaro) 2798^{P} 818^{11} **>22f<**
Melmac (SWE) **4** br c Diaglyphard-Sovereign Star (Comedy S $3044a^{2}$ **>102f<**
Melmoth (USA) **3** b c Nureyev (USA)-Memories (USA) (Hail the Pirates (USA)) 2460^{4} **>78f<**
Melodic Drive **5** b or br h Sizzling Melody-Gleneagle *1087^{8}* 1499^{3} (1668) (1918) **>44da 70f<**
Melody Dancer **4** b c Rambo Dancer (CAN)-Secret Song (Tudor Melody) *472^{7}* 2309^{7} 2484^{12} 2731^{7} **>56a 50f<**
Melody Wheel **3** b f Merdon Melody-Spare Wheel (Track Spare) 2469^{5} **>57f<**
Melos **2** b f Emarati (USA)-Double Stretch (Double-U-Jay) 650^{10} *1213^{6}* 3018^{5} *3953^{11}* **>12a 45f<**
Mels Baby (IRE) **2** br c Contract Law (USA)-Launch The Raft (Home Guard (USA)) 943^{9} 1176^{9} 1466^{4} 1665^{6} 1943^{5} 3417^{13} 3642^{7} 3975^{9} 4137^{6} **>55f<**
Melt The Clouds (CAN) **2** ch c Diesis-Population (General Assembly (USA)) 4188^{7} **>76+f<**
Members Welcome (IRE) **2** b c Eve's Error-Manuale Del Utente (Montekin) 1054^{11} 1197^{6} 1774^{3} 2153^{6} 2523^{8} 3988^{8} 4144^{10} **>51f<**
Memorable **4** b c Don't Forget Me-Jhansi Ki Rani (USA) (Far North (CAN)) 649^{6} 737^{4} 1470^{4} 1817^{9} 3705^{12} **>54f<**
Memory's Music **3** b c Dance of Life (USA)-Sheer Luck (Shergar) 1514^{12} 2032^{6} *2600^{4}* 3154^{6} *3514^{8}* 3745^{12} **>57a 58f<**
Menas Gold **3** b f Heights of Gold-Tolomena (Tolomeo) 620^{9} 933^{12} 1588^{4} 1923^{5} 2694^{7} **>100f<**
Mendip Mist **7** ch m Known Fact (USA)-Silver Surprise (Son of Silver) *172^{10}*
Mendip Son **5** b g Hallgate-Silver Surprise (Son of Silver) 741^{13} **>63df<**
Menoo Hal Batal (USA) **2** b c Gone West (USA)-Bank On Love (USA) (Gallant Romeo (USA)) 4239^{5} **>80f<**
Menshaar (USA) **3** b g Hawkster (USA)-Klassy Imp (USA) (Imp Society (USA)) 816^{10} 968^{9} 1147^{10} **>60f<**
Menshood (IRE) **3** b c Roi Danzig (USA)-Takhiyra (Vayrann) 428^{2} **>89f<**
Mentalasanythin **6** b g Ballacashtal (CAN)-Lafrowda (Crimson Beau) *66^{7} 108^{7} (240) 275^{4} 279^{2} 325^{6} 396^{3}* 423^{5} 430^{15} 879^{2} 905^{3} 1025^{2} 1160^{2} 1437^{2} (1596) (1686) 1744^{4} 2226^{2} 2427^{3} 3059^{2} 3665^{3} 3852^{5} **>80a 75f<**
Mental Pressure **2** ch c Polar Falcon (USA)-Hysterical (High Top) 3416^{8} 3713^{3} **>80f<**
Mentor (GR) **3** b c Wadood (USA)-Queen of the North (Northfields (USA)) *564^{6}* 694^{10} 1753^{2} 2014^{3} 2392^{4} **>71a 90f<**
Meranti **2** b c Puissance-Sorrowful (Moorestyle) 1123^{7} 1481^{6} 1938^{4} 3213^{8} 3538^{4} 3765^{4} 3893^{5} **>74f<**
Mercadier **4** ch c Rainbow Quest (USA)-Gerardmer (FR) 923^{4} (1243) **>96f<**
Merchant House (IRE) **7** ch h Salmon Leap (USA)-Persian Polly (Persian Bold) *1091^{9}* **>36a 52f<**
Merger Mania **3** b g Precocious-Scrummage (Workboy) 3060^{4} 3841^{8} **>8f<**
Meribel (IRE) **2** b f Nashwan (USA)-Dark Lomond 3939^{3} **>73+f<**
Merit (IRE) **3** b c Rainbow Quest (USA)-Fur Hat (Habitat) 715^{20} 881^{6} 4047^{12} 4136^{7} *(4223)* (4288) (4326) **>78+a 78+f<**
Merlin's Fancy **3** b f Caerleon (USA)-Smarten Up 752^{10} 2949^{6} 3442^{16} *3734^{9}* 4043^{7} 4242^{12} **>45a 70f<**
Merlin's Honour **2** ch f Crowning Honors (CAN)-Miss Merlin 615^{16} 699^{10} *1213^{2}* 3744^{10} 3975^{16} **>43a 37f<**
Merrie le Bow **3** b f Merdon Melody-Arch Sculptress (Arch Sculptor) *57^{2} 124^{3} 232^{3} 274^{3} 1032^{7}* 1549^{6} 2778^{9} 3034^{3} 3179^{4} 3640^{7} 4049^{4} 4194^{5} 4242^{8} **>51a 49f<**
Merrily **2** gr f Sharrood (USA)-Babycham Sparkle (So Blessed) 1375^{5} **>50f<**
Merry Festival (USA) **3** b f Private Account (USA)-Beat (USA) (Nijinsky (CAN)) 664^{7} 3183^{4} (3799) **>86f<**
Merry Mermaid **5** ch m Bairn (USA)-Manna Green (534) 757^{7} 1039^{2} 1252^{6} 1529^{12} **>15a 55f<**
Merseyside Man **9** b h My Dad Tom (USA)-Chanita (Averof) 1285^{23} *1459^{10}* **>44a f<**
Metal Boys **8** b h Krayyan-Idle Gossip (Runnett) 796^{9} 1271^{7} 1489^{9} 1756^{3} 2252^{10} 2326^{8} 2533^{8} 2665^{7} 2753^{3} 4278^{12} 4322^{16} **>64f<**
Metal Storm (FR) **7** b h *66^{8} 262^{3}* 439^{W} **>86a 89f<**
Mexican Dancer **6** b m Dance of Life (USA)-Mexican

Two Step (Gay Fandango (USA)) *288^{8} 416^{10} 588^{3}* **>25a 25f<**

Mezaan (IRE) 3 ch c Royal Academy (USA)-Arctic Heroine (USA) (Arctic Tern (USA)) 663^{5} (987) 1306^{4} 3164^{5} (3459) 3836^{7} **>101f<**

Mezzogiorno 2 b f Unfuwain (USA)-Aigue (High Top) 3339^{4} (3539) 3865^{2} **>94f<**

Mezzoramio 3 ch g Cadeaux Genereux-Hopeful Search (USA) (Vaguely Noble) *1087^{4} 1458^{3} 1762^{9} 2076^{6} 2587^{5} 2921^{8}* **>60a f<**

Mheanmetoo 4 ch g Roi Danzig (USA)-Spinster (Grundy) *202^{6} 287^{11} 371^{9}* **>23a 68df<**

Mhemeanles 5 br g Jalmood (USA)-Folle Idee (USA) (Foolish Pleasure (USA)) *186^{13}* 954^{8} 1161^{14} (1647) 1958^{4} 2263^{4} *2919^{16}* 3207^{4} 3402^{10} 3825^{3} 3987^{6} 4062^{7} **>7a 55f<**

Miami Banker 9 ch h Miami Springs-Banking Coyne *892^{5} 1214^{10}* 1595^{3} 2048^{2} 2338^{2} 2551^{2} (2686) (2850) 3219^{5} 3407^{4} 3554^{2} 3748^{19} 3961^{9} **>26a 59f<**

Miasma (USA) 3 b f Lear Fan (USA)-Syrian Circle (USA) (Damascus (USA)) 1729^{7} 3261^{2} 3399^{2} 3845^{3} **>90f<**

Michaelmas Park (IRE) 4 ch c Common Grounds-Fresh As A Daisy (Stanford) 1940^{13} 2342^{14} **>12f<**

Michel Georges 7 b m 1114a^{2} **>113f<**

Michelle's Ella (IRE) 3 b f Ela-Mana-Mou-Bustina (FR) 2086^{6} **>28f<**

Michellisa 4 b f Indian Ridge-Land Line (High Line) 555^{4} 789^{4} 2624^{3} 2786^{3} (3050) 3264^{2} 3506^{2} 3645^{4} 3941^{4} 4044^{3} 4171^{9} **>64f<**

Mick's Love (IRE) 2 b c Law Society (USA)-Flute (FR) (Luthier (FR)) (3463) (3709) **>93+f<**

Microlite (USA) 4 b f Lear Fan (USA)-Comicus (USA) (Northern Jove (CAN)) 661^{8} 931^{7} 1252^{4} 1416^{5} 2022^{5} 2224^{3} 2263^{3} 3367^{7} **>77f<**

Midas Gold 2 ch c Prince Sabo-So Rewarding (Never so Bold) 2315^{11} 2434^{7} 3895^{3} *4124^{6}* **>69a 65f<**

Middle East 2 b g Beveled (USA)-Godara (Bustino) (2354) 2833^{4} 3394^{3} 3612^{7} 3969^{14} **>64f<**

Midlin 5 ch m Midyan (USA)-Western Line (High Line) *83^{5} 120^{5} 166^{5} 592^{4}* 1350^{19} **>46da 32f<**

Midnight Blue 2 br f Be My Chief (USA)-Guyum (Rousillon (USA)) (4023) **>86+tf<**

Midnight Break 3 ch f Night Shift (USA)-Splintering (Sharpo) 727^{5} 1201^{3} (1546) (1783) 2079^{7} 2659^{5} 2973^{2} 3453^{5} 3624^{12} 3905^{9} **>68f<**

Midnight Cookie 2 b c Midyan (USA)-Midnight's Reward (Night Shift (USA)) 1054^{12} 2442^{17} 3558^{8} 3892^{12} 4144^{8} 4219^{7} 4276^{6} 4328^{9} **>54f<**

Midnight Escape 2 b c Aragon-Executive Lady (Night Shift (USA)) 1341^{4} (1938) 2315^{4} 2523^{3} **>76f<**

Midnight Jazz (IRE) 5 b h Shardari-Round Midnight (Star Appeal) 653^{9} 864^{8} 946^{3} 1344^{14} 1966^{4} (2718) 2979^{7} 3181^{6} 3664^{6} 4156^{11} **>82a 84f<**

Midnight Legend 4 b c Night Shift (USA)-Myth (Troy) 1385^{U} 1894^{2} 2323^{9} (2739) 3088^{2} 3498^{7} **>120f<**

Midnight Mass 3 b f Mandrake Major-Kirkby (Midsummer Night II) 779^{14} 1065^{11} 2480^{6} **>32f<**

Midnight Spell 3 ch f Night Shift (USA)-Bundled Up (USA) (Sharpen Up) 585^{2} 985^{9} *1953^{7}* 3466^{3} 3640^{6} 3878^{20} **>65a 76f<**

Midnight Walker 3 b f Exodal (USA)-Petite Butterfly (Absalom) 3023^{11} 3542^{11} 3762^{11} **>43f<**

Midtime (IRE) 2 b c Formidable (USA)-Between Time (Elegant Air) 2749^{4} 2995^{4} *3525^{6}* **>59a 75f<**

Midwich Cuckoo 3 b c Midyan (USA)-Portvasco (Sharpo) 694^{8} 1639^{3} (1876) 2240^{10} 2471^{2} 3488^{9} 4122^{11} **>89f<**

Midyan Blue (IRE) 5 ch h Midyan (USA)-Jarretiere (Star Appeal) 811^{2} (1109) 1300^{4} 1621^{3} 2238^{2} (2530) 2612^{5} 3162^{2} 3445^{5} 3730^{16} 4036^{4} **>63a 89f<**

Mighty Forum 4 b c Presidium-Mighty Flash (Rolfe (USA)) 4305a^{9} **>103f<**

Mighty Kingdom (IRE) 4 b f Mister Majestic-Great Land (USA) (Friend's Choice (USA)) *22^{7} 75^{5} 227^{12}* 2108^{4} (2246) 2490^{3} 2657^{9} 2946^{7} 3385^{6} 3515^{2} 3641^{14} 4079^{14} 4152^{5} 4209^{2} **>29a 53f<**

Mighty Marston 3 b c Mazilier (USA)-Thulium (Mansingh (USA)) 1312^{8} 1533^{8} (1904) 2199^{7} 2504^{2} 2864^{4} 3173^{7} **>74f<**

Mighty Phantom (USA) 2 b f Lear Fan (USA)-Migiyas (Kings Lake (USA)) 3495^{5} 3643^{7} **>74f<**

Mighty Squaw 3 b f Indian Ridge-Mighty Flash (Rolfe (USA)) 695^{5} 888^{5} 1053^{8} *1630^{7}* 1812^{6} 2167^{4} *2600^{2}* 2863^{6} 3756^{3} 3862^{8} 4096^{4} 4220^{4} **>64a 82df<**

Mignonnette (FR) 2 gr f Mtoto-Cut Velvet (USA) (Northern Dancer) 3136^{5} 4048^{15} **>52f<**

Migwar 2 b c Unfuwain (USA)-Pick of the Pops (High Top) 3900^{11} 4117^{5} **>65f<**

Mihriz (IRE) 3 b c Machiavellian (USA)-Ghzaalh (USA) (Northern Dancer) 813^{4} 962^{2} 1478^{5} 1753^{6} **>83f<**

Milbank Challenger 5 gr h Belfort (FR)-Princess Sharpenup (Lochnager) 784^{7} 926^{16} 1080^{8} **>40f<**

Miles Away (IRE) 3 ch f Ballad Rock-Far From Home (Habitat) 752^{8} 1146^{3} 1381^{8} **>55f<**

Miletrian City 2 gr c Petong-Blueit (FR) *1212^{11}* 2820^{7} 3647^{5} 3839^{4} **>21a 70df<**

Miletrian Refurb (IRE) 2 b br c Anita's Prince-Lady of Man (So Blessed) 1158^{5} 1562^{5} 1740^{2} 1943^{8} 2857^{5} 3417^{2} (3856) 4097^{5} **>65f<**

Milford Sound 2 b c Batshoof-Nafis (USA) (Nodouble (USA)) 4188^{10} **>63f<**

Millazure (USA) 3 b f Dayjur (USA)-Milligram (Mill Reef (USA)) 1796^{4} 2469^{3} 2708^{5} 3656^{6} **>68f<**

Mill Dancer (IRE) 3 b f Broken Hearted-Theatral (Orchestra) 1625^{7} 1824^{3} 2524^{3} (3060) 3429^{8} (3747) 3935^{6} 4071^{6} **>63df<**

Millemay 5 br m Respect-Ravenscraig (Impecunious) 594^{5} 877^{5} 992^{6} **>35f<**

Mill End Lady 2 b f Tina's Pet-Azelly (Pitskelly) 819^{6} 2498^{8} 3644^{14} 3806^{5} 4097^{17} **>63f<**

Millesime (IRE) 3 ch g Glow (USA)-Persian Myth (Persian Bold) 1040^{4} 1168^{10} 1405^{4} 1700^{5} 1949^{4} 2084^{3} (2267) (2513) 2850^{6} 2887^{2} 3376^{11} 3535^{3} 3622^{21} **>80f<**

Mill House Boy (IRE) 2 b g Astronef-Avantage Service (IRE) (Exactly Sharp (USA)) 1842^{11} 2195^{9} 2516^{13} **>24f<**

Million Dancer 3 b c Rambo Dancer (CAN)-Tea-Pot (Ragstone) 647^{13} 974^{11} 1407^{3} **>63a 55f<**

Millkom 4 b c Cyrano de Bergerac-Good Game (Mummy's Game) 607a^{5} 898a^{10} 3327a^{3} **>125f<**

Millridge (IRE) 4 ch f Indian Ridge-African Desert (African Sky) 503^{10} *624^{12}* 890^{6} **>44f<**

Millsolin (IRE) 7 b h Millfontaine-Isolin (Saulingo) *92^{4} 293^{5}* **>60da 60f<**

Millstock 5 b m Interrex (CAN)-Millingdale (Tumble

Wind (USA)) 1191[8] 1538[9] 2113[5] **>33f<**

Millstream (USA) **3** b f Dayjur (USA)-Aquaba (USA) (Damascus (USA)) 612[3] 921[4] 1364[2] (1703a) 1896[4] 2368[6] 2671[4] 3187[7] **>113f<**

Mill Thyme **3** b f Thowra (FR)-Milinetta (Milford) 747[9] 968[4] 1085[6] 1452[W] 1922[3] 2781[6] **>60f<**

Milltown Classic (IRE) **3** b f Classic Secret (USA)-Houwara (IRE) (Darshaan) 1155[4] 1523[6] 1873[7] 2582[6] 3302[6] 3722[9] **>39f<**

Millyant **5** ch m Primo Dominie-Jubilee Song 1112a[4] (1572a) 1896[7] 3187[5] 3689a[3] 4012a[6] (4253a) **>116f<**

Milngavie (IRE) **5** ch h Pharly (FR)-Wig And Gown (Mandamus) *15[5]* *88[3]* *131[5]* *178[0]* *246[7]* *370[7]* 495[8] 598[3] 840[10] 1957[2] 2127[3] 2734[6] 2835[2] 3002[2] 3114[5] 3311[4] 3724[14] (4331) **>66da 43f<**

Milos **4** b c Efisio-Elkie Brooks (Relkino) *20[3]* *191[3]* 2793[8] 3439[14] 3629[9] *3950[9]* **>62a 71f<**

Miltak **3** b f Risk Me (FR)-Tralee Maiden (IRE) (Persian Bold) 1445[11] 1718[5] 2149[3] 2582[8] *2959[7]* 3265[4] 4332[4] **>18a 49f<**

Milton **2** ch c Groom Dancer (USA)-Gold Flair (Tap On Wood) *4334[2]* **>75+a f<**

Mime Time (IRE) **2** ch c Classic Music (USA)-Beyond Words (Ballad Rock) 3592[17] **>5f<**

Mim-Lou-and **3** b c Glacial Storm (USA)-Tina's Melody (Tina's Pet) 453[4] 525[4] 1219[13] 1403[3] *1950[6]* 2174[9] 2334[2] 3058[3] 3402[4] **>35a 69f<**

Mimosa **2** ch f Midyan (USA)-Figini (Glint of Gold) 1223[P] 1511[5] 1849[10] 2552[11] 3933[2] 4218[11] **>72f<**

Min Alhawa (USA) **2** b f Riverman (USA)-Saffaanh (USA) (Shareef Dancer (USA)) 2025[2] (3364) **>74f<**

Mind Games **3** b c Puissance-Aryaf (CAN) (Vice Regent (CAN)) (612) (921) (1364) 1896[3] 3187[6] 3491[5] 4012a[8] **>121+f<**

Mindrace **2** b c Tina's Pet-High Velocity (Frimley Park) 1327[W] 3314[9] *3523[8]* 4132[6] 4224[3] **>15a 67f<**

Minds Music (USA) **3** ch c Silver Hawk (USA)-Misinskie (USA) (Nijinsky (CAN)) (635) 1129[2] 1301[2] 3609[2] (3923) **>119f<**

Min Elreeh (USA) **2** b f Danzig (USA)-Roseate Tern (Blakeney) 3069[6] **>82+f<**

Minervitta **3** b f Warrshan (USA)-Marie de Sologne (Lashkari) 291a[3] 488a[3]

Minneola **3** ch f Midyan (USA)-High Halo (High Top) 2790[13] 3294[12] **>36f<**

Minnesota Viking **4** b c Northern State (USA)-Miskin (Star Appeal) 1502[7] 1908[5] 2238[4] 2745[2] 3029[7] 4022[2] (4135) 4333[3] **>69f<**

Minnisam **2** ch c Niniski (USA)-Wise Speculation (USA) (Mr Prospector (USA)) 2741[8] 4146[4] 4246[9] **>52f<**

Minoletti **2** b g Emarati (USA)-French Plait (Thatching) 3988[5] **>60f<**

Minsterbeach **2** ch c Minster Son-China Beach (Superlative) 1752[7] 2320[16] 3215[5] 3620[16] 3894[14] 4192[9] **>64f<**

Minster Glory **4** b g Minster Son-Rapid Glory (Hittite Glory) *136[8]* *256[10]* *315[9]* 568[2] **>30a 47f<**

Mint a Million (IRE) **4** b g Thatching-Often (Ballymore) *377[4]* 582[9] *833[9]* 1350[10] 1594[7] 3569[12] 3676[12] **>37a 48f<**

Mirador **4** b f Town And Country-Wild Jewel 545[7] **>59f<**

Miriam **4** br f Forzando-Song of Hope (Chief Singer) 856[15] 1057[13] 1321[3] 1972[3] 2092[5] 2301[5] 2850[2] 3014[8] 3134[7] 3622[16] 3919[19] **>27a 54df<**

Mironov **2** b c Marju-Marquina (4348a)

Miroswaki (USA) **5** br h Miswaki (USA)-Miroswava (FR) (In Fijar (USA)) 1578[5] 1858[6] 1973[7] 2098[15] 2119[7] **>68a 75f<**

Misbelief **5** b or br m Shirley Heights-Misguided (Homing) 958[2] 1563[3] (2036) 2272[5] 3162[7] 3549[2] **>110f<**

Mischief Star **2** b f Be My Chief (USA)-Star Face 3089[13] 3474[4] 3633[7] **>59f<**

Mishaweer **2** b f Primo Dominie-Ideal Home (Home Guard (USA)) 3828[9] **>24f<**

Misinterrex **4** 2384a[3] (2720a)

Misky Bay **2** b c Shareef Dancer (USA)-Rain Date (Rainbow Quest (USA)) 4320[9] **>62f<**

Mislemani (IRE) **5** b h Kris-Meis El-Reem (Auction Ring (USA)) 887[13] 1126[9] 1426[3] *1630[2]* *1950[5]* 2549[3] (2685) 2946[6] 3706[14] 3771[2] 3943[10] **>54a 65f<**

Missal (IRE) **6** b m Alzao (USA)-Priors Mistress (Sallust) 4240[13]

Miss Aragon **7** b m Aragon-Lavenham Blue (Streetfighter) 1271[2] 1434[7] 1604[9] 1809[14] 2194[3] (2578) (2746) 3492[5] 3624[9] 3764[8] 3830[9] 3992[13] **>60df<**

Miss Biarritz **3** b f Be My Guest (USA)-Miss Bergerac (Bold Lad (IRE)) 552[P] **>29f<**

Miss Bigwig **2** b f Distinctly North (USA)-Jacqui Joy (Music Boy) (508) 718[4] 1833[5] (2735) 3064[6] 3335[2] (3753) 3962[4] **>84f<**

Miss Carottene **2** b f Siberian Express (USA)-Silk St James (Pas de Seul) 1348[9] 1536[10] 1938[7] 2135[7] 2809[2] 3132[7] 3423[2] 3568[3] 3623[9] 3858[14] 4211[9] **>57f<**

Miss Charlie **5** ch m Pharly (FR)-Close to You (Nebbiolo) *68[2]* *103[7]* *222[9]* *355[9]* 3226[2] **>43da 69f<**

Miss Ebene (FR) **2** f 2726a[6] **>81f<**

Missed Flight **5** b h Dominion-Loveskate (USA) (Overskate (CAN)) 425[3] (794) 1187[3] (3476a) 3589a[3] **>125f<**

Missed the Boat (IRE) **5** b h Cyrano de Bergerac-Lady Portobello (Porto Bello) 2037[9] (3521) 3710[10] **>40a 50f<**

Missel **3** b c Storm Bird (CAN)-Miss Demure (Shy Groom (USA)) 622[5] **>108df<**

Miss Electra **3** b f Superpower-Apocalypse (Auction Ring (USA)) 3475[17] 3681[19] **>20f<**

Miss Felixstowe (USA) **3** ch f Tejano (USA)-Sonseri (Prince Tenderfoot (USA)) 524[9] 908[4] 1945[8] 2744[3] 2955[4] 3099[2] 3259[5] **>58f<**

Miss Freebie (IRE) **4** b f Satco (FR)-Masina (Current Coin) *214[9]* *280[8]* **>19a 36f<**

Miss Greenyards **4** b f Stalker-Isle Maree (Star Appeal) 593[12]

Miss Gruntled **4** b f Arctic Lord-Sweet Move (Corvaro (USA)) 958[7] 1771[15] **>30a 51f<**

Miss Haversham **3** b f Salse (USA)-Rustic Stile (Rusticaro (FR)) 664[8] 868[7] 3239[2] 4052[3] **>84f<**

Miss Hotshot **2** ch f Chilibang-Emma's Double 983[8] 2023[7] 2185[12] 2735[6]

Missile **2** b g Rock City-Fast Chick (Henbit (USA)) 3663[8] 3869[2] (4137) **>68f<**

Missile Toe (IRE) **2** b c Exactly Sharp (USA)-Debach Dust (Indian King (USA)) 863[2] *1031[2]* 1540[5] 1871[6] (2608) 2940[5] 3271[5] 3803[5] 3947[3] **>59a 72f<**

Miss Impulse **2** b f Precocious-Dingle Belle (Dominion) 1288[3] 1503[3] *2382[8]* 2857[6] **>32a 43f<**

Miss Iron Heart (USA) **3** b f Minshaanshu Amad (USA)-Iron Franco (USA) (Barrera (USA)) 1541[13] 1961[6] *2923[10]* 3726[14] 4316[7] **>17a 50f<**

Miss Jemmima **3** b f Night Shift (USA)-Jenny Mere (Brigadier Gerard) *394[8]* *468[5]* 715[13] 1290[4] 1591[7] 3920[14] 4261[12] **>51a 64f<**

Miss Katie Louise **4** b f Monsanto (FR)-Shari Louise (Radetzky) *390[10]* **>27a 20f<**

Miss Laughter **3** b f Sulaafah (USA)-Miss Comedy (Comedy Star (USA)) 645[8] 1196[4] 1447[11] 2032[8] 2363[6] (2813) 3152[3] 3920[16] **>62f<**

Miss Mah-Jong **4** b f Absalom-Brookfield Miss *157[9]* 1092[6] **>37a 58f<**

Miss Mercy (IRE) **3** b f Law Society (USA)-Missing You (Ahonoora) 662[11] **>71f<**

Miss Movie World **6** b m Slim Jim-Regal Artist 1508[2] 1741[5] 2163[4] 2521[15] 2686[7] 3051[5] 3357[5] 3748[16] **>64f<**

Miss Offset **2** ch f Timeless Times (USA)-Farinara (Dragonara Palace (USA)) 490[2] 540[3] 903[6] *1089[2]* *1212[7]* *(1632)* (1734) 2765[8] 3168[5] 3684[8] **>67a 62df<**

Miss Parkes **6** ch m Mummy's Game-Bonne Baiser (Most Secret) 3896[13]

Miss Pickpocket (IRE) **2** b f Petorius-Fingers *3509[3]* 3816[5] 3988[6] **>60a 74f<**

Miss Pigalle **4** b f Good Times (ITY)-Panayr (Faraway Times (USA)) 877[7] 992[3] 1377[6] 1438[5] 1724[8] 2021[6] (2156) 2307[6] 2461[8] 2772[3] 2832[13] 3050[7] 3172[5] 3719[4] 3879[10] **>45f<**

Miss Pin Up **6** gr m Kalaglow-Allander Girl 2069[2] (2472) 2599[5] 2829[5] 3015[5] 3229[9] **>88f<**

Miss Pravda **2** ch f Soviet Star (USA)-Miss Paige (AUS) (Luskin Star (AUS)) 3948[15] 4102[3] **>58f<**

Miss Prism **2** b f Niniski (USA)-Reflected Glory (SWE) (Relko) 3364[5] 4050[15] **>37f<**

Miss Riviera **2** b f Kris-Miss Beaulieu (Northfields (USA)) (4314) **>90+f<**

Miss Roberto (IRE) **2** ch f Don Roberto (USA)-Frau Ahuyentante (ARG) (Frari (ARG)) 3763[20] 3955[6] 4244[6] 4327[16] **>39f<**

Miss Sacha (IRE) **4** b f Last Tycoon-Heaven High (High Line) 953[8] 3342[9] **>106f<**

Miss Satamixa (IRE) **3** gr f Linamix-Miss Satin (Satingo) (2727a) (3199a) 3589a[6] **>124f<**

Miss Siham (IRE) **6** ch m Green Forest (USA)-Miss Derby (USA) (Master Derby (USA)) *167[6]* *247[9]* 688[2] 926[9] 1023[4] 1721[8] (2502) 3116[14] **>28a 50+f<**

Miss Spent Youth **4** ch f Sylvan Express-Cedar Lady (Telsmoss) 2362[6] 3515[12] **>29f<**

Miss Springtime **4** b f Bluebird (USA)-Spring Lane (Forlorn River) 3493[15] 3808[29] *3952[12]* **>21a 38f<**

Miss Suzy **3** br f Kind of Hush-Pickwood Sue *5[7]* *51[8]* *90[10]* *185[5]* *292[5]* *339[8]* **>31a f<**

Miss Swing King (IRE) **2** b f Waajib-Hyland Rose (Steel Heart) 2964[6] 3346[3] 3450[5] **>63f<**

Miss Tahiti (IRE) **2** b f Tirol-Mini Luthe 3786a[2] (4013a) **>105f<**

Miss The Beat **3** b f Music Boy-Bad Start (USA) (Bold Bidder (USA)) *2493[7]* *2959[11]* *3522[12]* **>11a f<**

Miss Ticklepenny **3** b f Distant Relative-Aphrosina (Known Fact (USA)) 4214[4] **>42f<**

Miss Tipsy **4** b f Reprimand-Miss Alkie (Noalcoholic (FR)) *28[8]* *228[8]* **>34a 38f<**

Miss Toffee Nose (IRE) **3** b f Cyrano de Bergerac-Sweet Reprieve (Shirley Heights) *116[6]* *310[5]* **>9a f<**

Miss Tri Colour **3** b f Shavian-Bourgeonette (Mummy's Pet) 576[6] 1083[13] 2088[13] *2497[8]* **>17a 26f<**

Miss Universal (IRE) **2** ch f Lycius (USA)-Madame Nureyev (USA) (Nureyev (USA)) 3733[12] 3865[12] **>75f<**

Missus Murhill (IRE) **4** ch f Mon Tresor-Decoy Duck (Decoy Boy) *229[6]* *266[6]* 430[16] 776[5] 1529[8] (1744) 2064[7] 2305[3] 2759[6] 3297[5] **>30a 46f<**

Miss Vaxette **6** b m Norwick (USA)-Langton Herring (Nearly A Hand) 906[4] 1079[4] 2088[9] 2252[9] **>68df<**

Miss Waterline **2** br f Rock City-Final Shot (Dalsaan) 508[5] 617[3] 819[10] (1597) 1833[4] 3819[3] 3886[10] **>80?f<**

Miss Whittingham (IRE) **5** b m Fayruz-Windini (Windjammer (USA)) 491[8] 701[3] 789[3] 906[7] 1044[7] 2645[5] 2772[7] 2956[9] **>58da 59f<**

Miss Zanzibar **3** b f Kefaah (USA)-Circe (Main Reef) 674[11] (1824) *1952[2]* 2225[3] 2499[4] 2747[4] *2959[3]* 3151[3] 3396[12] **>63a 64f<**

Mister Aspecto (IRE) **2** b c Caerleon (USA)-Gironde (USA) (Raise A Native) 3416[7] 3666[6] 3827[7] 3967[9] **>68f<**

Mister Beat **4** b g Brustolon-Miss May (FR) (Northern Treat (USA)) *91[0]* **>68a 64f<**

Mister Blake **5** b g Damister (USA)-Larive (Blakeney) *82[11]* **>39a f<**

Mister Fire Eyes (IRE) **3** b c Petorius-Surfing (Grundy) *(324)* (437) 504[2] 775[5] 914[7] 1131[10] 1299[11] 1839[20] 2103[4] 2437[5] 2822[2] 3066[4] 3654[9] 3943[30] 4171[2] 4319[9] **>83a 81f<**

Mister Fox **4** b c Latest Model-Impromptu 2807[9] 3129[10] **>22f<**

Mister Joel **2** b g Risk Me (FR)-Net Call (Song) 3353[7] 3417[8] 3779[7] 3937[2] 3975[2] 4141[15] (4230) 4317[9] **>71f<**

Mister Jolson **6** br h Latest Model-Impromptu 434[9] 693[3] 922[17] 1316[3] 1614[12] 1895[23] 2570[5] 3359[8] 3717[18] 3961[4] 4068[24] 4145[14] **>81df<**

Mister O'Grady (IRE) **4** b c Mister Majestic-Judy O'Grady (Whistler) 975[6] 1402[5] 1716[5] (1940) 2657[10] (2842) 3320[4] **>39a 57f<**

Mister Raider **3** ch c Ballacashtal (CAN)-Martian Melody (Enchantment) *410[8]* 452[4] 580[2] 645[4] 855[10] 1016[7] 1164[4] 1545[5] 2793[7] 3055[4] 3139[4] **>53a 67df<**

Mister Rm **3** b c Dominion-La Cabrilla (Carwhite) 658[10] 853[11] (1467) 3706[2] 3813[27] 4035[14] **>38a 82f<**

Mister Sean (IRE) **2** b c Mac's Imp (USA)-Maid of Mourne (Fairy King (USA)) 1327[5] 1699[8] 1877[2] 2000[2] 2170[2] 2335[5] 3753[6] 3856[9] **>77f<**

Mistertopogigo (IRE) **5** b h Thatching-Decadence (Vaigly Great) 700[2] 921[9] 1703a[2] 1896[9] 2285[W] 2671[7] 3187[8] **>121df<**

Mister Westsound **3** b c Cyrano de Bergerac-Captivate (Mansingh (USA)) 904[4] 1157[14] 1461[8] 1723[5] 1822[2] 1936[2] 2024[2] 2160[3] 2475[3] 2736[8] (2930) (3000) 3172[2] 3310[6] 3719[12] 3807[4] 3855[2] 3980[2] 4236[6] 4280[7] **>71f<**

Mister Woodstick (IRE) **2** b c Distinctly North (USA)-Crannog 3465[15] 3592[12] **>41f<**

Mistinguett (IRE) **3** b f Doyoun-Sidama (FR) (Top Ville) 614[6] 717[6] 4071[2] **>82f<**

Mistle Cat (USA) **5** gr h Storm Cat (USA)-Mistle Toe (USA) (Maribeau) 814[2] (1284) 1706a[2] 2105[4] 2646[2]

3195a^{10} 4078^{4} 4324^{6} **>117f<**

Mistress Thames 3 br f Sharpo-Miss Thames (Tower Walk) 442^{3} 3829^{7} 3981^{3} 4134^{7} **>70f<**

Misty Melody 3 b f Digamist (USA)-Broken Melody (Busted) 1405^{5} 1719^{9} 2180^{4} **>57?f<**

Misty Silks 5 b m Scottish Reel-Silk St James (Pas de Seul) *318^{9}* (481) 724^{10} 885^{6} 1351^{8} 1617^{12} 2488^{7} 3601^{7} 3732^{6} 3984^{15} 4043^{2} 4227^{9} **>37a 83f<**

Misty Windows 5 ch g Starry Night (USA)-Hold Me Fast (USA) (Angle Light (USA)) 2798^{8}

Miswaki Belle (USA) 3 b f Miswaki (USA)-Belle et Deluree (USA) (The Minstrel (CAN)) 2469^{2} **>70+f<**

Mithraic (IRE) 3 b g Kefaah (USA)-Persian's Glory 643^{2} 777^{8} 1615^{6} 2479^{8} 2953^{3} **>67f<**

Mitsis 4 b c Picea-Edith Piaf (Thatch (USA)) 2179^{6} 2832^{6} 3079^{14} 3426^{9} **>12a 46f<**

Mixed Mood 3 br f Jalmood (USA)-Cool Combination (Indian King (USA)) *587^{5} (768) 1034^{4}* 1279^{5} 1541^{14} *(2497) 2923^{12} 3512^{13}* 3624^{16} *3950^{11}* 4054^{10} **>66da 45f<**

Mizag (IRE) 3 b c High Estate-Greatest Pleasure (Be My Guest (USA)) 1786^{10} **>60f<**

Mizyan (IRE) 7 b h Melyno-Maid of Erin (USA) (Irish River (FR)) *3^{2} 81^{4} (589)* 737^{2} (866) 1470^{6} **>75a 72f<**

Mnemonic 3 b f Mtoto-Neenah (Bold Lad (IRE)) 2056^{6} 2488^{9} 4043^{9} 4249^{9} **>60f<**

Mo-Addab (IRE) 5 b g Waajib-Tissue Paper (Touch Paper) 749^{3} 1183^{17} 1988^{3} 2321^{4} 2613^{2} (3113) 3732^{10} (3837) 4116^{2} 4267^{19} **>88f<**

Mobile King 2 ch c Colmore Row-Donosa (Posse (USA)) 2515^{9} *3077^{13}* 3378^{12} **>11a 40f<**

Moccasin Run (USA) 4 b c Topsider (USA)-Regal Heights (USA) (Forli (ARG)) 665^{6} 814^{8} (953) 1108^{10} 1618^{7} (2436) 3188^{15} 3358^{2} 3562^{4} 3813^{20} **>111f<**

Mockingbird 4 ch f Sharpo-Mountain Bluebird (USA) (Clever Trick (USA)) *233^{14} 267^{9} 312^{12}* **>20a 41f<**

Modajjaj 3 ch g Polish Precedent (USA)-Upend (Main Reef) 3618^{9} 4003^{4} 4072^{8} **>68f<**

Modern Day (USA) 2 b c Dayjur (USA)-Modena (USA) (Roberto (USA)) 1485^{3} (2667) 3301^{2} 3600^{5} **>86f<**

Modest Hope (USA) 8 b h Blushing Groom (FR)-Key Dancer (USA) (Nijinsky (CAN)) *35^{3} 77^{3} 166^{6} 271^{5} 312^{8} 340^{2} (421) 471^{2}* 568^{11} *771^{8}* 988^{8} *1029^{4}* 2861^{9} 3029^{4} 3435^{8} 3641^{6} *3951^{7}* 3970^{13} **>55a 56f<**

Mogin 2 ch f Komaite (USA)-Misdevious (USA) (Alleged (USA)) 2801^{9} 4048^{18} **>18f<**

Mogwai (IRE) 6 b h Alzao (USA)-Maltese Pet (Dragonara Palace (USA)) *73^{8} 175^{4} 200^{4}* **>41a 40f<**

Mohaajir (USA) 4 b c Sadler's Wells (USA)-Very Charming (USA) (Vagu 2219a^{3} **>112f<**

Mohannad (IRE) 2 b c Royal Academy (USA)-Pudibunda (Bold Lad (IRE)) 4080^{10} **>79f<**

Mohawk Trail 6 b h Midyan (USA)-Indian Wells 976^{13} 1183^{25} 1542^{12} **>76f<**

Mohican Brave (IRE) 5 ch h Salt Dome (USA)-Mrs Tittlemouse (Nonoalco (USA)) *845^{9}* **>64da 55f<**

Moi Canard 2 ch c Bold Owl-Royal Scots Greys (Blazing Saddles (AUS)) *(846) 1077^{2} (1213)* 1352^{3} 2153^{2} 2328^{7} 2750^{2} (2998) 3120^{2} 3314^{5} 3386^{4} 3895^{5} **>66a 66f<**

Mokaite 4 b f Komaite (USA)-Manhunt (Posse (USA)) 1434^{9} 1596^{19} **>1a 41f<**

Mokhtar (IRE) 4 b c Sadler's Wells (USA)-Flame of Tara (Artaius (USA)) (584) 938^{10} (1912) 2274^{10} 3489^{9} **>91f<**

Mokuti 3 b c Green Desert (USA)-Marie D'Argonne (FR) (Jefferson) 761^{4} 1312^{3} 1547^{3} **>82f<**

Moled Again 4 b c Then Again-Miss Milton (Young Christopher) 729^{10} *843^{7}* 1290^{W} **>12a 56f<**

Mollinsburn (IRE) 4 br c Tender King-Roundstone Lass (Montekin) *245^{9}* **>33df<**

Moltaire (GER) 3 c 3200a^{6} 4018a^{3} **>104f<**

Moments of Fortune (USA) 3 b c Timeless Moment (USA)-How Fortunate (USA) (What Luck (USA)) 438^{3} (720) (1010a) 1188^{5} 1872^{18} **>101f<**

Monaassib (IRE) 4 ch g Cadeaux Genereux-Pluvial (Habat) 719^{4} 1100^{7} 2699^{2} 3191^{9} 3979^{2} (4198) **>106f<**

Monaco Gold (IRE) 3 b c Durgam (USA)-Monaco Ville (Rheingold) 3669^{18} 3843^{9} **>50f<**

Monarch 3 b c Sadler's Wells (USA)-Bint Pasha (USA) (Affirmed (USA)) *592^{3}* (717) 995^{2} (1730) 1872^{3} 4047^{3} **>77a 92f<**

Mondragon 5 b h Niniski (USA)-La Lutine (My Swallow) 432^{13} 821^{3} 998^{7} 2098^{10} 2374^{3} 2907^{4} **>85f<**

Moneefa 4 br f Darshaan-Abha (Thatching) 1380^{4} *1568^{6}* (2482) 3611^{7} 4024^{6} 4227^{5} **>46a 90f<**

Moneghetti 4 ch g Faustus (USA)-The Victor Girls (Crofthall) 750^{3} *1091^{12} 1210^{7} (1630) 1884^{3} 2076^{3} (2377) 2923^{8}* **>50a 49f<**

Mongol Warrior (USA) 2 b c Deputy Minister (CAN)-Surely Georgie's (USA) (Alleged (USA)) 2408^{3} **>87f<**

Monica Cozzi (ITY) 0 01 f 1237a^{9} **>76f<**

Monica Maguire 3 ch f Prince Ragusa-Mary Maguire (Rapid River) 3272^{6} 3410^{7} **>7f<**

Moniques Venture 2 b f Midyan (USA)-Bumpkin (Free State) *3244^{6}* 3378^{6} 3570^{9} **>5a 37f<**

Monis (IRE) 4 ch c Waajib-Gratify (Grundy) 3222^{17} 3783^{17} 4068^{21} *4125^{9}* **>23a 47f<**

Monkey Boy (IRE) 4 b g Mazaad-Zareeta (Free State) *117^{13}* 818^{16} **>35da 59df<**

Monkey Face 4 gr f Clantime-Charming View (Workboy) 1355^{14} 2084^{8} 2220^{4} 2624^{10} 2972^{16} 3504^{5} **>40f<**

Monkey Wench (IRE) 4 b f Taufan (USA)-Northern Valkyrie (Glenstal (USA)) 597^{4} 905^{8} 991^{5} 1161^{2} 1420^{3} 1744^{6} 1957^{5} **>57f<**

Monkey Zanty (IRE) 2 b f Distinctly North (USA)-Achafalaya (USA) (Apalachee (USA)) *1879^{2}* 2302^{2} 2608^{7} 2773^{4} 3740^{8} **>44a 46f<**

Mono Lady (IRE) 2 b f Polish Patriot (USA)-Phylella (Persian Bold) 436^{7} 716^{4} 951^{6} 1443^{4} 4144^{15} **>64f<**

Mon Pere 2 b c Belfort (FR)-Lady Ever-so-Sure (Malicious) 2995^{8} 3436^{9} 3752^{8} 4211^{12} **>58f<**

Monrush (IRE) 4 b c Shirley Heights-Switched on (Known Fact (USA)) 1383^{13} 3384^{15} **>56f<**

Mons 2 b c Deploy-Morina (USA) (Lyphard (USA)) (1913) 2365^{2} (3068) (3812) 4199^{3} **>106f<**

Monsieur Culsyth 2 b c Mon Tresor-Regal Salute (Dara Monarch) 480^{5} (755) (1035) 1159^{4} 1740^{6} *2962^{8}* 3670^{12} **>37a 60f<**

Monsieur Petong 4 b c Petong-Little Madam (Habat) *2^{6} 31^{5} 50^{4} 157^{8} 267^{7} 314^{8} 348^{2} 393^{4} 419^{12}* 672^{12} 746^{9} *1087^{9}* **>47a 37f<**

Monsun (GER) 5 br h Konigsstuhl (GER)-Mosella (GER) (Surumu (GER)) 1398a^{6} (2046a) 3046a^{5} **>123f<**

Montagne 6 br m Midyan (USA)-La Masse (High Top) *624^{10}* **>4a f<**

Montague Dawson (IRE) 3 ch g Doulab (USA)-

Annacloy (Majority Blue) *(232) (319) 333^{4} 446^{3}* 681^{9} *1330^{5} 1882^{4} 2093^{3}* 3293^{13} *3512^{6} 3739^{8} 3954^{7} 4123^{4}* **>65a 47f<**

Montanelli (FR) **3** b c Dowsing (USA)-Honeymooning (USA) (Blushing Groom (FR)) *(64) (250) 360^{2}* 437^{14} 686^{6} 785^{10} *1953^{9} 2589^{6}* **>86a 63f<**

Mont d'Or (USA) **5** b g Devil's Bag (USA)-Most Precious (USA) (Nureyev (USA)) 1383^{12} 1905^{8} 2036^{5} **>38f<**

Monte Cavo **4** b g Bustino-Dance Festival (Nureyev (USA)) *592^{12}* 3457^{15} **>61a 65df<**

Montecristo **2** br c Warning-Sutosky (Great Nephew) 3398^{5} 3989^{10} 4058^{8} 4327^{12} **>65f<**

Montejurra **3** b c Belmez (USA)-Graphite (USA) (Mr Prospector (USA)) 691^{3} **>96f<**

Montendre **8** b h Longleat (USA)-La Lutine (My Swallow) (441) 659^{3} 934^{4} 2443^{4} 3834^{6} 4160^{10} 4324^{9} **>117f<**

Montenidoli(IRE) **0** 01 c Taufan-Travarica (Tissot) 1003a^{2}

Montjoy (USA) **3** b c Manila (USA)-Wendy's Ten (USA) (Tentam (USA)) 680^{2} 1121a^{2} 1848^{8} (2111) 2560a^{2} (3323a) 4120^{3} **>125f<**

Montone (IRE) **5** b h Pennine Walk-Aztec Princess (Indian King (USA)) 503^{3} 586^{2} 762^{2} 864^{2} 1048^{2} 1255^{8} 1745^{15} 2052^{2} 2222^{7} 2981^{3} 3234^{7} 3288^{6} *4298^{4}* **>61a 66df<**

Montrestar **2** ch c Mon Tresor-Wing of Freedom (Troy) (684) 1343^{4} 1678^{3} 3064^{8} 3284^{3} 3612^{16} 3803^{8} **>68f<**

Montserrat **3** b f Aragon-Follow the Stars (Sparkler) 850^{7} 1487^{5} 2369^{11} 2737^{14} 3466^{5} 3615^{15} 3964^{6} 4145^{5} 4266^{4} **>72f<**

Monty **3** ch g Colmore Row-Sussarando (Music Boy) 4055^{4} 4266^{5} **>58f<**

Monument **3** ch g Cadeaux Genereux-In Perpetuity (Great Nephew) 1615^{4} 2553^{13} (3105) 3348^{10} 3611^{12} **>85f<**

Moody **3** ch f Risk Me (FR)-Bocas Rose (Jalmood (USA)) 1172^{7} 1366^{15} 2112^{3} 3905^{12} **>66f<**

Moody's Cat (IRE) **2** b f Alzao (USA)-Zamayem (Sadler's Wells (USA)) 2420^{2} (3280) 4013a^{9} **>80f<**

Moofaji **4** b c Night Shift (USA)-Three Piece (Jaazeiro (USA)) 876^{11} 991^{10} 2307^{8} 2620^{4} 2994^{7} 4110^{9} 4275^{15} **>58df<**

Moonax (IRE) **4** ch c Caerleon (USA)-Moonsilk (Solinus) (1132) 1869^{2} 3789a^{2} 4008a^{2} **>125+f<**

Mooncusser **2** b g Forzando-Ragged Moon (Raga Navarro (ITY)) 684^{5} 1176^{7} *1454^{8}* 1992^{4} 3354^{5} 3882^{4} **>51a 59f<**

Moonee Valley **3** ch c Superlative-Superlife (USA) (Super Concorde (USA)) 449^{5} *560^{5}* **>32a 30f<**

Moon King (IRE) **3** ch c Cadeaux Genereux-Moon Drop (Dominion) 713^{3} 900a^{13} 1185^{2} (2015) 3910a^{9} (4087) 4198^{4} **>108f<**

Moonlight Air **4** b f Bold Owl-Havon Air (Celtic Cone) 1533^{10} 1683^{7} 3426^{10} 3862^{16} **>53df<**

Moonlight Calypso **4** ch f Jupiter Island-Moonlight Bay (Palm Track) *245^{5}* (905) 1252^{5} **>47a 53f<**

Moonlight Dance (USA) **4** b f Alysheba (USA)-Madelia (FR) 1002a^{5} **>113f<**

Moonlight Quest **7** gr h Nishapour (FR)-Arabian Rose (USA) (Lyphard (USA)) (556) 632^{2} 998^{11} 1416^{2} (1773) 1929^{6} 2256^{3} 2429^{2} (2799) 2996^{4} 3211^{5} 3930^{3} **>86f<**

Moonlight Saunter (USA) **3** ch f Woodman (USA)-Etoile D'Amore (USA) (The Minstrel (CAN)) (915) 1500^{4} 2001^{10} 2909^{7} 3175^{9} **>88f<**

Moon Magic **3** b f Polish Precedent (USA)-Castle Moon 3448^{3} 3543^{W} **>65f<**

Moon Mistress **4** br f Storm Cat (USA)-Spirit of The Wind (USA) (Little Current (USA)) 3611^{9} 3833^{9} **>90f<**

Moon Over Awir (IRE) **3** ch f Machiavellian (USA)-Shirley Reef (Shirley Heights) 1486^{7} 1701^{7} 1990^{8} **>65f<**

Moonshell (IRE) **3** b f Sadler's Wells (USA)-Moon Cactus (Kris) 933^{3} (1587) **>116f<**

Moonshine Dancer **5** b h Northern State (USA)-Double Birthday (Cavo Doro) *259^{9} 295^{7}* 3724^{5} 3971^{6} 4140^{5} **>41a 52f<**

Moon Strike (FR) **5** b or br h Strike Gold (USA)-Lady Lamia (USA) (Secreto (USA)) *(160) 262^{5}* (1070) 2369^{16} **>85a 82f<**

More Bills (IRE) **3** b g Gallic League-Lady Portobello (Porto Bello) *7^{7} 98^{4} 444^{12}* 1012^{11} *4293^{12}* **>40a 43f<**

More Royal (USA) **2** ch c Mt Livermore (USA)-Royal Run (USA) (Wavering Monarch (USA)) (1727) (2034) 2690^{3} (3483a) 3812^{2} 4010a^{5} **>96f<**

More Than You Know (IRE) **2** ch f Kefaah (USA)-Foston Bridge (Relkino) (3450) 4207^{2} **>91f<**

Morigi **4** b c Rousillon (USA)-Ibtidaar (USA) (Danzig (USA)) 4093a^{3} **>117f<**

Morjinski **5** ch m Myjinski (USA)-Morley (Hotfoot) *71^{11} 122^{9}* **>3a 8f<**

Morning Master **3** b g Jupiter Island-Hound Song 1317^{11} 1691^{14} 3747^{16} 3876^{10} 4131^{13} **>51f<**

Morning Sir **2** b c Southern Music-Morning Miss 4146^{6} **>38f<**

Morning Surprise **2** b br f Tragic Role (USA)-Fleur de Foret (USA) (Green Forest (USA)) 1327^{4} *2146^{10} (2382) 2629^{2}* 3289^{6} 3423^{3} 3623^{3} 3894^{8} **>68a 58f<**

Morocco (IRE) **6** b h Cyrano de Bergerac-Lightning Laser (Monseigneur (USA)) 1509^{8} 1664^{8} 1724^{10} (1742) 2016^{5} 2317^{12} 2510^{3} 2685^{15} 2983^{2} (3152) 3291^{4} 3439^{8} 3677^{3} 3771^{7} 3960^{2} 4115^{13} 4156^{5} 4242^{6} **>79df<**

Morski **6** ch h Morston (FR)-Lady Gainsborough (Sky Gipsy) 4062^{21}

Morstock **5** gr h Beveled (USA)-Miss Melmore (Nishapour (FR)) 454^{7} 4051^{10} **>52f<**

Moscow Mist (IRE) **4** b g Soviet Star (USA)-Ivory Dawn (USA) (Sir Ivor) 764^{6} 1167^{2} 1947^{2} **>76f<**

Moscow Road **4** b c Presidium-Missish (Mummy's Pet) *188^{3} 272^{6} 369^{5}* **>74a 69df<**

Moshaajir (USA) **5** b h Woodman (USA)-Hidden Trail (USA) (Gleaming (USA)) 737^{8} (1084) (1310) 1470^{2} 3804^{6} 3978^{5} 4166^{16} **>81df<**

Mo's Main Man (IRE) **3** b c Taufan (USA)-Broadway Rosie (Absalom) *59^{5}* 164a^{4} (209a) 488a^{12} 504^{19} 651^{8} 1166^{8} **>52a 65f<**

Mossalier **3** b f Mazilier (USA)-Mosso (Ercolano (USA)) 855^{11} 1012^{6} **>46f<**

Mo's Star **3** b f Most Welcome-Star Face 739^{3} 1405^{2} 1534^{5} 2317^{6} 2488^{3} 2807^{6} (3081) 3286^{7} 3383^{5} 3497^{13} 3605^{11} **>72f<**

Most Beautiful **4** ch f Most Welcome-Sorebelle *183^{5}* **>24a 49f<**

Most Becoming **3** b f Most Welcome-Tolomette (Tolomeo) 3401^{10} 3653^{15} 3799^{14} 4054^{14} 4225^{15} **>26f<**

Mo Stopher 3 ch f Sharpo-Red Gloves (Red God) 1692^{15} **>37f<**

Most Uppitty 3 gr f Absalom-Hyatti (Habitat) 507^{11} 646^{15} *842^{5} 1032^{3} 1331^{9} 1763^{2} 2144^{6} 2492^{5}* 3357^{8} *3522^{3}* 3783^{18} **>57da 33f<**

Most Welcome News 3 b c Most Welcome-In the Papers (Aragon) 651^{12} 867^{5} 1146^{7} 1548^{7} *1939^{6}* 3265^{6} **>47a 55f<**

Motakabber (IRE) 3 b c Sadler's Wells (USA)-High Spirited (Shirley Heights) 485^{2} (4003) **>90++f<**

Moujeeb (USA) 5 b h Riverman (USA)-Capricorn Belle (Nonoalco (USA)) 765^{4} 922^{12} 1071^{2} 1148^{4} 1321^{2} 1489^{3} *1566^{5}* 1700^{7} 2326^{9} 2909^{11} 3014^{5} 3219^{9} 3341^{6} 3376^{4} 3622^{11} 3764^{13} 3874^{9} 4122^{7} 4165^{2} 4238^{2} **>62a 71f<**

Moultazim (USA) 5 b h Diesis-Maysoon (Shergar) 3277^{8} *3529^{12}* 3759^{7} **>37f<**

Mouna El Arab 2 b f Governor General-Dancing May (Tina's Pet) 903^{5} 1282^{8} **>46f<**

Mountain Boy 4 b g Blakeney-Fire Mountain (Dragonara Palace (USA)) *190^{5} 290^{8} 352^{8}* **>34a f<**

Mountain Dream 2 b c Batshoof-Echoing (Formidable) 3536^{5} 3917^{9} **>75f<**

Mountain Holly 2 b f Shirley Heights-Ela Romara (Ela-Mana-Mou) 4262^{7} **>68f<**

Mountains of Mist (IRE) 3 b f Shirley Heights-Magic of Life (USA) (Seattle Slew (USA)) (1175) 4316^{4} **>79f<**

Mountain Valley 2 gr f Midyan (USA)-Glow Plug (Kalaglow) 1169^{3} 1662^{4} 1968^{4} 2964^{2} (3246) **>77f<**

Mountgate 3 b c Merdon Melody-Young Whip (Bold Owl) 1195^{6} 2188^{7} (2500) 2778^{U} 3598^{7} 3823^{10} 3973^{W} 4079^{3} 4194^{12} (4268) **>82f<**

Mourne Mountains 2 b c Scenic-Orlaith (Final Straw) 3536^{8} **>51f<**

Mousehole 3 b c Statoblest-Alo Ez (Alzao (USA)) 658^{12} 937^{9} 1302^{3} 1471^{2} (1847) 2067^{2} 2507^{4} 3637^{18} 4134^{13} **>77f<**

Move Darling 2 ch f Rock City-Larive (Blakeney) 2198^{8} 2683^{10} **>36f<**

Move Smartly (IRE) 5 b h Smarten (USA)-Key Maneuver (USA) (Key To Content (USA)) 749^{9} 988^{10} 1344^{5} 2061^{6} 2276^{2} 2611^{8} (2913) 3063^{2} 3396^{13} 3488^{11} 3808^{28} 4044^{15} 4275^{11} **>47a 62df<**

Move With Edes 3 b g Tragic Role (USA)-Good Time Girl (Good Times (ITY)) 880^{6} 1509^{5} 1824^{4} (2180) 4242^{10} **>71f<**

Moving Arrow 4 ch g Indian Ridge-Another Move (Farm Walk) 439^{2} 793^{4} 1217^{3} 1626^{9} 1851^{6} 2598^{10} (2933) 3188^{6} 3419^{8} 3924^{8} (3991) **>100f<**

Moving Up (IRE) 2 ch f Don't Forget Me-Our Pet (Mummy's Pet) 1790^{3} 2114^{2} 2351^{12} 3538^{7} 3915^{6} **>72f<**

Mowlaie 4 ch c Nashwan (USA)-Durrah (USA) (Nijinsky (CAN)) 961^{6} 1357^{10} 1933^{4} 2186^{6} 3433^{3} 3611^{14} 3645^{3} 4171^{14} *4298^{11}* **>58a 75f<**

Moylough Rebel 2 ch c Hotfoot-Stellajoe (Le Dauphin) 1752^{11} 2029^{5} 4045^{14} **>49f<**

Mr Abbot 5 b g Midyan (USA)-Abbotswood (Ahonoora) *4211^{0}* **>28a f<**

Mr Bean 5 b g Salse (USA)-Goody Blake (Blakeney) *22^{4} 304^{2} (340) 389^{3} (422) 517^{2} (1091) 1332^{3}* 1635^{3} **>67a 75f<**

Mr Bergerac (IRE) 4 b g Cyrano de Bergerac-Makalu (Godswalk (USA)) (2533) 3087^{3} (3219) 3551^{16} 3822^{3} 3964^{20} 4119^{7} **>85a 91f<**

Mr B Reasonable (IRE) 4 b c Reasonable (FR)-Dunbally (Dunphy) *139^{6} 182^{12} 220^{12} 269^{13}* **>31da 38f<**

Mr Browning (USA) 4 br c Al Nasr (FR)-Crinoline (Blakeney) *205^{4} 249^{5} 320^{10}* 545^{2} 744^{3} 884^{2} 1477^{2} (2050) 2792^{7} (3384) 4028^{9} 4201^{17} **>47a 79f<**

Mr Butch 5 b h Aragon-Kittycatoo Katango (USA) (Verbatim (USA)) 1644^{8} 2981^{10} **>64f<**

Mr Christie 3 b g Doulab (USA)-Hi There (High Top) 777^{6} 911^{3} 1270^{6} 1532^{4} 1825^{11} 2778^{6} 3447^{10} 3799^{10} 4000^{12} **>64?f<**

Mr Confusion (IRE) 7 b h Kafu-Mrs Foodbroker (Home Guard (USA)) 1135^{4} 1357^{7} 2118^{4} 2457^{16} **>96f<**

Mr Copyforce 5 gr h Sharrood (USA)-Cappuccilli *206^{5} 277^{6}* 3470^{14} **>56a 52f<**

Mr Cube (IRE) 5 ch h Tate Gallery (USA)-Truly Thankful (CAN) (Graustark (USA)) 820^{2} 976^{3} 1081^{8} 1351^{13} 1542^{3} 1644^{5} (1797) 1969^{7} 2081^{5} (2342) (2611) 2797^{3} 3050^{4} 3291^{8} 3661^{8} **>41a 70f<**

Mr Darcy 3 b c Dominion-Rose Chanelle (Welsh Pageant) 3317^{3} **>39f<**

Mr Devious 4 b c Superpower-Marton Maid (Silly Season) 738^{U} 1166^{12} **>59a 63f<**

Mr Eglantine 3 ch c Mr Fluorocarbon-Sweet Rosa (Absalom) 3099^{15} 3422^{13} 3805^{11} **>7f<**

Mr Frosty 3 b c Absalom-Chadenshe (Taufan (USA)) *(156) 251^{2}* 437^{3} 538^{10} 911^{4} *3319^{7}* **>66a 60f<**

Mr Geneaology (USA) 5 b h Procida (USA)-Que Mona (USA) 2514^{3} 2986^{2} 3263^{2} (3435) **>68f<**

Mr. Greeley (USA) 3 ch c Gone West (USA)-Long Legend (USA) *4303a^{2}* **>128a f<**

Mr. Ibrahim (DEN) 8 dk h Tshainik-Vibsen (DEN) (Hillbilly I 3044a^{3} **>101f<**

Mr Jasper 3 b g Colmore Row-Spic And Span 2180^{6} **>14a f<**

Mr Lowry, 3 b c Rambo Dancer (CAN)-Be Royal (Royal Palm) *38^{4} 251^{4} 283^{7} 1334^{9}* **>57a 39f<**

Mr Mactavish 3 ch g Salse (USA)-Sharmood (USA) (Sharpen Up) *(128) 301^{8} 626^{3}* 947^{7} 1289^{5} **>64da 76f<**

Mr Martini (IRE) 5 b h Pennine Walk-Arab Art (Artaius (USA)) *20^{6}* 439^{3} 665^{9} (793) 960^{3} (1586) 2105^{7} 2893a^{3} (3325a) 3562^{3} 3814^{5} **>78a 118f<**

Mr Medley 3 b g Merdon Melody-Hsian (Shantung) 2805^{3} 3105^{4} 3712^{2} 3958^{4} 4162^{7} **>80df<**

Mr Moriarty (IRE) 4 ch c Tate Gallery (USA)-Bernica (FR) *96^{5} 121^{2} 166^{3} 334^{5} 421^{5} 592^{5}* 649^{15} 1290^{12} *1459^{5} 1568^{7} 1762^{6} 1950^{4}* 2450^{10} 2956^{4} 3293^{15} 3649^{10} **>46a 33f<**

Mr Nevermind (IRE) 5 b h The Noble Player (USA)-Salacia *89^{5} 125^{3} 383^{4} 401^{2}* 450^{10} 1126^{2} 1534^{2} 2051^{3} 2602^{2} 3011^{8} 4157^{11} **>81a 70f<**

Mr Oscar 3 b c Belfort (FR)-Moushka (Song) (3103) (3535) **>101+f<**

Mr Personality 3 ch g Baim (USA)-Gentle Gain (Final Straw) 435^{9} 539^{17} 824^{10} 3060^{3} **>50f<**

Mr Poppleton 6 ch h Ballacashtal (CAN)-Greenstead Lady (Great Nephew) 2981^{11}

Mr Richard (IRE) 5 br h Fools Holme (USA)-Miss Markey (Gay Fandango (USA)) 1392a^{5} **>115f<**

Mr Rough 4 b c Fayruz-Rheinbloom (731) 1027^{3} 1438^{2} 1663^{7} 2979^{2} 3222^{6} 3664^{2} 4038^{16} *4297^{8}* **>55a 71f<**

Mrs Bizzybody 4 b f Efisio-Mrs Bizz *198^{4} 343^{8}* **>23a**

3f<

rs Jawleyford (USA) 7 b m Dixieland Band (USA)-Did he Agree (USA) (Restless Native) *45[5] 259[7] 295[9]* 4140[W] *336[16]* >55da 51f<

rs Jogglebury 4 b f Chilibang-Madame Bleu (Bruni) *3[7] 136[10]* 1737[5] >13f<

rs Keen 2 b f Beveled (USA)-Haiti Mill (Free State) 224[15] 4329[9] >15f<

r Slick 3 ch c Sharpo-Taj Victory (Final Straw) 596[4] 53[2] 966[13] >52a 53f<

rs McBadger 2 ch f Weldnaas (USA)-Scottish Lady Dunbeath (USA)) 650[4] 782[4] 1424[U] 2335[6] 3893[3] 4144[3] 329[6] >68f<

rs Nevermind 2 b f Sayf El Arab (USA)-Mana (GER) Windwurf (GER)) 1253[7] 3054[3] 3314[4] >49f<

r Speaker (IRE) 2 ch c Statoblest-Casting Vote (USA) Monteverdi) 825[11] *2958[8]* 3260[7] 3612[3] 3749[6] >37a 1f<

Mr Speculator 2 ch g Kefaah (USA)-Humanity Ahonoora) 3868[14] >65f<

Mrs Tigger 3 ch f Absalom-Steffi (Precocious) *59[9] 771[11] 1030[10]* 1428[7] 1692[14] 3055[8] >48a 38f<

Mrs. Yazzo (SWE) 4 b f National Zenith (SWE)-Svea Svan (SWE) (Harambe 3043a[3] >62f<

Mr Teddy 2 gr g Absalom-Chadenshe (Taufan (USA)) 4103[20] >58f<

Mr Teigh 3 b c Komaite (USA)-Khadino (Relkino) 1296[4] 1602[7] 1641[5] *1980[4]* 2108[6] >62a 76f<

Mr Towser 4 b c Faustus (USA)-Saltina (Bustino) *229[2] 271[4] (771)* 1505[4] 1844[5] >84a 73f<

Mr Woodman (GER) 3 c 3798a[7] 4094a[5] >106f<

Mr.Woodman (USA) 3 c 2215a[13] >75f<

Mu-Arrik 7 b or br h Aragon-Maravilla (Mandrake Major) 535[19] 646[7] 789[8] 1023[6] 1493[6] *2383[14]* 2784[10] 3467[13] 3830[5] 4115[10] 4236[10] >7a 49f<

Mua-Tab 2 ch f Polish Precedent (USA)-Alsabiha (Lord Gayle (USA)) 3948[4] >76f<

Mubariz (IRE) 3 b c Royal Academy (USA)-Ringtail (Auction Ring (USA)) 1065[2] >85f<

Mubhij (IRE) 2 ch c Mujtahid (USA)-Abhaaj (Kris) (825) 1868[3] 2243[3] 2704[2] (3165) 3610[2] (4032) >108f<

Muchtarak (IRE) 3 b c Try My Best (USA)-Secret Hideaway (USA) (Key To The Mint (USA)) 1069[2] 1487[17] 1787[5] (2437) 2803[W] 3214[8] 3408[7] >89f<

Much Too High 3 b c Salse (USA)-Hi-Li (High Top) 651[5] 851[13] 1535[2] 1696[3] 1997[4] 3676[5] 3986[8] >63f<

Mudlark 3 b g Salse (USA)-Mortal Sin (USA) (Green Forest (USA)) 880[3] 1463[3] *1762[5]* >34a 51f<

Mufarej (USA) 3 ch c Riverman (USA)-Azayim (Be My Guest (USA)) (3542) 3924[9] >84f<

Muferr (IRE) 3 b c Groom Dancer (USA)-Tiavanita (USA) (J O Tobin (USA)) (526) 618[F] (1192) >90f<

Muhab (USA) 3 b or br c Lyphard (USA)-Magic Slipper (Habitat) 945[4] 1145[5] 1837[9] 3608[11] 3814[6] >102df<

Muhandam (IRE) 2 b c Common Grounds-Unbidden Melody (USA) (Chieftain II) 2315[12] 2710[5] 3720[3] >74f<

Muhandis 2 b c Persian Bold-Night At Sea (Night Shift (USA)) 3933[3] 4103[15] >73+f<

Muhtadi (IRE) 2 br c Marju (IRE)-Moon Parade (Welsh Pageant) 2912[11] 3280[4] 3713[7] 4192[10] >77f<

Muhtarram (USA) 6 b h Alleged (USA)-Ballet De France (USA) (Northern Dancer) 1187[5] (1836) 2286[6] >126f<

Mukabir (USA) 2 b c Dayjur (USA)-Copper Creek (Habitat) 3185[7] 3371[7] >65f<

Mukallad (IRE) 3 ch c Unfuwain (USA)-Nouvelle Star (AUS) (Luskin Star (AUS)) 1337[5] >68f<

Mukhatab 3 b c Soviet Star (USA)-Azyaa (Kris) 1186[8] (1547) 3095[2] 3393[2] 3837[15] >87f<

Mukhlles (USA) 2 b c Diesis-Serenely (USA) (Alydar (USA)) 2408[5] >78f<

Muktabas (IRE) 3 b c Alzao (USA)-Welsh Fantasy (Welsh Pageant) 3027[2] (3261) 3602[3] 3845[5] >103df<

Mulciber 7 b h Head for Heights-Quisissanno (Be My Guest (USA)) *11[5]* 2139[6] 2298[4] >72a 69f<

Mulhollande Lad (IRE) 2 ch c Mulhollande (USA)-La Kumbha (FR) (Critique (USA)) 3018[11] 3502[12] 4059[4] >28f<

Mullagh Hill Lad (IRE) 2 b c Cyrano de Bergerac-Fantasise (FR) (General Assembly (USA)) *3077[6]* 3352[7] *3949[9]* 4097[3] 4243[4] >44a 51f<

Mullitover 5 ch h Interrex (CAN)-Atlantic Air (Air Trooper) *1[4] 89[11] 191[2]* 2010[6] 2414[4] (2979) (3159) 3348[4] (3545) 3943[5] (4122) >65a 93f<

Multi Franchise 2 ch c Gabitat-Gabibti (IRE) (Dara Monarch) 1047[9] 1184[12] 1981[3] *(2075)* 3533[8] *3675[11]* >65a 63f<

Munaadee (USA) 3 b c Green Dancer (USA)-Aliysa (Darshaan) 968[2] >74f<

Munakeb (FR) 2 b c Topsider (USA)-Antartica (FR) (Arctic Tern (USA)) 2615[W] 3053[6] (3352) 3612[8] 3990[14] >73f<

Muncie (IRE) 3 b f Sadler's Wells (USA)-Martingale (Luthier) (802a) (1238a) 1712a[5] 3694a[5] >113f<

Munif (IRE) 3 ch c Caerleon (USA)-Forest Lair (Habitat) (2559a) 3836[15] >87f<

Munketh (USA) 2 b c Red Ransom (USA)-Chewsy Suzy (USA) (Barachois (CAN)) 1184[8] 1856[2] 2485[3] 3090[6] (3266) 3516[7] 3780[3] 4151[10] >87f<

Munnasib (FR) 5 ch h Highest Honor (FR)-Parole Et Musique (USA) (Nureyev (USA)) *311[7]*

Muntafi 4 b c Unfuwain (USA)-Princess Sucree (USA) (Roberto (USA)) 1189[9] >85df<

Munwar 3 b c Kalaglow-Oatfield (679) (1068) 1611[9] 2218a[12] 3381[7] 4104[5] >114?f<

Murajja (USA) 3 ch c Silver Hawk (USA)-Halholah (USA) (Secreto (USA)) (614) (822) 1018[3] 1897[8] >103f<

Murheb 2 b g Mtoto-Masarrah (Formidable) 2912[10] 3340[2] >75f<

Murphy's Gold (IRE) 4 ch g Salt Dome (USA)-Winter Harvest (Grundy) *415[10]* 820[4] 1037[2] 1192[6] 1438[4] (1679) 2061[3] (2222) 2419[2] 2668[7] 3396[7] 3645[12] >27a 70f<

Murphys Way 6 br m Ardross-Choir (High Top) *4[4] 136[2] 259[4]* 556[6] 751[7] 840[6] 1036[4] *2919[8]* >57a 49f<

Murray's Mazda (IRE) 6 ch h M Double M (USA)-Lamya (Hittite Glory) 1342[4] 1493[7] 1721[15] 2124[5] 2475[6] 2645[2] 2784[4] 3098[4] 3357[12] 3667[10] 3879[2] 4280[12] >41f<

Muscat (IRE) 0 01 1228a[4] 2038a[6] 2721a[5]

Musetta (IRE) 3 b f Cadeaux Genereux-Monaiya (Shareef Dancer (USA)) 620[13] (932) 1101[3] 1587[4] 1867[3] 2563a[4] 2936[7] 3694a[9] 3944[7] >106df<

Museum (IRE) 4 b c Tate Gallery (USA)-Go Anywhere (Grundy) 1260[6] 1543[7] 3433[10] 3593[13] 3977[8] 4138[16] >70f<

Mushahadah (IRE) 2 ch f Ela-Mana-Mou-Mashteen

(USA) 3530^{P}
Mushahid (USA) 2 b c Wild Again (USA)-Playful Queen (USA) (Majestic Prince) (1298) 1727^{2} (2059) 2690^{4} 3215^{2} 3600^{2} 4139^{3} **>93f<**
Mushtak (USA) 2 b c Topsider (USA)-Informatique (USA) (Quack (USA)) 3536^{4} 3868^{20} 4143^{11} **>68f<**
Musica 3 ch f Primo Dominie-Show Home (Music Boy) 483^{3} 681^{6} 850^{5} 1181^{7} (1277) 1637^{8} 1924^{8} 3880^{5} **>84df<**
Musical Fantasy (IRE) 3 b f Gallic League-Trubbach (Vitiges (FR)) *173^{3} 278^{5}* **>45a 46f<**
Musical Heights (IRE) 2 b f Roaring Riva-Littleton Song (Song) 4132^{11} **>1f<**
Musical March 4 b f Daring March-Musical Princess (Cavo Doro) 1998^{6} 2620^{9} 2814^{7} **>26f<**
Musical Season 3 b c Merdon Melody-Earles-Field (Wolverlife) 828^{6} 1806^{5} 2120^{8} 2458^{2} 3087^{9} **>96f<**
Music Gold (IRE) 2 b br c Taufan (USA)-Nonnita (Welsh Saint) 3628^{2} 3892^{2} (3998) 4317^{2} **>87f<**
Music In Motion 2 b f Batshoof-Falaka (Sparkler) 3869^{10} **>12f<**
Musick House (IRE) 2 b c Sadler's Wells (USA)-Hot Princess (Hot Spark) 3456^{2} **>91+f<**
Music Maker 3 b f Unfuwain (USA)-Full Orchestra (Shirley Heights) 989^{3} *(1789) 2145^{7}* (2655) *2922^{8}* 3154^{2} 3657^{6} **>62a 69f<**
Music Mistress (IRE) 2 ch f Classic Music (USA)-Blue Scholar (Blue Cashmere or Hotfoot) 2011^{5} 2176^{2} 2403^{3} (2601) 2988^{2} 3233^{4} 3378^{3} 3858^{12} 4243^{12} **>56f<**
Music Theatre 2 b c Dancing Spree (USA)-Downshire (IRE) (Darshaan) *2633^{3} 2958^{2}* **>64a f<**
Musilumieres (FR) 3 b c Art Francais (USA)-Symphonie Girl (FR) (African Joy) (164a)
Mustaffa (IRE) 2 ch g Fayruz-Crimson Sunset (Red Sunset) *604^{4}* 740^{2} *1077^{3}* 1159^{5} 1640^{6} **>48a 57f<**
Mustang 0 S 3666^{10} 3881^{4} **>60f<**
Mustn't Grumble (IRE) 5 b g Orchestra-Gentle Heiress *20^{10}* 2585^{5} *3319^{11}* 3457^{6} 3800^{6} *3950^{8}* **>54a 63f<**
Mutabassim (IRE) 3 b c Green Desert (USA)-Almarai (USA) (Vaguely Noble) 658^{6} 1094^{22} 1380^{2} 1859^{4} 2602^{3} (3181) 3545^{10} 4156^{3} **>82f<**
Mutadarra (IRE) 2 ch c Mujtahid (USA)-Silver Echo (Caerleon (USA)) 4103^{2} **>91+f<**
Mu-Tadil 3 ch g Be My Chief (USA)-Inveraven (Alias Smith (USA)) 3618^{5} 3772^{12} **>75f<**
Mutahassin (USA) 2 b c Dixieland Band (USA)-Katie Lynn (USA) (Star de Naskra (USA)) 3625^{20} 3891^{2} **>64f<**
Mutakddim (USA) 4 ch c Seeking the Gold (USA)-Oscillate (USA) (Seattle Slew (USA)) 794^{3} 1187^{4} (1618) 2105^{8} 3931^{2} 4178a^{4} **>120f<**
Mutamanni (USA) 2 b c Caerleon (USA)-Mathkurh (USA) (Riverman (USA)) 4023^{2} 4244^{2} **>83?f<**
Mutammaddin 3 b br c Polish Precedent (USA)-Kadwah (USA) (Mr Prospector (USA)) 2944^{7} **>48f<**
Mutawali (IRE) 5 ch h Exactly Sharp (USA)-Ludovica (Bustino) 1350^{14} **>40f<**
Mutazz (USA) 3 b c Woodman (USA)-Ghashtah (USA) (Nijinsky (CAN)) 736^{4} 884^{3} 1093^{2} 1601^{2} **>71f<**
Mut (GB) 4 b c Stop the Music-Margamania 3585a^{3}
Mutiara 4 b f Never so Bold-Hello Cuddles (He Loves Me) *252^{8}* **>21a 49df<**
Mutinique 4 br f General Wade-Little Visitor (Tina's Pet) 731^{15} 882^{10} *1209^{10}* 1501^{6} 1545^{8} 2054^{9} 2538^{7} 3960^{6} 4157^{21} **>27a 50f<**
Muzrak (CAN) 4 ch c Forty Niner (USA)-Linda North (USA) (Northern Dancer) 558^{14} 676^{12} 1037^{13} 1295^{3} 1686^{3} 1875^{5} 2401^{2} **>65f<**
Muzz (IRE) 4 br c Gallic League-Cartier Bijoux (Ahonoora) *107^{10}* 701^{19} 877^{13} 1157^{15} **>47a 64df<**
My Abbey 6 b m Hadeer-Rose Barton (Pas de Seul) 639^{6} (926) 1152^{13} 1689^{6} 2163^{6} 2585^{8} 3116^{9} 3221^{3} 3424^{4} 3667^{27} **>59f<**
My Archie 2 b c Silver Arch-My Alma (IRE) (Reasonable (FR)) 3773^{7} 4067^{4} **>20f<**
Myasha (USA) 6 b h Imp Society (USA)-Mauna Loa (USA) 565^{7} 1537^{11} **>82f<**
My Best Valentine 5 b h Try My Best (USA)-Pas de Calais (Pas de Seul) *262^{7}* 665^{12} 1241^{4} 1614^{5} 1895^{27} 2764^{7} 2948^{9} 3359^{3} 3715^{17} **>50a 93f<**
Mybotye 2 br c Rambo Dancer (CAN)-Sigh (Highland Melody) 1134^{11} (1646) (3394) **>65+f<**
My Boy Josh 3 ch c Risk Me (FR)-Merry Kate (Shirley Heights) 553^{9} 673^{10} 1097^{16} *1628^{4} 2636^{2}* **>66a 54f<**
My Branch 2 b f Distant Relative-Pay the Bank (High Top) 2412^{2} (2619) 3032^{3} 3375^{2} (3548) (3702) 3866^{2} 4105^{3} **>106f<**
My Brave Girl 3 b f Never so Bold-Souadah (USA) (General Holme (USA)) 1549^{5} 1979^{12} 2319^{7} 3872^{13} **>50f<**
My Cadeaux 3 ch f Cadeaux Genereux-Jubilee Song 2576^{2} (2949) 3466^{7} **>83f<**
My Cherrywell 5 br m Kirchner-Cherrywood Blessin (Good Times (ITY)) *398^{8}* (475) 639^{10} 906^{2} *1032^{2} 1331^{5}* 1677^{5} 1741^{3} 2124^{9} *3524^{7}* 4057^{16} **>54a 49f<**
My Darlingdaughter 3 ch f Night Shift (USA)-Nicoletta 3653^{13} **>24f<**
My Dutch Girl 3 b f Midyan (USA)-Double Dutch (Nicholas Bill) 3756^{9} 3875^{16} **>46f<**
My Emma 2 b f Marju (IRE)-Pato (High Top) 4050^{7} **>64f<**
My Fiore 4 b f Midyan (USA)-My Tootsie (Tap On Wood) 1285^{19} **>41f<**
My First Romance 3 b f Danehill (USA)-Front Line Romance (Caerleon (USA)) 915^{6} **>70f<**
My Flag (USA) 2 ch f Easy Goer (USA)-Personal Ensign (USA) (Private Account (USA)) (4302a) **>110tf<**
Myfontaine 8 b h Persepolis (FR)-Mortefontaine (FR) 505^{8} 676^{9} 874^{5} (1324) (1543) (1658) 2139^{4} 2392^{5} 2658^{6} 3501^{2} 3659^{2} 3863^{14} **>70f<**
My Foxy Lady 5 b m Jalmood (USA)-La Petite Noblesse (Thatching) *14^{8} 139^{10} 212^{6}* **>7a 35f<**
My Gallery (IRE) 4 ch f Tate Gallery (USA)-Sententious (Kautokeino (FR)) 762^{9} *1209^{3} 1457^{5} 1633^{3}* 1873^{2} *(2141) (2290)* 2578^{9} 2797^{8} *2963^{5} 3072^{12}* 3719^{5} **>62a 58f<**
My Gina 3 ch f Be My Chief (USA)-Ginny Binny (Ahonoora) 1337^{4} 1507^{2} (1874) 2103^{7} 3497^{5} 3664^{4} (3840) **>83f<**
My Godson 5 br h Valiyar-Blessit (So Blessed) 578^{16} 753^{6} 1044^{4} 1153^{7} 1523^{5} 1843^{11} 2972^{10} 3504^{2} 3879^{16} **>29a 54f<**
My Handsome Prince 3 b c Handsome Sailor-My Serenade (USA) (Sensitive Prince (USA)) 1191^{3} 1412^{2} 1859^{5} 2081^{12} 2503^{11} 3227^{5} **>21a 57f<**

My Handy Man 4 ch c Out of Hand-My Home (Homing) *52^{2} 266^{8}* 785^{7} 909^{2} 1250^{14} 1438^{7} 1687^{7} 2228^{2} 2307^{5} 2543^{8} 4234^{14} **>64da 63f<**

My Happy Guest (IRE) 2 3584a^{8} **>62f<**

My Irish 5 b h Assert-Cremets (Mummy's Pet) (4092a) 4342a^{3} **>118f<**

My Jazzmyn 3 b f Chief Singer-Azaiyma (Corvaro (USA)) 3542^{12} 4054^{19}

Myjinka 5 gr m Myjinski (USA)-Royal Bat (Crowned Prince (USA)) *(39) 56^{7} 142^{4} 192^{3} 217^{2} (287) 320^{7}* 1274^{7} 1426^{8} 1516^{4} 2404^{8} 3079^{4} 3501^{8} **>42a 29f<**

My Kerry Dancer (USA) 5 ch h Seattle Dancer (USA)-Mumble Peg (General Assembly (USA)) 991^{11} 1934^{2} **>55f<**

My Kind 2 ch f Mon Tresor-Kind of Shy (Kind of Hush) (1503) 1829^{2} 2489^{5} 2757^{2} 3423^{5} 3749^{13} 3858^{4} 4141^{9} *4273^{13}* **>36a 65f<**

My Lady Brady 3 b f Risk Me (FR)-Miss Mischievous (Star Appeal) *363^{7}* 581^{4} 855^{4} *1032^{8}* 1445^{13} **>59a 55f<**

My Learned Friend 4 b or br g Broken Hearted-Circe (Main Reef) 1314^{3} (1616) (1908) 2577^{2} (3091) 3593^{6} 4201^{8} **>92f<**

My Lewicia (IRE) 2 b f Taufan (USA)-Christine Daae (Sadler's Wells (USA)) 3663^{14} **>47f<**

My Lifetime Lady (IRE) 4 ch f Indian Ridge-Liffey Reef (Main Reef) *177^{8} 217^{6} 302^{7} 341^{7} 355^{6}* 546^{8} 909^{8} **>37a 44df<**

My Lindianne 8 gr m Alias Smith (USA)-Lindrick Passion (Silly Season) 1191^{10} **>20f<**

My Mariam 2 ch f Salse (USA)-Birch Creek (Carwhite) (3371) 3680^{4} 3867^{9} 4206^{9} **>81f<**

My Melody Parkes 2 b f Teenoso (USA)-Summerhill Spruce (Windjammer (USA)) (638) 871^{6} 1849^{3} 3186^{2} 3692a^{3} 3702^{4} **>99f<**

My Millie 2 ch f Midyan (USA)-Madam Millie (Milford) 3110^{4} 3628^{17} 4050^{10} **>60f<**

My Minnie 5 b m Kind of Hush-Miami Mouse (Miami Springs) *27^{3} 100^{2} 161^{3} 330^{6} 414^{3} (517) (605) 771^{7}* **>75+a 52f<**

My Mother's Local (USA) 2 b f Local Talent (USA)-My Mother's Eyes (FR) (Saint Cyrien (FR)) 4312^{9} **>60f<**

My Mum Said 3 ch f Formidable-Moorland Lady (Swing Easy (USA)) 745^{12} 974^{8} **>52f<**

My Rossini 6 b g Ardross-My Tootsie (Tap On Wood) 3936^{3} **>53a 60f<**

Myrtle 2 b f Batshoof-Greek Goddess (Young Generation) 1169^{10} 2173^{2} 2594^{3} 3158^{3} (3306) 3561^{5} **>93f<**

Myrtle Quest 3 b c Rainbow Quest (USA)-Wryneck (Niniski (USA)) 694^{6} 1103^{5} 1839^{8} 2348^{4} **>86f<**

Myself 3 ch f Nashwan (USA)-Pushy (660) 933^{8} 1850^{7} 3564^{4} 3931^{3} 4178a^{9} **>119f<**

My Silversmith (IRE) 4 b f Cyrano de Bergerac-Golden Tears (Rheingold) 1157^{18} **>1f<**

Mysterious Times 2 b f Timeless Times (USA)-Misty Rocket (Roan Rocket) 554^{4} 699^{7} *770^{5}* 3231^{9} 3417^{12} 3806^{6} 4001^{11} 4141^{16} **>6a 51f<**

Mystery Matthias 2 b f Nicholas (USA)-Devils Dirge (Song) 852^{6} 1047^{6} 1163^{4} 1634^{5} 3655^{9} 3858^{6} **>65f<**

Mystic Dawn 2 b f Aragon-Ahonita (Ahonoora) 669^{10} 1653^{6} 3558^{7} 3749^{20} 4151^{9} **>60f<**

Mystic Hill 4 b c Shirley Heights-Nuryana (Nureyev (USA)) 1610^{3} 1853^{12} 2768^{3} (3107) 3836^{8} 4031^{7} **>97f<**

Mystic Knight 2 b c Caerleon (USA)-Nuryana (Nureyev (USA)) 2846^{6} 3672^{3} (3883) (4107) **>90+f<**

Mystic Lure 3 b f Green Desert (USA)-Splendid Girl (USA) (Golden Eagle) 1846^{4} 2576^{7} 2787^{4} **>76f<**

Mystic Memory 6 b m Ela-Mana-Mou-Mountain Memory (High Top) 751^{10} **>79f<**

Mystic Tempo (USA) 2 ch f El Gran Senor (USA)-Doubling Time (USA) (Timeless Moment (USA)) 970^{2} (1525) 2424^{3} 2674^{9} 4144^{5} *4294^{7}* **>56a 79f<**

Mystic Times 2 b f Timeless Times (USA)-Chikala (Pitskelly) 1413^{4} 1579^{7} 2542^{5} 2998^{2} 3160^{10} (3417) 3623^{17} **>60f<**

Mystique Smile 2 ch f Music Boy-Jay Gee Ell (Vaigly Great) 570^{3} 819^{4} (1017) 1395a^{7} 2442^{10} 3369^{4} 3824^{9} 4097^{16} **>76f<**

Mystoski 3 b f Petoski-Miss Adventure (Adonijah) 1990^{10} *2630^{8}* 3092^{6} **>26a 47f<**

Mytilene (IRE) 4 b f Soviet Star (USA)-Dancing Meg (USA) (Marshua's Dancer (USA)) 1345^{W} **>100f<**

Myttons Mistake 2 b g Rambo Dancer (CAN)-Hi-Hunsley (Swing Easy (USA)) (1903) (2223) 2432^{4} 3375^{11} 3714^{11} 3947^{14} **>85f<**

N

Naawy 5 b h Reference Point-Strike Home (Be My Guest (USA)) 649^{14} 1449^{2} 1667^{4} 1965^{7} **>32a 43f<**

Nabhaan (IRE) 2 b c In The Wings-Miss Gris (USA) (Hail the Pirates (USA)) 2005^{6} 2667^{4} (3503) 3701^{11} 4151^{12} **>90f<**

Nabjelsedr 5 b h Never so Bold-Klewraye (Lord Gayle (USA)) 548^{7} 780^{11} 1126^{18} 1472^{10} **>51f<**

Nador 2 ch c Rainbow Quest (USA)-Nadma (USA) (Northern Dancer) (3857) 4159^{9} **>85f<**

Nadwaty (IRE) 3 b f Prince Sabo-Faisalah (Gay Mecene (USA)) *197^{3} 236^{3} 392^{8} (420)* 754^{3} *1032^{10}* 1342^{3} *1566^{7}* 1660^{5} 1847^{10} *3522^{5}* 3783^{11} 4113^{14} **>40a 49f<**

Nafta 3 b c Music Boy-Single Bid (Auction Ring (USA)) 524^{10} 613^{5} 722^{7} 966^{8} 1377^{9} *3734^{12}* **>54a 67f<**

Naga (ITY) 3 b c Welnor-Nagalist (Brook) (3039a) **>100+f<**

Nagnagnag (IRE) 3 b f Red Sunset-Rubina Park 563^{11} 959^{5} 1138^{10} (1639) 2214a^{2} 2897a^{6} 3579a^{3} 3813^{23} 3932^{9} 4065^{5} **>104df<**

Nahla 5 b m Wassl-Bassita (Bustino) 1898^{5}

Nahri (USA) 4 ch c Riverman (USA)-Welden (USA) (Danzig (USA)) *45^{2} 295^{2}* 556^{9} 3435^{9} 3627^{15} **>68a 58f<**

Naissant 2 b f Shaadi (USA)-Nophe (USA) (Super Concorde (USA)) 1142^{4} 1384^{4} 2106^{6} 2675^{2} 3185^{5} 3763^{4} **>82f<**

Najeb (USA) 6 b h Chief's Crown (USA)-Modiste (USA) (Sir Ivor) 1965^{4} **>31a 38f<**

Najiya 2 b f Nashwan (USA)-The Perfect Life (IRE) (Try My Best (USA)) 2351^{3} (2934) (3452) 3866^{3} **>98f<**

Najmat Alshemaal (IRE) 3 b f Dancing Brave (USA)-Noretta (GER) (Cortez (GER)) 997^{3} 2547^{2} 2944^{3} (3338) 3549^{5} 3716^{6} **>105df<**

Najm Mubeen (IRE) 2 b c Last Tycoon-Ah Ya Zein (Artaius (USA)) (3672) 3925^{7} **>85f<**

Naked Emperor 2 b g Dominion Royale-Torville Gold (Aragon) 4161^{16} **>57f<**

Naked Welcome 3 ch c Most Welcome-Stripanoora

(Ahonoora) 1839^{4} (2457) 2738^{11} 3458^{3} 3945^{33} (4076) 4323^{4} **>110f<**

Nakhal 2 b c Puissance-Rambadale (Vaigly Great) 2767^{6} 3652^{4} 4221^{8} **>73f<**

Nakita 4 ch f Efisio-Ra Ra (Lord Gayle (USA)) 548^{3} *627*^{9} 790^{6} 976^{6} 1092^{12} 1291^{8} 1516^{8} 1692^{11} *2073*^{10} 2685^{7} *2923*^{15} **>53a 58f<**

Nameless 2 ch f Doc Marten-Opuntia (Rousillon (USA)) *604*^{2} *770*^{3} *(834)* *1077*^{6} *1632*^{2} 1810^{3} 1989^{2} *(2146)* 2281^{3} 2826^{5} 3651^{11} *4294*^{10} **>59a 59f<**

Name of Our Father (USA) 2 b c Northern Baby (CAN)-Ten Hail Marys (USA) (Halo (USA)) 3888^{4} 4073^{2} 4210^{8} **>76f<**

Name That Tune 3 ch f Fayruz-Gandoorah (Record Token) 502^{16} 522^{14} 1445^{6} *2627*^{7} 2858^{5} **>31a 49f<**

Name the Tune 4 b c Chief Singer-Try to Remember (Music Boy) 565^{4} 796^{4} 1106^{3} 1193^{2} 1304^{2} 1489^{4} 1765^{4} (2060) 2120^{3} (2570) 2935^{11} (3236) 3551^{10} 3717^{17} 4033^{23} 4197^{5} **>62da 91f<**

Nanny Doon 3 ch f Dominion-Sea Charm (Julio Mariner) *5*^{9} *98*^{7} **>17a f<**

Nanton Point (USA) 3 b c Darshaan-Migiyas (Kings Lake (USA)) 762^{14} 1093^{17} 1529^{9} (1986) (2177) (2355) (2374) 3351^{2} 3682^{4} 4036^{8} 4118^{2} **>88f<**

Napier Star 2 b f Inca Chief (USA)-America Star (Norwick (USA)) 3763^{23}

Napoleon's Law 3 b g Sharpo-Test Case 761^{14} 963^{9} 1846^{5} **>48f<**

Napoleon's Return 2 gr c Daring March-Miss Colenca (Petong) 943^{5} 1652^{4} 1977^{5} 2354^{2} 2541^{5} 3379^{5} 3612^{10} 3856^{4} (3975) 4111^{7} *4273*^{6} **>54a 66f<**

Napoleon Star (IRE) 4 ch g Mulhollande (USA)-Lady Portobello (Porto Bello) 765^{3} 949^{7} 1057^{5} 1411^{8} 1648^{4} 1815^{2} 2079^{5} 2764^{24} 3457^{4} 3629^{13} 3771^{11} 4041^{17} **>63da 72f<**

Narazyyani (FR) 3 b c Zayyani-Nara Queen (Emerson) (488a)

Narbonne 4 b g Rousillon (USA)-Historical Fact (Reform) 1148^{3} 1244^{8} 1651^{6} 1811^{2} 1911^{4} **>64f<**

Nardus 2 ch c Mujtahid (USA)-Al Najah (USA) (Topsider (USA)) 3536^{6} 3989^{14} **>64f<**

Naseem Alsahar 2 ch f Nashwan (USA)-El Fabulous (FR) (Fabulous Dancer (USA)) 4190^{2} **>76f<**

Nashaat (USA) 7 b h El Gran Senor (USA)-Absentia (USA) (Raise A Cup (USA)) 1052^{2} 1183^{4} 1626^{5} 2446^{8} 2994^{8} 3885^{7} (4060) (4240) **>74a 74f<**

Nashcash (IRE) 2 ch c Nashamaa-Six Penny Express (Bay Express) 3691a^{3} **>93f<**

Nashotah 3 ch f Nashwan (USA)-Haiati (USA) (Alydar (USA)) 1136^{4} 1755^{2} **>82f<**

Nash Terrace (IRE) 3 ch c Nashwan (USA)-Gay Hellene (Ela-Mana-Mou) 711^{3} 1127^{2} 1852^{8} 3728^{5} 3932^{2} 4069^{3} **>109f<**

Nashwanah 3 ch f Nashwan (USA)-Sharpina (Sharpen Up) 1270^{5} 1717^{11} **>62f<**

Nasrudin (USA) 2 b c Nureyev (USA)-Sunshine O'My Life (USA) (Graustark) 3881^{6} 4155^{2} **>68f<**

Natal Ridge 2 b c Indian Ridge-Song Grove 4210^{5} 4314^{15} **>55f<**

Natatari (IRE) 2 ch f Roi Danzig (USA)-Little Me (Connaught) 1336^{2} 3988^{14} 4148^{11} **>54f<**

National Grid 3 b c Warning-Current Raiser (Filiberto (USA)) 942^{6} **>65f<**

Natural Key 2 ch f Safawan-No Sharps Or Flats (USA) (Sharpen Up) 1536^{4} (1877) (2153) 2399^{2} 2424^{2} 3064^{10} 3670^{8} 3714^{8} **>74f<**

Natural Path 4 b f Governor General-Cuba Libre (Rum (USA)) 4275^{19} **>49f<**

Nautical Jewel 3 b g Handsome Sailor-Kopjes (Bay Express) *766*^{2} 882^{6} 1124^{17} *1568*^{2} 1911^{5} 2250^{3} 2503^{6} *2960*^{2} *3526*^{8} 3875^{5} **>58a 61f<**

Nautical Pet (IRE) 3 b c Petorius-Sea Mistress (Habitat) 803a^{2} (1233a) 1848^{7} **>111f<**

Nautiker (GER) 4 c 4094a^{9} **>99f<**

Naval Gazer (IRE) 2 b f Sadler's Wells (USA)-Naval Light (USA) (Majestic Light (USA)) (3955) **>72+f<**

Naval Hunter (USA) 2 ch c Jade Hunter (USA)-Navy Light (USA) (Polish Navy (USA)) 3663^{19} 4221^{7} **>48f<**

Navigate (USA) 2 ch c Diesis-Libras Shiningstar (USA) 617^{13} 683^{5} 1592^{2} 1752^{4} **>74f<**

Nawaasi 3 b f Green Desert (USA)-Mountain Memory (High Top) 1000^{2} (1701) 2679^{3} 3298^{3} 3964^{21} 4145^{17} **>78f<**

Nawar (FR) 5 b h Kahyasi-Nabita (FR) (Akarad (FR)) 958^{6} 1171^{6} 1479^{5} 1840^{12} 2284^{8} 2688^{5} **>91f<**

Neapolitano (GER) 3 b c Orfano-Nagaika (Chief) 902a^{2} **>95f<**

Nearly Honest 7 ch m Nearly A Hand-Miss Saddler (St Paddy) *158*^{10} **>25a 47f<**

Nebrangus (IRE) 3 ch c Nashamaa-Choral Park (Music Boy) 875^{6} 1433^{12} *1569*^{12} 2582^{13} 2927^{6} 3099^{16} 3747^{15} **>24f<**

Nec Plus Ultra (FR) 4 b c Kendor (FR)-Quintefolle (FR) (Luthier (FR)) (2558a) 3042a^{9} 3795a^{3} 4016a^{3} **>118f<**

Ned Al Sheeba 2 b c Taufan (USA)-Bold Polly (Bold Lad (IRE)) *1454*^{4} 1781^{3} (2182) 2779^{5} 3714^{13} 3956^{5} **>59a 82f<**

Ned's Bonanza 6 b h Green Ruby (USA)-Miss Display (Touch Paper) 723^{3} 926^{4} 1151^{3} 1193^{12} 1441^{4} 1461^{3} 1689^{11} (2252) 2326^{6} 2533^{9} (2758) 2930^{6} 3230^{9} 3418^{6} 3667^{20} 3878^{14} **>77f<**

Ned's Contessa (IRE) 2 ch f Persian Heights-Beechwood (USA) (Blushing Groom (FR)) 595^{5} 699^{9} 1665^{7} *2075*^{9} 2251^{7} 2516^{5} 2732^{2} 3353^{3} 3533^{10} 3721^{3} **>6a 53f<**

Needham Star (USA) 2 ch f Mt Livermore (USA)-Passing Gull (USA) (Arctic Tern (USA)) 1928^{4} 2442^{2} 3692a^{8} 4084^{15} 4203^{3} **>92f<**

Needle Gun (IRE) 5 b or br h Sure Blade (USA)-Lucayan Princess (High Line) 1836^{3} 2323^{6} (2891a) 3143^{4} 3690a^{5} **>121f<**

Needle Knot (IRE) 2 b c Don't Forget Me-Needlewoman (Moorestyle) 1652^{9} 1841^{3} 2192^{6} 4081^{9} 4263^{5} **>63f<**

Needle Match 2 ch c Royal Academy (USA)-Miss Tatting (USA) (Miswaki (USA)) 4255^{8} **>39f<**

Needwood Epic 2 b f Midyan (USA)-Epure (Bellypha) 2934^{5} 3397^{7} 3620^{6} **>70f<**

Needwood Fantasy 2 b f Rolfe (USA)-Needwood Nymph (Bold Owl) 2666^{5} 3643^{10} **>35f<**

Needwood Limelight 2 b c Rolfe (USA)-Lime Brook (Rapid River) 3720^{9} **>43f<**

Needwood Newt 3 ch f Rolfe (USA)-Lime Brook (Rapid River) *54*^{4} *118*^{5} *258*^{8} *314*^{5} **>45a 48f<**

Need You Badly 2 b f Robellino (USA)-Persian Tapestry

(Tap On Wood) 3892^{4} 4109^{4} 4212^{11} **>65f<**

Negative Equity 3 ch c Be My Chief (USA)-Rather Romantic (CAN) (Verbatim (USA)) 1093^{16} 1407^{2} 1696^{12} *1881^{12}* 2026^{7} 2682^{2} 3154^{5} **>21a 75df<**

Neither Nor 6 ch m Norwick (USA)-Leap in Time (Dance In Time (CAN)) 439^{22} 870^{13} 1362^{4} (1588) 1728^{6} **>101f<**

Nellie North 2 b f Northern State (USA)-Kimble Princess (Kala Shikari) 1123^{5} 1497^{2} 1779^{3} 2000^{3} (2487) 2740^{6} 3289^{7} 3766^{4} 4206^{8} **>80f<**

Nellyssia (FR) 3 b f Always Fair (USA)-Hecalene (FR) *1939^{11}* 2296^{5} 2650^{4} **>28a 58f<**

Nereus 2 b c Shareef Dancer (USA)-Lady of the Sea (Mill Reef (USA)) 3089^{11} **>57f<**

Nero Kris 3 ch c Kris-What A Pity (Blakeney) *564^{7}* 730^{8} 936^{5} 3761^{5} 3974^{7} 4136^{15} **>71f<**

Nessun Doro 3 b c Hallgate-Bamdoro (Cavo Doro) 1514^{7} *1761^{2}* 2361^{6} 3889^{12} 4051^{4} **>65a 71f<**

Neuwest (USA) 3 b c Gone West (USA)-White Mischief (Dance In Time (CAN)) 3829^{3} (4150) **>87f<**

Neverending (USA) 3 ch f Sabona (USA)-Play On And On (USA) (Stop The Music (USA)) 775^{6} 1130^{5} 1639^{9} 1862^{2} (3929) **>95f<**

Never Explain (IRE) 3 b f Fairy King (USA)-Purchasepaperchase (Young Generation) 1476^{7} 2446^{5} (2929) 3552^{11} 4319^{W} **>85f<**

Neverneyev (USA) 5 b h Nureyev (USA)-River Rose (FR) 608a^{2} 4178a^{5} **>121f<**

Never Say so 3 ch f Prince Sabo-So Rewarding (Never so Bold) 1040^{3} 1302^{4} 1559^{5} 2084^{12} 3649^{6} 3800^{20} **>37a 46f<**

Never So Fit 4 b g Never so Bold-Darine (Nonoalco (USA)) 539^{10} 593^{4} 1720^{4} 3183^{7} **>53f<**

Never so Rite (IRE) 3 b f Nordico (USA)-Nephrite (Godswalk (USA)) *289^{2} 384^{3} 448^{5}* 1534^{3} 1735^{2} (1811) 2033^{2} 2451^{3} 2831^{3} 3151^{2} 3383^{3} 3770^{12} **>54a 66f<**

Never so True 4 b f Never so Bold-Cottage Pie (Kalamoun) 578^{7} 642^{11} 876^{8} 990^{3} 1583^{6} 1720^{2} 2122^{5} 2232^{4} 2401^{3} (2874) 3118^{2} 3296^{4} 3410^{4} **>37da 54f<**

Never Such Bliss 3 b f Shavian-Donna Bold (Never so Bold) 522^{7} 772^{4} 1040^{2} 1453^{7} 1677^{11} 3972^{6} 4193^{7} **>61f<**

Never Think Twice 2 b c Never so Bold-Hope and Glory (USA) (Well Decorated (USA)) 561^{4} 1177^{3} 2131^{5} 2483^{6} 3133^{9} 3378^{2} 3570^{2} **>73f<**

Never Time (IRE) 3 b c Simply Great (FR)-Islet Time (Burslem) *33^{6} 255^{10}* 431^{12} 748^{13} 948^{9} 1285^{7} 1647^{3} 1824^{8} 3111^{3} 3464^{4} 3722^{6} 3805^{9} 4114^{3} **>29a 62f<**

New Albion (USA) 4 b or br c Pleasant Colony (USA)-Grand Bonheur (USA) (Blushing Groom (FR)) 1260^{7} 1661^{8} **>78f<**

New Broom (IRE) 3 b f Brush Aside (USA)-Qurrat Al Ain (Wolver Hollow) 3421^{4} 3799^{13} **>55f<**

Newbury Coat 5 b g Chilibang-Deanta in Eirinn (Red Sunset) (2038a) *3524^{3}* 3554^{11} *4125^{5} 4272^{11}* **>51a 60f<**

New Capricorn (USA) 5 ch h Green Forest (USA)-Size Six (USA) (Caerleon (USA)) 665^{13} 870^{22} 1143^{11} 1728^{7} 2117^{10} **>102f<**

New Century (USA) 3 gr c Manila (USA)-Casessa (USA) (Caro) 614^{5} 941^{7} 3924^{11} 3991^{6} 4236^{13} **>94f<**

New College 5 b h Niniski-Cut Loose (High Top) 4347a^{3} **>87f<**

Newgate Bubbles 4 b f Hubbly Bubbly (USA)-Streets Ahead (Ovid) 818^{15} 1149^{10} **>14?f<**

Newgate Hush 3 ch f Kind of Hush-Mummys Colleen 3722^{11} 3805^{15} 4232^{9} **>18f<**

New Herald 6 b h Heraldiste-New Mary (New Model) 1004a^{3} **>117f<**

New Herald (IRE) 6 b h Heraldiste-New Mary (New Model) 1577a^{3} 4093a^{8} **>108f<**

Newington Butts (IRE) 5 br m Dowsing (USA)-Cloud Nine *41^{9} 93^{12} 298^{3} 371^{4}* 450^{12} **>48a 45f<**

New Inn 4 b c Petoski-Pitroyal (Pitskelly) *246^{8} 325^{9}* 556^{11} (737) 866^{4} 1578^{3} 2186^{5} 3229^{7} 3641^{9} 4140^{8} **>72da 57f<**

Newlands Corner 2 b f Forzando-Nice Lady (Connaught) 3733^{15} 3915^{12} 4216^{10} **>48f<**

Newport Knight 4 ch c Bairn (USA)-Clara Barton (Youth (USA)) 2269^{3} 2682^{6} (3083) 3571^{5} 3898^{3} **>73f<**

New Reputation 4 b c Law Society (USA)-Reputation (Tower Walk) 998^{4} 1300^{2} (2352) 2799^{4} (3804) 4118^{P} **>103f<**

New Technique (FR) 2 br f Formidable (USA)-Dolly Bea Sweet (USA) (Super Concorde (USA)) 1977^{19}

Next Going (IRE) 3 b f Doulab-Regal Promise (Pitskelly) (3043a) **>84f<**

Nez Carrera 4 ch g Aragon-New Ribbons *6^{10} 32^{11}* **>36f<**

Nickitoto 3 gr f Mtoto-Nicholas Grey 950^{7} 1691^{11} 2341^{2} (2969) 3299^{2} **>72f<**

Nick the Biscuit 4 b g Nicholas Bill-Maryland Cookie (USA) (Bold Hour) *66^{10} 104^{2}* **>65a 69f<**

Nicky's Feelings 3 b f Feelings (FR)-Polly Potter (Pollerton) 1420^{6} 1819^{7} 2306^{5} **>33f<**

Nicolotte 4 b c Night Shift (USA)-Nicoletta 666^{4} 827^{2} 1385^{3} (1835) 2689^{4} 3199a^{7} (4093a) **>128f<**

Nicosie (USA) 3 c 1115a^{6} **>97f<**

Nigelschinapalace 6 b g Comrade in Arms-Ergo (Song) *68^{4} 103^{8}* 503^{8} *(588) 1075^{10} 1567^{7}* **>44a 10f<**

Nigel's Lad (IRE) 3 b g Dominion Royale-Back To Earth (FR) (Vayrann) *47^{3} (59) 151^{2} (189) 301^{4}* 538^{12} 614^{2} (736) 774^{3} (909) *1211^{6}* (1269) 2348^{11} 2616^{8} 2780^{5} 3101^{4} 3276^{2} 3469^{6} 3840^{2} (3926) **>81a 93f<**

Niggle 3 b f Night Shift (USA)-Enchanted 916^{2} 1473^{5} **>75f<**

Night Asset 6 b h Night Shift (USA)-Fine Asset (Hot Spark) 1050^{10} 1276^{2} (1429) 1700^{3} 1975^{P} **>59f<**

Night City 4 b c Kris-Night Secret (Nijinsky (CAN)) 1188^{4} 1851^{9} 2369^{8} 2703^{10} 3030^{2} 3594^{2} 3945^{15} (4147) **>106f<**

Night Dance 3 ch c Weldnaas (USA)-Shift Over (USA) (Night Shift (USA)) 618^{11} 829^{12} 1593^{2} 1839^{32} (2240) 2446^{3} 2669^{9} 3109^{2} (3813) (4035) 4267^{16} **>107f<**

Night Edition 5 b h Night Shift (USA)-New Chant (CAN) (New Providence) *73^{2} 100^{4} 158^{4} 4293^{7}* 4332^{14} **>44a 54f<**

Night Excellence 3 b c Night Shift (USA)-Briar Creek (Busted) *2141^{8}* **>29a 33f<**

Night Fantasy (IRE) 7 br m King of Clubs-Maria Renata (Jaazeiro (USA)) *1571^{1} 175^{6}* **>35a f<**

Night Flare (FR) 3 ch c Night Shift (USA)-Gold Flair (Tap On Wood) 715^{W} 2553^{4} 3016^{13} 3559^{4} 3921^{9} **>81f<**

Night Harmony (IRE) 2 ch c Digamist (USA)-Quaver (Song) 3604^{14} 3733^{21} 4132^{4} **>44f<**

Night Hero (USA) 3 ch c Mr Prospector (USA)-Lisaleen

(USA) (Northern Dancer) 1145^{4} 1365^{3} **>103f<**

Night in a Million 4 br g Night Shift (USA)-Ridalia *1571^{2}* 1693^{10} **>68a 66f<**

Night of Glass 2 b g Mazilier (USA)-Donna Elvira (Chief Singer) 1781^{7} 3371^{13} 4058^{11} **>48f<**

Night Parade (USA) 2 b c Rory's Jester (AUS)-Nocturnal Song (USA) (Northern Dancer) 683^{2} (996) 1868^{7} 2347^{9} 2740^{7} **>98f<**

Nightscene (IRE) 3 b f Scenic-Internet (Tender King) 957^{7} 1128^{10} 1473^{8} 1735^{4} **>68f<**

Night Silence 2 ch c Generous (IRE)-Exclusive Life (USA) (Exclusive Native (USA)) 4058^{13} 4155^{9} 4210^{6} **>50f<**

Night Time 3 b c Night Shift (USA)-Gathering Place (USA) (Hawaii) 783^{2} 1340^{7} 2314^{8} 2532^{3} 2781^{4} 3363^{4} 3634^{12} **>70f<**

Night Watch (USA) 2 b c Night Shift (USA)-Christchurch (FR) 2283^{4} 2741^{4} (3437) 3631^{4} (3782) **>94+f<**

Night Wink (USA) 3 ch c Rahy (USA)-Lady in White (Shareef Dancer (USA)) 1180^{17} 1524^{9} 3392^{4} 3431^{2} 3645^{11} 3920^{7} (4049) 4115^{3} (4234) 4268^{8} **>89f<**

Nijo 4 b c Top Ville-Nibabu (FR) (Nishapour (FR)) 1706a^{4} 1835^{2} 2646^{5} 3067^{2} 3562^{2} **>115f<**

Nikita's Star (IRE) 2 ch c Soviet Lad (USA)-Sally Chase (Sallust) 825^{7} 2846^{4} 3025^{7} 3540^{5} 3711^{14} 4081^{3} 4208^{12} **>76f<**

Niknaks Nephew 3 br c Tragic Role (USA)-Bubulina (Dunphy) 942^{8} 1173^{4} 1514^{16} 2768^{4} 3572^{10} 3769^{7} **>79f<**

Nilgiri Hills (IRE) 2 ch c Indian Ridge-Our Resolution (Caerleon (USA)) 1318^{3} 1992^{2} 2542^{3} 3749^{2} 3990^{2} **>79f<**

Nimble Boy (USA) 3 b g Arctic Tern (USA)-Blue Dance (Green Dancer) 1229a^{3}

Nimble Mind (USA) 3 ch f Lyphard-Nimble Folly (Cyane) 899a^{3} **>85?f<**

Nina From Pasadena 2 ch f Clantime-Abalone 1054^{6} 1481^{9} **>47f<**

Nineacres 4 b g Sayf El Arab (USA)-Mayor (Laxton) *6^{9} 39^{6} 69^{3} (102) 154^{5} 590^{10}* 639^{5} 688^{8} 926^{13} 994^{3} *3522^{6} 3739^{13}* **>62a 53f<**

Nine Barrow Down (IRE) 3 b c Danehill (USA)-Rising Spirits (Cure The Blues (USA)) 663^{7} (929) 1524^{6} 1872^{14} 3015^{4} 3343^{5} **>80f<**

Ninette (USA) 3 b f Alleged (USA)-Stellaria (USA) (Roberto (USA)) (2825) 3278^{2} 3932^{3} 4104^{4} **>106f<**

Ninety-Five 3 ch f Superpower-Vanishing Trick (Silly Season) 904^{2} 1181^{6} 1450^{2} 2527^{2} *3524^{4}* 3783^{6} 3992^{8} **>65f<**

Ninia (USA) 3 ch f Affirmed (USA)-Lajna (Be My Guest (USA)) *1939^{3}* (2020) 2181^{2} (2607) 2694^{4} (2952) (3305) (3506) 3607^{10} 3966^{3} 4116^{12} **>52a 80df<**

Ninotchka (USA) 2 b f Nijinsky (CAN)-Puget Sound (High Top) 4216^{5} **>70f<**

Nippers Boy 4 ch g Little Wolf-Just Bluffing (Green Shoon) 3282^{16}

Nirvana Prince 6 ch g Celestial Storm (USA)-Princess Sunshine (Busted) *245^{2}* **>72a f<**

Nisya 3 ch f Risk Me (FR)-Lompoa (Lomond (USA)) 522^{12} *768^{6}* **>28f<**

Nita's Choice 5 b m Valiyar-What's the Matter (High Top) 1128^{17} 1501^{4} *1951^{11}* 2246^{13} 2557^{6} **>37f<**

Nite-Owl Dancer 3 b f Robellino (USA)-Lady Tap (Red Sunset) *210^{3} 256^{2} 315^{5} 390^{3}* 746^{2} 1471^{4} 1559^{2} 2879^{2} (2916) 3166^{3} 3597^{11} **>51a 69f<**

Niteowl Raider (IRE) 2 ch c Standaan (FR)-Havana Moon (Ela-Mana-Mou) 2128^{7} 3300^{3} 4230^{5} **>58f<**

Nivasha 3 b f Shavian-Rheinza (Rheingold) 837^{3} 1379^{6} 1725^{5} *1950^{3}* 3876^{7} 4332^{13} **>39a 52f<**

Nizaal (USA) 4 ch c Diesis-Shicklah (USA) (The Minstrel (CAN)) 4038^{22} 4171^{20} 4319^{19} **>61f<**

Nkapen Rocks (SPA) 2 b c Risk Me (FR)-Debutina Park (Averof) 1652^{5} *2633^{4}* 3988^{7} **>49a 52f<**

No Animosity (IRE) 2 ch c Ajraas (USA)-Arctic Ford (FR) (Arctic Tern (USA)) (3587a) 4174a^{4} **>96f<**

Nobby Barnes 6 b h Nordance (USA)-Loving Doll (Godswalk (USA)) 839^{14} 1027^{4} 1081^{4} 1250^{12} 1438^{6} 1649^{3} 1855^{6} 2064^{4} 2276^{6} 2375^{3} 2668^{2} 2906^{3} 3101^{6} 3264^{3} 3447^{4} 4038^{4} 4234^{8} *4340^{9}* **>59a 52f<**

Nobby North 3 b g Northern State (USA)-One Degree (Crooner) 1514^{13} 2316^{4} 2790^{8} 3091^{7} 3572^{7} 3769^{10} **>67f<**

Noble Ballerina (USA) 3 b f Green Dancer (USA)-Noble Devorcee (USA) (Vaguely Noble) *2494^{4} 2921^{5} 3073^{9} 3527^{7}* 3669^{11} 3986^{18} **>49a 36f<**

Noble Canonire 3 b f Gunner B-Lucky Candy (Lucky Wednesday) *256^{12} 376^{7}* 3537^{8} 3747^{6} **>5a 51f<**

Noble Colours 2 b g Distinctly North (USA)-Kentucky Tears (USA) (Cougar (CHI)) 1670^{18} *2633^{7}* **>25a 25f<**

Noble Kingdom 3 b c Pharly (FR)-Certain Story (Known Fact (USA)) 662^{2} 914^{4} **>85f<**

Noblely (USA) 8 b g Lyphard (USA)-Nonoalco (USA) *195^{8}* 1716^{3} **>79da 74f<**

Noble Neptune 3 b c Governor General-Calibina *390^{4}* 813^{11} 1512^{5} (2778) 3408^{6} 3802^{8} 4116^{17} 4229^{6} **>47a 68f<**

Noble Rose (IRE) 4 b f Caerleon (USA)-Noble Lily (USA) (Vaguely Noble) 2272^{4} 3161^{7} (3549) 4009a^{4} **>115f<**

Noble Society 7 b h Law Society (USA)-Be Noble (Vaguely Noble) 1737^{4} **>35a 41f<**

Noble Spirit (IRE) 4 b g Cyrano de Bergerac-Grecian Sky (African Sky) *1033^{11}* 1438^{9} **>47a 28f<**

Noble Sprinter (IRE) 3 b c The Noble Player (USA)-Daybreaker (Thatching) 694^{7} 3654^{2} 3802^{3} 4038^{3} 4267^{6} **>87f<**

No Cliches 2 ch c Risk Me (FR)-Always on a Sunday (Star Appeal) 1246^{5} 1726^{9} 2408^{6} 3157^{6} (3546) **>79f<**

No Comebacks 7 b m Last Tycoon-Dead End (Bold Lad (IRE)) 1596^{10} 1808^{11} (2798) 3211^{4} 3700^{9} 3716^{4} 3852^{10} 4138^{8} 4259^{21} 4289^{5} **>75f<**

No Dancer (GER) 4 b c Shareef Dancer-Nice Gold (Pentathlon) 2567a^{3} 3798a^{6} **>111f<**

Noeprob (USA) 5 b m Majestic Shore (USA)-Heat Haze (USA) (Jungle Savage (USA)) 450^{11} 534^{9} 1202^{6} 1426^{4} 1644^{4} 1974^{4} (2081) **>30a 51f<**

No Extras (IRE) 5 b g Efisio-Parkland Rose (Sweet Candy (VEN)) 870^{20} 1241^{2} 1614^{11} 1895^{16} 2288^{14} 2764^{6} 3085^{5} (3359) 3615^{4} 3717^{2} 3813^{8} 4033^{3} 4160^{7} **>109f<**

No Hiding Place 2 ch c Nabeel Dancer (USA)-Blushing Pink (USA) (Blushing Groom (FR)) 3340^{17} **>43f<**

Noir Esprit 2 br c Prince Daniel (USA)-Danse D'Esprit (Lidhame) 2667^{8} 2995^{5} 3463^{11} 3780^{8} 3882^{6} **>57f<**

Nomadic Dancer (IRE) 3 b f Nabeel Dancer (USA)-Loveshine (USA) (Gallant Romeo (USA)) *146^{4} 237^{8} 274^{5}*

55^{2} 1125^{9} 1445^{7} 1750^{7} 2054^{5} 3205^{6} **>51a 51f<**

Nomogram 4 b g Nomination-Crosby Triangle (Windjammer (USA)) *22^{9}* **>8a 44f<**

No Monkey Nuts 2 ch g Clantime-Portvally (Import) (2230) 2423^{4} (3018) (3160) 3375^{9} 3990^{4} 4055^{2} 4317^{6} **>84f<**

No More Hassle (IRE) 2 ch g Magical Wonder (USA)-Friendly Ann (Artaius (USA)) 2995^{10} 3827^{9} 3968^{12} 4075^{14} 4285^{9} **>52f<**

Nonconformist (IRE) 2 ch g Nashamaa-Sperrin Mist (Camden Town) 2251^{6} 2715^{5} **>46f<**

Non Dimenticar Me (IRE) 3 b f Don't Forget Me-Amboselli (Raga Navarro (ITY)) (2527) 2836^{4} 2968^{4} 3365^{2} 3750^{13} **>71f<**

Nonios (IRE) 4 b c Nashamaa-Bosquet 2123^{8} 2544^{5} 3395^{6} **>61a 86df<**

Nononito (FR) 4 b c Nikos-Feuille D'Automne (FR) (Crystal Palace (FR)) 607a^{6} (1001a) 1239a^{2} 2890a^{5} 3329a^{2} 4008a^{3} **>122f<**

Non Vintage (IRE) 4 ch g Shy Groom (USA)-Great Alexandra (Runnett) *35^{5} 52^{3} 91^{7}* 2824^{5} 2981^{4} 3162^{19} 3274^{2} 3445^{12} 3659^{17} 3759^{3} 4189^{2} 4326^{4} **>63a 70f<**

Noon Air 4 b f Dark Harmony-Pride of Ayr (Recoil) *223^{6} 394^{13}*

Noonday Gun (IRE) 3 b c Bluebird (USA)-Soxoph (Hotfoot) 484^{3} 678^{F} **>69f<**

Noon (IRE) 2 b br f Treasure Kay-Tiempo (King of Spain) 1829^{4} 2204^{8} 4132^{7} **>39f<**

Noor El Houdah (IRE) 3 b f Fayruz-Moira My Girl (Henbit (USA)) *405^{8}* (482) 674^{7} *1033^{5}* 1263^{7} *1633^{5} 1883^{13}* 3624^{19} 3972^{16} **>56a 55f<**

Noosa (IRE) 3 b f Petorius-Miss Java (Persian Bold) *196^{8}* 581^{2} 861^{3} 1433^{11} 3467^{F} **>39a 75f<**

No Pattern 3 ch c Rock City-Sunfleet (Red Sunset) *(99) 176^{2} 250^{2}* 618^{4} 857^{4} 2199^{5} (2406) 3130^{4} 3959^{3} 4135^{4} **>88a 84f<**

Nordan Raider 7 ch m Domynsky-Vikris (Viking (USA)) *(93)* 1604^{6} *1953^{3}* 2187^{3} 3726^{12} 3830^{W} **>78a 64f<**

Nordansk 6 ch h Nordance (USA)-Free on Board (Free State) 3889^{16} **>23f<**

Nordesta (IRE) 3 b f Nordico (USA)-Braconda 1165^{13} 1660^{14} 1936^{5} 2239^{10} **>70f<**

Nordic Breeze (IRE) 3 b or br c Nordico (USA)-Baby Clair 435^{7} 613^{8} (1465) 1904^{2} 2003^{2} 2531^{3} 2778^{2} 2928^{2} 3802^{17} **>83f<**

Nordic Crown (IRE) 4 b f Nordico (USA)-Fit The Halo (Dance In Time (CAN)) 1349^{9} 1999^{4} **>45f<**

Nordic Doll (IRE) 3 ch f Royal Academy (USA)-Maculatus (USA) (Sharpen Up) (722) 911^{2} 1165^{12} 1474^{6} 2103^{10} 2376^{3} 2788^{7} 4194^{3} *4297^{11}* **>45a 77f<**

Nordic Mine (IRE) 5 b g Nordico (USA)-Tower Belle (Tower Walk) 1596^{6} *(3078)* 3710^{2} 4135^{7} **>53a 55f<**

Nordic Oak (IRE) 7 b g Nordico (USA)-Red Leaf (Carry Off) 609a^{3} **>101f<**

Nordico Princess 4 b f Nordico (USA)-Try Vickers (USA) (Fuzzbuster (USA)) *(177) 237^{5} 369^{2} 407^{2}* (452) (565) 1057^{3} 1376^{7} 3442^{17} 3748^{14} 3919^{13} 4165^{11} *4337^{7}* **>74a 58f<**

Nordinex (IRE) 3 b c Nordico (USA)-Debbie's Next (USA) (Arctic Tern (USA)) *(176) 360^{3}* (1693) 2103^{3} (2367) 2598^{5} 2941^{3} 3497^{3} 3973^{14} **>73a 86f<**

Nordisk Legend 3 b g Colmore Row-Nordic Rose (DEN) 3854^{6} **>45?f<**

Nord Lys (IRE) 4 b c Nordico (USA)-Beach Light (Bustino) *96^{16} 136^{11}* 578^{11} 818^{12} **>41f<**

Nordman Lass 3 b f Risk Me (FR)-Sundaysport Splash (Lord Gayle (USA)) 783^{9} 853^{15} 1094^{20} 1499^{14} 2137^{8} 2318^{14} **>43f<**

Nordoora (IRE) 6 b m Fayruz-African Cousin (Kampala) 2502^{16} 2879^{W} 3116^{12} **>64df<**

Nordross 7 b m Ardross-Noreena *1074^{6} 2072^{6} 2291^{10}* **>36a f<**

Norfolk Glory 3 ch c Weldnaas (USA)-Caviar Blini (What A Guest) *443^{8} 515^{8}* 1196^{6} 1447^{8} 2037^{11} 2171^{5} **>49a 67f<**

Norling (IRE) 5 ch g Nashamaa-Now Then (Sandford Lad) 1673^{8} 1832^{19} 2137^{11} 2448^{6} 3028^{3} 3139^{6} (3177) 3632^{W} 3874^{13} 4134^{14} 4215^{17} **>57df<**

Norman Prince (IRE) 3 b c Prince Rupert (FR)-Norme (FR) *513^{6}* **>54a 62f<**

Nornax Lad (USA) 7 b h Northern Baby (CAN)-Naxos (USA) (Big Spruce (USA)) 1058^{16} 1310^{7} 2733^{8} (2871) (3001) 3122^{2} **>74a 70f<**

Norsong 3 b c Northern State (USA)-Winsong Melody (Music Maestro) 1186^{13} 1515^{7} 2178^{5} (2602) 3095^{4} 3497^{9} 3654^{7} 3897^{12} **>60f<**

North Ardar 5 b h Ardar-Langwaite (Seaepic (USA)) 430^{19} 568^{5} 1378^{5} 1680^{2} (1844) (2159) 2663^{2} 2824^{2} 3189^{14} 3743^{4} *3951^{10}* **>63da 69f<**

Northern Ballet (IRE) 2 b f Sadler's Wells (USA)-Miranisa (Habitat) 2025^{7} **>40f<**

Northern Celadon (IRE) 4 b c Classic Secret (USA)-Exemplary *66^{3} 195^{7} 313^{4} 414^{8}* (503) *601^{6} 767^{2} 1087^{10} 1951^{5} 2291^{3} 2588^{2} 2922^{3} 3241^{11}* (3984) **>76a 75f<**

Northern Charmer 3 b g Charmer-Trading (Forlorn River) 613^{10} 908^{7} *1329^{5}* 4228^{8} **>30a 51f<**

Northern Chief 5 b h Chief Singer-Pacific Gull (USA) (Storm Bird (CAN)) *387^{12} 413^{8}* 505^{13} 672^{7} 1855^{11} 2310^{10} 2484^{8} 2733^{4} 3493^{12} **>37a 48f<**

Northern Clan 2 b c Clantime-Northern Line (Camden Town) 1063^{4} 1278^{4} 1356^{5} 1842^{10} 2914^{5} 3019^{10} 3749^{10} **>64f<**

Northern Emerald (USA) 5 b m Green Dancer (USA)-Tromphe de Naskra (USA) (Naskra (USA)) (3911a) **>116f<**

Northern Falcon 2 gr f Polar Falcon (USA)-Bishah (USA) (Balzac (USA)) 2666^{W} 3018^{8} 3306^{4} 3502^{7} 3721^{17} 4001^{10} **>62f<**

Northern Fan (IRE) 3 b c Lear Fan (USA)-Easy Romance (USA) (Northern Jove (CAN)) 585^{5} 907^{2} 3761^{2} 3974^{8} **>58a 79f<**

Northern Fleet 2 b c Slip Anchor-Kamkova (USA) (Northern Dancer) 4256^{4} **>88f<**

Northern Grey 3 gr c Puissance-Sharp Anne (Belfort (FR)) 1559^{7} *2071^{6} 2493^{6}* 2818^{3} 2997^{3} 3257^{2} 3508^{2} 3678^{U} 3800^{9} **>46a 54f<**

Northern Highlight 4 ch c Pharly (FR)-Unearthed (Electric) *3526^{3}* 3862^{14} **>51a 60f<**

Northern Judge 2 ch g Highest Honor (FR)-Nordica (Northfields (USA)) 4023^{8} 4155^{4} **>60f<**

Northern Kingdom (USA) 6 b h Graustark (USA)-Wonder Mar (USA) (Fire Dancer (USA)) 751^{4} 1295^{9} 1470^{3} 1826^{3} **>56f<**

Northern Law 3 gr c Law Society (USA)-Pharland (FR)

(Bellypha) 715^{7} 979^{7} 1490^{9} 2244^{4} 2520^{2} 2969^{W} (3052) (3355) 3425^{8} 3774^{6} **>82f<**

Northern Miracle (IRE) **2** b f Distinctly North (USA)-Danny's Miracle (Superlative) 4312^{18}

Northern Motto **2** b c Mtoto-Soulful (FR) (Zino) 3821^{11} 3967^{7} 4282^{9} **>55f<**

Northern Saga (IRE) **2** b c Distinctly North (USA)-Saga's Humour (Bustino) 849^{5} 3133^{7} 3386^{5} *3528^{5}* 3749^{16} 3858^{9} **>36a 37f<**

Northern Sky **2** b f North Col-Emma Wright (Skyliner) 3983^{16} 4045^{16} **>24f<**

Northern Soul (USA) **2** b c Tasso (USA)-Wajibird (USA) (Storm Bird (CAN)) 3994^{3} 4172^{2} 4320^{3} **>78f<**

Northern Spark **7** b h Trojan Fen-Heavenly Spark 789^{11} 1043^{2} (1433) 1666^{13} 2484^{3} 2698^{13} 2832^{15} 3467^{4} (4275) 4292^{4} **>58f<**

Northern Spruce (IRE) **3** ch g Astronef-Perle's Fashion (Sallust) 1092^{16} 1371^{11} 1659^{11} 1974^{22} 2134^{8} *2378^{9}* **>43f<**

Northern Spur (IRE) **4** b c Sadler's Wells (USA)-Fruition (Rheingold) 3576a^{10} (4307a) **>132f<**

Northern Spy (FR) **4** b g Comrade in Arms-Maple Sugar 3792a^{3} **>118f<**

Northern Trial (USA) **7** b h Far North (CAN)-Make An Attempt (USA) (Nashua) *414^{5} 471^{6}* **>42a f<**

Northern Trove (USA) **3** b c Northern Jove (CAN)-Herbivorous (USA) (Northern Jove (CAN)) 1150^{3} 1615^{5} 1947^{3} 2357^{2} 2518^{2} 2836^{3} 3169^{7} *3514^{10}* 4194^{18} 4284^{15} *4340^{16}* **>64f<**

Northern Union (CAN) **4** b c Alwasmi (USA)-Loving Cup (USA) (Big Spruce (USA)) 668^{9} (1661) 2559a^{B} **>88f<**

North Esk (USA) **6** ch h Apalachee (USA)-Six Dozen (USA) (What A Pleasure (USA)) 3455^{7} 3771^{10} 4170^{14} *4340^{8}* **>32a 63f<**

Northgate Raver **4** ch f Absalom-Real Party *233^{16}* 656^{10} 1677^{14} 2502^{17}

North Reef (IRE) **4** b c Danehill (USA)-Loreef (Main Reef) *(1980) (2407)* 2672^{9} **>79+a 81f<**

Northreel **4** ch g Scottish Reel-La Troienne (Henbit (USA)) 799a^{P} 2385a^{3}

North Star (IRE) **2** br c Distinctly North (USA)-King's Chase 1184^{14} 2534^{7} 4210^{11} **>54f<**

Northwise (IRE) **4** b f Northern Baby (CAN)-Infinite Wisdom (USA) (Sassafras (FR)) 2375^{9} 2955^{3} 3302^{8} **>50df<**

Norwegian Blue (IRE) **2** b c Mac's Imp (USA)-Opening Day (Day Is Done) 2029^{4} 2243^{5} 2704^{5} 3465^{2} 3699^{4} (3891) **>84f<**

Nose No Bounds (IRE) **2** b c Cyrano de Bergerac-Damezao (Alzao (USA)) 2453^{3} 3117^{3} *3525^{2} (3736)* 4001^{5} **>74a 74f<**

Nosey Native **2** b g Cyrano de Bergerac-Native Flair (Be My Native (USA)) 2467^{5} 3155^{2} 3752^{3} (4151) **>82f<**

Nosirrah **3** br f Rock City-Miss Alkie (Noalcoholic (FR)) 971^{8} 1124^{7} 1322^{11} 1498^{14} 1831^{9} 2451^{6} 2843^{11} **>52a 54f<**

No Speeches (IRE) **4** b c Last Tycoon-Wood Violet (USA) (Riverman (USA)) 634^{8} 935^{7} 1324^{8} 1757^{5} 2007^{7} 2310^{3} 3094^{5} 3238^{6} 3987^{9} 4028^{10} 4152^{2} *(4298)* **>63a 63df<**

Nostoi **2** b f Rock City-Norgabie (Northfields (USA)) (2852) 3228^{4} 3414^{3} 3516^{4} 3684^{5} 3956^{4} **>74f<**

No Submission (USA) **9** b h Melyno-Creeping Kate (USA) (Stop The Music (USA)) *30^{2} 94^{7} 117^{2} (211) 267^{2} (293) (336) (379) (399) 413^{2}* 493^{5} 738^{9} *767^{3} (1034)* 1286^{8} *1880^{5} 1951^{2} 2142^{3} (2291) 2588^{5} 2921^{4} 3241^{7}* 3825^{15} **>76a 74f<**

No Sympathy **2** ch f Ron's Victory (USA)-Ackcontent (USA) (Key To Content (USA)) 1163^{5} 1810^{5} 2047^{4} 2176^{4} *2382^{10}* 2838^{2} (3284) 3568^{12} **>16a 64f<**

Not for Sale **4** b f Hotfoot-Basic Bliss (Tumble Wind (USA)) *254^{5} 1762^{7}* **>31da 33f<**

Nothing Doing (IRE) **6** b g Sarab-Spoons (Orchestra) *35^{4} 178^{6} 260^{13} 288^{2} 346^{5} 514^{3} 833^{10} (1029)* 1694^{6} *2379^{8}* (2486) 3384^{13} 4135^{8} 4332^{2} **>44a 48f<**

Nothin' Leica Dane (AUS) **3** b c Danehill-Leica Pretender 4349a^{2}

Not in Doubt (USA) **6** b h Tom Rolfe-Trillionaire (USA) (Vaguely Noble) 661^{10} 869^{9} 1189^{10} **>94f<**

Not Quite Grey **2** gr c Absalom-Strawberry Song (Final Straw) 3436^{U} 3530^{6} 4172^{3} 4291^{5} **>69f<**

Not so Generous (IRE) **5** b m Fayruz-Ribero's Overture (Ribero) *70^{8}* **>55a 59f<**

Not Surprising (USA) **5** ch g Medieval Man (USA)-Tenderly Calling (USA) *4303a^{4}* **>123a f<**

Nottash (IRE) **3** ch f Royal Academy (USA)-Persian Polly (Persian Bold) 522^{3} 2708^{6} (3347) 3943^{29} **>78f<**

Not the Nadger **4** b g Aragon-Broken Accent (Busted) 503^{13} **>7a 55f<**

Nottonitejosephine **2** ch f Be My Chief (USA)-Josephine Gibney (High Top) 1627^{8} 2135^{8} 2526^{15} **>30f<**

Noufari (FR) **4** b g Kahyasi-Noufiyla *(15) (246) (325) 396^{4}* 432^{2} 506^{8} 751^{2} 998^{8} 1300^{3} 1840^{6} 2098^{4} 2352^{2} 2799^{3} **>85a 85f<**

Nouvelle Cuisine **7** b m Yawa-Radigo (Ragstone) 1681^{6} 1934^{3} 1998^{2} 2127^{4} 2355^{10} **>42a 57df<**

Novocento **5** b br h Nomination-Top Stream (Highland Melody) 685^{12}

Noyan **5** ch h Northern Baby (CAN)-Istiska (FR) (Irish River (FR)) (1025) (1160) 1268^{4} **>61f<**

Nuclear Express **8** b h Martinmas-Halka (Daring March) 2398^{8} 2642^{6} **>25a 61df<**

Nuclear Jewel **2** b f Superpower-Emerald Gulf (IRE) (Wassl) 2951^{10} 3231^{7} 3670^{18} **>31f<**

Nukud (USA) **3** b c Topsider (USA)-Summer Silence (USA) (Stop The Music (USA)) 2236^{13} **>6f<**

Nunnery Grove (IRE) **3** b f Waajib-Manela Lady (Ela-Mana-Mou) 867^{3} 1290^{5} 1830^{7} 2747^{11} 3383^{8} **>53f<**

Nunsharpa **2** b f Sharpo-Missed Blessing 4103^{10} **>70f<**

Nuriva (USA) **3** b f Woodman (USA)-Mesmerize (Mill Reef (USA)) 1116a^{14} 1870^{3} 2443^{3} **>114f<**

Nushka Babushka **3** b f Nishapour (FR)-Jessamine (Jalmood (USA)) 2884^{6} 3096^{6} 4062^{15} **>39f<**

Nutcracker **2** b f Rambo Dancer (CAN)-Fair Madame (Monseigneur (USA)) 3468^{6} 3806^{4} 3994^{13} *4339^{12}* **>36a 67f<**

Nuthatch (IRE) **3** b f Thatching-New Edition (Great Nephew) *149^{3} 239^{2} 322^{5} 766^{8} 847^{3} 1569^{8} 1883^{8}* 2054^{4} 2363^{10} 4131^{8} 4157^{6} **>52a 37f<**

Nuveen (IRE) **4** br c Al Nasr (FR)-Cactus Road (FR) (Iron Duke (FR)) 534^{11} *766^{14}* 1948^{6} **>34f<**

Nwaamis (USA) **3** b c Dayjur (USA)-Lady Cutlass (USA)

Cutlass (USA)) 680^{3} 920^{5} 1234a^{7} **>121f<**

Nyali Beach (IRE) 3 b f Treasure Kay-Gauloise Bleue (USA) (Lyphard's Wish (FR)) *515^{7}* 1012^{2} 1125^{6} 1428^{5} 1812^{8} *2093^{9}* 2574^{4} 2789^{W} 4261^{15} **>19a 60f<**

Nymph In The Ski (IRE) 2 br f Scenic-Al Mansoura (Honour Bound) 3197a^{10}

Oakbury (IRE) 3 ch c Common Grounds-Doon Belle (Ardoon) 651^{13} 1512^{7} 2037^{13} 2849^{2} 3126^{2} 3292^{3} 4196^{3} **>37a 75f<**

Oaks Star (USA) 4 b c Chief's Crown (USA)-Double Rock *26^{7}* **>20a f<**

Oare Budgie 2 ch f Midyan (USA)-Portvasco (Sharpo) 1790^{5} 2173^{7} 3093^{5} 3567^{3} 4243^{11} **>54f<**

Oare Sparrow 5 b m Night Shift (USA)-Portvasco (Sharpo) 3028^{9} 3359^{18} 3545^{7} (3874) (4134) 4268^{12} **>77f<**

Oatey 2 ch f Master Willie-Oatfield 1098^{7} 4212^{9} 4314^{8} **>64f<**

Obelos (USA) 4 ch c Diesis-Fair Sousanne (676) 841^{13} **>71f<**

Oberons Boy (IRE) 2 b c Fairy King (USA)-Bold Starlet (Precocious) 682^{6} 919^{2} 1311^{2} 1838^{12} 2058^{3} 2690^{6} 3733^{3} (3861) 4034^{3} 4207^{4} **>89f<**

Oberon's Dart (IRE) 2 b c Fairy King-Key Manoeuver 4005a^{3} 4222^{8} **>34f<**

Oblomov 2 b c Most Welcome-Flambera (FR) (Akarad (FR)) 1184^{16} 1662^{11} 2283^{11} (2529) 3215^{3} 3812^{8} 4107^{11} 4279^{2} **>78f<**

Obsessive (USA) 2 b br f Seeking the Gold (USA)-Secret Obsession (USA) (Secretariat (USA)) 3495^{2} (3662) 3942^{2} **>92f<**

Obsidian Grey 8 gr h Lyphard's Special (USA)-Marcrest (On Your Mark) *82^{5}* 578^{10} 748^{6} (790) 965^{4} 1044^{2} 1355^{13} 1433^{4} 1545^{7} 1819^{5} 1993^{8} **>40a 56f<**

Occupandiste (IRE) 2 b f Kaldoun-Only Seule (4251a)

Ocean Grove (IRE) 2 b f Fairy King (USA)-Leyete Gulf (IRE) (Slip Anchor) 1169^{6} 3364^{4} (3625) 3886^{4} **>79f<**

Ocean Park 4 b c Dominion-Chiming Melody (Cure The Blues (USA)) *1568^{0}* 3757^{8} 4171^{3} 4233^{3} **>69a 74f<**

Ocean Stream (IRE) 2 b c Waajib-Kilboy Concorde (African Sky) 3231^{4} 3456^{4} 3626^{5} 3839^{2} 3996^{4} 4255^{2} **>68f<**

Ochos Rios (IRE) 4 br g Horage-Morgiana (Godswalk (USA)) 559^{6} 876^{12} 1528^{2} 1679^{10} 3457^{5} 3645^{15} 3807^{5} 4041^{5} **>59a 65f<**

O'Connor (IRE) 3 b c Ela-Mana-Mou-Orillia (Red God) (1122a) **>104f<**

Office Hours 3 b c Danehill (USA)-Charmina (FR) (Nonoalco (USA)) 715^{4} 930^{7} 1072^{3} 1425^{3} 1747^{4} 2313^{2} 3448^{U} **>78f<**

Officer 3 ch c General Holme (USA)-Mode Classique (FR) (Top Ville) 1916^{3} 2331^{P} **>74f<**

Off'n'away (IRE) 3 ch c Be My Guest (USA)-Irish Edition (USA) (Alleged (USA)) *564^{3}* 2217a^{3} **>98a 116f<**

Off the Air (IRE) 4 b f Taufan (USA)-Milly Daydream (Hard Fought) *29^{2}* *(68)* *120^{4}* *152^{4}* *(226)* *308^{5}* *364^{11}* *3529^{14}* 3889^{15} 4054^{9} **>48a 36f<**

Oggi 4 gr c Efisio-Dolly Bevan (Another Realm) 434^{20} 565^{9} 877^{2} 1199^{3} (1411) 1510^{10} *3512^{4}* 3615^{5} 3964^{17} 4040^{12} **>71f<**

Oh Dearie Me 3 b f Puissance-Tyrian Princess (Comedy Star (USA)) 1564^{8} 3761^{13}

Oh So Handy 7 b g Nearly A Hand-Geordie Lass (Bleep-Bleep) 1737^{3} 2078^{3} 2268^{5} **>47f<**

Oh Whataknight 2 b f Primo Dominie-Carolside (Music Maestro) 2782^{4} 3444^{4} (3699) 4032^{6} **>83f<**

Oisin An Oir (IRE) 2 b c Alzao (USA)-Niamh Cinn Oir (IRE) (King of Clubs) 1597^{13} *2380^{4}* 3416^{10} 3713^{8} 3968^{9} **>34a 52f<**

Okavango (USA) 3 b c Riverman (USA)-Baby Duck (USA) (Quack (USA)) 663^{6} 824^{4} (1015) 1141^{5} 1478^{4} 1793^{8} **>88f<**

Okay Baby (IRE) 3 b f Treasure Kay-Miss Tuko (Good Times (ITY)) *156^{10}* 453^{11} 521^{14} 875^{3} 1155^{2} 1426^{9} 1548^{2} 1902^{2} (1956) 2776^{4} 2968^{7} 4152^{17} **>18a 63f<**

Oktan (IRE) 3 c 3910a^{6} **>97f<**

Old Comrades 8 ch g Music Boy-Miss Candine 1499^{4} 1828^{9} 1963^{4} *2074^{3}* *2383^{3}* **>51a 57df<**

Old Hat (IRE) 2 b c Thatching-Crystal Fountain (Great Nephew) 4023^{5} 4161^{10} **>72f<**

Old Hickory (IRE) 4 b c Alzao (USA)-Fabled Lifestyle (Kings Lake (USA)) 631^{8} 918^{4} 1135^{9} 1926^{4} 2241^{7} 2457^{15} **>110f<**

Old Irish 2 gr c Old Vic-Dunoof (Shirley Heights) 4169^{10} **>49f<**

Old Master (IRE) 4 b c Tate Gallery (USA)-Nancy Drew (Sexton Blake) 1771^{11} 3202^{4} **>36f<**

Old Provence 5 b h Rainbow Quest (USA)-Orange Hill (High Top) *(2072)* 3899^{5} **>71a 106df<**

Old Red (IRE) 5 ch h Ela-Mana-Mou-Sea Port (Averof) 3705^{4} (4118) 4326^{7} **>68a 83f<**

Old Rouvel (USA) 4 b c Riverman (USA)-Marie de Russy (FR) (Sassafras (FR)) *(290)* 610^{2} 869^{4} 1363^{2} 1869^{5} 3146^{5} 3563^{3} 3946^{4} (4191) 4258^{3} **>67a 113f<**

Old School House 2 ch c Polar Falcon (USA)-Farewell Letter (USA) (Arts And Letters) 3371^{12} 3683^{7} 3968^{10} 4151^{17} **>58f<**

Old Swinford (IRE) 3 b or br f Contract Law (USA)-Rockalong Rosie (Martinmas) 546^{5} *624^{6}* 1447^{5} 1625^{2} 1834^{3} 1962^{13} (2065) 2244^{2} 2452^{4} 2555^{6} (2650) 2868^{3} 3292^{4} 3569^{8} 3884^{13} **>40a 70df<**

Oleana (IRE) 2 b f Alzao (USA)-Buraida (Balidar) (4048) 4203^{5} **>84f<**

Oleron 3 b f Darshaan-Orangerie (FR) (Gay Mecene (USA)) 673^{16} 1150^{10} 1526^{9} 2279^{9} *2626^{2}* *2920^{4}* *3076^{6}* 3743^{6} **>56a 47f<**

Olifantsfontein 7 b h Thatching-Taplow (Tap On Wood) *2383^{15}* 2521^{13} 2665^{5} 2956^{6} 3051^{8} **>49a 57f<**

Olimpia Dukakis (ITY) 3 b f Isopach (USA)-Jaana (Cure The Blues (USA)) (809a) 1237a^{2} (2566a) 4020a^{2} **>100f<**

Oliver Rock 2 b c Shareef Dancer (USA)-Short Rations 3089^{7} 3280^{7} 3916^{9} **>68f<**

Oliver's Twist 3 b or br c Horatius-Heartful Star (Star de Na 1232a^{2} **>124f<**

Olivia Val 5 b m Valiyar-Traditional Miss (Traditionalist (USA)) *624^{4}* *1078^{5}* *1950^{10}* 2115^{10} **>21a 19f<**

Oliviero (FR) 2 dk f Vaguely Pleasant-My Green Eyes 4310a^{3}

Omara (USA) 2 b f Storm Cat (USA)-Alamosa (Alydar (USA)) 1142^{2} 1497^{5} **>73f<**

On a Pedestal (IRE) 3 b f Waajib-Lady Lane (Tanfirion) 538^{7} (786) 1347^{4} 1725^{4} 3469^{8} 3970^{11} **>61df<**

Once More for Luck (IRE) **4** b c Petorius-Mrs Lucky (Royal Match) 784^{4} 1291^{2} 1649^{10} 1946^{4} 2373^{4} 2678^{2} 2861^{2} 3061^{2} 3505^{2} 3593^{3} 3801^{14} 4002^{3} (4110) 4233^{8} **>75f<**

One Dream **2** b c Weldnaas (USA)-Superb Lady 4312^{16} **>28f<**

One False Move (IRE) **4** b f Don't Forget Me-Ninette de Valois (FR) (G 804a^{2} **>80f<**

One for Jeannie **3** b f Clantime-Miss Henry (Blue Cashmere) *42^{2} 105^{2} (146) 196^{7} (831) 891^{4}* 982^{6} 1265^{7} 1304^{8} 1564^{2} 1723^{6} **>72a 64f<**

One for the Chief **7** b h Chief Singer-Action Belle (Auction Ring (USA)) 840^{13}

Onefortheditch (USA) **2** gr f With Approval (CAN)-Wee Dram (USA) (Nostrum (USA)) 3948^{2} **>84+f<**

Onefourseven **2** b g Jumbo Hirt (USA)-Dominance (Dominion) 2526^{17} 2971^{8} *3243^{9}* **>40a 59f<**

Oneineverycolour **3** ch f Midyan (USA)-Matching Lines (Thatching) *284^{5} 363^{8}* 734^{6} 904^{7} 1164^{9} 1279^{13} *1763^{12}* 2124^{8} 2372^{7} **>5a 61f<**

One Life To Live (IRE) **2** gr c Classic Music (USA)-Fine Flame (Le Prince) *2381^{5}* 3432^{13} 3779^{11} **>55a 33f<**

One Off the Rail (USA) **5** b h Rampage (USA)-Catty Queen (USA) (Tom Cat) *66^{12} 106^{8} 206^{2} 396^{11} 403^{3} (496)* 1166^{10} (1518) 1694^{4} 2050^{4} 2439^{8} 3572^{4} 3769^{12} **>80a 50f<**

Oneoftheoldones **3** b c Deploy-Waveguide (Double Form) 747^{5} *(1761)* 2415^{8} 3802^{16} **>66a 62f<**

One Pound **2** b g Shareef Dancer (USA)-Beloved Visitor (USA) (Miswaki (USA)) 3089^{15} 3340^{14} 3652^{6} **>65f<**

One Shot (IRE) **2** b g Fayruz-La Gravotte (FR) (Habitat) 2548^{14} 2791^{5} 3080^{3} 3468^{12} **>64f<**

One Voice (USA) **5** ch h Affirmed (USA)-Elk's Ellie (USA) (Vaguely Noble) 3454^{3} **>72a 89f<**

One Wild Oat **4** b f Shareef Dancer (USA)-Short Rations *22^{10}* **>1a 59f<**

On Fair Stage (IRE) **2** b f Sadler's Wells (USA)-Fair Salinia (Petingo) 4262^{8} **>66f<**

Only Royale (IRE) **6** b m Caerleon (USA)-Etoile de Paris (Crowned Prince (USA)) (913) 1609^{2} 2213a^{3} **>123f<**

On the Carpet (IRE) **2** f 4004a^{10} 4320^{12} **>52f<**

On The Home Run **2** b f Governor General-In the Papers (Aragon) 3495^{15} **>16f<**

On The Off Chance **3** ch g French Gondolier (USA)-Off and on (Touching Wood (USA)) 3799^{16}

On The Wildside **2** ch f Charmer-No Control (Bustino) 4075^{18} 4263^{7} **>43f<**

On Y Va (USA) **8** ch m Victorious (USA)-Golden Moony (Northfields (USA)) *20^{9} 354^{7}* 1148^{10} *2923^{11}* **>56da 71f<**

Ooh Ah Cantona **4** b c Crofthall-Chablisse (Radetzky) 1344^{12} 1666^{4} 1875^{4} (2064) (2254) 2610^{2} (2954) 3462^{8} 3611^{11} **>75f<**

Oozlem (IRE) **6** b h Burslem-Fingers *50^{3}* 546^{9} 1426^{11} 1472^{5} 1745^{6} 1855^{10} 1940^{10} (3173) 3664^{8} 3770^{6} 3934^{10} 4209^{13} **>34a 45f<**

Opalette **2** b f Sharrood (USA)-Height of Folly (Shirley Heights) 4050^{6} **>66f<**

Opaque **3** b g Shirley Heights-Opale (Busted) 1147^{8} 1490^{6} **>61f<**

Opening Chorus **2** ch c Music Boy-One Sharper (Dublin Taxi) 1642^{5} 1919^{6} (3415) 3824^{7} 3969^{9} **>62f<**

Opera **2** ch f Forzando-Flattering (USA) (Nodouble (USA)) 2183^{4} (2434) 2765^{3} 3147^{13} 3546^{2} (3684) **>86f<**

Opera Buff (IRE) **4** br c Rousillon (USA)-Obertura (USA) (Roberto (USA)) *227^{6} 245^{3}* 423^{10} 649^{17} 2280^{3} 2511^{6} 3884^{2} (4168) 4288^{4} **>60a 76+f<**

Opera Fan (IRE) **3** b g Taufan (USA)-Shannon Lady (Monsanto (FR)) *105^{4} 174^{3}* 1290^{3} *1568^{9}* 2020^{4} 2250^{2} 2770^{4} 3152^{5} 3685^{14} 3920^{21} **>59a 59f<**

Opera Lover (IRE) **3** b f Sadler's Wells (USA)-Rensaler (USA) (Stop The Music (USA)) 868^{10} 3223^{4} 3549^{7} 3831^{5} **>103f<**

Operatic Dancer **4** b g Germont-Indian Dancer (Streak) 539^{13} 593^{9} 790^{7} 992^{10} **>33f<**

Options Open **3** b c Then Again-Zahiah 1848^{5} 2105^{5} **>106f<**

Opus One **4** b f Slip Anchor-Rustle of Silk (General Assembly (USA)) (2087) 2263^{2} 2545^{5} 3002^{3} *3735^{6}* **>53a 67f<**

Orange And Blue **2** br f Prince Sabo-Mazarine Blue (Bellypha) (644) 1035^{5} 1699^{5} 1841^{8} 3566^{8} *4339^{4}* **>59a 60tf<**

Orange Place (IRE) **4** ch g Nordance (USA)-Little Red Hut (Habitat) 3999^{6} 4160^{13} **>67f<**

Orange Walk (IRE) **2** b f Alzao-Belize Tropical 3692a^{9} **>83f<**

Orchard Gold **4** b c Glint of Gold-On The Top (High Top) 1044^{8} 1326^{8} **>55f<**

Orchestra Stall **3** b c Old Vic-Blue Brocade (Reform) 485^{3} **>80f<**

Orchidarma **3** b c Reprimand-My Fair Orchid (Roan Rocket) 618^{14} 1322^{6} 1490^{7} 1791^{4} 2065^{5} 2207^{4} 3422^{11} 3825^{8} **>62f<**

Orfijar (FR) **5** 3910a^{4} 4094a^{8} **>103f<**

Oriel Lad **2** b c Colmore Row-Consistent Queen (Queen's Hussar) 436^{8} 1047^{4} 1406^{4} 2077^{2} (2259) 2459^{4} 2644^{2} 2757^{3} 3147^{11} 3225^{4} 3394^{8} 3468^{2} 3701^{8} (3775) 3858^{5} 3990^{10} **>80f<**

Oriental Air (IRE) **4** b f Taufan (USA)-More Candy (Ballad Rock) 1668^{13} 1900^{4} 2160^{5} 2475^{4} 2585^{9} **>17a 55f<**

Oriental Song **6** ch m Battle Hymn-Miss Kung Fu (Caliban) *107^{12} 194^{4} 366^{11}* **>13da 32f<**

Orinoco River (USA) **2** ch c El Gran Senor (USA)-Miss Lilian (Sandford Lad) 3868^{7} 4080^{6} **>85f<**

Oriole **2** b c Mazilier (USA)-Odilese (Mummy's Pet) 533^{10} 615^{11} 878^{6} 1024^{2} 1440^{4} 1842^{9} 2259^{2} 2498^{7} (2757) 3354^{4} 3460^{6} 3809^{8} 4231^{10} **>62f<**

Orsay **3** b c Royal Academy (USA)-Bellifontaine (FR) (Bellypha) (553) **>75f<**

Orthorhombus **6** b h Aragon-Honeybeta (Habitat) *1^{2} 49^{5} 80^{2} 169^{5} 181^{5} 298^{6} 337^{2} 400^{9}* (450) *518^{2}* 579^{4} 702^{16} 922^{6} 1061^{7} 1148^{11} 1534^{12} 1956^{8} *2923^{16}* **>64a 67f<**

Ortolan **2** gr c Prince Sabo-Kala Rosa (Kalaglow) 436^{2} (940) 2442^{3} **>98+f<**

Oscar Rose **2** b c Aragon-Mossy Rose (King of Spain) 1751^{5} 2434^{4} 2801^{7} 3090^{12} **>56f<**

Oscar Schindler (IRE) **3** ch c Royal Academy (USA)-Saraday (Northfields (USA 708a^{2} 1234a^{6} 2218a^{4} 3789a^{3} **>122f<**

Oscar the Second (IRE) **5** b g Cyrano de Bergerac-El Cerrito 877^{16} 1042^{W} 1963^{22} 1993^{5} 2260^{4} 2784^{18} **>27da**

44f<

Oscilights Gift 3 b f Chauve Souris-Oscilight 3712^{15} 4049^{15} 4225^{19} **>21f<**

Ostia 0 D Aquino 3495^{14} **>25f<**

Ostwahl (IRE) 5 b m Waajib-Ostkonigin (GER) (Alpenkonig (GER)) 4094a^{3} **>105f<**

Ottavio Farnese 3 ch g Scottish Reel-Sense of Pride (Welsh Pageant) 1514^{6} 3559^{2} (3958) 4201^{19} **>82f<**

Otterbourne (IRE) 3 b c Royal Academy (USA)-Marwell (Habitat) 662^{3} 2235^{5} **>83f<**

Oubeck Princess 3 b f Puissance-Kalvee Dancer (Kalaglow) 2372^{9} 2818^{7} 3000^{7} 3257^{4} **>40f<**

Our Albert (IRE) 2 b c Durgam (USA)-Power Girl (Tyrant (USA)) 1781^{9} 3260^{5} 3644^{11} **>64f<**

Our Bairn 3 b f Bairn (USA)-Bewitched (African Sky) *133*^{9} 1801^{9} 2662^{8} **>16a 52f<**

Our Bessie 4 b f Persian Bold-Jamarj (Tyrnavos) *624*^{11} *1029*^{8} *1332*^{5} 1622^{4} 1863^{3} 2197^{2} 2546^{2} 2745^{9} *3078*^{3} **>45a 52+f<**

Our Dorothy 3 b f Aragon-Helewise (Dance In Time (CAN)) *156*^{11} *225*^{8} **>1a f<**

Our Eddie 6 ch g Gabitat-Ragusa Girl (Morston (FR)) *8*^{3} *145*^{8} *206*^{4} *445*^{6} **>68a 57f<**

Our Emblem (USA) 4 b c Mr Prospector (USA)-Personal Ensign (USA) (Private Account (USA)) *4303a*^{6} **>118a f<**

Our Kris 3 b c Kris-Our Reverie (USA) (J O Tobin (USA)) 3105^{5} 3438^{7} 3537^{6} 3818^{13} 3971^{8} (4108) **>76f<**

Our Little Lady 3 b f Queen's Soldier (USA)-Charlotte's Pearl (Monsanto (FR)) 2977^{6} 3183^{6} 3543^{4} *4128*^{12} **>11a 61f<**

Our Main Man 5 ch g Superlative-Ophrys (Nonoalco (USA)) 929^{7} 1291^{5} 1439^{4} 2224^{8} (2731) 2954^{3} 3102^{5} 3189^{15} 3743^{15} 4038^{19} (4138) *4335*^{3} **>62a 65f<**

Our Mica 5 gr h Belfort (FR)-Aristata (Habitat) *532*^{11} *602*^{7} *1214*^{8} 1565^{12} **>23a f<**

Our Rainbow 3 b f Primitive Rising (USA)-Cass Avon (Celtic Cone) 1059^{6} 1720^{3} 2129^{4} 2662^{5} 3099^{12} **>53f<**

Our Rita 6 b m Hallgate-Ma Pierrette (Cawston's Clown) 425^{5} 793^{9} 3332a^{9} 3608^{9} 3945^{36} 4267^{20} **>86f<**

Our Robert 3 b g Faustus (USA)-Duck Soup (Decoy Boy) 759^{4} 908^{3} 3461^{3} 3685^{11} 3802^{10} 4044^{11} **>39a 68f<**

Our Shadee (USA) 5 b h Shadeed (USA)-Nuppence *142*^{2} *(220)* *287*^{2} *(359)* *446*^{2} *499*^{8} 1975^{15} 2203^{3} 2504^{5} 2714^{5} 3139^{7} 3177^{3} *3319*^{9} 3638^{11} 3681^{2} *4217*^{4} 4240^{6} **>58a 52f<**

Our Tom 3 br c Petong-Boa (Mandrake Major) *(105)* *170*^{2} *210*^{8} *309*^{2} *(395)* *411*^{7} 538^{2} 647^{12} 4044^{14} 4261^{18} **>68a 61f<**

Our Tom's Boy 2 b c Colmore Row-Princess Silca Key (Grundy) 878^{9} *1090*^{4} *1570*^{7} 1734^{3} 2035^{6} 2153^{4} 2715^{3} *2962*^{6} 2988^{5} **>38a 54f<**

Our Topsie 8 b m My Dad Tom (USA)-Tops (Club House) 2721a^{3} (3322a) 3686a^{2} **>30f<**

Our Worley (IRE) 2 b f Mac's Imp (USA)-Castleforbes (Thatching) 970^{4} **>63f<**

Out of The Blue 3 b f Lochnager-Expletive (Shiny Tenth) 3762^{7} **>56f<**

Out of the Mist 4 b c Damister (USA)-Almitra (Targowice (USA)) 984^{18} 1291^{10} 1499^{5} 1963^{13} *2142*^{5} **>39a 47f<**

Out on a Promise (IRE) 3 b c Night Shift (USA)-Lovers' Parlour (Beldale Flutter (USA)) 504^{11} 829^{6} 1130^{6} 1351^{3} 1605^{3} 2240^{9} 2780^{2} 2980^{2} (3552) 4074^{7} 4163^{3} **>68a 96f<**

Outset (IRE) 5 ch h Persian Bold-It's Now Or Never (High Line) 4315^{4} **>74f<**

Outstayed Welcome 3 b g Be My Guest (USA)-Between Time (Elegant Air) 435^{11} 648^{10} 1221^{7} 1498^{10} (1863) 2233^{2} 2546^{3} 2824^{3} (3029) 3263^{4} 3710^{11} **>63f<**

Overbrook 3 b f Storm Cat (USA)-Spurned (USA) (Robellino (USA)) 633^{4} (959) 1138^{3} 1480^{4} 1795^{3} 3005^{4} **>97f<**

Overbury (IRE) 4 br c Caerleon (USA)-Overcall 666^{2} **>119f<**

Overpower 11 b h Try My Best (USA)-Just A Shadow (Laser Light) 1048^{11} (1484) 1519^{2} **>60f<**

Overruled (IRE) 2 b f Last Tycoon-Overcall 3339^{10} (4190) **>78+f<**

Oversman 2 b c Keen-Jamaican Punch (IRE) (Shareef Dancer (USA)) 1190^{8} *2381*^{3} 2681^{8} 3994^{9} **>75a 53f<**

Owdbetts (IRE) 3 b f High Estate-Nora Yo Ya (Ahonoora) *395*^{6} 1092^{4} 1404^{5} 1718^{7} (2522) 2807^{7} (3247) 3403^{6} 3726^{7} 3872^{7} **>64a 65f<**

Owington 4 b c Green Desert (USA)-Old Domesday Book (High Top) 921^{3} 1364^{3} 2368^{4} 3491^{3} *4303a*^{7} **>117a 118f<**

Oxalagu (GER) 3 c 2215a^{6} 3200a^{2} 3591a^{6} 4018a^{4} **>103f<**

Oxford Line (IRE) 3 b c Caerleon (USA)-Lorenza Bertini (Star Appeal) 1396a^{7} **>103f<**

Oxgang (IRE) 2 b c Taufan (USA)-Casla (Lomond (USA)) 2995^{12} *4338*^{3} **>70a 26f<**

Ozubeck (USA) 3 b f Deputy Minister (CAN)-Whitethroat (Artaius (USA)) 3239^{10} 3799^{11} 4052^{4} 4249^{11} 4289^{11} **>56f<**

Ozzie Jones 4 b c Formidable-Distant Relation (Great Nephew) *83*^{3} *121*^{4} *172*^{2} *215*^{5} *295*^{10} 1039^{9} **>51a 51df<**

P

Pab's Choice 4 ch f Telsmoss-Dido (Full of Hope) *499*^{9} 862^{7} 1021^{2} 1261^{10} 1638^{6} *2073*^{11} **>68a 68df<**

Pacific Girl (IRE) 3 b f Emmson-Power Girl (Tyrant (USA)) 1714^{17} 2202^{7} *2587*^{12} 2865^{3} 3123^{10} 3205^{5} 3426^{4} 3747^{8} 3844^{17} **>17a 48f<**

Pacific Grove 2 b f Persian Bold-Dazzling Heights (Shirley Heights) 1348^{6} 1497^{3} 1977^{4} 2756^{2} (3090) 3267^{4} (3516) (3867) 4203^{2} **>93f<**

Pacific Overture 3 br f Southern Music-Morning Miss 695^{18} 937^{11} 1337^{6} 1676^{19} 2081^{8} 3402^{13} 4054^{15} **>44f<**

Pacific Spirit 5 b m Governor General-Mossberry Fair (Mossberry) *603*^{5} 890^{3} *1209*^{7} 1323^{10} *1457*^{2} *1950*^{8} *3734*^{11} **>42a 50f<**

Paddys Cherub 3 b f Then Again-Lady Stock (Crofter (USA)) 2553^{15} 3542^{9} 4131^{10} **>33f<**

Paddy's Return (IRE) 3 b g Kahyasi-Bayazida (Bustino) 1198^{2} 1691^{3} **>84f<**

Paddy's Rice 4 ch c Hadeer-Requiem (Song) 542^{3} 765^{7} (1071) 1483^{5} 1910^{2} 2202^{3} 2685^{8} 3079^{2} 3534^{6} 3677^{9} **>74f<**

Paddy's Storm 3 b g Celestial Storm (USA)-Hot Tan (Hotfoot) 544^{8} 764^{23} 1275^{4} **>29f<**

Padre Mio (IRE) 7 b g The Parson-Mwanamio (Sole Mio (USA)) 2593^{7} **>65f<**

Pageboy 6 b h Tina's Pet-Edwin's Princess (Owen Dudley) *(23) 61^{2} 78^{5} 154^{9} 237^{6} 1076^{7}* 1193^{11} 1354^{10} 1689^{9} 2326^{3} 2578^{4} 2645^{3} 2930^{4} 3121^{7} *3512^{7}* 3783^{7} 3855^{4} **>69+a 65f<**

Painted Desert 3 b f Green Desert (USA)-Illusory (Kings Lake (USA)) 1373^{5} 1795^{6} 3005^{5} 3236^{3} 3407^{7} 3551^{14} **>90f<**

Painted Hall (USA) 3 br c Imperial Falcon (CAN)-Moon O'Gold (USA) (Slew O' Gold (USA)) 1514^{11} (1834) 2571^{6} 2902^{4} **>81f<**

Painter's Row (IRE) 3 b c Royal Academy (USA)-Road To The Top (Shirley Heights) (680) 920^{7} 2044a^{8} 2670^{P} **>112f<**

Paint It Black 2 ch c Double Schwartz-Tableaux (FR) (Welsh Pageant) 2846^{8} 3174^{3} (3553) 3886^{6} **>76f<**

Pair of Jacks (IRE) 5 ch h Music Boy-Lobbino (Bustino) *56^{8} 125^{9} 203^{6} 240^{W} 265^{5} 320^{11} 341^{8} 373^{2} 408^{2} 472^{4} 501^{3}* 541^{6} 882^{8} 1013^{9} 1255^{12} **>37a 46df<**

Pakol (IRE) 6 b m Martin John-Tamen John (African Sky) 2162^{3} 2784^{6} 2972^{14} 3365^{7} **>45a 44f<**

Palacegate Chief 2 b c Inca Chief (USA)-Sports Post Lady (IRE) (M Double M (USA)) 2817^{5} **>25f<**

Palacegate Episode (IRE) 5 b m Drumalis-Pasadena Lady (Captain James) 700^{5} 1572a^{4} 2039a^{3} 2671^{6} 3689a^{6} (3913a) 4006a^{6} 4181a^{2} **>112f<**

Palacegate Jack (IRE) 4 gr c Neshad (USA)-Pasadena Lady (Captain James) 441^{10} 1106^{7} (1451) 1909^{2} 3938^{5} 4119^{12} **>90df<**

Palacegate Jo (IRE) 4 b f Drumalis-Welsh Rhyme (Welsh Term) *66^{11} 91^{4} 137^{2} (186) (215) 229^{5} 266^{2} 351^{4} 517^{3} 589^{6} 771^{4} (843) 1029^{7} 1091^{7} 1955^{8} 2072^{3} (2293) 2379^{10} 2630^{5} 3240^{5} 3511^{12} 3737^{8}* **>59da 67f<**

Palacegate Touch 5 gr g Petong-Dancing Chimes (London Bells (CAN)) (535) 652^{5} 1100^{10} 1241^{9} *1953^{2}* 2001^{4} 2764^{26} 2823^{5} 3557^{5} 3717^{19} 3880^{4} 4281^{9} **>93a 86df<**

Palace Guard 3 br g Daring March-Royal Brush (King of Spain) 4162^{11} **>15f<**

Palace River (IRE) 7 b m Dragon Palace (USA)-Rosebrook (Brother Birdbrook) 2913^{7} 3256^{7} 4072^{11} **>45f<**

Palafairia (FR) 3 br f Always Fair-Palavera (Bikala) 1576a^{3} **>106f<**

Palamon (USA) 2 ch c Sanglamore (USA)-Gantlette (Run The Gantlet (USA)) 3868^{6} **>86f<**

Palatial Style 8 b g Kampala-Stylish Princess (Prince Tenderfoot (USA)) 3131^{5} 3374^{10} 3611^{10} **>94f<**

Palatine Boy (FR) 3 b c Caerwent-La Palatine 3580a^{2}

Paley Prince (USA) 9 b h Tilt Up (USA)-Apalachee Princess (USA) (Apalachee (USA)) 856^{9} 1057^{9} 1164^{13} 1265^{4} 1909^{6} 2079^{6} (2301) 2502^{3} 2867^{3} 2987^{6} 3205^{3} (3333) 3442^{5} **>48a 65f<**

Pallium (IRE) 7 b h Try My Best (USA)-Jungle Gardenia (Nonoalco (USA)) 1157^{12} 1441^{5} 1679^{14} 2124^{2} (2160) 2303^{8} 2521^{12} (2821) 2837^{6} 2992^{4} 3150^{5} 3667^{25} **>51a 62f<**

Palo Blanco 4 b f Precocious-Linpac Mapleleaf (Dominion) 1376^{4} 1604^{5} 3748^{6} 4040^{3} 4068^{3} **>80f<**

Paloma Bay (IRE) 2 b f Alzao (USA)-Adventurine (Thatching) (1142) 1871^{2} 2322^{P} **>87f<**

Pampas Breeze (IRE) 3 b f Darshaan-Pampas Miss (USA) (Pronto (ARG)) 764^{14} 2944^{2} 3224^{4} 3756^{4} 3899^{3} 4168^{2} **>74f<**

Pampered Guest (IRE) 4 b c Be My Guest (USA)-Miss Garuda (Persian Bold) 567^{10} **>77df<**

Panama Hat (IRE) 3 b c Thatching-Lady Donna (Dominion) 2133^{3} *2378^{10}* **>15f<**

Panchellita (USA) 6 b m Pancho Villa (USA)-Counselor's Pride (USA) (Good Counsel (USA)) *62^{9} 160^{8} 219^{6} 265^{4} 320^{3} 371^{5}* 1811^{10} 2017^{4} 2342^{10} 2685^{9} **>48a 40f<**

Panikin 7 gr g Red Sunset-Haunting 486^{9} **>73f<**

Panther (IRE) 5 ch h Primo Dominie-High Profile (High Top) *(165) 353^{3} 419^{5}* (594) *832^{3}* 877^{9} 1297^{10} 1828^{7} 2784^{3} 3098^{5} 3467^{9} 3719^{6} 3855^{5} 4115^{5} *4274^{8}* **>56a 54f<**

Paojiunic (IRE) 2 ch c Mac's Imp (USA)-Audenhove (GER) (Marduk (GER)) 1163^{7} **>35f<**

Paola (USA) 2 b f Lord Avie-Debutante Tea 4004a^{3}

Papagos (IRE) 4 b c Indian Forest (USA)-Our Katy (Dragonara Palace (USA)) *76^{8} 123^{5}* **>22a 42f<**

Papaha (FR) 2 b f Green Desert (USA)-Turban (Glint of Gold) 3626^{3} 3865^{4} 4105^{5} **>87f<**

Papaly (FR) 3 br g Balsamo (FR)-Rajania (FR) (Rheingold) 209a^{2}

Paper Cloud 3 b f Lugana Beach-Sweet Enough (Caerleon (USA)) 428^{4} 618^{9} 851^{16} 1382^{5} 2811^{3} 3641^{3} 3769^{6} **>71f<**

Papering (IRE) 2 b f Shaadi (USA)-Wrapping (Kris) 2370^{5} (2705) 3387^{2} **>92f<**

Paper Maze 2 b f Mazilier (USA)-Westonepaperchase (USA) (Accipiter (USA)) *1758^{3}* 2308^{4} 2817^{4} *3509^{10}* 3895^{6} **>50a 55f<**

Pappa Reale 2 ch f Indian Ridge-Daffodil Fields (Try My B (1395a)

Paradise Navy 6 b h Slip Anchor-Ivory Waltz (USA) 632^{12} 954^{2} 1144^{10} 1444^{3} 1840^{5} 1929^{3} 2284^{2} 2429^{5} 2996^{5} 3849^{2} 3971^{4} 4158^{5} 4326^{2} **>82f<**

Paradise Waters 3 gr f Celestial Storm (USA)-Gleaming Water (Kalaglow) 857^{5} 1083^{3} 1372^{2} 1674^{2} 2050^{5} (2658) 2969^{2} 3634^{4} 3927^{4} 4047^{10} **>69f<**

Parios (FR) 7 ch h Sicyos (USA)-Parga (FR) (Gay Mecene (USA)) 3484a^{3} **>98f<**

Paris Babe 3 b f Teenoso (USA)-Kala's Image (Kala Shikari) 551^{2} 660^{8} 959^{4} (1168) 1373^{3} (1698) 2066^{4} 2416^{5} (2748) 3342^{7} 3717^{16} 3922^{8} **>96f<**

Parish Walk (IRE) 4 ch g Pennine Walk-Baby Caroline (Martin John) 778^{6} 817^{9} 864^{10} 2224^{7} 2401^{4} (2465) *2592^{8}* **>5a 49f<**

Paris Joelle (IRE) 2 b f Fairy King (USA)-Gentle Freedom (Wolver Hollow) 1169^{11} **>62f<**

Park Charger 3 b f Tirol-Haitienne (Green Dancer) 1390a^{8} 3193a^{3} 3787a^{3} **>102f<**

Parklife (IRE) 3 ch g Double Schwartz-Silk Trade (Auction Ring (USA)) *128^{5}* 1195^{10} 1377^{5} 2021^{5} **>26a 44f<**

Park Ridge 3 b g Indian Ridge-Aspark (Sparkler) 1167^{6} 1446^{8} 1979^{8} 3402^{14} **>63f<**

Parks Pride 4 b f Hubbly Bubbly (USA)-Valentine Song (Pas de Seul) 3627^{20} **>36f<**

Parliament Piece 9 ch h Burslem-Sallywell (Manado) 1344^{9} (1902) 2358^{6} 2755^{5} (2945) 3431^{3} 3802^{6} 4041^{22} 4236^{15} **>55a 84f<**

Parme (USA) 4 b c Blushing Groom-Petroleuse (Habitat)

Pegs 4 b f Mandrake Major-Siouxsie 479^{8} 984^{15} **>72f<**

Pekay 2 b c Puissance-K-Sera 836^{3} 1418^{3} 1642^{2} 3465^{12} **>63f<**

Pelder (IRE) 5 b h Be My Guest (USA)-Sheer Audacity (Troy) 607a^{2} (898a) 1394a^{2} **>125f<**

Pelleman 3 b c Distant Relative-Lillemor (Connaught) (697) 914^{3} 1249^{7} 2405^{4} 2802^{3} 3534^{5} 4041^{10} 4156^{2} 4249^{10} **>75f<**

Pembridge Place 4 b c Niniski (USA)-Rose d'Amour (USA) (Lines of Power (USA)) 623^{8} 1477^{6} 1794^{6} 2445^{5} 3718^{7} **>81f<**

Pemley 3 b f Superpower-Redgrave Design (Nebbiolo) 754^{11} 1060^{12} 1677^{12} 2084^{10} 2372^{10} 3508^{5} 3678^{4} 3855^{16} **>24f<**

Penbola (IRE) 3 b c Pennine Walk-Sciambola (Great Nephew) 774^{7} 1601^{6} **>40a 56f<**

Pencilled In 2 b c Old Vic-Graphite (USA) (Mr Prospector (USA)) 4247^{3} 4320^{13} **>76f<**

Pendine 3 b f Pharly (FR)-Springwell (Miami Springs) *444^{9}* 521^{10} *1030^{12}* **>27a 40f<**

Pending 3 b g Shareef Dancer (USA)-Prelude (Troy) 764^{13} 942^{P} **>64f<**

Pendley Rose 2 ch f Prince Sabo-Rose Bouquet (General Assembly (USA)) 1348^{4} 1746^{5} *2958^{5}* 3721^{6} 3894^{4} **>45a 68f<**

Pendolino (IRE) 4 b g Thatching-Pendulina (Prince Tenderfoot (USA)) 559^{16} 749^{11} 876^{13} 1651^{5} 1817^{8} 3852^{12} 4002^{6} **>60f<**

Pengamon 3 b c Efisio-Dolly Bevan (Another Realm) 775^{3} 1474^{8} 1862^{4} 2746^{11} **>92f<**

Penmar 3 b c Reprimand-Latakia *2923^{3} 3514^{2} 3734^{2}* 3935^{7} *4128^{3}* 4292^{2} **>65a 64f<**

Pennekamp (USA) 3 b c Bering-Coral Dance (FR) (Green Dancer (USA)) (706a) (920) 1611^{11} **>131+f<**

Pennine Lad (IRE) 5 ch h Pennine Walk-Dominica (GER) (Zank) *3082^{7}* 3292^{6} **>59a 60f<**

Pennine Wind (IRE) 3 b c Pennine Walk-Wintina (Tumble Wind (USA)) *38^{5} 264^{2}* **>60a 65f<**

Penny a Day (IRE) 5 b g Supreme Leader-Mursuma (Rarity) (1357) 1585^{6} 3164^{9} 3864^{5} 4069^{4} **>106f<**

Pennycairn 3 b f Last Tycoon-Applecross (Glint of Gold) 857^{6} 1218^{5} 1547^{2} (2313) 2654^{2} 3214^{3} 3630^{10} 4083^{12} **>84f<**

Penny Dip 3 b f Cadeaux Genereux-Penny Blessing (1786) 2443^{5} 2748^{3} 3087^{2} 3615^{16} **>92f<**

Penny Drops 6 b m Sharpo-Darine (Nonoalco (USA)) 425^{6} (1004a) (3912a) (4019a) **>115f<**

Penny Ghent 2 b f Dominion-On The Top (High Top) 3093^{6} 3648^{11} 3763^{21} **>20f<**

Penny Jane 6 b m Charlotte's Dunce-Rebecca Sarah (Mansingh (USA)) 2798^{6}

Penny Parkes 2 ch f Clantime-Bonne Baiser (Most Secret) (429) 554^{2} *834^{3}* 983^{2} 1215^{W} **>32a 59tf<**

Penny Ramble (IRE) 4 b f Pennine Walk-Celestial Melody (USA) (The Minstrel (CAN)) *313^{14}* **>38f<**

Penny's Wishing 3 b f Clantime-Lady Pennington (Blue Cashmere) *354^{14}* 697^{4} 823^{7} 966^{9} 1216^{4} (1471) *1571^{14}* 3534^{18} 3750^{10} 3972^{9} 4115^{16} 4236^{12} **>63a 69df<**

Pent-House Baby 3 ch f Risk Me (FR)-Astral Suite (On Your Mark) *38^{9}* **>46a 27f<**

Pentire 3 b c Be My Guest (USA)-Gull Nook (Mill Reef (USA)) (826) (1018) (1224) (1897) 2595^{2} (3144) (3690a) **>129f<**

Pentre Ffynnon (IRE) 3 ch c Ballad Rock-One Better (Nebbiolo) (2649) 3150^{W} **>84f<**

People Direct 2 ch f Ron's Victory (USA)-Ayr Classic (Local Suitor (USA)) 3848^{U} 4137^{5} *4269^{6}* **>38a 43f<**

Pepitist 4 b g Bold Owl-Misoptimist (Blakeney) 4086^{11} **>57f<**

Peppers (IRE) 2 b f Bluebird (USA)-Pepilin (Coquelin (USA)) 2083^{7} 4048^{3} 4212^{7} **>68f<**

Perche No (FR) 3 dk c Akarad-Dancing Star 4187a^{3} **>114f<**

Percy Braithwaite (IRE) 3 b c Kahyasi-Nasseem (FR) 614^{10} 829^{8} 1524^{4} 1808^{2} 1862^{5} 3993^{6} 4083^{13} **>92f<**

Percy Park (USA) 2 br c Rajab (USA)-Clayton's Miss (USA) (Distinctive (USA)) 1190^{3} 1670^{5} 1857^{6} 3701^{14} 4231^{17} 4321^{11} **>56df<**

Percy Parrot 3 b c Lochnager-Soltago (Touching Wood (USA)) 689^{7} 1598^{7} 3745^{8} **>38f<**

Perdition (IRE) 5 b m Red Sunset-Free Rein (Sagaro) *30^{7} 91^{10}* 1401^{8} **>34a 44f<**

Perfect Bertie (IRE) 3 b g Cyrano de Bergerac-Perfect Chance (Petorius) 524^{15} 640^{5} 748^{5} 965^{8} 1414^{15} 1824^{14} 1962^{3} 2353^{3} 2503^{10} 2954^{7} 3099^{8} 3258^{3} 3422^{12} **>60f<**

Perfect Brave 4 b c Indian Ridge-Perfect Timing (Comedy Star (USA)) 887^{8} 1257^{2} (1750) 1975^{10} **>59a 62f<**

Perfect Ending 4 b g Never so Bold-Trinida (Jaazeiro (USA)) 1198^{13} *1759^{5} 2090^{4} 2495^{12}* **>50a 55tf<**

Perfect Gift 2 ch f Generous (IRE)-Knight's Baroness (Rainbow Quest (USA)) 2083^{8} 3397^{9} **>47f<**

Perfect Vintage 5 b h Shirley Heights-Fair Salinia (Petingo) 3910a^{7} **>97f<**

Perfect World 3 b c Puissance-More or Less 442^{6} 645^{5} 783^{8} *1034^{6} 1629^{3}* **>60a 67f<**

Perilous Plight 4 ch g Siberian Express (USA)-Loveskate (USA) (Overskate (CAN)) *2^{7} 63^{2} 157^{4} (187) (205) 275^{2} (320) (344) 383^{5} 401^{5}* 714^{18} 928^{5} *1049^{4}* 1517^{5} 1714^{11} 2016^{2} 2134^{6} **>81a 75f<**

Peripatetic 3 ch f Kris-Sweet Mover (USA) (Nijinsky (CAN)) 797^{W} 1283^{5} 1916^{2} **>70f<**

Periple 3 b c In The Wings-Dial Dream (Gay Mecene) 3479a^{3} **>82f<**

Periple (FR) 3 b c In The Wings-Dial Dream 4011a^{3} **>115f<**

Perpetual Light 2 b f Petoski-Butosky (Busted) 3644^{5} **>47f<**

Perryston View 3 b c Primo Dominie-Eastern Ember (Indian King (USA)) (639) (754) (1487) 1806^{9} (2324) 2823^{3} 3230^{6} 3717^{13} 4040^{7} **>93f<**

Perrywinkle Way (IRE) 2 b f Treasure Kay-Miss Moat (Dike (USA)) 4212^{17} 4329^{8} **>35f<**

Persephone 2 ch f Lycius (USA)-Elarrih (USA) (Sharpen Up) 3900^{22} **>39f<**

Persian Affair (IRE) 4 b c Persian Heights-Lady Chesterfield (USA) (In Reality (USA)) *365^{11} 386^{7}* 433^{18} 728^{8} 877^{4} (1013) 1179^{10} 1517^{4} 1689^{7} 1932^{8} 2229^{8} 2549^{11} 2906^{5} 3109^{3} 3212^{5} 3488^{8} 3719^{15} **>79a 72f<**

Persian Bailiwick (IRE) 3 ch f Persian Heights-A New Rose (IRE) (Saher) 3007^{9} 3177^{16} **>35f<**

Persian Brave (IRE) 5 b h Persian Heights-Commanche Belle (Shirley Heights) 631^{10} **>118f<**

Persian Bud (IRE) 7 b or br h Persian Bold-Awakening

Rose (Le Levanstell) *13^{6} 83^{6} 200^{7}* 534^{5} 1799^{2} 2052^{7} 3092^{5} **>27a 48f<**

Persian Butterfly 3 b f Dancing Dissident (USA)-Butterfly Kiss (Beldale Flutter (USA)) 664^{6} 3542^{5} **>86f<**

Persian Conquest (IRE) 3 b c Don't Forget Me-Alaroos (IRE) (Persian Bold) *59^{2} 135^{2} (190) 263^{3} 301^{5} 360^{5} 566^{2}* 655^{7} *(1320)* 1693^{4} 1978^{2} *(2145)* 2571^{4} 2792^{8} **>84a 66f<**

Persian Dawn 2 br f Anshan-Visible Form (Formidable) 4313^{15} **>46f<**

Persian Elite (IRE) 4 ch c Persian Heights-Late Sally (Sallust) 1140^{10} 1324^{5} 2490^{4} 2903^{3} (2967) 3374^{5} (3500) 3864^{4} 4036^{12} **>91f<**

Persian Fayre 3 b c Persian Heights-Dominion Fayre (Dominion) 640^{4} (989) 1687^{11} 1932^{5} 2123^{3} 2477^{2} 2770^{7} 3172^{6} 3310^{5} 4194^{16} **>71f<**

Persian Flower 3 b f Persian Heights-Edraianthus (Windjammer (USA)) 3030^{6} 4162^{5} *4271^{3}* **>38a 56f<**

Persian Heritage 4 ch c Persian Bold-Middleham Jewel (Swing Easy (USA)) 780^{20} 1368^{15} **>38f<**

Persian Linnet 4 b c Persian Heights-Swift Linnet (Wolver Hollow) 569^{6} 1359^{9} **>57f<**

Persian Saint (IRE) 4 b or br c Persian Bold-Santa Luciana (GER) (Luciano) 816^{5} 1198^{7} 2316^{2} 2790^{2} 3016^{5} (3517) 3730^{10} **>89f<**

Persian Secret (FR) 2 b f Persian Heights-Rahaam (USA) (Secreto (USA)) (1440) (1650) 2106^{2} 2554^{4} 3420^{3} 4203^{9} **>86f<**

Persiansky (IRE) 5 b g Persian Bold-Astra Adastra (Mount Hagen (FR)) 3148^{3} **>70df<**

Persian Smoke 4 b f Persian Bold-Gauloise 1254^{15} 1622^{10} (2439) 2713^{3} 3029^{10} 3217^{5} 3676^{9} 4259^{10} **>50f<**

Persian Soldier 8 b h Sandhurst Prince-Persian Case (Upper Case (USA)) 1505^{6} 1844^{2} 2002^{P} 2233^{4} 2584^{4} **>52f<**

Persistent (IRE) 3 b g Nashamaa-Reelin Elly (Pitskelly) 2225^{8} *2922^{7}* 3724^{16} **>71a 54f<**

Personal Love (USA) 2 b f Diesis-Personal Glory (Danzig) $3477a^{2}$

Personal Pride (IRE) 4 br c Personal Flag (USA)-Terracotta Hut (Habitat) *18^{12}* **>24a 48df<**

Personimus 5 b h Ballacashtal (CAN)-Sea Charm (Julio Mariner) *271^{8} 335^{8}* 976^{11} 1205^{11} 1378^{4} *1568^{3} 1950^{2}* 2276^{16} **>35a 35f<**

Persuasion 2 b f Batshoof-Primetta (Precocious) 4063^{7} **>65f<**

Persuasive 8 b m Sharpo-Queen's Eyot (Grundy) 494^{5} 1046^{2} 1435^{3} 1686^{4} 3391^{4} **>55f<**

Pesce D'Aprile 3 b f Mtoto-Neatfoot (Anfield) 886^{3} $1237a^{11}$ 1782^{6} 3728^{7} $4179a^{3}$ **>88f<**

Petal's Jarred 5 ro m Headin' Up-My Aisling (John de Coombe) *267^{8}* 578^{9} 818^{17} 1161^{17} 1873^{9} 1956^{7} 2165^{5} 2306^{4} 2355^{8} 2544^{9} **>15a 37df<**

Pete Afrique (IRE) 4 b c Petorius-Noir Afrique (African Sky) 535^{22} 685^{13} 1080^{11} 1582^{5} 2163^{10} 2521^{11} **>66df<**

Peter Monamy 3 ch c Prince Sabo-Revisit (Busted) *509^{3}* (654) 3401^{7} 4062^{20} **>40a 70f<**

Peterrex 2 b g Interrex (CAN)-Standard Rose (Ile de Bourbon (USA)) 2035^{3} 2176^{8} 3378^{9} **>53f<**

Peter Rowley 4 gr c Absalom-Tiszta Sharok (Song) 636^{17} 1052^{9} 1202^{9} 1472^{11} 1830^{8} **>63f<**

Peters Folly 2 b f King Among Kings-Santo Star (Monsanto (FR)) 2023^{4} 2185^{9} *3077^{5}* 3623^{14} 3742^{6} **>40a 40f<**

Petite Annie 2 b f Statoblest-Kuwait Night (Morston (FR)) 849^{6} 1047^{3} 1361^{6} 1590^{2} **>75f<**

Petite Bijou 4 b f Tina's Pet-Highland Lassie (Highland Melody) *96^{8} 136^{7}* **>29a 43f<**

Petite-D-Argent 6 b m Noalto-Honey To Spare 1299^{12} 1604^{10} 2096^{12} 2475^{5} 3667^{21} 3855^{13} **>58f<**

Petite Fantasy 3 b f Mansooj-Ride Bold (USA) (J O Tobin (USA)) $1703a^{3}$ $3198a^{2}$ $3689a^{2}$ **>107f<**

Petite Heritiere 2 b f Last Tycoon-Arianna Aldini (Habitat) 2846^{13} 3133^{6} 3495^{11} 3639^{10} **>50f<**

Petite Juliette 2 b f Salse (USA)-Cascade (Shirley Heights) 3948^{8} 4239^{8} **>70f<**

Petitjean (IRE) 4 b c Last Tycoon-Working Model (Ile de Bourbon (USA)) *389^{11}* **>36a 36f<**

Petit Point (IRE) 2 b f Petorius-Minnie Tudor (Tudor Melody) 3495^{4} 3763^{7} **>77f<**

Petit Poucet 3 b c Fairy King (USA)-City Ex (Ardross) $806a^{2}$ $1117a^{3}$ 1848^{10} $4016a^{2}$ **>119f<**

Petomi 3 ch f Presidium-Missish (Mummy's Pet) 985^{11} *2142^{6} 2493^{3}* 2776^{2} *3072^{4}* 3179^{6} 3492^{12} 3751^{2} (3764) **>65a 66f<**

Petonellajill 5 br m Petong-Crackerjill (Sparkler) 1344^{13} *2290^{5}* **>30a 63f<**

Petosiva (IRE) 3 b br c Petorius-Siva (FR) (Bellypha) 3594^{6} **>76f<**

Petova (IRE) 3 b f Petorius-Kirsova (Absalom) 1450^{8} 1847^{11} 2220^{10} *2925^{12}* **>29f<**

Petraco (IRE) 7 b h Petorius-Merrie Moira 507^{12} 656^{5} 972^{3} 1434^{2} (1499) 1975^{2} 2137^{5} 2448^{8} 2652^{7} 3055^{2} (3116) 3275^{8} 3359^{6} 3615^{22} 3783^{4} 3874^{2} 4142^{12} 4215^{6} 4280^{15} **>64da 72f<**

Petralona (IRE) 4 b f Alleged (USA)-Media Luna (Star Appeal) $703a^{3}$ **>102f<**

Petralona (USA) 4 b f Alleged (USA)-Media Luna (Star Appeal) $1239a^{4}$ **>107f<**

Petra's Star 3 b f Rock City-Meanieminymoe (Star Appeal) 1136^{18} 1476^{15} **>61f<**

Petrefuz (IRE) 2 b g Fayruz-Fifth Quarter (Cure The Blues (USA)) 1670^{17} 2696^{4} 3415^{7} 3877^{10} 4081^{7} **>66f<**

Petrico 3 b c Petong-Balearica (Bustino) 3725^{10} **>13f<**

Petros Pride 2 b f Safawan-Hala (Persian Bold) 1253^{11} 3887^{12} 4218^{7} **>61f<**

Peutetre 3 ch c Niniski (USA)-Marchinella (Daring March) *(204)* 792^{5} 2030^{3} 2571^{10} 3408^{8} 3781^{6} **>58+a 79f<**

Peveril Princess 4 b f Town And Country-Princess Siham (Chabrias (FR)) 885^{8} 1128^{12} 1254^{13} 3759^{16} **>57f<**

Pewter Lass 3 b f Dowsing (USA)-Ragged Moon (Raga Navarro (ITY)) 526^{14} 654^{10} 1093^{19} 1606^{4} 3658^{17} **>32f<**

Phanan 9 ch h Pharly (FR)-L'Ecossaise 1937^{6} 3898^{12} *4336^{11}* **>9a 33f<**

Phantom Creek 2 b f Mr Prospector (USA)-Danseur Fabuleux (USA) (Northern Dancer) 2322^{6} 3948^{7} **>89f<**

Phantom Dancer (IRE) 2 b c Distinctly North (USA)-Angel of Music (Burslem) 1063^{8} 2422^{4} 3048^{3} 3353^{4} 3937^{6} **>46f<**

Phantom Gold 3 b f Machiavellian (USA)-Trying for Gold (USA) (Northern Baby (CAN)) 868^{3} 1139^{6} (1867) 3161^{8} (4204) **>115f<**

Phantom Haze 2 gr g Absalom-Caroline Lamb 2820^{6}

2971^{7} 3231^{12} 4192^{4} 4285^{6} **>62f<**

Pharamineux 9 ch g Pharly (FR)-Miss Longchamp (Northfields (USA)) *37^{3} 97^{6}* (729) 1014^{6} 1149^{3} 1386^{8} (1594) 1749^{2} (2069) 2612^{3} 3127^{4} 3899^{11} 4205^{12} **>62da 73f<**

Pharaoh's Dancer 8 b h Fairy King (USA)-Marie Louise (King Emperor (USA)) *3242^{11} 3512^{8}* 3677^{2} 3960^{5} 4057^{13} **>48a 74f<**

Pharaoh's Joy 2 b f Robellino (USA)-Joyce's Best (Tolomeo) 1690^{6} 2277^{3} (2651) 3405^{5} 3749^{12} **>67f<**

Pharazini 4 b f Pharly (FR)-Arianna Aldini (Habitat) 928^{6} 1061^{9} 1291^{R} **>75f<**

Phar Closer 2 br f Phardante (FR)-Forever Together (Hawaiian Return (USA)) 3713^{10}

Pharly Dancer 6 b h Pharly (FR)-Martin-Lavell Mail (Dominion) *(35) (81) (377)* 423^{14} (757) 1109^{12} 3852^{7} *4270^{2}* **>84a 68f<**

Pharly Reef 3 b g Pharly (FR)-Hay Reef 715^{16} 1167^{5} 1446^{9} *1939^{7}* 2522^{6} **>55a 63f<**

Pharmacy 2 b f Mtoto-Anodyne (Dominion) 1670^{2} 2095^{4} 2542^{2} (3170) 3394^{7} 3990^{3} **>75f<**

Pharr 3 b f Reference Point-Pharian (USA) (Diesis) 1526^{15} **>27f<**

Pharsical 4 ch f Pharly (FR)-Brown Velvet (Mansingh (USA)) 1126^{3} 1335^{3} (1516) 1692^{3} 2017^{7} (2079) (2260) 2461^{10} **>79f<**

Phase One (IRE) 5 b m Horage-Fayes Ben (Don) *378^{13}* 1468^{6} 1855^{7} 2021^{2} 2229^{9} 3263^{5} (3370) 3506^{4} 3607^{15} 4043^{11} **>26a 62f<**

Philanthrop (FR) 0 (3038a) 3478a^{3} **>112f<**

Philgun 6 b h K-Battery-Andalucia *106^{3} 193^{8} 246^{6} 266^{3}* **>64a 75f<**

Philidor 6 b h Forzando-Philgwyn (Milford) (3332a) **>99f<**

Philistar 2 ch c Bairn (USA)-Philgwyn (Milford) 3337^{5} 3733^{20} 3933^{6} **>69f<**

Philmist 3 b f Hard Fought-Andalucia 787^{6} 1026^{4} 1162^{4} 1439^{7} 1816^{5} 1957^{8} *(2630) 2919^{2} 3318^{5} 3527^{5}* 3669^{15} 4086^{10} *4336^{7}* **>63a 48f<**

Philosopher (IRE) 2 b c Royal Academy (USA)-Flyaway Bride (USA) (Blushing Groom (FR)) 4312^{12} **>56f<**

Phils Fortune 3 ch f Kinglet-Crimson Sol (Crimson Beau) *2920^{7}* 3292^{10} **>18f<**

Phil's Time 4 b c Damister (USA)-Coca (Levmoss) 506^{4} 632^{15} 795^{13} 1840^{23} 2268^{3} 2514^{5} 3217^{11} **>79f<**

Phlirty 3 b f Pharly (FR)-Aim to Please (Gunner B) *2291^{12}* 4205^{15}

Phoenix House 2 ch c Formidable (USA)-Ladysave (Stanford) 2534^{10} (3080) 3727^{11} 3856^{8} **>66f<**

Phylian 4 b f Glint of Gold-Phylae (Habitat) 885^{10} 1539^{6} 1651^{4} 2482^{2} 2785^{4} 2845^{4} **>72f<**

Piccolo 4 b c Warning-Woodwind (FR) 921^{6} 1393a^{3} (1896) 2368^{2} **>129f<**

Pie Hatch (IRE) 6 b m Huntingdale-Small Is Beautiful (Condorcet (FR)) 2050^{8}

Pierre Blanco (USA) 6 b h Sovereign Don (USA)-Kiss Off (USA) (Princely Native (USA)) *260^{11}* **>6a f<**

Pierrot Solaire (FR) 2 ch c Dancing Spree-Mare Aux Fees (Kenmare) 2387a^{3} (2900a)

Pigalle Wonder 7 br h Chief Singer-Hi-Tech Girl (Homeboy) *62^{5} 71^{5} 205^{6} 320^{9} 471^{4}* 744^{10} **>39a 35f<**

Pigeon Hole 2 b f Green Desert (USA)-Cubby Hole (Town And Country) 1137^{7} **>61f<**

Pike Creek (USA) 2 b f Alwasmi (USA)-Regal Heights (USA) (Forli (ARG)) 3532^{4} **>74f<**

Pilib (IRE) 4 b c Salt Dome (USA)-Princess Elinor (Captain James) 763^{11} 2931^{6} **>61f<**

Pillow Talk (IRE) 4 b f Taufan (USA)-Concave (Connaught) *18^{2} 94^{11} 275^{5} 387^{6}* 1092^{7} 1403^{2} 1966^{13} 2165^{6} 2676^{3} 3303^{4} **>64a 63f<**

Pilsudski (IRE) 3 b c Polish Precedent (USA)-Cocotte (Troy) 1195^{2} 1872^{17} (2348) (2691) 3836^{3} **>108f<**

Pinatubo 4 ch g Nicholas Bill-Hi-Hunsley (Swing Easy (USA)) *226^{7}* **>56f<**

Pine Essence (USA) 4 ch f Green Forest (USA)-Paradise Coffee (Sharpo) 1432^{4} 1687^{8} (1917) 2954^{8} (3272) 3743^{8} 3987^{5} 4138^{14} 4284^{6} **>62f<**

Pine Needle 2 ch f Kris-Fanny's Cove (Mill Reef (USA)) 3532^{5} (3758) 4107^{5} **>82f<**

Pine Ridge Lad (IRE) 5 gr h Taufan (USA)-Rosserk (Roan Rocket) *(182) (267) 371^{7}* 491^{9} 535^{6} 928^{2} 1061^{8} 1179^{11} 1582^{3} 1828^{13} (1994) 2358^{3} 2517^{5} *3074^{3} 3241^{4}* 3457^{8} 3607^{6} 3977^{12} 4116^{13} 4234^{2} 4292^{5} **>72a 63f<**

Ping-Pong Ball 2 b f Statoblest-Desert Ditty (Green Desert (USA)) 650^{11}

Pink Brief (IRE) 4 b f Ela-Mana-Mou-Tumble Dale (Tumble Wind (USA)) 454^{10} 505^{3} 817^{11} 1543^{8} **>49da 69f<**

Pinkerton Polka 3 b f Shareef Dancer (USA)-Holy Day (Sallust) 779^{12} 1000^{12} 1383^{10} 1735^{10} 1811^{9} 4065^{7} 4228^{4} 4289^{12} **>59f<**

Pinkerton's Pal 4 ch c Dominion-White Domino 934^{9} 1108^{3} 1217^{5} 2235^{3} 2436^{10} 2703^{13} **>102f<**

Pink Petal 3 gr f Northern Game-Gratclo (Belfort (FR)) *185^{7} 331^{9}* 521^{6} 651^{7} 1718^{13} *2630^{11}* **>27a 28f<**

Pinocchio Boy (IRE) 2 b c Soviet Lad (USA)-Trust Sally (Sallust) 1938^{14} 2047^{7} 2656^{3} 2965^{3} (3135) 3233^{7} 3533^{17} *(3738)* 3767^{3} **>66a 63f<**

Pinzon (USA) 3 ch c El Gran Senor (USA)-Chalfont Place (USA) (Little Current (USA)) 715^{3} 924^{2} 1186^{3} 1337^{3} **>86f<**

Pioneer Princess 3 b or br f Prince Sabo-Bloom of Youth (IRE) (Last Tycoon) 745^{6} 1498^{18} 1539^{10} 1735^{9} 1962^{20} **>52f<**

Pipe Major (IRE) 3 b c Tirol-Annsfield Lady (Red Sunset) 920^{4} 1107^{4} (2105) 2646^{4} **>123f<**

Pipers Glen 3 ch g Domynsky-Linanhot (Hot Spark) 1464^{5} 1742^{10} 2021^{10} **>45f<**

Pip's Dream 4 b f Glint of Gold-Arabian Rose (USA) (Lyphard (USA)) *374^{13}* 884^{12} 1349^{2} 1539^{4} (2037) 2339^{3} **>3a 47f<**

Piquant 8 b or br h Sharpo-Asnoura (MOR) 1052^{5} 1244^{6} 1517^{3} 1745^{4} 2123^{7} (2510) 3276^{6} 4234^{4} **>80a 74f<**

Piquetnol (USA) 3 b f Private Account (USA)-Aviance (Northfields (USA)) 1116a^{13} **>101f<**

Pirates Gold (IRE) 5 ch h Vaigly Great-Hemline (Sharpo) *160^{7} 191^{4} 275^{8} 447^{4}* 731^{5} 1013^{3} 1426^{9} 1516^{3} 1815^{4} 2539^{5} 2641^{3} 2810^{2} **>56da 56f<**

Pistol (IRE) 5 ch h Glenstal (USA)-First Wind (Windjammer (USA)) 546^{7} 653^{12} 731^{2} 873^{4} 1141^{15} (1402) 1518^{5} 1908^{7} **>70f<**

Pistol River (IRE) 5 b h Simply Great (FR)-Pampala (Bold Lad (IRE)) 3817^{8} 4118^{9} **>93f<**

Pistols At Dawn (USA) **5** b h Al Nasr (FR)-Cannon Run (USA) (Cannonade (USA)) *(894) 1029^{3} 1086^{6} (1455) 1955^{4} 2145^{4}* **>71a 57f<**

Pitcroy **3** ch f Unfuwain (USA)-Reuval (Sharpen Up) (797) 1067^{4} 1729^{6} 3636^{6} 3944^{4} 4074^{6} **>105f<**

Pitter Patter **3** b f Shareef Dancer (USA)-Rain Date (USA) (Blushing Groom (FR)) 968^{8} 1346^{8} **>64f<**

Pivotal **2** ch c Polar Falcon (USA)-Fearless Revival (Cozzene (USA)) 4161^{9} (4276) (4328) **>95+f<**

Placid-Warrior **5** bl h Battle Hymn-Full of Love (Full of Hope) *311^{8} 375^{15}*

Plain Sailing (FR) **5** b g Slip Anchor-Lassalia (Sallust) 1449^{6} **>23f<**

Platini (IRE) **4** b c Gallic League-Tardy (USA) (Tom Rolfe) 550^{12} 1349^{3} 1513^{13} 3710^{16} **>54f<**

Platin Lady (IRE) **3** ch f Common Grounds-Paradise Bird (Sallust) 3045a^{2} **>112f<**

Plausilium **2** b c Ilium-Pause for Applause (Rolfe (USA)) 1640^{7} 2035^{4} *2496^{7}* 3135^{7} **>32a 43f<**

Playing Tricks **4** b f Elegant Air-Magic Kingdom (Kings Lake (USA)) *155^{10} 223^{5}* **>1a 39f<**

Playmaker **2** b c Primo Dominie-Salacious (Sallust) (533) 1556^{5} 1860^{2} 3803^{3} 4260^{6} **>78f<**

Pleading **2** b c Never so Bold-Ask Mama (Mummy's Pet) 3733^{10} 4161^{4} **>85f<**

Pleasant Memories **3** b f Danehill (USA)-Julip *72^{2} 282^{3}* 7791^{3} (2872) **>53a 60+f<**

Pleasant Surprise **2** b c Cadeaux Genereux-Quiet Week-End (Town And Country) 1134^{6} 2485^{2} 2667^{2} (2995) 3865^{17} **>85f<**

Please Suzanne **2** b f Cadeaux Genereux-Aquaglow (Caerleon (USA)) (3541) 3708^{2} 3816^{3} **>86f<**

Pleasure Beach **3** br g Pharly (FR)-Teacher's Game (Mummy's Game) *74^{3}* **>65a 45f<**

Pleasureland (IRE) **2** ch c Don't Forget Me-Elminya (IRE) (Sure Blade (USA)) *3525^{5}* 3890^{7} 4129^{9} **>59a 67f<**

Pleasure Time **2** ch c Clantime-First Experience (Le Johnstan) 424^{4} 533^{5} 810^{3} (1082) 1267^{5} 2085^{9} 2706^{5} (3064) 3213^{2} 3434^{2} 3568^{7} 3901^{10} **>74f<**

Pleasure Trick (USA) **4** br c Clever Trick (USA)-Pleasure Garden (USA) (Foolish Pleasure (USA)) 2061^{7} 2375^{10} (2755) 2994^{5} 3504^{4} **>70f<**

Plinth **4** b r Dowsing (USA)-Pedestal (High Line) 817^{5} (1166) 1402^{4} 1788^{2} 2298^{3} 2433^{4} 2842^{2} **>62a 66f<**

Plucky Pet **3** br f Petong-Lucky Flinders (Free State) *85^{7} 144^{7} 263^{10}* **>28a 46f<**

Plum Dennis **4** b g Robellino (USA)-Kaleidophone (Kalaglow) 1161^{11} 1435^{10} *1883^{11}* 2327^{14} **>44f<**

Plum First **5** b h Nomination-Plum Bold (Be My Guest (USA)) *400^{4}* 434^{5} 535^{10} 701^{5} (746) 877^{11} (972) 1297^{9} 1689^{3} 1827^{7} 1996^{8} 2096^{3} 2458^{6} 2585^{6} 2714^{4} 2992^{2} 3098^{7} 3230^{12} 3764^{14} **>39a 66f<**

Poddington **4** b g Crofthall-Bold Gift (Persian Bold) 2438^{3} **>80f<**

Poetic Dance (USA) **2** ch c Seattle Dancer (USA)-French Poem (USA) (Sharpen Up) 2681^{9} 3890^{11} **>52f<**

Poetry (IRE) **2** gr f Treasure Kay-Silver Heart (Yankee Gold) 4129^{3} **>58f<**

Pointer **3** b c Reference Point-Greenhill Lass 4162^{10} **>50f<**

Polar Champ **2** b c Polar Falcon (USA)-Ceramic (USA) (Raja Baba (USA)) 3340^{19} **>21f<**

Polar Eclipse **2** ch c Polar Falcon (USA)-Princess Zepoli (Persepolis (FR)) (4070) 4264^{3} **>94f<**

Polaris Flight (USA) **2** b c Northern Flagship (USA)-Anytimeatall (USA) (It's Freezing (USA)) (1779) 1893^{3} (2440) (2704) 3788a^{2} (4310a) **>101f<**

Polar Prince (IRE) **2** b c Distinctly North (USA)-Staff Approved (Teenoso (USA)) 2320^{5} 3089^{5} 3441^{2} (3821) 4107^{10} **>87f<**

Polar Queen **3** b f Polish Precedent (USA)-Rain Date (Rainbow Quest (USA)) (3023) 3728^{11} **>85f<**

Polar Refrain **2** ch f Polar Falcon (USA)-Cut No Ice (Great Nephew) 3647^{3} 3940^{8} 4109^{8} **>65+f<**

Polar Spirit **2** ch f Polar Falcon (USA)-Spirit of India (Indian King (USA)) 4048^{7} (4263) **>68f<**

Polhymnia **4** br f Chief Singer-Six Ashes (Bruni) *3524^{14}* 4240^{14} **>44f<**

Poliglote **3** b c Sadler's Wells (USA)-Alexandrie (USA) (Val de L'Orne (FR)) 801a^{3} 1008a^{2} 1574a^{2} 2044a^{5} 3696a^{2} 4185a^{15} **>121f<**

Polish Bear (IRE) **2** ch f Polish Patriot (USA)-Camarat (Ahonoora) 1054^{4} 1142^{9} 2135^{2} 2552^{10} 3132^{5} 3727^{2} 4206^{4} **>74f<**

Polish Consul **4** ch c Polish Precedent (USA)-Consolation (Troy) 1189^{6} 1600^{5} *2145^{5}* 3710^{6} **>66a 77f<**

Polish Lady (IRE) **2** b f Posen (USA)-Dame Ross (Raga Navarro (ITY)) 4100^{10} 4290^{8} **>38f<**

Polish Legion **2** b c Polish Precedent (USA)-Crystal Bright (Bold Lad (IRE)) (690) **>86+tf<**

Polish Saga **2** ch f Polish Patriot (USA)-Sagar (Habitat) 3170^{5} 3647^{10} 3828^{4} 3969^{12} 4231^{20} **>61?f<**

Polish Spring (IRE) **2** ch f Polish Precedent (USA)-Diavolina (USA) (Lear Fan (USA)) (3948) 4056^{4} 4200^{5} **>87f<**

Polish Widow **2** b f Polish Precedent (USA)-Widows Walk (Habitat) 4103^{5} **>75f<**

Pollen Count (USA) **6** b h Diesis-Apalachee Honey (USA) (Apalachee (USA)) 3478a^{4} 4016a^{6} **>121f<**

Polli Pui **3** b f Puissance-Wing of Freedom (Troy) *419^{14} 502^{4} 603^{6}* 701^{11} 867^{14} *1033^{8}* 4194^{19} **>33a 44f<**

Polly Garter **3** gr f Forzando-Dawn Dance (USA) (Grey Dawn II) *74^{4} 126^{2}* 727^{4} 1274^{6} 1469^{2} 1731^{4} **>46a 57f<**

Polly Golightly **2** ch f Weldnaas (USA)-Polly's Teahouse (Shack (USA)) (859) 1197^{4} 2328^{5} 2489^{3} 2765^{5} 3423^{4} 3548^{13} 4206^{3} (4317) **>80f<**

Polly Particular **3** b f Beveled (USA)-Ballafort (Ballacashtal (CAN)) 3597^{6} 3822^{15} 3992^{9} 4113^{10} **>76f<**

Polly Peculiar **4** b f Squill (USA)-Pretty Pollyanna (General Assembly (USA)) *186^{7} 361^{4}* (1323) 2115^{3} 2593^{6} 3619^{2} 3770^{3} (3872) 4061^{5} **>51a 73f<**

Polo Kit (IRE) **4** b c Trempolino (USA)-Nikitina (Nijinsky (CAN)) 506^{12} 661^{4} 795^{5} 1189^{4} **>89f<**

Polonez Prima **8** ch h Thatching-Taiga (Northfields (USA)) *94^{4}* 1037^{7} 1261^{5} 1415^{4} 1593^{4} 1775^{0} 1855^{4} 2051^{4} 2788^{5} 2979^{16} **>68a 70f<**

Polska (USA) **2** b f Danzig (USA)-Aquaba (USA) (Damascus (USA)) (3816) **>86+f<**

Poltarf (USA) **4** b c Alleged (USA)-La Polonaise (USA) (Danzig (USA)) 735^{3} 869^{2} **>112f<**

Poly By Staufan (IRE) **2** b f Taufan (USA)-Ana Gabriella (USA) (Master Derby (USA)) 3069^{22} 3379^{10} 3520^{6} 3651^{8} 3856^{2} 4109^{3} 4231^{9} **>60f<**

Polydamas **3** b c Last Tycoon-Graecia Magna (USA)

(Private Account (USA)) 764[7] 1382[2] 1589[9] 2571[2] (3016) 4076[7] >**92f**<

Poly Lane **3** b c Mazilier (USA)-Another Lane (Tina's Pet) *43[8] 90[3] 135[3] (185) 241[4] 270[4] 350[2] 366[7]* >**64a 62df**<

Poly Laureon (IRE) **3** b f Fairy King (USA)-Laureon (Caerleon (USA)) *43[2] 105[3] 196[6] 305[4] 363[2]* 524[18] *629[5]* 753[8] *891[3] 1331[6]* 1434[5] 1564[5] 2018[3] >**64a 56f**<

Poly Road **3** b f Most Welcome-Jump The Road (CAN) (Darby Creek Road (USA)) *10[4] (51) 141[3] 241[6] 339[2] (368) (388) 444[7]* 453[6] 538[5] (651) 851 974[2] 1093[3] 1218[7] >**64da 66f**<

Poly Screen **4** ch c Ballacashtal (CAN)-Scenic Villa (Top Ville) 3759[17] 4248[15] >**41a 50f**<

Poly Static (IRE) **2** b f Statoblest-Great Leighs (Vaigly Great) 429[4] 508[10] >**43f**<

Pommard (IRE) **2** b c Darshaan-Pont Aven (1752) >**83+f**<

Pomorie (IRE) **4** b f Be My Guest (USA)-Mpani (Habitat) 1025[7] 1973[3] 2248[3] 2569[11] >**72f**<

Pont Audemer (USA) **3** b f Chief's Crown (USA)-Peruvienne (3196a) >**99f**<

Pontynyswen **7** b h Ballacashtal (CAN)-Tropingay (Cawston's Clown) *(304) 396[10]* >**53a f**<

Poor Printer (IRE) **4** ch f Digamist (USA)-No Reproach (Northfields (USA)) 637[10] 887[16] >**27a 28f**<

Poplar Bluff (IRE) **3** b c Dowsing-Bleu Pale (FR) (El Gran S 608a[3] 895a[3] 1389a[3] 2040a[3] (3795a) (4178a) 4305a[13] >**123f**<

Popolare (IRE) **3** c 1396a[12] >**65f**<

Poppy Carew (IRE) **3** b f Danehill (USA)-Why so Silent (Mill Reef (USA)) 620[2] 1729[2] 2763[5] (3278) (3636) 3944[3] >**113f**<

Poppy My Love **2** ch f Clantime-Yankeedoodledancer (Mashhor Dancer (USA)) 925[8] 1497[8] 2023[5] 3124[5] *3244[5]* 3567[5] 4132[10] >**31a 32f**<

Pop to Stans **6** b h Gold Crest (USA)-Lady of Camelot (FR) (Bolkonski) *29[8] 68[6] 379[2] 413[7] 415[3] 497[4] 605[11]* 672[3] *1074[4]* (1523) 1854[2] 1911[10] 2334[10] 2528[3] 2744[7] 2983[5] 3202[3] 3426[6] 3658[16] 3825[4] 4152[6] 4209[9] >**59a 48f**<

Port Augusta (IRE) **3** b c Tirol-Sweet Adelaide (USA) (The Minstrel (CAN)) (502) >**70f**<

Porte Belloch **4** br f Belfort (FR)-Keyanloch (Lochnager) 817[2] 860[4] 1350[13] 1658[8] >**52df**<

Portelet **3** b f Night Shift (USA)-Noirmant (Dominion) *72[3] 156[2]* 524[2] *1032[4]* 1201[13] 1277[3] 1521[2] 1739[6] 3251[2] (3508) (3667) 3822[18] 4286[3] 4322[2] >**53a 85f**<

Portend **3** b c Komaite (USA)-Token of Truth (Record Token) *(33) (78) (118) 170[3] (210) 257[3] 380[3]* (426) (483) 828[5] >**79a 86f**<

Port Hedland **3** gr f Then Again-Port Na Blath (On Your Mark) *3514[13]* 3747[14] 3960[11] *4296[9]* >**8a 12f**<

Portite Sophie **4** b f Doulab (USA)-Impropriety (Law Society (USA)) 478[7] 1816[3] 2306[2] 2874[2] 3118[4] 3259[6] *3513[9]* >**22a 50f**<

Portland Way **3** b c Superpower-Broadway Stomp (USA) (Broadway Forli (USA)) *512[6]* 1092[20] 1428[6] 3426[14] 3619[17] >**24a 28f**<

Port Lucaya **5** ch h Sharpo-Sister Sophie (USA) (Effervescing (USA)) 609a[6] 1002a[4] 1236a[10] 3574a[8] >**117f**<

Portolano (FR) **4** b c Reference Point-Kottna (USA) (Lyphard (USA)) *161[8]* 866[18] 1285[20] 3426[11] >**38a 59f**<

Portscatho (IRE) **3** b g Common Grounds-Tweedling (USA) (Sir Ivor) 3756[8] 4072[14] >**43f**<

Port Sunlight (IRE) **7** ch h Tate Gallery (USA)-Nana's Girl *161[6] 254[2] 279[5] 367[6] 421[8]* 778[9] 905[12] *1074[9]* >**53a 75f**<

Portuguese Lil **2** ch f Master Willie-Sabonis (USA) (The Minstrel (CAN)) 3666[5] 4190[9] 4291[6] >**65f**<

Posen Gold (IRE) **2** b f Posen (USA)-Golden Sunlight (Ile de Bourbon (USA)) 1823[5] 2717[3] >**61f**<

Posidonas **3** b c Slip Anchor-Tamassos (Dance In Time (CAN)) (711) 1122a[8] (3603) (3790a) 4176a[5] >**114f**<

Posing (IRE) **3** b f Sadler's Wells (USA)-Glancing (Grundy) 987[3] 1383[5] 1732[8] 3004[3] 3395[4] 3621[2] 3885[14] >**74f**<

Positive Result (IRE) **3** ch f Doulab (USA)-Second Service (Red Regent) *363[9]* 855[17] 1445[15] >**2a 10f**<

Positivo **4** br c Robellino (USA)-Primetta (Precocious) 762[7] 1245[8] *1320[6]* 2115[2] >**70+a 75f**<

Possessive Artiste **2** b f Shareef Dancer (USA)-Possessive (Posse (USA)) 3069[5] 3339[8] >**85+f**<

Possibility **4** b f Robellino (USA)-Bentinck Hotel *62[7] 205[7] (265) 373[3] 406[5]* >**44a 57f**<

Possibly Perfect (USA) **5** b m Northern Baby (CAN)-Avasand (USA) (Avatar (USA)) (3480a) >**120f**<

Postage Stamp **8** ch h The Noble Player (USA)-Takealetter (Wolver Hollow) 2413[8] >**9f**<

Posted Abroad (IRE) **3** b g Cyrano de Bergerac-Postie (Sharpo) *(149) 257[2] (294)* >**71a f**<

Potenza **2** b g Puissance-Indivisible (Remainder Man) *2633[8] 3077[11] 4124[9]* >**36a f**<

Pourquoi Pas (IRE) **3** b f Nordico-Mystery Lady (4020a) >**101f**<

Pourville (USA) **3** f 1238a[5] >**43f**<

Powder Bowl (USA) **3** f 2045a[4] 3035a[2] >**97f**<

Power **4** b c Bustino-Pushy *(252) 377[2] 403[9]* 653[11] >**78a 79f**<

Power Dee **2** b f Superpower-Linn O' Dee (King of Spain) 429[6] 554[8] 755[4] 983[7] >**26f**<

Power Don **2** ch c Superpower-Donalee (Don) 2483[3] 2773[2] *3243[5]* 3417[3] 3670[5] 3856[3] >**56a 64f**<

Power Game **2** b c Puissance-Play the Game (Mummy's Game) 1278[3] 1492[2] 1685[5] 2619[5] 2904[3] 3468[9] 3838[3] 4098[3] >**72f**<

Power Mouse **3** ch g Hubbly Bubbly (USA)-Targuette 772[13] >**4f**<

Power of Polly (USA) **5** br h Green Dancer (USA)-Polly Daniels (USA) (Clever Trick (USA)) 1397a[3] >**94f**<

Power Princess **2** b f Superpower-Hyde Princess (Touch Paper) 3231[16] 3430[6] 3647[7] 3824[12] 3937[15] >**48f**<

Power Share **4** ch g Superpower-Collegian (Stanford) *373[10]* >**12a 45f**<

Poyle Jezebelle **4** ch f Sharpo-Hithermoor Lass (Red Alert) 862[6] 1126[4] 1344[4] 1649[5] 2088[5] (2404) 2659[12] 3028[10] 3624[2] 3874[4] 4057[17] 4215[11] >**56f**<

Praglia (IRE) **3** b f Darshaan-Nazanin (Sharpo) 2350[6] 3634[10] 3801[16] >**65f**<

Prague Spring **3** b f Salse (USA)-Wassl's Sister (Troy) 1128[5] (2653) 2989[3] >**75tf**<

Prairie Grove **5** b h Primo Dominie-Fairy Fans *235[10] 277[12]* >**14a 42f**<

Prancing 2 br f Prince Sabo-Valika (Valiyar) 1928^2 (3022) 3680^2 4084^5 **>89f<**

Pratique (USA) 4 ch f Known Fact (USA)-Scierpan (USA) (Sharpen Up) *119^8* **>64f<**

Precede 3 b c Polish Precedent (USA)-Height of Passion (Shirley Heights) (886) 1396a^3 **>104f<**

Precious Girl 2 ch f Precious Metal-Oh My Oh My (Ballacashtal (CAN)) (490) 993^5 1267^8 2131^3 (2424) 3809^{13} 4066^2 4243^6 4321^6 **>78f<**

Precious Times 3 b c Emarati (USA)-Massawa (FR) (Tennyson (FR)) *107^7 132^5 305^9 348^9* 904^8 **>39a 33f<**

Precious Wonder 6 b h Precocious-B M Wonder (Junius (USA)) 505^9 586^{12} 4027^5 4135^{16} **>46f<**

Predictable 9 ch h Music Boy-Piccadilly Etta *302^{10} 370^{12}* **>16a f<**

Premazing 3 ch c Precocious-Amazing Journey (USA) (Spectacular Bid (USA)) 1407^6 2050^6 *3318^8* 3899^{15} **>22a 38f<**

Premier Blues (FR) 5 b m Law Society (USA)-Etoile d'Ocean (USA) (Northern Dancer) *96^9 1086^{13}* 1555^4 1974^5 2486^{12} 3129^5 3258^5 3658^{12} **>20a 48f<**

Premier Dance 8 ch h Bairn (USA)-Gigiolina (King Emperor (USA)) *(131) 227^3 367^3 389^2 412^{11} 530^6 833^3 1075^3* 1328^5 1686^5 *2495^2 3245^2 4126^6* **>70a 52f<**

Premier Generation (IRE) 2 b c Cadeaux Genereux-Bristle (Thatch (USA)) 3916^{10} 4169^{11} **>58f<**

Premier League (IRE) 5 gr h Don't Forget Me-Kilmara (USA) (Caro) 2169^8 **>80f<**

Premier Star 5 ch g Precocious-Grove Star *82^{15}* **>34da 41df<**

Premium Gift 3 ch f Most Welcome-Emerald Eagle (Sandy Creek) 772^6 1302^2 (1602) 3166^{12} **>71f<**

Prends Ca (IRE) 2 b f Reprimand-Cri de Coeur (USA) (Lyphard (USA)) (1746) 2106^7 (4025) 4203^4 **>86f<**

Prenonamoss 7 b h Precocious-Nonabella (Nonoalco (USA)) 430^6 634^U 975^9 1183^{12} 1940^8 *2377^6 3075^{12}* (3605) 3837^9 3920^2 **>55a 64f<**

Present Arms (USA) 2 b c Affirmed (USA)-Au Printemps (USA) (Dancing Champ (USA)) 3888^{11} 3955^3 4146^3 **>74f<**

Presenting 3 br c Mtoto-D'Azy (Persian Bold) (619) (912) 1107^3 1611^3 2323^3 (2670) (3088) 4185a^{14} **>121+f<**

Present 'n Correct 2 ch g Cadeaux Genereux-Emerald Eagle (Sandy Creek) 4070^9

Present Situation 4 ch c Cadeaux Genereux-Storm Warning (Tumble Wind (USA)) *160^4 (298) 344^2 1633^7* 2317^{13} 3771^4 4157^5 *4297^2* **>77a 59f<**

Presidential (FR) 4 b g Village Star (FR)-Pokhara (FR) (Kashmir) *4293^{11}* **>21a f<**

Press Again 3 ch f Then Again-Silver Empress (Octavo (USA)) 1675^{11} 1979^9 **>38f<**

Press the Bell 5 br g Belfort (FR)-Northern Empress (Northfields (USA)) *70^2 216^6 327^5* 2150^6 **>73a 80f<**

Presto Boy 3 b c Precocious-Dingle Belle (Dominion) *25^6 90^5 171^2 258^7* 1285^3 1427^2 1645^7 1970^4 2129^6 2830^3 3184^3 3265^5 **>59a 55f<**

Preston Guild (IRE) 5 b h Mazaad-Dying Craft (Thatching) 778^3 986^2 1161^3 1858^{13} 3987^{16} **>62a 60df<**

Pretonic 7 b m Precocious-Northern Ballerina (Dance In Time (CAN)) *44^8 134^6 417^5 501^4 518^5* **>49a 23f<**

Pretoria Dancer 3 b c Dancing Brave (USA)-Pretoria (Habitat) 1526^8 1755^9 1916^6 *3526^5* 3818^4 (3978) 4086^6 **>79f<**

Pretty Average 5 b m Skyliner-Marock Morley *2627^{11}* (2784) 2821^3 **>10a 38f<**

Pretty Chic 6 b g Kabour-Boom Shanty (Dragonara Palace (USA)) *348^5 2295^{10} 2925^{10}* **>29a f<**

Pretty Scarce 4 ch f Handsome Sailor-Not Enough (Balinger) *394^9* **>27a f<**

Prevail (USA) 2 b f Danzig-Primevere 4251a^3

Pricket (USA) 2 ch f Diesis-Cacti (USA) (Tom Rolfe) (3346) **>62+f<**

Prickwillow (USA) 3 b f Nureyev (USA)-Braiswick (King of Spain) 695^{10} 3377^2 3653^2 (3847) **>77+f<**

Priddy Fair 2 b f North Briton-Rainbow Ring (Rainbow Quest (USA)) 1497^6 1823^4 *2143^9* 3533^{12} 3642^9 4045^{12} **>27a 67f<**

Pride of Brixton 2 b c Dominion-Caviar Blini (What A Guest) 3765^3 3893^2 **>71f<**

Pride of Hayling (IRE) 4 ch f Bold Arrangement-Malham Tarn (Riverman (USA)) 1071^9 1538^6 (2054) (2539) 2685^4 3177^{12} 3751^{10} 3874^8 *4217^{13}* **>17a 67df<**

Pride of Kashmir 2 gr c Petong-Proper Madam (Mummy's Pet) 617^{11} 849^7 3821^4 3985^{10} 4111^8 4327^4 **>55f<**

Pride of May (IRE) 4 b c Law Society (USA)-Aztec Princess (Indian King (USA)) *15^3 87^2* 432^{14} 668^4 938^2 1144^4 1349^6 1594^6 2201^5 2391^2 2622^4 2854^5 *3527^{14}* **>72a 78f<**

Pride of Pendle 6 ro m Grey Desire-Pendle's Secret 433^{15} 724^9 (927) 1021^9 1179^5 1357^6 1638^5 (1808) 1926^{13} 2419^5 2788^2 2952^2 3113^2 (3222) 3419^6 3607^7 3945^{11} 4038^{11} 4116^{10} **>85f<**

Pride of Whalley (IRE) 2 b f Fayruz-Wilderness (Martinmas) 782^6 *1089^4* 1356^2 **>51a 51f<**

Pridwell 5 b h Sadler's Wells (USA)-Glowing With Pride (Ile de Bourbon (USA)) 998^{15} **>53f<**

Prima Cominna 3 ch f Unfuwain (USA)-Cominna (Dominion) 743^2 959^3 1374^4 1544^3 2067^9 2437^2 2647^6 **>85f<**

Prima Silk 4 b f Primo Dominie-Silk St James (Pas de Seul) *219^4 365^8 417^3* 563^5 1335^6 (1604) (1827) 2840^0 3112^{10} 3359^{16} 3418^9 3519^7 3624^7 3637^{10} 4057^8 4134^4 4215^4 4322^7 **>70a 73f<**

Prima Volta 2 b f Primo Dominie-Femme Formidable (Formidable) 3133^4 (3495) 3867^{12} 4077^7 **>86f<**

Prime Connections 2 b c Petoski-Qualitair Princess (Bay Express) 836^5 *3738^{11}* 3975^{26} 4045^{19} **>13f<**

Prime Lady (GER) 4 b f Esclavo (GER)-Prime Rose 3912a^3 **>102f<**

Primelta 2 b f Primo Dominie-Pounelta (Tachypous) 1536^6 2025^{10} 3625^{12} **>63f<**

Prime Match (IRE) 3 ch c Primo Dominie-Last Blessing (Final Straw) 1094^{18} (1360) 1806^{11} 2271^6 2764^{27} *3242^9* 3748^{23} **>76a 86df<**

Prime Partner 2 b c Formidable (USA)-Baileys by Name (Nomination) 2408^{12} 2552^6 2801^2 3003^5 3423^8 4144^{12} 4206^{14} **>71f<**

Prime Property (IRE) 3 b f Tirol-Busker (Bustino) *315^{11}* 573^9 759^{14} 966^{15} 1358^9 2166^9 *2630^{15}* 2832^{10} 3098^2 (3275) 3879^6 3980^{21} **>7a 41f<**

Prime Secret 2 ch c Primo Dominie-Secret Freedom (USA) (Secreto (USA)) 2978^8 3260^{11} **>11f<**

Prim Lass 4 b f Reprimand-Vague Lass (Vaigly Great)

1290^{19} 1583^{3} 1843^{8} *2377^{16}* >**46a 55f**<

Primo Lad 2 b c Primo Dominie-Zinzi (Song) 836^{6}

Primo Lara 3 ch c Primo Dominie-Clara Barton (Youth (USA)) 963^{2} 1312^{4} 1736^{6} 2253^{5} 3125^{3} 3619^{3} 4115^{4} >**49a 74f**<

Primo Panache 3 ch f Primo Dominie-Royal Agnes (Royal Palace) 1182^{7} >**31f**<

Primrose Path 2 b f Shaadi (USA)-Crimson Conquest (USA) (Diesis) 2351^{10} 3136^{3} 3758^{6} >**71f**<

Primula Bairn 5 b m Bairn (USA)-Miss Primula (Dominion) *14^{5} (107) (194) 306^{3} 398^{3} (510)* 723^{13} *831^{7} 3072^{8} 3524^{5}* 3667^{8} 3777^{8} 3783^{14} >**51a 50f**<

Prince Arthur (IRE) 3 b c Fairy King (USA)-Daniela Samuel (USA) (No Robbery) 677^{2} (900a) 1234a^{5} 3199a^{6} 4093a^{2} >**120f**<

Prince Aslia 2 b c Aragon-Aslia (Henbit (USA)) 951^{3} (1063) (1584) 1868^{9} 2740^{W} 3100^{2} 3324a^{2} 3610^{7} 4084^{8} >**97df**<

Prince Belfort 7 b g Belfort (FR)-Princess Sharpenup (Lochnager) *369^{8}* 579^{8} (688) 746^{3} 2521^{6} 2758^{P} >**51a 68f**<

Prince Danzig (IRE) 4 ch c Roi Danzig (USA)-Veldt (High Top) *(143) 235^{2} 318^{3} 396^{6} (403) 445^{3}* 1014^{3} 1166^{4} 1518^{2} 1773^{4} (2639) 2829^{2} 2989^{2} 3083^{5} 3769^{2} 3957^{4} >**84a 75f**<

Prince Equiname 3 gr c Dominion-Moments Peace (Adonijah) 824^{8} 1162^{3} 1308^{4} 1578^{8} *1880^{6}* 3723^{10} 3853^{7} >**59a 57f**<

Prince Kinsky 2 ch c Master Willie-Princess Lieven (Royal Palace) 3089^{9} 4080^{8} >**83f**<

Princely Affair 2 b c Prince Sabo-Shillay (Lomond (USA)) 3625^{13} 3892^{8} 4109^{13} >**49f**<

Princely Gait 4 b c Darshaan-Roussalka (Habitat) *221^{3} (303) (346)* >**80a 62f**<

Princely Hush (IRE) 3 b c Prince Sabo-So Kind (Kind of Hush) 1133^{7} >**115f**<

Princely Sound 2 b c Prince Sabo-Sound of the Sea (Windjammer (USA)) 671^{4} 849^{2} 2791^{7} >**64f**<

Princely Sword (USA) 2 ch g Sanglamore (USA)-Princess of Man 3437^{8} >**51f**<

Prince Mike (IRE) 2 b br c Anita's Prince-Kiss The Bride (Sweet Revenge) 2782^{11} >**14f**<

Prince of Andros (USA) 5 b h Al Nasr (FR)-Her Radiance (USA) (Halo (USA)) (827) (1235a) 1708a^{2} 2286^{7} 3576a^{7} 3811^{8} >**120f**<

Prince of Florence (IRE) 2 ch c Bluebird (USA)-Seme de Lys (Slew O' Gold (USA)) 1176^{4} 1413^{3} 2183^{5} 2674^{2} 3281^{2} 3613^{7} 3861^{2} 4151^{2} >**87f**<

Prince of India 3 b c Night Shift (USA)-Indian Queen (Electric) 826^{8} 1185^{3} 1586^{5} 2105^{2} 2889a^{6} 4198^{3} 4345a^{5} >**122df**<

Prince of My Heart 2 ch c Prince Daniel (USA)-Blue Room (Gorytus (USA)) 1726^{11} 3089^{8} 3398^{3} 3821^{3} (3994) 4139^{6} >**77f**<

Prince of Spades 3 ch c Shavian-Diamond Princess (Horage) 2102^{5} (2309) 2532^{7} (2811) 3026^{7} 3860^{6} 4138^{9} >**70f**<

Prince Palacio 5 ch g Legend of France (USA)-Thatchville (Thatch (USA)) *46^{10}* >**40da f**<

Prince Pellinore 3 b c Prince Sabo-Pellinora (USA) (King Pellinore (USA)) 648^{19} *1334^{8} 1569^{10}* 2033^{8} 2491^{7} 2844^{4} 3515^{4} 3980^{12} 4131^{9} >**25a 46f**<

Prince Rodney 6 gr h King of Spain-Dancing Diana (Raga Navarro (ITY)) *39^{7}* 848^{12} *1034^{11}* >**34a 32f**<

Prince Rudolf (IRE) 3 b g Cyrano de Bergerac-Princess Raisa (Indian King (USA)) *7^{3} 146^{2} 220^{4} 251^{3} 300^{3} 319^{5} 420^{4}* 482^{8} *842^{7}* 966^{10} 1521^{3} 1963^{14} 2239^{7} 2540^{3} 2813^{4} 2885^{3} >**54a 59f**<

Princerullah 4 gr c Prince des Coeurs (USA)-Chevrullah (Grisaille) *58^{11}* >**23f**<

Prince's Feather (IRE) 3 ch f Cadeaux Genereux-Amaranthus (Shirley Heights) 1294^{5} 1692^{5} 1991^{8} 3058^{6} >**80df**<

Prince Songline 5 b h Prince Sabo-Question Mark 1206^{7} >**57a 58df**<

Princess Bilbao 2 br f Highest Honor-Princess Player 3328a^{3} >**80f**<

Princess Briana 2 b f Daring March-Jersey Maid (On Your Mark) 3253^{8} 3806^{14} 4098^{11} >**6f**<

Princess Danielle 3 b f Prince Daniel (USA)-Bells of St Martin (Martinmas) 1172^{13} 1541^{3} (1859) 2778^{5} 3095^{3} (3889) 4261^{9} >**68f**<

Princesse Abigail 4 b f Esprit du Nord (USA)-Princesse Vali (FR) (Val de L'Orne (FR)) 884^{15} 1058^{17} 1535^{14} 1788^{8} >**38f**<

Princess Efisio 2 b f Efisio-Cutlass Princess (USA) (Cutlass (USA)) 2000^{5} 2275^{6} >**41f**<

Princess Gay (IRE) 3 b f Fairy King (USA)-Tripoli (Great Heron (USA)) 522^{15} >**15f**<

Princess in Blue (IRE) 3 b f Bluebird (USA)-Parkeen Princess (He Loves Me) *146^{9}* >**19a 36f**<

Princess Kamina 3 b f Nomination-Danaka (FR) (Val de Loir) *95^{9} 292^{9}* >**29a 38f**<

Princess Maxine (IRE) 6 b m Horage-Sallywell (Manado) 493^{10} 567^{6} 724^{5} 785^{8} 1251^{11} 1995^{8} 2258^{2} 2484^{4} 2733^{2} 2814^{4} 2906^{4} 2999^{9} 3467^{16} 3800^{3} 3941^{7} 4060^{6} >**58f**<

Princess Oberon (IRE) 5 b or br m Fairy King (USA)-Flash of Gold (Pardao) 1106^{9} (1489) 1766^{4} 2060^{6} 2617^{2} 2746^{4} 3236^{7} >**91f**<

Princess Pamgaddy 2 gr f Petong-Edwin's Princess (Owen Dudley) 1223^{3} 1653^{5} 2185^{7} 3415^{6} (3744) 3851^{6} 3975^{4} 4075^{10} >**64f**<

Princess Renata (IRE) 2 ch f Maelstrom Lake-Sajanjal (Dance In Time (CAN)) *1031^{9}* 1399^{6} 1652^{6} 2715^{6} >**45f**<

Princess Sadie 3 ch f Shavian-Princess Zepoli (Persepolis (FR)) 2512^{3} 2742^{5} 3298^{5} 4278^{13} 4322^{20} >**81df**<

Princess Shera (IRE) 4 b f Prince Rupert (FR)-Crown Coral (Main Reef) *63^{11}* 2396^{11} 2913^{6} 3272^{7} >**29da 35df**<

Princethorpe 8 b g Ring Bidder-Sparkling Jenny (Sparkler) *1951^{10} 3073^{10} 4270^{10}* >**14a f**<

Prince Zizim 2 b c Shareef Dancer (USA)-Possessive Lady (Dara Monarch) 3371^{11} 3955^{4} >**65f**<

Principal Boy (IRE) 2 br g Cyrano de Bergerac-Shenley Lass (Prince Tenderfoot (USA)) 2608^{5} 2971^{4} 3463^{10} 3671^{5} 3882^{9} 4097^{12} 4287^{6} >**62df**<

Printers Quill 3 b g Squill (USA)-On Impulse (Jellaby) 3653^{10} 3847^{3} 4164^{9} >**59f**<

Priolo Prima 2 b c Priolo (USA)-Jungle Rose (Shirley Heights) 3779^{2} >**78+f**<

Priory Belle (IRE) 2 ch f Priolo (USA)-Ingabelle (Taufan (USA)) (3692a) >**101f**<

Private Audience (USA) 2 b c Private Account (USA)-

Monroe (USA) 4037^{6} **>52f<**
Private Fixture (IRE) 4 ch c The Noble Player (USA)-Pennyala (Skyliner) *293^{4}* 820^{17} 1542^{6} *2588^{7}* **>68a 69f<**
Private Line (USA) 3 ch f Private Account (USA)-Miss Summer (Luthier (FR)) 1500^{3} (2006) (3235) 3693a^{8} **>103f<**
Private Song (USA) 2 b c Private Account (USA)-Queen of Song (USA) (His Majesty (USA)) 4312^{2} **>83+f<**
Privileged 2 ch c Efisio-Prejudice (Young Generation) 2619^{6} (2820) **>72+f<**
Privity (USA) 14 ch h Empery (USA)-Information (USA) 1110a^{3} 1704a^{3} (2045a) 3694a^{8} **>112f<**
Prizefighter 4 b c Rambo Dancer (CAN)-Jaisalmer (Castle Keep) 1148^{7} 1995^{9} 2123^{6} 2668^{6} (3011) 3182^{8} 4038^{18} **>70f<**
Prize Giving 2 ch c Most Welcome-Glowing With Pride (Ile de Bourbon (USA)) 2370^{6} 3010^{2} 3340^{3} (4154) **>74f<**
Prize Pupil (IRE) 3 b c Royal Academy (USA)-Bestow (Shirley Heights) 675^{2} 2319^{5} (2568) 3066^{3} 3459^{7} 3926^{14} **>81f<**
Profit Release (IRE) 4 b f Dowsing (USA)-Going Digital (USA) (Northern Baby (CAN)) *2^{10} 31^{3} 127^{4} 179^{2} 219^{3} 255^{3} (302) 365^{10}* 481^{10} 672^{2} 784^{2} 927^{7} (1044) 1381^{3} 1421^{6} 1809^{2} 1828^{3} 1932^{6} 2088^{4} (2229) **>63a 67f<**
Progression 4 b c Reprimand-Mainmast (Bustino) 762^{3} 986^{8} 1314^{7} 1553^{4} 2175^{3} *2379^{5}* (2768) (3189) 3336^{2} 3547^{6} 3836^{16} **>50a 81+f<**
Projection (USA) 2 b c Topsider (USA)-Image of Reality (USA) (In Reality (USA)) (4103) **>91+f<**
Prolific Lady (IRE) 3 b f Nabeel Dancer (USA)-Aljood (Kris) 435^{4} 585^{4} (742) 985^{7} 1263^{2} 1564^{7} 1924^{6} 1982^{2} 2271^{5} 2697^{2} 3250^{3} 3637^{17} **>78f<**
Promise Fulfilled (USA) 4 b f Bet Twice (USA)-Kind Prospect (USA) (Mr Prospector (USA)) *364^{10}* 439^{15} 1021^{14} 1217^{4} 1560^{4} 2117^{11} 3700^{10} 3941^{11} **>71a 78f<**
Promitto 5 ch m Roaring Riva-I Don't Mind (Swing Easy (USA)) 1944^{5} 2132^{7} **>27f<**
Promptly (IRE) 2 b f Lead on Time (USA)-Ghariba (Final Straw) 3371^{2} **>74+f<**
Proper Blue (USA) 2 b c Proper Reality (USA)-Blinking (USA) (Tom Rolfe) 1781^{4} 2182^{3} 2434^{3} 3009^{2} (3267) **>92f<**
Property Man 3 gr c Clantime-Cool Number (Swing Easy (USA)) 3913a^{3} **>40ta 95f<**
Prophets Honour 3 ch g Deploy-Cat's Claw (USA) (Sharpen Up) 670^{4} 1097^{13} 3338^{4} 3618^{4} 3772^{4} 4082^{3} **>83f<**
Propolis Power (IRE) 2 ch g Simply Great (FR)-Now Then (Sandford Lad) 1063^{7} 1215^{5} 1841^{12} 2251^{10} **>32f<**
Proposing (IRE) 3 b c Rainbow Quest (USA)-La Romance (USA) (Lyphard (USA)) *(500) 564^{2}* **>98a f<**
Prosarch (IRE) 2 ch f Archway (IRE)-Biddy Mulligan (Ballad Rock) 3628^{20} 3988^{11} **>31f<**
Prosequendo (USA) 8 b h Robellino (USA)-Allegedly (USA) (Sir Ivor) *109^{8}* 2280^{9} 3676^{19} **>56da 44f<**
Prospector's Cove 2 b c Dowsing (USA)-Pearl Cove (Town And Country) (4290) **>83+f<**
Prospero 2 b g Petong-Pennies to Pounds (Ile de Bourbon (USA)) 4080^{12} **>70f<**
Protektor (GER) 6 b h Acatenango (GER)-Prioritat (FR) (Frontal) 2046a^{5} 2729a^{5} 3046a^{6} 3914a^{3} **>120f<**
Proton 5 b h Sure Blade (USA)-Banket (Glint of Gold) 634^{15} 961^{5} 1260^{3} 1853^{7} 2768^{2} 3091^{2} (3406) 3730^{15} 4325^{14} **>89f<**
Proud Brigadier (IRE) 7 b h Auction Ring (USA)-Naughty One Gerard (Brigadier Gerard) 3984^{19} **>69f<**
Proud Destiny 3 b f Green Desert (USA)-Pumpona (USA) (Sharpen Up) 695^{8} 1312^{2} 1554^{2} (2265) 2488^{4} 2848^{3} 3373^{2} 3488^{6} **>88f<**
Proud Image 3 b c Zalazl (USA)-Fleur de Foret (USA) (Green Forest (USA)) 715^{15} 973^{2} 1097^{20} 1353^{5} *1568^{8}* 1904^{4} 2191^{4} 2503^{5} (2620) (2807) 2945^{3} 3372^{7} **>41a 78f<**
Proud Monk 2 gr c Aragon-Silent Sister (Kind of Hush) 1318^{4} 1715^{6} 2299^{3} 2674^{5} 3655^{6} 3858^{3} 3956^{3} (4208) 4321^{3} **>78f<**
Provence 8 ch h Rousillon (USA)-Premier Rose (Sharp Edge) 954^{7} 1268^{7} **>86df<**
Prudent Pet 3 b f Distant Relative-Philgwyn (Milford) 573^{7} *847^{5}* 1724^{7} 1945^{2} (2332) *(3529)* 3700^{14} 4071^{15} 4171^{18} **>67a 67f<**
Prudent Princess 3 b f Puissance-Princess Story 2469^{4} 2949^{5} 3138^{3} *3734^{4}* 4049^{3} **>60a 71f<**
Prussia 4 b c Roi Danzig (USA)-Vagrant Maid (USA) (Honest Pleasure (USA)) 3759^{14} 3936^{13} 4248^{12} **>42f<**
Prussian Blue (USA) 3 b c Polish Navy (USA)-Lit'l Rose (USA) (Mr Prospector (USA)) 663^{3} (1062) 1872^{13} **>90f<**
Prussian Flag 3 b c Infantry-What A Present (Pharly (FR)) 2030^{4} 2436^{11} 3026^{8} 4170^{18} **>85df<**
Public Acclaim 2 ch f Weldnaas (USA)-Sure Victory (IRE) (Stalker) 1336^{7} *2496^{8}* **>27a 23f<**
Public Offering 2 b f Warrshan (USA)-Money Supply (Brigadier Gerard) 3767^{16} 3895^{16} **>21f<**
Public Reproof 2 b g Reprimand-Zelda (USA) (Sharpen Up) 4312^{15} **>32f<**
Puerto Escondido (USA) 4 b c Polish Navy-Relasure (Relaunch) 1392a^{4} 4092a^{3} 4342a^{2} **>110f<**
Puffy 8 ch g Wolverlife-Eskaroon (Artaius (USA)) *34^{3} 80^{3} 308^{8} 378^{3}* 478^{6} 818^{6} 1191^{7} 1523^{4} *(1762) 1884^{5} 2377^{4}* **>52a 50f<**
Pulga Circo 2 b f Tina's Pet-Pulga (Blakeney) *1212^{12} 1570^{3} 2075^{5} 2496^{2}* 3533^{19} *3738^{4}* 4045^{7} *4127^{10} 4273^{12}* **>57a 43f<**
Pulmicort 5 b g Red Sunset-Finesse (Miralgo) 1513^{17} 1659^{7} 1757^{11} **>49f<**
Pumice 3 ch f Salse (USA)-Horseshoe Reef (Mill Reef (USA)) 1296^{7} (2880) 3189^{6} 3552^{5} 4071^{8} 4248^{7} **>80f<**
Punch 3 b c Reprimand-Cartooness (USA) (Achieved) 1417^{5} 1725^{3} 1997^{3} 2312^{4} (3153) 3299^{4} 3669^{10} 3843^{8} **>62f<**
Punkah (USA) 2 b c Lear Fan (USA)-Gentle Persuasion (Bustino) 3890^{5} 4161^{18} **>76f<**
Purbeck Centenary 5 b h Lidhame-Double Stitch (Wolver Hollow) *192^{2} 287^{3} 359^{2} 446^{10}* 688^{11} 856^{16} 1164^{7} 1321^{8} 2054^{3} **>50a 44f<**
Pure Grain 3 b f Polish Precedent (USA)-Mill Line (Mill Reef (USA)) (1101) 1587^{3} (2563a) (3161) 4014a^{5} **>120f<**
Purple Fling 4 ch c Music Boy-Divine Fling (Imperial Fling (USA)) *1214^{5}* 1411^{5} 1802^{2} 1827^{2} *(1882)* 2079^{2} 2326^{7} (2700) (2819) *3242^{8}* 3619^{7} **>73a 82f<**
Purple Memories 2 b c Don't Forget Me-Tyrian Belle (Enchantment) (2422) 2696^{3} **>58f<**
Purple Rain (FR) 0 D Zino 3697a^{3} **>115f<**
Purple Splash 5 b h Ahonoora-Quay Line (High Line)

506^{3} (1621) 2413^{7} 3616^{3} 3730^{6} 4158^{3} **>92f<**

Pursuance (IRE) **3** b c Glenstal (USA)-Pocket (Tumble Wind (USA)) *42^{3} 210^{4} 232^{5} (2071) 2295^{4}* 2680^{8} 3622^{15} *(3739) 3954^{3} 4123^{8}* 4194^{11} **>68a 51f<**

Pursuit of Glory **4** b f Shirley Heights-Propensity (Habitat) 2008^{7} (2780) 3007^{7} 3237^{10} 3555^{8} **>89f<**

Pusey Street Boy **8** ch h Vaigly Great-Pusey Street (Native Bazaar) 780^{4} 1070^{5} 1323^{7} 1714^{10} 2246^{2} 2455^{9} 3619^{5} 3885^{10} 4060^{8} 4209^{5} **>52a 59f<**

Put Off **2** b f Hadeer-Dame Margot (USA) (Northern Dancer) 2351^{13} 2964^{7} **>57f<**

Pyramus (USA) **4** b c Danzig (USA)-Royal Honoree (USA) (Round Table (USA)) 1354^{9} 1648^{8} (2053) (2187) (2517) 2797^{10} **>81+f<**

Pytchley Night **8** b h Red Sunset-Lili Bengam (Welsh Saint) *1087^{3}* **>71a f<**

Q

Qaffal (USA) **5** b h Seattle Dancer (USA)-Samalex (Ela-Mana-Mou) 1535^{10} **>19f<**

Q Factor **3** br f Tragic Role (USA)-Dominiana (Dominion) 999^{3} 1222^{9} 1673^{4} 2009^{4} 2848^{7} 3715^{15} 4145^{6} 4319^{12} **>60a 76f<**

Quadrant **6** b h Shirley Heights-Sextant (Star Appeal) *260^{7} 329^{6} 469^{P}* **>49a 27f<**

Quakers Field **2** b c Anshan-Nosey (Nebbiolo) 2552^{8} (3104) 3746^{2} (3917) 4159^{6} **>99f<**

Qualitair Pride **3** b f Siberian Express (USA)-Qualitairess (Kampala) 722^{11} 1249^{10} *2140^{6}* 3099^{10} 3302^{9} **>37a 56f<**

Qualitair Ridge **3** ch f Indian Ridge-Comtec Princess (Gulf Pearl) *32^{8} 241^{7}* **>41a 55f<**

Quality (IRE) **2** b c Rock City-Queens Welcome (Northfields (USA)) 2777^{4} *3525^{4}* 3625^{2} 3779^{6} 3870^{5} (4081) 4151^{7} (4279) 4321^{8} **>66a 80f<**

Quandary (USA) **4** b f Blushing Groom (FR)-Lost Virtue (USA) 764^{2} 981^{9} 1905^{2} (2438) 3659^{0} (4031) (4257) **>103f<**

Quango **3** b g Charmer-Quaranta *(844)* 1178^{4} 1374^{2} (1807) 2457^{14} **>71+a 97f<**

Queenbird **4** b or br f Warning-Song Test (USA) (The Minstrel (CAN)) 665^{20} 2066^{8} 2455^{8} 2652^{8} 3565^{8} 3629^{12} 3770^{10} 3960^{9} 4229^{11} **>69f<**

Queen Emma (IRE) **2** b f Mac's Imp (USA)-Hinari Disk Deck (Indian King (USA)) 1443^{8} 3848^{7} 4212^{16} **>44f<**

Queenfisher **3** b or br f Scottish Reel-Mavahra (Mummy's Pet) 933^{11} 1066^{4} 2006^{4} 2409^{5} 2673^{10} (3399) 3564^{10} **>90f<**

Queen of Shannon (IRE) **7** b m Nordico (USA)-Raj Kumari (Vitiges (FR)) *76^{7} 91^{13}* **>46da 43f<**

Queens Check **2** b f Komaite (USA)-Ski Baby (Petoski) 3647^{8} 3838^{5} 4109^{6} (4287) **>69?f<**

Queens Consul (IRE) **5** gr m Kalaglow-Queens Connection (Bay Express) *1^{5} 30^{6} 94^{5}* 433^{21} 558^{6} 724^{2} 749^{2} *845^{10}* 927^{2} 1179^{7} 1357^{8} 1638^{7} (1845) 1969^{3} 2222^{2} 2703^{9} **>59a 87f<**

Queens Contractor **5** b h Formidable-Salazie (Ile de Bourbon (USA)) 884^{7} 1622^{13} 1937^{5} (1985) 2327^{9} 3384^{11} **>54da 46f<**

Queen's Insignia (USA) **2** b f Gold Crest (USA)-Years (USA) (Secretariat (USA)) 1098^{5} 1671^{4} (1829) (3928) 4151^{13} **>71f<**

Queen's Music (USA) **2** ch f Dixieland Band (USA)-Sticky Habit (Habitat) 1137^{5} 1511^{7} 1746^{6} 3136^{7} 3516^{6} 3760^{7} **>69f<**

Queen's Ransom (IRE) **3** b f Last Tycoon-Never so Fair (Never so Bold) 902a^{6} 3630^{11} *4297^{12}* **>48a 72f<**

Queens Stroller (IRE) **4** b f Pennine Walk-Mount Isa (Miami Springs) *(387)* (454) 550^{7} 738^{6} 909^{7} 1484^{10} 2528^{4} 2861^{W} 3004^{2} 3402^{7} 3658^{9} 3710^{21} 4259^{16} **>72a 62f<**

Queens Theatre **3** ch f Old Vic-Hello Cuddles (He Loves Me) 715^{17} 3438^{4} **>74f<**

Quest Again **4** ch g Then Again-Eagle's Quest (Legal Eagle) 1367^{10} 1813^{2} (2792) 3156^{4} 3470^{7} 3676^{13} 3836^{18} 4248^{3} 4333^{4} **>74f<**

Questionaire **2** b f Northern State (USA)-Broken Melody (Busted) 3672^{8} 3891^{11} **>41f<**

Question Ali **3** b f Petoski-Wild Lover (USA) (Lyphard (USA)) 2973^{6} 3298^{6} 3726^{9} 3879^{19} 3980^{23} **>52f<**

Questrill **3** ch f Rainbow Quest (USA)-Krill (Kris) 4162^{13} **>77f<**

Quick Million **4** b f Thowra (FR)-Miss Quick (Longleat (USA)) *36^{3} 117^{11} 343^{5}* 3884^{P} **>56da 41f<**

Quick Ransom **7** ch h Hostage (USA)-Run Amber Run (Run The Gantlet (USA)) 4349a^{4} **>106f<**

Quick Thinker (IRE) **3** ch g Carmelite House (USA)-Snap Decision (Bay Express) 1157^{16} 1471^{6} **>35a 45f<**

Quiet Mission **4** ch c Hubbly Bubbly (USA)-Woodlands Arabella VII *28^{7} 205^{11}* 722^{14} 874^{17} **>22a 45f<**

Quiet Moments (IRE) **2** b c Ron's Victory (USA)-Saint Cynthia (Welsh Saint) 2791^{12} 3379^{21} 3625^{15} 4144^{13} **>41f<**

Quilling **3** ch c Thatching-Quillotern (USA) (Arctic Tern (USA)) 1085^{4} 1249^{5} 1380^{5} 1847^{4} 2500^{5} 2624^{2} 2786^{4} 3649^{3} 3807^{W} (3980) 4068^{15} (4236) 4268^{2} 4319^{13} **>88f<**

Quillon Rose **3** ch f Sure Blade (USA)-Grey Walls (Habitat) 1097^{21} 1598^{6} 1692^{6} (2425) (3079) 3159^{4} 3920^{19} **>67f<**

Quillwork (USA) **3** b f Val de L'Orne (FR)-Quaff (USA) (Raise A Cup (USA)) 1986^{8} *2604^{3}* 3921^{4} 4162^{3} **>53a 68f<**

Quinntessa **2** ch f Risk Me (FR)-Nannie Annie (Persian Bold) 3982^{9} **>49f<**

Quinta Boy **2** b c Puissance-Figment (Posse (USA)) 1646^{6} 2354^{7} **>33f<**

Quintiliani (IRE) **4** b c Conquering Hero (USA)-Quilting (Mummy's Pet) 609a^{7} **>110df<**

Quintus Decimus **3** b c Nordico (USA)-Lemon Balm (High Top) 621^{7} 829^{5} 1130^{3} 3348^{5} 3813^{12} 4035^{4} 4163^{9} **>79f<**

Quinwood (USA) **3** ch f Woodman (USA)-Qirmazi (USA) (Riverman (USA)) 761^{6} (1736) **>85f<**

Quinzii Martin **7** b h Song-Quaranta *44^{7} (55) 94^{10} 130^{2} (231) 307^{3} 354^{11} 512^{U} 627^{10} 835^{3} 1088^{9}* 1516^{6} *1760^{6} 2073^{12} 2290^{8}* **>64a 51f<**

Quivira **4** ch f Rainbow Quest (USA)-Nobly Born (USA) (The Minstrel (CAN)) 1347^{6} 1513^{2} (1865) 1875^{3} (2139) 2694^{3} 3007^{8} 3229^{2} 3496^{2} 3659^{12} 4038^{20} 4316^{3} **>80f<**

Quiz Time **3** b f Efisio-Explosiva (USA) 2394^{2} 2742^{3} 3236^{2} 3376^{5} 3551^{17} 3815^{9} **>91f<**

Quorum **2** c 4310a^{5}

R

Raah Algharb (USA) **3** b c Gone West (USA)-Pharlette (FR) (Pharly (FR)) 921^{8} 1133^{6} 1364^{4} 2671^{11} 3067^{7} 3902^{9} **>105f<**

Raahin (USA) **10** ch h Super Concorde (USA)-Bonnie Hope (USA) (Nijinsky (CAN)) 795^{16} **>17f<**

Raased **3** b c Unfuwain (USA)-Sajjaya (USA) (Blushing Groom (FR)) (544) 756^{3} 1589^{11} **>85f<**

Raayaat (USA) **3** b br c Phone Trick (USA)-Badge of Courage (USA) (Well Decorated (USA)) 670^{9} 937^{10} 1216^{6} *1569^{3}* 1818^{4} **>59a 67tf<**

Rabican (IRE) **2** b c Distinctly North (USA)-Kaysama (FR) (Kenmare (FR)) 1318^{2} (1670) 1838^{11} (2779) (3328a) 3375^{4} 4250a^{9} **>87f<**

Racing Brenda **4** b f Faustus (USA)-Icecapped (Caerleon (USA)) 981^{10} 1351^{5} 1528^{3} 1783^{6} 2088^{6} (2862) 3101^{8} 3645^{2} 4043^{16} **>78a 63f<**

Racing Hawk (USA) **3** ch c Silver Hawk (USA)-Lorn Lady (Lorenzaccio) 2208^{5} *2494^{2}* 3896^{8} **>66a 69f<**

Racing Telegraph **5** b h Claude Monet (USA)-Near Enough (English Prince) 1714^{12} *2377^{14}* 2528^{8} 2685^{3} 3661^{3} 4157^{4} 4268^{15} **>24a 49f<**

Racing Wings (FR) **3** ch f In The Wings-Racing Home (FR) (Dom Racine (FR)) 2341^{4} **>53f<**

Rad **5** b h Valiyar-Phlox *12^{8} 157^{5} (212) 255^{7} 313^{7} 379^{8} 416^{9}* 2021^{4} 2528^{10} 2808^{5} 2983^{3} 3272^{4} 4152^{8} 4209^{7} **>59a 58f<**

Radevore **2** ch c Generous-Bioudan 4010a^{3} **>100f<**

Radiance (IRE) **3** b f Thatching-Dazzlingly Radiant (Try My Best (USA)) 2265^{7} 2488^{8} 3344^{17} **>58f<**

Radiant Star **2** b c Rainbow Quest (USA)-Miss Kuta Beach (Bold Lad (IRE)) 4313^{8} **>66f<**

Radio Caroline **7** b g 1324^{9} *1459^{11}* 1797^{14} *1951^{12}*

Radmore Brandy **2** b f Derrylin-Emerin 4277^{9} **>41f<**

Raed **2** b c Nashwan (USA)-Awayed (USA) (Sir Ivor) 2767^{2} 3873^{7} **>80f<**

Rafter-J **4** b or br g Petoski-Coming Out (Fair Season) *313^{11}* 984^{7} 1092^{5} (1291) 1351^{12} 4209^{18} 4284^{14} **>31a 55f<**

Rafters **6** b g Celestial Storm (USA)-Echoing (Formidable) 3820^{13} **>66f<**

Ragazzo (IRE) **5** b g Runnett-Redecorate (USA) (Hatchet Man (USA)) *16^{5} (41) 150^{5} 219^{2} 265^{7} 349^{10}* 450^{16} 848^{11} 882^{14} 1013^{7} 1996^{4} 2156^{13} 2397^{6} 2461^{12} 2913^{4} 3118^{6} 3830^{12} **>53da 44f<**

Ragmar (FR) **2** ch c Tropular-Reggae 4310a^{2}

Ragsak Jameel (USA) **2** b g Northern Baby (CAN)-Dream Play (USA) (Blushing Groom (FR)) 4312^{7} **>66f<**

Ragtime Song **6** b h Dunbeath (USA)-Kelowna (USA) (Master Derby (USA)) *9^{9} 88^{4} 147^{6} 346^{11}* 545^{16} 729^{6} *1319^{9}* 1427^{11} 1659^{12} **>29f<**

Raheen (USA) **2** b c Danzig (USA)-Belle de Jour (USA) 2370^{2} 2693^{3} 3185^{4} **>83f<**

Rahy Zoman (USA) **3** b c Rahy (USA)-Micki Bracken (USA) (Baldski (USA)) (1264) 1753^{3} 2068^{2} 2348^{5} 2691^{15} **>87f<**

Rain and Hail (ITY) **5** ch m Vacarme-Rose Stocking 4179a^{2} **>88f<**

Rainbow Dancer (FR) **4** b c Rainbow Quest (USA)-Ramanouche (FR) 1709a^{5} 4176a^{3} **>116f<**

Rainbow Reef **7** b h Rainbow Quest-Madigan Mill (4017a) **>94f<**

Rainbows Rhapsody **4** b f Handsome Sailor-Rainbow Trout (Comedy Star (USA)) *198^{5} 416^{3}* 479^{6} *766^{7}* 3726^{18} **>48a 22f<**

Rainbow Tiara **3** ch f Night Shift (USA)-Loreef (Main Reef) 1258^{13} **>62f<**

Rainbow Walk (IRE) **5** ch h Rainbow Quest (USA)-Widows Walk (Habitat) *66^{13} 152^{6} 246^{9}* 439^{14} 931^{W} **>75a 92df<**

Raincheck (GB) **0** S 1905^{6} 2438^{7} 2805^{5} 3056^{11} **>48f<**

Rain Cloud **2** ch f Totem (USA)-Cool Number (Swing Easy (USA)) 4073^{7} *4338^{8}* **>16a 38f<**

Raindeer Quest **3** ch f Hadeer-Rainbow Ring (Rainbow Quest (USA)) 575^{6} 3751^{20} **>49f<**

Rainelle **3** ch f Rainbow Quest (USA)-Dame Ashfield (Grundy) 797^{8} 1062^{3} 1283^{6} 3438^{11} 3634^{11} **>71f<**

Rainfest (FR) **4** ch f Rainbow Quest (USA)-Rockfest (USA) (Stage Door Johnny) 1408^{6} 1912^{5} 3804^{3} **>91f<**

Rain Warrior **5** br g Lidhame-Rainbow Star (Star Appeal) 1659^{10} **>47f<**

Rainy Day Song **2** br f Persian Bold-Sawaki (Song) 4212^{8} **>64f<**

Rainy Day Woman **3** ch f Sure Blade (USA)-Hocus (High Top) *509^{6} 628^{4}* **>54a f<**

Raisa Point **4** ch f Raised Socially (USA)-To The Point (Sharpen Up) 856^{4} 1050^{7} 1546^{5} 2301^{3} 2659^{13} 3139^{12} **>52f<**

Raise A Prince (FR) **2** b c Machiavellian (USA)-Enfant D'Amour (USA) (Lyphard (USA)) 3900^{5} **>80+f<**

Raise the Stakes **3** ch c Forzando-Timely Raise (USA) (Raise A Man (USA)) 572^{5} 1979^{2} 2319^{2} 2707^{3} 2880^{2} 3105^{2} 3409^{2} 3559^{3} 3770^{4} 3974^{9} **>83f<**

Raisonnable **2** b f Common Grounds-Salvora 3786a^{3} 4251a^{2} **>101f<**

Rakis (IRE) **5** b or br h Alzao (USA)-Bristle (Thatch (USA)) 3439^{11} *3510^{5}* 3638^{10} **>49a 58f<**

Rambling Bear **2** ch c Sharrood (USA)-Supreme Rose (Frimley Park) 1406^{2} (2660) 3165^{2} (3499) 3610^{4} **>97f<**

Rambo Delight **2** b c Rambo Dancer (CAN)-Light the Way (Nicholas Bill) (1642) 1860^{4} (2459) 2706^{4} **>81f<**

Rambold **4** b f Rambo Dancer (CAN)-Boldie (Bold Lad (IRE)) *23^{5}* 1537^{9} 1832^{11} 2448^{2} *2943^{7}* 3359^{17} 3624^{18} *3954^{9}* 4215^{10} **>61a 70df<**

Rambollina **4** b f Rambo Dancer (CAN)-Midriff (Busted) *335^{4} 378^{8} 422^{8}* **>38a 49f<**

Ramborette **3** b f Rambo Dancer (CAN)-Petiller (Monsanto (FR)) 966^{6} 1249^{6} 1434^{6} 1822^{6} 1936^{7} 2303^{3} 2463^{3} 2736^{11} 2837^{4} 3116^{3} 3256^{2} 3313^{6} 3667^{19} **>54f<**

Rambo's Hall **10** b g Crofthall-Murton Crags (No Argument) 2428^{6} 2948^{13} 3433^{5} 3608^{5} 3945^{24} 4163^{10} **>90f<**

Rambo's Rumtime **3** b f Rambo Dancer (CAN)-Errol Emerald (Dom Racine (FR)) 2018^{8} 2357^{7} 3167^{5} **>37f<**

Rambo Waltzer **3** b c Rambo Dancer (CAN)-Vindictive Lady (USA) (Foolish Pleasure (USA)) 427^{16} 573^{5} 1498^{5} 1945^{6} 2586^{4} *3074^{7} 3241^{3}* **>77a 62f<**

Rambrino **3** b c Robellino (USA)-Ballerine (USA) (Lyphard's Wish (FR)) 713^{5} 1018^{4} 1848^{12} 3594^{5} **>98f<**

Ramooz (USA) **2** b c Rambo Dancer (CAN)-My Shafy (Rousillon (USA)) 1913^{2} 2264^{2} 2796^{2} (3460) (3711) 4029^{4} **>100f<**

Ramsdens (IRE) **3** b c Danehill (USA)-To The Limit (Junius (USA)) 1065^{3} 3725^{7} 3897^{14} 4261^{2} 4333^{16} **>81f<**

Ramsey Hope 2 b c Timeless Times (USA)-Marfen (Lochnager) 424^{7} 533^{2} 615^{4} 788^{4} 993^{4} 1440^{2} (1685) 2131^{4} 2328^{4} 2523^{2} 2833^{3} 3100^{3} (3228) 3612^{14} 3714^{7} 3990^{8} **>84f<**

Random 4 ch f Beveled (USA)-Martian Melody (Enchantment) *328*^{5} *498*^{4} 734^{5} 1057^{10} 1538^{5} 1972^{7} *2402*^{3} 2743^{2} 3177^{4} 3519^{5} 3800^{12} **>64a 69f<**

Ranger Sloane 3 ch c Gunner B-Lucky Amy (Lucky Wednesday) *893*^{2} *1881*^{9} 3464^{9} 3778^{12} **>51a 24f<**

Rankaidade 4 b f Governor General-Keep Cool (FR) (Northern Treat (USA)) 535^{14} 1152^{10} 1376^{6} 1604^{8} 1809^{18} 3667^{16} 4193^{18} **>25a 38f<**

Ranosh (USA) 3 ch f Rahy (USA)-Knoosh (USA) (Storm Bird (CAN)) 2553^{5} 3016^{3} 3392^{3} 3537^{2} 3712^{7} **>79f<**

Rapid Liner 2 b c Skyliner-Stellaris (Star Appeal) 615^{5} 1190^{6} 1356^{11} 2926^{4} 3969^{17} **>62f<**

Rapid Mover 8 ch g Final Straw-Larive (Blakeney) 597^{6} **>37f<**

Rapier Point (IRE) 4 gr c Cyrano de Bergerac-Renzola (Dragonara Palace (USA)) *78*^{10} *129*^{6} *192*^{7} 701^{8} 2321^{13} 2945^{4} 3365^{6} *3524*^{10} 3764^{10} **>47a 63f<**

Rapporteur (USA) 9 b g His Majesty (USA)-Sweet Rapport (USA) (Round Table (USA)) *206*^{7} *303*^{7} 430^{5} 549^{4} 737^{6} 879^{16} 1937^{7} **>65da 65f<**

Rasas (IRE) 3 b or br c Lead on Time (USA)-Hufoof (Known Fact (USA)) 697^{5} 982^{5} (1249) (2311) (2802) **>92f<**

Rasayel (USA) 5 b m Bering-Reham (Mill Reef (USA)) *514*^{11} *600*^{6} 864^{3} 975^{2} (1200) 1295^{6} 1496^{6} 2126^{2} 2327^{6} 2798^{3} 3207^{3} (3462) 3700^{6} 3820^{12} **>56da 61f<**

Rash Gift 2 ch f Cadeaux Genereux-Nettle (Kris) 2749^{2} **>78+f<**

Rasmi (CAN) 4 ch c Riverman (USA)-Snow Blossom (CAN) (The Minstrel (CAN)) 630^{5} 739^{5} 1250^{6} 2269^{5} 3475^{16} 3565^{19} **>74f<**

Raticosa 3 b f Hallgate-Rose Meadow (Mummy's Game) 524^{19} 641^{6} **>29f<**

Rattle 16 br m Riverman (USA)-Kassa (Kashir II) 2869^{3} 3415^{4} 3671^{10} *3738*^{5} 3937^{4} 4141^{12} **>43a 52f<**

Raven's Roost (IRE) 4 b c Taufan (USA)-Al Zumurrud (Be My Guest (USA)) 1314^{9} 1664^{12} 2016^{R} **>62f<**

Rave-on-Hadley (IRE) 5 b g Commanche Run-Fleet Fact (Known Fact (USA)) *387*^{8} 430^{20} 820^{15} **>46a 26f<**

Ravier (ITY) 4 gr c Highest Honor (FR)-Revarola (ITY) (Marracci) 4093a^{10} **>109f<**

Rawi 2 ch c Forzando-Finally (Final Straw) 1123^{P} 1318^{9} 3404^{8} 3604^{6} 3765^{6} 3985^{18} **>65f<**

Rawya (USA) 4 ch f Woodman (USA)-Dance It (USA) (Believe It (USA)) *8*^{2} *145*^{2} **>82a 77df<**

Rawy (USA) 3 b c Rahy (USA)-Triple Kiss (Shareef Danc 709a^{3} **>93f<**

Rayner (IRE) 2 b c Lycius (USA)-Rosati (USA) (Caro) 2529^{6} 4221^{5} **>67f<**

Ray of Hope 3 b f Rainbow Quest (USA)-Widows Walk (Habitat) 485^{10} 745^{14} **>53f<**

Razana (IRE) 3 b f Kahyasi-Raysiya (Cure The Blues (USA)) (2151) 2547^{6} **>83f<**

R Dragon 3 ch f Insan (USA)-Hyde Princess (Touch Paper) 543^{7} 848^{14} 1125^{20} **>28f<**

Reach for Glory 6 b h Reach-Carlton Glory (Blakeney) (1449) *1759*^{3} **>44a 54+f<**

React 2 b f Reprimand-Shehana (USA) (The Minstrel (CAN)) 1375^{2} (1697) 2106^{3} 3387^{5} 3867^{15} **>82f<**

Readypower 3 b g Newski (USA)-Bay Runner (Bay Express) 3921^{15}

Readyspex 5 b g Kala Shikari-Set To Work 1533^{13} 1947^{6} 2086^{7} 2355^{11} 2698^{18} **>27f<**

Ready Teddy (IRE) 2 b f Fayruz-Racey Naskra (USA) (Star de Naskra (USA)) 2773^{5} 3670^{11} 3838^{8} **>33f<**

Reaganesque (USA) 3 b c Nijinsky (CAN)-Basoof (USA) (Believe It (USA)) 1526^{11} 1916^{5} 2329^{5} 3759^{10} 4086^{9} **>64f<**

Real Gem 2 b f Formidable (USA)-Emerald Ring (Auction Ring (USA)) 2651^{3} *3509*^{6} 3767^{5} 3915^{10} **>45a 64f<**

Realities (USA) 5 ch h Cozzene (USA)-Alquizar (USA) (Star de Naskra (USA)) 439^{23} 665^{17} 870^{14} 1143^{2} (1851) 2241^{4} 2703^{2} 3360^{3} 3473^{2} 3904^{5} **>116f<**

Reality Park 4 b c Dreams to Reality (USA)-Everingham Park (Record Token) 798a^{4} 2384a^{5} 2720a^{4} 3322a^{4} **>41f<**

Really A Dream (IRE) 2 br f Last Tycoon-Ancestry (Persepolis (FR)) 4262^{4} **>74+f<**

Real Madrid 4 b g Dreams to Reality (USA)-Spanish Princess (King of Spain) 2317^{15} 2593^{13} 3079^{5} 3674^{8} 3984^{12} 4157^{12} **>56df<**

Realms of Glory (IRE) 2 b c Reprimand-Wasaif (IRE) (Lomond (USA)) 3848^{6} 4064^{8} **>59f<**

Real Popcorn (IRE) 4 ch f Jareer (USA)-Avidal Park (Horage) *370*^{11} **>5a 56df<**

Reason Prevails (USA) 4 3908a^{2} **>97f<**

Rebeccas Secret (IRE) 4 ch c Classic Secret (USA)-Cordon (Morston (FR)) 476^{4} 1863^{11} **>67f<**

Rebel County (IRE) 2 b f Maelstrom Lake-Haven Bridge 2308^{5} 2651^{4} 3012^{2} 3430^{2} (3538) 3895^{2} 4211^{7} **>76f<**

Recall To Mind 2 b g Don't Forget Me-Northern Notion (USA) (Northern Baby (CAN)) 2542^{11} 2995^{7} 3307^{4} 4081^{12} **>64f<**

Reclaimed 2 ch f Tina's Pet-Far Claim (USA) (Far North (CAN)) 1481^{10} *2939*^{6} 3080^{6} **>29a 35f<**

Recluse 4 b c Last Tycoon-Nomadic Pleasure (Habitat) 3238^{8} 3505^{11} **>67f<**

Record Lover (IRE) 5 b h Alzao (USA)-Spun Gold (Thatch (USA)) 1596^{17} 1826^{4} 1929^{11} 2184^{7} 2875^{6} 3047^{7} 3274^{4} 3435^{11} 3936^{11} 4140^{4} **>69da 40f<**

Recovery Lad (IRE) 3 b g Prince Rupert (FR)-Hill of Tara *90*^{6} *241*^{3} *339*^{3} 654^{2} *1029*^{12} 1289^{6} 1581^{2} 1737^{2} 2244^{8} **>59a 69f<**

Red Acuisle (IRE) 2 br c Soviet Lad (USA)-Scottish Gaelic (USA) (Highland Park (USA)) 2091^{3} 2230^{2} 2487^{7} 3032^{5} 3290^{6} 3749^{5} 3937^{14} *4273*^{2} **>63a 63f<**

Red Admiral 5 ch g Formidable-Dancing Meg (USA) (Marshua's Dancer (USA)) *177*^{3} *244*^{8} 765^{15} 1050^{12} (1700) 2203^{5} 2539^{3} 2641^{2} 2887^{5} *2943*^{4} (3055) 3123^{5} **>66da 67f<**

Red Azalea 3 b f Shirley Heights-Cerise Bouquet (Mummy's Pet) (1976) 2547^{4} 3413^{8} 3636^{10} **>94f<**

Red Beacon 8 b g Red Sunset-Mount of Light (Sparkler) 1578^{6} 1997^{6} **>31f<**

Red Bishop (USA) 7 b or br h Silver Hawk (USA)-La Rouquine (Silly Season) (606a) 2286^{3} **>123f<**

Redbrook Lady 2 ch f Clantime-Silently Yours (USA) (Silent Screen (USA)) 2782^{10} 2970^{5} 3626^{19} 3824^{14} *3953*^{12} **>5a 50?f<**

Red Bustaan 3 b c Aragon-Red Rose Garden (Electric) 647^{5} 851^{2} (1281) 2284^{4} 2701^{3} 2996^{2} 3412^{3} 3817^{12} **>93f<**

Red Carnival (USA) 3 b f Mr Prospector (USA)-Seaside Attraction (USA) (Seattle Slew (USA)) 660^{3} 3904^{2} 4078^{3} **>115f<**

Red Dragon 3 b c Caerleon (USA)-Soemba (General Assembly (USA)) 635^{17} 1383^{11} 1755^{10} 2181^{8} 3218^{8} **>71f<**

Red Five 4 b g Clantime-Miami Dolphin (Derrylin) *532^{10}* 594^{6} 3964^{13} 4193^{15} **>29a 42f<**

Red Hassett (IRE) 3 b c Red Sunset-Rekolette *95^{12}* **>12a 55f<**

Red Hot Risk 3 b g Risk Me (FR)-Hot Sunday Sport (Star Appeal) 685^{10} 759^{11} 1355^{10} 1669^{11} 1824^{10} **>60f<**

Red Indian 9 ch h Be My Native (USA)-Martialette (Welsh Saint) *(296) 351^{5} 516^{4} 843^{3}* 1192^{9} 1557^{5} *1880^{4}* **>68a 50f<**

Red Light 3 b c Reprimand-Trull (Lomond (USA)) 3214^{6} 3959^{6} 4035^{5} 4205^{6} **>76f<**

Red March Hare 4 b f Daring March-Happy Harriet (Red Sunset) *31^{7}* **>33a 33f<**

Red Misty (IRE) 2 b f Red Sunset-Decoy Duck (Decoy Boy) 2025^{11} 2515^{6} 3283^{2} 3386^{6} 3642^{6} 3937^{11} 4075^{16} **>62f<**

Red Morning 3 b f Warning-Beautiful Dawn (USA) (Grey Dawn II) 1136^{9} 1473^{7} 1755^{7} 2711^{10} 3016^{14} 3218^{4} **>68f<**

Red Nose (IRE) 2 b c Cyrano de Bergerac-Crimson Glen (Glenstal (USA)) 682^{5} 1047^{5} 2183^{7} 2467^{3} 2847^{2} 3032^{4} 3720^{2} 4195^{5} **>75f<**

Red Nymph 2 b f Sharpo-Red Gloves (Red God) 2615^{3} (2978) 3420^{4} 3865^{16} **>83+f<**

Red O'Reilly 3 ch g Hubbly Bubbly (USA)-Name the Game (Fair Season) 442^{19} *519^{7}* 732^{10} 861^{5} 1371^{13} *1569^{11}* **>19a 53f<**

Red Owa Lady (IRE) 3 b f Jareer (USA)-The Woman in Red (Red Regent) *144^{9} 241^{8}* **>8a f<**

Red Paper (IRE) 3 b c Emmson-Gold Slipper (Glint of Gold) 2388a^{3} **>109f<**

Red Phantom (IRE) 3 ch g Kefaah (USA)-Highland Culture (Lomond (USA)) *2142^{4} 2378^{3} (2626) (2959)* **>75a f<**

Red Raja 2 b c Persian Heights-Jenny Splendid 2005^{P} 2320^{15} 4103^{19} 4208^{18} **>62f<**

Red Rita (IRE) 4 ch f Kefaah (USA)-Katie Roche (Sallust) 1065^{4} 2066^{7} (2337) 2803^{3} 3109^{5} 3557^{6} 3943^{26} **>81f<**

Red River Rose (IRE) 3 b f Red Sunset-Salonniere (FR) (Bikala) 648^{11} *1030^{4}* 1155^{3} 1412^{8} 3096^{7} 3305^{7} 3344^{16} **>50da 48f<**

Red River Valley 2 br g Belfort (FR)-Play For Time (Comedy Star (USA)) 878^{2} (1158) 1492^{3} 1860^{3} 2423^{2} (2914) 3354^{2} 3714^{16} 4084^{6} **>82f<**

Red Robbo (CAN) 2 b c Red Ransom (USA)-Aunt Jobiska (USA) (What Luck (USA)) (3449) 4207^{5} **>85f<**

Red Robin (IRE) 2 c 4174a^{5} **>92f<**

Red Rusty (USA) 2 ch g The Carpenter (USA)-Super Sisters (AUS) (Call Report (USA)) *4334^{7}* **>41a f<**

Red Simba 2 ch c Absalom-Plie (Superlative) 490^{3} 644^{4} *1632^{3} 2075^{4} (2294) 2496^{5}* 2857^{7} 3417^{9} *3528^{7} 3675^{8}* **>60a 55f<**

Red Sky Delight (IRE) 2 b f Skyliner-Blazing Sunset (Blazing Saddles (AUS)) 455^{7} 849^{9} 1272^{6} 1590^{13} 1981^{10} 4133^{16} **>35f<**

Red Slaney (IRE) 4 ch c Mazaad-Carrick Slaney 1153^{10} 1499^{19} **>56f<**

Red Spectacle (IRE) 3 b c Red Sunset-Buz Kashi *10^{6} (133) 141^{9} 605^{6}* 1166^{16} 1645^{8} 2122^{3} 2396^{2} 2774^{2} 3001^{4} 3047^{8} (3254) (3299) **>59a 65f<**

Redstella (USA) 6 ch h Theatrical-Orange Squash 1616^{5} 1767^{4} **>75f<**

Red Stream (USA) 2 b f Red Ransom (USA)-Beetwentysix (USA) (Buckaroo (USA)) (1341) 1530^{5} 3210^{2} 3548^{3} 3775^{2} **>83f<**

Red Tie Affair (USA) 2 b c Miswaki (USA)-Quiet Rendezvous (USA) (Nureyev (USA)) 4063^{15} **>39f<**

Red Time 2 br g Timeless Times (USA)-Crimson Dawn (Manado) 1336^{5} 1646^{5} **>36f<**

Red Valerian 4 b c Robellino (USA)-Fleur Rouge (Pharly (FR)) *(89) 125^{2} 262^{2} 383^{6}* 433^{12} 505^{2} 634^{7} 1908^{4} 2395^{2} 2433^{3} 2661^{3} **>90a 93f<**

Red Whirlwind 5 b h Shadeed (USA)-Red Red Rose (USA) (Blushing Groom (FR)) *96^{15} 370^{2} 514^{2}* 582^{6} *833^{2}* **>68a 56f<**

Redwood Falls (IRE) 3 b f Dancing Brave-Robertet (Roberto) (3035a)

Reed My Lips (IRE) 4 br c Thatching-Taunsa (Nishapour (FR)) 430^{27} 672^{10} 839^{17} 1044^{6} 1206^{3} 1523^{10} 1797^{2} 1873^{12} 2191^{3} 2484^{5} 2698^{9} 3493^{11} 3745^{5} 3965^{8} **>52da 49f<**

Reefa's Mill (IRE) 3 b c Astronef-Pharly's Myth (Pharly (FR)) 1979^{7} 2255^{2} 2583^{5} 2623^{2} 3958^{5} **>78df<**

Reef Raider 2 gr c Siberian Express (USA)-Superior Quality (Star Appeal) 1134^{10} 1670^{11} 2192^{10} 3851^{8} 4172^{13} 4247^{11} **>54f<**

Reeling 9 br m Relkino-Mother Brown *1950^{11}* 2268^{12} **>14f<**

Reem Dubai (IRE) 3 ch f Nashwan (USA)-Gesedeh (Ela-Mana-Mou) 2944^{5} 3224^{3} 3438^{5} 3971^{19} **>72f<**

Regal Aura (IRE) 5 ch g Glow (USA)-Dignified Air (FR) (Wolver Hollow) 3898^{13} 4022^{12} **>46f<**

Regal Chimes 6 gr h Another Realm-London Cries (FR) (Bellman (FR)) 441^{9} 571^{10} 693^{10} **>98f<**

Regal Eagle 2 b c Shirley Heights-On The Tiles (Thatch (USA)) 3068^{8} **>11f<**

Regal Fanfare (IRE) 3 b f Taufan (USA)-Tender Time (Tender King) 620^{12} 1066^{5} 1923^{10} 2941^{2} 3286^{5} 3531^{6} 3769^{9} **>75f<**

Regal Parade 11 br h Hello Gorgeous (USA)-Danseuse Classique (CAN) (Northern Dancer) 3332a^{2} **>93f<**

Regal Portrait (IRE) 3 b f Royal Academy (USA)-Regal Beauty (USA) (Princely Native (USA)) 2553^{6} 4316^{6} **>66f<**

Regal Pursuit (IRE) 4 b f Roi Danzig (USA)-Pursue (Auction Ring (USA)) *26^{2} 84^{3} 252^{6} 290^{2} 352^{5} 374^{4}* 1058^{11} 1200^{8} 1799^{4} **>58a 52f<**

Regal Rambler (CAN) 4 ch c Regal Classic (CAN)-Rushing Rachel (USA) (Breezing On (USA)) *45^{11} 179^{6} 304^{6}* **>22a 49f<**

Reggae Beat 10 b g Be My Native (USA)-Invery Lady (Sharpen Up) *108^{4}* **>52a f<**

Regiment (IRE) 2 gr c Shaadi (USA)-Rossaldene (1662) 2242^{2} **>87+f<**

Reigning Royal 4 ch f Tina's Pet-Regency Brighton

(Royal Palace) *1762^{14}* 2546^{11} **>14f<**

Reimei **6** b g Top Ville-Brilliant Reay 4028^{3} 4325^{15} **>72f<**

Reinaldo (FR) **3** b c Green Desert-Ghariba (Final Straw) 4181a^{3} **>105f<**

Reinhardt (IRE) **2** b c Bluebird (USA)-Rhein Bridge (Rheingold) 2741^{3} 3089^{2} 3587a^{9} 3666^{2} 3846^{3} **>80?f<**

Reiterate **2** b f Then Again-Indubitable (Sharpo) 3708^{5} **>59f<**

Rejects Reply **5** b g Balliol-Fair Dino *166^{7}* 534^{2} 879^{14} *1319^{6}* 1622^{7} *2090^{8}* *3078^{6}* **>35a 39f<**

Relatively Clever (USA) **2** gr c Clever Trick (USA)-Cousin Jen (USA) (Age Quod Agis (USA)) 2116^{4} 2371^{4} 2542^{7} **>57+f<**

Relaunchrette (CAN) **5** ro g Relaunch (USA)-Futurette (USA) (Sevastopol (USA)) 208a^{3}

Relentless (IRE) **3** b c Fayruz-Scotch Rocket (Roan Rocket) 3750^{7} 4049^{8} **>62f<**

Relentless Pursuit (IRE) **7** b h Thatching-Daring Way (USA) (Alydar (USA)) 3442^{10} **>50f<**

Reliable Edie **2** ch f Hadeer-Ever Welcome (Be My Guest (USA)) 1223^{6}

Remaadi Sun **3** gr c Cadeaux Genereux-Catch The Sun (Kalaglow) 815^{12} 1175^{9} 1417^{4} 1745^{17} **>63f<**

Remember This (IRE) **5** b g Don't Forget Me-Regal Twin (USA) *240^{6}* *285^{5}* *321^{6}* *374^{8}* *496^{5}* 729^{5} 1745^{11} 1937^{11} 2535^{4} *3078^{7}* **>48a 47df<**

Remontant (IRE) **3** ch f Al Hareb (USA)-Red Red Rose (USA) (Blushing Groom (FR)) *528^{3}* 1379^{5} *1628^{9}* *2072^{5}* 2280^{8} 2480^{2} 2662^{3} 2990^{3} 3153^{4} 3805^{3} 4167^{6} *4270^{8}* **>43a 53f<**

Rennyholme **4** ch c Rich Charlie-Jacqui Joy (Music Boy) 746^{11} 1469^{10} 1647^{14} **>25da 10f<**

Renown **3** b g Soviet Star (USA)-Starlet (Teenoso (USA)) *250^{4}* *(332)* *395^{2}* **>69a 58f<**

Repatriate (AUS) **2** ch f Rory's Jester (AUS)-Turkish Trousers (Kings Lake (USA)) 2412^{3} 3086^{5} 3647^{2} (3940) 4077^{15} 4317^{8} **>74f<**

Repertory **2** b c Anshan-Susie's Baby (Balidar) 562^{2} 996^{2} (1123) **>89f<**

Reploy **2** gr f Deploy-Nelly Do Da 4148^{4} **>56f<**

Reponist **3** b f Reprimand-Dragonist (Dragonara Palace (USA)) *48^{6}* *185^{6}* **>36a 53f<**

Reported (IRE) **6** ch h Heraldiste (USA)-Peach Melba (So Blessed) *(1074)* 1291^{3} *(1458)* 1801^{3} 2002^{4} *2145^{6}* **>78a 73f<**

Reprehend **4** br c Reprimand-Lake Ormond (Kings Lake (USA)) 1482^{4} 1728^{11} 2057^{3} (2661) 2766^{10} 4193^{2} **>92f<**

Requested **8** b g Rainbow Quest (USA)-Melody Hour (Sing Sing) 549^{16} 696^{10} 866^{3} (1144) 1386^{2} 1794^{2} 2284^{5} 3884^{12} 4026^{12} 4166^{14} 4248^{6} 4331^{7} **>60f<**

Resolute Bay **9** b h Crofthall-Spinner (Blue Cashmere) 672^{8} 1523^{3} 1873^{10} 2390^{3} (2586) 2733^{6} 2972^{7} 3118^{3} 3295^{6} 3504^{10} 3825^{12} 4170^{15} **>51df<**

Resounder (USA) **2** b c Explodent (USA)-Rub Al Khali (USA) (Mr Prospector (USA)) 1485^{7} (1726) 2029^{2} 3731^{4} 3903^{5} (4039) 4200^{2} **>97f<**

Respectable Jones **9** ch h Tina's Pet-Jonesee (Dublin Taxi) *71^{2}* *177^{7}* *202^{4}* *265^{3}* *402^{8}* 526^{6} 748^{10} 1155^{5} 1426^{5} 1797^{10} (1993) 2428^{8} **>50a 50f<**

Respect A Secret **3** ch f Respect-Pendle's Secret 2236^{10} 2649^{4} 3356^{4} 3507^{8} 3855^{11} **>33f<**

Restless Carl (IRE) **2** br c Caerleon-Restless Kara (Akarad) 3483a^{3} 3793a^{6} **>94f<**

Restraint **5** b m Bustino-Queens Message 1863^{14} 2021^{11}

Restructure (IRE) **3** b c Danehill (USA)-Twine (Thatching) 853^{8} 1136^{2} (1312) 1839^{7} (2616) 3164^{3} (4104) **>116f<**

Retender (USA) **6** br h Storm Bird (CAN)-Dandy Bury (FR) (Exbury) 558^{3} 668^{13} 4333^{9} **>70f<**

Ret Frem (IRE) **2** b c Posen (USA)-New Light (Reform) 1842^{8} 4154^{7} 4255^{7} **>56f<**

Return To Brighton **3** b f Then Again-Regency Brighton (Royal Palace) 730^{10} 881^{11} 1337^{11} **>33f<**

Reve Parisien (USA) **4** b c Trempolino-Madonna Sprite (Saint Cyrien (FR)) 4187a^{2} **>113f<**

Reverand Thickness **4** b c Prince Sabo-Wollow Maid (Wollow) *315^{3}* (479) *(627)* 780^{3} 1421^{4} 1809^{16} 2613^{3} 3447^{6} 3601^{4} 3810^{13} 3945^{16} 4079^{5} **>71a 79f<**

Revere (IRE) **5** b h Dancing Brave (USA)-Bint Pasha (USA) (Affirmed (USA)) (2008) 2476^{3} 2936^{6} (3932) 4204^{9} **>118df<**

Reveuse de Jour (IRE) **2** b f Sadler's Wells (USA)-Magic of Life (USA) (Seattle Slew (USA)) 3900^{16} **>57f<**

Rey (FR) **3** b c Solicitor (FR)-Reine Morte (FR) (Polyfoto) 163a^{2}

Rhumba Dancer **2** b f Aragon-Battle of Flowers (Shernazar) 508^{9} 650^{7} (2077) 2489^{2} 2779^{4} 3711^{3} 4025^{3} 4107^{3} **>83f<**

Rhythmic Ball **2** ch f Classic Music (USA)-Chrisanthy (So Blessed) *2633^{6}* 3720^{5} 3838^{7} **>28a 59f<**

Rhythmic Dancer **7** b h Music Boy-Stepping Gaily 1304^{16} 1451^{3} 2364^{5} 2521^{9} 2665^{2} 2865^{4} (3424) *(3524)* (3919) **>78a 71f<**

Ribot's Secret (IRE) **2** b f Danehill (USA)-Glim (USA) (Damascus (U 2216a^{3} 2594^{2} 3197a^{8} **>92f<**

Ricana **3** ch f Rich Charlie-Woolcana 477^{4} 576^{3} 596^{2} 875^{8} 1207^{9} 1453^{4} 1742^{8} 1818^{3} 2125^{3} 2156^{14} 2304^{3} 2769^{4} 4289^{9} **>62?f<**

Richard House Lad **2** b c Warrshan (USA)-Sirenivo (USA) 523^{7} 615^{9} 2346^{6} *2635^{6}* 4169^{6} *4273^{7}* *4339^{10}* **>55a 57f<**

Richard of York **5** b h Rainbow Quest (USA)-Triple First 898a^{3} 3194a^{3} 3614^{4} 3811^{2} 4173a^{4} **>118f<**

Richelieu (IRE) **3** ch c Kris-Madame Dubois (Legend of France (USA)) 2151^{2} (4072) **>94f<**

Rich Glow **4** b g Rich Charlie-Mayglow (Sparkling Boy) 475^{8} 688^{7} 789^{2} (994) 1271^{3} (1461) 1809^{11} (1900) 2060^{5} 2194^{8} 2418^{2} 2475^{2} 2609^{4} 2935^{5} 3145^{13} 3359^{2} 3615^{8} 3715^{20} 3878^{13} 3992^{10} **>22a 70f<**

Ricochet (IRE) **2** b g West China-Waajib's Song (IRE) (Waajib) *3243^{11}* *3738^{10}* *4339^{15}*

Ridgewood Ben **4** b c Indian Ridge-Ben's Pearl (Tap On Wood) 609a^{2} 794^{2} 2217a^{5} **>118f<**

Ridgewood Pearl **3** ch f Indian Ridge-Ben's Pearl (Tap On Wood) (804a) (1390a) (1850) (3589a) 3814^{2} (4305a) **>132f<**

Rifapour (IRE) **3** b c Shahrastani-Rifada (1008a) 1574a^{8} 3486a^{3} 3794a^{3} **>120f<**

Rififi **2** ch c Aragon-Bundled Up (USA) (Sharpen Up) 4064^{5} 4130^{8} **>67f<**

Rightacres Lad **4** ch g Librate-Sue Clare (Busted) 3426^{15} **>29f<**

Righteous Gent 2 b g Superpower-Golden (Don) 3441^{6} 3625^{11} 4263^{6} *4339^{8}* **>54a 57f<**

Right Win (IRE) 5 br h Law Society (USA)-Popular Win (Lorenzaccio) 712^{4} 898a^{8} 2323^{7} 3088^{5} 3591a^{3} 4182a^{7} **>117df<**

Ringmaster (IRE) 4 b c Taufan (USA)-Salustrina (Sallust) 1135^{10} 1558^{6} 2241^{6} 2457^{2} 2672^{11} 3374^{3} 3729^{8} 3836^{11} **>94f<**

Ring of Vision (IRE) 3 br g Scenic-Circus Lady (High Top) 969^{7} (1358) 1645^{5} **>52f<**

Ring the Chief 3 b c Chief Singer-Lomond Ring (Lomond (USA)) 1202^{7} *1633^{2}* 1963^{10} *2383^{2}* *2590^{3}* *3072^{7}* *3319^{6}* **>60a 43f<**

Rinus Magic 2 ch c Timeless Times (USA)-Callace (Royal Palace) 3967^{13}

Rinus Manor (IRE) 4 b c Ballad Rock-Never Never Land *603^{13}* 1545^{6} 1797^{5} 3370^{11} 3751^{6} **>38a 56f<**

Rio Duvida 2 ch c Salse (USA)-Fluctuate (Sharpen Up) (1551) (2029) 2347^{4} 3596^{2} (3865) **>99f<**

Riparius (USA) 4 b c Riverman (USA)-Sweet Simone (FR) (Green Dancer (USA)) 668^{5} (1558) 1853^{17} 2525^{5} 3091^{3} 3801^{11} 4026^{10} **>85f<**

Ripsnorter (IRE) 6 ch h Rousillon (USA)-Formulate 738^{21} 1472^{15} *3529^{6}* **>49a 29f<**

Risalah 2 b f Marju (IRE)-Alsaaybah (USA) (Diesis) 1253^{6} **>43f<**

Rise Up Singing 7 ch h Noalto-Incarnadine (Hot Spark) 2108^{2} 2321^{14} 3341^{3} 3457^{17} **>63f<**

Rising Dough (IRE) 3 br c Dowsing (USA)-Shortning Bread (Blakeney) 1317^{2} 1748^{2} (2094) 2405^{5} (2827) 3408^{4} **>85f<**

Rising River 3 b f Warning-Double River (USA) (Irish River (FR)) 1240^{9} 1425^{4} 1748^{5} **>28f<**

Rising Spray 4 ch c Waajib-Rose Bouquet (General Assembly (USA)) 668^{14} 884^{10} 1140^{11} 1256^{6} 1664^{3} 2342^{8} 3605^{9} 3677^{12} 3844^{3} 3934^{3} 4061^{11} **>59f<**

Rising Stream 2 b f Pharly (FR)-River's Rising (FR) (Mendez (FR)) 4218^{12} **>28f<**

Risk a Million 3 ch f Risk Me (FR)-Romana (Roman Warrior) 797^{14} 1275^{3} **>45f<**

Riskie Things 4 ch f Risk Me (FR)-Foolish Things (Song) *192^{10}* 1071^{12} 1534^{13} 1942^{6} 2202^{9} 3134^{10} **>55da 47f<**

Risking 2 b f Risk Me (FR)-Dark Kristal (IRE) (Gorytus (USA)) *3509^{11}* **>25a f<**

Risk Master 6 b h Risk Me (FR)-Trigamy 425^{8} 872^{3} 1188^{7} 4202^{10} **>99f<**

Risky 4 b f Risk Me (FR)-Dona Krista (King of Spain) 1572a^{11} 2430^{5} 3707^{6} **>95f<**

Risky Romeo 3 b g Charmer-Chances Are (He Loves Me) 437^{4} 504^{16} 648^{13} 1052^{4} 1180^{8} 2068^{9} 2531^{4} 2747^{5} 2979^{15} (3429) 3732^{17} 3980^{13} 4249^{8} **>87+a 68f<**

Risky Rose 3 b f Risk Me (FR)-Moharabuiee (Pas de Seul) *51^{6}* *90^{4}* *270^{5}* 521^{5} (837) 1059^{4} (1581) 2129^{5} 2511^{7} 2751^{3} 3148^{4} **>40a 60f<**

Risky Royal 3 ch g Risk Me (FR)-Royal Clover (Mansingh (USA)) 4057^{15} 4194^{14} **>59a 40f<**

Risky Tu 4 ch f Risk Me (FR)-Sarah Gillian (USA) (Zen (USA)) *186^{11}* *259^{2}* *295^{3}* *374^{3}* 423^{3} *771^{5}* 1477^{10} *2919^{14}* *3076^{7}* **>71a 63f<**

Rita's Joy 4 ch f Jalmood (USA)-Cash Limit *58^{10}* **>53da 46f<**

Rita's Sofa 4 b f Sulaafah (USA)-Rainbow Springs (Silly Season) 1771^{17}

Rithab 2 b f Shaadi-Lawahed 3692a^{6} **>96f<**

Riva-Deva 3 b c Roaring Riva-Hilly's Daughter (Hillandale) 1452^{10} *3735^{12}*

Rival Bid (USA) 7 b h Cannonade (USA)-Love Triangle (USA) (Nodouble (USA)) 935^{12} 1166^{6} 1519^{4} 1940^{5} 2678^{5} 3108^{2} 3406^{10} *3529^{5}* 3658^{3} 3759^{2} (3987) 4061^{4} (4229) *4335^{6}* **>56a 74f<**

Rival Queen (IRE) 3 ch f Royal Academy (USA)-Maria Stuarda (Royal And Regal (USA)) 1990^{5} 4164^{4} **>76f<**

Riva Rock 5 b g Roaring Riva-Kivulini (Hotfoot) 1402^{6} *1939^{8}* 2174^{6} 2535^{2} **>23a 43f<**

Riva's Book (USA) 4 b c Mari's Book (USA)-Riva's Revenge (USA) (Riva Ridge (USA)) *279^{9}* **>63f<**

Riverbank Red 4 ch f Lighter-Gypsy Louise (Ascendant) 1339^{9} **>43f<**

River Board 5 b h Dominion-Miss Thames (Tower Walk) 1217^{2} 1851^{26} **>96f<**

River Divine (USA) 2 ch f Irish River (FR)-Etoile D'Amore (USA) (The Minstrel (CAN)) 4277^{8} **>44f<**

River Garnock 3 br c Dowsing (USA)-Duboff 1249^{12} 1689^{12} **>81f<**

River Island (USA) 7 b h Spend A Buck (USA)-Promising Risk (USA) (Exclusive Native (USA)) 1340^{5} **>52f<**

River Keen (IRE) 3 ch c Keen-Immediate Impact (Caerleon (USA)) 552^{4} 914^{9} 1793^{6} (2571) 2707^{11} 3659^{14} 4028^{5} 4149^{17} **>85f<**

River May 3 b f Sulaafah (USA)-Five Diamonds (FR) (Sir Gaylord) 1979^{17} 3023^{10} 3537^{12} 3844^{14} **>47f<**

River North (IRE) 5 ch h Lomond (USA)-Petillante (USA) (Riverman (USA)) 712^{8} **>122f<**

Rivero (GER) 3 c 2215a^{15} **>58f<**

River Tern 2 b c Puissance-Millaine (Formidable) 1190^{7} 1722^{3} 3877^{4} **>57f<**

River Wye (IRE) 3 b c Jareer (USA)-Sun Gift (Guillaume Tell (USA)) 643^{5} 818^{8} 1824^{5} 2310^{7} 3621^{10} **>49f<**

Riviera Rainbow 7 b h Rainbow Quest (USA)-Miss Beaulieu (Northfields (USA)) 799a^{2} **>56f<**

Riviere Rouge 2 ch f Forzando-Furry Dance (USA) (Nureyev (USA)) 1253^{10} 1938^{13} **>21f<**

Riyadian 3 ch c Polish Precedent (USA)-Knight's Baroness (Rainbow Quest (USA)) 635^{3} (764) 1068^{2} 1611^{7} (3594) (3811) 4120^{2} **>125+f<**

Riyama (IRE) 3 b f Doyoun-Riyda (Be My Guest) 2563a^{8} **>69f<**

Roadsweeper (FR) 3 b c Bold Arrangement-Sweeperette (High Line) *372^{10}* *509^{4}* 654^{6} 1254^{19} 1436^{5} 1659^{3} **>36a 63f<**

Roar on Tour 6 b h Dunbeath (USA)-Tickled Trout (Red Alert) *(30)* *(94)* *138^{4}* *(230)* *(255)* *269^{3}* *349^{8}* 493^{8} **>74a 50f<**

Robamaset (IRE) 2 b c Caerleon (USA)-Smageta (High Top) 3530^{5} 3797a^{11} 4080^{4} **>87f<**

Robaty's Law (IRE) 3 b c Be My Native (USA)-River Low (IRE) (Lafontaine (USA)) *315^{6}* 880^{11} 1157^{17} 1248^{10} **>36a f<**

Robellina 3 b g Faustus (USA)-Express Edition (Comedy Star (USA)) 477^{6} 3805^{13} **>24f<**

Robellion 4 b c Robellino (USA)-Tickled Trout (Red Alert) 984^{10} 1070^{4} 1411^{3} 1777^{2} 2079^{4} 2288^{5} 2410^{2}

(2551) 2992^{7} 3087^{4} 3219^{8} 3376^{2} 3622^{19} 3783^{10} 3992^{18} 4145^{20} 4215^{9} *4295^{8}* **>50a 67f<**

Roberty Lea **7** b h Alleging (USA)-Rosy Lee (FR) 432^{3} (751) 3971^{12} 4118^{16} **>76f<**

Robingo (IRE) **6** b h Bob Back (USA)-Mill's Girl (Le Levanstell) 1621^{7} 2284^{7} 3343^{W} **>87f<**

Robin Island **3** b c Robellino (USA)-Irish Isle 1051^{4} 1290^{8} 1553^{6} 1914^{9} **>61df<**

Robins (IRE) **3** b c Scenic-Roman Walk (Petorius) 900a^{3} (3796a) 4093a^{9} **>106f<**

Robo Magic (USA) **3** b c Tejano (USA)-Bubble Magic (USA) (Clever Trick (USA)) *60^{3} 105^{7} (236) 300^{5}* 1165^{7} 1541^{4} 1832^{4} 1963^{7} 2318^{11} *(2943)* 3293^{7} 3677^{14} **>73a 60f<**

Robsera (IRE) **4** b c Robellino (USA)-Que Sera (Music Boy) 439^{12} 728^{9} 927^{11} 1638^{9} 1969^{8} *2291^{4}* 2510^{5} 2979^{9} 3984^{7} 4171^{4} **>62a 75f<**

Roc de Fer (IRE) **2** br c Polar Falcon (USA)-Miss Blitz (Formidable) 1964^{8} 4244^{7} **>41f<**

Rockafaba(GER) **3** f 1009a^{9} **>88f<**

Rockcorry Rose (IRE) **2** b f Magical Wonder-Tir-An-Oir 3197a^{7} 3692a^{13} **>73f<**

Rockcracker (IRE) **3** ch c Ballad Rock-Forest Blaze (USA) (Green Forest (USA)) *392^{4} 411^{10}* 524^{5} 3972^{10} 4165^{17} **>55a 61f<**

Rock Daisy **2** b br f Rock City-New Pastures (Formidable) 4161^{19} **>46f<**

Rocketeer (IRE) **4** ch c Bluebird (USA)-Chive *(20) 242^{7} 345^{6} 365^{9}* (2112) 2330^{3} (2585) 2909^{3} 3212^{7} 3545^{9} **>90a 78f<**

Rocket Grounds (IRE) **2** b f Common Grounds-Ginosa (Amen (FR)) 3982^{8} *4339^{13}* **>30a 50f<**

Rockfield Lady (IRE) **3** b f Dancing Dissident (USA)-Come True (FR) *85^{10} 98^{8}* **>20a f<**

Rockforce **3** ch c Rock City-Sleepline Princess (Royal Palace) (618) 829^{W} (2199) 2571^{8} (2822) 3066^{5} **>93f<**

Rock Foundation **3** b c Rock City-Runelia (Runnett) 686^{5} 907^{8} 2102^{7} (2769) (2873) **>64a 63++f<**

Rock Group **3** b c Rock City-Norska (Northfields (USA)) 1372^{12} 2781^{3} **>62f<**

Rock Oyster **3** b c Ballad Rock-Bombshell 715^{19} 867^{12} 1512^{15} 1831^{3} 1978^{8} 2037^{14} 3455^{6} 4227^{13} **>59f<**

Rock Rambler **3** ch g Rock City-Moonwalker (Night Shift (USA)) 1125^{13} 1554^{6} 3761^{11} **>50f<**

Rock Scene (IRE) **3** b c Scenic-Rockeater *1761^{5} 2588^{4} 2959^{5}* **>68a f<**

Rock Sharp **2** b c Rock City-Keen Melody (USA) (Sharpen Up) 2277^{8} 2548^{3} (2971) (3281) 3775^{4} **>78f<**

Rockstine (IRE) **4** b f Ballad Rock-Huldine (Cure The Blues (USA)) *18^{3} 76^{3} 217^{3} 240^{3} 3082^{13}* 3385^{2} *3529^{3}* 3871^{8} *3951^{11}* **>52a 47f<**

Rock Symphony **5** ch h Ballad Rock-Shamasiya (FR) (Vayrann) 1316^{10} 1614^{4} 1895^{25} 2096^{6} (2823) 3145^{9} 3230^{7} 4119^{8} **>95f<**

Rock The Barney (IRE) **6** b h 550^{13} 817^{3} 1368^{5} (1757) (2007) 2289^{9} 2845^{3} 4000^{15} 4135^{11} 4333^{5} **>65f<**

Rockusa **3** b f Rock City-Miss Derby (USA) (Master Derby (USA)) 1473^{10} 2747^{9} *3514^{4}* 3859^{3} 4049^{5} 4261^{19} **>67f<**

Rockville Pike (IRE) **3** b c Glenstal (USA)-Sound Pet (Runnett) 633^{9} 2324^{4} 2677^{4} **>85f<**

Rocky Bay **6** ch m Bold Owl-Overseas (Sea Hawk II) *304^{4} 600^{7}* **>27a 13f<**

Rocky Forum **3** ch f Deploy-Beau's Delight (USA) (Lypheor) *264^{5} 316^{4} 372^{6}* 453^{2} 1093^{6} 1382^{4} (1601) 2026^{6} *2604^{2}* (2942) **>48a 70+f<**

Rocky Oasis (USA) **2** b c Gulch (USA)-Knoosh (USA) (Storm Bird (CAN)) 3560^{3} **>75+f<**

Rocky's Meteor **2** b c Emarati (USA)-Hoop la (Final Straw) 2608^{2} *3509^{9}* **>36a 57+f<**

Rocky Two **4** b c Cree Song-Holloway Wonder (Swing Easy (USA)) *244^{2}* 452^{6} *602^{5} 892^{7} 1076^{9}* 1400^{9} 1832^{5} 2137^{9} 2793^{3} 2850^{5} 3134^{6} 3622^{10} 3961^{11} **>59a 56df<**

Rocky Waters (USA) **6** b or br h Rocky Marriage (USA)-Running Melody (Rheingold) *123^{3} 248^{2} 336^{3} 404^{2} 499^{5}* 728^{10} *1629^{4}* 2414^{9} 2743^{7} 3065^{8} 3439^{16} 3632^{10} **>74da 64f<**

Rocquaine Bay **8** b m Morston (FR)-Queen's Royale (Tobrouk (FR)) 884^{4} 1254^{12} 1674^{4} 2007^{5} 2439^{5} (2687) (3006) 3287^{3} **>48f<**

Roderick Hudson **3** b c Elmaamul (USA)-Moviegoer (Pharly (FR)) 637^{6} 1072^{2} 1425^{2} (1731) 2240^{5} 2737^{15} **>90f<**

Roger the Butler (IRE) **5** ch h Ahonoora-Indian Jubilee (Indian King (USA)) 1100^{4} (1480) 1870^{10} 2097^{7} 3198a^{9} **>111f<**

Roi de la Mer (IRE) **4** b c Fairy King (USA)-Sea Mistress (Habitat) 433^{9} 550^{10} 634^{16} 975^{4} 1472^{7} 1940^{9} 2134^{3} (2528) 3106^{13} 3605^{6} 3885^{5} 4171^{5} **>72f<**

Roi Estate (IRE) **2** b c High Estate-Dear Lorraine 3788a^{6} **>89f<**

Roi Ho (FR) **4** br c Holst (USA)-Reine Ka (FR) (Kaldoun (FR)) (253a)

Roisin Clover **4** ch f Faustus (USA)-Valiyen (Valiyar) (763) 961^{3} 2845^{2} 3156^{7} 3406^{4} 3657^{8} **>77f<**

Roka **3** br f Rock City-Kalandariya (Kris) 695^{15} 1168^{8} 1476^{11} **>59f<**

Rokeby Bowl **3** b c Salse (USA)-Rose Bowl (USA) (Habitat) 442^{4} 585^{7} 775^{2} 1130^{11} (1524) (1793) 2118^{2} 2457^{4} 2691^{2} 3459^{2} 3836^{10} 4031^{5} **>103f<**

Roll a Dollar **9** b g Spin of a Coin-Handy Dancer (Green God) 3593^{12} 3730^{20} **>66f<**

Rolling (IRE) **3** gr f Last Tycoon-Faakirah (Dragonara Palace (USA)) 697^{3} 1201^{8} 1550^{7} 1906^{5} **>72df<**

Rolling Settlement (IRE) **3** b f Contract Law (USA)-Ellaline (Corvaro (USA)) 4049^{11} 4225^{16} **>9f<**

Rolling the Bones (USA) **6** b h Green Dancer (USA)-Davelle's Bid (USA) 556^{2} (741) (1036) *1086^{4}* 1535^{9} 3978^{7} **>35a 52f<**

Rolling Waters **5** b h Robellino (USA)-Idle Waters *(835) 1029^{11}* 1166^{9} *1332^{2}* 1658^{7} *1955^{5} (2147)* 2407^{3} *2605^{2}* 2942^{4} *3082^{6} 3245^{5} 3951^{8}* **>69a 69f<**

Romalito **5** b g Robellino (USA)-Princess Zita (Manado) *183^{3}* 696^{7} 1328^{8} 1607^{8} (2280) 2530^{5} 2713^{5} 2860^{6} 3435^{5} 3627^{8} 3849^{5} 3986^{11} **>47a 54f<**

Roman Gold (IRE) **2** b c Petorius-Saffron (FR) (Fabulous Dancer (USA)) 2005^{5} 2408^{8} 2534^{4} 3003^{6} 3147^{4} 3345^{3} 3752^{2} **>69f<**

Roman Reel (USA) **4** ch c Sword Dance-Our Mimi (USA) (Believe It (USA)) *125^{6} 195^{9} (318) 406^{10} 470^{4}* 586^{3} 873^{15} 1048^{4} (2115) 2682^{5} 2808^{2} *3082^{11}* 3977^{3} 4227^{8} *4298^{8}* **>64a 77f<**

Romansh **6** b h Shernazar-Romara 2979^{12} 3234^{9} 3288^{9} **>59f<**

Romantic Folly 3 b f Thowra (FR)-Beaver Skin Hunter (Ballacashtal (CAN)) 651^{15} **>17f<**
Romanzof 3 ch c Kris-Russian Countess (USA) (Nureyev (USA)) (777) 1224^{4} 1370^{2} 2030^{W} (2471) 3013^{2} **>110f<**
Romios (IRE) 3 ch c Common Grounds-Domino's Nurse (Dom Racine (FR)) 1103^{3} 1322^{7} (1619) 2348^{10} 4031^{2} **>95f<**
Ron's Gem 2 b g Ron's Victory (USA)-Crystal Gael (Sparkler) 1620^{6} 2371^{6} *4339^{W}* **>46f<**
Ron's Secret 3 br f Efisio-Primrose Bank 1240^{5} 1428^{3} (1907) 2199^{4} (2694) 3106^{3} 3388^{9} 3630^{4} (3966) 4065^{3} 4267^{26} **>99f<**
Roodmas (IRE) 4 b f Sharrood (USA)-Taustaff (Taufan (USA)) *31^{8}* **>31df<**
Rood Music 4 ro g Sharrood (USA)-Rose Music (Luthier (FR)) 1649^{14} (3063) 3367^{9} 3534^{8} 3802^{9} 3977^{11} 4292^{6} *(4340)* **>62a 56f<**
Rookery Girl 3 b f Pharly (FR)-Persian Grey (Persepolis (FR)) *316^{10}* 547^{8} 761^{7} 1172^{12} 1692^{9} **>7a 67f<**
Rory 4 b c Dowsing (USA)-Crymlyn (Welsh Pageant) 558^{4} 634^{13} 1225^{5} 1626^{7} 2593^{5} 4038^{6} 4227^{6} **>86f<**
Rory John 7 ch g Country Classic-Rasimareem (Golden Mallard) *256^{11} 296^{6}* **>20a f<**
Rosa Bonheur 3 b f Absalom-Masirah (Dunphy) 733^{7} 1914^{5} 2180^{2} 2404^{2} (2712) 2905^{5} 3372^{3} 3624^{13} 3972^{8} **>54f<**
Roscommon Joe (IRE) 5 b g Simply Great (FR)-Kilvarnet (Furry Glen) 874^{14} 991^{8} 1997^{5} **>40f<**
Roscommon Lad (IRE) 3 b c Groom Dancer (USA)-Preoccupy (Habitat) 428^{11} 978^{11} 1526^{16} 2133^{4} 2754^{3} **>40f<**
Roseate Lodge 9 b h Habitat-Elegant Tern (USA) *379^{5}* (548) 748^{4} 848^{2} 1191^{2} 1291^{4} 1432^{5} 1808^{8} 2620^{5} 3493^{13} 3565^{14} 3704^{3} 3807^{13} 3920^{10} **>80a 60f<**
Roseberry Avenue (IRE) 2 b c Sadler's Wells (USA)-Lady's Bridge (USA) (Sir Ivor) 3900^{19} 4046^{6} 4226^{5} **>69f<**
Roseberry Ray (IRE) 3 b c High Estate-Rained Off (Welsh Pageant) 2553^{7} 2880^{3} (3119) 3659^{11} 3973^{10} **>86f<**
Rosebud 3 b f Indian Ridge-Tiszta Sharok (Song) (752) 1172^{3} 1487^{6} **>84f<**
Rose Chime (IRE) 3 b or br f Tirol-Repicado Rose (USA) (Repicado (CHI)) *47^{5} 85^{5} 180^{4}* 1028^{6} 1548^{8} 1920^{5} *2072^{4}* 2306^{6} **>39a 50f<**
Rose of Cadence 3 gr f Chief Singer-Couleur de Rose (Kalaglow) 1625^{4} **>66f<**
Rose of Glenn 4 b f Crofthall-May Kells (Artaius (USA)) *9^{3} 161^{4} 277^{3} 375^{8} 1759^{4}* (2078) 2514^{6} 2860^{10} 3202^{2} 3627^{3} 3884^{7} *4270^{6}* 4331^{8} **>55a 57f<**
Rose of Siberia (USA) 2 gr f Siberian Express (USA)-Exuberine (FR) (Be My Guest (USA)) 903^{4} 1842^{5} 3093^{2} 3538^{6} 3760^{4} (4172) **>66f<**
Roses In The Snow (IRE) 2 gr f Be My Guest (USA)-Desert Bluebell (Kalaglow) 791^{2} 1098^{4} 2315^{2} 2594^{6} 3133^{2} 3404^{2} 3865^{8} 4235^{2} **>80f<**
Rose Tint (IRE) 2 b f Salse (USA)-Sally Rose (Sallust) 2412^{6} **>46f<**
Rosevear (IRE) 3 b f Contract Law (USA)-Caimanite (Tap On Wood) *1034^{7} 1209^{4}* 1663^{12} *2140^{3} 3076^{4}* **>47a 49f<**
Rosie Sweetheart (IRE) 3 b f Sadler's Wells (USA)-Passamaquoddy (USA) (Drone) 942^{4} 1717^{4} 2312^{3} **>76f<**
Rosina's Folly 4 b f Tina's Pet-Rosie Dickins (Blue Cashmere) *32^{2} 92^{5} 119^{6} 214^{7} 267^{10} 402^{9}* 548^{8} 672^{14} 1153^{6} 1350^{6} 1647^{5} 1873^{11} *2587^{11}* **>58a 49f<**
Rosi Zambotti (IRE) 3 f 1237a^{5} 2566a^{2} 4020a^{4} **>98f<**
Rosscoyne 5 b m Ardross-Banking Coyne 545^{12} *1319^{12}* **>47df<**
Rossel (USA) 2 b c Blushing John (USA)-Northern Aspen (USA) (Northern Dancer) 3900^{12} 4241^{5} **>67f<**
Rossini Blue 4 ch c Music Boy-Miss Rossi (Artaius (USA)) *65^{7} 365^{12} 407^{4}* 685^{2} 870^{17} 1021^{3} 1261^{13} 1421^{12} *1630^{8}* 1931^{U} 2194^{6} 2428^{3} (2624) 3145^{17} 3230^{10} 3492^{3} 3719^{3} 3807^{2} 4041^{12} 4068^{12} 4193^{4} **>62a 80f<**
Rostaq 2 b c Keen-American Beauty 2526^{3} 2971^{2} **>79f<**
Rosy Hue (IRE) 3 b f Shaadi (USA)-Sally Rose (Sallust) 1473^{3} 1770^{3} 3630^{3} (3921) 4071^{7} **>81f<**
Rosy Lydgate 4 br f Last Tycoon-Sing Softly (Luthier (FR)) *30^{9}* **>7a 51f<**
Rotherfield Park (IRE) 3 b f High Estate-Alriyaah (Shareef Dancer (USA)) *33^{5} 146^{10} 278^{4}* 1975^{14} *2627^{13}* 3442^{14} 3748^{9} 3972^{14} **>43a 34f<**
Rothley Imp (IRE) 2 b f Mac's Imp (USA)-Valediction (Town Crier) 1098^{8} 1540^{9} 2346^{5} 2908^{6} 3124^{2} 3290^{2} 3749^{15} **>60f<**
Roufontaine 4 gr f Rousillon (USA)-Bellifontaine (FR) (Bellypha) 815^{2} 1128^{14} 2316^{5} 2547^{5} 2759^{5} 3006^{4} **>90f<**
Rouge Rancon (USA) 2 b f Red Ransom (USA)-Lady O'Lyph (Lyphard (USA)) (2351) 3692a^{5} 3835^{4} **>101f<**
Roushan 2 ch c Anshan-Fleur Rouge (Pharly (FR)) 3604^{10} **>54f<**
Rousitto 7 ch h Rousillon (USA)-Helenetta (Troy) *(34) 81^{3} 120^{2} 4270^{5}* **>65a 50f<**
Roussi (USA) 3 b c Nureyev (USA)-Iva Reputation (USA) (Sir Ivor) 3921^{3} 4072^{9} 4162^{4} **>72f<**
Roving Minstrel 4 ch c Cree Song-Klairove (Averof) (439) 714^{14} 870^{10} 1108^{7} 1728^{2} 2598^{4} 3222^{12} 3608^{2} 3945^{21} **>62a 95f<**
Rowhome 2 b c Colmore Row-Stride Home (Absalom) 644^{6} *1632^{4}* 2035^{8} *2294^{4} 2496^{6}* **>33a 25f<**
Rowlandsons Charm (IRE) 2 b f Fayruz-Magic Gold (Sallust) 1481^{3} 1690^{12} 1938^{10} 3213^{7} 3471^{3} 3628^{8} 3869^{7} 4130^{9} **>64f<**
Rowlandsons Links 2 b c Picea-Charlotte Piaf (Morston (FR)) 3673^{12} 3915^{13} **>32f<**
Rowlandsons Silver (FR) 3 b c Reprimand-African Dash (African Sky) *24^{5} 98^{5} 189^{5} 263^{9}* 2684^{6} **>37a 61f<**
Rowlandsons Stud (IRE) 2 b br c Distinctly North (USA)-Be My Million (Taufan (USA)) 2403^{5} 2656^{8} **>18f<**
Roxanian (IRE) 4 b c Cyrano de Bergerac-Sassanian 3632^{13} **>73df<**
Roxy River 6 ch m Ardross-Royal Yacht (USA) (Riverman (USA)) 2197^{8} 2501^{3} 2734^{7} **>37f<**
Royal Abjar (USA) 4 b c Gone West (USA)-Encorelle (FR) (Arctic Tern (USA)) 2389a^{2} **>122f<**
Royal Acclaim 10 ch h Tender King-Glimmer (Hot Spark) *68^{5} 169^{4} 312^{5} 341^{5} 387^{3} 408^{5}* 430^{9} 586^{7} 738^{16} *3240^{8}* **>50a 41f<**
Royal Addiction (IRE) 3 b c Prince Rupert (FR)-Opium Queen (King's Troop) *90^{12} 270^{8}* 2165^{9}

Royal Applause **2** b c Waajib-Flying Melody (Auction Ring (USA)) (1406) (1838) (3163) (3903) **>115f<**
Royal Ballerina (IRE) **5** b m Sadler's Wells (USA)-Fremanche (FR) 2211a^{4} 3161^{4} 3591a^{P} 4182a^{2} **>116f<**
Royal Canaska **2** ch c Royal Academy (USA)-North Telstar (Sallust) 4239^{3} **>86f<**
Royal Carlton (IRE) **3** b g Mulhollande (USA)-Saintly Angel 1982^{6} 2410^{7} 2686^{8} 3748^{17} 4268^{14} **>61f<**
Royal Ceilidh (IRE) **2** b f Prince Rupert (FR)-Isa (Dance In Time (CAN)) (1247) 1530^{6} 1769^{3} 2059^{5} 3701^{15} (4111) **>75df<**
Royal Circle **3** b f Sadler's Wells (USA)-Queen Midas (Glint of Gold) 691^{2} (2350) 3088^{6} 3831^{4} 4030^{4} 4323^{5} **>99f<**
Royal Circus **6** b h Kris-Circus Ring (High Top) *9^{7} (75) 122^{2} 178^{4} 221^{4} (285) 321^{7} 356^{2}* 1254^{10} 1496^{2} 1686^{9} 2109^{5} 2226^{7} **>43a 46f<**
Royal Citizen (IRE) **6** b h Caerleon (USA)-Taking Steps (Gay Fandango (USA)) *35^{2} 91^{2} 121^{5} (223) (280) 375^{2} 514^{5}* 866^{7} **>67a 55f<**
Royal College (IRE) **3** b c Sadler's Wells (USA)-Lady Capulet (USA) (Sir Ivor) 854^{8} 1015^{3} **>75f<**
Royal Comedian **6** gr m Jester-Royal Huntress *419^{16}* (992) *1334^{11}* 1843^{3} 2390^{4} 2685^{16} 3506^{5} 3726^{17} 3941^{8} 4234^{10} **>32a 50f<**
Royal Dancer **3** ch f Dancing Dissident (USA)-Aquarula (Dominion) *4296^{10}* **>31a 39f<**
Royal Diversion (IRE) **2** b f Marju (IRE)-Royal Recreation (USA) (His Majesty (USA)) 3891^{6} 4218^{2} **>68f<**
Royal Dome (IRE) **3** b c Salt Dome (USA)-Brook's Dilemma (Known Fact (USA)) 577^{3} *768^{5}* 2084^{13} 2372^{2} 2680^{4} (2858) 3150^{2} (3783) 3905^{2} (3992) **>18a 76f<**
Royale Figurine (IRE) **4** ch f Dominion Royale-Cree's Figurine (Creetown) (693) 1019^{6} 1475^{3} 1895^{7} 2570^{4} 3342^{2} (3717) (4121) 4253a^{2} 4324^{3} **>109f<**
Royal Expose (USA) **2** ch c Unzipped (USA)-Royal Tasha (USA) (Northern Prospect (USA)) 3592^{14} **>28f<**
Royal Expression **3** b c Sylvan Express-Edwin's Princess (Owen Dudley) 1204^{3} 1452^{4} (1720) 2312^{2} 2427^{5} **>66f<**
Royal Hill **4** b c Danehill (USA)-Royal Caprice (USA) (Swaps) 439^{5} 714^{9} 870^{2} 1851^{8} **>70++a 91f<**
Royal Jade **2** b f Last Tycoon-Imperial Jade (Lochnager) 2934^{3} **>91+f<**
Royal Mark (IRE) **2** b c Fairy King (USA)-Take Your Mark (USA) (Round Table (USA)) 2116^{3} (2464) (2911) 3281^{2} 3865^{13} **>85+f<**
Royal Oddsox **2** ch c Dominion Royale-Kevin's Pet (Petorius) *3525^{10}*
Royal Philosopher **3** b c Faustus (USA)-Princess Lucy (Local Suitor (USA)) 1315^{3} 1586^{7} 3598^{2} 3728^{9} **>104df<**
Royal Print (IRE) **6** ch h Kings Lake (USA)-Reprint (Kampala) *45^{10}* **>44a 44f<**
Royal Rabbit **3** b c Prince Daniel (USA)-Lirchur (Lir) *444^{6}* (1254) 1401^{4} *1628^{5} 2378^{8}* 2806^{3} 2976^{9} 3265^{2} 3722^{4} **>50a 58f<**
Royal Rapport **2** ch c Rich Charlie-Miss Camellia (Sonnen Gold) 615^{8} 788^{5} 1540^{11} 3644^{16} 3803^{13} **>58df<**
Royal Rebuke **3** br f Reprimand-Noble Lustre (USA) (Lyphard's Wish (FR)) (914) 1131^{3} 1923^{2} 2436^{4} 2703^{5} **>98f<**
Royal Rigger **2** gr f Reprimand-Overdraft (Bustino) 574^{5} 699^{8} *846^{3}* 3760^{11} **>29a 35f<**
Royal Romance **2** b f Crowning Honors (CAN)-Bali Sunset (Balidar) 2185^{W} 2516^{14} 2756^{U}
Royal Scimitar (USA) **3** ch c Diesis-Princess of Man 657^{2} (787) 979^{6} 1396a^{10} 1782^{3} 2415^{4} 4325^{7} **>101f<**
Royal Solo (IRE) **3** b c Sadler's Wells (USA)-Sharp Castan 677^{5} (978) (2560a) 3323a^{4} 3482a^{9} **>120f<**
Royal Sovereign (IRE) **3** b f Royal Academy (USA)-Adjarida 1168^{14} **>20f<**
Royal Uprising (IRE) **3** b f Red Sunset-Wilderness (Martinmas) *146^{8} 251^{5} 382^{5}* **>30a 39f<**
Royal York **3** b f Bustino-Rustle of Silk (General Assembly (USA)) 968^{6} (1669) (2312) 2937^{2} 3189^{12} 3669^{14} **>79f<**
Roy Boy **3** b c Emarati (USA)-Starky's Pet (Mummy's Pet) 437^{5} 572^{6} 697^{2} 772^{3} 1360^{4} 1550^{8} **>81f<**
Royrace **3** b g Wace (USA)-Royal Tycoon (Tycoon II) 3772^{10} 4047^{11} 4168^{8} **>56f<**
Rozalina Lady **3** b f Alzao (USA)-Diavolina (USA) (Lear Fan (USA)) 957^{9} 1167^{12} 1735^{8} 2037^{17} 2582^{11} 3259^{8} **>57f<**
Rozel Bay **2** ch f Kadir Cup 1024^{5} *3243^{2} 3738^{7} 4127^{5} 4273^{8}* **>53a f<**
Rubadub **4** b f Kalaglow-Ravens Peak (High Top) 973^{7} 1198^{8} 1519^{5} 1799^{5} 2245^{10} 2400^{5} 2549^{14} 2640^{7} **>52f<**
Rubhahunish (IRE) **4** b c Darshaan-Captive Island (Northfields (USA)) 1118a^{6} 1392a^{6} **>112f<**
Rubislaw **3** ch g Dunbeath (USA)-Larnem (Meldrum) *418^{11}* 1046^{5} 1379^{12} 1824^{9} 2396^{4} 2655^{9} **>19a 54f<**
Ruby Estate (IRE) **4** b f High Estate-Tuesday Morning (Sadler's Wells (USA)) 2613^{13} 2747^{12} **>64a 61f<**
Ruby Heights **4** b f Shirley Heights-Hence (USA) (Mr Prospector (USA)) 2028^{3} 2174^{2} 2577^{4} (3302) 3572^{5} 3889^{3} 4259^{4} **>65da 65f<**
Rubylee **3** ch f Persian Bold-Miss Merlin *468^{6}* 1825^{8} 2037^{8} 2317^{14} **>49a 65f<**
Ruby Rock **3** b f Rock City-Resonation (CAN) (Coastal (USA)) 1804^{4} 2086^{5} 2357^{8} 3504^{8} 3722^{10} **>33f<**
Ruby Two Shoes **2** b f Revlow-Miss Burgundy (Gambling Debt) 3883^{15} 4143^{10} **>47f<**
Ruby Venture **3** br f Ballad Rock-Sherkraine (Shergar) 797^{11} 950^{6} 1340^{6} **>67f<**
Ruddigore **3** ch c Old Vic-Sea Saga (Dara Monarch) 1286^{7} 1776^{5} 1970^{7} 2282^{4} 2812^{5} 3747^{10} 3984^{11} 4209^{19} **>59df<**
Rug **3** ch c Persian Bold-Golden Form (Formidable) 677^{6} (924) **>81f<**
Rumba Rhythm (CAN) **2** ch f Thorn Dance (USA)-Skoblikova (USA) (Phone Trick (USA)) 940^{5} 1169^{4} 1751^{4} **>77f<**
Rumi **4** ch f Nishapour (FR)-Seldom (Rarity) 661^{13} 860^{7} **>92f<**
Rumpelstiltskin **3** ch c Sharpo-Ouija 637^{9} 888^{11} 1337^{8} **>56f<**
Rumpipumpy **2** b f Shirley Heights-Wanton (Kris) 2025^{5} 2581^{2} 3346^{4} 3867^{2} **>85f<**
Rumpus (IRE) **5** b m Kahyasi-Helietta (Tyrnavos) 1058^{14} 1200^{7} **>42f<**
Run-Do-Run **3** b f Gabitat-Do-Run-Do (Palm Track) 1065^{7} 1512^{6} 2037^{16} 4043^{R} 4249^{20} 4332^{R} **>56df<**
Runforaction (IRE) **3** b f Contract Law (USA)-Prissy

Miss (Free State) 5^{4} 51^{4} 90^{9} 180^{3} 292^{6} 339^{7} 1569^{7} 1863^{9} 2129^{12} **>44a 48f<**

Run High **12** b h Thatch (USA)-Fleet Noble (USA) 1794^{9} 2090^{10} 2280^{5} **>43a 52f<**

Runic Symbol **4** b g Warning-Pagan Deity (Brigadier Gerard) 546^{3} 1202^{5} 1472^{4} 2276^{12} 2807^{3} 3063^{6} 3402^{6} 3664^{11} **>37f<**

Running Green **4** b c Green Desert (USA)-Smeralda (GER) (Dschingi's Khan) 593^{3} **>57f<**

Runrig (IRE) **5** b m Jalmood (USA)-Bluethroat (Ballymore) 876^{10} 992^{8} 1724^{3} 1816^{2} 1958^{5} 2126^{5} 2232^{6} 2396^{8} 3370^{5} **>49f<**

Runs in the Family **3** b f Distant Relative-Stoneydale (Tickled Pink) 733^{5} 862^{15} 1199^{14} 1483^{6} 2144^{8} 2497^{4} 2963^{11} 3667^{3} 3919^{18} 4057^{14} **>44a 56f<**

Rupert's Princess (IRE) **3** b f Prince Rupert (FR)-Llanelli (Welsh Saint) 482^{6} 629^{6} 732^{4} 1033^{2} 1279^{14} **>59a 57f<**

Rupiana (IRE) **3** b f Prince Rupert (FR)-Webbiana (African Sky) 873^{23} 1172^{15} 1447^{12} **>79df<**

Rushaway **4** b c Robellino (USA)-Brush Away (Ahonoora) 485^{6} 817^{7} 1256^{5} **>67f<**

Rushcutter Bay **2** br c Mon Tresor-Llwy Bren (Lidhame) 1652^{W} 1879^{4} (2135) 2978^{3} 3375^{6} **>41a 71f<**

Rushen Raider **3** br g Reprimand-Travel Storm (Lord Gayle (USA)) 1060^{8} (1153) 1465^{6} 1598^{5} 2655^{6} (2953) 2993^{5} 3169^{5} **>71f<**

Rusk **2** b c Pharly (FR)-Springwell (Miami Springs) 4037^{4} **>72f<**

Russian Heroine **3** b f Domynsky-Actress (Known Fact (USA)) 40^{5} 118^{3} 210^{7} 420^{2} 482^{3} 591^{4} 701^{2} 823^{9} 904^{3} 1033^{3} 1414^{12} (1469) 1541^{7} (1719) (1961) (2003) (2188) 2455^{3} 2500^{4} 2737^{7} 3212^{4} 3291^{7} 3457^{16} 3972^{15} **>73da 78f<**

Russian Maid **3** ch f Cadeaux Genereux-Tsar Maiden (USA) (Nijinsky (CAN)) 547^{4} (2583) 3214^{2} 3565^{4} 3922^{9} **>87f<**

Russian Music **2** b g Forzando-Sunfleet (Red Sunset) 3185^{3} 3456^{3} **>84f<**

Russian Rascal (IRE) **2** b g Soviet Lad (USA)-Anglo Irish (Busted) 615^{17} (1266) 2328^{3} 2644^{3} 3019^{2} 3780^{P} **>65f<**

Russian Revival (USA) **2** ch c Nureyev (USA)-Memories (USA) (Hail the Pirates (USA)) (1184) 1838^{2} $3330a^{4}$ **>105f<**

Russian Snows (IRE) **3** b f Sadler's Wells (USA)-Arctique Royale (Royal And Regal (USA)) $2211a^{2}$ $2563a^{2}$ $3326a^{2}$ (4009a) **>117f<**

Rustavi (IRE) **4** b g Entitled-Sweet Tones (Lord Gayle (USA)) 3849^{12}

Rustic League (IRE) **4** b g Gallic League-Walnut Lass (Tap On Wood) 148^{7} 199^{3} 353^{4} 419^{13} 452^{3} 519^{8} 726^{10} 1368^{13} 1883^{7} **>36a 35f<**

Rustic Song (IRE) **2** b f Fayruz-Red Note (Rusticaro (FR)) 671^{10} 3022^{3} 3509^{8} 3824^{2} 3901^{9} 4243^{13} **>37a 51f<**

Ruthy's Romance **4** b f Then Again-What's the Matter (High Top) 1092^{21} 1383^{W}

Ruwy **2** b f Soviet Star (USA)-Psylla (Beldale Flutter (USA)) 4218^{3} **>67f<**

Ruznama (USA) **2** ch f Forty Niner (USA)-Last Feather (USA) (Vaguely Noble) 3069^{7} (3339) 3561^{3} (3942) **>98+f<**

Rye Hill Queen (IRE) **5** b br m Wassl-Jendeal (Troy) 10861^{4}

Rymer's Rascal **3** b g Rymer-City Sound 823^{12} 999^{5} 1180^{12} 1249^{2} 1624^{3} 1723^{7} 3783^{15} 3964^{16} 4125^{10} **>21a 67f<**

S

Saafi (IRE) **4** b c Primo Dominie-Baby's Smile (Shirley Heights) 1254^{7} 1513^{7} 3024^{7} 3178^{5} **>63f<**

Saahi (USA) **6** b h Lyphard (USA)-Dumtadumtadum (USA) (Grey Dawn II) 763^{15} 1210^{5} 1594^{9} **>29a 34f<**

Saatchmo **3** b c Forzando-Into the Fire (Dominion) 732^{3} 758^{5} 1201^{9} 3514^{9} 3808^{26} **>38a 55f<**

Sabaah Elfull **2** ch f Kris-Putupon (Mummy's Pet) 3069^{11} 3643^{3} **>73f<**

Sabella **4** ch f Prince Sabo-Pour Moi (Bay Express) 2142^{9} 2492^{10} 3734^{8} **>34a 66df<**

Sabicas **3** b c High Kicker (USA)-Spanish Estates (Firestreak) 38^{7} 133^{6} **>45da 45f<**

Sabot **2** b c Polar Falcon (USA)-Power Take Off (Aragon) 3185^{6} 3606^{2} 4103^{4} **>83f<**

Sacha Star **5** b m Green Ruby (USA)-Rymerstar (Rymer) 2082^{6} **>65f<**

Sacho (IRE) **2** b c Sadler's Wells (USA)-Oh So Sharp (Kris) 4080^{2} **>93+f<**

Sacrament **4** b c Shirley Heights-Blessed Event (Kings Lake (USA)) 913^{4} **>120f<**

Sacramento (IRE) **2** c $2726a^{8}$ 4032^{7} **>69f<**

Sacred Mirror (IRE) **4** b f Shaadi (USA)-Heavenly Abode (FR) (Habitat) 313^{10} 347^{5} 389^{7} 454^{5} 860^{5} **>55da 68f<**

Sadarah (USA) **3** b c Dixieland Band (USA)-Chriso (USA) (Highland Blade (USA)) 4150^{10}

Saddlehome (USA) **6** b h Aragon-Kesarini (USA) (Singh (USA)) (398) 535^{2} 723^{6} 922^{11} 1106^{2} (1614) 2764^{25} 3221^{6} **>85a 82f<**

Saderlina (IRE) **3** b f Sadler's Wells-Dinalina (Top Ville) $3035a^{3}$

Sadler's Image (IRE) **4** b c Sadler's Wells (USA)-Exclusive Order (USA) (Exclusive Native (USA)) 1171^{2} **>118f<**

Sadler's Pearl **3** b f Thowra (FR)-Queens Pearl 695^{13} 779^{10} 957^{8} 1322^{9} 1628^{6} 1784^{7} 1937^{8} 2197^{6} 2592^{9} **>51a 63f<**

Sadler's Realm **2** b c Sadler's Wells (USA)-Rensaler (USA) (Stop The Music (USA)) 4247^{6} **>74f<**

Sadler's Walk **4** b c Sadler's Wells (USA)-Widows Walk (Habitat) 550^{4} 864^{5} 981^{2} 1926^{3} (2343) 2672^{4} 3729^{12} 3993^{2} **>86f<**

Sadly Sober (IRE) **3** b f Roi Danzig (USA)-Overcall 1916^{4} 4071^{13} **>65f<**

Safecracker **2** ch c Sayf El Arab (USA)-My Polished Corner (IRE) (Tate Gallery (USA)) 3441^{7} 3672^{12} **>52f<**

Safe Secret **4** b f Seclude (USA)-Safe Passage 1349^{10} 1513^{14} 1663^{10} 2246^{10} 2549^{12} 2983^{7} **>23a 61f<**

Safety Factor (USA) **4** b c Known Fact (USA)-Sookera (USA) 1786^{6} 2708^{3} **>83f<**

Safey Ana (USA) **4** b c Dixieland Band (USA)-Whatsoraire (USA) (Mr Prospector (USA)) 539^{6} 749^{5} 935^{15} 1183^{3} (1380) 2130^{7} (2414) 2602^{5} 3109^{6} 3457^{3} 3706^{8} 3943^{13} **>77f<**

Safio 2 ch c Efisio-Marcroft (Crofthall) (718) 1104[6] 1343[3] 1893[8] 2223[5] 3375[10] 3727[9] **>99f<**

Safwan 3 b c Primo Dominie-French Plait (Thatching) 3712[18]

Sagar Pride (IRE) 2 br f Jareer (USA)-Sagar Island (USA) (Sagace) 1849[8] **>87f<**

Sagasan 4 b c Rousillon (USA)-Scholastika (GER) (Alpenkonig (GER)) *1861[2] 311[2] 367[10] 843[4]* 1513[11] **>68a 66f<**

Sagebrush Roller 7 br h Sharpo-Sunita (Owen Dudley) 434[7] 563[3] 1021[10] 1299[10] 2099[6] 2428[4] 3719[2] 3943[15] 4041[11] 4319[15] **>90f<**

Sagitta's Reel (HOL) 4 b f Scottish Reel-Sagitta's Choice (Welsh Pageant) 3573[7] **>34f<**

Sahhar 2 ch c Sayf El Arab (USA)-Native Magic (Be My Native (USA)) 4314[10] **>63f<**

Sahil (IRE) 3 b c Taufan (USA)-Bouffant (High Top) 816[4] (1038) 1478[8] **>88f<**

Saibot (USA) 6 ch g Riverman (USA)-Arabev (USA) (Damascus (USA)) 1610[6] **>98f<**

Saifan 6 ch h Beveled (USA)-Superfrost (Tickled Pink) 486[7] 873[2] 1183[18] 1626[3] (2181) 2321[6] 2468[2] 2952[4] (3291) 3732[14] 4116[9] 4227[11] 4267[15] **>84f<**

Sailormaite 4 ch c Komaite (USA)-Marina Plata (Julio Mariner) 434[2] 535[4] 812[14] (1599) *(1953)* 2570[2] 3551[19] 3717[22] **>90a 90f<**

Sailors Moon 3 ch f Indian Ridge-Premiere Moon (Bold Owl) *156[6]* 521[16] 689[8] **>32a 39f<**

Sails Legend 4 b c Hotfoot-Miss Polly Peck (March Past) 795[14] 1189[8] 3876[8] 3986[16] **>57f<**

Saint Amigo 3 gr c Presidium-Little Token (Shack (USA)) 839[12] 1644[7] 1873[15] 1993[6] 2540[12] 3467[8] 3972[7] 4170[19] 4275[14] **>59a 57f<**

Saint Ciel (USA) 7 b h Skywalker (USA)-Holy Tobin (USA) (J O Tobin (USA)) 3759[8] **>56f<**

Saint Express 5 ch g Clantime-Redgrave Design (Nebbiolo) 1489[2] (1765) 2285[2] 2671[3] 3342[4] 3550[7] 3880[3] 4121[7] **>107df<**

Saint Rosalina 2 b f Common Grounds-Saint Systems (Uncle Pokey) 2249[3] *2591[2]* 2857[2] 4144[19] **>50a 49f<**

Sakharov 6 b h Bay Express-Supreme Kingdom (Take A Reef) *532[2] 590[6]* 789[10] 1493[3] 1724[2] 1994[3] 2310[2] **>60a 66f<**

Sakti (AUS) 2 b f Kenmare (FR)-Sakala (NZ) (Gold and Ivory (USA)) 740[4] **>28f<**

Sakura Chitose O (JPN) 5 b h Tony Bin-Sakura Clare (Northern Ta 1120a[2] **>123f<**

Sakura (IRE) 4 ch f Dominion-Ariadne (Bustino) 3052[6] **>31a 35f<**

Salamander King 3 b c Distant Relative-Spirit of The Wind (USA) (Little Current (USA)) 1136[19] **>46f<**

Salaman (FR) 3 b c Saumarez-Merry Sharp (Sharpen Up) 485[9] 687[3] 1730[5] (1973) (2256) (2429) 2688[3] (3274) 4118[11] **>97f<**

Salbus 5 b h Salse (USA)-Busca (USA) (Mr Prospector (USA)) *19[2] (104) 193[5] 308[4] 389[10]* **>70a 42f<**

Salduba 3 b f Fijar Tango (FR)-Silver Ore (FR) (Silver Hawk (USA)) 1463[5] 2425[6] 2873[4] 3841[5] **>32f<**

Saleel (IRE) 3 b c Salse (USA)-Kentfield (Busted) 673[7] 815[4] 1038[2] (2754) (3142) 3547[2] 4118[5] 4258[4] **>102f<**

Salfrill (IRE) 3 b f Salt Dome (USA)-Frill (Henbit (USA)) 1325[4] 1659[9] **>64f<**

Salilian Twilight 2 b f Bairn (USA)-Salilia (Nishapour (FR)) 2666[6] 2838[5] **>46f<**

Salinger 7 b h Rousillon (USA)-Scholastika (GER) (Alpenkonig (GER)) *255[4] 520[9]* 649[11] 866[6] (3047) (3297) 3462[10] **>36a 52f<**

Sallyoreally (IRE) 4 b f Common Grounds-Prosapia (USA) (Our Native (USA)) 676[13] 757[8] 967[7] 1651[10] 1875[7] 2064[5] 2310[15] 2545[6] 3741[6] 4110[10] 4234[13] **>43f<**

Sally Slade 3 b f Dowsing (USA)-Single Gal (Mansingh (USA)) *498[5]* 621[13] (850) 982[8] 1550[2] 1924[9] **>69a 84f<**

Sally State 2 b f Northern State (USA)-Cadenza (Radetzky) 3054[4] 3570[8] 3758[10] **>5f<**

Sally's Twins 2 b f Dowsing (USA)-Bird of Love (Ela-Mana-Mou) 3673[9] 3887[6] 4046[7] **>72f<**

Sally Weld 3 ch f Weldnaas (USA)-Sallytude (Tudor Music) 1094[4] 1201[10] 1660[8] 1982[5] 2404[6] (2831) 3390[10] 3677[10] 3771[5] **>64a 62f<**

Salmis 2 b f Salse (USA)-Misguided (Homing) (3869) 4067[2] **>81f<**

Salmon Ladder (USA) 3 b c Bering-Ballerina Princess (USA) (Mr Prospector (USA)) 1107[6] 1611[10] 4204[5] **>103f<**

Salsian 2 b f Salse (USA)-Phylae (Habitat) 4063[8] 4247[9] **>61f<**

Salska 4 b f Salse (USA)-Anzeige (GER) *18[10]* 1966[7] 2148[4] 2655[7] 2875[8] 3094[2] 3297[3] 3388[6] 3531[8] 3759[5] (3818) 4166[17] **>41a 56f<**

Saltando (IRE) 4 b g Salt Dome (USA)-Ange de Feu (Double Form) 1168[12] 1786[11] 1967[4] 2613[10] 3475[3] 3685[4] 3863[18] 3920[3] 4027[3] 4079[7] 4229[7] 4333[14] **>59f<**

Saltis (IRE) 3 ch g Salt Dome (USA)-Mrs Tittlemouse (Nonoalco (USA)) 1512[14] *1939[4]* 2363[4] 2946[4] 3159[10] 3475[12] 3897[4] 4194[10] **>59a 65df<**

Salt Lake 4 b c Mtoto-Bluebook (USA) (Secretariat (USA)) 704a[6] 1188[2] (1926) 2241[2] 2936[8] 3381[4] 3716[3] **>110f<**

Salty Girl (IRE) 2 b f Scenic-Sodium's Niece (Northfields (USA)) 2351[5] 2705[3] 3713[4] 3939[2] 4129[6] **>77f<**

Saltz (IRE) 3 b c Salt Dome (USA)-Heather Hut (Shack (USA)) *342[5] 398[13]* 966[18] 1302[5] 2191[5] 2624[7] 2881[2] (3264) 3429[7] **>52a 72f<**

Salutation (IRE) 4 b g Salt Dome (USA)-Salvationist (Mill Reef (USA)) *421[7]* **>32a f<**

Salvatore Giuliano 5 ch h Superlative-Bonny Bright Eyes (Rarity) 2842[6] 3178[6] *3544[3]* 3757[10] 3844[5] *4223[8]* **>48a 54f<**

Samah 5 ch h Pennine Walk-Ghanayim (USA) (Sharpen Up) 433[5] 749[12] 1183[15] 1808[12] (2321) (3457) 3565[9] 3703[8] 3715[8] 3813[7] (3943) 4041[18] **>83f<**

Samaka Hara (IRE) 3 b g Taufan (USA)-Aunt Hester (IRE) (Caerleon (USA)) 578[6] *767[6]* (875) 1028[5] 1207[4] *1569[2]* 2503[3] 2731[2] 3462[14] 3825[14] **>43a 64f<**

Samana Cay 3 ch f Pharly (FR)-Brown's Cay (Formidable) *33[4] 48[2] 95[4] 116[3] 185[3]* 2309[4] 2480[5] 2815[5] 2873[3] 2972[9] **>63a 46f<**

Samara (IRE) 2 ch f Polish Patriot (USA)-Smeralda (GER) (Dschingi's Khan) 3733[11] 3893[7] 4212[2] **>73f<**

Samara Song 2 ch c Savahra Sound-Hosting (Thatching) 2315[8] 3398[8] 3886[7] **>57f<**

Samba Sharply 4 b c Rambo Dancer (CAN)-Sharper Still 1183[13] 1617[2] 2031[2] 2468[5] 3545[3] 3837[13] (4171) 4267[23] **>86f<**

Sam Coles (USA) **2** br f Pirate Army (USA)-Ancora (GER) (Cortez (GER)) 650[8] (725) 852[7] **>53tf<**

Samim (USA) **2** b c Nureyev (USA)-Histoire (FR) (Riverman (USA)) 2107[6] 2749[3] 3307[3] (3809) 4001[4] **>86f<**

Samraan (USA) **2** br c Green Dancer (USA)-Sedra (Nebbiolo) 4117[4] **>66f<**

Samsolom **7** b g Absalom-Norfolk Serenade (Blakeney) 535[11] 765[12] 922[15] 1276[4] 1429[4] 1738[6] (1910) 2168[3] 2203[2] 2578[7] (2714) 2840[2] 3230[14] 3359[4] 4040[20] 4156[6] 4240[11] **>79a 76f<**

Samson-Agonistes **9** b h Bold Fort-Hello Cuddles (He Loves Me) *14[6] 70[3] 107[2] 154[7] 224[7] 391[3] 404[9]* **>64a 46df<**

Samsonesque **4** ch f Unfuwain (USA)-Fatal Distraction (Formidable) 539[4] 776[3] 991[6] 1367[9] **>70f<**

Samsung Lovelylady (IRE) **3** b f Petorius-Kentucky Wildcat (Be My Guest (USA)) 522[13] 758[12] 1040[6] 1419[7] 1739[4] *2071[9]* 2624[12] **>33a 55f<**

Samuel Scott **2** b g Shareef Dancer (USA)-Revisit (Busted) 2615[9] **>48f<**

Samwar **3** b c Warning-Samaza (USA) (Arctic Tern (USA)) 677[4] 937[4] 1168[6] **>77f<**

Sandabar **2** b c Green Desert (USA)-Children's Corner (FR) (Top Ville) 3174[7] **>42+f<**

Sandblaster **2** ch f Most Welcome-Honeychurch (USA) (Bering) 1356[8] 1646[8] 1842[12] 4109[7] 4231[4] **>50f<**

Sandicliffe (USA) **2** b f Imp Society (USA)-Sad Song (USA) (Roberto (USA)) 4050[12] **>46f<**

Sandmoor Chambray **4** ch c Most Welcome-Valadon (High Line) 433[7] (559) 927[12] 1415[2] 1617[4] 2117[6] 3607[16] 3807[8] **>77f<**

Sandmoor Denim **8** b g Red Sunset-Holernzaye *1[3] 55[6] 349[7]* (486) *601[5]* 749[8] *2922[2] 3075[7]* 3645[7] 3984[8] **>71a 72f<**

Sandmoor Velvet **3** b f Primo Dominie-Rectitude 1677[4] 2084[4] 2303[11] 2521[16] 3116[13] **>60df<**

Sandpiper **2** b f Green Desert (USA)-Sojourn (Be My Guest (USA)) 3888[12] **>9f<**

Sandpit (BRZ) **6** ch h Baynoun-Sand Dancer (FR) (Green Dancer (USA)) 3576a[2] **>122f<**

Sandra Dee (IRE) **3** ch f Be My Guest (USA)-Adventurine (Thatching) *60[2] 289[3] 332[5] 390[9] 401[6]* 739[9] 1050[W] 1521[5] 1785[5] 1906[7] *2093[8] 3544[13]* 4049[16] **>31a 35df<**

Sand Reef **4** b c Reference Point-Reine D'Egypte (USA) (Val de L'Orne (FR)) 1387a[2] **>112f<**

Sand Star **3** b f Lugana Beach-Overseas (Sea Hawk II) *64[9] 149[4] 225[2] (286) 360[6] 847[2] 1076[10] 1209[8]* **>61da f<**

Sandy Floss (IRE) **2** b c Green Desert (USA)-Mill on the Floss (Mill Reef (USA)) 2005[4] **>46f<**

Sandy Hollow **3** f 1705a[8]

Sangria (USA) **2** ch f El Gran Senor-Champagne Cocktail (Rober (2896a) 3330a[8] **>66f<**

Sanmartino (IRE) **3** b c Salse (USA)-Oscura (USA) (Caro) 663[4] 978[2] (1308) 2691[5] (3162) 4011a[4] **>110f<**

Sannkaya (IRE) **3** f 803a[5] **>98f<**

Sanoosea (USA) **3** b c Storm Bird (CAN)-Nobiliare (USA) (Vaguely Noble) 431[3] (613) 792[2] 1018[2] 4213[5] **>105df<**

San Pietra (IRE) **3** b f Caerleon (USA)-La Koumia (FR) (Kaldoun (FR)) 663[9] (1770) 2411[7] 2691[13] **>78f<**

Santa Fan (IRE) **3** b f Taufan (USA)-Les Saintes (Kris) 694[11] 885[4] 2152[3] 2411[5] 2532[4] **>82f<**

Santana Lady (IRE) **6** b m Blakeney-Santalina *137[6]* 2007[6] 2413[3] 2792[6] 3229[3] **>76da 70df<**

Santella Boy (USA) **3** b c Turkoman (USA)-Dream Creek (USA) (The Minstrel (CAN)) 762[18] 1093[11] 1730[2] 1937[2] 2439[3] 2603[3] 3056[2] 3521[3] 3862[13] 4136[5] **>68f<**

Santillana (USA) **2** ch c El Gran Senor (USA)-Galway (FR) (Irish River (FR)) 3900[3] (4291) **>82+f<**

Sapiston **2** b c Waajib-Camera Girl (Kalaglow) 3868[3] **>92+f<**

Sapphire Son (IRE) **3** ch g Maelstrom Lake-Gluhwein (Ballymoss) *518[12]* 1012[3] 1125[2] 1366[3] 1654[6] 2776[9] 2968[8] *3510[9]* 3638[16] **>16a 68f<**

Saracen Prince (USA) **3** ch c War (USA)-My Gallant Duchess (USA) (My Gallant (USA)) *(4271) 4340[13]* **>60a 54f<**

Sarah's Guest (IRE) **2** ch f Be My Guest (USA)-Lady Bennington (Hot Grove) 3865[20] **>63f<**

Sarasi **3** ch c Midyan (USA)-Early Call (Kind of Hush) *(24) 99[4] 324[5] 360[4]* 3447[11] **>77da 61f<**

Sarasonia **4** b f Dunbeath (USA)-La Graciosa (Comedy Star (USA)) 2404[10] 2843[7] 3057[6] 3681[9] **>39a 21f<**

Sarasota Storm **3** b c Petoski-Challanging (Mill Reef (USA)) (477) 717[8] 1281[4] 2103[12] 2613[6] 2778[7] 3531[12] **>66f<**

Sarawat **7** b h Slip Anchor-Eljazzi (Artaius (USA)) 558[11] 821[9] 1109[9] 1310[8] **>90f<**

Sarazar (USA) **6** ch g Shahrastani (USA)-Sarshara (Habitat) 1058[8] 1444[7] 1929[8] 2514[4] 2942[6] 3092[8] **>56f<**

Sari Marais **3** ch f Most Welcome-Willowbank (Gay Fandango (USA)) 1990[9] **>53f<**

Sariyaa **4** b f Persian Bold-Bedouin Veil (USA) (Shareef Dancer (USA)) 721[5] 2482[5] 2759[3] 2871[5] 3505[7] 3646[3] *3951[5]* **>64a 68f<**

Sarmatian (USA) **4** br c Northern Flagship (USA)-Tracy L (USA) (Bold Favorite (USA)) 493[2] 1179[3] 1299[9] 1687[2] 2397[3] (2999) **>74f<**

Sarrans **2** b c Noblequest-Levantene (In Fijar) 3583a[2] **>79f<**

Saseedo (USA) **5** ch h Afleet (CAN)-Barbara's Moment (USA) (Super Moment (USA)) 665[16] (922) 1143[7] 1316[6] 1895[12] 2369[12] 2746[6] 3706[11] 3815[5] 3924[4] 4033[6] 4119[11] (4238) **>93f<**

Sassetta (IRE) **2** ch f Soviet Lad (USA)-Sun Gift (Guillaume Tell (USA)) 2651[11] 2957[5] 3502[8] 3806[9] 3975[21] **>47f<**

Sassiver (USA) **5** b h Riverman (USA)-Sassabunda *45[4] 79[3] 108[8] 153[4] 514[8] 1086[10]* **>54a 42f<**

Sastrugi (IRE) **3** br c Bluebird (USA)-Royal Wolff (Prince Tenderfoot (USA)) 1625[6] 2574[5] *2959[6]* 3292[9] *3513[11]* **>44a 38f<**

Sasuru **2** b c Most Welcome-Sassalya 3180[2] 3449[2] 3709[3] **>89f<**

Satellite Star (IRE) **2** b f Red Sunset-Coffee Bean (Doulab (USA)) 650[5] (725) 940[3] 1137[2] 1293[3] (1492) 3375[14] 3711[15] 3901[8] **>69df<**

Saterne Lady **3** b f Deploy-Alghabrah (Lomond (USA)) 2296[4] 3747[7] 3844[16] **>57a 50f<**

Satin Secret (IRE) **2** ch f Thatching-Silky (USA) (Nijinsky (CAN)) 1525[6] 3339[13] **>74f<**

Saturiba (USA) **2** b c Fighting Fit (USA)-My Popsicle

(USA) (Raja Baba (USA)) 490^{7} 1935^{6} 3012^{7} 3468^{10} 4141^{6} **>48f<**

Saucy Maid (IRE) 4 ch f Sure Blade (USA)-Gay Milly (FR) 1128^{16} 2082^{4} 2314^{10} 3455^{2} 3685^{13} **>73f<**

Savage (IRE) 2 b f Polish Patriot-Special Meeting (Persian 3584a^{2} **>92f<**

Sava River (IRE) 2 ch c Lycius (USA)-Slava (USA) (Diesis) 2777^{3} (3093) 3315^{2} 3711^{2} 3842^{3} **>91f<**

Sav-Ed 6 b h Today and Tomorrow-Ole Flo (Frimley Park) *50^{9} 139^{8} 167^{11}* **>20f<**

Savinio (USA) 5 ch g The Minstrel (USA)-Fabulous Native (USA) (Le Fabuleux) 4305a^{5} **>117f<**

Sawa-Id 2 b br c Anshan-Bermuda Lily (Dunbeath (USA)) 4320^{11} **>57f<**

Saxon Heir (IRE) 3 b g Anita's Prince-Royal Accord (King of Spain) *226^{5} 283^{9} 342^{7}* 1516^{10} **>30da 47f<**

Saxon King (IRE) 5 ch g Ahonoora-My Therape *532^{4}* 646^{12} 1546^{3} 1756^{6} **>56a 46f<**

Saxon Magic 5 ch m Faustus (USA)-Wessex Kingdom (Vaigly Great) *335^{7}* 2174^{10} **>32a 42f<**

Saxon Maid 4 b f Sadler's Wells (USA)-Britannia's Rule 1243^{4} 1585^{3} (2104) (2456) 2702^{6} 3162^{17} 3549^{3} 3831^{2} 4030^{2} **>111f<**

Sayeh (IRE) 3 b c Fools Holme (USA)-Piffle (Shirley Heights) 720^{3} 1129^{5} 1807^{3} (3030) (3556) 3932^{7} **>103f<**

Sayitagain 3 b c Bering-Casey (Caerleon (USA)) 553^{6} 764^{16} **>67f<**

Sayyed Alraqs (USA) 3 b c Seattle Dancer (USA)-Glamorous Siren (USA) (Raise A Native) 816^{8} 1038^{4} 1162^{2} (1495) 1825^{6} 2525^{10} **>69f<**

Sayyedati 5 b m Shadeed (USA)-Dubian (High Line) 1389a^{2} 1835^{5} (2689) 3199a^{2} 3589a^{4} 4305a^{3} **>125f<**

Scale the Summit 3 b c Distant Relative-Top Heights (High Top) *1329^{3} 1569^{4} 1881^{10} 2378^{5}* **>50a 42f<**

Scalp 'em (IRE) 7 b g Commanche Run-Supremely Royal *75^{2} 131^{2} 161^{2} 227^{2} 280^{7} 833^{6}* 1039^{3} 1160^{4} *1332^{7} 1759^{2}* 1965^{2} 2355^{5} *2592^{3}* **>62a 52f<**

Scandinavian (FR) 4 b c Always Fair (USA)-Sarietta (GER) (Windwurf (GER)) 1002a^{6} **>115f<**

Scaraben 7 b g Dunbeath (USA)-Varushka (Sharpen Up) (493) 1491^{3} (1666) (1911) (2061) (3368) 3607^{2} (3703) 4116^{15} **>82+f<**

Scarlet Plume 2 b f Warning-Circus Plume (High Top) 1746^{2} 3364^{3} (3633) (4180a) **>96+f<**

Scathebury 2 b c Aragon-Lady Bequick 684^{2} 951^{4} *1212^{2} 1454^{2}* 2063^{7} *2381^{6} (2633)* 3271^{11} 4001^{2} 4151^{18} **>73a 67f<**

Scboo 6 b g Full Extent (USA)-Maygo (Maystreak) 2016^{10} 2661^{9} **>6f<**

Scenic Air 2 ch f Hadeer-Shark Song (Song) 2161^{10} 2447^{6} **>34f<**

Scenic Dancer 7 b h Shareef Dancer (USA)-Bridestones 1166^{3} 1513^{3} 1733^{4} 2138^{3} 2546^{9} 2745^{7} 3083^{4} 3303^{7} (3641) 4062^{4} 4332^{12} **>59f<**

Scenic Heights (IRE) 3 b c Scenic-Evangola (Persian Bold (USA)) 3013^{4} 3706^{15} **>87f<**

Scenicris (IRE) 2 b f Scenic-Princesse Smile (Balidar) 1278^{11} 2666^{3} 2964^{5} 3225^{2} 3427^{2} 3775^{5} 3988^{3} 4195^{3} 4290^{2} **>69f<**

Scent of Power 5 b g Fairy King (USA)-Agreloui (Tower Walk) *419^{10}* 479^{4} *766^{11}* 992^{U} (1290) 1523^{11} **>44a 38f<**

Scharnhorst 3 b g Tacheron-Stardyn (Star Appeal) 502^{11} *587^{9}* (882) (1366) 1676^{2} 1907^{3} 3175^{8} 3656^{7} 3929^{8} 4157^{23} *4297^{9}* **>55a 74f<**

School Boy 2 b c Aragon-Grovehurst (Homing) 3663^{15} 3873^{2} 4084^{25} **>72f<**

School Clock 2 b c Puissance-Village Idol 3662^{8} **>51f<**

School of Science 5 b h Then Again-Girl's Brigade (Brigadier Gerard) 4232^{12} **>38f<**

Scissor Ridge 3 ch g Indian Ridge-Golden Scissors (Kalaglow) *333^{6} 382^{4} 411^{4}* 482^{13} *560^{6}* 1255^{15} 1447^{7} 1906^{4} *2144^{3}* 3619^{16} 3751^{9} 4131^{6} 4194^{2} *4217^{7}* **>62a 53f<**

Scoffera 5 b m Scottish Reel-Single Bid (Auction Ring (USA)) *138^{10} 179^{5} 255^{6}* **>32a 55f<**

Scorched Air 5 b m Elegant Air-Misfire (Gunner B) *67^{9}* 1555^{8} 3759^{11} **>49a 68f<**

Scored Again 5 b h Music Boy-Thorner Lane (Tina's Pet) *69^{6} (154) (244) 327^{4} 398^{5} 602^{2}* **>62a 52f<**

Scorpius 5 b h Soviet Star (USA)-Sally Brown (Posse (USA)) 2945^{5} 3159^{12} 3641^{16} 3872^{14} **>66f<**

Scotoni 9 ch h Final Straw-Damiya (FR) (Direct Flight) 3384^{9} **>29f<**

Scotsky (IRE) 3 b c Astronef-Lady Heather (Manado) 3027^{5} 3419^{7} 3813^{25} **>96f<**

Scots Law 8 b h Law Society (USA)-Tweedling (USA) (Sir Ivor) *148^{9} 220^{14} 265^{11} 302^{11} 408^{10}* **>6a 1f<**

Scottish Bambi 7 ch g Scottish Reel-Bambolona (Bustino) 864^{12} 1095^{6} 1543^{5} 1801^{8} **>80f<**

Scottish Park 6 ch m Scottish Reel-Moss Agate (Alias Smith (USA)) *(73) 222^{10} 470^{6}* 550^{9} *605^{9}* 738^{10} *845^{6} 1091^{11}* 1244^{3} 1531^{6} 1745^{9} 2056^{7} 2310^{14} **>49a 50f<**

Screech 5 b m Daring March-Songless (Song) 800a^{3} 2038a^{2} 2384a^{2} 2720a^{2}

Scribano 5 b h Pharly (FR)-Biograph (USA) (Riverman (USA)) 1387a^{5} 1890a^{4} 4182a^{6} **>111f<**

Scud Missile (IRE) 4 b or gr c Persian Heights-Desert Bluebell (Kalaglow) 1401^{7} **>56f<**

Scylla 3 b f Rock City-Hearten (Hittite Glory) *133^{7}* 1218^{10} 1412^{9} 1944^{6} 2129^{10} **>28a 42f<**

Sea-Ayr (IRE) 5 ch m Magical Wonder (USA)-Kunuz (Ela-Mana-Mou) 559^{2} 749^{13} 1528^{7} 2088^{2} 2484^{9} **>30a 53f<**

Sea Dane 2 b c Danehill (USA)-Shimmering Sea (Slip Anchor) (1246) 1838^{6} (2131) 3560^{4} 3886^{9} **>98f<**

Sea Danzig 2 ch g Roi Danzig (USA)-Tosara (Main Reef) 4154^{9} 4255^{4} 4314^{6} **>68f<**

Sea-Deer 6 ch g Hadeer-Hi-Tech Girl (Homeboy) 1174^{7} 1316^{7} 1765^{5} 1895^{8} 2410^{4} 2746^{8} **>94f<**

Sea Devil 9 gr h Absalom-Miss Poinciana (Averof) *65^{2} 140^{2} 182^{2} 233^{2} (314) (366) 410^{2}* 548^{4} *625^{2} (1033)* **>78a 63f<**

Seaford Star (IRE) 2 ch c Waajib-Frensham Manor (Le Johnstan) 2077^{5} 2548^{2} 2932^{4} 3025^{6} 3553^{7} 3894^{9} **>66f<**

Sea Freedom 4 b c Slip Anchor-Rostova (Blakeney) 764^{9} 1140^{8} 1410^{9} 1623^{2} 2284^{6} 3178^{3} 3470^{2} 3616^{4} 3817^{7} 4026^{4} 4118^{8} 4248^{5} **>78f<**

Sea God 4 ch c Rainbow Quest (USA)-Sea Pageant 4152^{19} *4335^{11}* **>21a 60f<**

Sea Gone (USA) 3 b c 801a^{6} 1117a^{8} **>65f<**

Sealed With a Kiss 5 ch m High Line-The Crying Game (Manor Farm Boy) 879^{18} **>55f<**

Sea of Blue **2** b f Superlative-Persian Joy (Persian Bold) 1678^{7} 1841^{10} *2382^{12}* **>36f<**

Seaside Minstrel **7** ch h Song-Blackpool Belle (The Brianstan) 1057^{11} 1199^{4} 1304^{14} **>40a 53f<**

Seasonal Splendour (IRE) **5** b m Prince Rupert (FR)-Snoozy Time (Cavo Doro) (2012) 2274^{4} 3091^{6} 3406^{7} 3930^{0} 4158^{10} **>98f<**

Sea Spouse **4** ch c Jalmood (USA)-Bambolona (Bustino) *378^{10} (516) 771^{9} 1029^{14}* 1368^{7} 1663^{2} 1830^{10} 3664^{13} 4054^{7} 4170^{13} **>67a 52f<**

Sea Spray (IRE) **2** b f Royal Academy (USA)-Sailor's Mate (Shirley Heights) (3474) 4013a^{10} **>79f<**

Sea Thunder **3** gr f Salse (USA)-Money Moon (Auction Ring (USA)) 1240^{2} 1544^{2} 2576^{3} (2708) 3359^{5} 3615^{19} 3929^{3} 4068^{18} **>85f<**

Seattle Alley (USA) **2** b c Seattle Dancer (USA)-Alyanaabi (USA) (Roberto (USA)) 3666^{9} 3877^{6} 4064^{7} 4211^{7} **>64+f<**

Seattle John (USA) **3** c Seattle John (USA)-Jane Austen (Arts and Let 1010a^{2} 1396a^{8} **>103f<**

Seattle Special (USA) **2** b f Nureyev-O'Slewmova 4250a^{3} **>88f<**

Sea Victor **3** b c Slip Anchor-Victoriana (USA) (Storm Bird (CAN)) (428) 756^{4} 1589^{7} 2266^{7} 2555^{7} 2621^{6} 3635^{3} 3741^{3} 4062^{3} (4099) 4140^{2} (4166) 4326^{3} **>90f<**

Sebastian **3** b c Sadler's Wells (USA)-Sandy Island (Mill Reef (USA)) (657) 917^{2} (1127) (4069) **>122+f<**

Seckar Vale (USA) **3** ch c Elmaamul (USA)-Both Sides Now (USA) (Topsider (USA)) 679^{7} 927^{10} 3232^{W} 3552^{4} 3729^{7} (3864) 4076^{2} **>100+f<**

Second Cello **3** ch f Music Boy-Tufty Lady (Riboboy (USA)) 783^{3} 1165^{6} 1660^{6} (2032) 2206^{2} 3637^{11} 3972^{5} **>70f<**

Second Chance (IRE) **5** ch h Digamist (USA)-Flash Donna (USA) (Well Decorated (USA)) *66^{6} 383^{2}* 439^{20} 1070^{6} 1638^{4} (2056) 2343^{4} 2766^{6} 3382^{5} 3556^{8} 3601^{3} 3837^{2} 4202^{4} **>80a 93f<**

Second Colours (USA) **5** b or br h Timeless Moment (USA)-Ruffled Silk (USA) (Our Hero (USA)) *366^{3} (413)* 559^{7} *601^{2} 767^{8}* 1469^{5} (1644) 1687^{5} 1966^{5} (2019) (2227) 2479^{2} 2707^{5} (2994) *(3241)* (3443) 3704^{6} **>77a 78f<**

Seconds Away **4** b g Hard Fought-Keep Mum (Mummy's Pet) 594^{17} 1995^{7} 2156^{4} 2479^{9} 2872^{4} 3172^{8} 3855^{3} **>19a 35f<**

Second Time Lucky (IRE) **2** b c Digamist (USA)-Sallymiss (Tanfirion) 2552^{4} 2791^{2} 3628^{6} (3982) 4208^{2} **>78f<**

Secret Aly (CAN) **5** b h Secreto (USA)-Bouffant (USA) (Alydar (USA)) *89^{9} 145^{3} (249) 318^{2}* 634^{4} 1357^{9} (1792) 1926^{12} 2321^{7} (2669) 3222^{14} 3601^{13} 3945^{14} 4038^{7} (4227) **>86a 89f<**

Secret Assignment (USA) **5** ch g Naevus (USA)-Swedish Ivy (USA) (Northjet (USA)) *187^{9} 248^{7} 331^{7} 497^{6}* 741^{14} 1058^{13} 1657^{4} 1965^{9} 4331^{11} **>38a 33f<**

Secret Ballad (IRE) **3** b c Classic Secret (USA)-Bally (Balidar) 2317^{4} 2657^{11} **>70f<**

Secret Commander **2** ch c Ron's Victory (USA)-Louise 849^{10}

Secret Energy (USA) **3** ch f Alwuhush (USA)-Energy Square (Air Forbes 2042a^{3} **>99f<**

Secret Miss **3** ch f Beveled (USA)-Zamindara (Crofter (USA)) 502^{10} 522^{8} 862^{5} 1094^{8} 1546^{2} 1660^{12} 2239^{6} 2502^{11} 2624^{6} 2858^{8} 3467^{7} (3678) 3919^{16} *4274^{5}* **>44a 62+f<**

Secret Optimist (IRE) **2** c 3906a^{2}

Secret Pleasure (IRE) **2** ch f Classic Secret (USA)-Abbessingh (Mansingh (USA)) 1253^{5} 1481^{4} 3673^{3} 3887^{7} 4077^{16} **>72f<**

Secret Quest **3** b f Rainbow Quest-Secret Dancer (Fabulous D (899a) 1238a^{3} 3040a^{3} **>102f<**

Secret Serenade **4** b g Classic Secret (USA)-Norfolk Serenade (Blakeney) *67^{4} (108)* 506^{5} 2429^{7} **>79a 81f<**

Secret Service (IRE) **3** b c Classic Secret (USA)-Mystery Bid (Auction Ring (USA)) 3621^{7} 3704^{15} (3970) 4325^{3} **>83f<**

Secret Spring (FR) **3** b c Dowsing (USA)-Nordica (Northfields (USA)) *443^{2}* 585^{3} 1353^{2} 3618^{3} 3712^{5} 4162^{8} **>71a 81f<**

Secret Voucher **2** b c Vouchsafe-Welsh Secret (Welsh Captain) 977^{6} 2817^{3} 3290^{5} (3430) 3824^{3} **>65f<**

Sedbergh (USA) **2** b c Northern Flagship (USA)-Crumbaugh Pike (USA) (Within Hail (USA)) 2192^{11} *2625^{2}* 3463^{6} 3882^{3} **>59a 63f<**

Sedvicta **3** b g Primitive Rising (USA)-Annes Gift (Ballymoss) 537^{7} 905^{2} 1379^{7} **>62f<**

Seeking Destiny (IRE) **2** b c Two Timing (USA)-Heads We Called (IRE) (Bluebird (USA)) 1278^{12} 1781^{8} 3940^{10} 4154^{10} **>37f<**

Seeking Fortune (USA) **2** b f Seeking the Gold (USA)-Gabfest (USA) (Tom Rolfe) 3900^{6} **>71+f<**

Seenthelight **3** ch f Rich Charlie-Ackabarrow *33^{7}* 594^{15} 875^{7} 1279^{10} 2162^{4} 2425^{9} 2818^{8} **>65f<**

See You Again **3** b c Then Again-Down the Valley (Kampala) *38^{6}* 1983^{5} 2831^{6} 2984^{5} 3249^{2} 3638^{9} 4060^{20} **>49a 63f<**

Segala (IRE) **4** b c Petorius-Cerosia (Pitskelly) *2634^{3}* 3601^{8} 3840^{4} **>80a 83f<**

Segovia **3** b f Groom Dancer (USA)-Sedova (USA) (Nijinsky (CAN)) (1417) 1867^{5} 3190^{2} **>99f<**

Seigneurial **3** b c Primo Dominie-Spinner (Blue Cashmere) 1489^{10} 4033^{15} 4197^{8} 4281^{2} 4322^{18} **>87f<**

Seirenes **2** b f Formidable (USA)-Seriema (Petingo) 3816^{4} **>79f<**

Seize the Day (IRE) **7** b h Lomond (USA)-Cheerful Heart (Petingo) 649^{2} 741^{12} (954) 1310^{6} **>69f<**

Sejaal (IRE) **3** b c Persian Heights-Cremets (Mummy's Pet) 1136^{7} 1874^{3} 2319^{3} (3201) 3674^{7} **>75f<**

Select Few **2** b c Alzao (USA)-Elect (USA) (Vaguely Noble) 3340^{11} 3620^{5} (3916) **>89f<**

Selenia (IRE) **2** b f Danehill-Mimicry (Thatch) 1889a^{3} 2725a^{2} **>61f<**

Self Expression **7** b h Homing-Subtlety (Grundy) *378^{2}* 526^{13} 642^{8} 785^{6} *1088^{4}* 1323^{19} 1523^{2} 1531^{3} 1649^{9} 2254^{2} 2664^{6} **>59a 62f<**

Self Reliance **3** b f Never so Bold-Tahilla (Moorestyle) 547^{5} *768^{3}* 1196^{3} 1428^{4} (1812) 2003^{4} 2737^{8} *3075^{4}* **>62a 77f<**

Self Styled (IRE) **3** b g Taufan (USA)-Swinging Gold (Swing Easy (USA)) 1846^{6} 2357^{5} 3103^{5} 3357^{13} **>53f<**

Selhurstpark Flyer (IRE) **4** b g Northiam (USA)-Wisdom to Know (Bay Express) 611^{12} 922^{9} 1179^{4} 1870^{11} 2099^{7} 3212^{9} 3715^{7} 4068^{19} 4322^{10} **>78f<**

Selmeston (IRE) **3** b g Double Schwartz-Baracuda (FR)

(Zeddaan) 715[22] **>46f<**

Semi Serious 3 b c Midyan (USA)-Modica *174[4] 264[7] 591[13]* 3980[27] 4275[20] **>55a f<**

Semper (IRE) 2 b c Soviet Lad-Classic Dilemma (Sandhurs (1889a) 2454[3] 2775[4] **>76f<**

Senaan 3 b c Faustus (USA)-Frighten The Life (Kings Lake (USA)) 853[13] 1072[10] 1512[18] 1859[7] 2178[7] **>51f<**

Senebrova 4 b f Warning-Stemegna (Dance In Turn) 2566a[3] 4019a[3] 4093a[5] **>108f<**

Senneville (USA) 3 c 2560a[6] **>102f<**

Senorita Dinero (USA) 3 ch f Ferdinand (USA)-Martha's Fastmoney (USA) (Fast (USA)) (1128) 1505[3] (1988) (2269) 2903[2] 3021[4] **>95f<**

Sense of Priority 6 ch g Primo Dominie-Sense of Pride (Welsh Pageant) *2[11] 140[3] 233[4] 348[3]* 1080[13] 1248[6] 1809[15] 1993[4] (2162) *(2493)* 2758[5] 2832[5] 2913[5] *3074[9]* **>67a 63f<**

Senso (IRE) 4 b c Persian Heights-Flosshilde 2426[4] **>68?f<**

Sepoy (IRE) 2 ch c Common Grounds-Song of The Glens (Horage) 1620[7] 2619[2] 3699[5] (3838) **>84f<**

Seraphic 4 b f Slip Anchor-Cephira (FR) (Abdos) *103[9] 304[11]* 1377[15] 1854[13] 2157[6] **>29a 72f<**

Serendipity (FR) 2 b c Mtoto-Bint Damascus (USA) (Damascus (USA)) 2741[5] 4320[5] **>77f<**

Seren Quest 5 b m Rainbow Quest (USA)-Serenesse (Habat) 860[2] 1140[6] **>87f<**

Sergeyev (IRE) 3 ch c Mulhollande (USA)-Escape Path (Wolver Hollow) (543) (633) (1138) (1848) 2368[8] 2646[7] **>113+f<**

Sergio (IRE) 3 ch c Doubletour (USA)-Shygate (Shy Groom (USA)) *51[10] 90[11] 168[5] 213[8]* 837[7] **>35a 42f<**

Serif (USA) 2 b c Diesis-Ribbon (USA) (His Majesty (USA)) 1597[10] *2380[3] 2958[3]* 3749[19] **>57a 59f<**

Serious 5 b h Shadeed (USA)-Azallya (FR) (Habitat) 870[18] 1225[6] 1409[7] 1851[22] 3820[2] 4031[11] 4267[2] **>91f<**

Serious Fact 3 b c Aragon-Plain Tree (Wolver Hollow) 4278[8] **>25a 39f<**

Serious Hurry 7 ch h Forzando-Lady Bequick 475[11] 1023[8] 1157[3] 1304[12] 1461[7] 1689[10] 2160[2] 2303[9] 2475[9] 2736[7] (2997) 3150[4] (3252) 3313[2] 3855[14] 4113[19] **>54a 55f<**

Serious Option (IRE) 4 b c Reprimand-Top Bloom (Thatch (USA)) 486[10] 922[21] 1126[10] 1381[4] 2602[7] 2661[4] 3083[3] **>89df<**

Serious Trust 2 b c Alzao (USA)-Mill Line (Mill Reef (USA)) 2667[5] 2995[9] 3208[5] 3613[8] 4111[16] **>60f<**

Set Table (USA) 6 gr h Caro-Room For The Sauce (USA) (Sauce Boat (USA)) 433[2] 563[6] 984[3] **>76f<**

Set the Fashion 6 br h Green Desert (USA)-Prelude (Troy) 873[19] 1183[20] 3837[16] 4122[8] *(4217) (4297)* **>80a 67f<**

Seven Crowns (USA) 2 b c Chief's Crown (USA)-Ivory Dance (USA) (Sir Ivor) 1246[6] 2529[4] 3266[5] 3437[6] **>65f<**

Seven Kisses (IRE) 2 b f Kefaah (USA)-Avidal Park (Horage) 429[8]

Seventeens Lucky 3 gr c Touch of Grey-Westminster Waltz (Dance In Time (CAN)) 1094[14] 1504[2] 1812[2] 2103[11] 2500[3] 2831[2] 3109[4] 3286[6] 3973[3] (4038) 4163[16] **>77f<**

Severn Gale 5 br m Strong Gale-Miss Apex (Wolverlife) *103[4] 245[8] 322[6]* **>48a f<**

Seyouf (USA) 3 ch c Woodman (USA)-Lady in Silver (USA) (Silver Hawk (USA)) 1547[7] **>54f<**

Shaamit (IRE) 2 b c Mtoto-Shomoose (Habitat) 3868[4] (4320) **>88+f<**

Shaanxi (USA) 3 ch f Zilzal (USA)-Rich and Riotous (Empery) 807a[2] 1116a[3] 1712a[6] 2897a[2] 3199a[3] 3589a[2] (4016a) 4305a[11] **>120f<**

Shaarid (USA) 7 b h El Gran Senor (USA)-Summer Silence (USA) (Stop The Music (USA)) 586[4] 1048[3] **>72f<**

Shabanaz 10 b h Imperial Fling (USA)-Claironcita 744[4] 935[13] 1149[2] (1403) (1519) 1659[2] *1880[2]* 1926[9] 2359[4] (2976) 3108[3] (3426) (4232) *4293[6]* **>67a 72f<**

Shades of Jade 7 gr m General Wade-Gellifawr 856[17] 1071[13] 1265[11] 1321[7] 1538[8] 1595[10] **>28a 28f<**

Shadirwan (IRE) 4 b c Kahyasi-Shademah (Thatch (USA)) 696[2] (1156) 1840[4] 2098[12] 3616[8] 3817[13] 4118[15] **>91df<**

Shadow Jury 5 ch h Doulab (USA)-Texita (Young Generation) *78[4] 165[3] 184[3] (268) 407[5] 419[9]* 701[6] 1152[3] (1376) (1689) 2060[3] 2120[2] (2234) (2475) *(2627)* 2652[5] 2714[2] 2753[2] 2935[12] 3150[6] *3242[6]* 3376[9] 3597[7] 3748[13] 3878[18] 4278[6] 4322[6] **>75a 72f<**

Shadow Leader 4 br c Tragic Role (USA)-Hush it Up (Tina's Pet) 423[2] 623[2] 763[5] 938[4] 1140[7] 1853[3] 2274[3] 3162[6] 3489[3] 3730[13] **>89f<**

Shady Deed (USA) 3 ch f Shadeed (USA)-Sum Sharp Lady (USA) (Sharpen Up) 697[11] 1591[5] 1988[D] 2279[5] 2638[2] (2984) 3128[3] 3429[6] 3860[3] **>72f<**

Shady Girl (IRE) 2 b f Shaadi (USA)-Octavia Girl (Octavo (USA)) 3625[8] 3816[7] 4085[5] **>67f<**

Shady Link (IRE) 2 b c Mujtahid (USA)-Lady In Green (Shareef Dancer (USA)) 3663[9] **>64f<**

Shaffic (FR) 8 b h Auction Ring (USA)-Tavella (FR) *3[3]* **>47a f<**

Shaffishayes 3 ch g Clantime-Mischievous Miss (Niniski (USA)) (577) 675[3] 984[12] 3807[7] **>68f<**

Shafir (IRE) 2 b f Shaadi (USA)-Cheese Soup (USA) (Spectacular Bid (USA)) 964[3] 1158[4] (1448) 3699[9] 4112[5] **>67f<**

Shaft of Light 3 gr g Sharrood (USA)-Reflection (Mill Reef (USA)) *38[2] 128[2] (213) (384)* (2197) 2445[2] 2701[2] 3142[3] **>75a 92f<**

Shaha 2 b c Polish Precedent (USA)-Height of Passion (Shirley Heights) 1485[6] 3398[6] **>56f<**

Shahid 3 b c Green Desert (USA)-Roussalka (Habitat) (640) (775) (1069) (1222) 1848[2] (2646) 3360[5] 3562[5] 3931[7] 4078[5] **>113f<**

Shahrani 3 b c Lear Fan (USA)-Windmill Princess (Gorytus (USA)) 1446[5] 4061[15] 4228[9] **>67f<**

Shake the Yoke 2 b f Caerleon-Bermuda Classic (3786a) 4013a[2] **>108f<**

Shakiri 6 b m Sizzling Melody-Aspark (Sparkler) 1023[14]

Shakiyr (FR) 4 gr c Lashkari-Shakamiyn (Nishapour (FR)) *(4) 121[6] (193) (530) 833[4]* 1022[2] 1505[7] 3801[7] 4036[7] 4201[14] **>72a 66f<**

Shamaka 4 b f Kris-Sharka (Shareef Dancer (USA)) *96[10] 138[13]* **>31a 63df<**

Shamand (USA) 2 br c Minshaanshu Amad (USA)-Rose And Betty (USA) (Dare To Command) 2005[7] 2529[7] 3089[21] 3760[16] **>45f<**

Shamanic 3 b c Fairy King (USA)-Annie Albright (USA) (Verbatim (USA)) (883) 1480[8] 1870[9] 2409[9] 3027[6] 3166[10] 3557[2] 4040[6] 4324[7] **>102f<**

Shamardar (IRE) **3** c 2386a[5] >**91f**<

Shambo **8** b h Lafontaine (USA)-Lucky Appeal (Star Appeal) 712[3] 1020[2] 1132[3] >**122f**<

Shamekh **3** b c In The Wings-Troyanos (Troy) 673[9] 1289[8] 1527[8] 1696[8] 1978[R] >**62f**<

Shamokin **3** b c Green Desert (USA)-Shajan (Kris) 3974[18] >**10f**<

Shamrock Dancer (IRE) **5** b m Dance of Life (USA)-Practical (Ballymore) 1518[10]

Shamrock Fair (IRE) **3** ch f Shavian-Fair Country (Town And Country) 1544[4] 1907[5] >**70f**<

Shamshadal (IRE) **5** b g Darshaan-Shabarana (FR) (Nishapour (FR)) 866[9] 2154[8] >**64df**<

Shamwari (USA) **4** ch f Shahrastani (USA)-Exotic Treat (USA) (Vaguely Noble) *45[9] 96[2] 136[4] 352[2]* >**58da 71df**<

Shandine (USA) **3** b c Riverman (USA)-Proflare (USA) (Mr Prospector (USA)) 1306[7] 1728[10] >**90f**<

Shanghai Lil **3** b f Petong-Toccata (USA) *(830)* 1456[9] 1692[12] 2054[7] 2246[15] 2789[11] >**48a 35f**<

Shanghai Venture (USA) **4** br c Unfuwain (USA)-Intrepid Lady (USA) (Bold Ruler) 793[6] 1061[11] 1225[8] 1543[3] 2051[5] *2634[4] 3075[3] (3511)* 3679[14] >**80+a 81df**<

Shaniko (IRE) **2** b c Shaadi (USA)-Homely Touch (Touching Wood (USA)) 1893[6] (2408) 2740[5] 3606[4] 4084[13] >**95f**<

Shannjar **3** dk c Doyoun-Shanjarina (Blushing Groo 2889a[3] >**117f**<

Shanoora (IRE) **2** gr f Don't Forget Me-Shalara (Dancers Image (USA)) 455[5] *(770) 1077[5]* 1336[3] 3533[11] 3642[11] 3780[10] *4127[6] 4339[6]* >**56ta 57f**<

Shansi (IRE) **4** b g Shaadi (USA)-Chic Belle (USA) (Mr Prospector (USA)) *(158) 205[3] 330[5] 445[10] 501[9] 605[7] 2292[4]* 3207[9] >**50a 30f**<

Shanuke (IRE) **3** b f Contract Law (USA)-Auntie Ponny (Last Fandango) 544[4] *626[9]* 885[9] 1407[4] 1657[7] >**7a 42f**<

Sharaar (USA) **5** ch h Bering-Trasimeno (Kings Lake (USA)) 550[15] 738[20] >**22a 76df**<

Sharaf (IRE) **2** b c Sadler's Wells (USA)-Marie de Flandre (FR) (Crystal Palace (FR)) 3592[7] 3827[5] 4146[2] >**84f**<

Sharazi (USA) **4** ch c Shahrastani (USA)-Rio Rita (USA) (Secretariat (USA)) 584[8] 929[5] 1623[5] 2612[6] 3294[6] 3571[7] 3876[4] >**75f**<

Shareda (IRE) **2** ch f Anshan-Mawaal Habeebee (Northfields (USA)) 4050[16] 4155[10] >**31f**<

Shared (IRE) **3** b br c Doyoun-Fenjaan (Trojan Fen) 431[10] *513[7]* 3178[8] 3618[8] 3860[5] 4225[12] >**53f**<

Shared Risk **3** ch c Risk Me (FR)-Late Idea (Tumble Wind (USA)) *419[7] 587[2]* 839[19] *1569[9] 1881[4] 2378[2] 2921[2] 3527[12]* 3759[21] *3951[9]* >**66da 40f**<

Shareoftheaction **4** gr c Sharrood (USA)-Action Belle (Auction Ring (USA)) 1420[2] *1567[P]* 1858[12] *2292[10] 3952[8] 4340[14]* >**32a 62f**<

Share the Secret **3** b c Dowsing (USA)-Baino Fit (USA) (Fit To Fight (USA)) 544[5] 884[14] 1204[7] 1645[15] 1824[11] 1962[14] >**47f**<

Sharkashka (IRE) **5** ch m Shardari-Kashka (USA) (The Minstrel (CAN)) 1416[6] 1558[10] 1863[10] 2482[8] >**72f**<

Sharmoor **3** b f Shardari-Linpac North Moor (Moorestyle) 1379[15] 1647[11] >**24f**<

Sharp At Six (IRE) **5** ch g Sure Blade (USA)-Sixpenny (English Prince) 3665[11]

Sharp Conquest **4** ch c Sharpo-Likeness (Young Generation) *(103) 195[10] 313[12]* 433[17] 567[3] 701[15] >**69a 78df**<

Sharp Consul (IRE) **3** br c Exactly Sharp (USA)-Alicia Markova 1486[11] 1796[6] 1979[3] 3534[13] 3706[18] (3897) 4227[7] >**78f**<

Sharpening **4** ch f Sharpo-False Lift (Grundy) *80[6] 265[9]* >**43da 53f**<

Sharpest Image (IRE) **3** b c Exactly Sharp (USA)-Tycoon's Drama (IRE) 163a[3] (207a) 291a[2] 2889a[2] 3038a[2] 3323a[5] >**117f**<

Sharp Falcon (IRE) **4** gr f Shaadi (USA)-Honey Buzzard (Sea Hawk II) 550[5] 668[3] 935[6] 1260[2] (1655) 2069[4] 3836[12] 4028[3] >**81f**<

Sharp Gazelle **5** ch m Beveled (USA)-Shadha (Shirley Heights) *117[5] 226[3] 302[12] 416[12]* 1427[7] 1771[3] 2052[9] 2334[5] 2842[11] >**50a 54f**<

Sharp Holly (IRE) **3** b f Exactly Sharp (USA)-Children's Hour (Mummy's Pet) *322[4] 392[2] 527[3]* 551[4] *830[5] 891[6]* 1641[3] 1982[4] 2239[8] 2527[5] 3751[14] 4060[19] >**52a 55f**<

Sharpical **3** b g Sharpo-Magical Spirit (Top Ville) 585[11] 777[3] 963[4] 2103[13] (3218) 3363[2] 3497[2] 3605[3] >**80f**<

Sharp Imp **5** b h Sharpo-Implore (Ile de Bourbon (USA)) *55[2] 142[3]* 1255[13] 1676[12] 2342[6] (2641) 2685[5] *2943[3]* 3057[4] (3139) 3268[2] 3439[5] >**52a 56f**<

Sharp Matt **4** ch c Sharpo-Matoa (Tom Rolfe) (3044a) >**110f**<

Sharp Monty **2** b c Mon Tresor-Sharp Anne (Belfort (FR)) 533[13] 615[3] 718[5] 1540[4] 1992[3] 2161[2] 3260[9] >**69f**<

Sharp Night **2** ch c Sharpo-Midnight Owl (FR) (Ardross) 617[20] 859[6] 3650[9] 3767[10] >**49f**<

Sharp 'n' Shady **2** b f Sharpo-Shadiliya (Red Alert) 4212[15] 4314[9] >**60f**<

Sharp 'n Smart **3** ch c Weldnaas (USA)-Scottish Lady (Dunbeath (USA)) 449[2] *527[2]* 739[7] (2049) 2491[11] 2840[4] (3674) 3768[7] 4035[20] >**57a 82f**<

Sharp N' Smooth **8** ch h Sharpo-Winning Look (Relko) *44[9]* 476[6] 578[2] 642[9] 965[7] 1206[5] 1438[3] 1688[P] >**26a 56f**<

Sharp Pearl **2** ch c Sharpo-Silent Pearl (USA) (Silent Screen (USA)) 3371[8] 3606[5] 3893[4] 4206[11] >**69f**<

Sharp Point (IRE) **3** ch f Royal Academy (USA)-Nice Point (Sharpen Up) 707a[3] (2888a) 3187[4] >**111f**<

Sharp Prod (USA) **5** ch h Sharpo-Gentle Persuasion (Bustino) 441[2] 1119a[11] 3707[3] 3834[12] 4095a[2] 4345a[6] >**112f**<

Sharp Prospect **5** ch h Sharpo-Sabatina (USA) (Verbatim (USA)) (433) 714[8] >**86f**<

Sharp Rebuff **4** b c Reprimand-Kukri (Kris) 486[3] 579[2] 876[2] 1148[2] (1542) 2414[5] 3706[3] 4035[12] >**79f**<

Sharp Review (IRE) **7** b h Sharpen Up-Pleasant Review (USA) (The Minstrel (CAN)) 4267[30] >**95f**<

Sharp Sensation **5** ch g Crofthall-Pink Sensation (Sagaro) *83[8] 153[6] 227[5] 312[9]* 1957[3] 2734[4] >**47a 47f**<

Sharp Shuffle (IRE) **2** ch c Exactly Sharp (USA)-Style (Homing) 725[5] 3379[18] 4075[2] 4172[5] 4263[2] >**73f**<

Sharp Spring **4** ch c Beveled (USA)-Sea Farer Lake (Gairloch) 1771[6] 2528[18] 2843[4] 2984[8] >**60a 45f**<

Sharp Stock **2** b c Tina's Pet-Mrewa (Runnymede) 4132[2] 4219[4] >**67f**<

Sharp Thrill **4** ch c Squill (USA)-Brightelmstone (Prince

Regent (FR)) *46^{2} 120^{9} 245^{6}* 4332^{5} **>51a 47f<**

Shartel **3** b c Sharpo-Hinari Televideo (Caerleon (USA)) *43^{9} 146^{5} 842^{8}* 1559^{8} 1583^{9} **>34a f<**

Shashi (IRE) **3** br f Shaadi (USA)-Homely Touch (Touching Wood (USA)) 1181^{2} 1277^{2} 1550^{5} 2092^{3} 2252^{3} 2609^{3} 2867^{7} 3905^{10} **>80df<**

Shawahin **3** b c Nashwan (USA)-Bempton 657^{12} (2331) 2937^{9} 3445^{13} **>84f<**

Shawanni **2** gr f Shareef Dancer (USA)-Negligent (Ahonoora) (3663) 3835^{5} **>95f<**

Shaw House **2** ch f Shavian-Spinelle (Great Nephew) *2939^{3}* 3157^{5} **>52a 48f<**

Shayim (USA) **3** b or br c Storm Cat (USA)-Bundler (USA) (Raise A Native) (1216) 1698^{5} 2253^{2} 3433^{8} 3802^{12} **>84f<**

Shaynes Domain **4** b c Dominion-Glen Na Smole (Ballymore) *627^{11}* 762^{13} 882^{4} 1202^{8} 1255^{2} 1676^{17} 1991^{11} 4209^{11} **>46a 53f<**

Shazanni (IRE) **3** gr f Durgam (USA)-Donna Katrina (Kings Lake (USA)) *591^{5}* 924^{7} 1040^{10} 1358^{14} 2540^{13} 3201^{3} 3270^{2} 3428^{4} **>47a 52f<**

Sheama (USA) **3** ch f Miswaki (USA)-Perl (USA) (Graustark (USA)) 779^{4} (1154) 1561^{5} 2115^{4} 2376^{5} 2778^{8} 3770^{8} **>69f<**

Sheath Kefaah **2** ch c Kefaah (USA)-Wasslaweyeh (USA) (Damascus (USA)) 3530^{8} 4075^{11} **>63f<**

Shedansar (IRE) **3** b g In The Wings-Evening Kiss (Kris) 853^{19} **>19f<**

Sheemore (IRE) **2** b c Don't Forget Me-Curie Abu (Crofter (USA)) 2192^{9} 3416^{9} 3779^{9} **>39f<**

Sheer Danzig (IRE) **3** b c Roi Danzig (USA)-Sheer Audacity (Troy) *(418)* 678^{3} 1130^{10} 1839^{11} 2240^{13} (2613) 3447^{2} 3703^{5} (3993) 4163^{18} **>73a 93f<**

Shefoog **3** ch f Kefaah (USA)-Masarrah (Formidable) 620^{5} 868^{8} 1145^{6} 1754^{3} 3062^{2} 3706^{5} 3922^{7} (4214) **>95f<**

Sheilana (IRE) **2** b f Bluebird (USA)-Shadia (USA) (Naskra (USA)) 2315^{10} 3093^{3} 3404^{5} 3623^{2} 3947^{11} **>68f<**

Sheilas Dream **2** b f Inca Chief (USA)-Windlass (Persian Bold) 4216^{11} **>39f<**

Sheila's Secret (IRE) **5** b m Bluebird (USA)-Exemplary 1100^{13} **>98f<**

Shelter **8** b h Teenoso (USA)-Safe House (Lyphard (USA)) 1974^{9} 2052^{6} **>27f<**

Sheltered Cove (IRE) **4** ch c Bold Arrangement-Racing Home (FR) (Dom Racine (FR)) *178^{5} (277) 346^{2} 370^{9}* 632^{14} 795^{15} 1058^{7} **>62a 57f<**

Shemaq (USA) **3** b f Blushing John (USA)-Geraldine's Store (USA) (Exclusive Native (USA)) 2417^{2} (3013) 3413^{5} 3904^{10} (4065) **>100f<**

Shemaran (IRE) **3** b c Kahyasi-Sherzana (Great Nephew) 1113a^{2} (1708a) 2217a^{7} (3326a) **>121f<**

Shemozzle (IRE) **2** b f Shirley Heights-Reactress (USA) (Sharpen Up) (4102) (4277) **>73f<**

Shen Yang (USA) **3** ch c Fighting Fit (USA)-Our Mimi (USA) (Believe It (USA)) *468^{2}* 697^{10} (1405) 1639^{10} 1941^{4} 2362^{5} 2802^{4} 2941^{4} **>75a 81f<**

Shepherd Market (IRE) **4** b c Common Grounds-Dame Solitaire (CAN) (Halo (USA)) *11^{7} 125^{7} 205^{9}* 450^{3} 563^{2} 728^{2} 873^{11} 1261^{2} (1409) 1560^{3} 1638^{3} 2369^{17} 2685^{11} 3439^{15} 3619^{15} 3771^{9} 3874^{6} 4053^{3} 4215^{14} **>59a 66f<**

Shepherds Dean (IRE) **2** b f Tirol-Royal Episode (Royal Match) 819^{13} **>12f<**

Shepherds Rest (IRE) **3** b g Accordion-Mandy's Last (Krayyan) 816^{12} 1097^{18} 1198^{9} 1658^{4} 2007^{13} 2359^{5} *2636^{5}* **>26a 53f<**

Sheppard's Cross **4** b f Soviet Star (USA)-Cutlers Corner (Sharpen Up) 433^{6} (563) 714^{12} 1143^{5} 1895^{22} 3924^{7} **>89f<**

Sheraka (IRE) **2** b f Doyoun-Sherzana 4174a^{2} **>98f<**

Sheraz (IRE) **3** b c Persian Bold-Miss Siddons (Cure The Blues (USA)) 2794^{9} 3183^{2} 3537^{3} **>84?f<**

Sherblu **4** ch c Cigar-Glyn Blue (Fine Blue) *220^{5} 347^{4} 373^{5} 402^{2} 447^{5} 627^{7}* 1446^{7} **>53a 59f<**

Sheriff **4** b c Midyan (USA)-Daisy Warwick (USA) 1612^{10} 2233^{3} **>75f<**

Sherman (IRE) **4** b c Caerleon (USA)-Aghsan (Lord Gayle (USA)) 918^{6} (1135) 1610^{8} 2457^{9} 3164^{8} **>106f<**

Shermood **2** b f Shere Khan-Jalebird Blues (Jalmood (USA)) *3243^{7}* 3427^{7} **>39a 51f<**

Shernadeed (FR) **2** b f Shernazar-A Kiss In Deed (USA) (Shadeed (USA)) 2705^{6} 2964^{3} 3366^{5} **>66f<**

Sheroot **3** b c Cigar-Act of Treason (Absalom) 965^{14} 3507^{7} 3805^{17} 4193^{10} 4275^{13} **>50f<**

Sherqy (IRE) **3** br c Persian Bold-Turkish Treasure (USA) 962^{3} 1524^{3} 1946^{2} 2329^{2} (2643) 3021^{9} 3723^{4} **>87f<**

Sherrington **3** b f Thatching-Pertinent (Persepolis (FR)) 2331^{8} 2790^{14} 3239^{5} 3497^{10} **>60df<**

She Said No **3** ch f Beveled (USA)-She Said Yes (Local Suitor (USA)) 742^{8} 1258^{9} 1522^{5} *2140^{2} (2600)* **>62a 54f<**

She's a Madam **4** b f Kabour-Mrs Buzby (Abwah) *510^{4}* **>36a 10tf<**

She's Dynamite (IRE) **3** b f Danehill (USA)-Flaxen Hair (Thatch (USA)) 2748^{2} 3209^{6} 3564^{7} 3813^{24} **>89f<**

She's My Love **2** ch f Most Welcome-Stripanoora (Ahonoora) (2277) 2886^{3} 3345^{4} 3917^{7} **>76f<**

She's Simply Great (IRE) **2** b f Simply Great (FR)-Petrine (IRE) (Petorius) 2580^{4} 3170^{4} 3850^{7} **>54f<**

Shift Again (IRE) **3** b f Siberian Express (USA)-Pushkinia (FR) (Pharly (FR)) 761^{5} 1000^{3} (1428) 1845^{5} 2664^{8} 3020^{6} 3757^{9} 4071^{4} 4149^{3} **>73f<**

Shifting Moon **3** b c Night Shift (USA)-Moonscape 694^{9} 980^{5} 1180^{7} 1804^{3} (2361) 2537^{2} 2766^{2} **>93f<**

Shikari's Son **8** br h Kala Shikari-Have Form (Haveroid) (541) 728^{11} 1021^{5} 1261^{4} 1614^{3} 1895^{9} 2169^{2} 2428^{5} (2764) 3085^{11} 3358^{7} 3717^{F} **>103f<**

Shinerolla **3** b g Thatching-Primrolla (Relko) 426^{3} 483^{4} 640^{2} 813^{2} (839) 1130^{2} (1294) 1524^{2} 1687^{4} 3368^{12} 3607^{9} (3973) 4116^{3} **>48a 91f<**

Shining Candle (USA) **3** b f Bering-Reham (Mill Reef (USA)) 1000^{9} **>54f<**

Shining Cloud **2** ch f Indian Ridge-Hardiheroine (Sandhurst Prince) 1443^{3} 1751^{2} **>81f<**

Shining Dancer **3** b f Rainbow Quest (USA)-Strike Home (Be My Guest (USA)) 1473^{6} 2520^{5} 3501^{7} 3875^{11} **>72f<**

Shining Edge **3** ch c Beveled (USA)-Lustrous (Golden Act (USA)) 572^{8} 1180^{14} 1358^{3} 1524^{5} 1945^{9} 2253^{3} 2503^{2} 2822^{6} 3101^{9} 3808^{2} 3973^{5} **>65a 62f<**

Shining Example **3** ch c Hadeer-Kick the Habit (Habitat) 813^{10} 1366^{5} 1532^{3} *3526^{2}* 3965^{2} (4261) **>83f<**

Shining High 3 b f Shirley Heights-Padelia (Thatching) 647^{10} 1674^{3} (2284) 2907^{2} 3412^{8} 4118^{17} **>96f<**

Shining Molly (FR) 2 b f Shining Steel-Molly Martine (Lou Piquet 2210a^{2} 2726a^{2} 3330a^{5} **>96f<**

Ship of the Line 5 ch h High Line-Corvette (AUS) *103*^{3} *222*^{6} **>55a 72f<**

Ship's Dancer 2 b f Shareef Dancer (USA)-Sunderland (Dancers Image (USA)) 3339^{11} 3758^{7} 4063^{10} **>75f<**

Shirlaty 2 b f Shirley Heights-Jameelaty (USA) (Nureyev (USA)) 3948^{17} 4216^{14} **>44f<**

Shirley's Train (USA) 6 br h Malinowski (USA)-Tiger Trap (USA) (Al Hattab (USA)) 2197^{4} **>39f<**

Shirley Sue 2 b f Shirley Heights-Dame Ashfield (Grundy) 4048^{14} 4190^{8} **>53f<**

Shock-A-Lot (IRE) 2 ch c Fayruz-Vote Barolo (Nebbiolo) 2058^{4} 2615^{4} 2978^{6} 3281^{4} 3711^{11} **>66f<**

Shonara's Way 4 b f Slip Anchor-Favorable Exchange (USA) (Exceller (USA)) 3343^{2} 3730^{17} 3930^{2} 4118^{10} 4258^{5} **>102f<**

Shontaine 2 b c Pharly (FR)-Hinari Televideo (Caerleon (USA)) 1597^{3} (2116) 2328^{9} (2644) 3147^{12} 3394^{2} 3714^{15} 4111^{10} **>78f<**

Shoodah (IRE) 4 ch g Common Grounds-Tunguska (Busted) 853^{16} 1337^{12} **>30f<**

Shoofk 4 ch c Dunbeath (USA)-River Reem (USA) (Irish River (FR)) 454^{8} 586^{6} 653^{4} 778^{12} **>61f<**

Shooter 3 b c Salse (USA)-Debbie Harry (USA) (Alleged (USA)) 1097^{9} 2466^{4} *3514*^{6} 3658^{4} **>68a 63f<**

Shooting Light (IRE) 2 b c Shernazar-Church Light (Caerleon (USA)) 4320^{22} **>30f<**

Shot At Love (IRE) 4 br f Last Tycoon-Cooliney Dancer (Dancers Image (USA)) 2287^{9} 2694^{5} 2933^{6} **>89f<**

Shotley Again 5 b h Then Again-Sweet Candice (African Sky) 701^{15} 789^{15} 992^{5} *1088*^{13} 1297^{13} **>36a 31df<**

Shot the Sheriff 3 b c Warning-Dearest (Alzao (USA)) 648^{12} 882^{17} 3531^{14} 4131^{7} **>61a 41f<**

Showery 3 b f Rainbow Quest (USA)-Anodyne (Dominion) 555^{2} 759^{2} (1279) 1414^{3} 2909^{4} 3298^{2} 3964^{23} **>79+f<**

Show Faith (IRE) 5 ch h Exhibitioner-Keep the Faith (Furry Glen) 550^{3} 634^{9} 793^{3} 1280^{3} 1851^{13} (2446) 2672^{12} 3374^{7} 3729^{3} 3945^{4} 4202^{11} **>95f<**

Show Flair (IRE) 3 ch g Exhibitioner-Tudor Loom (Sallust) 616^{9} 2499^{6} **>32f<**

Shrewd Alibi 4 gr c Sharrood (USA)-Alsiba (Northfields (USA)) 929^{6} 1339^{6} 1623^{3} 1840^{15} 2154^{5} **>80f<**

Shrewd Idea 5 b h Alleged (USA)-Domludge (USA) (Lyphard (USA)) 4252a^{2} **>119f<**

Shropshire Blue 5 gr m Risk Me (FR)-Six Ashes (Bruni) 578^{14} 784^{8} 877^{17} 1684^{4}

Shu Gaa (IRE) 2 ch c Salse (USA)-River Reem (USA) (Irish River (FR)) 2995^{6} 3883^{8} **>72f<**

Shujan (USA) 6 b h Diesis-Linda's Magic (USA) (Far North (CAN)) 998^{14} **>85f<**

Shuttlecock 4 ch c Pharly (FR)-Upper Sister (Upper Case (USA)) *(31) (117) 169*^{8} *293*^{3} *349*^{5} *378*^{6} *767*^{7} 864^{6} 967^{5} 1328^{9} 1645^{4} 1855^{3} 2390^{7} *2628*^{5} **>75da 54f<**

Shuttlingslow 4 b f Celestial Storm (USA)-Sharanella (Shareef Dancer (USA)) *470*^{7} *589*^{7} **>51a 54f<**

Shy Paddy (IRE) 3 b g Shy Groom (USA)-Griqualand (Connaught) *59*^{10} *309*^{3} 1289^{9} *1628*^{10} 2657^{13} **>54a 64f<**

Sian Wyn 5 ch m Hotfoot-Curzon House (Green God) *409*^{3} 1622^{12} **>53a 15f<**

Sibbertoft (IRE) 2 b f Shaadi (USA)-Rossnagran (Ardross) 1781^{2} 2579^{2} **>76f<**

Siberian Grey 3 gr c 1121a^{9} 2389a^{8} 3195a^{2} 3582a^{5} **>111f<**

Siberian Henry 2 b g Siberian Express (USA)-Semperflorens (Don) 3968^{8} **>43f<**

Siberian Mystic 2 gr f Siberian Express (USA)-Mystic Crystal (IRE) (Caerleon (USA)) 782^{10} 1017^{6} 1540^{10} 1943^{10} **>57f<**

Sicarian 3 b c Kris-Sharka (Shareef Dancer (USA)) 3618^{7} 3799^{7} **>67f<**

Sidanora (IRE) 5 ch g Montekin-Lady of Eilat (Cut Above) 2798^{2}

Side Bar 5 b h Mummy's Game-Joli's Girl (Mansingh (USA)) *(201) 260*^{9} *288*^{10} 1403^{7} **>40da 31f<**

Siege Perilous (IRE) 2 b c Taufan (USA)-Carado (Manado) 3620^{14} 3821^{9} 3968^{7} **>49f<**

Sieve of Time (USA) 4 br c Arctic Tern (USA)-Got A Cold (USA) (Drone) *195*^{3} **>86a 90df<**

Sigama (USA) 9 ch h Stop The Music (USA)-Lady Speedwell (USA) (Secretariat (USA)) *(305) 369*^{6} 475^{4} *510*^{2} 685^{4} 746^{6} 944^{4} 1248^{4} 1451^{4} 1827^{9} 2124^{7} 2521^{7} **>62a 61f<**

Siger Water 2 ch f Rakaposhi King-Kates Fling (USA) (Quiet Fling (USA)) 638^{7}

Sight'n Sound 4 b f Chief Singer-Optaria (Song) 696^{9} 884^{8} **>63f<**

Signal Tap (USA) 4 b c Fappiano (USA)-South Sea Dancer (USA) (Northern Dancer) 4307a^{11} **>99f<**

Signature 3 b f Sadler's Wells (USA)-Riverstreak (USA) 2082^{3} **>76f<**

Sign From Heaven 2 b c Keen-Sarah's Love (Caerleon (USA)) 1913^{7} 3868^{19} **>50f<**

Signoretto (FR) 8 b h Mille Balles-Sardagnola 4016a^{5} 4300a^{2} **>115f<**

Signs 3 ch f Risk Me (FR)-Sunday Sport Star (Star Appeal) 692^{7} 828^{9} 1227^{5} 1613^{2} 2066^{5} 2325^{4} 2737^{12} 3382^{11} **>100f<**

Signs R Us (IRE) 2 b c Al Hareb (USA)-O La Bamba (IRE) (Commanche Run) 3157^{11} 3430^{10} 4075^{26} **>26f<**

Sihafi (USA) 2 ch c Elmaamul (USA)-Kit's Double (USA) (Spring Double) 3337^{8} 3996^{2} **>74+f<**

Sikosarki (USA) 2 ch f Inishpour-Miss Sarcastic (USA) (Vitriolic (USA)) 1159^{6} 3353^{8} *4127*^{12} **>23f<**

Silca Blanka (IRE) 3 b c Law Society (USA)-Reality (Known Fact (USA)) 667^{10} 920^{9} 1138^{5} (1613) 1848^{14} 2893a^{2} **>104f<**

Silence in Court (IRE) 4 b c Law Society (USA)-Fair Flutter (Beldale Flutter (USA)) 610^{3} 869^{3} **>110f<**

Silent Expression 5 gr m Siberian Express (USA)-Silent Sun (Blakeney) *(61) 383*^{7} (1261) 1604^{4} (1777) 2001^{3} 2764^{10} 3145^{5} (3451) 3564^{11} **>86a 92f<**

Silent Guest (IRE) 2 b c Don't Forget Me-Guest House 3838^{6} 4070^{5} 4188^{11} 4327^{14} **>61f<**

Silent Lake (GER) 4 2046a^{7} 2567a^{2} **>111f<**

Silently 3 b c Slip Anchor-Land of Ivory (USA) (The Minstrel (CAN)) (538) 647^{9} 941^{4} 1382^{7} 1825^{2} (2132) (2298) 2639^{5} 2878^{4} 3433^{6} 3781^{3} 3993^{5} **>86f<**

Silent Sky 3 b f Then Again-Summer Sky (Skyliner) 855^{15} 1718^{16} **>38a 30f<**

Silent Soprano **2** b f Kind of Hush-Musical Note (Sharpo) 964^{2} 1203^{4} 1440^{6} 1821^{4} 1899^{5} 2732^{4} 3168^{2} (3309) 3546^{17} 3744^{8} **>54f<**

Silent Sovereign **6** ch g Kind of Hush-Regency Brighton (Royal Palace) 1339^{11}

Silent Warrior (IRE) **3** b c 2560a^{5} (2889a) 3323a^{3} **>120f<**

Silhouette (IRE) **2** gr f Standaan (FR)-Frill (Henbit (USA)) 3450^{10} 3765^{14} 3856^{6} 4132^{8} **>41f<**

Silk Cottage **3** b c Superpower-Flute Royale (Horage) 3166^{9} 3357^{14} 3649^{7} 3783^{5} 3878^{5} 3992^{4} *4123*^{2} 4165^{7} 4322^{5} *4337*^{9} **>66a 68f<**

Silk Masque (USA) **2** b f Woodman (USA)-Silk Slippers (USA) (Nureyev (USA)) (2675) **>83+f<**

Silks and Studs **3** b c Danehill (USA)-Gild the Lily (Ile de Bourbon (USA)) 730^{7} 1512^{12} 1776^{6} 3987^{14} **>59f<**

Silktail (IRE) **3** b f Jalmood (USA)-Silky (USA) (Nijinsky (CAN)) 450^{9} 648^{4} 851^{3} 935^{9} *1329*^{6} 1452^{7} 2282^{2} (2781) (2902) 3189^{11} 3388^{5} 3957^{3} 4149^{15} **>29a 79f<**

Sil Sila (IRE) **2** b f Marju (IRE)-Porto Alegre (Habitat) (3983) (4203) **>101f<**

Silver Academy (IRE) **3** gr c Standaan (FR)-Right Cash (Right Tack) 937^{15} 1125^{18} 1802^{5} 2112^{6} 2267^{4} **>49f<**

Silver Bird (IRE) **3** b f Vision (USA)-Caralia (Caracolero (USA)) 1372^{14} **>26f<**

Silver Border **2** ch c Kris-Silver Fling (USA) (The Minstrel (CAN)) 2095^{3} **>78f<**

Silver Brief **4** gr g Sulaafah (USA)-Briefing (Rusticaro (FR)) *73*^{10} **>5a 43f<**

Silverdale Count **3** b g Nomination-Its My Turn (Palm Track) 1194^{10} 3052^{5} (3171) **>57f<**

Silverdale Fox **8** ch h Sweet Monday-Its My Turn (Palm Track) 3853^{5} **>40f<**

Silverdale Knight **2** b c Nomination-Its My Turn (Palm Track) 810^{8} 863^{3} 1440^{3} (1494) 1556^{6} 2131^{6} 2424^{4} (2541) 2855^{7} 3019^{6} 3168^{4} 3721^{10} 3851^{9} 3969^{8} **>84f<**

Silver Dome (USA) **2** b br c Silver Hawk (USA)-Pink Topaze (FR) (Djakao (FR)) (4080) **>96+f<**

Silver Groom (IRE) **5** gr h Shy Groom (USA)-Rustic Lawn (Rusticaro (FR)) 2241^{9} (2672) 3106^{7} 3388^{3} 3729^{5} 3945^{13} 4163^{4} **>85f<**

Silver Harrow **2** ch c Belmez (USA)-Dancing Diana (Raga Navarro (ITY)) 1540^{2} 1715^{4} 2526^{4} 2756^{3} 2998^{3} 3314^{6} 4133^{3} **>78df<**

Silver Hunter (USA) **4** b c Silver Hawk (USA)-Martha Queen (USA) (Nijinsky (CAN)) 668^{16} 935^{11} 1205^{8} 1694^{8} 2069^{7} 3470^{5} 3627^{10} 4135^{12} **>67f<**

Silver Prey (USA) **2** b c Silver Hawk (USA)-Truly My Style (USA) (Mount Hagen (FR)) 2320^{3} (3089) **>80f<**

Silver Rondo (USA) **3** b f Diesis-Silver Dollar (Shirley Heights) *256*^{6} *372*^{3} 1128^{11} 2282^{3} *2630*^{3} 2874^{3} **>55a 59f<**

Silver Samurai **6** b h Alleging (USA)-Be My Lady (Be My Guest (USA)) *421*^{9} 558^{13} *771*^{15} **>18a 46f<**

Silver Singer **3** gr f Pharly (FR)-Bustling Nelly (Bustino) 3573^{4} 3799^{4} 4072^{16} **>71f<**

Silver Sleeve (IRE) **3** b c Taufan (USA)-Sable Coated (Caerleon (USA)) 4164^{13} **>69f<**

Silver Sting **3** ch c Nashwan (USA)-Silver Fling (USA) (The Minstrel (CAN)) 431^{2} 637^{3} 937^{2} **>93f<**

Silver Tzar **3** gr g Dominion-Altaia (FR) (Sicyos (USA)) 1778^{9} 2003^{8} 2491^{10} 2641^{5} **>76+f<**

Silver Wedge (USA) **4** ch c Silver Hawk (USA)-Wedge Musical (What A Guest) 3581a^{3} 3811^{6} **>83a 108f<**

Silver Welcome **2** ch g Most Welcome-Silver Ore (FR) (Silver Hawk (USA)) 2259^{3} 2619^{4} 2852^{2} 3149^{2} (3502) 3775^{6} 3985^{7} 4111^{5} 4263^{10} **>66f<**

Silver Will **5** gr g Skyliner-Silver Cygnet 753^{13} **>29f<**

Silver Wing (USA) **2** b f Silver Hawk (USA)-Cojinx (USA) (Crafty Prospector (USA)) 2579^{5} 3827^{4} 4037^{2} **>72f<**

Silvicolous (USA) **3** ch c Woodman (USA)-Golden Oriole (USA) (Northern Dancer) 955^{2} 1150^{4} (1464) **>83f<**

S'Il Vous Plait(GER) **3** b f Dashing Blade-Silver Form (Formidable) 1009a^{2} 1705a^{6} **>107f<**

Simafar (IRE) **4** b g Kahyasi-Sidama (FR) (Top Ville) 661^{12} 1386^{6} 1840^{7} 3616^{10} 3817^{10} **>81f<**

Simand **3** b f Reprimand-Emmylou (Arctic Tern (USA)) 759^{8} 969^{6} 1207^{8} 1463^{2} *1880*^{8} 2332^{4} (2582) (2815) 3151^{4} 3704^{9} **>25a 61f<**

Simon Harold **2** b c Mazilier (USA)-Alison Rose (Jaazeiro (USA)) *889*^{4} **>25a f<**

Simply Dashing (IRE) **4** br g Simply Great (FR)-Qurrat Al Ain (Wolver Hollow) 3282^{3}

Simply (IRE) **6** b g Simply Great (FR)-Be A Dancer (Be Friendly) 741^{8} **>44f<**

Simply Miss Chief (IRE) **2** b f Mac's Imp (USA)-Wolverhants (Wolver Hollow) 3520^{4} 3628^{16} 3982^{13} *4294*^{8} **>36a 55f<**

Simply Silly (IRE) **2** b f Simply Great (FR)-Zany (Junius (USA)) 1352^{4} 1798^{10} 3432^{10} 3720^{4} 3877^{11} 4137^{7} **>59f<**

Simply Simon **3** b c Today and Tomorrow-Hamrahi (Final Straw) 482^{11} 736^{6} *1030*^{8} 1092^{9} 1583^{7} 2049^{7} **>27a 42f<**

Simply Tricky (USA) **4** b c Clever Trick (USA)-Simply Divine (USA) (Danzig (USA)) 1002a^{8} 1394a^{8} **>104f<**

Simposa (IRE) **3** b c Simply Great (FR)-Mariposa (Cure The Blues (USA)) *372*^{4} *418*^{7} *509*^{7} 3805^{4} 4062^{22} 4225^{13} **>46a 55f<**

Sinclair Lad (IRE) **7** ch h Muscatite-Kitty Frisk (Prince Tenderfoot (USA)) 1285^{10} 1513^{8} 1645^{3} 1854^{6} 2314^{7} 2450^{5} **>62a 55f<**

Sing And Dance **2** b f Rambo Dancer (CAN)-Musical Princess (Cavo Doro) 3881^{9} 4277^{10} **>37f<**

Singing Patriarch (IRE) **2** b c Marju (IRE)-Busker (Bustino) 2767^{7} 3530^{2} 3784^{2} 3865^{9} (4098) 4328^{3} **>82f<**

Singing Rock (IRE) **3** ch f Ballad Rock-Swift Pursuit (Posse (USA)) 662^{6} 1094^{9} 1366^{6} 1663^{9} 2178^{6} 2539^{6} **>69f<**

Singoalla (IRE) **2** b f Alwuhush (USA)-Broadway Gal (USA) (Foolish Pleasure (USA)) 1348^{3} 1671^{2} 1968^{2} 3870^{3} **>69f<**

Singspiel (IRE) **3** b c In The Wings-Glorious Song (CAN) (Halo (USA)) 826^{2} 979^{4} 2044a^{2} 2286^{2} 3144^{2} (3595) **>128f<**

Sing Up **3** b c Sizzling Melody-Hellene (Dominion) 3706^{21} 3845^{6} 4164^{10} **>50f<**

Sing With the Band **4** b f Chief Singer-Ra Ra Girl (Shack (USA)) 555^{3} *603*^{2} 772^{8} *(1032)* *1214*^{6} *1566*^{4} *(1763)* 2234^{5} *3242*^{3} 3783^{2} 4057^{11} *4125*^{2} **>77a 61f<**

Sinking Sun **2** gr f Danehill (USA)-Oscura (USA) (Caro) 4190^{5} **>65f<**

Sinyar **3** b or br c 1121a^{7} 3910a^{5} **>99f<**

Sir Arthur Hobbs **8** b h Lyphard's Special (USA)-Song

Grove 1724[4] 2132[6] 2227[2] 2906[2] 2999[5] **>67f<**

Sir Dickie Cox (IRE) 4 b c Nordico (USA)-Arthur's Daughter (Artaius (USA)) 556[16] 879[9] 986[6] **>54?f<**

Sirius (IRE) 3 br c Skyliner-Shantung Lassie (FR) (Shantung) 1514[19] 4331[14] **>37f<**

Sir Joey (USA) 6 ch h Honest Pleasure (USA)-Sougoli (Realm) 693[6] 796[10] 922[3] 1106[6] 1673[3] 1895[11] (2150) 2764[5] 3145[12] 3279[5] 3717[20] 4033[10] 4145[10] **>89df<**

Sir King (GER) 3 c 2215a[4] 4018a[8] 4254a[2] **>119f<**

Sir Norman Holt (IRE) 6 b h Ela-Mana-Mou-Ploy (Posse (USA)) 873[22] 2174[7] *4293[2]* **>67a 62f<**

Sir Silver Sox (USA) 3 gr c Corwyn Bay-Sox In The Box (USA) (Cresta Rider (USA)) 803a[6] 3717[24] **>101f<**

Sir Tasker 7 b h Lidhame-Susie's Baby (Balidar) *(16) 69[10] 188[5] (237) 345[5] (404) (446)* 646[9] 926[10] 1152[5] 1508[11] 1809[19] 2234[2] 2303[2] 2753[7] 2956[2] (3341) 3492[19] *3522[4]* 3681[13] *3950[6]* 4142[14] 4280[19] *4337[6]* **>65a 62df<**

Sir Thomas Beecham 5 b g Daring March-Balinese (Balidar) *13[2]* 506[9] 741[11] **>68a 67f<**

Sis Garden 2 b f Damister (USA)-Miss Nanna (Vayrann) 3449[9] 4277[4] *4338[6]* **>62a 54f<**

Siska (USA) 3 ch f Diesis-Kind Hope (USA) (Chieftain II) 1675[12] **>26f<**

Sison (IRE) 5 b h Vacarme (USA)-Silent Sail *65[8] 216[3] 305[8] 328[4]* 734[3] 856[11] 1400[7] 1738[3] 1942[4] **>58a 61f<**

Sistar Act 2 b f Salse (USA)-Unsuitable (Local Suitor (USA)) 2572[4] 3069[19] **>59tf<**

Sister Kit (IRE) 2 b f Glacial Storm (USA)-Good Holidays (Good Times (ITY)) 3758[8] 3887[4] 4063[14] **>72f<**

Six Clerks (IRE) 2 b c Shadeed (USA)-Skidmore Girl (USA) (Vaguely Noble) 2526[10] 2876[4] 3231[3] 4001[9] **>63f<**

Six for Luck 3 b c Handsome Sailor-Fire Sprite (Mummy's Game) 748[2] 861[4] 1723[8] 3854[5] 4278[9] **>64f<**

Sizzling 3 b c Sizzling Melody-Oriental Splendour (Runnett) 645[6] (1201) 1400[5] 1975[8] 2318[4] 2491[3] 3014[4] 3919[6] (4215) **>69f<**

Sizzling Romp 3 b f Sizzling Melody-Its A Romp (Hotfoot) *1033[9]* 1302[7] 1546[7] *2071[12]* 2887[6] **>35a 40f<**

Sizzling Serenade 2 gr f Sizzling Melody-Trynova (Tyrnavos) 3648[8] 3975[20] **>29f<**

Sizzling Symphony 2 b c Sizzling Melody-Polly Worth (Wolver Hollow) 1278[8] 1670[10] (1943) 2541[4] **>72+f<**

Skedaddle 3 b f Formidable (USA)-Norfolk Serenade (Blakeney) 758[4] 1000[11] 1554[4] 1845[4] 2225[4] *2630[9]* 3422[10] 3722[3] **>22a 60f<**

Skelton Countess (IRE) 2 ch f Imperial Frontier (USA)-Running Brook (Run The Gantlet (USA)) 570[8] 782[12] 1017[7] 1646[4] 1823[3] *1879[6]* 2128[3] **>4a 56f<**

Skelton Princess (IRE) 4 b f Carmelite House (USA)-Fariha (Mummy's Pet) *1950[12]* **>9a f<**

Sketchbook 2 ch g Sharpo-Cape Chestnut 1726[7] 2315[5] 3465[4] (3779) 4159[4] **>96f<**

Ski Academy (IRE) 2 b c Royal Academy (USA)-Cochineal (USA) (Vaguely Noble) (3398) 3600[3] 3865[29] **>89f<**

Ski Chalet 3 b f Petoski-Silver Lodge (Homing) *2378[7]* **>15a f<**

Skiddaw Samba 6 b m Viking (USA)-Gavea (African Sky) 2165[4] 2544[8] **>48f<**

Ski For Gold 2 b f Shirley Heights-Quest (USA) (The Minstrel (CAN)) 3541[4] 3916[6] (4148) **>65f<**

Skillington (USA) 2 b c Danzig (USA)-Annie Edge (Nebbiolo) 2573[2] 3089[6] 3280[3] 3592[2] **>80f<**

Skiptamaloo 4 b f Northern State (USA)-Pronetta (USA) (Mr Prospector (USA)) 555[10] 701[18] 877[15] 1080[14] 1355[12] 1677[9] 2084[2] 2624[13] 2956[8] 3508[15] 3649[5] **>7a 56?f<**

Skip to Somerfield 3 ch f Shavian-St Isadora (Lyphard (USA)) 2006[7] 2330[12] **>74f<**

Skolern 11 b h Lochnager-Piethorne (Fine Blade (USA)) 534[16] **>24a f<**

Skram 2 b c Rambo Dancer (CAN)-Skarberg (FR) (Noir Et Or) 3436[10] 3626[14] 3989[12] **>58f<**

Sky Diver 4 b c Salse (USA)-Sutosky (Great Nephew) 1255[9] 1971[7] 2113[4] **>21a 46f<**

Sky Dome (IRE) 2 ch c Bluebird (USA)-God Speed Her (Pas de Seul) 617[6] (788) 1556[4] **>74tf<**

Sky Girl 3 b f Statoblest-Alpine Sunset (Auction Ring (USA)) 3282[4] 3507[4] **>64f<**

Sky Music 4 ch f Absalom-On the Record (Record Token) 2096[5] 2369[2] 2647[4] **>88f<**

Slaney Project (IRE) 3 b c Project Manager-Sundrive (Status Seeker) 3106[11] 3388[13] 3801[8] 3936[7] 4047[14] **>71f<**

Slapy Dam 3 b g Deploy-Key to the River (USA) (Irish River (FR)) *51[5] 95[5]* 521[2] (575) 947[9] 1093[12] 2655[8] 2861[3] 3061[4] 3759[4] (3875) (4047) 4149[6] **>60a 66f<**

Slasher Jack (IRE) 4 b c Alzao (USA)-Sherkraine (Shergar) 440[10] 558[10] 757[6] (956) 1621[5] 1805[2] 2241[3] 2421[3] **>93f<**

Sleep Standing (IRE) 2 b f Standaan (FR)-Sleeping Car (Scorpio (FR)) *2382[11]* **>3a f<**

Sleeptite (FR) 5 gr g Double Bed (FR)-Rajan Grey (Absalom) *(260) 321[2] 374[2] 412[3]* 556[23] *600[3] 3951[4]* **>77a 10f<**

Sleepy Boy 2 br g Zero Watt (USA)-Furnace Lass VII (Damsire Unregistered) 4235[4] **>11f<**

Slicious 3 b c Slip Anchor-Precious Jade 3790a[2] 4176a[2] **>110f<**

Slip a Coin 4 b f Slip Anchor-Luck Penny (Bustino) *32[3] 80[10] 103[2] 199[4] (308) 364[2] 387[7] 414[12] 3952[13]* **>65a 54f<**

Sliparis 2 b f Slip Anchor-Parisian Express (FR) (Siberian Express (USA)) 3883[17] **>7f<**

Slivovitz 5 b h Petoski-Hiding 887[17] 1174[14] 1354[11] 1832[16] 3028[8] 3293[17] 4113[3] 4280[3] **>61f<**

Slmaat 4 ch f Sharpo-Wasslaweyeh (USA) (Damascus (USA)) *(137) 186[3] 325[8]* 549[2] 811[4] 1022[9] 3723[9] 4201[13] 4289[13] **>71a 69f<**

Sloe Brandy 5 b m Hotfoot-Emblazon *2379[7]* **>16a f<**

Slybird 3 b f Precocious-Demerger (Dominion) *98[9] 264[8] 274[6]* **>9a f<**

Sly's Fancy 2 gr f Rambo Dancer (CAN)-Fancy Flight (FR) (Arctic Tern (USA)) 3670[10] **>25f<**

Slytly Beveled 3 ch c Beveled (USA)-Bright Sunlight (Alzao (USA)) *349[11] 401[4] 447[8] 513[4] 587[6]* (880) 1028[4] 1191[5] 3264[6] 3385[10] **>66a 63f<**

Smart Debutante (IRE) 6 b m Glenstal (USA)-Cecily *19[9]*

Smarter Charter 2 br c Master Willie-Irene's Charter (Persian Bold) 3626[10] 3940[9] **>51+f<**

Smart Family (USA) 4 ch c Homebuilder (USA)-Enceinte (USA) (Forli (ARG)) 2901[2] **>82f<**

Smart Generation 4 b c Cadeaux Genereux-Gull Nook (Mill Reef (USA)) (1141) 1853[15] 3945[12] 4031[4] (4202)

>102f<
Smart Guest 3 ch g Be My Guest (USA)-Konbola (Superlative) 667^{11} (1146) 1613^{4} 1839^{31} 2240^{14} **>98f<**
Smart Teacher (USA) 5 b or br h Smarten (USA)-Finality (USA) (In Reality (USA)) *361^{6}* *408^{11}* 1509^{12} 2220^{9} **>33a 57f<**
Smile Forever (USA) 2 b f Sunshine Forever (USA)-Awenita (Rarity) 3136^{2} 3758^{5} 4262^{15} **>75f<**
Smiley Face 3 b g Colmore Row-Count On Me (No Mercy) 855^{14} **>44f<**
Smiling Bess 2 b f Salse (USA)-Wanda (Taufan (USA)) 3626^{18} 3940^{7} **>24f<**
Smiling Thru 3 b c Reference Point-Ever Genial (Brigadier Gerard) 654^{12} **>53f<**
Smilin N Wishin (USA) 2 b f Lyphard's Wish (FR)-Smilin Michele (USA) (Sharpen Up) 4143^{2} **>79?f<**
Smithereens 2 ch f Primo Dominie-Splintering (Sharpo) 3948^{12} 4328^{2} **>72f<**
Smocking 5 ch m Night Shift (USA)-Sue Grundy (Grundy) 3047^{2} 3288^{5} 3641^{4} 4259^{14} 4332^{7} **>47da 43f<**
Smolensk (IRE) 3 b c Ela-Mana-Mou-Merry Twinkle (Martinmas) 616^{7} 854^{5} 1154^{6} *1571^{4}* *1952^{3}* 2125^{4} **>67a 67f<**
Smolensk (USA) 3 b f Danzig (USA)-Blush with Pride (USA) (Blushing Groom (FR)) 705a^{2} 1116a^{4} (1576a) 1850^{2} (2897a) 3199a^{8} 3589a^{5} **>120f<**
Smooth Hound 4 b c Petong-Ocean Hound (Main Reef) 1771^{9} 2081^{9} **>50f<**
Smuggler's Point (USA) 5 b g Lyphard (USA)-Smuggly (USA) (Caro) 737^{9} 3569^{11} **>73f<**
Smuggling 4 b c Slip Anchor-Strigida (Habitat) 506^{2} (795) (1189) 1840^{3} **>95f<**
Snake Plissken (IRE) 4 ch g Reasonable (FR)-Shalie (Windjammer (USA)) 3063^{4} *3514^{5}* 3703^{18} **>48a 50f<**
Snickersnee 7 b h Kris-Cat Girl (USA) (Grey Dawn II) *2592^{12}*
Snipe Hall 4 b f Crofthall-Geopelia (Raffingora) 571^{7} 700^{4} 934^{6} 1100^{8} **>94f<**
Snitch 2 ch g Blow the Whistle-Whispering Sea (Bustino) *770^{6}* 983^{5} 1282^{7} 1740^{5} 2185^{2} 4097^{18} 4317^{11} **>54f<**
Snow Domino (IRE) 2 ch g Habyom-Magic Picture 3975^{28} *4334^{5}* **>43a f<**
Snow Dream 5 b m Siberian Express (USA)-National Dress (Welsh Pageant) *252^{9}* *340^{5}* 582^{4} 879^{13} *1086^{5}* (1328) (1470) 1607^{6} 2087^{9} **>35a 57f<**
Snow Falcon 2 b g Polar Falcon (USA)-Cameroun (African Sky) 2107^{3} 2681^{6} 3404^{6} 3711^{7} **>75f<**
Snow Foot 3 b f Formidable-Able Mabel (Absalom) 1624^{10} *2071^{7}* **>41a 47tf<**
Snowing 4 gr f Tate Gallery (USA)-Biding 4119^{3} **>93f<**
Snowpoles 2 b f High Estate-Bronzewing (Beldale Flutter (USA)) 3673^{7} **>62f<**
Snow Princess (IRE) 3 b f Ela-Mana-Mou-Karelia (USA) (Sir Ivor) 635^{7} 3799^{6} (3965) (4149) (4259) (4325) **>90f<**
Snow Queen (USA) 3 b f Gone West (USA)-Lady Ice (CAN) (Vice Regent (CAN)) 1486^{8} **>39f<**
Snowtown (IRE) 3 b f Alzao (USA)-Golden Bough (USA) (Graustark (USA)) 997^{4} 1242^{8} 1729^{5} 3831^{3} 4030^{5} 4311a^{2} **>105f<**
Snow Valley 3 b c Shirley Heights-Mountain Lodge (Blakeney) 663^{13} 929^{3} 1194^{6} 3130^{6} 3317^{2} 3896^{7} **>84f<**
Snowy Petrel (IRE) 3 b c Petorius-Bronzewing (Beldale Flutter (USA)) 618^{12} 962^{7} 1693^{3} 2068^{4} 2525^{4} (2975) 3229^{4} 3616^{7} 3918^{2} 4051^{5} 4189^{8} **>86f<**
Soaking 5 b h Dowsing (USA)-Moaning Low *405^{2}* 702^{12} 882^{5} *1049^{6}* 1714^{15} *1980^{5}* (2113) 2342^{2} 2685^{2} 2979^{11} 3159^{7} 3629^{5} 3885^{9} **>74a 60f<**
So Amazing 3 b f Hallgate-Jussoli (Don) 1417^{6} 2188^{4} 2974^{4} 3257^{3} 4194^{6} **>65f<**
Soba Guest (IRE) 6 ch h Be My Guest (USA)-Brazilian Princess (Absalom) *224^{9}* *248^{6}* *308^{6}* *358^{4}* *1457^{10}* 1799^{8} 1965^{10} **>41a 45f<**
Soba Up 5 ch m Persian Heights-Soba (Most Secret) 757^{3} 874^{3} 1064^{6} 1529^{10} (1817) (1958) (2002) 2159^{2} (2305) (2392) 2584^{2} 2798^{2} 3223^{3} 3774^{W} 4036^{13} 4248^{10} 4289^{4} **>81f<**
Sobeloved 3 gr g Beveled (USA)-Miss Solo 449^{3} 908^{10} 1124^{12} 1512^{9} 1718^{2} 1962^{19} 2149^{5} 3081^{4} 3249^{4} 3515^{14} 4157^{26} **>42f<**
Sobering Thoughts 9 ch g Be My Guest (USA)-Soba (Most Secret) 702^{4} 838^{6} 949^{4} 1043^{4} 1668^{7} 1996^{W} **>66df<**
Social Register 3 ch c Unfuwain (USA)-Bluebook (USA) (Secretariat (USA)) 616^{10} 1290^{16} 1649^{15} 2084^{5} **>59f<**
Society Girl 2 b f Shavian-Sirene Bleu Marine (USA) (Secreto (USA)) 1525^{8} (1841) (2346) 2541^{2} 2911^{3} 3468^{3} 3548^{15} 4279^{6} **>78f<**
Society Magic (USA) 2 b g Imp Society (USA)-Lady Kirtling (USA) (Kirtling) 3994^{5} 4143^{6} **>53f<**
Society Sue (IRE) 2 b f Mac's Imp (USA)-Ivory Wisdom (USA) (Sir Ivor) 1665^{14} 2128^{9} 2354^{5} 2852^{4} 3253^{2} 3312^{W} **>44f<**
Soda Popinski (USA) 7 b h Sir Ivor-Four Runs (USA) (Reviewer (USA)) *415^{14}* *2495^{9}*
So Discreet (USA) 7 b h Secreto (USA)-I'll Be Around (USA) (Isgala) *201^{2}* *260^{6}* *288^{6}* **>50a f<**
So Factual (USA) 5 b h Known Fact (USA)-Sookera (USA) 1133^{2} (1870) 2368^{7} (3187) **>127f<**
So Intrepid (IRE) 5 ch h Never so Bold-Double River (USA) (Irish River (FR)) *65^{9}* *314^{4}* 434^{6} 611^{9} 877^{6} (1248) 1545^{2} (1802) 2079^{7} 2533^{3} (2609) 2700^{4} 3221^{9} 3359^{13} 3637^{6} 3822^{14} **>44a 79f<**
Solano (IRE) 3 ch c Aragon-Hard to Stop (Hard Fought) 742^{9} **>45f<**
Solar Crystal (IRE) 2 b f Alzao (USA)-Crystal Spray (Beldale Flutter (USA)) (1348) 2106^{4} 2554^{2} (3561) 4013a^{3} **>101f<**
Solar Flight 3 b c Soviet Star (USA)-Fanciful (FR) (Gay Mecene (USA)) (670) 912^{4} (2205) 2762^{5} 3904^{12} **>90f<**
Solar One (FR) 3 b c Alleged (USA)-Nouvelle Lune (FR) (Be My Guest (USA)) 801a^{2} 1115a^{2} **>109f<**
Solatium (IRE) 3 b c Rainbow Quest (USA)-Consolation (Troy) 657^{7} 4003^{5} 4167^{9} **>64+f<**
Solazzi (FR) 3 b f Saint Cyrien (FR)-Sunclad (FR) (Tennyson (FR)) 1514^{15} **>38f<**
Soldier Cove (USA) 5 ch g Manila (USA)-Secret Form (Formidable) 3632^{4} 3754^{5} 4002^{7} 4215^{13} **>70f<**
Soldier Mak 2 ch g Infantry-Truly Blest 3379^{19} 3663^{17} 4241^{7} 4327^{10} **>64f<**
Soldier's Leap (FR) 3 b c Warning-Thalestria (FR) (Mill Reef (USA)) *59^{8}* *176^{3}* *(241)* *(289)* *564^{4}* 678^{6} 1661^{3} 1925^{4} **>85a 80f<**
Solianna 3 ch f Beveled (USA)-Reclusive (Sunley

Builds) *286^{3}* *332^{3}* *381^{6}* 727^{7} 2032^{4} (2164) *2497^{2}* 2513^{3} 2712^{5} 3000^{6} **>60a 66f<**

Solid Illusion (USA) **4** b c Cozzene (USA)-Polly's Harde (FR) (Lyphard (USA)) 1709a^{2} 2213a^{6} **>120f<**

Solidoun (FR) **4** gr c Kaldoun-Solidarite (Far North) 2041a^{3} 3036a^{2} **>117f<**

Solomon's Dancer (USA) **5** b or br h Al Nasr (FR)-Infinite Wisdom (USA) (Sassafras (FR)) 821^{5} 954^{6} 1558^{11} 2238^{6} 2785^{2} 2854^{W} **>82f<**

Solon (GER) **3** b c Local Suitor-Scilla (Alpenkonig) (2567a) (3486a) (3914a) **>124f<**

Solo Prize **3** b c Chief Singer-Raffle (Balidar) 850^{9} 999^{9} 1279^{8} 1550^{9} 1614^{14} **>38a 73f<**

Solor Dancer **3** b c Rambo Dancer (CAN)-Just Super (Star Appeal) *17^{5}* *213^{9}* 525^{7} 641^{7} 990^{13} **>17a 20f<**

Solo Symphony (IRE) **2** ch f Fayruz-Keen Note (Sharpo) 508^{3} **>53f<**

Solva Mist **2** gr f Sharrood (USA)-Irish Ditty (Derrylin) 561^{6} 740^{3} 1272^{4} 1369^{3} 1590^{5} 1810^{4} 2335^{7} *2591^{7}* **>9a 54f<**

Sombreffe **3** b f Polish Precedent (USA)-Somfas (USA) (What A Pleasure (USA)) 3829^{5} 3981^{2} *4296^{2}* **>63a 71f<**

Some Horse (IRE) **2** ch c Astronef-Daniela Lepida (ITY) (El-Muleta) 1646^{2} *2143^{11}* (3465) (3612) 3776^{4} 4195^{4} **>21a 99f<**

Somer Solo **2** b f Prince Daniel (USA)-Shift Over (USA) (Night Shift (USA)) 2964^{9} 3136^{6} 3541^{3} 3928^{8} 4241^{13} **>62f<**

Somerton Boy (IRE) **5** b h Thatching-Bonnie Bess (Ardoon) 749^{10} (1250) 1603^{6} (2477) 3411^{2} 3813^{22} 4041^{15} 4319^{6} **>83f<**

Something Speedy (IRE) **3** b f Sayf El Arab (USA)-Fabulous Pet (Somethingfabulous (USA)) *133^{5}* *292^{C}* *339^{9}* *893^{4}* *1628^{8}* **>50a 37f<**

Sommersby (IRE) **4** b c Vision (USA)-Echoing (Formidable) 676^{4} *1029^{2}* *(1332)* *1955^{2}* *2145^{3}* *2379^{6}* *3737^{3}* *(3951)* 4000^{8} *4126^{9}* **>75a 54f<**

Sonderise **6** br h Mummy's Game-Demderise (Vaigly Great) 475^{2} 639^{4} 753^{9} 994^{7} 1152^{7} 1304^{11} **>54f<**

Sondos **2** b f Dowsing (USA)-Krameria (Kris) 2791^{3} 3379^{4} **>68f<**

Soneeto **9** b h Teenoso (USA)-Flying Bid (Auction Ring (USA)) *19^{6}* *53^{7}* *161^{10}* **>40da f<**

Song of Tara (IRE) **3** b c Sadler's Wells (USA)-Flame of Tara (Artaius (USA)) (1339) (2722a) 3696a^{4} **>117f<**

Song of Years (IRE) **4** b f Shareef Dancer (USA)-Seattle Serenade (USA) (Seattle Slew (USA)) *218^{2}* *347^{3}* 1452^{6} 2037^{2} 2228^{3} 2745^{4} 2980^{7} 3872^{9} **>41a 65f<**

Songsheet **2** b f Dominion-Songstead (Song) 3998^{2} 4219^{2} 4328^{5} **>79f<**

Song Song Blue (IRE) **2** b br g Ballad Rock-Bluethroat (Ballymore) 2195^{8} 3827^{13} **>26f<**

Sonic Boy **3** b c Celestial Storm (USA)-Sharanella (Shareef Dancer (USA)) 667^{6} (945) 1129^{3} (1306) 1586^{4} 2558a^{6} 2936^{3} 3381^{9} 3458^{2} **>114f<**

Sonic Mail **2** b c Keen-Martin-Lavell Mail (Dominion) 617^{5} 760^{2} (1054) 1511^{3} 3176^{4} **>78f<**

Sonny Place **4** br g Glebe Place (USA)-Out To Lunch 3292^{11} 4062^{17} **>24f<**

Son of Anshan **2** b g Anshan-Anhaar (Ela-Mana-Mou) 3713^{W} 4070^{7} **>40f<**

Son of Sharp Shot (IRE) **5** b or br h Sharp Shot-Gay Fantasy (Troy) (653) (981) (1260) (1853) 2739^{4} 3162^{4} 3836^{9} 4076^{5} **>109f<**

Sonya Marie **2** b f Green Ruby (USA)-Sûsie Hall 1413^{11} 2257^{4} 2820^{8} 3937^{17} **>45f<**

Soojama (IRE) **5** b h Mansooj-Pyjama Game (Cavo Doro) (582) 741^{2} 866^{5} 1058^{5} (1535) 1657^{2} 1858^{4} 1929^{10} 3986^{2} 4135^{2} *4336^{13}* **>20a 57f<**

Sooki Sooki (IRE) **2** ch f Be My Guest-Somalia 4343a^{3} **>92?f<**

Sooty (IRE) **3** br f Caerleon (USA)-Aghsan (Lord Gayle (USA)) 658^{11} 867^{13} 2239^{9} 2786^{8} *4296^{8}* **>37a 76df<**

Sooty Tern **8** br h Wassl-High Tern (High Line) *529^{4}* 762^{5} 873^{6} 1021^{6} 1250^{8} (1472) (1517) *1884^{7}* 2080^{5} 2266^{4} (2397) 2586^{5} 2607^{5} 2797^{2} 3222^{15} *3319^{2}* 3664^{9} 3732^{15} **>55a 87f<**

Sophism (USA) **6** b g Al Nasr (FR)-Over The Waves (Main Reef) 1622^{6} 1773^{5} 4166^{18} **>59f<**

Sorbie Tower (IRE) **2** b c Soviet Lad (USA)-Nozet (Nishapour (FR)) 3832^{8} 3982^{2} **>72f<**

Soreze (IRE) **3** br f Gallic League-Run Bonnie (Runnett) 609a^{4} **>98f<**

Sorisky **3** ch c Risk Me (FR)-Minabella (Dance In Time (CAN)) 851^{9} 1245^{9} 1371^{9} 2661^{7} **>45f<**

So Select **2** ch f Northern State (USA)-Zamindara (Crofter (USA)) 3290^{11} 3468^{13} 3670^{16} 4133^{10} **>31f<**

Sotoboy (IRE) **3** b c Danehill (USA)-Fire Flash (Bustino) 622^{7} 912^{3} 1728^{8} 2121^{3} 2616^{9} 3209^{5} 3565^{13} 3755^{7} 4079^{6} **>81f<**

Sottises (IRE) **4** b f Northern State (USA)-Doppio (Dublin Taxi) 569^{7} 776^{10} 965^{13} **>35f<**

Soul of Honour (FR) **2** b c Highest Honor (FR)-Wink Beauty (USA) (Shahrastani (USA)) 1642^{4} 1857^{4} 2619^{8} 3049^{2} 3147^{6} 3612^{6} 3780^{4} **>64f<**

Soul of the Matter (USA) **4** dk b c Private Terms (USA)-Soul Light (USA) (T.V.Commercial (USA)) *4308a^{4}* **>131a 126f<**

Soul Risk **2** ch c Risk Me (FR)-Farras (Song) 2135^{9} 3379^{23} 3628^{18} **>34f<**

Sound Check **2** b f Formidable (USA)-Imperatrice (USA) (Kings Lake (USA)) 669^{11} 791^{8} 1253^{4} 1540^{3} 1798^{2} (2447) 3345^{7} 3516^{9} **>66df<**

Sound the Trumpet (IRE) **3** b c Fayruz-Red Note (Rusticaro (FR)) 1641^{6} 1918^{6} 3424^{6} *3522^{8}* 3597^{17} *4274^{13}* **>42a 49f<**

Sound Trick (USA) **3** b f Phone Trick (USA)-Lettre d'Amour (USA) (Caro) 1317^{7} 1547^{5} *1952^{6}* 2522^{5} 3657^{19} 3980^{24} **>41a 33f<**

Souperficial **4** gr g Petong-Duck Soup (Decoy Boy) *393^{5}* *(419)* *(532)* *590^{3}* 702^{2} *769^{8}* *(1334)* 1603^{7} 1828^{2} 1994^{4} (2330) 2578^{6} 3112^{12} *3242^{2}* 3492^{10} *3739^{11}* 4044^{17} **>70a 68df<**

Soupreme **3** ch f Northern State (USA)-Soupcon (King of Spain) 2953^{4} 4096^{5} **>65df<**

Source of Light **6** b h Rainbow Quest (USA)-De Stael (USA) (Nijinsky (CAN)) 1585^{4} 1853^{6} 2274^{7} 2739^{3} (3223) (3454) 3946^{6} **>111f<**

Southampton **5** b g Ballacashtal (CAN)-Petingo Gold (Pitskelly) 549^{9} 3217^{3} 3818^{14} **>23a 44f<**

South Eastern Fred **4** b c Primo Dominie-Soheir (Track Spare) *(8)* *(66)* 817^{4} 1061^{4} 1542^{5} 1788^{4} 2979^{14} 3182^{6} 3677^{8} 4138^{11} **>86a 59df<**

Southern Dominion **3** ch c Dominion-Southern Sky

(Comedy Star (USA)) *831^{5}* (855) 1201^{2} *1331^{10}* 1445^{3} 1741^{7} 2231^{2} *2492^{2}* *2627^{4}* 2692^{5} 2742^{4} 3121^{4} 3310^{4} 3667^{13} 3800^{2} 3919^{7} *4123^{3}* **>53a 68f<**

Southern Memories (IRE) 5 b h Don't Forget Me-Our Pet (Mummy's Pet) (3385) 4060^{7} **>60f<**

Southern Power (IRE) 4 b c Midyan (USA)-Tap The Line (Tap On Wood) 558^{2} 653^{3} 757^{4} 967^{2} 1064^{3} **>89f<**

Southern Ridge 4 b c Indian Ridge-Southern Sky (Comedy Star (USA)) 2168^{7} 2578^{12} 2979^{21} **>27a 70f<**

South Forest (IRE) 4 b c Pennine Walk-Route Royale (Roi Soleil) *315^{2}* *337^{4}* 502^{6} *(519)* *845^{11}* 3764^{15} **>67a 56f<**

South Pagoda (IRE) 2 b c Distinctly North (USA)-Lamya (Hittite Glory) 3337^{4} 3587a^{22} 4129^{10} **>70f<**

South Rock 3 b f Rock City-South Shore (Caerleon (USA)) 697^{6} 1809^{6} (2278) 2482^{6} 3113^{8} (3488) 3656^{2} (3823) 4121^{5} (4299a) **>103f<**

South Salem (USA) 2 b c Salem Drive (USA)-Azzurrina (Knightly Manner (USA)) (810) (1343) 1838^{3} **>104f<**

South Sands 9 ch h Sayf El Arab (USA)-Collegian (Stanford) *277^{5}* *288^{4}* **>40a f<**

South Sea Bubble (IRE) 3 b f Bustino-Night At Sea (Night Shift (USA)) 3958^{6} 4245^{3} **>79f<**

South Sound (IRE) 3 b c Petorius-Randolina (Wolver Hollow) 524^{7} 681^{8} 733^{14} 1165^{11} 1447^{3} 2033^{5} 2528^{17} 2983^{6} **>66tf<**

Sovereign Page (USA) 6 ch h Caro-Tashinsky (USA) (Nijinsky (CAN)) 935^{2} 981^{4} 1192^{3} **>88f<**

Sovereign Prince (IRE) 2 b c Bluebird (USA)-Everything Nice (Sovereign Path) 3709^{7}

Sovereign's Crown (USA) 2 br c Chief's Crown (USA)-Beau Prospector (USA) (Mr Prospector (USA)) 1551^{3} (3733) 3925^{3} 4084^{9} **>99f<**

Sovereigns Parade 3 ch g Chromite (USA)-Queen's Visit (Top Command (USA)) 1258^{8} 1520^{2} 1979^{16} 2537^{7} 3182^{4} 3685^{2} 3863^{4} 4136^{10} **>69f<**

Soviet Bride (IRE) 3 b f Soviet Star (USA)-Nihad (Alleged (USA)) 648^{5} 1124^{5} (2536) (2682) 2811^{2} 3006^{2} 3154^{4} 3555^{W} 3769^{4} 4047^{4} 4149^{7} **>70f<**

Soviet King (IRE) 2 b c Soviet Lad (USA)-Finessing (Indian King (USA)) 3617^{3} 3846^{6} 4172^{12} **>65f<**

Soviet Line (IRE) 5 b h Soviet Star (USA)-Shore Line (High Line) (1187) 1835^{3} 2689^{5} 3814^{3} 4078^{2} 4305a^{6} **>129f<**

Soviet Sakti (IRE) 2 b c Soviet Lad (USA)-Hill's Realm (USA) (Key to the Kingdom (USA)) 2277^{9} 2548^{6} 3158^{8} 3587a^{28} 3651^{12} 3760^{10} 4151^{19} **>47f<**

Soviet Style (AUS) 2 b g Rory's Jester (AUS)-Kitty Russe (Nureyev (USA)) 2423^{3} (2940) (3100) 3444^{3} 3668^{11} **>95f<**

Soviet Union 3 b g Soviet Star (USA)-Chalon (Habitat) *2142^{10}*

Sovitaka (IRE) 2 br f Soviet Lad (USA)-Pitaka (Pitskelly) 1082^{5} 1466^{3} 1665^{5} *2075^{6}* (2251) 2541^{8} 3048^{6} 3642^{16} 3780^{12} **>47a 54f<**

Sozzled 4 gr c Absalom-The High Dancer (High Line) *203^{9}* **>53a 65df<**

Spain Lane (USA) 4 b or br f Seeking the Gold (USA)-Regent's Walk (CAN) (Vice Regent (CAN)) 1112a^{2} 1572a^{5} **>115f<**

Spa Lane 2 ch c Presidium-Sleekit (Blakeney) 3441^{11} 3765^{9} 4063^{12} 4224^{17} **>44f<**

Spandrel 3 ch f Pharly (FR)-Oxslip (Owen Dudley) 3023^{9} **>47f<**

Spaniards Close 7 b h King of Spain-Avon Belle (Balidar) 693^{9} *(3522)* (3632) (3815) 4160^{2} **>83+a 102f<**

Spanish Girl (USA) 3 b f Alwuhush (USA)-Nat's Pleasure (USA) (Mr Prospector (USA)) *180^{0}* **>51a f<**

Spanish Luck 2 b f Mazilier (USA)-Spanish Heart (King of Spain) 1336^{4} 1642^{6} (2249) 2637^{7} 3008^{8} 3233^{6} 3566^{6} 3937^{9} **>49f<**

Spanish Steps (IRE) 3 b c Danehill (USA)-Belle Enfant (Beldale Flutter (USA)) 689^{3} 786^{8} 969^{5} 1269^{3} **>66f<**

Spanish Stripper (USA) 4 b c El Gran Senor (USA)-Gourmet Dinner (USA) (Raise A Cup (USA)) *82^{7}* *119^{4}* *169^{2}* *228^{7}* *256^{3}* *313^{5}* *334^{7}* *378^{12}* *592^{8}* 722^{4} 841^{9} 987^{6} *1088^{8}* (1377) 1534^{7} 1827^{3} 2108^{10} 2718^{3} 3020^{5} 4242^{7} **>48a 70f<**

Spanish Verdict 8 b h King of Spain-Counsel's Verdict (Firestreak) 579^{6} 642^{3} 785^{2} 927^{8} 1280^{7} 1432^{2} 1995^{2} 2307^{3} 2397^{5} 2607^{2} (2814) 3101^{5} 3255^{2} (3419) 3703^{12} 3977^{7} 4083^{9} 4234^{9} **>79f<**

Spanking Roger 2 ch c Unfuwain (USA)-Hi-Tech Girl (Homeboy) 3340^{16} 3592^{5} **>59f<**

Spara Tir 3 b c Dowsing (USA)-Jetelle (USA) (Northjet (USA)) 722^{5} 1279^{3} 1847^{3} 2084^{6} **>62f<**

Sparkling Roberta 4 b f Kind of Hush-Hitesca *1078^{3}* 1286^{3} 1553^{5} 1830^{9} *2961^{2}* *3076^{5}* 3871^{7} 4000^{7} **>40a 45f<**

Sparrowhawk (IRE) 3 b f Doyoun-Sparrow's Air (USA) (Assert) 1101^{4} 1615^{2} 1931^{2} (2297) 2738^{13} 3552^{6} 3927^{11} 4047^{5} 4213^{6} **>80df<**

Spartan Heartbeat 2 b c Shareef Dancer (USA)-Helen's Dream (Troy) 4226^{10} 4320^{19} **>50f<**

Special Beat 3 b f Bustino-Special Guest (Be My Guest (USA)) 2167^{5} 2653^{4} 2977^{5} 3521^{5} 3634^{14} **>68f<**

Special Dawn (IRE) 5 ch h Be My Guest (USA)-Dawn Star (High Line) (634) 918^{9} (1753) (2577) 3601^{10} 3729^{9} 4031^{12} **>102f<**

Specialize 3 b c Faustus (USA)-Scholastika (GER) (Alpenkonig (GER)) 651^{10} 976^{8} 1645^{9} 2282^{10} **>17a 59df<**

Special-K 3 br f Treasure Kay-Lissi Gori (FR) (Bolkonski) 1414^{2} 1723^{3} 2018^{2} (2357) (2499) 2679^{6} 3050^{6} 3305^{3} (3431) **>74f<**

Special Risk (IRE) 5 br g Simply Great (FR)-Ahonita (Ahonoora) 737^{10} **>55a 56f<**

Spectacle Jim 6 b h Mummy's Game-Welsh Blossom (Welsh Saint) *39^{3}* 1510^{6} 1832^{18} 1975^{3} 2317^{7} 2578^{11} 3139^{2} 4035^{18} 4134^{11} 4268^{13} **>46a 53f<**

Spectrum (IRE) 3 b c Rainbow Quest (USA)-River Dancer (Irish River (FR)) (792) (1234a) 1611^{13} 3794a^{2} (4120) **>128f<**

Speedster 3 c 2215a^{7} 2894a^{8} **>99f<**

Speed to Lead (IRE) 3 b f Darshaan-Instant Desire (USA) (Northern Dancer) 2208^{2} 4213^{3} **>83f<**

Speedybird (IRE) 3 b f Danehill (USA)-Mille Fleurs (USA) (Jacinto) *276^{4}* *332^{8}* 552^{6} (783) **>51a 73+f<**

Speedy Classic (USA) 6 br g Storm Cat (USA)-Shadows Lengthen (Star Appeal) *177^{2}* *272^{3}* *369^{4}* *446^{4}* 542^{8} 2793^{6} *4125^{4}* *4295^{2}* **>64a 64df<**

Speedy Snapper 4 ch g Hotfoot-Pearling *29^{7}* *588^{10}*

>21a 47f<

Speedy Snaps Pride 3 gr g Hallgate-Pineapple's Pride (John de Coombe) *294^{3} 394^{11}* 482^{5} *587^{3} 830^{3} 1457^{3}* 1664^{10} *2497^{5}* 2522^{3} 2761^{2} 3475^{8} 3844^{4} **>45a 51f<**

Spencer's Revenge 6 ch g Bay Express-Armour of Light (Hot Spark) *(71) (191) (323) 358^{2} 401^{3} 1049^{7}* (1255) *(3950)* (4156) 4240^{2} **>80a 79f<**

Spender 6 b or br g Last Tycoon-Lady Hester *61^{3} 123^{2} (188) 272^{4} 369^{3} 446^{6} (498)* 656^{3} 926^{2} 1106^{12} (2867) 3087^{7} 3376^{6} 3777^{9} 4113^{8} **>82a 74f<**

Sphinx Levelv (IRE) 2 ch c Digamist (USA)-Fantoccini (Taufan (USA)) 1540^{P} *2143^{4} 2380^{6}* 2857^{3} 3233^{9} 3612^{13} *4339^{7}* **>55a 52f<**

Spice and Sugar 5 ch m Chilibang-Pretty Miss (So Blessed) 778^{W} *1075^{7}* **>40a 43f<**

Spillo 2 b c Midyan (USA)-Myth (Troy) 3663^{18} 3868^{8} 4070^{3} **>84f<**

Spinning Mouse 2 b f Bustino-Minute Waltz (Sadler's Wells (USA)) 4169^{9} 4320^{16} **>48f<**

Spiral Flyer (IRE) 2 b br f Contract Law (USA)-Souveniers (Relko) 3157^{13} 3765^{13} 4050^{11} **>49f<**

Spirito Libro (USA) 2 b f Lear Fan (USA)-Teeming Shore (USA) (L'Emigrant (USA)) 2542^{4} 2771^{4} 3008^{3} (3312) (3570) 3721^{8} 3894^{11} 4075^{7} **>65f<**

Spirituelle 3 b f Distant Relative-Haunting 431^{9} 573^{6} 3311^{5} 3704^{17} **>57f<**

Spitfire Bridge (IRE) 3 b c Cyrano de Bergerac-Maria Renata (Jaazeiro (USA)) *560^{3} 626^{5}* 818^{3} *1320^{4}* 1509^{6} (1771) 3889^{8} 3987^{3} **>48a 60f<**

Splash of Salt (IRE) 5 b m Salt Dome (USA)-Indian Splash (Prince Tenderfoot (USA)) *39^{8} 134^{4} 165^{9} 287^{6} 359^{4} 499^{6}* 541^{10} 1321^{9} 1785^{9} 2054^{8} 2338^{4} **>42a 42f<**

Splicing 2 ch f Sharpo-Soluce (Junius (USA)) 1653^{2} 2011^{4} 3228^{3} 3548^{7} **>73f<**

Splintercat (USA) 3 ch f Storm Cat (USA)-My Cherie Amour (USA) (Sham (USA)) 613^{4} 2393^{3} (3226) 3451^{2} 3823^{4} **>88f<**

Splinter (IRE) 2 b c Warning-Sharpthorne (USA) (Sharpen Up) (2515) **>80+f<**

Sporting Fantasy 2 b c Primo Dominie-Runelia (Runnett) 617^{9} 760^{8} 1590^{3} 2047^{2} (2158) 2483^{9} 2735^{4} *3953^{9}* **>22a 61f<**

Sporting Risk 3 b g Risk Me (FR)-Sunday Sport's Pet (Mummy's Pet) 761^{10} 1124^{18} 1512^{8} 2033^{3} 2503^{13} 2881^{4} *3075^{5}* 3455^{14} 3685^{7} **>46a 53f<**

Sporting Spirit 5 br g Dunbeath (USA)-Silent Plea (Star Appeal) 1863^{12} 2254^{8} **>35da 1f<**

Sports View 6 b h Mashhor Dancer (USA)-Persian Express (Persian Bold) 582^{15} **>27f<**

Spot Prize (USA) 4 ch f Seattle Dancer (USA)-Lucky Brook (USA) (What Luck (USA)) 1056^{3} 1408^{5} 1636^{3} 1805^{4} **>102df<**

Spotted Eagle 2 ch g Risk Me (FR)-Egnoussa (Swing Easy (USA)) 1406^{5} **>61f<**

Spout 3 b f Salse (USA)-Arderelle (FR) (Pharly (FR)) 620^{10} (1139) 1729^{3} (3831) 4030^{3} **>111f<**

Spread The Word 3 b f Deploy-Apply (Kings Lake (USA)) 1473^{9} 1691^{9} 2568^{3} 3657^{9} 3898^{2} 4135^{14} **>67f<**

Spring Campaign (IRE) 2 b c Sayaarr (USA)-March The Second (Millfontaine) 3436^{5} 3994^{4} 4172^{4} **>68f<**

Spring Loaded 4 b c Last Tycoon-Time For Romance (Cure The Blues (USA)) *227^{8} 279^{8}* **>30a 62f<**

Spring Silhouette 2 b f Kind of Hush-Hasland (Aragon) 1821^{5} 2185^{8} 2542^{8} 2951^{8} 4100^{12} 4230^{8} **>34f<**

Springtime Affair 4 br f Danzig Connection (USA)-Springtime Sugar (USA) (Halo (USA)) *46^{9}* 1349^{7} 3986^{9} **>7a 56f<**

Spumante 3 ch g Executive Man-Midier (Comedy Star (USA)) 1979^{10} 2278^{2} 2654^{6} 4156^{14} 4249^{19} **>43a 69f<**

Squandamania 2 b c Ela-Mana-Mou-Garden Pink (FR) (Bellypha) 4320^{17} **>52f<**

Squire Corrie 3 b g Distant Relative-Fast Car (FR) (Carwhite) 621^{11} 850^{12} 1982^{3} 2199^{10} 3341^{2} 3681^{7} (3905) 4142^{3} *4295^{4}* **>64a 70f<**

Squires Mount 3 b f Sharpo-Plaything (High Top) 522^{10} **>30f<**

St Adele (USA) 2 b f Pleasant Colony (USA)-Northern Sunset (Northfields (USA)) 4241^{10} **>55f<**

Staffin 2 b f Salse (USA)-Fetlar (Pharly (FR)) 1670^{3} (2083) 2947^{2} 3216^{2} 3561^{7} **>90f<**

Stage Struck (IRE) 3 b f Sadler's Wells (USA)-Sun Princess (English Prince) 797^{3} (1717) 2110^{F} 2738^{14} 3156^{2} 3388^{11} **>87f<**

Stalled (IRE) 5 b h Glenstal (USA)-Chauffeuse (Gay Fandango (USA)) 423^{8} 632^{0} 795^{10} *1086^{7}* 1349^{5} 1622^{3} (1937) 2197^{3} *2592^{4} 4336^{6}* **>65a 63f<**

Stamshaw 6 ch m Noalto-Saint Motunde (Tyrant (USA)) 4232^{7} **>49da 26f<**

Standman 3 ch c Never so Bold-Sister Sophie (Effervesci $902a^{3}$ **>86f<**

Standown 2 b c Reprimand-Ashdown (Pharly (FR)) (1177) 1772^{3} 2483^{2} 2706^{9} (3651) 3901^{4} 3990^{6} 4077^{4} 4279^{7} **>73f<**

Stand Tall 3 b c Unfuwain (USA)-Antilla (Averof) 431^{7} 616^{6} 1150^{7} 1524^{8} 2425^{8} 3492^{18} 3783^{12} 4280^{4} **>53f<**

Stand Your Ground 2 b c Common Grounds-Proserpina (FR) (Shafaraz (FR)) 2801^{6} 3895^{9} **>45f<**

Star And Garter 2 ch f Soviet Star (USA)-On Show (Welsh Pageant) 3133^{3} 3495^{3} 3763^{6} 4085^{4} **>77f<**

Star Anise 3 ch f Prince Daniel (USA)-Elmajarrah (CAN) (Caro) 3409^{5} 3559^{7} **>38f<**

Star Carnival (USA) 4 b c Nashwan (USA)-Tell Me Sumthing (USA) (Summing (USA)) $2389a^{9}$ **>109f<**

Starfida 2 b f Soviet Star (USA)-Stufida (Bustino) 3948^{16} **>45f<**

Star Fighter 3 gr c Siberian Express (USA)-Eezepeeze (Alzao (USA)) *59^{4} 189^{4} (273) 301^{7} 529^{5}* 654^{4} *1030^{7}* 1254^{4} 1529^{6} 1696^{6} 3182^{7} *4298^{6}* **>54a 58f<**

Star Finch (FR) 2 b c $3793a^{7}$ **>60f<**

Star Information 3 ch f Mazilier (USA)-Mary Miller (Sharpo) *60^{4} 85^{9} 189^{8} 258^{12}* **>30a 20f<**

Starlight Flyer 8 b h In Fijar (USA)-Nareen (USA) (The Minstrel (CAN)) 586^{9} 729^{8} 1048^{7} *1078^{4}* 3234^{11} 3385^{5} 3619^{12} **>30da 45?f<**

Star Manager (USA) 5 b h Lyphard (USA)-Angel Clare (FR) (Mill Reef (USA)) (714) 1851^{14} 2419^{4} 2672^{7} 3729^{13} 4035^{6} 4227^{3} **>90f<**

Starmaniac (USA) 2 b c Septieme Ciel-Silver Lane (Silver Hawk) $3483a^{2}$ $4250a^{2}$ **>96f<**

Star of Gold 3 b c Night Shift (USA)-Sure Gold (Glint of Gold) 1094^{21} 1354^{8} 1679^{6} 1859^{2} 2278^{3} 2537^{4} 2979^{3} (3128) 3439^{6} 3980^{16} 4157^{17} **>74f<**

Starofgreatintent (USA) 3 ch c Lomond (USA)-Soliciting (USA) (Sassafras (FR)) 1173^{8} 1486^{10} **>64f<**

Star of Persia (IRE) 3 ch or gr c Persian Bold-Caranina (USA) (Caro) 1755^{5} (2086) 2571^{7} (2950) (3374) **>54+a 96+f<**

Star of Ring (IRE) 2 b c Taufan (USA)-Karine (Habitat) 1752^{6} 2529^{5} **>71f<**

Star of the Glen 9 b h Glenstal (USA)-Bamstar 2280^{4} 2452^{6} **>37f<**

Star of Zilzal (USA) 3 b c Zilzal (USA)-Tell Me Sumthing (USA) (Summing (USA)) (1370) 1837^{8} 2105^{6} 3191^{10} 3473^{4} (3845) 4257^{3} **>110f<**

Star Performer (IRE) 4 b c Petorius-Whitstar (Whitstead) *2290^{7}* 2611^{4} 2955^{6} 3396^{5} 3685^{15} 3808^{19} **>26a 55f<**

Star Player 9 ch h Simply Great (FR)-Star Girl 998^{13} 1313^{7} 1840^{17} 3817^{9} 4026^{8} 4166^{5} **>59f<**

Star Quest 8 b h Rainbow Quest (USA)-Sarah Siddons (Le Levanstell) *9^{5}* **>52a 58f<**

Star Rage (IRE) 5 b h Horage-Star Bound (Crowned Prince (USA)) 1558^{5} 1768^{7} 1840^{24} 2098^{11} 2238^{5} (2854) (2996) 3071^{5} 3162^{11} 3262^{2} (3412) 3445^{7} 3774^{4} 3849^{4} 3978^{4} 4036^{3} 4118^{13} **>77a 91f<**

Starry Eyed 3 b f Warning-Star of the Future (USA) (El Gran Senor (USA)) (3282) 3598^{6} 4319^{2} **>90f<**

Starry Typhoon 5 b h Double Schwartz-Cathedra (So Blessed) 901a^{3} **>104f<**

Starsport (IRE) 4 ch g Salt Dome (USA)-Ivory Smooth (USA) (Sir Ivor) 541^{9} 739^{12} 1426^{14} **>59f<**

Star Standard (USA) 3 b c Risen Star-Hoist Emy's Flag (Hoist t 1710a^{2} *4308a^{5}* **>122a 115f<**

Star Talent (USA) 4 b c Local Talent (USA)-Sedra (Nebbiolo) (652) 814^{5} 883^{7} **>114df<**

Star Tulip 3 b f Night Shift (USA)-Silk Petal (Petorius) 621^{4} 939^{8} (1305) 2443^{10} **>97f<**

Star Witness (IRE) 3 b c Contract Law (USA)-Star Heading (Upper Case (USA)) *99^{5}* **>42a 76f<**

Stash the Cash (IRE) 4 b c Persian Bold-Noble Girl (Be Friendly) 593^{2} **>84df<**

Statajack (IRE) 7 b g King of Clubs-Statira 623^{15} 918^{3} 1314^{4} **>96f<**

State Approval 2 b c Pharly (FR)-Tabeeba (Diesis) *1570^{2}* 1690^{7} *2075^{2}* 3701^{12} 3985^{11} 4263^{3} **>64a 69f<**

State Crystal (IRE) 4 b f High Estate-Crystal Spray (Beldale Flutter (USA)) 1235a^{7} **>113f<**

State Law 3 b c Law Society (USA)-Miss Zadig 618^{3} (1814) 2343^{2} 2738^{4} 3066^{7} 3500^{2} 3926^{3} **>97f<**

Stately 2 ch f Be My Chief (USA)-Lady Barrister (Law Society (USA)) 1375^{3} 1670^{12} *2958^{9}* 3546^{10} (3721) 3985^{3} 4151^{15} **>31a 56f<**

Stately Dancer 2 b f Be My Guest (USA)-Wild Pavane (Dancing Brave (USA)) 4103^{17} 4212^{3} **>69f<**

Stately Home (IRE) 4 b or br c Fools Holme (USA)-Water Splash (USA) (Little Current (USA)) 1638^{11} 1771^{4} 2050^{3} (2175) 2452^{2} 2569^{7} **>66f<**

State of Caution 2 b c Reprimand-Hithermoor Lass (Red Alert) 3900^{17} 4058^{5} **>71f<**

State Theatre (IRE) 2 b c Sadler's Wells (USA)-Fruition (Rheingold) 3868^{9} **>80+f<**

State Visitor 2 b c Be My Guest (USA)-Totham (Shernazar) 1184^{17} **>42f<**

Static Love 2 b f Statoblest-Run for Love (Runnett) 554^{7} *604^{6}* 4155^{11} **>7a 19f<**

Statistician 3 b g Statoblest-Sharp Lady 924^{4} 1150^{8} 1515^{3} 1949^{2} (2190) **>76f<**

Statius 3 ch c Statoblest-Kuwait Night (Morston (FR)) *315^{4}* 442^{10} *603^{3}* 722^{3} 966^{2} 1094^{2} 1151^{2} 1380^{6} (2786) 3112^{2} 3230^{4} 3715^{11} 4040^{8} (4142) **>57a 83f<**

Statomist 3 ch f Statoblest-Misty Arch (Starch Reduced) 754^{9} *1214^{11}* 1265^{12} 1679^{16} 1972^{8} *2295^{11}* 3622^{22} **>4a 32f<**

Statoyork 2 b c Statoblest-Ultimate Dream (Kafu) 2693^{5} 3340^{6} **>62f<**

Steadfast Elite (IRE) 4 b f Glenstal (USA)-Etching (Auction Ring (USA)) 839^{20} 3665^{7} **>35f<**

Steady Ready Go (IRE) 3 b c Night Shift (USA)-Smeralda (GER) (Dschingi's Khan) 1010a^{4} 1178^{2} (1888a) **>105f<**

Steady Risk 4 ch c Risk Me (FR)-Greenstead Lass (Double-U-Jay) 2832^{18} 3098^{10} 3305^{10} **>7a 24df<**

Steal 'Em 2 b f Efisio-Eastern Ember (Indian King (USA)) 1597^{8} *2143^{W}* 3210^{5} 3339^{15} 3821^{4} **>70f<**

Stealth Attack (IRE) 2 b c Fayruz-Adivara (Tyrnavos) 436^{10} 859^{4} 1562^{2} 1857^{5} 3300^{4} 3937^{22} **>65df<**

Steamroller Stanly 2 b c Shirley Heights-Miss Demure (Shy Groom (USA)) 3873^{9}

Steepholme 3 ch f Fools Holme (USA)-Shalati (FR) (High Line) 1125^{8} 1371^{8} 1719^{8} 4131^{11} *4270^{11}* **>46f<**

Steinway (SWE) 2 c 3909a^{2} **>71f<**

Stellar Line (USA) 2 ch c Zilzal (USA)-Stellaria (USA) (Roberto (USA)) 1726^{8} 3494^{4} 3821^{2} **>72f<**

Stelvio 3 b c Shirley Heights-Beveridge (USA) (Spectacular Bid (USA)) 711^{4} (1099) (1852) **>102f<**

Step Aloft 3 b f Shirley Heights-Pas de Deux 853^{10} 1339^{4} 3016^{2} 3756^{2} 4003^{2} 4201^{2} **>88f<**

Stephanentse 5 gr m Another Realm-Stephandre *183^{6}* **>23a 35f<**

Stephensons Rocket 4 ch g Music Boy-Martian Princess (Cure The Blues (USA)) 639^{8} 723^{12} 1193^{7} 3719^{10} 4041^{20} **>67f<**

Step On Degas 2 b f Superpower-Vivid Impression (Cure The Blues (USA)) 1938^{5} 2552^{9} 3379^{3} 3538^{2} **>68f<**

Stereo Dancer 2 b c Groom Dancer (USA)-Trystero (Shareef Dancer (USA)) 3352^{8} **>26f<**

Sterling Fellow 2 b c Pharly (FR)-Favorable Exchange (USA) (Exceller (USA)) 3672^{11} 4222^{5} **>45f<**

Sternkonig (IRE) 5 gr h Kalaglow-Sternwappen (3698a) 3914a^{2} 4182a^{3} **>123f<**

Stevie's Wonder (IRE) 5 ch h Don't Forget Me-Azurai (Dance In Time (CAN)) *(36) (121) 193^{2} 246^{2}* 811^{9} 1254^{5} (1502) 1844^{4} 2658^{8} *(2920) 3245^{4}* 3646^{9} (3884) *4126^{2} 4270^{4}* **>76a 69f<**

Sticks and Stones (IRE) 3 b c Waajib-Maiacourt (Malacate (USA)) 1130^{8} 1299^{7} 1619^{4} 1907^{4} **>83f<**

Sticks Mckenzie 2 ch c Hadeer-Tithing (USA) (Nureyev (USA)) 2408^{13} 2615^{5} 2926^{5} 3780^{7} 3985^{15} **>63f<**

Stiffelio (IRE) 3 ch c Be My Guest (USA)-Ivor's Honey 711^{5} 979^{5} 1636^{2} 1925^{3} 2273^{4} 2936^{5} (3131) **>105f<**

Stiletto Blade 3 b c Dashing Blade-On The Tiles (Thatch (USA)) 622^{3} 792^{3} 945^{3} 1107^{8} **>104f<**

Still Here (IRE) 2 b g Astronef-Covey's Quick Step (Godswalk (USA)) *2962^{9} 3243^{4} 3509^{5} 3738^{3}* 3937^{20} **>60a 7f<**

Stinging Reply 3 ch f Belmez (USA)-Nettle (Kris) (779) 1183^{22} 1793^{5} 2152^{2} 2411^{6} 2864^{3} **>81f<**

Stipple 4 ch f Blushing Scribe (USA)-April *158*^{9} *218*^{5} 1016^{14} 1404^{8} **>26a 44df<**

St Kitts 4 b f Tragic Role (USA)-T Catty (USA) (Sensitive Prince (USA)) 4331^{6} **>51f<**

St Louis Lady 4 gr f Absalom-Pearl Cove (Town And Country) 2832^{8} 3181^{3} 3439^{10} **>61f<**

St Mawes (FR) 2 ch c Shahrastani (USA)-Exemina (USA) (Slip Anchor) 2320^{9} (3009) **>75+f<**

Stoleamarch 2 br c Daring March-Pennine Star (IRE) (Pennine Walk) 964^{6} 1266^{6} 1665^{10} **>42f<**

Stolen Kiss (IRE) 3 b or br f Taufan (USA)-Sweet Goodbye (Petorius) 674^{4} 823^{5} 966^{4} 1342^{2} 1453^{2} (1677) 1924^{5} 2252^{2} 2394^{5} 3166^{5} 3667^{2} 3715^{3} 3878^{15} 4033^{14} **>79f<**

Stolen Melody 3 b f Robellino (USA)-Song of Hope (Chief Singer) 3755^{9} 3943^{28} 4122^{5} 4156^{9} **>79f<**

Stolen Music (IRE) 2 b f Taufan (USA)-Causa Sua (Try My Best (USA)) 4048^{13} **>47f<**

Stone Cross (IRE) 3 b c Pennine Walk-Micro Mover (Artaius (USA)) 477^{2} 698^{5} **>66f<**

Stoneham Girl 3 b f Nomination-Persian Tapestry (Tap On Wood) 453^{10} 1974^{20} 3958^{7} **>5f<**

Stone Ridge (IRE) 3 b c Indian Ridge-Cut in Stone (USA) (Assert) 635^{10} (730) 962^{6} 2240^{7} 2616^{5} 3214^{5} 3732^{7} (4116) 4267^{13} **>95f<**

Stoney End (USA) 2 b c High Brite (USA)-Cranareen (USA) (Nice Dancer (CAN)) 2615^{8} **>52f<**

Stoney Valley 5 b h Caerleon (USA)-Startino (Bustino) 632^{8} 795^{7} 1144^{9} 1386^{7} **>84df<**

Stoop To Conquer 2 b c Machiavellian (USA)-Chesnut Tree (USA) (Shadeed (USA)) 2320^{11} 2796^{5} **>63f<**

Stoppes Brow 3 b c Primo Dominie-So Bold (Never so Bold) *(40) (74) 196*^{3} *(345) 498*^{W} 621^{15} 2067^{7} 2491^{6} 2641^{4} 2831^{4} (3390) 3619^{4} 3771^{3} 4134^{2} **>87a 77f<**

Stop Play (IRE) 2 b f Distinctly North (USA)-Church Mountain (Furry Glen) 1361^{5} 1579^{5} (2508) 2779^{7} 2991^{3} 4077^{2} 4206^{5} 4243^{7} 4321^{5} **>76f<**

Stoproveritate 6 ch m Scorpio (FR)-Luscinia (Sing Sing) 430^{8} 568^{7} 1252^{2} *2630*^{4} **>68a 51f<**

Storiths (IRE) 5 b h Double Schwartz-Atlantic Dream (USA) (Muscovite (USA)) 652^{3} 953^{2} 1108^{4} 1284^{5} 2097^{6} 2699^{3} 3191^{4} **>115f<**

Stormaway (ITY) 3 ch c Glenstal (USA)-Smurfiusa (USA) (Sharpen Up) 635^{9} 1173^{11} 1383^{6} 1922^{4} 2177^{5} 2439^{7} **>71f<**

Storm Bidder 4 b g Gabitat-Queen's Bidder (Auction Ring (USA)) *122*^{7} *402*^{7} 1323^{20} 1756^{7} **>41da 40f<**

Storm Bid (USA) 3 b br c Storm Cat (USA)-Slam Bid (USA) (Forli (ARG)) 761^{2} (1258) 1698^{4} **>87f<**

Storm Flash 3 b f Green Desert (USA)-Storm Warning (Tumble Wind (USA)) 4249^{18} **>43a 64+f<**

Storm Leader 4 br c Squill (USA)-African Dash (African Sky) **>30f<**

Stormless 4 b g Silly Prices-Phyl's Pet 1205^{6} 3743^{12} 3852^{3} 4000^{6} **>43f<**

Storm Trooper (USA) 2 b c Diesis-Stormette (USA) (Assert) 2846^{5} 3416^{2} (3620) 4029^{2} **>100f<**

Storm Wind (IRE) 2 ch c Digamist (USA)-Hilton Gateway (Hello Gorgeous (USA)) 3821^{16} 3989^{16} **>28f<**

Story Line 2 ch f In The Wings-Known Line (Known Fact (USA)) (3832) **>97+f<**

Stotfold Boy (IRE) 2 b c Cyrano de Bergerac-Princess Biddy 1857^{10} 2498^{10} **>17f<**

Straight Thinking (USA) 2 ch c Bering-Sharp Perception (USA) (Sharpen Up) 2597^{4} **>62f<**

Strategic Choice (USA) 4 b c Alleged (USA)-Danlu (USA) (712) 1890a^{3} 2595^{3} 3591a^{9} (3789a) 4014a^{14} **>125f<**

Strategic Ploy 2 b f Deploy-Wryneck (Niniski (USA)) 3881^{5} 4085^{10} 4282^{8} **>53f<**

Strath Kitten 4 ch f Scottish Reel-Elemis (USA) (Sir Ivor) *1319*^{10} **>2a 30df<**

Strathtore Dream (IRE) 4 b or br f Jareer (USA)-Beyond Words (Ballad Rock) 479^{9} 594^{8} 877^{14} 1438^{8} 3667^{23} 3745^{13} 3855^{8} **>38f<**

Strat's Legacy 8 b g Chukaroo-State Romance (Free State) *13*^{7} 1937^{4} (2546) 2745^{6} 3401^{5} 3710^{4} 4135^{10} **>60a 51f<**

Straw Thatch 6 b h Thatching-Lashing (USA) (Storm Bird (CAN)) (1292) 1437^{4} 1557^{7} 2064^{2} 3258^{8} 3410^{6} 3658^{15} 3825^{7} 4062^{12} **>42a 52f<**

Stray Rein 3 gr f Lochnager-Olibanum 3115^{5} 3805^{16}

Streaky Hawk (USA) 3 b c Hawkster (USA)-Veroom Maid (USA) (Distinctive (USA)) 691^{10} 2849^{3} *3245*^{7} *3526*^{4} 3710^{9} 3818^{12} **>54a 71df<**

Streete Dancer (IRE) 2 b f Alzao (USA)-Dwell (USA) (Habitat) 2173^{3} 2705^{4} **>73f<**

Street Lady 5 b m Street Kafu-Lonely Dawn (USA) (Plenty Old (USA)) 1309^{7} 1456^{11} **>25f<**

Streetwise Sid 3 b g Presidium-New Street (USA) (Our Native (USA)) 1906^{9} **>37f<**

Streisand 4 b f Unfuwain (USA)-Maria Isabella (FR) (Young Generation) 4020a^{7} **>102f<**

Strictly Personal (USA) 5 b or br h Secreto (USA)-Tash (USA) (Never Bend) *19*^{3} 1435^{9} 1767^{6} 4000^{19} **>71a 46f<**

Striffolino 3 b c Robellino (USA)-Tizona (Pharly (FR)) (1945) 2062^{5} 2788^{3} 2974^{5} 3396^{11} 3704^{4} **>79f<**

Strike-a-Pose 5 ch m Blushing Scribe (USA)-My Bushbaby 1965^{6} **>46a 37f<**

Strip Cartoon (IRE) 7 ch g Tate Gallery (USA)-Reveal (Pitskelly) 3751^{19} **>49a f<**

Strolling Minstrel (IRE) 4 b c Fayruz-Airy Queen (USA) (Sadair) *96*^{17} **>41f<**

Stronz (IRE) 2 b c Classic Music (USA)-Carnival Fugue 1662^{3} 3025^{5} 3337^{0} 3553^{4} 3873^{5} 4075^{P} **>71f<**

Struggler 3 b c Night Shift (USA)-Dreamawhile (Known Fact (USA)) (608a) (1112a) 1572a^{3} 1896^{2} 2671^{10} **>121f<**

Strumming (IRE) 3 ch f Ballad Rock-Casla (Lomond (USA)) (3227) 3654^{5} **>82f<**

Strutting (IRE) 3 b f Ela-Mana-Mou-Taking Steps (Gay Fandango (USA)) 868^{6} 1139^{3} 1867^{6} 3636^{9} 3932^{6} (4052) 4265^{7} 4316^{2} **>98f<**

Studio Thirty 3 gr c Rock City-Chepstow Vale (USA) (Key To The Mint (USA)) *624*^{8} 1060^{9} 1368^{11} *1459*^{4} 1649^{8} *(1950) 2292*^{U} *2961*^{6} 3207^{6} *4223*^{11} **>50a 50f<**

Stuffed 3 ch c Clantime-Puff Pastry (Reform) 1580^{2} 1847^{2} 3992^{15} 4142^{2} 4280^{2} **>67f<**

Stunning Prospect (USA) 2 b c Gold Seam (USA)-Stunning Native (USA) (Our Native (USA)) 4320^{20} **>49f<**

St Valery 3 b f Statoblest-Fleur du Val (Valiyar) 1522^{3} **>74f<**

Stylish Interval 3 ch g Interrex (CAN)-Super Style (Artaius (USA)) 854^{6} 1124^{16} 1498^{17} 3515^{16} **>37a 66f<**

Stylish Ways (IRE) **3** b c Thatching-Style Of Life (USA) (1373) 1806^{3} 2105^{3} 2205^{5} 4121^{8} **>110f<**
Sualtach (IRE) **2** b c Marju (IRE)-Astra Adastra (Mount Hagen (FR)) 996^{3} 1134^{4} 1715^{2} (1964) 2131^{7} 4042^{4} 4200^{7} **>87df<**
Suave Tern (USA) **4** b c Arctic Tern (USA)-Suavite (USA) (Alleged (USA)) 607a^{8} 1387a^{6} 1709a^{3} **>118f<**
Subfusk **2** b f Lugana Beach-Hush it Up (Tina's Pet) *(1077)* 1259^{5} 1503^{10} 1740^{3} *(1954)* 3858^{13} 4056^{7} *4294^{9}* **>61a 61f<**
Subterfuge **2** br f Machiavellian (USA)-Sandy Island (Mill Reef (USA)) (2749) **>78t+f<**
Subtle One (IRE) **2** b f Polish Patriot (USA)-Subtle Change (IRE) (Law Society (USA)) 3566^{4} 3767^{15} 3915^{14} 4045^{11} **>59f<**
Subya **3** b f Night Shift (USA)-Ashshama (USA) (Arctic Tern (USA)) (620) 1009a^{4} (1242) 2211a^{7} 2763^{6} 3636^{7} **>105f<**
Subzero **3** b c Thatching-Cut No Ice (Great Nephew) 3660^{3} 3854^{2} 3979^{3} (4055) **>101f<**
Sudden Spin **5** b h Doulab (USA)-Lightning Legacy (USA) (Super Concorde (USA)) *(77) 121^{3}* 1292^{6} 1578^{4} *(1880) 2379^{3}* 3047^{4} *3511^{2} 3737^{6}* 3778^{3} *(3952)* **>70a 63f<**
Suedoro **5** b m Hard Fought-Barndoro (Cavo Doro) 642^{14} 753^{5} 776^{9} 1433^{9} (1493) 1996^{6} 2229^{4} 2461^{13} (2772) 2870^{4} (3121) 3726^{8} 3855^{10} **>52f<**
Sue Me (IRE) **3** b or br c Contract Law (USA)-Pink Fondant (Northfields (USA)) *599^{2}* 796^{7} 1094^{5} 1487^{16} 3492^{2} 3615^{9} 4068^{11} 4145^{15} *4337^{12}* **>66a 75f<**
Sue's Artiste **4** b f Damister (USA)-Sedova (USA) (Nijinsky (CAN)) 440^{7} 634^{6} 918^{8} 1851^{18} 2419^{3} 2672^{10} (3611) 3945^{6} (4316) **>98+f<**
Sue's Return **3** b f Beveled (USA)-Return to Tara (Homing) 662^{7} 1306^{2} 1478^{6} 2030^{W} 2287^{5} 2694^{2} 3188^{10} 3374^{8} 3608^{7} 3945^{18} 4087^{3} **>88f<**
Sugarland Express (IRE) **4** br c Roi Danzig (USA)-Island Time (USA) (Bold Hour) 1118a^{10} 2388a^{2} **>117f<**
Sugar Mill **5** b g Slip Anchor-Great Tom 673^{3} 816^{9} 1417^{7} 1767^{3} 3818^{2} (4189) 4326^{12} **>79f<**
Suile Mor **3** b f Satin Wood-Ra Ra (Lord Gayle (USA)) 1124^{13} 1447^{6} 2110^{3} 2450^{2} 2655^{4} 3206^{3} 3426^{5} **>60f<**
Suitor **2** b c Groom Dancer (USA)-Meliora 4080^{14} 4241^{8} **>62f<**
Suivez **5** b h Persian Bold-Butterfly Kiss (Beldale Flutter (USA)) *131^{6} 222^{4} 271^{3} (312) (351) 517^{5}* **>64a 64f<**
Suivez La (USA) **3** ch f Trempolino (USA)-Arisen (USA) (Mr Prospector (USA)) 4309a^{2} **>110f<**
Sujud (IRE) **3** b br f Shaadi (USA)-Sit Elnaas (USA) (Sir Ivor) 2469^{6} 2880^{7} 3573^{5} 3862^{11} 4167^{2} **>56f<**
Sulb (USA) **3** b c El Gran Senor (USA)-Stricly (ARG) (Dancing Moss) (761) (2030) 2689^{6} 3188^{14} **>101f<**
Sul Fosso **3** b c Skyliner-Sveltissima (Dunphy) 479^{5} 596^{3} 880^{9} **>39f<**
Sullamell **4** b g Sulaafah (USA)-Melody Lane (Horage) *1601^{10}*
Sultan's Son **9** b h Kings Lake (USA)-Get Ahead *833^{11}* **>10a f<**
Summerhill Special (IRE) **4** b f Roi Danzig (USA)-Special Thanks (Kampala) 4163^{13} **>68f<**
Summer Retreat (USA) **3** b f Gone West (USA)-Devon Diva (USA) (The Minstrel (CAN)) 442^{13} 1240^{3} 3347^{2} (3656) 3802^{5} **>83f<**
Summertown (USA) **3** ch f Diesis-Solar 630^{2} 2265^{4} **>76f<**
Summer Villa **3** b f Nomination-Maravilla (Mandrake Major) *270^{3} (310) (326) 384^{8}* 1873^{8} 2582^{2} 2733^{3} 2927^{4} 2972^{12} **>57a 55f<**
Summit **4** b c Salse (USA)-Reltop 1780^{5} **>109f<**
Sun Circus **3** b f Statoblest-Carmen Maria (Bold Lad (IRE)) 3762^{12} 4049^{12} 4162^{6} **>48f<**
Sunday Maelstrom (IRE) **2** b f Distinctly North (USA)-Make Your Mark (On Your Mark) 878^{7} 1440^{7} 2302^{5} **>38f<**
Sunday Mail Too (IRE) **3** b f Fayruz-Slick Chick 475^{6} 594^{11} 904^{9} 966^{11} 1450^{6} 1461^{9} 1721^{9} 1819^{4} 1961^{5} 2124^{10} 2160^{6} 2229^{5} 2398^{6} 2463^{7} 2772^{6} 2818^{5} 2997^{6} 3313^{7} 3855^{7} **>44f<**
Sunday News'n'echo (USA) **4** b f Trempolino (USA)-Icy Pop (USA) *271^{12}* 991^{7} (1252) 1310^{2} 1552^{2} 3723^{8} 4000^{18} 4288^{10} **>44a 66f<**
Sunderland Echo **6** br h Daring March-Incarnadine (Hot Spark) 423^{20} 811^{13} 967^{4} 2101^{4} 2392^{7} 3801^{9} 3963^{3} 4205^{4} **>68f<**
Sun Dreamer **6** ch m Dreams to Reality (USA)-Erica Alba (Yukon Eric (CAN)) 3847^{9}
Sundries **5** ch g Kabour-Tolly's Best (Hittite Glory) *3524^{15}* 3649^{12} 3829^{10} **>11f<**
Sungai Mas (USA) **3** ch c Lomond (USA)-Slow March 3294^{10} 3537^{10} 3761^{12} 4099^{6} **>61df<**
Sunley Secure **2** b g Warrshan (USA)-Brown Velvet (Mansingh (USA)) 3652^{2} 3850^{5} **>76f<**
Sun Mark (IRE) **4** ch g Red Sunset-Vivungi (USA) 1150^{11} 1557^{3} 1680^{6} **>60f<**
Sun of Spring **5** b h Green Desert (USA)-Unsuspected 3343^{7} 4118^{14} **>77f<**
Sunoma Valley **3** ch g Hubbly Bubbly (USA)-Empress Valley (Gay Fandango (USA)) 715^{23} 3218^{7} 3448^{5} 3818^{20} **>53f<**
Sunrise Song (FR) **4** ch f General Holme (USA)-Marissiya (Nishapour (FR)) 1709a^{4} (3041a) 3482a^{3} 4014a^{16} 4252a^{3} **>116f<**
Sunrise Special (IRE) **2** b c Petorius-Break of Day 2340^{7} 2693^{7} 3133^{8} 3858^{10} *4273^{5}* **>50a 50f<**
Sunset Harbour (IRE) **2** br f Prince Sabo-City Link Pet (Tina's Pet) 2011^{6} 2412^{5} 2552^{5} 2683^{4} 3520^{3} 3727^{8} **>62f<**
Sunset Reigns (IRE) **2** b f Taufan (USA)-More Candy (Ballad Rock) 2564a^{3} 3197a^{5} **>90f<**
Sunshack **4** b c Rainbow Quest (USA)-Suntrap (USA) (Roberto (USA)) (1387a) (1609) 2213a^{5} (4252a) **>126f<**
Sunshine Belle **3** b f Belfort (FR)-Bali Sunset (Balidar) 685^{7} *1032^{6}* 1164^{3} 1580^{9} 1739^{2} 2024^{7} 2124^{U} **>29a 59f<**
Supamova (USA) **2** b f Seattle Slew (USA)-Maximova (FR) (Green Dancer (USA)) 3708^{3} 3866^{5} **>86f<**
Suparoy **2** b c Midyan (USA)-Champ d'Avril (Northfields (USA)) 2809^{W} 3104^{5} 3266^{3} 3592^{9} 3760^{18} **>61f<**
Super Assignation (IRE) **4** ch f Bold Arrangement-Sabrine (Mount Hagen (FR)) *58^{4} 201^{6}* 1058^{20} **>43a 64f<**
Super Baron **2** b c Emarati (USA)-Carmen Maria (Bold Lad (IRE)) 3883^{18} 4075^{22} **>23f<**
Super Benz **9** ch h Hello Gorgeous (USA)-Investiture *(2) 55^{4} 92^{3} 117^{3} 184^{6} 211^{3}* (2518) 2836^{2} 2853^{2} 3230^{8}

3411[13] 4236[3] 4319[3] **>66a 73f<**

Superbit 3 b c Superpower-On A Bit (Mummy's Pet) *42[5] 132[3] 210[2] 258[3] 305[10]* 502[7] *629[9]* 855[7] *1033[10]* (1445) 1802[3] 2502[9] 2513[4] 2858[6] 3123[11] 3424[13] 3751[7] **>51da 51f<**

Supercool 4 ch g Superlative-Florentynna Bay (Aragon) *80[9] 225[4]* 503[16] **>42a 68f<**

Superensis 5 ch h Sayf El Arab (USA)-Superlife (USA) (Super Concorde (USA)) (2384a) 2720a[3] **>52f<**

Superflex 3 b f Jupiter Island-Off The Mark (On Your Mark) 552[9] 761[16] **>40f<**

Superfrills 2 b f Superpower-Pod's Daughter (IRE) (Tender King) 819[W] 1877[8] 2221[7] 2371[3] 2773[6] 3742[3] 3824[10] *3953[10]* 4230[10] **>10a 46f<**

Supergal 2 b f Superpower-Spinney Hill (Dominion) 595[6] 925[6] 983[6] **>29f<**

Super Gascon 3 b c Lesotho-Superstition (Touching Wo 3038a[3] 4090a[2] **>114f<**

Super Gentle (IRE) 3 b c Fast Gold-Gay Bentley (Riverman) 1229a[2]

Super Gift (IRE) 2 b f Darshaan-Speciality Package 4091a[2]

Super Heights 7 b h Superlative-Shadha (Shirley Heights) *374[14] 414[6] 512[4] 600[5]* **>54a f<**

Super High 3 b c Superlative-Nell of The North (USA) (Canadian Gil (CAN)) 783[6] *(1088) (1952)* 3125[10] 3605[5] 3677[13] 3872[2] 4136[4] 4249[3] 4292[9] **>77a 75f<**

Superior Force 2 ch c Superlative-Gleeful (Sayf El Arab (USA)) 3891[4] 4129[7] **>58f<**

Superlao (BEL) 3 b f Bacalao (USA)-Princess of Import (Import) *173[4] 216[2]* **>59a f<**

Superlativemaximus (IRE) 7 ch h Superlative-Samra (Welsh Saint) 583[9] *2627[8] 2925[P]* **>64da 48f<**

Super Look 3 b f Superlative-False Look (USA) (Alleged (USA)) 1302[6] 1602[10] *2141[10]* **>42f<**

Superluminal 4 b c Unfuwain (USA)-Branitska (Mummy's Pet) 550[2] 935[4] 1256[2] **>80f<**

Supermick 4 ch g Faustus (USA)-Lardana 2747[14] 3344[8] 3475[13] **>49a 23f<**

Supermister 2 br c Damister (USA)-Superfina (USA) (Fluorescent Light (USA)) 2420[5] 2667[9] 3231[5] 3503[4] **>53f<**

Superoo 9 b h Superlative-Shirleen (Daring Display (USA)) 928[8] 1061[3] 1323[3] 1679[7] (1843) 2222[9] 3607[11] 4115[12] *4272[10]* **>41a 75f<**

Super Park 3 b c Superpower-Everingham Park (Record Token) 2697[4] 3166[11] 3466[8] 3777[7] 3878[10] 4113[16] 4236[11] **>70f<**

Superpride 3 b c Superpower-Lindrake's Pride (Mandrake Major) 426[7] 1152[2] 1508[3] 1806[8] 4068[22] 4236[14] 4322[15] **>71f<**

Super Rocky 6 b h Clantime-Starproof (Comedy Star (USA)) *107[9]* (1342) 1461[6] 2179[2] (2338) (2736) (2992) 3279[10] 3878[11] 4113[5] **>56da 80f<**

Super Serenade 6 b h Beldale Flutter (USA)-Super Melody (Song) 1975[12] 2317[3] 2549[9] 2789[7] 2979[5] 3173[2] 3455[4] **>64tf<**

Super Sharp (NZ) 7 ch g Brilliant Invader (AUS)-Aspen Annie (NZ) (Amalgam (USA)) 485[16] **>8f<**

Super Sonata 3 b f Interrex (CAN)-Super Lady *2295[8]* 2665[6] 2877[3] 3051[9] *3522[10]* **>39a 60f<**

Supertop 7 b or br h High Top-Myth (Troy) 905[6] 4101[8] **>61f<**

Super Vite (USA) 3 b f Septieme Ciel (USA)-Erin on your Toes (USA) (Irish River (FR)) 2899a[2] **>108f<**

Supreme Desire 7 gr m Grey Desire-Fire Mountain (Dragonara Palace (USA)) 685[11] 1023[9] 1434[13] 1677[13] 1963[19] 2220[11] **>1a 29f<**

Supreme Power 2 ch c Superpower-Spinner (Blue Cashmere) 2487[6] 2660[8] (3012) 3568[4] 3753[4] 4084[19] 4206[10] **>75f<**

Supreme Scholar 2 b f Superpower-Double Decree (Sayf El Arab (USA)) 1356[12] 1503[8]

Supreme Star (USA) 4 b c Gulch (USA)-Just A Game (Tarboosh (USA)) 1513[10] (1799) 2007[3] (2713) 3024[2] (3238) 3384[2] 3616[2] 3817[3] 4026[6] 4166[2] 4326[11] **>63a 82f<**

Supreme Thought 3 b f Emarati (USA)-Who's That Girl (Skyliner) 1476[2] 1786[5] 2512[5] 3678[5] 3919[22] **>67df<**

Supreme (USA) 3 b f Lomond (USA)-Suprematie (FR) (Gay Mecene (USA)) 957[11] 3392[5] 3725[8] 3843[7] **>57f<**

Suranom (IRE) 3 b c Alzao (USA)-Gracieuse Majeste (Saint (1229a) 1886a[2] (3791a) 4347a[2] **>105f<**

Surcoat 8 b h Bustino-Mullet (Star Appeal) *295[13]* 1444[12] **>11f<**

Sure Care 4 ch f Caerleon (USA)-Sure Gold (Glint of Gold) 1198[4] (2391) 2672[14] 2979[19] 3137[7] **>72f<**

Sure Pride (USA) 7 b h Bates Motel (USA)-Coquelicot (CAN) *374[5]* 1535[11] *1784[5]* **>54a 11f<**

Sure to Win (IRE) 6 ch h Sure Blade (USA)-Mahabba (USA) (Elocutionist (USA)) *138[11]* 738[15] **>12a 18f<**

Surgiva 3 b f Presidium-Miss Skindles (Taufan (USA)) 673[14] 881[9] 1202[13] 1719[10] 2149[6] **>40f<**

Surprise Guest (IRE) 4 ch c Be My Guest (USA)-Olderfleet *8[4] 36[2] 97[4]* 884[16] *1075[8]* 1612[14] 1858[11] 2248[4] *3951[12]* **>60da 46f<**

Surprise Mission 3 ch g Clantime-Indigo (Primo Dominie) 772[9] 1040[8] (1302) (1641) 1936[3] **>73f<**

Surrey Dancer 7 b h Shareef Dancer (USA)-Juliette Marny 721[3] 3993[11] **>75a 75f<**

Surtees 2 b c Easy Goer (USA)-In Full Cry (USA) (Seattle Slew (USA)) 1726[6] 2777[2] 3003[3] 3765[2] **>73f<**

Survey King (NZ) 5 gr g Rough-Cast-Hamana (Namnan) 606a[3] **>116f<**

Susan-H 3 ch f Clantime-Just a Spark (Sparkler) 2162[10] **>29f<**

Suselja (IRE) 4 b f Mon Tresor-Stifen (Burslem) 3808[20] 4101[5] *4336[7]* **>35a 43f<**

Sushi Bar (IRE) 4 gr c Petorius-Sashi Woo (Rusticaro (FR)) 558[12] *1091[2]* (1997) **>64a 63f<**

Suvalu (USA) 3 b c Woodman (USA)-Danlu (USA) 888[3] 3016[10] 3338[5] 3403[4] **>79f<**

Sveltana 3 b f Soviet Star (USA)-Sally Brown (Posse (USA)) (2469) 3598[4] 3926[11] **>87f<**

Swain (IRE) 3 b c Nashwan-Love Smitten (Key to the (1885a) (3194a) (3482a) 4014a[3] **>128f<**

Swallowdale 3 ch f Statoblest-Rambadale (Vaigly Great) *1566[14]* 1942[8] **>13a 37f<**

Swallow Ridge (IRE) 6 ch m Martin John-Sheil-Na-Gig (Ridan (USA)) *56[6] 148[3] 205[2] 341[2] 501[10]* **>34a f<**

Swallows Dream (IRE) 4 ch g Bluebird (USA)-Gay Fantasy (Troy) 956[2] 1303[2] 1621[4] 2012[3] 2599[3] 3593[9] 4028[8] 4163[14] **>90df<**

Swan At Whalley 3 b c Statoblest-My Precious Daisy

(Sharpo) *398^{10}* 426^{4} 754^{10} 1641^{4} 1822^{4} 2024^{4} 3919^{20} 3992^{22} **>58a 64df<**

Swandale Flyer 3 ch g Weldnaas (USA)-Misfire (Gunner B) 1195^{9} 2479^{7} 3063^{5} 3469^{10} 3935^{12} **>44f<**

Swan Flyer 4 b f Hadeer-Fly The Coop (Kris) 1048^{10} 1403^{6} 1622^{9} 2209^{6} 2486^{15} **>47f<**

Swangrove (IRE) 2 b f Classic Music (USA)-Nishapours Baby (Nishapour (FR)) *1077^{8}*

Swaynes Lad 3 b g Sulaafah (USA)-Swaynes Lady 3129^{12} 3618^{11}

Sweet Allegiance 5 b m Alleging (USA)-Child of Grace (King's Leap) 2977^{7} 3347^{4} 3542^{6} 3726^{16} 4043^{17} 4157^{10} **>53f<**

Sweet Amoret 2 b f Forzando-Primrose Way (Young Generation) 2351^{14} 2876^{10} 3495^{W} 3643^{11} **>44f<**

Sweet Caroline 4 br f Squill (USA)-Think Ahead *13^{9} 21^{3} 84^{5} 136^{9} 201^{7}* **>37a 35f<**

Sweet Cheap Pet 3 b f Petong-Westonepaperchase (USA) (Accipiter (USA)) *51^{9} 258^{10} 283^{3} 326^{6}* 789^{13} 880^{8} 1080^{12} 1434^{12} 1824^{12} 2129^{11} **>50a 30f<**

Sweet Disorder (IRE) 5 br m Never so Bold-Mists of Avalon (USA) (Nureyev (USA)) (799a) 1518^{9} **>68f<**

Sweet Glow (FR) 8 b g Crystal Glitters (USA)-Very Sweet (Bellypha) 1840^{14} 4158^{9} **>86f<**

Sweetlittlemystery 4 ch f Gabitat-Bildara (Balidar) 839^{15} 1422^{8} *1951^{W}* 2744^{10} **>22a 45f<**

Sweet Magic 4 ch g Sweet Monday-Charm Bird (Daring March) 796^{2} 1241^{3} 2060^{2} (2617) 3087^{6} **>87f<**

Sweet Mate 3 ch c Komaite (USA)-Be My Sweet *48^{7} 95^{3} 135^{6} 587^{W} (842) 1033^{4}* 1344^{6} *1569^{6}* 1679^{8} 1963^{5} 2491^{2} 2680^{7} 2879^{5} 3750^{5} 3980^{4} 4194^{7} **>63a 55f<**

Sweet Mignonette 7 b m Tina's Pet-Ixia 430^{11} 3462^{5} 3621^{4} (3778) 3993^{4} **>75f<**

Sweet Nature (IRE) 2 b f Classic Secret (USA)-So Kind (Kind of Hush) 2508^{2} 3628^{11} *(3949)* 4077^{18} **>74+a 68f<**

Sweetness Herself 2 ch f Unfuwain (USA)-No Sugar Baby (FR) (Crystal Glitters (USA)) 3620^{3} 3983^{4} **>68f<**

Sweet Pavlova (USA) 3 b f Zilzal (USA)-Meringue Pie (USA) (Silent Screen (USA)) 752^{6} 976^{9} 1442^{2} 1984^{2} (2863) 3571^{10} **>76f<**

Sweet Robin (IRE) 2 b f Mujtahid (USA)-La Romance (USA) (Lyphard (USA)) (1176) 1849^{7} 2216a^{2} 2564a^{2} 3186^{3} 3561^{4} **>96f<**

Sweet Supposin (IRE) 4 b c Posen (USA)-Go Honey Go (General Assembly (USA)) *12^{3} 52^{5} 157^{2} (248) (358) 405^{3} 499^{3}* 636^{7} 784^{3} 1534^{8} *(1951) (2142)* 2797^{7} *(3073)* 3770^{9} *3950^{7}* **>87a 67f<**

Sweet Times 2 ch f Riverman (USA)-Affection Affirmed (USA) (Affirmed (USA)) 3983^{12} 4216^{6} **>64f<**

Sweet Trentino (IRE) 4 b g High Estate-Sweet Adelaide (USA) (The Minstrel (CAN)) *364^{9}* 1323^{14} 1596^{8} 2002^{6} 2269^{4} 2593^{8} *3240^{10}* **>53a 70f<**

Sweet Water (IRE) 3 b f Fayruz-Stamina (Star Appeal) 1453^{6} 1812^{9} **>22ta 50f<**

Sweet Whisper 4 gr f Petong-Softly Spoken (Mummy's Pet) *192^{5} 220^{2} 359^{5} 386^{6}* **>50a 20f<**

Sweet Wilhelmina 2 b f Indian Ridge-Henpot (IRE) (Alzao (USA)) 4218^{9} **>55f<**

Swift Fandango (USA) 2 b c Lear Fan (USA)-Danlu (USA) (2107) 2454^{2} **>82+f<**

Swift Maiden 2 gr f Sharrood (USA)-Gunner Girl (Gunner B) 2791^{6} 3397^{3} 3887^{3} 4208^{13} 4321^{10} **>75f<**

Swift Move 3 ch f Move Off-Phyl's Pet 3853^{12}

Swift Nick Nevison 4 b c Grey Desire-Bunnyloch (Lochnager) *247^{8}* 502^{14} **>38a 35f<**

Swifty Nifty (IRE) 2 b f Runnett-Swift Verdict (My Swallow) 650^{9} 943^{10} 1203^{7} 3940^{5} 4109^{11} **>41f<**

Swingalong Girl 2 ch f Weldnaas (USA)-Singalong Lass (Bold Lad (IRE)) 3895^{14} 4137^{12} 4218^{13} **>20f<**

Swinging Sixties (IRE) 4 b c Fairy King (USA)-La Bella Fontana (Lafontaine (USA)) 2363^{8} 3079^{9} (3920) 4044^{4} **>67f<**

Swinging Tich 6 b m Swing Easy (USA)-Little Tich (Great Nephew) *78^{6} 134^{3} 165^{2} 233^{7} 314^{7} 1760^{8}* 2246^{6} *2377^{13}* 2450^{9} 3871^{9} **>48da 47f<**

Swing Mania (IRE) 2 b f Polish Patriot (USA)-Exclusive Melody (CAN) (Commemorate (USA)) 1298^{5} 2580^{3} *3077^{3} 3244^{4} 3528^{12}* 3744^{5} 3975^{14} **>47a 59f<**

Swish 2 b c Primo Dominie-Honey Pot 1134^{12} 1597^{15} 3307^{7} 3503^{5} 3620^{15} 3809^{15} **>43f<**

Swiss Bank 3 b f Robellino (USA)-Granny's Bank (Music Boy) 3023^{5} 3859^{4} **>76f<**

Swiss Mountain 5 b or br m Formidable-Helvetique (FR) 1529^{13} 2245^{3} **>33f<**

Swiss Valley Lady 2 b f Tout Ensemble-Jokers High (USA) (Vaguely Noble) 429^{2} *(531)* 781^{2} 1035^{2} 1267^{4} **>55a 65f<**

Swivel 3 ch f Salse (USA)-Spin Turn (Homing) 1097^{7} 1283^{3} 1505^{5} 1986^{2} 2184^{2} 3217^{2} 3669^{19} **>78f<**

Swordking (IRE) 6 ch g Kris-Reine Mathilde (USA) (Vaguely Noble) *375^{5} 412^{12} 514^{9} 589^{4}* (649) 737^{12} 866^{10} *1075^{2}* 1552^{6} 1643^{5} *2147^{4} 2495^{3} 2919^{17}* **>57a 54f<**

Sword Master 6 b h Sayf El Arab (USA)-Swordlestown Miss (USA) (Apalachee (USA)) 661^{7} **>73f<**

Swynford Dream 2 b c Statoblest-Qualitair Dream (Dreams to Reality (USA)) 2859^{5} (3670) (3824) 3901^{2} (4097) 4260^{7} **>84f<**

Swynford Flyer 6 b m Valiyar-Qualitairess (Kampala) *387^{9} 397^{2} 421^{4} 530^{7} 605^{10} 835^{11}* 1285^{13} *1762^{8}* 2081^{4} 2310^{6} 2486^{7} 2789^{12} 3258^{4} 3396^{10} 4170^{10} **>45a 45f<**

Sycamore Lodge (IRE) 4 ch g Thatching-Bell Tower 702^{3} 927^{6} 1297^{2} 1421^{2} 1808^{6} 1944^{2} 2373^{2} 2610^{4} 3232^{5} **>78f<**

Sylvan Celebration 4 b f Sylvan Express-Footstool (Artaius (USA)) 905^{7} 1025^{8} 1161^{6} 2396^{9} 2769^{5} 2874^{5} 3171^{4} **>15a 34f<**

Sylvandra 3 b f Mazilier (USA)-Pattis Pet (Mummy's Pet) 694^{14} 939^{6} 1263^{4} 1474^{11} 2266^{6} 2451^{5} 2709^{2} 3175^{6} 3497^{11} 3624^{17} 3972^{4} 4157^{20} 4319^{11} **>66f<**

Sylvan Point 4 b c Reference Point-Sovereign Dona (Sovereign Path) 3798a^{2} 4088a^{2} 4311a^{3} **>119f<**

Sylvan Princess 2 b f Sylvan Express-Ela-Yianni-Mou (Anfield) 3436^{12} 3968^{14} **>20f<**

Sylvan Starlight 5 b or br m Sylvan Express-Kakisa (Forlorn River) 3402^{11} **>41f<**

Sylva Paradise (IRE) 2 b c Dancing Dissident (USA)-Brentsville (USA) (Arctic Tern (USA)) 2182^{6} 2442^{6} 3404^{4} (3873) **>77f<**

Sylvella 2 b f Lear Fan (USA)-Suprematie (FR) (Gay Mecene (USA)) 3948^{13} 4262^{14} **>59f<**

Synergetic (FR) 3 2730a^{6} **>103f<**

Syrian Queen 3 b f Slip Anchor-Rimosa's Pet (Petingo) 1175^{2} 1526^{3} (3537) 4020a^{8} **>82f<**

Syvanie (FR) 3 b f Sicyos-Avanie 4009a^{9} 4254a^{3}

>107f<
Szloto 2 ch c Polish Patriot (USA)-Swinging Gold (Swing Easy (USA)) 2782^{5} 3352^{5} 3666^{11} 3882^{7} **>56f<**

T

Taahhub (IRE) 5 b h Nordico (USA)-Undiscovered (Tap On Wood) 19^{4} 497^{7} 731^{4} 1801^{4} 2002^{8} **>53a 52f<**
Tabard Garden 3 ch f Scottish Reel-Wigeon 1060^{11} 1645^{13} **>28a 42f<**
Tabdeel 3 b c Warrshan (USA)-Tartique Twist (USA) (Arctic Tern (USA)) 673^{6} 3016^{15} (3304) 3705^{8} **>81f<**
Tablets of Stone (IRE) 2 b c Contract Law (USA)-Remember Mulvilla (Ballad Rock) 2791^{15} 3003^{9} 4169^{12} 4285^{12} **>43f<**
Tabook (IRE) 4 b c Cadeaux Genereux-Al Najah (USA) (Topsider (USA)) 2699^{5} 3033^{3} 3446^{6} 3551^{9} 3943^{22} 4160^{6} **>93f<**
Tabriz 2 b f Persian Heights-Faisalah (Gay Mecene (USA)) 1356^{3} 2161^{3} 2608^{3} 3147^{2} 3867^{6} 4192^{6} 4290^{4} **>73f<**
Tachycardia 3 ch f Weldnaas (USA)-Gold Ducat (Young Generation) 25^{4} 59^{7} 144^{5} 287^{8} 319^{7} 473^{7} 832^{5} 1400^{3} (1521) 1660^{13} 1942^{2} 2054^{6} 2642^{3} 2943^{11} 3919^{24} **>44a 59f<**
Tadellal (IRE) 4 ch f Glint of Gold-Meissarah (USA) (Silver Hawk (USA)) 584^{5} 1065^{5} 1367^{7} 2089^{5} 2407^{7} 2747^{7} (3082) 3402^{3} 3735^{5} 4223^{4} 4298^{2} **>70a 63f<**
Tadeo 2 ch c Primo Dominie-Royal Passion (Ahonoora) 684^{4} 836^{2} (1041) 1197^{2} 1584^{2} 1893^{5} 2243^{6} 3220^{3} 3369^{2} 3434^{5} 3668^{3} 4039^{4} (4219) **>99f<**
Tadjoni 3 b c Mtoto-Nobly Born (USA) (The Minstrel (CAN)) 635^{8} 854^{P} **>74f<**
Tael of Silver 3 b f Today and Tomorrow-Schula (Kala Shikari) 43^{6} 381^{5} 411^{6} (732) 862^{9} 1094^{15} 1832^{6} (1972) 2137^{2} 2190^{3} 2229^{6} 3072^{11} 3624^{3} 3800^{19} 4165^{16} **>56a 68f<**
Tafahhus 3 b c Green Desert (USA)-Mileeha (USA) (Blushing Groom (FR)) 524^{4} (727) 1013^{5} (1276) 1429^{3} 1624^{7} (1982) (2168) 2507^{5} 2802^{7} 3316^{6} **>88f<**
Taffeta Silk (USA) 4 b f Clever Trick (USA)-Silk Sari (USA) (Raja Baba (USA)) 1342^{5} 1700^{4} 1975^{5} 2344^{3} 2659^{3} 4125^{8} **>41a 70f<**
Tafia (IRE) 4 ch f Pharly (FR)-Tafila (Adonijah) 2638^{4} 3030^{5} 3810^{15} 4223^{14} **>28a 59f<**
Tagatay 2 b g Nomination-Salala (Connaught) 4338^{10} **>16a f<**
Tagula (IRE) 2 b c Taufan (USA)-Twin Island (IRE) (Standaan (FR)) 1184^{5} (1485) 1838^{4} (2347) (3330a) 4106^{3} **>112f<**
Tahya (USA) 2 ch f Elmaamul (USA)-Tatwij (USA) (Topsider (USA)) 2487^{10} 3892^{5} 4109^{10} **>62f<**
Taibhseach (USA) 3 b f Secreto-Ribonette (Ribot) 1390a^{9} 1708a^{4} **>99f<**
Taiki Blizzard (USA) 0 01 c Seattle Slew-Tree of Knowledge (Sassaf 1120a^{3} **>121f<**
Taipan (IRE) 3 b c Last Tycoon-Alidiva (Chief Singer) 619^{8} 1103^{4} 1619^{2} 1872^{9} **>96f<**
Tajannub (USA) 3 ch f Dixieland Band (USA)-Empress Jackie (USA) (Mount Hagen (FR)) 659^{4} 921^{12} 1488^{6} 1895^{17} (2416) (3358) **>109f<**
Tajar (USA) 3 b c Slew O' Gold (USA)-Mashaarif (USA) (Mr Prospector (USA)) 815^{11} 1147^{6} 1504^{7} 2503^{4} 2993^{3} 3657^{10} 3872^{5} **>67f<**
Tajawall (USA) 3 b c Dixieland Band-Conjinx 1121a^{5} **>102f<**
Takadou (IRE) 4 br c Double Schwartz-Taka (Blakeney) 1795^{4} 2060^{7} 2288^{8} 2823^{6} 3279^{7} 3777^{5} (3880) 3938^{3} 4033^{20} 4119^{2} 4197^{7} 4324^{8} **>97f<**
Takapuna (IRE) 2 ch f Be My Native (USA)-Tenoria (Mansingh (USA)) 570^{4} 644^{3} (1226) 3019^{5} 3267^{5} 3858^{8} **>67f<**
Take A Left 2 b c Formidable (USA)-Casamurrae (Be My Guest (USA)) 1134^{8} (1413) 1556^{3} 1838^{7} 2347^{2} 3163^{3} 3596^{3} **>99f<**
Takeapull 3 ch c Clantime-Dayana (Burglar) 1040^{9} 1559^{6} 1762^{16} **>54df<**
Take A Right 3 b g Skyliner-Miss Colenca (Petong) 2643^{3}
Take Liberties 3 b f Warning-Libertine (IRE) 705a^{3} 1116a^{15} 2561a^{2} 3040a^{2} 3331a^{3} **>114f<**
Take Note (IRE) 2 b c Don't Forget Me-Verthumna (Indian King (USA)) 3009^{6} 3441^{8} **>52f<**
Takeshi (IRE) 3 b f Cadeaux Genereux-Taplow (Tap On Wood) 722^{2} 989^{2} 1692^{10} 2188^{2} 2363^{2} 3057^{5} 3396^{6} 3534^{9} 3685^{6} **>68f<**
Take Two 7 b h Jupiter Island-Dancing Daughter (Dance In Time (CAN)) 3129^{6} **>75?f<**
Takhlid (USA) 4 b c Nureyev (USA)-Savonnerie (USA) (Irish River (FR)) 761^{3} 1168^{3} 1309^{2} 2100^{3} 2803^{5} (3268) (3755) **>90f<**
Taklif (IRE) 3 b c Sadler's Wells (USA)-Porphyrine (FR) (Habitat) 691^{6} 1764^{4} 3730^{3} 3896^{2} 4072^{2} 4220^{3} **>94f<**
Talented Ting (IRE) 6 ch h Hatim (USA)-An Tig Gaelige (Thatch (USA)) 526^{16} 601^{11} 820^{11} 988^{15} 1192^{10} (1491) (1687) 1724^{5} 1742^{6} 2068^{7} 2397^{2} 2999^{3} 3119^{2} 3240^{9} 3255^{4} 3840^{7} **>47a 78df<**
Talent Lady (USA) 2 dk f Personal Flag-Patient One 4175a^{2}
Talk Back (IRE) 3 br c Bob Back (USA)-Summit Talk (Head for Heights) 2316^{8} **>70f<**
Talloires (USA) 5 ch h Trempolino (USA)-Logiciel (Known Fact (USA)) 4307a^{13} **>94f<**
Tallulah Belle 2 b f Crowning Honors (CAN)-Fine a Leau (USA) (Youth (USA)) 3093^{8} 3244^{2} 3523^{6} 3740^{7} 3949^{5} 4231^{11} **>59a 46f<**
Talos (IRE) 7 b h Taufan (USA)-Jovial Josie (USA) 3963^{11} 4166^{10} 4288^{15} **>61f<**
Tamandu 5 b m Petoski-Gohar (USA) (Barachois (CAN)) 4293^{4} **>45a f<**
Tamarind Cove 2 ch g Safawan-Sayf As Houses (Sayf El Arab (USA)) 2635^{8} **>7a f<**
Tamarpour (USA) 8 b h Sir Ivor-Tarsila (High Top) 938^{8} 1328^{3} 1444^{4} 1840^{18} (2154) 2688^{6} 2860^{8} **>73f<**
Tamayaz (CAN) 3 b c Gone West (USA)-Minstrelsy (USA) (The Minstrel (CAN)) (2762) 3199a^{4} **>119f<**
Tamhid (USA) 2 b c Gulch (USA)-Futuh (USA) (Diesis) (2597) 3163^{5} 3886^{2} (4153) **>95f<**
Tamise 8 br m Dominion-Miss Thames (Tower Walk) 1712a^{11} (4309a) **>114f<**
Tamnia 2 br f Green Desert (USA)-Tanouma (USA) (Miswaki (USA)) 1726^{2} (2275) (2554) 3578a^{4} 3692a^{2} 3865^{5} **>99f<**
Tamure (IRE) 3 b c Sadler's Wells (USA)-Three Tails (Blakeney) (691) (917) (1129) 1611^{2} (3794a) 4120^{4}

4307a^{4} **>128f<**

Tanah Merah (IRE) 4 b c Alzao (USA)-Lady's Bridge (USA) (Sir Ivor) *103^{10} 256^{13} 312^{13}* 494^{2} 597^{3} 821^{10} 1596^{18} 4191^{3} **>27a 69df<**

Tanami 3 br f Green Desert (USA)-Propensity (Habitat) 1488^{4} 1870^{6} 2470^{3} **>106f<**

Tancred Mischief 4 b f Northern State (USA)-Mischievous Miss (Niniski (USA)) 672^{15} 2543^{4} 2759^{4} 3052^{3} **>42df<**

Tannerrun (IRE) 3 b f Runnett-Six Penny Express (Bay Express) 904^{11} 1465^{10} 1723^{9} **>76df<**

Tanseeq 4 b c Green Desert (USA)-Kawkeb (USA) (Vaguely Noble) 642^{12} 762^{17} 1081^{5} **>64f<**

Tapatch (IRE) 7 b h Thatching-Knees Up (USA) (Dancing Champ (USA)) *317^{3}* **>73a 62f<**

Tapestry Rose 4 ch f Arrasas (USA)-Sharelle (Relko) 3573^{8} 3876^{11}

Tapintime (USA) 2 b c Timeless Moment (USA)-Dancinmyway (USA) (Far North (CAN)) 617^{4} 2200^{5} 2912^{7} 3613^{4} 3928^{5} 4081^{5} **>69f<**

Tapis Rouge (IRE) 6 ch h Irish River (FR)-Marie Noelle (FR) (Brigadier Gerard) *18^{7} 67^{6} 106^{7}* **>62a 57f<**

Tap On Tootsie 3 b f Faustus (USA)-My Tootsie (Tap On Wood) 1736^{5} 2319^{13} 3294^{11} 3875^{9} **>60f<**

Tappen Lady (IRE) 3 ch f Doulab (USA)-Tappen Zee (Sandhurst Prince) *258^{13} 310^{7}* **>23da 35f<**

Tappeto 3 b g Liboi (USA)-Persian Carpet (FR) (Kalamoun) 2151^{4} 2438^{4} 2790^{3} (3094) 3469^{7} 4051^{6} **>82f<**

Tapping Feet 3 b f Dominion-Vitry (Vitiges (FR)) *47^{7} 141^{4} 243^{7} 468^{9}* 1545^{10} 1771^{12} 2511^{8} **>42a 14f<**

Tara Colleen (IRE) 3 b f Petorius-Peace Mission (Dunbeath (USA)) *10^{5}* 1172^{14} 1366^{10} 1512^{16} 1962^{18} 2318^{8} 2491^{13} *2963^{P}* **>56da 54f<**

Tarajan (USA) 3 ch g Shahrastani (USA)-Tarafa (Akarad (FR)) 2559a^{3}

Tarawa (IRE) 3 br g Caerleon (USA)-Sagar (Habitat) 1186^{8} (3712) 4035^{3} (4079) (4267) **>104f<**

Tarf (USA) 2 ch f Diesis-Tadwin (Never so Bold) 1163^{2} 1530^{3} 1772^{2} 3053^{2} (3176) 3668^{8} **>95f<**

Tarhelm (IRE) 3 br c Helm Reef-Tarabella (Dance In Time (CAN)) 1396a^{5} **>104f<**

Tarhelm (ITY) 0 3790a^{6} **>102f<**

Tarhhib 3 br f Danzig (USA)-Cancan Madame (USA) (Mr Prospector (USA)) (695) 930^{3} 1138^{8} **>94+f<**

Tarian (USA) 3 b c Lyphard (USA)-Chain Fern (USA) (Blushing Groom (FR)) 4245^{7} **>58f<**

Ta Rib (USA) 2 ch f Mr Prospector (USA)-Madame Secretary (USA) (Secretariat (USA)) 3339^{2} 3832^{3} **>95+f<**

Tarjumaan (USA) 4 b or br g Private Account (USA)-Etoile D'Amore (USA) (The Minstrel (CAN)) *332^{9} 357^{8} 500^{6}* 731^{12} **>55a f<**

Tarneem (USA) 2 b f Zilzal (USA)-Willowy Mood (USA) (Will Win (USA)) 3604^{5} 3816^{2} 4188^{2} **>83f<**

Tarn Lane (IRE) 3 b f Fools Holme (USA)-Amber Lightning (On Your Mark) 1377^{13} *2631^{10}* **>14a 49f<**

Taro Card (IRE) 4 b g Lancastrian-More Chat (Torenaga) 675^{5}

Tarouсca (IRE) 3 b f Tirol-Glendora (Glenstal (USA)) 3761^{9} **>72f<**

Taroudant 8 b g Pharly (FR)-Melbourne Miss (Chaparral (FR)) *108^{5} 295^{4} 412^{5}* **>74a 82df<**

Tarragon (IRE) 5 ch g Good Thyne (USA)-Vanda (Florescence) 3282^{5}

Tarry 2 b f Salse (USA)-Waitingformargaret (Kris) 1977^{14} 2683^{9} (2908) 3345^{6} 3546^{11} 3639^{8} 4141^{2} 4285^{3} **>65f<**

Tarsid 3 ch c Indian Forest (USA)-Small Fee (Blue Cashmere) *420^{13}* 596^{7}

Tart 2 b f Tragic Role (USA)-Fee (Mandamus) 4262^{13} **>60f<**

Tart and a Half 3 b f Distant Relative-Vaigrant Wind (Vaigly Great) 828^{8} 982^{4} 1055^{2} 1277^{4} 1487^{14} 1924^{10} 2067^{3} 2451^{4} 2593^{12} 3166^{4} 3407^{3} 3453^{3} **>85f<**

Tartan Dancer 6 b h Ballacashtal (CAN)-Waltzing Willow (Swing Easy (USA)) 2134^{10}

Tartan Express (IRE) 2 b g New Express-Running Feud (Prince Tenderfoot (USA)) 2336^{5} *2625^{6}* 3080^{7} 3427^{11} **>30f<**

Tartan Gem (IRE) 4 ch c Lomond (USA)-Red Jade 3945^{30} 4163^{20} **>73+a 86f<**

Tarte Aux Pommes (FR) 2 gr f Noblequest-Battle Lady (Persepolis) (2043a) 3584a^{6} 4013a^{6} **>91f<**

Tarthooth (IRE) 4 ch c Bob Back (USA)-Zoly (USA) (Val de L'Orne (FR)) 696^{5} 1058^{4} (1607) 1840^{10} 2248^{2} 2569^{12} **>76f<**

Tarvisio (IRE) 8 b h Northern Baby-Bold And Bright (FR) (Bold Lad (USA)) 1888a^{2} **>99f<**

Tascilla (GER) 3 dk f Kamiros-Tawinja (Windwurf) 1705a^{2} 4018a^{2} **>102f<**

Tasdik 2 ch f Unfuwain (USA)-Stay Sharpe (USA) (Sharpen Up) 4050^{3} 4246^{2} **>75f<**

Tashjir (USA) 2 ch f Slew O' Gold (USA)-Mashaarif (USA) (Mr Prospector (USA)) 3900^{23} 4048^{10} 4247^{10} **>55f<**

Tasliya (USA) 2 ch f Gulch (USA)-Aghani (USA) (Blushing Groom (FR)) 1627^{7} 1964^{7} 4103^{9} 4279^{3} **>71f<**

Tassagh Bridge (IRE) 5 b m Double Schwartz-Kasarose (Owen Dudley) *28^{9}* **>19a 22df<**

Tatika 5 ch h Tate Gallery (USA)-Independentia (Home Guard (USA)) *394^{2}* 559^{3} 812^{2} 928^{4} 1299^{8} 2010^{11} 2330^{6} **>74a 78f<**

Tatjana 4 ch f Soviet Star (USA)-Dancing Crystal (Kris) 2510^{7} **>64df<**

Taufan Blu (IRE) 6 b m Taufan (USA)-Engage *337^{7}* **>49a 89df<**

Taufan Boy 2 b c Taufan (USA)-Lydia Maria (Dancing Brave (USA)) 2242^{3} 2681^{3} *(3525)* 3809^{7} 4111^{11} **>80a 80f<**

Taufan's Melody 4 b g Taufan (USA)-Glorious Fate (Northfields (USA)) 918^{2} 1135^{5} 1853^{8} 2596^{2} 3164^{2} (3836) (4187a) (4346a) **>115f<**

Taurean Fire 2 ch c Tina's Pet-Golden Decoy (Decoy Boy) 1356^{10} 2951^{5} 3124^{7} 3670^{9} 4231^{12} **>52f<**

Tauten (IRE) 5 br m Taufan (USA)-Pitaka (Pitskelly) 4209^{14} 4332^{9} **>37f<**

Tawaaded (IRE) 2 ch f Nashwan (USA)-Thaidah (CAN) (Vice Regent (CAN)) 4023^{7} **>57tf<**

Tawafek (USA) 2 br c Silver Hawk (USA)-Tippy Tippy Toe (USA) (Nureyev (USA)) 4063^{13} 4226^{3} **>69f<**

Tawafij (USA) 6 ch h Diesis-Dancing Brownie (USA) (Nijinsky (CAN)) 486^{8} 870^{9} 1299^{2} (2099) 2369^{5} 2647^{5} 2948^{5} 3188^{13} 3411^{10} 3703^{14} **>89df<**

Tawkil (USA) 2 b c Riverman (USA)-Lyphette (FR)

(Lyphard (USA)) 2741[2] (3208) **>92+f<**
Taylord 3 ch c Cadeaux Genereux-Figini (Glint of Gold) 442[5] 502[15] 1016[3] 2067[6] 2692[8] 3640[8] 3678[13] **>61a 73f<**
Taylor (GER) 3 c 4018a[5] **>103f<**
Tazamisha 6 b m Blakeney-Ardverikie (Red Alert) 2300[4]
Te Amo (IRE) 3 b c Waajib-Avebury Ring (Auction Ring (USA)) 829[11] 1222[5] 1941[2] 2616[6] 3755[3] 3926[15] 4202[8] **>87f<**
Tea Service (IRE) 3 b f Roi Danzig (USA)-Tea House (Sassafras (FR)) 2211a[8] **>97f<**
Technological Risk 4 ch c Risk Me (FR)-Technology (FR) (Top Ville) *2290[10]* **>29a f<**
Tec's Champ (IRE) 3 c 808a[5] **>86f<**
Tedburrow 3 b c Dowsing (USA)-Gwiffina (Welsh Saint) 1249[3] 1414[8] (1936) (2239) (2556) (2697) 3166[6] 3411[6] 3715[14] **>88f<**
Tee-Emm 5 b h Lidhame-Tower Glades (Tower Walk) *188[4]* *247[3]* *328[3]* 656[8] 1050[6] 1265[10] 1400[6] (1942) 2092[7] 2521[14] 2887[4] 3123[4] 3333[8] *4295[3]* **>58a 45f<**
Teejay'n'aitch (IRE) 3 b c Maelstrom Lake-Middle Verde (USA) (Sham (USA)) 989[6] 1204[6] 1423[4] 1723[2] 1932[7] 2425[3] 2611[7] 2770[6] 3000[5] 3370[8] 3719[8] 3745[6] 3879[3] 3980[18] **>45f<**
Teen Jay 5 b h Teenoso (USA)-Spoilt Again (Mummy's Pet) 430[3] 1477[5] 2391[3] 2678[3] 3641[10] 3810[14] *4126[4]* **>63a 76f<**
Tee Tee Too (IRE) 3 ch g Hatim (USA)-Scottish Welcome (Be My Guest (USA)) *33[2]* *105[5]* *196[5]* 437[13] 535[4] 823[11] 1023[2] 1157[13] 1580[4] 1847[13] 1956[3] 2425[W] 2540[6] 2784[17] 3000[3] 3098[11] **>77da 67df<**
Teeton Thomas 6 b g Sunley Builds-Royal Darwin (Royal Palm) 3282[9]
Teetotaller (IRE) 4 gr c Taufan (USA)-Mainly Dry (The Brianstan) (765) 922[20] 1174[13] 1599[3] **>73f<**
Tejano Run (USA) 3 ch c Tejano (USA)-Royal Run (USA) (Wavering Monarch (USA)) 1006a[2] **>120f<**
Telasco (GER) 5 ch h Sharpo-Tschagra (Quick Fling) 1236a[3] **>95f<**
Telephus 6 b g Efisio-Mrs Bizz *321[8]* *403[8]* 817[18] **>50a 49f<**
Tellurium (USA) 4 b g Timeless Moment-Chinguetti (Green Dancer) 2558a[3] **>106f<**
Telmo (IRE) 3 b c Alleged (USA)-Chilly Welcome (General Assembly (USA)) 1600[7] 4003[6] 4167[10] **>61f<**
Telopea 4 b f Teenoso (USA)-Orlaith (Final Straw) 738[7] 1324[6] 1693[7] 2266[8] **>83f<**
Temora (IRE) 3 b f Ela-Mana-Mou-Romara 1983[2] (2329) 3636[8] **>92f<**
Tempering 9 b h Kris-Mixed Applause (USA) *(83)* *91[3]* *186[6]* *421[2]* *517[4]* *771[14]* *4335[12]* **>64a 26f<**
Tempting (IRE) 3 b f Waajib-Balela (African Sky) 797[15] 1053[5] **>63f<**
Temptress 2 br f Kalaglow-Circe (Main Reef) 3452[3] 3643[8] 3869[8] **>36f<**
Tennyson Bay 3 b c Allazzaz-Richards Folly (Hotfoot) 585[13] 884[18] **>27f<**
Tenor 4 b c Music Boy-Songstead (Song) *32[6]* *93[6]* *167[7]* *184[7]* *(247)* *(328)* *498[3]* 639[2] (723) 796[8] 926[6] 1152[6] 1271[4] 1461[5] 1508[7] 1765[10] 3667[26] 3783[16] 3878[12] 3992[11] **>68a 54f<**
Tenorio 3 b c Law Society (USA)-One Life (USA) (L'Emigrant (USA)) (1782) 1852[9] (2415) 3595[3] **>104f<**
Ten Past Six 3 ch c Kris-Tashinsky (USA) (Nijinsky (CAN)) (955) 1107[7] 2121[2] 3728[10] **>101f<**
Tenpenny 3 ch f Hadeer-Tithing (USA) (Nureyev (USA)) 484[6] **>25f<**
Teofilo Stephenson (IRE) 2 1889a[10]
Teoroma 5 ch h Teofane-Poppy Kelly (Netherkelly) *1319[3]* 1607[10] *2090[5]* 2268[6] **>33a 25f<**
Terdad (USA) 2 ch c Lomond (USA)-Istiska (FR) (Irish River (FR)) 3449[5] 3709[5] **>83f<**
Tereshkova (USA) 3 b f Mr Prospector (USA)-Lypatia (FR) (Lyphard (USA)) 705a[4] 1116a[10] 3785a[2] **>118f<**
Termon 2 b f Puissance-Alipura (Anfield) 1460[6] 1685[3] 2192[5] 2424[5] 3671[4] 3809[11] 3838[2] 4279[4] **>63f<**
Tertium (IRE) 3 b c Nordico (USA)-Nouniya (Vayrann) 670[2] (963) 1301[6] 1839[25] 3706[16] 4083[6] **>88df<**
Tervel (USA) 4 b g Chief's Crown (USA)-Eurobird (Ela-Mana-Mou) *252[4]* **>62a f<**
Tessajoe 3 ch g Clantime-Busted Love (Busted) 538[6] (687) 1194[5] (2166) (2427) (2622) 3505[5] 3935[4] 4201[11] **>78f<**
Tethys (USA) 4 b f Topsider (USA)-Tide (USA) (Coastal (USA)) 1300[6] (1805) 2098[17] 2456[5] 3162[16] 3489[4] 3593[5] 3826[3] 3995[3] 4258[7] 4289[6] **>96f<**
Texanne (BEL) 4 b f Efisio-Texan Rose (FR) (Margouillat (FR)) 2409[R] **>51f<**
Texas Cowgirl (IRE) 5 ch m Salt Dome (USA)-Cloven Dancer (USA) (Hurok (USA)) 452[5] 1400[2] *2943[5]* **>39a 46f<**
Texas Tramp 2 gr f Formidable (USA)-Katy Lou (Nishapour (FR)) 3917[11] 4130[12] **>17f<**
Thabit (USA) 4 b c Alleged (USA)-Close Comfort (USA) (Far North (CAN)) 1365[4] 2446[6] 3382[8] 3807[10] **>91df<**
Thagus (GER) 5 ro h Acatenango (GER)-Tiputip (GER) (Nebos (GER)) (3585a)
Thai Morning 2 gr c Petong-Bath (Runnett) 424[8] 523[3] 1662[6] 2277[7] (3567) 3824[4] 4260[4] **>70f<**
Thaleros 5 b h Green Desert (USA)-Graecia Magna (USA) (Private Account (USA)) *(53)* *215[3]* *246[3]* *303[9]* *396[9]* 556[10] 967[6] 1767[5] 1921[2] 2064[10] (2165) 2327[5] 2544[3] 2875[5] 3101[2] (3232) 3367[8] 3433[7] 3840[5] 4038[21] **>76a 65df<**
Thaljanah (IRE) 3 ch c In The Wings-Dawn is Breaking (Import) 504[14] 774 (1194) (1681) 2172[4] (2555) 3015[2] 3343[3] **>96f<**
Thames (FR) 4 b c Fabulous Dancer (USA)-Three Terns (USA) (Arctic Tern (USA)) 1394a[4] 2894a[9] **>117f<**
Thames Side 4 gr g Beveled (USA)-Free Range (Birdbrook) *218[4]* *497[3]* 729[9] 1092[3] 1404[4] 1519[3] 1974[11] 2538[2] 2640[2] 3129[2] 3362[4] 3679[15] (3844) 4061[0] 4229[5] **>45a 70f<**
Thara(GER) 3 f 1009a[7] **>92f<**
Tharwa (IRE) 3 b f Last Tycoon-Victory Kingdom (CAN) (Viceregal (CAN)) 524[13] 850[3] 1050[3] 1483[4] (1738) 2027[2] 2179[3] (2203) 2578[10] 3373[10] **>66f<**
Thatched (IRE) 5 b h Thatching-Shadia (USA) (Naskra (USA)) 568[6] (642) 820[3] 1037[6] 1378[6] 1506[5] 1995[3] (2123) 2310[4] 2788[4] 2999[4] (3255) 3368[2] 3840[10] 4038[14] 4083[4] 4234[5] **>65f<**
Thatcherella 4 br f Thatching-Ella Mon Amour (Ela-Mana-Mou) (887) 1174[3] (1335) 1614[2] 2288[9] 2743[5] 2764[W] 3359[22] 3615[26] 3961[5] 4113[9] 4268[10] **>73df<**

Thatcher's Era (IRE) 3 ch f Never so Bold-Prima Domina (FR) (Dominion) 1431[3] 1930[2] 2356[7] 3935[11] 4043[5] **>69f<**

Thatchmaster (IRE) 4 b c Thatching-Key Maneuver (USA) (Key To Content (USA)) 975[8] 1126[19] 1244[4] 2321[10] 2657[7] 3440[8] 3605[4] 3920[15] **>57f<**

Tha Tidja (FR) 3 b f Cricket Ball (USA)-Tarativa (USA) (Sensitive Prince (USA)) 164a[2]

That Man Again 3 ch c Prince Sabo-Milne's Way (The Noble Player (USA)) 426[5] *498[6]* 828[4] 1241[5] 1537[5] 1924[3] (2288) (2512) (2935) 3550[4] 3815[13] 4197[3] **>73a 105f<**

That Old Feeling (IRE) 3 b c Waajib-Swift Reply (He Loves Me) 792[4] 1315[4] 1605[6] 1976[2] 3473[6] 3754[2] 4074[9] **>103f<**

Thats Showbusiness 5 ch m Celtic Cone-Cauchemar (Hot Brandy) 2798[9]

The Archorian 6 b g Sula Bula-My Name Is Nobody (Push On) 3282[10]

The Aspecto Girl (IRE) 3 b f Alzao (USA)-North Telstar (Sallust) *24[6]* *448[8]* **>25a 36f<**

Theatre Magic 2 b c Sayf El Arab (USA)-Miss Orient (Damister (USA)) 836[4] 1642[3] 1877[6] 3434[8] 3642[10] **>60f<**

Theatrician (USA) 6 b h Theatrical-Suprina (Vaguely Noble) 3485a[2] **>99f<**

Thea (USA) 2 br f Marju (IRE)-Switched on (Known Fact (USA)) 4320[6] **>72f<**

The Banshee (FR) 3 b c Shernazar-Strident Note (The Minstrel (CAN)) 747[6] **>54+f<**

The Barnsley Belle (IRE) 2 b f Distinctly North (USA)-La Tanque (USA) (Last Raise (USA)) *3509[7]* 3828[7] *3949[6]* 4100[5] 4231[7] **>58a 51f<**

The Bizzo 4 b f Malaspina-Kingmon's Girl (Saucy Kit) 2798[7]

The Black Dubh (IRE) 2 b g Classic Secret (USA)-Coral Cave 2750[4] 3048[7] 3253[4] **>58f<**

The Boozing Brief (USA) 2 b c Turkoman (USA)-Evening Silk (USA) (Damascus (USA)) 3955[2] 4155[5] **>74f<**

The Butterwick Kid 2 ch g Interrex (CAN)-Ville Air (Town Crier) 1841[2] (2483) 3809[14] 3969[18] **>69f<**

The Cape Doctor (IRE) 3 b c Distant Relative-Yldizlar (Star Appeal) *25[3]* *128[6]* 733[16] 1290[10] 1647[7] 2540[4] *2959[10]* **>64da 64f<**

The Chairman (IRE) 4 b c Last Tycoon-Bhama (FR) (Habitat) *592[13]* 1328[12] 1622[21] 2981[8] 3173[9] **>66a 74df<**

The Clan 2 b f Clantime-Scottish Tina (Scottish Reel) 1981[8] 2403[6] **>40f<**

The Cottonwool Kid 3 b c Blakeney-Relatively Smart (Great Nephew) 1725[7] *1880[10]* 2004[5] *2632[3]* **>50a 46f<**

The Country Dancer 5 br m Mashhor Dancer (USA)-Slip The Ferret (Klairon) *94[14]* *147[7]* *343[10]* *361[7]* **>24da 35f<**

The Deaconess 4 b f Minster Son-Haddon Anna (Dragonara Palace (USA)) 3621[11] 3762[8] 4170[16] **>14a 56f<**

The Dilettanti (USA) 2 br c Red Ransom (USA)-Rich Thought (USA) (Rich Cream (USA)) 3888[8] **>39f<**

The Fed 5 ch g Clantime-Hyde Princess (Touch Paper) 507[16] 926[7] 1152[11] 1721[4] 1864[3] 2120[9] 2163[8] 2736[4] 2858[3] 2992[9] 3622[4] 3748[15] 4113[12] 4165[18] 4280[14] **>53f<**

The Flying Fiddle 3 ch f Northern State (USA)-Miss Flossa (FR) (Big John (FR)) 1736[8] 1990[7] 2466[3] 2744[11] **>53f<**

The Flying Phantom 4 gr c Sharrood (USA)-Miss Flossa (FR) (Big John (FR)) 735[5] 998[3] 1363[4] 1869[6] 2098[13] 2456[3] 3361[2] 3688a[6] **>108f<**

The French Friar (IRE) 4 b g Carmelite House (USA)-Netweight (FR) (Pampabird (FR)) 1141[8] 1477[3] 2241[10] 2457[10] 3106[6] **>83f<**

The Frisky Farmer 2 b c Emarati (USA)-Farceuse (Comedy Star (USA)) (554) 718[2] 1650[2] 2541[9] 2904[2] 3132[9] **>73f<**

The Frog Lady (IRE) 4 ch f Al Hareb (USA)-Lady Bettina (Bustino) *122[4]* *3078[9]* **>40a 56f<**

The Frog Princess 2 ch f Crowning Honors (CAN)-Sally Tadpole (Jester) 3767[11] 3915[17] **>39f<**

The Fullbangladesh 2 ch f Hubbly Bubbly (USA)-Oakhurst (Mandrake Major) 4277[6] *4339[2]* **>59a 46f<**

The Happy Fox (IRE) 3 ch c Ballad Rock-Amanzi (African Sky) 982[3] 1450[4] 1924[7] 2247[5] 2394[6] 2680[2] (2877) 3145[14] 3466[4] 4197[4] **>76a 89f<**

The Happy Loon (IRE) 4 b c Mazaad-Skimmer (Skymaster) *378[11]* 493[4] 984[13] 1250[9] 1421[5] 1528[8] 2156[6] 2461[3] 3050[5] 3855[6] **>33a 57f<**

Thehillsarealive (IRE) 3 b g Tirol-Hillbrow (Swing Easy (USA)) 1731[6] 2712[8] 3424[9] 3632[12] **>51f<**

The Imps (IRE) 2 b c Mac's Imp (USA)-Claire's Thatch (Thatch (USA)) 617[10] 1485[8] 1640[2] (1989) 2176[3] 2505[6] *3077[4]* *3675[4]* 3937[3] **>54a 58f<**

The Institute Boy 5 b h Fairy King (USA)-To Oneiro (Absalom) *306[2]* *328[2]* *393[6]* *407[7]* *532[8]* 701[13] 1042[5] *1214[2]* *1331[4]* 1434[3] *1566[6]* 2160[4] 2303[5] 2502[13] *2631[8]* 3123[6] 3252[7] 3357[4] 3622[20] **>58a 49df<**

The Jolly Barmaid (IRE) 2 b f Don't Forget Me-Gay Broad (Gay Fandango (USA)) 3763[10] 3988[13] **>30f<**

The Jotter 3 b f Night Shift (USA)-Note Book (Mummy's Pet) 551[3] 667[12] 939[5] 1305[8] 3637[4] 3922[6] **>94f<**

The Kastarbids (IRE) 2 b g Red Sunset-All Alright (Alzao (USA)) *2143[10]* 2346[9] 2505[2] 2908[8] 3135[5] 3350[7] **>25a 62f<**

The Kings Ransom 3 b g Cadeaux Genereux-The Kings Daughter (Indian King (USA)) 507[8] 733[3] 966[3] (1043) 1433[5] (1828) 2239[3] 2556[2] (2753) **>86f<**

The Leaf Sweeper 4 b f Tinoco-Queen's Royale (Tobrouk (FR)) *252[11]* *343[11]*

The Legions Pride 2 b c Rambo Dancer (CAN)-Immaculate Girl (Habat) 1184[9] 2198[4] 2526[9] 3090[5] 3281[5] 3928[7] **>65f<**

The Little Ferret 5 ch h Scottish Reel-Third Movement (Music Boy) *56[5]* *148[2]* *275[7]* *298[2]* *373[9]* 1517[9] *1789[2]* 2053[6] 2538[5] *2605[4]* 3268[6] **>64a 72?f<**

The Little Thief (FR) 4 b c Ela-Mana-Mou-Oui Papa (FR) (Riverman (USA)) 1001a[2] (1239a) 1869[P] **>119f<**

The Lone Dancer 4 b c Mashhor Dancer (USA)-Solo Vacation (Pas de Seul) 841[8] 1095[7] **>83f<**

The Man 2 b c Marju (IRE)-Mirkan Honey (Ballymore) 3003[7] 3371[3] 3558[2] (3720) 3776[3] 3886[3] 4032[3] **>86f<**

The Merry Monk 4 ch g Balidar-Floret (Monsanto (FR)) 503[11] **>8f<**

The Mestral 3 br f Formidable-Lariston Gale (Pas de Seul) 733[6] 1660[11] 1783[2] 2048[4] 2318[13] 2718[4] 2862[4] 3383[2] 3844[2] 3980[9] **>50f<**

Them Times (IRE) 6 b m Petorius-Atropine (Beldale

Flutter (USA)) 1645^{11} 1974^{17} 2450^{16} 3050^{9} 3293^{16} **>24a 27f<**
The Noble Oak (IRE) 7 ch h The Noble Player (USA)-Sea Palace 726^{13} 1023^{10} 1257^{6} 1508^{10} 1975^{9} 2301^{2} 2551^{7} 2793^{4} 3134^{9} 3139^{11} 3333^{6} 3453^{7} **>45a 42f<**
Thenorthernplayboy (IRE) 2 gr c Distinctly North (USA)-Monetary Wish (Wishing Star) 4244^{8} **>22f<**
The Oil Baron 9 gr h Absalom-Ruby's Chance 1622^{19} 2486^{10} 2806^{4} 2976^{8} **>38f<**
The Old Chapel 6 b h Lomond (USA)-Chapel Cottage (Homing) *393^{2}* 535^{3} 611^{4} (812) *(1076)* 1354^{6} 1599^{8} **>76a 66f<**
Theophanu (USA) 4 ch f The Minstrel (CAN)-Ticket to Paradise (USA) (Alydar (USA)) 1398a^{9} **>113+f<**
The Power of One 6 b h Bellypha-Biding *1951^{11}* **>54a f<**
The Premier Expres 5 gr h Siberian Express (USA)-Home And Away 423^{21} 494^{3} (598) 905^{9} **>21a 65f<**
The Puzzler (IRE) 4 b or br g Sharpo-Enigma (Ahonoora) 1706a^{3} **>114f<**
The Real Whizzbang (IRE) 4 b or br c New Express-Gail's Crystal (Crofter (USA)) *82^{14} 134^{5} 231^{7} 255^{W} 519^{3} 590^{4} 769^{7} (892) 1214^{3}* 1456^{12} 1565^{5} *2627^{3} 2925^{11}* 3777^{13} **>52a 41f<**
Therhea (IRE) 2 b c Pennine Walk-Arab Art (Artaius (USA)) 1123^{3} 2487^{3} 3003^{4} 3225^{5} 3587a^{7} 3711^{6} 3848^{2} 4084^{18} **>80f<**
The Right Time 10 b h King of Spain-Noddy Time 965^{11} 1248^{7} 1499^{6} **>48df<**
The Scythian 3 ch c Komaite (USA)-City to City (Windjammer (USA)) (823) 999^{11} (1414) 1876^{2} 2271^{3} 2556^{4} **>76f<**
The Stager (IRE) 3 b c Danehill (USA)-Wedgewood Blue (USA) (Sir Ivor) (573) 775^{4} 962^{4} 1180^{10} 2103^{6} 2361^{4} 2437^{6} 2691^{11} 3286^{4} 3390^{2} **>78f<**
The Swan 2 ch f Old Vic-El Vino (Habitat) 3673^{4} 3883^{9} 4169^{8} **>71f<**
The Vid (USA) 5 ch h World Appeal (USA)-Siren Song 3576a^{3} 4305a^{12} **>98f<**
The Wad 2 b c Emarati (USA)-Fair Melys (FR) 1670^{13} 2251^{9} 2756^{8} 3430^{7} 3642^{2} 4001^{7} 4111^{6} **>56f<**
Thick as Thieves 3 b c Shavian-Vivienda (Known Fact (USA)) 685^{5} 823^{W} 952^{4} 1151^{9} 3466^{9} 3597^{16} 3972^{17} **>49f<**
Think of England 3 ch f Night Shift (USA)-Final Thought (Final Straw) *2600^{7}* **>37f<**
Thisonesforalice 7 b g Lochnager-Bamdoro (Cavo Doro) 874^{9} 1027^{9} 1958^{2} 2122^{2} 2396^{7} 3311^{2} 3665^{8} **>46f<**
Thomas Crown (IRE) 3 ch c Last Tycoon-Upward Trend (Salmon Leap (USA)) 715^{21} 1124^{15} **>67f<**
Thomire 3 ch c Be My Chief (USA)-Timarete (ITY) (Green Dancer (USA)) 900a^{2} 1396a^{11} 3796a^{2} **>104f<**
Thordis 2 b g Mazilier (USA)-Doppio (Dublin Taxi) 3625^{5} *3949^{2}* (4224) **>71a 71f<**
Thorniwama 4 b f Hadeer-Hidden Asset (Hello Gorgeous (USA)) *26^{4} 84^{6} 175^{5} 218^{3} 290^{7} 347^{8}* **>38a 20f<**
Thorntoun Estate (IRE) 2 b g Durgam (USA)-Furry Friend (USA) (Bold Bidder (USA)) *3736^{5}* 3850^{4} 4045^{4} *4273^{3}* **>63a 70f<**
Thorntoun Jewel (IRE) 2 b f Durgam (USA)-Blue Bouquet (Cure The Blues (USA)) 699^{5} 755^{2} (1159) 2328^{6} 2541^{3} 2855^{5} 3623^{13} 3721^{16} 3937^{23} **>61f<**
Thorny Bishop 4 b g Belfort (FR)-Hill of Fare (Brigadier Gerard) *23^{6} 61^{5} 272^{5}* **>38a 39f<**
Thousla Rock (IRE) 6 ch h Thatching-Resooka (Godswalk (USA)) 2443^{9} **>113f<**
Thracian 2 b f Green Desert (USA)-Triple First 2675^{6} (3763) (3997) 4203^{7} **>103f<**
Three Arch Bridge 3 ch f Sayf El Arab (USA)-Alanood (Northfields (USA)) *294^{2} 333^{2} 411^{9} 448^{4} 518^{3} (587)* 839^{9} 969^{2} 1028^{3} 1060^{2} 1180^{13} 1465^{4} 1735^{3} 1920^{2} (2228) 2503^{7} *2589^{2}* (2770) 2862^{2} 2999^{6} 3255^{3} 3393^{6} (3645) 3837^{10} 3973^{6} **>68a 71f<**
Three Hills 2 b c Danehill (USA)-Three Stars (Star Appeal) 3773^{5} 4080^{3} **>92f<**
Three of Hearts 4 b f Governor General-Friendly Miss *78^{13}* **>51da 62f<**
Threesocks 2 ch f Weldnaas (USA)-Jeethgaya (USA) (Critique (USA)) *2958^{6}* 3397^{5} 3633^{6} **>35a 72f<**
Threesome (USA) 2 ch f Seattle Dancer (USA)-Triode (USA) (Sharpen Up) 2912^{3} 3339^{5} 3857^{2} **>91f<**
Three Stops (USA) 3 b c Nureyev (USA)-Smart Angle (USA) (Quadrangle) (1040) 1487^{7} 2737^{2} 3703^{17} 3943^{18} **>88f<**
Three Weeks 2 ch c Formidable (USA)-Zilda (FR) (Zino) 3494^{11} 3650^{8} **>26f<**
Three Wild Days 3 b g Nishapour (FR)-Golden Curd (FR) (Nice Havrais (USA)) 3799^{12} 4072^{7} **>58f<**
Threshfield (USA) 9 b h Northern Prospect (USA)-French Cutie (USA) (Vaguely Noble) 1714^{19} 2108^{5} 2317^{11} (3258) 3759^{15} 4152^{7} **>57f<**
Thrilling Day 2 b f Groom Dancer (USA)-Pushoff (USA) (Sauce Boat (USA)) 1142^{3} 2275^{2} (2580) 3186^{4} (3691a) 4105^{6} (4200) **>94f<**
Thrower 4 b g Thowra (FR)-Atlantic Line (Capricorn Line) 1349^{4} 1643^{10} 1801^{2} 2002^{5} 2289^{7} 2327^{7} 3061^{7} 3818^{3} 3884^{3} **>50f<**
Thrushwood 3 b f Move Off-Spring Garden (Silly Prices) 758^{14} 990^{10} **>12f<**
Thunder Gulch(USA) 3 ch c Gulch-Line of Thunder (Storm Bi (1006a) 1232a^{3} (1710a) **>124f<**
Thunderheart 4 b c Celestial Storm (USA)-Lorelene (FR) 661^{2} 998^{12} 1156^{3} 1386^{5} 1929^{2} 2087^{6} 2352^{3} 4166^{9} 4326^{P} **>77f<**
Thunder River (IRE) 5 ch h Thatching-In For More (Don) 2342^{11} 2698^{7} 3457^{11} (3661) 3808^{7} 4157^{8} 4268^{6} **>70f<**
Thwaab 3 b c Dominion-Velvet Habit (Habitat) 2304^{5} 2518^{3} 2968^{6} 3745^{11} 4275^{4} **>57f<**
Tiama (IRE) 2 b f Last Tycoon-Soyata (Bustino) 3541^{5} 3891^{8} 4048^{11} **>58f<**
Tibersen 3 b f Posen-Tiberly 1712a^{12} **>101f<**
Tibetan 3 b g Reference Point-Winter Queen (Welsh Pageant) 764^{5} 1175^{4} 1600^{4} 2413^{2} 4220^{2} **>92f<**
Ticka Ticka Timing 2 b c Timeless Times (USA)-Belltina (Belfort (FR)) 1466^{9} 1665^{10} 1943^{11} 2195^{6} *(2629)* 2951^{6} *3528^{14}* 3937^{10} *4339^{3}* **>69?a 44f<**
Tickerty's Gift 5 b h Formidable-Handy Dancer (Green God) 4333^{18} **>40a 59f<**
Tidal Reach (USA) 3 b f Kris S (USA)-Davie Lady (USA) (Bold And Brave (USA)) 614^{7} 980^{9} 2433^{6} *2589^{4}* **>63a 72f<**

Tiddy Oggie 4 b g Nomination-Careless Whisper (USA) (Broadway Forli (USA)) *336^{5} 518^{9}* 646^{17} 1070^{3} 1323^{16} 1785^{11} **>65a 48f<**

Tigana 3 b f Lugana Beach-Tina's Beauty (Tina's Pet) 2486^{17} 3081^{5} **>52f<**

Tiger Shoot 8 b g Indian King (USA)-Grand Occasion (Great Nephew) *52^{4} 221^{5} 1029^{6}* **>67+a 63f<**

Tigersong (USA) 5 b h Seattle Song (USA)-Tovalop (USA) (Northern Dancer) 4166^{19} 4248^{16}

Tiheros 3 ch c Risk Me (FR)-Farras (Song) (451) 507^{18} 1276^{10} 1445^{12} 1909^{5} 3681^{20} 4134^{15} **>49a 61df<**

Tikkanen (USA) 4 b c Cozzene (USA)-Reiko (FR) (Targowice (USA)) 913^{2} 1609^{4} 2213a^{4} **>132f<**

Tilaal (USA) 3 ch c Gulch (USA)-Eye Drop (USA) (Irish River (FR)) 824^{3} 1755^{4} 2086^{3} 2415^{6} 3115^{3} 3276^{4} 3810^{10} **>77f<**

Tiler (IRE) 3 br c Ballad Rock-Fair Siobahn (Petingo) 437^{2} 662^{10} 914^{5} 1131^{7} 2669^{8} (3145) 3209^{2} 3359^{19} 3715^{12} 3929^{10} 4281^{3} **>41a 87f<**

Tillandsia (IRE) 3 b f Unfuwain (USA)-Till You (USA) (Exclusive Native (USA)) 777^{2} (950) 1242^{2} 1867^{2} 2614^{3} 3331a^{2} 3636^{5} **>115f<**

Tilly Owl 4 b f Formidable-Tilly Tavi (Welsh Pageant) *80^{7} 94^{9} 231^{2} (307) 512^{5} 2630^{10}* **>50a 38f<**

Tilly Tupgill 2 ch f Domynsky-Sarsta Grai (Blakeney) 2516^{12} *2924^{8}*

Tilthams 3 br g Prince Sabo-Sparkling Sovereign (Sparkler) 867^{17} 1125^{12} 1322^{12} **>30f<**

Tilty (USA) 5 b h Linkage (USA)-Entiempo (USA) *45^{7}* 4166^{12} 4248^{9} **>43a 67f<**

Timarida (IRE) 3 gr f Kalaglow-Triumphant 3325a^{3} (3693a) (4015a) (4184a) **>120f<**

Timber Country (USA) 3 b c Woodman (USA)-Fal Aspen (USA) (Pretense (USA)) 1006a^{3} (1232a) **>125f<**

Time Again 5 b h Then Again-Vaula (Henbit (USA)) 3704^{20} 3840^{9} **>46f<**

Time Allowed 2 b f Sadler's Wells (USA)-Time Charter (Saritamer (USA)) 3089^{17} **>44f<**

Time Clash (IRE) 2 b f Timeless Times (USA)-Ash Amour (Hotfoot) *1758^{6}* 1981^{4} 2548^{5} (2965) 3711^{10} 3915^{9} 4144^{11} **>28a 58f<**

Time for Action (IRE) 3 b c Alzao (USA)-Beyond Words (Ballad Rock) 995^{9} 1170^{4} 1872^{8} 2415^{2} 4245^{4} 4325^{11} **>91f<**

Time For A Glass 2 b f Timeless Times (USA)-Marie Zephyr (Treboro (USA)) 2735^{5} 3366^{4} 3666^{W} **>17f<**

Time For Tea (IRE) 2 ch f Imperial Frontier (USA)-Glowing Embers (Nebbiolo) 2308^{7} 3157^{2} 3283^{4} 4137^{3} 4237^{3} *4294^{2}* **>67a 70f<**

Time Is Money (IRE) 3 br c Sizzling Melody-Tiempo (King of Spain) 1405^{6} 1550^{6} 1700^{6} 2239^{5} 2502^{10} 2887^{3} 3467^{12} *4123^{12}* 4165^{25} **>50f<**

Time Lapse 6 ch m The Noble Player (USA)-Low Line (High Line) 800a^{2} 3322a^{2} **>63df<**

Time Leader 3 ch c Lead on Time (USA)-Green Leaf (USA) (Alydar (USA)) 677^{8} 816^{11} 1914^{4} 2102^{9} **>71f<**

Timeless 3 b f Royal Academy (USA)-Glory of Hera (Formidable) 3438^{6} 3921^{5} 4150^{3} **>77f<**

Timely Example (USA) 4 ch c Timeless Moment (USA)-Dearest Mongo (USA) (Mongo) *307^{7}* **>34a 69f<**

Time of Night (USA) 2 gr ro f Night Shift (USA)-Tihama (USA) (Sassafras (FR)) 3155^{5} 3397^{4} 3625^{6} 3877^{3} **>73f<**

Times of Times (IRE) 2 b f Distinctly North (USA)-Lady Fandet (Gay Fandango (USA)) *1089^{6}* (2336) *2591^{3}* (2857) (3054) 3314^{3} (3423) 3566^{2} (3767) 3956^{6} (4231) 4328^{6} **>53a 81f<**

Time Star (USA) 4 b c Manila (USA)-Valdemosa (ARG) (Ringaro (USA)) 913^{3} 1609^{3} 1894^{6} 2323^{8} **>125f<**

Time To Fly 2 b c Timeless Times (USA)-Dauntless Flight (Golden Mallard) 925^{5} 1877^{7} 2852^{3} 3110^{5} 3149^{3} 4097^{7} 4231^{2} **>64f<**

Time to Move (IRE) 5 b m Cyrano de Bergerac-June Goddess (Junius (USA)) 3321a^{3}

Time To Tango 2 b f Timeless Times (USA)-Tangalooma (Hotfoot) 4109^{5} 4230^{2} **>66f<**

Timson 2 ch c Timeless Times (USA)-Pickwood Sue 1215^{7} *1570^{4} 1954^{7} 2381^{9} 2629^{10}* **>38a 12f<**

Tina Katerina 2 ch f Executive Man-Tria Romantica (Another Realm) 3763^{12} 3900^{18} **>52f<**

Tina's Charm (IRE) 6 b m Hatim (USA)-Tinas Image (He Loves Me) *100^{11}* 430^{10} **>46f<**

Tinashaan (IRE) 3 b f Darshaan-Catina 664^{2} 868^{2} 1346^{2} (2208) 2614^{2} (3496) 3831^{8} **>99f<**

Tina's Ridge 2 ch c Indian Ridge-Polly's Pear (USA) (Sassafras (FR)) 3003^{2} (3404) **>82f<**

Tinker Amelia 3 b f Damister (USA)-Miss Primula (Dominion) *258^{9} 274^{2} 392^{5} 410^{6}* **>49a f<**

Tinker Osmaston 4 br f Dunbeath (USA)-Miss Primula (Dominion) 856^{10} 1050^{9} (1199) 1335^{5} 1510^{2} 1777^{3} 2017^{6} 2551^{4} 3615^{21} 3919^{4} (4057) 4145^{2} 4165^{20} 4322^{10} **>78f<**

Tinklers Folly 3 ch c Bairn (USA)-Lucky Straw (Tumble Wind (USA)) 759^{15} 969^{4} 1207^{7} 1818^{2} 1961^{2} 2356^{4} (2733) 2974^{3} 3119^{4} 3310^{3} 3808^{18} **>58f<**

Tin Man 2 b c Tina's Pet-April Flower (Parva Stella) 1197^{5} 1779^{6} 2859^{8} 3124^{6} **>44f<**

Tinners Way (USA) 5 ch h Secretariat (USA)-Devon Diva (USA) (The Minstrel (CAN)) 3576a^{5} *4308a^{7}* **>116a f<**

Tino Tere 6 ch h Clantime-Blueit (FR) 1271^{6} 1508^{12} 1864^{7} **>55f<**

Tintara (IRE) 2 b f Caerleon (USA)-Justsayno (USA) (Dr Blum (USA)) 3900^{14} 4188^{9} **>62f<**

Tiny Astro 2 b c Superpower-Moonwalker (Night Shift (USA)) 574^{6} **>21f<**

Tip the Dove 6 br m Riberetto-Nimble Dove (Starch Reduced) *276^{6}* 485^{11} 610^{7} **>62f<**

Tira Heights (USA) 3 gr c Bering-Tira (FR) (Bellypha) 619^{10} 1127^{5} 3730^{21} 3926^{20} **>76f<**

Tirlie (IRE) 3 b g Tirol-Lisa's Favourite (Gorytus (USA)) 552^{10} **>44f<**

Tirolean Gold 3 b f Tirol-Pale Gold (FR) 1874^{4} **>20f<**

Tirolette (IRE) 3 b f Tirol-Etage (Ile de Bourbon (USA)) 948^{7} 1498^{3} (1733) 1984^{5} (3277) 3464^{8} 4259^{9} **>66f<**

Tirollac (IRE) 3 br f Tirol-Lago Real (Kings Lake (USA)) 1519^{7} 2149^{4} 2813^{3} 3385^{4} 3619^{8} 3860^{7} **>51f<**

Tirolling (IRE) 3 b f Tirol-Tanbure (Law Society) 1116a^{9} **>97f<**

Tirols Tyrant (IRE) 2 b g Tirol-Justitia (Dunbeath (USA)) 3340^{8} **>58f<**

Tish 3 b f Kabour-Boldera (Persian Bold) *420^{6}* 482^{17} 555^{6} 732^{17} *842^{6} 1030^{11}* **>27a 29f<**

Tissue of Lies (USA) 2 b br c Ascot Knight (CAN)-Choral Group (CAN) (Lord Durham (CAN)) 3827^{6} 3968^{5}

>72f<

Titania's Dance (IRE) 4 br f Fairy King (USA)-Camden Dancer (Camden Town) *94^{13} 205^{10}* **>23a f<**

Titanium Honda (IRE) 4 gr c Doulab (USA)-Cumbrian Melody (Petong) *150^{6} 187^{4} 341^{4} 378^{5} 419^{2} 520^{5} (766) 832^{7} 1034^{12}* 1297^{12} 1499^{9} *1762^{3}* 1991^{7} *2383^{6}* 3515^{11} 3638^{14} **>50a 42f<**

Titus Livius (FR) 2 ch c Machiavellian (USA)-Party Doll 2896a^{3} (3687a) 3793a^{4} (4250a) **>108+f<**

T'Niel 4 ch f Librate-Classy Colleen (St Paddy) *1074^{12}* 2832^{17} 3258^{10} **>29f<**

Toaff (IRE) 3 b c Nordico (USA)-Sunley Saint (Artaius (USA)) 3039a^{3} **>87f<**

Toasted 3 b f Statoblest-Load Line (High Line) 1602^{8} 2113^{2} **>71f<**

Toat Chieftain 3 b c Puissance-Tribal Lady (Absalom) 1136^{15} 1264^{8} 2177^{7} 3676^{17} **>55f<**

Tobago Boy 3 b g Colmore Row-Perfect Double (Double Form) 759^{9} 1207^{10} 1350^{17} 1725^{8} **>26f<**

Tocco Jewel 5 br m Reesh-Blackpool Belle (The Brianstan) 1161^{8} 1285^{17} 1350^{8} 1548^{9} 2334^{6} 2976^{10} **>41da 24f<**

Today's Fancy 7 b h Today and Tomorrow-Fancy Pages (Touch Paper) *3544^{14}*

Today Tonite 3 b f Adbass (USA)-Meet Again (Lomond (USA)) 1548^{4} 1718^{15} 2246^{9} (2466) 2976^{3} 3265^{3} **>49a 57f<**

Todd (USA) 4 b g Theatrical-Boldara (USA) (Alydar (USA)) 1048^{14} 4333^{12} **>49f<**

Toe Tappin Music (USA) 2 b c Show Dancer (USA)-Miss Garrett (USA) (Speak John) 3012^{6} 3625^{19} 4132^{9} **>40f<**

Toffee 2 ch f Midyan (USA)-Vaula (Henbit (USA)) 1697^{5} 3306^{2} 3553^{9} 3867^{11} **>80?f<**

Tokanda 11 ch h Record Token-Andalucia *58^{5} 201^{10}*

Tolent (IRE) 3 b f Taufan (USA)-Green Bonnet (FR) (Green Dancer (USA)) 449^{7} **>51f<**

Tolls Choice (IRE) 6 ch g Sun Valley-Creativity (Creative Plan (USA)) 559^{4} 672^{13} 820^{8} 1037^{4} (1081) 1250^{4} 1415^{6} 1531^{4} 1873^{4} 2611^{6} 3305^{5} 3808^{25} **>61f<**

Tomal 3 b c King Among Kings-Jacinda (Thatching) 1050^{13} 1975^{11} 2239^{12} *2631^{6}* 2831^{5} 3057^{2} 3429^{3} 3497^{7} 3757^{6} 3980^{5} 4131^{5} 4240^{7} **>37a 53f<**

Tomba La Bomba (USA) 2 b br c Green Dancer (USA)-Easter Mary (USA) (Lord Avie (USA)) 3868^{17} **>62f<**

Tom Morgan 4 b c Faustus (USA)-Pirate Maid (Auction Ring (USA)) 1409^{10} 2477^{5} 3706^{10} 3943^{27} **>84f<**

Tommy Cooper 4 br c Macmillion-My Charade (Cawston's Clown) 1643^{6} 1973^{5} 2268^{2} 2860^{2} 3217^{6} 3627^{9} 3849^{6} **>55f<**

Tommyknocker (IRE) 3 ch c Woodman (USA)-Repercutionist (USA) (Beaudelaire (USA)) 453^{5} 525^{5} 1379^{11} 2603^{4} **>42f<**

Tommy Tempest 6 ch g Northern Tempest (USA)-Silently Yours (USA) (Silent Screen (USA)) *14^{7} 69^{11} 154^{8} 194^{3} 247^{4} 892^{10}* 1538^{10} *1763^{6} 2074^{9} 2295^{9} (2402) 2627^{6}* 2867^{2} 3221^{12} 3453^{6} 3519^{14} **>54a 42f<**

Tom Swift (IRE) 2 b c Law Society (USA)-Debbie's Next (USA) (Arctic Tern (USA)) 4154^{11} 4313^{9} **>58f<**

Tondres (USA) 4 br c Chief's Crown (USA)-Icing *8^{6} 84^{4} 318^{8}* 1367^{4} 1612^{8} 2289^{10} 2445^{8} 2657^{8} 3217^{10} **>64a 79f<**

Tonka 3 b c Mazilier (USA)-Royal Meeting (Dara Monarch) *116^{5} 241^{9}* 655^{3} (773) 995^{5} 1407^{5} 1831^{U} 2298^{5} 2980^{6} 3363^{5} 3634^{2} 3872^{3} 4136^{6} 4333^{11} **>45a 71f<**

Tonnerre 3 b c Unfuwain (USA)-Supper Time 698^{4} (1600) 2550^{4} 3718^{9} 3963^{5} **>81f<**

Tonto 2 b c Nomination-Brigado (Brigadier Gerard) 4291^{8}

Tony's Delight (IRE) 7 b g Krayyan-Tinas Image (He Loves Me) *1074^{11}* **>6a f<**

Tony's Fen 6 b h Trojan Fen-Ladyfish (Pampapaul) 817^{6} (1095) 1410^{4} 1612^{4} (2101) 3611^{15} 3729^{6} **>83f<**

Tonys Gift 3 b f Midyan (USA)-Harmonical (USA) (Lyphard's Wish (FR)) 1515^{4} 1602^{9} 2017^{2} 2404^{3} 2712^{3} (3409) 3771^{8} 3984^{3} (4225) **>76f<**

Tony's Mist 5 b h Digamist (USA)-Tinas Image (He Loves Me) 653^{8} 975^{10} 1716^{8} 1971^{2} 2254^{6} **>78da 78df<**

Too Hasty 2 b c Dunbeath (USA)-Suggia (Alzao (USA)) 1670^{4} 1842^{2} (2161) 3147^{10} 3414^{6} 3714^{4} 4111^{14} **>78f<**

T O O Mamma's (IRE) 4 ch f Classic Secret (USA)-Bohemian Rhapsody *50^{8} 214^{5} 279^{7} 308^{2} 399^{4} 413^{4}* **>55a 42f<**

Topaglow (IRE) 2 ch c Topanoora-River Glow 615^{14} 810^{9} 1190^{9} *2924^{10}* 4143^{7} **>46f<**

Topanga 3 b c Dancing Brave (USA)-Trampship (High Line) 1691^{4} 1987^{3} **>81f<**

Top Banana 4 ch g Pharly (FR)-Oxslip (Owen Dudley) 870^{3} 1183^{11} (1544) (2027) (2410) 2764^{2} 3230^{3} 3717^{14} **>94f<**

Top Cat (FR) 2 ch f Be My Chief (USA)-Pussy Foot (Red Sunset) 638^{2} 819^{2} (1287) (1530) 1849^{9} 3086^{6} 3548^{17} 3668^{9} 3962^{5} **>86f<**

Top Cees 5 b g Shirley Heights-Sing Softly (Luthier (FR)) 423^{6} 661^{5} (998) 1840^{19} 3547^{4} 4118^{3} **>93+f<**

Top Fella (USA) 3 b or br g Horatius (USA)-Annapurna (USA) (Blade (USA)) *316^{3} 443^{6} 520^{3} 592^{7} 844^{3}* 948^{4} 1219^{10} *(1568)* 2282^{7} *2628^{3}* 2881^{3} *3082^{9} 3526^{7}* **>61a 60f<**

Top Guide (USA) 4 ch c Diesis-Raahia (CAN) (Vice Regent (CAN)) 665^{18} 960^{10} 1280^{6} 3393^{9} **>88f<**

Topical (USA) 2 b c Topsider (USA)-Meteoric (High Line) 3915^{18} **>5f<**

Top Lady (IRE) 3 b f Shirley Heights-Happy Kin (USA) (Bold Hitter (USA)) 854^{3} 1194^{2} 2622^{2} 2882^{3} 3224^{2} 3555^{2} (3756) 3957^{7} (4082) **>87f<**

Top of The Stack 2 b c Thatching-Prima Domina (FR) (Dominion) 2283^{7} 3558^{6} 3625^{16} **>63f<**

Top Pearl 3 ch f Superlative-Believe The Chick (USA) (Believe It (USA)) *629^{10}* 850^{15} 1165^{16} **>24a 59f<**

Top Pet (IRE) 5 br g Petong-Pounelta (Tachypous) 728^{7} 1013^{6} 1381^{5} 1534^{4} 1714^{4} 1937^{3} 2197^{5} 2804^{3} 3094^{4} 3619^{10} 3771^{15} 3920^{11} **>56f<**

Top Prize 7 b h High Top-Raffle (Balidar) *3^{6} 2919^{11}* 3017^{4} (3092) (3303) 3569^{9} 3705^{9} 3971^{16} **>40da 52f<**

To Prove a Point 3 b c Weldnaas (USA)-Run Little Lady (USA) (J O Tobin (USA)) 789^{12} 908^{9} 990^{5} 1285^{5} 1669^{10} **>39f<**

Top Royal 6 br h High Top-Maria Isabella (FR) (Young Generation) 2472^{5} 3470^{9} **>61f<**

Top Shiel 7 b h Top Ville-Gelder Shiel *29^{3} 120^{12}* **>79da 72f<**

Top Shop 3 ch f Nashwan (USA)-Select Sale (Auction

Ring (USA)) 950[2] (1283) **>82f<**

Top Show (IRE) 4 b c Digamist (USA)-Acquire *625[6]* 1080[4] 1355[8] **>56f<**

Top Skipper (IRE) 3 b g Nordico (USA)-Scarlet Slipper (Gay Mecene (USA)) 1486[6] 1547[6] 1947[5] 2460[7] 3679[11] 3823[11] 4152[18] **>70f<**

Top Spin 6 b h Niniski (USA)-Spin 632[17] **>44f<**

Top Tycoon (IRE) 4 b or br c Last Tycoon-Pounelta (Tachypous) 1070[15] 1164[8] 1483[7] **>53f<**

Toraja 3 b g Petoski-Helvetique (FR) 641[2] 1026[2] 1600[3] (2300) 2550[5] 2996[6] **>83f<**

Torch Dancer (IRE) 4 b c Sadler's Wells (USA)-River Dancer (Irish River (FR)) 973[6] **>54f<**

Torch Ochre (USA) 2 b c Seattle Dancer (USA)-Paris Jewel (USA) (Well Decorated (USA)) 3560[8] 3709[8]

Torch Vert (IRE) 3 b c Law Society (USA)-Arctic Winter (CAN) (Briartic (CAN)) 657[6] 1099[7] (1682) 2462[2] 2701[5] 3547[5] (3718) 4118[6] **>89f<**

Torreglia (IRE) 3 ch f Elmaamul (USA)-Dance Machine (Green Dancer (USA)) 1175[7] 1717[6] 2082[2] 2481[2] 2860[4] 3304[2] 3818[10] **>78f<**

Torrential (USA) 3 b c Gulch (USA)-Killaloe (USA) (Dr Fager) (431) (536) 826[5] (1575a) 2044a[4] 2730a[2] **>118f<**

Torrey Pines (IRE) 3 b g Red Sunset-Yukon Baby (USA) (Northern Dancer) *357[7]* *628[3]* *1762[12]* 1854[11] 2901[3] 3401[4] **>59a 61f<**

Torrismondo (USA) 4 b or br c Tasso (USA)-Miss Cabell Co (USA) (Junction (USA)) 1118a[7] **>103f<**

Toshiba Talk (IRE) 3 ch c Horage-Court Ballet (Barrons Court) 427[14] 492[3] (1083) 1358[6] 1669[7] 3462[12] 3710[18] **>54f<**

Toskano 3 b c Salse (USA)-Kukri (Kris) 2568[5] 2805[4] 3097[3] 3898[7] **>55f<**

Total Aloof 2 b f Groom Dancer (USA)-Bashoosh (USA) (Danzig (USA)) 2651[8] 2932[2] **>64f<**

Totality 4 b f Dancing Brave (USA)-Slightly Dangerous (USA) (Roberto (USA)) 1780[2] 2272[2] 3041a[6] 3549[4] **>109f<**

Total Joy (IRE) 4 gr c Persian Bold-Caranina (USA) (Caro) 550[11] 653[7] (778) 1014[5] 1410[6] 1695[5] 1937[13] 2175[6] 2535[3] **>74f<**

Totally Different 2 b c Totem (USA)-Bold Difference (Bold Owl) 1943[12] 4312[17] **>21f<**

Total Rach (IRE) 3 b f Nordico (USA)-Miss Kelly (Pitskelly) 526[8] 3108[10] 3288[8] 3685[5] 3987[8] 4043[6] (4152) *4298[12]* **>46a 63f<**

Total Stranger 3 b c Puissance-Jaisalmer (Castle Keep) 483[2] (982) 1193[3] 1489[8] 2394[4] 2692[9] 3221[14] **>84f<**

To the Roof (IRE) 3 b c Thatching-Christine Daae (Sadler's Wells (USA)) 2469[7] 2786[2] *3072[3]* 3293[3] 3681[6] 4057[2] **>65a 72f<**

To The Whire 2 br f Rock City-Free Dance (FR) (Green Dancer (USA)) 852[4] (1047) 1259[3] 1634[4] 4328[7] **>81f<**

Totostar 3 b f Mtoto-Prospector's Star (USA) (Mr Prospector (USA)) 1237a[8] **>81f<**

Tot Ou Tard (IRE) 5 b h Robellino (USA)-She's My Lovely (Sharpo) (703a) (896a) (1709a) 2213a[7] 3695a[3] 4014a[12] 4252a[7] **>120f<**

Touch Above 9 b h Touching Wood (USA)-B A Poundstretcher (Laser Light) 1037[12] 1378[3] 1557[4] 1816[6] 1966[12] 2254[5] 3232[3] 3367[5] **>53f<**

Touch a Million (USA) 3 b c Mr Prospector (USA)-Magic Gleam (USA) (Danzig (USA)) 1796[2] (2100) 2367[5] **>88f<**

Touching Times 7 b h Touching Wood (USA)-Pagan Deity (Brigadier Gerard) 3569[10] **>28f<**

Touch of Fantasy 2 b f Never so Bold-Brera (IRE) (Tate Gallery (USA)) 740[6] 1448[3] 1640[5] *2146[4]* *2382[3]* 2706[12] *3953[4]* **>54a 49f<**

Touch of Snow 2 b f Touch of Grey-Snow Huntress (Shirley Heights) 3054[5] *3738[8]* 4129[14] **>14a 4f<**

Toujours Riviera 5 ch h Rainbow Quest (USA)-Miss Beaulieu (Northfields (USA)) 1225[10] (2468) 2703[19] 3113[4] 3382[6] 3837[4] 4035[7] 4104[7] **>96f<**

Tourandot (IRE) 4 b g Emarati (USA)-Tomard (Thatching) 2888a[3] **>100f<**

Tour Leader (NZ) 6 ch h Nassipour (USA)-Colleen (NZ) (Karayar) 3676[10] 3971[10] **>38f<**

Tousle (FR) 3 b f Highest Honor-Ruffle 4299a[3] **>94f<**

Tout de Val 6 b m Tout Ensemble-Julie Emma (Farm Walk) 1274[5] 1542[10] 1854[3] *2090[9]* 2334[9] 2842[4] 3206[2] 3402[9] **>17a 37f<**

Tovarich 4 b c Soviet Star (USA)-Pretty Lucky (Shirley Heights) *256[5]* *313[6]* *520[10]* 568[13] (820) 1081[3] 1250[15] *1884[4]* *2293[2]* 2445[6] *2920[3]* *(3513)* *3737[2]* *4126[12]* **>72a 63f<**

Tower Green 4 b c Aragon-Pilley Green 2807[8] 4157[15] **>75df<**

Toy Princess (USA) 3 b f Arctic Tern (USA)-Princess Toy (Prince Tenderfoot (USA)) *376[2]* *448[3]* 538[3] (655) 947[5] 2184[4] 2882[2] **>71a 75f<**

Traceability 2 b c Puissance-Miss Petella (Dunphy) 615[12] (1665) 2059[4] 2541[7] (2732) (3008) (3345) **>70f<**

Traci's Castle (IRE) 2 b f Ajraas (USA)-Mia Gigi (Hard Fought) 3765[12] **>24f<**

Track Gal (USA) 4 b f Track Barron (USA)-Golden Galaxy (USA) *4303a[11]* **>79a f<**

Trade Wind 4 br g Rambo Dancer (CAN)-Cadasi (Persian Bold) 763[8] (1245) 1477[7] 1594[4] (2490) 2792[5] 3863[16] 4022[5] **>79f<**

Trafalgar Lady (USA) 2 b f Fairy King (USA)-Tremulous (USA) (Gregorian (USA)) 2351[W] (3933) 4056[2] **>88f<**

Tragic Hero 3 b c Tragic Role (USA)-Pink Mex (Tickled Pink) 1167[4] 1532[5] 2037[7] 2524[6] 2789[2] (2983) (3363) 4044[19] **>64f<**

Traikey (IRE) 3 b c Scenic-Swordlestown Miss (USA) (Apalachee (USA)) 1301[3] **>106f<**

Trail of Tears 5 ch g Kings Lake (USA)-Spring Water (USA) (Effervescing (USA)) *29[4]* *120[10]* 534[17] **>41a 23f<**

Trainglot 8 ch h Dominion-Mary Green 3804[8] **>92f<**

Tranquillity 3 b f Night Shift (USA)-Quiet Week-End (Town And Country) 957[3] (1446) 1793[9] 2367[6] 2848[5] 4038[12] **>76f<**

Transom (USA) 4 b or br c Private Account (USA)-Trestle (USA) (Tom Rolfe) 869[7] **>101f<**

Trans Siberia 4 gr c Siberian Express (USA)-Olivian (Hotfoot) 661[11] 1144[2] (1300) 1768[6] 2098[2] **>93f<**

Trapeze 4 br g Shirley Heights-Fiesta Fun (Welsh Pageant) 584[10] *1074[7]* 1198[10] **>39a 51f<**

Trauma (IRE) 3 b f Broken Hearted-Remoosh (Glint of Gold) 428[10] *515[6]* **>32a 29f<**

Travel Out 3 b f Presidium-Travel Bye (Miller's Mate) *54[7]* *134[8]* *257[5]* **>25a 38+f<**

Trazl (IRE) 3 b f Zalazl (USA)-Triple Reef (Mill Reef

USA)) 797^{10} 1154^{3} 1442^{3} (1901) (2201) (2452) 2986^{3} 3262^{3} (3826) 4082^{2} **>92f<**

Treasure Keay **3** b or br f Treasure Kay-Doppio (Dublin Taxi) 1053^{10} 1660^{16} 2032^{9} **>55f<**

Tregaron (USA) **4** b c Lyphard (USA)-Klarifi (Habitat) 539^{5} 873^{3} 1280^{10} 2419^{6} 3703^{16} **>82df<**

Tremendisto **5** b h Petoski-Misty Halo (High Top) 1596^{5} *2147*^{6} 3743^{2} *3951*^{3} 4101^{4} 4288^{2} **>57a 64f<**

Tremolante **4** b f Governor General-Glimmer (Hot Spark) *222*^{5} *269*^{6} *334*^{3} *414*^{4} *517*^{6} 1285^{22} **>33a 4f<**

Tremplin (USA) **3** b c Trempolino (USA)-Stresa (Mill Reef (USA)) 826^{7} **>95f<**

Tres Heureux (GER) **5** b h Konigsstuhl-Tres Magnifique (4094a) **>115f<**

Tria Kemata **2** b c Kris-Third Watch (Slip Anchor) 2441^{3} 3174^{6} 3560^{2} (3746) 4042^{3} **>85f<**

Triarius (USA) **5** ch h Trempolino (USA)-Noble Decretum (USA) (Noble Decree (USA)) (3458) (3614) 4007a^{3} **>119+f<**

Tribal Peace (IRE) **3** ch g Red Sunset-Mirabiliary (USA) (Crow (FR)) *(264)* *301*^{2} 614^{4} 962^{8} 3362^{2} 3531^{9} 3679^{7} (3934) 4136^{13} 4202^{6} **>75a 77f<**

Trible Pet **2** b f Petong-Fire Sprite (Mummy's Game) 1590^{4} 1790^{4} 2047^{6} *2382*^{2} 2601^{5} 3290^{7} *3675*^{6} **>55a 60f<**

Trickledown **2** b f Dowsing (USA)-Pillowing (Good Times (ITY)) 819^{5} 1190^{4} 1525^{7} 2259^{W} 4133^{15} **>65f<**

Trilby **2** b f In The Wings-Fur Hat (Habitat) 4190^{4} **>68+f<**

Trillo (ITY) **3** b c Church Lyric-Tia 3791a^{2} **>63f<**

Trimming (IRE) **3** b f Thatching-Tatouma (USA) (The Minstrel (CAN)) 660^{7} **>83+f<**

Trina **4** b f Malaspina-Tremmin (Horage) 1050^{11} 1265^{9} 1546^{9} 1993^{2} 2018^{7} 2363^{3} 2624^{8} 2789^{3} 2946^{9} 2976^{6} 3173^{10} **>45f<**

Trioming **9** b g Homing-Third Generation (Decoy Boy) 3116^{6} 3204^{7} **>38da 44f<**

Triple Joy **4** b f Most Welcome-Triple Reef (Mill Reef (USA)) *89*^{3} *(272)* 659^{2} 1488^{3} 2097^{3} **>99a 110f<**

Triple Tie (USA) **4** ch f The Minstrel (CAN)-Tea And Roses (USA) (Fleet Nasrullah) 632^{19} 811^{12} 1788^{7} 2028^{6} 2339^{6} 3127^{5} 3936^{17} 4051^{12} **>56df<**

Triple Tricks (IRE) **3** ch f Royal Academy (USA)-Tricky Note (Song) 1258^{4} 1624^{8} 1859^{3} 2125^{2} 2361^{7} 3661^{17} **>73f<**

Triquetti (IRE) **3** b c Royal Academy (USA)-Marie Noelle (FR) (Brigadier Gerard) 936^{2} (1167) 1782^{2} 2738^{12} 3556^{5} **>94f<**

Tristano **3** b c Colmore Row-Tura (Northfields (USA)) 1121a^{8} 2389a^{4} 4345a^{3} **>110f<**

Tristan's Comet **8** br h Sayf El Arab (USA)-Gleneagle *53*^{4} 556^{15} **>66a 34f<**

Trojan Risk **2** ch c Risk Me (FR)-Troyes (Troy) 3472^{4} 3672^{4} 3869^{4} 4130^{2} *4269*^{4} **>66a 78f<**

Trood **0** 3797a^{3}

Troon **5** gr h Beveled (USA)-Cestrefeld (Capistrano) (1707a) 4006a^{3} **>100f<**

Trooping (IRE) **6** b h Auction Ring (USA)-Tunguska (Busted) 876^{5} 1064^{7} **>71f<**

Tropical Beach **2** b g Lugana Beach-Hitravelscene (Mansingh (USA)) (574) 699^{4} 4066^{7} 4231^{15} **>58f<**

Tropical Dance (USA) **2** ch f Thorn Dance (USA)-Missuma (USA) (Procida (USA)) 617^{7} 919^{3} (1098) 1849^{5} (2136) (2489) 2947^{5} (3210) 3499^{5} **>88f<**

Tropical Jungle (USA) **5** b g Majestic Shore (USA)-Diamond Oyster (Formidable) *26*^{3} *127*^{7} *497*^{2} 569^{2} (818) 1422^{2} 1771^{2} 1971^{3} *3544*^{2} **>66a 64f<**

Troubadour Song **3** b g King of Clubs-Silver Singing (USA) (Topsider (USA)) 2794^{6} 3115^{2} 3294^{4} 3645^{19} 3844^{11} **>79f<**

Troysend **2** b c Dowsing (USA)-Way to Go (Troy) 3587a^{2} **>75f<**

Truancy **2** b c Polar Falcon (USA)-Zalfa (Luthier (FR)) 1551^{7} (1856) 3925^{6} 4039^{5} **>85f<**

True Ballad **3** ch g Ballad Rock-Ajuga (USA) (The Minstrel (CAN)) 3973^{P}

True Bird (IRE) **3** b f In The Wings-I Want My Say (USA) (Tilt Up (USA)) 698^{2} 1105^{6} 1439^{0} 3818^{8} 4099^{2} 4288^{W} **>69f<**

Truly a Dream (IRE) **4** b f Darshaan-Truly Special 607a^{10} 897a^{3} 1709a^{8} 3041a^{5} 4015a^{9} **>119f<**

Truly Madly Deeply **3** b f Most Welcome-Council Rock (General Assembly (USA)) 1186^{16} *1761*^{7} *1880*^{12} *2497*^{7} *2627*^{10} 2927^{7} **>24a 25f<**

Trumble **3** b c Tragic Role (USA)-Sideloader Special (Song) 1294^{4} 1465^{8} 1824^{2} 1962^{10} 2582^{4} 3111^{2} 3254^{2} (3410) 3722^{5} 4283^{5} **>60f<**

Truth **2** b f Prince Sabo-Pursuit of Truth (USA) (Irish River (FR)) 4212^{12} *4269*^{5} **>45a 59f<**

Truthful Image **6** b m Reesh-Token of Truth (Record Token) 535^{12} 636^{16} **>74df<**

Try Again Jane **5** ch m Alias Smith (USA)-Jane Again (Spartan General) *293*^{6} **>12a 42f<**

Try-Haitai (IRE) **4** ch g Colmore Row-Grain of Sand (Sandford Lad) 1168^{11} 1520^{3} 1786^{12} 2613^{12} 4053^{12} **>47f<**

Try My Segnor **2** b c Tirol-Carillon Miss (The Minstr (1391a) 2043a^{3}

Try Omnipotent **3** b g Nomination-Try G's (Hotfoot) 1625^{5} 1771^{5} 2065^{8} 2981^{5} 3184^{6} 3722^{2} 3875^{18} **>56f<**

Tryph **3** b f Pharly (FR)-Troja (Troy) 1615^{9} **>62f<**

Tryphosa (IRE) **3** b f Be My Guest (USA)-Thekla (GER) (Prince Ippi (GER)) (1009a) 1712a^{3} 2286^{8} 2894a^{3} 4015a^{8} **>113f<**

Tryst (IRE) **4** b c Thatching-Finalist (Star Appeal) *4128*^{8} **>47a 53f<**

Try to Please (IRE) **3** br c Try My Best (USA)-Amiga Irlande (Whistling Deer) 850^{10} 1876^{3} 2271^{8} 2802^{6} *3242*^{13} **>19a 85f<**

Tsarnista **2** b f Soviet Star (USA)-Princess Genista (Ile de Bourbon (USA)) 3069^{4} 3339^{7} 3766^{2} (4218) 4318^{6} **>87f<**

Tsarskaya (USA) **2** ch f Elmaamul (USA)-Wyandra (So Blessed) 3662^{5} **>58f<**

Tshusick **4** b f Dancing Brave (USA)-Infanta Real (Formidable) 535^{8} 1174^{10} **>83f<**

Ttyfran **5** b h Petong-So it Goes (Free State) 569^{8} 649^{16} **>29a 40f<**

Tucan (USA) **3** ch c Storm Bird (CAN)-Tuca Tuca (USA) (Miswaki (USA)) 647^{11} **>74f<**

Tudor Island **6** b h Jupiter Island-Catherine Howard (Tower Walk) (661) 931^{8} 2284^{3} 2530^{2} 3162^{14} 3547^{3} (4036) 4189^{10} **>89f<**

Tuesday's Special (USA) **5** b h Irish River-Cielo's Love

(Conquistado) (489a) 607a^3 898a^7 **>119f<**
Tuigamala 4 b g Welsh Captain-Nelliellamay (Super Splash (USA)) 762^{19} 2685^{14} (2843) 3011^9 3248^7 **>44f<**
Tukano (CAN) 4 ch c Halo (USA)-Northern Prancer (USA) (Northern Dancer) 1794^{11} 1929^9 2184^5 2352^5 **>88f<**
Tulu 4 ch f Nicholas Bill-Falcrello (3700) 3820^6 **>53+a 83f<**
Tumbleweed Ridge 2 ch c Indian Ridge-Billie Blue (Ballad Rock) 1485^2 1893^4 (2091) 3163^2 3925^2 (4159) **>101f<**
Tu Opes 4 ch g Most Welcome-Axiana (FR) (Akarad (FR)) *18^6 94^6 127^2 195^2 271^2 414^2* 935^{10} 1205^4 1506^6 1865^3 2022^2 (2184) 2374^2 2530^3 2799^5 **>76a 81f<**
Turbo North 2 b g Nordico (USA)-Turbo Rose (Taufan (USA)) 1356^7 1670^{15} 3648^7 **>38f<**
Turfman (IRE) 2 c (3906a)
Turfmans Vision 5 b h Vision (USA)-Persian Alexandra (Persian Bold) *245^4 295^{11} 375^9 421^3* 534^7 *588^6 1075^5* 1449^P **>58a 32f<**
Turia 2 b f Slip Anchor-Tura (Northfields (USA)) 4050^{14} **>37f<**
Turk Passer (USA) 5 b h Turkoman (USA)-Insilca (USA) 4307a^9 **>104f<**
Turner Prize (IRE) 5 b h Tate Gallery (USA)-Pansoverina *2919^{10}* **>42a f<**
Turnpole (IRE) 4 br g Satco (FR)-Mountain Chase (Mount Hagen (FR)) 673^5 815^{10} 968^5 2648^2 (2917) 3970^2 **>77f<**
Turquoise Sea (USA) 3 b f Shirley Heights-Aminata 635^{11} 1347^2 2026^5 (3705) 3849^8 4026^7 4158^7 **>87f<**
Turret 4 b f Shirley Heights-Moogie (Young Generation) 1444^{10} **>79f<**
Turrill House 3 b f Charmer-Megabucks *1074^8 1458^4* 1791^8 **>34a 24f<**
Turtle Power 5 ch g May Be This Time-Miss Chianti (Royben) *18^{11} 370^{13}*
Tuscan Dawn 5 ch h Clantime-Excavator Lady (Most Secret) 1019^5 1106^{10} 1637^9 2060^8 2609^7 2686^6 3221^{11} **>70f<**
Tuscania 5 ch m Faustus (USA)-The Shrew (Relko) *96^4 136^3 1567^5* 1965^8 **>51a 16f<**
Tutu Sixtysix 4 br f Petong-Odilese (Mummy's Pet) 838^{10} 994^5 1151^{17} 1441^8 1668^8 1996^5 2252^7 2502^{12} 2772^2 2879^7 3275^9 **>50f<**
Twice as Sharp 3 ch c Sharpo-Shadiliya (Red Alert) 658^2 (1296) 1648^3 2240^{15} 3637^7 (3878) 4033^{24} **>90f<**
Twice in Bundoran (IRE) 4 ch f Bold Arrangement-Asturiana (Julio Mariner) *78^{15} 167^8 269^{11} 404^3* 503^{14} 646^{10} 701^{17} 862^3 (1271) 1677^2 1972^5 2252^5 2609^8 3624^{23} 3748^{20} 3878^7 4115^{18} **>44a 53f<**
Twice Knightly 4 b c Double Bed (FR)-Charter Belle 1051^5 1401^9 **>66df<**
Twice Purple (IRE) 3 b c Then Again-Tyrian Belle (Enchantment) 1136^{16} 1476^8 3475^6 3654^4 4044^6 **>63f<**
Twice Removed 2 b f Distant Relative-Nigel's Dream (Pyjama Hunt) 1746^7 **>48f<**
Twice the Groom (IRE) 5 b h Digamist (USA)-Monaco Lady (Manado) 2392^3 3963^{12} **>66f<**
Twice Two (IRE) 2 ch f Double Schwartz-Ever so (Mummy's Pet) 1989^7 **>6f<**
Twilight Hour (USA) 3 b f Majestic Light (USA)-If Winter Comes (USA) (Dancing Champ (USA)) 2426^2 2790^4 3421^2 3818^{18} **>68f<**
Twilight Patrol 3 b f Robellino (USA)-Warning Light (High Top) 829^9 1066^3 1306^6 (2103) 2367^2 2737^4 3235^6 (3373) 3564^9 **>101f<**
Twilight Sleep (USA) 3 b c Shadeed (USA)-Sleeping Beauty (Mill Reef (USA)) 438^6 619^9 1672^P **>83f<**
Twin Creeks 4 b c Alzao (USA)-Double River (USA) (Irish River (FR)) *181^6 (256) 337^6* 1021^{15} 1433^7 1679^{12} 2021^3 2276^5 (2396) 2946^8 3879^8 **>59a 58f<**
Two Chalk 3 b c Mazilier (USA)-Feast-Rite *146^6 197^9* **>44a 29f<**
Two Four Sports (IRE) 2 b g Red Sunset-Golden Empress 3881^{10} 4064^{11} **>34f<**
Two Moves in Front (IRE) 5 ch h Ballad Rock-Kentucky Wildcat (Be My Guest (USA)) 434^{17} 838^5 877^{10} 1421^{10} 1648^9 1900^7 4142^9 **>60f<**
Two O'Clock Jump (IRE) 3 b c Be My Guest (USA)-Magic Spell (FR) (Dancers Image (USA)) (622) 826^6 1121a^4 1573a^4 2565a^3 (3478a) **>112f<**
Two Socks 2 ch c Phountzi (USA)-Mrs Feathers (Pyjama Hunt) 690^9 1318^8 1662^{12} 1829^8 *2635^4 2924^3 3736^2* 3776^5 4129^8 *4338^9* **>73a 53f<**
Two Timer 2 ch c Clantime-Two's Up (Double Jump) 3149^4 3720^8 *3949^8* **>39a 48f<**
Two Way Stretch 3 b f Prince Daniel (USA)-Playtex (Be Friendly) *144^{11} 339^4 444^8 893^5* 1125^5 1350^9 **>45a 47f<**
Tykeyvor (IRE) 5 b h Last Tycoon-Ivoronica 848^5 (1256) 1808^3 (3440) 3729^{15} 3945^{22} 4201^5 **>87f<**
Tymeera 2 b f Timeless Times (USA)-Dear Glenda (Gold Song) *604^3 1031^4* (2047) (2859) 3651^6 **>39a 69f<**
Typhoon Eight (IRE) 3 b c High Estate-Dance Date (IRE) (Sadler's Wells (USA)) 691^9 1198^6 3349^5 3593^4 3817^{15} **>84f<**
Tyreless (IRE) 3 ch f Milk of The Barley-Sigwell's Gold (Sonnen Gold) *54^5 141^5 168^4 185^9* **>42a 19f<**
Tyrian Purple (IRE) 7 b h Wassl-Sabrine (Mount Hagen (FR)) *16^4 71^4 140^4 (202) (331) 386^2 446^{11} 510^3* 541^8 1429^7 2338^3 (2642) 2810^3 *3522^9* 3874^{10} **>65a 62f<**
Tyrone Flyer 6 b h Celestial Storm (USA)-Dance a Jig (Dance In Time (CAN)) *231^8 255^8 312^{11} 354^{13}* 702^{13} 890^4 *1076^2 1087^2* 1469^6 1582^7 *1760^{11} 2290^4* 2832^{12} *2923^5* 4134^8 4165^{22} **>73a 63f<**
Tzar Rodney (FR) 3 b c Assert-Laquifan (USA) (Lear Fan (USA)) 207a^2 488a^2 808a^4 (1230a) 2560a^7 2890a^2 3482a^7 **>113f<**

U

Uckerby Lad 4 b g Tobin Lad (USA)-Chomolonga (High Top) *4^2 53^8 136^5 215^8 335^3 379^7 415^9* **>53a f<**
Ulanowa (GER) 3 f 1705a^4 **>97f<**
Ultimate Warrior 5 b g Master Willie-Fighting Lady (Chebs Lad) *145^9 (218) 320^8* 1095^3 *2605^3 3082^5 3735^{10}* **>66a 83df<**
Ultra Barley 2 ch c Beveled (USA)-Chapter One (Hello Gorgeous (USA)) 1352^5 *(2962)* (3120) 3271^4 3354^3 3468^7 *(4124)* **>87+a 74+f<**
Ultra Beet 3 b c Puissance-Cassiar (Connaught) *42^4 (86) (132) (173) (342) (363)* 426^{10} 754^5 *831^2* 1564^3 (1723) 1741^6 3905^{14} **>85a 79f<**
Ultra Finesse 3 b f Rahy-Suavite (Alleged) 2045a^2 3196a^3 **>99f<**

Ultra Power 2 ch g Sharpo-Scottish Legend (Legend of France (USA)) 1959^{4} 3415^{5} 3670^{17} **>45f<**
Umberston (IRE) 2 b c Nabeel Dancer (USA)-Pivotal Walk (IRE) (Pennine Walk) 3340^{18} 3683^{8} 4172^{7} **>53f<**
Unaccounted For (USA) 4 b c Private Account (USA)-Mrs Jenney (USA) (The Minstrel (CAN)) *4308a^{3}* **>132a f<**
Unanimous Vote (IRE) 3 ch c Roi Danzig (USA)-Sally Chase (Sallust) 2730a^{3} **>118f<**
Unbridled's Song (USA) 2 ro c Unbridled (USA)-Trolley Song (USA) (Caro) *(4306a)* **>124ta f<**
Unchanged 3 b f Unfuwain (USA)-Favorable Exchange (USA) (Exceller (USA)) 2339^{2} 2812^{4} (3569) (3774) 3971^{2} **>83f<**
Uncharted Waters 4 b f Celestial Storm (USA)-Try the Duchess (Try My Best (USA)) *330^{7} 412^{10}* 860^{3} 1014^{2} 1200^{6} 1518^{6} 1674^{5} 2289^{5} 2530^{10} 2687^{7} 3872^{4} 4051^{15} **>58a 64f<**
Uncle Doug 4 b c Common Grounds-Taqa (Blakeney) 821^{2} 1109^{4} 1416^{3} 1840^{9} 3724^{10} **>66f<**
Uncle George 2 ch c Anshan-Son Et Lumiere (Rainbow Quest (USA)) 523^{5} 2876^{9} (3180) 3684^{6} 3947^{10} **>73f<**
Uncle Oswald 4 ch c Nashwan (USA)-Riviere Bleue (Riverman (USA)) 423^{15} 634^{5} 873^{5} 1183^{6} 1661^{2} 1853^{18} 2269^{2} 2980^{5} **>92f<**
Unconditional Love (IRE) 2 b f Polish Patriot (USA)-Thatcherite (Final Straw) 474^{2} (570) (871) 1137^{3} 1849^{4} 2243^{7} **>91+f<**
Undawaterscubadiva 3 ch g Keen-Northern Scene (Habitat) 643^{7} 758^{13} 861^{8} 3508^{11} 3750^{11} **>40f<**
Unforeseen 3 ch c Unfuwain (USA)-Eversince (USA) (Foolish Pleasure (USA)) *4271^{7}* **>49a 64f<**
Unforgiving Minute 6 b h Bellypha-Kindjal (Kris) 2241^{13} 2457^{7} 3611^{5} 3810^{5} 4028^{13} **>88f<**
Unfuwaanah 3 ch f Unfuwain (USA)-Jeema (Thatch (USA)) 2583^{4} 3023^{12} (3640) 3905^{16} **>73f<**
Unihoc Ball 2 ch f Indian Ridge-Soon to Be (Hot Spark) 2116^{8} **>6f<**
Unison 4 gr c Merdon Melody-Bri-Ette (Brittany) 1456^{10} *1630^{4} 2076^{10}* **>24a 31f<**
United Force (IRE) 3 b c High Estate-Exuberine (FR) (Be My Guest (USA)) 691^{11} 1173^{2} 1526^{2} 1852^{11} 3338^{3} 3448^{P} **>87f<**
United Front 3 br c Be My Chief (USA)-Julia Flyte (Drone) 854^{2} (1085) 1478^{7} 4047^{18} 4158^{11} **>76?f<**
U-No-Harry (IRE) 2 b c Mansooj-Lady Roberta (USA) (Roberto (USA)) 671^{7} *889^{2} 1073^{2} 1212^{9}* (1352) 1665^{4} 2023^{3} (2185) 2800^{2} 2988^{4} 3064^{7} 3290^{3} 3434^{3} 3612^{11} 3803^{2} 3990^{9} 4260^{5} **>61a 69f<**
Un Parfum de Femme (IRE) 4 b c Mill Native (USA)-Hail To You (USA) (Kirtling) 505^{6} 653^{6} 811^{5} 1410^{7} 2069^{6} 2472^{2} 2713^{2} 3024^{5} **>77f<**
Unprejudice 4 b c North Briton-Interviewme (USA) 749^{6} 1126^{8} 1561^{2} 1801^{6} 3993^{12} 4138^{3} 4284^{10} **>73f<**
Unreal City (IRE) 2 b c Rock City-Tolmi 4154^{2} **>73+f<**
Unsold 2 b c Green Desert (USA)-Shoot Clear (Bay Express) 1551^{2} 3180^{4} 3604^{8} 3947^{4} **>77f<**
Unspoken Prayer 2 br f Inca Chief (USA)-Dancing Doll (USA) (Buckfinder (USA)) 3763^{18} 3893^{8} **>16f<**
Uoni 2 ch f Minster Son-Maid of Essex (Bustino) 1361^{7} **>64f<**
Upex le Gold Too 3 ch g Precocious-Restless Star (Star Appeal) 722^{10} 990^{4} 1059^{7} 1522^{7} 1742^{4} 1995^{13} 2122^{6} (2761) 3295^{5} 3661^{6} **>40a 50f<**
Up in Flames (IRE) 4 br c Nashamaa-Bella Lucia (Camden Town) 559^{10} 642^{5} (1280) (1638) 2117^{3} 2672^{13} **>87f<**
Uplift 2 ch f Bustino-Relatively Easy (Relkino) 3983^{14} 4048^{16} 4190^{11} **>35f<**
Uppance 7 b m Kabour-Final Cast (Saulingo) 475^{7} 789^{18} 994^{9} 1739^{8} 2463^{6} 2736^{6} 2930^{10} 2997^{10} 3313^{10} **>31df<**
Upper Heights (GER) 7 b h Head for Heights-Utika (GER) (Frontal) 3798a^{9} **>112?f<**
Upper Mount Clair 5 b m Ela-Mana-Mou-Sun Street (Ile de Bourbon (USA)) *67^{7} 109^{5} 201^{4} 288^{3} 346^{10}* (432) 632^{20} 751^{8} (1552) 1840^{26} 2429^{3} 2688^{2} 3425^{4} 3682^{2} **>55a 73f<**
Upper Torrish 3 b f Sharrood (USA)-Upper Caen (High Top) 1182^{5} **>65f<**
Urania 3 b f Most Welcome-Aonia (Mummy's Pet) 3239^{7} 3428^{2} 3573^{3} 3958^{2} **>71f<**
Urgent Swift 2 ch c Beveled (USA)-Good Natured (Troy) 1662^{5} 1903^{4} 2283^{9} 2765^{2} 3147^{7} 4001^{8} 4130^{5} **>66f<**
Ur Only Young Once 5 b m Pitpan-H and K Hattrick (Green Shoon) (2798)
Utmost Zeal (USA) 2 b c Cozzene (USA)-Zealous Lady (USA) (Highland Blade (USA)) 3010^{5} **>67f<**
Utrillo (USA) 6 b g Dahar (USA)-Waltz Me Sue (USA) (Olden Times) 2314^{13} **>17f<**
Utr (USA) 3 ch f Mr Prospector (USA)-Hasbah (Kris) 2576^{10} 2949^{7} 3783^{13} **>62tf<**

V

Vade Retro Satanas (FR) 3 b c Holst (USA)-Praise Be Given (Kings Lake (USA)) *5^{8} 90^{8}* 428^{12} **>36da 53df<**
Vadlamixa (FR) 3 gr f Linamix-Vadlava (Bikala) 1116a^{7} 1712a^{10} (3579a) 4015a^{5} **>111f<**
Vaguely Gay 3 b c Bering-Solveig (Gay Mecene) 1230a^{4} 2560a^{3} 3323a^{6} **>113f<**
Vague Spirit 2 ch c Vague Shot-Dawn Vigil VII (UR*) 2161^{9} 2912^{12} 3752^{7} **>41f<**
Vaigly Sunthyme 5 ch g Vaigly Great-Red Roses (FR) (Roi Dagobert) *589^{8}* 879^{10} 1496^{5} **>45f<**
Vain Prince 8 b h Sandhurst Prince-Vain Deb (Gay Fandango (USA)) 1036^{2} 1156^{5} (1359) 1643^{9} (1957) (2127) 2501^{4} (3002) 3355^{3} **>62f<**
Valanour(IRE) 3 b c Lomond-Vearia (Mill Reef) (1007a) 1575a^{6} (2044a) 3690a^{6} **>120f<**
Valclub (IRE) 6 ch m King of Clubs-Winfarthing (Reform) (4179a) **>91f<**
Vales Ales 2 b g Dominion Royale-Keep Mum (Mummy's Pet) 490^{6} 755^{5} 2158^{4} 2230^{3} 3851^{10} **>35f<**
Valetta 4 b f Faustus (USA)-Mrewa (Runnymede) 1326^{6} 1520^{4} 1967^{5} 3159^{9} **>41f<**
Valiant Man 4 br c Valiyar-Redcross Miss (Tower Walk) *31^{6}* **>49a 52f<**
Valiant Toski 4 b c Petoski-Corvelle (Reliance II) 1799^{3} *2090^{2}* (2535) **>50a 63f<**
Valinco 4 b f Malaspina-Sagareina (Sagaro) 1167^{14} 1539^{8} 1674^{9} 1974^{18} **>38f<**
Valise 2 b f Salse (USA)-Secret Valentine (Wollow) 2354^{4} 2773^{3} 3671^{7} **>46f<**
Valjess 2 b f Today and Tomorrow-Emmer Green

(Music Boy) 4023[11]
Valley of Gold (FR) **3** dk f Shirley Heights-Lustre (Halo) 802a[3] (1110a) (1237a) 2563a[3] 3694a[2] **>114f<**
Valley of Time (FR) **7** br m In Fijar (USA)-Vallee Sarthoise (FR) (Val de Loir) 1493[8] 1721[16] 1742[9] 2258[4] 2304[6] 2769[6] **>38f<**
Valsodo (USA) **3** ro c Alleged (USA)-Rainbow Morning (USA) (Super Concorde (USA)) 3790a[5] **>102f<**
Vanborough Lad **6** b g Precocious-Lustrous (Golden Act (USA)) 882[3] 1027[5] (1202) 1506[8] 1830[2] 2276[4] 2549[5] 2979[4] 3605[12] **>60f<**
Vanessa Rose **4** ro f Simply Great (FR)-Phoenix Rose 765[17] **>28a 58f<**
Van Gurp **2** ch c Generous (IRE)-Atlantic Flyer (USA) (Storm Bird (CAN)) 3494[3] 3832[7] **>68f<**
Vanishing Point **2** ch c Rock City-Lady River (FR) (Sir Gaylord) 436[11] 1424[2] 2135[10] (2765) 3019[4] 3267[3] 3613[W] (3780) 3985[17] 4151[4] **>86f<**
Vanola **3** b f Salse (USA)-Salilia (Nishapour (FR)) 1764[5] 1987[8] 2845[6] 3140[6] 3627[16] 3896[15] **>37f<**
Vanroy **11** b h Formidable-Princess Tavi 1509[7] 1663[6] **>60a 61df<**
Vaporize **3** ch g Handsome Sailor-Belle Appeal (Teenoso (USA)) 937[13] 1196[12] 1731[7] 2550[6] **>31f<**
Varnishing Day (IRE) **3** b c Royal Academy (USA)-Red Letter Day 2015[3] **>88f<**
Varsavia (USA) **4** br f Nureyev (USA)-Header Card (USA) (Quack (USA)) 1851[32] **>61++a 93f<**
Varvarka **3** b f Soviet Star (USA)-Helen Street (Troy) (1431) 2006[8] 2679[4] 3413[9] **>81f<**
Vasetto **2** b c Midyan (USA)-Canna (Caerleon (USA)) 2534[4] 2820[2] 3266[2] 3553[3] **>69f<**
Vasiliev **7** b h Sadler's Wells (USA)-Poquito Queen (CAN) (Explodent (USA)) 737[11] **>67df<**
Vaslav Nijinsky **3** b c Hadeer-Pacific Gull (USA) (Storm Bird (CAN)) *213[7] 316[2] 418[6] 587[8]* 1541[15] **>63a 11f<**
Vaugrenier (IRE) **3** b c Scenic-Church Mountain (Furry Glen) 657[10] 1097[3] (1275) 1912[4] 2172[2] 2691[6] 4149[8] 4283[3] **>87f<**
Vavona **3** ch f Ballad Rock-Savahra (Free State) 1786[9] 2137[6] 2318[5] 2491[8] **>62f<**
Vax New Way **2** gr c Siberian Express (USA)-Misty Arch (Starch Reduced) 1327[6] *(3509)* 3824[5] 3990[5] 4144[14] 4243[3] **>71a 63f<**
Vayello **4** b c Mtoto-Khalkeva (FR) (Vayrann) 1555[9] *1759[8]* **>43a 37f<**
Veesey **2** b f Rock City-Travel On (Tachypous) 1399[4] 1857[9] 2442[12] 3727[5] 3901[10] 3982[3] 4230[7] **>61f<**
Veiled Dancer (IRE) **2** b f Shareef Dancer (USA)-Fatal Distraction (Formidable) 3010[9] 3633[3] **>74f<**
Veloce (IRE) **7** b h Kafu-Joanns Goddess (Godswalk (USA)) *44[10] 71[8] 148[5] 211[5] 248[3] 323[5] 341[6]* 434[10] 559[5] 785[4] 870[21] 1021[11] (1155) (1355) 1561[3] (1754) 1915[8] 2369[6] 2477[9] 2744[2] 3063[7] 3207[5] 3222[9] **>51a 77f<**
Velvet Jones **2** b gr c Sharrood (USA)-Cradle of Love (USA) (Roberto (USA)) 1977[13] 2601[2] *2962[2]* 3132[6] 3350[2] 3533[3] 3767[4] 3858[7] 4045[6] **>52a 66f<**
Vena (IRE) **3** b f Danehill (USA)-Massawippi (Be My Native (USA)) 664[5] 957[5] (1473) 2028[4] 2411[4] (2707) 3007[3] 3413[2] 3945[37] **>101f<**
Vendetta **2** b f Belmez (USA)-Storm Warning (Tumble Wind (USA)) 1726[13] **>39f<**
Vengan **3** ch f Efisio-La Crima (Runnymede) 1515[8] *1763[10] 2071[11] 2493[5]* 2905[W] **>42a 50f<**
Venice Beach **3** b c Shirley Heights-Bold and Beautiful (Bold Lad (IRE)) 1804[2] 2100[4] 2929[2] 4164[D] **>86df<**
Veni Vidi Vici (IRE) **2** b c Fayruz-Divine Apsara (Godswalk (USA)) 3989[5] 4084[26] **>68f<**
Venture Capitalist **6** ch g Never so Bold-Brave Advance (USA) (Bold Laddie (USA)) 441[6] 571[4] (719) 953[4] (1100) 1482[5] 1895[4] 2097[4] 3191[6] 3446[2] 3551[7] 3717[9] **>114f<**
Venture Fourth **6** b h Hotfoot-Four Lawns *28[5] 120[11] 255[11]* 534[12] 784[6] 1161[9] 1688[4] 2165[8] 2769[7] **>32da 54f<**
Vera's First (IRE) **2** b f Exodal (USA)-Shades of Vera (Precocious) 791[11] 1536[5] 2011[2] 2173[6] 2674[3] 2847[3] 3080[2] 3969[4] 4144[4] 4243[5] **>72f<**
Verde Luna **3** b g Green Desert (USA)-Mamaluna (USA) (Roberto (USA)) 853[7] 1216[2] 1464[2] 1825[10] 2103[9] 2455[4] 2654[3] 3497[8] 3704[11] 3897[16] **>71f<**
Veronica Franco **2** b f Darshaan-Maiden Eileen (Stradavinsky) 4188[20] **>38f<**
Verro (USA) **8** ch h Irish River (FR)-Royal Rafale (USA) (Reneged) *894[8] 2090[3]* 2280[13] *2592[9]* **>20a 32f<**
Verulam (IRE) **2** b br c Marju (IRE)-Hot Curry (USA) (Sharpen Up) 3089[19] 3398[4] 3644[8] 4146[10] **>63f<**
Very Dicey **7** b g Tremblant-Party Game (Red Alert) *(14) 154[6] 194[2] 305[3] 391[2] 510[P]* **>67a 78df<**
Verzen (IRE) **3** ch c Salse (USA)-Virelai (Kris) (1374) 1839[10] (2948) 3813[16] 3991[3] **>103f<**
Veshca Lady (IRE) **2** b f Contract Law (USA)-Genzyme Gene (Riboboy (USA)) 819[8] 943[3] (1215) *1570[8]* 1740[4] 1943[6] 2155[2] 2516[3] 2855[3] (3048) 3309[3] 3975[12] 4111[12] **>61f<**
Vetheuil (USA) **3** ch c Riverman-Venise 4007a[7] **>99f<**
Vettori (IRE) **3** b c Machiavellian (USA)-Air Distingue (USA) (Sir Ivor) (1117a) 1611[6] 1837[3] **>118f<**
Veuve Hoornaert (IRE) **3** gr f Standaan (FR)-Hazy Lady (Habitat) 959[6] 1138[4] 1373[6] 2827[2] 3637[9] **>82f<**
Vezelay (USA) **3** b f Diesis-Vexation (USA) (Vice Regent (CAN)) 957[10] 1473[11] 1701[11] *2587[7]* **>34a 54f<**
Viardot (IRE) **6** b h Sadler's Wells (USA)-Vive La Reine (Vienna) 2391[5] 3899[7] **>67a 89df<**
Vibro (IRE) **3** b c Sharp Victor (USA)-Binnissima (USA) (Tilt Up (USA)) *7[8]* **>31a f<**
Vicenza **3** ch f Old Vic-Ela Romara (Ela-Mana-Mou) 4245[8] **>53f<**
Viceroy Ruler **4** gr c Faustus (USA)-Viceroy Princess (Godswalk (USA)) 1970[9] **>42f<**
Victim of Love **2** b f Damister (USA)-Tantalizing Song (CAN) (The Minstrel (CAN)) 4262[18] **>54f<**
Victoria Day **3** b f Reference Point-Victoress (USA) (Conquistador Cielo (USA)) 787[7] 2004[4] 3224[5] 3669[16] **>54f<**
Victoria Hall **5** b m Hallgate-Thorganby Victory *187[7] 233[11] 306[8]* **>34a 59f<**
Victoria Princess **8** b m King of Spain-Renira (Relkino) *71[12]* 541[11] **>4a 28f<**
Victoria Regia (IRE) **2** b f Lomond (USA)-Will of Victory (Dancers Image (USA)) 3069[9] 3339[3] 3650[3] (3996) **>95f<**
Victoria Sioux **2** ch f Ron's Victory (USA)-Blues Indigo (Music Boy) 1176[6] 1964[4] 2750[5] 3623[11] **>66f<**
Victoria's Secret (IRE) **3** b f Law Society (USA)-Organdy (Blakeney) 888[8] 2028[9] 2532[2] 3006[3] 3521[12] 4136[8] **>71f<**

Victoria Venture 2 b f Ron's Victory (USA)-Leafy Garland (USA) (Lypheor) 650[6] 1142[6] 1287[4] *2075*[3] 2242[8] *(2496)* *2635*[3] 2908[5] 3533[13] *3738*[2] *4127*[7] **>59a 58f<**

Victor Laszlo 3 b c Ilium-Report 'em (USA) (Staff Writer (USA)) 2426[3] 3421[5] 3722[8] **>55f<**

Victory Commander 2 b c Efisio-Gay Hostess (FR) (Direct Flight) 1662[14] 1938[12] 3441[12] **>32f<**

Victory Team (IRE) 3 b c Danehill (USA)-Hogan's Sister (USA) (Speak John) 637[7] 2319[4] 2553[12] 3377[3] 3497[15] 3875[6] **>72f<**

Vielle Rose (IRE) 3 f 2045a[6] **>93f<**

View From Above 9 b m Dara Monarch-Organdy (Blakeney) *8*[7] *106*[5] *193*[7] *285*[6] **>73a 84f<**

Vilaine 2 b f Reprimand-Mumtaz Highflyer (High Top) 3590a[2]

Vilander (GER) 3 c 1713a[9] 2215a[10] **>91f<**

Vilayet 2 ch c Machiavellian (USA)-Vilikaia (USA) (Nureyev (USA)) (2420) 3215[4] **>78f<**

Village King (IRE) 2 b c Roi Danzig (USA)-Honorine (USA) (Blushing Groom (FR)) 4080[7] 4320[7] **>84f<**

Village Native (FR) 2 ch c Village Star (FR)-Zedative (FR) (Zeddaan) 2320[14] 2487[2] 2740[W] 3628[3] 3765[5] 4208[W] 4211[5] (4330) **>76f<**

Village Opera 2 gr f Rock City-Lucky Song (Lucky Wednesday) 788[10] 1413[10] 3713[9] **>41f<**

Villeggiatura 2 b c Machiavellian (USA)-Hug Me (Shareef Dancer (USA)) 2070[2] 2320[10] (3010) 3414[4] **>87f<**

Vindaloo 3 ch c Indian Ridge-Lovely Lagoon (Mill Reef (USA)) *185*[2] *263*[5] *309*[4] *444*[4] (578) 759[5] (969) 1207[6] (1371) (1553) (1645) (1801) 1825[4] (1946) 2062[3] 2101[2] (2263) (2525) *(2589)* *(2604)* 2701[4] 3021[7] 3189[3] *3319*[3] 3433[2] 3459[4] 3659[4] 3781[2] 3840[3] 3926[9] **>74a 95f<**

Vin St Koola 3 b c Vin St Benet-Nikoola Eve (Roscoe Blake) *(372)* *566*[6] 822[3] 1170[7] 1626[12] 3531[13] 3863[15] 3970[10] **>57a 61f<**

Vintage Crop 8 ch g Rousillon (USA)-Overplay (Bustino) 1869[4] (2219a) (3481a) 3789a[4] 4349a[3] **>124f<**

Vintage Taittinger (IRE) 3 b c Nordico (USA)-Kalonji (Red Alert) 502[17] *(626)* 905[5] *1628*[3] *1881*[2] *1955*[10] **>50a 44f<**

Viridis (USA) 2 b f Green Dancer-Vachti (FR) (Crystal Palace (FR)) 4247[4] **>70f<**

Virkon Venture (IRE) 7 b g Auction Ring (USA)-Madame Fair (Monseigneur (USA)) 494[4] **>67df<**

Virtual Reality 4 b c Diamond Shoal-Warning Bell (Bustino) 1141[2] 1357[2] 1926[5] 2457[6] 2780[7] 3659[3] 3945[39] 4163[11] **>88df<**

Vishnu (USA) 5 b h Storm Bird (CAN)-Vachti (FR) (Crystal Palace (FR)) *15*[8] *206*[6] *295*[8] *374*[9] 751[9] **>62a 64f<**

Visual Illusion (IRE) 3 b f Hatim (USA)-Trompe D'Oeil (Longleat (USA)) *5*[11] *51*[7] *168*[6] **>9a f<**

Vital Evidence 2 br f Today and Tomorrow-Vital Witness (Garda's Revenge (USA)) *2962*[5] 3080[4] **>30a 59f<**

Vitus 3 b c Dancing Brave (USA)-Sancta (So Blessed) 691[7] **>85f<**

Viva Nureyev (USA) 3 ch c Nureyev (USA)-Viva Zapata (Affirmed (US 706a[3] 1117a[7] **>94f<**

Viyapari (IRE) 3 b c Last Tycoon-Rowa (Great Nephew) 552[2] 677[7] 2794[5] 3461[2] 3889[17] **>76f<**

Vizard (IRE) 3 ch c Old Vic-Impudent Miss (Persian Bold) 655[4] 851[12] 1093[15] 1379[2] 1696[4] 2268[9] **>73f<**

Vlaanderen (IRE) 3 b f In The Wings-Marie de Flandre (FR) (Crystal Palace (FR)) 1383[7] 1987[6] **>60f<**

Vladivostok 5 gr h Siberian Express (USA)-Tsungani (Cure The Blues (USA)) 1513[20] 4152[10] **>37a 30f<**

Vocal Command 3 b c Chief Singer-To Oneiro (Absalom) *4123*[11] *4340*[7] **>53a 59f<**

Voila Premiere (IRE) 3 b c Roi Danzig (USA)-Salustrina (Sallust) 524[16] 733[13] (908) 1251[2] 3469[5] **>73f<**

Volare 2 b f Prince Sabo-Nazmiah (Free State) 1653[3] **>60f<**

Vola Via (USA) 2 b br c Known Fact (USA)-Pinking Shears (USA) (Sharpen Up) 1134[7] 1511[4] 1856[5] (2299) 2710[4] 3090[3] 3405[2] 3711[12] 3865[10] **>83f<**

Volochine (IRE) 4 ch c Soviet Star (USA)-Harmless Albatross 606a[2] 1118a[5] 4007a[2] 4185a[7] **>122f<**

Volona 0 3583a[3] **>71f<**

Volunteer (IRE) 3 b c Midyan (USA)-Sistabelle (Bellypha) 854[4] 1097[11] 3653[7] 3889[4] **>71f<**

W

Wacky (IRE) 4 b or br f Petorius-Zany (Junius (USA)) 2832[16] **>7a 19f<**

Wadada 4 b or br c Adbass (USA)-No Rejection (Mummy's Pet) 423[18] 548[13] **>45a 37f<**

Waders Dream (IRE) 6 b h Doulab (USA)-Sea Mistress (Habitat) *71*[7] *140*[7] *220*[11] *287*[5] *331*[5] 1070[12] 1164[6] 1499[10] 1785[12] 3055[3] 3139[3] 3293[6] 3681[11] 4240[9] **>39a 53f<**

Wahem (IRE) 5 b h Lomond (USA)-Pro Patria *8*[8] *73*[9] *169*[7] 4284[2] **>35da 45f<**

Wahiba Sands 2 b g Pharly (FR)-Lovely Noor (USA) (Fappiano (USA)) (4312) **>84+f<**

Waikiki Beach (USA) 4 ch c Fighting Fit (USA)-Running Melody (Rheingold) 665[19] 1365[8] 1728[12] 2803[8] 3109[9] 3674[3] 3960[7] *4297*[7] **>60a 70f<**

Wainwright (USA) 6 ch h Bering-Crystal Bright (Bold Lad (IRE)) 2118[7] 2936[F] **>112f<**

Waiting 4 b c Polish Precedent (USA)-Just You Wait (Nonoalco (USA)) 750[2] (1479) 1585[2] 2104[3] 2360[2] **>112f<**

Waitingforwalnuts (IRE) 2 b f Fayruz-Centre Travel (Godswalk (USA)) *1090*[7] *2146*[9] *2924*[9] 3290[10] **>17f<**

Wakeel (USA) 3 b c Gulch (USA)-Raahia (CAN) (Vice Regent (CAN)) 1301[5] 1782[5] 2068[5] 3382[2] 3556[6] 3729[10] 3945[27] 4267[17] **>95f<**

Waking (CAN) 4 ch c Rahy (USA)-Dreamsend (USA) (Herbager) 3818[19] **>60df<**

Waldo 4 ch g Northern State (USA)-One Degree (Crooner) *89*[15] *249*[3] *313*[8] 2010[9] *2292*[6] 2661[2] 2808[3] *3082*[3] 3757[3] 3934[5] 4079[17] **>68a 76f<**

Wali (USA) 5 b h Lomond (USA)-Magic Slipper (Habitat) 593[7] 790[8] *1087*[11] **>73a 75f<**

Walk In The Wild 3 b f Bold Owl-Tripolitaine (FR) 3704[16] **>26f<**

Walk on Mix (FR) 3 gr c Linamix (FR)-Walk on Air (Cure The Blues (USA)) (801a) 1574a[9] 4176a[4] **>112f<**

Walk the Beat 5 b h Interrex (CAN)-Plaits (Thatching) *16*[2] *65*[4] *150*[2] *182*[6] *366*[6] (890) 1021[12] *2073*[7] 2736[3] 2870[2] 2930[2] 2997[4] 4057[19] **>65a 67f<**

Walnut Burl (IRE) 5 b h Taufan (USA)-Hay Knot (Main Reef) 728[4] 1013[2] 1261[8] 1516[5] 2342[7] 2539[4] (2840)

3268^{4} 3771^{6} 3960^{8} **>65f<**

Walsham Whisper (IRE) 4 b f Taufan (USA)-Papsie's Pet (Busted) 558^{9} 668^{8} 938^{13} **>85f<**

Walter Willy (IRE) 4 b c Sadler's Wells (USA)-Whakilyric (USA) (Miswaki (USA)) 1005a^{3} 1387a^{7} **>113f<**

Wandering Minstrel (IRE) 3 ch c Ballad Rock-Priddy Blue (Blue Cashmere) 813^{6} 1165^{2} 1512^{2} 1778^{8} 3181^{4} 3545^{13} 3823^{14} 4044^{13} **>64f<**

Wandering Star (USA) 2 b f Red Ransom (USA)-Beautiful Bedouin (USA) (His Majesty (USA)) 2351^{9} **>72f<**

Wannaplantatree 4 b f Niniski (USA)-Cataclysmic (Ela-Mana-Mou) *193^{6}* 506^{14} 1058^{12} 1695^{2} 2201^{4} 2452^{3} *2919^{5}* (3262) 3804^{4} **>61a 79f<**

Warbrook 2 b c Warrshan (USA)-Bracey Brook (Gay Fandango (USA)) 1715^{5} 2283^{8} 3436^{3} 3780^{2} (3968) 4139^{2} **>93f<**

Wardara 3 ch f Sharpo-Ward One (Mr Fluorocarbon) 3359^{21} 3545^{10} 3677^{5} 3715^{21} **>77f<**

Warhurst (IRE) 4 b g Nordance (USA)-Pourboire (Star Appeal) *1^{8} 82^{4} 117^{8} 308^{3}* **>55a 62f<**

Warluskee 3 b f Dancing Brave (USA)-Walesiana (GER) (Star Appeal) *(376)* 947^{12} 3343^{9} **>72a 60f<**

Warm Hearted (USA) 3 ch g Known Fact (USA)-Lovin' Lass (USA) (Cutlass (USA)) 1445^{U}

Warming Trends 2 b g Warning-Sunny Davis (USA) (Alydar (USA)) 2876^{8} 3003^{8} 3180^{7} (3749) (3858) (3894) **>81?f<**

Warm Spell 5 b g Northern State (USA)-Warm Wind (Tumble Wind (USA)) *(356)* 1716^{2} 2445^{7} 3406^{9} 3555^{5} 3730^{5} 3957^{10} **>78a 81f<**

Warning Order 3 b c Warrshan (USA)-Bell Toll (High Line) 619^{3} 1062^{2} 1925^{2} (2316) 2738^{10} 3107^{4} 3374^{3} 3556^{2} (3754) 3923^{3} 4074^{2} **>111f<**

Warning Reef 2 b c Warning-Horseshoe Reef (Mill Reef (USA)) 1752^{5} 1903^{2} 2441^{7} 3090^{4} **>82f<**

Warning Shadows (IRE) 3 ch f Cadeaux Genereux-Silent Movie (Shirley Heights) (664) 1145^{2} 1390a^{2} 1850^{4} 2349^{5} 2763^{2} 3323a^{2} 3498^{4} 3693a^{3} (3944) 4184a^{7} **>116f<**

Warning Shot 3 b c Dowsing (USA)-Warning Bell (Bustino) 930^{6} 1474^{4} 1754^{7} 2737^{16} 3028^{11} *3242^{10}* 3493^{7} 4053^{6} 4165^{23} **>25a 61f<**

Warning Star 3 b f Warning-Blade of Grass (Kris) (952) 1475^{7} 1848^{13} 2285^{3} 3476a^{2} 3550^{5} 4121^{11} **>106df<**

Warning Time 2 b c Warning-Ballad Island (Ballad Rock) (1751) 2441^{6} (2710) 3731^{3} 4039^{2} **>93f<**

Warren Knight 2 b c Weldnaas (USA)-Trigamy 4023^{9} **>55tf<**

War Requiem (IRE) 5 b h Don't Forget Me-Ladiz (Persian Bold) *3544^{5}* 3657^{18} **>37a 49?f<**

Warrgem 3 b f Warrshan (USA)-Flying Flynn (Vaigly Great) 1270^{10} 1430^{7} 1667^{10} **>13f<**

Warrior Lady (IRE) 3 ch f Al Hareb (USA)-Lady Bettina (Bustino) *141^{2} 261^{5} 350^{6} 444^{11}* 1219^{11} *1628^{7} 1881^{5}* **>56a 44f<**

War Shanty 2 b f Warrshan (USA)-Daring Ditty (Daring March) 4320^{23} **>15f<**

Warwick Mist (IRE) 3 ch f Digamist (USA)-Flash Donna (USA) (Well Decorated (USA)) *135^{4} 180^{2}* **>35a 38f<**

Warwick Warrior (IRE) 4 b g Reasonable (FR)-Almost Heaven (Corvaro (USA)) *6^{5} 102^{6} (139) 184^{2} 297^{6}* 636^{12} 765^{13} **>72a 66f<**

Wasblest 3 b f Statoblest-Safety First (Wassl) *40^{3} 86^{2} 159^{2} 629^{8}* 1972^{2} 2013^{4} 2092^{2} 2163^{2} 2303^{4} **>57a 62f<**

Washington Reef (USA) 2 b c Seattle Dancer (USA)-Broken Wave (Bustino) 3883^{14} 4063^{17} **>53f<**

Wassl's Guest (IRE) 4 b f Be My Guest (USA)-Wassl's Sister (Troy) 929^{11} 1149^{9} **>16f<**

Wassl's Nanny (IRE) 6 b m Wassl-Granny's Bank (Music Boy) *379^{10}* 478^{5} 672^{21} **>14a 48f<**

Wassl Street (IRE) 3 b c Dancing Brave (USA)-One Way Street (Habitat) 1526^{14} 3438^{8} 3896^{14} **>67f<**

Watani (USA) 4 ch c Riverman (USA)-Azayim (Be My Guest (USA)) 1577a^{7} **>92f<**

Watch Me Go (IRE) 6 b h On Your Mark-Nighty Night 3305^{6} *(3544)* **>55a 42f<**

Watch Me (IRE) 2 b f Green Desert (USA)-Fenny Rough (Home Guard (USA)) 1169^{2} 1497^{4} 3069^{10} **>83f<**

Watch My Lips 3 b g Vin St Benet-Manor Farm Toots (Royalty) 1914^{8} 2065^{9} 2744^{6} 3344^{15} 3658^{10} **>55f<**

Watch the Clock 3 b f Mtoto-Brilliant Timing (USA) (The Minstrel (CAN)) 932^{4} 1105^{2} 1800^{5} **>97f<**

Water Bebe (IRE) 3 b f Persian Bold-Bebe Altesse (GER) (Alpenkonig (GER)) *10^{2} 47^{4} (54) 98^{0}* **>66+a 51df<**

Water Chestnut 2 ch g Most Welcome-Water Pageant *4334^{12}* **>24a f<**

Water Diviner 5 b g Dowsing (USA)-Prudence (Grundy) 3658^{14} **>19a 48f<**

Water Hazard (IRE) 3 b c Maelstrom Lake-Simply Inch (Simply Great (FR)) *(85) 99^{3} 176^{4} (251) 333^{5}* 813^{14} 1165^{8} 1472^{13} *1789^{5} 2407^{2}* 2522^{8} 2828^{3} *3082^{4}* (3265) 3288^{3} 3959^{2} **>62a 59f<**

Waterland (USA) 2 ch f Explodent (USA)-Water Angel (USA) (Halo (USA)) 3009^{5} (3397) 3518^{3} **>81f<**

Waterloo Belle 4 ch f Kind of Hush-Afrabela (African Sky) *1567^{8}* 1971^{10} 2506^{5} **>12f<**

Waterlord (IRE) 5 b h Bob Back (USA)-Ringtail (Auction Ring (USA)) *417^{9}* 559^{17} 672^{16} 820^{7} 992^{4} 1027^{10} 3825^{13} 4170^{9} **>46a 55f<**

Water Music Melody 2 b f Sizzling Melody-Raintree Venture (Good Times (ITY)) 2515^{8} 2866^{3} **>40f<**

Wathbat Mtoto 3 b f Mtoto-Alwathba (USA) (Lyphard (USA)) 1128^{4} (1273) 1661^{9} (2752) 2902^{2} 3413^{4} **>94f<**

Watheeqah (USA) 4 b f Topsider (USA)-Reyah (Young Generation) *6^{7}* **>42a 64f<**

Wave Hill 6 b h Sizzling Melody-Trikymia (Final Straw) 2766^{7} 2979^{6} **>63a 75f<**

Waverley Star 10 br h Pitskelly-Quelle Blague (Red God) *23^{4} 237^{2} 287^{9} 331^{6} 348^{8} 404^{6} 501^{8}* 541^{3} 887^{11} 2398^{7} 2463^{5} 2956^{7} 3121^{8} *3522^{13}* **>41da 50f<**

Wavey 2 b f Kris-Throw Away Line (USA) (Assert) (3643) 3832^{4} 4105^{8} **>81f<**

Wave Your Flag (USA) 8 (3908a) **>100f<**

Wavian 3 b c Warning-Vian (USA) (Far Out East (USA)) 612^{2} 921^{7} 1480^{7} 2097^{5} 3316^{2} 3557^{4} **>102f<**

Wayfarers Way (USA) 4 ch c Manastash Ridge-Miss Daytona (USA) (Nashua) 1792^{4} 2010^{10} 3234^{2} 3362^{6} **>73f<**

Wayne County (IRE) 5 b h Sadler's Wells (USA)-Detroit (FR) (Riverman (USA)) (558) 623^{5} 712^{10} 913^{7} 1260^{4} 1385^{4} 1780^{6} (3070) 3498^{3} 3614^{3} 3811^{4} **>68a 116f<**

Waypoint 2 b f Cadeaux Genereux-Princess Athena (Ahonoora) 4070^{6} **>43f<**

Way West (FR) 5 b h Gone West (USA)-Greenway (FR) (Targowice (USA)) 1112a[3] 1572a[8] **>108f<**
Weather Break 4 b c Mtoto-Favourite Girl (Mummy's Pet) 652[7] 1531[5] 1754[8] 2051[2] 2414[10] **>86f<**
Weaver Bird 5 b m Master Willie-Sweet Snow (USA) (Lyphard (USA)) 960[6] 1351[2] (2031) 2703[18] 3026[3] (3382) 3945[9] 4267[14] **>95f<**
Weaver George (IRE) 5 b g Flash of Steel-Nephrite (Godswalk (USA)) 1025[4] 1359[4] **>39f<**
Web of Intrigue 3 ch f Machiavellian (USA)-Catawba (Mill Reef (USA)) 779[7] **>69f<**
Wedding Gift 2 b f Always Fair-Such Style (Sassafras) 3578a[3]
Wedding Gift (FR) 2 b f Always Fair-Such Style 4013a[7] **>89f<**
Wee Hope (USA) 2 b c Housebuster (USA)-Tell Me Sumthing (USA) (Summing (USA)) 2615[6] 3626[2] 3784[3] **>77f<**
Weet-A-Minute (IRE) 2 ro c Nabeel Dancer (USA)-Ludovica (Bustino) 2681[5] 3208[3] 3463[3] (3644) (4001) (4139) 4264[2] **>101f<**
Wee Tinkerbell 2 ch f Timeless Times (USA)-Kiveton Komet (Precocious) 1203[3] 1448[6] 1685[4] **>66f<**
Weetman's Weigh (IRE) 2 b c Archway (IRE)-Indian Sand (Indian King (USA)) *1089[3] 1454[5]* 1690[2] *2143[2]* 2548[4] (2817) 3271[6] 3969[2] 4077[9] **>66a 68f<**
Welcome Lu 2 ch f Most Welcome-Odile (Green Dancer (USA)) 3976[7] 4224[19]
Welcome Royale (IRE) 2 ch c Be My Guest (USA)-Kirsova (Absalom) 2116[5] 2420[4] 2995[11] 3701[6] 3928[3] 4081[4] **>76f<**
Well and Truly 8 b m Rousillon (USA)-Altana (Grundy) *(45) 108[3] 259[12] 295[6]* **>60a 41f<**
Well Arranged (IRE) 4 ch c Bold Arrangement-Eurynome (Be My Guest (USA)) 632[11] 1109[7] 2530[11] 2768[7] 3986[7] **>75f<**
Well Beloved 4 b c Sadler's Wells (USA)-Sancta (So Blessed) 661[3] 998[9] **>91f<**
Well Drawn 2 b c Dowsing (USA)-Classic Design (Busted) 3340[10] **>52f<**
Wellsian (USA) 3 b c Sadler's Wells (USA)-My Darling One (USA) (Exclusive Native (USA)) 1988[4] 2321[15] 2678[4] (3102) 3349[2] **>81f<**
Well Suited 5 b h Elegant Air-Gay Appeal (Star Appeal) *29[5]* **>24a 14f<**
Wells Whisper (FR) 3 b f Sadler's Wells (USA)-Whakilyric (USA) (Miswaki (USA)) 797[4] 997[7] 1990[3] 2411[3] 2798[4] 3031[3] **>82f<**
Wellsy Lad (USA) 8 ch h El Baba (USA)-Iwishiknew (USA) (Damascus (USA)) *78[14] 231[5] 338[4] 400[2]* 478[2] *590[11] 769[13] 845[12] 1034[2] 1459[3] 1571[6] (1760) 1884[2]* **>46a 52f<**
Welsh Column 9 b m Welsh Captain-Bally's Step (Ballynockan) *2076[9]* 2148[6] **>11a 7f<**
Welsh Heritage (IRE) 5 b m Slip Anchor-Mohibbah (USA) (Conquistador Cielo (USA)) *130[7] 199[5]* **>21a 39?f<**
Welsh Liberty (IRE) 6 b h Caerleon-Bernica 4186a[2] **>89f<**
Welshman 9 ch h Final Straw-Joie de Galles 998[17] 2429[6] 3211[2] 3425[7] 3774[9] **>103f<**
Welsh Melody 2 b f Merdon Melody-Young Whip (Bold Owl) 1287[7] *(2591) 2962[10] 3738[6]* 3937[18] *4127[9]* **>53a 31f<**
Welsh Mill (IRE) 6 b h Caerleon (USA)-Gay Milly (FR) 3801[13] 4000[20] **>66f<**
Welsh Mist 4 b f Damister (USA)-Welwyn (Welsh Saint) 571[12] 659[6] 934[3] 1870[5] 2285[7] 2416[3] 2671[5] 3191[5] 3446[11] 3551[13] **>107f<**
Welsh Mountain 2 b c Welsh Captain-Miss Nelski (Most Secret) 825[5] 1047[2] 1247[3] (2335) 2779[9] 3064[2] 3369[3] **>84f<**
Welsh Owl 2 ch f Bold Owl-Thabeh (Shareef Dancer (USA)) 2035[7] *2635[7]* 3054[6] **>37a 32f<**
Welsh Wizzard 3 b g Robellino (USA)-My Greatest Star (Great Nephew) *204[5] 270[6]* **>22a f<**
Welton Arsenal 3 b c Statoblest-Miller's Gait (Mill Reef (USA)) 438[5] 633[2] 858[4] 980[8] 1131[4] 1373[2] 1487[11] 1806[14] **>102f<**
Welville 2 b c Most Welcome-Miss Top Ville (FR) (Top Ville) 810[7] 1063[2] (3604) **>84f<**
Wendals Touch 4 gr f Touch of Grey-Snow Huntress (Shirley Heights) 2337[6] 3750[15] 3859[7] **>36f<**
Wendy's Way 3 b f Merdon Melody-Piccadilly Rose *54[8] 105[6] 171[10]* **>41a 50f<**
Wentbridge Lad (IRE) 5 b h Coquelin (USA)-Cathryn's Song (Prince Tenderfoot (USA)) 505[5] 568[4] 839[3] *1074[2]* 1202[2] 1323[2] 1491[5] *(1629)* 1714[3] *1953[5]* 1995[12] *2142[2] 2291[5] (2588)* (2797) 2875[3] 3063[3] 3113[5] 3222[4] 3393[5] 3611[3] 3802[13] 3837[5] 3963[6] 3993[8] 4038[9] 4325[12] **>82a 74f<**
We're Joken 3 b f Statoblest-Jay Gee Ell (Vaigly Great) *528[6]* 578[12] (753) 862[8] *(891)* (1453) 1564[4] 1876[5] 3830[13] *4274[11]* **>50a 57f<**
Wessam Prince 4 b c Soviet Star (USA)-Clare Bridge (USA) (Little Current (USA)) (895a) (1393a) 1870[4] 2562a[3] 3042a[3] 3582a[3] 3834[5] 4178a[7] **>118f<**
Wesshaun 5 b m Shaunicken-Wessex Flyer (Pony Express) *1762[11]* **>34f<**
West Austria (IRE) 2 b c Tirol-Labwa (USA) (Lyphard (USA)) 1597[6] 3228[7] **>66f<**
Westcoast 4 b g 503[17] *605[13]* **>3a 54f<**
Westcourt Magic 2 b c Emarati (USA)-Magic Milly (Simply Great (FR)) 1413[8] 1877[9] 2485[7] (2606) (2991) (3213) (3354) 3444[2] (3668) 4032[2] **>107f<**
Westcourt Princess 3 b f Emarati (USA)-Petrol (Troy) *587[10] 768[4]* 1414[10] 1669[8] 1945[4] (2225) 2503[8] 2993[2] (3422) 3462[4] 3935[10] 4038[8] **>41a 65+f<**
Western Country 3 ch c Beveled (USA)-Country Singer (Town And Country) 963[8] 1198[17] **>27f<**
Western Fame (USA) 3 b c Gone West (USA)-Fariedah (USA) (Topsider (USA)) 715[9] 987[7] (1778) 2321[3] (3411) 3813[3] 3999[2] 4267[7] **>98f<**
Western Fleet (USA) 4 ch c Westheimer (USA)-Fleetwood Fancy (Taufan (USA)) *530[9]* **>12a 63df<**
Western General 4 ch c Cadeaux Genereux-Patsy Western (Precocious) (749) 1061[10] 1415[9] 1616[3] 2117[7] 4002[2] 4196[4] **>88f<**
Western Horizon (USA) 3 ch f Gone West (USA)-Norette (Northfields (USA)) 449[4] *560[4]* 745[5] 1218[9] 1696[9] 2305[4] 2842[5] 3137[4] 3521[2] 3772[11] 3896[6] 4086[3] *4223[12]* **>33a 59f<**
Western Playboy 3 b c Law Society (USA)-Reine D'Beaute (Caerleon (USA)) 635[14] **>60f<**

Western Ploy **3** b f Deploy-Westerlake (Blakeney) *48^{9}* **>14f<**

Western Reel (USA) **3** b f Gone West (USA)-River Jig (USA) (Irish River (FR)) 865^{7} (1675) 1923^{3} 2763^{4} 3331a^{11} 3636^{4} **>110f<**

Western Sal **3** b f Salse (USA)-Patsy Western (Precocious) 1701^{3} 2265^{2} 2794^{3} (3294) 3863^{19} **>77f<**

Western Valley **5** ch m Valiyar-Another Western (Good Times (ITY)) 3363^{8} 3638^{8} 3661^{14} **>27a 41f<**

Western Venture (IRE) **2** ch c Two Timing (USA)-Star Gazing (IRE) (Caerleon (USA)) 2336^{3} 2498^{3} (3053) 3568^{13} **>68f<**

West Farm Boy **3** b g Full Extent (USA)-La Melodie 1993^{11} 2582^{14} 2818^{11} **>36f<**

Westfield Moves (IRE) **7** b h Montelimar (USA)-Rathcoffey Daisy (Pampapaul) *91^{11}* **>35a 57f<**

West Humble **2** ch f Pharly (FR)-Humble Pie (Known Fact (USA)) 3983^{3} **>74f<**

West Memphis (USA) **2** ch c Gone West-Dancing Slippers (Nijinsk 2896a^{2}

Westminster (IRE) **3** ch c Nashamaa-Our Galadrial (Salmon Leap (USA)) 687^{2} (1026) 1219^{4} 2139^{5} **>71f<**

Wet Patch (IRE) **3** b or br c Common Grounds-Disco Girl (FR) (Green Dancer (USA)) 745^{7} 1498^{2} 1664^{4} 1978^{4} 2557^{2} 2804^{4} (3154) 3531^{5} 4261^{14} **>72f<**

Whackford Squeers **3** ch g Komaite (USA)-Manhunt (Posse (USA)) *(174) 250^{5}* 2103^{8} **>72a 55f<**

Whalley Abbey **2** ch f Mon Tresor-Last Note (Welsh Pageant) 2487^{5} 2651^{10} *2939^{2}* 3887^{10} **>60a 60f<**

Wharfedale Music **4** ch f Grey Desire-Flute Royale (Horage) 1771^{13} 2450^{3} **>36f<**

What a Nightmare (IRE) **3** gr c Petorius-Mysterious Lady (Melyno) *324^{4} 388^{3} 417^{2} 591^{8} 767^{4} 1087^{6} 1334^{2} (1571) 1760^{2} (2073)* (2390) (2832) 3050^{3} 3807^{15} *3950^{3} 4272^{8}* **>73a 69f<**

Whatever's Right (IRE) **6** b g Doulab (USA)-Souveniers (Relko) 731^{14} *(1049)* 1244^{5} (1541) 1676^{3} 2342^{3} 3159^{2} 3439^{3} 3534^{4} 3943^{21} **>65a 80f<**

What Fun **2** b c Petong-State Romance (Free State) 849^{3} (977) 1838^{9} 4034^{4} 4084^{22} 4200^{6} **>80f<**

What Jim Wants (IRE) **2** b g Magical Strike (USA)-Sally Gone (IRE) (Last Tycoon) *3243^{10}* 3670^{15} 3975^{24} 4073^{6} 4172^{9} 4290^{11} **>50f<**

Whatone Bell **5** b h Presidium-Betbellof *36^{4} 142^{9} 265^{12} 341^{12}* **>32df<**

What's Secreto (USA) **3** gr c Secreto (USA)-What A Shack (USA) (Al Hattab (USA)) 1147^{11} 3653^{9} 3899^{12} 4205^{10} *4293^{3}* **>58a 62f<**

What's the Verdict (IRE) **3** b g Law Society (USA)-Cecina (Welsh Saint) *59^{3}* 687^{5} 1325^{2} (1463) **>75a 81f<**

Where's Margaret **2** b f Jareer (USA)-Dancing Chimes (London Bells (CAN)) 1690^{9} 1938^{2} 2336^{2} 2552^{2} 2706^{8} 3335^{4} *(3675)* 3894^{6} 4077^{6} **>61f<**

Whicksey Perry **2** b g Presidium-Phamilla (IRE) (Bellypha) (474) (562) (1096) 1384^{3} 1868^{6} 3668^{7} 4066^{8} **>85f<**

Whispering Dawn **2** b f Then Again-Summer Sky (Skyliner) 878^{4} 1169^{7} (1336) 1650^{4} 3546^{7} (3701) 3760^{15} **>68f<**

Whispering Loch (IRE) **4** ch c Lomond (USA)-Why so Silent (Mill Reef (USA)) 1732^{4} 1855^{9} 2246^{7} 2486^{5} **>46f<**

Whitechapel (USA) **7** br g Arctic Tern (USA)-Christchurch (FR) 1140^{4} 1853^{14} 3162^{13} (3730) 3836^{4} 4076^{3} 4204^{3} 4325^{9} **>109f<**

White Emir **2** b g Emarati (USA)-White African (Carwhite) 1203^{9} (1356) 2459^{2} 2523^{6} 3160^{2} (3655) 3727^{10} 4077^{3} **>86f<**

White Ensign (IRE) **2** b c Imperial Frontier (USA)-Markon 1662^{8} 1842^{3} 2340^{2} **>76f<**

White Flash **4** b f Sure Blade (USA)-Princess Matilda 1974^{15} 2134^{4} 2528^{15} 2983^{4} 3129^{4} **>60df<**

Whitegatesprincess (IRE) **4** b f Valiyar-Whitegates Lady (Le Coq d'Or) 2676^{7} 2913^{11}

White Heat **3** b f Last Tycoon-Sweeping (Indian King (USA)) 1312^{5} 2319^{10} 2657^{12} 3605^{16} 4043^{18} **>47f<**

White Knowle **5** b m Governor General-Teresa Way 987^{11} 1155^{8} **>18f<**

Whitelock Quest **7** b h Rainbow Quest (USA)-Sagar (Habitat) *(415) 520^{8} (1078)* **>45a 20f<**

White On Red(GER) **3** f 1009a^{6} 1705a^{7} **>94f<**

White Palace **3** b f Shirley Heights-Blonde Prospect (USA) (Mr Prospector (USA)) (865) 1139^{8} 1946^{6} **>87f<**

White Plains (IRE) **2** b c Nordico (USA)-Flying Diva (Chief Singer) 3900^{21} 4255^{5} (4329) **>70f<**

White Sea (IRE) **2** ch f Soviet Lad (USA)-Bilander (High Line) 2526^{2} 2717^{4} 3441^{3} (3887) 4208^{9} **>83f<**

White Settler **2** b c Polish Patriot (USA)-Oasis (Valiyar) 2107^{5} 3104^{3} 3662^{7} **>61f<**

White Sorrel **4** ro c Chilibang-Midnight Imperial (Night Shift (USA)) *(297) (400)* 434^{21} 1151^{5} 1565^{2} 2060^{12} 2930^{3} *3242^{7}* 3681^{17} *4337^{15}* **>82a 69f<**

White Whispers **2** gr f Absalom-Love Talk (Hotfoot) 791^{5} 1169^{9} (2035) 2242^{5} 2594^{4} 2947^{6} 3216^{4} 3452^{2} 3548^{4} 3702^{6} 3886^{5} **>83f<**

White Willow **6** br h Touching Wood (USA)-Dimant Blanche (USA) (Gummo (USA)) 556^{3} 821^{4} 1621^{U} **>90a 76f<**

Whitley Grange Boy **2** b g Hubbly Bubbly (USA)-Choir (High Top) 3592^{10} 4037^{5} *4334^{3}* **>67a 62f<**

Whittingham Girl **3** b f Primo Dominie-Snub (Steel Heart) *43^{3} (134) (197) 278^{6} 306^{4} 392^{7}* **>66a 29f<**

Whittle Rock **2** b f Rock City-Lurking (Formidable) 424^{10} 533^{3} 669^{5} 903^{2} (1562) 1849^{12} 2800^{3} 3210^{3} 3668^{4} 3962^{2} **>81?f<**

Whittle Woods Girl **4** b f Emarati (USA)-Flitteriss Park (Beldale Flutter (USA)) 535^{17} 611^{8} *769^{10}* **>54a 80f<**

Who's Tef (IRE) **7** b g Muscatite-Eternal Optimist (Relko) 3021^{8} 3232^{6} **>49f<**

Who's the Best (IRE) **5** b h Wassl-Rip Roaring (Royal And Regal (USA)) *172^{3} 186^{2} 215^{2} (259) 295^{5} 514^{6}* 741^{5} *1086^{3}* 1444^{14} *1567^{3} (1759) 2147^{7} 2919^{3} (3527)* 3705^{10} **>57a 33f<**

Whothehellisharry **2** ch g Rich Charlie-Ballagarrow Girl (North Stoke) 2932^{10} 3307^{5} 3463^{8} *4334^{4}* **>51a 55f<**

Wickins **5** b h Petong-Bo' Babbity (Strong Gale) 798a^{3} 1228a^{2} **>57f<**

Wicklow Boy (IRE) **4** b c Roi Danzig (USA)-Pickety Place (Prince Tenderfoot (USA)) *9^{6} 96^{3} 166^{11} 285^{8}* **>43da 44f<**

Wick Pound **9** b h Niniski (USA)-Hors Serie (USA) (Vaguely Noble) 3710^{15} **>5f<**

Wigberto (IRE) **3** ch c Old Vic-Royal Loft (Homing) 3929^{11} 4147^{3} **>76a 102?f<**

Wight **2** gr f Sharrood-Wrangbrook (Shirley Heights)

(4004a) 4117^{3} >**67f**<
Wijara (IRE) 3 b c Waajib-Nawara (Welsh Pageant) 679^{5} 1224^{5} 3585a^{4} (3728) 4104^{3} >**112f**<
Wilawander 2 ch c Nashwan (USA)-Wilayif (USA) (Danzig (USA)) 2573^{5} 2912^{2} 3746^{4} >**79f**<
Wilcuma 4 b c Most Welcome-Miss Top Ville (FR) (Top Ville) 793^{5} 1225^{3} 1626^{4} 1851^{21} 3601^{6} (3802) 3945^{17} 4202^{2} >**102f**<
Wild Adventure 6 b or br g Kabour-Magic Mover (Julio Mariner) *1^{W} 519^{9} 766^{10}* 992^{12} 1161^{15} >**28a 16f**<
Wild Bluebell (IRE) 3 b f Bluebird (USA)-Ingabelle (Taufan (USA)) (4021a) >**116f**<
Wildfire (SWI) 4 br c Beldale Flutter (USA)-Little White Star 763^{12} 1340^{3} 1694^{9} 2439^{13} >**63f**<
Wild Humour (IRE) 2 b f Fayruz-Nous 2412^{7} 3133^{5} 3465^{10} 3623^{20} 4066^{11} >**53f**<
Wild Palm 3 b c Darshaan-Tarasova (USA) (Green Forest (USA)) 2977^{4} 3537^{5} (3762) 3984^{6} >**84f**<
Wild Prospect 7 b h Homing-Cappuccilli 1432^{8} 1506^{13} >**40f**<
Wild Rice 3 b c *(239) (276)* 2437^{3} (2848) (3209) 3813^{26} >**82+a 93f**<
Wild Rita 3 ch f Risk Me (FR)-Ma Pierrette (Cawston's Clown) 1196^{2} 1353^{3} 1675^{3} 2411^{8} (3769) 3957^{5} 4071^{3} 4149^{4} >**79f**<
Wild Rose of York 4 gr f Unfuwain (USA)-Chepstow Vale (USA) (Key To The Mint (USA)) 2427^{7} 2731^{W} 3001^{3} 3171^{2} 3308^{2} >**61a 58f**<
Wild Rumour (IRE) 2 b f Sadler's Wells (USA)-Gossiping (USA) (Chati (USA)) (3708) >**82+f**<
Wild Strawberry 6 ro m Ballacashtal (CAN)-Pts Fairway *346^{4}* 632^{7} 795^{4} 961^{4} 1200^{2} 1635^{2} (1695) 1929^{4} 2201^{2} 2439^{6} 3769^{3} 4118^{18} >**77a 73f**<
Wildwood Flower 2 b f Distant Relative-Tolstoya (Northfields (USA)) 3495^{9} 3892^{6} 4056^{3} (4212) >**82f**<
Wilfull Lad (IRE) 2 b g Distinctly North (USA)-Lisa's Music (Abwah) 1798^{9} (2773) 3064^{12} 3271^{8} 3516^{5} >**72f**<
Willie Conquer 3 ch c Master Willie-Maryland Cookie (USA) (Bold Hour) 543^{3} 694^{5} 3943^{12} >**75f**<
Willie Rushton 2 ch f Master Willie-Amberush (No Rush) 2011^{7} 2346^{4} 2637^{3} 3233^{2} 3533^{4} (4045) >**62f**<
Willisa 2 ch f Polar Falcon (USA)-Ghassanah (Pas de Seul) 1413^{6} 2275^{3} 2934^{4} 3714^{12} 3947^{8} 4208^{10} >**72f**<
Willow Dale (IRE) 2 b f Danehill (USA)-Miss Willow Bend (USA) (Willow Hour (USA)) 1253^{9} 1653^{4} (2011) (3471) 3548^{6} (3727) 3886^{8} 4105^{7} >**84f**<
Willshe Gan 5 b m Precocious-Quisissanno (Be My Guest (USA)) 724^{6} (928) 1079^{2} 1468^{2} 1668^{4} 1918^{5} 2358^{4} 2519^{P} >**28a 55f**<
Winagins (IRE) 4 b f Roi Danzig (USA)-Mallee (Malinowski (USA)) *30^{10} 79^{11}* >**29f**<
Windi Imp (IRE) 2 b f Mac's Imp (USA)-Windini (Windjammer (USA)) 1361^{9} 1857^{3} 2170^{4} 2487^{W} 2847^{8} 2982^{6} 3133^{10} 3284^{6} >**60f**<
Wind in Her Hair (IRE) 4 b f Alzao (USA)-Burghclere 1408^{3} 1894^{5} 2575^{2} (3046a) 3161^{3} >**115f**<
Windmachine (SWE) 4 br f Riverscape (USA)-Miami Flyer (Miami Springs) 659^{9} 921^{14} 1475^{10} 1637^{10} 3407^{11} (4006a) >**105f**<
Window Display 4 gr c Chilibang-Stubble (Balidar) *2290^{6}* >**35a 42?f**<
Windrush Boy 5 br h Dowsing (USA)-Bridge Street Lady (Decoy Boy) 656^{6} 972^{9} 1050^{4} 1164^{11} 1538^{2} 1942^{5} 2247^{2} 2551^{3} 2793^{5} (3123) 3376^{7} 3961^{10} *4295^{10}* >**36a 66f**<
Windrush Lady 5 ch m Risk Me (FR)-Pusey Street (Native Bazaar) 440^{11} 634^{20} 1141^{9} 1616^{6} 2444^{4} 3611^{8} 3801^{15} >**76f**<
Windswept (IRE) 2 b f Taufan (USA)-Sutica 716^{3} (970) 1259^{4} 2489^{6} 3176^{5} 3548^{5} 3947^{12} >**81f**<
Windyedge (USA) 2 ch c Woodman (USA)-Abeesh (USA) (Nijinsky (CAN)) 4188^{13} >**58f**<
Winged Love (IRE) 3 b c In The Wings-J'ai Deux Amours (Top Vil 1574a^{3} (2218a) 2595^{4} 3696a^{3} >**125f**<
Winged Prince 2 b c Prince Daniel (USA)-Phyl (Ballad Rock) 2548^{11} 2846^{9} 3089^{14} 3546^{13} >**55f**<
Wingnut (IRE) 2 ch f Digamist (USA)-Royal Cloak 791^{12} 970^{5} *1212^{10}* 1640^{3} *2146^{3}* (2176) 2335^{3} 2523^{7} 3054^{2} 3284^{5} 3753^{3} *3953^{8}* >**39a 66f**<
Wings Cove 5 b h Elegant Air-Bel Esprit (Sagaro) 737^{5} 938^{3} >**87f**<
Wings of Desire (IRE) 3 b c Grey Desire-Minizen Lass (Hittite Glory) *48^{4} 134^{9}* >**39a 59df**<
Wings of Freedom (IRE) 7 b h Fairy King (USA)-Wingau (FR) 840^{7} >**24f**<
Winning Wonder 3 b f Charmer-Salchow (Niniski (USA)) *149^{6}*
Winn's Pride (IRE) 4 b c Indian Ridge-Blue Bell Girl (Blakeney) *227^{7} 312^{3} 340^{3} 389^{5} 1332^{10} 1955^{7} 2293^{8} 2495^{8}* 3970^{6} >**56a 53f**<
Winsome Wooster 4 ch f Primo Dominie-Bertrade (Homeboy) 856^{3} 1057^{2} 1411^{4} 1777^{7} 2009^{7} 2202^{4} 2659^{2} 2909^{12} 3204^{4} 3451^{3} 3629^{10} 4268^{5} 4319^{4} >**70f**<
Winston 2 b c Safawan-Lady Leman (Pitskelly) 2116^{6} 2526^{11} >**47f**<
Winterbottom 3 gr c Reference Point-Snowing (USA) (Icecapade (USA)) *78^{12} 189^{7} 270^{7}* >**19a f**<
Winter Gem 6 b m Hasty Word-Masami (King Log) *311^{6}*
Winter Quarters (USA) 2 ch c El Gran Senor (USA)-Refill (Mill Reef (USA)) 1726^{5} 2315^{3} (2846) (3477a) 3613^{2} 3907a^{2} *4306a^{6}* >**95ta 96f**<
Winter Romance 2 ch c Cadeaux Genereux-Island Wedding (USA) (Blushing Groom (FR)) 3663^{12} 3890^{3} 4058^{2} >**90f**<
Winters Cottage (IRE) 7 ch g Sandalay-Hilltown Yvonne (Avocat) 2331^{5} >**61f**<
Winter Scout (USA) 7 ch g It's Freezing (USA)-His Squaw (USA) (Tom Rolfe) 1355^{3} 2611^{5} 2905^{4} (3365) 3638^{5} >**18+a 63f**<
Wire Act (USA) 2 gr c Gate Dancer (USA)-Giovanelli (USA) (Monteverdi) 3174^{8} 3463^{4} 3592^{11} 3894^{7} *3949^{3}* 4081^{10} >**67a 63f**<
Wisam 2 b c Shaadi (USA)-Moon Drop (Dominion) (1223) 1838^{13} 2704^{4} >**91f**<
Wisdom 3 b c Insan (USA)-Emaline (FR) (Empery (USA)) *168^{2} 213^{3} 264^{3} (339)* >**65a 35f**<
Wise Brave 3 ch g Be My Chief (USA)-Fair and Wise (High Line) 3712^{16} 4164^{12} >**42f**<
Wishing (USA) 4 b c Lyphard's Wish (FR)-Vivre Libre (USA) (Honest Pleasure (USA)) (623) 931^{9} 1243^{2} 1585^{5} (1768) 2739^{5} 3162^{18} 3489^{7} >**105f**<
Witchfinder (USA) 3 b c Diesis-Colonial Witch (USA) (Pleasant Colony (USA)) 3799^{5} >**79f**<

Witch of Fife (USA) 2 b f Lear Fan (USA)-Fife (IRE) (Lomond (USA)) (2777) 2947^{3} 3561^{10} (3819) **>89f<**
With Fascination (USA) 2 dk f Dayjur-Fran's Valentine (Saros) (3037a) $3330a^{2}$ $3793a^{2}$ $4012a^{10}$ **>103f<**
With Gusto 8 b h Taufan (USA)-Finesse (Miralgo) *215^{7}* **>13a 37f<**
With Intent 3 b g Governor General-Don't Loiter (Town And Country) 937^{7} 1476^{6} 2049^{5} 2711^{9} 3159^{11} 3475^{14} **>58df<**
Without a Flag (USA) 5 ch h Stately Don (USA)-Northerly Cheer (USA) (Northjet (USA)) 623^{16} **>72f<**
With the Fairies 3 b f Fairy King (USA)-Upper Circle (Shirley Heights) 660^{5} 1488^{7} 2443^{6} $2727a^{7}$ $3693a^{4}$ **>103f<**
Witney-de-Bergerac (IRE) 3 b c Cyrano de Bergerac-Spy Girl (Tanfirion) *144^{3} 176^{5} 263^{4} 273^{3} 384^{7}* 2033^{4} 2317^{10} 2792^{3} (3710) 3817^{14} 4205^{7} **>61a 69f<**
Wizard King 4 b c Shaadi (USA)-Broomstick Cottage (Habitat) 2436^{2} 2598^{3} (3193a) 3191^{11} (3787a) $4021a^{2}$ **>119f<**
Wizzard Star 3 ch f Prince Sabo-Wizzard Art (Wolver Hollow) 1979^{15} **>30f<**
Wizzy Lizzy (IRE) 4 ch f Waajib-Ladiz (Persian Bold) 764^{22} 1200^{3} 1513^{15} 2078^{4} 2300^{3} 2511^{5} **>57df<**
Wolf Cleugh (IRE) 2 b f Last Tycoon-Santa Roseanna (Caracol (FR)) 4262^{11} **>64f<**
Wollboll 5 b g Layal-Top of the Barley (Oats) *361^{5}* $3321a^{2}$ **>42a 43f<**
Wollstonecraft (IRE) 2 b f Danehill (USA)-Ivory Thread (USA) (Sir Ivor) 1361^{3} **>79f<**
Wonderful Day 4 b f Niniski (USA)-Zipperti Do (Precocious) (776) 1252^{3} 1558^{2} 2648^{4} 4229^{9} **>76f<**
Woodborough (USA) 2 ch c Woodman (USA)-Performing Arts (The Minstrel (CAN)) 690^{8} (2693) $3197a^{2}$ (3586a) $3793a^{3}$ 3903^{2} **>104f<**
Woodbury Lad (USA) 2 c $3328a^{7}$ 3465^{8} **>64f<**
Woodcrest 3 b f Niniski (USA)-Cryptomeria 1173^{3} 1526^{7} (2082) 2599^{7} (3130) 3718^{5} **>88f<**
Woodlands Electric 5 b g Rich Charlie-Hallowed (Wolver Hollow) *16^{7} 65^{13}* 2761^{6} 3079^{6} 3293^{10} 3678^{9} **>3a 20f<**
Woodlands Energy 4 b f Risk Me (FR)-Hallowed (Wolver Hollow) 2449^{5} 2977^{10} 3294^{9} 3679^{10} 3987^{18} **>56f<**
Woodlands Lad Too 3 b c Risk Me (FR)-Hallowed (Wolver Hollow) 2760^{3} 3653^{16} 3847^{8} **>12f<**
Wood Magic 2 b g Shaadi (USA)-Majenica (USA) (Majestic Light (USA)) 3010^{4} *(3523)* (3776) **>78+a 86f<**
Woodmans Lady 3 b f Midyan (USA)-Diva Madonna (Chief Singer) 4062^{12} 4167^{11} **>46f<**
Woodrising 3 b f Nomination-Bodham (Bustino) 451^{3} 576^{2} *847^{7}* 1146^{2} 1791^{3} 2245^{5} (2532) 2687^{12} (2884) (3126) **>37a 70f<**
Woolaw Girl 7 br m Sayf El Arab (USA)-Pacific Princess (Dom Racine (FR)) 3103^{7} 3370^{13}
Woolverstone Hall (IRE) 3 b f Roi Danzig (USA)-Silver Mantle (Bustino) *319^{8} 473^{4}* 1016^{8} *2600^{5}* **>47a 66f<**
Wordsmith (IRE) 5 b h Cyrano de Bergerac-Cordon (Morston (FR)) *1029^{9}* 1206^{9} 1523^{9} *1880^{7}* 2620^{6} 3272^{2} 3658^{11} **>57da 63f<**
Words of Wisdom (IRE) 5 b g Petorius-Never So Lovely *(148) (217) 298^{4} 344^{5} 501^{6}* 731^{7} *832^{2}* 887^{4} 1261^{12} 1429^{5} *1571^{9} 1789^{3} 1980^{3}* 2202^{8} *2605^{6} 3074^{8}* **>66a 48f<**
Workingforpeanuts (IRE) 5 ch m Entitled-Tracy's Sundown (Red Sunset) 1622^{15} **>44a 25f<**
World Express (IRE) 5 b h Jareer (USA)-Eight Mile Rock (Dominion) *2293^{12}* **>6a 71f<**
Worldnews Extra (USA) 3 ch c Elmaamul (USA)-Wrap It Up (Mount Hagen (FR)) *500^{2}* (747) 1544^{5} 2014^{4} 2171^{4} **>77a 80f<**
World Premier 2 b c Shareef Dancer (USA)-Abuzz (Absalom) (424) 871^{2} 1104^{5} 1608^{2} (1871) 2347^{3} $3330a^{6}$ **>100f<**
World Traveller 4 ch c Most Welcome-Prudence (Grundy) *41^{5} 89^{14} 1034^{5} 1088^{7}* 1280^{11} 1541^{12} 2181^{4} 2747^{8} **>74a 64f<**
Worldwide Elsie (USA) 2 b f Java Gold (USA)-Tender Camilla (Prince Tenderfoot (USA)) 436^{6} 562^{3} *(1454)* 1871^{8} 4111^{9} (4211) 4327^{2} **>68a 74f<**
Wot-If-We (IRE) 3 b c Alzao (USA)-Awatef (Ela-Mana-Mou) (756) 1099^{6} 1852^{4} $2386a^{4}$ $2898a^{4}$ 3389^{2} 3946^{7} **>99f<**
Wottashambles 4 b or br c Arrasas (USA)-Manawa (Mandamus) *22^{2} 75^{6} 109^{6} 277^{8} 367^{4}* 2007^{4} (2359) 2687^{13} 3024^{3} 3470^{4} 3572^{2} 3970^{14} *4223^{9}* **>47a 53f<**
Wrays (USA) 2 b f Known Fact (USA)-Sunshine Law (USA) (Tisab (USA)) 2498^{2} 2666^{4} 3628^{13} 3895^{4} 3975^{11} **>68f<**
Written Agreement 7 ch g Stanford-Covenant (Good Bond) *122^{10} 172^{7} 200^{6} 234^{7}* **>12a 33f<**
Wurlitzer (USA) 3 ch c Riverman (USA)-Wedge Musical (What A Guest) 824^{6} 1175^{5} 1439^{2} 2026^{8} 2352^{4} **>79f<**
Wychwood-Palace 3 ch f Presidium-Cardinal Palace (Royal Palace) 908^{11} 1196^{13} **>62f<**
Wychwood Sandy 4 b c Mansingh (USA)-Do-Run-Do (Palm Track) 3678^{11} 4215^{21} **>55f<**
Wydale 2 b c Rich Charlie-Julia Mawe (Dominion) 964^{8} 1203^{8} 1646^{10} **>7f<**
Wyedean 2 ch c Faustus (USA)-Coleford (USA) (Secreto (USA)) *4269^{11}* **>12a f<**

X

Xenophon of Cunaxa (IRE) 2 b g Cyrano de Bergerac-Annais Nin (Dominion) 2340^{5} (3203) $3587a^{9}$ **>80f<**

Y

Yaakum 6 b h Glint of Gold-Nawadder (Kris) 1607^{11} 2186^{9} 2465^{3} **>54a 41f<**
Yaa Wale 3 br c Persian Bold-Starr Danias (USA) (Sensitive Prince (USA)) 555^{9} (2363) (2549) 2737^{11} 3348^{7} 3770^{2} **>89f<**
Yacht 3 ch c Warning-Bireme 678^{7} 1661^{12} **>70a 76f<**
Yahmi (IRE) 5 b h Law Society (USA)-Hogan's Sister (USA) (Speak John) 1339^{10} 3898^{10} **>43f<**
Ya Malak 4 b g Fairy King (USA)-La Tuerta (Hot Spark) 700^{3} 1220^{2} (1475) $2039a^{2}$ 2430^{6} $2899a^{4}$ 3187^{2} 3550^{6} **>122f<**
Ya Marhaba 2 b g Efisio-Ichnusa (Bay Express) 3648^{10} 3892^{10} **>43f<**
Yamuna (USA) 2 b f Forty Niner (USA)-Nimble Feet (USA) (Danzig (USA)) 1169^{5} **>73f<**
Yarn (IRE) 3 b f Don't Forget Me-Domiciliate (Kings Lake (USA)) (881) 997^{2} 1242^{3} 1729^{8} 2348^{12} **>96f<**

Yarob (IRE) 2 ch c Unfuwain (USA)-Azyaa (Kris) (2801) 3068^{2} 3606^{7} **>91f<**

Yarrow (IRE) 3 b c Danehill (USA)-Alyara (USA) (Alydar (USA)) 1383^{3} 1770^{2} 2086^{2} 3863^{13} 4163^{15} **>80f<**

Yavari (USA) 2 b f Danzig-Lake Valley (Mr Prospecto 2727a^{2} **>96f<**

Yaverland (IRE) 3 b c Astronef-Lautreamont (Auction Ring (USA)) 3761^{7} 3974^{10} **>66f<**

Yeast 3 b g Salse (USA)-Orient (Bay Express) 3507^{6} 3542^{3} 3829^{2} **>83f<**

Yeath (IRE) 3 ch c Exhibitioner-Grain of Sand (Sandford Lad) 1796^{9} 2319^{6} 2794^{8} 3214^{9} 3679^{12} **>59f<**

Yellow Dragon (IRE) 2 b c Kefaah (USA)-Veldt (High Top) 424^{11} 3752^{6} 4045^{3} **>57f<**

Yengema 4 b f Petoski-Bundu (FR) (Habitat) 1535^{15} 2719^{10} **>14a 25f<**

Yet Again 3 ch g Weldnaas (USA)-Brightelmstone (Prince Regent (FR)) *264^{6}* 544^{2} 1554^{5} (1813) 3500^{10} 3659^{10} 3885^{13} **>47a 56f<**

Yet More Roses 4 b c Gallic League-Ominous (Dominion) 636^{4} 812^{4} 1900^{3} 2533^{10} 2867^{6} *3242^{4}* *3512^{10}* **>63a 73f<**

Yezza (IRE) 2 b f Distinctly North (USA)-Small Paradise (Habat) 4314^{5} **>67f<**

Yo Kiri-B 4 b f Night Shift (USA)-Briar Creek (Busted) *1320^{5}* 1539^{3} 1811^{6} 2246^{5} (2334) 3108^{5} 4229^{10} **>33a 61f<**

Yo-Mate 4 b c Komaite (USA)-Silent Sun (Blakeney) 1749^{5} *2632^{4}* 2806^{7} **>48a 63f<**

Yosif (IRE) 3 b c High Estate-Respectfully (USA) (The Minstrel (CAN)) 715^{24} 1186^{12} 1383^{9} 1754^{5} 2199^{11} **>60f<**

You and I (USA) 4 b c Kris S (USA)-La Chaposa (USA) *4303a^{10}* **>108a f<**

Youcanstoplooking (IRE) 4 ch c Krayyan-Juju (Dragonara Palace (USA)) *71^{10}* *123^{6}* **>16a 30f<**

Youdontsay 3 ch f Most Welcome-Fabulous Luba (Luthier (FR)) 850^{2} (1094) 1201^{4} 1537^{4} (1832) 2009^{2} 2556^{5} 3929^{2} 4033^{12} 4122^{9} **>89f<**

Yougo 3 b g Good Times (ITY)-Young Wilkie (Callernish) 3304^{3} 3772^{3} 3896^{9} 4099^{4} **>79f<**

Yougoa 2 ch f Mon Tresor-Our Mable (Posse (USA)) 2483^{8} 2580^{5} 2951^{2} 3271^{7} 3670^{14} 3740^{5} **>54f<**

Young Ben (IRE) 3 ch g Fayruz-Jive (Ahonoora) 1360^{6} 1683^{5} 1846^{8} 3508^{10} 3750^{16} **>47f<**

Young Benson 3 b c Zalazl (USA)-Impala Lass (Kampala) 955^{5} 1216^{3} 1533^{5} 1778^{7} 2236^{2} 2583^{3} 2880^{4} 3095^{5} 3356^{3} 3565^{11} 4171^{16} *4337^{14}* **>17a 79df<**

Young Buster (IRE) 7 b h Teenoso (USA)-Bustara (Busted) 631^{3} 2008^{2} 2476^{4} 2936^{2} 3381^{6} 3614^{6} **>116f<**

Young Butt 2 ch c Bold Owl-Cymbal 849^{8} 1318^{7} 1752^{8} 1981^{9} *2496^{3}* *3528^{6}* 3915^{4} 4045^{2} *(4273)* **>65a 62f<**

Young Clifford (USA) 4 b or br c Lear Fan (USA)-Smile For Awhile (USA) (Norcliffe (CAN)) 1339^{8} 1973^{6} 2268^{8} **>67f<**

Young Dalesman 2 br c Teenoso (USA)-Fabulous Molly (Whitstead) 3827^{10} 4063^{16} 4246^{7} **>56f<**

Young Duke (IRE) 7 gr h Double Schwartz-Princess Pamela (Dragonara Palace (USA)) 1969^{2} **>72a 74f<**

Younger Days (IRE) 4 b g Desert of Wind (USA)-Schlarigna (Kings Lake (USA)) 1023^{13} 1377^{14} *1763^{11}* *2071^{5}* 2502^{6} 2624^{14} **>27a 38f<**

Young Ern 5 b h Efisio-Stardyn (Star Appeal) (814) 1187^{2} 1586^{6} 1835^{4} 3042a^{2} 3795a^{2} 3834^{2} 4178a^{10} **>125f<**

Young Frederick (IRE) 2 ch g Polish Patriot (USA)-Notre Histoire (Habitat) 4130^{11}

Young Freeman (USA) 6 b h Nijinsky (CAN)-Committed (USA) (Hagley (USA)) *(330) 385^{2} (445)* **>99a 79f<**

Young Mazaad (IRE) 2 b c Mazaad-Lucky Charm (IRE) (Pennine Walk) 3765^{15} 3916^{13} **>21f<**

Young Saffy 2 ch c Safawan-Miss Pisces (Salmon Leap (USA)) 3463^{12} 3620^{18} 4073^{8} **>43f<**

Young Sensation 3 ch c Arrasas (USA)-Jianna (Godswalk (USA)) 883^{8} *1078^{7}* 1265^{13} **>5a 38f<**

Young Steven 4 b c Singing Steven-Adoration (FR) (Dancers Image (USA)) 750^{4} 968^{7} 1160^{11} 1435^{11} **>49f<**

Young Vic 3 b f Old Vic-Loralane 1526^{10} **>60f<**

Your Most Welcome 4 b f Most Welcome-Blues Player (Jaazeiro (USA)) 2929^{3} 3438^{10} 3762^{6} **>58f<**

Yoush (IRE) 3 ch c Dominion-Astra Adastra (Mount Hagen (FR)) *418^{3}* *566^{7}* 813^{3} (1097) (1589) (2241) 2457^{3} 3728^{3} 3945^{31} **>62a 108f<**

Yoxall Lodge 5 b h Aragon-Opal Fancy 559^{9} 749^{7} 909^{9} 1603^{3} 1792^{2} *2922^{4}* **>44a 67f<**

Yubralee (USA) 3 ch c Zilzal (USA)-Kentucky Lill (USA) (Raise A Native) 435^{5} 630^{7} 857^{9} (1381) 1644^{3} 1801^{5} 4054^{13} **>79f<**

Yuppy Girl (IRE) 2 ch f Salt Dome (USA)-Sloane Ranger (Sharpen Up) 1823^{6} 2651^{2} 2971^{5} 3502^{2} 3644^{4} 3982^{4} 4137^{4} **>60f<**

Z

Zaaheyah (USA) 5 ch m Irish River (FR)-Shoag (USA) (Affirmed (USA)) *53^{9} 79^{4} 153^{2} 280^{4} 375^{12}* (495) 598^{2} 879^{5} 1025^{6} **>46a 55f<**

Zaaleff (USA) 3 ch c Zilzal (USA)-Continual (USA) 1796^{7} 2319^{9} **>60f<**

Zabadi (IRE) 3 b g Shahrastani (USA)-Zerzaya (Beldale Flutter) 709a^{2} **>93f<**

Zacaroon 4 b f Last Tycoon-Samaza (USA) (Arctic Tern (USA)) *145^{5} 275^{3} 349^{3} 470^{2}* 988^{2} 2139^{3} (2557) 2752^{2} 2967^{5} 3778^{4} *4128^{4}* 4233^{5} **>65a 75f<**

Zadok 3 ch g Exodal (USA)-Glenfinlass (Lomond (USA)) 4062^{18} 4220^{6} **>58f<**

Zaforum 2 b c Deploy-Beau's Delight (USA) (Lypheor) 3437^{5} 3631^{5} 4046^{5} 4264^{4} **>94+f<**

Zahid (USA) 4 ch c Storm Cat (USA)-Time An' Care (USA) (Twin Time (USA)) 430^{24} 582^{16} 954^{4} 1970^{5} 2174^{4} 2334^{3} 3108^{4} 3234^{6} 3295^{4} **>65f<**

Zahran (IRE) 4 b c Groom Dancer (USA)-Welsh Berry (USA) (Sir Ivor) *63^{4} 169^{6} 313^{9} 343^{2} 387^{4} 402^{4} (501) 601^{12}* 780^{17} *1049^{10}* 1351^{7} 1501^{2} 1771^{8} *1951^{6}* 2081^{2} 2246^{3} 2528^{9} 2885^{4} (3118) 3258^{6} *3544^{4}* 3658^{6} **>56a 66f<**

Zahwa 3 ch f Cadeaux Genereux-Peace Girl 2576^{6} 3347^{3} 3656^{3} 4156^{17} **>76f<**

Zajko (USA) 5 b h Nureyev (USA)-Hope For All (USA) (Secretariat (USA)) 873^{12} (1183) 1926^{8} 3837^{8} 4041^{8} 4227^{2} **>87f<**

Zalament 3 b f Zalazl (USA)-Key to Enchantment (Key To Content (USA)) 691^{14} 1308^{5} 1498^{8} 1694^{3} 2193^{5} 3756^{12} 4000^{21} **>65df<**

Zalotti (IRE) 2 ch f Polish Patriot (USA)-Honest Penny

(USA) (Honest Pleasure (USA)) (1460) **>83+f<**
Zamalek (USA) 3 b c Northern Baby (CAN)-Chellingoua (USA) (Sharpen Up) 1345[4] 1807[4] 2121[5] **>90f<**
Zamhareer (USA) 4 b c Lear Fan (USA)-Awenita (Rarity) 598[5] 3724[13] 3818[6] 3936[5] **>54f<**
Zanzara (IRE) 4 ch f Efisio-Slick Chick *267[3] 349[6] 520[11]* 676[14] 839[7] *1088[5]* 1651[7] 2132[4] *2379[9]* (2834) 3114[2] *3527[13]* (4114) 4288[16] **>49a 64f<**
Zaralaska 4 ch c Shernazar-Eskimo Spring (USA) (Riverman (USA)) 539[7] 841[2] (1140) 1853[2] **>101f<**
Zatopek 3 b or br c Reprimand-Executive Lady (Night Shift (USA)) 1072[5] 1167[10] 1542[4] 4157[9] **>66f<**
Zdenka 2 b f Dominion-Short And Sharp (Sharpen Up) 2025[9] 2447[2] 2717[2] 3427[5] 3870[2] 3985[6] **>71f<**
Zeb (IRE) 3 b c Cyrano de Bergerac-Bap's Miracle (Track Spare) (616) 920[10] 1133[5] 1305[3] 1806[13] **>101f<**
Zeetaro 4 b c Taufan (USA)-Gem Bracelet (USA) (Sir Ivor) 2863[2] (3058) 3232[4] 3440[4] 3679[3] (3810) **>87f<**
Zelaya (IRE) 2 b f Shaadi (USA)-Zizania (Ahonoora) 1169[8] **>68f<**
Zelda Zonk 3 b f Law Society (USA)-Massive Powder (Caerleon (USA)) 1186[10] 1675[5] 3712[3] 3929[7] 4079[4] 4268[3] **>71f<**
Zeliba 3 br f Doyoun-Zia (USA) (Shareef Dancer (USA)) *156[9] 251[6]* 2843[9] **>24a 33f<**
Zelzelah (USA) 2 b f Timeless Moment (USA)-Allevition (USA) (Alleged (USA)) (2441) 3692a[10] 3835[6] **>84+f<**
Zermatt (IRE) 5 b h Sadler's Wells (USA)-Chamonis (USA) (Affirmed (USA)) 634[18] 1610[9] (1775) 2080[2] 2266[3] 2613[4] 3113[10] 3237[5] 3382[9] 3820[5] 3934[8] **>70f<**
Zesti 3 br g Charmer-Lutine Royal (Formidable) *17[3] 72[8] 1330[7]* 1664[9] 1962[11] **>33a 56f<**
Zidac 3 b or br c Statoblest-Sule Skerry 764[4] 1097[5] 1264[4] 1514[4] 3921[8] 4149[10] **>77f<**
Zifta (USA) 4 ch f Zilzal (USA)-Shoalih (USA) (Alydar (USA)) 636[15] 953[7] (1079) 1261[14] 2436[9] 2647[8] **>85f<**
Ziggy's Dancer (USA) 4 b c Ziggy's Boy (USA)-My Shy Dancer (USA) (Northjet (USA)) *18[9] 119[3] (198) 307[2] (393)* 434[18] (789) 922[2] (1220) 1766[7] 1895[14] 2001[2] 2237[4] (2430) 2570[6] 3446[12] 3689a[9] 3938[6] 4040[16] 4119[5] 4197[6] **>75a 92f<**
Zilayah (USA) 3 ch f Zilzal (USA)-Welsh Garden 914[8] 1362[9] **>73f<**
Zilzal Zamaan (USA) 4 b c Zilzal (USA)-Iva Reputation (USA) (Sir Ivor) 712[7] (1020) 1894[4] 3482a[2] 3789a[7] 4182a[5] **>121f<**
Zinbaq 9 ch h Ahonoora-Zaiyundeen (FR) (Exbury) *56[4] 205[5] 320[5] 373[7] 501[5]* 1426[6] 1991[10] 2178[3] 3057[7] **>32a 36f<**
Zine Lane 3 ch g Minster Son-Pine (Supreme Sovereign) 585[8] 2316[6] 3756[6] 4149[11] **>69f<**
Zingibar 3 b c Caerleon (USA)-Duende (High Top) 678[8] 2269[6] 2613[9] 2654[4] 3440[9] 3493[4] **>71f<**
Ziro (IRE) 3 b g Alzao (USA)-Nazeera (FR) (Lashkari) 1198[16] 1600[6] 2151[6] **>64f<**
Zitziana (IRE) 3 ch f Salse (USA)-Zizania (Ahonoora) 865[8] 1701[10] **>50f<**
Zohar (GER) 6 br h Nebos (GER)-Zalucca (GER) (Luciano) 1004a[2] **>117f<**
Zonk 5 ch h Nishapour (FR)-Liberty Tree (Dominion) *201[9]* **>47a 49f<**
Zuhair 2 ch c Mujtahid (USA)-Ghzaalh (USA) (Northern Dancer) 1726[3] (2070) 2347[5] **>94f<**
Zuiena (USA) 3 ch f Sunshine Forever (USA)-Hattab Voladora (USA) (Dewan (USA)) 950[4] 1182[4] 1674[6] 2300[2] (2481) 3140[2] 3569[6] **>76f<**
Zuno Flyer (USA) 3 br c Lyphard (USA)-Triple Tipple (USA) (Raise A Cup (USA)) 585[9] 730[6] 937[12] 1498[12] 1776[7] 3475[11] 3875[17] 4240[9] **>44df<**
Zuno Noelyn 4 b f Most Welcome-Artist's Glory (Rarity) *(76) 158[3] 321[5] 406[2] 445[9]* (2640) **>59a 63f<**
Zuno Princess (IRE) 2 br f Distinctly North (USA)-Flash Donna (USA) (Well Decorated (USA)) 508[13] 1653[9] 2985[4] 3290[13] *4127[11]* **>14a 36f<**
Zusha 4 b f Kind of Hush-Zamandra (Foggy Bell) 1417[8] 1948[7] **>21f<**
Zygo (USA) 3 b c Diesis-La Papagena (Habitat) 987[4] **>76f<**

CORRECTION

Race 1568: **Ashkernazy (IRE)**: has been disqualified (prohibited substances (procaine and sulphadimidine) in urine). The second, third, fourth and fifth have been promoted.

Due to binding restrictions, we have unfortunately been unable to include Raceform Record Times, Raceform Standard Times and Raceform Speed Figures in this annual.

RACEFORM TOP RATED HORSES OF 1995

THREE-YEAR-OLDS AND UPWARDS

Lake Coniston (IRE)	134
Bahri (USA)	134
Freedom Cry	132
Ridgewood Pearl	132
Lammtarra (USA)	132
Northern Spur (IRE)	132
Celtic Swing	131
Pennekamp (USA)	131
Carnegie (IRE)	130
Halling (USA)	130
Green Tune (USA)	129
Pentire	129
Piccolo	129
Soviet Line (IRE)	129
Luso	128
Nicolotte	128
Flemensfirth (USA)	128
Tamure (IRE)	128
Spectrum (IRE)	128
Singspiel (IRE)	128
Swain (IRE)	128
Double Trigger (IRE)	127
So Factual (USA)	127

TWO-YEAR-OLDS

Alhaarth (IRE)	121
Bosra Sham (USA)	118
Royal Applause	115
Danehill Dancer (IRE)	115
Blue Duster (USA)	113
Tagula (IRE)	112
Bint Shadayid (USA)	111
Manninamix	110
Kahir Almaydan (IRE)	109
Mubhij (IRE)	108
Lord of Men	108
Titus Livius (FR)	108
Le Triton (USA)	108
Westcourt Magic	107
Beauchamp King	107
Dovebrace	106
Mons	106
My Branch	106
Russian Revival (USA)	105
Dance Sequence (USA)	105
Miss Tahiti (IRE)	105
Woodborough (USA)	104
South Salem (USA)	104

LEADING FLAT SIRES, 1995

First prizes in Great Britain and Ireland only

	Races Won	Stakes £	Last Year
1. Nijinsky (CAN)	5	801,087	-
2. Rainbow Quest (USA)	37	572,904	12
3. Salse (USA)	36	567,652	31
4. Sadler's Wells (USA)	57	507,926	1
5. Indian Ridge	44	463,751	-
6. Danehill (USA)	57	442,211	9
7. Polish Precedent (USA)	26	411,924	-
8. In The Wings	15	407,955	-
9. Riverman (USA)	17	395,083	-
10. Diesis	17	391,103	15
11. Caerleon (USA)	39	386,455	5
12. Green Desert (USA)	58	375,749	4
13. Be My Guest (USA)	20	367,796	26
14. Ela-Mana Mou	22	360,802	-
15. Cadeaux Genereux	53	343,095	36
16. Taufan (USA)	54	311,796	16
17. Mtoto	31	301,285	-
18. Bluebird (USA)	40	281,879	11
19. Night Shift (USA)	38	280,792	8
20. Danzig (USA)	27	272,042	6
21. Warning	32	266,102	13
22. Petong	33	264,574	-
23. Unfuwain (USA)	24	254,577	32
24. Waajib	16	249,283	-
25. Alleged (USA)	19	244,534	45
26. Gulch (USA)	12	239,940	-
27. Efisio	40	222,012	35
28. Primo Dominie	45	208,442	-
29. Woodman (USA)	25	205,793	38
30. Shirley Heights	29	205,078	7
31. Royal Academy (USA)	33	204,524	-
32. Midyan (USA)	22	204,437	40
33. Soviet Star (USA)	23	202,416	41
34. Persian Bold	33	200,591	42
35. Alzao (USA)	38	190,458	10
36. Most Welcome	35	188,463	-
37. Dominion	26	187,179	-
38. Kahyasi (IRE)	24	183,546	-
39. Fairy King (USA)	36	179,967	44
40. Nashwan (USA)	17	166,887	34
41. Rock City (IRE)	41	166,224	-
42. Dowsing (USA)	43	158,729	50
43. Shadeed (USA)	12	156,683	-
44. Puissance	22	156,368	-
45. Dancing Brave (USA)	14	153,557	-
46. Bering	10	152,918	27
47. Nordico (USA)	29	152,411	-
48. Cyrano De Bergerac (IRE)	34	146,407	-
49. Shaadi (USA)	32	146,135	29
50. Known Fact (USA)	12	145,108	-

LEADING FLAT JOCKEYS, 1995

	Win £	1st	2nd	3rd	Unpl	Total Mts	Per cent	£1 Level stake
1. L. Dettori	1,977,574	211	164	135	475	985	21.4	- 128.60
2. K. Darley	776,673	148	125	123	516	912	16.2	- 161.66
3. J. Weaver	907,107	144	135	127	552	958	15.0	- 195.32
4. W. Carson	1,708,290	139	91	93	391	714	19.5	- 157.96
5. Pat Eddery	1,188,213	125	79	74	369	647	19.3	- 96.83
6. T. Quinn	657,729	111	97	107	519	834	13.3	- 200.78
7. J. Reid	1,159,222	101	96	84	412	693	14.6	- 130.76
8. R. Cochrane	488,833	98	95	101	493	787	12.5	- 158.55
9. K. Fallon	395,841	91	100	87	357	635	14.3	- 17.82
10. W. Ryan	422,717	87	89	69	318	563	15.5	- 150.87
11. J. Carroll	354,364	76	77	64	394	611	12.4	- 173.44
12. M. Hills	679,071	74	56	62	326	518	14.3	**+ 56.19**
13. D. Holland	488,312	71	81	59	251	462	15.4	**+ 10.19**
14. R. Hills	494,429	70	61	57	289	477	14.7	- 134.78
15. M. Roberts	467,195	64	47	50	277	438	14.6	**+ 2.22**
16. R. Hughes	494,433	64	72	55	309	500	12.8	- 61.14
17. G. Carter	285,117	63	75	76	425	639	9.9	- 287.32
18. B. Doyle	481,186	62	57	62	366	547	11.3	- 63.44
19. D. Harrison	343,737	62	73	77	423	635	9.8	- 220.82
20. W. R. Swinburn	1,617,799	60	68	53	239	420	14.3	- 112.83
21. G. Duffield	242,998	58	57	57	427	599	9.7	- 252.29
22. Paul Eddery	356,878	56	63	69	397	585	9.6	- 238.21
23. S. Sanders	267,012	54	56	56	362	528	10.2	- 57.63
24. T. Ives	219,567	53	57	50	319	479	11.1	- 194.31
25. M. Fenton	191,265	51	54	44	380	529	9.6	- 201.20
26. J. Quinn	225,341	48	72	68	525	713	6.7	- 274.89
27. J. Fortune	184,379	46	55	65	283	449	10.2	- 170.68
28. P. Robinson	253,542	41	55	49	262	407	10.1	- 66.62
29. W. Woods	136,188	41	37	48	253	379	10.8	- 140.98
30. J. Stack	172,893	41	44	31	316	432	9.5	- 194.37
31. T. Williams	138,794	38	51	44	390	523	7.3	- 259.77
32. T. Sprake	143,795	37	24	19	213	293	12.6	**+ 95.60**
33. S. Whitworth	144,819	37	32	35	276	380	9.7	- 106.08
34. L. Charnock	184,884	36	37	32	340	445	8.1	- 200.72
35. M. Rimmer	138,501	36	32	23	217	308	11.7	- 69.43
36. D. R. McCabe	173,806	35	31	35	199	300	11.7	- 14.93
37. G. Hind	151,837	34	38	24	239	335	10.2	- 158.58
38. A. Mackay	125,176	34	37	48	376	495	6.9	- 263.91
39. J. Tate	170,164	33	27	37	235	332	9.9	- 118.81
40. Dane O'Neill	196,387	33	42	38	232	345	9.6	- 48.75
41. D. McKeown	112,183	31	28	47	384	490	6.3	- 256.67
42. M. Henry	148,388	30	34	35	196	295	10.2	- 39.47
43. M. J. Kinane	455,969	28	33	25	98	184	15.2	- 46.53
44. A. McGlone	115,120	28	27	20	245	320	8.8	- 166.17
45. B. Thomson	159,529	28	28	32	205	293	9.6	- 78.11
46. G. Bardwell	105,859	28	20	26	345	419	6.7	- 173.50
47. N. Varley	86,515	26	32	43	301	402	6.5	- 160.05
48. C. Rutter	91,309	26	13	24	208	271	9.6	- 84.31
49. P. McCabe	96,490	25	21	23	154	223	11.2	**+ 30.58**
50. S. Drowne	106,373	25	26	33	303	387	6.5	- 112.50

LEADING FLAT TRAINERS, 1995

	Races Won	Stakes £	£1 level profit	Last Year
1. J. L. Dunlop	26	2,019,765	-102.92	2
2. S bin Suroor	14	1,879,194	**+ 30.91**	-
3. M. R. Stoute	73	1,362,759	- 78.05	1
4. R. Hannon	110	1,219,356	-291.12	5
5. J. H. M. Gosden	82	1,105,662	- 66.05	4
6. M. Johnston	97	1,081,559	-128.92	6
7. B. W. Hills	74	994,325	- 94.27	11
8. H. R. A. Cecil	83	975,835	- 44.58	3
9. P. F. I. Cole	75	882,955	- 57.43	7
10. C. E. Brittain	39	748,231	- 52.77	35
11. P. W. Chapple-Hyam	37	640,512	- 95.70	27
12. G. Wragg	30	640,338	**+ 51.49**	10
13. D. R. Loder	44	590,944	**+ 5.31**	17
14. L. M. Cumani	39	576,387	- 91.37	8
15. M. R. Channon	68	535,648	-143.48	16
16. Major W. R. Hern	21	525,158	- 33.50	34
17. R. Akehurst	49	523,566	-114.08	14
18. R. Charlton	40	513,220	- 53.30	22
19. I. A. Balding	41	478,567	-128.09	12
20. J. Berry	65	453,669	-346.58	9
21. G. Lewis	37	437,758	- 64.20	24
22. Mrs M. Reveley	60	420,969	-224.12	23
23. Mrs J. R. Ramsden	50	403,807	- 90.34	26
24. Lady Herries	26	367,294	- 18.01	20
25. J. R. Fanshawe	29	360,743	- 27.85	43
26. B. J. Meehan	42	348,453	- 85.50	-
27. B. Hanbury	35	334,490	- 31.02	40
28. M. Bell	38	307,295	-140.33	18
29. A. Fabre,France	3	293,446	**+ 7.60**	15
30. M. A. Jarvis	16	292,527	**+ 3.08**	-
31. H. ThomsonJones	36	280,238	- 8.19	25
32. D. Morley	21	278,463	- 17.80	28
33. A. C. Stewart	27	258,877	**+ 37.64**	36
34. R. W. Armstrong	31	253,934	**+ 12.42**	13
35. R. Hollinshead	40	237,342	-214.15	-
36. S. Dow	26	228,486	- 72.42	-
37. M. H. Tompkins	22	221,004	- 46.02	39
38. P. T. Walwyn	26	214,544	- 62.85	46
39. Sir Mark Prescott	36	208,060	- 82.88	19
40. B. A. McMahon	18	204,252	- 39.38	49
41. J. Oxx,Ireland	1	204,222	- 0.50	-
42. T. D. Barron	22	194,649	- 2.31	37
43. G. Harwood	9	192,801	- 51.42	32
44. P. J. Makin	24	183,937	- 11.14	-
45. E. A. L. Dunlop	17	183,700	- 86.94	-
46. G. L. Moore	27	182,656	- 40.68	-
47. P. W. Harris	24	178,707	- 41.41	48
48. M. J. Fetherston-Godley	9	177,145	- 14.75	-
49. Lord Huntingdon	15	173,140	- 15.63	30
50. P. C. Haslam	21	162,275	- 24.62	-

LEADING FLAT OWNERS, 1995

	Races Won	Stakes £	Last Year
1. Hamdan Al Maktoum	171	2,616,849	1
2. Sheikh Mohammed	113	1,828,102	2
3. Godolphin	14	966,139	15
4. Saeed Maktoum Al Maktoum	2	783,260	19
5. Maktoum Al Maktoum	42	706,478	3
6. Mr K. Abdullah	39	592,397	4
7. Mollers Racing	9	436,242	-
8. Prince Fahd Salman	33	432,411	11
9. Lord Weinstock & The Hon Simon Weinstock	18	416,338	20
10. Cheveley Park Stud	28	413,408	5
11. Mr George Strawbridge	12	319,621	38
12. Mr P. D. Savill	38	318,433	6
13. Mr R. E. Sangster	28	309,220	7
14. Mr Wafic Said	14	298,568	-
15. Sheikh Ahmed Al Maktoum	30	280,123	14
16. Mr E. Penser	8	256,255	-
17. Mr R. W. Huggins	8	256,221	-
18. Mrs Anne Coughlan	1	204,222	-
19. Mr J. D. Abell	21	193,470	41
20. Maktoum Al Maktoum/Godolphin	1	189,673	-
21. The Queen	16	188,083	44
22. Highclere Thoroughbred Racing Ltd	8	172,110	21
23. Hesmonds Stud	22	169,659	50
24. Mr M. A. Jarvis	4	160,761	-
25. Mr Saeed Manana	7	159,522	-
26. Mr Martin Myers	10	149,560	-
27. Mr R. Barnett	3	137,345	-
28. Mr Mana Al Maktoum	9	135,720	-
29. Mr J. C. Smith	12	133,167	8
30. Lord Carnarvon	10	132,139	36
31. Windflower Overseas Holdings Inc	11	117,047	-
32. Mr Mohamed Obaida	1	113,807	-
33. Lady Rothschild	8	111,230	-
34. Mr R. M. Cyzer	5	106,841	-
35. Mr K. Higson	14	105,654	45
36. Mr M. Arbib	4	105,566	-
37. Mr I. A. N. Wight	3	102,435	-
38. Elite Racing Club	12	101,000	-
39. Prince A. A. Faisal	11	100,421	-
40. Lucayan Stud	10	97,646	-
41. Bloomsbury Stud	5	97,234	-
42. Mrs E. H. Vestey	3	96,798	-
43. Sir Philip Oppenheimer (deceased)	11	96,748	35
44. Mr A. S. Reid	19	94,965	-
45. Mr Robert Hughes	4	93,867	-
46. John White and Partners	1	93,295	-
47. Mr Roy Taiano	1	87,326	-
48. Mr S. S. Niarchos	3	86,105	-

REVIEW OF THE YEAR

by Richard Onslow

The season of 1995 will be remembered as the one in which the policy of wintering horses in the warmth of the Middle East paid rich dividends almost from start to finish. After Balanchine had been successful in the Oaks in 1994, Sheikh Mohammed's experiment in sending her to Dubai for the close-season seemed an interesting innovation. By the time Lammtarra triumphed in the Derby, refuge from the English winter in the milder climate of the Emirates was being acclaimed a winning formula.

During the course of more than 200 years, no colt has won the Derby in quite such poignant circumstances as did **Lammtarra**, carrying the colours of Saeed Maktoum Al Maktoum, a nephew of Sheikh Mohammed. As a juvenile, Lammtarra was trained by Alex Scott at Newmarket and, on his only appearance, won the Washington Singer Stakes at Newbury in August. Scott had immense faith in the potential of Lammtarra, but tragically never lived to see it fulfilled.

Only a matter of weeks before the Derby, it seemed unlikely that Lammtarra would even be in the field. After developing an abscess on a lung, he was still a sick horse in March, before gradually recovering in the Dubai Equine Centre under treatment supervised by Michael Hauser, who had flown in from Kentucky.

Lammtarra comes with a late swoop to take Europe's premier Classic

Following the Derby, Lammtarra scaled heights that even Alex Scott had probably never envisaged, in becoming the first Derby winner since Mill Reef in 1971 to go on to win the King George VI and Queen Elizabeth Diamond Stakes, and the Prix de l' Arc de Triomphe. Early in October, Lammtarra was retired to the Dalham Hall Stud, Newmarket as the unbeaten winner of just four races. Sheikh Mohammed considered that the Breeders' Cup Turf at Belmont Park on 28th October, his only remaining objective, would come too soon after Longchamp.

During the autumn of 1994, members of the Maktoum family flew 70 of their horses, selected from stables all over England, to Dubai. In April, the 40 most outstanding prospects returned to England to be trained by Saeed bin Suroor in the Moulton Paddocks Stables at Newmarket, under the management of Simon Crisford, to race under the banner of Godolphin Racing.

GROUP GLORY GALORE FOR GODOLPHIN

Between April 1st and the middle of May, Godolphin won no fewer than six Group One races in four different countries, including the French 2000 Guineas with **Vettori**. Further success followed at the York Spring Meeting, where Classic Cliché won the Dante Stakes, and Moonax triumphed in the Yorkshire Cup. As a two-year-old, **Classic Cliché** had been trained by Henry Cecil to win for Ivan Allan at Newmarket before being sold to Godolphin. Unlike Classic Cliché and others repatriated from Dubai, **Moonax** did not stay with Saeed bin Suroor. Instead he rejoined Barry Hills, the man responsible for training him to win the St Leger and the Prix Royal Oak.

Classic victory for Cliché

Moonshell, who had been third in the 1000 Guineas, landed the first leg of the Epsom classic double for Godolphin, winning the Oaks from the two Michael Stoute-trained fillies **Dance a Dream** and **Pure Grain**. The extent to which Cecil's Warren Place stable had been weakened by the assembly of the Godolphin team was becoming only too clear. Like Classic Cliché and French Classic winner Vettori, Moonshell had been with him as a juvenile, winning readily at Doncaster in October on her only appearance.

In the middle of the summer, the Godolphin horses continued to make their presence felt at the highest level. Whereas the likes of Lammtarra, notwithstanding his serious illness, and Moonshell had evidently thrived in the desert sunshine between their first and second seasons, the four-year-old **Halling** seemed to have made a good deal more than average improvement while winning three races on the sand. When under the care of Sheikh Mohammed's one-time private trainer John Gosden, Halling had defied a penalty in the Cambridgeshire of 1994 and, on resuming his activities in England somewhat belatedly in July, tackled a very much more formidable task in the Group 1 Eclipse Stakes but, in leading from start to finish, readily showed that he was a great deal better than the average Cambridgeshire winner.

Halling (left) powers on to hold Sheikh Mohammed's Singspiel

Next time out, Halling confirmed that he had returned from Dubai as the best of the older middle-distance horses by taking the measure of Bahri in the Juddmonte International at the York Summer Festival. Two days later, **So Factual** showed that sprinters also flourish in the desert by disposing of some of the fastest horses in the country in the Nunthorpe Stakes, to add to the variety of championship races won by the Godolphin operation.

SHEIKH UP FOR CECIL

The following month Classic Cliché became Godolphin's third English classic winner of the season by beating **Minds Music**, trained by Henry Cecil, in the St Leger. At this time the next consignment of aspirants to championship status were being selected for shipment to Dubai. Among the leading candidates for transportation was **Mark of Esteem**, whom Henry Cecil was obliged to withdraw from the Royal Lodge Stakes at the Ascot

Festival of Racing, on the instructions of Sheikh Mohammed. Over the following week it became obvious that there was increasingly serious disagreement between the owner and Cecil, who has been champion trainer ten times. On October 3rd, 40 horses belonging to Sheikh Mohammed were removed from Warren Place, matters having been brought to a head by the discovery that Mark of Esteem was suffering from an injury to a knee on arrival in Dubai.

The splendid training complex in Dubai, where the likes of Lammtarra, Halling and Moonshell had spent the winter, was not the only modern establishment to have sheltered some of the outstanding winners of 1995. Major Dick Hern, who assumed control of the newly constructed Kingwood House Stables in Lambourn in 1991, returned to his place amongst the leading trainers as a result of his skilful development of the abilities of Harayir and of the two-year-old Alhaarth, both owned by Sheikh Hamdan Al Maktoum. For his part, Barry Hills was fully entitled to be satisfied with the results obtained during his first season in the Faringdon Place Stables, which he had built at a cost in excess of a million pounds in another part of Lambourn.

ANOTHER CLASSIC YEAR FOR HERN

At 74 years of age, Major Hern obtained his 16th success in an English Classic when **Harayir** came home a length and a half clear of **Aqaarid** in the 1000 Guineas, a third of a century after winning his first classic, the St Leger of 1962 with Hethersett. As first jockey to Sheikh Hamdan, Willie Carson, who has ridden three Derby winners for Major Hern, had the choice of partnering either Harayir or Aqaarid. Making one of his few errors of judgement when presented with such an option, Carson elected to ride Aqaarid, leaving Richard Hills to win his first classic, which was also the first to be run in England on a Sunday.

Harayir went next to the Irish 1000 Guineas and a clash with much-touted **Ridgewood Pearl**. With the soft ground against her and, as it turned out very much in the favour of the Irish filly, Harayir never looked like winning. Ridgewood Pearl went on to further victories in the Coronation Stakes at the Royal Meeting, the Prix du Moulin and most memorably the Breeders' Cup Mile. Ending the season the winner of four Group One races, she was Raceform's top-rated European filly, and is expected to stay in training.

ALHAARTH WAY THERE

Unlike many potentially top-class colts of recent seasons, **Alhaarth** was thoroughly exposed as a two-year-old, and readily answered every question put to him. After beating Mark of Esteem by a neck in the Strutt & Parker Stakes at Newmarket's July meeting first time out, the bay son of Unfuwain impressed when overcoming quite serious difficulties that were not of his own making at Glorious Goodwood, where he was hampered along the rail two furlongs from home in the Lanson Champagne Vintage Stakes. After being switched towards the outside with a furlong to run, he found an impressive turn of speed to beat **Allied Forces** by a length. Following a third success in the Solario Stakes, Alhaarth had little opportunity to shine when obliged to make all his own running to beat two rivals in Doncaster's Laurent Perrier Champagne Stakes, but he then turned in a scintillating performance when storming home two and a half lengths clear of dual Group One winner **Danehill Dancer** in the Dewhurst.

Alhaarth in winning action, as he was five times in 1995

The two-year-old **Royal Applause**, who is owned by Sheikh Maktoum Al Maktoum, supplied more than one of the highlights of the season for Barry Hills. After being successful over an extended five furlongs at Newbury in late May when much touted, this unbeaten bay colt by Waajib became the first since Crocket in 1962 to complete the treble of the Coventry Stakes at Royal Ascot, the Gimcrack Stakes at York and the Middle Park Stakes at Newmarket. In doing so, Royal Applause left the widespread impression that his class was likely to stand him in better stead as a sprinter than a miler.

FLIGHT GOES EVEN FURTHER

In the autumn, Barry Hills made history when training the grey **Further Flight** to win the Jockey Club Cup for the fifth consecutive season. No other horse has won the same pattern race more than four times and, on returning, Further Flight, owned and bred by former MP and Navy Minister Major Simon Wingfield Digby, was loudly cheered while led on a lap of honour round the paddock. As usual, Further Flight was ridden by Michael Hills, who was winning his nineteenth race, and tenth pattern race on the nine-year-old.

Among the races that Further Flight won earlier in his career was the Ebor

Handicap. In August, Barry Hills won the Ebor again with the lightly-raced **Sanmartino**, who was making only his fifth appearance in public, and just his second in a handicap.

SWING LAID LOW

Long before the Godolphin operation, Major Hern and Barry Hills had achieved the feats recounted above, Peter Savill's unbeaten colt **Celtic Swing**, trained by Lady Herries in Angmering Park in Sussex, had been widely expected to dominate the classics on the strength of the spectacular manner of his success in the Racing Post Trophy in the autumn of 1994. Having been supplemented for the Derby at a cost of £6,000 in March, Celtic Swing showed that he had trained on well, by winning the Greenham Stakes in a time that was only two-fifths of a second outside the course record, despite the quarter of an inch of rain that had fallen on the Newbury course during the morning. On the strength of that performance Celtic Swing became still hotter favourite for the 2000 Guineas, the only apparent threat to him coming from Sheikh Mohammed's pair Pennekamp and Diffident.

The big showdown is won by France as Pennekamp outsprints Celtic Swing

The Guineas proved to be a superb duel between the remorseless gallop of Celtic Swing and the breathtaking acceleration of **Pennekamp**, almost as though the irresistible force was meeting the immovable object. Celtic Swing stormed past the Bushes with an apparently winning lead, yet speed carried the day as, almost as soon as Thierry Jarnet asked Pennekamp for an effort, it was evident that the colt would reach top gear with time enough to spare in which to settle the issue conclusively. Only a very high-class horse can produce acceleration of that order.

INJURY BLOW FOR CLASSIC COLTS

Sadly, though, we were to witness no more of the excellence of Pennekamp, who pulled up with a hairline fracture of the fetlock after the Derby. Celtic Swing, defeated, but anything but disgraced in the Guineas, was also to succumb to injury. On May 7th he was taken out of the betting for the Derby, connections letting it be known that he might well opt for the French equivalent. On June 1st, owner Peter Savill reluctantly announced that Celtic Swing would indeed run in the Prix du Jockey-Club, as he felt that the colt was likely to be better suited by the Chantilly course than the more testing undulations at Epsom, and would probably find the better going in France.

Celtic Swing duly won the French Derby, before failing to do himself justice in the Irish Derby. Less than a week after his defeat at The Curragh came the announcement that he had injured a knee. As it would be impossible to prepare him for the St Leger, he was to be retired for the season to give him time to make a full recovery, and ensure that he would be able to remain in training as a four-year-old.

BAIRD TAKES OPENING TURF RACE

The Raceform Apprentice Handicap, the opening race of the Turf Season at Doncaster, was won by **Achilles Heel**, ridden by Mark Baird, a 20-year-old from Hamilton. After completing his course at the Newmarket Racing School, Baird had a spell with Mark Johnston, for whom he won races on Luks Akura - a sure sign of a good jockey - before returning to Newmarket to join Mick Ryan.

When winning the William Hill Lincoln, **Roving Minstrel** brought to fruition a plan first tentatively conceived by Tamworth trainer Bryan McMahon after the four-year-old had been runner-up over seven furlongs at Haydock Park the previous September. Roving Minstrel was bred by the trainer's wife Joy, and is owned by her, in partnership with Tommy Staunton of Castlebar, Co. Meath. Although the winner was returned at 33/1, the result was far from a good one for the sponsors, as Roving Minstrel had been substantially backed by connections at 40/1, and again at SP.

Prince of Andros, who had given David Loder his first Group success in the Cumberland Lodge Stakes at Ascot in September 1993, was a worthy winner of the Gordon Richards Stakes at Sandown Park in late April on his seasonal debut. As a result of returning from Frankfurt with an injury to his near-hind in the middle of July, Prince of Andros had been off the course throughout the second half of the 1994 season.

Mark Johnston's Middleham stable, bedevilled by coughing during the first six weeks of the season, struck form at Ascot in early May. **Double Trigger**, who had been third in the St Leger, showed that he would be a major factor in the Cup races by battling on to win the Insulpak Sagaro Stakes, and juvenile **Unconditional Love** landed the Garter Stakes. Earlier Johnston had been in charge of another of the season's memorable performers in the shape of **Vindaloo**, who left for Jimmy Harris after being claimed and went on to equal the 20th century record of nine handicap successes in a season.

PUNTERS 'CEE' RED

The outcome of the Chester Cup gave rise to a great deal of ill-feeling, and left a bad taste in too many mouths. After beating Harlestone Brook by five lengths with any amount in hand, **Top Cees**, trained by Mrs Lynda Ramsden and ridden by Kieran Fallon, made his way to the winner's enclosure amidst a stony silence from racegoers, resentful of a blatant reversal of form. Three weeks earlier Top Cees, ridden again by Fallon, had finished fifth to Tudor Island, Thunderheart and Well Beloved over a mile and six at Newmarket, where he had lain a long way out of his ground early on. A stewards' enquiry found no evidence of breach of the rules. At Chester though, Top Cees finished more than ten lengths clear of Well Beloved, who was ninth, and Thunderheart, who was twelfth, and there was no stewards' enquiry.

Harlestone Brook obtained handsome compensation for his controversial defeat at the hands of Top Cees when making his contribution to the triumphs enjoyed by John Dunlop at Royal Ascot. Although standing well under sixteen hands, this game five-year-old carried the welter weight of 9st 8lbs successfully over the two and a half miles of the Ascot Stakes, thereby completing a first-day treble for Dunlop, who had already won the Group One St James's Palace Stakes with Bahri and the Britannia Handicap with **Medaille Militaire**. The following day Dunlop won the Bessborough Handicap with **Son of Sharp Shot** and, on the last of the four days, took the Hardwicke Stakes with **Beauchamp Hero**, running at the insistence of owner Erik Penser, the Swedish financier, despite his trainer's misgivings that he was at a 16lb disadvantage with any other runner on handicap ratings. Those five winners, from only ten runners, made John Dunlop leading trainer at the Royal meeting. Together with two runner-ups, they had earned £289,512 for the Arundel stable during the four days.

Among others to enjoy a first success at the fixture was 22-year-old Richard Hughes, who won the Jersey Stakes on Richard Hannon's **Sergeyev**. The son of Dessie Hughes, who won the Champion Hurdle on Monksfield in 1979, Richard is probably the tallest Flat jockey riding at 5 ft 9 ins, but rides with decided style.

Astrac, ridden by top apprentice Seb Sanders, came out best in an exciting race for the Wokingham Stakes. Twice a winner on the Fibresand at Southwell at the backend of his two-year-old days, Astrac improved steadily after joining Reg Akehurst's Epsom stable.

DOUBLE TRIGGER DIFFERENT CALIBRE

Mark Johnston, rather characteristically, went into the top league to obtain his first success at the Royal Meeting by winning the Gold Cup with Double Trigger. Quite indifferent to the firmish ground, Double Trigger made all the running to become the first Northern-trained winner of the season's premier test of stayers during the present century.

Double Trigger adopts his favourite front-running tactics

The meeting opened on an unexpected note with **Nicolotte** winning the Queen Anne Stakes, although it transpired that he was doing no more than belatedly fulfilling his potential. His trainer, Geoff Wragg, explained that he had been fancied for the 2000 Guineas after being more than useful as a two-year-old, but had cracked a hock in his winding-up gallop.

Also successful for Mollers Racing was **Pentire**, who was winning his fourth race in succession in taking the King Edward VII Stakes. The colt was later to run Lammtarra close in the King George before landing his biggest prize when touching off subsequent Arc runner-up **Freedom Cry** in the Irish Champion Stakes. Pentire stays in training.

The young Newmarket trainer James Fanshawe and his recently appointed stable jockey David Harrison shared an important success early in their association when **Bold Gait** won the Northumberland Plate at Newcastle. By defying 9st 10lb Bold Gait equalled the weight-carrying record for the race set by the mighty Barcaldine in 1883 and emulated by Karadar in 1984. Coincidentally, Fanshawe occupies the stable built by Barcaldine's rider Fred Archer, and he was formerly assistant to Karadar's trainer Michael Stoute.

HAT-TRICK IN FALMOUTH

At Newmarket's picturesque July Meeting, the Queen's Racing Manager Lord Carnarvon and Richard Hannon completed a remarkable treble with **Caramba** in the Falmouth Stakes. Owner and trainer had won the race with Lemon Soufflé, a half-sister to Caramba, in 1994 and with Niche in 1993.

Another popular winner at the July meeting was **Lake Coniston**, who landed the July Cup. Lake Coniston was providing a first training success in a Group One race for Geoff Lewis, who won any number of such events during his riding days, including the July Cup of thirty-two years earlier on Secret Step and of course the Derby on Mill Reef in 1971.

Consolidating his position as the season's leading stayer, Double Trigger prevailed in a memorable race for the Goodwood Cup by securing a neck verdict over **Double Eclipse**. Not only is Double Eclipse a stablemate of Double Trigger in Mark Johnston's Kingsley House yard at Middleham, but he is also his younger brother.

At five years of age, **Sayyedati**, heroine of the 1993 1000 Guineas, finally justified the perseverance of her trainer Clive Brittain by beating the wonderfully consistent Bahri in the Sussex Stakes. Sayyedati, second in the race in 1993 and fourth in 1994, had not won since beating Ski Paradise in the Prix Jacques le Marois at Deauville in August 1993, but Clive Brittain was certain her days of stardom were not numbered. She was a first Group One winner for 22-year-old Brett Doyle, who had begun riding out for Brittain while a schoolboy of thirteen years of age, before joining the 'Carlburg' Stables as an apprentice.

CONTINUED SUCCESS FOR GOLF IN EUROPE

With the going at Goodwood distinctly on the firm side, stopwatches were always liablę to go on short time. **Hever Golf Rose**, who won a total of eight races in five different coutries throughout the season, culminating with success in the Prix de l'Abbaye, set a new record time for the five furlongs of the King George Stakes, and at the same time provided Epsom trainer Joe

Jason Weaver and Hever Golf Rose struck up a memorable partnership

Naughton with his first success in a British Pattern race. **Brief Glimpse** broke the record for Goodwood's seven furlongs in the Oak Tree Stakes and became the first winner trained by Major David Chappell at the meeting. James Toller also saddled his first winner at this prestigious fixture, landing his biggest stake to date, when **Jalfrezi** gave Seb Sanders his thirty-third success of the season in the Volvo Truck Finance Spitfire H'cap.

The eight-year-old **Shikari's Son**, a 40/1 chance, became the oldest horse to win the Stewards' Cup, first run in 1840, and saved the bookmakers from paying out an estimated £3 million on favourite Top Banana. Trained by John White near Wendover in Buckinghamshire and ridden by Richard Hughes at 4lb overweight, the veteran was enhancing his record in Sussex, as he had already won nine times at nearby Brighton.

As is almost invariably the case, the Yorkshire Oaks provided one of the highlights of the summer Festival on the Knavesmire. As the Irish Oaks winner **Pure Grain** took the lead off **Magical Retreat** with more than two furlongs to run, all seemed set to be plain sailing, but Magical Retreat rallied to such good effect that Pure Grain only scraped home by a head, to provide the preferred result for Belfast breeder Robert Barnett. Not only is Robert Barnett the owner-breeder of Pure Grain, but he also bred Magical Retreat, who was in foal to Shirley Heights.

HELLO AGAIN FOR VETERAN

At Doncaster, **Hello Mister** won the Portland Handicap for the second year running for 88-year-old Jack O'Donoghue, the oldest licensed trainer. The last horse to win the race in consecutive seasons was Shalfleet in 1935 and 1936. Double Trigger gave another splendid exhibition of front-running to take the Doncaster Cup, thus becoming the fifth horse this century to complete the great stayers' treble, following successes in the Goodwood Cup and Ascot Gold Cup.

Henry Cecil won his 300th European Pattern Race when **Solar Crystal** enhanced the trainer's remarkable record in Doncaster's May Hill Stakes. It was the ninth time that he had won the race since his first success with Formulate in 1978.

GODLEY SCOOPS THE CREAM

Royal Figurine became the fifth of her sex to win the Ayr Gold Cup in six years, getting home by a neck from No Extras. Her triumph reflected further credit on Martin Fetherston-Godley, who has only sixteen horses in his East Ilsley stable in Berkshire, as he had won the Magnet Cup with **Naked Welcome** earlier in the season. Royal Figurine is owned and bred by Scots born Craig Pearman. Her dam Cree's Figurine was bought by Fetherston-Godley for 2,100 guineas and was the second winner that he saddled.

The enterprising tactics adopted by 52-year-old Willie Carson played a big part in the success of **Bahri** in the Queen Elizabeth II Stakes at the Ascot Festival of Racing. Taking the longest route for the first part of the race, Carson took Bahri to the far rail straight away, was ahead of his rivals after a furlong, and had extended his lead to some three lengths as he switched to the inside rail on the turn into the straight. He won going away, beating Ridgewood Pearl by six lengths.

24-year-old American jockey Corey Nakatani, on a working sabbatical in Europe, rode his first winner in Britain when displaying good judgement in getting up close home on **Cool Jazz** to beat Young Ern by a short head in the Diadem Stakes. One of the outstandingly successful riders in the United States, Nakatani had already won races worth $10 million, including seven of the ten of graded status at Santa Anita between January and April.

SHAM PAIN FOR DUSTER?

Wafic Said's filly **Bosra Sham**, who was the most expensive yearling in Britain in 1994, showed she was not necessarily expensive, even at 530,000 guineas, providing Henry Cecil with a belated first Group One success of the season in beating Bint Shadayid by a most convincing three and a half lengths in the Fillies Mile. A chestnut daughter of Woodman out of the Riverman mare Korveya, Bosra Sham is a sister to Hector Protector, winner of the French 2000 Guineas in 1991.

Newmarket handler David Loder, in only his third full season, reached yet another landmark by obtaining his first Group One success with **Blue Duster** in the Cheveley Park Stakes at Newmarket in late September. A little over three months earlier, the same filly had been Loder's first winner at Royal Ascot and, once again, Blue Duster decided the issue with brilliant speed. All the same, her relaxed style of racing created the impression that she could be fully effective over the mile of the 1000 Guineas, and her clash with Bosra Sham remains eagerly awaited.

David Loder's unbeaten Blue Duster

A little over half an hour before Blue Duster maintained her unbeaten record in the Cheveley Park, David Loder had initiated a notable double with

Rio Duvida in the Tattersalls Houghton Sales Conditions Stakes. Having cost 36,000 guineas at the relevant sales, Rio Duvida was establishing himself as one of the best bargains amongst the yearlings of 1994, as he collected prize money and bonuses worth in excess of £110,000 after earning more than £25,000 on his previous appearances. That performance on the part of Rio Duvida was a compliment to Alhaarth, who had given him 4lbs and a beating in the Champagne Stakes at Doncaster.

RECORD-BREAKING PERFORMANCE

After being unraced in 1994, **Cap Juluca** continued to make up for lost time in no uncertain manner by winning the Cambridgeshire under a record weight for a three-year-old during the 20th century. By achieving a fifth consecutive success with Cap Juluca, trainer Roger Charlton, who had been responsible for the rapid improvement the colt had made since winning a maiden race at a Windsor evening meeting less than three months previously, deserves immense credit. Jason Weaver had been booked to ride Cap Juluca in the Cambridgeshire but, having renewed his association with Mark Johnston in late August, he was required for Double Trigger in the Prix du Cadran. Consequently Richard Hughes came in for the ride and supplemented his success in the Stewards' Cup by winning another of the season's most important handicaps.

Richard Hughes and Cap Juluca after their Cambridgeshire victory

The Champion Stakes was a somewhat peculiar race as the amount of prize money secured by one of the beaten horses was almost as important as the thoroughly deserved success of **Spectrum**, whom Peter Chapple-Hyam had brought back to peak form. By finishing fifth, Bahri earned £6,398, thereby ensuring that 56-year-old John Dunlop would crown his thirtieth season in the famous Castle Stables at Arundel, Sussex, by being champion trainer. His only rival, Godolphin's Saeed bin Suroor was to have no more runners.

Peter Chapple-Hyam had always entertained a high opinion of Spectrum and this was first justified by Lord Weinstock's colt winning the Irish 2000 Guineas. The trainer had been bitterly disappointed by his defeat in the Derby, but the reason for that failure soon became apparent. Not only was he found to be jarred on his return to Manton, but he had developed a serious muscular problem in his back. By nursing him back to win this Group One prize, Chapple-Hyam was understandably delighted.

Mary Reveley's long-held belief in **Old Red** was rewarded with victory in the Cesarewitch. Although anxious to buy him as a yearling, she could not go to the 60,000 guineas that he fetched, but was able to acquire him on his subsequent appearance in a horses-in-training sales. Old Red had long enjoyed the reputation of a hard puller, but Mrs Reveley had taught him to settle during the previous winter by giving him plenty of steady cantering.

DUNLOP TAKES FINAL BRITISH GROUP ONE

A week after the Champion Stakes John Dunlop consolidated his position at the top of the trainers' table in singularly worthy fashion when Erik Penser's grey colt **Beauchamp King** won the Racing Post Trophy at Doncaster. Beauchamp King, who had been supplemented at a cost of £15,000, gave connections a handsome dividend by earning £87,736 when beating Even Top a length and a half.

No fewer than three jockeys rode their 1,000th domestic winner during the season. One of them was the Champion jockey Frankie Dettori, who took his tally to the millennium in real style by landing the St Leger on Classic Cliché. Kevin Darley was wearing Peter Savill's colours on Busy Banana at Carlisle when bringing one of his mounts into the winner's enclosure for the 1,000th time on April 28th, and Richard Quinn reached the four figure mark on Just Fizzy at Chepstow on 4th July.

With Sheikh Hamdan Al Maktoum at the top of the owners list, and John Dunlop leading trainer, Frankie Dettori retained the Jockeys' Championship, having reached his double century for the second successive season on Sheer Danzig at York. Fred Archer and Gordon Richards are the only other jockeys to have ridden 200 winners in a British season more than once.

In the contest for the Raceform Apprentices' Championship, Seb Sanders went three ahead of John Stack by bringing his score to twenty-four when completing a treble at Folkestone on June 30th, and increased his advantage to eight with a double at Brighton on 20th July. It was also at Brighton that Sanders rode out his claim on Crystal Heights, his 50th winner of the season on October 1st.

END OF AN ERA

Lester Piggott finally hung up his saddle for good. Although he did not ride in this country in 1995, he enjoyed some success on a round the world tour before bringing down the curtain on a glittering career in September on the run up to his 60th birthday. Mrs Meg Mullion died in March. Along with her husband, John, she owned many good horses, including Ragusa, who won the St Leger and King George VI and Queen Elizabeth Stakes in 1963. Raymond Clifford-Turner was 89 at the time of his death in May. A solicitor by profession, he was one of the first owners to send horses to Michael Stoute, who won the Ayr Gold Cup with Blue Cashmere for him in 1973. Lord White died at the age of 72 in August, and Sir Philip Oppenheimer was 83 when he died in October. Both made important contributions to the welfare of Racing.

Lord White, whose colours were carried by the Champion Stakes winner Legal Case in 1989, was responsible for Ever Ready being the first firm to sponsor the Derby in 1984. Sir Philip Oppenheimer obtained the permission of the Queen for De beers to sponsor the King George and Queen Elizabeth Stakes in 1975. Among the home-bred horses raced by Sir Philip was On the House, winner of the 1000 Guineas in 1982.

Jack Holt, who was 67 when he died in October, had a reputation for training sprinters in his small stable near Basingstoke, and was consistently successful with inexpensive horses. With Sweet Monday, who cost just 2,100 guineas, he won the Mill Reef Stakes at Newbury in 1980, while Argentum won the Cornwallis Stakes at Ascot in 1989, and the King George Stakes at Goodwood the following year. Jimmy Thompson died at the age of 77 in March. Having been champion apprentice in France, he rode for 'Rufus' Beasley in England, and later trained at Malton, before taking charge of one of Sir David Robinson's private stables at Newmarket.

Colonel Tom Nickalls died at the great age of 91 in June. After being a soldier of considerable distinction, Tom Nickalls joined The Sporting Life in 1946, and soon acquired a reputation for his fearless denunciation of sharp practice, no matter how exalted the connections of a horse might be. John Tyrrel was only 60 when he died in May. As well as having been a member of the Channel 4 racing team, he was a knowledgeable historian of the Turf, whose meticulously researched books included Racecourses on the Flat. George Blackwell, whose father and namesake trained the 1903 Triple Crown winner Rock Sand, died in March. A bloodstock agent with an international reputation and an independent turn of mind, he was responsible for the purchase of the 1980 Derby winner Henbit, Nonoalco and other high class horses.

START OF AN ERA

The meetings at Newmarket and Salisbury on May 7th ushered in a new era of Sunday racing with off-course betting. While the meetings were a great success with racegoers - the fixture at Chester in July attracted an estimated 35,000 people - the innovation proved less popular with betting shop customers.